W9-BXL-283

Heterick Memorial Library
Ohio Northern University
Ada, Ohio 45810

THE AUTHORITY SINCE 1868

THE WORLD ALMANAC®

AND BOOK OF FACTS

1995

WORLD ALMANAC
AN IMPRINT OF FUNK & WAGNALLS CORPORATION

THE WORLD ALMANAC AND BOOK OF FACTS 1995

Editor: Robert Famighetti
Deputy Editor: Patricia Coleman
Associate Editors: Christina Cheddar, Michael Northrop
Assistant Editor: Judith Leale
Desktop Publishing Associate: Melissa Janssens
Chronology Editor: Donald Young
Index: AEIOU Inc.

Funk & Wagnalls

Editorial Director: Leon L. Bram
Director of Editorial Production: Andrea J. Pitluk
Copy Editors: Matthew Friedlander, Lori Wiesenfeld
Desktop Publishing Assistant: Hana Shaki

World Almanac Books

Publisher: Richard W. Eiger
Sales Manager: James R. Keenley **Publicity Manager:** Joyce H. Stein

---

The editors acknowledge with thanks the many letters of helpful comment and criticism from readers of THE WORLD ALMANAC. Because of the volume of mail directed to the editorial offices, it is not possible to reply to each letter writer. However, every communication is read by the editors and all comments and suggestions receive careful attention.

THE WORLD ALMANAC does not decide wagers.

The first edition of THE WORLD ALMANAC, a 120-page volume with 12 pages of advertising, was published by the New York World in 1868. Annual publication was suspended in 1876. Joseph Pulitzer, publisher of the New York World, revived THE WORLD ALMANAC in 1886 with the goal of making it a "compendium of universal knowledge." It has been published annually since then.

THE WORLD ALMANAC and BOOK OF FACTS 1995
Copyright © 1994 by Funk & Wagnalls Corporation
The World Almanac and The World Almanac and Book of Facts
are registered trademarks of Funk & Wagnalls Corporation.
Library of Congress Catalog Card Number 4-3781
International Standard Serial Number (ISSN) 0084-1382
ISBN (softcover) 0-88687-766-0
ISBN (hardcover) 0-88687-767-9
Microform Edition: University Microfilms Intl.
Printed in the United States of America
The softcover and hardcover editions are distributed to the trade in the United States
by St. Martin's Press.

WORLD ALMANAC
An Imprint of Funk & Wagnalls Corporation
One International Boulevard, Suite 444
Mahwah, New Jersey 07495-0017

R
031
W92W
1995

CONTENTS

General Index 4

The Top 10 News Stories 33

FEATURE ARTICLES 33

Election '94 33
By Donald Young

The Information Superhighway 35
By Vice President Al Gore

World War II Remembered 37
By Stephen E. Ambrose

The Health-Care Reform Debate 38
By Mary Hager

Chronology of the Year's Events 40

Notable Supreme Court Decisions, 1993-94 70

The 1994 Nobel Prizes 70

Major Actions of the 103d Congress 71

United States Government 72

Cabinets of the U.S. 98

Notable Quotes in 1994 104

Historical Anniversaries 105

Economics 107

Agriculture 134

Employment 142

National Defense 155

Energy 164

Science and Technology 169

Meteorology 179

Environment 187

1994 in Pictures 193

Trade and Transportation 201

Crime 213

Education 219

Astronomy and Calendar 251

Aerospace 292

Arts and Media 300

Awards, Medals, Prizes 314

Noted Personalities 331

United States Population 373

United States History 438

Biographies of U.S. Presidents 471

Flags and Maps 481

United States Facts 497

World History 508

Historical Figures 534

World Exploration and Geography 543

Weights and Measures 557

Disasters 565

Associations and Societies 575

Postal Information 587

Language 592

Presidential Elections 601

Taxes 636

States and Other Areas of the U.S. 643

Cities of the U.S. 674

Buildings, Bridges, Tunnels, Dams 684

Social Security 696

Health 701

Consumer Information 712

Religious Information 729

Nations of the World 740

1994 in Pictures *(continued)* 777

Sports 852

Vital Statistics 957

Obituaries 973

Offbeat News Stories of 1994 975

Miscellaneous Facts 975

Quick Reference Index 976

GENERAL INDEX

Note: Page numbers in *italics* indicate photos.

—A—

Abbreviations
Canada, postal . . . 589
Common . . . 594
International organizations . . . 844-45
States, postal . . . 589
UN agencies . . . 847
A-bomb. *See* Atomic bomb
Abortion
Clinic access legislation (1994) . . . 71
Clinic shooting (1994) . . . 62
Legalized (1973) . . . 447, 465
Number, by state . . . 959-60
Restraints (1989) . . . 449
Restrictions overturned (1993) . . . 45
Supreme Court rulings (1993-94) . . . 70
Academy Awards (Oscars) . . . 327-29, *781*
Accidents and disasters . . . 565-74
Assassinations . . . 573-74
Aviation . . . 69, 296, 566-67, 965
Blizzards . . . 569
Deaths (number, causes) . . . 959, 964-65
Earthquakes (1989, 1994) . . . 48, 51, 54, 196, 449-50, 572
Explosions . . . 570-71
Fires (1993, 1994) . . . 41, 63-64, 570
Floods (1993, 1994) . . . 63, 451, 569
Home . . . 965
Hurricanes . . . 569
Kidnappings . . . 574
Mining . . . 568
Motor vehicle . . . 959, 964
Nuclear (1979) . . . 448, 531, 571
Occupational . . . 147, 965
Oil spills (1989, 1994). 57, 66, 449, 571-72
Railroad . . . 567-68
Ship (1915, 1989) . . . 443, 449, 565-66
Space exploration (1986) . . . 293, 294, 449
Storms . . . 569
Tidal waves . . . 569
Tornadoes . . . 568
Typhoons . . . 569
Volcanic eruptions (1980) . . . 448, 546
Acquired Immune Deficiency Syndrome
Chronology (1993-94) . . . 53
Deaths, new cases (1985-93) . . . 53, 971
Epidemic (1986) . . . 449
Hotline . . . 710
Reported, estimated cases worldwide . 842
Actors, actresses
Birthplaces, birth dates . . . 357-70
Death and birth dates . . . 367-70
Movies (1993-94) . . . 300
Movie, theater, TV awards. . . 325, 327-29
New York theater (1993-94). . . . 300, *780*
Original names . . . 370-72
Adams, John . . . 634, 635
Biography . . . 471
Burial site . . . 480
Cabinet . . . 98-100
Electoral vote . . . 633
Adams, John Quincy . . . 634
Biography . . . 472
Burial site . . . 480
Cabinet . . . 98-100
Popular, electoral votes . . . 633
Address, forms of . . . 597
Addresses
Abbreviations, postal
Canada . . . 589
States . . . 589
Armed forces, U.S. . . . 159
Associations and societies . . . 575-86
Businesses, major U.S. and foreign . 713-18
Colleges and universities . . . 226-50
Labor unions . . . 153-54
Religious groups, U.S. . . . 730-31
Sports, pro organizations . . . 904-5
Television, cable networks . . . 312
U.S. government departments . . . 72-75
U.S. independent agencies . . . 75-76
U.S. judiciary . . . 86-89
ZIP codes . . . 387-417, 436
Admirals, USN . . . 155
Address, forms of . . . 597
Personal salutes, honors. . . . 156
Adopted children . . . 962
Adventist churches . . . 729, 730
Advertising . . . 313
Aerospace. *See* Aviation; Space developments
Afghanistan . . . 532, 533, 740, 848, 851
AFL. *See* American Football League
AFL-CIO *See* American Federation of Labor and Congress of Industrial Organizations
Africa
Area . . . 839
Gold production . . . 131
Highest, lowest points . . . 556
History . . 511, 515, 517, 529-30, 532, 533
Lakes . . . 555
Languages . . . 598-99
Map . . . 494-95
Mountain peaks . . . 547
Population . . . 839, 840-41
Religions . . . 731
Volcanoes . . . 545
Waterfalls . . . 556
see also specific countries
African Americans. *See* Blacks
Agencies
United Nations . . . 847
U.S. government . . . 75-76, 107-8, 148
Agricultural Marketing Act (1929) . . . 444
Agriculture . . . 134-41
Acreage, number of farms . . . 134
Employment . . . 134, 143, 145
Minimum hourly rates. . . . 151
Social Security benefits . . . 698
Exports . . . 137, 141, 202
Foreign production . . . 141, 740-839
Imports . . . 137, 141, 202
Income . . . 124, 137
Land grants (1862) . . . 441
Legislation (1916, 1929) . . . 443, 444
Occupational injuries . . . 147
Population . . . 134
Prices received . . . 140
Production . . . 135, 138-39, 141
Real estate debt . . . 138
By state . . . 134, 135, 138
Subsidies . . . 136
U.S. programs . . . 136
see also Food; Grains
Agriculture, Department of . . . 73
Employees, payroll . . . 148
Expenditures . . . 107
Secretaries . . . 72, 73, 101
Chronology . . . 68
Aid
U.S. foreign . . . 851
Truman Doctrine (1947) . . 445, 477, 529
see also Welfare
AIDS. *See* Acquired Immune Deficiency Syndrome
Air
Composition, temperature . . . 270
Density . . . 270, 562
Pollution . . . 187
Air Commerce Act (1926) . . . 444
Air conditioning . . . 166
Aircraft. *See* Aviation
Air Force, Department of the . . . 148
Air Force, U.S.
Academy . . . 157, 236
Address for information . . . 159
Enlisted adviser, senior . . . 161
Flights, notable . . . 299
Generals, active duty . . . 155
Insignia . . . 157
Military units . . . 156
Personnel, active duty . . . 158
Secretary of the . . . 73
Training centers . . . 156
Women, active duty . . . 159
see also Armed forces, U.S.
Airlines, leading . . . 297
see also Aviation
Air mail . . . 589, 590-91
Airports, busiest
International . . . 296
U.S. . . . 296
Airships . . . 299, 566
Akron, OH . . . 674
Mayor . . . 89
Population . . . 381, 408, 674
Alabama . . . 643
Abortions reported . . . 959
Admission, area, capital . . . 499, 500, 643
Agriculture . . . 134-39
Altitudes (high, low) . . . 498
Birth, death statistics . . . 958
Budget . . . 113
Cities . . . 675, 679-80
Congressional representation . . . 76, 78, 376
Courts, U.S. . . . 87
Crime, prisons, death penalty . . . 216, 217, 218
Debt . . . 113
Energy consumption . . . 166
Geographic center . . . 500
Governor, state officials . . . 93, 94
As immigrants' intended residence . . . 386
Indians, American (population) . . . 507
Interest laws, rates . . . 720, 721
Marriage, divorce laws . . . 727, 728
Motor vehicle statistics . . . 207
Name origin, nickname . . . 501, 643
Population . . . 376-77, 379
Cities, towns . . . 387, 675, 679
Counties, county seats . . . 418
Density . . . 379
Port traffic . . . 203
Presidential elections . . . 601, 602, 630
Schools . . . 220, 222, 224
Taxes . . . 113, 207, 641, 642
Unemployment benefits . . . 142
Welfare assistance . . . 384
Alaska . . . 643-44
Abortions reported . . . 959
Accession . . . 502
Admission, area, capital (1959) . 446, 499, 500, 643, 644
Agriculture . . . 134-38
Altitudes (high, low) . . . 498
Birth, death statistics . . . 958
Budget . . . 113
Cities . . . 674
Congressional representation . 76, 78, 376
Courts, U.S. . . . 87
Crime, prisons, death penalty . . . 216, 218
Debt . . . 113
Energy consumption . . . 166
Geographic center . . . 500
Governor, state officials . . . 93, 94
As immigrants' intended residence . . 386
Indians, American (population) . . . 507
Interest laws, rates . . . 720, 721
Marriage, divorce laws . . . 727, 728
Motor vehicle statistics . . . 207
Name origin, nickname . . . 501, 643
Population . . . 376-77, 379
Census divisions . . . 418
Cities, towns . . . 387, 674
Density . . . 379
Port traffic . . . 203
Presidential elections . . . 601, 602-3, 630
Schools . . . 220, 222, 224
Taxes . . . 113, 207, 641
Time zones . . . 290
Unemployment benefits . . . 142
Welfare assistance . . . 384
Albania . . . 62, 740-41, 848, 851
Albany, NY . . . 89, 684
Albuquerque, NM . . . 674
Mayor . . . 89
Population . . . 381, 406, 674
Alcohol boiling point . . . 562
Alcoholic beverages. *See* Liquor
Alcohol, Tobacco, and Firearms, Bureau of (1993, 1994) . . 49-50, 59, 73, 76, 451
Aleutian Islands . . . 549
Alexander the Great . . . 511
Algeria . . . 741, 848, 851
Aliens
Admissions, exclusions, U.S. . . . 842-43
Illegal, amnesty (1988) . . . 449
Legislation (1952, 1990) . . . 445, 842-43
Naturalization . . . 843
Passports, visas . . . 842-43
Allen, Ethan (1775) . . . 339, 439
Allentown, PA
Mayor . . . 89
Population . . . 411
Alps . . . 547-48
Altitudes
Cities . . . 550-52
Highest, lowest
U.S. . . . 498
World . . . 555-56
Mountains . . . 546-48
Aluminum . . . 129, 131
Amazon River . . . 553
Ambassadors and envoys . . . 848-50
Address, form of . . . 597
Salute to (artillery) . . . 156
"America" ("My Country 'Tis of Thee") . . . 469
American Federation of Labor and Congress of Industrial Organizations
Address, affiliates . . . 153-54
AFL formed (1886) . . . 442
CIO formed (1935) . . . 444
Merger (1955) . . . 445
American Football League
Conference leaders (1960-69) . . . 874
Division champions . . . 873
Professional records . . . 879-80
see also Football, pro
American Kennel Club registration . . 192
American League (baseball) . . . 939-45, 949-51, 953
American Revolution (1775-83) . . . 521
Articles of Confederation (1777) . 439, 455
Battlefields, monuments . . . 503-4

Battles (1775, 1776, 1777, 1779, 1780, 1781) . . . 439
Black troops . . . 334
Casualties, numbers serving . . . 163
Costs . . . 160
Declaration of Independence (1776) . 439, 453-54
Liberty Bell . . . 469-70
Military leaders . . . 339-40
Americans, notable . . . 331-72
Actors, actresses . . . 327-29, 357-70
Architects . . . 335-36
Artists . . . 344-46
Athletes . . . 926-28
Blacks . . . 326, 332-34
Business leaders . . . 351-52
Cartoonists . . . 319-20, 325, 336
Composers . . . 352-54
Economists . . . 316, 348-49
Educators . . . 347-48
Historians . . . 321-22, 348-49
Industrialists . . . 351-52
Jazz artists . . . 354-55
Living personalities . . . 331-32
Lyricists . . . 354
Military leaders . . . 339-40
Obituaries (1993-94) . . . 973-74
Philanthropists . . . 351-52
Philosophers . . . 347
Playwrights . . . 321, 325, 334-35, 341-44
Poets . . . 323
Political leaders . . . 337-39
Religionists . . . 347
Rock & Roll musicians . . . 325, 355-56
Scientists . . . 314, 349-50
Social reformers . . . 347-48
Social scientists . . . 348-49
Statesmen, stateswomen . . . 316, 337-39
Writers . . . 315-16, 321, 334-35, 341-44
American Samoa. *See* Samoa, American
American's Creed . . . 466
American Stock Exchange
Address . . . 585
Volume, transactions . . . 127
America's Cup (yachting) . . . 937
"America, the Beautiful" . . . 469
Ames, Aldrich (1994) . . . 49, 55, 66, 196
Ames, Rosario . . . 68
Amnesty
Confederate citizens (1872) . . . 442
Illegal aliens (1988) . . . 449
Vietnam draft evaders (1977) . . . 448
Anaheim, CA . . . 674
Mayor . . . 89
Population . . . 381, 388, 674
Anchorage, AL . . . 674
Mayor . . . 89
Population . . . 381, 387, 674
Ancient civilizations . . . 508-13
Historical figures . . . 534
Measures . . . 562
Seven Wonders . . . 512
Andaman Sea . . . 552
Andes . . . 547
Andorra . . . 741
Angkor Wat temple . . . 516
Anglicanism . . . 53-54, 831
Angola . . . 201, 532, 742, 848, 851
Anguilla . . . 832
Animals
American Kennel Club . . . 192
Cat breeds . . . 192
Classification . . . 192
Collectives, names for . . . 594
Endangered species . . . 188, 189
Farm (*see* Livestock)
Gestation, incubation . . . 189
Longevity . . . 189
Speeds . . . 189
Venomous, major . . . 190
Westminster Kennel Club . . . 920
Young, names for . . . 595
Zoos, major U.S. . . . 191
Annapolis (MD) (Naval Academy) 55, 157, 237
Anniversaries
Historical events (1895, 1945, 1970) 105-6
Holidays . . . 291
Wedding . . . 725
Antarctica
Area . . . 839
Australian Territory . . . 744
British Territory . . . 833
Explorations . . . 543-45
French . . . 768
Highest, lowest points . . . 556
Mountain peaks . . . 548
Volcanoes . . . 545
Antigua and Barbuda . . . 549, 742, 848
Antilles. *See* Netherlands Antilles
Antoinette Perry Awards (Tonys) . . . 325
Apartheid . . . 56, 57, 533, 820
Aphelion, perihelion . . . 259-60, 268
Apogee of moon . . . 268
Apollo missions (1969) . . . 292-93, 447
Appliances, home . . . 166
Appomattox Court House (1865) . 441, 503
Apportionment, Congressional . . . 376
Arabia. *See* Middle East; Saudi Arabia
Arab-Israeli conflict
Lebanon . . . 532, 533, 788, 794
October War (1973) . . . 447, 532, 764, 788, 816
Palestinian self-rule (1993, 1994) . 40, 42, 45, 47, 50, 53, 55-56, 57-58, 62, 65, 69, *779*, 788
Palestinian uprising . . . 533, 788
Six-Day War (1967) . . 531, 764, 788, 816
Arab League . . . 530, 844
Archery . . . 866
Architects, notable . . . 325, 326, 335-36
Archives, National . . . 672-73
Arctic explorations . . . 543-44
Arctic Ocean
Area, depth . . . 552
Coast length, U.S. . . . 498
Islands, areas . . . 549
Area codes, telephone . . . 387-417
Areas (geographical)
Continents . . . 839
Earth . . . 269
Islands . . . 549
Lakes . . . 555
Largest country (Russia) . . . 813
National parks . . . 71, 503-4
National recreation . . . 502, 506
Nations, world . . . 740-839
Oceans . . . 552
United States . . . 437, 497, 499
Counties, by state . . . 418-36
States . . . 643-68
Territories . . . 436, 502, 669-71
Areas (mathematical)
Mathematical formulas . . . 564
Measures (units) . . . 557-64
Arenas, stadiums
Baseball . . . 954
Basketball . . . 914
Football . . . 880
Argentina . . . 742-43
Aid, U.S. . . . 851
Ambassadors, envoys . . . 848
History . . . 530, 532
Nuclear power . . . 168
Arizona . . . 644
Abortions reported . . . 959
Admission, area, capital . . . 499, 500, 644
Agriculture . . . 134-39
Altitudes (high, low) . . . 498
Birth, death statistics . . . 958
Budget . . . 113
Cities . . . 679, 681, 683
Congressional representation 76, 78, 376
Courts, U.S. . . . 87
Crime, prisons, death penalty 216, 217, 218
Debt . . . 113
Energy consumption . . . 166
Geographic center . . . 500
Governor, state officials . . . 93, 94
As immigrants' intended residence . . . 386
Indians, American (population) . . . 507
Interest laws, rates . . . 720, 721
Marriage, divorce laws . . . 727, 728
Mineral production . . . 129
Motor vehicle statistics . . . 207
Name origin, nickname . . . 501, 644
Population . . . 376-77, 379
Cities, towns . . . 387-88, 679, 681, 683
Counties, county seats . . . 418
Density . . . 379
Presidential elections . . . 601, 603, 630
Schools . . . 220, 222, 224
Taxes . . . 113, 207, 641
Unemployment benefits . . . 142
Welfare assistance . . . 384
Arkansas . . . 643-44
Abortions reported . . . 959
Admission, area, capital . . . 499, 500, 644
Agriculture . . . 134-39
Altitudes (high, low) . . . 498
Birth, death statistics . . . 958
Budget . . . 113
Cities . . . 678
Congressional representation 76, 78, 376
Courts, U.S. . . . 87
Crime, prisons, death penalty 216, 217, 218
Debt . . . 113
Energy consumption . . . 166
Geographic center . . . 500
Governor, state officials . . . 93, 94
As immigrants' intended residence . . . 386
Indians, American (population) . . . 507
Interest laws, rates . . . 721
Marriage, divorce laws . . . 727, 728
Motor vehicle statistics . . . 207
Name origin, nickname . . . 501, 644
Population . . . 376-77, 379
Cities, towns . . . 388, 678
Counties, county seats . . . 418-19
Density . . . 379
Presidential elections . . . 601, 603, 630
Schools . . . 220, 222, 224
Taxes . . . 113, 207, 641, 642
Unemployment benefits . . . 142
Welfare assistance . . . 384
Arkansas River . . . 553
Arlington National Cemetery (VA) . . . 673
Arlington, TX . . . 89, 381, 674
Armed forces (general)
Leaders, notable past . . . 339-40
Military strength (by country) . . . 161
Per 1,000 persons (by country) . . . 161
see also specific countries
Armed forces, U.S. . . . 155-63
Academies, service . . . 55, 157, 236, 237
Address, forms of . . . 597
Address for information . . . 159
Base closings (1993) . . . 70, 451
Battlefields and parks, national . . . 504
Black troops . . . 334
Casualties, by wars . . . 163
Commands . . . 155
Defense contracts . . . 159
Enlisted advisers, senior . . . 161
Expenditures . . . 107
Generals . . . 155
Homosexual issues (1993) . . . 42, 451
Insignia . . . 157
Joint Chiefs of Staff (1989) . . . 73, 449
Chairmen . . . 155, 162
Leaders, past notable . . . 339-40
Medal of Honor . . . 160
Military strength . . . 160, 161
Pay scales . . . 162
Personnel . . . 155, 158, 159, 160, 161
Salutes . . . 156
Secretaries . . . 73, 99-100
Time, 24-hour . . . 290
Training centers . . . 155-56
Troop strength, by wars . . . 163
Units . . . 156
Veterans . . . 159-60
Women, active duty . . . 159
Combat eligibility (1993) . . . 451
First general (1970) . . . 447
see also Weapons; *specific branches*
Armenia . . . 743, 848, 851
Arms control . . . 162
Bush reduction proposal (1992) . . . 450
Limitations of Armaments Conference (1921) . . . 443
Mid-range missiles ban . . . 162
Nuclear test-ban treaty (1963) . . 162, 446
Pacifist pacts (1920s) . . . 527
SALT (1972, 1979) . . . 162
START (1991, 1993) . . . 162
Army, Department of the
Employees, payroll . . . 148
Secretary . . . 73
Army, U.S.
Academy (West Point) . . . 157, 237
Address for information . . . 159
Enlisted adviser, senior . . . 161
Generals . . . 155
Address, form of . . . 597
Salutes, honors . . . 156
Women, first (1970) . . . 447
Insignia . . . 157
Leaders . . . 339-40
Personnel, active duty . . . 58
Secretary . . . 73
Training centers . . . 155-56
Units . . . 156
Women, active duty . . . 159
Art
Abstract . . . 527, 528
Artists, notable . . . 344-46
Baroque . . . 519
Beaux Arts . . . 524
Gothic . . . 517, 522
Impressionist . . . 524
Last Judgment restoration . . . 56
Neoclassical . . . 521
Pop . . . 531
Renaissance . . . 518, 519
Rococo . . . 521
Romanesque . . . 517
Romanticism . . . 522
Arthur, Chester A. . . . 634, 635
Biography . . . 474-75
Burial site . . . 480
Cabinet . . . 98-101
Articles of Confederation (1777) . 439, 455
Artillery salutes . . . 156

Artists, notable . . . 344-46
Aruba . . . 549, 805
Ascension Island . . . 549, 833
ASEAN. *See* Association of Southeast Asian Nations
Ashmore and Cartier Islands . . . 744
Ash Wednesday . . . 732, 733
Asia
Area . . . 839
Highest, lowest points . . . 555
Lakes . . . 555
Languages . . . 598-99
Map . . . 492-93
Mountain peaks . . . 546, 548
Population . . . 839, 840-41
Religions . . . 731
Trade . . . 201
Volcanoes . . . 546
Waterfalls . . . 556
see also specific countries
Asians, U.S.
Population . . . 375, 382
Social, economic characteristics . . . 378
Assassinations . . . 573-74
Attempts . . . 574
Ford, Gerald R. (1975) . . . 574
John Paul II, Pope (1981) . . . 574
Reagan, Ronald (1981) . . . 448, 574
Truman, Harry S. (1950) . . . 445, 574
Wallace, George C. (1972) . . . 447, 574
International
Gandhi, Indira (1984) . . . 533, 573
Gandhi, Rajiv (1991) . . . 573
Karami, Rashid (1987) . . . 533, 573
Ngo Dinh Diem (1963) . . . 446
Palme, Olaf (1986) . . . 573
Premadasa, Ranasinghe (1993) . . . 573
Sadat, Anwar al- (1981) . . . 533, 573
Zia ul-Haq, Mohammed (1988) . . . 533
Presidents, U.S.
Garfield, James A. (1881) . . 442, 474, 573
Kennedy, John F. (1963) . . 446, 478, 573
Lincoln, Abraham (1865) . . 441, 474, 573
McKinley, William (1901) . . 442, 475, 573
United States
Kennedy, Robert F. (1968) . . 447, 573
King, Martin Luther (1968) . . . 447, 573
Lennon, John (1980) . . . 448
Long, Huey (1935) . . . 444, 573
Assemblies of God . . . 730
Association of Southeast Asian Nations . 844
Associations and societies . . . 575-86
Health care . . . 710-11
Sports . . . 905
Astrological signs . . . 268
Astronauts
First on moon (1969) . . . 447
First orbit (1962) . . . 446
First women (1983) . . . 292, 293, 448
Hall of Fame . . . 97
Missions . . . 292-94
Astronomy . . . 251-85
Achievements, discoveries, (1994) . . . 169
Auroras . . . 266
Calendar (1995) . . . 274-85
Celestial highlights . . . 251-54
Constants . . . 264
Constellations . . . 264-65
Earth . . . 269-71
Eclipses (1995) . . . 266
Eclipses, total (1940-2000) . . . 273
Moon . . . 251-54, 263, 266, 268-69
Planetary configurations . . 251-54, 259-60
Planets visible . . . 254-59, 259-62
Signs and symbols . . . 259
Star tables . . . 263-64
Morning, evening . . . 272
Sun . . . 254, 263, 266, 267-68
Time . . . 259, 270
Twilight . . . 268, 272-73
Athletics. *See specific sports*; Sports
Atlanta, GA . . . 674
Airport traffic . . . 296
Buildings, tall . . . 684
Mayor . . . 89
Population . . . 381, 394, 674
Atlantic cable, first (1858) . . . 441
Atlantic Charter (1941) . . . 444
Atlantic Ocean
Area, depth . . . 552
Coasts, U.S.
Highest point . . . 497
Length . . . 498
Ports . . . 203, 204
Crossings, notable (1819) . . . 299, 440
Islands, areas . . . 549
Atmosphere (air pressure) . . . 564
Atmosphere (earth's) . . . 270
Atolls . . . 549, 671
Atomic bomb (1945) . . . 445, 529
see also Nuclear arms
Atomic clock . . . 271
Atomic energy. *See* Nuclear energy
Atomic weights . . . 177-78
Attila . . . 514
Attorneys general, U.S. . . . 100
Clinton administration . . . 72, 73, 100
Aunu'u Island . . . 669
Aurora, CO . . . 89, 381, 674
Auroras . . . 266, 512
Austin, TX . . . 674
Buildings, tall . . . 684
Mayor . . . 89
Population . . . 380, 413, 674
Australia . . . 525, 743-44
Ambassadors, envoys . . . 848
Area . . . 839
Gold production . . . 131
Great Barrier Reef . . . 512
Highest, lowest points . . . 556
Lakes . . . 555
Map . . . 496
Merchant fleet . . . 205
Mountain peaks . . . 547
Population . . . 839, 840, 841
Territories . . . 744
Waterfalls . . . 556
Australian Antarctic . . . 744
Australian Open (tennis) . . . 931
Austral Islands . . . 768
Austria . . . 744
Ambassadors, envoys . . . 848
History . . . 518, 522
Rulers . . . 538
World War I . . . 526
Authors, notable. *See* Writers, notable
Automobiles
Accidents, deaths . . . 959, 964
Commuters . . . 210
Drivers
Licensed (by age) . . . 209
By state . . . 207
Expenditures, driver . . . 210
Exports, imports . . . 202, 203
First cross-country trip (1903) . . . 443
Fuel
Consumption . . . 207, 210
Prices, retail . . . 167
Tax . . . 207
History . . . 525
Inventions . . . 174
Production
By country . . . 208
Registration . . . 207
Safety belt laws
By country . . . 209
By U.S. states . . . 207
Sales . . . 207, 208, 209
Theft . . . 214, 217
Top-selling . . . 209
Auto racing . . . 931-33
Autumn . . . 270-71
Autumnal Equinox . . . 253, 260, 271
Aviation
Accidents . . . 296, 566-67, 965
Air cargo . . . 296
Air Commerce Act (1926) . . . 444
Aircraft operation statistics . . . 297
Airlines, leading . . . 297
Air mail . . . 589, 590-91
Air mileage, between world cities . . . 212
Airships . . . 299, 566
Balloon flights . . . 298
Earhart lost (1937) . . . 444
Federal agency . . . 74, 76, 107
Flight attendants strike (1993) . . . 42
Flights, notable . . . 299
Gliders . . . 298
Hall of Fame . . . 297
Helicopters . . . 298
Inventions . . . 174
Wright brothers (1903) . . . 443, 525
Jet, first U.S. passenger (1958) . . . 446
Records, 1993 . . . 298
Safety . . . 296
Traffic . . . 296
Traffic controllers strike (1981) . . . 448
Transatlantic, first flight (1919) . . 299, 443
Transatlantic, first nonstop flight (1927) . . . 299, 444
Transcontinental, first flight (1911) . . . 443
Travel survey . . . 296
Avoirdupois measures . . . 558-60
Awards, prizes . . . 314-30
Baseball . . . 940, 944, 945
Broadcasting . . . 325
Football . . . 877, 887, 888-89, 896
Hockey, ice . . . 895-97
Journalism . . . 316-20, 324-25
Literature . . . 70, 315-16, 321-23, 324, 330
Medal of Honor . . . 160
Miscellaneous . . . 325-26
Miss America . . . 326
Movies . . . 325, 327-29
Music . . . 323-24, 329-30
National Medal of Science . . . 174
Nobel Prizes . . . 70, 314-16
Pulitzer Prizes . . . 316-24
Recording . . . 309, 329-30
Spingarn Medal . . . 326
Theater . . . 325
Video, music . . . 309
Azerbaijan . . . 744-45
Azores . . . 549, 812
Aztecs . . . 520, 543

— B —

Badminton . . . 866
Baha'i Faith . . . 729, 730, 731
Bahamas . . . 205, 549, 745, 848
Bahrain . . . 549, 745, 848
Baker Islands . . . 671
Bakersfield, CA . . . 89, 381, 674
Balance of trade . . 123, 132, 201, 202, 533
Balearic Islands . . . 549, 821
Bali . . . 549
Balloon flights, 1993 records . . . 298
Baltic Sea . . . 549, 552
Baltimore, MD . . . 675-76
Buildings, tall . . . 684
Commuters . . . 210
Mayor . . . 89
Population . . . 380, 399, 674
Port traffic . . . 203
Unemployment rate . . . 145
Bangladesh . . . 745-46, 848, 851
Bank of North America (1781) . . . 439
Bankruptcy . . . 112
Banks . . . 114-16
Charter, First (1781) . . . 439
Charter, Second (1816) . . . 440
Closed (1933) . . . 444
Deposits, U.S. . . . 114-15
Failures . . . 115
Farm credit . . . 138
Federal Reserve System (1913) 75, 116, 443
Financial panics (1873, 1893, 1907) 442, 443
Gold reserves (world) . . . 125
International . . . 847
Interstate . . . 71
Largest, U.S. . . . 115
Modern, beginning of . . . 519
Mortgages . . . 725, 726
Number, U.S. . . . 114-15
Savings and loan crisis (1989) . . 115, 449
Baptist churches
Addresses, U.S. headquarters . . . 730
Beliefs, practices . . . 738-39
Membership . . . 729
Barbados . . . 746, 848
Barley production . . . 138, 139, 140
Baseball
Addresses, team . . . 904
All-Star games . . . 952
Batting records . . . 943-44, 946-51, 953
Cy Young Award . . . 944
First black major league player (1947) 445
Gold Glove Awards (1993) . . . 940
Hall of Fame, museum . . . 659, 952
Home-run leaders . . . 941-42, 953, 954
Leaders
All-time . . . 944, 954
League (1994) . . . 953
Most Valuable Players . . . 945
Olympic champions (1992) . . . 866
Pennant, division winners . . . 939-40
Pitching records . . . 944, 946, 949, 953, 954
Players' strike (1994) . . 65-66, 67, *783*, 939
RBI leaders . . . 942-43, 953
Rookies of the Year . . . 945
Stadiums . . . 954
Triple Crown hitters . . . 944
World Series . . . 41, 955
Basketball
Addresses, team . . . 904
All-time leaders . . . 913, 914
Hall of Fame . . . 914
NBA . . . 907-13
Arenas . . . 914
Champions (1947-94) . . . 908
Championship (1994) . . . 783, 907
Coaching victories . . . 914
Most Valuable Players . . . 914
Player draft (1994) . . . 913
Rookie of the Year (1954-93) . . . 910
NCAA . . . 915-20
Coaches, Division 1 . . . 919
Tournament champions . . . 782, 916-18
Women's champions . . . 918

Wooden Award 918
Olympic champions (1992) 866
Baton Rouge, LA 675
Buildings, tall 684
Mayor 89
Population 381, 398, 675
Port traffic 203
Battlefields, national 504
Beans. *See* Legumes
Beef
Consumption 135
Nutritive value 702
Prices, farm 140
Production 135
Belarus 746-47, 848, 851
Belgian Congo. *See* Zaire
Belgium 747
Ambassadors, envoys 848
Gold reserves 125
Nuclear power 167, 168
Rulers 540, 747
Belize 747, 848, 851
Bell, Alexander Graham (1915) 443
Belmont Stakes 899
Benin 747-48, 848, 851
Bering, Vitus (1741) 438, 544
Bering Sea 552
Berlin, Germany
Blockade, airlift (1948) 445, 477, 529
Population 840
Riots, East sector (1953) 530
Wall built, opened (1961, 1989) 531, 533, 770
Bermuda 205, 549, 832-33
Bert Bell Memorial Trophy 877
Beverages
Nutritive value 702-3
see also specific kinds
Bhutan 748, 848
Bhutto, Benazir (1993) 40
Biafra 807
Biathlon 853
Bible, books of the 734
Biblical measures 562
Bicycles. *See* Cycling
Bill of Rights (1791) 439, 460
Bioethics 709
Biology
Animal, plant classification 192
Discoveries 169, 176-77
Birmingham, AL 675
Buildings, tall 684
Mayor 90
Population 381, 387, 675
Births
Certificates, records, rate 722, 957, 958
Infant mortality rates 958, 959
Life expectancy 972
Notable personalities, birth dates 331-72
Number, rate 957
By country (*see specific countries*)
By states 958
Birthstones 725
Black Death 518
Black Friday (1869) 442
Blacks
Bus boycott (1955) 445
Civil Rights Act (1875) 442
Civil Rights Act (1964) 446, 531
Civil rights amendments 461-62
Civil rights bill (1957) 446
Civil rights workers (1964) 446
Companies, leading (1993) 121
Disabled people 382
Education 219, 221, 223
Employment, unemployment 145, 150
Evers murder (1994) 49
First astronauts 293, 294
First governor since Reconstruction (1989) 450
First in colonies (1619) 438
First Joint Chiefs chairman (1989) 449
First major league baseball player (1947) 445
First senator since Reconstruction (1966) 446
First Supreme Court justice (1967, 1991) 447, 450
First woman representative (1968) 447
First woman senator (1992) 450
Households 960, 961, 962
Income distribution 383
Ku Klux Klan (1866, 1921) 441, 443
March on Washington (1963) 446
Notable personalities 332-34
Population 373, 375, 382, 437
Poverty rates 383
Race riots (1943, 1965, 1967, 1992) 444, 446-47, 450
Salaries and wages 149
Seminarian enrollment 736
Sit-ins (1960) 446
Spingarn Medal 326
Voting rights (1957, 1965) 446
War service 334
see also Desegregation; Slavery
Black Sea 552
Blended families 962
Blindness
Associations 576, 710
Diabetes-caused 709
Income tax deduction 638
Blizzards 569
Characteristics 179
Great (1888) 442, 569
Boat racing
America's Cup 937
Olympic champions (1992) 868
Power boat 925
Bobsledding 852
Body weight tables 705, 972
Boer War (1899-1902) 524
Boiling points 562
Bolivia 748
Aid, U.S. 851
Ambassadors, envoys 848
History 530, 532
Bonaire 805
Bonaparte, Napoleon (1798, 1803) 440, 521, 522
Bonds
Glossary 132, 133
Portraits on U.S. 117
Yields 126
Books
Awards 70, 315-16, 321-23, 330
Best selling (1993) 303
Copyright law, U.S. 723-25
Notable (1993) 303, 304
Postal rates 588
Writers, notable 334-35, 341-44
Booth, John Wilkes (1865) 441, 474, 573
Borneo 549, 776
Bosnia and Herzegovina 748-49, 848, 851
Chronology (1993-94) 50, 52, 55, 58, 60, 63, 65
Map 490
Boston, MA 675
Buildings, tall 684
Education, compulsory (1636) 438
Historical sites 503
Massacre (1770) 438, 471
Mayor 90
News Letter (1704) 438
Police strike (1919) 443
Population 380, 400, 675
Port traffic 203
Tea Party (1773) 439
Botany
Plant classification 192
Botswana 749, 848, 851
Boulder Dam (1936) 444
Boundary lines, U.S 500
Webster-Ashburton Treaty (1842) 441
Bourbon, House of 537
Bowl games (football)
College 882-84
Super Bowl 782, 873
Bowling 901-2
Boxer Rebellion (1900) 442
Boxing
Champions (by class) 934-36
Heavyweight title bouts 936
Olympic champions 865-66
Boy Scouts
Address 576
Founded (1910) 443
Brady Bill (1993) 42, 71, 213, 451
Branch Davidians (1993, 1994) 49-50, 59, 451
Braun, Carol Moseley (1992) 334, 450
Brazil 749-50
Aid, U.S. 851
Ambassadors, envoys 848
History 520, 522
Merchant fleet 205
Military strength 161
Nuclear power 168
Rio de Janiero harbor 512
Trade 201, 749
Bread
Nutritive value 702
Breeders' Cup 900
Brethren churches 729, 730
Breyer, Stephen 57, 61-62
Brezhnev, Leonid 532, 542
Bridge (card game) 564
Bridges 690-93
Britain. *See* United Kingdom
British Antarctic Territory 833
British Honduras. *See* Belize
British Indian Ocean Territory 833
British Isles. *See* United Kingdom
British West Indies 832
Broadcasting. *See* Radio; Television
Broadway. *See* Theater
Bronx, NY 191, 428
Brooklyn, NY 428
Brooklyn Bridge (1883) 442, 690
Brunei 750, 848
Bubonic plague 518
Buchanan, James 631, 634
Biography 473
Burial site 480
Cabinet 98-101
Popular, electoral votes 633
Buddhism
Address, U.S. headquarters 730
Adherents, world, U.S. 729, 731
Beliefs, practices 737
History 511, 519, 532
Budget
Federal 107-8
Balanced-budget amendment (1994) 51
Deficit (1993) 40, 109, 132
Deficit reduction legislation (1993) 451
First trillion-dollar (1987) 449
Proposed, 1995 fiscal year 49
Reconciliation Act (1993) 71
Glossary 132
States 113, 114
see also specific countries
Buenos Aires 742, 840
Buffalo, NY 675
Buildings, tall 684
Mayor 90
Population 381, 406, 675
Buildings, tall 684-90
Bulgaria 750-51
Aid, U.S. 851
Ambassadors, envoys 848
Merchant fleet 205
Nuclear power 167, 168
Bull Moose Party 475
Bull Run, Battle of (1861) 441
Bunker Hill, Battle of (1775) 439
Bureau of the Census 74, 76, 107, 374, 375
Bureau of Engraving and Printing 672
Bureau of the Mint 117
Burglaries 214, 215, 217, 218
Burkina Faso 751, 848, 851
Burma. *See* Myanmar
Burr, Aaron 440, 634, 635
Burundi 55, 751, 848, 851
Buses
Boycott, desegregation (1955) 445
Commuters 210
Bush, George 634, 635
Biography 479
Cabinet 97-102
Popular, electoral votes 601-30, 631, 633
Business
Advertising expenditures 313
Air travel 296
Black-owned, leading (1993) 121
Capital gains tax 122
Consumer products, parent company 719
Corporate tax rates 122
Defense contracts 159
Directory 713-18
Franchises, fastest growing (1993) 121
International transactions, U.S. 123
Leaders, notable 351-52
Leading (1993) 119, 121
Mergers/acquisitions
1994 51, 66
Largest 120
Multinational companies 121
Occupational injuries 147
Profits (by industry) 116
Rotary club, first (1905) 443
Sales, largest (1993) 120
Sherman Antitrust Act (1890) 442
Supreme Court rulings (1994) 70
Tax deductions 636, 637, 638
U.S. investments abroad 125
see also Banks; Economics; Industries, U.S.; Stocks
Butter
Nutritive value 701, 702
Byzantine Empire 515

— C —

Cabinet, U.S. 97-102
Address, form of 597
Clinton administration 97-102
Personal salutes, honors 156
Salute (artillery) 156
Cable (measure) 558
Cable television 310
Advertising expenditures 313
Network addresses, phone numbers 312
In schools 221

Cabrera Island 821
Caicos Island 832
Cairo, Egypt 763, 840
Calcium (dietary) 701, 702-3, 705
Calendar
Celestial (1995) 251-54
Daily astronomical (1995) 274-85
Days between two dates 289
Episcopal Church 732
Eras, cycles (1995) 272
Greek Orthodox Church 732
Gregorian 288
Islamic 732
Jewish 733
Julian 288, 289
Leap years 288
Lenten 732, 733
Lunar 289
Perpetual 286-87
Twilight (1993) 272-73
Year 270
Caliber (measure) 561
California 645
Abortions reported 959
Admission, area, capital 499, 645
Agriculture 134-39
Altitudes (high, low) 498
Birth, death statistics 958
Budget 113
Cities 674, 677, 678-79, 680, 681, 682, 683
Congressional representation 76, 78-79, 376
Courts, U.S. 87-88
Crime, prisons, death penalty 216, 217, 218
Debt 113
Desert Protection Act (1994) 71
Earthquake (1994) 48, 51, 54, 196
Energy consumption 166
Fire damage (1993) 41
Geographic center 500
Governor, state officials 93, 94
As immigrants' intended residence 386
Indians, American (population) 507
Interest laws, rates 720, 721
Marriage, divorce laws 727, 728
Mineral production 129
Motor vehicle statistics 207
Name origin, nickname 501, 645
Population 376-77, 379
Cities, towns 388-89, 674, 677, 678, 680, 681, 682, 683
Counties, county seats 419
Density 379
Port traffic 203
Presidential elections 601, 604, 630
Schools 20, 222, 224
Taxes 113, 207, 641, 642
Unemployment benefits 142
Welfare assistance 384
California, Gulf of 552
Calories 701, 702-3
Labels, nutrition 704
Calvin, John 347, 519
Cambodia 751-52, 848
Aid, U.S. 851
Devastation, Vietnamese invasion 532
Independence 530
Mayaguez seized (1975) 448
U.S. invasion (1970) 447
Cameroon 752, 848, 851
Canada 752-53
Aid, U.S. 851
Altitudes 550-51
Ambassadors, envoys 848
Buildings, tall 684, 685-86, 687, 688, 689, 690
Chronology (1993-94) 40, 41, 42
Distances to ports 204
Football 881
French and Indian War (1754-63) 438
Gold production, reserves 125, 131
Grey Cup 881
Islands 549
Lakes, largest 555
Latitudes, longitudes 550-51
Map 485
Mineral resources 129, 130
Mountain peaks 547
Nuclear power 167, 168
Postal codes, rates 589, 590, 591
Prime ministers 753
First woman (1993) 40
Provinces, territories 753
Religions 736
Rivers 553-54
St. Lawrence Seaway (1959) 446
Trade 201, 753
NAFTA 42-43, 44, 71, 204
Trains, passenger 206
Waterfalls 556
Zoos 191
Canadian Football League 881
Canals
Erie (1825) 440
Panama (1978) 139, 448, 809
Suez 530, 764
Canary Islands 549, 821
Cancer
Deaths, new cases 970
Help organizations 710
Medical discoveries (1994) 67, 169
Prevention 705, 708
Warning signals 708
Canoeing 866
Cape Verde 754, 848, 851
Capital gains 122, 132
Capital punishment. *See* Death penalty
Capitals
States, U.S. 499
U.S. (*see* Washington, DC)
World (*see specific countries*)
Capitol, U.S. 672
Burned (1814) 440
Carat (measure) 561
Carbohydrates 701, 702-3
Cardinals, Roman Catholic 734
Cardiovascular disease 970
Cards, playing (odds) 564
Caribbean Community (CARICOM) 844
Caribbean Sea
Area, depth 552
Islands, area 549, 670-71
Map 485
Volcanoes 546
Carlsbad Caverns (NM) 503, 658
Caroline Islands 549, 671
Carolingian dynasty 538
Cars. *See* Automobiles
Carter, Jimmy 631, 634, 635
Biography 478-79
Cabinet 97-102
Haiti junta ouster (1994) 67
North Korea nuclear dispute (1994) 60
Popular, electoral votes 633
Cartier and Ashmore Islands 744
Cartoonists
Awards 319-20, 325
Notable American 336
Castro, Fidel 530, 759-60
Casualties, U.S. wars 163
Cat breeds 192
Catholic Church. *See* Roman Catholicism
Cattle. *See* Livestock; Meats
Caucasus Mountains 548
Caves
Carlsbad, NM 503, 658
Mammoth, KY 503, 651
Wind, SD 503, 664
Cayman Islands 832
CD-ROM
Glossary 170
Household computers with 173
School usage 221
Software, top selling 173
Celebes 549
Celebrities. *See* Notable personalities; *specific fields*
Celestial events (1995) 251-54
Celsius scale 562
Cemeteries
Arlington National (VA) 673
Presidential burial sites 480
Census, U.S. *See* Population, U.S.; Population, world
Census Act (1790) 439
Central African Republic 754, 848, 851
Central America 533
Common Market 201
Maps 485,488
Volcanoes 545, 546
see also specific countries
Central Intelligence Agency 75
Ames spy case (1994) 49, 55, 66, *196*
Directors 103
Century, defined 288
Cereals
Nutritive value 701, 702
Ceuta 821
Ceylon. *See* Sri Lanka
Chad 754-55
Aid, U.S. 851
Ambassadors, envoys 848
History 517, 532
Challenger (space shuttle) (1983, 1984, 1986) 293, 294, 448, 449
Chambers of Commerce. *See* Cities, U.S.; States, U.S.
Champlain, Samuel de (1609) 438, 543
Channel Islands 549, 832
Charlemagne 515, 536
Charlotte, NC 675
Buildings, tall 684
Mayor 90
Population 381, 408, 675
Chatham Islands 549, 805
Cheese
Nutritive value 701, 702
Chemicals
Exports, imports 202
Toxic 187
Chemistry
Discoveries 176-77
Elements (atomic weights, numbers) 177-78
Nobel Prizes 70, 314-15
Chess 41, 956
Chesterfield Islands 768
Chiang Kai-shek 527
Chicago, IL 675
Airport traffic 296
Buildings, tall 684-85
Commuters 210
Fire (1871) 441, 570
Mayor 90
Population 380, 395, 675
Port traffic 203
Unemployment rate 145
Chickens
Nutritive value 702
Prices, farm 140
Children
Adoptees 962
Average height, weight 972
Child care 374, 961
Child support 374
Cost of raising 721
Immunization schedule 707
Living with grandparents 960, 962
School enrollment 219
Single-parent families 960, 961
Social Security benefits 697
Unmarried-couple households 962
Welfare assistance 384
Children's books
Awards 324, 330
Notable (1993) 304
Chile 755
Aid, U.S. 851
Ambassadors, envoys 848
History 532
Rulers 541
China, dynastic 524, 525
Boxer Rebellion (1900) 442
Chou 509, 511, 542
Great Wall 511, 512
Han 513, 542
Kuomintang 526, 527, 529
Manchu 520, 526, 542
Ming 519, 542
Open Door Policy (1899) 442
Opium War (1839-1842) 522-23
Revolution (1911) 526
Seven Wonders, Middle Ages 512
Shang 509, 542
Sung 516, 542
Tang 516, 542
Yuan 517
China, People's Republic of 755-56
Aid, U.S. 851
Ambassadors, envoys 848
Chronology (1993-94) 43, 47, 53, 58, 67
Gold production 131
History 529, 530, 531, 533, 756
Leaders 531-32, 542, 756
Maoism 531, 531-32, 756
Map 492-93
Merchant fleet 205
Military strength 161
Nixon visit (1972) *200*, 447
Nuclear power 168
Population 839
Tiananmen Square 533
Trade, U.S. 43, 47, 53, 58, 201
U.S. immigration 386
China, Republic of. *See* Taiwan
China Sea 552
Chinese lunar calendar 289
Cholesterol
Heart disease 707
Labels, nutrition 704
Chou Dynasty 509, 511, 542
Christ. *See* Jesus Christ
Christianity
Denominations 729-32, 738-39
History 513-14, 516-17, 519
Population, world 731
Christmas Day 291
Christmas Island 549, 744
Chromium 129, 130
Chronological eras, cycles (1995) 272
Chronology of 1993-94 40-69
Chunnel. *See* English Channel Tunnel

Churches
Addresses, U.S. headquarters 730-31
Calendars 732-33
Denominations 738-39
Feast, fast, holy days 730-31
Memberships 729-30, 731-32
Number, U.S. 729-30
Churchill, Sir Winston 337
Yalta Agreement (1945) 445
Church of Christ, Scientist 729, 730
Church of England 831
Church of Jesus Christ of Latter-Day Saints. *See* Latter-Day Saints, Church of
CIA. *See* Central Intelligence Agency
Cigarettes. *See* Smoking
Cincinnati, OH 675
Buildings, tall 685
City manager 90
Population 381, 409, 675
Cinema. *See* Movies
CIO. *See* American Federation of Labor and Congress of Industrial Organizations
Circle
Mathematical formulas 564
Circulation (newspapers, magazines) . . . 305-6
Circumference
Formula 564
Circumnavigation 299
Cities, U.S. 674-83
Air pollutants 187
Altitudes 550-51
Area codes, telephone 387-417
Buildings, tall 684-90
Climatological data 179-84, 185
Commuters 210
Consumer price indexes 110-11
Farthest east, north, south, west 497
Housing prices 726
Immigrants (1993) 385
Latitudes 550-51
Libraries, public 225
Longitudes 550-51
Mayors, managers 89-92
Mileage tables
Air 212
Road 211
Newspaper circulation 305
Orchestras, opera companies 307-8
Population 387-417, 674-83
Decline 381
100 largest 380-81
Ports 203-4
Precipitation 180-82
Salaries and wages 146
Stadiums, arenas 880, 914, 954
Temperatures 180-84
Time differences 291
Unemployment rates 145
Wind velocities 179, 182
ZIP codes 387-417
Cities, world
Air mileage 212
Altitudes 552
Bridges, buildings 690, 693
Latitudes, longitudes 552
Population (by country) 740-839
Population of largest 840
Port distances 204
Time differences 290
Citizenship, U.S.
American Indians (1924) 443
Fourteenth Amendment 461-62
Naturalization process 843
Civil rights
Act (1875) 442
Act (1964) 446, 531
Bill signed (1957) 446
Bill vetoed (1990) 450
Commission 75
Constitutional amendments . . 461-62, 463
Disabilities Act (1990) 450
see also Desegregation; Elections, voting rights; Women
Civil War, U.S. (1861-65) 441, 523
Amnesty Act (1872) 442
Appomattox Court House (1865) . . 441, 503
Battlefields 504
Black troops 334
Bull Run (1861) 441
Casualties, numbers serving 163
Confederate States (1861) 441, 464
Costs 160
Draft riots (1863) 441
Emancipation Proclamation (1863) . 441, 474
Ft. Sumter (1861) 441
Gettysburg Address (1863) 441, 464
Historical parks, sites 503, 504-5
Lincoln assassination (1865) . . 441, 474, 573
Military leaders 339, 340
Secession of states 464
Sherman's March (1864) 441
Classification, animal/plant 192
Clergy, forms of address 597
Cleveland, Grover 631, 634
Biography 475
Burial site 480
Cabinet 98-101
Popular, electoral votes 633
Cleveland, OH 675
Buildings, tall 685
Mayor 90
Population 380, 409, 675
Unemployment rate 145
Climate, U.S. 179-86
Annual data 182
Clinton, Bill
Administration 44, 59-60, 66, 72-75, 634, 635
Back-tax payment (1994) 54
Biography 479-80
Cabinet 44, 45, 72, 97-102
Election (1994) 33-34
European trips (1994) 47, 60, 62-63
First year (1993) 36-39, 451
Foster suicide (1993, 1994) . . . 44, 51, 59, 64, 451
Health-care reform (1993, 1994) . . 38-39, 49, 61, 64, 66-67, *195*, 451
Inauguration (1993) 451
Mideast peace process *779*
Presidential election (1992) . . 450, 601-31, 631, 633
Popular, electoral votes . . . 601-31, 633
Salary 72
Sexual harassment suit (1994) 56-57, 60, 64
State of the Union (1994) 46
Whitewater scandal (1993, 1994) . 44, 46, 49, 51-52, 59, 60, 62, 64, *194*, 451
Clinton, Hillary Rodham 480
Back-tax payment (1994) 54
Health-care reform (1993) 38, 451
Whitewater scandal (1993, 1994) . 44, 46, 49, 51-52, 59, 60, 62, 64, *194*, 451
Clothing
Exports, imports 202
Price index 109, 110
Clubs, organizations 575-86
Coal
Exports, imports 164, 202
Mining strikes (1922, 1946) 443, 445
Production, consumption 164
Coastal warnings 179
Coast Guard, U.S. 76
Academy 157
Address for information 159
Commandants 155
Insignia 157
Personnel, active duty 158
Women, active duty 159
Coastlines, U.S. 498
Cobain, Kurt 56, *780*
Cobalt 129, 130
Cocoa
Exports, imports 202
Cocos (Keeling) Island 744
Coffee
Exports, imports 202
Coinage 117-18
Cold War 529, 532-33
Colleges and universities . . . 221, 222-24, 226-50
ACT scores 223
Addresses 226-50
Basketball 782, 915-20
Coeducation, first (1833) 440
Colors 885-87
Desegregation (1962) 446
Enrollment 221, 226-50
Faculty, number 226-50
Football 882-89
Founding dates 226-50
Four-year 226-40
Freshman attitudes 250
Governing officials 226-50
Hockey, ice 897
Land Grant Act (1862) 441
Professors' salaries 224
SAT scores 223-24
State university, first (1795) 439
Team nicknames 885-87
Tuition and costs 222, 223
Loan repayment legislation (1993) . . 71
Two-year 240-50
Women's, first (1821) 440
Wrestling champions 905
Colombia 757
Aid, U.S. 851
Ambassadors, envoys 848
Gold production 131
Rulers 541
Colorado 645-46
Abortions reported 959
Admission, area, capital . . 499, 500, 645, 646
Agriculture 134-39
Altitudes (high, low) 498
Birth, death statistics 958
Budget 113
Cities 674, 675, 676
Congressional representation. . . 76, 79, 376
Courts, U.S. 88
Crime, prisons, death penalty . . . 217, 218
Debt 113
Energy consumption 166
Geographic center 500
Governor, state officials 93, 94
As immigrants' intended residence . . 386
Indians, American (population) 507
Interest laws, rates 720, 721
Marriage, divorce laws 727, 728
Motor vehicle statistics 207
Name origin, nickname 501, 645
Population 376-77, 379
Cities, towns 391, 674, 675, 676
Counties, county seats 419
Density 379
Presidential elections . . . 601, 604-5, 630
Schools 220, 222, 224
Taxes 113, 207, 641
Unemployment benefits 142
Welfare assistance 384
Colorado River 438, 543, 553
Colorado Springs, CO 675
Mayor 90
Population 381, 391, 675
Colors
Colleges and universities 885-87
Of spectrum 563
Columbia (space shuttle) (1981, 1982) . . . 293, 294, 448
Columbia River 553
Columbium 129, 130
Columbus, Christopher (1492) 438, 518, 543
Columbus, GA 90, 381, 676
Columbus, OH 676
Buildings, tall 685
Mayor 90
Population 380, 409, 676
Columbus Day 291
Comecon 530
Commands, U.S. 155
Commerce. *See* Commodities; Exports, imports; Shipping
Commerce, Department of 73-74
Employees, payroll 148
Expenditures 107
Secretaries 72, 73, 101-2
Commission on Civil Rights 75
Committee for Industrial Organization. *See* American Federation of Labor and Congress of Industrial Organizations
Commodities
Exports, imports 202
Price indexes 109-11
Production 135, 138, 139, 140
Common Market. *See* European Community
Common Sense (Paine)
Excerpt 452
Commonwealth of Independent States. . 844
Commonwealth of Nations 844
Communications
Information superhighway 35-36, *198*
Inventions 174-76
Satellite, first (1962) 446
Television 310-12, 313
Communism
Post-World War II 529
Russian revolution (1917) 526
Soviet Bloc shakeup (1989) 533
U.S.
Red scare (1920) 443
Trials, convictions (1949) 445
see also Cold War
Communist China. *See* China, People's Republic of
Community colleges 240-50
Commuters 210
Comoros 757, 848
Composers, notable 352-54
Compound interest table 562
Computers
CD-ROM households 173
CD-ROM software 173
Glossary 170-72
Information superhighway 35-36, *198*
Internet 173
Sales, ownership 173
School usage 221
Concentration camps 528, 529

Cone
Volume formula 564
Confederate States of America
Amnesty Act (1872) 442
Battlefield memorials 504
Civil War (1861-65) 441, 523
Casualties, numbers serving 163
Davis, Jefferson (1861) 337, 441, 464
Flags 464
Government 464
Lee, Robert E. (1865) 340, 441, 666
Secession 464
Confucianism
Adherents 731, 732
Confucius (551 BC) 511
Congo, Democratic Republic of. *See* Zaire
Congo, Republic of 757-58, 848
Congo (Zaire) River 553
Congregational churches 729
Congress, U.S. 76-85
Address, forms of 597
Apportionment 376
Bill-into-law process 463
Bills vetoed (1789-1993) 463
Black members (1992) 334, 450
Chronology 40, 46, 64, 66-67, 68
Committees 84-85
Constitutional powers 457
Elections (1992) 76-84, 450
Employees, payroll 148
Expenditures 107
House of Representatives 78-85
Bank scandal (1991, 1993) 450, 451
Black members 334
Committees 84, 85
Constitutional powers 456-57
First woman (1916) 443
Members 78-84
Party representation 85
Revenue bills origination 457
Salaries, term 78
Speakers 103
Legislation (1993-94) 71
Nonvoting members 84
Political division 85
Presidents, vice presidents 634-35
Qualifications 456
Salary amendment (1992) 450, 463
Senate 76-77
Committees 84
Election of senators 456, 462
First black woman (1992) 450
Floor leaders 103
Mitchell resignation (1994) 52
Members 76-77
Party representation 85
Salaries, term 76
Visitors, admission of 672
Women members (1916, 1992) 334, 443, 450
see also Continental Congress; Library of Congress
Congress of Industrial Organizations. *See* American Federation of Labor and Congress of Industrial Organizations
Congress of Vienna (1814-15) 522
Connecticut 646
Abortions reported 959
Admission, area, capital 499, 646
Agriculture 134-39
Altitudes (high, low) 498
Birth, death statistics 958
Budget 113
Congressional representation 76, 79, 376
Courts, U.S. 88
Crime, prisons, death penalty 216, 217
Debt 113
Energy consumption 166
Geographic center 500
Governor, state officials 93, 94
As immigrants' intended residence 386
Indians, American (population) 507
Interest laws, rates 720, 721
Marriage, divorce laws 727, 728
Motor vehicle statistics 207
Name origin, nickname 501, 646
Population 376-77, 379
Cities, towns 391-92
Counties, county seats 419
Density 379
Presidential elections 601, 605, 630
Schools 220, 222, 224
Taxes 113, 207, 641, 642
Unemployment benefits 142
Welfare assistance 384
Conservation. *See* Environment
Constantinople 515
Constants, astronomical 264
Constellations 264-65
Constitution, U.S. 456-63
Amendments 460-63
Balanced budget (1994) 51
ERA proposed (1972, 1982) 447, 448
Poll tax barred 463
Procedure for 459
Prohibition (1917, 1933) 443, 444, 462, 527
Reconstruction 461-62
Slavery abolished (1865) 441, 461
27th ratified (1992) 450
Voting age (1971) 447, 463
Bill of Rights 460
Origin 455
Preamble 456
Ratification (1787) 439, 455
Constitutional Convention (1787) 439, 455
Construction industry
Occupational injuries 147
Consumer Price Indexes 109-11
Consumer Product Safety Commission 75
Consumers and consumption
Business directory 713-18
Catalogues 712-13
Credit 118, 720-21
Debt 118
Energy 164, 165, 166
Food
Labeling, nutrition 704
Meats 135
Nutritive values 701-3
Housing prices 726
Information 712-28
Loan rates 720
Mortgages 725, 726
Personal expenditures 128
Price indexes 109-11
Products
Parent companies 719
Pure Food and Drug Act (1906) 443
Safety Commission 75
Transportation 207, 208, 210
Continental Congress
Articles of Confederation (1777) 439, 455
Declaration of Independence (1776) 439, 453-54
First (1774) 439
Great Seal of the U.S. 466
Northwest Ordinance (1787) 439
Presidents, meetings 452
Stars and Stripes (1777) 439, 466-67
Continental Divide 499
Continents 543-48
Altitudes (highest, lowest) 555-56
Areas 839
Lakes 555
Mountain peaks 546-48
Population 839
Religions 731
Rivers 553-54
Volcanoes 545-46
Waterfalls 556
see also specific continents
Convention sites, political 632
Cook Islands 805
Coolidge, Calvin 632, 634, 635
Biography 476
Burial site 480
Cabinet 98-101
Popular, electoral votes 633
Cooperstown (NY) (Baseball Hall of Fame) 659, 952
Copper
Production, reserve 129, 130, 131
Copyright law, U.S. 723-25
Corn
Exports, imports 141, 202
Nutritive value 703
Prices, farm 140
Production 138, 139, 141
Coronado, Francisco (1540) 438, 543
Corporation for Public Broadcasting 108
Corporations
Largest sales 120
Leading 119
Multinational 121
Profits (by industry) 116
Tax rates 122
see also Business
Corpus Christi, TX 676
City manager 90
Population 381, 414, 676
Port traffic 203
Corsica 549, 767
Cortes, Hernando 520, 543
Cosmonauts 49, 292-94
Costa Rica 758, 848, 851
Cost of living 109-11, 132
Cote d'Ivoire (Ivory Coast) 758-59, 848, 851
Cotton
Exports, imports 202
Prices, farm 140
Production 138, 139
Cotton Bowl 883
Counterfeiting 217
Counties, U.S. 378
Areas and county seats 418-36
Density 380
Elections (1988, 1992) 601-30
Highest growth rates 379
Largest, by population 380
Largest population declines 379
Largest, smallest 497
Population over 1 million 378
Courts. *See* Judiciary, U.S.; World Court
CPI. *See* Consumer Price Indexes
Credit
Consumer outstanding 118
Farm 138
Glossary 132
Laws, rates 720, 721
Compound interest table 562
Prime rate 133
Mortgages 725, 726
Rating (how to check) 721
Credit cards 720, 721
Crime 213-18
Arrests 217
Assassinations 533, 573-74
Chronology (1993-94) 45, 48, 49, 51, 56, 58-59, 61, 62, 63, 64
Crime Bill (1994) 64, 71, *194*, 213
Death penalty (1890, 1977) 70, 213, 216-17, 442, 448
Index, by crime, population, region 214
Law enforcement officers 213, 215
Prison population 70, 216-17
Rates, by type, region, state 215, 217-18
Sentences versus time served 218
see also War crimes
Crimean War (1853-56) 523
Croatia 759, 848, 851
Crozet Archipelago 768
Crude oil. *See* Petroleum
Crusades 516
Cuba 759-60, 848
Area 549
Bay of Pigs (1961) 446, 530
Castro, revolution (1959) 530
Map 488
Military strength 161
Missile crisis (1962) 446, 478
Nuclear power 168
Refugee exodus (1994) 65, 67, *778*
Spanish-American War (1898) 442, 524
Cube
Volume formula 564
Curacao 549, 805
Currency, U.S. 117-18
Circulation, amount in 118
Denominations discontinued 117
Engraving, printing 672
Foreign exchange rates 122, 125
Gold Standard dropped (1933) 444
Mint 117
Money supply 133
Portraits on 117
Silver coinage 117
Current Population Survey 142
Customs, U.S. 73, 76
Exemptions, advice 721-22
U.S. receipts 107
Cycles, chronological 272
Cycling 866
Tour de France (1994) 928
Cyclones 179, 569
Cylinder
Volume formula 564
Cyprus 205, 760, 848, 851
Cy Young awards 944
Czechoslovakia 529, 533, 760-61, 851
Czech Republic 168, 760-61, 848

— D —

Dahomey. *See* Benin
Dairy products
Exports, imports 202
Nutritive value 701, 702
Prices, farm 140
Dallas, TX 676
Airport traffic 296
Buildings, tall 685
City manager 90
Commuters 210
Population 380, 414, 676
Unemployment rate 145

Dams, major 694-95
Boulder (1936) 444
Dance companies 306-7
Dates
Days between two 289
Days of week, to find 286-87
Gregorian calendar 288
History, U.S. 438-51
History, world 508-33
International line 290
Julian calendar 288
Julian period 289
Davis, Jefferson (1861) 337, 441, 464
Davis Cup (tennis) 930
Daylight Saving Time 290
Days
Between two dates 289
Holidays 291
Length of 290
Names, non-English languages 596
Dayton, OH 676
Buildings, tall 685
City manager 90
Population 381, 409, 676
D-Day 50th anniversary 37, 61, *199*
Death penalty
Crime Bill (1994) 64, 71, *194*, 213
Electrocution, first (1890) 442
Gilmore execution (1977) 448
Rates, U.S. 216-17
States with 216-17
Supreme Court rulings (1994) 70
Death records, sources 722
Deaths
Accidental 959, 964-65
AIDS 971
Aviation 566-67, 965
Cancer 970
Cardiovascular disease 970
By execution 216-17
Firearms 964, 965
Fires 570, 964, 965, 966
Infant rates 958, 959
Leading causes 959, 964
Motor vehicles 959, 964, 965
Obituaries (1993-94) 973-74
Occupational 147, 965
Presidents, U.S. (dates) 634
Rates, U.S. 957
By states, regions 958
Ship disasters 565-66
Suicides 959, 960, 965
Survivor benefits 697
United States 957, 959, 964-65
see also Accidents and disasters; Murders
Debt
Consumer 118
Farm, U.S. 138
National 109, 133
State 113
Decathlon
Olympic champions 860
World record 868
Decibel (measure) 561
Decimals 563
Declaration of Independence
Adopted (1776) 439, 453
Signers 454-55
Text 453-54
Defense, Department of 73
Employees, payroll 148
Expenditures 107
Pentagon 673
Personal salutes, honors 156
Secretaries 44, 45, 72, 73, 99
Defense, national. *See* Armed forces, U.S.; Weapons
Defense contracts 159
Deficits, U.S. budget (1993) 40, 109, 132, 451
Delaware 646-47
Abortions reported 959
Admission, area, capital 499, 646
Agriculture 134-39
Altitudes (high, low) 498
Birth, death statistics 958
Budget 113
Congressional representation 76, 79, 376
Courts, U.S. 88
Crime, prisons, death penalty 216, 217, 218
Debt 113
Energy consumption 166
Geographic center 500
Governor, state officials 93, 94-95
As immigrants' intended residence 386
Indians, American (population) 507
Interest laws, rates 720, 721
Marriage, divorce laws 727, 728
Motor vehicle statistics 207
Name origin, nickname 501, 646
Population 376-77, 379
Cities, towns 392
Counties, county seats 419-20
Density 379
Presidential elections 601, 605, 630
Schools 220, 222, 224
Taxes 113, 207, 641, 642
Unemployment benefits 142
Welfare assistance 384
Democratic Party
Chronology (1993-94) 64
Convention sites 632
Elections (by county) 602-30
Presidential, vice presidential candidates 632-33, 633
Denmark 205, 539, 761, 848
Denominations, religious 729-32, 738-39
Density
Air 270, 562
Earth 267, 269
Gases 562
Planets 267
Sun 267
Denver, CO 676
Airport traffic 296
Buildings, tall 685
Mayor 90
Population 380, 391, 676
Departments, U.S.
Employees, payroll 148
Executive personnel 72-75
Expenditures 107-8
Secretaries 44, 45, 72-75, 97-102
see also specific departments, name inverted
Depression, economic
Glossary 132
Panic (1873) 442
Stock Market crash (1929) 444, 527
Worldwide (1929-39) 527-28
Desegregation
Baseball (1947) 445
Bus boycott (1955) 445
Mississippi, University of (1962) 446
Public schools (1954) 445
Sit-ins (1960) 446
Supreme Court (1954, 1955, 1956). 445, 446
Deserts, world 556
Des Moines, IA 676
Buildings, tall 685
City manager 90
Population 381, 397, 676
De Soto, Hernando (1539) 438, 543
Detroit, MI 676
Buildings, tall 685
Commuters 210
Mayor 90
Population 380, 401, 676
Port traffic 203
Riots (1943, 1967) 444, 446-47
Unemployment rate 145
Diabetes 708-9, 710
Dice (odds) 564
Diet. *See* Nutrition
Directories. *See* Addresses
Dirigibles
Hindenburg burned (1937) 566
Notable trips 299
Disability insurance 696-700
Disabled people
Anti-discrimination act (1990) 450
Ethnic, racial distribution 382
School programs 219
Disasters. *See* Accidents and disasters
Disciples of Christ Church
Address, headquarters 730
Beliefs, practices 738-39
Membership 729
Discoveries 174-78, 349-50
Chemical elements 177-78
Drugs 176-77
Explorers 543-45
Medicine 169, 176-77
Science, technology (1994) 169
Discus throw
Olympic champions 860, 862
World records 868, 869
Diseases. *See* Health and medicine; *specific diseases*
District Courts, U.S. 87-89
District of Columbia. *See* Washington, DC
Diving
Olympic champions 863-64, 865, 866
Divorce
Laws (by states) 728
Rates, patterns 957
Djibouti 761-62, 848, 851
DNA testing 56
Doctors
Age, sex, specialty 966
Patient visits 969
Revenues 968
Documents. *See* Laws and documents
Dogs
American Kennel Club 192
Iditarod sled race 920
Westminster Kennel Club 920
Dole, Bob 33-34
Dominica 549, 762, 848
Dominican Republic 762-63
Aid, U.S. 851
Ambassadors, envoys 848
U.S. military government (1916) 443
U.S. troops (1965) 446
Dow Jones Industrial Average
Components 127
Glossary 132
Milestones 127
Record drop (1987) 449
Draft, U.S.
NYC riots (1863) 441
Peacetime, first (1940) 444
Selective Service System 75
Vietnam-era end (1973) 447
Vietnam evaders pardoned (1977) 448
Drake, Sir Francis (1579) 438, 543
Dram (measure) 557-61
Drama. *See* Theater
Dred Scott decision (1857) 441, 464, 473
Drownings 964
Drug abuse
Arrests, sentences 217, 218
Usage 963
Drugs, therapeutic
AIDS (1986) 449
Consumer protection (1906) 443
Discoveries 176-77
Most frequently prescribed 969
Duran, Francisco 68
Dutch East Indies. *See* Indonesia
Duties. *See* Customs, U.S.
Duty-free imports 721-22

— E —

Earhart, Amelia
Lost (1937) 444
Notable flights 299
Earnings. *See* Salaries and wages
Earth 269-71
Area 269
Atmosphere 270
Climate zones 270
Dimensions 269
Latitude, longitude 270
Poles 271
Rotation 271
Seasons 270-71
Solar system 267
Sun, distance from 254, 267
Time 270
Earth science 169
Earthquakes, major 572
Los Angeles (1994) 48, 51, 54, *196*
San Francisco (1906, 1989) 443, 449-50, 572
East China Sea 552
Eastern Atoll 671
Eastern Europe 533
see also specific countries
Eastern Orthodox churches
Addresses, U.S. headquarters 730, 731
Beliefs, practices 738-39
Church calendar 732
Membership 729, 730
Russian church established 517
Easter Sunday 732, 733
East Germany. *See* Germany
EC. *See* European Community
Eclipse Awards 900
Eclipses 266, 273
Ecology. *See* Environment
Economic indicators, leading
Chronology (1993-94) 41, 44, 48, 51, 54, 56, 59, 61, 64
Glossary 132
Index 111
Economics 107-33
Banking statistics 114-16
Bankruptcy 112
Budget, U.S. 107-8
Business leaders, notable 351-52
Chronology (1993-94) 41, 44, 46, 48-49, 51, 54, 56, 59, 61, 64, 66, 68
Consumer credit 118
Consumer Price Indexes 109-11
Depressions (1873, 1929-39) 442, 444, 527-28
Dow Jones Average 127, 132
Economists, notable 348-49
(continued)

Economics *(continued)*
GDP, GNP . . . 111, 112
Glossary of terms . . . 132-33
Gold reserves . . . 125, 129
Income, national . . . 111, 124
Investments abroad . . . 125
Nobel Prizes . . . 70, 316
Reagan boom (1980s) . . . 533
State finances . . . 113
Stocks, bonds . . . 126-28
U.S. net receipts . . . 107, 108
World Bank . . . 847
see also Stocks
Ecuador . . . 763, 848, 851
Edison, Thomas A. . . . 350, 442
National historic site (NJ) . . . 504
Education . . . 219-50
Attainment
Annual earnings correlate . . . 149
By labor force status, occupation . . 145
Awards . . . 326
Black enrollment . . . 219, 221, 223
Computers, technology in schools . 35-36, 221
Day schools, full-time . . . 220
Desegregation, Supreme Court rulings (1954, 1955, 1956) . . . 445, 446
Disabled, programs for the . . . 219
Educators, notable . . . 347-48
Enrollment . . . 219, 220
Elementary, high schools . . . 219
Preprimary schools . . . 219
Public, private schools . . . 219
Food program costs . . . 136
Graduates, high school . . . 220, 221, 373
Historical summary (1909-92) . . . 219
Revenues, public schools . . . 222
SAT, ACT scores . . . 223-24
School prayer ban (1963, 1984) . 446, 449
Spending per student . . . 220, 373
see also Colleges and universities
Education, Department of . . . 75
Employees, payroll . . . 148
Expenditures . . . 107
Secretaries . . . 72, 75, 102
EEC. *See* European Community
EEOC. *See* Equal Employment Opportunity Commission
EFTA. *See* European Free Trade Association
Eggs
Exports, imports . . . 202
Nutritive value . . . 701, 702
Prices
Farm . . . 140
Per dozen, by state . . . 135
Production, by state . . . 135
Egypt . . . 763-64
Aid, U.S. . . . 851
Ambassadors, envoys . . . 848
Ancient . . . 509, 511
Seven Wonders . . . 512
Aswan Dam . . . 695, 764
Distances to ports . . . 204
Middle Ages . . . 512
Military strength . . . 161
Nasser, Gamal Abdel . . . 338, 764
Sadat, Anwar al- . . . 339, 764
Assassinated (1981) . . . 533, 573
Eisenhower, Dwight D. . . 631, 632, 634, 635
Biography . . . 477
Burial site . . . 480
Cabinet . . . 97-102
Popular, electoral votes . . . 633
Elba . . . 522, 549, 789
Elderly (over 65)
Living arrangements . . . 961
Medicare enacted . . . 446, 698, 712
Social Security . . . 696-700
Election Day . . . 291
Elections, U.S. . . . 33-34
Chronology (1993-94) . . . 41-42, 46, 66, 68, *197*
Congressional (1994) . . . 76-84
Gubernatorial (1994) . . . 94
Presidential
Electoral College . . . 632
Official results (1992) . . . 631
Party nominees (1844-92) . . . 632-33
Popular, electoral vote (1789-1992) . . . 601-30, 633
Voter participation
By age (1992) . . . 631
Characteristics (1992) . . . 631-32
Population percentage (1932-92) . 631
Voting rights
Act signed, interpreted (1965, 1994) . . . 70, 446
Black males (1870) . . . 462
18-year-olds (1971) . . . 447, 463
Motor-voter bill (1993) . . . 71, 451
Turnout (1932-92) . . . 631
Washington (DC) residents (1961) . . . 463, 668
Women (1869, 1920) . . . 442, 443, 462
Electoral College . . . 632
Apportionment . . . 376
Constitution on . . . 457-58, 461
Map . . . 630
Electrical appliance use . . . 166
Electric power
Blackout, northeastern U.S. (1965) . . . 446
Hydroelectric plants . . . 694
Nuclear plants . . . 168
Production, consumption . . . 164, 166, 167
Units measurements . . . 561
Elements, chemical . . . 177-78
Elevations, continental . . . 546-48
Elizabeth II, Queen (UK) . . . 198, 535, 830
Ellice Islands. *See* Tuvalu
Ellis Island (NYC) . . . 470
El Paso, TX . . . 676
Mayor . . . 90
Population . . . 380, 414, 676
El Salvador . . . 764, 848, 851
Em (measure) . . . 561
Emancipation Proclamation (1863) . . . 441
Emigration. *See* Immigration, emigration; *specific countries*
Emmy Awards . . . 325
Empire State Building (NYC)
Height . . . 687
Opened (1931) . . . 444
Employment . . . 142-54
Agricultural . . . 134, 143, 145
Benefit programs . . . 144, 151
By cities (selected) . . . 674-83
Commuters . . . 210
Current Population Survey . . . 142
Earnings . . . 150, 151, 152
By educational attainment . . . 145
Employer costs . . . 151
Family and Medical Leave Act (1993) . . . 71, 451
Full . . . 132
Government . . . 71, 148
Immigration based on . . . 842-43
Insurance . . . 142, 144
Military . . . 158, 159, 160
By nation (*see specific country*)
Occupational injuries, fatalities . . 147, 965
Occupations . . . 143, 145, 146, 373
Population percentage . . . 373
Rates . . . 143
Social Security benefits . . . 696-700
Supreme Court rulings (1993, 1994) . . 70
Training services, wage . . . 144
Unemployment . . . 142, 143, 144, 145
Women . . . 143, 145, 149, 150, 152, 961
see also Labor unions; Salaries and wages
Endangered species . . . 188, 189
Endeavour (space shuttle) (1993) . . . 43-44, 294, 451
Energy . . . 164-68
Consumption . . . 164, 165, 166
Exports, imports . . . 164, 165
Production . . . 164, 165, 167
see also specific countries, sources, types
Energy, Department of . . . 74
Employees, payroll . . . 148
Expenditures . . . 107
Nuclear radiation testing (1993) . . 44, 451
Secretaries . . . 72, 74, 102
England
History . . . 518, 520, 521, 831
Poets Laureate . . . 341
Prime ministers . . . 536
Rulers . . . 534-35
see also United Kingdom
English Channel Tunnel . . . 59, *198*, 694
Engraving and Printing, Bureau of . . 73, 672
Enlightenment (18th century) . . . 520
Entertainers
Awards . . . 325, 327-30
Birthplaces, birth dates . . . 357-70
Death and birth dates . . . 367-70
Original names . . . 370-72
see also Actors, actresses
Environment . . . 187-92
Endangered species . . . 188, 189
Hazardous waste sites . . . 187
Legislation (1994) . . . 71
Supreme Court rulings (1994) . . . 70
Toxic chemical releases . . . 187
Environmental Protection Agency . . . 75
Employees, payroll . . . 148
Expenditures . . . 107
Second-hand smoke warning . . . 46
Envoys. *See* Ambassadors and envoys
EPA. *See* Environmental Protection Agency
Ephemeris time . . . 270
Epiphany . . . 732
Episcopal Church
Address, headquarters . . . 730
Beliefs, practices . . . 738-39
Calendar, fast days . . . 732
Church of England . . . 53-54, 831
Membership . . . 729
Eponyms . . . 592
Equal Employment Opportunity Commission . . . 75, 108, 148
Equal Rights Amendment (1972, 1982) . . . 447, 448
Equatorial Guinea . . . 764-65, 848
Equestrian sports . . . 866
Equinoxes (1995) . . . 252, 253, 260, 271
ERA. *See* Equal Rights Amendment
Eras, chronological (1995) . . . 272
Erie, Lake . . . 555
Erie Canal (1825) . . . 440
Eriksson, Leif . . . 516
Eritrea . . . 765, 848, 851
Eskimos . . . 375
Esperanto . . . 599
Estate taxes. *See* Inheritance taxes
Estonia . . . 765, 848
Ethiopia . . . 765-66
Aid, U.S. . . . 851
Ambassadors, envoys . . . 848
History . . . 532
Italian war (1935-37) . . . 528, 789
Kingdoms . . . 515, 517
Ethnic, racial distribution (U.S.) 382, 437, 507
Disabled people . . . 382
Etna, Mt. . . . 546, 789
Europe
Area . . . 839
Highest, lowest points . . . 556
Islands . . . 549
Lakes . . . 555
Languages . . . 598-99
Map . . . 490
Mountain peaks . . . 547-48
Population . . . 839, 840-41
Religions . . . 731
Rivers . . . 553
Rulers . . . 534-41
Trade, U.S. . . . 201
Volcanoes . . . 545, 546
Waterfalls . . . 556
see also specific countries
European Community . . . 42, 201, 530, 532, 533, 844
European Free Trade Association . . . 201, 530, 532, 844
Evangelical churches . . . 532, 729, 730
Evening stars (1995) . . . 272
Events and anniversaries. *See* Anniversaries; Chronology of 1993-94
Everest, Mt. . . . 512, 546, 548
Everglades National Park (FL) . . . 503, 647
Evolution theory . . . 523
Exchange rates, foreign . . . 122, 125
Executions, U.S. *See* Death penalty
Executive agencies, U.S. . . . 72
Executive Office of the President . . 72, 107
Exercise
Heart rate . . . 701
Expenditures, federal . . . 107-8
Explorations, expeditions
Antarctic . . . 544-45
Arctic . . . 543-44
European . . . 518, 520
Major explorers (1497-1906) . . . 543-44
Space . . . 292-95
Explosions . . . 570-71
Exports, imports . . . 201-3
Agricultural . . . 137, 141, 202
Automobiles . . . 202, 203
Balance of trade . . . 123, 132, 201, 202, 533
Coal, coke . . . 202
Commodities . . . 202
Energy . . . 164, 165
GATT . . . 43, 45, 205, 530, 847
International transactions, U.S. . . . 123
Manufactures . . . 202
Merchant fleets . . . 205
NAFTA (1993) . . . 42-43, 44, 71, 204, 451
Petroleum . . . 164, 165, 202
Value . . . 202
Express Mail . . . 587

— F —

FAA. *See* Federal Aviation Administration
Faeroe Islands . . . 549, 761
Fahrenheit scale . . . 562
Falkland Islands . . . 549, 832-33
Families . . . 960
Blended . . . 962

Child care 374, 961
Child support 374
Immigrant preference system 842-43
Living arrangements 960, 961, 962
One-parent 960, 961
Poverty level 383
Profile, 1993 960
Unmarried couples 960, 962
Welfare assistance 384
see also Households
Family and Medical Leave Act (1993) 71, 451
FAO. *See* Food and Agriculture Organization
Farms. *See* Agriculture
Fastest trips
Air travel 298-99
Train, passenger 206
Fathom (measurement) 558
Fats and oils 701, 702
Labels, nutrition 704
FBI. *See* Federal Bureau of Investigation
FCC. *See* Federal Communications Commission
FDIC. *See* Federal Deposit Insurance Corporation
Federal agencies
Budget receipts, outlays 107-8
Civilian employment 148
Political activities legislation (1993) . . 71
Directory 75-76
see also specific agencies
Federal Aviation Administration . . . 74, 76, 107
Federal Bureau of Investigation
Directors 73
Expenditures 107
Headquarters 76, 672
Federal Communications Commission . . 75, 108
Federal Deposit Insurance Corporation . . 75, 108, 115
Employees, payroll 148
Glossary 132
Federal government. *See* Government, U.S.
Federal Reserve System 75, 116
Discount rate 115-16
Formed (1913) 443
Glossary 132
Federal taxes. *See* Taxes, federal
Federal Trade Commission 75, 108
Fencing 866
Fertility rate 957
Fiber
Labels, nutrition 704
Field hockey 867
Figure skating. *See* Skating
Fiji 549, 766, 848, 851
Fillmore, Millard 634, 635
Biography 473
Burial site 480
Cabinet 98-101
Films. *See* Movies
Finance. *See* Banks; Business; Economics; Stocks
Finland 766
Aid, U.S. 851
Ambassadors, envoys 848
Nuclear power 167, 168
Trade 201
World War II 529
Firearms
Crime Bill (1994) 64, 71, 194, 213
Deaths involving 964, 965
Gun control legislation (1993-94) . . 42, 71, 213, 451
Gun gauge, caliber 561
Rifle, pistol champions (1994) 925
Fires
Chicago, IL (1871) 442, 570
Deaths 570, 964, 965, 966
Major 41, 63-64, 570
Property loss 966
First aid 706
First ladies 480
Clinton, Hillary Rodham 194, 480
Onassis, Jacqueline Kennedy (1994) . 59, 200, 974
Fish and fishing
Exports, imports 202
Game fish records 921-22
Nutritive value 701, 702
see also specific countries
Flags
Confederacy 464
United States 466-68
Display 467-68
History 466-67
Pledge to 468
21-gun-salute to 156
World (color) 481-84
Flaxseed production 139
Fleets, merchant 205
Flights. *See* Aviation
Floods
Characteristics 179
Georgia (1994) 63
Johnstown (PA) (1889) 442
Mississippi R. region
Great Flood (1993) 451, 569
Historic 185
Worldwide 569
Florida 647
Abortions reported 959
Accession (1819) 440, 502, 647
Admission, area, capital . . . 499, 500, 647
Agriculture 134-39
Altitudes (high, low) 498
Birth, death statistics 958
Budget 113
Cities 677, 678, 679, 682, 683
Congressional representation . 76, 79, 376
Courts, U.S. 88
Crime, prisons, death penalty . 216, 217, 218
Debt 113
Energy consumption 166
Geographic center 500
Governor, state officials 93, 95
As immigrants' intended residence . . . 386
Indians, American (population) 507
Interest laws, rates 720, 721
Marriage, divorce laws 727, 728
Mineral production 129
Motor vehicle statistics 207
Name origin, nickname 501, 647
Population 376-77, 379
Cities, towns 392-94, 677, 678, 679, 682, 683
Counties, county seats 420
Density 379
Port traffic 203
Presidential elections . . . 601, 605-6, 630
Schools 220, 222, 224
Taxes 113, 207, 641
Territory 500, 502
Unemployment benefits 142
Welfare assistance 384
Fluid measures 557, 558, 559, 561, 562
Folger Shakespeare Library (DC) 672
Food 701-5
Exports, imports 202
Federal assistance programs . . . 107, 136
Labels, nutrition 704
Nutritive values 701-5
Dietary allowances 701, 705
Price indexes 109, 110
Production (world) 141
Pure Food and Drug Act (1906) 443
Food and Agriculture Organization (UN) 847
Food stamp program 107, 136
Football, Canadian 881
Football, college 882-89
Bowl games 882-84
Coaching 888
Conference champions 889
Heisman Trophy 887
National champions 888
Outland Award 887
Teams, Division I 885-87
Winning percentage leaders 888
Winning streaks 889
Football, pro 870-80
Addresses, teams 905
All-time records 879-80
All-time team 880
Bert Bell trophy 877
Champions 870-72
Expansion teams 870
George Halas Trophy 877
Hall of Fame 878
Head coaches (1994) 872
Jim Thorpe Trophy 877
Player draft (1993) 878
Stadiums 880
Standings, final (1993) 870
Statistical leaders (1993) 876-77
Statistical leaders (by years) 874-75
Super Bowl 48, 782, 873
Force, pressure measures 564
Ford, Gerald R. 631, 634, 635
Biography 478
Cabinet 97-102
Popular, electoral votes 633
Foreign aid, U.S.
By country 851
Truman Doctrine (1947) . . . 445, 477, 529
Foreign investment
By U.S. abroad 125
In U.S. companies 123
Foreign trade. *See* Exports, imports
Foreign words, phrases 593
Forests
Giant trees (U.S.) 190
Forgery 217
Forms of address 597
Formulas, mathematical 564
Fort Wayne, IN 676
Buildings, tall 686
Mayor 90
Population 381
Fort Worth, TX 676-77
Buildings, tall 686
City manager 90
Population 380, 414, 676
Foster, Vincent 44, 51, 59, 64, 451
Four Freedoms (1941) 444, 477
Fractions-to-decimals reduction 563
France 767-68
Ambassadors, envoys 848
Departments, overseas 767
English Channel Tunnel . . . 59, 198, 694
Gold reserves 125
History 518, 520, 521, 522, 524, 528, 532, 533
French and Indian War (1754-63) . . 438
French Revolution (1789) 521, 522
New World settlements (1699) . . . 438
Merchant fleet 205
Military strength 161
Nuclear power 167, 168
Rulers 520, 521, 536-37
Territories 768
Trade 201
Franchises 121
Franconia, House of 538
Franklin, Benjamin 337
Almanac (1732) 438
Declaration of Independence (1776) . . 453, 454
Kite experiment (1752) 438
Freedom Statue (U.S. Capitol) 672
Freezing point, water 562
Freight statistics
Air cargo 296
Merchant marine 205
Fremont, CA 381, 677
Fremont, John C. (1856) 441
French Antarctica 768
French Guiana 767
French and Indian War (1754-63) 438
French Open (tennis) 931
French Polynesia 768
French Revolution (1789) 521, 522
Fresno, CA 677
City manager 90
Population 381, 389, 677
Friends, Society of (Quakers) . . . 729, 730
Fruits
Exports, imports 202
Nutritive values 701, 702
Prices, farm 140
Production 139
FTC. *See* Federal Trade Commission
Fuel. *See* Energy; *specific kinds*
Fulton, Robert (1807) 440
Futuna-Alofi Island 768
Futures contract 133

— G —

Gabon 201, 768, 848
Gadsden Purchase (1853) 473, 502
Galapagos Islands 549, 763
Galileo 519, 520
Gambia 768-69, 848, 851
Gambier Islands 768
Gandhi, Indira 533, 573, 776
Gandhi, Mohandas 528, 529, 573, 776
GAO. *See* General Accounting Office
Garfield, James A. 632, 634
Assassinated (1881) 442, 474, 573
Biography 474
Burial site 480
Cabinet 98-101
Popular, electoral votes 633
Garland, TX 90, 381, 677
Gas, natural. *See* Natural gas
Gas appliance use 166
Gases (densities) 562
Gasoline
Arab embargo (1973) 447
Automobile consumption 207, 210
Prices retail 167
Taxes (by state) 207
GATT. *See* General Agreement on Tariffs and Trade
Gauge (measure) 561
Gays. *See* Homosexuality
GDP. *See* Gross Domestic Product
General Accounting Office 76, 148
General Agreement on Tariffs and Trade 43, 45, 205, 530, 847

Generals, U.S. 155
Address, form of 597
Insignia 157
Pay scale 162
Personal salutes, honors 156
Women, first (1970) 447
General Services Administration 75, 107, 148
Genetic fingerprinting 56
Geneva Conventions 847
Genghis Khan 517
Geodetic datum point 497
Geography 497-502, 543-49
Geographic centers, U.S. 500
International boundary lines, U.S. 500
Superlative statistics, U.S. 497
George Halas Trophy 877
George Washington Bridge (NY-NJ) 690
Georgia 647-48
Abortions reported 959
Admission, area, capital 499, 647
Agriculture 134-39
Altitudes (high, low) 498
Birth, death statistics 958
Budget 113
Cities 674, 676
Congressional representation 76, 79, 376
Courts, U.S. 88
Crime, prisons, death penalty 216, 217, 218
Debt 113
Energy consumption 166
Floods (1994) 63
Geographic center 500
Governor, state officials 93, 95
As immigrants' intended residence 386
Indians, American (population) 507
Interest laws, rates 720, 721
Marriage, divorce laws 727, 728
Mineral production 129
Motor vehicle statistics 207
Name origin, nickname 501, 647
Population 376-77, 379
Cities, towns 394-95, 674, 676
Counties, county seats 420-21
Density 379
Port traffic 203
Presidential elections 601, 606-7, 630
Schools 220, 222, 224
Taxes 113, 207, 641
Unemployment benefits 142
Welfare assistance 384
Georgia, Republic of 47, 50, 769, 848
Germany 769-70
Ambassadors, envoys 848
Chronology (1993-94) 63, 69
Gold reserves 125
History 516, 518, 521, 522, 523, 528, 533
Munich Olympics (1972) 532
Riots, East Germany (1953) 530
Merchant fleet 205
Military strength 161
Nuclear power 167, 168
Reunification (1990) 770
Rulers 516, 518, 537-38, 770
Submarine warfare (1917) 443, 526
Third Reich (Nazi) 528, 529, 538, 770
Surrender (1945) 445
Trade 201, 769
Weimar Republic 527, 770
see also Berlin, Germany
Gestation, incubation 189
Gettysburg Address (1863) 441, 464
Ghana 770-71
Aid, U.S. 851
Ambassadors, envoys 848
Gold production 131
History 515
GI Bill of Rights (1944) 444
Gibraltar 832
Gift taxes 640
Gingrich, Newt 33-34
Girl Scouts
Address 579
Founded (1912) 443
Glendale, CA 90, 381, 677
Glenn, John H., Jr. (1962) 292, 297, 446
Gliders (1993 records) 298
GNP. *See* Gross National Product
Gold
Black Friday (1869) 442
Carats in pure 561
Discovered, U.S. (1835, 1848) 440, 441
Production 129, 130, 131
Reserves 125, 129
Golden Gate Bridge (CA) 690
Golf 923-25
Good Friday 291, 732
Gorbachev, Mikhail 532, 542, 814
Nobel Peace Prize 316
Summit talks (1985, 1987) 162, 449, 533
Gore, Albert, Jr. (1992, 1993) 35-36, 43, 72, *198*, 450
Government, U.S. 72-89
Agencies 75-76, 107-8, 148
Branches 72
Clinton administration 44, 59-60, 66, 72-75
Publications 712-13
Revenue and expenditures 107-8
Governors, state 93-97
Address, form of 597
Black (1989) 334, 450
First women (1924) 444
Grains
Exports, imports 141, 202
Nutritive value 701, 702-3
Production, U.S. 138, 139, 141
Production, world (by country) 141
Storage capacities 140
Grammy Awards 329-30
Grand Canyon (AZ) 503, 512, 644
Grand Coulee Dam 695
Grand Rapids, MI 90, 381, 677
Grant, Ulysses S. 632, 634
Biography 474
Burial site 480
Cabinet 98-101
Popular, electoral votes 633
Gravity
Atmosphere, effect on 270
Planets (relative) 267
Great Barrier Reef 512
Great Britain. *See* United Kingdom
Great Lakes 555
Great Seal of the U.S. 466
Great White Fleet (1907) 443
Greece 771-72
Aid, U.S. 851
Ambassadors, envoys 848
History 532
Merchant fleet 205
Greece, ancient
City-states 509
Hellenistic Era 511, 513
Leading figures 534
Measures 562
Minoan civilization 509
Philosophers 509
Seven Wonders 512
Greek Orthodox Church. *See* Eastern Orthodox churches
Greenland 516, 549, 761
Greensboro, NC 381, 677
Greenwich meridian 290
Greenwich sidereal time (1995) 259
Gregorian calendar 288
Grenada 772
Ambassadors, envoys 848
Invasion (1983) 449, 533, 772
Grenadines 815, 849
Grey Cup 881
Gross Domestic Product, U.S. 111, 112, 132
Gross National Product, U.S. 111
Group of Seven (G-7) 63, 844
Guadalcanal 549
Battle for (1942) 444, 529
Guadeloupe 549, 767
Guam 669
Accession 502
Altitudes (high, low) 498
Area 502, 549
Congressional delegate 84
Courts 89
As immigrants' intended residence 386
Population 436
Guatemala 772, 848, 851
Guernsey 832
Guiana, French 767
Guinea, Republic of 772-73, 848, 851
Guinea-Bissau 773, 848, 851
Gulf Coast
Length 498
Gulfs 552
Gulf War. *See* Persian Gulf War
Guns. *See* Firearms
Guyana 773, 848, 851
Gymnastics
Olympic champions (1992) 867
Rhythmic 867
World championship (1994) 928

— H —

Haiti 773-74
Aid, U.S. 851
Ambassadors, envoys 848
Chronology (1993-94) 40, 58, 60, 62, 65, 67, *193*
Map 488
U.S. occupation (1915-34) 443, 444
Halas Trophy 877
Haldeman, H. R. (1973, 1975) 447, 448, 973
Hale, Nathan (1776) 439
Hall of Fame
Aviation 297
Baseball 659, 952
Basketball 914
Bowling 901
Football, pro 878
Women's 372
Hambletonian 901
Hammer throw
Olympic champions 860
World record 868
Hammurabi 508
Handball 867
Hanover, House of 535
Hapsburg dynasty 518, 523, 538
Harbors. *See* Ports
Harding, Warren G. 632, 634, 635
Biography 476
Burial site 480
Cabinet 98-101
Popular, electoral votes 633
Harness racing 901
Harrison, Benjamin 632, 634
Biography 475
Burial site 480
Cabinet 98-101
Popular, electoral votes 633
Harrison, William Henry 634
Biography 472
Burial site 480
Cabinet 98-100
Popular, electoral votes 633
Tippecanoe (1811) 440
Hartford, CT 686
Hart Memorial Trophy 897
Harvest moon 269
Hawaii 648
Abortions reported 959
Accession (1898) 442, 502
Admission, area, capital (1959) 446, 499, 500, 648
Agriculture 134-39
Altitudes (high, low) 498
Area 549
Birth, death statistics 958
Budget 113
Cities 677
Congressional representation 76, 79, 376
Courts, U.S. 88
Crime, prisons, death penalty 217, 218
Debt 113
Energy consumption 166
Geographic center 500
Governor, state officials 93, 95
As immigrants' intended residence 386
Indians, American (population) 507
Interest laws, rates 720, 721
Marriage, divorce laws 727, 728
Motor vehicle statistics 207
Name origin, nickname 501, 648
Population 376-77, 379
Cities, towns 395, 677
Counties, county seats 421
Density 379
Presidential elections 601, 607, 630
Schools 220, 222, 224
Taxes 113, 207, 641, 642
Unemployment benefits 142
Volcanoes 546
Waterfalls 556
Welfare assistance 384
Wettest spot, U.S. 181
Hayes, Rutherford B. 632, 634
Biography 474
Burial site 480
Cabinet 98-101
Popular, electoral votes 633
Hay production 138, 139, 140
Hazardous waste sites 187
H-Bomb. *See* Hydrogen bomb
Health-care reform 38-39, *195*
Chronology 46, 49, 61, 64, 66
Health and Human Services, Department of 74
Employees, payroll 148
Expenditures 107
Secretaries 72, 74, 102
Surgeon General 76
see also Social Security Administration
Health insurance
Coverage 373, 967
Disability benefits 696-700
Medicare (1966) 446, 698, 712
Reform efforts (1993, 1994) 38-39, 49, 61, 64, 66-67, 195, 451
Health and medicine 701-11
AIDS (1986, 1994) 53, 449, 842, 971
Anesthesia (1842) 441
Black Death 518
Cancer 67, 169, 705, 708, 712, 970

Diabetes . . . 708-9
Disabled people . . . 382
Discoveries . . . 169, 176-77
Doctor-office visits . . . 969
Doctors . . . 966
Drug abuse . . . 963
Emergency room visits . . . 969
Ethics, terminally ill . . . 709
Expenditures . . . 968
Family and Medical Leave Act (1993) . 71, 451
First aid . . . 706
Heart, blood vessels . . . 707
Artificial implant (1982) . . . 448
Diabetes . . . 709
Rate targets . . . 701
Help organizations . . . 710-11
Immunization . . . 707
Influenza (1918) . . . 443
Legionnaires' disease (1976) . . . 448
Life expectancy . . . 972
Medical discoveries . . . 169, 176-77
Nobel Prizes . . . 70, 315
Nursing school, first (1873) . . . 442
Occupational injuries, fatalities . 147, 965
Price Indexes . . . 109, 110
Revenue . . . 968
Smoking risk reduction . . . 705
see also Deaths
Heart disease . . . 707, 709, 970
Heart rate . . . 701
Heat Index . . . 186
Hebrews. *See* Judaism
Hebrides . . . 832
Height, weight (average adult, child) . 705, 972
Heisman Trophy . . . 887
Helgoland . . . 770
Helicopters (1993 records) . . . 298
Henry, Patrick (1775) . . . 439, 452
Heptathlon . . . 861, 869
Herzegovina. *See* Bosnia and Herzegovina
Hialeah, FL . . . 381, 677
Hieroglyphic writing . . . 509
High jump
Olympic champions . . . 859, 861-62
World indoor, outdoor records . . 868, 869
High schools
Commputer, technology usage . 35-36, 221
Drug usage . . . 963
Enrollment . . . 219
Graduates . . . 219, 220, 221
Revenues, public schools . . . 222
Test scores . . . 223-24
Highways. *See* Roads
Himalayas . . . 546, 548
Hindenburg (dirigible) . . . 299, 566
Hinduism
Adherents, U.S. . . . 729
Beliefs, practices . . . 737
India . . . 532
Population, world . . . 731
Hiroshima bombing (1945) . . . 445, 529
Hispanics
Disabled people . . . 382
Education . . . 219, 221
Employment, unemployment . . . 145
Households . . . 960, 961, 962
Population . . . 375
Poverty rates . . . 383
Salaries and wages . . . 149, 150
Hiss, Alger (1948) . . . 445
Historic sites, national . . . 504-5
History
Anniversaries . . . 105-6
Historians, notable . . . 348-49
Leading figures . . . 534-42
Parks, National . . . 503-6
Pulitzer Prizes . . . 321-22
U.S. . . . 438-51
World . . . 508-33
Hitler, Adolf . . . 338, 528, 538, 770
Hockey, field . . . 867
Hockey, ice . . . 890-97
Addresses, teams . . . 904-5
Goals (by season) . . . 897
Individual leaders . . . 891, 895
NCAA champions . . . 897
1994-95 season postponed . . . 69
Olympic champions . . . 853
Stanley Cup . . . *782*, 890
Trophy winners . . . 895-97
Hog production . . . 134, 135, 140
Holidays
Foreign, selected . . . 291
Legal, public (U.S.) . . . 291
Flag display . . . 467
Religious . . . 732-33
Holland. *See* Netherlands
Holocaust Memorial Museum . . . 672
Holy days . . . 732-33
Holy Roman Empire . . . 516
Home-accident deaths . . . 965
Homes. *See* Housing
Homestead Act (1862) . . . 441
Homosexuality
Chronology . . . 42, 44, 61, 68
Colorado rights ban (1993) . . . 44
Military conduct (1993) . . . 42, 451
Rights march (1993) . . . 451
Stonewall anniversary (1994) . . . 61
Honduras . . . 774, 848, 851
Honduras, British. *See* Belize
Hong Kong . . . 205, 549, 833, 840
Honolulu, HI . . . 677
Buildings, tall . . . 686
Mayor . . . 91
Population . . . 381, 395, 677
Hoover, Herbert . . . 631, 632, 634, 635
Biography . . . 476-77
Burial site . . . 480
Cabinet . . . 98-101
Popular, electoral votes . . . 633
Hoover Dam . . . 694, 695
Horsepower . . . 561
Horse racing
American thoroughbred . . . 898-901
Belmont Stakes . . . 899
Breeders' Cup . . . 900
Eclipse awards (1993) . . . 900
Horses of Year . . . 901
Jockey, annual leading . . . 899
Kentucky Derby . . . 898
Preakness . . . 898-99
Triple Crown winners . . . 898
Trotting, pacing . . . 901
see also Equestrian sports
Hospital Insurance Trust Fund . . . 700
Household furnishings
Appliances in use . . . 166
Price index . . . 109, 110
Households
Average number in . . . 373
Composition of . . . 960, 961, 962
Housing units . . . 373
Median net worth . . . 384
Non-English-speaking Americans . 599-600
Population (by type) . . . 378
Poverty level . . . 383
Single-parent . . . 960, 961
Single-person . . . 960, 961
Unmarried-couple . . . 960, 962
House of Representatives. *See* Congress, U.S.
Housing
Homeowners . . . 373
Mortgages . . . 373, 725, 726
Price Indexes . . . 109, 110
Prices . . . 373, 726
Rental . . . 373
Units . . . 373
Housing and Urban Development, Department of . . . 74
Employees, payroll . . . 148
Expenditures . . . 107
Scandal (1993, 1994) . . . 40, 49
Secretaries . . . 72, 74, 102
Houston, TX . . . 677
Buildings, tall . . . 686
Commuters . . . 210
Mayor . . . 91
Population . . . 380, 414, 677
Port traffic . . . 203
Unemployment rate . . . 145
Howland Island . . . 671
Hubble Space Telescope (1993, 1994) . . . 43-44, 63, 169, *198*, 294, 451
HUD. *See* Housing and Urban Development, Department of
Hudson, Henry (1609) . . . 438, 543
Hudson Bay . . . 552
Hudson River . . . 553
Hundred Years' War (1338-1453) . . . 518
Hungary . . . 774-75
Aid, U.S. . . . 851
Ambassadors, envoys . . . 848
Chronology (1993-94) . . . 60
History . . . 516, 518, 519, 527, 533
Nuclear power . . . 167, 168
Revolt (1956) . . . 530
Rulers . . . 538
Hunter's moon . . . 269
Huntington Beach, CA . . . 677
Mayor . . . 91
Population . . . 381, 389, 677
Huon Islands . . . 768
Huron, Lake . . . 555
Hurricanes . . . 569
Characteristics . . . 179
Names of (1995) . . . 185
Hussein, Saddam . . . 786
Hussein I . . . *779*, 790
Hydroelectric plants . . . 164, 694
Hydrogen bomb (1950, 1952) . . . 445, 530
see also Nuclear arms

— I —

IAEA. *See* International Atomic Energy Agency
Ibiza . . . 821
IBM
Sales (1993) . . . 120
ICAO. *See* International Civil Aviation Organization
ICC. *See* Interstate Commerce Commission
Ice hockey. *See* Hockey, ice
Iceland . . . 516, 775, 848
Ice skating. *See* Skating
IDA. *See* International Development Association
Idaho . . . 648-49
Abortions reported . . . 959
Admission, area, capital . . . 499, 500, 648
Agriculture . . . 134-39
Altitudes (high, low) . . . 498
Birth, death statistics . . . 958
Budget . . . 113
Congressional representation . 76, 79, 376
Courts, U.S. . . . 88
Crime, prisons, death penalty . . . 217, 218
Debt . . . 113
Energy consumption . . . 166
Geographic center . . . 500
Governor, state officials . . . 93, 95
As immigrants' intended residence . . 386
Indians, American (population) . . . 507
Interest laws, rates . . . 720, 721
Marriage, divorce laws . . . 727, 728
Motor vehicle statistics . . . 207
Name origin, nickname . . . 501, 648
Population . . . 376-77, 379
Cities, towns . . . 395
Counties, county seats . . . 421
Density . . . 379
Presidential elections . . . 601, 607-8, 630
Schools . . . 220, 222, 224
Taxes . . . 113, 207, 641, 642
Unemployment benefits . . . 142
Welfare assistance . . . 384
Idioms
Foreign . . . 595
Meanings, derivations . . . 596
Iditarod sled race . . . 920
IFC. *See* International Finance Corporation
Illinois . . . 649
Abortions reported . . . 959
Admission, area, capital . . . 499, 500, 649
Agriculture . . . 134-39
Altitudes (high, low) . . . 498
Birth, death statistics . . . 958
Budget . . . 113
Cities . . . 675
Congressional representation . . 76, 79-80, 376
Courts, U.S. . . . 88
Crime, prisons, death penalty . . 216, 217, 218
Debt . . . 113
Energy consumption . . . 166
Geographic center . . . 500
Governor, state officials . . . 93, 95
As immigrants' intended residence . . 386
Indians, American (population) . . . 507
Interest laws, rates . . . 720, 721
Marriage, divorce laws . . . 727, 728
Motor vehicle statistics . . . 207
Name origin, nickname . . . 501, 649
Population . . . 376-77, 379
Cities, towns . . . 395-96, 675
Counties, county seats . . . 421-22
Density . . . 79
Port traffic . . . 203
Presidential elections . . . 601, 608, 630
Schools . . . 220, 222, 224
Taxes . . . 113, 207, 641, 642
Unemployment benefits . . . 142
Welfare assistance . . . 384
ILO. *See* International Labor Organization
IMF. *See* International Monetary Fund
Immigration Act (1990) . . . 842-43
Immigration and Naturalization Act (1952) . . . 445
Immigration, emigration
Ellis Island (1892) . . . 442, 470
Illegal aliens amnesty (1988) . . . 449
Immigrants admitted
Country of origin . . . 386
Intended residence area . . . 385
By type, admission class . . . 385
Naturalization . . . 843

(continued)

Immigration, emigration *(continued)*
Non-English-speaking Americans . 599, 600
Quota system (1921, 1965) . . . 443, 446
Regulations, U.S. . . . 842-43
Immunization schedule . . . 707
IMO. *See* International Maritime Organization
Impeachment
Articles of . . . 456, 458
Johnson, Andrew (1868) . . . 442, 474
Nixon hearings (1974) . . . 447-48, 478
Imports. *See* Exports, imports
Incomes
Distribution . . . 124, 383
Educational level correlate . . . 373
Farm . . . 124, 137
Glossary . . . 132, 133
Minimum wage
Enacted (1938) . . . 444
Hourly rates (1950-1991) . . . 151
Increased (1989) . . . 450
National, U.S. . . . 111, 124
Pay differential, male/female . . . 149
Per capita income
Defined . . . 133
By foreign countries . . . 740-839
By U.S. states . . . 643-68
Personal, U.S. . . . 111
Distribution of total . . . 124
Poverty rate . . . 374, 383
Wage, salary workers . . . 150, 152
Welfare, by states . . . 384
Income taxes . . . 636-42
Federal . . . 636-40
Amendment authorizing . . . 462
Audits . . . 640
Changes, developments (1994) . . 636-37
Children . . . 636, 639
Deductions . . . 636, 637-39
Estimated . . . 636
Forms . . . 639-40
Gift . . . 640
Individual rates (1994) . . . 637
Medicare . . . 636
Paycheck withholding (1943) . . . 444
Reform Law (1986) . . . 449
Revenues . . . 107
Social Security . . . 636
Taxpayers' rights . . . 640
State . . . 113, 641-42
Death . . . 640-41
Incubation, gestation . . . 189
Index numbers
Consumer prices . . . 109-11
Economic indicators . . . 111
Heat . . . 186
Production (by industries) . . . 126
India . . . 775-76
Aid, U.S. . . . 851
Ambassadors, envoys . . . 848
Gandhi, Indira . . . 573, 776
Gandhi, Mohandas . . . 528, 529, 573, 776
History . . . 517, 518, 522, 524, 528, 529, 532
Gupta monarchs (320) . . . 513
Indus civilization . . . 509
Map . . . 492
Merchant fleet . . . 205
Military strength . . . 161
Nuclear power . . . 168
Trade . . . 201, 776
Indiana . . . 649-50
Abortions reported . . . 959
Admission, area, capital . . . 499, 500, 649
Agriculture . . . 134-39
Altitudes (high, low) . . . 498
Birth, death statistics . . . 958
Budget . . . 113
Cities . . . 676, 678
Congressional representation . 76, 80, 376
Courts, U.S. . . . 88
Crime, prisons, death penalty . 216, 217, 218
Debt . . . 113
Energy consumption . . . 166
Geographic center . . . 500
Governor, state officials . . . 93, 95
As immigrants' intended residence . . . 386
Indians, American (population) . . . 507
Interest laws, rates . . . 720, 721
Marriage, divorce laws . . . 727, 728
Motor vehicle statistics . . . 207
Name origin, nickname . . . 501, 649
Population . . . 376-77, 379
Cities, towns . . . 396-97, 676, 678
Counties, county seats . . . 422
Density . . . 379
Port traffic . . . 203
Presidential elections . . . 601, 608-9, 630
Schools . . . 220, 222, 224
Taxes . . . 113, 207, 641, 642
Unemployment benefits . . . 142
Welfare assistance . . . 384
Indianapolis, IN . . . 678
Buildings, tall . . . 686
Commuters . . . 210
Mayor . . . 91
Population . . . 380, 397, 678
Unemployment rate . . . 145
Indianapolis 500 (auto race) . . . 931
Indian Ocean
Area, depth . . . 552
Islands, areas . . . 549
Indians, American
Custer's last stand (1876) . . . 442
Geronimo surrender (1886) . . . 442
Gold discovered (1835) . . . 440
Population . . . 375, 382, 507
Reservations . . . 507
Sacagawea (1804) . . . 440
Sand Creek Massacre (1864) . . . 441
Seminole War (1835) . . . 440
Tippecanoe battle (1811) . . . 440
Tribes . . . 507
U.S. citizenship (1924) . . . 443
Wounded Knee, Battle of (1890) . . . 442
Individual Retirement Account . . 132, 638
Indochina. *See* Cambodia; Laos; Vietnam
Indochina War (1953) . . . 445, 531
see also Vietnam War
Indonesia . . . 776, 785
Aid, U.S. . . . 851
Ambassadors, envoys . . . 848
Independence . . . 805
Merchant fleet . . . 205
Military strength . . . 161
Trade . . . 201, 785
Volcanoes . . . 545, 546
Industrialists, notable . . . 351-52
Industrial Revolution . . . 521, 523
Industries, U.S.
Business directory . . . 713-18
Corporate tax rates . . . 122
Employees . . . 143, 151
Manufacturing, mining . . . 126
Mineral production . . . 129-31
Multinational companies . . . 121
National income by . . . 124
Occupational injuries, fatalities . . 147, 965
Production index . . . 126
Profits . . . 116
Sales . . . 120
see also Business; *specific types*
Infant mortality . . . 958-59
Inflation . . . 132
Influenza epidemic (1918) . . . 443
Information superhighway . . . 35-36, 198
Inheritance taxes . . . 640
Injuries
Accidental . . . 964, 965
Cost of unintentional . . . 965
Occupational . . . 965
Fatalities . . . 147
By industry, type . . . 147
Inner Mongolia . . . 756
Insects, venomous . . . 190
Insignia, military . . . 157
Insurance
Life . . . 967
Medical (1966) . . . 373, 446, 698, 700, 967
Medical, Reform efforts (1993, 1994) . . 38-39, 49, 61, 64, 66-67, 195, 451
Social Security . . . 696-700
Unemployment . . . 107, 142, 144
Interest
Compound, table of . . . 562
Glossary . . . 132
Laws, rates . . . 720, 721
Prime rate . . . 133
Interior, Department of the . . . 73
Employees, payroll . . . 148
Expenditures . . . 107
Secretaries . . . 72, 73, 101
Internal Revenue Service . . . 73, 76
Audits . . . 640
Expenditures . . . 107
see also Income taxes
International Atomic Energy Agency . . 52, 847
International Bank . . . 847
International boundary lines, U.S. . . . 500
International bridges, structures . 690, 693
International Civil Aviation Organization . . . 847
International Court of Justice . . . 847
International Date Line . . . 290
International Development Association . . 847
International Finance Corporation . . . 847
International Fund for Agricultural Development . . . 847
International Labor Organization . . . 847
International Maritime Organization . . 847
International Monetary Fund . . . 847
International organizations . . . 844-47
International postage . . . 590-91
International System (measurement) . . 557
International Telecommunication Union . . . 847
Internet . . . 173
Interpol . . . 844
Interstate Commerce Commission . 75, 108
Intolerable Acts (1774) . . . 439
Inventions . . . 174-77
Investment
Foreign
In U.S. companies . . . 123
By U.S companies . . . 125
Glossary . . . 132-33
IRAs . . . 638
see also Business; Stocks
Iowa . . . 650
Abortions reported . . . 959
Admission, area, capital . . . 499, 500, 650
Agriculture . . . 134-39
Altitudes (high, low) . . . 498
Birth, death statistics . . . 958
Budget . . . 113
Cities . . . 676
Congressional representation . 77, 80, 376
Courts, U.S. . . . 88
Crime, prisons, death penalty . . . 216, 218
Debt . . . 113
Energy consumption . . . 166
Geographic center . . . 500
Governor, state officials . . . 93, 95
As immigrants' intended residence . . 386
Indians, American (population) . . . 507
Interest laws, rates . . . 720, 721
Marriage, divorce laws . . . 727, 728
Motor vehicle statistics . . . 207
Name origin, nickname . . . 501, 650
Population . . . 376-77, 379
Cities, towns . . . 397, 676
Counties, county seats . . . 422-23
Density . . . 379
Presidential elections . . 601, 609-10, 630
Schools . . . 220, 222, 224
Taxes . . . 113, 207, 641, 642
Unemployment benefits . . . 142
Welfare assistance . . . 384
IRA. *See* Individual Retirement Account
Iran . . . 785-86, 848
Map . . . 492
Merchant fleet . . . 205
Military strength . . . 161
Nuclear power . . . 168
Persia . . . 511, 514, 518, 527
Revolution (1979-80) . . . 532, 785-86
Terrorism, international . . . 533
U.S. embassy seizure (1979, 1980) . . 448, 479, 785-86
Iran-contra affair (1986, 1987, 1989, 1991, 1993, 1994) . . . 46, 52, 449, 450
Iran-Iraq War (1980-88) . . . 533, 786
Iraq . . . 786, 848
Gulf War (1991) . . . 450, 786, 793, 817
Kuwait invasion (1990) . . 450, 786, 793, 817
Map . . . 492
Military buildup (1994) . . . 69
Military strength . . . 161
U.S. helicopter tragedy (1994) . . 56, 62, 66
Ireland, Northern . . . 43, 45, 47-48, 65, 67, 69, 532, 549, 832
Map . . . 490
Ireland, Republic of . . . 786-87
Aid, U.S. . . . 851
Ambassadors, envoys . . . 848
Area . . . 549
Chronology (1993-94) . . . 67
History . . . 515, 526
Map . . . 490
Iron
Exports, imports . . . 202
Production . . . 129, 130, 131
Reserve base, world . . . 129
Iron (dietary) . . . 701, 702-3, 705
IRS. *See* Internal Revenue Service
Islam
Address, U.S. headquarters . . . 730
Adherents, U.S. . . . 729
Beliefs, practices . . . 737
Calendar . . . 732
History . . . 514, 515, 517, 532
Population, world . . . 731
Islands
Area, ownership . . . 549
U.S. trusteeship . . . 671
Isle of Man . . . 205, 549, 832
Isle of Pines . . . 768
Isle of Skye . . . 832
Israel . . . 787-88
Aid, U.S. . . . 851
Ambassadors, envoys . . . 848

Formed (1948) . . . 529
Jordanian peace treaty (1994) . 62, 69, *779*, 788, 790
Map . . . 492
Military strength . . . 161
Palestinian militancy, uprising . . 532, 533, 788
Palestinian self-rule (1993, 1994) . . 40, 42, 45, 47, 50, 53, 55-56, 57-58, 62, 65, *779*, 788
Israeli-Arab wars. *See* Arab-Israeli conflict
Italo-Ethiopian War (1935-37) . . . 528, 789
Italy . . . 788-89
Ambassadors, envoys . . . 848
Chronology (1993-94) . . . 53, 58
Gold reserves . . . 125
History . . . 518, 523, 527, 528, 533
Merchant fleet . . . 205
Military strength . . . 161
Nuclear power . . . 168
Rulers . . . 540-41
Trade . . . 201, 788
Vatican City . . . 834-35, 849
ITU. *See* International Telecommunication Union
Ivory Coast. *See* Cote d'Ivoire
Iwo Jima
Area . . . 549
Battle (1945) . . . 445, 529
Memorial (statue) . . . 673

— J —

Jackson, Andrew . . . 634
Biography . . . 472
Burial site . . . 480
Cabinet . . . 98-100
Popular, electoral votes . . . 633
Jackson, Michael . . . 43, 45, 48
Jackson, MS . . . 678
Mayor . . . 91
Population . . . 381, 403, 678
Jacksonville, FL . . . 678
Buildings, tall . . . 686
Commuters . . . 210
Mayor . . . 91
Population . . . 380, 393, 678
Jamaica . . . 789, 848, 851
Jamestown, VA (1607) . . . 438
Japan . . . 789-90
Ambassadors, envoys . . . 848
Automobile production . . . 206, 208
Chronology (1993-94) . . . 43, 47, 50, 56, 60-61
Gold reserves . . . 125
Historical periods . . . 536
History . . . 515-16, 519, 520, 524, 533
Peace treaty, U.S. (1951) . . . 445, 790
Perry treaty (1853) . . . 441
World War I (1914-18) . . . 526
World War II (1941-45) . . . 444-45, 529
Islands, areas . . . 549
Map . . . 493
Merchant fleet . . . 205
Military strength . . . 161
Nuclear power . . . 167, 168
Space technology . . . 169
Trade . . . 50, 201, 790
Japan, Sea of . . . 552
Jarvis Island . . . 671
Java . . . 549, 776, 785
Javelin throw
Olympic champions . . . 860-61, 862
World records . . . 868, 869
Jazz artists, notable . . . 354-55
Jefferson, Thomas . . . 634, 635
Biography . . . 471
Burial site . . . 480
Cabinet . . . 98-100
Declaration of Independence . . . 439, 453-54, 455
Electoral votes . . . 633
Memorial (DC) . . . 672
Jehovah's Witnesses . . . 729, 730, 738-39
Jersey, Isle of . . . 549, 832
Jersey City, NJ . . . 678
Mayor . . . 91
Population . . . 381, 405, 678
Jerusalem . . . 511, 788
Jesuits . . . 519
Jesus Christ . . . 514
Jewelry
Birthstones . . . 725
Wedding anniversaries . . . 725
Jewish people. *See* Judaism
Jim Thorpe Trophy . . . 877
Job Corps . . . 144
Jobs. *See* Employment
Jockeys, leading . . . 899
John Paul II, Pope (1981) . . . 574, 735, 834
Johnson, Andrew . . . 632, 634, 635
Biography . . . 474
Burial site . . . 480
Cabinet . . . 98-101
Impeachment (1868) . . . 442
Johnson, Lyndon B. . . . 631, 632, 633, 634, 635
Biography . . . 478
Burial site . . . 480
Cabinet . . . 97-102
Popular, electoral votes . . . 633
Johnston Atoll . . . 671
Johnstown (PA) flood (1889) . . . 442
Joint Chiefs of Staff . . . 73
Chairmen . . . 155, 162
Personal salutes, honors . . . 156
Jordan . . . 790
Aid, U.S. . . . 851
Ambassadors, envoys . . . 848
Israeli peace treaty (1994) . . . 62, *779*, 788, 790
Map . . . 492
Joule (electrical unit) . . . 561
Journalism awards . . . 316-20, 324-25
see also Magazines; Newspapers
Judaism
Addresses, U.S. headquarters . . . 731
Ancient Hebrews . . . 509, 511, 562
Beliefs, practices . . . 737
Holy days . . . 733
Population, U.S., world . . . 729, 731, 732
Judiciary, U.S.
Address, forms of . . . 597
Court addresses, judges . . . 87-89
Employment, payroll . . . 148
Expenditures . . . 107
Supreme Court justices . . . 86-87
Judo . . . 867
Julian calendar . . . 288
Julian Period . . . 289
Junior colleges . . . 240-50
Jupiter (planet) . . . 256-57
Morning, evening stars . . . 272
Position by month . . . 251-54, 259-60
Rises, sets . . . 262
Solar system . . . 267
Struck by comet fragments (1994) . . . 63
Sun, distance from . . . 254, 267
Justice, Department of . . . 73
Attorneys general . . . 72, 73
First woman (1993) . . . 451
Employees, payroll . . . 148
Expenditures . . . 107

— K —

Kampuchea. *See* Cambodia
Kansas . . . 650-51
Abortions reported . . . 959
Admission, area, capital . . . 499, 500, 650
Agriculture . . . 134-39
Altitudes (high, low) . . . 498
Birth, death statistics . . . 958
Budget . . . 113
Cities . . . 683
Congressional representation . 77, 80, 376
Courts, U.S. . . . 88
Crime, prisons, death penalty . . 216, 218
Debt . . . 113
Energy consumption . . . 166
Geographic center . . . 500
Governor, state officials . . . 93, 95
As immigrants' intended residence . . . 386
Indians, American (population) . . . 507
Interest laws, rates . . . 720, 721
Marriage, divorce laws . . . 727, 728
Motor vehicle statistics . . . 207
Name origin, nickname . . . 501, 650
Population . . . 376-77, 379
Cities, towns . . . 397-98, 683
Counties, county seats . . . 423
Density . . . 379
Presidential elections . . . 601, 610-11, 630
Schools . . . 220, 222, 224
Taxes . . . 113, 207, 641, 642
Unemployment benefits . . . 142
Welfare assistance . . . 384
Kansas City, MO . . . 678
Buildings, tall . . . 686
Mayor . . . 91
Population . . . 380, 403, 678
Kansas-Nebraska Act (1854) . . . 441, 473
Karami, Rashid . . . 533
Kayaking . . . 866
Kazakhstan . . . 168, 790-91, 851
Kellogg-Briand Pact (1928) . . . 527
Kennedy, Ted . . . 33
Kennedy, John F. . . . 631, 632, 634, 635
Assassination (1963) . . . 446, 478, 573
Warren Commission (1964) . . . 446
Biography . . . 477-78
Burial site . . . 480, 673
Cabinet . . . 97-102
Popular, electoral votes . . . 633
Kennedy, John F., Center for the Performing Arts (DC) . . . 672
Kennedy, Robert F.
Assassinated (1968) . . . 447, 573
Burial site . . . 673
Kentucky . . . 651
Abortions reported . . . 959
Admission, area, capital . . . 499, 651
Agriculture . . . 134-39
Altitudes (high, low) . . . 498
Birth, death statistics . . . 958
Budget . . . 113
Cities . . . 678, 679
Congressional representation . 77, 80, 376
Courts, U.S. . . . 88
Crime, prisons, death penalty . . . 216, 218
Debt . . . 113
Energy consumption . . . 166
Geographic center . . . 500
Governor, state officials . . . 93, 95
As immigrants' intended residence . . 386
Indians, American (population) . . . 507
Interest laws, rates . . . 720, 721
Marriage, divorce laws . . . 727, 728
Motor vehicle statistics . . . 207
Name origin, nickname . . . 501, 651
Population . . . 376-77, 379
Cities, towns . . . 398, 678, 679
Counties, county seats . . . 423
Density . . . 379
Presidential elections . . . 601, 611, 630
Schools . . . 220, 222, 224
Taxes . . . 113, 207, 641, 642
Unemployment benefits . . . 142
Welfare assistance . . . 384
Kentucky Derby . . . 898
First (1875) . . . 442
Kenya . . . 791, 848, 851
Kerguelen Archipelago . . . 768
Kevorkian, Jack . . . 41, 43, 45, 58
Key, Francis Scott . . . 468
Khmer Empire . . . 516
Khomeini, Ayatollah . . . 785
Khrushchev, Nikita S. . . . 446, 542, 814
Kidnappings, notable . . . 574
Hearst, Patty (1975) . . . 448, 574
Lindbergh baby (1932) . . . 444, 574
Kilowatt-hour (electrical unit) . . . 561
Kim Il Sung . . . 63, *778*, 973
King, Martin Luther, Jr. . . . 333
Assassinated (1968) . . . 447, 573
Birthday (legal holiday) (1986) . . 291, 449
"I have a dream" speech (1963) . . . 446
King, Rodney (1992, 1993, 1994) . . 40, 55, 450, 451
King George's War (1744) . . . 438
Kingman Reef . . . 671
Kiribati . . . 791-92, 849
Knot (measurement) . . . 561
Koran . . . 514, 737
Korea, North (Democratic People's Republic of) . . . 792, 848
Chronology (1993-94) 42, 47, 52, 60, 65, 69
Established . . . 529, 530
Invaded South Korea (1950) . . . 445, 530
Kim Il Sung death (1994) . . . 63, *778*
Map . . . 493
Military strength . . . 161
Pueblo incident (1968) . . . 447
Korea, South (Republic of) . . . 792
Aid, U.S. . . . 851
Ambassadors, envoys . . . 849
Established . . . 529, 530
Invaded by North Korea (1950) . . 445, 530
Map . . . 493
Merchant fleet . . . 205
Military strength . . . 161
Nuclear power . . . 167, 168
Trade . . . 201
U.S. force (1945-1950) . . . 445, 530
Korean War (1950-53) . . . 530
Beginning (1950) . . . 445, 530
Casualties, U.S. forces . . . 163
Costs . . . 160
MacArthur removal (1951) . . . 445
Medal of Honor . . . 160
Veteran population . . . 159
Koresh, David (1993) . . . 451
Kosovo . . . 837
Krakatau volcano . . . 545, 546
Kublai Khan . . . 517
Ku Klux Klan (1866, 1921) . . . 441, 443
Kuomintang (China) . . . 526, 527, 529, 756

Kuwait 792-93
Ambassadors, envoys 849
Gulf War (1991) 450, 786, 793, 817
Iraqi invasion (1990) 450, 786, 793, 817
Map 492
Merchant fleet 205
Trade 201
Kyrgyzstan 793, 849, 851

— L —

Labor. *See* Employment; Labor unions
Labor, Department of 74
Employees, payroll 148
Expenditures 107
Secretaries 72, 74, 101
Labor unions
AFL-CIO merger (1955) 445
AFL formed (1886) 442
CIO formed (1935) 444
Contracts, first major (1937) 444
Directory 153-54
Haymarket riot (1886) 442
Knights of Labor (1869) 442
Membership (1930-93) 154
Salary, wage correlate 152
Taft-Hartley act (1947) 445
see also Strikes
Lacrosse 933
Lake Champlain, Battle of (1814) 440
Lakes 555
Lamb
Consumption 135
Nutritive value 702
Prices, farm 140
Production 135
Land (public, federal) 502
Homestead Act (1862) 441
Land Grant Act (1862) 441
Language 592-600
Abbreviations, common 594
Animal names 594, 595
Commonly confused words 596
Commonly misspelled words 597
Computer glossary 170-72
Days of week 596
Economic, financial glossary 132-33
Eponyms 592
Esperanto 599
Forms of address 597
Idioms 595-96
National Spelling Bee 593
New words, English 592
Non-English-speaking Americans 599
World languages 593, 595, 598-600
Laos (1964) 446, 530, 532, 793-94, 849
Lard 135
Las Vegas, NV 678
Buildings, tall 686
Mayor 91
Population 381
Latin America. *See* Central America; South America
Latinos. *See* Hispanics
Latitude
Cities (U.S., world) 550-52
Position, reckoning 270
Latter-Day Saints, Church of
Address, headquarters 730
Beliefs, practices 738-39
Membership 729
Organized (1830) 440
Utah (1846) 441
Latvia 205, 794, 849
Law enforcement
Crime Bill (1994) 64, 71, 194, 213
Officers 215
Laws and documents
Bill of Rights (1791) 439, 460
Civil rights (1875, 1964, 1990) 442, 446, 450, 531
Constitution 456-63
Consumer finance 720
Copyright 723-25
Crime Bill (1994) 64, 71, 194, 213
Declaration of Independence 439, 453-54
Disabilities, anti-discrimination (1990) 450
Divorce (by states) 728
Immigration (1952, 1990) 445, 842-43
Lend-lease (1941) 444
Marriage (by states) 727
Mayflower Compact (1620) 452
Personal records, obtaining 722
Safety belt (by countries) 209
Social Security (1935, 1994) 71, 444, 696-700
Supreme Court, landmark decisions 464-65
Tax reform (1986, 1993, 1994) 449, 451, 636-37
Voting rights (1957, 1965) 446
Lazarus, Emma 470
Lead production 129, 130, 131
League of Arab States 530, 844
League of Nations (1920) 443, 476, 527
Leap years 288
Lebanon 794
Aid, U.S. 851
Ambassadors, envoys 849
Israeli-Palestinian conflicts 532, 533, 788, 794
Terrorism (1983) 448, 794
U.S. Marines (1958, 1983) 446, 448, 794
Lee, Robert E. 340
Birthplace, grave (VA) 666
Surrender (1865) 441
Leeward Islands 832
Legal holidays 291
Legislation. *See* Laws and documents
Legislatures, state 89-92
Legumes
Nutritive value 701, 703
Production 139
Lend-Lease Act (1941) 444
Lent 732, 733
Lesotho 794-95, 849, 851
Lewis and Clark expedition (1804) 440, 471
Lexington, KY 678
Buildings, tall 686
Mayor 91
Population 381, 398, 678
Liberia 205, 795, 849, 851
Liberty Bell 469-70
Libraries, public 225
Postal rates 588
Library of Congress 76, 672
Employees, payroll 148
Librarians 103
Libya 795-96, 848
U.S. bombing (1986) 449, 533, 796
Liechtenstein 796, 848
Life expectancy 972
Animal longevity 189
Life insurance 967
Light, speed of 264
Lincoln, Abraham 632, 634
Assassinated (1865) 441, 474, 573
Biography 473-74
Birthday (legal holiday) 291
Burial site 480
Cabinet 98-101
Emancipation Proclamation (1863) 441
Gettysburg Address (1863) 441, 464
Memorial (DC) 672
Popular, electoral votes 633
Lincoln, NE 678
Mayor 91
Population 381, 404, 678
Lindbergh, Charles A.
Flight (1927) 299
Son kidnapped (1932) 444, 574
Linear measures 557-60, 562
Lipari Islands 789
Liquid measures 557-63
Liquor
Abuse 963
Duty-free 721-22
Exports, imports 202
Measures 563
Prohibition (1917-33) 443, 444, 462, 527
Liter (measure) 557, 559, 561
Literature
Awards 70, 315-16, 321-23, 330
Notable (1993) 303-4
Pen names 598
Writers, notable 334-35, 341-44
Lithuania 168, 796, 849, 851
Little Big Horn, Battle of (1876) 442
Little Rock, AR 678
Buildings, tall 686
Mayor 91
Population 381
School desegregation (1957) 446
Livestock 134, 135, 137, 140
see also Dairy products; Meats
Living wills 709
Lizards, poisonous 190
Loans. *See* Credit
London 830, 840
Long Beach, CA 678
Mayor 91
Population 380, 389, 678
Port traffic 203
Longevity, animal 189
Long Island, NY (1776) 439, 549
Longitude
Cities (U.S., world) 550-52
Position, reckoning 270
Long jump
Olympic champions 859, 862
World indoor, outdoor records 868, 869
Los Angeles, CA 678-79
Buildings, tall 686
Commuters 210
Earthquake (1994) 48, 51, 54, 196
King case (1992, 1993, 1994) 40, 55, 450, 451
Mayor 91
Population 380, 389, 678
Port traffic 203
Riots
Los Angeles (1992, 1993) 40, 450
Watts (1965) 446
Unemployment rate 145
Louisiana 651-52
Abortions reported 959
Admission, area, capital 499, 500, 651, 652
Agriculture 134-39
Altitudes (high, low) 498
Birth, death statistics 958
Budget 113
Cities 675, 680, 682
Congressional representation 77, 80, 376
Courts, U.S. 88
Crime, prisons, death penalty 216, 217, 218
Debt 113
Energy consumption 166
Geographic center 500
Governor, state officials 93, 95
As immigrants' intended residence 386
Indians, American (population) 507
Interest laws, rates 720, 721
Marriage, divorce laws 727, 728
Motor vehicle statistics 207
Name origin, nickname 501, 651
Population 376-77, 379
Cities, towns 398-99, 675, 680, 682
Density 379
Parishes, parish seats 424
Port traffic 203
Presidential elections 601, 612, 630
Schools 220, 222, 224
Taxes 113, 207, 641
Territory 500, 502
Unemployment benefits 142
Welfare assistance 384
Louisiana Purchase (1803) 440, 471, 502
Louisville, KY 679
Buildings, tall 687
Mayor 91
Population 381, 398, 679
Loyalty Islands 768
Lubbock, TX 679
City Manager 91
Population 381, 414, 679
Luge (sledding) 853
Lunar calendar 289
***Lusitania*, sinking of** (1915) 443, 565
Luther, Martin 347, 738
Lutheran churches
Addresses, headquarters 730-31
Beliefs, practices 738-39
Membership 729
Luxembourg 205, 796-97, 849
Lyricists, notable 354

— M —

MacArthur, Douglas (1945, 1951) 340, 445
Macau 812
Macedonia 50, 511, 797, 851
Madagascar 549, 797, 849, 851
Madeira Islands 549, 812
Madison, James 634
Biography 471
Burial site 480
Cabinet 98-100
Electoral votes 633
Madison, WI 91, 381, 679
Madura 549
Magazines
Advertising expenditures 313
Circulation 306
Journalism awards 316-20, 324-25
Mailing rate 588
Magna Carta (1215) 518
Magnetic poles 271
Mailing information 587-91
Maine 652
Abortions reported 959
Admission, area, capital 499, 652
Agriculture 134-39
Altitudes (high, low) 498
Birth, death statistics 958
Budget 113
Congressional representation 77, 80, 376
Courts, U.S. 88
Crime, prisons, death penalty 216, 217
Debt 113
Energy consumption 166
Geographic center 500
Governor, state officials 93, 95
As immigrants' intended residence 386
Indians, American (population) 507

Interest laws, rates 720, 721
Marriage, divorce laws 727, 728
Motor vehicle statistics 207
Name origin, nickname 501, 652
Population 376-77, 379
Cities, towns 399
Counties, county seats 424
Density 379
Port traffic 203
Presidential elections 601, 612, 630
Schools 220, 222, 224
Taxes 113, 207, 641
Unemployment benefits 142
Welfare assistance 384
Majorca 821
Malagasy Republic. *See* Madagascar
Malawi 58, 797-98, 849, 851
Malaysia 201, 205, 798, 849
Maldives 798, 848
Mali 798-99, 849, 851
Malta 205, 799, 849
Man, Isle of 549, 832
Management and Budget, Office of . . . 72
Employees, payroll 148
Expenditures 107
Manchuria 756
Mandela, Nelson (1994) 50, 56, 57, 69, *777*, 820
Manganese 129, 130
Manhattan, NY, (1624) 428, 438, 549
Manua Islands 669
Manufactures
Employees (by industry) 143
Exports, imports 202
Index numbers 126
Personal consumption expenditures . . 128
Workers' statistics 142-54
Occupational injuries 147
see also specific industries
Mao Zedong (Mao Tse-tung) 531-32, 542, 756
Maps (color) 485-96
World, time zones 484
Marathon
Boston 956
New York 956
Olympic champions 859, 862
World records 868, 869
Mardi Gras 652
Mariana Islands 502, 669-70, 671
As immigrants' intended residence . . . 386
Population 436
Zip codes 436
Marine Corps, U.S.
Address for information 159
China (1927) 444
Enlisted adviser, senior 161
Generals (active duty) 155
Grenada (1983) 449
Guadalcanal (1942) 444
Insignia 157
Iwo Jima (1945) 445
Lebanon (1958, 1983) 446, 448, 794
Nicaragua (1912) 443
Organization bases 156
Personnel, active duty 158
Training centers 156
War memorial 673
Women, active duty 159
Marquesas Islands 549, 768
Marriage
Age, lawful (by states) 727
Blood test requirements 727
Number, rate 957, 960
Records, obtaining 722
Spousal Social Security benefits 697
Wedding anniversaries 725
Mars (planet) 256
Morning, evening stars 272
Position by months 251-54, 259-60
Rises, sets 261
Solar system 267
Space exploration (1976) 295, 448
Sun, distance from 254, 267
Viking I and II (1976) 295, 448
Marshall, Thurgood (1967, 1991) . 447, 450
Marshall Islands 205, 549, 671, 799, 849, 851
Martinique 549, 767
Maryland 652-53
Abortions reported 959
Admission, area, capital . . . 499, 652, 653
Agriculture 134-39
Altitudes (high, low) 498
Birth, death statistics 958
Budget 113
Cities 674-75
Congressional representation . 77, 80, 376
Courts, U.S. 88
Crime, prisons, death penalty . . 216, 218
Debt 113
Energy consumption 166
Geographic center 500
Governor, state officials 93, 95
As immigrants' intended residence . . . 386
Indians, American (population) 507
Interest laws, rates 720, 721
Marriage, divorce laws 727, 728
Motor vehicle statistics 207
Name origin, nickname 501, 652
Population 376-77, 379
Cities, towns 399-400, 674
Counties, county seats 424-25
Density 379
Port traffic 203
Presidential elections . . . 601, 612-13, 630
Schools 220, 222, 224
Taxes 113, 207, 641, 642
Unemployment benefits 142
Welfare assistance 384
Mass, units of 557, 559, 560
Massachusetts 653
Abortions reported 959
Admission, area, capital 499, 653
Agriculture 134-39
Altitudes (high, low) 498
Birth, death statistics 958
Budget 113
Cities 675
Congressional representation . 77, 80, 376
Courts, U.S. 88
Crime, prisons, death penalty . . 216, 217
Debt 113
Energy consumption 166
Geographic center 500
Governor, state officials 93, 95
As immigrants' intended residence . . . 386
Indians, American (population) 507
Interest laws, rates 720, 721
Marriage, divorce laws 727, 728
Motor vehicle statistics 207
Name origin, nickname 501, 653
Population 376-77, 379
Cities, towns 400-401, 675
Counties, county seats 425
Density 379
Presidential elections 601, 613, 630
Schools 220, 222, 224
Taxes 113, 207, 641, 642
Unemployment benefits 142
Welfare assistance 384
Mathematics
Formulas 564
Fractions, decimals 563
Matsu 825
Mauritania 799-800, 849, 851
Mauritius 800, 849
Mayans 511, 516
Mayflower Compact (1620) 438, 452
Mayors 89-92
Address, form of 597
Black 334
First (1967) 447
Mayotte 767-68
McCarthy, Joseph (1954) 445
McKinley, Mt. 497, 547
McKinley, William 632, 634
Assassination (1901) 442, 475, 573
Biography 475
Burial site 480
Cabinet 98-101
Popular, electoral votes 633
Mean time 270
Measures 557-64
Meats
Consumption 135
Exports, imports 202
Inspection Act (1906) 443
Nutritive values 701, 702
Prices, farm 140
Production 134, 135
Medal of Honor 160
Media. *See* Magazines; Newspapers; Radio; Television
Medicare
Enacted (1966) 446
Federal tax 636
Program summary 698
Medicine. *See* Health and medicine
Mediterranean Sea
Area, depth 552
Islands, areas 549
Melilla 821
Memorial Day 291
Memorials, national 504, 672-73
Memphis, TN 679
Buildings, tall 687
Mayor 91
Population 380, 413, 679
Men
Employment 143, 145
Height, weight 705, 972
Life expectancy 972
Living alone 960, 961
Marital status 960
Median net worth 384
One-parent families 960, 961
Poverty rates 383
Salaries and wages
Annual earnings average 149
Hourly rates 150
Pay differential, male/female 149
Weekly earnings median 152
Mennonite churches 729, 731
Mercantilism 520
Merchant Marine
Academy 157
Fleets, by country 205
Mercury (planet) 254-55
Morning, evening stars 272
Position by month 251-54, 259-60
Solar system 267
Sun, distance from 254, 267
Mergers
Corporate, largest 120
Defense contractors (1994) 66
Labor unions (1955) 445
Phone-cable (1994) 51
Sherman Antitrust Act (1890) 442
Takeovers, defined 133
Mesa, AZ 679
Mayor 91
Population 381, 388, 679
Metals
Exports, imports 202
Production 130, 131
Reserve base, world 129
Meteorology 179-86
Methodist churches
Addresses, U.S. headquarters 731
Beliefs, practices 738-39
Membership 729-30
Metric measures 557-61
Mexican War (1846-48) 441
Casualties, U.S. forces 163
Costs 160
Mexico 800-801
Aid, U.S. 851
Ambassadors, envoys 849
Cession to U.S. (1846) 441, 502
Chronology (1993-94) 46-47, 52, 53, 65, 69
Cortes conquest 520
Gold production 131
Map 486
Mountain peaks 547
NAFTA 42-43, 44, 71, 204
Nuclear power 168
Olmec civilization 509, 516, 543
Paricutin volcano 512
Prehistory 543
Revolution (1910) 526-27
U.S. forces (1916) 443
U.S. immigration 386
Mexico, Gulf of 552
Mexico City, Mex. 800, 840
Miami, FL 679
Buildings, tall 687
City manager 91
Population 381, 393, 679
Michelangelo 56
Michigan 653-54
Abortions reported 959
Admission, area, capital . 499, 500, 653, 654
Agriculture 134-39
Altitudes (high, low) 498
Birth, death statistics 958
Budget 113
Cities 676, 677
Congressional representation. 77, 80-81, 376
Courts, U.S. 88
Crime, prisons, death penalty . . . 216, 218
Debt 113
Energy consumption 166
Geographic center 500
Governor, state officials 93, 95-96
As immigrants' intended residence . . 386
Indians, American (population) 507
Interest laws, rates 720, 721
Marriage, divorce laws 727, 728
Mineral production 129
Motor vehicle statistics 207
Name origin, nickname 501, 653
Population 376-77, 379
Cities, towns 401-2, 676, 677
Counties, county seats 425
Density 379
Port traffic 203
Presidential elections . . 601, 613-14, 630
Schools 220, 222, 224
Taxes 113, 207, 641, 642
Unemployment benefits 142
Welfare assistance 384
Michigan, Lake 555
Micronesia 671, 801, 849, 851

Middle East
History . . . 514, 515, 527, 531
see also Arab-Israeli conflict; Persian Gulf War; *specific countries*
Midway, Battle of (1942) . . . 444, 529
Midway Atoll . . . 671
Mileage
Air . . . 212
Road . . . 211
Sea lanes . . . 204
Miles (measurement) . . . 557, 558, 560
Military. *See* Armed forces, U.S.; *specific branches*
Military Academy, U.S. (West Point, NY) . . . 157, 237
Military leaders, notable . . . 339-40
Military parks, national . . . 504
Military strength
By country . . . 161
U.S. . . . 160, 161
Military time (24-hour) . . . 290
Military training centers . . . 155-56
Milk
Nutritive value . . . 701, 702
Prices, farm . . . 140
Milwaukee, WI . . . 679
Buildings, tall . . . 687
Mayor . . . 91
Population . . . 380, 417, 679
Unemployment rate . . . 145
Minerals . . . 129-31, 202
Minerals (dietary) . . . 701, 702-3, 705
Minimum wage, U.S.
Enacted (1938) . . . 444
Hourly rates (1950-91) . . . 151
Increased (1989) . . . 450
Mining
Coal . . . 164
Disasters, U.S. . . . 568
Gold, silver . . . 125, 129, 130, 131
Index numbers . . . 126
Occupational injuries . . . 147
Minneapolis, MN . . . 679
Buildings, tall . . . 687
Mayor . . . 91
Population . . . 381, 402, 679
Minnesota . . . 654
Abortions reported . . . 959
Admission, area, capital . . . 499, 500, 654
Agriculture . . . 134-39
Altitudes (high, low) . . . 498
Birth, death statistics . . . 958
Budget . . . 113
Cities . . . 679, 682
Congressional representation . 77, 81, 376
Courts, U.S. . . . 88
Crime, prisons, death penalty . . 216, 218
Debt . . . 113
Energy consumption . . . 166
Geographic center . . . 500
Governor, state officials . . . 93, 96
As immigrants' intended residence . . . 386
Indians, American (population) . . . 507
Interest laws, rates . . . 720, 721
Marriage, divorce laws . . . 727, 728
Mineral production . . . 129
Motor vehicle statistics . . . 207
Name origin, nickname . . . 501, 654
Population . . . 376-77, 379
Cities, towns . . . 402-3, 679, 682
Counties, county seats . . . 425-26
Density . . . 379
Port traffic . . . 203
Presidential elections . . . 601, 614-15, 630
Schools . . . 220, 222, 224
Taxes . . . 113, 207, 641
Territory . . . 500
Unemployment benefits . . . 142
Welfare assistance . . . 384
Minoans . . . 509
Minorca . . . 821
Mint, Bureau of the . . . 117
Minuit, Peter (1626) . . . 438
Miquelon Island . . . 768
Miscellaneous facts . . . 975
Miss America . . . 326
Missiles, rockets. *See* Nuclear arms; Space developments
Mississippi . . . 654-55
Abortions reported . . . 959
Admission, area, capital . . . 499, 500, 654, 655
Agriculture . . . 134-39
Altitudes (high, low) . . . 498
Birth, death statistics . . . 958
Budget . . . 113
Cities . . . 678
Congressional representation . 77, 81, 376
Courts, U.S. . . . 88
Crime, prisons, death penalty . 216, 217, 218
Debt . . . 113
Energy consumption . . . 166
Geographic center . . . 500
Governor, state officials . . . 93, 96
As immigrants' intended residence . . . 386
Indians, American (population) . . . 507
Interest laws, rates . . . 720, 721
Marriage, divorce laws . . . 727, 728
Motor vehicle statistics . . . 207
Name origin, nickname . . . 501, 654
Population . . . 376-77, 379
Cities, towns . . . 403, 678
Counties, county seats . . . 426
Density . . . 379
Port traffic . . . 203
Presidential elections . . . 601, 615, 630
Schools . . . 220, 222, 224
Taxes . . . 113, 207, 641
Unemployment benefits . . . 142
Welfare assistance . . . 384
Mississippi River . . . 553, 554
Bridges spanning . . . 690-92
First railroad crossing (1855) . . . 441
Commerce . . . 203
Discovered (1539) . . . 438, 543
Floods, historic (1993) . . . 185, 451
Missouri . . . 655
Abortions reported . . . 959
Admission, area, capital . . . 499, 500, 655
Agriculture . . . 134-39
Altitudes (high, low) . . . 498
Birth, death statistics . . . 958
Budget . . . 113
Cities . . . 678, 681
Congressional representation 77, 81, 376
Courts, U.S. . . . 88
Crime, prisons, death penalty . 216, 217, 218
Debt . . . 113
Energy consumption . . . 166
Geographic center . . . 500
Governor, state officials . . . 93, 96
As immigrants' intended residence . . . 386
Indians, American (population) . . . 507
Interest laws, rates . . . 720, 721
Marriage, divorce laws . . . 727, 728
Motor vehicle statistics . . . 207
Name origin, nickname . . . 501, 655
Population . . . 376-77, 379
Cities, towns . . . 403-4, 678, 681
Counties, county seats . . . 426-27
Density . . . 379
Port traffic . . . 203
Presidential elections . . . 601, 615-16, 630
Schools . . . 220, 222, 224
Taxes . . . 113, 207, 641, 642
Unemployment benefits . . . 142
U.S. center of population . . . 377
Welfare assistance . . . 384
Missouri Compromise (1820) . . . 440
Missouri River . . . 553, 554
Bridges spanning . . . 691-92
Flood (1993) . . . 451
Mobile, AL . . . 679
Mayor . . . 91
Population . . . 381, 387, 679
Mohammed. *See* Muhammad
Moldova . . . 801, 849, 851
Moluccas . . . 549
Monaco . . . 801
Money. *See* Currency, U.S.; Exchange rates, foreign
Mongolia . . . 801-2, 849, 851
Mongolia, Inner . . . 756
Mongols . . . 517
Monroe, James . . . 634
Biography . . . 472
Burial site . . . 480
Cabinet . . . 98-100
Electoral votes . . . 633
Monroe Doctrine (1823) . . . 440
Montana . . . 655-56
Abortions reported . . . 959
Admission, area, capital . 499, 500, 655, 656
Agriculture . . . 134-39
Altitudes (high, low) . . . 498
Birth, death statistics . . . 958
Budget . . . 113
Congressional representation . 77, 81, 376
Courts, U.S. . . . 88
Crime, prisons, death penalty . . 217, 218
Debt . . . 113
Energy consumption . . . 166
Geographic center . . . 500
Governor, state officials . . . 93, 96
As immigrants' intended residence . . . 386
Indians, American (population) . . . 507
Interest laws, rates . . . 720, 721
Marriage, divorce laws . . . 727, 728
Motor vehicle statistics . . . 207
Name origin, nickname . . . 501, 655
Population . . . 376-77, 379
Cities, towns . . . 404
Counties, county seats . . . 427
Density . . . 379
Presidential elections . . 601, 616-17, 630
Schools . . . 220, 222, 224
Taxes . . . 113, 207, 641, 642
Unemployment benefits . . . 142
Welfare assistance . . . 384
Montgomery, AL . . . 679-80
Mayor . . . 91
Population . . . 381, 387, 679-80
Montserrat . . . 832
Monuments, national . . . 505-6, 672-73
Largest U.S. . . . 497
Moon . . . 268-69
Apogee, perigee . . . 268
Apollo missions (1969) . . . 292-93, 447
Chinese lunar calendar . . . 289
Conjunctions . . . 251-54, 259-60
Eclipses (1995) . . . 266
First man on (1969) . . . 292, 447
Full . . . 274-85
Harvest, Hunter's . . . 269
Occultations . . . 251-54
Phases of . . . 269
Position by month (1995) . . . 251-54
Rises, sets (1995) . . . 263, 274-85
Tides, effects on . . . 185, 269
Moravian churches . . . 730, 731
Mormons. *See* Latter-Day Saints, Church of
Morning stars (1995) . . . 272
Morocco . . . 161, 802, 849, 851
Mortgages
Farm . . . 138
Income needed . . . 726
Tables . . . 725
Motion pictures. *See* Movies
Motor vehicles
Accidents and deaths . . . 959, 964
Commuters . . . 210
Production . . . 206, 208
see also Automobiles; Buses
Motor-Voter bill (1993) . . . 71, 451
Motto, U.S. . . . 466
Mountains . . . 546-48
Highest, Canada . . . 547
Highest, U.S. . . . 497, 498, 547, 548
Volcanoes . . . 545-46
Mt. Etna . . . 546, 789
Mt. Everest . . . 512, 546, 548
Mt. McKinley . . . 497, 498, 547
Mt. Rushmore . . . 504, 663
Mt. St. Helens (1980) . . . 448, 546
Mt. Vesuvius . . . 545, 546
Mount Vernon (VA) . . . 666, 673
Movies
Awards . . . 325, 327-29, *781*
Jazz Singer (1927) . . . 444
Kinetoscope (1894) . . . 442
National Film Registry . . . 302
Notable (1993-94) . . . 300, *781*
Sound-on-film, first (1923) . . . 443
Stars, directors 300, . . . 357-70
Talking (1927) . . . 444
Top 50 films, 1993 . . . 301
Top grossing, all-time . . . 301
Top videos (1993) . . . 302
Moynihan, Daniel Patrick . . . 33
Mozambique . . . 802-3, 849, 851
Muhammad . . . 514, 732, 737
Municipal bonds . . . 133
Murders
Arrests, sentences . . . 217, 218
Assassinations . . . 533, 574
Incidence . . . 214, 215, 965
Muscat and Oman. *See* Oman
Museums (Washington, DC) . . . 672-73
Music and musicians
Awards . . . 323-24, 325, 329-30
Chronology (1993-94) . . . 43, 45, 48, 56
Composers, works . . . 352-54
Dance companies . . . 306-7
Jazz artists . . . 354-55
Lyricists . . . 354
Musicians, singers . . . 354-70, *780, 781*
Opera, operetta . . . 308, 352-54
Pulitzer Prizes . . . 323-24
Recordings . . . 309, 329-30
Rock & Roll notables . 56, 325, 355-56, *780*
Symphony orchestras . . . 307-8
Theater . . . 353-54
Videos . . . 309
Muslim calendar . . . 732
Muslims. *See* Islam
Mutual funds . . . 126, 133
Myanmar (Burma) . 161, 529, 803, 849, 851

— N —

NAACP. *See* National Association for the Advancement of Colored People

NAFTA. *See* North American Free Trade Agreement
Nagasaki bombing (1945) 445, 529
Names
Animal collective 594
Animal young 595
Days, foreign languages 596
Original, actors and actresses 370-72
Pen names 598
States, origin and nicknames 501, 643-68
Namibia 803, 849, 851
Napoleon Bonaparte (1798, 1803) 440, 521, 522
NASA. *See* National Aeronautics and Space Administration
NASCAR (auto racing) 933
Nashville, TN 680
Buildings, tall 687
Mayor 91
Population 380, 413, 680
Nasser, Gamal Abdel 338, 764
National Aeronautics and Space Administration 75
Employees, payroll 148
Expenditures 107
National Anthem
Composed (1814) 440
Text 469
National Archives 672-73
National Association for the Advancement of Colored People
Director dismissed (1994) 64-65
Founding (1909) 443
Spingarn Medal 326
National Basketball Association *783*, 907-13
Addresses, teams 904
National debt 109, 133
National Film Registry 302
National Football League *782*, 870-80
Addresses, teams 905
National Foundation on the Arts and Humanities 75, 108
National Gallery of Art (DC) 673
National historic sites 504-5
National Hockey League *782*, 890-97
Addresses, teams 904-5
National income, U.S. 111, 124
National Information Infrastructure .. 35-36
National Labor Relations Board .. 75, 108
National League (baseball) ... 939-48, 953
National Medal of Science 174
National monuments 505-6, 672-73
Largest 497
National park system, U.S. 71, 503-6
Visitors, number (1993) 506
National recreation areas 502, 506
National Science Foundation 75, 108, 173, 174
National seashores 506
National Service Bill (1993) 71
National Spelling Bee 593
Nations of the World 740-839
Aid, U.S. 851
Ambassadors and envoys 848-50
Cities (population) 840
Embassies 740-839
Energy production, consumption. 165, 167
Exchange rates 122, 125
Flags 481-84
Investment in U.S. 123
Map 485-96
Merchant fleets 205
Military strength 161
Rulers 534-42
Safety belt laws 209
Stock exchanges 122
UN members 845-46
Native Americans. *See* Indians, American
NATO. *See* North Atlantic Treaty Organization
Natural gas
Exports, imports 164, 202
Production, consumption 164
Reserves 167
Naturalization 843
Barriers removed (1952) 445
see also Aliens
Nauru 803-4, 849
Nautilus (nuclear submarine) (1954) ... 445
Naval Academy, U.S. (Annapolis, MD) . 55, 157, 237
Naval disasters 565-66
Lusitania, sinking of (1915) 443, 565
Naval Expansion Act (1938) 444
Naval leaders, notable 339-40
Navassa Island 671
Navigation Act (1660) 438
Navy, Department of the
Employees, payroll 148
Secretaries 73, 99-100
Navy, U.S.
Academy 55, 157, 237
Address for information 159
Admirals (active duty) 155
Enlisted adviser, senior 161
Expansion Act (1938) 444
Insignia 157
Leaders, notable 339, 340
Personnel, active duty 158
Tailhook scandal (1994) 49, 55
Training centers 156
Women, active duty 159
Nazis
Rise of 528
Surrender (1945) 445
Third Reich 538, 770
World War II 529
NBA. *See* National Basketball Association
Nebraska 656
Abortions reported 959
Admission, area, capital ... 499, 500, 656
Agriculture 134-39
Altitudes (high, low) 498
Birth, death statistics 958
Budget 113
Cities 678, 680
Congressional representation 77, 81, 376
Courts, U.S. 88
Crime, prisons, death penalty .. 216, 218
Debt 113
Energy consumption 166
Geographic center 500
Governor, state officials 93, 96
As immigrants' intended residence ... 386
Indians, American (population) 507
Interest laws, rates 720, 721
Marriage, divorce laws 727, 728
Motor vehicle statistics 207
Name origin, nickname 501, 656
Population 376-77, 379
Cities, towns 404, 678, 680
Counties, county seats 427-28
Density 379
Presidential elections 601, 617, 630
Schools 220, 222, 224
Taxes 113, 207, 641, 642
Unemployment benefits 142
Welfare assistance 384
Necrology (1993-94) 973-74
Neolithic Revolution 508
Nepal 804, 849
Neptune (planet) 258
Morning, evening stars 272
Position by months 251-54, 259-60
Solar system 267
Sun, distance from 254, 267
Netherlands 804-5
Ambassadors, envoys 849
Gold reserves 125
History 518, 520
New World settlements (1624, 1626, 1664) 438
Indonesian independence 805
Merchant fleet 205
Nuclear power 168
Rulers 540
Netherlands Antilles 805
Nevada 656-57
Abortions reported 959
Admission, area, capital. 499, 500, 656, 657
Agriculture 134-39
Altitudes (high, low) 498
Birth, death statistics 958
Budget 113
Cities 678
Congressional representation. 77, 81, 376
Courts, U.S. 88
Crime, prisons, death penalty . 216, 217, 218
Debt 113
Energy consumption 166
Geographic center 500
Governor, state officials 93, 96
As immigrants' intended residence ... 386
Indians, American (population) 507
Interest laws, rates 720, 721
Marriage, divorce laws 727, 728
Mineral production 129
Motor vehicle statistics 207
Name origin, nickname 501, 656
Population 376-77, 379
Cities, towns 404, 678
Counties, county seats 428
Density 379
Presidential elections 601, 617, 630
Schools 220, 222, 224
Taxes 113, 207, 641
Territory 500
Unemployment benefits 142
Welfare assistance 384
Nevis 815, 849
New Amsterdam (1664) 438
Newark, NJ 680
Buildings, tall 687
Mayor 91
Population 381, 405, 680
Riots (1967) 446
Newbery Medal 324, 330
New Britain 549
New Caledonia 549, 768
New Deal (1933) 444
Newfoundland 549
New Guinea. *See* Papua New Guinea
New Hampshire 657
Abortions reported 959
Admission, area, capital 499, 657
Agriculture 134-39
Altitudes (high, low) 498
Birth, death statistics 958
Budget 113
Congressional representation . 77, 81, 376
Courts, U.S. 88
Crime, prisons, death penalty ... 216, 217
Debt 113
Energy consumption 166
Geographic center 500
Governor, state officials 93, 96
As immigrants' intended residence .. 386
Indians, American (population) 507
Interest laws, rates 720, 721
Marriage, divorce laws 727, 728
Motor vehicle statistics 207
Name origin, nickname 501, 657
Population 376-77, 379
Cities, towns 404
Counties, county seats 428
Density 379
Presidential elections .. 601, 617-18, 630
Schools 220, 222, 224
Taxes 113, 207, 641, 642
Unemployment benefits 142
Welfare assistance 384
New Ireland 549
New Jersey 657-58
Abortions reported 959
Admission, area, capital ... 499, 657, 658
Agriculture 134-39
Altitudes (high, low) 498
Birth, death statistics 958
Budget 113
Cities 678, 680
Congressional representation . 77, 81, 376
Courts, U.S. 88
Crime, prisons, death penalty ... 216, 218
Debt 113
Energy consumption 166
Geographic center 500
Governor, state officials 93, 96
As immigrants' intended residence .. 386
Indians, American (population) 507
Interest laws, rates 720, 721
Marriage, divorce laws 727, 728
Motor vehicle statistics 207
Name origin, nickname 501, 657
Population 376-77, 379
Cities, towns 404-6, 678, 680
Counties, county seats 428
Density 379
Port traffic 203
Presidential elections 601, 618, 630
Schools 220, 222, 224
Taxes 113, 207, 641, 642
Unemployment benefits 142
Welfare assistance 384
New Mexico 658
Abortions reported 959
Admission, area, capital ... 499, 500, 658
Agriculture 134-39
Altitudes (high, low) 498
Birth, death statistics 958
Budget 113
Cities 674
Congressional representation . 77, 81, 376
Courts, U.S. 88
Crime, prisons, death penalty ... 217, 218
Debt 113
Energy consumption 166
Geographic center 500
Governor, state officials 93, 96
As immigrants' intended residence .. 386
Indians, American (population) 507
Interest laws, rates 720, 721
Marriage, divorce laws 727, 728
Motor vehicle statistics 207
Name origin, nickname 501, 658
Population 376-77, 379
Cities, towns 406, 674
Counties, county seats 428
Density 379
Presidential elections .. 601, 618-19, 630
Schools 220, 222, 224
Taxes 113, 207, 641
(continued)

- **New Mexico** *(continued)*
  - Territory 500
  - Unemployment benefits 142
  - Welfare assistance 384
- **New Orleans, LA** 680
  - Buildings, tall 687
  - Mardi Gras 651
  - Mayor 91
  - Population 380, 398, 680
  - Port traffic 203
- **Newport News, VA** 91, 381, 680
- **Newspapers**
  - Advertising expenditures 313
  - *Boston News Letter* (1704) 438
  - Dailies
    - First U.S. (1784) 439
    - Top U.S. 305
  - Journalism awards 316-20, 324-25
  - Muckrakers 525
  - Offbeat stories (1994) 975
  - Pulitzer Prize winners 316-20
- **News photos** (1994) *193-200, 777-84*
- **New Testament** 734
- **Newton, Sir Isaac** 350
- **New words in English** 592
- **New World**
  - Central, South America 520
  - Explorers 518, 520, 543
  - Jamestown (VA) colony (1607) 438
  - Mayflower Compact (1620) 438, 452
  - New Netherland colony (1664) 438
- **New Year, Chinese** 289
- **New Year, Jewish** 733
- **New Year's Day** 291
- **New York** (state) 658-59
  - Abortions reported 960
  - Admission, area, capital 499, 658, 659
  - Agriculture 134-39
  - Altitudes (high, low) 498
  - Birth, death statistics 958
  - Budget 113
  - Cities 675, 680, 681, 683
  - Congressional representation 77, 81-82, 376
  - Courts, U.S. 88
  - Crime, prisons, death penalty 216, 218
  - Debt 113
  - Energy consumption 166
  - Geographic center 500
  - Governor, state officials 93, 96
  - As immigrants' intended residence 386
  - Indians, American (population) 507
  - Interest laws, rates 720, 721
  - Marriage, divorce laws 727, 728
  - Motor vehicle statistics 207
  - Name origin, nickname 501, 658
  - Population 376-77, 379
    - Cities, towns 406-8, 675, 680, 681, 683
    - Counties, county seats 428-29
    - Density 379
  - Port traffic 203
  - Presidential elections 601, 619, 630
  - Schools 220, 222, 224
  - Taxes 113, 207, 641, 642
  - Unemployment benefits 142
  - Welfare assistance 384
- **New York City** 680
  - Bridges, tunnels 690, 692
  - Buildings, tall 687-88
  - Commuters 210
  - Dutch surrender (1664) 438
  - Ellis Island 470
  - Harlem riots (1943) 444
  - Mayor 91
  - Mileage to foreign ports 204
  - Population 380, 407, 680
  - Port traffic 203
  - Statue of Liberty (1886) 442, 470
  - Theater openings (1993-94) 300, 780
  - Unemployment rate 145
  - United Nations 845
  - Verrazano exploration (1524) 438
  - World's Fair (1939) 444
  - World Trade Center bombing (1993, 1994) 52, 57, 451
- **New York Stock Exchange**
  - Address 585
  - Bomb exploded (1920) 443
  - Volume, transactions 127
  - *see also* Stocks
- **New Zealand** 525, 805
  - Ambassadors, envoys 849
  - Islands, areas 549
  - Mountain peaks 547
- **Niagara Falls** 556
- **Nicaragua** 805-6
  - Aid, U.S. 851
  - Ambassadors, envoys 849
  - CIA mining of harbors 533
  - Iran-contra (1986) 449, 533
  - Sandinistas 533
  - U.S. Marines (1912) 443
- **Nickel** 129, 130
- **Nicknames**
  - College football teams 885-87
  - U.S. states 643-68
- **Niger** 806, 849, 851
- **Nigeria** 806-7
  - Aid, U.S. 851
  - Ambassadors, envoys 849
  - History 511, 517, 530
  - Trade 201, 806
- **Nile River** 553
- **Niue Island** 805
- **Nixon, Richard M.** 631, 632, 633, 634, 635
  - Biography 478
  - Burial site 480
  - Cabinet 97-102
  - China visit (1972) *200*, 447
  - Death (1994) 54, *200*, 974
  - Impeachment hearings (1974) 447-48, 478
  - Moscow summit (1972) 447
  - Popular, electoral votes 633
  - Resigned (1974) *200*, 448, 531
  - Watergate (1973, 1974) 447, 448
- **Nobel Prizes** 70, 314-16
- **Nobility, forms of address** 597
- **Norfolk, VA** 680
  - Mayor 91
  - Population 381, 416, 680
  - Port traffic 203
- **Norfolk Island** 744
- **Noriega, Manuel** (1989) 450
- **Normandy, House of** 534
- **Normandy Invasion** (1944) 444
- **North, Oliver** 33
- **North America**
  - Area 839
  - Bridges 690-92
  - Buildings, tall 684-90
  - Cities 380-81, 550-51, 674-83
  - Explorations 543
  - Gold production 131
  - Highest, lowest points 556
  - Lakes 555
  - Map 485
  - Mountain peaks 547, 548
  - Population 839, 840-41
    - Religions 731
  - Rivers 553-54
  - Trade 42-43, 71, 201
  - Tunnels 693
  - Volcanoes 545, 546
  - Waterfalls 556
  - *see also* Canada; Mexico; United States
- **North American Free Trade Agreement** (1993) 42-43, 44, 71, 451
  - Provisions 204
- **North Atlantic Treaty Organization** 844
  - Bosnian civil war (1994) 50, 55, 65
  - Established (1949) 445
  - Expansion (1994) 47
  - International commands 155
  - Russian participation (1994) 60
- **North Carolina** 659
  - Abortions reported 960
  - Admission, area, capital 499, 659
  - Agriculture 134-39
  - Altitudes (high, low) 498
  - Birth, death statistics 958
  - Budget 113
  - Cities 675, 677, 681
  - Congressional representation 77, 82, 376
  - Courts, U.S. 88
  - Crime, prisons, death penalty 216, 217, 218
  - Debt 113
  - Energy consumption 166
  - Geographic center 500
  - Governor, state officials 93, 96
  - As immigrants' intended residence 386
  - Indians, American (population) 507
  - Interest laws, rates 720, 721
  - Marriage, divorce laws 727, 728
  - Motor vehicle statistics 207
  - Name origin, nickname 501, 659
  - Population 376-77, 379
    - Cities, towns 408, 675, 677, 681
    - Counties, county seats 429
    - Density 379
  - Presidential elections 601, 619-20, 630
  - Schools 220, 222, 224
  - Taxes 113, 207, 641, 642
  - Unemployment benefits 142
  - Welfare assistance 384
- **North Dakota** 660
  - Abortions reported 960
  - Admission, area, capital 499, 500, 660
  - Agriculture 134-39
  - Altitudes (high, low) 498
  - Birth, death statistics 958
  - Budget 113
  - Congressional representation 77, 82, 376
  - Courts, U.S. 88
  - Crime, prisons, death penalty 216, 218
  - Debt 113
  - Energy consumption 166
  - Geographic center 500
  - Governor, state officials 93, 96
  - As immigrants' intended residence 386
  - Indians, American (population) 507
  - Interest laws, rates 720, 721
  - Marriage, divorce laws 727, 728
  - Motor vehicle statistics 207
  - Name origin, nickname 501, 660
  - Population 376-77, 379
    - Cities, towns 408
    - Counties, county seats 429
    - Density 379
  - Presidential elections 601, 620-21, 630
  - Schools 220, 222, 224
  - Taxes 113, 207, 641, 642
  - Unemployment benefits 142
  - Welfare assistance 384
- **Northern Cyprus, Turkish Republic of** 760
- **Northern Ireland** 532, 832
- **Northern Lights** 266, 512
- **Northern Mariana Islands** 502, 669-70, 671
  - As immigrants' intended residence 386
  - Population 436
  - Zip codes 436
- **Northern Sung Dynasty** 516
- **North Island** 549, 805
- **North Korea.** *See* Korea, North (Democratic People's Republic of)
- **North Pole**
  - Discovery (1909) 443
  - Explorations 544
  - Magnetic force 271
- **North Sea** 552
- **Northwest Ordinance** (1787) 439
- **Northwest Territory, U.S.** (1787) 439, 500
- **Norway** 807
  - Ambassadors, envoys 849
  - Merchant fleet 205
  - Rulers 539
  - Trade 201
- **Notable personalities** 331-72
  - International figures 372
  - Obituaries (1993-94) 973-74
  - Sports 926-28
- **Novelists, notable.** *See* Writers, notable
- **NRC.** *See* Nuclear Regulatory Commission
- **Nubia** 511
- **Nuclear arms**
  - A-bomb dropped (1945) 445, 529
  - A-bomb experiments (1939) 444
  - Chinese test (1993) 76
  - H-bomb (1950, 1952) 445, 530
  - *Nautilus* submarine (1954) 445
  - Treaties, negotiations (1963-93) 44, 162, 446, 447, 449
- **Nuclear energy**
  - Accidents, major 571
    - Chernobyl (1986) 571
    - Three Mile Island (1979) 448, 531
  - First chain reaction (1942) 444
  - Power production 164, 167, 168
    - By U.S. states 643-68
  - Testing (1993) 44, 451
  - Uranium 177, 178
- **Nuclear Regulatory Commission** 75
  - Employees, payroll 148
  - Outlays, receipts 108
- **Numbers, large** 564
- **Numerals, roman** 564
- **Nurses**
  - First school (1873) 442
- **Nutrition** 701-5
  - Federal program costs 136
  - Labels 44, 704
- **Nuts**
  - Nutritive value 701, 703
  - Prices, farm 140
  - Production 139

— O —

- **Oakland, CA** 680
  - Buildings, tall 688
  - City manager 91
  - Population 381, 390, 680
- **OAS.** *See* Organization of American States
- **Oat production** 138, 139, 140
- **OAU.** *See* Organization of African Unity
- **Obesity** 972
- **Obituaries** (1993-94) 973-74
- **Occupations**
  - By age, sex 143
  - Educational attainment 145
  - Injuries, fatalities 147, 965
  - Leading, U.S. 373
  - Projections
    - Fastest-growing (1992-2005) 146

Occupational group growth (1992-2005) . . . 146
Oceans and seas
Areas, depths . . . 552
Crossings, notable . . . 299
Islands . . . 549
Territorial extent, U.S. . . . 502
Odds (cards, dice) . . . 564
OECD. *See* Organization for Economic Co-operation and Development
Offbeat news stories (1994) . . . 975
Ofu Island . . . 669
Ohio . . . 660-61
Abortions reported . . . 960
Admission, area, capital . . . 499, 500, 660
Agriculture . . . 134-39
Altitudes (high, low) . . . 498
Births, death statistics . . . 958
Budget . . . 113
Cities . . . 674, 675, 676, 683
Congressional representation . 77, 82, 376
Courts . . . 88-89
Crime, prisons, death penalty . . 216, 218
Debt . . . 113
Energy consumption . . . 166
Geographic center . . . 500
Governor, state officials . . . 93, 96
As immigrants' intended residence . . . 386
Indians, American (population) . . . 507
Interest laws, rates . . . 720, 721
Marriage, divorce laws . . . 727, 728
Motor vehicle statistics . . . 207
Name origin, nickname . . . 501, 660
Population . . . 376-77, 379
Cities, towns . . . 408-10, 674, 675, 676, 683
Counties, county seats . . . 429-30
Density . . . 379
Port traffic . . . 203
Presidential elections . . . 601, 621, 630
Schools . . . 220, 222, 224
Taxes . . . 113, 207, 641, 642
Unemployment benefits . . . 142
Welfare assistance . . . 384
Ohio River . . . 553, 554
Ohm (electrical unit) . . . 561
Oil. *See* Petroleum
Oil spills . . . 571-72
Exxon *Valdez* (1989, 1994) 57, 66, 449, 571
Okhotsk, Sea of . . . 552
Okinawa Island . . . 529, 549, 790
Oklahoma . . . 661
Abortions reported . . . 960
Admission, area, capital . . . 499, 500, 661
Agriculture . . . 134-39
Altitudes (high, low) . . . 498
Birth, death statistics . . . 958
Budget . . . 113
Cities . . . 680, 683
Congressional representation . 77, 82, 376
Courts . . . 89
Crime, prisons, death penalty . 216, 217, 218
Debt . . . 113
Energy consumption . . . 166
Geographic center . . . 500
Governor, state officials . . . 93, 96-97
As immigrants' intended residence . . . 386
Indians, American . . . 507
Interest laws, rates . . . 720, 721
Marriage, divorce laws . . . 727, 728
Motor vehicle statistics . . . 207
Name origin, nickname . . . 501, 661
Population . . . 376-77, 379
Cities, towns . . . 410, 680, 683
Counties, county seats . . . 430
Density . . . 379
Presidential elections . . . 601, 621-22, 630
Schools . . . 220, 222, 224
Taxes . . . 113, 207, 641, 642
Unemployment benefits . . . 142
Welfare assistance . . . 384
Oklahoma City, OK . . . 680
Buildings, tall . . . 688
City manager . . . 91
Population . . . 380, 410, 680
Old-age insurance. *See* Social Security Administration
Old Ironsides (1797) . . . 439
Old Testament . . . 734
Olmec civilization . . . 509, 516, 543
Olosega Island . . . 669
Olympic games
History, symbolism . . . 857, 868
Summer . . . 857-68
Games sites . . . 857
Medal standings (1992) . . . 857
Winter . . . 50-51, *784*, 852-56
Games sites . . . 852
Medal standings (1994) . . . 856
see also under specific sports
Olympics, Special . . . 956
Omaha, NE . . . 680
Buildings, tall . . . 688
Mayor . . . 91
Population . . . 381, 404, 680
Oman . . . 807-8, 849, 851
Omnibus Budget Reconciliation Act (1993) . . . 71
Omnibus Violent Crime Control and Prevention Act (1994) 64, 71, 194, 213
Onassis, Jacqueline Kennedy (1994) . 59, *200*, 974
Ontario, Lake . . . 555
OPEC. *See* Organization of Petroleum Exporting Countries
Open Door Policy (1899) . . . 442
Opera
Companies . . . 308
Composers . . . 352-54
Opium War . . . 523
Orange Bowl . . . 882
Orbits, planetary . . . 267
Orchestras, symphony . . . 307-8
Oregon . . . 661-62
Abortions reported . . . 960
Admission, area, capital . . . 499, 500, 661
Agriculture . . . 134-39
Altitudes (high, low) . . . 498
Birth, death statistics . . . 958
Budget . . . 113
Cities . . . 681
Congressional representation 77, 82, 376
Courts . . . 89
Crime, prisons, death penalty . . 217, 218
Debt . . . 113
Energy consumption . . . 166
Geographic center . . . 500
Governor, state officials . . . 93, 96-97
As immigrants' intended residence . . . 386
Indians, American (population) . . . 507
Interest laws, rates . . . 720, 721
Marriage, divorce laws . . . 727, 728
Motor vehicle statistics . . . 207
Name origin, nickname . . . 501, 661
Population . . . 376-77, 379
Cities, towns . . . 410-11, 681
Counties, county seats . . . 430-31
Density . . . 379
Port traffic . . . 203
Presidential elections . . . 601, 622, 630
Schools . . . 220, 222, 224
Taxes . . . 113, 207, 641, 642
Territory . . . 500, 502
Unemployment benefits . . . 142
Welfare assistance . . . 384
Organization for Economic Cooperation and Development . . . 201, 845
Organization of African Unity . . . 845
Organization of American States . . . 845
Founded (1948) . . . 445, 529
Organization of Petroleum Exporting Countries . . . 164, 165, 845
Organizations. *See* Associations and societies; International organizations
Orinoco River . . . 553
Orkney Islands . . . 549, 832
Orlando, FL . . . 91, 393, 688
Orleans, House of . . . 537
Orthodox churches. *See* Eastern Orthodox churches
Oscars. *See* Academy Awards
Ottoman Empire . . . 517, 523, 525
Outland Award . . . 887
Outlying areas, U.S. . . . 669-71
Population . . . 436
Ozone layer . . . 41

— P —

Pacific Islanders, U.S.
Population . . . 375, 382
Social, economic characteristics . . . 378
Pacific Ocean
Area, depth . . . 552
Coast, U.S.
Length . . . 498
Ports, cargo, volume . . . 203, 204
Crossings, notable . . . 299
Discovery . . . 543
Islands, areas . . . 549
Islands, U.S. . . . 549, 669-71
Map . . . 493
Pacing, trotting . . . 901
Packwood, Robert (1993, 1994) . . . 40, 41, 44, 46, 52
Paine, Thomas . . . 452
Painted Desert (AZ) . . . 556, 644
Painters, notable . . . 344-46
Pakistan . . . 808
Aid, U.S. . . . 851
Ambassadors, envoys . . . 849
Bhutto returned (1993) . . . 40
History . . . 529, 532
Military strength . . . 161
Nuclear power . . . 168
Palau . . . 436, 502, 671, 851
Paleontology . . . 169, 510
Palestine. *See* Israel; Middle East
Palestine Liberation Organization . . . 790
Gaza, West Bank self-rule 40, 42, 45, 47, 50 53, 55-56, 57-58, 62, 65, *779*, 788
Palestinian uprising . . . 533, 788
Palm Sunday . . . 732
Palmyra (atoll) . . . 671
Panama . . . 808-9
Aid, U.S. . . . 851
Ambassadors, envoys . . . 849
Distances to ports . . . 204
Merchant fleet . . . 205
Treaties, U.S. (1903, 1978) . . . 442-43, 448, 809
U.S. invasion (1989) . . . 450, 809
Panama Canal . . . 809
Employees, federal . . . 148
Opened (1914) . . . 443
Treaties (1903, 1978) . . 442-43, 448, 809
Pantelleria Island . . . 789
Paper
Exports, imports . . . 202
Invention . . . 513
Measures . . . 561
Papua New Guinea . . . 549, 809, 849, 851
Paraguay . . . 809-10, 849
Parcel post rates . . . 587-91
Parenthood . . . 721, 960
see also Households
Paricutin volcano . . . 512
Paris . . . 767, 840
Parks, national . . . 71, 503-6
Parliament
British . . . 831
Oldest (Iceland) . . . 775
Parthenon . . . 509
Parthians . . . 513
Passport regulations, U.S. . . . 722
Pay. *See* Salaries and wages
Peace Prizes, Nobel . . . 70, 316
Peale Atoll . . . 671
Peanut production . . . 139, 140
Pearl Harbor (1941) . . . 444
Peary, Robert E. (1909) . . . 443, 544
Peking Man . . . 508
Peloponnesian Wars . . . 509
Pemba . . . 826
Pendleton Act (1883) . . . 442
Penghu (Pescadores) . . . 825
Penn, William (1683) . . . 438
Pen names . . . 598
Pennsylvania . . . 662
Abortions reported . . . 960
Admission, area, capital . . . 499, 662
Agriculture . . . 134-39
Altitudes (high, low) . . . 498
Birth, death statistics . . . 958
Budget . . . 113
Cities . . . 680-81
Congressional representation. 77, 82-83, 376
Courts, U.S. . . . 89
Crime, prisons, death penalty . . . 216, 218
Debt . . . 113
Energy consumption . . . 166
Geographic center . . . 500
Governor, state officials . . . 93, 97
As immigrants' intended residence . . 386
Indians, American (population) . . . 507
Interest laws, rates . . . 720, 721
Marriage, divorce laws . . . 727, 728
Mineral production . . . 129
Motor vehicle statistics . . . 207
Name origin, nickname . . . 501, 662
Population . . . 376-77, 379
Cities, towns . . . 411-12, 680
Counties, county seats . . . 431
Density . . . 379
Port traffic . . . 203
Presidential elections . . 601, 622-23, 630
Schools . . . 220, 222, 224
Taxes . . . 113, 207, 641, 642
Unemployment benefits . . . 142
Welfare assistance . . . 384
Pensions
Veterans . . . 160
see also Social Security Administration
Pentagon . . . 673
Pentagon Papers (1971) . . . 447
Pentathlon . . . 867
Pentecostal churches
Address, U.S. headquarters . . . 731
Beliefs, practices . . . 738-39
Membership . . . 730

Per capita income. *See under* Incomes
Per capita public debt (U.S.) 109
Perigee of moon 268
Perihelion. *See* Aphelion, perihelion
Peron, Juan 530
Perot, H. Ross (1992, 1993) 43, 450, 601-30, 631, 633
Perpetual calendar 286-87
Perry, Matthew C. (1853) 441
Perry, Oliver H. (1813) 440
Pershing, John J. (1916) 443
Persia. *See under* Iran
Persian Gulf
Area, depth 552
Map 492
Persian Gulf War (1991) . . 450, 786, 793, 817
Black troops 334
Casualties, U.S. forces 163
Kuwait invaded (1990) . 450, 786, 793, 817
Personal consumption, U.S 109-11
Personal income, U.S. 111, 124
Personalities, notable. *See* Notable personalities
Peru 810
Aid, U.S. 851
Ambassadors, envoys 849
Ancient civilizations 511
Coup (1976) 532
Pizarro conquest 520, 543
Pescadores (Penghu) 825
Petroleum
Arab embargo (1973) 447
Exports, imports 164, 165, 202
First well (PA) (1859) 441
Oil spills (1989, 1994). 57, 66, 449, 571-72
OPEC 164, 165, 845
Production, consumption, U.S. 164
Reserves, crude oil 167
U.S. dependence on 164, 165
see also Gasoline
Phases of moon 269
Philadelphia, PA 680-81
Buildings, tall 688
Capital of U.S. (1790) 439
Commuters 210
Independence Hall 469-70
Liberty Bell 469-70
Mayor 91
Population 380, 412, 680
Port traffic 203
Unemployment rate 145
Philanthropists, notable 351-52
Philippines, Republic of the 810-11
Accession, U.S. (1898) 442, 811
Aid, U.S. 851
Ambassadors, envoys 849
Gold production 131
Independence (1946) 445, 529, 811
Insurrection (1899) 442
Islands, areas 549
Merchant fleet 205
Trade 201
U.S. immigration 386
World War II (1944) 444, 529, 811
Philosophers, notable 347, 509
Phoenicians 508, 509
Phoenix, AZ 681
Buildings, tall 688
City manager 91
Commuters 210
Population 380, 388, 681
Unemployment rate 145
Photographers, notable 344-46
Photographs of the year (1994) . *193-200, 777-84*
Photography
Inventions, notable 174, 175
Pulitzer Prizes 320
Physicians. *See* Doctors
Physics
Discoveries 169, 176-77
Nobel Prizes 70, 314
Physiology, Nobel Prize in 70, 315
Pierce, Franklin 634
Biography 473
Burial site 480
Cabinet 98-101
Popular, electoral votes 633
Pig iron production 131
Pinochle (odds) 564
Pistol champions (1994) 925
Pitcairn Island 833
Pittsburgh, PA 681
Buildings, tall 688
Mayor 91
Population 381, 412, 681
Pizarro, Francisco 520, 543
Planets 251-62
Configurations 251-54, 259-60
Earth 269-71
Morning, evening stars 272
Rising, setting 261-62
Solar System 267
Sun relationship 254
see also Space developments
Plantagenet, House of 534
Plants, classification 192
Platinum 129, 130
Playing cards (odds) 564
Plays. *See* Theater
Playwrights, notable . 325, 334-35, 341-44
Pulitzer Prizes 321
Pledge of allegiance 468
PLO. *See* Palestine Liberation Organization
Pluto (planet) 258-59
Position by months 252-54, 259-60
Solar system 267
Sun, distance from 254, 267
Plymouth colony (1620) 438, 520
Poets, notable 341-44
Awards 315-16, 323, 324
Laureates 341
Poison gas 964, 965
Poisons
Animals, major 190
Chemical pollution 187
Death rates 964, 965
Poker odds 564
Poland 811-12
Aid, U.S. 851
Ambassadors, envoys 849
History 516, 520, 521, 522, 533
Merchant fleet 205
Military strength 161
Rulers 539
Solidarity (1982) 448, 533, 811-12
World War II 528-29, 811
Polar explorations 543-45
Poles of the earth 271
Pole vault
Olympic champions 860
World indoor, outdoor records . . 868, 869
Police 213, 215
Political convention sites 632
Political leaders, notable 337-39
Polk, James K. 634
Biography 473
Burial site 480
Cabinet 98-100
Popular, electoral votes 633
Pollution. *See* Environment
Polynesia, French 768
Ponce de Leon (1513) 438, 543
Pony Express (1860) 441
Poor Richard's Almanac (1732) 438
Popes 734, 735
see also John Paul II, Pope
Population, U.S. 373-436
Asian-Pacific Islander 375, 378, 382
Birth, death statistics 957-60, 964-65
Black 373, 375, 382, 437
Census (1790-1990) 376-77
Census Act (1790) 439
Census Bureau 74, 76, 107, 374, 375
Census Test (1995) 374
Center (1790-present) 377
Cities 380-81, 387-417, 674-83
Colonies (1630-1780) 374
Congressional apportionment 376
Counties 378, 379-80, 418-36
Density
By county 380
By largest counties 380
By state 379
Disabled people 382
Distribution (by age) 437
Drug use 963
Educational level 220
Elderly (over 65) 382, 961
Election statistics 631
Ethnic, racial distribution. 375, 382, 437, 507
Farm 134
Hispanic 375
Immigration, by intended residence . . . 386
Indian, American 375, 382, 507
Languages spoken 599-600
More than 5,000 (by state) 387-417
Net worth, median 384
Poverty statistics 374, 383
Projections (1995-2050)
By age 382
By race 382
Religious groups 729-31
Sex, race, residence, median age (1790-1990) 378, 437
States 379, 418-36, 643-68
Census (1790-1990) 376-77
Veterans 159-60
Youth (under age 18) 382
Population, world
Cities
By country 740-839
By largest 840
Continents 839, 840-41
Growth (AD 1-1993) 510
Growth rate (by country) 740-839
International conference (1994) 67
Projections 840-41
Religions 731
Pork
Consumption 135
Nutritive value 702
Prices, farm 140
Production 135
Portland, OR 681
Buildings, tall 688
Mayor 92
Population 380, 410, 681
Ports 203, 204
Portugal 812
Aid, U.S. 851
Ambassadors, envoys 849
History 526, 527, 532
Possessions, U.S. 669-71
Governors 93, 97
Populations 436
ZIP codes 436
Postage stamps
First adhesive (1847) 441
Postal cards
First U.S. (1873) 442
International rates 591
Postal information 587-91
Abbreviations
Canadian 589
State 589
Domestic rates 587
International rates 590-91
Parcel post rates 587-91
Priority Mail 587
ZIP codes 387-417, 436
Postal Service, U.S. 75, 587-91
Abbreviations 589
Employees, payroll 148
Established (1970) 447, 587
Rates 587-91
Potatoes
Nutritive value 703
Prices, farm 140
Production 138, 139
Poultry products
Egg production 135
Nutritive value 701, 702
Prices
Farm 140
Per dozen, by state 135
Pound (measure) 558, 559
Poverty
Rate, level 374, 383
War on (1964) 446
Welfare assistance 384
Powell, Colin 67, 162, 334, 449
Power-boat racing 925
Preakness Stakes 898-99
Precipitation
International 184
Normal 180, 181
By U.S. cities 180-82
By U.S. states 181
Wettest spot 181
see also Blizzards
Presbyterian churches
Addresses, U.S. headquarters 731
Beliefs, practices 738-39
Membership 730
Presidential elections 601-33
Clinton elected (1992) 450
Returns 601-30, 631, 633
Electoral College 376, 457-58, 461, 630, 632
National Convention sites 632
Party nominees 632-33
Popular, electoral votes 601, 633
Returns (by states, counties) 602-30
Voter participation 631-32
Presidents, U.S.
Address, form of 597
Ages 634
Aides 72
Appointment powers 458
Assassinations 441, 442, 446, 474, 475, 478, 573
Biographies 471-80
Birth, death dates 634
Burial sites 480
Cabinets 72, 97-102
Children, number of 480
Clinton administration 72-75
Congresses 634-35
Constitutional powers 458

Disability . . . 458, 466
Election (*see* Presidential elections)
Inauguration . . . 462
Oath of office . . . 458, 466
Party . . . 632-33, 633
Salary . . . 72
Salutes, honors . . . 156
Succession law . . . 463, 466
Term beginning, limit . . . 72, 462-63
Vetoes . . . 86
Vice presidents . . . 634-35
Voter turnout . . . 631-32
White House . . . 66, 673
Wives . . . 480
see also specific presidents
Press. *See* Magazines; Newspapers
Pressure and force measures . . . 564
Price index
Consumer . . . 109-11
Producer . . . 133
Priest, form of address . . . 597
Prime interest rate . . . 133
Príncipe. *See* São Tomé and Príncipe
Printer's measures . . . 561
Priority Mail . . . 587
Prism, rectangular, volume . . . 564
Prisoners of war
Geneva Conventions . . . 847
Prison population . . . 70, 216-17
Prizes. *See* Awards, prizes
Probability (cards, dice) . . . 564
Prohibition (1917-33) . . 443, 444, 462, 527
Property rights . . . 70
Protein . . . 701, 702-3
Protestant churches
Beliefs, practices . . . 738-39
Books of the Bible . . . 734
Membership . . . 729-30, 731, 736
Reformation . . . 519
see also specific denominations
Protestant Episcopal Church. *See* Episcopal Church
Providence, RI . . . 92, 688
Prussia . . . 521, 523
Public debt . . . 109, 113, 133
Public holidays . . . 291
Public lands . . . 441, 502
Public libraries, U.S. . . . 225
Public schools. *See* Education
Puerto Rico . . . 670
Accession . . . 502
Altitudes (high, low) . . . 498
Area . . . 502, 549
Cities (population) . . . 436
Congressional delegate . . . 84
Courts . . . 89
Government . . . 97, 670
Governor . . . 93, 97
As immigrants' intended residence . . . 386
Interest laws, rates . . . 720, 721
Marriage, divorce laws . . . 727, 728
Name origin . . . 501
Port traffic . . . 203
Statehood defeated (1993) . . . 42, 451
Unemployment benefits . . . 142
Zip codes . . . 436
Pulitzer Prizes . . . 316-24
Punic Wars (264-146 BC) . . . 513
Pure Food and Drug Act (1906) . . . 443
Pyramid, volume . . . 564
Pyramids . . . 512
Pyrenees . . . 548

— Q —

Qatar . . . 812, 849
Quakers (Society of Friends) . . . 729, 730
Queen Anne's War (1701-13) . . . 438
Queens, NY . . . 428
Quemoy . . . 549, 825
Quire (measure) . . . 561
Quotes, notable (1994) . . . 104

— R —

Rabin, Yitzhak . . . *779*, 788
Race
Distribution . . . 375, 437, 507
Disabled people . . . 382
Projections (1995-2050) . . . 382
By state . . . 643-68
Population projections (1995-2050) . . 382
see also Asians, U.S.; Blacks; Indians, American; Pacific Islanders, U.S.
Racing
Airplane . . . 298
Automobile . . . 931-33
Bicycle . . . 866, 928
Bobsled . . . 853
Harness . . . 901
NASCAR . . . 933
Power boat . . . 925
Rowing . . . 867
Skiing . . . 853, 854-55, 920
Sled dog . . . 920
Speed skating . . . 855-56
Swimming . . . 862-65, 906
Thoroughbred . . . 898-900
Track and field . . . 858-62, 868-69
Yacht . . . 868, 937
Radiation, nuclear (1993) . . . 44, 451
Radio
Advertising expenditures . . . 313
Broadcast, first (1920) . . . 443
Inventions, notable . . . 175
Notable personalities . . . 357-70
Transatlantic, first (1901) . . . 525
War of the Worlds scare (1938) . . . 444
Railroads, U.S.
Accidents, deaths . . . 567-68
Army seizes (1950) . . . 445
Fastest runs . . . 206
First locomotive . . . 175
First Mississippi R. crossing (1855) . . 441
First passenger (1828) . . . 440
Growth (19th-century) . . . 523
Strike (1877) . . . 442
Transcontinental (1869) . . . 442
Railroads, world
Canadian . . . 206
Growth (19th-century) . . . 523
Tunnels
English Channel . . . 59, 198, 694
World's longest . . . 693
see also specific countries
Rainfall. *See* Precipitation
Raleigh, NC . . . 681
Buildings, tall . . . 688
Mayor . . . 92
Population . . . 381
Ramayana . . . 511
Rape . . . 214, 215, 217, 218
Reader's Digest (1922) . . . 443
Reagan, Ronald . . . 631, 633, 634, 635
Biography . . . 479
Cabinet . . . 97-102
Iran-contra (1994) . . . 52
Popular, electoral votes . . . 633
Ream (measure) . . . 561
Recession . . . 133
see also Depression, economic
Recommended Daily Dietary Allowances . . . 701, 705
Reconstruction Era (1866) . . . 441
Constitutional amendments . . . 461-62
Recordings . . . 309
Awards . . . 309, 329-30
Recreation areas, national . . . 502, 506
Rectangle
Area . . . 564
Red Sea . . . 552
Reformation, Protestant . . . 519
Reformed churches . . . 730, 731
Refrigerators . . . 166
Refugees, world . . . 842
Religion . . . 729-39
Addresses, U.S. headquarters . . . 730-31
Beliefs, practices . . . 737-39
Bible . . . 734
Census of U.S. groups . . . 729-30
Christian denominations . . . 738-39
Cultists found dead (1994) . . . 69
Holy days . . . 732-33
Major world . . . 737-39
Population (U.S., world) . . . 729-30, 731
Religionists, notable . . . 326, 347
Roman Catholic hierarchy . . . 734
School prayer banned (1963, 1984) . 446, 449
Religious wars (16th-17th centuries) . . . 519
Rembrandt . . . 345, 519
Renaissance . . . 518
Reno, Janet (1993) . . . 72, 73, 451
Rents
Consumer price index . . . 109, 110
Housing units . . . 373
Reporters. *See* Journalism awards
Republican Party
Convention sites . . . 632
Elections (by county) . . . 602-30
First presidential nominee (1856) . . . 441
Formed (1854) . . . 441
Presidential, vice presidential candidates . . . 632-33
Reservoirs . . . 695
Reunion Island . . . 549, 767
Revenue sharing . . . 107-8
Revere, Paul (1775) . . . 439
Revolutionary War. *See* American Revolution
Rheumatic heart disease . . . 970
Rhode Island . . . 662-63
Abortions reported . . . 960
Admission, area, capital . . . 499, 662
Agriculture . . . 134-39
Altitudes (high, low) . . . 498
Birth, death statistics . . . 958
Budget . . . 113
Congressional representation . 77, 83, 376
Courts, U.S. . . . 89
Crime, prisons, death penalty . . . 216, 217
Debt . . . 113
Energy consumption . . . 166
Geographic center . . . 500
Governor, state officials . . . 93, 97
As immigrants' intended residence . . 386
Indians, American (population) . . . 507
Interest laws, rates . . . 720, 721
Marriage, divorce laws . . . 727, 728
Motor vehicle statistics . . . 207
Name origin, nickname . . . 501, 662
Population . . . 376-77, 379
Cities, towns . . . 412
Counties, county seats . . . 431
Density . . . 379
Presidential elections . . . 601, 623, 630
Schools . . . 220, 222, 224
Taxes . . . 113, 207, 641, 642
Unemployment benefits . . . 142
Welfare assistance . . . 384
Rhodesia. *See* Zimbabwe
Rice production . . . 139, 140, 141
Richmond, VA . . . 681
Buildings, tall . . . 689
City manager . . . 92
Confederate capital . . . 464
Population . . . 381, 416, 681
Richmond County, NY . . . 428
Ride, Sally (1983) . . . 293, 448
Rifle champions (1994) . . . 925
Rig Veda . . . 509
Ring of Fire volcanoes . . . 545
Rio de Janeiro . . . 512, 840
Rio Grande . . . 553, 554
Riots
Detroit (1943, 1967) . . . 444, 446-47
East Berlin (1953) . . . 530
Haymarket (1886) . . . 442
Herrin (IL) strike (1922) . . . 443
Los Angeles
King case (1992, 1993) . . . 40, 450
Watts (1965) . . . 446
Newark (NJ) (1967) . . . 446
New York City
Draft (1863) . . . 441
Harlem (1943) . . . 444
Poznan (1956) . . . 530
Slave revolt (1712) . . . 438
Rivers
North American . . . 553-54
St. Lawrence Seaway (1959) . . . 446
World . . . 553
see also specific rivers
Riverside, CA . . . 681
Mayor . . . 92
Population . . . 381, 390, 681
Roads
Interstate system (1956) . . . 446
Mileage . . . 211
Robberies . . . 214, 215, 217, 218
Brink's (1950) . . . 445
Rochester, NY . . . 681
Buildings, tall . . . 689
City manager . . . 92
Population . . . 381, 407, 681
Rock & Roll notables . 56, 325, 355-56, *780*
Rockets. *See* Nuclear arms; Space developments
Rodeo champions . . . 937
Roe v. Wade (1973, 1989) . . . 447, 449, 465
Rogers, Will (1935) . . . 444
Roman Catholicism
Address, U.S. headquarters . . . 731
Beliefs, practices . . . 738-39
Books of the Bible . . . 734
Clergy, forms of address . . . 597
Hierarchy . . . 734
Pope John Paul II . . . 735, 834
Popes (chronological list) . . . 735
Population, U.S., world . . . 730, 731
Vatican City . . . 834-35, 849
Romania . . . 812-13
Aid, U.S. . . . 851
Ambassadors, envoys . . . 849
History . . . 527, 533
Merchant fleet . . . 205
Military strength . . . 161
Nuclear power . . . 168
Roman numerals . . . 564
Romans, ancient
Historical figures . . . 534

(continued)

Romans, ancient *(continued)*
Measures . . . 562
Rulers, emperors . . . 513, 540
Rome
Founding . . . 513
Population . . . 840
Seven Wonders, Middle Ages . . . 512
Roosevelt, Franklin D. . . . 631, 632, 634, 635
Biography . . . 477
Burial site . . . 480
Cabinet . . . 98-102
Library (Hyde Park, NY) . . . 659
New Deal (1933) . . . 444
Popular, electoral votes . . . 633
World War II (1939, 1941, 1945) . . . 444, 445
Roosevelt, Theodore . . . 632, 634, 635
Biography . . . 475
Burial site . . . 480
Cabinet . . . 98-101
Popular, electoral votes . . . 633
Rose Bowl . . . 882
Rose Island . . . 669
Ross, Betsy . . . 467
Ross Dependency . . . 805
Rostenkowski, Dan . . . 52, 57, *194*
Rowing . . . 867
Royalty . . . 534-42
Address, forms of . . . 597
British (1993, 1994) . . . 45, 61
Russian tsars . . . 517, 542
Rubber . . . 202
Rural Credits Act (1916) . . . 443
Rushmore, Mt. *See* Mt. Rushmore
Russia . . . 813-14
Aid, U.S. . . . 851
Ambassadors, envoys . . . 849
Area . . . 813, 839
Chronology (1993-94) . . . 42, 45, 47, 50, 51, 60, 67
Democratic reform efforts (1993, 1994) 42, 45, 47, *779*
Islands, areas . . . 549
Merchant fleet . . . 205
Military strength . . . 161
Mineral resources . . . 129, 130, 813
Nuclear power . . . 47, 167, 168
Russian Federation . . . 814
see also Soviet Union
Russian Empire (pre-1917) . . . 517
Alaska (1741, 1867) . . . 438, 442
Congress of Vienna . . . 522
Crimean War (1853-56) . . . 523
Japanese War (1904-5) . . . 525
Orthodox Church . . . 517
Tsars . . . 517, 542
see also Russia; Soviet Union (*for later history*)
Russian Federation. *See* Russia
Russian Orthodox churches. *See* Eastern Orthodox churches
Russian Revolution (1917) . . . 526
Russo-Japanese War (1904-5) . . . 525
Rwanda . . . 814-15
Aid, U.S. . . . 851
Ambassadors, envoys . . . 849
Ethnic violence (1994) . . . 55, 57, 60, 62, 65, *778*
Rye production . . . 139

— S —

Saba Island . . . 805
SAC. *See* Strategic Air Command
Sacco-Vanzetti case (1920) . . . 443
Sacramento, CA . . . 681
Buildings, tall . . . 689
City manager . . . 92
Population . . . 381, 390, 681
Sadat, Anwar al- (1981) . . . 533, 573, 764
Saints. *See name, inverted*
St. Augustine, FL (1565) . . . 438, 647
St. Croix Island . . . 436, 670-71
St. Eustatius Island . . . 805
St. Helena Island . . . 549, 833
St. Helens volcano (1980) . . . 448, 546
St. John Island . . . 436, 670-71
St. Kitts and Nevis . . . 815, 849
St. Lawrence River
Discovered . . . 543
Length, outflow . . . 553, 554
St. Lawrence Seaway (1959) . . . 446
St. Louis, MO . . . 681
Buildings, tall . . . 689
Mayor . . . 92
Population . . . 381, 403, 681
Port traffic . . . 203
Unemployment rate . . . 145
St. Lucia . . . 815, 849
St. Maarten . . . 805
St. Paul, MN . . . 682
Buildings, tall . . . 689
Mayor . . . 92
Population . . . 381, 402, 682
St. Petersburg, FL . . . 682
City manager . . . 92
Population . . . 381, 393, 682
St. Pierre and Miquelon . . . 768
St. Thomas Island . . . 436, 670-71
St. Valentine's Day Massacre (1929) . . . 444
St. Vincent and the Grenadines . . . 205, 815, 849
Salaries and wages
Armed Forces scale . . . 162
Average
By education, sex, race . . . 149
By metropolitan area . . . 146
College professors . . . 224
Earnings . . . 149, 150, 151, 152
Employer costs . . . 151
Governors, state officials . . . 93-97
Hourly rates . . . 150
Judges . . . 87, 89
Minimum wage
Enacted (1938) . . . 444
Hourly rates . . . 151
Increased (1989) . . . 450
Pay, average . . . 150, 152
Paycheck withholding tax (1943) . . . 444
Pay differential, male/female . . . 149
President, U.S. . . . 72
Representatives, U.S. . . . 78
Senators, U.S. . . . 76
Supreme Court justices . . . 86
Teachers . . . 220, 224
Vice president, U.S. . . . 72
see also Income taxes
Sales taxes (by states) . . . 643-68
SALT I and II. *See* Strategic Arms Limitation Treaty, I and II
Salt Lake City, UT . . . 92, 689
Salutations, persons of rank . . . 597
Salutes and honors . . . 156
Salvation Army . . . 730, 731
Samoa, American . . . 669
Accession . . . 502
Altitudes (high, low) . . . 498
Area . . . 502, 549
Congressional delegate . . . 84
Population . . . 436
Samoa, Western . . . 549, 836, 849
San Antonio, TX . . . 682
Buildings, tall . . . 689
Commuters . . . 210
Mayor . . . 92
Population . . . 380, 414, 682
Unemployment rate . . . 145
Sand Atoll . . . 671
Sand Creek Massacre (1864) . . . 441
San Diego, CA . . . 682
Buildings, tall . . . 689
City manager . . . 92
Commuters . . . 210
Population . . . 380, 390, 682
Unemployment rate . . . 145
San Francisco, CA . . . 682
Buildings, tall . . . 689
Commuters . . . 210
Earthquake (1989) . . . 449-50, 572
Earthquake, fire (1906) . . . 443, 572
Mayor . . . 92
Mileage to foreign ports . . . 204
Population . . . 380, 390, 682
Unemployment rate . . . 145
San Jose, CA . . . 682
City manager . . . 92
Commuters . . . 210
Population . . . 380, 390, 682
San Marino . . . 815-16
Santa Ana, CA . . . 682
City manager . . . 92
Population . . . 381, 390, 682
Santa Fe, NM (1609) . . . 438
São Tomé and Príncipe . . . 816, 849
Sardinia . . . 549, 789
Sark Islands . . . 549, 832
Satellites, space. *See* Space developments
Saturn (planet) . . . 257
Morning, evening stars . . . 272
Position by months . . . 251-54, 259-60
Rises, sets . . . 262
Solar system . . . 267
Sun, distance from . . . 254, 267
Saudi Arabia . . . 816-17
Ambassadors, envoys . . . 849
History . . . 527, 531
Map . . . 492
Persian Gulf War (1991) . . . 450, 817
Trade . . . 201
Savings and loan crisis . . . 115
Bailout bill (1989) . . . 449
Keating convictions (1991, 1993) . . . 450
Savings bonds, U.S. . . . 117
Scandinavia . . . 527
see also Denmark; Norway; Sweden
School prayer ban (1963, 1984) . . . 446, 449
Schools. *See* Education
Science and technology . . . 169-78
Achievements, discoveries (1994) . . . 169
Awards . . . 314-15, 326
Chemical elements . . . 177-78
Computers . . . 170-73, 221
Genetic fingerprinting . . . 56
Information superhighway . . . 35-36, 198
Inventions, discoveries . . . 174-77
National Medal winners . . . 174
Scientific Revolution (1500-1700) . . . 519
Scientists, notable . . . 314-15, 349-50
Scorpions, poisonous . . . 190
Scotland . . . 535, 831-32
see also United Kingdom
Sculptors, notable . . . 344-46
Sea creatures, venomous . . . 190
Seas. *See* Oceans and seas
Seashores, national . . . 506
Seasons . . . 259-60, 270-71
SEATO. *See* Southeast Asia Treaty Organization
Seattle, WA . . . 682
Buildings, tall . . . 689
Floating bridge . . . 692
Mayor . . . 92
Population . . . 380, 416, 682
Secret Service, U.S. . . . 73, 76
Securities and Exchange Commission . . . 75, 108, 148
Seeds
Nutritive value . . . 703
Segregation. *See* Desegregation
Selective Service System. *See* Draft, U.S.
Self-employment
Social Security benefits . . . 697-98
Seminole War (1835) . . . 440
Senate. *See* Congress, U.S.
Senegal . . . 817, 849, 851
Sentences, prison . . . 218
Seventh-Day Adventists . . . 729
Seven Wonders of the World . . . 512
Seward, William H. (1867) . . . 442, 644
Sexual harassment
Clinton accuser (1994) . . . 56-57, 60, 64
Packwood accusers (1993, 1994) . . . 40, 41, 44, 46, 52
Supreme Court rulings (1993) . . . 70
Tailhook scandal (1994) . . . 49, 55
Thomas accuser (1991) . . . 450
Seychelles . . . 817, 849
Shakespeare, William . . . 343, 518
Folger Library . . . 672
Shalikashvili, John . . . 73
Shang Dynasty . . . 509, 542
Shapiro, Robert . . . *195*
Shay's Rebellion (1787) . . . 439
Sheep . . . 134, 135, 140
Shepard, Alan B., Jr. (1961) . . . 292, 446
Sherman, William (1864, 1865) . . . 441
Sherman Antitrust Act (1890) . . . 442
Shetland Islands . . . 549, 832
Shi'ites. *See* Islam
Shintoism . . . 515, 731
Shipping
Distances . . . 204
Merchant fleets . . . 205
Tonnage at ports . . . 203, 205
Ships
Disasters (1915, 1987) . . . 443, 449, 565-66
Frigates, famous U.S. (1797) . . . 439
Great White Fleet (1907) . . . 443
Steamboats
First Atlantic crossing (1819) . . . 440
Fulton's (1807) . . . 440
Inventors . . . 175-76
see also Submarine
Shipwrecks . . . 565-66
Shooting (sport)
Olympic champions (1992) . . . 867
Rifle, pistol champions (1994) . . . 925
Shot put
Olympic champions . . . 860, 862
World indoor, outdoor records . . . 868, 869
Shreveport, LA . . . 682
Mayor . . . 92
Population . . . 381, 398, 682
Siam. *See* Thailand
Sicily . . . 549, 789
Sidereal day, year, time . . . 259, 270
Sierra Leone . . . 817-18, 849, 851
Signs and symbols
Astronomical . . . 259
Chemical elements . . . 177-78
Zodiac . . . 268
Sikhism . . . 518, 522, 731
Silver
Production . . . 129, 130, 131

Reserve base, world 129
Value in coins 117
Simpson, O. J. 61, 63, 67, *195*
Singapore 818
Aid, U.S. 851
Ambassadors, envoys 849
Area 549
Chronology (1993-94) 58-59
Distances to ports 204
Merchant fleet 205
Trade 201
Singers, notable 354-70
Single-parent households 960, 961
Sioux Indian War (1876) 442
Skating
Figure
Kerrigan assault (1994) . 48, 50-51, 54, 61
Olympic champions (1908-94). . . 50-51, *784*, 853
U.S., world champions 903
Speed
Olympic champions (1924-94) . . . 855-56
Skiing
Olympic champions (1924-94) . 853, 854-55
World Cup Alpine Champions 920
Skye, Isle of 832
Skylab 293
Slavery
Abolished, 13th Amendment (1865) . 441, 461
Abolitionist raids (1856, 1859) 441
Dred Scott decision (1857) . 441, 464, 473
Emancipation Proclamation (1863) . . . 441
Importation outlawed (1808) 440
Introduced into America (1619) 438
Kansas-Nebraska Act (1854) . . 441, 473
Missouri Compromise (1820) 440
Rebellions (1712, 1831) 438, 440
Slovakia 168, 818, 849
Slovenia 168, 818-19, 849
Small Business Administration . . 75, 108
Small Craft Advisory 179
Smith, Adam 521
Smith, Captain John (1607) 438
Smithsonian Institution 76, 108, 673
Smoking
Benefits of quitting 705
Heart disease 707
High school students 963
House hearings (1994) 54
Smythe Trophy 897
Snakes, poisonous 190
Snowfall
Blizzard of 1888 . . . . . 442, 569
Cities, U.S. 182
Mean annual 181
Soccer
Olympic champions (1992) 867
World Cup 61, 63, *783*, 937, 938
Social reformers, notable 347-48
Social scientists, notable 348-49
Social Security Administration . . . 71, 76, 696-700
Act passed (1935) 444
Medicare (1966) 446, 698, 712
Tax revenues 107
Societies. *See* Associations and societies
Sodium (dietary)
Labels, nutrition 704
Nutritive value 702-3
Software, CD-ROM 173
Solar day 270
Solar system 251-62, 267-71
Solidarity (Poland) (1982) . 448, 533, 811-12
Solomon Islands 819, 848
Solstices (1995) 252, 254, 260, 271
Somalia 819, 849, 851
Map 494-495
U.S. military force (1992, 1993, 1994) . 40, 42, 44, 53, 450
Somerset Island 549
Sorghum production 139, 140
Soto, Hernando de. *See* De Soto, Hernando
Sound, speed of 563
South Africa 819-20
Aid, U.S. 851
Ambassadors, envoys 849
Apartheid 56, 57, 533, 820
Boer War (1899-1902) 820
Distances to ports 204
Gold production 131
Mandela election (1994) 50, 56, 57, *777*, 820
Map 495
Nuclear power 167, 168
Self-government (1910) 525
Transitional government (1993, 1994) . 43, 52-53
U.S. sanctions (1986) 449
South America
Area 839
Gold production 131
Highest, lowest points 555
Lakes 555
Languages 598-99
Largest country 749-50
Liberation wars, leaders 530
Map 488-489
Mountain peaks 547
Population 839, 840-41
Religions 731-32
Trade 201
Volcanoes 545, 546
Waterfalls 556
see also specific countries
South Carolina 663
Abortions reported 960
Admission, area, capital 499, 663
Agriculture 134-39
Altitudes (high, low) 498
Birth, death statistics 958
Budget 113
Congressional representation . 77, 83, 376
Courts, U.S. 89
Crime, prisons, death penalty . 216, 217, 218
Debt 113
Energy consumption 166
Geographic center 500
Governor, state officials 93, 97
As immigrants' intended residence . . . 386
Indians, American (population) 507
Interest laws, rates 720, 721
Marriage, divorce laws 727, 728
Motor vehicle statistics 207
Name origin, nickname 501, 663
Population 376-77, 379
Cities, towns 412-13
Counties, county seats 431
Density 379
Presidential elections . . . 601, 623-24, 630
Schools 220, 222, 224
Taxes 113, 207, 641
Unemployment benefits 142
Welfare assistance 384
South China Sea 552
South Dakota 663-64
Abortions reported 960
Admission, area, capital . . . 499, 500, 663
Agriculture 134-39
Altitudes (high, low) 498
Birth, death statistics 958
Budget 113
Congressional representation 77, 83, 376
Courts, U.S. 89
Crime, prisons, death penalty . . 216, 218
Debt 113
Energy consumption 166
Geographic center 500
Governor, state officials 93, 97
As immigrants' intended residence . . . 386
Indians, American (population) 507
Interest laws, rates 720, 721
Marriage, divorce laws 727, 728
Motor vehicle statistics 207
Name origin, nickname 501, 663
Population 376-77, 379
Cities, towns 413
Counties, county seats 431-32
Density 379
Presidential elections 601, 624, 630
Schools 220, 222, 224
Taxes 113, 207, 641
Unemployment benefits 142
Welfare assistance 384
Southeast Asia
Map 493
see also Vietnam War; *specific countries*
Southeast Asia Treaty Organization (1954) 445
South Island 549, 805
South Korea. *See* Korea, South
South Pole
Exploration 544-45
Magnetic force 271
South Yemen. *See* Yemen
Soviet Union 814
Berlin blockade (1948) 445
Chernobyl disaster (1986) 571
Cold War 529, 532-33
Cuban crisis (1962) 446
Eastern Bloc revolt (1989) 532-33
Glasnost 532-33, 814
Gold production 131
Gorbachev Peace Prize 316
History 526, 527, 528
Hungarian revolt (1956) 530
Leaders 542
Nixon visit (1972) 447
Perestroika 532-33, 814
Space exploration 292-95, 530
Summit talks (1972, 1985, 1987). 447, 449
U.S. immigration 386
World War I 526
World War II 528-29
Yalta (1945) 445
see also Arms control; Russia; Russian Empire; *other former republics*
Soybean production 138, 139, 140
Space developments 292-95
Apollo missions (1969) 292-93, 447
Astronauts 292-94, 297
Cosmonauts 49, 292-94
Explorer 1 (1958) 446
First men in space (1961) . . 292, 293, 446
First women in space (1983) . . 292, 293, 448
Goddard's rockets demonstration, (1926) 444
Hall of Fame 297
Hubble telescope (1993, 1994) . 43-44, 63, 169, 198, 294, 451
Japanese rocket project 169
Mars *Viking* landings (1976) 448
Missions, proposed 295
Moonwalk, U.S. (1969) 292, 447
Outer Space Treaty (1967) 162
Payloads, worldwide 295
Planetary missions 295
Skylab 293
Space shuttles
Challenger (1983, 1984, 1986) 293, 294, 448, 449
Columbia (1981, 1982) . . . 293, 294, 448
Discovery 49, 293, 294
Endeavour (1993) 43-44, 294, 451
Missions 293-94
Sputnik satellite 530
Spain 820-21
Aid, U.S. 851
Ambassadors, envoys 849
History 515, 516, 518, 528, 532
Merchant fleet 205
Military strength 161
Nuclear power 168
Rulers 541
Spanish-American War (1898) . . . 442, 524
Casualties, U.S. forces 163
Costs 160
Spanish Armada 518
Spanish Civil War (1936-39) 528
Spanish Sahara 532
Spectrum, colors of 563
Speech, freedom of 70, 460
Speed
Of animals 189
Of light 264
Of sound 563
Speedboat racing 925
Speed skating. *See* Skating
Spelling
Commonly misspelled words 597
Spelling Bee, National 593
Sphere (formulas) 564
Spiders, poisonous 190
Spingarn Medal 326
Spirits. *See* Liquor
Spokane, WA 92, 381, 682
Sports 852-955
Directory 904-5
Dramatic events (1993-94) 852
Highlights (1994) 782-84
Personalities, notable 926-28
see also specific sports
Spring (season) 270-71
Sputnik (1957) 530
Square
Area 564
Sri Lanka (Ceylon) 821-22
Aid, U.S. 851
Ambassadors, envoys 849
Area 549
Trade 201
Stadiums, arenas
Baseball 954
Basketball 914
Football 880
Stalin, Joseph V. 529, 530, 814
Stamp Act (1765) 438
Stamps. *See* Postage stamps
Standard time 290, 291
Stanley Cup *782*, 890
Stars
Morning, evening 272
Tables 263-64
"Star-Spangled Banner" (1814) . . 440, 469
START I and II. *See* Strategic Arms Reduction Treaty, I and II
State, Department of 72
Employees, payroll 148
Expenditures 107
Secretaries 72, 98
Staten Island, NY 428, 549

- **States, U.S.** 643-68
  - Abbreviations, postal 589
  - Abortions 959-60
  - Admission of new (law) 459
  - Admitted to Union 499, 500, 643-68
  - Agriculture 134-41
  - Altitudes (high, low) 498
  - Area, rank 497, 499
  - Area codes, telephone 387-417
  - Automobile data 207
  - Births, deaths 958
  - Bridges 690-92
  - Budget 113, 114
  - Capitals 499
  - Census 375-77, 379, 387-436
  - Census Test (1995) 374
  - Chambers of Commerce 643-68
  - Climate 181, 183-84, 186
  - Coastline, in miles 498
  - Congressional representation 76-84
  - Construction, value of 643-68
  - Contiguous 48 497
  - Counties, county seats 378, 379-80, 418-36
  - Courts 87-89
  - Crime, prisons, death penalty 216-18
  - Death penalty 216-17
  - Deaths, births 958
  - Debt 113
  - Education 220, 222, 223-24
  - Electoral votes 601, 630
  - Energy consumption 166
  - Famous natives 643-68
  - Finances 113
  - Forested land 643-68
  - Geographic centers 500
  - Governors, state officials 93-97
  - Immigrants' intended residence 386
  - Income, per capita 643-68
  - Indian reservations, population 507
  - Inland water area 499
  - Languages spoken at home 599-600
  - Legislatures 94-97
  - Marriage, divorce laws 727, 728
  - Mineral production 129
  - Motor vehicle registration 207
  - Mountain peaks 547, 548
  - Names, origin of 501
  - Nicknames 643-68
  - Original 13 374, 499
  - Population, by states 376-77, 379, 643-68
    - Cities, more than 5,000 387-417
    - Density 379
    - Ethnic, racial distribution 382, 507, 643-68
  - Precipitation 181
  - Presidential elections 601-30
  - Public lands
    - Parks 71, 503-6
    - Recreation areas 502, 506
  - Public school costs, revenues 220, 222
  - Revenues, expenditures 114
  - Rivers 553-54
  - Secession 464
  - Settlement dates 499
  - Taxes 113, 207, 641-42
  - Temperatures 181, 183-84
  - Territories, former 500
  - Tornadoes 186
  - Tourist attractions 643-68
  - Unemployment benefits 142
  - Union entry dates 499, 500
  - Volcanoes 546
  - Welfare assistance 384
  - Zip codes 387-417
- **Statesmen and stateswomen, notable** 316, 337-39
- **Statistical Abstract of the United States** 497
- **Statue of Liberty** 470
  - Dedicated (1886) 442
  - Ellis Island 470
- **Steamships** (1807, 1819) 175, 440
- **Steel**
  - Discoveries 175
  - Exports, imports 202
  - Production 131
  - Strikes (1892, 1952) 442, 445
- **Steeplechase** (track and field)
  - Olympic champions 858
  - World records 868
- **Stewart Island** 549, 805
- **Stocks** 126-28
  - Dow Jones Average 127
  - Exchanges, global 122
  - Exchanges, U.S. 127, 585
  - Foreign, U.S. holdings 128
  - Glossary 132, 133
  - Market crash (1929) 444, 527-28
  - Market crash (1987) 449
  - Mutual funds 126, 133
  - Trading 127, 133
- **Stockton, CA** 92, 381, 683
- **Stonehenge** 512
- **Storms, notable** (1888) 442, 569
- **Storm warnings** 179
- **Strategic Air Command** 155
- **Strategic Arms Limitation Treaty, I and II** (1972, 1979) 162
- **Strategic Arms Reduction Treaty, I and II** (1991, 1993) 162
- **Stratosphere** 270
- **Strikes**
  - Air traffic controllers (1981) 448
  - Baseball players (1994) 65-66, 67, *783*, 939
  - Coal miners (1922, 1946) 443, 445
  - Flight attendants (1993) 42
  - Homestead (1892) 442
  - Number, days idle (1956-93) 152
  - Police (Boston) (1919) 443
  - Railroad (1877) 442
  - Shoe workers (1860) 441
  - Steel mill seizure (1952) 445
  - Steel workers (1892) 442
  - Women weavers (1824) 440
- **Strokes**
  - Deaths 970
  - Diabetes 709
  - Medical discoveries (1994) 169
  - Warning signs 699, 707
- **Students.** *See* Colleges and universities; Education
- **Submarine**
  - Invention 175
  - *Nautilus* (1954) 445
  - Sinkings 565-66
  - Warfare (1917) 443, 526
- **Subway accidents** 567-68
- **Succession, presidential** 463, 466
- **Sudan** 822, 849, 851
- **Suez Canal** 530, 764
- **Suffrage, woman**
  - Amendment (1920) 443, 462
- **Sugar**
  - Calories 703
  - Exports, imports 202
  - Labels, nutrition 704
  - Production 139
- **Sugar Bowl** 882
- **Suicides**
  - Chronology (1993-94) 41, 43, 45, 58
  - By firearms 965
  - Number 959, 960
  - Physician-assisted 709
- **Sullivan Trophy** 902
- **Sumatra** 549
- **Sumeria** 508
- **Summer** (season) 270-71
- **Summer Olympics.** *See* Olympic games
- **Summer Solstice** 252, 260, 271
- **Sun** 267-68
  - Eclipses (1995) 266, 273
  - Planets' distance from 254, 267
  - Rises, sets 263, 274-85
  - Twilight 268, 272-73
- **Sung Dynasty** 516, 542
- **Sunspots** 267-68
- **Super Bowl** 48, *782*, 873
- **Superconducting Supercollider** 40
- **Superior, Lake** 555
- **Superlative statistics, U.S.** 497
- **Supplemental Security Income (SSI)** 699
- **Supply-side economics** 133
- **Supreme Court, U.S.**
  - Abortion rulings
    - Antiabortion protests (1993-94) 70
    - Legalization (1973) 447, 465
    - Restraints (1989) 449
  - Address, form of 597
  - Appointments, salaries 86
  - Created (1789) 439
  - Decisions, notable 70, 464-65
    - *Dred Scott* (1857) 441, 464
    - *Marbury* v. *Madison* (1803) 440, 464
    - *Plessy* v. *Ferguson* (1896) 442, 464
  - Employees, payroll 148
  - First black justice (1967) 447
  - First woman justice (1981) 448
  - Judicial powers (law) 458
  - Justices 86-87
    - Blackmun retires (1994) 54
    - Breyer appointed (1994) 57, 61-62
    - White retires (1993) 451
  - Packing (1937) 444
  - Schools
    - Desegregation (1954, 1955, 1956) 445, 446
    - Prayer ban (1963, 1984) 446, 449
    - Special districts (1994) 70
- **Suriname** 822, 849, 851
- **Surveyor's chain measure** 558
- **Survivor insurance** 697, 699
- **Svalbard Islands** 807
- **Swahili** 517
- **Swains Island** 669
- **Swaziland** 823, 849, 851
- **Sweden** 823
  - Ambassadors, envoys 849
  - History 516, 520, 532
  - Merchant fleet 205
  - Nuclear power 167, 168
  - Rulers 539, 823
  - Trade 201
- **Sweet-potato production** 139
- **Swimming**
  - Olympic champions 862-65
  - Synchronized 867
  - World records 906
- **Switzerland** 823-24
  - Alps 547-48
  - Ambassadors, envoys 849
  - Gold reserves 125
  - Nuclear power 167, 168
- **Symbols.** *See* Signs and symbols
- **Symphony orchestras** 307-8
- **Syria** 47, 161, 824, 849

— T —

- **Table tennis** 867
- **Tacoma, WA** 92, 381, 683
- **Taft, William H.** 632, 634
  - Biography 476
  - Burial site 480
  - Cabinet 98-101
  - Popular, electoral votes 633
- **Taft-Hartley Act** (1947) 445
- **Tahiti** 549, 768
- **Taiwan** 824-25, 848
  - Aid, U.S. 851
  - Area 549
  - Map 493
  - Merchant fleet 205
  - Military strength 161
  - Nuclear power 167
  - Trade 201, 825
- **Tajikistan** 825, 849, 851
- **Taj Mahal** 518
- **Tall buildings** 684-90, 690
- **Talmud** 514
- **Tammany Hall** 475, 476
- **Tampa, FL** 683
  - Buildings, tall 689
  - Mayor 92
  - Population 381, 394, 683
- **Tanganyika** 826
- **Tang Dynasty** 516, 542
- **Tantalum** 129, 130
- **Tanzania** 825-26, 849, 851
- **Taoism** 511, 513
- **Tariff of Abominations** (1828) 440
- **Tariffs.** *See* Customs, U.S.
- **Ta'u Island** 669
- **Taxes, federal** 636-40
  - Audits 640
  - Capital gains 122
  - Corporate 122
  - Credits 636, 639
  - Deductions 636, 637-39
  - Estate 640-41
  - Estimated 636
  - Expenditures 107-8
  - Filing 639-40
  - Forms 639-40
  - Gift 640
  - Income tax 636-40
    - Amendment authorizing 462
  - Inheritance 640
  - Law changes (1986, 1993, 1994) 449, 451, 636-37
  - Receipts 107, 108
  - Social Security 107, 636, 696-700
  - Taxpayers' rights 640
- **Taxes, state**
  - Death 640-41
  - Gasoline 207
  - Income (by states) 641-42
  - Per capita 113
  - Sales (by states) 643-68
- **Tax Reform Law** (1986) 449
- **Taylor, Zachary** 634
  - Biography 473
  - Burial site 480
  - Cabinet 98-101
  - Popular, electoral votes 633
- **Teachers**
  - Awards 326
  - College, university 226-50
  - Pay, average 220, 224
  - Public schools 219, 220
- **Technology.** *See* Science and technology
- **Telecommunications** 35-36

Telegraph
Atlantic cable (1858) . . . 441
First message (1844) . . . 441
Inventions . . . 176, 523
Transcontinental (1861) . . . 441
Telephone
Area codes . . . 387-417
AT&T breakup (1982) . . . 448
First exchange (1878) . . . 442
First transcontinental talk (1915) . . . 443
International direct dial codes . . . 850
Inventions . . . 176
Transatlantic cable (1956) . . . 446
Television . . . 780
Actors, actresses . . . 357-70
Advertising expenditures . . . 313
Awards . . . 325
Cable networks . . . 310, 312, 313
Inventions . . . 176
Network addresses, phone numbers . 312
Programs, favorite . . . 311-12
Sets, number of . . . 312
Time spent viewing . . . 310
Transcontinental, first (1951) . . . 445
Viewing shares . . . 310
Temperature (weather)
Celsius-Fahrenheit conversion . . . 562
Heat index . . . 186
Highest, lowest recorded . . . 181
International . . . 184
U.S. normal, highs, lows . . . 180-84
Ten Commandments . . . 734
Tennessee . . . 664
Abortions reported . . . 960
Admission, area, capital . . . 499, 500, 664
Agriculture . . . 134-39
Altitudes (high, low) . . . 498
Birth, death statistics . . . 958
Budget . . . 113
Cities . . . 679, 680
Congressional representation . 77, 83, 376
Courts, U.S. . . . 89
Crime, prisons, death penalty . . 216, 218
Debt . . . 113
Energy consumption . . . 166
Geographic center . . . 500
Governor, state officials . . . 93, 97
As immigrants' intended residence . . . 386
Indians, American (population) . . . 507
Interest laws, rates . . . 720, 721
Marriage, divorce laws . . . 727, 728
Motor vehicle statistics . . . 207
Name origin, nickname . . . 501, 664
Population . . . 376-77, 379
Cities, towns . . . 413, 679, 680
Counties, county seats . . . 432
Density . . . 379
Port traffic . . . 203
Presidential elections . . . 601, 624-25, 630
Schools . . . 220, 222, 224
Taxes . . . 113, 207, 641, 642
Unemployment benefits . . . 142
Welfare assistance . . . 384
Tennessee Valley Authority . . 75, 108, 148
Tennis . . . *783*, 929-31
Olympic champions (1992) . . . 867
Teotihuacan . . . 516
Territorial sea, U.S. . . . 502
Territories, U.S.
Accession of . . . 502
Altitudes (high, low) . . . 498
Areas . . . 436
External . . . 436, 669-71
Populations . . . 436
Statehood . . . 500
Zip codes . . . 436
Terrorism
"Carlos" captured (1994) . . . 65
Crime Bill (1994) . . . 64, 71, 194, 213
International (1980-89) . . . 533
Lebanon (1983) . . . 448, 794
World Trade Center bombing (1993, 1994) . . . 52, 57, 451
see also Assassinations
Texas . . . 664-65
Abortions reported . . . 960
Accession . . . 502, 665
Admission, area, capital . . . 499, 665
Agriculture . . . 134-39
Altitudes (high, low) . . . 498
Birth, death statistics . . . 958
Budget . . . 113
Cities . . . 674, 676-77, 679, 682
Congressional representation . 77, 83, 376
Courts, U.S. . . . 89
Crime, prisons, death penalty . 216, 217, 218
Debt . . . 113
Energy consumption . . . 166
Geographic center . . . 500
Governor, state officials . . . 93, 97
As immigrants' intended residence . . . 386
Independence (1836) . . . 440
Indians, American (population) . . . 507
Interest laws, rates . . . 720, 721
Marriage, divorce laws . . . 727, 728
Mineral production . . . 129
Motor vehicle statistics . . . 207
Name origin, nickname . . . 501, 664
Population . . . 376-77, 379
Cities, towns . . . 413-15, 674, 676-77, 679, 682
Counties, county seats . . . 432-34
Density . . . 379
Port traffic . . . 203
Presidential elections . . . 601, 625-26, 630
Schools . . . 220, 222, 224
Taxes . . . 113, 207, 641
Unemployment benefits . . . 142
Welfare assistance . . . 384
Textiles . . . 202
Thailand (Siam) . . . 826
Aid, U.S. . . . 851
Ambassadors, envoys . . . 849
Military strength . . . 161
Trade . . . 201, 826
World War II . . . 529
Thames River . . . 553
Thanksgiving Day . . . 291
Theater . . . 300-301
Actors, actresses . . . 357-70
Awards . . . 325
Composers . . . 353-54
Dance companies . . . 306-7
First in colonies (1716) . . . 438
Long runs . . . 301
Nonprofit professional . . . 307
Notable openings (1993-94) . . . 300, *780*
Playwrights . . . 325, 334-35, 341-44
Pulitzer Prizes . . . 321
Theft . . . 214, 215, 217
Third Reich. *See under* Germany
Thirteen colonies . . . 499
Thirty Years War (1618-48) . . . 519
Thorpe Trophy . . . 877
Thunderstorms, characteristics . . . 179
Tiahuanaco . . . 516
Tibet . . . 516, 756
Ticonderoga, Ft. (1777) . . . 439
Tidal waves . . . 569
Tides . . . 185, 269
Tierra del Fuego . . . 549, 755
Tilden, Samuel J. (1876) . . . 442
Timbuktu . . . 517, 799
Time
Cities
North American . . . 291
World . . . 290
Computation . . . 270
Daylight Saving . . . 290
Differences, cities . . . 290, 291
Earth's rotation . . . 271
Greenwich . . . 259, 290
International Date Line . . . 290
Mean, apparent . . . 270
Military . . . 290
Sidereal . . . 259, 270
Solar . . . 270
Standard . . . 290, 291
24-hour . . . 290
Zones (map) . . . 484
Timor . . . 549
Tippecanoe Battle (1811) . . . 440, 472
Titanium . . . 129
Tobacco production . . . 138, 139
Exports, imports . . . 202
see also Smoking
Tobago. *See* Trinidad and Tobago
Togo . . . 826-27, 849, 851
Tokelau Island . . . 805
Tokyo . . . 789, 840
Toledo, OH . . . 683
Buildings, tall . . . 689
City manager . . . 92
Population . . . 381, 410, 683
Toltec civilization . . . 543
Ton (measure) . . . 558-60
Tonga . . . 827, 849
Tonkin Resolution (1964) . . . 446
Tonnage, gross, deadweight . . . 205
Tony Awards . . . 325
Tornadoes
Characteristics . . . 179
Notable . . . 568
Occurrence, by state . . . 186
Tour de France (1994) . . . 928
Tourism
Air travel survey . . . 296
Expenditures (by states) . . . 643-68
Foreign to U.S. . . . 123
National parks, monuments . . . 71, 503-6
States, territories, cities . . . 643-71
U.S. regulations . . . 721-22
Washington (DC) sites . . . 672-73
Townshend Acts (1767) . . . 438
Toxic chemical pollution . . . 187
Track and field
Olympic champions . . . 858-62
World indoor, outdoor records . . . 868-69
Trade. *See* Exports, imports
Traffic
Airline . . . 296
Motor vehicle . . . 959, 964
Ports, major U.S. . . . 203
Trails, national scenic . . . 506
Training Services, U.S. . . . 144
Trains. *See* Railroads, U.S.; Railroads, world
Transportation . . . 204-12
Expenditures, consumer . . . 210
Occupational injuries . . . 147
Price Indexes . . . 109, 110
see also specific types
Transportation, Department of . . . 74
Employees, payroll . . . 148
Expenditures . . . 107
Secretaries . . . 72, 74, 102
Trapezoid
Area . . . 564
Travel, foreign. *See* Tourism
Treasury, Department of . . . 73
Bonds . . . 117, 126
Employees, payroll . . . 148
Expenditures . . . 107
Mint . . . 117
Secretaries . . . 72, 73, 98-99
Waco (TX) standoff (1993, 1994) . . 49-50, 59, 451
see also Currency; *specific bureaus*
Treaties. *See* Arms control; *specific treaties*
Trees
Giant (U.S.) . . . 190
Official (by states) . . . 643-68
Triangle
Area . . . 564
Trieste . . . 789
Trinidad and Tobago . . . 827, 849, 851
Triple Crown winners . . . 898
Triple jump
Olympic champions . . . 860
World indoor, outdoor records . . 868, 869
Tripoli-U.S. War (1801) . . . 440
Tristan da Cunha . . . 549, 833
Tropical year . . . 270
Trotsky, Leon . . . 339, 573
Trotting, pacing . . . 901
Troy weight (measure) . . . 558-60
Trucks. *See* Motor vehicles
Truman, Harry S. . . . 631, 632, 634, 635
Biography . . . 477
Burial site . . . 480
Cabinet . . . 98-102
Popular, electoral votes . . . 633
Truman Doctrine (1947) . . . 445, 477, 529
Trust Territory, U.S. . . . 436, 671
Tsars, Russian . . . 517, 542
Tucson, AZ . . . 683
City manager . . . 92
Population . . . 380, 388, 683
Tudor, House of . . . 518, 535
Tuition, U.S. college . . . 222, 223
Tulsa, OK . . . 683
Buildings, tall . . . 690
Mayor . . . 92
Population . . . 381, 410, 683
Tunisia . . . 827-28, 849, 851
Tunnels . . . 693
English Channel . . . 59, 198, 694
Turkey . . . 828
Aid U.S. . . . 851
Ambassadors, envoys . . . 849
History . . . 517, 523, 525, 526, 532
Merchant fleet . . . 205
Military strength . . . 161
Turkeys . . . 140
Turkmenistan . . . 828, 849, 851
Turks and Caicos Islands . . . 832
Turner, Nat (1831) . . . 440
Tutuila Island . . . 669
Tuvalu . . . 828-29, 849
TV. *See* Television
TVA. *See* Tennessee Valley Authority
Tweed, Boss (1873) . . . 442
21st century, start of . . . 288
24-hour time . . . 290
21 gun salute . . . 156
Twilight . . . 268, 272-73
2-year colleges . . . 240-50
Tyler, John . . . 634
Biography . . . 472-73
Burial site . . . 480
Cabinet . . . 98-100
Typhoons . . . 569

— U —

Uganda 829, 849, 851
Ukraine 829-30
Aid, U.S. 851
Ambassadors, envoys 849
Chronology (1993-94) 47, 63
Military strength 161
Nuclear power 47, 167, 168
Ulster. *See* Northern Ireland
UN. *See* United Nations
Unemployment, U.S.
By city 145
Current Population Survey 142
By educational attainment 145
Rates, indicators 143, 145
Chronology (1993-94) 44, 46, 48, 51, 54, 56, 59, 61, 64, 66
Highest (1982) 448
Training services 144
Unemployment insurance 107, 142, 144
UNESCO. *See* United Nations Educational, Scientific, and Cultural Organization
UNICEF. *See* United Nations Children's Fund
Unified defense commands, U.S. 155
Union of Soviet Socialist Republics. *See* Soviet Union
Unions. *See* Labor unions
Unitarian churches 730, 731
United Arab Emirates 830, 849
United Arab Republic. *See* Egypt
United Church of Christ 730, 731, 738-39
United Kingdom 830-33
Aid, U.S. 851
Ambassadors, envoys 849
Area, capital, population 830
Chronology (1993-94) 43, 45, 53-54, 58, 63
Commonwealth 844
English Channel Tunnel 59, *198*, 694
Gold reserves 125
History 525, 527, 528, 533
Inflation 531
Islands, areas 549
Merchant fleet 205
Military strength 161
Monarchs 534-35
Northern Ireland 43, 45, 47-48, 65, 67, 532, 549, 832
Nuclear power 167, 168
Poets Laureate 341
Prime ministers 536
Royal family (1993, 1994) 45, 61
Scotland 831-32
Stonehenge 512
Wales 831
World War I 526
World War II 529
Yalta Conference (1945) 445
see also England
United Mine Workers
Membership 153
Strikes (1922, 1946) 443, 445
United Nations 845-47
Agencies 847
Charter (1945) 529, 845
Headquarters 845
Members 845-46
Secretaries General 846
U.S. Representatives 846
United Nations Children's Fund 847
United Nations Educational, Scientific, and Cultural Organization 847
United Nations High Commissioner for Refugees 847
United States of America 833
Accessions 502
Agencies, government 75-76
Altitudes 498, 550-51
Ambassadors, envoys 848-50
Anthem, national 468-69
Area codes 387-417
Areas (square miles) 437, 497, 499
Banks 114-16
Bicentennial (1976) 448
Births, deaths 957-60, 964-65, 971
Boundaries 500
Budget 107-8
Cabinets 72, 97-102
Capital 668-69, 672-73, 683
Cities 380-81, 674-83, 840
State capitals 643-68
Clinton administration 72-75
Coastline (by states) 498
Congress 76-85
Constitution 456-63
Contiguous 48 497
Continental Divide 499
Copyright law 723-25
Courts 86-89
Crime 213-18
Currency 117-18
Customs (traveler exemptions) 721-22
Dams 695
Debt, national 109
Declaration of Independence 453-54
Education 219-50
Energy 164, 165, 166, 167
Federal government employment, payroll 71, 148
Flag 466-68
Foreign aid 851
Foreign investment in 123
Foreign relations (*see* State, Department of; *specific countries*)
Geographic centers 500
Geographic superlatives 497
Gold production, reserves 125, 131
Government 72-89
Gross National/Domestic Products 111-12
Historic parks, sites 503-6
History 438-51
Holidays 291
Immigration 385-86, 842-43
Income, national 111, 124
Income taxes 107, 113, 636-42
Indian reservations 507
Investments abroad 125
Island trusteeships 671
Joint Chiefs of Staff 73, 155, 162
Judiciary 86-89
Labor force 143
Lakes 555
Land, public and federal 502
Latitudes, longitudes 550-51
Libraries 225
Manufacturing, mining indexes 126
Map 485
Memorials, national 504
Merchant fleet 205
Military 155-63
Mineral production 129-31
Monuments, national 505-6
Motto, national 466
Mountains 547-48
Naturalization 843
Nuclear arms treaties 162
Nuclear power 167, 168
Outlying areas 436, 669-71
Parks, national 71, 503-4
Passports 722
Petroleum production, consumption 164
Poets Laureate 341
Population 373-436
Postal information 387-417, 587-91
Presidential elections 601-33
Presidents 471-80, 634-35
Recreation areas 502, 506
Religions 729-31
Reservoirs 695
Social Security 696-700
Space program 292-95
Statehood dates 499, 500
States, individual 643-68
Superlative statistics 497
Trade 42-43, 44, 71, 123, 201-5
Veterans 159-60
Vice presidents 634-35
Vital statistics 957-72
Wars
American Revolution 439, 521
Casualties 163
Civil War 442, 523
Costs in dollars 160
Gulf War 450, 786, 793, 817
Korean War 445, 530
Mexican War 441
Spanish-American War 442, 524
Vietnam War 530, 531, 836
War of 1812 440
World War I 443, 526
World War II 37, 444-45, 529
Water area 437, 499
Waterfalls 556
Weather 179-86
Zip codes 387-417, 436
Units
Capacity 561
Electrical 561
Measurement 560-61
Universal Postal Union 847
Universities. *See* Colleges and universities
Unknown Soldier's Tomb 673
Upanishads 511
Upper Volta. *See* Burkina Faso
UPU. *See* Universal Postal Union
Uranium 177, 178
Uranus (planet) 258
Morning, evening stars 272
Position by months 251-54, 259-60
Solar system 267
Sun, distance from 254, 267
Urban areas. *See* Cities
Urban Development, Department of. *See* Housing and Urban Development, Department of
Uruguay 833-34, 849
U.S. Open (tennis) 929
USSR. *See* Soviet Union
Utah 665
Abortions reported 960
Admission, area, capital 499, 500, 665
Agriculture 134-39
Altitudes (high, low) 498
Birth, death statistics 958
Budget 113
Congressional representation 77, 83, 376
Courts, U.S. 89
Crime, prisons, death penalty 217, 218
Debt 113
Energy consumption 166
Geographic center 500
Governor, state officials 93, 97
As immigrants' intended residence 386
Indians, American (population) 507
Interest laws, rates 720, 721
Marriage, divorce laws 727, 728
Mineral production 129
Motor vehicle statistics 207
Name origin, nickname 501, 665
Population 376-77, 379
Cities, towns 415
Counties, county seats 434
Density 379
Presidential elections 601, 626-27, 630
Schools 220, 222, 224
Taxes 113, 207, 641, 642
Unemployment benefits 142
Welfare assistance 384
Uzbekistan 834, 849

— V —

Valdez, AK 203
Valois, House of 537
Vanadium 129
Van Buren, Martin 634, 635
Biography 472
Burial site 480
Cabinet 98-100
Popular, electoral votes 633
Vanuatu 205, 834, 848
Varangians 516
Vatican City 834-35
Ambassadors, envoys 849
Popes 734, 735
Veal
Consumption 135
Nutritive value 702
Prices, farm 140
Production 135
Vegetables
Nutritive value 701, 703
Production 139
Venezuela 835
Ambassadors, envoys 849
Rulers 541
Trade 201
Venomous animals 190
Venus (planet) 255-56
Morning, evening stars 272
Position by months 251-54, 259-60
Rises, sets 261
Solar system 267
Sun, distance from 254, 267
Vermont 665-66
Abortions reported 960
Admission, area, capital 499, 665
Agriculture 134-39
Altitudes (high, low) 498
Birth, death statistics 958
Budget 113
Congressional representation 77, 83, 376
Courts, U.S. 89
Crime, prisons, death penalty 216, 217
Debt 113
Energy consumption 166
Geographic center 500
Governor, state officials 93, 97
As immigrants' intended residence 386
Indians, American (population) 507
Interest laws, rates 720, 721
Marriage, divorce laws 727, 728
Motor vehicle statistics 207
Name origin, nickname 501, 665
Population 376-77, 379
Cities, towns 415
Counties, county seats 434
Density 379
Presidential elections 601, 627, 630

Schools 220, 222, 224
Taxes 113, 207, 641, 642
Unemployment benefits 142
Welfare assistance 384
Vernal Equinox 252, 260, 271
Verrazano, Giovanni da (1524) . . 438, 543
Versailles conference (1919) 526
Vesuvius 545, 546
Veterans, U.S. 159-60
Agent Orange suit (1984) 449
GI Bill (1944) 444
Veterans Affairs, Department of 75
Employees, payroll 148
Expenditures 107
Secretaries 72, 75, 102
Veterans' Day 291
Vice presidents, U.S. 632-33, 634-35
Nominees 449, 632
Presidential succession 463, 466
Salary 72
Salutes, honors 156
Victoria Falls 512
Videos
Movies, most popular (1993) 302
Music awards 309
Vietnam 835-36, 848
Division (1954) 530
Military strength 161
Nam-Viet Kingdom 516
Refugees (1975) 448, 532
U.S. advisers, aid (1950) 445
U.S. immigration 386
U.S. trade embargo (1994) 50
Vietnam War 836
Agent Orange suit (1984) 449
Black troops 334
Bombings (1965, 1966, 1971, 1972) . 446, 447
Bombings halted (1968) 447
Casualties, U.S. forces 163
Costs 160
Demonstrations against (1969) 447
End (1975) 448, 532
Indochina War (1953) 445, 530
Medal of Honor 160
Memorial 673
Mylai massacre (1969, 1971) 447
Participants 531
Peace pacts (1973) 447
Peace talks (1969) 447
Pentagon Papers (1971) 447
Tet offensive (1968) 447
Tonkin Resolution (1964) 446
Troop withdrawal (1973) 447
Veteran population 159
Women's memorial 673
Viking I and II (spacecraft) (1976) 295, 448
Vikings 516, 543
Virginia 666
Abortions reported 960
Admission, area, capital 499, 666
Agriculture 134-39
Altitudes (high, low) 498
Appomattox Court House (1865) 441
Birth, death statistics 958
Budget 113
Cities 680, 681, 683
Congressional representation . . 77, 83-84, 376
Courts, U.S. 89
Crime, prisons, death penalty . 216, 217, 218
Debt 113
Energy consumption 166
Geographic center 500
Governor, state officials 93, 97
As immigrants' intended residence . . . 386
Indians, American (population) 507
Interest laws, rates 720, 721
Marriage, divorce laws 727, 728
Memorials, monuments 673
Motor vehicle statistics 207
Name origin, nickname 501, 666
Population 376-77, 379
Cities, towns . . . 415-16, 680, 681, 683
Counties, county seats 434-35
Density 379
Port traffic 203
Presidential elections . . . 601, 627-28, 630
Schools 220, 222, 224
Taxes 113, 207, 641
Unemployment benefits 142
Welfare assistance 384
Virginia Beach, VA 683
Mayor 92
Population 381, 416, 683
Virgin Islands, British 549, 832
Virgin Islands, U.S. 670-71
Accession (1916) 443, 502
Altitudes (high, low) 498
Area, capital, population . . . 502, 549, 670
Cities (population) 436
Citizenship 670
Congressional delegate 84
Courts 89
As immigrants' intended residence . . . 386
Unemployment benefits 142
Vital statistics 957-72
Vitamins 701, 702-3, 705
Vojvodina 838
Volcanoes 545-46
Mt. St. Helens (1980) 448
Paricutin 512
Volleyball 867
Volume
Mathematical formulas 564
Measures, dry, fluid 557, 559, 561
Sun and planets 267
Voting rights. *See* Elections
Voting Rights Act (1965) 70, 446

—W—

Waco (TX) standoff (1993, 1994) . . . 49-50, 59, 451
Wages. *See* Salaries and wages
Wake Atoll 671
Wales 831
Walesa, Lech 533, 812
Freed (1982) 448
Nobel Peace Prize 316
Walking, Olympic champions 859
Wallis and Futuna Islands 768
Wall Street. *See* Stocks
Walvis Bay 803
War, Department of 99
see also Defense, Department of
War crimes
Geneva Conventions 847
Nuremberg trials (1946) 529
Warehouse Act (1916) 443
War of 1812 (1812-15) 440
Casualties, numbers serving 163
Costs 160
War on Poverty (1964) 446
Warren Commission (1964) 446
Wars
Battlefields, military parks 504
Casualties, U.S. 163
Costs, U.S. dollars 160
Geneva Conventions 847
Religious (16th-17th century) 519
Revolutions of 1848 523
Veterans, U.S. 159-60
see also specific wars
Wars of the Roses (1455-85) 518
War of the Worlds (broadcast) (1938) . . 444
Washington (state) 666-67
Abortions reported 960
Admission, area, capital . . . 499, 500, 666
Agriculture 134-39
Altitudes (high, low) 498
Birth, death statistics 958
Budget 113
Cities 682, 683
Congressional representation 77, 84, 376
Courts, U.S. 89
Crime, prisons, death penalty . . 216, 217, 218
Debt 113
Energy consumption 166
Geographic center 500
Governor, state officials 93, 97
As immigrants' intended residence . . . 386
Indians, American (population) 507
Interest laws, rates 720, 721
Marriage, divorce laws 727, 728
Motor vehicle statistics 207
Name origin, nickname 501, 666
Population 376-77, 379
Cities, towns 416-17, 682, 683
Counties, county seats 435
Density 379
Port traffic 203
Presidential elections . . . 601, 628-29, 630
Schools 220, 222, 224
Taxes 113, 207, 641
Unemployment benefits 142
Welfare assistance 384
Washington, Booker T. (1881) . . 334, 442
Washington, DC 668-69, 683
Abortions reported 959
Altitudes (high, low) 498
Area, population 420, 499
Birth, death, statistics 958
British burning of (1814) 440
Budget 108
Congressional delegate 84
Courts 88
Crime, prisons, death penalty . . 216, 218
Energy consumption 166
Federal workers 148
Geographic center 500
As immigrants' intended residence . . 386
Interest laws, rates 720, 721
Marches
Antiwar (1969) 447
Black civil rights (1963) 446
Gay activists (1993) 451
Marriage, divorce laws 727, 728
Mayor 92
Memorials, monuments 672-73
Motor vehicle statistics 207
Museums, libraries 672-73
Name origin 501
Population 376-77, 379, 380, 392, 420, 683
Density 379
Presidential elections 601, 605, 630
Public buildings 672-73
Schools 220, 222, 224
Taxes 207, 641
Unemployment benefits 142
Unemployment rate 145
Voting rights 463, 668
Welfare assistance 384
White House 66, 673
Washington, George 634
Biography 471
Birthday (legal holiday) 291
Burial site 480
Cabinet 98-100
Commander-in-chief (1775) 439
Constitutional convention (1787) 439
Delaware crossing (1776) 439
Electoral votes 633
Farewell Address (1796) 439
Monument (DC) 673
Mount Vernon 666, 673
Waste disposal 187
Water
Area (U.S.) 437, 499
Boiling, freezing points 562
Dams, reservoirs 694-95
Health, nutrition 701
Oceans, seas 552
Pollution 187
Usage 192
Weights 562
Waterfalls 556
Watergate 478, 531
Break-in (1972) 447
Convictions (1973) 447
Coverup (1973, 1975) 447, 448
Impeachment hearings (1974) . . . 447-48
Nixon resignation (1974) . . . 200, 448, 531
"Plumbers" (1974) 447
Tapes (1973, 1974) 447-48
Waterloo, Battle of (1815) 522
Water polo 867
Waterways. *See* Canals
Watt (electrical unit) 561
Weapons
Arrests, sentences 217, 218
Defense contracts 159
Firearms 213, 561, 964, 965
see also Nuclear arms
Weather 179-86
Annual climatological data 182
Blizzards 179, 569
By cities, foreign 184
By cities and states, U.S. 180-84
Coastal warnings 179
Floods (1993, 1994) . 63, 179, 185, 451, 569
Heat index 186
Hurricanes 179, 185, 569
Precipitation 180-82, 184
Storms 569
Temperatures 180-84, 186
Thunderstorms 179
Tornadoes 179, 186, 568
Typhoons 569
Watches, warnings 179
Wettest spot 181
Wind chill 186
Winds, velocities 179, 182
Webster, Noah (1783, 1828) 439, 440
Wedding anniversaries 725
Weight, body
Children, average 972
Heart disease, impact on 707
Overweight adults 972
Recommended 705
Weight lifting 867
Weights, measures, numbers 557-64
Atomic 177-78
Electrical units 561
Energy measures 561
Equivalents, table of 558-59
Gases 562
Human 705, 707, 972
Metric 557-61

(continued)

Weights, measures, numbers *(continued)*
Table of U.S. Customary 557-58
Temperature conversion 562
Water 562
Weimar Republic (1919) 527
Welfare
Families with Dependent Children (by state) 384
Food stamps 107, 136
Supplemental programs 699
Western Samoa. *See* Samoa, Western
West Germany. *See* Germany
West Indies, British 832
Westminster Kennel Club 920
West Point Military Academy . . . 157, 237
West Virginia 667
Abortions reported 960
Admission, area, capital 499, 667
Agriculture 134-39
Altitudes (high, low) 498
Birth, death statistics 958
Budget 113
Congressional representation . 77, 84, 376
Courts, U.S. 89
Crime, prisons, death penalty. . . 216, 218
Debt 113
Energy consumption 166
Geographic center 500
Governor, state officials 93, 97
As immigrants' intended residence . . . 386
Indians, American (population) 507
Interest laws, rates 720, 721
Marriage, divorce laws 727, 728
Motor vehicle statistics 207
Name origin, nickname 501, 667
Population 376-77, 379
Cities, towns 417
Counties, county seats 435
Density 379
Port traffic 203
Presidential elections 601, 629, 630
Schools 220, 222, 224
Taxes 113, 207, 641
Unemployment benefits 142
Welfare assistance 384
Wheat
Exports, imports 141, 202
Prices, farm 140
Production 138, 139, 141
White House 673
Burning (1814) 440
Employees, payroll 148
Expenditures 107
Plane crash (1994) 66
Staff 72
Whitewater scandal (1993, 1994) . . 44, 45, 49, 51-52, 59, 60, 62, *194*, 451
WHO. *See* World Health Organization
Wichita, KS 683
City manager 92
Population 381, 398, 683
Wilkes Atoll 671
Wills, living 709
Wilson, Woodrow 632, 634
Biography 476
Burial site 480
Cabinet 98-101
Popular, electoral votes 633
Wimbledon (tennis tournament) . . 783, 930
Wind chill factor 186
Windsor, House of . . . 45, 61, 535, 831-32
Wind speeds, U.S. 179, 182
Windward Islands. *See* Dominica; St. Lucia; St. Vincent and the Grenadines
Winston-Salem, NC 690
Winter (season) 270-71
Winter Olympics. *See* Olympic games
Winter Solstice 254, 260, 271
WIPO. *See* World Intellectual Property Organization
Wisconsin 667-68
Abortions reported 960
Admission, area, capital . . . 499, 500, 667
Agriculture 134-39
Altitudes (high, low) 498
Birth, death statistics 958
Budget 113
Cities 679
Congressional representation . 77, 84, 376
Courts, U.S. 89
Crime, prisons, death penalty . . 216, 218
Debt 113
Energy consumption 166
Geographic center 500
Governor, state officials 93, 97
As immigrants' intended residence . . . 386
Indians, American (population) 507
Interest laws, rates 720, 721
Marriage, divorce laws 727, 728
Motor vehicle statistics 207
Name origin, nickname 501, 667
Population 376-77, 379
Cities, towns 417, 679
Counties, county seats 435-36
Density 379
Port traffic 203
Presidential elections 601, 629-30
Schools 220, 222, 224
Taxes 113, 207, 641, 642
Unemployment benefits 142
Welfare assistance 384
WMO. *See* World Meteorological Organization
Women
Armed forces 159
Combat eligibility (1993) 451
Generals, first U.S. (1970) 447
Vietnam memorial 673
Astronauts, first (1983) 292, 293, 448
Attorney general, first (1993) 451
Child care arrangements 374, 961
Child support payments 374
College, first (1821) 440
Congresswoman, first (1916) 443
Election winners (1992) 450
Employment 143, 145, 149, 961
Equal Rights Amendment (1972, 1982) 447, 448
Equal rights convention (1848) 441
Feminist revival (1960s) 531
First ladies 480
Governor, first U.S. (1924) 444
Hall of Fame 372
Life expectancy 972
Living alone 960, 961
Marital status 960
Median net worth 384
Nobel Prize winners 314-16
Poverty rates 383
Salaries and wages
Annual earnings average 149
Hourly rates 150
Pay differential, male/female 149
Weekly earnings median 152
Seminarians 736
Single household heads 960, 961
Strikers, first (1824) 440
Suffrage (1869, 1920) 442, 443, 462
Supreme Court justices (1981, 1993). 448, 451
Unemployment 145
Vice-presidential nominee, first (1984) . . . 449
Weight, height 705, 972
Wooden Award 918
Woodstock anniversary (1994) 66
Wool prices (farm) 140
World Almanac, The, First (1868) 442
World Bank 847
World Court 847
World Cup
Skiing 920
Soccer 61, 63, *783*, 937, 938
World Health Organization 847
World history 508-33
World Intellectual Property Organization 847
World Meteorological Organization . . . 847
World population 839-41
World religions 731, 737-39
World Series 41, 955
World Trade Center bombing (1993, 1994) 52, 57, 451
World Trade Organization 205
World War I (1914-18) 526
Armistice (1918) 443
Black troops 334
Casualties, U.S. forces 163
Costs 160
Medal of Honor 160
Troop strength 163, 443
U.S. neutrality (1914) 443
Versailles conference (1919) 526
Veteran population 159
World War II (1939-45) 444-45, 529
Atomic bombs (1945) 445, 529
Black troops 334
Casualties, U.S. forces 163
Costs 160
50th anniversary remembrance . 37, 61, *199*
Medal of Honor 160
Peace treaties, Japan (1951) 445
Pearl Harbor attack (1941) 444
Troop strength 163
Veteran population 159
Wounded Knee, Battle of (1890) 442
Wrestling
NCAA champions 905
Olympic champions (1992) 867-68
Wright brothers
Flights (1903) 443, 525
Memorial (NC) 504, 659
Writers, notable 334-35, 341-44, *781*
Best-selling, notable books (1993) . . 303
Children's books (1993) 304
Living 334-35
Newbery Medal 324, 330
Nobel Prizes 70, 315-16
Past 341-44
Pen names 598
Poets Laureate
England 340
U.S. 341
Pulitzer Prizes 316-24
Special awards 324, 330
Wyoming 668
Abortions reported 960
Admission, area, capital . . . 499, 500, 668
Agriculture 134-39
Altitudes (high, low) 498
Birth, death statistics 958
Budget 113
Congressional representation . 77, 84, 376
Courts, U.S. 89
Crime, prisons, death penalty . . . 217, 218
Debt 113
Energy consumption 166
Geographic center 500
Governor, state officials 93, 97
As immigrants' intended residence . . 386
Indians, American (population) 507
Interest laws, rates 720, 721
Marriage, divorce laws 727, 728
Motor vehicle statistics 207
Name origin, nickname 501, 668
Population 376-77, 379
Cities, towns 417
Counties, county seats 436
Density 379
Presidential elections 601, 630
Schools 220, 222, 224
Taxes 113, 207, 641
Territory 500
Unemployment benefits 142
Welfare assistance 384
see also States, U.S.

—X—

X ray discovery (1895) 177

—Y—

Yacht racing
America's Cup 937
Olympic champions (1992) 868
Yalta Conference (1945) 445
Year
Calendar, perpetual 286-87
Chronological eras 272
Holidays 291
Sidereal, tropical 259, 270
Year in pictures (1994) . . . *193-200, 777-84*
Yellow Sea 552
Yellowstone National Park 503, 668
Founded (1872) 442
Yeltsin, Boris 42, 47, 67, 814
Yemen 58, 836-37, 850, 851
Yonkers, NY 683
Mayor 92
Population 381, 408, 683
York, House of 535
Young, Brigham (1846) 441
Yuan Dynasty 517, 542
Yugoslavia 67, 837-38, 850, 851
Yukon River 553, 554

—Z—

Zaire 838
Aid, U.S. 851
Ambassadors, envoys 850
Gold production 131
History 532
Rwandan refugees (1994) 65, *778*
Zaire (Congo) River 553
Zambia 838-39, 850, 851
Zanzibar 549, 826
Zen Buddhism 519
Zeppelins 299
Zero coupon bond 133
Zhirinovsky, Vladimir *779*
Zia ul-Haq, Mohammed 533
Zimbabwe 532, 839, 850, 851
Zinc production 129, 130, 131
ZIP codes
Colleges and universities 226-50
U.S. outlaying areas 436
U.S. states 387-417
Zodiac signs 268
Zones of earth 270
Zoological parks 191
Zoroaster 511

The World Almanac

and Book of Facts 1995

The Top 10 News Stories

On Election Day 1994, the Republicans won a resounding victory—taking control of both houses of Congress for the first time in 40 years and ending the day in control of some three-fifths of the nation's governorships, including seven of the eight largest states.

The Middle East peace process continued: Under Israeli-Palestine Liberation Organization agreements, limited Palestinian autonomy began in the Gaza Strip and the West Bank. Soon after, Israel and Jordan formally ended the 46-year state of war between them and signed a peace treaty.

Haiti's President Jean-Bertrand Aristide, who had been in exile since he was overthrown by the Haitian military in 1991, was restored to power with the aid of 15,000 U.S. troops.

In one of the most widely publicized criminal cases in American history, former football great O. J. Simpson was arrested and put on trial for allegedly murdering his ex-wife Nicole Brown Simpson and her friend Ronald Goldman.

Ethnic violence on a massive scale between Rwanda's Hutu majority and Tutsi minority left at least 500,000 people dead and caused millions to flee the country to refugee camps, where many succumbed to starvation and disease.

Multiracial democracy became a reality in South Africa, as more than 22 million eligible voters lined up over a 4-day period to cast their ballots in the first election open to all races, and Nelson Mandela, the black nationalist leader who had been imprisoned for 27 years under apartheid, was inaugurated as president.

President Bill Clinton's ambitious and controversial health-care reform plan, the major legislative issue of the year, stalled and eventually died in Congress, despite repeated attempts to reach a compromise.

Millions of sports fans were stunned and dismayed when a Major League Baseball players' strike led to cancellation of the World Series, and soon after, National Hockey League owners locked out the players on what would have been the first day of the 1994-95 hockey season.

A powerful earthquake, measuring 6.8 on the Richter scale, struck the Los Angeles area, resulting in 61 deaths and at least $4 billion in property damage.

Kurt Cobain, 27, lead singer of the influential rock band Nirvana, committed suicide. Touted as a spokesperson for his generation, a role he publicly rejected, Cobain had surprise success with his pained and disenchanted music and helped popularize other so-called alternative bands.

Election '94

By Donald Young

The Republican Party captured control of both houses of Congress in the Nov. 8, 1994, elections. The margins were narrow, but the results nonetheless constituted a revolution in American politics. A majority of Americans were not born when the GOP last won control of both houses, in 1952. Even more distant in time were 1947 and 1948, the most recent years in which Republicans held both the Senate and the House during a Democratic administration.

Nearly complete unofficial returns gave the Republicans a 52-48 majority in the Senate and an advantage of 230-204, with 1 independent, in the House. The Senate margin shifted to 53-47 when Sen. Richard Shelby of Alabama, who was not up for reelection in 1994, announced Nov. 9 that he was switching from the Democratic to the Republican Party.

The outcome of the election meant that two of Pres. Bill Clinton's most articulate and skillful adversaries would dominate the 104th Congress when it convened in January 1995. Sen. Bob Dole (KS) would become the Senate majority leader, and Rep. Newt Gingrich (GA) the Speaker of the House.

The Republicans also came out of the voting with a sizable majority of the nation's governorships.

Voter discontent fueled the Republican bandwagon. Clinton was not a very popular president. Americans were anxious about crime, the major issue of the campaign, and polls showed that they believed Republicans would be tougher on criminals. Also, voters held Congress in very low esteem, and candidates of the majority party inevitably became the target of voters wanting change. Republicans also benefited from the enthusiastic and well-organized support of conservative Christians, who were concerned about social issues, including abortion.

In the Senate, the Democrats held a 56-44 majority before the voting, and the Republicans needed to pick up 7 seats to take control. Five Democrats, including Majority Leader George Mitchell (ME), had decided not to seek reelection, and in Oklahoma a special election was held to fill Democrat David Boren's seat because he had announced he would resign to become president of the University of Oklahoma. The Republicans swept all 6 of these open Democratic seats.

As well, they retained all their own seats. All ten Republican incumbents, including such veterans as Richard Lugar (IN), Trent Lott (MS), and Orrin Hatch (UT), won. Additionally, the Republicans held the three seats left vacant by retiring GOP senators.

In each of the remaining 16 contests, a Democrat was standing for reelection, and the Republicans needed to replace at least one of them. This was accomplished in Pennsylvania, where Rep. Rick Santorum turned out Harris Wofford, who had been elected to fill a vacancy in 1991. The Republicans also ousted Sen. Jim Sasser (TN), who had been the front-runner to succeed Mitchell as Democratic leader. The winner was Bill Frist, a surgeon.

The 14 surviving Democratic incumbents included such veterans as Daniel Patrick Moynihan (NY) and Ted Kennedy (MA), a liberal icon who had once been thought vulnerable. Both won easily. Democrats also prevailed in the nation's 2 nastiest and most publicized contests. In Virginia, Charles Robb narrowly won again, defeating retired Marine Lt. Col. Oliver North, who was supported avidly by conservatives in general and by the Christian Coalition in particular. Robb had been obliged to apologize repeatedly for personal peccadillos, and North had been convicted—convictions overturned on a technicality—of felonies in the

Iran-contra affair. In California, Rep. Michael Huffington spent at least $25 million of his Texas oil fortune in an unsuccessful bid to unseat Sen. Dianne Feinstein, who spent $14 million, making this the most expensive congressional election in U.S. history. The two excoriated each other in television ads. The race was extremely close—and Huffington did not immediately concede—but he may have lost when he acknowledged that he and his wife had employed an illegal alien as a housekeeper.

The House of Representatives also went to the Republicans. In the 103d (outgoing) Congress, Democrats held a 256-178 majority, with 1 independent. On the morning after the election, with several races still in doubt, it appeared that the Republicans had picked up more than 50 seats and would have a majority of about 25.

Many of the Republican gains were in the South, and the party of Lincoln actually won about half the seats in the 11 former Confederate states. In Washington state, the Speaker of the House, Tom Foley, first elected to Congress in 1964 and long a target of conservative critics who said that he epitomized all that was wrong with one-party domination of the House, was narrowly defeated by Republican challenger George Nethercutt. No Speaker had been defeated for reelection since 1860.

Rep. Dan Rostenkowski (IL), who had been the subject of a 17-count indictment related to activities in his congressional offices, was defeated by Michael Flanagan in his Chicago district. The most familiar Republican face that would be missing in 1995 was that of Rep. Robert Michel (IL), his party's House leader for many years, who had retired. Genial, accommodating, and nonthreatening, Michel displayed a personal style far different from that of Gingrich, who would inherit the Speakership that had always been denied his predecessor.

An unprecedented number of black Republicans, mostly with conservative views, ran for office in 1994. Much attention had focused on J. C. Watts, who had played football for the University of Oklahoma. Watts was elected to the House from Oklahoma.

The gubernatorial elections provided more bad news for the Democrats. Before the voting, they had held a 29-19 advantage in statehouses, with 2 independents. The Republicans had envisioned winning the elections for governor in all of the nation's eight largest states—all these states were electing governors in 1994—and they nearly pulled off this unprecedented (for them) achievement.

In New York, Mario Cuomo failed in his attempt for a 4th term as governor, despite the endorsement of Mayor Rudolph Giuliani of New York City, a Republican, who said that Cuomo would be the best governor for the city. The winner was State Sen. George Pataki, who had promised to cut taxes and impose the death penalty, which Cuomo had long opposed.

In two other major states, sons of former Pres. George Bush ran for governor, with mixed results. In Florida, Lawton Chiles, the Democratic incumbent, defeated Jeb Bush. In Texas, on the other hand, Democratic Governor Ann Richards, who had high approval ratings, nonetheless lost to George W. Bush. Both brothers had waged forceful campaigns, stressing crime and the need to run state government in new and more creative ways.

The Republicans picked up another big state, Pennsylvania, where Tom Ridge won the gubernatorial office being vacated by Robert Casey, a Democrat. The Republicans easily held the statehouses in Massachusetts and in three major Midwestern states— Illinois, Michigan, and Ohio.

The executive mansion in California stayed in the hands of Pete Wilson, a Republican. He defeated State Treasurer Kathleen Brown, whose father and brother had been governors of the state.

In a closely watched election in the nation's capital, former Mayor Marion Barry, convicted and imprisoned for drug use only a few years earlier, completed a comeback by winning his old job, though not by a big margin.

Voters on Nov. 8 also considered various ballot initiatives. In California, they approved a proposition that would bar illegal aliens from attending public schools or receiving welfare or nonemergency medical aid; Proposition 187 faced immediate court challenges. Term limits for public officials were approved in several states.

Months before the voters actually cast their ballots on Nov. 8, tensions related to the election began to build in the nation's capital. It seemed that hardly any vote was cast on the Senate or House floor without some calculation as to how it might affect the midterm election. In the Senate, the GOP leadership rediscovered the filibuster. Sen. Dole, as minority leader, was able to prevent passage of a number of bills, principally in the campaign-reform and environmental areas. The Democrats, with only 56 senators, needed 60 votes to invoke cloture and bring a bill to a vote.

In the House, the filibuster option was not available for the GOP, and the Democrats commanded a lopsided, if not always united, majority. But in Gingrich, the heir apparent to Robert Michel, the White House had its most acerbic critic. More conservative than Dole, and more outspoken, Gingrich criticized the president constantly for—as he saw it—raising taxes, advocating big government, and running a White House characterized by ineptitude and ethical relativism.

The acrimony in Washington, communicated to the general public to a large degree in sound-bite epithets from the principals on evening television newscasts, contributed to a sour mood among the electorate. Americans seemed generally unmoved by the steadily strengthening economy. Unemployment continued to decline, interest rates remained low, the federal budget deficits were dropping faster than hardly anyone had dared predict, and the stock market remained buoyant. None of this lifted Clinton's approval rating, which remained below 50 percent in almost every public opinion survey.

The stabilizing world climate—the gradual emergence of what George Bush had envisioned as a New World Order—finally gave Clinton a lift in the polls in October. He went to the Israeli-Jordanian border for the signing of a peace treaty between those two countries. The administration had played a role in that agreement, as well as earlier accords between Israel and the Palestine Liberation Organization. Clinton could also cite progress in North Korea, where a nuclear threat was defused; in Haiti, where the U.S. had forced out a murderous junta; and in Cuba, where he got an accord with Pres. Fidel Castro on refugees. On Election Day, however, foreign affairs did not seem to be a major issue for most of the electorate.

Giving a positive spin to the Republican campaign, Gingrich assembled more than 300 GOP House candidates on the grounds of the U.S. Capitol, Sept. 27, where they signed a "Contract With America." They pledged that, on the election of a Republican majority, they would pass a balanced budget amendment to the U.S. Constitution, cut taxes, and increase defense spending. Democrats said this platform resembled the Reaganomics of the 1980s that, they contended, had ballooned the federal budget deficits.

The president campaigned vigorously in the last weeks before the election in states where Democrats were willing to appear with him, but his strenuous efforts apparently had little impact.

The Information Superhighway: What It Will Mean

By Vice President Al Gore

With the term "information superhighway" and advances in communications technology continually in the news, The World Almanac *asked Vice President Al Gore, who has made this a subject of special interest and expertise, to describe how he sees the coming technological changes affecting the average person and what he believes the role of government in this area should be.*

Futurist Alvin Toffler has written about three "waves" of civilization. In the First Wave, agriculture enabled nomadic peoples to settle into villages and cities. In the Second Wave, the industrial revolution made possible the modern industrial state. According to Toffler, a Third Wave has begun in which computing and telecommunications technologies will transform the global economy and have political and societal impacts every bit as profound as those of the First and Second Waves.

The Third Wave really began almost 50 years ago with ENIAC (Electronic Numerical Integrator And Computer), the first all-electronic computer, built at the University of Pennsylvania. Containing thousands of vacuum tubes, it filled a large room and was less powerful than a $10 pocket calculator today. Since then, computers have gone from being one-of-a-kind research tools to being part of everyday life. We use and rely on dozens of computers every day—when we go to the bank, use the telephone, buy groceries. No one can deny that computers have improved productivity and the quality of our lives.

Yet the impact of the computer, as pervasive as it has been, will be dwarfed by the impact of new digital telecommunications technologies—technologies that will enable us to quickly, effortlessly, and inexpensively transmit huge amounts of information to almost any place on the globe. The high-speed telecommunications links being built today will enable us to tie together millions of computers and effectively harness the computing power and information contained in all of them. These networks will multiply a thousandfold our ability to find, use, and process information.

Critical Changes

The rapid advances in computer and fiber optic technology that made the Third Wave possible are fostering three critical developments: digital wireless technologies, convergence, and policy reform.

Digital Wireless Technologies

Cellular telephones are just the beginning. We now have wireless computer networks, direct-broadcast satellite television, digital wireless cable TV networks, global telephone service, and global positioning systems that can pinpoint an individual's location to a few inches. New, innovative technologies are making these services cheaper, more reliable, and easier to use.

Convergence

The rapid advances in telecommunications and computer technology are causing the information and telecommunications industries to converge. Everything is going digital—telephones, televisions, radios. Soon it will be difficult or impossible to distinguish between a cable television company and a telephone company. Both will be providing high-speed, two-way, digital video services as well as ordinary phone service.

Policy Reform

In the United States and several other countries around the world, governments have recognized the fundamental changes being wrought by information technology and are changing their telecommunications policies accordingly. In the United States, Congress and the administration are working together to overhaul the 1934 Communications Act in order to spur competition in the telecommunications industry and to accelerate investment and innovation.

A Network of Networks

These developments are making possible a new global telecommunications system. In the course of just a few years, a network of networks will help to bring all of the communities of the world together through the information superhighway. This global information infrastructure will allow people from every continent in almost every country in all corners of the world to interact in a way that has never before been possible. For example, videoconferencing could become as commonplace and affordable as faxing is today. Most important, through this infrastructure we will be able to get the information we need—when and where we want it.

Consider that, according to one author, the average Sunday newspaper contains more information than a peasant in medieval England encountered in an entire lifetime. To deal with this explosion of information, we can use the computer and communications technology to help us sort it, store it, transport it, and, most important of all, understand it. In the future, supercomputers that store a small library's worth of information will make it all accessible in seconds; database software will shift through millions of pages of text to find the one needed paragraph; high-speed computer networks will ship all the information in a multivolume encyclopedia from coast to coast in seconds; and high-definition television systems will display super-sharp images and provide hundreds of channels of programming.

Already, access to a wide range of information has been greatly expanded. Using today's technologies—a $1,000 computer and a modem—anyone can get weather forecasts for major cities around the globe, read the latest news wire stories, plan a vacation, shop hundreds of on-line catalogs, and access thousands of other information services. Still, these services are limited because they provide only text or text and simple graphics.

The National Information Infrastructure

In the United States, President Bill Clinton has made the development of the National Information Infrastructure a top priority. The National Information Infrastructure will generate economic growth and improve the quality of life in myriad ways. It will improve education, make government at all levels more cost-effective and user friendly, reduce health-care costs while improving quality, help businesses compete more effectively in world markets, and give communities new ways to address problems such as crime and pollution. Put simply, the National Information Infrastructure will help move the United States into the 21st century.

The National Information Infrastructure will consist of four parts:

(1) telecommunication networks—fiber optic networks, telecommunications satellites, wireless systems, cable TV networks—that can carry hundreds, even thousands, of times as much information as today's networks;

(2) telephones, fax machines, televisions, and other "information appliances" attached to the networks;

(3) information stored in "digital libraries" and databases filled with millions of pages of text, images, and videos;

(4) the people who will design, build, and maintain this infrastructure.

The key attribute of this new information infrastructure will be choice. People will be able to choose the information they want from thousands, perhaps millions, of different information providers, just as they can choose today from millions of different books and magazines. Each viewer will be able to dial up the programming he or she wants. That's the power of a two-way, high-speed network.

The private sector will build the National Information Infrastructure. Private companies will provide the telecommunications services, the information appliances, and the information services. But the public sector has several important roles to play as well. President Clinton and I believe strongly that government should work with industry to promote development of the National Information Infrastructure in the following areas: research and development, pilot projects, government applications, information policy, and telecommunications policy.

Research and Development

The federal government has a key role to play in funding research on the fundamental technologies needed for the National Information Infrastructure. In part because of federal investment during the past 30 years, U.S. companies have led the way in advanced computing, high-speed networking, and software—the technological foundations upon which the National Information Infrastructure will rest.

Pilot Projects

Federal, state, and local governments can provide funding for pilot projects in schools, libraries, and hospitals to demonstrate how the National Information Infrastructure can help the nonprofit sector. For instance, linking classrooms to the Internet provides teachers and students with a powerful new learning tool that will enable students to access information from digital libraries around the world. Recently I visited a high school in California where a student was exchanging electronic mail with an "electronic pen pal" in Germany. Not only did this provide a new, exciting way to learn German, it was an excellent way to build cultural bridges and learn about another country.

Government Applications

Government can also use the National Information Infrastructure to better carry out its own mission. Government is in the information business. It collects, processes, and disseminates information—everything from tax forms to scientific data to weather forecasts. Unfortunately, in the past, the federal government has been slow to take advantage of the power of information technology. Many agencies are using outdated computer systems, while the ones available today are not only more powerful but also much less expensive to buy and maintain.

Information technology can play a key role in making government work better and cost less. The National Information Infrastructure will give government employees the tools they need to do their jobs more effectively and efficiently and help to make more information available to their customers—the American people.

Information Policy

Information policy includes protecting the privacy and intellectual property of National Information Infrastructure users. Today, most people spend less than a half hour a day on the phone. But in the future, many workers will telecommute to the office. They may even conduct most of their working day on-line. As this change takes place, National Information Infrastructure users must know that their conversations and their electronic mail are private and secure, that no one is listening in on personal conversations or stealing company secrets. For this reason, the administration is working with the the private sector to develop technologies and policies that protect National Information Infrastructure users.

Telecommunications Policy

And finally, the government has a critical role to play in telecommunications policy. Ever since the invention of the telegraph, government has had a hand in regulating telecommunications. But because of rapid advances in technology, telecommunications policy has not kept pace in the United States. That is why the Clinton administration and Congress have made reform of U.S. telecommunications policy a top priority.

New legislation is needed to promote private sector investment in the National Information Infrastructure and to remove barriers to full competition in the marketplace. Today, for example, it is illegal in many states to compete with the local phone company.

In 1983, the courts broke up AT&T's monopoly over the long-distance telephone market. As a result, long-distance phone rates have decreased more than 50 percent, service has improved, and customers can now choose from among dozens of long-distance companies. The administration and Congress plan to do the same for local phone and cable TV service so that subscribers have a choice. Any company should be free to offer any service to any customer. When competition replaces regulation, consumers will have more choice, better service, and much lower prices.

Ensuring Equal Access

Of course, some regulation will remain necessary to protect consumers and to ensure that all Americans—rich and poor, urban and rural—have access to the benefits of the National Information Infrastructure. As a nation we cannot tolerate, nor in the long run can we afford, a society in which some patients benefit from shared medical expertise and others do not, in which some children become fully educated and others do not, in which some adults have access to lifetime learning and others do not.

This type of government regulation can work. Today, more than 93 percent of all Americans have telephones, in part because of government regulations that ensure affordable phone service even in remote or poor areas. Advanced communications must be just as widely available.

Government policies should also ensure that network owners charge nondiscriminatory prices to anyone who wants to use their networks to distribute programming or information services. In this way, we can help to create the broadest range of information services and a fully competitive marketplace for information. Are these principles unique to the United States? Hardly. Many are accepted international principles as well. I believe these principles can inform and aid the development of the global information infrastructure, and I encourage other countries to incorporate and expand upon them as they develop their own information infrastructures.

Because it is impossible to predict exactly how technologies and policies will evolve, we cannot foresee exactly the end result of Toffler's Third Wave. But we do know the tremendous potential of the communications revolution. We do know that its impact will forever change the way we live, learn, work, and communicate with one another here in the United States and around the world.

With future-looking policies and a shared vision, the United States and other countries can seize this historic opportunity. We can accelerate economic development, dramatically improve the quality of people's lives, and protect and promote democracies throughout the world through the information infrastructure. We simply cannot afford to do otherwise.

World War II Remembered

By Stephen E. Ambrose

For the 50th anniversary, in 1995, of the end of World War II, The World Almanac *asked the noted historian Stephen E. Ambrose to describe the impact on Americans and on their nation of this critical period in history. Stephen E. Ambrose is the Director of the Eisenhower Center at the University of New Orleans, where he is the Boyd Professor of History. He is the author of numerous books, including the definitive, two-volume biography of Dwight D. Eisenhower and the best-selling* D-Day, June 6, 1944: The Climactic Battle of World War II.

For millions of people, World War II was the greatest catastrophe in history. But for most Americans, the war was a boon. They were spared the physical destruction that obliterated great cities in Europe and Asia, and fewer than 300,000 American soldiers, sailors, and airmen were killed in battle out of a total of some 16 million people who served in the armed forces, a ratio far lower than that of the other belligerents.

Around the world, the most common emotion during the war was fear, while the most common sensation was hunger. In the U.S., fear and hunger were nearly absent. During the six-year war (1939-45), no elections were held in Europe, Asia, Africa, or the Middle East. But in the U.S. during those six years there were two presidential, three congressional, and hundreds of state elections, all of them hotly contested.

The war transformed the world, and America too. It was a unique time; the half decade 1940-45 did more to shake America out of its past and to shape its future than any comparable period except the Civil War era. The biggest difference between the 1930s and the war years was that in the latter everyone had jobs and money in the bank. The next biggest difference was in the extent of travel. During the war, millions of young men and thousands of young women in the armed services went overseas, a new experience for nearly all of them–indeed, most had never been out of their home state, or even their home county. Within the U.S., more that 15 million civilians moved, more than half of them to new states. With 17 percent of the population on the move in the four-year period (1941-45) that America was a combatant, this was a mass migration that dwarfed even the westward movement of the 19th century. Most of those who moved were between 18 and 35 years of age, which means that nearly everyone in that age group moved at least once. This had a tremendously broadening effect on American politics and culture, as the internal migration helped break down regional prejudices and provincialism. Yankees and westerners who moved to the South, where most of the army bases were located, or southerners who moved to the West or North, where most of the war industries were located, learned to tolerate or understand, if not approve of, the different mores they encountered.

The generation who fought the war reinvented America after it was won. In the armed services, or in munitions plants or other war-related industries, young Americans had learned to work together as a team. As college students on the GI Bill of Rights, they learned skills. In the late 1940s and through the 1950s, they built a new America–superhighways, suburbs, skyscrapers, station wagons, semiconductors, a sky full of commercial airplanes.

The war dramatically changed political attitudes. In the 1930s most Americans were isolationists. Neutrality and disarmament were the dominant policies. It was thought that those policies would keep America out of the next war. They did not. In the 1940s it came to be recognized that the way to prevent future wars was through collective security and military preparedness.

The role of women, especially young women, changed just as dramatically. They entered the work force in record numbers, something that is so well known that one need only mention "Rosie the Riveter" to make the point. There were millions of hasty marriages–teenagers got married because, in the moral atmosphere of the day, if they wanted to have a sexual experience before one of them went off to war, they had to stand in front of a preacher first. Most of the marriages worked. The girls became women. They traveled alone, or with their infants, to distant places on hot and stuffy or cold and overcrowded trains. They became proficient cooks and housekeepers, managed the finances, learned to fix the car, and worked the night shift.

For African-Americans and Japanese-Americans, it was a terrible war. The armed services, the national capital, and the former Confederate states all maintained a strict segregation that was degrading to blacks–and things were not much if any better in New York or Chicago. U.S.-born Japanese-American citizens (nisei) were shipped from the West Coast to concentration camps in the western desert or as far away as the Arkansas delta.

Despite the mistreatment of minorities, American self-satisfaction during the war ran very high. Americans congratulated one another on living in the best, the freest, the richest, and the most democratic country in the world. It was also the most productive–by far. At a time when the country achieved the greatest single feat of industrial production in history, the making of the atomic bomb, it also manufactured countless products and weapons in incredible numbers. The raw figures for just one industry give some idea of the scope of the achievement. In 1939 American factories produced 5,856 aircraft. In 1944 American factories produced 96,318 aircraft, many of them gigantic four-engine bombers. The total number of planes produced for the war was more than 250,000. The figures were roughly similar for trucks, jeeps, and tanks, all of which came off the assembly line in a never-ending stream.

Another miracle was the creation of the armed forces. The army hardly existed at the beginning of 1940 (175,000 men) and was virtually without equipment. Five years later, at more than 8 million strong, it was far and away the best-equipped army in the world.

The theme of the war was teamwork. "We are all in this together" was a phrase heard almost as frequently as "Don't you know there's a war on?" In the Great Depression people felt isolated, alone, fearful. In the war people felt a sense of belonging. There was a commitment to the notion that society's needs come before individual desires. Americans were faced with a great challenge, they met it, they overcame all obstacles, and they won.

Another feature of the war experience was deferred gratification. The theme of almost all advertising and much government propaganda was the rewards that were coming after victory was attained. All the hardships of today–rationing, no tires, no new cars, no washing machines, three families to a single apartment–would disappear once the job was done. Tomorrow was worth saving for and delicious to dream about.

On V-J Day, Marjorie Haselton spoke for her generation in a letter to her soldier husband in the Pacific: "You and I were brought up to think cynically of patriotism by the bitter, realistic writers of the twenties and thirties. This war has taught me–I love my country, and I'm not ashamed to admit it anymore. I am proud of the men of my generation. Brought up in false prosperity and then degrading depression, they have overcome these handicaps. None of you fellows wanted the deal life handed you–but just about everyone of you gritted your teeth and hung on. You boys proved that teamwork couldn't be beaten."

In these days of the "me" generation and instant gratification, it is no wonder that those of us over sixty years of age look back with a certain nostalgia and think of World War II as "the good war."

The Health-Care Reform Debate

By Mary Hager

Mary Hager is a correspondent for Newsweek*'s Washington, DC, bureau. She specializes in health, medical, science, and environmental issues.*

From the start, 1994 was billed as the year Bill Clinton would achieve what no president since Harry Truman had been able to do: reform the American health-care system. It was commonly believed that the timing was ideal. Public pressure for change was mounting, employers wanted help in controlling the soaring costs of health care, and the nation had a leader committed to ensuring that all Americans had health insurance.

But those who believed health-care reform would happen in 1994 failed to account for the clout of the dozens, if not hundreds, of interest groups with a stake in the health-care system—which, after all, represents one-seventh of the U.S. economy and is one of its largest employers. Nor did they take account of the sharp divisions among the members of Congress about what reforming the American health-care system really meant. Even public support for reform was suspect, as polls showed that, although many people said they favored reform, they were unclear on what it meant and were, by and large, satisfied with the status quo.

As rhetoric escalated during the year and as the president's standing in the opinion polls plunged, the prospects for passing reform legislation worsened. By the time Congress belatedly adjourned for an abbreviated summer break in August, it looked as if the year for health reform might eventually end with nothing more than minor adjustments, at best. But even that prospect vanished once members were again in Washington after Labor Day. By autumn, health reform, large or small, was pronounced dead—at least for 1994.

Why Reform the Health-Care System?

Pressure for change in the health-care system had grown for years as annual costs steadily increased to the trillion dollar mark, defying continuing efforts to hold them in check, and as a growing number of Americans—at latest count something like 39 million—found themselves without health insurance, placing the burden of their care on the government, on those who do have health insurance and can pay the bills, or on health-care providers.

Many employers who do provide insurance coverage have found ways to hold down their own costs. Some have trimmed back coverage and/or increased the amount employees pay for their health insurance. Some large corporations have turned to negotiating for volume discounts with participating physicians, hospitals, and suppliers. Still other employers have turned to some form of managed care. In a managed-care system, costs are kept low by requiring that participating individuals receive all or most of their health care from a selected group of doctors and other medical personnel who have agreed to accept a standard fee from the insurer for the services they provide.

At the same time, with new technology, the ability of the American system to provide care continued to grow. Americans came to expect state-of-the-art care as a right, regardless of cost—especially if they were not paying all or most of their own bills.

In many parts of the country, it seemed as if the system was already reforming itself without waiting for Washington to act. In growing numbers, doctors and hospitals formed provider networks, and health-related businesses began to consolidate. The trend, especially pronounced in California and Minnesota, was making strong inroads in the Northeast and appeared to be spreading throughout the country. At the same time, many states embarked on their own versions of reform, but they slowed their efforts because of uncertainty over what course, if any, Washington would follow.

The Debate Begins

The tensions within the system that fueled the reform movement had festered beneath the surface for years, hardly an issue politicians were willing to confront. That changed in 1991 when Democrat Harris Wofford of Pennsylvania ran for the Senate on a platform that called for health-care reform, and won. This surprise victory by a candidate widely considered an underdog signaled a major change. Concern about losing health insurance, especially at a time of widespread unemployment, permeated the middle class. In addition, frustration grew over the number of regulations that insurance companies were beginning to establish; for example, companies were reluctant to insure persons who had preexisting medical conditions, such as diabetes, heart disease, or epilepsy. Even though polls showed that more than 80 percent of Americans were satisfied with their care, the need to reform the system had become, almost overnight, a politically viable, mainstream issue.

During the 1992 presidential campaign, the candidates seized the issue and talked about the need to provide insurance coverage for all Americans through an employer-based system—much as Richard Nixon had advocated in his pre-Watergate days. Above all, they cited the imperative to control the soaring costs of health care, which some forecasters warned could consume one-fifth of the nation's resources by the end of the century.

President George Bush proposed a system of tax rebates and deductions to give employers incentives to expand coverage; Clinton advocated an employer-based system that would guarantee all Americans a package of basic insurance benefits and control costs by injecting competition into the health-care market. In his campaign, Clinton stated that all this would be achieved without imposing new general taxes or compromising the high quality of care citizens expected.

But turning campaign promises into a workable plan once Clinton was elected proved a formidable challenge. The new president appointed, in January 1993, his wife, Hillary Rodham Clinton, to take charge of the effort to produce a health-care reform plan within 100 days. This decision immediately sparked criticism because no other first lady had ever assumed such a major public role. Her task force's way of operating was also controversial. Working in secrecy, a group of more than 500 anonymous experts met, analyzed, and finally honed the options that were ultimately refined into the Clinton plan. The task force, however, failed to meet the 100-day deadline.

When the president unveiled his plan officially in September 1993 before a joint session of Congress, he stressed the need to provide "health security" for all Americans with a basic package of insurance benefits and stated that he would not sign a bill that did not ensure universal coverage. In his speech, Clinton outlined a plan that required all employers to pay part of the costs of coverage for their employees, but offered government subsidies to small businesses, the self-employed, and the unemployed. To control costs, health insurance would be purchased from insurance providers or from groups of health-care providers by large "health alliances." Health alliances would be either regional groups run by the states and overseen by the federal government, and representing large numbers of people and smaller companies, or corporate alliances established by any employer with more than 5,000 workers. The health alliances, or insurance companies contracting with them, would negotiate with networks of hospitals and physicians to provide the mandated package of benefits at competitive prices. Individuals, including Medicaid recipients, would select from an array of insurance plans offered by the health alliances. Clinton's plan worked on the belief that insurers' costs would be lowered by spreading the risk over a larger group of people. Also, insurance and health-care providers would be forced to keep their prices low to compete with other providers vying for the large group of customers represented by a health alliance.

The Bill Moves to Capitol Hill

The Clinton plan was anything but simple. By the time the 1,300-plus page bill that contained the details for the plan was finally delivered to Congress in late October 1993, pundits had already pronounced it "Dead on Arrival." The plan, they warned, was too costly and too complex and would introduce too much new government intrusion into the private sector. The proposed health alliances were particularly controversial. Few quibbled with the stated goals of universal coverage, cost control, and quality care, but with the exception of the president's most stalwart supporters, almost no one agreed with his ambitious approach to meeting those goals. More than one expert contended that the three goals were contradictory; any two might be achieved, but not all three.

As Congress held hearings and then began to debate the issues seriously, support splintered even further. Republicans, many miffed because crafting the Clinton plan had been a strictly partisan effort, were unwilling partners but slow to come up with proposals of their own. Even Democrats were split, with nearly 100 members on record favoring a Canadian-style single-payer system in which the government would collect payroll taxes to fund universal coverage, and another contingent reluctant to mandate that employers pay the bill.

Interest Groups Voice Their Opinions

A record number of interest groups with a vested stake in the outcome of reform converged on Congress, all pleading their special cause. To maintain support of hospitals and physicians, the backbone of any health-care system, the administration had targeted the pharmaceutical industry and the health-insurance industry as the "bad guys" responsible for escalating costs. Both fought back. The pharmaceutical industry warned that the advances in therapy would be fewer and farther between if the ability to fund research through profits were hampered. The insurance industry began its fight with a series of aggressive television advertisements featuring the characters Harry and Louise. In the commercials, this fictional middle-class couple questioned what Clinton-style reform would mean for them and other average Americans.

Small-business groups led a grassroots campaign, cautioning members that the costs of providing health coverage for all workers, even with government subsidies, would inevitably lead to job loss and could force many to shut down. The fundamental question of who should pay for coverage dominated congressional discussion, pushing concerns about controlling the costs of health care—the initial starting point for the whole debate—and about maintaining the quality of care far to the background.

Still no side yielded. In his January 1994 State of the Union message, the president again threatened to veto any reform legislation reaching his desk that failed to guarantee insurance coverage for all Americans. Although the administration in public said it was ready to negotiate on all other parts of the plan, the original proposal remained intact, parceled out to five congressional committees—Energy and Commerce, Education and Labor, and Ways and Means in the House of Representatives; Finance, and Labor and Human Resources in the Senate.

The Plan Falters

All five groups thrashed through the issues and came up with independent proposals, but only the House Education and Labor plan and the Senate Labor and Human Resources plan bore much resemblance to the Clinton package. Both relied on an employer mandate to reach the goal of universal coverage, with requirements that employers pay 80 percent of the insurance premiums for workers and their families, although they differed in details. Energy and Commerce deadlocked on the issue of mandating that employers pay most of their workers' health insurance costs and failed to reach consensus on a draft proposal.

The administration lost strong support on the House Ways and Means Committee when Chairman Dan Rostenkowski (D, IL) stepped down in May 1994 after he was indicted on 17 criminal charges linked to the House Post Office scandal. In his absence, the committee passed a version of a subcommittee proposal creating a new entitlement program, Medicare Part C, to cover the existing Medicaid population as well as employees in small firms and anyone else falling between the cracks, with an employer mandate providing coverage for all other workers. In the Senate, the pivotal Finance Committee struggled with the employer mandate issue and finally produced a proposal that called for universal coverage without the mandate, but with a clause for revisiting the issue if the universal coverage target was not met.

The efforts of the five committees were eventually turned over to congressional leaders who would consolidate the recommendations and come up with consensus proposals. The House Democratic leadership did unveil a consolidated reform proposal on July 29, 1994. However, the House essentially opted to hold back, waiting to see what happened in the Senate, where Majority Leader George Mitchell (D, ME), a lame duck who had decided not to seek reelection, had insisted passage of health-care reform was his top priority, one he saw as a fitting finale to his Senate career. On August 2, Mitchell introduced a proposal—admittedly only a starting point for debate—that sparked criticism from members of both parties and was deemed, as all other proposals before it, too costly by Congressional Budget Office reviewers. Meanwhile, a middle-of-the-road group of senators from both parties struggled to come up with an approach that would gain bipartisan support. Tired, and having reached a stalemate, the Senate finally adjourned, August 12, for the summer recess, leaving a core group of members and staff to revisit the issues during the 4-week hiatus and, they hoped, come up with a workable proposal.

Reform Pronounced Dead

But the die had already been cast. To no one's surprise, last-minute efforts to craft a modest, mid-ground proposal foundered. By the end of September, Majority Leader Mitchell conceded that health reform was dead for the year, and even those who pushed for modest changes found themselves out of time.

Even though reform was officially proclaimed dead, few lamented, but no one cheered. Democrats blamed the intransigence of the Republicans who, they charged, did not want to give the president a victory on his major issue in an election year. Republicans blamed the Democrats for trying to get too much and to craft what they feared could become another massively expensive federal program.

No doubt much of the credit or blame for the failure of reform lay with the well-financed interest groups—hospitals, doctors, insurers, and hosts of others. All backed changes that would control costs and expand coverage, but according to their own prescriptions and favoring their constituencies.

While the White House struggled to salvage what it could for a return to health reform in 1995, congressional staffers braced for a renewed but, in all probability, more modest effort with new members of the 104th Congress. Clinton-style health reform might be dead, but the underlying problems of soaring costs and uninsured Americans that had sparked the health-care debate had far from vanished.

CHRONOLOGY OF THE YEAR'S EVENTS

Reported Month by Month in 3 Categories: National, International, and General
Oct. 16, 1993, to Oct. 31, 1994

OCTOBER

National

Verdict Given in L.A. Riot Incident—In Los Angeles in October, a County Superior Court jury reached a decision on most of the charges related to a well–publicized incident that occurred during the spring 1992 riots. A jury at that time had acquitted 4 police officers in the beating of Rodney King. Shortly thereafter, in footage shown widely on television, a white truck driver, Reginald Denny, was severely beaten. In verdicts announced **Oct. 18** and **20**, the jury found 2 black men, Damian Williams and Henry Watson, not guilty of attempted murder but guilty of lesser charges for attacks on Denny and others. Judge John Ouderkirk declared a mistrial on one remaining assault charge against Watson after the jury became deadlocked. In an agreement with prosecutors, **Nov. 2**, Watson pleaded guilty to a felony count of assault that had resulted from the beating of Larry Tarvin, another truck driver. Ouderkirk, **Dec. 7**, sentenced Williams to prison for 10 years on his convictions, and Watson was put on probation until 1997. Watson would also perform community service.

Superconducting Supercollider Canceled—Congress in October canceled the Superconducting Supercollider (SSC), 4 years after authorizing it. The SSC, which had been under construction near Waxahachie, TX, would have permitted scientists to study collisions of atomic particles at high speeds in an attempt to better understand the nature of matter. About $2 billion had been spent on the SSC; the total cost had once been estimated at $4.4 billion but was now projected at $11 billion. In June the U.S. House voted to kill the SSC, but the Senate later approved funds for it. The House then voted, 242-143, on **Oct 19**, to order Senate–House conferees working on the appropriations bill for energy projects to cancel the SSC. The conference committee complied, **Oct. 21**, but left $640 million in the bill for the 1994 fiscal year to help cover the costs of closing down the SSC.

Committee Subpoenas Senator's Diaries—The Senate Ethics Committee voted unanimously, **Oct. 20**, to subpoena the full diaries of Sen. Robert Packwood (R, OR). For nearly a year the committee had been investigating complaints by 26 women that Packwood had made unwanted sexual advances toward them. Packwood had allowed the committee to examine portions of his diaries but objected that it was seeking to examine entries unrelated to the allegations. Packwood's attorney, James Fitzpatrick, said, **Oct. 22**, that the diaries that Packwood had withheld included accounts of romantic affairs involving other members of Congress. Sen. Richard Bryan (D, NV) released a statement, **Oct. 28**, asserting that the diaries "raised questions about a possible violation of one or more laws, including criminal laws."

Another Ex-HUD Official Convicted—Deborah Gore Dean, once the executive assistant to then–Secretary of Housing and Urban Development Samuel Pierce, was convicted on 12 felony counts in U.S. District Court in Washington, DC, **Oct. 26**. Found guilty of defrauding the government, lying to Congress, and accepting a bribe, Dean was the 11th person to be convicted in the HUD scandal, which had involved funneling construction and renovation contracts, in the 1980s, to consultants and developers with close ties to Republican Party leaders.

Federal Budget Deficit Declines—The government, **Oct. 28**, put the federal budget deficit for the 1993 fiscal year at $254.9 billion, far below estimates and also sharply lower than the 1992 deficit of $290.2 billion. During the 1993 fiscal year, which ended Sept. 30, federal spending had risen 1.9%, to $1.408 trillion, while revenues had climbed 5.8%, to $1.153 trillion. In another encouraging report, the Commerce Dept. said, **Oct. 28**, that the GDP had grown at an annual rate of 2.8% during the 3d quarter, compared with 1.9% during the 2d quarter. Buoyed by strong corporate earnings reports and other evidence of an improving economy, on **Oct. 28** the Dow Jones Industrial Average finished at an all–time high of 3,687.86.

International

UN Renews Embargo on Haiti—The international community again confronted Haiti in October after the Haitian military and police indicated that they would not permit implementation of an agreement brokered by the United Nations to restore exiled Pres. Jean–Bertrand Aristide to office by Oct. 30. The UN Security Council voted unanimously, **Oct. 16**, to impose a naval blockade. Nine U.S. and Canadian warships put the blockade into effect, **Oct. 19**. A UN arms and oil embargo, approved earlier, was reinstituted, **Oct. 19**.

Israel Frees 600 Palestinians—Israeli and Palestinian negotiators continued during October to discuss the details of the accord on limited Palestinian self–rule that had been announced in September. During a week–long period beginning **Oct. 19**, Israel freed some 600 Palestinians being held in Israeli jails. Negotiators at the Egyptian resort of Taba agreed, **Oct 21**, on the terms of the first large–scale release of Palestinians in nearly 10 years. On **Oct. 26**, Palestine Liberation Organization officials called on Israel to free more of some 10,000 Palestinians that it still held. The abduction, **Oct. 29**, and subsequent murder of a Jewish settler in the West Bank triggered widespread violent demonstrations by thousands of settlers.

U.S. Army Rangers Leave Somalia—The U.S. took a step back from the tense situation in Somalia, **Oct 19**, when Pres. Bill Clinton announced that the 750 U.S. Army Rangers would be withdrawn immediately. Clinton said he was committed to pursuing negotiations aimed at finding a political solution in Somalia.

Bhutto Returns as Pakistani Leader—Benazir Bhutto completed a political comeback, **Oct. 19**, when she was elected prime minister of Pakistan. The army had helped oust Bhutto as prime minister in 1990 for alleged corruption and incompetency, but in early October her Pakistan People's Party had led in voting for seats in the Parliament. With the support of her party and of smaller parties and independents, Bhutto was returned to power by a parliamentary vote of 121-72.

Liberals Sweep to Victory in Canada—A political earthquake shook Canada, **Oct. 25**, when the opposition Liberal Party won a stunning landslide victory in national elections to the House of Commons. The results ensured that the Liberal Party leader, Jean Chrétien, would become the next prime minister. He would succeed Kim Campbell, who had headed the Progressive Conservative government only since June, when Brian Mulroney retired. The initial popularity of Campbell, Canada's first woman prime minister, had faded in the face of an 11% unemployment rate and the apparent desire by voters for a change of government after 9 years of Conservative leadership. Chrétien promised job creation and a public–works program. The Liberals captured 177 seats in the 295-member House, and the Conservatives were nearly wiped out, plunging from 154 seats to just 2. Campbell lost her own seat. The Bloc Quebecois, committed to taking Quebec out of the Canadian confederation, won 54 seats. Another regional grouping, the Reform Party, based primarily in Alberta and British Columbia, won 52 seats on a right–of–center platform. Further to the left, the New Democratic Party fell from 43 seats to just 9. One independent candidate was elected.

General

Toronto Wins 2d Straight World Series—The Toronto Blue Jays repeated as champions of baseball's World Series in October. The Jays, the American League champions, defeated the Philadelphia Phillies, the National League pennant–winners, 4 games to 2. The 4th game, played in Philadelphia, **Oct. 20**, was the longest (4 hr, 14 min) and highest scoring in Series history. Trailing 14-9, the Jays scored the last 6 runs of the game in the top of the 8th inning, with Devon White's triple driving in the final 2 runs in the 15-14 victory. That gave Toronto a 3-1 lead in the Series. The Phillies' Curt Schilling shut out the Jays, 2-0, **Oct. 21**. In Toronto, **Oct. 23**, the Phillies led, 6–5, going into the last of the 9th, but with 2 runners on base, outfielder Joe Carter hit a home run off Mitch Williams to give the home team the game and the Series. For only the 2d time a Series had ended with a home run. No team had won 2 titles in succession since the New York Yankees in 1977 and 1978.

Chess Title in Dispute—The world chess title was a matter of controversy in October as rival organizations sponsored matches between leading players. After a procedural dispute led the International Chess Federation (FIDE) to decline to sponsor a match between them, Gary Kasparov of Russia (who had been the FIDE–recognized world champion) and Nigel Short of Great Britain (who had been the FIDE–designated challenger) created the Professional Chess Association. They then played each other under its auspices, with Kasparov prevailing, 12.5 to 7.5, in a match that concluded in London, **Oct. 21**. Meanwhile, FIDE matched former world champion Anatoly Karpov of Russia and Jan Timman of the Netherlands, with Karpov winning, 12.5 to 8.5, in a contest that concluded in Jakarta, Indonesia, **Nov. 1**.

"Dr. Death" Assists in 19th Suicide—In October, Dr. Jack Kevorkian, who had been nicknamed "Doctor Death" and the "Suicide Doctor," for the 19th time helped an ill person commit suicide. At the time he was free on bail after being charged with violating Michigan's law against assisted suicides. On **Oct. 22** he helped Merian Frederick, who was suffering from amyotrophic lateral sclerosis (also known as Lou Gehrig's disease), to take her own life by inhaling carbon monoxide gas.

California Fires Cause Great Damage—Fires driven by hot dry Santa Ana winds caused widespread damage in 6 counties in Southern California in late October and early November. Arson was suspected as a major cause. By **Oct. 27** fires were burning in several places between Ventura Co. and the Mexican border, and Pres. Bill Clinton, **Oct. 28**, declared 5 counties disaster areas. The fires flourished in scrub forests and in dense dry brush. The state, **Oct. 31**, put damage at $500 million, with some 1,000 homes destroyed and more than 25,000 people left homeless. On **Nov. 2**, new fires swept into Malibu, a prosperous beach town that was home to may celebrities. Some 300 homes were destroyed in that area. Three persons died, and dozens of firefighters and others were reported injured. The fires were reported to be under control, **Nov. 4**. An insurance industry group reported, **Nov. 17**, that an estimated $950 million in insured damage had been caused by the fires that had occurred throughout the region.

NOVEMBER

National

Senate Confronts Packwood on Diaries—The Senate, **Nov. 1**, opened debate on whether to back up its Ethics Committee, which had asked Sen. Robert Packwood (R, OR) to surrender all his personal diaries. The diaries were of interest in the sexual–harassment complaints against Packwood and also as possible evidence of criminal violation by the senator. Before the Senate, Packwood and his supporters contended that it would violate his privacy to provide materials unrelated to the sexual–misconduct allegations. Packwood and Richard Bryan (D, NV), chairman of the Ethics Committee, both said, **Nov. 2**, that the committee was investigating whether Packwood had made any promises in return for job offers for his wife. Sen. Robert Byrd (D, WV) expressed his dismay, **Nov. 2**, at the embarrassment he said Packwood was bringing to the Senate and called on him to resign. The Senate, **Nov. 2**, voted, 94–6, to authorize legal action to compel Packwood to honor the subpoena for his diaries.

GOP Wins Top Offices in Elections—One year after they lost the White House, Republicans made an impressive comeback in off–year elections, **Nov. 2.** In the only 2 governorship contests, the GOP took both statehouses away from the Democrats. And a Republican, Rudolph Giuliani, unseated the incumbent Democratic major of New York City, David Dinkins. Giuliani, a former U.S. Attorney, had lost to Dinkins in 1989 but prevailed this time by 51% to 48%. Giuliani overcame a 5-1 margin in Democratic voter registration by stressing the city's weak economy, Dinkins's alleged weakness as a manager, and the precarious state of relations among the races. In New Jersey, Christine Todd Whitman defeated Jim Florio, who had promised when running for governor 4 years earlier that he would not raise taxes, only to push through a large increase in sales and personal income taxes once elected. For her part, Whitman promised to cut income taxes, and she won by 49% to 48%. In Virginia, where Gov. L. Douglas Wilder was not eligible to run again, the winner was George F. Allen, a lawyer and a former U.S. Representative. Allen, son of former Washington Redskins football coach George Allen, campaigned on an anticrime platform and defeated the Democratic candidate, Mary Sue Terry, by a 58–41 margin. In Minneapolis, Sharon Sayles Belton, a Democrat, became the first woman and first black to be elected mayor.

Economic Indicators Point Upward—In a signal that the economy was continuing to gain momentum, the Commerce Dept. reported, **Nov. 2**, that the index of leading economic indicators had moved up by 0.5% in September The Labor Dept., **Nov. 5**, put the October unemployment rate at 6.8%. The department said, **Nov. 10**, that the consumer price index had risen 0.4% in October, but it reported, **Nov. 11**, that prices charged by producers for finished goods had edged downward 0.2% in the same month. Anticipating that Congress would approve the North American Free Trade Agreement, investors pushed the Dow Jones Industrial Average to an all–time closing high of 3,710.77 on **Nov. 16**. The Commerce Dept. said, **Nov. 19**, that the merchandise trade deficit had grown to $10.89 billion in September. This figure was 8.3% higher than the revised August gap of $10.05 billion.

Alleged Vote Payoffs Stun New Jersey—Edward Rollins, the campaign manager for Christine Todd Whitman, the successful Republican candidate for governor of New Jersey, created a furor, **Nov. 9**, when he said that the campaign had paid out $500,000 to black ministers and Democratic workers in return for their help in suppressing voter turnout among blacks. Rollins, a former top strategist for Pres. Ronald Reagan and other leading Republicans, told reporters that the money was spent in urban neighborhoods, with the ministers being promised donations to their favorite charities if they did not appeal from their pulpits for a big Election Day vote. Whitman, **Nov. 10**, denied that any such payoffs had been made, and she released a statement from Rollins in which he called his previous comments "an exaggeration that turned out to be inaccurate." Whitman has defeated the incumbent governor, Jim Florio, by just 26,000 votes. Black ministers denounced Rollins and denied receiving any cash. The U.S. Justice Dept. and the State Attorney General's office began criminal investigations, **Nov. 12**. In a deposition, **Nov. 19**, Rollins called his initial claim a fabrication, created as his way of getting in a dig at his rival campaign manager, James Carville. No significant evidence in support of Rollins' original boast was discovered, and the Democratic Party, **Nov. 29**, dropped a civil lawsuit challenging Whitman's election. Federal and state prosecutors said, **Jan. 12**, that they had discontinued their investigations.

"Brady Bill" on Handguns Enacted—The Brady Handgun Violence Prevention Act, commonly called the Brady bill, became law in November. It was named for James Brady, the White House press secretary who was badly wounded during the attempt on Pres. Ronald Reagan's life in 1981. Since then, Brady and his wife, Sarah, had lobbied vigorously for adoption of a law that would require a waiting period for the purchase of a handgun. The National Rifle Association led the opposition to the Brady bill, but in Nov. first the House, **Nov. 10**, and then the Senate, **Nov. 20**, adopted different versions of the bill. The House accepted a compromise conference committee report, **Nov. 23**, and the Senate did the same, **Nov. 24**, after the Republican leader, Bob Dole (KS) abandoned delaying tactics. The law, which Pres. Bill Clinton signed, **Nov. 30**, provided for a 5–day waiting period and established a national computer network as a means to check the backgrounds of gun buyers.

Puerto Ricans Oppose Statehood—In a plebiscite, **Nov. 14**, Puerto Ricans voted to continue their commonwealth status with the U.S. The statehood option was defeated, though by a margin of only 48 to 46%. Four percent of the voters favored independence for the island. Puerto Ricans pay no federal taxes and cannot vote in presidential elections. To stimulate the island's economy, the U.S. government had exempted U.S. businesses from paying taxes on much of what they earned in Puerto Rico.

Court Rebuffs Pentagon on Homosexuals—A 3–judge panel of the U.S. Court of Appeals for the District of Columbia, **Nov. 16**, struck down the Pentagon policy barring homosexuals from military service. The case involved Joseph Steffan, a former midshipman at the U.S. Naval Academy, who was forced to resign 6 weeks before his 1987 graduation after he acknowledged that he was gay. The Pentagon had long maintained that homosexuality was incompatible with maintaining good order and discipline within the armed forces. Chief Judge Abner Mikva wrote, "A cardinal principle of equal protection law holds that the Government cannot discriminate against a certain class in order to give effect to the prejudice of others." The court ordered the Navy to award Steffan a diploma and a commission. Although the ruling applied to a long–established policy, it raised the prospect that new Clinton administration rules on homosexuals in the military would face a similar challenge in the courts.

Clinton Helps End Airline Strike—Members of the Association of Professional Flight Attendants went on strike at American Airlines, **Nov. 18**. The airline had lost almost $1 billion in 1992 and had announced plans to cut 5,000 jobs by the end of 1994. Employees were displeased with their salaries, work rules, and the company's efforts to get them to help pay for health insurance and other benefits. Training replacement workers quickly, American sought to keep its planes in the air, with mixed success. Thousands of would–be travelers saw their plans disrupted during the busy days preceding the Thanksgiving holiday. On **Nov. 22**, Pres. Bill Clinton and members of his administration got the airline and the attendants to agree to submit their differences to arbitration, and the employees returned to work, **Nov. 23**.

International

Treaty on European Union in Effect—After a ratification process that required almost 2 years, the European Community's Treaty on European Union became effective, **Nov. 1**. Leaders of 12 EC nations had approved the treaty in a meeting in Maastricht, the Netherlands, in Dec. 1991. In Oct. 1993, Germany had been the final nation to complete ratification. The nations of the newly titled European Union would work toward establishing common defense and foreign policies and, ultimately, a common currency.

North Korea Nuclear Impasse Continues—Hans Blix, director general of the International Atomic Energy Agency, told the UN, **Nov. 1**, that North Korea was still not cooperating with his agency's efforts to inspect its nuclear installations. He said that the IAEA was losing its capacity to monitor declared sites because cameras were running out of film and inspectors were not allowed access. Blix said North Korea had also denied inspectors access to undeclared nuclear sites. On **Nov. 3**, North Korea canceled scheduled talks with South Korea concerning the nuclear controversy and other military matters.

Israeli–PLO Self–Rule Talks Falter—Talks between Israel and the Palestine Liberation Organization stalled in early November. Israeli delegates, **Nov. 1**, proposed a withdrawal from Palestinian urban areas and refugee camps in the Gaza Strip, but with the redeployment of troops near 3 Israeli settlements. The Septebmer accord that had provided for limited Palestinian self–rule had established that Israel was responsible for security in Israeli settlements, but Palestinian negotiators, **Nov. 2**, objected to the redeployment plan and walked out of the talks. Although the talks later resumed, the increasing violence in the Gaza Strip, including killings on both sides, created new tensions. Lt. Gen. Ehud Barak, the Israeli army's chief of staff, apologized, **Nov. 30**, for what he called the inadvertent killing of a young Palestinian who had spoken out against violence by Palestinians. Israeli generals and PLO leaders met, **Nov. 30**, in Gaza to seek ways to restore calm in the area.

Chrétien Takes Office in Canada—Jean Chrétien, leader of the triumphant Liberal Party in the Oct. elections, was sworn in as Canada's 20th prime minister, **Nov. 4**. His cabinet appointments indicated that the new government might be more oriented toward the concerns of business than Liberal governments of the past. Chrétien, **Nov. 4**, canceled a contract with European and North American companies for the purchase of 43 helicopters, whose cost (US$3.6 billion) had been an issue in his campaign against the previous Conservative government.

Draft Russian Constitution Unveiled—Pres. Boris Yeltsin of Russia, **Nov. 6**, announced that he would serve out his term until 1996, reversing an earlier statement that presidential elections would be held in June 1994. On **Nov. 8**, he signed a new draft constitution, which, if approved by the voters in December, would replace a Communist–era constitution that had been in effect from 1978 until Sept. 1993, when its use was suspended by Yeltsin. The draft strengthened the hand of the president, who could appoint the premier as well as top judges and military commanders and who could dissolve Parliament under certain circumstances. The president could veto legislation, but Parliament could not block the president's decrees. The draft also protected the right to own private property, including land. Overall, the document increased the power of the central government at the expense of individual republics and other political units.

UN Abandons Pursuit of Somali Leader—The fugitive Somali warlord Gen. Mohammed Farah Aidid said, **Nov. 7**, that he would not participate in peace negotiations with the UN, which he called an obstacle to peace and responsible for Somalia's problems. He called on the UN Security Council to withdraw its warrant for his arrest and urged that his aides who had been seized be released. The U.S. House, following the Senate's lead, endorsed, **Nov. 9**, Pres. Bill Clinton's timetable for withdrawal of all U.S. forces in Somalia by the end of March 1994. The Security Council, **Nov. 16**, voted to drop its attempt to arrest Aidid. Eight Aidid aids were also released, **Nov. 16**.

U.S., Mexico Ratify Free Trade Agreement—The U.S. and Mexico, in November, ratified the North American

Free Trade Agreement, which was scheduled to go into effect Jan. 1, 1994. Canada, the third party to the agreement, which had been signed in 1992, had already ratified. Public opinion in the U.S. was sharply divided over NAFTA, and the differing views were represented in a televised debate, **Nov. 9**, between Vice Pres. Al Gore, speaking for an administration that supported it, and Ross Perot, an indepenent candidate for president in 1992, who had been campaigning across the country against it. Perot echoed the concerns of most American labor union leaders, who warned that jobs would disappear as companies took advantage of free trade by moving south of the border to employ Mexicans at low wages. Gore contended that creation of the world's largest low–tariff trading zone would improve economies throughout North America and that a more prosperous Mexico would sharply increase its purchase of goods from the U.S. Perot warned that companies would also be attracted to Mexico because of its lax environmental controls, but Gore countered that if NAFTA was defeated, the U.S. would lose its leverage over Mexico with respect to environmental standards. The debate over NAFTA in the U.S. House was fierce, with Pres. Bill Clinton exerting great pressure on individual members. Nonetheless, the Democratic leadership was divided, with Majority Leader Richard Gephardt (MO) opposing NAFTA. The House majority whip, David Bonier (MI), said, **Nov. 17**, ". . . it's not fair to ask American workers to compete against Mexican workers who earn $1 an hour." In the House vote, **Nov. 17**, a majority of Democrats opposed NAFTA, but Republicans overwhelmingly supported it, and the final total stood at 234–200 in favor. The U.S. Senate gave its approval, 61–38, **Nov. 20** The passage of NAFTA was considered Clinton's greatest legislative achievement so far. The Mexican Senate, **Nov. 22**, approved NAFTA by a vote of 56-2.

South Africans Draft Constitution—Representatives of some 20 South African parties, **Nov. 18**, approved a new constitution, to take effect after the April 1994 elections that would be open to voters of all races. Both black and white parties, including the ruling National Party, participated in writing the constitution. It provided for a 400–seat National Assembly and a 90–seat Senate that would write a permanent constitution under the coalition government that would run the country from 1994 to 1999. Under the new draft, the president would be elected by the National Assembly. The president's cabinet would contain members of all parties receiving at least 5% of the national vote. The president would also have the power to choose 11 members of a Constitutional Court. Members appointed to this high court would serve 7–year terms and would decide constitutional questions. The constitution gave full political rights to blacks and forbade discrimination on the basis of race, sex, sexual orientation, age, or physical disability. Parliament, **Dec. 22**, approved the constitution, 237–45.

Pacific Rim Leaders Meet—The presidents or prime ministers of 12 countries attended a summit meeting of the Asia–Pacific Economic Cooperation organization in Seattle in November. Altogether, delegates from 15 so–called Pacific Rim economies attended the summit, which was primarily concerned with issues relating to international trade. On **Nov. 19**, the day the summit began, Pres. Bill Clinton met for the first time with Pres. Jiang Zemin of China. Clinton told Jiang that, because of concerns about human rights abuses in China, the U.S. might not extend so–called most–favored–nation trading status with China beyond June 1994. The summit leaders endorsed the reduction or elimination of tariffs on a wide range of goods to facilitate work on the General Agreement on Tariffs and Trade, scheduled for completion in December.

Political Reform Moves Forward in Japan—Japan's new ruling coalition achieved a breakthrough, **Nov. 18**, when the lower house of the Diet (Parliament) approved a package of political reforms. The approval of the 4 bills, by a vote of 270–226, was a defeat for the Liberal Democratic Party, which had lost its longtime majority in Parliament earlier in the year because of public displeasure with repeated revelations of political corruption. Premier Morihiro Hosokawa orchestrated adoption of the reforms, which included a ban on direct contributions to candidates by corporations. Public funding for campaigns was authorized. The legislation created a new Parliament with a 500–seat lower house in which 274 members would be chosen in single–seat districts and 226 seats would be apportioned to parties based on their share of the total national vote. Each voter would cast 2 votes, one for an individual candidate and one for a preferred party. The reform bills would now be considered by the upper house of Parliament.

British Officials Communicate With IRA—The British government confirmed, **Nov. 28**, that for several years it had been in contact, through intermediaries, with the outlawed Irish Republican Army. The government had denied that it was negotiating with the IRA, but transcripts of exchanged messages, which it released, **Nov. 29**, indicated that the parties were exploring ways by which the violence related to the dispute over Northern Ireland could be ended. The transcripts, if accurate, indicated that the IRA was willing to end its terrorist bombings and participate in a dialogue that would lead to peace. Prime Minister John Major said, **Nov. 30**, that he wished to continue the contacts.

General

Dr. Kevorkian Imprisoned Twice—Dr. Jack Kevorkian, the so–called suicide doctor, was imprisoned in Wayne County Jail in Detroit, **Nov. 5**, for his alleged role in the suicides of 2 men in Aug. and Sept., and he then began a hunger strike. He was freed, **Nov. 8**, when a lawyer who did not know him paid $2,000 bail. Kevorkian assisted in a 20th suicide, **Nov. 22**. He was charged, **Nov. 29**, in Oakland County with helping Merian Frederick take her life in Oct. and was imprisoned in Pontiac, MI, **Nov. 30**.

Michael Jackson Treated for Addiction—Pop superstar Michael Jackson, **Nov. 12**, canceled the remainder of a worldwide concert tour in order, he said in a taped statement, to seek treatment for drug addiction. PepsiCo Inc., sponsor of the tour, said, **Nov. 14**, that it was ending its promotional agreement with the singer. Bertram Fields, Jackson's lawyer, said, **Nov. 15**, that Jackson was being treated at an undisclosed location for addiction to painkillers, which he had been taking since being burned during taping of a Pepsi–Cola commercial in 1984. Fields blamed the addiction on Jackson's "rage and humiliation and embarrassment" over a lawsuit filed earlier in the year on behalf of a 13–year–old boy who claimed Jackson had molested him. Jackson had denied the allegation and had not been charged with any crime.

DECEMBER

National

Shuttle Crew Repairs Space Telescope—The space shuttle *Endeavour*, with a crew of 7, was launched from Cape Canaveral, FL., **Dec. 2**. The mission was to repair the Hubble Space Telescope, which, because of a flaw in its main mirror, was not providing sharp photographs of objects as much as 15 billion mi distant, as intended. The mission commander, Col. Richard Covey, piloted the shuttle to within 30 ft of the telescope, **Dec. 4**, and the astronauts, in pairs, did the necessary work during 5 spacewalks, a record for a single mission. Four of the telescope's 6 gyroscopes were replaced, **Dec. 5.** The 2 solar panels, which had been vibrating as a result of extreme changes in temperature, were replaced, **Dec. 5-6.** Two astronauts, replaced, **Dec. 6-7**, the Hubble's primary camera, which had the flawed mirror, and also replaced 2 magnetic sensors, which measured the telescope's position in the magnetic field.

The shuttle landed at Cape Canaveral on **Dec. 13**, but astronomers would not see the first photographs from the repaired telescope for another month. On **Jan. 13**, NASA officials released photographs taken after the repairs; these images were much clearer that those taken earlier. One subject of the new photographs was the core of a galaxy 50 million light years distant.

Unemployment Rate Declines—The unemployment rate stood at 6.4% in November, the Labor Dept. reported, **Dec. 3**. This was a decline of 0.4 of a percentage point from October, the largest one-month decline in 10 years. The Commerce Dept. reported, **Dec. 3**, that the index of leading economic indicators had jumped 0.5% in October. Prices charged by producers for finished goods remained level in November, the Labor Dept. said, **Dec. 9**. The department reported, **Dec. 10**, that consumer prices had risen 0.2% in November. The Commerce Dept. said, **Dec. 16**, that the merchandise trade deficit in October was $10.46 billion. Leon Panetta, director of the White House Office of Management and Budget, said, **Dec. 22**, that the budget deficit for the 1995 fiscal year would be about $190 billion. This figure, lower than any previous projection, was attributed to the improvement in the economy. The Commerce Dept. said, **Dec. 29**, that the index of leading economic indicators had jumped another 0.5% in November. On Wall Street, the Dow Jones Industrial Average closed, **Dec. 31**, at 3,754.09, up 13.7% for the year.

Radiation Experiments Used Humans—Secret aspects of the nuclear past in the U.S. were revealed in December. Sec. of Energy Hazel O'Leary said, **Dec. 7**, that 204 underground nuclear tests had been conducted in Nevada from 1963 to 1990, without any notice to the public. Although safety guidelines were followed, at least 36 tests leaked trace radiation aboveground. Some 800 other tests had been previously acknowledged. The Energy Dept. said, **Dec. 8**, that radioactive substances had been fed to pregnant women in tests at Vanderbilt Univ. in the 1940s to study the effects on the fetuses. The Portland *Oregonian* reported that researchers had exposed the testicles of prisoners to radiation to study its effect on sperm. *The Boston Globe* reported, **Dec. 26**, that Harvard and MIT scientists from 1946 to 1956 had given doses of radiation in milk to 19 mentally retarded boys to study the digestive system. The Dept. of Energy said, **Dec. 28**, that some 800 people had been exposed to radiation in government experiments from the 1940s to the 1960s.

Colorado Judge Kills Gay Rights Ban—A judge in Colorado, **Dec. 14**, issued a permanent injunction barring implementation of a law that would have forbidden communities from passing ordinances protecting homosexuals from discrimination. Voters in Colorado had approved the anti-gay measure in a statewide referendum in 1992. The law would have had the effect of overturning existing ordinances in Aspen, Boulder, and Denver that protected homosexuals' rights in employment and housing. In January 1993, state District Court Judge Jeffrey Bayless issued a temporary injunction against the 1992 measure. The state Supreme Court held, in July, that it violated the U.S. Constitution's guarantee of equal protection of the law. When, in his view, supporters of the 1992 measure failed to demonstrate any "compelling state interest" justifying its enforcement, Bayless issued his permanent injunction.

Aspin Resigns as Defense Secretary—Les Aspin announced, **Dec. 15**, that he would resign as defense secretary, effective in January. The first member of the Clinton cabinet to bow out, Aspin had presided over the Pentagon during a storm-tossed year. U.S. military policy in Somalia, Bosnia, and elsewhere had seemed uncertain at times in direction and implementation. The secretary had been criticized for declining to reinforce U.S. troops in Somalia just before a bloody clash in which 18 U.S. Army Rangers died. Aspin had lifted restrictions on women flying combat missions, and he had struggled to reach a compromise under which homosexuals could serve in uniform. Pres. Bill Clinton, **Dec. 16**, announced that Adm. Bobby Ray Inman (ret.), who had a broad background in U.S. intelligence services, would be nominated to succeed Aspin.

Packwood Gives Diaries to Judge—Sen. Robert Packwood (R, OR) surrendered his diaries to a judge, **Dec. 16**, after the judge, Thomas Jackson of Federal District Court in Washington, DC, ordered him to give them up. Jackson would determine whether Packwood would have to give the diaries to the Senate Ethics Committee, which was investigating allegations against him. In a deposition released **Dec. 16,** a secretary for Packwood said the senator had altered some of the diary tapes.

Clintons Provide Records to Investigators—A real estate investment dating from the 1980s appeared to present a potential problem for Pres. and Mrs. Clinton in December. Bill and Hillary Rodham Clinton, along with a political supporter, James McDougal, had been co-owners of Whitewater Development Co., a now-defunct real estate firm in Arkansas. McDougal also owned the Madison Guaranty Savings and Loan, which failed in 1989. The Justice Dept. was investigating whether McDougal had diverted money illegally from Madison to the campaigns of Bill Clinton, who was then governor, and of other Arkansas political figures. When the Clintons sold their Whitewater holdings to McDougal, the details were handled by Vincent Foster, a lawyer who joined the White House staff in 1993. Foster committed suicide in July 1993. U.S. Park Police officials investigated Foster's death, but White House Counsel Bernard Nussbaum removed Foster's Whitewater files before they visited his office. This fact was confirmed by the White House only on **Dec. 20,** and on **Dec. 23** the White House said that the Clintons had instructed their attorneys to provide federal investigators with all their legal documents and financial records relating to Whitewater.

International

Police Kill Drug Kingpin Escobar—Pablo Escobar, multibillionaire boss of the Medellín cocaine cartel, was killed by Colombian police and soldiers in December. At its peak, the Medellín operation had provided most of the cocaine that reached the U.S. Escobar had been a fugitive since escaping from a comfortable prison in 1992. Many of his associates had been killed or captured, and a rival cartel operating out of Cali had come to dominate the Colombian cocaine trade. Escobar had become concerned about the safety of his wife and children, who had just returned to Colombia after being denied entry into Germany. While he talked with them by phone, **Dec. 2**, authorities using monitoring devices were able to locate his hideout in Medellín. As the task force assigned to track him down closed in, **Dec. 2**, Escobar attempted to flee but was shot to death. One of his lieutenants was also killed. In Medellín, many people mourned the death of Escobar, who had spent large sums on houses, roads, and other assistance for the poor.

Canada Gives Final OK on NAFTA—Prime Minister Jean Chrétien said, **Dec. 2**, that he had gotten the assurances he wanted on the North American Free Trade Agreement, and that his government now gave full support to NAFTA. In supplemental accords announced by Chrétien, the U.S., Canada, and Mexico said they would agree on antidumping measures by the end of 1995, and the 3 signatories also agreed that NAFTA rules would not require any nation to export water resources against its will. The pact was signed into U.S. law by Pres. Clinton on **Dec. 8**. It was scheduled to take effect January 1.

U.S. Flies Aidid to Talks on Somalia—Just 2 months after his forces killed 18 Americans and wounded 70 in battle, Somali warlord Mohammed Farah Aidid was a guest on a U.S. military plane, **Dec. 2**. The U.S. government, believing that talks in Addis Ababa, Ethiopia, were critical to a breakthrough on Somalia, provided the plane for Gen. Aidid. For weeks, Aidid had declined to join UN negotiations on the future of Somalia, but with his reversal of position all 15 Somali factions were represented at the meetings in the Ethiopian capital. The talks broke up, **Dec. 12**, without any agreement.

Ultranationalists Run Strongly in Russia—Russian voters, **Dec. 12**, approved, by about a 4-3 margin, the new draft constitution supported by Pres. Boris Yeltsin. Voting at the same time also determined the makeup of the 450-seat State Duma, the lower house of the new Parliament. Half the seats were to be distributed on the basis of party preferences expressed by the voters, and half went to the winners of single-constituency races. The results astounded most observers. The Liberal Democratic Party was the most successful in the party preference voting, winning 23% of the vote. The party's leader, Vladimir Zhirinovsky, was an outspoken nationalist whose provocative comments included ethnic insults and appeals for restoration of the historical boundaries of Russia stretching from Finland to Alaska. Yeltsin's reform party, Russia's Choice, won about 15%, and the Communists won about 13% of the party preference vote. U.S. Vice Pres. Al Gore, during a visit to Moscow, **Dec. 15**, called Zhirinovsky's views, including his advocacy of the use of nuclear weapons, "reprehensible and anathema to all freedom-loving people." Yeltsin responded to the apparent shift in the political winds. The government, **Dec. 17**, approved a scaled-back program for privatizing state-owned enterprises. Also on **Dec. 17**, Yeltsin authorized $120 million in cheap subsidized loans to farmers and announced new controls on immigration and the employment of non-Russians. The president said, **Dec. 21**, that the poor had supported the Liberal Democrats as a protest against poverty, and on **Dec. 22** he acknowledged that the voting had constituted a repudiation of some of his policies. As the tabulation came in slowly on the single-constituency elections, the reform parties improved their showing. In final results published **Dec. 28**, the Liberal Democrats had won 64 seats, Russia's Choice 58, the Communists 48, the Agrarian Party 33, Women of Russia 23, and the Yabloko ("Apple") bloc 22. Other parties held many seats, and 130 deputies claimed no party affiliation.

Northern Ireland Peace Plan Offered—Prime Ministers John Major of Great Britain and Albert Reynolds of Ireland, **Dec. 15**, set forth a "framework for lasting peace" in Northern Ireland. In their joint declaration, which they announced in London, the leaders agreed that the future of Northern Ireland should be decided by majority sentiment of the people who lived there. As part of an overall settlement, the Irish government agreed to seek changes in its constitution in which dominion over Ulster is claimed. Major agreed that Sinn Fein, the political wing of the outlawed Provisional Irish Republican Army, could join talks on the future of Northern Ireland 3 months after a permanent cease-fire took effect.

Broad World Tariff Cuts Approved—Peter Sutherland, director general of the General Agreement on Tariffs and Trade, declared, **Dec. 15**, that the Uruguay Round of global trade talks had been completed. Seven years of discussion among GATT's 117 members and a flurry of last-minute negotiations had resulted in an agreement that provided for sweeping reductions in tariffs on a wide range of goods and services. The agreement would become effective in July 1995. Successive rounds of negotiations under GATT's aegis, since 1947, had already brought a substantial lowering of tariffs. Under the new agreement, tariffs on most industrial imports were reduced by at least one-third, and many were eliminated altogether. Intellectual property, including patents, trademarks, and copyrights, was protected. Quotas and limitations on imports of textiles and apparel would be phased out over a decade. Subsidies and import quotas on agricultural products would be cut substantially within 6 years. GATT would have greater authority to resolve disputes over dumping. In the U.S., approval of GATT rested with Congress, which, however, could not amend the text.

Arafat Rejects Israeli Self-Rule Plan—Negotiations continued in December between the Israeli government and the Palestine Liberation Organization over implementation of Palestinian self-rule in the occupied territories. During the month, the 2 sides met in Norway, France, and Egypt. In a draft proposal presented **Dec. 29**, Israel offered the PLO joint control of border checkpoints and proposed to increase the area of Palestinian autonomy around Jericho to 43 sq mi. PLO Chairman Yasir Arafat rejected this compromise, **Dec. 29**, and the Palestinians continued to insist on a greater sphere of autonomy and sole control of border crossings from Egypt and Jordan.

General

Violent Crimes Alarm Public—Several violent crimes in the U.S. made headlines in December, and public-opinion surveys showed that crime had become the No. 1 public concern of Americans. A jobless man who reportedly had been denied unemployment benefits shot and killed 3 people and wounded 4 others at an unemployment office in Oxnard, CA, **Dec. 2**. During a subsequent chase he killed a policeman before being killed himself. The body of a 12-year-old girl, Polly Klaas, who had been abducted in October, was found, **Dec. 4**, in Cloverdale, CA. A suspect was arrested, and it was revealed that he had previously been questioned while holding the girl prisoner but had been released. The FBI reported, **Dec. 5**, that preliminary figures actually showed a decline of 3% in violent crime during the first 6 months of 1993. On **Dec. 7**, a man using a 9-mm handgun shot and killed 4 passengers on a crowded rush-hour Long Island Rail Road train as it approached a Garden City, NY, station. He also wounded 21, 2 of whom subsequently died. The suspect, Colin Ferguson, was subdued by 3 passengers. Pres. Bill Clinton, **Dec. 8**, asked Atty. Gen. Janet Reno to consider a program to register all guns. On **Dec. 15** a man shot and killed 4 employees and wounded another at a Chuck E Cheese restaurant in Aurora, CO. The suspect had been fired by the restaurant. Six bombs, 4 of which exploded, sent by courier or through the mail, killed 5 people and wounded 2 in western New York state, **Dec. 28**. All the bombs were delivered to relatives of the girlfriend of one of the 2 suspects arrested **Dec. 29**.

Princess of Wales Curtails Activities—In Great Britain, Diana, the Princess of Wales, announced, **Dec. 3**, that she would curtail her busy schedule of public appearances. Since her separation from her husband, Prince Charles, in 1992, Diana had been publicly active on behalf of charities assisting those who were ill, handicapped, or homeless. In her announcement, Diana criticized the press. "Twelve years ago, I understood that the media might be interested in what I did," she said, "but I was not aware of how overwhelming that attention would become." Charles had recently complained that "soap opera" coverage of him and Diana was hampeing his efforts to promote various causes.

Suicide Ruling Supports Kevorkian—Dr. Jack Kevorkian, an advocate of physician-assisted suicide for the terminally ill, won one round in Wayne County (MI) Circuit Court, **Dec. 13**. Judge Richard Kaufman held that gravely ill people with little prospect for recovery and a poor quality of life had a "constitutionally protected right" to take their own life. He found sections of Michigan's law forbidding assisted suicides to violate the Michigan state constitution. On **Dec. 14**, he dismissed charges against Kevorkian for assisting in a September suicide. Kevorkian, **Dec. 17**, was released from jail but still faced similar charges in a neighboring Michigan county. Appeals to higher courts were anticipated.

Michael Jackson Denies Allegations—Michael Jackson, who had been in seclusion for more than a month, spoke out, **Dec. 22**, and denied that he had molested a young boy. He read a 4-min statement that was broadcast live by satellite from his ranch near Santa Barbara, CA. The singer said that officers from the Santa Barbara County Sheriff Dept. and the Los Angeles Police Dept. had photographed his body, an experience Jackson called "the most humiliating ordeal of my life." The boy who had accused Jackson of abuse had given a detailed description of his body. Jackson called the boy's story "disgusting" and "totally false." He faced both a civil suit and a criminal investigation.

JANUARY

National

Prosecutor Named in Whitewater Affair—Attorney Gen. Janet Reno in January appointed an independent counsel, or special prosecutor, to investigate the so-called Whitewater affair. The White House said, **Jan. 5**, that in late December the Justice Dept. had subpoenaed documents belonging to Pres. Bill Clinton and First Lady Hillary Rodham Clinton concerning their dealings with James McDougal, an Arkansas financier who was under investigation. In the face of clamor from some members of Congress, Clinton, **Jan. 12**, asked Reno to appoint an independent counsel to conduct an inquiry into the Clintons' involvement with McDougal's failed Whitewater real estate venture. Reno, **Jan. 20**, appointed Robert Fiske, a former U.S. attorney from New York City, to head the inquiry.

Inman Pulls Out as Defense Nominee—Adm. Bobby Ray Inman (ret.), who in December 1993 had accepted Pres. Bill Clinton's invitation to become secretary of defense, withdrew in January as the nominee for the cabinet position. In a letter to Clinton, **Jan. 14**, Inman contended that Sen. Bob Dole (R, KS), the minority leader, planned to make his nomination, which required Senate approval, a partisan issue. In his letter, and at a press conference, **Jan. 18**, Inman asserted that elements of the media and political leadership would rather destroy reputations that work to effectively govern the country. Clinton, **Jan. 24**, nominated Deputy Defense Sec. William Perry to be defense secretary. Perry, once a member of the faculty of the school of engineering at Stanford, had served as undersecretary of defense under Pres. Jimmy Carter and had played a major role in the development of cruise missiles, laser-guided bombs, and stealth aircraft. On **Feb. 3**, the Senate confirmed Perry's nomination, 97-0.

Inflation Put at 7-Year Low—Data released in January showed that the U.S. inflation rate was at its lowest level in 7 years. Earlier, **Jan. 7**, the Labor Dept. said that the unemployment rate had edged downward 0.1 percentage point in December to 6.4%. The department reported, **Jan 12**, that the index of prices charged by producers for finished goods had declined 0.1% in December and that for all of 1993 the index had risen only 0.2%. The department said, **Jan. 13**, that consumer prices had advanced by only 2.7% during 1993, the smallest increase for any year since 1986. The Commerce Dept. said, **Jan. 19**, that the merchandise trade deficit had narrowed slightly in November to $10.17 billion. The Commerce Dept. reported, **Jan. 20**, that housing starts had climbed 7.1% in 1993 to their highest level since 1989. At the end of 1993, housing starts had been increasing for 5 consecutive months. The Commerce Dept. said, **Jan. 28**, that the initial figures for the gross domestic product had shown growth at an annual rate of 5.9% during the 4th quarter of 1993. This was the biggest quarterly surge in 6 years. The Dow Jones industrial average closed, **Jan. 31**, at an all-time high of 3,978.36.

Final Iran-Contra Report Released—Lawrence Walsh, the independent counsel who had headed the investigation of the Iran-contra scandal, issued his final report, **Jan. 18**. For the most part, it summarized facts and evidence already known. During the 6½-year, $37 million investigation, Walsh and his colleagues had brought charges against 14 men and obtained convictions or guilty pleas in 11 situations. But the convictions of 2 were overturned, and Pres. George Bush had pardoned 6 others who had been tried or were facing trial. In his report, Walsh said he had found evidence of complicity in the affair and in the subsequent cover-up among Pres. Ronald Reagan, Sec. of State George Shultz, Sec. of Defense Caspar Weinberger, Attorney Gen. Edwin Meese, and CIA Dir. William Casey. Of these, only Weinberger had faced charges, but he had been pardoned. Walsh cited evidence indicating that Meese had told others to tell the public and Congress that Reagan had known about illegal arms sales to Iran via Israel only after the fact. At a press conference, **Jan. 18**, Walsh rebuked Bush for the pardons and said his investigation had been handicapped by Congress, which had granted immunity to key witnesses for their testimony in congressional hearings.

Subpoena Upheld on Packwood Diaries—Federal District Court Judge Thomas Jackson, **Jan. 24**, upheld a subpoena from the Senate Ethics Committee for the diaries of Sen. Robert Packwood (R, OR). The subpoena sought access to all entries made from 1989 on. Jackson took custody of the diaries in December 1993 after Packwood sued to block the subpoena. Pointing out that the ethics committee would allow a mediator to examine the diaries to make sure that only information relevant to the investigation would be seen by the investigators, Jackson held that the subpoena did not unduly violate Packwood's privacy. The inquiry concerned allegations of sexual harassment and other possible misconduct by Packwood.

Clinton Addresses Congress—Pres. Bill Clinton, **Jan. 25**, delivered his first State of the Union address to a joint session of Congress. He cited the accomplishments of his administration, including passage of a deficit-reduction act. He reaffirmed his commitment to "health security for all" and said he would veto any health-care reform bill that "does not guarantee every American private health insurance that can never be taken away." He said he would introduce a bill to reform the federal welfare system that would give the poor "a second chance, not a way of life." He said he would seek to limit to 2 years the time during which heads of households could get welfare benefits. To fight crime, Clinton called for a ban on assault weapons and federal aid to permit local hiring of 100,000 new police officers. He endorsed a "3 strikes, you're out" provision in a Senate anticrime bill that would put anyone convicted of 3 violent felonies in prison for life. Sen. Bob Dole (R, KS), the Senate minority leader, gave a televised response to the president. He questioned the need for drastic action on health care, saying that "our country has health-care problems, but no health-care crisis."

Oliver North Seeks Senate Seat—Oliver North, one of the central figures in the Iran-contra affair, declared his candidacy for the Republican nomination for U.S. senator from Virginia, **Jan. 27**. North, then a colonel in the Marine Corps, had been assigned to the White House in the mid-1980s as a staff member of the National Security Council. He had orchestrated a secret effort to sell American weapons to Iran and divert the income to right-wing guerrillas in Nicaragua. His defense of his actions, in Senate hearings in 1987, made him a hero to conservatives. In 1989 he was convicted of obstructing Congress, destroying documents, and receiving an illegal gratuity. The convictions were set aside on a technicality, and the charges were subsequently dropped. In declaring his candidacy for the Senate, he depicted himself as a conservative and an outsider who was committed to family values. North's Senate bid divided Virginia Republicans. Sen. John Warner (R, VA) said North sent a bad signal concerning crime to the younger generation.

International

Mexican Rebels Launch Bloody Attacks—Mexican peasants in the southeastern state of Chiapas issued a declaration of war against the government in January, and initiated armed attacks that left more that 100 persons dead. The Zapatista National Liberation Army, a previously unknown organization, seized 4 towns, **Jan. 1**, including San Cristóbal de las Casas, the 2d-largest in the state. The rebels, in a statement, objected to the expulsion of Indians from communal farmlands and to the North American Free Trade Agreement, which they said would benefit only the wealthy. They called for the resignation of Pres. Carlos Salinas de Gortari and for fair elections. The government sent in soldiers and tanks, and by **Jan. 4** the ZNLA had withdrawn to nearby mountains. The government asserted, **Jan. 4**, that some of the rebels were from other countries. Bombs and grenades exploded in Mexico City and other places, **Jan. 8**. Salinas, **Jan. 10**, dismissed Interior Minister Patrocinio González Garrido, an unpopular former governor of Chiapas, and replaced him with Attorney Gen. Jorge Carpizo McGregor, an advocate of human rights. The government, **Jan. 12**, adopted a unilateral cease-fire. The death toll in the uprising was put at 107 by government officials. Salinas, **Jan. 16**, asked Congress to approve a general amnesty. The government said, **Jan. 18**, that it would address the concerns raised by the rebels. On **Jan. 28**, the government freed 38 prisoners accused of involvement in the revolt.

Limited Expansion of NATO Underway—The North Atlantic Treaty Organization, established in 1949 as a bulwark against the Soviet military threat, found itself in a time of transition in January. Several Eastern European states, including Slovakia and Lithuania on **Jan. 4**, were seeking membership in NATO as a means of protection against any future military threat from Russia. Responding, NATO leaders developed the concept of a "partnership for peace," in which nonmember nations could obtain limited association with NATO. Such nations, however, would not be given the full security guarantee that current members enjoyed. (NATO's basic principle was that an attack on any member was considered an attack on all, and all members would support the attacked nation.) The invitation to join the partnership for peace included Russia and Ukraine, both of whom had nuclear arsenals. Hungary, **Jan. 8**, Slovakia, **Jan. 9**, and the Czech Republic and Poland, **Jan. 10**, accepted the proposal. NATO leaders, at a summit in Brussels, **Jan. 10**, formally approved the plan.

U.S., North Korea Reach Agreement—A U.S. State Dept. official said, **Jan. 5**, that the U.S. and North Korea had agreed, in principle, that the latter would allow inspections of its 7 declared nuclear facilities. Officials of the International Atomic Energy Agency would be allowed to replace film and batteries in surveillance cameras. North Korea also promised to resume a dialogue with South Korea. The U.S., in return, would cancel its annual military exercise with South Korea.

Ex-President of Georgia Dead—It was reported, **Jan. 5**, that former Pres. Zviad Gamsakhurdia had died, but the circumstances of his death were unclear. Gamsakhurdia had led an unsuccessful revolt in late 1993 against the government of Pres. Eduard Shevardnadze. According to his wife, the former president had committed suicide Dec. 31, but a paramilitary group said he had been wounded in a skirmish, Dec. 31, and had died **Jan. 5**. Another conflict within the country appeared to ease, **Jan. 13**, when Georgia and its secessionist region of Abkhazia agreed to the deployment of UN peacekeeping troops who would police a cease-fire agreement.

U.S., China Agree on Textiles—The U.S. warned China, **Jan. 6**, that it would reduce by $1 billion its quota of textile imports from China unless a new agreement was negotiated. The U.S. State Dept. said, **Jan. 11**, in a preliminary report, that China had not yet made enough progress in the area of human rights to earn U.S. renewal of most-favored-nation trading status. Pres. Jiang Zemin told 6 visiting members of the U.S. House, **Jan. 15**, that China would make an effort to improve its human rights record. The U.S. and China, **Jan. 17**, reached an agreement in Beijing on textiles under which the 1994 quota would be frozen at the 1993 level and would increase by only 1% in each of the 2 following years.

Middle East Talks Make Headway—Israeli and Palestine Liberation Organization negotiators resumed talks, **Jan. 10**, in the Egyptian resort of Taba on the transfer of authority in selected areas of the occupied territories. The sticking points continued to be the size of the autonomous Jericho enclave, security for Israeli settlers, and control of border crossings. At a joint press conference in Geneva, **Jan. 16**, with Pres. Bill Clinton, Pres. Hafez al-Assad of Syria indicated a willingness to negotiate a peace treaty with Israel.

Clinton Visits Eastern Europe—Pres. Bill Clinton arrived in Prague, capital of the Czech Republic, **Jan. 11**, beginning a trip to Eastern Europe. In meetings, **Jan. 12**, with the presidents of the Czech Republic, Hungary, Poland, and Slovakia, Clinton said that the U.S. was committed to the security of their countries. Clinton also met, **Jan. 12**, with Pres. Leonid Kravchuk in Kiev, the capital of Ukraine. The 2 presidents reconfirmed a commitment they had made with Russian Pres. Boris Yeltsin under which Ukraine would give up its nuclear arsenal in return for compensation and security guarantees. Clinton met with Yeltsin in Moscow, **Jan. 13**. U.S. officials described Yeltsin as still pro–reform despite political setbacks. In Moscow, **Jan. 14**, Clinton, Kravchuk, and Yeltsin signed the agreement on Ukrainian weapons. Ukraine agreed to deactivate all of its strategic missiles and ship at least 200 warheads to Russia, all within 10 months. Russia would dismantle the warheads and return the uranium to Ukraine for civilian uses. Within 7 years, Ukraine would send the rest of its warheads to Russia for dismantling. The U.S. agreed to increase its financial aid to Ukraine, which also got pledges from Russia and the U.S. to come to its aid in the event of an outside attack. However, approval of the pact by the Ukrainian parliament remained uncertain. In a separate agreement with Russia, the U.S. would buy, over a period of 20 years, 500 tons of uranium from Soviet weapons, uranium worth $12 billion currently. Clinton and Yeltsin said, **Jan. 14**, that none of their strategic weapons would be aimed, after **May 30**, at the territory of any country. Clinton, **Jan. 14**, talked with Russian young people at a televised assembly. In Belarus, **Jan. 15**, Clinton honored the memory of more than 1 million persons who had died at the hands of the Nazis during World War II, and he also visited the mass grave of some 200,000 victims of Stalin's 1937–41 purges.

Pro-Reform Russian Ministers Resign—Russia's first deputy premier and economics minister, Yegor Gaidar, resigned, **Jan. 16**, saying that the government had not approved some of his pro–reform policies. Pres. Boris Yeltsin, **Jan. 17**, reaffirmed his commitment to reform, but Premier Viktor Chernomyrdin said, **Jan. 20**, that his government would seek to "correct the course of reforms." Another reformer. Finance Minister Boris Fyodorov, resigned, **Jan. 20**, after blaming the loose monetary policy of the central bank for the rising rate of inflation. Fyodorov, **Jan. 26**, declined an appeal from Yeltsin that he reconsider, and he said that it was unacceptable "that people who have done immense economic and political harm to the state" were serving in the cabinet.

Japan's Parliament Approves Reform Plan—The Japanese parliament in January approved a watered–down version of Premier Morihiro Hosokawa's political–reform package. The upper house of the Diet, the House of Councilors, **Jan. 21**, rejected, 130–118, the original package that had been approved by the lower house. Hosokawa's coalition government appeared in danger of falling after some members of one of his coalition partners, the Social Democrats, joined the Liberal Democrats in opposition. Hosokawa and the Liberal Democrats then worked out a compromise that was approved overwhelmingly in both houses, **Jan. 29**. It provided for a 500–member lower house in which 300 members would be elected from single–seat districts; the rest of the seats would be allocated according to the share of the vote obtained by each party. Representation from urban areas would be increased. Corporate contributions to individual candidates would be limited to 500,000 yen (about $4,500) annually. Hosokawa had sought to eliminate such contributions altogether. State subsidies would make up for the reduction of private donations.

IRA Leader Visits U.S.—Gerry Adams, leader of Sinn Fein, the political arm of the Irish Republican Army, traveled to the U.S. in January. He had long sought in vain to obtain a visa to visit the U.S. Clinton administration officials said, **Jan. 27**, that Adams would be admitted if the IRA renounced violence as part of its long campaign to force Great Britain to leave Northern Ireland. At a meeting with U.S. State Dept. officials in Belfast, **Jan. 28**, Adams, while not renouncing violence, was conciliatory enough to prompt the issuance of a visa, **Jan. 30**. Adams arrived in New York City, **Jan. 31**, and was limited to meetings and interviews in the metropolitan area. He appeared on television's *Larry King Live*, **Jan. 31**. Clinton, **Feb. 1**, said he had approved the visa in the hope that the U.S. would have a constructive role in the peace talks between the British government and the Republic of Ireland. Adams left New York, **Feb. 2**, when his visa expired.

General

Rival Linked to Attack on Skater—U.S. figure skater Nancy Kerrigan was clubbed with a blunt instrument in January, and within a week authorities began arresting suspects in the case who had ties to Kerrigan's leading American rival, Tonya Harding. On **Jan 6**, Kerrigan had just finished a practice session in Detroit when a man struck her on the right knee and then fled. Her knee badly bruised, Kerrigan withdrew from the U.S. Figure Skating Championship, which she had been favored to win. Harding won the competition in Detroit, **Jan 8**, and thus qualified for the Winter Olympic Games, scheduled for February. The U.S. Figure Skating Association, **Jan. 8**, added Kerrigan to the Olympic team, assuming her recovery. An unidentified woman told Detroit police she had heard others discuss an assault on Kerrigan. On **Jan. 13**, the Sheriff's Dept. in Portland, OR, Harding's home, arrested her bodyguard, Shawn Eckhardt, in connection with the attack. A 2d man, Derrick Smith, was also arrested, **Jan 13**. Shane Stant, whom authorities believed carried out the attack on Kerrigan, surrendered in Phoenix, **Jan. 14.** Jeff Gillooly, Harding's former husband, was arrested, **Jan. 19**, and charged with conspiracy in the attack on Kerrigan. Harding and Gillooly had divorced in 1993 but were again living together. On **Jan. 27**, Harding, in a statement, said that she had learned several days after the attack on Kerrigan that "persons that were close to me" had been involved. She acknowledged that she had not told authorities what she had learned until some days later.

Brothers Tried in Parents' Deaths—The 6–month murder trial of Lyle and Erik Menendez ended inconclusively in January. On Aug. 20, 1989, the brothers, now 26 and 23, respectively, had shot and killed their parents, Jose and Kitty Menendez, in their Beverly Hills, CA, home. They denied the shootings at the time but later told their therapist, L. Jerome Oziel, who taped their statements, that they had committed the act. A third party later heard the tapes and reported what she had heard to the police. The brothers then were charged with the murders. At the trial, in Los Angeles Superior Court, prosecutors said Lyle and Erik had killed their parents in order to inherit their $14 million estate. The brothers testified that they had been subjected to years of sexual and emotional abuse from their parents. The trial was carried in full on Court TV and was otherwise widely covered by the media. Separate juries, forced to choose between first–degree murder, second–degree murder, voluntary manslaughter, and involuntary manslaughter, were unable to reach verdicts. A mistrial was declared in Erik's case, **Jan. 13**, and in Lyle's case, **Jan. 28**. Prosecutors said that the young men would be tried again.

Los Angeles Earthquake Kills 61—A pre–dawn earthquake struck the Los Angeles area, **Jan. 17**, claiming 61 lives and causing widespread devastation. The epicenter was in the Northridge section of Los Angeles, about 20 miles northwest of the downtown area. Seismologists believed that the quake was caused by a fault 9 miles beneath Northridge. The main jolt, which lasted about 30 seconds and measured 6.8 on the Richter scale, was followed by hundreds of aftershocks in the subsequent days and weeks. More than 9,300 injuries were reported, and almost 45,000 residences were damaged or destroyed. The heaviest death toll, 16, occurred at the collapse of a 3–story apartment building in Northridge. The collapse of 3 heavily traveled overpasses created chaos for highway commuters, who would have to find alternate routes to work while repairs were made. Gov. Pete Wilson, **Jan. 19**, estimated the damage in the quake at $15 billion to $30 billion. Pres. Bill Clinton visited the earthquake area, **Jan. 19**. On **Jan. 21**, the National Guard began setting up tent cities to accommodate the homeless. The Clinton administration said, **Jan. 25**, that it would seek $6.6 billion in emergency aid from Congress.

Wife Acquitted in Mutilation of Husband—A Virginia woman was found not guilty by reason of temporary insanity, **Jan. 21**, on charges of malicious and unlawful wounding. The woman, Lorena Bobbitt, had cut off the penis of her husband, John Bobbitt, as he slept. It had been reattached after surgery. In November 1993, John Bobbitt had been tried for marital sexual assault, and his wife testified that she had attacked her husband as a result of his abuse of her that morning and on other occasions. Bobbitt, who denied any sexual assault of his wife, was found not guilty. After a jury found Lorena Bobbitt not guilty, Prince William County Circuit Court Judge Herman Whisenant ordered that she be given a psychiatric examination.

Dallas Wins Super Bowl Again—The Dallas Cowboys won their 2d straight pro football title in January. The Cowboys, **Jan. 23**, advanced to the Super Bowl by defeating San Francisco, 38–21, for the National Conference championship. Also on **Jan. 23**, the Buffalo Bills defeated Kansas City, 30–13, for their 4th consecutive American Conference title. For the Bills, this victory was only a prelude to their 4th straight defeat in the Super Bowl. In 1993, they had fallen to the Cowboys, 52–17, but in 1994, on **Jan. 30**, the contest was closer. The Bills led at the half, 13–6, but within the first minute of the 3d quarter Dallas safety James Washington picked up a fumble and ran 46 yards for a touchdown. Dallas took the lead later in the 3d quarter on a 64–yard drive in which Emmitt Smith, who was named the game's most valuable player, carried the ball 7 times and scored. Smith scored again in the 4th quarter. The final score was 30–13.

Jackson Pays Millions in Abuse Case—The performer Michael Jackson, **Jan. 25**, reached an out–of–court settlement with a boy, now 14, who had accused him of sexual molestation. The terms were not made public, but sources said Jackson had agreed to a payment of $10-20 million. Although the settlement brought an end to the civil suit, Jackson was still the subject of a criminal investigation.

FEBRUARY

National

Investors Watch Interest Rates—The Federal Reserve Board increased a key interest rate in February, and many investors responded by selling stocks. The Commerce Dept. reported, **Feb. 2**, that the index of leading economic indicators had jumped 0.7% in December. On **Feb. 4**, the Fed increased the federal funds rate, the interest rate banks charged each other on overnight loans, by 0.25% to 3.25%. This rate had not been increased in 5 years. The objective was to suppress any inflationary tendencies, but investors feared that higher interest rates could kill the economic recovery, and the Dow Jones industrial average, **Feb. 4**, tumbled 96.24 points, or 2.43%. The Labor Dept. said, **Feb. 4**, that the unemployment rate stood at 6.7% in January, 0.3% higher than in December, although the increase was attributed to a refinement in the survey. The department reported, **Feb. 11**, that the index of prices charged by producers for finished goods had risen 0.2% in January. In a report released **Feb. 14**, the White House's Council of Economic Advisers warned that the growing income gap between rich and poor Americans was "a threat to the social fabric that has long bound Americans together." The Council forecast continued steady economic growth, low interest rates, and low rates of inflation through the 1990s. The Labor Dept. said, **Feb. 17**, that consumer prices held steady in January. The Commerce Dept. reported, **Feb. 17**, that the U.S. merchandise trade deficit in 1993 was $115.78 billion, the highest in 5 years.

Whitewater Investigation Widens—The investigation into the so-called Whitewater affair took on an extra dimension as a result of a controversial meeting in early February. Deputy Treasury Secretary Roger Altman met, **Feb. 2**, with White House counsel Bernard Nussbaum. Margaret Williams, chief of staff for First Lady Hillary Rodham Clinton, and Harold Ickes, an adviser to Pres. Bill Clinton, were also present. Altman was also acting head of the Resolution Trust Corp., the federal agency responsible for disposing of the assets of insolvent savings and loan institutions. In testimony before the Senate Banking Committee, **Feb. 24**, Altman said he had briefed the others on actions the RTC could take in filing claims against Madison Guaranty, a failed Arkansas S&L. The Whitewater investigation, now headed by an independent counsel appointed by the U.S. attorney general, focused on whether money was diverted illegally from Madison to Clinton's political campaigns or to the Whitewater Development Corp., a real estate venture in which the Clintons had been partners. Altman received wide criticism for discussing an ongoing investigation with representatives of the Clintons, whose conduct and possible financial gain were under scrutiny.

Corporate Leaders Oppose Clinton on Health—The Business Roundtable, whose members were the chief executives of the nation's leading companies, voted, **Feb. 2**, to endorse a health-care bill opposed by the Clinton administration. The bill favored by the executives, introduced by Rep. Jim Cooper (D, TN), would require employers to make health insurance available, but small businesses would not have to pay for it, and larger businesses would not have to join cooperatives to buy insurance. In particular, the business leaders opposed the requirement in the Clinton plan that employers pay 80% of workers' health-insurance premiums. The president and his supporters said that the Cooper bill did not guarantee universal coverage. The nonpartisan Congressional Budget Office stated, **Feb. 8**, that a plan guaranteeing universal coverage would increase federal budget deficits in the short term, contrary to claims by the administration. The CBO did say, however, that the Clinton plan could contribute to deficit reduction by the year 2004.

Russian Flies on U.S. Shuttle—A Russian, Sergei Krikalev, became in February the first astronaut from his country to fly aboard a U.S. spacecraft. He joined the crew of the space shuttle *Discovery*, which was launched from Cape Canaveral, FL, **Feb. 3**. Krikalev had spent 15 months on the Russian space station. The shuttle crew did not succeed in one of its major objectives, the deployment of a science satellite. The orbiter landed in Florida, **Feb. 11**.

White Man Guilty in Evers Murder—Byron De La Beckwith, a white supremacist, was convicted in February of the 1963 murder of civil rights leader Medgar Evers. Evers, Mississippi field secretary for the National Association for the Advancement of Colored People, had been shot in front of his home in Jackson, MS. A rifle found at the scene contained Beckwith's fingerprints, but there were no witnesses, and two 1964 trails of Beckwith before all-white juries ended in deadlocks. On the basis of new evidence, Beckwith was indicted again, and at his latest trial 6 witnesses testified that he had boasted of killing Evers. This time the jury, which included 8 blacks and 4 whites, found Beckwith guilty, **Feb. 5**, and he was sentenced to life in prison.

Clinton Presents $1.52 Trillion Budget—Pres. Bill Clinton, **Feb. 7**, sent Congress his administration's budget for the 1995 fiscal year, starting October 1. He proposed expenditures of $1.52 trillion, with a deficit of $165.1 billion, assuming passage of his health-care plan. Although he proposed increases in spending for education, job training, and some other social programs, he also called for cutbacks elsewhere, including the elimination of 115 programs. His only proposed change in taxes was an increase in the federal excise tax on cigarettes from 24 to 99 cents a pack.

Admiral Linked to Scandal Resigns—Adm. Frank Kelso, the Chief of Naval Operations, announced in February that he would retire in April, 2 months before his scheduled retirement date. On **Feb. 8** a Navy Judge, Capt. William Vest, Jr., dismissed cases against 3 Navy officers implicated in the Tailhook scandal and held, in his ruling, that Kelso had used "unlawful command influence" to "manipulate" the investigation "in a manner designed to shield his personal involvement." Witnesses had testified that Kelso had observed misbehavior at the Tailhook convention in Las Vegas in 1991. Lt. Paula Coughlin, the officer who had exposed the scandal by reporting an assault against herself, had resigned from the Navy, the service announced **Feb. 10**. In her letter of resignation, Coughlin said that the attack on her and the "covert attacks" that followed prevented her from serving in the Navy. Kelso, **Feb. 10**, angrily denied the court testimony and Vest's assertions. Defense Sec. William Perry said, **Feb. 15**, that he had found no credible evidence that Kelso knew of misconduct at the convention and no evidence that he had sought to thwart the subsequent investigation. Kelso, announcing his early retirement, **Feb. 15**, said he had become a "lightning rod" for Tailhook.

Texas Senator Acquitted—The trial of U.S. Senator Kay Bailey Hutchison (R, TX) ended abruptly in February with her acquittal. She had been charged with misusing state funds and employees for political purposes, while serving as Texas state treasurer. Hutchison denied the allegations. Her trial opened in Fort Worth, **Feb. 11**, with a dispute over documents seized in a raid on her office in 1993. Her attorneys contended that any evidence the documents contained was not admissible because investigators had not had a search warrant. Judge John Onion declined, before the trial, to rule on the admissibility of the evidence. After Travis County District Attorney Ronnie Earle then refused to open his case, Onion directed the jury to find the defendant not guilty, which it did, **Feb. 11**.

Ex-Treasurer Guilty in HUD Case—A former U.S. Treasurer, Catalina Vasquez Villalpando, pleaded guilty, **Feb. 17**, to obstructing the investigation of influence peddling at the Dept. of Housing and Urban Development during the 1980s. Villalpando had served as U.S. treasurer from 1989 to 1993. The 12th person to be convicted or to plead guilty in connection with the HUD scandal, Villalpando also pleaded guilty to a charge unrelated to HUD, income tax evasion.

CIA Officer Accused of Spying—A longtime counterintelligence officer in the CIA was arrested, along with his wife, **Feb. 21**, and charged with selling information to the Soviet Union and Russia. Aldrich Ames and Maria del Rosario Casas Ames were arraigned, **Feb. 22**. Aldrich Ames's field of specialty had been counterintelligence against the Soviet Union and Eastern Europe, and authorities believed that at least 10 Soviet citizens working for U.S. intelligence had been executed by the Soviet Union after Ames identified them. Prosecutors estimated, **Feb. 28**, that Ames and his wife had been paid $2.5 million by the Soviet and Russian governments.

Texas Cultists Acquitted of Murder—Eleven members of the Branch Davidian religious cult were found not guilty in February of murder and conspiracy charges. In February 1993 federal agents had attacked the cult's compound near Waco, TX. Four agents had been killed by shots fired from within the compound. In April 1993 about 80 cultists had died when agents launched a heavier attack with tanks. The 11 cult members had been charged in connection with the deaths of the agents in the February incident. At their trial, defense lawyers played a 911 telephone call in which a member of the cult pleaded with a dispatcher to tell agents to cease the attack, which the caller said was endangering women and children. On **Feb. 26**, the jury found all 11 defendants not guilty of murder and conspiracy, but 5 were found guilty of aiding and abetting the voluntary manslaughter of federal officials, and 2 were found guilty of weapons charges.

International

South Africa Campaign Begins—Nelson Mandela, president of the African National Congress, formally opened his campaign, **Jan. 28**, for president of South Africa. The incumbent president, F. W. de Klerk, officially announced, **Feb. 2**, that the election, in which people of all races would choose national and regional assemblies, would be held Apr. 26-28. De Klerk, **Feb. 2**, also launched his own campaign for reelection.

U.S. Ends Vietnam Trade Embargo—Pres. Bill Clinton announced, **Feb. 3**, that the U.S. was lifting its trade embargo against Vietnam. During the past 19 years, successive U.S. administrations had maintained the embargo as a means of pressing Vietnam to assist in finding the remains of 2,238 Americans still missing from the war. Clinton said Vietnam had been helpful in searching for U.S. service personnel, and he said he was convinced that lifting the embargo was the best means of furthering that effort. Organizations representing veterans contended, however, that the U.S. had given away its most effective leverage on Vietnam. On **Feb. 7**, the Vietnamese government turned over to U.S. officials what were believed to be the remains of 12 U.S. soldiers.

Russia, Georgia Sign Agreements—The presidents of Russia and Georgia, Boris Yeltsin and Eduard Shevardnadze, signed a military treaty and other agreements, **Feb. 3**, that promised to ease tensions between the 2 countries. The treaty permitted Russia to keep 3 existing military bases in Georgia, and Russia agreed to train and equip the Georgian army. Russia also agreed to a large ruble loan for Georgia. The treaty encountered opposition in both countries.

Serbs Bow to NATO Ultimatum—Bosnian Serb forces that had been besieging Sarajevo, the capital of Bosnia and Herzegovina, pulled back in February after the North Atlantic Treaty Organization threatened to take military action. On **Feb. 5**, a mortar shell fired from the hills overlooking Sarajevo exploded in a market in the city, killing 68 people and injuring more than 200. The Serbs denied responsibility for the attack. The UN secretary general, Boutros Boutros–Ghali, **Feb. 6**, asked NATO for authority to order air strikes against Serb artillery positions. NATO, **Feb. 9**, gave the Serbs 10 days to pull back or face air strikes. Russian Deputy Foreign Minister Vitaly Churkin announced in Bosnia, **Feb. 17**, that the Serbs had agreed to withdraw in exchange for the deployment of 800 Russian peacekeeping troops. By **Feb. 23** almost all Serb gun positions had been abandoned or brought under control of UN monitors. Bosnia's Croats and Muslims signed a cease–fire, **Feb. 23**, and the Croats agreed to pull back from Mostar, a Muslim city they had brought under siege. On **Feb. 28**, for the first time in its 45–year history, NATO was involved in actual combat. Six Bosnian Serb aircraft violated the UN–imposed no–fly zone in central Bosnia. Some or all dropped bombs on a town containing a munitions factory, but they succeeded only in hitting a hospital and storage depot. After the Serb planes ignored radio warnings, 4 of them were shot down by U.S. fighter planes operating under NATO auspices.

Massacre Jolts Palestinian Talks—An act of extreme violence disrupted the Middle East peace negotiations in February. On **Feb. 9** in Cairo, Palestine Liberation Organization Chairman Yasir Arafat and Foreign Minister Shimon Peres of Israel initialed an agreement that resolved some contentious issues. They agreed that the area of Palestinian self-rule in the Jericho area would consist of about 21 sq mi. To protect Jewish settlements in Gaza, Israel would control joint Israeli-Palestinian patrols on 3 roads linking the settlements to Israel. Also in Gaza, Israel would control a small zone around the settlements, but Palestinians would control most of the Gaza Strip. On **Feb. 25**, a Jewish settler entered a mosque and shrine in Hebron known as the Cave of the Patriarchs, in the occupied West Bank, and fired into worshippers with an automatic rifle. The gunman, U.S.–born Baruch Goldstein, a physician, killed 29, and 3 more were trampled to death in the rush to escape. Some 150 people were wounded or injured. Goldstein was overpowered and beaten to death. Israeli Prime Minister Yitzhak Rabin denounced the assault as "loathsome." Arafat, **Feb. 25**, asked the UN to send an international force to protect Palestinians in the occupied territories. Goldstein had been a supporter of the late Rabbi Meir Kahane, a radical opponent of the Arabs, who had been assassinated in 1990. Goldstein's murderous assault triggered widespread violent demonstrations by Palestinians, some 20 of whom were killed in the next week in street clashes with Israeli soldiers. Israel, **Feb. 27**, took action to disarm and arrest settlers deemed to be dangerous. The PLO, meanwhile, had broken off peace talks and said, **Feb. 28**, that Israel must disarm all the settlers and keep them out of areas of Palestinian concentration.

U.S. Recognizes Macedonia—On **Feb. 9**, the U.S. extended diplomatic recognition to The Former Yugoslav Republic of Macedonia. Although a number of other nations had done the same, Greece continued to express concern that the new nation was seeking to unite with Macedonians living in northern Greece.

U.S.-Japanese Trade Talks Break Down—On **Feb. 11**, at a joint news conference in Washington, DC, with Prime Minister Morihiro Hosokawa of Japan, Pres. Bill Clinton announced that trade talks between the 2 countries had failed to reach an agreement. The U.S. had wanted Japan to set target domestic market shares for foreign products, but Japan had rejected that approach as "managed trade" involving inappropriate intervention by the government. U.S. Trade Representative Mickey Kantor said, **Feb. 15**, that the U.S. would seek to impose sanctions on Japanese manufacturers of cellular telephones. An American corporation, Motorola, had claimed that Japan had violated an agreement granting access to the Japanese cellular-phone market.

Leaders of Coups Freed in Russia—The lower house of the Russian parliament, the State Duma, voted, **Feb. 23**, 253–67, with 28 abstentions, to grant amnesties to leaders of 1991 and 1993 plots against the government. Pres. Boris Yeltsin had no authority to prevent the release of the plotters from prison. The action was heavily supported by communists and ultranationalists in parliament who opposed the president. One of the freed men, former Vice Pres. Aleksandr Rutskoi, said he planned to run for president in 1996.

General

Further Developments in Kerrigan Assault—The attack on U.S. figure skater Nancy Kerrigan, who had been clubbed with a blunt instrument in January, continued to make headlines in February. On **Feb. 1**, Jeff Gillooly, the former husband of figure skater Tonya Harding, pleaded guilty in Portland, OR, to a charge of racketeering for his role in planning the attack on Kerrigan. In testimony by Gillooly released in Multnomah County Circuit Court, **Feb. 1**, he said Harding had helped plan the assault. After the U.S. Olympic Committee announced, **Feb. 8**, that it would hold a hearing on whether Harding should be permitted to compete in the Winter Olympics, to beheld in Norway later in the month, Harding, **Feb. 9**, filed a $25 million lawsuit against the USOC. The committee, **Feb. 12**, agreed to allow Harding to compete. In the Olympic women's figure skating competition,

Feb. 23 and 25, the gold medal was won by 16-year-old Oksana Baiul of Ukraine. Four of the 9 judges gave higher marks to Kerrigan, who thus narrowly missed the championship and was awarded the silver medal for 2d place. Harding finished 8th. Public interest in the Kerrigan-Harding story in the U.S. was intense, and the 126.6 million Americans who, it was estimated, watched the first figure-skating program, **Feb. 23**, on CBS constituted the 4th largest television audience ever in the U.S.

$8.6 Billion Voted for Quake Victims—California officials, **Feb. 8**, lowered their damage estimate for the Jan. 17 earthquake in the Los Angeles area. The revised figure was $13-20 billion, down from initial estimates of $15-30 billion. Insured losses were put at $2.5 billion. Pres. Bill Clinton, **Feb. 12**, signed a bill providing $8.6 billion in aid to California.

Olympic Winter Games Held—The 17th Olympic Winter Games opened, **Feb. 12**, held in Lillehammer, Norway, featuring 1,884 athletes from 67 countries, including 11 former Soviet republics now competing as independent countries. Team USA captured 13 medals, the most overall in U.S. Winter Olympic history. U.S. skier Tommy Moe took the gold in the men's downhill, **Feb. 13**. Teammate Diann Roffe-Steinrotter followed, **Feb. 15**, with an upset victory in the women's super giant slalom. Switzerland's Vreni Schneider became the first woman to win 3 gold medals in alpine skiing when she added to her 2 golds in 1988 by winning the women's slalom, **Feb. 26.** U.S. speedskater Bonnie Blair won the women's 500-meter race, **Feb. 19**, and the 1,500-meter, **Feb. 23**. Blair's career total of 5 gold medals was the most of any female U.S. Olympic athlete. Host-country Norway won a games-high 26 medals, including 3 Olympic record-breaking performances by speedskater Johann Olav Koss, who won the men's 1,500, 5,000, and 10,000-meter races. Dan Jansen of the U.S. ended his Olympic drought, **Feb. 18**, with a win in the men's 1,000-meter speedskating event. In a thrilling shoot-out, Sweden took the gold, **Feb. 27**, over Canada in the hockey finals. After regulation time and overtime, the teams had been tied 2-2. They remained tied at 2 after 5 penalty shots each against the opposing goaltender, and the game went to a sudden-death shoot-out. Sweden won the gold when Peter Forsberg scored on the 7th shot. In perhaps the most watched event of the Olympics, the women's figure skating championship went to Ukraine's Oksana Baiul, **Feb. 25**. Aleksei Urmanov of Russia captured the gold in the men's figure-skating event, **Feb. 19**, and Russian pairs skaters Ekaterina Gordeeva and Sergei Grinkov placed first in their event, **Feb. 15**. Cross-country skier Manuela Di Centa of Italy won 5 medals at Lillehammer, the most by one athlete. The Games closed **Feb. 27**.

Serial Killer of 55 Executed—Andrei Chikatilo, a convicted serial killer who had admitted murdering 55 girls, boys, and women, was executed by firing squad in a prison in the Rostov-on-Don region of Russia, **Feb. 14**. Many of Chikatilo's victims had been mutilated or cannibalized. Prior to his arrest in 1990, he had eluded capture for many years.

Viacom Wins Control of Paramount—A long, fierce corporate struggle ended in February when Viacom Inc. won control of Paramount Communications Inc. Viacom's components included popular cable television channels such as MTV and Nickelodeon. Viacom and Paramount had agreed to merge in 1993, but QVC Network Inc., the home-shopping network, obtained a court injunction in November that forced Paramount to consider other offers. Paramount accepted a QVC offer in December, then switched to a sweetened proposal from Viacom. Viacom broadened its holdings in January, agreeing to buy Blockbuster Entertainment Corp., the video-rental company, for $8.4 billion. The contest for Paramount featured 3 of the entertainment industry's most colorful figures—Sumner Redstone (Viacom), Barry Diller (QVC), and Martin Davis (Paramount). Viacom's ultimately successful bid for Paramount was valued at just under $10 billion in cash and stock. Claiming victory, **Feb. 15**, Viacom said nearly 75% of Paramount's stock had been tendered to it. Paramount's assets, in addition to the movie studio, included book publisher Simon & Schuster, Madison Square Garden, the New York Knicks basketball team, and the New York Rangers hockey team. Among entertainment conglomerates, only Time Warner Inc. would be bigger.

Big Corporate Merger Called Off—The Bell Atlantic Corporation and Tele-Communications Inc., **Feb. 23**, abandoned their effort to complete one of the biggest corporate mergers ever, the purchase by Bell of TCI and the Liberty Media Corporation. The proposed merger, announced in October 1993 and valued then at $33 billion, could have prompted a revolution in technologies related to home entertainment and information. Since October, however, the value of Bell and TCI stock had declined sharply, and the federal government's rollback of cable-television rates threatened the profitability of TCI.

MARCH

National

Balanced-Budget Amendment Fails—Senators supporting a balanced-budget amendment to the U.S. Constitution fell short, **Mar. 1**, in their latest effort to pass the measure. The vote in favor of the amendment was 63-37, 4 short of the required two-thirds margin. The proposal, if also approved by the House and three-fourths of the states, would have required that the federal budget be balanced by the year 2001.

Economic Growth Estimate Revised Upward—The Commerce Dept., **Mar. 1**, revised upward its estimate of the growth in gross domestic product for the 4th quarter of 1993, putting it at an annual rate of 7.5%. This was the largest quarterly increase since 1984. The department said, **Mar. 4**, that the index of leading economic indicators had risen 0.3% in January. This was the 6th straight monthly gain for the index. The Labor Dept. reported, **Mar. 4**, that the unemployment rate had fallen to 6.5% in February. The department said, **Mar. 15**, that the prices charged by producers for finished goods had jumped 0.5% in February. It reported, **Mar. 16**, that the index of consumer prices had risen 0.3% in February. Using a new formula that combined trade in services with merchandise trade, the Commerce Dept. reported, **Mar. 22**, that the U.S. had posted a $6.3 billion trade deficit in January. Because the U.S. was running a surplus in trade in services, the effect of the new calculation would be to produce lower deficits. In its final revision of 4th quarter GDP, the department said, **Mar. 31**, that the economy had grown at an annual rate of 7.0% during the last 3 months of 1993.

Whitewater Costs White House Counsel His Job—White House counsel Bernard Nussbaum resigned in March following a furor over briefings received by White House aides from Treasury Dept. officials concerning the investigations of the Madison Guaranty Savings and Loan. Pres. Bill Clinton and First Lady Hillary Rodham Clinton were subjects of the inquiry. White House officials acknowledged that a Treasury Dept. representative had told Nussbaum in September 1993 that the Clintons would be named as possible beneficiaries of the alleged diversion of funds from the Arkansas savings and loan. Pres. Clinton conceded, **Mar. 3**, that "it would have been better" if no meetings had taken place. Robert Fiske, the independent counsel investigating the so-called Whitewater affair, issued subpoenas, **Mar. 4**, for 9 White House and Treasury officials who had participated in questionable briefings, and he also subpoenaed Lisa Caputo, Hillary Clinton's press secretary. Nussbaum, who had also been criticized for removing Whitewater-related papers from the office of White House deputy counsel Vincent Foster, who had apparently committed suicide in 1993, resigned, **Mar. 5**. Fiske, **Mar. 7**, stated his opposition to congressional hearings on Whitewater, because of his concern that witnesses granted immunity for their testimony might escape subsequent prosecution. Pres. Clinton, **Mar. 8**, named Lloyd Cutler, who had served as White House counsel for Pres. Jimmy Carter, to succeed Nussbaum. Republican senators assured Fiske, **Mar. 9**, that immunity to witnesses would not be granted. Associate Attorney Gen. Webster Hubbell, a close friend of the Clintons, resigned, **Mar. 14**. The resignation was not directly related to Whitewater, but he left to focus on a dispute with his former partners at the Rose Law Firm, in Little Rock, AR, which had been marginally linked to the Whitewater investigation. David Hale, a former municipal judge in Little Rock who had accused Bill Clinton of wrongdoing with respect to land and financial dealings, pleaded guilty in Little Rock, **Mar. 22**, to conspiring to defraud the Small Business Administration, and he agreed to cooperate with prosecutors. Rep. Jim Leach (R, IA) charged, **Mar. 24**, that James McDougal had skimmed federally insured deposits from Madison Guaranty, which he owned, and that the Clintons had probably known and benefited from the diversion of the funds. At a press conference, **Mar. 24**, Clinton said he had no knowledge of any diversion of Madison funds to his gubernatorial campaigns. Tax returns for 1977-79 and other documents made public by the Clintons, **Mar. 25**, showed that they had lost $46,635 on their Whitewater investment, which was less than the amount they had previously claimed ($68,800).

Four Guilty in World Trade Center Bombing— Four men were found guilty, **Mar. 4**, of a total of 38 charges related to the 1993 bombing at the World Trade Center in New York City. Six people had died in the explosion. The trial was held in U.S. District Court in Manhattan. Prosecutors had charged that Mohammed Salameh had rented the apartment where the chemicals used in the bombing were mixed and had rented the van in which the bomb was transported. Ahmad Ajaj had been accused of bringing bomb-making manuals into the country, Nidal Ayyad of obtaining chemicals used in the bombing, and Mahmud Abouhalima of being present when the chemicals were mixed. Three additional suspects in the bombing plot had not been tried. Two, Ramzi Ahmed Yousef and Abdul Rahman Yasin, were at large and were thought to have left the U.S. The third suspect, Bilal Alkaisi, would be tried at a later date.

Senate Majority Leader to Retire—Sen. George Mitchell (D, ME), the Senate majority leader, announced, **Mar. 4**, that he would not seek reelection in 1994. Mitchell, 60, had served in the Senate since 1980 and had been majority leader since 1989. He said he thought it appropriate that he limit his length of service and said the time was right to consider other challenges.

Packwood Gives Up Fight Over Diaries—On **Mar. 14**, Sen. Robert Packwood (R, OR) dropped a court battle to prevent a Senate committee from gaining access to his diaries. The committee, investigating sexual harassment and influence–peddling charges, had subpoenaed the diaries, and a federal judge had upheld the subpoena in January.

Rostenkowski Wins Renomination—Rep. Dan Rostenkowski (D, IL), chairman of the House Ways and Means Committee and one of the most powerful members of Congress, won a hard-fought battle for renomination in his Chicago district in March. Rostenkowski, the subject of an ongoing criminal investigation into his financial affairs, was considered by many to be an indispensable ally to Pres. Bill Clinton in the latter's efforts to reform health care. On **Feb. 28**, 2 weeks before the primary election, Clinton made several appearances with Rostenkowski in Chicago, although the president's staff avoided saying that Clinton was campaigning for the congressman. On primary day, **Mar. 15**, Rostenkowski won renomination, capturing 50% of the vote against 4 challengers.

Reagan Disputes Oliver North's Claims—In March, former Pres. Ronald Reagan disputed assertions relevant to the Iran-contra affair made by a former member of his national security staff, Oliver North. North was currently seeking the Republican nomination for the U.S. Senate from Virginia. In his autobiography and in interviews, North had said that Reagan "knew everything" about the Iran-contra operation and that the president had told him to lie to Congress. In a letter made public **Mar. 17** by James Miller, who was opposing North in the primary, Reagan said he was "steamed" by North's statements and denied that he had known about the diversion of money to the contras or that he had ever told anyone in his administration to mislead Congress.

International

Bosnia's Muslims, Croats Form Federation—The government of Bosnia and Herzegovina, dominated by Muslims, and Bosnia's Croats, **Mar. 1**, agreed to a federation embracing portions of the war-torn country under their control. The Muslims and Croats, who had been fighting against each other as well as against Bosnia's Serbs, had agreed to a cease-fire in February. Together, the Muslims and Croats controlled about one-third of Bosnia, and the Bosnian Serbs held the rest. The Bosnian government and the Bosnian Serbs, **Mar. 17**, reached an agreement to permit civilians freely to cross siege lines in Sarajevo for the first time in almost 2 years. The Muslims and Croats signed their agreement in Washington, DC, **Mar. 18**, and under a 2d agreement the new entity would form a confederation with Croatia. The UN, U.S., and Russia had pressured the parties to reach their agreement. The Serbs lifted the 5–month siege of Maglaj, a Muslim enclave in north-central Bosnia, **Mar. 19**, and UN convoys carrying 90 tons of flour and beans arrived, **Mar. 20**. The Serbs, **Mar. 29**, stepped up their bombardment of Gorazde, 35 miles southeast of Sarajevo, which they had first surrounded in May 1993. Gorazde had been intended to be one of 6 "safe areas" established under a UN agreement in May 1993, but few steps had been taken to protect the city.

Mexico, Zapatistas Reach Agreement—The government of Mexico reached a tentative agreement, **Mar. 2**, with the Zapatista National Liberation Army, which had launched an insurrection in January. The draft did not contain the commitment to democratic reform that the Zapatistas had sought, but assurances were given that a congressional session would be sought for the purpose of codifying the reforms. Under the draft accord, public works projects would bring employment to the Mayan Indians of Chiapas state and laws would be approved to protect the Indians from discrimination. The government promised to track the impact of the North American Free Trade Agreement (NAFTA) on Chiapas. The accord would be presented to the supporters of the Zapatistas for approval.

UN Agency Confronts North Korea—North Korea and the International Atomic Energy Agency appeared to be on a collision course in March. On **Mar. 3**, believing that North Korea would meet the IAEA's demands for inspection of its nuclear sites, the U.S. had suspended planning for the Team Spirit military exercises with South Korea. Then, on **Mar. 16**, the IAEA announced that its inspectors who had visited North Korea during the previous 2 weeks had been prevented from conducting a full inspection at one of the Communist nation's 7 targeted sites. The IAEA demanded, **Mar. 21**, that North Korea allow the inspection to go forward, and the U.S. signaled its desire to go ahead with the Team Spirit exercises. In response, North Korea, **Mar. 21**, threatened to pull out of the Nuclear Nonproliferation Treaty.

Killings Mar Run-up to South African Election—The weeks prior to South Africa's first universal-suffrage election were marred by bloodshed. On **Mar. 7**, Pres. Lucas Mangope of the nominally independent black homeland of Bophuthatswana refused to allow his homeland to participate in the April election. According to the negotiated constitution that was planned to take effect on the date of the election, the nominally independent homelands would be reincorporated into South Africa. White extremists poured into Bophuthatswana to support Mangope's stand, and dozens of people were killed in the next few days in clashes between proponents and opponents of the election. Many people in the homeland took to the streets to demand reincorporation into South Africa, and Mangope's government collapsed, **Mar. 10**. Mangope agreed to participate in the election on **Mar. 11**, changed his mind on **Mar. 12**, and was deposed, **Mar. 13**, by the South African government, the African National Congress (ANC), and the Transitional Executive Committee. South Africa imposed direct rule on Bophuthatswana. Elsewhere, the Inkatha Freedom Party, led by the Zulu chief Mangosuthu Buthelezi, was demanding that the KwaZulu homeland be declared a sovereign monarchy and excluded from the election. Fighting among the Zulu nationalists, the ANC, and the police claimed 53 lives in Johannesburg, **Mar. 28**, and 300 were wounded. It was reported, **Mar. 28**, that the dispute over the future of the Zulus had left more than 150 people dead in Natal province during the past 11 days. South Africa's president, F. W. de Klerk, declared a state of emergency in KwaZulu, **Mar. 31**.

PLO Agrees to Resume Talks With Israel—The Palestine Liberation Organization (PLO) agreed in March to resume discussions with Israel on the implementation of Palestinian limited self-rule in the occupied territories. Talks had broken off in February following the massacre in a mosque in Hebron committed by an Israeli settler. Maj. Gen. Danny Yatom, the Israeli army commander on the West Bank, told investigators, **Mar. 8**, that the army had not prepared a strategy for countering Jewish terrorists and that 5 of the 6 Israeli soldiers assigned to the mosque had not been at their posts at the time of the massacre. The Israeli cabinet, **Mar. 13**, banned extremist groups that called for the expulsion of Arabs from "the biblical Land of Israel." Israeli police, **Mar. 14**, confiscated weapons from some settlers in Hebron. The UN Security Council, **Mar. 18**, called for protective measures for the Palestinians and urged Israel to disarm the settlers. The PLO, **Mar. 31**, resumed talks with Israel after the latter agreed to permit the deployment of lightly armed foreign observers in Hebron. The observers would have no power to settle disputes.

China Rebuffs U.S. on Human Rights—Meetings in Beijing in March between Chinese leaders and U.S. Sec. of State Warren Christopher failed to resolve American concerns about human-rights abuses in China. The Clinton administration had linked this issue with the continuation of China's most-favored-nation trading status. The Chinese complained that a meeting in late February between Asst. Sec. of State for Human Rights John Shattuck and a prominent Chinese dissident, Wei Jingsheng, constituted an interference in their internal affairs. Christopher met with Premier Li Peng, **Mar. 12**, and with Pres. Jiang Zemin, **Mar. 13**, but without any reported progress on the human-rights controversy.

Presidential Candidate Slain in Mexico—The nominee of the ruling party for president of Mexico was shot to death, **Mar. 23**, just after delivering a campaign speech in Tijuana. The candidate, Luis Donaldo Colosio Murrieta, had served as secretary of social development in the administration of Pres. Carlos Salinas de Gortari. In 1993, the latter had designated Colosio as the presidential candidate of the governing Institutional Revolutionary Party (PRI), which had won every presidential election since the 1930s. Colosio was shot in the head at close range while surrounded by supporters, and he died soon thereafter. A suspect believed to be the gunman was seized immediately. Ernesto Zedillo Ponce de Leon was chosen, **Mar. 29**, as the PRI's new candidate. In the cabinet he had served as secretary of the budget and then of education. A second suspect was arrested, **Mar. 29**, by Mexican federal agents in Tijuana.

Last U.S. Troops Leave Somalia—The last U.S. soldiers in the UN peacekeeping force left Somalia in March. During the 15 months since Americans had first landed in Somalia, the specter of famine had been checked, and the level of clan violence had subsided. No government had been set up, however, and armed men were still disrupting the delivery of humanitarian aid. The UN mission could count the setting up of schools and a vaccination program among its successes, but 102 peacekeepers from all nations participating in the mission had been killed in sporadic clashes with the clans, and 262 had been wounded. Thirty U.S. soldiers had been killed in combat and 175 wounded. The most powerful clan leaders, Mohammed Farah Aidid and Ali Mahdi, signed a peace agreement in Nairobi, Kenya, **Mar. 24**, that called for a cease-fire and repudiated violence. The last of the American peacekeepers left Mogadishu, the capital, **Mar. 25**, though about 50 soldiers remained to protect U.S. diplomats, and an additional 12 soldiers remained to provide logistical support to UN forces in the Somalian capital. Some 19,000 other UN peacekeepers were still in Somalia.

Conservatives Run Well in Italian Elections—On **Mar. 27** and **28**, Italians participated in their first general election since the adoption of a new electoral law that had been approved in reaction to widespread political corruption. Under the new rules, three-fourths of the seats in both houses of the national parliament were to be filled from single-seat constituencies. The rest were to be assigned proportionally based on the relative popular strength of the parties. A coalition of 3 conservative parties, the Alliance for Freedom, ran well ahead in the voting. The coalition garnered 43% of the vote for the Chamber of Deputies (the lower house of parliament), with half of that going to Forza Italia, led by Silvio Berlusconi, owner of 3 television networks. Berlusconi had waged an antiestablishment campaign and promised to cut taxes. The smallest of the conservative coalition parties, the National Alliance, regarded as being neo-fascist, won 8% of the vote. The Communist-dominated Progressive Alliance had 34% popular support, and a centrist party coalition, led by the Popular Party (the renamed, long-dominant Christian Democrats), was backed by only 16% of the voters.

General

New AIDS Cases Doubled in U.S. in 1993—The U.S. Centers for Disease Control and Prevention reported, **Mar. 10**, that the number of new AIDS cases had more than doubled in the U.S. in 1993, to 103,500, from 49,016 in 1992. A broadened definition of the disease accounted for most of the increase. Although heterosexual transmission accounted for only 9,288 of the new cases (less than 9%), this was a 130% jump from 1992. Cases continued to increase more rapidly among women than among men, and blacks and Hispanics continued to be disproportionately represented in the totals.

Anglican Church Ordains Women Priests—The Church of England ordained its first women priests in March, ending a bitter debate that began when the ordination of women was found theologically unobjectionable by the General Synod of the Anglican Church in 1975. Thirty-two female deacons gathered, **Mar. 12**, at the historic Bristol Cathedral in London for the laying on of hands by the bishop, the Rt. Rev. Barry Rogerson. They became the first women in the 460-year history of the Church of England to become priests. Although the ordination of women had become common in the Anglican Communion in other countries, opposition in the home church of international Anglicanism was strong. Although many supported the decision, at least 700 clergy members, some of them retired, had indicated their objection to the decision and had announced their intention to convert to Roman

Catholicism. Thirty-five priests had announced their resignation. There were a total of 10,200 priests in the church.

Harding Admits Role in Kerrigan Attack—Tonya Harding pleaded guilty, **Mar. 16**, in Portland, OR, to helping cover up the plot to assault her fellow figure skater Nancy Kerrigan. She acknowledged having conspired with her former husband, Jeff Gillooly, and her former bodyguard, Shawn Eckhardt, to conceal from investigators what she knew. Harding continued to assert that she had no foreknowledge of the attack. Harding was fined $100,000 and court costs, and she agreed to establish a $50,000 fund for the Special Olympics and contribute 500 hours of community service. She also agreed to resign from the U.S. Figure Skating Assn., thus ending her amateur career. Gillooly had already pleaded guilty to racketeering, and on **Mar. 21,** 3 other men previously arrested, including Eckhardt, were indicted in the case.

Strong Aftershock Hits Los Angeles—By late March, 5,000 aftershocks had been recorded in southern California since the major January earthquake, and the strongest of these, measuring 5.3 on the Richter scale, was reported **Mar. 20**. It caused minor damage. It was reported, **Mar. 21** and **22**, that the insurance industry had raised its estimate of insured losses from the quake to as much as $4 billion. The Santa Monica Freeway, which had been badly damaged, reopened **Apr. 11**.

Coach of Super Bowl Champs Quits—Jimmy Johnson, who had led the Dallas Cowboys from a 1-15 record in 1989 to 2 consecutive Super Bowl titles after the 1992 and 1993 seasons, resigned in March. Tensions had long run high between Johnson and Jerry Jones, owner of the Cowboys, in part over who deserved credit for the team's success. Johnson announced, **Mar. 29**, that he was stepping down. The Cowboys named, **Mar. 30**, Barry Switzer, the former Oklahoma University coach, to succeed Johnson.

APRIL

National

Large Number of New Jobs Created—The unemployment rate held level in March at 6.5%, the Labor Dept. reported, **Apr. 1**, but it also said that 456,000 nonfarm jobs were added in March, the largest such one-month increase since February 1988. The stock market, in early April, continued a decline begun in late March that appeared to be based on investors' concerns about inflation. On **Apr. 4**, the Dow Jones industrial average stood at 3,593.35, almost 10% below its level less than 2 weeks earlier. Then, however, the average rebounded, climbing 82.06 to close at 3,675.41 on **Apr. 5**. The Commerce Dept. reported, **Apr. 5**, that the index of leading economic indicators had slipped 0.1% in February. The Labor Dept. said, **Apr. 12**, that an index of prices charged by producers for finished goods had risen 0.1% to 56.7% in March. The department reported, **Apr. 13**, that the index of consumer prices had risen 0.3% in March. The Federal Reserve Board, **Apr. 18**, raised the federal funds rate—the interest rate banks charged each other on overnight loans—from 3.5% to 3.75%, the third such increase in 3 months. The increase apparently reflected the Fed's continuing concern about the threat of inflation. In response, several leading banks raised their prime lending rates to 6.75%. The prime rate is used by commercial banks for a variety of purposes, and the interest rates for some adjustable rate mortgages and credit cards are tied to the prime rate. The Commerce Dept. said, **Apr. 19**, that the U.S. trade deficit in February had been $9.71 billion. The Commerce Dept. reported, **Apr. 28**, that the gross domestic product had grown 2.6% at an annual rate during the first quarter, a sharp fall off from the 7.0% increase for the last quarter of 1993. The GDP figure was subject to revision.

Justice Blackmun Announces Retirement—Justice Harry A. Blackmun, who had served on the U.S. Supreme Court since being chosen by Pres. Richard Nixon in 1970, announced his retirement, **Apr. 6**. Blackmun, who was 85, said that he had decided to step down because of his age. In his best-known written decision, in *Roe* v. *Wade* (1973), he spoke for a 7-2 Court majority that had voted to uphold a woman's right to have an abortion under certain circumstances. Blackmun, who would continue to serve for the remainder of the current term, was the most liberal member of the present Court. Earlier in 1994, he said that he had concluded that the death penalty was unconstitutional. Senate Majority Leader George Mitchell (D, ME) said, **Apr. 12**, that he had declined an offer from Pres. Bill Clinton to appoint him to succeed Blackmun.

Clintons Pay Back Taxes—On **Apr. 11**, Pres. Bill Clinton and First Lady Hillary Rodham Clinton paid $14,615 in federal and Arkansas back taxes and interest. The payments related to profits in 1980 in a commodity trading account maintained by Hillary Clinton, profits that she and her husband had not previously reported. At a televised press conference, **Apr. 22**, Hillary Clinton answered questions concerning her and the president's investments. She said that they had no knowledge of any impropriety related to their accounts and that no partners or associates had received any preferential treatment during the time Bill Clinton was governor of Arkansas. She gave new information on her trading between 1978 and 1980, during which time she had shown profits of nearly $100,000. She acknowledged that she had gotten investment advice from James Blair, who was, at the time of the investments, a counsel for Tyson Foods Inc.—one of Arkansas' largest employers and a company subject to regulation by the state government.

Tobacco Executives Testify—Executives representing 7 major tobacco companies encountered generally hostile questioning, **Apr. 14**, when they testified before the House Energy and Commerce subcommittee on health and the environment. They all stated that they did not believe that cigarettes were addictive and said they did not know if cigarettes caused or contributed to major illnesses. They acknowledged that their companies could control the nicotine content of cigarettes through the blending of different tobaccos but said that the blending was done to enhance flavor, not to make cigarettes addictive. The executives denied assertions by committee members that the companies were targeting their advertising at young people.

Former President Richard Nixon Dies—Richard Milhous Nixon, the 37th president of the U.S., died in April. His career had been one of the most dramatic in the history of American politics. He had risen from humble origins to serve in the House and Senate, as vice president, and as president. Nixon was the only U.S. president to resign his office. His downfall came in 1974, when he resigned after a House committee voted to recommend his impeachment for various abuses of power related to the Watergate scandal. During the past 20 years, he had remained active, meeting frequently with world leaders and writing a number of books on world affairs. Nixon, who was 81, suffered a stroke, **Apr. 18**, at his home in Park Ridge, NJ. He was taken to New York Hospital-Cornell Medical Center in Manhattan, where his condition declined, and he died **Apr. 22**. The tributes to Nixon in the following days tended to focus on his achievements, including the opening of diplomatic ties with China and the establishment of détente with the Soviet Union. Pres. Bill Clinton, **Apr. 23**, declared the day of his funeral, **Apr. 27**, a national day of mourning. Nixon was buried next to his wife, Thelma Ryan (Pat) Nixon, on the grounds of the Richard Nixon Library and Birthplace in Yorba Linda, CA. Clinton gave one of the eulogies. First Lady Hillary Rodham Clinton was present, as were all 4 living former presidents, Gerald Ford, Jimmy Carter, Ronald Reagan, and George Bush, and their wives.

Rodney King Awarded Damages—Rodney King, the victim in a widely publicized beating incident in Los Angeles in 1991, was awarded $3,816,535.45 in compensatory damages from the city of Los Angeles, **Apr. 19**. The award, by a U.S. District Court jury in Los Angeles, came in a civil lawsuit filed by King, who had turned down a pretrial offer from the city of $1.25 million. The jury had heard testimony that King would lose up to $1 million in lifetime earnings because of his physical condition. Two policemen who had beaten King had been sentenced to prison for violating his civil rights.

Admiral Survives Dispute Over Retirement—Adm. Frank Kelso, Chief of Naval Operations, retired in April after weathering another dispute linked to the Tailhook scandal. Kelso a d attended the Tailhook convention in Las Vegas in 1991 but had denied—after some allegations to the contrary—that he had seen any sexual assaults on women. He later agreed to take early retirement, but the law required that the Senate approve his retirement at 4-star rank or he would revert to 2-star rank with a reduced retirement income. No military chief of staff had ever been denied retirement at an attained rank, but the 7 women members of the Senate led a fight to reduce his rank. Kelso's defenders contended that whatever happened in Tailhook should not outweigh his 38 years of distinguished service. Critics said that making an example of Kelso would send a strong message on sexual harassment. Kelso's retirement with 4 stars was approved, 54-43, **Apr. 19**. The Senate, **Apr. 21**, approved Pres. Bill Clinton's nominee to replace Kelso, Adm. Jeremy Boorda, and Boorda formally succeeded Kelso on **Apr. 23**.

Academy Midshipmen Expelled—The Navy, **Apr. 28**, expelled 24 midshipmen from the U.S. Naval Academy in what was said to be the biggest cheating scandal in Annapolis history. Originally, 134 students who had taken an electrical engineering examination in 1992 had been accused of obtaining advance information, and some had been accused of lying about what they had done.

Ex-CIA Official Pleads Guilty to Spying—Aldrich Ames, a former high official in the Central Intelligence Agency, pleaded guilty, **Apr. 28**, to a charge of spying for the Soviet Union and Russia. He also pleaded guilty to a charge of income-tax evasion. Ames and his wife, Rosario, had been arrested in February. Under a plea bargain with the government, Aldrich Ames received a life sentence in prison and agreed to cooperate with investigators. In return, Rosario Ames, who also pleaded guilty to espionage and tax evasion, **Apr. 28**, would receive a lenient sentence. The couple had a 5-year-old son. The sentence on Aldrich Ames was imposed in federal court in Washington, DC, **Apr. 28**, and the couple was also required to give up his pension, their house, 2 cars, and the contents of all their bank accounts. At his hearing, Aldrich Ames said he had named at least 12 agents operating in the Soviet bloc whom the CIA had recruited and whom he had betrayed. They had been killed or imprisoned, or they had disappeared. Ames said that he had initially accepted money from the Soviet Union because he was in debt and that he had provided the names of agents because he disapproved of a "shift to the extreme right" within the U.S. government. He called espionage "a self-serving sham" by career bureaucrats who had deceived policy-makers and the American public about the importance of their work.

International

Serbs Withdraw After NATO Bombing—Serb forces pulled back from the predominantly Muslim enclave of Gorazde, in Bosnia and Herzegovina, in April after their positions were bombed by NATO aircraft and after NATO issued another warning. Earlier in the month, U.S. Defense Sec. William J. Perry said, **Apr. 3**, that the Clinton administration would not take military action to save Gorazde, and UN officials indicated, beginning **Apr. 3**, that they were not prepared to launch any attack on the Serbs. The Serbs broke through Bosnian army defense lines at Gorazde, **Apr. 5**. U.S. National Security Adviser Anthony Lake said, **Apr. 7**, that the use of air power had not been ruled out. The Serbs made new gains, **Apr. 8**, and continued to pound Gorazde with artillery. UN Secretary Gen. Boutros Boutros-Ghali warned them, **Apr. 9**, to pull back. A 1993 UN Security Council resolution permitted peacekeepers to use force to protect 6 designated "safe areas" in Bosnia, including Gorazde. The NATO attack began, **Apr. 10**, when 2 U.S. aircraft bombed and destroyed a Serb command post. This was the first-ever NATO air attack against ground targets. After the Serbs again attacked Gorazde, **Apr. 11**, bombs from 2 U.S. planes destroyed a Serb tank and 2 armored personnel carriers. The Serbs called a halt to their shelling. UN aid workers reported, **Apr. 12**, that the Serb attacks had caused almost 1,000 casualties in the city. The Russian envoy in the Balkans, Vitaly Churkin, said, **Apr. 13**, that the Serbs had promised to end their attacks; however, the next day, **Apr. 14**, 3 children were reported killed as a result of suspected Serbian fire. The Serbs, **Apr. 16**, used a surface-to-air missile to down a British reconnaissance and attack jet as the British jet was attempting to fire on a Serbian tank. The pilot parachuted to safety. Resuming their offensive, the Serbs broke through to the center of Gorazde, **Apr. 17**. A Serb attack, **Apr. 20**, destroyed much of the town's hospital. Following another NATO ultimatum on **Apr. 22**, the Serbs began to pull back **Apr. 23**, even while continuing to shell the town and destroy Muslim homes. Clashes between Serbs and UN personnel occurred. British troops killed 3 Serbs, **Apr. 29**, inside the exclusion zone near Gorazde, and Danish troops killed 9 Serbs near Tuzla, in northeastern Bosnia, **Apr. 29** and **30**.

Two Presidents Killed in Plane Crash—Pres. Cyprien Ntaryamira of Burundi and Pres. Juvenal Habyarimana of Rwanda were killed, **Apr. 6**, when their plane crashed in Kigali, the capital of Rwanda. They were returning from Tanzania, after attending a conference with other African leaders that had sought to end the prolonged and bloody conflict in Burundi and Rwanda between members of the Hutu and Tutsi ethnic groups. The Burundi ambassador to the UN said, **Apr. 6**, that the plane had been struck by rocket fire. In succeeding days, violence became widespread in Kigali, with those killed including Rwanda's premier as well as Jesuit priests and Belgian peacekeeping soldiers. Within a week, fighting in Rwanda between Hutu and Tutsi had claimed up to 20,000 lives. On **Apr. 10**, France reported that its paratroopers had evacuated 525 French expatriates from Rwanda, and 800 Belgian paratroopers arrived to evacuate the estimated 1,500 Belgian citizens who had lived there. On **Apr. 26**, separate cease-fires declared by the Hutus and Tutsis took effect, but fighting flared anew, **Apr. 27**. Estimates of those killed, mostly civilians, rose to 100,000 and then to 200,000. Large numbers of civilians fled into neighboring countries. On **Apr. 29** alone, it was estimated that 250,000 people crossed the border from Rwanda to Tanzania.

Israel, Palestinians Reach Agreement—Israeli and Palestine Liberation Organization negotiators worked out details in April on the transfer of authority in designated areas of the occupied territories. More terrorist acts added to the tense atmosphere. Seven people were killed, **Apr. 6**, when a Palestinian driving a car outfitted with a bomb drove into a school bus in Afula. An agreement reached **Apr. 12**, in Cairo, provided that 9,000 Palestinian police would be stationed in Jericho and the Gaza Strip after the Israeli military withdrawal. Most would be drawn from Palestinian forces based in Jordan. Israel agreed to release 5,000 (out of some 8,500) Palestinian prisoners that it held. Five Israelis died and about 30 were wounded, **Apr. 13**, when another Palestinian suicide bomber detonated explosives in a bus station in Hadera.

Japanese Prime Minister Resigns—Morihiro Hosokawa, who had been elected prime minister of Japan in August 1993 on an anticorruption platform, resigned in April after a question was raised about his own integrity. Hosokawa had formed a coalition government after voters denied a parliamentary majority to the Liberal Democratic Party, which had held power for decades. The major achievement in his 8 months in office had been the approval by parliament of a political-reform bill that was intended to reduce the influence of money in the public sphere. His policies had been thwarted repeatedly because of conflicts among parties in his coalition. Hosokawa announced his resignation, subject to the selection of a successor, **Apr. 8**, after allegations were made that he had profited illegally from a 100 million yen loan from a trucking company in 1982. Hosokawa said he had repaid the loan but acknowledged that he had not repaid interest on the loan. The Diet (parliament), **Apr. 25**, elected Tsutomu Hata of the Japan Renewal Party (Shinseito) as Hosokawa's successor. He was deputy premier and foreign minister in the outgoing government. Hata abruptly faced a crisis when the Social Democratic Party of Japan pulled out of the ruling coalition, **Apr. 26**. The Social Democrats said they believed that they were going to be squeezed out of the government. The other parties in the coalition were more conservative. Their defection left the Hata government without a majority in the lower house of the Diet.

South Africa Holds Election Open to All—South Africa in April conducted its first universal-suffrage election. The big question mark hanging over the election was the participation of the Zulu-based Inkatha Freedom Party. The party's leader, Chief Mangosuthu Buthelezi, had opposed participation. On **Apr. 12**, former U.S. Sec. of State Henry Kissinger and former British Foreign Secretary Lord Carrington joined other negotiators in Johannesburg seeking to resolve the impasse. Pres. F. W. de Klerk and his leading challenger for the presidency, African National Congress head Nelson Mandela, debated each other on television and radio, **Apr. 14**. On **Apr. 19**, Buthelezi dropped his demands that KwaZulu be declared a sovereign monarchy and agreed to compete in the election. Election-related bombings, **Apr. 24-27**, claimed 21 lives, and 31 people linked to white-separatist groups were arrested in these attacks. The election was held, as scheduled, **Apr. 26-28**, and was extended to **Apr. 29** because of the heavy turnout and because of the inexperience of many officials overseeing the balloting. Nineteen parties contested the election, in which members of a 400-seat National Assembly and a 90-vote Senate were chosen. Mandela cast his first vote ever, **Apr. 27**. Blacks in great numbers formed long lines at the polls and participated in a spirit of celebration. More than 300 monitors from other nations observed the election and reported that it had been free and fair. It was apparent that the system of racial separation, called apartheid, which had been in place since 1948, was at an end.

U.S. Planes Down 2 U.S. Helicopters—In a tragic error, 2 U.S. war planes shot down 2 U.S. Army helicopters in northern Iraq's so-called no-fly zone, **Apr. 14**. The helicopters had been mistaken for Russian-built Iraqi military aircraft. They had been engaged in a UN humanitarian mission in behalf of Iraq's Kurdish minority. All 26 aboard, including 15 Americans, were killed. Defense Sec. William J. Perry said, **Apr. 15**, that the jets had not been able to receive radio confirmation of the identity of the helicopters because the latter's transponders apparently had not been functioning. He said that the pilots' decision to fire without warning had been authorized by the rules of engagement.

General

Kurt Cobain Dead at Age 27—Kurt Cobain, the lead singer of the influential rock band Nirvana, was found dead in April of a self-inflicted gunshot wound to the head. An electrician who had come to install a security system in Cobain's Seattle home discovered the singer's body in a greenhouse above the garage, **Apr. 8**. A 20-gauge shotgun and a note addressed to Cobain's wife, Courtney Love, and the couple's 19-month-old daughter, Frances Bean, was found near Cobain's body. The King County Medical Examiner's Office later reported that Cobain had died on **Apr. 5**. In an emotional taped message, Love read parts of Cobain's suicide note to the 5,000 grieving fans who had gathered, **Apr. 10**, outside the Seattle Center for a memorial service. Cobain had struggled with depression and drug addiction for years and had made a failed suicide attempt in early March while in Rome for a performance. The group's groundbreaking 1991 album *Nevermind* had thrust the band into the spotlight and sold more than 10 million copies. Cobain was said to be a founder of so-called grunge rock, a new musical genre that combined elements of punk, heavy metal, and contemporary alternative music.

Michelangelo's Fresco Restored—The restored 16th-century fresco *The Last Judgment*, created by a team of artists led by Michelangelo Buonarroti in Rome's Sistine Chapel, was formally unveiled by Pope John Paul II, **Apr. 8**. The fresco, 7 stories tall, depicted Jesus surrounded by many figures, some ascending into heaven and others being cast into hell. The restoration, which had taken 4 years, had removed dust and candle smoke that had darkened Michelangelo's brilliant colors. The restorers also removed from some nude figures the drapes that had been added after Michelangelo's death.

Murderer Executed on Basis of DNA Tests—For the first time a murderer was executed in a case in which DNA-matching technology had been used to obtain a conviction. The technology is commonly called genetic fingerprinting. Timothy Spencer had been tried in Virginia in the raping and strangling of 4 women in 1987. The prosecution had no confession, no witnesses, and no fingerprints, but DNA tests linked semen at the crime scene with Spencer's blood. Scientists have testified that DNA matches can be confirmed with an extremely high level of certainty, and such evidence had been used in the U.S. since 1986. Spencer was executed in the Greensville Correctional Center, south of Richmond, **Apr. 27**.

MAY

National

Short-Term Interest Rates Increased— Continuing to confront potential inflationary pressures, the Federal Reserve Board in May increased 2 key short-term interest rates. The Commerce Dept. reported, **May 3**, that the index of leading economic indicators had risen 0.7% in March. The Federal Reserve Board said, **May 4**, that much of the U.S. was experiencing "solid economic growth." The Labor Dept. reported, **May 6**, that the unemployment rate edged downward 0.1% in April to 6.4%. The department said, **May 13**, that an index of consumer prices had risen 0.1% in April. The Fed, **May 17**, raised the interest rate charged by banks on overnight loans to each other for the 4th time in 1994—from 3.75% to 4.25%. The discount rate, the rate the Fed charged on loans to commercial banks, was increased, **May 17**, from the 3% at which it had stood for almost 2 years to 3.5%. The Commerce Dept. reported, **May 19**, that the U.S. trade deficit had declined in March to $7.46 billion.

Suit Alleges Harassment by Clinton—A former Arkansas state employee filed a suit in May that accused Pres. Bill Clinton of sexual harassment. The White House said, **May 3**, that Clinton had hired Robert Bennett, a prominent attorney in Washingnton, DC, to defend him. The federal civil lawsuit, filed, **May 6**, in Little Rock by Paula Corbin Jones, charged that Clinton, then governor of Arkansas, had made an unwanted sexual advance during a meeting with Jones in a hotel room in Arkansas in 1991. In her suit, Jones asked for a public apology from Clinton and $700,000 in damages from Clinton and from Danny Ferguson, an Arkansas state trooper, whom she said had given a false account of her meeting with Clinton. Jones maintained that because she had rejected Clinton's overture she had been denied promotion. The suit was believed to be the first of its kind ever filed against a sitting president.

Exxon Back in Court Over Alaska Oil Spill—The long legal struggle growing out of the 1989 *Exxon Valdez* oil spill in Alaska continued in May and June. The Exxon Corp. tanker had spilled 11 million gallons of oil into Prince William Sound, causing serious and widespread environmental damage. In the current legal phase, some 10,000 fishermen, property owners, and native Alaskans were suing Exxon and the *Valdez* captain, Joseph Hazelwood, for $1.5 billion. In U.S. District Court in Anchorage, **May 10**, Hazelwood testified that Exxon knew he had been treated for alcoholism but allowed him to return to duty without monitoring his alcohol consumption. Hazelwood, who had been acquitted in 1990 of operating the *Valdez* while drunk, testified, **May 11**, that he had had 3 vodkas just hours before the accident. This repudiated his previous assertion that he had drunk just one beer. The federal jury, **June 13**, concluded that Exxon Corp. had been reckless in allowing Hazelwood to captain the *Valdez*. The jury found Hazelwood both negligent and reckless. The rulings, which marked the end of the first phase of a four–part trial, permitted the 10,000 plaintiffs to pursue their litigation and seek compensation for their losses.

Federal Judge Nominated for Supreme Court—Pres. Bill Clinton, **May 13**, announced that he was nominating Judge Stephen Breyer, a member of the U.S. Court of Appeals for the First Circuit, in Boston, to succeed Justice Harry A. Blackmun on the U.S. Supreme Court. Blackmun, in April, had announced his intention to retire. A graduate of Stanford and Harvard Law School, Breyer had taught law at Harvard and had served as an assistant special prosecutor during the Watergate investigation. He had been chief counsel to the Senate Judiciary Committee and, since 1980 on appointment by Pres. Jimmy Carter, a member of the appeals court. The nomination of Judge Breyer, whose decisions appeared free of any ideological persuasion, was applauded by political conservatives as well as liberals.

Trade Center Bombers Get Stiff Sentences—Four men convicted in March of the 1993 bombing of the World Trade Center in New York City received prison terms of 240 years each in May. In announcing his sentences, **May 24**, Judge Kevin Duffy of the U.S. District Court in Manhattan called the men "cowards" and explained that 180 years of their sentences were based on the life expectancies of the 6 people killed in the blast and the balance of the sentences was for charges related to assault on a federal officer. The sentences, which stated that there would be no possibility for parole, ensured that the men would spend the rest of their lives in prison.

Rostenkowski Indicted—Rep. Dan Rostenkowski (D, IL), chairman of the House Ways and Means Committee and one of the most powerful members of Congress, was the subject of a 17-count felony indictment in May. In an investigation that had begun in 1992, he had been implicated in an embezzlement scheme involving the House Post Office. After noticing some evidence of additional wrongdoing, the prosecutors broadened their inquiry into Rostenkowski's finances. Rejecting a proposed plea-bargain agreement, Rostenkowski, **May 30**, declared his innocence. U.S. Attorney Eric Holder announced the indictment, **May 31**. It was charged that from 1971 to 1992 the congressman had put 14 people on his payroll who did little or no work and who, in some cases, performed personal services for Rostenkowski and members of his family. In other counts, Rostenkowski was accused of embezzling $50,000 from the House Post Office, tampering with a witness in the investigation, and improperly charging $40,000 worth of gifts to friends to his congressional expense account. Under the rules of the Democratic caucus, Rostenkowski, on being indicted, stepped down as chairman of his committee. Rep. Sam Gibbons (D, FL) succeeded him as interim chairman, **May 31**. As committee chairman, Rostenkowski had been a forceful advocate of Pres. Bill Clinton's health reform bill, which was now perceived to be in greater difficulty in Congress.

International

Mandela Becomes S. Africa's 1st Black President—Concluding a remarkable ascent to power after spending 27 years in prison, Nelson Mandela was inaugurated in May as the first black president of South Africa. Blacks also held a majority in the new parliament, and the system of required racial separation, called apartheid, which had been imposed by white governments since the 1940s, ceased to exist. Mandela, a black nationalist leader who had been imprisoned for sabotage and treason, claimed victory, **May 2**, in the elections held in late April that had been open to citizens of all races. The runner-up in the election, the incumbent Pres. F. W. de Klerk, had been instrumental in freeing Mandela and bringing him into the political process. In election results announced **May 6**, Mandela's African National Congress (ANC) received 63% of the vote and de Klerk's National Party 20%. The Inkatha Freedom Party, which had agreed just before the election to participate, captured 10%. Seats in the 400-member National Assembly, which would choose the new president, were apportioned according to the vote for each party. The new assembly took office, **May 9**, and Mandela was the only candidate nominated for president. A throng of 100,000 heard Mandela speak, **May 9**, in Cape Town, and another large crowd, including 45 heads of state and other dignitaries from 130 countries, attended his inauguration, **May 10**. Vice Pres. Al Gore led the U.S. delegation. Mandela praised South Africa for having overcome the "extraordinary human disaster" of apartheid. The many white citizens who attended the ceremonies joined in the festival atmosphere. Mandela named de Klerk as one of his vice presidents. The cabinet was completed **May 11**. Its members included 18 from the ANC, 6 from the National Party, and 3 from Inkatha.

Civil War Continues in Rwanda—The bloody civil war in Rwanda between Hutu and Tutsi continued in May. Estimates of the death toll ran as high as 500,000. The floodtide of refugees into neighboring countries also continued. The U.S., **May 2**, pledged $15 million in humanitarian aid to Rwanda. The UN Security Council, **May 17**, approved sending a force of 500 Ghanaians to secure the airport at Kigali, the Rwandan capital, and, later, an additional 5,500 troops, drawn mostly from other African nations, would be sent to facilitate the establishment of a cease-fire. Rebels seized the airport at Kigali, **May 22**. In Uganda, up to 40,000 bodies of Rwandan massacre victims had washed up on the shores of Lake Victoria by **May 22**. The bodies had floated 60 miles dowstream on the Kagera River.

Israel, PLO Sign Self-Rule Accord—Israeli Prime Minister Yitzhak Rabin and Yasir Arafat, chairman of the Palestine Liberation Organization (PLO), signed an agreement, **May 4** in Cairo, establishing the terms for the implementation of limited Palestinian self-rule in the Gaza Strip and Jericho. Some issues, related to the size of the Jericho enclave and the presence of Palestinian police at border crossings, remained unresolved. Arafat balked, until getting further assurances from Rabin, at signing one map annexed to the agreement because Arafat feared that the PLO would be committed to particular boundaries for the Jericho enclave. The agreement provided for a 24-member Palestinian National Authority headed by Arafat to oversee the self-rule area. Israel would withdraw its troops from the designated areas within 3 weeks but would remain responsible for foreign relations and the security of Jewish settlements. Israel also agreed to release about 5,000 Palestinian prisoners over a period of 5 weeks. The transfer of power began, **May 11**, when about 150 Palestinian police took over security responsibilities in a town in the Gaza Strip. Israel completed its withdrawal from Jericho, **May 13**, 460 Palestinian policemen arrived from Jordan, and joint Israeli-PLO patrols got underway. As the last Israeli soldiers pulled out of Gaza, **May 18**, Palestinian police took their places. On **May 20**, Islamic militants shot and killed 2 Israeli soldiers at a border checkpoint in Gaza.

Civil War Flares in Yemen—Growing strife in Yemen culminated, **May 5**, in the onset of civil war between a northern faction loyal to the president and a southern faction supportive of the vice president. In 1990, 2 separate nations had united to form the present Yemen, but clan-based rivalries had prevented complete transition to a single state. The new fighting featured bombing raids and exchanges between tanks and artillery. By **May 6**, the northerners were advancing on the southern port city of Aden. The U.S. State Dept., **May 8**, asked some 5,000 Americans in Yemen to leave the country.

UN OKs Tougher Embargo on Haiti—The UN Security Council, **May 6**, voted to impose a tougher trade embargo on Haiti if the nation's military rulers did not yield power within 2 weeks. Only food, medicine, and cooking oils would be exempt from the embargo. Reports out of Haiti continued to indicate that the regime was engaged in widespread human-rights abuses. Modifying American policy, Pres. Bill Clinton said, **May 8**, that Haitian refugees intercepted in international waters while en route to the U.S. would be given asylum interviews and would be granted asylum if they could demonstrate the prospect of political persecution in Haiti. Randall Robinson, a Washington, DC-based lobbyist on African and Caribbean issues, ended a fast, **May 8**, that he had begun as a protest against the U.S. policy of turning back all refugees. Haiti's military leaders succeeded, **May 11**, in installing as provisional president Emil Jonassaint, a Supreme Court justice. The embargo, backed up by U.S. naval vessels and Coast Guard cutters, went into effect **May 22**.

Billionaire Heads Italian Government—Conservatives took control of the government of Italy in May. As a result of the election in late March, the 3 leading conservative parties held 366 seats in the 630-seat Chamber of Deputies, the lower house of parliament, and were just 6 seats shy of a majority in the Senate. Silvio Berlusconi, billionaire owner of 3 television networks and leader of Forza Italia, the leading conservative party, was sworn in as premier, **May 11**. His cabinet included 5 members of the neo-fascist National Alliance.

Muslims, Croats Agree on Bosnian Federation—Meeting in Vienna, **May 11**, representatives of the Muslim-dominated Bosnian government and Bosnian Croat leaders agreed to form a federation. Under the plan, 4 provinces would be heavily Muslim, 2 would be heavily Croat, and 2 would be ethnically mixed. The Bosnian Serbs, who controlled about two-thirds of the republic's land, were not a party to the agreement. On **May 13**, the U.S., Russia, and 5 European countries proposed a partitioning of Bosnia and Herzegovina, with about 51% going to the new federation and 49% to the Bosnian Serbs. Economic sanctions against Serbia would be lifted while the partition was being implemented. UN officials said, **May 23**, that the Bosnian Serbs had not removed all their troops from the 2-mile exclusion zone around Gorazde. The continuing Serb deployment defied edicts from NATO and the UN.

British Labour Party Leader Dies—John Smith, leader of Britain's opposition Labour Party, died, **May 12**, after suffering a heart attack in London. Smith, 55, had succeeded Neil Kinnock as party leader in 1992. Labour had subsequently enjoyed a resurgence in popularity, and Smith had been seen by many as Britain's next prime minister.

30-Year Dictatorship Ends in Malawi—Pres. Hastings Banda of Malawi, one of the world's most durable leaders, fell from power in May. His effort to win independence for Nyasaland from Great Britain ended in success in 1964, when the newly named Republic of Malawi won its freedom. Malawi became a one-party dictatorship, with Banda serving as president from 1966. He lived lavishly while most of the people suffered extreme poverty. In 1993, parliament legalized all political parties, and in the first multiparty election, held **May 17**, Banda, who was thought to be in his 90s, was defeated by Bakili Muluzi, leader of the opposition United Democratic Front. Muluzi was sworn in as president on **May 21**.

Clinton Grants China Favored Trade Status—Changing his mind on a key foreign policy issue, Pres. Bill Clinton decided in May to extend most-favored-nation (MFN) trading status to China for another year. This is the status that the U.S. generally accords to almost all of its trading partners. Clinton had said in 1993 that he would not renew MFN for China when it came up for renewal in 1994 unless China demonstrated significant improvement in its human-rights record. Since then, China's progress in this field had been spotty at best, but U.S. business leaders and their representatives in Congress, concerned about being shut out of the immense Chinese market, had brought great pressure on Clinton to renew MFN. In announcing his extension, **May 26**, Clinton said that his approach would permit the U.S. government to maintain greater leverage with China and would advance the cause of human rights in the long run. He also said China was too large and powerful to isolate, although he did ban the importation of guns and ammunition from China.

General

Suicide Doctor's Legal Battles Continue—Legal disputes involving the so-called suicide doctor, Jack Kevorkian, continued in May. A Wayne County, MI, jury, **May 2**, acquitted Kevorkian of violating a state law forbidding assisted suicides. Kevorkian had been present at the death of Thomas Hyde, who was terminally ill. Hyde inhaled a lethal dose of carbon monoxide gas. Several jurors said they believed that the doctor was only trying to alleviate Hyde's suffering. On **May 3**, in Seattle, U.S. District Judge Barbara Rothstein struck down Washington's assisted-suicide law, holding that it violated the 14th amendment protection against infringement by government of an individual's rights. The Michigan Court of Appeals, **May 10**, overturned Michigan's law. At the same time, however, this court ensured further legal confrontation by reinstating murder charges against Kevorkian in the 1991 suicide deaths of 2 women.

U.S. Teenager Caned in Singapore—An American, Michael Fay, age 18, was subjected to a severe caning in Singapore in May, following an international debate over the merits of corporal punishment. Fay lived with his mother and stepfather in Singapore, a small city-state that prided itself on its low crime rate and that imposed sentences harsh by Western standards on a wide range of offenses. Fay, who had no previous criminal record, and other young men had been arrested in 1993 for spray-painting cars and other acts of vandalism. Fay confessed but said later that he did so only after he was beaten by police in prison. His sentence included 4 months in prison, a $2,250 fine, and 6 strokes on the bare buttocks with a rattan cane. Caning, common in Singapore, was very painful and usually drew blood and left permanent scars. Human rights groups protested the caning. Pres. Bill Clinton called it extreme and appealed for clemency. Public opinion in the U.S. was divided, with many people saying that corporal punishment would reduce crime rates. The government of

Singapore, **May 4**, rejected Clinton's appeal but reduced the caning sentence to 4 strokes. This sentence was carried out **May 5**. Fay was released from prison, **June 21**, and returned to the U.S., **June 22**, to live with his father.

"Chunnel" Links Britain, France—The Channel Tunnel, a railway under the English Channel between Britain and France, was inaugurated, **May 6**. Queen Elizabeth II and Pres. François Mitterrand participated in the inaugural ceremony, but paying customers were not expected to have access to the so-called chunnel for months. High speed trains would transport passengers and automobiles from Folkestone, England, to Calais, France, a distance of 31 miles.

Serial Killer of 33 Executed—John Wayne Gacy, who had been convicted of killing 33 young men and boys between 1972 and 1978, was executed by lethal injection at the Stateville Correctional Center in Joliet, IL, in May. Twenty-seven bodies had been found buried under Gacy's home in Des Plaines near Chicago. Prosecutors said Gacy had assaulted his victims sexually and then strangled them. He had confessed, then recanted, and had fought to prevent his execution. Legal appeals were exhausted, **May 9**, and Gacy was executed **May 10**.

Jacqueline Kennedy Onassis Dies—Former First Lady Jacqueline Kennedy Onassis, one of the most admired women in the U.S., died in May at age 64 after a brief illness. Born to wealth, Jacqueline Bouvier had grown up among the social elite of the Northeast. After graduating from Georgetown, she became a newspaper reporter and met Sen. John Kennedy of Massachusetts. They married in 1953. Kennedy was elected president in 1960. Jacqueline Kennedy, initially renowned for her glamor, was also acclaimed for her tasteful and elegant restoration of the White House. She was riding with the president when he was assassinated in Dallas in 1963. Her poise and dignity during the next few days was credited with helping the nation get through a traumatic experience. The Kennedys had 2 children, Caroline and John, Jr., who survived infancy. Jacqueline Kennedy was married to the Greek shipping owner Aristotle Onassis from 1968 until his death in 1975. She then worked as a book editor in New York. She was diagnosed as having non-Hodgkins lymphoma in January 1994, and her condition worsened in March. She left the hospital for the last time, **May 18**, and died in her home on Fifth Avenue in Manhattan, **May 19**. After funeral services in Manhattan, **May 23**, she was buried next to her first husband in Arlington National Cemetery in Virginia.

JUNE

National

Unemployment Rate Down Sharply—The nation's unemployment rate had fallen sharply, according to data released in June. After a big advance in March, the index of leading economic indicators was unchanged in April, the Commerce Dept. reported, **June 2**. The Labor Dept. said, **June 3**, that the unemployment rate had declined from 6.4% in April to 6.0% in May. The department reported, **June 10**, that an index of prices charged by producers for finished goods had fallen 0.1% in May from April, but on **June 14** it said that the consumer price index had edged upward 0.2% in May. For the first time since World War II the U.S. dollar, **June 21**, fell in value to less than 100 Japanese yen on international currency markets.

Oliver North Nominated for Senate—Oliver North, whose convictions on several charges in connection with the Iran-contra affair had later been overturned, won the nomination of the Virginia Republican Party for the U.S. Senate, **June 4**. At the GOP state convention, North won 55% of the vote against James C. Miller 3d, who had served as White House budget director under Pres. Ronald Reagan. Some Virginia Republicans balked at endorsing North after he was nominated. Sen. John Warner (R, VA), said he was prepared to support former State Attorney Gen. Marshall Coleman, a Republican who was circulating petitions to run as an independent. Former Gov. L. Douglas Wilder, a Democrat, was also planning an independent campaign. The 3 candidates were seeking to unseat Sen. Charles Robb, a Democrat, whose popularity had declined as a result of questions about ethics and character. Coleman qualified for the ballot, **June 13**. On **June 14**, Virginia Democrats renominated Robb, but he got only 58% of the vote. Wilder, with whom Robb had long feuded, turned in his petitions, **June 14**, and declared his candidacy, **June 18**.

Nominees Chosen for General Election—Nominees for Congress and state offices were being chosen throughout the country during the spring and summer. In California, **June 7**, Republicans renominated Gov. Pete Wilson, but a conservative held him to 62% of the vote. Democrats chose as his opponent Kathleen Brown, the state treasurer and the daughter and sister of 2 former governors. The contest for governor in Minnesota warmed up, **June 17**, when the Republican state convention rejected the candidacy of the incumbent GOP governor, Arne Carlson, and endorsed Allen Quist, a farmer and creationist. Carlson had angered conservatives by supporting abortion rights and civil rights for homosexuals. Quist and Carlson would next compete in a party primary in September.

Whitewater Counsel Issues 1st Report—Robert Fiske, the special counsel investigating matters related to the Whitewater affair, issued his first report in June. Fiske took sworn depositions from Pres. Bill Clinton and First Lady Hillary Rodham Clinton, **June 12**, at the White House. This was believed to be the first time that a sitting president had responded directly to questions in a legal case relating to his official conduct, and also the first time that a first lady had given testimony about her conduct while residing in the White House. The Senate, **June 14**, and the House, **June 15**, approved hearings on Whitewater. In his first report, released **June 30**, Fiske said he had not found substantial evidence that Clinton aides and Treasury Dept. officials had "acted with the intent to corruptly influence" an investigation by the Resolution Trust Corp. into the collapse of the Madison Guaranty Savings and Loan, in Arkansas. Fiske investigated more than 20 contacts related to Madison among White House and Treasury officials. Deputy Treasury Sec. Roger Altman was acting director of the RTC. In his report, Fiske also concluded that the death of former Clinton White House aide Vincent Foster in July 1993 was a suicide, as originally reported. There was speculation that Foster's death was somehow linked to Whitewater.

Texas Cult Members Sentenced to Prison—U.S. District Court Judge Walter Smith, **June 17**, sentenced members of the Branch Davidian cult who had been convicted of charges in February 1994 in connection with the February 1993 federal raid on their compound near Waco, TX. The 8 cultists, who had been found not guilty on some charges, all received prison terms. Five were sentenced to 10 years for aiding and abetting the voluntary manslaughter of federal officers and 30 years on weapons charges that the judge had reinstated. Three other Davidians received lesser prison terms and fines. The judge ordered the defendants to pay more than $1.1 million in fines and restitution.

Clinton Names New Chief of Staff—Apparently responding to concerns that his staff was providing him with indecisive and ineffective support on both foreign and domestic policy, Pres. Bill Clinton, **June 27**, made several changes in his White House team. He chose Leon Panetta, director of the White House Office of Management and Budget, to succeed Thomas McLarty, his boyhood friend, as chief of staff. Panetta, a former member of the U.S. House, was seen as having considerable skill in working with Congress and the bureaucracy. McLarty would stay on as a counselor to the president. Alice Rivlin, deputy OMB director, was named to succeed Panetta. David Gergen, who had been serving as an adviser to Clinton, was given new responsibilities in foreign policy as an adviser to both the president and Sec. of State Warren Christopher.

Clinton Seeks Immunity in Harassment Case—Pres. Bill Clinton's attorneys in June filed motions in federal district court in Little Rock, AK, asking for a delay in the sexual harassment suit filed by a former Arkansas state employee. Earlier, on **June 10**, an Arkansas state trooper, Danny Ferguson, filed court papers denying allegations by Clinton's accuser, Paula Corbin Jones, that he had arranged the meeting, at Clinton's request, between the then-governor and Jones in May 1991. It was at this meeting that the alleged sexual harassment occurred. He acknowledged that he had taken Jones to Clinton's hotel room. He said that Jones had later offered to become Clinton's girlfriend and had given him her phone number for him to relay to Clinton. In a motion filed **June 27**, Clinton's lawyer, Robert Bennett, contended that presidents were entitled to immunity during their terms to ensure that their attention would not be diverted from their constitutional duties.

Clintons Establish Legal Defense Fund—Pres. Bill Clinton and First Lady Hillary Rodham Clinton established a legal defense fund, **June 28**, to help cover legal expenses that would be connected with the Whitewater investigation and with the sexual harassment lawsuit filed against the president. Legal expenses for the Clintons could run into the millions of dollars. Individuals would be allowed to contribute up to $1,000, and lists of donors would be disclosed every 6 months. The creation of such a fund for a sitting president was unprecedented.

International

Clinton Visits European Countries—While in Europe to help observe the 50th anniversary of D-Day, Pres. Bill Clinton visited several other countries. He met with Pope John Paul II at the Vatican, **June 2**, to discuss abortion, birth control, and related family issues. The president also spoke to American seminary students. Clinton met in Rome, **June 2**, with Italian Premier Silvio Berlusconi—the latter's first meeting with a major Western head of state. Addressing the French National Assembly, Clinton said, **June 7**, that the Bosnian crisis represented a critical test of the resolve of the Western nations. He publicly backed a partition plan formulated by European nations that would give 49% of Bosnia to the Bosnian Serbs. On **June 8**, Clinton received an honorary degree from Oxford University, which he had attended as a Rhodes scholar.

N. Koreans, Carter Discuss Nuclear Dispute—Former Pres. Jimmy Carter met with leaders of North Korea in Pyongyang in June as part of the effort to defuse the international controversy over the North's nuclear-development sites. Inspectors for the International Atomic Energy Agency had been trying to ascertain whether North Korea was developing plutonium for use in weapons. U.S. officials, **June 3**, initiated discussions at the UN concerning new economic sanctions against North Korea. The latter, which said it would view such sanctions as an act of war, reiterated, **June 7**, its refusal to allow inspection of 2 sites. Carter, accepting a standing invitation from Pres. Kim Il Sung to visit North Korea, arrived in Pyongyang, the capital, **June 15**, accompanied by his wife, Rosalynn. He was not representing the U.S. government. Traveling to South Korea, **June 18**, Carter persuaded South Korean Pres. Kim Young Sam to agree to meet with Pres. Kim Il Sung. A breakthrough occurred, **June 22**, when Clinton and North Korea accepted Carter's plan, which included resumption of high-level talks between their 2 countries. North Korea also agreed to essentially close the disputed nuclear complex at Yongbyon during the duration of the talks. Negotiators from North and South Korea announced, **June 28**, that their presidents would meet in Pyongyang in late July—at a summit that had no precedent.

Ex-Communists Win in Hungary—On **June 4**, the Hungarian Socialist Party—led by communists and formally called the Hungarian Socialist Workers' Party—chose its leader, Gyula Horn, to be the country's next premier. The party had won a majority in parliamentary elections held in May. Right-wing parties had led the country since 1990, but economic hardship had been one result of the government's effort to move from a state-run system to private enterprise. Frustration with economic change had also prompted a return to leadership by former communists in Lithuania, Poland, Romania, and Slovenia.

More Sanctions Instituted for Haiti—The international community got tougher on the Haitian regime in June. The Organization of American States, **June 7**, urged further steps to make life difficult for Haiti's wealthier citizens, who tended to support the government. Responding, Pres. Bill Clinton, **June 10**, froze most financial transactions between the U.S. and Haiti. Joined by Canada, Clinton, **June 10**, also suspended commercial flights to Haiti, effective **June 25**.

Bosnian Cease-Fire Takes Effect—Representatives of the 2 major warring factions in Bosnia and Herzegovina, the Muslim-Croat federation and the Bosnian Serbs, signed a cease-fire agreement, **June 8**, in Geneva, Switzerland. The UN Protection Force would monitor the cease-fire, although it had no authority to enforce the truce. The U.S. House of Representatives, **June 9**, voted, 244-178, to require the Clinton administration to cease participating in the UN-sponsored arms embargo against the Bosnian government. The Muslim government had been hard pressed to obtain sufficient arms to mount an effective defense. The new cease-fire went into effect **June 10**.

Rwandan Rebels Make Further Gains—The Rwandan Patriotic Front, the rebel fighting force composed primarily of Tutsi, made further gains in Rwanda's civil war in June. At the beginning of the month, some of the Hutu-dominated government troops were retreating from Kigali, the capital, and falling back toward an interim capital established at Gitarama. It was reported, **June 13**, that the rebels had overrun Gitarama. Although a cease-fire was reached, **June 14**, fighting continued. The UN Security Council approved, **June 22**, a French intervention plan, and the French forces crossed, **June 23**, from Zaire into Rwanda with the objective of protecting civilians from the combatants. As the rebels advanced, the French troops and UN personnel found thousands of bodies buried in mass graves, apparently the victims of atrocities committed by the Hutus.

Russia Joins NATO "Partnership"—Russia joined the North Atlantic Treaty Organization's Partnership for Peace program, **June 22**. Russia and 20 other countries, including other former Communist states, had enrolled as NATO partners, under which they could participate in limited joint military exercises and peacekeeping missions. The full NATO members were not obliged to come to the defense of the so-called partners if they were attacked.

Socialist Named Premier of Japan—Japan got its 3d premier of the year in June. Tsutomu Hata had headed a shaky reform coalition since April, but on **June 23** the opposition Liberal Democratic Party (LDP) in the lower house of the Diet (parliament) filed a motion of no-confidence in his government. Hata faced an unusual alliance between the LDP and the Social Democratic Party of Japan (SDPJ), decades-long rivals who had little in common except hostility to electoral reforms that the governing coalition had supported under ex-Premier Morihiro Hosokawa. Hata chose not to risk defeat on the motion, which would oblige him to call new elections that would be held under the pre-reform rules. He therefore resigned, **June 25**, and on **June 29** the LDP and the SDPJ combined forces in the Diet to elect Tomiichi Murayama, the Socialist leader, as premier. Murayama, **June 30**, announced his cabinet, which was dominated by members of the LDP.

Massacre Found to Be Act of One Man—An Israeli investigative panel said, **June 26**, that a Jewish settler, Baruch Goldstein, had acted alone in shooting worshippers in Hebron in February.

General

World War II Allies Remember D-Day—National leaders and elderly veterans in June commemorated the 50th anniversary of the Allied landing in Normandy on June 6, 1944, which marked the beginning of the final phase of the struggle against Nazi Germany in World War II. Pres. and Mrs. Bill Clinton joined Queen Elizabeth II, the prime ministers of Britain, Canada, Australia, and New Zealand, and other dignitaries at Portsmouth, England, **June 5**, for a religious service at the site where the invasion forces embarked for France. More than 300 warships passed in review outside Portsmouth. The national leaders, **June 6**, participated in ceremonies at several landing sites in France. At the American cemetery near Omaha Beach, Clinton paid tribute to "the fathers we never knew, the uncles we never met, the friends who never returned, the heroes we can never repay."

O. J. Simpson Charged in 2 Murders—O. J. Simpson, one of the most successful running backs in the history of collegiate and professional football, was charged in June with the murders of his former wife Nicole Brown Simpson and a friend of hers, Ronald Goldman. At the Univ. of Southern California, Simpson had won the Heisman trophy, awarded annually to the best college football player. He had then starred with the Buffalo Bills and the San Francisco 49ers and had remained in the public eye as an actor and television sportscaster. O. J. and Nicole Simpson, who had 2 children, were divorced in 1992. After midnight on **June 13**, the 2 victims were found stabbed to death outside Nicole Simpson's condominium in the Brentwood section of Los Angeles. O. J. Simpson, who lived 2 miles away, had left late on the previous evening for a long-planned trip to Chicago. On being informed of his ex-wife's death, he returned to Los Angeles, **June 13**, and was questioned by police. Simpson, with his children, attended Nicole's funeral, **June 16**. On **June 17**, police charged Simpson with 2 counts of murder and said that he had reneged on an agreement to turn himself in. He had disappeared from a house in the San Fernando Valley where police went to pick him up. A friend, Robert Kardashian, read a letter from Simpson, **June 17**, in which the latter proclaimed his innocence. Later that day police found Simpson riding in a white Ford Bronco driven by a friend and former teammate, Al Cowlings, on an interstate highway south of Los Angeles. Cowlings, on a cellular phone, reported that Simpson was holding a gun to his head and threatening suicide. Helicopters filmed the 60-mile police chase, which was shown live on all major television networks to a large national audience. Large numbers of people gathered along the highways or at overpasses, many of them cheering for Simpson. Police allowed Simpson to return to his home, where he remained in the car for an hour before being taken into custody. Simpson, **June 20**, entered a plea of not guilty to the murders in Los Angeles Municipal Court. He was held without bail in the Los Angeles jail.

U.S. Hosts World Soccer Competition—For the first time ever, the U.S. played host in June and July to the World Cup soccer tournament. Soccer, or football as it was known elsewhere, was wildly popular in many countries but had never been a leading sport in the U.S. Competition, scheduled for 9 sites across the country opened, **June 17**. As host country, the U.S. had qualified automatically for the 24-team tournament. In a major upset, the U.S. defeated Colombia, 2-1, **June 22**. The winners' first goal was scored when a Colombian defender, Andres Escobar, unintentionally knocked the ball into his own net.

Homosexuals Mark Anniversary of Protest—Homosexuals from across the U.S. and from other countries came to New York City in June to commemorate the 25th anniversary of a protest demonstration that marked the beginning of the gay-rights movement. In June 1969, police had raided the Stonewall Inn, a gay bar in Greenwich Village, and patrons had resisted the incursion. As part of the anniversary observation, the Gay Games, an Olympic-style competition, opened, **June 18**, in New York. Some 500,000 spectators watched 11,000 athletes perform during the next week. In a parade, **June 26**, gays and their supporters carried a rainbow-colored flag one mile in length through the streets to a rally in Central Park attended by at least 100,000 people. The mood of celebration was shadowed by the concern over the still-expanding AIDS epidemic.

Prince Charles Admits Adultery—In a taped interview presented on British television, **June 29**, Prince Charles spoke candidly of his marriage to Diana, the Princess of Wales. He said he had been faithful to her until the marriage "became irretrievably broken down, us both having tried." He said that divorce, if it should occur, would not be an impediment to his becoming king. Although as king he would be the head of the Church of England, which opposed divorce, Charles said that the sovereign had to represent subjects of all faiths, not just Protestant Anglicans.

Skating Title Taken From Harding—The U.S. Figure Skating Association (USFSA), **June 30**, took its 1994 national championship away from Tonya Harding, who had previously pleaded guilty to a conspiracy charge related to an assault on her rival Nancy Kerrigan. After Kerrigan's injury, Harding had won the title in January. The USFSA concluded that Harding had "prior knowledge" of the incident. Harding also was banned from its ranks for life. Four men had admitted roles in the attack.

JULY

National

Important Economic Data Unchanged—The Commerce Dept. said, **July 1**, that the index of leading economic indicators had remained unchanged from April to May. The Labor Dept. reported, **July 8**, that the unemployment rate had held at 6.0% in June. A survey of business payrolls revealed, however, that nonfarm employment had increased by a surprisingly strong 379,000 in June. The department said, **July 12**, that the prices charged by producers for finished goods had also stayed level in June. The Labor Dept. said, **July 13**, that consumer prices had risen 0.3% in June. The Commerce Dept. said, **July 19**, that the trade deficit had increased slightly in May to $9.17 billion. The department said, **July 29**, that the gross domestic product had grown at an annual rate of 3.7% during the second quarter, up from a revised rate of 3.3% for the first quarter.

Clinton Signals Flexibility on Health Care—Pres. Bill Clinton appeared in July to back off from his pledge to veto any health-care bill that did not provide universal coverage. By **July 2**, 4 of the 5 congressional committees working on health-care reform had approved bills, but they varied in scope and method of financing. Democratic governors, **July 18**, endorsed universal coverage but declined to support requiring businesses to pay for most of their employees' health insurance, which Clinton favored. At the meeting of the National Governors' Association, **July 19**, Clinton said he could accept a compromise that would guarantee coverage to somewhere around 95% of the population. Some members of Congress who were pushing for universal coverage expressed dismay at Clinton's statement.

Senate Approves Supreme Court Nominee—The U.S. Senate in July approved Pres. Bill Clinton's nomination of federal judge Stephen Breyer to the U.S. Supreme Court. Earlier, **July 12-15**, the Senate Judiciary Committee had conducted hearings on the nomination, during which Breyer had declined to answer questions concerning how he would vote on specific issues likely to come before the Supreme Court. The committee, **July 19**, approved the nomination unanimously. The Senate, **July 29**, approved the nomination, 87-9. Breyer was sworn in, **Aug. 3**, as the 108th Supreme Court justice in a private ceremony at the Vermont home of Chief Justice William Rehnquist.

Human Errors Blamed in Copter Tragedy—A Defense Dept. report, **July 13**, blamed human errors for the downing, in April, of 2 U.S. helicopters over Iraq by 2 U.S. fighter jets. All 26 persons on the copters were killed. A fighter pilot sent an IFF (Identify Friend or Foe) message to the helicopters, but their frequencies were set for Turkey, not Iraq. The crew of a U.S. AWACS (Airborne Warning and Control System) plane picked up IFF signals from the copters but did not inform the fighter pilots. The lead fighter pilot saw the copters and concluded incorrectly that they were Russian-built Iraqi aircraft. The second fighter pilot was unable to identify the copters but gave a signal that the first pilot took as confirmation. Two minutes later, missiles from the first fighter brought down both helicopters. The Defense Dept. report said that the pilots had not been adequately trained to distinguish between U.S. and Iraqi helicopters.

Military College Told to Admit Woman—The Citadel, a state-financed military college in Charleston, SC, was ordered by a U.S. District Court judge in July to open its doors to a woman who had applied for admission. Since its founding in 1842, the school had never admitted women to its corps of cadets. Supporters of this policy had contended that only a single-sex school could preserve the traditions of male bonding and harsh discipline for which the Citadel was well known. In 1993, the application of Shannon Faulkner had been accepted before the school realized that she was not a male. After the Citadel withdrew its offer, Faulkner filed suit. Subsequently, a court order had allowed her to attend classes but not participate in cadet activities. Then, on **July 22**, Judge C. Weston Houck held that by excluding women the Citadel was in violation of the equal-protection provisions of the 14th Amendment. In upholding Faulkner, Houck also told the Citadel to come up with a plan for admitting more women. The school said it would appeal.

Committees Open Whitewater Hearings—The House Banking Committee, **July 26**, and the Senate Banking Committee, **July 29**, began their hearings into the Whitewater affair. Their principal focus related to contacts between the White House and Treasury Dept. officials at a time when the Resolution Trust Corp. was investigating a failed Arkansas savings and loan that had ties with then-Gov. Bill Clinton and Hillary Rodham Clinton. Roger Altman, the deputy Treasury secretary and a long-time friend of the Clintons, was also acting head of the RTC.

2 Shot to Death at Abortion Clinic—John Bayard Britton, a doctor who performed abortions, and James Barrett, an escort for Britton, were shot to death outside an abortion clinic in Pensacola, FL, **July 29**. Barrett's wife, June, was wounded slightly. In 1993, Dr. David Gunn had been shot to death at Pensacola's other abortion clinic. In the latest killings, police arrested, **July 29,** Paul Hill, an outspoken opponent of abortions who had said that killing a doctor who performed them was "justifiable homicide." Hill was charged, **July 30**, with 2 counts of first-degree murder and one count of attempted murder.

International

UN Authorizes Invasion of Haiti—The likelihood grew in July that the dispute over the government of Haiti would be resolved by force. As the number of people attempting to flee Haiti grew into the tens of thousands, Pres. Bill Clinton, **June 28**, opened a refugee processing station at the U.S. naval base at Guantánamo Bay, Cuba. The U.S., **July 5**, stopped accepting refugees and said that other countries would be asked to provide them with "safe havens." Panama, however, pulled out of a plan, **July 7**, under which it would have accepted up to 10,000 refugees. William Gray, Clinton's special adviser on Haiti, said, **July 7**, that 3 small Caribbean nations had agreed to accept refugees. Gray said that Haiti was becoming a major crisis and that the coup leaders who had ousted Pres. Jean-Bertrand Aristide in 1991 would not be allowed to prevent the restoration of democracy. Haiti, **July 11**, ordered human-rights monitors from the UN and the Organization of American States to leave the country. The UN Security Council, **July 31**, voted, 12-0, to authorize a U.S.-led force to invade Haiti, oust the coup leaders, and restore Aristide.

Israel, Jordan End State of War—Israel and Jordan in July formally ended their state of war. Earlier, on **July 1**, Yasir Arafat, chairman of the Palestine Liberation Organization, crossed from Egypt into the Gaza Strip, stepping onto Palestinian soil for the first time in 27 years. Addressing more than 100,000 people, Arafat hailed the Israeli-PLO peace process and urged Palestinians to work for a united and democratic Palestinian state with a capital in East Jerusalem. On **July 5**, in Jericho on the West Bank, he took the oath as head of the new Palestinian National Authority. Arafat then swore in 12 of the 19 people he had named to the PNA. In Paris, **July 6** and **7**, Arafat met with Israeli Prime Minister Yitzhak Rabin and Foreign Minister Shimon Peres to discuss the next steps toward Palestinian self-rule. Arafat and his wife took up permanent residence in the Gaza Strip, **July 12**. Palestinian workers, **July 17**, became annoyed by delays at an Israeli checkpoint. They threw rocks at Israeli soldiers, and Israelis and Palestinian police exchanged gunfire. Two people were killed and about 100 injured during day-long rioting. Palestinian militants shot and killed an Israeli soldier in the Gaza Strip, **July 19**. In Washington, DC, **July 25**, Rabin and King Hussein signed a declaration that ended the 46-year state of war between Israel and Jordan. The 2 leaders supported a "just, lasting and comprehensive peace between Israel and its neighbors." They both addressed Congress, **July 26**.

Rwanda Rebels Claim Victory—The Rwandan Patriotic Front, consisting mainly of members of the minority Tutsi ethnic group, claimed victory over the Hutu-run government in July. The UN Security Council, **July 1**, authorized a commission to investigate "acts of genocide" in Rwanda. French forces in Rwanda established, **July 4**, a security zone to protect refugees. The rebels, **July 4**, captured the nation's second largest city and occupied government installations in Kigali, the capital. On **July 5**, they agreed to respect the security zone, to which 600,000 refugees had fled. The Patriotic Front declared victory, **July 18**. Up to 500,000 people in Rwanda's population of 8 million had been killed during the fighting. Most were civilians slaughtered by the government forces. Up to 2 million had fled into Zaire. The UN, **July 22**, urged refugees to return home. Dysentery and cholera were taking a heavy toll of life among the refugees. Pres. Bill Clinton, **July 22**, ordered the Pentagon to mount a major relief effort. U.S. Army Engineers, **July 29**, began pumping fresh water from Lake Kivu to the refugees. Clinton, **July 29**, ordered U.S. troops to open the Kigali airport, and 200 U.S. military personnel arrived at the airport **July 31**.

Ex-President of Albania Convicted—Ramiz Alia, the last Communist president of Albania, was convicted, **July 2**, by a court in Tirana of abuse of power and the violation of citizens' rights. He was sentenced to 9 years in prison. Democratic forces had forced Alia from power in 1992, and he was arrested in 1993. Nine other former leaders of the Communist era had been convicted on similar charges.

Clinton Visits European Countries—Before and after

the "Group of 7" meeting in Naples, Pres. Bill Clinton visited other European countries. His trip to Latvia, **July 6**, was the first ever by an American president to the Baltic region. He met there with the presidents of Latvia, Estonia, and Lithuania. In Poland, **July 7**, Clinton addressed the parliament, pledging an increase in international aid, and he visited memorials to uprisings by Jews and others in 1943 and 1944 against Nazi rule. He met with Chancellor Helmut Kohl of Germany in Bonn, **July 10** and **11**, and addressed a large crowd at the Brandenburg Gate in Berlin, **July 12**.

North Korea's Pres. Kim Il Sung Dies—Pres. Kim Il Sung, 82, leader of North Korea since its founding in 1948, died, **July 8**, in Pyongyang, the capital. Though born in Pyongyang, Kim had spent much of his early life in Manchuria, where he studied and embraced Communist doctrine. He was forced into the Soviet Union by the invading Japanese in 1940 and remained there until 1945, when he returned to Korea and took control of the Communist Party with Soviet support. His attempt to seize South Korea in 1950 was ultimately thwarted by a U.S.-led international force. A personality cult had been built up around Kim, who was known as the Great Leader. Tensions on the Korean peninsula had grown in 1994 after Kim's regime refused UN inspectors access to nuclear-development sites. On **July 8**, however, North Korean and U.S. officials had begun talks in Geneva, but these were suspended after Kim died. Kim's death eliminated the historic summit meeting with South Korean Pres. Kim Young Sam, scheduled for later in July. In 1980, Kim Il Sung had designated his son, Kim Jong Il, as his successor, and on **July 13** the state radio confirmed that the younger Kim, about whom not much was known, had been named his father's sole successor. Kim's funeral was held **July 19**. Hundreds of thousands attended an outdoor service, **July 20**, at which top North Korean officials pledged their support to Kim Jong Il.

"Group of 7" Heads of Government Meet—The presidents and prime ministers of the leading industrialized nations, the "Group of 7," met in July in Naples. The U.S. dollar had been slumping against other currencies, and, on **July 8**, the first day of the summit, it dipped as low as 97.77 Japanese yen after Pres. Bill Clinton said that he would not seek to halt the dollar's decline for fear of blocking economic growth. The leaders, **July 9**, rejected Clinton's proposal to reduce tariffs beyond the cuts approved in the recently signed Uruguay Round of the General Agreement on Tariffs and Trade. In a communiqué, **July 9**, the leaders acknowledged that unemployment was too high in their countries and pledged actions to create jobs. Pres. Boris Yeltsin of Russia was once again a guest of the "7," and for the first time, **July 10**, he participated in the leaders' annual political discussion. During currency trading, **July 12**, the U.S. dollar fell to 96.60 yen, a post-World War II low.

Ukraine Elects New President—Ukraine chose a new president, **July 10**, when the challenger, Leonid Kuchma, edged out the incumbent president, Leonid Kravchuk, in a runoff election. Kuchma, who had called for a closer association with Russia, won overwhelmingly in Russian-speaking areas of the country. A decline in industrial production and high unemployment also hurt Kravchuk.

Court Opens Door for German Military—The Federal Constitutional Court, Germany's highest court, ruled, **July 12**, that Germany's armed forces could participate in international military missions providing that the lower house of parliament approved. The 1949 West German constitution had banned all military activities except those that related to collective security. The court's ruling related to a German role in UN miliary activities in Somalia, Yugoslavia, and Bosnia and Herzegovina.

Jews Are Targets in Bombing Attacks—A car bomb exploded in Buenos Aires, Argentina, **July 18**, killing some 100 people in or near a building that housed Jewish organizations. Another bomb exploded near the Israeli embassy in London, **July 26**, injuring a dozen people. A 3d bombing, **July 27**, at an Israeli fund-raising office in London, injured 5. In May, Muslim extremists had vowed retaliation for the kidnapping of a Muslim guerrilla leader by Israel.

Bosnian Serbs Reject Partition Plan—On **July 20**, the Bosnian Serb leadership rejected a plan backed by major countries that would have given them 49% of Bosnian territory. The Serbs held 72% of Bosnia and Herzegovina. The plan's authors—the U.S., Germany, Britain, France, and Russia—decided, **July 30**, to tighten economic sanctions on the Serb-dominated government in what remained of Yugoslavia.

Labour Party Chooses New Leader—Britain's opposition Labour Party, **July 21**, chose Tony Blair to succeed John Smith as its leader. Smith had died in May. Blair, 41, was the youngest leader the party had ever had. He was expected to continue his predecessor's policy of moving the party toward the political center.

General

Brazil Wins Soccer Title—Brazil in July won the first World Cup soccer competition ever held in the U.S. The sports world was stunned when, **July 2**, the Colombian player Andres Escobar was shot to death in Medellín, Colombia. Escobar had inadvertently deflected the ball into his own net, scoring a goal for the U.S., in a 2-1 loss by Colombia earlier in the tournament. Escobar's assailants reportedly rebuked him for contributing to his team's defeat. Brazil, **July 4**, eliminated the U.S. from contention, 1-0. The final game, played **July 17** in Pasadena, CA, between Brazil and Italy, was watched by 94,194 spectators and by 2 billion on television around the world. For the first time ever, a championship game was scoreless. Brazil won in the penalty kick round, 3-2.

Georgia Hard-Hit by Floods—Tropical storm Alberto brought heavy rains and flooding to parts of the South in July. The storm stalled over Georgia, **July 3**, after crossing Florida, when a high-pressure system to the east prevented further movement. Sixteen people died in Americus, GA, where 21.1 in of rainfall was reported, **July 7**. In Albany, the Flint River crested at 28 ft above flood stage, **July 10**. Water covered 1 million acres of farmland in the Southeast. Pres. Bill Clinton toured the area, **July 13**, and announced $66 million in federal aid. The death toll was put at 30 in Georgia, 1 in Alabama.

O. J. Simpson Faces Trial in Murders—O. J. Simpson was ordered in July to stand trial for the murders of his ex-wife and a friend of hers. At the pretrial hearing, **July 6**, 2 policemen testified that they had jumped a fence on O. J. Simpson's property on the night of the murders after a bloodstain was discovered on a van parked outside his estate. Los Angeles Municipal Court Judge Kathleen Kennedy-Powell, **July 7**, denied a motion by the defense to suppress evidence that police officers had obtained during their subsequent search. Kennedy-Powell, **July 8**, said there was "ample evidence to establish strong suspicion of the guilt" of Simpson, and she ordered that he stand trial on 2 counts of first-degree murder. At his arraignment, **July 22**, Simpson said he was "absolutely 100% not guilty."

Jupiter Struck by Fragments of Comet—In a dramatic event forecast by astronomers, up to 21 fragments of the Shoemaker-Levy 9 comet struck Jupiter, **July 16–22**. The U.S. Hubble Space Telescope and other space-based cameras recorded the scene. The impacts, at speeds of 130,000 mph, produced huge plumes of dust and gas and dark discolorations on the planet's surface. One fragment hit with a force of 250 million megatons of TNT.

Fires Rage in Western U.S.—High temperatures and dry conditions created an environment for forest fires in the western U.S. in July, and lightning set off blazes that burned 240,000 acres in 11 states. Fourteen firefighters died near Glenwood Springs, CO, **July 6**, when a gust of wind caused them to be surrounded by fire. Two firefighters and a pilot were killed, **July 12**, when a helicopter crashed in New Mexico.

AUGUST

National

Hopes for Health-Care Reform Fade—It became increasingly likely in August that Congress would not approve sweeping health-care reform in 1994. The House and Senate Democratic leadership, on **July 29** and **Aug. 2**, respectively, introduced health-care bills. The latter, introduced by Senate Majority Leader George Mitchell (D, ME), would cover 95% of Americans by the year 2000. The expenses would be borne by a cigarette tax and other taxes. Employers would be required to offer their employees a choice of health plans. Pres. Bill Clinton, who had previously backed coverage for all Americans, endorsed the Mitchell plan, **Aug. 3**. Republicans criticized the Mitchell plan for its emphasis on taxes and an increased bureaucracy. A bipartisan "mainstream coalition" in the Senate agreed, **Aug. 18**, on a plan that sought to cover 93% of Americans by 1999, while cutting $100 billion from the federal budget over 10 years. However, by the time Congress recessed, **Aug. 25**, it appeared likely that only limited health-reform measures, if any, were likely to pass in 1994.

New Whitewater Prosecutor Named—A panel of 3 federal judges named a new Whitewater prosecutor in August. Earlier, at separate hearings conducted by Senate and House committees, Treasury and White House officials contradicted one another about details concerning contacts they had when the Resolution Trust Corp. was investigating the failed Madison Guaranty Savings and Loan, linked to the Clintons. Jean Hanson, the Treasury Dept. general counsel, testified **Aug. 1** that she had contacted the White House at the request of Roger Altman, Treasury Dept. deputy secretary. The White House acknowledged, **Aug. 2**, that a file from the office of Deputy White House Counsel Vincent Foster had been kept at the White House for 5 days after he committed suicide in 1993. Altman, **Aug. 2** and **3**, denied that any testimony he had given in February was false. Treasury Sec. Lloyd Bentsen denied, **Aug. 3**, that he had any knowledge of contacts between the White House and his department on Madison. The federal judges, **Aug. 5**, named Kenneth Starr, solicitor general under Pres. George Bush, as independent prosecutor investigating Whitewater. He succeeded Robert Fiske, who had been appointed to investigate the case before the independent counsel law was renewed. The judges made the change because they concluded that Fiske was technically an appointee of the administration. Meanwhile, the hearings in Congress focused on why Altman, a friend of the Clintons, had taken so long to recuse himself from the Madison investigation. A number of members of Congress rebuked Altman and some of his aides for alleged poor judgment and lack of candor. Altman submitted his resignation, **Aug. 17**, and Hanson did likewise, **Aug. 18**. The federal judges who had appointed Starr declined, **Aug. 18**, to reconsider their action; some Democrats had complained that Starr, a conservative Republican, could not be impartial.

Job Growth Remains Strong—The Commerce Dept. said, **Aug. 3**, that the index of leading economic indicators had advanced 0.2% in June. The Labor Dept. reported, **Aug. 5**, that 259,000 nonfarm jobs were created in July, following an even larger revised total for June, 356,000. These totals overshadowed the unemployment rate actually edging upward 0.1% in July to 6.1%. The department said, **Aug. 12**, that consumer prices rose 0.3% in July. As an anti-inflation move, the Federal Reserve Board, **Aug. 16**, increased 2 short-term interest rates, the federal funds rate and the discount rate. The Commerce Dept. said, **Aug. 18**, that the trade deficit in goods and services had been $9.37 billion in June. The department reported, **Aug. 31**, that the index of leading economic indicators was unchanged in July.

Arkansas Executes 3 on Same Day—The state of Arkansas, **Aug. 3**, executed 3 men by lethal injection on the same evening at a state prison in Varner. All 3 were convicted of killing the same man in 1981. A 4th man was convicted in the case, but his death sentence was commuted to life in prison. Hoyt Clines, Darryl Richley, and James Holmes were executed in that order, about an hour apart.

Democratic Chairman to Resign—The chairman of the Democratic National Committee, David Wilhelm, announced, **Aug. 9**, that he would resign after the November elections. In scattered elections in 1993 and 1994, the Democrats had suffered a string of defeats, and polls indicated the likelihood of big Republican gains in November. Wilhelm announced that former Rep. Tony Coelho (D, CA) had joined the committee as its chief strategist for the campaign.

Clinton Seeks Dismissal of Suit—In a brief filed in Little Rock, AR, **Aug. 10**, lawyers for Pres. Bill Clinton sought dismissal, for the duration of his presidency, of a lawsuit brought against him by Paula Jones, a former Arkansas state employee. The suit, which charged Clinton with sexual harassment, was before the federal district court.

Congress Approves Crime Bill—After a fierce conflict in both houses, Congress in August approved a crime bill supported by the Clinton administration. Earlier, the Senate and the House had approved different versions of the bill, which then went to a conference committee. The Senate-House conferees, **July 28**, approved a $30.2 billion bill that included funds to hire 100,000 police officers over 6 years and build new state prisons. The cost of the bill would be covered by the elimination of 250,000 federal jobs over 6 years. The federal death penalty would be expanded to apply to about 60 crimes, and 19 kinds of semiautomatic assault weapons would be banned. The bill also contained the popular "3 strikes and you're out" provision that would send to prison for life anyone convicted of a federal felony who had 2 other serious felony convictions. Many Republicans and some conservative Democrats opposed the weapons ban, and they also ridiculed some social programs, including midnight basketball games in high-crime areas. Some members of the Congressional Black Caucus opposed the expansion of the death penalty and the dropping from the bill of a provision that would let death-row prisoners use statistics to challenge their sentences as discriminatory. The House defeated, **Aug. 11**, the conference report, 225-210. Pres. Bill Clinton then accepted compromises to reverse the outcome. The money allocated for community programs was sharply reduced. Provisions were added allowing accusations of past sexual offenses to be introduced in federal criminal trials and requiring that a community be notified when a convicted sex offender moved there. The House approved the revised version, 235-195, on **Aug. 21**. Senate Republicans then sought to block the bill through parliamentary maneuvering, but the effort failed, and the Senate gave its approval, 61-38, on **Aug. 25**. The passage of the bill was regarded as one of Clinton's biggest victories in Congress.

NAACP Removes Executive Director—The board of directors of the National Association for the Advancement of Colored People dismissed its executive director in August. The leader, Benjamin Chavis, had been elected to his post in April 1993. He had been criticized for his friendship with Louis Farrakhan, leader of the Nation of Islam, whom some regarded as racist and anti-Semitic, and for his lack of success in improving the NAACP's difficult financial situation. Chavis had also reportedly agreed to pay more than $330,000 of the organization's money to a former employee who had threatened to file a sex-discrimination suit against him. The directors removed Chavis, **Aug. 20**, and named Earl Shinhoster as his interim replacement. Chavis, **Aug. 22**, sought a temporary restraining order to prevent his removal, but a Washington, DC, superior court denied, **Aug. 24**, the request.

International

Haiti Declares State of Siege—Haiti's de facto president, Emile Jonassaint, responding to a UN Security Council resolution authorizing an invasion of Haiti, declared, **Aug. 1**, that his country was under a state of siege. Constitutional guarantees were suspended and civilian authority transferred to the military. Pres. Bill Clinton said, **Aug. 3**, that there were no immediate plans to invade Haiti. After a supporter of exiled Pres. Jean-Bertrand Aristide was shot to death, **Aug. 28**, in Port-au-Prince, the U.S. State Dept. said, **Aug. 29**, that the incident would "strengthen our resolve to rid Haiti" of the perpetrators. The UN Security Council, **Aug. 30**, condemned the violations of international law and human rights by the Haitian government.

Some Refugees Return to Rwanda—Rwanda's new coalition government said, **Aug. 2**, that it would prosecute those responsible for the massacres occurring in recent months. By **Aug. 3**, 90,000 refugees had returned to Rwanda from Zaire, but the number returning declined thereafter under pressure from Hutu leaders. It was estimated, **Aug. 8**, that 40,000 refugees had died, mostly of cholera and dysentery, in the Zairian camps. The last French soldiers withdrew from the "safe zone" in southwestern Rwanda, **Aug. 21**. Forces of the victorious Rwandan Patriotic Front had said they would occupy the zone. As of **Aug. 24**, about 100,000 of the 2.5 million Rwandan refugees had returned home.

NATO Attacks Bosnian Serbs Again—U.S. jets under NATO command attacked a Bosnian Serb position again in August. Earlier, on **Aug. 2**, Serbian Pres. Slobodan Milosevic threatened to break off relations with the Bosnian Serbs if they did not accept a peace plan put forward by the U.S. and European nations. The Bosnian Serbs, however, rejected the plan again, **Aug. 3**, and said a referendum would be held on it. Milosevic said, **Aug. 4**, that Yugoslavia (Serbia and Montenegro) was ending economic and political relations with the Bosnian Serb republic. On **Aug. 5**, Bosnian Serbs seized vehicles and an anti-aircraft gun from a UN weapons depot near Sarajevo. This violation of the exclusion zone near the capital brought a quick response from 2 U.S. ground-attack jets, which destroyed a Bosnian Serb antitank vehicle south of Sarajevo. The Bosnian Serbs returned, **Aug. 6**, what they had seized **Aug. 5**. Meanwhile, the army of the predominantly Muslim Bosnian government was gaining ground on the military fronts. On **Aug. 27-28**, by a reported 90% majority, Bosnian Serb voters rejected the international peace plan.

U.S. Acts to Halt Cuban Exodus—Cubans anxious to escape from the Castro regime created a crisis in Cuban-American relations in August. Beginning in late July, Cubans attempted in large numbers to reach the U.S. by water. Opponents of Castro clashed with police in Havana, **Aug. 5**. Pres. Fidel Castro, **Aug. 5**, blamed the unrest on U.S. radio broadcasts to the island. He warned that the government might stop putting obstacles in the way of those who sought to leave. Gov. Lawton Chiles (D) of Florida pressed the Clinton administration to do something about the prospective flood of immigrants from Cuba. Pres. Bill Clinton announced, **Aug. 19**, that he was ending the 28-year U.S. policy of allowing Cuban refugees to take up U.S. residence if they reached the country. He said that refugees would now be picked up at sea and put in holding camps at the U.S. base at Guantánamo Bay, Cuba, or in the U.S. Clinton deployed 2 warships to waters between the U.S. and Cuba. Within a week after Clinton's announcement, more than 7,000 would-be refugees were intercepted at sea.

U.S., North Korea Reach Agreement—Negotiators for the U.S. and North Korea signed, **Aug. 13**, an agreement in Geneva in which North Korea agreed to allow UN monitors to inspect a secret nuclear laboratory. Western nations believed that North Korea had been planning to build nuclear weapons. Talks leading to the agreement had been broken off in July after the death of Pres. Kim Il Sung. In other terms of the August accord, North Korea agreed not to reprocess any more spent fuel rods from nuclear reactors, a process used to extract plutonium that could be utilized in weapons, and agreed not to withdraw from the Nuclear Nonproliferation Treaty; the U.S. and North Korea would move toward full diplomatic relations; and the U.S. would help North Korea build light-water nuclear reactors, a less accessible source of weapons-grade plutonium. South Korean Pres. Kim Young Sam said, **Aug. 15**, that his government would offer North Korea aid to build the light-water reactors.

Notorious Terrorist "Carlos" Captured—The veteran international terrorist Ilich Ramirez Sanchez, known as "Carlos" and "the Jackal," was seized in Sudan, **Aug. 14**. Born in Venezuela, Carlos had become a legend in the 1970s and 1980s, and his name was linked with many acts of violence, some of which he had nothing to do with. In 1975, he led a team representing the Popular Front for the Liberation of Palestine that seized 11 oil ministers of petroleum-exporting countries and held them hostage. Carlos, who was given sanctuary by several Communist countries, was tried in absentia in 1992 in France and convicted of murders committed there. He had also been sought by France in connection with bombings at transportation stations that killed 11 people. French Interior Minister Charles Pasqua said, **Aug. 15**, that Carlos had claimed to have killed 83 people. He was extradited to France, **Aug. 15**.

Ruling Party Candidate Wins in Mexico—Mexico elected a president on **Aug. 21**, and the candidate of the Institutional Revolutionary Party (PRI) prevailed again, as in every election since 1929. The winner, Ernesto Zedillo Ponce de Leon, had become his party's candidate after the original nominee, Luis Donaldo Colosio Murrieta, was assassinated in March. Zedillo won 50% of the vote, lowest ever for a PRI candidate. Diego Fernandez de Cevallos of the National Action Party received 27%, and Cuauhtemoc Cardenas of the Democratic Revolutionary Party, 17%. The PRI also maintained majorities in both houses of the national legislature. Fraud had marred the 1988 presidential election, but the latest contest was believed to be relatively clean.

Israel, PLO Sign New Accord—In an agreement signed, **Aug. 29**, by Israel and the Palestine Liberation Organization, Israel agreed to shift administrative functions throughout the West Bank to the Palestinian National Authority. The PNA, which would assume responsibilities in the areas of health, welfare, education, tourism, and taxation, promised to establish an effective means of collecting taxes.

IRA Announces a Cease-Fire—Six months of mostly secret negotiations culminated, **Aug. 31**, in a cease-fire declaration by the Irish Republican Army. The IRA, which had struggled for decades to end British rule in Northern Ireland, asserted in a statement that it was now time to seek a political solution. British Prime Minister John Major said, **Aug. 31**, that his government had made no concessions to the IRA. In the past 25 years, more than 3,000 persons had been killed as a result of the conflict, in both Northern Ireland and Britain. Protestant extremists were responsible for many of the deaths.

General

Baseball Players Strike—Major league baseball players went on strike, following the conclusion of the **Aug. 11** games. The principal issue was the attempt by owners to impose a cap on the teams' overall salary levels. A 4-year collective bargaining agreement had expired in 1993, and negotiations had continued since then between the owners and the Major League Baseball Players' Association. The owners had proposed to give the players 50% of the collective revenue of the 28 teams. The players currently got about 58%. Players wanted to raise the minimum salary to at least $175,000 from the current $109,000. The strike interrupted an exciting season during which several players were pursuing records or other major achievements.

Concert Marks Woodstock's 25th Year—A concert was held in Saugerties, NY, **Aug. 12-14**, to mark the 25th anniversary of the Woodstock Music and Art Fair concert in Bethel, NY, in 1969. That concert has been considered one of the most important cultural events in recent U.S. history. Some 500,000 had turned out in 1969, and attendance at Saugerties was put at up to 350,000. As in 1969, rain came down, turning the grounds into a mess. Some performers from 1969, including Joe Cocker and Crosby, Stills and Nash, appeared again at the 1994 concert. The concert was held on an 840-acre farm.

Lockheed, Martin Marietta Merge—The Lockheed and Martin Marietta corporations agreed, **Aug. 30**, to a merger that would create the largest U.S. defense contractor. The company would be called Lockheed Martin. The 2 existing companies had annual sales of nearly $23 billion.

SEPTEMBER

National

Jobless Rate Holds Steady—The Labor Dept. reported, **Sept. 2**, that the unemployment rate had remained unchanged at 6.1% in August. The department said, **Sept. 9**, that prices charged by producers for finished goods had risen 0.6% in August. It reported, **Sept. 13**, that consumer prices were up 0.3% in August. The Commerce Dept. reported, **Sept. 20**, that the merchandise trade deficit in July—$10.99 billion—was the second highest ever. In its final revision, the department said, **Sept. 29**, that the U.S. gross domestic product had grown at an annual rate of 4.1% in the second quarter of 1994, compared with an annual rate of 3.3% percent in the first quarter.

Primary Elections Bring More Surprises—The 1994 primary election season neared its conclusion in September, amid more unexpected results. On **Sept. 8**, in Florida, Jeb Bush, son of former President George Bush, ran well ahead in the voting to select the Republican opponent for incumbent Democratic Gov. Lawton Chiles. Although Bush did not quite get a majority, the second-place finisher withdrew, eliminating the need for a runoff and giving the nomination to Bush. Another son of the former president, George W. Bush, Jr., had already won the Republican nomination for governor of Texas. In a major comeback, former Washington, DC, Mayor Marion Barry won, **Sept. 13**, the Democratic nomination for mayor and thus became a strong favorite to get his old job back in the November election. The incumbent mayor, Sharon Pratt Kelly, finished third. Barry was released from prison in 1992 after a misdemeanor conviction for possession of crack cocaine. He said that his recovery from addiction would help him become a role model. On **Sept. 13**, another Democratic incumbent, Rhode Island's Gov. Bruce Sundlun, was defeated for renomination, and a Republican member of Congress, David Levy (NY) lost in another primary. Also on **Sept. 13,** in Minnesota, Gov. Arne Carlson, whose nomination bid had been rejected by the Republican state convention in favor of Allen Quist, a conservative, rebounded to win the GOP primary. On **Sept. 15**, former Gov. L. Douglas Wilder, trailing in the polls, dropped out of the contest for governor of Virginia, leaving 3 men still running there. On **Sept. 20,** House Speaker Tom Foley (D, WA) got only 35% of the vote in an open primary, although that was enough to get him into the November general election. Rep. Mike Synar (D, OK), whose support of Pres. Bill Clinton, gun control, and higher tobacco taxes had antagonized conservatives, lost a primary election to an unknown.

Charges Filed in "Friendly Fire" Accident—The Department of Defense said, **Sept. 8**, that a pilot, Lt. Col. Randy May, had been charged with 26 counts of negligent homicide in connection with the accidental downing of 2 U.S. helicopters over Iraq in April. Investigators had announced in July that errors by a number of U.S. airmen had contributed to the tragedy. May had flown one of the 2 fighter planes involved in the downing. The Air Force also filed charges against 5 crew members on an AWACS plane involved in the accident.

Pilot Crashes Plane at White House—A pilot crashed his small plane on the White House lawn, **Sept. 12**, killing himself and creating an alarm over presidential security. The pilot, Frank Corder, was an unemployed truck driver who had been treated for alcoholism and who was described as despondent by his family. He had taken off in a Cessna from Aberdeen, MD, and crash-landed on the South Lawn at 1:49 AM. The skidding plane struck the White House below Pres. Bill Clinton's second-floor bedroom. The Clinton family was staying at Blair House, across the street, while the White House was undergoing repairs. Air space above the White House was in a restricted zone and was monitored from National Airport, outside Washington, DC. Corder's route had been recorded on radar, but traffic controllers apparently had not been watching that screen.

Alaska Jury Orders Exxon to Pay $5 Billion—The Exxon Corp., **Sept. 16**, was hit with the 2d largest assessment for punitive damages ever directed at one corporation, and the largest ever in a pollution case. A Federal court jury in Anchorage ordered the company to pay $5 billion to more than 34,000 fishermen and natives whose livelihoods had been impacted by the oil spill from the *Exxon Valdez* in 1989. The jury ordered Joseph Hazelwood, captain of the vessel, to pay $5,000 in punitive damages. Exxon and Hazelwood plan to appeal the verdict.

Press Secretary Survives White House Reshuffle—The latest White House personnel realignment proved less drastic than some had anticipated, when Dee Dee Myers, the presidential press secretary, not only kept her job but was also named an assistant to the president. Chief of Staff Leon Panetta announced, **Sept. 23**, changes that he said were intended to bring "greater discipline" to the White House. Myers reportedly appealed directly to Pres. Bill Clinton to save her job. In another change, Mark Gearan stepped down as communications director and became an assistant to Panetta.

No CIA Heads Roll in Ames Scandal—James Woolsey, director of the Central Intelligence Agency, said in September that no CIA officials would be dismissed as a result of the spy scandal involving Aldrich Ames. News stories said, **Sept. 24**, that Ames had exposed 55 secret U.S. and allied operations to the Soviet Union and Russia. CIA Inspector General Frederick Hitz, the source of that information, blamed Ames's success in betraying his country to "almost complete indifference of senior CIA supervisors." Woolsey, **Sept. 28**, told the House Intelligence Committee that letters of reprimand would be sent to 11 present and retired CIA officers who bore indirect responsibility for Ames's actions, but he said that no one would be demoted or dismissed. Many members of Congress criticized the letters of reprimand as too mild a discipline.

Health-Care Reform Fails in Congress—Senate Majority Leader George Mitchell (D, ME) abandoned, **Sept. 26**, his effort to get a health-care reform bill through the Senate in 1994. Mitchell blamed the insurance industry and the Republican leadership for the failure of the reform effort. Senate Minority Leader Bob Dole (R, KS) said the

American people had "feared an overdose of government control." Pres. Bill Clinton's original proposal, which had included universal health-insurance coverage, had gradually lost support as a result of opposition from business and from the insurance and medical industries.

International

China and Russia Sign Agreements—Pres. Jiang Zemin of China visited Moscow in September and signed several agreements with Pres. Boris Yeltsin of Russia. No Chinese head of state had visited Moscow since 1957. In one agreement signed **Sept. 3**, the 2 presidents pledged to reduce the number of troops each had massed along their nations' common border. They also promised not to aim nuclear weapons at each other.

Irish Prime Minister, IRA Leader Meet—On **Sept. 6**, 6 days after the Irish Republican Army had declared a truce, Irish Prime Minister Albert Reynolds met with Gerry Adams, president of Sinn Fein, the IRA's political wing. They declared that their goal was a lasting agreement on the future of Northern Ireland that all parties could accept. British Prime Minister John Major met, **Sept. 6**, with Ian Paisley, a Protestant militant from Northern Ireland. The meeting ended when Paisley declined to accept Major's assurance that no secret deal had been struck with the IRA.

Haitian Junta Yields to U.S. Show of Force—The leaders of the military junta in Haiti, facing the imminent reality of a U.S. armed invasion, agreed in September to surrender power to Jean-Bertrand Aristide, whom they had ousted from the presidency in 1991. U.S. Secretary of State Warren Christopher declared, **Sept. 7**, that "one way or another" the junta would be unseated. Amid evidence of a U.S. military buildup, Pres. Bill Clinton, denounced, **Sept. 15**, on television the military leaders as brutal and told them to "leave now" or be forced out. Clinton sent, **Sept. 17**, a 3-man delegation, headed by former Pres. Jimmy Carter, to Haiti in a final effort to negotiate a transfer of authority. Sen. Sam Nunn (D, GA) and Gen. Colin Powell (ret.), former chairman of the Joint Chiefs of Staff, were the other 2 members of the delegation. The Americans met with Lt. Gen. Raoul Cedras, the junta leader; Brig. Gen. Philippe Biamby, the military chief of staff; and the president installed by the junta, Emile Jonassaint. Their discussions were inconclusive until the Haitians learned that U.S. airborne forces were actually en route to the Caribbean nation. Powell notified Clinton on the afternoon of **Sept. 18**, 9 hours before the invasion was to begin, that the junta would step down by Oct. 15 in favor of Aristide in return for the enactment of a general amnesty by the Haitian parliament. It was also agreed that the UN economic embargo and sanctions would be lifted. The terms did not avert the arrival of the U.S. military. On **Sept. 19**, the first 3,000 U.S. troops entered Port-au-Prince, the capital, and 1,800 landed, **Sept. 20**, at Cap-Haitien. They met no resistance and were greeted enthusiastically by thousands of Aristide supporters. Under orders not to intervene, Americans watched while Haitian military personnel and police assaulted the pro-democracy demonstrators. Clinton said, **Sept. 21**, that such violence would not be tolerated. In a clash, **Sept. 24**, with pro-junta forces, U.S. Marines killed 10 Haitians in Cap-Haitien. Addressing the UN General Assembly, **Sept. 26**, Clinton announced that the U.S. would lift most of its unilateral sanctions against Haiti. U.S. forces took control, **Sept. 27**, of the parliament building and began paying Haitians to turn in guns in order to reduce the firepower on the streets. By **Sept. 28**, 15,679 American military personnel were deployed in Haiti. The parliament convened **Sept. 28**, with Aristide supporters divided over the issue of granting amnesty. On **Sept. 29** and **30**, supporters of the junta killed 13 pro-Aristide demonstrators.

U.S., Cuba Reach Refugee Agreement—U.S.-Cuban negotiations opened in New York City in September on the refugee issue. An agreement signed **Sept. 9** provided that the U.S. would accept a minimum of 20,000 refugees a year, and Cuba agreed to attempt to discourage its citizens from fleeing to the U.S. on rafts and other vessels. Pres. Fidel Castro of Cuba announced, **Sept. 9**, that Cubans would have until Sept. 13 to remove rafts from Cuban beaches. Under the agreement, 30,000 refugees now at the U.S. base at Guantánamo Bay, Cuba, or in Panama could stay where they were or return to Cuba. They could apply for a U.S. visa only from Cuba. The U.S. made no concession on ending its economic embargo of Cuba.

UN Lifts Some Yugoslav Sanctions—Responding to Pres. Slobodan Milosevic's decision to cut off most supplies to the Bosnian Serbs, the UN Security Council, **Sept. 23**, voted, 11-2, to lift some sanctions it had imposed on Yugoslavia. Milosevic had also supported the international plan for the partition of Bosnia and Herzegovina and had agreed to allow international observers along the Yugoslav-Bosnian border.

Yeltsin Visits U.S.—Pres. Boris Yeltsin of Russia, in an address to the UN General Assembly in New York City, **Sept. 26**, defended Russia's right to maintain troops in some former Soviet republics. He met with Pres. Bill Clinton in Washington, DC, **Sept. 27** and **28**. They agreed to speed up implementation of the 2d Strategic Arms Reduction Treaty.

General

Population Stability Is Conference's Goal—A broad plan aimed at stabilizing the world's population was approved in September at the 3d UN International Conference on Population and Development, held in Cairo, Egypt. The Vatican had strongly criticized draft language on abortion and sexuality, and some Muslim nations objected on religious grounds to the emphasis on the status and rights of women. The document that the conference approved, **Sept. 13**, declared that the use of contraceptives as well as "gender equity and the empowerment of women" were the primary means of controlling population. The text on abortion was revised and included the assertion, "In no case should abortion be promoted as a method of family planning." All 179 delegations present endorsed the draft plan by consensus, although the Vatican and some 20 other countries declared their reservations.

Baseball's World Series Canceled—For the first time since 1904, there would be no World Series champion in baseball in 1994. On **Sept. 14**, Allan H. (Bud) Selig, the acting major league baseball commissioner, announced that the remainder of the regular season, the playoffs, and the World Series would be canceled because of the strike by players. He said that 26 of 28 team owners had signed a statement blaming intransigence by the players' union for the strike. Losses to the teams could run to $500 million or more, with the income lost by players running about half of that. The players had refused to accept a salary cap desired by the owners, and negotiations since the strike began in August had proved unsuccessful

Gene Related to Breast Cancer Found—A team of scientists from several U.S. and Canadian institutions reported, **Sept. 14**, that they had found a gene believed responsible for almost half of all breast cancer cases linked to heredity. This would represent 2% to 5% of all cases. Women having a defective form of the gene faced a high risk of developing breast cancer, which was the 2d leading cause of death by cancer among women.

Jury Selection Begins in Simpson Trial—The trial of O. J. Simpson on 2 counts of murder got underway officially, **Sept. 26**, in Los Angeles. The first phase would be the selection of 12 jurors and 8 alternates. The process was anticipated to be protracted because of the difficulty of finding men and women not already familiar with the case.

OCTOBER

National

Louisiana Reelects All 7 in House—A supposed national tide against incumbents failed to materialize in Louisiana on **Oct. 1**. In open primaries, all 7 members of the U.S. House delegation from Louisiana, 4 Democrats and 3 Republicans, won a majority and therefore would not be required to run again in the November general election. First Lady Hillary Rodham Clinton campaigned, **Oct. 1**, in Florida, in support of her brother, Hugh Rodham, a candidate for the Democratic nomination for the U.S. Senate. Rodham won a runoff, **Oct. 4**, and would oppose incumbent Sen. Connie Mack (R) in November. The final weeks of the fall campaign were enlivened by some unexpected endorsements. On **Oct. 21**, former Democratic Gov. L. Douglas Wilder of Virginia endorsed his long-time bitter intraparty rival, Sen. Charles Robb, who was seeking reelection in a tight contest with Oliver North. On **Oct. 24**, Rudolph Giuliani, the Republican mayor of New York City, endorsed Gov. Mario Cuomo, a Democrat, for reelection. Mayor Richard Riordan of Los Angeles, a Republican, announced, **Oct. 30**, that he was supporting Sen. Dianne Feinstein, a Democrat, for reelection.

Under Investigation, Secretary Espy Resigns—Agriculture Secretary Mike Espy announced his resignation, **Oct. 3**, effective at the end of the year. An independent counsel and the Agriculture Department's inspector general's office were investigating gifts that Espy had accepted. These included travel, accommodations, and tickets from Tyson Foods, Inc., an Arkansas company that was the largest U.S. supplier of poultry. Espy's girlfriend had also received an academic scholarship from Tyson. Espy had been accused of delaying implementation of Agriculture Dept. rules for poultry inspection. Espy denied violating any laws or ethics rules but admitted he had been careless.

Downtrend in Unemployment Continues—The Labor Dept. reported, **Oct. 7**, that the unemployment rate had inched down again, to 5.9% in September. The department said, **Oct. 13**, that prices charged by producers for finished goods had plunged 0.5% in September. It reported, **Oct. 14**, that consumer prices had risen 0.2% in September. The Commerce Dept. reported, **Oct. 28**, that the gross domestic product had grown 3.4% at an annual rate during the 3d quarter (the figure was subject to revision).

Congress Ends Session in Gridlock—The regular 1994 session of the 103d Congress ended, **Oct. 8**, amid acrimony as bills failed in the face of Republican filibusters. GOP senators, sometimes supported by conservative Democrats, had made use of filibusters and other delaying tactics to prevent adoption of bills that appeared to have majority approval, acting in the apparent belief that they would be in a stronger position to influence legislation after the November election. A lobbying-reform bill that would have barred most gifts from lobbyists to members of Congress fell by the wayside, **Oct. 7**, as did a bill to restrict spending in congressional campaigns and special-interest contributions to campaigns. The latter bill would have provided some public matching funds. Congress also abandoned changes in the 1872 Mining Act that would have required companies to pay royalties and comply with new environmental standards. Changes in the Superfund—which provided money to clean up hazardous-waste sites—to deal with rising litigation costs were also thwarted. An effort to reform the Safe Drinking Water Act also failed, **Oct. 7**.

Congress Approves California Desert Bill—The California Desert Protection Bill barely survived a Republican filibuster in the Senate, **Oct. 8**. As previously approved by a Senate-House conference committee and then by the House, the bill provided for the upgrading and expansion of Death Valley and Joshua Tree national monuments to national park status, as well as the creation of the Mojave National Preserve and several large wilderness areas in the desert. Senate Republicans then sought to filibuster the bill to death, but several Democrats who had left Washington as the congressional session wound down flew back to the capital to join in a 68-23 vote to impose cloture. The bill was then passed. Affecting 6 million acres, the legislation was the largest land-conservation bill ever enacted for the U.S. outside Alaska.

Colorado's Anti-Gay Law Struck Down—The Colorado Supreme Court, **Oct. 11**, struck down a law, Amendment 2, approved by the state's voters in 1992 that forbade local governments from enacting laws protecting homosexuals from discrimination in employment and housing. Subject to legal challenge from the time it was enacted, Amendment 2 had not gone into effect, and it had provoked an economic boycott against the state. The court's 6-1 majority found that the law denied gays equal participation in the political process and that it violated the equal protection clauses of the state and federal constitutions.

Mrs. Ames Sentenced in Spying Case—Rosario Ames, the wife of confessed spy Aldrich Ames, was sentenced, **Oct. 21**, in a federal district court to 63 months in prison for her role in collaborating with her husband.

Gunman Shoots at White House—A resident of Colorado Springs was seized, **Oct. 29**, after he sprayed the White House with bullets from an assault rifle. Pres. Bill Clinton was inside at the time, watching a football game on television. No one was injured. The suspect, Francisco Duran, was overpowered by bystanders. He had fired from the sidewalk alongside Pennsylvania Ave. Duran was charged, **Oct. 31**, with possession of a firearm as a convicted felon, destruction of federal property, assaulting a federal officer, and using a firearm in the commission of a violent crime.

International

Aristide Reclaims Presidency of Haiti—Three years after he was ousted from the presidency in a military coup, Jean-Bertrand Aristide returned in triumph to Haiti in October and assumed his office again. Earlier, responding to the murder of 16 civilians in late September, U.S. troops raided, **Oct. 3**, the headquarters in Port-au-Prince of a paramilitary group that had been linked to the killings of hundreds of Aristide supporters in the past 3 years. Forty people were detained, as were 75 in a similar raid in Cap-Haitien. Lt. Col. Joseph Michel François, chief of police in Port-au-Prince and leader of the group of enlisted men who had overthrown Aristide in 1991, left Haiti for the Dominican Republic, **Oct. 4**. The National Assembly, **Oct. 7**, completed action on a bill that would allow Aristide to pardon those accused of political offenses, but this option was not extended to murder and other human rights abuses. Thus, the general amnesty visualized in the accord reached in September between Haitian and U.S. negotiators did not materialize. Lt. Gen. Raoul Cedras, commander in chief of the Haitian armed forces, formally resigned **Oct. 10**. His chief aide, Brig. Gen. Philippe Biamby, had resigned **Oct. 8**. The 2 men chose to go into exile, and they and 14 family members arrived, **Oct. 13**, in Panama on a plane chartered by the U.S. military. Another plane carried 23 more relatives and friends to the U.S. The White House announced that some 600 military leaders in the Cedras regime would gain access to $79 million in frozen U.S. bank accounts. At the White House, **Oct. 14**, Aristide thanked Pres. Bill Clinton for his support in ousting the junta. Returning to Haiti, **Oct. 15**, Aristide received an emotional welcome from throngs of celebrating supporters. In an address, he pledged "no to violence, no to vengeance, yes to reconciliation."

Economist Elected President of Brazil—Fernando Enrique Cardoso, the finance minister who had received much of the credit for curbing his country's runaway inflation, was elected president of Brazil, **Oct. 3**. Once barred from teaching by the military regime then in power, Cardoso then co-wrote a book that blamed Brazil's economic underdevelopment on its dependence on capital and technology from other nations. Returning to Brazilian politics, he served in parliament and then as foreign minister and as finance minister. In the last position he developed an anti-inflation plan that proved highly successful in the months before the election.

Mandela Visits U.S.—Pres. Nelson Mandela of South Africa addressed the UN General Assembly, **Oct. 3**, and then met with Pres. Bill Clinton, **Oct. 4** and **5**. During his U.S. visit, Mandela stressed the need for business investment in South Africa. Clinton announced, **Oct. 5**, a program of aid that included funds for southern Africa, including South Africa, to aid small and medium-size businesses. He also pledged money for health care and electrification. Mandela addressed a joint session of Congress, **Oct. 6.**

U.S. Confronts Iraq Again in Gulf—Pres. Bill Clinton announced, **Oct. 7**, that he was sending the U.S. Navy and Marines to the Persian Gulf area in response to an Iraqi military buildup along the Iraq-Kuwait border. Tensions had not been so high in the region since allied forces had pushed the Iraqis out of Kuwait in 1991. With Army troops also being deployed, the U.S. personnel commitment stood at 36,000 by **Oct. 9**. In a televised address, **Oct. 10**, Clinton said that Pres. Saddam Hussein of Iraq could not be trusted and that economic sanctions against Iraq would not be lifted until Iraq complied fully with UN resolutions. The Pentagon reported, **Oct. 11** and **12**, that the Iraqis were pulling back from the border. The 6 countries in the Gulf Cooperation Council—Bahrain, Kuwait, Oman, Qatar, Saudi Arabia, and the United Arab Emirates—agreed, **Oct. 12**, to pay much of the cost for the deployment of the U.S. forces. Defense Sec. William Perry said, **Oct. 15**, in Kuwait, that the immediate danger of war seemed over. During his Middle East trip, Clinton visited U.S. troops in Kuwait, **Oct. 28**.

Ulster Protestants Announce Cease-Fire—Another possible step toward peace in Ulster (Northern Ireland) took place in October when Protestant paramilitaries announced a cease-fire. The Irish Republican Army had announced a cease-fire in August. At a news conference, **Oct. 13**, Augustus Spence, a Protestant leader who had been imprisoned for 19 years for killing a Catholic bartender in 1966, read a statement on behalf of the Combined Loyalist Military Command, an umbrella military organization. The statement expressed "abject and true remorse" to the families of "innocent victims" of the conflict in Northern Ireland, which had claimed some 3,000 lives over 25 years.

Killings Mar Peace Prize Award—The killing of an abducted Israeli soldier by Palestinian extremists during a failed rescue effort and the deaths of 4 others in the shootout cast a pall in October over the awarding of the Nobel Peace Prize to Israeli leaders Yitzhak Rabin and Shimon Peres and Palestine Liberation Organization leader Yasir Arafat. The soldier was held for several days by Hamas, a militant Palestinian group that opposed the PLO-Israeli accord providing limited autonomy for Palestinians in Gaza and the West Bank. On **Oct. 14**, the Israelis attacked the kidnappers' hideout in the West Bank near Jerusalem. The soldier, Cpl. Nahshon Waxman, was found shot to death. Another Israeli soldier and 3 kidnappers were killed in the battle. Also on **Oct. 14**, the Nobel Prize was awarded to Prime Minister Rabin and Foreign Minister Peres of Israel and to PLO chairman Arafat. Terrorist attacks continued with the explosion of a bomb on a bus in Tel Aviv, **Oct. 19**, which killed more than 20 people. Islamic militants took responsibility for the bus bombing, which was the deadliest single terrorist attack in Israel since 1978.

Kohl Retains Power in Germany—Chancellor Helmut Kohl retained his office in Germany's parliamentary elections in October, but he saw his majority in the lower house of Parliament dwindle from 134 seats to just 10. His governing coalition, led by the Christian Democrats, won 48.4% of the popular vote on **Oct. 16** to 48.1% for the opposition coalition led by the Social Democrats.

U.S., North Korea Reach Nuclear Accord—The Clinton Administration announced, **Oct. 17**, that the U.S. and North Korea had reached an agreement that would freeze the latter's nuclear weapons program and permit international inspections of its facilities. U.S. allies would build 2 nuclear power plants in North Korea, and the inspection of 2 suspicious nuclear sites in North Korea would be delayed. The latest agreement was an extension of terms announced in August. The 2 countries signed the agreement in Geneva, **Oct. 21.**

Israel, Jordan Sign Peace Treaty—The second peace treaty between Israel and an Arab state (the first had been signed with Egypt in 1979) was concluded between Israel and Jordan in October. The approval of a draft treaty took place, **Oct. 17**, in Amman, the capital of Jordan. The treaty was signed, **Oct. 26**, at a desert site along the Israeli-Jordanian border. Pres. Bill Clinton attended the ceremony. In their agreement, the 2 countries settled long-standing disputes over land and water, agreed to work together to build tourism, and pledged that no other group or organization could launch military attacks from Israel or Jordan. Clinton met with Pres. Hafez al-Assad in Syria, **Oct. 27**, hoping to promote progress in Israel-Syrian peace talks.

Mexican Candidate's Assassin Sentenced—Mario Aburto Martínez, the 23-year-old factory worker who admitted that he shot and killed Mexican presidential candidate Luis Donaldo Colosio in March, was convicted of murder, **Oct. 31**, in a nonjury trial; he was sentenced to 42 years in prison.

General

Opening of Hockey Season Postponed—The National Hockey League did not open its 1994-95 season on **Oct. 1**, as scheduled. The NHL commissioner, Gary Bettman, said it was being postponed because owners and players could not agree on a new contract. Some teams were losing money, and owners proposed a tax on the payrolls of teams with large salaries as a means of revenue sharing. Players objected to what they saw as a salary cap. By **Oct. 11**, each side had rejected the other side's latest proposal. At month's end, some games had been canceled, none had been played, and the dispute remained unresolved.

53 Religious Cultists Found Dead—Fifty-three members of a secretive religious cult, the Order of the Solar Temple, were found dead, victims of murder or suicide, in October. Police found 23 dead, **Oct. 5**, in a farmhouse in Cheiry, Switzerland. Some, wearing ceremonial robes, were lying on the floor in a circle. Most had bullet wounds, some were bound, and some were drugged. Twenty-five more bodies were found in 3 chalets in Granges-sur-Salvan. Those victims included Luc Jouret, a Belgian homeopathic doctor who had founded the cult, and Joseph di Mambro, an influential figure in the cult. Canadian authorities found 5 more victims in adjoining residences in Morin Heights, Quebec, 2 on **Oct. 5** and 3 on **Oct. 6**. Fires had been set at all the locations, utilizing timers and telephone lines. The order had been established in 1984 by Jouret, whose teachings involved a mixture of astrology, New Age spiritualism, and Christianity.

Crash of Commuter Plane Kills 68—A twin-engine commuter airplane, carrying 64 passengers and 4 crew members, crashed, **Oct. 31**, into a soybean field 30 miles south of Gary, IN. American Eagle Flight 4184 had been in a holding pattern in a heavy rainstorm waiting to land at Chicago's O'Hare International Airport when it disappeared from air-traffic radar at 4:15 PM. The crash was the 3d major air disaster in the U.S. in 1994. In September, a USAir jetliner crashed on approach to Pittsburgh International Airport, killing all 132 on board, and a July crash of a USAir jet near Charlotte, NC, left 37 of the 57 people aboard dead.

Notable Supreme Court Decisions, 1993-94

The Supreme Court's 1993-94 term began Oct. 4, 1993, and ended June 30, 1994, with the Court issuing signed decisions in only 84 cases, the fewest in almost 40 years. Of these decisions, one-third were unanimous, a slight decrease from the 1992-93 Court term. Only 14 cases were decided by 5-4 votes. The justices were most at odds in cases dealing with religion and race.

Justices Clarence Thomas and Antonin Scalia were most likely to vote together; they did so in 79% of the cases that were not unanimous. Justices Thomas and Harry A. Blackmun were least likely to agree; the pair voted the same way in only 10% of the divided opinions. Justice Anthony M. Kennedy most often cast the swing vote. He was in the majority in 13 of the Court's 5-4 decisions. In cases in which the Court was split either 5-4 or 6-3, Justice Kennedy was in the majority 85% of the time. Justice Blackmun, who served his last term on the Court, was the most frequent dissenter. He voted with the majority in only 35% of the split decisions. Some of the most notable decisions are described below.

Abortion: Although the Court declined to hear cases dealing with the fundamental right to an abortion, 2 cases were decided that dealt with protests outside abortion clinics. In a unanimous decision, the Court ruled (Jan. 24) that clinics could invoke the Racketeer-Influenced and Corrupt Organizations Act (RICO), a federal racketeering law, to sue violent antiabortion protesters for damages. In a 6-3 decision (June 30), the Court upheld a Florida state court decision to create a 36-ft buffer zone around abortion clinics in which no antiabortionists could demonstrate. Chief Justice William H. Rehnquist, in writing for the majority, expressed the view that creating the buffer zone did not place more of an undue burden on the protesters' freedom of speech than was necessary to protect the well-being of patients.

Business and Finance: Taking away a major legal defense sometimes used by investors in securities fraud cases, the Court decided (Apr. 19), 5-4, to sharply limit the conditions under which investors can sue their financial advisers. In a separate decision, the Court upheld (June 20) California's unitary tax law, which required multinational corporations to base their state taxes on their worldwide income. In another decision, the Court upheld (June 24), 7-2, the right of judges to review punitive damage awards to prevent juries from requiring corporations to pay excessive damages.

Death Penalty: Justice Blackmun wrote (June 30) a majority opinion upholding, 5-4, the right of a federal district judge to issue a stay of execution for death-row inmates who had exhausted their state appeals but wished to obtain legal representation to pursue a federal appeal.

The Environment: With increasing pressure on states to balance environmental concerns and waste disposal, it was not suprising that the Court was called on to decide several cases concerning the transport of garbage. In one case, the Court decided (Apr. 4), 7-2, that states could not impose higher taxes on waste imported from outside the state than on waste generated in-state. In another 7-2 ruling, the Court decided (May 2) that ash from incinerators had to be treated as hazardous waste. The Court struck down (May 16), 6-3, a law that required garbage haulers to deliver trash to a designated facility, citing the prohibition on state and local governments' regulating interstate commerce, a power given strictly to Congress by the Constitution.

Freedom of Speech: The Court unanimously ruled (Mar. 7) that song parody was constitutionally protected free expression, exempt from copyright law restrictions on reuse of the original songs. In another unanimous decision (June 13), the Court overturned a Missouri suburb's prohibition on residents' posting signs on their property expressing their personal or political views.

Military Base Closures: Sen. Arlen Specter (R, PA) lost a case he brought to and argued before the Court. In a unanimous decision (May 23), the Court upheld the government's method for selecting military bases to close. Specter had wanted the decisions on base closings to be subject to judicial review.

Prisoners' Rights: The Court's unanimous decision (June 6) made it easier for prisoners attacked by other inmates to prove that jail officials had been negligent.

Property: In a 5-4 decision (June 24), the Court curbed the rights of municipalities to require businesses to give up part of their property for public use, citing the Fifth Amendment's restriction on the taking of private property by government.

Religion and Schools: In a 5-4 decision (June 27), the Court declared unconstitutional a public school district created solely for the learning-disabled or otherwise handicapped children of a Hasidic Jewish community.

Sexual Harassment and Worker Discrimination: The Court removed a barrier to proving sexual harassment when it unanimously ruled (Nov. 9) that workers do not have to offer evidence of serious psychological damage to win their case. Issuing two 8-1 rulings (Apr. 26), the Court barred retroactive use of the Civil Rights Act of 1991, which makes it easier for workers to file bias suits.

Voting Districts: The Court delivered (June 30) 2 opinions regarding the interpretation of Section 2 of the Voting Rights Act of 1965, which guarantees minorities the right to "participate in the political process and to elect representatives of their choice." In the first decision, the Court ruled, 7-2, that states could create only as many minority districts as would be proportional to the minority population. In the second decision, the Court held, 5-4, that the Voting Rights Act could not be used to challenge the size of a governing body.

The 1994 Nobel Prizes

Each 1994 Nobel Prize, awarded in October, consisted of a large solid gold medal and a cash award of more than $900,000. For prizes shared by more than one recipient, the names are in alphabetical order.

Chemistry: George A. Olah, an American, won the prize for his early contributions to the field of hydrocarbon research. Olah's work led to the discovery of new ways to break apart and rebuild compounds of carbon and hydrogen, facilitating (among other things) development of higher-octane gasoline.

Memorial Prize in Economic Science: Two Americans—John C. Harsanyi and John F. Nash—and Reinhard Selten, a German, shared the prize for their pioneering work in the field of game theory.

Literature: Kenzaburo Oe, a Japanese writer most known for his powerful accounts of the atomic bombing of Hiroshima, won the prize. His works include *The Catch, A Personal Matter, The Silent Cry,* and *Hiroshima Notes.*

Peace: Yasir Arafat, the Palestine Liberation Organization (PLO) chairman, Shimon Peres, foreign minister of Israel, and Yitzhak Rabin, prime minister of Israel, shared the prize "for their efforts to create peace in the Middle East."

Physics: Bertram N. Brockhouse, a Canadian, and Clifford G. Shull, an American, shared the prize. Brockhouse and Shull developed and refined techniques for using neutron probes to explore the atomic structure of matter.

Physiology or Medicine: Two Americans, Alfred G. Gilman and Martin Rodbell, shared the prize. Working separately, Gilman and Rodbell conducted research important to the discovery of natural substances (G-proteins) that help cells convert signals from the environment and within the body to control fundamental life processes.

Major Actions of the 103d Congress

The 103d Congress convened Jan. 5, 1993, and adjourned for the year on Nov. 26, 1993. Reconvening on Jan. 25, 1994, Congress adjourned for the 1994 elections on Oct. 8, with a postelection "lame duck" session scheduled for Nov. to consider legislation implementing a new 117-nation trade pact. One of the first acts of the 103d Congress, on Jan. 6, 1993, was to count the Electoral College votes and certify the election of Bill Clinton as 42d president and Al Gore as vice president. The following is a summary of major actions of the 103d Congress in the first 2 years of the Clinton administration.

1993

Family and Medical Leave Act, the first major legislation passed by the 103d Congress. It permits some workers to take up to 12 weeks of unpaid leave in any 12-month period for the birth or adoption of a child, to care for a sick relative, or to deal with their own serious illness. Businesses with fewer than 50 employees are exempted. Similar bills were vetoed twice by Pres. George Bush. Passed the Senate Feb. 4, 71-27; passed the House Feb. 4, 247-152; signed by Pres. Clinton, Feb. 5; took effect Aug. 5, 1993.

Voter Registration, the so-called motor-voter bill. It requires states to allow eligible citizens to register to vote when they apply for or renew their driver's license; states must also permit registration by mail and must make forms available at certain public-assistance agencies. Passed the House May 5, 259-164; passed the Senate May 11, 62-36; signed by Pres. Clinton, May 20; takes effect 1995.

Omnibus Budget Reconciliation Act, approved in the House on Aug. 5 with no votes to spare, 218-216, and in the Senate on Aug. 6, with Vice President Al Gore casting a yes vote to break a 50-50 tie. Signed by Pres. Clinton on Aug. 10. The measure essentially approved the president's plan to reduce the budget deficits by $496 billion over 5 years through a combination of spending cuts and tax increases.

National Service Bill, establishes a federal program to allow young people to repay college loans from the federal government through community service. The $1.5 billion, 3-year program will enable about 100,000 young people to perform community service, offering as much as $4,725 a year for 2 years. Passed the House Aug. 6; passed the Senate Sept. 8, 57-40; signed by Pres. Clinton Sept. 21.

Hatch Act Revisions, revised a 1939 law that barred most federal employees from participating in partisan political activities. It allows most federal employees to endorse, solicit votes for, and otherwise campaign for partisan candidates outside the work place. Passed the Senate July 20, 68-31; passed the House Sept. 21, 339-85; signed by Pres. Clinton Oct. 6.

Gun Control, the so-called Brady Bill (named for James Brady, press secretary to Pres. Ronald Reagan, who was seriously injured when he was shot during a 1981 assassination attempt against Reagan). The measure imposes a 5-day waiting period for the purchase of handguns and provides for the creation of a national computer network to check the backgrounds of gun buyers. Passed the House Nov. 23, 238-187; passed the Senate Nov. 24, voice vote; signed by Pres. Clinton, Nov. 30; took effect Mar. 1994.

NAFTA, legislation to implement the North American Free Trade Agreement, which gradually abolishes nearly all trade barriers between the U.S., Mexico, and Canada. The implementing legislation was approved by the House on Nov. 17, 234-200. The Senate gave its approval on Nov. 20, 61-38. Pres. Clinton signed the measure Dec. 8. NAFTA officially took effect Jan. 1, 1994. *For more information on NAFTA, see p. 204.*

Superconducting Supercollider, designed to allow physicists to create and study high-speed collisions of atomic particles, killed when Congress did not include continued funding for it in the relevant appropriations bill. The supercollider was originally approved by Congress in 1989 and at that time was estimated to cost $4.4 billion. By the time the project was killed in Oct. 1993, the cost to date was $2 billion, and estimates to complete the project were at $11 billion.

Student Loans, a new program that enables students to borrow directly from the government, instead of from banks, and gives them 5 repayment options.

1994

Freedom of Access to Clinic Entrances Act, makes it a federal crime to use or attempt to use force, threats, or physical obstruction to injure or interfere with anyone providing or receiving abortions and other reproductive health services. It also bars protesters from making uninvited approaches to patients within 300 ft of the clinic. Passed the House May 5, 241-174; passed the Senate May 12, 69-30; signed by Pres. Clinton May 26.

Omnibus Violent Crime Control and Prevention Act, a $30.2 billion package that provides for 100,000 new police officers, expands the death penalty to cover more than 50 federal crimes, bans the sale and possession of 19 types of assault weapons, and authorizes $6.9 billion for prevention programs. Passed the House Aug. 21, 235-195; passed the Senate Aug. 25, 61-38; signed by Pres. Clinton Sept. 13. *For more information on the crime bill, see p. 213.*

Independent Counsel, reinstates the independent counsel law, which had expired in 1992, providing for a prosecutor from outside the government to be appointed by a panel of 3 federal judges to investigate accusations of criminal wrongdoing made against high government officials. Passed the Senate May 25, voice vote; passed the House June 21, 317-105; signed by Pres. Clinton June 30.

Social Security Bill, a law that makes the Social Security Administration, currently part of the Department of Health and Human Services, an independent government agency. Passed by the Senate Aug. 5, voice vote; passed by the House Aug. 11, 431-0; signed by Pres. Clinton, Aug. 15; takes effect Mar. 31, 1995.

Interstate Banking, allows banks to operate branches across the nation. It eliminates the remaining barriers to interstate banking in a dozen states and eliminates the requirement that banks operate separate subsidiaries in each state. The bill will make banking more convenient for Americans who live in one state and work in another. Big banks are virtually required, at least for the next few years, to buy a bank in another state before opening branches there. Passed the House Aug. 4, voice vote; passed the Senate Sept. 13, 94-4; signed by Pres. Clinton, Sept. 29.

California Desert Protection, designates 9.4 million acres of desert in California as national park land and preserves, which creates the largest wilderness area outside Alaska. Passed the House Oct. 7; passed the Senate Oct. 8.

UNITED STATES GOVERNMENT

EXECUTIVE BRANCH	LEGISLATIVE BRANCH	JUDICIAL BRANCH
PRESIDENT **Vice President Cabinet** **Executive Office of the President** White House Office Office of Management and Budget Council of Economic Advisers National Security Council Office of the U.S. Trade Representative Council on Environmental Quality Office of Science and Technology Policy Office of National Drug Control Policy Office of Administration	**CONGRESS** **Senate House** Architect of the Capitol U.S. Botanic Garden General Accounting Office Government Printing Office Library of Congress Office of Technology Assessment Congressional Budget Office	**Supreme Court of the United States** Courts of Appeals District Courts Territorial Courts Court of International Trade Court of Federal Claims Court of Military Appeals Tax Court Court of Veterans Appeals Administrative Office of the Courts Federal Judicial Center Sentencing Commission

The Clinton Administration

As of mid-1994; all mailing addresses listed are for Washington, DC

Terms of office of the president and vice president: Jan. 20, 1993, to Jan. 20, 1997. No person may be elected president of the United States for more than two 4-year terms.

President — Bill Clinton of Arkansas receives salary of $200,000 a year taxable; in addition an expense allowance of $50,000 to assist in defraying expenses resulting from his official duties. Also there may be expended not exceeding $100,000, nontaxable, a year for travel expenses and $20,000 for official entertainment available for allocation within the Executive Office of the President.

Vice President — Albert Gore, Jr., of Tennessee receives salary of $171,500 a year and $10,000 for expenses, all of which is taxable.

The Cabinet

(Salary: $148,400 per annum)

Secretary of State — Warren M. Christopher
Secretary of Treasury — Lloyd Bentsen
Secretary of Defense — William J. Perry
Attorney General — Janet Reno
Secretary of Interior — Bruce Babbitt
Secretary of Agriculture — Mike Espy
Secretary of Commerce — Ronald H. Brown
Secretary of Labor — Robert B. Reich
Secretary of Health and Human Services — Donna E. Shalala
Secretary of Housing and Urban Development — Henry G. Cisneros
Secretary of Transportation — Federico F. Peña
Secretary of Energy — Hazel R. O'Leary
Secretary of Education — Richard W. Riley
Secretary of Veterans Affairs — Jesse Brown

The White House Staff

1600 Pennsylvania Ave. NW 20500

Chief of Staff — Leon Panetta
Asst. to the President & Deputy Chief of Staff for Policy and Political Affairs — Harold Ickes
Asst. to the President & Deputy Chief of Staff for Operations —Erskine Bowles
Counselor to the President — Thomas F. McLarty 3d
Special Adviser to the President — David Gergen[1]
Senior Adviser on Policy and Strategy — George Stephanopoulos
Assistants to the President:
  Counsel to the President — Abner Mikva
  Domestic Policy Council — Carol Rasco
  Presidential Personnel — J. Veronica Biggins
  Press Secretary — Dee Dee Myers
  Legislative Affairs — Patrick Griffin
  Strategic Planning — Mark Gearan
  National Economic Policy — Robert E. Rubin
  Intergovernmental Affairs — Marcia Hale
  National Security — W. Anthony Lake
  Staff Secretary — John Podesta
  Political Affairs — Joan Baggett
  Public Liaison — Alexis Herman

(1) Gergen resigned in November 1994. (He had also served as Special Adviser to the Secretary of State, a non–career position that did not require Senate approval.)

Executive Agencies

Council of Economic Advisers — Laura D'Andrea Tyson, chmn.
Office of Administration — Patsy Thomasson, dir.
Office of Science & Technology Policy — John H. Gibbons
Office of National Drug Control Policy — Lee P. Brown
Office of Management and Budget — Alice Rivlin, dir.
U.S. Trade Representative — Michael Kantor
Council on Environmental Policy — vacant

Department of State

2201 C St. NW 20520

Secretary of State — Warren M. Christopher
Deputy Secretary — Strobe Talbott
Under Sec. for Political Affairs — Peter Tarnoff
Under Sec. for International Security Affairs — Lynn Davis
Under Secretary for Management — Richard Moose
Under Sec. for Global Affairs — Timothy Wirth
Legal Adviser — Conrad K. Harper
Assistant Secretaries for:
  Administration — Patrick F. Kennedy
  African Affairs — George E. Moose
  Consular Affairs — Mary A. Ryan
  Diplomatic Security — Tony Quainton
  East Asian & Pacific Affairs — Winston Lord
  Economic & Business Affairs — Daniel Tarullo
  European & Canadian Affairs — Richard Holbrooke
  Human Rights & Humanitarian Affairs — John H. F. Shattuck
  Intelligence & Research — Tobi Gati
  Inter-American Affairs — Alexander Watson
  International Narcotics Matters — Robert S. Gelbard
  International Organization Affairs — Douglas J. Bennett Jr.
  Legislative Affairs — Wendy R. Sherman
  Near-Eastern & S. Asian Affairs — Edward Djerejian
  Oceans, International Environmental & Scientific Affairs — Elinor G. Constable
  Politico-Military Affairs — vacant
  Public Affairs — Thomas Dinilon
  South Asian Affairs — Robin Raphel

Department of the Treasury

1500 Pennsylvania Ave. NW 20220

Secretary of the Treasury — Lloyd Bentsen
Deputy Sec. of the Treasury — Frank N. Newman
Under Sec. for Domestic Finance — vacant
Under Sec. for International Affairs — Lawrence Summers
General Counsel — Edward Knight
Assistant Secretaries for:
Economic Policy — Alicia Hancock Munnell
Enforcement — vacant
Fiscal Affairs — Gerald Murphy
International Affairs — Jeffrey Shafer
Legislative Affairs — Michale B. Levy
Public Affairs — Joan Louge–Kinder
Tax Policy — Leslie B. Samuels
Bureaus:
Alcohol, Tobacco & Firearms — John Magaw, dir.
Comptroller of the Currency — Eugene A. Ludwig, comm.
Customs — George J. Weise, comm.
Engraving & Printing — Peter H. Daley, dir.
Federal Law Enforcement Training Center — Charles F. Rinkevich, dir.
Financial Management Service — Russell Morris, comm.
Internal Revenue Service — Margaret Milner Richardson, comm.
Mint — Philip Diehl, dir.
Public Debt — Richard L. Gregg, comm.
Treasurer of the U.S. — Mary Ellen Withrow
U.S. Secret Service — Eljay B. Bowron, dir.

Department of Defense

The Pentagon 20301

Secretary of Defense — William J. Perry
Deputy Secretary — John Deutch
Under Sec. for Acquisition and Technology — Paul Kaminski
Under Sec. for Policy — Frank Wisner
Asst. Secretaries for:
Command, Control, Communications & Intelligence — Emmett Paige Jr.
Personnel and Readiness — Edwin Dorn
Health Affairs — Stephen C. Joseph
International Security Policy — Ashton B. Carter
Legislative Affairs — Sandra Stuart
Policy & Plans — Graham T. Allison
Products & Logistics — vacant
Program Analysis & Evaluation — vacant
Public Affairs — Kenneth Bacon
Reserve Affairs — Deborah Lee
Special Operations & Low Intensity Conflict— H. Allen Holmes
Comptroller— John Hamre
General Counsel — Judith Miller
Administration — Ann Reese, dir.
Operational Test & Evaluation — Phillip E. Coyle
Chairman, Joint Chiefs of Staff — Gen. John Shalikashvili
Secretary of the Army — Togo West
Secretary of the Navy — John Dalton
Secretary of the Air Force — Sheila Widnall

Department of Justice

Constitution Ave. & 10th St. NW 20530

Attorney General — Janet Reno
Deputy Attorney General — Jamie Gorelick
Associate Attorney General — John Schmidt
Solicitor General — Drew S. Days 3d
Office of Inspector General — Michael R. Bromwich
Assistants:
Antitrust Division — Anne K. Bingaman
Civil Division — Frank Hunger
Civil Rights Division — Deval Patrick
Criminal Division — Jo Ann Harris
Environment & Natural Resources Division — Lois Schiffer
Justice Programs — Laurie Robinson
Legal Counsel — Walter Dellinger
Policy Development — Eleanor Acheson
Legislative Affairs — Sheila Anthony
Administration — Steve Colgate
Tax Division — Loretta Argrett
Office of Public Affairs — Carl Stern
Office of Information and Privacy — Richard L. Huff/Daniel J. Metcalf
Fed. Bureau of Investigation — Louis J. Freeh, dir.
Exec. Off. for Immigration Review — Tony Moscato, dir.
Bureau of Prisons — Kathleen M. Hawk, dir.
Comm. Relations Service — Jeffrey Weiss, act. dir.
Drug Enforcement Adm. — Tom Constantine
Office of Intelligence Policy and Review — Richard Scruggs, act. counsel
Office of Professional Responsibility — Michael E. Shaheen Jr.
Exec. Off. for U.S. Trustees — William Baity, act. dir.
Exec. Off. for U.S. Attorneys — Carol DiBattiste, dir.
Immigration and Naturalization Service — Doris Meissner
Pardon Attorney — Margaret C. Love
U.S. Parole Commission — Edward F. Reilly Jr., chmn.
U.S. Marshals Service — Eduardo Gonzalez, dir.
U.S. Natl. Central Bureau of INTERPOL — Shelley G. Altenstadtero, chief

Department of the Interior

1849 C St. NW 20240

Secretary of the Interior — Bruce Babbitt
Deputy Secretary — vacant
Assistant Secretaries for:
Fish, Wildlife, and Parks — George T. Framton Jr.
Indian Affairs — Ada E. Deer
Land & Minerals — Robert Armstrong
Policy, Budget, and Management — Bonnie R. Cohen
Territorial & Intl. Affairs — Leslie Turner
Water & Science — Elizabeth A. Reike
Bureau of Land Management — Michael Dombeck, act. dir.
Bureau of Mines — Rhea Graham, dir.
Bureau of Reclamation — Daniel T. Beard, comm.
Fish & Wildlife Service — Mollie Beattie, dir.
Geological Survey — Gordon P. Eaton, dir.
National Park Service — Roger Kennedy, dir.
Communications — Kevin Sweeney, dir.
Office of Congressional and Legislative Affairs — Stephanie Solien
Solicitor — John D. Leshy

Department of Agriculture

14th St. and Independece Ave. SW 20250

Secretary of Agriculture — Mike Espy[1]
Deputy Secretary — Richard Rominger
Assistant Secretaries for:
Administration — Wardell Townsend Jr.
Congressional Relations — Fred Slabach
Economics — Keith Collins, act.
Food & Consumer Services — Ellen Haas
Intl. Affairs & Commodity Programs — Eugene Moos
Marketing & Inspection Services — Patricia Jensen, act.
Natural Resources & Environment — James Lyons
Science & Education — R. D. Plowman, act.
General Counsel — James Gilliland
Inspector General — Charles Gillum, act.
Communications — Ali Webb
Press Secretary — vacant

(1) Announced resignation Oct. 3, 1994, effective Dec. 31, 1994.

Department of Commerce

14th St. between Constitution & Pennsylvania Ave. NW 20230

Secretary of Commerce — Ronald H. Brown
Deputy Secretary — David Barram
Chief of Staff — Robert Stein
General Counsel — Ginger Lew
Assistant Secretaries for:
Chief Financial Officer & Asst. for Administration — Thomas Bloom
Economic Development Adm. — William Ginsberg

Export Enforcement — John Despres
Import Administration — Susan Esserman
Intl. Economic Policy — Charles Meissner
Legislative Affairs — Loretta Dunn
Natl. Telecommunications Information Adm. — Clarence Irving Jr.
Oceans & Atmosphere — Douglas K. Hall
Patent & Trademark Office & Act. Asst. Comm. — Bruce Lehman
Trade Development — Raymond Vickery Jr.
Bureau of the Census — vacant
Bureau of Economic Analysis — Carol S. Carson, dir.
Under Sec. for International Trade — Jeffrey Garten
Under Sec. for Econ. Affairs — Everett Ehrlich
Under Sec. for Technology — Mary Lowe Good
Natl. Technical Info. Service — Donald Johnson
Natl. Institute for Standards & Technology — Arati Prabhakar, dir.
Minority Business Development Agency — Michael Rogers
Public Affairs — Jill Schuker

Department of Labor

200 Constitution Ave. NW 20210

Secretary of Labor — Robert B. Reich
Deputy Secretary — Thomas P. Glynn
Chief of Staff — Kathryn Higgins
Assistant Secretaries for:
Administration and Management — Cynthia A. Metzler
Congressional & Intergovernmental Affairs — Geri Palast
Employment & Training — Doug Ross
Employment Standards — Bernard E. Anderson
Occupational Safety & Health — Joseph A. Dear
Mine Safety & Health—Davitt McAteer
Office of American Workplace—Charles L. Smith, act.
Pension & Welfare Benefits — E. Olena Berg
Policy — Leslie Lobie, act.
Public Affairs — Anne H. Lewis
Veterans Employment & Training — Preston M. Taylor Jr.
Solicitor of Labor — Thomas S. Williamson Jr.
Bureau of International Affairs — Joaquin F. Otero
Women's Bureau — Karen Nussbaum
Inspector General — Charles C. Masten
Bureau of Labor Statistics — Katharine G. Abraham

Department of Health and Human Services

200 Independence Ave. SW 20201

Secretary of HHS — Donna E. Shalala, Ph.D.
Deputy Secretary — Walter D. Broadnax, Ph.D.
Chief of Staff — Kevin L. Thurm
Assistant Secretaries for:
Health — Jerry D. Klepner
Legislation — Jerry D. Klepner
Management & Budget — Kenneth S. Apfel
Personnel Administration — Thomas S. McFee
Planning & Evaluation — David T. Ellwood
Public Affairs — Avis LaVelle
General Counsel — Harriet Rabb
Inspector General — June Gibbs Brown
Office of Civil Rights — Dennis Hayashi
Surgeon General — Joycelyn Elders, M.D.
Social Security Adm. — Shirley Sears Chater[1]
Office of Consumer Affairs — Polly Baca
Administration on Aging—Fernando Torres–Gil
Health Care Financing Adm. — Bruce C. Vladeck
Administration for Children & Families — Mary Jo Bane

(1) Effective Mar. 31, 1995, the Social Security Administration will become an independent agency.

Department of Housing and Urban Development

451 7th St. SW 20410

Secretary of Housing & Urban Development — Henry G. Cisneros.
Deputy Secretary — Dwight P. Robinson, act.
Asst. to Dep. Sec. for Field Mgt.—John Wilson
Assistant Secretaries for:
Administration — Marilynn A. Davis
Community Planning & Development — Andrew Cuomo
Fair Housing & Equal Opportunity — Roberta Achtenberg
Housing & Federal Housing Commissioner — Nicolas P. Retsinas
Labor Relations — vacant
Congressional & Intergovernmental Relations — William J. Gilmartin
Policy Development & Research — Michael Stegman
Public Affairs — Jean Nolan
Public & Indian Housing — Joseph Shuldiner
General Counsel — Nelson Diaz
Inspector General — Susan Gaffney

Department of Transportation

400 7th St. SW 20590

Secretary of Transportation — Federico F. Peña
Deputy Secretary — Mortimer L. Downey
Assistant Secretaries for:
Administration — Jon H. Seymour
Budget & Programs — Louise F. Stoll
Governmental Affairs — Steven O. Palmer
Aviation & International Affairs — Raymond Romero
Transportation—Frank E. Kreusi
Public Affairs — Richard I. Mintz
U.S. Coast Guard Commandant — Adm. Robert E. Kramek
Federal Aviation Admin. — David R. Hinson
Federal Highway Admin. — Rodney E. Slater
Federal Railroad Admin. — Jolene Molitoris
Maritime Admin. — Albert Herberger
National Highway Traffic Safety Adm. — Ricardo Martinez
Federal Transit Admin. — Gordon J. Linton
Research & Special Programs Admin. — Dharmendra K. Sahama
Saint Lawrence Seaway Development Corp. — Stan E. Parris

Department of Energy

1000 Independence Ave. SW 20585

Secretary of Energy — Hazel R. O'Leary
Deputy Sec. — William H. White
Under Secretary — Charles B. Curtis
Chief of Staff — Richard Rosenzweig
Deputy Chief of Staff —Dan Reicher
General Counsel — Robert Nordhaus
Inspector General — John C. Layton
Assistant Secretaries for:
Congressional & Intergovernmental Affairs — William Taylor
Energy Efficiency & Renewable Energy — Christine Ervin
Defense Programs — Victor Reis
Policy, Planning, and Program Evaluation — Susan F. Tierney
Environmental Restoration and Waste Management — Thomas Grumbly
Administration and Human Resource Management — Archer L. Durham
Environment, Safety & Health — Tara Jeanne O'Toole
Fossil Energy — Patricia Godley
Nuclear Energy — Terry Lash, dir.
Energy Information Adm. — Jay E. Hakes, adm.
Economic Impact and Diversity — Corlis Moody, dir.
Federal Energy Regulatory Comm. — Elizabeth Moler, chair.
Hearings & Appeals — George Breznay, dir.
Energy Research — Martha Krebs
Civilian Radioactive Waste Management — Daniel A. Dreyfuss
Intelligence and National Security — John Keliher, dir.
Education & Technical Information — Terry Cornwell Rumsey, dir.
Public and Consumer Affairs — Mike Gauldin, dir.
Chief Financial Officer — Joseph F. Vivona
Associate Dep. Sec. for Field Management —Don Pearman

Department of Education

400 Maryland Ave. SW 20202

Secretary of Education — Richard W. Riley
Deputy Secretary — Madeleine Kunin
Under Secretary — Marshall S. Smith
Chief of Staff — Frank Holleman
Inspector General — James B. Thomas Jr.
General Counsel — Judith Winston
Assistant Secretaries for:
Adult & Vocational Education — Augusta Kappner
Civil Rights — Norma V. Cantu
Educational Research and Improvement — Sharon Porter Robinson
Elementary and Secondary Education — Thomas W. Payzant
Intergovernmental & Interagency Affairs — Mario Moreno
Legislation & Congressional Affairs — Kay Casstevens
Management — Rod McCowan
Postsecondary Education — David Longanecker
Special Education and Rehabilitative Services — Judith Heumann
Bilingual & Minority Language Affairs — Eugene Garcia, dir.
Rehabilitation Services Admin. — Frederic K. Schroeder, comm.

Department of Veterans Affairs

810 Vermont Ave. NW 20420

Secretary of Veterans Affairs — Jesse Brown
Deputy — Hershel W. Gober
Assistant Secretaries for:
Acquisition & Facilities — Gary Krump, act.
Congressional Affairs — Edward P. Scott
Finance & Information Resources Mgmt. — D. Mark Catlett
Human Resources & Adm. — Eugene Brickhouse
Policy & Planning — H. David Burge, act.
Public & Intergovernmental Affairs — Kathy E. Jurado
Inspector General — Stephen Trodden
Under Sec. for Benefits — R. John Vogel
Under Sec. for Health — Kenneth W. Kizer, M.D.
National Cemetery System — Jerry W. Bowen, dir.
General Counsel — Mary Lou Keener
Board of Veterans Appeals — Charles L. Cragin, chmn.

Notable U.S. Government Independent Agencies

Source: *The U.S. Government Manual*, National Archives and Records Administration

All addresses are Washington, DC, unless otherwise noted; as of mid-1994

Administrative Conference of the United States — Sally Katzen, act. chmn. (Suite 500, 2120 L St. NW, 20037).
Central Intelligence Agency — R. James Woolsey, dir. (Wash., DC 20505).
Commission on Civil Rights — Mary Frances Berry, chmn. (624 9th St. NW, 20425).
Commodity Futures Trading Commission — Barbara P. Holum, act. chmn. (2033 K St. NW, 20581).
Consumer Product Safety Commission — Ann Brown, chmn. (East West Towers, 4330 East West Hwy., Bethesda, MD 20814).
Environmental Protection Agency — Carol M. Browner, adm. (401 M St. SW, 20460).
Equal Employment Opportunity Commission — Tony E. Gallegos, act. chmn. (1801 L St. NW, 20507).
Export-Import Bank of the United States — Kenneth D. Brody, pres. and chmn. (811 Vermont Ave. NW, 20571).
Farm Credit Administration — Billy Ross Brown, chmn., Farm Credit Administration Board (1501 Farm Credit Drive, McLean, VA 22102).
Federal Communications Commission — Reed E. Hundt, chmn. (1919 M St. NW, 20554).
Federal Deposit Insurance Corporation — Ricki R. Tigert, act. chmn. (550 17th St. NW, 20429).
Federal Election Commission — Trevor Potter, chmn. (999 E St. NW, 20463).
Federal Emergency Management Agency — James Lee Witt, dir. (500 C St. SW, 20472).
Federal Housing Finance Board — vacant, chmn. (1777 F St. NW, 20006).
Federal Labor Relations Authority — Jean McKee, chmn. (607 14th St. NW, 20424).
Federal Maritime Commission — William D. Hathaway, chmn. (800 N. Capitol St. NW, 20573).
Federal Mediation and Conciliation Service — Joan Calhoun Weils, dir. (2100 K St. NW, 20427).
Federal Mine Safety & Health Review Commission — Arlene Holen, chmn. (1730 K St. NW, 20006).
Federal Reserve System — Alan Greenspan, chairman, Board of Governors (20th St. & Constitution Ave. NW, 20551).
Federal Retirement Thrift Investment Board — James H. Atkins, act. chmn. (1250 H St. NW, 20005).
Federal Trade Commission — Janet D. Steiger, chmn. (Pennsylvania Ave. at 6th St. NW, 20580).
General Services Administration — Roger W. Johnson, adm. (18th & F Sts. NW, 20405).
Inter-American Foundation — Frank D. Yturria, chmn. (901 N. Stuart St., Arlington, VA 22203).
Interstate Commerce Commission — Gail C. McDonald, chmn. (12th St. & Constitution Ave. NW, 20423).
Merit Systems Protection Board — Benjamin L. Erdreich, chmn. (1120 Vermont Ave. NW, 20419).
National Aeronautics and Space Administration — Daniel S. Goldin, adm. (300 E St. SW, 20546).
National Archives & Records Administration — Trudy H. Peterson, act. archivist (7th St. & Pennsylvania Ave. NW, 20408).
National Credit Union Administration — Norman E. D'Amours, chmn. (1775 Duke St., Alexandria, VA 22314).
National Foundation on the Arts and the Humanities — Jane Alexander, chmn. (arts) 1100 Pennsylvania Ave. NW, 20506; Sheldon Hackney, chmn. (humanities) same address; Linda Bell, act. dir. (museum services) same address.
National Labor Relations Board — William B. Gould IV, chmn. (1099 14th St. NW, 20570).
National Mediation Board — Ernest W. DuBester, chmn. (Suite 250 East, 1301 K St. NW, 20572).
National Railroad Passenger Corporation (Amtrak) — Thomas M. Downs, chmn. (60 Massachusetts Ave. NE, 20002).
National Science Foundation — James J. Duderstadt, chmn., National Science Board (4201 Wilson Blvd., Arlington, VA 22230).
National Transportation Safety Board — Carl W. Vogt, chmn. (490 L'Enfant Plaza SW, 20594).
Nuclear Regulatory Commission — Ivan Selin, chmn. (1717 H St. NW, 20555).
Occupational Safety and Health Review Commission — Stuart E. Weisberg, chmn. (1120 20th St. NW, 20036).
Office of Government Ethics — Stephen D. Potts, dir. (1201 New York Ave. NW, 20005).
Office of Personnel Management — James B. King, dir. (1900 E St. NW, 20415).
Office of Special Counsel — Kathleen Day Koch, sp. counsel (1730 M St. NW, 20036).
Peace Corps — Carol Bellamy, dir. (1990 K St. NW, 20526).
Pension Benefit Guaranty Corporation — Robert B. Reich, chm., Board of Directors (1200 K St. NW, 20005).
Postal Rate Commission — Edward J. Gleiman, chmn. (1333 H St. NW, 20268).
Railroad Retirement Board — Glen L. Bower, chmn. (Main Office: 844 N. Rush St., Chicago, IL 60611).
Resolution Trust Corporation — John E. Ryan, act. chm. (801 17th St. NW, 20434).
Securities and Exchange Commission — Arthur Levitt, chmn. (450 5th St. NW, 20549).
Selective Service System — G. Huntington Banister, act. dir. (National Headquarters, Arlington, VA 20435).
Small Business Administration — Erskine B. Bowles, adm. (409 Third St. SW, 20416).
Tennessee Valley Authority — Craven Crowell, chm., Board of Directors (400 W. Summit Hill Dr., Knoxville, TN 37902, and One Mass. Ave. NW, 20444).
Thrift Depositor Protection Oversight Board — Lloyd Bentsen, chm., Board of Directors (808 17th St. NW, 20232).
Trade and Development Agency — J. Joseph Grand Maison, dir. (State Annex 16, 20523).
United States Arms Control & Disarmament Agency — John D. Holum, dir. (320 21st St. NW, 20451).
United States Information Agency — Joseph D. Duffey, dir. (301 4th St. SW, 20547).
United States International Trade Commission — Don E. Newquist, chmn. (500 E St. SW, 20436).
United States Postal Service — Marvin Runyon, Postmaster General (475 L'Enfant Plaza SW, 20260).

Other Notable U.S. Agencies

Source: *The U.S. Government Manual,* National Archives and Records Administration; unless otherwise noted, all addresses are Washington, DC

Bureau of Alcohol, Tobacco, and Firearms — John W. Magaw, dir. (Dept. of Treasury, 650 Mass. Ave NW, 20226).

Bureau of the Census — vacant, dir. (Dept. of Commerce, 20233).

Bureau of Economic Analysis — Carol S. Carson, dir. (Dept. of Commerce, 20230).

Bureau of Indian Affairs — Ada E. Deer, asst. sec. (Dept. of the Interior, 20240).

Bureau of Prisons — Kathleen M. Hawk, dir. (Dept. of Justice, 320 First St. NW, 20534).

Centers for Disease Control & Prevention — David Satcher, dir. (Dept. of HHS, 1600 Clifton Rd. NE, Atlanta, GA 30333).

Federal Aviation Administration — David R. Hinson, adm. (Dept. of Transportation, 800 Independence Ave. SW, 20591).

Federal Bureau of Investigation — Louis J. Freeh, dir. (Dept. of Justice, 9th St. and Pennsylvania Ave. NW, 20535).

Federal Highway Administration — Rodney E. Slater, adm. (Dept. of Trans., 400 7th St. SW, 20590).

Fish & Wildlife Service — Mollie Beattie, dir. (Dept. of the Interior, 20240).

Food and Drug Administraton — David A. Kessler, comm. (Dept. of HHS, 5600 Fishers Ln., Rockville, MD 20857).

Forest Service — Jack W. Thomas, chief (Dept. of Agriculture, PO Box 96090, 20090).

General Accounting Office — (congressional agency) Charles A. Bowsher, comptroller gen. (441 G St. NW, 20548).

Government Printing Office — (congressional agency) Michael F. DiMario, public printer (N. Capitol and H. Sts. NW, 20401).

Immigration & Naturalization Service — Doris Meissner, comm. (Dept. of Justice, 425 I St. NW, 20536).

Internal Revenue Service — Margaret Milner Richardson, comm. (Dept. of Treas., 1111 Constitution Ave. NW, 20224).

Library of Congress — (congressional agency) James H. Billington, Librarian of Congress (101 Independence Av. SE, 20540).

National Institutes of Health — Harold E. Varmus, dir. (Dept. of HHS, 9000 Rockville Pike, Bethesda, MD 20892).

National Oceanic and Atmospheric Administration — Sigmund R. Petersen, dir. (Dept. of Commerce, 20230).

National Park Service — Roger G. Kennedy, dir. (Dept. of the Interior, 20240).

Social Security Administration — Shirley Sears Chater, comm. (Dept. of HHS, 6401 Security Blvd., Baltimore, MD 21235).[1]

Smithsonian Institution — (quasi-official agency) Robert McC. Adams, sec. (1000 Jefferson Dr. SW, 20560).

Surgeon General — Joycelyn Elders (Public Health Service, Dept. of HHS, 200 Independence Ave. SW, 20201& 5600 Fishers Ln., Rockville, MD 20857).

U.S. Customs Service — George J. Weise, comm. (Dept. of the Treasury, 1301 Constitutional Ave. NW, 20229).

U.S. Coast Guard — Adm. Robert E. Kramek, commandant, (Dept. of Trans., 2100 2d St. SW, 20593).

U.S. Mint — Philip Diehl, dir. (Dept. of Treas., 633 3d St. NW, 20220).

U.S. Secret Service — Eljay B. Bowron, dir. (Dept. of Treas., 1800 G St. NW, 20223).

(1) Effective Mar. 31, 1995, the Social Security Administration will become an independent agency.

The One Hundred and Fourth Congress

With Preliminary 1994 Election Results

Source: Voter News Service; World Almanac research; data subject to change, pending official election results.

The 104th Congress convenes in January 1995.

The Senate

Rep., 53; Dem., 47; Total, 100. *Incumbent. Boldface denotes the 1994 election winner.

Terms are for 6 years and end Jan. 3 of the year preceding the senator's name in the following table. Annual salary, $133,600; President Pro Tempore, Majority Leader, and Minority Leader, $148,400. To be eligible for the U.S. Senate a person must be at least 30 years of age, a citizen of the United States for at least 9 years, and a resident of the state from which he or she is chosen. The Congress must meet annually on Jan. 3, unless it has, by law, appointed a different day.

The ZIP code of the Senate is 20510; the telephone number is 202-224-3121.

Senate officials in 1993-94 (103d Congress) were: President Pro Tempore, Robert C. Byrd; Majority Leader, George J. Mitchell; Majority Whip, Wendell H. Ford; Minority Leader, Bob Dole; Minority Whip, Alan K. Simpson.

D-Democrat; R-Republican; ACP-A Connecticut Party; I-Independent; L-Liberal; C-Conservative

Term ends	Senator (Party)/Service from[1]	1994 Election
	Alabama	
1997	Howell Heflin (D)/1979	
1999	Richard C. Shelby (R)[2]/1987	
	Alaska	
1997	Ted Stevens (R)/12/24/68	
1999	Frank H. Murkowski (R)/1981	
	Arizona	
1999	John McCain (R)/1987	
2001	**Jon Kyl** (R)	**577,934**
	Sam Coppersmith (D)	427,285
	Arkansas	
1997	David H. Pryor (D)/1979	
1999	Dale Bumpers (D)/1975	
	California	
1999	Barbara Boxer (D)/1993	
2001	**Dianne Feinstein*** (D)/11/10/92	**3,593,069**
	Michael Huffington (R)	3,481,840
	Colorado	
1997	Hank Brown (R)/1991	
1999	Ben Nighthorse Campbell (D)/1993	
	Connecticut	
1999	Christopher J. Dodd (D)/1981	
2001	**Joe Lieberman*** (D,ACP)/1989	**697,911**
	Jerry Labriola (R)	324,405
	Delaware	
1997	Joseph R. Biden, Jr. (D)/1973	
2001	**William V. Roth, Jr.*** (R)/1/2/71	**110,886**
	Charles M. Oberly (D)	84,465
	Florida	
1999	Bob Graham (D)/1987	
2001	**Connie Mack*** (R)/1989	**2,874,873**
	Hugh E. Rodham (D)	1,205,460
	Georgia	
1997	Sam Nunn (D)/1973	
1999	Paul Coverdell (R)/1993	
	Hawaii	
1999	Daniel K. Inouye (D)/1963	
2001	**Daniel K. Akaka*** (D)/5/16/90	**256,189**
	Maria M. Hustace (R)	86,320
	Idaho	
1997	Larry E. Craig (R)/1991	
1999	Dirk Kempthorne (R)/1993	
	Illinois	
1997	Paul Simon (D)/1985	
1999	Carol Moseley-Braun (D)/1993	
	Indiana	
1999	Daniel R. Coats (R)/1989	
2001	**Richard G. Lugar*** (R)/1977	**1,029,421**
	James Jontz (D)	467,715
	Iowa	
1997	Tom Harkin (D)/1985	
1999	Charles E. Grassley (R)/1981	

Term ends	Senator (Party)/Service from[1]	1994 Election
	Kansas	
1997	Nancy Landon Kassebaum (R)/12/23/78	
1999	Bob Dole (R)/1969	
	Kentucky	
1997	Mitch McConnell (R)/1985	
1999	Wendell H. Ford (D)/12/28/74	
	Louisiana	
1997	J. Bennett Johnston (D)/11/14/72	
1999	John B. Breaux (D)/1987	
	Maine	
1997	William S. Cohen (R)/1979	
2001	**Olympia J. Snowe** (R)	**304,516**
	Thomas H. Andrews (D)	185,210
	Maryland	
1999	Barbara A. Mikulski (D)/1987	
2001	**Paul S. Sarbanes*** (D)/1977	**788,052**
	William Brock (R)	538,326
	Massachusetts	
1997	John F. Kerry (D)/1/2/85	
2001	**Edward M. Kennedy*** (D)/11/7/62	**1,257,945**
	W. Mitt Romney (R)	888,435
	Michigan	
1997	Carl Levin (D)/1979	
2001	**Spencer Abraham** (R)	**1,577,865**
	Bob Carr (D)	1,298,726
	Minnesota	
1997	Paul David Wellstone (D)/1991	
2001	**Rod Grams** (R)	**869,568**
	Ann Wynia (D)	781,496
	Mississippi	
1997	Thad Cochran (R)/12/27/78	
2001	**Trent Lott*** (R)/1989	**411,733**
	Ken Harper (D)	184,986
	Missouri	
1999	Christopher "Kit" Bond (R)/1987	
2001	**John Ashcroft** (R)	**1,058,320**
	Alan Wheat (D)	633,941
	Montana	
1997	Max Baucus (D)/12/15/78	
2001	**Conrad Burns*** (R)/1989	**212,823**
	Jack Mudd (D)	128,996
	Nebraska	
1997	J. James Exon (D)/1979	
2001	**Bob Kerrey*** (D)/1989	**314,442**
	Jan Stoney (R)	258,417
	Nevada	
1999	Harry M. Reid (D)/1987	
2001	**Richard H. Bryan*** (D)/1989	**193,444**
	Hal Furman (R)	155,547
	New Hampshire	
1997	Robert Smith (R)/1991	
1999	Judd Gregg (R)/1993	
	New Jersey	
1997	Bill Bradley (D)/1979	
2001	**Frank R. Lautenberg*** (D)/12/27/82	**1,017,751**
	Garabed "Chuck" Haytaian (R)	950,415
	New Mexico	
1997	Pete V. Domenici (R)/1973	
2001	**Jeff Bingaman*** (D)/1983	**243,759**
	Colin R. McMillan (R)	205,334
	New York	
1999	Alfonse M. D'Amato (R)/1981	
2001	**Daniel Patrick Moynihan*** (D,L)/1977	**2,549,012**
	Bernadette Castro (R,C)	1,940,345
	North Carolina	
1997	Jesse Helms (R)/1973	
1999	Lauch Faircloth (R)/1993	

Term ends	Senator (Party)/Service from[1]	1994 Election
	North Dakota	
1999	Byron L. Dorgan (D)/12/14/92	
2001	**Kent Conrad*** (D)/1987	**135,668**
	Ben Clayburgh (R)	98,069
	Ohio	
1999	John Glenn (D)/12/24/74	
2001	**Mike DeWine** (R)	**1,818,126**
	Joel Hyatt (D)	1,330,287
	Oklahoma	
1997	**James M. Inhofe** (R)[3]	**542,390**
	Dave McCurdy (D)	392,488
1999	Don Nickles (R)/1981	
	Oregon	
1997	Mark O. Hatfield (R)/1/10/67	
1999	Bob Packwood (R)/1969	
	Pennsylvania	
1999	Arlen Specter (R)/1981	
2001	**Rick Santorum** (R)	**1,729,614**
	Harris Wofford* (D)/5/8/91	1,642,199
	Rhode Island	
1997	Claiborne Pell (D)/1961	
2001	**John H. Chafee*** (R)/12/29/76	**213,896**
	Linda J. Kushner (D)	118,411
	South Carolina	
1997	Strom Thurmond (R)/11/7/56	
1999	Ernest F. "Fritz" Hollings (D)/11/9/66	
	South Dakota	
1997	Larry Pressler (R)/1979	
1999	Thomas A. Daschle (D)/1987	
	Tennessee	
1997	**Fred Thompson** (R)[4]	**878,443**
	Jim Cooper (D)	559,358
2001	**Bill Frist** (R)	**828,975**
	Jim Sasser* (D)/1977	616,043
	Texas	
1997	Phil Gramm (R)/1985	
2001	**Kay Bailey Hutchison*** (R)/6/5/93	**2,596,508**
	Richard Fisher (D)	1,635,885
	Utah	
1999	Robert F. Bennett (R)/1993	
2001	**Orrin G. Hatch*** (R)/1977	**356,345**
	Patrick A. Shea (D)	146,731
	Vermont	
1999	Patrick J. Leahy (D)/1975	
2001	**Jim Jeffords*** (R)/1989	**102,978**
	Jan Backus (D)	84,833
	Virginia	
1997	John W. Warner (R)/1/2/79	
2001	**Charles S. Robb*** (D)/1989	**925,500**
	Oliver L. "Ollie" North (R)	873,954
	J. Marshall Coleman (I)	232,278
	Washington	
1999	Patty Murray (D)/1993	
2001	**Slade Gorton*** (R)/1989	**796,233**
	Ron Sims (D)	654,357
	West Virginia	
1997	John D. Rockefeller IV (D)/1/15/85	
2001	**Robert C. Byrd*** (D)/1959	**288,353**
	Stan Klos (R)	129,458
	Wisconsin	
1999	Russell D. Feingold (D)/1993	
2001	**Herbert H. Kohl*** (D)/1989	**912,826**
	Robert T. Welch (R)	637,103
	Wyoming	
1997	Alan K. Simpson (R)/1979	
2001	**Craig Thomas** (R)	**118,061**
	Mike Sullivan (D)	79,553

(1) Jan. 3, unless otherwise noted. (2) Democratic Sen. Richard C. Shelby announced Nov. 9, 1994, that he changed his party designation to Republican. (3) A special election was held, Nov. 8, 1994, to fill the seat left vacant by the resignation of Sen. David Boren (D) to become president of the Univ. of Oklahoma. The winner will serve the remainder of Boren's term. (4) A special election was held, Nov. 8, 1994, to fill the seat left vacant by the resignation of Al Gore, Jr., to become vice president in 1993. The winner will serve the remainder of Gore's term.

The House of Representatives

Rep. 230; Dem. 204; Ind., 1; Total, 435. *Incumbent. Boldface denotes the 1994 election winner.

Members' terms to Jan. 3, 1997. Annual salary, $133,600; Speaker of the House, $171,500; Majority Leader and Minority Leader, $148,400. To be eligible for membership, a person must be at least 25 years of age, a U.S. citizen for at least 7 years, and a resident of the state from which he or she is chosen. The ZIP code of the House is 20515; the telephone number is 202-225-3121.

House officials in 1993-94 (103d Congress) were: Speaker, Thomas S. Foley; Majority Leader, Richard A. Gephardt; Majority Whip, David E. Bonior; Minority Leader, Robert H. Michel; Minority Whip, Newt Gingrich.

D-Democrat; R-Republican; ACP-A Connecticut Party; B-Libertarian; C-Conservative; CC-Change Congress; GR-Green; I-Independent; IF-Independent Fusion; IN-Independent Neighbors; L-Liberal; LI-Long Island First; PF-Peace & Freedom; T-Right to Life; TX-Taxpayers; WE-We the People.

Dist.	Representative (Party)	1994[1] Election
	Alabama	
1.	**H. L. "Sonny" Callahan*** (R)	**101,956**
	Don Womack (D)	49,671
2.	**Terry Everett*** (R)	**124,525**
	Brian Dowling (D)	44,694
3.	**Glen Browder*** (D)	**93,795**
	Ben Hand (R)	53,706
4.	**Tom Bevill*** (D)	**Unopposed**
5.	**Bud Cramer*** (D)	**88,542**
	Wayne Parker (R)	86,717
6.	**Spencer Bachus*** (R)	**152,757**
	Larry Fortenberry (D)	40,659
7.	**Earl F. Hilliard*** (D)	**113,985**
	Alfred J. Middleton, Sr. (R)	34,649
	Alaska	
	Don Young* (R),	**101,839**
	Tony Smith (D)	58,601
	Joni Whitmore (GR)	18,112
	Arizona	
1.	**Matt Salmon** (R)	**97,513**
	Chuck Blanchard (D)	68,661
2.	**Ed Pastor*** (D)	**59,925**
	Robert MacDonald (R)	31,411
3.	**Bob Stump*** (R)	**141,600**
	Howard Lee Sprague (D)	60,903
4.	**John Shadegg** (R)	**111,961**
	Carol Cure (D)	68,055
5.	**Jim Kolbe*** (R)	**139,330**
	Gary Auerbach (D)	58,906
6.	**J. D. Hayworth** (R)	**105,005**
	Karan English* (D)	80,362
	Arkansas	
1.	**Blanche M. Lambert*** (D)	**94,841**
	Warren Dupwe (R)	82,053
2.	**Ray Thornton*** (D)	**97,463**
	Bill Powell (R)	72,419
3.	**Tim Hutchinson*** (R)	**129,623**
	Berta L. Seitz (D)	61,766
4.	**Jay Dickey*** (R)	**87,461**
	Jay Bradford (D)	81,372
	California	
1.	**Frank Riggs** (R)	**100,819**
	Dan Hamburg* (D)	88,242
2.	**Wally Herger*** (R)	**131,775**
	Mary Jacobs (D)	53,229
3.	**Vic Fazio*** (D)	**86,825**
	Tim Lefever (R)	83,729
4.	**John T. Doolittle*** (R)	**132,482**
	Katie Hirning (D)	75,134
5.	**Robert T. Matsui*** (D)	**118,463**
	Robert S. Dinsmore (R)	50,363
6.	**Lynn C. Woolsey*** (D)	**125,117**
	Michael J. Nugent (R)	81,342
7.	**George Miller*** (D)	**107,794**
	Charles V. Hughes (R)	42,154
8.	**Nancy Pelosi*** (D)	**119,095**
	Elsa C. Cheung (R)	26,232
9.	**Ronald V. Dellums*** (D)	**117,818**
	Deborah Wright (R)	36,914
10.	**Bill Baker*** (R)	**126,295**
	Ellen Schwartz (D)	82,555
11.	**Richard Pombo*** (R)	**86,252**
	Randy A. Perry (D)	48,833
12.	**Tom Lantos*** (D)	**102,273**
	Deborah Wilder (R)	49,580
13.	**Fortney "Pete" Stark*** (D)	**88,999**
	Larry Molton (R)	42,026
14.	**Anna G. Eshoo*** (D)	**109,149**
	Ben Brink (R)	70,801
15.	**Norm Mineta*** (D)	**109,475**
	Robert Wick (R)	74,455
16.	**Zoe Lofgren** (D)	**68,778**
	Lyle J. Smith (R)	37,359
17.	**Sam Farr*** (D)	**76,521**
	Bill McCampbell (R)	66,537
18.	**Gary A. Condit*** (D)	**79,767**
	Tom Carter (R)	39,690
19.	**George P. Radanovich** (R)	**92,979**
	Rick Lehman* (D)	64,246
20.	**Cal Dooley*** (D)	**47,857**
	Paul Young (R)	37,682
21.	**Bill Thomas*** (R)	**104,472**
	John L. Evans (D)	41,599
22.	**Andrea Seastrand** (R)	**90,612**
	Walter Holden Capps (D)	89,643
23.	**Elton Gallegly*** (R)	**99,022**
	Kevin Ready (D)	41,453
24.	**Anthony C. Beilenson*** (D)	**84,080**
	Rich Sybert (R)	80,879
25.	**Howard "Buck" McKeon*** (R)	**97,613**
	James H. Gilmartin (D)	47,554
26.	**Howard L. Berman*** (D)	**48,840**
	Gary E. Forsch (R)	25,101
27.	**Carlos J. Moorhead*** (R)	**75,566**
	Doug Kahn (D)	61,967
28.	**David Dreier*** (R)	**99,342**
	Tommy Randle (D)	45,402
29.	**Henry A. Waxman*** (D)	**113,023**
	Paul Stepanek (R)	46,226
30.	**Xavier Becerra*** (D)	**38,712**
	David A. Ramirez (R)	16,269
31.	**Matthew G. Martinez*** (D)	**45,503**
	John V. Flores (R)	31,156
32.	**Julian C. Dixon*** (D)	**88,007**
	Ernie A. Farhat (R)	19,469
33.	**Lucille Roybal-Allard*** (D)	**30,350**
	Kermit Booker (PF)	6,953
34.	**Esteban E. Torres*** (D)	**65,598**
	Albert J. Nunez (R)	36,039
35.	**Maxine Waters*** (D)	**60,446**
	Nate Truman (R)	16,802
36.	**Susan Brooks** (R)	**82,415**
	Jane Harman* (D)	82,322
37.	**Walter R. Tucker III*** (D)	**58,693**
	Guy Wilson (B)	16,777
38.	**Steve Horn*** (R)	**76,399**
	Peter Mathews (D)	47,672
39.	**Ed Royce*** (R)	**105,602**
	R. O. "Bob" Davis (D)	46,169
40.	**Jerry Lewis*** (R)	**111,738**
	Donald M. "Don" Rusk (D)	46,360

Dist.	Representative (Party)	1994[1] Election
41.	**Jay Kim*** (R)	**77,393**
	Ed Tessier (D)	47,271
42.	**George E. Brown, Jr.*** (D)	**56,924**
	Rob Guzman (R)	54,496
43.	**Ken Calvert*** (R)	**77,152**
	Mark A. Takano (D)	54,129
44.	**Sonny Bono** (R)	**87,728**
	Steve Clute (D)	60,134
45.	**Dana Rohrabacher*** (R)	**116,177**
	Brett Williamson (D)	51,964
46.	**Robert K. "Bob" Dornan*** (R)	**46,460**
	Michael P. "Mike" Farber (D)	29,976
47.	**Christopher Cox*** (R)	**143,060**
	Gary Kingsbury (D)	49,557
48.	**Ron Packard*** (R)	**132,319**
	Andrei Leschick (D)	40,150
49.	**Brian P. Bilbray** (R)	**83,743**
	Lynn Schenk* (D)	79,029
50.	**Bob Filner*** (D)	**55,015**
	Mary Alice Acevedo (R)	34,119
51.	**Randy "Duke" Cunningham*** (R)	**124,557**
	Rita K. Tamerius (D)	51,785
52.	**Duncan Hunter*** (R)	**99,825**
	Janet M. Gastil (D)	48,411
	Colorado	
1.	**Patricia Schroeder*** (D)	**92,639**
	William F. Eggert (R)	61,399
2.	**David Skaggs*** (D)	**103,690**
	Patricia "Pat" Miller (R)	78,777
3.	**Scott McInnis*** (R)	**145,304**
	Linda Powers (D)	63,281
4.	**Wayne Allard*** (R)	**136,789**
	Cathy Kipp (D)	52,070
5.	**Joel Hefley*** (R)	**Unopposed**
6.	**Dan Schaefer*** (R)	**124,079**
	John Hallen (D)	49,701
	Connecticut	
1.	**Barbara Bailey Kennelly*** (D,ACP)	**136,997**
	Douglas T. Putnam (R)	46,085
2.	**Sam Gejdenson*** (D)	**80,924**
	Edward W. Munster (R)	80,082
	David Bingham (ACP)	28,304
3.	**Rosa L. DeLauro*** (D)	**105,065**
	Susan Johnson (R,ACP)	60,372
4.	**Christopher Shays*** (R)	**97,977**
	Jonathan D. Kantrowitz (D)	32,128
5.	**Gary A. Franks*** (R)	**92,487**
	James H. Maloney (D,ACP)	80,220
6.	**Nancy L. Johnson*** (R)	**121,895**
	Charlotte Koskoff (D,ACP)	60,145
	Delaware	
	Michael N. Castle* (R)	**137,646**
	Carol Ann DeSantis (D)	51,784
	Florida	
1.	**Joe Scarborough** (R)	**106,140**
	Vince Whibbs, Jr. (D)	67,191
2.	**Pete Peterson*** (D)	**115,748**
	Carole Griffin (R)	72,050
3.	**Corrine Brown*** (D)	**62,650**
	Marc Little (R)	45,390
4.	**Tillie K. Fowler*** (R)	**Unopposed**
5.	**Karen L. Thurman*** (D)	**125,780**
	Don "Big Daddy" Garlits (R)	94,093
6.	**Clifford B. "Cliff" Stearns*** (R)	**Unopposed**
7.	**John L. Mica*** (R)	**131,705**
	Edward D. Goddard (D)	47,742
8.	**Bill McCollum*** (R)	**Unopposed**
9.	**Michael Bilirakis*** (R)	**Unopposed**
10.	**C. W. Bill Young*** (R)	**Unopposed**
11.	**Sam M. Gibbons*** (D)	**76,774**
	Mark Sharpe (R)	72,062
12.	**Charles T. Canady*** (R)	**105,737**
	Robert Connors (D)	57,018

Dist.	Representative (Party)	1994[1] Election
13.	**Dan Miller*** (R)	**Unopposed**
14.	**Porter J. Goss*** (R)	**Unopposed**
15.	**Dave Weldon** (R)	**117,026**
	Sue Munsey (D)	100,512
16.	**Mark Foley** (R)	**122,734**
	John Comerford (D)	88,646
17.	**Carrie P. Meek*** (D)	**Unopposed**
18.	**Ileana Ros-Lehtinen*** (R)	**Unopposed**
19.	**Harry Johnston*** (D)	**147,591**
	Peter J. Tsakanikas (R)	75,779
20.	**Peter Deutsch*** (D)	**114,615**
	Beverly "Bev" Kennedy (R)	72,516
21.	**Lincoln Diaz-Balart*** (R)	**Unopposed**
22.	**Clay Shaw*** (R)	**119,690**
	Hermine L. Wiener (D)	69,215
23.	**Alcee L. Hastings*** (D)	**Unopposed**
	Georgia	
1.	**Jack Kingston*** (R)	**88,658**
	Raymond Beckworth (D)	27,671
2.	**Sanford Bishop*** (D)	**64,980**
	John Clayton (R)	33,415
3.	**Mac Collins*** (R)	**93,647**
	Fred Overby (D)	49,264
4.	**John Linder*** (R)	**90,063**
	Comer Yates (D)	66,366
5.	**John Lewis*** (D)	**85,094**
	Dale Dixon (R)	37,999
6.	**Newt Gingrich*** (R)	**119,550**
	Ben Jones (D)	66,681
7.	**Bob Barr** (R)	**70,801**
	George "Buddy" Darden* (D)	65,481
8.	**Saxby Chambliss** (R)	**88,977**
	Craig Mathis (D)	52,977
9.	**Nathan Deal*** (D)	**78,892**
	Robert L. Castello (R)	57,477
10.	**Charlie Norwood** (R)	**99,511**
	Don Johnson* (D)	51,192
11.	**Cynthia McKinney*** (D)	**71,935**
	Woodrow Lovett (R)	37,556
	Hawaii	
1.	**Neil Abercrombie*** (D)	**94,754**
	Orson Swindle (R)	76,623
2.	**Patsy Takemoto Mink*** (D)	**124,431**
	Robert H. (Lopaka) Garner (R)	42,891
	Idaho	
1.	**Helen Chenoweth** (R)	**111,768**
	Larry LaRocco* (D)	89,824
2.	**Mike Crapo*** (R)	**143,076**
	Penny Fletcher (D)	48,425
	Illinois	
1.	**Bobby L. Rush*** (D)	**107,000**
	William J. Kelly (R)	34,807
2.	**Mel Reynolds*** (D)	**Unopposed**
3.	**William O. Lipinski*** (D)	**90,699**
	Jim Nalepa (R)	77,125
4.	**Luis V. Gutierrez*** (D)	**44,235**
	Steven Valtierra (R)	14,699
5.	**Michael Patrick Flanagan** (R)	**73,340**
	Dan Rostenkowski* (D)	61,152
6.	**Henry J. Hyde*** (R)	**115,286**
	Tom Berry (D)	37,017
7.	**Cardiss Collins*** (D)	**86,894**
	Charles "Chuck" Mobley (R)	23,156
8.	**Philip M. Crane*** (R)	**88,084**
	Robert C. Walberg (D)	47,539
9.	**Sidney R. Yates*** (D)	**92,794**
	George Edward Larney (R)	47,469
10.	**John E. Porter*** (R)	**114,806**
	Andrew M. Krupp (D)	38,152
11.	**Gerald C. "Jerry" Weller** (R)	**96,986**
	Frank Giglio (D)	62,779
12.	**Jerry F. Costello*** (D)	**101,391**
	Jan Morris (R)	52,417
13.	**Harris W. Fawell*** (R)	**124,312**
	William A. Riley (D)	45,709

Dist.	Representative (Party)	1994[1] Election
14.	**J. Dennis Hastert*** (R)	**109,681**
	Steve Denari (D)	33,885
15.	**Thomas W. Ewing*** (R)	**108,857**
	Paul Alexander (D)	50,874
16.	**Donald Manzullo*** (R)	**117,238**
	Pete Sullivan (D)	48,736
17.	**Lane Evans*** (D)	**95,312**
	Jim Anderson (R)	79,471
18.	**Ray LaHood** (R)	**119,838**
	G. Douglas Stephens (D)	78,332
19.	**Glenn Poshard*** (D)	**115,045**
	Brent Winters (R)	81,995
20.	**Richard J. Durbin*** (D)	**108,034**
	Bill Owens (R)	88,964

Indiana

Dist.	Representative (Party)	1994[1] Election
1.	**Peter J. Visclosky*** (D)	**67,527**
	John Larson (R)	52,233
2.	**David M. McIntosh** (R)	**93,592**
	Joseph H. Hogsett (D)	78,241
3.	**Tim Roemer*** (D)	**72,491**
	Richard Burkett (R)	58,878
4.	**Mark Edward Souder** (R)	**87,665**
	Jill L. Long* (D)	70,744
5.	**Steve Buyer*** (R)	**110,917**
	J. D. Beatty (D)	45,180
6.	**Dan Burton*** (R)	**134,471**
	Natalie M. Bruner (D)	40,244
7.	**John T. Myers*** (R)	**102,140**
	Michael M. Harmless (D)	55,856
8.	**John Hostettler** (R)	**93,167**
	Frank McCloskey* (D)	84,751
9.	**Lee H. Hamilton*** (D)	**90,148**
	Jean Leising (R)	83,642
10.	**Andrew Jacobs, Jr.*** (D)	**55,491**
	Marvin Bailey Scott (R)	48,363

Iowa

Dist.	Representative (Party)	1994[1] Election
1.	**Jim Leach*** (R)	**109,975**
	Glen Winekauf (D)	69,240
2.	**Jim Nussle*** (R)	**110,639**
	Dave Nagle (D)	86,024
3.	**Jim Ross Lightfoot*** (R)	**110,528**
	Elaine Baxter (D)	78,251
4.	**Greg Ganske** (R)	**110,522**
	Neal Smith* (D)	97,513
5.	**Tom Latham** (R)	**112,908**
	Sheila McGuire (D)	72,525

Kansas

Dist.	Representative (Party)	1994[1] Election
1.	**Pat Roberts*** (R)	**167,881**
	Terry L. Nichols (D)	49,229
2.	**Sam Brownback** (R)	**135,617**
	John Carlin (D)	70,958
3.	**Jan Meyers*** (R)	**102,107**
	Judy Hancock (D)	78,207
4.	**Todd Tiahrt** (R)	**111,105**
	Dan Glickman* (D)	98,801

Kentucky

Dist.	Representative (Party)	1994[1] Election
1.	**Edward Whitfield** (R)	**64,659**
	Tom Barlow* (D)	62,225
2.	**Ron Lewis** (R)	**90,363**
	David Adkisson (D)	60,797
3.	**Mike Ward** (D)	**67,637**
	Susan B. Stokes (R)	67,210
	Richard Lewis (TX)	17,577
4.	**Jim Bunning*** (R)	**96,464**
	Sally Harris Skaggs (D)	33,713
5.	**Harold "Hal" Rogers*** (R)	**82,276**
	Walter "Doc" Blevins (D)	21,309
6.	**Scotty Baesler*** (D)	**70,082**
	Matthew Eric Wills (R)	49,030

Louisiana

Dist.	Representative (Party)	1994[1] Election
1.	**Robert L. "Bob" Livingston*** (R)	
2.	**William J. Jefferson*** (D)	
3.	**W. J. "Billy" Tauzin*** (D)	
4.	**Cleo Fields*** (D)	
5.	**Jim McCrery*** (R)	
6.	**Richard Baker*** (R)	
7.	**James A. "Jimmy" Hayes*** (D)	

In Louisiana, all candidates of all parties run against each other in an open primary, unless they are unopposed incumbents in which case they are declared elected. All candidates who receive more than 50 percent of the primary vote are also declared elected and do not appear on the general election ballot.

Maine

Dist.	Representative (Party)	1994[1] Election
1.	**James B. Longley, Jr.** (R)	**136,560**
	Dennis L. Dutremble (D)	125,467
2.	**John Baldacci** (D)	**108,793**
	Richard A. Bennett (R)	96,952

Maryland

Dist.	Representative (Party)	1994[1] Election
1.	**Wayne T. Gilchrest*** (R)	**115,838**
	Ralph T. Gies (D)	55,725
2.	**Robert L. Ehrlich, Jr.** (R)	**121,165**
	Gerry L. Brewster (D)	72,333
3.	**Benjamin L. Cardin*** (D)	**113,009**
	Robert Ryan Tousey (R)	46,231
4.	**Albert R. Wynn*** (D)	**91,021**
	Michele Dyson (R)	29,620
5.	**Steny H. Hoyer*** (D)	**95,550**
	Donald Devine (R)	66,765
6.	**Roscoe Bartlett*** (R)	**118,297**
	Paul Muldowney (D)	61,031
7.	**Kweisi Mfume*** (D)	**93,170**
	Kenneth Kondner (R)	21,879
8.	**Constance A. Morella*** (R)	**138,010**
	Steven Van Grack (D)	58,476

Massachusetts

Dist.	Representative (Party)	1994[1] Election
1.	**John W. Olver*** (D)	**Unopposed**
2.	**Richard E. Neal*** (D)	**114,826**
	John M. Briare (R)	71,018
3.	**Peter I. Blute*** (R)	**116,286**
	Kevin O'Sullivan (D)	93,704
4.	**Barney Frank*** (D)	**Unopposed**
5.	**Martin T. Meehan*** (D)	**141,144**
	David E. Coleman (R)	60,628
6.	**Peter G. Torkildsen*** (R)	**120,743**
	John F. Tierney (D)	113,289
7.	**Edward J. Markey*** (D)	**145,966**
	Brad Bailey (R)	80,629
8.	**Joseph P. Kennedy II*** (D)	**Unopposed**
9.	**John Joseph Moakley*** (D)	**143,530**
	Michael M. Murphy (R)	60,737
10.	**Gerry E. Studds*** (D)	**171,585**
	Keith Jason Hemeon (R)	78,055

Michigan

Dist.	Representative (Party)	1994[1] Election
1.	**Bart Stupak*** (D)	**121,138**
	Gil Ziegler (R)	89,745
2.	**Peter Hoekstra*** (R)	**146,666**
	Marcus Hoover (D)	46,184
3.	**Vernon J. Ehlers*** (R)	**135,819**
	Betsy J. Flory (D)	43,485
4.	**Dave Camp*** (R)	**143,821**
	Damion Frasier (D)	49,899
5.	**James A. Barcia*** (D)	**126,522**
	William T. Anderson (R)	61,385
6.	**Fred Upton*** (R)	**121,925**
	David Taylor (D)	42,373
7.	**Nick Smith*** (R)	**113,721**
	Kim McCaughtry (D)	57,393
8.	**Dick Chrysler** (R)	**109,663**
	Bob Mitchell (D)	95,383
9.	**Dale E. Kildee*** (D)	**97,024**
	Megan O'Neill (R)	89,091
10.	**David E. Bonior*** (D)	**121,516**
	Donald J. Lobsinger (R)	73,671

Dist.	Representative (Party)	1994[1] Election
11.	**Joe Knollenberg*** (R)	**155,158**
	Mike Breshgold (D)	69,337
12.	**Sander Levin*** (D)	**103,420**
	John Pappageorge (R)	92,625
13.	**Lynn Nancy Rivers** (D)	**87,445**
	John A. Schall (R)	75,889
14.	**John Conyers, Jr.*** (D)	**129,850**
	Richard Charles Fournier (R)	26,417
15.	**Barbara-Rose Collins*** (D)	**119,328**
	John W. Savage II (R)	20,039
16.	**John D. Dingell*** (D)	**105,301**
	Ken Larkin (R)	70,429

Minnesota

Dist.	Representative (Party)	1994[1] Election
1.	**Gil Gutknecht** (R)	**115,328**
	John C. Hottinger (D)	93,234
2.	**David Minge*** (D)	**118,077**
	Gary B. Revier (R)	103,234
3.	**Jim Ramstad*** (R)	**173,190**
	Bob Olson (D)	62,193
4.	**Bruce F. Vento*** (D)	**115,775**
	Dennis Newinski (R)	88,302
5.	**Martin Olav Sabo*** (D)	**121,507**
	Dorothy LeGrand (R)	73,258
6.	**William P. "Bill" Luther** (D)	**113,736**
	Tad Jude (R)	113,187
7.	**Collin C. Peterson*** (D)	**108,025**
	Bernie Omann (R)	102,653
8.	**James L. Oberstar*** (D)	**153,152**
	Phil Herwig (R)	79,767

Mississippi

Dist.	Representative (Party)	1994[1] Election
1.	**Roger Wicker** (R)	**80,108**
	Bill Wheeler (D)	46,443
2.	**Bennie G. Thompson*** (D)	**66,224**
	Bill Jordan (R)	48,508
3.	**G. V. "Sonny" Montgomery*** (D)	**80,038**
	Dutch Dabbs (R)	38,516
4.	**Mike Parker*** (D)	**81,316**
	Mike Wood (R)	37,458
5.	**Gene Taylor*** (D)	**71,720**
	George Barlos (R)	47,530

Missouri

Dist.	Representative (Party)	1994[1] Election
1.	**William "Bill" Clay, Sr.*** (D)	**97,191**
	Donald R. Counts (R)	50,426
2.	**James M. Talent*** (R)	**154,895**
	Pat Kelly (D)	70,488
3.	**Richard A. Gephardt*** (D)	**117,598**
	Gary Gill (R)	80,978
4.	**Ike Skelton*** (D)	**138,351**
	James A. Noland, Jr. (R)	66,308
5.	**Karen McCarthy*** (D)	**100,059**
	Ron Freeman (R)	76,807
6.	**Pat "Patsy Ann" Danner*** (D)	**140,074**
	Tina Tucker (R)	71,619
7.	**Melton D. "Mel" Hancock*** (R)	**110,397**
	James R. Fossard (D)	77,040
8.	**Bill Emerson*** (R)	**129,728**
	James L. "Jay" Thompson (D)	49,897
9.	**Harold L. Volkmer*** (D)	**98,401**
	Kenny Hulshof (R)	86,883

Montana

Dist.	Representative (Party)	1994[1] Election
	Pat Williams* (D)	**167,271**
	Cy Jamison (R)	145,440

Nebraska

Dist.	Representative (Party)	1994[1] Election
1.	**Doug Bereuter*** (R)	**117,014**
	Patrick Combs (D)	69,946
2.	**Jon Christensen** (R)	**91,658**
	Peter Hoagland* (D)	89,839
3.	**Bill Barrett*** (R)	**153,492**
	Gil Chapin (D)	41,766

Nevada

Dist.	Representative (Party)	1994[1] Election
1.	**John Ensign** (R)	**73,768**
	James H. Bilbray* (D)	72,332
2.	**Barbara F. Vucanovich*** (R)	**141,943**
	Janet Greeson (D)	65,291

New Hampshire

Dist.	Representative (Party)	1994[1] Election
1.	**Bill Zeliff*** (R)	**97,658**
	Bill Verge (D)	42,919
2.	**Charles Bass** (R)	**82,919**
	Dick Swett* (D)	74,098

New Jersey

Dist.	Representative (Party)	1994[1] Election
1.	**Robert E. Andrews*** (D)	**105,196**
	James N. Hogan (R)	40,301
2.	**Frank A. LoBiondo** (R)	**101,455**
	Louis N. Magazzu (D)	55,636
3.	**Jim Saxton*** (R)	**112,296**
	James B. Smith (D)	53,000
4.	**Christopher H. Smith*** (R)	**107,617**
	Ralph Walsh (D)	48,723
5.	**Marge Roukema*** (R)	**139,217**
	Bill Auer (D)	41,042
6.	**Frank Pallone, Jr.*** (D)	**89,049**
	Mike Herson (R)	55,235
7.	**Bob Franks*** (R)	**93,733**
	Karen Carroll (D)	61,819
8.	**Bill Martini** (R)	**69,886**
	Herb Klein (D)	67,879
9.	**Robert G. Torricelli*** (D)	**99,202**
	Peter J. Russo (R)	57,396
10.	**Donald M. Payne*** (D)	**72,345**
	Jim Ford (R)	20,858
11.	**Rodney Frelinghuysen** (R)	**127,626**
	Frank Herbert (D)	50,036
12.	**Dick Zimmer*** (R)	**124,581**
	Joseph D. Youssouf (D)	56,087
13.	**Robert Menendez*** (D)	**67,169**
	Fernando A. Alonso (R)	23,726

New Mexico

Dist.	Representative (Party)	1994[1] Election
1.	**Steven H. Schiff*** (R)	**110,255**
	Peter L. Zollinger (D)	39,791
2.	**Joseph R. Skeen*** (R)	**89,511**
	Benjamin Anthony Chavez (D)	45,381
3.	**Bill Richardson*** (D)	**99,306**
	F. Gregg Bemis, Jr. (R)	53,052

New York

Dist.	Representative (Party)	1994[1] Election
1.	**Michael P. Forbes** (R/WE,C,T)	**90,036**
	George J. Hochbrueckner* (D,LI)	78,620
2.	**Rick A. Lazio*** (R/WE,C)	**97,745**
	James L. Manfre (D, LI)	40,520
3.	**Peter T. King*** (R,C)	**114,787**
	Norma Grill (D)	76,701
4.	**Daniel Frisa** (R)	**86,613**
	Philip M. Schiliro (D)	64,536
5.	**Gary L. Ackerman*** (D,L)	**91,177**
	Grant M. Lally (R,C)	72,630
6.	**Floyd H. Flake*** (D)	**66,414**
	Denny D. Bhagwandin (R,C)	16,329
7.	**Thomas J. Manton*** (D)	**56,608**
	Robert E. Hurley (C)	8,134
8.	**Jerrold L. Nadler*** (D,L)	**101,693**
	David L. Askren (R)	20,543
9.	**Charles E. Schumer*** (D,L)	**91,250**
	James P. McCall (R,C)	36,653
10.	**Edolphus Towns*** (D,L)	**72,479**
	Amelia Smith Parker (R)	7,617
11.	**Major R. Owens*** (D,L)	**59,068**
	Gary S. Popkin (R,B)	6,551
12.	**Nydia M. Velazquez*** (D,L)	**38,324**
	Genevieve R. Brennan (C)	2,671
13.	**Susan Molinari*** (R,C)	**93,393**
	Tyrone G. Butler (D,L)	33,456
14.	**Carolyn B. Maloney*** (D,IN)	**92,390**
	Charles Millard (R,L)	52,754
15.	**Charles B. Rangel*** (D,L)	**73,517**
	Jose Suero (T,IF)	2,816
16.	**José E. Serrano*** (D,L)	**57,245**
	Michael Walters (C)	1,371

Dist.	Representative (Party)	1994[1] Election
17.	**Eliot L. Engel*** (D,L)	**66,838**
	Edward T. Marshall (R)	16,138
18.	**Nita M. Lowey*** (D)	**83,965**
	Andrew C. Hartzell, Jr. (R,C)	60,359
19.	**Sue W. Kelly** (R)	**96,239**
	Hamilton Fish, Jr. (D)	66,330
	Joseph J. DioGuardi (C,T)	19,023
20.	**Benjamin A. Gilman*** (R)	**113,239**
	Gregory B. Julian (D)	48,950
21.	**Michael R. McNulty*** (D,C)	**144,794**
	Joseph Gomez (R)	56,239
22.	**Gerald B. H. Solomon*** (R,C,T)	**154,346**
	L. Robert Lawrence, Jr. (D)	55,975
23.	**Sherwood L. Boehlert*** (R)	**118,359**
	Charles W. Skeele, Jr. (D)	39,231
24.	**John M. McHugh*** (R,C)	**119,935**
	Danny M. Francis (D)	33,083
25.	**James T. Walsh*** (R,C)	**110,242**
	Rhea Jezer (D,CC)	82,186
26.	**Maurice D. Hinchey*** (D,L)	**90,998**
	Bob Moppert (R,C)	89,920
27.	**Bill Paxon*** (R,C,T)	**151,155**
	William A. Long, Jr. (D)	51,491
28.	**Louise M. Slaughter*** (D)	**109,947**
	Renee Forgensi Davison (R,C)	77,948
29.	**John J. LaFalce*** (D,L)	**101,921**
	William E. Miller, Jr. (R,C)	79,603
30.	**Jack Quinn*** (R,C)	**122,233**
	David A. Franczyk (D,L)	60,390
31.	**Amo Houghton*** (R,C)	**114,718**
	Gretchen S. McManus (T)	21,102
	North Carolina	
1.	**Eva M. Clayton*** (D)	**66,521**
	Ted Tyler (R)	42,477
2.	**David Funderburk** (R)	**79,666**
	Richard Moore (D)	62,108
3.	**Walter B. Jones, Jr.** (R)	**72,247**
	H. Martin Lancaster* (D)	65,003
4.	**Frederick Kenneth Heineman** (R)	**77,770**
	David E. Price* (D)	76,457
5.	**Richard Burr** (R)	**84,580**
	A. P. "Sandy" Sands (D)	63,105
6.	**Howard Coble*** (R)	**Unopposed**
7.	**Charles G. Rose III*** (D)	**62,396**
	Robert C. Anderson (R)	58,572
8.	**W. G. "Bill" Hefner*** (D)	**62,882**
	Sherrill Morgan (R)	57,099
9.	**Sue Myrick** (R)	**81,409**
	Rory Blake (D)	44,352
10.	**T. Cass Ballenger*** (R)	**107,479**
	Robert Wayne Avery (D)	42,722
11.	**Charles H. Taylor*** (R)	**113,207**
	Maggie Palmer Lauterer (D)	75,104
12.	**Mel Watt*** (D)	**57,592**
	Joseph A. "Joe" Martino (R)	29,910
	North Dakota	
	Earl Pomeroy* (D)	**121,631**
	Gary Porter (R)	104,651
	Ohio	
1.	**Steve Chabot** (R)	**92,451**
	David Mann* (D)	72,263
2.	**Rob Portman*** (R)	**149,249**
	Les Mann (D)	43,471
3.	**Tony P. Hall*** (D)	**104,608**
	David A. Westbrock (R)	71,638
4.	**Michael G. Oxley*** (R)	**Unopposed**
5.	**Paul E. Gillmor*** (R)	**134,581**
	Jarrod Tudor (D)	48,914
6.	**Frank A. Cremeans** (R)	**90,401**
	Ted Strickland* (D)	86,892
7.	**David L. Hobson*** (R)	**Unopposed**
8.	**John A. Boehner*** (R)	**Unopposed**
9.	**Marcy Kaptur*** (D)	**117,237**
	R. Randy Whitman (R)	38,442

Dist.	Representative (Party)	1994[1] Election
10.	**Martin R. Hoke*** (R)	**94,499**
	Francis E. Gaul (D)	70,547
	Joseph J. Jacobs, Jr. (I)	17,586
11.	**Louis Stokes*** (D)	**112,914**
	James J. Sykora (R)	33,361
12.	**John R. Kasich*** (R)	**107,627**
	Cynthia L. Ruccia (D)	63,033
13.	**Sherrod Brown*** (D)	**92,535**
	Gregory A. White (R)	85,763
14.	**Thomas C. Sawyer*** (D)	**95,510**
	Lynn Slaby (R)	88,427
15.	**Deborah Pryce*** (R)	**110,892**
	Bill Buckel (D)	51,503
16.	**Ralph Regula*** (R)	**136,375**
	J. Michael Finn (D)	45,423
17.	**James A. Traficant, Jr.*** (D)	**147,849**
	Mike G. Meister (R)	43,067
18.	**Bob Ney** (R)	**100,929**
	Greg L. DiDonato (D)	88,230
19.	**Steven C. LaTourette** (R)	**99,392**
	Eric D. Fingerhut* (D)	89,162
	Oklahoma	
1.	**Steve Largent** (R)	**107,085**
	Stuart Price (D)	63,753
2.	**Tom Coburn** (R)	**82,479**
	Virgil R. Cooper (D)	75,943
3.	**Bill K. Brewster*** (D)	**115,731**
	Darrel Dewayne Tallant (R)	41,147
4.	**J. C. Watts** (R)	**80,251**
	David Perryman (D)	67,237
5.	**Ernest Istook*** (R)	**136,877**
	Tom Keith (I)	38,270
6.	**Frank Lucas*** (R)	**106,961**
	Jeffrey S. Tollett (D)	45,399
	Oregon	
1.	**Elizabeth Furse*** (D)	**96,125**
	Bill Witt (R)	85,652
2.	**Wes Cooley** (R)	**100,335**
	Sue C. Kupillas (D)	71,576
3.	**Ron Wyden*** (D)	**132,271**
	Everett Hall (R)	31,183
4.	**Peter DeFazio*** (D)	**138,059**
	John D. Newkirk (R)	65,427
5.	**Catherine Webber** (D)	**88,213**
	Jim Bunn (R)	85,823
	Pennsylvania	
1.	**Thomas M. Foglietta*** (D)	**97,283**
	Roger F. Gordon (R)	22,553
2.	**Chaka Fattah** (D)	**117,754**
	Lawrence R. Watson (R)	19,849
3.	**Robert A. Borski*** (D)	**92,013**
	James C. Hasher (R)	54,723
4.	**Ron Klink*** (D)	**118,907**
	Ed Peglow (R)	66,391
5.	**William F. "Bill" Clinger, Jr.*** (R)	**Unopposed**
6.	**Tim Holden*** (D)	**89,184**
	Fred Levering (R)	67,308
7.	**Curt Weldon*** (R)	**137,177**
	Sara Nichols (D)	59,777
8.	**Jim Greenwood*** (R)	**110,239**
	John P. Murray (D)	45,057
9.	**Bud Shuster*** (R)	**Unopposed**
10.	**Joseph M. McDade*** (R)	**105,663**
	Daniel J. Schreffler (D)	50,112
11.	**Paul E. Kanjorski*** (D)	**100,956**
	J. Andrew Podolak (R)	50,389
12.	**John P. Murtha*** (D)	**117,783**
	Bill Choby (R)	57,113
13.	**Jon D. Fox** (R)	**96,431**
	Marjorie Margolies Mezvinsky* (D)	88,173
14.	**William J. Coyne*** (D)	**104,600**
	John Robert Clark (R)	53,250
15.	**Paul McHale*** (D)	**71,751**
	Jim Yeager (R)	71,545

Dist.	Representative (Party)	1994[1] Election
16.	**Robert S. Walker*** (R)	**109,487**
	Bill Chertok (D)	47,569
17.	**George W. Gekas*** (R)	**Unopposed**
18.	**Mike Doyle** (D)	**101,396**
	John McCarty (R)	83,714
19.	**Bill Goodling*** (R)	**Unopposed**
20.	**Frank R. Mascara** (D)	**95,340**
	Mike McCormick (R)	83,900
21.	**Phil English** (R)	**89,367**
	Bill Leavens (D)	84,817
	Rhode Island	
1.	**Patrick J. Kennedy** (D)	**86,904**
	Kevin Vigilante (R)	73,527
2.	**John F. Reed*** (D)	**115,246**
	A. John Elliot (R)	53,937
	South Carolina	
1.	**Mark Sanford** (R)	**97,878**
	Robert Barber (D)	47,849
2.	**Floyd D. Spence*** (R)	**Unopposed**
3.	**Lindsey Graham** (R)	**90,061**
	James E. Bryan, Jr. (D)	59,846
4.	**Bob Inglis*** (R)	**109,613**
	Jerry L. Fowler (D)	39,389
5.	**John Spratt*** (D)	**77,007**
	Larry Bigham (R)	70,314
6.	**James E. Clyburn** (D)	**88,700**
	Gary McLeod (R)	50,225
	South Dakota	
	Tim Johnson* (D)	**183,038**
	Jan Berkhout (R)	112,100
	Tennessee	
1.	**James H. "Jimmy" Quillen*** (R)	**101,508**
	J. Carr "Jack" Christian (D)	34,591
2.	**John J. Duncan, Jr.*** (R)	**127,831**
	Randon J. Krieg (I)	6,783
	Greg Samples (I)	6,612
3.	**Zach Wamp** (R)	**84,346**
	Randy Button (D)	73,602
4.	**Van Hilleary** (R)	**81,328**
	Jeff Whorley (D)	60,800
5.	**Bob Clement*** (D)	**94,005**
	John Osborne (R)	60,710
6.	**Bart Gordon*** (D)	**90,720**
	Steve Gill (R)	88,644
7.	**Ed Bryant** (R)	**101,733**
	Harold Byrd (D)	65,777
8.	**John Tanner*** (D)	**96,513**
	Neal R. Morris (R)	55,100
9.	**Harold E. Ford*** (D)	**94,804**
	Rod DeBerry (R)	69,224
	Texas	
1.	**Jim Chapman*** (D)	**86,420**
	Mike Blankenship (R)	63,884
2.	**Charles Wilson*** (D)	**87,553**
	Donna Peterson (R)	65,947
3.	**Sam Johnson*** (R)	**157,011**
	Tom Donahue (B)	15,611
4.	**Ralph M. Hall*** (D)	**99,315**
	David L. Bridges (R)	67,264
5.	**John Bryant*** (D)	**61,342**
	Pete Sessions (R)	58,608
6.	**Joe Barton*** (R)	**152,011**
	Terry Jesmore (D)	44,394
7.	**Bill Archer*** (R)	**Unopposed**
8.	**Jack Fields*** (R)	**147,890**
	Russ Klecka (I)	12,752
9.	**Steve Stockman** (R)	**81,353**
	Jack Brooks* (D)	71,643
10.	**Lloyd Doggett** (D)	**113,738**
	A. Jo Baylor (R)	80,382
11.	**Chet Edwards*** (D)	**76,589**
	Jim Broyles (R)	52,824
12.	**Pete Geren*** (D)	**96,576**
	Ernest J. Anderson, Jr. (R)	43,957

Dist.	Representative (Party)	1994[1] Election
13.	**William M. "Mac" Thornberry** (R)	**79,418**
	Bill Sarpalius* (D)	63,724
14.	**Greg Laughlin*** (D)	**85,899**
	Jim Deats (R)	68,791
15.	**E. "Kika" de la Garza*** (D)	**61,889**
	Tom Haughey (R)	40,755
16.	**Ronald Coleman*** (D)	**49,815**
	Bobby Ortiz (R)	37,409
17.	**Charles W. Stenholm*** (D)	**83,486**
	Phil Boone (R)	72,000
18.	**Sheila Jackson Lee** (D)	**84,802**
	Jerry Burley (R)	28,156
19.	**Larry Combest*** (R)	**Unopposed**
20.	**Henry B. Gonzalez*** (D)	**59,257**
	Carl Bill Colyer (R)	35,895
21.	**Lamar Smith*** (R)	**165,425**
	Kerry L. Lowry (I)	18,471
22.	**Tom DeLay*** (R)	**119,296**
	Scott Douglas Cunningham (D)	38,823
23.	**Henry Bonilla*** (R)	**72,868**
	Rolando L. Rios (D)	43,727
24.	**Martin Frost*** (D)	**65,177**
	Ed Harrison (R)	58,039
25.	**Ken Bentsen** (D)	**61,945**
	Gene Fontenot (R)	53,309
26.	**Dick Armey*** (R)	**135,397**
	LeEarl Ann Bryant (D)	39,765
27.	**Solomon P. Ortiz*** (D)	**64,454**
	Erol A. Stone (R)	44,200
28.	**Frank Tejeda*** (D)	**73,900**
	David C. Slatter (R)	28,745
29.	**Gene Green*** (D)	**44,090**
	Harold "Oilman" Eide (R)	15,948
30.	**Eddie Bernice Johnson** (D)	**73,166**
	Lucy Cain (R)	25,848
	Utah	
1.	**James V. Hansen*** (R)	**104,740**
	Bobbie Coray (D)	57,583
2.	**Enid Greene Waldholtz** (R)	**85,479**
	Karen Shepherd* (D)	66,883
	Merrill Cook (I)	34,174
3.	**Bill Orton*** (D)	**91,091**
	Dixie Thompson (R)	61,377
	Vermont	
	Bernard Sanders* (I)	**103,201**
	John Carroll (R)	95,995
	Virginia	
1.	**Herbert H. "Herb" Bateman*** (R)	**142,927**
	Mary F. Sinclair (D)	44,804
2.	**Owen B. Pickett*** (D)	**78,524**
	J. L. "Jim" Chapman IV (R)	54,623
3.	**Robert C. "Bobby" Scott*** (D)	**108,091**
	Thomas E. "Tom" Ward (R)	28,042
4.	**Norman Sisisky*** (D)	**115,236**
	A. George Sweet III (R)	71,176
5.	**L. F. Payne, Jr.*** (D)	**94,955**
	George C. Landrith III (R)	83,135
6.	**Robert W. "Bob" Goodlatte*** (R)	**Unopposed**
7.	**Thomas J. "Tom" Bliley, Jr.*** (R)	**176,650**
	Gerald E. "Jerry" Berg (I)	33,123
8.	**James P. Moran, Jr.*** (D)	**116,602**
	Kyle E. McSlarrow (R)	77,088
9.	**Frederick C. "Rick" Boucher*** (D)	**102,329**
	S. H. "Steve" Fast (R)	72,021
10.	**Frank R. Wolf*** (R)	**150,421**
	Alan R. Ogden (I)	13,320
	Robert L. "Bob" Rilee (I)	8,147
11.	**Thomas M. Davis III** (R)	**91,622**
	Leslie L. Byrne* (D)	80,729
	Washington	
1.	**Rick White** (R)	**82,912**
	Maria Cantwell* (D)	80,948
2.	**Jack Metcalf** (R)	**89,765**
	Harriet A. Spanel (D)	76,295
3.	**Linda Smith** (R)	**86,072**
	Jolene Unsoeld* (D)	74,713

Dist.	Representative (Party)	1994[1] Election
4.	**Doc Hastings** (R)	**76,483**
	Jay Inslee* (D)	69,338
5.	**George Nethercutt** (R)	**99,622**
	Thomas S. Foley* (D)	97,448
6.	**Norm Dicks*** (D)	**90,822**
	Benjamin Gregg (R)	64,648
7.	**Jim McDermott*** (D)	**127,758**
	Keith Harris (R)	39,791
8.	**Jennifer Dunn*** (R)	**118,572**
	Jim Wyrick (D)	57,779
9.	**Randy Tate** (R)	**64,434**
	Mike Kreidler* (D)	61,642
	West Virginia	
1.	**Alan B. Mollohan*** (D)	**102,605**
	Sally Rossy Riley (R)	43,291
2.	**Bob Wise*** (D)	**90,063**
	Sam Cravotta (R)	51,224
3.	**Nick Joe Rahall II*** (D)	**74,344**
	Ben Waldman (R)	41,972
	Wisconsin	
1.	**Mark W. Neumann** (R)	**83,935**
	Peter W. Barca* (D)	82,537
2.	**Scott L. Klug*** (R)	**133,802**
	Thomas C. Hecht (D)	55,398
3.	**Steve Gunderson*** (R)	**89,271**
	Harvey Stower (D)	65,755
4.	**Gerald D. Kleczka*** (D)	**93,801**
	Tom Reynolds (R)	77,701
5.	**Tom Barrett*** (D)	**88,040**
	Stephen B. Hollingshead (R)	51,443
6.	**Thomas E. Petri*** (R)	**Unopposed**
7.	**David R. Obey*** (D)	**97,184**
	Scott West (R)	81,697
8.	**Toby Roth*** (R)	**114,021**
	Stan Gruszynski (D)	65,218
9.	**F. James Sensenbrenner, Jr.*** (R)	**Unopposed**
	Wyoming	
	Barbara Cubin (R)	**104,229**
	Bob Schuster (D)	80,964

The following members of Congress are nonvoting: Carlos Romero Barceló (D), resident commissioner, Puerto Rico; Eleanor Holmes Norton (D), District of Columbia; Robert Underwood (D), Guam; Eni F. H. Faleomavaega (D), American Samoa. A run-off election between Eileen R. Petersen (D) and Victor D. Frazer (I) was scheduled for Nov. 22, 1994, for the nonvoting delegate position for the Virgin Islands.

(1) Results are preliminary and subject to change, pending official results.

Congressional Committees

Senate Standing Committees

(As of Apr. 1994)

Agriculture, Nutrition, and Forestry
Chairman: Patrick J. Leahy, Vt.
Ranking Rep.: Richard G. Lugar, Ind.

Appropriations
Chairman: Robert C. Byrd, W.V.
Ranking Rep.: Mark O. Hatfield, Ore.

Armed Services
Chairman: Sam Nunn, Ga.
Ranking Rep.: Strom Thurmond, S.C.

Banking, Housing, and Urban Affairs
Chairman: Donald W. Riegle, Jr., Mich.
Ranking Rep.: Alfonse D'Amato, N.Y.

Budget
Chairman: Jim Sasser, Tenn.
Ranking Rep.: Pete V. Domenici, N.M.

Commerce, Science, and Transportation
Chairman: Ernest F. Hollings, S.C.
Ranking Rep.: John C. Danforth, Mo.

Energy and Natural Resources
Chairman: J. Bennett Johnston, La.
Ranking Rep.: Malcolm Wallop, Wyo.

Environment and Public Works
Chairman: Max Baucus, Mon.
Ranking Rep.: John H. Chafee, R.I.

Finance
Chairman: Daniel Patrick Moynihan, N.Y.
Ranking Rep.: Bob Packwood, Ore.

Foreign Relations
Chairman: Claiborne Pell, R.I.
Ranking Rep.: Jesse Helms, N.C.

Governmental Affairs
Chairman: John Glenn, Ohio
Ranking Rep.: William V. Roth, Jr., Del.

Judiciary
Chairman: Joseph R. Biden, Jr., Del.
Ranking Rep.: Orrin G. Hatch, Ut.

Labor and Human Resources
Chairman: Edward M. Kennedy, Mass.
Ranking Rep.: Nancy Landon Kassebaum, Kan.

Rules and Administration
Chairman: Wendell H. Ford, Ky.
Ranking Rep.: Ted Stevens, Alas.

Small Business
Chairman: Dale Bumpers, Ark.
Ranking Rep.: Larry Pressler, S.D.

Veterans' Affairs
Chairman: John D. Rockefeller IV, W.V.
Ranking Rep.: Frank H. Murkowski, Alas.

Senate Other, Select, and Special Committees

(As of Apr. 1994)

Aging
Chairman: David H. Pryor, Ark.
Ranking Rep.: William S. Cohen, Me.

Ethics
Chairman: Richard H. Bryan, Nev.
V. Chairman: Mitch McConnell, Ky.

Indian Affairs
Chairman: Daniel K. Inouye, Ha.
Ranking Rep.: John McCain, Ariz.

Intelligence
Chairman: Dennis DeConcini, Ariz.
V. Chairman: John W. Warner, Va.

House Select Committees

(As of May 1994)

Intelligence
Chairman: Bill Richardson, N.M.
Ranking Rep.: Larry Combest, Tex.

Joint Committees of Congress

(As of May 1994)

Economic
Chairman: Rep. David R. Obey, Wis.
V. Chairman: Sen. Paul S. Sarbanes, Md.

Library
Chairman: Rep. Charles C. "Charlie" Rose, N.C.
V. Chairman: Sen. Claiborne Pell, R.I.

Organization of Congress
Co-Chairman: Sen. David L. Boren, Okla.
Co-Chairman: Rep. Lee H. Hamilton, Ind.
V. Chairman: Sen. Pete V. Domenici, N.M.
V. Chairman: Rep. David Dreier, Cal.

Printing
Chairman: Sen. Wendell H. Ford, Ky.
V. Chairman: Rep. Charles C. "Charlie" Rose, N.C.

Taxation
Chairman: Rep. Sam Gibbons, Fla., act.[1]
V. Chairman: Sen. Daniel Patrick Moynihan, N.Y.

House Standing Committees

(As of May 1994)

Agriculture
Chairman: E. "Kika" de la Garza, TX
Ranking Rep.: Pat Roberts, KS

Appropriations
Chairman: David R. Obey, WI
Ranking Rep.: Joseph M. McDade, PA

Armed Services
Chairman: Ronald V. Dellums, CA
Ranking Rep.: Floyd D. Spence, SC

Banking, Finance, and Urban Affairs
Chairman: Henry B. Gonzalez, TX
Ranking Rep.: James A. "Jim" Leach, IA

Budget
Chairman: Martin Olav Sabo, MN
Ranking Rep.: John R. Kasich, OH

District of Columbia
Chairman: Fortney "Pete" Stark, CA
Ranking Rep.: Thomas J. "Tom" Bliley, Jr., VA

Education and Labor
Chairman: William D. Ford, MI
Ranking Rep.: William F. Goodling, PA

Energy and Commerce
Chairman: John D. Dingell, MI
Ranking Rep.: Carlos J. Moorhead, CA

Foreign Affairs
Chairman: Lee H. Hamilton, IN
Ranking Rep.: Benjamin A. Gitman, NY

Government Operations
Chairman: John Conyers, Jr., MI
Ranking Rep.: William F. "Bill" Clinger, Jr., PA

House Administration
Chairman: Charles C. "Charlie" Rose, NC
Ranking Rep.: William M. "Bill" Thomas, CA

Judiciary
Chairman: Jack Brooks, TX
Ranking Rep.: Hamilton Fish, Jr., NY

Merchant Marine and Fisheries
Chairman: Gerry E. Studds, MA
Ranking Rep.: Jack Fields, TX

Natural Resources
Chairman: George Miller, CA
Ranking Rep.: Don Young, AK

Post Office and Civil Service
Chairman: William "Bill" Clay, MO
Ranking Rep.: John T. Meyers, IN

Public Works and Transportation
Chairman: Norman Y. Mineta, CA
Ranking Rep.: Bud Shuster, PA

Rules
Chairman: John Joseph Moakley, MA
Ranking Rep.: Gerald B. H. Solomon, NY

Science, Space, and Technology
Chairman: George E. Brown, Jr., CA
Ranking Rep.: Robert S. Walker, PA

Small Business
Chairman: John J. LaFalce, NY
Ranking Rep.: Jan Meyers, KS

Standards of Official Conduct
Chairman: Jim McDermott, WA
Ranking Rep.: Fred Grandy, IA

Veterans' Affairs
Chairman: G. V. "Sonny" Montgomery, MS
Ranking Rep.: Bob Stump, AZ

Ways and Means
Chairman: Sam Gibbons, FL, act.[1]
Ranking Rep.: Bill Archer, TX

(1) Dan Rostenkowski resigned his position on May 31, 1994.

Political Divisions of the U.S. Senate and House of Representatives, 1965-95

Source: Clerk of the House of Representatives; Secretary of the Senate; Voter News Service

		Senate					House of Representatives				
Congress	Years	Number of Senators	Democrats	Republicans	Other parties	Vacant	Number of Representatives	Democrats	Republicans	Other parties	Vacant
89th . . .	1965-67	100	68	32			435	295	140		
90th . . .	1967-69	100	64	36			435	248	187		
91st . . .	1969-71	100	58	42			435	243	192		
92d. . . .	1971-73	100	54	44	2		435	255	180		
93d. . . .	1973-75	100	56	42	2		435	242	192	1	
94th . . .	1975-77	100	61	37	2		435	291	144		
95th . . .	1977-79	100	61	38	1		435	292	143		
96th . . .	1979-81	100	58	41	1		435	277	158		
97th . . .	1981-83	100	46	53	1		435	242	190		3
98th . . .	1983-85	100	46	54			435	269	166		
99th . . .	1985-87	100	47	53			435	253	182		
100th. . .	1987-89	100	54	46			435	258	177		
101st. . .	1989-91	100	57	43			435	262	173		
102d . . .	1991-93	100	57	43			435	266	164	1	4
103d . . .	1993-95	100	56	44			435	256	178	1	
104th. . .	1995-97	100	47[1]	53[1]			435	204[1]	230[1]	1[1]	

(1) As of preliminary 1994 election results; data subject to change pending official election results.

Congressional Bills Vetoed, 1789-1994

Source: Senate Library; Oct. 1994

	Regular vetoes	Pocket vetoes	Total vetoes	Vetoes over-ridden
Washington	2	—	2	—
John Adams	—	—	—	—
Jefferson	—	—	—	—
Madison	5	2	7	—
Monroe	1	—	1	—
John Q. Adams	—	—	—	—
Jackson	5	7	12	—
Van Buren	—	1	1	—
William Harrison	—	—	—	—
Tyler	6	4	10	1
Polk	2	1	3	—
Taylor	—	—	—	—
Fillmore	—	—	—	—
Pierce	9	—	9	5
Buchanan	4	3	7	—
Lincoln	2	5	7	—
Andrew Johnson	21	8	29	15
Grant	45	48	93	4
Hayes	12	1	13	1
Garfield	—	—	—	—
Arthur	4	8	12	1
Cleveland	304	110	414	2

	Regular vetoes	Pocket vetoes	Total vetoes	Vetoes over-ridden
Benjamin Harrison	19	25	44	1
Cleveland	42	128	170	5
McKinley	6	36	42	—
Theodore Roosevelt	42	40	82	1
Taft	30	9	39	1
Wilson	33	11	44	6
Harding	5	1	6	—
Coolidge	20	30	50	4
Hoover	21	16	37	3
Franklin Roosevelt	372	263	635	9
Truman	180	70	250	12
Eisenhower	73	108	181	2
Kennedy	12	9	21	—
Lyndon Johnson	16	14	30	—
Nixon	26	17	43	7
Ford	48	18	66	12
Carter	13	18	31	2
Reagan	39	39	78	9
Bush[1]	29	15	44	1
Clinton	—	—	—	—
Total[1]	**1,467**	**1,066**	**2,514**	**104**

(1) Excluded from the figures are 2 additional bills, which Pres. Bush claimed to be vetoed but Congress considered enacted into law because the President failed to return them to Congress during a recess period.

Judiciary of the U.S.

Data as of mid-1994

Justices of the United States Supreme Court

The Supreme Court comprises the chief justice of the U.S. and 8 associate justices, all appointed by the president with advice and consent of the Senate. Salaries: chief justice $171,500 annually, associate justice $164,100. The Supreme Court is located at the U.S. Supreme Court Bldg., 1 First St. NE, Washington, DC 20543.

Members of the Supreme Court at the start of the 1994-95 term (Oct. 3, 1994): *Chief justice:* William H. Rehnquist; *associate justices:* Stephen Breyer, Ruth Bader Ginsburg, Anthony M. Kennedy, Sandra Day O'Connor, Antonin Scalia, David H. Souter, John Paul Stevens, Clarence Thomas.

Name[1], apptd from	Service Term	Yrs.	Born	Died
John Jay, NY	1789-1795	5	1745	1829
John Rutledge, SC	1789-1791	1	1739	1800
William Cushing, MA	1789-1810	20	1732	1810
James Wilson, PA	1789-1798	8	1742	1798
John Blair, VA	1789-1796	6	1732	1800
James Iredell, NC	1790-1799	9	1751	1799
Thomas Johnson, MD	1791-1793	1	1732	1819
William Paterson, NJ	1793-1806	13	1745	1806
John Rutledge, SC	1795[2]	—	1739	1800
Samuel Chase, MD	1796-1811	15	1741	1811
Oliver Ellsworth, CT	1796-1800	4	1745	1807
Bushrod Washington, VA	1798-1829	31	1762	1829
Alfred Moore, NC	1799-1804	4	1755	1810
John Marshall, VA	1801-1835	34	1755	1835
William Johnson, SC	1804-1834	30	1771	1834
Henry B. Livingston, NY	1806-1823	16	1757	1823
Thomas Todd, KY	1807-1826	18	1765	1826
Joseph Story, MA	1811-1845	33	1779	1845
Gabriel Duval, MD	1811-1835	22	1752	1844
Smith Thompson, NY	1823-1843	20	1768	1843
Robert Trimble, KY	1826-1828	2	1777	1828
John McLean, OH	1829-1861	32	1785	1861
Henry Baldwin, PA	1830-1844	14	1780	1844
James M. Wayne, GA	1835-1867	32	1790	1867
Roger B. Taney, MD	1836-1864	28	1777	1864
Philip P. Barbour, VA	1836-1841	4	1783	1841
John Catron, TN	1837-1865	28	1786	1865
John McKinley, AL	1837-1852	15	1780	1852
Peter V. Daniel, VA	1841-1860	19	1784	1860
Samuel Nelson, NY	1845-1872	27	1792	1873
Levi Woodbury, NH	1845-1851	5	1789	1851
Robert C. Grier, PA	1846-1870	23	1794	1870
Benjamin R. Curtis, MA	1851-1857	6	1809	1874
John A. Campbell, AL	1853-1861	8	1811	1889
Nathan Clifford, ME	1858-1881	23	1803	1881
Noah H. Swayne, OH	1862-1881	18	1804	1884
Samuel F. Miller, IA	1862-1890	28	1816	1890
David Davis, IL	1862-1877	14	1815	1886
Stephen J. Field, CA	1863-1897	34	1816	1899
Salmon P. Chase, OH	1864-1873	8	1808	1873
William Strong, PA	1870-1880	10	1808	1895
Joseph P. Bradley, NJ	1870-1892	21	1813	1892
Ward Hunt, NY	1872-1882	9	1810	1886
Morrison R. Waite, OH	1874-1888	14	1816	1888
John M. Harlan, KY	1877-1911	34	1833	1911
William B. Woods, GA	1880-1887	6	1824	1887
Stanley Matthews, OH	1881-1889	7	1824	1889
Horace Gray, MA	1881-1902	20	1828	1902
Samuel Blatchford, NY	1882-1893	11	1820	1893
Lucius Q.C. Lamar, MS	1888-1893	5	1825	1893
Melville W. Fuller, IL	1888-1910	21	1833	1910
David J. Brewer, KS	1889-1910	20	1837	1910
Henry B. Brown, MI	1890-1906	15	1836	1913
George Shiras Jr., PA	1892-1903	10	1832	1924
Howell E. Jackson, TN	1893-1895	2	1832	1895
Edward D. White, LA	1894-1910	16	1845	1921
Rufus W. Peckham, NY	1895-1909	13	1838	1909
Joseph McKenna, CA	1898-1925	26	1843	1926
Oliver W. Holmes, MA	1902-1932	29	1841	1935
William R. Day, OH	1903-1922	19	1849	1923
William H. Moody, MA	1906-1910	3	1853	1917
Horace H. Lurton, TN	1909-1914	4	1844	1914
Charles E. Hughes, NY	1910-1916	5	1862	1948
Willis Van Devanter, WY	1910-1937	26	1859	1941
Joseph R. Lamar, GA	1910-1916	5	1857	1916
Edward D. White, LA	1910-1921	10	1845	1921
Mahlon Pitney, NJ	1912-1922	10	1858	1924
James C. McReynolds, TN	1914-1941	26	1862	1946
Louis D. Brandeis, MA	1916-1939	22	1856	1941
John H. Clarke, OH	1916-1922	5	1857	1945
William H. Taft, CT	1921-1930	8	1857	1930
George Sutherland, UT	1922-1938	15	1862	1942
Pierce Butler, MN	1922-1939	16	1866	1939
Edward T. Sanford, TN	1923-1930	7	1865	1930
Harlan F. Stone, NY	1925-1941	16	1872	1946
Charles E. Hughes, NY	1930-1941	11	1862	1948
Owen J. Roberts, PA	1930-1945	15	1875	1955
Benjamin N. Cardozo, NY	1932-1938	6	1870	1938
Hugo L. Black, AL	1937-1971	34	1886	1971
Stanley F. Reed, KY	1938-1957	19	1884	1980
Felix Frankfurter, MA	1939-1962	23	1882	1965
William O. Douglas, CT	1939-1975	36	1898	1980
Frank Murphy, MI	1940-1949	9	1890	1949
Harlan F. Stone, NY	1941-1946	5	1872	1946
James F. Byrnes, SC	1941-1942	1	1879	1972
Robert H. Jackson, NY	1941-1954	12	1892	1954
Wiley B. Rutledge, IA	1943-1949	6	1894	1949
Harold H. Burton, OH	1945-1958	13	1888	1964
Fred M. Vinson, KY	1946-1953	7	1890	1953
Tom C. Clark, TX	1949-1967	18	1899	1977
Sherman Minton, IN	1949-1956	7	1890	1965
Earl Warren, CA	1953-1969	16	1891	1974
John Marshall Harlan, NY	1955-1971	16	1899	1971
William J. Brennan Jr., NJ	1956-1990	33	1906	—
Charles E. Whittaker, MO	1957-1962	5	1901	1973
Potter Stewart, OH	1958-1981	23	1915	1985
Byron R. White, CO	1962-1993	31	1917	—
Arthur J. Goldberg, IL	1962-1965	3	1908	1990
Abe Fortas, TN	1965-1969	4	1910	1982
Thurgood Marshall, NY	1967-1991	24	1908	1993
Warren E. Burger, VA	1969-1986	17	1907	—
Harry A. Blackmun, MN	1970-1994	24	1908	—
Lewis F. Powell Jr., VA	1972-1987	15	1907	—
William H. Rehnquist, AZ	1972-1986	14	1924	—
John Paul Stevens, IL	1975-	—	1920	—
Sandra Day O'Connor, AZ	1981-	—	1930	—
William H. Rehnquist, AZ	1986-	—	1924	—
Antonin Scalia, VA	1986-	—	1936	—
Anthony M. Kennedy, CA	1988-	—	1936	—
David H. Souter, NH	1990-	—	1939	—
Clarence Thomas, VA	1991-	—	1948	—
Ruth Bader Ginsburg, DC	1993-	—	1933	—
Stephen Breyer, MA	1994-	—	1938	—

(1) Chief justices in italics. (2) Rejected Dec. 15, 1795.

U.S. Courts of Appeals

(Salaries, $141,700. CJ means Chief Judge)

Federal Circuit — Glenn L. Archer, Jr., CJ; Helen W. Nies, Giles S. Rich, Pauline Newman, H. Robert Mayer, Paul R. Michel, S. Jay Plager, Alan D. Lourie, Raymond C. Clevenger III, Randall F. Rader, Alvin A. Schall; Clerk's Office, Washington, DC 20439.

District of Columbia — Harry T. Edwards, CJ; Patricia M. Wald, Laurence H. Silberman, James L. Buckley, Stephen F. Williams, Douglas Ginsburg, David B. Sentelle, Karen LeCraft Henderson, A. Raymond Randolph, Judith W. Rogers, David S. Tatel; Clerk's Office, Washington, DC 20001.

First Circuit (ME, MA, NH, RI, Puerto Rico) — Juan R. Torruella CJ; Bruce M. Selya, Conrad K. Cyr, Michael Boudin, Norman H. Stahl; Clerk's Office, Boston, MA 02109.

Second Circuit (CT, NY, VT) — Jon O. Newman, CJ; Amalya Lyle Kearse, Ralph K. Winter, Roger J. Miner, Frank X. Altimari, J. Daniel Mahoney, John M. Walker Jr., Joseph M. McLaughlin, Dennis G. Jacobs, Pierre N. Leval, Guido Calabresi, Jose A. Cabranes; Clerk's Office, New York, NY 10007.

Third Circuit (DE, NJ, PA, Virgin Islands) — Dolores K. Sloviter, CJ; Edward R. Becker, Carol Los Mansmann, Walter K. Stapleton, Morton I. Greenberg, Anthony J. Scirica, William D. Hutchinson, Robert E. Cowen, Richard L. Nygaard, Samuel A. Alito Jr., Jane R. Roth, Timothy K. Lewis, Theodore A. McKee; Clerk's Office, Philadelphia, PA 19106.

Fourth Circuit (MD, NC, SC, VA, WV) — Sam J. Ervin 3d, CJ; Kenneth K. Hall, Donald Stuart Russell, H. Emory Widener Jr., Francis D. Murnaghan Jr., J. Harvie Wilkinson 3d, William W. Wilkins Jr., Paul V. Niemeyer, Clyde H. Hamilton, J. Michael Luttig, Karen J. Williams, M. Blane Michael, Diana G. Motz; Clerk's Office, Richmond, VA 23219.

Fifth Circuit (LA, MS, TX) — Henry A. Politz, CJ; Carolyn Dineen King, Will Garwood, E. Grady Jolly, Patrick E. Higginbotham, W. Eugene Davis, Jerry E. Smith, Edith Hollan Jones, John M. Duhé Jr., Rhesa A. Barksdale, Jacques L. Wiener Jr., Emilio M. Garza, Harold R. DeMoss Jr., Fortunato P. Benavides, Carl E. Stewart, Robert M. Parker; Clerk's Office, New Orleans, LA 70130.

Sixth Circuit (KY, MI, OH, TN) — Gilbert S. Merritt, CJ; Damon J. Keith, Boyce F. Martin Jr., Nathaniel R. Jones, Cornelia G. Kennedy, H. Ted Milburn, David A. Nelson, James L. Ryan, Danny J. Boggs, Alan E. Norris, Richard H. Suhrheinrich, Eugene E. Siler Jr., Alice M. Batchelder, Martha Craig Daughtrey; Clerk's Office, Cincinnati, OH 45202.

Seventh Circuit (IL, IN, WI) — Richard A. Posner, CJ; William J. Bauer, Walter J. Cummings, Richard D. Cudahy, John L. Coffey, Joel M. Flaum, Frank H. Easterbrook, Kenneth F. Ripple, Daniel A. Manion, Michael S. Kanne, Ilana D. Rovner, Wilbur F. Pell Jr., Thomas E. Fairchild, Harlington Wood, Jesse E. Eschbach; Clerk's Office, Chicago, IL 60604.

Eighth Circuit (AR, IA, MN, MO, NE, ND, SD) — Richard S. Arnold, CJ; Theodore McMillian, George C. Fagg, Pasco M. Bowman, Roger L. Wollman, Frank J. Magill, C. Arlen Beam, James B. Loken, David R. Hansen, Morris S. Arnold; Clerk's Office, St. Louis, MO 63101.

Ninth Circuit (AK, AZ, CA, HI, ID, MT, NV, OR, WA, Guam, N. Mariana Islands) — J. Clifford Wallace, CJ; James R. Browning, Procter Hug Jr., Jerome Farris, Betty B. Fletcher, Mary M. Schroeder, Harry Pregerson, Cecil F. Poole, Dorothy W. Nelson, William C. Canby Jr., Stephen Reinhardt, Robert R. Beezer, Cynthia M. Hall, Charles E. Wiggins, Melvin Brunetti, Alex Kozinski, David R. Thompson, John T. Noonan, Diarmuid F. O'Scannlain, Edward Leavy, Stephen S. Trott, Ferdinand F. Fernandez, Pamela Ann Rymer, Thomas G. Nelson, Andrew J. Kleinfeld, Michael D. Hawkins; Clerk's Office, San Francisco, CA 94119.

Tenth Circuit (CO, KS, NM, OK, UT, WY) — Stephanie K. Seymour, CJ; John P. Moore, Stephen H. Anderson, Deanell R. Tacha, Bobby R. Baldock, Wade Brorby, David M. Ebel, Paul J. Kelly Jr., Robert H. Henry; Clerk's Office, Denver, CO 80294.

Eleventh Circuit (AL, FL, GA) — Gerald B. Tjoflat, CJ; Peter T. Fay, Phyllis A. Kravitch, Joseph W. Hatchett, R. Lanier Anderson 3d, J. L. Edmondson, Emmett R. Cox, Stanley F. Birch Jr., Joel F. Dubina, Susan H. Black, Edward E. Carnes; Clerk's Office, Atlanta GA 30303.

U.S. District Courts

(Salaries, $133,600. CJ means Chief Judge)

Alabama — **Northern:** Sam C. Pointer Jr., CJ; James Hughes Hancock, Robert B. Propst, U. W. Clemon, William M. Acker Jr., Edwin L. Nelson, Sharon Lovelace Blackburn; Clerk's Office, Birmingham 35203. **Middle:** Myron H. Thompson, CJ; W. Harold Albritton, Ira Dement; Clerk's Office, Montgomery 36101. **Southern:** Charles R. Butler Jr., CJ; Alex T. Howard Jr., Richard W. Vollmer Jr.; Clerk's Office, Mobile 36602.

Alaska — H. Russel Holland, CJ; James K. Singleton, John W. Sedwick; Clerk's Office, Anchorage 99513.

Arizona — William D. Browning, CJ; Richard M. Bilby, Earl H. Carroll, Paul G. Rosenblat, Robert C. Bloomfield, Roger G. Strand, Stephen M. McNamee, John M. Roll; Clerk's Office, Phoenix 85025.

Arkansas — **Eastern:** Stephen M. Reasoner, CJ; Henry Woods, George Howard Jr., Susan Weber Wright, G. Thomas Eisele, Elsiejane Trimble Roy, William R. Wilson, Jr.; Clerk's Office, Little Rock 72203. **Western:** H. Franklin Waters, CJ; George Howard Jr., Jimm Larry Hendren, Harry F. Barnes; Clerk's Office, Fort Smith 72902.

California — **Northern:** Thelton E. Henderson, CJ; Alfonso J. Zirpoli, Stanley A. Weigel, Samuel Conti, Spencer Williams, William H. Orrick, Jr., William A. Ingram, William W Schwarzer, Robert P. Aguilar, Marilyn H. Patel, Eugene F. Lynch, Charles A. Legge, D. Lowell Jensen, Fern M. Smith, Vaughn R. Walker, James Ware, Saundra Brown Armstrong, Ronald J. Whyte, Claudia Wilken; Clerk's Office, San Francisco 94102. **Eastern:** Robert E. Coyle, CJ; Lawrence K. Karlton, Edward J. Garcia, William B. Shubb, David F. Levi, Oliver W. Wanger, Garland E. Burrell Jr., Milton Schwartz; Clerk's Office, Sacramento 95814. **Central:** Wm. Matthew Byrne Jr., CJ; Manuel L. Real, Robert M. Takasugi, Mariana R. Pfaelzer, Terry J. Hatter Jr., A. Wallace Tashima, Consuelo Bland Marshall, David V. Kenyon, Richard A. Gadbois, Edward Rafeedie, Harry L. Hupp, Alicemarie H. Stotler, James M. Ideman, William J. Rea, William D. Keller, Stephen V. Wilson, J. Spencer Letts, Dickran M. Tevrizian Jr., John G. Davies, Ronald S.W. Lew, Gary L. Taylor, Linda Hodge McLaughlin, Lourdes G. Baird, Audrey B. Collins, Richard A. Paez, Robert J. Timlin, Stephen V. Wilson; Clerk's Office, Los Angeles 90012. **Southern:** Judith N. Keep, CJ; Gordon Thompson Jr., Rudi M. Brewster, John S. Rhoades Sr., Marilyn L. Huff, Irma E. Gonzalez, Napoleon A. Jones, Jr.; Clerk's Office, San Diego 92101.

Colorado — Richard P. Matsch, CJ; Sherman G. Finesilver, John L. Kane Jr., Jim R. Carrigan, Zita L. Weinshienk, Lewis T. Babcock, Edward W. Nottingham, Daniel B. Sparr; Clerk's Office, Denver 80294.

Connecticut — Peter C. Dorsey, CJ; T.F. Gilroy Daly, Alan H. Nevas, Alfred V. Covello, Warren W. Eginton, Ellen Bree Burns; Clerk's Office, New Haven 06510.

Delaware — Joseph J. Longobardi, CJ; Joseph J. Farnan Jr., Sue L. Robinson, Roderick R. McKelvie; Clerk's Office, Wilmington 19801.

District of Columbia — John Garrett Penn, CJ; Charles R. Richey, Harold H. Greene, Joyce Hens Green, Norma Holloway Johnson, Thomas P. Jackson, Thomas F. Hogan, Stanley S. Harris, Stanley Sporkin, Royce C. Lamberth, Gladys Kessler, Paul L. Friedman, Ricardo M. Urbina, Emmet G. Sullivan; Clerk's Office, Washington DC 20001.

Florida — Northern: Maurice M. Paul, CJ; C. Roger Vinson, Lacey A. Collier, William H. Stafford; Clerk's Office, Tallahassee 32301. **Middle:** John H. Moore 2d, CJ; William Terrell Hodges, Elizabeth A. Kovachevich, George K. Sharp, Patricia C. Fawsett, Harvey E. Schlesinger, Ralph W. Nimmons Jr., Anne C. Conway, Steven D. Merry Day, Susan C. Bucklew, Henry L. Adams Jr.; Clerk's Office, Jacksonville 32201. **Southern:** Norman C. Roettger, CJ; Jose A. Gonzalez Jr., Edward B. Davis, Lenore C. Nesbitt, Stanley Marcus, William J. Zloch, Kenneth L. Ryskamp, Federico A. Moreno, Shelby Highsmith, Donald L. Graham, K. Michael Moore, Ursula Ungaro-Benages, Wilkie D. Ferguson Jr., Daniel T. K. Hurley; Clerk's Office, Miami 33128.

Georgia — Northern: William C. O'Kelley, CJ; Harold L. Murphy, G. Ernest Tidwell, Orinda D. Evans, Robert L. Vining Jr., J. Owen Forrester, Jack T. Camp, Julie E. Carnes, Clarence Cooper, Frank M. Hull; Clerk's Office, Atlanta 30335. **Middle:** Wilbur D. Owens Jr., CJ; J. Robert Elliott, Duross Fitzpatrick, W. Louis Sands; Clerk's Office, Macon 31202. **Southern:** B. Avant Edenfield, CJ; Dudley H. Bowen Jr., Anthony A. Alaimo; Clerk's Office, Savannah 31412.

Hawaii — Alan C. Kay, CJ; Harold M. Fong, David A. Ezra; Clerk's Office, Honolulu 96850.

Idaho — Edward J. Lodge, CJ; Clerk's Office, Boise 83724.

Illinois — Northern: James B. Moran, CJ; Marvin E. Aspen, Charles P. Kocoras, William T. Hart, Paul E. Plunkett, Charles R. Norgle Sr., James F. Holderman, Ann C. Williams, Brian Barnett Duff, Harry D. Leinenweber, James B. Zagel, James H. Alesia, Suzanne B. Conlon, George M. Marovich, George W. Lindberg, Wayne R. Andersen, Philip G. Reinhard, Ruben Castillo, Blanche M. Manning; Clerk's Office, Chicago 60604. **Central:** Michael M. Mihm, CJ; Richard Mills, Joe Billy McDade; Clerk's Office, Springfield 62705. **Southern:** J. Phil Gilbert, CJ; William D. Stiehl, William L. Beatty, James L. Foreman; Clerk's Office, E. St. Louis 62201.

Indiana — Northern: Allen Sharp, CJ; William C. Lee, James T. Moody, Robert L. Miller Jr., Rudy Lozano; Clerk's Office, South Bend 46601. **Southern:** Gene E. Brooks, CJ; S. Hugh Dillin, Sarah E. Barker, Larry J. McKinney, John D. Tinder; Clerk's Office, Indianapolis 46204.

Iowa — Northern: Michael J. Melloy, CJ; Clerk's Office, Cedar Rapids 52401. **Southern:** Charles R. Wolle, CJ; Harold D. Vietor, R. E. Longstaff; Clerk's Office, Des Moines 50309.

Kansas — Patrick F. Kelly, CJ; Sam A. Crow, C. Thomas Van Bebber, John W. Lungstrum, Monti L. Belot, Kathryn H. Vritil; Clerk's Office, Wichita 67202.

Kentucky — Eastern: William Bertelsman, CJ; Henry R. Wilhoit Jr., Karl S. Forester, Joseph M. Hood, Jennifer B. Coffman; Clerk's Office, Lexington 40596-3074. **Western:** Ronald E. Meredith, CJ; Charles R. Simpson 3d, Edward H. Johnstone, John G. Heyburn 3d, Jennifer B. Coffman; Clerk's Office, Louisville 40202.

Louisiana — Eastern: Morley L. Sear, CJ; Adrian A. Duplantier, Veronica D. Wicker, Peter Beer, A. J. McNamara, Martin L. C. Feldman, Marcel Livaudais Jr., Edith Brown Clement, Charles Schwartz Jr., Frederick J. R. Heebe, Ginger Berrigan, Henry A. Mentz Jr., Patrick E. Carr; Clerk's Office, New Orleans 70130. **Middle:** John V. Parker, CJ; Frank J. Polozola; Clerk's Office, Baton Rouge 70821. **Western:** John M. Shaw, CJ; F. A. Little Jr., Donald E. Walter, Richard Haiks, James T. Trimble, Rebecca F. Doherty, Tucker L. Melancon; Clerk's Office, Shreveport 71101.

Maine — Gene Carter, CJ; D. Brock Hornby, Martin A. Brody; Clerk's Office, Portland 04112.

Maryland — J. Frederick Motz, CJ; Frederic N. Smalkin, William M. Nickerson, Marvin J. Garbis, Benson Everett Legg, Deborah K. Chasanow, Peter J. Messitte, Alexander Williams Jr.; Clerk's Office, Baltimore 21201.

Massachusetts — Joseph L. Tauro, CJ; Robert E. Keeton, Rya W. Zobel, William G. Young, Mark L. Wolf, Douglas P. Woodlock, Edward F. Harrington, Nathaniel M. Gorton, Richard G. Stearns, Reginald C. Lindsay, Patti B. Saris, Nancy Gertner; Clerk's Office, Boston 02109.

Michigan — Eastern: Julian A. Cook Jr., CJ; Stewart A. Newblatt, Avern Cohn, Anna Diggs Taylor, George E. Woods, George La Plata, Barbara K. Hackett, Lawrence P. Zatkoff, Patrick J. Duggan, Bernard A. Friedman, Paul V. Gadola, Gerald E. Rosen, Robert H. Cleland, Nancy G. Edmunds, Denise Page-Hood, Paul D. Borman, John Corbett O'Meara; Clerk's Office, Detroit 48226. **Western:** Benjamin F. Gibson, CJ; Richard A. Enslen, Robert H. Bell, David W. McKeague, Gordon J. Quist; Clerk's Office, Grand Rapids 49503.

Minnesota — Diana E. Murphy, CJ; Paul A. Magnuson, James M. Rosenbaum, David S. Doty, Richard H. Kyle, Michael J. Davis; Clerk's Office, St. Paul 55101.

Mississippi — Northern: L. T. Senter Jr., CJ; Neal Biggers, Glen H. Davidson; Clerk's Office, Oxford 38655. **Southern:** William H. Barbour Jr., CJ; Henry T. Wingate, Tom S. Lee, Walter J. Gex 3d, Charles W. Pickering Sr., David Bramlette; Clerk's Office, Jackson 39201.

Missouri — Eastern: Edward L. Filippine, CJ; Stephen N. Limbaugh, George F. Gunn Jr., Jean Hamilton, Donald J. Stohr, Carol E. Jackson, Charles A. Shaw; Clerk's Office, St. Louis 63101. **Western:** Joseph E. Stevens Jr., CJ; D. Brook Bartlett, Dean Whipple, Fernando J. Gaitan Jr.; Clerk's Office, Kansas City 64106.

Montana — Paul G. Hatfield, CJ; Charles C. Lovell, Jack D. Shanstrom; Clerk's Office, Billings 59101.

Nebraska — William G. Cambridge, CJ; Lyle E. Strom, Richard G. Kopf, Thomas M. Shanahan; Clerk's Office, Omaha 68101.

Nevada — Lloyd D. George, CJ; Howard D. McKibben, Philip M. Pro, David W. Hagen; Clerk's Office, Las Vegas 89101, Reno 89509.

New Hampshire — Joseph A. DiClerico, CJ; Paul J. Barbadaro, Steven J. McAuliffe; Clerk's Office, Concord 03301.

New Jersey — Anne E. Thompson, CJ; John F. Gerry, H. Lee Sarokin, John W. Bissell, Maryanne Trump Barry, Joseph H. Rodriguez, Garrett E. Brown Jr., Alfred J. Lechner Jr., Nicholas H. Politan, Alfred M. Wolin, John C. Lifland, William G. Bassler, Mary Little Parell, Jerome E. Simandle, Joseph E. Irenas; Clerk's Office, Newark 07102.

New Mexico — John E. Conway, CJ; James A. Parker, C. Leroy Hansen, Martha Vazquez; Clerk's Office, Albuquerque 87103.

New York — Northern: Thomas J. McAvoy, CJ; Con G. Cholakis, Frederick J. Scullin Jr., Rosemary S. Pooler; Clerk's Office, Syracuse 13261-7367. **Eastern:** Thomas C. Platt Jr., CJ; Charles P. Sifton, Eugene H. Nickerson, I. Leo Glasser, Raymond J. Dearie, Leonard D. Wexler, Edward R. Korman, Reena Raggi, Arthur D. Spatt, Carol Bagley Amon, Sterling Johnson Jr., Denis R. Hurley, David G. Trager, Joanna Seybert, Allyne Ross, John Gleeson, Fredric Block; Clerk's Office, Brooklyn 11201. **Southern:** Thomas P. Griesa, CJ; David N. Edelstein, Charles L. Brieant, Kevin Thomas Duffy, Leonard B. Sand, Gerard L. Goettel, Charles S. Haight Jr., John E. Sprizzo, Shirley Wohl Kram, John F. Keenan, Peter K. Leisure, Louis L. Stanton, Miriam G. Cedarbaum, Lewis A. Kaplan, Michael B. Mukasey, Kimba Wood, Robert P. Patterson Jr., Lawrence McKenna, John S. Martin Jr., Loretta A. Preska, Sonia Sotomayer, Harold Baer Jr., Deborah A. Batts, Denny Chin, Denise L. Cote, John Koeltl, Allen G. Schwartz; Clerk's Office, New

York City 10007. **Western:** Michael A. Telesca, CJ; Richard J. Arcara, David G. Larimer, William M. Skretny, John T. Curtin, John T. Elfvin; Clerk's Office, Buffalo 14202.

North Carolina — Eastern: James C. Fox, CJ; W. Earl Britt, Terrence W. Boyle, Malcolm J. Howard; Clerk's Office, Raleigh 27611. **Middle:** Frank W. Bullock, CJ; N. Carlton Tilley Jr., William L. Osteen Sr.; Clerk's Office, Greensboro 27402. **Western:** Richard L. Voorhees, CJ; Graham C. Mullen; Clerk's Office, Asheville 28801.

North Dakota — Rodney S. Webb, CJ; Patrick A. Conmy; Clerk's Office, Bismarck 58502.

Ohio — Northern: Thomas D. Lambros, CJ; George W. White, Ann Aldrich, David D. Dowd Jr., Sam H. Bell, Paul R. Matia, Lesley Brooks Wells, Solomon Oliver Jr., John Manos, James Carr; Clerk's Office, Cleveland 44114. **Southern:** John D. Holschuh, CJ; Carl B. Rubin, Walter Herbert Rice, S. Arthur Spiegel, Herman J. Weber, James L. Graham, George C. Smith, Sandra S. Beckwith; Clerk's Office, Columbus 43215.

Oklahoma — Northern: Thomas R. Brett, CJ; Terry C. Kern, Michael Burrage; Clerk's Office, Tulsa 74103. **Eastern:** Frank H. Shey, CJ; Michael Burrage; Clerk's Office, Muskogee 74401. **Western:** Lee R. West, CJ; Ralph G. Thompson, Wayne Alley, David L. Russell, Robin Cauthron, Timothy D. Leonard; Clerk's Office, Oklahoma City 73102.

Oregon — James A. Redden, CJ; Helen J. Frye, Malcolm F. Marsh, Robert E. Jones, Michael R. Hogan, Ancer L. Haggerty; Clerk's Office, Portland 97205.

Pennsylvania — Eastern: Edward N. Cahn, CJ; Norma L. Shapiro, James T. Giles, James McGirr Kelly, Thomas N. O'Neill Jr., Marvin Katz, Edmund V. Ludwig, Robert F. Kelly, Franklin S. Van Antwerpen, Robert S. Gawthrop III, Lowell A. Reed Jr., Jan E. Dubois, Herbert J. Hutton, Jay C. Waldman, Ronald L. Buckwalter, Stewart Dalzell, William H. Yohn Jr., Harvey Battle 3d, John R. Padova, J. Curtis Joyner, Eduardo C. Robreno, Anita B. Brody, Marjorie O. Rendell; Clerk's Office, Philadelphia 19106. **Middle:** Sylvia H. Rambo, CJ; Edward M. Kosik, James F. McClure Jr., Thomas I. Vanaskie; Clerk's Office, Scranton 18501. **Western:** Donald E. Ziegler, CJ; Maurice B. Cohill Jr., Alan N. Bloch, William L. Standish, D. Brooks Smith, Donald J. Lee, Donetta W. Ambrose, Gary L. Lancaster; Clerk's Office, Pittsburgh 15230.

Rhode Island — Ronald R. Lagueux, CJ; Ernest C. Torres, Mary M. Lisi; Clerk's Office, Providence 02903.

South Carolina — C. Weston Houck, CJ; Matthew J. Perry Jr., George R. Anderson Jr., Joseph F. Anderson Jr., David C. Norton, Dennis W. Shedd, Henry M. Herlong Jr., William B. Traxler, Cameron M. Currie; Clerk's Office, Columbia 29201.

South Dakota — Richard H. Battey, CJ; John Baily Jones, Lawrence L. Piersol; Clerk's Office, Sioux Falls 57102.

Tennessee — Eastern: James H. Jarvis, CJ; Thomas G. Hull, R. Allan Edgar, Leon Jordan; Clerk's Office, Knoxville 37901. **Middle:** John T. Nixon, CJ; Thomas A. Wiseman Jr., Thomas A. Higgins, Robert L. Echols; Clerk's Office, Nashville 37203. **Western:** Julia S. Gibbons, CJ; Odell Horton, James D. Todd, Jerome Turner, Jon Phipps McCalla; Clerk's Office, Memphis 38103.

Texas — Northern: Barefoot Sanders, CJ; Mary Lou Robinson, Jerry Buchmeyer, A. Joe Fish, Robert B. Maloney, Sidney A. Fitzwater, Samuel R. Cummings, John H. McBryde, Jorge A. Solis, Terry Means, Joe Kendall; Clerk's Office, Dallas 75242. **Southern:** Norman W. Black, CJ; George P. Kazen, Filemon B. Vela, Hayden W. Head Jr., Ricardo H. Hinojosa, Lynn N. Hughes, David Hittner, Kenneth M. Hoyt, Simeon T. Lake 3d, Melinda Harmon, John D. Rainey, Samuel B. Kent, Ewing Werlein Jr., Lee H. Rosenthal, Janis Graham Jack, Vanessa Gilmore; Clerk's Office, Houston 77208. **Eastern:** Richard A. Schell, CJ; William Wayne Justice, Howell Cobb, Paul N. Brown, John Hannah Jr., Joe J. Fisher; Clerk's Office, Tyler 75702. **Western:** Harry Lee Hudspeth, CJ; Hipolito F. Garcia, James R. Nowlin, Edward C. Prado, Walter S. Smith Jr., Sam Sparks, W. Royal Furgeson, Fred Biery, Orlando L. Garcia; Clerk's Office, San Antonio 78206.

Utah — David K. Winder, CJ; J. Thomas Greene, David Sam, Dee Benson; Clerk's Office, Salt Lake City 84101.

Vermont — Fred I. Parker, CJ; Clerk's Office, Burlington 05402.

Virginia — Eastern: James C. Cacheris, CJ; Robert G. Doumar, Claude M. Hilton, James R. Spencer, Thomas S. Ellis 3d, Rebecca Beach Smith, Henry Coke Morgan Jr., Robert E. Payne, Raymond A. Jackson, Leonie M. Brinkema; Clerk's Office, Alexandria 22320. **Western:** Jackson L. Kiser, CJ; James C. Turk, James H. Michael Jr., Samuel G. Wilson; Clerk's Office, Roanoke 24006.

Washington — Eastern: Justin L. Quackenbush, CJ; Alan A. McDonald; Fred Van Sickle, William Fremming Nielsen; Clerk's Office, Spokane 99210. **Western:** Carolyn R. Dimmick, CJ; Barbara J. Rothstein, John C. Coughenour, Robert J. Bryan, William L. Dwyer, Thomas Zilly, Franklin D. Burgess; Clerk's Office, Seattle 98104.

West Virginia — Northern: Frederick P. Stamp Jr., CJ; Robert Earl Maxwell, Irene M. Keeley; Clerk's Office, Elkins 26241. **Southern:** Charles H. Haden 2d, CJ; Robert J. Staker, John T. Copenhaver Jr., Elizabeth V. Hallanan, David A. Faber; Clerk's Office, Charleston 25329.

Wisconsin — Eastern: Terence T. Evans, CJ; Thomas J. Curran, J. P. Stadtmueller, Rudolph T. Randa, Aaron E. Goodstein, Patricia J. Gorence; Clerk's Office, Milwaukee 53202. **Western:** Barbara B. Crabb, CJ; John C. Shabaz; Clerk's Office, Madison 53701.

Wyoming — Alan B. Johnson, CJ; Clarence A. Brimmer, William F. Downes; Clerk's Office, Cheyenne 82001.

U.S. Territorial District Courts

Guam — John S. Unpingco, CJ; Clerk's Office, Agana 96910.

Puerto Rico — Carmen Consuelo Cerezo, CJ; Gilberto Gierbolini, Juan M. Perez-Gimenez, Jaime Pieras Jr., Raymond L. Acosta, Hector M. Laffitte, Jose Antonio Fuste; Clerk's Office, Hato Rex, 00918.

Virgin Islands — Thomas K. Moore, CJ; Raymond L. Finch; Clerk's Office, St. Croix, V.I. 00820.

U.S. Court of International Trade

New York, NY 10007 (Salaries, $133,600)

Chief Judge — Dominick L. DeCarlo.

Judges — Gregory W. Carmen, Jane A. Restani, Thomas J. Aquilino Jr., Nicholas Tsoucalas, R. Kenton Musgrave, Richard W. Goldberg.

U.S. Court of Federal Claims

Washington, DC 20005 (Salaries, $133,600)

Chief Judge — Loren A. Smith.

Judges — James F. Merow, John P. Wiese, Robert J. Yock, Reginald W. Gibson, Lawrence S. Margolis, Christine Odell Cook Miller, Moody R. Tidwell 3d, Marian Blank Horn, Eric G. Bruggink, Bohdan A. Futey, Wilkes C. Robinson, Roger B. Andewelt, James T. Turner, Robert H. Hodges Jr., Diane Gilbert Weinstein.

U.S. Tax Court

Washington, DC 20217 (Salaries, $133,600)

Chief Judge — Lapsley W. Hamblen Jr.

Judges — Renato Beghe, Herbert L. Chabot, Edna G. Parker, Mary Ann Cohen, John O. Colvin, Joel Gerber, Julien I. Jacobs, Carolyn Miller Parr, Robert P. Ruwe, James S. Halpern, Carolyn P. Chiechi, David Laro, Stephen Swift, Thomas Wells, Laurence J. Whalen, Lawrence A. Wright.

U.S. Court of Veterans Appeals

Washington, DC 20004 (Salaries, $133,600)

Chief Judge — Frank Q. Nebeker.

Judges — Kenneth B. Kramer, John J. Farley 3d, Hart T. Mankin, Ronald M. Holdaway, Donald L. Ivers, Jonathan R. Steinberg.

Mayors of Selected U.S. Cities

Reflects Nov. 8, 1994, election results. The expiration date for the mayor's term of office appears next to each name.

D, Democrat; R, Republican; N-P, Non-Partisan; I, Independent

City	Name	Term
Abilene, TX	Gary McCaleb, N-P	**1996, May**
Akron, OH	D. L. Plusquellic, D	**1996, Jan.**
Alameda, CA	E. William Withrow Jr., N-P	**1995, Apr.**
Albany, GA	Paul Keenan, D	**1996, Jan.**
Albany, NY	Gerald D. Jennings, D	**1997, Dec.**
Albuquerque, NM	Martin Chavez, D	**1997, Nov.**
Alexandria, LA	Edward Randolph Jr., D	**1998, Nov.**
Alexandria, VA	Patricia Ticer, D	**1997, June**
Alhambra, CA	Boyd G. Condie, N-P	**1995, Feb.**
Allentown, PA	William Heydt, R	**1997, Dec.**
Amarillo, TX	Kel Seliger, N-P	**1995, May**
Ames, IA	Larry R. Curtis, N-P	**1997, Dec.**
Anaheim, CA	Tom Daly, N-P	**1998, Nov.**
Anchorage, AK	Rick Mystrom, R	**1997, July**
Anderson, IN	J. Mark Lawler, D	**1995, Dec.**
Anderson, SC	Darwin Wright, D	**1998, June**
Ann Arbor, MI	Ingrid B. Sheldon, R	**1996, Nov.**
Appleton, WI	Richard De Broux, N-P	**1996, Apr.**
Arcadia, CA	Mary B. Young, N-P	**1995, Apr.**
Arlington, MA	Donald R. Marquis, N-P	**1995, Nov.**
Arlington, TX	Richard Greene, N-P	**1995, May**
Arlington Hts., IL	Arlene J. Mulder, N-P	**1997, Apr.**
Arvada, CO	Robert Eric, N-P	**1995, Nov.**
Asheville, NC	Russel Martin, N-P	**1995, Dec.**
Athens, GA	Gwen O'Looney, D	**1998, Dec.**
Atlanta, GA	Bill Campbell, D	**1997, Dec.**
Atlantic City, NJ	Jim Whelan, N-P	**1998, July**
Augusta, GA	Charles Devaney, N-P	**1998, Jan.**
Aurora, CO	Paul E. Tauer, N-P	**1995, Nov.**
Aurora, IL	David L. Pierce, N-P	**1997, Apr.**
Austin, TX	Bruce Todd, N-P	**1997, June**
Bakersfield, CA	Bob Price, N-P	**1996, Dec.**
Baldwin Park, CA	Fidel Vargas, N-P	**1996, Apr.**
Baltimore, MD	Kurt Schmoke, D	**1995, Dec.**
Baton Rouge, LA	Tom E. McHugh, D	**1996, Dec.**
Battle Creek, MI	John Gallagher	**1994, Nov.**
Bayonne, NJ	Leonard P. Kiczek, N-P	**1998, June**
Baytown, TX	Pete C. Alfaro, N-P	**1995, May**
Beaumont, TX	David W. Moore, N-P	**1996, May**
Belleville, IL	Roger C. Cook, I	**1997, May**
Belleville, NJ	Jim Messina, D	**1998, May**
Bellevue, WA	Don Davidson, N-P	**1995, Dec.**
Bellingham, WA	Tim Douglas, N-P	**1995, Nov.**
Bellflower, CA	Ken Cleveland, N-P	**1995, Apr.**
Berkeley, CA	Jeffrey Leiter, N-P	**1994, Dec.**
Bethlehem, PA	Kenneth Smith, R	**1997, Dec.**
Beverly Hills, CA	Vicki Reynolds, N-P	**1995, Apr.**
Billings, MT	Richard L. Larsen, N-P	**1995, Dec.**
Biloxi, MS	A. J. Holloway, R	**1997, July**
Binghamton, NY	Richard Bucci, R	**1997, Dec.**
Birmingham, AL	Richard Arrington Jr., D	**1995, Oct.**
Bismarck, ND	Bill Sorensen, R	**1998, June**
Bloomfield, NJ	James P. Norton, R	**1995, Dec.**
Bloomington, IL	Jesse Smart, R	**1997, May**
Bloomington, IN	Tomilea Allison, D	**1996, Jan.**
Bloomington, MN	Neil Peterson, N-P	**1995, Dec.**
Boca Raton, FL	Bill Smith Jr., N-P	**1995, Apr.**
Boise, ID	H. Brent Coles, N-P	**1997, Dec.**
Bossier City, LA	George Dement, N-P	**1997, May**
Boston, MA	Thomas M. Menino, D	**1998, Jan.**
Boulder, CO	Leslie L. Durgin, N-P	**1995, Nov.**
Bridgeport, CT	Joseph Ganim, D	**1995, Dec.**
Bristol, CT	Frank N. Nicastro, D	**1995, Nov.**
Brockton, MA	Winthrop Farwell Jr., D	**1996, Jan.**
Broken Arrow, OK	Jim Reynolds, N-P	**1995, Apr.**
Brooklyn Park, MN	Grace Arborgast	**1998, Dec.**
Brownsville, TX	Pat Ahumada, N-P	**1995, Nov.**
Bryan, TX	Marvin Tate, N-P	**1995, May**
Buena Park, CA	Donald L. Bone	**1994, Dec.**
Buffalo, NY	Anthony Masiello, D	**1997, Dec.**
Burbank, CA	Bill Wiggins, N-P	**1995, May**
Burlington, VT	Peter C. Brownell, R	**1995, Apr.**
Calumet City, IL	Gerry P. Genova, I	**1997, Apr.**
Camarillo, CA	Charles K. Gose, N-P	**1998, Dec.**
Cambridge, MA	Kenneth Reeves, N-P	**1995, Dec.**
Camden, NJ	Arnold Webster, D	**1996, Dec.**
Canton, OH	Richard Watkins, R	**1995, Nov.**
Cape Coral, FL	Roger G. Butler, N-P	**1996, Nov.**
Carlsbad, CA	Claude Lewis, N-P	**1998, Dec.**
Carson, CA	Michael Mitoma, N-P	**1995, Apr.**
Casper, WY	Michael E. Reed, N-P	**1995, Jan.**
Cedar Rapids, IA	Larry Serbousek, N-P	**1995, Dec.**
Champaign, IL	Dan McCollum, N-P	**1995, May**
Chandler, AZ	Jay Tibshraeny, N-P	**1996, Mar.**
Charleston, SC	Joseph P. Riley Jr., D	**1996, Jan.**
Charleston, WV	Kent S. Hall, R	**1995, Apr.**
Charlotte, NC	Richard Vinroot, R	**1995, Dec.**
Charlottesville, VA	David Toscano, D	**1996, June**
Chattanooga, TN	Gene Roberts, R	**1997, Apr.**
Chesapeake, VA	William Ward, N-P	**1996, June**
Chester, PA	Barbara Bohannan-Shepperd, D	**1996, Dec.**
Cheyenne, WY	Leo Pando, N-P	**1997, Jan.**
Chicago, IL	Richard M. Daley, D	**1995, Apr.**
Chicopee, MA	Joseph Chessey, D	**1995, Dec.**
Chino, CA	Eunice M. Ulloa, R	**1996, Nov.**
Chula Vista, CA	Shirley Horton, I	**1998, Nov.**
Cicero, IL	Betty L. Maltese, R	**1997, Apr.**
Cincinnati, OH	Roxanne Qualis, D	**1995, Nov.**
Clarksville, TN	Don Trotter, N-P	**1999, Jan.**
Clearwater, FL	Rita Garvey, N-P	**1996, Apr.**
Cleveland, OH	Michael White, D	**1997, Dec.**
Cleveland Hts., OH	Carol Edwards, N-P	**1994, Dec.**
Clifton, NJ	James Anzaldi, R	**1998, July**
Colorado Spgs., CO	Robert M. Isaac, N-P	**1995, Apr.**
Columbia, MO	Mary Ann McCollum, N-P	**1995, Apr.**
Columbia, SC	Robert Coble, N-P	**1998, June**
Columbus, GA	Bobby Peters, D	**1999, Jan.**
Columbus, OH	Gregory Lashutka, R	**1995, Dec.**
Compton, CA	Omar Bradley, N-P	**1995, June**
Concord, CA	Michael Pastrick, N-P	**1994, Dec.**
Coon Rapids., MN	William Thompson, N-P	**1995, Dec.**
Coral Gables, FL	Raul Valdes-Sauli, N-P	**1996, Mar.**
Corona, CA	William Miller, N-P	**1994, Dec.**
Corpus Christi, TX	Mary Rhodes, N-P	**1995, Apr.**
Costa Mesa, CA	Sandy Genis, N-P	**1994, Dec.**
Council Bluffs, IA	Tom Hanafan, N-P	**1997, Dec.**
Covington, KY	Denny Bowman, D	**1996, Jan.**
Cranston, RI	Michael Traficante, R	**1998, Dec.**
Cuyahoga Falls, OH	Donald L. Robart, R	**1997, Dec.**
Dallas, TX	Steve Bartlett, N-P	**1995, May**
Daly City, CA	Madolyn L. Agrimonti, N-P	**1994, Nov.**
Danbury, CT	Gene Eriquez, D	**1995, Nov.**
Danville, VA	F. S. Anderson Jr., N-P	**1996, July**
Davenport, IA	Patrick J. Gibbs, R	**1995, Dec.**
Davis, CA	Dave Rosenberg, N-P	**1996, July**
Dayton, OH	Michael R. Turner, N-P	**1998, Jan.**
Daytona Beach, FL	Paul A. Carpenella, N-P	**1995, Nov.**
Dearborn , MI	Michael Guido, N-P	**1998, Jan.**
Dearborn Hts., MI	Ruth A. Canfield, N-P	**1997, Dec.**
Decatur, IL	Erik K. Brechnitz, N-P	**1995, May**
Delray Beach, FL	Thomas E. Lynch, N-P	**1996, Mar.**
Denton, TX	Bob Castleberry, N-P	**1996, May**
Denver, CO	Wellington Webb, N-P	**1995, May**
Des Moines, IA	John Dorrian, D	**1995, Dec.**
Des Plaines, IL	Ted Sherwood, N-P	**1997, Apr.**
Detroit, MI	Dennis W. Archer, D	**1997, Dec.**
Dothan, AL	Alfred Saliba, N-P	**1997, July**
Downey, CA	Barbara Riley, N-P	**1998, July**
Dubuque, IA	Terrance M. Duggan, N-P	**1997, Dec.**
Duluth, MN	Gary L. Doty, N-P	**1996, Jan.**
Durham, NC	Sylvia S. Kerckhoff, N-P	**1995, Dec.**
East Hartford, CT	Robert DeCrescenzo, D	**1995, Nov.**
East Lansing, MI	Robert J. Phipps, N-P	**1995, Nov.**
East Orange, NJ	Cardell Cooper, D	**1996, Dec.**
Eau Claire, WI	Mark Lewis, N-P	**1995, Apr.**
Edison, NJ	George Spadoro, D	**1997, Dec.**
Edmond, OK	Randel Shadid, N-P	**1995, Apr.**
El Cajon, CA	Joan Shoemaker, N-P	**1998, July**
El Monte, CA	Patricia Wallach, D	**1996, Apr.**
El Paso, TX	Larry Francis, N-P	**1995, June**
Elgin, IL	George Van De Voorde, N-P	**1995, Apr.**
Elizabeth, NJ	J. C. Bollwage, D	**1996, Dec.**
Elkhart, IN	James Perron, D	**1996, Jan.**
Elyria, OH	Michael Keys, D	**1995, Dec.**
Enfield, CT	Ann M. Petronella, N-P	**1995, Nov.**
Enid, OK	Norman Grey, N-P	**1995, May**
Erie, PA	Joyce Savocchio, D	**1997, Dec.**
Escondido, CA	Sid Hollins, N-P	**1996, June**
Euclid, OH	David Lynch, R	**1996, Jan.**
Eugene, OR	Ruth Bascom, N-P	**1997, Jan.**
Evanston, IL	Lorraine Morton, N-P	**1997, Apr.**
Evansville, IN	Frank McDonald, D	**1995, Dec.**

City	Name	Term
Everett, WA	Edward D. Hansen, N-P	**1997, Dec.**
Fairfield, CA	Chuck Hamond, N-P	**1997, Jan.**
Fairfield, CT	Paul A. Audley, R	**1995, Nov.**
Fall River, MA	John Mitchell, D	**1996, Jan.**
Fargo, ND	Bruce Furness, N-P	**1998, May**
Farmington Hills, MI	Lawrence Lichtman, N-P	**1995, Nov.**
Fayetteville, NC	J. L. Dawkins, N-P	**1995, Nov.**
Fitchburg, MA	Jeffrey Bean, D	**1997, Jan.**
Flagstaff, AZ	Christopher Bavasi, N-P	**1996, Apr.**
Flint, MI	Woodrow Stanley, D	**1995, Nov.**
Florissant, MO	James J. Eagan, N-P	**1995, Apr.**
Fontano, CA	David Eshleman, D	**1998, Nov.**
Ft. Collins, CO	Ann Azari, N-P	**1995, Apr.**
Ft. Lauderdale, FL	Jim Naugle, N-P	**1997, Mar.**
Ft. Smith, AR	Ray Baker, N-P	**1998, Dec.**
Ft. Wayne, IN	Paul Helmke, R	**1996, Jan.**
Ft. Worth, TX	Kay Granger, N-P	**1995, May**
Fountain Valley, CA	John Collins, N-P	**1994, Dec.**
Fremont, CA	Gus Morrison, N-P	**1996, Nov.**
Fresno, CA	Jim Patterson, N-P	**1997, Mar.**
Fullerton, CA	Julie Sa, N-P	**1994, Dec.**
Gadsden, AL	Steve Means, N-P	**1998, Oct.**
Gainesville, FL	Paula DeLaney, N-P	**1995, Mar.**
Galveston, TX	Barbara K. Crews, N-P	**1996, May**
Gardena, CA	Donald L. Dear, N-P	**1996, Apr.**
Garden Grove, CA	Bruce Broadwater, N-P	**1996, Dec.**
Garland, TX	James B. Ratliff, N-P	**1996, May**
Gary, IN	Thomas Barnes, D	**1996, Jan.**
Gastonia, NC	James B. Garland, N-P	**1997, Nov.**
Glendale, AZ	Elaine Scruggs, N-P	**1996, Apr.**
Glendale, CA	Larry Zarian, N-P	**1997, Apr.**
Grand Forks, ND	Michael Polovitz, D	**1996, June**
Grand Prairie, TX	Charles V. England, N-P	**1996, May**
Grand Rapids, MI	John Logie, N-P	**1996, Jan.**
Greeley, CO	William Morton, N-P	**1995, Nov.**
Green Bay, WI	Samuel Halloin, N-P	**1995, July**
Greenville, SC	William D. Workman III, R	**1995, June**
Greenwich, CT	John Margenot, R	**1995, Dec.**
Groton, CT	Dolores Hauber, N-P	**1995, Nov.**
Gulfport, MS	Ken Combs, R	**1997, June**
Hamden, CT	Lillian Clayman, D	**1995, Nov.**
Hamilton, OH	Charles R. Furmon, N-P	**1995, Dec.**
Hammond, IN	Duane W. Dadelow, R	**1996, Jan.**
Hampton, VA	James L. Eason, N-P	**1996, June**
Harrisburg, PA	Stephen Reed, D	**1997, Dec.**
Hartford, CT	Mike Peters, N-P	**1995, Dec.**
Haverhill, MA	James Rurak, D	**1995, Dec.**
Hawthorne, CA	Larry Guidi, N-P	**1995, Nov.**
Hayward, CA	Roberta Cooper, N-P	**1998, Apr.**
Henderson, NV	Robert A. Groesbeck, N-P	**1997, June**
Hesperia, CA	Michael Lampignano, R	**1994, Dec.**
Hialeah, FL	Raul Martinez, R	**1997, Nov.**
High Point, NC	Rebecca R. Smothers, N-P	**1995, Dec.**
Hollywood, FL	Mara Giulianti, N-P	**1996, Mar.**
Holyoke, MA	William Hamilton, R	**1995, Dec.**
Honolulu, HI	Frank Fasi, R	**1997, Jan.**
Houston, TX	Bob Lanier, N-P	**1995, Dec.**
Huntington, WV	Jean Dean, R	**1997, June**
Huntington Beach, CA	Victor Leipzig	**1996, Dec.**
Huntington Park, CA	Richard V. Loya, R	**1995, Apr.**
Huntsville, AL	Steve Hettinger, N-P	**1996, Oct.**
Idaho Falls, ID	Linda Milam, N-P	**1998, Jan.**
Independence, MO	Ron Stewart, N-P	**1998, Apr.**
Indianapolis, IN	Steve Goldsmith, R	**1995, Dec.**
Inglewood, CA	Edward Vincent, D	**1999, Jan.**
Iowa City, IA	Susan M. Horowitz, N-P	**1996, Jan.**
Irving, TX	Bobby Joe Raper, N-P	**1995, May**
Irvington, NJ	Sara A. Bost, D	**1998, July**
Jackson, MS	Kane Ditto, D	**1997, July**
Jacksonville, FL	Ed Austin, D	**1995, July**
Janesville, WI	Steven Sheiffer, N-P	**1996, Apr.**
Jersey City, NJ	Bret Schundler, R	**1997, May**
Johnson City, TN	Jeff Anderson, N-P	**1995, May**
Joliet, IL	Arthur Schultz, N-P	**1995, May**
Kalamazoo, MI	Edward Annen, N-P	**1995, Nov.**
Kansas City, KS	Joe Steineger, N-P	**1995, Apr.**
Kansas City, MO	Emanuel Cleaver, D	**1995, Apr.**
Kenner, LA	Aaron F. Broussard, D	**1998, July**
Kenosha, WI	John Antaramian, D	**1996, Apr.**
Kettering, OH	Richard Hartmann, R	**1997, Dec.**
Killeen, TX	Raul Villaronga, N-P	**1996, May**
Knoxville, TN	Victor Ashe, R	**1995, Dec.**
Kokomo, IN	Robert Sargent, D	**1995, Dec.**
LaCrosse, WI	Patrick Zielke, N-P	**1997, Apr.**
La Habra, CA	David Cheverton, N-P	**1994, Dec.**
La Mesa, CA	Arthur Madrid, N-P	**1998, Nov.**
La Mirada, CA	Bob Chaotiner, N-P	**1995, Apr.**
Lafayette, IN	James Riehle, D	**1995, Dec.**

City	Name	Term
Lafayette, LA	Kenneth Bowen, D	**1996, June**
Lake Charles, LA	Willie L. Mount, D	**1997, June**
Lakeland, FL	Ralph L. " Buddy" Fletcher	**1996, Dec.**
Lakewood, CA	Joseph Esquirel, N-P	**1995, May**
Lakewood, CO	Linda Morton, N-P	**1995, Nov.**
Lakewood, OH	David Harbarger, R	**1995, Dec.**
Lancaster, PA	Janice Stork, D	**1997, Dec.**
Lansing, MI	David Hollister, N-P	**1997, Dec.**
Laredo, TX	Saul N. Ramirez Jr., N-P	**1998, May**
Largo, FL	Thomas Feaster, N-P	**1997, Apr.**
Las Cruces, NM	Ruben A. Smith, D	**1995, Nov.**
Las Vegas, NV	Jan Laverty Jones, D	**1995, June**
Lauderhill, FL	Ilene Lieberman, D	**1996, Mar.**
Lawrence, KS	Jolene Andersen, N-P	**1995, Apr.**
Lawrence, MA	Mary Claire Kennedy, N-P	**1997, Dec.**
Lawton, OK	John T. Marley, N-P	**1995, Apr.**
Lexington, KY	Pam Miller, N-P	**1998, Dec.**
Lima, OH	David Berger, N-P	**1997, Dec.**
Lincoln, NE	Mike Johanns, R	**1995, May**
Little Rock, AR	Jim Dailey, N-P	**1999, Jan.**
Livermore, CA	Cathie Brown, N-P	**1995, Nov.**
Livonia, MI	Robert Bennett, N-P	**1996, Jan.**
Lodi, CA	Jack Sieglock, N-P	**1994, Dec.**
Long Beach, CA	Beverly O'Neill, N-P	**1998, July**
Longmont,CO	Leona Stoecker, N-P	**1995, Nov.**
Longview, TX	I. J. Patterson Jr., N-P	**1996, May**
Lorain, OH	Alex Olejko, D	**1995, Dec.**
Los Angeles, CA	Richard Riordan, N-P	**1997, June**
Louisville, KY	Jerry Abramson, D	**1997, Dec.**
Lowell, MA	Richard Howe, N-P	**1996, Jan.**
Lubbock, TX	David Langston, N-P	**1996, May**
Lynchburg, VA	James Whitaker, N-P	**1996, July**
Lynn, MA	Patrick McManus, D	**1995, Dec.**
Lynwood, CA	Paul Richards, III, N-P	**1995, Dec.**
Macon, GA	Tommy Olmstead, D	**1995, Dec.**
Madison, WI	Paul Soglin, R	**1995, Apr.**
Malden, MA	Edwin C. Lucey, D	**1995, Dec.**
Manchester, CT	Stephen Cassano, N-P	**1995, Nov.**
Manchester, NH	Ray Wieczorek, R	**1996, Jan.**
Mansfield, OH	Lydia J. Reid, D	**1995, Nov.**
Marietta, GA	Ansley L. Meaders, D	**1997, Dec.**
McAllen, TX	Othal Brand, R	**1997, May**
Medford, MA	Michael McGlynn, D	**1996, Jan.**
Medford, OR	Jerry Lausman, N-P	**1996, Dec.**
Melbourne, FL	Joseph F. Mullins, N-P	**1996, Nov.**
Memphis, TN	W. W. Herenton, D	**1995, Dec.**
Mentor, OH	James F. Struna, N-P	**1995, Dec.**
Merced, CA	Richard Bernasconi, N-P	**1995, Nov.**
Meriden, CT	Joseph Marinan, Jr., N-P	**1995, Dec.**
Meridian, MS	John Robert Smith, R	**1997, June**
Mesa, AZ	Willie Wong, N-P	**1996, June**
Mesquite, TX	Cathye Ray, N-P	**1995, May**
Miami, FL	Steve Clark, N-P	**1997, Nov.**
Miami Beach, FL	Seymour Gelber, D	**1995, Nov.**
Midland, TX	Robert E. Burns, N-P	**1996, June**
Midwest City, OK	Eddie O. Reed, N-P	**1998, Apr.**
Milford, CT	Frederick Lisman, R	**1995, Nov.**
Milpitas, CA	Peter McHugh, N-P	**1996, Nov.**
Milwaukee, WI	John Norquist, D	**1996, Apr.**
Minneapolis, MN	Sharon Sayles Belton, D	**1997, Dec.**
Minnetonka, MN	Karen J. Anderson, N-P	**1995, Dec.**
Mobile, AL	Michael Dow, R, I	**1997, Oct.**
Modesto, CA	Richard Lang, N-P	**1995, Nov.**
Monroe, LA	Robert Powell, D	**1996, July**
Montclair, NJ	James Bishop, R	**1996, July**
Montebello, CA	Art Payan, D	**1995, Nov.**
Monterey Park, CA	Judy Chu, N-P	**1995, Apr.**
Montgomery, AL	Emory Folmar, R	**1995, Nov.**
Mt. Prospect, IL	Gerald "Skip" Farley, N-P	**1997, May**
Mt. Vernon, NY	Ronald Blackwood, D	**1995, Nov.**
Mountain View, CA	Bob Schatz, N-P	**1995, Apr.**
Muncie, IN	David M. Dominick, R	**1995, Dec.**
Muskogee, OK	Kathy Hewitt, N-P	**1996, May**
Napa, CA	Ed Solomon, R	**1996, July**
Naperville, IL	Samuel MacCrane, N-P	**1995, May**
Nashua, NH	Rob Wagner, D	**1996, Jan.**
Nashville, TN	Philip Bredesen, D	**1995, Sept.**
National City, CA	George H. Waters, R	**1998, Nov.**
New Bedford, MA	Rosemary Tierney, D	**1996, Jan.**
New Britain, CT	Linda Blogoslawski, R	**1995, Nov.**
New Haven, CT	John DeStafano, D	**1995, Dec.**
New Orleans, LA	Marc Morial, D	**1998, May**
New Rochelle, NY	Timothy Idoni, D	**1996, Jan.**
New York, NY	Rudolph Giuliani, R	**1997, Dec.**
Newark, NJ	Sharpe James, D	**1998, July**
Newport, RI	David S. Roderick, N-P	**1996, Jan.**

City	Name	Term
Newport Beach, CA	Clarence Turner, N-P	**1994, Nov.**
Newport News, VA	Barry E. Duval, N-P	**1996, Nov.**
Newton, MA	Thomas Concannon, N-P	**1997, Dec.**
Niagara Falls, NY	Jacob A. Palillo, R	**1996, Jan.**
Norfolk, VA	Paul D. Fraim, N-P	**1996, July**
Norman, OK	William Nation, MD, N-P	**1995, Apr.**
North Charleston, SC	Bobby Kinard, R	**1995, July**
N. Little Rock, AR	Patrick Hayes, D	**1996, Dec.**
Norwalk, CA	Michael Mendez, N-P	**1995, Apr.**
Norwalk, CT	Frank Esposito, R	**1995, Nov.**
Novato, CA	Cynthia Murray, N-P	**1995, Nov.**
Oak Park, IL	Lawrence Christmas, N-P	**1997, Apr.**
Oak Ridge, TN	Edmund A. Nephew, N-P	**1995, June**
Oakland, CA	Elihu Mason Harris, N-P	**1999, Jan.**
Oceanside, CA	Dick Lyon, N-P	**1996, Dec.**
Odessa, TX	Lorraine Perryman, N-P	**1996, Apr.**
Ogden, UT	Glenn Mecham, N-P	**1995, Dec.**
Oklahoma City, OK	Ronald Norick, N-P	**1995, Apr.**
Omaha, NE	P. J. Morgan, R	**1997, June**
Ontario, CA	Gus James Skropos, N-P	**1998, Nov.**
Orange, CA	Joanne Coontz, N-P	**1996, Nov.**
Orlando, FL	Glenda E. Hood, N-P	**1996, Oct.**
Oshkosh, WI	Richard A. Wollangk, N-P	**1995, Apr.**
Overland Park, KS	Ed Eilert, R	**1997, Apr.**
Owensboro, KY	David C. Adkisson, N-P	**1995, Dec.**
Oxnard, CA	Manuel M. Lopez, N-P	**1996, Nov.**
Palm Springs, CA	Lloyd Maryanov, N-P	**1996, Apr.**
Palo Alto, CA	Liz Kniss, N-P	**1994, Dec.**
Parma, OH	Gerald M. Blodt, D	**1996, Jan.**
Pasadena, CA	Rick Cole, N-P	**1995, May**
Pasadena, TX	Johnny Isbell, N-P	**1997, June**
Passaic, NJ	Margie Semler, N-P	**1997, June**
Paterson, NJ	William Pascrell, D	**1998, July**
Pawtucket, RI	Robert Metivier, D	**1995, Dec.**
Peabody, MA	Peter Torigian, D	**1997, Jan.**
Pembroke Pines, FL	Charles W. Flanagan, N-P	**1996, Mar.**
Pensacola, FL	John Fogg, N-P	**1995, June**
Peoria, IL	James A. Maloof, N-P	**1997, May**
Philadelphia, PA	Edward Rendell, D	**1996, Jan.**
Phoenix, AZ	Thelda Williams, N-P	**1995, Dec.**
Pico Rivera, CA	Beatrice Proo, N-P	**1995, Apr.**
Pine Bluff, AR	Jerry Taylor, I	**1996, Dec.**
Pittsburgh, PA	Tom Murphy, D	**1997, Dec.**
Pittsfield, MA	Edward Reilly, N-P	**1995, Dec.**
Plainfield, NJ	Mark Fury, N-P	**1997, Dec.**
Plano, TX	James N. Muns, N-P	**1996, May**
Plantation, FL	Frank Veletri, D	**1995, Mar.**
Plymouth, MA	George Cameron, N-P	**1995, May**
Pocatello, ID	Peter Angstadt, N-P	**1997, Dec.**
Pomona, CA	Eddie Cortez, N-P	**1995, Apr.**
Pompano Beach, FL	E. Pat Larkins, N-P	**1995, Mar.**
Pontiac, MI	Charles Harrison Jr., N-P	**1997, Dec.**
Port Arthur, TX	Mary Ellen Summerlin, D	**1995, May**
Portland, ME	Richard Paulson Jr., N-P	**1995, June**
Portland, OR	Vera Katz, D	**1996, Dec.**
Portsmouth, VA	Gloria O. Webb, N-P	**1996, June**
Poughkeepsie, NY	Sheila Newman, N-P	**1995, Dec.**
Providence, RI	Vincent Cianci Jr., R, I	**1998, Dec.**
Provo, UT	George O. Stewart, N-P	**1997, Dec.**
Quincy, IL	Charles W. Scholz, D	**1997, Apr.**
Quincy, MA	James Sheets, D	**1996, Jan.**
Racine, WI	N. Owen Davies, N-P	**1995, Apr.**
Raleigh, NC	Tom Fetzer, N-P	**1995, Dec.**
Rapid City, SD	Edward McGlaughlin, N-P	**1995, May**
Reading, PA	Warren Haggerty Jr., D	**1995, Dec.**
Redding, CA	Robert Anderson, N-P	**1995, Apr.**
Redondo Beach, CA	Brad Parton, N-P	**1997, May**
Redwood City, CA	Judy Buchan, N-P	**1994, Nov.**
Reno, NV	Peter J. Sferrazza, N-P	**1995, June**
Rialto, CA	John Longville, N-P	**1996, Nov.**
Richardson, TX	Gary Slagel, N-P	**1995, May**
Richmond, CA	Rosemary Corbin, D	**1997, Nov.**
Richmond, VA	Leonidas B. Young, N-P	**1998, July**
Riverside, CA	Ronald O. Loveridge, N-P	**1997, Dec.**
Roanoke, VA	David Bowers, D	**1996, June**
Rochester, MN	Chuck Hazama, N-P	**1995, June**
Rochester, NY	Bill Johnson, D	**1997, Dec.**
Rochester Hills, MI	Billie Ireland, R	**1995, Nov.**
Rock Hill, SC	Elizabeth D. Rhea, N-P	**1997, Dec.**
Rock Island, IL	Mark W. Schwiebert, N-P	**1997, Apr.**
Rockford, IL	Charles Box, D	**1997, Apr.**
Rockville, MD	James F. Coyle, N-P	**1995, Nov.**
Rome, NY	Joseph Griffo, R	**1995, Dec.**
Rosemead, CA	Robert W. Bruesch, N-P	**1997, Mar.**
Roseville, MI	Gerald K. Alsip, N-P	**1997, Nov.**
Roswell, NM	Thomas Jennings, N-P	**1998, Mar.**
Royal Oak, MI	Dennis G. Cowan, N-P	**1995, Dec.**
Sacramento, CA	Joseph Serna Jr., N-P	**1996, June**
Saginaw, MI	Gary L. Loster, N-P	**1995, Nov.**
St. Charles, MO	Grace M. Nichols, N-P	**1995, Apr.**
St. Clair Shores, MI	Ted B. Wahby, N-P	**1995, Nov.**
St. Cloud, MN	Charles Winkleman, N-P	**1997, Nov.**
St. Joseph, MO	Larry Stobbs, N-P	**1998, Mar.**
St. Louis, MO	Freeman R. Bosley Jr., D	**1997, Apr.**
St. Louis Park, MN	Lyle Hanks, N-P	**1995, Dec.**
St. Paul, MN	Norm Coleman, N-P	**1997, Dec.**
St. Petersburg, FL	David Fischer, N-P	**1997, Mar.**
Salem, OR	Roger Gertenrich, N-P	**1996, Dec.**
Salinas, CA	Alan Styles, N-P	**1995, June**
Salt Lake City, UT	Deedee Corradini, D	**1995, Dec.**
San Angelo, TX	Dick Funk, N-P	**1995, May**
San Antonio, TX	Nelson Wolff, N-P	**1995, May**
San Bernardino, CA	Tom Minor, R	**1997, June**
San Diego, CA	Susan Golding, R	**1996, Dec.**
San Francisco, CA	Frank Jordan, D	**1996, Jan.**
San Jose, CA	Susan Hammer	**1999, Jan.**
San Leandro, CA	Ellen M. Corbett, N-P	**1998, May**
San Mateo, CA	Claire Mack, N-P	**1995, Dec.**
San Rafael, CA	Albert J. Boro, N-P	**1995, Nov.**
Sandy, UT	Thomas M. Dolan, N-P	**1998, Jan.**
Santa Ana, CA	Miguel Pulido, N-P	**1996, Nov.**
Santa Barbara, CA	Hal Conklin, N-P	**1997, Dec.**
Santa Clara, CA	Judy Nadler, N-P	**1998, Nov.**
Santa Cruz, CA	Scott Kennedy, N-P	**1994, Nov.**
Santa Fe, NM	Debbie Jaramillo, N-P	**1998, Mar.**
Santa Maria, CA	Roger Bunch, N-P	**1996, Nov.**
Santa Monica, CA	Judy Abdo, N-P	**1994, Nov.**
Santa Rosa, CA	Bill Knight, N-P	**1994, Dec.**
Sarasota, FL	Nora Patterson, N-P	**1995, Mar.**
Savannah, GA	Susan Weiner, N-P	**1995, Dec.**
Schaumburg, IL	Al Larson, N-P	**1995, Apr.**
Schenectady, NY	Frank Duci, R	**1995, Dec.**
Scottsdale, AZ	Herbert Drinkwater, R	**1996, Apr.**
Scranton, PA	James Connors, R	**1997, Dec.**
Seattle, WA	Norman Rice, D	**1997, Dec.**
Sheboygan, WI	Richard Schneider, N-P	**1997, Apr.**
Shreveport, LA	Robert W. Williams, R	**1998, Nov.**
Simi Valley, CA	Greg Stratton, N-P	**1996, Nov.**
Sioux City, IA	Robert Scott, N-P	**1997, Dec.**
Sioux Falls, SD	Jack White, R	**1996, June**
Skokie, IL	Jacqueline B. Gorell, N-P	**1997, Apr.**
Somerville, MA	Michael Capuano, D	**1996, Jan.**
South Bend, IN	Joseph Kernan, D	**1995, Dec.**
South Gate, CA	Albert Robles, N-P	**1995, Apr.**
Southfield, MI	Donald F. Fracassi, R	**1997, Dec.**
Sparks, NV	Bruce Breslow, N-P	**1995, June**
Spartanburg, SC	James E. Talley, N-P	**1998, Jan.**
Spokane, WA	Jack Geraghty, N-P	**1997, Dec.**
Springfield, IL	Ossie Langfelder, D	**1995, Apr.**
Springfield, MA	Robert Markel, D	**1996, Jan.**
Springfield, MO	N. L. McCartney, N-P	**1995, Apr.**
Springfield, OH	Dale A. Henry, N-P	**1995, Dec.**
Stamford, CT	Stanley Esposito, R	**1995, Dec.**
Sterling Hts., MI	Richard J. Notte, N-P	**1995, Nov.**
Stockton, CA	Joan Darrah, N-P	**1996, Dec.**
Stratford, CT	Rudolf Weiss, N-P	**1995, Nov.**
Sunnyvale, CA	Frances Rowe, N-P	**1995, Nov.**
Suffolk, VA	S. Chris Jones, N-P	**1995, July**
Sunrise, FL	Steve Effman, N-P	**1997, Mar.**
Syracuse, NY	Roy A. Bernardi, R	**1997, Dec.**
Tacoma, WA	Harold G. Moss, N-P	**1995, Dec.**
Tallahassee, FL	Penny Shaw Herman, N-P	**1995, Mar.**
Tampa, FL	Sandra Freedman, N-P	**1995, Mar.**
Taunton, MA	Robert Nunes, D	**1995, Dec.**
Taylor, MI	Cameron Priebe, D	**1997, Nov.**
Tempe, AZ	Neil Giuliano, N-P	**1996, July**
Temple, TX	J. W. Perry, N-P	**1996, May**
Terre Haute, IN	Pete Chalos, D	**1995, Dec.**
Thornton, CO	Margaret Carpenter, N-P	**1995, Nov.**
Thousand Oaks, CA	Elois Zeanah	**1994, Dec.**
Titusville, FL	Tom Mariani, N-P	**1996, Nov.**
Toledo, OH	Carty Finkbeiner, N-P	**1998, Jan.**
Topeka, KS	Butch Felker, R	**1997, Apr.**
Torrance, CA	Dee Hardison, N-P	**1998, Mar.**
Trenton, NJ	Douglas Palmer, N-P	**1998, July**
Troy, MI	Jeanne M. Stine, N-P	**1995, Apr.**
Troy, NY	Eugene Eaton, R	**1996, Jan.**
Tucson, AZ	George Miller, D	**1995, Dec.**
Tulsa, OK	M. Susan Savage, D	**1998, Mar.**
Tuscaloosa, AL	Alvin DuPont, D	**1997, Oct.**
Tyler, TX	Smith P. Reynolds Jr., N-P	**1996, May**
Union City, NJ	Bruce D. Walter, D	**1996, May**
Upland, CA	Robert R. Nolan, N-P	**1996, Nov.**
Utica, NY	Louis La Polla, R	**1995, Dec.**
Vacaville, CA	David A. Fleming, N-P	**1998, Nov.**
Vallejo, CA	Anthony Intintoli Jr., N-P	**1995, Dec.**
Vancouver, WA	Bruce E. Hagensen, N-P	**1995, Dec.**
Vineland, NJ	Joseph Romano, I	**1996, June**
Virginia Beach, VA	Meyera E. Oberndorf, I	**1996, June**
Visalia, CA	Basil A. Perch, N-P	**1995, Nov.**
Vista, CA	Gloria McClellan, R	**1998, Dec.**

City	Name	Term
Waco, TX	Robert Sheehy Jr., N-P	**1996, May**
Walnut Creek, CA	Ron Beagley, N-P	**1994, Nov.**
Waltham, MA	William Stanley, D	**1996, Jan.**
Warren, MI	Ronald Bonkowski, N-P	**1995, Nov.**
Warren, OH	Daniel Sferra, D	**1996, Jan.**
Warwick, RI	Lincoln D. Chafee, R	**1996, Dec.**
Washington, DC	Marion Barry, D	**1999, Jan.**
Waterbury, CT	Edward D. Bergin, D	**1995, Nov.**
Waterloo, IA	John Rooff III, R	**1995, Dec.**
Waukegan, IL	William F. Durkin, D	**1997, Apr.**
Waukesha, WI	Carol Opel, N-P	**1998, Apr.**
Wauwatosa, WI	Maricolette Walsh, N-P	**1996, Apr.**
W. Allis, WI	John Turck, N-P	**1996, Apr.**
W. Covina, CA	Brad McFadden, N-P	**1995, Apr.**
W. Hartford, CT	Sandy Klebanoff, D	**1995, Nov.**
W. Haven, CT	H. Richard Borer Jr., D	**1995, Dec.**
W. Palm Beach, FL	Nancy M. Graham, N-P	**1995, Mar.**
Westland, MI	Robert Thomas, D	**1997, Dec.**
Westminster, CA	Charles V. Smith, N-P	**1996, Nov.**
Westminster, CO	Nancy Heil, N-P	**1995, Nov.**
Wheaton, IL	Gwendolyn Henry, N-P	**1995, May**
White Plains, NY	S. J. Schulman, D	**1997, Dec.**
Whittier, CA	Michael Sullens, N-P	**1996, Apr.**
Wichita, KS	Elma Broadfoot, N-P	**1995, Apr.**
Wichita Falls, TX	Michael Lam, N-P	**1996, May**
Wilkes-Barre, PA	Lee Namey, D	**1996, Jan.**
Wilmington, DE	Jim Sills, D	**1996, Dec.**
Wilmington, NC	Don Betz, N-P	**1995, Dec.**
Winston-Salem, NC	Martha S. Wood, N-P	**1997, Dec.**
Woodbridge, NJ	James McGreevey, D	**1996, Jan.**
Woonsocket, RI	Francis Lanctot, N-P	**1995, Dec.**
Worcester, MA	Raymond V. Mariano, N-P	**1996, Jan.**
Wyandotte, MI	James R. DeSana, D	**1995, Apr.**
Wyoming, MI	Jack Magnuson, N-P	**1995, Nov.**
Yakima, WA	Pat Berndt, N-P	**1996, Jan.**
Yonkers, NY	Terence Zaleski, D	**1995, Dec.**
York, PA	C. Robertson D	**1997, Dec.**
Youngstown, OH	Patrick Ungaro, D	**1997, Dec.**
Yuma, AZ	Marilyn R. Young, N-P	**1997, Dec.**

Governors of States and Possessions

(as of preliminary election results Nov. 1994)

State	Capital, Zip Code	Governor	Party	Term years	Term expires	Annual salary[1]
Alabama	Montgomery 36130	Fob James Jr.	Rep.	4	Jan. 1999	$81,151
Alaska	Juneau 99811	Tony Knowles	Dem.	4	Dec. 1998	81,648
Arizona	Phoenix 85007	Fife Symington	Rep.	4	Jan. 1999	75,000
Arkansas	Little Rock 72201	Jim Guy Tucker	Dem.	4	Jan. 1999	60,000
California	Sacramento 95814	Pete Wilson	Rep.	4	Jan. 1999	120,000
Colorado	Denver 80203	Roy Romer	Dem.	4	Jan. 1999	70,000
Connecticut	Hartford 06106	John G. Rowland	Rep.	4	Jan. 1999	78,000
Delaware	Dover 19901	Thomas R. Carper	Dem.	4	Jan. 1997	95,000
Florida	Tallahassee 32399	Lawton Chiles	Dem.	4	Jan. 1999	101,764
Georgia	Atlanta 30334	Zell Miller	Dem.	4	Jan. 1999	91,092
Hawaii	Honolulu 96813	Ben Cayetano	Dem.	4	Dec. 1998	94,780
Idaho	Boise 83720	Phil Batt	Rep.	4	Jan. 1999	75,000
Illinois	Springfield 62706	Jim Edgar	Rep.	4	Jan. 1999	103,097
Indiana	Indianapolis 46204	Evan Bayh	Dem.	4	Jan. 1997	77,200
Iowa	Des Moines 50319	Terry E. Branstad	Rep.	4	Jan. 1999	76,700
Kansas	Topeka 66612	Bill Graves	Rep.	4	Jan. 1999	76,476
Kentucky	Frankfort 40601	Brereton C. Jones	Dem.	4	Dec. 1995	86,352
Louisiana	Baton Rouge 70804	Edwin W. Edwards	Dem.	4	May 1996	73,440
Maine	Augusta 04333	Angus King	Ind.	4	Jan. 1999	70,000
Maryland	Annapolis 21401	Parris N. Glendening	Dem.	4	Jan. 1999	120,000
Massachusetts	Boston 02113	William F. Weld	Rep.	4	Jan. 1999	75,000
Michigan	Lansing 48909	John Engler	Rep.	4	Jan. 1999	112,025
Minnesota	St. Paul 55155	Arne H. Carlson	Rep.	4	Jan. 1999	109,053
Mississippi	Jackson 39205	Kirk Fordice	Rep.	4	Jan. 1996	75,600
Missouri	Jefferson City 65102	Mel Carnahan	Dem.	4	Jan. 1997	90,312
Montana	Helena 59620	Marc Racicot	Rep.	4	Jan. 1997	55,502
Nebraska	Lincoln 68509	Ben Nelson	Dem.	4	Jan. 1999	65,000
Nevada	Carson City 89710	Bob Miller	Dem.	4	Jan. 1999	90,000
New Hampshire	Concord 03301	Steve Merrill	Rep.	2	Jan. 1997	86,235
New Jersey	Trenton 08625	Christine Todd Whitman	Rep.	4	Jan. 1998	85,000
New Mexico	Santa Fe 87503	Gary Johnson	Rep.	4	Jan. 1999	90,000
New York	Albany 12224	George E. Pataki	Rep.	4	Jan. 1999	130,000
North Carolina	Raleigh 27603	James B. Hunt Jr.	Dem.	4	Jan. 1997	123,300
North Dakota	Bismarck 58505	Edward T. Schafer	Rep.	4	Jan. 1997	68,280
Ohio	Columbus 43215	George V. Voinovich	Rep.	4	Jan. 1999	115,752
Oklahoma	Oklahoma City 73105	Frank Keating	Rep.	4	Jan. 1999	70,000
Oregon	Salem 97310	John Kitzhaber	Dem.	4	Jan. 1999	80,000
Pennsylvania	Harrisburg 17120	Tom Ridge	Rep.	4	Jan. 1999	105,000
Rhode Island	Providence 02903	Lincoln C. Almond	Rep.	4	Jan. 1999	69,900
South Carolina	Columbia 29211	David Beasley	Rep.	4	Jan. 1999	101,959
South Dakota	Pierre 57501	William J. Janklow	Rep.	4	Jan. 1999	74,649
Tennessee	Nashville 37243	Don Sundquist	Rep.	4	Jan. 1999	85,000
Texas	Austin 78711	George W. Bush	Rep.	4	Jan. 1999	99,122
Utah	Salt Lake City 84114	Michael O. Leavitt	Rep.	4	Jan. 1997	70,000
Vermont	Montpelier 05609	Howard Dean	Dem.	2	Jan. 1997	85,977
Virginia	Richmond 23219	George F. Allen	Rep.	4	Jan. 1998	110,000
Washington	Olympia 98504	Mike Lowry	Dem.	4	Jan. 1997	121,000
West Virginia	Charleston 25305	Gaston Caperton	Dem.	4	Jan. 1997	90,000
Wisconsin	Madison 53707	Tommy G. Thompson	Rep.	4	Jan. 1999	92,283
Wyoming	Cheyenne 82002	Jim Geringer	Rep.	4	Jan. 1999	70,000
Puerto Rico	San Juan 00936	Pedro J. Rosselló	—	4	Jan. 1996	—

(1) Salary in effect in 1994.

The Race for Governor, 1994

Source: Voter News Service

(preliminary returns, subject to change, pending official results)

State	Democrat	Vote	Republican	Vote	Other	Vote
AL	Jim Folsom*	590,091	**Fob James, Jr.**	**601,822**		
AK	**Tony Knowles**	**78,308**	James O. Campbell	77,969	John Coghill (AI)	23,969
AZ	Eddie Basha	484,307	**Fife Symington***	**570,501**		
AR	**Jim Guy Tucker***	**427,970**	Sheffield Nelson	287,649		
CA	Kathleen Brown	3,178,081	**Pete Wilson***	**4,351,584**		
CO	**Roy Romer***	**616,521**	Bruce Benson	430,252		
CT	Bill Curry	372,210	**John G. Rowland**	**411,887**	Eunice Groark (ACP)	215,596
FL	**Lawton Chiles***	**2,125,984**	Jeb Bush	2,051,407		
GA	**Zell Miller***	**787,835**	Guy Millner	756,412		
HI	**Ben Cayetano**	**134,978**	Patricia "Pat" Saiki	107,908	Frank Fasi (BP)	113,158
ID	Larry EchoHawk	181,471	**Phil Batt**	**215,751**		
IL	Dawn Clark Netsch	1,051,068	**Jim Edgar***	**1,973,239**		
IA	Bonnie J. Campbell	411,495	**Terry E. Branstad***	**562,918**		
KS	Jim Slattery	294,516	**Bill Graves**	**524,624**		
ME	Joseph E. Brennan	171,787	Susan M. Collins	116,344	**Angus King (I)**	**178,606**
MD	**Parris N. Glendening**	**683,995**	Ellen R. Sauerbrey	677,808		
MA	Mark Roosevelt	606,648	**William F. Weld***	**1,521,561**		
MI	Howard Wolpe	1,186,559	**John Engler***	**1,893,520**		
MN	John Marty	591,350	**Arne H. Carlson***	**1,101,345**		
NE	**Ben Nelson***	**420,048**	Gene Spence	146,971		
NV	**Bob Miller***	**199,891**	Jim Gibbons	156,637		
NH	Wayne D. King	79,493	**Steve Merrill***	**216,755**		
NM	Bruce King*	182,154	**Gary Johnson**	**224,411**	R. Mondragon (GR)	47,080
NY	Mario M. Cuomo*	2,286,117	**George E. Pataki**	**2,477,882**		
OH	Robert L. Burch, Jr.	829,859	**George Voinovich***	**2,382,591**		
OK	Jack Mildren	294,936	**Frank Keating**	**466,740**	Wes Watkins (I)	233,336
OR	**John Kitzhaber**	**501,539**	Denny Smith	386,484		
PA	Mark S. Singel	1,422,072	**Tom Ridge**	**1,622,835**	Peg Luksik (I)	458,206
RI	Myrth York	151,861	**Lincoln C. Almond**	**164,130**		
SC	Nick Theodore	446,289	**David Beasley**	**469,595**		
SD	Jim Beddow	126,258	**William J. Janklow**	**172,500**		
TN	Phil Bredesen	659,844	**Don Sundquist**	**801,664**		
TX	Ann W. Richards*	2,014,399	**George W. Bush**	**2,350,493**		
VT	**Howard Dean***	**142,998**	David F. Kelley	39,703		
WI	Chuck Chvala	480,343	**Tommy Thompson***	**1,052,776**		
WY	Kathy Karpan	80,383	**Jim Geringer**	**117,491**		

boldface = winner. *Incumbent. ACP = A Connecticut Party. AI = Alaska Independence. BP = Best Party. GR = Green Party. I = Independent.

State Officials, Salaries, Party Membership

As of mid-1994; † ind. or other party.

Alabama

Governor — Jim Folsom, D, $81,151.
Lt. Gov. — vacant.
Sec. of State — Jim Bennett, D, $57,203.
Atty. Gen. — Jimmy Evans, D, $90,474.
Treasurer — George Wallace Jr., D, $57,203.

Legislature: meets annually the 3d Tuesday in Apr. (first year of term of office), first Tuesday in Feb. (2d and 3d years), 2d Tuesday in Jan. (4th year) at Montgomery. Members receive $10 a day salary, plus $50 a day expenses, plus $2,280 per month expenses and mileage of 10¢ per mile.

Senate — Dem., 27; Rep., 8. Total, 35.
House — Dem., 82; Rep., 23. Total, 105.

Alaska

Governor — Walter Hickel, †, $81,648.
Lt. Gov. — John B. Coghill, †, $76,188.
Atty. General — Bruce Botelho, R, $79,860.

Legislature: meets annually in January at Juneau, for 120 days with a 10-day extension possible upon 2/3 vote. First session in odd years. Members receive $22,872 per year plus $80 a day per diem.

Senate — Dem., 10; Rep., 10. Total, 20.
House — Dem., 20; Rep., 18; 2 other. Total, 40.

Arizona

Governor — Fife Symington, R, $75,000.
Sec. of State — Richard Mahoney, D, $54,600.
Atty. Gen. — Grant Woods, R, $76,440.
Treasurer — Tony West, R, $54,600.

Legislature: meets annually in January at Phoenix. Each member receives an annual salary of $15,000.

Senate — Dem., 12; Rep., 18. Total, 30.
House — Dem., 25; Rep., 35. Total, 60.

Arkansas

Governor — Jim Guy Tucker, D, $60,000.
Lt. Gov. — Mike Huckabee, R, $29,000.
Sec. of State — W. J. "Bill" McCuen, D, $37,500.
Atty. Gen. — Winston Bryant, D, $50,000.
Treasurer — Jimmie Lou Fisher, D, $37,500.
Auditor — Julia Hughes Jones, D, $37,500.

General Assembly: meets odd years in January at Little Rock. Members receive $12,500 per year.

Senate — Dem., 30; Rep., 5. Total, 35.
House — Dem., 88; Rep., 11; 1 ind. Total, 100.

California

Governor — Pete Wilson, R, $120,000.
Lt. Gov. — Leo T. McCarthy, D, $90,000.
Sec. of State — vacant.
Controller — Gray Davis, D, $90,000.
Atty. Gen. — Dan Lungren, R, $102,000.

Legislature: meets at Sacramento; regular sessions commence on the first Monday in Dec. of every even-numbered year; each session lasts 2 years. Members receive $52,500 per year plus mileage and $100 per diem.

Senate — Dem., 22; Rep., 15; 2 ind.; 1 vac. Total, 40.
Assembly — Dem., 47; Rep. 33. Total, 80.

Colorado

Governor — Roy Romer, D, $70,000.
Lt. Gov. — Sam Cassidy, D, $48,500.
Sec. of State — Natalie Meyer, R, $48,500.
Atty. Gen. — Gale Norton, R, $60,000.
Treasurer — Gail Schoettler, D, $48,500.

General Assembly: meets annually in January at Denver. Members receive $17,500 annually.

Senate — Dem., 16; Rep., 19. Total, 35.
House — Dem., 31; Rep., 34. Total, 65.

Connecticut

Governor — Lowell Weicker, †, $78,000.
Lt. Gov. — Eunice S. Groark, †, $55,000.
Sec. of State — Pauline R Kezer, R, $50,000.
Treasurer — Joseph M. Suggs, Jr., D, $50,000.
Comptroller — William E. Curry Jr., D, $50,000.
Atty. Gen. — Richard Blumenthal, D, $60,000.
General Assembly: meets annually odd years in January and even years in February at Hartford. Salary $15,200 per year plus $4,500 (senator), $3,500 (representative) per year for expenses, plus travel allowance.
Senate — Dem., 19; Rep., 17. Total, 36.
House — Dem., 86; Rep., 65. Total, 151.

Delaware

Governor — Thomas R. Carper, D, $95,000.
Lt. Gov. — Ruth Ann Minner, D, $39,500.
Sec. of State — Edward J. Freel, D, $83,100.
Atty. Gen. — Charles Oberly III, D, $91,600.
Treasurer — Janet C. Rzewnicki, R, $73,700.
General Assembly: session beginning the 2d Tuesday in January until June 30. Members receive $26,200 base salary, plus $5,500 expense account.
Senate — Dem., 14; Rep., 7. Total, 21.
House — Dem., 18; Rep., 23. Total, 41.

Florida

Governor — Lawton Chiles, D, $101,764.
Lt. Gov. — Kenneth "Buddy" McKay, D, $97,479.
Sec. of State — Jim Smith, R, $100,735.
Comptroller — Gerald Lewis, D, $100,735.
Atty. Gen. — Robert Butterworth, D, $100,735.
Treasurer — Tom Gallagher, R, $100,735.
Legislature: meets annually at Tallahassee. Members receive $22,560 per year plus expense allowance while on official business.
Senate — Dem., 20; Rep., 20. Total, 40.
House — Dem., 71; Rep., 49. Total, 120.

Georgia

Governor — Zell Miller, D, $91,092.
Lt. Gov. — Pierre Howard, D, $59,145.
Sec. of State — Max Cleland, D, $72,966.
Insurance Comm. — Tim Ryles, D, $72,954.
Atty. Gen. — Michael J. Bowers, R, $74,645.
General Assembly: meets annually at Atlanta. Members receive $10,509 per year, $59 per diem, and $4,800 expense reimbursement. During session $59 per day for expenses.
Senate — Dem., 38; Rep., 17; 1 vac. Total, 56.
House — Dem., 128; Rep., 51; 1 vac. Total, 180.

Hawaii

Governor — John Waihee, D, $94,780.
Lt. Gov. — Benjamin Cayetano, D, $90,041.
Atty. Gen. — Robert Marks, $85,302.
Comptroller — Robert Takushi, $85,302.
Dir. of Budget & Finance — Yukio Takemoto, $85,302.
Legislature: meets annually on 3d Wednesday in January at Honolulu. Members receive $27,000 per year plus expenses.
Senate — Dem., 22; Rep., 3. Total, 25.
House — Dem., 47; Rep., 4. Total, 51.

Idaho

Governor — Cecil D. Andrus, D, $75,000.
Lt. Gov. — C. L. "Butch" Otter, R, $20,000.
Sec. of State — Pete T. Cenarrusa, R, $62,500.
Treasurer — Lydia Justice Edwards, R, $62,500.
Atty. Gen. — Larry EchoHawk, D, $67,500.
Legislature: meets annually the Monday on or nearest the 9th of January at Boise. Members receive $12,000 per year plus $70 per day during session if required to maintain a 2d residence; $40 if no 2d residence, plus $50.00 per day when engaged in legislative business when legislature is not in session.
Senate — Dem., 12; Rep., 23. Total, 35.
House — Dem., 20; Rep., 50. Total, 70.

Illinois

Governor — Jim Edgar, R, $103,097.
Lt. Gov. — Bob Kustra, R, $71,069.
Sec. of State — George H. Ryan, R, $88,836.
Comptroller — Dawn Clark Netsch, D, $78,839.
Atty. Gen. — Roland W. Burris, D, $88,836.
Treasurer — Patrick Quinn, D, $78,839.
General Assembly: meets annually in January at Springfield. Members receive $39,420 per annum.
Senate — Dem., 27; Rep., 32. Total, 59.
House — Dem., 67; Rep., 51. Total, 118.

Indiana

Governor — Evan Bayh, D, $77,200 plus discretionary expenses.
Lt. Gov. — Frank O'Bannon, D, $64,000 plus discretionary expenses.
Sec. of State — Joseph Hogsett, D, $46,000.
Atty. Gen. — Pamela Carter, D, $59,200.
Treasurer — Marjorie H. O'Laughlin, R, $46,000.
Auditor — Ann G. DeVore, R, $46,000.
General Assembly: meets annually in January. Members receive $11,600 per year plus $105 per day while in session, $25 per day while not in session.
Senate — Dem., 22; Rep., 28. Total, 50.
House — Dem., 55; Rep., 45. Total, 100.

Iowa

Governor — Terry E. Branstad, R, $76,700.
Lt. Gov. — Joy Corning, R, $60,000.
Sec. of State — Elaine Baxter, D, $60,000.
Atty. Gen. — Bonnie Campbell, D, $73,600.
Treasurer — Michael L. Fitzgerald, D, $60,000.
Auditor — Richard D. Johnson, R, $60,000.
Sec. of Agriculture — Dale M. Cochran, D, $60,000.
General Assembly: meets annually in January at Des Moines. Members receive $18,100 annually plus expense allowance.
Senate — Dem., 27; Rep., 23. Total, 50.
House — Dem., 49; Rep., 51. Total, 100.

Kansas

Governor — Joan Finney, D, $76,476.
Lt. Gov. — James Francisco, D, $76,125.
Sec. of State — Bill Graves, R, $59,112.
Atty. Gen. — Robert T. Stephan, R, $68,328.
Treasurer — Sally Thompson, D, $59,406.
Legislature: meets annually in January at Topeka. Members receive $63 a day plus $73 a day expenses while in session, plus $600 per month while not in session.
Senate — Dem., 13; Rep., 27. Total, 40.
House — Dem., 59; Rep., 66. Total, 125.

Kentucky

Governor — Brereton C. Jones, D, $86,352.
Lt. Gov. — Paul Patton, D, $73,411.
Sec. of State — Bob Babbage, D, $73,411.
Atty. Gen. — Chris Gorman, D, $73,411.
Treasurer — Francis J. Mills, D, $73,411.
Auditor — Ben Chandler, D, $73,411.
General Assembly: meets even years in January at Frankfort. Members receive $100 per day and $75 per day during session and $950 per month for expenses for interim.
Senate — Dem., 23; Rep., 14; 1 vac. Total, 38.
House — Dem., 71; Rep., 29; 2 vac. Total, 100.

Louisiana

Governor — Edwin W. Edwards, D, $73,440.
Lt. Gov. — Melinda Schwegmann, D, $63,367.
Sec. of State — Fox McKeithen, R, $60,169.
Atty. Gen. — Richard Ieyoub, D, $60,169.
Treasurer — Mary Landrieu, D, $60,169.
Legislature: meets annually for 60 legislative days commencing on the last Monday in March. Members receive $75 per day and mileage plus annual salary of $16,800.
Senate — Dem., 33; Rep., 6. Total, 39.
House — Dem., 86; Rep., 17; 1, ind.; 1 vac. Total, 105.

Maine

Governor — John R. McKernan Jr., R, $70,000.
Sec. of State — G. William Diamond, D, $48,152.
Atty. Gen. — Michael E. Carpenter, D, $61,152.
Treasurer — Samuel Shapiro, D, $61,200.
Legislature: meets annually the first Wednesday in December at Augusta, and the Wednesday after the first Tuesday in Jan. in even numbered years. Members receive $10,500 for first regular session, $7,500 for second regular session plus expenses; presiding officers receive 50% more.
Senate — Dem., 20; Rep., 15. Total, 35.
House — Dem., 90; Rep., 61. Total, 151.

Maryland

Governor — William Donald Schaefer, D, $120,000.
Lt. Gov. — Melvin Steinberg, D, $100,000.
Comptroller — Louis L. Goldstein, D, $100,000.
Atty. Gen. — J. Joseph Curran Jr., D, $100,000.
Sec. of State — Tyras S. Athey, D, $70,000.
Treasurer — Lucille Maurer, D, $100,000.
General Assembly: meets 90 consecutive days annually beginning on the 2d Wednesday in January at Annapolis. Members receive $27,000 per year plus expenses.
Senate — Dem., 38; Rep., 9. Total, 47.
House — Dem., 117; Rep., 24. Total, 141.

Massachusetts

Governor — William F. Weld, R, $75,000.

Lt. Gov. — A. Paul Cellucci, R, $60,000.
Sec. of State — Michael Joseph Connolly, D, $60,000.
Atty. Gen. — L. Scott Harshbarger, D, $65,000.
Treasurer — Joseph Malone, R, $60,000.
Auditor — A. Joseph DeNucci, D, $60,000.
General Court (Legislature): meets each January in Boston. Salaries $30,000 per annum.
Senate — Dem., 31; Rep., 9. Total, 40.
House — Dem., 124; Rep., 35; 1 ind. Total, 160.

Michigan

Governor — John Engler, R, $112,025, plus $30,000 expense allowance.
Lt. Gov. — Connie Binsfeld, R, $84,315, plus $9,000 expense allowance.
Sec. of State — Richard H. Austin, D, $111,200.
Atty. Gen. — Frank J. Kelley, D, $111,200.
Treasurer — Doug Roberts, appointed, $87,300.
Legislature: meets annually in January at Lansing. Members receive $47,723 per year, plus $8,925 expense allowance.
Senate — Dem., 15; Rep., 22; 1 vac. Total, 38.
House — Dem., 55; Rep., 55. Total, 110.

Minnesota

Governor — Arne H. Carlson, R, $109,053.
Lt. Gov. — Joanell Dyrstad, IR, $59,981.
Sec. of State — Joan Anderson Growe, DFL, $59,981.
Atty. Gen. — Hubert H. Humphrey 3d, DFL, $85,194.
Treasurer — Michael McGrath, DFL, $59,981.
Auditor — Mark Dayton, IR, $65,437.
Legislature: meets for a total of 120 days within every 2 years at St. Paul. Members receive $27,979 per year, plus expense allowance during session.
Senate — DFL, 45; IR, 22. Total, 67.
House — DFL, 85; IR, 49. Total, 134.
(DFL means Democratic-Farmer-Labor. IR means Independent Republican.)

Mississippi

Governor — Kirk Fordice, R, $75,600.
Lt. Gov. — Eddie Briggs, R, $40,800.
Sec. of State — Dick Molpus, D, $59,400.
Atty. Gen. — Mike Moore, D, $68,400.
Treasurer — Marshall Bennett, D, $59,400.
Legislature: meets annually in January at Jackson. Members receive $10,000 per regular session plus travel allowance, and $800 per month while not in session.
Senate — Dem., 37; Rep., 15. Total, 52.
House — Dem., 90; Rep., 30; 2 ind. Total, 122.

Missouri

Governor — Mel Carnahan, D, $90,312.
Lt. Gov. — Roger Wilson, D, $54,343.
Sec. of State — vacant, $72,327.
Atty. Gen. — Jeremiah W. Nixon, D, $78,322.
Treasurer — Bob Holden, D, $72,327.
State Auditor — Margaret Kelly, R, $72,327.
General Assembly: meets annually in Jefferson City on the first Wednesday after first Monday in January. Members receive $22,862 annually.
Senate — Dem., 19; Rep., 14; 1 vac. Total, 34.
House — Dem., 95; Rep., 67; 1 vac. Total, 163.

Montana

Governor — Marc Racicot, R, $55,502.
Lt. Gov. — Dennis Rehberg, R, $40,466.
Sec. of State — Mike Cooney, D, $37,526.
Atty. Gen. — Joe Mazurek, D, $50,841.
Legislative Assembly: meets odd years in January at Helena. Members receive $55.50 per legislative day plus $50 per day for expenses while in session.
Senate — Dem., 30; Rep., 20. Total, 50.
House — Dem., 46; Rep., 53; 1 vac. Total, 100.

Nebraska

Governor — Ben Nelson, D, $65,000.
Lt. Gov. — Kim Robak, D, $47,000.
Sec. of State — Allen J. Beermann, R, $52,000.
Atty. Gen. — Don Stenberg, R, $64,500.
Treasurer — Dawn Rockey, D, $49,500.
Legislature: meets annually in January at Lincoln. Members receive salary of $12,000 annually plus expenses.
Unicameral body composed of 49 members who are elected on a nonpartisan ballot and are called senators.

Nevada

Governor — Bob Miller, D, $90,000.
Lt. Gov. — Sue Wagner, R, $20,000.
Sec. of State — Cheryl Lau, R, $62,500.
Comptroller — Darrel Daines, R, $62,500.
Atty. Gen. — Frankie Sue Del Papa, D, $85,000.
Treasurer — Bob Seale, R, $62,500.
Legislature: meets odd years in January at Carson City. Members receive $130 per day for 60 days (20 days for special sessions).
Senate — Dem., 10; Rep., 11. Total, 21.
Assembly — Dem., 29; Rep., 13. Total, 42.

New Hampshire

Governor — Steve Merrill, R, $86,235.
Sec. of State — William M. Gardner, D, $68,768.
Atty. Gen. — Jeffrey Howard, R, $72,888.
Treasurer — Georgie A. Thomas, R, $68,768.
General Court (Legislature): meets every year in January at Concord. Members receive $200; presiding officers $250.
Senate — Dem., 11; Rep., 13. Total, 24.
House — Rep., 257; Dem., 137; 5 ind. & other; 1 vac. Total, 400.

New Jersey

Governor — Christine Todd Whitman, R, $85,000.
Sec. of State — Lonna R. Hooks, R, $100,225.
Atty. Gen. — Deborah T. Poritz, R, $100,225.
Treasurer — Bryan W. Clymer, R, $100,225.
Legislature: meets throughout the year at Trenton. Members receive $35,000 per year, except president of Senate and speaker of Assembly who receive 1/3 more.
Senate — Dem., 13; Rep., 27. Total, 40.
Assembly — Dem., 27; Rep., 53. Total, 80.

New Mexico

Governor — Bruce King, D, $90,000.
Lt. Gov. — Casey Luna, D, $65,000.
Sec. of State — Stephanie Gonzales, D, $65,000.
Atty. Gen. — Tom Udall, D, $72,500.
Treasurer — David King, D, $65,000.
Legislature: meets on the 3d Tuesday in January at Santa Fe; odd years for 60 days, even years for 30 days. Members receive $75 per day while in session.
Senate — Dem., 26; Rep., 15; 1 ind. Total, 42.
House — Dem., 53; Rep., 17. Total, 70.

New York

Governor — Mario M. Cuomo, D, $130,000.
Lt. Gov. — Stan Lundine, D, $110,000.
Sec. of State — Gail S. Shaffer, D, $90,832.
Comptroller — Edward V. Regan, R, $110,000.
Atty. Gen. — G. Oliver Koppell, D, $110,000.
Legislature: meets annually in January at Albany. Members receive $57,500 per year.
Senate — Dem., 26; Rep., 35. Total, 61.
Assembly — Dem., 102; Rep., 48; Total, 150.

North Carolina

Governor — James B. Hunt Jr., D, $123,300 plus $11,500 per year expenses.
Lt. Gov. — Dennis Wicker, D, $75,774 plus expenses.
Sec. of State — Rufus L. Edmisten, D, $87,000.
Atty. Gen. — Michael Easley, D, $75,252.
Treasurer — Harlan E. Boyles, D, $75,252.
General Assembly: meets odd years in January at Raleigh. Members receive $12,504 annual salary and $6,624 annual expense allowance, plus $81 per diem subsistence and travel allowance while in session.
Senate — Dem., 39; Rep., 11. Total, 50.
House — Dem., 78; Rep., 42. Total, 120.

North Dakota

Governor — Edward T. Schafer, R, $68,280.
Lt. Gov. — Rosemarie Myrdal, R, $56,112.
Sec. of State — Alvin A. Jaeger, R, $51,752.
Atty. Gen. — Heidi Heitkamp, D, $57,936.
Treasurer — Kathi Gilmore, D, $51,744.
Legislative Assembly: meets odd years in January at Bismarck. Members receive $90 per day expenses during session and $180 per month.
Senate — Dem., 25; Rep., 24. Total, 49.
House — Dem., 33; Rep., 65. Total, 98.

Ohio

Governor — George V. Voinovich, R, $115,752.
Lt. Gov. — Michael DeWine, R, $59,841.
Sec. of State — Bob Taft, R, $85,508.
Atty. Gen. — Lee Fisher, D, $77,563.
Treasurer — Mary Ellen Withrow, D, $85,508.
Auditor — Thomas E. Ferguson, D, $81,432.
General Assembly: meets odd years at Columbus on first Monday in January; no limit on session. Members receive $42,426 per annum.
Senate — Dem., 13; Rep., 20. Total, 33.
House — Dem., 53; Rep., 46. Total, 99.

Oklahoma

Governor — David Walters, D, $70,000.
Lt. Gov. — Jack Mildren, D, $62,500.
Sec. of State — John Kennedy, D, $42,500.
Atty. Gen. — Susan Loving, D, $75,000.
Treasurer — Claudette Henry, R, $70,000.
Auditor— Clifton Scott, D, $50,000.
Legislature: meets annually the first Monday in Feb. at Oklahoma City. Members receive $32,000 annually.
Senate — Dem., 37; Rep., 11. Total, 48.
House — Dem., 68; Rep., 33. Total, 101.

Oregon

Governor — Barbara Roberts, D, $80,000.
Sec. of State — Phil Keisling, D, $61,500.
Atty. Gen. — Ted Kulongoski, D, $66,000.
Treasurer — Jim Hill, D, $61,500.
Legislative Assembly: meets odd years in January at Salem. Members receive $1,029 monthly and $73 expenses per day both during & out of session.
Senate — Dem., 16; Rep., 14. Total, 30.
House — Dem., 32; Rep., 28. Total, 60.

Pennsylvania

Governor — Robert Casey, D, $105,000.
Lt. Gov. — Mark S. Singel, D, $83,000.
Sec. of the Commonwealth — Robert N. Grant, D, $72,000.
Atty. Gen. — Ernest R. Preate, R, $84,000.
Treasurer — Catherine Baker Knoll, D, $84,000.
General Assembly — convenes annually in January at Harrisburg. Members receive $47,000 per year plus expenses.
Senate — Dem., 26; Rep., 24. Total, 50.
House — Dem., 102; Rep., 101. Total, 203.

Rhode Island

Governor — Bruce Sundlun, D, $69,900.
Lt. Gov. — Robert A. Weygand, D, $52,000.
Sec. of State — Barbara M. Leonard, R, $52,000.
Atty. Gen. — Jeffrey B. Pine, R, $55,000.
Treasurer — Nancy J. Mayer, R, $52,000.
General Assembly: meets annually in January at Providence. Members receive $5 per day for 60 days, and travel allowance of 8¢ per mile.
Senate — Dem., 39; Rep., 11. Total, 50.
House — Dem., 85; Rep., 15. Total, 100.

South Carolina

Governor — Carroll A. Campbell Jr., R, $101,959.
Lt. Gov. — Nick Theodore, D, $44,737.
Sec. of State — Jim Miles, R, $92,007.
Comptroller Gen. — Earle E. Morris Jr., D, $92,007.
Atty. Gen. — T. T. Medlock, D, $92,007.
Treasurer — G. L. Patterson Jr., D, $85,000.
General Assembly: meets annually in January at Columbia. Members receive $10,400 per year and expense allowance of $79 per day, plus travel and postage allowance.
Senate — Dem., 30; Rep., 16. Total, 46.
House — Dem., 73; Rep., 50; 1 ind. Total, 124.

South Dakota

Governor — Walter Dale Miller, R, $74,649.
Lt. Gov. — vacant.
Sec. of State — Joyce Hazeltine, R, $50,721.
Treasurer — G. Homer Harding, R, $50,721.
Atty. Gen. — Mark Barnett, R, $63,402.
Auditor — Vernon Larson, R, $50,721.
Legislature: meets annually in January at Pierre. Members receive $4,267 for 40-day session in odd-numbered years, and $3,733 for 35-day session in even-numbered years, plus $75 per legislative day.
Senate — Dem., 20; Rep., 15. Total, 35.
House — Dem., 29; Rep., 41. Total, 70.

Tennessee

Governor — Ned Ray McWherter, D, $85,000.
Lt. Gov. — John S. Wilder, D, $49,500.
Sec. of State — Riley C. Darnell, D, $80,700.
Comptroller — William Snodgrass, D, $80,700.
Atty. Gen. — Charles W. Burson, D, $93,540.
General Assembly: meets annually in January at Nashville. Members receive $16,500 yearly plus $78.00 per diem plus office expenses.
Senate — Dem., 19; Rep., 14. Total, 33.
House — Dem., 63; Rep., 36. Total, 99.

Texas

Governor — Ann W. Richards, D, $99,122.
Lt. Gov. — Bob Bullock, D, $7,200.
Sec. of State — Ronald Kirk, D, $76,966.
Comptroller — John Sharp, D, $79,246.
Atty. Gen. — Dan Morales, D, $79,246.
Treasurer — Martha Whitehead, D, $79,246.
Railroad Commissioner — James G. Nugent
Legislature: meets odd years in January at Austin. Members receive annual salary not exceeding $7,200, per diem while in session, and travel allowance.
Senate — Dem., 18; Rep., 13. Total, 31.
House — Dem., 92; Rep., 58. Total, 150.

Utah

Governor — Michael O. Leavitt, R, $70,000.
Lt. Gov. — Olene S. Walker, R, $52,500.
Atty. Gen. — Jan Graham, D, $56,000.
Treasurer — Edward T. Alter, R, $53,000.
Legislature: convenes for 45 days on 2d Monday in January each year; members receive $25 per day, $15 daily expenses, and mileage.
Senate — Dem., 11; Rep., 18. Total, 29.
House — Dem., 26; Rep., 49. Total, 75.

Vermont

Governor — Howard Dean, D, $85,977.
Lt. Gov. — Barbara W. Snelling, R, $35,842.
Sec. of State — Donald M. Hooper, D, $54,102.
Atty. Gen. — Jeffrey Amestoy, R, $64,991.
Treasurer — Paul W. Ruse Jr., D, $54,102.
Auditor of Accounts — Edward S. Flanagan, D, $54,102.
General Assembly: meets in January at Montpelier (annual and biennial session). Members receive $510 per week while in session plus $100 per day for special session, plus specified expenses.
Senate — Dem., 14; Rep., 16. Total, 30.
House — Dem., 87; Rep., 59; Prog. Coalition, 2; 2 ind. Total, 150.

Virginia

Governor — George F. Allen, R, $110,000.
Lt. Gov. — Donald S. Beyer Jr., D, $32,000.
Atty. Gen. — James S. Gilmore III, R, $97,500.
Sec. of the Commonwealth — Elizabeth Beamer, R, $73,023.
Treasurer — Ronald L. Tillett, $89,500.
General Assembly: meets annually in January at Richmond. Members receive $18,000 annually plus expense and mileage allowances.
Senate — Dem., 22; Rep., 18. Total, 40.
House — Dem., 58; Rep., 41; 1 ind. Total, 100.

Washington

Governor — Mike Lowry, D, $121,000.
Lt. Gov. — Joel Pritchard, R, $62,700.
Sec. of State — Ralph Munro, R, $64,300.
Atty. Gen. — Christine Gregoire, D, $92,000.
Treasurer — Daniel K. Grimm, D, $79,500.
Legislature: meets annually in January at Olympia. Members receive $25,900 annually plus $66 per diem and 28¢ per mile while in session, and $66 per diem for attending meetings during interim.
Senate — Dem., 28; Rep., 21. Total, 49.
House — Dem., 65; Rep., 33. Total, 98.

West Virginia

Governor — Gaston Caperton, D, $90,000.
Sec. of State — Ken Hechler, D, $65,000.
Atty. Gen. — Darrell McGraw, D, $75,000.
Treasurer — Larrie Bailey, D, $65,000.
Comm. of Agric. — Gus Douglass, D, $70,000.
Auditor — Glen B. Gainer 3d, D, $70,000.
Legislature: meets annually in January at Charleston. Members receive $15,000.
Senate — Dem., 32; Rep., 2. Total, 34.
House — Dem., 79; Rep., 21. Total, 100.

Wisconsin

Governor — Tommy G. Thompson, R, $92,283.
Lt. Gov. — Scott McCallum, R, $49,673.
Sec. of State — Douglas La Follette, D, $45,088.
Treasurer — Cathy S. Zeuske, R, $45,088.
Atty. Gen. — James E. Doyle, D, $82,706.
Superintendent of Public Instruction — John T. Benson, $72,337.
Legislature: meets in January at Madison. Members receive $35,070 annually plus $64 per day expenses.
Senate — Dem., 16; Rep., 17. Total, 33.
Assembly — Dem., 52; Rep., 47. Total, 99.

Wyoming

Governor — Mike Sullivan, D, $70,000.
Sec. of State — Kathy Karpan, D, $52,500.
Atty. Gen. — Joseph Meyer, $52,500.
Treasurer — Stan Smith, R, $52,500.
Auditor — Dave Ferrari, R, $52,500.
Legislature: meets odd years in January, even years in February, at Cheyenne. Members receive $75 per day while in session, plus $60 per day for expenses.
Senate — Dem., 10; Rep., 20. Total, 30.
House — Dem., 19; Rep., 45. Total, 64.

Puerto Rico

Governor — Pedro J. Rosselló.
Legislature: composed of a Senate of 27 members and a House of Representatives of 53 members. Majority of the members of both chambers belongs to the New Progressive Party. They meet annually on the 2d Monday in January to May 31, and on the 2d Monday o September to October 30 in San Juan.

CABINETS OF THE U.S.

Role of the Cabinet

The Cabinet as a governmental institution is not provided for in the U.S. Constitution. It developed as an advisory body out of the desire of presidents to consult the heads of the executive departments on policy issues and problems. Aside from its role as a consultative and advisory body, the cabinet has no function and wields no executive authority. The president may or may not consult the cabinet and is not bound by its advice. Most presidents also consult numerous advisers outside the cabinet. A group of regular informal advisers to the president has been known in American history as a "kitchen cabinet." The formal cabinet meets at times set by the president, often once a week. Members of Pres. Bill Clinton's Cabinet listed here are as of Oct. 1994.

Secretaries of State

The Department of Foreign Affairs was created by act of Congress July 27, 1789, and the name changed to Department of State on Sept. 15.

President	Secretary	Home	Apptd.
Washington	Thomas Jefferson	Va.	1789
"	Edmund Randolph	Va.	1794
"	Timothy Pickering	Pa.	1795
Adams, J.	Timothy Pickering	Pa.	1797
"	John Marshall	Va.	1800
Jefferson	James Madison	Va.	1801
Madison	Robert Smith	Md.	1809
"	James Monroe	Va.	1811
Monroe	John Quincy Adams	Mass.	1817
Adams, J.Q.	Henry Clay	Ky.	1825
Jackson	Martin Van Buren	N.Y.	1829
"	Edward Livingston	La.	1831
"	Louis McLane	Del.	1833
"	John Forsyth	Ga.	1834
Van Buren	John Forsyth	Ga.	1837
Harrison, W.H.	Daniel Webster	Mass.	1841
Tyler	Daniel Webster	Mass.	1841
"	Abel P. Upshur	Va.	1843
"	John C. Calhoun	S.C.	1844
Polk	John C. Calhoun	S.C.	1845
"	James Buchanan	Pa.	1845
Taylor	James Buchanan	Pa.	1849
"	John M. Clayton	Del.	1849
Fillmore	John M. Clayton	Del.	1850
"	Daniel Webster	Mass.	1850
"	Edward Everett	Mass.	1852
Pierce	William L. Marcy	N.Y.	1853
Buchanan	William L. Marcy	N.Y.	1857
"	Lewis Cass	Mich.	1857
"	Jeremiah S. Black	Pa.	1860
Lincoln	Jeremiah S. Black	Pa.	1861
"	William H. Seward	N.Y.	1861
Johnson, A.	William H. Seward	N.Y.	1865
Grant	Elihu B. Washburne	Ill.	1869
"	Hamilton Fish	N.Y.	1869
Hayes	Hamilton Fish	N.Y.	1877
"	William M. Evarts	N.Y.	1877
Garfield	William M. Evarts	N.Y.	1881
"	James G. Blaine	Me.	1881
Arthur	James G. Blaine	Me.	1881
"	F.T. Frelinghuysen	N.J.	1881
Cleveland	F.T. Frelinghuysen	N.J.	1885
"	Thomas F. Bayard	Del.	1885
Harrison, B.	Thomas F. Bayard	Del.	1889
Harrison, B.	James G. Blaine	Me.	1889
"	John W. Foster	Ind.	1892
Cleveland	Walter Q. Gresham	Ind.	1893
"	Richard Olney	Mass.	1895
McKinley	Richard Olney	Mass.	1897
"	John Sherman	Oh.	1897
"	William R. Day	Oh.	1898
"	John Hay	D.C.	1898
Roosevelt, T.	John Hay	D.C.	1901
"	Elihu Root	N.Y.	1905
"	Robert Bacon	N.Y.	1909
Taft	Robert Bacon	N.Y.	1909
"	Philander C. Knox	Pa.	1909
Wilson	Philander C. Knox	Pa.	1913
"	William J. Bryan	Neb.	1913
"	Robert Lansing	N.Y.	1915
"	Bainbridge Colby	N.Y.	1920
Harding	Charles E. Hughes	N.Y.	1921
Coolidge	Charles E. Hughes	N.Y.	1923
"	Frank B. Kellogg	Minn.	1925
Hoover	Frank B. Kellogg	Minn.	1929
"	Henry L. Stimson	N.Y.	1929
Roosevelt, F.D.	Cordell Hull	Tenn.	1933
"	E.R. Stettinius Jr.	Va.	1944
Truman	E.R. Stettinius Jr.	Va.	1945
"	James F. Byrnes	S.C.	1945
"	George C. Marshall	Pa.	1947
"	Dean G. Acheson	Conn.	1949
Eisenhower	John Foster Dulles	N.Y.	1953
"	Christian A. Herter	Mass.	1959
Kennedy	Dean Rusk	N.Y.	1961
Johnson, L.B.	Dean Rusk	N.Y.	1963
Nixon	William P. Rogers	N.Y.	1969
"	Henry A. Kissinger	D.C.	1973
Ford	Henry A. Kissinger	D.C.	1974
Carter	Cyrus R. Vance	N.Y.	1977
"	Edmund S. Muskie	Me.	1980
Reagan	Alexander M. Haig Jr.	Conn.	1981
"	George P. Shultz	Cal.	1982
Bush	James A. Baker 3d.	Tex.	1989
"	Lawrence S. Eagleburger	Mich.	1992
Clinton	Warren M. Christopher	Cal.	1993

Secretaries of the Treasury

The Treasury Department was organized by act of Congress Sept. 2, 1789.

President	Secretary	Home	Apptd.
Washington	Alexander Hamilton	N.Y.	1789
"	Oliver Wolcott	Conn.	1795
Adams, J.	Oliver Wolcott	Conn.	1797
"	Samuel Dexter	Mass.	1801
Jefferson	Samuel Dexter	Mass.	1801
"	Albert Gallatin	Pa.	1801
Madison	Albert Gallatin	Pa.	1809
"	George W. Campbell	Tenn.	1814
"	Alexander J. Dallas	Pa.	1814
"	William H. Crawford	Ga.	1816
Monroe	William H. Crawford	Ga.	1817
Adams, J.Q.	Richard Rush	Pa.	1825
Jackson	Samuel D. Ingham	Pa.	1829
"	Louis McLane	Del.	1831
"	William J. Duane	Pa.	1833
"	Roger B. Taney	Md.	1833
"	Levi Woodbury	N.H.	1834
Van Buren	Levi Woodbury	N.H.	1837
Harrison, W.H.	Thomas Ewing	Oh.	1841
Tyler	Thomas Ewing	Oh.	1841
"	Walter Forward	Pa.	1841
"	John C. Spencer	N.Y.	1843
Tyler	George M. Bibb	Ky.	1844
Polk	Robert J. Walker	Miss.	1845
Taylor	William M. Meredith	Pa.	1849
Fillmore	Thomas Corwin	Oh.	1850
Pierce	James Guthrie	Ky.	1853
Buchanan	Howell Cobb	Ga.	1857
"	Phillip F. Thomas	Md.	1860
"	John A. Dix	N.Y.	1861
Lincoln	Salmon P. Chase	Oh.	1861
"	William P. Fessenden	Me.	1864
"	Hugh McCulloch	Ind.	1865
Johnson, A.	Hugh McCulloch	Ind.	1865
Grant	George S. Boutwell	Mass.	1869
"	William A. Richardson	Mass.	1873
"	Benjamin H. Bristow	Ky.	1874
"	Lot M. Morrill	Me.	1876
Hayes	John Sherman	Oh.	1877
Garfield	William Windom	Minn.	1881
Arthur	Charles J. Folger	N.Y.	1881
"	Walter Q. Gresham	Ind.	1884
"	Hugh McCulloch	Ind.	1884

President	Secretary	Home	Apptd.
Cleveland	Daniel Manning	N.Y.	1885
"	Charles S. Fairchild	N.Y.	1887
Harrison, B.	William Windom	Minn.	1889
"	Charles Foster	Oh.	1891
Cleveland	John G. Carlisle	Ky.	1893
McKinley	Lyman J. Gage	Ill.	1897
Roosevelt, T.	Lyman J. Gage	Ill.	1901
"	Leslie M. Shaw	Ia.	1902
"	George B. Cortelyou	N.Y.	1907
Taft	Franklin MacVeagh	Ill.	1909
Wilson	William G. McAdoo	N.Y.	1913
"	Carter Glass	Va.	1918
"	David F. Houston	Mo.	1920
Harding	Andrew W. Mellon	Pa.	1921
Coolidge	Andrew W. Mellon	Pa.	1923
Hoover	Andrew W. Mellon	Pa.	1929
"	Ogden L. Mills	N.Y.	1932
Roosevelt, F.D.	William H. Woodin	N.Y.	1933
"	Henry Morgenthau, Jr.	N.Y.	1934
Truman	Fred M. Vinson	Ky.	1945
Truman	John W. Snyder	Mo.	1946
Eisenhower	George M. Humphrey	Oh.	1953
"	Robert B. Anderson	Conn.	1957
Kennedy	C. Douglas Dillon	N.J.	1961
Johnson, L.B.	C. Douglas Dillon	N.J.	1963
"	Henry H. Fowler	Va.	1965
"	Joseph W. Barr	Ind.	1968
Nixon	David M. Kennedy	Ill.	1969
"	John B. Connally	Tex.	1971
"	George P. Shultz	Ill.	1972
"	William E. Simon	N.J.	1974
Ford	William E. Simon	N.J.	1974
Carter	W. Michael Blumenthal	Mich.	1977
"	G. William Miller	R.I.	1979
Reagan	Donald T. Regan	N.Y.	1981
"	James A. Baker 3d	Tex.	1985
"	Nicholas F. Brady	N.J.	1988
Bush	Nicholas F. Brady	N.J.	1989
Clinton	Lloyd Bentsen	Tex.	1993

Secretaries of Defense

The Department of Defense, originally designated the National Military Establishment, was created Sept. 18, 1947. It is headed by the secretary of defense, who is a member of the president's cabinet.

The departments of the army, of the navy, and of the air force function within the Department of Defense, and since 1947 their respective secretaries are not members of the president's cabinet.

President	Secretary	Home	Apptd.
Truman	James V. Forrestal	N.Y.	1947
"	Louis A. Johnson	W.Va.	1949
"	George C. Marshall	Pa.	1950
"	Robert A. Lovett	N.Y.	1951
Eisenhower	Charles E. Wilson	Mich.	1953
"	Neil H. McElroy	Oh.	1957
"	Thomas S. Gates Jr.	Pa.	1959
Kennedy	Robert S. McNamara	Mich.	1961
Johnson, L.B.	Robert S. McNamara	Mich.	1963
"	Clark M. Clifford	Md.	1968
Nixon	Melvin R. Laird	Wis.	1969
"	Elliot L. Richardson	Mass.	1973
"	James R. Schlesinger	Va.	1973
Ford	James R. Schlesinger	Va.	1974
"	Donald H. Rumsfeld	Ill.	1975
Carter	Harold Brown	Cal.	1977
Reagan	Caspar W. Weinberger	Cal.	1981
"	Frank C. Carlucci	Pa.	1987
Bush	Richard B. Cheney	Wyo.	1989
Clinton	Les Aspin	Wis.	1993
"	William J. Perry	Cal.	1994

Secretaries of War

The War Department (which included jurisdiction over the navy until 1798) was created by act of Congress Aug. 7, 1789, and Gen. Henry Knox was commissioned secretary of war under that act Sept. 12, 1789.

President	Secretary	Home	Apptd.
Washington	Henry Knox	Mass.	1789
"	Timothy Pickering	Pa.	1795
"	James McHenry	Md.	1796
Adams, J.	James McHenry	Md.	1797
"	Samuel Dexter	Mass.	1800
Jefferson	Henry Dearborn	Mass.	1801
Madison	William Eustis	Mass.	1809
"	John Armstrong	N.Y.	1813
"	James Monroe	Va.	1814
"	William H. Crawford	Ga.	1815
Monroe	John C. Calhoun	S.C.	1817
Adams, J.Q.	James Barbour	Va.	1825
"	Peter B. Porter	N.Y.	1828
Jackson	John H. Eaton	Tenn.	1829
"	Lewis Cass	Mich.	1831
"	Benjamin F. Butler	N.Y.	1837
Van Buren	Joel R. Poinsett	S.C.	1837
Harrison, W.H.	John Bell	Tenn.	1841
Tyler	John Bell	Tenn	1841
"	John C. Spencer	N.Y.	1841
"	James M. Porter	Pa.	1843
"	William Wilkins	Pa.	1844
Polk	William L. Marcy	N.Y.	1845
Taylor	George W. Crawford	Ga.	1849
Fillmore	Charles M. Conrad	La.	1850
Pierce	Jefferson Davis	Miss.	1853
Buchanan	John B. Floyd	Va.	1857
"	Joseph Holt	Ky.	1861
Lincoln	Simon Cameron	Pa.	1861
"	Edwin M. Stanton	Pa.	1862
Johnson, A.	Edwin M. Stanton	Pa.	1865
"	John M. Schofield	Ill.	1868
Grant	John A. Rawlins	Ill.	1869
"	William T. Sherman	Oh.	1869
"	William W. Belknap	Ia.	1869
"	Alphonso Taft	Oh.	1876
"	James D. Cameron	Pa.	1876
Hayes	George W. McCrary	Ia.	1877
"	Alexander Ramsey	Minn.	1879
Garfield	Robert T. Lincoln	Ill.	1881
Arthur	Robert T. Lincoln	Ill.	1881
Cleveland	William C. Endicott	Mass.	1885
Harrison, B.	Redfield Proctor	Vt.	1889
"	Stephen B. Elkins	W.Va.	1891
Cleveland	Daniel S. Lamont	N.Y.	1893
McKinley	Russel A. Alger	Mich.	1897
"	Elihu Root	N.Y.	1899
Roosevelt, T.	Elihu Root	N.Y.	1901
"	William H. Taft	Oh.	1904
"	Luke E. Wright	Tenn.	1908
Taft	Jacob M. Dickinson	Tenn.	1909
"	Henry L. Stimson	N.Y.	1911
Wilson	Lindley M. Garrison	N.J.	1913
"	Newton D. Baker	Oh.	1916
Harding	John W. Weeks	Mass.	1921
Coolidge	John W. Weeks	Mass.	1923
"	Dwight F. Davis	Mo.	1925
Hoover	James W. Good	Ill.	1929
"	Patrick J. Hurley	Okla.	1929
Roosevelt, F.D.	George H. Dern	Ut.	1933
"	Harry H. Woodring	Kan.	1937
"	Henry L. Stimson	N.Y.	1940
Truman	Robert P. Patterson	N.Y.	1945
"	*Kenneth C. Royall	N.C.	1947

* Last member of Cabinet. The War Department became the Department of the Army and became a branch of the Department of Defense, created Sept. 18, 1947.

Secretaries of the Navy

The Navy Department was created by act of Congress Apr. 30, 1798.

President	Secretary	Home	Apptd.
Adams, J.	Benjamin Stoddert	Md.	1798
Jefferson	Benjamin Stoddert	Md.	1801
"	Robert Smith	Md.	1801
Madison	Paul Hamilton	S.C.	1809
"	William Jones	Pa.	1813
"	Benjamin W. Crowninshield	Mass.	1814

President	Secretary	Home	Apptd.
Monroe	Benjamin W. Crowninshield	Mass. .	1817
"	Smith Thompson	N.Y.. . .	1818
"	Samuel L. Southard . .	N.J. . . .	1823
Adams, J.Q.	Samuel L. Southard . .	N.J. . . .	1825
Jackson . . .	John Branch	N.C. . .	1829
"	Levi Woodbury.	N.H. . .	1831
"	Mahlon Dickerson. . . .	N.J. . . .	1834
Van Buren. .	Mahlon Dickerson. . . .	N.J. . . .	1837
"	James K. Paulding . . .	N.Y.. . .	1838
Harrison, W.H.	George E. Badger . . .	N.C. . .	1841
Tyler.	George E. Badger . . .	N.C. . .	1841
"	Abel P. Upshur.	Va. . . .	1841
"	David Henshaw	Mass. .	1843
"	Thomas W. Gilmer . . .	Va. . . .	1844
"	John Y. Mason.	Va. . . .	1844
Polk	George Bancroft.	Mass. .	1845
"	John Y. Mason.	Va. . . .	1846
Taylor	William B. Preston . . .	Va. . . .	1849
Fillmore. . . .	William A. Graham . . .	N.C. . .	1850
"	John P. Kennedy	Md. . . .	1852
Pierce	James C. Dobbin	N.C. . .	1853
Buchanan . .	Isaac Toucey	Conn. .	1857
Lincoln	Gideon Welles	Conn. .	1861
Johnson, A. .	Gideon Welles	Conn. .	1865
Grant	Adolph E. Borie	Pa. . . .	1869
"	George M. Robeson . .	N.J. . . .	1869
Hayes.	Richard W. Thompson	Ind.	187
"	Nathan Goff Jr.	W.Va. . .	188
Garfield. . . .	William H. Hunt	La.	188
Arthur	William E. Chandler . .	N.H. . . .	188
Cleveland . .	William C. Whitney . . .	N.Y. . . .	188
Harrison, B. .	Benjamin F. Tracy . . .	N.Y. . . .	188
Cleveland . .	Hilary A. Herbert	Ala.	189
McKinley. . .	John D. Long.	Mass. . .	189
Roosevelt, T.	John D. Long	Mass. . .	190
"	William H. Moody	Mass. . .	190
"	Paul Morton.	Ill.	190
"	Charles J. Bonaparte .	Md.	190
"	Victor H. Metcalf.	Cal.	190
"	Truman H. Newberry .	Mich. . . .	190
Taft	George von L. Meyer .	Mass. . .	190
Wilson	Josephus Daniels. . . .	N.C. . . .	191
Harding. . . .	Edwin Denby	Mich. . . .	192
Coolidge . . .	Edwin Denby	Mich. . . .	192
"	Curtis D. Wilbur	Cal.	192
Hoover	Charles Francis Adams	Mass. . .	192
Roosevelt, F.D.	Claude A. Swanson . .	Va.	193
"	Charles Edison	N.J.	194
"	Frank Knox	Ill.	194
"	James V. Forrestal . . .	N.Y. . . .	194
Truman. . . .	*James V. Forrestal . .	N.Y. . . .	194

* Last member of Cabinet. The Navy Department became a branch of the Department of Defense, created Sept. 18, 1947.

Attorneys General

The office of attorney general was organized by act of Congress Sept. 24, 1789. The Department of Justice was created June 22, 1870.

President	Attorney General	Home	Apptd.
Washington. .	Edmund Randolph . .	Va.. . . .	1789
"	William Bradford. . . .	Pa.. . . .	1794
"	Charles Lee	Va.. . . .	1795
Adams, J. . . .	Charles Lee	Va.. . . .	1797
Jefferson. . . .	Levi Lincoln	Mass.. .	1801
"	John Breckenridge . .	Ky.. . . .	1805
"	Caesar A. Rodney . .	Del. . . .	1807
Madison	Caesar A. Rodney . .	Del. . . .	1807
"	William Pinkney	Md. . . .	1811
"	Richard Rush.	Pa.. . . .	1814
Monroe	Richard Rush.	Pa.. . . .	1817
"	William Wirt	Va.. . . .	1817
Adams, J.Q. .	William Wirt	Va.. . . .	1825
Jackson	John M. Berrien	Ga. . . .	1829
"	Roger B. Taney	Md. . . .	1831
"	Benjamin F. Butler . .	N.Y. . . .	1833
Van Buren. . .	Benjamin F. Butler . .	N.Y. . . .	1837
"	Felix Grundy	Tenn. . .	1838
"	Henry D. Gilpin.	Pa.. . . .	1840
Harrison, W.H.	John J. Crittenden . .	Ky.. . . .	1841
Tyler.	John J. Crittenden . .	Ky.. . . .	1841
"	Hugh S. Legare	S.C. . . .	1841
"	John Nelson.	Md. . . .	1843
Polk	John Y. Mason.	Va.. . . .	1845
"	Nathan Clifford	Me. . . .	1846
"	Isaac Toucey	Conn.. .	1848
Taylor	Reverdy Johnson . . .	Md. . . .	1849
Fillmore.	John J. Crittenden . .	Ky.. . . .	1850
Pierce	Caleb Cushing	Mass.. .	1853
Buchanan . . .	Jeremiah S. Black . .	Pa.. . . .	1857
"	Edwin M. Stanton . . .	Pa.. . . .	1860
Lincoln	Edward Bates	Mo. . . .	1861
"	James Speed.	Ky.. . . .	1864
Johnson, A. . .	James Speed.	Ky.. . . .	1865
"	Henry Stanbery	Oh. . . .	1866
"	William M. Evarts . . .	N.Y. . . .	1868
Grant	Ebenezer R. Hoar. . .	Mass.. .	1869
"	Amos T. Akerman. . .	Ga. . . .	1870
"	George H. Williams. .	Ore. . . .	1871
"	Edwards Pierrepont .	N.Y. . . .	1875
"	Alphonso Taft.	Oh. . . .	1876
Hayes	Charles Devens	Mass.. .	1877
Garfield.	Wayne MacVeagh . .	Pa.. . . .	1881
Arthur	Benjamin H. Brewster	Pa.. . . .	1882
Cleveland . . .	Augustus Garland. . .	Ark. . . .	1885
Harrison, B. . .	William H. H. Miller . .	Ind. . . .	1889
Cleveland . . .	Richard Olney	Mass.. .	1893
"	Judson Harmon	Oh. . . .	1895
McKinley. . . .	Joseph McKenna . . .	Cal. . . .	1897
"	John W. Griggs	N.J. . . .	1898
"	Philander C. Knox . .	Pa. . . .	1901
Roosevelt, T. .	Philander C. Knox . .	Pa. . . .	1901
"	William H. Moody . . .	Mass.. .	1904
"	Charles J. Bonaparte	Md. . . .	1906
Taft	George W. Wicker-sham.	N.Y. . . .	1909
Wilson	J.C. McReynolds . . .	Tenn. . .	1913
"	Thomas W. Gregory .	Tex. . . .	1914
"	A. Mitchell Palmer . .	Pa. . . .	1919
Harding.	Harry M. Daugherty .	Oh. . . .	1921
Coolidge	Harry M. Daugherty .	Oh. . . .	1923
"	Harlan F. Stone	N.Y. . . .	1924
"	John G. Sargent. . . .	Vt.	1925
Hoover	William D. Mitchell . .	Minn. . .	1929
Roosevelt, F.D.	Homer S. Cummings	Conn. . .	1933
"	Frank Murphy	Mich. . .	1939
"	Robert H. Jackson . .	N.Y. . . .	1940
"	Francis Biddle	Pa. . . .	1941
Truman.	Thomas C. Clark . . .	Tex. . . .	1945
"	J. Howard McGrath .	R.I. . . .	1949
"	J.P. McGranery	Pa. . . .	1952
Eisenhower. .	Herbert Brownell Jr. .	N.Y. . . .	1953
"	William P. Rogers. . .	Md. . . .	1957
Kennedy	Robert F. Kennedy. .	Mass.. .	1961
Johnson, L.B.	Robert F. Kennedy. .	Mass.. .	1963
"	N. de B. Katzenbach	Ill.	1964
"	Ramsey Clark	Tex. . . .	1967
Nixon	John N. Mitchell	N.Y. . . .	1969
"	Richard G. Kleindi-enst	Ariz. . . .	1972
"	Elliot L. Richardson .	Mass.. .	1973
"	William B. Saxbe . . .	Oh. . . .	1974
Ford	William B. Saxbe . . .	Oh. . . .	1974
"	Edward H. Levi	Ill.	1975
Carter.	Griffin B. Bell	Ga. . . .	1977
"	Benjamin R. Civiletti .	Md. . . .	1979
Reagan.	William French Smith	Cal. . . .	1981
"	Edwin Meese 3d . . .	Cal. . . .	1985
"	Richard Thornburgh .	Pa	1988
Bush.	Richard Thornburgh .	Pa. . . .	1989
"	William P. Barr.	N.Y. . . .	1991
Clinton	Janet Reno	Fla. . . .	1993

Secretaries of the Interior

The Department of the Interior was created by act of Congress Mar. 3, 1849.

President	Secretary	Home	Apptd.
Taylor	Thomas Ewing	Oh.	1849
Fillmore	Thomas M. T. McKennan	Pa.	1850
"	Alex H. H. Stuart	Va.	1850
Pierce	Robert McClelland	Mich.	1853
Buchanan	Jacob Thompson	Miss.	1857
Lincoln	Caleb B. Smith	Ind.	1861
"	John P. Usher	Ind.	1863
Johnson, A.	John P. Usher	Ind.	1865
"	James Harlan	Ia.	1865
"	Orville H. Browning	Ill.	1866
Grant	Jacob D. Cox	Oh.	1869
"	Columbus Delano	Oh.	1870
"	Zachariah Chandler	Mich.	1875
Hayes	Carl Schurz	Mo.	1877
Garfield	Samuel J. Kirkwood	Ia.	1881
Arthur	Henry M. Teller	Col.	1882
Cleveland	Lucius Q.C. Lamar	Miss.	1885
"	William F. Vilas	Wis.	1888
Harrison, B.	John W. Noble	Mo.	1889
Cleveland	Hoke Smith	Ga.	1893
"	David R. Francis	Mo.	1896
McKinley	Cornelius N. Bliss	N.Y.	1897
"	Ethan A. Hitchcock	Mo.	1898
Roosevelt, T.	Ethan A. Hitchcock	Mo.	1901
"	James R. Garfield	Oh.	1907
Taft	Richard A. Ballinger	Wash.	1909

President	Secretary	Home	Apptd.
Taft	Walter L. Fisher	Ill.	1911
Wilson	Franklin K. Lane	Cal.	1913
"	John B. Payne	Ill.	1920
Harding	Albert B. Fall	N.M.	1921
"	Hubert Work	Col.	1923
Coolidge	Hubert Work	Col.	1923
"	Roy O. West	Ill.	1929
Hoover	Ray Lyman Wilbur	Cal.	1929
Roosevelt, F.D.	Harold L. Ickes	Ill.	1933
Truman	Harold L. Ickes	Ill.	1945
"	Julius A. Krug	Wis.	1946
"	Oscar L. Chapman	Col.	1949
Eisenhower	Douglas McKay	Ore.	1953
"	Fred A Seaton	Neb.	1956
Kennedy	Stewart L. Udall	Ariz.	1961
Johnson, L.B.	Stewart L. Udall	Ariz.	1963
Nixon	Walter J. Hickel	Alas.	1969
"	Rogers C.B. Morton	Md.	1971
Ford	Rogers C.B. Morton	Md.	1971
"	Stanley K. Hathaway	Wyo.	1975
"	Thomas S. Kleppe	N.D.	1975
Carter	Cecil D. Andrus	Ida.	1977
Reagan	James G. Watt	Col.	1981
"	William P. Clark	Cal.	1983
"	Donald P. Hodel	Ore.	1985
Bush	Manuel Lujan	N.M.	1989
Clinton	Bruce Babbitt	Ariz.	1993

Secretaries of Agriculture

The Department of Agriculture was created by act of Congress May 15, 1862. On Feb. 8, 1889, its commissioner was renamed secretary of agriculture and became a member of the cabinet.

President	Secretary	Home	Apptd.
Cleveland	Norman J. Colman	Mo.	1889
Harrison, B.	Jeremiah M. Rusk	Wis.	1889
Cleveland	J. Sterling Morton	Neb.	1893
McKinley	James Wilson	Ia.	1897
Roosevelt, T.	James Wilson	Ia.	1901
Taft	James Wilson	Ia.	1909
Wilson	David F. Houston	Mo.	1913
"	Edwin T. Meredith	Ia.	1920
Harding	Henry C. Wallace	Ia.	1921
Coolidge	Henry C. Wallace	Ia.	1923
"	Howard M. Gore	W.Va.	1924
"	William M. Jardine	Kan.	1925
Hoover	Arthur M. Hyde	Mo.	1929
Roosevelt, F.D.	Henry A. Wallace	Ia.	1933
"	Claude R. Wickard	Ind.	1940

President	Secretary	Home	Apptd.
Truman	Clinton P. Anderson	N.M.	1945
"	Charles F. Brannan	Col.	1948
Eisenhower	Ezra Taft Benson	Ut.	1953
Kennedy	Orville L. Freeman	Minn.	1961
Johnson, L.B.	Orville L. Freeman	Minn.	1963
Nixon	Clifford M. Hardin	Ind.	1969
"	Earl L. Butz	Ind.	1971
Ford	Earl L. Butz	Ind.	1974
"	John A. Knebel	Va.	1976
Carter	Bob Bergland	Minn.	1977
Reagan	John R. Block	Ill.	1981
"	Richard E. Lyng	Cal.	1986
Bush	Clayton K. Yeutter	Neb.	1989
"	Edward Madigan	Ill.	1991
Clinton	Mike Espy[1]	Miss.	1993

(1) Announced resignation Oct. 3, 1994, effective Dec. 31, 1994.

Secretaries of Commerce and Labor

The Department of Commerce and Labor, created by Congress Feb. 14, 1903, was divided by Congress Mar. 4, 1913, into separate departments of Commerce and Labor. The secretary of each was made a cabinet member.

President	Secretary	Home	Apptd.
Secretaries of Commerce and Labor			
Roosevelt, T.	George B. Cortelyou	N.Y.	1903
"	Victor H. Metcalf	Cal.	1904
"	Oscar S. Straus	N.Y.	1906
Taft	Charles Nagel	Mo.	1909
Secretaries of Labor			
Wilson	William B. Wilson	Pa.	1913
Harding	James J. Davis	Pa.	1921
Coolidge	James J. Davis	Pa.	1923
Hoover	James J. Davis	Pa.	1929
"	William N. Doak	Va.	1930
Roosevelt, F.D.	Frances Perkins	N.Y.	1933
Truman	L.B. Schwellenbach	Wash.	1945
"	Maurice J. Tobin	Mass.	1949
Eisenhower	Martin P. Durkin	Ill.	1953
"	James P. Mitchell	N.J.	1953
Kennedy	Arthur J. Goldberg	Ill.	1961
"	W. Willard Wirtz	Ill.	1962
Johnson, L.B.	W. Willard Wirtz	Ill.	1963

President	Secretary	Home	Apptd.
Nixon	George P. Shultz	Ill	1969
"	James D. Hodgson	Cal.	1970
"	Peter J. Brennan	N.Y.	1973
Ford	Peter J. Brennan	N.Y.	1974
"	John T. Dunlop	Cal.	1975
"	W.J. Usery Jr.	Ga.	1976
Carter	F. Ray Marshall	Tex.	1977
Reagan	Raymond J. Donovan	N.J.	1981
"	William E. Brock	Tenn.	1985
"	Ann D. McLaughlin	D.C.	1987
Bush	Elizabeth Hanford Dole	N.C.	1989
"	Lynn Martin	Ill.	1991
Clinton	Robert B. Reich	Mass.	1993
Secretaries of Commerce			
Wilson	William C. Redfield	N.Y.	1913
"	Joshua W. Alexander	Mo.	1919
Harding	Herbert C. Hoover	Cal.	1921
Coolidge	Herbert C. Hoover	Cal.	1923
"	William F. Whiting	Mass.	1928
Hoover	Robert P. Lamont	Ill.	1929
"	Roy D. Chapin	Mich.	1932

President	Secretary	Home	Apptd.
Roosevelt, F.D.	Daniel C. Roper	S.C.	1933
"	Harry L. Hopkins	N.Y.	1939
"	Jesse Jones	Tex.	1940
"	Henry A. Wallace	Ia.	1945
Truman	Henry A. Wallace	Ia.	1945
"	W. Averell Harriman	N.Y.	1947
"	Charles Sawyer	Oh.	1948
Eisenhower	Sinclair Weeks	Mass.	1953
"	Lewis L. Strauss	N.Y.	1958
"	Frederick H. Mueller	Mich.	1959
Kennedy	Luther H. Hodges	N.C.	1961
Johnson, L.B.	Luther H. Hodges	N.C.	1963
"	John T. Connor	N.J.	1965
"	Alex B. Trowbridge	N.J.	1967
Johnson, L.B.	Cyrus R. Smith	N.Y.	1968
Nixon	Maurice H. Stans	Minn.	1969
"	Peter G. Peterson	Ill.	1972
"	Frederick B. Dent	S.C.	1973
Ford	Frederick B. Dent	S.C.	1974
"	Rogers C.B. Morton	Md.	1975
"	Elliot L. Richardson	Mass.	1975
Carter	Juanita M. Kreps	N.C.	1977
"	Philip M. Klutznick	Ill.	1979
Reagan	Malcolm Baldrige	Conn.	1981
"	C. William Verity Jr.	Oh.	1987
Bush	Robert A. Mosbacher	Tex.	1989
"	Barbara H. Franklin	Pa.	1992
Clinton	Ronald H. Brown	D.C.	1993

Secretaries of Housing and Urban Development

The Department of Housing and Urban Development was created by act of Congress Sept. 9, 1965.

President	Secretary	Home	Apptd.
Johnson, L.B.	Robert C. Weaver	Wash.	1966
"	Robert C. Wood	Mass.	1969
Nixon	George W. Romney	Mich.	1969
"	James T. Lynn	Oh.	1973
Ford	James T. Lynn	Oh.	1974
"	Carla Anderson Hills	Cal.	1975
Carter	Patricia Roberts Harris	D.C.	1977
"	Moon Landrieu	La.	1979
Reagan	Samuel R. Pierce Jr.	N.Y.	1981
Bush	Jack F. Kemp	N.Y.	1989
Clinton	Henry G. Cisneros	Tex.	1993

Secretaries of Transportation

The Department of Transportation was created by act of Congress Oct. 15, 1966.

President	Secretary	Home	Apptd.
Johnson, L.B.	Alan S. Boyd	Fla.	1966
Nixon	John A. Volpe	Mass.	1969
"	Claude S. Brinegar	Cal.	1973
Ford	Claude S. Brinegar	Cal.	1974
"	William T. Coleman Jr.	Pa.	1975
Carter	Brock Adams	Wash.	1977
Carter	Neil E. Goldschmidt	Ore.	1979
Reagan	Andrew L. Lewis Jr.	Pa.	1981
"	Elizabeth Hanford Dole	N.C.	1983
"	James H. Burnley	N.C.	1987
Bush	Samuel K. Skinner	Ill.	1989
"	Andrew H. Card Jr.	Mass.	1992
Clinton	Federico F. Peña	Col.	1993

Secretaries of Energy

The Department of Energy was created by federal law Aug. 4, 1977.

President	Secretary	Home	Apptd.
Carter	James R. Schlesinger	Va.	1977
"	Charles Duncan Jr.	Wyo.	1979
Reagan	James B. Edwards	S.C.	1981
Reagan	Donald P. Hodel	Ore.	1982
"	John S. Herrington	Cal.	1985
Bush	James D. Watkins	Cal.	1989
Clinton	Hazel R. O'Leary	Minn.	1993

Secretaries of Health, Education, and Welfare

The Department of Health, Education, and Welfare, created by Congress Apr. 11, 1953, was divided by Congress Sept. 27, 1979, into separate departments of Education and of Health and Human Services. The secretary of each is a cabinet member.

President	Secretary	Home	Apptd.
Eisenhower	Oveta Culp Hobby	Tex.	1953
"	Marion B. Folsom	N.Y.	1955
"	Arthur S. Flemming	Oh.	1958
Kennedy	Abraham A. Ribicoff	Conn.	1961
"	Anthony J. Celebrezze	Oh.	1962
Johnson, L.B.	Anthony J. Celebrezze	Oh.	1963
"	John W. Gardner	N.Y.	1965
"	Wilbur J. Cohen	Mich.	1968
Nixon	Robert H. Finch	Cal.	1969
"	Elliot L. Richardson	Mass.	1970
"	Caspar W. Weinberger	Cal.	1973
Ford	Caspar W. Weinberger	Cal.	1974
"	Forrest D. Mathews	Ala.	1975
Carter	Joseph A. Califano, Jr.	D.C.	1977
"	Patricia Roberts Harris	D.C.	1979

Secretaries of Health and Human Services

President	Secretary	Home	Apptd.
Carter	Patricia Roberts Harris	D.C.	1979
Reagan	Richard S. Schweiker	Pa.	1981
"	Margaret M. Heckler	Mass.	1983
Reagan	Otis R. Bowen	Ind.	1985
Bush	Louis W. Sullivan	Ga.	1989
Clinton	Donna E. Shalala	Wis.	1993

Secretaries of Education

President	Secretary	Home	Apptd.
Carter	Shirley Hufstedler	Cal.	1979
Reagan	Terrel Bell	Ut.	1981
"	William J. Bennett	N.Y.	1985
"	Lauro F. Cavazos	Tex.	1988
Bush	Lauro F. Cavazos	Tex.	1989
"	Lamar Alexander	Tenn.	1991
Clinton	Richard W. Riley	S.C.	1993

Secretaries of Veterans Affairs

The Department of Veterans Affairs was created Oct. 25, 1988, when Pres. Reagan signed a bill that made the Veterans Administration into a cabinet post as of Mar. 15, 1989.

President	Secretary	Home	Apptd.
Bush	Edward J. Derwinski	Ill.	1989
Clinton	Jesse Brown	Ill.	1993

Central Intelligence Agency

On June 13, 1942, President Roosevelt established the Office of Strategic Services (OSS) and named William J. Donovan as its director. The OSS was disbanded Oct. 1, 1945, and its functions absorbed by the State and War departments. President Truman, Jan. 22, 1946, established the Central Intelligence Agency Group (CIG) to operate under the direction of the National Intelligence Authority (NIA). The National Security Act of 1947 replaced the NIA with the National Security Council and the CIG with the Central Intelligence Agency.

Director	Served	Appointed by President
Adm. Sidney W. Souers	1946	Truman
Gen. Hoyt S. Vandenberg	1946-1947	Truman
Adm. Roscoe H. Hillenkoetter	1947-1950	Truman
Gen. Walter Bedell Smith	1950-1953	Truman
Allen W. Dulles	1953-1961	Eisenhower
John A. McCone	1961-1965	Kennedy
Adm. William F. Raborn Jr.	1965-1966	Johnson
Richard Helms	1966-1973	Johnson
James R. Schlesinger	1973	Nixon
William E. Colby	1973-1976	Nixon
George Bush	1976-1977	Ford
Adm. Stansfield Turner	1977-1981	Carter
William J. Casey	1981-1987	Reagan
William H. Webster	1987-1991	Reagan
Robert M. Gates	1991-1993	Bush
R. James Woolsey	1993-	Clinton

Speakers of the House of Representatives

Party designations: A, American; D, Democratic; DR, Democratic-Republican; F, Federalist; R, Republican; W, Whig (as of Oct. 1994)

Name	Party	State	Tenure
Frederick Muhlenberg	F	Pa.	1789-1791
Jonathan Trumbull	F	Conn.	1791-1793
Frederick Muhlenberg	F	Pa.	1793-1795
Jonathan Dayton	F	N.J.	1795-1799
Theodore Sedgwick	F	Mass.	1799-1801
Nathaniel Macon	DR	N.C.	1801-1807
Joseph B. Varnum	DR	Mass.	1807-1811
Henry Clay	DR	Ky.	1811-1814
Langdon Cheves	DR	S.C.	1814-1815
Henry Clay	DR	Ky.	1815-1820
John W. Taylor	DR	N.Y.	1820-1821
Philip P. Barbour	DR	Va.	1821-1823
Henry Clay	DR	Ky.	1823-1825
John W. Taylor	D	N.Y.	1825-1827
Andrew Stevenson	D	Va.	1827-1834
John Bell	D	Tenn.	1834-1835
James K. Polk	D	Tenn.	1835-1839
Robert M. T. Hunter	D	Va.	1839-1841
John White	W	Ky.	1841-1843
John W. Jones	D	Va.	1843-1845
John W. Davis	D	Ind.	1845-1847
Robert C. Winthrop	W	Mass.	1847-1849
Howell Cobb	D	Ga.	1849-1851
Linn Boyd	D	Ky.	1851-1855
Nathaniel P. Banks	A	Mass.	1856-1857
James L. Orr	D	S.C.	1857-1859
William Pennington	R	N.J.	1860-1861
Galusha A. Grow	R	Pa.	1861-1863
Schuyler Colfax	R	Ind.	1863-1869
Theodore M. Pomeroy	R	N.Y.	1869
James G. Blaine	R	Me.	1869-1875
Michael C. Kerr	D	Ind.	1875-1876
Samuel J. Randall	D	Pa.	1876-1881
Joseph W. Keifer	R	Oh.	1881-1883
John G. Carlisle	D	Ky.	1883-1889
Thomas B. Reed	R	Me.	1889-1891
Charles F. Crisp	D	Ga.	1891-1895
Thomas B. Reed	R	Me.	1895-1899
David B. Henderson	R	Ia.	1899-1903
Joseph G. Cannon	R	Ill.	1903-1911
Champ Clark	D	Mo.	1911-1919
Frederick H. Gillett	R	Mass.	1919-1925
Nicholas Longworth	R	Oh.	1925-1931
John N. Garner	D	Tex.	1931-1933
Henry T. Rainey	D	Ill.	1933-1935
Joseph W. Byrns	D	Tenn.	1935-1936
William B. Bankhead	D	Ala.	1936-1940
Sam Rayburn	D	Tex.	1940-1947
Joseph W. Martin Jr.	R	Mass.	1947-1949
Sam Rayburn	D	Tex.	1949-1953
Joseph W. Martin Jr.	R	Mass.	1953-1955
Sam Rayburn	D	Tex.	1955-1961
John W. McCormack	D	Mass.	1962-1971
Carl Albert	D	Okla.	1971-1977
Thomas P. O'Neill Jr.	D	Mass.	1977-1987
James Wright	D	Tex.	1987-1989
Thomas S. Foley	D	Wash.	1989-

Floor Leaders in the U.S. Senate

(as of Oct. 1994)

Majority Leaders

Name	Party	State	Tenure
Charles Curtis	R	Kan.	1925-1929
James E. Watson	R	Ind.	1929-1933
Joseph T. Robinson	D	Ark.	1933-1937
Alben W. Barkley	D	Ky.	1937-1947
Wallace H. White	R	Me.	1947-1949
Scott W. Lucas	D	Ill.	1949-1951
Ernest W. McFarland	D	Ariz.	1951-1953
Robert A. Taft	R	Oh.	1953
William F. Knowland	R	Cal.	1953-1955
Lyndon B. Johnson	D	Tex.	1955-1961
Mike Mansfield	D	Mont.	1961-1977
Robert C. Byrd	D	W.Va.	1977-1981
Howard H. Baker Jr.	R	Tenn.	1981-1985
Robert J. Dole	R	Kan.	1985-1987
Robert C. Byrd	D	W.Va.	1987-1989
George J. Mitchell[1]	D	Me.	1989-1995

(1) Retirement announced as of the end of the 103d Congress.

Minority Leaders

Name	Party	State	Tenure
Oscar W. Underwood	D	Ala.	1920-1923
Joseph T. Robinson	D	Ark.	1923-1933
Charles L. McNary	R	Ore.	1933-1944
Wallace H. White	R	Me.	1944-1947
Alben W. Barkley	D	Ky.	1947-1949
Kenneth S. Wherry	R	Neb.	1949-1951
Henry Styles Bridges	R	N.H.	1952-1953
Lyndon B. Johnson	D	Tex.	1953-1955
William F. Knowland	R	Cal.	1955-1959
Everett M. Dirksen	R	Ill.	1959-1969
Hugh D. Scott	R	Penn.	1969-1977
Howard H. Baker Jr.	R	Tenn.	1977-1981
Robert C. Byrd	D	W.Va.	1981-1987
Robert J. Dole	R	Kan.	1987-

Librarians of Congress

Librarian	Served	Appointed by President
John J. Beckley	1802-1807	Jefferson
Patrick Magruder	1807-1815	Jefferson
George Watterston	1815-1829	Madison
John Silva Meehan	1829-1861	Jackson
John G. Stephenson	1861-1864	Lincoln
Ainsworth Rand Spofford	1864-1897	Lincoln
John Russell Young	1897-1899	McKinley
Herbert Putnam	1899-1939	McKinley
Archibald MacLeish	1939-1944	F. Roosevelt
Luther H. Evans	1945-1953	Truman
L. Quincy Mumford	1954-1974	Eisenhower
Daniel J. Boorstin	1975-1987	Ford
James H. Billington	1987-	Reagan

Notable Quotes in 1994

"Never, never . . . shall it be that this beautiful land will again experience the oppression of one by another and suffer the indignity of being the skunk of the world."
Nelson Mandela, the first South African president selected in an election in which people of all races were allowed to vote

"It's as if someone upset a beehive around here. Every time we stick our heads up, we get stung."
A *White House aide* lamenting a series of Clinton administration setbacks

"Did you read . . . that there's two new suspects in the case—Ben & Jerry?"
Judge *Lance Ito,* presiding over the O. J. Simpson trial, joking about the cup of ice cream reportedly found at the murder scene

"World War I couldn't stop the World Series. Neither could World War II. Even an earthquake couldn't stop it. . . . It's almost too much to comprehend."
Al Martin, a Pittsburgh Pirates player representative, on the premature end of the baseball season because of a players' strike

"Going back or staying here, either way we die."
Wilson Ndabateze, a Rwandan refugee living in a cholera-infested refugee camp in Zaire, speaking on the grim choice facing displaced victims of his country's civil war

"I begged them to send troops. . . . Unfortunately, let us say with great humility, I failed. It is a scandal. I am the first one to say it."
UN Secretary-Gen. *Boutros Boutros-Ghali,* admitting the failure of UN efforts to halt the Rwanda slaughter

"It looks like someone sat on it."
Hockey Hall of Fame spokesperson *Phil Pritchard,* on the condition of the Stanley Cup after NY Rangers' celebrations

"Be Cool in School! Good Grades Has Its Rewards."
A sign at *Wendy's* fast-food restaurants

"It's all true. We are space aliens. I'm amazed that it's taken you so long to find out."
Sen. *Phil Gramm* of Texas, on a supermarket-tabloid story headlined 12 SENATORS ARE FROM OUTER SPACE!

"I hate to say this, but I believe my children will be safer in Bujumbura [capital of Burundi] than in Washington, DC."
Former Sen. *Bob Krueger,* on his appointment as ambassador to Burundi, next door to Rwanda

"We cannot solve every such outburst of civil strife or militant nationalism simply by sending in our forces."
Pres. *Bill Clinton,* on the conflict in Rwanda

"I feel like the Susan Lucci of the administration."
Interior Secretary *Bruce Babbitt,* after nearly being nominated to the Supreme Court on two occasions, comparing himself to the perennial soap-opera Emmy also-ran

"He's caning Madonna."
Dan Rather, on why David Letterman could not appear to accept his Broadcaster of the Year award from the International Radio and Television Society

"Can I answer every question that anybody might ever ask me about something that happened 10, 15, 17 years ago on the spur of the moment and have total recall of that while trying to be president? No sir, I cannot."
Pres. *Bill Clinton,* responding to an editor who said his Whitewater explanation sounded evasive

"You lived to tell the tale, did you?"
Prince Charles to a well-wisher who told the prince that she had met his estranged wife, Diana

"I don't have to ride in that bus, do I?"
Michael Jordan, on seeing a run-down White Sox minor league team vehicle (he later bought the team a new bus)

"Goodness knows what you all would be saying if we had made money on it."
First Lady Hillary Rodham Clinton, responding to the intense media interest in the president's and her Whitewater investment

"I was a bit surprised. Maybe my endorsement of him caused him to withdraw."
Senate Republican leader *Bob Dole,* on Sen. George Mitchell's surprise decision to remove himself from consideration as a Supreme Court candidate

"It was obvious that the size of your chest was in direct proportion to the size of your salary."
Indiana exotic dancer *Cynthia Hess,* explaining why she sought—successfully—to have her size 56FF breast implants declared a tax-deductible business expense

"If she had turned to Mickey Mouse and said, 'Hey you're a jerk,' that would have been one thing."
Nancy Kerrigan's agent, *Jerry Solomon,* defending Kerrigan after she complained, "This is so corny. This is so dumb. I hate it," while riding in a Disney World parade

"Well, for one thing, I find that I no longer win every golf game I play."
George Bush, on life after the presidency

"Times are tough. I don't know if they're that tough, though."
Marsha Anderson, spokeswoman for the Ft. Worth, TX, Public Library, on the destruction caused when hundreds of people stormed the library looking for money a local disc jockey had announced he'd hidden in the stacks

"I am not sure what speech is in the TelePrompTer tonight, but I hope we can talk about the State of the Union."
Pres. *Bill Clinton,* in a joking reference to his previous address before Congress, for which the wrong speech had been mistakenly loaded into the machine

"I sometimes think the media has dreamed our history up."
Director *Oliver Stone,* who has been criticized for distorting history in his movies, in a commencement address

"There haven't been this many executives sweating over one woman since Heidi Fleiss, baby."
Whoopi Goldberg, on her role as master of ceremonies at the Academy Awards

"We all thought he was a boxers man."
Laetitia Thompson, a 17-year-old from Potomac, MD, who asked Pres. Clinton during an MTV forum on youth and violence whether he preferred boxer shorts or briefs

"I'll take 'Things I don't really want to know' for $500, Alex."
David Letterman, on Pres. Clinton's admission that he usually wears briefs

"Chairman Arafat, our partner in a very difficult journey: We did it!"
Israeli Foreign Minister *Shimon Peres* after he and Palestine Liberation Organization Chairman Yasir Arafat signed an accord for Palestinian self-rule

"You mean after Bill and Hillary put all those new bureaucrats and taxes on us, we're still all going to die?"
Pres. *Bill Clinton* to Hillary Rodham Clinton, in a spoof, at the Washington press corps' Gridiron dinner, of the "Harry and Louise" TV ads opposing his health-care reform plan

"This is the best drink after the longest drought in my life."
Director *Steven Spielberg,* on winning the Academy Award for best director for *Schindler's List* (which also won for best picture)

Historical Anniversaries

By Jacqueline Laks Gorman

1895 — 100 Years Ago

Severe economic depression continued in the U.S. A financial crisis appeared to be developing early in the year, when U.S. Treasury gold reserves fell to $41 million, but was averted when a syndicate led by J. P. Morgan underwrote a $62 million bond issue. This led to a public outcry over the spectacle of a private banker saving the country from bankruptcy and helped discredit the administration of Pres. Grover Cleveland.

Cuban nationalist rebels began fighting Spain for independence in **February,** proclaiming an independent republic **July 15.** The revolt was suppressed, but guerrilla warfare continued until the Spanish-American War of 1898.

The Treaty of Shimonoseki, ending the Sino-Japanese War, was signed **Apr. 17.** China was forced to recognize the independence of Korea and to cede Formosa (Taiwan) and other territory to Japan.

The Supreme Court, **May 20,** declared unconstitutional the federal income tax provision of the 1894 Wilson-Gorman Tariff Act.

Black leader Booker T. Washington, in a speech **Sept. 18,** proposed the "Atlanta Compromise," calling upon blacks to stop fighting segregation and second-class citizenship and to concentrate instead on learning useful skills; he asked whites to help these efforts.

Sir Leander Starr Jameson, supported by the British, launched an unsuccessful raid **Dec. 29** into the Transvaal to overthrow its Boer government.

Wilhelm Roentgen discovered X rays. Guglielmo Marconi invented the wireless telegraph system (radio signals). The diesel engine was invented by Rudolf Diesel. King C. Gillette created the disposable safety razor.

In Paris, Auguste and Louis Lumière put on the first public film show, demonstrating their new cinématographe, the first commercially successful motion picture projector.

Literature: *Studies in Hysteria* by Viennese doctors Sigmund Freud and Josef Breuer; *The Time Machine* by H. G. Wells; *The Red Badge of Courage* by Stephen Crane; *Jude the Obscure* by Thomas Hardy; *Quo Vadis* by Henryk Sienkiewicz; *Poems* by W. B. Yeats.

Journalism: *The Denver Post,* which employed sensationalism while crusading for the public good, began publication; *Collier's Weekly* magazine debuted, challenging *The Saturday Evening Post.*

Art: Winslow Homer's "Northeaster"; Kathe Kollwitz's "Revolt of the Weavers"; Auguste Rodin's "The Burghers of Calais."

Theater: *The Importance of Being Earnest* by Oscar Wilde, in London. It was Wilde's last major achievement; on **May 25** he was convicted of homosexuality and indecent acts and sentenced to 2 years at hard labor.

Ballet: *Swan Lake,* with music by Russian composer Petr Ilich Tchaikovsky and choreography by Marius Petipa, in St. Petersburg.

Popular Songs: "The Band Played On" by John F. Palmer and Charles B. Ward; "America the Beautiful" by Katharine Lee Bates, to the music of Samuel A. Ward.

Sports: The American Bowling Congress was founded. The first 18-hole golf course in the U.S. opened, in Chicago. The first U.S. automobile race took place, on Thanksgiving between Chicago and Milwaukee; only 6 of the 80 entries were able to start, and they averaged of 5.25 mph.

Miscellaneous: The first U.S. pizzeria opened, in New York City.

1945 — 50 Years Ago

World War II came to an end, leaving some 45 million dead (including almost 300,000 U.S. servicemen and women who died in battle) and changing the political order of the world.

In Europe, Allied offensives into Germany that began in 1944 continued. On **Mar. 7,** U.S. troops, moving eastward into Germany, established a bridgehead at Remagen and crossed the Rhine. Russian troops drove westward, and German cities began to fall almost daily thereafter. The 2 Allied forces made contact at Torgau on the Elbe, **Apr. 25.** As the Russians shelled Berlin, Adolf Hitler committed suicide **Apr. 30.** Germany surrendered **May 7; May 8** was proclaimed V-E Day.

In the Pacific, U.S. forces took 2 crucial islands from the Japanese in major battles—at Iwo Jima, **Feb. 19-Mar. 16** (where the U.S. flag was raised on Mt. Suribachi, **Feb. 23**), and at Okinawa, **Apr. 1-June 21.** A heavy bombing offensive was launched from these bases, devastating Japanese industry and the navy. The dropping of atomic bombs (tested successfully on **July 16** at Alamogordo, NM) on Hiroshima, **Aug. 6,** and Nagasaki, **Aug. 9,** forced Japan to surrender, **Aug. 14. Sept. 2,** the day the Japanese signed the official surrender, was proclaimed V-J Day.

Franklin D. Roosevelt was inaugurated as U.S. president (for an unprecedented 4th term), and Harry S. Truman as vice president, **Jan. 20.**

Pres. Roosevelt, British Prime Min. Winston Churchill, and Russian leader Joseph Stalin, attending the Yalta Conference in the Crimea, **Feb. 4-11,** outlined postwar plans and agreed to Russian entry into the war against Japan in exchange for specific territory in Eastern Europe.

The League of Arab States was founded, **Mar. 22.**

Pres. Roosevelt died of a cerebral hemorrhage at Warm Springs, Ga., **Apr. 12.** Vice Pres. Truman was sworn in as 33d U.S. president.

The UN Charter was drawn up by delegates from 50 nations at the United Nations Conference on International Organization in San Francisco, **Apr. 25-June 26.** The charter was ratified **July 28** by the U.S. Senate, 89-2, and went into effect **Oct. 24.** Congress named Eleanor Roosevelt a U.S. delegate to the UN, **Dec. 19.**

Benito Mussolini was captured and killed by Italian partisans, **Apr. 28.**

Tensions surfaced between Russia and the West when Pres. Truman, Stalin, and Clement Attlee (who replaced Churchill as British prime minister **July 26** when Labour won an upset election victory) attended the Potsdam Conference outside Berlin, **July 17-Aug. 2.** They agreed to try Nazi leaders as war criminals, made plans to exact reparations from Germany, and confirmed the division of Germany into occupation zones administered by the Americans, British, Russians, and French.

An Army B-25 bomber struck the Empire State Building in New York City, **July 28,** killing 13.

Russian troops occupied Korea north of the 38th parallel, **Aug. 10;** U.S. forces arrived **Sept. 8** to occupy the southern part of the former Japanese territory.

The Democratic Republic of Vietnam was founded, **Sept. 2,** with Ho Chi Minh as president.

The trial of some 20 Nazi leaders accused of war crimes opened in Nuremberg, Germany, **Nov. 20.**

In a message to Congress, **Dec. 3,** Pres. Truman proposed a plan to curb strikes, as U.S. labor unrest increased following the end of the war.

The Bretton Woods Agreement was ratified by representatives of 28 nations, **Dec. 27,** establishing the International Monetary Fund and the International Bank for Reconstruction and Development (the World Bank) to promote loans and investment for needy countries.

The antibiotics bacitracin and streptomycin were developed, and penicillin was introduced on a commercial basis. Vitamin A was synthesized. A New Orleans doctor noted a link between lung cancer and cigarettes. Grand Rapids, MI, became the first U.S. city to fluoridate its water supply.

Meet the Press debuted on a New York radio station in **Oct.;** it began airing on television in 1947. *Ebony* magazine began publication.

Literature: *Animal Farm* by George Orwell; *Cannery Row* by John Steinbeck; *Forever Amber* by Kathleen Winsor; *Brideshead Revisited* by Evelyn Waugh; *The Age of Reason* by Jean-Paul Sartre; *Christ Stopped at Eboli* by Carlo Levi; *Black Boy* by Richard Wright.

Art: "If This Be Not I" by Philip Guston; "For Internal Use Only" by Stuart Davis; "Red Pyramid" by Alexander Calder; "Family Group" by Henry Moore.

Theater: *The Glass Menagerie* by Tennessee Williams; *The Madwoman of Chaillot* by Jean Giraudoux, in Paris.

Musicals: *Carousel,* with John Raitt, Jan Clayton; music by Richard Rodgers, lyrics by Oscar Hammerstein II; songs including "If I Loved You," "June Is Bustin' Out All Over," and "You'll Never Walk Alone."

Movies: Billy Wilder's *The Lost Weekend,* with Ray Milland, Jane Wyman; John Ford's *They Were Expendable,* with Robert Montgomery, Donna Reed; Elia Kazan's *A Tree Grows in Brooklyn,* with Dorothy McGuire, Joan Blondell; Alfred Hitchcock's *Spellbound,* with Ingrid Bergman, Gregory Peck; Vincente Minnelli's *The Clock,* with Judy Garland, Robert Walker; *Mildred Pierce,* with Joan Crawford.

Popular Songs: "It's Been a Long, Long Time"; "Till the End of Time"; "For Sentimental Reasons"; "Let It Snow! Let It Snow! Let It Snow!"

Sports: Eddie Arcaro won the Kentucky Derby for the 3d of 5 times. Jackie Robinson was signed to a contract with the Brooklyn Dodgers' minor league Montreal team, the first black to sign with a team in organized baseball.

Miscellaneous: Chemist Earl S. Tupper introduced the first commercial product (a water tumbler) made of a plastic called polyethylene. He soon began large-scale marketing of such products, calling them Tupperware.

1970 — 25 Years Ago

For a second year, the Paris peace talks failed to end the Vietnam War. Mounting public pressure in the U.S.—including a huge antiwar rally in Washington, DC, **May 9** and the closing of hundreds of colleges and universities by protesting students—forced Pres. Richard Nixon to reduce the number of U.S. troops in Vietnam to 400,000. Prior to that, Pres. Nixon announced an escalation of the war **Apr. 30,** sending U.S. troops into Cambodia (until **June 29**) to destroy North Vietnamese sanctuaries there. Bombing of North Vietnam also resumed.

The "Chicago 7" were found innocent of conspiring to incite riots during the 1968 Democratic National Convention but 5 were found guilty **Feb. 20** of crossing state lines with the intent to incite riots.

Millions of Americans marched and rallied in support of environmental protection, **Apr. 22,** the first Earth Day.

Ohio National Guardsmen, called in to control demonstrators at Kent State Univ., fired into the crowd and killed 4 students, **May 4.** Mississippi state police fired on a dormitory at Jackson State Coll., **May 15,** killing 2.

The Senate, **May 12,** approved the nomination of Harry A. Blackmun to the Supreme Court. The Senate had rejected Pres. Nixon's 2 previous nominees, Clement Haynsworth and G. Harrold Carswell.

Two women generals, the first in U.S. history, were named by Pres. Nixon, **May 15.**

Pres. Nixon signed into law, **June 22,** a measure lowering the voting age from 21 to 18.

The Postal Reorganization Act was signed **Aug. 12,** converting the Post Office Department into an independent government agency, the U.S. Postal Service. Postal workers had gone on strike for the first time ever on **Mar. 18.**

Congress passed the Rail Passenger Service Act **Oct. 14,** creating the National Rail Passenger Corporation (Amtrak).

The Environmental Protection Agency was created by Congress, **Dec. 2,** to set and enforce U.S. pollution standards. Pres. Nixon signed the Occupational Safety and Health Act, **Dec. 29,** and the Clean Air Act, **Dec. 31.**

Floppy disks to store computer data, invented by IBM researchers, were introduced. The first complete synthesis of a gene was announced by Univ. of Wisconsin scientists.

The first jumbo jet, a Boeing 747, began regular passenger service.

Paul McCartney left the Beatles. Rock music stars Jimi Hendrix and Janis Joplin both died of drug-related causes.

Literature: *Play It as It Lays* by Joan Didion; *Deliverance* by James Dickey; *Love Story* by Erich Segal; *Jonathan Livingston Seagull* by Richard Bach; *The Making of a Counter-Culture* by Theodore Roszak; *The Greening of America* by Charles Reich; *Up the Organization* by Robert Townsend; *Future Shock* by Alvin Toffler; *Hard Times* by Studs Terkel; *Sexual Politics* by Kate Millett; *Everything You Always Wanted to Know About Sex (But Were Afraid to Ask)* by David Reuben.

Art: "Andy Warhol" by Alice Neel; "Patchwork Quilt" by Romare Bearden.

Theater: *Child's Play* by Robert Marasco; *Sleuth* by Anthony Shaffer, in London; *The Effect of Gamma Rays on Man-in-the-Moon Marigolds* by Paul Zindel.

Musicals: *Applause,* with Lauren Bacall; music by Charles Strouse, lyrics by Lee Adams, book by Betty Comden and Adolph Green; *Company,* music and lyrics by Stephen Sondheim.

Movies: Bob Rafelson's *Five Easy Pieces,* with Jack Nicholson, Karen Black, Susan Anspach; Arthur Penn's *Little Big Man,* with Dustin Hoffman, Faye Dunaway; Robert Altman's *M*A*S*H,* with Elliott Gould, Donald Sutherland, Sally Kellerman; *Patton,* with George C. Scott; *Woodstock,* a documentary about the giant 1969 concert.

Popular Songs: "Bridge Over Troubled Water" by Simon and Garfunkel; "Your Song" by Elton John; "Close to You" by The Carpenters.

Sports: The Seattle Pilots baseball franchise moved to Milwaukee and became the Brewers. Jim Bouton's tell-all book about baseball, *Ball Four,* was a best-seller. Pitcher Denny McLain was suspended, first for gambling ties and later for gun possession. Margaret Smith Court won the Grand Slam of tennis—the Australian, French, Wimbledon, and U.S. singles titles. The first New York Marathon was run in **Sept.**

Miscellaneous: Garry Trudeau's comic strip *Doonesbury* had its debut in 30 newspapers.

Jacqueline Laks Gorman is a writer and editor specializing in current affairs, history, and business topics.

ECONOMICS

U.S. Budget Receipts and Outlays—1990-93

Source: Financial Management Service, U.S. Dept. of the Treasury
(Fiscal year ends Sept. 30)
(millions of dollars; some figures may not add due to independent rounding)
(outlays incl. selected departments and agencies)

Classification	Fiscal 1990	Fiscal 1991	Fiscal 1992	Fiscal 1993
Net Receipts				
Individual income taxes	$466,884	$467,827	$476,465	$509,680
Corporation income taxes	93,507	98,086	100,270	117,520
Social insurance taxes and contributions:				
Federal old-age and survivors insurance	255,031	265,503	273,137	281,735
Federal disability insurance	26,625	28,382	29,289	30,199
Federal hospital insurance	68,556	72,842	79,109	81,224
Railroad retirement fund	3,679	3,799	3,957	3,781
Total employment taxes and contributions	**353,891**	**370,526**	**385,491**	**396,939**
Other insurance and retirement:				
Unemployment	21,635	20,922	23,410	26,556
Federal employees retirement	4,405	4,459	4,683	4,709
Non-federal employees	117	108	105	96
Total social insurance taxes and contributions	**380,047**	**396,016**	**413,689**	**428,300**
Excise taxes	35,345	42,402	45,570	48,057
Estate and gift taxes	11,500	11,138	11,143	12,577
Customs duties	16,607	15,949	17,359	18,802
Deposits of earnings-Federal Reserve Banks	24,319	19,158	22,920	14,908
All other miscellaneous receipts	2,997	3,688	4,275	3,331
Net Budget Receipts	**$1,031,308**	**$1,054,265**	**$1,091,692**	**$1,153,175**
Net Outlays				
Legislative Branch	$2,244	$2,296	$2,677	$2,406
The Judiciary	1,641	1,989	2,295	2,579
Executive Office of the President:				
The White House Office	30	32	36	40
Office of Management and Budget	44	53	54	55
Total Executive Office	**157**	**193**	**190**	**194**
Funds appropriated to the President:				
International security assistance	8,352	9,531	7,203	7,322
Multilateral assistance	1,695	1,520	1,717	1,547
Agency for International Development	1,773	1,835	2,142	2,145
International Development Assistance	3,528	3,444	4,029	3,856
Total funds appropriated to the President	**10,086**	**11,724**	**11,108**	**11,527**
Agriculture Department:				
Food stamp program	15,923	19,649	22,800	24,602
Farmers Home Admin.	6,713	6,629	4,455	2,042
Forest service	2,934	3,001	3,293	3,292
Total Agriculture Department	**46,012**	**54,119**	**56,436**	**63,143**
Commerce Department:				
Bureau of the Census	1,575	451	302	346
Total Commerce Department	**3,734**	**2,585**	**2,567**	**2,798**
Defense Department (military):				
Military personnel	75,622	83,439	81,171	75,904
Operation and maintenance	88,340	101,769	92,042	94,105
Procurement	80,972	82,028	74,881	69,936
Research, development, test, evaluation	37,458	34,589	34,632	36,958
Military construction	5,080	3,497	4,262	4,831
Total Defense Department (military)	**289,755**	**261,925**	**286,632**	**278,576**
Defense Department (civil)	24,975	26,543	28,265	29,262
Education Department	23,109	25,339	26,047	30,414
Energy Department	12,023	12,459	15,439	16,801
Health and Human Services Department:				
Food and Drug Administration	553	648	752	733
National Institutes of Health	7,492	7,677	8,376	9,543
Public Health Service	14,007	15,348	17,447	18,865
Health Care Financing Adm.	184,893	205,776	239,366	266,452
Total Health and Human Services Dept.	**193,679**	**217,969**	**257,961**	**282,774**
Social Security (Off Budget)	244,998	266,395	281,418	298,349
Housing and Urban Development Department	20,167	22,751	24,470	25,185
Interior Department	5,795	6,096	6,555	6,728
Justice Department:				
Federal Bureau of Investigation	1,473	1,695	1,832	1,975
Total Justice Department	**6,507**	**8,244**	**9,826**	**10,197**
Labor Department:				
Unemployment Trust Fund	20,250	28,434	41,294	39,869
Total Labor Department	**25,316**	**34,040**	**47,193**	**44,738**
State Department	3,979	4,252	5,007	5,384
Transportation Department:				
Federal Aviation Adm.	6,391	7,241	8,155	8,800
Total Transportation Department	**28,637**	**30,503**	**32,560**	**34,457**
Treasury Department:				
Internal Revenue Service	12,053	13,689	17,904	18,472
Interest on the public debt	264,853	285,472	292,330	292,502
Total Treasury Department	**255,264**	**276,352**	**293,428**	**298,711**
Veterans Affairs Department	28,998	31,214	33,737	35,487
Environmental Protection Agency	5,108	5,770	5,932	5,925
General Services Administration	–123	487	469	743
National Aeronautics and Space Administration	12,429	13,878	13,961	14,305

(continued)

Classification	Fiscal 1990	Fiscal 1991	Fiscal 1992	Fiscal 1993
Office of Personnel Management	$31,949	$34,808	$35,596	$36,794
Small Business Administration	692	613	394	937
Other independent agencies:				
Action	169	192	194	208
Board for International Broadcasting	208	228	210	246
Corporation for Public Broadcasting	229	299	327	319
District of Columbia	578	671	691	698
Equal Employment Opportunity Commission	181	192	209	218
Export-Import Bank of the United States	357	–88	–119	–747
Federal Communications Commission	79	66	78	94
Federal Deposit Insurance Corporation	6,429	7,363	3,666	–8,412
Federal Trade Commission	57	60	71	64
Interstate Commerce Comm.	43	45	40	41
Legal Services Corporation	291	344	329	389
National Archives & Records Adm.	157	172	226	269
National Foundation on the Arts and Humanities	307	325	331	343
National Labor Relations Board	141	143	155	171
National Science Foundation	1,838	2,081	2,249	2,452
Nuclear Regulatory Commission	221	–1	50	–19
Railroad Retirement Board	4,477	4,358	4,843	4,782
Securities and Exchange Commission	129	143	117	99
Smithsonian Institution	302	340	378	395
Tennessee Valley Authority	–312	740	1,469	1,629
U.S. Information Agency	888	1,001	1,050	1,088
Total other independent agencies	73,666	81,217	18,876	–10,631
Undistributed offsetting receipts	–99,025	–110,005	–117,118	–119,662
Net Budget Outlays	**1,251,776**	**1,323,757**	**1,381,895**	**1,408,122**
Less net receipts	1,031,308	1,054,265	1,091,692	1,153,175
Deficit	**$–220,469**	**$–269,492**	**$–290,204**	**$–254,948**

Summary of Receipts, Outlays, and Surpluses or Deficits, 1936-89

Source: Financial Management Service, U.S. Dept. of the Treasury

(millions of dollars)

Year[1]	Receipts	Total Outlays	Surplus or Deficit (–)	Year[1]	Receipts	Total Outlays	Surplus or Deficit (–)
1936	$3,923	$8,228	$–4,304	1964	$112,613	$118,528	$–5,915
1937	5,387	7,580	–2,193	1965	116,817	118,228	–1,411
1938	6,751	6,840	–89	1966	130,835	134,532	–3,698
1939	6,295	9,141	–2,846	1967	148,822	157,464	–8,643
1940	6,548	9,468	–2,920	1968	152,973	178,134	–25,161
1941	8,712	13,653	–4,941	1969	186,882	183,640	3,242
1942	14,634	35,137	–20,503	1970	192,807	195,649	–2,842
1943	24,001	78,555	–54,554	1971	187,139	210,172	–23,033
1944	43,747	91,304	–47,557	1972	207,309	230,681	–23,373
1945	45,159	92,712	–47,553	1973	230,799	245,707	–14,908
1946	39,296	55,232	–15,936	1974	263,224	269,359	–6,135
1947	38,514	34,496	4,018	1975	279,090	332,332	–53,242
1948	41,560	29,764	11,796	1976	298,060	371,779	–73,719
1949	39,415	38,835	580	Transition quarter[2]	81,232	95,973	–14,741
1950	39,443	42,562	–3,119	1977	355,559	409,203	–53,644
1951	51,616	45,514	6,102	1978	399,561	458,729	–59,168
1952	66,167	67,686	–1,519	1979	463,302	503,464	–40,162
1953	69,608	76,101	–6,493	1980	517,112	590,920	–73,808
1954	69,701	70,855	–1,154	1981	599,272	678,209	–78,936
1955	65,451	68,444	–2,993	1982	617,766	745,706	–127,940
1956	74,587	70,640	3,947	1983	600,562	808,327	–207,764
1957	79,990	76,578	3,412	1984	666,457	851,781	–185,324
1958	79,636	82,405	–2,769	1985	734,057	946,316	–212,260
1959	79,249	92,098	–12,849	1986	769,091	990,231	–221,140
1960	92,492	92,191	301	1987	854,143	1,003,804	– 149,661
1961	94,388	97,723	–3,335	1988	908,166	1,063,318	–155,151
1962	99,676	106,821	–7,146	1989	990,701	1,144,020	–153,319
1963	$106,560	$111,316	$–4,756				

(1) Fiscal years: 1936 to 1976, July 1-June 30; starting with 1977, Oct. 1-Sept. 30. (2) Transition quarter covers July 1, 1976-Sept. 30, 1976.

Net Receipts and Outlays, 1789-1935

Source: U.S. Dept. of the Treasury; annual statements for year ending June 30

(thousands of dollars)

Yearly average	Receipts	Outlays	Yearly average	Receipts	Outlays	Yearly average	Receipts	Outlays
1789-1800[1]	$5,717	$5,776	1866-1870	$447,301	$377,642	1901-1905	$559,481	$535,559
1801-1810[2]	13,056	9,086	1871-1875	336,830	287,460	1906-1910	628,507	639,178
1811-1820[2]	21,032	23,943	1876-1880	288,124	255,598	1911-1915	710,227	720,252
1821-1830[2]	21,928	16,162	1881-1885	366,961	257,691	1916-1920	3,483,652	8,065,333
1831-1840[2]	30,461	24,495	1886-1890	375,448	279,134	1921-1925	4,306,673	3,578,989
1841-1850[2]	28,545	34,097	1891-1895	352,891	363,599	1926-1930	4,069,138	3,182,807
1851-1860	60,237	60,163	1896-1900	434,877	457,451	1931-1935	2,770,973	5,214,874
1861-1865	160,907	683,785						

(1) Average for period March 4, 1789, to Dec. 31, 1800. (2) Years ended Dec. 31, 1801 to 1842; average for 1841-1850 is for the period Jan. 1, 1841, to June 30, 1850.

Public Debt of the U.S.

Source: Bureau of Public Debt, U.S. Dept. of the Treasury

Fiscal year	Debt (billions)	Per. cap. (dollars)	Interest paid (billions)	% of federal outlays
1870	$2.4	$61.06	—	—
1880	2.0	41.60	—	—
1890	1.1	17.80	—	—
1900	1.2	16.60	—	—
1910	1.1	12.41	—	—
1920	24.2	228	—	—
1930	16.1	131	—	—
1940	43.0	325	$1.0	10.5
1945	258.7	1,849	3.8	4.1
1950	256.1	1,688	5.7	13.4
1955	272.8	1,651	6.4	9.4
1960	284.1	1,572	9.2	10.0
1965	313.8	1,613	11.3	9.6
1970	370.1	1,814	19.3	9.9
1975	533.2	2,475	32.7	9.8
1976	620.4	2,852	37.1	10.0
1977	698.8	3,170	41.9	10.2
1978	$771.5	$3,463	$48.7	10.6
1979	826.5	3,669	59.8	11.9
1980	907.7	3,985	74.9	12.7
1981	997.9	4,338	95.6	14.1
1982	1,142.0	4,913	117.4	15.7
1983	1,377.2	5,870	128.8	15.9
1984	1,572.3	6,640	153.8	18.1
1985	1,823.1	7,598	178.9	18.9
1986	2,125.3	8,774	190.2	19.2
1987	2,350.3	9,615	195.4	19.5
1988	2,602.3	10,534	214.1	20.1
1989	2,857.4	11,545	240.9	21.0
1990	3,233.3	13,000	264.8	21.1
1991	3,665.3	14,436	285.4	21.5
1992	4,064.6	15,846	292.3	21.1
1993	4,351.2	16,689	292.5	20.8

Note: Through 1976 the fiscal year ended June 30. From 1977 on, the fiscal year ends Sept. 30.

Consumer Price Index

The Consumer Price Index (CPI) is a measure of the average change in prices over time of basic consumer goods and services. From Jan. 1978, the Bureau of Labor Statistics began publishing CPI's for 2 population groups: (1) a CPI for all urban consumers (CPI-U), which covers about 80% of the total population; and (2) a CPI for urban wage earners and clerical workers (CPI-W), which covers about 32% of the total population. The CPI-U includes, in addition to wage earners and clerical workers, groups such as professional, managerial, and technical workers, the self-employed, short-term workers, the unemployed, retirees, and others not in the labor force.

The CPI is based on prices of food, clothing, shelter, fuels, transportation fares, charges for doctors' and dentists' services, drugs, and prices of the other goods and services bought for day-to-day living. The index measures price changes from a designated reference period, 1982-84, which equals 100.0.

Use of this reference period began in Jan. 1988.

Consumer Price Indexes, 1994

Source: Bureau of Labor Statistics, U.S. Dept. of Labor

	CPI-U				CPI-W			
	Unadjusted indexes	Unadjusted percent change to Aug. 1994 from		Seasonally adjusted percent change from	Unadjusted indexes	Unadjusted percent change to Aug. 1994 from		Seasonally adjusted percent change from
(1982-84=100)	Aug. 1994	Aug. 1993	July 1994	July to Aug.	Aug. 1994	Aug. 1993	July 1994	July to Aug.
Food, beverages	145.3	2.7	0.3	0.3	144.9	2.6	0.3	0.4
Housing	145.9	2.5	0.3	0.3	143.0	2.5	0.4	0.4
Apparel, upkeep	131.1	–0.6	0.2	–1.0	130.2	–0.2	0.3	–0.9
Transportation	135.9	4.4	1.0	1.0	135.2	4.5	1.0	1.0
Medical care	212.2	4.6	0.3	0.4	211.5	4.5	0.3	0.4
Entertainment	150.2	3.0	0.0	0.0	148.3	2.9	–0.1	0.0
Other goods, services	199.4	3.1	0.7	0.2	197.5	2.5	0.6	0.4
Services	164.2	3.3	0.5	0.4	161.6	3.3	0.4	0.4
Special indexes								
All items less food	149.8	2.9	0.5	0.3	146.8	2.9	0.5	0.4
Commodities less food	128.4	2.1	0.5	0.2	128.4	2.3	0.5	0.4
Nondurables	137.4	2.2	0.6	0.6	137.3	2.3	0.7	0.7
Energy	108.5	3.1	1.6	1.4	108.2	3.4	1.8	1.6
All items less energy	154.6	2.9	0.4	0.3	151.9	2.8	0.3	0.3

Consumer Price Indexes[1] Annual Percent Change

Source: Bureau of Labor Statistics, U.S. Dept. of Labor

	1982[2]	1983	1984	1985	1986	1987	1988	1989	1990	1991	1992	1993
All items	6.2	3.2	4.3	3.6	1.9	3.6	4.1	4.8	5.4	4.2	3.0	3.0
Food	4.1	2.1	3.8	2.3	3.2	4.1	4.1	5.8	5.8	2.9	1.2	2.2
Shelter	7.1	2.3	4.9	5.6	5.5	4.7	4.8	4.5	5.4	4.5	3.3	3.0
Rent, residential	7.6	5.8	5.2	6.2	5.8	4.1	3.8	3.9	5.6	6.1	2.5	2.3
Fuel & other utilities	9.8	5.6	4.6	1.6	–2.3	–1.1	–1.4	3.3	3.5	3.3	2.2	3.0
Apparel and upkeep	2.6	2.5	1.9	2.8	0.9	4.4	4.3	2.8	4.6	3.7	2.5	1.4
Private transportation	3.5	2.3	4.3	2.5	–4.7	–3.0	3.3	4.9	5.2	2.6	2.2	2.3
New cars	3.9	2.6	2.9	3.2	4.2	3.6	2.0	2.0	1.8	3.8	2.5	2.4
Gasoline	–5.3	–3.3	–1.6	0.8	–21.9	–4.0	0.9	9.5	14.1	–1.8	–0.2	–1.3
Public transportation	10.9	4.8	6.2	4.5	5.9	3.5	1.8	5.0	10.1	4.4	1.7	10.3
Medical care	11.6	8.8	6.2	6.3	7.5	6.6	6.5	7.7	9.0	8.7	7.4	5.9
Entertainment	6.5	4.3	3.7	3.9	3.4	3.3	4.3	5.2	4.7	4.5	2.8	2.5
Commodities	4.1	2.9	3.4	2.1	–0.9	3.2	3.5	4.7	5.2	4.2	2.0	1.9

(1) The Consumer Price Index (CPI-U) measures the average change in prices of goods and services purchased by all urban consumers. (2) Change from 1981.

Consumer Price Indexes for Selected Items and Groups

Source: Bureau of Labor Statistics, U.S. Dept. of Labor
(all urban consumers = CPI-U)
(1982-84 = 100. Annual averages of monthly figures)

	1970	1975	1980	1985	1990	1991	1992	1993
All Items	**38.8**	**53.8**	**82.4**	**107.6**	**130.7**	**136.2**	**140.3**	**144.5**
Food and beverages	**40.1**	**60.2**	**86.7**	**105.6**	**132.1**	**136.8**	**138.7**	**141.6**
Food	39.2	59.8	86.8	105.6	132.4	136.3	137.9	140.9
Food at home	39.9	61.8	88.4	104.3	132.3	135.8	136.8	140.1
Cereals, bakery prods.	37.1	62.9	83.9	107.9	140.0	145.8	151.5	156.6
Meats, poultry, fish, eggs	44.6	67.0	92.0	100.1	130.0	132.6	130.9	135.5
Dairy prods.	44.7	62.6	90.9	103.2	126.5	125.1	128.5	129.4
Fruits, vegetables	37.8	56.9	82.1	106.4	149.0	155.8	155.4	159.0
Sugar, sweets	30.5	65.3	90.5	105.8	124.7	129.3	133.1	133.4
Fats, oils	39.2	73.5	89.3	106.9	126.3	131.7	129.8	130.0
Nonalcoholic beverages	27.1	41.3	91.4	104.3	113.5	114.1	114.3	114.6
Other prepared foods	39.6	58.9	83.6	106.4	131.2	137.1	140.1	143.7
Food away from home	37.5	54.5	83.4	108.3	133.4	137.9	140.7	143.2
Alcoholic beverages	52.1	65.9	86.4	106.4	129.3	142.8	147.3	149.6
Housing	**36.4**	**50.7**	**81.1**	**107.7**	**128.5**	**133.6**	**137.5**	**141.2**
Shelter	35.5	48.8	81.0	109.8	140.0	146.3	151.2	155.7
Rent	46.5	58.0	80.9	111.8	146.7	155.6	160.9	165.0
Maintenance, repairs	35.8	54.1	82.4	106.5	122.2	126.3	128.6	130.6
Fuel, other utilities	29.1	45.4	75.4	106.5	111.6	115.3	117.8	121.3
Energy services	31.8	50.0	75.8	106.9	117.4	112.6	114.8	118.5
Household furnishings & operation	46.8	63.4	86.3	103.8	113.3	116.0	118.0	119.3
House furnishings	55.5	69.8	88.5	101.7	106.7	107.5	109.0	109.5
Apparel & upkeep	**59.2**	**72.5**	**90.9**	**105.0**	**124.1**	**128.7**	**131.9**	**133.7**
Apparel commodities	63.3	76.7	92.9	104.0	122.0	126.4	129.4	131.0
Men's & boys'	62.2	75.5	89.4	105.0	120.4	124.2	126.5	127.5
Women's & girls'	71.8	85.5	96.0	104.9	122.6	127.6	130.4	132.6
Footwear	56.8	69.6	91.8	102.3	117.4	120.9	125.0	125.9
Transportation	**37.5**	**50.1**	**83.1**	**106.4**	**120.5**	**123.8**	**126.5**	**130.4**
Private	37.5	50.6	84.2	106.2	118.8	121.9	124.6	127.5
New cars	53.0	62.9	88.4	106.1	121.4	126.0	128.4	131.5
Used cars	31.2	43.8	62.3	113.7	117.6	118.1	123.2	133.9
Gasoline	27.9	45.1	97.5	98.6	101.0	99.2	99.0	97.7
Public	35.2	43.5	69.0	110.5	142.6	148.9	151.4	167.0
Medical care	**34.0**	**47.5**	**74.9**	**113.5**	**162.8**	**177.0**	**190.1**	**201.4**
Entertainment	**47.5**	**62.0**	**83.6**	**107.9**	**132.4**	**138.4**	**142.3**	**145.8**
Other goods & services	**40.9**	**53.9**	**75.2**	**114.5**	**159.0**	**171.6**	**183.3**	**192.9**
Tobacco products	43.1	54.7	72.0	116.7	181.5	202.7	219.8	228.4
Personal care	43.5	57.9	81.9	106.3	130.4	134.9	138.3	141.5
Toilet goods	42.7	58.0	79.6	107.6	128.2	132.8	136.5	139.0
Personal care services	44.2	57.7	83.7	108.9	132.8	137.0	140.0	144.0
Personal, educational expenses	35.5	48.7	70.9	119.1	170.2	183.7	197.4	210.7

Consumer Price Index by Region and Selected Cities

Source: Bureau of Labor Statistics, U.S. Dept. of Labor

	CPI-U Indexes			Percent change	CPI-W Indexes			Percent change
Area (1982-84 = 100)	**June 1994**	**July 1994**	**Aug. 1994**	**Aug. 1993-Aug. 1994**	**June 1994**	**July 1994**	**Aug. 1994**	**Aug. 1993-Aug. 1994**
U.S. city average	**148.0**	**148.4**	**149.0**	**2.9**	**145.4**	**145.8**	**146.5**	**2.9**
Northeast urban	**154.8**	**155.2**	**155.9**	**2.8**	**152.3**	**152.7**	**153.4**	**2.7**
More than 1,200,000	155.4	155.7	156.6	2.7	151.9	152.2	153.1	2.7
500,000 to 1,200,000	153.5	154.3	154.8	3.0	151.4	152.3	152.8	3.0
50,000 to 500,000	153.2	152.9	153.8	2.7	154.6	154.4	155.2	2.6
North Central urban	**144.0**	**144.3**	**145.2**	**3.4**	**140.9**	**141.3**	**142.2**	**3.3**
More than 1,200,000	145.1	145.4	146.3	3.2	141.4	141.6	142.6	3.2
360,000 to 1,200,000	143.0	143.6	144.4	3.8	139.5	140.1	141.0	4.0
50,000 to 360,000	144.7	145.0	145.9	3.4	142.2	142.6	143.6	3.5
Less than 50,000	139.8	140.2	140.8	4.1	138.4	138.9	139.5	3.9
South urban	**144.7**	**145.0**	**145.5**	**2.8**	**143.2**	**143.6**	**144.1**	**2.8**
More than 1,200,000	145.3	145.3	145.7	2.6	143.4	143.6	144.1	2.6
450,000 to 1,200,000	146.6	147.1	147.9	3.4	143.2	143.7	144.5	3.4
50,000 to 450,000	143.5	143.8	144.3	2.6	143.3	143.7	144.2	2.6
Less than 50,000	142.5	142.7	142.9	2.5	142.7	142.9	143.2	2.6
West urban	**148.9**	**149.5**	**150.1**	**2.7**	**146.1**	**146.7**	**147.2**	**2.5**
More than 1,250,000	150.4	150.9	151.3	2.4	146.0	146.5	146.9	2.2
50,000 to 330,000	148.6	150.0	151.1	4.0	146.4	147.7	148.6	3.8
Selected areas								
Chicago, IL–Gary-Lake County, IL–IN–WI	148.1	148.3	149.8	2.5	143.6	143.7	145.1	2.5
L.A.–Anaheim, Riverside, CA	151.3	151.7	152.0	1.4	146.1	146.5	146.8	1.3
New York, NY–Northern NJ, Long Island, NY–NJ–CT	157.8	158.2	159.1	2.4	154.2	154.4	155.3	2.4
Philadelphia, Wilmington, Trenton, PA–NJ–DE–MD	154.6	155.3	155.7	3.4	154.2	154.9	155.3	3.3
San Francisco–Oakland, San Jose, CA	148.1	148.9	149.4	2.2	145.7	146.6	147.1	2.2
Baltimore, MD	—	148.2	—	—	—	147.3	—	—

Area (1982-84 = 100)	CPI-U Indexes June 1994	July 1994	Aug. 1994	Percent change Aug. 1993-Aug. 1994	CPI-W Indexes June 1994	July 1994	Aug. 1994	Percent change Aug. 1993-Aug. 1994
Boston, Lawrence, Salem, MA–NH	—	153.9	—	—	—	152.9	—	—
Cleveland, Akron, Lorain, OH	—	143.7	—	—	—	136.3	—	—
Miami, Ft. Lauderdale, FL	—	143.4	—	—	—	141.4	—	—
St. Louis, E. St. Louis, MO–IL	—	141.9	—	—	—	141.4	—	—
Washington, DC–MD–VA	—	151.8	—	—	—	149.4	—	—
Dallas–Fort Worth, TX	141.4	—	142.2	3.0	140.6	—	141.6	2.6
Detroit, Ann Arbor, MI	144.8	—	145.3	3.9	140.2	—	141.0	3.9
Houston, Galveston, Brazoria, TX	137.4	—	139.2	4.7	137.0	—	138.8	4.6
Pittsburgh-Beaver Valley, PA	144.0	—	145.7	3.8	137.8	—	139.4	3.9

Percent Change in Consumer Prices in Selected Countries

Source: International Monetary Fund

Country	1975-1980, avg.	1980-1985, avg.	1988-1989, avg.	1989-1990, avg.	1990-1991, avg.	1991-1992, avg.	1992-1993, avg.
Canada	8.7	7.4	5.0	4.8	5.6	1.5	1.8
France	10.5	9.6	3.5	3.4	3.1	2.4	2.1
Germany	4.1	3.9	2.8	2.7	3.5	4.0	4.1
Italy	16.3	13.7	6.3	6.5	6.4	5.6	4.2
Japan	6.5	2.7	2.3	3.1	3.3	1.7	1.3
Spain	18.6	12.2	6.8	6.7	5.9	5.8	4.6
Sweden	10.5	9.0	6.4	10.5	9.3	2.3	4.6
Switzerland	2.3	4.3	3.2	5.4	5.8	4.0	3.3
United Kingdom	14.4	7.2	7.8	9.5	5.9	3.7	1.6
United States	8.9	5.5	4.8	5.4	4.2	3.0	3.0

Index of Leading Economic Indicators

Source: Bureau of Economic Analysis, U.S. Dept. of Commerce

The index of leading economic indicators is used to project the U.S. economy's performance 6 months or a year ahead. The index is made up of 11 measurements of economic activity that tend to change direction long before the overall economy does.

Components

Average work week of production workers in manufacturing
Average weekly claims for state unemployment insurance
New orders for consumer goods and materials, adjusted for inflation
Vendor performance (companies receiving slower deliveries from suppliers)
Contracts and orders for plant and equipment, adjusted for inflation
New building permits issued
Change in manufacturers' unfilled orders, durable goods
Change in sensitive materials prices
Index of stock prices
Money supply: M-2, adjusted for inflation
Index of consumer expectations

Gross Domestic Product, Gross National Product, Net National Product, National Income, and Personal Income

Source: Bureau of Economic Analysis, U.S. Dept. of Commerce

(billions of dollars)

	1960	1970	1980	1990	1992	1993
Gross domestic product	—	—	—	$5,546.1	$6,020.2	$6,343.3
Gross national product	$515.3	$1,015.5	$2,732.0	5,567.8	6,025.8	6,347.8
Less: Capital consumption allowances	46.4	88.8	303.8	602.7	658.5	669.1
Equals: Net national product	468.9	926.6	2,428.1	4,965.1	5,367.3	5,678.7
Less: Indirect business tax and nontax liability	45.3	94.0	213.3	444.0	504.4	525.3
Business transfer payments	2.0	4.1	12.1	26.8	28.1	28.7
Statistical discrepancy	–2.8	–1.1	4.9	7.8	8.8	2.3
Plus: Subsidies less current surplus of government enterprises	.4	2.9	5.7	4.5	3.5	9.0
Equals: National income	424.9	832.6	2,203.5	4,491.0	4,829.5	5,131 .4
Less: Corporate profits with inventory valuation and capital consumption adjustment	49.5	74.7	177.2	380.6	405.1	485.8
Net interest	11.3	41.2	200.9	463.7	420.0	399.5
Contributions for social insurance	21.9	62.2	216.5	503.1	556.4	585.6
Wage accruals less disbursement	.0	.0	.0	.1	–20.0	20.0
Plus: Government transfer payments to persons	27.5	81.8	312.6	666.3	837.9	892.6
Personal interest income	24.9	69.3	271.9	698.2	665.2	637.9
Personal dividend income	12.9	22.2	52.9	144.4	161.0	181.3
Business transfer payments	2.0	4.1	12.1	21.3	22.3	22.8
Equals: Personal income	409.4	831.8	2,258.5	4,673.8	5,154.3	5,375.1

Gross Domestic Product

Source: Bureau of Economic Analysis, U.S. Dept. of Commerce

(billions of dollars)

	1992	1993	First Quarter 1994[1]
Gross domestic product	**6,020.2**	**6,343.3**	**6,574.7**
Personal consumption expenditures	**4,136.9**	**4,378.2**	**4,535.0**
Durable goods	492.7	538.0	576.2
Nondurable goods	1,295.5	1,339.2	1,368.9
Services	2,348.7	2,501.0	2,589.9
Gross private domestic investment	**788.3**	**882.0**	**966.6**
Fixed investment	785.2	866.7	942.5
Nonresidential	561.4	616.1	665.4
Structures	171.1	173.4	172.7
Producers' durable equipment	390.3	442.7	492.7
Residential	223.8	250.6	277.1
Change in business inventories	3.0	15.4	24.1
Nonfarm	–2.7	20.1	22.3
Farm	5.7	–4.7	1.8
Net exports of goods and services	**–30.3**	**–65.3**	**–86.7**
Exports	638.1	659.1	674.2
Imports	668.4	724.3	760.9
Government purchases	**1,125.3**	**1,148.4**	**1,159.8**
Federal	449.0	443.6	437.8
National defense	314.2	302.7	291.7
Nondefense	134.8	140.9	146.1
State and local	676.3	704.7	722.0

(1) Seasonally adjusted at annual rates.

Chapter 11

Chapter 11 refers to the provisions in the Federal Bankruptcy Act for court-supervised reorganization of debtor companies. A company files for Chapter 11 protection when it can no longer pay its creditors or when it expects future liabilities it cannot hope to pay, like product liability damage awards. In 1991, the U.S. Supreme Court ruled that the provision of federal bankruptcy law that permits corporations to reorganize while continuing to operate was also available for use by individuals. The Bankruptcy Reform Act of 1994 further amended Chapter 11.

Process

1. Judge issues automatic stay.

- Creditors cannot file or continue suits for repayment.
- Debts are frozen and creditors generally must stop collection actions. This is called the "automatic stay."
- Debtor's day-to-day operations continue.
- Spending, borrowing, and asset sales that are outside of the debtor's normal course of business must be approved by the court.
- Secured creditors can ask the court for hardship exemption from the automatic stay to undertake or continue debt collection under some circumstances.

2. Unsecured creditors form a committee.

- The U.S. trustee appoints the committee, which ordinarily consists of the 7 largest unsecured creditors who are willing to serve on the panel.
- The U.S. trustee can appoint additional committees to represent other creditors and shareholders.
- The committee chooses representatives to deal with the debtor company.
- The committee and U.S. trustee oversee the debtor's business operations.
- Creditors and the U.S. trustee can ask the court to appoint an examiner to investigate possible fraud or mismanagement.
- Creditors and the U.S. trustee can ask the court to order the appointment of a case trustee to run the debtor company.
- If the court orders the appointment, the U.S. trustee selects the case trustee unless a party asks that creditors be allowed to elect the case trustee.

3. The committee, other creditors, and the debtor company negotiate a reorganization plan.

- Parties negotiate a plan for the reorganization of the debtor's business and repayment of frozen debts. This step can take months or years.
- Only the debtor can file a reorganization plan with the court for the first 120 days of the bankruptcy case. The court can extend the so-called "exclusivity" period and often does so.
- If the debtor does not file a plan during the exclusivity period, if the debtor's plan is not approved by the court, or if a trustee is appointed, any party can file a plan.
- The proponent of the plan prepares a disclosure statement, which must be approved by the court at a separate hearing.

4. Creditors and shareholders vote on the plan.

- Only creditors and shareholders whose claims and interests are impaired or affected by the plan vote on it.
- A class of creditors accepts the plan if the plan is approved by creditors who hold more than half of the claims in the class by number and at least two-thirds of the claims by amount.
- A class of shareholders accepts the plan if the plan is approved by shareholders who hold at least two-thirds of the equity interest in the class by amount.

5. Judge considers the plan.

- The bankruptcy judge approves the plan if it complies with the Bankruptcy Code and all impaired classes approve.
- If at least one of the impaired classes approves the plan and it meets certain statutory tests, the judge can confirm the plan in a so-called "cramdown" even if all impaired classes do not approve.

6. Reorganized company emerges.

- Generally, the debtor's debts are discharged.
- The debtor and creditors must comply with the confirmed plan.
- The automatic stay ends.
- The reorganized debtor operates like a normal company.
- Only 17% of the debtors who file Chapter 11 cases get their plans confirmed.

Expedited Procedure for Small Businesses

- The Bankruptcy Reform Act of 1994 included an expedited confirmation process to be used in Chapter 11 cases filed by small businesses.
- The debtor can elect to use the new process if it has less than $2 million in debts and its primary business is not owning and operating real estate.
- The court can order that a creditors' committee not be appointed.
- Unless the court orders otherwise, the debtor's exclusivity period for filing a plan is shortened to 100 days and all plans must be filed within 160 days.
- The court may conditionally approve the disclosure statement. This saves time by combining the court hearing on the disclosure statement with the hearing on confirmation of the plan.

State Finances

Revenue, Expenditures, Debt, and Taxes

Source: Census Bureau, U.S. Dept. of Commerce

(fiscal year 1992)

State	Revenue (millions)	Expenditures (millions)	Debt (millions)	Per cap.[1] debt	Per cap.[1] taxes	Per cap.[1] expenditures
Alabama	$10,536	$9,651	$4,129	$998	$1,019	$2,333
Alaska	6,327	5,255	4,942	8,418	2,730	8,952
Arizona	9,551	9,096	2,849	743	1,259	2,373
Arkansas	5,864	5,478	1,942	809	1,145	2,283
California	100,154	97,079	37,824	1,225	1,494	3,145
Colorado	9,079	7,492	2,977	857	1,018	2,159
Connecticut	11,784	11,627	11,957	3,644	1,846	3,543
Delaware	2,848	2,504	3,542	5,140	1,944	3,634
Florida	28,311	27,089	12,295	911	1,068	2,008
Georgia	14,761	14,054	4,471	662	1,076	2,081
Hawaii	5,299	5,301	4,687	4,040	2,335	4,570
Idaho	2,902	2,604	1,292	1,210	1,303	2,440
Illinois	27,865	26,832	18,742	1,611	1,157	2,306
Indiana	13,490	12,341	5,172	913	1,143	2,179
Iowa	7,520	7,227	1,884	669	1,280	2,569
Kansas	5,794	5,484	486	192	1,110	2,173
Kentucky	10,640	10,154	6,619	1,762	1,353	2,704
Louisiana	11,842	11,750	9,994	2,331	991	2,740
Maine	3,755	3,722	2,637	2,135	1,347	3,013
Maryland	13,730	13,004	8,335	1,698	1,324	2,649
Massachusetts	20,456	20,368	24,008	4,002	1,651	3,395
Michigan	26,298	25,509	10,357	1,097	1,195	2,703
Minnesota	15,090	13,526	4,143	924	1,662	3,019
Mississippi	6,177	5,762	1,626	621	954	2,204
Missouri	11,619	10,446	6,301	1,213	988	2,011
Montana	2,661	2,460	1,868	2,266	1,153	2,984
Nebraska	3,751	3,624	1,754	1,092	1,176	2,256
Nevada	3,948	3,826	1,934	1,457	1,369	2,883
New Hampshire	2,727	2,871	4,313	3,882	770	2,584
New Jersey	28,922	29,316	19,786	2,540	1,643	3,763
New Mexico	5,582	4,972	1,605	1,015	1,415	3,144
New York	74,931	73,153	55,868	3,083	1,661	4,037
North Carolina	17,664	16,046	3,819	558	1,316	2,344
North Dakota	2,072	2,001	1,027	1,615	1,186	3,145
Ohio	35,590	30,425	12,193	1,106	1,099	2,761
Oklahoma	8,379	8,183	3,657	1,138	1,206	2,547
Oregon	10,025	7,979	6,295	2,114	1,113	2,680
Pennsylvania	36,699	33,622	12,962	1,079	1,354	2,799
Rhode Island	3,609	3,968	5,151	5,125	1,270	3,948
South Carolina	9,897	9,428	4,685	1,300	1,092	2,616
South Dakota	1,756	1,565	1,889	2,657	794	2,200
Tennessee	11,126	10,406	2,806	558	900	2,071
Texas	36,763	33,894	8,001	453	964	1,919
Utah	4,917	4,481	2,153	1,187	1,096	2,471
Vermont	1,898	1,841	1,543	2,706	1,339	3,230
Virginia	15,292	13,921	7,403	1,160	1,101	2,182
Washington	17,366	17,316	7,192	1,400	1,648	3,371
West Virginia	5,452	5,262	2,594	1,431	1,297	2,903
Wisconsin	17,131	13,596	7,299	1,457	1,380	2,715
Wyoming	2,007	1,925	895	1,920	1,386	4,131
United States	**$741,857**	**$699,432**	**$371,901**	**$1,461**	**$1,288**	**$2,748**

(1) Per capita amounts are based on population figures of the resident U.S. population (excluding the District of Columbia) as of July 1, 1992.

State and Local Government Receipts and Expenditures

Source: Bureau of Economic Analysis, U.S. Dept. of Commerce

(billions of dollars)

	1992	1993	First Quarter 1994[1]
Receipts	**842.9**	**891.0**	**919.1**
Personal tax and nontax receipts	159.1	166.1	172.9
Income taxes	118.1	123.3	128.7
Nontaxes	21.8	22.7	23.5
Other	19.1	20.1	20.7
Corporate profits tax accruals	24.2	30.3	32.3
Indirect business tax and nontax accruals	423.1	440.7	454.2
Sales taxes	202.1	212.4	220.7
Property taxes	177.5	184.0	188.0
Other	43.5	44.3	45.6
Contributions for social insurance	64.5	67.8	69.7
Federal grants-in-aid	172.2	186.1	190.0
Expenditures	**818.1**	**864.7**	**893.9**
Purchases	676.3	704.7	722.0
Compensation of employees	461.7	483.0	497.1
Other	214.6	221.7	224.9
Transfer payments to persons	229.0	250.4	264.3
Net interest paid	–53.1	–53.4	–54.1
Interest paid	64.8	65.1	65.3
Less: Interest received by government	117.9	118.4	119.4
Less: Dividends received by government	10.1	10.4	10.7
Subsidies less current surplus of government enterprises	–24.0	–26.7	–27.7
Subsidies	0.4	0.4	0.4
Less: Current surplus of government enterprises	24.4	27.1	28.1
Less: Wage accruals less disbursements	0.0	0.0	0.0
Surplus or deficit (–), national income and product accounts	**24.8**	**26.3**	**25.2**

(1) Seasonally adjusted at annual rates.

State and Local Government Expenditures by Type and Function

Source: Bureau of Economic Analysis, U.S. Dept. Of Commerce

(millions of dollars)

	1992			1993		
	Expendi ures	Purchases	Transfer payments and net interest paid less dividends	Expenditures	Purchases	Transfer payments and net interest paid less dividends
Total	**818,115**	**676,331**	**165,831**	**864,696**	**704,749**	**186,689**
Central executive, legislative, and judicial activities	**50,522**	**49,831**	**691**	**52,755**	**52,033**	**722**
Administrative, legislative, and judicial activities	27,672	27,672	...	28,996	28,996	...
Tax collection and financial management	22,850	22,159	691	23,759	23,037	722
Civilian safety	**80,708**	**80,639**	**69**	**84,492**	**84,418**	**74**
Police	35,927	35,927	...	37,529	37,529	...
Fire	14,814	14,814	...	15,538	15,538	...
Correction	29,967	29,898	69	31,425	31,351	74
Education	**307,996**	**301,707**	**6,289**	**321,073**	**314,282**	**6,791**
Elementary and secondary	236,026	236,026	...	247,414	247,414	...
Higher	54,315	54,315	...	55,070	55,070	...
Libraries	4,120	4,120	...	4,276	4,276	...
Other	13,535	7,246	6,289	14,313	7,522	6,791
Health and hospitals	**27,937**	**27,629**	**308**	**25,621**	**25,296**	**325**
Health	20,617	20,617	...	21,505	21,505	...
Hospitals	7,320	7,012	308	4,116	3,791	325
Income support, social security, and welfare	**187,009**	**34,894**	**152,115**	**206,257**	**37,342**	**168,915**
Government employees retirement and disability	–11,495	3,407	–14,902	–8,621	3,971	–12,592
Workers' Compensation and temporary disability insurance	9,839	1,593	8,246	10,339	1,792	8,547
Medical care	122,520	...	122,520	135,817	...	135,817
Welfare and social services	66,145	29,894	36,251	68,722	31,579	37,143
Veterans benefits and services	**182**	**168**	**14**	**190**	**174**	**16**
Housing and community services	**14,986**	**24,649**	**...**	**15,733**	**26,723**	**...**
Housing, community development, and urban renewal	3,052	3,196	...	2,475	3,280	...
Water	1,843	7,520	...	2,633	8,682	...
Sewerage	4,571	8,413	...	4,544	8,680	...
Sanitation	5,520	5,520	...	6,081	6,081	...
Recreational and cultural activities	**12,192**	**12,192**	**...**	**12,467**	**12,467**	**...**
Energy	**–5,393**	**3,608**	**...**	**–5,377**	**4,171**	**...**
Gas utilities	–58	459	...	–47	518	...
Electric utilities	–5,335	3,149	...	–5,330	3,653	...
Agriculture	**3,793**	**3,793**	**...**	**3,884**	**3,884**	**...**
Natural resources	**7,666**	**7,666**	**...**	**8,336**	**8,336**	**...**
Transportation	**76,402**	**72,487**	**...**	**79,909**	**76,042**	**...**
Highways	60,911	63,304	...	64,499	67,035	...
Water	143	686	...	137	727	...
Air	1,359	3,815	...	1,053	3,750	...
Transit and railroad	13,989	4,682	...	14,220	4,530	...
Economic development, regulation, and services	**6,299**	**6,299**	**...**	**6,387**	**6,387**	**...**
Labor training and services	**5,646**	**4,528**	**1,118**	**5,904**	**4,802**	**1,102**
Commercial activities	**–8,981**	**317**	**...**	**–9,764**	**307**	**...**
Publicly owned liquor store systems	–545	9	...	–550	8	...
Government-administered lotteries and parimutuels	–8,539	...	...	–9,257	...	...
Other	103	308	...	43	299	...
Net interest paid[1]	**5,227**	**...**	**5,227**	**8,744**	**...**	**8,744**
Other and unallocable	**45,924**	**45,924**	**...**	**48,085**	**48,085**	**...**

(1) Excludes interest received by social insurance funds, which is netted against expenditures for the appropriate functions.

All Banks in U.S.—Number, Deposits

Source: Federal Reserve System

Comprises all national banks in the U.S. and all state commercial banks, trust companies, mutual stock savings banks, private and industrial banks, and special types of institutions that are treated as banks by the federal bank supervisory agencies. Data as of June 30 prior to 1975.

	Number of banks						Total deposits (millions of dollars)					
		F.R.S. members			Nonmembers			F.R.S. members			Nonmembers	
Year	Total all banks	Total	Nat'l	State	Mutual savings	Other	Total all banks	Total	Nat'l	State	Mutual savings	Other
1925	**26,479**	9,538	8,066	1,472	621	18,320	**$51,641**	$32,457	$19,912	$12,546	$7,089	$12,095
1930	**23,855**	8,315	7,247	1,068	604	14,936	**59,828**	38,069	23,235	14,834	9,117	12,642
1935	**16,047**	6,410	5,425	985	569	9,068	**51,149**	34,938	22,477	12,461	9,830	6,381
1940	**14,955**	6,398	5,164	1,234	551	8,008	**70,770**	51,729	33,014	18,715	10,631	8,410
1945	**14,542**	6,840	5,015	1,825	539	7,163	**151,033**	118,378	76,534	41,844	14,413	18,242
1950	**14,674**	6,885	4,971	1,914	527	7,262	**163,770**	122,707	82,430	40,277	19,927	21,137
1955	**14,309**	6,611	4,744	1,867	525	7,173	**208,850**	154,670	98,636	56,034	27,310	26,870
1960	**14,006**	6,217	4,542	1,675	513	7,276	**249,163**	179,519	116,178	63,341	35,316	34,328

Year	Number of banks						Total deposits (millions of dollars)					
		F.R.S. members			Nonmembers			F.R.S. members			Nonmembers	
	Total all banks	Total	Nat'l	State	Mutual savings	Other	Total all banks	Total	Nat'l	State	Mutual savings	Other
1965	**14,295**	6,235	4,803	1,432	504	7,556	**362,611**	259,743	171,528	88,215	50,980	51,889
1970	**14,167**	5,805	4,638	1,167	496	7,866	**502,542**	346,289	254,322	91,967	69,285	86,968
1975	**15,108**	5,787	4,741	1,046	475	8,846	**896,879**	590,999	447,590	143,409	110,569	195,311
1980	**15,145**	5,422	4,425	997	460	9,263	**1,333,399**	843,030	651,848	191,182	150,000	340,369
1985	**14,713**	6,044	4,964	1,080	344	8,325	**1,973,816**	1,285,562	1,033,631	251,931	137,535	500,179
1990	**12,736**	5,034	4,012	1,022	361	7,341	**2,522,492**	1,679,654	1,374,004	305,650	183,522	659,316
1991	**12,312**	4,808	3,823	985	358	7,146	**2,546,753**	1,694,124	1,380,379	313,745	178,231	674,398
1992	**11,927**	4,599	3,632	967	428	6,900	**2,573,346**	1,720,678	1,369,262	351,416	177,856	674,813
1993	**11,508**	4,332	3,354	978	504	6,672	**2,588,073**	1,735,431	1,363,675	371,756	180,001	672,642

Largest U.S. Commercial Banks

Source: *American Banker* (as of Dec. 31, 1993)

Bank	Assets (millions)	Bank	Assets (millions)
Citibank, New York	$175,712.0	First Fidelity Bank, New Jersey, Newark	$20,065.4
Bank of America, San Francisco	136,692.5	State Street Bank & Trust Co., Boston	18,783.9
Chemical Bank, New York	115,510.0	Bank One, Texas, Dallas	18,173.4
Morgan Guaranty Trust Co., New York	101,902.3	Core States Bank, Philadelphia	17,628.8
Chase Manhattan Bank, New York	84,189.4	Marine Midland Bank, Buffalo	17,455.2
Bankers Trust Co., New York	68,134.0	National Westminster Bank USA, New York	16,675.2
Wells Fargo Bank, San Francisco	50,924.7	Union Bank, San Francisco	16,526.5
PNC Bank, Pittsburgh	40,615.0	First Bank, Minneapolis	15,803.6
Nations Bank of Texas, Dallas	37,109.1	NationsBank of Georgia, Atlanta	15,308.2
Bank of New York	36,068.1	Norwest Bank Minnesota, Minneapolis	15,294.6
First National Bank, Chicago	34,491.5	Seattle Fleet National Bank	15,083.6
Republic National Bank of New York	29,697.3	Shawmut Bank Connecticut, Hartford	14,508.1
First National Bank, Boston	29,551.7	Key Bank of New York, Albany	13,607.8
Mellon Bank, Pittsburgh	29,254.1	Northern Trust Co., Chicago	13,538.1
First Union National Bank of Florida, Jacksonville	27,765.1	Shawmut Bank, Boston	12,584.4
NBD Bank, Detroit	25,354.7	Meridian Bank, Reading, Pennsylvania	12,358.7
National Bank of North Carolina, Charlotte	25,014.2	Wachovia Bank of Georgia, Atlanta	11,975.5
Comerica Bank, Detroit	24,335.3	Huntington National Bank, Columbus, Ohio	11,846.3
Continental Bank, Chicago	22,331.0	NationsBank of Virginia, Richmond	11,578.0
First Union National Bank of North Carolina, Charlotte	21,955.6	Crestar Bank, Richmond	11,417.4
Society National Bank, Cleveland	21,803.2	Maryland National Bank, Baltimore	11,375.6
NationsBank of Florida, Tampa	21,391.5	United States National Bank, Portland, Ore.	11,345.4
Texas Commerce Bank, Houston	21,387.4	Bank of Hawaii, Honolulu	11,288.9
First Interstate Bank of California, Los Angeles	20,514.8	Bank One, Arizona, Phoenix	11,178.1
Wachovia Bank of North Carolina, Winston-Salem	20,286.8	Banco Popular de Puerto Rico, San Juan	10,987.2

Bank Failures

Source: Federal Deposit Insurance Corp.

Year	Closed or assisted	Year	Closed or assisted	Year	Closed or assisted	Year	Closed or assisted
1934	61	1961	9	1973	6	1985	120
1935	32	1963	2	1975	14	1986	145
1936	72	1964	8	1976	17	1987	184
1937	84	1965	9	1978	7	1988	221
1938	81	1966	8	1979	10	1989	207
1939	72	1967	4	1980	10	1990	169
1940	48	1969	9	1981	10	1991	127
1955	5	1970	8	1982	42	1992	122
1959	3	1971	6	1983	48	1993	42
1960	2	1972	3	1984	72		

Federal Deposit Insurance Corporation (FDIC)

The primary purpose of the Federal Deposit Insurance Corporation (FDIC) is to insure deposits in all banks approved for insurance coverage benefits under the Federal Deposit Insurance Act. The major functions of the FDIC are to protect depositors of insured banks, to act as receiver for all national banks placed in receivership and for state banks placed in receivership when appointed receiver by state authorities, and to ensure the continuance or development of safe and sound banking practices. The FDIC's income consists of assessments on insured banks and income from investments; it receives no appropriations from Congress. It may borrow from the U.S. Treasury not to exceed $30 billion outstanding, but has made no such borrowings since it was organized in 1933. The FDIC deficit (Deposit Insurance Fund) as of June 30, 1994, was $17.5 billion.

The Savings and Loan Crisis

Congress has authorized $105 billion for resolving insolvent savings institutions that failed between 1989 and the Resolution Trust Corporation (RTC) sunset date of Dec. 31, 1995. The RTC currently estimates the S&L cleanup will cost no more than $105 billion and based on current economic conditions could total approximately $90 billion. This does not include $60 billion spent before 1989.

Federal Reserve Board Discount Rate

The discount rate is the rate of interest set by the Federal Reserve that member banks are charged when borrowing money through the Federal Reserve System. Data are as of Oct. 1994.

Effective date	Rate	Effective date	Rate	Effective date	Rate	Effective date	Rate
1980: Feb. 15	13	June 13	11	Sept. 26	11	Dec. 5	13
May 30	12	July 28	10	Nov. 17	12	**1981:** May 5	14

(continued)

	Effective date	Rate
	Nov. 2	13
	Dec. 4	12
1982:	July 20	11½
	Aug. 2	11
	Aug. 16	10½
	Aug. 27	10
	Oct. 12	9½
	Nov. 22	9
	Dec. 15	8½
1984:	April 9	9
	Nov. 21	8½
	Dec. 24	8
1985:	May 20	7½
1986:	March 7	7
	April 21	6½
	July 11	6
	Aug. 21	5½
1987:	Sept. 4	6
1988:	Aug. 9	6½
1989:	Feb. 24	7
1990:	Dec. 18	6½
1991:	Apr. 30	5½
	Sept. 13	5
	Nov. 6	4½
	Dec. 20	3½
1992:	July 3	3
1994:	May 17	3½
	Aug. 16	4

Federal Reserve System

(as of Aug. 1994)

The Federal Reserve System is the central bank for the U.S. The system was established on Dec. 23, 1913, originally to give the country an elastic currency, to provide facilities for discounting commercial paper, and to improve the supervision of banking. Since then, the system's responsibilities have been broadened. Over the years, stability and growth of the economy, a high level of employment, stability in the purchasing power of the dollar, and reasonable balance in transactions with other countries have come to be recognized as primary objectives of governmental economic policy.

The Federal Reserve System consists of the Board of Governors, the 12 District Reserve Banks and their branch offices, and the Federal Open Market Committee. Several advisory councils help the board meet its varied responsibilities.

The hub of the system is the 7-member Board of Governors in Washington. The members of the board are appointed by the president and confirmed by the Senate, to serve 14-year terms. The president also appoints the chairman and vice chairman of the board from among the board members for 4-year terms that may be renewed. Currently, the board members are: Alan Greenspan, Chairman; Alan S. Blinder, Vice Chairman; Edward W. Kelley, Jr.; John P. La Ware; Lawrence B. Lindsey; Susan M. Phillips; and Janet Yellen.

The board is the policy-making body. In addition to its policy-making responsibilities, it supervises the budget and operations of the Reserve Banks, approves the appointments of their presidents, and appoints 3 of each District Bank's directors, including the chairman and vice chairman of each Reserve Bank's board.

The 12 Reserve Banks and their branch offices serve as the decentralized portion of the system, carrying out day-to-day operations such as circulating currency and coin and providing fiscal agency functions and payments mechanism services. The District Banks are in Boston, New York, Philadelphia, Cleveland, Richmond, Atlanta, Chicago, St. Louis, Minneapolis, Kansas City, Dallas, and San Francisco.

The system's principal function is monetary policy, which it controls using 3 tools: reserve requirements, the discount rate, and open market operations. Uniform reserve requirements, set by the board, are applied to the transaction accounts and nonpersonal time deposits of all depository institutions. Responsibility for setting the discount rate (the interest rate at which depository institutions can borrow money from the Reserve Banks) is shared by the Board of Governors and the Reserve Banks. Changes in the discount rate are recommended by the individual boards of directors of the Reserve Banks and are subject to approval by the Board of Governors. The most important tool of monetary policy is open market operations (the purchase and sale of government securities). Responsibility for influencing the cost and availability of money and credit through the purchase and sale of government securities lies with the Federal Open Market Committee (FOMC). This committee is composed of the 7 members of the Board of Governors, the president of the Federal Reserve Bank of New York, and 4 other Federal Reserve Bank presidents, who serve one-year terms on a rotating basis. The committee bases its decisions on current economic and financial developments and outlook, setting yearly growth objectives for key measures of money supply and credit. The decisions of the committee are carried out by the Domestic Trading Desk of the Federal Reserve Bank of New York.

The Federal Reserve Act prescribes a Federal Advisory Council, consisting of one member from each Federal Reserve District, elected annually by the Board of Directors of each of the 12 Federal Reserve Banks. They meet with the Federal Reserve Board 4 times a year to discuss business and financial conditions and to make advisory recommendations.

The Consumer Advisory Council is a statutory body, including both consumer and creditor representatives, which advises the Board of Governors on its implementation of consumer regulations and other consumer-related matters.

Following the passage of the Monetary Control Act of 1980, the Board of Governors established the Thrift Institutions Advisory Council to provide information and views on the special needs and problems of thrift institutions. The group is composed of representatives of mutual savings banks, savings and loan associations, and credit unions.

U.S. Corporate Profits by Industry

Source: Bureau of Economic Analysis, U.S. Dept. of Commerce

(billions of dollars)

	1992	1993	First quarter[1] 1994
Corporate profits with inventory valuation and capital consumption adjustments	**405.1**	**485.8**	**508.2**
Domestic industries	**344.5**	**420.5**	**447.1**
Financial	67.9	89.5	74.9
Nonfinancial	276.6	330.9	372.2
Rest of the world	**60.6**	**65.3**	**61.1**
Receipts from the rest of the world	65.4	74.2	77.6
Less: Payments to the rest of the world	4.8	8.9	16.6
Corporate profits with inventory valuation adjustment	**389.4**	**456.2**	**471.2**
Domestic industries	**328.8**	**391.0**	**410.1**
Financial	81.9	103.7	89.6
Federal Reserve banks	17.8	16.0	16.0
Other	64.2	87.7	73.6
Nonfinancial	246.9	287.3	320.5
Manufacturing	94.5	114.2	145.1
Durable goods	35.5	49.4	71.4
Primary metal industries	–0.4	0.2	0.2
Fabricated metal prods.	7.5	6.8	9.0
Industrial machinery and equip.	6.1	7.4	9.3
Electronic and other electric equip.	9.0	11.9	16.6
Motor vehicles and equip.	–1.5	4.1	14.4
Other	14.8	19.0	21.8
Nondurable goods	58.9	64.9	73.8
Food and kindred prods.	17.5	16.9	20.9
Chemicals and allied prods.	15.8	17.5	18.4
Petroleum and coal prods.	–1.4	4.7	5.5
Other	27.1	25.8	29.0
Transportation and public utilities	55.6	65.0	63.4
Wholesale and retail trade	54.8	61.2	59.0
Other	42.0	46.9	53.0
Rest of the world	**60.6**	**65.3**	**61.1**

(1) Seasonally adjusted at annual rates.

United States Mint

Source: United States Mint, U.S. Dept. of the Treasury

The United States Mint was created by an act of Congress on April 2, 1792, which established the U.S. national coinage system. Supervision of the mint was a function of the secretary of state, but in 1799 the mint became an independent agency reporting directly to the president. The mint was made a statutory bureau of the Treasury Department in 1873, with a director appointed by the President to oversee its operations.

The mint manufactures and ships all U.S. coins for circulation to the Federal Reserve banks and branches, which issue coins to the public and the business community through depository institutions. The mint also safeguards the Treasury Department's stored gold and silver and other monetary assets.

The composition of dimes, quarters, and half dollars, traditionally produced from silver, was changed by the Coinage Act of 1965, which mandated that these coins be minted from a cupronickel-clad alloy and reduced the silver content of the half dollar to 40%. In 1970, legislative action mandated that the half dollar and a dollar coin be minted from the same cupronickel-clad alloy.

The Eisenhower dollar was minted from 1971 through 1978, when legislation called for the minting of the smaller Susan B. Anthony dollar coin. The Anthony dollar, which was minted from 1979 through 1981, marked the first time that a woman, other than a mythical figure, appeared on a U.S. coin produced for general circulation.

Mint headquarters is in Washington, DC. Mint production facilities are in Philadelphia, Denver, San Francisco, and West Point, NY. In addition, the mint is responsible for the U.S. Bullion Depository at Fort Knox, KY.

Proof coin sets, silver proof coin sets, and uncirculated coin sets are available annually from the mint. The mint also produces ongoing series of national and historic medals in honor of outstanding persons or events and sites of special meaning to the American people.

Since 1982, the mint has produced the following congressionally authorized commemorative coins: the 1982 George Washington commemorative half dollar; 1984 U.S. Olympic coins; 1986 U.S. Statue of Liberty coins; 1987 Bicentennial of the U.S. Constitution coins; 1989 U.S. Congressional coins; the 1990 Eisenhower Centennial coin; the 1991 United Services Organization 59th Anniversary coin; the 1991 Korean War Memorial coin; 1991 Mount Rushmore Anniversary coins; 1992 U.S. Olympic coins; the 1992 White House 200th Anniversary coin; 1992 Christopher Columbus Quincentenary coins; 1993 Bill of Rights coins; 1993 World War II 50th Anniversary coins; 1994 World Cup USA coins; the Thomas Jefferson 250th Anniversary coin; the U.S. Veterans Commemorative coins (featuring the Prisoner of War coin, the Vietnam Veterans Memorial coin, and the Women in Military Service for America coin); and the Bicentennial of the U.S. Capitol Commemorative Silver Dollar.

The 1996 Atlanta Centennial Olympic coins, scheduled for sale in 1995 and 1996, will help support staging of the 1996 Olympic Games in Atlanta. Sales of the 1995 Civil War Battlefield coins will benefit the Civil War Trust, for the preservation of historically significant Civil War battlefields.

The congressionally authorized American eagle gold and silver bullion coins produced by the mint are available through dealers worldwide. The gold eagles are sold in one-ounce, half-ounce, quarter-ounce, and one-tenth-ounce sizes; the price of the coins fluctuates with the daily market value of gold. The American eagle silver bullion coin contains one troy ounce of .999 fine silver and is priced according to the daily market value of silver. These coins also are available in proof condition, separately priced.

The mint offers free public tours and operates sales centers at the U.S. mints in Denver and Philadelphia. The mint also operates a museum and sales center at the old mint in San Francisco and a sales center at Union Station in Washington, DC.

Information about mint programs and products is available from the United States Mint, Customer Service Center, 10001 Aerospace Rd., Lanham, MD 20706. Telephone: (301) 436-7400.

Portraits on U.S. Treasury Bills, Bonds, Notes, and Savings Bonds

Denomination	Savings bonds	Treas. bills	Treas. bonds	Treas. notes
50	Washington		Jefferson	
75	Adams			
100	Jefferson		Jackson	
200	Madison			
500	Hamilton		Washington	
1,000	Franklin	H. McCulloch	Lincoln	Lincoln
5,000	Revere	J.G. Carlisle	Monroe	Monroe
10,000	J. Wilson	J. Sherman	Cleveland	Cleveland
50,000		C. Glass		
100,000		A. Gallatin	Grant	Grant
1,000,000		O. Wolcott	T. Roosevelt	T. Roosevelt
100,000,000				Madison
500,000,000				McKinley

Large Denominations of U.S. Currency Discontinued

The largest denomination of U.S. currency now being issued is the $100 bill. Issuance of currency in denominations larger than $100 was discontinued in 1969.

As large denomination bills reach the Federal Reserve Bank, they are removed from circulation.

Because some discontinued currency is expected to be in the hands of holders for many years, the description of the various denominations below is continued.

Amt.	Portrait	Embellishment on back
$ 1	Washington	Great Seal of U.S.
2	Jefferson	Signers of Declaration
5	Lincoln	Lincoln Memorial
10	Hamilton	U.S. Treasury
20	Jackson	White House
50	Grant	U.S. Capitol
100	Franklin	Independence Hall

Amt.	Portrait	Embellishment on back
$ 500	McKinley	Ornate denominational marking
1,000	Cleveland	Ornate denominational marking
5,000	Madison	Ornate denominational marking
10,000	Chase	Ornate denominational marking
100,000*	W. Wilson	Ornate denominational marking

* For use only in transactions between Federal Reserve System and Treasury Department.

U.S. Currency and Coin

Source: Financial Management Service, U.S. Dept. of the Treasury (Mar. 31, 1994)

Amounts Outstanding and in Circulation

Currency	Total currency and coin	Total currency	Federal Reserve notes[1]	U.S. notes	Currency no longer issued
Amounts outstanding	$436,851,905,801	$415,118,434,903	$414,534,245,484	$322,539,016	$261,650,403
Less amounts held by:					
Treasury	370,119,615	43,505,646	4,894,012	38,412,539	199,095
Federal Reserve banks	65,016,004,698	64,580,975,097	64,580,968,174	582	6,341
Amounts in circulation	**$371,465,781,488**	**$350,493,954,160**	**$349,948,383,298**	**$284,125,895**	**$261,444,967**

Coins[2]	Total	Dollars[3]	Fractional coins
Amounts outstanding	$21,733,470,898	$2,024,703,898	$19,708,767,000
Less amounts held by:			
Treasury	326,613,969	295,406,091	31,207,878
Federal Reserve banks	435,029,601	83,327,313	351,702,288
Amounts in circulation	**$20,971,827,328**	**$1,645,970,494**	**$19,325,856,834**

Currency in Circulation by Denominations

Denomination	Total currency in circulation	Federal Reserve notes[1]	U.S. notes	Currency no longer issued
1 Dollar	$5,674,996,280	$5,525,259,374	$143,481	$149,593,425
2 Dollars	973,910,720	841,185,004	132,712,924	12,792
5 Dollars	6,672,449,500	6,526,963,310	111,110,370	34,375,820
10 Dollars	13,205,056,280	13,181,595,210	5,950	23,455,120
20 Dollars	75,061,576,480	75,041,466,700	3,380	20,106,400
50 Dollars	41,046,149,300	41,034,649,200	—	11,500,100
100 Dollars	207,539,210,500	207,477,209,500	40,149,700	21,851,300
500 Dollars	146,120,500	145,932,000	—	188,500
1,000 Dollars	169,259,000	169,053,000	—	206,000
5,000 Dollars	1,775,000	1,720,000	—	55,000
10,000 Dollars	3,450,000	3,350,000	—	100,000
Fractional parts	485	—	—	485
Partial notes[4]	115	—	90	25
Total currency	**$350,493,954,160**	**$349,948,383,298**	**$284,125,895**	**$261,444,967**

Comparative Totals of Money in Circulation — Selected Dates

Date	Dollars (in millions)	Per capita[5]	Date	Dollars (in millions)	Per capita[5]	Date	Dollars (in millions)	Per capita[5]
Mar. 31, 1994	371,466.0	1,428.37	June 30, 1975	81,196.4	380.08	June 30, 1940	7,847.5	59.40
Mar. 31, 1993	332,822.7	1,293.58	June 30, 1970	54,351.0	265.39	June 30, 1935	5,567.1	43.75
Mar. 31, 1992	303,215.0	1,219.15	June 30, 1965	39,719.8	204.14	June 30, 1930	4,522.0	36.74
Mar. 31, 1991	286,675.0	1,138.62	June 30, 1960	32,064.6	177.47	June 30, 1925	4,815.2	41.56
Mar. 31, 1990	257,664.4	1,028.71	June 30, 1955	30,229.3	182.90	June 30, 1920	5,467.6	51.36
June 30, 1985	185,890.7	778.58	June 30, 1950	27,156.3	179.03	June 30, 1915	3,319.6	33.01
June 30, 1980	127,097.2	558.28	June 30, 1945	26,746.4	191.14	June 30, 1910	3,148.7	34.07

(1) Issued on and after July 1, 1929. (2) Excludes coin sold to collectors at premium prices. (3) Includes $481,781,898 in standard silver dollars. (4) Represents value of certain partial denominations not presented for redemption. (5) Based on Bureau of the Census estimates of population.

The requirement for a gold reserve against U.S. notes was repealed by Public Law 90-269 approved Mar. 18, 1968. Silver certificates issued on and after July 1, 1929, became redeemable from the general fund on June 24, 1968. The amount of security after those dates has been reduced accordingly.

Consumer Credit Outstanding, 1970 to 1992

Source: Federal Reserve System

(billions of dollars)

Estimated amounts of credit outstanding as of end of year. Not seasonally adjusted (unless noted).

Type of Credit	1970	1975	1980	1985	1988	1989	1990	1991	1992
Credit outstanding	**133.8**	**207.5**	**355.4**	**601.6**	**742.1**	**799.5**	**813.0**	**799.9**	**809.2**
Ratio to disposable personal income[1] (percent)	18.5	18.0	18.2	20.4	20.9	20.6	19.5	18.5	17.8
Installment	**105.5**	**168.7**	**302.1**	**526.2**	**673.5**	**736.3**	**752.9**	**749.0**	**756.9**
Automobile paper	36.3	57.2	111.9	210.4	285.4	292.4	284.9	261.2	260.0
Revolving	5.1	15.0	58.5	128.9	184.0	209.4	234.8	256.9	267.9
All other loans[2]	64.1	99.7	131.6	213.8	181.3	239.2	238.4	236.5	229.0
Commercial banks	48.7	82.9	147.0	245.1	324.8	342.8	347.1	340.7	331.9
Finance companies	27.6	32.7	62.3	111.7	144.7	138.9	133.3	121.9	117.1
Credit unions	13.0	25.7	44.0	72.7	88.3	93.1	93.1	92.7	97.6
Retailers[3]	13.9	18.2	28.7	43.0	48.4	44.2	43.5	39.8	42.1
Other[4]	2.3	9.2	20.1	53.8	67.1	67.2	57.0	50.3	47.8
Noninstallment	**28.3**	**38.8**	**53.3**	**75.3**	**68.7**	**63.2**	**60.1**	**50.9**	**52.3**

(1) Based on fourth quarter seasonally adjusted disposable personal income at annual rates as published by the U.S. Bureau of Economic Analysis. (2) Comprises mobile home loans and all other installment loans not incl. in automobile or revolving credit, such as loans for education, boats, trailers, or vacations. (3) Excludes 30-day charge credit held by travel and entertainment companies. (4) Comprises savings institutions and gasoline companies.

Leading U.S. Businesses in 1993

Source: FORTUNE Magazine

(millions of dollars in sales)

Aerospace	
Boeing	$25,285
United Technologies	20,736
McDonnell-Douglas	14,487
Lockheed	13,071
Allied-Signal	11,827
Martin Marietta	9,436
Textron	8,669
Northrop	5,063
General Dynamics	4,661
Grumman	3,225
Apparel	
Levi Strauss	$5,892
VF	4,320
Berkshire Hathawa	3,099
Fruit of the Loom	1,884
Kellwood	1,078
Russell	931
Hartmarx	732
Warnaco Group	704
Leslie Fay	662
Beverages	
Pepsico	$25,021
Coca-Cola	13,957
Anheuser-Busch	11,505
Coca-Cola Enterprises	5,465
J.E. Seagram	3,799
Whitman	2,530
Adolph Coors	1,582
Brown-Forman	1,415
Dr Pepper/Seven-Up	707
Coca-Cola Bottling Cons.	687
Building Materials, Glass	
Corning	$4,005
American Standard	3,830
Owens-Illinois	3,535
Owens-Corning	2,944
Armstrong World Ind.	2,525
USG	1,916
Lafarge	1,495
Anchor Glass Container	1,126
Chemicals	
E.I. Du Pont De Nemours	$32,621
Dow Chemical	18,060
Occidental Petroleum	8,116
Monsanto	7,902
Hoechst Celanese	6,899
Miles	6,586
PPG Industries	5,754
W.R. Grace	5,737
BASF	5,202
Union Carbide	4,640
Computers, Office Equip.	
IBM	$62,716
Hewlett-Packard	29,317
Digital Equipment	14,027
Apple Computer	7,977
Unisys	7,743
Compaq Computer	7,191
Sun Microsystems	4,309
Pitney Bowes	3,543
Seagate Technology	3,044
Conner Peripherals	2,152
Electronics, Electrical Equip.	
General Electric	$60,823
Motorola	16,963
Westinghouse Electric	11,564
Rockwell International	10,840
Raytheon	9,201
Intel	8,782
Texas Instruments	8,523
Emerson Electric	8,174
Whirlpool	7,533
Cooper Industries	6,274
Food	
Philip Morris	$50,521
Conagra	21,519
Sara Lee	14,580
IBP	11,671
Archer Daniels Midland	9,811
General Mills	8,135
Ralston Purina	7,902
H.J. Heinz	7,103
CPC International	6,738
Borden	6,700
Forest and Paper Products	
International Paper	$13,685
Georgia-Pacific	12,330
Weyerhaeuser	9,545
Kimberly-Clark	6,973
Champion International	5,069
Stone Container	5,060
Mead	4,790
Scott Paper	4,749
James River (VA)	4,650
Boise Cascade	3,958
Furniture	
Interco	$1,657
Leggett & Platt	1,527
Herman Miller	856
Hon Industries	780
Kimball International	722
La-Z-Boy Chair	684
Sealy	683
Industrial and Farm Equip.	
Tenneco	$13,255
Caterpillar	11,615
Deere	7,694
Black & Decker	4,882
Cummins Engine	4,248
Dresser Industries	4,216
Ingersoll-Rand	4,021
Baker Hughes	2,702
Parker Hannifin	2,489
Dover	2,484
Metal Products	
Gillette	$5,411
Crown Cork & Seal	4,163
Masco	3,886
Tyco International	3,115
Ball	2,508
Stanley Works	2,273
McDermott	1,970
Mascotech	1,775
Newell	1,645
Hillenbrand Industries	1,448
Metals	
Alcoa	$9,056
Reynolds Metals	5,269
Bethlehem Steel	4,323
LTV	4,163
Inland Steel Industries	3,888
Phelps Dodge	2,611
National Steel	2,419
Alumax	2,347
Nucor	2,254
Maxxam	2,031
Motor Vehicles and Parts	
General Motors	$133,622
Ford Motor	108,521
Chrysler	43,600
TRW	7,948
Dana	5,460
Navistar International	4,694
Eaton	4,401
Paccar	3,379
Varity	3,375
Echlin	1,944
Petroleum Refining	
Exxon	$97,825
Mobil	56,576
Texaco	34,359
Chevron	32,123
Amoco	25,336
Shell Oil	20,853
Atlantic Richfield	17,189
USX	16,844
Phillips Petroleum	12,309
Coastal	10,136
Pharmaceuticals	
Johnson & Johnson	$14,138
Bristol-Myers Squibb	11,413
Merck	10,498
Abbott Laboratories	8,408
American Home Products	8,305
Pfizer	7,478
Eli Lilly	6,452
Warner-Lambert	5,794
American Cyanamid	5,306
Schering-Plough	4,341
Publishing & Printing	
R.R. Donnelley & Sons	$4,388
Times Mirror	3,714
Gannett	3,642
Reader's Digest Assn.	2,869
Knight-Ridder	2,451
McGraw-Hill	2,195
New York Times	2,020
Tribune	1,953
Dow Jones	1,932
American Greetings	1,672
Rubber and Plastic Prods.	
Goodyear Tire	$11,643
Illinois Tool Works	3,159
Premark International	3,097
Rubbermaid	1,960
M.A. Hanna	1,561
Mark IV Industries	1,222
Cooper Tire & Rubber	1,194
Standard Products	764
Foamex	696
A. Schulman	693
Scientific, Photographic, and Control Equip.	
Eastman Kodak	$20,059
Xerox	14,981
Minnesota Mining & Mfg.	14,020
Baxter International	8,879
Johnson Controls	6,182
Honeywell	5,963
EG&G	2,698
Becton Dickinson	2,465
Polaroid	2,245
Bausch & Lomb	1,872
Soaps, Cosmetics	
Procter & Gamble	$30,433
Colgate-Palmolive	7,141
Avon Products	4,008
Clorox	1,807
Intl. Flavors & Fragr.	1,189
Helene Curtis Industries	1,168
Alberto-Culver	1,148
Safety-Kleen	795
Stanhome	751
Mary Kay Cosmetics	737
Textiles	
Shaw Industries	$2,321
Collins & Aikman Group	2,225
Burlington Ind. Equity	2,058
Springs Industries	2,023
West Point Stevens	1,501
UNIFI	1,332
TRIARC	1,232
Fieldcrest Cannon	1,000
JPS Textile Group	886
Cone Mills	769
Tobacco	
RJR Nabisco Holdings	$15,104
American Brands	8,288
Universal	3,047
Standard Commercial	1,239
UST	1,076
Dibrell Brothers	1,065
Toys, Sporting Goods	
Hasbro	$2,747
Mattel	2,704
Tyco Toys	730
Transportation Equip.	
Brunswick	$2,354
Trinity Industries	1,540
Coltec Industries	1,335
Harley-Davidson	1,217
Huffy	758

U.S. Industrial Corporations With Largest Sales in 1993

Source: FORTUNE Magazine

(millions of dollars)

Company, headquarters	Sales	Company, headquarters	Sales
General Motors, Detroit, MI	$133,622	Chevron, San Francisco, CA	$32,123
Ford Motor, Dearborn, MI	108,521	Procter & Gamble, Cincinnati, OH	30,433
Exxon, Irving, TX	97,825	Amoco, Chicago, IL	25,336
IBM, Armonk, NY	62,716	Boeing, Seattle, WA	25,285
General Electric, Fairfield, CT	60,823	Pepsico, Purchase, NY	25,021
Mobil, Fairfax, VA	56,576	Conagra, Omaha, NE	21,519
Philip Morris, New York, NY	50,621	Shell Oil, Houston, TX	20,853
Chrysler, Highland Park, MI	43,600	United Technologies, Hartford, CT	20,736
Texaco, White Plains, NY	34,359	Hewlett-Packard, Palo Alto, CA	20,317
E.I. Du Pont de Nemours, Wilmington, DE	32,621	Eastman Kodak, Rochester, NY	20,059

U.S. Diversified Service Coporations With Largest Sales in 1993

Source: FORTUNE Magazine

(millions of dollars)

Company, headquarters	Sales	Company, headquarters	Sales
America Telephone & Telegraph, New York, NY	$67,156	Enron, Houston, TX	$7,973
Fleming, Oklahoma City, OK	13,092	Fluor, Irvine, CA	7,971
Supervalu, Eden Prairie, MN	12,568	Marriott International, Washington, DC	7,430
MCI Communications, Washington, DC	11,921	Bergen Brunswig, Orange, CA	6,824
McKesson, San Francisco, CA	11,672	Alco Standard, Wayne, PA	6,591
Sprint, Westwood, KS	11,368	Time Warner, New York, NY	6,581
Sysco, Houston, TX	10,022	Halliburton, Dallas, TX	6,351
WMX Technologies, Oak Brook, IL	9,136	Capital Cities/ABC, New York, NY	5,674
Walt Disney, Burbank, CA	8,529	Columbia Healthcare, Louisville, KY	5,653
Electronic Data Systems, Plano, TX	8,507	Hospital Corp. Of Amer., Nashville, TN	5,122

Largest Corporate Mergers or Acquisitions in U.S.

(as of Oct. 1994; most recent mergers and acquisitions may not be complete)

Company	Acquirer	Dollars	Year
RJR Nabisco	Kohlberg Kravis Roberts	24.9 bil	1988
Warner Communications	Time	13.9 bil	1989
Gulf Oil	Chevron	13.3 bil	1984
Kraft	Philip Morris	13.1 bil	1988
McCaw Cellular	AT&T	12.6 bil	1993
Squibb	Bristol-Myers	11.5 bil	1989
Getty Oil	Texaco	10.1 bil	1984
Lockheed	Martin Marietta	10.0 bil	1994
Paramount	Viacom	9.7 bil	1994
American Cyanamid	American Home Products	9.7 bil	1994
Conoco	DuPont	8.0 bil	1981
Standard Oil	British Petroleum	7.9 bil[1]	1987
Blockbuster	Viacom	7.7 bil	1994
Federated Dept. Stores	Campeau	7.4 bil	1988
NCR	AT&T	7.4 bil	1991
MCA	Matsushita	6.5 bil	1990
Marathon Oil	U.S. Steel	6.5 bil	1981
Contel	GTE	6.2 bil	1990
Beatrice	Kohlberg Kravis Roberts	6.2 bil	1986
RCA	General Electric	6.2 bil	1986
Medco	Merck	6.0 bil	1993
Superior Oil	Mobil Oil	5.7 bil	1984
Pillsbury	Grand Metropolitan	5.7 bil	1988
General Foods	Philip Morris	5.6 bil	1986
Syntex	Roche Holding	5.4 bil	1994
Safeway Stores	Kohlberg Kravis Roberts	5.3 bil	1986
Farmers Group	B.A.T. Industries	5.2 bil	1988
Southern Pacific	Santa Fe Railroad	5.2 bil	1983
Southland	J.T. Acquisition	5.1 bil	1987
Hughes Aircraft	General Motors	5.0 bil	1985
Nabisco	R.J. Reynolds	4.9 bil	1985
Signal Cos.	Allied Corp.	4.9 bil	1986
Sperry	Burroughs	4.8 bil	1986
Connecticut General	INA	4.3 bil	1981
Borg-Warner	AV Holdings	4.2 bil	1987
Texasgulf	Elf Aquitaine	4.2 bil	1981
Cities Service	Occidental Petroleum	4.0 bil	1982
Security Pacific	BankAmerica	4.0 bil	1991
Travelers	Primerica	4.0 bil	1993
PCS Health Systems	Eli Lilly	4.0 bil	1994
Dome Petroleum	Amoco	3.8 bil	1987
Gerber	Sandoz	3.7 bil	1994
R.H. Macy	various investors	3.7 bil	1986
American Hospital	Baxter Travenol	3.7 bil	1986
Owens-Illinois	Kohlberg Kravis Roberts	3.6 bil	1987
Belridge Oil	Shell Oil	3.6 bil	1979
NWA	Checchi Group	3.6 bil	1988
Allied Stores	Campeau	3.5 bil	1986
Fort Howard Paper	Morgan Stanley Group	3.5 bil	1988
ABC Broadcasting	Capital Cities Comm.	3.5 bil	1985
Columbia Pictures	Sony	3.4 bil	1989
Viacom	National Amusements	3.4 bil	1987
LIN Broadcasting	McCaw Cellular	3.3 bil[2]	1989
Panhandle Eastern	Texas Eastern	3.2 bil	1989
Chesebrough-Ponds	Unilever N.V.	3.1 bil	1987
Kemper	Conseco	3.0 bil	1994
MidCon	Occidental Petroleum	3.0 bil	1986
American Med. Intl.	IMA Holdings	3.0 bil	1989
Texas Oil and Gas	USX Corp.	3.0 bil	1986
Emhart	Black & Decker	2.8 bil	1989
Carnation	Nestle	2.8 bil	1984
Celanese	American Hoechst	2.7 bil	1987
Esmark	Beatrice Foods	2.7 bil	1984
G.D. Searle	Monsanto	2.7 bil	1986
Continental Group	Kiewit-Murdock	2.7 bil	1984
St. Joe Minerals	Fluor	2.6 bil	1981
Electronic Data Systems	General Motors	2.6 bil	1984
Firestone Tire	Bridgestone	2.6 bil	1988
Macmillan	Maxwell Comm.	2.6 bil	1988
Associated Dry Goods	May Dept. Stores	2.5 bil	1986
WilTel	LDDS Communications	2.5 bil	1994
Times Mirror Cable Unit	Cox Enterprises	2.3 bil	1994
BB&T Financial	Southern National	2.2 bil	1994
Grumman	Northrop	2.1 bil	1994
Borden	Kohlberg Kravis Roberts	2.0 bil	1994

(1) For the 45% of Standard Oil that British Petroleum did not already own. (2) For about 42% of LIN's shares.

U.S Multinational Companies[1], 1982-92

Source: Bureau of Economic Analysis, U.S. Dept. of Commerce

	MNCs worldwide[2]	U.S. Parent Companies	Foreign Affiliates
Total assets			
Millions of dollars:			
1982	**3,493,105**	2,741,619	751,486
1983	**3,653,616**	2,902,793	750,823
1984	**3,820,025**	3,060,031	759,994
1985	**4,297,034**	3,462,398	834,636
1986	**4,723,294**	3,792,001	931,293
1987	**5,285,962**	4,175,308	1,110,654
1988	**5,569,767**	4,363,441	1,206,326
1989	**6,182,401**	4,852,373	1,330,028
1990	**6,510,086**	4,951,048	1,559,038
1991	**6,861,631**	5,183,286	1,678,345
1992	**7,317,221**	5,570,464	1,746,757
Percent change at annual rates:			
1982-92	**7.7**	7.3	8.8
1990-91	**5.4**	4.7	7.7
1991-92	**6.6**	7.5	4.1
Sales			
Millions of dollars:			
1982	**3,284,168**	2,348,388	935,780
1983	**3,263,802**	2,377,488	886,314
1984	**3,407,337**	2,508,779	898,558
1985	**3,482,155**	2,586,695	895,460
1986	**3,473,354**	2,544,439	928,915
1987	**3,742,022**	2,689,227	1,052,795
1988	**4,022,942**	2,828,209	1,194,733
1989	**4,421,731**	3,136,837	1,284,894
1990	**4,737,147**	3,243,721	1,493,426
1991	**4,794,100**	3,252,534	1,541,566
1992	**4,931,700**	3,353,017	1,578,683
Percent change at annual rates:			
1982-92	**4.1**	3.6	5.4
1990-91	**1.2**	0.3	3.2
1991-92	**2.9**	3.1	2.4
Number of employees			
Thousands:			
1982	**25,344.8**	18,704.6	6,640.2
1983	**24,782.6**	18,399.5	6,383.1
1984	**24,548.4**	18,130.9	6,417.5
1985	**24,531.9**	18,112.6	6,419.3
1986	**24,082.0**	17,831.8	6,250.2
1987	**24,255.4**	17,985.8	6,269.6
1988	**24,141.1**	17,737.6	6,403.5
1989	**25,387.5**	18,765.4	6,622.1
1990	**25,263.6**	18,429.7	6,833.9
1991	**24,837.1**	17,958.9	6,878.2
1992	**24,344.7**	17,617.2	6,727.5
Percent change at annual rates:			
1982-92	**–0.4**	–0.6	0.1
1990-91	**–1.7**	–2.6	0.6
1991-92	**–2.0**	–1.9	–2.2

(1) Banks not included. (2) The MNC totals for assets and sales contain duplication because they do not exclude positions and transactions between parent companies and foreign affiliates.

Fastest Growing Franchises in 1993[1]

Source: Reprinted with permission from *Entrepreneur* Magazine, January 1994

Company	Business	Minimum start-up cost[2]
7-Eleven Convenience Stores	convenience stores	$12,500
Subway	submarine sandwiches	38,900
Snap-On Tools	retail hardware	12,600
Maico Tools	retail hardware	42,500
McDonald's	hamburgers	varies
Chem-Dry Carpet Drapery & Upholstery Cleaning	carpet, upholstery, and drapery services	3,550
Little Caesars Pizza	pizza	170,000
Burger King Corp.	hamburgers	73,000
Coverall North America Inc.	commercial cleaning services	3,250
Mail Boxes Etc.	postal and business services	28,180
CleanNet USA Inc.	commercial cleaning services	425
Jani-King	commercial cleaning services	2,500
Dunkin' Donuts	donuts	175,000
Coldwell Banker Residential Affiliates Inc.	real estate services	4,000-117,000
Jazzercise Inc.	weight-control/fitness centers	1,360
Tower Cleaning Systems	commercial cleaning services	$1,190
Miracle Ear	health-care equipment	20,000
Play It Again Sports	sports equipment and apparel	56,700
GNC Franchising Inc.	health foot/vitamin stores	66,700
Super 8 Motels Inc.	hotels and motels	300,000
Choice Hotels Int'l.	hotels and motels	1,500,000
Jackson Hewitt Tax Service	Income tax/financial services	13,000
Blimpie Co.	submarine sandwiches	63,920
Re/Max Int'l. Inc.	real estate services	60,000
O.P.E.N. Cleaning Systems	commercial cleaning services	500
Decorating Den	misc. decorative products and services	8,900
Baskin-Robbins USA Co.	ice cream, frozen yogurt, & shaved ice	92,000
Holiday Inn Worlwide	hotels and motels	varies
SuperGlass Windshield Repair	windshield and glass repair	500+
Hardee's	hamburgers	502,200

(1) Based on the number of new franchise units added. (2) Not including franchise fee, which varies.

Largest U.S. Black-Owned Companies in 1993

Source: *Black Enterprise* Magazine

Company (Business)	Location	Sales (millions)
TLC Beatrice International Holdings Inc. (international food processor & distributor)	New York	$1,700.0
Johnson Publishing Co. Inc. (publishing, broadcasting, TV prod., cosmetics, hair care)	Chicago	293.8
Philadelphia Coca-Cola Bottling Co. Inc.	Philadelphia	290.0
H.J. Russell & Co. (construction, communications)	Atlanta	152.4
RMS Technologies Inc. (computer & tech. services)	Marlton, NJ	$115.2
The Anderson-Dubose Co. (food distributor)	Solon, OH	115.0
Gold Line Refining Ltd. (oil refinery)	Houston	108.1
Threads 4 Life (apparel manufacturer)	Commerce, CA	97.0
Soft Sheen Products Inc. (hair care products)	Chicago	96.6
Garden State Cable TV (cable TV operator)	Cherry Hill, NJ	96.0

Capital Gains Tax

Source: U.S. Chamber of Commerce

The following shows how the top effective tax rate on capital gains has changed since 1960.

Year	Effective rate (percent)	Year	Effective rate (percent)	Year	Effective rate (percent)	Year	Effective rate (percent)
1960	25.0	1970	32.2	1976	49.1	1987	28.0
1968	26.9	1971	34.4	1979	28.0	1988	33.0
1969	27.5	1972	45.5	1981	20.0	1991	28.0

1994 Federal Corporate Tax Rates

Taxable Income Amount	Tax Rate	Taxable Income Amount	Tax Rate
Not more than $50,000	15%	$335,001 to $10,000,000	34%
$50,001 to $75,000	25%	$10,000,001 to $15,000,000	35%
$75,001 to $100,000	34%	$15,000,001 to $18,333,333	38%
$100,001 to $335,000	39%	More than $18,333,333	35%

Personal service corporations (used by professional individuals such as attorneys and doctors) pay a flat rate of 35%.

Global Stock Markets

Source: Bureau of Economic Analysis, U.S. Dept. Of Commerce; not seasonally adjusted

Stock price indexes (1967=100):	1993	1994 Jan.	Feb.	Mar.	Apr.	May	June	July	Aug.
United States	491.0	514.5	513.0	504.5	486.5	490.5	494.8	491.0	505.0
Japan	1,381.4	1,376.0	1,445.1	1,466.9	1,457.0	1,488.6	1,526.2	1,498.5	1,494.6
Germany	312.2	374.2	372.7	380.2	396.9	399.8	373.1	372.0	389.4
France	970.2	(p)1,145.8	(p)1,141.4	(p)1,095.8	(p)1,072.1	(p)1,075.8	(p)987.1	(p)998.2	(p)1,030.6
United Kingdom	1,375.0	1,584.3	1,584.3	1,520.6	1,488.3	1,472.6	1,409.9	(p)1,426.4	(p)1,495.7
Italy	575.2	646.8	703.3	699.9	815.6	823.9	757.1	(r)738.5	(p)721.2
Canada	441.1	514.7	499.9	489.2	482.2	488.9	454.8	472.2	491.5

(p) = preliminary. (r)= revised.

Foreign Exchange Rates: 1970 to 1993

Source: International Monetary Fund

(National currency units per dollar except as indicated; data are annual averages)

Year	Australia[1] (dollar)	Austria (schilling)	Belgium (franc)	Canada (dollar)	Denmark (krone)	France (franc)	Germany[2] (deutsche mark)	Greece (drachma)
1970	1.1136	25.880	49.680	1.0103	7.489	5.5200	3.6480	30.00
1975	1.3077	17.443	36.799	1.0175	5.748	4.2876	2.4613	32.29
1980	1.1400	12.945	29.237	1.1693	5.634	4.2250	1.8175	42.62
1985	.7003	20.690	59.378	1.3655	10.596	8.9852	2.9440	138.12
1987	.7009	12.643	37.334	1.3260	6.840	6.0107	1.7974	135.43
1988	.7842	12.243	36.768	1.2307	6.732	5.9569	1.7562	141.89
1989	.7925	13.231	39.404	1.1840	7.310	6.3801	1.8800	162.42
1990	.7813	11.370	33.418	1.1668	6.189	5.4453	1.6157	158.51
1991	.7791	11.676	34.148	1.1457	6.396	5.6421	1.6595	182.27
1992	.7353	10.989	32.150	1.2087	6.036	5.2938	1.5617	190.62
1993	.6801	11.632	34.597	1.2901	6.484	5.6632	1.6533	229.25

Year	India (rupee)	Ireland[1] (pound)	Italy (lira)	Japan (yen)	Malaysia (ringgit)	Netherlands (guilder)	Norway (kroner)	Portugal (escudo)
1970	7.576	2.3959	623	357.60	3.0900	3.5970	7.1400	28.75
1975	8.409	2.2216	653	296.78	2.4030	2.5293	5.2282	25.51
1980	7.887	2.0577	856	226.63	2.1767	1.9875	4.9381	50.08
1985	12.369	1.0656	1,909	238.54	2.4830	3.3214	8.5972	170.39
1987	12.962	1.4881	1,296	144.64	2.5196	2.0257	6.7375	140.88
1988	13.917	1.5261	1,301	128.15	2.6188	1.9766	6.5170	143.95
1989	16.226	1.4190	1,372	137.96	2.7088	2.1207	6.9045	157.46
1990	17.504	1.6585	1,198	144.79	2.7048	1.8209	6.2597	142.55
1991	22.742	1.6155	1,240	134.71	2.7501	1.8697	6.4829	144.48
1992	25.918	1.7053	1,232	126.65	2.5474	1.7585	6.2145	135.00
1993	30.493	1.4671	1.574	111.20	2.5741	1.8573	7.0941	160.80

Year	Singapore (dollar)	South Korea (won)	Spain (peseta)	Sweden (krona)	Switzerland (franc)	Thailand (baht)	United[1] Kingdom (pound)
1970	3.0800	310.57	69.72	5.1700	4.3160	21.000	2.3959
1975	2.3713	484.00	57.43	4.1530	2.5839	20.379	2.2216
1980	2.1412	607.43	71.76	4.2309	1.6772	20.476	2.3243
1985	2.2002	870.02	170.04	8.6039	2.4571	27.159	1.2963
1987	2.1059	822.57	123.48	6.3404	1.4912	25.723	1.6389
1988	2.0124	731.57	116.49	6.1272	1.4633	25.294	1.7813
1989	1.9508	671.46	118.38	6.4469	1.6359	25.702	1.6897
1990	1.8125	707.76	101.93	5.9188	1.3892	25.585	1.7847
1991	1.7276	733.35	103.91	6.0475	1.4340	25.517	1.7694
1992	1.6290	780.65	102.38	5.8238	1.4062	25.400	1.7655
1993	1.6158	802.67	127.26	7.7834	1.4776	25.319	1.5020

(1) Value of one unit of foreign currency in dollars. (2) W. Germany prior to 1991.

Tourism: International Visitors to the U.S., 1993

Source: U.S. Travel & Tourism Administration; Bureau of Economic Analysis

Country of origin	Visitors (millions)	Expenditures (billions)	Expenditures per visitor	Country of origin	Visitors (millions)	Expenditures (billions)	Expenditures per visitor
Japan	3.5	$13.7	$3,914	France	.8	$2.9	$3,431
Canada	17.3	8.5	491	Italy	.6	1.9	3,167
Mexico	9.8	5.7	582	Australia	.4	1.8	4,009
United Kingdom	3.0	8.5	2,833	Netherlands	.4	.8	2,000
Germany	1.8	5.3	2,944	**All countries**	**45.8**	**74.4**	**1,624**

Excludes international passenger fare payments and cruise travel. Numbers may not add up due to rounding

Foreign Direct Investment[1] in the U.S. by Selected Countries

Source: Bureau of Economic Analysis; U.S. Dept. of Commerce

(millions of dollars)

	1992	1993
All countries[2]	**$425,636**	**$445,268**
Canada	37,845	39,408
Europe[2]	251,206	270,767
Austria	518	557
Belgium	4,288	4,589
Denmark	1,508	833
Finland	1,416	1,500
France	25,459	28,470
Germany	29,603	34,667
Ireland	2,750	2,593
Italy	274	1,229
Netherlands	65,323	68,477
Spain	1,546	623
Sweden	6,850	8,077
Switzerland	20,635	21,384
United Kingdom	89,073	95,415
South and Central America[2]	7,790	6,604
Brazil	574	714
Mexico	$1,230	$1,039
Panama	5,040	4,754
Venezuela	440	–398
Other Western Hemisphere[2]	13,308	13,739
Bahamas	2,779	1,184
Bermuda	1,473	1,442
Middle East[2]	4,786	5,027
Israel	1,284	1,712
Kuwait	1,643	1,555
Saudi Arabia	1,688	1,591
United Arab Emirates	93	107
Asia and Pacific[2]	109,978	108,918
Australia	7,069	7,278
Hong Kong	1,842	2,015
Japan	97,537	96,213
Singapore	873	228
Taiwan	1,117	1,272

(1) The book value of foreign direct investors' equity in, and net outstanding loans to, their U.S. affiliates. A U.S. affiliate is a U.S. business enterprise in which a single foreign direct investor owns at least 10% of the voting securities or the equivalent. (2) Totals include countries not shown.

U.S. International Transactions

Source: Bureau of Economic Analysis, U.S. Dept. of Commerce

(millions of dollars)

	1965	1970	1975	1980	1985	1990	1992	1993
Exports of goods, services, and income[1]	**$42,722**	**$68,387**	**$157,936**	**$344,440**	**$380,051**	**$680,890**	**$731,373**	**$755,533**
Merchandise, adjusted, excluding military[2]	26,461	42,469	107,088	224,250	215,915	388,705	440,361	456,866
Services	8,824	14,171	25,497	47,584	73,026	148,638	176,563	184,811
Income receipts on U.S. assets abroad	7,437	11,748	25,351	71,388	82,282	143,547	114,449	113,856
Imports of goods, services, and income	**–32,708**	**–59,901**	**–33,745**	**–333,774**	**–473,998**	**–738,401**	**–767,217**	**–827,312**
Merchandise, adjusted, excluding military[2]	–21,510	–39,866	–98,185	–249,750	–338,088	–497,558	–536,458	–589,441
Services	–9,111	–14,520	–4,795	–21,996	–41,491	–116,583	–120,850	–127,961
Income payments on foreign assets in the U.S.	–2,088	–5,515	–12,564	–45,532	–67,875	–124,261	–109,909	–109,910
Unilateral transfers, net	**–4,583**	**–6,156**	**–7,075**	**–8,349**	**–22,950**	**–32,916**	**–32,042**	**–32,117**
U.S. assets abroad, net (increase/capital outflow [-])	**–5,716**	**–9,337**	**–39,703**	**–86,967**	**–34,069**	**–56,321**	**–61,510**	**–147,898**
U.S. official reserve assets, net	1,225	2,481	–849	–8,155	–3,858	–2,158	3,901	–1,379
U.S. Government assets, other than official reserve assets, net	–1,605	–1,589	–3,474	–5,162	–2,821	–2,304	–1,652	–306
U.S. private assets, net	–5,336	–10,229	–35,380	–73,651	–27,391	–56,467	–63,759	–146,213
Foreign assets in U.S., net (increase/capital inflow [+])	**742**	**6,359**	**15,670**	**58,112**	**130,012**	**99,379**	**146,504**	**230,698**
Statistical discrepancy (sum of above items with sign reversed)	**–457**	**–219**	**5,917**	**25,386**	**24,825**	**47,370**	**–17,108**	**21,096**
Memorandum:								
Balance on current account	5,431	2,331	18,116	2,317	–121,721	–90,428	–67,886	–103,896

(1) Excludes transfers of goods and services under U.S. military grant programs. (2) Excludes exports of goods under U.S. military agency sales contracts identified in Census export documents, excludes imports of goods under direct defense expenditures identified in Census import documents, and reflects various other adjustments.

National Income by Industry

Source: Bureau of Economic Analysis, U.S. Dept. of Commerce

(billions of dollars)

	1960	1970	1975	1980	1990	1992	1993
National income without capital consumption adjustment	**$428.6**	**$835.1**	**$1,315.0**	**$2,263.9**	**$4,497.5**	**$4,880.3**	**$5,172.7**
Domestic industries	**425.1**	**827.8**	**1,297.4**	**2,216.3**	**4,486.7**	**4,873.0**	**5,172.5**
Private industries	**371.6**	**695.4**	**1,088.3**	**1,894.5**	**3,828.9**	**4,138.5**	**4,407.2**
Agriculture, forestry, fisheries	17.8	25.9	46.5	61.4	97.1	100.9	105.3
Mining	5.6	8.4	21.2	43.8	38.1	38.5	40.1
Construction	22.5	47.4	69.9	126.6	234.4	212.8	228.0
Manufacturing	125.3	215.6	317.5	532.1	846.9	895.3	928.2
Durable goods	73.4	127.7	185.0	313.7	484.3	501.7	522.6
Nondurable goods	52.0	87.9	132.5	218.4	362.6	393.6	405.6
Transportation, public utilities	35.8	64.4	101.1	177.3	328.7	356.1	376.1
Transportation	18.5	31.5	48.0	85.8	139.4	151.0	161.8
Communications	8.2	17.6	26.8	48.1	96.4	103.7	107.4
Electric, gas, and sanitary services	9.1	86.8	90.2	43.4	92.9	101.5	106.9
Wholesale trade	25.0	47.5	83.0	143.3	263.6	283.6	297.7
Retail trade	41.3	79.9	123.1	189.4	392.1	416.7	444.9
Finance, insurance, and real estate	51.3	96.4	143.9	279.5	679.8	748.9	816.0
Services	46.9	109.8	182.1	341.0	948.3	1,085.8	1,171.0
Government	**53.5**	**132.4**	**209.1**	**321.8**	**657.9**	**734.5**	**765.3**

National Income by Type of Income

Source: Bureau of Economic Analysis, U.S. Dept. of Commerce

(billions of dollars)

	1960	1970	1980	1990	1991	1992	1993
National income[1]	**$424.9**	**$832.6**	**$2,203.5**	**$4,459.6**	**$4,544.2**	**$4,743.4**	**$5,131.4**
Compensation of employees	**296.7**	**618.3**	**1,638.2**	**3,290.3**	**3,390.8**	**3,525.2**	**3,780.4**
Wages and salaries	272.8	551.5	1,372.0	2,738.9	2,812.2	2,916.6	3,100.8
Government	49.2	117.1	260.1	514.0	543.5	562.5	583.8
Other	223.7	434.3	1,111.8	2,224.9	2,268.7	2,354.1	2,517.0
Supplements to wages, salary	23.8	66.8	266.3	551.4	578.7	608.6	679.6
Employer contrib. for social ins.	12.6	34.3	127.9	277.3	290.4	302.9	324.3
Other labor income	11.2	32.5	138.4	274.0	288.3	305.7	355.3
Propietors' income	**52.1**	**80.2**	**180.7**	**373.2**	**368.0**	**404.5**	**441.6**
Farm	11.6	14.7	20.5	42.5	35.8	39.5	37.3
Nonfarm	40.5	65.4	160.1	330.7	332.2	364.9	404.3
Rental income of persons with capital consump. adjust.	**15.3**	**18.2**	**6.6**	**–12.9**	**–10.4**	**4.7**	**24.1**
Corp. profits with inventory adjustment	**49.8**	**69.5**	**194.0**	**319.0**	**346.3**	**393.8**	**456.2**
Corp. profits before tax	49.9	76.0	237.1	332.3	334.7	371.6	462.4
Corp. profits tax liability	22.7	34.4	84.8	135.3	124.0	140.2	173.2
Corp. profits after tax	27.2	41.7	152.3	197.0	210.7	231.4	289.2
Dividends	12.9	22.5	54.7	133.7	146.5	149.3	191.7
Undistributed profits	14.3	19.2	97.6	63.3	64.2	82.1	97.5
Inventory valuation adjustment	–0.2	–6.6	–43.1	–14.2	3.1	–7.4	–6.2
Net interest	**11.3**	**41.2**	**200.9**	**490.1**	**449.5**	**415.2**	**399.5**

(1) National income is the aggregate of labor and property earnings that arises in the current production of goods and services. It is the sum of employee compensation, proprietors' income, rental income, corporate profits, and net interest. It measures the total factor costs of the goods and services produced by the economy. Income is measured before deduction of taxes on income.

Distribution of Total Personal Income[1]

Source: Bureau of Economic Analysis, U.S. Dept. of Commerce

(billions of dollars)

					Personal Savings	
Year	Personal income	Personal taxes	Disposable personal income	Personal outlays	Amount	As pct. of disposable income
1960	$ 402.3	$50.4	$ 352.0	$332.3	$19.7	5.6%
1965	40.7	64.9	475.8	442.1	33.7	7.1
1970	811.1	115.8	695.3	639.5	55.8	8.0
1975	1,265.0	168.9	1,096.1	1,001.8	94.3	8.6
1980	2,165.3	336.5	1,828.9	1,718.7	110.2	6.0
1981	2,429.5	387.7	2,041.7	1,904.3	137.4	6.7
1982	2,584.6	404.1	2,180.5	2,044.5	136.0	6.2
1983	2,838.6	410.5	2,428.1	2,297.4	130.6	5.4
1984	3,108.7	440.2	2,668.6	2,504.5	164.1	6.1
1985	3,325.3	486.6	2,838.7	2,713.3	125.4	4.4
1986	3,526.2	512.9	3,013.3	2,888.5	124.9	4.1
1987	3,776.6	571.7	3,205.9	3,104.1	101.8	3.2
1988	4,070.8	591.6	3,479.2	3,333.6	145.6	4.2
1989	4,384.3	658.8	3,725.5	3,553.7	171.8	4.6
1990	4,679.8	621.0	4,058.8	3,853.1	205.8	5.1
1991	4,828.4	618.7	4,209.6	4,009.9	199.6	4.7
1992	5,058.1	627.3	4,430.6	4,218.1	212.6	4.8
1993	5,375.1	686.4	4,688.7	4,496.2	192.6	4.1

(1) Figures may not add because of rounding.

U.S. Direct Investment[1] Abroad in Selected Countries

Source: Bureau of Economic Analysis, U.S. Dept. of Commerce

(millions of dollars)

	1990	1992	1993
All countries[2]	**$424,096**	**$498,991**	**$548,644**
Africa[2]	NA	4,440	5,297
Egypt	1,465	1,337	1,374
Nigeria	161	301	527
S. Africa	956	879	925
Asia and Pacific (excl. Japan)[2]	NA	53,394	60,876
China	—	516	877
Hong Kong	6,187	8,730	10,457
India	513	485	759
Indonesia	3,226	4,472	5,031
Malaysia	1,384	1,598	1,928
Philippines	1,629	1,724	1,770
Singapore	3,385	6,728	8,782
South Korea	2,178	2,850	3,001
Taiwan	2,014	2,910	3,096
Thailand	1,585	2,595	2,893
Australia	14,846	16,885	18,437
Bermuda	21,737	25,668	28,153
Canada	67,033	68,832	70,395
European Union	177,642	207,170	224,587
Belgium	9,050	11,115	11,552
Denmark	1,597	1,676	1,797
France	18,874	24,709	23,565
Germany	27,259	33,578	37,524
Greece	288	372	424
Ireland	6,880	7,686	9,575
Italy	13,117	13,899	13,920
Luxembourg	1,390	1,783	2,314
Netherlands	22,658	20,142	19,887
Portugal	598	1,225	1,162
Spain	7,704	8,345	6,437
United Kingdom	68,224	82,641	96,430
Other Europe[2]	33,552	39,058	44,569
Austria	889	1,378	1,384
Finland	551	364	336
Norway	3,815	3,824	4,353
Sweden	1,600	1,887	1,802
Switzerland	25,199	29,190	32,901
Turkey	494	674	1,023
Japan	20,997	26,590	31,393
South America[2]	23,760	28,360	30,921
Argentina	2,956	3,399	4,355
Brazil	14,918	16,343	16,908
Chile	1,368	2,655	2,869
Colombia	1,728	2,436	2,542
Ecuador	387	294	511
Peru	410	620	631
Venezuela	1,490	1,977	2,295
Central America[2]	17,719	25,863	28,966
Mexico	9,398	13,723	15,413
Panama	7,409	11,329	12,575
Middle East[2]	3,973	5,644	6,459
Israel	756	1,358	1,660
Saudi Arabia	1,981	2,351	2,567
United Arab Emirates	519	429	537

(1) The book value of U.S. direct investors' equity in, and net outstanding loans to, their foreign affiliates. A foreign affiliate is a foreign business enterprise in which a single U.S. investor owns at least 10% of the voting securities or the equivalent. (2) Total includes countries not shown. NA = not available.

Gold Reserves of Central Banks and Governments

Source: IMF, *International Financial Statistics;* million fine troy ounces

Year end	All countries[1]	United States	Canada	Japan	Belgium	France	Germany	Italy	Netherlands	Switzerland	United Kingdom
1975	1,018.71	274.71	21.95	21.11	42.17	100.93	117.61	82.48	54.33	83.20	21.03
1976	1,014.23	274.68	21.62	21.11	42.17	101.02	117.61	82.48	54.33	83.28	21.03
1977	1,029.19	277.55	22.01	21.62	42.45	101.67	118.30	82.91	54.63	83.28	22.23
1978	1,036.82	276.41	22.13	23.97	42.59	101.99	118.64	83.12	54.78	83.28	22.83
1979	944.44	264.60	22.18	24.23	34.21	81.92	95.25	66.71	43.97	83.28	18.25
1980	952.99	264.32	20.98	24.23	34.18	81.85	95.18	66.67	43.94	83.28	18.84
1981	953.72	264.11	20.46	24.23	34.18	81.85	95.18	66.67	43.94	83.28	19.03
1982	949.16	264.03	20.26	24.23	34.18	81.85	95.18	66.67	43.94	83.28	19.01
1983	947.84	263.39	20.17	24.23	34.18	81.85	95.18	66.67	43.94	83.28	19.01
1984	946.79	262.79	20.14	24.23	34.18	81.85	95.18	66.67	43.94	83.28	19.03
1985	949.39	262.65	20.11	24.33	34.18	81.85	95.18	66.67	43.94	83.28	19.03
1986	949.11	262.04	19.72	24.23	34.18	81.85	95.18	66.67	43.94	83.28	19.01
1987	944.49	262.38	18.52	24.23	33.63	81.85	95.18	66.67	43.94	83.28	19.01
1988	944.92	261.87	17.14	24.23	33.67	81.85	95.18	66.67	43.94	83.28	19.00
1989	938.95	261.93	16.10	24.23	30.23	81.85	95.18	66.67	43.94	83.28	18.99
1990	940.29	261.91	14.76	24.23	30.23	81.85	95.18	66.67	43.94	83.28	18.94
1991	939.58	261.91	12.96	24.23	30.23	81.85	95.18	66.67	43.94	83.28	18.89
1992	930.30	261.91	9.94	24.23	25.04	81.85	95.18	66.67	43.94	83.28	18.61
1993	911.77	261.79	6.05	24.23	25.04	81.85	95.18	66.67	33.66	83.28	18.45

(1) Covers IMF members with reported gold holdings. For countries not listed above, see *International Financial Statistics*, a monthly publication of the International Monetary Fund.

Trade-Weighted Index of Foreign Currency Value of the Dollar

Source: Office of Foreign Exchange Operations, U.S. Dept. of the Treasury

These indices are presented to provide measures of the general foreign exchange value of the dollar that are broader than those provided by single exchange rate levels. They do not purport to represent a guide to measuring the impact of exchange rate levels on U.S. international transactions. The indices are computed as geometric averages of individual currency levels with weights derived from the share of each country's trade with the U.S. during 1982-83.

End of period (Dec. 1980 = 100)	Index of industrial country currencies[1]	End of period (Dec. 1980 = 100)	Index of industrial country currencies[1]	End of period (Dec. 1980 = 100)	Index of industrial country currencies[1]
1984	140.8	1990	94.4	Feb.	102.0
1985	127.8	1991	93.7	Mar.	101.8
1986	114.4	1992	101.1	Apr.	101.4
1987	97.8	1993	103.3	May	101.5
1988	98.4	1994		June	99.6
1989	100.0	Jan.	102.8	July	99.5

(1) Each index covers (a) 22 currencies of countries represented in the Organization for Economic Cooperation and Development (OECD): Australia, Austria, Belgium-Luxembourg, Canada, Denmark, Finland, France, Germany, Greece, Iceland, Ireland, Italy, Japan, the Netherlands, New Zealand, Norway, Portugal, Spain, Sweden, Switzerland, Turkey, and the United Kingdom; and (b) currencies of four major trading economies outside the OECD: Hong Kong, Korea, Singapore, and Taiwan. Exchange rates are drawn from the International Monetary Fund's "International Financial Statistics" when available.

Industrial Production Indexes,[1] by Industry Groups

Source: Bureau of Economic Analysis, U.S. Dept. of Commerce

Industry Groups	1991	1992	1993
Mining	**100.4**	**97.6**	**97.3**
Metal mining	156.7	161.8	167.6
Coal	109.3	105.5	103.8
Oil and gas extraction	96.0	92.6	92.2
Crude oil	89.1	85.7	....
Natural gas	107.0	106.7	....
Stone and earth minerals	94.2	93.8	93.8
Utilities	**111.9**	**111.9**	**116.2**
Electric	112.7	111.6	115.9
Gas	109.0	112.9	117.2
Manufacturing	**103.7**	**106.9**	**111.7**
Durable	103.9	108.2	114.3
Lumber and products	90.5	96.4	100.6
Furniture and fixtures	94.0	98.9	103.3
Clay, glass, and stone products	92.6	95.9	98.7
Primary metals	98.5	101.2	106.5
Iron and steel	100.7	104.8	111.6
Nonferrous	95.5	96.2	99.5
Fabricated metal products	95.0	96.8	99.5
Machinery and computer equipment	113.8	124.9	144.1
Electrical machinery	112.8	120.0	127.5
Transportation equipment	102.0	102.7	104.2
Motor vehicles and parts	94.8	105.0	120.7
Instruments	105.4	104.3	104.0
Nondurable	103.5	105.4	108.7
Foods	105.3	106.0	108.6
Tobacco products	96.7	99.6	91.0
Textile mill products	96.9	104.7	107.8
Apparel products	91.8	92.6	93.1
Paper and products	106.2	108.2	112.3
Printing and publishing	96.8	95.0	101.3
Chemicals and products	111.3	115.0	117.8
Petroleum products	101.6	102.0	104.9
Rubber and plastics products	104.5	109.7	115.9
Leather and products	87.9	92.5	85.0

(1) 1987 = 100.

Average Yields of Long-Term Treasury, Corporate, and Municipal Bonds

Source: Office of Market Finance, U.S. Dept. of the Treasury

Period	Treasury 30-Year Bonds	New Aa Corporate Bonds[1]	New Aa Municipal Bonds[2]
1982			
June	13.92	15.96	12.14
Dec.	10.54	12.15	9.84
1983			
June	10.93	11.90	9.08
Dec.	11.88	12.87	9.77
1984			
June	13.44	14.49	10.44
Dec.	11.52	12.47	9.65
1985			
June	10.45	11.33	8.46
Dec.	9.54	10.42	8.44
1986			
June	7.57	9.39	7.75
Dec.	7.37	8.87	6.70
1987			
June	8.57	9.64	7.69
Dec.	9.12	10.22	7.83
1988			
June	9.00	10.08	7.67
Dec.	9.01	10.05	7.40
1989			
June	8.27	9.24	6.94
Dec.	7.90	9.23	6.76
1990			
June	8.46	9.69	6.98
Dec.	8.24	9.55	6.85
1991			
June	8.47	9.37	6.90
Dec.	7.70	8.55	6.43
1992			
Jan.	7.58	8.36	6.29
Apr.	7.96	8.59	6.54
Sept.	7.34	7.99	6.05
Dec.	7.44	8.12	6.02
1993			
Jan.	7.34	7.91	6.05
Feb.	7.09	7.73	5.74
Mar.	6.82	7.39	5.54
Apr.	6.85	7.48	5.64
May	6.92	7.52	5.61
June	6.81	7.48	5.54
July	6.63	7.35	5.40
Aug.	6.32	7.04	5.50
Sept.	6.00	6.88	5.44
Oct.	5.94	6.88	5.23
Nov.	6.21	7.17	5.19
Dec.	6.25	7.22	5.27
1994			
Jan.	6.29	7.16	5.19
Feb.	6.49	7.27	5.16
Mar.	6.91	7.64	5.47

(1) Treasury series based on 3-week moving average of reoffering yields of new corporate bonds rated Aa by Moody's Investors Service with an original maturity of at least 20 years. (2) Index of new reoffering yields on 20-year general obligations rated Aa by Moody's Investors Service. Source: U.S. Treasury, 1982-1990; Moody's, 1991-1994.

Performance of Mutual Funds by Type

Source: Morningstar Inc.

Fund type	Fund objective	1-Yr Total Return No.	1-Yr Total Return Avg.	5-Yr Total Return No.	5-Yr Total Return Avg.
Stock	Aggressive growth	43	17.81	37	17.81
	Equity income	53	13.68	32	12.32
	Financial	11	18.24	8	21.34
	Growth	354	12.14	212	15.15
	Growth and income	203	11.62	128	13.41
	Health care	11	1.22	9	19.35
	Natural resource	14	20.46	11	9.70
	Other specialized	16	21.31	8	19.49
	Precious metals	21	92.44	19	7.51
	Small company	124	17.21	72	17.15
	Technology	20	24.90	16	18.98
	Utility industry	38	16.08	18	14.29
International stock	Worldwide	52	32.29	26	10.75
	Pacific area	25	57.31	10	6.80
	European	17	29.28	8	8.22
	Other foreign	94	42.14	31	11.08
Hybrid	Asset allocation	51	15.48	30	11.54
	Balanced	87	10.96	40	12.61
	Convertible bond	17	16.24	14	13.81
	Income	33	12.74	19	11.95
Bond	Adjustable rate mortgage	44	3.78	5	7.62
	California municipal	73	12.28	43	9.69
	General corporate	147	10.69	56	10.71
	General government	155	7.89	93	9.79
	High-quality corporate	94	8.43	45	9.94
	High-yield bond	69	19.47	56	11.37
	Mortgage	70	6.85	41	9.87
	National municipal	212	11.27	146	9.31
	New York municipal	60	12.18	36	9.81
	Other state municipal	268	12.12	115	9.46
	Treasury bond	40	11.39	24	11.12
International bond	World bond	56	17.26	19	10.31

Dow Jones Industrial Average Since 1961

High			Year	Low		
Dec.	13	734.91	**1961**	Jan.	3	610.25
Jan.	3	726.01	**1962**	June	26	535.76
Dec.	18	767.21	**1963**	Jan.	2	646.79
Nov.	18	891.71	**1964**	Jan.	2	766.08
Dec.	31	969.26	**1965**	June	28	840.59
Feb.	9	995.15	**1966**	Oct.	7	744.32
Sept.	25	943.08	**1967**	Jan.	3	786.41
Dec.	3	985.21	**1968**	Mar.	21	825.13
May	14	968.85	**1969**	Dec.	17	769.93
Dec.	29	842.00	**1970**	May	6	631.16
Apr.	28	950.82	**1971**	Nov.	23	797.97
Dec.	11	1036.27	**1972**	Jan.	26	889.15
Jan.	11	1051.70	**1973**	Dec.	5	788.31
Mar.	13	891.66	**1974**	Dec.	6	577.60
July	15	881.81	**1975**	Jan.	2	632.04
Sept.	21	1014.79	**1976**	Jan.	2	858.71
Jan.	3	999.75	**1977**	Nov.	2	800.85
Sept.	8	907.74	**1978**	Feb.	28	742.12
Oct.	5	897.61	**1979**	Nov.	7	796.67
Nov.	20	1000.17	**1980**	Apr.	21	759.13
Apr.	27	1024.05	**1981**	Sept.	25	824.01
Dec.	27	1070.55	**1982**	Aug.	12	776.92
Nov.	29	1287.20	**1983**	Jan.	3	1027.04
Jan.	6	1286.64	**1984**	July	24	1086.57
Dec.	16	1553.10	**1985**	Jan.	4	1184.96
Dec.	2	1955.57	**1986**	Jan.	22	1502.29
Aug.	25	2722.42	**1987**	Oct.	19	1738.74
Oct.	21	2183.50	**1988**	Jan.	20	1879.14
Oct.	9	2791.41	**1989**	Jan.	3	2144.64
July	16	2999.75	**1990**	Oct.	11	2365.10
Dec.	31	3168.83	**1991**	Jan.	9	2470.30
June	1	3413.21	**1992**	Oct.	9	3136.58
Dec.	29	3794.33	**1993**	Jan.	20	3241.95
Jan.	31	3978.36	**1994***	Apr.	4	3593.35

*As of Oct. 1

Components of Dow Jones Industrial Average

Allied-Signal
Aluminum Co. of Amer. (Alcoa)
American Express
AT&T
Bethlehem Steel
Boeing
Caterpillar
Chevron
Coca-Cola
Disney
DuPont
Eastman Kodak
Exxon
General Electric
General Motors
Goodyear
IBM
International Paper
McDonald's
Merck
Minn. Mining & Manuf.
Morgan (J.P.)
Philip Morris
Procter & Gamble
Sears
Texaco
Union Carbide
United Technologies
Westinghouse
Woolworth

Components of Dow Jones Transportation Average

AMR Corp.
Airborne Freight
Alaska Air
American President
Burlington Northern
CSX
Carolina Freight
Consolidated Freightways
Consolidated Rail
Delta Air Lines
Federal Express
Norfolk Southern
Roadway Services
Ryder System
Santa Fe Pacific
Southwest Air Lines
UAL
Union Pacific
USAir Group
XTRA Corp

Components of Dow Jones Utility Average

American Electric Power
Centerior Energy
Consolidated Edison
Consolidated Natural Gas
Detroit Edison
Houston Industries
Niagara Mohawk Power
NorAm Energy
Pacific Gas & Electric
Panhandle Eastern
Peoples Energy
Philadelphia Electric
Public Service Enterprises
SCE
Unicom

Milestones of the Dow Jones Industrial Average

First close over...	
100	Jan. 12, 1906
500	March 12, 1956
1,000	Nov. 14, 1972
1,500	Dec. 11, 1985
2,000	Jan. 8, 1987
2,500	July 17, 1987
3,000	April 17, 1991
3,500	May 19, 1993
3,600	Aug. 18, 1993
3,700	Nov. 16, 1993
3,800	Jan. 6, 1994
3,900	Jan. 21, 1994

Most Active Common Stocks in 1993

New York Exchange

	Volume (millions of shares)
Merck	728.6
RJR Nabisco	685.3
Philip Morris	642.9
Wal-Mart Stores	600.4
Teléfonos de Mexico	584.1
General Motors	578.6
I.B.M.	566.9
Chrysler	542.4
Citicorp	523.9
Glaxo Holdings	480.5
A.T.&T.	469.6
Ford Motor	379.0
Home Depot	378.2
Eastman Kodak	377.9
Bristol-Myers Squibb	375.5

American Exchange

	Volume (millions of shares)
Echo Bay Mines	265.9
Royal Oak Mines	234.6
Energy Services	181.4
Amdahl	83.7
Cheyenne Software	69.5
Atari	66.8
Interdigital Comm.	60.3
Hasbro	59.9
Nabors Industries	58.2
NTN Communications	57.3
Pegasus Gold	57.3
New York Times "A"	53.0
S. & P. units-"Spiders"	51.7
Ivax	50.3
Weaterhford Int'l.	48.8

NASDAQ

	Volume (millions of shares)
Intel	894.1
Novell	735.8
Tele-Comm. "A"	620.3
Synoptics Comm.	571.0
Cisco Systems	554.9
MCI Communications	549.9
Microsoft	503.5
Apple Computer	494.1
Amgen	459.6
Oracle Systems	448.9
Spectrum Info. Tech.	428.3
Sun Microsystems	403.5
Dell Computer	360.5
Newbridge Networks	345.1
Adobe Systems	341.0

U.S. Holdings of Foreign Stocks

Source: Bureau of Economic Analysis, U.S. Dept. Of Commerce

(billions of dollars)

	1992	1993
Total holdings	**178.1**	**297.7**
Western Europe	90.9	123.4
Of which: United Kingdom	29.0	41.9
Germany	14.5	23.0
Netherlands	11.6	18.0
France	11.5	16.3
Canada	14.8	23.1
Japan	28.9	42.7
Latin America	15.2	35.8
Other countries	28.3	72.7

Selected Personal Consumption Expenditures in the U.S.

Source: Bureau of Economic Analysis, U.S. Dept. of Commerce

(billions of dollars)

	1987	1988	1989	1990	1991	1992	1993
Personal consumption expenditures	**$3,009.4**	**$3,296.1**	**$3.523.1**	**$3,761.2**	**$3,906.4**	**$4,139.9**	**4,378.2**
Food & Tobacco	**566.4**	**569.8**	**605.6**	**648.2**	**666.8**	**684.5**	**700.3**
Food purchased for off-premise consumption	353.7	351.7	373.7	400.2	411.1	418.0	422.2
Purchased meals and beverages	165.5	171.7	180.6	193.1	198.5	203.5	215.2
Tobacco products	35.6	36.2	40.5	43.4	45.4	50.9	50.5
Clothing, accessories, jewelry	**222.3**	**231.8**	**248.7**	**259.3**	**264.3**	**282.4**	**293.9**
Shoes	25.9	27.4	30.1	31.4	31.3	32.3	33.0
Clothing and accessories less shoes	152.5	158.9	170.1	175.7	181.6	195.7	202.1
Jewelry and watches	24.7	28.8	29.7	31.3	31.6	34.0	36.2
Personal care	**44.4**	**51.4**	**55.8**	**59.2**	**60.9**	**63.2**	**65.8**
Toilet articles, preparations	26.3	31.8	34.1	36.8	38.2	39.3	41.1
Barbershops, beauty parlors, health clubs	18.2	19.6	21.6	22.4	22.6	23.9	24.6
Housing	**468.9**	**484.2**	**514.4**	**547.5**	**574.4**	**600.0**	**629.0**
Owner-occupied nonfarm dwellings space rent	316.9	334.1	355.8	379.5	399.1	417.8	438.3
Tenant-occupied nonfarm dwellings rent	123.6	125.3	132.6	141.1	147.7	153.8	160.2
Rental value of farm dwellings	10.3	4.9	5.0	5.2	5.3	5.3	5.6
Household operation	**363.3**	**398.9**	**422.6**	**437.3**	**452.7**	**475.2**	**508.2**
Furniture, incl. bedding	31.8	34.0	36.9	36.7	36.8	40.0	42.5
Kitchen, other household appliances	26.7	24.1	25.7	26.4	27.1	29.2	31.3
China, glassware, tableware, utensils	15.3	16.4	17.9	18.7	19.4	21.0	22.1
Other durable house furnishings	33.5	37.7	40.2	42.0	41.9	45.2	47.2
Semidurable house furnishings	16.0	19.4	20.4	21.2	21.9	23.6	25.2
Household utilities	125.8	127.3	134.1	136.7	145.3	149.9	159.3
Telephone, telegraph	44.1	50.2	51.7	53.8	56.2	58.7	68.2
Medical care	**399.0**	**487.7**	**536.4**	**597.8**	**651.7**	**704.6**	**760.5**
Drug preparations, sundries	32.3	50.8	55.0	60.6	64.4	65.9	69.0
Physicians	94.0	110.6	121.6	133.8	144.0	153.1	165.6
Dentists	25.0	27.9	30.0	31.6	32.9	36.4	38.6
Hospitals and nursing homes	166.3	190.9	209.5	231.3	255.3	279.6	346.8
Health insurance	25.3	26.4	31.2	36.6	40.0	45.9	46.2
Personal business	**215.4**	**255.0**	**272.2**	**296.0**	**323.4**	**356.0**	**373.3**
Brokerage charges, investment counseling	20.5	19.3	21.6	22.0	24.3	28.5	34.8
Bank service charges, trust services, safe deposit box	14.6	19.8	22.0	23.7	25.2	27.6	31.2
Legal services	35.0	41.7	45.5	49.2	49.9	54.0	56.1
Funeral, burial expenses	7.0	7.8	7.9	8.5	9.0	9.6	10.4
Transportation	**379.7**	**413.2**	**437.3**	**453.9**	**434.6**	**463.1**	**504.2**
User-operated transportation	346.3	376.9	399.6	414.0	395.5	423.9	461.9
New autos	93.5	101.0	99.9	96.6	79.5	87.3	93.4
Used autos	38.5	30.5	32.5	33.1	36.7	39.5	45.9
Repair, greasing, washing, parking, storage, rental, leasing	55.9	73.5	79.1	82.6	82.4	89.5	98.4
Gasoline and oil	75.3	86.9	96.2	108.4	102.9	103.4	105.6
Tolls	1.9	1.8	2.1	2.0	2.0	2.1	2.5
Insurance premiums less claims paid	15.4	16.8	16.8	18.1	22.7	24.6	27.5
Purchased local transportation	8.2	8.3	8.1	8.9	9.1	9.2	9.3
Mass transit systems	4.0	5.4	5.3	5.7	5.7	5.9	5.9
Taxicab	3.5	2.9	2.8	3.2	3.4	3.3	3.4
Purchased intercity transportation	25.5	28.0	29.5	30.9	30.0	30.0	33.0
Railway (excl. commutation)	0.7	0.6	0.7	0.7	0.7	0.7	0.7
Bus	1.4	2.2	1.7	1.4	1.5	1.5	1.3
Airline	20.8	23.0	24.7	26.4	25.6	25.7	28.5
Recreation	**223.2**	**246.8**	**266.0**	**285.7**	**299.4**	**318.8**	**339.9**
Books, maps	9.5	14.6	15.8	17.5	18.3	20.2	20.8
Magazines, newspapers, sheet music	15.4	20.8	22.0	23.8	24.7	25.4	26.8
Nondurable toys and sport supplies	26.2	27.5	30.0	32.1	33.5	35.2	37.4
Wheel goods, durable toys, sports equipment, boats, pleasure aircraft	33.2	30.0	31.0	31.3	31.4	34.0	33.0
Video & audio prods., computers, musical instruments	—	44.5	47.3	50.4	55.4	59.1	65.7
Flowers, seeds, potted plants	7.0	9.3	10.1	10.3	10.4	11.0	12.4
Admissions to specified spectator amusements	11.3	11.1	12.1	14.0	14.9	16.1	16.8
Motion picture theaters	4.2	3.6	3.9	4.7	5.0	5.5	5.6
Legitimate theater, opera	4.0	3.6	3.9	4.5	4.7	5.1	5.5
Spectator sports	3.0	3.9	4.3	4.9	5.2	5.5	5.7
Clubs, fraternal organizations	5.5	7.6	8.0	8.4	8.6	9.0	9.5
Commercial participant amusements	17.1	19.1	20.5	23.1	23.8	25.7	28.0
Education & Research	**50.9**	**71.6**	**79.4**	**86.2**	**91.8**	**98.2**	**105.5**
Higher education	17.7	36.7	40.3	44.0	47.3	50.8	56.1
Nursery, elementary and secondary schools	15.5	17.1	19.2	19.8	20.6	21.6	22.1
Religious and welfare activities	**68.1**	**86.0**	**92.7**	**101.6**	**105.7**	**116.2**	**123.0**

Minerals

Source: Bureau of Mines, U.S. Dept. of the Interior; as of mid-1994

Aluminum: the second most abundant metallic element in the earth's crust. Bauxite is the main source of aluminum; convert to aluminum equivalent by multiplying by 0.232. Guinea and Australia have 49% of the world's reserves. Aluminum is used in the U.S. principally in packaging (35%), transportation (25%), and building (20%).

Chromium: some two-thirds of the world's production of chromite, the chief source of chromium, is in Kazakhstan and South Africa. The chemical and metallurgical industries use about 90% of the chromite consumed in the world.

Cobalt: used in superalloys for jet engines, chemicals (paint dryers, catalysts, magnetic coatings), permanent magnets, and cemented carbides for cutting tools. Principal cobalt-producing countries include Zaire, Zambia, and Russia. The U.S. uses about one-third of total world consumption. Although its resources are relatively large, the U.S. has not produced cobalt since 1971; most cobalt resources are low grade, and production from these deposits is not economically feasible.

Columbium: used mostly as an additive in steelmaking and in superalloys. Brazil and Canada are the world's leading producers. There is no U.S. columbium mining industry.

Copper: main uses of copper in the U.S. are in building construction (42%), electrical and electronic products (24%), industrial machinery and equipment (13%), transportation (11%), and consumer and general products (10%). The leading producer is Chile, followed by the U.S., Canada, Russia, Zambia, Australia, Poland, and China. Principal mining states are Arizona, New Mexico, and Utah.

Gold: used in the U.S. in jewelry and the arts (71%), the electronics and other industries (22%), and dentistry (7%). South Africa has about half of the world's resources; significant quantities are also present in the U.S., Canada, the former USSR, and Brazil. Gold mining in the U.S. takes place in nearly all of the western states and Alaska.

Iron ore: the source of primary iron for the world's iron and steel industries. Major iron ore producers include the former USSR, Brazil, Australia, and China.

Lead: the U.S., Australia, China, Peru, and Canada are the world's largest producers of lead. Transportation accounts for the major end use in the U.S., with 83% used in batteries, bearings, casting metals, and solders. Other uses include emergency power supply batteries, construction sheeting, sporting ammunition, and power cable coverings. The U.S. produces and consumes more than 20% of the world's lead metal.

Manganese: essential to iron and steel production. The U.S., Japan, and Western Europe have all nearly exhausted their economically minable manganese resources. South Africa and the former USSR have over 80% of the world's reserves.

Nickel: vital to the stainless steel industry and played a key role in the development of the chemical and aerospace industries. Leading producers include Russia, Canada, Australia, New Caledonia, and Indonesia.

Platinum-Group Metals: the platinum group consists of 6 closely related metals: platinum, palladium, rhodium, ruthenium, iridium, and osmium. They commonly occur together in nature and are among the scarcest of the metallic elements. They are consumed in the U.S. by the following industries: automotive, electrical and electronic, chemical, and dental and medical. The automotive, chemical, and petroleum-refining industries use platinum-group metals mainly as catalysts. The former USSR and South Africa have nearly all the world's reserves.

Silver: used in the following U.S. industries: photography; electrical and electronic products; sterlingware, electroplated ware, and jewelry. Silver is mined in more than 60 countries. Nevada produces over 43% of U.S. silver, Idaho 12%.

Tantalum: a refractory metal with unique electrical, chemical, and physical properties; it is used in the U.S. mostly to produce electronic components, mainly tantalum capacitors. Australia, Brazil, Canada, and Thailand are the leading producers. There is no U.S. tantalum mining industry.

Titanium: a metal that is mostly used in jet engines, airframes, and space and missile applications. It is produced in Ukraine, Russia, Kazakhstan, Japan, the western and central U.S., the United Kingdom, and China.

Vanadium: used as an alloying element in steel, as an alloying agent in aerospace titanium alloys, and as a catalyst in the production of sulfuric acid and maleic anhydride. The former USSR and South Africa are the world's largest producers.

Zinc: used as a protective coating on steel, as diecastings, as an alloying metal with copper to make brass, and as a component of chemical compounds in rubber and paints. It is mined in over 50 countries, with Canada the leading producer, followed by Australia, China, the former USSR, Peru, and the U.S. In the U.S., mine production comes mostly from Alaska, Tennessee, New York, and Missouri.

World Mineral Reserve Base

Source: Bureau of Mines, U.S. Dept. of the Interior; as of mid-1994

Mineral	Reserve Base[1]
Aluminum	28,000 mil metric tons[2]
Chromium	6,700 mil metric tons
Cobalt	8.8 mil metric tons
Columbium	4,200 mil kilograms
Copper	520 mil metric tons
Gold	57,000 metric tons
Iron ore	230,000 mil metric tons[3]
Lead	130 mil metric tons
Manganese	4,800 mil metric tons
Nickel	110 mil metric tons
Platinum-Group Metals	66 mil kilograms
Silver	420,000 metric tons
Tantalum	35 mil kilograms
Titanium	595 mil metric tons[4]
Vanadium	27 mil metric tons
Zinc	330 mil. metric tons

(1) Includes demonstrated resources that are currently economic (reserves) or marginally economic (marginal reserves) and some of those that are currently subeconomic. (2) Bauxite. (3) Crude ore. (4) Titanium dioxide (TiO_2) content.

U.S. Nonfuel Mineral Production—10 Leading States in 1993

Source: Bureau of Mines, U.S. Dept. of the Interior

Rank/State	Value (millions)	Percent of U.S. total	Principal minerals
1. Arizona	$2,742	8.69	Copper, sand & gravel (construction), cement, molybdenum
2. Nevada	2,734	8.67	Gold, sand & gravel (construction), silver, diatomite
3. California	2,282	7.24	Sand & gravel (construction), cement, gold, boron minerals
4. Georgia	1,691	5.36	Clays (kaolin), stone (crushed), clays (Fuller's earth), cement
5. Michigan	1,408	4.46	Iron ore, cement, sand & gravel (construction), stone (crushed)
6. Texas	1,394	4.42	Cement, stone (crushed), magnesium metal, sand & gravel (construction)
7. Utah	1,350	4.28	Copper, gold, magnesium metal, cement
8. Minnesota	1,323	4.19	Iron ore, sand & gravel (construction), stone (crushed), sand & gravel (industrial)
9. Florida	1,297	4.11	Phosphate rock, stone (crushed), cement, sand & gravel (construction)
10. Pennsylvania	893	2.83	Stone (crushed), cement, lime, sand & gravel (construction)

U.S. Nonfuel Mineral Production

Source: Bureau of Mines, U.S. Dept. of the Interior

Production as measured by mine shipments, sales, or marketable production (including consumption by producers)

Mineral	Unit	1988	1989	1990	1991[1]	1992[1]	1993[1]
Antimony (ore and concentrate)		W	W	W	W	W	W
Bauxite	thousand metric tons, dried equivalent	588	W	W	W	W	W
Beryllium (metal equivalent)	metric tons	212	184	182	174	193	198
Copper (recoverable content of ores, etc.)	thousand metric tons	1,417	1,498	1,588	1,631	1,765	1,801
Gold (recoverable content of ores, etc.)	metric tons	200.9	265.7	294.2	294.1	330.2	331
Iron ore, usable (includes byproduct material)	million metric tons	57.5	59.0	56.4	56.8	55.6	55.7
Lead (in concentrate)	thousand metric tons	394	420	495	477	407	362
Magnesium metal (primary)	thousand metric tons	142	152	139	131	137	132
Molybdenum (content of ore and concentrate)	metric tons	43,051	63,105	61,611	53,364	49,725	36,803
Nickel (content of ore and concentrate)	metric tons	—	—	330	5,523	6,671	2,464
Silver (recoverable content of ores, etc.)	metric tons	1,661	2,008	2,121	1,855	1,804	1,645
Tungsten (content of ore and concentrate)	metric tons	W	W	W	W	W	W
Zinc (recoverable content of ores, etc.)	thousand metric tons	244	276	515	518	523	488
Asbestos	thousand metric tons	18	17	W	20	16	14
Barite	thousand metric tons	404	290	430	448	326	315
Boron minerals	thousand metric tons	578	562	608	626	554	574
Bromine	million kilograms	163	175	177	170	171	177
Cement (portland, masonry, etc.)	thousand short tons	76,867	77,189	77,111	73,585	77,354	83,000[E]
Clays	thousand metric tons	44,515	42,254	42,904	41,017	40,237	41,074
Diatomite	thousand metric tons	629	617	631	610	595	599
Feldspar	thousand metric tons	650	655	630	580	725	770
Fluorspar	thousand metric tons	64	66	64	58	51	60
Garnet (industrial)	metric tons	42,506	42,605	47,009	50,860	54,139	43,995
Gem stones	million dollars	43.5	42.9	52.9	84.4	52.1	75.6
Gypsum	thousand short tons	16,390	17,624	16,406	15,456	16,269	16,900[E]
Helium (extracted from natural gas)	million cubic meters	63.3	66.3	64.6	86.4	92.0	96.7[E]
Helium (Grade A)	million cubic meters	71.4	79.9	84.8	88.1	94.4	93.1[E]
Iodine	thousand kilograms	1,015	1,508	1,973	1,999	1,995	1,935
Lime	thousand metric tons	15,469	15,560	15,832	15,667	16,199	16,932
Mica (scrap & flake)	thousand metric tons	130	119	109	103	85	88
Peat	thousand metric tons	766	690	692	632	599	616
Perlite (sold and used by producers)	thousand metric tons	523	545	576	514	541	569
Phosphate rock (marketable product)	thousand metric tons	45,389	49,817	46,343	48,096	46,965	35,494
Pumice and pumicite	thousand metric tons	353	424	443	401	481	469
Salt	thousand metric tons	35,326	35,250	36,916	35,902	34,784	38,665
Sand and gravel (construction)	thousand short tons	923,400	897,300[E]	913,500	780,300[E]	919,300	957,600
Sand and gravel (industrial)	thousand metric tons	25,837	26,494	25,769	23,224	25,195	26,220
Soda ash (sodium carbonate)	thousand metric tons	8,738	8,995	9,156	9,005	9,379	8,959
Sodium sulfate (natural)	thousand metric tons	361	340	349	354	337	322
Stone (crushed)	million short tons	1,248[E]	1,213	1,222[E]	1,103	1,162	1,230
Stone (dimension)[1]	thousand short tons	1,159[E]	1,238	1,232	1,275	1,169	1,362
Sulfur	thousand metric tons	10,746	11,592	11,560	10,820	10,663	10,959
Talc and pyrophyllite	thousand metric tons	1,234	1,253	1,267	1,037*	997*	968*
Vermiculite	thousand metric tons	276	249	209[E]	180	190	190

(E) Estimated. (W) Withheld to avoid disclosing company proprietary data. (—) No production. *Talc only. (1) 1991, 1992, and 1993 production includes Puerto Rico.

U.S. Reliance on Foreign Supplies of Minerals

Source: Bureau of Mines, U.S. Dept. of the Interior

Mineral	Percent imported in 1993	Major sources (1989-93)	Major uses
Bauxite and alumina	100%	Australia, Jamaica, Guinea, Brazil, Guyana	Aluminum production, abrasives, refractories
Columbium	100	Brazil, Canada, Germany	Steelmaking and aerospace alloys
Graphite	100	Mexico, China, Canada, Madagascar, Brazil	Refractories, brake linings, packings
Manganese	100	South Africa, France, Australia, Brazil	Steelmaking
Mica (sheet)	100	India, Belgium, Brazil, China	Electronic and electrical equipment
Strontium (celestite)	100	Mexico	Television picture tubes, pyrotechnics
Diamonds (industrial)	98	Ireland, Britain, Zaire, South Africa	Machinery for grinding and cutting
Fluorspar	89	Mexico, China, South Africa, Canada, Morocco	Hydrofluoric acid production, steelmaking
Platinum group	88	South Africa, Britain, former USSR	Catalytic converters for autos, electrical and electronic equipment
Tantalum	86	Germany, Australia, Canada, Brazil	Electronic components
Tungsten	84	China, Bolivia, Peru, Germany	Machinery, lamps and lighting
Chromium	82	South Africa, Turkey, Zimbabwe, Yugoslavia	Ferroalloys, chemicals, refractories
Tin	81	Brazil, Bolivia, China, Indonesia, Malaysia	Cans, electrical, construction
Cobalt	75	Zambia, Zaire, Canada, Norway	Aerospace alloys, catalysts, paint dryers, magnetic alloys
Potash	71	Canada, Israel, former USSR, Germany	Fertilizer
Cadmium	66	Canada, Mexico, Australia, France	Batteries, plating and coating of metals, pigments
Nickel	64	Canada, Norway, Australia, Dominican Rep.	Stainless steel and other alloys
Barite	58	China, India, Mexico	Oil and gas well drilling fluids
Silver	NA	Mexico, Canada, Britain, Peru	Photography, electrical and electronic products

NA = not available.

U.S. Copper, Lead, and Zinc Production, 1950-92

Source: Bureau of Mines, U.S. Dept. of the Interior

Year	Copper		Lead		Zinc	
	Quantity (metric tons)	Value ($1,000)	Quantity (metric tons)	Value ($1,000)	Quantity (metric tons)	Value ($1,000)
1950	827	379,122	390,839	113,078	565,516	167,000
1960	1,037	733,706	223,774	57,722	395,013	112,365
1965	1,226	957,028	273,196	93,959	554,429	178,284
1970	1,560	1,984,484	518,698	178,609	484,560	163,650
1975	1,282	1,814,763	563,783	267,230	425,792	366,097
1980	1,181	2,666,931	550,366	515,189	317,103	261,671
1985	1,105	1,631,000	413,955	174,008	226,545	201,607
1987	1,244	2,262,000	311,381	246,720	216,281	200,529
1988	1,417	3,764,000	384,983	315,222	244,314	324,249
1989	1,497	4,323,000	410,915	356,476	275,883	499,103
1990	1,586	4,310,000	483,704	490,750	515,355	847,485
1991	1,631	3,931,000	465,931	343,907	517,804	602,426
1992	1,705	4,180,000	397,923	307,922	523,430	673,800

U.S. Pig Iron and Raw Steel Output, 1940-93

Source: American Iron and Steel Institute (net tons)

Year	Total pig iron	Raw steel
1940	46,071,666	66,982,686
1945	53,223,169	79,701,648
1950	64,586,907	96,836,075
1960	66,480,648	99,281,601
1965	88,184,901	131,461,601
1970	91,435,000	131,514,000
1975	101,208,000	116,642,000
1980	68,721,000	111,835,000
1985	50,446,000	88,259,000
1986	43,952,000	81,606,000
1987	48,410,000	89,151,000
1988	55,745,000	99,924,000
1989	55,873,000	97,943,000
1990	54,750,000	98,906,000
1991	48,637,000	87,896,000
1992	52,224,000	92,949,000
1993	53,082,000	97,877,000

Steel figures include only that portion of the capacity and production of steel for castings used by foundries that were operated by companies producing steel ingots.

World Gold Production, 1972-92

Source: Bureau of Mines, U.S. Dept. of the Interior
(troy ounces)

		Africa			North and South America				Other			
Year	World prod.	South Africa	Ghana	Zaire[r]	United States	Canada	Mexico	Colombia	Australia	China	Philippines	USSR
1972	44,843,374	29,245,273	724,051	80,377	1,449,943	2,078,567	146,061	188,137	754,866	NA	606,730	NA
1975	38,476,371	22,937,820	523,889	115,743	1,052,252	1,653,611	144,710	308,864	526,821	NA	502,577	NA
1977	38,906,145	22,501,886	480,884	96,452	1,100,347	1,733,609	212,709	257,070	624,270	NA	558,554	NA
1978	38,983,019	22,648,558	402,034	32,151	998,832	1,735,077	202,003	246,446	647,579	NA	586,531	NA
1979	38,768,978	22,617,179	362,000	73,947	964,390	1,644,265	190,364	269,369	596,910	NA	535,166	NA
1980	39,197,315	21,669,468	353,000	96,452	969,782	1,627,477	195,991	510,439	547,591	NA	753,452	8,425,000
1982	43,082,814	21,355,111	331,000	135,033	1,465,686	2,081,230	214,349	472,674	866,815	1,800,000	834,439	8,550,000
1984	46,929,444	21,860,933	287,000	321,507	2,084,615	2,682,786	270,998	730,670	1,295,963	1,900,000	827,149	8,650,000
1985	49,283,691	21,565,230	299,363	257,206	2,427,232	2,815,118	265,693	1,142,385	1,881,491	1,950,000	1,062,997	8,700,000
1986	51,534,056	20,513,665	287,127	257,206	3,739,015	3,364,700	250,615	1,285,878	2,413,842	2,100,000	1,296,400	8,850,000
1987	53,033,614	19,176,500	327,598	385,809	4,947,040	3,724,000	256,822	853,600	3,558,954	2,300,000	1,048,081	8,850,000
1988	60,308,973	19,965,611	355,620	401,884	6,459,534	4,334,338	292,508	932,822	5,046,059	2,507,758	980,019	8,925,046
1989	65,335,998	19,530,290	429,470	340,798	8,543,449	5,127,850	276,914	948,640	6,544,702	2,893,567	964,265	9,773,826
1990	68,632,896	19,454,414	541,419	299,002	9,458,395	5,381,166	268,073	943,689	7,849,186	3,215,074	790,619	9,709,524
1991	69,083,682	19,323,014	845,886	282,927	9,542,501	5,676,278	287,331	1,120,260	7,530,283	3,858,089	801,775	8,359,193
1992	72,269,724	19,737,341	997,670	257,206	10,581,581	5,081,393	321,507	1,189,578	7,716,178	4,501,104	771,618	8,101,987*

NA=not available. r=revised to reflect improved data. *USSR as constituted prior to Dec. 1991.

U.S. and World Silver Production, 1930-92

Source: Bureau of Mines, U.S. Dept. of the Interior
(metric tons)

Largest production of silver in the United States in 1915—2,332 metric tons.

Year	United States	World
1930 . . .	1,578	7,736
1935 . . .	1,428	6,865
1940 . . .	2,164	8,565
1945 . . .	904	5,039
1950 . . .	1,347	6,323
1955 . . .	1,134	6,967
1960 . . .	1,120	7,505
1965 . . .	1,238	8,007
1970 . . .	1,400	9,670
1975 . . .	1,087	9,428
1980 . . .	1,006	10,556
1985 . . .	1,227	13,051
1986 . . .	1,074	12,970
1987 . . .	1,241	14,019
1988 . . .	1,661	15,484
1989 . . .	2,008	16,041
1990 . . .	2,121	16,216
1991 . . .	1,855	15,692
1992 . . .	1,804	15,345

Aluminum Summary, 1980 to 1992

Source: Bureau of Mines, U.S. Dept. of the Interior

Item	Unit	1980	1985	1988	1989	1990	1991	1992
U.S. production.	1,000 metric ton. .	5,914	5,262	6,066	6,084	6,441	6,407	6,799
Primary aluminum	1,000 metric ton. .	4,654	3,500	3,944	4,030	4,048	4,121	4,042
Secondary aluminum[1]	1,000 metric ton. .	1,260	1,762	2,122	2,054	2,393	2,286	2,757
Primary aluminum value.	Bil. dol	7.3	6.3	9.5	7.8	6.6	5.4	5.1
Price (Primary alum.)[2]	Cents/lb	71.6	81.0	110.1	87.8	74.0	59.5	57.5
Imports for consumption[3]	1,000 metric ton. .	647	1,420	1,620	1,470	1,514	1,490	1,725
Exports[3]	1,000 metric ton. .	1,346	908	1,247	1,613	1,659	1,762	1,453
World production.	1,000 metric ton. .	15,383	15,398	18,495	19,104	19,292	19,528	19,219

(1) Recoverable metal content from purchased scrap, old and new. (2) Average prices for primary aluminum, quoted by *Metals Week.* (3) Crude and semicrude (including metal and alloys, plates, bars, etc., and scrap).

Economic and Financial Glossary

Acquisition: The purchase of one company by another.

Arbitrage: A form of hedged investment meant to capture slight differences in the prices of two related securities—for example, buying gold in London and selling it at a higher price in New York.

Balanced budget: A government budget is balanced when receipts are equal to current expenditure.

Balance of payments: The difference between all payments made to and from foreign countries over a set period of time. A *favorable* balance exists when more payments are coming in than going out; an *unfavorable* balance, when the reverse is true. Payments include gold, the cost of merchandise and services, interest and dividend payments, money spent by travelers, and repayment of principal on loans.

Balance of trade (trade gap): The difference between exports and imports, in both actual funds and credit. A nation's balance of trade is *favorable* when exports exceed imports and *unfavorable* when the reverse is true.

Bear market: A market in which prices are falling.

Bearer bond: A bond issued in bearer form rather than being registered in the owner's name. Ownership is determined by possession.

Bond: A written promise or IOU by the issuer to repay a fixed amount of borrowed money on a specified date and to pay a set annual rate of interest in the meantime, usually at semi-annual intervals. Bonds are generally considered safe because the borrower (whether a company or the government) usually must make interest payments before the money is spent on anything else.

Bull market: A market in which prices are on the rise.

Capital gain (loss): An increase (decrease) in the market value of an asset above (below) the price originally paid, at the time the asset is sold.

Commercial paper: An extremely short-term corporate IOU, generally due in 270 days or less. Available in face amounts of $100,000, $250,000, $500,000, $1,000,000 and combinations thereof.

Convertible bond: A corporate bond (see below) that may be converted into a stated number of shares of common stock. Its price tends to fluctuate along with fluctuations in the price of the stock and with changes in interest rates.

Corporate bond: Evidence of debt by a corporation. The bond normally has a stated life and pays a fixed rate of interest. Considered safer than the common or preferred stock of the same company.

Cost of living: The cost of maintaining a standard of living measured in terms of purchased goods and services. A rise in the cost of living mirrors the rate of inflation.

Cost-of-living benefits: Benefits that go to those persons whose money receipts increase automatically as prices rise.

Credit crunch (liquidity crisis): The period when cash for lending to business and consumers is in short supply.

Debenture: An unsecured long-term debt obligation backed only by the general credit of the issuing corporation.

Deficit spending: The practice whereby a government goes into debt to finance some of its expenditures.

Depression: A long period of economic decline when prices are low, unemployment is high, and there are many business failures.

Derivatives: Custom-designed financial contracts whose values are based on, or *derived* from, a financial market like stocks, interest rates, or currencies.

Devaluation: The official lowering of a nation's currency, decreasing its value in relation to foreign currencies.

Discount rate: The rate of interest set by the Federal Reserve that member banks are charged when borrowing money through the Federal Reserve System.

Disposable income: Income after taxes which is available to persons for spending and saving.

Dividend: Payment by a corporation to its shareholders, usually in the form of cash, stock shares, or other property.

Dow-Jones Industrial Average: A measure of stock market prices, based on 30 leading companies on the New York Stock Exchange.

Econometrics: The application of mathematical and statistical methods to the study of economic and financial data.

Economic growth: The steady process of increasing productive capacity of the economy, and hence of increasing national income.

Federal Deposit Insurance Corporation (FDIC): A government-sponsored corporation that insures accounts in national banks and other qualified institutions.

Federal Reserve System: The entire banking system of the U.S., incorporating 12 Federal Reserve banks (one in each of 12 Federal Reserve districts), 24 Federal Reserve branch banks, all national banks and state-chartered commercial banks, and trust companies that have been admitted to its membership. The system greatly influences the nation's monetary and credit policies.

Full employment: The economy is said to be at full employment when only fractional unemployment exists. That is, everyone who wishes to work at the going wage-rate for his type of labor is employed. Since it takes time to switch from one job to another, there will be at any given time a small amount of unemployment.

Golden parachute: Provisions in the employment contracts of executives guaranteeing substantial severance benefits if they lose their position in a corporate takeover.

Government bond: An IOU of the U.S. Treasury, considered the safest security in the investment world. They are divided into two categories, those that are not marketable and those that are. *Savings Bonds* cannot be bought and sold once the original purchase is made. These include the familiar Series EE bonds. You buy them at 50 percent of their face value and when they mature, 12 years later, they will pay you back 100 percent of face value if you cash them in. Another type, Series H, are not discounted, but issued in amounts of $500, $1,000, $5,000, and $10,000 and pay their interest in semiannual checks. Marketable bonds fall into 12 categories. *Treasury Bills* are short-term U.S. obligations, maturing in 3, 6, or 12 months. They are sold at a discount of the face value, and the minimum denomination is $10,000. *Treasury Notes* mature in up to 10 years. Denominations range from $500, $1,000 to $5,000, $10,000 and up. *Treasury Bonds* mature in 10 to 30 years. The minimum investment is $1,000.

Greenmail: A company buys back its own shares from a suitor for more than the going market price to avoid a hostile takeover.

Gross domestic product (GDP): The market value of all goods and services that have been bought for final use during a year. It became the official measure of the U.S. economy in 1991, and replaced the *Gross National Product (GNP),* which had been in use since 1941. The GDP covers workers and capital employed within the nation's borders. The GNP covers production by American residents, regardless of location. The switch aligned the U.S. with most other industrialized countries, making comparisons easier.

Hedge fund: A flexible investment fund for a limited number of large investors (the minimum investment is typically $1 million). Hedge funds can use almost any investment technique, including those not allowed for mutual funds, such as short-selling and heavy leveraging.

Hedging: Taking two positions that will offset each other if prices change, in order to limit financial risk.

Individual retirement account (IRA): A self-funded retirement plan that allows employed individuals to contribute a maximum yearly sum toward their retirement. Interest earned in the account is tax deferred.

Inflation: An increase in the average level of prices.

Insider information: Important facts about the condition or plans of a corporation that have not been released to the general public.

Interest: Money paid for the use of money. There are two kinds of interest. Simple interest is interest that is earned and paid. Compound interest is the accumulated interest that is added to the principal amount.

Junk bonds: Debt securities that sell at relatively low prices, because of the low credit rating of their issuers.

Leading indicators: A series of eleven indicators from different segments of the economy used by the Commerce Department to foretell what will happen in the economy in the near future.

Leverage: A way to amplify the potential gain or loss of an investment, usually by investing with borrowed money.

Leveraged buy-out: An acquisition of a publicly traded company by a small group, often including the company's management, which takes the company private. Much of the purchase price is borrowed, with the debt repaid from company profits or by selling company assets.

Liquid assets: Assets that include cash or those items that are easily converted into cash.

Margin account: A brokerage account that allows a person to trade securities on credit. A **margin call** is a demand for more collateral on the account.

Money supply: The currency held by the public plus checking accounts in commercial banks and savings institutions.

Mortgage-backed securities: Created when a bank, builder, or government agency gathers together a group of mortgages and then sells bonds to other institutions and the public. The investors receive their proportionate share of the interest payments on the loans as well as the principal payments. Usually, these mortgages are guaranteed by the government.

Municipal bond: Issued by governmental units such as states, cities, local taxing authorities, and other agencies. Interest is exempt from U.S.—and sometimes state and local—income tax. *Municipal Bond Unit Investment Trusts* allow you to invest in a portfolio of many different municipal bonds chosen by professionals. The income is exempt from federal income taxes.

Mutual fund: A portfolio, or selection, of professionally bought and managed stocks in which you pool your money along with thousands of other people. A share price is based on net asset value, or the value of all the investments owned by the funds, less any debt, and divided by the total number of shares. The major advantage is less risk — it is spread out over many stocks and, if one or two do badly, the remainder may shield you from the losses. *Bond Funds* are mutual funds that deal in the bond market exclusively. *Money Market Mutual Funds* buy in the so-called "Money Market" — institutions that need to borrow large sums of money for short terms. Usually the individual investor cannot afford the denominations required in the "Money Market" (i.e. treasury bills, commercial paper, certificates of deposit), but through a money market mutual fund he can take advantage of these instruments when interest rates are high. These funds offer special checking account advantages.

National debt: The debt of the national government as distinguished from the debts of the political subdivisions of the nation and private business and individuals.

National debt ceiling: Limit set by Congress beyond which the national debt cannot rise. This limit is periodically raised by congressional vote.

Option: A contractual agreement between a buyer and a seller to buy or sell shares of a security. A **Call** option contract gives the right to purchase shares of a specific stock at a stated price within a given period of time. A **Put** option contract gives the buyer the right to sell shares of a specific stock at a stated price within a given period of time.

Per capita income: The nation's total income divided by the number of people in the nation.

Prime interest rate: The rate charged by banks on short-term loans to large commercial customers with the highest credit rating.

Producer price index: A statistical measure of the change in the price of wholesale goods. It is reported for 3 different stages of the production chain: crude, intermediate, and finished goods.

Program trading: A term used for trading techniques involving large numbers and large blocks of stocks, usually used in conjunction with computer programs. Techniques include *Index Arbitrage,* in which traders profit from price differences between stocks and futures contracts on stock indexes, and *Portfolio Insurance,* which is the use of stock-index futures to protect stock investors from large losses when the market drops.

Public debt: The total of the nation's debts owed by state, local, and national government. This is considered a good measure of how much of the nation's spending is financed by borrowing rather than taxation.

Recession: A mild decrease in economic activity marked by a decline in real GDP, employment, and trade, usually lasting 6 months to a year, and marked by widespread decline in many sectors of the economy.

Savings Association Insurance Fund (SAIF): Created in 1989 to insure accounts in savings and loan associations up to $100,000.

Seasonal adjustment: Statistical changes made to compensate for regular fluctuations in data that are so great they tend to distort the statistics and make comparisons meaningless. For instance, seasonal adjustments are made in mid-winter for a slowdown in housing construction and for the rise in farm income in the fall after the summer crops are harvested.

Short-selling: Borrowing shares of stock from a brokerage firm and selling them, hoping to buy the shares back at a lower price, return them, and realize a profit from the decline in prices.

Stagnation: A period of economic slowdown in which there is little growth in GDP, capital investment, and real income.

Stock: *Common Stocks* are shares of ownership in a corporation; they are the most direct way to participate in the fortunes of a company. There can be wide swings in the prices of this kind of stock. *Preferred Stock* is a type of stock on which a fixed dividend must be paid before holders of common stock are issued their share of the issuing corporation's earnings. Prices are higher and yields lower than comparable bonds. However, they are attractive to corporate investors because 85 percent of preferred dividends are tax exempt to corporations. *Convertible Preferred Stock* can be converted into the common stock of the company that issued the preferred. This stock has the advantage of producing a higher yield than common stock and it also has appreciation potential. *Over-the-Counter Stock* is not traded on the major or regional exchanges, but rather through dealers from whom you buy directly. *Blue Chip* stocks are so called because they have been leading stocks for a long time. *Growth* stocks are stocks whose earnings have grown over several years.

Stock-index futures: A futures contract is an agreement to buy or sell a specific amount of a commodity or financial instrument at a particular price at a set date. Futures on a stock index (such as the Standard & Poor's 500) are bets on the future price of that group of stocks.

Supply-side economics: The school of economic thinking that stresses the importance of the costs of production as a means of revitalizing the economy. Advocates policies that raise capital and labor output by increasing the incentives to produce.

Takeover: The passing of control of one company by another company or group by sale or merger. A friendly takeover occurs when the acquired company's management is agreeable to the merger; when managementis opposed to the merger it is an unfriendly takeover. Takeover **arbitrage** is the purchase and/or selling of the securities of companies involved in takeover situations in order to realize a profit.

Tender offer: A public offer to buy a company's stock; usually priced at a premium above the market.

Unit investment trust: A portfolio of many different corporate bonds, preferred stocks, government-backed securities, or utility common stocks in which you can invest with as little as $1,000. Professional managers choose the securities, arrange for safekeeping, and collect the income. You receive your pro rata share of income every month.

Zero coupon bond: A corporate or government bond that is issued at a deep discount from the maturity value and pays no interest during the life of the bond. It is redeemable at face value.

AGRICULTURE

The U.S. Farm Population

Source: Bureau of the Census, U.S. Dept. of Commerce

The total estimated number of persons living on U.S. farms in 1992 was 4,665,000, about the same as in 1991. As late as 1950, about 23 mil people lived on U.S. farms. The farm population peaked at about 32 mil in the 1910-20 period. When the first reports of farm population were published in 1945, 20% of Americans were farm residents. In 1992, only about 2% of Americans were farm residents. In 1992, farm residence was no longer a reliable indication of whether someone was involved in farming: 30% of farm managers were not farm residents, and 86% of farm workers lived elsewhere. The Midwest was home to a larger proportion of the nation's farm population—48%—than any other region of the country in 1992. Whites constituted most of the U.S. farm population (97%). Approximately 29% of men living on farms had some college education, compared with 46% of men who did not live on farms.

Persons in Farm Occupations, 1850-1992

Source: Economic Research Service, U.S. Dept. of Agriculture; Bureau of the Census, U.S. Dept. of Commerce; in thousands

Year	Total workers*	Farm occupations: Number	Farm occupations: % of total
1850	7,697	4,902	63.7
1870	12,925	6,850	53.0
1900	29,030	10,888	37.5
1920	42,206	11,390	27.0
1930	48,686	10,321	21.2
1940	51,742	8,995	17.4
1950	59,230	6,858	11.6
1960	67,990	4,132	6.1
1970	79,802	2,881	3.6
1980	104,058	2,818	2.7
1985 (March)	106,214	2,949	2.8
1990 (March)	117,491	2,864	2.4
1991 (March)	116,000	2,848	2.5
1992 (March)	116,442	2,936	2.5

* Total workers for 1985 to 1992 are employed workers ages 15 years and older; total workers for 1970 and 1980 are members of the experienced civilian labor force ages 16 years and older; total workers for 1900 to 1960 are members of the experienced civilian labor force ages 14 years and older; and total workers for 1850 to 1890 are gainfully employed workers ages 10 years and older.

Farms–Number and Acreage by State, 1983 and 1993

Source: National Agricultural Statistics Service, U.S. Dept. of Agriculture

State	Farms (1,000) 1983	Farms (1,000) 1993	Acreage (mil) 1983	Acreage (mil) 1993	Acreage per farm 1983	Acreage per farm 1993
U.S.	**2,379**	**2,068**	**1,023**	**978**	**430**	**473**
Alabama	54	47	12	10	215	213
Alaska	1	1	1	1	2,333	1,759
Arizona	8	8	38	36	4,573	4,557
Arkansas	56	46	16	15	288	335
California	82	76	33	30	404	391
Colorado	27	26	35	33	1,289	1,286
Connecticut	4	4	1	(Z)	116	103
Delaware	4	3	1	1	186	220
Florida	40	39	13	10	318	264
Georgia	55	45	14	12	249	269
Hawaii	5	4	2	2	422	389
Idaho	25	21	15	14	608	659
Illinois	100	80	29	28	287	354
Indiana	84	63	17	16	198	254
Iowa	115	100	34	33	293	333
Kansas	75	65	48	48	644	735
Kentucky	103	91	15	14	141	155
Louisiana	36	29	10	9	282	297
Maine	8	7	2	1	195	200
Maryland	18	15	3	2	150	147
Massachusetts	6	7	1	1	108	98
Michigan	64	52	11	11	178	206
Minnesota	102	87	30	30	298	341
Mississippi	51	39	14	13	280	333
Missouri	118	106	31	30	264	285
Montana	24	25	61	60	2,544	2,445
Nebraska	62	55	47	47	765	856
Nevada	3	2	9	9	3,179	3,708
New Hampshire	3	3	1	(Z)	159	174
New Jersey	10	8	1	1	105	104
New Mexico	14	14	46	44	3,286	3,274
New York	49	38	10	8	194	216
North Carolina	83	59	11	9	133	159
North Dakota	37	33	41	40	1,123	1,224
Ohio	92	76	16	15	173	200
Oklahoma	73	71	34	34	459	479
Oregon	38	37	18	18	480	473
Pennsylvania	59	51	9	8	147	155
Rhode Island	1	1	(Z)	(Z)	91	90
South Carolina	29	24	6	5	200	212
South Dakota	37	35	45	44	1,203	1,281
Tennessee	95	86	13	12	141	144
Texas	194	185	137	130	706	703
Utah	14	13	12	11	857	862
Vermont	8	7	2	2	227	219
Virginia	58	43	10	9	169	200
Washington	38	36	16	16	429	444
West Virginia	23	20	4	4	175	185
Wisconsin	88	79	18	17	207	216
Wyoming	9	9	35	35	3,804	3,742

(Z) Fewer than 500 farms or 500,000 acres

Livestock on Farms in the U.S., 1900-94

Source: National Agricultural Statistics Service, U.S. Dept. of Agriculture (in thousands)

Year (On Jan. 1)	All cattle	Milk cows	Sheep	Hogs[1]
1900	59,739	16,544	48,105	51,055
1910	58,993	19,450	50,239	48,072
1920	70,400	21,455	40,743	60,159
1925	63,373	22,575	38,543	55,770
1930	61,003	23,032	51,565	55,705
1935	68,846	26,082	51,808	39,066
1940	68,309	24,940	52,107	61,165
1945	85,573	27,770	46,520	59,373
1950	77,963	23,853	29,826	58,937
1955	96,592	23,462	31,582	50,474
1960	96,236	19,527	33,170	59,026
1965[2]	109,000	16,981	25,127	56,106
1970	112,369	12,091	20,423	57,046
1980	111,242	10,758	12,699	67,318
1985	109,582	10,777	10,716	54,073
1990	98,162	10,153	11,363	53,821
1991	98,896	10,156	11,200	54,477
1992	99,559	9,913	10,750	57,684
1993	100,892	9,844	10,174	59,016
1994[3]	101,749	9,638	9,079	57,938

(1) As of Dec. 1 of preceding year. (2) From 1965, milk cows and heifers that have calved. (3)Total estimated value on farms as of Jan. 1, 1994, was (avg. value per head in parentheses): cattle & calves $66,968,048 ($659.00); sheep & lambs $638,564 ($70.30); hogs & pigs $4,368,525 ($75.40).

U.S. Farms, 1940-93

Source: U.S. Dept. of Agriculture

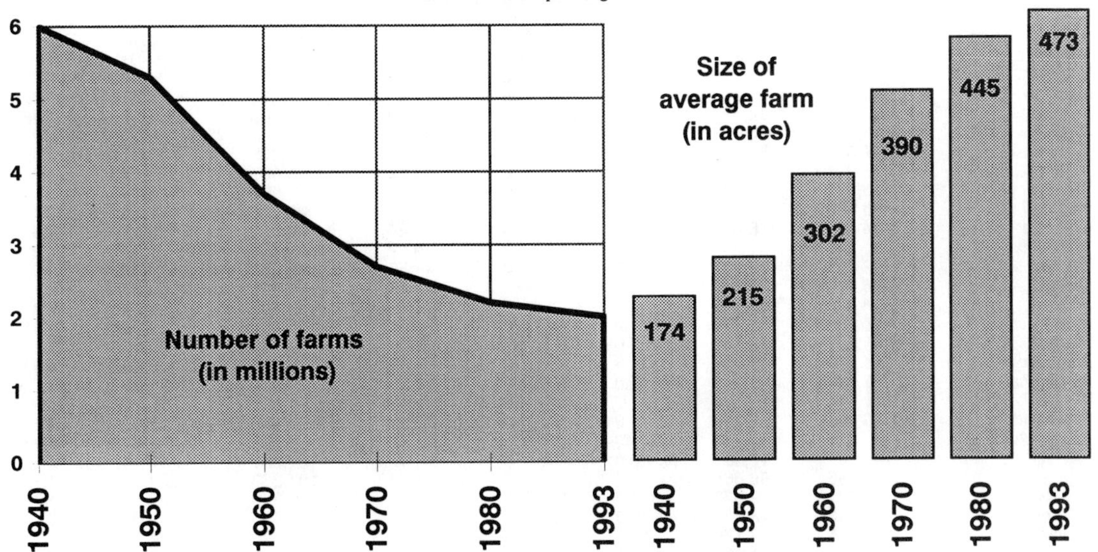

Eggs: U.S. Production, Price, and Value, 1992-93[1]

Source: Economic Research Service, U.S. Dept. of Agriculture

State	Eggs produced[2] 1992 (million)	Eggs produced[2] 1993 (million)	Price per dozen 1992 (cents)	Price per dozen 1993 (cents)	Value of production 1992 (1,000 dollars)	Value of production 1993 (1,000 dollars)
AL	2,512	2,538	81.3	103.0	170,188	217,845
AK	0.5	0.5	169.0	179.0	70	75
AZ	85	88	49.7	50.6	3,520	3,711
AR	3,601	3,638	88.3	94.1	264,974	285,280
CA	7,007	6,501	47.6	49.2	277,944	266,541
CO	837	837	61.4	68.8	42,827	47,988
CT	940	988	96.9	103.0	75,905	84,803
DE	164	162	107.0	106.0	14,623	14,310
FL	2,341	2,475	46.7	51.8	91.104	106,838
GA	4,326	4,449	74.8	74.6	269.654	276,580
HI	222.4	210.6	85.5	85.5	15,846	15,005
ID	214	232	62.6	66.4	11,164	12,837
IL	801	807	48.0	59.0	32,040	39,678
IN	5,207	5,281	48.8	55.9	211,751	246,007
IA	2,902	3,328	39.4	45.1	95,282	125,077
KS	355	334	38.3	44.1	11,330	12,275
KY	588	629	61.7	68.0	30,233	35,643
LA	316	450	97.0	92.3	25,543	34,613
ME	1,078	1,204	89.5	96.1	80,401	96,420
MD	855	831	62.2	57.6	44,318	39,888
MA	213	202	97.0	103.0	17,218	17,338
MI	1,398	1,401	40.4	46.0	47,066	53,705
MN	2,805	2,692	41.0	46.0	95,838	103,193
MS	1,408	1,433	82.1	88.5	96,331	105,684
MO	1,633	1,644	41.0	45.8	55,794	62,746
MT	160	125	49.0	63.0	6,533	6,563
NE	1,777	2,027	36.0	43.0	53,310	72,634
NV	1.5	1.1	38.8	41.3	49	38
NH	63	45	104.0	105.0	5,460	3,938
NJ	515	526	70.0	76.0	30,042	33,313
NM	303	313	58.0	64.0	14,645	16,693
NY	1,040	1,028	53.9	60.7	46,713	52,000
NC	3,026	3,082	71.4	76.0	180,047	195,193
ND	41	58	41.0	43.0	1,401	2,078
OH	5,021	5,066	40.7	48.1	170,296	203,062
OK	873	880	96.0	100.0	69,840	73,333
OR	686	673	76.6	79.0	43,790	44,306
PA	5,513	5,642	42.9	51.0	197,090	239,785
RI	57	53	91.0	98.1	4,323	4,333
SC	1,447	1,282	57.3	65.0	69,094	69,442
SD	622	636	32.5	37.5	16,846	19,875
TN	282	258	55.0	50.0	12,925	10,750
TX	3,462	3,569	63.0	68.1	181,755	202,541
UT	493	498	53.0	57.0	21,774	23,655
VT	31	30	98.0	104.0	2,532	2,600
VA	1,008	926	75.3	84.8	63,252	65,437
WA	1,305	1,283	63.4	69.8	68,948	74,628
WV	180	206	104.0	110.0	15,600	18,883
WI	831	820	42.5	47.0	29,431	32,117
WY	1.7	1.6	65.5	74.0	93	99
U.S.	70,541	71,391	57.6	63.4	3,386,753	3,771,376

(1) Estimates cover the 12 month period from Dec. 1 of the previous year through Nov. 30. (2) States may not total to U.S. due to rounding.

U.S. Meat Production and Consumption, 1940-93

Source: Economic Research Service, U.S. Dept. of Agriculture
(in millions of pounds)

Year	Beef Production	Beef Consumption[2]	Veal Production	Veal Consumption[2]	Lamb and mutton Production	Lamb and mutton Consumption[2]	Pork (exclud. lard) Production	Pork (exclud. lard) Consumption[2]	All meats[1] Production	All meats[1] Consumption[2]	Lard Production	Lard Consumption[3]
1940	7,175	7,257	981	981	876	873	10,044	9,701	19,076	18,812	2,288	1,901
1950	9,534	9,529	1,230	1,206	597	596	10,714	10,390	22,075	21,721	2,631	1,891
1960	14,728	15,465	1,109	1,118	769	857	13,905	14,057	30,511	31,497	2,562	1,358
1970	21,684	23,451	588	613	551	669	14,699	14,957	37,522	39,689	1,913	939
1980	21,643	23,560	400	420	318	351	16,617	16,838	38,978	41,701	1,207	588
1990	22,743	24,031	327	325	363	397	15,354	16,031	38,787	40,784	(4)	(4)
1991	22,917	24,113	306	305	363	396	15,999	16,399	39,585	41,214	(4)	(4)
1992	23,086	24,261	310	312	348	388	17,233	17,474	40,977	42,435	(4)	(4)
1993	23,049	24,006	285	286	337	381	17,088	18,213	40,759	42,092	(4)	(4)

(1) Meats may not add to total. (2) Includes shipments. (3) Direct use. Excludes lard used in such products as table spreads and shortenings. (4) Data collection discontinued.

Government Agricultural Payments by State, 1993[1]

Source: Economic Research Service, U.S. Dept. of Agriculture; in thousands of dollars

State	Feed Grain	Wheat	Rice	Cotton	Wool Act	Conservation[2]	Miscellaneous[3]	Total
Alabama	6,327	4,572	0	47,707	105	30,614	47,915	137,240
Alaska	131	0	0	0	3	1,170	485	1,789
Arizona	2,988	5,263	0	82,204	1,897	1,662	19,864	113,878
Arkansas	12,045	34,321	257,938	79,016	340	17,709	303,298	704,667
California	15,093	30,023	127,013	138,427	8,915	14,144	188,531	522,146
Colorado	67,371	73,212	0	0	7,054	85,229	17,387	250,253
Connecticut	911	0	0	0	32	603	1,346	2,892
Delaware	3,585	406	0	0	9	509	1,735	6,244
Florida	3,566	781	288	5,104	7	22,573	78,361	110,680
Georgia	24,062	16,468	0	46,249	28	32,522	106,164	225,493
Hawaii	0	0	0	0	19	1,990	1,122	3,131
Idaho	22,521	72,937	0	0	4,455	43,081	16,322	159,316
Illinois	706,713	36,749	0	0	643	67,869	39,216	851,190
Indiana	315,829	16,445	0	0	289	38,455	7,935	378,953
Iowa	916,663	356	0	0	2,504	185,497	124,524	1,229,544
Kansas	245,269	328,468	0	57	1,694	157,789	50,686	783,963
Kentucky	54,479	8,635	8	0	169	30,937	2,469	96,697
Louisiana	7,457	5,448	103,360	105,898	36	14,094	131,064	367,357
Maine	844	1	0	0	88	4,608	14,126	19,667
Maryland	15,206	2,358	0	0	116	2,699	5,910	26,289
Massachusetts	311	0	0	0	52	602	2,678	3,643
Michigan	140,984	17,551	0	0	747	24,651	57,409	241,342
Minnesota	418,196	86,865	0	0	1,697	107,283	209,209	823,250
Mississippi	5,903	9,622	49,538	169,729	21	42,303	106,675	383,791
Missouri	136,742	43,226	19,995	26,296	1,276	114,810	113,019	455,364
Montana	45,115	148,179	0	0	10,538	110,096	24,080	338,008
Nebraska	601,962	71,262	0	0	1,448	83,600	48,001	806,273
Nevada	227	700	0	0	1,380	951	3,755	7,013
New Hampshire	243	0	0	0	55	1,060	584	1,942
New Jersey	3,702	461	0	0	31	632	2,472	7,298
New Mexico	14,025	9,164	0	7,729	7,851	21,261	16,412	76,442
New York	39,089	4,013	0	0	440	8,381	20,363	72,286
North Carolina	39,889	7,982	0	24,192	94	10,537	49,754	132,448
North Dakota	107,244	284,749	0	0	2,724	110,839	58,975	564,531
Ohio	192,042	27,545	0	0	1,162	32,776	11,849	265,374
Oklahoma	15,823	167,738	215	28,448	2,617	54,751	54,357	323,949
Oregon	5,816	42,533	0	0	2,766	30,023	11,668	92,806
Pennsylvania	25,561	1,359	0	0	574	10,253	7,404	45,151
Rhode Island	3	0	0	0	4	132	1	140
South Carolina	17,547	9,309	0	19,774	2	14,760	41,120	102,512
South Dakota	165,187	83,370	0	0	8,515	75,221	100,131	432,424
Tennessee	22,535	9,100	111	51,160	86	28,158	49,474	160,624
Texas	200,584	117,058	91,212	392,947	77,941	185,131	355,957	1,420,830
Utah	3,710	5,668	0	0	7,522	11,122	8,592	36,614
Vermont	815	1	0	0	148	1,914	499	3,377
Virginia	17,594	4,794	0	681	699	7,130	15,448	46,346
Washington	23,249	112,249	0	0	814	57,851	13,045	207,208
West Virginia	2,381	124	0	0	371	2,220	1,163	6,259
Wisconsin	171,948	2,444	0	0	534	52,215	83,027	310,168
Wyoming	4,522	5,853	0	0	12,737	12,274	7,827	43,213
United States	**4,844,009**	**1,909,362**	**649,678**	**1,225,618**	**173,249**	**1,966,691**	**2,633,408**	**13,402,015**

(1) Includes both cash payments and payment-in-kind (PIK). (2) Includes amount paid under agriculture and conservation programs (Conservation Reserve, Agriculture Conservation, Emergency Conservation, and Great Plains Program). (3) The programs included Rural Clean Water, Forestry Incentive, Water Bank, Dairy Indemnity, Extended Warehouse Storage, Extended Farm Storage, Colorado River Salinity, Livestock Emergency Assistance, Interest Penalty Payments, Disaster, Loan Deficiency, Market Gains, Naval Stores Conservation, Interest on CCC-6S, Option Pilot, Rice Marketing Expense, Arkansas Beaver Lake, Wetland Reserve Program-Cost Shares, 90 Day Rule, and Potato Diversion.

Federal Food Assistance Programs[1], 1984-93

Source: Food and Nutrition Service, U.S. Dept. of Agriculture; in millions of dollars

Program	1984	1985	1986	1987	1988	1989	1990	1991	1992	1993
Food Stamps[2]	$11,579	$11,703	$11,638	$11,605	$12,317	$12,932	$15,491	$18,770	$22,462	$23,652
P.R. Nutr. Asst.[3]	825	825	820	853	879	908	937	963	1,002	1,040
Natl. School Lunch[4]	3,335	3,380	3,537	3,685	3,730	3,770	3,834	4,224	4,564	4,751
School Breakfast	364	379	406	447	482	513	596	685	787	869
WIC[5]	1,388	1,489	1,583	1,680	1,798	1,911	2,122	2,301	2,597	2,829
Summer Food Svc.[4]	96	112	115	129	133	146	164	182	204	218
Child/Adult Care[4]	407	452	496	548	628	703	820	950	1,099	1,228
Special Milk	16	16	16	15	19	18	19	20	20	19
Nutrition for the Elderly[4]	127	134	137	139	146	146	142	144	151	153
Food Distrib. to Indian Reserv.	51	60	60	63	62	65	66	65	62	62
Commodity Supp. Food [4,6]	48	48	48	56	62	73	85	93	105	113
Food Dist.—Charitable Instit.[7]	190	170	240	158	159	136	104	93	115	92
Emergency Food Assistance	1,075	1,026	895	895	645	276	257	256	236	238
Soup Kitchens/Food Banks	0	0	0	0	0	34	77	45	36	35
Other Costs[8]	52	56	60	62	58	68	71	73	88	100
Total[9]	**$19,552**	**$19,851**	**$20,051**	**$20,335**	**$21,118**	**$21,698**	**$24,783**	**$28,864**	**$33,528**	**$35,398**

(1) Data are for fiscal (not calendar) years. (2) Includes the federal share of state administrative expenses and other federal costs. (3) Puerto Rico participated in the Food Stamp Program from FY 1975 until July 1982, when it initiated a separate grant program. (4) Includes the value of commodities (entitlement, bonus, and cash in lieu). (5) Special Supplemental Pgm. for Women, Infants, and Children includes program studies and farmers market demonstration projects. (6) Includes elderly feeding projects. (7) Includes summer camps. (8) Includes child nutrition state admin. expenses, nutrition studies, nutrition education and training, and nutrition assistance to the Northern Marianas. (9) Excludes food program administration (FPA) costs.

Farm Marketings by State, 1992-93

Source: Economic Research Service, U.S. Dept. of Agriculture

(in thousands of dollars)

	1992 Farm marketings			1993 Farm marketings		
State/Rank	**Total**	**Crops**	**Livestock and products**	**Total**	**Crops**	**Livestock and products**
Alabama (24)	2,815,689	768,223	2,047,466	2,911,935	728,065	2,183,870
Alaska (50)	25,795	19,699	6,096	26,622	20,754	5,868
Arizona (31)	1,841,047	948,471	892,576	1,925,525	1,040,729	884,796
Arkansas (13)	4,665,797	1,955,778	2,710,019	4,382,606	1,480,810	2,901,796
California (1)	18,857,811	13,802,212	5,055,599	19,358,464	14,112,061	5,246,403
Colorado (16)	3,801,146	1,055,419	2,745,727	4,070,301	1,191,683	2,878,618
Connecticut (41)	506,431	252,851	253,580	521,072	263,064	258,008
Delaware (40)	628,052	177,398	450,654	622,070	159,098	462,972
Florida (8)	6,092,153	4,932,558	1,159,595	5,749,009	4,547,424	1,201,585
Georgia (15)	4,086,812	1,781,347	2,305,465	4,216,786	1,644,715	2,572,071
Hawaii (43)	520,222	431,068	89,154	490,443	405,080	85,363
Idaho (25)	2,774,403	1,601,121	1,173,282	2,856,731	1,689,350	1,167,381
Illinois (5)	7,598,993	5,345,886	2,253,107	7,914,735	5,665,617	2,249,118
Indiana (11)	4,462,562	2,638,592	1,823,970	5,117,558	3,185,824	1,931,734
Iowa (3)	10,409,111	4,809,503	5,599,608	10,002,876	4,174,185	5,828,691
Kansas (6)	7,169,462	2,386,946	4,782,516	7,361,010	2,490,846	4,870,164
Kentucky (21)	3,203,692	1,562,948	1,640,744	3,376,632	1,656,884	1,719,748
Louisiana (33)	1,911,038	1,299,336	611,702	1,761,274	1,073,432	687,842
Maine (45)	495,967	204,173	291,794	471,828	197,597	274,231
Maryland (35)	1,365,234	576,244	788,990	1,364,553	558,611	805,942
Massachusetts (42)	495,083	360,845	134,238	496,325	374,154	122,171
Michigan (20)	3,220,119	1,909,500	1,310,619	3,384,959	2,009,132	1,375,827
Minnesota (7)	7,023,049	3,412,871	3,610,178	6,574,569	2,800,134	3,774,435
Mississippi (27)	2,637,494	1,282,378	1,355,116	2,607,471	1,030,555	1,576,916
Missouri (17)	4,178,613	1,992,262	2,186,351	4,053,406	1,783,796	2,269,610
Montana (32)	1,705,745	807,980	897,765	1,781,082	842,735	938,347
Nebraska (4)	8,782,851	3,107,431	5,675,420	8,909,778	3,067,712	5,842,066
Nevada (47)	276,417	74,701	201,716	288,516	102,014	186,502
New Hampshire (48)	142,730	80,596	62,134	162,472	97,635	64,837
New Jersey (39)	653,534	463,208	190,326	706,261	507,581	198,680
New Mexico (34)	1,514,983	476,177	1,038,806	1,605,437	470,713	1,134,724
New York (26)	2,923,102	1,016,434	1,906,668	2,823,327	935,801	1,887,526
North Carolina (9)	5,177,284	2,378,801	2,798,483	5,456,868	2,256,242	3,200,626
North Dakota (23)	2,984,113	2,234,172	749,941	2,933,436	2,226,981	706,455
Ohio (14)	4,244,801	2,695,030	1,549,771	4,340,992	2,667,672	1,673,320
Oklahoma (18)	3,665,101	1,112,451	2,552,650	3,866,503	1,104,921	2,761,582
Oregon (28)	2,450,377	1,652,540	797,837	2,459,694	1,721,230	738,464
Pennsylvania (19)	3,600,518	1,046,114	2,554,404	3,715,806	1,094,184	2,621,622
Rhode Island (49)	73,007	60,279	12,728	79,137	66,842	12,295
South Carolina (36)	1,197,062	651,808	545,254	1,233,332	634,107	599,225
South Dakota (22)	3,188,790	1,224,468	1,964,322	3,317,518	1,144,730	2,172,788
Tennessee (30)	2,121,450	1,063,165	1,058,285	2,038,611	1,027,000	1,011,611
Texas (2)	11,618,578	4,094,363	7,524,215	12,750,083	4,407,861	8,342,222
Utah (38)	752,808	194,927	557,881	805,775	179,471	626,304
Vermont (44)	460,666	72,369	388,297	482,664	80,092	402,572
Virginia (29)	2,140,094	779,015	1,361,079	2,070,004	686,546	1,383,458
Washington (12)	4,436,516	2,888,787	1,547,729	4,587,823	3,027,071	1,560,752
West Virginia (46)	343,243	76,122	267,121	405,525	77,847	327,678
Wisconsin (10)	5,469,824	1,158,196	4,311,628	5,248,517	1,084,348	4,164,169
Wyoming (37)	773,720	167,169	606,551	816,492	159,517	656,975
United States	**171,483,089**	**85,083,932**	**86,399,157**	**174,504,413**	**83,954,453**	**90,549,960**

Value of U.S. Agricultural Exports and Imports, 1974-93

Source: Economic Research Service, U.S. Dept. of Agriculture

(in billions of dollars, except percent)

Year	Trade balance	Exports, domestic products	Percentage of all exports	Imports for consumption	Percentage of all imports
1974	11.8	22.0	23	10.2	10
1975	12.6	21.9	21	9.3	10
1976	12.0	23.0	20	11.0	9
1977	10.2	23.6	20	13.4	9
1978	14.6	29.4	21	14.8	9
1979	18.0	34.7	19	16.7	8
1980	23.9	41.2	19	17.4	7
1981	26.6	43.3	18	16.8	6
1982	21.2	36.6	17	15.4	6
1983	19.5	36.1	18	16.6	6
1984	18.5	37.8	17	19.3	6
1985	9.1	29.0	13	20.0	6
1986	4.8	26.2	13	21.5	6
1987	8.3	28.7	12	20.4	6
1988	16.1	37.1	12	21.0	5
1989	18.2	39.9	11	21.7	5
1990	16.6	39.4	10	22.8	5
1991	16.5	39.2	10	22.7	5
1992	18.3	42.9	10	24.6	5
1993	17.6	42.6	10	25.0	4

Farm Real Estate Debt Outstanding by Lender Groups[1], 1960-93

Source: Economic Research Service, U.S.Dept. of Agriculture

(in thousands of dollars)

		Amounts held by principal lender groups				
Dec. 31	Total farm real estate debt[2]	Federal land banks[2]	Farmers Home Adminis-tration[3]	Life in-surance com-panies[4]	All commer-cial banks	Other[5]
1960	$12,867,524	$2,539,000	$723,000	$2,975,000	$1,592,000	$5,039,000
1970	30,492,357	7,145,363	2,440,043	5,610,300	3,772,377	11,524,000
1980	97,486,996	36,196,103	8,163,270	12,927,800	8,563,457	31,636,000
1985	105,739,201	44,583,842	10,426,971	11,830,400	11,384,920	27,507,000
1986	95,879,799	37,757,626	10,348,597	10,940,200	12,710,650	24,123,000
1987	87,717,601	32,637,687	10,083,239	9,895,800	14,455,162	20,646,000
1988	82,952,518	30,326,707	9,606,796	9,581,700	15,416,700	18,020,000
1989	80,482,189	28,506,713	8,719,822	9,597,900	16,646,179	17,011,577
1990	78,903,115	27,390,156	8,092,982	10,186,300	17,227,171	16,006,500
1991	78,304,937	26,760,206	7,462,411	10,029,300	18,436,918	16,616,072
1992	80,419,686	26,886,261	6,779,546	9,208,000	19,862,622	17,683,259
1993	80,739,299	26,460,450	6,216,178	9,000,000	20,861,671	18,201,000

(1)Includes operator households. (2)Includes data for joint stock land banks and real estate loans by Agricultural Credit Assn. (3)Includes loans made directly by FmHA for farm ownership, soil and water loans to individuals, Native American tribe land acquisition, grazing associations, and half of economic emergency loans. Also includes loans for rural housing on farm tracts and labor housing. (4)American Council of Life Insurance. (5)Estimated by ERS, USDA. Includes Commodity Credit Corporation storage and drying facility loans.

Grain, Hay, Potato, Cotton, Soybean, Tobacco Production, by State, 1993

Source: Economic Research Service, U.S. Dept. of Agriculture

1993 State	Barley (1,000 bu)	Corn, grain (1,000 bu)	Cotton lint (1,000 b)	All Hay (1,000 t)	Oats (1,000 bu)	Potatoes (1,000 cwt)	Soybeans (1,000 bu)	Tobacco (1,000 lb)	All Wheat (1,000 bu)
Alabama	—	13,750	460.0	1,440	1,350	1,058	7,080	—	3,23[illegible]
Alaska	—	—	—	—	—	—	—	—	—
Arizona	2,900	1,600	895.0	1,236	—	1,485	—	—	7,79[illegible]
Arkansas	—	8,190	1,120.0	2,390	1,360	—	86,250	—	40,00[illegible]
California	13,000	28,050	3,155.0	7,590	2,400	14,932	—	—	43,80[illegible]
Colorado	7,650	99,000	—	4,275	1,984	27,680	—	—	96,99[illegible]
Connecticut	—	—	—	163	—	—	—	2,097	—
Delaware	2,275	13,600	—	45	—	750	4,945	—	3,59[illegible]
Florida	—	6,500	85.0	660	—	7,580	1,250	18,720	82[illegible]
Georgia	—	39,200	720.0	1,140	3,000	—	8,160	96,320	13,68[illegible]
Hawaii	—	—	—	—	—	—	—	—	—
Idaho	60,000	5,625	—	4,844	1,200	121,460	—	—	110,35[illegible]
Illinois	—	1,300,000	—	4,106	4,590	1,170	374,100	—	68,20[illegible]
Indiana	—	712,800	—	2,282	2,240	1,050	213,400	17,415	34,84[illegible]
Iowa	—	880,000	—	4,803	9,000	105	246,000	—	1,00[illegible]
Kansas	690	216,000	0.6	6,430	1,020	—	51,800	—	388,50[illegible]
Kentucky	1,072	126,880	—	5,452	—	—	37,950	471,825	23,03[illegible]
Louisiana	—	19,950	1,110.0	600	—	—	28,750	—	2,37[illegible]
Maine	—	—	—	399	1,950	20,540	—	—	—
Maryland	4,761	32,760	—	550	424	322	14,820	13,300	10,80[illegible]
Massachusetts	—	—	—	186	—	615	—	635	—
Michigan	1,512	236,500	—	5,790	7,150	15,280	54,720	—	22,14[illegible]
Minnesota	37,700	322,000	—	5,970	23,750	14,230	110,000	—	7,19[illegible]
Mississippi	—	14,820	1,560.0	1,728	—	—	42,900	—	6,93[illegible]
Missouri	—	166,500	345.0	7,333	686	1,508	117,150	5,600	53,20[illegible]
Montana	63,800	840	—	5,229	4,550	2,700	—	—	204,48[illegible]
Nebraska	1,216	785,200	—	7,573	6,880	3,638	87,500	—	73,50[illegible]
Nevada	500	—	—	1,385	—	2,926	—	—	80[illegible]
New Hampshire	—	—	—	140	—	—	—	—	—
New Jersey	300	7,680	—	231	—	627	4,263	—	1,41[illegible]
New Mexico	—	14,025	107.0	1,434	—	3,950	—	—	6,21[illegible]
New York	—	60,900	—	3,605	6,510	7,693	—	—	3,91[illegible]
North Carolina	1,200	55,250	415.0	715	1,800	3,234	28,800	596,285	23,52[illegible]
North Dakota	117,600	16,425	—	5,043	37,100	19,980	9,180	—	335,06[illegible]
Ohio	—	360,800	—	3,745	9,000	1,140	153,520	18,900	52,52[illegible]
Oklahoma	280	15,400	265.0	4,248	875	—	6,240	—	162,00[illegible]
Oregon	11,250	2,945	—	3,066	3,000	23,277	—	—	64,96[illegible]
Pennsylvania	5,985	93,120	—	4,728	10,000	4,600	11,505	20,300	7,42[illegible]
Rhode Island	—	—	—	15	—	237	—	—	—
South Carolina	266	9,600	210.0	414	1,500	—	7,800	110,760	9,88[illegible]
South Dakota	15,120	160,650	—	8,450	26,520	1,066	35,700	—	111,52[illegible]
Tennessee	—	46,200	550.0	3,478	—	—	30,690	129,140	13,94[illegible]
Texas	308	212,750	5,148.0	7,506	7,420	2,935	3,895	—	118,40[illegible]
Utah	9,350	2,860	—	2,530	1,014	1,643	—	—	7,27[illegible]
Vermont	—	—	—	654	—	—	—	—	—
Virginia	5,695	17,100	30.0	2,491	—	1,760	9,870	101,405	13,51[illegible]
Washington	23,115	15,200	—	2,835	2,040	85,500	—	—	177,58[illegible]
West Virginia	—	3,655	—	1,059	240	—	—	3,550	47[illegible]
Wisconsin	3,220	216,200	—	6,260	24,150	22,240	20,300	8,630	4,66[illegible]
Wyoming	9,460	3,520	—	2,608	1,550	504	—	—	6,54[illegible]
United States	**400,225**	**6,344,045**	**16,175.6**	**148,854**	**206,253**	**419,415**	**1,808,538**	**1,614,882**	**2,402,05[illegible]**

Production of Principal U.S. Crops, 1980-93

Source: National Agricultural Statistics Service, U.S. Dept. of Agriculture

Year	Corn for grain (1,000 bu)	Oats (1,000 bu)	Barley (1,000 bu)	Sorghum for grain (1,000 bu)	All Wheat (1,000 bu)	Rye (1,000 bu)	Flax-seed (1,000 bu)	Cotton lint (1,000 b)	Cotton-seed (1,000 t)
1980....	6,639,396	458,792	361,135	579,343	2,380,934	15,958	7,728	11,122	4,470
1982....	8,235,101	592,630	515,935	835,083	2,764,967	19,533	10,278	11,963	4,744
1985....	8,875,453	518,490	590,213	1,120,271	2,424,115	20,373	8,293	13,432	5,279
1986....	8,225,764	384,996	608,532	938,869	2,090,570	19,067	11,538	9,731	3,801
1987....	7,131,300	373,713	521,499	730,809	2,107,685	19,526	7,444	14,760	5,769
1988....	4,928,681	217,600	289,994	576,686	1,812,201	14,689	1,615	15,412	6,062
1989....	7,525,493	373,587	404,203	615,420	2,036,618	13,647	1,215	12,196	4,677
1990....	7,934,028	357,524	422,196	573,303	2,736,428	10,176	3,812	15,505	5,969
1991....	7,475,480	243,451	464,326	584,860	1,981,139	9,761	6,200	17,614	6,926
1992....	9,481,688	294,764	457,910	884,010	2,458,948	11,952	3,288	16,218	6,230
1993...	6,344,045	206,253	400,225	567,867	2,402,055	10,340	3,480	16,175	6,271

Year	Tobacco (1,000 lb)	All Hay (1,000 t)	Beans dry edible (1,000 cwt)	Peas dry edible (1,000 cwt)	Peanuts (1,000 lb)	Soy-beans (1,000 bu)	Potatoes (1,000 cwt)	Sweet potatoes (1,000 cwt)
1980........	1,786,225	130,740	26,729	3,285	2,302,762	1,797,543	303,905	10,953
1982........	1,994,494	149,241	25,563	NA	3,440,255	2,190,297	355,131	14,833
1985........	1,511,638	148,719	22,298	NA	4,122,787	2,099,056	407,109	14,573
1986........	1,161,940	155,385	22,960	3,196	3,697,085	1,942,558	361,511	12,368
1987........	1,188,868	147,319	26,031	3,385	3,616,010	1,938,087	385,774	11,611
1988........	1,369,500	126,010	19,253	3,868	3,980,917	1,548,841	356,438	10,945
1989........	1,367,188	145,512	23,729	3,883	3,989,995	1,923,666	370,444	11,358
1990........	1,626,380	146,820	32,379	2,372	3,602,770	1,925,947	402,110	12,594
1991........	1,664,372	153,325	33,765	3,715	4,926,570	1,986,539	417,622	11,203
1992........	1,721,671	148,863	22,615	2,535	4,284,306	2,187,904	425,367	12,005
1993........	1,614,882	148,854	21,842	3,292	3,326,500	1,808,538	419,415	11,791

Year	Rice (1,000 cwt)	Sugar-cane (1,000 t)	Sugar beets (1,000 t)	Pecans (1,000 t)	Almonds (1,000 t)	Wal-nuts (1,000 t)	Hazel-nuts[1] (1,000 t)	Oranges[2] (1,000 bx)	Grape-fruit[2] (1,000 bx)
1980......	146,150	26,963	23,502	91.8	264.4	197.0	15.4	273,630	73,200
1982......	153,637	29,770	20,894	109.3	283.5	234.0	18.8	176,690	70,550
1985......	134,913	28,213	22,529	122.2	375.6	219.0	24.6	158,350	56,150
1986......	133,356	30,311	25,150	136.4	201.3	180.0	15.1	175,440	57,870
1987......	129,603	29,218	28,072	131.1	519.0	247.0	21.8	181,175	63,775
1988......	159,897	29,904	24,810	154.1	451.9	209.0	16.5	200,250	68,700
1989......	154,487	29,426	25,131	125.3	394.7	229.0	13.0	209,050	69,500
1990......	156,088	28,136	27,513	102.5	519.7	227.0	21.7	186,075	48,600
1991......	157,457	30,252	28,203	149.5	385.8	259.0	25.5	178,950	55,500
1992......	179,658	30,363	29,143	83.0	454.4	203.0	27.7	209,610	55,265
1993.....	156,110	30,525	26,396	182.5	401.0	260.0	38.2	257,660	68,675

NA=Not available. (1)Formerly called filberts. (2)Crop year ending in year cited.

Principal U.S. Crops: Area Planted and Harvested, 1990-93

Source: Natl. Agricultural Statistics Service, U.S. Dept. of Agriculture

(in thousand acres)

State	Area planted[1] 1991	1992	1993	Area harvested[1] 1991	1992	1993	State	Area planted[1] 1991	1992	1993	Area harvested[1] 1991	1992	1993
AL	2,354	2,246	2,256	2,229	2,130	2,116	NE	19,009	19,276	18,733	18,366	18,330	17,917
AZ	778	744	710	770	736	695	NV	502	407	530	495	403	527
AR	8,180	8,310	8,425	7,863	8,110	8,165	NH	94	105	108	92	103	106
CA	4,872	4,916	4,792	4,396	4,459	4,403	NJ	431	446	455	380	391	413
CO	6,023	5,868	6,014	5,591	5,395	5,625	NM	1,287	1,301	1,266	1,042	1,051	995
CT	132	134	131	125	128	125	NY	3,541	3,325	3,236	3,443	3,185	3,150
DE	568	531	512	556	515	499	NC	4,666	4,757	4,432	4,397	4,519	4,127
FL	1,104	1,130	1,103	1,048	1,071	1,046	ND	21,338	21,732	21,932	20,655	21,011	19,782
GA	4,185	4,039	4,053	3,777	3,693	3,523	OH	10,229	10,429	10,279	9,972	10,087	10,037
HI	74	68	64	74	68	64	OK	11,185	11,112	10,777	8,518	9,392	8,771
ID	4,311	4,177	4,506	4,079	4,006	4,322	OR	2,367	2,236	2,337	2,260	2,147	2,260
IL	23,695	23,940	23,325	22,906	23,237	21,934	PA	4,182	4,176	4,111	4,067	4,065	4,035
IN	11,813	12,219	12,038	11,527	11,709	11,767	RI	10	11	12	10	11	12
IA	23,877	24,222	23,562	23,356	23,666	21,916	SC	1,945	1,988	1,837	1,824	1,885	1,603
KS	21,901	21,916	21,869	20,712	20,266	20,454	SD	16,328	17,047	15,381	15,606	15,858	14,223
KY	5,770	5,647	5,663	5,495	5,419	5,419	TN	4,567	4,522	4,640	4,379	4,326	4,408
LA	4,010	4,150	3,865	3,665	4,029	3,729	TX	23,501	23,820	22,512	17,714	18,769	18,524
ME	369	386	390	351	375	373	UT	1,040	1,050	1,083	973	990	1,031
MD	1,626	1,679	1,627	1,562	1,619	1,569	VT	442	473	443	434	463	434
MA	141	140	139	136	135	134	VA	2,833	2,858	2,831	2,656	2,705	2,659
MI	6,918	7,059	6,922	6,733	6,817	6,751	WA	5,469	4,233	4,378	3,861	3,957	4,227
MN	19,294	19,905	19,277	18,692	19,301	16,940	WV	630	652	630	615	639	621
MS	4,716	4,990	4,840	4,478	4,855	4,708	WI	8,830	8,668	8,016	8,449	8,096	7,498
MO	13,204	13,201	12,826	12,900	12,904	11,542	WY	1,960	1,789	1,888	1,899	1,723	1,804
MT	9,680	9,320	9,466	8,687	8,369	8,891	**U.S.[2]**	**326,032**	**327,409**	**320,276**	**303,864**	**307,171**	**295,918**

(1)Crops included in area planted are corn, sorghum, oats, barley, winter wheat, rye, durum wheat, other spring wheat, rice, soybeans, peanuts, sunflower, cotton, dry edible beans, potatoes, and sugar beets. Harvested acreage is used for all hay, tobacco, and sugarcane in computing total area planted. Includes double-cropped acres and unharvested small grains planted as cover crops. (2)State figures do not add to U.S. totals due to sunflower and sugar-beet unallocated acreage.

Average Prices Received by U.S. Farmers, 1940-93

Source: Natl. Agricultural Statistics Service, U.S. Dept. of Agriculture

The figures represent dollars per 100 lb for hogs, beef cattle, veal calves, sheep, lamb, and milk (wholesale); dollars per head for milk cows; cents per lb for chickens, broilers, turkeys, and wool; cents per dozen for eggs.

Weighted calendar year prices for livestock and livestock products other than wool. For 1943-63, wool prices are weighted on marketing year basis. The marketing year was changed in 1964 from a calendar year to a Dec.-Nov. basis for hogs, chickens, broilers, and eggs.

Year	Hogs	Cattle (beef)	Calves (veal)	Sheep	Lambs	Milk cows	Milk	Chickens (excl. broilers)	Broilers	Turkeys	Eggs	Wool
1940	5.39	7.56	8.83	3.95	8.10	61	1.82	13.0	17.3	15.2	18.0	28.4
1950	18.00	23.30	26.30	11.60	25.10	198	3.89	22.2	27.4	32.8	36.3	62.1
1960	15.30	20.40	22.90	5.61	17.90	223	4.21	12.2	16.9	25.4	36.1	42.0
1970	22.70	27.10	34.50	7.51	26.40	332	5.71	9.1	13.6	22.6	39.1	35.4
1975	46.10	32.20	27.20	11.30	42.10	412	8.75	9.9	26.3	34.8	54.5	44.8
1979	41.80	66.10	88.80	26.30	66.70	1,040	12.00	14.4	25.9	41.3	58.3	86.3
1980	38.00	62.40	76.80	21.30	63.60	1,190	13.05	11.0	27.7	41.3	56.3	88.1
1984	47.10	57.30	59.90	16.40	60.10	895	13.46	15.9	33.7	48.9	72.3	79.5
1985	44.00	53.70	62.10	23.90	67.70	860	12.76	14.8	30.1	49.1	57.1	63.3
1986	49.30	52.60	61.10	25.60	69.00	820	12.51	12.5	34.5	47.1	61.6	66.8
1987	51.20	61.10	78.50	29.50	77.60	920	12.54	11.0	28.7	34.8	54.9	91.7
1988	42.30	66.60	89.20	25.60	69.10	990	12.26	9.2	33.1	38.6	52.8	1.4
1989	42.50	69.50	90.80	24.40	66.10	1,030	13.56	14.9	36.6	40.9	68.9	1.2
1990	53.70	74.60	95.60	23.20	55.50	1,160	13.74	9.3	32.6	39.4	70.9	80.0
1991	49.10	72.70	98.00	19.70	52.20	1,100	12.27	7.1	30.8	38.4	67.8	55.0
1992	41.60	71.30	89.00	25.80	59.50	1,130	13.15	8.6	31.8	37.7	57.6	74.0
1993	45.20	72.60	91.20	28.60	64.40	1,160	12.86	9.4	34.0	39.0	63.4	51.0

The figures represent cents per lb for cotton, apples, and peanuts; dollars per bushel for oats, wheat, corn, barley, and soybeans; dollars per 100 lb for rice, sorghum, and potatoes; dollars per ton for cottonseed and baled hay.

Weighted crop year prices. Crop years are as follows: apples, June-May; wheat, oats, barley, hay, and potatoes, July-June; cotton, rice, peanuts, and cottonseed, August-July; soybeans, September-August; and corn and sorghum grain, October-September.

Year	Corn	Wheat	Upland cotton*	Oats	Barley	Rice	Soy-beans	Sor-ghum	Pea-nuts	Cotton-seed	Hay	Pota-toes	Apples
1940	0.62	0.67	9.8	0.30	0.39	1.80	0.89	0.87	3.7	21.70	9.78	0.85	...
1950	1.52	2.00	39.9	0.79	1.19	5.09	2.47	1.88	10.9	86.60	21.10	1.50	...
1960	1.00	1.74	30.1	0.60	0.84	4.55	2.13	1.49	10.0	42.50	21.70	2.00	2.7
1970	1.33	1.33	21.9	0.62	0.97	5.17	2.85	2.04	12.8	56.40	26.10	2.21	6.5
1975	2.54	3.55	51.1	1.45	2.42	8.35	4.92	4.21	19.0	97.00	52.10	4.48	8.8
1979	2.52	3.78	62.3	1.36	2.29	10.50	6.28	4.18	20.6	121.00	59.50	3.43	15.4
1980	3.11	3.91	74.4	1.79	2.86	12.80	7.57	5.25	25.1	129.00	71.00	6.55	12.1
1984	2.63	3.39	58.7	1.67	2.29	8.04	5.84	4.15	27.9	99.50	72.70	5.69	15.5
1985	2.23	3.08	56.8	1.23	1.98	6.53	5.05	3.45	24.4	66.00	67.60	3.92	17.3
1986	1.50	2.42	51.5	1.21	1.61	3.75	4.78	2.45	29.2	80.00	59.70	5.03	19.1
1987	1.94	2.57	63.7	1.56	1.81	7.27	5.88	3.04	28.0	82.50	65.00	4.38	12.7
1988	2.54	3.72	55.6	2.61	2.80	6.83	7.42	4.05	28.0	118.00	85.20	6.02	17.4
1989	2.36	3.72	63.6	1.49	2.42	7.35	5.69	3.75	28.0	105.00	85.40	7.36	13.9
1990	2.28	2.61	67.1	1.14	2.14	6.68	5.74	3.79	34.7	121.00	80.60	6.08	20.9
1991	2.37	3.00	56.8	1.21	2.10	7.58	5.58	4.01	28.3	71.00	71.20	4.96	25.1
1992	2.07	3.24	53.7	1.32	2.04	5.89	5.56	3.38	3.0	87.50	74.30	5.52	19.0
1993	2.55	3.26	57.4	1.36	1.99	8.50	6.45	4.30	2.9	113.00	81.60	6.22	18.2

*Beginning in 1964, 480 lb net weight bales.

Grain Storage Capacity at Principal U.S. Grain Centers, Aug. 1994

Source: Chicago Board of Trade Market Information Department

(in bushels)

Cities	Capacity
Atlantic Coast	**12,800,000**
Great Lakes	
Toledo, OH	63,100,000
Duluth, MN	57,600,000
Chicago, IL	52,400,000
Buffalo, NY	15,200,000
Milwaukee, WI	6,600,000
River Points	
Kansas City, MO	95,200,000
Minneapolis, MN	82,100,000
St. Joseph, MO	22,300,000
St. Louis, MO	17,700,000
Atchison, KS	16,900,000
Omaha-Council Bluffs, NE	8,200,000
Sioux City, IA	3,800,000

Cities	Capacity
Southwest	
Enid, OK	79,700,000
Texas High Plains	72,700,000
Fort Worth, TX	68,000,000
Gulf Points	
South Mississippi Region	46,600,000
Texas Gulf	45,800,000
Plains	
Topeka, KS	53,300,000
Salina, KS	49,500,000
Hutchinson, KS	42,000,000
Wichita, KS	37,400,000
Lincoln, NE	33,700,000
Hastings-Grand Island, NE	25,600,000
Pacific NW	
Puget Sound (incl. Portland)	35,100,000
California Ports	NA

Atlantic Coast — Albany, NY, Philadelphia, PA, Baltimore, MD, Norfolk, VA; **Gulf Points, South Mississippi Region** — New Orleans, Baton Rouge, Ama, Belle Chasse, LA, Mobile, AL; **Texas Gulf** — Houston, Galveston, Beaumont, Port Arthur, Corpus Christi, Brownsville; **Pacific NW** — Seattle, Taçoma, WA, Portland, OR, Columbia River; **Texas High Plains** — Amarillo, Lubbock, Hereford, Plainview, TX. NA = not available.

World Wheat, Rice, and Corn Production, 1991

Source: UN Food and Agriculture Organization
(in thousands of metric tons)

Country	Wheat	Rice	Corn
World, total	**550,993**	**519,869**	**478,775**
Afghanistan	1,726	335	420
Argentina	9,000	347	7,768
Australia	9,633	726	159
Austria	1,341	—	1,524
Bangladesh	1,004	28,575	3
Belgium-Lux	1,620	—	62
Brazil	3,007	9,503	22,604
Bulgaria	4,503	27	2,718
Cambodia	—	2,400	50
Canada	32,822	—	7,319
Chile	1,589	117	836
China	95,003	187,450	93,350
Colombia	94	1,739	1,274
Cuba	—	430	95
Czechoslovakia	6,205	—	862
Denmark	3,629	—	—
Ecuador	28	841	665
Egypt	4,483	3,152	5,270
Ethiopia	890	—	1,590
Finland	431	—	—
France	34,483	109	12,787
Germany	4,721	—	1,928
Greece	2,750	127	1,700
Hungary	5,954	38	7,509
India	54,522	110,945	8,200
Indonesia	—	44,321	6,409
Iran	8,900	2,100	7
Iraq	525	125	74
Ireland	703	—	—
Israel	160	—	3
Italy	9,289	1,236	6,208
Japan	860	12,005	1
Korea, North	195	5,100	4,500
Korean, South	1	7,478	75
Laos	—	1,400	60
Madagascar	1	2,200	150
Malaysia	—	1,500	36
Mexico	4,115	354	13,527
Myanmar	123	13,201	190
Nepal	836	3,600	1,235
Netherlands	916	—	5
New Zealand	176	—	195
Pakistan	14,505	4,903	1,190
Panama	—	180	94
Peru	128	814	669
Philippines	—	9,670	4,655
Poland	9,269	—	340
Portugal	323	153	677
Romania	5,442	31	10,493
South Africa	2,245	3	8,200
Spain	5,392	582	3,151
Sri Lanka	—	2,397	34
Sweden	1,524	—	2,397
Switzerland	574	—	225
Syria	2,135	—	185
Thailand	—	20,040	3,990
Turkey	20,400	200	2,100
United Kingdom	14,300	—	—
United States	53,915	7,006	189,867
Uruguay	136	540	124
Former USSR	80,000	2,200	8,500
Venezuela	—	608	1,100
Vietnam	—	19,428	652
Yugoslavia	6,530	32	8,800

Note: Some figures are estimates. Where production is small or nonexistent, — is indicated.

Wheat, Rice, and Corn—Exports and Imports of 10 Leading Countries

Source: UN Food and Agriculture Organization
(in thousands of metric tons)

Wheat

Leading exporters	Exports[1] 1980	1990	1992	Leading importers	Imports[1] 1980	1990	1992
U.S.	41,199	29,064	35,205	Former USSR	16,000	15,650	20,950
Canada	16,262	21,731	23,878	China	13,789	9,500	11,621
France	13,423	18,600	19,761	Italy	3,028	5,500	6,332
Australia	9,577	11,760	8,203	Japan	5,840	5,622	5,979
Argentina	3,845	5,592	6,268	Egypt	5,423	5,668	*5,886
Germany	1,502	3,295	5,754	Brazil	3,910	4,444	4,655
Turkey	530	544	4,489	Algeria	2,294	4,600	*3,666
United Kingdom	1,100	4,165	4,088	South Korea	2,095	4,200	3,546
Italy	1,620	2,700	2,604	India	—	640	*3,000
Saudi Arabia	27	1,661	2,001	Indonesia	1,474	2,300	2,510

Rice

Leading exporters	1980	1990	1992	Leading importers	1980	1990	1992
Thailand	3,049	3,993	5,151	Iran	583	565	950
U.S.	3,028	2,317	2,164	Former USSR	1,283	400	850
Vietnam	5	1,000	1,950	Saudi Arabia	356	525	525
Pakistan	1,163	1,320	1,511	Brazil	0	800	480
China	580	689	1,034	Malaysia	167	355	443
Italy	475	580	739	Hong Kong	362	368	401
India	900	500	560	Côte d'Ivoire	275	310	380
Australia	468	443	518	South Africa	126	346	361
Uruguay	184	270	328	Senegal	340	430	356
Spain	45	210	219	United Kingdom	—	258	282

Corn

Leading exporters	1980	1990	1992	Leading importers	1980	1990	1992
U.S.	60,737	43,807	43,235	Japan	13,989	16,042	16,382
China	125	6,571	10,313	Former USSR	11,800	8,720	*8,100
France	2,380	5,300	7,042	South Korea	2,355	5,571	6,612
Argentina	9,098	4,000	6,092	South Africa	0	375	3,594
Hungary	300	500	*2,100	Netherlands	2,638	1,869	1,911
Greece	0	400	652	Malaysia	717	1,490	1,816
Canada	1,056	142	398	Spain	4,251	1,523	1,790
Former Yugoslavia	300	21	F300	United Kingdom	2,349	1,250	1,690
Germany	—	—	254	Egypt	—	*1,900	1,443
Thailand	2,142	1,193	145	Zimbabwe	0	100	*1,300

Note: * unofficial figure. F=Food and Agriculture Organization (FAO) estimate. (1)Marketing years.

EMPLOYMENT

Redesigning the Current Population Survey

Source: Bureau of Labor Statistics, U.S. Dept. of Labor

The Current Population Survey (CPS) is the source of the nation's statistics on the labor force, total employment, unemployment, and persons not in the labor force. Beginning in Jan. 1994, data collected from the CPS will reflect the results of a major redesign of the survey that has affected virtually every aspect of the survey, including the questionnaire, the methods of data collection, the processing of collected data, and the size of the sample. As a result of these changes, data collected prior to Jan. 1994 will be incompatible with data collected since that time.

This redesign was the first significant change to the CPS since 1967. It better reflects labor market trends such as the following: continuing growth in service-sector employment; the more prominent role of women, particularly mothers, in the labor force; and shifts in the nature of employment, including more part-time workers and less permanent attachment of employees to their employers. Also, in the past quarter-century, advances in survey research techniques and in data collection procedures have facilitated the development of more precise measurement methods that were not utilized in the old CPS. Finally, a 1979 presidential commission made recommendations concerning the way discouraged workers were measured in the old CPS that were not implemented because of the lack of funding.

The redesigned CPS is the result of a collaborative effort between the Bureau of Labor Statistics and the Bureau of the Census that began in the late 1980s. The new survey replaces the pencil-and-paper data collection method with an entirely automated process (mostly via laptop computers). This method has several clear advantages over the pencil-and-paper method. First, it allows for complicated skip patterns, standardized follow-up questions, and customized questions that are tailored to the individual's situation, without placing an undue burden on either the respondent or the interviewer. Also, responses can be entered directly into an electronic database. All these techniques reduce the possibility for error.

In addition to improving the quality of the data collected, the redesigned CPS will collect important new information. For the first time, the CPS will track the number of employed persons who have two or more jobs each month and will yield estimates of counts and changes over time in the full-time and part-time job markets.

Selected Unemployment Insurance Data, by State

Source: Employment and Training Admin., U.S. Dept. of Labor

Calendar year 1993, state programs only

State	Monitarily eligible claimants	First payments	Final payments	Initial claims	Benefits paid	Average weekly benefit amount	Employers subject to state law
AL	183,099	158,910	32,085	361,598	$188,949,890	$128.66	79,209
AK	45,498	40,689	20,292	89,446	103,360,420	170.83	14,150
AZ	105,249	79,119	31,575	168,852	177,215,070	149.26	82,590
AR	111,088	81,248	30,568	202,517	163,526,340	157.53	52,621
CA	1,633,253	1,258,112	610,131	3,091,809	3,425,421,800	155.92	767,736
CO	107,974	71,717	31,480	147,931	167,987,740	186.45	98,119
CT	144,817	150,871	58,547	276,707	539,140,930	224.02	91,673
DE	30,338	25,463	6,640	50,213	61,427,080	182.67	20,624
DC	29,285	25,092	15,385	35,175	112,176,180	222.76	21,948
FL	345,447	276,244	147,827	514,800	692,892,420	167.16	326,718
GA	275,253	202,002	70,637	402,702	298,087,520	149.80	148,482
HI	46,296	36,259	14,626	79,524	156,394,430	251.79	27,041
ID	47,996	41,134	14,689	101,897	78,532,944	162.36	29,347
IL	477,235	349,227	150,244	822,450	1,250,158,500	194.98	255,509
IN	168,707	112,426	38,038	255,984	195,933,250	141.69	113,284
IA	103,890	82,565	24,855	158,989	178,519,390	176.65	64,080
KS	78,417	62,530	23,684	126,039	175,925,790	188.61	59,967
KY	139,080	116,527	24,871	274,208	208,780,500	155.84	73,882
LA	110,661	81,599	30,877	200,554	161,119,900	119.42	83,409
ME	52,507	45,517	18,924	109,911	102,383,940	162.94	35,036
MD	166,116	121,665	32,299	247,731	360,753,600	180.48	114,665
MA	253,022	211,407	91,669	401,138	811,443,010	233.61	145,470
MI	540,183	394,677	121,488	848,176	1,050,078,600	215.02	190,383
MN	132,114	118,615	40,715	210,446	377,736,580	209.66	105,016
MS	80,895	55,856	19,892	159,570	98,502,576	126.50	46,808
MO	212,393	153,214	60,182	428,346	320,099,040	149.03	130,077
MT	32,081	26,289	9,288	55,720	50,257,360	150.90	25,384
NE	39,125	29,937	8,768	63,472	47,310,240	137.57	39,941
NV	73,017	54,465	19,433	106,009	133,879,820	175.01	30,737
NH	40,381	26,743	3,734	49,734	40,505,188	141.66	31,767
NJ	335,086	287,089	164,930	556,444	1,220,005,200	233.70	200,791
NM	35,554	26,360	10,717	63,532	64,573,668	144.12	35,591
NY	600,301	556,420	289,269	1,103,237	2,163,543,000	200.13	431,035
NC	232,856	154,622	40,152	447,778	274,949,630	168.03	139,575
ND	17,116	13,675	5,000	29,182	26,428,272	149.70	18,029
OH	328,167	264,731	92,054	576,065	739,507,070	183.24	213,721
OK	68,917	52,685	23,420	123,765	123,019,550	164.22	67,684
OR	144,411	128,269	47,859	318,674	354,540,260	180.22	82,776
PA	536,160	434,761	166,111	1,038,330	1,523,581,600	210.41	233,057
RI	57,155	48,603	23,735	112,081	157,609,790	210.58	32,235
SC	157,926	106,390	31,417	340,440	176,135,550	146.75	73,170
SD	10,464	7,946	1,119	19,195	11,675,555	131.22	19,656
TN	228,504	154,405	51,826	405,857	237,865,310	131.31	97,544
TX	523,332	387,462	194,521	787,705	1,105,428,900	183.65	340,403
UT	43,072	32,274	11,387	59,363	73,429,584	181.37	37,040
VT	25,947	22,441	6,452	42,436	56,518,424	162.81	19,358
VA	164,728	98,718	36,698	292,684	215,203,470	168.77	135,320
WA	258,556	221,048	75,986	519,651	728,270,270	191.93	150,573
WV	65,871	52,530	15,035	94,751	122,198,770	166.98	36,184
WI	220,881	197,203	44,627	429,957	420,768,380	183.13	107,952
WY	15,418	10,421	3,409	26,247	24,164,136	163.58	16,053
PR	141,497	132,793	63,768	274,659	207,345,460	88.98	48,781
VI	4,354	3,361	962	4,740	7,704,743	177.15	2,475
U.S.	**10,021,670**	**7,884,326**	**3,203,897**	**17,708,421**	**$21,762,966,640**	**$171.52**	**5,844,676**

Employment and Unemployment in the U.S.

Source: Bureau of Labor Statistics, U.S. Dept. of Labor
(Civilian labor force, persons 16 years of age and older; in thousands)

Year[1]	Employed	Unemployed	Unemployment rate	Year[1]	Employed	Unemployed	Unemployment rate
1940[2]	47,520	8,120	14.6%	1985	107,150	8,312	7.2%
1950	58,918	3,288	5.0	1986[3]	109,597	8,237	7.0
1960	65,778	3,852	5.5	1987	112,440	7,425	6.2
1970	78,678	4,093	4.9	1988	114,988	6,701	5.5
1980	99,303	7,637	7.1	1989	117,342	6,528	5.3
1981	100,397	8,273	7.6	1990	117,914	6,874	5.5
1982	99,526	10,678	9.7	1991	116,877	8,426	6.7
1983	100,834	10,717	9.6	1992	117,598	9,384	7.4
1984	105,005	8,539	7.5	1993	119,306	8,734	6.8

(1) **Early unemployment rates:** 1915, 9.7; 1916, 4.8; 1917, 4.8; 1918, 1.4; 1919, 2.3; 1920, 4.0; 1921, 11.9; 1922, 7.6; 1923, 3.2; 1924, 5.5; 1925, 4.0; 1926, 1.9; 1927, 4.1; 1928, 4.4; 1929, 3.2; 1930, 8.7; 1931, 15.9; 1932, 23.6; 1933, 24.9; 1934, 21.7; 1935, 20.1; 1936, 16.9; 1937, 14.3; 1938, 19.0; 1939, 17.2. (2) Persons 14 years of age and older. (3) Not strictly comparable with prior years.

Employed Persons, by Occupation, Sex, and Age

Source: Bureau of Labor Statistics, U.S. Dept. of Labor
(in thousands)

Occupation	Total 16 years and older		Men 16 years and older		Women 16 years and older	
	1992	1993	1992	1993	1992	1993
Total	**117,598**	**119,306**	**63,805**	**64,700**	**53,793**	**54,606**
Managerial and professional specialty	31,153	32,280	16,416	16,839	14,736	15,441
Executive, administrative, and managerial	14,767	15,376	8,641	8,923	6,126	6,452
Officials and administrators, public administration	619	659	361	380	258	278
Other executive, administrative, and managerial	10,187	10,561	6,384	6,578	3,802	3,984
Management-related occupations	3,961	4,155	1,896	1,965	2,065	2,190
Professional specialty	16,386	16,904	7,775	7,916	8,611	8,988
Engineers	1,751	1,716	1,603	1,568	148	148
Mathematical and computer scientists	935	1,051	622	711	313	340
Natural scientists	459	531	334	371	125	160
Health diagnosing occupations	914	909	747	723	167	186
Health assessment and treating occupations	2,517	2,602	332	353	2,184	2,249
Teachers, college and university	737	772	435	444	302	328
Teachers, except college and university	4,216	4,397	1,062	1,093	3,154	3,304
Lawyers and judges	788	814	620	629	167	185
Other professional specialty occupations	4,068	4,111	2,018	2,024	2,050	2,087
Technical, sales, and administrative support	36,808	36,814	13,269	13,311	23,539	23,503
Technicians and related support	4,253	4,014	2,169	1,985	2,084	2,028
Health technologists and technicians	1,517	1,522	278	288	1,239	1,233
Engineering and science technicians	1,160	1,131	913	879	247	253
Technicians, except health, engineering and science	1,576	1,361	978	818	598	543
Sales occupations	13,919	14,245	7,252	7,389	6,667	6,857
Supervisors and proprietors	3,879	4,016	2,529	2,552	1,349	1,463
Sales representatives, finance and business services	2,247	2,317	1,348	1,378	899	939
Sales representatives, commodities, except retail	1,571	1,538	1,229	1,215	342	323
Sales workers, retail and personal services	6,129	6,281	2,113	2,206	4,016	4,075
Sales-related occupations	93	93	32	37	61	57
Administrative support, including clerical	18,636	18,555	3,848	3,937	14,788	14,618
Supervisors	759	778	329	323	430	455
Computer equipment operators	664	603	242	230	423	373
Secretaries, stenographers, and typists	4,315	4,174	70	75	4,245	4,099
Financial records processing	2,335	2,272	219	229	2,117	2,043
Mail and message distributing	902	953	564	594	338	359
Other administrative support, including clerical	9,660	9,775	2,424	2,486	7,236	7,289
Service occupations	16,096	16,522	6,494	6,688	9,602	9,833
Private household	876	912	37	44	840	868
Protective service	2,096	2,152	1,745	1,783	351	370
Service, except private household and protective	13,124	13,457	4,712	4,861	8,411	8,596
Food service	5,459	5,691	2,243	2,370	3,215	3,321
Health service	2,105	2,213	237	279	1,868	1,934
Cleaning and building service	2,988	2,959	1,760	1,711	1,228	1,248
Personal service	2,573	2,594	473	501	2,100	2,092
Precision production, craft, and repair	13,128	13,326	12,000	12,185	1,128	1,141
Mechanics and repairers	4,441	4,416	4,293	4,261	147	156
Construction trades	4,790	5,004	4,702	4,909	89	95
Other precision production, craft, and repair	3,897	3,906	3,005	3,015	892	890
Operators, fabricators, and laborers	16,957	17,038	12,720	12,862	4,237	4,176
Machine operators, assemblers, and inspectors	7,524	7,415	4,535	4,548	2,989	2,868
Manufacturing industries	6,136	6,014	3,645	3,664	2,492	2,350
Nonmanufacturing industries	1,387	1,401	890	884	497	518
Transportation and material moving occupations	4,878	5,004	4,451	4,539	427	465
Handlers, equipment cleaners, helpers, and laborers	4,556	4,619	3,734	3,776	821	843
Farming, forestry, and fishing	3,456	3,326	2,905	2,814	551	512
Farm operators and managers	1,232	1,170	1,042	1,003	190	167
Other farming, forestry, and fishing occupations	2,224	2,156	1,864	1,811	361	344

Note: Data for 1992 and 1993 are not fully comparable because of the introduction of the occupational classification system used in the 1990 census and new surveying methodology.

Employment and Training Services and Unemployment Insurance

Source: Employment and Training Administration, U.S. Dept. of Labor; September 1994

Employment Service

The Federal-State Employment Service consists of the United States Employment Service and affiliated state employment services that make up the nation's public employment service system. From July 1, 1992, to June 30, 1993, the public employment service listed 5.6 million job openings and placed more than 2.6 million people in jobs.

The employment service refers employable applicants to job openings that use their highest skills and helps the unemployed obtain services or training to make them employable. It also provides special attention to handicapped workers, migrants and seasonal farmworkers, workers who lose their jobs because of foreign trade competition, and other worker groups. Veterans receive priority services including referral to jobs and training. During program year 1992, 398,551 veterans were placed in jobs.

Job Training

The Job Training Partnership Act (JTPA), which became fully operational on Oct. 1, 1983, provides job training and employment services for economically disadvantaged youths and adults, dislocated workers, and others who face significant employment barriers. The goal of the act is to move as many jobless workers as possible into permanent, unsubsidized, self-sustaining employment.

As of the end of program year 1992, JTPA had provided approximately 10 million Americans with training and employment services since its inception. Its placement rate is almost 69%, making it one of the most successful job and training efforts ever undertaken.

Title I of the act's 5 titles basically establishes an administrative structure for the delivery of job and training services. Generally, state governors receive bloc grants from the Labor Department, and the funds are then distributed to Service Delivery Areas—areas of 200,000 population or more where local elected officials work with Private Industry Councils to plan and conduct local training projects.

Title II is in 3 parts, with Title II-A spelling out the act's provision of employment and training projects for the economically disadvantaged. In program year 1992 (July 1, 1992, to June 30, 1993), these projects served nearly 1 million people.

Title II-B outlines a summer youth program offering basic and remedial education, institutional and on-the-job training, work experience, and supportive services. This program had nearly 633,221 participants in program year 1993. Beginning July 1, 1993, a new Title II-C provided for a year-round youth training program.

Title III, Economic Dislocation and Worker Adjustment Assistance, provides for job and training help for dislocated workers—workers who lose jobs and are unlikely to return to their previous industries or occupations. This includes workers who lose their jobs because of plant closings or mass layoffs; long-term unemployed persons with limited local opportunities for jobs in their fields; farmers, ranchers, and other self-employed persons who become jobless due to general economic conditions or natural disasters; and, under certain circumstances, displaced homemakers. Such assistance benefitted 311,876 workers in program year 1992.

Title IV authorizes programs to address the employment and training needs of specific groups facing significant barriers to productive employment, including Native Americans, migrant and seasonal farmworkers, and the disabled. In program year 1992, these programs served 25,126 Native Americans; 37,949 migrant and seasonal farmworkers; 97,456 older workers; and more than 7,000 disabled persons.

In addition, Title IV includes the Job Corps, which each year enrolls approximately 100,000 young people between the ages of 16 and 21 in 107 residential job training centers throughout the U.S.; the National Commission for Employment Policy; and nationally administered programs for technical assistance, labor market information, research and evaluation, and pilots and demonstrations.

With recent amendments to JTPA, Title V is now the Jobs for Employable Dependent Individuals (JEDI) Incentive Bonus Program. Title VI provides for new state human resources investment councils, and Title VII covers transition provisions and technical conforming amendments.

Trade Adjustment Assistance for Workers

Trade Adjustment Assistance (TAA) is available to workers who lose their jobs or whose hours of work and wages are reduced as a result of increased imports. TAA includes a variety of benefits and reemployment services to help unemployed workers prepare for and obtain suitable employment. Workers may be eligible for training, job search, relocation, and other reemployment services. Additionally, weekly trade readjustment allowances (TRA) may be payable to eligible workers following their exhaustion of unemployment insurance benefits. In fiscal year 1993, about 9,566 workers received $50.5 million in TRA payments; 19,454 workers entered training; 796 workers were involved in job search visits; and 1,961 workers relocated in order to obtain long term jobs.

The TAA program is administered by the Employment and Training Administration's Office of Trade Adjustment Assistance. State employment security agencies serve as agents of the U.S., under an agreement with the Secretary of Labor, for administering the TAA benefit provisions in the Trade Act of 1974, as amended.

Unemployment Insurance

Unlike old-age and survivors insurance, entirely a federal program, the unemployment insurance program is a federal-state system that provides insured wage earners with partial replacement of wages lost during involuntary unemployment. The program protects most workers. During calendar year 1993, an estimated 107 million workers in commerce, industry, agriculture, and government, including the armed forces, were covered under the federal-state system.

Each state, as well as the District of Columbia, Puerto Rico, and the Virgin Islands, has its own law and operates its own program. The amount and duration of the weekly benefits are determined by state laws, based on prior wages and length of employment. States are required to extend the duration of benefits when unemployment rises to and remains above specified state levels; costs of extended benefits are shared by the state and federal governments.

Under the Federal Unemployment Tax Act, the federal tax rate is 6.2% on the first $7,000 paid to each employee of employers with one or more employees in 20 weeks of the year or a quarterly payroll of $1,500. A credit of up to 5.4% is allowed for taxes paid under state unemployment insurance laws that meet certain criteria, leaving the net federal rate at 0.8% of taxable wages. Subject employers also pay a state unemployment tax.

The secretary of labor certified states for administrative grants to operate the program (under the Social Security Act) and for employer tax credit (under the Federal Unemployment Tax Act).

Benefits are financed solely by employer contributions, except in Alaska, Pennsylvania, and New Jersey where employees also contribute. Benefits are paid through the states' public employment offices, at which unemployed workers must register for work and to which they must report regularly for referral to a possible job during the time when they are drawing weekly benefit payments. During the fiscal year 1993, $21.9 billion in benefits was paid under state unemployment insurance programs to 7.8 million beneficiaries. They received an average weekly payment of $178.58 for total unemployment for an average of 16.4 weeks.

U.S. Labor Force, Employment and Unemployment

Source: Bureau of Labor Statistics, U.S. Dept. of Labor; seasonally adjusted

Selected Unemployment Indicators

Category	1991			1992				1993				1994	
Characteristic	II	III	IV	I	II	III	IV	I	II	III	IV	I	II
Total (all civilian workers)	6.7	6.7	7.0	7.3	7.5	7.5	7.3	7.0	7.0	6.7	6.5	6.6	6.2
Men, 20 years and older	6.4	6.4	6.5	7.0	7.2	7.1	6.9	6.6	6.5	6.4	6.0	5.9	5.4
Women, 20 years and older	5.7	5.5	5.9	6.1	6.2	6.4	6.2	6.0	5.9	5.8	5.7	5.9	5.4
Both sexes, 16 to 19 years	18.5	19.0	19.2	19.7	20.6	20.6	19.4	19.6	19.8	18.2	18.3	18.0	18.4
White	6.0	6.0	6.2	6.4	6.6	6.6	6.4	6.2	6.1	5.9	5.8	5.7	5.4
Black and other	11.1	10.9	11.5	12.4	12.8	12.7	12.7	12.3	12.1	11.5	11.0	11.4	10.5
Black	12.5	12.2	12.8	13.9	14.3	14.1	14.1	13.6	13.3	12.6	12.0	12.8	11.5
Hispanic origin	9.6	10.2	10.2	11.2	11.3	11.7	11.6	11.3	10.3	10.2	10.7	10.2	10.2
Married men, spouse present	4.4	4.3	4.5	4.9	5.0	5.2	4.9	4.6	4.5	4.4	4.1	4.2	3.7
Married women, spouse present	4.5	4.4	4.7	4.9	5.1	5.1	5.0	4.6	4.7	4.6	4.5	4.4	4.1
Women who maintain families	9.2	9.0	9.3	9.4	10.0	10.1	10.0	9.8	9.7	9.2	9.5	9.6	8.9
Occupation[1]													
Managerial and professional specialty	2.8	2.9	2.9	3.0	3.1	3.3	3.2	3.3	3.0	2.7	2.9	2.8	2.6
Technical, sales, and administrative support	5.2	5.0	5.3	5.7	5.8	5.9	5.8	5.4	5.5	5.3	5.2	5.5	5.2
Precision production, craft, and repair	7.8	8.3	8.3	9.3	8.7	8.6	8.6	8.1	8.3	7.9	7.3	7.0	6.4
Operators, fabricators, and laborers	10.7	10.2	10.4	11.2	11.2	11.1	10.6	10.1	9.9	10.2	9.4	9.4	9.0
Farming, forestry, and fishing	7.3	7.6	7.8	7.6	8.0	8.6	8.4	8.5	8.0	7.8	8.2	9.2	7.5
Industry													
Nonagricultural private wage and salary workers	7.0	7.0	7.3	7.6	7.7	7.8	7.6	7.3	7.2	7.0	6.8	6.9	6.3
Goods-producing industries	9.1	8.8	9.2	9.6	9.8	9.8	9.5	8.9	9.0	9.0	8.1	7.7	7.0
Mining	7.6	8.4	9.1	7.7	8.1	8.8	6.9	6.8	8.5	6.9	6.9	4.9	6.9
Construction	15.0	15.5	16.5	17.5	16.8	16.5	15.5	14.8	15.0	14.9	12.9	13.6	12.0
Manufacturing	7.5	6.9	7.2	7.5	7.8	7.9	7.9	7.3	7.2	7.3	6.7	6.1	5.5
Durable goods	7.9	7.1	7.1	7.6	7.8	8.2	8.3	7.2	7.2	7.2	6.6	5.5	5.3
Nondurable goods	6.9	6.7	7.3	7.3	7.8	7.6	7.3	7.5	7.2	7.5	6.9	7.0	5.9
Service-producing industries	6.2	6.2	6.4	6.8	6.9	7.0	6.8	6.6	6.5	6.2	6.2	6.6	6.1
Transportation and public utilities	5.4	5.1	5.6	5.5	5.2	5.5	5.7	4.9	5.0	5.2	5.3	5.1	4.9
Wholesale and retail trade	7.4	7.7	7.8	8.4	8.4	8.7	8.0	7.9	8.0	7.5	7.7	8.0	7.3
Finance, insurance, and real estate	4.2	4.1	4.2	4.3	4.5	4.6	4.7	4.3	4.3	4.0	3.7	3.4	3.6
Services	5.8	5.8	6.0	6.4	6.6	6.4	6.7	6.4	6.0	5.9	5.9	6.5	6.0
Government workers	3.1	3.2	3.5	3.7	3.5	3.4	3.5	3.6	3.3	3.2	3.1	3.6	3.6
Agricultural wage and salary workers	11.4	11.2	11.7	11.0	12.7	13.2	12.7	12.2	11.5	11.3	11.1	13.9	9.1

Note: Data for 1994 are not directly comparable with data for 1993 and earlier years due to a major redesign of the survey used.
(1) Seasonally adjusted data for service occupations are not available because the seasonal components are small relative to the trend-cycle and/or irregular components and consequently cannot be separated with sufficient precision.

Unemployment Rates, by Selected City, 1992

Source: Bureau of Labor Statistics, U.S. Dept of Labor

Cities	Unemployment rate[1]	Cities	Unemployment rate[1]
Baltimore, MD	13.5	New York, NY	9.7
Chicago, IL	9.7	Philadelphia, PA	10.3
Cleveland, OH	9.8	Phoenix, AZ	7.8
Dallas, TX	7.9	St. Louis, MO	15.1
Detroit, MI	15.8	San Antonio, TX	7.0
Houston, TX	8.7	San Diego, CA	7.3
Indianapolis, IN	6.0	San Francisco, CA	7.8
Los Angeles, CA	9.3	Washington, DC	7.9
Milwaukee, WI	8.4		

(1) Average annual unemployment rates include self-employed and unpaid family workers and mining, but do not include persons with no previous work experience or agricultural workers.

Educational Attainment by Labor Force Status and Occupation, March 1993

Source: Bureau of the Census, Dept. of Commerce

Characteristics	Number of persons (1000)	Percentage with: High school degree or more	Some college or more	Bachelor's degree or more
Civilian labor force, 25 years and older				
Employed	100,152	88.9	54.1	27.8
Not employed	6,716	76.3	36.1	13.6
Not in the labor force	55,268	64.7	28.9	11.9
Total, employed persons, 25-64 years old	**96,908**	**89.3**	**54.5**	**28.0**
Executive, admin., and managerial	14,125	97.4	75.0	47.8
Professional specialty occupations	15,373	99.1	92.7	75.2
Technicians and related support occupations	3,439	98.1	78.0	30.9
Sales occupations	10,777	94.0	58.3	29.2
Administrative support occupations, includ. clerical	14,894	96.1	52.3	14.7
Private household occupations	555	62.4	25.4	7.2
Other service occupations	11,188	79.5	33.7	7.8
Farming, forestry, and fishing	2,280	68.7	27.7	9.5
Precision products, craft, and repair	10,965	82.5	34.2	6.3
Machine operators, assemblers, and inspectors	6,208	73.1	21.0	4.3
Transportation and material moving	4,218	77.8	25.0	4.4
Handlers, equipment cleaners, helpers, and laborers	2,888	73.1	20.4	4.2

Projected Fastest-Growing Occupations, 1992-2005

Source: Bureau of Labor Statistics, U.S. Dept. of Labor

Occupation	Change in employment, 1992-2005 Percentage	Number
Chefs, cooks, and other kitchen workers	38	1,190,000
School teacher—kindergarten, elementary, and secondary	34	1,113,000
Information clerks	32	429,000
Adjusters, investigators, and collectors	28	397,000
General maintenance mechanics	35	319,000
Gardeners and groundskeepers	34	311,000
Receptionists	32	305,000
Accountants and auditors	40	304,000
Licensed practical nurses	32	261,000
Barbers and cosmetologists	28	239,000
Lawyers and judges	35	197,000
Physicians	40	195,000
Social workers	38	191,000
Services sales representatives	32	185,000
Adult education teachers	30	172,000
Computer programmers	36	169,000
Marketing, advertising, and public relations managers	32	156,000
Personnel, training, and labor relations specialists and managers	29	150,000
Painters and paperhangers	32	128,000
Employment interviewers processing managers	37	106,000
Social scientists and urban planners	36	95,000
Counter and rental clerks	35	88,000
Property and real estate managers	38	85,000
Recreation workers	39	78,000
Dental assistants	40	72,000

Occupational Group Projections, 1992-2005

Source: Bureau of Labor Statistics, U.S. Dept. of Labor

(in thousands)

	1992		2005		Change 1992-2005	
	Number	Percentage	Number	Percentage	Number	Percentage
Total, all occupations	**121,099**	**100.0**	**147,482**	**100.0**	**26,383**	**21.8**
Administrative support occupations, including clerical	22,349	18.5	25,406	17.2	3,057	13.7
Agricultural, forestry, fishing, and related occupations	3,530	2.9	3,650	2.5	120	3.4
Executive	12,066	10.0	15,195	10.3	3,129	25.9
Marketing and sale occupations	12,993	10.7	15,664	10.6	2,671	20.6
Operators, fabricators, and laborers	16,349	13.5	17,902	12.1	1,553	9.5
Precision production, craft, and repair occupations	13,580	11.2	15,380	10.4	1,800	13.3
Professional speciality occupations	16,592	13.7	22,801	15.5	6,209	37.4
Service occupations	19,358	16.0	25,820	17.5	6,462	33.4
Technicians and related support occupations	4,282	3.5	5,664	3.8	1,382	32.2

Top 15 Metropolitan Areas, by Average Annual Salary, 1992

Source: Bureau of Labor Statistics, U.S. Dept. of Labor

Rank	Metropolitan area	Average annual salary[1]
1.	Bridgeport-Stamford-Norwalk-Danbury, CT	$ 39,006
2.	New York, NY	38,802
3.	San Jose, CA	37,068
4.	Middlesex-Somerset-Hunterdon, NJ	34,826
5.	Newark, NJ	34,712
6.	San Francisco, CA	34,358
7.	Trenton, NJ	33,960
8.	Bergen-Passaic, NJ	33,592
9.	Anchorage, AK	$ 33,007
10.	Washington, DC-MD-VA	32,899
11.	Hartford-New Britain-Middletown-Bristol, CT	31,967
12.	Boston-Lawrence-Salem-Lowell-Brockton, MA	31,872
13.	Jersey City, NJ	31,628
14.	Los Angeles-Long Beach, CA	31,267
15.	Chicago, IL	30,692

(1) Data are preliminary and may include workers covered by Unemployment Insurance and Unemployment Components for Federal Employees programs. **Note:** Jacksonville, NC, recorded the lowest annual pay level in 1992—$15,624—followed by McAllen-Edinburg-Mission, TX ($16,583), Yakima, WA ($17,210), Brownsville-Harlingen, TX ($17,294), and Yuma, AZ ($17,438). The average annual salary in the 5 bottom-ranked metropolitan areas averaged 36-43% below the nationwide metropolitan average of $25,903. A total of 33 metropolitan areas reported average pay levels below $20,000 annually.

Top 20 Metropolitan Areas, by Fastest Growing Average Annual Salary, 1991-92

Source: Bureau of Labor Statistics, U.S. Dept. of Labor

Rank	Metropolitan area	Average annual salary 1991	1992[1]	Percentage change 1991-92
1.	New York, NY	$ 35,073	$ 38,802	10.6
2.	Fort Smith, AR-OK	19,062	20,755	8.9
2.	Jersey City, NJ	29,045	31,628	8.9
4.	Bridgeport-Stamford-Norwalk-Danbury, CT	35,998	39,006	8.4
5.	Seattle, WA	27,327	29,586	8.3
6.	Janesville-Beloit, WI	22,235	24,062	8.2
7.	Fort Pierce, FL	20,216	21,821	7.9
8.	Newark, NJ	32,231	34,712	7.7
9.	Laredo, TX	16,414	17,660	7.6
9.	San Jose, CA	34,462	37,068	7.6
11.	Reno, NV	23,099	24,802	7.4
11.	Bergen-Passaic, NJ	31,292	33,592	7.4
13.	Las Vegas, NV	22,862	24,527	7.3
13.	Bremerton, WA	22,578	24,221	7.3
13.	Manchester-Nashua, NH	26,448	28,372	7.3
13.	San Francisco, CA	32,031	34,358	7.3
13.	Sioux City, IA-NE	18,993	20,376	7.3
18.	Santa Cruz, CA	21,667	23,219	7.2
18.	Orange County, NY	22,981	24,646	7.2
20.	Middlesex-Somerset-Hunterdon, NJ	32,523	34,826	7.1

(1) Data are preliminary and may include workers covered by Unemployment Insurance and Unemployment Components for Federal Employees programs.

Occupational Illnesses, by Industry and Type of Illness, 1992

Source: Bureau of Labor Statistics, U.S. Dept. of Labor

(Incidence rate per total injuries and illnesses)

Occupational illness	Private sector[1]	Agri-culture[2]	Min-ing[3]	Con-struc-tion	Manu-facturing	Trans. and pub. utilities	Trade Whole-sale	Trade Retail	Fin-ance[4]	Service
Total [2,331,100 cases]	100.0	100.0	100.0	100.0	100.0	100.0	100.0	100.0	100.0	100.0
Nature of injury, illness:										
Sprains, strains	43.9	38.8	41.1	37.7	39.8	50.5	46.7	41.3	40.1	50.1
Bruises, contusions	9.6	8.0	10.7	7.8	9.4	10.5	10.2	10.5	8.2	9.4
Cuts, lacerations	7.4	9.5	5.9	9.2	8.1	4.3	6.9	11.1	6.8	4.7
Fractures	6.2	6.9	11.1	10.0	6.1	6.5	6.5	5.0	7.4	5.0
Heat burns	1.8	0.6	1.3	1.2	1.5	0.6	1.0	3.9	0.7	1.6
Carpal tunnel syndrome	1.4	0.5	0.3	0.5	2.8	0.7	0.8	0.9	3.2	1.0
Chemical burns	0.7	0.7	0.9	0.6	0.9	0.5	0.6	0.6	0.5	0.6
Amputations	0.5	1.4	0.8	0.5	1.0	0.2	0.5	0.3	0.4	0.2
Multiple injuries	2.9	3.1	6.4	3.4	2.8	3.1	3.1	2.7	2.9	2.7
All other	25.7	30.3	21.2	29.1	27.7	23.1	23.8	23.6	29.7	24.7
Event or exposure:										
Contact with object/equip.	27.4	32.6	41.0	34.6	32.5	23.0	28.2	28.7	18.7	19.4
Struck by object	12.9	16.1	21.4	17.8	13.3	10.4	13.2	15.3	8.8	9.6
Struck against object	7.3	7.1	8.5	8.1	7.8	6.5	7.0	8.6	5.6	6.0
Caught in object	4.4	5.8	9.4	3.7	7.8	3.2	5.0	2.8	2.4	2.3
Fall to lower level	5.0	7.1	8.2	11.9	3.3	6.3	5.5	3.7	7.2	4.0
Fall to same level	10.3	8.8	7.1	6.5	7.2	8.8	8.1	14.8	15.2	12.9
Slips, trips	3.5	3.9	1.1	3.1	2.9	4.6	3.0	3.6	5.0	3.7
Overexertion	28.3	20.6	28.7	23.0	26.8	29.1	31.4	26.3	22.2	33.4
Overexertion in lifting	17.1	12.1	11.8	13.4	15.2	16.8	20.8	18.2	13.3	19.8
Repetitive motion	3.9	2.3	0.7	1.5	8.0	1.9	2.1	2.4	7.0	2.4
Exposed to harmful substance	4.8	5.4	4.6	4.2	5.1	3.1	3.2	6.0	4.2	5.0
Transportation accidents	2.9	3.8	1.5	2.4	1.4	7.8	5.2	2.0	3.2	2.8
Fires, explosions	0.2	0.1	0.5	0.4	0.2	0.2	0.3	0.2	0.5	0.1
Assault, by person	1.0	0.3	(5)	0.1	0.1	0.4	0.3	1.1	1.4	2.6
All other	12.8	15.1	6.6	12.5	12.3	14.7	12.7	11.2	15.4	13.7
Source of injury, illness:										
Chemicals/chem. products	2.0	2.1	5.8	1.5	2.5	1.2	1.9	1.6	2.3	1.9
Containers	15.1	11.9	5.8	5.7	15.1	20.4	23.9	22.2	12.2	9.3
Furniture, fixtures	4.2	0.7	0.6	1.7	3.0	2.3	2.9	6.5	6.6	5.9
Machinery	6.9	8.2	12.2	6.6	11.1	2.9	6.3	6.5	5.0	4.3
Parts and materials	11.1	7.4	17.6	25.0	16.5	9.3	12.5	6.2	5.9	4.2
Worker motion or position	13.4	12.4	4.9	10.3	17.3	12.9	10.9	11.4	16.1	12.8
Floor, ground surface	14.8	14.8	13.9	17.2	10.1	15.1	13.6	17.6	24.3	16.5
Tools, instruments, equip.	6.3	9.1	8.5	10.8	6.7	3.9	4.1	7.0	5.2	5.1
Vehicles	6.7	6.7	6.1	4.3	4.3	16.6	11.3	5.4	5.0	6.1
Health care patient	4.5	(5)	(5)	(5)	(5)	0.8	(5)	(5)	0.3	18.8
All other	15.1	26.8	24.5	16.9	13.3	14.6	12.7	15.7	17.2	15.1

Note: Components may not add to totals due to rounding. All injuries and illnesses reported involved days away from work. (1) Private sector includes all industries except government, but excludes farms with fewer than 11 employees. (2) Agriculture includes forestry and fishing, but excludes farms with fewer than 11 employees. (3)Mining includes quarrying and oil and gas extraction. (4) Finance includes insurance and real estate. (5) Fewer than 0.05.

Fatal Occupational Injuries, 1993

Source: Bureau of Labor Statistics, U.S. Dept. of Labor

Event or exposure	Fatalities Number	Fatalities Percentage
Total	**6,271**	**100**
Transportation incidents	**2,482**	**40**
Highway	1,232	20
Collision between vechicles	652	10
Vehicle struck stationary object	188	3
Noncollision	333	5
Nonhighway (farm, industrial premises)	392	6
Aircraft	280	4
Worker struck by a vehicle	361	6
Water vehicle	119	2
Railway	85	1
Assaults and violent acts	**1,309**	**21**
Homicide	1,063	17
Shooting	874	14
Stabbing	95	2
Self-inflicted injury	215	3
Contact with objects and equipment	**1,039**	**17**
Struck by object	563	9
Struck by falling object	345	6
Struck by flying object	81	1
Caught in or compressed by equipment or objects	308	5
Caught in or crushed by collapsing materials	138	2
Falls	**611**	**10**
Fall to lower level	530	8
Fall on same level	46	1
Exposure to harmful substances or environments	**590**	**9**
Contact with electric current	324	5
Exposure to caustic, noxious, or allergenic substances	116	2
Oxygen deficiency	111	2
Drowning, submersion	89	1
Fires and explosions	**201**	**3**
Other events or exposures[1]	**39**	**1**

Note: Totals for major categories may include subcategories not shown separately. Percentage, based on incidence rate per total fatalities, may not add to totals because of rounding. (1) Includes the category "Bodily reaction and exertion."

Civilian Employment of the Federal Government in May 1994

Source: Workforce Analysis and Statistics Division, U.S. Office of Personnel Management

(Payroll in thousands of dollars, for the month of May, 1994)

Agency	All Areas		United States		Wash., DC MSA		Overseas	
	Employ-ment	Payroll	Employ-ment	Payroll	Employ-ment	Payroll	Employ-ment	Payroll
Total, all agencies[1]	**$2,984,597**	**$9,406,448**	**$2,872,564**	**$9,074,407**	**$370,520**	**$1,407,129**	**$112,033**	**$332,041**
Legislative Branch	**36,949**	**126,570**	**36,896**	**126,337**	**34,932**	**118,681**	**53**	**233**
Congress	20,405	66,871	20,405	66,871	20,405	66,871	—	—
U.S. Senate	7,581	24,728	7,581	24,728	7,581	24,728	—	—
House of Rep Summary	12,807	42,086	12,807	42,086	12,807	42,086	—	—
Comm. on Scty & Coop in Eur	17	57	17	57	17	57	—	—
Architect of the Capitol	2,229	5,958	2,229	5,958	2,229	5,958	—	—
Botanic Garden	54	154	54	154	54	154	—	—
Comm. on Legal Immi. Reform	9	28	9	28	9	28	—	—
Competit Policy Council	7	32	7	32	7	32	—	—
Congressional Budget Ofc	223	1,068	223	1,068	223	1,068	—	—
General Accounting Ofc	4,546	20,214	4,499	20,021	2,994	13,545	47	193
Government Printing Ofc	4,352	14,828	4,352	14,828	3,928	13,751	—	—
John C Stennis Ctr Pub Dev	8	18	8	18	—	—	—	—
Library of Congress	4,605	15,166	4,599	15,126	4,578	15,073	6	40
Ofc Technology Assessment	206	830	206	830	206	830	—	—
Physician Payment Rev. Comm.	1	10	1	10	—	—	—	—
Prosptv Paymt. Assessmt. Comm.	—	14	—	14	—	14	—	—
U.S. Tax Court	304	1,379	304	1,379	299	1,357	—	—
Judicial Branch	**27,945**	**139,740**	**27,646**	**138,287**	**2,010**	**11,223**	**299**	**1,453**
Supreme Court	362	1,122	362	1,122	362	1,122	—	—
U.S. Courts	27,500	138,302	27,201	136,849	1,565	9,785	299	1,453
U.S. Court of Vets Appeals	83	316	83	316	83	316	—	—
Executive Branch	**2,919,703**	**9,140,138**	**2,808,022**	**8,809,783**	**333,578**	**1,277,225**	**111,681**	**330,355**
Exec Ofc of the President	1,595	7,297	1,589	7,260	1,589	7,260	6	37
White House Office	396	1,545	396	1,545	396	1,545	—	—
Ofc of Vice President	20	107	20	107	20	107	—	—
Ofc of Mgt & Budget	531	2,802	531	2,802	531	2,802	—	—
Office of Administration	188	660	188	660	188	660	—	—
Council Economic Advisors	31	143	31	143	31	143	—	—
Council on Environ Qual	3	13	3	13	3	13	—	—
Ofc of Policy Development	40	200	40	200	40	200	—	—
Exec Residence at WH	87	427	87	427	87	427	—	—
National Security Council	55	267	55	267	55	267	—	—
Ofc of Natl Drug Control	26	138	26	138	26	138	—	—
Ofc of Sci and Tech Policy	35	183	35	183	35	183	—	—
Ofc of U.S. Trade Rep.	183	812	177	775	177	775	6	37
Executive Departments	**1,928,651**	**6,180,341**	**1,836,624**	**5,902,096**	**251,368**	**954,755**	**92,027**	**278,245**
State	25,819	105,225	9,542	38,021	8,515	33,235	16,277	67,204
Treasury	162,058	506,401	160,937	501,913	23,991	95,814	1,121	4,488
Defense, Total	898,154	2,649,144	832,557	2,471,188	86,474	278,462	65,597	177,956
Dept of the Army	288,728	680,905	261,800	612,179	25,354	45,826	26,928	68,726
Army, Mil Func Total	258,505	604,421	231,676	535,976	24,178	42,310	26,829	68,445
Army, Civil Func Total	30,223	76,484	30,124	76,203	1,176	3,516	99	281
Corps of Engineers	30,099	76,170	30,000	75,889	1,052	3,202	99	281
Cemeterial Expenses	124	314	124	314	124	314	—	—
Dept of the Navy	264,628	894,000	252,743	859,938	34,803	123,908	11,885	34,062
Dept of the Air Force	191,936	615,750	182,997	585,759	5,867	23,315	8,939	29,991
Defense Log Agcy	56,787	168,627	56,047	167,050	2,925	12,521	740	1,577
Other Defense Activities	96,075	289,862	78,970	246,262	17,525	72,892	17,105	43,600
Justice	97,712	362,759	95,755	355,201	21,269	83,130	1,957	7,558
Interior	80,058	294,528	79,706	293,383	9,675	45,238	352	1,145
Agriculture	115,542	352,139	114,118	348,571	12,959	49,242	1,424	3,568
Commerce	37,333	127,832	36,400	124,153	20,371	76,621	933	3,679
Labor	17,072	60,083	17,033	59,941	6,033	22,543	39	142
Health and Human Services	129,374	419,789	128,712	417,769	30,392	114,585	662	2,020
Housing & Urban Dev	13,019	45,999	12,907	45,616	3,450	14,660	112	383
Transportation	65,293	372,157	64,750	369,342	10,140	54,300	543	2,815
Energy	20,056	89,820	20,050	89,779	7,237	38,425	6	41
Education	4,687	24,817	4,683	24,801	3,280	17,491	4	16
Veterans Affairs	262,474	769,648	259,474	762,418	7,582	31,009	3,000	7,230
Independent Agencies[1]	**989,457**	**2,952,500**	**969,809**	**2,900,427**	**80,621**	**315,210**	**19,648**	**52,073**
Environmtl Protect Agcy	18,250	69,564	18,228	69,482	6,060	25,434	22	82
Equal Employ Opp Comm	2,917	9,984	2,917	9,984	737	2,884	—	—
Federal Deposit Ins Corp.	19,596	80,507	19,588	80,467	3,964	19,337	8	40
Fed Emergency Mgmt Agcy	6,006	16,321	5,912	16,095	1,584	5,817	94	226
General Svcs Admin.	19,677	61,622	19,572	61,337	6,485	24,149	105	285
Natl Archives & Recds Admin.	3,160	6,737	3,160	6,737	1,271	3,634	—	—
Natl Aero Space Admin	23,437	106,165	23,427	106,098	5,349	31,865	10	67
Nuclear Regulatory Comm	3,386	18,597	3,386	18,597	2,266	12,923	—	—
Office of Personnel Mgmt.	5,866	16,061	5,845	16,022	2,511	8,804	21	39
Panama Canal Commission	8,478	18,961	19	82	7	53	8,459	18,879
Securities & Exchnge Comm	2,698	11,305	2,698	11,305	1,737	7,232	—	—
Small Business Admin	7,515	24,657	7,416	24,348	906	3,732	99	309
Smithsonian, Summary	5,506	15,790	5,327	15,349	4,931	14,051	179	441
Tennessee Valley Auth	18,990	77,473	18,990	77,473	9	50	—	—
U.S. Information Agency	8,085	26,375	4,120	16,924	3,862	15,509	3,965	9,451
U.S. Intnatl Dev Coop Agcy	4,183	18,073	2,294	9,977	2,291	9,959	1,889	8,096
U.S. Postal Service	809,369	2,286,916	805,512	2,274,771	22,305	70,431	3,857	12,145

(1) Included in total are other independent agencies with fewer than 2,500 employees.

10 Facts About Women Workers

Source: Women's Bureau, U.S. Dept. of Labor

1. Of the 101 million women 16 and older in the U.S., 58 million were labor force participants (working or looking for work) during 1993. Women accounted for 60% of labor force growth between 1982 and 1993.
2. Women represented 46% of all persons in the civilian labor force in 1993. Women are projected to comprise 48% of the labor force by the year 2005.
3. Teenage women (16-19 years old) are not as active in the labor force as adult women (20 years of age and older). Only 50% were in the labor force, compared with 58% of adult women. In addition, teenage women's unemployment rate was 3 times as high as that of adult women—17.4% and 5.9%, respectively.
4. The unemployment rate for all women in the labor force was 6.5% in 1993. Teenage black and Hispanic women continued to experience very high unemployment rates—37.5% and 26.4%, respectively.
5. Of the 55 million employed women in the U.S. in 1993, 41 million worked full time (35 or more hours per week); nearly 14 million, or 25% of all women workers, held part-time jobs. Two-thirds (66%) of all part-time workers were women.
6. Women have made substantial progress in obtaining jobs in virtually all managerial and professional specialty occupations. In 1983 they held 40% (9.7 million) of these high-paying jobs; in 1993 they held 48% (15.4 million). Women employed in managerial and professional specialty occupations had 1993 median weekly earnings between $347 and $1,015.
7. Women are still overrepresented in low-paying jobs. Almost half (43%) of employed women work in technical, sales, and administrative support jobs—23.5 million women. Even though the earnings gap between men and women is slowly closing, women earn only 77 cents for every dollar earned by men when comparing 1993 median weekly earnings of full-time workers ($395 for women and $514 for men). The 5 most lucrative occupations for women are lawyer, physician, pharmacist, engineer, and computer systems analyst. (This list excludes any occupation at which fewer than 50,000 females are employed.)
8. Median earnings for female high school graduates age 25 and older (with no college) working year-round, full time in 1992 were less than those of fully employed men who were high school dropouts—$18,648 and $21,179, respectively. During the 10-year period 1982-92, the earnings gap between the 2 groups has slowly declined from $4,256 to $2,537. Female high school graduates (with no college) continue to earn substantially less than their male counterparts—$18,648 versus $26,766. In addition, men with an associate's degree working year-round, full time earned nearly the same as similarly employed women with a master's degree—$32,349 and $33,018, respectively.
9. Of the approximately 67 million families in the U.S. in 1993, 12 million (18%) were maintained by women. In black families, women maintained 48%; in Hispanic families, 24%; and in white families, 18%. The median weekly earnings of families maintained by women in 1993 was $393, compared with $804 for married-couple families and $523 for families maintained by men.
10. In 1992 women represented 62% of all persons 18 years and older who were living below the poverty level. The poverty rate for families maintained by women with no husband present was 6 times as high as for married-couple families—34.9% and 6.5%, respectively. Women maintained 52% of all poor families in 1992. Women maintained 75% of poor black families, about 43% of poor Hispanic families, and 43% of poor white families.

Earnings Difference Between Women and Men, 1983 and 1992

Source: Women's Bureau, U.S. Dept. of Labor

Occupational class	Women's earnings as a percentage of men's		Women as a percentage of total employment	
	1992	1983	1992	1983
Total (all occupational classes)	**75.4**	**66.7**	**43.1**	**40.4**
Registered nurses	104.7	99.5	93.5	94.4
Pharmacists	90.1	NA	42.7	27.8
Therapists	95.8	NA	76.0	75.1
Teachers, secondary school	90.3	88.6	53.9	49.1
Cashiers	94.8	84.3	75.7	80.9
Scheduling supervisors/clerks	92.9	NA	30.7	20.1
Secretaries, stenographers, typists	91.6	76.7	98.5	98.5
Records processing, except financial	90.4	76.2	79.7	82.0
Postal clerks, except mail carriers	94.6	93.4	42.9	32.2
Mail carriers, postal service	97.0	NA	25.2	14.3
Mail clerks, except postal service	93.2	89.0	48.5	48.9
Data-entry keyers	95.0	NA	86.6	93.5
Guards/police, except public service	94.2	91.2	14.8	11.1
Waiters/waitresses, assistants	97.2	NA	38.3	36.9
Miscellaneous food occupations	105.6	102.5	39.9	48.8
Nurses aids, orderlies, attendants	96.0	81.0	87.9	86.8
Mechanics/repairers	105.4	89.4	3.3	3.4
Textile sewing machine operators	91.9	NA	87.2	94.0
Packaging/filling machine operators	90.0	78.5	61.5	64.2
Stock handlers, baggers	97.4	91.9	24.5	19.0
Hand packers/packagers	94.6	91.6	63.3	66.4

NA = not available. **Note:** Earnings data are not developed for occupations with fewer than 50,000 employees.

Annual Earnings, by Education Attainment, Sex, Race, and Hispanic Origin, 1992

Source: Bureau of the Census, U.S. Dept. of Commerce; averages per person

Characteristic	Total	Not a high school graduate	High school graduate	Some college or an associate degree	Bachelor's degree	Advanced degree
Total	$23,227	$12,809	$18,737	$20,866	$32,629	$48,653
Male	28,448	14,934	22,978	25,660	40,039	58,324
Female	17,145	9,311	14,128	16,023	23,991	33,814
White	23,932	13,193	19,265	21,357	33,092	49,346
Black	17,416	11,077	15,260	17,768	27,457	39,088
Hispanic origin[1]	16,824	11,836	16,714	19,215	28,260	41,296

(1) May be of any race.

Distribution of Wage and Salary Workers Paid Hourly Rates

Source: Bureau of Labor Statistics, U.S. Dept. of Labor; unpublished tabulations from Current Population Survey, 1993.

(in thousands)

Sex and age	Total paid hourly rates	$4.25[1] or less	Less than $10.00	$10.00 or more
Total, 16 years and older	**63,316**	**4,186**	**40,639**	**22,677**
16 to 24 years	**14,331**	2,241	13,178	1,153
20 to 24 years	9,310	932	8,221	1,090
25 years and older	48,984	1,946	27,457	21,527
25 to 54 years	42,597	1,588	23,553	19,045
25 to 34 years	17,566	806	10,915	6,651
35 to 44 years	15,354	500	7,481	7,873
45 to 54 years	9,677	282	4,762	4,915
55 years and older	6,387	357	3,906	2,481
55 to 64 years	5,041	209	2,838	2,203
65 years and older	1,346	148	1,070	276
Men, 16 years and older	31,699	1,583	17,512	14,187
16 to 24 years	7,385	966	6,666	719
20 to 24 years	4,853	366	4,178	675
25 years and older	24,314	618	10,845	13,469
Women, 16 years and older	31,617	2,603	23,126	8,491
16 to 24 years	6,946	1,275	6,514	432
20 to 24 years	4,457	566	4,042	415
25 years and older	24,671	1,328	16,613	8,058
Family relationship				
Husbands	16,611	298	NA	NA
Wives	15,659	748	NA	NA
Women who maintain families	4,277	329	NA	NA
Men who maintain families	1,307	35	NA	NA
Race and Hispanic origin				
White				
Total, 16 years and older	52,971	3,467	33,370	19,601
Men	26,656	1,290	14,241	12,415
Women	26,315	2,177	19,129	7,186
Black				
Total, 16 years and older	8,078	572	5,777	2,301
Men	3,915	234	4,714	1,333
Women	4,163	338	3,195	968
Hispanic origin				
Total, 16 years and older	6,047	544	4,491	1,556
Men	3,642	295	2,535	1,107
Women	2,405	248	1,954	451
Full- and part-time status and sex				
Full-time workers				
Total, 16 years and older	47,125	1,448	26,901	20,224
Men	26,557	600	12,955	13,602
Women	20,567	848	13,946	6,621
Part-time workers				
Total, 16 years and older	16,191	2,739	13,737	2,454
Men	5,142	984	4,557	585
Women	11,050	1,755	9,182	1,868

NA = not available. **Note:** Data exclude the incorporated self-employed. (1) $4.25 = minimum wage from April 1, 1991.

Average Hours and Earnings of Production Workers, 1965-93

Source: Bureau of Labor Statistics, U.S. Dept. of Labor

(annual averages)

Year	Weekly hours	Total private[1] Hourly earnings	Weekly earnings	Year	Weekly hours	Total private[1] Hourly earnings	Weekly earnings
1965	38.8	$2.46	$95.45	1980	35.3	$6.66	$235.10
1966	38.6	2.56	98.82	1981	35.2	7.25	255.20
1967	38.0	2.68	101.84	1982	34.8	7.68	267.26
1968	37.8	2.85	107.73	1983	35.0	8.02	280.70
1969	37.7	3.04	114.61	1984	35.2	8.32	292.86
1970	37.1	3.23	119.83	1985	34.9	8.57	299.09
1971	36.9	3.45	127.31	1986	34.8	8.76	304.85
1972	37.0	3.70	136.90	1987	34.8	8.98	312.50
1973	36.9	3.94	145.39	1988	34.7	9.28	322.02
1974	36.5	4.24	154.76	1989	34.6	9.66	334.24
1975	36.1	4.53	163.53	1990	34.5	10.01	345.35
1976	36.1	4.86	175.45	1991	34.3	10.32	353.98
1977	36.0	5.25	189.00	1992	34.4	10.57	363.61
1978	35.8	5.69	203.70	1993	34.5	10.83	373.64
1979	35.7	6.16	219.91				

(1) Data relate to production workers in mining and manufacturing; construction workers in construction; and nonsupervisory workers in transportation and public utilities; wholesale and retail trade; finance, insurance, and real estate; and services.

Employer Costs for Employee Compensation, March 1994

Source: Bureau of Labor Statistics, U.S. Dept. of Labor; dollar figures are costs per hour worked

The following table discusses average employee compensation costs for all civilian employees (private industry and state and local governments).

In private industry, March 1994 employer compensation costs averaged $17.08 per hour worked. This figure was composed of $12.14 per hour in straight-time wages and $4.94 per hour in benefits costs, including legally required benefits. Compensation costs averaged more for workers in goods-producing industries ($20.85 per hour worked) than for those in service-producing industries ($15.82 per hour worked).

During the same period, employer compensation costs for state and local government employees averaged $25.27 per hour worked. Of this amount, costs for straight-time wages and salaries averaged $17.57 per hour, and benefit costs, including legally required benefits, averaged $7.71 per hour. Among work activities, average compensation costs were higher per hour worked in services (i.e., health and educational services) than in public administration ($26.94 per hour and $22.11 per hour, respectively). These 2 categories account for most state and local government employment.

	Total compensation	Wages and salaries	Benefit Costs					
			Total[1]	Paid leave	Supplemental pay	Insurance	Retirement and savings	Legally required benefits
Civilian workers	**$18.43**	**$13.06**	**$5.37**	**$1.23**	**$0.40**	**$1.38**	**$0.73**	**$1.59**
Occupational group:								
White-collar occupations	21.86	15.85	6.01	1.55	.38	1.55	.88	1.60
Professional specialty and technical	29.15	21.37	7.77	1.94	.37	1.99	1.46	1.96
Executive, administrative, and managerial	31.28	22.44	8.84	2.69	.71	1.84	1.21	2.24
Administrative support including clerical	14.90	10.41	4.49	1.13	.26	1.41	.51	1.17
Blue-collar occupations	17.09	11.38	5.70	1.02	.57	1.48	.67	1.91
Service occupations	10.00	7.18	2.82	.58	.16	.70	.37	1.00
Industry group:								
Services	19.68	14.39	5.29	1.29	.26	1.40	.84	1.49
Health services	19.29	13.64	5.66	1.57	.54	1.44	.57	1.53
Hospitals	20.57	14.37	6.20	1.75	.62	1.63	.60	1.58
Educational services	25.62	18.87	6.75	1.51	.06	1.98	1.62	1.57
Elementary and secondary education	25.52	18.80	6.72	1.40	.04	2.08	1.65	1.52
Higher education	28.14	20.60	7.54	1.91	.11	1.97	1.83	1.72
			Percent of Total Compensation					
Civilian workers	**100%**	**70.9%**	**29.1%**	**6.7%**	**2.2%**	**7.5%**	**4.0%**	**8.6%**
Occupational group:								
White-collar occupations	100.0	72.5	27.5	7.1	1.8	7.1	4.0	7.3
Professional specialty and technical	100.0	73.3	26.7	6.7	1.3	6.8	5.0	6.7
Executive, administrative, and managerial	100.0	71.7	28.3	8.6	2.3	5.9	3.9	7.2
Administrative support including clerical	100.0	69.9	30.1	7.6	1.7	9.5	3.4	7.9
Blue-collar occupations	100.0	66.6	33.4	6.0	3.3	8.7	3.9	11.2
Service occupations	100.0	71.8	28.2	5.8	1.6	7.0	3.7	10.0
Industry group:								
Services	100.0	73.1	26.9	6.5	1.3	7.1	4.3	7.6
Health services	100.0	70.7	29.3	8.1	2.8	7.5	2.9	7.9
Hospitals	100.0	69.8	30.2	8.5	3.0	7.9	2.9	7.7
Educational services	100.0	73.7	26.3	5.9	.2	7.7	6.3	6.1
Elementary and secondary education	100.0	73.7	26.3	5.5	.2	8.2	6.5	6.0
Higher education	100.0	73.2	26.8	6.8	.4	7.0	6.5	6.1

(1) Includes severance pay and supplemental unemployment benefits, not listed separately.

Federal Minimum Hourly Wage Rates Since 1950

Source: U.S. Dept. of Labor

The Fair Labor Standards Act of 1938 and subsequent amendments provide for minimum wage coverage applicable to specified nonsupervisory employment categories. Exempt from coverage are executives and administrators or professionals.

Minimum Rates for Nonfarm Workers

Effective date	Laws prior to 1966[1]	Percent, avg earnings[2]	1966 and later[3]	Minimum rates for farm workers[4]
Jan. 25, 1950	$.75	54	NA	NA
Mar. 1, 1956	1.00	52	NA	NA
Sept. 3, 1961	1.15	50	NA	NA
Sept. 3, 1963	1.25	51	NA	NA
Feb. 1, 1967	1.40	50	$1.00	$1.00
Feb. 1, 1968	1.60	54	1.15	1.15
Feb. 1, 1969	(5)	(5)	1.30	1.30
Feb. 1, 1970	(5)	(5)	1.45	(5)
Feb. 1, 1971	(5)	(5)	1.60	(5)
May 1, 1974	2.00	46	1.90	1.60
Jan. 1, 1975	$2.10	45	$2.00	$1.80
Jan. 1, 1976	2.30	46	2.20	2.00
Jan. 1, 1977	(5)	(5)	2.30	2.20
Jan. 1, 1978	2.65	44	2.65	2.65
Jan. 1, 1979	2.90	45	2.90	2.90
Jan. 1, 1980	3.10	43	3.10	3.10
Jan. 1, 1981	3.35	42	3.35	3.35
Apr. 1, 1990	3.80[6]	35	3.80[6]	3.80[6]
Apr. 1, 1991	4.25[6]	38	4.25[6]	4.25[6]

NA = not applicable. (1) Applies to workers covered prior to 1961 Amendments and, after Sept. 1965, to workers covered by 1961 Amendments. Rates set by 1961 Amendments were: Sept. 1961, $1.00; Sept. 1964, $1.15; and Sept. 1965, $1.25. (2) Percent of gross average hourly earnings of production workers in manufacturing. (3) Applies to workers newly covered by Amendments of 1966, 1974, and 1977, and Title IX of Education Amendments of 1972. (4) Included in coverage as of 1966, 1974, and 1977 Amendments. (5) No change in rate. (6) Training wage for workers age 16-19 in first six months of first job: 1990, $3.35; 1991, $3.62 and from Apr. 1, 1991, additional requirements refer to subsequent employment by a different employer for an additional 90 days. The training wage expired Mar. 31, 1993.

Median Weekly Earnings of Full-Time Wage and Salary Workers by Age, Sex, and Union Affiliation

Source: Bureau of Labor Statistics, U.S. Dept. of Labor

	1992				1993			
Sex and age	Total	Members of unions[1]	Represented by unions[2]	Non-union	Total	Members of unions[1]	Represented by unions[2]	Non-union
Total, 16 years and older	$445	$547	$541	$413	$463	$575	$569	$426
16 to 24 years	277	352	346	272	283	377	366	277
25 years and older	480	559	554	450	493	585	581	468
25 to 34 years	424	506	499	410	439	520	514	420
35 to 44 years	504	576	572	484	519	595	593	499
45 to 54 years	523	601	601	496	543	622	620	507
55 to 64 years	483	552	549	447	492	576	573	462
65 years and older	378	495	493	354	394	467	462	381
Men, 16 years and older	505	589	586	480	514	608	606	490
16 to 24 years	285	374	367	279	289	393	383	283
25 years and older	539	597	596	515	559	617	616	524
25 to 34 years	470	535	528	449	478	555	549	459
35 to 44 years	584	609	608	570	598	623	623	586
45 to 54 years	636	636	638	633	656	670	671	641
55 to 64 years	578	597	598	557	586	610	612	564
65 years and older	421	571	557	400	453	529	524	434
Women, 16 years and older	381	484	481	361	395	504	500	374
16 to 24 years	267	319	322	263	274	344	340	270
25 years and older	400	491	489	383	416	511	508	396
25 to 34 years	383	451	445	374	396	481	474	383
35 to 44 years	419	504	503	399	437	526	524	412
45 to 54 years	417	519	518	391	441	540	537	407
55 to 64 years	376	461	460	355	396	482	480	372
65 years and older	328	409	419	310	335	400	399	316

(1) Data refer to members of a labor union or an employee association similar to a union. (2) Data refer to members of a labor union or an employee association similar to a union as well as workers who report no union affiliation but whose jobs are covered by a union or an employee association contract. **Note:** Data refer to the sole or principal job of full-time workers. Excluded are self-employed workers whose businesses are incorporated although they technically qualify as wage and salary workers.

Work Stoppages (Strikes) in the U.S., 1956-93

Source: Bureau of Labor Statistics, U.S. Dept. of Labor
(involving 1,000 workers or more)

	Number stoppages[1]	Workers involved[1] (thousands)	Work days idle[1] (thousands)		Number stoppages[1]	Workers involved[1] (thousands)	Work days idle[1] (thousands)
1960	222	896	13,260	1979	235	1,021	20,409
1965	268	999	15,140	1980	187	795	20,844
1966	321	1,300	16,000	1981	145	729	16,908
1967	381	2,192	31,320	1982	96	656	9,061
1968	392	1,855	35,567	1983	81	909	17,461
1969	412	1,576	29,397	1984	62	376	8,499
1970	381	2,468	52,761	1985	54	324	7,079
1971	298	2,516	35,538	1986	69	533	11,861
1972	250	975	16,764	1987	46	174	4,481
1973	317	1,400	16,260	1988	40	118	4,364
1974	424	1,796	31,809	1989	51	452	16,996
1975	235	965	17,563	1990	44	185	5,926
1976	231	1,519	23,962	1991	40	392	4,584
1977	298	1,212	21,258	1992	35	364	3,989
1978	219	1,006	23,774	1993	35	182	3,981

(1) The number of stoppages and workers relate to stoppages that began in the year. Days of idleness include all stoppages in effect. Workers are counted more than once if they were involved in more than one stoppage during the year.

Work Stoppages Involving 5,000 Workers or More Beginning in 1993

Source: Bureau of Labor Statistics, U.S. Dept. of Labor

Employer, location, and union	Began	Ended	Workers involved[1]	Estimated days idle in 1993[1]
Boeing Co., Seattle, WA, Engineers	1/19	1/19	21,000	21,000
Bituminous Coal Operators Association, interstate, Mine Workers	2/2	3/2	6,700	103,400
Douglas Aircraft Co., California, Machinists	3/2	3/3	6,800	13,600
Kaiser Permanente, California, Service Employees	4/1	4/1	12,000	12,000
Retail food stores (Shoprite, Pathmark, Grand Union, and Foodtown), NJ/NY, Food and Commercial Workers	5/7	5/29	23,800	246,200
Bituminous Coal Operators Association, interstate, Mine Workers	5/10	12/14	16,800	2,203,000
Los Angeles Depart. of Water and Power, Los Angeles, CA, Electrical Workers (IBEW) and Engineers and Architects	9/1	9/9	9,000	54,000
Southern California Gas Co., California, Utility Workers and Chemical Workers	10/1	10/1	6,000	6,000
Boston public schools, Boston, MA, Teachers (AFT)	10/27	10/27	5,700	5,700
Caterpillar, Inc., IL, CO, and PA, Automobile Workers	11/11	11/14	14,000	14,000
American Airlines, interstate, Flight Attendants	11/18	11/22	19,000	57,000

(1) Workers and days idle are rounded to the nearest 100.

Labor Union Directory

Source: Bureau of Labor Statistics, U.S. Dept. of Labor; World Almanac questionnaire

(*) Independent union; all others affiliated with AFL-CIO.

American Federation of Labor & Congress of Industrial Organizations (AFL-CIO), 815 16th St. NW, Washington, DC 20006; founded 1955; Lane Kirkland, Pres. (since 1979); 13.3 mil. members.

Actors and Artistes of America, Associated (AAAA), 165 W 46th St., New York, NY 10036; founded 1919; Theodore Bikel, Pres.; no individual members, 7 National Performing Arts Unions are affiliates; approx. 100,000 combined membership.

Actors' Equity Association, 165 W 46th St., New York, NY 10036; founded 1913; Ron Silver, Pres. (since 1991); 32,000 active members.

Air Line Pilots Association, 1625 Massachusetts Ave. NW, Washington, DC 20036; founded 1933; J. Randolph Babbitt, Pres. (since 1990); 44,000 members.

Aluminum, Brick & Glass Workers International Union (ABGWIU), 3362 Hollenberg Drive, Bridgeton, MO 63044; founded 1953; Ernie J. Labaff, Pres. (since 1985); 44,000 members, 375 locals.

Automobile, Aerospace & Agricultural Implement Workers of America, International Union, United (UAW), 8000 E Jefferson Ave., Detroit, MI 48214; founded 1935; Owen Bieber, Pres. (since 1983); 1.3 mil. members, 1,181 locals.

Bakery, Confectionery & Tobacco Workers International Union (BC&T), 10401 Connecticut Ave., Kensington, MD 20895; founded 1886; Frank Hurt, Pres. (since 1992); 125,000 members.

Boilermakers, Iron Ship Builders, Blacksmiths, Forgers and Helpers, International Brotherhood of (IBBISB/BF&H), 570 New Brotherhood Bldg., 753 State Ave., Kansas City, KS 66101; founded 1880; Charles W. Jones, Pres. (since 1982); 90,000 members, 350 locals.

Bricklayers and Allied Craftsmen, International Union of, 815 15th St. NW, Washington, DC 20005; founded 1865; John T. Joyce, Pres.; 100,000 members, 400 locals.

Carpenters and Joiners of America, United Brotherhood of, 101 Constitution Ave. NW, Washington, DC 20001; founded 1881; Sigurd Lucassen, Gen. Pres. (since 1988); 500,000 members, 3,200 locals.

Chemical Workers Union, International (ICWU), 1655 West Market St., Akron, OH 44313; founded 1944; Frank D. Martino, Pres. (since 1975); 50,000 members, 350 locals.

Clothing and Textile Workers Union, Amalgamated (ACTWU), 15 Union Square, New York, NY 10003; founded 1976 (by merger of 2 unions); Jack Sheinkman, Pres. (since 1987); 26,500 members.

Communications Workers of America (CWA), 501 3d St. NW, Washington, DC 20001-2797; founded 1938; Morton Bahr, Pres. (since 1985); 600,000 members, 1,200 locals.

Distillery, Wine & Allied Workers International Union (DWU), 66 Grand Ave., Englewood, NJ 07631; founded 1940; George J. Orlando, Pres. (since 1984).

***Education Association, National,** 1201 16th St. NW, Washington, DC 20036; Keith Geiger, Pres. (since 1989); 2.2 mil. members, 13,250 affiliates.

Electrical Workers, International Brotherhood of (IBEW), 1125 15th St. NW, Washington, DC 20005; founded 1891; John J. Barry, Int'l Pres. (since 1986); 800,000 members, 1,500 locals.

Electronic, Electrical, Salaried, Machine and Furniture Workers, International Union of (IUE), 1126 16th St. NW, Washington, DC 20036; founded 1949; William H. Bywater, Pres. (since 1982); 140,000 members, 500 locals.

Farm Workers of America, United (UFW), 29700 Woodfoel Tehachapi Rd., PO Box 62, Keene, CA 93531; founded 1962; Arturo S. Rodríguez, Pres. (since 1993); 50,000 members, 32 locals.

***Federal Employees, National Federation of (NFFE),** 1016 16th St. NW, Washington, DC 20036; founded 1917; Sheila K. Velazco, Pres.; 148,000 members, 392 locals.

Fire Fighters, International Association of, 1750 New York Ave. NW, Washington, DC 20006; founded 1918; Alfred K. Whitehead, Gen. Pres. (since 1988); 200,000 members, 2,280 locals.

Firemen and Oilers, International Brotherhood of, 1100 Circle 75 Parkway, Suite 350, Atlanta, GA 30339; founded 1899; Jimmy L. Walker, Pres.; 25,000 members, 210 locals.

Food and Commercial Workers International Union, United (UFCW), 1775 K St. NW, Washington, DC 20006-1598; founded 1979 following merger; Douglas H. Dority, Int'l Pres. (since 1994); 1.4 mil. members, 660 locals.

Garment Workers of America, United (UGWA), 4207 Lebanon Rd., Hermitage, TN 37076; founded 1891; Dave Johnson, Gen. Pres. (since 1991); 20,000 members, 120 locals.

Glass, Molders, Pottery, Plastics & Allied Workers Intl. Union (GMP), 608 E Baltimore Pike, PO Box 607, Media, PA 19063; founded 1842; James E. Hatfield, Int'l Pres. (since 1977); 72,000 members, 450 locals.

Government Employees, American Federation of (AFGE), 80 F St. NW, Washington, DC 20001; founded 1932; John N. Sturdivant, Natl. Pres. (since 1988); 200,000 members, 1,200 locals.

Grain Millers, American Federation of (AFGM), 4949 Olson Memorial Hwy., Minneapolis, MN 55422; founded 1936; Larry R. Jackson, Gen. Pres. (since 1991); 28,000 members, 200 locals.

Graphic Communications International Union (GCIU), 1900 L St. NW, Washington, DC 20036; founded 1983; James J. Norton, Pres. (since 1985); 165,000 members, 450 locals.

Hotel Employees and Restaurant Employees International Union, 1219 28th St. NW, Washington, DC 20007; Edward T. Henley, Gen. Pres.(since 1973); 400,000 members, 190 locals.

Industrial Workers of America, International Union, Allied (AIW), merged with the United Paperworkers International Union, Jan. 1, 1994.

Iron Workers, International Association of Bridge, Structural and Ornamental, 1750 New York Ave. NW, Washington, DC 20006; founded 1896; Jake West, Gen. Pres. (since 1989); 140,000 members, 300 locals.

Laborers' International Union of North America (LIUNA), 905 16th St. NW, Washington, DC 20006; founded 1903; Arthur A. Coia, Gen. Pres. (since 1993); 700,000 members.

Ladies' Garment Workers' Union, International (ILGWU), 1710 Broadway, New York, NY 10019; founded 1900; Jay Mazur, Pres. (since 1986); 150,000 members, 245 locals.

Leather Goods, Plastic and Novelty Workers' Union, International, 265 W 14th St., New York, NY 10011; Andrew McKenzie, Gen. Pres. (since 1992); 6,000 members, 85 locals.

Letter Carriers, National Association of (NALC), 100 Indiana Ave. NW, Washington, DC 20001; founded 1889; Vincent R. Sombrotto, Pres. (since 1978); 310,000 members, 3,190 locals.

***Locomotive Engineers, Brotherhood of (BLE),** The Standard Bldg., 1370 Ontario Ave., Cleveland, OH 44113-1702; founded 1863; Ronald P. McLaughlin, Pres. (since 1991); 50,500 members, 610 divisions.

Longshoremen's Association, International, 17 Battery Pl., New York, NY 10004; John Bowers, Pres., (since 1987); 65,000 members, 331 locals.

***Longshoremen's & Warehousemen's Union, International (ILWU),** 1188 Franklin St., San Francisco, CA 94109; founded 1937; Brian McWilliams, Pres. (since 1994); 45,000 members, 58 locals.

Machinists and Aerospace Workers, International Association of (IAM), 9000 Machinist Pl., Upper Marlboro, MD 20772-2687; founded 1888; George J. Kourpias, Int'l Pres. (since 1989); 731,780 members, 1,370 locals.

Maintenance of Way Employees, Brotherhood of (BMWE), 26555 Evergreen Rd., Suite 200, Southfield, MI 48076; founded 1887; Mac A. Fleming, Pres. (since 1990); 50,000 members, 801 locals.

Marine & Shipbuilding Workers of America, Industrial Union of (IUMSWA), 5101 River Rd., #110, Bethesda, MD 20816; founded 1934; merged with Machinists and Aerospace Workers, Dec. 1, 1990.

Marine Engineer Beneficial Assn. (MEBA), 444 N Capitol St. NW, Suite 800, Washington, DC 20001; founded 1875; Joel E. Bem, Pres. (1994); 4,242 members, 25 locals.

Maritime, National, Union (NMU), 1125 15th St. NW, Suite 501, Washington, DC 20005; Louis Parise, Pres.; 50,000 members.

***Mine Workers of America, United (UMWA),** 900 15th St. NW, Washington, DC 20005; founded 1890; Richard L. Trumka, Int'l Pres. (since 1982); 240,000 members, 900 locals.

Musicians of the United States and Canada, American Federation of (AF of M), 1501 Broadway, Suite 600, New York, NY 10036; founded 1896; Mark Tully Massagli, Pres. (since 1991); 150,000 members, 340 locals.

Newspaper Guild, The (TNG), 8611 Second Ave., Silver Spring, MD 20910; founded 1933; Charles B. Dale, Pres. (since 1987); 32,000 members, 76 locals.

***Nurses Association, American (ANA),** 600 Maryland Ave. SW, Suite 100W, Washington, DC 20024-2571; Virginia Trotter-Betts, JD, RN, Pres. (since 1992); 210,000 members, 53 constituent state assns.

Office and Professional Employees International Union (OPEIU), 265 W 14th St., New York, NY 10011; founded 1945 (AFL Charter); Michael Goodwin, Int'l Pres. (since 1994); 130,000 members, 250 locals.

Oil, Chemical and Atomic Workers International Union (OCAW), 255 Union Blvd., PO Box 281200, Lakewood, CO 80228; Robert E. Wages, Pres. (since 1991); 87,000 members, 384 locals.

Operating Engineers, International Union of (IUOE), 1125 17th St. NW, Washington, DC 20036; founded 1896; Frank Hanley, Gen. Pres.; 400,000 members, 200 locals.

Painters and Allied Trades, International Brotherhood of (IBPAT), 1750 New York Ave. NW, Washington, DC 20006; founded 1887; A. L. "Mike" Monroe, Gen. Pres.; 128,243 members, 550 locals.

Paperworkers International Union, United (UPIU), 3340 Perimeter Hill Dr., Nashville, TN 37211; founded 1872; Wayne E. Glenn, Pres. (since 1978); 265,000 members, 1,425 locals.

***Plant Guard Workers of America, International Union, United (UPGWA),** 25510 Kelly Rd., Roseville, MI 48066; founded 1948; Gene McConville, Pres.; 28,000 members, 176 locals.

Plasterers' and Cement Masons' International Association of the United States & Canada; Operative, 1125 17th St. NW, 6th Fl., Washington, DC 20036; founded 1864; Dominic A. Martell, Gen. Pres.; 40,000 members, 250 locals.

Plumbing and Pipefitting Industry of the United States and Canada, United Association of Journeymen and Apprentices of the, 901 Massachusetts Ave. NW, Washington, DC 20001; founded 1889; Marvin J. Boede, Pres. (since 1982); 297,000 members, 437 locals.

***Police, Fraternal Order of,** 1410 Donelson Pike, Nashville, TN 37217; Dewey R. Stokes, Natl. Pres., and Jerry Atnip, Natl. Secy.; 253,000 members, 1,860 affiliates.

***Postal Supervisors, National Association of,** 1727 King St., Suite 400, Alexandria, VA 22314-2753; Vincent Palladino, Pres. (since 1992); 37,464 members, 407 locals.

Postal Workers Union, American (APWU), 1300 L St. NW, Washington, DC 20005; founded 1971; Moe Biller, Pres. (since 1980); 350,000 members, 1,850 locals.

Railway Carmen Division of Transportation Communications Int'l. Union (BRC Division/TCU), 3 Research Pl., Rockville, MD 20850; founded 1888; R. P. Wojtowicz, Gen. Pres. (since 1992); 50,000 members, 265 locals.

Retail, Wholesale and Department Store Union, 30 E 29th St., New York, NY 10016; Lenore Miller, Pres.; 100,000 members, 157 locals.

Roofers, Waterproofers & Allied Workers, United Union of, 1125 17th St. NW, Washington, DC 20036; founded 1903; Earl J. Kruse, Pres. (since 1985); 25,000 members, 110 locals.

Rubber, Cork, Linoleum and Plastic Workers of America, United (URW), 570 White Pond Dr., Akron, OH 44320-1156; founded 1935; Kenneth L. Coss, Int'l Pres. (since 1990); 90,000 members, 360 locals.

***Rural Letter Carriers' Association, National,** 1630 Duke St., 4th floor, Alexandria, VA 22314; founded 1903; Scottie B. Hicks, Pres. (since 1994); 48,000 members; 50 state organizations.

Seafarers International Union of North America (SIUNA), 5201 Auth Way, Camp Springs, MD 20746; founded 1938; Michael Sacco, Pres. (since 1988); 85,000 members.

Service Employees International Union (SEIU), 1313 L St. NW, Washington, DC 20005; founded 1921; John J. Sweeney, Pres. (since 1980); 1 mil. members, 290 locals.

Sheet Metal Workers' International Association (SMWIA), 1750 New York Ave. NW, Washington, DC 20006; founded 1888; Arthur Moore, Gen. Pres. (since 1993); 135,000 members, 213 locals.

State, County and Municipal Employees, American Federation of, 1625 L St. NW, Washington, DC 20036; Gerald McEntee, Pres. (since 1981); 1.3 mil. members, 3,515 locals.

Steelworkers of America, United (USWA), 5 Gateway Center, Pittsburgh, PA 15222; founded 1936; George Becker, Int'l Pres. (since 1994); 550,000 members, 2,300 locals.

Teachers, American Federation of (AFT), 555 New Jersey Ave. NW, Washington, DC 20001; founded 1916; Albert Shanker, Pres. (since 1974); 852,200 members, 2,255 locals.

Teamsters, Chauffeurs, Warehousemen and Helpers of America, International Brotherhood of (IBT), 25 Louisiana Ave. NW, Washington, DC 20001; founded 1903; Ronald R. Carey, Pres. (since 1992); 1.4 mil. members, 615 locals.

Television and Radio Artists, American Federation of, 260 Madison Ave., New York, NY 10016; founded 1937; Shelby Scott, Pres.; 77,000 members, 30 locals.

Textile Workers of America, United (UTWA), 2 Echelon Plaza, Suite 200, Laurel Rd., Voorhees, NJ 08043; founded 1901; Ron Myslowka, Intl. Pres. (since 1992); 30,000 members, 125 locals.

Theatrical Stage Employees and Moving Picture Machine Operators of the United States and Canada, International Alliance of (IATSE), 1515 Broadway, Suite 601, New York, NY 10036; founded 1893; Alfred W. Di Tolla, Pres.; 75,000 members, 552 locals.

Transit Union, Amalgamated (ATU), 5025 Wisconsin Ave. NW, Washington, DC 20016; founded 1892; James La Sala, Intl. Pres. (since 1986); 160,000 members, 275 locals.

Transport Workers Union of America, 80 West End Ave., New York, NY 10023; founded 1934; Sonny Hall, Int'l Pres. (since 1993); 125,000 members, 92 locals.

Transportation Communications International Union (TCU), 3 Research Place, Rockville, MD 20850; founded 1899; Robert A. Scardelletti, Int'l Pres. (since 1991); 123,081 members, 920 locals.

***Transportation Union, United (UTU),** 14600 Detroit Ave., Cleveland, OH 44107; founded 1969; G. Thomas DuBose, Pres. (since 1991); 134,000 members, 712 locals.

***Treasury Employees Union, National (NTEU),** 901 E St. NW, Suite 600, Washington, DC 20004; founded 1938; Robert M. Tobias, Natl. Pres. (since 1983); 150,000 represented, 250 chapters.

***University Professors, American Association of (AAUP),** 1012 14th St. NW, Washington, DC 20005; founded 1915; James Perley, Pres.; 44,000 members, 1,000 chapters.

Utility Workers Union of America (UWUA), 815 16th St. NW, Suite 605, Washington, DC 20006; founded 1945; Marshall M. Hicks, Natl. Pres. (since 1991); 50,000 members, 210 locals.

International Woodworkers of America—U.S. (IWA—U.S.), merged with the International Association of Machinists and Aerospace Workers, May 1, 1994.

U.S. Union Membership, 1930-93

Source: Bureau of Labor Statistics, U.S. Dept. of Labor

Year	Labor[1] force (thousands)	Union[2] members (thousands)	Percentage	Year	Labor[1] force (thousands)	Union[2] members (thousands)	Percentage
1930	29,424	3,401	11.6	1984	92,194	17,340	18.8
1935	27,053	3,584	13.2	1985	94,521	16,996	18.0
1940	32,376	8,717	26.9	1986	96,903	16,975	17.5
1945	40,394	14,322	35.5	1987	99,303	16,913	17.0
1950	45,222	14,267	31.5	1988	101,407	17,002	16.8
1955	50,675	16,802	33.2	1989	103,480	16,960	16.4
1960	54,234	17,049	31.4	1990	103,905	16,740	16.1
1965	60,815	17,299	28.4	1991	102,786	16,568	16.1
1970	70,920	19,381	27.3	1992	103,688	16,390	15.8
1975	76,945	19,611	25.5	1993	105,067	16,598	15.8
1980	90,564	19,843	21.9				

(1) Does not include agricultural employment; from 1984 data do not include self-employed or unemployed persons. (2) From 1930 to 1980 data are the number of dues-paying members of traditional trade unions with members counted regardless of employment status; from 1984 members include employee associations that engage in collective bargaining with employers.

NATIONAL DEFENSE

Data as of mid-1994

Chairman, Joint Chiefs of Staff
Gen. John M. Shalikashvili

Vice Chairman
Adm. David E. Jeremiah

The Joint Chiefs of Staff consists of the Chairman and Vice Chairman of the Joint Chiefs of Staff; the Chief of Staff, U.S. Army; the Chief of Naval Operations; the Chief of Staff, U.S. Air Force; and the Commandant of the Marine Corps.

Army

Chief of Staff—Gordon R. Sullivan

Generals	Date of Rank		
Downing, Wayne A.	May	20,	1993
Franks, Frederick M., Jr.	Aug.	23,	1991
Joulwan, George A.	Nov.	21,	1990
Luck, Gary E.	July	1,	1993
Maddox, David M.	July	9,	1992
McCaffrey, Barry R.	Feb.	17,	1994
Peay, J.H. Binford III	Mar.	26,	1993
Reimer, Dennis J.	June	21,	1991
Salomon, Leon E.	Feb.	11,	1994
Shalikashvili, John M.	Jun.	24,	1992

Air Force

Chief of Staff—Merrill A. McPeak, until Oct. 1994*

Generals	Date of Rank		
Ashy, Joseph W.	July	15,	1994
Boyd, Charles G.	Dec.	1,	1992
Carns, Michael P.C.	May	16,	1991
Davis, James B.	June	1,	1992
*Fogleman, Ronald R.	Sept.	1,	1992
Jamerson, James L.	July	15,	1994
Loh, John M.	June	1,	1990
Moorman, Thomas S.	July	15,	1994
Rutherford, Robert L.	Feb.	1,	1993
Viccellio, Henry, Jr.	Dec.	10,	1992
Yates, Ronald W.	Apr.	1,	1990

Navy

Chief of Naval Operations
Adm. Jeremy M. Boorda (surface warfare)

Admirals	Date of Rank		
Arthur, Stanley R. (aviator)	July	6,	1992
Chiles, Henry G., Jr. (submariner)	Feb.	14,	1992
Demars, Bruce (submariner)	Nov.	1,	1988
Kelly, Robert J. (aviator)	Mar.	1,	1991
Larson, Charles R. (submariner)	Mar.	1,	1990
Mauz, Henry H., Jr. (surface warfare)	Aug.	1,	1992
Miller, Paul D. (surface warfare)	Feb.	1,	1991
Owens, William A. (submariner)	Mar.	1,	1994
Smith, Leighton W., Jr. (aviator)	May	1,	1994

Marine Corps

Corps Commandant, with rank of General

Carl E. Mundy, Jr. . . . . . July 1, 1991

Assistant Commandant (ACMC)

Walter E. Boomer . . . . . . Sept. 1, 1992

Coast Guard

Commandant, with rank of Admiral

Robert E. Kramek . . . . . . June 1, 1994

Vice Commandant, with rank of Vice Admiral

Arthur E. Henn . . . . . . June 17, 1994

Unified Defense Commands Commanders in Chief

(as of mid-1994)

U.S. European Command, Brussels, Belgium — Gen. George A. Joulwan (USA) (concurrently NATO Supreme Allied Commander, Europe)

U.S. Southern Command, Quarry Heights, Panama Canal Zone — Gen. Barry R. McCaffrey (USA)

U.S. Atlantic Command, Norfolk, Virginia — Adm. Paul D. Miller (USN) (concurrently NATO Supreme Allied Commander, Atlantic)

U.S. Pacific Command, Honolulu, Hawaii — Adm. Richard C. Macke (USN)

U.S. Space Command, Peterson AFB, Colo. — Gen. Joseph W. Ashy (USAF)

U.S. Strategic Command, Omaha, Neb. — Adm. Henry G. Chiles, Jr. (USN)

U.S. Forces Command, Fort McPherson, Ga. — Gen. Dennis J. Reimer (USA)

U.S. Transportation Command, Scott AFB, Ill. — Gen. Ronald R. Fogleman* (USAF)

U.S. Special Operations Command, Fort Walton Beach, Fla. — Gen. Wayne A. Downing (USA)

U.S. Central Command, MacDill AFB, Fla. — Gen. J.H. Binford Peay, III (USA)

* In Aug. 1994, Gen. Fogleman was nominated to replace Gen. McPeak as Air Force Chief of Staff, following McPeak's scheduled Oct. retirement.

North Atlantic Treaty Organization International Commands

(as of mid-1994)

Supreme Allied Commander, Europe (SACEUR) — Gen. George A. Joulwan (USA)

Deputy Supreme Allied Commander, Europe (DSACEUR) — Gen. Sir John Waters (UKA)

Commander in Chief Allied Forces Northern Europe — Air Chief Marshall Richard Johns (UKAF)

Commander in Chief Allied Forces Central Europe — Gen. Helge Hansen (GEA)

Commander in Chief Allied Forces Southern Europe — Adm. Leighton W. Smith, Jr. (USN)

Chairman, NATO Military Committee — Field Marshall Sir Richard Vincent (UKA)

Principal U.S. Military Training Centers

Army

Name, P.O. address	Zip	Nearest city
Aberdeen Proving Ground, MD	21005	Aberdeen
Carlisle Barracks, PA	17013	Carlisle
Fort Benning, GA	31905	Columbus
Fort Bliss, TX	79916	El Paso
Fort Bragg, NC	28307	Fayetteville
Fort Devens, MA	01433	Ayer
Fort Dix, NJ	08640	Trenton
Fort Eustis, VA	23604	Newport News
Fort Gordon, GA	30905	Augusta
Fort Benjamin Harrison, IN	46216	Indianapolis
Fort Sam Houston, TX	78234	San Antonio
Fort Huachuca, AZ	85613	Sierra Vista
Fort Jackson, SC	29207	Columbia
Fort Knox, KY	40121	Louisville
Fort Leavenworth, KS	66027	Leavenworth
Fort Lee, VA	23801	Petersburg
Fort McClellan, AL	36205	Anniston
Fort Monmouth, NJ	07703	Red Bank
Fort Rucker, AL	36362	Dothan
Fort Sill, OK	73503	Lawton

(continued)

Name, P.O. address	Zip	Nearest city	Name, P.O. address	Zip	Nearest city
Fort Leonard Wood, MO	65473	Rolla	The Judge Advocate General School, VA	22901	Charlottesville
Joint Readiness, Ft. Chaffee, AR	72905	Fort Smith	U.S. Military Acad., NY	10996	West Point
National Training Center	92311	Barstow, CA			

Navy

Name, P.O. address	Zip	Nearest city	Name, P.O. address	Zip	Nearest city
Atlantic Fleet	02841	Norfolk, VA	Naval Education & Training Ctr.	02841	Newport, RI
Pacific Fleet	92147	San Diego, CA	Naval Submarine School	06349	Groton, CT
Great Lakes, IL	60088	North Chicago	Naval Training Center	92133	San Diego, CA
Naval Air Training	78419	Corpus Christi, TX	Naval Training Center	32813	Orlando, FL

Marine Corps

Name, P.O. address	Zip	Nearest city	Name, P.O. address	Zip	Nearest city
MCB Camp Lejeune, NC	28542	Jacksonville	MCAS Kaneohe Bay, Oahu, HI	San Francisco 96863	Kailua
MCB Camp Pendleton, CA	92055	Oceanside			
MCAGCC Twentynine Palms, CA	92278	Palm Springs			
MCCDC Quantico, VA	22134	Quantico			
MCRD Parris Island, SC	29905	Beaufort			
MCAS Cherry Point, NC	28533	Havelock	MCAS Beaufort, SC	29904	Beaufort
MCAS Tustin, CA	92780	Santa Ana	MCAS Yuma, AZ	85369	Yuma
MCAS New River, NC	28545	Jacksonville	MCMWTC Bridgeport, CA	93517	Bridgeport

MCB = Marine Corps Base. MCCDC = Marine Corps Combat Development Command. MCAS = Marine Corps Air Station. MCRD = Marine Corps Recruit Depot. MCAGCC = Marine Corps Air-Ground Combat Center. MCMWTC = Marine Corps Mountain Warfare Training Center.

Air Force

Name, P.O. address	Zip	Nearest city	Name, P.O. address	Zip	Nearest city
Goodfellow AFB, TX	76908	San Angelo	Lackland AFB, TX	78236	San Antonio
Gunter AFB, AL	36114	Montgomery	Maxwell AFB, AL	36112	Montgomery
Keesler AFB, MS	39534	Biloxi	Sheppard AFB, TX	76311	Wichita Falls

All are Air Education and Training Command Bases.

Personal Salutes and Honors

The United States national salute, 21 guns, is also the salute to a national flag. The independence of the U. S. is commemorated by the salute to the Union — one gun for each state — fired at noon on July 4, at all military posts provided with suitable artillery.

A 21-gun salute on arrival and departure, with 4 ruffles and flourishes, is rendered to the President of the United States, to an ex-President, and to a President-elect. The national anthem or "Hail to the Chief" as appropriate, is played for the President, and the national anthem for the others. A 21-gun salute on arrival and departure, with 4 ruffles and flourishes, also is rendered to the sovereign or chief of state of a foreign country or a member of a reigning royal family; the national anthem of his or her country is played. The music is considered an inseparable part of the salute and will immediately follow the ruffles and flourishes without pause. Regarding the Honors March, generals receive the "General's March," admirals receive the "Admiral's March," and all others receive the 32-bar medley of "The Stars and Stripes Forever."

Grade, title, or office	Salute—guns Arrive	Leave	Ruffles and flourishes	Music
Vice President of United States	19		4	Hail Columbia
Speaker of the House	19		4	Honors March
American or foreign ambassador	19		4	Nat. anthem of official
Premier or prime minister	19		4	Nat. anthem of official
Secretary of Defense, Army, Navy, or Air Force	19	19	4	Honors March
Other Cabinet members, Senate President pro tempore, Governor, or Chief Justice of U.S.	19		4	Honors March
Chairman, Joint Chiefs of Staff	19	19	4	
Army Chief of Staff, Chief of Naval Operations, Air Force Chief of Staff, Marine Commandant	19	19	4	Honors March
General of the Army, General of the Air Force, Fleet Admiral	19	19	4	
Generals, Admirals	17	17	4	
Assistant secretaries of Defense, Army, Navy, or Air Force	17	17	4	Honors March
Chairman of a committee of Congress	17		4	Honors March

Other salutes (on arrival only) include 15 guns, along with 3 ruffles and flourishes, for U.S. envoys or ministers and foreign envoys or ministers accredited to the U.S.; 15 guns, for a lieutenant general or vice admiral; 13 guns, along with 2 ruffles and flourishes, for a major general or rear admiral (upper half) and for U.S. ministers resident and ministers resident accredited to the U.S.; 11 guns, along with 1 ruffle and flourish, for a brigadier general or rear admiral (lower half) and for U.S. charges d'affaires and like officials accredited to the U.S.; and 11 guns, and no ruffles and flourishes, for consuls general accredited to the U.S.

Military Units, U.S. Army and Air Force

Army Units. Squad. In infantry usually 10 enlisted personnel under a staff sergeant. **Platoon.** In infantry 4 squads under a lieutenant. **Company.** Headquarters section and 4 platoons under a captain. (Company-size unit in the artillery is a battery; in the cavalry, a troop.) **Battalion.** Hdqts. and 4 or more companies under a lieutenant colonel. (Battalion-size unit in the cavalry is a squadron.) **Brigade.** Hdqts. and 3 or more battalions under a colonel. **Division.** Hdqts. and 3 brigades with artillery, combat support, and combat service support units under a major general. **Army Corps.** Two or more divisions with corps troops under a lieutenant general. **Field Army.** Hdqts. and two or more corps with field Army troops under a general.

Air Force Units. Flight. Numerically designated flights are the lowest level unit in the Air Force. They are used primarily where there is a need for small mission elements to be incorporated into an organized unit. **Squadron.** A squadron is the basic unit in the Air Force. It is used to designate the mission units in operational commands. **Group.** The group is a flexible unit composed of two or more squadrons whose functions may be either tactical, support, or administrative in nature. **Wing.** An operational wing normally has two or more assigned mission squadrons in an area such as combat, flying training, or airlift. **Numbered Air Forces.** Normally an operationally oriented agency, the numbered air force is designed for the control of two or more air divisions or units of comparable strength. It is a flexible organization and may be of any size. Its wings may be assigned to air divisions or directly under the numbered air force. **Major Command.** A major subdivision of the Air Force that is assigned a major segment of the USAF mission.

The Federal Service Academies

U.S. Military Academy, West Point, NY. Founded 1802. Awards B.S. degree and Army commission for a 5-year service obligation. For admissions information, write Admissions Office, USMA, West Point, NY 10996.

U.S. Naval Academy, Annapolis, MD. Founded 1845. Awards B.S. degree and Navy or Marine Corps commission for a 5-year service obligation. For admissions information, write Dean of Admissions, Naval Academy, Annapolis, MD 21402.

U.S. Air Force Academy, Colorado Springs, CO. Founded 1954. Awards B.S. degree and Air Force commission for a 5-year service obligation. For admissions information, write Registrar, U.S. Air Force Academy, CO 80840.

U.S. Coast Guard Academy, New London, CT. Founded 1876. Awards B.S. degree and Coast Guard commission for a 5-year service obligation. For admissions information, write Director of Admissions, Coast Guard Academy, New London, CT 06320.

U.S. Merchant Marine Academy, Kings Point, NY. Founded 1943. Awards B.S. degree, a license as a deck, engineer, or dual officer, and a U.S. Naval Reserve commission. Service obligations vary according to options taken by the graduate. For admissions information, write Admission Office, U.S. Merchant Marine Academy, Kings Point, NY 11024.

U.S. Army and Air Force Insignia and Chevrons

Source: Department of the Army, U.S. Dept. of Defense

Army

General of the Armies

General John J. Pershing, the only person to have held this rank, was authorized to prescribe his own insignia, but never wore in excess of four stars. The rank originally was established by Congress for George Washington in 1799, and he was promoted to the rank by joint resolution of Congress, approved by Pres. Gerald Ford, Oct. 19, 1976.

General of Army... Five silver stars fastened together in a circle and the coat of arms of the United States in gold color metal with shield and crest enameled.

General	Four silver stars
Lieutenant General	Three silver stars
Major General	Two silver stars
Brigadier General	One silver star
Colonel	Silver eagle
Lieutenant Colonel	Silver oak leaf
Major	Gold oak leaf
Captain	Two silver bars
First Lieutenant	One silver bar
Second Lieutenant	One gold bar

Warrant Officers

Grade Four—Silver bar with 4 enamel black squares.
Grade Three—Silver bar with 3 enamel black squares.
Grade Two—Silver bar with 2 enamel black squares.
Grade One—Silver bar with 1 enamel black squares.

Noncommissioned Officers

Sergeant Major of the Army (E-9). Same as Command Sergeant Major (below) but with 2 stars. Also wears distinctive red and white shield on lapel.

Command Sergeant Major (E-9). Three chevrons above three arcs with a 5-pointed star with a wreath around the star between the chevrons and arcs.

Sergeant Major (E-9). Three chevrons above three arcs with a five-pointed star between the chevrons and arcs.

First Sergeant (E-8). Three chevrons above three arcs with a lozenge between the chevrons and arcs.

Master Sergeant (E-8). Three chevrons above three arcs.

Sergeant First Class (E-7). Three chevrons above two arcs.

Staff Sergeant (E-6). Three chevrons above one arc.

Sergeant (E-5). Three chevrons.

Corporal (E-4). Two chevrons.

Specialists

Specialist (E-4). Eagle device only.

Other enlisted

Private First Class (E-3). One chevron above one arc.

Private (E-2). One chevron.

Private (E-1). None.

Air Force

Insignia for Air Force officers are identical to those of the Army. The insignia for enlisted personnel are worn on both sleeves and consist of a star and an appropriate number of rockers. Chevrons appear above six rockers for the top three noncommissioned officer ranks, as follows (in ascending order): Senior Master Sergeant, 1 chevron; Chief Master Sergeant, 2 chevrons; Chief Master Sergeant of the Air Force, 2 chevrons, a wreath around the star design.

U.S. Navy, Marine Corps, and Coast Guard Insignia

Source: Dept. of the Navy, U.S. Dept. of Defense

Navy

Stripes and corps device are of gold embroidery.

Stripes

Fleet Admiral	1 two inch with 4 one-half inch.
Admiral	1 two inch with 3 one-half inch.
Vice Admiral	1 two inch with 2 one-half inch.
Rear Admiral (upper half)	1 two inch with 1 one-half inch.
Rear Admiral (lower half)	1 two inch.
Captain	4 one-half inch.
Commander	3 one-half inch.
Lieut. Commander	2 one-half inch with 1 one-quarter inch between.
Lieutenant	2 one-half inch.
Lieutenant (j.g.)	1 one-half inch with one-quarter inch above.
Ensign	1 one-half inch.

Warrant Officers—One ½″ broken with ½″ intervals of blue as follows:

Warrant Officer W-4 — 1 break
Warrant Officer W-3 — 2 breaks, 2″ apart
Warrant Officer W-2 — 3 breaks, 2″ apart

The breaks are symmetrically centered on outer face of the sleeve.

Enlisted personnel (noncommissioned petty officers)—A rating badge worn on the upper left arm, consisting of a spread eagle, appropriate number of chevrons, and centered specialty mark.

Marine Corps

Marine Corps and Army officer insignia are similar. Marine Corps and Army enlisted insignia, although basically similar, differ in color and design, and there are fewer Marine Corps subdivisions. The Marine Corps' distinctive cap and collar ornament is a combination of the American eagle, a globe, and an anchor.

Coast Guard

Coast Guard insignia follow Navy custom, with certain minor changes such as the officer cap insignia. The Coast Guard shield is worn on both sleeves of officers and on the right sleeve of all enlisted personnel.

U.S. Army Personnel on Active Duty[1]

Source: Department of the Army, U.S. Dept. of Defense

Date[2]	Total strength	Commissioned officers			Warrant officers		Enlisted personnel		
		Total	Male	Female[3]	Male[4]	Female	Total	Male	Female
1940	267,767	17,563	16,624	939	763	—	249,441	249,441	—
1942	3,074,184	203,137	190,662	12,475	3,285	—	2,867,762	2,867,762	—
1943	6,993,102	557,657	521,435	36,222	21,919	0	6,413,526	6,358,200	55,325
1944	7,992,868	740,077	692,351	47,726	36,893	10	7,215,888	7,144,601	71,287
1945	8,266,373	835,403	772,511	62,892	56,216	44	7,374,710	7,283,930	90,780
1946	1,889,690	257,300	240,643	16,657	9,826	18	1,622,546	1,605,847	16,699
1950	591,487	67,784	63,375	4,409	4,760	22	518,921	512,370	6,551
1955	1,107,606	111,347	106,173	5,174	10,552	48	985,659	977,943	7,716
1960	871,348	91,056	86,832	4,224	10,141	39	770,112	761,833	8,279
1965	967,049	101,812	98,029	3,783	10,285	23	854,929	846,409	8,520
1970	1,319,735	143,704	138,469	5,235	23,005	13	1,153,013	1,141,537	11,476
1975	781,316	89,756	85,184	4,572	13,214	22	678,324	640,621	37,703
1980 (Sept 30)	772,661	85,339	77,843	7,496	13,265	113	673,944	612,593	61,351
1985 (Sept. 30)	776,244	94,103	83,563	10,540	15,296	288	666,557	598,639	67,918
1990 (Mar. 31)	746,220	91,330	79,520	11,810	15,177	470	639,713	567,015	72,698
1991 (Mar. 31)	740,023	89,448	77,489	11,959	14,771	505	635,299	564,180	71,119
1992 (Mar. 31)	661,391	85,953	74,326	11,627	13,840	494	561,104	496,335	64,769
1993 (Mar. 31)	590,324	76,714	66,336	10,378	12,359	441	500,810	443,942	56,868
1994	553,627	74,956	64,281	10,675	12,448	535	465,688	405,664	60,024

(1) Represents strength of the active Army, including Philippine Scouts, retired Regular Army personnel on extended active duty, and National Guard and Reserve personnel on extended active duty; excludes U.S. Military Academy cadets, contract surgeons, and National Guard and Reserve personnel not on extended active duty.

(2) June 30, unless otherwise noted; data for 1940 to 1946 include personnel in the Army Air Forces and its predecessors (Air Service and Air Corps).

(3) Includes women doctors, dentists, and Medical Service Corps officers for 1946 and subsequent years, women in the Army Nurse Corps for all years, and the Women's Army Corps and Women's Medical Specialists Corps (dietitians, physical therapists, and occupational specialists) for 1943 and subsequent years.

(4) Act of Congress approved April 27, 1926, directed the appointment as warrant officers of field clerks still in active service. Includes flight officers as follows: 1943, 5,700; 1944, 13,615; 1945, 31,117; 1946, 2,580.

U.S. Navy Personnel on Active Duty

Date	Officers	Nurses	Enlisted	Officer Candidates	Total
1940 (June)	13,162	442	144,824	2,569	160,997
1945 (June)	320,293	11,086	2,988,207	61,231	3,380,817
1950 (June)	42,687	1,964	331,860	5,037	381,538
1960 (June)	67,456	2,103	544,040	4,385	617,984
1970 (June)	78,488	2,273	605,899	6,000	692,660
1980 (June)	63,100[1]	—	464,100[2]	—	527,200
1990 (Sept.)	74,429[1]	—	530,133[2]	—	604,562
1992 (Mar.)	71,826[1]	—	500,459[2]	—	572,285
1993 (Mar.)	66,787[1]	—	445,409[2]	—	512,196
1994 (Apr.)	64,430[1]	—	418,378[2]	—	512,196

(1) Nurses are included. (2) Officer candidates are included.

U.S. Marine Corps Personnel on Active Duty

(midyear personnel figures)

Year	Officers	Enlisted	Total
1955	18,417	186,753	205,170
1960	16,203	154,418	170,621
1965	17,258	172,955	190,213
1970	24,941	234,796	259,737
1980	18,198	170,271	188,469
1985	20,175	177,850	198,025
1990	19,958	176,694	196,652
1991	19,753	174,297	194,050
1992	19,132	165,397	184,529
1993	18,878	161,205	180,083
1994	18,430	159,949	178,379

U.S. Air Force Personnel on Active Duty

Year[1]	Strength
1907	3
1918	195,023
1920	9,050
1930	13,531
1940	51,165
1941	152,125
1942	764,415
1943	2,197,114
1944	2,372,292
1945	2,282,259
1950	411,277
1960	814,213
1970	791,078
1980	557,969
1986	608,200
1988	575,603
1989	570,965
1990	535,200
1991	508,500
1992	486,800
1993	444,351
1994	425,700

(1) Prior to 1947, data are for U.S. Army Air Corps and Air Service of the Signal Corps.

U.S. Coast Guard Personnel on Active Duty

Year	Total	Officers	Cadets	Enlisted
1970	37,689	5,512	653	31,524
1975	36,788	5,630	1,177	29,981
1980	39,381	6,463	877	32,041
1981	39,760	6,519	981	32,260
1982	38,248	6,431	902	30,915
1983	39,708	6,535	811	32,362
1984	38,705	6,790	759	31,156
1985	38,595	6,775	733	31,087
1986	37,284	6,577	754	29,953
1987	38,576	6,644	859	31,073
1988	37,723	6,530	887	30,306
1990	37,308	6,475	820	29,860
1991	38,280	7,095	900	30,285
1992	39,185	7,348	919	30,918
1993	38,832	7,724	691	30,417

Defense Contracts

Source: U.S. Dept. of Defense; thousands of dollars

The 50 companies (including their subsidiaries) receiving the largest dollar volume of prime contract awards from the Department of Defense during fiscal 1993.

McDonnell Douglas	$7,539,806	Bath Holding	997,183	Bell Boeing JV	472,224
Lockheed	6,910,871	Texas Instruments	967,934	Allied Signal	453,540
Martin Marietta	4,727,071	Textron	954,890	Teledyne	435,362
General Motors	4,075,618	Tenneco	906,097	Mitre	431,929
Raytheon	3,232,856	AT&T	870,480	Computer Sciences	422,134
United Technologies	3,083,185	IBM	849,136	Exxon	418,513
Northrop	3,004,238	Foundation Health	817,832	Renco Group	398,045
General Dynamics	2,146,816	Science Application Intl.	786,411	Black & Decker	382,307
Loral	1,729,230	E-Systems	753,704	Harris	377,510
Grumman	1,705,363	Unisys	716,719	Olin	368,559
Boeing	1,664,421	GTE	713,981	MIT	365,694
General Electric	1,605,616	ITT	614,184	Oshkosh Truck	361,662
Westinghouse Electric	1,569,528	Alliant Techsystems	612,014	Johnson Controls	353,629
Litton Industries	1,554,889	Avondale Industries	587,224	Royal Dutch Shell Group	351,504
Natl. Steel & Shipbuilding	1,398,037	FMC	508,211	Coastal	339,477
Rockwell International	1,316,610	Tracor	492,879	Chevron	320,995
TRW	1,160,499	Dyncorp	491,889		

Women in the Armed Forces

Source: U.S. Dept. of Defense

Women in the Army, Navy, Air Force, Marines, and Coast Guard are all fully integrated with male personnel. Expansion of military women's programs began in the Department of Defense in fiscal year 1973.

As of June 1993, women made up 11.6 percent of the armed forces. Almost 25 percent of medical and dental specialists were women; of active duty women personnel, fewer than 1 percent served in the infantry, in gun crews, or aboard ship.

Under new rules instituted in 1993, women are allowed to fly combat aircraft and to serve aboard warships. Women are still restricted from service in ground combat units.

Admission of women to the service academies began in the fall of 1976.

Women Active Duty Troops in 1994

Service	% Women
Army	12.8
Navy	11.5
Marines	4.5
Air Force	14.7
Coast Guard (1993)	8.3

Women on Active Duty, All Services: 1973-1993

Year	% Women	Year	% Women
1973	2.5	1983	9.3
1975	4.6	1987	10.2
1981	8.9	1993	11.6

For Further Information on the U.S. Armed Forces

Army — Information: Chief, Office of Public Affairs, Dept. of the Army, Wash., DC 20310.

Navy — Information: Chief of Information, Dept. of the Navy, Wash., DC 20350-2000.

Air Force — Information: Office of Public Affairs, Air Force, 1690 Pentagon, Wash., DC 20330-1690.

Marine Corps — Information: Commandant of the Marine Corps (Code PA), Headquarters, Marine Corps, Wash., DC 20380-0001.

Coast Guard — Information: Commandant (G-PRJ), U.S. Coast Guard, 2100 Second St. SW, Wash., DC 20593-0001.

Veteran Population

Source: U.S. Dept. of Veterans Affairs; as of July 1993; in thousands

Total veterans in civilian life[a,b]	**26,789**
Total wartime veterans	**20,675**
Total Persian Gulf War	1,027
Persian Gulf War with service in Vietnam era	164
Persian Gulf War with no prior wartime service	863
Total Vietnam era	8,287
Vietnam era with service in Korean conflict	547
Vietnam era with no prior wartime service	7,740
Total Korean conflict	4,692
Korean conflict with service in WWII	795
Korean conflict with no prior wartime service	3,897
World War II	8,150
World War I	25
Total peacetime veterans	**6,114**
Total post-Vietnam era	3,054
Service between Korean conflict and Vietnam era only	1,886
Other peacetime	173

NOTE: Detail may not add to total shown due to rounding. (a) The category "Wartime veterans" equals the sum of Persian Gulf War (no service in Vietnam era), Vietnam era (no service in Korean conflict), Korean conflict (no service in World War II), World War II, and World War I. The data refer only to veterans living in the U.S. and Puerto Rico since data on veterans living elsewhere are not available. (b) There are an indeterminate number of Mexican Border period veterans, 41 of whom were receiving benefits in May 1994.

Veterans Compensation and Pension Case Payments

Fiscal year	Living veteran cases (no.)	Deceased veteran cases (no.)	Total cases (no.)	Total dis-bursement (dollars)
1900	752,510	241,019	993,529	138,462,130
1910	602,622	318,461	921,083	159,974,056
1920	419,627	349,916	769,543	316,418,029
1930	542,610	298,223	840,833	418,432,808
1940	610,122	239,176	849,298	429,138,465
1950	2,368,238	658,123	3,026,361	2,009,462,298
1960	3,008,935	950,802	3,959,737	3,314,761,383
1970	3,127,338	1,487,176	4,614,514	5,113,649,490
1980	3,195,395	1,450,785	4,646,180	11,045,412,000
1990	2,746,329	837,596	3,583,925	15,535,069,000
1991	2,709,500	799,677	3,509,177	15,975,440,000
1992	2,673,833	753,981	3,427,814	16,145,203,000
1993	2,660,030	713,758	3,373,788	16,881,938,000

Active Duty U.S. Military Personnel Strengths, Worldwide

Source: U.S. Dept. of Defense

(As of Sept. 30, 1993)

U.S. Territories & Special Locations	
U.S., 48 contiguous states	1,127,242
Alaska	22,015
Hawaii	42,958
Guam	7,424
Johnston Atoll	268
Puerto Rico	3,739
Transients	38,527
Afloat	154,823
Total[1]	**1,397,083**
Western & Southern Europe	
Belgium	1,808
Germany	105,254
Greece	807
Greenland	131
Iceland	2,878
Italy	10,333
Netherlands	2,226
Norway	196
Portugal	1,320
Spain	3,820
Turkey	4,049
United Kingdom	16,100
Afloat	16,968
Total[1]	**166,249**
East Asia & Pacific	
Australia	339
Japan	46,131
Philippines	53
Rep. of Korea	34,830
Singapore	162
Thailand	106
Afloat	17,150
Total[1]	**99,022**
North Africa, Middle East & South Asia	
Bahrain	379
Diego Garcia	1,233
Egypt	605
Kuwait	233
Saudi Arabia	950
Afloat	7,803
Total[1]	**11,490**
Sub-Saharan Africa	**6,864**
Other Western Hemisphere	
Bermuda	527
Canada	547
Cuba (Guantánamo)	2,189
Honduras	696
Panama	10,542
Afloat	2,698
Total[1]	**17,758**
Total Worldwide	**1,705,103**

(1) Area totals include countries with fewer than 100 assigned U.S. military members.

Estimates of Total Dollar Costs of American Wars

Source: *The Military Budget and National Economic Priorities,* revised and updated by James L. Clayton

(millions of dollars, except percent)

Item	World War II	Vietnam Conflict	Korean Conflict	World War I	Civil War: Union	Civil War: Confed-eracy	Spanish American War	American Revolution	War of 1812	Mexican War
Original increment, direct costs:[1]										
Current dollars	360,000	140,600	50,000	32,700	2,300	1,000	270	100-140	89	82
Constant (1967) dollars	816,300	148,800	69,300	100,000	8,500	3,700	1,100	400-680	170	300
Percent 1 year's GNP	188	14	15	43	74	123	2	104	14	4
Service-connected veterans' benefits[2]	96,666	32,288	19,512	19,580	3,290	—	2,111	28	20	26
Interest, pmts. on war loans[3]	(5)	(5)	(5)	11,000	1,200	(5)	60	20	14	10
Current cost to 1990[4]	466,000	179,000	72,000	63,500	6,790	(5)	2,441	170	120	120

(1) Figures are rounded and taken from Claudia D. Goldin, *Encyclopedia of American Economic History.* (2) Total cost to Oct. 1, 1990. For World War I and later wars, benefits are actual service-connected figures from *Annual Report* of Veterans Administration. For earlier wars, service-connected veterans' benefits are estimated at 40 percent of total, the approximate ratio of service-connected to total benefits since World War I. (3) Total cost to 1990. Interest payments are a very rough approximation based on the percentage of the original costs of each war financed by money creation and debt, the difference between the level of public debt at the beginning of the war and at its end, and the approximate time required to pay off the war debts. (4) Figures are rounded estimates. (5) Unknown.

The Medal of Honor

The Medal of Honor is the highest military award for bravery that can be given to any individual in the United States. The first Army Medals were awarded on March 25, 1863, and the first Navy Medals went to sailors and Marines on April 3, 1863.

The Medal of Honor, established by Joint Resolution of Congress, July 12, 1862 (amended by Acts of Congress, July 9, 1918, and July 25, 1963), is awarded in the name of Congress to a person who, while a member of the Armed Forces, distinguishes himself or herself conspicuously by gallantry and intrepidity at the risk of life above and beyond the call of duty while engaged in an action against any enemy of the United States; while engaged in military operations involving conflict with an opposing foreign force; or while serving with friendly foreign forces engaged in an armed conflict against an opposing armed force in which the United States is not a belligerent party. The deed performed must have been one of personal bravery or self-sacrifice so conspicuous as to clearly distinguish the individual above his or her comrades and must have involved risk of life. Incontestable proof of the performance of service is required, and each recommendation for award of this decoration is considered on the standard of extraordinary merit.

Prior to World War I, the 2,625 Army Medal of Honor awards up to that time were reviewed to determine which past awards met new stringent criteria. The Army removed 911 names from the list, most of them former members of a volunteer infantry group during the Civil War who had been induced to extend their enlistments when they were promised the Medal.

Since that review Medals of Honor have been awarded in the following numbers:

World War I	96	Korean War	131
World War II	432	Vietnam War	238

Armed Services Senior Enlisted Advisers

The U.S. Army, Navy, and Air Force in 1966-1967 each created a new position of senior enlisted adviser, whose primary job is to represent the point of view of the services' enlisted men and women on matters of welfare, morale, and any problems concerning enlisted personnel. The senior adviser has direct access to the military chief of the service and policy-making bodies. The senior enlisted adviser for each service as of mid-1994 is:

Army—Sgt. Major of the Army Richard A. Kidd.

Navy—Master Chief Petty Officer of the Navy John Hagan.

Air Force—Chief Master Sgt. of the Air Force Gary R. Pfingston.

Marines—Sgt. Major of the Marine Corps Harold G. Overstreet.

Armed Forces Per 1,000 Persons, 1992[1]

Source: U.S. Arms Control and Disarmament Agency

Country	Per 1,000	Country	Per 1,000	Country	Per 1,000
Argentina	2.0	India	1.4	Pakistan	4.5
Australia	3.9	Indonesia	1.5	Philippines	1.7
Austria	6.6	Iran	8.9	Poland	7.7
Belgium	8.1	Iraq	20.3	Portugal	5.6
Bolivia	4.1	Israel	33.4	Romania	8.6
Brazil	2.0	Italy	6.2	Russia	18.2
Bulgaria	11.9	Japan	2.0	Singapore	1.9
Canada	3.0	Jordan	27.3	South Africa	1.9
Chile	6.8	Korea, North	50.9	Spain	5.6
China	2.6	Korea, South	14.5	Sweden	8.8
Colombia	4.1	Kuwait	9.8	Switzerland	0.2
Cuba	16.1	Lebanon	13.1	Syria	32.4
Denmark	5.7	Libya	19.1	Taiwan	17.4
Egypt	7.3	Mexico	2.1	Thailand	5.0
El Salvador	8.0	Mongolia	7.1	Turkey	9.6
Finland	6.5	Morocco	7.5	United Kingdom	5.1
France	7.5	Netherlands	6.1	Venezuela	3.7
Germany	5.6	Nicaragua	3.6	Vietnam	12.4
Greece	15.5	Norway	7.6		
Hungary	7.8	Oman	21.8		

(1) Includes active-duty personnel performing national security functions. Does not include reserves or paramilitary forces.

Nations With Largest Armed Forces, by Active-Duty Troop Strength, 1992

Source: *The Military Balance, 1993-94* (Internatl. Institute for Strategic Studies, published by Brassey's U.K.)

		Troop strength				Navy			
		Active troops (thousands)	Reserve troops (thousands)	Defense expend. ($mil)	Tanks (MBT)	Cruisers/ Frigates/ Destroyers	Sub-marines	Combat aircraft FGA (air force only)	Combat aircraft fighters (air force only)
1	**China**	3,030.0	1,200	$22,364	7,500-8,500	38F/18D	47	500	4000 est.
2	**Russia**	2,720.0	3,000.0	39,680	25,000	29C/114F/24D*	219	1,800	1,200
3	**USA**	1,913.8	1,784.1	242,717	15,120	52C/59F/38D*	110	57 tactical ftr. sqn	
4	India	1,265.0	655.0	7,550	3,400	17F/5D	15	374	303
5	N. Korea	1,132.0	540.0	5,087	3,700	3F	25	334	360
6	Vietnam	857.0	NA	1,750	1,300	7F	-	65	175
7	S. Korea	633.0	4,500.0	7,189	1,800	29F/9D	4	238	96
8	Pakistan	580.0	513.0	3,252	1,890+	11F/3D	6	126	210
9	Turkey	560.3	1,107.0	3,423	4,835	8F/11D	15	19 sqn	2 sqn
10	Iran	528.0	350.0	NA	700+	5F/3D	2	140	115
11	Germany	447.0	904.7	19,252	4,778	8F/6D	20	15 sqn	7 sqn
12	**France**	431.7	374.0	21,898	1,000	1C/35F/4D*	19	11 sqn	11 sqn
13	Egypt	410.0	604.0	3,427	3,167	4F/1D	2	126	340
14	Syria	408.0	400.0	NA	4,500	2	3	170	302
15	Taiwan	390.0	1,657.5	5,373	309	11F/22D	4	418 total FGA/ftr.	
16	Iraq	382.5	650.0	NA	2,200	1F	-	130 est.	180 est.
17	Italy	354.0	584.0	10,690	1,210	1C/22F/4D*	8	240	6 sqn
18	Brazil	296.7	1,515.0	1,643	†	13F/6D	4	77	18
19	Poland	296.5	435.2	2,279	2,545	1F/1D	3	124	262
20	**U.K.**	293.5	353.0	20,726	1,126	26F/12D*	18	13 sqn	7 sqn
21	Myanmar	286.0	NA	269	56	-	-	-	12
22	Indonesia	283.0	400.0	2,003	†	17F	2	40	14
23	Thailand	283.0	500.0	1,937	203	9F	-	30	44
24	Japan	246.0	48.4	16,901	1,200	55F/7D	17	94	230
25	**Ukraine**	230.0	1,000.0	4,320	5,700	-	-	184	509
26	Spain	217.0	498.0	3,735	1,148	15F*	8	4 sqn	8 sqn
27	Romania	200.0	593.0	955	2,869	5F/1D	1	150	235
28	Morocco	195.5	100.0	692	284	1F	-	29	15
29	Cuba	175.0	1,435.0	1,272	1,575	3F	3	20	106
30	**Israel**	175.0	430.0	3,984	3,960	-	3	600 total FGA/ftr.	

Bold face denotes nations with strategic nuclear capability; MBT=main battle tank; FGA=fighter, ground attack; sqn= squadron (18-24 aircraft); †= light tanks only; * denotes navies with aircraft carriers, as follows: Russia 2, USA 12, France 2, Italy 1, U.K. 2, Spain 1. NA = not available.

Nuclear Arms Treaties and Negotiations: An Historical Overview

Aug. 5, 1963—Limited Test Ban Treaty signed in Moscow by the U.S., USSR, and Great Britain; prohibited testing of nuclear weapons in space, above ground, and under water.

Jan. 27, 1967—Outer Space Treaty banned the introduction of nuclear weapons and other weapons of mass destruction into space.

July 1, 1968—Nuclear Nonproliferation Treaty, with U.S., USSR, and Great Britain as major signers, limited the spread of military nuclear technology by agreement not to assist nonnuclear nations in getting or making nuclear weapons.

May 26, 1972—Strategic Arms Limitation Treaty (SALT I) — interim agreement — signed in Moscow by U.S. and USSR. The treaty imposed a 5-year freeze on testing and deployment of intercontinental ballistic missiles (ICBMs) and submarine-launched ballistic missiles (SLBMs). An interim short-term agreement putting a ceiling on numbers of offensive nuclear weapons was also signed. SALT I was in effect until Oct. 3, 1977. In the area of defensive nuclear weapons, the separate **ABM Treaty** limited antiballistic missiles to 2 sites of 100 antiballistic missile launchers in each country (amended in 1974 to one site in each country).

July 3, 1974—ABM Treaty Revision (protocol on antiballistic missile systems) and **Threshold Test Ban Treaty** on limiting underground testing of nuclear weapons to 150 kilotons were signed by U.S. and USSR in Moscow.

Sept. 1977—U.S. and USSR agreed to continue to abide by SALT I, despite its expiration date.

June 18, 1979—SALT II, signed in Vienna by the U.S. and USSR, constrained offensive nuclear weapons, limiting each side to 2,400 missile launchers and heavy bombers with that ceiling to apply until Jan. 1, 1985. The treaty also set a subceiling of 1,320 ICBMs and SLBMs with multiple warheads on each side. Although approved by the U.S. Senate Foreign Relations Committee, the treaty never reached the Senate floor for ratification because Pres. Jimmy Carter withdrew his support for the treaty following the Dec. 1979 invasion of Afghanistan by Soviet troops.

Dec. 8, 1987—Intermediate-Range Nuclear Forces (INF) Treaty signed in Washington, D.C., by USSR leader Mikhail Gorbachev and U.S. Pres. Ronald Reagan, eliminating all medium- and shorter-range nuclear missiles from Europe; ratified with conditions by U.S. Senate on May 27, 1988.

July 31, 1991—Strategic Arms Reduction Treaty (START I) signed in Moscow by Soviet Pres. Mikhail Gorbachev and U.S. Pres. George Bush to reduce strategic offensive arms by approximately 30 percent in three phases over seven years. START I was the first treaty to mandate reductions by the superpowers. The treaty was approved by the U.S. Senate Oct. 1, 1992. With the breakup of the Soviet Union in December 1991, four former Soviet republics became independent nations with strategic nuclear weapons on their territory—Russia, Ukraine, Kazakhstan, and Belarus. The last 3 agreed in principle in 1992 to transfer their nuclear weapons to Russia and ratify START I. The Russian Supreme Soviet voted to ratify Nov. 4, 1992, but Russia decided not to provide the instruments of ratification until Ukraine, Kazakhstan, and Belarus each ratified START I and acceded to the Nuclear Nonproliferation Treaty (NPT) as nonnuclear nations. By late 1993, Belarus and Kazakhstan had ratified START I and acceded to the nonproliferation treaty. In February 1994, Ukraine ratified START II, but it had not yet acceded to the NPT.

Jan. 3, 1993—START II signed in Moscow by U.S. Pres. George Bush and Russian Pres. Boris Yeltsin. Potentially the broadest disarmament pact in history, it called for both sides to reduce their long-range nuclear arsenals to about one-third of their then-current levels within a decade and would entirely eliminate land-based multiple-warhead missiles. Action will not be taken on START II until START I enters into force. START II will require ratification only by the U.S. Senate and the legislature of Russia, which would, under the guidelines for START I finalization, be the only remaining nuclear republic of the former Soviet Union.

Monthly Military Pay Scale

Source: U.S. Dept. of Defense; effective Jan. 1, 1994

	Years of Service						
Rank/Grade	**2**	**4**	**8**	**12**	**16**	**20**	**26**
General—0-10	$7,040.70	$7,040.70	$7,311.00	$7,716.00	$8,267.70	$8,821.50	$9,371.10
Lt. General—0-9	6,185.70	6,317.40	6,478.20	6,747.60	7,311.00	7,716.00	8,267.70
Major General—0-8	5,623.50	5,756.70	6,185.70	6,478.20	6,747.60	7,311.00	7,491.30
Brig. General—0-7	4,845.00	4,845.00	5,062.20	5,355.60	6,185.70	6,611.10	6,611.10
Colonel—0-6	3,694.20	3,936.30	3,936.30	3,936.30	4,713.60	5,062.20	5,806.60
Lt. Colonel—0-5	3,157.50	3,375.90	3,665.40	3,665.40	4,203.90	4,579.50	4,739.40
Major—0-4	2,760.30	2,944.50	3,533.10	3,533.10	3,856.50	3,962.70	3,962.70
Captain—0-3	2,355.30	2,785.80	3,345.00	3,345.00	3,427.20	3,427.20	3,427.20
1st Lt.—0-2	2,005.80	2,491.20	2,542.80	2,542.80	2,542.80	2,542.80	2,542.80
2d Lt.—0-1	1,659.90	2,005.80	2,005.80	2,005.80	2,005.80	2,005.80	2,005.80
Chief Warrant—W-4	2,302.50	2,355.30	2,866.20	2,866.20	3,290.40	3,290.40	3,665.40
Warrant Officer—W-1	1,632.00	1,768.20	1,927.50	2,088.90	2,410.20	2,410.20	2,410.20
Sgt. Major—E-9	0.00	0.00	2,552.70	2,552.70	2,783.40	2,783.40	3,214.20
Master Sgt.—E-8	0.00	0.00	2,210.40	2,210.40	2,439.60	2,439.60	2,870.40
Sgt. 1st class—E-7	1,578.00	1,693.80	1,923.30	1,923.30	2,152.20	2,152.20	2,582.70
Staff Sgt.—E-6	1,370.70	1,488.60	1,744.20	1,744.20	1,885.20	1,885.20	1,885.20
Sergeant—E-5	1,201.20	1,314.30	1,571.40	1,571.40	1,599.90	1,599.90	1,599.90
Corporal—E-4	1,087.20	1,239.90	1,288.80	1,288.80	1,288.80	1,288.80	1,288.80
Pvt. 1st class—E-3	1,023.00	1,105.80	1,105.80	1,105.80	1,105.80	1,105.80	1,105.80
Private—E-2	933.30	933.30	933.30	933.30	933.30	933.30	933.30
Recruit—E-1	832.80	832.80	832.80	832.80	832.80	832.80	832.80

Chairmen of the Joint Chiefs of Staff

Gen. of the Army Omar N. Bradley, USA	8/16/49–8/14/53
Adm. Arthur W. Radford, USN	8/15/53–8/14/57
Gen. Nathan F. Twining, USAF	8/15/57 – 9/30/60
Gen. Lyman L. Lemnitzer, USA	10/1/60 – 10/30/62
Gen. Maxwell D. Taylor, USA	10/1/62 – 7/3/64
Gen. Earle G. Wheeler, USA	7/3/64 – 7/2/70
Adm. Thomas H. Moorer, USN	7/3/70 – 6/30/74
Gen. George S. Brown, USAF	7/1/74 – 6/20/78
Gen. David C. Jones, USAF	6/21/78 – 6/18/82
Gen. John W. Vessey Jr., USA	6/18/82 – 9/30/85
Adm. William J. Crowe, Jr., USN	10/1/85 – 9/30/89
Gen. Colin L. Powell, USA	10/1/89 – 9/30/93
Gen. John M. Shalikashvili, USA	10/1/93 –

Casualties in Principal Wars of the U.S.

Source: U.S. Dept. of Defense

Data prior to World War I are based on incomplete records in many cases. Casualty data are confined to dead and wounded personnel and therefore exclude personnel captured or missing in action who were subsequently returned to military control. Dash (—) indicates information is not available.

War	Branch of service	Number serving	Casualties: Battle deaths	Other deaths	Wounds not mortal[7]	Total
Revolutionary War	**Total**	**—**	**4,435**	**—**	**6,188**	**—**
1775-1783	Army	184,000	4,044	—	6,004	—
	Navy	to	342	—	114	—
	Marines	250,000	49	—	70	—
War of 1812	**Total**	**286,730[8]**	**2,260**	**—**	**4,505**	**6,765**
1812-1815	Army	—	1,950	—	4,000	5,950
	Navy	—	265	—	439	704
	Marines	—	45	—	66	111
Mexican War	**Total**	**78,718[8]**	**1,733**	**11,550**	**4,152**	**17,435**
1846-1848	Army	—	1,721	11,500	4,102	17,373
	Navy	—	1	—	3	4
	Marines	—	11	—	47	58
Civil War	**Total**	**2,213,363[8]**	**140,414**	**224,097**	**281,881**	**646,392**
Union forces	Army	2,128,948	138,154	221,374	280,040	639,568
1861-1865	Navy	—	2,112	2,411	1,710	6,233
	Marines	84,415	148	312	131	591
Confederate forces	**Total**	**—**	**74,524**	**59,297**	**—**	**133,821**
(estimate)[1]	Army	600,000	—	—	—	—
1863-1866	Navy	to	—	—	—	—
	Marines	1,500,000	—	—	—	—
Spanish-American War	**Total**	**306,760**	**385**	**2,061**	**1,662**	**4,108**
1898	Army[3]	280,564	369	2,061	1,594	4,024
	Navy	22,875	10	0	47	57
	Marines	3,321	6	0	21	27
World War I	**Total**	**4,743,826**	**53,513**	**63,195**	**204,002**	**320,710**
April 6, 1917-	Army[4]	4,057,101	50,510	55,868	193,663	300,041
Nov. 11, 1918	Navy	599,051	431	6,856	819	8,106
	Marines	78,839	2,461	390	9,520	12,371
	Coast Guard	8,835	111	81	—	192
World War II	**Total**	**16,353,659**	**292,131**	**115,185**	**670,846**	**1,078,162**
Dec. 7, 1941-	Army[5]	11,260,000	234,874	83,400	565,861	884,135
Dec. 31, 1946[2]	Navy[6]	4,183,466	36,950	25,664	37,778	100,392
	Marines	669,100	19,733	4,778	67,207	91,718
	Coast Guard	241,093	574	1,343	—	1,917
Korean War[9]	**Total**	**5,764,143**	**33,651**	**—**	**103,284**	**—**
June 25, 1950-	Army	2,834,000	27,709	—	77,596	—
July 27, 1953	Navy	1,177,000	474	176	1,576	2,226
	Marines	424,000	4,270	339	23,744	28,353
	Air Force	1,285,000	1,198	298	368	1,864
	Coast Guard	44,143	—	—	—	—
Vietnam War[10]	**Total**	**8,744,000**	**47,369**	**10,799**	**153,303**	**211,471**
Aug. 4, 1964-	Army	4,368,000	30,911	7,274	96,802	134,987
Jan. 27, 1973	Navy	1,842,000	1,631	927	4,178	6,736
	Marines	794,000	13,083	1,754	51,392	66,229
	Air Force	1,740,000	1,739	842	931	3,512
	Coast Guard	—	5	2	—	7
Persian Gulf War	**Total**	**467,539[11]**	**148**	**145**	**467**	**760**
1991	Army	246,682	98	105	—	—
	Navy	98,852	6	8	—	—
	Marines	71,254	24	26	—	—
	Air Force	50,751	20	6	—	—

(1) Authoritative statistics for the Confederate forces are not available. An estimated 26,000-31,000 Confederate personnel died in Union prisons.

(2) Data are for the period Dec. 1, 1941 through Dec. 31, 1946 when hostilities were officially terminated by Presidential Proclamation, but few battle deaths or wounds not mortal were incurred after the Japanese acceptance of Allied peace terms on Aug. 14, 1945. Numbers serving Dec. 1, 1941-Aug. 31, 1945 were: Total—14,903,213; Army—10,420,000; Navy—3,883,520; and Marine Corps—599,693.

(3) Number serving covers the period April 21-Aug. 13, 1898, while dead and wounded data are for the period May 1-Aug. 31, 1898. Active hostilities ceased on Aug. 13, 1898, but ratifications of the treaty of peace were not exchanged between the United States and Spain until April 11, 1899.

(4) Includes Army Air Forces battle deaths and wounds not mortal, as well as casualties suffered by American forces in Northern Russia to Aug. 25, 1919, and in Siberia to April 1, 1920. Other deaths covered the period April 1, 1917-Dec. 31, 1918.

(5) Includes Army Air Forces.

(6) Battle deaths and wounds not mortal include casualties incurred in Oct. 1941 due to hostile action.

(7) Marine Corps data for World War II, the Spanish-American War, and prior wars represent the number of individuals wounded, whereas all other data in this column represent the total number (incidence) of wounds.

(8) As reported by the Commissioner of Pensions in his Annual Report for Fiscal Year 1903.

(9) Battle deaths and other deaths associated with the conflict differ from previously reported figures due to a reexamination of individual files by the U.S. Dept. of Defense.

(10) Number serving covers the period Aug. 4, 1964-Jan. 27, 1973 (date of ceasefire). Number of casualties incurred in connection with the conflict in Vietnam covers the period Jan. 1, 1961-Sept. 30, 1977. Includes casualties incurred in Mayaguez Incident. Wounds not mortal exclude 150,375 persons not requiring hospital care.

(11) Estimated, because deployment figures changed continually.

ENERGY

World Energy Production and Consumption Trends

Source: Energy Information Administration, U.S. Dept. of Energy, *International Energy Annual 1992*

Since 1983, the world's total output of primary energy—petroleum, natural gas, coal, hydroelectricity, and nuclear electricity—has increased steadily at an average annual rate of 2.3%. World production increased from 279 quadrillion Btu in 1983 to 343 quadrillion Btu in 1992. In 1992 world production of petroleum was about 67 million barrels per day, or 137 quadrillion Btu. During the period from 1983 to 1992, petroleum was the world's most heavily used source of energy. Between 1983 and 1992, petroleum production increased by nearly 9 million barrels per day. In that period, production by OPEC (Organization of Petroleum Exporting Countries) increased by 7.9 million barrels per day, while production in North America declined by 0.8 million barrels per day.

In 1992 three countries—the U.S., Russia, and China—were the leading producers and consumers of energy. These 3 countries produced 42% and consumed 42% of the world totals. Russia and the U.S. were the world's largest producers of energy in 1992, supplying 33% of the world total. The U.S. accounted for 24% of the world's total energy consumption—more than any other country. The U.S. consumed 23% more than it produced—an imbalance of 15.5 quadrillion Btu.

U.S. Energy Summary

Source: Energy Information Administration, U.S. Dept. of Energy, *Annual Energy Review 1993*

In 1993, a gradually reviving domestic economy, low energy prices, and a return to normal weather contributed to the second consecutive year of growth in U.S. total energy consumption, which rose to a record 84 quadrillion Btu. The increase came as a result of increases in the consumption of petroleum, natural gas, coal, and hydroelectric power. Consumption of nuclear power, however, declined for the first time in 13 years. The improvement in the economy and continued low prices for crude oil led to a modest increase in petroleum consumption. Petroleum consumption rose 0.2 million barrels per day to 17 million barrels per day. This was primarily the result of increased demand in the transportation sector, which relies on petroleum so heavily that even a small 1.9% increase in its consumption affected the total. Consumption of petroleum by electric utilities rose 9.5%, while consumption by the residential and commercial sector rose very little, and consumption by the industrial sector declined.

Energy consumption per dollar of gross domestic product (GDP) declined for the second consecutive year in 1993. About 16,000 Btu of energy were consumed for each dollar in 1993, compared with 23,000 Btu per dollar in the early 1970s (1987 dollars used throughout).

U.S. total energy production declined in 1993 for the third consecutive year, down 1.6% to 66 quadrillion Btu. Most of the decline was attributed to lower crude oil production, which fell 0.7 quadrillion Btu to 14 quadrillion Btu, and to lower coal production. A strike by the United Mine Workers of America caused coal production to decline by 1.1 quadrillion Btu to 20 quadrillion Btu. Crude oil production dropped to 6.8 million barrels per day, down 4.6%. Hydroelectric power production rose to 269 billion kilowatt-hours from 244 billion kilowatt-hours in 1992, a year of persistent drought in western states.

U.S. net imports of energy rose to 17 quadrillion Btu in 1993, an increase of 15% from the 1992 level and the highest net import volume since 1978. Petroleum net imports rose 8.2% to 16 quadrillion Btu, natural gas net imports rose 10% to 2.1 quadrillion Btu, and coal net exports declined 32% to 1.8 quadrillion Btu. U.S. net imports of petroleum totaled 7.5 million barrels per day in 1993. Members of OPEC supplied 4.3 million barrels per day, well over half the total. Despite a sharp decline from the 1992 level, coal remained the primary U.S. energy export. Coal exports totaled 75 million short tons in 1993.

U.S. Energy Overview, 1960-93

Source: Energy Information Administration, U.S. Dept. of Energy, *Annual Energy Review 1993*; in quadrillion Btu

Activity and energy source	1960	1965	1970	1975	1980	1985	1990	1992	1993P
Production	**41.49**	**49.34**	**62.07**	**59.86**	**64.76**	**64.87**	**67.85**	**66.85 R**	**65.81**
Coal	10.82	13.06	14.61	14.99	18.60	19.33	22.46	21.59 R	20.49
Natural gas (dry)	12.66	15.78	21.67	19.64	19.91	16.98	18.36	18.38 R	18.98
Crude oil[1]	14.93	16.52	20.40	17.73	18.25	18.99	15.57	15.22 R	14.48
Natural gas plant liquids	1.46	1.88	2.51	2.37	2.25	2.24	2.17	2.36	2.40
Nuclear electric power	0.01	0.04	0.24	1.90	2.74	4.15	6.16	6.61 R	6.52
Hydroelectric power[2]	1.61	2.06	2.63	3.15	2.90	2.97	2.93	2.50 R	2.76
Other[3]	(4)	0.01	0.02	0.07	0.11	0.21	0.20	0.19	0.18
Imports	**4.23**	**5.92**	**8.39**	**14.11**	**15.97**	**12.10**	**18.99**	**19.65 R**	**21.19**
Natural gas	0.16	0.47	0.85	0.98	1.01	0.95	1.55	2.16 R	2.29
Crude oil[5]	2.20	2.65	2.81	8.72	11.19	6.81	12.77	13.25 R	14.63
Petroleum products[6]	1.80	2.75	4.66	4.23	3.46	3.80	4.35	3.71 R	3.67
Other[7]	0.07	0.04	0.07	0.19	0.31	0.54	0.32	0.52 R	0.60
Exports	**1.48**	**1.85**	**2.66**	**2.36**	**3.72**	**4.23**	**4.91**	**5.02 R**	**4.31**
Coal	1.02	1.38	1.94	1.76	2.42	2.44	2.77	2.68	1.95
Crude oil	0.43	0.39	0.55	0.44	1.16	1.66	1.82	2.01	2.11
Other[8]	0.03	0.09	0.18	0.16	0.14	0.14	0.31	0.33 R	0.25
Adjustments[9]	**–0.43**	**–0.72**	**–1.37**	**–1.07**	**–1.05**	**1.24**	**–0.67**	**0.66 R**	**1.27**
Consumption	**43.80**	**52.68**	**66.43**	**70.55**	**75.96**	**73.98**	**81.26**	**82.14 R**	**83.96**
Coal	9.84	11.58	12.26	12.66	15.42	17.48	19.10	18.87 R	19.63
Natural gas[10]	12.39	15.77	21.79	19.95	20.39	17.83	19.30	20.13 R	20.79
Petroleum[11]	19.92	23.25	29.52	32.73	34.20	30.92	33.55	33.53 R	33.77
Nuclear electric power	0.01	0.04	0.24	1.90	2.74	4.15	6.16	6.61 R	6.52
Hydroelectric power[12]	1.66	2.06	2.65	3.22	3.12	3.40	2.95	2.79	3.06
Other[13]	(4)	–0.01	–0.04	0.09	0.08	0.20	0.21	0.22	0.20

(1) Includes lease condensate. (2) Electric utility and industrial generation. (3) "Other" production is electricity generated for distribution from wood, waste, geothermal, wind, photovoltaic, and solar thermal energy. (4) Less than 0.005 quadrillion Btu. (5) Includes imports of crude oil for the Strategic Petroleum Reserve, which began in 1977. (6) Includes imports of unfinished oils and natural gas plant liquids. (7) "Other" imports are coal, electricity, and coal coke. (8) "Other" exports are natural gas, petroleum products, electricity, and coal coke. (9) A balancing item. Includes stock changes, losses, gains, miscellaneous blending components, and unaccounted for supply. (10) Includes supplemental gaseous fuels. (11) Petroleum products supplied, including natural gas plant liquids and crude oil burned as fuel. (12) Electric utility and industrial generation, and net imports of electricity. (13) "Other" consumption is net imports of coal coke and electricity generated for distribution from wood, waste, geothermal, wind, photovoltaic, and solar thermal energy. R= Revised data. P= Preliminary data. **Notes:** Due to a lack of consistent historical data, some renewable energy sources are not included. For 1992 consumption, 3.0 quadrillion Btu of renewable energy consumed by U.S. electric utilities to generate electricity for distribution is included, but an estimated 3.0 quadrillion Btu of renewable energy used by other sectors in the U.S. is not included. Sum of components may not equal total due to independent rounding.

World's Major Producers of Primary Energy, 1992

Source: Energy Information Administration, *International Energy Annual*, 1992; Quadrillion Btu

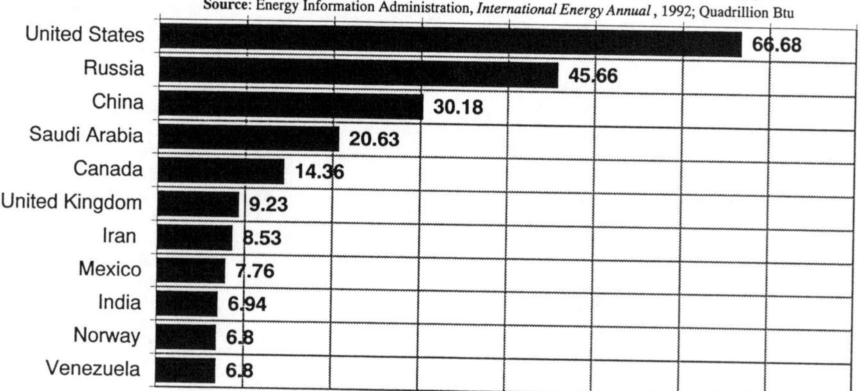

World's Major Consumers of Primary Energy, 1992

Source: Energy Information Administration, International Energy Annual 1992; Quadrillion Btu

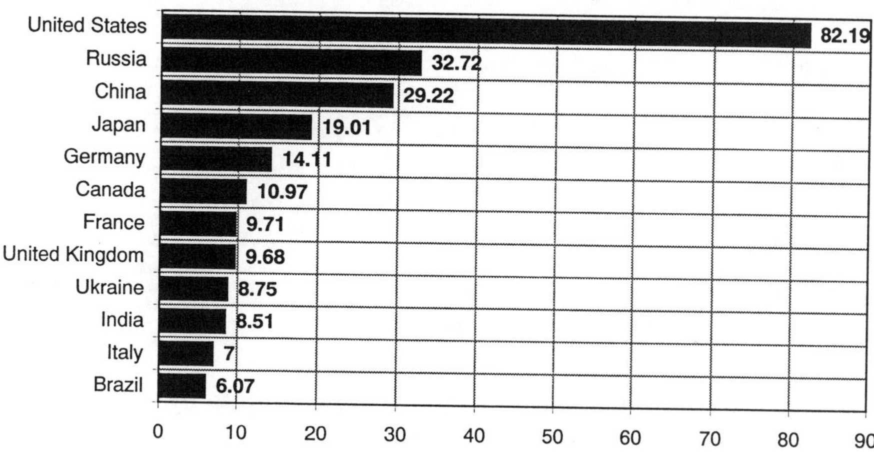

U.S. Net Imports of Petroleum, 1973-93

Source: Energy Information Administration, U.S. Dept. of Energy, *Monthly Energy Review,* June 1994; thousand barrels per day

Average annual rate	Net Imports[1] From Arab OPEC[2]	Net Imports[1] From OPEC[3]	Net Imports[1] From all countries	Petroleum products supplied
1973	914	2,991	6,025	17,308
1974	752	3,277	5,892	16,653
1975	1,382	3,599	5,846	16,322
1976	2,423	5,063	7,090	17,461
1977	3,184	6,190	8,565	18,431
1978	2,962	5,747	8,002	18,847
1979	3,054	5,633	7,985	18,513
1980	2,549	4,293	6,365	17,056
1981	1,844	3,315	5,401	16,058
1982	852	2,136	4,298	15,296
1983	630	1,843	4,312	15,231
1984	817	2,037	4,715	15,726
1985	470	1,821	4,286	15,726
1986	1,160	2,828	5,439	16,281
1987	1,272	3,053	5,914	16,665
1988	1,837	3,513	6,587	17,283
1989	2,128	4,124	7,202	17,325
1990	2,243	4,285	7,161	16,988
1991	2,057	4,064	6,626	16,714
1992	1,972	4,071	6,938	17,033
1993......	1,995[R]	4,253[R]	7,618[R]	17,237[R]

R= Revised. (1) Net Imports is imports minus exports. Imports from members of the Organization of Petroleum Exporting Countries (OPEC) exclude indirect imports, which are petroleum products primarily from Caribbean and West European areas and refined from crude oil produced by OPEC.(2) The Arab members of OPEC are Algeria, Iraq, Kuwait Libya, Qatar, Saudi Arabia, and the United Arab Emirates. Net imports from the Neutral Zone between Kuwait and Saudi Arabia are included in net imports from Arab OPEC.(3) OPEC currently consists of Gabon, Indonesia, Iran, Nigeria, and Venezuela, as well as the Arab members; prior to 1993, it also included Ecuador. **Notes:** Beginning in October 1977, Strategic Petroleum Reserves are included. Geographic coverage is the 50 states and the District of Columbia.

Appliance Use in U.S. Households, 1978-90

Source: Energy Information Administration, U.S. Dept. of Energy, *Annual Energy Review 1993*

(percentage of households)

Appliance	1978	1980	1982	1984	1987	1990	Change 1980-90
Total households	100	100	100	100	100	100	—
Type of appliances							
Electric appliances							
Television set (color)	NA	82	85	88	93	96	14
Television set (B/W)	NA	51	47	43	36	31	–20
Clothes washer	75	75	72	74	76	76	1
Range (stove-top burner)	53	54	53	54	57	58	4
Oven, regular or microwave	54	59	59	63	79	88	29
Oven, microwave	8	14	21	34	61	79	65
Clothes dryer	45	47	45	46	51	53	6
Separate freezer	35	38	37	37	34	35	–3
Dishwasher	35	37	36	38	43	45	8
Dehumidifier	NA	9	9	9	10	12	3
Waterbed heaters	NA	NA	NA	10	14	15	NA
Window or ceiling fan	NA	NA	28	35	46	51	NA
Whole house fan	NA	NA	8	8	9	10	NA
Evaporative cooler	NA	4	4	4	3	4	–[1]
Personal computer	NA	NA	NA	NA	NA	16	NA
Pump for well water	NA	NA	NA	NA	NA	15	NA
Swimming-pool pump[2]	NA	4	3	NA	NA	5	1
Gas appliances[3]							
Range (stove-top burner)	48	46	47	45	43	42	–4
Oven	47	42	42	42	41	41	–1
Clothes dryer	14	14	15	16	15	16	2
Outdoor gas grill	NA	9	11	13	20	26	17
Outdoor gas light	2	2	2	1	1	1	–1
Swimming pool heater[4]	NA	NA	NA	1	1	2	NA
Refrigerators[5]							
One	86	86	86	88	86	84	–2
Two or more	14	14	13	12	14	15	1
Air Conditioning							
Central[6]	23	27	28	30	36	39	12
Individual room units[6]	33	30	30	30	30	29	–1
None	44	43	42	40	36	32	–11
Portable Kerosene Heaters	–[1]	–[1]	3	6	6	5	5

(1) Less than 0.5%. (2) All reported swimming pools were assumed to have an electric pump for filtering and circulating the water. (3) Includes natural gas or liquefied petroleum gases. (4) In 1984, 1987, and 1990, also includes heaters for jacuzzis and hot tubs. (5) Fewer than 0.5% of the households do not have a refrigerator. (6) Households with both central and individual room units are counted only under central. NA= not available. **Note:** No data are available for years not shown except 1979.

Energy Consumption and Consumption per Capita by State, 1992

Source: Energy Information Administration, U.S. Dept. of Energy, *Annual Energy Review 1993*

Consumption

Rank	State	Trillion Btu	Rank	State	Trillion Btu
1.	Texas	9,915.1	27.	Mississippi	967.5
2.	California	7,092.3	28.	Colorado	958.9
3.	Ohio	3,732.6	29.	Arizona	944.5
4.	New York	3,616.0	30.	Oregon	942.4
5.	Pennsylvania	3,597.0	31.	Iowa	926.7
6.	Louisiana	3,557.5	32.	Arkansas	796.0
7.	Illinois	3,487.3	33.	West Virginia	794.2
8.	Florida	3,066.4	34.	Connecticut	761.7
9.	Michigan	2,784.1	35.	Alaska	611.5
10.	Indiana	2,407.8	36.	New Mexico	584.3
11.	New Jersey	2,401.0	37.	Utah	556.8
12.	Georgia	2,094.7	38.	Nebraska	505.8
13.	North Carolina	2,018.9	39.	Wyoming	422.3
14.	Washington	1,991.2	40.	Nevada	411.5
15.	Virginia	1,853.3	41.	Idaho	386.6
16.	Tennessee	1,792.7	42.	Maine	370.3
17.	Alabama	1,653.2	43.	Montana	340.5
18.	Kentucky	1,532.4	44.	North Dakota	327.2
19.	Missouri	1,499.2	45.	Hawaii	263.1
20.	Wisconsin	1,404.3	46.	Rhode Island	246.8
21.	Massachusetts	1,369.5	47.	New Hampshire	244.1
22.	Minnesota	1,369.1	48.	Delaware	240.6
23.	Oklahoma	1,302.0	49.	South Dakota	204.9
24.	South Carolina	1,224.3	50.	District of Columbia	174.0
25.	Maryland	1,203.7	51.	Vermont	139.9
26.	Kansas	1,013.5		**Total United States**	**82,128.2**

Consumption per Capita

Rank	State	Million Btu	Rank	State	Million Btu
1.	Alaska	1040.0	27.	Utah	307.4
2.	Wyoming	908.1	28.	New Jersey	307.0
3.	Louisiana	831.4	29.	Minnesota	306.4
4.	Texas	560.7	30.	Illinois	300.3
5.	North Dakota	516.1	31.	Pennsylvania	299.9
6.	West Virginia	439.0	32.	North Carolina	299.7
7.	Indiana	425.6	33.	Maine	299.6
8.	Montana	414.3	34.	District of Columbia	297.4
9.	Kentucky	408.2	35.	Michigan	295.1
10.	Oklahoma	406.2	36.	Virginia	289.8
11.	Kansas	403.0	37.	South Dakota	289.4
12.	Alabama	399.5	38.	Missouri	288.8
13.	Washington	387.2	39.	Wisconsin	281.2
14.	Mississippi	370.0	40.	Colorado	276.8
15.	New Mexico	369.3	41.	Rhode Island	246.6
16.	Idaho	362.6	42.	Arizona	246.5
17.	Tennessee	356.7	43.	Vermont	244.9
18.	Delaware	343.7	44.	Maryland	244.8
19.	South Carolina	339.8	45.	Connecticut	232.3
20.	Ohio	338.7	46.	California	229.6
21.	Arkansas	332.5	47.	Massachusetts	228.5
22.	Iowa	330.6	48.	Hawaii	227.6
23.	Oregon	317.1	49.	Florida	227.4
24.	Nebraska	315.9	50.	New Hampshire	218.9
25.	Georgia	309.3	51.	New York	199.7
26.	Nevada	308.0		**Total United States**	**322.0**

World Crude Oil and Natural Gas Reserves, Jan. 1, 1993

Source: Energy Information Administration, U.S. Dept. of Energy, *Annual Energy Review 1993; Oil and Gas Journal,* Penn Well Publishing Company, Dec. 1992; *World Oil,* Gulf Publising Company, Aug., 1993

Region and country	Crude oil (billion barrels)		Natural gas (trillion cubic feet)	
	Oil and Gas Journal	*World Oil*	*Oil and Gas Journal*	*World Oil*
North America	**80.3**	**80.6**	**331.6**	**329.2**
Canada	5.3	5.7	95.7	94.1
Mexico	51.3	51.2	70.9	70.0
United States	23.7	23.7	165.0	165.0
Central and South America	**72.5**	**74.3**	**188.6**	**189.0**
Argentina	1.6	1.6	22.7	23.8
Bolivia	0.1	0.1	4.1	4.2
Brazil	3.0	3.7	4.4	4.8
Colombia	1.9	1.6	7.2	3.9
Ecuador	1.6	2.0	3.9	4.0
Trinidad and Tobago	0.6	0.5	8.7	8.5
Venezuela	62.7	63.3	126.5	128.9
Other	1.0	1.3	11.1	10.9
Western Europe	**16.1**	**24.0**	**194.7**	**215.6**
Denmark	0.7	0.7	4.0	3.6
Germany	0.4	0.2	12.1	7.8
Italy	0.7	0.8	13.0	12.7
Netherlands	0.1	0.3	68.9	68.1
Norway	8.8	16.8	70.6	97.3
United Kingdom	4.1	4.6	19.1	21.5
Other	1.0	0.6	7.0	4.5
Eastern Europe and Former U.S.S.R.	**59.0**	**188.5**	**1,960.4**	**2049.3**
Former U.S.S.R.	57.0	186.9	1,942.3	2033.4
Other[1]	2.0	1.6	18.1	15.9
Middle East	**661.8**	**596.3**	**1,520.1**	**1,365.6**
Bahrain	0.1	0.1	5.8	5.6
Iran	92.9	61.3	699.2	610.0
Iraq	100.0	99.8	109.5	109.3
Kuwait	96.5	94.8	52.9	51.6
Oman	4.5	4.7	16.9	17.0
Qatar	3.7	4.3	227.0	165.0
Saudi Arabia	260.3	261.0	183.1	185.3
United Arab Emirates	98.1	65.1	204.6	198.4
Other	5.7	5.0	21.1	23.4
Africa	**61.9**	**74.7**	**346.9**	**326.0**
Algeria	9.2	10.4	128.0	128.9
Cameroon	0.4	0.3	3.9	3.9
Egypt	6.2	3.6	15.4	12.3
Libya	22.8	38.2	46.2	43.5
Nigeria	17.9	18.2	120.0	121.9
Tunisia	1.7	0.5	3.0	0.9
Other	3.7	3.6	30.4	14.6
Far East and Oceania	**44.6**	**54.0**	**341.0**	**342.7**
Australia	1.8	3.2	18.3	73.9
Brunei	1.4	1.1	14.0	13.1
China	24.0	29.6	49.4	45.0
India	6.0	5.9	26.0	23.9
Indonesia	5.8	8.4	64.4	48.5
Malaysia	3.7	4.3	67.8	66.9
New Zealand	0.2	0.2	3.4	3.1
Pakistan	0.4	0.1	31.0	23.7
Thailand	0.2	0.2	8.5	8.2
Other	1.1	1.0	58.4	36.3
World	**996.1**	**1,092.4**	**4,883.3**	**4,817.3**

(1) Albania, Bulgaria, former Czechoslovakia, Hungary, Poland, and Romania. **Notes:** Data for Kuwait and Saudi Arabia include one-half of the reserves in the Neutral Zone between Kuwait and Saudi Arabia. All reserve figures except those for the former U.S.S.R. and natural gas reserves in Canada are proved reserves recoverable with present technology and prices. Former U.S.S.R. figures are "explored reserves," which include proved, probable, and some possible. The Canadian natural gas figure includes proved and some probable. The latest Energy Information Administration data for the United States are for December 31, 1992. Sum of components may not equal total due to rounding.

Gasoline Retail Prices, U.S. City Average, 1973-93

Source: Energy Information Administration, U.S. Dept. of Energy, *Monthly Energy Review,* June 1994
(cents per gallon, including taxes)

Average	Leaded Regular	Unleaded Regular	Unleaded Premium	All Types[1]
1973	38.8	NA	NA	NA
1974	53.2	NA	NA	NA
1975	56.7	NA	NA	NA
1976	59.0	61.4	NA	NA
1977	62.2	65.6	NA	NA
1978	62.6	67.0	NA	65.2
1979	85.7	90.3	NA	88.2
1980	119.1	124.5	NA	122.1
1981[2]	131.1	137.8	147.0[3]	135.3
1982	122.2	129.6	141.5	128.1
1983	115.7	124.1	138.3	122.5
1984	112.9	121.2	136.6	119.8
1985	111.5	120.2	134.0	119.6
1986	85.7	92.7	108.5	93.1
1987	89.7	94.8	109.3	95.7
1988	89.9	94.6	110.7	96.3
1989	99.8	102.1	119.7	106.0
1990	114.9	116.4	134.9	121.7
1991	NA	114.0	132.1	119.6
1992	NA	112.7	131.6	119.0
1993	NA	110.8	130.2	117.3

(1) Also includes types of motor gasoline not shown separately. (2) In Sept. 1981, the Bureau of Labor Statistics changed the weights used in the calculation of average motor gasoline prices. From Sept. 1981 forward, gasohol is included in the average for all types, and unleaded premium is weighted more heavily. (3) Based on Sept. through Dec. data only. **Notes:** Geographic coverage for 1973-77 is 56 urban areas; for 1978 forward, 85 urban areas. NA = not available.

Nuclear Electricity Gross Generation by Selected Country, March 1994

Source: Energy Information Administration, U.S. Dept. of Energy; *Monthly Energy Review,* June 1994
(billion kilowatt hours)

Belgium	3.6
Bulgaria	1.4
Canada	10.4
Finland	1.8
France	30.5
Germany	12.7
Hungary	1.2
Japan	18.6
Russia	9.5
South Africa	0.8
South Korea	4.6
Spain	4.1
Sweden	7.2
Switzerland	2.3
Taiwan	2.9
Ukraine	6.5
United Kingdom	7.9
United States	51.3

World Nuclear Power

Source: International Atomic Energy Agency, Dec. 31, 1993

Country	Reactors in operation No. of units	Reactors in operation Total MW(e)[1]	Reactors under construction No. of units	Reactors under construction Total MW(e)[1]	Nuclear electricity supplied in 1993 TW(e).h	Nuclear electricity supplied in 1993 % of total	Total operating experience to Dec. 31, 1993 Years	Total operating experience to Dec. 31, 1993 Months
Argentina	2	935	1	692	7.2	14.2	30	7
Belgium	7	5,527	—	—	39.5	58.9	121	7
Brazil	1	626	1	1,245	0.4	0.2	11	9
Bulgaria	6	3,538	—	—	14.0	36.9	71	1
Canada	22	15,755	—	—	88.6	17.3	304	11
China	2	1,194	1	906	2.5	0.3	2	5
Cuba	—	—	2	816	—	—	—	—
Czech Republic	4	1,648	2	1,824	12.6	29.2	30	8
Finland	4	2,310	—	—	18.8	32.4	59	4
France	57	59,033	4	5,815	350.2	77.7	766	5
Germany	21	22,657	—	—	145.0	29.7	469	1
Hungary	4	1,729	—	—	13.0	43.3	34	2
India	9	1,593	5	1,010	5.4	1.9	110	3
Iran	—	—	2	2,392	—	—	—	—
Italy	—	—	—	—	—	—	—	—
Japan	48	38,029	6	5,645	246.3	30.9	603	7
Kazakhstan	1	70	—	—	0.4	0.5	20	6
Korea, South	9	7,220	7	5,770	55.4	40.3	81	1
Lithuania	2	2,370	—	—	12.3	87.2	16	6
Mexico	1	654	1	654	3.7	3.0	4	9
Netherlands	2	504	—	—	3.7	5.1	45	9
Pakistan	1	125	1	300	0.4*	0.9*	22	3
Romania	—	—	5	3,155	—	—	—	—
Russia	29	19,843	4	3,375	119.2	12.5	468	6
South Africa	2	1,842	—	—	7.2	4.5	18	3
Slovakia	4	1,632	4	1,552	11.0	53.6	53	5
Slovenia	1	632	—	—	3.8	35.5	12	3
Spain	9	7,105	—	—	53.6	36.0	128	8
Sweden	12	10,002	—	—	58.9	42.0	195	2
Switzerland	5	2,985	—	—	22.0	37.9	93	10
Ukraine	15	12,679	6	5,700	75.2*	32.9	143	11
United Kingdom	35	11,909	1	1,188	79.8	26.3	994	2
United States	109	98,784	2	2,330	610.3	21.2	1,810	8
Total[2]	**430**	**337,820**	**55**	**44,369**	**2,093.4**	**—**	**6,902**	**2**

(1) 1 terawatt-hour (TW(e).h) = 10^6 megawatt-hour (MW(e).h). For an average power plant, 1 TW(e).h = 0.39 megatonnes of coal equivalent (input) and 0.23 megatonnes of oil equivalent (input). (2) Includes Taiwan data. *IAEA estimate.

U.S. Nuclear Power Plant Operations

Source: Energy Information Administration, U.S. Dept. of Energy, *Monthly Energy Review,* June 1994

	Operable reactors number	Nuclear-based electricity generation million net kilowatt-hours	Nuclear portion of domestic electricity generation percent
1976	61	191,104	9.4
1977	65	250,883	11.8
1978	70	276,403	12.5
1979	68	255,155	11.4
1980	70	251,116	11.0
1981	74	272,674	11.9
1982	77	282,773	12.6
1983	80	293,677	12.7
1984	86	327,634	13.6
1985	95	383,691	15.5
1986	100	414,038	16.6
1987	107	455,270	17.7
1988	108	526,973	19.5
1989	110	529,355	19.0
1990	111	576,862	20.5
1991	111	612,565	21.7
1992	109	618,776	22.1
1993	109	610,291	21.2

Status of U.S. Nuclear Reactor Units

Source: Energy Information Administration, U.S. Dept. of Energy, *Monthly Energy Review,* June 1994

	Licensed for operation		Construction permits					Total design capacity million net kilowatts
	Operable	In startup	Granted	Pending	On order	Announced	Total	
	Number of reactor units							
1980	70	2	82	12	3	0	169	163
1981	74	0	75	11	3	0	163	157
1982	77	2	60	3	2	0	144	135
1983	80	3	53	0	2	0	138	129
1984	86	6	38	0	2	0	132	123
1985	95	3	30	0	2	0	130	121
1986	100	7	19	0	2	0	128	119
1987	107	4	14	0	2	0	127	119
1988	108	3	12	0	0	0	123	115
1989	110	1	10	0	0	0	121	113
1990	111	0	8	0	0	0	119	111
1991	111	0	8	0	0	0	119	111
1992	109	0	8	0	0	0	117	111
1993	109	0	7	0	0	0	116	110

SCIENCE AND TECHNOLOGY

Scientific Achievements and Discoveries, 1994

Anthropology and Paleontology

- Fossil fragments, believed to belong to the oldest human ancestors, were found in Aramis, Ethiopia. If genetic research is correct, the fossils belong to a new species of apelike creatures that lived 4.4 million years ago, taking scientists back 800,000 years in reconstructing the prehuman fossil record.
- Skull fragments of *Homo erectus* found on the Indonesian island of Java were estimated to be about about 1.8 million years old, making them as old as the oldest fossils ever found in Africa.
- More fossil evidence of the early apelike human ancestor *Australopithecus afarensis* was uncovered. Scientists had always been slightly skeptical about the 1974 discovery of the famous "Lucy" skeleton, which belongs to this species, because the skeleton was not complete. The new evidence found in the Maka area of the Middle Awash River valley in Ethiopia supported earlier findings.
- An ancient "lost city" was discovered 60 mi northwest of the modern city of Veracruz, Mexico. The temple mounds, ball courts, and other traces of the city, now named El Pital for a nearby village, were overgrown with vegetation and had been thought to be natural hills. Scientists will need time to determine more about the people who lived at this once flourishing seaport between AD 100 and 600.
- Bones of a previously unknown species of meat-eating dinosaur that roamed Antarctica 200 million years ago, when it had a warmer climate, were uncovered. The animal, *Cryolophosaurus elioti* (frozen crested reptile), measured nearly 25 ft, walked on large hindlegs, and had small forefeet, a long tail, and large, powerful jaws.

Earth Science

- With the constant danger of quakes and rock falls, the Dante 2, an advanced robot outfitted with scientific instruments and monitors, picked its way 650 ft into the active Mount Spurr volcano in Alaska and studied the volcano floor where no human has ever been. It took 4 days for the 1,700-lb robot to descend in a crablike motion into the pit of the volcano. On its return, Dante slipped and toppled to its side 400 ft from the volcano rim. In a daring move, the $1.7 million robot was plucked from the crater. Despite this accident, the robot had proven that it could perform functions in situations too dangerous for humans.

Biology

- Vu Quang Nature Reserve in the Nhe Tinh Province of Vietnam was the sight of a newly discovered mammal species—the giant Muntjac (or barking) deer.
- Although biologists had believed that all bacteria are microscopic, researchers announced the discovery of a strain so large that it can been seen with the unaided eye. The newly identified organism, *Epulopiscium fishelsoni*, was found inside a fish caught off the coast of Australia.
- In a remote mountainous region of Indonesia, researchers found another member of the marsupial family, a new species of tree kangaroo. This primitive animal has black and white pandalike patterns in its thick fur and is about the size of a medium dog.

Astronomy

- The first planets to be found outside the solar system were discovered in orbit around a pulsar star located 1,500 light-years from earth. By observing irregularities in the otherwise regularly pulsating radio signals projected from the star, scientists confirmed what they believe to be the existence of 3 planets. Preliminary findings indicate the existence of a 4th may also be likely.
- With newly corrected vision, the Hubble Space Telescope relayed important data to earth. First, bizarre, unexplainable gas rings were spotted wobbling around the Supernova 1987A. NASA astrophysicists then announced that information relayed from the telescope provided "seemingly conclusive evidence" that a black hole exists at the center of the M87 galaxy, which is 50 million light-years away in the constellation Virgo. Hubble also found the strongest evidence yet that material present in Orion Nebula could form planets in the future.

Medicine

- Research indicated that certain types of peptic ulcers caused by the bacterium *Helicobacter pylori* can be cured—not just treated—with antibiotics. Studies indicated that *H. pylori* may also play a role in certain forms of stomach cancer.
- The search for the hormone that stimulates a person's bone marrow to produce platelets ended successfully. If clinical trials prove successful and the hormone works as expected in humans, patients such as cancer victims undergoing radiation therapy would benefit.
- A second gene linked to colon cancer was found. This discovery may enable scientists to create a screening test that would identify 90% of those people at risk for inherited forms of the disease.
- Mice with immune systems altered through genetic engineering so that they are capable of producing human antibodies were bred for the first time. Scientists hope that the mice can be used as factories to produce human antibodies that can in turn be used to make disease-fighting drugs.
- The discovery of a mutant gene tied to the development of 10% of all hereditary breast cancer cases was announced. Scientists involved in this research believe that those with the mutant gene may have an 85% lifetime risk of developing the disease by age 50.
- A carotid endarterectomy, a controversial operation that is performed to remove the fatty deposits from a major artery in the neck, was found to sharply reduce the risk of stroke in individuals with an artery blockage restricting 70-99% of the blood flow.
- Two chemical agents—called netrins—that are responsible for laying down the tracks of the human nervous system when the human fetus is less than one month old were identified. Diffusing outward from their point of origin, the netrins stimulate the growth and direct the organization of the axons of nerve cells.

Physics

- A team of 439 scientists working at the Fermi National Accelerator Laboratory in Batavia, IL, announced that they believed they had discovered evidence proving the existence of the top quark, the 6th and last of the quarks to be identified by physicists. Quarks are the basic particles postulated, in the so-called Standard Model, to be the foundation of all matter. Since ordinary matter is composed of 2 of the 6 quarks and the other more elusive particles are believed to have existed at the creation of the universe, scientists have had to recreate the remaining 4 particles to prove their existence.
- Physicists recently cooled cesium atoms to 700 nanokelvins (700 billionths of a degree above absolute zero), the coldest temperature ever recorded for matter.

Technology

- On Feb. 4, 1994, Japan launched its first large rocket built entirely using Japanese technology. The 164-ft rocket cost about $2.4 billion to build and represented many years of effort on the part of Japan's space agency to build a rocket that could be used to launch communications and earth-observing satellites.

Computer Glossary

Source: *Electronic Computer Glossary* by Alan Freedman, © 1994, The Computer Language Co. Inc., Point Pleasant, PA 18950

access: to place data on and to retrieve data from a disk or other storage device connected to a computer.
analog: of or relating to the representation of an object that resembles the original.
application: a computer program that does work, for example, word-processing software or an electronic spreadsheet.
arithmetic logic unit (ALU): a part of the *central processing unit (CPU)* that performs arithmetic operations and logical comparisons.
artificial intelligence (AI): a broad range of computer applications that resemble human intelligence and that can mimic human behaviors, such as understanding speech, making judgments, and learning.
ASCII: an acronym for American Standard Code for Information Interchange; a widely used binary code for storing and transferring data.
assembly language: a low-level, CPU-specific programming language that represents machine-language instructions as mnemonics.
authorization code: an identification number or a password that a user must enter to access a computer system.

back up (verb); back-up (noun): to copy data (verb); a copy of data (noun).
BASIC: an acronym for Beginner's All-purpose Symbolic Instruction Code, a widely used, high-level programming language.
baud rate: the speed at which data is transmitted over a modem.
binary code: a representation of the base-2 number system in which the only allowable digits are 0 and 1.
bit: short for binary digit (0 or 1), the smallest unit of information stored in a computer.
board: short for printed circuit board; a flat board that holds chips and other electronic components connected by electronically conductive pathways that are "printed" on the board layers.
boot: short for bootstrap, to start the computer.
bps: short for bits per second, the unit of measure for the speed of modems and printers.
buffer: a reserved, temporary place in which information is stored while being processed.
bug: a software or hardware error that causes the system to malfunction.
bus: a common channel, or pathway, between hardware devices.
byte: an 8-bit sequence of binary digits. Each byte corresponds to 1 character of data, representing a single letter, number, or symbol.

C: a high-level programming language often used to write commercial products because of its transportability among different computer systems.
C++: an object-oriented version of the C programming language.
CAD/CAM: abbreviation for computer-aided design/computer-aided manufacturing.
CD-ROM: an acronym for Compact Disc-Read Only Memory; an optical disc, widely used for *multimedia* and interactive applications. A laser beam retrieves data by scanning tracks of microscopic holes in the disc. The disc can store more than 600 megabytes (the equivalent of 250,000 pages of text).
central processing unit (CPU): the part within the computer that interprets and executes the instructions the user gives the system. It is composed of an arithmetic logic unit, a control unit, and some memory. In a personal computer, it is a single chip.
chip: short for integrated circuit chip, a collection of interconnected microminiature electronic components.
CISC: an acronym for Complex Instruction Set Computer, a computer architecture used by the older Intel microprocessors; requires more extensive instructions than the newer *RISC* architecture. Computers with CISC architecture often require additional circuit boards to handle more complicated tasks.
client: a single-user workstation in a network.
clipper chip: the nickname for the controversial microprocessor that uses the Data Encryption Standard designed by the National Security Agency (NSA). Using a powerful algorithm, the chip offers advanced data encryption; however, one of the *keys* would be held by the federal government. NSA has recommended that it become the universal standard.
COBOL: an acronym for Common Business Oriented Language; one of the first high-level programming languages; widely used for writing financial applications.
code: a set of machine symbols that represents data or instructions; also to write a program.
common carrier: a regulated organization that provides telecommunications services for public use.
communications protocol: software that manages the delivery of messages between stations on a network.
computer: a programmable machine that accepts, processes, and displays data.
connect time: the time a user at a workstation is logged-on to a computer network or on-line service.
cursor: the movable symbol on the computer monitor that is the contact point between the user and the data.
cybernetics: the comparative study of human and machine processes in order to understand the similarities and differences.

database: a large amount of data stored in a well-organized format electronically and managed by a program that allows access to the information.
Data Encryption Standard (DES): the encryption algorithm endorsed by the U.S. National Institute of Standards and Technology.
data glove: a glove used to report the position of a user's hand in *virtual reality* systems.
debug: to correct a problem within computer hardware or software.
desktop publishing: the production of printed matter by means of a desktop computer having a layout program that integrates text and graphics.
digital: of or relating to the representation, manipulation, or transmission of data by discrete signals.
disk: a direct access storage device. See also *CD-ROM*, *floppy disk*, and *hard disk*.
disk drive: a peripheral machine that rotates a magnetic or optical storage disk in order to read or record information.
DOS: an acronym for disk operating system; a single-user operating system used on IBM-compatible personal computers.
download: to transmit data between remote computers, from a file server to a workstation, or from a computer to a floppy disk; usually means receiving data. See also *upload*.

dump: a printout of the contents of memory or of a file.

electronic mail: transmission of memos and messages over a *network*. Also called e-mail.
emoticon: a coded shorthand often used within e-mail messages to give emotion to the computer message in networked conversations, for example, :). Also called smileys.
encryption: encoding data for security purposes.

field: the physical unit of data in a record.
file: any collection of data treated as a single unit.
file server: a computer that stores data and programs shared by network users.
fire walls: security barriers on the Internet.
flamed: to get bombarded with hundreds of angry electronic messages for a breach in the unwritten code of conduct on the Internet; the result for the recipient is jammed telephone lines and a busy, temporarily inoperable computer.
floppy disk: a small, inexpensive removable magnetic disk used to record and store information; commonly used to transfer data from one machine to another or to back up files.
font: a set of type characters of a particular design.
format: the arrangement by which data are stored or displayed.
FORTRAN: an acronym for Formula Translator; a high-level computer language widely used for scientific, engineering, or mathematical purposes.
fuzzy search: a method of data retrieval that does not depend upon the user knowing the exact information being sought; it can get results when the exact spelling is not known or help users obtain information that is loosely related to a topic.

global memory: the shared central memory of a multiple-processor system.
graphical user interface: a method originally popularized by the Macintosh computer that employs graphical symbols to represent instructions and commands to the computer for ease in operating by less-experienced users.
groupware: software designed to allow several users to work together, in synchronization, on one project.

hard copy: printed computer output.
hard disk: a metal or glass platter covered with a magnetic recording surface. Hard disks have become the primary storage device of a personal computer.
hardware: the physical apparatus that makes up a computer: chips, transformers, boards, and wires. Also used to describe various pieces of equipment used with a computer including the keyboard, mouse, printer, modem, disk drives, and speakers.
hexadecimal: the base-16 number system, which is used to condense binary-based codes, such as bytes, for more efficient computer processing.

integrated circuit (IC): the formal name for a *chip*.
Intel: a major manufacturer of integrated circuits used in many personal computers. Intel makes the 8086 family of microprocessors and its derivatives. See also *x86*.
interactive: a type of computing that does not have a predetermined outcome; instead, the operator may interrupt the program to make choices that affect the course of the program.
interface: a connection and interaction between hardware, software, and the user.
Internet: a network of computer networks involving millions of users.

joystick: a handheld lever that can be tilted in different directions to control the movement of the cursor on the terminal screen.

K: abbreviation for kilobyte, used to denote 1,024 units of stored matter.
key: the code that will open encrypted data.
keyboard: a set of input keys; also used as a verb meaning to type data into a computer for processing.
kludge: an inelegant solution to a technical problem.

language: any set of related commands or instructions that a computer understands.
light pen: an input device that gives directions to the computer when touching the terminal screen.
load: the actual operation of putting information and data into the computer or memory.
local area network (LAN): a computer system that links computers, printers, and other devices in a confined area, such as a building or a campus.
log on/log off: to connect to or disconnect from another computer system or file server.

machine language: binary-code instructions that are directly understood by a computer.
machine readable: any paper form or storage medium that a computer can read.
Macintosh: a family of personal computers from Apple Computer that use the Motorola 680x0 processor or PowerPC CPUs; these computers (also called Macs) popularized the graphical user interface.
mainframe computer: the largest type of computer, usually capable of processing data quickly and able to serve many users simultaneously.
memory: the computer's internal storage capacity.
menu: programs, functions, or other choices displayed in a list on the monitor for user selection.
microcomputer: a computer that uses a microprocessor for its CPU. Personal computers are microcomputers.
microprocessor: a complete CPU on a single chip.
minicomputer: an intermediate computer system sized between the microcomputer and the mainframe computer.
modem: an acronym for modulator-demodulator; a device that enables data to be transmitted between computers, generally over telephone lines, but sometimes via fiber-optic cable or wireless radio frequency.
monitor: a high-resolution screen used to display the output of a computer.
mouse: a handheld input device that can be rolled across a flat surface.
multimedia: a software format that utilizes a CD-ROM to disseminate information via a combination of audio, text, graphics, animation, and full-motion video.
multitasking: the ability to run more than one program on one computer at the same time.

network: in communications, terminals and computers linked together with the ability to interact with one another. See also *local area network* and *wide area network*. In database management, a database design.
network operating system: an operating system that supports multiple, simultaneous users. Examples include NetWare, UNIX, LANtastic, LAN Manager, Windows 95, and Windows NT.

nibble: one-half byte, or 4 bits.
noise: extraneous, random disturbances that degrade or disrupt electronic signals in a communication network or electronic device.

objects: self-contained software modules used in object-orientated programming languages; contain reusable and interoperable instructions to complete specified tasks in multiple applications.
object-oriented programming: a programming method with formalized rules for developing self-contained software routines, or *objects*, that can be reused in other applications for greater programming flexibility.
on-line: immediately accessible by a computer's CPU.
open architecture: an electronic system whose architecture is made available to the public, for example, the Apple II and the Macintosh.
open system: an operating system, such as UNIX, that is designed to interoperate with other products and whose architecture is designed by numerous vendors.
operating system: a master control program that runs the computer. It provides the user interface and routines that let the user load and run software.
optical character reader (OCR): a device capable of recognizing characters in a special typeface.
optical fiber: an ultrathin strand of glass that can carry billions of bits of encoded data per second when pulses of laser light are beamed through it.
optoelectronics: a technology that joins light and electricity. OCRs, laser printers, and CD-ROMs are examples of optoelectronic devices.

Pascal: a popular high-level programming language.
PC: an abbreviation for personal computer.
peripheral: any hardware device that provides input, output or storage for a computer, such as keyboards, monitors, disks, or printers.
pixel: an acronym for picture element; the smallest display element on a video display screen.
port: the channel or interface between the *microprocessor* and *peripherals.*
PowerPC: a family of RISC-based CPU chips from Motorola and IBM. It was also designed by Apple. The PowerMac was the first personal computer to use the PowerPC chip.
printer: a device that converts computer output into printed images.
program: a sequence of detailed, coded instructions telling a computer how to perform a specific function.

RAM: an acronym for Random Access Memory; same as *memory*. The user can retrieve and alter contents of RAM.
random access: the ability to retrieve records in a file directly without reading any previous records.
record: a group of related fields that store data about a subject.
RISC: an acronym for Reduced Instruction Set Computer; a computer architecture that is less complicated and generally requires fewer instructions than the traditonal *CISC* (Complex Instruction Set Computer) architecture. Used by PowerPCs, RISC architecture is better suited for programs involving speech recognition and multimedia.
ROM: an acronym for Read Only Memory; a permanent memory, the contents of which can be read, but not altered.

sector: a defined portion of a concentric track on a disk.
software: the programs, or sets of instructions, that tell the computer what to do.
supercomputer: the fastest, most powerful computers at a given time; typically supercomputers can manipulate large amounts of data.

telecommuting: working at home and communicating with the office by computer via modem, fax, and other electronic means.
teleconferencing: to communicate with a number of people simultaneously via telephone lines or radio signals with audio, video, or computer connections.
terminal: a keyboard and a display unit (usually a monitor) that allow a person to communicate with a computer.
timesharing: the simultaneous use of a computer by more than one person, as in a *local area network.*
track: a concentric band on a magnetic disk that contains a specified amount of data. Tracks are broken into *sectors.*

UNIX: a multiuser operating system that runs on a variety of computers. It is most often used by the academic and engineering professions and in the business world on network servers.
upload: to transmit data between remote computers, from a file server to a workstation, or from a computer to a floppy disk; usually refers to transmitting, rather than receiving data. See also *download.*
user-friendly: easy to learn and use.

virtual memory: the use of hard disk storage to expand effective memory capability.
virtual reality: interaction with a computer to create an artificial reality that projects the user into a 3-dimensional space.
virus: a destructive program that is secretly attached to an existing program; once run, it alters or deletes data or causes a computer system to malfunction whenever the preexisting program is run.

wide area network (WAN): a communications network that spans large geographic distances and usually relies on transmission facilities from telephone companies and other common carriers.
window: a separate viewing area on a display screen.
word: a computer's basic storage unit; a sequence of bits—8 to 64—occupying a single storage location and processed as a unit by the computer.
word processor: a text creation and editing program or system that allows electronic writing and correcting of documents.
workstation: a high-performance, single-user microcomputer or minicomputer; or in a *local area network*, a personal computer that serves a single user.
write-access: authorization to record or alter data stored in a computer.

x86: short for the 8086 family of Intel microprocessors, which are the CPUs in IBM-compatible personal computers. It includes the 8086, 8088, 80286, 80386, 80486, and Pentium.

680x0: a family of microprocessors from Motorola that are the CPUs in the Macintosh and a variety of workstations.

U.S. Computer Sales and Ownership, 1982-95

Source: *Electronic Industries Association Consumer Electronic U.S. Sales*, 1982-94

(sales through retail consumer channels)

Year	Unit sales to dealers (thousands)	Dollar sales to dealers (millions)	Percentage of households with owners	Year	Unit sales to dealers (thousands)	Dollar sales to dealers (millions)	Percentage of households with owners
1982	1,550	1,375	NA	1989	3,900	3,711	22
1983	3,750	2,070	7	1990[1]	4,000	4,187	27
1984	3,975	2,385	13	1991[1]	3,900	4,287	29
1985	3,200	2,175	15	1992[1]	4,875	5,575	34
1986	2,950	3,060	16	1993[1]	5,850	6,921	35
1987	3,125	3,100	20	1994[1]	6,552	8,021	37
1988	3,500	3,340	21	1995[1]	7,340	8,514	NA

NA = not available. (1) Estimated figures.

U.S. Households With Computers With Installed CD-ROM Drives, 1993-97

Source: Inteco, Norwalk CT

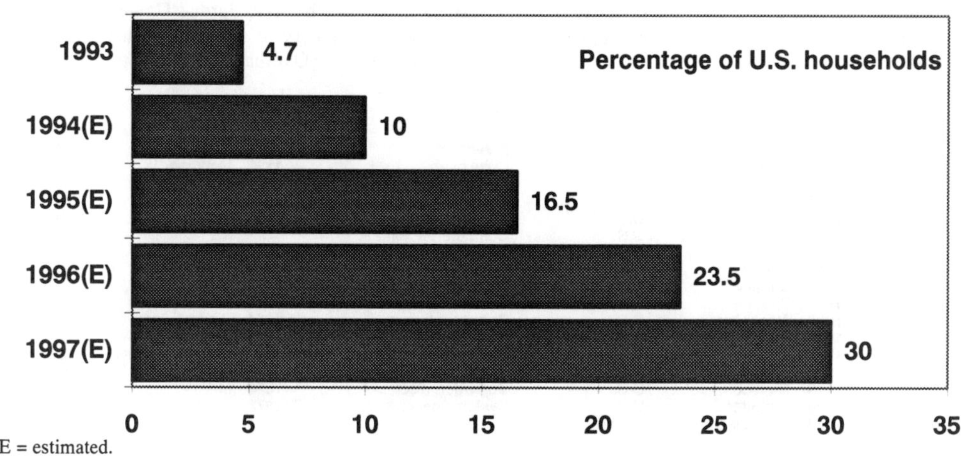

E = estimated.

Top-Selling CD-ROM Software, 1994

Source: PC Data, Reston, VA; based on average sales, Jan.-June 1994

Rank	Title	Manufacturer
1.	Myst	Brøderbund
2.	Star Wars Rebel Assault	LucasArts
3.	5Ft. 10 Pack	Sirius
4.	Microsoft Encarta	Microsoft
5.	7th Guest	Virgin
6.	Grolier's Encyclopedia	Grolier
7.	Microsoft Bookshelf	Microsoft
8.	Street Atlas USA	DeLorme
9.	Print Shop Delux CD Ensemble	Brøderbund
10.	Just Grandma and Me	Living Books
11.	Gabriel Knight	Sierra On-Line
12.	Commanche Maximum Overkill	Nova Logic
13.	Tortoise and the Hare	Living Books
14.	Microsoft Cinemania	Microsoft
15.	Quicken CD-ROM Deluxe	Intuit
16.	MegaRace	Software Toolworks
17.	Return to Zork	LucasArts
18.	Microsoft Golf	Microsoft
19.	Ultima VIII	Origin
20.	Lands of Lore	Virgin

The Internet

The Internet links people together via computer terminals and telephone lines (and in some cases wireless radio connections) in a web of networks and shared software, allowing users to communicate with one another wherever they are in the "net." Among the services available through the Internet are telnet, which grants users access to more powerful computers; usenet newsgroups, allowing open discussion between users; archives with access to scientific and government research; and electronic mail.

Originally created by the Pentagon, the Internet is now subsidized by the National Science Foundation, which controls the Internet's core computer network. Although it is impossible to get a true count of the number of people currently accessing the Internet, it is thought that 15 million people in the U.S. and 25 million worldwide access the Internet regularly. Despite the increasing accessibility through some public libraries, computer bulletin boards, and software packages, the primary users remain government officials, scientists, and corporate researchers.

To access the Internet, the requirements are a personal computer (preferably one able to use Windows software or the Macintosh operating system), a modem (with a speed of at least 9,000 bps), a communications program, access to a telephone line, and an account with an Internet service provider. More information about the Internet is available through Internet Network Information Center (Internic), a federally sponsored service, by calling (800) 444-4345.

National Medal of Science Winners, 1994

Source: National Science Foundation, Arlington, VA 22230

Authorized by Congress in 1959, the National Medal of Science is the highest award for outstanding contributions to the physical, biological, mathematical, behavioral, and engineering sciences. Winners are selected periodically by the president of the U.S. from a list of candidates recommended by the National Science Foundation. Among the 8 winners for 1994 was the first sociologist to win the medal, **Dr. Robert K. Merton**. Dr. Merton, a professor at Columbia University, founded the study of the sociology of science and is well known for introducing the focused-interview technique, now popularly used in the field of marketing. The other winners are:

- **Dr. Thomas Eisner**, Cornell University, pioneered the study of chemical ecology in plants and animals.
- **Dr. Ray Clough**, University of California at Berkeley (retired), structural engineering, designed earthquake-proof structures.
- **Dr. John Cocke**, IBM (retired), computer science, pioneered the development of reduced instruction set computer (RISC) architecture.
- **Dr. Frank Press**, Carnegie Institution of Washington, geophysicist, completed research dealing with the nature of the earth's deepest interior and the mitigation of natural disasters. He is also the former president of the National Academy of Sciences.
- **Dr. George Hammond**, Bowling Green State University, created the field of organic photochemistry.
- **Dr. Elizabeth Neufeld**, University of California at Los Angeles, human biochemical genetics, advanced the understanding of lysosomal storage diseases.
- **Dr. Albert Overhauser**, Purdue University, physicist, developed the theory of dynamic nuclear polarization, also known as the Overhauser Effect.

Inventions

Invention	Date	Inventor	Nation
Adding machine	**1642**	Pascal	French
Adding machine	**1885**	Burroughs	U.S.
Aerosol spray	**1926**	Rotheim	Norwegian
Air brake	**1868**	Westinghouse	U.S.
Air conditioning	**1911**	Carrier	U.S.
Air pump	**1654**	Guericke	German
Airplane, automatic pilot	**1912**	Sperry	U.S.
Airplane, experimental	**1896**	Langley	U.S.
Airplane jet engine	**1939**	Ohain	German
Airplane with motor	**1903**	Wright bros.	U.S.
Airplane, hydro	**1911**	Curtiss	U.S.
Airship	**1852**	Giffard	French
Airship, rigid dirigible	**1900**	Zeppelin	German
Arc welder	**1919**	Thomson	U.S.
Aspartame	**1965**	Schlatter	U.S.
Autogyro	**1920**	de la Cierva	Spanish
Automobile, differential gear	**1885**	Benz	German
Automobile, electric	**1892**	Morrison	U.S.
Automobile, exp'mtl	**1864**	Marcus	Austrian
Automobile, gasoline	**1889**	Daimler	German
Automobile, gasoline	**1892**	Duryea	U.S.
Automobile magneto	**1897**	Bosch	German
Automobile muffler	...	Maxim, H.P.	U.S.
Automobile self-starter	**1911**	Kettering	U.S.
Babbitt metal	**1839**	Babbitt	U.S.
Bakelite	**1907**	Baekeland	Belg., U.S.
Balloon	**1783**	Montgolfier	French
Barometer	**1643**	Torricelli	Italian
Bicycle, modern	**1885**	Starley	English
Bifocal lens	**1780**	Franklin	U.S.
Block signals, railway	**1867**	Hall	U.S.
Bomb, depth	**1916**	Tait	U.S.
Bottle machine	**1895**	Owens	U.S.
Braille printing	**1829**	Braille	French
Burner, gas	**1855**	Bunsen	German
Calculating machine	**1833**	Babbage	English
Calculator, electronic pocket	**1972**	Merryman, Van Tassel	U.S.
Camera, Kodak	**1888**	Eastman, Walker	U.S.
Camera, Polaroid Land	**1948**	Land	U.S.
Car coupler	**1873**	Janney	U.S.
Carburetor, gasoline	**1893**	Maybach	German
Card time recorder	**1894**	Cooper	U.S.
Carding machine	**1797**	Whittemore	U.S.
Carpet sweeper	**1876**	Bissell	U.S.
Cash register	**1879**	Ritty	U.S.
Cassette, audio	**1963**	Philips Co.	Dutch
Cassette, videotape	**1969**	Sony	Japanese
Cathode ray oscilloscope	**1897**	Braun	German
Cathode ray tube	**1878**	Crookes	English
CAT, or CT, scan (computerized tomography)	**1973**	Hounsfield	English
Cellophane	**1908**	Brandenberger	Swiss
Celluloid	**1870**	Hyatt	U.S.
Cement, Portland	**1824**	Aspdin	English
Chronometer	**1761**	Harrison	English
Circuit breaker	**1925**	Hilliard	U.S.
Circuit, integrated	**1959**	Kilby, Noyce, Texas Instr.	U.S.
Clock, pendulum	**1657**	Huygens	Dutch
Coaxial cable system	**1929**	Affel, Espensched	U.S.
Coke oven	**1893**	Hoffman	Austrian
Compressed air rock drill	**1871**	Ingersoll	U.S.
Comptometer	**1887**	Felt	U.S.
Computer, automatic sequence	**1944**	Aiken, et al.	U.S.
Computer, mini	**1960**	Digital Corp	U.S.
Condenser microphone (telephone)	**1916**	Wente	U.S.
Contraceptive, oral	**1954**	Pincus, Rock	U.S.
Corn, hybrid	**1917**	Jones	U.S.
Cotton gin	**1793**	Whitney	U.S.
Cream separator	**1878**	DeLaval	Swedish
Cultivator, disc	**1878**	Mallon	U.S.
Cystoscope	**1878**	Nitze	German
Diesel engine	**1895**	Diesel	German
Disk, compact	**1972**	RCA	U.S.
Disk, floppy	**1970**	IBM	U.S.
Disk player, compact	**1979**	Sony, Philips Co.	Japan., Dutch
Disk, video	**1972**	Philips Co.	Dutch
Dynamite	**1866**	Nobel	Swedish
Dynamo, continuous current	**1871**	Gramme	Belgian
Dynamo, hydrogen cooled	**1915**	Schuler	U.S.
Electric battery	**1800**	Volta	Italian
Electric fan	**1882**	Wheeler	U.S.
Electrocardiograph	**1903**	Einthoven	Dutch
Electroencephalograph	**1929**	Berger	German
Electromagnet	**1824**	Sturgeon	English
Electron spectrometer	**1944**	Deutsch, Elliott, Evans	U.S.
Electron tube multigrid	**1913**	Langmuir	U.S.
Electroplating	**1805**	Brugnatelli	Italian
Electrostatic generator	**1929**	Van de Graaff	U.S.
Elevator brake	**1852**	Otis	U.S.
Elevator, push button	**1922**	Larson	U.S.
Engine, automatic transmission	**1910**	Fottinger	German
Engine, coal-gas 4-cycle	**1876**	Otto	German
Engine, compression ignition	**1883**	Daimler	German
Engine, electric ignition	**1883**	Benz	German
Engine, gas, compound	**1926**	Eickemeyer	U.S.
Engine, gasoline	**1872**	Brayton, Geo.	U.S.
Engine, gasoline	**1889**	Daimler	German
Engine, jet	**1930**	Whittle	English
Engine, steam, piston	**1705**	Newcomen	English
Engine, steam, piston	**1769**	Watt	Scottish
Engraving, half-tone	**1852**	Talbot	U.S.
Fiberglass	**1938**	Owens-Corning	U.S.
Fiber optics	**1955**	Kapany	English
Filament, tungsten	**1913**	Coolidge	U.S.
Flanged rail	**1831**	Stevens	U.S.
Flatiron, electric	**1882**	Seely	U.S.
Food, frozen	**1924**	Birdseye	U.S.
Freon (low-boiling fluorine compounds)	**1930**	Midgley, et al.	U.S.
Furnace (for steel)	**1858**	Siemens	German
Galvanometer	**1820**	Sweigger	German
Gas discharge tube	**1922**	Hull	U.S.

Invention	Date	Inventor	Nation
Gas lighting	1792	Murdoch	Scottish
Gas mantle	1885	Welsbach	Austrian
Gasoline (lead ethyl)	1922	Midgley	U.S.
Gasoline, cracked	1913	Burton	U.S.
Gasoline, high octane	1930	Ipatieff	Russian
Geiger counter	1913	Geiger	German
Glass, laminated safety	1909	Benedictus	French
Glider	1853	Cayley	English
Gun, breechloader	1811	Thornton	U.S.
Gun, Browning	1897	Browning	U.S.
Gun, magazine	1875	Hotchkiss	U.S.
Gun, silencer	1908	Maxim, H.P.	U.S.
Guncotton	1847	Schoenbein	German
Gyrocompass	1911	Sperry	U.S.
Gyroscope	1852	Foucault	French
Harvester-thresher	1818	Lane	U.S.
Heart, artificial	1982	Jarvik	U.S.
Helicopter	1939	Sikorsky	U.S.
Hydrometer	1768	Baume	French
Hydrogen bomb	1952	U.S. government scientists	U.S
Ice-making machine	1851	Gorrie	U.S.
Iron lung	1928	Drinker, Slaw	U.S.
Kaleidoscope	1817	Brewster	Scottish
Kinetoscope	1889	Edison	U.S.
Lacquer, nitrocellulose	1921	Flaherty	U.S.
Lamp, arc	1847	Staite	English
Lamp, flourescent	1938	General Electric, Westinghouse	U.S.
Lamp, incandescent	1879	Edison	U.S.
Lamp, incand., frosted	1924	Pipkin	U.S.
Lamp, incand., gas	1913	Langmuir	U.S.
Lamp, klieg	1911	Kliegl, A. & J.	U.S.
Lamp, mercury vapor	1912	Hewitt	U.S.
Lamp, miner's safety	1816	Davy	English
Lamp, neon	1909	Claude	French
Lathe, turret	1845	Fitch	U.S.
Launderette	1934	Cantrell	U.S.
Lens, achromatic	1758	Dollond	English
Lens, fused bifocal	1908	Borsch	U.S.
Leyden jar (condenser)	1745	von Kleist	German
Lightning rod	1752	Franklin	U.S.
Linoleum	1860	Walton	English
Linotype	1884	Mergenthaler	U.S.
Lock, cylinder	1851	Yale	U.S.
Locomotive, electric	1851	Vail	U.S.
Locomotive, exp'mtl	1802	Trevithick	English
Locomotive, exp'mtl	1812	Fenton, et al.	English
Locomotive, exp'mtl	1813	Hedley	English
Locomotive, exp'mtl	1814	Stephenson	English
Locomotive, practical	1829	Stephenson	English
Locomotive, 1st U.S.	1830	Cooper, P.	U.S.
Loom, power	1785	Cartwright	English
Loudspeaker, dynamic	1924	Rice, Kellogg	U.S.
Machine gun	1861	Gatling	U.S.
Machine gun, improved	1872	Hotchkiss	U.S.
Machine gun (Maxim)	1883	Maxim, H.S.	U.S., Eng.
Magnet, electro	1828	Henry	U.S.
Mantle, gas	1885	Welsbach	Austrian
Mason jar	1858	Mason, J.	U.S.
Match, friction	1827	John Walker	English
Mercerized textiles	1843	Mercer, J.	English
Meter, induction	1888	Shallenberg	U.S.
Metronome	1816	Malezel	German
Microcomputer	1973	Truong, et al.	French
Micrometer	1636	Gascoigne	English
Microphone	1877	Berliner	U.S.
Microprocessor	1971	Intel Corp.	U.S.
Microscope, compound	1590	Janssen	Dutch
Microscope, electronic	1931	Knoll, Ruska	German
Microscope, field ion	1951	Mueller	German
Monitor, warship	1861	Ericsson	U.S.
Monotype	1887	Lanston	U.S.
Motor, AC	1892	Tesla	U.S.
Motor, DC	1837	Davenport	U.S.
Motor, induction	1887	Tesla	U.S.
Motorcycle	1885	Daimler	German
Movie machine	1894	Jenkins	U.S.
Movie, panoramic	1952	Waller	U.S.
Movie, talking	1927	Warner Bros.	U.S.
Mower, lawn	1831	Budding, Ferrabee	English
Mowing machine	1822	Bailey	U.S.
Neoprene	1930	Carothers	U.S.
Nylon synthetic	1930	Carothers	U.S.
Nylon	1937	Du Pont lab	U.S.
Oil cracking furnace	1891	Gavrilov	Russian

Invention	Date	Inventor	Nation
Oil filled power cable	1921	Emanueli	Italian
Oleomargarine	1869	Mege-Mouries	French
Ophthalmoscope	1851	Helmholtz	German
Paper	105	Lun	Chinese
Paper machine	1809	Dickinson	U.S.
Parachute	1785	Blanchard	French
Pen, ballpoint	1938	Biro	Hungarian
Pen, fountain	1884	Waterman	U.S.
Pen, steel	1780	Harrison	English
Pendulum	1583	Galileo	Italian
Percussion cap	1807	Forsythe	Scottish
Phonograph	1877	Edison	U.S.
Photo, color	1892	Ives	U.S.
Photo film, celluloid	1893	Reichenbach	U.S.
Photo film, transparent	1884	Eastman, Goodwin	U.S.
Photoelectric cell	1895	Elster	German
Photographic paper	1835	Talbot	English
Photography	1835	Talbot	English
Photography	1835	Daguerre	French
Photography	1816	Niepce	French
Photophone	1880	Bell	U.S.-Scot.
Phototelegraphy	1925	Bell Labs	U.S.
Piano	1709	Cristofori	Italian
Piano, player	1863	Fourneaux	French
Pin, safety	1849	Hunt	U.S.
Pistol (revolver)	1836	Colt	U.S.
Plow, cast iron	1785	Ransome	English
Plow, disc	1896	Hardy	U.S.
Pneumatic hammer	1890	King	U.S.
Powder, smokeless	1884	Vieille	French
Printing press, rotary	1845	Hoe	U.S.
Printing press, web	1865	Bullock	U.S.
Propeller, screw	1804	Stevens	U.S.
Propeller, screw	1837	Ericsson	Swedish
Pulsars	1967	Bell	English
Punch card accounting	1889	Hollerith	U.S.
Quasars	1963	Schmidt	U.S.
Radar	1940	Watson-Watt	Scottish
Radio amplifier	1906	De Forest	U.S.
Radio beacon	1928	Donovan	U.S.
Radio crystal oscillator	1918	Nicolson	U.S.
Radio receiver, cascade tuning	1913	Alexanderson,	U.S.
Radio receiver, heterodyne	1913	Fessenden	U.S.
Radio transmitter triode modulation	1914	Alexanderson	U.S.
Radio tube diode	1905	Fleming	English
Radio tube oscillator	1915	De Forest	U.S.
Radio tube triode	1906	De Forest	U.S.
Radio, signals	1895	Marconi	Italian
Radio, magnetic detector	1902	Marconi	Italian
Radio FM, 2-path	1933	Armstrong	U.S.
Rayon (acetate)	1895	Cross	English
Rayon (cuprammonium)	1890	Despeissis	French
Rayon (nitrocellulose)	1884	Chardonnet	French
Razor, electric	1917	Schick	U.S.
Razor, safety	1895	Gillette	U.S.
Reaper	1834	McCormick	U.S.
Record, cylinder	1887	Bell, Tainter	U.S.
Record, disc	1887	Berliner	U.S.
Record, long playing	1947	Goldmark	U.S.
Record, wax cylinder	1888	Edison	U.S.
Refrigerator car	1868	David	U.S.
Resin, synthetic	1931	Hill	English
Richter scale	1935	Richter	U.S.
Rifle, repeating	1860	Spencer	U.S.
Rocket engine	1926	Goddard	U.S.
Rubber, vulcanized	1839	Goodyear	U.S.
Saccharin	1879	Remsen, Fahlberg	U.S.
Saw, band	1808	Newberry	English
Saw, circular	1777	Miller	English
Sewing machine	1846	Howe	U.S.
Shoe-sewing machine	1860	McKay	U.S.
Shrapnel shell	1784	Shrapnel	English
Shuttle, flying	1733	Kay	English
Sleeping-car	1865	Pullman	U.S.
Slide rule	1620	Oughtred	English
Soap, hardwater	1928	Bertsch	German
Spectroscope	1859	Kirchoff, Bunsen	German
Spectroscope (mass)	1918	Dempster	U.S.
Spinning jenny	c. 1764	Hargreaves	English
Spinning mule	1779	Crompton	English
Steamboat, exp'mtl	1778	Jouffroy	French
Steamboat, exp'mtl	1785	Fitch	U.S.
Steamboat, exp'mtl	1787	Rumsey	U.S.
Steamboat, exp'mtl	1788	Miller	Scottish
Steamboat, exp'mtl	1803	Fulton	U.S.

(continued)

Invention	Date	Inventor	Nation
Steamboat, exp'mtl	**1804**	Stevens	U.S.
Steamboat, practical	**1802**	Symington	Scottish
Steamboat, practical	**1807**	Fulton	U.S.
Steam car	**1770**	Cugnot	French
Steam turbine	**1884**	Parsons	English
Steel (converter)	**1856**	Bessemer	English
Steel alloy	**1891**	Harvey	U.S.
Steel alloy, high-speed	**1901**	Taylor, White	U.S.
Steel, electric	**1900**	Heroult	French
Steel, manganese	**1884**	Hadfield	English
Steel, stainless	**1916**	Brearley	English
Stereoscope	**1838**	Wheatstone	English
Stethoscope	**1819**	Laennec	French
Stethoscope, binaural	**1840**	Cammann	U.S.
Stock ticker	**1870**	Edison	U.S.
Storage battery, rechargeable	**1859**	Plante	French
Stove, electric	**1896**	Hadaway	U.S.
Submarine	**1891**	Holland	U.S.
Submarine, even keel	**1894**	Lake	U.S.
Submarine, torpedo	**1776**	Bushnell	U.S.
Superconductivity (BCS theory)	**1957**	Bardeen, Cooper, Schreiffer	U.S.
Tank, military	**1914**	Swinton	English
Tape recorder, magnetic	**1899**	Poulsen	Danish
Teflon	**1938**	Du Pont	U.S.
Telegraph, magnetic	**1837**	Morse	U.S.
Telegraph, quadruplex	**1864**	Edison	U.S.
Telegraph, railroad	**1887**	Woods	U.S.
Telegraph, wireless high frequency	**1895**	Marconi	Italian
Telephone	**1876**	Bell	U.S.-Scot.
Telephone amplifier	**1912**	De Forest	U.S.
Telephone, automatic	**1891**	Stowger	U.S.
Telephone, radio	**1900**	Poulsen, Fessenden	Danish
Telephone, radio	**1906**	De Forest	U.S.
Telephone, radio, l. d.	**1915**	AT&T	U.S.
Telephone, recording	**1898**	Poulsen	Danish
Telephone, wireless	**1899**	Collins	U.S.
Telescope	**1608**	Lippershey	Neth.
Telescope	**1609**	Galileo	Italian
Telescope, astronomical	**1611**	Kepler	German
Teletype	**1928**	Morkrum, Kleinschmidt	U.S.
Television, iconoscope	**1923**	Zworykin	U.S.
Television, electronic	**1927**	Farnsworth	U.S.
Television, mech. scanner	**1923**	Baird	Scottish
Thermometer	**1593**	Galileo	Italian
Thermometer	**1730**	Reaumur	French
Thermometer, mercury	**1714**	Fahrenheit	German
Time recorder	**1890**	Bundy	U.S.
Time, self-regulator	**1918**	Bryce	U.S.
Tire, double-tube	**1845**	Thomson	Scottish
Tire, pneumatic	**1888**	Dunlop	Scottish
Toaster, automatic	**1918**	Strite	U.S.
Tool, pneumatic	**1865**	Law	English
Torpedo, marine	**1804**	Fulton	U.S.
Tractor, crawler	**1904**	Holt	U.S.
Transformer, AC.	**1885**	Stanley	U.S.
Transistor	**1947**	Shockley, Brattain, Bardeen	U.S.
Trolley car, electric	**1884-87**	Van DePoele, Sprague	U.S.
Tungsten, ductile	**1912**	Coolidge	U.S.
Tupperware	**1945**	Tupper	U.S.
Turbine, gas	**1849**	Bourdin	French
Turbine, hydraulic	**1849**	Francis	U.S.
Turbine, steam	**1884**	Parsons	English
Type, movable	**1447**	Gutenberg	German
Typewriter	**1867**	Sholes, Soule, Glidden	U.S.
Vacuum cleaner, electric	**1907**	Spangler	U.S.
Velcro	**1948**	de Mestral	Swiss
Video game ("Pong")	**1972**	Buschnel	U.S.
Video home system (VHS)	**1975**	Matsushita, JVC	Japanese
Washer, electric	**1901**	Fisher	U.S.
Welding, atomic hydrogen	**1924**	Langmuir, Palmer	U.S.
Welding, electric	**1877**	Thomson	U.S.
Wind tunnel	**1912**	Eiffel	French
Wire, barbed	**1874**	Glidden	U.S.
Wire, barbed	**1875**	Haisn	U.S.
Wrench, double-acting	**1913**	Owen	U.S.
X-ray tube	**1913**	Coolidge	U.S.
Zipper	**1891**	Judson	U.S.

Discoveries and Innovations: Chemistry, Physics, Biology, Medicine

	Date	Discoverer	Nation
Acetylene gas	**1862**	Berthelot	French
ACTH	**1927**	Evans, Long	U.S.
Adrenalin	**1901**	Takamine	Japanese
Aluminum, electrolytic process	**1886**	Hall	U.S.
Aluminum, isolated	**1825**	Oersted	Danish
Anesthesia, ether	**1842**	Long	U.S.
Anesthesia, local	**1885**	Koller	Austrian
Anesthesia, spinal	**1898**	Bier	German
Aniline dye	**1856**	Perkin	English
Anti-rabies	**1885**	Pasteur	French
Antiseptic surgery	**1867**	Lister	English
Antitoxin, diphtheria	**1891**	Von Behring	German
Argyrol	**1897**	Bayer	German
Arsphenamine	**1910**	Ehrlich	German
Aspirin	**1889**	Dresser	German
Atabrine	...	Mietzsch, et al.	German
Atomic numbers	**1913**	Moseley	English
Atomic theory	**1803**	Dalton	English
Atomic time clock	**1948**	Lyons	U.S.
Atomic time clock, cesium beam	**1948**	Essen	English
Atom-smashing theory	**1919**	Rutherford	English
Bacitracin	**1945**	Johnson, et al.	U.S.
Bacteria (described)	**1676**	Leeuwenhoek	Dutch
Barbital	**1903**	Fischer	German
Bleaching powder	**1798**	Tennant	English
Blood, circulation	**1628**	Harvey	English
Bordeaux mixture	**1885**	Millardet	French
Bromine from sea	**1924**	Edgar Kramer	U.S.
Calcium carbide	**1888**	Wilson	U.S.
Calculus	**1670**	Newton	English
Camphor synthetic	**1896**	Haller	French
Canning (food)	**1804**	Appert	French
Carbomycin	**1952**	Tanner	U.S.
Carbon oxides	**1925**	Fisher	German
Chloamphenicol	**1947**	Burkholder	U.S.
Chlorine	**1774**	Scheele	Swedish
Chloroform	**1831**	Guthrie, S.	U.S.
Chlortetracycline	**1948**	Duggen	U.S.
Classification of plants and animals	**1735**	Linnaeus	Swedish
Cocaine	**1860**	Niermann	German
Combustion explained	**1777**	Lavoisier	French
Conditioned reflex	**1914**	Pavlov	Russian
Cortisone	**1936**	Kendall	U.S.
Cortisone, synthesis	**1946**	Sarett	U.S.
Cosmic rays	**1910**	Gockel	Swiss
Cyanamide	**1905**	Frank, Caro	German
Cyclotron	**1930**	Lawrence	U.S.
DDT (not applied as insecticide until 1939)	**1874**	Zeidler	German
Deuterium	**1932**	Urey, Brickwedde, Murphy	U.S.
DNA (structure)	**1951**	Crick	English
		Watson	U.S.
		Wilkins	English
Electric resistance (law)	**1827**	Ohm	German
Electric waves	**1888**	Hertz	German
Electrolysis	**1852**	Faraday	English
Electromagnetism	**1819**	Oersted	Danish
Electron	**1897**	Thomson, J.	English
Electron diffraction	**1936**	Thomson, G.	English
		Davisson	U.S.
Electroshock treatment	**1938**	Cerletti, Bini	Italian
Erythromycin	**1952**	McGuire	U.S.
Evolution, natural selection	**1858**	Darwin	English
Falling bodies, law	**1590**	Galileo	Italian
Gases, law of combining volumes	**1808**	Gay-Lussac	French
Geometry, analytic	**1619**	Descartes	French
Gold (cyanide process for extraction)	**1887**	MacArthur, Forest	British
Gravitation, law	**1687**	Newton	English
Holograph	**1948**	Gabor	British
Human heart transplant	**1967**	Barnard	S. African
Human immunodeficiency virus identified	**1984**	Montagnier, Gallo	French, U.S.

	Date	Discoverer	Nation
Indigo, synthesis of	1880	Baeyer	German
Induction, electric	1830	Henry	U.S.
Insulin	1922	Banting, Best, Macleod	Canadian, Scottish
Intelligence testing	1905	Binet, Simon	French
In vitro fertilization	1978	Steptoe, Edwards	English
Isoniazid	1952	Hoffman-La-Roche Domagk	U.S. German
Isotopes, theory	1912	Soddy	English
Laser (light amplification by stimulated emission of radiation)	1958	Townes, Schawlow	U.S.
Light, velocity	1675	Roemer	Danish
Light, wave theory	1690	Huygens	Dutch
Lithography	1796	Senefelder	Bohemian
Lobotomy	1935	Egas Moniz	Portuguese
LSD-25	1943	Hoffman	Swiss
Mendelian laws	1866	Mendel	Austrian
Mercator projection (map)	1568	Mercator(Kremer)	Flemish
Methanol	1661	Boyle	Irish
Milk condensation	1853	Borden	U.S.
Molecular hypothesis	1811	Avogadro	Italian
Motion, laws of	1687	Newton	English
Neomycin	1949	Waksman, Lechevalier	U.S.
Neutron	1932	Chadwick	English
Nitric acid	1648	Glauber	German
Nitric oxide	1772	Priestley	English
Nitroglycerin	1846	Sobrero	Italian
Oil cracking process	1891	Dewar	U.S.
Oxygen	1774	Priestley	English
Oxytetracycline	1950	Finlay, et al.	U.S.
Ozone	1840	Schonbein	German
Paper, sulfite process	1867	Tilghman	U.S.
Paper, wood pulp, sulfate process	1884	Dahl	German
Penicillin	1929	Fleming	Scottish
practical use	1941	Florey, Chain	English
Periodic law and table of elements	1869	Mendeleyev	Russian
Planetary motion, laws	1609	Kepler	German
Plutonium fission	1940	Kennedy, Wahl, Seaborg, Segre	U.S.
Polymyxin	1947	Ainsworth	English
Positron	1932	Anderson	U.S.
Proton	1919	Rutherford	N. Zealand
Psychoanalysis	1900	Freud	Austrian
Quantum theory	1900	Planck	German
Quasars	1963	Matthews, Sandage	U.S.
Quinine synthetic	1946	Woodward, Doering	U.S.

	Date	Discoverer	Nation
Radioactivity	1896	Becquerel	French
Radiocarbon dating	1947	Libby	U.S.
Radium	1898	Curie, Pierre Curie, Marie	French Pol.-Fr.
Relativity theory	1905	Einstein	German
Reserpine	1949	Jal Vaikl	Indian
Schick test	1913	Schick	U.S.
Silicon	1823	Berzelius	Swedish
Smallpox eradication	1979	World Health Organization	United Nations
Streptomycin	1945	Schatz, Waksman	U.S.
Sulfanilamide	1935	Bovet, Trefouel	French
Sulfanilamide theory	1908	Gelmo	German
Sulfapyridine	1938	Ewins, Phelps	English
Sulfathiazole	...	Fosbinder, Walter	U.S.
Sulfuric acid	1831	Phillips	English
Sulfuric acid, lead	1746	Roebuck	English
Thiacetazone	1950	Belmisch, Mietzsch, Domagk	German
Tuberculin	1890	Koch	German
Uranium fission (theory)	1939	Hahn, Meitner, Strassmann Bohr Fermi Einstein, Pegram, Wheeler	German Danish Italian U.S.
Uranium fission, atomic reactor	1942	Fermi, Szilard	U.S.
Vaccine, measles	1954	Enders, Peebles	U.S.
Vaccine, meningitis (first conjugate)	1987	Gordon, et. al., Connaught Lab., Inc.	U.S.
Vaccine, polio	1955	Salk	U.S.
Vaccine, polio, oral	1955	Sabin	U.S.
Vaccine, rabies	1885	Pasteur	French
Vaccine, smallpox	1796	Jenner	English
Vaccine, typhus	1909	Nicolle	French
Van Allen belts, radiation	1958	Van Allen	U.S.
Vitamin A	1913	McCollum, Davis	U.S.
Vitamin B	1916	McCollum	U.S.
Vitamin C	1928	Szent-Gyorgyi, King	U.S.
Vitamin D	1922	McCollum	U.S.
Wassermann test	1906	Wassermann	German
Xerography	1938	Carlson	U.S.
X ray	1895	Roentgen	German

Chemical Elements, Atomic Weights, Discoverers

Atomic weights, based on the exact number 12 as the assigned atomic mass of the principal isotope of carbon, carbon 12, are provided through the courtesy of the International Union of Pure and Applied Chemistry and Butterworth Scientific Publications.

For the radioactive elements, with the exception of uranium and thorium, the mass number of either the isotope of longest half-life (*) or the better known isotope (**) is given.

Chemical element	Symbol	Atomic number	Atomic weight	Year discov.	Discoverer
Actinium	Ac	89	227*	1899	Debierne
Aluminum	Al	13	26.9815	1825	Oersted
Americium	Am	95	243*	1944	Seaborg, et al.
Antimony	Sb	51	121.75	1450	Valentine
Argon	Ar	18	39.948	1894	Rayleigh, Ramsay
Arsenic	As	33	74.9216	13th c.	Albertus Magnus
Astatine	At	85	210*	1940	Corson, et al.
Barium	Ba	56	137.34	1808	Davy
Berkelium	Bk	97	249**	1949	Thompson, Ghiorso, Seaborg
Beryllium	Be	4	9.0122	1798	Vauquelin
Bismuth	Bi	83	208.980	15th c.	Valentine
Boron	B	5	10.811a	1808	Gay-Lussac, Thenard
Bromine	Br	35	79.904b	1826	Balard
Cadmium	Cd	48	112.40	1817	Stromeyer
Calcium	Ca	20	40.08	1808	Davy
Californium	Cf	98	251*	1950	Thompson, et al.
Carbon	C	6	12.01115a	B.C.	unknown
Cerium	Ce	58	140.12	1803	Klaproth
Cesium	Cs	55	132.905	1860	Bunsen, Kirchhoff
Chlorine	Cl	17	35.453b	1774	Scheele
Chromium	Cr	24	51.996b	1797	Vauquelin
Cobalt	Co	27	58.9332	1735	Brandt
Copper	Cu	29	63.546b	B.C.	unknown
Curium	Cm	96	247*	1944	Seaborg, James, Ghiorso
Dysprosium	Dy	66	162.50*	1886	Boisbaudran

(continued)

Chemical element	Symbol	Atomic number	Atomic weight	Year discov.	Discoverer
Einsteinium	Es	99	254*	1952	Ghiorso, et al.
Erbium	Er	68	167.26	1843	Mosander
Europium	Eu	63	151.96	1901	Demarcay
Fermium	Fm	100	257*	1953	Ghiorso, et al.
Fluorine	F	9	18.9984	1771	Scheele
Francium	Fr	87	223*	1939	Perey
Gadolinium	Gd	64	157.25	1886	Marignac
Gallium	Ga	31	69.72	1875	Boisbaudran
Germanium	Ge	32	72.59	1886	Winkler
Gold	Au	79	196.967	B.C.	unknown
Hafnium	Hf	72	178.49	1923	Coster, Hevesy
Hahnium	Ha	105	262*	1970	Ghiorso, et al.
Hassium	Hs	108	265*	1984	Münzenberg, et al.
Helium	He	2	4.0026	1868	Janssen, Lockyer
Holmium	Ho	67	164.930	1878	Soret, Delafontaine
Hydrogen	H	1	1.00797a	1766	Cavendish
Indium	In	49	114.82	1863	Reich, Richter
Iodine	I	53	126.9044	1811	Courtois
Iridium	Ir	77	192.2	1804	Tennant
Iron	Fe	26	55.847b	B.C.	unknown
Krypton	Kr	36	83.80	1898	Ramsay, Travers
Lanthanum	La	57	138.91	1839	Mosander
Lawrencium	Lr	103	262*	1961	Ghiorso, T. Sikkeland, A.E. Larsh, and R.M. Latimer
Lead	Pb	82	207.19	B.C.	unknown
Lithium	Li	3	6.939	1817	Arfvedson
Lutetium	Lu	71	174.97	1907	Welsbach, Urbain
Magnesium	Mg	12	24.312	1829	Bussy
Manganese	Mn	25	54.9380	1774	Gahn
Meitnerium	Mt	109	266*	1982	Münzenberg, et al.
Mendelevium	Md	101	258*	1955	Ghiorso, et al.
Mercury	Hg	80	200.59	B.C.	unknown
Molybdenum	Mo	42	95.94	1782	Hjelm
Neodymium	Nd	60	144.24	1885	Welsbach
Neon	Ne	10	20.183	1898	Ramsay, Travers
Neptunium	Np	93	237*	1940	McMillan, Abelson
Nickel	Ni	28	58.71	1751	Cronstedt
Nielsbohrium	Ns	107	262*	1981	Münzenberg, et al.
Niobium[1]	Nb	41	92.906	1801	Hatchett
Nitrogen	N	7	14.0067	1772	Rutherford
Nobelium	No	102	259*	1958	Ghiorso, et al.
Osmium	Os	76	190.2	1804	Tennant
Oxygen	O	8	15.9994a	1774	Priestley, Scheele
Palladium	Pd	46	106.4	1803	Wollaston
Phosphorus	P	15	30.9738	1669	Brand
Platinum	Pt	78	195.09	1735	Ulloa
Plutonium	Pu	94	242**	1940	Seaborg, et al.
Polonium	Po	84	210**	1898	P. and M. Curie
Potassium	K	19	39.102	1807	Davy
Praseodymium	Pr	59	140.907	1885	Welsbach
Promethium	Pm	61	147**	1945	Glendenin, Marinsky, Coryell
Protactinium	Pa	91	231*	1917	Hahn, Meitner
Radium	Ra	88	226*	1898	P. and M. Curie, Bemont
Radon	Rn	86	222*	1900	Dorn
Rhenium	Re	75	186.2	1925	Noddack, Tacke, Berg
Rhodium	Rh	45	102.905	1803	Wollaston
Rubidium	Rb	37	85.47	1861	Bunsen, Kirchhoff
Ruthenium	Ru	44	101.07	1845	Klaus
Rutherfordium	Rf	104	261*	1969	Ghiorso, et al.
Samarium	Sm	62	150.35	1879	Boisbaudran
Scandium	Sc	21	44.956	1879	Nilson
Seaborgium	Sg	106	266*	1974	Ghiorso, et al.
Selenium	Se	34	78.96	1817	Berzelius
Silicon	Si	14	28.086a	1823	Berzelius
Silver	Ag	47	107.868b	B.C.	unknown
Sodium	Na	11	22.9898	1807	Davy
Strontium	Sr	38	87.62	1790	Crawford
Sulfur	S	16	32.064a	B.C.	unknown
Tantalum	Ta	73	180.948	1802	Ekeberg
Technetium	Tc	43	99**	1937	Perrier and Segre
Tellurium	Te	52	127.60	1782	Von Reichenstein
Terbium	Tb	65	158.924	1843	Mosander
Thallium	Tl	81	204.37	1861	Crookes
Thorium	Th	90	232.038	1828	Berzelius
Thulium	Tm	69	168.934	1879	Cleve
Tin	Sn	50	118.69	B.C.	unknown
Titanium	Ti	22	47.90	1791	Gregor
Tungsten (Wolfram)	W	74	183.85	1783	d'Elhujar
Uranium	U	92	238.03	1789	Klaproth
Vanadium	V	23	50.942	1830	Sefstrom
Xenon	Xe	54	131.30	1898	Ramsay, Travers
Ytterbium	Yb	70	173.04	1878	Marignac
Yttrium	Y	39	88.905	1794	Gadolin
Zinc	Zn	30	65.37	B.C.	unknown
Zirconium	Zr	40	91.22	1789	Klaproth

(1) Formerly Columbium. (a) Atomic weights so designated are known to be variable because of natural variations in isotopic composition. The observed ranges are: hydrogen±0.0001; boron±0.003; carbon±0.005; oxygen±0.0001; silicon±0.001; sulfur±0.003. (b) Atomic weights so designated are believed to have the following experimental uncertainties: chlorine±0.001; chromium±0.001; iron±0.003; copper±0.001; bromine±0.001; silver±0.001.

METEOROLOGY

National Weather Service Watches and Warnings

Source: National Weather Service, NOAA, U.S. Dept. of Commerce; *Glossary of Meteorology,* American Meteorological Society

National Weather Service forecasters issue a Severe Thunderstorm or Tornado Watch for a specific area where threatening weather is most likely to occur during the valid time of the watch. A Severe Thunderstorm Watch is issued for a specific area where severe thunderstorms are most likely. A Severe Thunderstorm Warning indicates that a severe thunderstorm has been sighted or indicated by radar. A Tornado Watch is issued when severe thunderstorms that produce tornadoes are likely to occur in a specific area. A Watch alerts people to check for threatening weather, make plans for action, and listen for a Tornado Warning. A Tornado Warning means that a tornado has been sighted or indicated by radar and that safety precautions should be taken at once. A Hurricane Watch means that an existing hurricane poses a threat to coastal and inland communities, within 24-36 hours, in the area specified by the Watch. A Hurricane Warning means hurricane force winds and/or dangerously high water and exceptionally high waves are expected in a specified coastal area within 24 hours.

Tornado—A violent rotating column of air in contact with the ground and pendant from a thundercloud, usually recognized as a funnel-shaped vortex accompanied by a loud roar. With rotating winds est. up to 300 mph., on a local scale, it is the most destructive storm. Tornado paths have varied in length from a few feet to nearly 300 miles (avg. 5 mi.); diameter from a few feet to over a mile (average 220 yards); average forward speed, 30 mph.

Cyclone—An atmospheric circulation of winds rotating counterclockwise in the northern hemisphere and clockwise in the southern hemisphere. Tornadoes, hurricanes, and the lows shown on weather maps are all examples of cyclones having various sizes and intensities. Cyclones are usually accompanied by precipitation or stormy weather.

Hurricane—A severe cyclone originating over tropical ocean waters and having sustained winds 74 miles an hour or higher. (West of the international date line, in the western Pacific, such storms are known as typhoons.) The area of hurricane-force winds takes the form of a circle or an oval, sometimes as much as 300 miles in diameter. In the lower latitudes hurricanes usually move toward the west or northwest at 10 to 15 mph. When the center approaches 25° to 30° North Latitude, direction of motion often changes to northeast, with increased forward speed.

Blizzard—A severe weather condition characterized by strong winds bearing a great amount of snow. The National Weather Service specifies winds of 35-miles an hour or higher and sufficient falling and/or blowing snow to frequently reduce visibility to less than ¼ mile for a duration of at least three hours.

Severe Thunderstorm—A thunderstorm with winds of 58 mph. or greater and/or hail three-fourths of an inch or larger in diameter.

Flood—The condition that occurs when water overflows the natural or artificial confines of a stream or other body of water, or accumulates by drainage over low-lying areas.

National Weather Service Marine Warnings and Advisories

Small Craft Advisory: A Small Craft Advisory alerts mariners to sustained (exceeding two hours) weather and/or sea conditions, either present or forecast, potentially hazardous to small boats. Although there is no definition of a small craft, hazardous conditions generally include winds of 18 to 33 knots and/or dangerous wave conditions. It is the responsibility of the mariner, based on experience and on the location and size or type of boat, to determine if the conditions are hazardous. When a mariner becomes aware of a Small Craft Advisory, he or she should immediately obtain the latest marine forecast to determine the reason for the Advisory.

Gale Warning indicates that winds within the range 34 to 47 knots, not directly associated with a tropical storm, are forecast for the area.

Tropical Storm Warning indicates that winds of 34 to 63 knots are forecast in a specified coastal area within 24 hours or less. Only issued for winds of tropical weather systems.

Storm Warning indicates that winds 48 knots or above, not directly associated with a tropical storm, are forecast for the area.

Hurricane Warning indicates that winds 64 knots or greater are forecast for the area. Only issued for winds produced by tropical weather systems.

Special Marine Warning: A warning for potentially hazardous weather conditions, usually of short duration (2 hours or less) and producing wind speeds of 34 knots or more, not adequately covered by existing marine warnings.

Primary sources of dissemination are commercial radio, TV, U.S. Coast Guard radio stations, and NOAA VHF-FM broadcasts. These broadcasts on 162.40 to 162.55 MHz can usually be received 20-40 miles from the transmitting antenna site, depending on terrain and quality of the receiver used. Where transmitting antennas are on high ground, the range may be somewhat greater, reaching 60 miles or more.

Speed of Winds in the U.S.

Source: National Climatic Data Center, NESDIS, NOAA, U.S. Dept. of Commerce

Miles per hour — average through 1992. High through 1992. Wind velocities in true values.

Station	Avg.	High	Station	Avg.	High	Station	Avg.	High
Albuquerque, NM	9.0	(b)90	Helena, MT	7.7	73	Mt. Washington, NH	35.3	231
Anchorage, AK	7.0	75	Honolulu, HI	11.4	(b)67	New Orleans, LA	8.2	(b)98
Atlanta, GA	9.1	60	Houston, TX	7.9	51	New York, NY(c)	9.4	(b)70
Baltimore, MD	9.2	80	Indianapolis, IN	9.6	46	Omaha, NE	10.6	(b)109
Bismarck, ND	10.2	(b)72	Jacksonville, FL	7.9	(b)82	Philadelphia, PA	9.6	73
Boston, MA	12.5	(b)61	Kansas City, MO	10.8	(b)70	Phoenix, AZ	6.3	(b)86
Buffalo, NY	11.9	91	Lexington, KY	9.2	46	Pittsburgh, PA	9.1	58
Cape Hatteras, NC	11.1	(b)110	Little Rock, AR	7.8	65	Portland, OR	7.9	88
Casper, WY	12.9	81	Los Angeles, CA	6.2	49	St. Louis, MO	9.7	(b)60
Chicago, IL	10.4	58	Louisville, KY	8.4	(b)61	Salt Lake City, UT	8.8	71
Cleveland, OH	10.6	(b)74	Memphis, TN	8.8	46	San Diego, CA	7.0	56
Dallas, TX	10.7	73	Miami, FL	9.3	(a)86	San Francisco, CA	8.7	47
Denver, CO	8.7	(b)56	Milwaukee, WI	11.5	54	Seattle, WA	9.0	66
Detroit, MI	10.4	48	Minneapolis, MN	10.6	(b)92	Spokane, WA	8.9	59
Galveston, TX	11.0	(d)100	Mobile, AL	9.0	63	Washington, DC	9.4	(b)78

(a) Highest velocity ever recorded in Miami area was 132 mph, at former station in Miami Beach in September 1926. (b) Previous location. (c) Data for Central Park; Battery Place data through 1960, avg. 14.5, high 113. (d) Recorded before anemometer blew away. Estimated high 120.

Monthly Normal Temperature and Precipitation

Source: National Climatic Data Center, NESDIS, NOAA, U.S. Dept. of Commerce

The normal temperatures below are based on records for the 30-year period 1961-90 inclusive. For stations that did not have continuous records from the same instrument site for the entire 30 years, the means have been adjusted to the record at the present site.

Airport station; *city stations. † for the period 1951-80. T, temperature in Fahrenheit; P, precipitation in inches; L, less than 0.05 inch.

	Jan.		Feb.		Mar.		Apr.		May		June		July		Aug.		Sept.		Oct.		Nov.		Dec.	
Station	T.	P.	T.	P.	T.	P.	T.	P.	T.	P.	T.	P.	T.	P.	T.	P.	T.	P.	T.	P.	T.	P.	T.	P.
Albany, NY	21	2.4	24	2.3	34	2.9	46	3.0	58	3.4	67	3.6	72	3.2	70	3.5	61	3.0	50	2.8	40	3.2	27	2.9
Albuquerque, NM	34	0.4	40	0.5	47	0.5	55	0.5	64	0.5	74	0.6	79	1.4	76	1.6	69	1.0	57	0.9	44	0.4	35	0.5
Anchorage, AK	15	0.8	19	0.8	26	0.7	36	0.7	47	0.7	54	1.1	58	1.7	56	2.4	48	2.7	35	2.0	21	1.1	16	1.1
Asheville, NC	36	3.3	39	3.9	47	4.6	55	3.4	63	4.4	69	4.2	73	4.5	72	4.7	66	3.9	56	3.6	48	3.6	40	3.5
Atlanta, GA	41	4.8	45	4.8	54	5.8	62	4.3	69	4.3	76	3.6	79	5.0	78	3.7	73	3.4	62	3.1	53	3.9	45	4.3
Atlantic City, NJ	31	3.5	33	3.1	42	3.6	50	3.6	60	3.3	69	2.6	75	3.8	73	4.1	66	2.9	55	2.8	46	3.6	36	3.3
Baltimore, MD	32	3.1	35	3.1	44	3.4	53	3.1	63	3.7	73	3.7	77	3.7	76	3.9	69	3.4	57	3.0	47	3.3	37	3.4
Barrow, AK	-13	0.2	-18	0.2	-15	0.2	-2	0.2	19	0.2	34	0.3	39	0.9	38	1.0	31	0.6	14	0.5	-2	0.3	-11	0.2
Birmingham, AL	42	5.1	46	4.7	54	6.2	62	5.0	69	4.9	76	3.7	80	5.3	79	3.6	73	3.9	63	2.8	53	4.3	45	5.1
Bismarck, ND	9	0.5	16	0.4	28	0.8	43	1.7	55	2.2	64	2.7	71	2.1	68	1.7	57	1.5	46	0.9	29	0.5	14	0.5
Boise, ID	29	1.5	36	1.2	43	1.3	49	1.2	58	1.1	67	1.8	74	0.4	73	0.4	63	0.8	52	0.8	40	1.5	30	1.4
Boston, MA	29	3.6	30	3.6	39	3.7	48	3.6	58	3.3	68	3.1	74	2.8	72	3.2	65	3.1	55	3.3	45	4.2	34	4.0
Buffalo, NY	24	2.7	25	2.3	34	2.7	45	2.9	57	3.1	66	3.6	71	3.1	69	4.2	62	3.5	51	3.1	41	3.8	29	3.7
Burlington, VT	16	1.8	18	1.6	31	2.2	44	2.8	56	3.1	65	3.5	71	3.7	68	4.1	59	3.3	48	2.9	37	3.1	23	2.4
Caribou, ME	9	2.4	12	1.9	25	2.4	38	2.5	51	3.1	61	2.9	66	4.0	63	4.1	54	3.5	43	3.1	31	3.6	15	3.2
Charleston, SC	48	3.5	51	3.3	58	4.3	65	2.7	73	4.0	78	6.4	82	6.8	81	7.2	76	4.7	67	2.9	58	2.5	51	3.2
Chicago, IL	21	1.5	25	1.4	37	2.7	49	3.6	59	3.3	69	3.8	73	3.7	72	4.2	64	3.8	53	2.4	40	2.9	27	2.5
Cleveland, OH	25	2.0	27	2.2	37	2.9	48	3.1	58	3.5	68	3.7	72	3.5	70	3.4	64	3.4	53	2.5	43	3.2	31	3.1
Columbus, OH	26	2.2	30	2.2	41	3.3	51	3.2	61	3.9	69	4.0	73	4.3	72	3.7	66	3.0	54	2.2	43	3.2	32	2.9
Dallas-Ft. Worth, TX	43	1.8	48	2.2	57	2.8	66	3.5	73	4.9	81	3.0	85	2.3	85	2.2	77	3.4	67	3.5	56	2.3	47	1.8
Denver, CO	30	0.5	33	0.6	39	1.3	48	1.7	57	2.4	67	1.8	74	1.9	71	1.5	62	1.2	51	1.0	39	0.9	31	0.6
Des Moines, IA	19	1.0	25	1.1	37	2.3	51	3.4	62	3.7	72	4.5	77	3.8	74	4.2	65	3.5	54	2.6	39	1.8	24	1.3
Detroit, MI	23	1.8	25	1.7	36	2.6	47	3.0	58	2.9	68	3.6	72	3.2	71	3.4	63	2.9	51	2.1	40	2.7	28	2.8
Dodge City, KS†	30	0.5	35	0.5	42	1.5	54	1.8	64	3.3	75	3.0	80	3.1	78	2.5	69	1.9	58	1.3	43	0.8	34	0.5
Duluth, MN	7	1.2	12	0.8	24	1.9	39	2.3	51	3.0	60	3.8	66	3.6	64	4.0	54	3.8	44	2.5	28	1.8	13	1.2
Fairbanks, AK	-10	0.5	-4	0.4	11	0.4	31	0.3	49	0.6	60	1.4	63	1.9	57	2.0	46	1.0	25	0.9	3	0.8	-7	0.9
Fresno, CA	46	2.0	51	1.8	55	1.9	61	1.0	69	0.3	77	0.1	82	L	80	L	75	0.2	65	0.5	54	1.4	45	1.4
Galveston, TX*	53	3.3	55	2.3	62	2.2	69	2.4	76	3.6	81	4.4	83	4.0	84	4.5	80	5.9	73	2.8	64	3.4	56	3.5
Grand Junction, CO†	26	0.6	34	0.5	42	0.8	52	0.7	62	0.8	72	0.4	79	0.5	76	0.9	67	0.7	55	0.9	40	0.6	28	0.6
Gr. Rapids, MI	22	1.8	24	1.4	34	2.6	46	3.4	58	3.1	67	3.7	72	3.2	70	3.6	61	4.2	50	2.8	38	3.3	27	2.9
Hartford, CT	25	3.4	28	3.2	38	3.6	49	3.9	60	4.1	69	3.8	74	3.2	72	3.7	63	3.8	52	3.6	42	4.0	30	3.9
Helena, MT	20	0.6	26	0.4	34	0.7	43	1.0	53	1.8	62	1.9	69	1.1	67	1.3	55	1.2	45	0.6	32	0.5	21	0.6
Honolulu, HI	73	3.6	73	2.2	74	2.2	76	1.5	78	1.1	79	0.5	81	0.6	81	0.4	81	0.8	80	2.3	77	3.0	74	3.8
Houston, TX	50	3.2	54	3.3	61	2.7	68	4.2	75	4.7	80	4.0	83	3.3	82	3.7	78	4.9	70	3.7	61	3.4	54	3.7
Huron, SD	13	0.4	19	0.8	32	1.2	46	2.0	58	2.7	68	3.3	74	2.3	72	2.0	61	1.4	49	1.4	32	0.7	18	0.5
Indianapolis, IN	26	2.3	30	2.5	41	3.8	52	3.7	63	4.0	72	3.5	75	4.5	73	3.6	67	2.9	55	2.6	43	3.2	31	3.3
Jackson, MS	44	5.2	48	4.7	57	5.8	65	5.6	72	5.1	79	3.2	82	4.5	81	3.8	76	3.6	65	3.3	56	4.8	48	5.9
Jacksonville, FL	52	3.3	55	3.9	61	3.7	67	2.8	73	3.6	79	5.7	82	5.6	81	7.9	78	7.0	70	2.9	62	2.1	55	2.7
Juneau, AK†	22	3.7	28	3.7	31	3.3	39	2.9	46	3.4	53	3.0	56	4.1	55	5.0	49	6.4	42	7.7	33	5.2	27	4.7
Kansas City, MO	26	1.1	31	1.1	43	2.5	55	3.1	64	5.0	73	4.7	79	4.4	76	4.0	68	4.9	57	3.3	43	1.9	30	1.6
Knoxville, TN	36	4.2	40	4.1	49	5.1	58	3.7	65	4.1	73	4.0	77	4.7	76	3.1	70	3.1	58	2.8	49	3.8	40	4.5
Lander, WY	20	0.5	25	0.6	34	1.2	43	2.1	53	2.3	63	1.5	71	0.8	69	0.5	58	1.1	47	1.1	31	0.8	21	0.6
Lexington, KY	31	2.9	35	3.2	45	4.4	55	3.9	64	4.5	72	3.7	76	5.0	75	3.9	68	3.2	57	2.6	46	3.4	36	4.0
Little Rock, AR	39	3.9	44	4.4	53	5.3	62	6.2	70	7.0	78	7.8	82	8.2	81	8.1	74	7.4	63	6.3	52	5.2	43	4.3
Los Angeles, CA*	58	2.9	60	3.1	61	2.6	63	1.0	66	0.2	70	L	74	L	75	0.1	74	0.5	70	0.3	63	2.0	58	2.0
Louisville, KY	32	2.9	36	3.3	46	4.7	56	4.2	65	4.6	73	3.5	77	4.5	76	3.5	70	3.2	58	2.7	47	3.7	37	3.6
Marquette, MI*	12	2.2	14	1.7	24	2.8	37	2.6	50	3.0	59	3.5	65	2.9	63	3.4	54	4.1	44	3.6	30	2.9	17	2.6
Memphis, TN	40	3.7	44	4.4	53	5.4	63	5.5	71	5.0	79	3.6	83	3.8	81	3.4	74	3.5	63	3.0	53	5.1	44	5.7
Miami, FL	67	2.0	69	2.1	72	2.4	75	2.9	79	6.2	81	9.3	83	5.7	83	7.6	82	7.6	78	5.6	74	2.7	69	1.8
Milwaukee, WI	19	1.6	23	1.5	33	2.7	44	3.5	55	2.8	35	3.2	71	3.5	69	3.5	62	3.4	50	2.4	38	2.5	24	2.3
Minneapolis, MN	12	1.0	18	0.9	31	1.9	46	2.4	59	3.4	68	4.1	74	3.5	71	3.6	61	2.7	49	2.2	33	1.6	18	1.1
Mobile, AL	50	4.8	53	5.5	61	6.4	68	4.5	75	5.7	80	5.0	82	6.9	82	7.0	78	5.9	68	2.9	60	4.1	53	5.3
Moline, IL	20	1.5	25	1.2	37	3.0	50	3.9	61	4.3	71	4.3	75	5.0	73	4.2	65	4.0	53	2.9	40	2.5	25	2.2
Nashville, TN	36	3.6	40	3.8	50	4.9	59	4.4	68	4.9	76	3.6	79	4.0	78	3.5	72	3.5	60	2.6	50	4.1	41	4.6
Newark, NJ	31	3.4	33	3.0	42	3.9	52	3.8	63	4.1	73	3.2	78	4.5	76	3.9	69	3.7	58	3.1	47	3.9	36	3.5
New Orleans, LA	51	5.1	54	6.0	62	4.9	69	4.5	75	4.6	80	5.8	82	6.1	82	6.2	78	5.5	69	3.1	61	4.4	55	5.8
New York, NY*	32	3.4	34	3.3	42	4.1	53	4.2	63	4.4	72	3.7	77	4.4	76	4.0	68	3.9	58	3.6	48	4.5	37	3.9
Norfolk, VA	39	3.8	41	3.5	49	3.7	57	3.1	66	3.8	74	3.8	78	5.1	77	4.8	72	3.9	61	3.2	53	2.9	44	3.2
Okla. City, OK†	36	1.0	41	1.3	49	2.1	60	2.9	68	5.5	77	3.9	82	3.0	81	2.4	73	3.4	62	2.7	49	1.5	40	1.2
Omaha, NE	21	0.7	27	0.8	39	2.0	52	2.7	62	4.5	72	3.9	77	3.5	74	3.2	65	3.7	53	2.3	39	1.5	25	1.0
Philadelphia, PA	30	3.2	33	2.8	42	3.5	52	3.6	63	3.8	72	3.7	77	4.3	76	3.8	68	3.4	56	2.6	46	3.3	36	3.4
Phoenix, AZ	54	0.7	58	0.7	62	0.9	70	0.2	79	0.1	88	0.1	94	0.8	92	1.0	86	0.9	75	0.7	62	0.7	54	1.0
Pittsburgh, PA	26	2.5	29	2.4	39	3.4	50	3.2	60	3.6	68	3.7	72	3.8	71	3.2	64	3.0	52	2.4	42	2.9	32	2.9
Portland, ME	21	3.5	23	3.3	33	3.7	43	4.1	53	3.6	62	3.4	69	3.1	67	2.9	59	3.1	49	3.9	39	5.2	27	4.6
Portland, OR	40	5.4	44	3.9	47	3.6	51	2.4	57	2.1	64	1.5	68	0.6	69	1.1	63	1.8	55	2.7	46	5.3	40	6.1
Providence, RI	28	4.1	30	3.7	37	4.3	47	4.0	57	3.5	67	2.8	73	3.0	71	4.0	64	3.5	54	3.8	44	4.2	33	4.5
Raleigh, NC	39	3.6	42	3.4	50	3.7	59	2.9	67	3.7	74	3.7	78	4.4	77	4.4	71	3.3	60	2.7	51	2.9	43	3.1
Rapid City, SD	22	0.4	27	0.5	34	1.0	45	1.9	55	2.7	65	3.1	72	2.0	71	1.7	60	1.2	49	1.1	35	0.6	24	0.5
Reno, NV	33	1.1	38	1.0	43	0.7	49	0.4	57	0.7	65	0.5	72	0.3	70	0.3	60	0.4	51	0.4	40	0.9	33	1.0
Richmond, VA	37	3.2	39	3.2	48	3.6	57	3.0	66	3.8	74	3.6	78	5.0	77	4.4	70	3.3	59	3.5	50	3.2	40	3.3
St. Louis, MO	29	1.8	34	2.1	45	3.6	57	3.5	66	4.0	75	3.7	80	3.9	78	2.9	70	3.1	58	2.7	46	3.3	34	3.0
Salt Lake City, UT	28	1.1	34	1.2	42	1.9	50	2.1	59	1.8	69	0.9	78	0.8	76	0.9	65	1.3	53	1.4	41	1.3	30	1.4
San Antonio, TX	49	1.7	54	1.8	62	1.5	69	2.5	76	4.2	82	3.8	85	2.2	85	2.5	79	3.4	70	3.2	60	2.6	52	1.5
San Diego, CA	57	1.8	59	1.5	60	1.8	62	0.8	64	0.2	67	0.1	71	L	73	0.1	71	0.2	68	0.4	62	1.5	57	1.6
San Francisco, CA	49	4.4	52	3.2	53	3.1	56	1.4	58	0.2	62	0.1	63	L	64	0.1	65	0.2	61	1.2	55	2.9	49	3.1
San Juan, PR†	77	3.0	77	2.0	78	2.3	80	3.6	79	5.6	80	4.7	82	4.9	82	5.9	82	6.0	81	5.9	80	5.6	78	4.7
Sault Ste. Marie, MI*	13	2.4	14	1.7	24	2.3	38	2.4	51	2.7	58	3.1	64	2.7	63	3.6	55	3.7	45	3.2	33	3.5	19	2.9
Savannah, GA	49	3.6	52	3.2	59	3.8	66	3.0	74	4.1	79	5.7	82	6.4	81	7.4	77	4.5	67	2.4	59	2.2	52	3.0
Scottsbluff, NE	25	0.5	30	0.5	36	1.1	47	1.6	56	2.8	67	2.6	74	2.1	72	1.1	61	1.1	50	0.8	36	0.6	26	0.6
Seattle, WA	41	5.4	44	4.0	47	3.8	50	2.5	56	1.8	61	1.6	65	0.9	66	1.2	61	1.9	54	3.3	46	5.7	42	6.0
Spokane, WA	27	2.0	33	1.5	39	1.5	46	1.2	54	1.4	62	1.3	69	0.7	68	0.7	59	0.7	47	1.0	35	2.2	28	2.4
Springfield, MO	31	1.8	36	2.2	46	3.9	56	4.2	65	4.4	73	5.1	78	2.9	77	3.5	69	4.6	58	3.6	46	3.8	35	3.2
Syracuse, NY	22	2.3	24	2.2	34	2.8	46	3.3	57	3.3	65	3.8	70	3.8	68	3.5	62	3.8	51	3.2	41	3.7	28	3.2
Tampa, FL	60	2.0	62	3.1	67	3.0	71	1.2	77	3.1	81	5.5	82	6.6	82	7.6	81	6.0	75	2.0	68	1.8	62	2.2
Washington, DC	31	2.7	34	2.8	43	3.2	53	3.1	62	4.0	71	3.9	76	3.5	74	3.9	67	3.4	55	3.2	45	3.3	35	3.2
Wilmington, DE	31	3.0	33	2.9	43	3.4	52	3.4	63	3.8	72	3.6	76	4.2	75	3.4	68	3.4	56	2.9	46	3.3	36	3.5

Normal High and Low Temperatures, Precipitation

Source: National Climatic Data Center, NESDIS, NOAA, U.S. Dept. of Commerce

The normal temperatures below are based on records for the 30-year period 1961-90. The extreme temperatures (through 1990) are listed for the stations shown and may not agree with the states records shown on pages 182-83.

Airport stations; * designates city stations. The minus (–) sign indicates temperatures below zero. Fahrenheit thermometer registration.

State	Station	Normal temperature January Max.	January Min.	July Max.	July Min.	Extreme temperature Highest	Extreme temperature Lowest	Normal annual precipitation (inches)
Alabama	Mobile	60	40	91	73	104	3	63.96
Alaska	Anchorage	21	8	65	52	85	–34	15.91
Alaska	Barrow	–7	–19	45	34	79	–56	4.49
Arizona	Phoenix	66	41	106	81	122	17	7.66
Arkansas	Little Rock	49	29	92	72	112	-5	72.10
California	Los Angeles*	68	49	84	65	112	28	14.77
California	San Diego	66	49	76	66	111	29	9.9
California	San Francisco	56	42	72	54	106	20	19.70
Colorado	Denver	43	16	88	59	104	–30	15.40
Connecticut	Hartford	33	16	85	62	102	–26	44.14
Delaware	Wilmington	39	22	86	67	102	–14	40.84
Dist. of Col.	Washington - National	42	27	89	71	104	–5	38.63
Florida	Jacksonville	64	41	91	72	105	7	51.32
Florida	Miami	75	59	89	76	98	30	55.91
Georgia	Atlanta	50	32	88	70	105	–8	50.77
Georgia	Savannah	60	38	91	72	105	3	49.22
Hawaii	Honolulu	80	66	88	74	94	53	22.02
Idaho	Boise	36	22	90	58	111	–25	12.11
Illinois	Chicago	29	13	84	63	104	–27	35.82
Illinois	Moline	28	11	86	65	106	-27	39.08
Indiana	Indianapolis	34	17	86	65	104	–23	39.94
Iowa	Des Moines	28	11	87	67	108	–24	33.12
Lexington	Kentucky	39	22	86	66	103	–21	44.55
Kentucky	Louisville	40	23	87	67	105	–20	44.39
Louisiana	New Orleans	61	42	91	73	102	11	61.88
Maine	Caribou	19	–2	77	55	96	–41	36.60
Maine	Portland	30	11	79	58	103	–39	44.34
Maryland	Baltimore	40	23	87	67	105	–7	40.76
Massachusetts	Boston	36	22	82	65	102	–12	41.51
Michigan	Detroit	30	16	83	61	104	–21	32.62
Michigan	Sault Ste. Marie*	21	5	76	51	98	–36	34.23
Minnesota	Duluth	16	–2	77	55	97	–39	30.00
Minnesota	Minn.-St. Paul	21	3	84	63	105	–34	28.32
Mississippi	Jackson	56	33	92	71	106	2	55.37
Missouri	Kansas City	35	17	89	68	109	–23	37.62
Missouri	St. Louis	38	21	89	70	107	–18	37.51
Montana	Helena	30	10	85	53	105	–42	11.60
Nebraska	Omaha	31	11	88	66	114	–23	29.86
Nebraska	Scottsbluff	38	12	90	59	109	–42	15.27
Nevada	Reno	45	21	92	51	105	–16	7.53
New Jersey	Atlantic City	40	21	85	65	106	–11	40.29
New Mexico	Albuquerque	47	22	93	64	105	–17	8.88
New York	Albany	30	11	84	60	100	–28	36.17
New York	Buffalo	30	17	80	62	99	–20	38.58
New York	New York-La Guardia	37	26	84	69	107	–3	42.12
No. Carolina	Asheville	47	25	83	62	100	–16	47.59
No. Carolina	Raleigh	49	29	88	68	105	–9	41.43
No. Dakota	Bismarck	20	–2	84	56	109	–44	15.47
Ohio	Cleveland	32	18	82	61	104	–19	36.63
Ohio	Columbus	34	19	84	63	102	–19	38.09
Oregon	Portland	45	34	80	57	107	–3	36.30
Pennsylvania	Philadelphia	38	23	86	67	104	–7	41.41
Pennsylvania	Pittsburgh	34	19	83	62	103	–18	36.85
Rhode Island	Providence	37	19	82	63	104	–13	45.53
So. Carolina	Charleston	58	38	90	73	104	6	51.53
So. Dakota	Huron	24	2	87	62	112	–39	20.08
So. Dakota	Rapid City	34	11	86	58	110	–30	16.64
Tennessee	Memphis	49	31	92	73	108	–13	52.10
Tennessee	Nashville	46	27	90	69	107	–17	47.30
Texas	Galveston*	58	47	87	79	101	8	42.28
Texas	Houston	61	40	93	72	107	7	46.07
Utah	Salt Lake City	36	19	92	64	107	–30	16.18
Vermont	Burlington	25	8	81	60	101	–30	34.47
Virginia	Norfolk	47	31	86	70	104	–3	44.64
Virginia	Richmond	46	26	88	68	105	–12	43.16
Washington	Seattle–Tacoma	45	35	75	55	99	0	37.19
Washington	Spokane	33	21	83	54	108	–25	16.49
Wisconsin	Milwaukee	26	12	80	62	103	–26	32.93
Wyoming	Lander	31	8	86	56	101	–37	13.01

Mean Annual Snowfall (inches) based on record through 1990: Boston, Mass., 42; Sault Ste. Marie, Mich., 113; Albany, N.Y., 65.2; Burlington, Vt., 78.6; Lander, Wyo., 66; Juneau, Alas., 105.8.

Wettest Spot: Mount Waialeale, Ha., on the island of Kauai, is the rainiest place in the world, according to the National Geographic Society, with an average annual rainfall of 460 inches.

Highest Temperature: A temperature of 136° F observed at Azizia, Tripolitania in northern Africa on Sept. 13, 1922, is generally accepted as the world's highest temperature recorded under standard conditions.

The record high in the United States was 134° F in Death Valley, Cal., July 10, 1913.

Lowest Temperature: A record low temperature of –128.6° F was recorded at the Soviet Antarctica station Vostok on July 21, 1983.

The record low in the United States was –80° F at Prospect Creek, Alas., Jan. 23, 1971.

The lowest official temperature on the North American continent was recorded at –81° F in February 1947, at a lonely airport in the Yukon called Snag.

These are the meteorological champions—the official temperature extremes—but there are plenty of other claimants to thermometer fame. However, sun readings are unofficial records, since meteorological data to qualify officially must be taken on instruments in a sheltered and ventilated location.

Annual Climatological Data

Source: National Climatic Data Center, NESDIS, NOAA, U.S. Dept. of Commerce

1993		Temperature °F				Precipitation[1]			Sleet or snow			Fastest[2] Wind		No. of days			
Station	Elev. ft.	Highest	Date	Lowest	Date	Total (in.)	Greatest in 24 hours	Date	Total (in.)	Greatest in 24 hours	Date	MPH	Date	Clear*	Cloudy*	Prec. .01 in. or more	Snow, sleet 1 in. or more
Albany, N.Y.	275	95	7/8	–14	2/7	41.25	3.42	7/29	85.6	26.6	3/13	32	7/29	60	178	138	15
Albuquerque, N.M.	5311	100	7/7	13	12/23	9.03	0.90	8/28	7.3	3.7	11/15	39	7/29	155	109	65	3
Anchorage, Alas.	114	80	7/12	–22	2/2	16.89	0.92	9/16	59.1	9.1	2/5	40	2/3	51	247	124	16
Asheville, N.C.	2140	95	7/29	2	3/15	37.97	2.46	11/26	29.2	16.5	3/12	48	3/13	91	158	109	4
Atlanta, Ga.	1010	102	7/22	18	3/14	48.05	2.81	10/29	7.0	4.2	3/13	49	7/27	123	144	104	2
Atlantic City, N.J.	11	101	7/10	4	2/7	38.7	2.54	3/4	13.2	2.9	3/13	38	3/13	77	156	112	6
Baltimore, Md.	148	100	7/9	9	12/31	42.50	2.54	12.4	25.8	11.9	3/13	37	3/13	89	158	118	5
Barrow, Alas.	31	79	7/13	–52	2/1	5.33	0.30	8/1	51.3	2.9	1/12	43	10/11	107	223	109	12
Birmingham, Ala.	678	102	7/23	2	3/14	39.20	2.48	9/2	13.0	13.0	3/12	—	—	—	—	110	2
Bismarck, N.D.	1647	93	6/21	–30	12/27	26.99	5.27	7/15	64.6	10.8	11/24	45	8/11	76	179	97	16
Boise, Ida.	2838	102	7/28	0	11/24	12.76	0.89	3/17	27.3	6.2	1/8	35	5/25	126	162	100	9
Boston, Mass.	15	99	7/10	2	2/7	43.21	2.95	12/4	85.2	12.8	3/13	54	3/13	87	162	134	19
Buffalo, N.Y.	705	95	7/5	–9	12/27	40.66	2.12	9/27	98.0	17.2	3/13	38	10/21	59	206	159	23
Burlington, Vt.	332	94	7/7	–27	2/7	32.86	1.42	8/24	129.6	22.4	3/13	35	5/6	60	204	155	31
Caribou, Me.	624	90	7/7	–28	2/21	40.00	2.02	8/17	83.5	14.6	3/13	30	1/25	—	—	169	22
Charleston, S.C.	40	100	7/29	24	12/31	52.69	3.90	1/12	T	T	12/23	46	3/13	97	160	104	0
Chicago, Ill.	658	94	8/27	–5	2/24	44.90	2.90	7/18	42.1	6.5	1/9	32	8/9	52	207	136	16
Cleveland, Oh.	777	96	7/28	–5	2/25	40.63	1.82	9/2	96.5	14.8	2/23	35	7/28	46	222	154	25
Columbus, Oh.	812	96	8/26	–2	2/18	37.85	2.89	7/1	34.8	5.4	2/15	30	7/10	53	215	141	9
Dallas-Ft. Worth, Tex.	551	104	8/1	23	11/26	32.83	2.31	9/13	0.3	0.3	11/25	38	11/14	120	152	84	0
Denver, Co.	5283	99	7/31	–9	2/17	14.78	1.33	10/17	63.0	6.0	11/13	46	7/8	115	121	97	21
Des Moines, Ia.	938	92	8/26	–6	2/24	55.88	4.01	8/28	30.9	5.3	1/11	59	4/10	80	198	149	10
Detroit, Mich.	633	96	8/27	–2	2/25	30.63	2.17	6/25	48.8	7.5	3/10	36	10/21	58	203	142	10
Duluth, Minn.	1428	87	8/25	–25	12/26	32.35	2.16	6/23	88.4	9.7	1/23	36	11/19	77	192	156	24
Fairbanks, Alas.	436	93	7/15	–58	2/2	11.33	0.80	9/18	90.4	10.1	1/13	30	1/14	57	209	107	32
Fresno, Cal.	328	108	6/26	26	1/4	13.75	1.61	6/4	0.0	0.0	—	39	1/14	188	97	48	0
Galveston, Tex.	7	93	9/10	37	11/27	47.12	4.34	10/12	T	T	1/25	32	3/12	—	—	86	0
Grand Rapids, Mich.	784	93	7/4	–12	2/25	46.47	3.19	10/16	64.2	9.2	12/23	36	10/21	48	222	159	19
Hartford, Conn.	169	99	8/28	–3	2/7	45.09	2.13	12/4	62.1	14.8	3/13	30	1/30	91	165	130	17
Helena, Mont.	3828	95	7/29	–23	1/6	18.81	1.10	6/15	46.1	11.7	2/18	47	12/12	71	188	118	13
Honolulu, Ha.	7	93	10/6	54	2/4	5.84	1.13	10/24	0.0	0.0	—	33	12/5	119	58	76	0
Houston, Tex.	96	101	8/16	27	11/27	57.99	3.68	4/3	T	T	5/9	35	4/7	84	161	111	0
Huron, S.D.	1281	94	8/9	–22	2/24	30.01	2.09	7/17	53.8	6.9	11/24	41	7/21	97	169	104	17
Indianapolis, Ind.	792	94	7/28	–9	2/18	50.76	4.15	11/13	32.4	7.4	2/25	39	4/15	68	216	148	10
Jackson, Miss.	291	99	6/15	19	3/14	48.02	3.78	11/14	1.6	106	3/12	33	12/13	—	—	107	1
Jacksonville, Fla.	26	100	6/7	26	2/19	50.12	4.05	10/30	T	T	12/25	44	3/13	90	157	125	0
Kansas City, Mo.	1014	98	7/31	–6	2/18	51.46	3.15	9/13	32.6	10.8	2/24	38	7/31	100	169	137	6
Knoxville, Tenn.	979	100	7/28	6	3/15	45.09	4.02	12/3	16.4	14.1	3/12	29	4/15	97	158	122	3
Lander, Wyo.	5557	94	7/29	–21	2/17	16.54	2.48	6/2	90.9	9.4	11/13	37	6/21	119	135	90	27
Lexington, Ky.	966	96	7/25	3	2/18	45.58	2.60	6/4	26.5	6.5	3/13	35	4/15	69	192	140	5
Little Rock, Ark.	257	106	7/31	15	2/18	43.77	2.71	1/4	T	T	10/30	—	—	—	—	95	0
Los Angeles, Cal.	97	98	9/26	42	1/5	23.50	2.90	1/6	—	—	—	—	—	—	—	39	—
Louisville, Ky.	477	97	8/29	2	2/18	47.39	1.95	8/17	23.0	7.9	2/25	40	11/14	92	183	127	4
Marquette, Mich.	1415	88	8/25	–17	2/26	33.01	2.34	9/13	170.3	17.4	4/15	—	—	—	—	146	50
Memphis, Tenn.	258	99	8/20	16	2/18	44.00	2.95	12/3	T	T	10/31	38	2/21	99	167	119	0
Miami, Fla.	7	97	8/21	44	3/15	62.79	5.73	11/8	0.0	0.0	—	38	3/13	54	118	126	0
Milwaukee, Wis.	672	95	8/27	–2	2/25	36.84	2.46	4/19	49.1	8.0	11/28	38	4/24	51	215	128	13
Minneapolis, Minn.	834	89	8/26	–16	1/1	32.21	1.94	6/16	36.9	6.2	1/12	38	8/18	80	189	127	10
Mobile, Ala.	211	97	8/19	21	3/14	60.40	5.04	1/20	2.7	2.7	3/12	36	3/12	104	152	124	1
Moline, Ill.	582	94	8/26	–9	2/24	50.79	3.70	6/24	26.2	4.5	1/9	35	6/29	76	198	142	11
Nashville, Tenn.	590	99	7/28	12	2/18	44.38	2.99	12/3	9.4	3.5	2/15	35	4/15	85	152	125	3
Newark, N.J.	7	105	7/10	5	2/7	42.51	2.80	3/13	32.2	12.6	3/13	41	11/20	77	166	112	7
New Orleans, La.	4	98	7/31	27	12/31	52.71	3.56	5/1	T	T	3/12	36	3/12	99	158	114	0
New York, N.Y.	132	99	7/10	5	2/7	43.16	2.69	8/12	41.6	11.7	3/13	52	3/13	104	151	112	8
Norfolk, Va.	24	103	7/29	16	12/31	36.03	2.11	9/4	7.8	3.9	12/23	36	3/13	90	159	114	3
Omaha, Neb.	997	95	8/14	–7	2/17	42.72	2.93	7/21	33.0	3.1	1/9	35	12/24	76	191	133	13
Philadelphia, Pa.	5	101	7/10	9	2/7	42.18	2.60	9/17	25.2	12.0	3/13	52	3/13	86	157	111	5
Phoenix, Ariz.	1110	114	8/1	35	12/23	13.34	2.16	11/14	T	T	1/18	29	3/26	214	68	46	0
Pittsburgh, Pa.	1137	98	8/26	–1	2/25	38.26	1.89	4/25	76.7	23.8	3/13	35	1/13	52	213	163	16
Portland, Me.	43	98	7/10	–16	2/7	43.85	1.76	12/21	123.2	18.6	3/13	37	3/13	83	172	153	24
Portland, Ore.	21	97	8/4	18	11/24	30.36	1.52	1/19	9.5	6.5	2/18	38	12/8	66	222	134	2
Providence, R.I.	51	100	7/10	–2	2/7	42.16	3.02	12/4	46.2	10.2	3/13	37	3/14	89	164	126	15
Raleigh, N.C.	434	99	7/29	14	12/31	38.05	2.75	3/3	5.6	3.1	12/22	153	7/10	108	145	115	1
Rapid City, S.D.	3162	95	7/30	–21	2/17	19.79	1.88	6/6	55.1	8.1	1/8	46	12/23	96	146	117	17
Reno, Nev.	4404	100	8/2	–3	1/3	6.58	1.15	10/4	36.2	4.2	1/17	45	12/8	163	131	53	13
Richmond, Va.	164	102	7/8	8	12/31	42.25	2.36	3/3	14.4	4.0	12/28	29	8/20	85	173	121	5
Scottsbluff, Neb.	3957	97	7/29	–20	2/17	24.82	2.84	6/2	63.5	8.9	2/10	48	7/26	90	160	109	20
St. Louis, Mo.	535	97	8/19	–1	2/18	54.76	3.17	8/11	32.9	11.7	2/24	35	7/31	58	200	129	8
Salt Lake City, Ut.	4221	96	7/28	–4	1/5	—	1.53	10/7	82.0	9.7	1/2	48	6/21	130	149	116	22
San Antonio, Tex.	788	101	9/8	23	11/27	32.00	6.26	5/5	T	T	10/30	25	123	91	151	86	0
San Diego, Cal.	13	87	9/27	39	1/4	17.26	2.54	1/15	0.0	0.0	—	40	2/18	131	99	49	0
San Francisco, Cal.	8	100	8/1	33	1/4	23.51	3.00	1/12	0.0	0.0	—	41	1/12	153	123	76	0
Sault Ste. Marie, Mich.	721	88	8/25	–31	12/26	33.93	2.08	9/13	88.3	7.6	12/27	31	10/21	62	223	166	29
Savannah, Ga.	46	103	7/29	25	12/31	48.05	4.44	9/6	0.2	0.2	3/13	41	3/13	115	146	100	0
Seattle, Wash.	400	95	8/4	19	11/24	28.80	1.98	3/22	2.7	1.4	2/20	47	1/20	82	201	137	1
Spokane, Wash.	2356	92	5/12	–5	11/24	13.63	0.82	5/3	46.1	11.0	2/19	35	1/20	88	204	109	11
Springfield, Mo.	1268	97	8/27	–6	2/18	55.78	6.27	9/24	21.8	11.2	2/15	31	9/19	100	182	129	6
Syracuse, N.Y.	410	94	7/6	–13	2/7	43.61	2.91	8/24	212.9	35.6	3/13	37	11/20	—	—	175	42
Tampa, Fla.	19	97	8/9	35	3/15	37.53	1.89	3/12	0.0	0.0	—	40	3/13	102	111	109	0
Washington, D.C.	10	100	7/28	11	2/19	41.41	4.03	11/27	3.3	6.6	3/12	46	5/16	77	178	116	4
Wilmington, Del.	74	98	7/10	5	2/7	46.75	2.60	6/1	27.7	13.1	3/13	38	11/28	100	166	112	7

* To get partly cloudy days deduct the total of clear and cloudy days from 365 (1 yr.). T—trace. (1) Date shown is the starting date of the storm (in some cases it lasted more than one day). (2) Sustained for at least 1 minute, not peak gust.

Record Temperatures by State Through 1992

Source: National Climatic Data Center, NESDIS, NOAA, U.S. Dept. of Commerce

State	Lowest °F	Highest	Latest date	Station	Approximate elevation in feet
Alabama	–27		Jan. 30, 1966	New Market	760
		112	*Sept. 5, 1925*	*Centerville*	*345*
Alaska	–80		Jan. 23, 1971	Prospect Creek Camp	1,100
		100	*June 27, 1915*	*Fort Yukon*	*420*
Arizona	–40		Jan. 7, 1971	Hawley Lake	8,180
		127	*July 7, 1905*[1]	*Parker*	*345*
Arkansas	–29		Feb. 13, 1905	Pond	1,250
		120	*Aug. 10, 1936*	*Ozark*	*396*
California	–45		Jan. 20, 1937	Boca	5,532
		134	*July 10, 1913*	*Greenland Ranch*	*–178*
Colorado	–61		Feb. 1, 1985	Maybell	5,920
		118	*July 11, 1888*	*Bennett*	*5,484*
Connecticut	–32		Feb. 16, 1943	Falls Village	585
		105	*July 21, 1991*[1]	*Danbury*	*450*
Delaware	–17		Jan. 17, 1893	Millsboro	20
		110	*July 21, 1930*	*Millsboro*	*20*
Dist. of Col.	–15		Feb. 11, 1899	Washington	112
		106	*July 20, 1930*	*Washington*	*112*
Florida	–2		Feb. 13, 1899	Tallahassee	193
		109	*June 29, 1931*	*Monticello*	*207*
Georgia	–17		Jan. 27, 1940	CCC Camp F-16	1,000
		112	*Jul. 24, 1952*	*Louisville*	*132*
Hawaii	12		May 17, 1979	Mauna Kea	13,770
		100	*Apr. 27, 1931*	*Pahala*	*850*
Idaho	–60		Jan. 18, 1943	Island Park Dam	6,285
		118	*July 28, 1934*	*Orofino*	*1,027*
Illinois	–35		Jan. 22, 1930	Mount Carroll	817
		117	*July 14, 1954*	*E. St. Louis*	*410*
Indiana	–35		Feb. 2, 1951	Greensburg	954
		116	*July 14, 1936*	*Collegeville*	*672*
Iowa	–47		Jan. 12, 1912	Washta	1,157
		118	*July 20, 1934*	*Keokuk*	*614*
Kansas	–40		Feb. 13, 1905	Lebanon	1,812
		121	*July 24, 1936*[1]	*Alton (near)*	*1,651*
Kentucky	–34		Jan. 28, 1963	Cynthiana	684
		114	*July 28, 1930*	*Greensburg*	*581*
Louisiana	–16		Feb. 13, 1899	Minden	194
		114	*Aug. 10, 1936*	*Plain Dealing*	*268*
Maine	–48		Jan. 19, 1925	Van Buren	510
		105	*July 10, 1911*[1]	*North Bridgton*	*450*
Maryland	–40		Jan. 13, 1912	Oakland	2,461
		109	*July 10, 1936*[1]	*Cumberland and Frederick*	*623; 325*
Massachusetts	–35		Jan. 12, 1981	Chester	640
		107	*Aug. 2, 1975*	*Chester and New Bedford*	*120; 640*
Michigan	–51		Feb. 9, 1934	Vanderbilt	785
		112	*July 13, 1936*	*Mio*	*963*
Minnesota	–59		Feb. 16, 1903[1]	Pokegama Dam	1,280
		114	*July 6, 1936*[1]	*Moorhead*	*904*
Mississippi	–19		Jan. 30, 1966	Corinth	420
		115	*July 29, 1930*	*Holly Springs*	*600*
Missouri	–40		Feb. 13, 1905	Warsaw	700
		118	*July 14, 1954*[1]	*Warsaw and Union*	*687; 560*
Montana	–70		Jan. 20, 1954	Rogers Pass	5,470
		117	*July 5, 1937*	*Medicine Lake*	*1,950*
Nebraska	–47		Feb. 12, 1899	Camp Clarke	3,700
		118	*July 24, 1936*[1]	*Minden*	*2,169*
Nevada	–50		Jan. 8, 1937	San Jacinto	5,200
		122	*June 26, 1990*[1]	*Laughlin*	*680*
New Hampshire	–46		Jan. 28 1925	Pittsburgh	1,575
		106	*July 4, 1911*	*Nashua*	*125*
New Jersey	–34		Jan. 5, 1904	River Vale	70
		110	*July 10, 1936*	*Runyon*	*18*
New Mexico	–50		Feb. 1, 1951	Gavilan	7,350
		116	*July 14, 1934*[1]	*Orogrande*	*4,171*
New York	–52		Feb. 18, 1979	Old Forge	1,720
		108	*July 22, 1926*	*Troy*	*35*
North Carolina	–34		Jan. 21, 1985	Mt. Mitchell	6,525
		110	*Aug. 21, 1983*	*Fayetteville*	*213*
North Dakota	–60		Feb. 15, 1936	Parshall	1,929
		121	*July 6, 1936*	*Steele*	*1,857*
Ohio	–39		Feb. 10, 1899	Milligan	800
		113	*July 21, 1934*	*Gallipolis (near)*	*673*
Oklahoma	–27		Jan. 18, 1930[1]	Watts	958
		120	*July 26, 1943*[1]	*Tishmomingo*	*670*
Oregon	–54		Feb. 10, 1933[1]	Seneca	4,700
		119	*Aug. 10, 1898*	*Pendleton*	*1,074*
Pennsylvania	–42		Jan. 5, 1904	Smethport	1,500
		111	*July 10, 1936*[1]	*Phoenixville*	*100*
Rhode Island	–23		Jan. 11, 1942	Kingston	100
		104	*Aug. 2, 1975*	*Providence*	*51*
South Carolina	–19		Jan. 21, 1985	Caesar's Head	3,100
		111	*June 28, 1954*[1]	*Camden*	*170*
South Dakota	–58		Feb. 17, 1936	McIntosh	2,277
		120	*July 5, 1936*	*Gannvalley*	*1,750*

State	Lowest °F	Highest	Latest date	Station	Approximate elevation in feet
Tennessee	-32		Dec. 30, 1917	Mountain City	2,471
		113	*Aug. 9, 1930*[1]	*Perryville*	*377*
Texas	-23		Feb. 8, 1933	Seminole	3,275
		120	*Aug. 12, 1936*	*Seymour*	*1,291*
Utah	-69		Feb. 1, 1985	Peter's Sink	8,092
		117	*Jul. 5, 1985*	*Saint George*	*2,880*
Vermont	-50		Dec. 30, 1933	Bloomfield	915
		105	*July 4, 1911*	*Vernon*	*310*
Virginia	-30		Jan. 22, 1985	Mountain Lake Bio. Station	3,870
		110	*July 15, 1954*	*Balcony Falls*	*725*
Washington	-48		Dec. 30, 1968	Mazama and Winthrop	2,120; 1,765
		118	*Aug. 5, 1961*[1]	*Ice Harbor Dam*	*475*
West Virginia	-37		Dec. 30, 1917	Lewisburg	2,200
		112	*July 10, 1936*[1]	*Martinsburg*	*435*
Wisconsin	-54		Jan. 24, 1922	Danbury	908
		114	*July 13, 1936*	*Wisconsin Dells*	*900*
Wyoming	-63		Feb. 9, 1933	Moran	6,770
		114	*July 12, 1900*	*Basin*	*3,500*

(1) Also on earlier dates at the same or other places.

International Temperature and Precipitation

Source: Environmental Data Service, U.S. Dept. of Commerce

A standard period of 30 years has been used to obtain the average daily maximum and minimum temperatures and precipitation. The length of record of extreme maximum and minimum temperatures includes all available years of data for a given location and is usually for a longer period.

		Temperature F°						Average annual precipitation (inches)
		Average Daily				Extreme		
	Elev.	January		July				
Station	Feet	Max.	Min.	Max.	Min.	Max.	Min.	
Addis Ababa, Ethiopia	8,038	75	43	69	50	94	32	48.7
Algiers, Algeria	194	59	49	83	70	107	32	30.0
Amsterdam, Netherlands	5	40	34	69	59	95	3	25.6
Athens, Greece	351	54	42	90	72	109	20	15.8
Auckland, New Zealand	23	73	60	56	46	90	33	49.1
Bangkok, Thailand	53	89	67	90	76	104	50	57.8
Beirut, Lebanon	111	62	51	87	73	107	30	35.1
Berlin, Germany	187	35	26	74	55	96	−15	23.1
Bogotá, Colombia	8,355	67	48	64	50	75	30	41.8
Bombay, India	27	88	62	88	75	110	46	71.2
Bucharest, Romania	269	33	20	86	61	105	−18	22.8
Budapest, Hungary	394	35	26	82	61	103	−10	24.2
Buenos Aires, Argentina	89	85	63	57	42	104	22	37.4
Cairo, Egypt	381	65	47	96	70	117	34	1.1
Capetown, South Africa	56	78	60	63	45	103	28	20.0
Caracas, Venezuela	3,418	75	56	78	61	91	45	32.9
Casablanca, Morocco	164	63	45	79	65	110	31	15.9
Copenhagen, Denmark	43	36	29	72	55	91	−3	23.3
Damascus, Syria	2,362	53	36	96	64	113	21	8.6
Dublin, Ireland	155	47	35	67	51	86	8	29.7
Geneva, Switzerland	1,329	39	29	77	58	101	−1	33.9
Havana, Cuba	80	79	65	89	75	104	43	48.2
Hong Kong	109	64	56	87	78	97	32	85.1
Istanbul, Turkey	59	45	36	81	65	100	17	31.5
Jerusalem, Israel	2,654	55	41	87	63	107	26	19.7
Lagos, Nigeria	10	88	74	83	74	104	60	72.3
La Paz, Bolivia	12,001	63	43	62	33	80	26	22.6
Lima, Peru	394	82	66	67	57	93	49	1.6
London, England	149	44	35	73	55	99	9	22.9
Madrid, Spain	2,188	47	33	87	62	102	14	16.5
Manila, Philippines	49	86	69	88	75	101	58	82.0
Mexico City, Mexico	7,340	66	42	74	54	92	24	23.0
Montreal, Canada	187	21	6	78	61	97	−35	40.8
Moscow, Russia	505	21	9	76	55	96	−27	24.8
Nairobi, Kenya	5,971	77	54	69	51	87	41	37.7
Oslo, Norway	308	30	20	73	56	93	−21	26.9
Paris, France	164	42	32	76	55	105	1	22.3
Prague, Czech Republic	662	34	25	74	58	98	−16	19.3
Reykjavik, Iceland	92	36	28	58	48	74	4	33.9
Rome, Italy	377	54	39	88	64	104	20	29.5
San Salvador, El Salvador	2,238	90	60	89	65	105	45	70.0
Santiago, Chile	1,706	85	53	59	37	99	24	14.2
Sao Paolo, Brazil	2,628	77	63	66	53	100	32	57.3
Shanghai, China	16	47	32	91	75	104	10	45.0
Singapore		86	73	88	75	97	66	95.0
Stockholm, Sweden	146	31	23	70	55	97	−26	22.4
Sydney, Australia	62	78	65	60	46	114	35	46.5
Tehran, Iran	3,937	45	27	99	72	109	−5	9.7
Tokyo, Japan	19	47	29	83	70	101	17	61.6
Toronto, Canada	379	30	16	79	59	105	−26	32.2
Tripoli, Libya	72	61	47	85	71	114	33	15.1
Vienna, Austria	664	34	26	75	59	98	−14	25.6
Warsaw, Poland	294	30	21	75	56	98	−22	22.0

Tides and Their Causes

Source: U.S. Dept. of Commerce, (NOAA) Natl. Oceanic & Atmospheric Admin., (NOS) Natl. Ocean Service

The tides are a natural phenomenon involving the alternating rise and fall in the large fluid bodies of the earth caused by the combined gravitational attraction of the sun and moon. The combination of these two variable force influences produces the complex recurrent cycle of the tides. Tides may occur in both oceans and seas, to a limited extent in large lakes, the atmosphere, and, to a very minute degree, in the earth itself. The period between succeeding tides varies as the result of many factors and force influences.

The tide-generating force represents the difference between (1) the centrifugal force produced by the revolution of the earth around the common center-of-gravity of the earth-moon system and (2) the gravitational attraction of the moon acting upon the earth's overlying waters. Since, on the average, the moon is only 238,852 miles from the earth compared with the sun's much greater distance of 92,956,000 miles, this closer distance outranks the much smaller mass of the moon compared with that of the sun, and the moon's tide-raising force is, accordingly, 1/5; times that of the sun.

The effect of the tide-generating forces of the moon and sun acting tangentially to the earth's surface (the so-called "tractive force") tends to cause a maximum accumulation of the waters of the oceans at two diametrically opposite positions on the surface of the earth and to withdraw compensating amounts of water from all points 90° removed from the positions of these tidal bulges. As the earth rotates beneath the maxima and minima of these tide-generating forces, a sequence of two high tides, separated by two low tides, ideally is produced each day (semidiurnal tide).

Twice in each lunar month, when the sun, moon, and earth are directly aligned, with the moon between the earth and the sun (at new moon) or on the opposite side of the earth from the sun (at full moon), the sun and the moon exert their gravitational force in a mutual or additive fashion. The highest high tides and lowest low tides are produced. These are called *spring* tides. At two positions 90° in between, the gravitational forces of the moon and sun — imposed at right angles— tend to counteract each other to the greatest extent, and the range between high and low tides is reduced. These are called *neap* tides. This semi-monthly variation between the spring and neap tides is called the *phase inequality*.

The inclination of the moon's monthly orbit to the equator and the inclination of the sun during the earth's yearly orbit to the equator produce a difference in the height of succeeding high tides and in the extent of depression of succeeding low tides that is known as the diurnal inequality. In most cases, this produces a type of tide called a mixed tide. In extreme cases, these phenomena can result in only one high tide and one low tide each (diurnal tide). There are also other monthly and yearly variations in the tide due to the elliptical shape of the orbits themselves.

The datum for Charting and Predictions is (MLLW) Mean Lower Low Water. This became effective January 1989 according to the convention of 1980 which prescribed that datums on all United States coastlines would be the same. Namely (MHHW) Mean Higher High Water, (MHW) Mean High Water, (MTL) Mean Tide Level, (MSL) Mean Sea Level, (MLW) Mean Low Water, (MLLW) Mean Lower Low Water. Diurnal range of tide is the difference in height between mean higher high water and mean lower low water. Mean range of tide is the difference in height between mean high water and mean low water.

The actual range of tide in the waters of the open oceans may amount to only one to three feet. However, as the ocean tide approaches shoal waters and its effects are augmented the tidal range may be greatly increased. In Nova Scotia along the narrow channel of the Bay of Fundy, the range of tides, or difference between high and low waters, may reach 43 1/2 feet or more (under spring tide conditions) due to resonant amplification.

At New Orleans, the periodic rise and fall of the diurnal tide is affected by the seasonal stages of the Mississippi River, being about 10 inches at low stage and zero at high. The Canadian Tide Tables for 1972 gave a maximum range of nearly 50 feet at Leaf Basin, Ungava Bay, Quebec.

In every case, actual high or low tide can vary considerably from the average, due to weather conditions such as strong winds, abrupt barometric pressure changes, or prolonged periods of extreme high or low pressure.

The Average Rise and Fall of Tides[1]

Places	Ft.	In.	Places	Ft.	In.	Places	Ft.	In.
Baltimore, Md.	1	8	Mobile, Ala.	1	6	San Diego, Cal.	5	9
Boston, Mass.	10	4	New London, Conn.	3	1	Sandy Hook, N.J.	5	2
Charleston, S.C.	5	10	Newport, R.I.	3	11	San Francisco, Cal.	5	10
Cristobal, Panama	1	1	New York, N.Y.	5	1	Savannah, Ga.	8	3
Eastport, Me.	19	4	Old Pt. Comfort, Va.	3	0	Seattle, Wash.	11	4
Galveston, Tex.	1	5	Philadelphia, Pa.	6	9	Tampa, Fla.	2	10
Halifax, N.S.	4	5[2]	Portland, Me.	9	11	Vancouver, B.C.	10	6
Key West, Fla.	1	10	St. John's, Nfld.	2	7[2]	Washington, D.C.	3	2

(1) Diurnal range. (2) Mean range.

Hurricane Names in 1995

Source: National Weather Service, NOAA, U.S. Dept. of Commerce

Names assigned to Atlantic hurricanes, 1995 — Allison, Barry, Chantal, Dean, Erin, Felix, Gabrielle, Humberto, Iris, Jerry, Karen, Luis, Marilyn, Noel, Opal, Pablo, Roxanne, Sebastien, Tanya, Van, Wendy.

Names assigned to Eastern Pacific hurricanes, 1995 — Adolph, Barbara, Cosme, Dalila, Erick, Flossie, Gil, Henriette, Ismael, Juliette, Kiko, Lorena, Manuel, Narda, Octave, Priscilla, Raymond, Sonia, Tico, Velma, Wallis, Xina, York, Zelda.

Historic Floods of the Mississippi River Region

Source: U.S. Army Corps of Engineers, Vicksburg, Miss.

Year	Location	Volume (cu. ft./ sec.)	Damage (1993 dollars)
1844	upper Mississippi	1.3 million	NA
1913	lower Mississippi	1.97 million	NA
1927	upper and lower Mississippi	2.3 million	$4.4 billion
1937	lower Mississippi and Ohio valleys	2.0 million	$150 million
1945	upper and lower Mississippi	1.9 million	NA
1950	lower Mississippi	1.96 million	NA
1973	upper and lower Mississippi	1.9 million	$11.54 billion
1983	upper and lower Mississippi	1.8 million	$1.15 billion
1993	upper Mississippi	1.0 million	$15 billion

NA = not available

Tornado Occurrence by State, 1962-91

Source: National Severe Storm Forecast Center

State	Total	Average per year	State	Total	Average per year	State	Total	Average per year
AL	668	22	LA	831	28	OH	463	15
AK	0	0	ME	50	2	OK	1,412	47
AZ	106	4	MD	86	3	OR	34	1
AR	596	20	MA	89	3	PA	310	10
CA	148	5	MI	567	19	RI	7	0
CO	781	26	MN	607	20	SC	307	10
CT	37	1	MS	775	26	SD	864	29
DE	31	1	MO	781	26	TN	360	12
FL	1,590	53	MT	175	6	TX	4,174	139
GA	615	21	NE	1,118	37	UT	58	2
HI	25	1	NV	41	1	VT	21	1
ID	80	3	NH	56	2	VA	188	6
IL	798	27	NJ	78	3	WA	45	2
IN	604	20	NM	276	9	WV	69	2
IA	1,079	36	NY	169	6	WI	625	21
KS	1,198	40	NC	435	15	WY	356	12
KY	296	10	ND	621	21			

Wind Chill Table

Source: National Weather Service, NOAA, U.S. Dept. of Commerce

Both temperature and wind cause heat loss from body surfaces. A combination of cold and wind makes a body feel colder than the actual temperature. The table shows, for example, that a temperature of 20 degrees Fahrenheit, plus a wind of 20 miles per hour, causes a body heat loss equal to that in minus 10 degrees with no wind. In other words, the wind makes 20 degrees feel like minus 10.

Top line of figures shows actual temperatures in degrees Fahrenheit. Column at left shows wind speeds.

MPH	35	30	25	20	15	10	5	0	-5	-10	-15	-20	-25	-30	-35	-40	-45
5	33	27	21	16	12	7	0	-5	-10	-15	-21	-26	-31	-36	-42	-47	-52
10	22	16	10	3	-3	-9	-15	-22	-27	-34	-40	-46	-52	-58	-64	-71	-77
15	16	9	2	-5	-11	-18	-25	-31	-38	-45	-51	-58	-65	-72	-78	-85	-92
20	12	4	-3	-10	-17	-24	-31	-39	-46	-53	-60	-67	-74	-81	-88	-95	-103
25	8	1	-7	-15	-22	-29	-36	-44	-51	-59	-66	-74	-81	-88	-96	-103	-110
30	6	-2	-10	-18	-25	-33	-41	-49	-56	-64	-71	-79	-86	-93	-101	-109	-116
35	4	-4	-12	-20	-27	-35	-43	-52	-58	-67	-74	-82	-89	-97	-105	-113	-120
40	3	-5	-13	-21	-29	-37	-45	-53	-60	-69	-76	-84	-92	-100	-107	-115	-123
45	2	-6	-14	-22	-30	-38	-46	-54	-62	-70	-78	-85	-93	-102	-109	-117	-125

(Wind speeds greater than 45 mph have little additional chilling effect.)

Heat Index

The index is a measure of the contribution that high humidity makes with abnormally high temperatures in reducing the body's ability to cool itself. For example, the index shows that for an actual air temperature of 100 degrees Fahrenheit and a relative humidity of 50 percent, the effect on the human body would be same as 120 degrees. Sunstroke and heat exhaustion are likely when the heat index reaches 105. This index is a measure of what hot weather "feels like" to the average person for various temperatures and relative humidities.

	Air Temperature*										
	70	**75**	**80**	**85**	**90**	**95**	**100**	**105**	**110**	**115**	**120**
Relative Humidity	**Apparent Temperature***										
0%	64	69	73	78	83	87	91	95	99	103	107
10%	65	70	75	80	85	90	95	100	105	111	116
20%	66	72	77	82	87	93	99	105	112	120	130
30%	67	73	78	84	90	96	104	113	123	135	148
40%	68	74	79	86	93	101	110	123	137	151	
50%	69	75	81	88	96	107	120	135	150		
60%	70	76	82	90	100	114	132	149			
70%	70	77	85	93	106	124	144				
80%	71	78	86	97	113	136					
90%	71	79	88	102	122						
100%	72	80	91	108							

*Degrees Fahrenheit.

ENVIRONMENT

Hazardous Waste Sites in the U.S.

Source: Environmental Protection Agency, *Natl. Priorities List,* May 1994

State/Territory	General	Federal	Total*
Alabama	9	3	13
Alaska	2	6	8
Arizona	7	3	10
Arkansas	12	0	12
California	69	22	96
Colorado	13	3	18
Connecticut	14	1	16
Delaware	18	1	19
District of Columbia	0	0	0
Florida	49	5	57
Georgia	11	2	13
Hawaii	0	3	4
Idaho	6	2	10
Illinois	33	4	37
Indiana	32	0	33
Iowa	16	1	19
Kansas	9	1	10
Kentucky	19	1	20
Louisiana	11	1	13
Maine	7	3	10
Maryland	8	4	13
Massachusetts	22	8	30
Michigan	76	0	77
Minnesota	37	3	41
Mississippi	2	0	4
Missouri	20	3	23
Montana	8	0	8
Nebraska	7	1	10
Nevada	1	0	1
New Hampshire	16	1	17
New Jersey	101	6	108
New Mexico	7	2	11
New York	79	4	85
North Carolina	20	1	22
North Dakota	2	0	2
Ohio	31	3	38
Oklahoma	9	1	11
Oregon	9	1	12
Pennsylvania	95	5	101
Rhode Island	10	2	12
South Carolina	22	1	24
South Dakota	2	1	4
Tennessee	12	3	17
Texas	25	4	30
Utah	8	4	16
Vermont	8	0	8
Virginia	19	5	25
Washington	34	20	56
West Virginia	4	2	6
Wisconsin	40	0	40
Wyoming	2	1	3
American Samoa	0	0	0
Guam	1	1	2
Northern Marianas	0	0	0
Palau	0	0	0
Puerto Rico	8	1	9
Virgin Islands	0	0	2
Total	**1,082**	**150**	**1,286***

* Includes proposed sites

Toxics Release Inventory, 1992

Source: Environmental Protection Agency

Reported industrial releases of toxic chemicals into the nation's environment by major manufacturing facilities (excluding power plants and mining facilities) continued to decrease in 1992, according to the EPA's Toxics Release Inventory (TRI). The pollutants reported released in 1992 represented a decrease of 7% from the 1991 figure and a decrease of 35% from the figure in 1988, the baseline year.

1992 pollutant releases	3,182 million pounds
Air releases	1,845 million pounds
Water releases	273 million pounds
Underground injection	726 million pounds
Land releases	338 million pounds
1992 pollutant transfers	4,368 million pounds
To publicly owned treatment works	381 million pounds
To treatment/disposal/other	669 million pounds
To recycling	2,840 million pounds
To energy recovery	478 million pounds
Top states, total releases (air, water, land, and underground injection):	
Louisiana	465 million pounds
Texas	420 million pounds
Tennessee	194 million pounds
Ohio	144 million pounds
Indiana	124 million pounds
Top industries, total releases	
Chemicals	1,536 million pounds
Primary metals	345 million pounds
Paper	233 million pounds
Plastics	138 million pounds
Transportation equipment	137 million pounds
Top chemicals, total releases	
Ammonia	464 million pounds
Hydrochloric acid	287 million pounds
Methanol	242 million pounds
Phosphric acid	207 million pounds
Toluene	193 million pounds

Releases of Toxic Substances, 1988-92

Source: Environmental Protection Agency

	Percent Change 1991-92	Percent Change 1988-92
Total releases	-7	-35
Air releases	-9	-32
Water releases[1]	+12	-12
Underground injection	+2	-46
Land releases	-19	-34
Transfers for treatment/ disposal	-19	—[2]
To publicly owned treatment works	-12	—[2]
To other treatment facilities	-6	—[2]
To disposal facilities	-32	—[2]

(1) The net increase in water releases from 1991 to 1992 is largely attributable to increased runoff from four fertilizer facilities in Louisiana and Texas. Excluding those increases, reported water releases would have decreased by 11.5% from 1991 to 1992. (2) 1992 transfers cannot be directly compared to 1988 transfers because of a change in reporting requirements.

"Urban Air": Soot in Selected Cities, 1990[1]

Source: Environmental Protection Agency

(Micograms per cubic meter of air of suspended particles that are 10 microns or less in diameter)

Area	High[2]	Average
Anaheim-Santa Ana, CA	108	48
Atlanta, GA	110	51
Chicago	149	45
Detroit	114	35
Los Angeles-Long Beach	132	55
Minneapolis-St. Paul, MN-WI	140	34
New York	103	37
Oakland, CA	118	33
Pittsburgh	191	43
Riverside-San Bernardino, CA	278	80
St. Louis	164	82

(1) Figures are for metropolitan areas. (2) The EPA treats the reading from the highest day as a statistical anomaly and reports the reading for the second highest day of the year.

Some Endangered Species

Source: Fish and Wildlife Service, U.S. Dept. of Interior; as of Aug. 23,1993. For a complete list of threatened and endangered species, write to: Publications Unit, U.S. Fish and Wildlife Service (110 WEBB), Washington, DC 20240.

Common name	Scientific name	Range
Mammals		
Asian wild ass	Equus hemionus	Southwestern & Central Asia
Point Arena mountain beaver	Aplodontia rufa nigra	U.S. (Cal.)
Bobcat	Felis rufus escuinapae	Central Mexico
Ozark big-eared bat	Plecotus townsendii ingens	U.S. (Mo., Okla., Ariz.)
Brown or grizzly bear	Ursus arctos horribilis	U.S. (48 conterminous states)
Cheetah	Acinonyx jubatus	Africa to India
Eastern cougar	Felis concolor couguar	Eastern N.A.
Columbian white-tailed deer	Odocoileus virginianus leucurus	U.S. (Wash., Ore.)
Chinese river dolphin	Lipotes vexillifer	China
Asian elephant	Elephas maximus	Southcentral, Southeast Asia
San Joaquin kit fox	Vulpes macrotis mutica	U.S. (Cal.)
Gorilla	Gorilla gorilla	Central & W Africa
Leopard	Panthera pardus	Africa, Asia
Asiatic lion	Panthera leo persica	Turkey to India
Howler monkey	Alouatta pigra	Mexico to S. America
Salt marsh harvest mouse	Reithrodontomys raviventris	U.S. (Cal.)
Ocelot	Felis pardalis	U.S. (Tex., Ariz.) to C. and S. America
Marine otter	Lutra felina	Peru south to Straits of Magellan
Giant panda	Ailuropoda melanoleuca	China
Florida panther	Felis concolor coryi	U.S. (La., Ark. east to S.C., Fla.)
Lower keys rabbit	Sylvilagus palustris hefneri	U.S. (Fla.)
Black rhinoceros	Diceros bicornis	Sub-Saharan Africa
Stellar sea lion	Eumetopias jubatus	U.S. (Alaska, Cal., Ore., Wash.), N Pacific Ocean
Carolina northern flying squirrel	Glaucomys sabrinus coloratus	U.S. (N.C., Tenn.)
Tiger	Panthera tigris	Asia
Hualapai Mexican vole	Microtus mexicanus hualpaiensis	U.S. (Ariz.)
Gray whale	Eschrichtius robustus	N Pacific Ocean
Red wolf	Canis rufus	U.S. (Southeast to central Tex.)
Wild yak	Bos grunniens	China (Tibet), India
Mountain zebra	Equus zebra zebra	South Africa
Birds		
Masked bobwhite (quail)	Colinus virginianus ridgwayi	U.S. (Ariz.), Mexico (Sonora)
California condor	Gymnogyps californianus	U.S. (Ore., Cal.)
Hooded crane	Grus monacha	Japan, Russia
White-necked crow	Corvus leucognaphalus	U.S. (P.R.), Dominican Rep., Haiti
Eskimo curlew	Numenius borealis	Alaska and N Canada
American peregrine falcon	Falco peregrinus anatum	Canada to Mexico
Hawaiian hawk	Buteo solitarius	U.S. (Hawaii)
Japanese crested ibis	Nipponia nippon	China, Japan, Russia, Korea
Indigo macaw	Anodorhynchus leari	Brazil
West African ostrich	Struthio camelus spatzi	Western Sahara
Golden parakeet	Aratinga guarouba	Brazil
Imperial parrot	Amazona imperialis	West Indies (Dominica)
Attwater's greater prairie-chicken	Tympanuchus cupido attwateri	U.S. (Tex.)
Bachman's warbler (wood)	Vermivora bachmanii	U.S. (Southeast), Cuba
Kirtland's warbler (wood)	Dendroica kirtlandii	U.S., Canada, Bahama Is.
Ivory-billed woodpecker	Campephilus principalis	U.S. (Southcentral and Southeast), Cuba
Reptiles		
American alligator	Alligator mississippiensis	U.S (Southeastern)
American crocodile	Crocodylus acutus	U.S. (Fla.), Mexico, C. and S. America
Leatherback sea turtle	Dermochelys coriacea	Tropical, temperate, and subpolar seas
Plymouth red-bellied turtle	Pseudemys rubiventris bangsi	U.S. (Mass.)
Fishes		
Bonytail chub	Gila elegans	U.S. (Ariz., Cal., Col., Nev., Ut., Wyo.)
Gila trout	Salmo gilae	U.S. (Ariz., N.M.)
Sockeye (red) salmon	Oncorhynchus nerka	N Pacific basin, U.S. to Russia
Plants		
Florida golden aster	Chrysopsis floridana	U.S. (Fla.)
Autumn buttercup	Ranunculus acriformis var aestivalis	U.S. (Ut.)
Bakersfield cactus	Opuntia treleasei	U.S. (Cal.)
Robbins' cinquefoil	Potentilla robbinsiana	U.S. (N.H., Vt.)
Santa Cruz cypress	Cupressus abramsiana	U.S. (Cal.)
Maguire daisy	Erigeron maguirei var maguirei	U.S. (Ut.)
Short's goldenrod	Solidago shortii	U.S. (Ky.)
Mountain golden heather	Hudsonia montana	U.S. (N.C.)
Cooley's meadowrue	Thalictrum cooleyi	U.S. (N.C., Fla.)
Wheeler's peperomia	Peperomia wheeleri	U.S. (P.R.)
Chapman rhododendron	Rhododendron chapmanii	U.S. (Fla.)
Texas wild-rice	Zizania texana	U.S. (Tex.)

U.S. List of Endangered and Threatened Species

Source: Fish and Wildlife Service, U.S. Dept. of Interior; as of Aug. 4, 1994.

	Endangered			Threatened			
Group	**U.S. Only**	**U.S. & Foreign**	**Foreign Only**	**U.S. Only**	**U.S. & Foreign**	**Foreign Only**	**Total Listed Species**
Mammals	36	20	251	5	4	22	338
Birds	57	16	153	8	9	0	243
Reptiles	8	8	63	15	4	14	112
Amphibians	6	0	8	4	1	0	19
Fishes	60	4	11	32	6	0	113
Snails	14	0	1	7	0	0	22
Clams	50	0	2	6	0	0	58
Crustaceans	11	0	0	2	0	0	13
Insects	16	3	4	9	0	0	32
Arachnids	4	0	0	0	0	0	4
Animals, Total	**262**	**51**	**493**	**88**	**24**	**36**	**954**
Plants	**378**	**10**	**1**	**75**	**9**	**2**	**475**
Total	**640**	**61**	**494**	**163**	**33**	**38**	**1,429**

Note: When separate populations of a species are listed as endangered and as threatened, those species are tallied twice. The 10 species so counted are chimpanzee, grizzly bear, leopard, gray wolf, bald eagle, piping plover, roseate tern, Nile crocodile, green sea turtle, and olive ridley sea turtle. In addition, 9 species of lemurs; 9 of gibbons; 2 each of musk deer, sifakas, and uakaris; and 29 to 41 of Oahu tree snails are each counted as 1 species above.

Gestation, Longevity, and Incubation of Animals

Information reviewed and updated as of mid-1994 by Ronald M. Nowak, ed. *Walker's Mammals of the World* (5th ed., Johns Hopkins University Press, 1991). Average longevity figures were supplied by Ronald T. Reuther. They refer to animals in captivity; the potential life span of animals is rarely attained in nature. Figures on gestation and incubation are averages based on estimates by leading authorities.

Animal	**Gestation** (days)	**Average longevity** (years)	**Maximum longevity** (yrs.-mos.)
Ass	365	12	47
Baboon	187	20	45
Bear: Black	219	18	36-10
Grizzly	225	25	50
Polar	240	20	38
Beaver	105	5	50
Bison	285	15	40
Camel (Bactrian)	406	12	50
Cat (domestic)	63	12	28
Chimpanzee	230	20	53
Chipmunk	31	6	8
Cow	284	15	30
Deer (white-tailed)	201	8	20
Dog (domestic)	61	12	20
Elephant (African)	660	35	70
Elephant (Asian)	645	40	77
Elk	250	15	26-8
Fox (red)	52	7	14
Giraffe	425	10	33-7
Goat (domestic)	151	8	18
Gorilla	258	20	54
Guinea pig	68	4	8
Hippopotamus	238	41	54-4
Horse	330	20	50
Kangaroo (gray)	36	7	24
Leopard	98	12	23
Lion	100	15	30
Monkey (rhesus)	166	15	37
Moose	240	12	27
Mouse (meadow)	21	3	4
Mouse (dom. white)	19	3	6
Opossum (American)	13	1	5
Pig (domestic)	112	10	27
Puma	90	12	20
Rabbit (domestic)	31	5	13
Rhinoceros (black)	450	15	45
Rhinoceros (white)	480	20	50
Sea lion (California)	350	12	30
Sheep (domestic)	154	12	20
Squirrel (gray)	44	10	23-6
Tiger	105	16	26-3
Wolf (maned)	63	5	13
Zebra (Grant's)	365	15	50

Incubation time (days)

Chicken	21
Duck	30
Goose	30
Pigeon	18
Turkey	26

Speeds of Animals

Source: Natural History magazine, March 1974. Copyright © The American Museum of Natural History, 1974.

Animal	**Mph**
Cheetah	70
Pronghorn antelope	61
Wildebeest	50
Lion	50
Thomson's gazelle	50
Quarterhorse	47.5
Elk	45
Cape hunting dog	45
Coyote	43
Gray fox	42
Hyena	40
Zebra	40
Mongolian wild ass	40
Greyhound	39.35
Whippet	35.50
Rabbit (domestic)	35
Mule deer	35
Jackal	35
Reindeer	32
Giraffe	32
White-tailed deer	30
Wart hog	30
Grizzly bear	30
Cat (domestic)	30
Human	27.89
Elephant	25
Black mamba snake	20
Six-lined race runner	18
Wild turkey	15
Squirrel	12
Pig (domestic)	11
Chicken	9
Spider (Tegenaria atrica)	1.17
Giant tortoise	0.17
Three-toed sloth	0.15
Garden snail	0.03

Most of these measurements are for maximum speeds over approximate quarter-mile distances. Exceptions are the lion and elephant, whose speeds were clocked in the act of charging; the whippet, which was timed over a 200-yard course; the cheetah, timed over a 100-yard distance; the human, timed for a 15-yard segment of a 100-yard run (of 13.6 seconds); and the black mamba, six-lined race runner, spider, giant tortoise, three-toed sloth, and garden snail, which were measured over various small distances.

Major Venomous Animals

Snakes

Coral snake - 2 to 5 ft. long, in Americas south of Canada; bite may be painless; slow onset of paralysis, impaired breathing; mortalities rare, but high without antivenom and mechanical respiration.

Rattlesnake - 2 to 6 ft. long, throughout W. Hemisphere. Rapid onset of severe pain, swelling; mortality low, but amputation of affected digits is sometimes necessary; antivenom. Mojave rattler may produce temporary paralysis.

Cottonmouth water moccasin - up to 5 ft. long, wetlands of southern U.S. from Virginia to Texas. Rapid onset of severe pain, swelling; mortality low, but tissue destruction can be extensive; antivenom.

Copperhead - less than 4 ft. long, from New England to Texas; pain and swelling; very seldom fatal; antivenom seldom needed.

Bushmaster - up to 12 ft. long, wet tropical forests of C. and S. America; few bites occur, but mortality rate is high.

Barba Amarilla or **Fer-de-lance** - up to 7 ft. long, from tropical Mexico to Brazil; severe tissue damage common; moderate mortality; antivenom.

Asian pit vipers - from 2 to 5 ft. long, throughout Asia; reactions and mortality vary, but most bites cause tissue damage and mortality is generally low.

Sharp-nosed pit viper or **One Hundred Pace Snake** - up to 5 ft. long, in S Vietnam and Taiwan, China; the most toxic of Asian pit vipers; very rapid onset of swelling and tissue damage, internal bleeding; moderate mortality; antivenom.

Boomslang - under 6 ft. long, in African savannahs; rapid onset of nausea and dizziness, often followed by slight recovery and then sudden death from internal hemorrhaging; bites rare, mortality high; antivenom.

European vipers - from 1 to 3 ft. long; bleeding and tissue damage; mortality low; antivenoms.

Puff adder - up to 5 ft. long, fat; south of the Sahara and throughout the Middle East; rapid large swelling, great pain, dizziness; moderate mortality often from internal bleeding; antivenom.

Gaboon viper - over 6 ft. long, fat; 2-inch fangs; south of the Sahara; massive tissue damage, internal bleeding; few recorded bites.

Saw-scaled or carpet viper - up to 2 ft. long, in dry areas from India to Africa; severe bleeding, fever; high mortality, causes more human fatalities than any other snake; antivenom.

Desert horned viper - in dry areas of Africa and western Asia; swelling and tissue damage; low mortality; antivenom.

Russell's viper or **tic-polonga** - over 5 ft. long, throughout Asia; internal bleeding; moderate mortality rate; bite reports common; antivenom.

Black mamba - up to 14 ft. long, fast-moving; S and C Africa; rapid onset of dizziness, difficulty breathing, erratic heart-beat; mortality high, nears 100% without antivenom.

Kraits - up to 5 ft. long, in S Asia; rapid onset of sleepiness; numbness; up to 50% mortality even with antivenom.

Common or Asian cobra - 4 to 8 ft. long, throughout S Asia; considerable tissue damage, sometimes paralysis; mortality probably not more than 10%; antivenom.

King cobra - up to 16 ft. long, throughout S Asia; rapid swelling, dizziness, loss of consciousness, difficulty breathing, erratic heartbeat; mortality varies sharply with amount of venom involved, most bites involve nonfatal amounts; antivenom.

Yellow or Cape cobra - 7 ft. long, in southern Africa; most toxic venom of any cobra; rapid onset of swelling, breathing and cardiac difficulties; mortality high without treatment; antivenom.

Ringhals, or spitting, cobra - 5 ft. and 7 ft. long; S Africa; squirt venom through holes in front of fangs as a defense; venom is severely irritating and can cause blindness.

Australian brown snakes - 4 to 7 ft. long; very slow onset of cardiac or respiratory distress; moderate mortality, but because death can be sudden and unexpected, it is the most dangerous of the Australian snakes; antivenom.

Tiger snake - 2 to 6 ft. long, S Australia; pain, numbness, mental disturbances with rapid onset of paralysis; may be the most deadly of all land snakes though antivenom is quite effective.

Death adder - less than 3 ft. long, Australia; rapid onset of faintness, cardiac and respiratory distress; at least 50% mortality without antivenom.

Taipan - up to 11 ft. long, in Australia and New Guinea; rapid paralysis with severe breathing difficulty; mortality nears 100% without antivenom.

Sea snakes - throughout Pacific, Indian oceans except NE Pacific; almost painless bite, variety of muscle pain, paralysis; mortality rate low, many bites are not envenomed; some antivenoms.

Notes: Not all bites by venomous snakes are actually envenomed. Any animal bite, however, carries the danger of tetanus, and anyone suffering a venomous snake bite should seek medical attention. Antivenoms do not cure; they are only an aid in the treatment of bites. Mortality rates above are for envenomed bites; low mortality, up to 2% result in death; moderate, 2–5%; high, 5–15%.

Lizards

Gila monster - up to 24 inches long with heavy body and tail, in high desert in SW U.S. and N Mexico; immediate severe pain and transient low blood pressure; no recent mortality.

Mexican beaded lizard - similar to Gila monster, Mexican west coast; reaction and mortality rate similar to Gila monster.

Insects

Ants, bees, wasps, hornets, etc. Global distribution. Usual reaction is piercing pain in area of sting. Not directly fatal, except in cases of massive multiple stings. Many people suffer allergic reactions — swelling and rashes — and a few may die within minutes from severe sensitivity to the venom (anaphylactic shock).

Spiders, Scorpions

Black widow - small, round-bodied with red hour-glass marking; the widow and its relatives are found in tropical and temperate zones; severe musculoskeletal pain, weakness, breathing difficulty, convulsions; may be more serious in small children; low mortality; antivenom. The **redback** spider of Australia has the hour-glass marking on its back, rather than on its front, but is otherwise identical to the black widow.

Recluse or fiddleback and brown spiders - small, oblong body; throughout U.S.; pain with later ulceration at place of bite; in severe cases fever, nausea, and stomach cramps; ulceration may last months; very low mortality.

Atrax spiders - also known as funnel whip spiders; several varieties, often large, in Australia; slow onset of breathing, circulation difficulties; low mortality; antivenom.

Tarantulas - large, hairy spiders found around the world; American tarantulas, and probably all others, are **harmless,** though their bite may cause some pain and swelling.

Scorpions - crab-like body with stinger in tail, various sizes, many varieties throughout tropical and subtropical areas; various symptoms may include severe pain spreading from the wound, numbness, severe agitation, cramps; severe reaction may include respiratory failure; low mortality, usually in children; antivenoms.

Sea Life

Sea wasps - jellyfish, with tentacles up to 30 ft., in the S. Pacific; very rapid onset of circulatory problems; high mortality because of speed of toxic reaction; antivenom.

Portuguese man-of-war - jellyfish-like, with tentacles up to 70 ft. long, in most warm water areas; immediate severe pain; not fatal, though shock may cause death in rare cases.

Octopi - global distribution, usually in warm waters; all varieties produce venom but only a few can cause death; rapid onset of paralysis with breathing difficulty.

Stingrays - several varieties of differing sizes, found in tropical and temperate seas and some fresh water; severe pain, rapid onset of nausea, vomiting, breathing difficulties; wound area may ulcerate, gangrene may appear; seldom fatal.

Stonefish - brownish fish that lies motionless as a rock on bottom in shallow water; throughout S. Pacific and Indian oceans; extraordinary pain, rapid paralysis; low mortality; antivenom available, amount determined by number of puncture wounds; warm water relieves pain.

Cone-shells - mollusks in small, beautiful shells in the S Pacific and Indian oceans; shoot barbs into victims; paralysis; low mortality.

Giant Trees of the U.S.

Source: The American Forestry Assn., Washington, D.C.

Approximately 850 native and naturalized species of trees are grown in the U.S. The oldest living thing on earth is believed to be a bristlecone pine tree in California named Methusalah, estimated to be 4,700 years old. The world's largest living thing, the General Sherman sequoia in California, weighs more than 1,400 tons—as much as 9 blue whales or 360 elephants.

The American Forestry Assn. recognizes and lists the National Champion (largest by total mass) of each U. S. tree species. Anyone can nominate candidates for this National Register of Big Trees. For information, write to American Forestry Assn., P.O. Box 2000, Washington, DC 20013.

Major U.S. Public Zoological Parks

Source: World Almanac questionnaire, 1994; budget and attendance in millions.

Zoo	Budget	Attendance	Acres	Species	Major attractions
Arizona-Sonora Desert Museum (Tucson)	$4.7	0.6	30	300	"Living" museum, 90% outdoors, hummingbird aviary *for further information: (602) 883-2702.*
Audubon (New Orleans)	7.8	0.9	58	500	White alligators, Louisiana Swamp, Reptile Encounter *for further information: (504) 861-2537.*
Bronx (N.Y.C.)	24.6	2.0	265	670	Himalayan Highlands, Jungle World, baboon reserve, endangered species *for further information: (718) 367-1010.*
Buffalo	3.2	0.5	23	183	Gorilla Habitat, World of Wildlife Building *for further information: (716) 837-3900.*
Chicago (Brookfield)	27.0	2.0	215	400+	7 Seas Seascape, Tropic World, Africa! *for further information: (708) 485-0263.*
Cincinnati	12.0	1.3	67	761	Gorilla World, white Bengal tigers, Jungle Trails *for further information: (513) 281-4701.*
Cleveland	8.1	1.4	165	564	Rain Forest—600 animals, 7,000 plants *for further information: (216) 661-7511.*
Dallas	6.4	0.4	70	350	25-acre Wilds of Africa with monorail, nature trail, Gorilla Center, major aquarium nearby *for further information: (214) 946-5145.*
Denver	10.0	1.4	80	600	Tropical Discovery, Northern Shores *for further information: (303) 331-4100.*
Detroit	9.0	1.0	125	250	Penguinarium, chimpanzee habitat *for further information: (810) 398-0900.*
Houston	6.6	1.4	55	605	Bird Garden, white tigers, African lion savannah *for further information: (713) 525-3300.*
Lincoln Park (Chicago)	16.0	4.0	35	250	Great Ape House, Bird House, Lion House, Farm-in-the-Zoo *for further information: (312) 294-2492.*
Los Angeles	17.2	1.6	80	400	Koala House, World of Birds, Tiger Falls *for further information: (213) 666-4090.*
Louisville	5.1	0.6	74	395	American wildcat exhibit, Australian Walkabout *for further information: (502) 451-0440.*
Memphis	5.7	0.7	70	445	Cat Country, Primate World, The Forest, aquarium *for further information: (901) 725-3400.*
Miami Metrozoo	7.0	0.8	290	281	Koalas, aviary, cageless exhibits, Asian River Life *for further information: (305) 251-0400.*
Milwaukee	14.0	1.3	200	500	Sea lion exhibit, wolf woods, bear dens *for further information: (414) 256-5414.*
Minnesota	13.7	1.2	500	450	Dolphin shows, World of Birds *for further information: (612) 431-9200.*
National (Wash., DC)	13.0	3.0	163	509	Giant pandas, Komodo dragon lizards, gorillas (zoo has not provided up-to-date information) *for further information: (202) 673-4800.*
Oklahoma City	12.0	0.6	110	500	Dolphin, sea lion shows, Great EscApe, Children's Discovery *for further information: (405) 424-3344.*
Omaha/Henry Doorly Zoo	6.0	1.1	140	462	Indoor rainforest, free-flight aviary, cat complex *for further information: (402) 733-8401.*
Philadelphia	15.0	1.3	42	437	Carnivore Kingdom, white lions, red pandas *for further information: (215) 243-1100.*
Phoenix	8.0	1.0	125	327	Tropical rainforest, Arizona Trail, 200 endangered animals *for further information: (602) 273-1341.*
Gladys Porter (Brownsville, TX)	2.3	0.3	31	392	Free-flight aviary, Herpetarium, 4 geographic areas *for further information: (210) 546-7187.*
Rio Grande (Albuquerque)	4.3	0.6	63	260	Sea lion pool, white Bengal tigers *for further information: (505) 843-7413.*
Riverbanks (Columbia, SC)	4.0	0.9	170	480	Aquarium Reptile Complex, Riverbanks Farm *for further information: (803) 779-8730.*
St. Louis	15.0	2.7	83	665	Living World, Bear Pits, Jungle of the Apes *for further information: (314) 781-0900.*
San Antonio	7.3	1.0	40	700	Australian Walkabout, Amazonia, aquarium *for further information: (210) 734-7184.*
San Diego	56.0	3+	100	800	Tiger River, koalas, Komodo dragons *for further information: (619) 234-3153.*
San Diego (Wild Animal Park)	15.0	1.5	2,100	400+	Mixed-species enclosures, exotic species, monorail with 50-minute, narrated tour *for further information: (619) 234-6541.*
San Francisco	11.0	1.0	140	270	Primate Discovery Center, Koala Crossing, Gorilla World, Penguin Island, Children's Zoo *for further information: (415) 753-7061.*
Toledo	7.8	0.9	30	460	Hippoquarium, African savanna, Kingdon of the Apes *for further information: (419) 385-5721.*
Washington Park (Portland, OR)	18.0	1.2	65	166	Alaska tundra, Penguinarium, African rainforest *for further information: (503) 226-1561.*
Woodland Park (Seattle)	9.2	1.0	92	273	African savanna, gorillas, Asian Elephant Forest *for further information: (206) 684-4800.*

Major Canadian Public Zoological Parks

Source: World Almanac questionnaire, 1994; budget in millions of dollars (Canadian), attendance in millions.

Zoo	Budget	Attendance	Acres	Species	Major attractions
Calgary	NA	0.8	132	316	Canadian Wilds, Prehistoric Park *for further information: (403) 232-9300.*
Granby (Quebec)	5.0	0.4	70	225	Reptile House, Bear Mountain, Big Cats Pavilion *for further information: (514) 372-9113.*
Toronto	9.6	1.2	710	559	Indoor Zoo, South American Waterfall, Underground Zoo *for further information: (416) 392-5900.*
Vancouver Aquarium	5.9 (U.S.)	0.8	2	591	Killer Whale Habitat, beluga whale, Amazon gallery *for further information: (604) 685-3364.*
Winnipeg	2.5	0.5	59	250	Rare colder climate animals *for further information: (204) 986-6920.*

Top 50 American Kennel Club Registrations

Source: American Kennel Club, New York, NY; dogs registered Jan. 1, 1993, to Dec. 31, 1993.

Breed	Rank	Number Regis-tered 1993	Rank	Number Regis-tered 1992	Breed	Rank	Number Regis-tered 1993	Rank	Number Regis-tered 1992
Labrador Retrievers	1	124,899	1	120,879	Pekingese	26	16,869	23	18,218
Rottweilers	2	104,160	2	95,445	Collies	27	15,952	26	17,081
Geman Shepherd Dogs	3	79,936	4	76,941	Pugs	28	15,722	27	16,008
Cocker Spaniels	4	75,882	3	91,925	Miniature Pinschers	29	14,987	30	13,353
Golden Retrievers	5	68,125	6	69,850	German Shorthaired Pointers	30	13,931	29	13,737
Poodles	6	67,850	5	73,449	Brittanys	31	13,635	28	14,901
Beagles	7	61,051	7	60,661	Bichons Frises	32	12,120	31	12,172
Dachshunds	8	48,573	8	50,046	Bulldogs	33	12,105	32	12,046
Dalmatians	9	42,816	15	38,927	Akitas	34	11,574	33	11,383
Shetland Sheepdogs	10	41,113	9	43,449	Great Danes	35	10,929	34	11,067
Pomeranians	11	40,805	12	42,488	West Highland White Terriers	36	9,459	35	10,015
Yorkshire Terriers	12	39,827	14	39,904	Scottish Terriers	37	6,724	36	7,914
Shih Tzu	13	39,773	11	42,561	Pembroke Welsh Corgis	38	6,707	38	6,501
Miniature Schnauzers	14	37,267	13	41,058	Samoyeds	39	6,172	37	7,267
Chow Chows	15	33,824	10	42,670	Saint Bernards	40	5,595	43	4,863
Chihuahuas	16	32,435	16	31,301	Weimaraners	41	5,590	44	4,758
Boxers	17	30,757	17	30,123	Alaskan Malamutes	42	5,451	41	5,644
Siberian Huskies	18	25,565	18	26,057	Cairn Terriers	43	5,386	40	6,141
Doberman Pinschers	19	21,469	20	22,113	Australian Shepherds	44	5,364	53	2,767
English Springer Spaniels	20	19,989	19	22,183	Chesapeake Bay Retrievers	45	5,361	42	5,295
Basset Hounds	21	19,982	21	21,137	Keeshonden	46	5,125	39	6,177
Chinese Shar-Pei	22	19,465	NR*	90,081	Great Pyrenees	47	4,005	46	3,776
Maltese	23	17,491	24	17,615	Airedale Terriers	48	3,889	45	4,236
Lhasa Apsos	24	17,124	22	20,616	Mastiffs	49	3,567	48	3,294
Boston Terriers	25	17,091	25	17,271	Schipperkes	50	3,519	47	3,752

* Breed recognized by AKC only as of 1992; will not be officially ranked for first time until 1993.

Cat Breeds

Source: Cat Fanciers' Assn., Manasquan, NJ

Only a small percentage of house cats in the U.S. are pedigreed, or registered with one of the official registering bodies, the largest of which is the Cat Fanciers' Assn., sponsor of more than 600 clubs. The Cat Fanciers' Assn. recognized 37 breeds as of mid-1994 (in order of registration totals): Persian, Maine Coon Cat, Siamese, Abyssinian, Exotic, Scottish Fold, Oriental Shorthair, American Shorthair, Birman, Burmese, Cornish Rex, Tonkinese, Ocicat, Manx (includes Cymric), Somali, Devon Rex, Russian Blue, Colorpoint Shorthair, British Shorthair, Japanese Bobtail, Ragdoll, Balinese, Egyptian Mau, Norwegian Forest Cat, Chartreux, American Curl, Javanese, Turkish Angora, Korat, Bombay, Singapura, Havana Brown, American Wirehair, Turkish Van, Oriental Longhair, Selkirk Rex, and European Burmese.

Classification

Source: Funk & Wagnalls New Encyclopedia.

In biology, classification is the identification, naming, and grouping of organisms into a formal system. The two fields that are most directly concerned with classification are taxonomy and systematics. Although the two disciplines overlap considerably, taxonomy is more concerned with nomenclature (naming) and with constructing hierarchical systems, and systematics with uncovering evolutionary relationships. Two kingdoms of living forms, Plantae and Animalia, have been recognized since Aristotle established the first taxonomy in the 4th century BC. In addition, there are the following 3 kingdoms: Protista (one-celled organisms), Monera (bacteria and blue-green algae), also known as the kingdom Procaryotae, and Fungi. The 7 basic categories of classification (from most general to most specific) are: kingdom, phylum (division), class, order, family, genus, and species. Below are 2 examples:

Zoological hierarchy

Kingdom	Phylum	Class	Order	Family	Genus	Species Name	Common name
Animalia	Chordata	Mammalia	Primates	Hominidae	Homo	Homo sapiens	Human

Botanical hierarchy

Kingdom	Division*	Class	Order	Family	Genus	Species Name	Common name
Plantae	Magnoliophyta	Magnoliopsida	Magnoliales	Magnoliaceae	Magnolia	M. virginiana	Sweet Bay

* In botany, the division is generally used in place of phylum.

How Much Water Is Used...?

Source: American Water Works Assn.

Total freshwater withdrawals for all offstream uses in the U.S. were estimated to be 339 billion gallons per day during 1990, about the same as during 1985. Offstream use is defined as water withdrawn or diverted from a ground- or surface-water source for public water supply; domestic, commercial, or industrial use; irrigation; livestock; mining; and thermoelectric power.

Total water withdrawals in 1990 from lakes, reservoirs, streams, wells, and springs were estimated at 408 billion gallons per day, including 69 billion gallons per day of salt water.

The following are some answers to the question "How much water is used...?"

1. In the average residence during a year? **110,000**
2. By an average person daily? **123 gallons**
3. To flush a non low-flow toilet? **5-7 gallons**
4. To take a shower? **15-30 gallons**
5. To brush your teeth (water running)? **1-2 gallons**
6. To shave (water running)? **10-15 gallons**
7. To wash dishes by hand? **20 gallons**
8. To run a dishwasher? **9-12 gallons**
9. To manufacture a new car? **39,090 gallons**
10. To refine one barrel of crude oil? **1,851 gallons**

1994 IN PICTURES

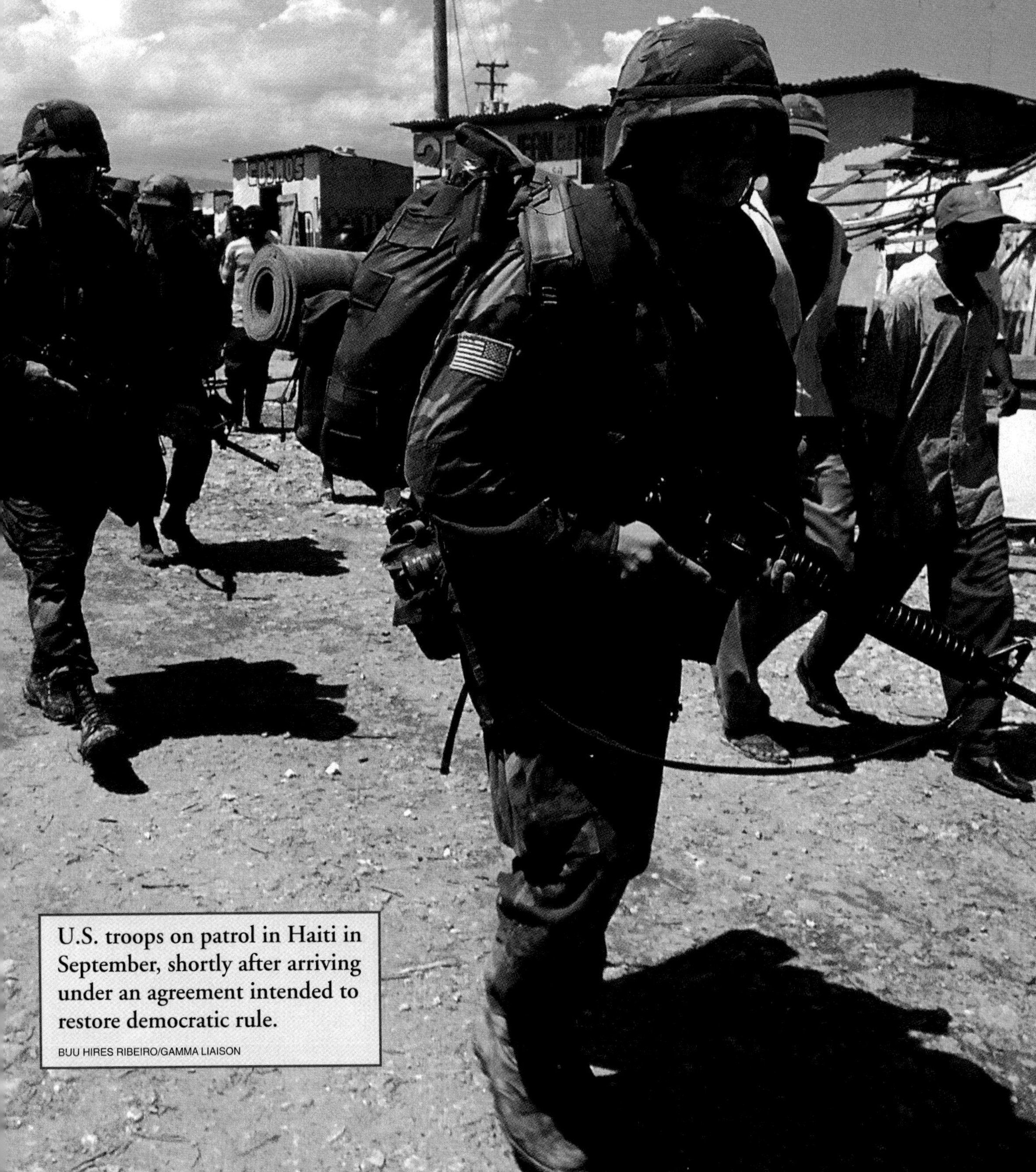

U.S. troops on patrol in Haiti in September, shortly after arriving under an agreement intended to restore democratic rule.

BUU HIRES RIBEIRO/GAMMA LIAISON

National Scene

Members of Congress look over a "Street Sweeper" on Capitol Hill. Congress passed an assault weapons ban in August, as part of a major anticrime bill.

AP/WIDE WORLD PHOTOS

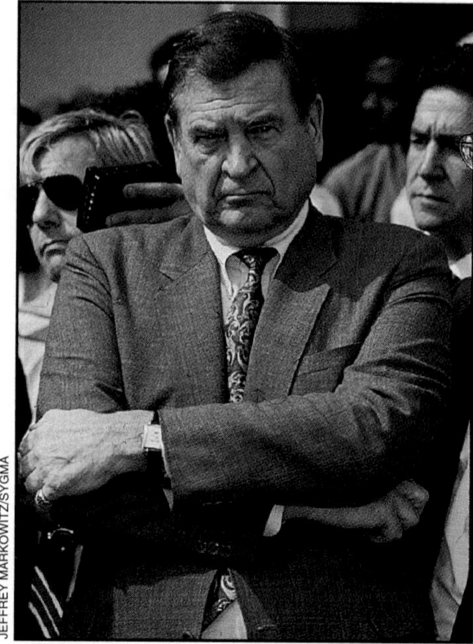

JEFFREY MARKOWITZ/SYGMA

Representative Dan Rostenkowski was forced to resign his powerful committee chairmanship after being indicted in May for alleged misuse of federal funds.

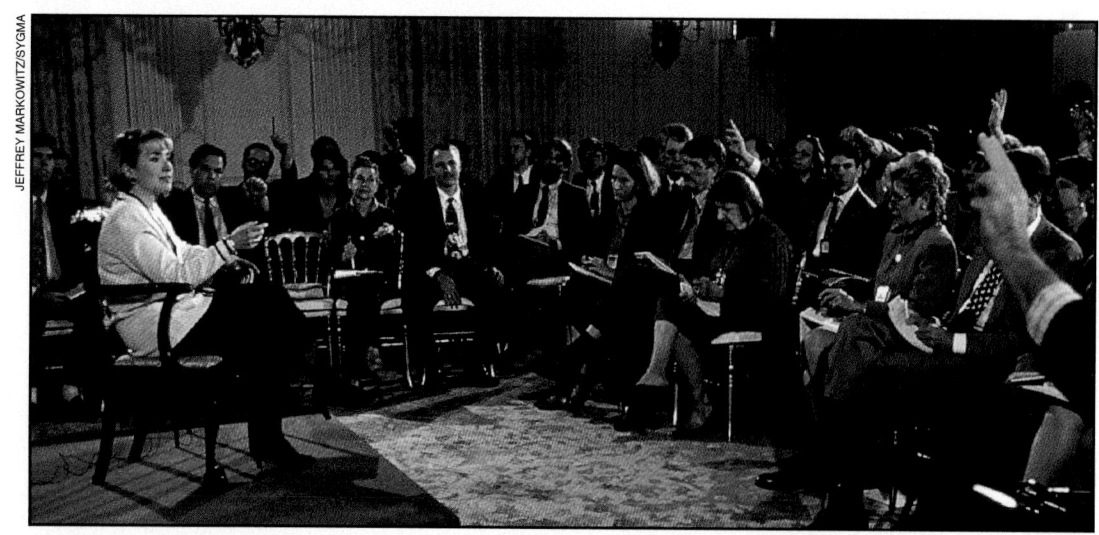

JEFFREY MARKOWITZ/SYGMA

In April, at her first press conference as first lady, Hillary Rodham Clinton answers questions about the Clintons' involvement in the Whitewater affair.

GIBOUX/GAMMA LIAISON; INSET TED SOQUI/SYGMA

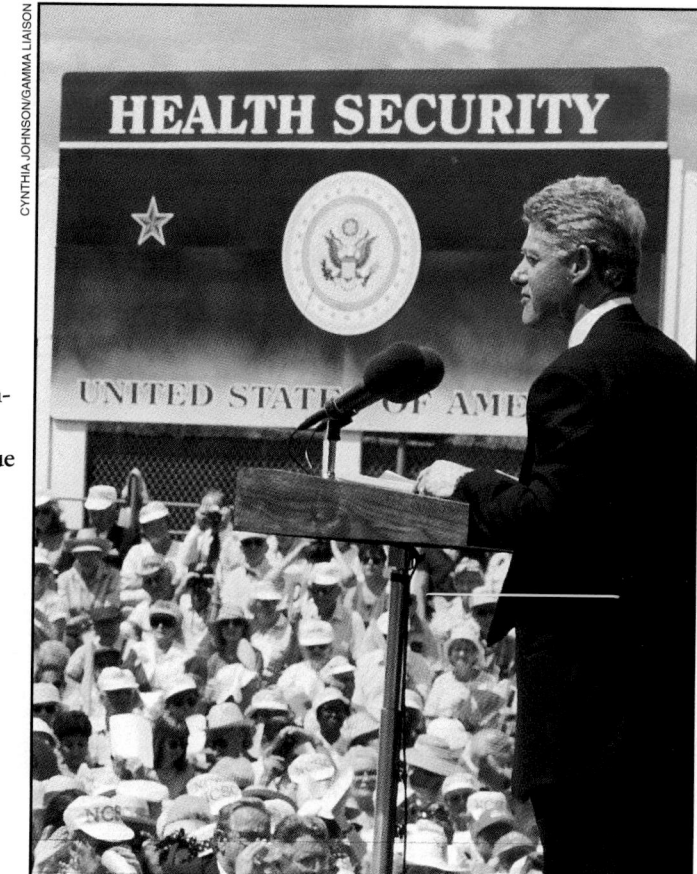

Ex-football great O. J. Simpson led police on a chase in a white Ford Bronco, before being arrested and charged with murdering his ex-wife and a male friend of hers. (Inset, Simpson with lawyer Robert Shapiro.)

CYNTHIA JOHNSON/GAMMA LIAISON

President Clinton presses for health-care reform, his primary domestic initiative for 1994. Though the issue was hotly debated in Congress and in the nation, no major legislation was enacted.

NATIONAL SCENE

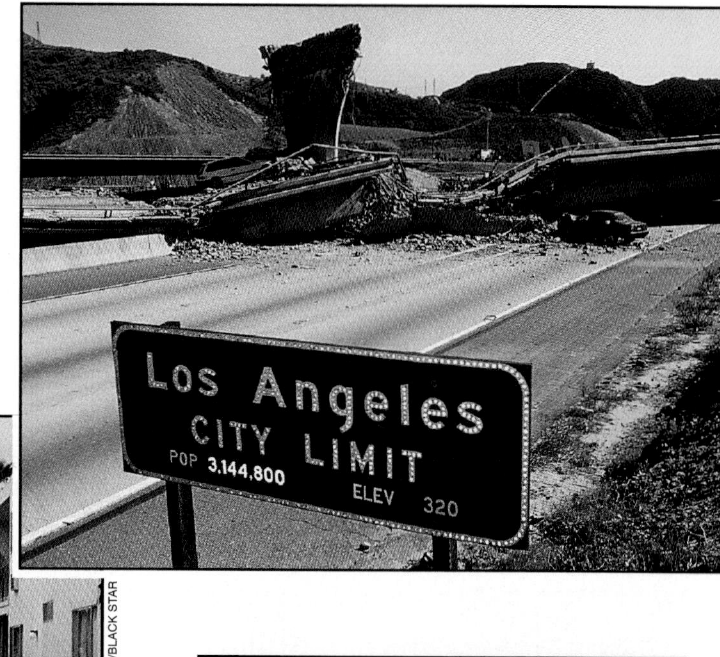

A powerful earthquake hit the Los Angeles area January 17, killing 61 people and causing heavy damage, as illustrated by the collapsed roadway at right and the row of smashed cars below.

BOTH PHOTOS, C. DAVID BUTOW/BLACK STAR

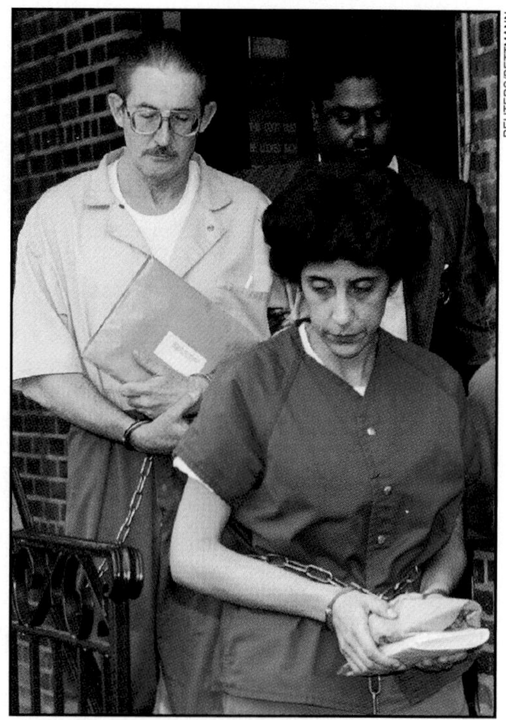

REUTERS/BETTMANN

CIA official Aldrich Ames and his wife, Rosario, pleaded guilty in April to selling secrets to the Soviet Union and Russia.

ELECTION '94

The Virginia Senate candidates debate on *Larry King Live:* (left to right) incumbent Charles Robb (D); ex-governor L. Douglas Wilder (I), who dropped out of the race in mid-September; Marshall Coleman (I); and Iran-contra figure Oliver North (R).

AP/WIDE WORLD PHOTOS

In California, incumbent Pete Wilson (R) and State Treasurer Kathleen Brown (D), the daughter and sister of former California governors, fought a high-cost, closely watched race for governor of the nation's largest state.

AP/WIDE WORLD PHOTOS

REUTERS/BETTMANN

Science and Technology

Queen Elizabeth II and French President François Mitterrand at the official inauguration of the Channel Tunnel, May 6 in Calais, France. Behind them is a huge tunnel-boring machine.

THIERRY ORBAN/SYGMA

NASA

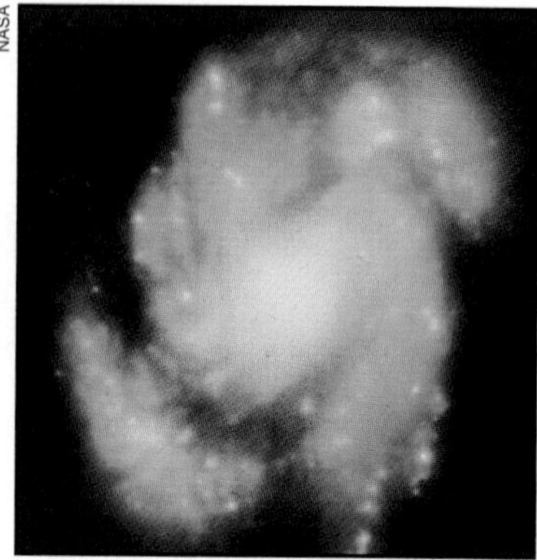

Very different photos of a remote galaxy, taken by the Hubble Space Telescope before (top) and after it was repaired by astronauts.

NASA

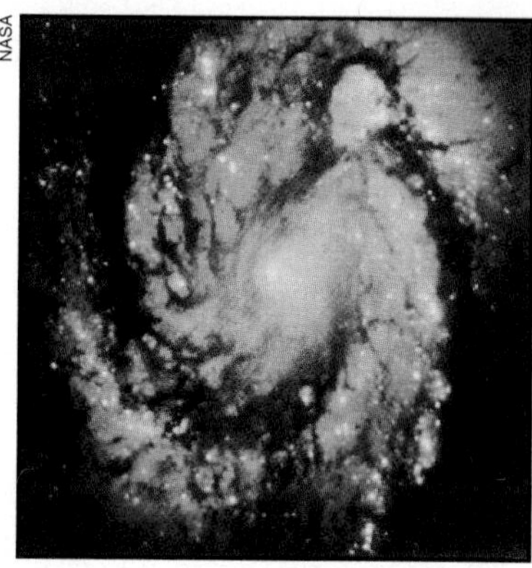

PHIL HUMNICKY/THE WHITE HOUSE

Vice President Al Gore, Jr., in January, holds the first White House electronic news conference, responding via computer and modem to questioners from around the world.

Remembering D-Day

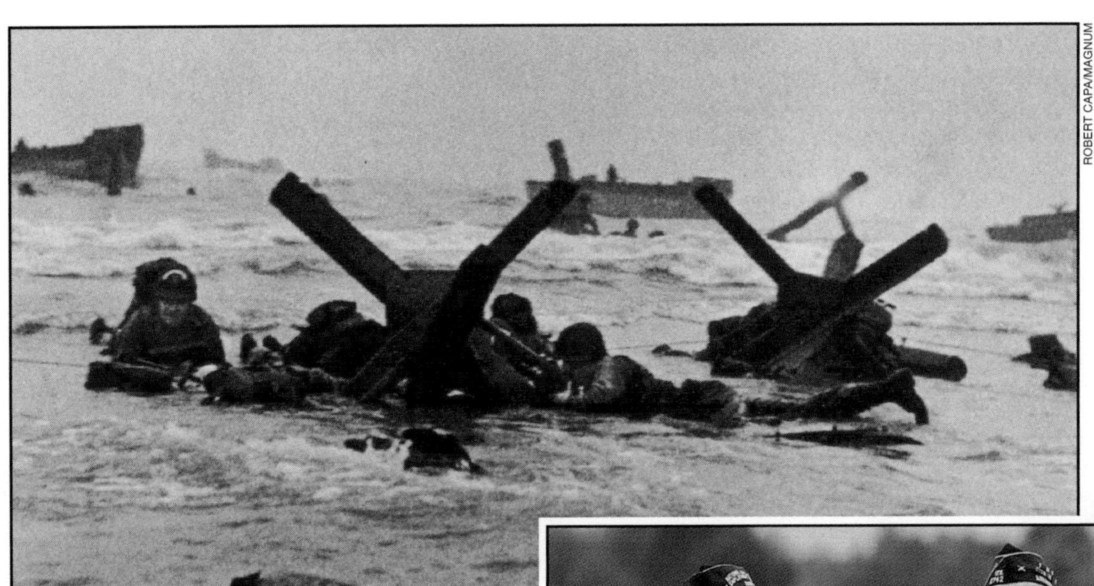

ROBERT CAPA/MAGNUM

Fifty years after the Allied invasion of Normandy on June 6, 1944 (above, a photo of the landing on Omaha Beach), veterans (right) and other visitors returned to pay tribute to those who fell in combat and are buried there (below).

LEFT, AP/WDE WORLD PHOTOS;
ABOVE, © 1994 PETER TURNLEY/NEWSWEEK/BLACK STAR

TRANSITIONS

The death of Richard Nixon on April 22 revived contrasting memories. At right, President Nixon, with his wife, Pat, visits the Great Wall of China. Below, after resigning because of Watergate, he takes leave of the American people, August 9, 1974.

AP/WIDE WORLD PHOTOS

DENNIS BRACK/BLACK STAR

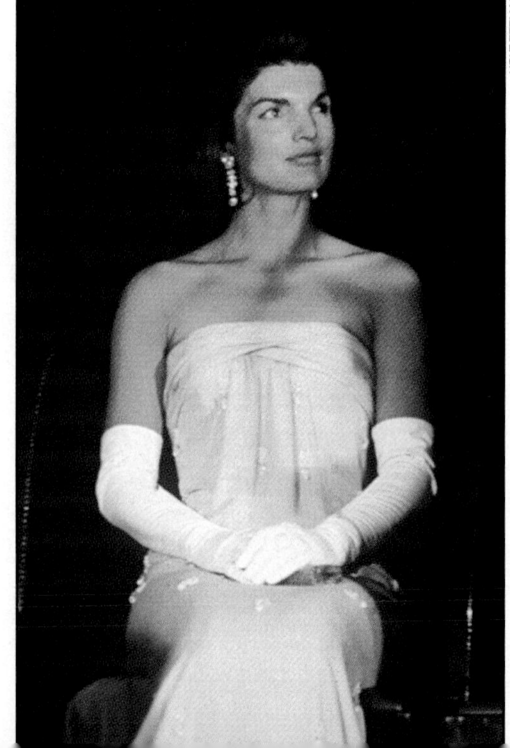

UPI/BETTMANN

On May 19, Jacqueline Kennedy Onassis, widow of President John F. Kennedy and one of the nation's most elegant and admired first ladies, died at the age of 64.

Photos continue on page 777

TRADE AND TRANSPORTATION

U.S. Trade With Leading Countries and Areas, 1993

Source: Office of Trade and Economic Analysis, U.S. Dept. of Commerce
(millions of dollars, not seasonally adjusted)

Country/Area	Trade balance	Rank	Exports	Rank	Imports	Rank
Total	**$-115,568.4**	**(X)**	**$465,091.0**	**(X)**	**$580,659.4**	**(X)**
Japan	-59,354.9	1	47,891.5	2	102,246.4	2
China	-22,777.1	2	8,762.8	13	31,539.9	4
Canada	-10,772.1	3	100,444.3	1	111,216.4	1
Germany	-9,629.9	4	18,932.2	5	28,562.1	5
Taiwan	-8,933.7	5	16,167.8	6	25,101.5	6
Italy	-6,751.9	6	6,463.8	17	13,215.6	10
Thailand	-4,775.4	7	3,766.2	24	8,541.5	14
Malaysia	-4,498.6	8	6,064.4	18	10,563.0	12
Nigeria	-4,406.7	9	894.7	52	5,301.4	21
Venezuela	-3,549.7	10	4,590.2	20	8,139.8	15
Indonesia	-2,665.1	11	2,770.3	30	5,435.4	20
Korea	-2,336.0	12	14,782.0	7	17,118.0	8
Sweden	-2,180.0	13	2,353.7	34	4,533.7	25
France	-2,012.5	14	13,266.8	8	15,279.3	9
Angola	-1,918.4	15	173.8	86	2,092.2	32
India	-1,775.6	16	2,778.1	29	4,553.7	24
Brazil	-1,420.8	17	6,058.0	19	7,478.8	17
Philippines	-1,364.4	18	3,529.2	25	4,893.6	23
Singapore	-1,120.2	19	11,678.0	10	12,798.2	11
Saudi Arabia	-1,046.6	20	6,661.2	16	7,707.8	16
Gabon	-912.8	21	48.2	123	961.0	49
Kuwait	-819.0	22	999.4	48	1,818.5	35
Sri Lanka	-798.5	23	203.2	84	1,001.7	48
Finland	-760.7	24	847.6	55	1,608.3	38
Norway	-745.1	25	1,212.4	42	1,957.5	33
North America	-9,108.4	(X)	142,025.4	(X)	151,133.8	(X)
Western Europe	-1,876.0	(X)	113,680.6	(X)	115,556.7	(X)
European Community (EC)	-967.2	(X)	96,973.4	(X)	97,940.6	(X)
European Free Trade Association	-3,112.1	(X)	12,703.8	(X)	15,815.9	(X)
Eastern Europe	2,578.4	(X)	6,104.2	(X)	3,525.7	(X)
Former Soviet Republics	1,889.7	(X)	3,983.8	(X)	2,094.2	(X)
Organization for Economic Cooperation & Development (OECD) in Europe	-1,856.3	(X)	113,114.1	(X)	114,970.3	(X)
Pacific Rim Countries	-97,956.6	(X)	131,595.4	(X)	229,551.9	(X)
Asia—Near East	1,433.8	(X)	16,820.9	(X)	15,387.1	(X)
Asia—(NICS)	-12,070.5	(X)	52,501.6	(X)	64,572.2	(X)
Asia—South	-3,370.1	(X)	4,062.8	(X)	7,432.9	(X)
Assn. of Southeast Asian Nations (ASEAN)	-13,981.4	(X)	28,280.6	(X)	42,262.0	(X)
South/Central America	2,385.6	(X)	36,841.9	(X)	34,456.3	(X)
Twenty Latin American Republics	2,281.7	(X)	73,547.8	(X)	71,266.1	(X)
Central American Common Market	511.0	(X)	4,777.0	(X)	4,265.9	(X)
Latin American Free Trade Association (LAFTA)	1,108.1	(X)	65,002.7	(X)	63,894.5	(X)
Organization of Petroleum Exporting Countries (OPEC)	-12,239.6	(X)	19,499.5	(X)	31,739.2	(X)
Unidentified[1]	343.8	(X)	343.8	(X)	(X)	(X)

(1) The export totals reflect shipments of certain grains, oilseeds, and satellites that are not included in the country/area totals. (X) Not applicable. **Note:** Details may not equal totals due to rounding.

Definitions of areas:

North America - Canada, Mexico.
Western Europe - Andorra, Austria, Belgium, Bosnia and Herzegovina, Croatia, Cyprus, Denmark, Finland, France, Germany, Greece, Iceland, Ireland, Italy, Liechtenstein, Luxembourg, Macedonia, Malta and Gozo, Monaco, Netherlands, Norway, Portugal, San Marino, Slovenia, Spain, Sweden, Switzerland, Turkey, United Kingdom, Vatican City, Yugoslavia.
European Community - Belgium, Denmark, France, Germany, Greece, Ireland, Italy, Luxembourg, Netherlands, Portugal, Spain, United Kingdom.
European Free Trade Association - Austria, Finland, Iceland, Liechtenstein, Norway, Sweden, Switzerland.
Eastern Europe - Albania, Armenia, Azerbaijan, Belarus, Bulgaria, Czech Republic, Estonia, Georgia, Hungary, Kazakhstan, Kyrgyzstan, Latvia, Lithuania, Moldova, Poland, Romania, Russia, Slovakia, Tajikistan, Turkmenistan, Ukraine, Uzbekistan.
Former Soviet Republics - Armenia, Azerbaijan, Belarus, Estonia, Georgia, Kazakhstan, Kyrgyzstan, Latvia, Lithuania, Moldova, Russia, Tajikistan, Turkmenistan, Ukraine, Uzbekistan.
OECD - Austria, Belgium, Denmark, Finland, France, Germany, Greece, Iceland, Ireland, Italy, Liechtenstein, Luxembourg, Monaco, Netherlands, Norway, Portugal, San Marino, Spain, Sweden, Switzerland, Turkey, United Kingdom.
Pacific Rim Countries - Australia, Brunei, China, Hong Kong, Indonesia, Japan, South Korea, Macao, Malaysia, New Zealand, Papua New Guinea, Philippines, Singapore, Taiwan.
Asia Near East - Bahrain, Iran, Iraq, Israel, Jordan, Kuwait, Lebanon, Oman, Qatar, Saudi Arabia, Syria, United Arab Emirates, Yemen.
Asia NICS - Hong Kong, South Korea, Singapore, Taiwan.
Asia South - Afghanistan, Bangladesh, India, Nepal, Pakistan, Sri Lanka.
ASEAN - Brunei, Indonesia, Malaysia, Philippines, Singapore, Thailand.
South/Central America - Anguilla, Antigua and Barbuda, Argentina, Aruba, Bahamas, Barbados, Belize, Bermuda, Bolivia, Brazil, British Virgin Islands, Cayman Islands, Chile, Colombia, Costa Rica, Cuba, Dominica, Dominican Republic, Ecuador, El Salvador, Falkland Islands, French Guiana, Grenada, Guadeloupe, Guatemala, Guyana, Haiti, Honduras, Jamaica, Martinique, Montserrat, Netherlands Antilles, Nicaragua, Panama, Paraguay, Peru, St. Kitts and Nevis, St. Lucia, St. Vincent and the Grenadines, Suriname, Trinidad and Tobago, Turks and Caicos Islands, Uruguay, Venezuela.
Twenty Latin American Republics - Argentina, Bolivia, Brazil, Chile, Colombia, Costa Rica, Cuba, Dominican Republic, Ecuador, El Salvador, Guatemala, Haiti, Honduras, Mexico, Nicaragua, Panama, Paraguay, Peru, Uruguay, Venezuela.
Central American Common Market - Costa Rica, El Salvador, Guatemala, Honduras, Nicaragua.
LAFTA - Argentina, Bolivia, Brazil, Chile, Colombia, Ecuador, Mexico, Paraguay, Peru, Uruguay, Venezuela.
OPEC - Algeria, Gabon, Indonesia, Iran, Iraq, Kuwait, Libya, Nigeria, Qatar, Saudi Arabia, United Arab Emirates, Venezuela.

U.S. Exports and Imports by Principal Commodity Groupings, 1993

Source: Office of Trade and Economic Analysis, U.S. Dept. of Commerce
(millions of dollars, not seasonally adjusted, current dollar basis)

Item	Exports	Imports
Total	**$465,091.0**	**$580,659.4**
Agricultural commodities	**41,938.3**	**23,640.6**
Animal feeds	3,463.6	367.5
Bulbs	106.7	216.7
Cereal flour	1,098.5	801.9
Cocoa	39.0	738.6
Coffee	31.6	1,382.7
Corn	4,504.1	60.7
Cotton, raw and linters	1,574.8	12.4
Dairy products; eggs	820.0	544.4
Fur skins, raw	97.6	59.0
Grains, unmilled	683.0	156.6
Hides and skins	1,186.6	119.3
Live animals	519.0	1,535.9
Meat and preparations	4,353.3	2,791.8
Oils/fats, animal	472.5	21.2
Oils/fats, vegetable	733.8	859.2
Plants	111.8	91.8
Rice	791.2	106.3
Seeds	294.0	153.7
Soybeans	4,580.2	22.2
Sugar	1.6	605.5
Tobacco, unmanufactured	1,299.5	942.2
Vegetables and fruit	6,007.9	5,665.5
Wheat	4,678.9	213.3
Other agricultural	4,489.0	6,172.1
Manufactured goods	**364,848.7**	**479,897.6**
ADP equipment; office mach.	21,176.7	43,192.8
Airplanes	21,270.4	3,805.5
Airplane parts	9,486.7	2,613.3
Aluminum	2,309.8	3,277.0
Artwork/antiques	951.5	2,673.0
Basketware, etc.	1,644.0	2,391.5
Chemicals - cosmetics	3,047.3	1,808.4
Chemicals - dyeing	2,014.1	1,699.6
Chemicals - fertilizers	1,798.5	1,135.9
Chemicals - inorganic	3,810.4	3,284.4
Chemicals - medicinal	5,750.5	4,134.8
Chemicals - organic	11,075.7	9,279.4
Chemicals - plastics	10,743.5	4,848.0
Chemicals - other	6,835.3	2,941.4
Clothing	4,814.5	33,779.7
Copper	1,200.4	1,733.3
Electrical machinery	36,817.3	46,735.3
Footwear	604.9	11,172.7
Furniture and parts	2,947.9	6,249.0
Gem diamonds	152.9	5,102.6
General industrial mach.	19,515.4	17,082.1
Glass	1,340.7	1,004.2
Glassware	501.5	1,031.5
Gold, nonmonetary	9,115.1	2,014.3
Iron and steel mill products	3,330.3	9,027.1
Lighting, plumbing	$1,096.5	$1,762.1
Metal manufactures	5,975.5	7,646.7
Metalworking machinery	3,255.7	3,683.2
Motorcycles, bicycles	1,433.2	2,160.6
Nickel	199.2	685.9
Optical goods	797.1	1,682.6
Paper and paperboard	6,463.0	8,640.0
Photographic equipment	2,932.4	4,266.8
Plastic articles	2,988.0	3,936.8
Platinum	339.4	1,255.4
Pottery	110.3	1,436.3
Power generating mach.	19,166.5	17,125.1
Printed materials	3,994.7	2,026.0
Records/magnetic media	5,316.9	3,442.7
Rubber articles	678.8	1,013.8
Rubber tires and tubes	1,465.0	2,736.4
Scientific instruments	15,222.9	8,457.1
Ships, boats	975.6	968.6
Silver and bullion	203.0	390.5
Spacecraft	392.9	0.2
Specialized ind. mach.	17,625.7	13,564.6
Telecommunications equip.	13,122.0	27,297.4
Textile yarn, fabric	5,894.6	8,438.3
Toys/games/sporting goods	2,706.8	11,636.9
Travel goods	199.5	2,652.9
Vehicles/new cars - Canada	6,350.1	17,653.9
Vehicles/new cars - Japan	981.9	21,581.2
Vehicles/new cars - other	4,914.2	12,022.5
Vehicles/trucks	4,144.3	10,109.0
Vehicles/chassis/bodies	369.7	406.3
Vehicles/parts	19,307.1	17,653.2
Watches/clocks/parts	236.0	2,545.9
Wood manufactures	1,475.3	2,869.4
Zinc	39.6	735.6
Other manufactured goods	26,220.1	35,397.0
Mineral fuel	**9,756.0**	**55,899.8**
Coal	3,197.4	513.8
Crude oil	20.1	38,469.4
Petroleum preparations	3,919.7	10,789.4
Liquefied propane/butane	228.7	951.5
Natural gas	241.3	3,677.7
Electricity	102.4	661.9
Other mineral fuels	2,046.5	836.1
Selected commodities:		
Fish and preparations	2,991.3	5,820.3
Cork, wood, lumber	5,785.5	5,633.4
Pulp and waste paper	2,978.0	1,886.2
Metal ores; scrap	3,227.3	3,030.2
Crude fertilizers	1,345.0	935.9
Cigarettes	3,918.6	491.0
Alcoholic bev., distilled	342.7	1,737.1
All other	**2,715.9**	**1,687.4**

Note: Details may not equal totals due to rounding.

U.S. Exports, Imports, and Merchandise Trade Balance, 1950-93

Source: Office of Trade and Economic Analysis, U.S. Dept. of Commerce
(millions of dollars)

	Principal Census trade totals					Other Census totals		
Year	U.S. exports and reexports excluding military grant-aid	U.S. general imports f.a.s. transaction values[1]	U.S. merchandise balance f.a.s.[1]	U.S. general imports c.i.f.	U.S. balance exports f.a.s. imports c.i.f.	Military grant-aid shipments	Exports of domestic merchandise	Re-exports
1950	$9,997	$8,954	$1,043	$ —	$ —	$282	$10,146	$133
1955	14,298	11,566	2,732	—	—	1,256	15,426	128
1960	19,659	15,073	4,586	—	—	949	20,408	201
1965	26,742	21,520	5,222	—	—	779	27,178	343
1970	42,681	40,356	2,325	42,833	−152	565	42,612	634
1975	107,652	98,503	9,149	105,935	1,716	461	106,622	1,490
1980	220,626	244,871	−24,245	256,984	−36,358	156	216,668	4,115
1985	213,133	345,276[2]	−132,143	361,626	−148,493	13	206,925	6,221
1990	394,030	495,042[2]	−101,012	516,987	−122,957	15	375,606	18,439
1991	421,730	485,453[2]	−66,723	508,363	−86,633	NA	401,109	20,621
1992	448,164	532,665[2]	−84,501	554,023	−105,859	NA	425,737	22,427
1993	465,091	580,659	−115,568	603,583	−138,492	NA	439,847	25,244

Note: Export values include both commercially financed shipments and shipments under government-financed programs such as AID and PL-480. (1) Prior to 1974, imports are customs values, i.e., generally at prices in principal foreign markets. (2) In 1981 import value changes back to customs value. NA=not available.

New Passenger Cars Imported Into the U.S., by Country of Origin,[1] 1964-90

Source: Bureau of the Census, U.S. Dept. of Commerce

	Japan	West Germany	Italy	United Kingdom	Sweden	France	South Korea	Mexico	Canada	Total[2]
1964 ..	16,023	364,683	10,843	77,548	18,562	39,532	N.A.	N.A.	9,201	536,725
1965 ..	25,538	376,950	9,509	66,565	26,010	24,941	N.A.	N.A.	33,378	563,673
1966 ..	56,050	527,137	14,110	81,870	34,632	33,122	N.A.	N.A.	152,333	899,895
1967 ..	70,304	472,360	16,928	67,928	43,371	25,454	N.A.	N.A.	323,638	1,020,618
1968 ..	169,849	707,972	33,843	96,787	52,515	39,551	N.A.	N.A.	500,881	1,620,452
1969 ..	260,005	642,157	41,569	104,050	41,008	24,457	N.A.	N.A.	691,146	1,846,717
1970 ..	381,338	674,945	42,523	76,257	57,844	37,114	N.A.	N.A.	692,783	2,013,420
1971 ..	703,672	770,807	51,469	106,710	61,925	23,316	N.A.	0	802,281	2,587,484
1972 ..	697,788	676,967	64,614	72,038	64,541	14,713	N.A.	9	842,300	2,485,901
1973 ..	624,805	677,465	56,102	64,140	58,626	8,219	N.A.	4,469	871,557	2,437,345
1974 ..	791,791	619,757	107,071	72,512	60,817	21,331	N.A.	3,914	817,559	2,572,557
1975 ..	695,573	370,012	102,344	67,106	51,993	15,647	N.A.	0	733,766	2,074,653
1976 ..	1,128,936	349,804	82,500	77,190	37,466	21,916	N.A.	0	825,590	2,536,749
1977 ..	1,341,530	423,492	55,437	56,889	39,370	19,215	N.A.	N.A.	849,814	2,790,144
1978 ..	1,563,047	416,231	69,689	54,478	56,140	28,502	N.A.	6	833,061	3,024,982
1979 ..	1,617,328	495,565	72,456	46,911	65,907	27,887	N.A.	4	677,008	3,005,523
1980 ..	1,991,502	338,711	46,899	32,517	61,496	47,386	N.A.	1	594,770	3,116,448
1981 ..	1,911,525	234,052	21,635	12,728	68,042	42,477	N.A.	1	563,943	2,856,286
1982 ..	1,801,185	259,385	9,402	13,023	89,231	50,032	N.A.	27	702,495	2,926,407
1983 ..	1,871,192	239,807	5,442	17,261	114,726	40,823	N.A.	2	835,665	3,133,836
1984 ..	1,948,714	335,032	8,582	19,833	114,854	37,788	N.A.	N.A.	1,073,425	3,559,427
1985 ..	2,527,467	473,110	8,689	24,474	142,640	42,882	N.A.	13,647	1,144,805	4,397,679
1986 ..	2,618,711	451,699	11,829	27,506	148,700	10,869	169,309	41,983	1,162,226	4,691,297
1987 ..	2,417,509	377,542	8,648	50,059	138,565	26,707	399,856	126,266	926,927	4,589,010
1988 ..	2,123,051	264,249	6,053	31,636	108,006	15,990	455,741	148,065	1,191,357	4,450,213
1989 ..	2,051,525	216,881	9,319	29,378	101,571	4,885	270,609	133,049	1,151,122	4,042,728
1990 ..	1,867,794	245,286	11,045	27,271	93,084	1,976	201,475	215,986	1,220,221	3,944,602

(1) Excludes passenger cars assembled in U.S. foreign trade zones. (2) Includes countries not shown separately.

50 Busiest U.S. Ports, 1992

Source: Corps of Engineers, Dept. of the Army, U.S. Dept. of Defense

(ports ranked by tonnage handled, all figures in tons)

Rank	Port	Total	Domestic	Foreign	Imports	Exports
1	South Louisiana, LA, Port of	199,665,010	104,751,527	94,913,483	28,236,107	66,677,376
2	Houston, TX	137,663,612	64,879,273	72,784,339	45,959,450	26,824,889
3	New York, NY and NJ	115,310,756	74,741,170	40,569,586	33,042,416	7,527,170
4	Valdez, AK	93,736,659	93,721,497	15,162	13,051	2,111
5	Baton Rouge, LA	84,699,463	48,302,305	36,397,158	20,722,871	15,674,287
6	New Orleans, LA	66,441,189	37,500,345	28,940,844	11,638,524	17,302,320
7	Corpus Christi, TX	60,866,092	24,565,493	36,300,599	31,018,397	5,282,202
8	Plaquemine, LA, Port of	58,473,474	40,202,638	18,270,836	4,256,047	14,014,789
9	Norfolk Harbor, VA	53,496,276	9,518,718	43,977,558	4,758,785	39,216,773
10	Long Beach, CA	52,048,625	22,731,354	29,317,271	12,850,838	16,466,433
11	Tampa, FL	46,434,233	28,415,386	18,018,847	5,100,055	12,918,792
12	Lake Charles, LA	44,038,688	18,921,457	25,117,231	19,413,184	5,704,047
13	Texas City, TX	43,104,101	18,746,369	24,357,732	21,968,536	2,389,196
14	Mobile, AL	40,482,387	20,570,265	19,912,102	7,635,758	12,276,344
15	Los Angeles, CA	40,103,692	16,671,084	23,432,608	12,401,748	11,030,860
16	Philadelphia, PA	39,667,259	14,558,134	25,109,125	24,424,378	684,747
17	Duluth-Superior, MN and WI	39,303,709	31,099,910	8,203,799	915,531	7,288,268
18	Baltimore, MD	37,655,691	12,344,559	25,311,132	11,231,800	14,079,332
19	Pittsburgh, PA	34,320,725	34,320,725	0	0	0
20	Port Arthur, TX	33,524,964	8,231,475	25,293,489	21,966,200	3,327,289
21	St. Louis, MO and IL	31,947,230	31,947,230	0	0	0
22	Pascagoula, MS	29,245,347	9,467,649	19,777,698	16,136,042	3,641,656
23	Portland, OR	28,226,591	11,521,174	16,705,417	3,211,774	13,493,643
24	Marcus Hook, PA	26,569,805	13,984,909	12,584,896	12,409,926	174,970
25	Newport News, VA	24,450,445	3,696,646	20,753,799	810,072	19,943,727
26	Beaumont, TX	22,701,500	15,809,048	6,892,452	4,148,139	2,744,313
27	Chicago, IL	22,153,979	19,623,164	2,530,815	1,716,704	814,111
28	Seattle, WA	21,883,200	8,119,525	13,763,675	6,464,121	7,299,554
29	Huntington, WV	21,833,428	21,833,428	0	0	0
30	Richmond, CA	21,042,244	15,886,366	5,155,878	1,537,395	3,618,483
31	Paulsboro, NJ	20,254,199	9,775,689	10,478,510	10,383,730	94,780
32	Tacoma, WA	20,116,344	6,290,604	13,825,740	4,747,359	9,078,381
33	Boston, MA	19,207,776	9,093,322	10,114,454	9,408,260	706,194
34	Jacksonville, FL	17,208,707	9,825,536	7,383,171	5,153,381	2,229,790
35	Detroit, MI	16,303,234	12,976,873	3,326,361	2,954,863	371,498
36	Indiana Harbor, IN	15,325,931	15,225,074	100,857	66,945	33,912
37	Anacortes, WA	15,259,637	13,463,393	1,796,244	556,152	1,240,092
38	Freeport, TX	14,952,599	7,587,161	7,365,438	6,254,491	1,110,947
39	Port Everglades, FL	14,507,888	10,226,190	4,281,698	3,155,801	1,125,897
40	San Juan, PR	14,330,502	8,440,718	5,889,784	5,306,574	583,210
41	Savannah, GA	13,988,735	2,307,319	11,681,416	4,958,623	6,722,793
42	Cleveland, OH	13,653,652	11,807,350	1,846,302	1,583,585	262,717
43	Lorain, OH	13,282,176	13,145,012	137,164	110,391	26,773
44	Memphis, TN	13,281,285	13,281,285	0	0	0
45	Oakland, CA	13,211,391	4,592,808	8,618,583	3,690,444	4,928,139
46	Toledo, OH	12,721,749	6,795,608	5,926,151	983,428	4,942,723
47	Portland, ME	12,511,340	2,190,554	10,320,786	10,219,598	101,188
48	Galveston, TX	12,317,599	3,948,570	8,369,029	6,152,422	2,216,607
49	Cincinnati, OH	11,852,263	11,852,263	0	0	0
50	New Castle, DE	11,831,119	5,440,820	6,390,299	6,370,922	19,377

Shortest Navigable Distances[1] Between Ports

Source: Defense Mapping Agency, Hydrographic/Topographic Center, June 1994

Distances shown are in nautical mi (1,852 m or about 6,076.115 ft). For statute mi, multiply by 1.15.

From	To	Distance
New York, New York	Barcelona, Spain	3,714
"	Cape Town, South Africa	6,786
"	Cherbourg, France	3,134
"	Copenhagen, Denmark	3,720
"	Galveston, Texas	1,935
"	Glasgow, Scotland	3,065
"	Hamburg, Germany	3,654
"	Havana, Cuba	1,186
"	Helsinki, Finland	4,257
"	Oslo, Norway	3,644
"	Piraeus, Greece	4,688
"	Southampton, England	3,169
Montreal, Canada	Algiers, Algeria	3,842
"	Barcelona, Spain	3,939
"	Cape Town, South Africa	7,118
"	Gibraltar[2]	3,429
"	Halifax, Nova Scotia	895
"	Havana, Cuba	3,326
"	Istanbul, Turkey	5,226
"	Kingston, Jamaica	3,269
"	Lagos, Nigeria	6,505
"	Marseille, France	4,116
"	Naples, Italy	4,406
"	Oslo, Norway	3,957
"	Piraeus, Greece	4,856
"	Port Said, Egypt	5,348
"	Southampton, England	3,397
Colón,[3] Panama	Buenos Aires, Argentina	5,385
Colón,[3] Panama	Copenhagen, Denmark	5,233
"	Galveston, Texas	1,508
"	Gibraltar[2]	4,332
"	Hamburg, Germany	5,061
"	Helsinki, Finland	5,036
"	Lagos, Nigeria	7,495
"	Lisbon, Portugal	4,152
"	Oslo, Norway	5,053
"	Piraeus, Greece	5,759
"	Port Said, Egypt	6,251
"	St. John's, Nfld.	2,695
"	Southampton, England	4,576
San Francisco, Calif.	Bombay, India	9,794
"	Calcutta, India	9,384
"	Colón, Panama	3,285
Vancouver, Canada	Calcutta, India	8,727
"	Melbourne, Australia	7,365
Panama, Panama	Jakarta, Indonesia	10,603
Port Said, Egypt	Ho Chi Minh City, Vietnam	5,684
"	Hong Kong	6,489
"	Manila, Philippines	6,365
"	Melbourne, Australia	7,886
"	Singapore	5,035
"	Yokohama, Japan	7,924
Cape Town,[4] S. Africa	Jakarta, Indonesia	5,276
"	Melbourne, Australia	5,719
"	Singapore	5,614
Singapore	Jakarta, Indonesia	525

(1) Traveling through station points. (2) Gibraltar (port) is 24 nautical mi E of the Strait of Gibraltar. (3) Colón on the Atlantic is 44 nautical mi from Panamá (port) on the Pacific. (4) Cape Town is 35 nautical mi NW of the Cape of Good Hope.

North American Free Trade Agreement

The U.S., Canada, and Mexico announced the conclusion of negotiations for a comprehensive plan for free trade across North America on Aug. 12, 1992, and portrayed it as an opportunity for greater economic growth for all 3 nations. The North American Free Trade Agreement (NAFTA) was greeted enthusiastically by business groups generally, but U.S. labor unions, long opposed to opening the southern border, contended that the accord would send jobs to Mexico, where labor costs were lower and environmental regulations laxer than in the U.S.

The 3 countries attempted to satisfy some of the NAFTA opposition by concluding side agreements, announced on Aug. 13, 1993. These additional agreements called for the establishment of a 5-step procedure to enforce existing labor and environmental laws in the U.S., Canada, and Mexico. Secretariats to process, investigate, and enforce this procedure would be established, one in Canada to handle environmental complaints and the other in Dallas to deal with labor issues. Failure to comply with a decision of a secretariat could result in fines of as much as $20 million in 1994 on national governments and limited trade sanctions. The maximum fine is adjusted annually. The side agreements were signed (separately) by Canada on Sept. 13, 1993, and by the U.S. and Mexico on Sept. 14, 1993.

Before it could take effect, NAFTA had to be ratified by the legislatures of the 3 nations. The Canadian Senate ratified the agreement June 23, 1993. On Nov. 17, 1993, the U.S. House of Representatives voted 234-200 in favor of NAFTA, and the Senate gave its approval on Nov. 20, 1993, voting 61-38. On Nov. 22, 1993, the Mexican Senate approved NAFTA by a vote of 56-2. NAFTA officially took effect Jan. 1, 1994.

Key Provisions

Agriculture—Tariffs on all farm products will be eliminated over 15 years. All 3 countries agreed to allow domestic price-support systems, provided that they did not distort trade.

Automobiles—After 8 years, at least 62.5% of an automobile's value must have been produced in North America for it to qualify for duty-free status. Tariffs will be phased out over 10 years.

Banking—U.S. and Canadian banks are now allowed to acquire Mexican commercial banks accounting for as much as 8% of the industry's capital. All limits on bank ownership will end Jan. 1, 2004.

Disputes—Special judges will be empaneled to resolve disagreements within strict timetables.

Energy—Mexico will not alter its constitution, which prohibits foreign ownership of its oil fields, but after 10 years U.S. and Canadian companies can bid on contracts offered by Mexican oil and electricity monopolies.

Environment—The agreement encourages effective enforcement of environmental laws; it cannot be used to overrule national and state environmental, health, or safety laws.

Immigration—All 3 countries will ease restrictions on the movement of business executives and professionals.

Jobs—Current barriers designed to limit Mexican migration to the U.S. will remain in force.

Patent and copyright protection—Mexico strengthened its laws providing protection to intellectual property. It now honors foreign patents for pharmaceuticals for 20 years.

Textiles—A strict "rule of origin" provision requires most garments to be made from yarn and fabric also produced in North America. Most tariffs will be phased out over 5 years.

Tariffs—Tariffs on 10,000 customs goods will be eliminated over 15 years. One-half of U.S. exports to Mexico will be considered duty-free within 5 years.

Trucking—Trucks will be allowed free access on cross-border routes and throughout the 3 countries by the end of 1999.

General Agreement on Tariffs and Trade

Following World War II, the major economic powers of the world, recognizing that obstacles to trade hindered economic development and growth, negotiated a set of rules for reducing and limiting barriers to trade and for settling trade disputes. These rules were called the General Agreement on Tariffs and Trade (GATT).

Although the world benefited enormously from the original GATT rules, global commerce changed so rapidly that the rules increasingly were out of step. For example, they did not cover many areas of trade such as intellectual property and services; they were not meaningful for aspects of trade such as agriculture; and they did not bring about the prompt settlement of disputes.

Periodically, rounds of multilateral trade negotiations have been carried out since the late 1940s. The 8th round began in 1986 in Punta del Este, Uruguay, and is usually referred to as the Uruguay Round.

The Uruguay Round concluded on Dec. 15, 1993, when 117 countries completed a new trade-liberalization agreement.

Key Provisions of the 1993 Agreement

- Cuts tariffs on many manufactured products by more than one-third
- Protects the intellectual property of entrepreneurs in industries such as pharmaceuticals, entertainment, and software
- Ensures open markets for exporters of services such as accounting, advertising, computer services, tourism, engineering, and construction
- Expands export opportunities for agricultural products by limiting the ability of governments to restrict trade through tariffs, quotas, subsidies, and other domestic policies and regulations
- Ensures that developing and developed countries follow the same trade rules
- Establishes rules for settling disputes promptly
- Creates the World Trade Organization (WTO) to implement the agreements

As of mid-September 1994, 26 GATT nations had approved the trade pact. The pact has a formal deadline for ratification of July 1, 1995.

Major Merchant Fleets of the World

Source: Maritime Administration, U.S. Dept. of Commerce (tonnage in thousands)

Fleets of oceangoing steam and motor ships totaling 1 million gross tons or more as of Jan. 1, 1993. Excludes ships operating exclusively on the Great Lakes and inland waterways and special types such as channel ships, icebreakers, cable ships, and merchant ships owned by any military force. Gross tonnage is a volume measurement; each cargo gross ton represents 100 cubic ft of enclosed space. Deadweight tonnage is the carrying capacity of a ship in long tons (2,240 lb). Tonnage figures may not add, due to rounding.

	Total			Type of vessel: Freighters			Bulk carriers			Tankers		
	No. of ships	Gross tons	Dwt tons	No. of ships	Gross tons	Dwt tons	No. of ships	Gross tons	Dwt tons	No. of ships	Gross tons	Dwt tons
All countries[1]	23,753	402,217	656,591	12,339	101,635	123,179	5,420	138,712	246,983	5,642	156,683	285,009
United States[2]	603	15,406	22,500	349	6,824	7,232	23	574	991	220	7,825	14,180
Privately owned[3]	384	12,611	18,774	167	4,648	4,498	21	536	929	193	7,349	13,320
Government owned	219	2,795	3,726	182	2,176	2,734	2	38	62	27	476	860
Australia	74	2,313	3,495	21	241	271	30	1,007	1,685	23	1,065	1,539
Bahamas	818	19,412	32,173	380	4,003	5,213	147	4,343	7,690	242	10,062	19,034
Bermuda	62	3,150	5,369	18	177	200	9	204	347	35	2,769	4,822
Brazil	220	5,131	8,783	59	543	698	77	2,434	4,250	83	2,153	3,834
*Bulgaria	117	1,266	1,880	59	371	463	37	603	949	19	290	468
*China	1,231	12,631	19,388	752	5,364	7,438	285	5,433	9,181	170	1,661	2,685
Cyprus	1,251	20,050	35,630	616	4,085	5,996	488	10,858	19,840	140	5,046	9,766
Denmark	281	4,335	6,309	189	2,294	2,563	14	555	1,029	78	1,486	2,717
France	106	3,020	4,742	45	1,003	1,084	6	103	153	48	1,853	3,485
Germany	419	4,462	5,672	351	3,475	4,263	22	522	853	39	327	513
Greece	904	24,431	46,101	193	1,540	2,258	458	11,834	22,134	231	10,898	21,639
Hong Kong	200	7,085	11,981	64	1,135	1,286	104	4,821	8,839	31	1,039	1,853
India	296	6,029	10,036	97	914	1,339	119	2,928	4,994	77	2,162	3,693
Indonesia	365	1,588	2,514	247	842	1,310	19	181	268	92	549	922
Iran	124	4,421	8,228	38	385	533	50	1,058	1,757	36	2,978	5,938
Isle of Man	68	1,498	2,583	28	275	314	12	311	543	28	912	1,726
Italy	468	6,411	9,737	172	1,346	1,355	60	2,317	4,208	217	2,473	4,110
Japan	913	21,109	32,562	351	3,849	3,077	251	8,653	15,992	296	8,407	13,437
Korea, South	422	6,383	10,238	225	1,996	2,307	130	3,869	7,013	67	518	918
Kuwait	43	2,208	3,792	13	281	370	0	0	0	30	1,927	3,422
Latvia	118	1,023	1,316	75	431	425	0	0	0	43	592	891
Liberia	1,568	55,139	97,173	367	5,911	6,363	540	17,333	32,001	639	31,143	58,679
Luxembourg	51	1,609	2,605	16	199	225	17	881	1,630	17	496	745
Malaysia	185	1,865	2,779	107	666	926	24	468	842	54	731	1,011
Malta	752	10,569	17,971	343	2,286	3,313	255	5,209	9,163	147	3,002	5,468
Marshall Islands	31	2,031	4,002	4	86	102	18	625	1,163	9	1,320	2,737
Netherlands	367	3,240	4,265	285	1,950	2,403	19	393	638	58	766	1,206
Norway	737	20,230	35,371	193	1,860	2,049	219	6,114	11,079	311	11,866	22,173
Panama	3,171	49,589	79,414	1,719	13,966	16,325	717	17,115	29,587	704	18,169	33,375
Philippines	534	7,979	13,420	239	1,382	1,833	251	6,202	10,871	39	360	699
Poland	212	2,780	4,046	119	980	1,111	85	1,671	2,740	5	109	185
Romania	255	2,701	4,135	193	1,147	1,535	50	1,110	1,820	12	444	780
Russia	1,363	10,036	13,370	1,006	5,509	6,369	135	2,092	3,209	211	2,378	3,781
Saint Vincent	431	4,344	7,114	285	1,625	2,313	97	1,881	3,286	47	823	1,503
Singapore	493	9,525	15,377	227	2,706	3,168	82	2,514	4,480	184	4,305	7,729
Spain	222	2,116	3,904	130	350	558	30	530	959	61	1,234	2,384
Sweden	172	2,467	3,157	90	1,079	1,035	10	220	374	67	1,011	1,723
Taiwan	215	5,955	9,146	134	2,444	2,852	60	2,537	4,622	21	974	1,672
Turkey	339	3,817	6,583	189	715	1,039	93	2,239	3,987	54	849	1,551
United Kingdom	154	2,749	3,081	58	1,062	1,032	19	139	209	59	1,159	1,731
Vanuatu	119	2,018	3,021	55	644	599	52	1,115	1,948	11	253	472

(1) Includes combination passenger & cargo ships. (2) Excludes nonmerchant type and/or navy-owned vessels that are currently in the National Reserve Fleet. (3) Includes 18 integrated tug/barge vessels of 637,000 dwt tons. * Source material limited.

Fastest Scheduled Passenger Train Runs in the U.S. and Canada

Source: Darrell J. Smith, Natl. Railroad Passenger Corp.; 1994 timetables

Railroad	Train	From	To	Mi	Min	MPH
Amtrak	Eight Metroliner Service trains	Wilmington	Baltimore	68.4	42	97.7
Amtrak	16 Metroliner Service trains	Baltimore	Wilmington	68.4	43	95.0
Amtrak	Express Metroliner Service train 203	Metropark	Baltimore	160.0	103	93.0
Amtrak	Express Metroliner Service train 202	New Carrollton	New York City	216.0	141	91.9
Amtrak	Express Metroliner Service train 220	Washington	Philadelphia	135.0	88	91.8
Amtrak	Express Metroliner Service train 223	New York	Baltimore	185.0	123	90.2
Amtrak	Two Metroliner Service trains	Newark	Philadelphia	80.7	55	87.7
Amtrak	Nine Metroliner Service trains	Newark	Philadelphia	80.7	56	86.8
VIA	Renaissance	Dorval	Kingston	165.0	117	84.6
VIA	York	Kingston	Cornwall	108.0	77	84.4
Amtrak	Three Metroliner Service trains	Philadelphia	Newark	80.7	58	83.2
VIA	York	Cornwall	Kingston	108.0	78	83.1
VIA	Renaissance	Kingston	Dorval	165.0	120	82.5

Notes: The fastest scheduled passenger train runs in the world are those of France's TGV Atlantique, between Paris and various cities in western France, at 186.4 mph. On Dec. 12, 1992, Amtrak operated the Swedish X-2000 train at 155 mph, and on July 18, 1993, operated the German ICE train at 162 mph, both on a portion (in northern New Jersey) of the Northeast Corridor. The runs were part of Amtrak's program to test high-speed equipment for use on the Washington-Boston Northeast Corridor.

Passenger Car Production, U.S. Plants

Source: American Automobile Manufacturers Assn.

	1992	1993
Chrysler Corp.		
Neon	0	1,522
Acclaim	70,768	52,460
Sundance	64,953	101,326
Total Plymouth	**135,721**	**155,308**
LeBaron	9,755	27,359
LeBaron J	45,235	32,601
Fifth Avenue Y	40,436	11,185
Imperial	6,635	3,286
New Yorker C	21,339	10,388
Total Chrysler-Plymouth	**259,121**	**240,127**
Neon	0	2,754
Shadow	93,920	126,153
Daytona	14,544	2,055
Spirit	68,068	64,724
Dynasty	86,697	27,466
Intrepid	0	29,341
Viper	310	1,953
Total Dodge	**263,539**	**254,446**
Total Chrysler Corp.	**522,660**	**494,573**
Ford Motor Co.		
Thunderbird	97,822	125,659
Taurus	427,621	428,718
Tempo	129,334	157,460
Escort	179,143	208,263
Mustang	88,568	106,238
Total Ford	**922,488**	**1,026,338**
Cougar	61,042	76,901
Sable	123,531	137,262
Topaz	57,961	64,795
LincolnTown Car	117,789	114,491
Mark	11,468	35,688
Continental	39,299	34,224
Total Lincoln-Mercury	**411,090**	**463,361**
Total Ford Motor Co.	**1,333,578**	**1,489,699**
General Motors Corp.		
Caprice	103,594	93,941
Corvette	20,839	22,578
Beretta-Corsica	187,441	202,819
Camaro	47,757	0
Cavalier	212,117	287,790
Geo Prizm	75,479	84,988
Total Chevrolet	**647,227**	**692,116**
Grand Prix	110,465	119,847
Grand Am	251,822	230,070
Firebird	14,786	0
Bonneville H	98,748	91,285
Sunbird	86,119	111,745
Total Pontiac	**561,940**	**552,947**
88 Royale	66,620	70,132
Oldsmobile 98	26,154	24,351
Achieva	87,372	51,665
Cutless Supreme	76,855	101,037
Ciera	133,140	151,566
Total Oldsmobile	**359,974**	**398,717**
LeSabre	157,790	157,125
Roadmaster	50,566	33,092
Park Avenue	58,587	65,875
Riviera	11,801	0
Century	88,820	93,379
Skylark	60,351	52,918
Total Buick	**427,915**	**402,389**
DeVille C	122,844	71,883
DeVille K	0	42,066
Fleetwood	17,384	29,744
Brougham	2,170	0
Eldorado	29,866	23,621
Seville	46,440	45,231
Allante	2,408	2,262
Total Cadillac	**221,112**	**214,807**
Saturn	212,122	281,479
Total General Motors Corp.	**2,466,290**	**2,542,455**
Diamond Star		
Mitsubishi Eclipse	72,367	54,694
Mitsubishi Mirage	10,140	0
Mitsubishi Galant	0	42,896
Plymouth Laser	21,993	11,571
Eagle Talon	31,802	26,874
Eagle Summit	3,481	0
Total Diamond Star	**139,783**	**136,035**
Honda		
Accord	356,382	283,038
Civic	101,872	120,737
Total Honda	**458,254**	**403,775**
Auto Alliance		
Probe	80,086	103,323
Mazda MX-6/626	88,773	115,773
Total Auto Alliance	**168,859**	**219,096**
Nissan		
Altima	52,166	155,563
Sentra	119,238	136,619
Total Nissan	**171,404**	**292,182**
Subaru Legacy	**57,623**	**47,117**
Toyota		
Corolla	105,370	122,054
Camry	240,382	234,060
Total Toyota	**345,752**	**356,114**
Total Passenger Cars	**5,664,203**	**5,981,046**

Selected Motor Vehicle Statistics

Source: Federal Highway Administration; U.S. Dept. of Transportation; Insurance Institute for Highway Safety; 1992 figures unless otherwise specified.

State	Driver's age Jan. 1, 1994 (1) Regular	Driver's age Jan. 1, 1994 (2) Juvenile	State gas tax cents/gal. (Jan. 1, 1994)	Safety belt use law[3] (Aug. 1, 1994)	Licensed drivers per 1,000 resident population	Registered motor vehicles per 1,000 resident population	Licensed drivers per registered motor vehicle	Gallons of fuel used per vehicle	Miles per gallon	Annual miles driven per vehicle	Vehicle miles per licensed driver
Alabama	16	—	18	S	720	799	0.90	822	16.84	13,850	15,370
Alaska	16	—	8	S	690	828	0.83	587	13.47	7,902	9,482
Arizona	16	—	18	S	654	731	0.89	749	16.71	12,513	13,986
Arkansas	16	—	18.7	S	714	626	1.14	1,088	14.12	15,372	13,480
California	16/18	14	17	P	652	719	0.91	688	17.18	11,825	13,055
Colorado	18	16	22	S	689	840	0.82	592	16.77	9,923	12,092
Connecticut	16/18	—	29	P	719	783	0.92	584	17.63	10,299	11,223
Delaware	16/18	—	22	S	728	791	0.92	717	17.63	12,646	13,746
Dist. of Col.	18	16	20	S	597	435	1.37	738	18.81	13,892	10,129
Florida	16	—	11.8	S	781	759	1.03	667	16.74	11,172	10,848
Georgia	16	—	7.5	S*	681	874	0.78	745	17.72	13,205	16,937
Hawaii	15	—	16	P	618	667	0.93	512	20.33	10,420	11,257
Idaho	17	15	21	S	676	969	0.70	589	17.67	10,407	14,930
Illinois	16/18	—	19	S	637	686	0.93	677	16.22	10,980	11,826
Indiana	16/18	—	15	S	671	798	0.84	746	16.95	12,638	15,017
Iowa	16/18	—	20	P	661	962	0.69	596	14.83	8,843	12,873
Kansas	16	14	18	S	671	761	0.88	740	16.99	12,581	14,282
Kentucky	16	—	15.4	S	654	794	0.82	797	16.01	12,759	15,491
Louisiana	15/17	15	20	S	610	722	0.85	712	15.37	10,943	12,937
Maine	16/17	16	19	No	743	792	0.94	715	17.37	12,423	13,237
Maryland	16/18	16	23.5	S	659	752	0.88	649	17.51	11,357	12,956
Massachusetts	17/18	16½	21	S**	695	611	1.14	707	18.27	12,925	11,354
Michigan	16/18	14	15	S	687	775	0.89	657	17.53	11,520	12,995
Minnesota	16/18	15	20	S	586	778	0.75	679	17.40	11,815	15,680
Mississippi	15	—	18.4	S	623	748	0.83	822	16.34	13,429	16,116
Missouri	16	—	13.03	S	665	771	0.86	850	15.64	13,300	15,416
Montana	15/16	13	24	S	725	1,100	0.66	625	15.05	9,401	14,279
Nebraska	16	14	24.4	S	703	844	0.83	723	14.92	10,790	12,952
Nevada	16	14	24	S	721	694	1.04	903	13.11	11,833	11,382
New Hampshire	16/18	16	18.7	No	765	804	0.95	629	17.91	11,265	11,842
New Jersey	17	16	10.5	S	679	718	0.95	643	16.51	10,625	11,241
New Mexico	15/16	—	23	P	712	855	0.83	774	17.63	13,651	16,384
New York	17/18	16	22.89	P	572	540	1.06	641	17.53	11,236	10,606
North Carolina	16/18	—	22	P	680	776	0.88	734	17.34	12,726	14,507
North Dakota	16	14	18	S	681	1,030	0.66	644	14.39	9,265	14,019
Ohio	16/18	14	22	S	832	820	1.02	606	17.39	10,545	10,385
Oklahoma	16	—	17	S	712	852	0.84	750	17.10	12,831	15,356
Oregon	16	14	24	P	815	868	0.94	648	16.69	10,810	11,513
Pennsylvania	17/18	16	22.35	S	668	681	0.98	675	16.16	10,906	11,124
Rhode Island	16/18	—	28	S	682	619	1.10	650	18.99	12,340	11,203
South Carolina	16	15	16	S	666	722	0.92	842	16.01	13,476	14,604
South Dakota	16	14	18	S**	701	1,012	0.69	676	14.84	10,029	14,491
Tennessee	16	14	20	S	694	925	0.75	658	16.35	10,763	14,341
Texas	16/18	15	20	P	648	723	0.90	780	16.41	12,793	14,280
Utah	16/18	—	19	S	630	691	0.91	747	17.43	13,022	14,267
Vermont	18	16	16	S	743	815	0.91	748	17.31	12,949	14,213
Virginia	16/19	—	17.5	S	737	822	0.90	688	17.61	12,111	13,508
Washington	16/18	—	23	S	706	870	0.81	604	18.31	11,059	13,615
West Virginia	16/18	16	25.35	S	725	702	1.03	809	15.99	12,945	12,538
Wisconsin	16/18	14	23.2	S	708	746	0.95	689	18.51	12,753	13,444
Wyoming	16	14	9	S	736	1,036	0.71	967	13.32	12,877	18,127
Average					**679**	**746**	**0.91**	**698**	**16.85**	**11,766**	**12,938**

(1) Unrestricted operation of private passenger car. When 2 ages are shown, license is issued at lower age upon completion of approved driver education course. (2) Juvenile license issued with consent of parent or guardian. (3) P = an officer may stop a vehicle for a violation (primary); S = an officer may only issue a seat belt citation when the vehicle is stopped for another moving violation (secondary); *Although the Georgia law is secondary, for persons 4-18 years of age it is enforced primarily; **The seat belt laws in Massachusetts and South Dakota were subject to referenda in November 1994.

U.S. Car Sales by Vehicle Size and Type, 1983-93

Source: American Automobile Manufacturers Assn.

Year	Small (%)	Midsize (%)	Large (%)	Luxury (%)	Total (%)
1993	32.8	43.3	11.1	12.8	100.0
1992	32.9	44.5	9.2	13.4	100.0
1991	33.0	44.9	8.3	13.9	100.0
1990	32.8	44.8	9.4	13.0	100.0
1989	36.6	41.9	11.9	11.6	100.0
1988	37.6	42.5	10.0	9.9	100.0
1987	38.4	42.3	9.1	10.2	100.0
1986	37.6	42.5	9.8	10.1	100.0
1985	37.9	42.1	9.8	10.2	100.0
1984	39.1	39.6	11.6	9.7	100.0
1983	38.8	40.6	10.7	9.9	100.0

U.S. Car Sales by Type of Buyer, 1980-93

Source: American Automobile Manufacturers Assn.

Year	Sales in thousands				% of total sales	
	Consumer	Business	Government	Total	Consumer	Business
1993	4,672	3,943	100	8,715	53.6	45.2
1992	4,558	3,683	113	8,354	54.6	44.1
1991	4,538	3,752	97	8,387	54.1	44.8
1990	5,768	3,567	149	9,484	60.8	37.6
1989	6,375	3,402	136	9,913	64.3	34.3
1988	6,802	3,699	138	10,639	63.9	34.8
1987	6,748	3,395	135	10,278	65.7	33.0
1986	7,658	3,666	127	11,450	66.9	32.0
1985	7,083	3,822	134	11,039	64.2	34.6
1984	6,590	3,669	135	10,394	63.4	35.3
1983	6,054	3,006	119	9,179	66.0	32.7
1982	5,285	2,593	102	7,980	66.2	32.5
1981	5,623	2,787	116	8,535	66.0	32.7
1980	6,062	2,791	126	8,979	67.5	31.1

Domestic and Imported Retail Car Sales in the U.S., 1980-93

Source: American Automobile Manufacturers Assn.

Calendar year	Domestic	Imports				Total U.S. sales	Import %		U.S.-sponsored imports
		From Japan	From Germany	Other countries	Total imports		Total	Japan	
1980	6,581,307	1,905,968	305,219	186,700	2,397,887	8,979,194	26.7	21.2	223,310
1981	6,208,760	1,858,896	282,881	185,502	2,327,279	8,536,039	27.3	21.8	174,665
1982	5,758,586	1,801,969	247,080	174,508	2,223,557	7,982,143	27.9	22.6	139,767
1983	6,795,295	1,915,621	279,748	191,403	2,386,772	9,182,067	26.0	20.9	138,798
1984	7,951,523	1,906,206	344,416	188,220	2,438,842	10,390,365	23.5	18.3	116,965
1985	8,204,542	2,217,837	423,983	195,925	2,837,745	11,042,287	25.7	20.1	206,252
1986	8,214,897	2,382,614	443,721	418,286	3,244,621	11,459,518	28.3	20.8	314,358
1987	7,080,858	2,190,405	347,881	657,465	3,195,751	10,276,609	31.1	21.3	348,154
1988	7,526,038	2,022,602	280,099	700,991	3,003,692	10,529,730	28.5	19.2	393,412
1989	7,072,902	1,897,143	248,561	553,660	2,699,364	9,772,266	27.6	19.4	340,425
1990	6,896,888	1,719,384	265,116	418,823	2,403,323	9,300,211	25.8	18.5	296,778
1991	6,136,757	1,500,309	192,776	344,814	2,037,899	8,174,656	24.9	18.4	254,572
1992	6,276,557	1,452,737	200,851	283,939	1,937,527	8,214,084	23.6	17.7	228,927
1993	6,734,491	1,328,448	186,177	268,746	1,783,371	8,517,862	20.9	15.6	185,284

World Motor Vehicle Production, 1950-92

Source: American Automobile Manufacturers Assn.
(in thousands)

Year	United States	Canada	Europe	Japan	Other	World total	U.S. %of world total
1992	9,702	1,968	17,244	12,499	5,964	47,377	20.5
1991	8,811	1,873	17,527	13,245	5,040	46,496	19.0
1990	9,783	1,928	18,651	13,487	4,496	48,345	20.2
1985	11,653	1,933	16,015	12,271	2,939	44,811	26.0
1980	8,010	1,324	15,445	11,043	2,692	38,514	20.8
1970	8,284	1,160	13,033	5,289	1,637	29,403	28.2
1960	7,905	398	6,837	482	866	16,488	47.9
1950	8,006	388	1,991	32	160	10,577	75.7

Note: As far as can be determined, production refers to vehicles locally manufactured.

Motor Vehicle Production by Selected Countries, 1993

Source: American Automobile Manufacturers Assn.

Country	Passenger cars	Commercial vehicles	Total
Argentina	286,964	55,386	342,350
Australia	348,509	131,272	479,781
Austria	40,777	3,942	44,719
Belgium	347,427	56,528	403,955
Brazil	1,102,119	288,142	1,390,261
Canada	1,349,081	888,652	2,237,733
China	221,390	1,088,610	1,310,000
Commonwealth of Independent States	1,207,500	599,500	1,807,000
Czech Republic/ Slovakia	210,100	23,950	234,050
France	2,836,280	319,437	3,155,717
Germany	3,753,341	237,309	3,990,650
Hungary[1]	10,600	5,110	15,710
India	199,571	172,059	371,630
Italy	1,117,009	150,186	1,267,195
Japan	8,497,094	2,730,451	11,227,545
Korea, South	1,592,669	457,389	2,050,058
Malaysia	115,000	0	115,000
Mexico	835,079	245,065	1,080,144
Netherlands	80,246	18,946	99,192
Poland	266,000	38,000	304,000
Spain	1,505,949	261,691	1,767,640
Sweden	279,002	58,384	337,386
Taiwan	277,900	105,000	382,900
United Kingdom	1,375,524	193,410	1,568,934
United States	5,981,046	4,883,157	10,864,203
Yugoslavia[2]	7,359	954	8,313
Total	**33,843,536**	**13,012,530**	**46,856,066**[3]

(1) Estimated. (2) Federal Republic of Yugoslavia (Serbia and Montenegro) only. (3) Includes countries not listed.

Top-Selling Passenger Cars in the U.S. by Calendar Year, 1990-93 (Domestic and Import)

Source: American Automobile Manufacturers Assn.

1993

Rank	Car	Sales
1.	Ford Taurus	360,448
2.	Honda Accord	330,030
3.	Toyota Camry	299,737
4.	Chevrolet Cavalier	273,617
5.	Ford Escort	269,034
6.	Honda Civic	255,579
7.	Saturn	229,356
8.	Chevrolet Lumina	219,683
9.	Ford Tempo	217,644
10.	Pontiac Grand Am.	214,761
11.	Toyota Corolla	193,749
12.	Chevrolet Corsica/Beretta	171,794
13.	Nissan Sentra	167,351
14.	Buick LeSabre	149,299
15.	Oldsmobile Ciera	143,699
16.	Nissan Altima	133,879
17.	Ford Thunderbird	122,415
18.	Mercury Sable	120,977
19.	Dodge Shadow	119,262
20.	Buick Century	116,034

1992

Rank	Car	Sales
1.	Ford Taurus	409,751
2.	Honda Accord	393,477
3.	Toyota Camry	286,602
4.	Ford Escort	236,622
5.	Honda Civic/CRX	219,228
6.	Chevrolet Lumina	218,114
7.	Chevrolet Cavalier	212,374
8.	Pontiac Grand Am	210,332
9.	Ford Tempo	207,173
10.	Saturn	196,126

1991

Rank	Car	Sales
1.	Honda Accord	399,297
2.	Ford Taurus	299,659
3.	Toyota Camry	263,818
4.	Chevrolet Cavalier	259,385
5.	Ford Escort	247,864
6.	Chevrolet Corsica/Beretta	231,227
7.	Chevrolet Lumina	217,555
8.	Honda Civic	205,715
9.	Toyota Corolla	199,083
10.	Ford Tempo	189,457

1990

Rank	Car	Sales
1.	Honda Accord	417,179
2.	Ford Taurus	313,274
3.	Chevrolet Cavalier	295,123
4.	Ford Escort	288,727
5.	Toyota Camry	284,595
6.	Chevrolet Corsica/Beretta	277,176
7.	Toyota Corolla	228,211
8.	Honda Civic	220,852
9.	Chevrolet Lumina	218,288
10.	Ford Tempo	215,290

Licensed Drivers, by Age

Source: Federal Highway Administration, U.S. Dept. of Transportation

	1992				Estimated 1993			
Age	Male	Female	Total	Percent male	Male	Female	Total	Percent change total drivers 1982-92
Under 16	24,423	21,859	46,282	52.77	24,809	22,208	47,017	-62.37
16	740,132	668,452	1,408,584	52.54	751,841	679,134	1,430,975	-14.27
17	1,103,410	989,201	2,092,611	52.73	1,120,866	1,005,009	2,125,875	-17.42
18	1,312,095	1,169,121	2,481,216	52.88	1,332,852	1,187,804	2,520,656	-21.06
19	1,439,869	1,280,991	2,720,860	52.92	1,462,648	1,301,462	2,764,110	-23.27
(19 and under)	4,619,929	4,129,624	8,749,553	52.80	4,693,016	4,195,617	8,888,633	-20.38
20	1,535,185	1,402,462	2,937,647	52.26	1,559,472	1,424,874	2,984,346	-18.87
21	1,707,044	1,579,160	3,286,204	51.95	1,734,049	1,604,396	3,338,445	-14.60
22	1,802,467	1,674,017	3,476,484	51.85	1,830,982	1,700,769	3,531,751	-12.08
23	1,805,860	1,676,310	3,482,170	51.86	1,834,429	1,703,098	3,537,527	-12.92
24	1,780,780	1,648,083	3,428,863	51.94	1,808,952	1,674,420	3,483,372	-14.06
(20-24)	8,631,336	7,980,032	16,611,368	51.96	8,767,884	8,107,557	16,875,441	-14.43
25-29	9,744,089	9,195,731	18,939,820	51.45	9,898,240	9,342,682	19,240,922	-3.61
30-34	10,606,522	10,243,747	20,850,269	50.87	10,774,317	10,407,447	21,181,764	16.53
35-39	10,125,683	9,892,700	20,018,383	50.58	10,285,872	10,050,790	20,336,662	33.18
40-44	9,117,586	8,908,721	18,026,307	50.58	9,261,826	9,051,087	18,312,913	52.39
45-49	7,587,131	7,366,321	14,953,452	50.74	7,707,160	7,484,038	15,191,198	48.35
50-54	5,932,365	5,716,990	11,649,355	50.92	6,026,215	5,808,350	11,834,565	17.27
55-59	5,017,712	4,801,433	9,819,145	51.10	5,097,092	4,878,162	9,975,254	-0.36
60-64	4,784,396	4,585,290	9,369,686	51.06	4,860,085	4,658,565	9,518,650	6.84
65-69	4,413,771	4,323,981	8,737,752	50.51	4,483,597	4,393,080	8,876,677	25.67
70 and over	7,806,828	7,593,478	15,400,306	50.69	7,930,332	7,714,826	15,645,158	56.54
Total	**88,387,348**	**84,738,048**	**173,125,396**	**51.05**	**89,785,636**	**86,092,201**	**175,877,837**	**15.24**

Some Countries With Safety Belt Use Laws

Source: American Automobile Manufacturers Assn.

Country	Effective Date
Australia	1/72
Austria	7/76
Belgium	6/75
Brazil	6/72
Bulgaria	1976
Canadian Provinces	
Alberta	7/87
British Columbia	10/77
Manitoba	4/84
Newfoundland	7/82
New Brunswick	11/83
Nova Scotia	1/85
Ontario	1/76
Prince Edward Island	1/88
Quebec	7/76
Saskatchewan	7/77
Denmark	1/76
Finland	7/75
France	10/79
Greece	12/79
Hong Kong	10/83
Hungary	7/77
Iceland	10/81
Ireland	2/79
Israel	7/75
Ivory Coast	1970
Japan	12/71
Jordan	12/83
Luxembourg	6/75
Malaysia	4/79
Netherlands	6/75
New Zealand	6/72
Norway	9/75
Poland	1/84
Portugal	1/78
Singapore	7/81
South Africa	12/77
Spain	10/74
Sweden	1/75
Switzerland	1/76
Turkey	10/84

How Americans Get to Work in the 15 Largest U.S. Cities

Source: Bureau of the Census, U.S. Dept. of Commerce; as of 1990 Census

City, State	Population	Drive[1] (%)	Use public transportation (%)	Other[2] (%)	Average travel time to work (min)
New York, NY	7,322,564	32.5	53.4	14.0	36.5
Los Angeles, CA	3,485,557	80.6	10.5	8.9	26.5
Chicago, IL	2,783,726	61.1	29.7	9.2	31.5
Houston, TX	1,629,902	87.2	6.5	6.3	24.7
Philadelphia, PA	1,585,577	57.9	28.7	13.5	27.4
San Diego, CA	1,110,623	83.5	4.2	12.3	20.4
Detroit, MI	1,027,974	83.9	10.7	5.4	24.7
Dallas, TX	1,007,618	87.7	6.7	5.7	24.0
Phoenix, AZ	983,403	88.8	3.3	7.9	23.0
San Antonio, TX	935,393	88.9	4.9	6.2	21.7
San Jose, CA	782,224	91.5	3.5	5.0	25.5
Baltimore, MD	736,014	67.7	22.0	10.2	26.0
Indianapolis, IN	731,327	91.4	3.3	5.2	20.8
San Francisco, CA	723,959	50.0	33.5	16.5	26.9
Jacksonville, FL	635,230	89.7	2.7	7.6	21.6

Note: Percentages may not total 100% due to independent rounding. (1) Includes driving alone and carpooling. (2) Includes walking, working at home, and other means.

How Americans Get to Work[1]

Source: Bureau of the Census, U.S. Dept. of Commerce

Means of transportation	1990 Number	1990 Percent	1980 Number	1980 Percent
Workers 16 years and over	115,070,274	100.0	96,617,296	100.0
Car, truck, or van	99,592,932	86.5	81,258,496	84.1
Drove alone	84,215,298	73.2	62,193,449	64.4
Carpool	15,377,634	13.4	19,065,047	19.7
Public transportation	6,069,589	5.3	6,175,061	6.4
Bus or trolley bus[2]	3,445,000	3.0	3,924,787	4.1
Streetcar or trolley car[2]	78,130	0.1	—	—
Subway or elevated	1,755,476	1.5	1,528,852	1.6
Railroad	574,052	0.5	554,089	0.6
Ferryboat	37,497	0.0	—	—
Taxicab	179,434	0.2	167,133	0.2
Motorcycle	237,404	0.2	419,007	0.4
Bicycle	466,856	0.4	468,348	0.5
Walked	4,488,886	3.9	5,413,248	5.6
Other means	808,582	0.7	703,273	0.7
Worked at home	3,406,025	3.0	2,179,863	2.3

(1) Means of transportation used to commute to and from work. (2) This category was "Bus or streetcar" in 1980.

Personal Consumption Expenditures for Transportation

Source: American Automobile Manufacturers Assn.; Bureau of Economic Analysis, U.S. Dept. of Commerce; in millions of dollars

	1982	1984	1986	1988	1990	1991	1992	1993
User-operated transportation								
New autos	$53,336	$77,560	$100,328	$101,041	$96,692	$79,530	$87,265	$91,319
Net purchases of used autos	13,551	21,152	25,356	30,532	33,663	36,659	39,453	43,008
Other motor vehicles*	15,605	28,589	40,818	45,577	49,586	46,020	53,879	62,443
Tires, tubes, accessories and parts	15,230	17,302	18,353	20,685	22,483	23,339	23,687	25,540
Repair, greasing, washing, parking, storage, and rental	37,903	49,723	60,695	73,531	82,538	82,371	89,468	97,344
Gasoline and oil	94,125	94,532	79,699	86,899	108,471	102,879	103,444	103,727
Bridge, tunnel, ferry, and road tolls	1,306	1,387	1,794	1,774	2,024	2,048	2,116	2,260
Insurance premiums, less claims paid	9,150	10,099	12,724	16,842	18,066	22,678	24,572	29,706
Total user-operated transportation	**$240,206**	**$300,344**	**$339,767**	**$376,881**	**$413,523**	**$395,524**	**$423,885**	**$455,347**
Purchased local transportation								
Transit systems	$3,839	$4,244	$4,913	$5,377	$5,707	$5,707	$5,940	$5,762
Taxicabs	1,513	2,498	2,998	2,935	3,209	3,351	3,285	3,372
Total purchased local transportation	**$5,352**	**$6,742**	**$7,911**	**$8,312**	**$8,916**	**$9,058**	**$9,225**	**$9,134**
Purchased intercity transportation								
Railway excluding commutation	$317	$415	$472	$588	$708	$722	$698	$692
Bus	1,665	1,632	1,469	2,181	1,396	1,521	1,451	1,412
Airline	14,706	17,721	18,993	22,993	26,467	25,609	25,684	27,062
Other	1,173	1,360	1,737	2,229	2,644	2,185	2,185	2,428
Total purchased intercity transportation	**$17,861**	**$21,128**	**$22,671**	**$27,991**	**$31,215**	**$30,037**	**$30,018**	**$31,594**
Total transportation expenditures	**$263,419**	**$328,214**	**$370,349**	**$413,184**	**$453,654**	**$434,619**	**$463,128**	**$496,075**
Total personal consumption expenditures	**$2,059,179**	**$2,460,288**	**$2,850,553**	**$3,296,126**	**$3,748,417**	**$3,906,353**	**$4,139,901**	**$4,391,790**

* New and used trucks, recreation vehicles, etc.

Road Mileage Between Selected U.S. Cities

	Atlanta	Boston	Chicago	Cincin-nati	Cleve-land	Dallas	Denver	Des Moines	Detroit	Houston
Atlanta, Ga.	...	1,037	674	440	672	795	1,398	870	699	789
Boston, Mass..	1,037	...	963	840	628	1,748	1,949	1,280	695	1,804
Chicago, Ill.	674	963	...	287	335	917	996	327	266	1,067
Cincinnati, Oh.	440	840	287	...	244	920	1,164	571	259	1,029
Cleveland, Oh.	672	628	335	244	...	1,159	1,321	652	170	1,273
Dallas Tex.	795	1,748	917	920	1,159	...	781	684	1,143	243
Denver, Col.	1,398	1,949	996	1,164	1,321	781	...	669	1,253	1,019
Detroit, Mich.	699	695	266	259	170	1,143	1,253	584	...	1,265
Houston, Tex.	789	1,804	1,067	1,029	1,273	243	1,019	905	1,265	...
Indianapolis, Ind.. . .	493	906	181	106	294	865	1,058	465	278	987
Kansas City, Mo.. . .	798	1,391	499	591	779	489	600	195	743	710
Los Angeles, Cal. . .	2,182	2,979	2,054	2,179	2,367	1,387	1,059	1,727	2,311	1,538
Memphis, Tenn. . . .	371	1,296	530	468	712	452	1,040	599	713	561
Milwaukee, Wis. . . .	761	1,050	87	374	422	991	1,029	361	353	1,142
Minneapolis, Minn. .	1,068	1,368	405	692	740	936	841	252	671	1,157
New Orleans, La. . .	479	1,507	912	786	1,030	496	1,273	978	1,045	356
New York, N.Y.. . . .	841	206	802	647	473	1,552	1,771	1,119	637	1,608
Omaha, Neb.	986	1,412	459	693	784	644	537	132	716	865
Philadelphia, Pa.. . .	741	296	738	567	413	1,452	1,691	1,051	573	1,508
Pittsburgh, Pa.	687	561	452	287	129	1,204	1,411	763	287	1,313
Portland Ore.	2,601	3,046	2,083	2,333	2,418	2,009	1,238	1,786	2,349	2,205
St. Louis, Mo.	541	1,141	289	340	529	630	857	333	513	779
San Francisco	2,496	3,095	2,142	2,362	2,467	1,753	1,235	1,815	2,399	1,912
Seattle, Wash.	2,618	2,976	2,013	2,300	2,348	2,078	1,307	1,749	2,279	2,274
Tulsa, Okla.	772	1,537	683	736	925	257	681	443	909	478
Washington, D.C. . .	608	429	671	481	346	1,319	1,616	984	506	1,375

	India-napolis	Kansas City	Los Angeles	Louis-ville	Memphis	Mil-waukee	Minne-apolis	New Orleans	New York	Omaha
Atlanta, Ga.	493	798	2,182	382	371	761	1,068	479	841	986
Boston, Mass..	906	1,391	2,979	941	1,296	1,050	1,368	1,507	206	1,412
Chicago, Ill.	181	499	2,054	292	530	87	405	912	802	459
Cincinnati, Oh.	106	591	2,179	101	468	374	692	786	647	693
Cleveland Oh..	294	779	2,367	345	712	422	740	1,030	473	784
Dallas, Tex.	865	489	1,387	819	452	991	936	496	1,552	644
Denver, Col.	1,058	600	1,059	1,120	1,040	1,029	841	1,273	1,771	537
Detroit, Mich.	278	743	2,311	360	713	353	671	1,045	637	716
Houston, Tex..	987	710	1,538	928	561	1,142	1,157	356	1,608	865
Indianapolis, Ind.. . .	...	485	2,073	111	435	268	586	796	713	587
Kansas City, Mo.. . .	485	...	1,589	520	451	537	447	806	1,198	201
Los Angeles, Cal. . .	2,073	1,589	...	2,108	1,817	2,087	1,889	1,883	2,786	1,595
Memphis, Tenn. . . .	435	451	1,817	367	...	612	826	390	1,100	652
Milwaukee, Wis. . . .	268	537	2,087	379	612	...	332	994	889	493
Minneapolis, Minn. .	586	447	1,889	697	826	332	...	1,214	1,207	357
New Orleans, La. . .	796	806	1,883	685	390	994	1,214	...	1,311	1,007
New York, N.Y.. . . .	713	1,198	2,786	748	1,100	889	1,207	1,311	...	1,251
Omaha, Neb.	587	201	1,595	687	652	493	357	1,007	1,251	...
Philadelphia, Pa.. . .	633	1,118	2,706	668	1,000	825	1,143	1,211	100	1,183
Pittsburgh, Pa.	353	838	2,426	388	752	539	857	1,070	368	895
Portland, Ore..	1,227	1,809	959	2,320	2,259	2,010	1,678	2,505	2,885	1,654
St. Louis, Mo.	235	257	1,845	263	285	363	552	673	948	449
San Francisco	2,256	1,835	379	2,349	2,125	2,175	1,940	2,249	2,934	1,683
Seattle, Wash.	2,194	1,839	1,131	2,305	2,290	1,940	1,608	2,574	2,815	1,638
Tulsa, Okla.	631	248	1,452	659	401	757	695	647	1,344	387
Washington, D.C. . .	558	1,043	2,631	582	867	758	1,076	1,078	233	1,116

	Phila-delphia	Pitts-burgh	Port-land	St. Louis	Salt Lake City	San Fran-cisco	Seattle	Toledo	Tulsa	Wash., D.C.
Atlanta, Ga.	741	687	2,601	541	1,878	2,496	2,618	640	772	608
Boston, Mass..	296	561	3,046	1,141	2,343	3,095	2,976	739	1,537	429
Chicago, Ill.	738	452	2,083	289	1,390	2,142	2,013	232	683	671
Cincinnati, Oh.	567	287	2,333	340	1,610	2,362	2,300	200	736	481
Cleveland Oh..	413	129	2,418	529	1,715	2,467	2,348	111	925	346
Dallas, Tex.	1,452	1,204	2,009	630	1,242	1,753	2,078	1,084	257	1,319
Denver, Col.	1,691	1,411	1,238	857	504	1,235	1,307	1,218	681	1,616
Detroit, Mich.	576	287	2,349	513	1,647	2,399	2,279	59	909	506
Houston, Tex..	1,508	1,313	2,205	779	1,438	1,912	2,274	1,206	478	1,375
Indianapolis, Ind.. . .	633	353	2,227	235	1,504	2,256	2,194	219	631	558
Kansas City, Mo.. . .	1,118	838	1,809	257	1,086	1,835	1,839	687	248	1,043
Los Angeles, Cal. . .	2,706	2,426	959	1,845	715	379	1,131	2,276	1,452	2,631
Memphis, Tenn. . . .	1,000	752	2,259	285	1,535	2,125	2,290	654	401	867
Milwaukee, Wis. . . .	825	539	2,010	363	1,423	2,175	1,940	319	757	758
Minneapolis, Minn. .	1,143	857	1,678	552	1,186	1,940	1,608	637	695	1,076
New Orleans, La. . .	1,211	1,070	2,505	673	1,738	2,249	2,574	986	647	1,078
New York, N.Y.. . . .	100	368	2,885	948	2,182	2,934	2,815	578	1,344	233
Omaha, Neb.	1,183	895	1,654	449	931	1,683	1,638	681	387	1,116
Philadelphia, Pa.. . .	...	288	2,821	868	2,114	2,866	2,751	514	1,264	133
Pittsburgh, Pa.	288	...	2,535	588	1,826	2,578	2,465	228	984	221
Portland, Ore..	2,821	2,535	...	2,060	767	636	172	2,315	1,913	2,754
St. Louis, Mo.	868	588	2,060	...	1,337	2,089	2,081	454	396	793
San Francisco	2,866	2,578	636	2,089	752	...	808	2,364	1,760	2,799
Seattle, Wash.	2,751	2,465	172	2,081	836	808	...	2,245	1,982	2,684
Tulsa, Okla.	1,264	984	1,913	396	1,172	1,760	1,982	850	...	1,189
Washington, D.C. . .	133	221	2,754	793	2,047	2,799	2,684	447	1,189	...

Air Distances Between Selected World Cities in Statute Miles

Point-to-point measurements are usually from City Hall.

	Bangkok	Beijing	Berlin	Cairo	Cape Town	Caracas	Chicago	Hong Kong	Honolulu	Lima
Bangkok	...	2,046	5,352	4,523	6,300	10,555	8,570	1,077	6,609	12,244
Beijing	2,046	...	4,584	4,698	8,044	8,950	6,604	1,217	5,077	10,349
Berlin	5,352	4,584	...	1,797	5,961	5,238	4,414	5,443	7,320	6,896
Cairo	4,523	4,698	1,797	...	4,480	6,342	6,141	5,066	8,848	7,726
Cape Town	6,300	8,044	5,961	4,480	...	6,366	8,491	7,376	11,535	6,072
Caracas	10,555	8,950	5,238	6,342	6,366	...	2,495	10,165	6,021	1,707
Chicago	8,570	6,604	4,414	6,141	8,491	2,495	...	7,797	4,256	3,775
Hong Kong	1,077	1,217	5,443	5,066	7,376	10,165	7,797	...	5,556	11,418
Honolulu	6,609	5,077	7,320	8,848	11,535	6,021	4,256	5,556	...	5,947
London	5,944	5,074	583	2,185	5,989	4,655	3,958	5,990	7,240	6,316
Los Angeles	7,637	6,250	5,782	7,520	9,969	3,632	1,745	7,240	2,557	4,171
Madrid	6,337	5,745	1,165	2,087	5,308	4,346	4,189	6,558	7,872	5,907
Melbourne	4,568	5,643	9,918	8,675	6,425	9,717	9,673	4,595	5,505	8,059
Mexico City	9,793	7,753	6,056	7,700	8,519	2,234	1,690	8,788	3,789	2,639
Montreal	8,338	6,519	3,740	5,427	7,922	2,438	745	7,736	4,918	3,970
Moscow	4,389	3,607	1,006	1,803	6,279	6,177	4,987	4,437	7,047	7,862
New York	8,669	6,844	3,979	5,619	7,803	2,120	714	8,060	4,969	3,639
Paris	5,877	5,120	548	1,998	5,786	4,732	4,143	5,990	7,449	6,370
Rio de Janeiro	9,994	10,768	6,209	6,143	3,781	2,804	5,282	11,009	8,288	2,342
Rome	5,494	5,063	737	1,326	5,231	5,195	4,824	5,774	8,040	6,750
San Francisco	7,931	5,918	5,672	7,466	10,248	3,902	1,859	6,905	2,398	4,518
Singapore	883	2,771	6,164	5,137	6,008	11,402	9,372	1,605	6,726	11,689
Stockholm	5,089	4,133	528	2,096	6,423	5,471	4,331	5,063	6,875	7,166
Tokyo	2,865	1,307	5,557	5,958	9,154	8,808	6,314	1,791	3,859	9,631
Warsaw	5,033	4,325	322	1,619	5,935	5,559	4,679	5,147	7,366	7,215
Washington, D.C.	8,807	6,942	4,181	5,822	7,895	2,047	596	8,155	4,838	3,509

	London	Los Angeles	Madrid	Melbourne	Mexico City	Montreal	Moscow	New Delhi	New York	Paris
Bangkok	5,944	7,637	6,337	4,568	9,793	8,338	4,389	1,813	8,669	5,877
Beijing	5,074	6,250	5,745	5,643	7,753	6,519	3,607	2,353	6,844	5,120
Berlin	583	5,782	1,165	9,918	6,056	3,740	1,006	3,598	3,979	548
Cairo	2,185	7,520	2,087	8,675	7,700	5,427	1,803	2,758	5,619	1,998
Cape Town	5,989	9,969	5,308	6,425	8,519	7,922	6,279	5,769	7,803	5,786
Caracas	4,655	3,632	4,346	9,717	2,234	2,438	6,177	8,833	2,120	4,732
Chicago	3,958	1,745	4,189	9,673	1,690	745	4,987	7,486	714	4,143
Hong Kong	5,990	7,240	6,558	4,595	8,788	7,736	4,437	2,339	8,060	5,990
Honolulu	7,240	2,557	7,872	5,505	3,789	4,918	7,047	7,412	4,969	7,449
London	...	5,439	785	10,500	5,558	3,254	1,564	4,181	3,469	214
Los Angeles	5,439	...	5,848	7,931	1,542	2,427	6,068	7,011	2,451	5,601
Madrid	785	5,848	...	10,758	5,643	3,448	2,147	4,530	3,593	655
Melbourne	10,500	7,931	10,758	...	8,426	10,395	8,950	6,329	10,359	10,430
Mexico City	5,558	1,542	5,643	8,426	...	2,317	6,676	9,120	2,090	5,725
Montreal	3,254	2,427	3,448	10,395	2,317	...	4,401	7,012	331	3,432
Moscow	1,564	6,068	2,147	8,950	6,676	4,401	...	2,698	4,683	1,554
New York	3,469	2,451	3,593	10,359	2,090	331	4,683	7,318	...	3,636
Paris	214	5,601	655	10,430	5,725	3,432	1,554	4,102	3,636	...
Rio de Janeiro	5,750	6,330	5,045	8,226	4,764	5,078	7,170	8,753	4,801	5,684
Rome	895	6,326	851	9,929	6,377	4,104	1,483	3,684	4,293	690
San Francisco	5,367	347	5,803	7,856	1,887	2,543	5,885	7,691	2,572	5,577
Singapore	6,747	8,767	7,080	3,759	10,327	9,203	5,228	2,571	9,534	6,673
Stockholm	942	5,454	1,653	9,630	6,012	3,714	716	3,414	3,986	1,003
Tokyo	5,959	5,470	6,706	5,062	7,035	6,471	4,660	3,638	6,757	6,053
Warsaw	905	5,922	1,427	9,598	6,337	4,022	721	3,277	4,270	852
Washington, D.C.	3,674	2,300	3,792	10,180	1,885	489	4,876	7,500	205	3,840

	Rio de Janeiro	Rome	San Francisco	Singapore	Stockholm	Tehran	Tokyo	Vienna	Warsaw	Wash., D.C.
Bangkok	9,994	5,494	7,931	883	5,089	3,391	2,865	5,252	5,033	8,807
Beijing	10,768	5,063	5,918	2,771	4,133	3,490	1,307	4,648	4,325	6,942
Berlin	6,209	737	5,672	6,164	528	2,185	5,557	326	322	4,181
Cairo	6,143	1,326	7,466	5,137	2,096	1,234	5,958	1,481	1,619	5,822
Cape Town	3,781	5,231	10,248	6,008	6,423	5,241	9,154	5,656	5,935	7,895
Caracas	2,804	5,195	3,902	11,402	5,471	7,320	8,808	5,372	5,559	2,047
Chicago	5,282	4,824	1,859	9,372	4,331	6,502	6,314	4,698	4,679	596
Hong Kong	11,009	5,774	6,905	1,605	5,063	3,843	1,791	5,431	5,147	8,155
Honolulu	8,288	8,040	2,398	6,726	6,875	8,070	3,859	7,632	7,366	4,838
London	5,750	895	5,367	6,747	942	2,743	5,959	771	905	3,674
Los Angeles	6,330	6,326	347	8,767	5,454	7,682	5,470	6,108	5,922	2,300
Madrid	5,045	851	5,803	7,080	1,653	2,978	6,706	1,128	1,427	3,792
Melbourne	8,226	9,929	7,856	3,759	9,630	7,826	5,062	9,790	9,598	10,180
Mexico City	4,764	6,377	1,887	10,327	6,012	8,184	7,035	6,320	6,337	1,885
Montreal	5,078	4,104	2,543	9,203	3,714	5,880	6,471	4,009	4,022	489
Moscow	7,170	1,483	5,885	5,228	716	1,532	4,660	1,043	721	4,876
New York	4,801	4,293	2,572	9,534	3,986	6,141	6,757	4,234	4,270	205
Paris	5,684	690	5,577	6,673	1,003	2,625	6,053	645	852	3,840
Rio de Janeiro	...	5,707	6,613	9,785	6,683	7,374	11,532	6,127	6,455	4,779
Rome	5,707	...	6,259	6,229	1,245	2,127	6,142	477	820	4,497
San Francisco	6,613	6,259	...	8,448	5,399	7,362	5,150	5,994	5,854	2,441
Singapore	9,785	6,229	8,448	...	5,936	4,103	3,300	6,035	5,843	9,662
Stockholm	6,683	1,245	5,399	5,936	...	2,173	5,053	780	494	4,183
Tokyo	11,532	6,142	5,150	3,300	5,053	4,775	...	5,689	5,347	6,791
Warsaw	6,455	820	5,854	5,843	494	1,879	5,689	347	...	4,472
Washington, D.C.	4,779	4,497	2,441	9,662	4,183	6,341	6,791	4,438	4,472	...

CRIME

1994 Crime Bill Summary

The 1994 Omnibus Violent Crime Control and Prevention Act was passed by Congress on Aug. 25, 1994, and signed by Pres. Bill Clinton on Sept. 13, 1994. Below is a summary of the act's major provisions (numbers may not add to totals due to rounding).

Violent Crime Reduction Trust Fund - $30.2 billion

Authorizes federal spending of $30.2 billion over six years through the newly created Violent Crime Reduction Trust Fund. Savings from reductions in the federal workforce are to provide the funds, to be used as follows:

Law Enforcement - $13.5 billion

State and Local - $10.8 billion, including:

Community policing: $8.8 billion to put 100,000 police officers on the streets in community policing programs.

Rural law enforcement: $245 million for rural anticrime and drug efforts.

Technical automation: $130 million for technical automation grants for law enforcement agencies.

Brady Bill: $150 million for implementation of the Brady Handgun Violence Prevention Act (passed in 1993).

Drug enforcement: $1 billion in grants.

DNA: $40 million for DNA testing research and programs.

Courts, prosecutors, and public defenders: $200 million.

Police Corps: $200 million for college scholarships for students who agree to serve as police officers, and for scholarships for in-service officers.

Federal - $2.6 billion, including:

FBI: $250 million. Drug Enforcement Administration: $150 million. Immigration enforcement: INS and Border Patrol: $1.2 billion. United States Attorneys: $50 million. Treasury Department: $550 million. Justice Department: $200 million. Federal courts: $200 million.

Prisons - $9.7 billion

Grants to states: $7.9 billion to build and operate prisons and incarceration alternatives such as boot camps.

$1.8 billion to states for the costs of incarcerating criminal illegal aliens.

Crime Prevention - $6.1 billion, including:

Violence Against Women Act: $1.6 billion to fight violence against women.

$90 million to create an interagency Ounce of Prevention Council to coordinate new and existing crime prevention programs.

Community schools: $567 million for after-school, weekend, and summer "safe haven" programs to provide children with alternatives to street life.

$243 million to provide in-school assistance to at-risk children, including education, mentoring, and other programs.

Local Partnership Act: $1.6 billion for direct funding to localities for anticrime efforts, such as drug treatment, education, and jobs.

Model Intensive Grants: $626 million for model crime prevention programs targeted at high crime neighborhoods.

Community Economic Partnership: $270 million for lines of credit to community development corporations to stimulate business and employment opportunities for low-income, unemployed and underemployed individuals.

Drug treatment: $383 million for drug treatment programs for state ($270 million) and federal ($113 million) prisoners. Creates a treatment schedule for all drug-addicted federal prisoners. Requires drug testing of federal prisoners on release.

Crime Prevention Block Grant: $377 million for a new Local Crime Prevention Block Grant program, the funds to be distributed to local governments to be used as local needs dictate for, among other things, the following purposes:

- Anti-gang programs.
- Sports leagues: To fund midnight sports leagues to give at-risk youths nightly alternatives to the streets, and for the U.S. Olympic Committee to develop supervised sports and recreation programs in high-crime areas.
- Boys and Girls Clubs.
- Partnerships between senior citizen groups and law enforcement agencies to combat crimes against elderly Americans.
- Partnerships between law enforcement and social service agencies to fight crimes against children, and for the creation of youth councils to combat crime.
- To provide jobs to young adults in high crime areas, conditioned on continued responsible behavior.

Drug Courts - $1 billion

Provides $1 billion to create drug courts, which could place nonviolent offenders with substance abuse problems in treatment programs, rather than in jail.

Other Provisions

Firearms

Assault weapons: Bans the manufacture of 19 named military-style assault weapons, assault weapons with specific combat features, "copy-cat" models, and high-capacity ammunition magazines ("clips") of more than ten rounds.

Prohibits the sale or transfer of a gun to a juvenile and possession of a gun by a juvenile.

Prohibits gun sales to, and possession by, persons subject to family violence restraining orders.

Strengthens federal licensing standards for firearms dealers.

Gangs and Youth Violence

Provides new, stiff penalties for violent and drug crimes committed by gangs.

Triples penalties for using children to deal drugs near schools and playgrounds.

Enhances penalties for all crimes using children and for recruiting or encouraging children to commit a crime.

Increases penalties for drug dealing in drug free zones — near playgrounds, schoolyards, video arcades, and youth centers.

Increases penalties for drug dealing near public housing.

Authorizes juveniles aged 13 and older to be tried as adults in federal courts for some violent crimes.

Death Penalty

Expands the federal death penalty to cover about 60 offenses, including terrorism, murder of a law enforcement officer, large-scale drug trafficking, drive-by shootings, and carjackings resulting in murder.

Other Penalties

Three strikes: Mandates life imprisonment for anyone convicted of a federal crime who has 2 prior convictions for serious state or federal felonies.

Miscellaneous: Increases or creates new penalties for over 70 federal criminal offenses, primarily covering violent crimes, drug trafficking, and gun crimes.

Terrorism

Increases penalties for any felony involving or promoting international terrorism.

Crime Victims

Right of allocution: Allows victims of violent and sex crimes to speak at the sentencing of their assailants.

Mandatory restitution: Requires sex offenders and child molesters to pay restitution to their victims.

Fraud

Strengthens penalties for telemarketing fraud, insurance fraud, and credit card fraud. Revises and expands computer crime offenses.

Summary of Spending

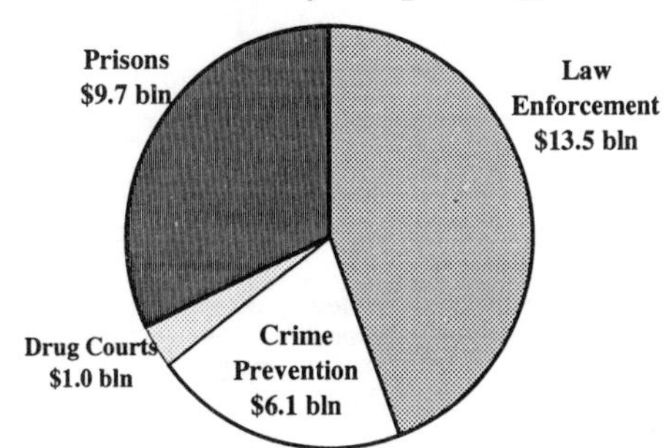

Crime Down Overall in 1993, But Murders Increase

Serious crimes reported to law enforcement agencies in the U.S. decreased 3% in 1993 compared to 1992, according to preliminary *Uniform Crime Reports* figures released by the Federal Bureau of Investigation. The decrease continued the trend from 1992, when overall crime was also down 3% from the previous year.

Serious crime is measured by the Crime Index, composed of 4 violent and 4 property crimes. Violent crime dropped 1% in 1993, and property crime (excluding arson) decreased 3%.

Of the 4 violent crimes in the Crime Index, 1 increased and 2 declined. The number of reported murders was up 3% in 1993 versus 1992; forcible rape fell 4%; robbery dropped 2%; and aggravated assault showed no change. In the property crime category, burglary and arson each dropped 6%; motor vehible theft fell 4%; and larceny-theft was down 2%.

Declines in overall Crime Index totals occurred in all regions: 5% in the northeast, 3% in the midwest, and 2% in the south and in the west.

There were Crime Index decreases in all population groupings during 1993. The greatest decline—5%—was recorded in cities with populations of more than 1 million. Rural county law enforcement agencies reported a decrease of 3%, and suburban county law enforcement agencies reported a decrease of 2%.

Crime Index Trends

Source: FBI, *Uniform Crime Reports,* 1993 Preliminary Annual Release

(Percentage change 1993 over 1992, offenses known to the police.)

Population group and area	No. of agencies[1]	Population (thousands)	Crime Index (total)	Violent crime	Property crime[2]	Murder	Forcible rape	Robbery	Aggravated assault	Burglary	Larceny-theft	Motor vehicle theft
Total U.S.	10,084	202,316	–3	–1	–3	+3	–4	–2	0	–6	–2	–4
Cities:												
Over 1,000,000	8	20,365	–5	–4	–6	–4	–4	–5	–3	–8	–3	–9
500,000 to 999,999	18	12,199	–2	+1	–2	+9	–2	0	+2	–5	0	–5
250,000 to 499,999	33	12,352	–2	0	–3	+8	–7	0	0	–7	–2	–1
100,000 to 249,999	124	18,467	–2	+2	–2	+12	–5	0	+3	–5	–1	–2
50,000 to 99,999	294	20,495	–3	–2	–3	+5	–6	–2	–1	–5	–2	–3
25,000 to 49,999	554	19,310	–3	0	–3	+13	–3	0	0	–5	–3	–2
10,000 to 24,999	1,231	19,401	–3	–1	–3	–9	+1	–2	–1	–4	–3	0
Under 10,000	4,791	16,717	–3	+2	–3	–1	–3	+1	+3	–4	–3	–4
Counties:												
Suburban[3]	1,079	43,374	–2	–1	–2	+2	–3	–4	0	–5	–2	+1
Rural[4]	1,952	19,637	–3	+4	–3	–3	+2	–2	+5	–5	–3	+1
Areas:												
Suburban area[5]	5,165	83,287	–3	–1	–3	+2	–3	–2	0	–5	–2	–1
Cities outside metropolitan areas	2,490	15,514	–2	+1	–3	+1	–2	0	+2	–4	–2	0

(1) Law–enforcement agencies. (2) Data for arson not included. (3) Includes crimes reported to sheriffs' departments, county police departments, and state police within Metropolitan Statistical Areas. (4) Includes crimes reported to sheriffs' departments, county police departments, and state police outside Metropolitan Statistical Areas. (5) Includes crimes reported to city, county, and state law enforcement agencies within Metropolitan Statistical Areas but outside the central cities.

Crime Index Trends by Geographic Region

Source: FBI, *Uniform Crime Reports,* 1993 Preliminary Annual Release

(Percentage change 1993 over 1992, offenses known to the police.)

Region	Crime Index (total)	Violent crime	Property crime[1]	Murder	Forcible rape	Robbery	Aggravated assault	Burglary	Larceny-theft	Motor vehicle theft
Total U.S.	–3	–1	–3	+3	–4	–2	0	–6	–2	–4
Northeast	–5	–2	–5	+5	–5	–4	0	–6	–4	–9
Midwest	–3	–1	–4	–1	–3	–1	–1	–7	–2	–4
South	–2	0	–3	+3	–2	–2	0	–7	–1	–4
West	–2	–1	–2	+4	–7	–3	+1	–3	–2	0

(1) Data for arson not included.

Crime Index Trends, 1990-93

Source: FBI, *Uniform Crime Reports,* 1993 Preliminary Annual Release

(Percentage change over previous year.)

Year	Crime Index (total)	Violent crime	Property crime[1]	Murder	Forcible rape	Robbery	Aggravated assault	Burglary	Larceny-theft	Motor vehicle theft
1990	+2	+11	0	+9	+9	+11	+11	–3	+1	+5
1991	+3	+5	+2	+7	+3	+8	+3	+3	+2	+2
1992	–3	+1	–4	–4	+2	–2	+3	–6	–3	–3
1993	–3	–1	–3	+3	–4	–2	0	–6	–2	–4

(1) Data for arson not included.

Crime in the U.S., 1973–92

Source: FBI, *Uniform Crime Reports,* 1992

Population[1]	Crime Index (total)[2]	Violent crime	Property crime[3]	Murder and non-negligent man-slaughter	Forcible rape	Robbery	Burglary	Larceny theft
				Number of offenses				
Population by year								
1973–209,851,000...	8,718,000	875,910	7,842,200	19,640	51,400	384,220	2,565,500	4,347,900
1974–211,392,000...	10,253,400	974,720	9,278,700	20,710	55,400	442,400	3,039,200	5,262,500
1975–213,124,000...	11,292,400	1,039,710	10,252,700	20,510	56,090	470,500	3,265,300	5,977,700
1976–214,659,000...	11,349,700	1,004,210	10,345,500	18,780	57,080	427,810	3,108,700	6,270,800
1977–216,332,000...	10,984,500	1,029,580	9,955,000	19,120	63,500	412,610	3,071,500	5,905,700
1978–218,059,000...	11,209,000	1,085,550	10,123,400	19,560	67,610	426,930	3,128,300	5,991,000
1979–220,099,000...	12,249,500	1,208,030	11,041,500	21,460	76,390	480,700	3,327,700	6,601,000
1980–225,349,264...	13,408,300	1,344,520	12,063,700	23,040	82,990	565,840	3,795,200	7,136,900
1981–229,146,000...	13,423,800	1,361,820	12,061,900	22,520	82,500	592,910	3,779,700	7,194,400
1982–231,534,000...	12,974,400	1,322,390	11,652,000	21,010	78,770	553,130	3,447,100	7,142,500
1983–233,981,000...	12,108,600	1,258,090	10,850,500	19,310	78,920	506,570	3,129,900	6,712,800
1984–236,158,000...	11,881,800	1,273,280	10,608,500	18,690	84,230	485,010	2,984,400	6,591,900
1985–238,740,000...	12,431,400	1,328,800	11,102,600	18,980	88,670	497,870	3,073,300	6,926,400
1986–241,077,000...	13,211,900	1,489,170	11,722,700	20,610	91,460	542,780	3,241,400	7,257,200
1987–243,400,000...	13,508,700	1,484,000	12,024,700	20,100	91,110	517,700	3,236,200	7,499,900
1988–245,807,000...	13,923,100	1,566,220	12,356,900	20,680	92,490	542,970	3,218,100	7,705,900
1989–248,239,000...	14,251,400	1,646,040	12,605,400	21,500	94,500	578,330	3,168,200	7,872,400
1990–248,709,873...	14,475,600	1,820,130	12,655,500	23,440	102,560	639,270	3,073,900	7,945,700
1991–252,177,000...	14,872,900	1,911,770	12,961,100	24,700	106,590	687,730	3,157,200	8,142,200
1992–255,082,000...	14,438,200	1,932,270	12,505,900	23,760	109,060	672,480	2,979,900	7,915,200
Percent change: number of offenses								
1992/1991	–2.9	+1.1	–3.5	–3.8	+2.3	–2.2	–5.6	–2.8
1992/1988	+3.7	+23.4	+1.2	+14.9	+17.9	+23.9	–7.4	+2.7
1992/1983	+19.2	+53.6	+15.3	+23.0	+38.2	+32.8	–4.8	+17.9
				Rate per 100,000 inhabitants				
Year								
1973.............	4,154.4	417.4	3,737.0	9.4	24.5	183.1	1,222.5	2,071.9
1974.............	4,850.4	461.1	4,389.3	9.8	26.2	209.3	1,437.7	2,489.5
1975.............	5,298.5	487.8	4,810.7	9.6	26.3	220.8	1,532.1	2,804.8
1976.............	5,287.3	467.8	4,819.5	8.8	26.6	199.3	1,448.2	2,921.3
1977.............	5,077.6	475.9	4,601.7	8.8	29.4	190.7	1,419.8	2,729.9
1978.............	5,140.3	497.8	4,642.5	9.0	31.0	195.8	1,434.6	2,747.4
1979.............	5,565.5	548.9	5,016.6	9.7	34.7	218.4	1,511.9	2,999.1
1980.............	5,950.0	596.6	5,353.3	10.2	36.8	251.1	1,684.1	3,167.0
1981.............	5,858.2	594.3	5,263.9	9.8	36.0	258.7	1,649.5	3,139.7
1982.............	5,603.6	571.1	5,032.5	9.1	34.0	238.9	1,488.8	3,084.8
1983.............	5,175.0	537.7	4,637.4	8.3	33.7	216.5	1,337.7	2,868.9
1984.............	5,031.3	539.2	4,492.1	7.9	35.7	205.4	1,263.7	2,791.3
1985.............	5,207.1	556.6	4,650.5	7.9	37.1	208.5	1,287.3	2,901.2
1986.............	5,480.4	617.7	4,862.6	8.6	37.9	225.1	1,344.6	3,010.3
1987.............	5,550.0	609.7	4,940.3	8.3	37.4	212.7	1,329.6	3,081.3
1988.............	5,664.2	637.2	5,027.1	8.4	37.6	220.9	1,309.2	3,134.9
1989.............	5,741.0	663.1	5,077.9	8.7	38.1	233.0	1,276.3	3,171.3
1990.............	5,820.3	731.8	5,088.5	9.4	41.2	257.0	1,235.9	3,194.8
1991.............	5,897.8	758.1	5,139.7	9.8	42.3	272.7	1,252.0	3,228.8
1992.............	5,660.2	757.5	4,902.7	9.3	42.8	263.6	1,168.2	3,103.0
Percent change: rate per 100,000 inhabitants								
1992/1991	–4.0	–0.1	–4.6	–5.1	+1.2	–3.3	–6.7	–3.9
1992/1988	–0.1	+18.9	–2.5	+10.7	+13.8	+19.3	–10.8	–1.0
1992/1983	+9.4	+40.9	+5.7	+12.0	+27.0	+21.8	–12.7	+8.2

(1) Populations are Bureau of the Census provisional estimates as of July 1, except 1980 and 1990, which are the decennial census counts. (2) Because of rounding, the offenses may not add to totals. (3) Data for arson not included.
Note: All rates were calculated on the offenses before rounding.

Law Enforcement Officers

Source: FBI, *Uniform Crime Reports,* 1992

The U.S. law enforcement community employed an average of 2.3 full–time officers for every 1,000 inhabitants as of October 31, 1992. Considering full–time civilians, the overall law enforcement employee rate was 3.1 per 1,000 inhabitants according to 13,032 city, county, and state police agencies. These agencies collectively offered law enforcement service to a population of over 241 million, employing 544,309 officers and 204,521 civilians.

The law enforcement employee average for all cities nationwide was 2.8 per 1,000 inhabitants. City law enforcement employee averages ranged from 3.4 per 1,000 inhabitants in those with populations of less than 10,000 to 3.6 for those with populations of 250,000 or more. Rural and suburban counties averaged full–time law enforcement employee rates of 3.9 and 3.6 per 1,000 population, respectively.

Regionally, the highest law enforcement employee rate was in the South, with 3.2, and lowest in the West, 2.4.

Nationally, males comprised 91 percent of all sworn employees. Ninety–three percent of the officers in rural counties and 91 percent of those in cities were males, while in suburban counties males accounted for 89 percent.

Civilians made up 27 percent of the total U.S. law enforcement employee force. They represented 22 percent of the police employees in cities, 34 percent of those in rural counties, and 36 percent in suburban counties.

Sixty–one law enforcement officers were feloniously slain in the line of duty in 1992, 10 fewer than in 1991. Another 66 officers were killed due to accidents occurring while performing official duties.

Prison Situation Among the States, 1993

Source: *Prisoners in 1993,* Bureau of Justice Statistics, U.S. Dept. of Justice; year–end 1993.

10 states with the largest 1993 prison populations	Number of inmates	10 states with the highest incarceration rates, 1993[1]	Prisoners per 100,000 residents	10 states with the largest % increases in prison population: 1992–93	% increase	1988–93	% increase
California	119,951	Texas	553	Connecticut	20.1	Washington	79.1
Texas	71,103	Oklahoma	506	Texas	16.2	Texas	75.8
New York	64,569	Louisiana	499	Minnesota	15.5	New Hampshire	74.2
Florida	53,048	South Carolina	489	Mississippi	15.2	Connecticut	71.0
Ohio	40,641	Nevada	438	Oklahoma	10.7	Tennessee	65.9
Michigan	39,529	Alabama	431	Georgia	9.9	Illinois	63.6
Illinois	34,495	Arizona	430	Florida	9.8	Iowa	61.4
Georgia	27,783	Michigan	416	California	9.5	Virginia	61.1
Pennsylvania	26,050	Delaware	397	Illinois	9.0	Minnesota	57.7
New Jersey	23,831	Georgia	387	Iowa	8.4	California	57.5

Note: The District of Columbia as a wholly urban jurisdiction is excluded. (1) Prisoners with sentences of more than 1 year.

State and Federal Prison Population; Death Penalty

Source: Prison population: Bureau of Justice Statistics, U.S. Dept. of Justice, Dec. 31, 1993; Death penalty: Bureau of Justice Statistics,as of Dec. 31, 1993.

The number of prisoners under the jurisdiction of federal or state correctional authorities at year–end 1993 reached a record high of 948,881. The states and the District of Columbia added 55,898 prisoners; the federal system, 9,327. The increase for 1993 brought total growth in the prison population since 1980 to 619,060—an increase of about 188% in the 13–year period. The 1993 growth rate of 7.4% was slightly greater than the percentage increase recorded during 1992 (7.0%), and the number of new prisoners added during 1993 was 7,188 more than the number added during the preceding year (58,037). The 1993 increase translated into a nationwide need for approximately 1,254 prison bedspaces per week, compared with the 1,116 prison bedspaces per week needed in 1992. In 1980, about 1 of every 15 court–committed entries to state prison was an offender convicted of a drug offense. In 1992, drug offenses accounted for about 1 in 3 new commitments to state prisons. During the same period, the percentage of prison admissions entering as violators of probation or parole conditions also increased—from 17% to about 30%.

	Sentenced to more than 1 yr: Final 1992	Advance 1993	% change 1992–93	Under sentence of death	Death penalty 1992: Executions	Death penalty
Total	**847,271**	**910,462**	**7.5%**	**2,575**	**31**	—
Federal institutions	**65,706**	**74,398**	**13.2**	**1**	**0**	**Yes**
State institutions	**781,565**	**836,064**	**7.0**	**2,574**	**31**	**36**
Northeast	**133,658**	**139,956**	**4.7**	**160**	**0**	—
Connecticut	8,794	10,508	19.5	4	0	Yes
Maine	1,492	1,446	–3.1	0	0	No
Massachusetts	9,665	9,315	–3.6	0	0	No
New Hampshire	1,777	1,775	–0.1	0	0	Yes
New Jersey	22,653	23,689	4.6	3	0	Yes
New York	61,736	64,569	4.6	0	0	No
Pennsylvania	24,966	26,045	4.3	153	0	Yes
Rhode Island	1,710	1,716	.4	0	0	No
Vermont	865	893	3.2	0	0	No
Midwest	**166,658**	**173,363**	**4.0**	**411**	**1**	—
Illinois	31,640	34,495	9.0	145	0	Yes
Indiana	13,791	14,364	4.2	50	0	Yes
Iowa	4,518	4,898	8.4	0	0	No
Kansas	6,028	5,727	–5.0	0	0	No
Michigan	39,113	39,529	1.1	0	0	No
Minnesota	3,822	4,415	15.5	0	0	No
Missouri	16,181	16,178	—	82	1	Yes
Nebraska	2,435	2,360	–3.1	12	0	Yes
North Dakota	428	446	4.2	0	0	No
Ohio	38,378	40,641	5.9	121	0	Yes
South Dakota	1,487	1,553	4.4	1	0	Yes
Wisconsin	8,837	8,757	–0.9	0	0	No
South	**315,167**	**343,451**	**9.0**	**1,439**	**25**	—
Alabama	16,938	18,169	7.3	124	2	Yes
Arkansas	8,195	8,567	4.5	32	2	Yes
Delaware	2,708	2,796	3.2	11	1	Yes
District of Columbia	7,528	8,908	18.3	0	0	No
Florida	48,285	53,041	9.8	312	2	Yes
Georgia	24,848	27,079	9.0	101	0	Yes
Kentucky	10,364	10,440	0.7	29	0	Yes
Louisiana	20,812	21,499	3.3	44	0	Yes
Maryland	18,808	19,121	1.7	15	0	Yes
Mississippi	8,593	9,798	14.0	42	0	Yes
North Carolina	19,965	21,358	7.0	76	1	Yes
Oklahoma	14,821	16,409	10.7	120	1	Yes
South Carolina	17,612	17,896	1.6	41	0	Yes
Tennessee	11,849	12,827	8.3	99	0	Yes
Texas	61,178	71,103	16.2	344	12	Yes
Virginia	20,989	22,635	7.8	49	4	Yes
West Virginia	1,674	1,805	7.8	0	0	No
West	**166,082**	**179,294**	**8.0**	**564**	**4**	—
Alaska	1,944	1,954	0.5	0	0	No
Arizona	15,850	17,160	8.3	103	1	Yes

	Sentenced to more than 1 yr			Death penalty 1992		
	Final 1992	Advance 1993	% change 1992–93	Under sentence of death	Executions	Death penalty
California	105,467	115,573	9.6	332	1	Yes
Colorado	8,997	9,462	5.2	3	0	Yes
Hawaii	1,922	2,026	5.4	0	0	No
Idaho	2,256	2,606	—	23	0	Yes
Montana	1,498	1,454	−2.9	8	0	Yes
Nevada	6,049	6,198	2.5	62	0	Yes
New Mexico	3,154	3,373	6.9	1	0	Yes
Oregon	5,236	5,118	−2.3	11	0	Yes
Utah	2,687	2,871	6.8	10	1	Yes
Washington	9,959	10,419	4.6	11	0	Yes
Wyoming	1,063	1,080	1.6	0	1	Yes

Note: Prisoner counts for 1992 may differ from those reported previously. Counts for 1993 are subject to revision.

Executions, by State and Method, 1977–92

Source: Bureau of Justice Statistics, *Capital Punishment 1992,* Dec. 1993

		Method of Execution			
State	Number executed	Lethal injection	Electrocution	Lethal gas	Firing squad
Total U.S.	**188**	**82**	**98**	**7**	**1**
Texas	54	54			
Florida	29		29		
Louisiana	20		20		
Georgia	15		15		
Virginia	17		17		
Alabama	10		10		
Missouri	7	7			
Nevada	5	4		1	
Mississippi	4			4	
North Carolina	5	5			
South Carolina	4		4		
Utah	4	3			1
Arkansas	4	3	1		
Indiana	2		2		
Illinois	1	1			
Oklahoma	3	3			
Arizona	1			1	
California	1			1	
Delaware	1	1			
Wyoming	1	1			

Note: This table shows the distribution of execution methods used since 1977. The most frequently used method, electrocution, was used in 52% of the executions carried out. Lethal injection accounted for 44% of the executions. Three states—Arkansas, Nevada, and Utah—employed 2 methods.

Total Estimated Arrests,[1] 1992

Source: FBI, *Uniform Crime Reports,* 1992

Total[2]	**14,075,100**
Murder and nonnegligent manslaughter	22,510
Forcible rape	39,100
Robbery	173,310
Aggravated assault	507,210
Burglary	424,000
Larceny–theft	1,504,500
Motor vehicle theft	197,600
Arson	19,900
Violent crimes[3]	**742,130**
Property crime[4]	**2,146,000**
Crime Index total[5]	**2,888,200**
Other assaults	1,074,700
Forgery and counterfeiting	105,400
Fraud	424,200
Embezzlement	13,700
Stolen Property: buying, receiving, possesseing	161,500
Vandalism	323,100
Weapons: carrying, possessing, etc.	239,300
Prostitution and commercialized vice	96,200
Sex offenses (except forcible rape and prostitution)	108,400
Drug abuse violations	1,066,400
Gambling	17,100
Offenses against family and children	109,200
Driving under the influence	1,624,500
Liquor laws	541,700
Drunkenness	832,300
Disorderly conduct	753,100
Vagrancy	34,300
All other offenses	3,389,500
Suspicion (not included in totals)	18,400
Curfew and loitering law violations	91,100
Runaways	181,300

(1) Arrest totals are based on all reporting agencies and estimates for unreported areas. (2) Because of rounding, figures may not add to totals. (3) Violent crimes are murder, forcible rape, robbery, and aggravated assault. (4) Property crimes are burglary, larceny–theft, motor vehicle theft, and arson. (5) Includes arson.

Crime Rates by Region, Geographic Division, and State, 1992

Source: FBI, *Uniform Crime Reports,* 1992
(Rate per 100,000)

Area	Total	Violent crime[1]	Property crime[2]	Murder	Rape	Robbery	Aggravated assault	Burglary	Larceny-theft	Motor vehicle theft
United States Total	**5,660.2**	**757.5**	**4,902.7**	**9.3**	**42.8**	**263.6**	**441.8**	**1,168.2**	**3,103.0**	**631.5**
Northeast	**4,836.7**	**731.5**	**4,105.2**	**7.8**	**29.5**	**335.9**	**358.2**	**934.9**	**2,443.2**	**727.2**
New England	**4,614.0**	**534.7**	**4,079.3**	**3.5**	**32.0**	**148.7**	**350.5**	**1,007.5**	**2,442.1**	**629.7**
Connecticut	5,052.9	495.3	4,557.6	5.1	26.9	210.9	252.5	1,108.6	2,726.7	722.3
Maine	3,523.6	130.9	3,392.7	1.7	23.8	23.3	82.0	822.3	2,426.4	144.0
Massachusetts	5,002.9	779.0	4,223.8	3.6	36.1	184.4	555.0	1,072.3	2,361.0	790.5
New Hampshire	3,080.6	125.7	2,954.8	1.6	38.2	33.0	52.9	621.9	2,138.1	194.9
Rhode Island	4,578.0	394.5	4,183.5	3.6	30.9	94.5	265.5	1,047.7	2,393.2	742.6
Vermont	3,410.0	109.5	3,300.5	2.1	24.9	8.9	73.5	825.6	2,369.6	105.3

Area	Total	Violent crime[1]	Property crime[2]	Murder	Rape	Robbery	Aggravated assault	Burglary	Larceny-theft	Motor vehicle theft
Middle Atlantic	**4,914.2**	**800.0**	**4,114.3**	**9.3**	**28.7**	**401.1**	**360.9**	**909.6**	**2,443.5**	**761.2**
New Jersey	5,064.4	625.8	4,438.5	5.1	30.7	285.2	304.8	969.4	2,653.6	815.6
New York	5,858.4	1,122.1	4,736.3	13.2	28.4	596.9	483.5	1,068.2	2,735.8	932.3
Pennsylvania	3,392.7	427.0	2,965.7	6.2	27.7	180.7	212.4	631.5	1,866.5	467.7
Midwest	**4,975.4**	**607.2**	**4,368.1**	**7.6**	**45.5**	**207.3**	**346.7**	**963.7**	**2,927.9**	**476.5**
East North Central	**5,135.6**	**671.0**	**4,464.6**	**8.6**	**49.9**	**242.6**	**370.0**	**974.1**	**2,952.4**	**538.0**
Illinois	5,765.3	977.3	4,788.1	11.4	37.1	412.5	516.4	1,077.3	3,091.9	618.8
Indiana	4,686.9	508.5	4,178.5	8.2	42.4	122.2	335.7	952.1	2,776.1	450.3
Michigan	5,610.6	770.1	4,840.5	9.9	80.0	221.5	458.6	1,041.2	3,173.5	625.8
Ohio	4,665.5	525.9	4,139.6	6.6	52.1	199.0	268.2	947.3	2,721.3	471.0
Wisconsin	4,319.0	275.7	4,043.3	4.4	26.3	119.8	125.3	691.9	2,919.9	431.5
West North Central	**4,594.0**	**455.5**	**4,138.5**	**5.4**	**35.2**	**123.4**	**291.5**	**938.9**	**2,869.5**	**330.1**
Iowa	3,957.1	278.0	3,679.2	1.6	18.8	39.6	218.0	753.8	2,766.3	159.1
Kansas	5,319.9	510.8	4,809.1	6.0	41.3	129.9	333.7	1,293.7	3,191.7	323.8
Minnesota	4,590.7	338.0	4,252.7	3.3	41.1	109.5	184.1	889.7	3,007.8	355.2
Missouri	5,097.1	740.4	4,356.7	10.5	36.5	226.9	466.5	1,100.1	2,759.3	497.4
Nebraska	4,324.0	348.6	3,975.5	4.2	31.4	56.7	256.2	714.6	3,060.0	200.8
North Dakota	2,903.3	83.3	2,820.0	1.9	23.3	7.9	50.3	391.0	2,279.6	149.4
South Dakota	2,998.9	194.5	2,804.4	0.6	51.8	16.9	125.3	541.4	2,161.9	101.1
South	**6,154.6**	**809.6**	**5,345.0**	**11.1**	**46.1**	**240.9**	**511.5**	**1,378.8**	**3,388.4**	**577.8**
South Atlantic	**6,428.3**	**867.1**	**5,561.2**	**10.6**	**45.2**	**276.1**	**535.2**	**1,429.8**	**3,572.2**	**559.2**
Delaware	4,848.5	621.2	4,227.3	4.6	85.8	151.2	379.5	957.6	2,963.6	306.1
District of Columbia	11,407.0	2,832.8	8,574.2	75.2	36.5	1,266.4	1,454.7	1,820.2	5,205.9	1,548.0
Florida	8,358.2	1,207.2	7,151.0	9.0	54.2	366.9	777.2	1,888.8	4,434.3	828.0
Georgia	6,405.4	733.2	5,672.3	11.0	45.3	249.8	427.1	1,442.8	3,653.1	576.4
Maryland	6,224.6	1,000.1	5,224.5	12.1	46.4	429.0	512.6	1,131.2	3,366.8	726.4
North Carolina	5,802.2	681.0	5,121.2	10.6	35.9	186.8	447.7	1,653.0	3,181.6	286.6
South Carolina	5,893.1	944.5	4,948.6	10.4	57.5	170.6	706.0	1,378.5	3,224.7	345.4
Virginia	4,298.5	374.9	3,923.6	8.8	31.5	137.8	196.8	709.1	2,909.0	305.6
West Virgina	2,609.7	211.5	2,398.2	6.3	21.7	43.5	140.0	622.9	1,611.5	163.8
East South Central	**4,589.2**	**672.3**	**3,916.8**	**9.7**	**41.6**	**156.5**	**464.5**	**1,118.1**	**2,406.9**	**391.8**
Alabama	5,268.1	871.7	4,396.4	11.0	41.2	164.9	654.6	1,186.0	2,848.2	362.3
Kentucky	3,323.5	535.5	2,788.1	5.8	32.2	87.2	410.4	729.1	1,842.5	216.5
Mississippi	4,282.5	411.7	3,870.7	12.2	44.6	124.5	230.4	1,282.8	2,251.4	336.5
Tennessee	5,135.8	746.2	4,389.6	10.4	47.3	218.2	470.3	1,267.2	2,546.5	575.9
West South Central	**6,588.9**	**792.7**	**5,796.2**	**12.5**	**50.1**	**230.9**	**499.2**	**1,442.2**	**3,640.8**	**713.1**
Arkansas	4,761.7	576.5	4,185.2	10.8	41.3	125.5	399.0	1,092.7	2,763.2	329.3
Louisiana	6,546.5	984.6	5,561.9	17.4	42.3	271.4	653.4	1,366.3	3,567.5	628.1
Oklahoma	5,431.6	622.8	4,808.8	6.5	48.4	136.2	431.6	1,359.8	2,932.1	516.8
Texas	7,057.9	806.3	6,251.6	12.7	53.4	252.5	487.7	1,523.2	3,906.8	821.7
West	**6,387.9**	**864.0**	**5,523.9**	**9.7**	**46.6**	**295.0**	**512.6**	**1,273.1**	**3,451.5**	**799.3**
Mountain	**6,011.9**	**563.1**	**5,448.8**	**6.6**	**46.2**	**126.5**	**383.8**	**1,149.9**	**3,791.4**	**507.5**
Arizona	7,028.6	670.8	6,357.8	8.1	43.0	153.1	466.6	1,411.7	4,124.6	821.5
Colorado	5,958.8	578.8	5,379.9	6.2	47.3	120.5	404.9	1,090.9	3,780.1	509.0
Idaho	3,996.2	281.4	3,714.7	3.5	31.8	21.5	224.7	743.6	2,813.8	157.4
Montana	4,596.1	169.9	4,426.2	2.9	25.5	26.9	114.6	643.9	3,548.9	233.4
Nevada	6,203.8	696.8	5,506.9	10.9	62.8	331.3	291.8	1,289.2	3,520.3	697.4
New Mexico	6,434.1	934.9	5,499.2	8.9	62.6	139.3	724.1	1,511.4	3,609.9	377.9
Utah	5,658.5	290.5	5,368.0	3.0	45.4	55.9	186.2	885.0	4,245.1	237.9
Wyoming	4,575.1	319.5	4,255.6	3.6	35.0	18.0	262.9	671.0	3,434.1	150.4
Pacific	**6,520.8**	**970.2**	**5,550.6**	**10.8**	**46.8**	**354.5**	**558.1**	**1,316.7**	**3,331.6**	**902.3**
Alaska	5,569.5	660.5	4,909.0	7.5	98.6	109.0	445.3	880.7	3,531.2	497.1
California	6,679.5	1,119.7	5,559.8	12.7	41.3	424.1	641.6	1,384.9	3,137.8	1,037.1
Hawaii	6,112.0	258.4	5,853.5	3.6	37.9	99.2	117.7	1,121.2	4,357.2	375.1
Oregon	5,820.9	510.2	5,310.7	4.7	53.1	151.4	301.1	1,106.7	3,670.6	533.5
Washington	6,172.8	534.5	5,638.3	5.0	72.0	139.8	317.8	1,121.7	4,045.1	471.5

(1) Populations are Bureau of the Census provisional estimates as of July 1, 1992, and are subject to change. (2) Violent crimes are murder, forcible rape, robbery, and aggravated assault. (3) Property crimes are burglary, larceny–theft, and motor vehicle theft. Data are not included for the property crime of arson. (4) The percentage representing area actually reporting will not coincide with the ratio between reported and estimated crime totals, since these data represent the sum of the calculations for individual states, which have varying populations, portions reporting, and crime rates.

Sentences vs. Time Served for Selected Crimes

Source: Bureau of Justice Statistics, *National Corrections Reporting Program, 1991,* February 1994

The following is a comparison of the average maximum sentence lengths (excluding both life and death sentences) and the actual time served for selected state–court convictions, based on 1991 data.

Crime	Sentence	Time served	Crime	Sentence	Time served
Murder	18 years, 11 months	8 years, 1 month	Burglary	6 years, 5 months	2 years, 2 months
Rape	10 years	4 years, 9 months	Drug Offenses	5 years	1 year, 6 months
Robbery	8 years, 10 months	3 years, 4 months	Weapons Offenses	4 years, 1 month	1 year, 9 months

EDUCATION

Historical Summary of Public Elementary and Secondary Schools

Source: National Center for Education Statistics, U.S. Dept. of Education

Pupils and teachers (thousands)	1919-20	1929-30	1939-40	1949-50	1959-60[1]	1969-70[1]	1979-80[1]	1989-90[1]	1990-91[1]	1991-92[1]
Total U.S. population	104,512	121,770	130,880	148,665	179,323	203,212	224,567	246,819	249,415	252,137
Population 5-17 years of age	27,556	31,417	30,150	30,168	43,881	52,490	48,041	44,949	45,311	45,918
Percentage 5-17 years of age	26.4	25.8	23.0	20.3	24.5	25.8	21.4	18.2	18.2	18.2
Enrollment (thousands)										
Elementary and secondary	21,578	25,678	25,434	25,111	36,087	45,619	41,645	40,543	41,217	42,036
Percentage pop. 5-17 enrolled	78.3	81.7	84.4	83.2	82.2	86.9	86.7	90.2	91.0	91.5
Percentage in high schools	10.2	17.1	26.0	22.7	23.5	28.5	32.9	28.1	27.5	27.4
High school graduates (thousands)	231	592	1,143	1,063	1,627	2,589	2,748	2,320	2,237	2,212
Average school term (in days)	161.9	172.7	175.0	177.9	178.0	178.9	178.5	—	179.8	—
Total instructional staff	678	880	912	962	1,464	2,253	2,441	—	—	3,104
Teachers, librarians, and other nonsupervisory instructional staff	657	843	875	920	1,393	2,195	2,300	2,860	2,924	2,975
Men	93	140	195	195	404	714	782	—	—	—
Women	585	703	681	724	989	1,484	1,518	—	—	—
Percentage men	14.1	16.6	22.2	21.3	29.0	32.4	34.0	—	—	—
Revenue & expenditures (millions)										
Total revenue	$970	$2,088	$2,260	$5,437	$14,746	$40,267	$96,881	$207,753	$222,823	$234,486
Total expenditures	1,036	2,316	2,344	5,837	15,613	40,683	95,962	212,100	228,933	241,567
Current elem. and secondary	861	1,843	1,941	4,687	12,239	34,218	86,984	187,558	201,550	211,216
Capital outlay	153	370	257	1,014	2,661	4,659	6,506	17,788	19,771	20,797
Interest on school debt	18	92	130	100	489	1,171	1,874	3,770	4,314	5,162
Other	3	9	13	35	132	636	598	2,985	3,298	4,392
Salaries and pupil cost	(Data in unadjusted dollars)									
Annual salary of instructional staff[2]	$871	$1,420	$1,441	$3,010	$5,174	$8,840	$16,715	$32,723	$34,385	$34,410
Expenditure per capita total pop.	9.91	19.03	17.91	39	87	200	427	859	918	958
Current expenditure per pupil ADA[3]	53.32	86.70	88.09	209	375	816	2,272	4,962	5,245	5,421

(1) Because of a modification in scope, "current expenditures for elementary and secondary schools" data for 1959-60 and later years are not entirely comparable with data for prior years. (2) Includes supervisors, principals, teachers, and nonsupervisory instructional staff. (3) ADA means average daily attendance in elementary and secondary day schools.

Preprimary School Enrollment, 1970-93

Source: Bureau of the Census, U.S. Dept. of Commerce

As of October. Civilian noninstitutional population. Includes public and nonpublic nursery school and kindergarten programs. Excludes 5-year-olds enrolled in elementary school.

Item	1975	1980	1985	1986	1987	1988	1989	1990	1991	1992	1993
Number of children (1,000)											
Population, 3 to 5 years old	**10,183**	**9,284**	**10,733**	**10,866**	**10,872**	**10,894**	**11,038**	**11,207**	**11,370**	**11,544**	**11,954**
Total enrolled[1]	**4,954**	**4,878**	**5,865**	**5,971**	**5,932**	**5,977**	**6,026**	**6,659**	**6,334**	**6,403**	**6,581**
Nursery school	1,745	1,981	2,477	2,545	2,555	2,621	2,825	3,378	2,824	2,857	2,984
Public	570	628	848	829	819	852	930	1,202	996	1,074	1,204
Private	1,174	1,353	1,631	1,715	1,736	1,770	1,894	2,177	1,827	1,784	1,779
Kindergarten	3,211	2,897	3,388	3,426	3,377	3,356	3,201	3,281	3,510	3,546	3,597
Public	2,682	2,438	2,847	2,859	2,842	2,875	2,704	2,767	2,968	2,996	3,020
Private	528	459	541	567	535	481	496	513	543	550	577
White	4,105	3,994	4,757	4,851	4,748	4,891	4,911	5,389	5,104	5,137	5,252
Black	731	725	919	892	893	814	872	964	928	966	976
Hispanic[2]	(NA)	370	496	593	587	544	520	642	675	728	726
3 years old	683	857	1,035	1,041	1,022	1,028	1,005	1,205	1,075	1,081	1,097
4 years old	1,418	1,423	1,765	1,772	1,717	1,768	1,882	2,086	1,993	1,982	2,197
5 years old	2,852	2,598	3,065	3,157	3,192	3,183	3,139	3,367	3,266	3,340	3,306
Enrollment rate											
Total enrolled[1]	**48.6**	**52.5**	**54.6**	**55.0**	**54.6**	**54.4**	**54.6**	**59.4**	**55.7**	**55.5**	**55.1**
White	48.6	52.7	54.7	55.2	54.1	55.4	55.0	59.7	56.2	55.8	55.8
Black	48.1	51.8	55.8	54.1	54.2	48.2	54.2	57.8	53.1	55.1	52.4
Hispanic[2]	(NA)	43.3	43.3	47.8	45.5	44.2	41.6	49.0	46.4	48.4	45.2
3 years old	21.5	27.3	28.8	28.9	28.6	27.6	27.1	32.6	28.2	27.7	27.1
4 years old	40.5	46.3	49.1	49.0	47.7	49.1	51.0	56.0	53.0	52.1	53.9
5 years old	81.3	84.7	86.5	86.7	86.1	86.6	86.4	88.8	86.0	87.2	85.7

(NA) Not available. (1) Includes races not shown separately. (2) Persons of Hispanic origin may be of any race. The method of identifying Hispanic children was changed in 1980 from allocation based on status of mother to status reported for each child. Using the new method, the number of Hispanic children is larger.

Programs for the Disabled, 1983-92

Source: Office of Special Education and Rehabilitative Services, U.S. Dept. of Education

Number of children 0 to 21 years old served annually in educational programs for the disabled; in thousands.

Type of Disability	1983-84	1984-85	1985-86	1986-87	1987-88	1988-89	1989-90	1990-91	1991-92
All disabilities	**4,298**	**4,315**	**4,317**	**4,374**	**4,446**	**4,544**	**4,641**	**4,771**	**4,949**
Learning disabilities	1,806	1,832	1,862	1,914	1,928	1,987	2,050	2,130	2,234
Speech impairments	1,128	1,126	1,125	1,136	953	967	973	987	997
Mental retardation	727	694	660	643	582	564	548	536	538
Serious emotional disturbance	361	372	375	383	373	376	381	391	399
Hearing impairments	72	69	66	65	56	56	57	58	60
Orthopedic impairments	56	56	57	57	47	47	48	49	51
Visual impairments	29	28	27	26	22	23	22	23	24
Deaf-blindness	2	2	2	2	12	2	2	1	1

Note: Counts are based on reports from the 50 states, District of Columbia, and Puerto Rico (i.e., figures from U.S. territories are not included). Details may not add to totals because of rounding.

Enrollment and Teachers in Full-Time Public Day Schools

Elementary and Secondary Day Schools, Fall 1992

Source: National Center for Education Statistics, U.S. Dept. of Education; National Education Assn.

	Local school districts	Classroom teachers	Total enrollment	Pupils per teacher	Teacher's average pay (1992-93)	Instructional aides	Expenditure per pupil
U.S.	**15,025**	**2,457,737**	**42,734,746**	**17.4**	**$35,027**	**427,220**	**$5,421**
Alabama	129	41,567	723,410	17.4	26,953	3,636	3,616
Alaska	56	7,282	122,487	16.8	46,019	1,775	8,450
Arizona	229	36,076	673,477	18.7	31,352	8,741	4,381
Arkansas	319	25,978	441,490	17.0	27,433	3,436	4,031
California	1,002	215,738	5,195,777	24.1	40,035	55,098	4,746
Colorado	176	33,419	612,635	18.3	33,541	4,662	5,172
Connecticut	166	34,193	488,476	14.3	48,343	6,592	8,017
Delaware	19	6,252	104,321	16.7	36,217	828	6,093
District of Columbia	1	6,064	80,937	13.3	38,702	344	9,549
Florida	67	107,590	1,981,407	18.4	31,172	20,858	5,243
Georgia	183	66,942	1,207,186	18.0	30,051	17,871	4,375
Hawaii	1	10,083	177,448	17.6	36,470	1,165	5,420
Idaho	114	11,827	231,668	19.6	27,011	1,578	3,556
Illinois	930	111,461	1,873,567	16.8	38,632	16,289	5,670
Indiana	296	54,552	960,630	17.6	35,066	13,265	5,074
Iowa	437	31,405	494,839	15.8	30,130	4,548	5,096
Kansas	304	29,753	451,536	15.2	32,863	3,716	5,007
Kentucky	176	37,868	655,041	17.3	31,115	8,381	4,719
Louisiana	66	47,024	797,985	16.6	27,617	8,989	4,354
Maine	283	15,375	216,453	14.1	30,250	3,548	5,652
Maryland	24	44,495	751,850	16.9	38,753	6,354	6,679
Massachusetts	345	57,225	859,948	15.0	38,223	9,814	6,408
Michigan	558	82,301	1,603,610	19.5	*43,604	13,461	6,268
Minnesota	413	45,050	793,724	17.6	35,093	7,798	5,409
Mississippi	149	27,829	506,668	18.2	24,367	8,416	3,245
Missouri	538	52,984	859,357	16.2	29,382	5,696	4,830
Montana	539	10,135	160,011	15.8	27,617	1,429	5,423
Nebraska	729	19,323	282,476	14.6	28,768	3,172	5,263
Nevada	17	11,953	222,974	18.7	34,119	1,325	4,926
New Hampshire	178	11,654	181,247	15.6	33,931	2,545	5,790
New Jersey	608	83,057	1,130,560	13.6	42,680	10,423	9,317
New Mexico	88	17,912	315,668	17.6	26,532	3,328	3,765
New York	716	176,375	2,689,686	15.2	44,999	23,356	8,527
North Carolina	133	66,630	1,114,083	16.7	29,315	20,127	4,555
North Dakota	270	7,794	118,734	15.2	25,211	1,227	4,441
Ohio	612	106,233	1,796,418	16.9	34,500	9,241	5,694
Oklahoma	568	38,433	597,096	15.5	25,918	6,022	4,078
Oregon	295	26,634	510,122	19.2	35,880	4,847	5,913
Pennsylvania	501	100,912	1,717,613	17.0	41,215	12,534	6,613
Rhode Island	36	10,069	143,798	14.3	37,933	1,316	6,546
South Carolina	95	37,295	633,419	17.0	29,224	6,727	4,436
South Dakota	178	8,767	134,573	15.3	24,289	1,605	4,173
Tennessee	140	43,566	845,618	19.4	28,960	7,807	3,692
Texas	1,048	225,207	3,535,871	15.7	29,935	36,734	4,632
Utah	40	19,191	463,870	24.2	27,239	4,097	3,040
Vermont	285	7,031	98,558	14.0	34,824	2,052	6,944
Virginia	141	64,769	98,558	14.0	*32,306	10,701	4,880
Washington	296	44,295	896,475	20.2	35,759	7,552	5,271
West Virginia	57	20,961	318,296	15.2	30,301	2,872	5,109
Wisconsin	427	53,387	829,415	15.5	35,926	8,105	6,139
Wyoming	58	5,821	100,313	17.2	30,080	1,217	5,812

* National Education Association estimate.

Public High School Graduation Rates, 1992

Source: National Center for Education Statistics, U.S. Dept. of Education

	Graduation rate	Rank
U.S.	**71.2 %**	
Alabama	66.1	(44)
Alaska	74.1	(29)
Arizona	72.7	(33)
Arkansas	78.3	(19)
California	68.6	(40)
Colorado	75.1	(28)
Connecticut	80.4	(16)
Delaware	69.6	(38)
D.C.	62.8	(47)
Florida	65.0	(45)
Georgia	63.7	(46)
Hawaii	78.1	(20)
Idaho	81.1	(12)
Illinois	78.6	(18)
Indiana	76.0	(27)
Iowa	87.6	(2)
Kansas	80.5	(15)
Kentucky	69.8	(37)
Louisiana	52.9	(51)
Maine	81.1	(12)
Maryland	76.1	(25)
Massachusetts	79.1	(17)
Michigan	70.9	(35)
Minnesota	89.2	(1)
Mississippi	62.1	(48)
Missouri	73.2	(32)
Montana	85.5	(5)
Nebraska	87.2	(4)
Nevada	70.7	(36)
New Hampshire	78.1	(20)
New Jersey	84.1	(7)
New Mexico	67.8	(42)
New York	66.6	(43)
North Carolina	68.5	(41)
North Dakota	87.5	(3)
Ohio	72.4	(34)
Oklahoma	76.3	(24)
Oregon	73.5	(31)
Pennsylvania	81.5	(11)
Rhode Island	76.8	(23)
South Carolina	58.1	(49)
South Dakota	85.3	(6)
Tennessee	68.7	(39)
Texas	56.0	(50)
Utah	81.1	(12)
Vermont	82.4	(9)
Virginia	74.0	(30)
Washington	76.1	(25)
West Virginia	77.0	(22)
Wisconsin	82.2	(10)
Wyoming	83.8	(8)

College Enrollment Rates of High School Graduates, by Race/Ethnicity and Sex, 1960-93

Source: American College Testing Program; Bureau of the Census, U.S. Department of Commerce; U.S. Department of Labor

(in thousands)

	High school graduates[1]						Enrolled in college[2]					
Year	Total	Male	Female	White[3]	Black[3,4]	Hispanic[4]	Total	Male	Female	White[3]	Black[3,4]	Hispanic[4]
1960..	1,679	756	923	1,565	—	—	758	408	350	717	—	—
1961..	1,763	756	923	1,612	—	—	847	445	402	840	—	—
1962..	1,838	872	966	1,660	—	—	900	488	420	840	—	—
1963..	1,741	794	947	1,615	—	—	784	415	420	736	—	—
1964..	2,145	997	1,148	1,964	—	—	1,037	570	467	967	—	—
1965..	2,659	1,254	1,405	2,417	—	—	1,354	718	636	1,249	—	—
1966..	2,612	1,207	1,405	2,403	—	—	1,309	709	600	1,243	—	—
1967..	2,525	1,142	1,383	2,267	—	—	1,311	658	653	1,202	—	—
1968..	2,606	1,184	1,422	2,303	—	—	1,444	748	696	1,304	—	—
1969..	2,842	1,352	1,490	2,538	—	—	1,516	812	704	2,538	—	—
1970..	2,757	1,343	1,414	2,461	—	—	1,427	741	686	1,280	—	—
1971..	2,872	1,369	1,503	2,461	—	—	1,535	788	747	1,402	—	—
1972..	2,961	1,420	1,541	2,614	—	—	1,457	749	708	1,292	—	—
1973..	3,101	1,491	1,610	2,707	—	—	1,425	730	695	1,302	—	—
1974..	3,101	1,491	1,610	2,736	—	—	1,474	736	738	1,288	—	—
1975..	3,186	1,513	1,673	2,825	—	—	1,615	796	819	1,446	—	—
1976..	2,987	1,450	1,537	2,640	320	152	1,458	685	773	1,291	134	80
1977..	3,140	1,482	1,658	2,768	335	156	1,590	773	817	1,403	166	80
1978..	3,161	1,485	1,676	2,750	352	133	1,584	758	826	1,378	161	57
1979..	3,160	1,474	1,686	2,776	324	154	1,559	743	816	1,376	147	69
1980..	3,089	1,500	1,589	2,682	361	129	1,524	701	823	1,339	151	68
1981..	3,053	1,490	1,563	2,626	359	146	1,646	816	830	1,434	154	76
1982..	3,100	1,508	1,592	2,644	384	174	1,568	739	829	1,376	140	75
1983..	2,964	1,390	1,574	2,496	392	138	1,562	721	841	1,372	151	75
1984..	3,012	1,429	1,583	2,514	438	185	1,662	800	862	1,455	176	82
1985..	2,666	1,286	1,380	2,241	333	141	1,539	754	785	1,332	141	72
1986..	2,786	1,331	1,455	2,307	386	169	1,499	744	755	1,292	141	75
1987..	2,647	1,278	1,369	2,207	337	176	1,503	746	757	1,249	175	59
1988..	2,673	1,334	1,339	2,187	382	179	1,575	761	814	1,328	172	102
1989..	2,454	1,208	1,245	2,051	337	168	1,463	696	767	1,238	178	93
1990..	2,355	1,169	1,185	1,921	341	112	1,410	676	735	1,182	158	53
1991..	2,276	1,139	1,137	1,867	320	154	1,420	656	763	1,207	146	88
1992..	2,398	1,216	1,182	1,900	353	199	1,479	725	754	1,204	169	109
1993..	2,338	1,118	1,219	1,910	302	200	1,464	668	797	1,200	168	125

(1) Individuals age 16 to 24 who graduated from high school during the preceding 12 months. (2) Enrollment in college as of October of each year for individuals age 16 to 24 who graduated from high school during the preceding 12 months. (3) Includes persons of Hispanic origin. (4) Due to the small sample size, data are subject to relatively large sampling errors. — Data not available.

Technology in Public Schools, 1992-94

Source: Quality Education Data, Inc., Denver, CO

Technology	Number of schools			Percentage of schools		
	1992	1993	1994	1992	1993	1994
Schools with interactive videodisk players[1]	**6,502**	**11,729**	**17,489**	**8.0**	**14.0**	**21.0**
Elementary[2]	2,921	5,986	9,247	6.0	12.0	18.0
Junior high[3]	1,258	2,386	3,580	10.0	18.0	26.0
Senior high[4]	2,106	3,129	4,548	14.0	19.0	27.0
Schools with modems[1]	**13,597**	**18,471**	**22,611**	**16.0**	**22.0**	**27.0**
Elementary[2]	5,831	8,492	10,878	11.0	17.0	21.0
Junior high[3]	2,608	3,431	4,246	20.0	26.0	31.0
Senior high[4]	5,001	6,371	7,402	30.0	38.0	44.0
Schools with networks[1]	**4,184**	**11,657**	**17,522**	**5.0**	**14.0**	**21.0**
Elementary[2]	1,583	4,683	7,545	3.0	9.0	15.0
Junior high[3]	776	2,030	3,220	6.0	15.0	24.0
Senior high[4]	1,736	4,895	6,576	10.0	29.0	39.0
Schools with CD-ROMs[1]	**5,706**	**11,021**	**20,943**	**7.0**	**13.0**	**25.0**
Elementary[2]	1,897	4,457	9,791	4.0	9.0	19.0
Junior high[3]	1,231	2,326	4,261	9.0	17.0	31.0
Senior high[4]	2,543	4,168	6,713	15.0	25.0	40.0
Schools with cable[1]	**(NA)**	**47,745**	**58,132**	**(X)**	**57.0**	**69.0**
Elementary[2]	(NA)	27,923	35,041	(X)	54.0	68.0
Junior high[3]	(NA)	9,266	10,611	(X)	69.0	78.0
Senior high[4]	(NA)	10,296	12,043	(X)	62.0	72.0

NA Not available. X Not applicable. (1) Includes schools for special and adult education, not shown separately. (2) Includes K-12, preschool, preschool through 3, K-6, and K-8. (3) Includes schools with grade spans of 4-8 and 7-9. (4) Includes 7-12, 9-12,10-12, vocational technical, and alternative high schools.

Revenues[1] for Public Elementary and Secondary Schools, by State, 1991-92

Source: National Center for Education Statistics, U.S. Dept. of Education

(numbers in thousands)

State	Total $	Federal Amount $	Federal %	State Amount $	State %	Local and intermediate Amount $	Local and intermediate %	Private[2] Amount $	Private[2] %
U.S.	234,485,729	15,493,330	6.6	108,792,779	46.4	103,975,705	44.3	6,223,916	2.7
Alabama	2,823,340	322,576	11.4	1,659,018	58.8	611,248	21.6	230,497	8.2
Alaska	1,120,970	128,612	11.5	762,663	68.0	205,615	18.3	24,530	2.2
Arizona	3,226,760	284,615	8.8	1,366,934	42.4	1,510,219	46.8	64,992	2.0
Arkansas	1,828,439	197,915	10.8	1,095,488	59.9	478,138	26.2	56,899	3.1
California	26,868,216	2,027,474	7.5	17,696,851	65.9	6,830,548	25.4	313,344	1.2
Colorado	3,058,633	152,090	5.0	1,307,982	42.8	1,510,328	49.4	88,233	2.9
Connecticut	3,891,217	126,225	3.2	1,583,668	40.7	2,063,543	53.0	117,781	3.0
Delaware	608,015	46,144	7.6	400,819	65.9	150,409	24.7	10,643	1.8
District of Columbia	711,172	66,508	9.4	—	—	641,350	90.2	3,314	0.5
Florida	10,810,522	788,420	7.3	5,227,256	48.4	4,350,167	40.2	444,679	4.1
Georgia	5,332,428	409,741	7.7	2,545,306	47.7	2,255,693	42.3	121,687	2.3
Hawaii	1,000,848	75,310	7.5	903,444	90.3	4,893	0.5	17,201	1.7
Idaho	861,955	69,859	8.1	532,475	61.8	242,120	28.1	17,501	2.0
Illinois	9,959,661	680,351	6.8	2,881,367	28.9	6,177,317	62.0	220,627	2.2
Indiana	5,127,888	272,355	5.3	2,710,144	52.9	1,975,429	38.5	169,960	3.3
Iowa	2,486,610	132,718	5.3	1,176,197	47.3	1,025,899	41.3	151,796	6.1
Kansas	2,264,365	123,564	5.5	959,173	42.4	1,112,810	49.1	68,817	3.0
Kentucky	2,939,351	296,573	10.1	1,969,899	67.0	651,896	22.2	20,984	0.7
Louisiana	3,377,064	363,958	10.8	1,848,734	54.7	1,068,290	31.6	96,082	2.8
Maine	1,246,798	73,876	5.9	621,026	49.8	548,461	44.0	3,435	0.3
Maryland	4,692,155	238,573	5.1	1,792,755	38.2	2,511,988	53.5	148,839	3.2
Massachusetts	5,621,629	296,702	5.3	1,728,360	30.7	3,483,002	62.0	113,565	2.0
Michigan	9,659,095	599,076	6.2	2,566,851	26.6	6,289,097	65.1	204,071	2.1
Minnesota	4,512,902	200,853	4.5	2,327,594	51.6	1,817,120	40.3	167,355	3.7
Mississippi	1,701,274	289,302	17.0	910,068	53.5	436,000	25.6	65,904	3.9
Missouri	4,053,529	258,032	6.4	1,538,752	38.0	2,088,076	51.5	168,668	4.2
Montana	821,111	72,483	8.8	343,293	41.8	373,016	45.4	32,318	3.9
Nebraska	1,506,050	93,705	6.2	517,098	34.3	761,716	50.6	133,530	8.9
Nevada	1,122,853	46,957	4.2	434,762	38.7	601,857	53.6	39,277	3.5
New Hampshire	1,015,187	31,098	3.1	86,597	8.5	871,238	85.8	26,253	2.6
New Jersey	10,523,002	436,024	4.1	4,438,939	42.2	5,451,200	51.8	196,838	1.9
New Mexico	1,368,013	169,616	12.4	1,009,593	73.8	154,408	11.3	34,395	2.5
New York	21,573,865	1,210,481	5.6	8,696,709	40.3	11,447,389	53.1	219,286	1.0
North Carolina	5,067,118	364,253	7.2	3,274,259	64.6	1,218,261	24.0	210,345	4.2
North Dakota	539,184	59,909	11.1	241,401	44.8	207,434	38.5	30,439	5.6
Ohio	9,736,287	571,416	5.9	3,974,682	40.8	4,797,389	49.3	392,800	4.0
Oklahoma	2,541,025	117,060	4.6	1,580,811	62.2	749,822	29.5	93,332	3.7
Oregon	2,869,231	183,784	6.4	877,897	30.6	1,722,487	60.0	85,063	3.0
Pennsylvania	11,561,337	664,767	5.7	4,788,825	41.4	5,874,822	50.8	232,923	2.0
Rhode Island	896,056	53,653	6.0	344,820	38.5	486,720	54.3	10,863	1.2
South Carolina	2,914,730	262,740	9.0	1,409,019	48.3	1,119,150	38.4	123,822	4.2
South Dakota	559,944	61,986	11.1	151,173	27.0	327,868	58.6	18,918	3.4
Tennessee	3,093,743	324,252	10.5	1,305,270	42.2	1,225,443	39.6	238,778	7.7
Texas	16,891,646	1,120,400	6.6	7,326,385	43.4	7,975,106	47.2	469,755	2.8
Utah	1,527,561	106,069	6.9	874,332	57.2	493,354	32.3	53,807	3.5
Vermont	645,751	32,761	5.1	204,369	31.6	395,643	61.3	12,978	2.0
Virginia	5,560,451	322,156	5.8	1,729,400	31.1	3,340,445	60.1	168,450	3.0
Washington	5,086,074	288,382	5.7	3,644,053	71.6	998,770	19.6	154,868	3.0
West Virginia	1,715,747	129,763	7.6	1,153,764	67.2	406,703	23.7	25,517	1.5
Wisconsin	4,966,200	216,430	4.4	1,958,288	39.4	2,693,730	54.2	97,752	2.0
Wyoming	598,728	31,762	5.3	314,216	52.5	242,527	40.5	10,222	1.7

(1) Excludes revenues for state education agencies. Because of rounding, details may not add to total. (2) Includes revenues from gifts and tuition and fees from patrons.

Institutions of Higher Education–Charges, 1970-93

Source: National Center for Education Statistics, U.S. Dept. of Education

Data are for the entire academic year ending in year shown. Figures for 1970 are average charges for full-time resident degree-credit students; figures for later years are average charges per full-time equivalent student. Room and board are based on full-time students.

Academic control and year	Tuition and required fees: All institutions	Tuition and required fees: 2-yr colleges	Tuition and required fees: 4-yr universities	Board rates: All institutions	Board rates: 2-yr colleges	Board rates: 4-yr universities	Dormitory charges: All institutions	Dormitory charges: 2-yr colleges	Dormitory charges: 4-yr universities
Public									
1970	$323	$178	$427	$511	$465	$540	$369	$308	$395
1980	583	355	840	867	894	898	715	572	749
1990	1,356	756	2,035	1,635	1,581	1,728	1,513	962	1,561
1991	1,454	824	2,159	1,691	1,594	1,767	1,612	1,050	1,658
1992	1,624	937	2,410	1,780	1,612	1,852	1,731	1,074	1,789
1993	1,787	1,018	2,352	1,843	1,660	1,857	1,764	1,115	1,820
Private									
1970	1,533	1,034	1,809	561	546	608	436	413	503
1980	3,130	2,062	3,811	955	924	1,078	827	769	999
1990	8,147	5,196	10,348	1,948	1,811	2,339	1,923	1,663	2,411
1991	8,772	5,570	11,379	2,074	1,989	2,470	2,063	1,744	2,654
1992	9,434	5,752	12,192	2,252	2,090	2,727	2,221	1,789	2,860
1993	10,031	6,101	10,393	2,353	1,925	2,363	2,357	2,157	2,372

Tuition and College Costs, 1993-94

Based on the *Peterson's Guides* Annual Survey of Undergraduate Institutions, the average cost of tuition, mandatory fees, and college room and board at four-year private colleges was $14,858 in the 1993–94 academic year. The average cost at four-year public colleges was $6,318 for state residents and $10,534 for nonresidents. Two-year public colleges were the least expensive group of institutions; tuition and fees averaged $1,646 for state residents and $4,025 for nonresidents. Tuition and fees at two-year private colleges averaged $6,108.

The most expensive four-year institutions, including tuition, mandatory fees, and college room and board, were Harvard University ($26,931); Barnard College ($26,770); Brandeis University ($26,580); Massachusetts Institute of Technology ($26,559); Yale University ($26,350); Sarah Lawrence College ($26,258); Tufts University ($26,172); Hampshire College ($26,145); University of Pennsylvania ($26,126); Bard College ($26,025). The least expensive four-year undergraduate institutions were the United States service academies, which are all free.

American College Testing (ACT) Program Mean Scores and Characteristics of College-Bound Students, 1980-93

Source: The American College Testing Program
(For school year ending in year shown.)

Type of test and mean test scores[1]	Unit	1980	1985	1986[2]	1987[2]	1988[2]	1989[2]	1990[2]	1991[2]	1992[2]	1993[2]
Composite	Points	18.5	18.6	20.8	20.8	20.8	20.6	20.6	20.6	20.6	20.7
Male	Points	19.3	19.4	19.6	19.5	19.6	19.3	21.0	20.9	20.9	21.0
Female	Points	17.9	17.9	18.1	18.1	18.1	18.0	20.3	20.4	20.5	20.5
English	Points	17.9	18.1	18.5	18.4	18.5	18.4	20.5	20.3	20.2	20.3
Male	Points	17.3	17.6	17.9	17.9	18.0	17.8	20.1	19.8	19.8	19.8
Female	Points	18.3	18.6	18.9	18.9	19.0	18.9	20.9	20.7	20.6	20.6
Math	Points	17.4	17.2	17.3	17.2	17.2	17.1	19.9	20.0	20.0	20.1
Male	Points	18.9	18.6	18.8	18.6	18.4	18.3	20.7	20.6	20.7	20.8
Female	Points	16.2	16.0	16.0	16.1	16.1	16.1	19.3	19.4	19.5	19.6
Participants											
Total	1,000	822	739	730	777	842	855	817	796	832	875
Male	Percent	45	46	46	46	46	46	46	45	45	45
White	Percent	83	82	82	81	81	80	79	79	79	79
Black	Percent	8	8	8	8	9	9	9	9	9	9
Obtaining composite scores of											
27 or above	Percent	13	14	14	14	14	14	12	11	12	12
18 or below	Percent	33	32	31	31	31	32	35	35	35	35

(1) Minimum score, 1; maximum score, 36. Test scores and characteristics of college-bound students based on a 10% sample prior to 1985. Beginning in 1985, these data are based on the performance of all ACT-tested students who graduated in the spring of a given school year and who took the ACT Assessment during junior or senior year of high school.

(2) Beginning with the Oct. 1989 test (1990 scores), an entirely new ACT Assessment was introduced. The Enhanced ACT Assessment increases the emphasis on rhetorical skills in the measurement of writing proficiency, increases the number of advanced math items, and includes a new reading test that features inferential and reasoning skills and a test designed to measure science reasoning. The Enhanced ACT also provides subscores in English, mathematics, and reading. The composite scores for 1986-89 have been converted to provide a basis of comparison; all 1990-93 scores are for the Enhanced ACT. It is not possible to compare direcly these data and data from earlier years.

SAT Mean Scores and Characteristics of College-Bound Seniors, 1975-94

Source: College Entrance Examination Board
(For school year ending in year shown)

Type of test and characteristic	Unit	1975	1980	1985	1987	1988	1989	1990	1991	1992	1993	1994
Test scores[1]												
Verbal, total[1]	Points	434	424	431	430	428	427	424	422	423	424	423
Male	Points	437	428	437	435	435	434	429	426	428	428	425
Female	Points	431	420	425	425	422	421	419	418	419	420	421
Math, total[1]	Points	472	466	475	476	476	476	476	474	476	478	479
Male	Points	495	491	499	500	498	500	499	497	499	502	501
Female	Points	449	443	452	453	455	454	455	453	456	457	460
Participants												
Total (thousands)		992	989	1,080	1,134	1,088	1,025	1,033	1,032	1,034	1,109	1,050
Male	Percent	49.9	48.2	48.3	48.0	48.0	48.0	48.0	48.0	48.0	47.0	47.0
White	Percent	86.0	82.1	80.0	78.0	77.0	75.0	73.0	72.0	71.0	70.0	69.0
Black	Percent	7.9	9.1	8.9	9.0	9.0	10.0	10.0	10.0	10.0	11.0	11.0
Obtaining scores of												
600 or above												
Verbal	Percent	7.9	7.2	7.0	8.0	7.0	7.8	7.0	7.0	7.0	7.0	7.0
Math	Percent	15.6	15.1	17.0	18.0	17.0	18.0	18.0	17.0	18.0	19.0	18.0
Below 400												
Verbal	Percent	37.8	41.8	40.0	40.0	42.0	40.5	41.0	43.0	42.0	42.0	42.0
Math	Percent	28.5	30.2	28.0	29.0	27.0	28.0	28.0	29.0	27.0	28.0	26.0

(1) Minimum score, 200; maximum score, 800.

SAT Mean Scores by State, 1990-94

Source: College Entrance Examination Board

	1990		1991		1992		1993		1994		% Graduates Taking
	Verbal	Math	Verbal	Math	Verbal	Math	Verbal	Math	Verbal	Math	SAT*
Alabama	470	514	476	515	476	520	480	526	482	529	8
Alaska	438	476	439	481	433	475	438	477	434	477	49
Arizona	445	497	442	490	440	493	444	497	443	496	26
Arkansas	470	511	482	523	474	516	478	519	417	518	6
California	419	484	415	482	416	484	415	484	413	482	46
Colorado	456	513	453	506	453	507	454	509	456	513	28
Connecticut	430	471	429	468	430	470	430	474	426	472	80
Delaware	433	470	428	464	432	463	429	465	428	464	68
Dist. of Columbia	409	441	405	435	405	437	405	441	406	443	53
Florida	418	466	416	466	416	468	416	466	413	466	49
Georgia	401	443	400	444	398	444	399	445	398	446	65
Hawaii	404	481	405	478	401	477	401	478	401	480	58
Idaho	466	502	463	505	460	503	465	507	461	508	16
Illinois	466	528	471	535	473	537	475	541	478	546	14
Indiana	408	459	408	457	409	459	409	460	410	466	60
Iowa	511	577	515	578	512	584	520	583	506	574	5
Kansas	492	548	493	546	487	546	494	548	494	550	10
Kentucky	473	521	473	520	470	518	476	522	474	523	11
Louisiana	476	517	476	518	471	520	481	527	481	530	9
Maine	423	463	421	458	422	460	422	463	420	463	68
Maryland	430	478	429	475	431	476	431	478	429	479	64
Massachusetts	427	473	426	470	428	474	427	476	426	475	79
Michigan	454	514	461	519	464	523	469	528	472	537	11
Minnesota	477	542	480	543	492	561	489	556	495	562	9
Mississippi	477	519	477	520	478	526	481	521	485	528	4
Missouri	473	522	476	526	475	529	481	532	485	532	10
Montana	464	523	464	518	465	523	459	516	463	523	21
Nebraska	484	546	481	543	478	540	479	544	482	543	9
Nevada	434	487	435	484	434	488	432	488	429	484	30
New Hampshire	442	486	440	481	440	483	442	487	438	486	69
New Jersey	418	473	417	469	420	471	419	473	418	475	71
New Mexico	480	527	474	522	475	521	478	525	475	528	12
New York	412	470	413	468	416	466	416	471	416	472	76
North Carolina	401	440	400	444	405	450	406	453	405	455	60
North Dakota	505	564	502	571	501	567	518	583	497	559	5
Ohio	450	499	450	496	450	501	454	505	456	510	24
Oklahoma	478	523	476	521	480	527	482	530	482	537	9
Oregon	439	484	439	483	439	486	441	492	436	491	53
Pennsylvania	420	463	417	459	418	459	418	460	417	462	70
Rhode Island	422	461	421	459	421	460	419	464	420	462	68
South Carolina	397	437	395	437	394	437	396	442	395	443	60
South Dakota	506	555	496	551	490	550	502	558	483	548	5
Tennessee	483	525	487	528	484	529	486	531	488	535	12
Texas	413	461	411	463	410	466	413	472	412	474	48
Utah	492	539	494	537	496	545	500	549	509	558	4
Vermont	431	466	424	466	429	468	426	467	427	472	68
Virginia	425	470	424	466	425	468	425	469	424	469	65
Washington	437	486	433	480	432	484	435	486	434	488	49
West Virginia	443	490	441	485	440	484	439	485	439	482	17
Wisconsin	476	543	481	542	481	548	485	551	487	557	9
Wyoming	458	519	466	514	462	516	463	507	459	521	12
National Average	**424**	**476**	**422**	**474**	**423**	**476**	**424**	**478**	**423**	**479**	**42**

* Based on number of high school graduates in 1994, as projected by the Western Interstate Commission for Higher Education, and number of students in the class of 1994 who took the SAT. **Note:** Comparing states or ranking them on the basis of SAT scores alone is invalid, and the College Entrance Examination Board strongly discourages doing so.

Salaries of College Professors, 1993-94

Source: American Association of University Professors

Type of institution (by highest degree offered)	Public	Private/ independent	Church related
Doctorate			
Professor	$64,860	$85,520	$72,000
Associate professor	47,170	54,880	51,990
Assistant professor	39,860	46,230	43,440
Master's			
Professor	$55,690	$59,610	$58,200
Associate professor	44,660	46,150	46,090
Assistant professor	37,220	37,790	38,160
4-year liberal arts			
Professor	$49,720	$56,780	$45,000
Associate professor	41,010	43,110	37,000
Assistant professor	34,320	35,690	31,490
2-year			
Professor	$49,120	38,190	$32,240
Associate professor	41,030	38,170	28,860
Assistant professor	34,670	35,090	29,540

Top 50[1] Public Libraries in the U.S. and Canada, 1993

Source: World Almanac questionnaire; Public Library Association

Population served	Library name and location	No. of branches	No. of bound volumes	Circulation	Annual acquisition expenditures
3,485,398	Los Angeles Public Library (CA)	63	5,500,000	10,137,087	$5,710,124
3,180,120	Los Angeles County Public Library (CA)	87	5,500,000	15,874,726	3,000,000
3,070,302	New York Public Library, The Branch Libraries (NY)	82	17,800,000	10,712,582	16,172,000
2,783,726	Chicago Public Library (IL)	81	6,037,756	7,455,063	6,384,942
2,300,664	Brooklyn Public Library (NY)	59	5,747,768	9,310,195	5,287,105
2,122,101	Maricopa County Library District (Phoenix, AZ)	12	523,960	1,518,678	1,160,000
1,951,598	Queens Borough Public Library (NY)	62	9,271,960	13,237,978	5,691,688
1,630,533	Houston Public Library (TX)	34	4,225,223	6,334,647	2,823,900
1,626,510	Miami-Dade Public Library System (FL)	31	3,000,000	7,800,000	5,000,000
1,585,577	Free Library of Philadelphia (PA)	52	5,062,771	6,226,330	5,858,156
1,336,449	Carnegie Library of Pittsburgh (PA)	18	1,963,557	3,051,851	1,300,000
1,322,044	Broward County Library System (Fort Lauderdale, FL)	32	1,949,600	6,542,576	4,205,144
1,185,394	San Antonio Public Library (TX)	17	1,811,542	3,347,472	2,000,000
1,149,600	San Diego Public Library (CA)	32	2,030,185	5,364,276	2,028,793
1,099,058	Sacramento Public Library (CA)	22	1,700,000	3,900,000	13,000,000
1,029,025	Riverside City and County Public Library (CA)	31	1,432,236	4,292,013	1,565,154
1,027,954	Detroit Public Library (MI)	25	2,655,754	1,557,298	2,402,837
1,025,000	Phoenix Public Library (AZ)	11	1,600,000	6,036,000	2,429,000
1,017,666	Montréal, Bibliothèque Municipale De (Que.)	25	2,841,413	4,465,510	[2]4,260,287
1,006,877	Dallas Public Library (TX)	19	2,301,069	4,191,263	1,607,570
1,003,464	Providence Public Library (RI)	9	700,000	643,734	391,734
995,675	San Bernardino County Library (CA)	27	1,059,000	5,800,000	800,000
968,584	Buffalo & Erie County Public Library (NY)	52	4,000,000	8,400,000	2,700,000
909,000	King County Library System (Seattle, WA)	39	2,900,000	11,600,000	4,500,000
908,580	San Diego County Library (CA)	31	2,013,472	2,845,685	738,500
866,228	Cincinnati & Hamilton County, Public Library of (OH)	41	4,542,300	11,701,885	6,332,378
847,419	Fairfax County Public Library (VA)	22	1,787,767	8,182,548	2,567,790
842,936	St. Louis County Library (MO)	17	2,013,472	9,456,144	3,095,022
835,054	Tampa-Hillsborough County Public Library (FL)	17	1,933,567	2,971,424	1,747,549
826,330	Memphis Shelby County Public Library (TN)	21	1,726,329	3,689,260	1,514,203
803,000	San Jose Public Library System (CA)	17	1,401,000	4,585,571	1,386,863
770,684	Indianapolis-Marion County Public Library (IN)	21	1,738,732	8,141,544	4,118,578
752,400	Montgomery County Dept. of Public Libraries (Rockville, MD)	21	2,042,305	8,188,500	3,560,200
747,500	Enoch Pratt Free Library (Baltimore, MD)	28	2,659,464	1,378,788	2,034,275
738,715	Jacksonville Public Libraries (FL)	18	2,022,429	2,942,763	1,239,541
728,729	Prince George's County Memorial Library System (Hyattsville, MD)	20	2,385,286	5,334,207	1,682,908
728,700	San Francisco Public Library (CA)	26	2,023,081	3,093,941	1,323,820
717,400	Macomb County Library (Mount Clemens, MI)	1	184,673	266,447	283,369
717,133	Calgary Public Library (Alb.)	0	1,524,245	9,603,295	[23]3,500,000
715,565	Contra Costa County Library (Pleasant Hill, CA)	21	1,002,000	3,944,000	1,070,000
713,968	Rochester Public Library (NY)	12	600,000	150,000	875,000
708,582	Columbus Metropolitan Library (OH)	20	2,100,000	10,600,000	6,400,000
703,034	Baltimore County Public Library (MD)	15	1,829,059	12,325,124	3,558,672
696,310	Fresno County Library (CA)	35	848,744	1,861,438	497,084
695,685	Tucson-Pima Library (AZ)	18	1,200,000	5,200,000	[3]1,800,000
694,338	Atlanta-Fulton Public Library (GA)	31	1,885,000	2,734,000	2,103,720
677,164	Las Vegas Clark County Library District (NV)	22	1,300,000	3,500,000	2,500,000
669,923	Orange County Library System (Orlando, FL)	11	1,580,000	500,000	1,500,000
664,937	Louisville Free Public Library (KY)	14	849,499	2,560,194	1,926,721
664,048	Hennepin County Library (Minnetonka, MN)	25	1,133,132	8,909,315	3,144,482

(1) By population served. (2) Canadian dollars. (3) 1994-95 estimate.

Public Library Operating Income, by State, 1992

Source: National Center for Education Statistics, U.S. Dept. of Education; (in thousands)

State	Income	State	Income	State	Income
U.S. Total	**$4,997,421**	Kansas	$42,899	North Carolina	$87,964
Alabama	$39,713	Kentucky	$41,417	North Dakota	$6,111
Alaska	$417,498	Louisiana	$60,011	Ohio	$356,314
Arizona	$62,718	Maine	$16,589	Oklahoma	$33,612
Arkansas	$18,080	Maryland	$116,749	Oregon	$58,874
California	$620,510	Massachusetts	$122,250	Pennsylvania	$152,649
Colorado	$78,333	Michigan	$164,317	Rhode Island	$17,433
Connecticut	$87,856	Minnesota	$96,825	South Carolina	$38,502
Delaware	$7,246	Mississippi	$21,210	South Dakota	$9,345
District of Columbia	$21,730	Missouri	$87,227	Tennessee	$46,632
Florida	$203,409	Montana	$9,155	Texas	$169,053
Georgia	$81,976	Nebraska	$21,959	Utah	$28,255
Hawaii	$23,875	Nevada	$31,746	Vermont	$8,882
Idaho	$12,608	New Hampshire	$23,898	Virginia	$120,301
Illinois	$473,792	New Jersey	$225,751	Washington	$123,819
Indiana	$142,044	New Mexico	$17,531	West Virginia	$16,571
Iowa	$48,153	New York	$569,202	Wisconsin	$103,952
				Wyoming	$10,874

American Colleges and Universities

General Information for the 1993-94 Academic Year

Source: Peterson's Guides, Copyright 1994

These listings include all accredited undergraduate degree-granting institutions in the United States and U.S. territories that have a total institutional enrollment of 1,000 or more. Four-year colleges (those that award a bachelor's as their highest undergraduate degree) are listed first, followed by two-year colleges (those that award an associate as their highest or primary undergraduate degree).

All institutions are coeducational except those where the zip code is directly followed by: (1)–men only, (2)–primarily men, (3)–women only, (4)–primarily women.

Year is that of founding.

Governing official is the chief executive officer.

Institutional control: 1–independent (nonprofit), 2–independent-religious, 3–proprietary (profit making), 4–federal, 5–state, 6–commonwealth (Puerto Rico), 7–territory (U.S. territories), 8–county, 9–district, 10–city, 11–state and local, 12–state related.

Highest degree offered: B–bachelor's, M–master's, F–first professional, D–doctorate.

Enrollment is the total number of matriculated undergraduate and (if applicable) graduate students.

Faculty is the total number of faculty members teaching undergraduate courses and (if available) graduate courses.

Any data not reported are indicated as NR.

Data reported for institutions that provided updated information on Peterson's Annual Survey of Undergraduate Institutions for the 1993-94 academic year.

Four-Year Colleges

Name, address	Year	Governing official, control, and highest degree offered		Enroll-ment	Faculty
Abilene Christian U, Abilene, TX 79699	1906	Dr. Royce Money	2-M	4,069	246
Acad of Art Coll, San Francisco, CA 94105-3410	1929	Ms. Elisa Stephens	3-M	2,736	303
Adams State Coll, Alamosa, CO 81102	1921	Dr. Marvin Motz	5-M	2,353	120
Adelphi U, Garden City, NY 11530	1896	Dr. Peter Diamandopoulos	1-D	8,194	675
Adrian Coll, Adrian, MI 49221-2575	1859	Dr. Stanley P. Caine	2-B	1,135	134
Alabama A&M U, Normal, AL 35762-1357	1875	Dr. David B. Henson	5-D	5,593	333
Alabama State U, Montgomery, AL 36101-0271	1874	Dr. C. C. Baker	5-M	5,800	270
Albany State Coll, Albany, GA 31705-2717	1903	Dr. Billy C. Black	5-M	3,257	150
Albion Coll, Albion, MI 49224-1831	1835	Dr. Melvin L. Vulgamore	2-B	1,674	127
Albright Coll, Reading, PA 19612-5234	1856	Dr. Ellen S. Hurwitz	2-B	1,105	124
Alcorn State U, Lorman, MS 39096	1871	Dr. Rudolph E. Waters	5-M	3,256	183
Alfred U, Alfred, NY 14802-1232	1836	Dr. Edward G. Coll, Jr.	1-D	2,326	197
Allegheny Coll, Meadville, PA 16335	1815	Dr. Daniel F. Sullivan	2-B	1,790	196
Allentown Coll of St Francis de Sales, Center Valley, PA 18034-9568	1962	Rev. Daniel Gambet, OSFS	2-M	2,216	98
Alma Coll, Alma, MI 48801-1599	1886	Dr. Alan J. Stone	2-B	1,334	109
Alvernia Coll, Reading, PA 19607-1799	1958	Dr. Daniel N. DeLucca	2-B	1,264	106
Alverno Coll, Milwaukee, WI 53234-3922 (3)	1887	Sr. Joel Read	2-B	1,503	215
Amber U, Garland, TX 75041-5595	1971	Dr. Douglas W. Warner	1-M	1,610	65
American International Coll, Springfield, MA 01109-3189	1885	Dr. Harry J. Courniotes	1-M	1,781	122
American Tech Inst, Brunswick, TN 38014-0008 (2)	1985	Dr. D. W. Jones	1-B	1,500	8
American U, Washington, DC 20016-8001	1893	Dr. Benjamin Ladner	2-D	11,708	1,335
Amherst Coll, Amherst, MA 01002	1821	Dr. Tom Gerety	1-B	1,585	156
Anderson Coll, Anderson, SC 29621-4035	1911	Dr. Mark L. Hopkins	2-B	1,131	73
Anderson U, Anderson, IN 46012-3495	1917	Dr. James L. Edwards	2-M	2,256	201
Andrews U, Berrien Springs, MI 49104	1874	Dr. Niels-Erik Andreasen	2-D	2,979	329
Angelo State U, San Angelo, TX 76909	1928	Dr. Lloyd Drexell Vincent	5-M	6,100	227
Anna Maria Coll, Paxton, MA 01612	1946	Sr. Rita Larivee, SSA	2-M	1,719	92
Appalachian State U, Boone, NC 28608	1899	Dr. Francis T. Borkowski	5-D	11,641	688
Aquinas Coll, Grand Rapids, MI 49506-1799	1886	Mr. R. Paul Nelson	2-M	2,476	195
Arizona State U, Tempe, AZ 85287	1885	Dr. Lattie F. Coor	5-D	41,250	1,705
Arizona State U West, Phoenix, AZ 85069-7100	1984	Dr. Ben R. Forsyth	5-M	2,026	249
Arkansas State U, State University, AR 72467-1630	1909	Dr. Robert L. Hoskins	5-D	9,888	470
Arkansas Tech U, Russellville, AR 72801-2222	1909	Dr. Robert C. Brown	5-M	4,730	250
Armstrong State Coll, Savannah, GA 31419-1997	1935	Dr. Robert A. Burnett	5-B	5,187	179
Art Ctr Coll of Design, Pasadena, CA 91103-1999	1930	Mr. David R. Brown	1-M	1,340	427
Asbury Coll, Wilmore, KY 40390-1198	1890	Dr. David J. Gyertson	2-B	1,157	114
Ashland U, Ashland, OH 44805-3702	1878	Dr. G. William Benz	2-M	5,583	202
Assumption Coll, Worcester, MA 01615-0005	1904	Dr. Joseph H. Hagan	2-M	2,792	228
Athens State Coll, Athens, AL 35611-1902	1822	Dr. Jerry F. Bartlett	5-B	3,234	182
Atlantic Union Coll, South Lancaster, MA 01561-1000	1882	Dr. James J. Londis	2-M	1,411	69
Auburn U, Auburn University, AL 36849-0001	1856	Dr. William V. Muse	5-D	21,363	1,215
Auburn U at Montgomery, Montgomery, AL 36117-3596	1967	Dr. Guinevera A. Nance	5-M	6,341	356
Audrey Cohen Coll, New York, NY 10014-4502	1964	Dr. Audrey C. Cohen	1-M	1,045	73
Augsburg Coll, Minneapolis, MN 55454-1351	1869	Dr. Charles S. Anderson	2-M	2,964	268
Augusta Coll, Augusta, GA 30904-2200	1925	Dr. William A. Bloodworth, Jr.	5-M	5,625	252
Augustana Coll, Rock Island, IL 61201-2296	1860	Dr. Thomas Tredway	2-B	1,988	175
Augustana Coll, Sioux Falls, SD 57197	1860	Dr. Ralph H. Wagoner	2-M	1,692	151
Aurora U, Aurora, IL 60506-4892	1893	Dr. Thomas H. Zarle	1-M	2,025	240
Austin Coll, Sherman, TX 75090-4440	1849	Dr. Oscar C. Page	2-M	1,193	99
Austin Peay State U, Clarksville, TN 37044-0001	1927	NR	5-M	8,207	477
Averett Coll, Danville, VA 24541-3692	1859	Dr. Frank R. Campbell	2-D	2,024	57
Avila Coll, Kansas City, MO 64145-1698	1916	Dr. Larry Kramer	2-M	1,389	150
Azusa Pacific U, Azusa, CA 91702-2701	1899	Dr. Richard E. Felix	2-M	3,869	337
Babson Coll, Babson Park, MA 02157-0310	1919	Mr. William F. Glavin	1-M	3,235	176
Baker Coll of Flint, Flint, MI 48507-5508	1911	Mr. Edward J. Kurtz	1-B	4,147	163
Baker Coll of Muskegon, Muskegon, MI 49442-3497	1888	Mr. Robert D. Jewell	1-B	1,712	93
Baker Coll of Owosso, Owosso, MI 48867-4400	1984	Dr. Rick Amidon	1-B	1,391	77
Baldwin-Wallace Coll, Berea, OH 44017-2088	1845	Dr. Neal Malicky	2-M	4,772	314
Ball State U, Muncie, IN 47306-1099	1918	Dr. John E. Worthen	5-D	20,717	1,151
Bard Coll, Annandale-on-Hudson, NY 12504	1860	Dr. Leon Botstein	1-M	1,178	135
Barnard Coll, New York, NY 10027-6598 (3)	1889	Prof. Judith R. Shapiro	1-B	2,190	242
Barry U, Miami Shores, FL 33161-6695	1940	Sr. Jeanne O'Laughlin, OP	2-D	6,850	500
Barton Coll, Wilson, NC 27893	1902	Dr. James B. Hemby	2-B	1,614	107

Name, address	Year	Governing official, control, and highest degree offered	Enroll-ment	Faculty
Baruch Coll of the City U of New York, New York, NY 10010-5585	1919	Dr. Matthew Goldstein . . . 11-D	14,796	820
Bates Coll, Lewiston, ME 04240-6028	1855	Dr. Donald W. Harward . . . 1-B	1,599	165
Baylor U, Waco, TX 76798	1845	Dr. Herbert H. Reynolds . . . 2-D	12,194	667
Beaver Coll, Glenside, PA 19038-3295	1853	Dr. Bette E. Landman . . . 2-M	2,387	185
Belhaven Coll, Jackson, MS 39202-1789	1883	Dr. Newton Wilson . . . 2-B	1,083	80
Bellarmine Coll, Louisville, KY 40205-0671	1950	Dr. Joseph J. McGowan, Jr. . 2-M	2,339	172
Bellevue U, Bellevue, NE 68005-3039	1965	Dr. John B. Muller . . . 1-M	2,093	83
Belmont U, Nashville, TN 37212-3757	1951	Dr. William E. Troutt . . . 2-M	2,871	298
Beloit Coll, Beloit, WI 53511-5596	1846	Mr. Victor E. Ferrall, Jr. . . 1-M	1,211	136
Bemidji State U, Bemidji, MN 56601-2699	1919	Dr. Linda Baer . . . 5-M	4,593	223
Bentley Coll, Waltham, MA 02154-4705	1917	Dr. Joseph M. Cronin . . . 1-M	5,400	360
Berea Coll, Berea, KY 40404	1855	Dr. John B. Stephenson . . . 1-B	1,591	128
Berklee Coll of Music, Boston, MA 02215-3693	1945	Dr. Lee Eliot Berk . . . 1-B	2,553	280
Berry Coll, Mount Berry, GA 30149-0159	1902	Dr. Gloria M. Shatto . . . 1-M	1,788	129
Bethel Coll, Mishawaka, IN 46545-5591	1947	Dr. Norman Bridges . . . 2-M	1,158	104
Bethel Coll, St Paul, MN 55112-6979	1871	Dr. George K. Brushaber . . . 2-M	2,101	190
Bethune-Cookman Coll, Daytona Beach, FL 32114-3099	1904	Dr. Oswald P. Bronson, Sr. . 2-B	2,210	212
Biola U, La Mirada, CA 90639-0001	1908	Dr. Clyde Cook . . . 2-D	2,865	219
Birmingham-Southern Coll, Birmingham, AL 35254	1856	Dr. Neal R. Berte . . . 2-M	1,673	146
Black Hills State U, Spearfish, SD 57799-9501	1883	Dr. Clifford M. Trump . . . 5-M	2,870	111
Bloomfield Coll, Bloomfield, NJ 07003-4895	1868	Dr. John F. Noonan . . . 2-B	2,036	112
Bloomsburg U of Pennsylvania, Bloomsburg, PA 17815-1905	1839	Dr. Jessica Kozloff . . . 5-M	7,375	398
Bluefield State Coll, Bluefield, WV 24701-2198	1895	Dr. Robert E. Moore . . . 5-B	2,601	178
Boise State U, Boise, ID 83725-0399	1932	Dr. Charles Ruch . . . 5-D	13,835	896
Boricua Coll, New York, NY 10032-1560	1974	Dr. Victor G. Alicea . . . 1-B	1,146	128
Boston Coll, Chestnut Hill, MA 02167-9991	1863	Rev. J. Donald Monan, SJ . . 2-D	14,440	967
Boston U, Boston, MA 02215	1839	Dr. John Silber . . . 1-D	28,594	2,480
Bowdoin Coll, Brunswick, ME 04011-2546	1794	Mr. Robert H. Edwards . . . 1-B	1,498	167
Bowie State U, Bowie, MD 20715-3318	1865	Dr. Nathanael Pollard, Jr. . . 5-M	4,946	193
Bowling Green State U, Bowling Green, OH 43403	1910	Dr. Paul J. Olscamp . . . 5-D	17,249	873
Bradley U, Peoria, IL 61625-0002	1897	Dr. John R. Brazil . . . 1-M	6,024	438
Brandeis U, Waltham, MA 02254-9110	1948	Dr. Jehuda Reinharz . . . 1-D	3,938	467
Brenau U, Gainesville, GA 30501-3697 (4)	1878	Dr. John S. Burd . . . 1-M	2,120	258
Brewton-Parker Coll, Mt Vernon, GA 30445	1904	Dr. Y. Lynn Holmes . . . 2-B	2,142	229
Briar Cliff Coll, Sioux City, IA 51104-2100	1930	Sr. Margaret Wick . . . 2-B	1,168	73
Bridgewater State Coll, Bridgewater, MA 02325-0001	1840	Dr. Adrian Tinsley . . . 5-M	8,590	376
Brigham Young U, Provo, UT 84602-1001	1875	Dr. Rex E. Lee . . . 2-D	30,547	1,660
Brigham Young U–Hawaii Cmps, Laie, Oahu, HI 96762-1294	1955	Dr. Eric Shumway . . . 2-B	2,023	159
Brooklyn Coll of the City U of New York, Brooklyn, NY 11210-2889	1930	Dr. Vernon E. Lattin . . . 11-M	13,832	850
Brown U, Providence, RI 02912	1764	Dr. Vartan Gregorian . . . 1-D	7,655	689
Bryant Coll, Smithfield, RI 02917-1287	1863	Dr. William E. Trueheart . . . 1-M	4,252	212
Bryn Mawr Coll, Bryn Mawr, PA 19010-2899 (4)	1885	Dr. Mary Patterson McPherson . . . 1-D	1,642	229
Bucknell U, Lewisburg, PA 17837	1846	Dr. Gary A. Sojka . . . 1-M	3,600	259
Buena Vista Coll, Storm Lake, IA 50588-1798	1891	Dr. Keith G. Briscoe . . . 2-B	1,023	82
Butler U, Indianapolis, IN 46208-3485	1855	Dr. Geoffrey Bannister . . . 1-M	3,733	374
Cabrini Coll, Radnor, PA 19087-3699	1957	Dr. Antoinette Iadarola . . . 2-M	1,867	146
Caldwell Coll, Caldwell, NJ 07006-6195	1939	Sr. Patrice Werner . . . 2-M	1,584	102
California Coll for Health Sciences, National City, CA 91950-6605	1977	Mr. Kenneth B. Scheiderman 3-M	4,200	9
California Coll of Arts and Crafts, Oakland, CA 94618	1907	NR . . . 1-M	1,178	203
California Inst of Tech, Pasadena, CA 91125-0001	1891	Dr. Thomas E. Everhart . . . 1-D	1,977	295
California Inst of the Arts, Valencia, CA 91355-2340	1961	Dr. Steven D. Lavine . . . 1-M	1,061	232
California Lutheran U, Thousand Oaks, CA 91360-2700	1959	Dr. Luther S. Luedtke . . . 2-M	2,963	257
California Polytechnic State U, San Luis Obispo, San Luis Obispo, CA 93407	1901	Dr. Warren J. Baker . . . 5-M	15,477	858
California State Polytechnic U, Pomona, Pomona, CA 91768-2557	1938	Dr. Bob Suzuki . . . 5-M	17,050	869
California State U, Bakersfield, Bakersfield, CA 93311-1022	1970	Dr. Tomas A. Arciniega . . . 5-M	5,243	337
California State U, Chico, Chico, CA 95929-0150	1887	Dr. Manuel A. Esteban . . . 5-M	14,706	845
California State U, Dominguez Hills, Carson, CA 90747-0001	1960	Dr. Robert Detweiler . . . 5-M	9,672	401
California State U, Fresno, Fresno, CA 93740	1911	Dr. John D. Welty . . . 5-D	18,017	968
California State U, Fullerton, Fullerton, CA 92634-9480	1957	Dr. Milton A. Gordon . . . 5-M	22,565	1,013
California State U, Hayward, Hayward, CA 94542-3000	1957	Dr. Norma Rees . . . 5-M	12,583	636
California State U, Long Beach, Long Beach, CA 90840-0119	1949	Dr. Robert C. Maxson . . . 5-M	27,073	1,441
California State U, Los Angeles, Los Angeles, CA 90032-4221	1947	Dr. James M. Rosser . . . 5-M	20,801	946
California State U, Northridge, Northridge, CA 91330-0001	1958	Dr. Blenda J. Wilson . . . 5-M	27,282	1,306
California State U, Sacramento, Sacramento, CA 95819-6048	1947	Dr. Donald R. Gerth . . . 5-M	23,319	1,171
California State U, San Bernardino, San Bernardino, CA 92407-2318	1965	Dr. Anthony H. Evans . . . 5-M	12,121	571
California State U, San Marcos, San Marcos, CA 92096	1990	Dr. Bill W. Stacy . . . 5-M	2,376	105
California State U, Stanislaus, Turlock, CA 95382	1957	Dr. Marvalene Hughes . . . 5-M	5,907	335
California U of Pennsylvania, California, PA 15419-1394	1852	Dr. Angelo Armenti, Jr. . . . 5-M	6,330	345
Calvin Coll, Grand Rapids, MI 49546-4388	1876	Dr. Anthony J. Diekema . . . 2-M	3,730	277
Cameron U, Lawton, OK 73505-6377	1908	Dr. Don Davis . . . 5-M	5,969	227
Campbellsville Coll, Campbellsville, KY 42718-2799	1906	Dr. Kenneth W. Winters . . . 2-M	1,163	73
Campbell U, Buies Creek, NC 27506-0546	1887	Dr. Norman A. Wiggins . . . 2-F	6,047	302
Canisius Coll, Buffalo, NY 14208-1098	1870	Rev. Vincent M. Cooke, S.J. . 2-M	4,807	374
Capital U, Columbus, OH 43209-2394	1830	Dr. Josiah H. Blackmore . . . 2-F	3,824	163
Cardinal Stritch Coll, Milwaukee, WI 53217-3985	1937	Sr. Mary Lea Schneider . . . 2-M	5,639	525
Carleton Coll, Northfield, MN 55057-4001	1866	Dr. Stephen R. Lewis, Jr. . . . 1-B	1,678	164
Carlow Coll, Pittsburgh, PA 15213-3165 (4)	1929	Dr. Grace Ann Geibel, RSM . 2-M	1,469	184
Carnegie Mellon U, Pittsburgh, PA 15213-3891	1900	Dr. Robert Mehrabian . . . 1-D	7,259	743
Carroll Coll, Helena, MT 59625-0002	1909	Dr. Matthew J. Quinn . . . 2-B	1,415	103
Carroll Coll, Waukesha, WI 53186-5593	1846	Dr. Frank Falcone . . . 2-M	2,154	126
Carson-Newman Coll, Jefferson City, TN 37760	1851	Dr. J. Cordell Maddox . . . 2-M	2,126	182
Carthage Coll, Kenosha, WI 53140-1994	1847	Dr. F. Gregory Campbell . . . 2-M	2,050	135
Case Western Reserve U, Cleveland, OH 44106	1826	Dr. Agnar Pytte . . . 1-D	9,276	1,807
Castleton State Coll, Castleton, VT 05735	1787	Dr. Martha K. Farmer . . . 5-M	2,089	179

Name, address	Year	Governing official, control, and highest degree offered	Enrollment	Faculty
Catawba Coll, Salisbury, NC 28144-2488	1851	Mr. J. Fred Corriher, Jr. 2-M	1,002	76
Catholic U of America, Washington, DC 20064	1887	Br. Patrick Ellis, FSC 2-D	6,147	681
Cedar Crest Coll, Allentown, PA 18104-6132 (4)	1867	Dr. Dorothy Gulbenkian Blaney 2-B	1,545	140
Cedarville Coll, Cedarville, OH 45314-0601	1887	Dr. Paul H. Dixon 2-B	2,278	170
Centenary Coll of Louisiana, Shreveport, LA 71134-1188	1825	Dr. Kenneth L. Schwab 2-M	1,026	107
Central Coll, Pella, IA 50219-1999	1853	Dr. William M. Wiebenga 2-B	1,501	131
Central Connecticut State U, New Britain, CT 06050-4010	1849	Dr. John W. Shumaker 5-M	10,105	729
Central Methodist Coll, Fayette, MO 65248-1198	1854	Dr. Joe A. Howell 2-B	1,068	80
Central Michigan U, Mount Pleasant, MI 48859	1892	Dr. Leonard E. Plachta 5-D	16,252	813
Central Missouri State U, Warrensburg, MO 64093	1871	Dr. Ed Elliott 5-M	11,282	526
Central State U, Wilberforce, OH 45384	1887	Dr. Arthur E. Thomas 5-M	3,068	147
Central Washington U, Ellensburg, WA 98926	1891	Dr. Ivory V. Nelson 5-M	8,423	344
Central Wesleyan Coll, Central, SC 29630-1020	1906	Dr. David J. Spittal 2-M	1,372	173
Chadron State Coll, Chadron, NE 69337	1911	Dr. Samuel H. Rankin 5-M	3,439	137
Chapman U, Orange, CA 92666-1011	1861	Dr. James Doti 2-M	2,930	296
Charleston Southern U, Charleston, SC 29423-8087	1964	Dr. Jairy C. Hunter, Jr. 2-M	2,485	131
Charter Oak State Coll, Newington, CT 06111-2646	1973	Dr. Merle W. Harris 5-B	1,144	NR
Chestnut Hill Coll, Philadelphia, PA 19118-2695 (3)	1924	Dr. Carol J. Vale, SSJ 2-M	1,213	122
Cheyney U of Pennsylvania, Cheyney, PA 19319	1837	Dr. Douglas Covington 5-M	1,519	93
Chicago State U, Chicago, IL 60628	1867	Dr. Dolores Cross 5-M	9,507	482
Christian Brothers U, Memphis, TN 38104-5581	1871	Dr. Michael J. McGinnis, FSC 2-M	1,517	149
Christopher Newport U, Newport News, VA 23606-2998	1961	Dr. Anthony R. Santoro 5-M	4,756	329
The Citadel, The Military Coll of South Carolina, Charleston, SC 29409 (1)	1842	Lt. Gen. Claudius E. Watts, III 5-M	3,600	166
City Coll of the City U of New York, New York, NY 10031	1847	Dr. Yolanda T. Moses 11-D	14,832	1,185
City U, Bellevue, WA 98004-6442	1973	Dr. Michael A. Pastore 1-M	2,791	811
Clarion U of Pennsylvania, Clarion, PA 16214	1867	Dr. Diane L. Reinhard 5-M	5,881	365
Clark Atlanta U, Atlanta, GA 30314	1869	Dr. Thomas Cole, Jr. 2-D	5,128	350
Clarkson U, Potsdam, NY 13699-5557	1896	Dr. Richard H. Gallagher 1-D	2,772	184
Clark U, Worcester, MA 01610-1477	1887	Dr. Richard P. Traina 1-D	2,706	262
Clayton State Coll, Morrow, GA 30260-0285	1969	NR 5-B	4,760	191
Cleary Coll, Ypsilanti, MI 48197-1788	1883	Mr. Thomas Sullivan 1-B	1,000	93
Clemson U, Clemson, SC 29634	1889	Dr. Max Lennon 5-D	16,614	1,268
Cleveland State U, Cleveland, OH 44115	1964	Dr. Claire A. Van Ummersen 5-D	17,137	859
Clinch Valley Coll of the U of Virginia, Wise, VA 24293	1954	Dr. L. Jay Lemons 5-B	1,547	89
Coastal Carolina U, Myrtle Beach, SC 29578-1954	1954	Dr. Ronald R. Ingle 5-M	4,416	285
Coe Coll, Cedar Rapids, IA 52402-5070	1851	Dr. John E. Brown 2-M	1,354	114
Colby Coll, Waterville, ME 04901	1813	William R. Cotter 1-B	1,755	176
Colgate U, Hamilton, NY 13346-1386	1819	Dr. Neil R. Grabois 1-M	2,693	254
Coll for Lifelong Learning of the U System of NH, Durham, NH 03824-6654	1972	Dr. Victor Montana 11-B	1,194	300
Coll Misericordia, Dallas, PA 18612-1098	1924	Dr. Carol A. Jobe 2-M	1,779	120
Coll of Aeronautics, Flushing, NY 11371 (2)	1932	Dr. Richard B. Goetze, Jr. 1-B	1,092	88
Coll of Charleston, Charleston, SC 29424-0002	1770	Dr. Alexander M. Sanders, Jr. 5-M	10,566	613
Coll of Great Falls, Great Falls, MT 59405	1932	Dr. Frederick W. Gilliard 2-M	1,440	88
Coll of Insurance, New York, NY 10007-2165	1962	Dr. Ellen Thrower 1-M	2,267	93
Coll of Mount St Joseph, Cincinnati, OH 45233-1670	1920	Sr. Francis Marie Thrailkill, OSU 2-M	2,621	230
Coll of Mount Saint Vincent, Riverdale, NY 10471-1093	1911	Dr. Mary C. Stuart 1-M	1,211	92
Coll of New Rochelle, New Rochelle, NY 10805-2308 (4)	1904	Sr. Dorothy Ann Kelly, OSU 1-M	2,468	173
Coll of Notre Dame, Belmont, CA 94002-1997	1851	Dr. Margaret Huber 2-M	1,647	179
Coll of Notre Dame of Maryland, Baltimore, MD 21210-2473 (3)	1873	Sr. Rosemarie Nassif 2-M	1,986	84
Coll of Saint Benedict, Saint Joseph, MN 56374 (3)	1887	Sr. Colman O'Connell, OSB 2-B	1,767	150
Coll of St Catherine, St Paul, MN 55105-1789 (3)	1905	Dr. Anita Pampusch 2-M	2,588	240
Coll of Saint Elizabeth, Morristown, NJ 07960-6989 (4)	1899	Sr. Jacqueline Burns 2-M	1,484	116
Coll of St Francis, Joliet, IL 60435-6188	1920	Dr. John C. Orr 2-M	1,888	124
Coll of Saint Mary, Omaha, NE 68124-2377 (3)	1923	Dr. Kenneth Nielsen 2-B	1,168	135
Coll of Saint Rose, Albany, NY 12203-1419	1920	Dr. Louis C. Vaccaro 1-M	3,905	241
Coll of St Scholastica, Duluth, MN 55811-4199	1912	Dr. Daniel H. Pilon 2-M	1,838	176
Coll of Santa Fe, Santa Fe, NM 87505	1947	Dr. James A. Fries 1-M	1,641	145
Coll of Staten Island of the City U of New York, Staten Island, NY 10314-6600	1955	Dr. Felix F. Cardegna 11-M	12,050	734
Coll of the Holy Cross, Worcester, MA 01610	1843	Rev. Gerard C. Reedy, SJ 2-B	2,675	281
Coll of the Ozarks, Point Lookout, MO 65726	1906	Dr. Jerry C. Davis 2-B	1,472	108
The Coll of West Virginia, Beckley, WV 25802-2830	1933	Dr. Charles H. Polk 1-B	1,940	115
Coll of William and Mary, Williamsburg, VA 23187-8795	1693	Mr. Timothy J. Sullivan 5-D	7,586	556
The Coll of Wooster, Wooster, OH 44691	1866	Dr. Henry J. Copeland 2-B	1,704	NR
Colorado Christian U, Lakewood, CO 80226-1053	1914	Dr. Ronald Schmidt 2-M	1,166	72
The Colorado Coll, Colorado Springs, CO 80903-3294	1874	Dr. Kathryn Mohrman 1-M	1,917	200
Colorado Sch of Mines, Golden, CO 80401-1887	1874	Dr. George S. Ansell 5-D	3,093	200
Colorado State U, Fort Collins, CO 80523	1862	Dr. Albert C. Yates 5-D	21,110	1,006
Colorado Tech Coll, Colorado Springs, CO 80907-3896	1965	Mr. David D. O'Donnell 3-M	1,487	73
Columbia Coll, Chicago, IL 60605-1997	1890	Mr. John B. Duff 1-M	7,327	853
Columbia Coll, New York, NY 10027	1754	Mr. Steven Marcus 1-B	3,447	475
Columbia Coll, Columbia, SC 29203-5998 (3)	1854	Dr. Peter T. Mitchell 2-M	1,237	76
Columbia U, Sch of Engineering & Applied Sci, New York, NY 10027	1864	Dr. David H. Auston 1-D	1,008	100
Columbia U, Sch of General Studies, New York, NY 10027	1754	Ms. Caroline W. Bynum 1-M	1,196	450
Columbia U, Sch of Nursing, New York, NY 10032-3702 (4)	1892	Dr. Mary O. Mundinger 1-D	549	40
Columbus Coll, Columbus, GA 31907-5645	1958	Dr. Frank D. Brown 5-M	5,241	228
Columbus Coll of Art and Design, Columbus, OH 43215-1758	1879	Mr. Joseph V. Canzani 1-B	1,695	108
Concord Coll, Athens, WV 24712-1000	1872	Dr. Jerry L. Beasley 5-B	2,801	150
Concordia Coll, Moorhead, MN 56562	1891	Dr. Paul J. Dovre 2-B	2,999	256
Concordia Coll, St Paul, MN 55104-5494	1893	Dr. Robert Holst 2-M	1,234	124
Concordia Coll, Portland, OR 97211-6099	1905	Dr. Charles E. Schlimpert 2-B	1,017	90
Concordia U, River Forest, IL 60305-1499	1864	Dr. Eugene L. Krentz 2-M	2,497	216
Concordia U Wisconsin, Mequon, WI 53097-2402	1881	Dr. R. John Buuck 2-M	2,722	135
Connecticut Coll, New London, CT 06320-4196	1911	Dr. Claire L. Gaudiani 1-M	1,947	228
Converse Coll, Spartanburg, SC 29302-0006 (3)	1889	Dr. Sandra C. Thomas 1-M	1,106	100
Cooper Union for the Advancement of Science & Art, New York, NY 10003-7120	1859	Mr. John Jay Iselin 1-M	1,045	235
Coppin State Coll, Baltimore, MD 21216-3698	1900	Dr. Calvin W. Burnett 5-M	3,267	153
Cornell Coll, Mount Vernon, IA 52314-1098	1853	Dr. Leslie H. Garner, Jr. 2-B	1,150	125
Cornell U, Ithaca, NY 14853-0001	1865	Dr. Frank H. T. Rhodes 1-D	18,449	1,594

Name, address	Year	Governing official, control, and highest degree offered		Enroll-ment	Faculty
Creighton U, Omaha, NE 68178-0001	1878	Rev. Michael G. Morrison, SJ	2-D	6,341	1,180
Culver-Stockton Coll, Canton, MO 63435-1299	1853	Dr. Edwin B. Strong, Jr.	2-B	1,104	75
Cumberland Coll, Williamsburg, KY 40769-1372	1889	Dr. James Taylor	2-M	1,518	108
Curry Coll, Milton, MA 02186-9984	1879	Dr. Catherine W. Ingold	1-M	1,249	148
Daemen Coll, Amherst, NY 14226-3592	1947	Dr. Robert S. Marshall	1-M	1,802	131
Dakota State U, Madison, SD 57042-1799	1881	Dr. Jerald Tunheim	5-B	1,563	68
Dallas Baptist U, Dallas, TX 75211-9299	1965	Dr. Gary R. Cook	2-M	2,803	179
Dartmouth Coll, Hanover, NH 03755	1769	Mr. James O. Freedman	1-D	5,475	468
Davenport Coll of Business, Grand Rapids, MI 49503	1866	Mr. Donald W. Maine	1-B	3,455	178
Davenport Coll of Business, Kalamazoo Cmps, Kalamazoo, MI 49006-2791 (4)	1866	Mr. C. Dexter Rohm	1-B	1,905	99
Davenport Coll of Business, Lansing Cmps, Lansing, MI 48933-2197	1979	Mr. Don Colizzi	1-B	1,619	104
David Lipscomb U, Nashville, TN 37204-3951	1891	Dr. Harold Hazelip	2-M	2,335	184
Davidson Coll, Davidson, NC 28036-1719	1837	Dr. John W. Kuykendall	2-B	1,607	140
Delaware State U, Dover, DE 19901-2277	1891	Dr. William B. DeLauder	5-M	2,935	182
Delaware Valley Coll, Doylestown, PA 18901-2697	1896	Mr. George F. West	1-B	1,468	106
Delta State U, Cleveland, MS 38733-0001	1925	Dr. F. Kent Wyatt	5-D	3,841	244
Denison U, Granville, OH 43023	1831	Dr. Michele Tolela Myers	1-B	1,940	165
DePaul U, Chicago, IL 60604-2287	1898	Rev. John P. Minogue, CM	2-D	16,477	1,065
DePauw U, Greencastle, IN 46135-1772	1837	Dr. Robert G. Bottoms	2-B	1,983	208
Detroit Coll of Business, Dearborn, MI 48126-3799	1962	Dr. James Mendola	1-B	2,513	142
Detroit Coll of Business, Warren Cmps, Warren, MI 48092-5209	1975	Ms. Janet Guggenheim	1-B	1,460	82
DeVry Inst of Tech, Phoenix, AZ 85021-2995	1967	Mr. James A. Dugan	3-B	2,645	88
DeVry Inst of Tech, Pomona, CA 91768-2642	1983	Dr. Rose Marie Dishman	3-B	2,620	100
DeVry Inst of Tech, Decatur, GA 30030-2198	1969	Dr. Ronald Bush	3-B	2,825	85
DeVry Inst of Tech, Addison, IL 60101-6106	1982	Mr. Jerry R. Dill	3-B	2,779	104
DeVry Inst of Tech, Chicago, IL 60618-5994	1931	Dr. E. Arthur Stunnard	3-B	3,025	113
DeVry Inst of Tech, Kansas City, MO 64131-3698	1931	Mr. Charles R. Levalley	3-B	1,907	69
DeVry Inst of Tech, Columbus, OH 43209-2764	1952	Mr. Richard A. Czerniak	3-B	2,798	78
DeVry Inst of Tech, Irving, TX 75038-2440	1969	Dr. Francis V. Cannon	3-B	2,033	100
Dickinson Coll, Carlisle, PA 17013-2896	1773	Dr. A. Lee Fritschler	1-B	1,951	187
Dickinson State U, Dickinson, ND 58601-4896	1918	Dr. Phillip W. Conn	5-B	1,613	98
Dillard U, New Orleans, LA 70122-3097	1869	Dr. Samuel DuBois Cook	2-B	1,584	124
Doane Coll, Crete, NE 68333-2430	1872	Dr. Frederic D. Brown	2-M	1,124	96
Dominican Coll of Blauvelt, Orangeburg, NY 10962-1210	1952	Sr. Kathleen Sullivan	1-M	1,540	112
Dominican Coll of San Rafael, San Rafael, CA 94901-8008	1890	Dr. Joseph R. Fink	2-M	1,098	144
Dordt Coll, Sioux Center, IA 51250-1697	1955	Dr. John B. Hulst	2-B	1,104	90
Dowling Coll, Oakdale, NY 11769-1999	1955	Dr. Victor P. Meskill	1-M	5,362	389
Drake U, Des Moines, IA 50311-4516	1881	Dr. Michael R. Ferrari	1-D	6,333	278
Drew U, Madison, NJ 07940-1493	1867	Mr. Thomas H. Kean	2-D	1,984	179
Drexel U, Philadelphia, PA 19104-2875	1891	Dr. Richard D. Breslin	1-D	10,210	841
Drury Coll, Springfield, MO 65802-3791	1873	Dr. John E. Moore, Jr.	2-M	1,406	129
Duke U, Durham, NC 27708-0586	1838	Dr. Nannerl O. Keohane	2-D	11,010	2,408
Duquesne U, Pittsburgh, PA 15282-0001	1878	Dr. John E. Murray, Jr.	2-D	8,637	716
Dyke Coll, Cleveland, OH 44115-1096	1848	Dr. John C. Corfias	1-B	1,447	92
D'Youville Coll, Buffalo, NY 14201-1084	1908	Dr. Denise A. Roche, GNSH	1-M	1,796	136
Earlham Coll, Richmond, IN 47374-4095	1847	Dr. Richard J. Wood	2-B	1,041	88
East Carolina U, Greenville, NC 27858-4353	1907	Dr. Richard Eakin	5-D	17,729	1,181
East Central U, Ada, OK 74820-6899	1909	Dr. Bill S. Cole	5-M	4,418	225
Eastern Coll, St Davids, PA 19087-3696	1932	Dr. Roberta Hestenes	2-M	1,842	168
Eastern Connecticut State U, Willimantic, CT 06226-2295	1889	Mr. David G. Carter	5-M	4,576	192
Eastern Illinois U, Charleston, IL 61920-3099	1895	Dr. David L. Jorns	5-M	11,395	662
Eastern Kentucky U, Richmond, KY 40475-3102	1906	Dr. Hanly Funderburk	5-M	16,391	829
Eastern Mennonite U, Harrisonburg, VA 22801-2462	1917	Dr. Joseph L. Lapp	2-F	1,102	106
Eastern Michigan U, Ypsilanti, MI 48197	1849	Dr. William E. Shelton	5-D	25,836	1,046
Eastern Nazarene Coll, Quincy, MA 02170-2999	1918	Dr. Kent R. Hill	2-M	1,374	66
Eastern New Mexico U, Portales, NM 88130	1934	Dr. Everett L. Frost	5-M	3,816	224
Eastern Oregon State Coll, La Grande, OR 97850-2899	1929	Mr. David E. Gilbert	5-M	1,899	145
East Stroudsburg U of Pennsylvania, East Stroudsburg, PA 18301-2999	1893	Dr. James Gilbert	5-M	5,403	265
East Tennessee State U, Johnson City, TN 37614-0734	1911	Dr. Roy S. Nicks	5-D	11,518	641
East Texas Baptist U, Marshall, TX 75670-1498	1912	Dr. Bob E. Riley	2-M	1,187	98
East Texas State U, Commerce, TX 75429-3011	1889	Dr. Jerry D. Morris	5-D	8,145	396
Eckerd Coll, St Petersburg, FL 33711	1958	Dr. Peter H. Armacost	2-B	1,418	139
Edgewood Coll, Madison, WI 53711-1998	1927	Dr. James A. Ebben	2-M	1,787	124
Edinboro U of Pennsylvania, Edinboro, PA 16444	1857	Mr. Foster F. Diebold	5-M	7,730	406
Elizabeth City State U, Elizabeth City, NC 27909-7806	1891	Dr. Jimmy R. Jenkins	5-B	2,130	136
Elizabethtown Coll, Elizabethtown, PA 17022-2298	1899	Dr. Gerhard E. Spiegler	2-B	1,788	147
Elmhurst Coll, Elmhurst, IL 60126-3296	1871	Dr. Ivan E. Frick	2-B	2,687	140
Elmira Coll, Elmira, NY 14901	1855	Dr. Thomas K. Meier	1-M	1,099	76
Elms Coll, Chicopee, MA 01013-2839 (3)	1928	Sr. Kathleen Keating	2-M	1,168	96
Elon Coll, Elon College, NC 27244	1889	Dr. J. Fred Young	2-M	3,279	193
Embry-Riddle Aeronautical U, Prescott, AZ 86301-3720	1978	Mr. Paul S. Daly	1-B	1,450	84
Embry-Riddle Aeronautical U, Daytona Beach, FL 32114-3900	1926	Dr. Steven M. Sliwa	1-M	4,357	267
Embry-Riddle Aeronautical U, Coll of Career Ed, Daytona Beach, FL 32114-3900	1970	Dr. Leon E. Flancher	1-M	5,403	1,975
Emerson Coll, Boston, MA 02116-1511	1880	Dr. Jacqueline W. Liebergott	1-D	2,776	246
Emmanuel Coll, Boston, MA 02115 (4)	1919	Sr. Janet Eisner, SND	2-M	1,471	137
Emory U, Atlanta, GA 30322-1100	1836	Dr. William M. Chace	2-D	10,367	1,983
Emporia State U, Emporia, KS 66801-5087	1863	Dr. Robert E. Glennen	5-D	6,090	290
Eugene Lang Coll, New Sch for Social Research, New York, NY 10011-8601	1985	Dr. Beatrice Banu	1-B	335	59
Evangel Coll, Springfield, MO 65802-2191	1955	Dr. Robert H. Spence	2-B	1,503	115
The Evergreen State Coll, Olympia, WA 98505	1967	Dr. Jane L. Jervis	5-M	3,672	177
Fairfield U, Fairfield, CT 06430	1942	Rev. Aloysius P. Kelley, SJ	2-M	4,777	320
Fairleigh Dickinson U, Florham-Madison Cmps, Madison, NJ 07940-1099	1942	Dr. Francis J. Mertz	1-D	7,963	628
Fairmont State Coll, Fairmont, WV 26554	1865	Dr. Robert J. Dillman	5-B	6,344	416
Fashion Inst of Tech, New York, NY 10001-5992	1944	Dr. Allan F. Hershfield	11-M	12,196	820
Faulkner U, Montgomery, AL 36109-3398	1942	Dr. Billy D. Hilyer	2-D	1,990	125
Fayetteville State U, Fayetteville, NC 28301	1867	Dr. Lloyd V. Hackley	5-M	4,032	240
Felician Coll, Lodi, NJ 07644-2198	1942	Sr. Theresa Martin	2-B	1,142	97

Name, address	Year	Governing official, control, and highest degree offered		Enroll-ment	Faculty
Ferris State U, Big Rapids, MI 49307	1884	Dr. Helen Popovich	5-F	11,188	751
Ferrum Coll, Ferrum, VA 24088	1913	Dr. Jerry M. Boone	2-B	1,132	102
Finch U of Health Sciences/Chicago Medical Sch, North Chicago, IL 60064-3037	1912	Mr. Herman M. Finch	1-D	1,204	23
Fitchburg State Coll, Fitchburg, MA 01420-2697	1894	Dr. Vincent J. Mara	5-M	5,208	293
Flagler Coll, St Augustine, FL 32085-1027	1968	Dr. William L. Proctor	1-B	1,345	117
Florida A&M U, Tallahassee, FL 32307	1887	Dr. Frederick Humphries	5-D	9,871	616
Florida Atlantic U, Boca Raton, FL 33431-0991	1961	Dr. Anthony James Catanese	5-D	15,700	548
Florida Inst of Tech, Melbourne, FL 32901-6988	1958	Dr. Lynn E. Weaver	1-D	4,982	446
Florida Southern Coll, Lakeland, FL 33801-5698	1885	Dr. Robert A. Davis	2-M	2,604	120
Florida State U, Tallahassee, FL 32306	1857	Dr. Talbot D'Alemberte	5-D	28,669	1,543
Fontbonne Coll, St Louis, MO 63105-3098	1917	Dr. Meneve Dunham	2-M	1,984	131
Fordham U, New York, NY 10458	1841	Rev. Joseph A. O'Hare, SJ	2-D	14,611	762
Fort Lewis Coll, Durango, CO 81301-3999	1911	Mr. Joel M. Jones	5-B	4,279	250
Fort Valley State Coll, Fort Valley, GA 31030-3262	1895	Dr. Oscar L. Prater	5-F	2,746	151
Framingham State Coll, Framingham, MA 01701-9101	1839	Dr. Paul F. Weller	5-M	5,292	228
Franciscan U of Steubenville, Steubenville, OH 43952-6701	1946	Rev. Michael Scanlan, TOR	2-M	1,901	133
Francis Marion U, Florence, SC 29501-0547	1970	Dr. Lee A. Vickers	5-M	4,103	215
Franklin and Marshall Coll, Lancaster, PA 17604-3003	1787	Dr. A. Richard Kneedler	1-B	1,844	165
Franklin Pierce Coll, Rindge, NH 03461-0060	1962	Dr. Walter Peterson	1-B	1,240	106
Franklin U, Columbus, OH 43215-5399	1902	Paul J. Otte	1-M	3,915	212
Freed-Hardeman U, Henderson, TN 38340-2399	1869	Dr. Milton R. Sewell	2-M	1,361	91
Fresno Pacific Coll, Fresno, CA 93702-4709	1944	Dr. Richard Kriegbaum	2-M	1,536	155
Frostburg State U, Frostburg, MD 21532-2302	1898	Dr. Catherine R. Gira	5-M	5,398	305
Furman U, Greenville, SC 29613	1826	Dr. David E. Shi	1-M	2,841	198
Gallaudet U, Washington, DC 20002-3625	1864	Dr. I. King Jordan	1-D	2,201	330
Gannon U, Erie, PA 16541	1925	Msgr. David A. Rubino, PhD	2-M	3,981	300
Gardner-Webb U, Boiling Springs, NC 28017	1905	Dr. M. Christopher White	2-M	2,327	174
Geneva Coll, Beaver Falls, PA 15010-3599	1848	Dr. John H. White	2-M	1,632	102
George Fox Coll, Newberg, OR 97132-2697	1891	Dr. Edward F. Stevens	2-D	1,557	133
George Mason U, Fairfax, VA 22030-4445	1957	Dr. George W. Johnson	5-D	21,300	1,151
Georgetown Coll, Georgetown, KY 40324-1696	1829	Dr. William H. Crouch, Jr.	2-M	1,382	105
Georgetown U, Washington, DC 20057	1789	Rev. Leo J. O'Donovan, SJ	2-D	12,321	1,808
The George Washington U, Washington, DC 20052	1821	Mr. Stephen J. Trachtenberg	1-D	16,072	2,425
Georgia Coll, Milledgeville, GA 31061	1889	Dr. Edwin G. Speir	5-M	5,668	264
Georgia Inst of Tech, Atlanta, GA 30332-0001	1885	Dr. John P. Crecine	5-D	12,846	615
Georgian Court Coll, Lakewood, NJ 08701-2697 (4)	1908	Sr. Barbara Williams	2-M	2,580	204
Georgia Southern U, Statesboro, GA 30460-8100	1906	Dr. Nicholas Henry	5-M	14,191	649
Georgia State U, Atlanta, GA 30303-3083	1913	Dr. Carl V. Patton	5-D	23,651	1,292
Gettysburg Coll, Gettysburg, PA 17325-1411	1832	Dr. Gordon A. Haaland	1-B	1,950	174
Glenville State Coll, Glenville, WV 26351-1200	1872	Dr. William K. Simmons	5-B	2,306	160
GMI Engineering & Management Inst, Flint, MI 48504-4898	1919	Dr. James E. A. John	1-M	3,204	150
Golden Gate U, San Francisco, CA 94105-2968	1853	Dr. Thomas M. Stauffer	1-D	6,934	454
Goldey-Beacom Coll, Wilmington, DE 19808-1999	1886	Mr. William R. Baldt	1-M	1,795	73
Gonzaga U, Spokane, WA 99258	1887	Rev. Bernard J. Coughlin, SJ	2-D	4,915	285
Gordon Coll, Wenham, MA 01984-1899	1889	Dr. R. Judson Carlberg	2-B	1,228	97
Goucher Coll, Baltimore, MD 21204-2794	1885	Dr. Judy J. Mohraz	1-M	1,001	138
Governors State U, University Park, IL 60466	1969	Dr. Paula Wolff	5-M	5,553	294
Graceland Coll, Lamoni, IA 50140	1895	Dr. William T. Higdon	2-B	1,105	81
Grand Canyon U, Phoenix, AZ 85017-3030	1949	Dr. Bill Williams	2-M	1,963	172
Grand Valley State U, Allendale, MI 49401-9403	1960	Mr. Arend D. Lubbers	5-M	13,384	660
Grand View Coll, Des Moines, IA 50316-1599	1896	Dr. Arthur E. Puotinen	2-B	1,389	137
Grinnell Coll, Grinnell, IA 50112-0805	1846	Dr. Pamela A. Ferguson	1-B	1,322	150
Grove City Coll, Grove City, PA 16127-2104	1876	Dr. Jerry H. Combee	2-B	2,248	143
Guilford Coll, Greensboro, NC 27410-4173	1837	Dr. William R. Rogers	2-B	1,225	108
Gustavus Adolphus Coll, St Peter, MN 56082-1498	1862	Dr. Axel D. Steuer	2-B	2,316	214
Gwynedd-Mercy Coll, Gwynedd Valley, PA 19437	1948	Dr. Linda M. Bevilacqua, OP	2-M	1,696	183
Hahnemann U, Philadelphia, PA 19102	1848	Mr. Sherif Abdelhak	1-D	1,758	752
Hamilton Coll, Clinton, NY 13323-1218	1812	Dr. Eugene M. Tobin	1-B	1,670	195
Hamline U, St Paul, MN 55104-1284	1854	Dr. Larry G. Osnes	2-F	2,562	245
Hampshire Coll, Amherst, MA 01002	1965	Dr. Gregory S. Prince, Jr.	1-B	1,079	100
Hampton U, Hampton, VA 23668	1868	Dr. William R. Harvey	1-D	5,704	390
Hanover Coll, Hanover, IN 47243	1827	Dr. Russell L. Nichols	2-B	1,051	101
Harding U, Searcy, AR 72149-0001	1924	Dr. David B. Burks, Jr.	2-M	3,552	209
Hardin-Simmons U, Abilene, TX 79698-0001	1891	Dr. Lanny Hall	2-M	1,974	142
Hartwick Coll, Oneonta, NY 13820-4020	1797	Dr. Richard A. Detweiler	1-B	1,456	157
Harvard U, Cambridge, MA 02138	1636	Dr. Neil Rudenstine	1-D	18,556	2,065
Hastings Coll, Hastings, NE 68902-0269	1882	Dr. Thomas J. Reeves	2-M	1,047	86
Haverford Coll, Haverford, PA 19041-1392	1833	Dr. Tom G. Kessinger	1-B	1,084	109
Hawaii Pacific U, Honolulu, HI 96813-2785	1965	Mr. Chatt Wright	1-M	7,526	394
Heidelberg Coll, Tiffin, OH 44883-2462	1850	Dr. Kenneth J. Porada	2-M	1,305	113
Henderson State U, Arkadelphia, AR 71999-0001	1890	Dr. Charles D. Dunn	5-M	3,832	173
High Point U, High Point, NC 27262-3598	1924	Dr. Jacob C. Martinson, Jr.	2-M	2,429	106
Hillsdale Coll, Hillsdale, MI 49242-1298	1844	Dr. George C. Roche, III	1-B	1,130	112
Hofstra U, Hempstead, NY 11550-1090	1935	Dr. James M. Shuart	1-D	11,998	979
Hollins Coll, Roanoke, VA 24020-1657 (3)	1842	Dr. Jane Margaret O'Brien	1-M	1,030	91
Holy Family Coll, Philadelphia, PA 19114-2094	1954	Sr. Francesca Onley	2-M	2,590	236
Hood Coll, Frederick, MD 21701-8575 (4)	1893	Dr. Martha E. Church	2-M	2,080	93
Hope Coll, Holland, MI 49422-9000	1862	Dr. John H. Jacobson, Jr.	2-B	2,713	245
Houghton Coll, Houghton, NY 14744	1883	Dr. Daniel R. Chamberlain	2-B	1,210	100
Houston Baptist U, Houston, TX 77074-3298	1960	Dr. E. Douglas Hodo	2-M	2,191	146
Howard Payne U, Brownwood, TX 76801-2715	1889	Dr. Don Newbury	2-B	1,467	108
Howard U, Washington, DC 20059-0002	1867	Dr. Joyce A. Ladner	1-D	10,736	2,021
Humboldt State U, Arcata, CA 95521-8299	1913	Dr. Alistair W. McCrone	5-M	7,122	509
Hunter Coll of the City U of New York, New York, NY 10021-5085	1870	Dr. Blanche D. Blank	11-M	18,390	696
Huron U, Huron, SD 57350-2798	1883	Dr. Norman L. Stewart	3-M	1,146	84
Husson Coll, Bangor, ME 04401-2999	1898	Dr. William H. Beardsley	1-M	1,871	75
ICI U, Irving, TX 75063-2631	1967	Dr. George M. Flattery	2-M	9,650	NR
Idaho State U, Pocatello, ID 83209	1901	Dr. Richard Bowen	5-D	10,779	635
Illinois Benedictine Coll, Lisle, IL 60532-0900	1887	Dr. Richard C. Becker	2-M	2,624	245
Illinois Inst of Tech, Chicago, IL 60616	1890	Mr. Lewis Collens	1-D	7,027	492
Illinois State U, Normal, IL 61761	1857	Dr. Thomas P. Wallace	5-D	20,610	953
Illinois Wesleyan U, Bloomington, IL 61702-2900	1850	Dr. Minor Myers, Jr.	1-B	1,841	178
Immaculata Coll, Immaculata, PA 19345-0900 (4)	1920	Sr. Marie Roseanne Bonfini	2-D	2,346	167

Name, address	Year	Governing official, control, and highest degree offered		Enroll-ment	Faculty
Incarnate Word Coll, San Antonio, TX 78209-6397	1881	Dr. Louis J. Agnese, Jr.	2-M	2,801	196
Indiana State U, Terre Haute, IN 47809-1401	1865	Dr. John W. Moore	5-D	12,181	667
Indiana U Bloomington, Bloomington, IN 47405	1820	Dr. Kenneth R. R. Gros Louis	5-D	35,551	1,557
Indiana U East, Richmond, IN 47374-1289	1971	Dr. Charlie Nelms	5-B	2,376	192
Indiana U Kokomo, Kokomo, IN 46904-9003	1945	Dr. Emita B. Hill	5-M	3,494	195
Indiana U Northwest, Gary, IN 46408-1197	1959	Dr. Hilda Richards	5-M	5,908	374
Indiana U of Pennsylvania, Indiana, PA 15705	1875	Dr. Lawrence K. Pettit	5-D	14,062	814
Indiana U–Purdue U Fort Wayne, Fort Wayne, IN 46805-1499	1917	Dr. Michael A. Wartell	5-M	11,701	667
Indiana U–Purdue U Indianapolis, Indianapolis, IN 46202-2896	1969	Mr. Gerald L. Bepko	5-D	27,552	2,187
Indiana U South Bend, South Bend, IN 46634-7111	1922	Dr. H. Daniel Cohen	5-M	7,582	557
Indiana U Southeast, New Albany, IN 47150-6405	1941	Dr. Leon Rand	5-M	5,770	403
Inter American U of PR, Arecibo Cmps, Arecibo, PR 00614-4050	1957	Dr. Zaida Vega	1-B	4,432	224
Inter American U of PR, San Germán Cmps, San Germán, PR 00683-5008	1912	Prof. Agnes Mojica	1-M	5,852	307
Iona Coll, New Rochelle, NY 10801-1890	1940	Br. John G. Driscoll, CFC	1-M	6,996	428
Iowa State U of Science and Tech, Ames, IA 50011-2010	1858	Dr. Martin C. Jischke	5-D	25,112	1,759
Ithaca Coll, Ithaca, NY 14850	1892	Dr. James J. Whalen	1-M	5,964	565
Jackson State U, Jackson, MS 39217	1877	Dr. James E. Lyons, Sr.	5-D	6,346	388
Jacksonville State U, Jacksonville, AL 36265-9982	1883	Dr. Harold J. McGee	5-M	7,506	354
Jacksonville U, Jacksonville, FL 32211-3394	1934	Dr. James J. Brady	1-M	2,407	246
James Madison U, Harrisonburg, VA 22807	1908	Dr. Ronald E. Carrier	5-M	11,354	686
Jamestown Coll, Jamestown, ND 58405	1883	Dr. James Walker	2-B	1,066	72
Jersey City State Coll, Jersey City, NJ 07305	1927	Dr. Carlos Hernandez	5-M	6,845	434
John Brown U, Siloam Springs, AR 72761-2121	1919	Dr. A. LeVon Balzer	2-B	1,060	95
John Carroll U, University Heights, OH 44118-4581	1886	Rev. Michael J. Lavelle, SJ	2-M	4,430	337
John F Kennedy U, Orinda, CA 94563-2689	1964	Mr. Charles E. Glasser	1-F	1,796	88
John Jay Coll of Criminal Justice of City U of NY, New York, NY 10019-1093	1964	Dr. Gerald Lynch	11-M	8,691	496
Johns Hopkins U, Baltimore, MD 21218-2699	1876	Dr. William C. Richardson	1-D	4,803	534
Johnson & Wales U, Providence, RI 02903-2807	1914	Dr. John A. Yena	1-M	8,690	312
Johnson & Wales U at Charleston, Charleston, SC 29403	1984	Dr. Barry L. Gleim	1-B	1,102	66
Johnson C Smith U, Charlotte, NC 28216	1867	Dr. Dorothy Cowser Yancy	1-B	1,391	91
Johnson State Coll, Johnson, VT 05656-9405	1828	Dr. Robert Hahn	5-M	1,758	140
Juniata Coll, Huntingdon, PA 16652-2119	1876	Dr. Robert W. Neff	1-B	1,118	104
Kalamazoo Coll, Kalamazoo, MI 49006-3295	1833	Dr. Lawrence Bryan	1-B	1,218	110
Kansas Newman Coll, Wichita, KS 67213-2084	1933	Sr. Tarcisia Roths	2-B	1,832	262
Kansas State U, Manhattan, KS 66506	1863	Dr. Jon Wefald	5-D	20,775	1,116
Kean Coll of New Jersey, Union, NJ 07083	1855	Dr. Elsa Gomez	5-M	12,497	824
Keene State Coll, Keene, NH 03431-4183	1909	Dr. Stanley J. Yarosewick	5-M	3,960	336
Kennesaw State Coll, Marietta, GA 30061-0444	1963	Dr. Betty L. Siegel	5-M	12,273	529
Kent State U, Kent, OH 44242-0001	1910	Dr. Carol A. Cartwright	5-D	22,700	1,340
Kentucky State U, Frankfort, KY 40601	1886	Dr. Mary L. Smith	12-M	2,487	158
Kenyon Coll, Gambier, OH 43022-9623	1824	Dr. Philip H. Jordan, Jr.	1-B	1,454	160
King's Coll, Wilkes-Barre, PA 18711-0801	1946	Rev. James Lackenmier, CSC	2-M	2,323	171
Kutztown U of Pennsylvania, Kutztown, PA 19530	1866	Dr. David E. McFarland	5-M	7,762	382
Lafayette Coll, Easton, PA 18042-1798	1826	Mr. Arthur J. Rothkopf	2-B	2,156	228
LaGrange Coll, LaGrange, GA 30240-2999	1831	Dr. Walter Y. Murphy	2-M	1,023	93
Lake Forest Coll, Lake Forest, IL 60045-2399	1857	Dr. David Spadafora	1-M	1,026	112
Lake Superior State U, Sault Sainte Marie, MI 49783	1946	Dr. Robert D. Arbuckle	5-M	3,244	112
Lamar U–Beaumont, Beaumont, TX 77705	1923	Dr. Rex Cottle	5-D	8,356	725
Lambuth U, Jackson, TN 38301	1843	Dr. Thomas F. Boyd	2-B	1,165	87
Lander U, Greenwood, SC 29649-2099	1872	Dr. William C. Moran	5-M	2,760	166
La Roche Coll, Pittsburgh, PA 15237-5898	1963	Msgr. William Kerr	2-M	1,813	126
La Salle U, Philadelphia, PA 19141-1199	1863	Br. Joseph Burke	2-M	5,900	324
La Sierra U, Riverside, CA 92515	1922	Dr. Lawrence T. Geraty	2-D	1,469	105
Lawrence Tech U, Southfield, MI 48075-1058	1932	Dr. Charles M. Chambers	1-M	4,503	307
Lawrence U, Appleton, WI 54912-0599	1847	Dr. Richard Warch	1-B	1,211	129
Lebanon Valley Coll, Annville, PA 17003-0501	1866	Mr. John A. Synodinos	2-M	1,682	104
Lee Coll, Cleveland, TN 37311-4475	1918	Dr. Paul Conn	2-B	2,011	163
Lehigh U, Bethlehem, PA 18015-3094	1865	Dr. Peter Likins	1-D	6,496	495
Le Moyne Coll, Syracuse, NY 13214	1946	Rev. Robert A. Mitchell, SJ	2-M	2,512	210
LeMoyne-Owen Coll, Memphis, TN 38126-6595	1862	Dr. Burnett Joiner	2-M	1,321	100
Lenoir-Rhyne Coll, Hickory, NC 28603	1891	Dr. Ryan A. LaHurd	2-M	1,425	120
Lesley Coll, Cambridge, MA 02138-2790 (3)	1909	Ms. Margaret A. McKenna	1-D	5,876	161
LeTourneau U, Longview, TX 75607-7001	1946	Dr. Alvin O. Austin	2-M	1,745	214
Lewis & Clark Coll, Portland, OR 97219-7879	1867	Dr. Michael J. Mooney	1-F	3,198	275
Lewis-Clark State Coll, Lewiston, ID 83501-2698	1893	NR	5-B	3,226	302
Lewis U, Romeoville, IL 60441	1932	Br. James Gaffney, FSC	2-M	4,343	160
Liberty U, Lynchburg, VA 24506-8001	1971	Dr. A. Pierre Guillermin	2-D	4,879	191
Lincoln Memorial U, Harrogate, TN 37752	1897	Dr. Scott D. Miller	1-M	1,904	113
Lincoln U, Jefferson City, MO 65102	1866	Dr. Wendell G. Rayburn, Sr.	5-M	3,623	251
Lincoln U, Lincoln University, PA 19352	1854	Dr. Niara Sudarkasa	12-M	1,477	138
Lindenwood Coll, St Charles, MO 63301-1695	1827	Dr. Dennis Spellmann	2-M	3,137	162
Lindsey Wilson Coll, Columbia, KY 42728-1298	1903	Dr. John B. Begley	2-B	1,170	55
Linfield Coll, McMinnville, OR 97128-6894	1849	Dr. Vivian A. Bull	2-M	1,613	133
Livingston U, Livingston, AL 35470	1835	Dr. Donald C. Hines	5-M	1,986	120
Lock Haven U of Pennsylvania, Lock Haven, PA 17745-2390	1870	Dr. Craig Dean Willis	5-M	3,687	226
Long Island U, Brooklyn Cmps, Brooklyn, NY 11201	1926	Dr. David J. Steinberg	1-D	7,681	507
Long Island U, C W Post Cmps, Brookville, NY 11548	1954	Dr. David J. Steinberg	1-D	8,110	719
Long Island U, Southampton Cmps, Southampton, NY 11968	1963	Dr. David J. Steinberg	1-M	1,727	120
Longwood Coll, Farmville, VA 23909-1800	1839	Dr. William F. Dorrill	5-M	3,360	205
Loras Coll, Dubuque, IA 52004-0178	1839	Dr. Kenneth K. Krans	2-M	1,914	130
Louisiana State U and A&M Coll, Baton Rouge, LA 70803-3103	1860	Dr. William E. Davis	5-D	25,369	1,252
Louisiana State U in Shreveport, Shreveport, LA 71115-2399	1965	Dr. John R. Darling, Jr.	5-M	4,465	218
Louisiana State U Medical Ctr, New Orleans, LA 70112-2223	1931	Dr. Mervin L. Trail	5-D	3,074	NR
Louisiana Tech U, Ruston, LA 71272	1894	Dr. Daniel D. Reneau	5-D	10,100	452

Name, address	Year	Governing official, control, and highest degree offered		Enroll-ment	Faculty
Lourdes Coll, Sylvania, OH 43560-2898	1958	Sr. Ann Francis Klimkowski, OSF	2-B	1,623	131
Loyola Coll, Baltimore, MD 21210-2699	1852	Rev. Harold Ridley, S.J.	2-D	6,169	436
Loyola Marymount U, Los Angeles, CA 90045-2699	1911	Rev. Thomas P. O'Malley, SJ	2-F	6,525	465
Loyola U Chicago, Chicago, IL 60611-2196	1870	Rev. John J. Piderit, SJ	2-D	14,361	1,107
Loyola U, New Orleans, New Orleans, LA 70118-6195	1912	Rev. James C. Carter, SJ	2-M	5,859	391
Lubbock Christian U, Lubbock, TX 79407-2099	1957	Dr. Ken Jones	2-M	1,117	97
Luther Coll, Decorah, IA 52101-1045	1861	Dr. H. George Anderson	2-B	2,354	193
Lycoming Coll, Williamsport, PA 17701-5192	1812	Dr. James E. Douthat	2-B	1,453	113
Lynchburg Coll, Lynchburg, VA 24501-3199	1903	Dr. Charles O. Warren, Jr.	2-M	2,244	196
Lyndon State Coll, Lyndonville, VT 05851	1911	Dr. Margaret R. Williams	5-M	1,178	107
Lynn U, Boca Raton, FL 33431-5598	1962	Dr. Donald E. Ross	1-M	1,550	75
Macalester Coll, St Paul, MN 55105-1899	1874	Dr. Robert M. Gavin, Jr.	2-B	1,836	195
Malone Coll, Canton, OH 44709-3897	1892	Dr. Ronald G. Johnson	2-M	1,924	141
Manhattan Coll, Riverdale, NY 10471	1853	Br. Thomas J. Scanlan	2-M	3,495	282
Manhattanville Coll, Purchase, NY 10577-2132	1841	Dr. Marcia A. Savage	1-M	1,502	207
Mankato State U, Mankato, MN 56002-8400	1868	Dr. Richard R. Rush	5-M	13,003	702
Mannes Coll of Music, New Sch for Social Research, New York, NY 10024-4402	1916	Dr. Charles Kaufman	1-M	256	216
Mansfield U of Pennsylvania, Mansfield, PA 16933	1857	Mr. Rod C. Kelchner	5-M	3,223	188
Marian Coll, Indianapolis, IN 46222-1997	1851	Dr. Daniel A. Felicetti	2-B	1,350	139
Marian Coll of Fond du Lac, Fond du Lac, WI 54935-4699	1936	Mr. Matthew G. Flanigan	2-M	2,404	103
Marietta Coll, Marietta, OH 45750-4000	1835	Dr. Patrick D. McDonough	1-M	1,379	110
Marist Coll, Poughkeepsie, NY 12601-1387	1929	Dr. Dennis J. Murray	1-M	4,288	348
Marquette U, Milwaukee, WI 53233-2278	1881	Rev. Albert J. DiUlio, SJ	2-D	10,764	1,000
Marshall U, Huntington, WV 25755-0001	1837	Dr. J. Wade Gilley	5-D	12,717	681
Mars Hill Coll, Mars Hill, NC 28754	1856	Dr. Fred B. Bentley	2-B	1,024	123
Mary Baldwin Coll, Staunton, VA 24401 (4)	1842	Dr. Cynthia H. Tyson	2-M	1,300	113
Marygrove Coll, Detroit, MI 48221-2599	1910	Dr. John E. Shay, Jr.	2-M	1,234	60
Marylhurst Coll, Marylhurst, OR 97036-0261	1893	Dr. Nancy A. Wilgenbusch	2-M	1,183	276
Marymount Coll, Tarrytown, NY 10591-3796 (4)	1907	Dr. Brigid Driscoll, RSHM	1-B	1,101	126
Marymount Manhattan Coll, New York, NY 10021-4597	1936	Dr. Regina Peruggi	1-B	1,759	200
Marymount U, Arlington, VA 22207-4299	1950	Sr. Eymard Gallagher, RSHM	2-M	3,965	385
Maryville U of Saint Louis, St Louis, MO 63141-7299	1872	Dr. Keith Lovin	1-M	3,764	321
Mary Washington Coll, Fredericksburg, VA 22401-5358	1908	Dr. William M. Anderson, Jr.	5-M	3,498	222
Marywood Coll, Scranton, PA 18509-1598	1915	Sr. Mary Reap, IHM	2-M	3,017	205
Massachusetts Coll of Art, Boston, MA 02115-5801	1873	Dr. William F. O'Neil	5-M	1,209	94
Mass Coll of Pharmacy and Allied Health Sciences, Boston, MA 02115-5896	1823	Dr. Sumner M. Robinson	1-D	1,436	122
Massachusetts Inst of Tech, Cambridge, MA 02139-4307	1861	Dr. Charles M. Vest	1-D	9,790	972
McKendree Coll, Lebanon, IL 62254-1299	1828	Dr. James M. Dennis	2-B	1,450	77
McMurry U, Abilene, TX 79697	1923	Dr. Robert E. Shimp	2-B	1,357	132
McNeese State U, Lake Charles, LA 70609-2495	1939	Dr. Robert D. Hebert	5-M	8,404	300
Medaille Coll, Buffalo, NY 14214-2695	1875	Mr. Kevin I. Sullivan	1-B	1,146	94
Medgar Evers Coll of the City U of New York, Brooklyn, NY 11225-2298	1969	Dr. Edison O. Jackson	11-B	5,200	272
Medical Coll of Georgia, Augusta, GA 30912-1003	1828	Dr. Francis J. Tedesco	5-D	2,077	751
Medical U of South Carolina, Charleston, SC 29425-0002	1824	Dr. James B. Edwards	5-D	2,310	2,435
Mercer U, Macon, GA 31207-0003	1833	Dr. R. Kirby Godsey	2-F	6,729	670
Mercer U, Cecil B Day Cmps, Atlanta, GA 30341-4155	1968	Dr. R. Kirby Godsey	2-D	1,530	97
Mercy Coll, Dobbs Ferry, NY 10522-9988	1951	Dr. Jay Sexter	1-M	6,242	670
Mercyhurst Coll, Erie, PA 16546	1926	Dr. William P. Garvey	2-M	2,317	154
Meredith Coll, Raleigh, NC 27607-5298 (3)	1891	Dr. John E. Weems	2-M	2,066	194
Merrimack Coll, North Andover, MA 01845-5800	1947	Mr. Richard J. Santagati	2-B	3,021	178
Mesa State Coll, Grand Junction, CO 81502-2647	1925	Dr. Ray N. Kieft	5-B	4,600	246
Messiah Coll, Grantham, PA 17027	1909	Dr. Rodney J. Sawatsky	2-B	2,311	196
Methodist Coll, Fayetteville, NC 28311-1420	1956	Dr. M. Elton Hendricks	2-B	1,508	85
Metropolitan State Coll of Denver, Denver, CO 80217-3362	1963	Dr. Sheila Kaplan	5-B	17,551	831
Metropolitan State U, St Paul, MN 55106-5000	1971	Dr. Susan A. Cole	5-M	5,320	531
Miami U, Oxford, OH 45056	1809	Dr. Paul G. Risser	5-D	16,202	874
Michigan State U, East Lansing, MI 48824-1020	1855	Dr. M. Peter McPherson	5-D	39,743	4,006
Michigan Tech U, Houghton, MI 49931-1295	1885	Dr. Curtis J. Tompkins	5-D	6,603	393
MidAmerica Nazarene Coll, Olathe, KS 66062-1899	1966	Dr. Richard Spindle	2-M	1,434	113
Middlebury Coll, Middlebury, VT 05753-6000	1800	Dr. John McCardell	1-D	1,960	243
Middle Tennessee State U, Murfreesboro, TN 37132	1911	Dr. James E. Walker	5-D	17,383	877
Midland Lutheran Coll, Fremont, NE 68025-4200	1883	Dr. Carl L. Hansen	2-B	1,117	70
Midwestern State U, Wichita Falls, TX 76308-2096	1922	Dr. Louis J. Rodriguez	5-M	5,794	258
Millersville U of Pennsylvania, Millersville, PA 17551-0302	1855	Dr. Joseph A. Caputo	5-M	6,299	406
Millikin U, Decatur, IL 62522-2084	1901	Dr. Curtis L. McCray	2-B	1,883	215
Millsaps Coll, Jackson, MS 39210-0001	1890	Dr. George M. Harmon	2-M	1,329	NR
Mills Coll, Oakland, CA 94613-1000 (3)	1852	Dr. Janet H. McKay	1-M	1,137	153
Milwaukee Sch of Engineering, Milwaukee, WI 53202-3109	1903	Dr. Hermann Viets	1-M	3,031	253
Minot State U, Minot, ND 58707-0002	1913	Dr. H. Erik Shaar	5-M	4,026	192
Mississippi Coll, Clinton, MS 39058	1826	Dr. Howell Todd	2-F	3,781	234
Mississippi State U, Mississippi State, MS 39762	1878	Dr. Donald W. Zacharias	5-D	13,651	830
Mississippi U for Women, Columbus, MS 39701-9998 (4)	1884	Dr. Clyda S. Rent	5-M	2,865	164
Mississippi Valley State U, Itta Bena, MS 38941-1400	1946	Dr. William W. Sutton	5-M	2,329	136
Missouri Baptist Coll, St Louis, MO 63141-8698	1968	Dr. Thomas S. Field	2-B	1,748	93
Missouri Southern State Coll, Joplin, MO 64801-1595	1937	Dr. Julio Leon	5-B	5,666	278
Missouri Valley Coll, Marshall, MO 65340-3197	1889	Dr. J. Kenneth Bryant	2-B	1,103	68
Missouri Western State Coll, St Joseph, MO 64507-2294	1915	Dr. Janet Gorman Murphy	5-B	5,121	311
Molloy Coll, Rockville Centre, NY 11570-1199	1955	Dr. Janet A. Fitzgerald, OP	1-M	2,075	188
Monmouth Coll, West Long Branch, NJ 07764-1898	1933	Dr. Rebecca Stafford	1-M	3,780	310
Montana State U-Billings, Billings, MT 59101-0298	1927	Dr. Ronald P. Sexton	5-M	3,732	200
Montana State U-Bozeman, Bozeman, MT 59717	1893	Dr. Michael P. Malone	5-D	10,798	660
Montana State U-Northern, Havre, MT 59501-7751	1929	Dr. William Daehling	5-M	1,742	113
Montana Tech of the U of Montana, Butte, MT 59701-8997	1895	Dr. Lindsay D. Norman, Jr.	5-M	1,992	139
Montclair State U, Upper Montclair, NJ 07043-1624	1908	Dr. Irvin D. Reid	5-M	13,203	769
Moorhead State U, Moorhead, MN 56563-0002	1885	Dr. Roland Barden	5-M	7,029	435
Moravian Coll, Bethlehem, PA 18018-6650	1742	Dr. Roger Harry Martin	2-M	1,385	124
Morehead State U, Morehead, KY 40351	1922	Dr. Ronald Eaglin	5-M	8,899	336
Morehouse Coll, Atlanta, GA 30314 (1)	1867	Dr. Leroy Keith, Jr.	1-B	2,990	178
Morgan State U, Baltimore, MD 21239	1867	Dr. Earl Richardson	5-D	5,858	297
Morningside Coll, Sioux City, IA 51106-1751	1894	Dr. Jerry Israel	2-M	1,291	124
Mount Aloysius Coll, Cresson, PA 16630-1900	1939	Dr. Edward F. Pierce	2-B	1,098	120
Mount Holyoke Coll, South Hadley, MA 01075-1414 (3)	1837	Mrs. Elizabeth T. Kennan	1-M	1,952	230
Mount Marty Coll, Yankton, SD 57078-3724	1936	Sr. Jacquelyn Ernster	2-M	1,097	81

Name, address	Year	Governing official, control, and highest degree offered		Enroll-ment	Faculty
Mount Mary Coll, Milwaukee, WI 53222-4597 (3)	1913	Sr. Ruth Hollenbach	2-M	1,533	153
Mount Mercy Coll, Cedar Rapids, IA 52402-4797	1928	Dr. Thomas R. Feld	2-B	1,349	110
Mount Saint Mary Coll, Newburgh, NY 12550-3494	1960	Sr. Ann Sakac	1-M	1,800	166
Mount St Mary's Coll, Los Angeles, CA 90049-1597 (4)	1925	Sr. Karen Kennelly	2-M	1,843	137
Mount Saint Mary's Coll, Emmitsburg, MD 21727-7799	1808	Mr. George R. Houston, Jr.	2-M	1,737	159
Mount Union Coll, Alliance, OH 44601-3929	1846	Dr. Harold M. Kolenbrander	2-B	1,407	92
Mount Vernon Nazarene Coll, Mount Vernon, OH 43050-9509	1964	Dr. E. LeBron Fairbanks	2-M	1,223	69
Muhlenberg Coll, Allentown, PA 18104-5586	1848	Mr. Arthur R. Taylor	2-B	1,687	164
Murray State U, Murray, KY 42071-0009	1922	Dr. Kern Alexander	5-M	8,120	371
Muskingum Coll, New Concord, OH 43762	1837	Dr. Samuel W. Speck, Jr.	2-M	1,222	116
National–Louis U, Evanston, IL 60201-1730	1886	Dr. Orley R. Herron	1-D	7,108	283
National U, San Diego, CA 92108-4107	1971	Dr. Jerry C. Lee	1-M	9,093	1,348
Nazareth Coll of Rochester, Rochester, NY 14618-3790	1924	Dr. Rose Marie Beston	1-M	2,800	180
Nebraska Wesleyan U, Lincoln, NE 68504-2796	1887	Dr. John W. White, Jr.	2-B	1,703	153
Neumann Coll, Aston, PA 19014	1965	Dr. Nan B. Hechenberger	2-M	1,214	122
New Hampshire Coll, Manchester, NH 03106-1045	1932	Dr. Richard A. Gustafson	1-M	2,800	175
New Jersey Inst of Tech, Newark, NJ 07102-1982	1881	Dr. Saul K. Fenster	12-D	7,551	467
New Mexico Highlands U, Las Vegas, NM 87701	1893	Dr. Gilbert Sanchez	5-M	2,768	134
New Mexico Inst of Mining and Tech, Socorro, NM 87801	1889	Dr. Daniel H. Lopez	5-D	1,726	108
New Mexico State U, Las Cruces, NM 88003-8001	1888	Dr. James E. Halligan	5-D	15,788	795
New Sch Bach of Arts, New Sch for Social Research, New York, NY 10011-8603	1919	Ms. Elizabeth D. Dickey	1-D	248	545
New York Inst of Tech, Old Westbury, NY 11568-8000	1955	Dr. Matthew Schure	1-F	9,187	934
New York U, New York, NY 10012-1019	1831	Dr. L. Jay Oliva	1-D	33,435	4,110
Niagara U, Niagara University, NY 14109	1856	Rev. Brian J. O'Connell, CM	1-M	2,836	257
Nicholls State U, Thibodaux, LA 70310	1948	Dr. Donald J. Ayo	5-M	7,076	265
Nichols Coll, Dudley, MA 01571	1815	Dr. Lowell C. Smith	1-M	1,239	47
Norfolk State U, Norfolk, VA 23504-3907	1935	Dr. Harrison B. Wilson	5-M	8,624	526
North Adams State Coll, North Adams, MA 01247-4100	1894	Dr. Thomas D. Aceto	5-M	1,725	136
North Carolina Ag and Tech State U, Greensboro, NC 27411	1891	Dr. Edward B. Fort	5-M	7,973	409
North Carolina Central U, Durham, NC 27707-3129	1910	Mr. Julius L. Chambers	5-F	5,635	381
North Carolina State U, Raleigh, NC 27695	1887	Dr. Larry K. Monteith	5-D	27,170	1,431
North Central Bible Coll, Minneapolis, MN 55404-1322	1930	Dr. Don H. Argue	2-B	1,059	68
North Central Coll, Naperville, IL 60566-7063	1861	Dr. Harold R. Wilde	2-M	2,453	167
North Dakota State U, Fargo, ND 58105	1890	Dr. Jim Ozbun	5-D	9,460	497
Northeastern Illinois U, Chicago, IL 60625-4699	1961	Dr. Gordon Lamb	5-M	10,306	506
Northeastern U, Boston, MA 02115-5096	1898	Dr. John A. Curry	1-D	29,712	2,457
Northeast Louisiana U, Monroe, LA 71209-0001	1931	Mr. Lawson L. Swearingen, Jr	5-D	11,571	537
Northeast Missouri State U, Kirksville, MO 63501	1867	Dr. Jack Magruder	5-M	6,153	457
Northern Arizona U, Flagstaff, AZ 86011	1899	Dr. Clara M. Lovett	5-D	18,817	733
Northern Illinois U, De Kalb, IL 60115-2864	1895	Dr. John E. LaTourette	5-D	23,177	1,210
Northern Kentucky U, Highland Heights, KY 41099	1968	Dr. Leon E. Boothe	5-F	10,809	697
Northern Michigan U, Marquette, MI 49855-5301	1899	Dr. William E. Vandament	5-M	8,896	363
Northern State U, Aberdeen, SD 57401-7198	1901	Dr. John Hutchinson	5-M	3,078	143
North Georgia Coll, Dahlonega, GA 30597-1001	1873	Dr. Delmas J. Allen	5-M	2,898	145
North Park Coll, Chicago, IL 60625-4895	1891	Dr. David G. Horner	2-D	1,417	80
Northwestern Coll, Orange City, IA 51041-1996	1882	Dr. James E. Bultman	2-M	1,110	91
Northwestern Coll, St Paul, MN 55113-1598	1902	Dr. Donald Ericksen	2-B	1,244	110
Northwestern Oklahoma State U, Alva, OK 73717-2799	1897	Dr. Joe J. Struckle	5-M	1,897	167
Northwestern State U of Louisiana, Natchitoches, LA 71497	1884	Dr. Robert A. Alost	5-M	8,552	335
Northwestern U, Evanston, IL 60208	1851	Dr. Arnold R. Weber	1-D	12,053	1,072
Northwest Missouri State U, Maryville, MO 64468-6001	1905	Dr. Dean L. Hubbard	5-M	5,814	274
Northwest Nazarene Coll, Nampa, ID 83686-5897	1913	Dr. Richard Hagood	2-M	1,288	121
Northwood U, Midland, MI 48640-2398	1959	Dr. David E. Fry	1-M	1,383	59
Norwich U, Northfield, VT 05663	1819	Dr. Richard Schneider	1-M	2,620	183
Notre Dame Coll, Manchester, NH 03104-2299	1950	Dr. Carol J. Descoteaux, CSC	2-M	1,300	90
Nova Southeastern U, Fort Lauderdale, FL 33314-7721	1964	Dr. Ovid C. Lewis	1-D	11,918	580
Oakland U, Rochester, MI 48309-4401	1957	Dr. Sandra Packard	5-D	12,895	618
Oakwood Coll, Huntsville, AL 35896	1896	Dr. Benjamin F. Reaves	2-B	1,451	122
Oberlin Coll, Oberlin, OH 44074	1833	Dr. Nancy Schrom Dye	1-B	2,669	217
Occidental Coll, Los Angeles, CA 90041-3392	1887	Dr. John B. Slaughter	1-M	1,661	187
Oglethorpe U, Atlanta, GA 30319-2797	1835	Dr. Donald S. Stanton	1-M	1,212	111
Ohio Dominican Coll, Columbus, OH 43219-2099	1911	Sr. Mary Andrew Matesich	2-B	1,594	96
Ohio Northern U, Ada, OH 45810	1871	Dr. DeBow Freed	2-F	2,964	224
Ohio State U, Columbus, OH 43210	1870	Dr. E. Gordon Gee	5-D	50,623	3,790
Ohio State U–Lima Cmps, Lima, OH 45804-3576	1960	Dr. Violet I. Meek	5-B	1,348	92
Ohio State U–Mansfield Cmps, Mansfield, OH 44906-1547	1958	Dr. John O. Riedl, Jr.	5-B	1,412	72
Ohio State U–Marion Cmps, Marion, OH 43302-5695	1957	Dr. Dominic Dottavio	5-B	1,046	75
Ohio State U–Newark Cmps, Newark, OH 43055-1797	1957	Dr. Rafael L. Cortado	5-B	1,675	110
Ohio U, Athens, OH 45701	1804	Dr. Robert Glidden	5-D	18,484	959
Ohio U–Chillicothe, Chillicothe, OH 45601-0609	1946	Dr. Delbert Meyer	5-B	1,866	84
Ohio U–Eastern, St Clairsville, OH 43950-9724	1957	Dr. James W. Newton	5-B	1,083	110
Ohio U–Zanesville, Zanesville, OH 43701-2695	1946	Dr. Craig D. Laubenthal	5-M	1,367	49
Ohio Wesleyan U, Delaware, OH 43015	1842	Dr. Thomas B. Courtice	2-B	1,828	173
Oklahoma Baptist U, Shawnee, OK 74801-2558	1910	Dr. Bob R. Agee	2-M	2,432	157
Oklahoma Christian U of Science and Arts, Oklahoma City, OK 73136-1100	1950	Dr. J. Terry Johnson	2-M	1,676	124
Oklahoma City U, Oklahoma City, OK 73106-1402	1904	Dr. Jerald C. Walker	2-F	4,481	268
Oklahoma Panhandle State U, Goodwell, OK 73939-0430	1909	Dr. Ron Meek	5-B	1,208	78
Oklahoma State U, Stillwater, OK 74078	1890	Dr. Ray M. Bowen	5-D	19,001	897
Old Dominion U, Norfolk, VA 23529	1930	Dr. James V. Koch	5-D	15,886	1,124
Olivet Nazarene U, Kankakee, IL 60901-0592	1907	Dr. John C. Bowling	2-M	2,194	120
Oral Roberts U, Tulsa, OK 74171-0001	1963	Mr. Richard Roberts	2-D	3,905	250
Oregon Health Sciences U, Portland, OR 97201-3098	1974	Dr. Peter O. Kohler	5-D	1,374	76
Oregon Inst of Tech, Klamath Falls, OR 97601-8801	1947	Dr. Lawrence J. Wolf	5-B	2,587	182
Oregon State U, Corvallis, OR 97331	1868	Dr. John V. Byrne	5-D	14,336	2,285
Otterbein Coll, Westerville, OH 43081	1847	Dr. C. Brent DeVore	2-M	2,584	158
Ouachita Baptist U, Arkadelphia, AR 71998-0001	1886	Dr. Ben M. Elrod	2-B	1,371	112

Name, address	Year	Governing official, control, and highest degree offered	Enroll-ment	Faculty
Our Lady of Holy Cross Coll, New Orleans, LA 70131-7399	1916	Rev. Thomas E. Chambers, CSC 2-M	1,276	99
Our Lady of the Lake U of San Antonio, San Antonio, TX 78207-4689	1895	Sr. Elizabeth Anne Sueltenfuss 2-D	3,103	194
Pace U, New York, NY 10038	1906	Dr. Patricia Ewers 1-D	12,256	1,088
Pacific Lutheran U, Tacoma, WA 98447	1890	Dr. Loren J. Anderson 2-M	3,349	319
Pacific Union Coll, Angwin, CA 94508	1882	Dr. D. Malcolm Maxwell 2-M	1,488	125
Pacific U, Forest Grove, OR 97116-1797	1849	Dr. Robert F. Duvall 1-F	1,787	214
Palm Beach Atlantic Coll, West Palm Beach, FL 33416-4708	1968	Dr. Paul R. Corts 2-M	1,867	110
Parsons Sch of Design, New Sch for Social Research, New York, NY 10011-8878	1896	Mr. Charles S. Olton 1-M	1,793	350
Pembroke State U, Pembroke, NC 28372-1510	1887	Dr. Joseph B. Oxendine 5-M	3,045	197
Penn State U at Erie, The Behrend Coll, Erie, PA 16563	1948	Dr. John M. Lilley 12-M	3,240	201
Penn State U at Harrisburg—The Capital Coll, Middletown, PA 17057-4898	1966	Dr. Ruth Leventhal 12-D	3,549	210
Penn State U Univ Park Cmps, University Park, PA 16802-1503	1855	Dr. Joab L. Thomas 12-D	37,658	2,091
Pepperdine U, Malibu, CA 90263-0001	1937	Dr. David Davenport 2-D	7,023	297
Peru State Coll, Peru, NE 68421	1867	Dr. Robert L. Burns 5-M	1,581	79
Pfeiffer Coll, Misenheimer, NC 28109-0960	1885	Dr. Zane E. Eargle 2-M	1,005	91
Philadelphia Coll of Bible, Langhorne, PA 19047-2990	1913	Dr. W. Sherrill Babb 2-M	1,017	93
Philadelphia Coll of Pharmacy and Science, Philadelphia, PA 19104-4495	1821	Dr. Allen Misher 1-D	1,882	198
Philadelphia Coll of Textiles and Science, Philadelphia, PA 19144-5497	1884	Dr. James P. Gallagher 1-M	3,297	113
Pittsburg State U, Pittsburg, KS 66762-5880	1903	Dr. Donald W. Wilson 5-M	6,589	289
Plymouth State Coll of the U System of NH, Plymouth, NH 03264-1600	1871	Dr. Donald P. Wharton 5-M	4,000	271
Point Loma Nazarene Coll, San Diego, CA 92106-2899	1902	Dr. Jim L. Bond 2-M	2,484	143
Point Park Coll, Pittsburgh, PA 15222-1984	1960	Dr. J. Matthew Simon 1-M	2,669	206
Polytechnic U, Brooklyn Cmps, Brooklyn, NY 11201-2990	1854	Dr. George Bugliarello 1-D	2,315	302
Pomona Coll, Claremont, CA 91711-6301	1887	Dr. Peter W. Stanley 1-B	1,389	188
Pontifical Catholic U of Puerto Rico, Ponce, PR 00732	1948	Rev. F. Tosello Giangiacomo 2-M	12,251	557
Portland State U, Portland, OR 97207-0751	1946	Dr. Judith Ramaley 5-D	14,486	629
Prairie View A&M U, Prairie View, TX 77446-2610	1878	Lt. Gen. Julius W. Becton, Jr. 5-M	5,848	303
Pratt Inst, Brooklyn, NY 11205-3899	1887	Dr. Thomas F. Schutte 1-M	2,886	519
Presbyterian Coll, Clinton, SC 29325	1880	Dr. Kenneth B. Orr 2-B	1,163	91
Princeton U, Princeton, NJ 08544-1019	1746	Mr. Harold T. Shapiro 1-D	6,444	869
Providence Coll, Providence, RI 02918	1917	Rev. John F. Cunningham, OP 2-D	6,103	312
Purchase Coll, State U of NY, Purchase, NY 10577-1400	1967	Mr. Bill Lacy 5-M	3,996	292
Purdue U, West Lafayette, IN 47907-1968	1869	Dr. Steven C. Beering 5-D	35,161	2,270
Purdue U Calumet, Hammond, IN 46323-2094	1951	Dr. James Yackel 5-M	8,285	457
Queens Coll, Charlotte, NC 28274-0002	1857	Dr. Billy O. Wireman 2-M	1,549	95
Queens Coll of the City U of New York, Flushing, NY 11367-1597	1937	Dr. Shirley Strum Kenny 11-M	17,921	1,274
Quincy U, Quincy, IL 62301-2699	1860	Rev. James Toal, OFM 2-M	1,202	101
Quinnipiac Coll, Hamden, CT 06518-1904	1929	Dr. John L. Lahey 1-F	4,634	333
Radford U, Radford, VA 24142	1910	Dr. Charles W. Owens 5-M	9,380	392
Ramapo Coll of New Jersey, Mahwah, NJ 07430-1681	1969	Dr. Robert A. Scott 5-B	4,683	276
Randolph-Macon Coll, Ashland, VA 23005-5505	1830	Dr. Ladell Payne 2-B	1,119	152
Reed Coll, Portland, OR 97202-8199	1909	Dr. Steven Koblik 1-M	1,277	124
Regis Coll, Weston, MA 02193-1571 (3)	1927	Sr. Sheila Megley, RSM 2-M	1,160	112
Regis U, Denver, CO 80221-1099	1877	Rev. Michael J. Sheeran, SJ 2-M	6,471	90
Rensselaer Polytechnic Inst, Troy, NY 12180-3590	1824	Dr. R. Byron Pipes 1-D	6,681	465
Rhode Island Coll, Providence, RI 02908-1924	1854	Dr. John Nazarian 5-M	9,509	502
Rhode Island Sch of Design, Providence, RI 02903-2784	1877	Mr. Roger Mandle 1-M	1,990	323
Rhodes Coll, Memphis, TN 38112-1690	1848	Dr. James H. Daughdrill, Jr. 2-M	1,409	147
Rice U, Houston, TX 77251-1892	1912	Dr. Malcolm Gillis 1-D	4,123	556
The Richard Stockton Coll of New Jersey, Pomona, NJ 08240-9988	1971	Dr. Vera King Farris 5-B	5,130	307
Rider U, Lawrenceville, NJ 08648-3001	1865	Dr. J. Barton Luedeke 1-M	5,317	413
Rivier Coll, Nashua, NH 03060-5086	1933	Sr. Jeanne Perreault 2-M	2,723	189
Roanoke Coll, Salem, VA 24153-3794	1842	Dr. David M. Gring 2-B	1,699	153
Robert Morris Coll, Coraopolis, PA 15108-1189	1921	Dr. Edward A. Nicholson 1-M	5,347	348
Roberts Wesleyan Coll, Rochester, NY 14624-1997	1866	Dr. William C. Crothers 2-M	1,115	110
Rochester Inst of Tech, Rochester, NY 14623-5604	1829	Dr. Albert J. Simone 1-D	12,637	1,083
Rockford Coll, Rockford, IL 61108-2393	1847	Dr. Bill Shields 1-M	1,610	135
Rockhurst Coll, Kansas City, MO 64110-2561	1910	Rev. Thomas J. Savage, SJ 2-M	2,674	221
Roger Williams U, Bristol, RI 02809	1948	Mr. Anthony J. Santoro 1-F	2,111	229
Rollins Coll, Winter Park, FL 32789-4499	1885	Dr. Rita Bornstein 1-M	3,352	271
Roosevelt U, Chicago, IL 60605-1394	1945	Dr. Theodore L. Gross 1-M	6,587	508
Rosary Coll, River Forest, IL 60305-1099	1901	Dr. Jean Murray, OP 2-M	1,920	124
Rose-Hulman Inst of Tech, Terre Haute, IN 47803-3920 (1)	1874	Dr. Samuel F. Hulbert 1-M	1,420	97
Rowan Coll of New Jersey, Glassboro, NJ 08028-1702	1923	Dr. Herman D. James 5-M	9,368	323
Rush U, Chicago, IL 60612-3832	1969	Dr. Leo M. Henikoff 1-D	1,344	170
Russell Sage Coll, Troy, NY 12180-4115 (3)	1916	Dr. Sara Chapman 1-M	1,130	170
Rust Coll, Holly Springs, MS 38635-2328	1866	Dr. David L. Beckley 2-B	1,180	65
Rutgers, State U of NJ, Camden Coll of Arts & Scis, Camden, NJ 08102-1401	1927	Dr. Robert A. Catlin 5-B	2,567	NR
Rutgers, State U of NJ, Coll of Engineering, Piscataway, NJ 08855-0909	1864	Dr. Ellis H. Dill 5-B	2,451	NR
Rutgers, State U of NJ, Coll of Nursing, Newark, NJ 07102-1803	1956	Ms. Dorothy J. DeMaio 5-D	428	NR
Rutgers, State U of NJ, Coll of Pharmacy, Piscataway, NJ 08855-0789	1927	Dr. John Louis Colaizzi 5-D	911	NR
Rutgers, State U of NJ, Cook Coll, New Brunswick, NJ 08903-2101	1921	Dr. Daryl B. Lund 5-B	2,931	NR
Rutgers, State U of NJ, Douglass Coll, New Brunswick, NJ 08903-0270 (3)	1918	Dr. Mary S. Hartman 5-B	2,990	NR
Rutgers, State U of NJ, Livingston Coll, New Brunswick, NJ 08903-2101	1969	Dr. Walton R. Johnson 5-B	3,686	NR

Name, address	Year	Governing official, control, and highest degree offered		Enroll-ment	Faculty
Rutgers, State U of NJ, Mason Gross Sch of Arts, New Brunswick, NJ 08903-0270	1976	Dr. Marilyn F. Somville	5-M	634	NR
Rutgers, State U of NJ, Newark Coll of Arts & Scis, Newark, NJ 07102-1801	1946	Dr. David Hosford	5-B	3,643	NR
Rutgers, State U of NJ, Rutgers Coll, New Brunswick, NJ 08903-2101	1766	Dr. Carl Kirschner	5-B	8,582	NR
Rutgers, State U of NJ, U Coll–Camden, Camden, NJ 08102-1401	1950	Dr. Robert A. Catlin	5-B	830	NR
Rutgers, State U of NJ, U Coll–Newark, Newark, NJ 07102-1896	1934	Dr. David Hosford	5-B	1,820	NR
Rutgers, State U of NJ, U Coll–New Brunswick, New Brunswick, NJ 08903	1934	Dr. Amy Cohen	5-B	3,232	NR
Sacred Heart U, Fairfield, CT 06432-1000	1963	Dr. Anthony J. Cernera	2-M	5,300	321
Saginaw Valley State U, University Center, MI 48710	1963	Dr. Eric R. Gilbertson	5-M	6,975	377
St Ambrose U, Davenport, IA 52803-2898	1882	Dr. Edward J. Rogalski	2-M	2,518	216
Saint Anselm Coll, Manchester, NH 03102-1310	1889	Rev. Jonathan DeFelice, OSB	2-B	1,873	155
Saint Augustine's Coll, Raleigh, NC 27610-2298	1867	Dr. Prezell R. Robinson	2-B	1,918	92
St Bonaventure U, St Bonaventure, NY 14778-2284	1858	Dr. Robert J. Wickenheiser	2-M	2,580	175
St Cloud State U, St Cloud, MN 56301-4498	1869	Dr. Robert Bess	5-M	15,118	742
St Edward's U, Austin, TX 78704-6489	1885	Dr. Patricia Hayes	2-M	3,107	211
St Francis Coll, Brooklyn Heights, NY 11201-4398	1884	Br. Donald Sullivan, OSF	1-B	2,257	151
Saint Francis Coll, Loretto, PA 15940-0600	1847	Rev. Christian R. Oravec	2-M	2,070	99
St John Fisher Coll, Rochester, NY 14618-3597	1948	Dr. William L. Pickett	2-M	2,291	212
Saint John's U, Collegeville, MN 56321 (1)	1857	Br. Dietrich Reinhart, OSB	2-M	1,859	181
St John's U, Jamaica, NY 11439	1870	Rev. Donald J. Harrington, CM	2-D	17,876	998
Saint Joseph Coll, West Hartford, CT 06117-2700 (3)	1932	Dr. Winifred E. Coleman	2-M	2,022	144
Saint Joseph's Coll, Rensselaer, IN 47978-0850	1889	Dr. Albert J. Shannon	2-M	1,037	88
St Joseph's Coll, New York, Brooklyn, NY 11205-3688	1916	Sr. George Aquin O'Connor	1-B	1,144	98
St Joseph's Coll, Suffolk Cmps, Patchogue, NY 11772-2399	1916	Sr. George Aquin O'Connor	1-B	2,039	170
Saint Joseph's U, Philadelphia, PA 19131-1376	1851	Rev. Nicholas S. Rashford, SJ	2-M	6,915	371
St Lawrence U, Canton, NY 13617-1455	1856	Dr. Patti McGill Peterson	1-M	2,068	174
Saint Leo Coll, Saint Leo, FL 33574-2008	1889	Msgr. Frank Mouch	2-B	1,000	100
Saint Louis U, St Louis, MO 63103-2097	1818	Rev. Lawrence Biondi, SJ	2-D	11,382	2,857
Saint Mary-of-the-Woods Coll, Saint Mary-of-the-Woods, IN 47876 (3)	1840	Dr. Barbara Doherty, SP	2-M	1,258	55
Saint Mary's Coll, Notre Dame, IN 46556 (3)	1844	Dr. William A. Hickey	2-B	1,550	190
Saint Mary's Coll of California, Moraga, CA 94575	1863	Br. Mel Anderson, FSC	2-M	4,087	167
St Mary's Coll of Maryland, St Mary's City, MD 20686	1840	Dr. Edward T. Lewis	5-B	1,348	156
Saint Mary's Coll of Minnesota, Winona, MN 55987-1399	1912	Br. Louis DeThomasis, FSC	2-M	7,009	262
St Mary's U of San Antonio, San Antonio, TX 78228-8507	1852	Rev. John Moder, SM	2-D	4,129	286
Saint Michael's Coll, Colchester, VT 05439	1904	Dr. Paul J. Reiss	2-M	2,486	174
St Norbert Coll, De Pere, WI 54115-2099	1898	Dr. Thomas A. Manion	2-M	2,059	151
St Olaf Coll, Northfield, MN 55057-1098	1874	Dr. Mark U. Edwards, Jr.	2-B	2,993	379
Saint Peter's Coll, Jersey City, NJ 07306	1872	Rev. Daniel A. Degnan, SJ	2-M	3,567	420
St Thomas Aquinas Coll, Sparkill, NY 10976	1958	Dr. Donald T. McNelis	1-M	1,454	115
St Thomas U, Miami, FL 33054-6459	1961	Rev. Msgr. Franklyn M. Casale	2-F	2,560	149
Saint Vincent Coll, Latrobe, PA 15650	1846	Rev. John F. Murtha, OSB	2-M	1,072	105
Saint Xavier U, Chicago, IL 60655-3105	1847	Dr. Colette Mahoney	2-M	3,850	226
Salem State Coll, Salem, MA 01970-5353	1854	Dr. Nancy D. Harrington	5-M	10,132	409
Salisbury State U, Salisbury, MD 21801-6837	1925	Dr. Thomas E. Bellavance	5-M	5,956	333
Salve Regina U, Newport, RI 02840-4192	1934	Dr. Therese Antone, RSM	2-D	2,022	286
Samford U, Birmingham, AL 35229-0002	1841	Dr. Thomas E. Corts	2-F	4,443	384
Sam Houston State U, Huntsville, TX 77341-2448	1879	Dr. Martin J. Anisman	5-D	12,800	502
San Diego State U, San Diego, CA 92182	1897	Dr. Thomas B. Day	5-D	27,573	2,139
San Francisco State U, San Francisco, CA 94132-1722	1899	Dr. Robert A. Corrigan	5-D	25,713	1,384
San Jose State U, San Jose, CA 95192-0001	1857	Mr. J. Handel Evans	5-M	27,057	1,552
Santa Clara U, Santa Clara, CA 95053-0001	1851	Rev. Paul L. Locatelli, SJ	2-D	7,678	577
Sarah Lawrence Coll, Bronxville, NY 10708	1926	Dr. Alice Stone Ilchman	1-M	1,242	226
Savannah Coll of Art and Design, Savannah, GA 31401-3146	1978	Mr. Richard G. Rowan	1-M	2,281	137
Sch of the Art Inst of Chicago, Chicago, IL 60603-3103	1866	G. David Pollick	1-M	1,729	304
Sch of Visual Arts, New York, NY 10010-3901	1947	Mr. David Rhodes	3-M	2,811	602
Seattle Pacific U, Seattle, WA 98119-1997	1891	Dr. E. Arthur Self	2-D	3,437	203
Seattle U, Seattle, WA 98122	1891	Rev. William J. Sullivan, SJ	2-D	5,060	356
Seton Hall U, South Orange, NJ 07079-2697	1856	Rev. Thomas R. Peterson, OP	2-D	9,938	676
Shawnee State U, Portsmouth, OH 45662-4344	1986	Dr. Clive Veri	5-B	3,312	266
Shenandoah U, Winchester, VA 22601-5195	1875	Dr. James A. Davis	2-M	1,537	204
Shepherd Coll, Shepherdstown, WV 25443	1871	Dr. Michael P. Riccards	5-B	3,565	256
Shippensburg U of Pennsylvania, Shippensburg, PA 17257	1871	Dr. Anthony F. Ceddia	5-M	6,487	352
Shorter Coll, Rome, GA 30165-4298	1873	Dr. Larry Lee McSwain	2-B	1,230	89
Siena Coll, Loudonville, NY 12211-1462	1937	Fr. William McConville, OFM	2-B	3,436	253
Simmons Coll, Boston, MA 02115 (3)	1899	Dr. Jean A. Dowdall	1-D	3,334	403
Simpson Coll, Indianola, IA 50125-1297	1860	Dr. Stephen G. Jennings	2-B	1,724	146
Skidmore Coll, Saratoga Springs, NY 12866-1661	1903	Dr. David H. Porter	1-M	2,132	220
Slippery Rock U of Pennsylvania, Slippery Rock, PA 16057	1889	Dr. Robert Aebersold	5-M	7,677	422
Smith Coll, Northampton, MA 01063 (3)	1871	Ms. Mary Maples Dunn	1-D	3,000	290
Sonoma State U, Rohnert Park, CA 94928-3609	1960	Dr. Ruben Arminana	5-M	6,570	424
South Dakota Sch of Mines and Tech, Rapid City, SD 57701-3995	1885	Dr. Richard J. Gowen	5-D	2,487	131
South Dakota State U, Brookings, SD 57007	1881	Dr. Robert T. Wagner	5-D	9,536	559
Southeastern Coll of the Assemblies of God, Lakeland, FL 33801-6099	1935	Dr. James Hennesy	2-B	1,143	86
Southeastern Louisiana U, Hammond, LA 70402	1925	Dr. G. Warren Smith	5-M	13,235	545
Southeastern Oklahoma State U, Durant, OK 74701	1909	Dr. Larry Williams	5-M	4,202	209
Southern Arkansas U–Magnolia, Magnolia, AR 71753	1909	Dr. Steven G. Gamble	5-M	2,918	167
Southern Coll of Seventh-day Adventists, Collegedale, TN 37315-0370	1892	Dr. Donald R. Sahly	2-B	1,531	99
Southern Coll of Tech, Marietta, GA 30060-2896	1948	Dr. Stephen R. Cheshier	5-M	3,960	210
Southern Connecticut State U, New Haven, CT 06515-1355	1893	Mr. Michael J. Adanti	5-M	12,144	726
Southern Illinois U at Carbondale, Carbondale, IL 62901-6806	1869	Dr. John C. Guyon	5-D	23,881	1,514

Name, address	Year	Governing official, control, and highest degree offered	Enrollment	Faculty
Southern Illinois U at Edwardsville, Edwardsville, IL 62026-0001	1957	Dr. Nancy G. Belck 5-F	11,263	720
Southern Methodist U, Dallas, TX 75275	1911	Mr. A. Kenneth Pye 2-D	8,931	640
Southern Nazarene U, Bethany, OK 73008-2694	1899	Dr. Loren P. Gresham 2-M	1,731	101
Southern Oregon State Coll, Ashland, OR 97520	1926	Dr. Joseph Cox 5-M	4,515	267
Southern U and A&M Coll, Baton Rouge, LA 70813	1880	Dr. Marvin L. Yates 5-D	10,000	603
Southern Utah U, Cedar City, UT 84720-2498	1897	Mr. Gerald R. Sherratt 5-M	4,592	200
Southwest Baptist U, Bolivar, MO 65613-2597	1878	Dr. Roy Blunt 2-M	3,136	208
Southwestern Oklahoma State U, Weatherford, OK 73096-3098	1901	Dr. Joe Anna Hibler 5-M	4,990	228
Southwestern U, Georgetown, TX 78626	1840	Dr. Roy B. Shilling, Jr. 2-B	1,220	135
Southwest Missouri State U, Springfield, MO 65804-0094	1905	Dr. John H. Keiser 5-M	18,160	859
Southwest State U, Marshall, MN 56258-3306	1963	Dr. Doug Sweetland 5-B	2,637	136
Southwest Texas State U, San Marcos, TX 78666	1899	Dr. Jerome Supple 5-M	21,302	902
Spalding U, Louisville, KY 40203-2188	1814	Dr. Thomas R. Oates 2-D	1,221	115
Spelman Coll, Atlanta, GA 30314-4399 (3)	1881	Dr. Johnnetta B. Cole 1-B	2,023	202
Springfield Coll, Springfield, MA 01109-3797	1885	Dr. Randolph W. Bromery 1-D	2,961	232
Spring Hill Coll, Mobile, AL 36608-1791	1830	Rev. William J. Rewak, SJ 2-M	1,106	84
Stanford U, Stanford, CA 94305-9991	1891	Mr. Gerhard Casper 1-D	14,002	1,398
State U of NY at Binghamton, Binghamton, NY 13902-6000	1946	Dr. Lois B. DeFleur 5-D	11,997	677
State U of NY at Buffalo, Buffalo, NY 14260	1846	Mr. William R. Greiner 5-D	23,470	1,915
State U of NY at Oswego, Oswego, NY 13126	1861	Dr. Stephen Weber 5-M	8,734	391
State U of NY at Stony Brook, Stony Brook, NY 11794	1957	Dr. Shirley Strum Kenny 5-D	17,205	1,568
State U of NY Coll at Brockport, Brockport, NY 14420-2997	1867	Dr. John E. Van de Wetering 5-M	7,867	524
State U of NY Coll at Cortland, Cortland, NY 13045	1868	Dr. James M. Clark 5-M	5,247	459
State U of NY Coll at Fredonia, Fredonia, NY 14063	1826	Dr. Donald A. MacPhee 5-M	4,838	285
State U of NY Coll at Geneseo, Geneseo, NY 14454-1401	1867	Dr. Carol C. Harter 5-M	5,630	328
State U of NY Coll at New Paltz, New Paltz, NY 12561-2449	1828	Dr. Alice Chandler 5-M	7,941	569
State U of NY Coll at Old Westbury, Old Westbury, NY 11568-0210	1965	Dr. L. Eudora Pettigrew 5-B	3,757	223
State U of NY Coll at Oneonta, Oneonta, NY 13820	1889	Dr. Alan B. Donovan 5-M	5,665	306
State U of NY Coll at Plattsburgh, Plattsburgh, NY 12901	1889	Dr. Horace A. Judson 5-M	5,829	384
State U of NY Coll at Potsdam, Potsdam, NY 13676	1816	Dr. William Merwin 5-M	4,333	273
State U of NY Coll of Environ Sci and Forestry, Syracuse, NY 13210-2779	1911	Dr. Ross S. Whaley 5-D	1,871	127
State U of NY Empire State Coll, Saratoga Springs, NY 12866-4391	1971	Dr. James W. Hall 5-M	5,751	305
State U of NY Inst of Tech at Utica/Rome, Utica, NY 13504-3050	1966	Dr. Peter J. Cayan 5-M	2,550	138
Stephen F Austin State U, Nacogdoches, TX 75962	1923	Dr. Daniel D. Angel 5-D	12,493	667
Stetson U, DeLand, FL 32720-3781	1883	Dr. H. Douglas Lee 1-F	2,955	193
Stevens Inst of Tech, Hoboken, NJ 07030	1870	Dr. Harold J. Raveche 1-D	2,876	250
Stonehill Coll, North Easton, MA 02357-0001	1948	Rev. Bartley MacPhaidin, CSC 2-B	1,999	182
Suffolk U, Boston, MA 02108-2770	1906	Mr. David J. Sargent 1-F	6,091	443
Sullivan Coll, Louisville, KY 40232	1864	Dr. A.R. Sullivan 3-B	2,019	71
Susquehanna U, Selinsgrove, PA 17870-1001	1858	Dr. Joel L. Cunningham 2-B	1,515	141
Swarthmore Coll, Swarthmore, PA 19081-1397	1864	Dr. Alfred H. Bloom 1-B	1,387	171
Syracuse U, Syracuse, NY 13244-0003	1870	Dr. Kenneth A. Shaw 1-D	14,743	1,694
Talladega Coll, Talladega, AL 35160	1867	Dr. Joseph B. Johnson 1-B	1,027	89
Tampa Coll, Tampa, FL 33614-5899	1890	Mr. David Zorn 3-M	1,200	57
Tarleton State U, Stephenville, TX 76402	1899	Dr. Dennis P. McCabe 5-M	6,455	307
Taylor U, Upland, IN 46989-1001	1846	Dr. Jay L. Kesler 1-B	1,849	131
Teikyo Marycrest U, Davenport, IA 52804-4096	1939	Dr. Sherry Manning 1-M	1,186	93
Teikyo Post U, Waterbury, CT 06723-2540	1890	Dr. Phyllis C. DeLeo 1-B	1,843	166
Temple U, Philadelphia, PA 19122	1884	Mr. Peter J. Liacouras 12-D	27,304	2,482
Tennessee State U, Nashville, TN 37209-1561	1912	Dr. James A. Hefner 5-D	7,851	430
Tennessee Tech U, Cookeville, TN 38505	1915	Dr. Angelo A. Volpe 5-D	8,341	494
Texas A&M International U, Laredo, TX 78040	1969	Dr. Leo Sayavedra 5-M	1,728	84
Texas A&M U, College Station, TX 77843-1244	1876	Dr. Ray M. Bowen 5-D	42,524	2,424
Texas A&M U–Corpus Christi, Corpus Christi, TX 78412-5503	1947	Dr. Robert R. Furgason 5-D	4,489	250
Texas A&M U–Kingsville, Kingsville, TX 78363	1925	Dr. Manuel L. Ibanez 5-D	6,574	333
Texas Christian U, Fort Worth, TX 76129-0002	1873	Dr. William E. Tucker 2-D	6,822	497
Texas Lutheran Coll, Seguin, TX 78155-5999	1891	Dr. Charles H. Oestreich 2-B	1,023	91
Texas Southern U, Houston, TX 77004-4584	1947	Dr. Joann Horton 5-D	10,872	514
Texas Tech U, Lubbock, TX 79409	1923	Dr. Robert W. Lawless 5-D	24,007	928
Texas Wesleyan U, Fort Worth, TX 76105-1536	1890	Dr. Jake B. Schrum 2-F	2,437	147
Texas Woman's U, Denton, TX 76204 (4)	1901	Dr. Carol Surles 5-D	9,702	576
Thomas Edison State Coll, Trenton, NJ 08608-1176	1972	Dr. George A. Pruitt 5-B	8,768	NR
Thomas Jefferson U, Philadelphia, PA 19107	1824	Dr. Paul C. Brucker 1-M	1,533	83
Thomas More Coll, Crestview Hills, KY 41017-3495	1921	Rev. William F. Cleves 2-B	1,258	130
Tiffin U, Tiffin, OH 44883-2161	1888	Dr. George Kidd, Jr. 1-M	1,092	55
Touro Coll, New York, NY 10010	1971	Dr. Bernard Lander 1-F	9,561	894
Towson State U, Towson, MD 21204-7097	1866	Dr. Hoke L. Smith 5-M	14,696	903
Trenton State Coll, Trenton, NJ 08650-4700	1855	Dr. Harold Eickhoff 5-M	7,013	556
Trevecca Nazarene Coll, Nashville, TN 37210-2834	1901	Dr. Millard Reed 2-M	1,256	127
Trinity Coll, Hartford, CT 06106-3100	1823	Dr. Borden W. Painter, Jr. 1-M	2,136	214
Trinity Coll, Washington, DC 20017-1094 (3)	1897	Ms. Patricia A. McGuire 2-M	1,197	110
Trinity Coll of Vermont, Burlington, VT 05401-1470 (4)	1925	Sr. Janice Ryan 2-M	1,075	99
Trinity U, San Antonio, TX 78212-7200	1869	Dr. Ronald K. Calgaard 2-M	2,465	270
Tri-State U, Angola, IN 46703	1884	Dr. R. John Reynolds 1-B	1,076	87
Troy State U, Troy, AL 36082	1887	Dr. Jack Hawkins, Jr. 5-M	5,050	205
Troy State U at Dothan, Dothan, AL 36304-0368	1961	Dr. Thomas Harrison 5-M	2,500	144
Troy State U in Montgomery, Montgomery, AL 36103-4419	1957	Dr. Glenda S. McGaha 5-M	3,469	185
Tufts U, Medford, MA 02155	1852	Dr. John A. DiBiaggio 1-D	7,998	1,660
Tulane U, New Orleans, LA 70118-5669	1834	Dr. Eamon M. Kelly 1-D	11,203	713
Tusculum Coll, Greeneville, TN 37743-9997	1794	Dr. Robert E. Knott 2-M	1,144	104
Tuskegee U, Tuskegee, AL 36088	1881	Dr. Benjamin F. Payton 1-F	3,371	271
Union Coll, Barbourville, KY 40906-1499	1879	Dr. Jack C. Phillips 2-M	1,018	65
Union Coll, Schenectady, NY 12308-2311	1795	Dr. Roger H. Hull 1-D	2,257	193
Union U, Jackson, TN 38305	1823	Dr. Hyran E. Barefoot 2-M	2,005	166
United States Air Force Acad, USAF Academy, CO 80840-5025	1954	Lt. Gen. Bradley C. Hosmer 4-B	4,000	517

Name, address	Year	Governing official, control, and highest degree offered		Enroll-ment	Faculty
United States International U, San Diego, CA 92131-1799	1952	Dr. Garry D. Hays	1-D	1,485	84
United States Military Acad, West Point, NY 10996	1802	Lt. Gen. Howard D. Graves	4-B	4,273	488
United States Naval Acad, Annapolis, MD 21402-5000 (2)	1845	Rear Adm. Thomas Lynch	4-B	4,125	650
Universidad Politécnica de Puerto Rico, Hato Rey, PR 00919	1966	Mr. Ernesto Vazquez-Barquet	1-M	5,056	222
U at Albany, State U of NY, Albany, NY 12222-0001	1844	Dr. H. Patrick Swygert	5-D	14,786	902
U of Akron, Akron, OH 44325-0001	1870	Dr. Peggy Gordon Elliott	5-D	26,032	1,722
U of Alabama, Tuscaloosa, AL 35487-0132	1831	Dr. E. Roger Sayers	5-D	19,516	1,165
U of Alabama at Birmingham, Birmingham, AL 35294	1969	Dr. J. Claude Bennett	5-D	16,788	1,833
U of Alabama in Huntsville, Huntsville, AL 35899	1950	Dr. Frank Franz	5-D	8,271	456
U of Alaska Anchorage, Anchorage, AK 99508-8060	1954	Dr. Donald F. Behrend	5-M	13,519	1,203
U of Alaska Fairbanks, Fairbanks, AK 99775-7480	1917	Dr. Joan K. Wadlow	5-D	5,072	717
U of Arizona, Tucson, AZ 85721	1885	Dr. Manuel T. Pacheco	5-D	35,279	1,652
U of Arkansas, Fayetteville, AR 72701	1871	Dr. Daniel E. Ferritor	5-D	14,407	837
U of Arkansas at Little Rock, Little Rock, AR 72204-1000	1927	Dr. Charles E. Hathaway	5-D	12,070	725
U of Arkansas at Monticello, Monticello, AR 71656	1909	Dr. Fred J. Taylor	5-B	2,512	126
U of Arkansas at Pine Bluff, Pine Bluff, AR 71601-2799	1873	Dr. Lawrence A. Davis, Jr.	5-M	4,075	193
U of Arkansas for Medical Sciences, Little Rock, AR 72205-7199	1879	Dr. Harry P. Ward	5-D	1,828	NR
U of Baltimore, Baltimore, MD 21201-5779	1925	Dr. H. Mebane Turner	5-F	5,487	287
U of Bridgeport, Bridgeport, CT 06601	1927	Dr. Edwin G. Eigel, Jr.	1-D	1,605	235
U of California at Berkeley, Berkeley, CA 94720	1868	Dr. Chang-Lin Tien	5-D	30,341	1,443
U of California, Davis, Davis, CA 95616	1905	Larry N. Vanderhoef	5-D	22,486	1,574
U of California, Irvine, Irvine, CA 92717-1425	1965	Ms. Laurel L. Wilkening	5-D	17,189	811
U of California, Los Angeles, Los Angeles, CA 90024-1301	1919	Dr. Charles E. Young	5-D	34,447	3,280
U of California, Riverside, Riverside, CA 92521-0102	1954	Dr. Raymond L. Orbach	5-D	8,677	709
U of California, San Diego, La Jolla, CA 92093-5003	1959	Dr. Richard C. Atkinson	5-D	17,870	1,384
U of California, Santa Barbara, Santa Barbara, CA 93106	1909	Dr. Henry Yang	5-D	18,581	880
U of California, Santa Cruz, Santa Cruz, CA 95064	1965	Dr. Karl S. Pister	5-D	10,173	559
U of Central Arkansas, Conway, AR 72035-0001	1907	Dr. Winfred L. Thompson	5-M	9,567	566
U of Central Florida, Orlando, FL 32816	1963	Dr. John C. Hitt	5-D	23,333	1,001
U of Central Oklahoma, Edmond, OK 73034-0172	1890	Mr. George Nigh	5-M	15,901	678
U of Charleston, Charleston, WV 25304-1099	1888	Dr. Edwin H. Welch	1-M	1,434	162
U of Chicago, Chicago, IL 60637-1513	1891	Mr. Hugo F. Sonneschein	1-D	10,855	1,855
U of Cincinnati, Cincinnati, OH 45221	1819	Dr. Joseph A. Steger	5-D	18,107	985
U of Colorado at Boulder, Boulder, CO 80309	1876	Dr. Judith E. N. Albino	5-D	25,013	1,081
U of Colorado at Colorado Springs, Colorado Springs, CO 80933-7150	1965	Dr. Linda Bunnell Shade	5-D	5,724	369
U of Colorado at Denver, Denver, CO 80217-3364	1912	Mr. John Buechner	5-D	9,614	500
U of Colorado Health Sciences Ctr, Denver, CO 80262	1883	Dr. Vincent A. Fulginiti	5-D	2,305	NR
U of Connecticut, Storrs, CT 06269	1881	Dr. Harry J. Hartley	5-D	18,399	1,250
U of Connecticut at Hartford, West Hartford, CT 06117-2620	1946	Dr. Russell F. Farnen	5-B	1,075	91
U of Connecticut at Stamford, Stamford, CT 06903-2899	1951	Dr. Karen Arms	5-M	1,600	93
U of Dallas, Irving, TX 75062-4799	1956	Dr. Robert F. Sasseen	2-D	2,901	117
U of Dayton, Dayton, OH 45469-1611	1850	Br. Raymond L. Fitz, SM	2-D	9,447	794
U of Delaware, Newark, DE 19716	1743	Dr. David P. Roselle	12-D	18,015	997
U of Denver, Denver, CO 80208	1864	Mr. Daniel Ritchie	1-D	8,339	392
U of Detroit Mercy, Detroit, MI 48219-0900	1877	Sr. Maureen A. Fay, OP	2-D	7,463	494
U of Dubuque, Dubuque, IA 52001-5099	1852	Dr. John J. Agria	2-M	1,042	64
U of Evansville, Evansville, IN 47722-0002	1854	Dr. James S. Vinson	2-M	3,009	175
The U of Findlay, Findlay, OH 45840-3653	1882	Dr. Kenneth E. Zirkle	2-M	3,378	250
U of Florida, Gainesville, FL 32611-8140	1853	Dr. John V. Lombardi	5-D	35,978	3,058
U of Georgia, Athens, GA 30602	1785	Dr. Charles B. Knapp	5-D	28,753	1,813
U of Guam, Mangilao, GU 96923	1952	Dr. John C. Salas	7-M	3,653	230
U of Hartford, West Hartford, CT 06117-1500	1877	Dr. Humphrey Tonkin	1-D	7,262	783
U of Hawaii at Hilo, Hilo, HI 96720-4091	1970	Dr. Kenneth Perrin	5-B	2,953	281
U of Hawaii at Manoa, Honolulu, HI 96822-2310	1907	Dr. Kenneth P. Mortimer	5-D	18,334	1,485
U of Houston, Houston, TX 77204	1927	Dr. James Pickering	5-D	32,124	2,280
U of Houston–Clear Lake, Houston, TX 77058-1098	1971	Dr. Glenn A. Goerke	5-M	7,194	374
U of Idaho, Moscow, ID 83843-4140	1889	Dr. Elisabeth Zinser	5-D	10,790	570
U of Illinois at Chicago, Chicago, IL 60680-5220	1946	Dr. James J. Stukel	5-D	25,170	2,545
U of Illinois at Urbana-Champaign, Champaign, IL 61820-5711	1867	Dr. Michael Aiken	5-D	36,436	2,158
U of Indianapolis, Indianapolis, IN 46227-3697	1902	Dr. G. Benjamin Lantz, Jr.	2-M	3,767	276
The U of Iowa, Iowa City, IA 52242	1847	Dr. Hunter R. Rawlings, III	5-D	27,051	1,783
U of Kansas, Lawrence, KS 66045	1866	Dr. Gene A. Budig	5-D	29,161	2,002
U of Kentucky, Lexington, KY 40506-0032	1865	Dr. Charles T. Wethington, Jr.	5-D	23,670	2,075
U of La Verne, La Verne, CA 91750-4443	1891	Dr. Stephen Morgan	1-D	1,113	165
U of Louisville, Louisville, KY 40292-0001	1798	Dr. Donald C. Swain	5-D	21,826	1,710
U of Maine, Orono, ME 04469	1865	Dr. Frederick E. Hutchinson	5-D	11,343	878
U of Maine at Farmington, Farmington, ME 04938-1911	1863	Dr. Sue Huseman	5-B	1,975	153
U of Maine at Presque Isle, Presque Isle, ME 04769-2888	1903	Dr. W. Michael Easton	5-B	1,477	106
U of Mary, Bismarck, ND 58504-9652	1959	Sr. Thomas Welder	2-M	1,893	118
U of Mary Hardin-Baylor, Belton, TX 76513	1845	Dr. Jerry G. Bawcom	2-M	2,117	113
U of Maryland Baltimore County, Baltimore, MD 21228-5398	1966	Dr. Freeman A. Hrabowski	5-D	10,667	696
U of Maryland Coll Park, College Park, MD 20742	1856	Dr. William E. Kirwan	5-D	32,441	1,518
U of Maryland Eastern Shore, Princess Anne, MD 21853	1886	Dr. William P. Hytche	5-D	2,700	154
U of Maryland U Coll, College Park, MD 20742	1947	Dr. T. Benjamin Massey	5-M	36,431	1,618
U of Massachusetts Amherst, Amherst, MA 01003-0001	1863	Dr. David K. Scott	5-D	21,912	1,275
U of Massachusetts Lowell, Lowell, MA 01854-2881	1894	Dr. William T. Hogan	5-D	13,618	604
The U of Memphis, Memphis, TN 38152	1912	Dr. V. Lane Rawlins	5-D	20,373	1,143
U of Miami, Coral Gables, FL 33124	1925	Mr. Edward T. Foote, II	1-D	13,558	1,639
U of Michigan, Ann Arbor, MI 48109	1817	Dr. James J. Duderstadt	5-D	36,845	3,369
U of Michigan–Dearborn, Dearborn, MI 48128-1491	1959	Dr. James C. Renick	5-M	7,318	385
U of Michigan–Flint, Flint, MI 48502-2186	1956	Dr. Lawrence Kugler	5-M	6,652	211
U of Minnesota, Crookston, Crookston, MN 56716-5001	1966	Dr. Donald G. Sargeant	5-B	1,457	73
U of Minnesota, Duluth, Duluth, MN 55812-2496	1947	Dr. Lawrence A. Ianni	5-M	7,616	436
U of Minnesota, Morris, Morris, MN 56267	1959	Dr. David C. Johnson	5-B	1,933	142
U of Minnesota, Twin Cities Cmps, Minneapolis, MN 55455-0213	1851	Dr. Nils Hasselmo	5-D	37,548	2,953
U of Mississippi, University, MS 38677	1844	Dr. R. Gerald Turner	5-D	10,369	524
U of Mississippi Medical Ctr, Jackson, MS 39216-4505	1955	Dr. Norman Crooks Nelson	5-D	1,731	646
U of Missouri–Columbia, Columbia, MO 65211	1839	Dr. Charles A. Kiesler	5-D	22,168	1,517
U of Missouri–Kansas City, Kansas City, MO 64110-2499	1929	Dr. Eleanor B. Schwartz	5-D	9,858	566
U of Missouri–Rolla, Rolla, MO 65401-0249	1870	Dr. John T. Park	5-D	5,681	348

Name, address	Year	Governing official, control, and highest degree offered	Enroll-ment	Faculty
U of Missouri–St Louis, St Louis, MO 63121-4499	1963	Dr. Blanche M. Touhill 5-D	11,868	923
U of Mobile, Mobile, AL 36663-0220	1961	Dr. Michael A. Magnoli 2-M	1,879	121
U of Montana, Missoula, MT 59812-0002	1893	Dr. George M. Dennison 5-D	10,828	566
U of Montevallo, Montevallo, AL 35115	1896	Dr. Robert M. McChesney 5-M	3,315	182
U of Nebraska at Kearney, Kearney, NE 68849-0001	1903	Dr. Gladys Styles Johnston 5-M	8,045	423
U of Nebraska at Omaha, Omaha, NE 68182	1908	Dr. Del D. Weber 5-D	16,536	690
U of Nebraska–Lincoln, Lincoln, NE 68588	1869	Dr. Graham B. Spanier 5-D	24,695	1,538
U of Nebraska Medical Ctr, Omaha, NE 68198-0001	1869	Dr. Carol A. Aschenbrener 5-D	2,703	489
U of Nevada, Las Vegas, Las Vegas, NV 89154-9900	1957	Dr. Kenny Guinn 5-D	19,682	1,001
U of Nevada, Reno, Reno, NV 89557	1874	Dr. Joseph N. Crowley 5-D	12,137	591
U of New England, Biddeford, ME 04005-9526	1939	Dr. Thomas Hedley Reynolds 1-F	1,389	147
U of New Hampshire, Durham, NH 03824	1866	Dr. Dale F. Nitzschke 5-D	12,397	867
U of New Haven, West Haven, CT 06516-1916	1920	Dr. Lawrence J. DeNardis 1-D	5,912	301
U of New Mexico, Albuquerque, NM 87131-2039	1889	Dr. Richard E. Peck 5-D	25,334	1,185
U of New Orleans, New Orleans, LA 70148	1958	Dr. Gregory M. O'Brien 5-D	15,570	728
U of North Alabama, Florence, AL 35632-0001	1872	Mr. Robert L. Potts 5-M	5,409	260
U of North Carolina at Asheville, Asheville, NC 28804-3299	1927	Dr. Lauren Wilson 5-M	3,165	243
U of North Carolina at Chapel Hill, Chapel Hill, NC 27599	1795	Mr. Paul Hardin, III 5-D	24,299	2,249
U of North Carolina at Charlotte, Charlotte, NC 28223	1946	Dr. James H. Woodward, Jr. 5-D	15,645	890
U of North Carolina at Greensboro, Greensboro, NC 27412-0001	1891	Dr. William E. Moran 5-D	12,114	724
U of North Carolina at Wilmington, Wilmington, NC 28403-3201	1947	Dr. James R. Leutze 5-M	8,157	426
U of North Dakota, Grand Forks, ND 58202	1883	Dr. Kendall Baker 5-D	12,029	711
U of Northern Colorado, Greeley, CO 80639	1890	Dr. Herman D. Lujan 5-D	10,458	556
U of Northern Iowa, Cedar Falls, IA 50614	1876	Dr. Constantine W. Curris 5-D	12,717	841
U of North Texas, Denton, TX 76203-6737	1890	Dr. Alfred F. Hurley 5-D	25,759	1,031
U of Notre Dame, Notre Dame, IN 46556	1842	Rev. Edward A. Malloy, CSC 2-D	10,000	900
U of Oklahoma, Norman, OK 73019	1890	Dr. David L. Boren 5-D	19,680	983
U of Oklahoma Health Sciences Ctr, Oklahoma City, OK 73190	1890	Dr. Jay H. Stein 5-D	3,209	838
U of Oregon, Eugene, OR 97403	1872	Mr. David Frohnmayer 5-D	16,593	1,118
U of Pennsylvania, Philadelphia, PA 19104	1740	Dr. Judith Rodin 1-D	22,469	4,209
U of Phoenix, Phoenix, AZ 85072-9382	1976	Mr. William Gibbs 3-M	15,341	1,500
U of Pittsburgh, Pittsburgh, PA 15260-0001	1787	Dr. J. Dennis O'Connor 12-D	27,528	3,344
U of Pittsburgh at Bradford, Bradford, PA 16701-2812	1963	Dr. Richard E. McDowell 12-B	1,261	99
U of Pittsburgh at Greensburg, Greensburg, PA 15601-5860	1963	Dr. George F. Chambers 12-B	1,445	89
U of Pittsburgh at Johnstown, Johnstown, PA 15904-2990	1927	Dr. David L. Dunlop 12-B	3,008	187
U of Portland, Portland, OR 97203-5798	1901	Rev. David T. Tyson, CSC 2-M	2,700	200
U of Puerto Rico at Ponce, Ponce, PR 00732-7186	1970	Ms. Ruth E. Calzada 6-B	2,552	131
U of Puerto Rico, Humacao U Coll, Humacao, PR 00791	1962	Dr. Rafael Aponte-Hernandez 6-B	3,825	239
U of Puerto Rico Medical Sciences Cmps, San Juan, PR 00936-5067	1950	Dr. Jorge L. Sanchez 6-D	2,956	754
U of Puget Sound, Tacoma, WA 98416-0005	1888	Dr. Susan Resneck Pierce 1-M	3,169	227
U of Redlands, Redlands, CA 92373-0999	1907	Dr. James R. Appleton 1-M	3,950	156
U of Rhode Island, Kingston, RI 02881	1892	Dr. Robert L. Carothers 5-D	11,280	717
U of Richmond, Richmond, VA 23173	1830	Dr. Richard L. Morrill 2-F	4,327	389
U of Rio Grande, Rio Grande, OH 45674	1876	Dr. Barry M. Dorsey 1-M	2,170	135
U of Rochester, Rochester, NY 14627-0001	1850	Mr. Thomas H. Jackson 1-D	8,401	1,376
U of St Thomas, St Paul, MN 55105-1089	1885	Rev. Dennis Dease 2-D	10,245	678
U of St Thomas, Houston, TX 77006-4694	1947	Mr. Joseph M. McFadden 2-D	2,284	173
U of San Diego, San Diego, CA 92110-2492	1949	Dr. Author E. Hughes 2-D	6,202	471
U of San Francisco, San Francisco, CA 94117-1080	1855	Rev. John P. Schlegel, SJ 2-D	7,662	874
U of Science and Arts of Oklahoma, Chickasha, OK 73018-0001	1908	Dr. Roy Troutt 5-B	1,613	75
U of Scranton, Scranton, PA 18510-4622	1888	Rev. J. A. Panuska, SJ 2-M	4,917	395
U of South Alabama, Mobile, AL 36688	1963	Dr. Frederick P. Whiddon 5-D	12,260	802
U of South Carolina, Columbia, SC 29208	1801	Dr. John M. Palms 5-D	26,567	1,466
U of South Carolina–Aiken, Aiken, SC 29801-6309	1961	Dr. Robert E. Alexander 5-B	3,284	232
U of South Carolina at Spartanburg, Spartanburg, SC 29303-4932	1967	Dr. William J. Whitener 5-B	3,265	240
U of South Dakota, Vermillion, SD 57069-2390	1862	Dr. Betty Turner Asher 5-D	7,707	480
U of Southern California, Los Angeles, CA 90089	1880	Dr. Steven B. Sample 1-D	27,201	2,336
U of Southern Colorado, Pueblo, CO 81001-4990	1933	Dr. Robert Shirley 5-M	4,583	278
U of Southern Indiana, Evansville, IN 47712-3590	1965	Dr. H. Ray Hoops 5-M	7,551	365
U of Southern Maine, Portland, ME 04103	1878	Dr. Richard L. Pattenaude 5-F	9,522	595
U of Southern Mississippi, Hattiesburg, MS 39406-5001	1910	Dr. Aubrey K. Lucas 5-D	11,487	670
U of South Florida, Tampa, FL 33620-9951	1956	Betty Castor 5-D	34,776	1,504
U of Southwestern Louisiana, Lafayette, LA 70504-1770	1898	Dr. Ray P. Authement 5-D	16,586	616
The U of Tampa, Tampa, FL 33606-1490	1931	Dr. David G. Ruffer 1-M	2,506	182
U of Tennessee at Chattanooga, Chattanooga, TN 37403-2504	1886	Dr. Frederick W. Obear 5-M	8,325	495
U of Tennessee at Martin, Martin, TN 38238-1000	1927	Dr. Margaret N. Perry 5-M	5,546	283
U of Tennessee, Knoxville, Knoxville, TN 37996	1794	Dr. William T. Snyder 5-D	25,890	1,191
U of Texas at Arlington, Arlington, TX 76019	1895	Dr. Ryan C. Amacher 5-D	23,749	940
U of Texas at Austin, Austin, TX 78712	1883	Dr. Robert M. Berdahl 5-D	48,555	2,342
U of Texas at El Paso, El Paso, TX 79968-0001	1913	Dr. Diana Natalicio 5-D	16,999	781
U of Texas at San Antonio, San Antonio, TX 78249-1130	1969	Dr. Samuel A. Kirkpatrick 5-D	17,097	660
U of Texas-Houston Health Science Ctr, Houston, TX 77225-0036	1943	Dr. M. David Low 5-D	3,279	136
U of Texas Medical Branch at Galveston, Galveston, TX 77555	1891	Dr. Thomas N. James 5-D	2,251	186
U of Texas–Pan American, Edinburg, TX 78539-2999	1927	Dr. Miguel A. Nevarez 5-D	13,298	478
U of Texas Southwestern Medical Ctr at Dallas, Dallas, TX 75235-9012	1943	Dr. C. Kern Wildenthal 5-D	1,680	344
U of the Arts, Philadelphia, PA 19102-4944	1870	Mr. Peter Solmssen 1-M	1,302	362
U of the District of Columbia, Washington, DC 20008-1175	1976	Dr. Tilden J. LeMelle 9-M	10,608	615
U of the Pacific, Stockton, CA 95211-0197	1851	Dr. Bill L. Atchley 1-D	4,140	322
U of the South, Sewanee, TN 37383-1000	1857	Dr. Samuel R. Williamson 2-D	1,230	128
U of the State of NY, Regents Coll, Albany, NY 12203-5159	1970	Mr. C. Wayne Williams 1-B	15,344	NR
U of the Virgin Islands, Charlotte Amalie, St Thomas, VI 00802-9999	1962	Dr. Orville Kean 7-M	2,942	266
U of Toledo, Toledo, OH 43606-3398	1872	Dr. Frank E. Horton 5-D	24,188	1,128
U of Tulsa, Tulsa, OK 74104-3126	1894	Dr. Robert H. Donaldson 2-D	4,810	454
U of Utah, Salt Lake City, UT 84112	1850	Dr. Arthur K. Smith 5-D	25,982	1,463
U of Vermont, Burlington, VT 05405-0160	1791	Mr. Thomas P. Salmon 5-D	9,341	999
U of Virginia, Charlottesville, VA 22906	1819	Mr. John T. Casteen, III 5-D	17,708	1,950

Name, address	Year	Governing official, control, and highest degree offered		Enroll-ment	Faculty
U of Washington, Seattle, WA 98195	1861	Mr. William P. Gerberding	5-D	34,008	3,558
U of West Florida, Pensacola, FL 32514-5750	1963	Dr. Morris L. Marx	5-M	7,800	255
U of Wisconsin–Eau Claire, Eau Claire, WI 54702-4004	1916	Dr. Larry Schnack	5-M	10,345	554
U of Wisconsin–Green Bay, Green Bay, WI 54311-7001	1968	Dr. Mark L. Perkins	5-M	5,403	256
U of Wisconsin–La Crosse, La Crosse, WI 54601-3742	1909	Dr. Judith L. Kuipers	5-M	8,659	450
U of Wisconsin–Madison, Madison, WI 53706-1380	1848	Dr. David Ward	5-D	40,556	2,325
U of Wisconsin–Milwaukee, Milwaukee, WI 53201-0413	1956	Dr. John H. Schroeder, Jr.	5-D	23,794	1,342
U of Wisconsin–Oshkosh, Oshkosh, WI 54901-3551	1871	Dr. John E. Kerrigan	5-M	10,088	535
U of Wisconsin–Platteville, Platteville, WI 53818-3099	1866	Dr. Robert G. Culbertson	5-M	4,915	280
U of Wisconsin–River Falls, River Falls, WI 54022-5013	1874	Dr. Gary A. Thibodeau	5-M	5,263	295
U of Wisconsin–Stevens Point, Stevens Point, WI 54481-3897	1894	Dr. Keith R. Sanders	5-M	8,545	462
U of Wisconsin–Stout, Menomonie, WI 54751	1891	Dr. Charles Sorensen	5-M	7,198	402
U of Wisconsin–Superior, Superior, WI 54880-2873	1893	Dr. Betty J. Youngblood	5-M	2,420	162
U of Wisconsin–Whitewater, Whitewater, WI 53190-1790	1868	Dr. H. Gaylon Greenhill	5-M	10,550	471
U of Wyoming, Laramie, WY 82071	1886	Dr. Terry P. Roark	5-D	12,012	748
Upper Iowa U, Fayette, IA 52142-1857	1857	Dr. Ralph L. McKay	1-B	2,780	230
Upsala Coll, East Orange, NJ 07019-1186	1893	Dr. Robert E. Karsten	2-M	1,534	116
Ursinus Coll, Collegeville, PA 19426-1000	1869	Dr. Richard P. Richter	2-B	1,148	120
Ursuline Coll, Pepper Pike, OH 44124-4398 (4)	1871	Anne Marie Diederich, OSU, PhD	2-M	1,563	141
Utah State U, Logan, UT 84322	1888	Dr. George H. Emert	5-D	17,555	784
Utah Valley State Coll, Orem, UT 84058-0001	1941	Dr. Kerry D. Romesburg	5-B	10,510	578
Utica Coll of Syracuse U, Utica, NY 13502-4892	1946	Dr. Michael K. Simpson	1-B	1,887	141
Valdosta State U, Valdosta, GA 31698	1906	Dr. Hugh C. Bailey	5-M	8,675	390
Valley City State U, Valley City, ND 58072	1890	Dr. Ellen Earle Chaffee	5-B	1,052	75
Valparaiso U, Valparaiso, IN 46383-6493	1859	Dr. Alan F. Harre	2-F	3,499	341
Vanderbilt U, Nashville, TN 37240-1001	1873	Mr. Joe B. Wyatt	1-D	9,853	1,881
Vassar Coll, Poughkeepsie, NY 12601	1861	Dr. Frances D. Fergusson	1-M	2,241	234
Villa Julie Coll, Stevenson, MD 21153	1952	Dr. Carolyn Manuszak	1-B	1,858	154
Villanova U, Villanova, PA 19085-1699	1842	Rev. Edmund J. Dobbin, OSA	2-D	11,039	872
Virginia Commonwealth U, Richmond, VA 23284-9005	1838	Dr. Eugene P. Trani	5-D	21,854	2,389
Virginia Military Inst, Lexington, VA 24450 (1)	1839	Maj. Gen. John W. Knapp	5-B	1,191	119
Virginia Polytechnic Inst and State U, Blacksburg, VA 24061-0202	1872	Dr. Paul E. Jorgensen	5-D	23,865	1,999
Virginia State U, Petersburg, VA 23806	1882	Mr. Eddie N. Moore, Jr.	5-M	4,000	224
Virginia Union U, Richmond, VA 23220-1170	1865	Dr. S. Dallas Simmons	2-D	1,549	139
Virginia Wesleyan Coll, Norfolk, VA 23502-5599	1961	Dr. William T. Greer, Jr.	2-B	1,547	94
Viterbo Coll, La Crosse, WI 54601-4797	1890	Dr. William J. Medland	2-M	1,401	107
Wagner Coll, Staten Island, NY 10301	1883	Dr. Norman R. Smith	1-M	1,781	177
Wake Forest U, Winston-Salem, NC 27109	1834	Dr. Thomas K. Hearn, Jr.	1-D	5,593	1,579
Walla Walla Coll, College Place, WA 99324-3000	1892	Dr. Niels-Erik Andreasen	2-M	1,771	172
Walsh Coll of Accountancy and Business Admin, Troy, MI 48007-7006	1922	Mr. David A. Spencer	1-M	3,578	102
Walsh U, North Canton, OH 44720-3396	1958	Rev. Richard Mucowski	2-M	1,550	113
Wartburg Coll, Waverly, IA 50677-1033	1852	Dr. Robert Vogel	2-B	1,400	141
Washburn U of Topeka, Topeka, KS 66621	1865	Dr. Hugh Thompson	10-F	6,574	430
Washington and Jefferson Coll, Washington, PA 15301-4801	1781	Dr. Howard J. Burnett	1-B	1,110	101
Washington and Lee U, Lexington, VA 24450	1749	Dr. John D. Wilson	1-F	1,947	167
Washington State U, Pullman, WA 99164	1890	Dr. Samuel H. Smith	5-D	18,822	1,105
Washington U, St Louis, MO 63130-4899	1853	Dr. William H. Danforth	1-D	10,164	3,385
Waynesburg Coll, Waynesburg, PA 15370-1222	1849	Mr. Timothy R. Thyreen	2-M	1,380	109
Wayne State Coll, Wayne, NE 68787	1910	Dr. Donald J. Mash	5-M	3,765	215
Wayne State U, Detroit, MI 48202	1868	Mr. David Adamany	5-D	34,280	2,649
Weber State U, Ogden, UT 84408-0002	1889	Dr. Paul H. Thompson	5-M	14,447	480
Webster U, St Louis, MO 63119-3194	1915	Dr. Richard S. Meyers	1-D	10,506	746
Wellesley Coll, Wellesley, MA 02181 (3)	1870	Ms. Diana Chapman Walsh	1-B	2,340	313
Wentworth Inst of Tech, Boston, MA 02115-5998	1904	Dr. John F. Van Domelen	1-B	2,387	222
Wesleyan U, Middletown, CT 06459-0260	1831	Dr. Joanne V. Creighton	1-D	3,324	337
Wesley Coll, Dover, DE 19901	1873	Dr. Reed M. Stewart	2-B	1,320	106
West Chester U of Pennsylvania, West Chester, PA 19383	1871	Dr. Madeleine Wing Adler	5-M	11,344	670
West Coast U, Los Angeles, CA 90020-1765	1909	Dr. Robert M. L. Baker, Jr.	1-M	1,600	250
Western Carolina U, Cullowhee, NC 28723	1889	Dr. Myron L. Coulter	5-M	6,368	488
Western Illinois U, Macomb, IL 61455-1396	1899	Dr. Donald S. Spencer	5-M	12,877	721
Western International U, Phoenix, AZ 85021-2718	1978	Mr. James Haynes	1-M	1,514	80
Western Kentucky U, Bowling Green, KY 42101-3576	1906	Dr. Thomas C. Meredith	5-M	15,335	769
Western Maryland Coll, Westminster, MD 21157-4390	1867	Dr. Robert H. Chambers	1-M	2,099	179
Western Michigan U, Kalamazoo, MI 49008	1903	Dr. Diether H. Haenicke	5-D	26,555	1,020
Western New England Coll, Springfield, MA 01119-2654	1919	Dr. Beverly W. Miller	1-F	4,674	306
Western Oregon State Coll, Monmouth, OR 97361	1856	Dr. Richard S. Meyers	5-M	3,936	282
Western State Coll of Colorado, Gunnison, CO 81231	1911	Dr. Kaye Howe	5-B	2,487	138
Western Washington U, Bellingham, WA 98225-5996	1893	Dr. Karen Morse	5-M	10,302	534
Westfield State Coll, Westfield, MA 01086	1838	Dr. Ronald L. Applbaum	5-M	5,026	330
West Georgia Coll, Carrollton, GA 30118	1933	Dr. Bruce W. Lyon	5-M	7,947	345
West Liberty State Coll, West Liberty, WV 26074	1837	Dr. Clyde D. Campbell	5-B	2,365	153
Westminster Coll, New Wilmington, PA 16172-0001	1852	Dr. Oscar E. Remick	2-M	1,575	118
Westminster Coll of Salt Lake City, Salt Lake City, UT 84105-3697	1875	Dr. Charles H. Dick	1-M	2,153	205
Westmont Coll, Santa Barbara, CA 93108-1099	1940	Dr. David K. Winter	2-B	1,285	115
West Texas A&M U, Canyon, TX 79016-0001	1909	Dr. Russell C. Long	5-M	6,738	332
West Virginia Inst of Tech, Montgomery, WV 25136	1895	Dr. John P. Carrier	5-M	2,859	214
West Virginia State Coll, Institute, WV 25112-1000	1891	Dr. Hazo W. Carter	5-B	4,757	229
West Virginia U, Morgantown, WV 26506	1867	Dr. Neil S. Bucklew	5-D	23,080	1,563
West Virginia Wesleyan Coll, Buckhannon, WV 26201	1890	Dr. G. Thomas Mann	2-M	1,755	132
Wheaton Coll, Wheaton, IL 60187-5571	1860	Dr. A. Duane Litfin	2-D	2,575	261
Wheaton Coll, Norton, MA 02766	1834	Dr. Dale Rogers Marshall	1-B	1,365	100
Wheeling Jesuit Coll, Wheeling, WV 26003-6295	1954	Fr. Thomas S. Acker, SJ	2-M	1,438	80
Wheelock Coll, Boston, MA 02215 (4)	1888	Dr. Marjorie Bakken	1-M	1,312	175
Whitman Coll, Walla Walla, WA 99362-2083	1859	Dr. Thomas Cronin	1-B	1,204	147
Whittier Coll, Whittier, CA 90608-0634	1887	Dr. James L. Ash, Jr.	1-F	1,922	118
Whitworth Coll, Spokane, WA 99251-0001	1890	Dr. William P. Robinson	2-M	1,839	95
Wichita State U, Wichita, KS 67260	1895	Dr. Eugene Morgan Hughes	5-D	14,892	487
Widener U, Chester, PA 19013-5792	1821	Dr. Robert J. Bruce	1-D	8,938	310
Wilkes U, Wilkes-Barre, PA 18766-0002	1933	Dr. Christopher N. Breiseth	1-M	3,257	236
Willamette U, Salem, OR 97301-3931	1842	Dr. Jerry E. Hudson	2-F	2,335	240

Name, address	Year	Governing official, control, and highest degree offered		Enroll-ment	Faculty
William Jewell Coll, Liberty, MO 64068-1843	1849	Dr. Jim E. Tanner	2-B	1,354	157
William Paterson Coll of New Jersey, Wayne, NJ 07470-8420	1855	Dr. Arnold Speert	5-M	9,798	320
Williams Coll, Williamstown, MA 01267	1793	Dr. Harry C. Payne	1-M	2,125	262
Wilmington Coll, New Castle, DE 19720-6491	1967	Dr. Audrey K. Doberstein	1-D	2,500	360
Wingate Coll, Wingate, NC 28174	1896	Dr. Jerry E. McGee	2-M	1,461	99
Winona State U, Winona, MN 55987-5838	1858	Dr. Darrell Krueger	5-M	7,500	350
Winston-Salem State U, Winston-Salem, NC 27110-0003	1892	Dr. Cleon F. Thompson, Jr.	5-B	2,817	172
Winthrop U, Rock Hill, SC 29733	1886	Dr. Anthony DiGiorgio	5-M	5,107	420
Wittenberg U, Springfield, OH 45501-0720	1845	Dr. William A. Kinnison	2-B	2,169	166
Wofford Coll, Spartanburg, SC 29303-3663	1854	Dr. Joab M. Lesesne	2-B	1,108	96
Woodbury U, Burbank, CA 91510	1884	Dr. Paul E. Sago	1-M	1,106	125
Worcester Polytechnic Inst, Worcester, MA 01609-2247	1865	Dr. Jon C. Strauss	1-D	3,218	345
Worcester State Coll, Worcester, MA 01602-2597	1874	Dr. Kalyan K. Ghosh	5-M	4,418	194
Wright State U, Dayton, OH 45435	1964	Dr. Harley E. Flack	5-D	17,295	950
Xavier U, Cincinnati, OH 45207-5311	1831	Rev. James E. Hoff, SJ	2-M	6,279	411
Xavier U of Louisiana, New Orleans, LA 70125-1098	1925	Dr. Norman C. Francis	2-F	3,391	250
Yale U, New Haven, CT 06520	1701	Mr. Richard C. Levin	1-D	10,844	2,035
Yeshiva U, New York, NY 10033-3201	1886	Dr. Norman Lamm	1-D	4,989	1,005
York Coll of Pennsylvania, York, PA 17405-7199	1787	Dr. George W. Waldner	1-M	4,817	310
York Coll of the City U of New York, Jamaica, NY 11451-0001	1967	Dr. Josephine D. Davis	11-B	6,869	200
Youngstown State U, Youngstown, OH 44555-0002	1908	Dr. Leslie H. Cochran	5-D	14,501	904

Two-Year Colleges

The highest undergraduate degree offered for all two-year colleges is the associate degree.

Name, address	Year	Governing official, control		Enroll-ment	Faculty
Abraham Baldwin Ag Coll, Tifton, GA 31794-2601	1933	Dr. Harold J. Loyd	5	2,773	113
Adirondack Comm Coll, Queensbury, NY 12804	1960	Dr. Roger Andersen	11	3,695	208
Aiken Tech Coll, Aiken, SC 29802-0600	1972	Mr. Donald B. Campbell	11	2,386	124
Aims Comm Coll, Greeley, CO 80632-0069	1967	Dr. George R. Conger	9	7,724	429
Alabama Southern Comm Coll, Monroeville, AL 36460	1965	Dr. John A. Johnson	5	1,866	107
Alamance Comm Coll, Graham, NC 27253-8000	1959	Dr. W. Ronald McCarter	5	3,572	145
Albuquerque Tech Vocational Inst, Albuquerque, NM 87106-4023	1965	Mr. Ted Martinez	5	14,841	603
Allan Hancock Coll, Santa Maria, CA 93454-6399	1920	Dr. Ann F. Stephenson	11	7,744	417
Allegany Comm Coll, Cumberland, MD 21502	1961	Dr. Donald L. Alexander	11	2,962	207
Allen County Comm Coll, Iola, KS 66749-1607	1923	Mr. John Masterson	11	1,766	135
Alpena Comm Coll, Alpena, MI 49707-1495	1952	Dr. Donald L. Newport	11	1,941	89
Alvin Comm Coll, Alvin, TX 77511-4898	1949	Dr. A. Rodney Allbright	11	4,085	141
Amarillo Coll, Amarillo, TX 79178-0001	1929	Dr. Luther Bud Joyner	11	6,687	384
Angelina Coll, Lufkin, TX 75902-1768	1968	Dr. Larry M. Phillips	11	3,478	151
Anne Arundel Comm Coll, Arnold, MD 21012-1895	1961	Dr. Thomas E. Florestano	11	12,387	577
Anoka-Ramsey Comm Coll, Coon Rapids, MN 55433-3499	1965	Dr. Patrick M. Johns	5	6,378	228
Arapahoe Comm Coll, Littleton, CO 80160-9002	1965	Dr. James F. Weber	5	7,165	298
Arizona Western Coll, Yuma, AZ 85366-0929	1962	Dr. James R. Carruthers	11	5,400	210
Arkansas State U–Beebe Branch, Beebe, AR 72012-1008	1927	Mr. William H. Owen, Jr.	5	1,962	71
Art Inst of Atlanta, Atlanta, GA 30326-1018	1949	Mr. Hal R. Griffith	3	1,365	104
Art Inst of Dallas, Dallas, TX 75231-5993	1978	Thomas M. Hauser	3	1,023	84
Art Inst of Fort Lauderdale, Fort Lauderdale, FL 33316-3000	1968	David Paul Dire	3	1,800	150
The Art Inst of Houston, Houston, TX 77056-4115	1978	Mr. Steve R. Gregg	3	1,083	91
The Art Inst of Philadelphia, Philadelphia, PA 19103-5198	1966	Mr. Robert P. Gioella	3	1,400	90
Art Inst of Pittsburgh, Pittsburgh, PA 15222-3269	1921	Ms. Saundra M. Van Dyke	3	2,259	106
Art Inst of Seattle, Seattle, WA 98121-1642	1982	Leslie E. Pritchard	3	1,605	101
Asheville-Buncombe Tech Comm Coll, Asheville, NC 28801-4897	1959	Mr. K. Ray Bailey	5	4,090	216
Asnuntuck Comm-Tech Coll, Enfield, CT 06082-3800	1972	Dr. Harvey S. Irlen	5	2,181	112
Athens Area Tech Inst, Athens, GA 30610-0399	1958	Dr. Kenneth C. Easom	5	1,658	100
Atlanta Metropolitan Coll, Atlanta, GA 30310-4498	1974	Dr. Edwin A. Thompson	5	1,819	100
Atlantic Comm Coll, Mays Landing, NJ 08330-2699	1966	Dr. John May	8	6,400	390
Austin Comm Coll, Austin, MN 55912-1407	1940	Dr. Vicky R. Smith	5	1,373	73
Austin Comm Coll, Austin, TX 78752-4342	1972	Dr. Bill Segura	9	25,275	1,388
Bainbridge Coll, Bainbridge, GA 31717	1972	Dr. Edward D. Mobley	5	1,049	39
Bakersfield Coll, Bakersfield, CA 93305-1299	1913	Dr. Richard Wright	11	12,267	496
Barstow Coll, Barstow, CA 92311-6699	1959	Dr. Judith Strattan	11	3,569	128
Barton County Comm Coll, Great Bend, KS 67530-9283	1969	Dr. Jimmie L. Downing	11	7,000	205
Bay de Noc Comm Coll, Escanaba, MI 49829-2511	1963	Dr. Dwight E. Link	8	2,354	143
Beaufort County Comm Coll, Washington, NC 27889-1069	1967	Dr. Ron Champion	5	1,192	95
Bee County Coll, Beeville, TX 78102-2197	1965	Dr. Norman Wallace	8	2,530	116
Belleville Area Coll, Belleville, IL 62221-5899	1946	Dr. Joseph Cipfl	9	16,869	1,088
Belmont Tech Coll, St Clairsville, OH 43950-9766	1971	Dr. Wesley R. Channell	5	1,758	101
Bergen Comm Coll, Paramus, NJ 07652-1595	1965	Dr. Jose Lopez-Isa	8	8,659	672
Berkeley Coll of Business, West Paterson, NJ 07424-3353	1931	Mr. Kevin L. Luing	3	1,608	110
Berkshire Comm Coll, Pittsfield, MA 01201-5786	1960	Dr. Barbara A. Viniar	5	2,585	149
Bessemer State Tech Coll, Bessemer, AL 35021-0308	1966	Dr. W. Michael Bailey	5	1,868	102
Big Bend Comm Coll, Moses Lake, WA 98837-3299	1962	Dr. Greg Fitch	5	1,850	147
Bishop State Comm Coll, Mobile, AL 36603-5898	1965	Dr. Yvonne Kennedy	5	4,478	258
Bismarck State Coll, Bismarck, ND 58501-1299	1939	Dr. Kermit Lidstrom	5	2,462	117
Black Hawk Coll, Moline, IL 61265-5899	1946	Dr. Judith A. Redwine	11	5,881	305
Blinn Coll, Brenham, TX 77833-4049	1883	Dr. Donald E. Voelter	11	8,715	324
Blue Mountain Comm Coll, Pendleton, OR 97801-1000	1962	Mr. Ronald L. Daniels	11	4,100	245
Blue Ridge Comm Coll, Weyers Cave, VA 24486-0080	1965	Dr. James R. Perkins	5	2,630	141
Borough of Manhattan Comm Coll of City U of NY, New York, NY 10007-1079	1963	Dr. Steven M. Curtis	11	16,878	1,080
Bowling Green State U–Firelands Coll, Huron, OH 44839-9791	1968	Dr. R. Darby Williams	5	1,403	75
Brainerd Comm Coll, Brainerd, MN 56401-3904	1938	Ms. Sally Jane Ihne	5	2,022	97
Bramson ORT Tech Inst, Forest Hills, NY 11375-4239	1977	NR	1	1,360	57
Brazosport Coll, Lake Jackson, TX 77566-3199	1948	Dr. John R. Grable	11	3,199	148
Brevard Comm Coll, Cocoa, FL 32922-6597	1960	Dr. Maxwell C. King	5	14,869	976
Briarcliffe–The Coll for Business & Tech, Woodbury, NY 11797-2015	1966	Mr. Richard Turan	3	1,223	112

Name, address	Year	Governing official, control		Enroll-ment	Faculty
Bristol Comm Coll, Fall River, MA 02720-7391	1965	Ms. Eileen Farley	5	3,143	183
Bronx Comm Coll of City U of NY, Bronx, NY 10453	1959	NR	11	6,472	390
Brookdale Comm Coll, Lincroft, NJ 07738	1967	Dr. Peter Burnham	8	12,809	443
Brookhaven Coll, Farmers Branch, TX 75244-4997	1978	Dr. Walter G. Bumphus	8	9,060	525
Broome Comm Coll, Binghamton, NY 13902-1017	1946	Dr. Donald A. Dellow	11	6,470	345
Broward Comm Coll, Fort Lauderdale, FL 33301-2298	1960	Dr. Willis N. Holcombe	5	28,433	775
Brunswick Coll, Brunswick, GA 31520-3644	1961	Dr. Dorothy L. Lord	5	2,029	74
Bucks County Comm Coll, Newtown, PA 18940-1525	1964	Dr. James J. Linksz	8	10,800	375
Bunker Hill Comm Coll, Boston, MA 02129	1973	Dr. C. Scully Stikes	5	6,002	145
Burlington County Coll, Pemberton, NJ 08068-1599	1966	Dr. Robert Messina	8	7,155	322
Butler County Comm Coll, El Dorado, KS 67042-3280	1927	Dr. Rodney V. Cox, Jr.	11	7,500	473
Butler County Comm Coll, Butler, PA 16003-1203	1965	Dr. Frederick F. Bartok	8	3,222	135
Caldwell Comm Coll and Tech Inst, Hudson, NC 28638-2397	1964	Dr. Eric B. McKeithan	5	2,730	174
Camden County Coll, Blackwood, NJ 08012-0200	1967	Dr. Phyllis Della Vecchia	11	15,585	639
Cape Cod Comm Coll, West Barnstable, MA 02668	1961	Dr. Richard A. Kraus	5	4,083	263
Cape Fear Comm Coll, Wilmington, NC 28401-3993	1959	NR	5	3,150	153
Capital Comm Tech Coll, Hartford, CT 06105-2354	1946	Dr. Conrad L. Mallett	5	3,773	130
Carl Albert State Coll, Poteau, OK 74953-5208	1934	Dr. Joe E. White	5	1,979	160
Carl Sandburg Coll, Galesburg, IL 61401-9576	1967	Dr. Donald G. Crist	11	3,200	208
Carteret Comm Coll, Morehead City, NC 28557-2989	1963	Dr. Donald W. Bryant	5	1,602	93
Casper Coll, Casper, WY 82601-4699	1945	Dr. LeRoy Strausner	9	2,758	185
Catawba Valley Comm Coll, Hickory, NC 28602-9699	1960	Dr. Cuyler A. Dunbar	11	3,600	235
Catonsville Comm Coll, Catonsville, MD 21228-5381	1957	Dr. Frederick J. Walsh	8	10,735	534
Cayuga County Comm Coll, Auburn, NY 13021-3099	1953	Dr. Lawrence H. Poole	11	2,515	225
Cazenovia Coll, Cazenovia, NY 13035	1824	Dr. Stephen M. Schneeweiss	1	1,036	117
Cecil Comm Coll, North East, MD 21901-1999	1968	Dr. Robert L. Gell	8	1,064	96
Cedar Valley Coll, Lancaster, TX 75134-3799	1977	Dr. Carol J. Spencer	5	3,136	130
Central Alabama Comm Coll, Alexander City, AL 35010-0699	1965	Dr. James H. Cornell	5	2,043	139
Central Carolina Comm Coll, Sanford, NC 27330-9000	1962	Dr. Marvin R. Joyner	11	2,953	189
Central Carolina Tech Coll, Sumter, SC 29150-2499	1963	Dr. Herbert C. Robbins	5	2,244	144
Central Comm Coll–Grand Island Cmps, Grand Island, NE 68802-4903	1976	Dr. William Giddings	11	1,450	163
Central Comm Coll–Hastings Cmps, Hastings, NE 68902-1024	1966	Dr. Judy Dresser	11	1,567	135
Central Comm Coll–Platte Cmps, Columbus, NE 68602-1027	1968	Dr. Roger Augspurger	11	1,615	120
Central Florida Comm Coll, Ocala, FL 34478-1388	1957	Dr. William J. Campion	11	5,616	178
Centralia Coll, Centralia, WA 98531-4099	1925	Dr. Henry P. Kirk	5	1,800	112
Central Ohio Tech Coll, Newark, OH 43055-1767	1971	Dr. Rafael L. Cortada	5	1,898	99
Central Oregon Comm Coll, Bend, OR 97701-5998	1949	Dr. Robert L. Barber	9	2,945	184
Central Piedmont Comm Coll, Charlotte, NC 28235-5009	1963	Mr. Paul A. Zeiss	11	15,336	1,220
Central Texas Coll, Killeen, TX 76542	1967	Dr. James R. Anderson	11	8,423	328
Central Virginia Comm Coll, Lynchburg, VA 24502-4907	1966	Dr. Belle S. Wheelan	5	4,087	120
Central Wyoming Coll, Riverton, WY 82501-2273	1966	Dr. JoAnne McFarland	11	1,498	147
Chaffey Coll, Rancho Cucamonga, CA 91737-3002	1883	Dr. Jerry W. Young	9	15,000	540
Champlain Coll, Burlington, VT 05402	1878	Dr. Roger H. Perry	1	2,051	117
Charles County Comm Coll, La Plata, MD 20646-0910	1958	Dr. John Sine	11	5,890	301
Charles Stewart Mott Comm Coll, Flint, MI 48503-2089	1923	Dr. Allen Arnold	9	10,877	489
Chattahoochee Valley State Comm Coll, Phenix City, AL 36869-7928	1974	Dr. Richard Federinko	5	1,989	96
Chattanooga State Tech Comm Coll, Chattanooga, TN 37406-1018	1965	Dr. James L. Catanzaro	5	8,756	599
Chemeketa Comm Coll, Salem, OR 97309-7070	1955	Dr. Gerard Berger	11	10,757	881
Chesapeake Coll, Wye Mills, MD 21679-0008	1965	Dr. John R. Kotula	11	2,114	106
Chesterfield-Marlboro Tech Coll, Cheraw, SC 29520-1007	1967	Dr. Ronald W. Hampton	11	1,022	65
Chipola Jr Coll, Marianna, FL 32446-3065	1947	Dr. Jerry W. Kandzer	5	2,604	142
Chippewa Valley Tech Coll, Eau Claire, WI 54701-6120	1912	Mrs. Judith M. Ristow	9	3,800	400
Cincinnati State Tech and Comm Coll, Cincinnati, OH 45223-2612	1966	Dr. James P. Long	5	5,562	317
Cisco Jr Coll, Cisco, TX 76437-9321	1940	Dr. Roger C. Schustereit	11	2,690	98
Citrus Coll, Glendora, CA 91741-1899	1915	Dr. Louis E. Zellers	11	10,296	361
City Colls of Chicago, Harold Washington Coll, Chicago, IL 60601-2420	1962	Ms. Nancy DeSombre	11	6,804	197
City Colls of Chicago, Harry S Truman Coll, Chicago, IL 60640-5616	1956	Dr. Wallace B. Appelson	11	5,175	160
City Colls of Chicago, Kennedy-King Coll, Chicago, IL 60621-3733	1935	Dr. Wayne Watson	11	2,630	106
City Colls of Chicago, Malcolm X Coll, Chicago, IL 60612-3145	1911	Ms. Zerrie D. Campbell	11	3,076	93
City Colls of Chicago, Olive-Harvey Coll, Chicago, IL 60628-1645	1970	Mr. Homer D. Franklin	11	3,591	133
City Colls of Chicago, Richard J Daley Coll, Chicago, IL 60652-1242	1960	Dr. Ted Martinez	11	5,557	155
City Colls of Chicago, Wilbur Wright Coll, Chicago, IL 60634-1591	1934	Mr. Raymond F. LeFevour	11	6,188	161
Clackamas Comm Coll, Oregon City, OR 97045-7998	1966	Dr. John S. Keyser	8	6,966	514
Clark Coll, Vancouver, WA 98663-3598	1933	Dr. Earl P. Johnson	5	10,300	320
Clark State Comm Coll, Springfield, OH 45501-0570	1962	Mr. Albert A. Salerno	5	2,962	175
Clatsop Comm Coll, Astoria, OR 97103	1958	Dr. John W. Wubben	8	2,265	165
Cleveland State Comm Coll, Cleveland, TN 37320-3570	1967	Dr. Owen Cargol	5	3,460	184
Clinton Comm Coll, Clinton, IA 52732-6299	1946	Dr. Desna L. Wallin	5	1,274	75
Clinton Comm Coll, Plattsburgh, NY 12901-9573	1969	Dr. Jay L. Fennell	11	2,183	179
Cloud County Comm Coll, Concordia, KS 66901-1002	1965	Dr. James P. Ihrig	11	3,018	225
Clovis Comm Coll, Clovis, NM 88101-8381	1971	Dr. Jay Gurley	5	3,328	NR
Coastal Carolina Comm Coll, Jacksonville, NC 28546-6877	1964	Dr. Ronald K. Lingle, Jr.	11	3,590	192
Coastline Comm Coll, Fountain Valley, CA 92708-2597	1976	Dr. Lily N. Purdy	11	13,760	437
Cochise Coll, Douglas, AZ 85607-9724	1962	Dr. Walter S. Patton	11	1,665	154
Cochise Coll, Sierra Vista, AZ 85635-2317	1977	NR	11	3,058	228
Coffeyville Comm Coll, Coffeyville, KS 67337-5063	1923	Dr. Dan Kinney	11	2,300	86
Colby Comm Coll, Colby, KS 67701-4099	1964	Dr. Mikel Ary	11	1,090	80
Coll of DuPage, Glen Ellyn, IL 60137	1967	Dr. Harold D. McAninch	11	31,132	1,842
Coll of Eastern Utah, Price, UT 84501-2699	1937	Dr. Michael A. Petersen	5	2,849	127
Coll of Lake County, Grayslake, IL 60030-1198	1967	Dr. Daniel J. La Vista	9	15,498	826
Coll of Marin, Kentfield, CA 94904	1926	Dr. James E. Middleton	11	8,845	464
Coll of Southern Idaho, Twin Falls, ID 83303-1238	1964	Mr. Gerald R. Meyerhoeffer	11	3,804	244

Name, address	Year	Governing official, control		Enroll-ment	Faculty
Coll of The Albemarle, Elizabeth City, NC 27906-2327	1960	Dr. Larry R. Donnithorne	5	1,999	117
Coll of the Canyons, Santa Clarita, CA 91355-1899	1969	Dr. Dianne G. Van Hook	11	6,250	229
Coll of the Mainland, Texas City, TX 77591-2499	1967	Mr. Larry L. Stanley	11	3,883	180
Coll of the Redwoods, Eureka, CA 95501-9300	1964	Dr. Cedric A. Sampson	11	6,928	376
Coll of the Sequoias, Visalia, CA 93277-2234	1925	NR	11	9,499	479
Coll of the Siskiyous, Weed, CA 96094-2899	1957	Dr. Martha Romero	11	2,145	146
Collin County Comm Coll, McKinney, TX 75070-2906	1985	Dr. John H. Anthony	11	10,057	540
Colorado Inst of Art, Denver, CO 80203-2903	1952	Dr. W. C. Bottoms	3	1,349	86
Columbia Basin Coll, Pasco, WA 99301-3397	1955	Dr. Marv Weiss	5	6,842	350
Columbia Coll, Sonora, CA 95370	1968	Dr. Kenneth White	11	3,618	121
Columbia-Greene Comm Coll, Hudson, NY 12534-0327	1969	Dr. Terry A. Cline	11	1,677	115
Columbia State Comm Coll, Columbia, TN 38402-1315	1966	Dr. Paul Sands	5	3,468	178
Columbus State Comm Coll, Columbus, OH 43216-1609	1963	Dr. Harold M. Nestor	5	17,042	842
Comm Coll of Allegheny County Allegheny Cmps, Pittsburgh, PA 15212-6003	1966	Dr. J. David Griffin	8	6,945	394
Comm Coll of Allegheny County Boyce Cmps, Monroeville, PA 15146-1348	1966	Dr. Jacqueline D. Taylor	8	4,332	230
Comm Coll of Allegheny County North Cmps, Pittsburgh, PA 15237-5353	1972	Dr. Fred F. Bartok	8	4,489	268
Comm Coll of Allegheny County South Cmps, West Mifflin, PA 15122-3029	1967	Dr. Thomas A. Juravich	8	5,512	276
Comm Coll of Aurora, Aurora, CO 80011-9036	1983	Dr. Larry Carter	5	4,695	197
Comm Coll of Beaver County, Monaca, PA 15061-2588	1966	Dr. Margaret Williams-Betlyn	5	2,800	150
Comm Coll of Denver, Denver, CO 80217-3363	1970	Dr. Byron McClenney	5	7,021	271
Comm Coll of Philadelphia, Philadelphia, PA 19130-3991	1964	Dr. Frederick W. Capshaw	11	19,786	1,182
Comm Coll of Rhode Island, Warwick, RI 02886-1807	1964	Mr. Edward Liston	5	11,732	719
Comm Coll of Southern Nevada, North Las Vegas, NV 89030-4296	1971	NR	5	17,118	925
Comm Coll of the Air Force, Maxwell Air Force Base, AL 36112-6655	1972	Col. Paul A. Reid	4	478,245	8,000
Comm Coll of Vermont, Waterbury, VT 05676-0120	1970	Dr. Michael Holland	5	2,807	527
Compton Comm Coll, Compton, CA 90221-5393	1927	Dr. Byron R. Skinner	11	5,700	347
Connors State Coll, Warner, OK 74469-9700	1908	Dr. Ronald D. Garner	5	2,379	110
Copiah-Lincoln Comm Coll, Wesson, MS 39191-0457	1928	Dr. Billy B. Thames	11	1,578	116
Corning Comm Coll, Corning, NY 14830-3297	1956	Dr. Donald H. Hangen	11	3,964	197
Cosumnes River Coll, Sacramento, CA 95823-5799	1970	Dr. Marc E. Hall	9	10,530	412
County Coll of Morris, Randolph, NJ 07869-2086	1966	Dr. Edward J. Yaw	8	10,006	553
Cowley County Comm Coll and Voc-Tech Sch, Arkansas City, KS 67005-2662	1922	Dr. Patrick J. McAtee	11	3,059	184
Crafton Hills Coll, Yucaipa, CA 92399-1799	1972	Dr. Luis S. Gomez	11	5,041	152
Craven Comm Coll, New Bern, NC 28562-4984	1965	Dr. Lewis S. Redd	5	2,391	211
Crowder Coll, Neosho, MO 64850-9160	1963	Dr. Kent A. Farnsworth	11	1,895	147
Cuesta Coll, San Luis Obispo, CA 93403-8106	1964	Dr. Grace N. Mitchell	9	7,444	314
Culinary Inst of America, Hyde Park, NY 12538-1499	1946	Mr. Ferdinand E. Metz	1	1,900	101
Cumberland County Coll, Vineland, NJ 08360-0517	1963	Dr. Roland J. Chapdelaine	11	2,783	118
Cuyahoga Comm Coll, Eastern Cmps, Highland Hills, OH 44122-6104	1971	Dr. Lawrence Simpson	11	5,858	225
Cuyahoga Comm Coll, Metropolitan Cmps, Cleveland, OH 44115-3123	1963	Dr. Alex Johnson	11	7,004	474
Cuyahoga Comm Coll, Western Cmps, Parma, OH 44130-5199	1966	Mr. Ronald M. Sobel	11	13,169	611
Dabney S Lancaster Comm Coll, Clifton Forge, VA 24422	1964	Dr. John F. Backels	5	1,653	NR
Dalton Coll, Dalton, GA 30720-3797	1963	Dr. Derrell C. Roberts	5	2,913	108
Danville Comm Coll, Danville, VA 24541-4088	1967	Dr. B. Carlyle Ramsey	5	3,990	142
Darton Coll, Albany, GA 31707-3098	1965	Dr. Peter J. Sireno	5	2,633	136
Davidson County Comm Coll, Lexington, NC 27293-1287	1958	Dr. J. Bryan Brooks	11	2,302	134
Daytona Beach Comm Coll, Daytona Beach, FL 32120-2811	1958	Dr. Philip R. Day, Jr.	5	10,936	981
Dean Coll, Franklin, MA 02038-1941	1865	Mr. John A. Dunn	1	1,756	126
DeKalb Coll, Decatur, GA 30034-3832	1964	Dr. Marvin M. Cole	5	16,349	1,038
Delaware County Comm Coll, Media, PA 19063-1094	1967	Dr. Richard D. De Cosmo	11	10,269	486
Delaware Tech & Comm Coll, Southern Cmps, Georgetown, DE 19947	1967	Mr. Jack F. Owens	5	3,563	159
Delaware Tech & Comm Coll, Stanton/Wilmington Cmps, Newark, DE 19702	1968	Dr. Orlando J. George, Jr.	5	6,273	348
Delaware Tech & Comm Coll, Terry Cmps, Dover, DE 19904	1972	Dr. Marguerite M. Johnson	5	1,997	105
Delgado Comm Coll, New Orleans, LA 70119-4324	1921	Dr. Ione Elioff	5	14,938	1,029
Del Mar Coll, Corpus Christi, TX 78404-3897	1935	Mr. B. R. Venters	11	11,825	512
Delta Coll, University Center, MI 48710	1961	Dr. Peter D. Boyse	9	10,650	508
Des Moines Area Comm Coll, Ankeny, IA 50021-8995	1966	Dr. Joseph Borgen	11	11,184	NR
DeVry Tech Inst, Woodbridge, NJ 07095-1407	1969	Mr. Robert Bocchino	3	2,214	79
Dixie Coll, St George, UT 84770-3876	1911	Dr. Robert Huddleston	5	2,542	107
Dodge City Comm Coll, Dodge City, KS 67801-2399	1935	Dr. Thomas E. Gamble	11	2,601	161
Doña Ana Branch Comm Coll, Las Cruces, NM 88003-8001	1973	Dr. James L. McLaughlin	11	3,615	158
Dundalk Comm Coll, Baltimore, MD 21222-4694	1970	Dr. Harold D. McAninch	8	3,314	224
Durham Tech Comm Coll, Durham, NC 27703-5023	1961	Dr. Phail Wynn, Jr.	5	5,003	271
Dutchess Comm Coll, Poughkeepsie, NY 12601-1595	1957	Dr. D. David Conklin	11	7,029	477
Dyersburg State Comm Coll, Dyersburg, TN 38025-0648	1969	Dr. Karen A. Bowyer	5	2,100	132
East Arkansas Comm Coll, Forrest City, AR 72335-9598	1974	Dr. Tom Spencer	5	1,821	89
East Central Coll, Union, MO 63084-0529	1968	Dr. Dale Gibson	9	3,008	155
East Central Comm Coll, Decatur, MS 39327-0129	1928	Dr. Eddie M. Smith	11	1,446	64
Eastern Arizona Coll, Thatcher, AZ 85552-0769	1888	Mr. Gherald L. Hoopes, Jr.	11	1,859	243
Eastern New Mexico U–Roswell, Roswell, NM 88202-6000	1958	Dr. Loyd R. Hughes	5	2,085	140
Eastern Oklahoma State Coll, Wilburton, OK 74578-4999	1907	NR	5	2,474	54
Eastern Wyoming Coll, Torrington, WY 82240-1699	1948	Dr. Jack L. Bottenfield	11	1,704	136
Eastfield Coll, Mesquite, TX 75150-2099	1970	Dr. Robert Aguero	11	9,569	NR
East Los Angeles Coll, Monterey Park, CA 91754-6001	1945	Dr. Ernest H. Moreno	11	13,423	450
East Mississippi Comm Coll, Scooba, MS 39358-0158	1927	Dr. Thomas L. Davis	11	1,363	70
Edgecombe Comm Coll, Tarboro, NC 27886-9399	1968	Dr. Hartwell H. Fuller, Jr.	11	1,827	125
Edison Comm Coll, Fort Myers, FL 33906-6210	1962	Dr. Kenneth Walker	11	9,836	724
Edison State Comm Coll, Piqua, OH 45356-9253	1973	Dr. Kenneth A. Yowell	5	3,297	183
Edmonds Comm Coll, Lynnwood, WA 98036-5999	1967	Mr. Thomas C. Nielsen	11	8,140	381
Elaine P Nunez Comm Coll, Chalmette, LA 70043-1249	1992	Dr. Carol S. Hopson	5	1,550	101
El Centro Coll, Dallas, TX 75202-3604	1966	Dr. Wright L. Lassiter, Jr.	8	6,328	331
Elgin Comm Coll, Elgin, IL 60123-7193	1949	Dr. Paul Heath	11	9,500	460

Name, address	Year	Governing official, control	Enroll-ment	Faculty
El Paso Comm Coll, El Paso, TX 79998-0500	1969	Dr. Adriana Barrera 8	18,845	1,098
Enterprise State Jr Coll, Enterprise, AL 36331-1300	1965	Dr. Joseph D. Talmadge 5	2,285	125
Erie Comm Coll, City Cmps, Buffalo, NY 14203-2601	1971	Dr. Louis M. Ricci 11	3,594	241
Erie Comm Coll, North Cmps, Williamsville, NY 14221-7095	1946	Dr. Louis M. Ricci 11	6,868	392
Erie Comm Coll, South Cmps, Orchard Park, NY 14127-2199	1974	Dr. Louis M. Ricci 11	3,427	316
Essex Comm Coll, Baltimore, MD 21237-3899	1957	Dr. Donald J. Slowinski 11	10,767	599
Essex County Coll, Newark, NJ 07102-1798	1966	Dr. Zachary Yamba 8	9,000	270
Eugenio Maria de Hostos Comm Coll of City U of NY, Bronx, NY 10451-5307	1968	Dr. Isaura Santiago 11	5,142	319
Everett Comm Coll, Everett, WA 98201-1390	1941	Dr. Susan C. Carroll 5	6,590	268
Evergreen Valley Coll, San Jose, CA 95135-1598	1975	Dr. Noella Vela 11	9,582	275
Fairleigh Dickinson U, Edward Williams Coll, Hackensack, NJ 07601-6112	1964	Mr. Kenneth T. Vehrkens 1	1,064	68
Fayetteville Tech Comm Coll, Fayetteville, NC 28303-0236	1961	Dr. Craig Allen 5	7,361	317
Fergus Falls Comm Coll, Fergus Falls, MN 56537-1009	1960	Mr. Dan F. True 5	1,300	60
Finger Lakes Comm Coll, Canandaigua, NY 14424-8395	1965	Dr. Daniel T. Hayes 11	4,028	234
Fiorello H LaGuardia Comm Coll of City U of NY, Long Island City, NY 11101-3071	1970	Dr. Raymond C. Bowen 11	10,303	914
Flathead Valley Comm Coll, Kalispell, MT 59901-2622	1967	Dr. Howard L. Fryett 11	1,658	108
Florence-Darlington Tech Coll, Florence, SC 29501-0548	1963	Dr. Charles W. Gould 5	2,639	201
Florida Comm Coll at Jacksonville, Jacksonville, FL 32202-4030	1963	Dr. Charles C. Spence 5	19,294	1,564
Florida Keys Comm Coll, Key West, FL 33040-4397	1965	Dr. William A. Seeker 5	2,200	94
Floyd Coll, Rome, GA 30162-1864	1970	Dr. H. Lynn Cundiff 5	2,986	66
Foothill Coll, Los Altos Hills, CA 94022-4599	1958	Dr. Bernadine Chuck Fong . . 11	16,147	578
Forsyth Tech Comm Coll, Winston-Salem, NC 27103-5197	1964	Dr. Bob H. Greene 5	4,959	574
Fort Scott Comm Coll, Fort Scott, KS 66701	1919	Dr. Laura Meeks 11	2,127	59
Fox Valley Tech Coll, Appleton, WI 54913-2277	1967	Dr. H. Victor Baldi 11	6,500	1,241
Frederick Comm Coll, Frederick, MD 21702-2097	1957	Dr. Lee J. Betts 11	4,336	267
Fresno City Coll, Fresno, CA 93741-0002	1910	Dr. Brice W. Harris 9	18,598	832
Front Range Comm Coll, Westminster, CO 80030-2105	1968	Dr. Thomas Gonzales 5	10,973	517
Fulton-Montgomery Comm Coll, Johnstown, NY 12095-3790	1964	Dr. Richard R. Teaff 11	1,953	94
Gadsden State Comm Coll, Gadsden, AL 35902-0227	1985	Dr. Victor Ficker 5	6,210	303
Gainesville Coll, Gainesville, GA 30503-1358	1964	Dr. J. Foster Watkins 5	2,632	104
Galveston Coll, Galveston, TX 77550-7496	1967	Dr. Marc A. Nigliazzo 11	2,331	121
Garden City Comm Coll, Garden City, KS 67846-6399	1919	Dr. James H. Tangeman 9	2,323	138
Garland County Comm Coll, Hot Springs, AR 71914-3470	1973	NR 11	2,164	122
Gaston Coll, Dallas, NC 28034-1499	1963	Dr. Paul R. Berrier 11	4,037	363
Gateway Comm Coll, Phoenix, AZ 85034-1795	1968	Dr. Phil Randolph 11	6,257	253
Gateway Comm-Tech Coll, New Haven, CT 06511-5918	1968	Dr. Antonio Perez 5	5,163	259
Gateway Tech Coll, Kenosha, WI 53144-1690	1911	Mr. William P. Nickolai 11	10,827	850
Gavilan Coll, Gilroy, CA 95020-9599	1919	Dr. Glenn E. Mayle 11	4,029	164
Genesee Comm Coll, Batavia, NY 14020-9704	1966	Dr. Stuart Steiner 11	4,219	235
George Corley Wallace State Comm Coll, Selma, AL 36702-1049	1966	Dr. Julius Ray Brown 5	1,800	78
George C Wallace State Comm Coll, Dothan, AL 36303	1949	Dr. Larry Beaty 5	4,060	180
Georgia Military Coll, Milledgeville, GA 31061	1879	Maj Gen. Peter J. Boylam, Jr. 11	2,549	179
Germanna Comm Coll, Locust Grove, VA 22508-0339	1970	Dr. Francis S. Turnage 5	2,535	135
Glendale Comm Coll, Glendale, AZ 85302-3090	1965	Dr. John R. Waltrip 11	17,520	656
Glen Oaks Comm Coll, Centreville, MI 49032-9719	1965	Dr. Philip G. Ward 11	1,334	114
Gloucester County Coll, Sewell, NJ 08080	1967	Dr. Richard H. Jones 8	5,362	230
Gogebic Comm Coll, Ironwood, MI 49938	1932	Dr. James R. Grote 11	1,376	91
Golden West Coll, Huntington Beach, CA 92647-2748	1966	Dr. Philip Westin 11	14,378	443
Gordon Coll, Barnesville, GA 30204-1762	1852	Dr. Jerry M. Williamson 5	2,241	121
Grand Rapids Comm Coll, Grand Rapids, MI 49503-3201	1914	Mr. Richard Calkins 9	13,636	550
Grays Harbor Coll, Aberdeen, WA 98520-7599	1930	Dr. Jewell Manspeaker 5	2,815	140
Grayson County Coll, Denison, TX 75020-8299	1964	Dr. Jim M. Williams 11	3,400	176
Greenfield Comm Coll, Greenfield, MA 01301-9739	1962	Dr. Katherine H. Sloan 5	1,954	131
Green River Comm Coll, Auburn, WA 98092-3699	1965	Mr. Richard A. Rutkowski 5	8,683	342
Greenville Tech Coll, Greenville, SC 29606-5616	1962	Dr. Thomas E. Barton, Jr. 5	8,782	480
Grossmont Coll, El Cajon, CA 92020-1799	1961	Dr. Richard M. Sanchez 11	15,038	600
Guilford Tech Comm Coll, Jamestown, NC 27282-0309	1958	Dr. Don Cameron 11	7,550	539
Gulf Coast Comm Coll, Panama City, FL 32401-1058	1957	Dr. Robert L. McSpadden 5	6,087	324
Hagerstown Jr Coll, Hagerstown, MD 21742-6590	1946	Dr. Norman P. Shea 8	3,064	177
Harford Comm Coll, Bel Air, MD 21015-1698	1957	Dr. Richard J. Pappas 11	5,520	330
Harrisburg Area Comm Coll, Harrisburg, PA 17110-2999	1964	Dr. Mary L. Fifield 11	11,304	575
Hartnell Coll, Salinas, CA 93901-1697	1920	Dr. Len Grandy 9	6,754	363
Hawkeye Comm Coll, Waterloo, IA 50704-8015	1967	Dr. Phillip O. Barry 11	2,552	163
Haywood Comm Coll, Clyde, NC 28721-9453	1964	Dr. Dan W. Moore 11	1,286	126
Henry Ford Comm Coll, Dearborn, MI 48128-1495	1938	Dr. Andrew A. Mazzara 9	15,307	780
Herkimer County Comm Coll, Herkimer, NY 13350	1966	Dr. Ronald F. Williams 11	2,577	129
Hesser Coll, Manchester, NH 03103-7245	1900	Mr. Linwood W. Galeucia 3	3,000	60
Hibbing Comm Coll, Hibbing, MN 55746-3300	1916	Dr. Anthony Kuznik 5	1,005	65
Highland Comm Coll, Freeport, IL 61032-9341	1962	Dr. Ruth Mercedes Smith . . . 11	2,824	159
Highland Comm Coll, Highland, KS 66035-0068	1858	Dr. Eric M. Priest 11	2,160	182
Highline Comm Coll, Des Moines, WA 98198-9800	1961	Dr. Edward M. Command 5	10,300	432
Hill Coll of the Hill Jr Coll District, Hillsboro, TX 76645-0619	1923	Dr. W. R. Auvenshine 9	2,000	80
Hillsborough Comm Coll, Tampa, FL 33631-3127	1968	Dr. Andreas A. Paloumpis 5	21,049	716
Hinds Comm Coll, Raymond, MS 39154	1917	NR 11	9,074	726
Hocking Tech Coll, Nelsonville, OH 45764-9588	1968	Dr. John J. Light 5	6,110	253
Holmes Comm Coll, Goodman, MS 39079-0369	1928	Dr. Starkey A. Morgan, Sr. . . . 11	2,370	125
Holyoke Comm Coll, Holyoke, MA 01040-1099	1946	Dr. David M. Bartley 5	3,646	222
Horry-Georgetown Tech Coll, Conway, SC 29526	1965	Dr. D. Kent Sharples 11	2,800	121
Housatonic Comm-Tech Coll, Bridgeport, CT 06608-2453	1966	Dr. Vincent S. Darnowski 5	2,691	105
Houston Comm Coll System, Houston, TX 77270-7849	1971	Dr. Charles Green 11	39,321	2,470
Howard Comm Coll, Columbia, MD 21044-3197	1966	Dr. Dwight A. Burrill 11	5,050	312
Hudson County Comm Coll, Jersey City, NJ 07306-4301	1974	Dr. Glen Gabert 11	3,076	198
Hudson Valley Comm Coll, Troy, NY 12180-6096	1953	Dr. Joseph J. Bulmer 11	10,374	544
Huertas Jr Coll, Caguas, PR 00625	1945	Dr. Felix Rodriguez Matos 3	2,220	91
Hutchinson Comm Coll, Hutchinson, KS 67501-5894	1928	Dr. Edward E. Berger 11	3,888	264

Name, address	Year	Governing official, control		Enroll-ment	Faculty
ICS Ctr for Degree Studies, Scranton, PA 18515	1975	Mr. Gary Keisling	3	20,363	5
Illinois Central Coll, East Peoria, IL 61635-0002	1967	Dr. Thomas K. Thomas	11	13,632	626
Illinois Eastern Comm Colls, Frontier Comm Coll, Fairfield, IL 62837-2601	1976	Mr. Richard Mason	11	1,890	148
Illinois Eastern Comm Colls, Lincoln Trail Coll, Robinson, IL 62454-9524	1969	Dr. John Arabatgis	11	1,152	67
Illinois Eastern Comm Colls, Olney Central Coll, Olney, IL 62450-1043	1962	Dr. Judith M. Hansen	11	1,481	92
Illinois Eastern Comm Colls, Wabash Valley Coll, Mount Carmel, IL 62863-2657	1960	Dr. Harry K. Benson	11	2,257	94
Illinois Valley Comm Coll, Oglesby, IL 61348-9691	1924	Dr. Alfred E. Wisgoski	9	4,541	176
Independence Comm Coll, Independence, KS 67301-0708	1925	Dr. Don Schoening	5	1,605	153
Indiana Business Coll, Indianapolis, IN 46204-1108	1902	Mr. Kenneth J. Konesco	3	1,700	70
Indiana Vocational Tech Coll–Central Indiana, Indianapolis, IN 46206-1763	1963	Dr. Meredith L. Carter	5	5,622	359
Indiana Vocational Tech Coll–Columbus, Columbus, IN 47203-1868	1963	Mr. Homer B. Smith	5	2,891	166
Indiana Vocational Tech Coll–Eastcentral, Muncie, IN 47302-9448	1968	Dr. Thomas C. Henry	5	2,470	167
Indiana Vocational Tech Coll–Kokomo, Kokomo, IN 46901-2548	1968	Dr. Shanon Christiansen	5	1,753	124
Indiana Vocational Tech Coll–Lafayette, Lafayette, IN 47903-6299	1968	Dr. Elizabeth J. Doversberger	5	1,672	128
Indiana Vocational Tech Coll–Northcentral, South Bend, IN 46619-3837	1968	Dr. Carl F. Lutz	5	2,741	225
Indiana Vocational Tech Coll–Northeast, Fort Wayne, IN 46805-1430	1969	Mr. Jon L. Rupright	5	3,971	265
Indiana Vocational Tech Coll–Northwest, Gary, IN 46409-1499	1963	Dr. Jerry Lacey	5	2,279	177
Indiana Vocational Tech Coll–Southcentral, Sellersburg, IN 47172-1829	1968	Mr. Jonathan W. Thomas	5	2,046	127
Indiana Vocational Tech Coll–Southwest, Evansville, IN 47710-3398	1963	NR	5	2,992	185
Indiana Vocational Tech Coll–Wabash Valley, Terre Haute, IN 47802	1966	Dr. Sam E. Borden	5	2,392	174
Indiana Vocational Tech Coll–Whitewater, Richmond, IN 47374-1220	1963	Mr. James Steck	5	1,055	96
Indian Hills Comm Coll, Ottumwa, IA 52501-1398	1966	Dr. Lyle A. Hellyer	11	3,387	137
Indian River Comm Coll, Fort Pierce, FL 34981-5599	1960	Dr. Edwin R. Massey	5	13,730	577
Inver Hills Comm Coll, Inver Grove Heights, MN 55076-3209	1969	Dr. Steve Wallace	5	5,574	220
Iowa Central Comm Coll, Fort Dodge, IA 50501-5798	1966	Dr. Jack L. Bottenfield	11	2,500	155
Iowa Lakes Comm Coll, Estherville, IA 51334-2725	1967	Mr. James E. Billings	11	1,574	40
Iowa Western Comm Coll, Council Bluffs, IA 51502	1966	Dr. Dan Kinney	9	3,571	160
Itasca Comm Coll, Grand Rapids, MN 55744	1922	Dr. Lawrence N. Dukes	5	1,169	73
Itawamba Comm Coll, Fulton, MS 38843-1099	1947	Dr. David Cole	11	3,500	102
ITT Tech Inst, Fort Wayne, IN 46825-5532	1967	Mr. Jack B. Cozad	3	1,024	36
ITT Tech Inst, Indianapolis, IN 46268-1119	1966	Mr. Larry L. Graphman	3	1,054	41
Jackson Comm Coll, Jackson, MI 49201-8399	1928	Dr. Lee Howser	8	8,100	435
Jackson State Comm Coll, Jackson, TN 38301-3797	1967	Dr. Walter L. Nelms	5	3,413	166
James Sprunt Comm Coll, Kenansville, NC 28349-0398	1964	Dr. Donald L. Reichard	5	1,062	99
Jamestown Comm Coll, Jamestown, NY 14701-1999	1950	Mr. Gary Winger	11	4,304	316
Jefferson Coll, Hillsboro, MO 63050-2441	1963	Dr. Gregory D. Adkins	11	4,220	190
Jefferson Comm Coll, Watertown, NY 13601	1961	Dr. John W. Deans	11	2,593	217
Jefferson State Comm Coll, Birmingham, AL 35215-3098	1965	Dr. Judy M. Merritt	5	7,370	317
Jefferson Tech Coll, Steubenville, OH 43952-3598	1966	Dr. Edward L. Florak	11	1,658	118
John A Logan Coll, Carterville, IL 62918	1967	Dr. Ray Hancock	11	4,895	237
John C Calhoun State Comm Coll, Decatur, AL 35609-2216	1965	Dr. Richard Carpenter	5	7,899	422
Johnson County Comm Coll, Overland Park, KS 66210-1299	1967	Dr. Charles J. Carlsen	11	15,353	694
Johnston Comm Coll, Smithfield, NC 27577-2350	1969	Dr. John L. Tart	5	2,804	235
John Tyler Comm Coll, Chester, VA 23831	1967	Dr. Marshall W. Smith	5	5,770	224
Joliet Jr Coll, Joliet, IL 60436-9352	1901	Dr. Raymond A. Pietak	11	10,427	591
Jones County Jr Coll, Ellisville, MS 39437-3901	1928	Dr. T. Terrell Tisdale	11	4,400	153
Jordan Coll, Cedar Springs, MI 49319-9699	1967	Dr. Lexie K. Coxon	2	2,115	188
Kalamazoo Valley Comm Coll, Kalamazoo, MI 49009-9606	1966	Dr. Marilyn J. Schlack	11	9,344	380
Kankakee Comm Coll, Kankakee, IL 60901-0888	1966	Dr. Larry D. Huffman	11	4,000	222
Kansas City Kansas Comm Coll, Kansas City, KS 66112-3003	1923	Dr. Thomas R. Burke	11	6,063	367
Kaskaskia Coll, Centralia, IL 62801-7878	1966	Dr. Alice Marie Mumaw	11	3,379	295
Kellogg Comm Coll, Battle Creek, MI 49017-3306	1956	Dr. Paul R. Ohm	11	9,256	328
Kelsey Jenney Coll, San Diego, CA 92101-4088	1863	Dr. Robert Evans	1	1,000	50
Kent State U, Ashtabula Cmps, Ashtabula, OH 44004-2299	1958	Dr. John K. Mahan	5	1,025	69
Kent State U, Stark Cmps, Canton, OH 44720-7599	1967	Dr. William G. Bittle	5	2,362	107
Kent State U, Trumbull Cmps, Warren, OH 44483-1998	1954	Dr. David A. Allen, Jr.	5	2,028	100
Kent State U, Tuscarawas Cmps, New Philadelphia, OH 44663-9447	1962	Mr. Harold D. Shade	5	1,267	84
Kilgore Coll, Kilgore, TX 75662-3299	1935	Dr. J. Frank Thornton	11	4,566	247
Kingsborough Comm Coll of City U of NY, Brooklyn, NY 11235	1963	Dr. Leon M. Goldstein	11	9,191	628
Kirkwood Comm Coll, Cedar Rapids, IA 52406-2068	1966	Dr. Norm Nielsen	11	9,664	456
Kirtland Comm Coll, Roscommon, MI 48653-9699	1966	Dr. Dorothy N. Franke	9	1,390	95
Kishwaukee Coll, Malta, IL 60150	1967	Dr. Norman L. Jenkins	11	3,388	NR
Labette Comm Coll, Parsons, KS 67357-4299	1923	Mr. Joseph C. Birmingham	11	2,598	261
Lackawanna Jr Coll, Scranton, PA 18505-1845	1894	Dr. Joseph Morelli	1	1,200	50
Lake City Comm Coll, Lake City, FL 32025	1962	Dr. Muriel Kay Heimer	5	3,038	223
Lake Land Coll, Mattoon, IL 61938-9366	1966	Dr. Robert K. Luther	11	4,763	361
Lakeland Comm Coll, Mentor, OH 44060-7595	1967	Dr. Ralph R. Doty	11	8,907	444
Lake Michigan Coll, Benton Harbor, MI 49022-1899	1946	Mr. Greg Koroch	9	3,816	240
Lakeshore Tech Coll, Cleveland, WI 53015-1414	1967	Dr. Dennis Ladwig	11	2,784	336
Lake-Sumter Comm Coll, Leesburg, FL 34788-8751	1962	Dr. Robert Westrick	11	2,394	117
Lakewood Comm Coll, White Bear Lake, MN 55110-5697	1967	Dr. James M. Meznek	5	6,251	189
Lamar U–Port Arthur, Port Arthur, TX 77641-0310	1909	Dr. Sam Monroe	5	2,363	111
Lane Comm Coll, Eugene, OR 97405-0640	1964	Dr. Jerry Moskus	11	10,060	543

Name, address	Year	Governing official, control		Enrollment	Faculty
Lansing Comm Coll, Lansing, MI 48901-7210	1957	Dr. Abel B. Sykes, Jr.	11	18,432	1,085
Laramie County Comm Coll, Cheyenne, WY 82007	1968	Dr. Charles Bohlen	8	4,272	255
Laredo Comm Coll, Laredo, TX 78040-4395	1946	Dr. Roger L. Worsley	11	6,716	297
Lawson State Comm Coll, Birmingham, AL 35221-1798	1965	Dr. Perry W. Ward	5	2,307	99
Lehigh Carbon Comm Coll, Schnecksville, PA 18078-2598	1967	Mr. James R. Davis	11	4,860	155
Lenoir Comm Coll, Kinston, NC 28501	1960	Dr. Lonnie H. Blizzard	5	2,069	163
Lewis and Clark Comm Coll, Godfrey, IL 62035-2466	1970	Dr. Dale T. Chapman	9	5,441	305
Lima Tech Coll, Lima, OH 45804-3597	1971	Dr. James J. Countryman	5	2,758	167
Lincoln Land Comm Coll, Springfield, IL 62794-9256	1967	Dr. Norman Stephens, Jr.	9	10,012	401
Linn-Benton Comm Coll, Albany, OR 97321	1966	Mr. Jon Carnahan	11	5,899	486
Long Beach City Coll, Long Beach, CA 90808-1780	1927	Miss Barbara A. Adams	5	27,000	763
Longview Comm Coll, Lee's Summit, MO 64081-2100	1969	Mr. Aldo W. Leker	11	8,959	409
Lorain County Comm Coll, Elyria, OH 44035	1963	Dr. Roy Church	11	7,753	339
Lord Fairfax Comm Coll, Middletown, VA 22645-0047	1969	Dr. Marilyn C. Beck	5	3,072	148
Los Angeles Harbor Coll, Wilmington, CA 90744-2311	1949	Mr. James L. Heinselman	11	9,200	350
Los Angeles Mission Coll, Sylmar, CA 91342-3200	1974	Dr. Jack Fujimoto	11	6,097	115
Los Angeles Pierce Coll, Woodland Hills, CA 91371-0001	1947	Dr. Mary E. Lee	11	18,314	519
Los Angeles Southwest Coll, Los Angeles, CA 90047-4810	1967	Dr. Carolyn G. Williams	11	6,557	250
Los Angeles Trade-Tech Coll, Los Angeles, CA 90015-4108	1925	Mr. Thomas L. Stevens, Jr.	11	11,398	445
Los Medanos Coll, Pittsburg, CA 94565-5197	1974	Mr. Stanley H. Chin	9	6,883	244
Louisiana State U at Alexandria, Alexandria, LA 71302-9121	1960	Dr. Robert Cavanaugh	5	2,622	87
Louisiana State U at Eunice, Eunice, LA 70535-1129	1967	Dr. Michael Smith	5	2,861	120
Lurleen B Wallace State Jr Coll, Andalusia, AL 36420-1418	1969	Dr. Seth Hammett	5	1,191	60
Luzerne County Comm Coll, Nanticoke, PA 18634-9804	1966	Mr. Donald R. Bronsard	8	7,281	512
Macon Coll, Macon, GA 31297	1968	Dr. S. Aaron Hyatt	5	4,907	141
Madison Area Tech Coll, Madison, WI 53704-2599	1911	Dr. Beverly S. Simone	9	11,622	1,960
Manatee Comm Coll, Bradenton, FL 34206-7046	1957	Dr. Stephen J. Korcheck	5	8,144	298
Maple Woods Comm Coll, Kansas City, MO 64156-1299	1969	Dr. Stephen R. Brainard	11	5,088	197
Maria Coll, Albany, NY 12208-1798	1958	Sr. Laureen Fitzgerald	1	1,003	60
Marion Tech Coll, Marion, OH 43302-5694	1971	Dr. John Richard Bryson	12	1,901	105
Marshalltown Comm Coll, Marshalltown, IA 50158-4760	1927	Dr. William Simpson	9	1,449	107
Marymount Coll, Palos Verdes, California, Rancho Palos Verdes, CA 90274-6299	1932	Dr. Thomas M. McFadden	2	1,087	86
Massachusetts Bay Comm Coll, Wellesley Hills, MA 02181-5359	1961	Mr. Roger A. Van Winkle	5	5,233	278
Massasoit Comm Coll, Brockton, MA 02402-3996	1966	Dr. Gerard F. Burke	5	7,500	427
McCook Comm Coll, McCook, NE 69001-2631	1926	Dr. Robert G. Smallfoot	11	1,100	64
McHenry County Coll, Crystal Lake, IL 60012-2761	1967	Mr. Robert C. Bartlett	11	4,368	161
McLennan Comm Coll, Waco, TX 76708-1499	1965	Dr. Dennis F. Michaelis	8	5,703	284
Mendocino Coll, Ukiah, CA 95482-0300	1973	Dr. Carl J. Ehmann	11	3,400	169
Merced Coll, Merced, CA 95348-2898	1962	Dr. E. Jan Moser	11	7,078	421
Mercer County Comm Coll, Trenton, NJ 08690-1004	1966	Dr. Thomas Sepe	11	8,805	356
Meridian Comm Coll, Meridian, MS 39307	1937	Dr. William F. Scaggs	11	2,872	236
Mesabi Comm Coll, Virginia, MN 55792	1918	Mr. John Harris	5	1,003	47
Mesa Comm Coll, Mesa, AZ 85202-4866	1965	Dr. Larry K. Christiansen	11	20,622	852
Metropolitan Comm Coll, Omaha, NE 68103-0777	1974	Dr. J. Richard Gilliland	11	10,301	373
Miami-Dade Comm Coll, Miami, FL 33132-2296	1960	Dr. Robert H. McCabe	11	52,814	2,147
Miami U–Hamilton Cmps, Hamilton, OH 45011-3399	1968	Dr. Harriet V. Taylor	5	2,798	114
Miami U–Middletown Cmps, Middletown, OH 45042-3497	1966	Dr. Michael P. Governanti	5	2,405	165
Middle Georgia Coll, Cochran, GA 31014-1599	1884	Dr. Joe Ben Welch	5	2,025	82
Middlesex Comm Coll, Bedford, MA 01730-1655	1970	Dr. Carole A. Cowan	5	7,113	295
Middlesex Comm Tech Coll, Middletown, CT 06457-4889	1966	Dr. Leila Gonzalez Sullivan	5	3,230	130
Middlesex County Coll, Edison, NJ 08818-3050	1964	Dr. Flora M. Edwards	8	12,500	287
Midland Coll, Midland, TX 79705-6399	1969	Dr. David E. Daniel	11	3,789	192
Midlands Tech Coll, Columbia, SC 29202-2408	1974	Dr. James L. Hudgins	11	9,140	650
Mid-Plains Comm Coll, North Platte, NE 69101-9420	1965	Dr. William A. Griffin, Jr.	9	2,024	91
Mid-State Tech Coll, Wisconsin Rapids, WI 54494-5599	1917	Dr. M. H. Schneeberg	11	2,808	86
Mineral Area Coll, Park Hills, MO 63601	1922	Dr. Dixie A. Kohn	9	3,064	128
Minneapolis Comm Coll, Minneapolis, MN 55403-1779	1965	Dr. Jacquelyn Belcher	5	4,535	256
Mission Coll, Santa Clara, CA 95054-1897	1977	Dr. Floyd M. Hogue	11	10,224	313
Mississippi County Comm Coll, Blytheville, AR 72316-1109	1975	Dr. John P. Sullins	5	1,680	95
Mississippi Delta Comm Coll, Moorhead, MS 38761-0668	1926	Dr. Bobby Garvin	9	2,546	128
Mississippi Gulf Coast Comm Coll, Perkinston, MS 39573-0067	1911	Dr. Richard Miller	9	8,721	753
Mitchell Comm Coll, Statesville, NC 28677-5293	1852	Dr. Douglas O. Eason	5	1,526	90
Moberly Area Comm Coll, Moberly, MO 65270-1392	1927	Dr. Andrew Komar, Jr.	11	1,846	95
Modesto Jr Coll, Modesto, CA 95350-5800	1921	Dr. Stanley L. Hodges	11	8,510	454
Mohave Comm Coll, Kingman, AZ 86401-1299	1971	Dr. Charles W. Hall	5	5,144	259
Mohawk Valley Comm Coll, Utica, NY 13501-5394	1946	Dr. Michael I. Schafer	11	6,500	353
Monroe Coll, Bronx, NY 10468-5407	1933	Mr. Stephen J. Jerome	3	2,400	100
Monroe Comm Coll, Rochester, NY 14623-5780	1961	Dr. Peter A. Spina	11	13,465	660
Monroe County Comm Coll, Monroe, MI 48161-9047	1964	Mr. Gerald D. Welch	8	4,057	178
Montcalm Comm Coll, Sidney, MI 48885-0300	1965	Dr. Donald C. Burns	11	1,834	134
Montgomery Coll–Germantown Cmps, Germantown, MD 20874	1975	Dr. Robert E. Parilla	11	4,200	185
Montgomery Coll–Rockville Cmps, Rockville, MD 20850-1196	1965	Dr. Robert E. Parilla	11	14,355	705
Montgomery Coll–Takoma Park Cmps, Takoma Park, MD 20912	1946	Dr. Robert E. Parilla	11	4,830	219
Montgomery County Comm Coll, Blue Bell, PA 19422-0796	1964	Dr. Edward M. Sweitzer	8	9,123	486
Moorpark Coll, Moorpark, CA 93021-1695	1967	Dr. James W. Walker	8	12,078	450
Moraine Park Tech Coll, Fond du Lac, WI 54936-1940	1967	Dr. John J. Shanahan	11	6,137	289
Moraine Valley Comm Coll, Palos Hills, IL 60465-0937	1967	Dr. Vernon O. Crawley	11	13,826	611
Morton Coll, Cicero, IL 60650-4398	1924	Mr. Charles P. Ferro	11	4,592	230
Motlow State Comm Coll, Tullahoma, TN 37388-8100	1969	Dr. A. Frank Glass	5	3,263	245
Mountain Empire Comm Coll, Big Stone Gap, VA 24219-0700	1972	Dr. Robert H. Sandel	5	2,700	133
Mountain View Coll, Dallas, TX 75211-6599	1970	Dr. Monique Amerman	8	6,306	268
Mt Hood Comm Coll, Gresham, OR 97030-3300	1966	Dr. Paul Kreider	11	7,960	549
Mount Ida Coll, Newton Centre, MA 02159-3310	1899	Dr. Bryan E. Carlson	1	1,901	177
Mt San Antonio Coll, Walnut, CA 91789-1399	1946	Dr. William H. Feddersen	9	23,294	821
Mt San Jacinto Coll, San Jacinto, CA 92583-2399	1963	Dr. Roy B. Mason, II	11	7,010	181
Mount Wachusett Comm Coll, Gardner, MA 01440-1000	1963	Dr. Daniel M. Asquino	5	2,200	112
Murray State Coll, Tishomingo, OK 73460-3130	1908	Dr. Glen Pedersen	5	1,674	69
Muscatine Comm Coll, Muscatine, IA 52761-5396	1929	Dr. Victor G. McAvoy	5	1,203	68

Name, address	Year	Governing official, control		Enroll-ment	Faculty
Muskegon Comm Coll, Muskegon, MI 49442-1493	1926	Dr. James L. Stevenson	11	5,169	150
Muskingum Area Tech Coll, Zanesville, OH 43701-2694	1969	Dr. Lynn H. Willett	11	2,701	104
Nash Comm Coll, Rocky Mount, NC 27804-0488	1967	Dr. J. Reid Parrott, Jr.	5	1,923	175
Nashville State Tech Inst, Nashville, TN 37209-4515	1970	Dr. George H. Van Allen	5	6,302	294
Nassau Comm Coll, Garden City, NY 11530-6793	1959	Dr. Sean A. Fanelli	11	22,347	1,440
National Ed Ctr–Brown Inst Cmps, Minneapolis, MN 55407-1932	1946	Ms. Bonnie M. Hugeback	3	1,180	79
Naugatuck Valley Comm–Tech Coll, Waterbury, CT 06708-3000	1967	Dr. Richard L. Sanders	5	6,008	114
Navajo Comm Coll, Tsaile, AZ 86556	1968	Dr. Tommy Lewis, Jr.	4	2,165	155
Navarro Coll, Corsicana, TX 75110-4899	1946	Dr. Gerald Burson	11	3,246	175
Neosho County Comm Coll, Chanute, KS 66720-2699	1936	Dr. Theodore W. Wischropp	11	1,950	117
The New England Banking Inst, Boston, MA 02111-2671	1909	NR	1	1,755	360
New England Inst of Tech, Warwick, RI 02886-2244	1940	Dr. Richard I. Gouse	1	1,950	134
New England Inst of Tech & Florida Culinary Inst, West Palm Beach, FL 33407-2384	1983	Mr. John Anderson	3	1,000	68
New Hampshire Tech Inst, Concord, NH 03301-7412	1964	Dr. David E. Larrabee, Sr.	5	1,544	145
New Mexico Jr Coll, Hobbs, NM 88240-9123	1965	Dr. Charles D. Hays	11	2,691	109
New Mexico State U–Alamogordo, Alamogordo, NM 88310	1958	Dr. Charles R. Reidlinger	5	1,786	109
New Mexico State U–Carlsbad, Carlsbad, NM 88220-3509	1950	Dr. Douglas E. Burghan	5	1,271	73
New Orleans Baptist Theological Sem, New Orleans, LA 70126-4858	1917	Dr. Landrum P. Leavell, II	2	1,917	18
New River Comm Coll, Dublin, VA 24084-1127	1969	Dr. Edwin L. Barnes	5	1,861	187
New York City Tech Coll of City U of NY, Brooklyn, NY 11201-2983	1946	Dr. Charles W. Merideth	11	10,600	750
Niagara County Comm Coll, Sanborn, NY 14132-9460	1962	Mr. Gerald L. Miller	11	5,663	467
Nicolet Area Tech Coll, Rhinelander, WI 54501-0518	1968	Dr. Adrian Lorbetske	11	1,700	84
Normandale Comm Coll, Bloomington, MN 55431-4399	1968	Dr. Thomas J. Horak	5	8,870	300
Northampton County Area Comm Coll, Bethlehem, PA 18017-7599	1967	Dr. Robert J. Kopecek	11	6,475	406
North Arkansas Comm/Tech Coll, Harrison, AR 72601	1974	Dr. Bill Baker	11	1,620	84
North Central Michigan Coll, Petoskey, MI 49770-8717	1958	Mr. Robert B. Graham	8	2,141	102
North Central Missouri Coll, Trenton, MO 64683-1824	1925	Dr. James Selby	9	1,144	70
North Central Tech Coll, Mansfield, OH 44901-0698	1961	Dr. Byron E. Kee	5	2,958	185
Northcentral Tech Coll, Wausau, WI 54401-1880	1912	Dr. Robert Ernst	9	4,881	211
North Central Texas Coll, Gainesville, TX 76240-4699	1924	Dr. Ronnie Glasscock	8	4,068	175
North Country Comm Coll, Saranac Lake, NY 12983-2046	1967	Dr. Gail Rogers Rice	11	1,823	140
North Dakota State Coll of Science, Wahpeton, ND 58076	1903	Dr. Jerry Olson	5	2,192	141
Northeast Alabama State Comm Coll, Rainsville, AL 35986-0159	1963	Dr. Charles M. Pendley	5	1,787	53
Northeast Comm Coll, Norfolk, NE 68702-0469	1973	Dr. Robert P. Cox	11	3,408	122
Northeastern Jr Coll, Sterling, CO 80751-2344	1941	Dr. Henry M. Milander	11	1,843	79
Northeastern Oklahoma A&M Coll, Miami, OK 74354-6434	1919	Dr. Jerry D. Carroll	5	2,600	133
Northeast Iowa Comm Coll, Peosta Cmps, Peosta, IA 52068-9776	1970	Ms. Karla Berns	11	1,450	66
Northeast Mississippi Comm Coll, Booneville, MS 38829	1948	Mr. Joe M. Childers	9	2,775	NR
Northeast State Tech Comm Coll, Blountville, TN 37617-0246	1966	Dr. R. Wade Powers	5	4,995	166
Northeast Texas Comm Coll, Mount Pleasant, TX 75456-1307	1985	Dr. Michael C. Bruner	11	2,105	93
Northern Essex Comm Coll, Haverhill, MA 01830	1960	Dr. John R. Dimitry	5	7,058	457
Northern Nevada Comm Coll, Elko, NV 89801-3348	1967	Dr. Ronald K. Remington	5	2,500	242
Northern New Mexico Comm Coll, Española, NM 87532	1909	Ms. Connie A. Valdez	5	1,654	154
Northern Oklahoma Coll, Tonkawa, OK 74653-0310	1901	Dr. Joe Kinzer	5	2,250	80
Northern Virginia Comm Coll, Annandale, VA 22003-3796	1965	Dr. Richard J. Ernst	5	38,530	1,452
North Florida Jr Coll, Madison, FL 32340-1602	1958	Dr. William H. McCoy	5	1,070	30
North Hennepin Comm Coll, Minneapolis, MN 55445-2231	1966	Dr. Janis H. Weiss	5	6,160	212
North Idaho Coll, Coeur d'Alene, ID 83814-2199	1933	Dr. C. Robert Bennett	11	3,312	181
North Iowa Area Comm Coll, Mason City, IA 50401-7299	1918	Dr. David Buettner	11	2,923	107
Northland Pioneer Coll, Holbrook, AZ 86025-0610	1974	Dr. John H. Anderson	11	4,779	400
North Seattle Comm Coll, Seattle, WA 98103-3599	1970	Dr. Peter Ku	5	9,200	290
North Shore Comm Coll, Danvers, MA 01923-4093	1965	Dr. George Traicoff	5	3,305	NR
NorthWest Arkansas Comm Coll, Bentonville, AR 72712-1408	1989	NR	11	1,979	124
Northwest Coll, Powell, WY 82435-1898	1946	Dr. John P. Hanna	11	2,082	176
Northwestern Coll, Lima, OH 45805-1498	1920	Mr. Loren R. Jarvis	1	1,650	59
Northwestern Connecticut Comm-Tech Coll, Winsted, CT 06098	1965	Dr. R. Eileen Baccus	5	2,096	87
Northwestern Michigan Coll, Traverse City, MI 49684-3061	1951	Dr. Timothy G. Quinn	11	4,140	231
Northwest Mississippi Comm Coll, Senatobia, MS 38668-1701	1927	Dr. David M. Haraway	11	4,200	180
Northwest-Shoals Comm Coll, Phil Campbell, AL 35581-9399	1961	Dr. Larry McCoy	5	2,049	83
Northwest State Comm Coll, Archbold, OH 43502-9542	1968	Dr. Larry G. McDougle	5	1,897	117
Norwalk Comm-Tech Coll, Norwalk, CT 06854-1655	1961	Dr. William H. Schwab	5	5,113	241
Oakland Comm Coll, Bloomfield Hills, MI 48304-2266	1964	Dr. Patsy J. Fulton	11	28,457	788
Oakton Comm Coll, Des Plaines, IL 60016-1268	1969	Dr. Thomas TenHoeve	9	11,254	495
Ocean County Coll, Toms River, NJ 08754-2001	1964	Dr. Milton Shaw	8	8,193	374
Ohio U–Southern Cmps, Ironton, OH 45638-2214	1956	Dr. Bill Dingus	5	2,390	122
Okaloosa-Walton Comm Coll, Niceville, FL 32578-1295	1963	Dr. James R. Richburg	11	5,820	297
Oklahoma City Comm Coll, Oklahoma City, OK 73159-4419	1969	Dr. Bobby Gaines	5	10,875	340
Oklahoma State U, Oklahoma City, Oklahoma City, OK 73107-6120	1961	Dr. James Hooper	5	4,357	205
Oklahoma State U, Okmulgee, Okmulgee, OK 74447-3901	1946	Dr. Robert Klabenes	5	2,221	138
Olympic Coll, Bremerton, WA 98337-1699	1946	Dr. Wallace A. Simpson	5	6,536	323
Onondaga Comm Coll, Syracuse, NY 13215	1962	Dr. Bruce H. Leslie	11	8,100	536
Orangeburg-Calhoun Tech Coll, Orangeburg, SC 29115-8299	1968	Mr. M. Rudolph Groomes	11	1,847	120
Orange Coast Coll, Costa Mesa, CA 92628-5005	1947	Mr. David A. Grant	11	25,043	763
Orange County Comm Coll, Middletown, NY 10940-6437	1950	Dr. William F. Messner	11	5,996	385
Owensboro Comm Coll, Owensboro, KY 42303-1899	1986	Dr. John McGuire	5	2,570	124
Owens Comm Coll, Toledo, OH 43699-1947	1966	Mr. Daniel H. Brown	5	7,770	483
Owens Comm Coll, Toledo, OH 43699-1947	1983	Mr. Daniel H. Brown	5	1,437	91
Palm Beach Comm Coll, Lake Worth, FL 33461-4796	1933	Dr. Edward M. Eissey	5	16,462	656

Name, address	Year	Governing official, control		Enroll-ment	Faculty
Palo Alto Coll, San Antonio, TX 78224-2499	1987	Dr. Joel E. Vela	11	6,666	317
Palomar Coll, San Marcos, CA 92069-1487	1946	Dr. George R. Boggs	11	22,926	1,097
Palo Verde Coll, Blythe, CA 92225-1118	1947	Dr. Wilford J. Beumel	11	1,200	69
Panola Coll, Carthage, TX 75633	1947	Dr. W. F. Edmondson	11	1,515	68
Paradise Valley Comm Coll, Phoenix, AZ 85032-1200	1985	Dr. Raul Cardenas	11	5,179	221
Paris Jr Coll, Paris, TX 75460-6298	1924	Mr. Bobby R. Walters	11	2,450	117
Parkland Coll, Champaign, IL 61821-1899	1967	Dr. Zelema M. Harris	9	8,869	673
Pasadena City Coll, Pasadena, CA 91106-2041	1924	Dr. Jack A. Scott	9	22,414	946
Pasco-Hernando Comm Coll, Dade City, FL 33525-7599	1972	Dr. Robert Judson, Jr.	5	3,717	204
Passaic County Comm Coll, Paterson, NJ 07505-1179	1968	Mr. Elliott Collins	8	3,738	225
Patrick Henry Comm Coll, Martinsville, VA 24115-5311	1962	Dr. Max Wingett	5	2,570	88
Paul D Camp Comm Coll, Franklin, VA 23851-0737	1971	Dr. Jerome J. Friga	5	1,553	59
Pearl River Comm Coll, Poplarville, MS 39470	1909	Dr. Ted J. Alexander	11	2,779	160
Pellissippi State Tech Comm Coll, Knoxville, TN 37933-0990	1974	Dr. Allen G. Edwards	5	7,866	444
Peninsula Coll, Port Angeles, WA 98362-2779	1961	Dr. Wallace Sigmar	5	2,904	149
Pennsylvania Coll of Tech, Williamsport, PA 17701-5778	1965	Dr. Robert Breuder	12	4,781	330
Penn State U Altoona Cmps, Altoona, PA 16601-3760	1929	Dr. Allen C. Meadors	12	2,470	132
Penn State U Berks Cmps, Reading, PA 19610-6009	1924	Dr. Frederick H. Gaige	12	1,726	104
Penn State U Delaware County Cmps, Media, PA 19063-5596	1966	Dr. Edward S. J. Tomezsko	12	1,389	88
Penn State U Hazleton Cmps, Hazleton, PA 18201-1291	1934	Dr. James J. Staudenmeier	12	1,220	77
Penn State U New Kensington Cmps, New Kensington, PA 15068-1798	1958	Dr. Roy Myers	12	1,126	71
Penn State U Ogontz Cmps, Abington, PA 19001-3918	1950	Dr. Karen Wiley Sandler	12	3,088	168
Penn State U Schuylkill Cmps, Schuylkill Haven, PA 17972-2208	1934	Dr. Wayne Lammie	12	1,110	65
Penn State U Shenango Cmps, Sharon, PA 16146-1537	1965	Dr. Albert N. Skomra	12	1,099	74
Penn State U Worthington Scranton Cmps, Dunmore, PA 18512-1699	1923	Dr. James D. Gallagher	12	1,299	89
Penn State U York Cmps, York, PA 17403-3298	1926	Dr. Donald A. Gogniat	12	1,913	125
Penn Valley Comm Coll, Kansas City, MO 64111	1969	Dr. E. Paul Williams	11	5,347	424
Pensacola Jr Coll, Pensacola, FL 32504-8998	1948	Dr. Horace E. Hartsell	5	13,000	950
Phillips County Comm Coll, Helena, AR 72342-0785	1965	Dr. Steven Jones	11	1,494	107
Phillips Jr Coll, New Orleans, LA 70123-3449	1970	NR	3	1,100	NR
Phoenix Coll, Phoenix, AZ 85013-4234	1920	Dr. Marie Pepicello	11	14,319	540
Piedmont Virginia Comm Coll, Charlottesville, VA 22902-8714	1972	Dr. Deborah M. DiCroce	5	4,316	262
Pierce Coll, Tacoma, WA 98498-1999	1967	Dr. George Delaney	5	9,830	492
Pikes Peak Comm Coll, Colorado Springs, CO 80906-5498	1968	Dr. Marijane Axtell Paulsen	5	6,568	417
Pitt Comm Coll, Greenville, NC 27835-7007	1961	Dr. Charles E. Russell	11	4,661	234
Pittsburgh Inst of Aeronautics, Pittsburgh, PA 15236-0897 (2)	1929	Mr. John Graham, II	1	1,012	56
Polk Comm Coll, Winter Haven, FL 33881-4299	1964	Dr. Maryly VanLeer Peck	5	6,100	260
Porterville Coll, Porterville, CA 93257-6058	1927	Dr. Bonnie L. Rogers	5	2,700	128
Portland Comm Coll, Portland, OR 97280-0990	1961	Dr. Daniel F. Moriarty	11	34,028	1,215
Potomac State Coll of West Virginia U, Keyser, WV 26726	1901	Dr. Lester K. Beavers	5	1,108	83
Prairie State Coll, Chicago Heights, IL 60411-1275	1958	Dr. T. Lightfield	11	5,461	289
Pratt Comm Coll, Pratt, KS 67124	1938	Dr. William Wojciechowski	9	2,064	48
Prince George's Comm Coll, Largo, MD 20772-2199	1958	Dr. Robert I. Bickford	8	12,955	600
Pueblo Comm Coll, Pueblo, CO 81004-1499	1979	Dr. Joe May	5	3,200	396
Queensborough Comm Coll of City U of NY, Bayside, NY 11364	1958	Dr. Kurt R. Schmeller	11	12,300	563
Quincy Coll, Quincy, MA 02169-4522	1958	Dr. Donald L. Young	10	2,331	69
Quinebaug Valley Comm-Tech Coll, Danielson, CT 06239-1440	1971	Ms. Dianne E. Williams	5	1,178	55
Quinsigamond Comm Coll, Worcester, MA 01606-2092	1963	Dr. Clifford S. Peterson	5	4,827	238
Randolph Comm Coll, Asheboro, NC 27204-1009	1962	Dr. Larry K. Linker	5	1,548	80
Rappahannock Comm Coll, Glenns, VA 23149-0287	1970	Dr. John H. Upton	11	2,089	129
Raritan Valley Comm Coll, Somerville, NJ 08876-1265	1965	Dr. Cary A. Israel	8	4,445	276
Reading Area Comm Coll, Reading, PA 19603-1706	1971	Dr. Gust Zogas	8	3,418	159
Redlands Comm Coll, El Reno, OK 73036	1938	Dr. Larry F. Devane	5	2,070	115
Red Rocks Comm Coll, Lakewood, CO 80401	1969	Dr. Dorothy A. Horrell	5	6,831	276
Rend Lake Coll, Ina, IL 62846-9801	1967	Mr. Mark S. Kern	5	4,511	201
Richard Bland Coll of the Coll of William and Mary, Petersburg, VA 23805-7100	1961	Dr. Clarence Maze, Jr.	5	1,206	47
Richland Coll, Dallas, TX 75243-2199	1972	Dr. Stephen Mittelstet	11	13,391	665
Richland Comm Coll, Decatur, IL 62521-8513	1971	Dr. Charles R. Novak	9	4,110	213
Richmond Comm Coll, Hamlet, NC 28345-1189	1964	Mr. Joseph W. Grimsley	5	1,035	100
Ricks Coll, Rexburg, ID 83460-4107	1888	Dr. Steven D. Bennion	2	8,217	387
Rio Hondo Coll, Whittier, CA 90608	1960	Mr. Tim Wood	11	14,500	710
Rio Salado Comm Coll, Phoenix, AZ 85003-1558	1978	Dr. Linda Thor	11	9,531	511
Riverside Comm Coll, Riverside, CA 92506-1293	1916	Dr. Salvatore Rotella	11	23,000	480
Roane State Comm Coll, Harriman, TN 37748-5011	1971	Dr. Sherry L. Hoppe	5	5,840	333
Robert Morris Coll, Chicago Cmps, Chicago, IL 60601-2501	1913	Mr. Richard D. Pickett	1	2,979	180
Rochester Comm Coll, Rochester, MN 55904-4999	1915	Dr. Karen E. Nagle	5	3,953	225
Rockingham Comm Coll, Wentworth, NC 27375-0038	1964	Dr. N. J. Owens, Jr.	5	2,033	114
Rockland Comm Coll, Suffern, NY 10901-3699	1959	Dr. Neal A. Raisman	11	8,044	792
Rock Valley Coll, Rockford, IL 61114-5699	1964	Dr. Karl J. Jacobs	9	9,238	224
Rogers State Coll, Claremore, OK 74017-2099	1909	Dr. Richard H. Mosier	5	3,875	270
Rogue Comm Coll, Grants Pass, OR 97527-9298	1970	Dr. Harvey Bennett	11	2,894	334
Rose State Coll, Midwest City, OK 73110-2799	1971	Dr. Larry Nutter	11	9,700	337
Rowan-Cabarrus Comm Coll, Salisbury, NC 28145-1595	1963	Dr. Richard L. Brownell	5	3,500	130
Sacramento City Coll, Sacramento, CA 95822-1386	1916	Dr. Robert M. Harris	11	15,648	420
Saddleback Coll, Mission Viejo, CA 92692-3697	1967	Dr. Ned Doffoney	11	20,103	638
Saint Augustine Coll, Chicago, IL 60640-3501	1980	Fr. Carlos A. Plazas	1	1,398	150
Saint Charles County Comm Coll, St Peters, MO 63376-0975	1986	Dr. Donald D. Shook	5	4,679	190
St Clair County Comm Coll, Port Huron, MI 48061-5015	1923	Dr. R. Ernest Dear	8	4,849	290
St Cloud Tech Coll, St Cloud, MN 56303-1240	1948	Dr. Larry Barnhardt	11	3,152	102
St Johns River Comm Coll, Palatka, FL 32177-3807	1958	Dr. R. L. McLendon, Jr.	5	3,391	157
St Louis Comm Coll at Florissant Valley, St Louis, MO 63135-1499	1963	Mr. Michael Maguire	9	9,651	440
St Louis Comm Coll at Forest Park, St Louis, MO 63110-1316	1962	Dr. Henry D. Shannon	9	8,122	367

Name, address	Year	Governing official, control	Enroll-ment	Faculty
St Louis Comm Coll at Meramec, Kirkwood, MO 63122-5720	1963	Mr. Richard A. Black 9	14,752	745
St Mary's Cmps of the Coll of St Catherine, Minneapolis, MN 55454-1494	1964	Dr. Anita M. Pampusch 2	1,171	119
St Paul Tech Coll, St Paul, MN 55102-1800	1922	Dr. Donovan Schwichtenberg . 11	3,570	565
St Petersburg Jr Coll, St Petersburg, FL 33733-3489	1927	Dr. Carl M. Kuttler, Jr. 11	23,488	861
St Philip's Coll, San Antonio, TX 78203-2098	1898	Mr. Hamice R. James,, Jr. 9	5,844	334
Salem Comm Coll, Carneys Point, NJ 08069-2799	1971	Dr. Linda C. Jolly 8	1,553	74
Salt Lake Comm Coll, Salt Lake City, UT 84130-0808	1948	Dr. Frank W. Budd 5	17,437	890
Sampson Comm Coll, Clinton, NC 28328-0318	1965	Dr. Clifton W. Paderick 11	1,065	99
San Antonio Coll, San Antonio, TX 78212-4299	1925	Dr. Ruth Burgos-Sasscer 11	19,908	847
Sandhills Comm Coll, Pinehurst, NC 28374-8299	1963	Dr. John Dempsey 11	2,498	125
San Diego City Coll, San Diego, CA 92101-4787	1914	Dr. Jerome Hunter 11	13,200	250
San Diego Mesa Coll, San Diego, CA 92111-4998	1964	Dr. Constance Carroll 9	21,917	791
San Diego Miramar Coll, San Diego, CA 92126-2999	1969	Dr. Louis C. Murillo 11	6,553	174
San Jacinto Coll–Central Cmps, Pasadena, TX 77501-2007	1961	Dr. Monte Blue 11	10,562	539
San Jacinto Coll–North Cmps, Houston, TX 77049-4599	1974	Dr. Edwin E. Lehr 11	3,939	190
San Jacinto Coll–South Cmps, Houston, TX 77089-6099	1979	Dr. Parker Williams 11	5,382	204
San Joaquin Delta Coll, Stockton, CA 95207-6370	1935	Dr. L. H. Horton, Jr. 9	15,777	579
San Jose City Coll, San Jose, CA 95128-2797	1921	Ms. Del M. Anderson 9	10,856	390
San Juan Coll, Farmington, NM 87402-4699	1958	Dr. James C. Henderson 8	4,182	165
Santa Barbara City Coll, Santa Barbara, CA 93109-2394	1908	Dr. Peter R. MacDougall 9	10,555	485
Santa Fe Comm Coll, Gainesville, FL 32606-6200	1966	Dr. Larry W. Tyree 11	11,813	539
Santa Fe Comm Coll, Santa Fe, NM 87502-4187	1983	Dr. Leonardo de la Garza . . . 11	4,316	353
Santa Monica Coll, Santa Monica, CA 90405-1644	1929	Dr. Richard L. Moore 11	24,196	664
Santa Rosa Jr Coll, Santa Rosa, CA 95401-4395	1918	Dr. Robert F. Agrella 11	24,526	1,371
Sauk Valley Comm Coll, Dixon, IL 61021	1965	Dr. Richard L. Behrendt 9	2,790	152
Schenectady County Comm Coll, Schenectady, NY 12305-2294	1968	Dr. Gabriel J. Basil 11	3,834	225
Schoolcraft Coll, Livonia, MI 48152-2696	1961	Dr. Richard W. McDowell 9	9,819	423
Scott Comm Coll, Bettendorf, IA 52722-6804	1966	Dr. Lenny E. Stone 11	4,000	235
Seattle Central Comm Coll, Seattle, WA 98122-2400	1966	Dr. Charles H. Mitchell 5	9,673	388
Seminole Comm Coll, Sanford, FL 32773-6199	1966	Dr. Earl S. Weldon 11	7,458	502
Seminole Jr Coll, Seminole, OK 74818-0351	1931	Dr. James J. Cook 5	1,844	76
Seward County Comm Coll, Liberal, KS 67905-1137	1969	Dr. James Grote 11	1,609	147
Shasta Coll, Redding, CA 96049-6006	1948	Dr. Douglas Treadway 11	12,820	424
Shawnee Comm Coll, Ullin, IL 62992-9725	1967	Dr. Jack D. Hill 11	2,500	194
Shelby State Comm Coll, Memphis, TN 38174-0568	1970	Dr. Lawrence M. Cox 5	7,018	339
Sheridan Coll, Sheridan, WY 82801-1500	1948	Dr. Stephen Maier 11	2,365	156
Shoreline Comm Coll, Seattle, WA 98133-5696	1964	Dr. Ronald E. Bell 5	8,575	333
Sierra Coll, Rocklin, CA 95677-3397	1936	Dr. Kevin M. Ramirez 5	13,735	510
Sinclair Comm Coll, Dayton, OH 45402-1453	1887	Dr. David H. Ponitz 11	20,948	932
Skagit Valley Coll, Mount Vernon, WA 98273-5899	1926	Dr. James M. Ford 5	6,236	325
Skyline Coll, San Bruno, CA 94066-1698	1969	Ms. Linda Graef Salter 8	7,908	268
Snead State Comm Coll, Boaz, AL 35957	1935	Dr. William H. Osborn 5	1,677	69
Snow Coll, Ephraim, UT 84627-1203	1888	Dr. Gerald Day 5	2,434	106
Solano Comm Coll, Suisun City, CA 94585-3197	1945	Dr. Virginia L. Holton 8	10,347	374
South Arkansas Comm Coll, El Dorado, AR 71731-7010	1975	Dr. Ben Whitfield 5	1,200	81
Southeast Comm Coll, Lincoln Cmps, Lincoln, NE 68520-1299	1973	NR 9	4,101	535
Southeastern Comm Coll, Whiteville, NC 28472-0151	1964	Dr. Stephen C. Scott 5	1,750	145
Southeastern Comm Coll, North Cmps, West Burlington, IA 52655-0605	1968	Dr. R. Gene Gardner 11	2,166	94
Southeastern Illinois Coll, Harrisburg, IL 62946-9804	1960	Dr. Ben Cullers 5	3,763	152
Southern Arkansas U Tech, Camden, AR 71701	1968	Dr. George J. Brown 5	1,197	114
Southern Maine Tech Coll, South Portland, ME 04106	1946	Dr. Wayne H. Ross 5	1,250	148
Southern State Comm Coll, Hillsboro, OH 45133-9487	1975	Dr. George R. McCormick 5	1,658	121
Southern Union State Comm Coll, Wadley, AL 36276	1922	Dr. Roy W. Johnson 5	3,274	168
Southern U, Shreveport–Bossier City Cmps, Shreveport, LA 71107	1964	Dr. Jerome G. Greene,, Jr. 5	1,054	75
Southern West Virginia Comm Coll, Logan, WV 25601-2900	1971	Dr. Harry J. Boyer 5	3,115	198
South Florida Comm Coll, Avon Park, FL 33825-9356	1965	Dr. Catherine P. Cornelius 5	1,500	266
South Georgia Coll, Douglas, GA 31533-5098	1906	Dr. Edward D. Jackson, Jr. . . .5	1,495	57
South Mountain Comm Coll, Phoenix, AZ 85040	1979	Dr. John A. Cordova 11	3,028	177
South Plains Coll, Levelland, TX 79336-6595	1958	Dr. Gary D. McDaniel 11	5,914	356
South Puget Sound Comm Coll, Olympia, WA 98512-6292	1970	Dr. Kenneth J. Minnaert 5	5,400	215
South Seattle Comm Coll, Seattle, WA 98106-1499	1970	Mr. Jerry M. Brockey 5	3,134	292
Southside Virginia Comm Coll, Alberta, VA 23821-9719	1970	Dr. John J. Cavan 5	1,973	169
South Suburban Coll, South Holland, IL 60473-1270	1927	Dr. Richard Fonte 11	7,783	332
Southwestern Coll, Chula Vista, CA 91910-7299	1961	Mr. Joseph M. Conte 11	16,039	646
Southwestern Comm Coll, Creston, IA 50801	1966	Mr. Richard L. Byerly 5	1,180	65
Southwestern Comm Coll, Sylva, NC 28779-9578	1964	Dr. Barry W. Russell 5	1,521	199
Southwestern Michigan Coll, Dowagiac, MI 49047-9793	1964	Mr. David C. Briegel 11	2,834	182
Southwest Mississippi Comm Coll, Summit, MS 39666	1918	NR 9	1,520	89
Southwest Texas Jr Coll, Uvalde, TX 78801-6296	1946	Mr. Billy Word 11	2,859	147
Southwest Virginia Comm Coll, Richlands, VA 24641	1968	Dr. Charles R. King 5	4,551	235
Southwest Wisconsin Tech Coll, Fennimore, WI 53809-9778	1967	Dr. Richard A. Rogers 11	1,500	101
Spartanburg Tech Coll, Spartanburg, SC 29305-4386	1961	Dr. Jack A. Powers 5	2,500	NR
Spokane Comm Coll, Spokane, WA 99207-5399	1963	Mr. Donald Kolb 5	6,776	481
Spokane Falls Comm Coll, Spokane, WA 99204-5288	1967	Dr. Vern Loland 5	6,685	656
Spoon River Coll, Canton, IL 61520-9801	1959	Dr. Felix T. Haynes 5	2,300	133
Springfield Tech Comm Coll, Springfield, MA 01105-1296	1967	Mr. Andrew M. Scibelli 5	3,973	234
Stanly Comm Coll, Albemarle, NC 28001-7458	1971	Dr. Jan J. Crawford 5	1,651	76
Stark Tech Coll, Canton, OH 44720-7299	1970	Dr. John J. McGrath 11	4,326	210
State Comm Coll of East St Louis, East St Louis, IL 62201-1100	1969	Dr. Robert Randolph 5	1,268	83
State Fair Comm Coll, Sedalia, MO 65301-2199	1966	Dr. Marvin Fielding 9	2,369	98
State Tech Inst at Memphis, Memphis, TN 38134-7693	1967	Dr. Charles Temple 5	11,117	527
State U of NY Coll of A&T at Cobleskill, Cobleskill, NY 12043	1916	Dr. Kenneth E. Wing 5	2,801	164
State U of NY Coll of A&T at Morrisville, Morrisville, NY 13408	1908	Dr. Frederick W. Woodward . . .5	3,289	171
State U of NY Coll of Tech at Alfred, Alfred, NY 14802	1908	Dr. William Rezak 5	3,391	176
State U of NY Coll of Tech at Canton, Canton, NY 13617	1906	Dr. Joseph L. Kennedy 5	2,278	107
State U of NY Coll of Tech at Delhi, Delhi, NY 13753	1913	Dr. Mary Ellen Duncan 5	2,285	144
State U of NY Coll of Tech at Farmingdale, Farmingdale, NY 11735	1912	Dr. Frank A. Cipriani 5	7,730	576

Name, address	Year	Governing official, control	Enroll-ment	Faculty
Suffolk County Comm Coll–Ammerman Cmps, Selden, NY 11784-2851	1962	Dr. John F. Cooper 11	13,154	782
Suffolk County Comm Coll–Eastern Cmps, Riverhead, NY 11901	1977	Dr. Elizabeth Blake 11	2,680	216
Suffolk County Comm Coll–Western Cmps, Brentwood, NY 11717	1974	Mr. Salvatore J. LaLima 11	6,097	349
Sullivan County Comm Coll, Loch Sheldrake, NY 12759-4002	1962	Dr. Jeffrey B. Willens 11	2,093	167
Surry Comm Coll, Dobson, NC 27017-0304	1965	Dr. Swanson Richards 5	3,036	98
Tacoma Comm Coll, Tacoma, WA 98465-1997	1965	Dr. Raymond Needham 5	5,517	369
Tallahassee Comm Coll, Tallahassee, FL 32304-2895	1966	Dr. James H. Hinson, Jr. 11	9,800	370
Tarrant County Jr Coll, Fort Worth, TX 76102-6599	1967	Mr. C. A. Roberson 8	27,352	988
Tech Coll of the Lowcountry, Beaufort, SC 29901-1288	1972	Dr. Anne S. McNutt 5	1,600	69
Temple Jr Coll, Temple, TX 76504-7435	1926	Dr. Marvin R. Felder 9	2,363	113
Terra State Comm Coll, Fremont, OH 43420-9670	1968	Dr. Charlotte J. Lee 5	2,940	148
Texarkana Coll, Texarkana, TX 75599-0001	1927	Dr. Carl M. Nelson 11	3,990	196
Texas State Tech Coll–Harlingen Cmps, Harlingen, TX 78550-3697	1967	Dr. J. Gilbert Leal 5	3,486	197
Texas State Tech Coll–Waco/Marshall Cmps, Waco, TX 76705-1695	1965	Mr. Don E. Goodwin 5	3,210	341
Thomas Nelson Comm Coll, Hampton, VA 23670-0407	1968	Dr. Robert G. Templin, Jr. 5	7,828	321
Three Rivers Comm Coll, Poplar Bluff, MO 63901-2393	1966	Dr. Stephen M. Poort 5	3,061	67
Three Rivers Comm-Tech Coll, Norwich, CT 06360	1969	Dr. Booker T. DeVaughn 5	4,275	128
Tidewater Comm Coll, Portsmouth, VA 23703	1968	Dr. Larry Whitworth 5	17,509	787
Tomball Coll, Tomball, TX 77375-4036	1988	Dr. Roy Lazenby 11	3,885	187
Tompkins Cortland Comm Coll, Dryden, NY 13053-9533	1968	Dr. Carl Haynes 11	2,899	196
Treasure Valley Comm Coll, Ontario, OR 97914-3423	1962	Dr. Berton L. Glandon 11	2,299	110
Tri-County Tech Coll, Pendleton, SC 29670-0587	1962	Dr. Don C. Garrison 5	3,308	250
Trident Tech Coll, Charleston, SC 29423-8067	1964	Dr. Mary Thornley 11	9,800	385
Trinidad State Jr Coll, Trinidad, CO 81082-2396	1925	Dr. Harold Deselms 5	1,676	111
Trinity Valley Comm Coll, Athens, TX 75751-2765	1946	Mr. Ron Baugh 11	4,786	224
Triton Coll, River Grove, IL 60171-1995	1964	Dr. George Jorndt 5	11,653	668
Trocaire Coll, Buffalo, NY 14220-2094	1958	Barbara Ciarico, RSM 1	1,162	106
Truckee Meadows Comm Coll, Reno, NV 89512-3901	1971	Dr. John Gwaltney 5	9,490	547
Tulsa Jr Coll, Tulsa, OK 74135-6198	1968	Dr. Dean P. VanTrease 5	22,702	700
Tunxis Comm Coll, Farmington, CT 06032-3026	1969	Dr. Cathryn Addy 5	2,465	175
Tyler Jr Coll, Tyler, TX 75711-9020	1926	Dr. Raymond M. Hawkins 11	7,984	364
Ulster County Comm Coll, Stone Ridge, NY 12484	1961	Mr. Robert T. Brown 11	2,319	194
Umpqua Comm Coll, Roseburg, OR 97470-0226	1964	Dr. James M. Kraby 11	2,300	145
Union County Coll, Cranford, NJ 07016-1528	1933	Dr. Thomas H. Brown 11	10,859	451
The U of Akron–Wayne Coll, Orrville, OH 44667-9192	1972	Dr. Peggy Gordon Elliott 5	1,461	109
U of Alaska Anchorage, Kenai Peninsula Coll, Soldotna, AK 99669-9732	1964	Ms. Ginger Steffy 5	1,817	87
U of Alaska Anchorage, Matanuska-Susitna Coll, Palmer, AK 99645-2889	1958	Mr. Glenn Massay 5	1,654	114
U of Alaska Southeast, Sitka Cmps, Sitka, AK 99835-9418	1962	Ms. Elaine Sunde 5	1,200	92
U of Cincinnati Clermont Coll, Batavia, OH 45103-1785	1972	Dr. Roger J. Barry 5	1,912	135
U of Cincinnati Raymond Walters Coll, Cincinnati, OH 45236-1007	1967	Dr. Barbara A. Bardes 5	2,690	226
U of Hawaii–Kapiolani Comm Coll, Honolulu, HI 96816-4421	1957	Mr. John F. Morton 5	7,356	239
U of Hawaii–Kauai Comm Coll, Lihue, HI 96766-9500	1965	Mr. David Iha 5	1,563	84
U of Hawaii–Leeward Comm Coll, Pearl City, HI 96782-3366	1968	Dr. Barbara B. Polk 5	6,342	264
U of Hawaii–Maui Comm Coll, Kahului, HI 96732	1967	Dr. Clyde Sakamoto 5	2,553	147
U of Hawaii–Windward Comm Coll, Kaneohe, HI 96744-3528	1972	Dr. Peter T. Dyer 5	1,550	80
U of Kentucky, Ashland Comm Coll, Ashland, KY 41101-3683	1937	Dr. Charles Dassance 5	3,168	150
U of Kentucky, Elizabethtown Comm Coll, Elizabethtown, KY 42701-3081	1964	Dr. Charles E. Stebbins 5	4,246	136
U of Kentucky, Hazard Comm Coll, Hazard, KY 41701-2403	1968	Dr. G. Edward Hughes 5	1,796	111
U of Kentucky, Henderson Comm Coll, Henderson, KY 42420-4623	1963	Dr. Patrick R. Lake 5	1,396	96
U of Kentucky, Hopkinsville Comm Coll, Hopkinsville, KY 42241-2100	1965	Dr. Jim Kerley 5	3,120	148
U of Kentucky, Jefferson Comm Coll, Louisville, KY 40202-2005	1968	Dr. Ronald J. Horvath 5	11,350	490
U of Kentucky, Lexington Comm Coll, Lexington, KY 40506-0235	1965	Dr. Janice N. Friedel 5	4,862	302
U of Kentucky, Madisonville Comm Coll, Madisonville, KY 42431-9185	1968	Dr. Arthur D. Stumpf 5	2,513	127
U of Kentucky, Maysville Comm Coll, Maysville, KY 41056	1967	Dr. James C. Shires 5	1,537	111
U of Kentucky, Paducah Comm Coll, Paducah, KY 42002-7380	1932	Dr. Leonard O'Hara 5	3,241	102
U of Kentucky, Prestonsburg Comm Coll, Prestonsburg, KY 41653-1815	1964	Dr. Deborah Lee Floyd 5	3,012	124
U of Kentucky, Somerset Comm Coll, Somerset, KY 42501-2973	1965	Dr. Rollin J. Watson 5	2,815	153
U of Kentucky, Southeast Comm Coll, Cumberland, KY 40823-1099	1960	Dr. W. Bruce Ayers 5	2,634	107
U of Maine at Augusta, Augusta, ME 04330-9410	1965	Dr. George P. Connick 5	5,476	172
U of New Mexico–Gallup Branch, Gallup, NM 87301-5603	1968	Dr. John M. Phillips 5	2,650	117
U of New Mexico–Valencia Cmps, Los Lunas, NM 87031-7633	1981	Dr. Ralph Sigala 5	1,367	93
U of South Carolina at Beaufort, Beaufort, SC 29902-4601	1959	Dr. Chris P. Plyler 5	1,159	64
U of South Carolina at Lancaster, Lancaster, SC 29721-0889	1959	Dr. Joseph Pappin 5	1,039	52
U of South Carolina at Sumter, Sumter, SC 29150-2498	1966	Dr. C. Leslie Carpenter 5	1,675	98
U of Wisconsin Ctr–Fox Valley, Menasha, WI 54952-1224	1933	Dr. James W. Perry 5	1,447	58
U of Wisconsin Ctr–Marathon County, Wausau, WI 54401-5396	1933	Dr. G. Dennis Massey 5	1,111	71
U of Wisconsin Ctr–Waukesha County, Waukesha, WI 53188-2720	1966	Dr. Mary S. Knudten 5	2,147	86
Valencia Comm Coll, Orlando, FL 32802-3028	1967	Dr. Paul C. Gianini, Jr. 5	23,260	947

Name, address	Year	Governing official, control		Enroll-ment	Faculty
Vance-Granville Comm Coll, Henderson, NC 27536-0917	1969	Dr. Ben F. Currin	5	2,652	178
Vernon Regional Jr Coll, Vernon, TX 76384-4092	1972	Dr. Wade Kirk	11	1,780	115
Victoria Coll, Victoria, TX 77901-4494	1925	Dr. Jimmy Goodson	8	3,451	120
Vincennes U, Vincennes, IN 47591-5202	1801	Dr. Phillip M. Summers	5	7,211	400
Vincennes U–Jasper Ctr, Jasper, IN 47546-9393	1970	Dr. Gerald J. Altstadt	5	1,198	62
Virginia Highlands Comm Coll, Abingdon, VA 24210-0828	1967	Dr. N. DeWitt Moore, Jr.	5	2,295	131
Virginia Western Comm Coll, Roanoke, VA 24038-4065	1966	Dr. Charles L. Downs	5	6,895	202
Volunteer State Comm Coll, Gallatin, TN 37066-3146	1970	Dr. Hal R. Ramer	5	5,920	308
Wake Tech Comm Coll, Raleigh, NC 27603-5696	1958	Dr. Bruce I. Howell	11	7,065	405
Wallace State Comm Coll, Hanceville, AL 35077-2000	1966	Dr. James C. Bailey	5	5,166	267
Walla Walla Comm Coll, Walla Walla, WA 99362-9270	1967	Dr. Steven L. VanAusdle	5	4,858	267
Walters State Comm Coll, Morristown, TN 37813-6899	1970	Dr. Jack E. Campbell	5	5,544	253
Washington State Comm Coll, Marietta, OH 45750-9225	1971	Dr. Carson K. Miller	5	2,187	132
Washtenaw Comm Coll, Ann Arbor, MI 48106	1965	Dr. Gunder A. Myran	11	10,954	757
Waterbury State Tech Coll, Waterbury, CT 06708-3000	1964	Dr. Richard L. Sanders	5	1,531	45
Waubonsee Comm Coll, Sugar Grove, IL 60554-9799	1966	Dr. John J. Swalec	9	7,569	494
Waukesha County Tech Coll, Pewaukee, WI 53072-4601	1923	Dr. Richard T. Anderson	11	4,700	520
Wayne Comm Coll, Goldsboro, NC 27533-8002	1957	Dr. Edward H. Wilson, Jr.	11	2,613	153
Wayne County Comm Coll, Detroit, MI 48226-3010	1967	Dr. Richard M. Turner, III	11	9,577	400
Weatherford Coll, Weatherford, TX 76086-5699	1869	Dr. Jim Boyd	5	2,277	94
Wenatchee Valley Coll, Wenatchee, WA 98801-1799	1939	Dr. Woody Ahn	11	3,419	168
Westark Comm Coll, Fort Smith, AR 72913-3649	1928	Mr. Joel R. Stubblefield	11	5,323	236
Westchester Comm Coll, Valhalla, NY 10595-1698	1946	Dr. Joseph N. Hankin	11	17,551	574
Western Iowa Tech Comm Coll, Sioux City, IA 51102-0265	1966	Dr. Robert E. Dunker	5	2,575	157
Western Nevada Comm Coll, Carson City, NV 89703-7316	1971	Dr. Anthony D. Calabro	5	4,775	358
Western Oklahoma State Coll, Altus, OK 73521-1397	1926	Dr. Stephen R. Hensley	5	1,738	78
Western Piedmont Comm Coll, Morganton, NC 28655-9978	1964	Dr. Jim A. Richardson	5	2,592	132
Western Texas Coll, Snyder, TX 79549-6189	1969	Dr. Harry L. Krenek	11	1,086	55
Western Wisconsin Tech Coll, La Crosse, WI 54602-0908	1911	Dr. James Lee Rasch	9	4,388	189
Western Wyoming Comm Coll, Rock Springs, WY 82902-0428	1959	Dr. T. L. Boggs	11	2,575	158
West Hills Comm Coll, Coalinga, CA 93210-1399	1932	Dr. Frank P. Gornick	5	2,810	160
West Los Angeles Coll, Culver City, CA 90230-3500	1969	Dr. Evelyn C. Wong	11	8,958	320
Westmoreland County Comm Coll, Youngwood, PA 15697	1970	Dr. Daniel C. Krezenski	8	6,911	390
West Shore Comm Coll, Scottville, MI 49454-9716	1967	Dr. William M. Anderson	9	1,522	71
West Virginia Northern Comm Coll, Wheeling, WV 26003	1972	Dr. Ron Hutkin	5	2,895	154
West Virginia U at Parkersburg, Parkersburg, WV 26101-9577	1971	Dr. Eldon L. Miller	5	3,782	161
Whatcom Comm Coll, Bellingham, WA 98226-8003	1970	Dr. Harold G. Heiner	5	2,608	132
Wilkes Comm Coll, Wilkesboro, NC 28697	1965	Dr. James R. Randolph	5	1,887	116
William Rainey Harper Coll, Palatine, IL 60067-7398	1965	Dr. Paul N. Thompson	11	15,859	1,018
Willmar Comm Coll, Willmar, MN 56201-0797	1961	Mr. Harold G. Conradi	5	1,468	71
Willmar Tech Coll, Willmar, MN 56201-1097	1961	Mr. Ronald Erpelding	11	1,201	90
Wilson Tech Comm Coll, Wilson, NC 27893-3310	1958	Dr. Frank L. Eagles	5	1,309	74
Wisconsin Indianhead Tech Coll, New Richmond Cmps, New Richmond, WI 54017-1738	1972	Ms. Marilyn McCarty	9	1,102	65
Wisconsin Indianhead Tech Coll, Rice Lake Cmps, Rice Lake, WI 54868-2435	1941	Ms. Mary Ellen Filkins	9	1,136	79
Wood Coll, Mathiston, MS 39752-0289	1886	Dr. Doyce W. Gunter	2	1,500	35
Wor-Wic Comm Coll, Salisbury, MD 21801	1976	Dr. Arnold H. Maner	11	1,834	94
Wytheville Comm Coll, Wytheville, VA 24382-3308	1967	Dr. William F. Snyder	5	1,651	137
Yakima Valley Comm Coll, Yakima, WA 98907-1647	1928	Dr. V. Philip Tullar	5	5,500	410
Yavapai Coll, Prescott, AZ 86301-3297	1966	Dr. Doreen Dailey	11	6,253	377
York Tech Coll, Rock Hill, SC 29730-3395	1961	Mr. Dennis F. Merrell	5	3,251	236
Yuba Coll, Marysville, CA 95901-7699	1927	Dr. Patricia L. Wirth	11	9,781	267

College Freshman Attitudes, 1993

According to the 28th annual survey of college freshmen conducted by the American Council on Education and UCLA, 65% of college freshmen (compared with 55% in 1992) planned to seek advanced degrees. For the first time in the history of the survey, women were more likely than men to pursue all major types of advanced degrees (master's, doctorate, medicine, and law). In 1967, 3 times as many men as women sought a high-level degree (26.7% v. 8.5%). In 1993, more women than men (27.3% v. 25.8%) sought such degrees.

Finances continued to matter in 1993. College freshmen reported, a "very important" reason for attending college was "to be able to make more money" (75.1%, an increase from 73.3% in 1992) or "to get a better job" (82.1% compared with 78.5% in 1992). Financial considerations were key in college selection. "Low tuition" was said to be a "very important" reason (32.0%, an increase from 30.0% in 1992) for choosing a college as was a student's being "offered financial assistance" (31.6%, compared with 28.3% in 1992). In 1993, more freshmen than ever depended on federal loans for financial assistance. Additionally, a record number of freshmen (5.6%) expected to work full-time while attending college.

A record number of students applied to 4 or more colleges (22.2%, an increase from 19.1% in 1992), which indicated increasing competitive pressures. Survey results suggest that college freshmen feel increasingly stressed. High percentages reported that they frequently "felt overwhelmed by all I have to do" (23.2%, compared with 22.0% in 1992) and frequently "felt depressed" (9.4%, an increase from 9.1% in 1992). Students' self-ratings on "emotional health" and "physical health" reached all-time lows. Problems at home may be a cause; record high percentages of freshmen reported their father's occupation as "unemployed" (3.7%).

For the 6th straight year, college freshmen showed strong interest in health professions (15.8%, an increase from 15.6% in 1992). In contrast, for the same period students' interest in business fields continued to decline (16.1%, a decrease from 16.3% in 1992).

College freshmen were more likely to identify themselves as being to the left or to the right of the political center, with those claiming to be "middle of the road" falling below half (49.9%) for the first time since 1972. Although this movement from the center went to both the left and the right, the right picked up the majority, increasing 2.6 percentage points to 22.9%. The percentage on the left was the highest since 1976 at 27.2%.

A record high percentage of college freshmen (81.8%, an increase from 80.4% in 1992) supported greater efforts to control handguns. Additionally, students' support for raising taxes to reduce the federal deficit hit an all-time high (31.4%, an increase from 26.9% in 1992). For the 6th successive year, student support for legislation to outlaw homosexuality declined (36.2%, a decrease from 37.6% in 1992). Support for the legalization of marijuana also increased for the 4th straight year (28.2%, compared with 23% in 1992).

ASTRONOMY AND CALENDAR

Edited by Dr. Kenneth L. Franklin, Astronomer Emeritus
American Museum of Natural History-Hayden Planetarium

Celestial Events Summary, 1995

(Greenwich Mean Time, or GMT)

In the morning sky at the beginning of the year, Venus, Mars, and Jupiter provide interest, but only Saturn attracts our attention in the evening, as Mercury is usually too close to the bright horizon for easy viewing. Mars is on stage from February practically until May, when Jupiter dominates the scene. Although Saturn is in the sky all night by fall, it is not at its usual brightness this year. The celestial drama for all to see, however, comes in November, when Venus, Mars, and Jupiter all pass one another from Nov. 16 to Nov. 22, and all are passed by the crescent moon on Nov. 24. This dance of the planets can be seen rather low in the southwest after the evening twilight has faded sufficiently.

About every 15 years, the earth and Saturn have an interesting interaction. As Saturn takes about 30 years to orbit the sun, it carries its rings along so that the plane in which the ring particles revolve about the planet always stays parallel to itself. Twice in that 30-year period, the ring plane passes across the orbit of the earth, thus across the earth itself, and across the sun too. On May 22, as the earth moves around the sun toward Saturn, the rings sweep across the earth's location so that the earth passes from the north side to the south side of the rings. At that time, even the most powerful telescopes on earth cannot discern the rings edge-on. Galileo's imperfect telescope led him to believe that Saturn "had ears." Imagine his surprise when a few years later he could see no "ears" at all. Huygens, working with better equipment about 40 years later, saw that Saturn had rings. As the earth approaches Saturn in their mutual excursions around the sun, the earth catches up to the ring plane again, crossing the plane from south to north on Aug. 10. Although the view of the south side of the rings is very narrow from earth, the sun is shining at a very low angle on their north side. The earth will get very little light from them; all that can be seen from earth is coming from the ball of the planet itself. Saturn will be in opposition to the sun on Sept. 14. On Nov. 19, the sun will lie in the ring plane, after which time its light will shine on the south side. This is a Saturnian autumnal equinox, during which the darker side of the rings will again be seen from earth. Earth will pass through the ring plane from north to south for the last time on Feb. 11, 1996, again the view from earth being the side illuminated by the sun. In the next 7 to 8 years, the rings will appear to widen, providing an ever enlarging screen to reflect sunlight, and Saturn will again be the bright beauty we all know. Look for a repeat performance with the rings in about 15 years.

In the following summary, events are reported that cannot actually be seen from your location. Take these as notices to view the objects at least a day or two before and after the event in order to see the two objects close together and to observe how they move in the sky and relative to each other. Although everything seems to move very slowly, and we can't feel our own motion through space, be aware that all is, indeed, in motion. We are watching moving planets from a moving platform. It is all complicated enough to be interesting.

Celestial Events Highlights, 1995

(GMT, or as indicated)

January

Mercury, at greatest eastern elongation on the 19th, may be visible about the end of evening twilight low in the western sky near where the sun sets this month, looking like a bright star of nearly magnitude –1 early in the month, to near zero by the end.

Venus is at greatest elongation in the morning sky on the 13th, passing Jupiter on the 14th.

Mars is stationary on the 4th, beginning its retrograde motion in Leo, brightening from near zero magnitude to near –1 during the month.

Jupiter, in Scorpius, 2.5 magnitudes fainter than Venus, passes Venus on the 14th and passes Antares on the 23d.

Saturn, appearing as a 1st magnitude star in Aquarius, is visible in the western sky after sunset.

Moon passes Saturn on the 5th, Mars on the 19th, occults Spica on the 23d, passes Jupiter on the 26th, occults Venus on the 27th, and passes Neptune on the 29th.

Jan. 2—Mercury is 3° south of Neptune.

Jan. 4—Mercury is 1.°7 south of Uranus; Mars stationary; the earth at perihelion, 91.4 million miles from the sun; Quadrantid meteor shower.

Jan. 5—Moon is 7° north of Saturn.

Jan. 13—Venus at greatest elongation, 47° west of the sun; Neptune in conjunction with the sun.

Jan. 14—Venus is 3° north of Jupiter.

Jan. 15—Venus is 8° north of Antares.

Jan. 17—Uranus in conjunction with the sun.

Jan. 19—Mercury at greatest elongation, 19° east of the sun; Mars 9° north of the moon; sun enters Capricornus.

Jan. 23—Jupiter is 5° north of Antares; the moon occults Spica.

Jan. 25—Mercury stationary, begins retrograde motion.

Jan. 26—Jupiter is 1.°7 south of the moon.

Jan. 27—Venus is 0.°2 south of the moon and is occulted.

Jan. 29—Neptune is 4° south of the moon.

February

Mercury is at inferior conjunction on the 3d, but may become visible in the morning sky, low and to the right of the rising sun, as a star brightening to near zero magnitude by month's end.

Venus, dominating the morning sky, passes 4° south of the crescent moon and 0.°7 north of 7.9 magnitude Neptune on the 26th.

Mars, attaining magnitude –1.2 at mid-month in Leo, passes closest to the earth on the 11th, and is at opposition to the sun on the 12th.

Jupiter, still in the morning sky in Scorpius, passes 2° south of the fat crescent moon on the 25th.

Saturn becomes very difficult to see in the evening twilight by month's end.

Moon passes Saturn on the 2d, Mars on the 15th, occults Spica on the 19th, passes Jupiter on the 23d, Neptune, Venus, and Uranus on the 26th, and Mercury on the 27th.

Feb. 2—Saturn is 6° south of the moon.

Feb. 3—Mercury at inferior conjunction, between the earth and the sun.

Feb. 11—Mars closest to the earth.

Feb. 12—Mars at opposition.

Feb. 15—Mars is 10° north of the moon; Mercury stationary.

Feb. 16—Sun enters Aquarius.

Feb. 19—Spica is occulted.

Feb. 23—Jupiter is 2° south of the moon.

Feb. 26—Neptune is 4° south of the moon; Venus is 4° south of the moon; Venus is 0.°7 north of Neptune; Uranus is 6° south of the moon.

Feb. 27—Mercury is 5° south of the moon.

March

Mercury is at greatest elongation on the 1st, brightening all month in the morning twilight to the right of the sunrise point; it passes 0.°6 south of Saturn on the 26th.

Venus is 1.°5 north of 5.6 magnitude Uranus on the 2d.

Mars, now in the evening sky, continues in its westerly, retrograde motion into Cancer until the 25th, when it is stationary, then resuming its direct motion.

Jupiter, as a –2.1 magnitude star, is prominent in Scorpius in the morning sky until outshined when Venus rises.

Saturn, a faint 1st magnitude, emerges from the morning twilight near the end of the month, after its conjunction with the sun on the 6th; Mercury, at –0.4 magnitude, may help point out Saturn on the 26th, when Saturn passes 0.°6 north of Mercury.

Moon passes Mars on the 14th, occults Spica on the 19th, passes Jupiter on the 22d, Neptune and Uranus on the 25th, Venus on the 28th, Saturn on the 29th, and Mercury on the 30th.

Mar. 1—Mercury is at greatest elongation, 27° west of the sun.

Mar. 2—Venus is 1.°5 north of Uranus.

Mar. 6—Saturn is in conjunction with the sun; Pluto is stationary, beginning its retrograde motion.

Mar. 11—Sun enters Pisces.

Mar. 14—Mars is 9° north of the moon.

Mar. 19—Spica is occulted by the recently full moon; see them very close on the evening of the 18th.

Mar. 21—Vernal equinox at 2:14 GMT, 21:14 of the 20th for EST; spring begins in the northern hemisphere.

Mar. 22—Jupiter is 2° south of the moon.

Mar. 25—Neptune is 5° south of the moon; Mars is stationary; Uranus is 6° south of the moon.

Mar. 26—Mercury is 0.°6 south of Saturn.

Mar. 28—Venus is 6° south of the moon.

Mar. 29—Saturn is 6° south of the moon.

Mar. 30—Mercury is 6° south of the moon.

April

Mercury passes superior conjunction with the sun on the 14th, thus in morning and evening twilight all month.

Venus passes very close to Saturn on the 13th, a good time to compare position changes from the morning of the 13th and the 14th.

Mars fades about half a magnitude this month as the earth continues to recede from the ruddy planet, which appears to leave Cancer for Leo this month.

Jupiter continues to be the brightest planet in the night sky, beginning its retrograde motion on the 1st, when it is stationary.

Saturn has a close encounter with Venus on the 13th.

Moon passes Mars on the 10th, occults Spica and is partially eclipsed on the 15th, passes Jupiter on the 18th, Neptune on the 21st, Uranus on the 22d, Saturn on the 26th, and Venus on the 27th, and produces an annular solar eclipse on the 29th.

Apr. 1—Jupiter is stationary, beginning retrograde motion.

Apr. 10—Mars is 8° north of the moon.

Apr. 13—Venus is 0.°6 north of Saturn.

Apr. 14—Mercury in superior conjunction with the sun.

Apr. 15—Spica is occulted by the moon; partial lunar eclipse.

Apr. 18—Jupiter is 3° south of the moon; sun enters Aries.

Apr. 21—Neptune is 5° south of the moon.

Apr. 22—Uranus is 6° south of the moon.

Apr. 26—Saturn is 6° south of the moon.

Apr. 27—Venus is 4° south of the moon; Neptune stationary, beginning retrograde.

Apr. 29—Annular solar eclipse.

May

Mercury is at greatest eastern elongation on the 12th and is stationary on the 24th, beginning its retrograde motion; in the early part of the month, Mercury may be visible in the evening twilight near the place the sun was seen to set.

Venus is still the brightest planet in the morning sky, heralding the rising of the sun.

Mars, continuing to fade, passes close to Regulus on the 24th.

Jupiter is master of the sky all night long, demonstrating why it was identified with the king of the gods; its magnitude at May's end is –2.6.

Saturn fades to magnitude 1.3 by mid-month, because on the 22d its rings will all but disappear in even the most powerful telescopes when the earth passes north to south through the plane of the rings; they will then be seen edge-on.

Moon passes Mercury on the 1st, Mars on the 8th, occults Spica on the 12th, passes Jupiter on the 16th, Neptune and Uranus on the 19th, Saturn on the 23d, and occults Venus on the 27th.

May 1—Mercury is 4° north of the moon.

May 5—Uranus is stationary, beginning its retrograde motion.

May 8—Mars is 7° north of the moon.

May 10—Mercury is 8° north of Aldebaran.

May 12—Mercury at greatest elongation, 22° east of the sun; moon occults Spica.

May 13—Sun enters Taurus.

May 16—Jupiter is 2° south of the moon.

May 19—Neptune is 5° south of the moon; Uranus is 6° south of the moon.

May 20—Pluto at opposition.

May 22—Earth passes from north to south through the plane of Saturn's rings.

May 23—Saturn 6° south of the moon.

May 24—Mars is 1.°1 north of Regulus.

May 27—Venus is occulted by the thin crescent moon about 3 AM EDT, before sunrise in most of the western hemisphere; look for Venus and the moon very close together when they do rise in the morning sky.

June

Mercury is at inferior conjunction, between the earth and the sun, on the 5th, not being visible in the morning sky until late in the month, when it is 22° west of the sun, greatest elongation.

Venus, while still bright, approaches the morning twilight all month, passing Mercury on the 19th.

Mars, hanging in the evening sky, looking like a 1st magnitude star, continues to speed toward the east, moving from Leo to Virgo.

Jupiter is at opposition on the 1st, appearing due south at local midnight, and passing Antares on the 14th.

Saturn begins to brighten almost imperceptibly as the rings begin to show an area that reflects sunlight.

Moon passes Mars on the 5th, occults Spica on the 9th, passes Jupiter on the 12th, Neptune and Uranus on the 15th, Saturn on the 19th, and Venus on the 26th.

June 1—Jupiter at opposition.

June 5—Mercury at inferior conjunction; Mars 6° north of the moon.

June 9—Spica occulted by the moon.

June 12—Jupiter 2° south of the moon.

June 14—Jupiter 5° north of Antares.

June 15—Neptune 5° south of the moon; Uranus 6° south of the moon; Mercury 1.°2 north of Aldebaran.

June 17—Mercury stationary, resuming direct motion.

June 18—Mercury 1.°1 north of Aldebaran.

June 19—Venus 5° north of Aldebaran; Mercury 4° south of Venus; Saturn is 6° south of the moon.

June 20—Sun enters Gemini.

June 21—Summer solstice at 20:34 GMT, 15:34 EST; summer begins in the northern hemisphere.

June 26—Mercury occulted by the moon; Venus 3° north of the moon.

June 29—Mercury at greatest elongation, 22° west of the sun.

July

Mercury may be visible in the morning twilight early in the month before entering the glare of the sun for its superior conjunction on the 28th.

Venus finally disappears into the morning twilight, preparing for its superior conjunction next month.

Mars is now fainter than a 1st magnitude star, moving rapidly to the east among the constellations, leaving Leo for Virgo.

Jupiter is the very prominent object in the eastern evening sky.

Saturn brightens slightly because more of the sunlit side of the rings can be seen from the earth and because Saturn and the earth are getting closer together; Saturn begins its retrograde motion on the 7th.

Moon passes Mars on the 4th, Jupiter on the 9th, Neptune on the 12th, Uranus on the 13th, and Saturn on the 17th.

July 4—Earth at aphelion, 94.4 million miles from the sun; Mars 4° north of the moon.

July 7—Saturn stationary, beginning retrograde motion.

July 9—Jupiter 2° south of the moon.

July 12—Neptune 4° south of the moon.

July 13—Uranus 6° south of the moon.

July 17—Saturn 6° south of the moon; Neptune at opposition.

July 20—Sun enters Cancer.

July 21—Uranus at opposition.

July 28—Mercury at superior conjunction.

August

Mercury is too close to the western horizon after sunset all month for easy sighting.

Venus is lost to sight all month, passing superior conjunction on the 21st.

Mars, nearly 1.4 magnitude, hovers between Jupiter and the western horizon all month.

Jupiter remains the bright evening star all month, resuming its direct motion on the 2d.

Saturn rises in the evening a few hours after sunset, a bit brighter than 1st magnitude.

Moon passes Mars on the 1st, Jupiter on the 5th, Neptune and Uranus on the 9th, Saturn on the 13th, Mercury on the 28th, and occults Mars on the 30th.

Aug. 1—Mars 2° north of the moon.

Aug. 2—Jupiter stationary.

Aug. 5—Jupiter 2° south of the moon.

Aug. 9—Neptune 5° south of the moon; Uranus 6° south of the moon; Mercury 1.°1 north of Regulus.

Aug. 10—Earth passes south to north through the plane of Saturn's rings, which become virtually invisible from the earth; sun enters Leo.

Aug. 11—Watch for Perseid meteor shower tonight and tomorrow night.

Aug. 12—Pluto stationary, resuming direct motion.

Aug. 13—Saturn 5° south of the moon.

Aug. 21—Venus in superior conjunction.

Aug. 27—Mars 2° north of Spica.

Aug. 28—Mercury 1.°8 north of the moon.

Aug. 30—Mars 0.°2 north of the moon for an occultation.

September

Mercury is at greatest eastern elongation from the sun on the 9th, but not in favorable viewing position.

Venus is lost in the glare of the sun all month.

Mars is still about halfway to the horizon, below Jupiter in the evening twilight, moving into Libra this month.

Saturn is at opposition on the 14th, a little brighter than 1st magnitude without the ring display to add to its glow.

Moon passes Jupiter on the 2d, Neptune and Uranus on the 5th, Saturn on the 9th, Mercury on the 25th, Mars on the 27th, and Jupiter again on the 29th.

Sep. 2—Jupiter is 2° south of the moon.

Sep. 5—Neptune is 5° south of the moon, and Uranus is 6° south of the moon.

Sep. 9—Mercury at greatest elongation, 27° east of the sun; Saturn is 6° south of the moon.

Sep. 14—Saturn at opposition.

Sep. 16—Sun enters Virgo.

Sep. 20—Jupiter 5° north of Antares.

Sep. 22—Mercury stationary, beginning its retrograde motion.

Sep. 23—Autumnal equinox at 12:13 GMT, 7:13 AM EST; fall begins in the northern hemisphere.

Sep. 25—Mercury is 3° south of the moon.

Sep. 27—Mars is 2° south of the moon.

Sep. 28—Mercury is 5° south of Venus.

Sep. 29—Jupiter is 3° south of the moon.

October

Mercury, after passing inferior conjunction on the 5th, may be visible just before sunrise toward the end of the month, when it passes north of Spica.

Venus slowly makes its way into the evening sky by mid-month.

Mars, by month's end having moved into Scorpius, looks like a moderately bright star lying between brilliant Jupiter, above, and dazzling Venus, closer to the western horizon.

Jupiter is gradually supplanted as the evening star when Venus becomes more prominent by the end of the month.

Saturn begins to fade slightly as it and the earth move apart.

Moon passes Neptune on the 2d, Uranus on the 3d, Saturn on the 6th, is in penumbral eclipse on the 8th, passes Mercury on the 22d, totally eclipses the sun on the 24th, passes Venus on the 25th, Mars on the 26th, Jupiter on the 27th, Neptune on the 29th, and Uranus on the 30th.

Oct. 2—Neptune is 5° south of the moon.

Oct. 3—Uranus is 6° south of the moon.

Oct. 4—Venus is 3° north of Spica.

Oct. 5—Neptune stationary, resuming direct motion; Mercury in inferior conjunction.

Oct. 6—Uranus stationary, resuming direct motion; Saturn 6° south of the moon.

Oct. 8—Penumbral eclipse of the moon.

Oct. 13—Mercury stationary, resuming direct motion.

Oct. 20—Mercury at greatest elongation, 18° west of the sun.

Oct. 21—Orionid meteor shower.

Oct. 22—Mercury 4° north of the moon.

Oct. 24—Total solar eclipse.

Oct. 25—Venus 1.°9 south of moon.

Oct. 26—Mars 4° south of the moon.

Oct. 27—Jupiter 4° south of the moon.

Oct. 29—Neptune 5° south of the moon.

Oct. 30—Uranus 6° south of the moon; Mercury 4° north of Spica; sun enters Libra.

November

Mercury is lost to view all month, passing superior conjunction on the 23d.

Venus passes close to Jupiter on the 19th and close to Mars on the 22d.

Mars passes close to Jupiter on the 16th and close to Venus on the 22d.

Jupiter passes close to Mars on the 16th and close to Venus on the 19th.

Saturn is stationary on the 22d, resuming direct motion.

Moon passes Saturn on the 3d, Jupiter, Mars, and Venus on the 24th, Neptune and Uranus on the 26th, and Saturn on the 30th.

Nov. 2—Mars 4° north of Antares.

Nov. 3—Saturn 6° south of the moon.

Nov. 10—Venus 4° north of Antares.

Nov. 16—Mars 1.°2 south of Jupiter.

Nov. 17—Leonid meteor shower.

Nov. 19—Venus 1.°3 south of Jupiter.

Nov. 22—Saturn stationary; Venus 0.°2 south of Mars; sun enters Scorpius.

Nov. 23—Mercury in superior conjunction; Pluto in conjunction with the sun.

Nov. 24—Jupiter 4° south of the moon; Mars 5° south of the moon; Venus 6° south of the moon.

Nov. 26—Neptune 5° south of the moon; Uranus 6° south of the moon.

Nov. 29—Sun enters Ophiuchus.

Nov. 30—Saturn 6° south of the moon.

December

Mercury is still in the evening glare of the sun until the last part of the month, when it passes close to Mars and then close to Neptune.

Venus, for many people, can take on the role of Christmas star, being the only bright starlike object in the low western sky of evening, but may provide a pointer to Neptune and Uranus, which it passes this month.

Mars, looking fainter than a 1st magnitude star, will become difficult to see, low in the evening twilight in Sagittarius.

Jupiter is gone for the month, passing conjunction on the 18th.

Saturn, another 1st magnitude star, may still be seen in the west to northwest after sunset.

Moon passes Mercury, Mars, and Neptune on the 23d, Uranus and Venus on the 24th, and Saturn on the 27th.

Dec. 13—Geminid meteor shower.

Dec. 16—Venus passes 2° south of Neptune; sun enters Sagittarius.

Dec. 18—Jupiter in conjunction.

Dec. 20—Venus passes 1.°3 south of Uranus.

Dec. 22—Winter solstice at 8:17 GMT, 3:17 AM EST; winter begins in the northern hemisphere.

Dec. 23—Mercury is 7° south of the moon; Mars is 6° south of the moon; Mercury is 1.°1 south of Mars; Neptune is 5° south of the moon.

Dec. 24—Uranus is 6° south of the moon; Venus is 7° south of the moon.

Dec. 27—Saturn is 5° south of the moon.

Dec. 28—Mercury is 2° south of Neptune.

Planets and the Sun

The planets of the solar system, in order of their mean distance from the sun, are Mercury, Venus, the earth, Mars, Jupiter, Saturn, Uranus, Neptune, and Pluto. Both Uranus and Neptune are visible through good field glasses, but Pluto is so distant and so small that only large telescopes or long-exposure photographs can make it visible.

Because Mercury and Venus are nearer to the sun than is the earth, their motions about the sun are seen from the earth as wide swings first to one side of the sun and then to the other, although they are both passing continuously around the sun in orbits that are almost circular. When their passage takes them either between the earth and the sun or beyond the sun as seen from the earth, they are invisible to us. Because of the laws that govern the motions of planets about the sun, both Mercury and Venus require much less time to pass between the earth and the sun than around the far side of the sun; so their periods of visibility and invisibility are unequal.

The planets that lie farther from the sun than does the earth may be seen for longer periods of time and are invisible only when they are so located in our sky that they rise and set at about the same time as the sun, when, of course, they are overwhelmed by the sun's great brilliance. None of the planets has any light of its own; each shines only by reflecting sunlight from its surface. Mercury and Venus, because they are between the earth and the sun, show phases very much as the moon does. The planets farther from the sun are always seen as full, although Mars does occasionally present a slightly gibbous phase — like the moon when not quite full.

The planets move rapidly among the stars because they are very much nearer to us. The stars are also in motion, some of them at tremendous speeds, but they are so far away that their motion does not change their apparent positions in the heavens sufficiently for anyone to perceive that change in a single lifetime. The very nearest star is about 7,000 times as far away as the most distant planet.

Planets of the Solar System

Mercury

Mercury, the nearest planet to the sun, is the second smallest of the 9 planets known to be orbiting the sun. Its diameter is 3,100 miles, and its mean distance from the sun is 36,000,000 miles.

Mercury moves with great speed in its journey about the sun, averaging about 30 miles a second to complete its circuit in 88 of our days. Mercury rotates upon its axis over a period of nearly 59 days, thus exposing all its surface periodically to the sun. It is believed that the surface passing before the sun may have a temperature of about 800° F. and that the temperature on the side turned temporarily away from the sun does not fall as low as might be expected. This night temperature has been described by Russian astronomers as "room temperature" — possibly about 70° F. This would contradict the former belief that Mercury did not possess an atmosphere, for some sort of atmosphere would be needed to retain the fierce solar radiation that strikes Mercury. A shallow but dense layer of carbon dioxide would produce the "greenhouse" effect, in which heat accumulated during exposure to the sun would not completely escape at night. The actual presence of a carbon dioxide atmosphere is in dispute. Other research, however, has indicated a nighttime temperature approaching –300° F.

This uncertainty about conditions on Mercury and its motion arise from its shorter angular distance from the sun as seen from the earth. Mercury is always too much in line with the sun to be observed against a dark sky, but is always seen during either morning or evening twilight.

Mariner 10 passed Mercury 3 times in 1974 and 1975. A large fraction of the surface was photographed from varying distances, revealing a degree of cratering similar to that of the moon. An atmosphere of hydrogen and helium may be made up of gases of the solar wind temporarily concentrated by the presence of Mercury. The discovery of a weak but permanent magnetic field was a surprise. It has been held that both a fluid core and rapid rotation were necessary for the generation of a planetary magnetic field. Mercury may demonstrate these conditions to be unnecessary, or the field may reveal something about the history of Mercury.

Venus

Venus, slightly smaller than the earth, moves about the sun at a mean distance of 67,000,000 miles in 225 of our days. Its synodical revolution — its return to the same relationship with the earth and the sun, which is a result of the combination of its own motion with that of the earth — is 584 days. Every 19 months, then, Venus will be nearer to the earth than any other planet in the solar system. The planet is covered with a dense, white, cloudy atmosphere that conceals whatever is below it. This same cloud reflects sunlight efficiently so that when Venus is favorably situated it is the third brightest object in the sky, exceeded only by the sun and the moon.

Spectral analysis of sunlight reflected from Venus's cloud tops has shown features that can best be explained by identifying material of the clouds as sulfuric acid (oil of vitriol). Infrared spectroscopy from a balloon-borne telescope nearly 20 miles above the earth's surface gave indications of a small amount of water vapor present in the same region of the atmosphere of Venus. In 1956, radio astronomers at the Naval Research Laboratories in Washington, D.C., found a temperature for Venus of about 600° F., in marked contrast to –125° F. previously found at the cloud tops. Subsequent radio work confirmed a high temperature and produced evidence for this temperature to be associated with the solid body of Venus. With this peculiarity in mind, space scientists devised experiments for the U.S. space probe *Mariner 2* to perform when it flew by in 1962. *Mariner 2* confirmed the high temperature and the fact that it pertained to the ground rather than to some special activity of the atmosphere. In addition, *Mariner 2* was unable to detect the existence of a magnetic field even as weak as 1/100,000 of that of the earth.

In 1967, a Russian space probe, *Venera 4*, and the American *Mariner 5* arrived at Venus within a few hours of each other. *Venera 4* was designed to allow an instrument package to land gently on the surface via parachute. It ceased to transmit information in about 75 minutes when its temperature reading went above 500° F. After considerable controversy, it was agreed that the instrument package still had 20 miles to go to reach the surface. *Mariner 5* went around the dark side of Venus at a distance of about 6,000 miles. Again, it detected no significant field, but its radio signals passed to earth through Venus's atmosphere twice —once on the night side and once on the day side. The results were startling. Venus's atmosphere is nearly all carbon dioxide and must exert a pressure at the planet's surface of as much as 100 times the earth's normal sea-level pressure of one atmosphere. Because the earth and Venus are about the same size and were presumably formed at the same time, by the same general process and from the same mixture of chemical elements, one is faced with the question: Which is the planet with the unusual history—the earth or Venus?

Radar astronomers using powerful transmitters as well as sensitive receivers and computers succeeded in determining the rotation period of Venus. It turns out to be 243 days clockwise—in other words, contrary to the spin of the other planets and to its own motion around the sun. If it were exactly 243.16 days, Venus would present the same face toward the earth at every inferior conjunction. This rate and sense of rotation allows a "day" on Venus of 117.4 earth days. Any part of Venus will receive sunlight on its clouds for more than 58 days and will be in darkness for 58 days. Earth-based radar observations have shown surface features below the clouds. Large craters, continent-sized highlands, and extensive, dry "ocean" basins were identified.

Mariner 10 passed Venus before traveling on to Mercury in 1974. The carbon dioxide molecule found in such abundance in the atmosphere is rather opaque to certain ultraviolet wavelengths, enabling sensitive television cameras to photograph the Venusian cloud cover. Photos radioed to earth showed a spiral pattern in the clouds from the equator to the poles.

In Dec. 1978, two U.S. *Pioneer* probes arrived at Venus. One went into orbit around Venus; the other split into 5 separate probes targeted for widely spaced entry points to sample different conditions. The instrument ensemble was selected on the basis of previous missions that had shown the range of conditions to be studied. The probes confirmed expected high surface temperatures and high winds aloft. Winds of about 200 miles per hour there may account for the transfer of heat into the night side despite the low rotation speed of the planet. Surface winds were light at the time, however. Atmosphere and cloud chemistries were examined in detail, providing much data for continued analysis. The probes detected 4 layers of clouds and more light on the surface than expected solely from sunlight. This light allowed Russian scientists to obtain at least 2 photos of rocks on the surface. Sulphur seems to play a large role in the chemistry of Venus, and reactions involving sulphur may be responsible for the glow. To learn more about the weather and atmospheric circulation on Venus, the orbiter took daily photos of the daylight-side cloud cover. It confirmed the cloud pattern and its circulation shown by *Mariner 10*. The ionosphere showed large variability. The orbiter's radar operated in 2 modes: one for ground elevation variability, and the second for ground reflectivity in 2 dimensions, thus "imaging" the surface. Radar maps of the entire planet showing the large features mentioned above were produced.

The Venus orbiter *Magellan* was launched May 5, 1989. It was equipped to observe Venus by a side-scanning radar system, together with one to gather data on the variations in elevations directly beneath the craft. *Magellan* mapped all but a small fraction of the planet. The side-looking radar illuminates the surface and its features with radio waves and records the strength and distance of the returning echoes. Computer processing produces what seems to be a view of the landscape as if seen through a clear atmosphere from above, near sunset, with a resolution better than about 500 feet on Venus. Information on vertical relief has a resolution of about 30 feet.

Craters more than 20 miles wide are believed to have been caused by impacting bodies. One 150-mile-wide crater has been named for Margaret Mead. Smaller craters are probably the result of volcanic action. One such caldera has been named Sakajawea. Many lava flows have been seen, and some old craters and plains seem to be filled with lava.

Most of the surface is believed to be younger than 1 billion to 500 million years old. Modifications of previously existing surface features have been caused by tectonic actions such as faulting and by weathering. Tectonic actions on Venus in general are distinctly different from such actions on earth. The intense heat at the surface of Venus can prevent the surface materials from cooling to the same brittle condition as on earth. The same actions may produce somewhat different results on earth than they would on Venus. No activity on Venus seems to be similar to the earth's moving tectonic plates, but local stretching and compressing may produce rift valleys and higher plains and mountains. Although no weathering is due to water on Venus, the action of the winds is in evidence. Extensive sand dunes have been seen, and windblown deposits indicate stable wind patterns for very long periods of time. Although there are deep regions, somewhat similar to earth's ocean basins, there is no water to fill them.

The tremendous amount of information about the topography of Venus's surface obtained by *Magellan* will keep teams of analysts and theoreticians busy for years. The orbit of *Magellan* has been adjusted to a nearly circular shape about 300 miles from the planet's surface. In this mode, variation in its orbital speed reveals information on irregularities in the gravitational field presumably due to details in the internal structure of the planet.

Mars

Mars is the first planet beyond the earth, away from the sun. Mars's diameter is about 4,200 miles, although a determination of the radius and mass of Mars by the space probe *Mariner 4*, which flew by Mars at a distance of less than 6,000 miles on July 14, 1965, indicated that these dimensions were slightly larger than had been previously estimated. Although Mars's orbit is nearly circular, it is somewhat more eccentric than the orbits of many of the other planets, and Mars is more than 30 million miles farther from the sun in some parts of its year than it is at others. Mars takes 687 of our days to make one circuit of the sun, traveling at about 15 miles a second. Mars rotates upon its axis in almost the same period of time that the earth does — 24 hours and 37 minutes. Mars's mean distance from the sun is 141 million miles; so the temperature on Mars would be lower than that on the earth even if Mars's atmosphere were about the same as ours. The atmosphere is not, however, for *Mariner 4* reported that atmospheric pressure on Mars is between 1% and 2% of the earth's atmospheric pressure. This thin atmosphere appears to be largely carbon dioxide. No evidence of free water was found.

There appears to be no magnetic field about Mars. This would eliminate the previous conception of a dangerous radiation belt around Mars. The same lack of a magnetic field would expose the surface of Mars to an influx of cosmic radiation about 100 times as intense as that on earth.

Deductions from years of telescopic observation indicate that 5/8 of the surface of Mars is a desert of reddish rock, sand, and soil. The rest of Mars is covered by irregular patches that appear generally green in hues that change through the Martian year. These were formerly held to be some sort of primitive vegetation, but with the findings of *Mariner 4* of a complete lack of water and oxygen, such growth does not appear possible. The nature of the green areas is now unknown. They may be regions covered with volcanic salts whose color changes with changing temperatures and atmospheric conditions, or they may be gray rather than green. When large gray areas are placed beside large red areas, the gray areas appear green to the eye.

Mars's axis of rotation is inclined from a vertical to the plane of its orbit about the sun by about 25°, and therefore Mars has seasons as does the earth, except that the Martian seasons are longer because Mars's year is longer. White caps form about the winter pole of Mars, growing in the winter and shrinking in the summer. These polar caps are now believed to be both water ice and carbon dioxide ice. It is the carbon dioxide that is seen to come and go with the seasons. The water ice is apparently in many layers with dust between them, indicating climatic cycles.

The canals of Mars have become more of a mystery than they were before the voyage of *Mariner 4*. Markings forming a network of fine lines crossing much of the surface of Mars have been seen there by those who have devoted much time to the study of the planet, but no canals have shown clearly enough in previous photographs to be universally accepted. A few of the 21 photographs sent back to earth by *Mariner 4* covered areas crossed by canals. The pictures show faint, ill-defined, broad, dark markings, but no positive identification of the nature of the markings.

Mariners 6 and *7* in 1969 sent back many more photographs of higher quality than those of the pioneering *Mariner 4*. These pictures showed cratering similar to the earlier views, but in addition showed 2 other types of terrain. Some regions seemed featureless for many square miles, but others were chaotic, showing high relief without apparent organization into mountain chains or craters.

Mariner 9, the first artificial body to be placed in an orbit about Mars, has transmitted more than 10,000 photographs covering 100% of the planet's surface. Preliminary study of these photos and other data shows that Mars resembles no other planet we know. Using terrestrial terms, however, scientists describe features that seem to be clearly of volcanic origin. One of these features is Nix Olympica (now called Olympus Mons), apparently a shield volcano whose caldera is more than 50 miles wide, whose outer slopes are more than 300 miles in diameter, and which stands about 90,000 feet above the surrounding plain. Some features may have been produced by cracking (faulting) of the surface and the sliding of one region over or past another. Many craters seem to have been produced by impacting bodies that may have come from the nearby asteroid belt. Features near the south pole may have been produced by glaciers that are no longer present. Flowing water, nonexistent on Mars at the present time, probably carved canyons, one 10 times longer and 3 times deeper than the Grand Canyon.

Although the Russians landed a probe on the Martian surface, it transmitted for only 20 seconds. In 1976, the U.S. landed 2 *Viking* spacecraft on the Martian surface. The landers had devices aboard to perform chemical analyses of the soil in search of evidence of life. The results have been inconclusive. The 2 *Viking* orbiters have returned the best pictures yet of Martian topographic features. Many features can be explained only if Mars once had large quantities of flowing water.

Mars's position in its orbit and its speed around that orbit in relation to the earth's position and speed bring Mars fairly close to the earth on occasions about 2 years apart and then move Mars and the earth too far apart for accurate observation and photography. Every 15-17 years, the close approaches are especially favorable to close observation.

Mars has 2 satellites, discovered in 1877 by Asaph Hall. The outer satellite, Deimos, revolves around Mars in about 31 hours. The inner satellite, Phobos, whips around Mars in a little more than 7 hours, making 3 trips around the planet each Martian day. *Mariner* and *Viking* photos show these bodies to be irregularly shaped and pitted with numerous craters. Phobos also shows a system of linear grooves, each about 1/3 mile across and roughly parallel. Phobos measures about 8 by 12 miles and Deimos about 5 by 7.5 miles.

Jupiter

Jupiter is the largest of the planets. Its equatorial diameter is 88,000 miles, 11 times the diameter of the earth. Its polar diameter is about 6,000 miles shorter. This is an equilibrium condition resulting from the liquidity of the planet and its extremely rapid rate of rotation: a Jupiter day is only 10 earth hours long. For a planet this size, this rotational speed is amazing, and it moves a point on Jupiter's equator at a speed of 22,000 miles an hour, as compared with 1,000 miles an hour for a point on the earth's equator. Jupiter is at an average distance of 480 million miles from the sun and takes almost 12 of our years to make one complete circuit of the sun.

The major observable chemical constituents of Jupiter's atmosphere are methane (CH_4) and ammonia (NH_3), but it is reasonable to assume the same mixture of elements available to make Jupiter as to make the sun. This would mean a large fraction of hydrogen and helium must be present also, as well as water (H_2O). The temperature at the tops of the clouds may be about –260° F. The clouds are probably ammonia ice crystals, becoming ammonia droplets lower down. There may be a space before water ice crystals show up as clouds: in turn, these become water droplets near the bottom of the entire cloud layer. The total atmosphere may be only a few hundred miles in depth, pulled down by the surface gravity (= 2.64 times earth's) to a relatively thin layer. Of course, the gases become denser with depth until they may turn into a slush or a slurry. Perhaps there is no surface — no real interface between the gaseous atmosphere and the body of Jupiter. *Pioneers 10* and *11* provided evidence for considering Jupiter almost entirely liquid hydrogen. Long before a rocky core about the size of the earth is reached, hydrogen mixed with helium becomes a liquid metal at very high temperature and pressure. Jupiter's cloudy atmosphere is a fairly good reflector of sunlight and makes it appear far brighter than any of the stars.

Fourteen of Jupiter's 17 or more satellites have been found through earth-based observations. Four of the moons are large and bright, rivaling the earth's moon and the planet Mercury in diameter, and may be seen through a field glass. They move rapidly around Jupiter, and their change of position from night to night is extremely interesting to watch. The other satellites are much smaller and in all but one instance much farther from Jupiter and cannot be seen except through powerful telescopes. The 4 outermost satellites are revolving around Jupiter clockwise as seen from the north, contrary to the motions of the great majority of the satellites in the solar system and to the direction of revolution of the planets around the sun. The reason for this retrograde motion is not known, but one theory is that Jupiter's tremendous gravitational power may have captured 4 of the minor planets or asteroids that move about the sun between Mars and Jupiter and that these would necessarily revolve backward. At the great distance of these bodies from Jupiter — some 14 million miles — direct motion would result in decay of the orbits, while retrograde orbits would be stable. Jupiter's mass is more than twice the mass of all the other planets put together, which accounts for Jupiter's tremendous gravitational field and so, probably, for its numerous satellites and its dense atmosphere.

In Dec. 1973, *Pioneer 10* passed about 80,000 miles from the equator of Jupiter and was whipped into a path that would take it beyond the system of planets on June 13, 1983, and out of the earth's solar system in about 50 years. In Dec. 1974, *Pioneer 11* passed within 30,000 miles of Jupiter, moving roughly from south to north, over the poles.

Photographs from both encounters were useful at the time but were far surpassed by those of *Voyagers I* and *II*, both of which were launched in 1977 and rendezvoused with Jupiter in 1979. Thousands of high-resolution multicolor pictures show rapid variations of features both large and small. The Great Red Spot exhibits its internal counterclockwise rotation. Much turbulence is seen in adjacent material passing north or south of it. The satellites Amalthea, Io, Europa, Ganymede, and Callisto were photographed, some in great detail. Each is individual and unique, with no similarities to other known planets or satellites. Io has active volcanoes that probably have ejected material into a doughnut-shaped ring enveloping its orbit about Jupiter. This is not to be confused with the thin flat disklike ring closer to Jupiter's surface.

Beginning July 6, 1994, the 21 large fragments of the comet Shoemaker-Levy 9 collided with Jupiter in a dramatic 6-day barrage. Moving at 134,000 mph, stretched out like a 21-car freight train, the fragments impacted one after another against the side of Jupiter facing away from the earth. The high speed of the planet's rotation, allowing the impact sites to rotate quickly into view, along with the sheer scope of the reactions provided a show unprecedented in astronomy. Massive plumes of gas erupted from the impact sites, forming brilliant fireballs and leaving dark blotches and smears behind. For example, one of the largest chunks, labeled the G fragment, impacted with the force of 6 million megatons of TNT, 100,000 times the power of the largest nuclear bomb ever detonated. It produced a plume 1,200-1,600 miles high and 5,000 miles wide and left a dark discoloration larger than the earth. These impacts, predicted a year in advance, were closely observed and produced a massive amount of data for scientists and astronomers to analyze, even as they continue to observe Jupiter for the event's aftermath.

Saturn

Saturn, last of the planets visible to the unaided eye, is almost twice as far from the sun as Jupiter, almost 900 million miles. It is second in size to Jupiter, but its mass is much smaller. Saturn's specific gravity is less than that of water. Its diameter is about 71,000 miles at the equator; its rotational speed spins it completely around in a little more than 10 hours, and its atmosphere is much like that of Jupiter, except that its temperature at the top of its cloud layer is at least 100° F. lower. At about 300° F. below zero, the ammonia would be frozen out of Saturn's clouds. The theoretical construction of Saturn resembles that of Jupiter; it is either all gas, or it has a small dense center surrounded by a layer of liquid and a deep atmosphere.

Until *Pioneer 11* passed Saturn in Sept. 1979, only 10 satellites of the planet were known. Data retrieved since that time have confused scientists. Added to data interpretations from the fly-by are earth-based observations using techniques employed while the rings were edge-on and virtually invisible. It was hoped that the *Voyager I* and *II* fly-bys would help scientists sort out the satellite system, but it is still not entirely understood. It is now believed that Saturn has at least 22 satellites, some sharing orbits.

Saturn's ring system begins about 7,000 miles above the visible disk of Saturn, lying above its equator and extending about 35,000 miles into space. The diameter of the ring system visible from earth is about 170,000 miles; the rings are estimated to be no thicker than 10 miles. In 1973, radar observation showed the ring particles to be large chunks of material averaging a meter on a side.

Voyager I and *II* observations showed the rings to be considerably more complex than had been believed, so much so that interpretation will take much time. To the untrained eye, the *Voyager* photographs could be mistaken for pictures of a colorful phonograph record.

Uranus

Voyager II, after passing Saturn in Aug. 1981, headed for a rendezvous with Uranus, culminating in a fly-by Jan. 24, 1986. This encounter answered many questions and raised others.

Uranus, discovered by Sir William Herschel on Mar. 13, 1781, lies at a distance of 1.8 billion miles from the sun, taking 84 years to make its circuit around our star. Uranus has a diameter of about 32,000 miles and spins once in some 16.8 hours, according to fly-by data. One of the most fascinating features of Uranus is how far over it is tipped. Its north pole lies 98° from being directly up and down to its orbit plane. Thus, its seasons are extreme. When the sun rises at the north pole, it stays up for 42 years; then it sets, and the north pole is in darkness (and winter) for 42 years.

The satellite system of Uranus consists of at least 15 moons (the 5 largest having been known before the fly-by), which have orbits lying in the plane of the planet's equator. In that plane there is also a complex of rings, 9 of which were discovered in 1978. Invisible from earth, the 9 original rings were found by observers watching Uranus pass before a star. As they waited, they saw their photoelectric equipment register several short eclipses of the star; then the planet occulted the star as expected. After the star came out from behind Uranus, the star winked out several more times. Subsequent observations and analyses indicated the 9 narrow, nearly opaque rings circling Uranus. Evidence from the *Voyager II* fly-by has shown the ring particles to be predominantly a yard or so in diameter.

In addition to the 10 new, very small satellites, *Voyager II* returned detailed photos of the 5 large satellites. As in the case of other satellites newly observed in the *Voyager* program, these bodies proved to be entirely different from one another and from any others. Miranda has grooved markings, reminiscent of Jupiter's Ganymede, but often arranged in a chevron pattern. Ariel shows rifts and channels. Umbriel is extremely dark, prompting some observers to regard its surface as among the oldest in the system. Titania has rifts and fractures, but not the evidence of flow found on Ariel. Oberon's main feature is its surface saturated with craters, unrelieved by other formations.

The structure of Uranus is subject to some debate. Basically, however, it may have a rocky core surrounded by a thick icy mantle on top of which is a crust of hydrogen and helium that gradually becomes an atmosphere. Perhaps continued analysis of the wealth of data returned by *Voyager II* will shed some light on this problem.

Neptune

Neptune, currently the most distant planet from the sun (until 1999), lies at an average distance of 2.8 billion miles. It was the last planet visited in *Voyager II*'s epic 12-year trek (1977-89) from earth. Although much new information was immediately perceived, much more must await analysis of the tremendous amount of data returned from the spacecraft.

As with the other giant planets, Neptune may have no solid surface to give real meaning to a measure of a diameter. However, a mean value of 30,600 miles may be assigned to a diameter between atmosphere levels where the pressure is about the same as sea level on earth, as determined by radio experimenters. A different radio observational technique gave evidence of a rotation period for the bulk of Neptune of 16.1 hours, a shorter value than the 18.2 hours given by the clouds seen in the blue atmosphere. Neptune orbits the sun in 164 years in nearly a circular orbit.

Voyager II, which passed 3,000 miles from Neptune's north pole, found a magnetic field that is considerably asymmetric to the planet's structure, similar to, but not so extreme as, that found at Uranus.

Neptune's atmosphere was seen to be quite blue, with quickly changing white clouds often suspended high above an apparent surface. In that apparent surface were found features, one of which was reminiscent of the Great Red Spot of Jupiter, even to the counterclockwise rotation expected in a high-pressure system in the southern hemisphere. Atmospheric constituents are mostly hydrocarbon compounds. Although lightning and auroras have been found on other giant planets, only the aurora phenomenon has been seen on Neptune.

Six new satellites were discerned around Neptune, one confirming a 1981 sighting that was then difficult to recover for proper identification. Five of these satellites orbit Neptune in a half day or less. Of the 8 satellites of Neptune, the largest, Triton, is in a retrograde orbit suggesting that it was captured rather than being coeval with Neptune. Triton's large size, sufficient to raise significant tides on Neptune, will one day, say 100 million years from now, cause Triton to come close enough to Neptune for it to be torn apart. Nereid was found in 1949 and is in a long looping orbit suggesting that it too was captured. Each of the satellites that has been photographed by the 2 *Voyagers* in the planetary encounters has been different from any of the other satellites, and certainly different from any of the planets. Only about half of Triton has been observed, but its terrain shows cratering and a strange regional feature described as resembling the skin of a cantaloupe. Triton has a tenuous atmosphere of nitrogen with a trace of hydrocarbons and has evidence of active geysers injecting material into it. At –238 degrees Celsius, Triton is one of the coldest objects in the solar system observed by *Voyager II*.

In addition to the satellite system, *Voyager II* confirmed the existence of at least 3 rings composed of very fine particles. There may be some clumpiness in their structure, but the known satellites may not contribute to the formation or maintenance of the rings, as they have in other systems.

As with the other giant planets, Neptune is emitting more energy than it receives from the sun, *Voyager* finding the excess to be 2.7 times the solar contribution. These excesses are thought to be cooling from internal heat sources and from the heat of formation of the planets.

Pluto

Although Pluto on the average stays about 3.6 billion miles from the sun, its orbit is so eccentric that its minimum distance of 2.7 billion miles is less than the current distance of Neptune. Thus, Pluto, until 1999, is temporarily planet number 8 from the sun. At its mean distance, Pluto takes 247.7 years to circumnavigate the sun, a $^{3}/_{2}$ resonance with Neptune. Until recently, this was about all that was known of Pluto.

About a century ago, a hypothetical planet was believed to lie beyond Neptune and Uranus because neither planet followed the paths predicted by astronomers even when all known gravitational influences were considered. Little more than a guess, a mass of one earth was assigned to the mysterious body, and mathematical searches were begun. Amid some controversy about the validity of the predictive process, Pluto was found nearly where it was predicted to be. It was found by Clyde Tombaugh at the Lowell Observatory in Flagstaff, AZ, in 1930.

At the U.S. Naval Observatory, also in Flagstaff, on

July 2, 1978, James Christy obtained a photograph of Pluto that was distinctly elongated. Repeated observations of this shape and its variation were convincing evidence of the discovery of a satellite of Pluto, now named Charon. Subsequent observations show it to be 750 miles across, at a distance of more than 12,000 miles from Pluto, and taking 6.4 days to move around Pluto. In this same length of time Pluto and Charon each rotate once around their individual axes. The Pluto-Charon system thus appears to rotate as virtually a ridged body. Gravitational laws allow these interactions to give the mass of Pluto as 0.0020 of the earth. This mass, together with a new diameter for Pluto of 1,430 miles, make the density about twice that of water. Theorists predict a rocky core for Pluto surrounded by a thick mantle of ice.

It is now clear that Pluto, the body found by Tombaugh, could not have influenced Neptune and Uranus to go astray. Theorists are again at work looking for a new planet X.

Because the rotational axis of the system is tipped from the reference plane of the solar system by about 98°.3, similar to that of Uranus, there is only a short interval every half solar period when Pluto and Charon alternately eclipse each other. Analysis of the variations in light in and out of the recent eclipses has led to the diameters quoted above and to interesting knowledge of other aspects of the system. Both components are approximately spherical, but they are otherwise different. Pluto is red, Charon gray. Charon's surface is identified as water ice; Pluto's surface is frozen methane. Large regions on Pluto are dark, others light; Pluto has spots and, perhaps, polar caps. Although extremely cold, Pluto's methane surface produces a tenuous atmosphere that may be slowly escaping into space, perhaps going to Charon. When Pluto occulted a star, the star's light faded in such a way as to have passed through a haze layer lying above the planet's surface, indicating an inversion of temperatures — 110°K above and 50°K below — suggesting Pluto has primitive weather.

There are tentative plans for a spacecraft reconnaissance of the Pluto system, thus completing direct, close-up observation of each planet of the solar system.

Greenwich Sidereal Time for 0^h GMT, 1995

(Add 12 hours to obtain Right Ascension of Mean Sun)

Date	d	h	m	Date	d	h	m	Date	d	h	m	Date	d	h	m
Jan.	1	06	40.7	Apr.	1	12	35.5	July	10	19	09.8	Oct.	8	01	06.5
	11	07	20.1		11	13	15.0		20	19	49.2		18	01	46.0
	21	07	59.6		21	13	54.4		30	20	28.7		28	02	25.4
	31	08	39.0	May	1	14	33.8	Aug.	9	21	08.1	Nov.	7	03	04.8
Feb.	10	09	18.4		11	15	13.2		19	21	47.5		17	03	44.2
	20	09	57.8		21	15	52.7		29	22	26.9		27	04	23.7
Mar.	2	10	37.3		31	16	32.1	Sept.	8	23	06.4	Dec.	7	05	03.1
	12	11	16.7	June	10	17	11.5		18	23	45.8		17	05	42.5
	22	11	56.1		20	17	51.0		28	00	25.2		27	06	21.9
					30	18	30.4								

Astronomical Signs and Symbols

☉	The Sun	⊕	The Earth	♅	Uranus	□	Quadrature
☽	The Moon	♂	Mars	♆	Neptune	☍	Opposition
☿	Mercury	♃	Jupiter	♇	Pluto	☊	Ascending Node
♀	Venus	♄	Saturn	☌	Conjunction	☋	Descending Node

Two heavenly bodies are in "conjunction" (☌) when they are due north and south of each other, either in Right Ascension (with respect to the north celestial pole) or in Celestial Longitude (with respect to the north ecliptic pole). If the bodies are seen near each other, they will rise and set at nearly the same time. They are in "opposition" (☍) when their Right Ascensions differ by exactly 12 hours, or when their Celestial Longitudes differ by 180°. One of the two objects in opposition will rise while the other is setting. "Quadrature" (□) refers to the arrangement when the coordinates of 2 bodies differ by exactly 90°. These terms may refer to the relative positions of any 2 bodies as seen from the earth, but one of the bodies is so frequently the sun that mention of the sun is omitted; otherwise, both bodies are named. The geocentric angular separation between sun and object is termed "elongation." Elongation is limited only for Mercury and Venus; the "greatest elongation" for each of these bodies is noted in the appropriate tables and is approximately the time for longest observation. When a planet is in its "ascending" (☊) or "descending" (☋) node, it is passing northward or southward, respectively, through the plane of the earth's orbit, across the celestial circle called the ecliptic. The term "perihelion" means nearest to the sun, and "aphelion," farthest from the sun. An "occultation" of a planet or a star is an eclipse of it by some other body, usually the moon.

Planetary Configurations, 1995

Greenwich Mean Time (0 designates midnight; 12 designates noon; ✳ = star; ☽ = moon)

Mo.	d.	h.	m.				
Jan.	2	02	-	☌	☿	♆	☿ 3° S
	4	01	-	☌	☿	♅	☿ 1°.7 S; ♂ Stationary
	4	11	-				⊕ closest to ☉; Perihelion
	5	17	-	☌	♄	☽	♄ 7° S
	13	12	-				♀ Gr. Elong; 47° W of ☉
	13	17	-	☌	♆	☉	
	14	09	-	☌	♀	♃	♀ 3° N
	15	22	-	☌	♀	✳	♀ 8° N of Antares
	17	00	-	☌	♅	☉	
	19	08	-				☿ Gr. Elong; 19° E of ☉
	19	19	-	☌	♂	☽	♂ 9° N
	23	01	-	☌	♃	✳	♃ 5° N of Antares
	23	11	-	☌	✳	☽	Spica 0°.6 S; Occultation
	25	12	-				☿ Stationary
	26	17	-	☌	♃	☽	♃ 1°.7 S
	27	12	-	☌	♀	☽	♀ 0°.2 S; Occultation
	28	18	-	☌	♂	✳	♂ 4° N of Regulus
	29	20	-	☌	♆	☽	♆ 4° S
Feb.	2	08	-	☌	♄	☽	♄ 6° S
	3	23	-	☌	☿	☉	Inferior Conj.
	11	14	-				♂ closest to ⊕
	12	03	-	☍	♂	☉	
	15	10	-	☌	♂	☽	♂ 10° N
	15	19	-				☿ Stationary
	19	17	-	☌	☽	✳	Spica 0°.9 S; Occultation
	23	05	-	☌	♃	☽	♃ 2° S

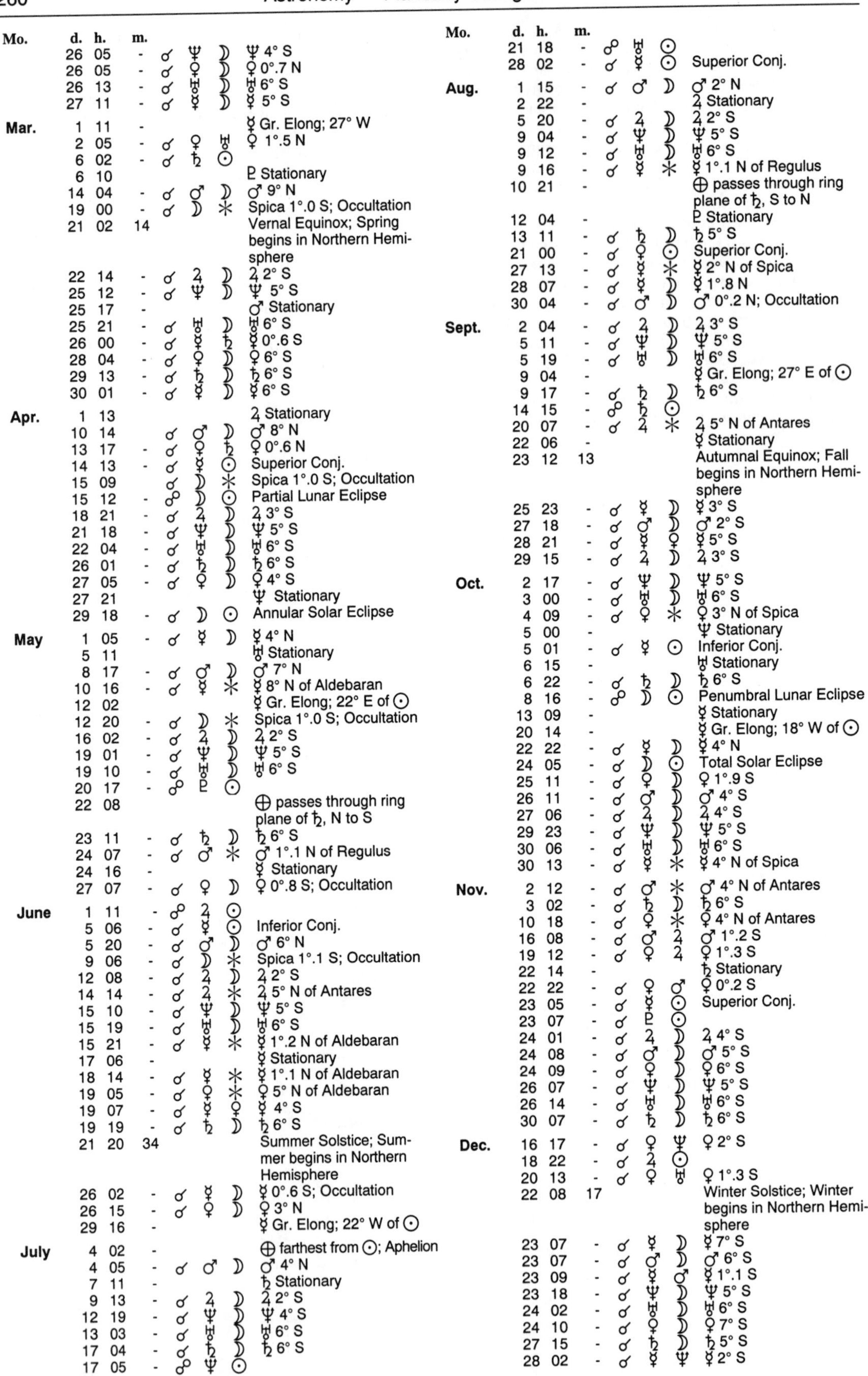

Mo.	d.	h.	m.				
	26	05	-	☌	♆	☽	♆ 4° S
	26	05	-	☌	♀	☽	♀ 0°.7 N
	26	13	-	☌	♅	☽	♅ 6° S
	27	11	-	☌	☿	☽	☿ 5° S
Mar.	1	11	-				☿ Gr. Elong; 27° W
	2	05	-	☌	♀	♅	♀ 1°.5 N
	6	02	-	☌	♄	☉	
	6	10					♇ Stationary
	14	04	-	☌	♂	☽	♂ 9° N
	19	00	-	☌	☽	✳	Spica 1°.0 S; Occultation
	21	02	14				Vernal Equinox; Spring begins in Northern Hemisphere
	22	14	-	☌	♃	☽	♃ 2° S
	25	12	-	☌	♆	☽	♆ 5° S
	25	17	-				♂ Stationary
	25	21	-	☌	♅	☽	♅ 6° S
	26	00	-	☌	☿	♄	☿ 0°.6 S
	28	04	-	☌	♀	☽	♀ 6° S
	29	13	-	☌	♄	☽	♄ 6° S
	30	01	-	☌	☿	☽	☿ 6° S
Apr.	1	13					♃ Stationary
	10	14		☌	♂	☽	♂ 8° N
	13	17	-	☌	♀	♄	♀ 0°.6 N
	14	13	-	☌	☿	☉	Superior Conj.
	15	09	-	☌	☽	✳	Spica 1°.0 S; Occultation
	15	12	-	☍	☽	☉	Partial Lunar Eclipse
	18	21	-	☌	♃	☽	♃ 3° S
	21	18	-	☌	♆	☽	♆ 5° S
	22	04	-	☌	♅	☽	♅ 6° S
	26	01	-	☌	♄	☽	♄ 6° S
	27	05	-	☌	♀	☽	♀ 4° S
	27	21					♆ Stationary
	29	18	-	☌	☽	☉	Annular Solar Eclipse
May	1	05	-	☌	☿	☽	☿ 4° N
	5	11					♅ Stationary
	8	17	-	☌	♂	☽	♂ 7° N
	10	16	-	☌	☿	✳	☿ 8° N of Aldebaran
	12	02					☿ Gr. Elong; 22° E of ☉
	12	20	-	☌	☽	✳	Spica 1°.0 S; Occultation
	16	02	-	☌	♃	☽	♃ 2° S
	19	01	-	☌	♆	☽	♆ 5° S
	19	10	-	☌	♅	☽	♅ 6° S
	20	17	-	☍	♇	☉	
	22	08					⊕ passes through ring plane of ♄, N to S
	23	11	-	☌	♄	☽	♄ 6° S
	24	07	-	☌	♂	✳	♂ 1°.1 N of Regulus
	24	16	-				☿ Stationary
	27	07	-	☌	♀	☽	♀ 0°.8 S; Occultation
June	1	11	-	☍	♃	☉	
	5	06	-	☌	☿	☉	Inferior Conj.
	5	20	-	☌	♂	☽	♂ 6° N
	9	06	-	☌	☽	✳	Spica 1°.1 S; Occultation
	12	08	-	☌	♃	☽	♃ 2° S
	14	14	-	☌	♃	✳	♃ 5° N of Antares
	15	10	-	☌	♆	☽	♆ 5° S
	15	19	-	☌	♅	☽	♅ 6° S
	15	21	-	☌	☿	✳	☿ 1°.2 N of Aldebaran
	17	06	-				☿ Stationary
	18	14	-	☌	☿	✳	☿ 1°.1 N of Aldebaran
	19	05	-	☌	♀	✳	♀ 5° N of Aldebaran
	19	07	-	☌	☿	♀	☿ 4° S
	19	19	-	☌	♄	☽	♄ 6° S
	21	20	34				Summer Solstice; Summer begins in Northern Hemisphere
	26	02	-	☌	☿	☽	☿ 0°.6 S; Occultation
	26	15	-	☌	♀	☽	♀ 3° N
	29	16	-				☿ Gr. Elong; 22° W of ☉
July	4	02	-				⊕ farthest from ☉; Aphelion
	4	05	-	☌	♂	☽	♂ 4° N
	7	11	-				♄ Stationary
	9	13	-	☌	♃	☽	♃ 2° S
	12	19	-	☌	♆	☽	♆ 4° S
	13	03	-	☌	♅	☽	♅ 6° S
	17	04	-	☌	♄	☽	♄ 6° S
	17	05	-	☍	♆	☉	
	21	18	-	☍	♅	☉	
	28	02	-	☌	☿	☉	Superior Conj.
Aug.	1	15	-	☌	♂	☽	♂ 2° N
	2	22	-				♃ Stationary
	5	20	-	☌	♃	☽	♃ 2° S
	9	04	-	☌	♆	☽	♆ 5° S
	9	12	-	☌	♅	☽	♅ 6° S
	9	16	-	☌	☿	✳	☿ 1°.1 N of Regulus
	10	21	-				⊕ passes through ring plane of ♄, S to N
	12	04	-				♇ Stationary
	13	11	-	☌	♄	☽	♄ 5° S
	21	00	-	☌	♀	☉	Superior Conj.
	27	13	-	☌	☿	✳	☿ 2° N of Spica
	28	07	-	☌	☿	☽	☿ 1°.8 N
	30	04	-	☌	♂	☽	♂ 0°.2 N; Occultation
Sept.	2	04	-	☌	♃	☽	♃ 3° S
	5	11	-	☌	♆	☽	♆ 5° S
	5	19	-	☌	♅	☽	♅ 6° S
	9	04	-				☿ Gr. Elong; 27° E of ☉
	9	17	-	☌	♄	☽	♄ 6° S
	14	15	-	☍	♄	☉	
	20	07	-	☌	♃	✳	♃ 5° N of Antares
	22	06	-				☿ Stationary
	23	12	13				Autumnal Equinox; Fall begins in Northern Hemisphere
	25	23	-	☌	☿	☽	☿ 3° S
	27	18	-	☌	♂	☽	♂ 2° S
	28	21	-	☌	☿	♀	☿ 5° S
	29	15	-	☌	♃	☽	♃ 3° S
Oct.	2	17	-	☌	♆	☽	♆ 5° S
	3	00	-	☌	♅	☽	♅ 6° S
	4	09	-	☌	♀	✳	♀ 3° N of Spica
	5	00	-				♆ Stationary
	5	01	-	☌	☿	☉	Inferior Conj.
	6	15	-				♅ Stationary
	6	22	-	☌	♄	☽	♄ 6° S
	8	16	-	☍	☽	☉	Penumbral Lunar Eclipse
	13	09	-				☿ Stationary
	20	14	-				☿ Gr. Elong; 18° W of ☉
	22	22	-	☌	☿	☽	☿ 4° N
	24	05	-	☌	☽	☉	Total Solar Eclipse
	25	11	-	☌	♀	☽	♀ 1°.9 S
	26	11	-	☌	♂	☽	♂ 4° S
	27	06	-	☌	♃	☽	♃ 4° S
	29	23	-	☌	♆	☽	♆ 5° S
	30	06	-	☌	♅	☽	♅ 6° S
	30	13	-	☌	☿	✳	☿ 4° N of Spica
Nov.	2	12	-	☌	♂	✳	♂ 4° N of Antares
	3	02	-	☌	♄	☽	♄ 6° S
	10	18	-	☌	♀	✳	♀ 4° N of Antares
	16	08	-	☌	♂	♃	♂ 1°.2 S
	19	12	-	☌	♀	♃	♀ 1°.3 S
	22	14	-				♄ Stationary
	22	22	-	☌	♀	♂	♀ 0°.2 S
	23	05	-	☌	☿	☉	Superior Conj.
	23	07	-	☌	♇	☉	
	24	01	-	☌	♃	☽	♃ 4° S
	24	08	-	☌	♂	☽	♂ 5° S
	24	09	-	☌	♀	☽	♀ 6° S
	26	07	-	☌	♆	☽	♆ 5° S
	26	14	-	☌	♅	☽	♅ 6° S
	30	07	-	☌	♄	☽	♄ 6° S
Dec.	16	17	-	☌	♀	♆	♀ 2° S
	18	22	-	☌	♃	☉	
	20	13	-	☌	♀	♅	♀ 1°.3 S
	22	08	17				Winter Solstice; Winter begins in Northern Hemisphere
	23	07	-	☌	☿	☽	☿ 7° S
	23	07	-	☌	♂	☽	♂ 6° S
	23	09	-	☌	☿	♂	☿ 1°.1 S
	23	18	-	☌	♆	☽	♆ 5° S
	24	02	-	☌	♅	☽	♅ 6° S
	24	10	-	☌	♀	☽	♀ 7° S
	27	15	-	☌	♄	☽	♄ 5° S
	28	02	-	☌	☿	♆	☿ 2° S

Rising and Setting of Planets, 1995

Greenwich Mean Time (0 designates midnight)

Venus, 1995

Date		20° N Latitude Rise	Set	30° N Latitude Rise	Set	40° N Latitude Rise	Set	50° N Latitude Rise	Set	60° N Latitude Rise	Set
Jan	1	3:09	14:28	3:22	14:15	3:39	13:59	4:01	13:36	4:36	13:01
	11	3:12	14:25	3:27	14:10	3:46	13:51	4:12	13:25	4:54	12:43
	21	3:18	14:25	3:35	14:08	3:56	13:47	4:26	13:18	5:14	12:29
	31	3:27	14:30	3:45	14:11	4:08	13:49	4:40	13:17	5:33	12:23
Feb	10	3:36	14:38	3:55	14:19	4:18	13:55	4:51	13:22	5:47	12:27
	20	3:45	14:48	4:04	14:29	4:27	14:06	4:59	13:34	5:53	12:40
Mar	2	3:53	15:00	4:10	14:43	4:32	14:22	5:01	13:52	5:50	13:03
	12	3:59	15:13	4:14	14:58	4:33	14:39	4:58	14:14	5:40	13:33
	22	4:03	15:26	4:15	15:14	4:30	14:59	4:50	14:39	5:23	14:07
Apr	1	4:04	15:39	4:13	15:30	4:24	15:19	4:39	15:05	5:02	14:43
	11	4:04	15:51	4:10	15:46	4:16	15:40	4:24	15:32	4:37	15:19
	21	4:03	16:03	4:05	16:02	4:06	16:01	4:08	15:59	4:11	15:56
May	1	4:02	16:15	3:59	16:18	3:56	16:21	3:51	16:26	3:44	16:34
	11	4:00	16:27	3:54	16:34	3:46	16:43	3:35	16:54	3:17	17:12
	21	4:00	16:41	3:50	16:51	3:37	17:04	3:19	17:23	2:51	17:52
	31	4:02	16:55	3:48	17:09	3:30	17:27	3:06	17:51	2:27	18:32
Jun	10	4:06	17:10	3:49	17:27	3:27	17:49	2:57	18:20	2:06	19:12
	20	4:13	10:49	17:25	17:45	3:29	18:10	2:53	18:46	1:51	19:49
	30	4:24	11:02	17:41	18:02	3:35	18:30	2:56	19:09	1:46	20:20
Jul	10	4:37	11:16	17:55	18:17	3:47	18:45	3:07	19:25	1:54	20:38
	20	4:52	11:30	18:08	18:29	4:04	18:55	3:26	19:34	2:17	20:42
	30	5:08	11:43	18:17	18:36	4:25	19:00	3:50	19:34	2:51	20:33
Aug	9	5:24	18:24	5:08	18:40	4:47	19:00	4:19	19:29	3:31	20:15
	19	5:40	18:28	5:27	18:40	5:11	18:56	4:49	19:18	4:13	19:52
	29	5:55	18:29	5:46	18:38	5:35	18:48	5:20	19:03	4:56	19:26
Sep	8	6:09	18:28	6:04	18:33	5:58	18:38	5:50	18:46	5:38	18:58
	18	6:22	18:27	6:22	18:27	6:21	18:28	6:20	18:28	6:19	18:29
	28	6:35	18:26	6:39	18:22	6:44	18:16	6:51	18:10	7:00	17:59
Oct	8	6:49	18:25	6:58	18:17	7:08	18:06	7:22	17:52	7:43	17:31
	18	7:04	18:26	7:17	18:14	7:32	17:58	7:53	17:37	8:26	17:04
	28	7:20	18:30	7:37	18:14	7:57	17:54	8:25	17:25	9:10	16:40
Nov	7	7:37	18:37	7:57	18:17	8:21	17:53	8:55	17:19	9:53	16:20
	17	7:55	18:47	8:17	18:25	8:44	17:58	9:23	17:19	10:32	16:10
	27	8:12	19:01	8:34	18:38	9:03	18:09	9:44	17:28	10:59	16:13
Dec	7	8:26	19:16	8:49	18:54	9:17	18:26	9:57	17:45	11:10	16:32
	17	8:38	19:33	8:59	19:12	9:25	18:46	10:02	18:10	11:06	17:05
	27	8:46	19:50	9:04	19:32	9:27	19:10	9:58	18:38	10:51	17:46

Mars, 1995

Date		20° N Latitude Rise	Set	30° N Latitude Rise	Set	40° N Latitude Rise	Set	50° N Latitude Rise	Set	60° N Latitude Rise	Set
Jan	1	21:16	10:04	21:04	10:16	20:49	10:32	20:28	10:53	19:54	11:27
	11	20:35	9:24	20:22	9:37	20:06	9:53	19:44	10:15	19:09	10:50
	21	19:47	8:40	19:34	8:54	19:17	9:11	18:53	9:35	18:15	10:13
	31	18:55	7:52	18:40	8:07	18:21	8:25	17:55	8:51	17:13	9:34
Feb	10	17:58	7:00	17:42	7:16	17:22	7:37	16:53	8:05	16:06	8:52
	20	17:01	6:07	16:44	6:25	16:22	6:46	15:51	7:17	14:59	8:09
Mar	2	16:07	5:16	15:49	5:34	15:26	5:57	14:54	6:29	13:58	7:24
	12	15:18	4:27	15:00	4:46	14:36	5:09	14:03	5:42	13:06	6:39
	22	14:35	3:44	14:16	4:02	13:53	4:25	13:20	4:58	12:24	5:55
Apr	1	13:57	3:04	13:39	3:22	13:17	3:45	12:45	4:17	11:50	5:11
	11	13:25	2:29	13:07	2:46	12:46	3:08	12:15	3:38	11:24	4:30
	21	12:56	1:57	12:40	2:13	12:19	2:33	11:51	3:02	11:03	3:49
May	1	12:30	1:27	12:15	1:42	11:56	2:01	11:30	2:27	10:47	3:10
	11	12:07	0:59	11:54	1:13	11:37	1:30	11:13	1:54	10:35	2:32
	21	11:46	0:33	11:34	0:45	11:19	1:00	10:58	1:21	10:25	1:55
	31	11:27	0:08	11:16	0:18	11:03	0:31	10:45	0:49	10:17	1:18
Jun	10	11:08	23:41	11:00	23:49	10:49	0:03	10:34	0:18	10:11	0:41
	20	10:51	23:17	10:44	23:24	10:36	23:32	10:24	23:44	10:06	0:05
	30	10:35	22:54	10:30	22:59	10:24	23:05	10:16	23:13	10:03	23:26
Jul	10	10:19	22:32	10:16	22:35	10:13	22:38	10:08	22:43	10:00	22:50
	20	10:04	22:10	10:04	22:11	10:03	22:11	10:01	22:13	9:59	22:15
	30	9:50	21:49	9:52	21:47	9:53	21:45	9:55	21:43	9:58	21:40
Aug	9	9:37	21:28	9:40	21:24	9:45	21:20	9:50	21:14	9:59	21:05
	19	9:24	21:08	9:30	21:02	9:37	20:55	9:46	20:45	10:01	20:31
	29	9:12	20:49	9:20	20:40	9:30	20:31	9:43	20:17	10:03	19:57
Sep	8	9:01	20:30	9:12	20:20	9:24	20:07	9:41	19:50	10:07	19:24
	18	8:51	20:13	9:04	20:01	9:19	19:45	9:39	19:24	10:12	18:52
	28	8:42	19:57	8:56	19:42	9:14	19:24	9:39	19:00	10:18	18:20
Oct	8	8:34	19:42	8:50	19:26	9:10	19:05	9:39	18:37	10:25	17:51
	18	8:26	19:29	8:44	19:10	9:07	18:48	9:39	18:16	10:32	17:23
	28	8:19	19:17	8:39	18:57	9:04	18:32	9:39	17:57	10:38	16:58
Nov	7	8:13	19:07	8:34	18:46	9:01	18:19	9:38	17:42	10:44	16:36
	17	8:07	18:58	8:29	18:36	8:57	18:08	9:36	17:29	10:46	16:19
	27	8:01	18:51	8:24	18:28	8:52	18:00	9:32	17:20	10:45	16:07
Dec	7	7:55	18:45	8:18	18:22	8:46	17:54	9:26	17:14	10:38	16:02
	17	7:48	18:40	8:10	18:18	8:38	17:50	9:17	17:11	10:26	16:02
	27	7:41	18:35	8:02	18:14	8:28	17:48	9:05	17:12	10:09	16:07

Jupiter, 1995

Date		20° N Latitude		30° N Latitude		40° N Latitude		50° N Latitude		60° N Latitude	
		Rise	Set	Rise	Set	Rise	Set	Rise	Set	Rise	Set
Jan	1	3:59	15:01	4:17	14:42	4:40	14:20	5:11	13:48	6:04	12:56
	11	3:28	14:29	3:47	14:10	4:10	13:47	4:42	13:15	5:36	12:21
	21	2:57	13:57	3:16	13:38	3:39	13:15	4:12	12:42	5:07	11:46
	31	2:25	13:24	2:44	13:05	3:08	12:41	3:41	12:08	4:38	11:12
Feb	10	1:53	12:51	2:12	12:31	2:36	12:07	3:09	11:34	4:07	10:36
	20	1:19	12:16	1:38	11:57	2:02	11:33	2:36	10:59	3:34	10:01
Mar	2	0:44	11:41	1:04	11:22	1:28	10:57	2:02	10:23	3:01	9:25
	12	0:08	11:05	0:28	10:45	0:52	10:21	1:27	9:47	2:25	8:48
	22	23:27	10:28	23:47	10:08	0:15	9:43	0:50	9:09	1:49	8:10
Apr	1	22:48	9:49	23:08	9:29	23:33	9:05	0:11	8:30	1:10	7:31
	11	22:08	9:09	22:28	8:49	22:52	8:25	23:27	7:51	0:30	6:52
	21	21:27	8:28	21:47	8:08	22:11	7:44	22:45	7:10	23:44	6:11
May	1	20:44	7:45	21:04	7:26	21:28	7:02	22:02	6:28	23:00	5:29
	11	20:01	7:02	20:20	6:43	20:44	6:19	21:18	5:45	22:16	4:47
	21	19:16	6:18	19:35	5:59	19:59	5:35	20:33	5:02	21:30	4:04
	31	18:31	5:34	18:50	5:15	19:14	4:51	19:47	4:18	20:44	3:21
Jun	10	17:46	4:49	18:05	4:31	18:29	4:07	19:02	3:34	19:57	2:38
	20	17:02	4:05	17:20	3:47	17:44	3:23	18:16	2:51	19:11	1:56
	30	16:18	3:22	16:36	3:03	17:00	2:40	17:32	2:08	18:26	1:13
Jul	10	15:35	2:39	15:53	2:21	16:16	1:58	16:48	1:26	17:43	0:32
	20	14:53	1:58	15:12	1:39	15:35	1:16	16:07	0:44	17:00	23:47
	30	14:13	1:17	14:31	0:59	14:54	0:36	15:26	0:04	16:20	23:06
Aug	9	13:34	0:38	13:52	0:20	14:15	23:53	14:47	23:21	15:41	22:27
	19	12:56	23:56	13:15	23:38	13:38	23:15	14:10	22:42	15:04	21:48
	29	12:20	23:19	12:38	23:01	13:02	22:37	13:34	22:05	14:29	21:10
Sep	8	11:45	22:44	12:03	22:25	12:27	22:01	13:00	21:28	13:56	20:33
	18	11:11	22:09	11:30	21:50	11:53	21:26	12:27	20:53	13:24	19:56
	28	10:37	21:35	10:57	21:16	11:21	20:52	11:55	20:18	12:53	19:20
Oct	8	10:05	21:02	10:25	20:43	10:49	20:18	11:24	19:44	12:23	18:45
	18	9:34	20:30	9:54	20:10	10:18	19:45	10:53	19:10	11:53	18:10
	28	9:03	19:58	9:23	19:38	9:48	19:13	10:24	18:38	11:25	17:36
Nov	7	8:33	19:27	8:53	19:07	9:18	18:41	9:54	18:06	10:57	17:03
	17	8:03	18:57	8:23	18:36	8:49	18:10	9:25	17:34	10:29	16:31
	27	7:33	18:27	7:54	18:06	8:20	17:40	8:57	17:03	10:01	15:59
Dec	7	7:04	17:57	7:25	17:36	7:51	17:10	8:28	16:33	9:33	15:28
	17	6:35	17:27	6:56	17:06	7:22	16:40	7:59	16:02	9:05	14:57
	27	6:05	16:57	6:26	16:36	6:53	16:10	7:30	15:33	8:36	14:27

Saturn, 1995

Date		20° N Rise	20° N Set	30° N Rise	30° N Set	40° N Rise	40° N Set	50° N Rise	50° N Set	60° N Rise	60° N Set
Jan	1	10:12	21:45	10:20	21:36	10:31	21:26	10:45	21:12	11:07	20:50
	11	9:35	21:09	9:43	21:01	9:54	20:51	10:07	20:37	10:28	20:16
	21	8:59	20:34	9:07	20:26	9:17	20:17	9:30	20:04	9:50	19:44
	31	8:23	20:00	8:31	19:52	8:40	19:43	8:52	19:30	9:11	19:11
Feb	10	7:47	19:25	7:55	19:18	8:03	19:09	8:15	18:58	8:33	18:39
	20	7:12	18:51	7:19	18:44	7:27	18:36	7:38	18:25	7:55	18:08
Mar	2	6:36	18:17	6:43	18:11	6:50	18:03	7:01	17:52	7:17	17:36
	12	6:01	17:43	6:07	17:37	6:14	17:30	6:24	17:20	6:39	17:05
	22	5:25	17:09	5:31	17:03	5:38	16:56	5:47	16:47	6:01	16:34
Apr	1	4:50	16:34	4:55	16:29	5:01	16:23	5:10	16:15	5:23	16:02
	11	4:14	16:00	4:19	15:55	4:25	15:49	4:33	15:42	4:44	15:30
	21	3:38	15:25	3:43	15:21	3:48	15:15	3:55	15:08	4:06	14:57
May	1	3:02	14:50	3:06	14:46	3:11	14:41	3:18	14:34	3:28	14:24
	11	2:26	14:15	2:29	14:11	2:34	14:06	2:40	14:00	2:50	13:50
	21	1:49	13:38	1:52	13:35	1:57	13:30	2:03	13:25	2:11	13:16
	31	1:11	13:02	1:15	12:58	1:19	12:54	1:25	12:49	1:33	12:40
Jun	10	0:34	12:25	0:37	12:21	0:41	12:17	0:47	12:12	0:55	12:04
	20	23:52	11:47	23:55	11:44	23:59	11:40	0:08	11:35	0:16	11:27
	30	23:13	11:08	23:16	11:05	23:20	11:01	23:25	10:56	23:33	10:48
Jul	10	22:34	10:29	22:37	10:26	22:41	10:22	22:46	10:17	22:54	10:09
	20	21:54	9:49	21:58	9:46	22:02	9:42	22:07	9:36	22:15	9:28
	30	21:14	9:09	21:18	9:05	21:22	9:01	21:27	8:55	21:36	8:47
Aug	9	20:34	8:27	20:37	8:24	20:42	8:19	20:48	8:13	20:56	8:05
	19	19:53	7:45	19:56	7:42	20:01	7:37	20:07	7:31	20:17	7:21
	29	19:11	7:03	19:15	6:59	19:20	6:54	19:27	6:48	19:37	6:38
Sep	8	18:30	6:21	18:34	6:16	18:39	6:11	18:46	6:04	18:57	5:53
	18	17:48	5:38	17:53	5:34	17:58	5:28	18:06	5:20	18:17	5:09
	28	17:06	4:56	17:11	4:51	17:17	4:45	17:25	4:37	17:37	4:25
Oct	8	16:25	4:13	16:30	4:08	16:36	4:02	16:45	3:54	16:57	3:41
	18	15:44	3:32	15:49	3:26	15:55	3:20	16:04	3:11	16:17	2:58
	28	15:03	2:50	15:08	2:45	15:15	2:38	15:24	2:29	15:37	2:16
Nov	7	14:22	2:09	14:28	2:04	14:35	1:57	14:44	1:48	14:58	1:34
	17	13:42	1:29	13:48	1:24	13:55	1:17	14:04	1:08	14:18	0:54
	27	13:03	0:50	13:09	0:44	13:15	0:38	13:24	0:29	13:38	0:15
Dec	7	12:24	0:11	12:30	0:06	12:36	23:56	12:45	23:47	12:59	23:33
	17	11:46	23:30	11:51	23:25	11:58	23:18	12:06	23:09	12:20	22:56
	27	11:08	22:53	11:13	22:48	11:20	22:42	11:28	22:33	11:41	22:21

Calculation of Rise Times

The *Daily Calendar* pages contain rise and set times for the sun and moon for the Greenwich Meridian at north latitudes 20°, 30°, 40°, 50°, and 60°. You probably live somewhere west of the Greenwich Meridian, 0° longitude, and within the range of latitudes in the table. Notice that from day to day, the values for the sun at any particular latitude do not change very much. This slow variation for the sun means that no important correction needs to be made from one day to the next, once a proper correction for your latitude has been made. Thus, whenever the sun rises or sets at the 0° meridian, that will also be the time of that phenomenon at your Standard Time meridian. Any correction necessary for you to be able to observe that phenomenon from your location will be to account for your distance from the Standard Time meridian and for your latitude.

The moon, however, moves its own diameter, about one-half degree, in an hour, or about 12°.5 in one complete turn of the earth—one day. Most of this is eastward against the background stars of the sky, but some is also north or south of the equator. If there is little change on the same day of the times over the range of latitudes, the moon is near the celestial equator. All this motion considerably affects the times of rise or set, as you can see from the adjacent entries in the table. Thus, it is necessary to take your longitude into account in addition to your latitude. If you have no need for total accuracy, simply note that the time will be between the 4 values you find surrounding your location and the dates of interest.

The process of finding more accurate corrections is called interpolation. In the example, linear interpolation involving simple differences is used. In extreme cases, higher order interpolation should be used. If such cases are important to you, it is suggested that you plot the times, draw smooth curves through the plots, and interpolate by eye between the relevant curves. Some people find this exercise fun.

Let's find the time of the July Full Moon at Springfield, MA.

First, where is Springfield, MA? Find Springfield's latitude and longitude on page 551.

I. Springfield, MA: 42° 06′ 21″ N
72° 35′ 32″ W

IA. Convert these values to decimals:
21 / 60 = 0.35
6 + .35 = 6.35
6.35 / 60 = 0.11
42 + .11 = 42.11
32 / 60 = 0.53
35 + .53 = 35.53
35.53 / 60 = 0.59
72 + .59 = 72.59

IB. The fraction that Springfield lies between 40° and 50°:
42.11 – 40 = 2.11; 2.11/10 = 0.211

IC. The fraction that the world must turn between Greenwich and Springfield:
72.59/360 = 0.202

ID. The EST meridian is 75°, thus 72.59 is 75 – 72.59 = 2.41 degrees east of the Eastern Standard Meridian. In 24 hours, there are 24 × 60 = 1440 minutes; 1440/360 = 4 minutes for every degree around the earth. Therefore, events happen 4 × 2.41 = 9.64 minutes earlier in Springfield than at the 75° meridian.

IE. The values IB and IC are interpolates for Springfield. ID is the time correction from local to Standard time for Springfield. These values need never be calculated again for Springfield.

IIA. We need the Greenwich times for moonrise at latitudes 40° and 50° and for July 12 and 13, the days of the Full Moon and the next day.

	40°	**Diff.**	**50°**
July 12	19:21	:25	19:46
July 13	20:06	:20	20:26

IIB. We want IB and the July 12 time difference:
0.211 × 25 = 5.3
Add this to the July 12, 40° time;
19:21 + 5.3 = 19:26.3
And for July 13:
0.211 × 20 = 4.2
Add this to the July 13 rise time:
20:06 + 4.2 = 20:10.2
These 2 times are for the latitude of Springfield, but for the Greenwich Meridian.

IIC. To get the time for Springfield, take the difference between the 2 times just determined,
20:10 – 19:26 = 56 minutes,
and find what fraction of this 24-hour change took place while the earth turned between Greenwich and Springfield (see IC), 0.202.
56 × 0.202 = 11.3 minutes after 19:26.
Thus, 19:26 + 11 = 19:37 is the time the Full Moon will rise in the local time of Springfield.

IID. But this is 10 minutes earlier than EST at Springfield (see ID), thus
19:37 – 10 = 19:27 EST.
But this is summer and Daylight Savings Time is in effect. Thus
19:27 + 1:00 = 20:27 EDT is the rise time for the Full Moon at Springfield the evening of July 12, 1995.

Star Tables

These tables include stars of visual magnitude 2.5 and brighter. Coordinates are for mid-1995. If no parallax figures are given, the trigonometric parallax figure is smaller than the margin for error, and the distance given is obtained by indirect methods. Stars of variable magnitude are designated by v.

To find the time when the star is on meridian, subtract Right Ascension of Mean Sun, from the sidereal time table on page 259, from the star's right ascension, first adding 24h to the latter, if necessary. Mark this result PM, if less than 12h; but if greater than 12, subtract 12h and mark the remainder AM.

	Star	Magnitude	Parallax ″	Light yrs.	Right ascen. h. m.	Declination ° ′
α	Andromedae (Alpheratz)	2.06	0.02	90	0 08.2	29 04
β	Cassiopeiae	2.27 v	0.07	45	0 08.9	59 07
α	Phoenicis	2.39	0.04	93	0 26.1	-42 20
α	Cassiopeiae (Schedir)	2.23	0.01	150	0 40.2	56 31
β	Ceti	2.04	0.06	57	0 43.4	-18 01
γ	Cassiopeiae	2.47 v	0.03	96	0 56.4	60 42
β	Andromedae	2.06	0.04	76	1 09.5	35 36
α	Eridani (Achernar)	0.46	0.02	118	1 37.5	-57 16
γ	Andromedae	2.26		260	2 03.6	42 18
α	Arietis	2.00	0.04	76	2 06.9	23 26
o	Ceti	2.00	0.01	103	2 19.1	-3 00
α	Ursae Min. (Pole Star)	2.02 v		680	2 26.4	89 15
β	Persei (Algol)	2.12 v	0.03	105	3 07.9	40 56
α	Persei	1.80	0.03	570	3 24.0	49 51
α	Tauri (Aldebaran)	0.85 v	0.05	68	4 35.7	16 30
β	Orionis (Rigel)	0.12 v		900	5 14.3	-8 12
α	Aurigae (Capella)	0.08	0.07	45	5 16.4	46 00
γ	Orionis (Bellatrix)	1.64	0.03	470	5 24.9	6 21
β	Tauri (El Nath)	1.65	0.02	300	5 26.0	28 36
δ	Orionis	2.23 v		1500	5 31.8	-0 18
ε	Orionis	1.70		1600	5 36.0	-1 12
ζ	Orionis	2.05	0.02	1600	5 40.5	-1 57
κ	Orionis	2.06	0.01	2100	5 47.5	-9 40
α	Orionis (Betelgeuse)	0.50 v		520	5 54.9	7 24
β	Aurigae	1.90	0.04	88	5 59.2	44 57
β	Canis Majoris	1.98	0.01	750	6 22.5	-17 57
α	Carinae (Canopus)	-0.72	0.02	98	6 23.9	-52 42
γ	Geminorum	1.93	0.03	105	6 37.5	16 24
α	Canis Majoris (Sirius)	-1.46	0.38	8.7	6 44.9	-16 43
ε	Canis Majoris	1.50		680	6 58.5	-28 58
δ	Canis Majoris	1.86		2100	7 08.2	-26 23
η	Canis Majoris	2.44		2700	7 23.9	-29 18
α	Geminorum (Castor)	1.99	0.07	45	7 34.3	31 54
α	Canis Minoris (Procyon)	0.38	0.29	11.3	7 39.1	5 14
β	Geminorum (Pollux)	1.14	0.09	35	7 45.0	28 02
ζ	Puppis	2.25		2400	8 03.4	-39 59
γ	Velorum	1.82		520	8 09.4	-47 19
ε	Carinae	1.86		340	8 22.4	-59 30
δ	Velorum	1.96	0.04	76	8 44.6	-54 42
λ	Velorum	2.21	0.02	750	9 07.8	-43 25
β	Carinae	1.68	0.04	86	9 13.2	-69 42
ι	Carinae	2.25		750	9 17.0	-59 15
κ	Velorum	2.50	0.01	470	9 22.0	-54 59
α	Hydrae	1.98	0.02	94	9 27.4	-8 38
α	Leonis (Regulus)	1.35	0.04	84	10 08.1	11 59
γ	Leonis	1.90	0.02	90	10 19.7	19 54
β	Ursae Majoris (Merak)	2.37	0.04	78	11 01.6	56 24
α	Ursae Majoris (Dubhe)	1.79	0.03	105	11 03.5	61 47
β	Leonis (Denebola)	2.14	0.08	43	11 48.8	14 36
γ	Ursae Majoris (Phecda)	2.44	0.02	90	11 53.6	53 43
α	Crucis	1.58		370	12 26.3	-63 04
γ	Crucis	1.63		220	12 30.9	-57 05
γ	Centauri	2.17		160	12 41.3	-48 56
β	Crucis	1.25 v		490	12 47.5	-59 40
ε	Ursae Majoris (Alioth)	1.77 v	0.01	68	12 53.8	55 59
ζ	Ursae Majoris (Mizar)	2.05	0.04	88	13 23.7	54 57
α	Virginis (Spica)	0.97 v	0.02	220	13 25.0	-11 08
ε	Centauri	2.30 v		570	13 39.6	-53 27
η	Ursae Majoris (Alkaid)	1.86		210	13 47.4	49 20
β	Centauri	0.61 v	0.02	490	14 03.5	-60 21
θ	Centauri	2.06	0.06	55	14 06.4	-36 21
α	Bootis (Arcturus)	-0.04	0.09	36	14 15.5	19 12
η	Centauri	2.31 v		390	14 35.2	-42 08
α	Centauri	-0.01	0.75	4.3	14 39.3	-60 49
α	Lupi	2.30 v		430	14 41.6	-47 22
ε	Bootis	2.40	0.01	103	14 44.8	27 06
β	Ursae Minoris	2.08	0.03	105	14 50.7	74 10
α	Coronae Borealis	2.23 v	0.04	76	15 34.5	26 44
δ	Scorpii	2.32		590	16 00.1	-22 37
α	Scorpii (Antares)	0.96 v	0.02	520	16 29.1	-26 25
α	Trianguli Australis	1.92	0.02	82	16 48.2	-69 01
ε	Scorpii	2.29	0.05	66	16 49.9	-34 17
η	Ophiuchi	2.43	0.05	69	17 10.1	-15 43
λ	Scorpii	1.63 v		310	17 33.3	-37 06
α	Ophiuchi	2.08	0.06	58	17 34.7	12 34
θ	Scorpii	1.87	0.02	650	17 37.0	-43 00
κ	Scorpii	2.41 v		470	17 42.2	-39 02
γ	Draconis	2.23	0.02	108	17 56.5	51 29
ε	Sagittarii	1.85	0.02	124	18 23.9	-34 23
α	Lyrae (Vega)	0.03	0.12	26.5	18 36.8	38 47
σ	Sagittarii	2.02		300	18 55.0	-26 18
α	Aquilae (Altair)	0.77	0.20	16.5	19 50.6	8 51
γ	Cygni	2.20		750	20 22.1	40 15
α	Pavonis	1.94		310	20 25.3	-56 45
α	Cygni (Deneb)	1.25		1600	20 41.3	45 16
ε	Cygni	2.46	0.04	74	20 46.0	33 57
α	Cephei	2.44	0.06	52	21 18.5	62 34
ε	Pegasi	2.39		780	21 44.0	9 51
α	Gruis	1.74	0.05	64	22 08.0	-46 59
β	Gruis	2.11 v		280	22 42.4	-46 54
α	Piscis Austrinis (Fomalhaut)	1.16	0.14	22.6	22 57.4	-29 39
β	Pegasi	2.42 v	0.02	210	23 03.6	28 03
α	Pegasi	2.49	0.03	109	23 04.5	15 11

Astronomical Constants; Speed of Light

The following were adopted in 1968, in accordance with the resolutions and recommendations of the International Astronomical Union (Hamburg 1964): Speed of light, 299,792.5 kilometers per second, or about 186,282.3976 statute miles per second; solar parallax, 8″.794; constant of nutation, 9″.210; and constant of aberration, 20″.496.

Constellations

Culturally, constellations are imagined patterns among the stars that, in some cases, have been recognized through millenia of tradition. In the early days of astronomy, knowledge of the constellations was necessary in order to function as an astronomer. For today's astronomers, constellations are simply areas on the entire sky in which interesting objects await observation and interpretation.

Because western culture has prevailed in establishing modern science, equally viable and interesting constellations and celestial traditions of other cultures (of Asia or Africa, for example) are not well known outside their regions of origin. Even the patterns with which we are most familiar today have undergone considerable change over the centuries, because the western heritage embraces teachings of cultures disparate in time as well as place.

Today, students of the sky the world over recognize 88 constellations that cover the entire celestial sphere. Many of these have their origins in ancient days; many are "modern," contrived out of unformed stars by astronomers a few centuries ago. Unformed stars were those usually too faint or inconveniently placed to be included in depicting the more prominent constellations.

When astronomers began to travel to South Africa in the 16th and 17th centuries, they found a sky that itself was unformed and showing numerous brilliant stars. Thus, we find constellations in the southern hemisphere like the "air pump," the "microscope," the "furnace," and other technological marvels of the time, as well as some arguably traditional forms, such as the "fly."

Many of the commonly recognized constellations had their origins in ancient Asia Minor—Syria, Babylon, etc. These were adopted by the Greeks and Romans, who translated their names and stories into their own languages, modifying some details in the process. After the declines of these cultures, most such knowledge entered oral tradition or remained hidden in monastic libraries. Beginning in the 8th century, the Muslim explosion spread through the Mediterranean world. Wherever possible, everything was translated into Arabic to be taught in the universities the Muslims established all over their new-found world.

In the 13th century, Alphonsus XX of Spain, an avid student of astronomy, succeeded in having Claudius Ptolemy's *Almagest,* as its Arabian title was known, translated into Latin. It thus became widely available to European scholars. In the process, the constellation names were translated, but the star names were retained in their Arabic forms. Transliterating Arabic into the Roman alphabet has never been an exact art, so many of the star names we use today only "seem" Arabic to all but scholars.

Names of stars often indicated what parts of the traditional figures they represented: Deneb, the tail of the swan; Betelgeuse, the armpit of the giant. Thus, the names were an indication of the position in the sky of a particular star, provided one recognized the traditional form of the mythic figure.

In English, usage of the Latin names for the constellations couples often inconceivable creatures, represented in unimaginable configurations, with names that often seem unintelligible. Avoiding traditional names, astronomers may designate the brighter stars in a constellation with Greek letters, usually in order of brightness. Thus, the " alpha star" is often the brightest star of that constellation. The "of" implies possession, so the genitive (possessive) form of the constellation name is used, as in Alpha Orionis, the first star of Orion (Betelgeuse). Astronomers usually use a 3-letter form for the constellation name, understanding it to be read as either the nominative or genitive case of the name.

Until the 1920s, astronomers used curved boundaries for the constellation areas. As these were rather arbitrary at best, the International Astronomical Union adopted boundaries that ran due north-south and east-west, filling the sky much as the contiguous states fill up the area of the "lower 48" United States.

Within these boundaries, and occasionally crossing them, popular "asterisms" are recognized: the Big Dipper is a small part of Ursa Major, the big bear; the Sickle is the traditional head and mane of Leo, the lion; one of the horntips of Taurus, the bull, properly belongs to Auriga, the charioteer; the northeast star of the Great Square of Pegasus is Alpha Andromedae.

It is unlikely that further change will occur in the realm of the celestial constellations.

Name	Genitive	Abbreviation	Meaning
Andromeda	Andromedae	And	Chained Maiden
Antlia	Antliae	Ant	Air Pump
Apus	Apodis	Aps	Bird of Paradise
Aquarius	Aquarii	Aqr	Water Bearer
Aquila	Aquilae	Aql	Eagle
Ara	Arae	Ara	Altar
Aries	Arietis	Ari	Ram
Auriga	Aurigae	Aur	Charioteer
Bootes	Bootis	Boo	Herdsmen
Caelum	Caeli	Cae	Chisel
Camelopardalis	Camelopardalis	Cam	Giraffe
Cancer	Cancri	Cnc	Crab
Canes Venatici	Canum Venaticorum	CVn	Hunting Dogs
Canis Major	Canis Majoris	CMa	Great Dog
Canis Minor	Canis Minoris	CMi	Little Dog
Capricornus	Capricorni	Cap	Sea-goat
Carina	Carinae	Car	Keel
Cassiopeia	Cassiopeiae	Cas	Queen
Centaurus	Centauri	Cen	Centaur
Cepheus	Cephei	Cep	King
Cetus	Ceti	Cet	Whale
Chamaeleon	Chamaeleontis	Cha	Chameleon
Circinus	Circini	Cir	Compasses (art)
Columba	Columbae	Col	Dove
Coma Berenices	Comae Berenices	Com	Berenice's Hair
Corona Australis	Coronae Australis	CrA	Southern Crown
Corona Borealis	Coronae Borealis	CrB	Northern Crown
Corvus	Corvi	Crv	Crow
Crater	Crateris	Crt	Cup
Crux	Crucis	Cru	Cross (southern)
Cygnus	Cygni	Cyg	Swan
Delphinus	Delphini	Del	Dolphin
Dorado	Doradus	Dor	Goldfish
Draco	Draconis	Dra	Dragon
Equuleus	Equulei	Equ	Little Horse
Eridanus	Eridani	Eri	River
Fornax	Fornacis	For	Furnace
Gemini	Geminorum	Gem	Twins
Grus	Gruis	Gru	Crane (bird)
Hercules	Herculis	Her	Hercules
Horologium	Horologii	Hor	Clock
Hydra	Hydrae	Hya	Water Snake (female)
Hydrus	Hydri	Hyi	Water Snake (male)
Indus	Indi	Ind	Indian
Lacerta	Lacertae	Lac	Lizard
Leo	Leonis	Leo	Lion
Leo Minor	Leonis Minoris	LMi	Little Lion
Lepus	Leporis	Lep	Hare
Libra	Librae	Lib	Balance
Lupus	Lupi	Lup	Wolf
Lynx	Lyncis	Lyn	Lynx
Lyra	Lyrae	Lyr	Lyre
Mensa	Mensae	Men	Table Mountain
Microscopium	Microscopii	Mic	Microscope
Monoceros	Monocerotis	Mon	Unicorn
Musca	Muscae	Mus	Fly
Norma	Normae	Nor	Square (rule)
Octans	Octantis	Oct	Octant
Ophiuchus	Ophiuchi	Oph	Serpent Bearer
Orion	Orionis	Ori	Hunter
Pavo	Pavonis	Pav	Peacock
Pegasus	Pegasi	Peg	Flying Horse
Perseus	Persei	Per	Hero
Phoenix	Phoenicis	Phe	Phoenix
Pictor	Pictoris	Pic	Painter
Pisces	Piscium	Psc	Fishes
Piscis Austrinius	Piscis Austrini	PsA	Southern Fish
Puppis	Puppis	Pup	Stern (deck)
Pyxis	Pyxidis	Pyx	Compass (sea)
Reticulum	Reticuli	Ret	Reticle
Sagitta	Sagittae	Sge	Arrow
Sagittarius	Sagittarii	Sgr	Archer
Scorpius	Scorpii	Sco	Scorpion
Sculptor	Sculptoris	Scl	Sculptor
Scutum	Scuti	Sct	Shield
Serpens	Serpentis	Ser	Serpent
Sextans	Sextantis	Sex	Sextant
Taurus	Tauri	Tau	Bull
Telescopium	Telescopii	Tel	Telescope
Triangulum	Trianguli	Tri	Triangle
Triangulum Australe	Trianguli Australis	TrA	Southern Triangle
Tucana	Tucanae	Tuc	Toucan
Ursa Major	Ursae Majoris	UMa	Great Bear
Ursa Minor	Ursae Minoris	UMi	Little Bear
Vela	Velorum	Vel	Sail
Virgo	Virginis	Vir	Maiden
Volans	Volantis	Vol	Flying Fish
Vulpecula	Vulpeculae	Vul	Fox

Aurora Borealis and Aurora Australis

The Aurora Borealis, also called the Northern Lights, is a broad display of rather faint light in the northern skies at night. The Aurora Australis, a similar phenomenon, appears at the same time in southern skies. The aurora appears in a wide variety of forms. Sometimes it is seen as a quiet glow, almost foglike in character; sometimes as vertical streamers in which there may be considerable motion; sometimes as a series of luminous expanding arcs. There are many colors, with white, yellow, and red predominating.

The auroras are most vivid and most frequently seen at about 20 degrees from the magnetic poles, along the northern coast of the North American continent and the eastern part of the northern coast of Europe. The Aurora Borealis has been seen as far south as Key West, and the Aurora Australis has been seen as far north as Australia and New Zealand. Such occurences are rare, however.

Although the cause of the auroras is not known beyond question, there does seem to be a definite correlation between auroral displays and sun-spot activity. It is thought that atomic particles expelled from the sun by the forces that cause solar flares speed through space at velocities of 400 to 600 miles per second. These particles are entrapped by the earth's magnetic field, forming what are termed the Van Allen belts. The encounter of these clouds of the solar wind with the earth's magnetic field weakens the field so that previously trapped particles are allowed to impact the upper atmosphere. The collisions between solar and terrestrial atoms result in the glow in the upper atmosphere called the aurora. The glow may be vivid where the lines of magnetic force converge near the magnetic poles.

The auroral displays appear at heights ranging from 50 to about 600 miles and have given us a means of estimating the extent of the earth's atmosphere.

The auroras are often accompanied by magnetic storms whose forces, also guided by the lines of force of the earth's magnetic field, disrupt electrical communication.

Eclipses, 1995

There are four eclipses: two of the sun, and two of the moon.

I. Partial lunar eclipse, April 15.

Only about 12% of the lunar diameter will be in the umbral shadow of the earth, an event entirely observable in the United States from about the Missouri River westward, as well as in Mexico, Alaska, the entire Pacific Ocean, New Zealand, Australia, the Philippines, Japan, Indonesia, India north of Sri Lanka, China except the far west, the Arctic Ocean north of the Bering Strait except the North Pole, and portions of Antarctica bordering the Pacific Ocean.

Circumstances of the Eclipse

Event	Date		h	m
Moon enters penumbra	April	15	10	7.9
Moon enters umbra		15	11	40.8
Middle of eclipse		15	12	18.1
Moon leaves umbra		15	12	55.1
Moon leaves penumbra		15	14	28.0

Magnitude of the eclipse: 0.1172.

II. Annular solar eclipse, April 29.

Partial phases of this eclipse are visible in the eastern South Pacific Ocean, Easter Island, Pitcairn Island, the Galápagos Islands, all of Central and South America south of Mexico City except Tierra del Fuego, Florida except the extreme north, the West Indies, and the southern portion of the North Atlantic Ocean.

The land path of annularity, central eclipse, begins in southern Ecuador, moves across northern Peru, southern Colombia, northern Brazil, and the Brazilian coast from Belém past Fortaleza.

Circumstances of the Eclipse

Event	Date		h	m
Eclipse begins	April	29	14	33.3
Central eclipse begins		29	15	39.8
Central eclipse at local noon		29	17	32.3
Central eclipse ends		29	19	25.0
Eclipse ends		29	20	31.5

Maximum duration: 6 min 36.9 sec.

III. Penumbral lunar eclipse, October 5.

The beginning of the penumbral phase is generally visible from central California, western Nevada, Oregon, Washington, western Canada, Alaska, the Pacific Ocean except Hawaii and eastward, and New Zealand; all of the event is visible from Australia, the East Indies, and Asia to the Caspian Sea; the end is visible from most of Saudi Arabia, Europe, and Africa except the far west.

Circumstances of the Eclipse

Event	Date		h	m
Moon enters penumbra	October	8	13	57.8
Middle of eclipse		8	16	4.1
Moon leaves penumbra		8	18	10.0

Penumbral magnitude of the eclipse: 0.85.

IV. Total solar eclipse, October 24.

The partial phases of this eclipse are visible from Pakistan, India, Asia except the northeast, Indochina, Indonesia, New Guinea, Australia except the southern part, and the Philippines, and the western Pacific Ocean.

The path of totality begins in Iran, passing over parts of Afghanistan, the Celebes Sea, into the south Pacific Ocean.

Circumstances of the Eclipse

Event	Date		h	m
Eclipse begins	October	24	1	51.9
Central eclipse begins		24	2	52.5
Central eclipse at local noon		24	4	22.5
Central eclipse ends		24	6	12.6
Eclipse ends		24	7	13.1

Maximum duration: 2 min 9.6 sec.

The Planets and the Solar System

Planet	Mean daily motion "	Orbital velocity miles per sec.	Sidereal revolution days	Synodical revolution days	Distance from sun in millions of mi Max.	Min.	Dist. from Earth. in millions of mi Max.	Min.	Light at[1] peri-helion	aphe-helion
Mercury. . . .	14732	29.75	88.0	115.9	43.4	28.6	136	50	10.58	4.59
Venus.	5768	21.76	224.7	583.9	67.7	66.8	161	25	1.94	1.89
Earth.	3548	18.51	365.3	—	94.6	91.4	—	—	1.03	0.97
Mars.	1886	14.99	687.0	779.9	155.0	128.5	248	35	0.524	0.360
Jupiter.	299	8.12	4331.8	398.9	507.0	460.6	600	368	0.0408	0.0333
Saturn.	120	5.99	10760.0	378.1	937.5	838.4	1031	745	0.01230	0.00984
Uranus	42	4.23	30684.0	369.7	1859.7	1669.3	1953	1606	0.00300	0.00250
Neptune . . .	21	3.38	60188.3	367.5	2821.7	2760.4	2915	2667	0.00114	0.00109
Pluto.	14	2.95	90466.8	366.7	4551.4	2756.4	4644	2663	0.00114	0.00042

(1) Light at perihelion and aphelion is solar illumination in units of mean illumination at earth.

Planet	Mean longitude of:* ascending node °	′	″	perihelion °	′	″	Inclination* of orbit to ecliptic °	′	″	Mean* distance**	Eccentricity* of orbit	Mean longitude at the epoch* °	′	″
Mercury . . .	48	16	51	77	23	36	7	0	18	.387098	.205631	51	34	28
Venus	76	38	31	131	30	16	3	23	41	.723330	.006774	277	25	49
Earth.	0	0	0	102	51	53	0	0	0	1.000001	.016710	18	8	3
Mars	49	31	32	335	58	57	1	50	59	1.523679	.093397	266	0	20
Jupiter	100	25	17	14	15	47	1	8	13	5.202603	.048488	265	57	29
Saturn	113	37	42	92	58	25	2	29	21	9.554910	.055523	358	20	24
Uranus. . . .	73	59	2	172	56	32	0	46	23	19.218446	.046297	295	52	40
Neptune . . .	131	44	15	48	3	48	1	46	13	30.110387	.008988	295	3	2
Pluto*** . . .	110	17	6	224	20	6	17	7	38	39.839800	.255354	232	9	40

* Consistent for the standard epoch: 1995 October 9 Ephemeris Time.

** Astronomical units.

*** Consistent for the standard epoch: 1994 September 4 Ephemeris Time.

Sun and planets	Semi-diameter at unit distance ′ ″	at mean least dist. ′ ″	in miles mean s.d.	Volume ⊕=1.	Mass. ⊕=1.	Density ⊕=1	Sidereal period of rotation d.	h.	m.	s.	Gravity at surface ⊕=1.	Reflecting power Pct.		Probable temperature °F.
Sun.	959.62	____	432449	1299370	332946	0.26	24	16	48		27.90	____	+	10,000
Mercury. . .	3.37	5.5	1515	0.0559	0.0553	1.00	58	15	30		0.37	0.11	+	620
Venus. . . .	8.34	30.1	3760	0.8541	0.8150	0.97	243	R			0.88	0.65	+	900
Earth.	____	____	3963	1.000	1.000	1.00		23	56	6.7	1.00	0.37	+	72
Moon	2.40	932.4	1080	0.020	0.0123	0.62	27	7	43		0.17	0.12	-	10
Mars.	4.69	8.95	2108.5	0.1506	0.1074	0.73		24	37	26	0.38	0.15	-	10
Jupiter. . . .	98.35	23.4	44419	1403	317.89	0.25		9	3	30	2.64	0.52	-	240
Saturn. . . .	82.83	9.7	37448	832	95.18	0.13		10	39	22	1.15	0.47	-	300
Uranus . . .	35.4	1.9	15881	63	14.54	0.23		17	14	R	1.15	0.40	-	340
Neptune . .	33.4	1.2	15387	55	17.15	0.30		16	6		1.12	0.35	-	370
Pluto.	1.9	0.05	714	0.006	0.0020	0.37	6	9	17		0.04	0.5	?	?

(R) Retrograde of Venus and Uranus.

The Sun

The sun, the controlling body of the earth's solar system, is a star whose dimensions cause it to be classified among stars as average in size, temperature, and brightness. Its proximity to the earth makes it appear tremendously large and bright. A series of thermonuclear reactions involving the atoms of the elements of which it is composed produces the heat and light that make life possible on earth.

The sun has a diameter of 864,000 miles and is distant, on the average, 92,900,000 miles from the earth. It is 1.41 times as dense as water. The light of the sun reaches the earth in 499.012 seconds, or in slightly more than 8 minutes. The average solar surface temperature has been measured by several indirect methods that agree closely on a value of 6,000° Kelvin, or about 10,000° F. The interior temperature of the sun is about 35,000,000° F.

When sunlight is analyzed with a spectroscope, it is found to consist of a continuous spectrum composed of all the colors of the rainbow in order, crossed by many dark lines. The "absorption lines" are produced by gaseous materials in the atmosphere of the sun. More than 60 of the natural terrestrial elements have been identified in the sun, all in gaseous form because of the intense heat of the sun.

Spheres and Corona

The radiating surface of the sun is called the **photosphere,** and just above it is the **chromosphere.** The chromosphere is visible to the naked eye only at times of total solar eclipses, appearing then to be a pinkish-violet layer with occasional great prominences projecting above its general level. With proper instruments the chromosphere can be seen or photographed whenever the sun is visible without waiting for a total eclipse. Above the chromosphere is the **corona,** also visible to the naked eye only at times of total eclipse. Instruments also permit the brighter portions of the corona to be studied whenever conditions are favorable. The pearly light of the corona surges millions of miles from the sun. Iron, nickel, and calcium are believed to be principal contributors to the composition of the corona, all in a state of extreme attenuation and high ionization that indicates temperatures on the order of a million degrees Fahrenheit.

Sunspots

There is an intimate connection between sunspots and the corona. At times of low sunspot activity, the fine streamers of the corona will be much longer above the sun's equator than over the polar regions of the sun; during high sunspot activity, the corona extends fairly evenly outward from all regions of the sun, but to a much greater distance in space. Sunspots are dark, irregularly shaped regions whose diameters may reach tens of thousands of miles. The average life of a sunspot group is from 2 to 3 weeks, but there have been groups that have lasted for more than a year, being carried repeatedly around as the sun rotated upon its axis. The record for the duration of a sunspot is 18 months. Sunspots reach a low point every 11.3 years, with a peak of activity occurring irregularly between 2 successive minima.

The sun is 400,000 times as bright as the full moon and gives the earth 6 million times as much light as do all the other stars put together. Actually, most of the stars that can be easily seen on any clear night are brighter than the sun.

The Zodiac

The sun's apparent yearly path among the stars is known as the **ecliptic.** The zone, 16° wide, 8° on each side of the ecliptic, is known as the **zodiac.** Inside this zone are the apparent paths of the sun, moon, earth, and major planets. Beginning at the point on the ecliptic that marks the position of the sun at the vernal equinox and proceeding eastward, the zodiac is divided into 12 signs of 30° each, as shown here.

These signs are named from the 12 constellations of the zodiac with which the signs coincided in the time of the astronomer Hipparchus, about 2,000 years ago. Owing to the precession of the equinoxes, that is to say, to the retrograde motion of the equinoxes along the ecliptic, each sign in the zodiac has, in the course of 2,000 years, moved backward 30° into the constellation west of it; the sign Aries is now in the constellation Pisces, for example, and so on.

The vernal equinox will move from Pisces into Aquarius about the middle of the 26th century. The signs of the zodiac with their Latin and English names are as follows:

Spring	1.	♈	Aries	The Ram
	2.	♉	Taurus	The Bull
	3.	♊	Gemini	The Twins
Summer	4.	♋	Cancer	The Crab
	5.	♌	Leo	The Lion
	6.	♍	Virgo	The Virgin
Autumn	7.	♎	Libra	The Balance
	8.	♏	Scorpius	The Scorpion
	9.	♐	Sagittarius	The Archer
Winter	10.	♑	Capricorn	The Goat
	11.	♒	Aquarius	The Water Bearer
	12.	♓	Pisces	The Fishes

Twilight

Twilight is that evening period of waning light from the time of sunset to dark, often termed dusk. Morning twilight, a time of increasing light, is called dawn. The source of this light is the sun shining on the atmosphere above the observer. Twilight is a time of very slowly changing sky illumination with no abrupt variations. Nevertheless, there are 3 commonly accepted divisions in this smooth continuum defined by the distance the sun lies below the astronomical horizon: civil twilight, nautical twilight, and astronomical twilight. The astronomical horizon is that great circle lying 90° from the zenith, the point directly over the observer's head. Twilight ends in the evening or begins in the morning at a particular time. Nominally, evening events are repeated in reverse order in the morning.

Civil twilight is the time between the moment of sunset, when the sun's apparent upper edge is just at the horizon, until the center of the sun is 6° directly below the horizon. In many states, this is the time in the evening when automobile headlights must be turned on, not to see better, but to be seen by other drivers. After this time, a newspaper becomes increasingly difficult to read in the absence of artificial light.

Nautical twilight ends when the sun's center is 12° below the horizon. By this time in the evening, the bright stars used by navigators have appeared, and the horizon may still be seen. After this time, the horizon is more difficult to perceive, preventing navigators from sighting stars.

Astronomical twilight ends in the evening when the sun is 18° below the horizon and when the sky is dark enough, at least away from the sun's location, to allow astronomical work to proceed. Sunlight, however, is still shining on the higher levels of the atmosphere from the observer's zenith to the horizon toward the sun. Although not named as a period of twilight, when the sun is 24° below the horizon, no part of the observer's atmosphere, even toward the sun, receives any sunlight.

In the tropics, the sun moves nearly vertically accomplishing its 6°, 12°, or 18° depression very quickly. In the polar regions, the sun's diurnal motion may actually be nearly along the horizon, prolonging the twilight period or even not permitting darkness to fall at all. In mid-latitudes, civil twilight may last about a half hour, nautical, an hour, and astronomers can go to work in about 90 minutes.

The twilight tables given in *The World Almanac* are for astronomical twilight and are presented for reference only. Although the instant of the sun's horizontal depression may be calculated precisely, the phenomena associated with the event are sufficiently imprecise that the table is not recalculated each year.

Moon's Perigee and Apogee, 1995

Perigee

Month	Day	h	Month	Day	h
Jan	27	23	Jul	11	10
Feb	22	2	Aug	8	14
Mar	20	13	Sep	5	1
Apr	17	8	Sep	30	4
May	15	15	Oct	26	21
Jun	13	1	Nov	23	23
			Dec	22	10

Apogee

Month	Day	h	Month	Day	h
Jan	11	22	Jul	23	20
Feb	8	18	Aug	20	12
Mar	8	15	Sep	17	6
Apr	5	10	Oct	15	2
May	3	1	Nov	11	21
May	30	8	Dec	9	10
Jun	26	11			

Perihelion

Month	Day	h
Jan	4	11

Aphelion

Month	Day	h
Jul	4	2

Moon Phases, 1995

Greenwich Mean Time

New Moon				First Q				Full Moon				Last Q			
Month	Day	h	m	Month	Day	h	m	Month	Day	h	m	Month	Day	h	m
Jan	1	10	56	Jan	8	15	46	Jan	16	20	26	Jan	24	4	58
Jan	30	22	48	Feb	7	12	54	Feb	15	12	15	Feb	22	13	4
Mar	1	11	48	Mar	9	10	14	Mar	17	1	26	Mar	23	20	10
Mar	31	2	9	Apr	8	5	35	Apr	15	12	8	Apr	22	3	18
Apr	29	17	36	May	7	21	44	May	14	20	48	May	21	11	36
May	29	9	27	Jun	6	10	26	Jun	13	4	3	Jun	19	22	1
Jun	28	0	50	Jul	5	20	2	Jul	12	10	49	Jul	19	11	10
Jul	27	15	13	Aug	4	3	16	Aug	10	18	15	Aug	18	3	4
Aug	26	4	31	Sep	2	9	3	Sep	9	3	37	Sep	16	21	9
Sep	24	16	55	Oct	1	14	36	Oct	8	15	52	Oct	16	16	26
Oct	24	4	36	Oct	30	21	17	Nov	7	7	20	Nov	15	11	40
Nov	22	15	43	Nov	29	6	28	Dec	7	1	27	Dec	15	5	31
Dec	22	22	2	Dec	28	19	6								

The Moon

The moon completes a circuit around the earth in a period whose mean or average duration is 27 days 7 hours 43.2 minutes. This is the moon's sidereal period. Because of the motion of the moon in common with the earth around the sun, the mean duration of the lunar month — the period from one new moon to the next new moon — is 29 days 12 hours 44.05 minutes. This is the moon's synodical period.

The mean distance of the moon from the earth according to the American Ephemeris is 238,857 miles. Because the orbit of the moon about the earth is not circular but elliptical, however, the maximum distance from the earth that the moon may reach is 252,710 miles and the least distance is 221,463 miles. All distances are from the center of one object to the center of the other.

The moon's diameter is 2,160 miles. If we deduct the radius of the moon, 1,080 miles, and the radius of the earth, 3,963 miles, from the minimum distance or perigee, given above, we shall have for the nearest approach of the bodies' surfaces 216,420 miles.

The moon rotates on its axis in a period of time exactly equal to its sidereal revolution about the earth — 27.321666 days. The moon's revolution about the earth is irregular because of its elliptical orbit. The moon's rotation, however, is regular, and this, together with the irregular revolution, produces what is called "libration in longitude," which permits us to see first farther around the east side and then farther around the west side of the moon. The moon's variation north or south of the ecliptic permits us to see farther over first one pole and then the other of the moon; this is called "libration in latitude." These two libration effects permit us to see a total of about 60% of the moon's surface over a period of time. The hidden side of the moon was photographed in 1959 by the Soviet space vehicle Lunik III. Since then, many excellent pictures of nearly all of the moon's surface have been transmitted to earth by Lunar Orbiters launched by the U.S.

The tides are caused mainly by the moon, because of its proximity to the earth. The ratio of the tide-raising power of the moon to that of the sun is 11 to 5.

Harvest Moon and Hunter's Moon

The Harvest Moon, the full moon nearest the Autumnal Equinox, ushers in a period of several successive days when the moon rises soon after sunset. This phenomenon gives farmers in temperate latitudes extra hours of light in which to harvest their crops before frost and winter come. The 1995 Harvest Moon falls on Sept. 9 GMT. Harvest Moon in the south temperate latitudes falls on Mar. 17.

The next full moon after Harvest Moon is called the Hunter's Moon, accompanied by a similar phenomenon but less marked; — Oct. 8, northern hemisphere; April 15, southern hemisphere.

The Earth: Size, Computation of Time, Seasons

Size and Dimensions

The earth is the fifth largest planet and the third from the sun. Its mass is 6 sextillion, 588 quintillion short tons. Using the parameters of an ellipsoid adopted by the International Astronomical Union in 1964 and recognized by the International Union of Geodesy and Geophysics in 1967, the length of the equator is 24,901.55 miles, the length of a meridian is 24,859.82 miles, the equatorial diameter is 7,926.41 miles, and the area of this reference ellipsoid is approximately 196,938,800 square miles.

The earth is considered a solid, rigid mass with a dense core of magnetic, probably metallic material. The outer part of the core is probably liquid. Around the core is a thick shell or mantle of heavy crystalline rock that in turn is covered by a thin crust forming the solid granite and basalt base of the continents and ocean basins. Over broad areas of the earth's surface the crust has a thin cover of sedimentary rock such as sandstone, shale, and limestone formed by weathering of the earth's surface and deposition of sands, clays, and plant and animal remains.

The temperature in the earth increases about 1° F. with every 100 to 200 feet in depth, in the upper 100 kilometers of the earth, and the temperature near the core is believed to be near the melting point of the core materials under the conditions at that depth. The heat of the earth is believed to be derived from radioactivity in the rocks, pressures developed within the earth, and original heat (if the earth in fact was formed at high temperatures).

Atmosphere of the Earth

The earth's atmosphere is a blanket composed of nitrogen, oxygen, and argon, in amounts of about 78%, 21%, and 1% by volume. Also present in minute quantities are carbon dioxide, hydrogen, neon, helium, krypton, and xenon.

Water vapor displaces other gases and varies from nearly zero to about 4% by volume. The height of the **ozone** layer varies from approximately 12 to 21 miles above the earth. Traces exist as low as 6 miles and as high as 35 miles. Traces of methane have been found.

The atmosphere rests on the earth's surface with the weight equivalent to a layer of water 34 ft. deep. For about 300,000 ft. upward the gases remain in the proportions stated. Gravity holds the gases to the earth. The weight of the air compresses it at the bottom so that the greatest density is at the earth's surface. Pressure, as well as density, decreases as height increases because the weight pressing upon any layer is always less than that pressing upon the layers below.

The temperature of the air drops with increased height until the **tropopause** is reached. This may vary from 25,000 to 60,000 ft. The atmosphere below the tropopause is the **troposphere;** the atmosphere for about 20 miles above the tropopause is the **stratosphere,** where the temperature generally increases with height except at high latitudes in winter. A temperature maximum near the 30-mile level is called the **stratopause.** Above this boundary is the **mesosphere,** where the temperature decreases with height to a minimum, the **mesopause,** at a height of 50 miles. Extending above the mesosphere to the outer fringes of the atmosphere is the **thermosphere,** a region where temperature increases with height to a value measured in thousands of degrees Fahrenheit. The lower portion of this region, extending from 50 to about 400 miles in altitude, is characterized by a high ion density and is thus called the **ionosphere.** The outer region is called the **exosphere;** this is the region where gas molecules traveling at high speed may escape into outer space, above 600 miles.

Latitude, Longitude

Position on the globe is measured by means of meridians and parallels. Meridians, which are imaginary lines drawn around the earth through the poles, determine **longitude.** The meridian running through Greenwich, England, is the **prime meridian of longitude,** and all others are either east or west. Parallels, which are imaginary circles parallel with the equator, determine **latitude.** The length of a degree of longitude varies as the cosine of the latitude. At the equator a degree is 69.171 statute miles; this is gradually reduced toward the poles. Value of a longitude degree at the poles is zero.

Latitude is reckoned by the number of degrees north or south of the equator, an imaginary circle on the earth's surface everywhere equidistant between the two poles. According to the International Astronomical Union ellipsoid of 1964, the length of a degree of latitude is 68.708 statute miles at the equator and varies slightly north and south because of the oblate form of the globe; at the poles it is 69.403 statute miles.

Definitions of Time

The earth rotates on its axis and follows an elliptical orbit around the sun. The rotation makes the sun appear to move across the sky from East to West. It determines day and night, and the complete rotation, in relation to the sun, is called the **apparent** or **true solar day.** This varies, but an average determines the **mean solar day** of 24 hours.

The mean solar day is in universal use for civil purposes. It may be obtained from apparent solar time by correcting observations of the sun for the equation of time, but when high precision is required, the mean solar time is calculated from its relation to sidereal time. These relations are extremely complicated, but for most practical uses, they may be considered as follows:

Sidereal time is the measure of time defined by the diurnal motion of the vernal equinox and is determined from observation of the meridian transits of stars. One complete rotation of the earth relative to the equinox is called the **sidereal day.** The **mean sidereal day** is 23 hours, 56 minutes, 4.091 seconds of mean solar time.

The **Calendar Year** begins at 12 o'clock midnight precisely local clock time, on the night of Dec. 31-Jan. 1. The day and the calendar month also begin at midnight by the clock. The interval required for the earth to make one absolute revolution around the sun is a **sidereal year;** it consisted of 365 days, 6 hours, 9 minutes, and 9.5 seconds of mean solar time (approximately 24 hours per day) in 1900 and is increasing at the rate of 0.0001 second annually.

The **Tropical Year,** on which the return of the seasons depends, is the interval between 2 consecutive returns of the sun to the vernal equinox. The tropical year consisted of 365 days, 5 hours, 48 minutes, and 46 seconds in 1900. It is decreasing at the rate of 0.530 second per century.

In 1956 the unit of time interval was defined to be identical with the second of **Ephemeris Time,** 1/31,556,925.9747 of the tropical year for 1900 January Od 12th hour E.T. A physical definition of the second based on a quantum transition of cesium (atomic second) was adopted in 1964. The atomic second is equal to 9,192,631,770 cycles of the emitted radiation. In 1967 this atomic second was adopted as the unit of time interval for the International System of Units.

The Zones and Seasons

The 5 zones of the earth's surface are Torrid, lying between the Tropics of Cancer and Capricorn; North Temperate, between Cancer and the Arctic Circle; South Temperate, between Capricorn and the Antarctic Circle; the Frigid Zones, between the polar Circles and the Poles.

The inclination or tilt of the earth's axis with respect to the sun determines the seasons. These are commonly marked in the North Temperate Zone, where spring begins at the vernal equinox, summer at the summer solstice, autumn at the autumnal equinox, and winter at the winter solstice.

In the South Temperate Zone, the seasons are reversed. Spring begins at the autumnal equinox, summer at the winter solstice, etc.

If the earth's axis were perpendicular to the plane of the earth's orbit around the sun, there would be no change of seasons. Day and night would be of nearly constant length, and there would be equable conditions of temperature. But the axis is tilted 23° 27′ away from a perpendicular to the orbit, and only in March and September is the axis at right angles to the sun.

The points at which the sun crosses the equator are the equinoxes, when day and night are most nearly equal. The points at which the sun is at a maximum distance from the equator are the solstices. Days and nights are then most unequal.

In June the North Pole is tilted 23° 27′ toward the sun, and the days in the northern hemisphere are longer than the nights, while the days in the southern hemisphere are shorter than the nights. In December the North Pole is tilted 23° 27′ away from the sun, and the situation is reversed.

The Seasons in 1995

In 1995 the 4 seasons will begin as follows: add one hour to EST for Atlantic Time; subtract one hour for Central, two hours for Mountain, 3 hours for Pacific, 4 hours for Yukon, 5 hours for Alaska-Hawaii, and 6 hours for Bering Time. Also shown is Greenwich Mean Time.

		Date	GMT	EST
Vernal Equinox	**Spring**	Mar. 21	2:14	21:14*
Summer Solstice	**Summer**	June 21	20:34	15:34
Autumnal Equinox	**Autumn**	Sept. 23	12:13	7:13
Winter Solstice	**Winter**	Dec. 22	8:17	3:17

*Previous Day

Poles of the Earth

The geographic (rotation) poles, or points where the earth's axis of rotation cuts the surface, are not absolutely fixed in the body of the earth. The pole of rotation describes an irregular curve about its mean position.

Two periods have been detected in this motion: (1) an annual period due to seasonal changes in barometric pressure, to load of ice and snow on the surface, and to other phenomena of seasonal character; (2) a period of about 14 months due to the shape and constitution of the earth.

In addition there are small but as yet unpredictable irregularities. The whole motion is so small that the actual pole at any time remains within a circle of 30 or 40 feet in radius centered at the mean position of the pole.

The pole of rotation for the time being is of course the pole having a latitude of 90° and an indeterminate longitude.

Magnetic Poles

The **north magnetic pole** of the earth is that region where the magnetic force is vertically downward, and the **south magnetic pole** is that region where the magnetic force is vertically upward. A compass placed at the magnetic poles experiences no directive force in azimuth.

There are slow changes in the distribution of the earth's magnetic field. These changes were at one time attributed in part to a periodic movement of the magnetic poles around the geographical poles, but later evidence refutes this theory and points, rather, to a slow migration of "disturbance" foci over the earth.

There appear shifts in position of the magnetic poles due to the changes in the earth's magnetic field. The center of the area designated as the north magnetic pole was estimated to be in about latitude 70.5° N and longitude 96° W in 1905; from recent nearby measurements and studies of the secular changes, the position in 1970 was estimated as latitude 76.2° N and longitude 101° W. Improved data rather than actual motion account for at least part of the change.

The position of the south magnetic pole in 1912 was near 71° S and longitude 150° E; the position in 1970 was estimated at latitude 66° S and longitude 139.1° E.

The direction of the horizontal components of the magnetic field at any point is known as magnetic north at that point, and the angle by which it deviates east or west of true north is known as the magnetic declination or, in the mariner's terminology, the **variation of the compass.**

A compass without error points in the direction of magnetic north. (In general, this is *not* the direction of the magnetic north pole.) If one follows the direction indicated by the north end of the compass, he or she will travel along a rather irregular curve that eventually reaches the north magnetic pole (though not usually by a great-circle route). However, the action of the compass should not be thought of as due to any influence of the distant pole, but simply as an indication of the distribution of the earth's magnetism at the place of observation.

Rotation of the Earth

The speed of rotation of the earth about its axis has been found to be slightly variable. The variations may be classified as:

(A) **Secular.** Tidal friction acts as a brake on the rotation and causes a slow secular increase in the length of the day, about 1 millisecond per century.

(B) **Irregular.** The speed of rotation may increase for a number of years, about 5 to 10, and then start decreasing. The maximum difference from the mean in the length of the day during a century is about 5 milliseconds. The accumulated difference in time has amounted to approximately 44 seconds since 1900. The cause is probably motion in the interior of the earth.

(C) **Periodic.** Seasonal variations exist with periods of 1 year and 6 months. The cumulative effect is such that each year the earth is late about 30 milliseconds near June 1 and is ahead about 30 milliseconds near Oct. 1. The maximum seasonal variation in the length of the day is about 0.5 millisecond. It is believed that the principal cause of the annual variation is the seasonal change in the wind patterns of the northern and southern hemispheres. The semiannual variation is due chiefly to tidal action of the sun, which distorts the shape of the earth slightly.

The secular and irregular variations were discovered by comparing time based on the rotation of the earth with time based on the orbital motion of the moon about the earth and of the planets about the sun. The periodic variation was determined largely with the aid of quartz-crystal clocks. The introduction of the cesium-beam atomic clock in 1955 made it possible to determine in greater detail than before the nature of the irregular and periodic variations.

Morning and Evening Stars, 1995

(GMT)

	Morning	Evening
Jan.	Venus Mars Jupiter Uranus, from Jan. 17 Neptune, from Jan. 13	Mercury Saturn Uranus, to Jan. 17 Neptune, from Jan. 13
Feb.	Mercury, from Feb. 3 Venus Mars, to Feb. 12 Jupiter Uranus Neptune	Mercury, to Feb. 3 Mars, from Feb. 12 Saturn, to Mar.6
Mar.	Mercury Venus Jupiter Saturn, from Mar. 6 Uranus Neptune	Mars Saturn, to Mar. 6
Apr.	Mercury, to Apr. 14 Venus Jupiter Saturn Uranus Neptune	Mercury, from Apr. 14 Mars
May	Venus Jupiter Saturn Uranus Neptune	Mercury Mars
Jun.	Mercury, from Jun. 5 Venus Jupiter, to Jun. 1 Saturn Uranus Neptune	Mercury, to Jun. 5 Mars Jupiter, from Jun. 1 Uranus, from Jul. 21 Neptune, from Jul. 17
Jul.	Mercury, to Jul. 28 Venus Saturn Uranus, to Jul. 21 Neptune, to Jul. 17	Mercury, from Jul. 28 Mars Jupiter Uranus, from Jul. 21 Neptune, from Jul. 17
Aug.	Venus, to Aug. 20 Saturn	Mercury Mars Jupiter Uranus Neptune
Sept.	Saturn, to Sept. 14	Mercury Venus Mars Jupiter Saturn, from Sept. 14 Uranus Neptune
Oct.	Mercury, from Oct. 5	Mercury, from Oct. 5 Venus Mars Jupiter Saturn Uranus Neptune
Nov.	Mercury, to Nov. 23	Mercury, from Nov. 23 Venus Mars Jupiter Saturn Uranus Neptune
Dec.	Jupiter, from Dec. 18	Mercury Venus Mars Jupiter, to Dec. 18 Saturn Uranus Neptune

Chronological Eras, 1995

The year 1995 of the Christian Era comprises the latter part of the 219th and the beginning of the 220th year of the independence of the U.S.

Era	Year	Begins in 1995
Byzantine	7504	Sept. 14
Jewish	5756	Sept. 24 (sunset)
Roman (Ab Urbe Condita)	2748	Jan.. 14
Nabonassar (Babylonian)	2744	Apr. 25
Japanese	2655	Jan.. 1
Grecian (Seleucidae)	2307	Sept. 14 or Oct. 14
Diocletian	1712	Sept. 12
Indian (Saka)	1917	Mar. 22
Mohammedan (Hegira)	1416	May 30

Chronological Cycles, 1995

Dominical Letter	A	Golden Number (Lunar Cycle)	I	Roman Indiction	3
Epact	29	Solar Cycle	16	Julian Period (year of)	6708

Astronomical Twilight—Meridian of Greenwich

Date 1993[1]		20° Begin h	m	End h	m	30° Begin h	m	End h	m	40° Begin h	m	End h	m	50° Begin h	m	End h	m	60° Begin h	m	End h	m
Jan.	1	5	16	**6**	**50**	5	30	**6**	**35**	5	45	**6**	**21**	6	00	**6**	**07**	6	18	**5**	**49**
	11	5	19	**6**	**56**	5	33	**6**	**43**	5	46	**6**	**30**	6	00	**6**	**17**	6	15	**6**	**01**
	21	5	21	**7**	**01**	5	32	**6**	**51**	5	43	**6**	**40**	5	55	**6**	**30**	6	06	**6**	**18**
Feb.	1	5	21	**7**	**07**	5	29	**6**	**58**	5	38	**6**	**51**	5	45	**6**	**44**	5	51	**6**	**38**
	11	5	18	**7**	**11**	5	24	**7**	**05**	5	29	**7**	**01**	5	32	**6**	**59**	5	32	**7**	**01**
	21	5	13	**7**	**15**	5	17	**7**	**12**	5	17	**7**	**12**	5	16	**7**	**14**	5	09	**7**	**23**
Mar.	1	5	08	**7**	**18**	5	08	**7**	**19**	5	06	**7**	**21**	4	59	**7**	**29**	4	44	**7**	**45**
	11	5	00	**7**	**21**	4	58	**7**	**24**	4	50	**7**	**32**	4	38	**7**	**46**	4	12	**8**	**12**

Date 1993[1]	20° Begin		20° End		30° Begin		30° End		40° Begin		40° End		50° Begin		50° End		60° Begin		60° End	
	h	m	h	m	h	m	h	m	h	m	h	m	h	m	h	m	h	m	h	m
21	4	52	**7**	**24**	4	45	**7**	**32**	4	33	**7**	**44**	4	14	**8**	**04**	3	37	**8**	**43**
Apr. 1	4	42	**7**	**28**	4	31	**7**	**39**	4	14	**7**	**57**	3	47	**8**	**25**	2	53	**9**	**21**
11	4	32	**7**	**32**	4	18	**7**	**47**	3	56	**8**	**09**	3	20	**8**	**47**	2	03	**10**	**10**
21	4	23	**7**	**36**	4	04	**7**	**54**	3	37	**8**	**23**	2	52	**9**	**11**	0	37	**11**	**47**
May 1	4	14	**7**	**41**	3	52	**8**	**04**	3	19	**8**	**37**	2	22	**9**	**39**				
11	4	08	**7**	**46**	3	41	**8**	**13**	3	03	**8**	**53**	1	49	**10**	**09**				
21	4	02	**7**	**52**	3	32	**8**	**22**	2	48	**9**	**07**	1	13	**10**	**46**				
June 1	3	58	**7**	**58**	3	26	**8**	**30**	2	36	**9**	**20**	0	21	**11**	**52**				
11	3	56	**8**	**03**	3	22	**8**	**36**	2	29	**9**	**30**								
21	3	57	**8**	**06**	3	22	**8**	**40**	2	28	**9**	**35**								
July 1	3	59	**8**	**07**	3	25	**8**	**41**	2	30	**9**	**35**								
11	4	03	**8**	**06**	3	30	**8**	**39**	2	40	**9**	**30**								
21	4	08	**8**	**03**	3	39	**8**	**33**	2	52	**9**	**18**	1	12	**11**	**23**				
Aug. 1	4	15	**7**	**56**	3	48	**8**	**23**	3	09	**9**	**01**	1	49	**10**	**20**				
11	4	20	**7**	**50**	3	56	**8**	**13**	3	22	**8**	**46**	2	21	**9**	**46**				
21	4	24	**7**	**41**	4	05	**8**	**01**	3	34	**8**	**27**	2	47	**9**	**15**				
Sept. 1	4	29	**7**	**31**	4	14	**7**	**46**	3	51	**8**	**08**	3	13	**8**	**43**	1	40	**10**	**02**
11	4	32	**7**	**20**	4	20	**7**	**33**	4	02	**7**	**50**	3	33	**8**	**16**	2	36	**9**	**12**
21	4	35	**7**	**11**	4	26	**7**	**19**	4	14	**7**	**31**	3	52	**7**	**52**	3	11	**8**	**31**
Oct. 1	4	38	**7**	**02**	4	33	**7**	**05**	4	25	**7**	**13**	4	10	**7**	**28**	3	41	**7**	**54**
11	4	40	**6**	**53**	4	40	**6**	**53**	4	35	**6**	**58**	4	26	**7**	**05**	4	07	**7**	**23**
21	4	43	**6**	**47**	4	45	**6**	**44**	4	45	**6**	**43**	4	41	**6**	**46**	4	32	**6**	**55**
Nov. 1	4	46	**6**	**41**	4	52	**6**	**34**	4	56	**6**	**30**	4	58	**6**	**27**	4	56	**6**	**27**
11	4	50	**6**	**38**	4	59	**6**	**28**	5	06	**6**	**21**	5	13	**6**	**14**	5	17	**6**	**08**
21	4	55	**6**	**36**	5	06	**6**	**25**	5	16	**6**	**15**	5	26	**6**	**04**	5	37	**5**	**52**
Dec. 1	5	00	**6**	**37**	5	13	**6**	**24**	5	25	**6**	**11**	5	38	**5**	**58**	5	53	**5**	**42**
11	5	06	**6**	**40**	5	20	**6**	**26**	5	34	**6**	**12**	5	48	**5**	**57**	6	06	**5**	**38**
21	5	11	**6**	**45**	5	25	**6**	**30**	5	39	**6**	**16**	5	55	**6**	**00**	6	15	**5**	**40**
31	5	15	**6**	**50**	5	30	**6**	**35**	5	44	**6**	**21**	6	00	**6**	**06**	6	18	**5**	**48**

(1)Although the instant of the sun's horizontal depression may be calculated precisely, the phenomena associated with astronomical twilight are sufficiently imprecise that the table is not recalculated each year.

Total Eclipses, 1940-2000

Date	Duration m	Duration s	Width miles	Path of Totality
1940 Oct. 1	5	35	135	Colombia, Brazil, Atlantic Ocean, S. Africa
1941 Sept. 21	3	21	88	Soviet Union, China, Pacific Ocean
1943 Feb. 4	2	39	142	Japan, Pacific Ocean, Alaska
1944 Jan. 25	4	08	90	Peru, Brazil, W. Africa
1945 July 9	1	15	57	US, Canada, Greenland, Scandinavia, USSR
1947 May 20	5	13	121	S. America, Atlantic Ocean, Africa
1948 Nov. 1	1	55	52	Africa, Indian Ocean
1950 Sept. 12	1	13	83	Arctic Ocean, Siberia, Pacific Ocean
1952 Feb. 25	3	09	85	Africa, Middle East, Soviet Union
1954 June 30	2	35	95	US, Canada, Iceland, Europe, Middle East
1955 June 20	7	07	157	SE Asia, Philippines, Pacific Ocean
1956 June 8	4	44	266	South Pacific Ocean
1958 Oct. 12	5	10	129	Pacific Ocean, Chile, Argentina
1959 Oct. 2	3	01	75	New England, Atlantic Ocean, Africa
1961 Feb. 15	2	45	160	Europe, Soviet Union
1962 Feb. 5	4	08	91	Borneo, New Guinea, Pacific Ocean
1963 July 20	1	39	63	Pacific Ocean, Alaska, Canada, Maine
1965 May 30	5	15	123	New Zealand, Pacific Ocean
1966 Nov. 12	1	57	52	Pacific Ocean, S. America, Atlantic Ocean
1968 Sept. 22	0	39	64	Soviet Union, China
1970 Mar. 7	3	27	95	Pacific Ocean, Mexico, Eastern US, Canada
1972 July 10	2	35	109	Siberia, Alaska, Canada
1973 June 30	7	03	159	Atlantic Ocean, Central Africa, Indian Ocean
1974 June 20	5	08	214	Indian Ocean, Australia
1976 Oct. 23	4	46	123	Africa, Indian Ocean, Australia
1977 Oct. 12	2	37	61	Pacific Ocean, Colombia, Venezuela
1979 Feb. 26	2	49	185	NW US, Canada, Greenland
1980 Feb. 16	4	08	92	Africa, Indian Ocean, India, Burma, China
1981 July 31	2	02	67	Soviet Union, Pacific Ocean
1983 June 11	5	10	123	Indian Ocean, Indonesia, New Guinea
1984 Nov. 22	1	59	53	New Guinea, Pacific Ocean
1985 Nov. 12	1	58	430	Antarctica
1986 Oct. 3h	0	01	1	North Atlantic Ocean
1987 Mar. 29h	0	07	3	South Atlantic Ocean, Africa
1988 Mar. 18	3	46	104	Sumatra, Borneo, Philippines, Pacific Ocean
1990 July 22	2	32	125	Finland, Soviet Union, Aleutian Islands
1991 July 11	6	53	160	Hawaii, Mexico, C. America, Colombia, Brazil
1992 June 30	5	20	182	South Atlantic Ocean
1994 Nov. 3	4	23	117	Peru, Bolivia, Paraguay, Brazil
1995 Oct. 24	2	09	48	Iran, India, SE Asia
1997 Mar. 9	2	50	221	Mongolia, Siberia
1998 Feb. 26	4	08	94	Galapagos Islands, Panama, Colombia, Venezuela
1999 Aug. 11	2	22	69	Europe, Middle East, India

(1) "h" indicates annular-total hybrid eclipse.

1st Month | **January 1995** | **31 days**

Greenwich Mean Time

NOTE: For each day, numbers on first line indicate Sun. *Italic* numbers on second line indicate *Moon.* Degrees are North Latitude.

FM = full moon; LQ = last quarter; NM = new moon; FQ = first quarter.

CAUTION: Must be converted to local time. For instructions see page 263.

Day of month week year	Sun on Meridian Moon Phase h m s	Sun's Declination °	20° Rise Sun Moon h m	20° Set Sun Moon h m	30° Rise Sun Moon h m	30° Set Sun Moon h m	40° Rise Sun Moon h m	40° Set Sun Moon h m	50° Rise Sun Moon h m	50° Set Sun Moon h m	60° Rise Sun Moon h m	60° Set Sun Moon h m
1 SU	12 3 26	-23 3	6: 35	17: 32	6: 56	17: 11	7: 22	16: 45	7: 59	16: 8	9: 2	15: 5
1	*10 56 NM*		*6: 20*	*17: 50*	*6: 38*	*17: 33*	*7: 1*	*17: 12*	*7: 32*	*16: 42*	*8: 23*	*15: 52*
2 MO	12 3 54	-22 58	6: 35	17: 33	6: 56	17: 12	7: 22	16: 46	7: 59	16: 9	9: 2	15: 6
2			*7: 16*	*18: 54*	*7: 32*	*18: 39*	*7: 51*	*18: 22*	*8: 17*	*17: 57*	*9: 0*	*17: 17*
3 TU	12 4 22	-22 53	6: 36	17: 33	6: 56	17: 13	7: 22	16: 47	7: 58	16: 11	9: 1	15: 8
3			*8: 7*	*19: 55*	*8: 19*	*19: 44*	*8: 34*	*19: 31*	*8: 55*	*19: 13*	*9: 26*	*18: 44*
4 WE	12 4 50	-22 47	6: 36	17: 34	6: 56	17: 13	7: 22	16: 48	7: 58	16: 12	9: 1	15: 9
4			*8: 53*	*20: 52*	*9: 2*	*20: 46*	*9: 12*	*20: 38*	*9: 26*	*20: 27*	*9: 47*	*20: 10*
5 TH	12 5 17	-22 41	6: 36	17: 34	6: 57	17: 14	7: 22	16: 49	7: 58	16: 13	9: 0	15: 11
5			*9: 36*	*21: 48*	*9: 40*	*21: 45*	*9: 45*	*21: 42*	*9: 52*	*21: 38*	*10: 3*	*21: 32*
6 FR	12 5 43	-22 34	6: 36	17: 35	6: 57	17: 15	7: 22	16: 50	7: 58	16: 14	8: 59	15: 13
6			*10: 16*	*22: 40*	*10: 16*	*22: 42*	*10: 16*	*22: 44*	*10: 17*	*22: 47*	*10: 18*	*22: 52*
7 SA	12 6 10	-22 27	6: 37	17: 36	6: 57	17: 16	7: 22	16: 50	7: 57	16: 15	8: 58	15: 14
7			*10: 54*	*23: 32*	*10: 51*	*23: 37*	*10: 46*	*23: 44*	*10: 41*	*23: 53*	*10: 32*	– –
8 SU	12 6 35	-22 20	6: 37	17: 36	6: 57	17: 16	7: 22	16: 51	7: 57	16: 16	8: 57	15: 16
8	*15 46 FQ*		*11: 32*	– –	*11: 25*	– –	*11: 16*	– –	*11: 4*	– –	*10: 46*	*0: 8*
9 MO	12 7 1	-22 12	6: 37	17: 37	6: 57	17: 17	7: 22	16: 52	7: 57	16: 18	8: 56	15: 18
9			*12: 11*	*0: 22*	*12: 0*	*0: 31*	*11: 47*	*0: 42*	*11: 30*	*0: 58*	*11: 2*	*1: 22*
10 TU	12 7 25	-22 3	6: 37	17: 38	6: 57	17: 18	7: 22	16: 53	7: 56	16: 19	8: 55	15: 20
10			*12: 51*	*1: 12*	*12: 37*	*1: 24*	*12: 20*	*1: 40*	*11: 58*	*2: 1*	*11: 21*	*2: 35*
11 WE	12 7 49	-21 54	6: 37	17: 38	6: 57	17: 19	7: 21	16: 54	7: 56	16: 20	8: 54	15: 22
11			*13: 33*	*2: 2*	*13: 17*	*2: 17*	*12: 57*	*2: 35*	*12: 29*	*3: 2*	*11: 45*	*3: 44*
12 TH	12 8 13	-21 45	6: 38	17: 39	6: 57	17: 20	7: 21	16: 55	7: 55	16: 22	8: 53	15: 24
12			*14: 17*	*2: 51*	*13: 59*	*3: 8*	*13: 37*	*3: 30*	*13: 6*	*4: 0*	*12: 16*	*4: 49*
13 FR	12 8 36	-21 35	6: 38	17: 40	6: 57	17: 20	7: 21	16: 57	7: 54	16: 23	8: 51	15: 26
13			*15: 4*	*3: 41*	*14: 45*	*3: 59*	*14: 22*	*4: 22*	*13: 49*	*4: 54*	*12: 55*	*5: 48*
14 SA	12 8 58	-21 25	6: 38	17: 40	6: 57	17: 21	7: 21	16: 58	7: 54	16: 25	8: 50	15: 29
14			*15: 53*	*4: 30*	*15: 34*	*4: 48*	*15: 11*	*5: 12*	*14: 39*	*5: 44*	*13: 45*	*6: 39*
15 SU	12 9 20	-21 15	6: 38	17: 41	6: 57	17: 22	7: 20	16: 59	7: 53	16: 26	8: 48	15: 31
15			*16: 44*	*5: 18*	*16: 27*	*5: 35*	*16: 5*	*5: 58*	*15: 35*	*6: 28*	*14: 45*	*7: 19*
16 MO	12 9 40	-21 4	6: 38	17: 42	6: 57	17: 23	7: 20	17: 0	7: 52	16: 27	8: 47	15: 33
16	*20 26 FM*		*17: 36*	*6: 4*	*17: 21*	*6: 20*	*17: 2*	*6: 40*	*16: 36*	*7: 7*	*15: 54*	*7: 52*
17 TU	12 10 1	-20 52	6: 38	17: 42	6: 56	17: 24	7: 19	17: 1	7: 51	16: 29	8: 45	15: 35
17			*18: 29*	*6: 48*	*18: 17*	*7: 2*	*18: 2*	*7: 18*	*17: 41*	*7: 41*	*17: 8*	*8: 17*
18 WE	12 10 20	-20 41	6: 38	17: 43	6: 56	17: 25	7: 19	17: 2	7: 51	16: 30	8: 44	15: 38
18			*19: 23*	*7: 31*	*19: 14*	*7: 41*	*19: 4*	*7: 54*	*18: 49*	*8: 11*	*18: 26*	*8: 37*
19 TH	12 10 39	-20 28	6: 38	17: 44	6: 56	17: 26	7: 18	17: 3	7: 50	16: 32	8: 42	15: 40
19			*20: 17*	*8: 12*	*20: 12*	*8: 19*	*20: 6*	*8: 27*	*19: 58*	*8: 38*	*19: 46*	*8: 54*
20 FR	12 10 57	-20 16	6: 38	17: 44	6: 56	17: 26	7: 18	17: 4	7: 49	16: 34	8: 40	15: 42
20			*21: 11*	*8: 53*	*21: 11*	*8: 55*	*21: 10*	*8: 59*	*21: 9*	*9: 3*	*21: 7*	*9: 10*
21 SA	12 11 14	-20 3	6: 38	17: 45	6: 55	17: 27	7: 17	17: 5	7: 48	16: 35	8: 38	15: 45
21			*22: 7*	*9: 33*	*22: 10*	*9: 32*	*22: 14*	*9: 30*	*22: 20*	*9: 28*	*22: 30*	*9: 25*
22 SU	12 11 31	-19 50	6: 38	17: 45	6: 55	17: 28	7: 17	17: 7	7: 47	16: 37	8: 36	15: 47
22			*23: 3*	*10: 15*	*23: 11*	*10: 10*	*23: 20*	*10: 3*	*23: 33*	*9: 54*	*23: 54*	*9: 40*
23 MO	12 11 47	-19 36	6: 38	17: 46	6: 55	17: 29	7: 16	17: 8	7: 46	16: 38	8: 34	15: 50
23			– –	*10: 59*	– –	*10: 49*	– –	*10: 38*	– –	*10: 22*	– –	*9: 58*
24 TU	12 12 2	-19 22	6: 37	17: 47	6: 54	17: 30	7: 16	17: 9	7: 45	16: 40	8: 32	15: 52
24	*4 58 LQ*		*0: 2*	*11: 46*	*0: 13*	*11: 33*	*0: 27*	*11: 16*	*0: 47*	*10: 54*	*1: 19*	*10: 20*
25 WE	12 12 16	-19 8	6: 37	17: 47	6: 54	17: 31	7: 15	17: 10	7: 43	16: 42	8: 30	15: 55
25			*1: 2*	*12: 36*	*1: 17*	*12: 20*	*1: 35*	*12: 0*	*2: 1*	*11: 33*	*2: 44*	*10: 48*
26 TH	12 12 30	-18 53	6: 37	17: 48	6: 54	17: 32	7: 14	17: 11	7: 42	16: 43	8: 28	15: 57
26			*2: 3*	*13: 31*	*2: 20*	*13: 13*	*2: 42*	*12: 51*	*3: 13*	*12: 19*	*4: 4*	*11: 26*
27 FR	12 12 42	-18 38	6: 37	17: 49	6: 53	17: 32	7: 13	17: 13	7: 41	16: 45	8: 26	16: 0
27			*3: 4*	*14: 30*	*3: 23*	*14: 11*	*3: 47*	*13: 48*	*4: 19*	*13: 15*	*5: 15*	*12: 19*
28 SA	12 12 54	-18 22	6: 37	17: 49	6: 53	17: 33	7: 13	17: 14	7: 40	16: 47	8: 24	16: 3
28			*4: 4*	*15: 32*	*4: 23*	*15: 14*	*4: 46*	*14: 51*	*5: 18*	*14: 20*	*6: 12*	*13: 26*
29 SU	12 13 6	-18 7	6: 37	17: 50	6: 52	17: 34	7: 12	17: 15	7: 38	16: 48	8: 22	16: 5
29			*5: 1*	*16: 34*	*5: 18*	*16: 18*	*5: 39*	*15: 59*	*6: 8*	*15: 31*	*6: 55*	*14: 46*
30 MO	12 13 16	-17 51	6: 36	17: 50	6: 52	17: 35	7: 11	17: 16	7: 37	16: 50	8: 20	16: 8
30	*22 48 NM*		*5: 54*	*17: 36*	*6: 8*	*17: 23*	*6: 25*	*17: 8*	*6: 49*	*16: 46*	*7: 26*	*16: 11*
31 TU	12 13 26	-17 34	6: 36	17: 51	6: 51	17: 36	7: 10	17: 17	7: 36	16: 52	8: 17	16: 10
31			*6: 42*	*18: 35*	*6: 53*	*18: 27*	*7: 5*	*18: 16*	*7: 23*	*18: 1*	*7: 50*	*17: 38*

2d Month — February 1995 — 28 days

Greenwich Mean Time

NOTE: For each day, numbers on first line indicate Sun. *Italic* numbers on second line indicate *Moon.* Degrees are North Latitude.

FM = full moon; LQ = last quarter; NM = new moon; FQ = first quarter.

CAUTION: Must be converted to local time. For instructions see page 263.

Day of month / week year	Sun on Meridian / Moon Phase (h m s)	Sun's Declination (° ′)	20° Rise Sun/Moon (h m)	20° Set Sun/Moon (h m)	30° Rise Sun/Moon (h m)	30° Set Sun/Moon (h m)	40° Rise Sun/Moon (h m)	40° Set Sun/Moon (h m)	50° Rise Sun/Moon (h m)	50° Set Sun/Moon (h m)	60° Rise Sun/Moon (h m)	60° Set Sun/Moon (h m)
1 WE	12 13 34	-17 17	6: 36	17: 52	6: 51	17: 37	7: 9	17: 19	7: 34	16: 53	8: 15	16: 13
32			*7: 27*	*19: 32*	*7: 34*	*19: 28*	*7: 41*	*19: 22*	*7: 52*	*19: 15*	*8: 8*	*19: 3*
2 TH	12 13 42	-17 0	6: 35	17: 52	6: 50	17: 38	7: 8	17: 20	7: 33	16: 55	8: 13	16: 16
33			*8: 9*	*20: 27*	*8: 12*	*20: 27*	*8: 14*	*20: 27*	*8: 18*	*20: 26*	*8: 24*	*20: 25*
3 FR	12 13 49	-16 43	6: 35	17: 53	6: 49	17: 39	7: 7	17: 21	7: 31	16: 57	8: 10	16: 18
34			*8: 49*	*21: 21*	*8: 48*	*21: 24*	*8: 46*	*21: 29*	*8: 43*	*21: 35*	*8: 39*	*21: 44*
4 SA	12 13 56	-16 25	6: 35	17: 53	6: 49	17: 39	7: 6	17: 22	7: 30	16: 59	8: 8	16: 21
35			*9: 28*	*22: 12*	*9: 23*	*22: 20*	*9: 16*	*22: 29*	*9: 7*	*22: 41*	*8: 54*	*23: 1*
5 SU	12 14 1	-16 8	6: 34	17: 54	6: 48	17: 40	7: 5	17: 23	7: 28	17: 0	8: 5	16: 24
36			*10: 8*	*23: 3*	*9: 59*	*23: 14*	*9: 47*	*23: 28*	*9: 33*	*23: 46*	*9: 10*	– –
6 MO	12 14 6	-15 49	6: 34	17: 54	6: 47	17: 41	7: 4	17: 25	7: 27	17: 2	8: 3	16: 26
37			*10: 47*	*23: 54*	*10: 35*	– –	*10: 20*	– –	*10: 0*	– –	*9: 28*	*0: 15*
7 TU	12 14 9	-15 31	6: 34	17: 55	6: 47	17: 42	7: 3	17: 26	7: 25	17: 4	8: 0	16: 29
38	*12 54 FQ*		*11: 29*	– –	*11: 14*	*0: 7*	*10: 55*	*0: 25*	*10: 30*	*0: 48*	*9: 50*	*1: 27*
8 WE	12 14 12	-15 12	6: 33	17: 56	6: 46	17: 43	7: 2	17: 27	7: 24	17: 5	7: 58	16: 31
39			*12: 12*	*0: 44*	*11: 55*	*1: 0*	*11: 34*	*1: 20*	*11: 5*	*1: 48*	*10: 17*	*2: 34*
9 TH	12 14 14	-14 53	6: 33	17: 56	6: 45	17: 44	7: 1	17: 28	7: 22	17: 7	7: 55	16: 34
40			*12: 57*	*1: 33*	*12: 39*	*1: 51*	*12: 17*	*2: 13*	*11: 45*	*2: 44*	*10: 53*	*3: 36*
10 FR	12 14 16	-14 34	6: 32	17: 57	6: 45	17: 44	7: 0	17: 29	7: 20	17: 9	7: 53	16: 37
41			*13: 45*	*2: 22*	*13: 27*	*2: 41*	*13: 4*	*3: 4*	*12: 32*	*3: 36*	*11: 38*	*4: 30*
11 SA	12 14 16	-14 15	6: 32	17: 57	6: 44	17: 45	6: 59	17: 31	7: 19	17: 11	7: 50	16: 39
42			*14: 35*	*3: 10*	*14: 18*	*3: 28*	*13: 55*	*3: 51*	*13: 25*	*4: 22*	*12: 33*	*5: 15*
12 SU	12 14 16	-13 55	6: 31	17: 58	6: 43	17: 46	6: 57	17: 32	7: 17	17: 12	7: 48	16: 42
43			*15: 27*	*3: 57*	*15: 11*	*4: 14*	*14: 51*	*4: 35*	*14: 24*	*5: 3*	*13: 38*	*5: 50*
13 MO	12 14 15	-13 35	6: 31	17: 58	6: 42	17: 47	6: 56	17: 33	7: 15	17: 14	7: 45	16: 45
44			*16: 20*	*4: 42*	*16: 7*	*4: 57*	*15: 50*	*5: 15*	*15: 27*	*5: 40*	*14: 50*	*6: 19*
14 TU	12 14 13	-13 15	6: 30	17: 59	6: 41	17: 48	6: 55	17: 34	7: 13	17: 16	7: 42	16: 47
45			*17: 14*	*5: 26*	*17: 4*	*5: 38*	*16: 52*	*5: 52*	*16: 34*	*6: 11*	*16: 7*	*6: 42*
15 WE	12 14 11	-12 55	6: 30	17: 59	6: 40	17: 48	6: 54	17: 35	7: 12	17: 18	7: 39	16: 50
46	*12 15 FM*		*18: 9*	*6: 9*	*18: 3*	*6: 17*	*17: 55*	*6: 27*	*17: 44*	*6: 40*	*17: 27*	*7: 1*
16 TH	12 14 8	-12 34	6: 29	18: 0	6: 40	17: 49	6: 52	17: 36	7: 10	17: 19	7: 37	16: 53
47			*19: 4*	*6: 51*	*19: 2*	*6: 55*	*18: 59*	*7: 0*	*18: 56*	*7: 7*	*18: 50*	*7: 17*
17 FR	12 14 4	-12 13	6: 28	18: 0	6: 39	17: 50	6: 51	17: 38	7: 8	17: 21	7: 34	16: 55
48			*20: 1*	*7: 32*	*20: 3*	*7: 32*	*20: 5*	*7: 33*	*20: 8*	*7: 33*	*20: 14*	*7: 33*
18 SA	12 13 59	-11 52	6: 28	18: 0	6: 38	17: 51	6: 50	17: 39	7: 6	17: 23	7: 31	16: 58
49			*20: 58*	*8: 15*	*21: 4*	*8: 11*	*21: 12*	*8: 6*	*21: 22*	*7: 59*	*21: 39*	*7: 49*
19 SU	12 13 54	-11 31	6: 27	18: 1	6: 37	17: 51	6: 48	17: 40	7: 4	17: 24	7: 29	17: 0
50			*21: 57*	*8: 58*	*22: 7*	*8: 50*	*22: 19*	*8: 41*	*22: 37*	*8: 27*	*23: 5*	*8: 7*
20 MO	12 13 48	-11 10	6: 27	18: 1	6: 36	17: 52	6: 47	17: 41	7: 2	17: 26	7: 26	17: 3
51			*22: 56*	*9: 45*	*23: 10*	*9: 33*	*23: 27*	*9: 18*	*23: 51*	*8: 59*	– –	*8: 28*
21 TU	12 13 41	-10 48	6: 26	18: 2	6: 35	17: 53	6: 46	17: 42	7: 0	17: 28	7: 23	17: 6
52			*23: 57*	*10: 34*	– –	*10: 19*	– –	*10: 0*	– –	*9: 35*	*0: 30*	*8: 54*
22 WE	12 13 34	-10 27	6: 25	18: 2	6: 34	17: 54	6: 44	17: 43	6: 58	17: 30	7: 20	17: 8
53	*12 4 LQ*		– –	*11: 27*	*0: 13*	*11: 10*	*0: 34*	*10: 48*	*1: 3*	*10: 18*	*1: 51*	*9: 29*
23 TH	12 13 26	-10 5	6: 25	18: 3	6: 33	17: 54	6: 43	17: 44	6: 56	17: 31	7: 17	17: 11
54			*0: 57*	*12: 23*	*1: 15*	*12: 5*	*1: 38*	*11: 42*	*2: 10*	*11: 9*	*3: 4*	*10: 15*
24 FR	12 13 18	-9 43	6: 24	18: 3	6: 32	17: 55	6: 42	17: 46	6: 55	17: 33	7: 14	17: 13
55			*1: 56*	*13: 22*	*2: 14*	*13: 4*	*2: 37*	*12: 41*	*3: 10*	*12: 9*	*4: 4*	*11: 15*
25 SA	12 13 9	-9 21	6: 23	18: 3	6: 31	17: 56	6: 40	17: 47	6: 53	17: 35	7: 12	17: 16
56			*2: 52*	*14: 22*	*3: 9*	*14: 6*	*3: 31*	*13: 45*	*4: 1*	*13: 16*	*4: 51*	*12: 28*
26 SU	12 12 59	-8 58	6: 22	18: 4	6: 30	17: 57	6: 39	17: 48	6: 51	17: 36	7: 9	17: 18
57			*3: 45*	*15: 22*	*4: 0*	*15: 8*	*4: 19*	*14: 51*	*4: 44*	*14: 27*	*5: 25*	*13: 48*
27 MO	12 12 49	-8 36	6: 22	18: 4	6: 29	17: 57	6: 37	17: 49	6: 49	17: 38	7: 6	17: 21
58			*4: 34*	*16: 21*	*4: 46*	*16: 11*	*5: 0*	*15: 58*	*5: 20*	*15: 40*	*5: 52*	*15: 12*
28 TU	12 12 38	-8 13	6: 21	18: 5	6: 28	17: 58	6: 36	17: 50	6: 47	17: 40	7: 3	17: 24
59			*5: 19*	*17: 19*	*5: 28*	*17: 12*	*5: 38*	*17: 4*	*5: 51*	*16: 53*	*6: 12*	*16: 36*

3d Month **March 1995** **31 days**

Greenwich Mean Time

NOTE: For each day, numbers on first line indicate Sun. *Italic* numbers on second line indicate *Moon.* Degrees are North Latitude.

FM = full moon; LQ = last quarter; NM = new moon; FQ = first quarter.

CAUTION: Must be converted to local time. For instructions see page 263.

Day of month week year	Sun on Meridian Moon Phase	Sun's Declination	20° Rise Sun Moon	20° Set Sun Moon	30° Rise Sun Moon	30° Set Sun Moon	40° Rise Sun Moon	40° Set Sun Moon	50° Rise Sun Moon	50° Set Sun Moon	60° Rise Sun Moon	60° Set Sun Moon
	h m s	° ′	h m	h m	h m	h m	h m	h m	h m	h m	h m	h m
1 WE	12 12 27	-7 51	6: 20	18: 5	6: 27	17: 59	6: 34	17: 51	6: 44	17: 41	7: 0	17: 26
60	*11 48 NM*		*6: 2*	*18: 14*	*6: 7*	*18: 12*	*6: 12*	*18: 9*	*6: 19*	*18: 5*	*6: 30*	*17: 59*
2 TH	12 12 15	-7 28	6: 20	18: 5	6: 26	17: 59	6: 33	17: 52	6: 42	17: 43	6: 57	17: 29
61			*6: 43*	*19: 8*	*6: 43*	*19: 10*	*6: 44*	*19: 12*	*6: 44*	*19: 15*	*6: 45*	*19: 19*
3 FR	12 12 3	-7 5	6: 19	18: 6	6: 24	18: 0	6: 31	17: 53	6: 40	17: 45	6: 54	17: 31
62			*7: 23*	*20: 1*	*7: 19*	*20: 7*	*7: 15*	*20: 14*	*7: 9*	*20: 23*	*7: 0*	*20: 38*
4 SA	12 11 51	-6 42	6: 18	18: 6	6: 23	18: 1	6: 30	17: 55	6: 38	17: 46	6: 51	17: 34
63			*8: 3*	*20: 53*	*7: 55*	*21: 2*	*7: 46*	*21: 13*	*7: 34*	*21: 29*	*7: 16*	*21: 54*
5 SU	12 11 38	-6 19	6: 17	18: 6	6: 22	18: 1	6: 28	17: 56	6: 36	17: 48	6: 48	17: 36
64			*8: 43*	*21: 44*	*8: 32*	*21: 56*	*8: 19*	*22: 12*	*8: 1*	*22: 33*	*7: 34*	*23: 7*
6 MO	12 11 24	-5 56	6: 16	18: 7	6: 21	18: 2	6: 27	17: 57	6: 34	17: 50	6: 45	17: 39
65			*9: 24*	*22: 35*	*9: 10*	*22: 50*	*8: 53*	*23: 8*	*8: 31*	*23: 34*	*7: 54*	– –
7 TU	12 11 10	-5 33	6: 16	18: 7	6: 20	18: 3	6: 25	17: 58	6: 32	17: 51	6: 42	17: 41
66			*10: 6*	*23: 25*	*9: 51*	*23: 42*	*9: 31*	– –	*9: 4*	– –	*8: 20*	*0: 17*
8 WE	12 10 55	-5 9	6: 15	18: 7	6: 19	18: 3	6: 24	17: 59	6: 30	17: 53	6: 39	17: 44
67			*10: 51*	– –	*10: 34*	– –	*10: 12*	*0: 3*	*9: 42*	*0: 32*	*8: 52*	*1: 21*
9 TH	12 10 41	-4 46	6: 14	18: 8	6: 18	18: 4	6: 22	18: 0	6: 28	17: 54	6: 36	17: 46
68	*10 14 FQ*		*11: 38*	*0: 14*	*11: 19*	*0: 32*	*10: 57*	*0: 54*	*10: 25*	*1: 26*	*9: 32*	*2: 18*
10 FR	12 10 25	-4 22	6: 13	18: 8	6: 17	18: 5	6: 20	18: 1	6: 26	17: 56	6: 33	17: 49
69			*12: 26*	*1: 2*	*12: 8*	*1: 20*	*11: 46*	*1: 43*	*11: 15*	*2: 14*	*10: 23*	*3: 7*
11 SA	12 10 10	-3 59	6: 12	18: 8	6: 15	18: 5	6: 19	18: 2	6: 24	17: 58	6: 30	17: 51
70			*13: 17*	*1: 49*	*13: 0*	*2: 6*	*12: 39*	*2: 27*	*12: 10*	*2: 57*	*11: 23*	*3: 46*
12 SU	12 9 54	-3 35	6: 11	18: 9	6: 14	18: 6	6: 17	18: 3	6: 21	17: 59	6: 27	17: 54
71			*14: 9*	*2: 34*	*13: 54*	*2: 50*	*13: 36*	*3: 9*	*13: 11*	*3: 35*	*12: 31*	*4: 18*
13 MO	12 9 38	-3 12	6: 11	18: 9	6: 13	18: 7	6: 16	18: 4	6: 19	18: 1	6: 24	17: 56
72			*15: 2*	*3: 18*	*14: 50*	*3: 31*	*14: 36*	*3: 47*	*14: 16*	*4: 9*	*13: 45*	*4: 43*
14 TU	12 9 21	-2 48	6: 10	18: 9	6: 12	18: 7	6: 14	18: 5	6: 17	18: 3	6: 21	17: 59
73			*15: 56*	*4: 1*	*15: 48*	*4: 11*	*15: 38*	*4: 23*	*15: 25*	*4: 39*	*15: 3*	*5: 4*
15 WE	12 9 5	-2 24	6: 9	18: 9	6: 11	18: 8	6: 13	18: 6	6: 15	18: 4	6: 18	18: 1
74			*16: 52*	*4: 44*	*16: 48*	*4: 50*	*16: 42*	*4: 57*	*16: 36*	*5: 7*	*16: 25*	*5: 22*
16 TH	12 8 48	-2 1	6: 8	18: 10	6: 9	18: 9	6: 11	18: 7	6: 13	18: 6	6: 15	18: 3
75			*17: 48*	*5: 26*	*17: 49*	*5: 28*	*17: 49*	*5: 30*	*17: 49*	*5: 34*	*17: 49*	*5: 38*
17 FR	12 8 30	-1 37	6: 7	18: 10	6: 8	18: 9	6: 9	18: 8	6: 11	18: 7	6: 12	18: 6
76	*1 26 FM*		*18: 47*	*6: 9*	*18: 51*	*6: 7*	*18: 56*	*6: 4*	*19: 4*	*6: 0*	*19: 16*	*5: 55*
18 SA	12 8 13	-1 13	6: 6	18: 10	6: 7	18: 10	6: 8	18: 9	6: 8	18: 9	6: 9	18: 8
77			*19: 46*	*6: 53*	*19: 55*	*6: 47*	*20: 6*	*6: 39*	*20: 20*	*6: 29*	*20: 44*	*6: 13*
19 SU	12 7 55	-0 50	6: 6	18: 11	6: 6	18: 10	6: 6	18: 10	6: 6	18: 11	6: 6	18: 11
78			*20: 48*	*7: 40*	*21: 0*	*7: 30*	*21: 15*	*7: 17*	*21: 37*	*7: 0*	*22: 11*	*6: 33*
20 MO	12 7 38	-0 26	6: 5	18: 11	6: 5	18: 11	6: 4	18: 11	6: 4	18: 12	6: 3	18: 13
79			*21: 49*	*8: 30*	*22: 5*	*8: 16*	*22: 24*	*7: 59*	*22: 52*	*7: 35*	*23: 36*	*6: 58*
21 TU	12 7 20	-0 2	6: 4	18: 11	6: 3	18: 12	6: 3	18: 12	6: 2	18: 14	6: 0	18: 16
80			*22: 51*	*9: 23*	*23: 9*	*9: 6*	*23: 31*	*8: 46*	– –	*8: 17*	– –	*7: 31*
22 WE	12 7 2	0 21	6: 3	18: 11	6: 2	18: 12	6: 1	18: 14	6: 0	18: 15	5: 57	18: 18
81			*23: 51*	*10: 19*	– –	*10: 1*	– –	*9: 38*	*0: 2*	*9: 7*	*0: 53*	*8: 14*
23 TH	12 6 44	0 45	6: 2	18: 12	6: 1	18: 13	6: 0	18: 15	5: 58	18: 17	5: 54	18: 21
82	*20 10 LQ*		– –	*11: 17*	*0: 9*	*10: 59*	*0: 32*	*10: 36*	*1: 4*	*10: 5*	*1: 58*	*9: 11*
24 FR	12 6 26	1 9	6: 1	18: 12	6: 0	18: 14	5: 58	18: 16	5: 55	18: 18	5: 51	18: 23
83			*0: 48*	*12: 17*	*1: 6*	*12: 0*	*1: 28*	*11: 39*	*1: 58*	*11: 9*	*2: 49*	*10: 19*
25 SA	12 6 8	1 32	6: 0	18: 12	5: 59	18: 14	5: 56	18: 17	5: 53	18: 20	5: 48	18: 25
84			*1: 41*	*13: 16*	*1: 57*	*13: 1*	*2: 16*	*12: 43*	*2: 43*	*12: 18*	*3: 27*	*11: 36*
26 SU	12 5 49	1 56	5: 59	18: 13	5: 57	18: 15	5: 55	18: 18	5: 51	18: 22	5: 45	18: 28
85			*2: 30*	*14: 14*	*2: 43*	*14: 3*	*2: 59*	*13: 48*	*3: 21*	*13: 29*	*3: 55*	*12: 57*
27 MO	12 5 31	2 20	5: 59	18: 13	5: 56	18: 15	5: 53	18: 19	5: 49	18: 23	5: 42	18: 30
86			*3: 16*	*15: 11*	*3: 25*	*15: 3*	*3: 37*	*14: 53*	*3: 53*	*14: 40*	*4: 17*	*14: 19*
28 TU	12 5 13	2 43	5: 58	18: 13	5: 55	18: 16	5: 51	18: 20	5: 47	18: 25	5: 39	18: 33
87			*3: 59*	*16: 6*	*4: 4*	*16: 2*	*4: 11*	*15: 57*	*4: 21*	*15: 50*	*4: 35*	*15: 40*
29 WE	12 4 55	3 7	5: 57	18: 13	5: 54	18: 17	5: 50	18: 21	5: 45	18: 26	5: 36	18: 35
88			*4: 40*	*16: 59*	*4: 41*	*16: 59*	*4: 44*	*16: 59*	*4: 47*	*17: 0*	*4: 51*	*17: 0*
30 TH	12 4 37	3 30	5: 56	18: 14	5: 53	18: 17	5: 48	18: 22	5: 42	18: 28	5: 33	18: 38
89			*5: 19*	*17: 52*	*5: 17*	*17: 56*	*5: 15*	*18: 1*	*5: 11*	*18: 8*	*5: 6*	*18: 18*
31 FR	12 4 19	3 53	5: 55	18: 14	5: 51	18: 18	5: 47	18: 23	5: 40	18: 29	5: 30	18: 40
90	*2 9 NM*		*5: 59*	*18: 44*	*5: 53*	*18: 51*	*5: 46*	*19: 1*	*5: 36*	*19: 14*	*5: 22*	*19: 34*

4th Month | **April 1995** | **30 days**

Greenwich Mean Time

NOTE: For each day, numbers on first line indicate Sun. *Italic* numbers on second line indicate *Moon.* Degrees are North Latitude.

FM = full moon; LQ = last quarter; NM = new moon; FQ = first quarter.

CAUTION: Must be converted to local time. For instructions see page 263.

Day of month week year	Sun on Meridian Moon Phase h m s	Sun's Declination ° ′	20° Rise Sun Moon h m	20° Set Sun Moon h m	30° Rise Sun Moon h m	30° Set Sun Moon h m	40° Rise Sun Moon h m	40° Set Sun Moon h m	50° Rise Sun Moon h m	50° Set Sun MOon h m	60° Rise Sun Moon h m	60° Set Sun Moon h m
1 SA	12 4 1	4 17	5: 54	18: 14	5: 50	18: 18	5: 45	18: 24	5: 38	18: 31	5: 27	18: 43
91			*6: 38*	*19: 35*	*6: 29*	*19: 46*	*6: 18*	*20: 0*	*6: 2*	*20: 19*	*5: 39*	*20: 49*
2 SU	12 3 44	4 40	5: 53	18: 14	5: 49	18: 19	5: 43	18: 25	5: 36	18: 33	5: 24	18: 45
92			*7: 19*	*20: 26*	*7: 7*	*20: 40*	*6: 52*	*20: 57*	*6: 31*	*21: 21*	*5: 58*	*22: 0*
3 MO	12 3 26	5 3	5: 52	18: 15	5: 48	18: 20	5: 42	18: 26	5: 34	18: 34	5: 21	18: 47
93			*8: 1*	*21: 17*	*7: 46*	*21: 33*	*7: 28*	*21: 53*	*7: 3*	*22: 21*	*6: 22*	*23: 7*
4 TU	12 3 8	5 26	5: 52	18: 15	5: 47	18: 20	5: 40	18: 27	5: 32	18: 36	5: 18	18: 50
94			*8: 45*	*22: 6*	*8: 29*	*22: 24*	*8: 8*	*22: 46*	*7: 39*	*23: 16*	*6: 52*	— —
5 WE	12 2 51	5 49	5: 51	18: 15	5: 45	18: 21	5: 39	18: 28	5: 29	18: 37	5: 15	18: 52
95			*9: 31*	*22: 55*	*9: 13*	*23: 13*	*8: 51*	*23: 35*	*8: 20*	— —	*7: 29*	*0: 7*
6 TH	12 2 34	6 11	5: 50	18: 16	5: 44	18: 21	5: 37	18: 29	5: 27	18: 39	5: 12	18: 55
96			*10: 19*	*23: 42*	*10: 1*	*23: 59*	*9: 38*	— —	*9: 7*	*0: 7*	*8: 15*	*0: 59*
7 FR	12 2 17	6 34	5: 49	18: 16	5: 43	18: 22	5: 35	18: 30	5: 25	18: 40	5: 9	18: 57
97			*11: 8*	— —	*10: 51*	— —	*10: 30*	*0: 21*	*10: 0*	*0: 51*	*9: 10*	*1: 42*
8 SA	12 1 60	6 57	5: 48	18: 16	5: 42	18: 23	5: 34	18: 31	5: 23	18: 42	5: 6	19: 0
98	*5 35 FQ*		*11: 58*	*0: 27*	*11: 43*	*0: 43*	*11: 24*	*1: 3*	*10: 57*	*1: 31*	*10: 14*	*2: 16*
9 SU	12 1 43	7 19	5: 47	18: 16	5: 41	18: 23	5: 32	18: 32	5: 21	18: 44	5: 3	19: 2
99			*12: 50*	*1: 11*	*12: 37*	*1: 25*	*12: 21*	*1: 42*	*11: 59*	*2: 6*	*11: 24*	*2: 43*
10 MO	12 1 27	7 42	5: 47	18: 17	5: 40	18: 24	5: 31	18: 33	5: 19	18: 45	5: 0	19: 5
100			*13: 43*	*1: 54*	*13: 33*	*2: 5*	*13: 21*	*2: 18*	*13: 5*	*2: 37*	*12: 39*	*3: 6*
11 TU	12 1 11	8 4	5: 46	18: 17	5: 38	18: 24	5: 29	18: 34	5: 17	18: 47	4: 57	19: 7
101			*14: 37*	*2: 35*	*14: 31*	*2: 43*	*14: 23*	*2: 53*	*14: 13*	*3: 5*	*13: 58*	*3: 25*
12 WE	12 0 55	8 26	5: 45	18: 17	5: 37	18: 25	5: 28	18: 35	5: 15	18: 48	4: 54	19: 9
102			*15: 32*	*3: 17*	*15: 30*	*3: 21*	*15: 28*	*3: 26*	*15: 25*	*3: 32*	*15: 20*	*3: 42*
13 TH	12 0 39	8 48	5: 44	18: 18	5: 36	18: 26	5: 26	18: 36	5: 12	18: 50	4: 51	19: 12
103			*16: 30*	*3: 59*	*16: 32*	*3: 59*	*16: 35*	*3: 59*	*16: 39*	*3: 59*	*16: 45*	*3: 58*
14 FR	12 0 24	9 10	5: 43	18: 18	5: 35	18: 26	5: 25	18: 37	5: 10	18: 51	4: 48	19: 14
104			*17: 29*	*4: 43*	*17: 36*	*4: 39*	*17: 44*	*4: 33*	*17: 55*	*4: 26*	*18: 13*	*4: 15*
15 SA	12 0 9	9 31	5: 43	18: 18	5: 34	18: 27	5: 23	18: 38	5: 8	18: 53	4: 45	19: 17
105	12 8 FM		*18: 31*	*5: 29*	*18: 42*	*5: 21*	*18: 55*	*5: 11*	*19: 13*	*4: 56*	*19: 43*	*4: 35*
16 SU	11 59 55	9 53	5: 42	18: 18	5: 33	18: 27	5: 22	18: 39	5: 6	18: 55	4: 42	19: 19
106			*19: 34*	*6: 19*	*19: 49*	*6: 7*	*20: 7*	*5: 52*	*20: 31*	*5: 31*	*21: 12*	*4: 58*
17 MO	11 59 40	10 14	5: 41	18: 19	5: 32	18: 28	5: 20	18: 40	5: 4	18: 56	4: 39	19: 22
107			*20: 39*	*7: 12*	*20: 55*	*6: 57*	*21: 17*	*6: 38*	*21: 46*	*6: 11*	*22: 35*	*5: 29*
18 TU	11 59 27	10 35	5: 40	18: 19	5: 31	18: 29	5: 19	18: 41	5: 2	18: 58	4: 36	19: 24
108			*21: 41*	*8: 9*	*22: 0*	*7: 52*	*22: 22*	*7: 30*	*22: 54*	*6: 59*	*23: 48*	*6: 9*
19 WE	11 59 13	10 56	5: 39	18: 19	5: 30	18: 29	5: 17	18: 42	5: 0	18: 59	4: 33	19: 27
109			*22: 41*	*9: 9*	*22: 59*	*8: 51*	*23: 22*	*8: 28*	*23: 53*	*7: 56*	— —	*7: 2*
20 TH	11 59 0	11 17	5: 39	18: 20	5: 28	18: 30	5: 16	18: 43	4: 58	19: 1	4: 30	19: 29
110			*23: 37*	*10: 10*	*23: 54*	*9: 53*	— —	*9: 31*	— —	*9: 0*	*0: 45*	*8: 9*
21 FR	11 58 48	11 37	5: 38	18: 20	5: 27	18: 31	5: 14	18: 44	4: 56	19: 2	4: 28	19: 32
111			— —	*11: 11*	— —	*10: 55*	*0: 14*	*10: 36*	*0: 42*	*10: 9*	*1: 28*	*9: 25*
22 SA	11 58 36	11 58	5: 37	18: 20	5: 26	18: 31	5: 13	18: 45	4: 54	19: 4	4: 25	19: 34
112	*3 18 LQ*		*0: 28*	*12: 10*	*0: 42*	*11: 57*	*0: 59*	*11: 42*	*1: 22*	*11: 20*	*1: 59*	*10: 46*
23 SU	11 58 24	12 18	5: 36	18: 21	5: 25	18: 32	5: 12	18: 46	4: 52	19: 5	4: 22	19: 37
113			*1: 15*	*13: 7*	*1: 26*	*12: 58*	*1: 38*	*12: 47*	*1: 56*	*12: 32*	*2: 23*	*12: 8*
24 MO	11 58 13	12 38	5: 36	18: 21	5: 24	18: 32	5: 10	18: 47	4: 50	19: 7	4: 19	19: 39
114			*1: 58*	*14: 1*	*2: 5*	*13: 56*	*2: 14*	*13: 50*	*2: 25*	*13: 42*	*2: 42*	*13: 28*
25 TU	11 58 2	12 58	5: 35	18: 21	5: 23	18: 33	5: 9	18: 48	4: 49	19: 9	4: 16	19: 42
115			*2: 39*	*14: 55*	*2: 42*	*14: 54*	*2: 46*	*14: 52*	*2: 51*	*14: 50*	*2: 58*	*14: 47*
26 WE	11 57 52	13 17	5: 34	18: 22	5: 22	18: 34	5: 7	18: 49	4: 47	19: 10	4: 13	19: 44
116			*3: 19*	*15: 47*	*3: 18*	*15: 49*	*3: 17*	*15: 53*	*3: 16*	*15: 57*	*3: 14*	*16: 5*
27 TH	11 57 42	13 37	5: 34	18: 22	5: 21	18: 34	5: 6	18: 50	4: 45	19: 12	4: 11	19: 47
117			*3: 57*	*16: 38*	*3: 53*	*16: 45*	*3: 47*	*16: 53*	*3: 40*	*17: 3*	*3: 29*	*17: 20*
28 FR	11 57 33	13 56	5: 33	18: 22	5: 20	18: 35	5: 5	18: 51	4: 43	19: 13	4: 8	19: 49
118			*4: 37*	*17: 29*	*4: 28*	*17: 39*	*4: 19*	*17: 51*	*4: 5*	*18: 8*	*3: 45*	*18: 35*
29 SA	11 57 25	14 15	5: 32	18: 23	5: 20	18: 36	5: 3	18: 52	4: 41	19: 15	4: 5	19: 52
119	*17 36 NM*		*5: 17*	*18: 20*	*5: 5*	*18: 33*	*4: 51*	*18: 49*	*4: 33*	*19: 11*	*4: 3*	*19: 47*
30 SU	11 57 16	14 34	5: 32	18: 23	5: 19	18: 36	5: 2	18: 53	4: 39	19: 16	4: 2	19: 54
120			*5: 58*	*19: 10*	*5: 44*	*19: 26*	*5: 27*	*19: 45*	*5: 3*	*20: 12*	*4: 25*	*20: 55*

5th Month — May 1995 — 31 days

Greenwich Mean Time

NOTE: For each day, numbers on first line indicate Sun. *Italic* numbers on second line indicate *Moon*. Degrees are North Latitude.

FM = full moon; LQ = last quarter; NM = new moon; FQ = first quarter.

CAUTION: Must be converted to local time. For instructions see page 263.

Day of month week year	Sun on Meridian Moon Phase h m s	Sun's Declination ° ′	20° Rise Sun Moon h m	20° Set Sun Moon h m	30° Rise Sun Moon h m	30° Set Sun Moon h m	40° Rise Sun Moon h m	40° Set Sun Moon h m	50° Rise Sun Moon h m	50° Set Sun Moon h m	60° Rise Sun Moon h m	60° Set Sun Moon h m
1 MO	11 57 9	14 52	5: 31	18: 23	5: 18	18: 37	5: 1	18: 54	4: 37	19: 18	3: 59	19: 57
121			6: 41	20: 0	6: 25	20: 18	6: 5	20: 39	5: 37	21: 9	4: 52	21: 58
2 TU	11 57 2	15 10	5: 31	18: 24	5: 17	18: 38	5: 0	18: 55	4: 36	19: 19	3: 57	19: 59
122			7: 26	20: 49	7: 9	21: 7	6: 47	21: 30	6: 17	22: 1	5: 27	22: 53
3 WE	11 56 55	15 28	5: 30	18: 24	5: 16	18: 38	4: 58	18: 56	4: 34	19: 21	3: 54	20: 2
123			8: 13	21: 37	7: 55	21: 55	7: 33	22: 17	7: 2	22: 48	6: 9	23: 39
4 TH	11 56 49	15 46	5: 29	18: 24	5: 15	18: 39	4: 57	18: 57	4: 32	19: 22	3: 51	20: 4
124			9: 2	22: 23	8: 44	22: 39	8: 23	23: 0	7: 52	23: 29	7: 1	– –
5 FR	11 56 44	16 3	5: 29	18: 25	5: 14	18: 40	4: 56	18: 58	4: 30	19: 24	3: 49	20: 6
125			9: 51	23: 7	9: 35	23: 21	9: 15	23: 40	8: 47	– –	8: 2	0: 16
6 SA	11 56 39	16 20	5: 28	18: 25	5: 13	18: 40	4: 55	18: 59	4: 29	19: 25	3: 46	20: 9
126			10: 42	23: 49	10: 28	– –	10: 11	– –	9: 47	0: 5	9: 8	0: 46
7 SU	11 56 34	16 37	5: 28	18: 26	5: 13	18: 41	4: 54	19: 0	4: 27	19: 27	3: 43	20: 11
127	21 44 FQ		11: 33	– –	11: 22	0: 1	11: 8	0: 16	10: 50	0: 37	10: 20	1: 9
8 MO	11 56 31	16 54	5: 27	18: 26	5: 12	18: 42	4: 53	19: 1	4: 26	19: 28	3: 41	20: 14
128			12: 25	0: 30	12: 18	0: 39	12: 8	0: 50	11: 55	1: 6	11: 35	1: 29
9 TU	11 56 27	17 10	5: 27	18: 26	5: 11	18: 42	4: 51	19: 2	4: 24	19: 30	3: 38	20: 16
129			13: 18	1: 10	13: 15	1: 16	13: 10	1: 23	13: 3	1: 32	12: 53	1: 46
10 WE	11 56 25	17 26	5: 26	18: 27	5: 10	18: 43	4: 50	19: 3	4: 22	19: 31	3: 36	20: 19
130			14: 13	1: 51	14: 14	1: 53	14: 14	1: 55	14: 14	1: 58	14: 15	2: 2
11 TH	11 56 23	17 42	5: 26	18: 27	5: 10	18: 43	4: 49	19: 4	4: 21	19: 33	3: 33	20: 21
131			15: 11	2: 33	15: 15	2: 31	15: 20	2: 28	15: 28	2: 24	15: 40	2: 19
12 FR	11 56 21	17 58	5: 25	18: 27	5: 9	18: 44	4: 48	19: 5	4: 19	19: 34	3: 31	20: 24
132			16: 10	3: 17	16: 19	3: 11	16: 30	3: 3	16: 44	2: 52	17: 8	2: 36
13 SA	11 56 20	18 13	5: 25	18: 28	5: 8	18: 45	4: 47	19: 6	4: 18	19: 36	3: 28	20: 26
133			17: 13	4: 5	17: 26	3: 54	17: 41	3: 41	18: 3	3: 24	18: 38	2: 57
14 SU	11 56 19	18 28	5: 25	18: 28	5: 8	18: 45	4: 46	19: 7	4: 16	19: 37	3: 26	20: 28
134			18: 18	4: 56	18: 34	4: 42	18: 53	4: 25	19: 21	4: 1	20: 6	3: 24
15 MO	11 56 19	18 42	5: 24	18: 29	5: 7	18: 46	4: 45	19: 8	4: 15	19: 39	3: 24	20: 31
135	12 8 FM		19: 23	5: 52	19: 41	5: 36	20: 3	5: 15	20: 34	4: 46	21: 27	3: 59
16 TU	11 56 20	18 56	5: 24	18: 29	5: 6	18: 47	4: 44	19: 9	4: 14	19: 40	3: 21	20: 33
136			20: 27	6: 53	20: 45	6: 35	21: 8	6: 12	21: 40	5: 40	22: 34	4: 47
17 WE	11 56 21	19 10	5: 23	18: 29	5: 6	18: 47	4: 44	19: 10	4: 12	19: 41	3: 19	20: 35
137			21: 27	7: 55	21: 44	7: 37	22: 6	7: 15	22: 35	6: 43	23: 24	5: 50
18 TH	11 56 23	19 24	5: 23	18: 30	5: 5	18: 48	4: 43	19: 11	4: 11	19: 43	3: 17	20: 38
138			22: 22	8: 59	22: 37	8: 42	22: 55	8: 22	23: 21	7: 53	– –	7: 6
19 FR	11 56 26	19 37	5: 23	18: 30	5: 5	18: 49	4: 42	19: 12	4: 10	19: 44	3: 15	20: 40
139			23: 12	10: 1	23: 24	9: 47	23: 38	9: 30	23: 58	9: 7	0: 1	8: 28
20 SA	11 56 28	19 50	5: 22	18: 31	5: 4	18: 49	4: 41	19: 12	4: 8	19: 45	3: 12	20: 42
140			23: 57	11: 0	– –	10: 50	– –	10: 37	– –	10: 20	0: 28	9: 53
21 SU	11 56 32	20 2	5: 22	11: 57	18: 31	18: 50	4: 40	19: 13	4: 7	19: 47	3: 10	20: 44
141	11 36 LQ		– –	11: 57	0: 5	11: 50	0: 15	11: 43	0: 29	11: 32	0: 49	11: 15
22 MO	11 56 36	20 15	5: 22	11: 57	18: 32	18: 50	4: 39	19: 14	4: 6	19: 48	3: 8	20: 47
142			0: 40	12: 51	0: 44	12: 49	0: 49	12: 46	0: 56	12: 42	1: 7	12: 36
23 TU	11 56 41	20 27	5: 22	11: 57	18: 32	18: 51	4: 39	19: 15	4: 5	19: 49	3: 6	20: 49
143			1: 20	13: 44	1: 20	13: 45	1: 20	13: 47	1: 21	13: 50	1: 22	13: 54
24 WE	11 56 46	20 38	5: 21	11: 57	18: 32	18: 52	4: 38	19: 16	4: 4	19: 51	3: 4	20: 51
144			1: 58	14: 35	1: 55	14: 40	1: 51	14: 47	1: 45	14: 56	1: 37	15: 10
25 TH	11 56 51	20 49	5: 21	11: 57	18: 33	18: 52	4: 37	19: 17	4: 3	19: 52	3: 2	20: 53
145			2: 37	15: 26	2: 30	15: 34	2: 21	15: 45	2: 10	16: 0	1: 53	16: 24
26 FR	11 56 58	21 0	5: 21	11: 57	18: 33	18: 53	4: 37	19: 18	4: 2	19: 53	3: 0	20: 55
146			3: 16	16: 16	3: 6	16: 28	2: 53	16: 43	2: 36	17: 3	2: 10	17: 36
27 SA	11 57 4	21 11	5: 21	11: 57	18: 34	18: 53	4: 36	19: 18	4: 1	19: 54	2: 58	20: 57
147			3: 57	17: 6	3: 44	17: 21	3: 27	17: 39	3: 5	18: 5	2: 30	18: 46
28 SU	11 57 11	21 21	5: 21	11: 57	18: 34	18: 54	4: 36	19: 19	4: 0	19: 55	2: 57	20: 59
148			4: 39	17: 56	4: 24	18: 13	4: 4	18: 34	3: 38	19: 3	2: 55	19: 50
29 MO	11 57 19	21 30	5: 20	11: 57	18: 34	18: 55	4: 35	19: 20	3: 59	19: 57	2: 55	21: 1
149	9 27 NM		5: 24	18: 46	5: 6	19: 3	4: 45	19: 26	4: 15	19: 57	3: 26	20: 48
30 TU	11 57 27	21 40	5: 20	11: 57	18: 35	18: 55	4: 34	19: 21	3: 58	19: 58	2: 53	21: 3
150			6: 10	19: 34	5: 52	19: 52	5: 30	20: 14	4: 58	20: 46	4: 6	21: 38
31 WE	11 57 36	21 49	5: 20	11: 58	18: 35	18: 56	4: 34	19: 22	3: 57	19: 59	2: 52	21: 5
151			6: 58	20: 20	6: 40	20: 38	6: 18	20: 59	5: 47	21: 29	4: 55	22: 18

6th Month **June 1995** **30 days**

Greenwich Mean Time

NOTE: For each day, numbers on first line indicate Sun. *Italic* numbers on second line indicate *Moon.* Degrees are North Latitude.

FM = full moon; LQ = last quarter; NM = new moon; FQ = first quarter.

CAUTION: Must be converted to local time. For instructions see page 263.

Day of month week year	Sun on Meridian Moon Phase h m s	Sun's Declination ° ′	20° Rise Sun Moon h m	20° Set Sun Moon h m	30° Rise Sun Moon h m	30° Set Sun Moon h m	40° Rise Sun Moon h m	40° Set Sun Moon h m	50° Rise Sun Moon h m	50° Set Sun Moon h m	60° Rise Sun Moon h m	60° Set Sun Moon h m
1 TH	11 57 44	21 57	5: 20	11: 58	18: 36	18: 56	4: 34	19: 22	3: 56	20: 0	2: 50	21: 7
152			*7: 47*	*21: 5*	*7: 30*	*21: 20*	*7: 10*	*21: 40*	*6: 41*	*22: 7*	*5: 52*	*22: 50*
2 FR	11 57 54	22 6	5: 20	11: 58	18: 36	18: 57	4: 33	19: 23	3: 56	20: 1	2: 49	21: 8
153			*8: 37*	*21: 47*	*8: 22*	*22: 1*	*8: 4*	*22: 17*	*7: 39*	*22: 40*	*6: 57*	*23: 15*
3 SA	11 58 3	22 13	5: 20	11: 58	18: 36	18: 57	4: 33	19: 24	3: 55	20: 2	2: 47	21: 10
154			*9: 28*	*22: 28*	*9: 16*	*22: 39*	*9: 0*	*22: 52*	*8: 40*	*23: 9*	*8: 6*	*23: 36*
4 SU	11 58 13	22 21	5: 20	11: 58	18: 37	18: 58	4: 32	19: 24	3: 54	20: 3	2: 46	21: 12
155			*10: 19*	*23: 8*	*10: 10*	*23: 15*	*9: 59*	*23: 24*	*9: 43*	*23: 36*	*9: 19*	*23: 54*
5 MO	11 58 24	22 28	5: 20	11: 58	18: 37	18: 58	4: 32	19: 25	3: 54	20: 4	2: 45	21: 13
156			*11: 10*	*23: 48*	*11: 5*	*23: 51*	*10: 58*	*23: 55*	*10: 49*	– –	*10: 35*	– –
6 TU	11 58 34	22 35	5: 20	11: 59	18: 37	18: 59	4: 32	19: 26	3: 53	20: 4	2: 43	21: 15
157	*10 26 FQ*		*12: 3*	– –	*12: 1*	– –	*11: 59*	– –	*11: 57*	*0: 1*	*11: 53*	*0: 10*
7 WE	11 58 45	22 41	5: 20	11: 59	18: 38	18: 59	4: 31	19: 26	3: 53	20: 5	2: 42	21: 16
158			*12: 57*	*0: 28*	*13: 0*	*0: 27*	*13: 3*	*0: 27*	*13: 7*	*0: 26*	*13: 13*	*0: 25*
8 TH	11 58 57	22 47	5: 20	11: 59	18: 38	19: 0	4: 31	19: 27	3: 52	20: 6	2: 41	21: 17
159			*13: 54*	*1: 9*	*14: 1*	*1: 5*	*14: 9*	*0: 59*	*14: 20*	*0: 52*	*14: 37*	*0: 41*
9 FR	11 59 8	22 52	5: 20	11: 59	18: 38	19: 0	4: 31	19: 27	3: 52	20: 7	2: 40	21: 19
160			*14: 54*	*1: 53*	*15: 4*	*1: 45*	*15: 17*	*1: 35*	*15: 35*	*1: 21*	*16: 4*	*0: 59*
10 SA	11 59 20	22 57	5: 20	11: 59	18: 39	19: 0	4: 31	19: 28	3: 51	20: 8	2: 40	21: 20
161			*15: 56*	*2: 42*	*16: 10*	*2: 29*	*16: 28*	*2: 14*	*16: 52*	*1: 54*	*17: 32*	*1: 22*
11 SU	11 59 32	23 2	5: 20	12: 0	18: 39	19: 1	4: 31	19: 28	3: 51	20: 8	2: 39	21: 21
162			*17: 1*	*3: 34*	*17: 17*	*3: 19*	*17: 39*	*3: 0*	*18: 8*	*2: 34*	*18: 57*	*1: 51*
12 MO	11 59 44	23 6	5: 20	12: 0	18: 39	19: 1	4: 31	19: 29	3: 51	20: 9	2: 38	21: 22
163			*18: 6*	*4: 32*	*18: 24*	*4: 15*	*18: 47*	*3: 53*	*19: 19*	*3: 22*	*20: 13*	*2: 32*
13 TU	11 59 56	23 10	5: 20	12: 0	18: 40	19: 2	4: 31	19: 29	3: 51	20: 10	2: 37	21: 23
164	*4 3 FM*		*19: 9*	*5: 34*	*19: 27*	*5: 16*	*19: 49*	*4: 53*	*20: 21*	*4: 21*	*21: 13*	*3: 27*
14 WE	12 0 8	23 14	5: 20	12: 0	18: 40	19: 2	4: 31	19: 30	3: 50	20: 10	2: 37	21: 24
165			*20: 8*	*6: 39*	*20: 24*	*6: 21*	*20: 45*	*6: 0*	*21: 12*	*5: 29*	*21: 58*	*4: 38*
15 TH	12 0 21	23 17	5: 20	12: 0	18: 40	19: 2	4: 31	19: 30	3: 50	20: 11	2: 36	21: 25
166			*21: 2*	*7: 44*	*21: 16*	*7: 28*	*21: 32*	*7: 9*	*21: 55*	*6: 43*	*22: 30*	*6: 0*
16 FR	12 0 34	23 19	5: 20	12: 1	18: 41	19: 3	4: 31	19: 31	3: 50	20: 11	2: 36	21: 25
167			*21: 52*	*8: 46*	*22: 1*	*8: 35*	*22: 13*	*8: 20*	*22: 29*	*7: 59*	*22: 55*	*7: 27*
17 SA	12 0 47	23 21	5: 21	12: 1	18: 41	19: 3	4: 31	19: 31	3: 50	20: 12	2: 36	21: 26
168			*22: 37*	*9: 46*	*22: 42*	*9: 39*	*22: 50*	*9: 29*	*22: 59*	*9: 15*	*23: 14*	*8: 53*
18 SU	12 0 60	23 23	5: 21	12: 1	18: 41	19: 3	4: 31	19: 31	3: 50	20: 12	2: 36	21: 27
169			*23: 18*	*10: 44*	*23: 20*	*10: 40*	*23: 23*	*10: 35*	*23: 26*	*10: 28*	*23: 30*	*10: 18*
19 MO	12 1 13	23 25	5: 21	12: 1	18: 41	19: 4	4: 31	19: 32	3: 50	20: 12	2: 36	21: 27
170	*22 1 LQ*		*23: 58*	*11: 38*	*23: 56*	*11: 38*	*23: 54*	*11: 38*	*23: 51*	*11: 38*	*23: 46*	*11: 38*
20 TU	12 1 26	23 26	5: 21	12: 1	18: 42	19: 4	4: 31	19: 32	3: 50	20: 13	2: 36	21: 27
171			– –	*12: 31*	– –	*12: 35*	– –	*12: 40*	– –	*12: 46*	– –	*12: 56*
21 WE	12 1 39	23 26	5: 21	12: 2	18: 42	19: 4	4: 31	19: 32	3: 51	20: 13	2: 36	21: 28
172			*0: 38*	*13: 22*	*0: 32*	*13: 30*	*0: 25*	*13: 39*	*0: 15*	*13: 52*	*0: 1*	*14: 12*
22 TH	12 1 52	23 26	5: 22	12: 2	18: 42	19: 4	4: 31	19: 32	3: 51	20: 13	2: 36	21: 28
173			*1: 17*	*14: 13*	*1: 8*	*14: 24*	*0: 56*	*14: 37*	*0: 41*	*14: 56*	*0: 18*	*15: 25*
23 FR	12 2 5	23 26	5: 22	12: 2	18: 42	19: 4	4: 32	19: 32	3: 51	20: 13	2: 36	21: 28
174			*1: 57*	*15: 3*	*1: 45*	*15: 17*	*1: 29*	*15: 34*	*1: 9*	*15: 58*	*0: 37*	*16: 36*
24 SA	12 2 18	23 25	5: 22	12: 2	18: 43	19: 5	4: 32	19: 33	3: 51	20: 13	2: 37	21: 28
175			*2: 38*	*15: 53*	*2: 24*	*16: 9*	*2: 5*	*16: 29*	*1: 40*	*16: 57*	*1: 0*	*17: 42*
25 SU	12 2 31	23 24	5: 22	12: 3	18: 43	19: 5	4: 32	19: 33	3: 52	20: 13	2: 37	21: 28
176			*3: 22*	*16: 42*	*3: 5*	*17: 0*	*2: 44*	*17: 22*	*2: 16*	*17: 52*	*1: 29*	*18: 43*
26 MO	12 2 43	23 23	5: 23	12: 3	18: 43	19: 5	4: 33	19: 33	3: 52	20: 13	2: 38	21: 28
177			*4: 7*	*17: 31*	*3: 50*	*17: 49*	*3: 27*	*18: 11*	*2: 56*	*18: 43*	*2: 5*	*19: 36*
27 TU	12 2 56	23 21	5: 23	12: 3	18: 43	19: 5	4: 33	19: 33	3: 52	20: 13	2: 38	21: 27
178			*4: 55*	*18: 18*	*4: 37*	*18: 36*	*4: 14*	*18: 58*	*3: 43*	*19: 28*	*2: 50*	*20: 19*
28 WE	12 3 9	23 18	5: 23	12: 3	18: 43	19: 5	4: 33	19: 33	3: 53	20: 13	2: 39	21: 27
179	*0 50 NM*		*5: 44*	*19: 4*	*5: 27*	*19: 20*	*5: 5*	*19: 40*	*4: 35*	*20: 8*	*3: 45*	*20: 54*
29 TH	12 3 21	23 16	5: 23	12: 3	18: 43	19: 5	4: 34	19: 33	3: 53	20: 13	2: 40	21: 26
180			*6: 34*	*19: 47*	*6: 18*	*20: 1*	*5: 59*	*20: 19*	*5: 32*	*20: 43*	*4: 48*	*21: 22*
30 FR	12 3 33	23 13	5: 24	12: 4	18: 43	19: 5	4: 34	19: 33	3: 54	20: 13	2: 41	21: 26
181			*7: 24*	*20: 29*	*7: 11*	*20: 40*	*6: 55*	*20: 54*	*6: 32*	*21: 14*	*5: 56*	*21: 44*

7th Month — July 1995 — 31 days

Greenwich Mean Time

NOTE: For each day, numbers on first line indicate Sun. *Italic* numbers on second line indicate *Moon.* Degrees are North Latitude.

FM = full moon; LQ = last quarter; NM = new moon; FQ = first quarter.

CAUTION: Must be converted to local time. For instructions see page 263.

Day of month week year	Sun on Meridian Moon Phase h m s	Sun's Declination ° ′	20° Rise Sun Moon h m	20° Set Sun Moon h m	30° Rise Sun Moon h m	30° Set Sun Moon h m	40° Rise Sun Moon h m	40° Set Sun Moon h m	50° Rise Sun Moon h m	50° Set Sun Moon h m	60° Rise Sun Moon h m	60° Set Sun Moon h m
1 SA	12 3 45	23 9	5: 24	12: 4	18: 43	19: 5	4: 35	19: 33	3: 55	20: 13	2: 42	21: 25
182			*8: 15*	*21: 9*	*8: 5*	*21: 17*	*7: 53*	*21: 27*	*7: 35*	*21: 41*	*7: 8*	*22: 2*
2 SU	12 3 56	23 5	5: 24	12: 4	18: 43	19: 5	4: 35	19: 33	3: 55	20: 12	2: 43	21: 24
183			*9: 7*	*21: 48*	*9: 0*	*21: 53*	*8: 51*	*21: 59*	*8: 40*	*22: 7*	*8: 22*	*22: 19*
3 MO	12 4 8	23 1	5: 25	12: 4	18: 44	19: 5	4: 36	19: 32	3: 56	20: 12	2: 44	21: 24
184			*9: 58*	*22: 27*	*9: 55*	*22: 28*	*9: 51*	*22: 30*	*9: 46*	*22: 31*	*9: 38*	*22: 34*
4 TU	12 4 19	22 56	5: 25	12: 4	18: 44	19: 5	4: 36	19: 32	3: 57	20: 12	2: 45	21: 23
185			*10: 51*	*23: 7*	*10: 52*	*23: 4*	*10: 53*	*23: 1*	*10: 54*	*22: 56*	*10: 57*	*22: 49*
5 WE	12 4 29	22 51	5: 25	12: 4	18: 44	19: 5	4: 37	19: 32	3: 57	20: 11	2: 46	21: 22
186	*20 2 FQ*		*11: 45*	*23: 49*	*11: 50*	*23: 42*	*11: 56*	*23: 34*	*12: 4*	*23: 23*	*12: 17*	*23: 6*
6 TH	12 4 40	22 45	5: 26	12: 5	18: 44	19: 5	4: 37	19: 32	3: 58	20: 11	2: 48	21: 21
187			*12: 42*	– –	*12: 50*	– –	*13: 1*	– –	*13: 16*	*23: 53*	*13: 40*	*23: 26*
7 FR	12 4 50	22 39	5: 26	12: 5	18: 44	19: 5	4: 38	19: 32	3: 59	20: 10	2: 49	21: 20
188			*13: 41*	*0: 34*	*13: 53*	*0: 23*	*14: 9*	*0: 10*	*14: 30*	– –	*15: 5*	*23: 51*
8 SA	12 4 59	22 33	5: 26	12: 5	18: 43	19: 5	4: 38	19: 31	4: 0	20: 10	2: 51	21: 18
189			*14: 42*	*1: 22*	*14: 58*	*1: 9*	*15: 17*	*0: 52*	*15: 44*	*0: 28*	*16: 29*	– –
9 SU	12 5 8	22 26	5: 27	12: 5	18: 43	19: 4	4: 39	19: 31	4: 1	20: 9	2: 52	21: 17
190			*15: 45*	*2: 16*	*16: 3*	*2: 0*	*16: 25*	*1: 39*	*16: 56*	*1: 11*	*17: 48*	*0: 24*
10 MO	12 5 17	22 19	5: 27	12: 5	18: 43	19: 4	4: 40	19: 30	4: 2	20: 8	2: 54	21: 16
191			*16: 48*	*3: 15*	*17: 7*	*2: 57*	*17: 30*	*2: 34*	*18: 2*	*2: 2*	*18: 55*	*1: 10*
11 TU	12 5 25	22 12	5: 27	12: 5	18: 43	19: 4	4: 40	19: 30	4: 3	20: 8	2: 55	21: 14
192			*17: 50*	*4: 17*	*18: 7*	*3: 59*	*18: 29*	*3: 36*	*18: 59*	*3: 5*	*19: 48*	*2: 11*
12 WE	12 5 33	22 4	5: 28	12: 6	18: 43	19: 4	4: 41	19: 30	4: 4	20: 7	2: 57	21: 13
193	*10 49 FM*		*18: 47*	*5: 22*	*19: 2*	*5: 5*	*19: 21*	*4: 45*	*19: 46*	*4: 16*	*20: 27*	*3: 27*
13 TH	12 5 40	21 55	5: 28	12: 6	18: 43	19: 3	4: 42	19: 29	4: 5	20: 6	2: 59	21: 11
194			*19: 40*	*6: 26*	*19: 51*	*6: 13*	*20: 6*	*5: 56*	*20: 26*	*5: 32*	*20: 56*	*4: 53*
14 FR	12 5 47	21 47	5: 29	12: 6	18: 43	19: 3	4: 43	19: 29	4: 6	20: 5	3: 1	21: 10
195			*20: 28*	*7: 29*	*20: 36*	*7: 19*	*20: 46*	*7: 7*	*20: 59*	*6: 49*	*21: 19*	*6: 22*
15 SA	12 5 54	21 38	5: 29	12: 6	18: 43	19: 3	4: 43	19: 28	4: 7	20: 4	3: 3	21: 8
196			*21: 13*	*8: 30*	*21: 17*	*8: 24*	*21: 21*	*8: 16*	*21: 28*	*8: 6*	*21: 37*	*7: 50*
16 SU	12 5 59	21 28	5: 29	12: 6	18: 43	19: 2	4: 44	19: 27	4: 8	20: 3	3: 4	21: 6
197			*21: 55*	*9: 27*	*21: 55*	*9: 25*	*21: 54*	*9: 23*	*21: 54*	*9: 20*	*21: 54*	*9: 15*
17 MO	12 6 5	21 19	5: 30	12: 6	18: 42	19: 2	4: 45	19: 27	4: 9	20: 2	3: 6	21: 4
198			*22: 35*	*10: 22*	*22: 31*	*10: 24*	*22: 26*	*10: 27*	*22: 20*	*10: 31*	*22: 9*	*10: 36*
18 TU	12 6 10	21 9	5: 30	12: 6	18: 42	19: 2	4: 46	19: 26	4: 10	20: 1	3: 8	21: 2
199			*23: 15*	*11: 15*	*23: 8*	*11: 21*	*22: 58*	*11: 29*	*22: 45*	*11: 39*	*22: 26*	*11: 55*
19 WE	12 6 14	20 58	5: 30	12: 6	18: 42	19: 1	4: 46	19: 26	4: 11	20: 0	3: 10	21: 1
200	*11 10 LQ*		*23: 56*	*12: 7*	*23: 45*	*12: 17*	*23: 31*	*12: 28*	*23: 13*	*12: 45*	*22: 44*	*13: 10*
20 TH	12 6 18	20 47	5: 31	12: 6	18: 42	19: 1	4: 47	19: 25	4: 13	19: 59	3: 13	20: 59
201			– –	*12: 58*	– –	*13: 11*	– –	*13: 26*	*23: 43*	*13: 48*	*23: 6*	*14: 23*
21 FR	12 6 21	20 36	5: 31	12: 6	18: 41	19: 0	4: 48	19: 24	4: 14	19: 58	3: 15	20: 57
202			*0: 37*	*13: 48*	*0: 23*	*14: 3*	*0: 6*	*14: 22*	– –	*14: 48*	*23: 32*	*15: 31*
22 SA	12 6 24	20 25	5: 32	12: 6	18: 41	19: 0	4: 49	19: 23	4: 15	19: 57	3: 17	20: 54
203			*1: 20*	*14: 38*	*1: 4*	*14: 55*	*0: 44*	*15: 16*	*0: 17*	*15: 45*	– –	*16: 34*
23 SU	12 6 26	20 13	5: 32	12: 6	18: 41	18: 59	4: 50	19: 23	4: 16	19: 56	3: 19	20: 52
204			*2: 5*	*15: 27*	*1: 47*	*15: 45*	*1: 26*	*16: 7*	*0: 55*	*16: 38*	*0: 6*	*17: 30*
24 MO	12 6 28	20 1	5: 32	18: 40	5: 14	18: 59	4: 51	19: 22	4: 18	19: 54	3: 21	20: 50
205			*2: 51*	*16: 15*	*2: 33*	*16: 33*	*2: 11*	*16: 55*	*1: 40*	*17: 26*	*0: 48*	*18: 17*
25 TU	12 6 29	19 48	5: 33	18: 40	5: 14	18: 58	4: 51	19: 21	4: 19	19: 53	3: 23	20: 48
206			*3: 40*	*17: 1*	*3: 22*	*17: 18*	*3: 0*	*17: 39*	*2: 30*	*18: 8*	*1: 39*	*18: 55*
26 WE	12 6 30	19 35	5: 33	18: 40	5: 15	18: 58	4: 52	19: 20	4: 20	19: 52	3: 26	20: 46
207			*4: 30*	*17: 45*	*4: 13*	*18: 0*	*3: 53*	*18: 19*	*3: 25*	*18: 45*	*2: 39*	*19: 26*
27 TH	12 6 29	19 22	5: 33	18: 39	5: 16	18: 57	4: 53	19: 19	4: 22	19: 50	3: 28	20: 43
208	*15 13 NM*		*5: 20*	*18: 28*	*5: 6*	*18: 41*	*4: 49*	*18: 56*	*4: 24*	*19: 17*	*3: 45*	*19: 50*
28 FR	12 6 29	19 8	5: 34	18: 39	5: 16	18: 56	4: 54	19: 18	4: 23	19: 49	3: 30	20: 41
209			*6: 12*	*19: 9*	*6: 0*	*19: 19*	*5: 46*	*19: 30*	*5: 27*	*19: 46*	*4: 57*	*20: 10*
29 SA	12 6 27	18 55	5: 34	18: 39	5: 17	18: 56	4: 55	19: 17	4: 24	19: 48	3: 32	20: 39
210			*7: 3*	*19: 49*	*6: 55*	*19: 55*	*6: 45*	*20: 3*	*6: 32*	*20: 13*	*6: 11*	*20: 28*
30 SU	12 6 25	18 40	5: 35	18: 38	5: 17	18: 55	4: 56	19: 16	4: 26	19: 46	3: 35	20: 36
211			*7: 55*	*20: 29*	*7: 51*	*20: 31*	*7: 45*	*20: 34*	*7: 38*	*20: 38*	*7: 27*	*20: 44*
31 MO	12 6 23	18 26	5: 35	18: 38	5: 18	18: 54	4: 57	19: 15	4: 27	19: 45	3: 37	20: 34
212			*8: 48*	*21: 8*	*8: 47*	*21: 7*	*8: 46*	*21: 5*	*8: 46*	*21: 3*	*8: 44*	*20: 59*

8th Month **August 1995** **31 days**

Greenwich Mean Time

NOTE: For each day, numbers on first line indicate Sun. *Italic* numbers on second line indicate *Moon.* Degrees are North Latitude.

FM = full moon; LQ = last quarter; NM = new moon; FQ = first quarter.

CAUTION: Must be converted to local time. For instructions see page 263.

Day of month week year	Sun on Meridian Moon Phase h m s	Sun's Declination ° ′	20° Rise Sun Moon h m	20° Set Sun Moon h m	30° Rise Sun Moon h m	30° Set Sun Moon h m	40° Rise Sun Moon h m	40° Set Sun Moon h m	50° Rise Sun Moon h m	50° Set Sun MOon h m	60° Rise Sun Moon h m	60° Set Sun Moon h m
1 TU	12 6 20	18 11	5: 35	18: 37	5: 19	18: 54	4: 58	19: 14	4: 28	19: 43	3: 39	20: 32
213			*9: 41*	*21: 49*	*9: 44*	*21: 44*	*9: 49*	*21: 37*	*9: 55*	*21: 29*	*10: 4*	*21: 15*
2 WE	12 6 16	17 56	5: 36	18: 37	5: 19	18: 53	4: 59	19: 13	4: 30	19: 42	3: 42	20: 29
214			*10: 36*	*22: 32*	*10: 43*	*22: 23*	*10: 52*	*22: 12*	*11: 5*	*21: 57*	*11: 25*	*21: 34*
3 TH	12 6 12	17 41	5: 36	18: 36	5: 20	18: 52	5: 0	19: 12	4: 31	19: 40	3: 44	20: 27
215	*3 16 FQ*		*11: 33*	*23: 18*	*11: 44*	*23: 6*	*11: 58*	*22: 50*	*12: 17*	*22: 29*	*12: 47*	*21: 56*
4 FR	12 6 7	17 25	5: 36	18: 36	5: 20	18: 51	5: 1	19: 11	4: 33	19: 39	3: 46	20: 24
216			*12: 32*	— —	*12: 46*	*23: 53*	*13: 4*	*23: 34*	*13: 29*	*23: 8*	*14: 9*	*22: 25*
5 SA	12 6 1	17 9	5: 37	18: 35	5: 21	18: 51	5: 2	19: 10	4: 34	19: 37	3: 49	20: 21
217			*13: 32*	*0: 8*	*13: 49*	— —	*14: 10*	— —	*14: 39*	*23: 54*	*15: 28*	*23: 4*
6 SU	12 5 55	16 53	5: 37	18: 35	5: 22	18: 50	5: 2	19: 9	4: 36	19: 35	3: 51	20: 19
218			*14: 33*	*1: 3*	*14: 51*	*0: 45*	*15: 14*	*0: 24*	*15: 45*	— —	*16: 38*	*23: 56*
7 MO	12 5 48	16 37	5: 37	18: 34	5: 22	18: 49	5: 3	19: 8	4: 37	19: 34	3: 54	20: 16
219			*15: 34*	*2: 1*	*15: 52*	*1: 43*	*16: 14*	*1: 21*	*16: 45*	*0: 49*	*17: 37*	— —
8 TU	12 5 40	16 20	5: 38	18: 33	5: 23	18: 48	5: 4	19: 6	4: 38	19: 32	3: 56	20: 14
220			*16: 32*	*3: 3*	*16: 48*	*2: 46*	*17: 8*	*2: 24*	*17: 36*	*1: 54*	*18: 21*	*1: 3*
9 WE	12 5 32	16 3	5: 38	18: 33	5: 23	18: 47	5: 5	19: 5	4: 40	19: 30	3: 58	20: 11
221			*17: 26*	*4: 7*	*17: 39*	*3: 52*	*17: 56*	*3: 33*	*18: 19*	*3: 6*	*18: 55*	*2: 23*
10 TH	12 5 23	15 46	5: 38	18: 32	5: 24	18: 46	5: 6	19: 4	4: 41	19: 28	4: 1	20: 8
222	*18 15 FM*		*18: 16*	*5: 10*	*18: 26*	*4: 58*	*18: 38*	*4: 43*	*18: 55*	*4: 22*	*19: 21*	*3: 49*
11 FR	12 5 14	15 28	5: 39	18: 32	5: 25	18: 45	5: 7	19: 3	4: 43	19: 27	4: 3	20: 6
223			*19: 3*	*6: 12*	*19: 9*	*6: 3*	*19: 16*	*5: 53*	*19: 26*	*5: 39*	*19: 41*	*5: 18*
12 SA	12 5 4	15 11	5: 39	18: 31	5: 25	18: 44	5: 8	19: 1	4: 44	19: 25	4: 6	20: 3
224			*19: 47*	*7: 11*	*19: 49*	*7: 7*	*19: 51*	*7: 2*	*19: 54*	*6: 55*	*19: 59*	*6: 45*
13 SU	12 4 54	14 53	5: 39	18: 30	5: 26	18: 44	5: 9	19: 0	4: 46	19: 23	4: 8	20: 0
225			*20: 29*	*8: 8*	*20: 27*	*8: 8*	*20: 25*	*8: 9*	*20: 21*	*8: 9*	*20: 16*	*8: 9*
14 MO	12 4 43	14 34	5: 40	18: 30	5: 26	18: 43	5: 10	18: 59	4: 47	19: 21	4: 10	19: 57
226			*21: 11*	*9: 3*	*21: 5*	*9: 8*	*20: 57*	*9: 13*	*20: 48*	*9: 20*	*20: 33*	*9: 31*
15 TU	12 4 32	14 16	5: 40	18: 29	5: 27	18: 42	5: 11	18: 57	4: 49	19: 19	4: 13	19: 54
227			*21: 52*	*9: 57*	*21: 42*	*10: 5*	*21: 31*	*10: 15*	*21: 15*	*10: 28*	*20: 51*	*10: 49*
16 WE	12 4 20	13 57	5: 40	18: 28	5: 28	18: 41	5: 12	18: 56	4: 50	19: 17	4: 15	19: 52
228			*22: 33*	*10: 50*	*22: 21*	*11: 1*	*22: 5*	*11: 15*	*21: 44*	*11: 34*	*21: 12*	*12: 4*
17 TH	12 4 7	13 38	5: 40	18: 28	5: 28	18: 40	5: 13	18: 55	4: 52	19: 15	4: 18	19: 49
229			*23: 16*	*11: 41*	*23: 1*	*11: 55*	*22: 43*	*12: 12*	*22: 17*	*12: 37*	*21: 36*	*13: 16*
18 FR	12 3 54	13 19	5: 41	18: 27	5: 29	18: 39	5: 14	18: 53	4: 53	19: 14	4: 20	19: 46
230	*3 4 LQ*		— —	*12: 32*	*23: 44*	*12: 48*	*23: 23*	*13: 8*	*22: 54*	*13: 36*	*22: 7*	*14: 21*
19 SA	12 3 41	12 60	5: 41	18: 26	5: 29	18: 38	5: 15	18: 52	4: 55	19: 12	4: 22	19: 43
231			*0: 0*	*13: 21*	— —	*13: 38*	— —	*14: 0*	*23: 36*	*14: 30*	*22: 46*	*15: 20*
20 SU	12 3 27	12 40	5: 41	18: 25	5: 30	18: 37	5: 16	18: 50	4: 56	19: 10	4: 25	19: 40
232			*0: 46*	*14: 9*	*0: 29*	*14: 27*	*0: 7*	*14: 49*	— —	*15: 20*	*23: 33*	*16: 11*
21 MO	12 3 13	12 21	5: 41	18: 25	5: 30	18: 35	5: 17	18: 49	4: 58	19: 8	4: 27	19: 37
233			*1: 34*	*14: 56*	*1: 17*	*15: 13*	*0: 55*	*15: 35*	*0: 24*	*16: 4*	— —	*16: 53*
22 TU	12 2 58	12 1	5: 42	18: 24	5: 31	18: 34	5: 18	18: 48	4: 59	19: 6	4: 30	19: 35
234			*2: 23*	*15: 41*	*2: 7*	*15: 57*	*1: 46*	*16: 16*	*1: 17*	*16: 43*	*0: 29*	*17: 27*
23 WE	12 2 42	11 41	5: 42	18: 23	5: 32	18: 33	5: 19	18: 46	5: 1	19: 4	4: 32	19: 32
235			*3: 14*	*16: 25*	*2: 59*	*16: 38*	*2: 40*	*16: 55*	*2: 15*	*17: 18*	*1: 33*	*17: 54*
24 TH	12 2 27	11 20	5: 42	18: 22	5: 32	18: 32	5: 20	18: 45	5: 2	19: 2	4: 35	19: 29
236			*4: 5*	*17: 7*	*3: 53*	*17: 17*	*3: 37*	*17: 30*	*3: 16*	*17: 48*	*2: 43*	*18: 16*
25 FR	12 2 11	10 60	5: 43	18: 22	5: 33	18: 31	5: 21	18: 43	5: 4	19: 0	4: 37	19: 26
237			*4: 57*	*17: 48*	*4: 48*	*17: 55*	*4: 36*	*18: 4*	*4: 21*	*18: 16*	*3: 56*	*18: 35*
26 SA	12 1 54	10 39	5: 43	18: 21	5: 33	18: 30	5: 21	18: 42	5: 5	18: 58	4: 39	19: 23
238	*4 31 NM*		*5: 49*	*18: 28*	*5: 44*	*18: 32*	*5: 37*	*18: 36*	*5: 27*	*18: 42*	*5: 12*	*18: 51*
27 SU	12 1 37	10 18	5: 43	18: 20	5: 34	18: 29	5: 22	18: 40	5: 7	18: 56	4: 42	19: 20
239			*6: 43*	*19: 8*	*6: 41*	*19: 8*	*6: 38*	*19: 8*	*6: 35*	*19: 8*	*6: 30*	*19: 8*
28 MO	12 1 20	9 57	5: 43	18: 19	5: 34	18: 28	5: 23	18: 39	5: 8	18: 54	4: 44	19: 17
240			*7: 37*	*19: 49*	*7: 39*	*19: 45*	*7: 41*	*19: 41*	*7: 45*	*19: 34*	*7: 50*	*19: 24*
29 TU	12 1 2	9 36	5: 44	18: 18	5: 35	18: 27	5: 24	18: 37	5: 10	18: 51	4: 46	19: 14
241			*8: 32*	*20: 32*	*8: 38*	*20: 24*	*8: 45*	*20: 15*	*8: 55*	*20: 2*	*9: 11*	*19: 42*
30 WE	12 0 44	9 15	5: 44	18: 17	5: 36	18: 25	5: 25	18: 36	5: 11	18: 49	4: 49	19: 11
242			*9: 28*	*21: 17*	*9: 38*	*21: 6*	*9: 50*	*20: 52*	*10: 7*	*20: 33*	*10: 34*	*20: 4*
31 TH	12 0 26	8 53	5: 44	18: 17	5: 36	18: 24	5: 26	18: 34	5: 13	18: 47	4: 51	19: 8
243			*10: 27*	*22: 6*	*10: 40*	*21: 52*	*10: 56*	*21: 34*	*11: 19*	*21: 9*	*11: 55*	*20: 30*

9th Month **September 1995** **30 days**

Greenwich Mean Time

NOTE: For each day, numbers on first line indicate Sun. *Italic* numbers on second line indicate *Moon.* Degrees are North Latitude.

FM = full moon; LQ = last quarter; NM = new moon; FQ = first quarter.

CAUTION: Must be converted to local time. For instructions see page 263.

Day of month week year	Sun on Meridian Moon Phase	Sun's Declination	20° Rise Sun Moon	20° Set Sun Moon	30° Rise Sun Moon	30° Set Sun Moon	40° Rise Sun Moon	40° Set Sun Moon	50° Rise Sun Moon	50° Set Sun Moon	60° Rise Sun Moon	60° Set Sun Moon
	h m s	° ′	h m	h m	h m	h m	h m	h m	h m	h m	h m	h m
1 FR	12 0 7	8 32	5: 44	18: 16	5: 37	18: 23	5: 27	18: 32	5: 14	18: 45	4: 54	19: 5
244			*11: 26*	*22: 58*	*11: 42*	*22: 42*	*12: 1*	*22: 21*	*12: 29*	*21: 52*	*13: 14*	*21: 5*
2 SA	11 59 48	8 10	5: 44	18: 15	5: 37	18: 22	5: 28	18: 31	5: 16	18: 43	4: 56	19: 2
245	*9 3 FQ*		*12: 26*	*23: 54*	*12: 43*	*23: 36*	*13: 5*	*23: 14*	*13: 36*	*22: 43*	*14: 27*	*21: 52*
3 SU	11 59 29	7 48	5: 45	18: 14	5: 38	18: 21	5: 29	18: 29	5: 17	18: 41	4: 58	18: 59
246			*13: 25*	– –	*13: 42*	– –	*14: 5*	– –	*14: 36*	*23: 43*	*15: 28*	*22: 51*
4 MO	11 59 9	7 26	5: 45	18: 13	5: 38	18: 20	5: 30	18: 28	5: 19	18: 39	5: 1	18: 56
247			*14: 22*	*0: 53*	*14: 38*	*0: 36*	*14: 59*	*0: 14*	*15: 28*	– –	*16: 16*	– –
5 TU	11 58 49	7 4	5: 45	18: 12	5: 39	18: 18	5: 31	18: 26	5: 20	18: 37	5: 3	18: 53
248			*15: 16*	*1: 54*	*15: 30*	*1: 38*	*15: 48*	*1: 18*	*16: 13*	*0: 50*	*16: 53*	*0: 4*
6 WE	11 58 29	6 42	5: 45	18: 11	5: 39	18: 17	5: 32	18: 24	5: 22	18: 34	5: 5	18: 50
249			*16: 6*	*2: 55*	*16: 18*	*2: 42*	*16: 32*	*2: 25*	*16: 51*	*2: 2*	*17: 21*	*1: 25*
7 TH	11 58 9	6 20	5: 46	18: 10	5: 40	18: 16	5: 33	18: 23	5: 23	18: 32	5: 8	18: 47
250			*16: 54*	*3: 56*	*17: 2*	*3: 46*	*17: 11*	*3: 34*	*17: 24*	*3: 17*	*17: 44*	*2: 50*
8 FR	11 57 48	5 57	5: 46	18: 10	5: 40	18: 15	5: 34	18: 21	5: 25	18: 30	5: 10	18: 44
251			*17: 39*	*4: 56*	*17: 43*	*4: 50*	*17: 47*	*4: 42*	*17: 54*	*4: 32*	*18: 3*	*4: 16*
9 SA	11 57 27	5 35	5: 46	18: 9	5: 41	18: 13	5: 35	18: 20	5: 26	18: 28	5: 12	18: 41
252	*3 37 FM*		*18: 22*	*5: 53*	*18: 22*	*5: 52*	*18: 21*	*5: 49*	*18: 21*	*5: 46*	*18: 21*	*5: 41*
10 SU	11 57 6	5 12	5: 46	18: 8	5: 42	18: 12	5: 36	18: 18	5: 27	18: 26	5: 15	18: 38
253			*19: 4*	*6: 50*	*19: 0*	*6: 52*	*18: 55*	*6: 55*	*18: 48*	*6: 58*	*18: 38*	*7: 4*
11 MO	11 56 45	4 49	5: 46	18: 7	5: 42	18: 11	5: 37	18: 16	5: 29	18: 24	5: 17	18: 35
254			*19: 45*	*7: 45*	*19: 38*	*7: 51*	*19: 28*	*7: 58*	*19: 15*	*8: 9*	*18: 56*	*8: 25*
12 TU	11 56 24	4 27	5: 47	18: 6	5: 43	18: 10	5: 37	18: 15	5: 30	18: 21	5: 19	18: 32
255			*20: 28*	*8: 38*	*20: 16*	*8: 48*	*20: 3*	*9: 0*	*19: 44*	*9: 16*	*19: 16*	*9: 42*
13 WE	11 56 3	4 4	5: 47	18: 5	5: 43	18: 9	5: 38	18: 13	5: 32	18: 19	5: 22	18: 29
256			*21: 10*	*9: 31*	*20: 57*	*9: 44*	*20: 40*	*9: 59*	*20: 16*	*10: 21*	*19: 39*	*10: 56*
14 TH	11 55 41	3 41	5: 47	18: 4	5: 44	18: 7	5: 39	18: 11	5: 33	18: 17	5: 24	18: 26
257			*21: 55*	*10: 23*	*21: 39*	*10: 38*	*21: 19*	*10: 57*	*20: 52*	*11: 23*	*20: 8*	*12: 5*
15 FR	11 55 20	3 18	5: 47	18: 3	5: 44	18: 6	5: 40	18: 10	5: 35	18: 15	5: 26	18: 23
258			*22: 40*	*11: 13*	*22: 23*	*11: 30*	*22: 2*	*11: 51*	*21: 32*	*12: 20*	*20: 43*	*13: 8*
16 SA	11 54 59	2 55	5: 47	18: 2	5: 45	18: 5	5: 41	18: 8	5: 36	18: 13	5: 29	18: 20
259	*21 9 LQ*		*23: 27*	*12: 2*	*23: 10*	*12: 19*	*22: 48*	*12: 41*	*22: 18*	*13: 12*	*21: 27*	*14: 2*
17 SU	11 54 37	2 32	5: 48	18: 1	5: 45	18: 4	5: 42	18: 6	5: 38	18: 10	5: 31	18: 17
260			– –	*12: 49*	*23: 59*	*13: 7*	*23: 38*	*13: 28*	*23: 8*	*13: 58*	*22: 19*	*14: 48*
18 MO	11 54 16	2 8	5: 48	18: 0	5: 46	18: 2	5: 43	18: 5	5: 39	18: 8	5: 33	18: 14
261			*0: 16*	*13: 35*	– –	*13: 51*	– –	*14: 11*	– –	*14: 39*	*23: 20*	*15: 24*
19 TU	11 53 55	1 45	5: 48	17: 59	5: 46	18: 1	5: 44	18: 3	5: 41	18: 6	5: 36	18: 11
262			*1: 6*	*14: 19*	*0: 50*	*14: 33*	*0: 31*	*14: 51*	*0: 4*	*15: 15*	– –	*15: 54*
20 WE	11 53 33	1 22	5: 48	17: 59	5: 47	18: 0	5: 45	18: 1	5: 42	18: 4	5: 38	18: 8
263			*1: 56*	*15: 1*	*1: 43*	*15: 13*	*1: 26*	*15: 28*	*1: 3*	*15: 47*	*0: 26*	*16: 18*
21 TH	11 53 12	0 59	5: 48	17: 58	5: 47	17: 59	5: 46	18: 0	5: 44	18: 2	5: 41	18: 4
264			*2: 47*	*15: 43*	*2: 37*	*15: 51*	*2: 24*	*16: 2*	*2: 6*	*16: 16*	*1: 38*	*16: 39*
22 FR	11 52 51	0 35	5: 49	17: 57	5: 48	17: 57	5: 47	17: 58	5: 45	17: 59	5: 43	18: 1
265			*3: 40*	*16: 23*	*3: 33*	*16: 29*	*3: 24*	*16: 35*	*3: 12*	*16: 44*	*2: 53*	*16: 56*
23 SA	11 52 30	0 12	5: 49	17: 56	5: 49	17: 56	5: 48	17: 56	5: 47	17: 57	5: 45	17: 58
266			*4: 33*	*17: 4*	*4: 29*	*17: 6*	*4: 25*	*17: 7*	*4: 19*	*17: 10*	*4: 11*	*17: 13*
24 SU	1 52 9	-0 11	5: 49	17: 55	5: 49	17: 55	5: 49	17: 55	5: 48	17: 55	5: 48	17: 55
267	*16 55 NM*		*5: 27*	*17: 46*	*5: 28*	*17: 43*	*5: 28*	*17: 40*	*5: 29*	*17: 36*	*5: 31*	*17: 30*
25 MO	11 51 48	-0 35	5: 49	17: 54	5: 50	17: 54	5: 50	17: 53	5: 50	17: 53	5: 50	17: 52
268			*6: 23*	*18: 29*	*6: 28*	*18: 22*	*6: 33*	*18: 15*	*6: 41*	*18: 4*	*6: 53*	*17: 48*
26 TU	11 51 28	-0 58	5: 50	17: 53	5: 50	17: 52	5: 51	17: 51	5: 51	17: 51	5: 52	17: 49
269			*7: 21*	*19: 14*	*7: 29*	*19: 4*	*7: 39*	*18: 52*	*7: 54*	*18: 35*	*8: 16*	*18: 9*
27 WE	11 51 7	-1 22	5: 50	17: 52	5: 51	17: 51	5: 52	17: 50	5: 53	17: 48	5: 55	17: 46
270			*8: 20*	*20: 3*	*8: 32*	*19: 49*	*8: 47*	*19: 33*	*9: 7*	*19: 10*	*9: 40*	*18: 35*
28 TH	11 50 47	-1 45	5: 50	17: 51	5: 51	17: 50	5: 53	17: 48	5: 54	17: 46	5: 57	17: 43
271			*9: 20*	*20: 55*	*9: 35*	*20: 39*	*9: 53*	*20: 19*	*10: 19*	*19: 52*	*11: 2*	*19: 7*
29 FR	11 50 27	-2 8	5: 50	17: 50	5: 52	17: 49	5: 54	17: 47	5: 56	17: 44	5: 59	17: 40
272			*10: 20*	*21: 50*	*10: 37*	*21: 33*	*10: 58*	*21: 11*	*11: 28*	*20: 41*	*12: 17*	*19: 51*
30 SA	11 50 7	-2 32	5: 50	17: 49	5: 52	17: 47	5: 55	17: 45	5: 58	17: 42	6: 2	17: 37
273			*11: 20*	*22: 48*	*11: 37*	*22: 30*	*12: 0*	*22: 8*	*12: 30*	*21: 38*	*13: 22*	*20: 46*

10th Month **October 1995** **31 days**

Greenwich Mean Time

NOTE: For each day, numbers on first line indicate Sun. *Italic* numbers on second line indicate *Moon*. Degrees are North Latitude.

FM = full moon; LQ = last quarter; NM = new moon; FQ = first quarter.

CAUTION: Must be converted to local time. For instructions see page 263.

Day of month week year	Sun on Meridian Moon Phase h m s	Sun's Declination ° ′	20° Rise Sun Moon h m	20° Set Sun Moon h m	30° Rise Sun Moon h m	30° Set Sun Moon h m	40° Rise Sun Moon h m	40° Set Sun Moon h m	50° Rise Sun Moon h m	50° Set Sun Moon h m	60° Rise Sun Moon h m	60° Set Sun Moon h m
1 SU	11 49 48	-2 55	5: 51	17: 49	5: 53	17: 46	5: 56	17: 43	5: 59	17: 40	6: 4	17: 34
274	*14 36 FQ*		*12: 17*	*23: 48*	*12: 34*	*23: 31*	*12: 55*	*23: 11*	*13: 25*	*22: 42*	*14: 14*	*21: 54*
2 MO	11 49 28	-3 18	5: 51	17: 48	5: 54	17: 45	5: 57	17: 42	6: 1	17: 37	6: 7	17: 31
275			*13: 11*	– –	*13: 26*	– –	*13: 45*	– –	*14: 11*	*23: 51*	*14: 54*	*23: 11*
3 TU	11 49 9	-3 41	5: 51	17: 47	5: 54	17: 44	5: 58	17: 40	6: 2	17: 35	6: 9	17: 28
276			*14: 2*	*0: 48*	*14: 14*	*0: 34*	*14: 30*	*0: 16*	*14: 51*	– –	*15: 24*	– –
4 WE	11 48 51	-4 5	5: 51	17: 46	5: 55	17: 43	5: 59	17: 38	6: 4	17: 33	6: 11	17: 25
277			*14: 49*	*1: 47*	*14: 58*	*1: 36*	*15: 9*	*1: 22*	*15: 24*	*1: 3*	*15: 48*	*0: 33*
5 TH	11 48 32	-4 28	5: 52	17: 45	5: 55	17: 41	6: 0	17: 37	6: 5	17: 31	6: 14	17: 22
278			*15: 34*	*2: 46*	*15: 39*	*2: 38*	*15: 45*	*2: 29*	*15: 54*	*2: 16*	*16: 8*	*1: 56*
6 FR	11 48 14	-4 51	5: 52	17: 44	5: 56	17: 40	6: 1	17: 35	6: 7	17: 29	6: 16	17: 19
279			*16: 16*	*3: 42*	*16: 18*	*3: 39*	*16: 19*	*3: 35*	*16: 22*	*3: 29*	*16: 25*	*3: 20*
7 SA	11 47 57	-5 14	5: 52	17: 43	5: 56	17: 39	6: 2	17: 34	6: 8	17: 27	6: 18	17: 16
280			*16: 58*	*4: 38*	*16: 56*	*4: 39*	*16: 52*	*4: 39*	*16: 48*	*4: 40*	*16: 42*	*4: 42*
8 SU	11 47 39	-5 37	5: 53	17: 43	5: 57	17: 38	6: 3	17: 32	6: 10	17: 25	6: 21	17: 13
281	*15 52 FM*		*17: 39*	*5: 33*	*17: 33*	*5: 37*	*17: 26*	*5: 43*	*17: 15*	*5: 50*	*17: 0*	*6: 2*
9 MO	11 47 23	-5 60	5: 53	17: 42	5: 58	17: 37	6: 4	17: 31	6: 11	17: 22	6: 23	17: 10
282			*18: 21*	*6: 27*	*18: 12*	*6: 35*	*18: 0*	*6: 45*	*17: 44*	*6: 59*	*17: 19*	*7: 20*
10 TU	11 47 6	-6 23	5: 53	17: 41	5: 58	17: 35	6: 5	17: 29	6: 13	17: 20	6: 26	17: 7
283			*19: 4*	*7: 20*	*18: 51*	*7: 32*	*18: 36*	*7: 46*	*18: 15*	*8: 5*	*17: 41*	*8: 36*
11 WE	11 46 50	-6 45	5: 53	17: 40	5: 59	17: 34	6: 6	17: 27	6: 15	17: 18	6: 28	17: 4
284			*19: 48*	*8: 13*	*19: 33*	*8: 27*	*19: 14*	*8: 44*	*18: 49*	*9: 9*	*18: 8*	*9: 48*
12 TH	11 46 35	-7 8	5: 54	17: 39	6: 0	17: 33	6: 7	17: 26	6: 16	17: 16	6: 31	17: 1
285			*20: 33*	*9: 4*	*20: 17*	*9: 20*	*19: 56*	*9: 40*	*19: 27*	*10: 8*	*18: 41*	*10: 54*
13 FR	11 46 20	-7 31	5: 54	17: 38	6: 0	17: 32	6: 8	17: 24	6: 18	17: 14	6: 33	16: 58
286			*21: 20*	*9: 54*	*21: 3*	*10: 11*	*20: 41*	*10: 33*	*20: 11*	*11: 2*	*19: 21*	*11: 52*
14 SA	11 46 6	-7 53	5: 54	17: 38	6: 1	17: 31	6: 9	17: 23	6: 19	17: 12	6: 35	16: 56
287			*22: 8*	*10: 42*	*21: 51*	*10: 59*	*21: 29*	*11: 21*	*21: 0*	*11: 51*	*20: 10*	*12: 41*
15 SU	11 45 52	-8 15	5: 55	17: 37	6: 1	17: 30	6: 10	17: 21	6: 21	17: 10	6: 38	16: 53
288			*22: 57*	*11: 28*	*22: 41*	*11: 45*	*22: 21*	*12: 6*	*21: 53*	*12: 35*	*21: 7*	*13: 22*
16 MO	11 45 39	-8 38	5: 55	17: 36	6: 2	17: 29	6: 11	17: 20	6: 23	17: 8	6: 40	16: 50
289	*16 26 LQ*		*23: 47*	*12: 13*	*23: 33*	*12: 28*	*23: 15*	*12: 47*	*22: 50*	*13: 12*	*22: 10*	*13: 54*
17 TU	11 45 26	-8 60	5: 55	17: 35	6: 3	17: 28	6: 12	17: 18	6: 24	17: 6	6: 43	16: 47
290			– –	*12: 55*	– –	*13: 8*	– –	*13: 24*	*23: 51*	*13: 46*	*23: 19*	*14: 20*
18 WE	11 45 14	-9 22	5: 56	17: 35	6: 3	17: 27	6: 13	17: 17	6: 26	17: 4	6: 45	16: 44
291			*0: 37*	*13: 36*	*0: 25*	*13: 46*	*0: 11*	*13: 59*	– –	*14: 16*	– –	*14: 41*
19 TH	11 45 2	-9 43	5: 56	17: 34	6: 4	17: 26	6: 14	17: 15	6: 27	17: 2	6: 48	16: 41
292			*1: 28*	*14: 17*	*1: 20*	*14: 24*	*1: 9*	*14: 32*	*0: 54*	*14: 43*	*0: 31*	*15: 0*
20 FR	11 44 52	-10 5	5: 56	17: 33	6: 5	17: 25	6: 15	17: 14	6: 29	17: 0	6: 50	16: 38
293			*2: 20*	*14: 57*	*2: 15*	*15: 0*	*2: 9*	*15: 4*	*2: 0*	*15: 9*	*1: 47*	*15: 17*
21 SA	11 44 42	-10 27	5: 57	17: 32	6: 5	17: 24	6: 16	17: 13	6: 31	16: 58	6: 53	16: 35
294			*3: 14*	*15: 38*	*3: 12*	*15: 37*	*3: 11*	*15: 37*	*3: 8*	*15: 36*	*3: 5*	*15: 34*
22 SU	11 44 32	-10 48	5: 57	17: 32	6: 6	17: 23	6: 17	17: 11	6: 32	16: 56	6: 55	16: 33
295			*4: 9*	*16: 21*	*4: 11*	*16: 16*	*4: 15*	*16: 10*	*4: 19*	*16: 3*	*4: 26*	*15: 51*
23 MO	11 44 23	-11 9	5: 57	17: 31	6: 7	17: 22	6: 18	17: 10	6: 34	16: 54	6: 58	16: 30
296			*5: 6*	*17: 6*	*5: 13*	*16: 57*	*5: 21*	*16: 47*	*5: 32*	*16: 33*	*5: 50*	*16: 11*
24 TU	11 44 15	-11 30	5: 58	17: 30	6: 8	17: 21	6: 19	17: 8	6: 36	16: 52	7: 0	16: 27
297	*4 36 NM*		*6: 6*	*17: 54*	*6: 16*	*17: 42*	*6: 29*	*17: 27*	*6: 47*	*17: 7*	*7: 16*	*16: 35*
25 WE	11 44 8	-11 51	5: 58	17: 30	6: 8	17: 20	6: 21	17: 7	6: 37	16: 50	7: 3	16: 24
298			*7: 7*	*18: 46*	*7: 21*	*18: 31*	*7: 38*	*18: 12*	*8: 2*	*17: 47*	*8: 41*	*17: 6*
26 TH	11 44 1	-12 12	5: 59	17: 29	6: 9	17: 19	6: 22	17: 6	6: 39	16: 49	7: 5	16: 22
299			*8: 10*	*19: 42*	*8: 26*	*19: 25*	*8: 46*	*19: 4*	*9: 15*	*18: 34*	*10: 2*	*17: 46*
27 FR	11 43 55	-12 33	5: 59	17: 29	6: 10	17: 18	6: 23	17: 5	6: 40	16: 47	7: 8	16: 19
300			*9: 11*	*20: 41*	*9: 29*	*20: 23*	*9: 51*	*20: 1*	*10: 22*	*19: 30*	*11: 13*	*18: 38*
28 SA	11 43 50	-12 53	5: 59	17: 28	6: 10	17: 17	6: 24	17: 3	6: 42	16: 45	7: 11	16: 16
301			*10: 11*	*21: 41*	*10: 29*	*21: 24*	*10: 50*	*21: 3*	*11: 21*	*20: 33*	*12: 11*	*19: 44*
29 SU	11 43 45	-13 13	6: 0	17: 27	6: 11	17: 16	6: 25	17: 2	6: 44	16: 43	7: 13	16: 13
302			*11: 7*	*22: 42*	*11: 23*	*22: 27*	*11: 43*	*22: 9*	*12: 11*	*21: 43*	*12: 55*	*21: 0*
30 MO	11 43 42	-13 33	6: 0	17: 27	6: 12	17: 15	6: 26	17: 1	6: 45	16: 41	7: 16	16: 11
303	*21 17 FQ*		*11: 59*	*23: 42*	*12: 13*	*23: 30*	*12: 29*	*23: 15*	*12: 52*	*22: 54*	*13: 28*	*22: 21*
31 TU	11 43 39	-13 53	6: 1	17: 26	6: 13	17: 14	6: 27	17: 0	6: 47	16: 40	7: 18	16: 8
304			*12: 48*	– –	*12: 58*	– –	*13: 10*	– –	*13: 27*	– –	*13: 54*	*23: 44*

11th Month **November 1995** **30 days**

Greenwich Mean Time

NOTE: For each day, numbers on first line indicate Sun. *Italic* numbers on second line indicate *Moon.* Degrees are North Latitude.

FM = full moon; LQ = last quarter; NM = new moon; FQ = first quarter.

CAUTION: Must be converted to local time. For instructions see page 263.

Day of month week year	Sun on Meridian Moon Phase h m s	Sun's Declination ° ′	20° Rise Sun Moon h m	20° Set Sun Moon h m	30° Rise Sun Moon h m	30° Set Sun Moon h m	40° Rise Sun Moon h m	40° Set Sun Moon h m	50° Rise Sun Moon h m	50° Set Sun Moon h m	60° Rise Sun Moon h m	60° Set Sun Moon h m
1 WE	11 43 36	-14 12	6: 1	17: 26	6: 13	17: 13	6: 28	16: 58	6: 49	16: 38	7: 21	16: 5
305			*13: 32*	*0: 41*	*13: 39*	*0: 32*	*13: 47*	*0: 21*	*13: 58*	*0: 7*	*14: 14*	– –
2 TH	11 43 35	-14 31	6: 2	17: 25	6: 14	17: 13	6: 30	16: 57	6: 50	16: 36	7: 23	16: 3
306			*14: 15*	*1: 37*	*14: 18*	*1: 32*	*14: 21*	*1: 26*	*14: 25*	*1: 18*	*14: 32*	*1: 6*
3 FR	11 43 34	-14 50	6: 2	17: 25	6: 15	17: 12	6: 31	16: 56	6: 52	16: 34	7: 26	16: 0
307			*14: 56*	*2: 32*	*14: 55*	*2: 31*	*14: 53*	*2: 30*	*14: 52*	*2: 29*	*14: 49*	*2: 27*
4 SA	11 43 34	-15 9	6: 3	17: 24	6: 16	17: 11	6: 32	16: 55	6: 54	16: 33	7: 29	15: 58
308			*15: 37*	*3: 26*	*15: 32*	*3: 29*	*15: 26*	*3: 33*	*15: 18*	*3: 38*	*15: 6*	*3: 46*
5 SU	11 43 35	-15 28	6: 3	17: 24	6: 17	17: 10	6: 33	16: 54	6: 55	16: 31	7: 31	15: 55
309			*16: 17*	*4: 19*	*16: 9*	*4: 26*	*15: 59*	*4: 34*	*15: 45*	*4: 46*	*15: 24*	*5: 4*
6 MO	11 43 37	-15 46	6: 4	17: 23	6: 17	17: 10	6: 34	16: 53	6: 57	16: 30	7: 34	15: 53
310			*16: 59*	*5: 12*	*16: 48*	*5: 22*	*16: 34*	*5: 35*	*16: 14*	*5: 52*	*15: 44*	*6: 20*
7 TU	11 43 40	-16 4	6: 4	17: 23	6: 18	17: 9	6: 35	16: 52	6: 59	16: 28	7: 36	15: 50
311	*7 20 FM*		*17: 43*	*6: 4*	*17: 28*	*6: 17*	*17: 11*	*6: 34*	*16: 47*	*6: 56*	*16: 9*	*7: 32*
8 WE	11 43 43	-16 22	6: 5	17: 23	6: 19	17: 8	6: 36	16: 51	7: 0	16: 26	7: 39	15: 48
312			*18: 27*	*6: 56*	*18: 11*	*7: 11*	*17: 51*	*7: 31*	*17: 24*	*7: 57*	*16: 39*	*8: 41*
9 TH	11 43 47	-16 39	6: 5	17: 22	6: 20	17: 8	6: 38	16: 50	7: 2	16: 25	7: 41	15: 45
313			*19: 14*	*7: 47*	*18: 57*	*8: 3*	*18: 35*	*8: 25*	*18: 5*	*8: 54*	*17: 16*	*9: 43*
10 FR	11 43 53	-16 57	6: 6	17: 22	6: 20	17: 7	6: 39	16: 49	7: 4	16: 23	7: 44	15: 43
314			*20: 1*	*8: 36*	*19: 44*	*8: 53*	*19: 22*	*9: 15*	*18: 52*	*9: 45*	*18: 2*	*10: 36*
11 SA	11 43 59	-17 13	6: 6	17: 22	6: 21	17: 6	6: 40	16: 48	7: 5	16: 22	7: 46	15: 41
315			*20: 50*	*9: 23*	*20: 33*	*9: 40*	*20: 13*	*10: 1*	*19: 44*	*10: 31*	*18: 56*	*11: 20*
12 SU	11 44 5	-17 30	6: 7	17: 21	6: 22	17: 6	6: 41	16: 47	7: 7	16: 21	7: 49	15: 38
316			*21: 39*	*10: 8*	*21: 24*	*10: 24*	*21: 5*	*10: 43*	*20: 39*	*11: 11*	*19: 56*	*11: 55*
13 MO	11 44 13	-17 46	6: 7	17: 21	6: 23	17: 5	6: 42	16: 46	7: 9	16: 19	7: 52	15: 36
317			*22: 29*	*10: 51*	*22: 16*	*11: 5*	*22: 0*	*11: 22*	*21: 38*	*11: 45*	*21: 2*	*12: 23*
14 TU	11 44 22	-18 2	6: 8	17: 21	6: 24	17: 5	6: 43	16: 45	7: 10	16: 18	7: 54	15: 34
318			*23: 19*	*11: 32*	*23: 9*	*11: 43*	*22: 56*	*11: 57*	*22: 39*	*12: 16*	*22: 12*	*12: 46*
15 WE	11 44 31	-18 18	6: 8	17: 20	6: 25	17: 4	6: 44	16: 44	7: 12	16: 17	7: 57	15: 32
319	*11 40 LQ*		– –	*12: 12*	– –	*12: 20*	*23: 54*	*12: 30*	*23: 43*	*12: 44*	*23: 25*	*13: 5*
16 TH	11 44 41	-18 33	6: 9	17: 20	6: 25	17: 4	6: 46	16: 43	7: 13	16: 15	7: 59	15: 30
320			*0: 9*	*12: 51*	*0: 2*	*12: 56*	– –	*13: 2*	– –	*13: 10*	– –	*13: 22*
17 FR	11 44 53	-18 49	6: 10	17: 20	6: 26	17: 3	6: 47	16: 43	7: 15	16: 14	8: 2	15: 27
321			*1: 1*	*13: 31*	*0: 57*	*13: 32*	*0: 54*	*13: 33*	*0: 48*	*13: 35*	*0: 40*	*13: 38*
18 SA	11 45 5	-19 3	6: 10	17: 20	6: 27	17: 3	6: 48	16: 42	7: 17	16: 13	8: 4	15: 25
322			*1: 54*	*14: 11*	*1: 54*	*14: 9*	*1: 55*	*14: 6*	*1: 56*	*14: 1*	*1: 58*	*13: 55*
19 SU	11 45 18	-19 18	6: 11	17: 20	6: 28	17: 2	6: 49	16: 41	7: 18	16: 12	8: 7	15: 23
323			*2: 49*	*14: 54*	*2: 53*	*14: 48*	*2: 59*	*14: 40*	*3: 7*	*14: 29*	*3: 19*	*14: 13*
20 MO	11 45 31	-19 32	6: 11	17: 19	6: 29	17: 2	6: 50	16: 41	7: 20	16: 11	8: 9	15: 21
324			*3: 47*	*15: 40*	*3: 55*	*15: 30*	*4: 6*	*15: 18*	*4: 20*	*15: 1*	*4: 43*	*14: 34*
21 TU	11 45 46	-19 45	6: 12	17: 19	6: 30	17: 2	6: 51	16: 40	7: 21	16: 10	8: 11	15: 19
325			*4: 47*	*16: 31*	*4: 59*	*16: 17*	*5: 15*	*16: 0*	*5: 36*	*15: 37*	*6: 9*	*15: 1*
22 WE	11 46 1	-19 59	6: 13	17: 19	6: 30	17: 1	6: 52	16: 39	7: 23	16: 9	8: 14	15: 18
326	*15 43 NM*		*5: 50*	*17: 26*	*6: 5*	*17: 10*	*6: 24*	*16: 49*	*6: 51*	*16: 22*	*7: 35*	*15: 36*
23 TH	11 46 17	-20 12	6: 13	17: 19	6: 31	17: 1	6: 54	16: 39	7: 24	16: 8	8: 16	15: 16
327			*6: 54*	*18: 25*	*7: 11*	*18: 7*	*7: 33*	*17: 45*	*8: 3*	*17: 15*	*8: 53*	*16: 24*
24 FR	11 46 34	-20 24	6: 14	17: 19	6: 32	17: 1	6: 55	16: 38	7: 26	16: 7	8: 19	15: 14
328			*7: 57*	*19: 27*	*8: 15*	*19: 10*	*8: 37*	*18: 48*	*9: 8*	*18: 17*	*10: 0*	*17: 26*
25 SA	11 46 52	-20 36	6: 15	17: 19	6: 33	17: 1	6: 56	16: 38	7: 28	16: 6	8: 21	15: 12
329			*8: 58*	*20: 31*	*9: 14*	*20: 15*	*9: 35*	*19: 55*	*10: 4*	*19: 27*	*10: 52*	*18: 41*
26 SU	11 47 10	-20 48	6: 15	17: 19	6: 34	17: 0	6: 57	16: 37	7: 29	16: 5	8: 23	15: 11
330			*9: 53*	*21: 34*	*10: 8*	*21: 20*	*10: 26*	*21: 4*	*10: 51*	*20: 41*	*11: 30*	*20: 3*
27 MO	11 47 30	-20 60	6: 16	17: 19	6: 35	17: 0	6: 58	16: 37	7: 30	16: 4	8: 25	15: 9
331			*10: 45*	*22: 34*	*10: 56*	*22: 24*	*11: 10*	*22: 12*	*11: 29*	*21: 55*	*11: 59*	*21: 28*
28 TU	11 47 49	-21 11	6: 16	17: 19	6: 35	17: 0	6: 59	16: 36	7: 32	16: 3	8: 28	15: 8
332			*11: 31*	*23: 32*	*11: 39*	*23: 26*	*11: 49*	*23: 19*	*12: 2*	*23: 9*	*12: 22*	*22: 52*
29 WE	11 48 10	-21 21	6: 17	17: 19	6: 36	17: 0	7: 0	16: 36	7: 33	16: 3	8: 30	15: 6
333	*6 28 FQ*		*12: 15*	– –	*12: 19*	– –	*12: 24*	– –	*12: 31*	– –	*12: 41*	– –
30 TH	11 48 31	-21 32	6: 18	17: 19	6: 37	17: 0	7: 1	16: 36	7: 35	16: 2	8: 32	15: 5
334			*12: 57*	*0: 28*	*12: 57*	*0: 26*	*12: 57*	*0: 24*	*12: 57*	*0: 20*	*12: 57*	*0: 14*

12th Month **December 1995** **31 days**

Greenwich Mean Time

NOTE: For each day, numbers on first line indicate Sun. *Italic* numbers on second line indicate *Moon*. Degrees are North Latitude.

FM = full moon; LQ = last quarter; NM = new moon; FQ = first quarter.

CAUTION: Must be converted to local time. For instructions see page 263.

Day of month week year	Sun on Meridian Moon Phase h m s	Sun's Declination ° '	20° Rise Sun Moon h m	20° Set Sun Moon h m	30° Rise Sun Moon h m	30° Set Sun Moon h m	40° Rise Sun Moon h m	40° Set Sun Moon h m	50° Rise Sun Moon h m	50° Set Sun Moon h m	60° Rise Sun Moon h m	60° Set Sun Moon h m
1 FR	11 48 53	-21 41	6: 18	17: 19	6: 38	17: 0	7: 2	16: 35	7: 36	16: 1	8: 34	15: 3
335			*13: 37*	*1: 22*	*13: 33*	*1: 24*	*13: 29*	*1: 26*	*13: 23*	*1: 29*	*13: 14*	*1: 34*
2 SA	11 49 16	-21 51	6: 19	17: 19	6: 39	17: 0	7: 3	16: 35	7: 37	16: 1	8: 36	15: 2
336			*14: 17*	*2: 15*	*14: 10*	*2: 21*	*14: 1*	*2: 28*	*13: 49*	*2: 37*	*13: 31*	*2: 52*
3 SU	11 49 39	-21 60	6: 20	17: 20	6: 39	17: 0	7: 4	16: 35	7: 39	16: 0	8: 38	15: 1
337			*14: 58*	*3: 7*	*14: 48*	*3: 17*	*14: 35*	*3: 28*	*14: 17*	*3: 43*	*13: 50*	*4: 7*
4 MO	11 50 2	-22 8	6: 20	17: 20	6: 40	17: 0	7: 5	16: 35	7: 40	16: 0	8: 40	15: 0
338			*15: 40*	*3: 59*	*15: 27*	*4: 11*	*15: 10*	*4: 27*	*14: 48*	*4: 47*	*14: 12*	*5: 21*
5 TU	11 50 27	-22 16	6: 21	17: 20	6: 41	17: 0	7: 6	16: 35	7: 41	15: 59	8: 42	14: 59
339			*16: 24*	*4: 51*	*16: 8*	*5: 5*	*15: 49*	*5: 24*	*15: 23*	*5: 49*	*14: 40*	*6: 30*
6 WE	11 50 52	-22 24	6: 21	17: 20	6: 42	17: 0	7: 7	16: 35	7: 42	15: 59	8: 43	14: 58
340			*17: 9*	*5: 41*	*16: 52*	*5: 58*	*16: 31*	*6: 18*	*16: 2*	*6: 47*	*15: 14*	*7: 34*
7 TH	11 51 17	-22 31	6: 22	17: 20	6: 42	17: 0	7: 8	16: 35	7: 44	15: 59	8: 45	14: 57
341	*1 27 FM*		*17: 57*	*6: 31*	*17: 39*	*6: 48*	*17: 17*	*7: 10*	*16: 47*	*7: 40*	*15: 56*	*8: 31*
8 FR	11 51 43	-22 38	6: 23	17: 21	6: 43	17: 0	7: 9	16: 35	7: 45	15: 59	8: 47	14: 56
342			*18: 45*	*7: 19*	*18: 28*	*7: 36*	*18: 6*	*7: 58*	*17: 36*	*8: 28*	*16: 47*	*9: 18*
9 SA	11 52 9	-22 45	6: 23	17: 21	6: 44	17: 0	7: 10	16: 35	7: 46	15: 58	8: 48	14: 56
343			*19: 34*	*8: 5*	*19: 18*	*8: 21*	*18: 58*	*8: 42*	*18: 31*	*9: 10*	*17: 45*	*9: 57*
10 SU	11 52 36	-22 51	6: 24	17: 21	6: 45	17: 1	7: 10	16: 35	7: 47	15: 58	8: 50	14: 55
344			*20: 23*	*8: 49*	*20: 9*	*9: 3*	*19: 52*	*9: 22*	*19: 28*	*9: 47*	*18: 50*	*10: 27*
11 MO	11 53 3	-22 56	6: 25	17: 22	6: 45	17: 1	7: 11	16: 35	7: 48	15: 58	8: 51	14: 54
345			*21: 13*	*9: 30*	*21: 2*	*9: 43*	*20: 48*	*9: 58*	*20: 28*	*10: 19*	*19: 58*	*10: 52*
12 TU	11 53 31	-23 1	6: 25	17: 22	6: 46	17: 1	7: 12	16: 35	7: 49	15: 58	8: 53	14: 54
346			*22: 3*	*10: 10*	*21: 54*	*10: 20*	*21: 44*	*10: 32*	*21: 30*	*10: 48*	*21: 9*	*11: 12*
13 WE	11 53 59	-23 6	6: 26	17: 22	6: 47	17: 1	7: 13	16: 35	7: 50	15: 58	8: 54	14: 54
347			*22: 52*	*10: 49*	*22: 48*	*10: 55*	*22: 42*	*11: 3*	*22: 34*	*11: 14*	*22: 21*	*11: 30*
14 TH	11 54 27	-23 10	6: 26	17: 23	6: 47	17: 2	7: 14	16: 35	7: 51	15: 58	8: 55	14: 53
348			*23: 43*	*11: 27*	*23: 42*	*11: 30*	*23: 41*	*11: 34*	*23: 39*	*11: 39*	*23: 36*	*11: 46*
15 FR	11 54 56	-23 14	6: 27	17: 23	6: 48	17: 2	7: 14	16: 36	7: 51	15: 58	8: 57	14: 53
349	*5 31 LQ*		– –	*12: 6*	– –	*12: 5*	– –	*12: 4*	– –	*12: 3*	– –	*12: 1*
16 SA	11 55 25	-23 17	6: 27	17: 23	6: 49	17: 2	7: 15	16: 36	7: 52	15: 58	8: 58	14: 53
350			*0: 36*	*12: 46*	*0: 38*	*12: 42*	*0: 42*	*12: 36*	*0: 46*	*12: 29*	*0: 53*	*12: 18*
17 SU	11 55 54	-23 20	6: 28	17: 24	6: 49	17: 3	7: 16	16: 36	7: 53	15: 59	8: 59	14: 53
351			*1: 30*	*13: 29*	*1: 37*	*13: 21*	*1: 45*	*13: 11*	*1: 56*	*12: 57*	*2: 13*	*12: 36*
18 MO	11 56 24	-23 22	6: 29	17: 24	6: 50	17: 3	7: 16	16: 36	7: 54	15: 59	9: 0	14: 53
352			*2: 28*	*14: 16*	*2: 38*	*14: 4*	*2: 51*	*13: 50*	*3: 8*	*13: 30*	*3: 36*	*12: 59*
19 TU	11 56 53	-23 24	6: 29	17: 25	6: 50	17: 3	7: 17	16: 37	7: 54	15: 59	9: 0	14: 53
353			*3: 28*	*15: 7*	*3: 42*	*14: 52*	*3: 59*	*14: 34*	*4: 22*	*14: 9*	*5: 0*	*13: 28*
20 WE	11 57 23	-23 25	6: 30	17: 25	6: 51	17: 4	7: 17	16: 37	7: 55	16: 0	9: 1	14: 54
354			*4: 31*	*16: 4*	*4: 47*	*15: 47*	*5: 8*	*15: 26*	*5: 36*	*14: 56*	*6: 23*	*14: 8*
21 TH	11 57 53	-23 26	6: 30	17: 26	6: 51	17: 4	7: 18	16: 38	7: 56	16: 0	9: 2	14: 54
355			*5: 35*	*17: 5*	*5: 53*	*16: 47*	*6: 15*	*16: 25*	*6: 46*	*15: 54*	*7: 38*	*15: 2*
22 FR	11 58 23	-23 26	6: 31	17: 26	6: 52	17: 5	7: 19	16: 38	7: 56	16: 1	9: 2	14: 55
356	*2 22 NM*		*6: 38*	*18: 10*	*6: 56*	*17: 53*	*7: 18*	*17: 31*	*7: 48*	*17: 1*	*8: 39*	*16: 11*
23 SA	11 58 53	-23 26	6: 31	17: 27	6: 52	17: 5	7: 19	16: 39	7: 57	16: 1	9: 3	14: 55
357			*7: 38*	*19: 15*	*7: 54*	*19: 0*	*8: 14*	*18: 42*	*8: 41*	*18: 16*	*9: 26*	*17: 33*
24 SU	11 59 23	-23 26	6: 32	17: 27	6: 53	17: 6	7: 19	16: 39	7: 57	16: 2	9: 3	14: 56
358			*8: 34*	*20: 19*	*8: 47*	*20: 8*	*9: 3*	*19: 53*	*9: 25*	*19: 33*	*10: 1*	*19: 1*
25 MO	11 59 53	-23 25	6: 32	17: 28	6: 53	17: 6	7: 20	16: 40	7: 57	16: 2	9: 3	14: 57
359			*9: 25*	*21: 21*	*9: 34*	*21: 13*	*9: 46*	*21: 4*	*10: 2*	*20: 50*	*10: 27*	*20: 29*
26 TU	12 0 23	-23 23	6: 33	17: 28	6: 54	17: 7	7: 20	16: 41	7: 58	16: 3	9: 3	14: 57
360			*10: 12*	*22: 20*	*10: 17*	*22: 16*	*10: 24*	*22: 12*	*10: 34*	*22: 5*	*10: 48*	*21: 55*
27 WE	12 0 53	-23 21	6: 33	17: 29	6: 54	17: 8	7: 21	16: 41	7: 58	16: 4	9: 4	14: 58
361			*10: 55*	*23: 16*	*10: 57*	*23: 17*	*10: 59*	*23: 17*	*11: 2*	*23: 18*	*11: 6*	*23: 18*
28 TH	12 1 22	-23 19	6: 33	17: 29	6: 55	17: 8	7: 21	16: 42	7: 58	16: 5	9: 4	14: 59
362	*19 6 FQ*		*11: 37*	– –	*11: 35*	– –	*11: 32*	– –	*11: 28*	– –	*11: 23*	– –
29 FR	12 1 52	-23 16	6: 34	17: 30	6: 55	17: 9	7: 21	16: 43	7: 58	16: 5	9: 3	15: 0
363			*12: 18*	*0: 11*	*12: 12*	*0: 15*	*12: 4*	*0: 20*	*11: 55*	*0: 27*	*11: 40*	*0: 38*
30 SA	12 2 21	-23 12	6: 34	17: 31	6: 55	17: 10	7: 21	16: 43	7: 59	16: 6	9: 3	15: 2
364			*12: 58*	*1: 4*	*12: 49*	*1: 12*	*12: 38*	*1: 21*	*12: 22*	*1: 35*	*11: 58*	*1: 55*
31 SU	12 2 50	-23 9	6: 35	17: 31	6: 56	17: 10	7: 22	16: 44	7: 59	16: 7	9: 3	15: 3
365			*13: 40*	*1: 56*	*13: 28*	*2: 7*	*13: 12*	*2: 21*	*12: 52*	*2: 39*	*12: 19*	*3: 9*

Perpetual Calendar

The number shown for each year indicates which Gregorian calendar to use. For 1583-1802, see "Gregorian Calendar" on page 288. For 1803-20, use numbers for 1983-2000, respectively. For Julian Calendar, see "Julian Calendar" on page 288.

1821 . . . 2	1847 . . . 6	1873 . . . 4	1899 . . . 1	1925 . . . 5	1951 . . . 2	1977 . . . 7	2003 . . . 4	2029 . . . 2	2055 . . . 6
1822 . . . 3	1848 . . . 14	1874 . . . 5	1900 . . . 2	1926 . . . 6	1952 . . . 10	1978 . . . 1	2004 . . . 12	2030 . . . 3	2056 . . . 14
1823 . . . 4	1849 . . . 2	1875 . . . 6	1901 . . . 3	1927 . . . 7	1953 . . . 5	1979 . . . 2	2005 . . . 7	2031 . . . 4	2057 . . . 2
1824 . . . 12	1850 . . . 3	1876 . . . 14	1902 . . . 4	1928 . . . 8	1954 . . . 6	1980 . . . 10	2006 . . . 1	2032 . . . 12	2058 . . . 3
1825 . . . 7	1851 . . . 4	1877 . . . 2	1903 . . . 5	1929 . . . 3	1955 . . . 7	1981 . . . 5	2007 . . . 2	2033 . . . 7	2059 . . . 4
1826 . . . 1	1852 . . . 12	1878 . . . 3	1904 . . . 13	1930 . . . 4	1956 . . . 8	1982 . . . 6	2008 . . . 10	2034 . . . 1	2060 . . 12
1827 . . . 2	1853 . . . 7	1879 . . . 4	1905 . . . 1	1931 . . . 5	1957 . . . 3	1983 . . . 7	2009 . . . 5	2035 . . . 2	2061 . . 7
1828 . . . 10	1854 . . . 1	1880 . . . 12	1906 . . . 2	1932 . . . 13	1958 . . . 4	1984 . . . 8	2010 . . . 6	2036 . . . 10	2062 . . 1
1829 . . . 5	1855 . . . 2	1881 . . . 7	1907 . . . 3	1933 . . . 1	1959 . . . 5	1985 . . . 3	2011 . . . 7	2037 . . . 5	2063 . . 2
1830 . . . 6	1856 . . . 10	1882 . . . 1	1908 . . . 11	1934 . . . 2	1960 . . . 13	1986 . . . 4	2012 . . . 8	2038 . . . 6	2064 . . 10
1831 . . . 7	1857 . . . 5	1883 . . . 2	1909 . . . 6	1935 . . . 3	1961 . . . 1	1987 . . . 5	2013 . . . 3	2039 . . . 7	2065 . . 5
1832 . . . 8	1858 . . . 6	1884 . . . 10	1910 . . . 7	1936 . . . 11	1962 . . . 2	1988 . . . 13	2014 . . . 4	2040 . . . 8	2066 . . 6
1833 . . . 3	1859 . . . 7	1885 . . . 5	1911 . . . 1	1937 . . . 6	1963 . . . 3	1989 . . . 1	2015 . . . 5	2041 . . . 3	2067 . . 7
1834 . . . 4	1860 . . . 8	1886 . . . 6	1912 . . . 9	1938 . . . 7	1964 . . . 11	1990 . . . 2	2016 . . . 13	2042 . . . 4	2068 . . 8
1835 . . . 5	1861 . . . 3	1887 . . . 7	1913 . . . 4	1939 . . . 1	1965 . . . 6	1991 . . . 3	2017 . . . 1	2043 . . . 5	2069 . . 3
1836 . . . 13	1862 . . . 4	1888 . . . 8	1914 . . . 5	1940 . . . 9	1966 . . . 7	1992 . . . 11	2018 . . . 2	2044 . . . 13	2070 . . 4
1837 . . . 1	1863 . . . 5	1889 . . . 3	1915 . . . 6	1941 . . . 4	1967 . . . 1	1993 . . . 6	2019 . . . 3	2045 . . . 1	2071 . . 5
1838 . . . 2	1864 . . . 13	1890 . . . 4	1916 . . . 14	1942 . . . 5	1968 . . . 9	1994 . . . 7	2020 . . . 11	2046 . . . 2	2072 . . 13
1839 . . . 3	1865 . . . 1	1891 . . . 5	1917 . . . 2	1943 . . . 6	1969 . . . 4	1995 . . . 1	2021 . . . 6	2047 . . . 3	2073 . . 1
1840 . . . 11	1866 . . . 2	1892 . . . 13	1918 . . . 3	1944 . . . 14	1970 . . . 5	1996 . . . 9	2022 . . . 7	2048 . . . 11	2074 . . 2
1841 . . . 6	1867 . . . 3	1893 . . . 1	1919 . . . 4	1945 . . . 2	1971 . . . 6	1997 . . . 4	2023 . . . 1	2049 . . . 6	2075 . . 3
1842 . . . 7	1868 . . . 11	1894 . . . 2	1920 . . . 12	1946 . . . 3	1972 . . . 14	1998 . . . 5	2024 . . . 9	2050 . . . 7	2076 . . 11
1843 . . . 1	1869 . . . 6	1895 . . . 3	1921 . . . 7	1947 . . . 4	1973 . . . 2	1999 . . . 6	2025 . . . 4	2051 . . . 1	2077 . . 6
1844 . . . 9	1870 . . . 7	1896 . . . 11	1922 . . . 1	1948 . . . 12	1974 . . . 3	2000 . . . 14	2026 . . . 5	2052 . . . 9	2078 . . 7
1845 . . . 4	1871 . . . 1	1897 . . . 6	1923 . . . 2	1949 . . . 7	1975 . . . 4	2001 . . . 2	2027 . . . 6	2053 . . . 4	2079 . . 1
1846 . . . 5	1872 . . . 9	1898 . . . 7	1924 . . . 10	1950 . . . 1	1976 . . . 12	2002 . . . 3	2028 . . . 14	2054 . . . 5	2080 . . 9

1

1995

JANUARY

S	M	T	W	T	F	S
1	2	3	4	5	6	7
8	9	10	11	12	13	14
15	16	17	18	19	20	21
22	23	24	25	26	27	28
29	30	31				

FEBRUARY

S	M	T	W	T	F	S
			1	2	3	4
5	6	7	8	9	10	11
12	13	14	15	16	17	18
19	20	21	22	23	24	25
26	27	28				

MARCH

S	M	T	W	T	F	S
			1	2	3	4
5	6	7	8	9	10	11
12	13	14	15	16	17	18
19	20	21	22	23	24	25
26	27	28	29	30	31	

APRIL

S	M	T	W	T	F	S
						1
2	3	4	5	6	7	8
9	10	11	12	13	14	15
16	17	18	19	20	21	22
23	24	25	26	27	28	29
30						

MAY

S	M	T	W	T	F	S
	1	2	3	4	5	6
7	8	9	10	11	12	13
14	15	16	17	18	19	20
21	22	23	24	25	26	27
28	29	30	31			

JUNE

S	M	T	W	T	F	S
				1	2	3
4	5	6	7	8	9	10
11	12	13	14	15	16	17
18	19	20	21	22	23	24
25	26	27	28	29	30	

JULY

S	M	T	W	T	F	S
						1
2	3	4	5	6	7	8
9	10	11	12	13	14	15
16	17	18	19	20	21	22
23	24	25	26	27	28	29
30	31					

AUGUST

S	M	T	W	T	F	S
		1	2	3	4	5
6	7	8	9	10	11	12
13	14	15	16	17	18	19
20	21	22	23	24	25	26
27	28	29	30	31		

SEPTEMBER

S	M	T	W	T	F	S
					1	2
3	4	5	6	7	8	9
10	11	12	13	14	15	16
17	18	19	20	21	22	23
24	25	26	27	28	29	30

OCTOBER

S	M	T	W	T	F	S
1	2	3	4	5	6	7
8	9	10	11	12	13	14
15	16	17	18	19	20	21
22	23	24	25	26	27	28
29	30	31				

NOVEMBER

S	M	T	W	T	F	S
			1	2	3	4
5	6	7	8	9	10	11
12	13	14	15	16	17	18
19	20	21	22	23	24	25
26	27	28	29	30		

DECEMBER

S	M	T	W	T	F	S
					1	2
3	4	5	6	7	8	9
10	11	12	13	14	15	16
17	18	19	20	21	22	23
24	25	26	27	28	29	30
31						

2

JANUARY

S	M	T	W	T	F	S
	1	2	3	4	5	6
7	8	9	10	11	12	13
14	15	16	17	18	19	20
21	22	23	24	25	26	27
28	29	30	31			

FEBRUARY

S	M	T	W	T	F	S
				1	2	3
4	5	6	7	8	9	10
11	12	13	14	15	16	17
18	19	20	21	22	23	24
25	26	27	28			

MARCH

S	M	T	W	T	F	S
				1	2	3
4	5	6	7	8	9	10
11	12	13	14	15	16	17
18	19	20	21	22	23	24
25	26	27	28	29	30	31

APRIL

S	M	T	W	T	F	S
1	2	3	4	5	6	7
8	9	10	11	12	13	14
15	16	17	18	19	20	21
22	23	24	25	26	27	28
29	30					

MAY

S	M	T	W	T	F	S
		1	2	3	4	5
6	7	8	9	10	11	12
13	14	15	16	17	18	19
20	21	22	23	24	25	26
27	28	29	30	31		

JUNE

S	M	T	W	T	F	S
					1	2
3	4	5	6	7	8	9
10	11	12	13	14	15	16
17	18	19	20	21	22	23
24	25	26	27	28	29	30

JULY

S	M	T	W	T	F	S
1	2	3	4	5	6	7
8	9	10	11	12	13	14
15	16	17	18	19	20	21
22	23	24	25	26	27	28
29	30	31				

AUGUST

S	M	T	W	T	F	S
			1	2	3	4
5	6	7	8	9	10	11
12	13	14	15	16	17	18
19	20	21	22	23	24	25
26	27	28	29	30	31	

SEPTEMBER

S	M	T	W	T	F	S
						1
2	3	4	5	6	7	8
9	10	11	12	13	14	15
16	17	18	19	20	21	22
23	24	25	26	27	28	29
30						

OCTOBER

S	M	T	W	T	F	S
	1	2	3	4	5	6
7	8	9	10	11	12	13
14	15	16	17	18	19	20
21	22	23	24	25	26	27
28	29	30	31			

NOVEMBER

S	M	T	W	T	F	S
				1	2	3
4	5	6	7	8	9	10
11	12	13	14	15	16	17
18	19	20	21	22	23	24
25	26	27	28	29	30	

DECEMBER

S	M	T	W	T	F	S
						1
2	3	4	5	6	7	8
9	10	11	12	13	14	15
16	17	18	19	20	21	22
23	24	25	26	27	28	29
30	31					

3

JANUARY

S	M	T	W	T	F	S
		1	2	3	4	5
6	7	8	9	10	11	12
13	14	15	16	17	18	19
20	21	22	23	24	25	26
27	28	29	30	31		

FEBRUARY

S	M	T	W	T	F	S
					1	2
3	4	5	6	7	8	9
10	11	12	13	14	15	16
17	18	19	20	21	22	23
24	25	26	27	28		

MARCH

S	M	T	W	T	F	S
					1	2
3	4	5	6	7	8	9
10	11	12	13	14	15	16
17	18	19	20	21	22	23
24	25	26	27	28	29	30
31						

APRIL

S	M	T	W	T	F	S
	1	2	3	4	5	6
7	8	9	10	11	12	13
14	15	16	17	18	19	20
21	22	23	24	25	26	27
28	29	30				

MAY

S	M	T	W	T	F	S
			1	2	3	4
5	6	7	8	9	10	11
12	13	14	15	16	17	18
19	20	21	22	23	24	25
26	27	28	29	30	31	

JUNE

S	M	T	W	T	F	S
						1
2	3	4	5	6	7	8
9	10	11	12	13	14	15
16	17	18	19	20	21	22
23	24	25	26	27	28	29
30						

JULY

S	M	T	W	T	F	S
	1	2	3	4	5	6
7	8	9	10	11	12	13
14	15	16	17	18	19	20
21	22	23	24	25	26	27
28	29	30	31			

AUGUST

S	M	T	W	T	F	S
				1	2	3
4	5	6	7	8	9	10
11	12	13	14	15	16	17
18	19	20	21	22	23	24
25	26	27	28	29	30	31

SEPTEMBER

S	M	T	W	T	F	S
1	2	3	4	5	6	7
8	9	10	11	12	13	14
15	16	17	18	19	20	21
22	23	24	25	26	27	28
29	30					

OCTOBER

S	M	T	W	T	F	S
		1	2	3	4	5
6	7	8	9	10	11	12
13	14	15	16	17	18	19
20	21	22	23	24	25	26
27	28	29	30	31		

NOVEMBER

S	M	T	W	T	F	S
					1	2
3	4	5	6	7	8	9
10	11	12	13	14	15	16
17	18	19	20	21	22	23
24	25	26	27	28	29	30

DECEMBER

S	M	T	W	T	F	S
1	2	3	4	5	6	7
8	9	10	11	12	13	14
15	16	17	18	19	20	21
22	23	24	25	26	27	28
29	30	31				

4

JANUARY

S	M	T	W	T	F	S
			1	2	3	4
5	6	7	8	9	10	11
12	13	14	15	16	17	18
19	20	21	22	23	24	25
26	27	28	29	30	31	

FEBRUARY

S	M	T	W	T	F	S
						1
2	3	4	5	6	7	8
9	10	11	12	13	14	15
16	17	18	19	20	21	22
23	24	25	26	27	28	

MARCH

S	M	T	W	T	F	S
						1
2	3	4	5	6	7	8
9	10	11	12	13	14	15
16	17	18	19	20	21	22
23	24	25	26	27	28	29
30	31					

APRIL

S	M	T	W	T	F	S
		1	2	3	4	5
6	7	8	9	10	11	12
13	14	15	16	17	18	19
20	21	22	23	24	25	26
27	28	29	30			

MAY

S	M	T	W	T	F	S
				1	2	3
4	5	6	7	8	9	10
11	12	13	14	15	16	17
18	19	20	21	22	23	24
25	26	27	28	29	30	31

JUNE

S	M	T	W	T	F	S
1	2	3	4	5	6	7
8	9	10	11	12	13	14
15	16	17	18	19	20	21
22	23	24	25	26	27	28
29	30					

JULY

S	M	T	W	T	F	S
		1	2	3	4	5
6	7	8	9	10	11	12
13	14	15	16	17	18	19
20	21	22	23	24	25	26
27	28	29	30	31		

AUGUST

S	M	T	W	T	F	S
					1	2
3	4	5	6	7	8	9
10	11	12	13	14	15	16
17	18	19	20	21	22	23
24	25	26	27	28	29	30
31						

SEPTEMBER

S	M	T	W	T	F	S
	1	2	3	4	5	6
7	8	9	10	11	12	13
14	15	16	17	18	19	20
21	22	23	24	25	26	27
28	29	30				

OCTOBER

S	M	T	W	T	F	S
			1	2	3	4
5	6	7	8	9	10	11
12	13	14	15	16	17	18
19	20	21	22	23	24	25
26	27	28	29	30	31	

NOVEMBER

S	M	T	W	T	F	S
						1
2	3	4	5	6	7	8
9	10	11	12	13	14	15
16	17	18	19	20	21	22
23	24	25	26	27	28	29
30						

DECEMBER

S	M	T	W	T	F	S
	1	2	3	4	5	6
7	8	9	10	11	12	13
14	15	16	17	18	19	20
21	22	23	24	25	26	27
28	29	30	31			

5

JANUARY

S	M	T	W	T	F	S
				1	2	3
4	5	6	7	8	9	10
11	12	13	14	15	16	17
18	19	20	21	22	23	24
25	26	27	28	29	30	31

FEBRUARY

S	M	T	W	T	F	S
1	2	3	4	5	6	7
8	9	10	11	12	13	14
15	16	17	18	19	20	21
22	23	24	25	26	27	28

MARCH

S	M	T	W	T	F	S
1	2	3	4	5	6	7
8	9	10	11	12	13	14
15	16	17	18	19	20	21
22	23	24	25	26	27	28
29	30	31				

APRIL

S	M	T	W	T	F	S
			1	2	3	4
5	6	7	8	9	10	11
12	13	14	15	16	17	18
19	20	21	22	23	24	25
26	27	28	29	30		

MAY

S	M	T	W	T	F	S
					1	2
3	4	5	6	7	8	9
10	11	12	13	14	15	16
17	18	19	20	21	22	23
24	25	26	27	28	29	30
31						

JUNE

S	M	T	W	T	F	S
	1	2	3	4	5	6
7	8	9	10	11	12	13
14	15	16	17	18	19	20
21	22	23	24	25	26	27
28	29	30				

JULY

S	M	T	W	T	F	S
			1	2	3	4
5	6	7	8	9	10	11
12	13	14	15	16	17	18
19	20	21	22	23	24	25
26	27	28	29	30	31	

AUGUST

S	M	T	W	T	F	S
						1
2	3	4	5	6	7	8
9	10	11	12	13	14	15
16	17	18	19	20	21	22
23	24	25	26	27	28	29
30	31					

SEPTEMBER

S	M	T	W	T	F	S
		1	2	3	4	5
6	7	8	9	10	11	12
13	14	15	16	17	18	19
20	21	22	23	24	25	26
27	28	29	30			

OCTOBER

S	M	T	W	T	F	S
				1	2	3
4	5	6	7	8	9	10
11	12	13	14	15	16	17
18	19	20	21	22	23	24
25	26	27	28	29	30	31

NOVEMBER

S	M	T	W	T	F	S
1	2	3	4	5	6	7
8	9	10	11	12	13	14
15	16	17	18	19	20	21
22	23	24	25	26	27	28
29	30					

DECEMBER

S	M	T	W	T	F	S
		1	2	3	4	5
6	7	8	9	10	11	12
13	14	15	16	17	18	19
20	21	22	23	24	25	26
27	28	29	30	31		

6

JANUARY

S	M	T	W	T	F	S
					1	2
3	4	5	6	7	8	9
10	11	12	13	14	15	16
17	18	19	20	21	22	23
24	25	26	27	28	29	30
31						

FEBRUARY

S	M	T	W	T	F	S
	1	2	3	4	5	6
7	8	9	10	11	12	13
14	15	16	17	18	19	20
21	22	23	24	25	26	27
28						

MARCH

S	M	T	W	T	F	S
	1	2	3	4	5	6
7	8	9	10	11	12	13
14	15	16	17	18	19	20
21	22	23	24	25	26	27
28	29	30	31			

APRIL

S	M	T	W	T	F	S
				1	2	3
4	5	6	7	8	9	10
11	12	13	14	15	16	17
18	19	20	21	22	23	24
25	26	27	28	29	30	

MAY

S	M	T	W	T	F	S
						1
2	3	4	5	6	7	8
9	10	11	12	13	14	15
16	17	18	19	20	21	22
23	24	25	26	27	28	29
30	31					

JUNE

S	M	T	W	T	F	S
		1	2	3	4	5
6	7	8	9	10	11	12
13	14	15	16	17	18	19
20	21	22	23	24	25	26
27	28	29	30			

JULY

S	M	T	W	T	F	S
				1	2	3
4	5	6	7	8	9	10
11	12	13	14	15	16	17
18	19	20	21	22	23	24
25	26	27	28	29	30	31

AUGUST

S	M	T	W	T	F	S
1	2	3	4	5	6	7
8	9	10	11	12	13	14
15	16	17	18	19	20	21
22	23	24	25	26	27	28
29	30	31				

SEPTEMBER

S	M	T	W	T	F	S
			1	2	3	4
5	6	7	8	9	10	11
12	13	14	15	16	17	18
19	20	21	22	23	24	25
26	27	28	29	30		

OCTOBER

S	M	T	W	T	F	S
					1	2
3	4	5	6	7	8	9
10	11	12	13	14	15	16
17	18	19	20	21	22	23
24	25	26	27	28	29	30
31						

NOVEMBER

S	M	T	W	T	F	S
	1	2	3	4	5	6
7	8	9	10	11	12	13
14	15	16	17	18	19	20
21	22	23	24	25	26	27
28	29	30				

DECEMBER

S	M	T	W	T	F	S
			1	2	3	4
5	6	7	8	9	10	11
12	13	14	15	16	17	18
19	20	21	22	23	24	25
26	27	28	29	30	31	

7 1994

JANUARY

S	M	T	W	T	F	S
						1
2	3	4	5	6	7	8
9	10	11	12	13	14	15
16	17	18	19	20	21	22
23	24	25	26	27	28	29
30	31					

FEBRUARY

S	M	T	W	T	F	S
		1	2	3	4	5
6	7	8	9	10	11	12
13	14	15	16	17	18	19
20	21	22	23	24	25	26
27	28					

MARCH

S	M	T	W	T	F	S
		1	2	3	4	5
6	7	8	9	10	11	12
13	14	15	16	17	18	19
20	21	22	23	24	25	26
27	28	29	30	31		

APRIL

S	M	T	W	T	F	S
					1	2
3	4	5	6	7	8	9
10	11	12	13	14	15	16
17	18	19	20	21	22	23
24	25	26	27	28	29	30

MAY

S	M	T	W	T	F	S
1	2	3	4	5	6	7
8	9	10	11	12	13	14
15	16	17	18	19	20	21
22	23	24	25	26	27	28
29	30	31				

JUNE

S	M	T	W	T	F	S
			1	2	3	4
5	6	7	8	9	10	11
12	13	14	15	16	17	18
19	20	21	22	23	24	25
26	27	28	29	30		

JULY

S	M	T	W	T	F	S
					1	2
3	4	5	6	7	8	9
10	11	12	13	14	15	16
17	18	19	20	21	22	23
24	25	26	27	28	29	30
31						

AUGUST

S	M	T	W	T	F	S
	1	2	3	4	5	6
7	8	9	10	11	12	13
14	15	16	17	18	19	20
21	22	23	24	25	26	27
28	29	30	31			

SEPTEMBER

S	M	T	W	T	F	S
				1	2	3
4	5	6	7	8	9	10
11	12	13	14	15	16	17
18	19	20	21	22	23	24
25	26	27	28	29	30	

OCTOBER

S	M	T	W	T	F	S
						1
2	3	4	5	6	7	8
9	10	11	12	13	14	15
16	17	18	19	20	21	22
23	24	25	26	27	28	29
30	31					

NOVEMBER

S	M	T	W	T	F	S
		1	2	3	4	5
6	7	8	9	10	11	12
13	14	15	16	17	18	19
20	21	22	23	24	25	26
27	28	29	30			

DECEMBER

S	M	T	W	T	F	S
				1	2	3
4	5	6	7	8	9	10
11	12	13	14	15	16	17
18	19	20	21	22	23	24
25	26	27	28	29	30	31

8

JANUARY

S	M	T	W	T	F	S
1	2	3	4	5	6	7
8	9	10	11	12	13	14
15	16	17	18	19	20	21
22	23	24	25	26	27	28
29	30	31				

FEBRUARY

S	M	T	W	T	F	S
			1	2	3	4
5	6	7	8	9	10	11
12	13	14	15	16	17	18
19	20	21	22	23	24	25
26	27	28	29			

MARCH

S	M	T	W	T	F	S
				1	2	3
4	5	6	7	8	9	10
11	12	13	14	15	16	17
18	19	20	21	22	23	24
25	26	27	28	29	30	31

APRIL

S	M	T	W	T	F	S
1	2	3	4	5	6	7
8	9	10	11	12	13	14
15	16	17	18	19	20	21
22	23	24	25	26	27	28
29	30					

MAY

S	M	T	W	T	F	S
		1	2	3	4	5
6	7	8	9	10	11	12
13	14	15	16	17	18	19
20	21	22	23	24	25	26
27	28	29	30	31		

JUNE

S	M	T	W	T	F	S
					1	2
3	4	5	6	7	8	9
10	11	12	13	14	15	16
17	18	19	20	21	22	23
24	25	26	27	28	29	30

JULY

S	M	T	W	T	F	S
1	2	3	4	5	6	7
8	9	10	11	12	13	14
15	16	17	18	19	20	21
22	23	24	25	26	27	28
29	30	31				

AUGUST

S	M	T	W	T	F	S
			1	2	3	4
5	6	7	8	9	10	11
12	13	14	15	16	17	18
19	20	21	22	23	24	25
26	27	28	29	30	31	

SEPTEMBER

S	M	T	W	T	F	S
						1
2	3	4	5	6	7	8
9	10	11	12	13	14	15
16	17	18	19	20	21	22
23	24	25	26	27	28	29
30						

OCTOBER

S	M	T	W	T	F	S
	1	2	3	4	5	6
7	8	9	10	11	12	13
14	15	16	17	18	19	20
21	22	23	24	25	26	27
28	29	30	31			

NOVEMBER

S	M	T	W	T	F	S
				1	2	3
4	5	6	7	8	9	10
11	12	13	14	15	16	17
18	19	20	21	22	23	24
25	26	27	28	29	30	

DECEMBER

S	M	T	W	T	F	S
						1
2	3	4	5	6	7	8
9	10	11	12	13	14	15
16	17	18	19	20	21	22
23	24	25	26	27	28	29
30	31					

9 1996

JANUARY

S	M	T	W	T	F	S
	1	2	3	4	5	6
7	8	9	10	11	12	13
14	15	16	17	18	19	20
21	22	23	24	25	26	27
28	29	30	31			

FEBRUARY

S	M	T	W	T	F	S
				1	2	3
4	5	6	7	8	9	10
11	12	13	14	15	16	17
18	19	20	21	22	23	24
25	26	27	28	29		

MARCH

S	M	T	W	T	F	S
					1	2
3	4	5	6	7	8	9
10	11	12	13	14	15	16
17	18	19	20	21	22	23
24	25	26	27	28	29	30
31						

APRIL

S	M	T	W	T	F	S
	1	2	3	4	5	6
7	8	9	10	11	12	13
14	15	16	17	18	19	20
21	22	23	24	25	26	27
28	29	30				

MAY

S	M	T	W	T	F	S
			1	2	3	4
5	6	7	8	9	10	11
12	13	14	15	16	17	18
19	20	21	22	23	24	25
26	27	28	29	30	31	

JUNE

S	M	T	W	T	F	S
						1
2	3	4	5	6	7	8
9	10	11	12	13	14	15
16	17	18	19	20	21	22
23	24	25	26	27	28	29
30						

JULY

S	M	T	W	T	F	S
	1	2	3	4	5	6
7	8	9	10	11	12	13
14	15	16	17	18	19	20
21	22	23	24	25	26	27
28	29	30	31			

AUGUST

S	M	T	W	T	F	S
				1	2	3
4	5	6	7	8	9	10
11	12	13	14	15	16	17
18	19	20	21	22	23	24
25	26	27	28	29	30	31

SEPTEMBER

S	M	T	W	T	F	S
1	2	3	4	5	6	7
8	9	10	11	12	13	14
15	16	17	18	19	20	21
22	23	24	25	26	27	28
29	30					

OCTOBER

S	M	T	W	T	F	S
		1	2	3	4	5
6	7	8	9	10	11	12
13	14	15	16	17	18	19
20	21	22	23	24	25	26
27	28	29	30	31		

NOVEMBER

S	M	T	W	T	F	S
					1	2
3	4	5	6	7	8	9
10	11	12	13	14	15	16
17	18	19	20	21	22	23
24	25	26	27	28	29	30

DECEMBER

S	M	T	W	T	F	S
1	2	3	4	5	6	7
8	9	10	11	12	13	14
15	16	17	18	19	20	21
22	23	24	25	26	27	28
29	30	31				

10

JANUARY

S	M	T	W	T	F	S
		1	2	3	4	5
6	7	8	9	10	11	12
13	14	15	16	17	18	19
20	21	22	23	24	25	26
27	28	29	30	31		

FEBRUARY

S	M	T	W	T	F	S
					1	2
3	4	5	6	7	8	9
10	11	12	13	14	15	16
17	18	19	20	21	22	23
24	25	26	27	28	29	

MARCH

S	M	T	W	T	F	S
						1
2	3	4	5	6	7	8
9	10	11	12	13	14	15
16	17	18	19	20	21	22
23	24	25	26	27	28	29
30	31					

APRIL

S	M	T	W	T	F	S
		1	2	3	4	5
6	7	8	9	10	11	12
13	14	15	16	17	18	19
20	21	22	23	24	25	26
27	28	29	30			

MAY

S	M	T	W	T	F	S
				1	2	3
4	5	6	7	8	9	10
11	12	13	14	15	16	17
18	19	20	21	22	23	24
25	26	27	28	29	30	31

JUNE

S	M	T	W	T	F	S
1	2	3	4	5	6	7
8	9	10	11	12	13	14
15	16	17	18	19	20	21
22	23	24	25	26	27	28
29	30					

JULY

S	M	T	W	T	F	S
		1	2	3	4	5
6	7	8	9	10	11	12
13	14	15	16	17	18	19
20	21	22	23	24	25	26
27	28	29	30	31		

AUGUST

S	M	T	W	T	F	S
					1	2
3	4	5	6	7	8	9
10	11	12	13	14	15	16
17	18	19	20	21	22	23
24	25	26	27	28	29	30
31						

SEPTEMBER

S	M	T	W	T	F	S
	1	2	3	4	5	6
7	8	9	10	11	12	13
14	15	16	17	18	19	20
21	22	23	24	25	26	27
28	29	30				

OCTOBER

S	M	T	W	T	F	S
			1	2	3	4
5	6	7	8	9	10	11
12	13	14	15	16	17	18
19	20	21	22	23	24	25
26	27	28	29	30	31	

NOVEMBER

S	M	T	W	T	F	S
						1
2	3	4	5	6	7	8
9	10	11	12	13	14	15
16	17	18	19	20	21	22
23	24	25	26	27	28	29
30						

DECEMBER

S	M	T	W	T	F	S
	1	2	3	4	5	6
7	8	9	10	11	12	13
14	15	16	17	18	19	20
21	22	23	24	25	26	27
28	29	30	31			

11

JANUARY

S	M	T	W	T	F	S
			1	2	3	4
5	6	7	8	9	10	11
12	13	14	15	16	17	18
19	20	21	22	23	24	25
26	27	28	29	30	31	

FEBRUARY

S	M	T	W	T	F	S
						1
2	3	4	5	6	7	8
9	10	11	12	13	14	15
16	17	18	19	20	21	22
23	24	25	26	27	28	29

MARCH

S	M	T	W	T	F	S
1	2	3	4	5	6	7
8	9	10	11	12	13	14
15	16	17	18	19	20	21
22	23	24	25	26	27	28
29	30	31				

APRIL

S	M	T	W	T	F	S
			1	2	3	4
5	6	7	8	9	10	11
12	13	14	15	16	17	18
19	20	21	22	23	24	25
26	27	28	29	30		

MAY

S	M	T	W	T	F	S
					1	2
3	4	5	6	7	8	9
10	11	12	13	14	15	16
17	18	19	20	21	22	23
24	25	26	27	28	29	30
31						

JUNE

S	M	T	W	T	F	S
	1	2	3	4	5	6
7	8	9	10	11	12	13
14	15	16	17	18	19	20
21	22	23	24	25	26	27
28	29	30				

JULY

S	M	T	W	T	F	S
			1	2	3	4
5	6	7	8	9	10	11
12	13	14	15	16	17	18
19	20	21	22	23	24	25
26	27	28	29	30	31	

AUGUST

S	M	T	W	T	F	S
						1
2	3	4	5	6	7	8
9	10	11	12	13	14	15
16	17	18	19	20	21	22
23	24	25	26	27	28	29
30	31					

SEPTEMBER

S	M	T	W	T	F	S
		1	2	3	4	5
6	7	8	9	10	11	12
13	14	15	16	17	18	19
20	21	22	23	24	25	26
27	28	29	30			

OCTOBER

S	M	T	W	T	F	S
				1	2	3
4	5	6	7	8	9	10
11	12	13	14	15	16	17
18	19	20	21	22	23	24
25	26	27	28	29	30	31

NOVEMBER

S	M	T	W	T	F	S
1	2	3	4	5	6	7
8	9	10	11	12	13	14
15	16	17	18	19	20	21
22	23	24	25	26	27	28
29	30					

DECEMBER

S	M	T	W	T	F	S
		1	2	3	4	5
6	7	8	9	10	11	12
13	14	15	16	17	18	19
20	21	22	23	24	25	26
27	28	29	30	31		

12

JANUARY

S	M	T	W	T	F	S
				1	2	3
4	5	6	7	8	9	10
11	12	13	14	15	16	17
18	19	20	21	22	23	24
25	26	27	28	29	30	31

FEBRUARY

S	M	T	W	T	F	S
1	2	3	4	5	6	7
8	9	10	11	12	13	14
15	16	17	18	19	20	21
22	23	24	25	26	27	28
29						

MARCH

S	M	T	W	T	F	S
	1	2	3	4	5	6
7	8	9	10	11	12	13
14	15	16	17	18	19	20
21	22	23	24	25	26	27
28	29	30	31			

APRIL

S	M	T	W	T	F	S
				1	2	3
4	5	6	7	8	9	10
11	12	13	14	15	16	17
18	19	20	21	22	23	24
25	26	27	28	29	30	

MAY

S	M	T	W	T	F	S
						1
2	3	4	5	6	7	8
9	10	11	12	13	14	15
16	17	18	19	20	21	22
23	24	25	26	27	28	29
30	31					

JUNE

S	M	T	W	T	F	S
		1	2	3	4	5
6	7	8	9	10	11	12
13	14	15	16	17	18	19
20	21	22	23	24	25	26
27	28	29	30			

JULY

S	M	T	W	T	F	S
				1	2	3
4	5	6	7	8	9	10
11	12	13	14	15	16	17
18	19	20	21	22	23	24
25	26	27	28	29	30	31

AUGUST

S	M	T	W	T	F	S
1	2	3	4	5	6	7
8	9	10	11	12	13	14
15	16	17	18	19	20	21
22	23	24	25	26	27	28
29	30	31				

SEPTEMBER

S	M	T	W	T	F	S
			1	2	3	4
5	6	7	8	9	10	11
12	13	14	15	16	17	18
19	20	21	22	23	24	25
26	27	28	29	30		

OCTOBER

S	M	T	W	T	F	S
					1	2
3	4	5	6	7	8	9
10	11	12	13	14	15	16
17	18	19	20	21	22	23
24	25	26	27	28	29	30
31						

NOVEMBER

S	M	T	W	T	F	S
	1	2	3	4	5	6
7	8	9	10	11	12	13
14	15	16	17	18	19	20
21	22	23	24	25	26	27
28	29	30				

DECEMBER

S	M	T	W	T	F	S
			1	2	3	4
5	6	7	8	9	10	11
12	13	14	15	16	17	18
19	20	21	22	23	24	25
26	27	28	29	30	31	

13

JANUARY

S	M	T	W	T	F	S
					1	2
3	4	5	6	7	8	9
10	11	12	13	14	15	16
17	18	19	20	21	22	23
24	25	26	27	28	29	30
31						

FEBRUARY

S	M	T	W	T	F	S
	1	2	3	4	5	6
7	8	9	10	11	12	13
14	15	16	17	18	19	20
21	22	23	24	25	26	27
28	29					

MARCH

S	M	T	W	T	F	S
		1	2	3	4	5
6	7	8	9	10	11	12
13	14	15	16	17	18	19
20	21	22	23	24	25	26
27	28	29	30	31		

APRIL

S	M	T	W	T	F	S
					1	2
3	4	5	6	7	8	9
10	11	12	13	14	15	16
17	18	19	20	21	22	23
24	25	26	27	28	29	30

MAY

S	M	T	W	T	F	S
1	2	3	4	5	6	7
8	9	10	11	12	13	14
15	16	17	18	19	20	21
22	23	24	25	26	27	28
29	30	31				

JUNE

S	M	T	W	T	F	S
			1	2	3	4
5	6	7	8	9	10	11
12	13	14	15	16	17	18
19	20	21	22	23	24	25
26	27	28	29	30		

JULY

S	M	T	W	T	F	S
					1	2
3	4	5	6	7	8	9
10	11	12	13	14	15	16
17	18	19	20	21	22	23
24	25	26	27	28	29	30
31						

AUGUST

S	M	T	W	T	F	S
	1	2	3	4	5	6
7	8	9	10	11	12	13
14	15	16	17	18	19	20
21	22	23	24	25	26	27
28	29	30	31			

SEPTEMBER

S	M	T	W	T	F	S
				1	2	3
4	5	6	7	8	9	10
11	12	13	14	15	16	17
18	19	20	21	22	23	24
25	26	27	28	29	30	

OCTOBER

S	M	T	W	T	F	S
						1
2	3	4	5	6	7	8
9	10	11	12	13	14	15
16	17	18	19	20	21	22
23	24	25	26	27	28	29
30	31					

NOVEMBER

S	M	T	W	T	F	S
		1	2	3	4	5
6	7	8	9	10	11	12
13	14	15	16	17	18	19
20	21	22	23	24	25	26
27	28	29	30			

DECEMBER

S	M	T	W	T	F	S
				1	2	3
4	5	6	7	8	9	10
11	12	13	14	15	16	17
18	19	20	21	22	23	24
25	26	27	28	29	30	31

14

JANUARY

S	M	T	W	T	F	S
						1
2	3	4	5	6	7	8
9	10	11	12	13	14	15
16	17	18	19	20	21	22
23	24	25	26	27	28	29
30	31					

FEBRUARY

S	M	T	W	T	F	S
		1	2	3	4	5
6	7	8	9	10	11	12
13	14	15	16	17	18	19
20	21	22	23	24	25	26
27	28	29				

MARCH

S	M	T	W	T	F	S
			1	2	3	4
5	6	7	8	9	10	11
12	13	14	15	16	17	18
19	20	21	22	23	24	25
26	27	28	29	30	31	

APRIL

S	M	T	W	T	F	S
						1
2	3	4	5	6	7	8
9	10	11	12	13	14	15
16	17	18	19	20	21	22
23	24	25	26	27	28	29
30						

MAY

S	M	T	W	T	F	S
	1	2	3	4	5	6
7	8	9	10	11	12	13
14	15	16	17	18	19	20
21	22	23	24	25	26	27
28	29	30	31			

JUNE

S	M	T	W	T	F	S
				1	2	3
4	5	6	7	8	9	10
11	12	13	14	15	16	17
18	19	20	21	22	23	24
25	26	27	28	29	30	

JULY

S	M	T	W	T	F	S
						1
2	3	4	5	6	7	8
9	10	11	12	13	14	15
16	17	18	19	20	21	22
23	24	25	26	27	28	29
30	31					

AUGUST

S	M	T	W	T	F	S
		1	2	3	4	5
6	7	8	9	10	11	12
13	14	15	16	17	18	19
20	21	22	23	24	25	26
27	28	29	30	31		

SEPTEMBER

S	M	T	W	T	F	S
					1	2
3	4	5	6	7	8	9
10	11	12	13	14	15	16
17	18	19	20	21	22	23
24	25	26	27	28	29	30

OCTOBER

S	M	T	W	T	F	S
1	2	3	4	5	6	7
8	9	10	11	12	13	14
15	16	17	18	19	20	21
22	23	24	25	26	27	28
29	30	31				

NOVEMBER

S	M	T	W	T	F	S
			1	2	3	4
5	6	7	8	9	10	11
12	13	14	15	16	17	18
19	20	21	22	23	24	25
26	27	28	29	30		

DECEMBER

S	M	T	W	T	F	S
					1	2
3	4	5	6	7	8	9
10	11	12	13	14	15	16
17	18	19	20	21	22	23
24	25	26	27	28	29	30
31						

Julian and Gregorian Calendars; Leap Year; Century

Calendars based on the movements of the sun and moon have been used since ancient times, but none has been perfect. The **Julian calendar**, under which Western nations measured time until AD 1582, was authorized by Julius Caesar in 46 BC, the year 709 of Rome. His expert was a Greek, Sosigenes. The Julian calendar, on the assumption that the true year was 365 1/4 days, gave every fourth year 366 days. The Venerable Bede, an Anglo-Saxon monk, announced in AD 730 that the 365 1/4-day Julian year was 11 min, 14 sec too long, a cumulative error of about a day every 128 years, but nothing was done about it for more than 800 years.

By 1582 the accumulated error was estimated to amount to 10 days. In that year Pope Gregory XIII decreed that the day following Oct. 4, 1582, should be called Oct. 15, thus dropping 10 days and initiating what became known as the **Gregorian calendar.**

However, with common years 365 days and a 366-day leap year every fourth year, the error in the length of the year would have recurred at the rate of a little more than 3 days every 400 years. Therefore, 3 of every 4 centesimal years (years ending in 00) were made common years, not leap years. Thus, 1600 was a leap year; 1700, 1800, and 1900 were not, but 2000 will be. **Leap years** are those years divisible by 4, except centesimal years, which are common unless divisible by 400.

The Gregorian calendar was adopted at once by France, Italy, Spain, Portugal, and Luxembourg. Within 2 years most German Catholic states, Belgium, and parts of Switzerland and the Netherlands were brought under the new calendar, and Hungary followed in 1587. The rest of the Netherlands, along with Denmark and the German Protestant states, made the change in 1699-1700 (German Protestants retained the old reckoning of Easter until 1776).

The British government imposed the Gregorian calendar on all its possessions, including the American colonies, in 1752. The British decreed that the day following Sept. 2, 1752, should be called Sept. 14, a loss of 11 days. All dates preceding were marked O.S., for Old Style. In addition, New Year's Day was moved to Jan. 1 from Mar. 25 (e.g., under the old reckoning, Mar. 24, 1700, had been followed by Mar. 25, 1701). George Washington's birthdate, which was Feb. 11, 1731, O.S., became Feb. 22, 1732, New Style (N.S.). In 1753 Sweden too went Gregorian, retaining the old Easter rules until 1844.

In 1793 the French revolutionary government adopted a calendar of 12 months of 30 days each with 5 extra days in September of each common year and a 6th extra day every 4th year. Napoleon reinstated the Gregorian calendar in 1806.

The Gregorian system later spread to non-European regions, first in the European colonies and then in the independent countries, replacing traditional calendars at least for official purposes. Japan in 1873, Egypt in 1875, China in 1912, and Turkey in 1917 made the change, usually in conjunction with political upheavals. In China, the republican government began reckoning years from its 1911 founding — e.g., 1948 was designated the year 37. After 1949, the Communists adopted the Common, or Christian Era, year count, even for the traditional lunar calendar.

In 1918 the revolutionary government in the Soviet Union decreed that the day after Jan. 31, 1918, O.S., would become Feb. 14, 1918, N.S. Greece followed in 1923. (The Russian Orthodox Church has retained the Julian calendar, as have various Middle Eastern Christian sects.) For the first time in history, all major cultures have one calendar.

To convert from the Julian to the Gregorian calendar, add 10 days to dates Oct. 5, 1582, through Feb. 28, 1700; after that date add 11 days through Feb. 28, 1800; 12 days through Feb. 28, 1900; and 13 days through Feb. 28, 2100.

A **century** consists of 100 consecutive calendar years. The 1st century AD consisted of the years 1 through 100. The 20th century consists of the years 1901 through 2000 and will end Dec. 31, 2000. The 21st century will begin Jan. 1, 2001.

Julian Calendar

To find which of the 14 calendars printed on pages 286-87 applies to any year, starting Jan. 1, under the Julian system, find the century for the desired year in the 3 leftmost columns below; read across. Then find the year in the 4 top rows; read down. The number in the intersection is the calendar designation for that year.

Year (last 2 figures of desired year)

				01	**02**	**03**	**04**	**05**	**06**	**07**	**08**	**09**	**10**	**11**	**12**	**13**	**14**	**15**	**16**	**17**	**18**	**19**	**20**	**21**	**22**	**23**	**24**	**25**	**26**	**27**	**28**
				29	**30**	**31**	**32**	**33**	**34**	**35**	**36**	**37**	**38**	**39**	**40**	**41**	**42**	**43**	**44**	**45**	**46**	**47**	**48**	**49**	**50**	**51**	**52**	**53**	**54**	**55**	**56**
				57	**58**	**59**	**60**	**61**	**62**	**63**	**64**	**65**	**66**	**67**	**68**	**69**	**70**	**71**	**72**	**73**	**74**	**75**	**76**	**77**	**78**	**79**	**80**	**81**	**82**	**83**	**84**
Century			**00**	**85**	**86**	**87**	**88**	**89**	**90**	**91**	**92**	**93**	**94**	**95**	**96**	**97**	**98**	**99**													
0	**700**	**1400**	12	7	1	2	10	5	6	7	8	3	4	5	13	1	2	3	11	6	7	1	9	4	5	6	14	2	3	4	12
100	**800**	**1500**	11	6	7	1	9	4	5	6	14	2	3	4	12	7	1	2	10	5	6	7	8	3	4	5	13	1	2	3	11
200	**900**	**1600**	10	5	6	7	8	3	4	5	13	1	2	3	11	6	7	1	9	4	5	6	14	2	3	4	12	7	1	2	10
300	**1000**	**1700**	9	4	5	6	14	2	3	4	12	7	1	2	10	5	6	7	8	3	4	5	13	1	2	3	11	6	7	1	9
400	**1100**	**1800**	8	3	4	5	13	1	2	3	11	6	7	1	9	4	5	6	14	2	3	4	12	7	1	2	10	5	6	7	8
500	**1200**	**1900**	14	2	3	4	12	7	1	2	10	5	6	7	8	3	4	5	13	1	2	3	11	6	7	1	9	4	5	6	14
600	**1300**	**2000**	13	1	2	3	11	6	7	1	9	4	5	6	14	2	3	4	12	7	1	2	10	5	6	7	8	3	4	5	13

Gregorian Calendar

Choose the desired year from the table below or from page 286 (for years 1803 to 2080). The number shown with each year designates which calendar to use for that year, as shown on pages 286-87. (The Gregorian calendar was inaugurated Oct. 15, 1582. From that date to Dec. 31, 1582, use calendar 6.)

1583-1802

Year	Cal.	Year	Cal.	Year	Cal.	Year	Cal.	Year	Cal.	Year	Cal.	Year	Cal.	Year	Cal.	Year	Cal.	Year	Cal.	Year	Cal.
1583	7	1603	4	1623	1	1643	5	1663	2	1683	6	1703	2	1723	6	1743	3	1763	7	1783	[illegible]
1584	8	1604	12	1624	9	1644	13	1664	10	1684	14	1704	10	1724	14	1744	11	1764	8	1784	[illegible]
1585	3	1605	7	1625	4	1645	1	1665	5	1685	2	1705	5	1725	2	1745	6	1765	3	1785	[illegible]
1586	4	1606	1	1626	5	1646	2	1666	6	1686	3	1706	6	1726	3	1746	7	1766	4	1786	[illegible]
1587	5	1607	2	1627	6	1647	3	1667	7	1687	4	1707	7	1727	4	1747	1	1767	5	1787	[illegible]
1588	13	1608	10	1628	14	1648	11	1668	8	1688	12	1708	8	1728	12	1748	9	1768	13	1788	[illegible]
1589	1	1609	5	1629	2	1649	6	1669	3	1689	7	1709	3	1729	7	1749	4	1769	1	1789	[illegible]
1590	2	1610	6	1630	3	1650	7	1670	4	1690	1	1710	4	1730	1	1750	5	1770	2	1790	[illegible]
1591	3	1611	7	1631	4	1651	1	1671	5	1691	2	1711	5	1731	2	1751	6	1771	3	1791	[illegible]
1592	11	1612	8	1632	12	1652	9	1672	13	1692	10	1712	13	1732	10	1752	14	1772	11	1792	[illegible]
1593	6	1613	3	1633	7	1653	4	1673	1	1693	5	1713	1	1733	5	1753	2	1773	6	1793	[illegible]
1594	7	1614	4	1634	1	1654	5	1674	2	1694	6	1714	2	1734	6	1754	3	1774	7	1794	[illegible]
1595	1	1615	5	1635	2	1655	6	1675	3	1695	7	1715	3	1735	7	1755	4	1775	1	1795	[illegible]
1596	9	1616	13	1636	10	1656	14	1676	11	1696	8	1716	11	1736	8	1756	12	1776	9	1796	[illegible]
1597	4	1617	1	1637	5	1657	2	1677	6	1697	3	1717	6	1737	3	1757	7	1777	4	1797	[illegible]
1598	5	1618	2	1638	6	1658	3	1678	7	1698	4	1718	7	1738	4	1758	1	1778	5	1798	[illegible]
1599	6	1619	3	1639	7	1659	4	1679	1	1699	5	1719	1	1739	5	1759	2	1779	6	1799	[illegible]
1600	14	1620	11	1640	8	1660	12	1680	9	1700	6	1720	9	1740	13	1760	10	1780	14	1800	[illegible]
1601	2	1621	6	1641	3	1661	7	1681	4	1701	7	1721	4	1741	1	1761	5	1781	2	1801	[illegible]
1602	3	1622	7	1642	4	1662	1	1682	5	1702	1	1722	5	1742	2	1762	6	1782	3	1802	[illegible]

The Julian Period

How many days have you lived? To determine this, you must multiply your age by 365, add the number of days since your last birthday until today, and account for all leap years. Chances are your answer would be wrong. Astronomers, however, find it convenient to express dates and long time intervals in days rather than in years, months, and days. This is done by placing events within the Julian period.

The Julian period was devised in 1582 by the French classical scholar Joseph Scaliger (1540-1609) and named after his father Julius Caesar Scaliger (1484-1558), not after the Julian calendar. Joseph Scaliger began Julian Day (JD) #1 at noon, Jan. 1, 4713 BC, the most recent time that 3 major chronological cycles began on the same day—(1) the 28-year solar cycle, after which dates in the Julian calendar (e.g., Feb. 11) return to the same days of the week (e.g., Monday); (2) the 19-year lunar cycle, after which the phases of the moon return to the same dates of the year; and (3) the 15-year indiction cycle, used in ancient Rome to regulate taxes. It will take 7,980 years to complete the period, the product of 28, 19, and 15.

Noon of Dec. 31, 1994, marks the beginning of JD 2,449,718; that many days will have passed since the start of the Julian period. The JD at noon of any date in 1995 may be found by adding to this figure the day of the year for that date, which is given in the left most column in the chart below. Simple JD conversion tables are used by astronomers.

Days Between Two Dates

Table covers period of 2 ordinary years. Example—Days between Feb. 10, 1989, and Dec. 15, 1990; subtract 41 from 714; answer is 673 days. For leap year, such as 1992, one day must be added: final answer is 674.

Date	Jan.	Feb.	Mar.	April	May	June	July	Aug.	Sept.	Oct.	Nov.	Dec.
1	1	32	60	91	121	152	182	213	244	274	305	335
2	2	33	61	92	122	153	183	214	245	275	306	336
3	3	34	62	93	123	154	184	215	246	276	307	337
4	4	35	63	94	124	155	185	216	247	277	308	338
5	5	36	64	95	125	156	186	217	248	278	309	339
6	6	37	65	96	126	157	187	218	249	279	310	340
7	7	38	66	97	127	158	188	219	250	280	311	341
8	8	39	67	98	128	159	189	220	251	281	312	342
9	9	40	68	99	129	160	190	221	252	282	313	343
10	10	41	69	100	130	161	191	222	253	283	314	344
11	11	42	70	101	131	162	192	223	254	284	315	345
12	12	43	71	102	132	163	193	224	255	285	316	346
13	13	44	72	103	133	164	194	225	256	286	317	347
14	14	45	73	104	134	165	195	226	257	287	318	348
15	15	46	74	105	135	166	196	227	258	288	319	349
16	16	47	75	106	136	167	197	228	259	289	320	350
17	17	48	76	107	137	168	198	229	260	290	321	351
18	18	49	77	108	138	169	199	230	261	291	322	352
19	19	50	78	109	139	170	200	231	262	292	323	353
20	20	51	79	110	140	171	201	232	263	293	324	354
21	21	52	80	111	141	172	202	233	264	294	325	355
22	22	53	81	112	142	173	203	234	265	295	326	356
23	23	54	82	113	143	174	204	235	266	296	327	357
24	24	55	83	114	144	175	205	236	267	297	328	358
25	25	56	84	115	145	176	206	237	268	298	329	359
26	26	57	85	116	146	177	207	238	269	299	330	360
27	27	58	86	117	147	178	208	239	270	300	331	361
28	28	59	87	118	148	179	209	240	271	301	332	362
29	29	—	88	119	149	180	210	241	272	302	333	363
30	30	—	89	120	150	181	211	242	273	303	334	364
31	31	—	90	—	151	—	212	243	—	304	—	365

Date	Jan.	Feb.	Mar.	April	May	June	July	Aug.	Sept.	Oct.	Nov.	Dec.
1	366	397	425	456	486	517	547	578	609	639	670	700
2	367	398	426	457	487	518	548	579	610	640	671	701
3	368	399	427	458	488	519	549	580	611	641	672	702
4	369	400	428	459	489	520	550	581	612	642	673	703
5	370	401	429	460	490	521	551	582	613	643	674	704
6	371	402	430	461	491	522	552	583	614	644	675	705
7	372	403	431	462	492	523	553	584	615	645	676	706
8	373	404	432	463	493	524	554	585	616	646	677	707
9	374	405	433	464	494	525	555	586	617	647	678	708
10	375	406	434	465	495	526	556	587	618	648	679	709
11	376	407	435	466	496	527	557	588	619	649	680	710
12	377	408	436	467	497	528	558	589	620	650	681	711
13	378	409	437	468	498	529	559	590	621	651	682	712
14	379	410	438	469	499	530	560	591	622	652	683	713
15	380	411	439	470	500	531	561	592	623	653	684	714
16	381	412	440	471	501	532	562	593	624	654	685	715
17	382	413	441	472	502	533	563	594	625	655	686	716
18	383	414	442	473	503	534	564	595	626	656	687	717
19	384	415	443	474	504	535	565	596	627	657	688	718
20	385	416	444	475	505	536	566	597	628	658	689	719
21	386	417	445	476	506	537	567	598	629	659	690	720
22	387	418	446	477	507	538	568	599	630	660	691	721
23	388	419	447	478	508	539	569	600	631	661	692	722
24	389	420	448	479	509	540	570	601	632	662	693	723
25	390	421	449	480	510	541	571	602	633	663	694	724
26	391	422	450	481	511	542	572	603	634	664	695	725
27	392	423	451	482	512	543	573	604	635	665	696	726
28	393	424	452	483	513	544	574	605	636	666	697	727
29	394	—	453	484	514	545	575	606	637	667	698	728
30	395	—	454	485	515	546	576	607	638	668	699	729
31	396	—	455	—	516	—	577	608	—	669	—	730

Lunar Calendar, Chinese New Year, Vietnamese Tet

The ancient Chinese lunar calendar is divided into 12 months of either 29 or 30 days (compensating for the lunar month's mean duration of 29 days, 12 hr, 44.05 min). The calendar is synchronized with the solar year by the addition of extra months at fixed intervals.

The Chinese calendar runs on a sexagenary cycle, i.e., a 60-year cycle. The cycles 1876-1935 and 1936-95, with the years grouped under their 12 animal designations, are printed below. A new cycle will begin in 1996 and last until 2055. The Year 1995 (Lunar Year 4693) is found in the 12th column, under Pig, and is known as a Year of the Pig. Readers can find the animal name for the year of their birth, marriage, etc., in the same chart. (Note: The first 3-7 weeks of each of the Western years belong to the previous Chinese year and animal designation.)

Both the Western (Gregorian) and traditional lunar calendars are used publicly in China and in North and South Korea, and 2 New Year's celebrations are held. In Taiwan, in overseas Chinese communities, and in Vietnam, the lunar calendar is used only to set the dates for traditional festivals, with the Gregorian system in general use.

The 4-day Chinese New Year, Hsin Nien, the 3-day Vietnamese New Year festival, Tet, and the 3-to-4-day Korean festival, Suhl, begin at the first new moon after the sun enters Aquarius. Because the date is fixed according to the date of the new moon in the Far East, which is west of the International Date Line, the date may be one day later than that of the new moon in the U.S. The day may fall, therefore, between Jan. 21 and Feb. 19 of the Gregorian calendar. Jan. 31, 1995, marks the start of the new Chinese year.

Rat	Ox	Tiger	Hare (Rabbit)	Dragon	Snake	Horse	Sheep (Goat)	Monkey	Rooster	Dog	Pig
1876	1877	1878	1879	1880	1881	1882	1883	1884	1885	1886	1887
1888	1889	1890	1891	1892	1893	1894	1895	1896	1897	1898	1899
1900	1901	1902	1903	1904	1905	1906	1907	1908	1909	1910	1911
1912	1913	1914	1915	1916	1917	1918	1919	1920	1921	1922	1923
1924	1925	1926	1927	1928	1929	1930	1931	1932	1933	1934	1935
1936	1937	1938	1939	1940	1941	1942	1943	1944	1945	1946	1947
1948	1949	1950	1951	1952	1953	1954	1955	1956	1957	1958	1959
1960	1961	1962	1963	1964	1965	1966	1967	1968	1969	1970	1971
1972	1973	1974	1975	1976	1977	1978	1979	1980	1981	1982	1983
1984	1985	1986	1987	1988	1989	1990	1991	1992	1993	1994	1995
1996	1997	1998	1999	2000	2001	2002	2003	2004	2005	2006	2007

Standard Time, Daylight Saving Time, and Others

Source: Defense Mapping Agency Hydrographic/Topographic Center; U.S. Dept. of Transportation

Standard Time

Standard Time is reckoned from Greenwich, England, recognized as the Prime Meridian of Longitude. The world is divided into 24 zones, each 15° of arc, or one hour in time apart. The Greenwich meridian (0°) extends through the center of the initial zone, and the zones to the east are numbered from 1 to 12 with the prefix "minus" indicating the number of hours to be subtracted to obtain Greenwich Time. Each zone extends 7½° on either side of its central meridian.

Westward zones are similarly numbered, but prefixed "plus" showing the number of hours that must be added to get Greenwich Time. Although these zones apply generally to sea areas, the Standard Time maintained in many countries does not coincide with zone time. A graphical representation of the zones is shown on the Standard Time Zone Chart of the World published by the Defense Mapping Agency, Attn: PR, 8613 Lee Highway, Fairfax, VA 22031-2137.

The U.S. and possessions are divided into 8 Standard Time zones, as set forth by the Uniform Time Act of 1966, which also provides for the use of Daylight Saving Time therein. Each zone is approximately 15° of longitude in width. All places in each zone use, instead of their own local time, the time counted from the transit of the "mean su " across the Standard Time meridian that passes near the middle of that zone.

These time zones are designated as Atlantic, Eastern, Central, Mountain, Pacific, Yukon, Alaska-Hawaii, and Bering (Samoa), and the time in these zones is basically reckoned from the 60th, 75th, 90th, 105th, 120th, 135th, 150th, and 165th meridians west of Greenwich. The line wanders to conform to local geographical regions. The time in the various zones is earlier than Greenwich Time by 4, 5, 6, 7, 8, 9, 10, and 11 hours respectively.

24-Hour Time

Twenty-four-hour time is widely used in scientific work throughout the world. In the U.S. it is used also in operations of the Armed Forces. In Europe it is frequently used by the transportation networks in preference to the 12-hour AM and PM system. With the 24-hour system, the day begins at midnight and is designated 0000 through 2359.

International Date Line

The Date Line is a zig-zag line that approximately coincides with the 180th meridian, and it separates the calendar dates. The date must be advanced one day when crossing in a westerly direction and set back one day when crossing in an easterly direction.

The line is deflected eastward through the Bering Strait and westward of the Aleutians to prevent separating these areas by date. The line is again deflected eastward of the Tonga and New Zealand Islands in the South Pacific for the same reason.

Daylight Saving Time

Daylight Saving Time is achieved by advancing the clock one hour. Since 1987, Daylight Saving Time in all U.S. states, the District of Columbia, and U.S. possessions begins at 2 AM on the first Sunday in Apr. and ends at 2 AM on the last Sunday in Oct.

Daylight Saving Time was first instituted in the Uniform Time Act, which became effective in 1967. At that time, all states, the District of Columbia, and U.S. possessions were to observe Daylight Saving Time beginning at 2 AM on the last Sunday in Apr. and ending at 2 AM on the last Sunday in October. Any state could, by law, exempt itself; a 1972 amendment to the act authorized states split by time zones to take that into consideration in exempting themselves. Arizona, Hawaii, Puerto Rico, the Virgin Islands, American Samoa, and part of Indiana are now exempt. Some local zone boundaries in Kansas, Texas, Florida, Michigan, and Alaska have been modified by the Dept. of Transportation, which oversees the act. To conserve energy, Congress put most of the nation on year-round Daylight Saving Time for 2 years effective Jan. 6, 1974, through Oct. 26, 1975, but another bill, signed in Oct. 1974, restored Standard Time from the last Sunday in that month to the last Sunday in Feb. 1975. At the end of 1975, Congress failed to renew this temporary legislation, and the nation returned to the older end-of-April to end-of-October Daylight Saving Time system.

On July 8, 1986, Pres. Ronald Reagan signed legislation moving up the start of Daylight Saving Time to the first Sunday in Apr. The law was effective beginning in 1987. The Dept. of Transportation estimated that the earlier starting date would help save more than $28 million in traffic accident costs and prevent more than 1,500 injuries and 20 deaths annually.

International

Adjusting clock time to be able to use the added daylight on summer evenings is common throughout the world.

Western Europe is on Daylight Saving Time generally from the last Sunday in March to the last Sunday in Sept.; however, the United Kingdom continues until the last Sunday in Oct.

Russia, which lies over 11 time zones, maintains its Standard Time 1 hour fast of the zone designation. Additionally, it proclaims Daylight Saving Time as does Europe.

China, which lies across 5 time zones, has decreed that the entire country be placed on Greenwich Time plus 8 hours, with Daylight Saving Time from Apr. 12 to Sept. 12.

Many countries in the Southern Hemisphere maintain Daylight Saving Time, generally from Oct. to March; however, most countries near the equator do not deviate from Standard Time.

Standard Time Differences—World Cities

The time indicated in the table is fixed by law and is called the legal time or, more generally, Standard Time. Use of Daylight Saving Time varies widely. * Indicates morning of the following day. At 12:00 noon, Eastern Standard Time, the Standard Time (in 24-hour time) in selected cities is as follows:

City	Time	City	Time	City	Time	City	Time
Addis Ababa	20 00	Cape Town	19 00	Lima	12 00	Santiago (Chile)	13 00
Alexandria	19 00	Caracas	13 00	Lisbon	17 00	Seoul	2 00*
Amsterdam	18 00	Casablanca	17 00	Liverpool	17 00	Shanghai	1 00*
Athens	19 00	Copenhagen	18 00	London	17 00	Singapore	1 00*
Auckland	5 00*	Delhi	22 30	Madrid	18 00	Stockholm	18 00
Baghdad	20 00	Dhaka	23 00	Manila	1 00*	Sydney (Australia)	3 00*
Bangkok	0 00	Dublin	17 00	Mecca (Saudi Arabia)	20 00	Tashkent	23 00
Beijing	1 00*	Gdánsk	18 00	Melbourne	3 00*	Teheran	20 30
Belfast	17 00	Geneva	18 00	Mexico City	11 00	Tel Aviv	19 00
Berlin	18 00	Havana	12 00	Montevideo	14 00	Tokyo	2 00*
Bogotá	12 00	Helsinki	19 00	Moscow	20 00	Valparaiso	13 00
Bombay	22 30	Ho Chi Minh City	0 00	Nagasaki	2 00*	Vladivostok	3 00*
Bremen	18 00	Hong Kong	1 00*	Oslo	18 00	Vienna	18 00
Brussels	18 00	Istanbul	19 00	Paris	18 00	Warsaw	18 00
Bucharest	19 00	Jakarta	0 00	Prague	18 00	Wellington (N.Z.)	5 00*
Budapest	18 00	Jerusalem	19 00	Rio de Janeiro	14 00	Yangon (Rangoon)	23 30
Buenos Aires	14 00	Johannesburg	19 00	Rome	18 00	Yokohama	2 00*
Cairo	19 00	Karachi	22 00	St. Petersburg	20 00	Zürich	18 00
Calcutta	22 30	Le Havre	18 00				

Standard Time Differences — North American Cities

At 12:00 noon, Eastern Standard Time, the Standard Time in North American cities is as follows:

Akron, Oh.	12	00	Noon
Albuquerque, N.M.	10	00	AM
Atlanta, Ga.	12	00	Noon
Austin, Tex.	11	00	AM
Baltimore, Md.	12	00	Noon
Birmingham, Ala.	11	00	AM
Bismarck, N.D.	11	00	AM
Boise, Ida.	10	00	AM
Boston, Mass.	12	00	Noon
Buffalo, N.Y.	12	00	Noon
Butte, Mon.	10	00	AM
Calgary, Alta.	10	00	AM
Charleston, S.C.	12	00	Noon
Charleston, W.Va.	12	00	Noon
Charlotte, N.C.	12	00	Noon
Charlottetown, P.E.I.	1	00	PM
Chattanooga, Tenn.	12	00	Noon
Cheyenne, Wy.	10	00	AM
Chicago, Ill.	11	00	AM
Cleveland, Oh.	12	00	Noon
Colorado Spr., Col.	10	00	AM
Columbus, Oh.	12	00	Noon
Dallas, Tex.	11	00	AM
*Dawson, Yuk.	9	00	AM
Dayton, Oh.	12	00	Noon
Denver, Col.	10	00	AM
Des Moines, Ia.	11	00	AM
Detroit, Mich.	12	00	Noon
Duluth, Minn.	11	00	AM
El Paso, Tex.	10	00	AM
Erie, Pa.	12	00	Noon
Evansville, Ind.	11	00	AM
Fairbanks, Alas.	8	00	AM
Flint, Mich.	12	00	Noon
*Fort Wayne, Ind.	12	00	Noon
Fort Worth, Tex.	11	00	AM
Frankfort, Ky.	12	00	Noon
Galveston, Tex.	11	00	AM
Grand Rapids, Mich.	12	00	Noon
Halifax, N.S.	1	00	PM
Hartford, Conn.	12	00	Noon
Helena, Mon.	10	00	AM
*Honolulu, Ha.	7	00	AM
Houston, Tex.	11	00	AM
*Indianapolis, Ind.	12	00	Noon
Jacksonville, Fla.	12	00	Noon
Juneau, Alas.	8	00	AM
Kansas City, Mo.	11	00	AM
Knoxville, Tenn.	12	00	Noon
Lexington, Ky.	12	00	Noon
Lincoln, Neb.	11	00	AM
Little Rock, Ark.	11	00	AM
Los Angeles, Cal.	9	00	AM
Louisville, Ky.	12	00	Noon
*Mexico City	11	00	AM
Memphis, Tenn.	11	00	AM
Miami, Fla.	12	00	Noon
Milwaukee, Wis.	11	00	AM
Minneapolis, Minn.	11	00	AM
Mobile, Ala.	11	00	AM
Montreal, Que.	12	00	Noon
Nashville, Tenn.	11	00	AM
New Haven, Conn.	12	00	Noon
New Orleans, La.	11	00	AM
New York, N.Y.	12	00	Noon
Nome, Alas.	8	00	AM
Norfolk, Va.	12	00	Noon
Okla. City, Okla.	11	00	AM
Omaha, Neb.	11	00	AM
Peoria, Ill.	11	00	AM
Philadelphia, Pa.	12	00	Noon
*Phoenix, Ariz.	10	00	AM
Pierre, S.D.	11	00	AM
Pittsburgh, Pa.	12	00	Noon
Portland, Me.	12	00	Noon
Portland, Ore.	9	00	AM
Providence, R.I.	12	00	Noon
*Regina, Sask.	11	00	AM
Reno, Nev.	9	00	AM
Richmond, Va.	12	00	Noon
Rochester, N.Y.	12	00	Noon
Sacramento, Cal.	9	00	AM
St. John's, Nfld.	1	30	PM
St. Louis, Mo.	11	00	AM
St. Paul, Minn.	11	00	AM
Salt Lake City, Ut.	10	00	AM
San Antonio, Tex.	11	00	AM
San Diego, Cal.	9	00	AM
San Francisco, Cal.	9	00	AM
Santa Fe, N.M.	10	00	AM
Savannah, Ga.	12	00	Noon
Seattle, Wash.	9	00	AM
Shreveport, La.	11	00	AM
Sioux Falls, S.D.	11	00	AM
Spokane, Wash.	9	00	AM
Tampa, Fla.	12	00	Noon
Toledo, Oh.	12	00	Noon
Topeka, Kan.	11	00	AM
Toronto, Ont.	12	00	Noon
*Tucson, Ariz.	10	00	AM
Tulsa, Okla.	11	00	AM
Vancouver, B.C.	9	00	AM
Washington, D.C.	12	00	Noon
Wichita, Kan.	11	00	AM
Wilmington, Del.	12	00	Noon
Winnipeg, Man.	11	00	AM

* Cities with an asterisk do not observe Daylight Saving Time. During much of the year, it is necessary to add one hour to the time in cities that do observe Daylight Saving Time to get the proper time relation.

Legal or Public Holidays, 1995

Technically, the U.S. observes no national holidays; each state has jurisdiction over its holidays, which are designated by legislative enactment or executive proclamation. In practice, however, most states observe the federal legal public holidays, even though the president and the U.S. Congress can legally designate holidays only for the District of Columbia and for federal employees. Federal legal public holidays are New Year's Day, Martin Luther King Day, Washington's Birthday, Memorial Day, Independence Day, Labor Day, Columbus Day, Veterans Day, Thanksgiving, and Christmas.

Chief Legal or Public Holidays

When a holiday falls on a Sunday or a Saturday, it is usually observed on the following Monday or the preceding Friday. For some holidays, government and business closing practices vary. In most states, the office of the Secretary of State can provide details for holiday closings. The following will be legal or public holidays in most states in 1995:

Jan. 1 (Sun.) — New Year's Day

Jan. 16 (3d Mon. in Jan.) — Martin Luther King Day

Feb. 12 (Sun.) — Lincoln's Birthday

Feb. 20 (3d Mon. in Feb.) — Washington's Birthday, or Presidents' Day, or Washington-Lincoln Day

May 29 (last Mon. in May) — Memorial Day, or Decoration Day

July 4 (Tues.) — Independence Day

Sept. 4 (1st Mon. in Sept.) — Labor Day

Oct. 9 (2d Monday in Oct.) — Columbus Day, or Discoverers' Day, or Pioneers' Day

Nov. 11 (Sat.) — Veterans Day

Nov. 23 (4th Thurs. in Nov.) — Thanksgiving Day

Dec. 25 (Mon.) — Christmas Day

In some states, the following will be legal or public holidays in 1995:

Apr. 4 (Fri.) — Good Friday. In some states, observed for half or part of day.

Nov. 7 (1st Tues. after 1st Mon. in Nov.) — Election Day

Selected International Holidays

Jan. 31 — Australia Day obsvd., Australia
Feb. 5 — Constitution Day, Mexico
Feb. 6 — Waitangi Day, New Zealand
Feb. 11 — National Foundation Day, Japan
Mar. 13 — Commonwealth Day, Canada
Mar. 17 — St. Patrick's Day, Ireland
Mar. 21 — Benito Juarez's Birthday, Mexico
Apr. 8 — Buddha's Birthday, Korea, Japan
Apr. 22 — Independence Day, Israel
Apr. 30 — Feast of Valborg (Walpurgis Night), Sweden
May 5 — Cinco de Mayo (Battle of Puebla Day), Mexico
May 14 — Joan of Arc's Day, France
May 22 — Victoria Day, Canada
June 10 — Day of Portugal, Portugal
July 1 — Canada Day, Canada
July 14 — Bastille Day, France
Sept. 15 — Respect for the Aged Day, Japan
Sept. 16 — Independence Day, Mexico
Sept. 19 — St. Gennaro, Italy
Sept. 28 — Confucius' Birthday/Teachers' Day, Taiwan
Oct. 9 — Thanksgiving Day, Canada
Nov. 1-2 — Day of the Dead, Mexico
Nov. 5 — Guy Fawkes Day, Great Britain
Nov. 11 — Remembrance Day, Canada
Dec. 12 — Jamhuri Day, Kenya; Guadalupe Day, Mexico
Dec. 26 — Boxing Day, Australia, Canada, United Kingdom

AEROSPACE

Memorable Moments in Human Spaceflight

Sources: National Aeronautics and Space Administration; Congressional Research Service; World Almanac research

Note: U.S. space missions are in **boldface**. Other missions were sponsored by the former Soviet Union or the Commonwealth of Independent States. EVA = extravehicular activity. ASTP = Apollo-Saturn Test Project.

DATES	VEHICLE NAME	CREW (no. of flights)	CREW DURATION (HR:MIN)	REMARKS
4/12/61	Vostok 1	Yuri A. Gagarin	1:48	1st human orbital flight
5/5/61	**Mercury-Redstone 3**	**Alan B. Shepard Jr.**	**0:15**	**1st American in space**
7/21/61	**Mercury-Redstone 4**	**Virgil I. Grissom**	**0:15**	**Spacecraft sank, Grissom rescued**
8/6/61-8/7/61	Vostok 2	Gherman S. Titov	25:18	1st spaceflight of more than 24 hrs
2/20/62	**Mercury-Atlas 6**	**John H. Glenn Jr.**	**4:55**	**1st American in orbit; 3 orbits**
5/24/62	**Mercury-Atlas 7**	**M. Scott Carpenter**	**4:56**	**Manual retrofire error caused 250-mi landing overshoot**
8/11/62-8/15/62	Vostok 3	Andrian G. Nikolayev	94:22	Vostok 3 and 4 made 1st group flight
8/12/62-8/15/62	Vostok 4	Pavel R. Popovich	70:57	On 1st orbit it came within 3 mi of Vostok 3
5/15/63-5/16/63	**Mercury-Atlas 9**	**L. Gordon Cooper**	**34:19**	**1st U.S. evaluation of effects of one day in space on a person; 22 orbits**
6/14/63-6/19/63	Vostok 5	Valery F. Bykovsky	119:06	Vostok 5 and 6 made 2d group flight
6/16/63-6/19/63	Vostok 6	Valentina V. Tereshkova	70:50	1st woman in space; passes within 3 mi of Vostok 5
10/12/64-10/13/64	Voskhod 1	Vladimir M. Komarov, Konstantin P. Feoktistov, Boris B. Yegorov	24:17	1st 3-man orbital flight; 1st without space suits
3/18/65-3/19/65	Voskhod 2	Pavel I. Belyayev, Aleksei A. Leonov	26:02	Leonov made 1st "space walk" (10 min)
3/23/65	**Gemini-Titan 3**	**Grissom (2), John W. Young**	**4:53**	**1st piloted spacecraft to change its orbital path**
6/3/65-6/7/65	**Gemini-Titan 4**	**James A. McDivitt, Edward H. White 2d**	**97:56**	**White was 1st American to "walk in space" (20 min)**
12/4/65-12/18/65	**Gemini-Titan 6**	**Frank Borman, James A. Lovell**	**330:35**	**Longest duration Gemini flight**
12/15/65-12/16/65	**Gemini-Titan 7**	**Schirra (2), Thomas P. Stafford**	**25:51**	**Completed world's 1st space rendezvous, with Gemini 8**
3/16/66-3/17/66	**Gemini-Titan 8**	**Neil A. Armstrong, David R. Scott**	**10:41**	**1st docking of one space vehicle with another; mission aborted, control malfunction; 1st Pacific landing**
7/18/66-7/21/66	**Gemini-Titan 10**	**Young (2), Michael Collins**	**70:47**	**1st use of Agena target vehicle's propulsion systems; 1st orbital docking**
9/12/66-9/15/66	**Gemini-Titan 11**	**Conrad (2), Richard F. Gordon Jr.**	**71:17**	**Docked with Agena rocket; made 2 revolutions of the earth tethered; set Gemini altitude record (739.2 mi.)**
11/11/66-11/15/66	**Gemini-Titan 12**	**Lovell (2), Edwin W. "Buzz" Aldrin Jr.**	**94:34**	**Final Gemini mission; record 5½ hr of EVA**
4/23/67-4/24/67	Soyuz 1	Komarov (2)	26:40	Crashed on reentry killing Komarov
10/11/68-10/22/68	**Apollo-Saturn 7**	**Schirra (3), Donn F. Eisele, R. Walter Cunningham**	**260:09**	**1st piloted flight of Apollo spacecraft command-service module only; live TV footage of crew**
10/26/69-10/30/68	Soyuz 3	Georgi T. Beregovoy	94:51	Made rendezvous with unpiloted Soyuz 2
12/21/68-12/27/68	**Apollo-Saturn 8**	**Borman (2), Lovell (3), William A. Anders**	**147:00**	**1st lunar orbit and piloted lunar return reentry (command-service module only); views of lunar surface televised to earth**
1/14/69-1/17/69	Soyuz 4	Vladimir A. Shatalov	71:21	Docked with Soyuz 5
1/15/69-1/18/69	Soyuz 5	Boris V. Volyanov, Aleksei S. Yeliseyev, Yevgeny V. Khrunov	72:54	Docked with 4; Yeliseyev and Khrunov transferred to Soyuz 4 via a spacewalk
3/3/69-3/13/69	**Apollo-Saturn 9**	**McDivitt (2), Scott (2), Russell L. Schweickart**	**241:00**	**1st piloted flight of lunar module**
5/18/69-5/26/69	**Apollo-Saturn 10**	**Stafford (3), Young (3), Cernan(2)**	**192:03**	**1st lunar module orbit of moon, 50,000 ft from moon surface**
7/16/69-7/24/69	**Apollo-Saturn 11**	**Armstrong (2), Collins (2), Aldrin (2)**	**195:18**	**1st lunar landing made by Armstrong and Aldrin (7/20/69); collected 48.5 lb of soil, rock samples; lunar stay time 21:36:21**
10/11/69-10/16/69	Soyuz 6	Georgi S. Shonin, Valery N. Kubasov	118:43	1st welding of metals in space
10/12/69-10/17/69	Soyuz 7	Anatoly V. Flipchenko, Vladislav N. Volkov, Viktor V. Gorbatko	118:40	Space lab construction test made; Soyuz 6, 7, and 8; 1st time 3 spacecraft, 7 crew members orbited the earth at once
10/13/69[1]	Soyuz 8	Shatalov (2), Yeliseyev (2)	118:51	Part of space lab construction team
11/14/69-11/24/69	**Apollo-Saturn 12**	**Conrad (3), Gordon (2), Alan L. Bean**	**244:36**	**Conrad and Bean made 2d moon landing; collected 74.7 lb of samples, lunar stay time 31:31**

DATES	VEHICLE NAME	CREW (no. of flights)	CREW DURATION (HR:MIN)	REMARKS
4/11/70-4/17/70	**Apollo-Saturn 13**	**Lovell (4), Fred W. Haise Jr., John L. Swigart Jr.**	**142:54**	**Aborted after service module oxygen tank ruptured; crew returned safely using lunar module**
1/31/71-2/9/71	**Apollo-Saturn 14**	**A. Shepard (2), Stuart A. Roosa, Edgar D. Mitchell**	**216:01**	**Shepard and Mitchell made 3d moon landing, collected 96 lb of lunar samples; lunar stay 33:31**
4/19/71[1]	Salyut 1[2]	(Occupied by Soyuz 11crew)		1st space station
4/22/71[1]	Soyuz 10	Shatalov (3), Yeliseyev (3), Nikolay N. Rukavishnikov	47:46	1st successful docking; failed to enter space station
6/6/71-6/30/71	Soyuz 11	Georgi T. Dobrovolskiy, V. Volkov (2), Viktor I. Patsayev	570:22	Docked and entered Salyut 1 space station; orbited in Salyut 1 for 23 days, crew died during reentry from loss of pressurization
7/26/71-8/7/71	**Apollo-Saturn 15**	**Scott (3), James B. Irwin, Alfred M. Worden**	**295:12**	**Scott and Irwin made 4th moon landing; 1st lunar rover use; 1st deep space walk; 170 lb of samples; 66:55 stay**
4/16/72-4/27/72	**Apollo-Saturn 16**	**Young (4), Charles M. Duke Jr., Thomas K. Mattingly**	**265:51**	**Young and Duke made 5th moon landing; colleced 213 lb of lunar samples; lunar stay 71:2**
12/7/72-12/19/72	**Apollo-Saturn 17**	**Cernan (3), Ronald E. Evans, Harrison H. Schmitt**	**301:51**	**Cernan and Schmitt made 6th piloted lunar landing; collected 243 lb of samples; record lunar stay of more than 75 hr**
5/14/73[1]	**Skylab 1[3]**	**(Occupied by Skylab 2, 3, and 4 crews)**		**1st U.S. space station**
5/25/73-6/22/73	**Skylab 2**	**Conrad (4), Joseph P. Kerwin, Paul J. Weitz**	**672:49**	**1st Amer. piloted orbiting space station; made long-flight tests, crew repaired damage caused during boost**
7/28/73-9/25/73	**Skylab 3**	**Bean (2), Owen K. Garriott, Jack R. Lousma**	**1,427:09**	**Crew systems and operational tests, exceeded pre-mission plans for scientific activities; EVA total 13:44**
11/16/73-2/8/74	**Skylab 4**	**Gerald P. Carr, Edward G. Gibson, William Pogue**	**2,017:15**	**Final Skylab mission; set then-record space walk of 7:1**
7/15/75-7/21/75	Soyuz 19 (ASTP)	Leonov (2), Kubasov (2)	143:31	U.S.-USSR joint flight; crews linked up in space (7/17), conducted experiments, shared meals, and held a joint news conference
7/15/75-7/24/75	**Apollo 18 (ASTP)**	**Vance Brand, Stafford (4), Donald K. Slayton**	**217:28**	**Joint flight with Soyuz 19**
12/10/77[1]	Soyuz 26	Yuri V. Romanenko, Georgiy M. Grechko (2)	2,314:00	1st multiple docking to a space station (Soyuz 26 and 27 docked at Salyut 6)
1/10/78[1]	Soyuz 27	Vladimir A. Dzhanibekov	142:59	*See Soyuz 26*
3/2/78[1]	Soyuz 28	Aleksei A. Gubarev (2), Vladimir Remek	190:16	1st international crew launch; Remek was 1st Czech in space
4/12/81-4/14/81	**Columbia**	**Young (5), Robert L. Crippen**	**54:21**	**1st space shuttle flight[4]**
11/11/82-11/16/82	**Columbia**	**Brand (2), Robert Overmyer, William Lenoir, Joseph Allen**	**122:14**	**1st reuse of space shuttle; 1st 4-person crew**
4/4/83-4/9/83	**Challenger**	**Weitz (2), Karol Bobko, Story Musgrave, Donald Peterson**	**120:24**	**1st Challenger flight**
6/18/83-6/24/83	**Challenger**	**Crippen (2), Frederick Hauck, Sally K. Ride, John W. Fabian, Norman Thagard**	**146:24**	**Ride was 1st U.S. woman in space; 1st 5-person crew**
6/27/83[1]	Soyuz T-9	Vladimir A. Lyakhov (2)	3,585:46	Docked at Salyut 7; 1st construction in space
8/30/83-9/5/83	**Challenger**	**Truly (2), Daniel Brandenstein, William Thornton, Guion Bluford, Dale Gardner**	**3,585:46**	**Bluford was 1st U.S. black in space**
11/28/83-12/8/83	**Columbia**	**Young (6), Brewster Shaw Jr., Robert Parker, Garriott (2), Byron Lichtenberg, Ulf Merbold**	**247:47**	**1st Columbia flight; Merbold was 1st German on U.S. mission; 1st 6-person crew**
2/3/84-2/11/84	**Challenger**	**Brand (3), Robert Gibson, Ronald McNair, Bruce McCandless, Robert Stewart**	**191:16**	**1st untethered EVA**
2/8/84-10/2/84	Soyuz T-10	Leonid Kizim (2), Vladmir Solovyov, Oleg Atkov	5,868:50	Docked at Salyut 7; set space endurance record (since broken)
4/6/84-4/13/84	**Challenger**	**Crippen (3), Francis R. Scobee, George D. Nelson, Terry J. Har, James D. Van Hoften**	**167:40**	**1st in-orbit satellite repair**
7/17/84[1]	Soyuz T-12	Dzhanibekov (4), Svetlana Y. Savitskaya (2), Igor P. Volk,	283:14	Docked at Salyut 7; Savitskaya was 1st woman to perform EVA
8/30/84-9/5/84	**Discovery**	**Hartsfield (2), Michael L. Coats, Steven A. Hawley, Judith A. Resnik, Richard M. Mullane, Charles D. Walker**	**144:57**	**1st flight of the Discovery**
10/5/84-10/13/84	**Challenger**	**Crippen (4), Jon A. McBride, Kathryn D. Sullivan, Ride (2), Marc Garneau, David C. Leestma, Paul D. Scully-Power**	**197:24**	**Garneau was 1st Canadian in space; 1st 7-person crew**

DATES	VEHICLE NAME	CREW (no. of flights)	CREW DURATION (HR:MIN)	REMARKS
11/8/84-11/16/84	**Discovery**	**Hauck (2); David M. Walker, Dr. Anna L. Fisher, J. Allen (2), D. Gardner (2)**	**191:45**	**1st satellite retrieval/repair**
4/12/85-4/19/85	**Discovery**	**Karol J. Bobko, Donald E. Williams, Jake Garn, Charles D. Walker, Jeffrey A. Hoffman, S. David Griggs, M. Rhea Seddon**	**167:55**	**Garn was 1st senator in space**
6/17/85-6/24/85	**Discovery**	**Brandenstein (2), John O. Creighton, Shannon W. Lucid, Steven R. Nagel, Fabian (2), Prince Sultan Salman al-Saud, Patrick Baudry**	**169:39**	**Launched 4 satellites; Salman al-Saud was 1st Arab in space; Baudry was 1st French person on U.S. mission**
10/3/85	**Atlantis**	**Bobko (3), Ronald J. Grabe, David C. Hilmers, Stewart (2), William A. Pailes**	**97:47**	**1st Atlantis flight**
10/30/85	**Challenger**	**Hartsfield (3), Steven R. Nagel, Buchli (2), Bluford (2), Bonnie J. Dunbar, Wubbo J. Ockels, Richard Furrer, Ernst Messerschmid**	**168:44**	**1st 8-person crew**
11/26/85	**Atlantis**	**Shaw (2), Bryan D. O'Connor, Sherwood C. Spring, Mary L. Cleave, Jerry L. Ross, C. Walker (3), Rodolfo Neri**	**165:05**	**Neri was 1st Mexican in space**
1/12/86	**Columbia**	**R. Gibson (2), Charles F. Bolden Jr., Hawley (2), G. Nelson (2), Franklin R. Chang-Diaz, Robert J. Cenker, Bill Nelson**	**146:04**	**B. Nelson was 1st congressman in space**
1/28/86	**Challenger**	**Scobee (2), Michael J. Smith, Resnik (2), Ellison S. Onizuka (2), Ronald E. McNair, Gregory B. Jarvis, Christa McAuliffe**		**Exploded 73 sec after liftoff; all were killed**
2/20/86[1]	Mir[2]	Space station with 6 docking ports		
3/13/86[1]	Soyuz T-15	Kizim (3), V. Solovyov (2)	3,000:01	Ferry between stations; docked at Mir
2/5/87-12/29/87	Soyuz TM-2	Romanenko (3), Aleksandr I. Laveikin	7,835:38	Romanenko remained at station Mir and set record Soviet single endurance flight in orbit (326.5 days)
12/21/87-12/21/88	Soyuz TM-4	V. Titov (2), Muso Manarov, Anatoly Levchenko	8,782:39	Docked at Mir; set team space endurance record (360 days)
9/29/88-10/3/88	**Discovery**	**Hauck (3), Richard O. Covey (2), Hilmers (2), G. Nelson (2), John M. Lounge (2)**	**97:00**	**Redesigned shuttle makes 1st flight**
4/24/90-4/29/90	**Discovery**	**McCandless (2), Sullivan (2), Loren J. Shriver (2), Bolden (2), Hawley (3)**	**121:15**	**Raunched Hubble telescope**
5/7/92-5/16/92	**Endeavour**	**Brandenstein (4), Kevin C. Chilton, Bruce E. Melnick (2), Pierre J. Thuot (2), Richard J. Hieb (2), Karen Thornton (2), Akers (2)**	**213:18**	**1st Endeavour flight; set EVA duration record (since broken); 1st 3-person EVA**
9/12/92-9/21/92	**Endeavour**	**R. Gibson (4), Curtis L. Brown Jr., Mark Lee (2), Jay Apt (2), N. Jan Davis, Mae Carol Jemison, Mamoru Mohri**	**190:30**	**50th shuttle mission; Jemison was 1st black woman in space; Mohri was 1st Japanese national; Lee and Davis were 1st married couple to travel together in space**
4/8/93-4/17/93	**Discovery**	**Kenneth D. Cameron, Stephen S. Oswald (2), C. Michael Foale (2), Ellen Ochoa, Kenneth D. Cockrell**	**222:08**	**Crew inc. the 300th human in space; launched tracking satellite; Ochoa was 1st Hispanic woman in space**
10/18/93-11/1/93	**Columbia**	**John Blaha, Richard A. Searfoss, William S. McArthur Jr., David A. Wolf, Seddon (3), Lucid (4), Martin J. Fettman**	**336:13**	**2d longest space shuttle flight; first dissection in space**
12/2/93-12/13/93	**Endeavour**	**Covey (3), Kenneth D. Bowersox (2), Claude Nicollier (2), Musgrave (5), Akers (3), K. Thornton (3), Hoffman (4)**	**259:58**	**Hubble space telescope repaired; Akers set new U.S. EVA duration record (29 hr, 40 min)**
2/3/94-2/11/94	**Discovery**	**Bolden (3), Kenneth S. Reightier Jr. (2), Davis, (2), Chang-Diaz (3), Ronald M. Sega, Sergei K. Krikalev**	**199:30**	**Krikalev was 1st Russian on U.S. shuttle; attempt to launch the Wake Shield facility (a device to create vacuums in space) failed**
3/4/94-3/18/94	**Columbia**	**John H. Casper, Andrew M. Allen (2), Thuot (3), Charles D. Gemar, Marsha S. Ivins (3)**	**335:17**	**Performed many scientific experiments**
4/9/94-4/20/94	**Endeavour**	**Sidney M. Guiterrez, Chilton (2), Michael R. Cliffordn (2), Linda Godwin, Apt (3), Thomas D. Jones**	**269:49**	**1st flight of space radar lab; mapped Earth surface in 3 dimensions; environmental studies conducted**
7/8/94-7/23/94	**Columbia**	**Robert D. Cabana (3), James D. Halsell Jr., Hieb (3), Carl E. Walz (2), Leroy Chiao, Donald A. Thomas; Chiaki Naito-Mukai**	**353:55**	**Set shuttle flight duration record; 2d flight of International Microgravity Laboratory; more than 80 experiments conducted**

Note: Four Soviets died in spaceflights: Komarov on Soyuz 1 (1967) when the parachute lines tangled during descent; the 3-man Soyuz 11 crew (1971) asphyxiated. Seven Americans died in the 1986 Challenger explosion; 3 astronauts, Virgil I. Grissom, Edward H. White, and Roger B. Chaffee, died in the Jan. 27, 1967, Apollo 204 fire on the ground at Cape Kennedy, FL. (1) Launch date. (2) Other Salyut launchings are not included on this list. Later Soyuz craft docked at the Salyut or Mir stations. Stations have been used to exchange crews since 1985. (3) Spacelab 1 deteriorated and fell from orbit without burning up upon entering the atmosphere. Pieces fell on Australia and the Indian Ocean; however, no one was injured. (4) As of July 1994, there have been 63 space shuttle flights; 38 since the Challenger explosion.

Summary of Worldwide Payloads, 1986-93

Source: National Aeronautics and Space Administration
(A payload is something carried into space by a rocket.)

Year	Total[1]	USSR/CIS[2]	United States	Japan	European Space Agency	India	China
1986	132	114	9	3	0	—	3
1987	133	116	9	3	1	—	1
1988	136	107	15	2	2	2	3
1989	129	95	22	4	2	0	0
1990	160	96	31	7	1	1	5
1991	156	101	30	2	4	1	1
1992	128	77	27	3	1	2	2
1993	93	59	29	1	2	1	1
Total	**4,393[3]**	**3,897**	**1,187**	**57**	**33**	**16**	**33**

(1) Includes launches sponsored by countries not shown.(2) Figures for 1986-91 are for the Soviet Union; 1992-93 figures are for the Commonwealth of Independent States.(3) Includes launches in prior years not shown.

Notable U.S. Planetary Science Missions

Source: National Aeronautics and Space Administration

Spacecraft	Launch date (GMT)	Mission	Remarks
Mariner 2	Aug. 27, 1962	Venus	Passed within 22,000 miles from Venus 12/14/62; contact lost 1/3/63 at 54 million miles
Ranger 7	July 28, 1964	Moon	Yielded over 4,000 photos
Mariner 4	Nov. 28, 1964	Mars	Passed behind Mars 7/14/65; took 22 photos from 6,000 miles
Ranger 8	Feb. 17, 1965	Moon	Yielded over 7,000 photos
Surveyor 3	Apr. 17, 1967	Moon	Scooped and tested lunar soil
Mariner 5	June 14, 1967	Venus	In solar orbit; closest Venus fly-by 10/19/67
Mariner 6	Feb. 24, 1969	Mars	Came within 2,000 miles of Mars 7/31/69; sent back data, photos
Mariner 7	Mar. 27, 1969	Mars	Came within 2,000 miles of Mars 8/5/69
Mariner 9	May 30, 1971	Mars	First craft to orbit Mars 11/13/71; sent back over 7,000 photos
Pioneer 10	Mar. 2, 1972	Jupiter	Passed Jupiter 12/3/73; exited the solar system 6/14/83; still operating in outer solar system
Mariner 10	Nov. 3, 1973	Venus, Mercury	Passed Venus 2/5/74; arrived Mercury 3/29/74. First time gravity of one planet (Venus) used to whip spacecraft toward another (Mercury)
Viking 1	Aug. 20, 1975	Mars	Landed on Mars 7/20/76; did scientific research, sent photos; functioned 6 ½ years
Viking 2	Sept. 9, 1975	Mars	Landed on Mars 9/3/76; functioned 3 ½ years
Voyager 1	Sept. 5, 1977	Jupiter, Saturn	Encountered Jupiter 3/5/79, provided evidence of Jupiter ring; passed near Saturn 11/12/80
Voyager 2	Aug. 20, 1977	Jupiter, Saturn, Uranus, Neptune	Encountered Jupiter 7/9/79; Saturn 8/26/81; Uranus 1/8 and 1/27/86; Neptune 8/24/89
Pioneer Venus 1	May 20, 1978	Venus	Entered Venus orbit 12/4/78; spent 14 years studying planet; ceased operating 10/19/92
Pioneer Venus 2	Aug. 8, 1978	Venus	Encountered Venus 12/9/78; probes impacted on surface
Magellan	May 4, 1989	Venus	Orbit and map Venus; monitoring geological activity on surface; first planetary spacecraft to lower its orbit by using planet's atmosphere (aerobraking) 5/25/93-8/3/93
Titan IV	June 14, 1989	Orbit Earth	First of 41 such rockets whose primary purpose is defense
Galileo	Oct. 18, 1989	Jupiter	Used Earth's gravity to propel it toward Jupiter; encountered Venus Feb. 1991
Mars Observer	Sept. 25, 1992	Mars	Communication was lost 8/21/93

Notable Proposed U.S. Space Missions

Source: National Aeronautics and Space Administration

Year	Mission	Purpose
1996	Mars Environmental Survey Pathfinder	Technical demonstration of Mars Environmental Survey
1996	X-ray Timing Explorer	Study temporal variability in compact X-ray emitting objects
1997	Cassini	Study of Saturn's atmosphere, rings, magnetosphere and moons
1998	Earth Observing System	Provide long-term data sets of interactions between earth's land, atmosphere, water, and life
1998, 1999	Advanced X-ray Astrophysics Facility (2 spacecraft)	Study of dark matter, stellar evolution, galactic clusters
TBD	Pluto Fast Flyby	First fly-by of Pluto for photographic survey and other studies
2001	Space Infrared Telescope Facility	High sensitivity observations of celestial sources

Note: All spacecraft to be launched by expendable rockets. TBD=To Be Determined.

Air Travel Survey, 1993

Source: Gallup/Air Transport Association Survey

Percentage of adults who have:	1983	1992	1993	Purpose of trips (%):	1983	1992	1993
Ever flown	66	76	77	Business	51	37	48
Flown in past 12 months	22	33	33	Pleasure/personal	49	63	52

Traffic at World Airports, 1993

Source: Airport Council International-North America

Airport	Total Passengers
London, UK (Heathrow)	47,898,526
Tokyo/Haneda, Japan (Tokyo Intl.)	41,562,084
Frankfurt, Germany	32,536,457
Paris, France (Charles De Gaulle)	26,114,633
Paris, France (Orly)	25,368,248
Hong Kong (Hong Kong Intl.)	25,129,070
Osaka, Japan (Osaka Intl.)	23,360,638
Seoul, South Korea	22,855,644
Tokyo/Narita, Japan (New Tokyo Intl.)	22,138,328
Amsterdam, Netherlands (Schiphol)	21,274,407
Toronto, Ontario (Lester B. Pearson Intl.)	20,484,431
London, UK (Gatwick)	20,159,285
Singapore (Changi)	20,011,816
Rome, Italy (Fiumicino)	19,273,178
Bangkok, Thailand (Bangkok Intl.)	19,130,581
Madrid, Spain (Barajas)	17,546,770
Sydney, Australia (Kingsford Smith)	16,580,110
Zurich, Switzerland (Zurich)	13,511,353
Manchester, UK (Manchester)	13,453,777
Dusseldorf, Germany (Dusseldorf)	13,056,485
Munich, Germany (Munich)	12,731,917
Stockholm, Sweden (Arlanda)	12,558,625
Palma De Mallorca, Spain (Palma De Mallorca)	12,513,653
Taipei, Taiwan (Chiang Kai Shek Intl.)	12,494,046

Traffic at U.S. Airports, 1993

Source: Air Transport Association of America

Airport	Passenger Arrivals and Departures
Chicago (O'Hare)	65,091,168
Dallas/Ft. Worth	49,654,730
Los Angeles	47,844,794
Atlanta	47,751,000
Denver	32,626,956
San Francisco	32,042,186
Miami	28,660,396
New York (JFK)	26,796,036
Newark	25,809,413
Detroit	24,170,570
Boston	24,038,178
Phoenix	23,542,372
Minneapolis/St. Paul	23,402,412
Las Vegas	22,492,156
Honolulu	22,061,953
Orlando	21,466,033
Houston	20,251,212
St. Louis	19,923,774
New York (La Guardia)	19,804,566
Seattle	18,800,524

U.S. Scheduled Airline Traffic, 1991-93

Source: Air Transport Association of America; in thousands

	1991	1992	1993
Passenger traffic			
Revenue passengers enplaned	452,301	475,108	487,249
Revenue passenger miles	447,954,829	478,553,708	489,137,135
Available seat miles	715,199,140	752,772,435	770,830,560
Revenue passenger load factor (%)	62.6	63.6	63.5
Cargo traffic (ton miles)	12,129,963	13,198,674	14,089,149
Revenue freight and express (ton miles)	10,225,199	11,129,962	11,914,794
Revenue U.S. Mail (ton miles)	1,904,764	2,068,962	2,174,355
Financial			
Passenger revenue	$57,091,675	$59,828,487	$63,950,548
Net profit	-$1,940,157	-$4,791,284	-$2,137,659
Employees	533,565	540,413	537,111

U.S. Airline Safety, Scheduled Commercial Carriers

Source: National Transportation Safety Board

	Departures (millions)	Fatal accidents	Fatalities	Fatal accidents per 100,000 departures
1978	5.0	5	160	0.100
1979	5.4	4	351	0.074
1980	5.4	0	0	0.000
1981	5.2	4	4	0.077
1982	5.0	4	233	0.060
1983	5.0	4	15	0.079
1984	5.4	1	4	0.018
1985	5.8	4	197	0.069
1986	6.4	2	5	0.016
1987	6.6	4(1)	231	0.046(1)
1988	6.7	3(1)	285	0.030(1)
1989	6.6	11	278	0.166
1990	6.9	6	39	0.087
1991	6.8	4	62	0.059
1992	7.1	4	33	0.057
1993	7.2	1	1	0.014

(1) Sabotage-caused accidents are included in the number of fatal accidents, but not in the calculation of accident rates.

Leading U.S. Passenger Airlines, 1993

Source: Air Transport Association of America; in thousands

Airline	Passengers	Airline	Passengers	Airline	Passengers
Delta	84,813	Trans World	18,938	Morris	2,232
American	82,536	America West	14,700	Air Wisconsin	2,066
United	69,672	Alaska	6,351	Business Express	2,207
USAir	53,679	Aloha	4,704	Reno	1,861
Northwest	44,098	Hawaiian	4,327	Atlantic Southeast	1,460
Southwest	37,517	Simmons	4,147	Trans States	1,388
Continental	37,280	Horizon Air	2,752		

Aircraft Operating Statistics, 1993

Source: Air Transport Association of America; figures are averages for most commonly used models

	Number of seats	Speed airborne	Flight length	Fuel (gallons per hour)	Aircraft operating cost per hour
B747-400	398	533	4,331	3,356	$6,939
B747-100	390	520	3,060	3,490	5,396
L-1011	288	496	1,498	2,384	4,564
DC-10-10	281	492	1,493	2,229	4,261
A300-600	266	473	1,207	1,938	4,332
MD-11	254	524	3,459	2,232	4,570
DC-10-30	248	520	2,947	2,612	4,816
B767-300ER	221	493	2,285	1,549	3,251
B757-200	186	457	1,086	1,004	2,303
B767-200ER	185	483	2,031	1,392	3,012
A320-100/200	149	445	974	771	1,816
B727-200	148	430	686	1,251	2,222
B737-400	144	406	615	775	1,779
MD-80	141	422	696	891	1,793
B737-300	131	414	613	748	1,818
DC-9-50	124	369	320	893	1,901
B737-500	113	408	532	708	1,594
B737-100/200	112	387	437	800	1,757
DC-9-30	100	383	447	798	1,690
F-100	97	366	409	737	1,681
DC-9-10	72	381	439	740	1,332

National Aviation Hall of Fame

The National Aviation Hall of Fame at Dayton, OH, is dedicated to honoring the outstanding pioneers of air and space.

Allen, William M.
Andrews, Frank M.
Armstrong, Neil A.
Arnold, Henry H. "Hap"
Atwood, John Leland

Balchen, Bernt
Baldwin, Thomas S.
Beachey, Lincoln
Beech, Olive A.
Beech, Walter H.
Bell, Alexander Graham
Bell, Lawrence D.
Bellanca, Giuseppe Mario
Bendix, Vincent T.
Boeing, William E.
Bong, Richard I.
Borman, Frank
Boyd, Albert
Bradley, Mark E.
Brown, George "Scratchley"
Byrd, Richard E.

Cessna, Clyde V.
Chamberlin, Clarence D.
Chanute, Octave
Chennault, Claire L.
Cochran (Odlum), Jacqueline
Collins, Michael
Conrad Jr., Charles
Crawford, Frederick C.
Crossfield, A. Scott
Cunningham, Alfred A.
Curtiss, Glenn H.

Davis Jr., Benjamin 0.
DeSeversky, Alexander P.
Doolittle, James H.
Douglas, Donald W.
Draper, Charles S.

Eaker, Ira C.
Earhart (Putnam), Amelia
Eielson, C. Benjamin
Ellyson, Theodore G.
Ely, Eugene B.
Everest, Frank K.

Fairchild, Sherman M.
Fleet, Reuben H.
Fokker, Anthony H.G.
Ford, Henry
Foss, Joseph
Foulois, Benjamin D.
Frye, Jack

Gabreski, Francis S.
Gilruth, Robert R.
Glenn Jr., John H.
Goddard, George W.
Goddard, Robert H.
Godfrey, Arthur
Goldwater, Barry M.
Grissom, Virgil I.
Gross, Robert E.
Grumman, Leroy R.
Guggenheim, Harry F.

Haughton, Daniel J.
Hegenberger, Albert F.
Heinemann, Edward H.
Hoover, Robert A.
Hughes, Howard R.

Ingalls, David S.

James Jr., Daniel "Chappie"
Jeppesen, Elrey B.
Johnson, Clarence L.
Johnston, Alvin M. "Tex"
Jones, Thomas V.

Kenney, George C.
Kettering, Charles F.
Kindelberger, James H.
Knabenshue, A. Roy
Knight, William J.

Lahm, Frank P.
Langley, Samuel P.
Lear Sr., William P.
LeMay, Curtis E.
LeVier, Anthony W.
Lindbergh, Anne M.
Lindbergh, Charles A.
Link, Edwin A.
Lockheed, Allan H.
Loening, Grover
Luke Jr., Frank

Macready, Carl B.
Macready, John A.
Martin, Glenn L.
McDonnell, James S.
Mitscher, Marc A.
Meyer, John C.
Mitchell, William "Billy"
Montgomery, John J.
Moorer, Thomas H.
Moss, Sanford A.

Neumann, Gerhard
Nichols, Ruth R.
Norden, Carl L.
Northrop, John K.

Patterson, William A.
Piper Sr., William T.
Post, Wiley H.

Read, Albert C.
Reeve, Robert C.
Rentschler, Frederick B.
Richardson, Holden C.
Rickenbacker, Edward V.
Rodgers, Calbraith P.
Rogers, Will

Rushworth, Robert A.
Ryan, T. Claude

Schirra, Walter M.
Schriever, Bernard A.
Selfridge, Thomas E.
Shepard Jr., Alan B.
Sikorsky, Igor I.
Six, Robert F.
Smith, C.R.
Spaatz, Carl A.
Sperry Sr., Elmer A.
Sperry Sr., Lawrence B.
Stanley, Robert M.
Stapp, John P.
Stearmam, Lloyd C.

Taylor, Charles E.
Thomas, Lowell
Towers, John H.
Trippe, Juan T.
Turner, Roscoe
Twining, Nathan F.

Vandenberg, Hoyt
von Braun, Wernher
von Karman, Theodore
von Ohain, Hans P.
Vought, Chance M.

Wade, Leigh
Walden, Henry W.
Wells, Edward
Wilson, Thornton A.
Woolman, Collett Everman "C.E."
Wright, Orville
Wright, Wilbur

Yeager, Charles E.
Young, John W.

Memorable Flight Records, 1993

Source: National Aeronautic Association of the USA

The National Aeronautics Association of the USA, 1815 North Fort Myer Dr., Arlington, VA 22209, is the U.S. representative of the Fédération Aéronautique Internationale, the certifying agency for world aviation and space records. The International Aeronautical Federation was formed in 1905 by representatives from Belgium, France, Germany, Great Britian, Spain, Italy, Switzerland, and the United States, with headquarters in Paris. Regulations for the control of official records were signed Oct. 14, 1905.

World abosolute records are defined as maximum performance, regardless of class or type of aircraft used. Absolute records for space flight are kept separately. All other records, also international in scope, are termed "World Class" records and are divided into 17 classes, including: Class A, free balloons; Class B, airships; Class C-1, airplanes; Class C-2, seaplanes; Class C-3, amphibians; Class D, gliders; and Class E, rotorcrafts, such as helicopters. Classes are subdivided into 4 groups based on their power source: Group I—piston engine, Group II—turboprop, Group III—jet engine, Group IV—rocket engine. Sometimes there are also further divisions for weight subclasses, such as Class C-1d, which is a light airplane weighing 3,858 to 6,614 lb.

In 1993, the NAA certified 125 aviation records. Of those records the NAA's Contest and Records Board selected several memorable record flights of 1993. They are as follows:

Balloons, Subclass AX-8 (3,000-4,000 m^3)

Distance — 755.50 mi — William E. Bussey, Thunder and Colt AX-8; Amarillo, TX-Milbank, SD, 1/24-1/25/93.
Duration — 29 hr 14 min 35 sec — William E. Bussey, Thunder and Colt AX-8; Amarillo, TX-Milbank, SD, 1/24-1/25/93.

Helicopters, Turbine Engine (6,614-9,920 lb)

Great circle distance without landing — 1,976.05 mi — Ron Williamson, Bell UH-1H; Oxnard, CA-Marietta, GA, 4/22/93.

Gliders, Single Place

Free Distance — 866.22 mi — Thomas L. Knauff, Schempp-Hirth Discus B; Julian, PA, 6/1/93.

Light Airplanes, Piston Engine (661-1,102 lb)

Speed over a 3 km (1.9 mi) course — 277.25 mph — Jon M. Sharp, Sharp DR90; Oshkosh, WI, 8/1/93.
Great circle distance without landing — 2,490.32 mi — F. Gary Hertzler, VariEze; Chandler, AZ-Perris, CA, 10/31/93.

Light Airplanes, Piston Engine (1,102-2,204 lb)

Speed over recognized course — 401.79 mph — Henry M. Bouley Jr., Questair Venture; Chicago-Boston, 1/26/93.

Light Airplanes, Piston Engine (2,204-3,858 lb)

Speed over recognized course, round trip — 198.27 mph — Stuart C. Goldberg, Beechcraft Bonanza V35B; New York-Los Angeles, 9/5-9/6/93.

Medium Airplanes, Turboprop (19,841-26,455 lb)

Altitude — 35,735 ft — William G. Walker, Wyatt C. Ingram, Marsh S-2F3T Turbotracker, 8/31/93.
Time to Climb — 3 min 40 sec — William G. Walker, Wyatt C. Ingram, Marsh S-2F3T Turbotracker, 8/30/93.
Closed Circuit — 282.43 mph — William G. Walker, Wyatt C. Ingram, Marsh S-2F3T Turbotracker, 8/31/93.

Heavy Airplanes, Jet Engine (132,276-176,386 lb)

Great circle distance without landing — 4,472.90 mi — Robert E. Siman, Hassan A. Al-Kandry, McDonnell Douglas MD-83, Washington, DC-Rome, 5/23/93.

Altitude with 2,000 kg (6.6 lb) payload — 36,900 ft — Robert E. Siman, Hassan A. Al-Kandry, McDonnell Douglas MD-83, Washington, DC-Rome, 5/23/93.

Altitude in horizontal flight — 36,900 ft — Robert E. Siman, Hassan A. Al-Kandry, McDonnell Douglas MD-83, Washington, DC-Rome, 5/23/93.

National Records

Fastest time to visit all the hard surface, public airports in Michigan (128) — 1 day 12 hr 5 min 3 sec —Patrick J. Curley, Juanita D. Curley, Piper PA-28-181, 6/29-6/30/93.

Other Notable Records

Dr. Morris Wortman set 3 World Records in 1993 with his Mooney TLS, a light airplane with a piston engine. His first record-setting flight occured on May 15 when he achieved an average speed of 227.43 mph on a recognized round-trip course from Rochester, NY, to New York City. On Oct. 22, he acheived an average speed of 336.60 mph over a recognized course from Chicago to New York City. He also set records on a round-trip course from Buffalo, NY, to New York City with an average speed of 212.74 mph on Nov. 30.

Pilot Bruce J. Mayes and his copilot, Jerry Procter, set 3 records in their Grumman Aerospace AA-5B, a piston-engine light airplane, on May 30. Flying from Kailua, HI, to Lihue, HI, they achieved an average speed of 160.67 mph. The same day, from Lihue, HI, to Kailua, HI, an average speed of 145.26 mph was maintained. On a recognized round-trip course from Kailua, HI to Lihue, HI, Mayes and Proctor averaged 133.53 mph. On Aug. 10, Mayes returned to Kailua with copilot Richard L. Potts in an Aérospatiale AS 350D, a subclass E-1.D helicopter (3,858-6,614 lb), and set another FAI course record. Mayes and Potts averaged 143.70 mph on their trip to Lihue.

Some other 1993 FAI course records set in light airplanes, with piston engines (2,204-3,858 lbs) were:

St. Louis, MO, to Augusta, GA — 201.30 mph — James R. Lyle, Piper PA-32R-301, 1/7/93.
Las Vegas, NV, to Salt Lake City, UT — 196.06 mph — Vincent F. Latona, Beechcraft Bonanza B36TC, 8/4/93.
Twentynine Palms, CA, to St. Charles, MO — 160.52 mph — Marvin A. Robinson, Kenneth Rapier, Mooney M20J, 7/17/93.
Los Angeles, CA, to Lakeland, FL — 363.45 mph — Dave Morss, Lancair IV, 4/18/93.

Notable Around-the-World and Intercontinental Trips

	From/To	Miles	Time	Date
Nellie Bly	New York/New York		72d 06h 11m	1889
George Francis Train	New York/New York		67d 12h 03m	1890
Charles Fitzmorris	Chicago/Chicago		60d 13h 29m	1901
J. W. Willis Sayre	Seattle/Seattle		54d 09h 42m	1903
J. Alcock-A.W. Brown [1]	Newfoundland/Ireland	1,960	16h 12m	June 14-15, 1919
Two U.S. Army airplanes	Seattle/Seattle	26,103	35d 01h 11m	1924
Richard E. Byrd [2]	Spitsbergen/N. Pole	1,545	15h 30m	May 9, 1926
Amundsen-Ellsworth-Nobile Expedition	Spitsbergen/Teller, Alaska		80h	May 11-14,1926
E.S. Evans and L. Wells (N.Y.World) [3]	New York/New York	18,410	28d 14h 36m 05s	June 16-July 14, 1926
Charles Lindbergh [4]	New York/Paris	3,610	33h 29m 30s	May 20-21, 1927
Amelia Earhart, W. Stultz, L. Gordon	Newfoundland/Wales		20h 40m	June 17-18, 1928
Graf Zeppelin	Friedrichshafen, Ger./Lakehurst, N.J.	6,630	4d 15h 46m	Oct. 11-15, 1928
Graf Zeppelin	Friedrichshafen, Ger./Lakehurst, N.J.	21,700	20d 04h	Aug. 14-Sept. 4, 1929
Wiley Post and Harold Gatty (Monoplane Winnie Mae)	New York/New York	15,474	8d 15h 51m	July 1, 1931
C. Pangborn-H. Herndon Jr. [5]	Misawa, Japan/Wenatchee, Wash.	4,458	41h 34m	Oct. 3-5, 1931
Amelia Earhart [6]	Newfoundland/Ireland	2,026	14h 56m	May 20-21, 1932
Wiley Post (Monoplane Winnie Mae) [7]	New York/New York	15,596	115h 36m 30s	July 15-22, 1933
Hindenburg Zeppelin	Lakehurst, N.J./Frankfort, Ger.		42h 53m	Aug. 9-11, 1936
H. R. Ekins (Scripps-Howard Newspapers in race) (Zeppelin Hindenburg to Germany, air-planes from Frankfurt)	Lakehurst, N.J./Lakehurst, N.J.	25,654	18d 11h 14m 33s	Sept, 30-Oct. 19, 1936
Howard Hughes and 4 assistants	New York/New York	14,824	3d 19h 08m 10s	July 10-13, 1938
Douglas Corrigan	New York/Dublin		28h 13m	July 17-18, 1938
Mrs. Clara Adams (Pan American Clipper)	Port Washington, N.Y./ Newark, N.J.		16d 19h 04m	June 28-July 15, 1939
Globester, U.S. Air Transport Command	Wash., D.C./Wash., D.C.	23,279	149h 44m	Oct. 4, 1945
Capt. William P. Odom (A-26 Reynolds Bombshell)	New York/New York	20,000	78h 55m 12s	Apr. 12-16, 1947
America, Pan American 4-engine Lockheed Constellation [8]	New York/New York	22,219	101h 32m	June 17-30, 1947
Col. Edward Eagan	New York/New York	20,559	147h 15m	Dec. 13, 1948
USAF B-50 Lucky Lady II (Capt. James Gallagher) [9]	Ft. Worth, Tex./Ft. Worth, Tex.	23,452	94h 01m	Feb. 26-Mar. 2, 1949
Col. D. Schilling, USAF [10]	England/Limestone, Me.	3,300	10h 01m	Sept. 22, 1950
C.F. Blair Jr.	Norway/Alaska	3,300	10h 29m	May 29, 1951
Two U.S. S-55	Massachusetts/Scotland	3,410	42h 30m	July 15-31, 1952
Canberra Bomber [11]	N. Ireland/Newfoundland	2073	04h 34m	Aug. 26, 1952
	Newfoundland/N. Ireland	2073	03h 25m	Aug. 26, 1952
Three USAF B-52 Stratofortresses [12]	Merced, Cal./Cal.	24,325	45h 19m	Jan. 15-18, 1957
Max Conrad	Chicago/Rome	5,000	34h 03m	Mar. 5-6, 1959
USSR TU-114 [13]	Moscow/New York	5,092	11h 06m	June 28, 1959
Boeing 707-320	New York/Moscow	c.5090	08h 54m	July 23, 1959
Peter Gluckmann (solo)	San Francisco/San Francisco	22,800	29d	Aug. 22-Sept. 20, 1959
Sue Snyder	Chicago/Chicago	21,219	62h 59m	June 22-24, 1960
Max Conrad (solo)	Miami/Miami	25,946	8d 18h 35m 57s	Feb. 28-Mar. 8, 1961
Sam Miller & Louis Fodor	New York/New York		46h 28m	Aug. 3-4, 1963
Robert & Joan Wallick	Manila/Manila	23,129	5d 06h 17m 10s	June 2-7, 1966
Arthur Godfrey, Richard Merrill Fred Austin, Karl Keller	New York/New York	23,333	86h 9m 01s	June 4-7, 1966
Trevor K. Brougham	Darwin, Australia/Darwin	24,800	5d 05h 57m	Aug. 5-10, 1972
Walter H. Mullikin, Albert Frink, Lyman Watt, Frank Cassaniti, Edward Shields	New York/New York	23,137	1d 22h 50s	May 1-3, 1976
David Kunst [14]	Waseca, Minn./Waseca, Minn.	14,500	4yrs 3mos 16d	June 10, 1970-Oct. 5, 1974
Arnold Palmer	Denver/Denver	22,985	57h 7m 12s	May 17-19, 1976
Boeing 747 [15]	San Francisco/San Francisco	26,382	57h 25m 42s	Oct. 28-31, 1977
Concorde	London/Wash., D.C.	1,023 mph	03h 34m 48s	May 29, 1976
Concorde	Paris/New York	1,037.50 mph	03h 30m 11s	Aug. 22, 1978
Richard Rutan&Jeana Yeager [16]	Edwards AFB, Cal.	24,986	09d 03m 44s	Dec. 14-23, 1986

(1) Non-stop transatlantic flight. (2) Polar flight. (3) Mileage by train and auto, 4,110; by plane, 6,300; by steamship, 8,000. (4) Solo transatlantic flight in the Ryan monoplane the "Spirit of St. Louis". (5) Non-stop Pacific flight. (6) Women's transoceanic solo flight. (7) First to fly solo around northern circumference of the world, also first to fly twice around the world. (8) Inception of regular commercial global air service. (9) First non-stop round-the-world flight, refueled 4 times in flight. (10) Non-stop jet transatlantic flight. (11) Transatlantic round trip on same day. (12) First non-stop global flight by jet planes; refueled in flight by KC-97 aerial tankers; average speed approx. 525 mph. (13) Non-stop between Moscow and New York. (14) First to circle the earth on foot. (15) Speed record around the world over both the earth's poles. (16) Circled the earth non-stop without refueling.

ARTS AND MEDIA

Notable Movies of the Year, Sept. 1993-Aug. 1994

Movie	Stars	Director
Ace Ventura: Pet Detective	Jim Carrey, Sean Young, Courtney Cox	Tom Shadyac
Addams Family Values	Anjelica Huston, Raul Julia, Christopher Lloyd	Barry Sonnenfeld
Age of Innocence, The	Daniel Day-Lewis, Michelle Pfeiffer, Winona Ryder	Martin Scorsese
Angels in the Outfield	Tony Danza, Ben Johnson, Joseph Gordon-Levitt	William Dear
A Perfect World	Clint Eastwood, Kevin Costner, Laura Dern	Clint Eastwood
Beverly Hills Cop III	Eddie Murphy, Judge Reinhold, Hector Elizondo	John Landis
Blown Away	Jeff Bridges, Tommy Lee Jones	Stephen Hopkins
Carlito's Way	Al Pacino, Sean Penn, Penelope Ann Miller	Brian De Palma
City Slickers II	Billy Crystal, Daniel Stern, Jon Lovitz, Jack Palance	Paul Weiland
Clear and Present Danger	Harrison Ford, Willem Dafoe, Anne Archer, James Earl Jones	Phillip Noyce
Client, The	Susan Sarandon, Tommy Lee Jones	Joel Schumacher
Crooklyn	Alfre Woodard, Delroy Lindo, Zelda Harris	Spike Lee
Crow, The	Brandon Lee, Ernie Hudson, Michael Wincott	Alex Proyas
Demolition Man	Sylvester Stallone, Wesley Snipes	Marco Brambilla
Flintstones, The	John Goodman, Rick Moranis, Elizabeth Perkins, Rosie O'Donnell	Brian Levant
Forrest Gump	Tom Hanks, Robin Wright, Gary Sinise, Sally Field	Robert Zemeckis
Four Weddings and a Funeral	Hugh Grant, Andie MacDowell, Simon Callow	Mike Newell
Getting Even With Dad	Macaulay Culkin, Ted Danson	Howard Deutch
Grumpy Old Men	Jack Lemmon, Walter Matthau, Ann-Margret, Daryl Hannah	Donald Petrie
Heaven and Earth	Tommy Lee Jones, Hiep Thi Le, Joan Chen, Haing S. Ngor	Oliver Stone
In the Name of the Father	Daniel Day-Lewis, Emma Thompson	Jim Sheridan
Jimmy Hollywood	Joe Pesci, Christian Slater, Victoria Abril	Barry Levinson
I Love Trouble	Julia Roberts, Nick Nolte	Charles Shyer
It Could Happen to You	Nicolas Cage, Bridget Fonda, Rosie Perez, Isaac Hayes	Andrew Bergman
Lassie	Thomas Guiry, Helen Slater, Jon Tenney, Frederic Forrest	Daniel Petrie
Lion King, The	Jeremy Irons, James Earl Jones, Matthew Broderick, Whoopi Goldberg, Cheech Marin	Roger Allers Rob Minkoff
Little Big League	Luke Edwards, Timothy Busfield, John Ashton	Andrew Scheinman
Little Buddha	Keanu Reeves, Ying Ruocheng, Chris Isaak, Bridget Fonda	Bernardo Bertolucci
Mask, The	Jim Carrey, Peter Riegart, Peter Greene	Charles Russell
Maverick	Mel Gibson, Jodie Foster, James Garner	Richard Donner
Mrs. Doubtfire	Robin Williams, Sally Field, Pierce Brosnan, Harvey Fierstein	Chris Columbus
My Life	Michael Keaton, Nicole Kidman	Bruce Joel Rubin
Naked Gun 33 1/3: The Final Insult	Leslie Nielsen, Priscilla Presley	Peter Segal
North	Jason Alexander, Alan Arkin, Dan Aykroyd	Rob Reiner
Paper, The	Michael Keaton, Glenn Close, Robert Fuvall, Marisa Tomei	Ron Howard
Pelican Brief, The	Julia Roberts, Denzel Washington	Alan J. Pakula
Philadelphia	Tom Hanks, Denzel Washington, Antonio Banderas	Jonathan Demme
Piano, The	Holly Hunter, Harvey Keitel, Sam Neill, Anna Paquin	Jane Campion
Reality Bites	Winona Ryder, Ethan Hawke, Ben Stiller	Ben Stiller
Schindler's List	Liam Neeson, Ben Kingsley, Ralph Fiennes	Steven Spielberg
Shadow, The	Alec Baldwin, John Lone, Penelope Ann Miller	Russell Mulcahy
Shadowlands	Anthony Hopkins, Debra Winger	Richard Attenborough
Speed	Keanu Reeves, Dennis Hopper, Sandra Bullock	Jan DeBont
Three Musketeers, The	Chris O'Donnell, Charlie Sheen, Kiefer Sutherland	Stephen Herek
Tim Burton's The Nightmare Before Christmas	Chris Sarandon, Catherine O'Hara, Paul Reubens	Henry Selick
True Lies	Arnold Schwarzenegger, Jamie Lee Curtis	James Cameron
Tombstone	Kurt Russell, Val Kilmer, Michael Biehn, Powers Boothe	George P. Cosmatos
Wayne's World 2	Mike Myers, Dana Carvey	Stephen Surjik
What's Eating Gilbert Grape	Johnny Depp, Juliette Lewis, Leonardo DiCaprio	Lasse Hallstrom
When a Man Loves a Woman	Andy Garcia, Meg Ryan, Lauren Tom, Ellen Burstyn	Luis Mandoki
Wolf	Jack Nicholson, Michelle Pfeiffer	Mike Nichols
Wrestling Ernest Hemingway	Robert Duvall, Richard Harris, Sandra Bullock	Randa Haine
Wyatt Earp	Kevin Costner, Dennis Quaid, Gene Hackman	Lawrence Kasdan

Notable New York Theater Openings, 1993-94 Season

Abe Lincoln in Illinois, Robert E. Sherwood's 1939 Pulitzer-Prize-winning drama about the life of President Abraham Lincoln; directed by Gerald Gutierrez; with Sam Waterston.

Angels in America: Perestroika, the second half of Tony Kushner's play about life in the age of AIDS; directed by George C. Wolfe; with Ron Leibman, Kathleen Chalfant, David Marshall Grant, Marcia Gay Harden, and Joe Mantello.

Any Given Day, a drama by Frank D. Gilroy; about 9 people living in New York during the early 1940s; directed by Paul Benedict; with Sada Thompson and Andrea Marcovicci.

Beauty and the Beast, a musical adaptation of the 1991 Walt Disney animated film; directed by Robert Jess Roth; music by Alan Menken; lyrics by Howard Ashman and Time Rice; with Susan Egan and Terrence Mann.

Broken Glass, an Arthur Miller drama set in 1938 Brooklyn, about a woman whose sudden paralysis baffles her husband and doctor; directed by John Tillinger; with Ron Rifkin, Amy Irving, and David Dukes.

Carousel, a revival of the 1945 Rodgers and Hammerstein musical; directed by Nicholas Hytner; with Michael Hayden.

Cyrano—The Musical, based on the Edmond Rostand play *Cyrano de Bergerac*; directed by Eddy Habbema; music by Ad van Dijk; with Bill van Dijk, Anne Runolfsson, and Paul Anthony Stewart.

Damn Yankees, a revival of the 1955 musical about a baseball fan who sells his soul to the Devil so that he can become the world's greatest baseball player and his team can win; directed by Jack O'Brien; music and lyrics by Richard Adler and Jerry Ross; with Victor Garber and Bebe Neuwirth.

Gray's Anatomy, Spalding Gray's autobiographical account of being diagnosed with an unusual visual disability; directed by Renée Sharfransky.

Grease, a revival of the 1972 rock-and-roll musical; produced by Tommy Tune; music and lyrics by Jim Jacobs and Warren Casey; directed and choreographed by Jeff Calhoun; with Rosie O'Donnell.

Hedda Gabler, a new translation of the Ibsen drama by Frank McGuinness; directed by Sarah Pia Anderson; with Kelly McGillis, Keith David, Jeffrey DeMunn, and Jim Abele.

An Inspector Calls, a revival of the 1946 mystery thriller by J. B. Priestley; directed by Stephen Daldry; with Rosemary Harris, Philip Bosco, and Kenneth Cranham.

Laughter on the 23rd Floor, Neil Simon's play about a group of New York comedy writers during the early days of television; directed by Jerry Zaks; with Nathan Lane, Randy Graff, and Mark Linn-Baker.

Passion, a Stephen Sondheim musical based on the 19th-century novel *Fosca* by Igino Tarchetti; directed by James Lapine; with Donna Murphy, Jere Shea, and Marin Mazzie.

Twilight: Los Angeles, 1992, a one-woman show by Anna Deavere Smith based on interviews with people who were affected by the Rodney King case and the subsequent Los Angeles riots; directed by George C. Wolfe.

Record Long-Run Broadway Plays[1]

Source: *Variety*

Play	Performances
Chorus Line	6,137
Oh, Calcutta (revival)	5,959
*Cats	4,917
42nd Street	3,486
Grease	3,388
Fiddler on the Roof	3,242
Life With Father	3,224
Tobacco Road	3,182
*Les Misérables	3,005
Hello Dolly	2,844
*Phantom of the Opera	2,717
My Fair Lady	2,717
Annie	2,377
Man of La Mancha	2,328
Abie's Irish Rose	2,327
Oklahoma!	2,212
Pippin	1,944
South Pacific	1,925
Magic Show	1,920
Deathtrap	1,792
Gemini	1,788
Harvey	1,775
Dancin'	1,774
La Cage aux Folles	1,761
Hair	1,750
The Wiz	1,672
Born Yesterday	1,642
Ain't Misbehavin'	1,604
Best Little Whorehouse in Texas	1,584
Mary, Mary	1,572
Evita	1,567
Voice of the Turtle	1,557
Barefoot in the Park	1,530
Dreamgirls	1,521
Mame	1,508
Same Time, Next Year	1,453
Arsenic and Old Lace	1,444
The Sound of Music	1,443
How to Succeed in Business Without Really Trying	1,417
Me and My Girl	1,412
Hellzapoppin	1,404
The Music Man	1,375
*Miss Saigon	1,361
Funny Girl	1,348
Mumenschanz	1,326
Oh! Calcutta! (original)	1,314
Brighton Beach Memoirs	1,299
Angel Street	1,295
Lightnin'	1,291
Promises, Promises	1,281
The King and I	1,246
Cactus Flower	1,234
Sleuth	1,222
Torch Song Trilogy	1,222
"1776"	1,217
Equus	1,209
Sugar Babies	1,208
Guys and Dolls	1,200
Amadeus	1,181
Cabaret	1,165
Mister Roberts	1,157
Annie Get Your Gun	1,147
Seven Year Itch	1,141

(1) Number of performances through July 17, 1994.* Still running July 17, 1994.

All-Time Top 50 American Movies

Source: *Variety,* May 1994

Rental figures are in absolute dollars, reflecting actual amounts received by the distributors (estimated for movies in current release) as of April 1994. Ticket price inflation favors recent films, but older films have the advantage of reissues.

Rank/Title/Date	Rentals (millions)
1. E.T. The Extra-Terrestrial* (1982)	$228.2
2. **Jurassic Park** (1993)	208.0
3. Star Wars (1977)	193.8
4. Return of the Jedi (1983)	169.2
5. Batman (1989)	150.5
6. The Empire Strikes Back (1980)	141.7
7. Home Alone (1990)	140.1
8. Ghostbusters (1984)	132.7
9. Jaws (1975)	129.5
10. Raiders of the Lost Ark (1981)	115.6
11. Indiana Jones and the Last Crusade (1989)	115.5
12. Terminator 2* (1991)	112.5
13. **Mrs. Doubtfire** (1993)	109.8
14. Indiana Jones and the Temple of Doom (1984)	109.0
15. Beverly Hills Cop (1984)	108.0
16. Back to the Future (1985)	105.5
17. **Home Alone 2** (1992)	$103.4
18. Batman Returns (1992)	100.1
19. Ghost (1990)	98.2
20. Grease (1978)	96.3
21. Tootsie (1982)	94.9
22. **The Fugitive** (1993)	92.6
23. The Exorcist (1973)	89.0
24. Rain Man (1989)	86.8
25. The Godfather (1972)	86.3
26. Robin Hood: Prince of Thieves (1991)	86.0
27. Superman (1978)	82.8
28. Close Encounters of the Third Kind (1977/1980)	82.8
29. **Aladdin** (1992)	82.5
30. Pretty Woman (1990)	81.9
31. Dances with Wolves (1990)	81.5
32. Three Men and a Baby (1987)	81.4
33. Who Framed Roger Rabbit (1988)	81.2
34. Beverly Hills Cop II (1987)	$80.9
35. Lethal Weapon 3 (1992)	80.0
36. The Sound of Music* (1965)	80.0
37. Gremlins (1984)	79.5
38. Lethal Weapon 2 (1989)	79.5
39. Top Gun (1986)	79.4
40. Gone With the Wind (1939)	79.4
41. Rambo: First Blood Part II (1985)	78.9
42. The Sting (1973)	78.2
43. **Snow White and the Seven Dwarfs** (1937)	77.2
44. **The Firm** (1993)	77.0
45. Rocky IV (1985)	76.0
46. Saturday Night Fever (1977)	74.1
47. Back to the Future, Part II (1989)	72.3
48. Honey, I Shrunk the Kids (1989)	72.0
49. **A Few Good Men** (1992)	71.0
50. National Lampoon's Animal House (1978)	70.8

Note: Boldface print = film new to list or significant improvement since previous year; * rentals adjusted since last report.

Top 50 Movies, 1993

Source: *Variety,* Jan. 1994

Rank/Title	Gross (millions)
1. Jurassic Park	$338.9
2. The Fugitive	179.3
3. The Firm	158.3
4. Sleepless in Seattle	126.5
5. Aladdin	118.9
6. Mrs. Doubtfire	111.8
7. Indecent Proposal	106.6
8. In the Line of Fire	102.3
9. Cliffhanger	84.0
10. A Few Good Men	78.2
11. Free Willy	77.7
12. Groundhog Day	70.9
13. Dave	63.3
14. Rising Sun	63.1
15. Scent of a Woman	63.1
16. Cool Runnings	61.1
17. The Crying Game	59.3
18. Demolition Man	56.5
19. Rookie of the Year	53.6
20. The Pelican Brief	52.0
21. Dennis the Menace	51.2
22. Sommersby	50.1
23. Last Action Hero	50.0
24. The Nightmare Before Christmas	48.9
25. The Three Musketeers	48.0
26. The Bodyguard	46.9
27. Malice	45.1
28. Made in America	44.9
29. The Good Son	44.4
30. Addams Family Values	44.4
31. Teenage Mutant Ninja Turtles	42.3
32. Homeward Bound	41.8
33. Snow White and the Seven Dwarfs	41.6
34. The Beverly Hillbillies	41.6
35. Falling Down	40.9
36. Hocus Pocus	39.5
37. What's Love Got to Do With It	39.1
38. Hot Shots! Part Deux	38.9
39. Home Alone 2	37.6
40. Wayne's World 2	37.2
41. Alive	36.7
42. Son-in-Law	36.4
43. Sliver	36.3
44. Robin Hood: Men in Tights	35.7
45. Sister Act 2: Back in the Habit	35.7
46. Dragon: Bruce Lee Story	35.1
47. Carlito's Way	34.1
48. Hard Target	32.5
49. The Sandlot	32.4
50. Cop and a Half	31.9

National Film Registry, 1989-93

"Culturally, historically, or esthetically significant" films placed on the National Film Registry, Library of Congress. Films selected in 1993 are in **boldface.** Titles are in alphabetic order.

Adam's Rib (1949)
All About Eve (1950)
All Quiet on the Western Front (1930)
An American in Paris (1951)
Annie Hall (1977)
Badlands (1973)
The Bank Dick (1940)
The Battle of San Pietro (1945)
The Best Years of Our Lives (1946)
Big Business (1929)
The Big Parade (1925)
The Birth of a Nation (1915)
The Black Pirate (1926)
Blade Runner (1982)
The Blood of Jesus (1941)
Bonnie and Clyde (1967)
Bringing Up Baby (1938)
Carmen Jones (1954)
Casablanca (1942)
Castro Street (1966)
Cat People (1942)
The Cheat (1915)
Chinatown (1974)
Chulas Fronteras (1976)
Citizen Kane (1941)
City Lights (1931)
The Crowd (1928)
David Holzman's Diary (1968)
Detour (1946)
Dodsworth (1936)
Dog Star Man (1964)
Double Indemnity (1944)
Dr. Strangelove (or, How I Learned to Stop Worrying and Love the Bomb) (1964)
Duck Soup (1933)
Eaux D'Artifice (1953)
Fantasia (1940)
Footlight Parade (1933)
Frankenstein (1931)
The Freshman (1925)
The General (1927)
Gertie the Dinosaur (1914)
Gigi (1958)
The Godfather (1972)
The Godfather, Part II (1974)
The Gold Rush (1925)
Gone with the Wind (1939)
The Grapes of Wrath (1940)
The Great Train Robbery (1903)
Greed (1924)
Harlan County, U.S.A. (1976)
High Noon (1952)
High School (1968)
His Girl Friday (1940)
How Green Was My Valley (1941)
I Am a Fugitive From a Chain Gang (1932)
Intolerance (1916)
It Happened One Night (1934)
It's a Wonderful Life (1946)
The Italian (1915)
Killer of Sheep (1977)
King Kong (1933)
Lassie Come Home (1943)
Lawrence of Arabia (1962)
The Learning Tree (1969)
Letter From an Unknown Woman (1948)
Love Me Tonight (1932)
Magical Maestro (1952)
The Magnificent Ambersons (1942)
The Maltese Falcon (1941)
March of Time: Inside Nazi Germany—1938 (1938)
Meshes of the Afternoon (1943)
Modern Times (1936)
Morocco (1930)
Mr. Smith Goes to Washington (1939)
My Darling Clementine (1946)
Nanook of the North (1922)
Nashville (1975)
A Night at the Opera (1935)
The Night of the Hunter (1955)
Ninotchka (1939)
Nothing But a Man (1964)
On the Waterfront (1954)
One Flew Over the Cuckoo's Nest (1975)
Out of the Past (1947)
Paths of Glory (1957)
A Place in the Sun (1951)
Point Of Order (1964)
The Poor Little Rich Girl (1917)
Primary (1960)
The Prisoner of Zenda (1937)
Psycho (1960)
Raging Bull (1980)
Rebel Without a Cause (1955)
Red River (1948)
Ride the High Country (1962)
The River (1937)
Salesman (1969)
Salt of the Earth (1954)
The Searchers (1956)
Shadow of a Doubt (1943)
Shadows (1959)
Shane (1953)
Sherlock, Jr. (1924)
Singin' in the Rain (1952)
Snow White and the Seven Dwarfs (1937)
Some Like It Hot (1959)
Star Wars (1977)
Sullivan's Travels (1941)
Sunrise (1927)
Sunset Boulevard (1950)
Sweet Smell of Success (1957)
Tevye (1939)
Top Hat (1935)
Touch of Evil (1958)
The Treasure of the Sierra Madre (1948)
Trouble in Paradise (1932)
2001: A Space Odyssey (1968)
Vertigo (1958)
What's Opera, Doc? (1957)
Where Are My Children? (1916)
The Wind (1928)
Within Our Gates (1920)
The Wizard of Oz (1939)
A Woman Under the Influence (1974)
Yankee Doodle Dandy (1942)

Most Popular Movie Videos, 1993

Source: Alexander & Associates/Video Flash

Top 10 Rentals

1. Sister Act
2. Under Siege
3. A Few Good Men
4. The Bodyguard
5. Beauty and the Beast
6. Aladdin
7. Unforgiven
8. Home Alone 2: Lost in New York
9. Lethal Weapon 3
10. Last of the Mohicans

Top 10 Sales

1. Aladdin
2. Pinocchio
3. Beauty and the Beast
4. Barney (various)
5. Homeward Bound: The Incredible Journey
6. Free Willy
7. Home Alone 2: Lost in New York
8. 101 Dalmatians
9. Sister Act
10. Ghost

Notable Books, 1993

Source: American Library Association

Fiction

In Troubled Waters, Beverly Coyle
The Virgin Suicides, Jeffrey Eugenides
A Lesson Before Dying, Ernest J. Gaines
The Pugilist at Rest, Thom Jones
Judge on Trial, Ivan Klima
Remembering Babylon, David Malouf
Here's Your Hat, What's Your Hurry, Elizabeth McCracken
Wolf Whistle, Lewis Nordan
The Shipping News, E. Annie Proulx
Nobody's Fool, Richard Russo
Montana 1948, Larry Watson

Poetry

Words Like Fate and Pain, Karen Fiser
If It Be Not I: Collected Poems, 1959-1982, Mona Van Duyn

Nonfiction

Before Night Falls, Reinaldo Arenas
The Warbugs, Ron Chernow
Having Our Say: The Delany Sisters' First 100 Years, Sarah and A. Elizabeth Delany
The Balkan Express: Fragments From the Other Side of War, Slavenka Drakulic
Balkan Ghosts: A Journey Through History, Robert D. Kaplan
Girl, Interrupted, Susanna Kaysen
Martyr's Day: Chronicle of a Small War, Michael Kelly
Preparing for the Twenty-first Century, Paul Kennedy
This Little Light of Mine: The Life of Fannie Lou Hamer, Kay Mills
Dead Man Walking: An Eyewitness Account of the Death Penalty in the United States, Helen Prejean
Lenin's Tomb: The Last Days of the Soviet Empire, David Remnick
The Last Panda, George B. Schaller
United States: Essays, 1952-1992, Gore Vidal

Best-Selling Books, 1993

Source: *Publishers Weekly*, Mar. 7, 1994. Rankings are determined by sales figures provided by publishers; numbers generally reflect reports of copies "shipped and billed" in 1993, but not final net sales.

Hardcover Fiction

1. *The Bridges of Madison County,* Robert James Waller
2. *The Client,* John Grisham
3. *Slow Waltz at Cedar Bend,* Robert James Waller
4. *Without Remorse,* Tom Clancy
5. *Nightmares and Dreamscapes,* Stephen King
6. *Vanished,* Danielle Steel
7. *Lasher,* Anne Rice
8. *Pleading Guilty,* Scott Turow
9. *Like Water for Chocolate,* Laura Esquivel
10. *The Scorpio Illusion,* Robert Ludlum
11. *The Golden Mean,* Nick Bantock
12. *I'll Be Seeing You,* Mary Higgins Clark
13. *A Dangerous Fortune,* Ken Follett
14. *Mr. Murder,* Dean Koontz
15. *Gai-Jin,* James Clavell

Hardcover Nonfiction

1. *See I Told You,* Rush Limbaugh
2. *Private Parts,* Howard Stern
3. *Seinlanguage,* Jerry Seinfeld
4. *Embraced by the Light,* Betty J. Eadie with Curtis Taylor
5. *Ageless Body, Timeless Mind,* Deepak Chopra
6. *Stop the Insanity,* Susan Powter
7. *Women Who Run With the Wolves,* Clarissa Pinkola
8. *Men Are From Mars, Women Are From Venus,* John Gray
9. *The Hidden Life of Dogs,* Elizabeth Marshall Thomas
10. *And If You Play Golf, You're My Friend,* Harvey Penick with Bud Shrake
11. *The Way Things Ought to Be,* Rush Limbaugh
12. *Beating the Street,* Peter Lynch with John Rothchild
13. *Harvey Penick's Little Red Book,* Harvey Penick with Bud Shrake
14. *Wouldn't Take Nothing for My Journey Now,* Maya Angelou
15. *Further Along the Road Less Traveled,* M. Scott Peck

Trade Paperback

1. *The T-Factor Fat Gram Counter,* Dr. Martin Katahn and Jamie Pope-Cordle
2. *Life's Little Instruction Book,* H. Jackson Brown, Jr.
3. *The Days Are Just Packed,* Bill Waterson
4. *The Age of Innocence,* Edith Wharton
5. *The Far Side Gallery 4,* Gary Larson
6. *Rare Air: Michael on Michael,* Michael Jordan
7. *The Chickens Are Restless,* Gary Larson
8. *Schindler's List,* Thomas Keneally
9. *Live and Learn and Pass It On,* H. Jackson Brown, Jr.
10. *Beavis & Butthead: This Book Sucks,* Mike Judge
11. *A Return to Love,* Marianne Williamson
12. *Submarine,* Tom Clancy
13. *A Thousand Acres,* Jane Smiley
14. *On the Pulse of the Morning,* Maya Angelou
15. *Not for Sale at Any Price,* Ross Perot

Mass-Market Paperback

1. *The Pelican Brief,* John Grisham
2. *The Firm,* John Grisham
3. *Jurassic Park,* Michael Crichton
4. *A Time to Kill,* John Grisham
5. *Rising Sun,* Michael Crichton
6. *Jewels,* Danielle Steel
7. *Mixed Blessings,* Danielle Steel
8. *Gerald's Game,* Stephen King
9. *All Around Town,* Mary Higgins Clark
10. *Dolores Claiborne,* Stephen King
11. *The Waste Lands,* Stephen King
12. *Congo,* Michael Crichton
13. *Stars Shine Down,* Sidney Sheldon
14. *Darkest Hour,* V. C. Andrews
15. *Dragon Tears,* Dean Koontz

Almanacs, Atlases, and Annuals

1. *The World Almanac and Book of Facts 1993,* ed. Mark Hoffman
2. *The World Almanac and Book of Facts 1994,* ed. Robert Famighetti
3. *J. K. Lasser's Your Income Tax, 1994*
4. *Mobil Travel Guide Series 1993,* ed. Alice M. Wisel
5. *The Ernst & Young Tax Guide 1993*

Notable Books for Children and Young Adults, 1993

Source: American Library Association

All Ages

From Sea to Shining Sea: A Treasury of American Folklore and Folksongs, Amy Cohn
Sculptor's Eye: Looking at Contempory American Art, Jan Greenberg and Sandra Jordan
Short Walk Around the Pyramids and Through the World of Art, Philip M. Isaacson
Santa Calls, William Joyce
Lives of the Musicians: Good Times, Bad Times (And What the Neighbors Thought), Kathleen Krull
Brown Angels: An Album of Pictures and Verse, Walter Dean Myers
Grandfather's Journey, Allen Say
We Are All in the Dumps with Jack and Guy, Maurice Sendak
A Color Sampler, Kathleen Westray

Younger Readers

Chin Yu Min and the Ginger Cat, Jennifer Armstrong
Peppe the Lamplighter, Elisa Bartone
In the Small, Small Pond, Denise Fleming
Number of Animals, Kate Green
Owen, Kevin Henkes
Julius, Angela Johnson
Pigs Aplenty, Pigs Galore! David McPhail
Uncle Jed's Barbershop, Margaree King Mitchell
The Outside Dog, Charlotte Pomerantz
Yo! Yes? Chris Raschka
Two by Two, Barbara Reid
Hunting the White Cow, Tres Seymour
The Three Little Wolves and the Big Bad Pig, Eugene Trivizas
Hop Jump, Ellen Stoll Walsh

Middle Grade Readers

Giants in the Land, Diana Applebaum
Amish Home, Raymond Bial
Tsugele's Broom, Valerie Scho Carey
Sadako, Eleanor Coerr
Lotus Seed, Sherry Garland
Grandaddy and Janetta, Helen V. Griffth
The Princess in the Kitchen Garden, Annemie Heymans and Margriet Heymans
A Gathering of Garter Snakes, Bianca Lavies
Hiding Out, Martin James
Raven: A Trickster Tale from the Pacific Northwest, Gerald McDermott
Maybe Yes, Maybe No, Maybe Maybe, Susan Patron
More Rootabagas, Carl Sandburg
A Small Tall Tale From the Far Far North, Peter Sis
The Sweetest Fig, Chris Van Allsburg
Matthew and the Sea Singer, Jill Paton Walsh
Scooter, Vera B. Williams

Junior High School Age Readers

Song of Be, Lesley Beake
Whaling Days, Carol Carrick
Tell Me Everything, Carolyn Coman
Crazy Lady! Jane Leslie Conly
The Boggart, Susan Cooper
A Bone From a Dry Sea, Peter Dickinson
Bull Run, Paul Fleischman
Eleanor Roosevelt: A Life of Discovery, Russell Freedman
Be Seated: A Book About Chairs, James Cross Giblin
Many Thousand Gone: African Americans from Slavery to Freedom, Virginia Hamilton
Plain City, Virginia Hamilton
It's Our World, Too! Stories of Young People Who Are Making a Difference, Phillip Hoose
Toning the Sweep, Angela Johnson
Hero of Lesser Causes, Julie Johnston
Owl in Love, Patrice Kindl
Alien Secrets, Annette Curtis Klause
The Great Migration: An American Story, Jacob Lawerence
I Was a Teenage Professional Wrestler, Ted Lewin
The Apprentice, Pilar Molina Llorente
The Giver, Lois Lowry
Starting Home: The Story of Horace Pippin, Painter, Mary E. Lyons
Baby, Patricia Maclachlan
The Oxboy, Anne Mazer
Across America on an Emigrant Train, Jim Murphy
Nightjohn, Gary Paulsen
Harper and Moon, Ramon Royal Ross
The Wainscott Weasel, Tor Seidler
Visions: Stories About Women Artists, Leslie Sills
Anne Frank: Beyond the Diary: A Photographic Remembrance, Rian Verhoeven and Ruud van der Rol
Peter, Kate Walker
Make Lemonade, Virgina Euwer Wolff
Dragon's Gate, Lawrence Yep
Learning by Heart, Ronder Thomas Young

Young Adult (Teenage)—Fiction

Singer to the Sea God, Vivien Alcock
Bus People, Rachel Anderson
Durable Goods, Elizabeth Berg
Missing Angel Juan, Francesca Lia Block
Here's to You, Rachel Robinson, Judy Blume
Dawn Land, Joseph Bruchac
Crazy Lady! Jane Leslie Conly
Whatever Happened to Janie? Caroline B. Cooney
Staying Fat for Sarah Byrnes, Chris Crutcher
Heart of a Champion, Carl Deuker
A Bone From a Dry Sea, Peter Dickinson
Like Water for Chocolate, Laura Esquivel
Bull Run, Paul Fleischman
A Lesson Before Dying, Ernest J. Gaines
Shadow of the Dragon, Sherry Garland
The Champion, Maurice Gee
Charms for an Easy Life, Kaye Gibbons
Shadow Man, Cynthia D. Grant
Uncle Vampire, Cynthia D. Grant
The Wind, Mary Downing Hahn
Right by My Side, David Haynes
Beardance, Will Hobbs
For the Life of Laetitia, Merle Hodge
Toning the Sweep, Angela Johnson
Winter of Fire, Sherryl Jordan
The TV Guidance Counselor, A. C. Le Mieux
The Giver, Lois Lowry
Shadow Boxer, Chris Lynch
Baby, Patricia MacLachlan
Who Is Eddie Leonard? Harry Mazer
Out of Control, Norma Fox Mazer
Deerskin, Robin McKinley
Shelter, Monte Merrick
White Lilacs, Carolyn Meyer
Shizuko's Daughter, Kyoko Mori
The Magic Circle, Donna Jo Napoli
Harris and Me: A Summer, Gary Paulsen
Nightjohn, Gary Paulsen
Freak the Mighty, Rodman Philbrick
Revolutions of the Heart, Marsha Qualey
The Crocodile Bird, Ruth Rendell
Detour for Emmy, Marilyn Reynolds
In My Father's House, Ann Rinaldi
Lady of the Forest: A Novel of Sherwood, Jennifer Roberson
Who Do You Think You Are? Hazel Rochman and Darlene Z. McCampbell
Miriam's Well, Lois Ruby
Oddballs, William Sleator
Thor, Wayne Smith
Haveli, Suzanne Fisher Staples
The Tiger Orchard, Joyce Sweeney
Fair Game, Erika Tamar
Timothy of the Cay, Theodore Taylor
Grab Hands and Run, Frances Temple
Walker of Time, Helen Hughes Vick
Peter, Kate Walker
Montana 1948, Larry Watson
Striking Out, Will Weaver
Lombardo's Law, Ellen Wittlinger
Make Lemonade, Virginia Euwer Wolff

Top 100 Daily Newspapers in the U.S.

Source: *1994 Editor & Publisher International Yearbook*
(circulation as of Sept. 30, 1993; m=morning, e=evening)

In 1993, the trends that began in the newspaper industry during the mid-1970s continued. The discontinuation or merging of 19 daily newspapers, offset by the addition of 5 new dailies, brought the total number of daily newspapers published in the U.S. as of Feb. 1, 1994, to 1,556, a net loss of 14 when compared with the same date in 1993. This net loss was an improvement over the same period in 1991-92 when 26 dailies either ceased publishing, merged with other competing papers, or switched to weekly distribution. When comparing the average daily circulation for the 6-month period ending Sept. 30, 1993, with the average for the same period in 1992, circulation dropped 352,905, from 60,164,499 to 59,811,594. The trend toward morning distribution also continued, as 31 evening dailies switched to morning distribution. The total number of morning papers rose to 623 over 1992's count of 596, while the number of evening papers dropped from 996 to 954. Continuing another trend, 8 daily newspapers added a Sunday edition during this time period; however, with the additional loss of other Sunday editions by daily newspapers that closed, the number of Sunday editions decreased to 884 from 891. Despite the net loss of Sunday editions, Sunday circulation increased from 62,159,971 to 62,565,574.

Newspaper		Circulation
1. *Wall Street Journal* (New York, NY)	(m)	1,818,562
2. *USA Today* (Arlington, VA)	(m)	1,494,929
3. *Times* (New York, NY)	(m)	1,141,366
4. *Times* (Los Angeles, CA)	(m)	1,089,690
5. *Post* (Washington, DC)	(m)	813,908
6. *Daily News* (New York, NY)	(m)	764,070
7. *Newsday* (Long Island/New York, NY)	(all day)	747,890
8. *Tribune* (Chicago, IL)	(m)	690,842
9. *Free Press* (Detroit, MI)	(m)	556,116
10. *Chronicle* (San Francisco, CA)	(m)	544,253
11. *Globe* (Boston, MA)	(m)	507,647
12. *Morning News* (Dallas, TX)	(m)	493,837
13. *Inquirer* (Philadelphia, PA)	(m)	486,586
14. *Star-Ledger* (Newark, NJ)	(m)	473,553
15. *Chronicle* (Houston, TX)	(all day)	413,448
16. *Star Tribune* (Minneapolis, MN)	(m)	410,754
17. *Herald* (Miami, FL)	(m)	403,555
18. *Plain Dealer* (Cleveland, OH)	(m)	395,791
19. *Post* (New York, NY)	(m)	394,431
20. *Union-Tribune* (San Diego, CA)	(all day)	383,827
21. *News* (Detroit, MI)	(e)	366,988
22. *Times* (St. Petersburg, FL)	(m)	356,909
23. *Sun-Times* (Chicago, IL)	(m)	353,793
24. *Arizona Republic* (Phoenix, AZ)	(m)	347,839
25. *Register* (Orange County, CA)	(m)	343,906
26. *Rocky Mountain News* (Denver, CO)	(m)	342,885
27. *Post-Dispatch* (St. Louis, MO)	(m)	342,340
28. *Sun* (Baltimore, MD)	(m)	338,322
29. *Oregonian* (Portland, OR)	(all day)	332,652
30. *Star* (Indianapolis, IN)	(m)	325,283
31. *Herald* (Boston, MA)	(m)	321,715
32. *News* (Buffalo, NY)	(all day)	302,490
33. *Constitution* (Atlanta, GA)	(m)	299,699
34. *Star* (Kansas City, MO)	(m)	291,299
35. *Tribune* (Tampa, FL)	(m)	285,330
36. *Post* (Denver, CO)	(m)	284,542
37. *Post* (Houston, TX)	(m)	284,220
38. *Mercury News* (San Jose, CA)	(all day)	282,488
39. *Sentinel* (Orlando, FL)	(all day)	280,994
40. *Bee* (Sacramento, CA)	(m)	269,665
41. *Dispatch* (Columbus, OH)	(m)	263,956
42. *Times-Picayune* (New Orleans, LA)	(all day)	263,657
43. *Sun-Sentinel* (Fort Lauderdale, FL)	(m)	256,136
44. *Star-Telegram* (Fort Worth, TX)	(all day)	252,008
45. *Post-Gazette* (Pittsburgh, PA)	(m)	250,204
46. *Express-News* (San Antonio, TX)	(all day)	242,623
47. *Courier-Journal* (Louisville, KY)	(m)	236,008
48. *Observer* (Charlotte, NC)	(m)	233,398
49. *Journal* (Milwaukee, WI)	(e)	232,438
50. *Courant* (Hartford, CT)	(m)	229,504
51. *Times* (Seattle, WA)	(e)	228,562
52. *World-Herald* (Omaha, NE)	(all day)	227,409
53. *Pioneer Press* (St. Paul, MN)	(m)	214,541
54. *Times-Dispatch* (Richmond, VA)	(m)	214,227
55. *Virginian-Pilot* (Norfolk, VA)	(m)	211,047
56. *Daily Oklahoman* (Oklahoma City, OK)	(m)	210,728
57. *Daily News* (Los Angeles, CA)	(m)	207,862
58. *Democrat and Chronicle* (Rochester, NY	(m)	203,160
59. *Post-Intelligencer* (Seattle, WA)	(m)	203,112
60. *Enquirer* (Cincinatti, OH)	(m)	201,415
61. *Daily News* (Philadelphia, PA)	(m)	198,163
62. *Journal* (Providence, RI)	(all day)	190,876
63. *Register* (Des Moines, IA)	(m)	187,746
64. *Commercial Appeal* (Memphis, TN)	(m)	183,185
65. *Times-Union* (Jacksonville, FL)	(m)	181,659
66. *Democrat-Gazette* (Little Rock, AR)	(m)	176,682
67. *Palm Beach Post* (West Palm Beach, FL)	(m)	176,221
68. *Sentinel* (Milwaukee, WI)	(m)	175,502
69. *American-Statesman* (Austin, TX)	(m)	173,105
70. *World* (Tulsa, OK)	(m)	171,833
71. *Daily News* (Dayton, OH)	(m)	171,699
72. *Press* (Asbury Park, NJ)	(e)	165,569
73. *Investor's Business Daily* (Los Angeles, CA)	(m)	163,580
74. *Press-Enterprise* (Riverside, CA)	(m)	157,784
75. *News* (Birmingham, AL)	(e)	157,656
76. *Beacon Journal* (Akron, OH)	(m)	157,229
77. *Record* (Hackensack, NJ)	(m)	155,849
78. *Blade* (Toledo, OH)	(m)	152,076
79. *Press* (Grand Rapids, MI)	(e)	149,452
80. *Bee* (Fresno, CA)	(m)	148,955
81. *News & Observer* (Raleigh, NC)	(m)	145,989
82. *Journal* (Atlanta, GA)	(e)	142,635
83. *Tennessean* (Nashville, TN)	(m)	141,793
84. *Review-Journal* (Las Vegas, NV)	(m)	138,302
85. *Morning Call* (Allentown, PA)	(m)	137,735
86. *The State* (Columbia, SC)	(m)	134,945
87. *Morning News Tribune* (Tacoma, WA)	(m)	128,051
88. *Examiner* (San Francisco, CA)	(e)	124,947
89. *News-Sentinel* (Knoxville, TN)	(m)	123,904
90. *News Journal* (Wilmington, DE)	(all day)	123,609
91. *Herald-Leader* (Lexington, KY)	(m)	123,373
92. *Press-Telegram* (Long Beach, CA)	(m)	123,076
93. *Spokesman-Review* (Spokane, WA)	(m)	122,692
94. *Herald-Tribune* (Sarasota, FL)	(m)	122,606
95. *Tribune* (Salt Lake City, UT)	(m)	121,373
96. *Daily Herald* (Chicago, IL)	(m)	121,091
97. *Journal* (Albuquerque, NM)	(m)	117,086
98. *Eagle* (Wichita, KS)	(m)	115,323
99. *Times & World-News* (Roanoke, VA)	(m)	114,486
100. *Telegram & Gazette* (Worcester, MA)	(m)	111,114

100 Best-Selling U.S. Magazines

Source: Audit Bureau of Circulations, Schaumburg, IL

General magazines, exclusive of groups and comics; also exclusive of magazines that failed to file reports to ABC by press time. Based on total average paid circulation during the 6 months prior to Dec. 31, 1993.

	Magazine	Circulation
1.	Reader's Digest	16,261,968
2.	TV Guide	14,122,915
3.	The Conde Nast Select	11,039,917
4.	National Geographic	9,390,787
5.	Better Homes & Gardens	7,600,960
6.	Good Housekeeping	5,162,597
7.	Ladies' Home Journal	5,153,565
8.	Family Circle	5,114,030
9.	Woman's Day	4,858,625
10.	McCall's	4,605,441
11.	Time	4,103,772
12.	People	3,446,569
13.	National Enquirer	3,403,330
14.	Playboy	3,402,617
15.	AAA World	3,400,807
16.	Sports Ilustrated	3,356,729
17.	Redbook	3,345,451
18.	Prevention	3,220,763
19.	Newsweek	3,156,192
20.	American Legion	3,004,913
21.	Star	2,957,915
22.	Cosmopolitan	2,627,491
23.	Southern Living	2,368,678
24.	Glamour	2,304,769
25.	U.S. News & World Report	2,281,369
26.	Smithsonian	2,212,418
27.	Motorland	2,130,374
28.	Money	2,100,039
29.	VFW	2,054,232
30.	Field & Stream	2,007,901
31.	Country Living	1,977,214
32.	Seventeen	1,940,061
33.	Popular Science	1,815,819
34.	Parents	1,776,470
35.	American Rifleman	1,733,679
36.	YM	1,701,615
37.	Popular Mechanics	1,656,951
38.	Life	1,625,096
39.	American Hunter	1,534,423
40.	Outdoor Life	1,502,676
41.	Golf Digest	1,461,556
42.	Sunset	1,441,506
43.	Soap Opera Digest	1,437,758
44.	Elks	1,346,030
45.	Self	1,314,315
46.	New Woman	1,314,294
47.	Bon Appetit	1,294,945
48.	First for Women	1,269,735
49.	Boys' Life	1,265,024
50.	Consumer's Digest	1,254,468
51.	True Story Plus	1,253,929
52.	Vogue	1,250,008
53.	Rolling Stone	1,236,525
54.	Golf	1,221,554
55.	Mademoiselle	1,218,985
56.	Woman's World	1,216,925
57.	Penthouse	1,201,692
58.	Sesame Street	1,187,862
59.	Teen	1,170,842
60.	Vanity Fair	1,157,725
61.	Cooking Light	1,119,811
62.	Us	1,110,056
63.	Kiplinger's	1,100,379
64.	Entertainment Weekly	1,066,141
65.	Country Home	1,061,226
66.	Car and Driver	1,055,403
67.	Home	1,043,964
68.	Family Handyman	1,040,372
69.	PC Magazine	1,039,720
70.	Weight Watchers	1,035,322
71.	Scouting	1,031,750
72.	Discover	1,031,496
73.	Home Mechanix	1,025,071
74.	Country America	1,021,777
75.	Mature Outlook	1,021,116
76.	Globe	1,011,117
77.	Travel & Leisure	1,010,939
78.	House Beautiful	1,009,446
79.	Architectural Digest	1,000,592
80.	Health	961,113
81.	Essence	954,351
82.	Motor Trend	932,881
83.	Endless Vacation	929,356
84.	Elle	924,429
85.	Men's Health	918,648
86.	PC World	915,326
87.	Victoria	913,691
88.	Gourmet	906,299
89.	Business Week, NA	883,718
90.	PC/Computing	875,768
91.	Conde Nast Traveler	866,557
92.	Nation's Business	861,402
93.	Midwest Living	825,412
94.	True Story	825,060
95.	American Health	820,087
96.	Tennis	814,490
97.	The New Yorker	808,545
98.	Workbench	807,810
99.	Parenting	805,512
100.	Working Woman	805,157

Some Notable U.S. Dance Companies

Source: Dance/USA, July 1994

African-American Dance Ensemble, Durham, NC
Alvin Ailey American Dance Theater, New York, NY
Aman Folk Ensemble, Los Angeles, CA
American Ballet Theatre, New York, NY
American Repertory Ballet Company, Princeton, NJ
Atlanta Ballet, GA
Avaz International Dance Theatre, Los Angeles, CA
Ballet Arizona, Phoenix, AZ
Ballet Austin, Austin, TX
Ballet Chicago, IL
Ballet Concierto de Puerto Rico, Santurce, PR
Ballet Florida, West Palm Beach, FL
Ballet Hispanico of New York, New York, NY
BalletMet, Columbus, OH
Ballet Oklahoma, Oklahoma City, OK
Ballet Omaha, NE
Ballet West, Salt Lake City, UT
Karen Bamonte Dance Works/Amphora, Philadelphia, PA
Tandy Beal and Company, Santa Cruz, CA
Maria Benitez Teatro Flamenco, Santa Fe, NM
Boston Ballet, Boston, MA
Trisha Brown Company, New York, NY
Donald Byrd/The Group, New York, NY
Caribbean Dance Company, St. Croix, VI
Chen & Dancers, New York, NY
Lucinda Childs Dance Company, New York, NY
Cincinnati Ballet, Cincinnati, OH
Cleveland/San Jose Ballet, Cleveland, OH
Colorado Ballet, Denver, CO
Contemporary Dance/Fort Worth, Ft. Worth TX
Contraband, San Francisco, CA
Cunningham Dance Foundation, New York, NY
Dallas Black Dance Theatre, Dallas, TX
Dance Alloy, Pittsburgh, PA
Dance Brigade, Oakland CA
Dance Exchange, Washington, DC
Dance Theatre of Harlem, New York, NY
DanceBrazil, New York, NY
Danceteller, Philadelphia, PA
Della Davidson Dance Company, San Francisco, CA
Dayton Ballet Association, Dayton, OH
Dayton Contemporary Dance Company, Dayton, OH
Laura Dean Musicians and Dancers, New York, NY
Douglas Dunn & Dancers, New York, NY
Eiko & Koma, New York, NY
Jan Erkert & Dancers, Chicago, IL
Eugene Ballet Company, Eugene, OR
Garth Fagan's Dance, Rochester, NY
Feld Ballet, New York, NY
Fort Worth Ballet, Fort Worth, TX
Joe Goode Performance Group, San Francisco, CA
David Gordon/Pick Up Co., New York, NY
Martha Graham Dance Co., New York, NY
Pat Graney Company, Seattle, WA
Hartford Ballet, Hartford, CT
Erick Hawkins Dance Co., New York, NY
Joseph Holmes Dance Theater, Chicago, IL
Houston Ballet, Houston, TX
Hubbard Street Dance, Chicago, IL
Indianapolis Ballet Theatre, Indianapolis, IN
Isaacs, McCaleb & Dancers, San Diego, CA
Jazz Tap Ensemble, Los Angeles, CA
Margaret Jenkins Dance Company, San Francisco, CA
The Joffrey Ballet, New York, NY
Bill T. Jones/Arnie Zane Company, New York, NY
Joseph Holmes Chicago Dance Theatre, Chicago, IL
Rebecca Kelly Dance Company, New York, NY
KHADRA International Folk Ballet, San Francisco, CA
Ko-Thi Dance Company, Bronx, NY
Ralph Lemon Company, New York, NY
Lewitzky Dance Company, Los Angeles, CA
Jose Limon Dance Company, New York, NY
LINES Contemporary Ballet, San Francisco, CA
Loretta Livingston & Dancers, Los Angeles, CA

Los Angeles Chamber Ballet, CA
Louisville Ballet, Louisville, KY
Lar Lubovitch Dance Company, New York, NY
Susan Marshall & Company, New York, NY
Miami City Ballet, Miami Beach, FL
Bebe Miller and Company, New York, NY
Milwaukee Ballet, Milwaukee, WI
Elisa Monte Dance Company, New York, NY
Montgomery Ballet, Montgomery, AL
Mordine & Company, Chicago, IL
Mark Morris Dance Group, New York, NY
Jennifer Muller/The Works, New York, NY
Muntu Dance Theater, Chicago, IL
Nai-Ni Chen, Fort Lee, NJ
Nashville Ballet, Nashville, TN
Nevada Dance Theatre, Las Vegas, NV
New York City Ballet, New York, NY
Rosalind Newman and Dancers, New York, NY
Nikolais/Louis Foundation for Dance, New York, NY
North Carolina Dance Theatre, Winston-Salem, NC
Oakland Ballet, Oakland, CA
ODC/San Francisco, San Francisco, CA
Ohio Ballet, Akron, OH
Oregon Ballet Theatre, Portland, OR
Pacific Northwest Ballet, Seattle, WA
The Parsons Dance Company, New York, NY
Pennsylvania Ballet, Philadelphia, PA
Pepatián, Bronx, NY
Stephen Petronio Dance Company, New York, NY
Philadanco, Philadelphia, PA
Pilobolus Dance Theater, Washington, CT
Stuart Pimsler Dance & Theater, Columbus, OH
Pittsburgh Ballet Theatre, Pittsburgh, PA
Pittsburgh Dance Alloy, Pittsburgh, PA
Repertory Dance Theatre, Salt Lake City, UT
Rhythm in Shoes, Spring Valley, OH
Richmond Ballet, Richmond, VA
Ririe-Woodbury Dance Company, Salt Lake City, UT
Kim Robards DANCE!, Denver, CO
Cleo Parker Robinson Dance Theater, Denver, CO
Nicholas Rodriguez and DanceCompass, Montclair, NJ
David Roussave/Reality, New York, NY
Betty Salamun's DANCECIRCUS, Milwaukee, WI
San Francisco Ballet, San Francisco, CA
Carlota Santana Spanish Dance Arts Co., New York, NY
Sarasota Ballet, FL
James Sewell Dance, Minneapolis, MN
Solomons Company/Dance, New York, NY
Southern Ballet Theater, Winter Park, FL
State Ballet of Missouri, Kansas City, MO
Elizabeth Streb Ringside, New York, NY
Paul Taylor Dance Company, New York, NY
Joyce Trisler Danscompany, New York, NY
Tulsa Ballet Theatre, Tulsa, OK
Urban Bush Women, New York, NY
Dan Wagoner and Dancers, New York, NY
Washington Ballet, Washington, DC
Lula Washington's L.A. Contemporary Dance Theatre, Los Angeles, CA
June Watanabe in Company, San Rafael, CA
Nina Wiener Dance Company, New York, NY
Zenon Dance Company, Minneapolis, MN
Zivili Kolo Ensemble, Granville, OH

Some Notable Nonprofit Professional Theaters in the U.S

Source: Theatre Communications Group, Inc., July, 1994

Theater	City	State
Actors Theatre of Louisville	Louisville	KY
Alabama Shakespeare Festival	Montgomery	AL
Alley Theater	Houston	TX
Alliance Theatre Company	Atlanta	GA
American Conservatory Theater	San Francisco	CA
American Repertory Theatre	Cambridge	MA
Arena Stage	Washington	DC
Asolo Center for the Performing Arts	Sarasota	FL
Children's Theatre Company, The	Minneapolis	MN
Cincinnati Playhouse in the Park	Cincinnati	OH
Cleveland Play House, The	Cleveland	OH
Denver Center Theatre Company	Denver	CO
Ford's Theatre	Washington	DC
Goodman Theatre	Chicago	IL
Guthrie Theater, The	Minneapolis	MN
Huntington Theatre Company	Boston	MA
La Jolla Playhouse	La Jolla	CA
Long Wharf Theatre	New Haven	CT
Manhattan Theatre Club	New York	NY
Mark Taper Forum	Los Angeles	CA
McCarter Theatre Center for the Performing Arts	Princeton	NJ
Milwaukee Repertory Theater	Milwaukee	WI
New York Shakespeare Festival	New York	NY
Old Globe Theatre	San Diego	CA
Oregon Shakespeare Festival	Ashland	OR
Seattle Repertory Theatre	Seattle	WA
Shakespeare Theatre, The	Washington	DC
South Coast Repertory	Costa Mesa	CA
Theatreworks/USA	New York	NY
Walnut Street Theatre Company, The	Philadelphia	PA

Symphony Orchestras of the U.S.

Source: American Symphony Orchestra League, 777 14th St. NW, Washington, DC 20005

(All orchestras listed had budgets in excess of $1.05 million in fiscal 1993.)

Symphony Orchestra[1]	Music Director[2]
Alabama (Birmingham)	Paul Polivnick
Atlanta (GA)	Yoel Levi
Austin (TX)	Sung Kwak
Baltimore (MD)	David Zinman
Boston (MA)	Seiji Ozawa
Brooklyn Philharmonic (NY)	Dennis Russell Davies
Buffalo Philharmonic (NY)	Maximiano Valdez
Cedar Rapids (IA)	Christian Tiemeyer
Charleston (SC)	David Stahl
Charlotte (NC)	Leo B. Driehuys
Chattanooga, & Opera Assn. (TN)	Robert Bernhardt
Chicago (IL)	Daniel Barenboim
Cincinnati (OH)	Jesus Lopez-Cobos
Cleveland (OH)	Christoph von Dohnanyi
Colorado (Denver)	David T. Abosch
Colorado Springs (CO)	Christopher P. Wilkins
Columbus (OH)	Alessandro Siciliani
Dallas (TX)	Andrew Litton
Dayton Philharmonic (OH)	Isaiah Jackson
Delaware (Wilmington)	Stephen Gunzenhauser
Detroit (MI)	Neeme Jarvi
The Florida Orchestra (Tampa)	Jahja Ling
Florida Philharmonic (Fort Lauderdale)	James Judd
Florida Symphonic Pops (Boca Raton)	Derek Stannard
Fort Wayne Philharmonic (IN)	Edward Chivzel
Fort Worth (TX)	John Giordano
Grand Rapids (MI)	Catherine Comet
Grant Park (Chicago, IL)	Catherine M. Cahill
Hartford (CT)	Michael Lankester
Honolulu (HI)	Donald Johanos
Houston (TX)	Christoph Eschenbach
Hudson Valley Philharmonic (Poughkeepsie, NY)	Randall Craig Fleischer
Indianapolis (IN)	Raymond Leppard
Jacksonville (FL)	Roger Nierenberg
Kansas City (MO)	William McGlaughlin
Knoxville (TN)	Kirk Trevor
Long Beach (CA)	JoAnn Falletta
Long Island Philharmonic (NY)	Marin Alsop

(continued)

Symphony Orchestra[1]	Music Director[2]
Los Angeles Chamber Or. (CA)	Christof Perick
Los Angeles Philharmonic (CA)	Esa-Pekka Salonen
The Louisville Orchestra (KY)	Lawrence Leighton Smith
Memphis (TN)	Alan Balter
Milwaukee (WI)	Zdenek Macal
The Minnesota Orchestra (Minneapolis)	Edo de Waart
Mississippi (Jackson)	Colman Pearce
Naples Philharmonic (FL)	Timothy W. Russell
The Nashville Symphony (TN)	Kenneth S. Schermerhorn
National (Washington, DC)	Mstislav Rostropovich
New Haven (CT)	Michael Palmer
New Jersey (Newark)	Zdenek Macal
New Mexico (Albuquerque)	Neal H. Stulberg
New World Symphony (Miami Beach, FL)	Michael Tilson Thomas
New York Chamber Sym. of the 92nd St. Y (NYC)	Gerard Schwarz
New York Philharmonic (NYC)	Kurt Masur
North Carolina (Raleigh)	Gerhardt Zimmermann
Ohio Chamber Orchestra (Cleveland)	Vacant
Oklahoma City Philharmonic (OK)	Joel A. Levine
Omaha (NE)	Bruce B. Hangen
Oregon (Portland)	James DePreist
Pacific Symphony (Irvine, CA)	Carl St. Clair
The Philadelphia Orchestra (PA)	Wolfgang Sawallisch
Phoenix (AZ)	James L. Sedares
Pittsburgh (PA)	Lorin Maazel
Portland (ME)	Toshiyuki Shimada
Puerto Rico (Santurce)	Roselin Pabon
Rhode Island Philharmonic Or. (Providence)	Zuohuang Chen
The Richmond Symphony (VA)	George Manahan
Rochester Philharmonic Or. (NY)	Mark Elder
Sacramento (CA)	Alasdair P. Neale
St. Louis (MO)	Leonard Slatkin
St. Paul Chamber Or. (MN)	Hugh Wolff
San Antonio (TX)	Christopher P. Wilkins
San Diego (CA)	Yoav Talmi
San Francisco (CA)	Herbert Blomstedt
San Jose (CA)	Leonid Grin
Savannah (GA)	Philip B. Greenberg
Seattle (WA)	Gerard Schwarz
Shreveport (LA)	Peter Leonard
Spokane (WA)	Vakhtang Jordania
Springfield (MA)	Raymond C. Harvey
Syracuse (NY)	Kazuyoshi Akiyama
Toldeo (OH)	Andrew Massey
Tucson (AZ)	Robert E. Bernhardt
Tulsa Philharmonic Or. (OK)	Bernard Rubenstein
Utah (Salt Lake City)	Joseph Silverstein
The Virginia Symphony (Norfolk)	JoAnn Falletta
West Virginia (Charleston)	Thomas B. Conlin
Wichita (KS)	Zuohuang Chen
Winston-Salem Piedmont Triad Symphony (NC)	Peter J. Perret

(1) Orchestra name=place name + Symphony Orchestra, unless otherwise noted; (2) General title; listed is highest-ranking member of conducting personnel.

U.S. Opera Companies With Budgets of $500,000 or More

Source: OPERA America, July 1994

(Companies listed alphabetically by state.)

Anchorage Opera; Peter Brown, gen. dir.
Arizona Opera Co. (Tucson); Glynn Ross, gen. dir.
Opera Theatre at Wildwood (AZ); Ann Chotard, art. dir.
Fullerton Civic Light Opera (CA); Griff Duncan, gen. mgr.
Long Beach Opera (CA); Michael Milenski, gen. dir.
Long Beach Civic Light Opera (CA); Pegge Logefeil, mng. dir.
L.A. Music Center Opera Assn.; Peter Hemmings, gen. dir.
Opera Pacific (Costa Mesa, CA); David DiChiera, gen. dir.
Sacramento Opera Assn. (CA); Marianne H. Oaks, gen. dir.
San Diego Civic Light Opera; C. E. Franks, exec. dir.
San Diego Opera Assn.; Ian Campbell, gen. dir.
San Francisco Opera; Lotfi Mansouri, gen. dir.
San Francisco Opera Center (inc. Western Opera Theater)
Opera San José (CA); Irene Dalis, art. dir.
San José Civic Light Opera (CA); Dianna Shuster, dir.
Central City Opera (Denver); Daniel Rule, gen. mgr.
Opera Colorado (Denver); Nathaniel Merrill, art. dir.
Connecticut Grand Opera & Stamford State Opera, Laurence Gilgore, art. dir.
Connecticut Opera (Hartford); George Osborne, gen. dir.
Goodspeed Opera House (E. Haddam, CT); Michael Price, exec. dir.
OperaDelaware (Wilmington); Leland Kimball, gen. dir.
Washington Opera (DC); Martin Feinstein, gen. dir.
Florida Grand Opera; Robert Heuer, gen. mgr.
Orlando Opera Co. (FL); Robert Swedberg, gen. dir.
Palm Beach Opera; Herbert P. Benn, gen. dir.
Sarasota Opera Assn. (FL); Deane Allyn, exec. dir.
The Atlanta Opera (GA); Alfred Kennedy, exec. dir.
Augusta Opera (GA); Edward Bradberry, gen. dir.
Hawaii Opera Theatre; J. Mario Ramos, gen. dir.
Chicago Opera Theater; Alan Stone, art. dir.
Lyric Opera of Chicago; Ardis Krainik, gen. dir.
Indianapolis Opera; Nando Scheller, gen. dir.
Des Moines Metro Opera (Indianola); Robert Larsen, art. dir.
Kentucky Opera Assn. (Louisville); Thomson Smillie, gen. dir.
New Orleans Opera Assn.; Arthur Cosenza, gen. dir.
Baltimore Opera Co.; Michael Harrison, gen. dir.
Opera Company of Boston; Sarah Caldwell, art. dir.
Boston Opera Theatre; Robert Canon, exec. dir.
Boston Lyric Opera of Chicago; Janice Mancini Del Sesto, mng. dir.
Michigan Opera Theatre (Detroit); David DiChiera, gen. dir.
Opera Grand Rapids (MI); Robert Lyall, gen. dir.
Minnesota Opera Co. (St. Paul); Kevin Smith, gen. dir.
Lyric Opera of Kansas City (MO); Russell Patterson, gen. dir. & art. dir.
Opera Theatre of St. Louis (MO); Charles MacKay, gen. dir.
Opera/Omaha (NE); Mary Robert, gen. dir.
Nevada Opera (Reno); Ted Puffer, art dir.
Opera Festival of NJ (Princeton Junction); Deborah S. Sandler, gen. dir.
New Jersey State Opera (Newark); Alfredo Silipigni, art. dir.
Albuquerque Civic Light Opera; Linda E. McVey, exec. dir.
Santa Fe Opera (NM); John Crosby, gen. dir.
Tri-Cities Opera (Binghamton, NY); Marilyn Altman and Marilyn Cotter, co-exec. dir.
St. Ann Center for Restoration and the Arts (Brooklyn, NY); Susan Feldman, art. dir.
Greater Buffalo Opera (NY); Judith Wolf, exec. dir.
Chautauqua Opera (NY); Linda Jackson, gen. dir.
Glimmerglass Opera (Cooperstown, NY); Paul Kellogg, gen. mgr.
Lake George Opera Festival (NY); Susan T. Danis, exec. dir.
Syracuse Opera; Julie Richard, mng. dir.
Metropolitan Opera Assn. (NYC); Joseph Volpe, gen. mgr.
Music-Theatre Group (NY & Stockbridge, MA); Lyn Austin, prod. dir.
New York City Opera; Christopher Keene, gen. dir.
New York City Opera Natl. Co.; Nancy Kelly, adm. dir.
Opera Orchestra of NY (NYC); Eve Queler, art dir.
Opera Carolina (Charlotte, NC); James Wright, gen. dir.
Cincinnati Opera Assn.; James deBlasis, art. dir.
Cleveland Opera; David Bamberger, gen. dir.
Lyric Opera Cleveland (OH); Michael McConnell, exec. dir.
Opera/Columbus (OH); William F. Russell, gen. dir.
Dayton Opera Assn. (OH); Jane Nelson, gen. dir.
Tulsa Opera (OK); Myrna S. Ruffner, gen. mgr.
Portland Opera Assn. (OR); Robert Bailey, exec. dir.
American Music Theater Festival (Phila.); Marjorie Samoff, prod. dir.
Opera Company of Philadelphia; Robert B. Driver, gen. dir.
Pittsburgh Civic Light Opera; Charles Gray, exec. dir.
Pittsburgh Opera; Tito Capobianco, gen. dir.
Knoxville Opera (TN); Robert Lyall, gen. dir.
Nashville Opera (TN); Kyle Ridout, gen. dir.
Opera Memphis (TN); Michael Ching, gen./art. dir
Austin Lyric Opera (TX); Walter Ducloux, art. dir.
Dallas Opera; Plato Karayanis, gen. dir.
Fort Worth Opera; William Walker, gen. dir.
Houston Grand Opera Assn.; David Gockley, gen. dir.
Texas Opera Theater (Houston); James Ireland, gen. mgr.
Utah Opera (Salt Lake City); Anne Ewers, gen. dir.
Virginia Opera (Norfolk); Peter Mark, gen. dir.
Wolf Trap Opera (Vienna, VA); Peter Russell, gen. dir.
Seattle Opera Assn.; Speight Jenkins, gen. dir.
Madison Opera (WI); Ann Stanke, exec. dir.
Florentine Opera of Milwaukee; Dennis Hanthorn, gen. mgr.
Skylight Opera Theatre (Milwaukee); Chas Rader-Shieber, art. dir.

Recordings and Music Videos

Source: Recording Industry Assn. of America, *Listening for Tomorrow,* 1993

The sound recording market became a more than $10 billion industry in 1993. Overall unit shipments (net after returns) in 1993 increased 6.7% over the previous year. The CD format increased its popularity. In 1993, slightly more than 61% of all prerecorded music sold was in CD format, 36% was in cassette format, LP format decreased to less than 1%, and music video rose to more than 2% of the market. With the Electronic Industries Association estimating that CD players were in 43% of all American households at the end of 1993, it is likely that sales for CD formats will continue to rise.

In 1993, Rock remained the top musical genre sold, with 32.6% of all musical recordings sold falling into this category. Country music continued its upward trend in popularity, with a 17.5% share of the market. Other popular musical styles were: Pop (11.7%), Urban Contemporary (9.9%), Rap (7.8%), Classical (4.0%), Jazz (3.3%), and Gospel (3.1%).

In 1993, Arista's *The Bodyguard* soundtrack was the biggest success of the year. By the end of 1993, sales had reached 10 million. Another noteworthy trend was the popularity of acoustic albums, spurred in part by the popular MTV "Unplugged" concert series. Several acts, including 10,000 Maniacs, Arrested Development, Eric Clapton, Mariah Carey, and Rod Stewart, added recordings of their acoustic performances from this program to 1993's gold and platinum certifications. Audiences were very open to new artists in 1993. Many acts, such as Blind Melon, The Cranberries, The Proclaimers, Radiohead, and The Sundays took home their first awards. Reggae artists received more attention as well. Inner Circle, Shabba Ranks, and Snow received their first certifications. Toni Braxton, with her double platinum self-titled album, was the best-selling new artist. Also noteworthy, Reba McEntire became the first female country artist to have five albums go multi-plantinum.

Gold and platinum full-length album tallies surpassed the previous year's, with 239 gold albums versus 213 in 1992; 149 platinum albums, up from 144 in 1992. In addition to *The Bodyguard,* other big multi-plantinum albums included Kenny G's *Breathless* and Janet Jackson's *janet.* With sales of 5 million, Kenny G and Janet Jackson were 1993's best-selling male and female solo artists. Michael Jackson reached the 22 million mark with his 1982 release *Thriller.* Sales for both Fleetwood Mac's *Rumours* and the Eagles' *Greatest Hits 1971-1975* reached 14 millon in 1993.

Multi-Platinum and Platinum Awards, 1993

To achieve platinum status an album must reach a minimum sale of 1 million units in LP's, tapes, and CD's with a (manufacturer's dollar volume of at least $2 million based on one-third of the suggested retail list price for each record, tape, or CD sold.) To achieve multi-platinum status an album must reach a minimum sale of at least 2 million units in LP's, tapes, and CD's, with a manufacturer's dollar volume of at least $4 million based on one-third of the list price. Singles must sell 1 million units to achieve a platinum award and must sell at least 2 million to achieve a multi-platinum award. EP singles count as two units. Music videos (long form) must sell 100,000 units to qualify for a platinum award and must sell more than 200,000 units to qualify for a multi-platinum award. Video singles, which must have a maximum running time of 15 minutes and no more than two songs per title, must sell 50,000 units to qualify for a platinum award and must sell at least 100,000 units to qualify for a multi-platinum award. Awards in 1993 were for albums and singles released in 1993 and for music videos released at any time. No multi-platinum singles were awarded for singles released in 1993. No multi-platinum music video singles were awarded in 1993.

Albums, Multi-Platinum

(Number in parentheses = millions sold)

Aerosmith, *Get A Grip* (2)
Barney, *Barney's Favorites, Volume I* (2)
Toni Braxton, *Toni Braxton* (2)
Brooks & Dunn, *Hard Workin' Man* (2)
Garth Brooks, *In Pieces* (3)
Mariah Carey, *Music Box* (4)
Janet Jackson, *janet* (5)
Billy Joel, *River of Dreams* (3)
Reba McEntire, *Greatest Hits, Volume II* (2)
Meat Loaf, *Bat Out of Hell II: Back Into Hell* (3)
Soundtrack, *Sleepless in Seattle* (2)
Rod Stewart, *Unplugged . . . And Seated* (2)
Sting, *Ten Summoner's Tales* (2)
U2, *Zooropa* (2)
Van Halen, *Right Here, Right Now* (2)
Various, *Common Threads: Songs of the Eagles* (2)

Albums, Platinum

Boys II Men, *Christmas Interpretations*
Phil Collins, *Both Sides*
The Cranberries, *Everybody Else Is Doing It, So Why Can't We*
Cypress Hill, *Cypress Hill*
Billy Ray Cyrus, *It Won't Bet the Last*
Def Leppard, *Retro Active*
Depeche Mode, *Songs of Faith and Devotion*
Duran Duran, *Duran Duran 2*
H-Town, *Fever for Da Flavor*
Wynonna Judd, *Tell Me Why*
Lenny Kravitz, *Are You Gonna Go My Way*
Tracy Lawrence, *Alibis*
John Mellencamp, *Human Wheels*
Naughty By Nature, *19NaughtyIII*
Nirvana, *In Utero*
Onyx, *Bacdafucup*
Dolly Parton, *Slow Dancing With the Moon*
Smashing Pumpkins, *Siamese Dream*
Snow, *12 Inches of Snow*
Soundtrack, *Last Action Hero*
George Strait, *Easy Come, Easy Go*
Barbra Streisand, *Back to Broadway*
Tony! Toni! Tone! *Sons of Soul*
UB-40, *Promises and Lies*
Luther Vandross, *Never Let Me Go*
Dwight Yoakam, *This Time*

Singles, Platinum

95 South, "Whoot, There It Is"
Ace of Base, "All That She Wants"
Mariah Carey, "Dreamlover"
Mariah Carey, "Hero"
D.R.S., "Gangsta Lean"
Dr. Dre, "Nuthin' but a 'G' Thang"
H-Town, "Knockin' the Boots"
Ice Cube, "Check Yo Self"
Janet Jackson, "Again"
Janet Jackson, "That's the Way Love Goes"
Meat Loaf, "I'd Do Anything for Love (But I Won't Do That)"
Naughty By Nature, "Hip Hop Hooray"
Onyx, "Slam"
S.W.V., "Weak"
Silk, "Freak Me"
Snow, "Informer"
Tag Team, "Whoomp! (There It Is)"
UB-40, "Can't Help Falling in Love"
Xscape, "Just Kickin' It"

Music Videos, Multi-Platinum

(Number in parenthesis = units sold)

Garth Brooks, *This Is Garth Brooks* (500,000)
Billy Ray Cyrus, *Live on Tour* (200,000)
Jan Hammer, *Beyond the Mind's Eye* (200,000)
Mary-Kate and Ashley Olsen, *Our First Video* (200,000)
James Reynold, *The Mind's Eye: Computer Animation Odyssey* (200,000)
Ray Stevens, *Comedy Video Classics* (300,000)

Top 20 Cable Video Networks

Source: *Cable Television Developments,* Natl. Cable Television Assn., April 1994; ranked by number of subscribers

Rank	Network[1]	Systems	Subscribers (millions)
1	**ESPN** (1979)	26,500[2]	63.1
2	**CNN** (1980)	11,608	62.6
3	**The Discovery Channel** (1985)	10,036	62.0
4	**USA** Network (1980)	12,000[2]	62.0
5	**TNN (The Nashville Network)** (1983)	13,540	61.7
6	**The Family Channel** (1977)	10,264	60.2
7	**TBS** (1976)	14,954[2]	60.0
8	**C-Span** (1979)	4,599	59.8
9	**Arts & Entertainment Network** (1984)	9,300	59.0
10	**Nickelodeon** (1979)	9,171	59.0
	Nick at Nite (1985)	4,381	
11	**TNT (Turner Network Television)** (1988)	8,731	59.0
12	**MTV: Music Television** (1981)	8,324	58.3
13	**LIFETIME Television** (1984)	5,800	57.0
14	**The Weather Channel** (1982)	5,550	55.4
15	**Headline News** (1982)	6,002	54.5
16	**CNBC** (1989)	4,000[2]	52.0
17	**VH-1 (Video Hits One)** (1985)	5,304	50.2
18	**QVC Network** (1986)	4,794	47.5
19	**AMC (American Movie Classics)** (1984)	NA	47.0
20	**BET (Black Entertainment Television)** (1980)	2,622	39.6

NA = Not available. (1) Date in parentheses is year service began. (2) Includes noncable affiliates.

U.S. Households With Cable Television, 1976-93

Source: *Cable Television Developments,* Natl. Cable Television Assn., Apr. 1994; figures as of Nov. 1993

Year	Basic cable subscribers	Percentage of households with TVs	Year	Basic cable subscribers	Percentage of households with TVs
1976	10,787,970	15.1	1985	39,872,520	46.2
1977	12,168,450	16.6	1986	42,237,140	48.1
1978	13,391,910	17.9	1987	44,970,880	50.5
1979	14,814,380	19.4	1988	48,636,520	53.8
1980	17,671,490	22.6	1989	52,564,470	57.1
1981	23,219,200	28.3	1990	54,871,330	59.0
1982	29,340,570	35.0	1991	55,786,390	60.6
1983	34,113,790	40.5	1992	57,211,600	61.5
1984	37,290,870	43.7	1993	58,834,440	62.5

Number of Cable TV Systems: 1971-94

Source: *Cable Television Developments,* Natl. Cable Television Assn., Apr. 1994; figures as of Jan. 1994

Year	Systems	Year	Systems	Year	Systems	Year	Systems
1971	2,639	1977	3,832	1983	5,600	1989	9,050
1972	2,841	1978	3,875	1984	6,200	1990	9,575
1973	2,991	1979	4,150	1985	6,600	1991	10,704
1974	3,158	1980	4,225	1986	7,500	1992	11,073
1975	3,506	1981	4,375	1987	7,900	1993	11,108
1976	3,681	1982	4,825	1988	8,500	1994	11,217

TV Viewing Shares: Broadcast Years 1984/85-1992/93[1]

Source: *Cable Television Developments,* Natl. Cable Television Assn., Apr. 1994; figures as of Jan. 1994

Total Television Households	'84/'85	'85/'86	'86/'87	'87/'88	'88/'89	'89/'90	'90/'91	'91/'92	'92/'93
Broadcast Network Affiliates	66	66	64	61	58	55	53	54	53
Independent TV Stations[2]	18	18	20	20	20	20	21	20	21
Public TV Stations	3	3	4	4	3	3	3	3	4
Basic Cable Networks[2]	11	11	13	15	17	21	24	24	25
Pay Cable Services	6	5	4	7	7	6	6	6	5

All Cable Households	'84/'85	'85/'86	'86/'87	'87/'88	'88/'89	'89/'90	'90/'91	'91/'92	'92/'93
Broadcast Network Affiliates	56	56	53	52	49	46	46	47	46
Independent TV Stations[2]	17	17	17	17	16	16	17	16	17
Public TV Stations	3	3	3	3	3	3	2	3	3
Basic Cable Networks[2]	19	19	23	25	28	32	35	35	36
Pay Cable Services	11	10	10	11	11	10	9	8	8

Pay Cable Households	'84/'85	'85/'86	'86/'87	'87/'88	'88/'89	'89/'90	'90/'91	'91/'92	'92/'93
Broadcast Network Affiliates	51	51	48	48	45	43	41	43	42
Independent TV Stations[2]	17	17	16	17	16	16	16	16	16
Public TV Stations	3	3	3	3	2	2	2	2	2
Basic Cable Networks[2]	19	19	23	24	27	30	34	33	35
Pay Cable Services	18	17	17	18	18	18	17	17	16

(1) For all television viewing Monday-Sunday, 24 hours/day. Due to multiset use and rounding off of numbers, totals are more than 100. (2) For broadcast years 1984/1985-1985/1986, superstation shares are divided between independent stations and basic cable networks categories; for broadcast years 1986/1987-1992/1993, TBS has been counted in the basic cable networks category. Independent shares include those for FOX.

Average Television Viewing Time, 1994

Source: Nielsen Media Research, May 1994 (Hours:Minutes per week)

		Mon.-Fri. 10 am-4:30 pm	Mon.-Fri. 4:30 pm-7:30 pm	Mon.-Sun. 8-11 pm	Sat. 7 am-1 pm	Mon.-Fri. 11:30 pm-1 am
Total		3:58	3:20	8:01	:41	1:15
Women	18+	5:28	3:57	9:19	:35	1:30
	18-24	4:45	2:49	6:34	:26	1:17
	25-54	4:31	3:10	8:36	:31	1:29
	55+	7:37	5:58	11:52	:37	1:36
Men	18+	3:07	2:54	8:20	:35	1:28
	18-24	3:15	2:15	5:43	:34	1:24
	25-54	2:28	2:19	7:54	:34	1:29
	55+	4:37	4:41	10:49	:36	1:29
Teens	12-17	2:01	2:59	6:14	:41	:47
Children	2-5	5:22	3:01	4:25	1:09	:21
	6-11	1:41	2:58	5:95	1:10	:20

America's Favorite Prime-Time Television Programs, 1993-94

Source: Nielsen Media Research

Regularly Scheduled Network Programs (Sept. 20, 1993-Apr. 17, 1994)

Average audience percentages, or ratings, are estimates based on the percentage of TV households and persons in TV households watching a program. Audience share percentages are estimates based on the total number of televisions that are turned on in TV households.

Rank	Program	Average audience (%)	Audience Share (%)	Rank	Program	Average Audience (%)	Audience Share (%)
1.	Home Improvement	21.9	33	26.	NBC Monday Night Movies	13.6	21
2.	60 Minutes	20.8	34	27.	Homicide	13.5	22
3.	Seinfeld	19.3	29	28.	CBS Tuesday Movie	13.2	21
4.	Roseanne	19.2	29	28.	Evening Shade	13.2	21
5.	These Friends of Mine	18.7	29	30.	Phenom	13.1	20
6.	Grace Under Fire	18.0	27	31.	ABC Sunday Night Movie	12.6	20
7.	Frasier	17.5	27	31.	Family Matters	12.6	23
8.	Coach	17.4	27	33.	Sister, Sister	12.5	22
9.	Murder, She Wrote	16.9	25	33.	Unsolved Mysteries	12.5	19
10.	NFL Monday Night Football	16.8	28	35.	Mad About You	12.3	20
11.	Murphy Brown	16.4	24	36.	Blossom	12.2	19
12.	CBS Sunday Movie	16.1	25	37.	Burke's Law	12.1	20
13.	Thunder Alley	15.9	25	38.	NBC Sunday Night Movie	12.0	19
14.	20/20	14.8	26	38.	Step by Step	12.0	21
15.	Love & War	14.5	22	40.	704 Hauser	11.9	19
16.	Northern Exposure	14.4	23	40.	Christy	11.9	20
17.	Wings	14.3	22	42.	Boy Meets World	11.8	21
18.	Full House	14.2	23	42.	L.A. Law	11.8	20
18.	Primetime Live	14.2	24	42.	Someone Like Me	11.8	18
20.	Dave's World	14.0	21	45.	ABC Monday Night Movie	11.6	18
21.	Dr. Quinn, Medicine Woman	13.9	24	45.	48 Hours	11.6	20
21.	NYPD Blue	13.9	23	45.	Hangin' With Mr. Cooper	11.6	20
21.	Rescue: 911	13.9	22	48.	Walker, Texas Ranger	11.5	21
24.	Turning Point	13.8	23	49.	Law and Order	11.4	19
25.	Fresh Prince of BelAir	13.7	21	49.	Matlock	11.4	17
				49.	The Simpsons	11.4	18

Favorite Syndicated Programs, 1993-94

Source: Nielsen Media Research, Aug. 30, 1993-Apr. 17, 1994

Average audience percentages, or ratings, are estimates based on the percentage of TV households and persons in TV households watching a program.

Rank	Program	Avg. audience (%)	Rank	Program	Avg. audience (%)
1.	Wheel of Fortune	14.7	12.	Hard Copy	6.7
2.	Jeopardy	12.6	13.	Current Affair	6.6
3.	Star Trek	10.8	14.	Baywatch	6.5
4.	Oprah Winfrey	9.7	15.	Action Pack Network	6.1
5.	Entertainment Tonight	8.4	16.	Family Matters	5.9
6.	Star Trek: Deep Space Nine	8.2	17.	Cops	5.7
7.	Roseanne	7.9	18.	World Wrestling Federation	5.7
8.	National Geographic on Assignment	7.5	19.	Sally Jessy Raphael	5.2
9.	Inside Edition	7.3	20.	Designing Women	5.1
10.	Wheel of Fortune-Weekend	7.2	20.	Donahue	5.1
11.	Married With Children	6.9			

All-Time Top Television Programs

Source: Nielsen Media Research; Jan. 1961-Feb. 27, 1994

Estimates exclude unsponsored or joint network telecasts or programs under 30 minutes long. Ranked by rating (percentage of average TV audience).

Rank	Program	Telecast date	Network	Rating (%)	Avg. audience (000)
1.	M*A*S*H (last episode)	2/28/83	CBS	60.2	50,150
2.	Dallas (Who Shot J.R.?)	11/21/80	CBS	53.3	41,470
3.	Roots-Pt. 8	1/30/77	ABC	51.1	36,380
4.	Super Bowl XVI	1/24/82	CBS	49.1	40,020
5.	Super Bowl XVII	1/30/83	NBC	48.6	40,480
6.	XVII Winter Olympics - 2d Wed.	2/23/94	CBS	48.5	45,690
7.	Super Bowl XX	1/26/86	NBC	48.3	41,490
8.	Gone With the Wind-Pt. 1	11/7/76	NBC	47.7	33,960
9.	Gone With the Wind-Pt. 2	11/8/76	NBC	47.4	33,750
10.	Super Bowl XII	1/15/78	CBS	47.2	34,410
11.	Super Bowl XIII	1/21/79	NBC	47.1	35,090
12.	Bob Hope Christmas Show	1/15/70	NBC	46.6	27,260
13.	Super Bowl XVIII	1/22/84	CBS	46.4	38,800
13.	Super Bowl XIX	1/20/85	ABC	46.4	39,390
15.	Super Bowl XIV	1/20/80	CBS	46.3	35,330
16.	ABC Theater (The Day After)	11/20/83	ABC	46.0	38,550
17.	Roots-Pt. 6	1/28/77	ABC	45.9	32,680
17.	The Fugitive	8/29/67	ABC	45.9	25,700
19.	Super Bowl XXI	1/25/87	CBS	45.8	40,030
20.	Roots-Pt. 5	1/27/77	ABC	45.7	32,540
21.	Super Bowl XXVIII	1/29/94	NBC	45.5	42,860
21.	Cheers (last episode)	5/20/93	NBC	45.5	42,360
23.	Ed Sullivan	2/9/64	CBS	45.3	23,240
24.	Super Bowl XXVII	1/31/93	NBC	45.1	41,990
25.	Bob Hope Christmas Show	1/14/71	NBC	45.0	27,050
26.	Roots-Pt. 3	1/25/77	ABC	44.8	31,900
27.	Super Bowl XI	1/9/77	NBC	44.4	31,610
27.	Super Bowl XV	1/25/81	NBC	44.4	34,540
29.	Super Bowl VI	1/16/72	CBS	44.2	27,450

(continued)

Rank	Program	Telecast date	Network	Rating (%)	Avg. audience (000)
30.	XVII Winter Olympics - 2d Fri.	2/25/94	CBS	44.1	41,540
30.	Roots-Pt. 2	1/24/77	ABC	44.1	31,400
32.	Beverly Hillbillies	1/8/64	CBS	44.0	22,570
33.	Roots-Pt. 4	1/26/77	ABC	43.8	31,190
33.	Ed Sullivan	2/16/64	CBS	43.8	22,445
35.	Super Bowl XXIII	1/22/89	NBC	43.5	39,320
36.	Academy Awards	4/7/70	ABC	43.4	25,390
37.	Thorn Birds-Pt. 3	3/29/83	ABC	43.2	35,990
38.	Thorn Birds-Pt. 4	3/30/83	ABC	43.1	35,900
39.	CBS NFC Championship	1/10/82	CBS	42.9	34,960
40.	Beverly Hillbillies	1/15/64	CBS	42.8	21,960
41.	Super Bowl VII	1/14/73	NBC	42.7	27,670
42.	Thorn Birds-Pt. 2	3/28/83	ABC	42.5	35,400

Top-Rated TV Shows of Each Season, 1950-51 to 1993-94

Source: Nielsen Media Research; regular series programs, Sept.-Apr. season

Season	Program	Rating	TV Households[1] (in thousands)	Season	Program	Rating	TV Households[1] (in thousands)
1950-51	Texaco Star Theatre	61.6	10,320	1972-73	All in the Family	33.3	64,800
1951-52	Godfrey's Talent Scouts	53.8	15,300	1973-74	All in the Family	31.2	66,200
1952-53	I Love Lucy	67.3	20,400	1974-75	All in the Family	30.2	68,500
1953-54	I Love Lucy	58.8	26,000	1975-76	All in the Family	30.1	69,600
1954-55	I Love Lucy	49.3	30,700	1976-77	Happy Days	31.5	71,200
1955-56	$64,000 Question	47.5	34,900	1977-78	Laverne & Shirley	31.6	72,900
1956-57	I Love Lucy	43.7	38,900	1978-79	Laverne & Shirley	30.5	74,500
1957-58	Gunsmoke	43.1	41,920	1979-80	60 Minutes	28.2	76,300
1958-59	Gunsmoke	39.6	43,950	1980-81	Dallas	31.2	79,900
1959-60	Gunsmoke	40.3	45,750	1981-82	Dallas	28.4	81,500
1960-61	Gunsmoke	37.3	47,200	1982-83	60 Minutes	25.5	83,300
1961-62	Wagon Train	32.1	48,555	1983-84	Dallas	25.7	83,800
1962-63	Beverly Hillbillies	36.0	50,300	1984-85	Dynasty	25.0	84,900
1963-64	Beverly Hillbillies	39.1	51,600	1985-86	Bill Cosby Show	33.8	85,900
1964-65	Bonanza	36.3	52,700	1986-87	Bill Cosby Show	34.9	87,400
1965-66	Bonanza	31.8	53,850	1987-88	Bill Cosby Show	27.8	88,600
1966-67	Bonanza	29.1	55,130	1988-89	Roseanne	25.5	90,400
1967-68	Andy Griffith	27.6	56,670	1989-90	Roseanne	23.4	92,100
1968-69	Rowan & Martin Laugh-In	31.8	58,250	1990-91	Cheers	21.6	93,100
1969-70	Rowan & Martin Laugh-In	26.3	58,500	1991-92	60 Minutes	21.7	92,100
1970-71	Marcus Welby, MD	29.6	60,100	1992-93	60 Minutes	21.6	93,100
1971-72	All in the Family	34.0	62,100	1993-94	Home Improvement	21.9	94,200

(1) Data prior to 1988-89 exclude Alaska and Hawaii.

U.S. Television Set Ownership

Source: Neilsen Media Research; May1994

Total households with TV: 94.2 million homes (98% of U.S. households) own at least one TV set.

Of TV households:

99% have color televisions
38% have 2 TV sets
28% have 3 or more TV sets
79% have a VCR
63% receive basic cable
28% receive pay cable

Some Television Addresses and Phone Numbers

BROADCAST

ABC–American Broadcasting Company
77 W 66th St.
New York, NY 10023 (212) 456-7777

CBS–Columbia Broadcasting System, Inc.
51 W 52nd St.
New York, NY 10019 (212) 975-4321

NBC–National Broadcasting Company
30 Rockefellar Plaza
New York, NY 10112 (212) 644-4444

Westinghouse Broadcasting and Cable Inc.
888 7th Ave.
New York, NY 10106 (212) 307-3000

Fox Television
205 E 67th St.
New York, NY 10021 (212) 452-5555

PBS–Public Broadcasting Service
1790 Broadway
New York, NY 10019 (212) 708-3000

CABLE

A&E–Arts & Enterntainment Network
235 E 45th St.
New York, NY 10017 (212) 661-4500

AMC, BRV–American Movie Classics, Bravo
Rainbow Programming Holdings, Inc.
150 Crossways Pk. W
Woodbury, NY 11797 (516) 364-2222

BET–Black Entertainment Television
1232 31st St. NW
Washington, DC 20007 (202) 337-5260

CNBC–Consumer News and Business Channel
2200 Fletcher Ave.
Fort Lee, NJ 07024 (201) 585-2622

CNN–Cable News Network
One CNN Center, Box 105366
Atlanta, GA 30348-5366 (404) 827-1500

C-SPAN–Cable-Satellite Public Affairs Network
400 N Capitol St. NW, Suite 650
Washington, DC 20001 (202) 737-3220

DIS–The Disney Channel
3800 W Alameda Ave.
Burbank, CA 91505 (818) 569-7500

ESPN–ESPN, Inc.
ESPN Plaza
Bristol, CT 06010-9454 (203) 585-2000

MTV–Music Television
MTV Networks, Inc.
1515 Broadway
New York, NY 10036 (212) 258-8000

NICK–Nickelodeon/Nick at Nite
MTV Networks, Inc.
1515 Broadway
New York, NY 10036 (212) 258-8000

SC–SportsChannel
3 Crossways Pk. W
Woodbury, NY 11797 (516) 921-3764

TBS–Turner Broadcasting System
1050 Techwood Dr. NW
Atlanta, GA 30318 404) 855-4396

TDC–The Discovery Channel
Discovery Networks
7700 Wisconsin Ave.
Bethesda, MD 20814-3522
(301) 986-1999

USA–USA Network
USA Networks
1230 Ave. of the Americas
New York, NY 10020 (212) 408-9100

100 Leading U.S. Advertisers, 1991-1992

Source: *Advertising Age,* Sept. 29, 1993 © Crain Communications Inc. 1993

Rank '92	Rank '91	Advertiser	Ad spending 1992
1.	1.	Procter & Gamble	$2,165.6
2.	2.	Philip Morris	2,024.1
3.	3.	General Motors	1,333.6
4.	4.	Sears, Roebuck	1,204.6
5.	5.	PepsiCo	928.6
6.	9.	Ford	794.5
7.	11.	Warner-Lambert	757.5
8.	21.	Chrysler	756.6
9.	8.	McDonald's	743.6
10.	14.	Nestlé	733.4
11.	10.	Eastman Kodak	686.0
12.	6.	Grand Metropolitan	688.2
13.	16.	Unilever NV	672.8
14.	7.	Johnson & Johnson	659.6
15.	13.	Toyota	648.9
16.	15.	Time Warner	637.9
17.	17.	Kellogg	630.3
18.	12.	AT&T	623.7
19.	20.	General Mills	571.2
20.	22.	Anheuser-Busch	555.8
21.	18.	Kmart	551.1
22.	30.	J.C. Penny	537.4
23.	24.	American Home Products	531.6
24.	23.	Walt Disney	524.6
25.	25.	Sony	507.9
26.	19.	RJR Nabisco	422.2
27.	27.	Ralston Purina	411.5
28.	29.	Coca-Cola	392.0
29.	28.	May Department Stores	390.9
30.	33.	Hershey Foods	383.0
31.	38.	Nissan	370.7
32.	37.	Sara Lee	356.9
33.	32.	Honda	349.1
34.	40.	U.S. Government	331.0
35.	41.	Mars	320.4
36.	31.	Colgate-Palmolive	$315.5
37.	34.	Matsushita Electric Industrial	304.2
38.	26.	H.J. Heinz	301.1
39.	43.	American Express	294.3
40.	36.	Bristol-Myers Squibb	280.1
41.	35.	R.H. Macy & Co.	270.4
42.	39.	Circuit City Stores	261.1
43.	52.	SmithKline Beecham	257.3
44.	45.	Quaker Oats	256.2
45.	53.	General Electric	250.7
46.	56.	Hasbro	245.3
47.	46.	Dayton Hudson	230.9
48.	47.	Nike	230.8
49.	48.	Federated Department Stores	225.9
50.	58.	Wal-Mart	222.4
51.	51.	Mazda	215.4
52.	57.	Schering-Plough	214.0
53.	82.	Levi Strauss	211.9
54.	65.	Campbell Soup	209.7
55.	49.	American Brands	208.6
56.	44.	S.C. Johnson & Sons	208.0
57.	70.	Sprint	207.6
58.	55.	American Stores	205.1
59.	66.	ITT	203.5
60.	54.	Adolph Coors	195.0
61.	63.	U.S. dairy farmers	189.6
62.	68.	Helene Curtis Industries	189.5
63.	87.	Dow Chemical	186.6
64.	42.	ConAgra	185.7
65.	97.	IBM	185.5
66.	50.	Tandy	185.1
67.	73.	News Corp.	181.3
68.	81.	Goodyear Tire & Rubber	178.1
69.	96.	Ciba-Geigy	$177.6
70.	75.	Joh. A. Benckiser GmBH	172.0
71.	72.	Montgomery Ward	169.9
72.	69.	Carter Hawley Hale Stores	166.4
73.	59.	Paramount Communications	166.3
74.	60.	Gillette	164.6
75.	74.	Phillips	161.5
76.	61.	Clorox	161.4
77.	71.	MCI Communications	156.2
78.	64.	Marriott	151.8
79.	62.	Delta AirLines	147.1
80.	79.	CPC International	145.4
81.	83.	Reebok International	143.0
82.	90.	Wendy's International	142.6
83.	67.	AMR	139.4
84.	95.	Upjohn	138.0
85.	88.	UAL	136.9
86.	89.	Wm. Wrigley Jr.	134.0
87.	85.	Dillard Department Stores	133.6
88.	*	Roll International	133.1
89.	94.	Revlon Group	131.7
90.	*	Hewlett-Packard	131.2
91.	77.	Loews	128.8
92.	*	Bayer	127.4
93.	*	Mattel	125.3
94.	76.	Slim-Fast Foods	122.0
95.	80.	Bell Atlantic	117.7
96.	99.	U.S. Shoe	117.3
97.	78.	Dr. Pepper/Seven-Up	115.3
98.	*	Brown-Ferman	113.7
99.	86.	Seagram	113.1
100.	*	Nynex	112.6

*Did not rank among 100 leading advertisers in 1991.

Total U.S. Ad Spending by Category and Medium, 1992

Source: *Advertising Age,* Sept. 29, 1993 © Crain Communications Inc. 1993
(in millions)

Category	Total ad spending	Magazine	Sunday magazines	Local newspaper	Network TV	Spot TV	Syndicated TV	Cable TV	Network radio
Retail	$7,696.7	$180.3	$127.5	$4,906.6	$441.5	$1,552.8	$27.4	$64.2	$71.3
Automotive	5,913.5	1,036.6	29.7	910.7	1,578.8	1,851.0	50.0	146.8	50.9
Business, consumer svcs.	4,675.8	500.6	33.8	1,353.9	851.3	1,106.1	56.5	145.4	78.5
Food	3,511.8	461.3	51.3	29.4	1,483.2	879.3	305.4	182.1	34.4
Entertainment	3,141.0	63.3	37.3	407.3	1,035.5	1,236.0	84.6	105.8	15.1
Toiletries & cosmetics	2,427.2	719.3	27.7	7.8	1,110.3	273.5	119.3	143.1	7.0
Travel & hotels	2,240.7	332.5	51.0	1,097.1	199.1	247.6	7.7	51.6	35.9
Drugs & remedies	2,087.4	276.2	26.6	80.3	935.4	370.8	154.1	108.3	95.2
Direct response cos.	1,402.2	616.3	377.6	99.2	72.9	89.6	26.6	32.0	36.7
Candy, snacks & soft drinks	1,234.2	64.5	4.0	13.2	566.7	299.1	113.2	89.6	30.5
Apparel, footwear	1,065.8	493.1	27.7	12.1	339.7	78.8	27.2	55.3	8.9
Insurance & real estate	979.7	135.6	11.3	403.9	167.3	119.3	7.1	22.9	15.5
Sporting goods, toys	885.6	169.6	3.4	6.3	241.8	259.6	107.4	91.9	0.7
Beer & wine	850.8	63.5	5.1	12.3	365.6	203.5	27.5	53.9	7.2
Publishing & media	804.2	202.3	14.7	237.9	39.2	162.7	7.3	25.1	22.2
Computers, office equip.	732.9	347.6	3.9	50.2	125.2	21.9	6.7	21.6	1.5
Household equipment	670.1	160.9	14.8	18.1	286.6	93.2	41.1	45.7	3.3
Soaps & cleansers	601.8	71.4	5.1	3.0	298.4	108.9	54.3	49.1	6.4
Electronic entertainment	413.0	112.5	4.1	34.2	116.9	68.5	23.1	34.8	8.3
Cigarettes	382.3	224.0	26.9	6.6	0.0	0.1	0.0	0.0	0.4
Building materials	344.5	83.5	8.1	50.2	87.5	67.2	6.4	27.4	2.8
Jewelry, optical	341.4	156.1	9.1	6.9	109.6	18.7	7.1	20.6	1.3
Gasoline & lubricants	304.0	17.9	0.9	9.5	70.7	135.0	4.5	16.7	0.6
Household furnishings	260.2	124.9	11.1	42.3	37.8	27.6	6.6	4.6	0.0
Liquor	236.3	185.4	8.8	8.4	0.0	2.1	0.0	0.0	1.4
Horticulture & farming	214.8	19.4	14.0	48.4	27.0	52.2	2.7	18.4	8.0
Pets & pet foods	170.3	34.0	1.8	6.1	68.8	27.5	12.2	16.8	1.8
Freight, industrial	152.1	34.8	0.0	6.3	54.4	32.5	0.0	4.8	0.2
Industrial materials	121.3	45.6	0.1	7.7	40.4	10.6	0.3	4.5	1.8
Business propositions	39.5	26.9	0.6	1.8	0.0	1.6	0.0	0.1	0.2
Airplanes (not travel)	21.9	12.3	0.0	2.7	0.0	0.5	0.0	1.0	0.0
Miscellaneous	333.8	132.6	4.0	39.5	0.5	2.9	0.5	6.6	1.0
Total	**44,256.7**	**7,105.1**	**941.9**	**9,920.1**	**10,752.5**	**9,399.7**	**1,286.6**	**1,590.5**	**549.1**

AWARDS — MEDALS — PRIZES

The Alfred B. Nobel Prize Winners

Alfred B. Nobel (1833-96), inventor of dynamite, bequeathed $9,000,000, the interest to be distributed yearly to those who had most benefited humankind in physics, chemistry, medicine-physiology, literature, and peace. Prizes in these 5 areas were first awarded in 1901. The first Nobel Memorial Prize in Economic Science was awarded in 1969, funded by the central bank of Sweden. If the year is omitted, no awards were given that year. In 1993, each prize was worth approximately $825,000.

Physics

1993 Joseph H. Taylor, Russell A. Hulse, both U.S.
1992 Georges Charpak, Pol.-Fr.
1991 Pierre-Giles de Gennes, French
1990 Richard E. Taylor, Can.; Jerome I. Friedman, Henry W. Kendall, both U.S.
1989 Norman F. Ramsey, U.S.; Hans G. Dehmelt, German-U.S.; Wolfgang Paul, German
1988 Leon M. Lederman, Melvin Schwartz, Jack Steinberger, all U.S.
1987 K. Alex Müller, Swiss; J. Georg Bednorz, W. German
1986 Ernest Ruska, German; Gerd Binnig, W. German; Heinrich Rohrer, Swiss
1985 Klaus von Klitzing, W. German
1984 Carlo Rubbia, Italian; Simon van der Meer, Dutch
1983 Subrahmanyan Chandrasekhar, William A. Fowler, both U.S.
1982 Kenneth G. Wilson, U.S.
1981 Nicolaas Bloembergen, Arthur Schaalow, both U.S.; Kai M. Siegbahn, Swedish
1980 James W. Cronin, Val L. Fitch, both U.S.
1979 Steven Weinberg, Sheldon L. Glashow, both U.S.; Abdus Salam, Pakistani
1978 Pyotr Kapitsa, USSR; Arno Penzias, Robert Wilson, both U.S.
1977 John H. Van Vleck, Philip W. Anderson, both U.S.; Nevill F. Mott, British
1976 Burton Richter, Samuel C.C. Ting, both U.S.
1975 James Rainwater, U.S.; Ben Mottelson, U.S.-Danish; Aage Bohr, Danish
1974 Martin Ryle, Antony Hewish, both British
1973 Ivar Giaever, U.S.; Leo Esaki, Japanese; Brian D. Josephson, British
1972 John Bardeen, Leon N. Cooper, John R. Schrieffer, all U.S.
1971 Dennis Gabor, British
1970 Louis Neel, French; Hannes Alfven, Swedish
1969 Murray Gell-Mann, U.S.
1968 Luis W. Alvarez, U.S.
1967 Hans A. Bethe, U.S.
1966 Alfred Kastler, French
1965 Richard P. Feynman, Julian S. Schwinger, both U.S.; Shinichiro Tomonaga, Japanese
1964 Nikolai G. Basov, Aleksander M. Prochorov, both USSR; Charles H. Townes, U.S.
1963 Maria Goeppert-Mayer, Eugene P. Wigner, both U.S.; J. Hans D. Jensen, German
1962 Lev. D. Landau, USSR
1961 Robert Hofstadter, U.S.; Rudolf L. Mossbauer, German
1960 Donald A. Glaser, U.S.
1959 Owen Chamberlain, Emilio G. Segre, both U.S.
1958 Pavel Cherenkov, Ilya Frank, Igor Y. Tamm, all USSR
1957 Tsung-dao Lee, Chen Ning Yang, both U.S.
1956 John Bardeen, Walter H. Bratain, William Shockley, all U.S.
1955 Polykarp Kusch, Willis E. Lamb, both U.S.
1954 Max Born, British; Walter Bothe, German
1953 Frits Zernike, Dutch
1952 Felix Bloch, Edward M. Purcell, both U.S.
1951 Sir John D. Cockroft, British; Ernest T. S. Walton, Irish
1950 Cecil F. Powell, British
1949 Hideki Yukawa, Japanese
1948 Patrick M. S. Blackett, British
1947 Sir Edward V. Appleton, British
1946 Percy Williams Bridgman, U.S.
1945 Wolfgang Pauli, U.S.
1944 Isidor Isaac Rabi, U.S.
1943 Otto Stern, U.S.
1939 Ernest O. Lawrence, U.S.
1938 Enrico Fermi, Italian-U.S.
1937 Clinton J. Davisson, U.S.; Sir George P. Thomson, British
1936 Carl D. Anderson, U.S.; Victor F. Hess, Austrian
1935 Sir James Chadwick, British
1933 Paul A. M. Dirac, British; Erwin Schrodinger, Austrian
1932 Werner Heisenberg, German
1930 Sir Chandrasekhara V. Raman, Indian
1929 Prince Louis-Victor de Broglie, French
1928 Owen W. Richardson, British
1927 Arthur H. Compton, U.S.; Charles T. R. Wilson, British
1926 Jean B. Perrin, French
1925 James Franck, Gustav Hertz, both German
1924 Karl M. G. Siegbahn, Swedish
1923 Robert A. Millikan, U.S.
1922 Niels Bohr, Danish
1921 Albert Einstein, Ger.-U.S.
1920 Charles E. Guillaume, French
1919 Johannes Stark, German
1918 Max K. E. L. Planck, German
1917 Charles G. Barkla, British
1915 Sir William H. Bragg, Sir William L. Bragg, both British
1914 Max von Laue, German
1913 Heike Kamerlingh-Onnes, Dutch
1912 Nils G. Dalen, Swedish
1911 Wilhelm Wien, German
1910 Johannes D. van der Waals, Dutch
1909 Carl F. Braun, German; Guglielmo Marconi, Italian
1908 Gabriel Lippmann, French
1907 Albert A. Michelson, U.S.
1906 Sir Joseph J. Thomson, British
1905 Philipp E. A. von Lenard, Ger.
1904 John W. Strutt, Lord Rayleigh, both British
1903 Antoine Henri Becquerel, Pierre Curie, both French; Marie Curie, Polish-French
1902 Hendrik A. Lorentz, Pieter Zeeman, both Dutch
1901 Wilhelm C. Roentgen, German

Chemistry

1993 Kary B. Mullis, U.S.; Michael Smith, British-Canadian
1992 Rudolph A. Marcus, Can.-U.S.
1991 Richard R. Ernst, Swiss
1990 Elias James Corey, U.S.
1989 Thomas R. Cech, Sidney Altman, both U.S.
1988 Johann Deisenhofer, Robert Huber, Hartmut Michel, all W. German
1987 Donald J. Cram, Charles J. Pedersen, both U.S.; Jean-Marie Lehn, French
1986 Dudley Herschbach, Yuan T. Lee, both U.S.; John C. Polanyi, Can.
1985 Herbert A. Hauptman, Jerome Karle, both U.S.
1984 Bruce Merrifield, U.S.
1983 Henry Taube, Canadian
1982 Aaron Klug, S. African
1981 Kenichi Fukui, Japan; Roald Hoffmann, U.S.
1980 Paul Berg, Walter Gilbert, both U.S.; Frederick Sanger, U.K.
1979 Herbert C. Brown, U.S.; George Wittig, German
1978 Peter Mitchell, British
1977 Ilya Prigogine, Belgian
1976 William N. Lipscomb, U.S.
1975 John Cornforth, Austral.-Brit.; Vladimir Prelog, Yugo.-Swiss
1974 Paul J. Flory, U.S.
1973 Ernst Otto Fischer, W. German; Geoffrey Wilkinson, British
1972 Christian B. Anfinsen, Stanford Moore, William H. Stein, all U.S.
1971 Gerhard Herzberg, Canadian
1970 Luis F. Leloir, Argentine
1969 Derek H. R. Barton, British; Odd Hassel, Norwegian
1968 Lars Onsager, U.S.
1967 Manfred Eigen, German; Ronald G. W. Norrish, George Porter, both British
1966 Robert S. Mulliken, U.S.
1965 Robert B. Woodward, U.S.
1964 Dorothy C. Hodgkin, British
1963 Giulio Natta, Italian; Karl Ziegler, German
1962 John C. Kendrew, Max F. Perutz, both British
1961 Melvin Calvin, U.S.
1960 Willard F. Libby, U.S.
1959 Jaroslav Heyrovsky, Czech.
1958 Frederick Sanger, British
1957 Sir Alexander R. Todd, British
1956 Sir Cyril N. Hinshelwood, British; Nikolai N. Semenov, USSR
1955 Vincent du Vigneaud, U.S.
1954 Linus C. Pauling, U.S.
1953 Hermann Staudinger, German
1952 Archer J. P. Martin, Richard L. M. Synge, both British
1951 Edwin M. McMillan, Glenn T. Seaborg, both U.S.
1950 Kurt Alder, Otto P. H. Diels, both German
1949 William F. Giauque, U.S.
1948 Arne W. K. Tiselius, Swedish
1947 Sir Robert Robinson, British
1946 James B. Sumner, John H. Northrop, Wendell M. Stanley, all U.S.
1945 Artturi I. Virtanen, Finnish
1944 Otto Hahn, German
1943 Georg de Hevesy, Hungarian
1939 Adolf F. J. Butenandt, German; Leopold Ruzicka, Swiss
1938 Richard Kuhn, German
1937 Walter N. Haworth, British; Paul Karrer, Swiss
1936 Peter J. W. Debye, Dutch

1935 Frederic Joliot-Curie, Irene Joliot-Curie, both French
1934 Harold C. Urey, U.S.
1932 Irving Langmuir, U.S.
1931 Friedrich Bergius, Karl Bosch, both German
1930 Hans Fischer, German
1929 Sir Arthur Harden, British; Hans von Euler-Chelpin, Swed.
1928 Adolf O. R. Windaus, German
1927 Heinrich O. Wieland, German
1926 Theodor Svedberg, Swedish
1925 Richard A. Zsigmondy, German
1923 Fritz Pregl, Austrian
1922 Francis W. Aston, British
1921 Frederick Soddy, British
1920 Walther H. Nernst, German
1918 Fritz Haber, German
1915 Richard M. Willstatter, German
1914 Theodore W. Richards, U.S.
1913 Alfred Werner, Swiss
1912 Victor Grignard, Paul Sabatier, both French
1911 Marie Curie, Polish-French
1910 Otto Wallach, German
1909 Wilhelm Ostwald, German
1908 Ernest Rutherford, British
1907 Eduard Buchner, German
1906 Henri Moissan, French
1905 Adolf von Baeyer, German
1904 Sir William Ramsay, British
1903 Svante A. Arrhenius, Swedish
1902 Emil Fischer, German
1901 Jacobus H. van't Hoff, Dutch

Physiology or Medicine

1993 Phillip A. Sharp, U.S.; Richard J. Roberts, British
1992 Edmond H. Fisher, Edwin G. Krebs, both U.S.
1991 Edwin Neher, Bert Sakmann, both German
1990 Joseph E. Murray, E. Donnall Thomas, both U.S.
1989 J. Michael Bishop, Harold E. Varmus, both U.S.
1988 Gertrude B. Elion, George H. Hitchings, both U.S; Sir James Black, British
1987 Susumu Tonegawa, Japanese
1986 Rita Levi-Montalcini, It.-U.S., Stanley Cohen, U.S.
1985 Michael S. Brown, Joseph L. Goldstein, both U.S.
1984 Cesar Milstein, Brit.-Argentine; Georges J. F. Koehler, German; Niels K. Jerne, Brit.-Danish
1983 Barbara McClintock, U.S.
1982 Sune Bergstrom, Bengt Samuelsson, both Swedish; John R. Vane, British
1981 Roger W. Sperry, David H. Hubel, Tosten N. Wiesel, all U.S.
1980 Baruj Benacerraf, George Snell, both U.S.; Jean Dausset, France
1979 Alian M. Cormack, U.S.; Geoffrey N. Hounsfield, British
1978 Daniel Nathans, Hamilton O. Smith, both U.S.; Werner Arber, Swiss
1977 Rosalyn S. Yalow, Roger C.L. Guillemin, Andrew V. Schally, all U.S.
1976 Baruch S. Blumberg, Daniel Carleton Gajdusek, both U.S.
1975 David Baltimore, Howard Temin, both U.S.; Renato Dulbecco, Ital.-U.S.
1974 Albert Claude, Lux.-U.S.; George Emil Palade, Rom.-U.S.; Christian Rene de Duve, Belgian
1973 Karl von Frisch, Ger.; Konrad Lorenz, Ger.-Austrian; Nikolaas Tinbergen, British
1972 Gerald M. Edelman, U.S.; Rodney R. Porter, British
1971 Earl W. Sutherland Jr., U.S.
1970 Julius Axelrod, U.S.; Sir Bernard Katz, British; Ulf von Euler, Swedish
1969 Max Delbrück, Alfred D. Hershey, Salvador Luria, all U.S.
1968 Robert W. Holley, H. Gobind Khorana, Marshall W. Nirenberg, all U.S.
1967 Ragnar Granit, Swedish; Haldan Keffer Hartline, George Wald, both U.S.
1966 Charles B. Huggins, Francis Peyton Rous, both U.S.
1965 François Jacob, Andre Lwoff, Jacques Monod, all French
1964 Konrad E. Bloch, U.S.; Feodor Lynen, German
1963 Sir John C. Eccles, Australian; Alan L. Hodgkin, Andrew F. Huxley, both British
1962 Francis H. C. Crick, Maurice H. F. Wilkins, both British; James D. Watson, U.S.
1961 Georg von Bekesy, U.S.
1960 Sir F. MacFarlane Bumet, Australian; Peter B. Medawar, British
1959 Arthur Kornberg, Severo Ochoa, both U.S.
1958 George W. Beadle, Edward L. Tatum, Joshua Lederberg, all U.S.
1957 Daniel Bovet, Italian
1956 Andre F. Cournand, Dickinson W. Richards Jr., both U.S.; Werner Forssmann, German
1955 Alex H. T. Theorell, Swedish
1954 John F. Enders, Frederick C. Robbins, Thomas H. Weller, all U.S.
1953 Hans A. Krebs, British; Fritz A. Lipmann, U.S.
1952 Selman A. Waksman, U.S.
1951 Max Theiler, U.S.
1950 Philip S. Hench, Edward C. Kendall, both U.S.; Tadeus Reichstein, Swiss
1949 Walter R. Hess, Swiss; Antonio Moniz, Portuguese
1948 Paul H. Müller, Swiss
1947 Carl F. Cori, Gerty T. Cori, both U.S.; Bernardo A. Houssay, Arg.
1946 Hermann J. Muller, U.S.
1945 Ernst B. Chain, Sir Alexander Fleming, Sir Howard W. Florey, all British
1944 Joseph Erlanger, Herbert S. Gasser, both U.S.
1943 Henrik C. P. Dam, Danish; Edward A. Doisy, U.S.
1939 Gerhard Domagk, German
1938 Corneille J. F. Heymans, Belg.
1937 Albert Szent-Gyorgyi, Hung.-U.S.
1936 Sir Henry H. Dale, British; Otto Loewi, U.S.
1935 Hans Spemann, German
1934 George R. Minot, William P. Murphy, G. H. Whipple, all U.S.
1933 Thomas H. Morgan, U.S.
1932 Edgar D. Adrian, Sir Charles S. Sherrington, both British
1931 Otto H. Warburg, German
1930 Karl Landsteiner, U.S.
1929 Christiaan Eijkman, Dutch; Sir Frederick G. Hopkins, British
1928 Charles J. H. Nicolle, French
1927 Julius Wagner-Jauregg, Austrian
1926 Johannes A. G. Fibiger, Danish
1924 Willem Einthoven, Dutch
1923 Frederick G. Banting, Canadian; John J. R. Macleod, Scottish
1922 Archibald V. Hill, British; Otto F. Meyerhof, German
1920 Schack A. S. Krogh, Danish
1919 Jules Bordet, Belgian
1914 Robert Barany, Austrian
1913 Charles R. Richet, French
1912 Alexis Carrel, French
1911 Allvar Gullstrand, Swedish
1910 Albrecht Kossel, German
1909 Emil T. Kocher, Swiss
1908 Paul Ehrlich, German; Elie Metchnikoff, French
1907 Charles L. A. Laveran, French
1906 Camillo Golgi, Italian; Santiago Ramon y Cajal, Spanish
1905 Robert Koch, German
1904 Ivan P. Pavlov, Russian
1903 Niels R. Finsen, Danish
1902 Sir Ronald Ross, British
1901 Emil A. von Behring, German

Literature

1993 Toni Morrison, U.S.
1992 Derek Walcott, West Indian
1991 Nadine Gordimer, South African
1990 Octavio Paz, Mexican
1989 Camilo José Cela, Spanish
1988 Naguib Mahfouz, Egyptian
1987 Joseph Brodsky, USSR-U.S.
1986 Wole Soyinka, Nigerian
1985 Claude Simon, French
1984 Jaroslav Siefert, Czech.
1983 William Golding, British
1982 Gabriel Garcia Marquez, Colombian-Mex.
1981 Elias Canetti, Bulgarian-British
1980 Czeslaw Milosz, Polish-U.S.
1979 Odysseus Elytis, Greek
1978 Isaac Bashevis Singer, U.S. (Yiddish)
1977 Vicente Aleixandre, Spanish
1976 Saul Bellow, U.S.
1975 Eugenio Montale, Italian
1974 Eyvind Johnson, Harry Edmund Martinson, both Swedish
1973 Patrick White, Australian
1972 Heinrich Böll, W. German
1971 Pablo Neruda, Chilean
1970 Aleksandr I. Solzhenitsyn, USSR
1969 Samuel Beckett, Irish
1968 Yasunari Kawabata, Japanese
1967 Miguel Angel Asturias, Guate.
1966 Samuel Joseph Agnon, Israeli; Nelly Sachs, Swedish
1965 Mikhail Sholokhov, USSR
1964 Jean Paul Sartre, French (Prize declined)
1963 Giorgos Seferis, Greek
1962 John Steinbeck, U.S.
1961 Ivo Andric, Yugoslavian
1960 Saint-John Perse, French
1959 Salvatore Quasimodo, Italian
1958 Boris L. Pasternak, USSR (Prize declined)
1957 Albert Camus, French
1956 Juan Ramon Jimenez, Spanish
1955 Halldor K. Laxness, Icelandic
1954 Ernest Hemingway, U.S.
1953 Sir Winston Churchill, British
1952 Francois Mauriac, French
1951 Par F. Lagerkvist, Swedish
1950 Bertrand Russell, British
1949 William Faulkner, U.S.
1948 T.S. Eliot, British
1947 Andre Gide, French
1946 Hermann Hesse, Swiss
1945 Gabriela Mistral, Chilean
1944 Johannes V. Jensen, Danish
1939 Frans E. Sillanpaa, Finnish
1938 Pearl S. Buck, U.S.
1937 Roger Martin du Gard, French

1936 Eugene O'Neill, U.S.
1934 Luigi Pirandello, Italian
1933 Ivan A. Bunin, USSR
1932 John Galsworthy, British
1931 Erik A. Karlfeldt, Swedish
1930 Sinclair Lewis, U.S.
1929 Thomas Mann, German
1928 Sigrid Undset, Norwegian
1927 Henri Bergson, French
1926 Grazia Deledda, Italian
1925 George Bernard Shaw, Irish-British
1924 Wladyslaw S. Reymont, Polish
1923 William Butler Yeats, Irish
1922 Jacinto Benavente, Spanish
1921 Anatole France, French
1920 Knut Hamsun, Norwegian
1919 Carl F. G. Spitteler, Swiss
1917 Karl A. Gjellerup, Henrik Pontoppidan, both Danish
1916 Verner von Heidenstam, Swed.
1915 Romain Rolland, French
1913 Rabindranath Tagore, Indian
1912 Gerhart Hauptmann, German
1911 Maurice Maeterlinck, Belgian
1910 Paul J. L. Heyse, German
1909 Selma Lagerlof, Swedish
1908 Rudolf C. Eucken, German
1907 Rudyard Kipling, British
1906 Giosue Carducci, Italian
1905 Henryk Sienkiewicz, Polish
1904 Frederic Mistral, French; Jose Echegaray, Spanish
1903 Bjornsterne Bjornson, Norw.
1902 Theodor Mommsen, German
1901 Rene F. A. Sully Prudhomme, French

Peace

1993 Frederik W. de Klerk, Nelson Mandela, both South African
1992 Rigoberta Menchú, Guatemalan
1991 Aung San Suu Kyi, Myanmarese
1990 Mikhail S. Gorbachev, USSR
1989 Dalai Lama, Tibetan
1988 United Nations Peacekeeping Forces
1987 Oscar Arias Sanchez, Costa Rican
1986 Elie Wiesel, Romanian-U.S.
1985 Intl. Physicians for the Prevention of Nuclear War, U.S.
1984 Bishop Desmond Tutu, South African
1983 Lech Walesa, Polish
1982 Alva Myrdal, Swedish; Alfonso Garcia Robles, Mexican
1981 Office of UN High Commissioner for Refugees
1980 Adolfo Perez Esquivel, Argentine
1979 Mother Teresa of Calcutta, Albanian-Indian
1978 Anwar Sadat, Egyptian; Menachem Begin, Israeli
1977 Amnesty International
1976 Mairead Corrigan, Betty Williams, both N. Ireland
1975 Andrei Sakharov, USSR
1974 Eisaku Sato, Japanese; Sean MacBride, Irish
1973 Henry Kissinger, U.S.; Le Duc Tho, N. Vietnamese (Tho declined)
1971 Willy Brandt, W. German
1970 Norman E. Borlaug, U.S.
1969 Intl. Labor Organization
1968 Rene Cassin, French
1965 U.N. Children's Fund (UNICEF)
1964 Martin Luther King Jr., U.S.
1963 International Red Cross, League of Red Cross Societies
1962 Linus C. Pauling, U.S.
1961 Dag Hammarskjold, Swedish
1960 Albert J. Luthuli, South African
1959 Philip J. Noel-Baker, British
1958 Georges Pire, Belgian
1957 Lester B. Pearson, Canadian
1954 Office of the UN High Commissioner for Refugees
1953 George C. Marshall, U.S.
1952 Albert Schweitzer, French
1951 Leon Jouhaux, French
1950 Ralph J. Bunche, U.S.
1949 Lord John Boyd Orr of Brechin Mearns, British
1947 Friends Service Council, British; American Friends Service Committee, U.S.
1946 Emily G. Balch, John R. Mott, both U.S.
1945 Cordell Hull, U.S.
1944 International Red Cross
1938 Nansen International Office for Refugees
1937 Viscount Cecil of Chelwood, Brit.
1936 Carlos de Saavedra Lamas, Arg.
1935 Carl von Ossietzky, German
1934 Arthur Henderson, British
1933 Sir Norman Angell, British
1931 Jane Addams, Nicholas Murray Butler, both U.S.
1930 Nathan Soderblom, Swedish
1929 Frank B. Kellogg, U.S.
1927 Ferdinand E. Buisson, French; Ludwig Quidde, German
1926 Aristide Briand, French; Gustav Stresemann, German
1925 Sir J. Austen Chamberlain, Brit.; Charles G. Dawes, U.S.
1922 Fridtjof Nansen, Norwegian
1921 Karl H. Branting, Swedish; Christian L. Lange, Norwegian
1920 Leon V.A. Bourgeois, French
1919 Woodrow Wilson, U.S.
1917 International Red Cross
1913 Henri La Fontaine, Belgian
1912 Elihu Root, U.S.
1911 Tobias M.C. Asser, Dutch; Alfred H. Fried, Austrian
1910 Permanent Intl. Peace Bureau
1909 Auguste M. F. Beernaert, Belg.; Paul H. B. B. d'Estournelles de Constant, French
1908 Klas P. Arnoldson, Swedish; Fredrik Bajer, Danish
1907 Ernesto T. Moneta, Italian; Louis Renault, French
1906 Theodore Roosevelt, U.S.
1905 Baroness Bertha von Suttner, Austrian
1904 Institute of International Law
1903 Sir William R. Cremer, British
1902 Elie Ducommun, Charles A. Gobat, both Swiss
1901 Jean H. Dunant, Swiss; Frederic Passy, French

Nobel Memorial Prize in Economic Science

1993 Robert W. Fogel, Douglass C. North, both U.S.
1992 Gary S. Becker, U.S.
1991 Ronald H. Coase, Br.-U.S.
1990 Harry M. Markowitz, William F. Sharpe, Merton H. Miller, all U.S.
1989 Trygve Haavelmo, Norwegian
1988 Maurice Allais, French
1987 Robert M. Solow, U.S.
1986 James M. Buchanan, U.S.
1985 Franco Modigliani, It.-U.S.
1984 Richard Stone, British
1983 Gerard Debreu, Fr.-U.S.
1982 George J. Stigler, U.S.
1981 James Tobin, U.S.
1980 Lawrence R. Klein, U.S.
1979 Theodore W. Schultz, U.S.; Sir Arthur Lewis, British
1978 Herbert A. Simon, U.S.
1977 Bertil Ohlin, Swedish; James E. Meade, British
1976 Milton Friedman, U.S.
1975 Tjalling Koopmans, Dutch-U.S.; Leonid Kantorovich, USSR
1974 Gunnar Myrdal, Swed.; Friedrich A. von Hayek, Austrian
1973 Wassily Leontief, U.S.
1972 Kenneth J. Arrow, U.S.; John R. Hicks, British
1971 Simon Kuznets, U.S.
1970 Paul A. Samuelson, U.S.
1969 Ragnar Frisch, Norwegian; Jan Tinbergen, Dutch

Pulitzer Prizes in Journalism, Letters, and Music

The Pulitzer Prizes were endowed by Joseph Pulitzer (1847-1911), publisher of the *New York World*, in a bequest to Columbia University and are awarded annually by the president of the university on recommendation of the Pulitzer Prize Board for work done during the preceding year. The administrator is Seymour Topping of Columbia University. All prizes are $3,000 (originally $500) in each category, except Meritorious Public Service, for which a gold medal is given. If a year is omitted, no award was given that year.

Journalism

Meritorious Public Service

For distinguished and meritorious public service by a United States newspaper.

1918—New York Times. Also special award to Minna Lewinson and Henry Beetle Hough
1919—Milwaukee Journal
1921—Boston Post
1922—New York World
1923—Memphis Commercial Appeal
1924—New York World
1926—Enquirer-Sun, Columbus, GA
1927—Canton (OH) Daily News
1928—Indianapolis Times
1929—New York Evening World
1931—Atlanta (GA) Constitution
1932—Indianapolis (IN) News
1933—New York World-Telegram
1934—Medford (OR) Mail-Tribune
1935—Sacramento (CA) Bee
1936—Cedar Rapids (IA) Gazette
1937—St.Louis Post-Dispatch
1938—Bismarck (ND) Tribune
1939—Miami (FL) Daily News
1940—Waterbury (CT) Republican and American
1941—St.Louis Post-Dispatch
1942—Los Angeles Times
1943—Omaha World Herald

1944—New York Times
1945—Detroit Free Press
1946—Scranton (PA) Times.
1947—Baltimore Sun
1948—St. Louis Post-Dispatch
1949—Nebraska State Journal
1950—Chicago Daily News; St. Louis Post-Dispatch
1951—Miami (FL) Herald and Brooklyn Eagle
1952—St. Louis Post-Dispatch
1953—Whiteville (NC) News Reporter; Tabor City (NC) Tribune
1954—Newsday (Long Island, NY)
1955—Columbus (GA) Ledger and Sunday Ledger-Enquirer
1956—Watsonville (CA) Register-Pajaronian
1957—Chicago Daily News
1958—Arkansas Gazette, Little Rock
1959—Utica (NY) Observer-Dispatch and Utica Daily Press
1960—Los Angeles Times
1961—Amarillo (TX) Globe-Times
1962—Panama City (FL) News-Herald
1963—Chicago Daily News
1964—St.Petersburg (FL) Times
1965—Hutchinson (KS) News
1966—Boston Globe
1967—Louisville Courier-Journal; Milwaukee Journal
1968—Riverside (CA) Press-Enterprise
1969—Los Angeles Times
1970—Newsday (Long Island, NY)
1971—Winston Salem (NC) Journal & Sentinel
1972—New York Times
1973—Washington Post
1974—Newsday (Long Island, NY)
1975—Boston Globe
1976—Anchorage Daily News
1977—Lufkin (TX) News
1978—Philadelphia Inquirer
1979—Point Reyes (CA) Light
1980—Gannett News Service
1981—Charlotte (NC) Observer
1982—Detroit News
1983—Jackson (MS) Clarion-Ledger
1984—Los Angeles Times
1985—Ft. Worth (TX) Star-Telegram
1986—Denver Post
1987—Pittsburgh Press
1988—Charlotte Observer
1989—Anchorage Daily News
1990—Philadelphia Inquirer, Gilbert M. Gaul; Washington (NC) Daily News
1991—Des Moines Register, Jane Schorer
1992—Sacramento Bee, Tom Knudson
1993—Miami Herald
1994—Akron Beacon Journal

Reporting

This category originally embraced all fields—local, national, and international. Later, separate categories were created for national and international reporting.

1917—Herbert Bayard Swope, New York World
1918—Harold A. Littledale, New York Evening Post
1920—John J. Leary Jr., New York World
1921—Louis Seibold, New York World
1922—Kirke L. Simpson, Associated Press
1923—Alva Johnston, New York Times
1924—Magner White, San Diego Sun
1925—James W. Mulroy and Alvin H. Goldstein, Chicago Daily News
1926—William Burke Miller, Louisville Courier-Journal
1927—John T. Rogers, St. Louis Post-Dispatch
1929—Paul Y. Anderson, St. Louis Post-Dispatch
1930—Russell D. Owens, New York Times. Also $500 to W.O. Dapping, Auburn (NY) Citizen
1931—A.B. MacDonald, Kansas City (MO) Star
1932—W.C. Richards, D.D. Martin, J.S. Pooler, F.D. Webb, J.N.W. Sloan, Detroit Free Press
1933—Francis A. Jamieson, Associated Press
1934—Royce Brier, San Francisco Chronicle
1935—William H. Taylor, New York Herald Tribune
1936—Lauren D. Lyman, New York Times
1937—John J. O'Neill, NY Herald Tribune; William L. Laurence, NY Times; Howard W. Blakeslee, AP; Gobind Behari Lal, Universal Service; and David Dietz, Scripps-Howard Newspapers
1938—Raymond Sprigle, Pittsburgh Post-Gazette
1939—Thomas L. Stokes, Scripps-Howard Newspaper Alliance
1940—S. Burton Heath, New York World-Telegram
1941—Westbrook Pegler, New York World-Telegram
1942—Stanton Delaplane, San Francisco Chronicle
1943—George Weller, Chicago Daily News
1944—Paul Schoenstein, New York Journal-American
1945—Jack S. McDowell, San Francisco Call-Bulletin
1946—William L. Laurence, New York Times
1947—Frederick Woltman, New York World-Telegram
1948—George E. Goodwin, Atlanta Journal
1949—Malcolm Johnson, New York Sun
1950—Meyer Berger, New York Times
1951—Edward S. Montgomery, San Francisco Examiner
1952—George de Carvalho, San Francisco Chronicle

(1) General or Spot; (2) Special or Investigative

1953—(1) Providence (RI) Journal and Evening Bulletin; (2) Edward J. Mowery, New York World-Telegram & Sun
1954—(1) Vicksburg (MS) Sunday Post-Herald; (2) Alvin Scott McCoy, Kansas City (MO) Star
1955—(1) Mrs. Caro Brown, Alice (TX) Daily Echo; (2) Roland K. Towery, Cuero (TX) Record
1956—(1) Lee Hills, Detroit Free Press; (2) Arthur Daley, New York Times
1957—(1) Salt Lake Tribune, Salt Lake City, UT; (2) Wallace Turner and William Lambert, Portland Oregonian
1958—(1) Fargo, (ND) Forum; (2) George Beveridge, Evening Star, Washington, DC
1959—(1) Mary Lou Werner, Washington Evening Star; (2) John Harold Brislin, Scranton (PA) Tribune, and The Scrantonian
1960—(1) Jack Nelson, Atlanta Constitution; (2) Miriam Ottenberg, Washington Evening Star
1961—(1) Sanche de Gramont, New York Herald Tribune; (2) Edgar May, Buffalo Evening News
1962—(1) Robert D. Mullins, Deseret News, Salt Lake City; (2) George Bliss, Chicago Tribune
1963—(1) Shared by Sylvan Fox, William Longgood, and Anthony Shannon, New York World-Telegram & Sun; (2) Oscar Griffin Jr., Pecos (TX) Independent and Enterprise
1964—(1) Norman C. Miller, Wall Street Journal; (2) Shared by James V. Magee, Albert V. Gaudiosi, and Frederick A. Meyer, Philadelphia Bulletin
1965—(1) Melvin H. Ruder, Hungry Horse News (Columbia Falls, MT); (2) Gene Goltz, Houston Post
1966—(1) Los Angeles Times Staff; (2) John A. Frasca, Tampa (FL) Tribune
1967—(1) Robert V. Cox, Chambersburg (PA) Public Opinion; (2) Gene Miller, Miami Herald
1968—Detroit Free Press Staff; (2) J. Anthony Lukas, New York Times
1969—(1) John Fetterman, Louisville Courier-Journal and Times; (2) Albert L. Delugach, St. Louis Globe Democrat, and Denny Walsh, Life
1970—(1) Thomas Fitzpatrick, Chicago Sun-Times; (2) Harold Eugene Martin, Montgomery Advertiser & Alabama Journal
1971—(1) Akron Beacon Journal Staff; (2) William Hugh Jones, Chicago Tribune
1972—(1) Richard Cooper and John Machacek, Rochester Times-Union; (2) Timothy Leland, Gerard M. O'Neill, Stephen A. Kurkjian and Anne De Santis, Boston Globe
1973—(1) Chicago Tribune; (2) Sun Newspapers of Omaha
1974—(1) Hugh F. Hough, Arthur M. Petacque, Chicago Sun-Times; (2) William Sherman, New York Daily News
1975—(1) Xenia (OH) Daily Gazette; (2) Indianapolis Star
1976—(1) Gene Miller, Miami Herald; (2) Chicago Tribune
1977—(1) Margo Huston, Milwaukee Journal; (2) Acel Moore, Wendell Rawls Jr., Philadelphia Inquirer
1978—(1) Richard Whitt, Louisville Courier-Journal; (2) Anthony R. Dolan, Stamford (CT) Advocate
1979—(1) San Diego (CA) Evening Tribune; (2) Gilbert M. Gaul, Elliot G. Jaspin, Pottsville (PA) Republican
1980—(1) Philadelphia Inquirer; (2) Stephen A. Kurkjian, Alexander B. Hawes Jr., Nils Bruzelius, Joan Vennochi, Robert M. Porterfield, Boston Globe
1981—(1) Longview (WA) Daily News staff; (2) Clark Hallas and Robert B. Lowe, Arizona Daily Star
1982—(1) Kansas City Star, Kansas City Times; (2) Paul Henderson, Seattle Times
1983—(1) Fort Wayne (IN) News-Sentinel; (2) Loretta Tofani, Washington Post
1984—(1) Newsday (NY); (2) Boston Globe
1985—(1) Thomas Turcol, Virginian-Pilot and Ledger-Star, Norfolk, VA; (2) William K. Marimow, Philadelphia Inquirer; Lucy Morgan & Jack Reed, St. Petersburg (FL) Times
1986—(1) Edna Buchanan, Miami Herald; (2) Jeffrey A. Marx & Michael M. York, Lexington (KY) Herald-Leader
1987—(1) Akron Beacon Journal; (2) Daniel R. Biddle, H.G. Bissinger, Fredric N. Tulsky, Philadelphia Inquirer; John Woestendiek, Philadelphia Inquirer
1988—(1) Alabama Journal; Lawrence (MA) Eagle-Tribune; (2) Walt Bogdanich, Wall Street Journal
1989—(1) Louisville Courier-Journal; (2) Bill Dedman, Atlanta Journal and Constitution

1990—(1) San Jose Mercury News; (2) Lon Kilzer, Chris Ison, Star Tribune, Minneapolis-St. Paul
1991—(1) Miami Herald; (2) Joseph T. Hallinan, Susan M. Headden, Indianapolis Star
1992—(1) New York Newsday; (2) Lorraine Adams, Dan Malone, Dallas Morning News
1993—(1) Los Angeles Times; Jeff Brazil, Steve Berry, Orlando Sentinel
1994—(1) New York Times staff; (2) Providence Journal-Bulletin staff

Criticism or Commentary

(1) Criticism; (2) Commentary

1970—(1) Ada Louise Huxtable, New York Times; (2) Marquis W. Childs, St. Louis Post-Dispatch
1971—(1) Harold C. Schonberg, New York Times; (2) William A. Caldwell, The Record, Hackensack, NJ
1972—(1) Frank Peters Jr., St. Louis Post-Dispatch; (2) Mike Royko, Chicago Daily News
1973—(1) Ronald Powers, Chicago Sun-Times; (2) David S. Broder, Washington Post
1974—(1) Emily Genauer, Newsday (NY); (2) Edwin A. Roberts Jr., National Observer
1975—(1) Roger Ebert, Chicago Sun Times; (2) Mary McGrory, Washington Star
1976—(1) Alan M. Kriegsman, Washington Post; (2) Walter W. (Red) Smith, New York Times
1977—(1) William McPherson, Washington Post; (2) George F. Will, Washington Post Writers Group
1978—(1) Walter Kerr, New York Times; (2) William Safire, New York Times
1979—(1) Paul Gapp, Chicago Tribune; (2) Russell Baker, New York Times
1980—(1) William A. Henry III, Boston Globe; (2) Ellen Goodman, Boston Globe
1981—(1) Jonathan Yardley, Washington Star; (2) Dave Anderson, New York Times
1982—(1) Martin Bernheimer, Los Angeles Times; (2) Art Buchwald, Los Angeles Times Syndicate
1983—(1) Manuela Hoelterhoff, Wall St. Journal; (2) Claude Sitton, Raleigh (NC) News & Observer
1984—Paul Goldberger, New York Times; (2) Vermont Royster, Wall St. Journal
1985—(1) Howard Rosenberg, Los Angeles Times; (2) Murray Kempton, Newsday (NY)
1986—(1) Donal J. Henahan, New York Times; (2) Jimmy Breslin, New York Daily News
1987—(1) Richard Eder, Los Angeles Times; (2) Charles Krauthammer, Washington Post
1988—(1) Tom Shales, Washington Post; (2) Dave Barry, Miami Herald
1989—(1) Michael Skube, News and Observer, Raleigh, NC; (2) Clarence Page, Chicago Tribune
1990—(1) Allan Temko, San Francisco Chronicle; (2) Jim Murray, Los Angeles Times
1991—(1) David Shaw, Los Angeles Times; (2) Jim Hoagland, Washington Post
1992—(1) No award; (2) Anna Quindlen, New York Times
1993—(1) Michael Dirda, Washington Post; (2) Liz Balmaseda, Miami Herald
1994—(1) Lloyd Schwartz, Boston Phoenix; (2) William Raspberry, Washington Post

National Reporting

1942—Louis Stark, New York Times
1944—Dewey L. Fleming, Baltimore Sun
1945—James B. Reston, New York Times
1946—Edward A. Harris, St. Louis Post-Dispatch
1947—Edward T. Folliard, Washington Post
1948—Bert Andrews, New York Herald Tribune; Nat S. Finney, Minneapolis Tribune
1949—Charles P. Trussell, New York Times
1950—Edwin O. Guthman, Seattle Times
1952—Anthony Leviero, New York Times
1953—Don Whitehead, Associated Press
1954—Richard Wilson, Des Moines Register
1955—Anthony Lewis, Washington Daily News
1956—Charles L. Bartlett, Chattanooga Times
1957—James Reston, New York Times
1958—Relman Morin, AP; Clark Mollenhoff, Des Moines Register & Tribune
1959—Howard Van Smith, Miami (FL) News
1960—Vance Trimble, Scripps-Howard, Washington, DC
1961—Edward R. Cony, Wall Street Journal
1962—Nathan G. Caldwell and Gene S. Graham, Nashville Tennessean
1963—Anthony Lewis, New York Times
1964—Merriman Smith, UPI
1965—Louis M. Kohlmeier, Wall Street Journal
1966—Haynes Johnson, Washington Evening Star
1967—Monroe Karmin and Stanley Penn, Wall Street Journal
1968—Howard James, Christian Science Monitor; Nathan K. Kotz, Des Moines Register
1969—Robert Cahn, Christian Science Monitor
1970—William J. Eaton, Chicago Daily News
1971—Lucinda Franks & Thomas Powers, UPI
1972—Jack Anderson, United Feature Syndicate
1973—Robert Boyd and Clark Hoyt, Knight Newspapers
1974—James R. Polk, Washington Star-News; Jack White, Providence Journal-Bulletin
1975—Donald L. Barlett and James B. Steele, Philadelphia Inquirer
1976—James Risser, Des Moines Register
1977—Walter Mears, Associated Press
1978—Gaylord D. Shaw, Los Angeles Times
1979—James Risser, Des Moines Register
1980—Charles Stafford, Bette Swenson Orsini, St. Petersburg (FL) Times
1981—John M. Crewdson, New York Times
1982—Rick Atkinson, Kansas City Times
1983—Boston Globe
1984—John Noble Wilford, New York Times
1985—Thomas J. Knudson, Des Moines (IA) Register
1986—Craig Flournoy & George Rodrigue, Dallas Morning News; Arthur Howe, Philadelphia Inquirer
1987—Miami Herald; New York Times
1988—Tim Weiner, Philadelphia Inquirer
1989—Donald L. Barlett & James B. Steele, Philadelphia Inquirer
1990—Ross Anderson, Bill Dietrich, Mary Ann Gwinn, Eric Nalder, Seattle Times
1991—Marjie Lundstrom, Rochelle Sharpe, Gannett News Service
1992—Jeff Taylor, Mike McGraw, Kansas City Star
1993—David Maraniss, Washington Post
1994—Eileen Welsome, Albuquerque Tribune

International Reporting

1942—Laurence Edmund Allen, Associated Press
1943—Ira Wolfert, North American Newspaper Alliance
1944—Daniel DeLuce, Associated Press
1945—Mark S. Watson, Baltimore Sun
1946—Homer W. Bigart, New York Herald Tribune
1947—Eddy Gilmore, Associated Press
1948—Paul W. Ward, Baltimore Sun
1949—Price Day, Baltimore Sun
1950—Edmund Stevens, Christian Science Monitor
1951—Keyes Beech and Fred Sparks, Chicago Daily News; Homer Bigart and Marguerite Higgins, New York Herald Tribune; Relman Morin and Don Whitehead, AP
1952—John M. Hightower, Associated Press
1953—Austin C. Wehrwein, Milwaukee Journal
1954—Jim G. Lucas, Scripps-Howard Newspapers
1955—Harrison Salisbury, New York Times
1956—William Randolph Hearst Jr., Frank Conniff, Hearst Newspapers; Kingsbury Smith, INS
1957—Russell Jones, United Press
1958—New York Times
1959—Joseph Martin and Philip Santora, New York Daily News
1960—A.M. Rosenthal, New York Times
1961—Lynn Heinzerling, Associated Press
1962—Walter Lippmann, New York Herald Tribune Syndicate
1963—Hal Hendrix, Miami (FL) News
1964—Malcolm W. Browne, AP; David Halberstam, New York Times
1965—J.A. Livingston, Philadelphia Bulletin
1966—Peter Arnett, AP
1967—R. John Hughes, Christian Science Monitor
1968—Alfred Friendly, Washington Post
1969—William Tuohy, Los Angeles Times
1970—Seymour M. Hersh, Dispatch News Service
1971—Jimmie Lee Hoagland, Washington Post
1972—Peter R. Kann, Wall Street Journal
1973—Max Frankel, New York Times
1974—Hedrick Smith, New York Times
1975—William Mullen and Ovie Carter, Chicago Tribune
1976—Sydney H. Schanberg, New York Times
1978—Henry Kamm, New York Times
1979—Richard Ben Cramer, Philadelphia Inquirer
1980—Joel Brinkley, Jay Mather, Louisville (KY) Courier-Journal
1981—Shirley Christian, Miami Herald
1982—John Darnton, New York Times
1983—Thomas L. Friedman, New York Times; Loren Jenkins, Washington Post
1984—Karen Elliot House, Wall St. Journal
1985—Josh Friedman, Dennis Bell, Ozler Muhammad, Newsday (NY)

1986—Lewis M. Simons, Pete Carey, Katherine Ellison, San Jose (CA) Mercury News
1987—Michael Parks, Los Angeles Times
1988—Thomas L. Friedman, New York Times
1989—Glenn Frankel, Washington Post; Bill Keller, New York Times
1990—Nicholas D. Kirstof, Sheryl WuDunn, New York Times
1991—Caryle Murphy, Washington Post; Serge Schmemann, New York Times
1992—Patrick J. Sloyan, Newsday (NY)
1993—John F. Burns, New York Times; Roy Gutman, Newsday (NY)
1994—Dallas Morning News team

Correspondence

For Washington or foreign correspondence. Category was merged with those in national and international reporting in 1948.
1929—Paul Scott Mowrer, Chicago Daily News
1930—Leland Stowe, New York Herald Tribune
1931—H.R. Knickerbocker, Philadelphia Public Ledger and New York Evening Post
1932—Walter Duranty, New York Times, and Charles G. Ross, St. Louis Post-Dispatch
1933—Edgar Ansel Mowrer, Chicago Daily News
1934—Frederick T. Birchall, New York Times
1935—Arthur Krock, New York Times
1936—Wilfred C. Barber, Chicago Tribune
1937—Anne O'Hare McCormick, New York Times
1938—Arthur Krock, New York Times
1939—Louis P. Lochner, Associated Press
1940—Otto D. Tolischus, New York Times
1941—Bronze plaque to commemorate work of American correspondents on war fronts
1942—Carlos P. Romulo, Philippines Herald
1943—Hanson W. Baldwin, New York Times
1944—Ernest Taylor Pyle, Scripps-Howard Newspaper Alliance
1945—Harold V. (Hal) Boyle, Associated Press
1946—Arnaldo Cortesi, New York Times
1947—Brooks Atkinson, New York Times

Editorial Writing

1917—New York Tribune
1918—Louisville (KY) Courier-Journal
1920—Harvey E. Newbranch, Omaha Evening World-Herald
1922—Frank M. O'Brien, New York Herald
1923—William Allen White, Emporia Gazette
1924—Frank Buxton, Boston Herald, Special Prize; Frank I. Cobb, New York World
1925—Robert Lathan, Charleston (SC) News and Courier
1926—Edward M. Kingsbury, New York Times
1927—F. Lauriston Bullard, Boston Herald
1928—Grover C. Hall, Montgomery Advertiser
1929—Louis Isaac Jaffe, Norfolk Virginian-Pilot
1931—Chas. Ryckman, Fremont (NE) Tribune
1933—Kansas City (MO) Star
1934—E. P. Chase, Atlantic (IA) News Telegraph
1936—Felix Morley, Washington Post; George B. Parker, Scripps-Howard Newspapers
1937—John W. Owens, Baltimore Sun
1938—W.W. Waymack, Des Moines (IA) Register and Tribune
1939—Ronald G. Callvert, Portland Oregonian
1940—Bart Howard, St. Louis Post-Dispatch
1941—Reuben Maury, Daily News, NY
1942—Geoffrey Parsons, New York Herald Tribune
1943—Forrest W. Seymour, Des Moines (IA) Register and Tribune
1944—Henry J. Haskell, Kansas City (MO) Star
1945—George W. Potter, Providence (RI) Journal-Bulletin
1946—Hodding Carter, Greenville (MS) Delta Democrat-Times
1947—William H. Grimes, Wall Street Journal
1948—Virginius Dabney, Richmond (VA) Times-Dispatch
1949—John H. Crider, Boston (MA) Herald; Herbert Elliston, Washington Post
1950—Carl M. Saunders, Jackson (MI) Citizen-Patriot
1951—William H. Fitzpatrick, New Orleans States
1952—Louis LaCoss, St. Louis Globe Democrat
1953—Vermont C. Royster, Wall Street Journal
1954—Don Murray, Boston Herald
1955—Royce Howes, Detroit Free Press
1956—Lauren K. Soth, Des Moines (IA) Register and Tribune
1957—Buford Boone, Tuscaloosa (AL) News
1958—Harry S. Ashmore, Arkansas Gazette
1959—Ralph McGill, Atlanta Constitution
1960—Lenoir Chambers, Norfolk Virginian-Pilot
1961—William J. Dorvillier, San Juan (Puerto Rico) Star
1962—Thomas M. Storke, Santa Barbara (CA) News-Press
1963—Ira B. Harkey Jr., Pascagoula (MS) Chronicle
1964—Hazel Brannon Smith, Lexington (MS) Advertiser
1965—John R. Harrison, Gainesville (FL) Sun
1966—Robert Lasch, St. Louis Post-Dispatch
1967—Eugene C. Patterson, Atlanta Constitution
1968—John S. Knight, Knight Newspapers
1969—Paul Greenberg, Pine Bluff (AR) Commercial
1970—Philip L. Geyelin, Washington Post
1971—Horance G. Davis Jr., Gainesville (FL) Sun
1972—John Strohmeyer, Bethlehem (PA) Globe-Times
1973—Roger B. Linscott, Berkshire Eagle, Pittsfield, MA
1974—F. Gilman Spencer, Trenton (NJ) Trentonian
1975—John D. Maurice, Charleston (WV) Daily Mail
1976—Philip Kerby, Los Angeles Times
1977—Warren L. Lerude, Foster Church, and Norman F. Cardoza, Reno (NV) Evening Gazette and Nevada State Journal
1978—Meg Greenfield, Washington Post
1979—Edwin M. Yoder, Washington Star
1980—Robert L. Bartley, Wall Street Journal
1982—Jack Rosenthal, New York Times
1983—Editorial board, Miami Herald
1984—Albert Scardino, Georgia Gazette
1985—Richard Aregood, Philadelphia Daily News
1986—Jack Fuller, Chicago Tribune
1987—Jonathan Freedman, Tribune (San Diego)
1988—Jane Healy, Orlando Sentinel
1989—Lois Wille, Chicago Tribune
1990—Thomas J. Hylton, Pottstown (PA) Mercury
1991—Ron Casey, Harold Jackson, Joey Kennedy, Birmingham (AL) News
1992—Maria Henson, Lexington (KY) Herald-Leader
1993—No award
1994—R. Bruce Dold, Chicago Tribune

Editorial Cartooning

1922—Rollin Kirby, New York World
1924—Jay N. Darling, Des Moines Register
1925—Rollin Kirby, New York World
1926—D. R. Fitzpatrick, St. Louis Post-Dispatch
1927—Nelson Harding, Brooklyn Eagle
1928—Nelson Harding, Brooklyn Eagle
1929—Rollin Kirby, New York World
1930—Charles Macauley, Brooklyn Eagle
1931—Edmund Duffy, Baltimore Sun
1932—John T. McCutcheon, Chicago Tribune
1933—H. M. Talburt, Washington Daily News
1934—Edmund Duffy, Baltimore Sun
1935—Ross A. Lewis, Milwaukee Journal
1937—C. D. Batchelor, New York Daily News
1938—Vaughn Shoemaker, Chicago Daily News
1939—Charles G. Werner, Daily Oklahoman
1940—Edmund Duffy, Baltimore Sun
1941—Jacob Burck, Chicago Times
1942—Herbert L. Block, Newspaper Enterprise Assn.
1943—Jay N. Darling, Des Moines Register
1944—Clifford K. Berryman, Washington Star
1945—Bill Mauldin, United Feature Syndicate
1946—Bruce Alexander Russell, Los Angeles Times
1947—Vaughn Shoemaker, Chicago Daily News
1948—Reuben L. (Rube) Goldberg, New York Sun
1949—Lute Pease, Newark (NJ) Evening News
1950—James T. Berryman, Washington Star
1951—Reginald W. Manning, Arizona Republic
1952—Fred L. Packer, New York Mirror
1953—Edward D. Kuekes, Cleveland Plain Dealer
1954—Herbert L. Block, Washington Post & Times-Herald
1955—Daniel R. Fitzpatrick, St. Louis Post-Dispatch
1956—Robert York, Louisville (KY) Times
1957—Tom Little, Nashville Tennessean
1958—Bruce M. Shanks, Buffalo Evening News
1959—Bill Mauldin, St. Louis Post-Dispatch
1961—Carey Orr, Chicago Tribune
1962—Edmund S. Valtman, Hartford Times
1963—Frank Miller, Des Moines Register
1964—Paul Conrad, Denver Post
1966—Don Wright, Miami News
1967—Patrick B. Oliphant, Denver Post
1968—Eugene Gray Payne, Charlotte Observer
1969—John Fischetti, Chicago Daily News
1970—Thomas F. Darcy, Newsday
1971—Paul Conrad, Los Angeles. Times
1972—Jeffrey K. MacNelly, Richmond News-Leader
1974—Paul Szep, Boston Globe
1975—Garry Trudeau, Universal Press Syndicate
1976—Tony Auth, Philadelphia Inquirer
1977—Paul Szep, Boston Globe
1978—Jeffrey K. MacNelly, Richmond News Leader
1979—Herbert L. Block, Washington Post
1980—Don Wright, Miami (FL) News
1981—Mike Peters, Dayton (OH) Daily News

1982—Ben Sargent, Austin American-Statesman
1983—Richard Lochner, Chicago Tribune
1984—Paul Conrad, Los Angeles Times
1985—Jeffrey K. MacNelly, Chicago Tribune
1986—Jules Feiffer, Village Voice (NY)
1987—Berke Breathed, Washington Post
1988—Doug Marlette, Atlanta Constitution, Charlotte Observer
1989—Jack Higgins, Chicago Sun-Times
1990—Tom Toles, Buffalo News
1991—Jim Borgman, Cincinnati Enquirer
1992—Signe Wilkinson, Philadelphia Daily News
1993—Stephen R. Benson, Arizona Republic
1994—Michael P. Ramirez, Commercial Appeal, Memphis, TN

Spot News Photography

1942—Milton Brooks, Detroit News
1943—Frank Noel, Associated Press
1944—Frank Filan, AP; Earl L. Bunker, Omaha World-Herald
1945—Joe Rosenthal, Associated Press, for photograph of planting American flag on Iwo Jima
1947—Arnold Hardy, amateur, Atlanta, GA
1948—Frank Cushing, Boston Traveler
1949—Nathaniel Fein, New York Herald Tribune
1950—Bill Crouch, Oakland (CA) Tribune
1951—Max Desfor, Associated Press
1952—John Robinson and Don Ultang, Des Moines Register and Tribune
1953—William M. Gallagher, Flint (MI) Journal
1954—Mrs. Walter M. Schau, amateur
1955—John L. Gaunt Jr., Los Angeles Times
1956—New York Daily News
1957—Harry A. Trask, Boston Traveler
1958—William C. Beall, Washington Daily News
1959—William Seaman, Minneapolis Star
1960—Andrew Lopez, UPI
1961—Yasushi Nagao, Mainichi Newspapers, Tokyo
1962—Paul Vathis, Associated Press
1963—Hector Rondon, La Republica, Caracas, Venezuela
1964—Robert H. Jackson, Dallas Times-Herald
1965—Horst Faas, Associated Press
1966—Kyoichi Sawada, UPI
1967—Jack R. Thornell, Associated Press
1968—Rocco Morabito, Jacksonville Journal
1969—Edward Adams, AP
1970—Steve Starr, AP
1971—John Paul Filo, Valley Daily News & Daily Dispatch of Tarentum & New Kensington, PA
1972—Horst Faas and Michel Laurent, AP
1973—Huynh Cong Ut, AP
1974—Anthony K. Roberts, AP
1975—Gerald H. Gay, Seattle Times
1976—Stanley Forman, Boston Herald American
1977—Neal Ulevich, Associated Press; Stanley Forman, Boston Herald American
1978—John H. Blair, UPI
1979—Thomas J. Kelly III, Pottstown (PA) Mercury
1980—UPI
1981—Larry C. Price, Ft. Worth (TX) Star-Telegram
1982—Ron Edmonds, Associated Press
1983—Bill Foley, AP
1984—Stan Grossfeld, Boston Globe
1985—The Register, Santa Ana, CA
1986—Carol Guzy & Michel duCille, Miami Herald
1987—Kim Komenich, San Francisco Examiner
1988—Scott Shaw, Odessa (TX) American
1989—Ron Olshwanger, St. Louis Post-Dispatch
1990—Oakland (CA) Tribune photo staff
1991—Greg Marinovich, Associated Press
1992—Associated Press staff
1993—Ken Geiger, William Snyder, Dallas Morning News
1994—Paul Watson, Toronto Star

Feature Photography

1968—Toshio Sakai, UPI
1969—Moneta Sleet Jr., Ebony
1970—Dallas Kinney, Palm Beach Post
1971—Jack Dykinga, Chicago Sun-Times
1972—Dave Kennerly, UPI
1973—Brian Lanker, Topeka Capitol-Journal
1974—Slava Veder, AP
1975—Matthew Lewis, Washington Post
1976—Louisville Courier-Journal and Louisville Times
1977—Robin Hood, Chattanooga News-Free Press
1978—J. Ross Baughman, AP
1979—Staff photographers, Boston Herald American
1980—Erwin H. Hagler, Dallas Times-Herald
1981—Taro M. Yamasaki, Detroit Free Press
1982—John H. White, Chicago Sun-Times
1983—James B. Dickman, Dallas Times-Herald
1984—Anthony Suad, Denver Post
1985—Stan Grossfeld, Boston Globe; Larry C. Price, Philadelphia Inquirer
1986—Tom Gralish, Philadelphia Inquirer
1987—David Peterson, Des Moines Register
1988—Michel duCille, Miami Herald
1989—Manny Crisostomo, Detroit Free Press
1990—David C. Turnley, Detroit Free Press
1991—William Snyder, Dallas Morning News
1992—John Kaplan, Block Newspapers (Toledo, OH)
1993—Associated Press staff
1994—Kevin Carter, New York Times

Special Citation

1938—Edmonton (Alberta) Journal, bronze plaque
1941—New York Times
1944—Byron Price and Mrs. William Allen White. Also to Richard Rodgers and Oscar Hammerstein 2d, for musical, Oklahoma!
1945—Press cartographers for war maps
1947—(Pulitzer centennial year.) Columbia Univ. and the Graduate School of Journalism, and St. Louis Post-Dispatch
1948—Dr. Frank Diehl Fackenthal
1951—Cyrus L. Sulzberger, New York Times
1952—Max Kase, New York Journal-American, Kansas City Star
1953—New York Times; Lester Markel
1957—Kenneth Roberts, for his historical novels
1958—Walter Lippmann, New York Herald Tribune
1960—Garrett Mattingly, for The Armada
1961—American Heritage Picture History of the Civil War
1964—Gannett Newspapers
1973—James T. Flexner, for biography of George Washington
1976—John Hohenberg, for services to American journalism
1977—Alex Haley, for Roots
1978—Richard Lee Strout, Christian Science Monitor and New Republic
—E.B. White
1984—Theodore Geisel ("Dr. Seuss")
1985—William Schuman, composer, educational leader
1987—Joseph Pulitzer Jr.
1992—Art Spiegelman, for Maus

Feature Writing

1979—Jon D. Franklin, Baltimore Evening Sun
1980—Madeleine Blais, Miami Herald Tropic Magazine; Janet Cooke, Washington Post
1981—Teresa Carpenter, Village Voice, New York City
1982—Saul Pett, Associated Press
1984—Peter M. Rinearson, Seattle Times
1985—Alice Steinbach, Baltimore Sun
1986—John Camp, St. Paul Pioneer Press & Dispatch
1987—Steve Twomey, Philadephia Inquirer
1988—Jacqui Banaszynski, St. Paul Pioneer Press Dispatch
1989—David Zucchino, Philadelphia Inquirer
1990—Dave Curtin, Colorado Springs Gazette Telegraph
1991—Sheryl James, St. Petersburg Times
1992—Howell Raines, New York Times
1993—George Lardner Jr., Washington Post
1994—Isabel Wilkerson, New York Times

Explanatory Journalism

1985—Jon Franklin, Baltimore Evening Sun
1986—New York Times staff
1987—Jeff Lyon & Peter Gorner, Chicago Tribune
1988—Daniel Hertzberg, James B. Stewart, Wall Street Journal
1989—David Hanners, William Snyder, Karen Blessen, Dallas Morning News
1990—David A. Vise, Steve Coll, Washington Post
1991—Susan C. Faludi, Wall Street Journal
1992—Robert S. Capers, Eric Lipton, Hartford (CT) Courant
1993—Mike Toner, Atlanta Journal-Constitution
1994—Ronald Kotulak, Chicago Tribune

Specialized Reporting

1985—Randall Savage, Jackie Crosby, Macon (GA) Telegraph and News
1986—Andrew Schneider & Mary Pat Flaherty, Pittsburgh Press
1987—Alex S. Jones, New York Times
1988—Dean Baquet, William Gaines, Ann Marie Lipinski, Chicago Tribune
1989—Edward Humes, Orange County (CA) Register
1990—Tamar Stieber, Albuquerque Journal
1991—Natalie Angier, New York Times
1992—Deborah Blum, Sacramento Bee
1993—Paul Ingrassia, Joseph B. White, Wall Street Journal
1994—Eric Friedman, Jim Mitzelfeld, Detroit News

Letters

Fiction

For fiction in book form by an American author, preferably dealing with American life.

1918—Ernest Poole, His Family
1919—Booth Tarkington, The Magnificent Ambersons
1921—Edith Wharton, The Age of Innocence
1922—Booth Tarkington, Alice Adams
1923—Willa Cather, One of Ours
1924—Margaret Wilson, The Able McLaughlins
1925—Edna Ferber, So Big
1926—Sinclair Lewis, Arrowsmith (Refused prize)
1927—Louis Bromfield, Early Autumn
1928—Thornton Wilder, Bridge of San Luis Rey
1929—Julia M. Peterkin, Scarlet Sister Mary
1930—Oliver LaFarge, Laughing Boy
1931—Margaret Ayer Barnes, Years of Grace
1932—Pearl S. Buck, The Good Earth
1933—T. S. Stribling, The Store
1934—Caroline Miller, Lamb in His Bosom
1935—Josephine W. Johnson, Now in November
1936—Harold L. Davis, Honey in the Horn
1937—Margaret Mitchell, Gone With the Wind
1938—John P. Marquand, The Late George Apley
1939—Marjorie Kinnan Rawlings, The Yearling
1940—John Steinbeck, The Grapes of Wrath
1942—Ellen Glasgow, In This Our Life
1943—Upton Sinclair, Dragon's Teeth
1944—Martin Flavin, Journey in the Dark
1945—John Hersey, A Bell for Adano
1947—Robert Penn Warren, All the King's Men
1948—James A. Michener, Tales of the South Pacific
1949—James Gould Cozzens, Guard of Honor
1950—A. B. Guthrie Jr., The Way West
1951—Conrad Richter, The Town
1952—Herman Wouk, The Caine Mutiny
1953—Ernest Hemingway, The Old Man and the Sea
1955—William Faulkner, A Fable
1956—MacKinlay Kantor, Andersonville
1958—James Agee, A Death in the Family
1959—Robert Lewis Taylor, The Travels of Jaimie McPheeters
1960—Allen Drury, Advise and Consent
1961—Harper Lee, To Kill a Mockingbird
1962—Edwin O'Connor, The Edge of Sadness
1963—William Faulkner, The Reivers
1965—Shirley Ann Grau, The Keepers of the House
1966—Katherine Anne Porter, Collected Stories of Katherine Anne Porter
1967—Bernard Malamud, The Fixer
1968—William Styron, The Confessions of Nat Turner
1969—N. Scott Momaday, House Made of Dawn
1970—Jean Stafford, Collected Stories
1972—Wallace Stegner, Angle of Repose
1973—Eudora Welty, The Optimist's Daughter
1975—Michael Shaara, The Killer Angels
1976—Saul Bellow, Humboldt's Gift
1978—James Alan McPherson, Elbow Room
1979—John Cheever, The Stories of John Cheever
1980—Norman Mailer, The Executioner's Song
1981—John Kennedy Toole, A Confederacy of Dunces
1982—John Updike, Rabbit Is Rich
1983—Alice Walker, The Color Purple
1984—William Kennedy, Ironweed
1985—Alison Lurie, Foreign Affairs
1986—Larry McMurtry, Lonesome Dove
1987—Peter Taylor, A Summons to Memphis
1988—Toni Morrison, Beloved
1989—Anne Tyler, Breathing Lessons
1990—Oscar Hijuelos, The Mambo Kings Play Songs of Love
1991—John Updike, Rabbit at Rest
1992—Jane Smiley, A Thousand Acres
1993—Robert Olen Butler, A Good Scent From a Strange Mountain
1994—E. Annie Proulx, The Shipping News

Drama

For an American play, preferably original and dealing with American life.

1918—Jesse Lynch Williams, Why Marry?
1920—Eugene O'Neill, Beyond the Horizon
1921—Zona Gale, Miss Lulu Bett
1922—Eugene O'Neill, Anna Christie
1923—Owen Davis, Icebound
1924—Hatcher Hughes, Hell-Bent for Heaven
1925—Sidney Howard, They Knew What They Wanted
1926—George Kelly, Craig's Wife
1927—Paul Green, In Abraham's Bosom
1928—Eugene O'Neill, Strange Interlude
1929—Elmer Rice, Street Scene
1930—Marc Connelly, The Green Pastures
1931—Susan Glaspell, Alison's House
1932—George S. Kaufman, Morrie Ryskind, and Ira Gershwin, Of Thee I Sing
1933—Maxwell Anderson, Both Your Houses
1934—Sidney Kingsley, Men in White
1935—Zoe Akins, The Old Maid
1936—Robert E. Sherwood, Idiot's Delight
1937—George S. Kaufman and Moss Hart, You Can't Take It With You
1938—Thornton Wilder, Our Town
1939—Robert E. Sherwood, Abe Lincoln in Illinois
1940—William Saroyan, The Time of Your Life
1941—Robert E. Sherwood, There Shall Be No Night
1943—Thornton Wilder, The Skin of Our Teeth
1945—Mary Chase, Harvey
1946—Russel Crouse and Howard Lindsay, State of the Union
1948—Tennessee Williams, A Streetcar Named Desire
1949—Arthur Miller, Death of a Salesman
1950—Richard Rodgers, Oscar Hammerstein 2d, and Joshua Logan, South Pacific
1952—Joseph Kramm, The Shrike
1953—William Inge, Picnic
1954—John Patrick, Teahouse of the August Moon
1955—Tennessee Williams, Cat on a Hot Tin Roof
1956—Frances Goodrich and Albert Hackett, The Diary of Anne Frank
1957—Eugene O'Neill, Long Day's Journey Into Night
1958—Ketti Frings, Look Homeward, Angel
1959—Archibald MacLeish, J. B.
1960—George Abbott, Jerome Weidman, Sheldon Harnick, and Jerry Bock, Fiorello
1961—Tad Mosel, All the Way Home
1962—Frank Loesser and Abe Burrows, How to Succeed in Business Without Really Trying
1965—Frank D. Gilroy, The Subject Was Roses
1967—Edward Albee, A Delicate Balance
1969—Howard Sackler, The Great White Hope
1970—Charles Gordone, No Place to Be Somebody
1971—Paul Zindel, The Effect of Gamma Rays on Man-in-the-Moon Marigolds
1973—Jason Miller, That Championship Season
1975—Edward Albee, Seascape
1976—Michael Bennett, James Kirkwood, Nicholas Dante, Marvin Hamlisch, and Edward Kleban, A Chorus Line
1977—Michael Cristofer, The Shadow Box
1978—Donald L. Coburn, The Gin Game
1979—Sam Shepard, Buried Child
1980—Lanford Wilson, Talley's Folly
1981—Beth Henley, Crimes of the Heart
1982—Charles Fuller, A Soldier's Play
1983—Marsha Norman, 'night, Mother
1984—David Mamet, Glengarry Glen Ross
1985—Stephen Sondheim and James Lapine, Sunday in the Park With George
1987—August Wilson, Fences
1988—Alfred Uhry, Driving Miss Daisy
1989—Wendy Wasserstein, The Heidi Chronicles
1990—August Wilson, The Piano Lesson
1991—Neil Simon, Lost in Yonkers
1992—Robert Schenkkan, The Kentucky Cycle
1993—Tony Kushner, Angels in America: Millennium Approaches
1994—Edward Albee, Three Tall Women

History

For a book on the history of the United States.

1917—J. J. Jusserand, With Americans of Past and Present Days
1918—James Ford Rhodes, History of the Civil War
1920—Justin H. Smith, The War With Mexico
1921—William Sowden Sims, The Victory at Sea
1922—James Truslow Adams, The Founding of New England
1923—Charles Warren, The Supreme Court in United States History
1924—Charles Howard McIlwain, The American Revolution: A Constitutional Interpretation
1925—Frederick L. Paxton, A History of the American Frontier
1926—Edward Channing, A History of the U.S.
1927—Samuel Flagg Bemis, Pinckney's Treaty
1928—Vernon Louis Parrington, Main Currents in American Thought

1929—Fred A. Shannon, The Organization and Administration of the Union Army, 1861-65
1930—Claude H. Van Tyne, The War of Independence
1931—Bernadotte E. Schmitt, The Coming of the War, 1914
1932—Gen. John J. Pershing, My Experiences in the World War
1933—Frederick J. Turner, The Significance of Sections in American History
1934—Herbert Agar, The People's Choice
1935—Charles McLean Andrews, The Colonial Period of American History
1936—Andrew C. McLaughlin, The Constitutional History of the United States
1937—Van Wyck Brooks, The Flowering of New England
1938—Paul Herman Buck, The Road to Reunion, 1865-1900
1939—Frank Luther Mott, A History of American Magazines
1940—Carl Sandburg, Abraham Lincoln: The War Years
1941—Marcus Lee Hansen, The Atlantic Migration, 1607-1860
1942—Margaret Leech, Reveille in Washington
1943—Esther Forbes, Paul Revere and the World He Lived In
1944—Merle Curti, The Growth of American Thought
1945—Stephen Bonsal, Unfinished Business
1946—Arthur M. Schlesinger Jr., The Age of Jackson
1947—James Phinney Baxter 3d, Scientists Against Time
1948—Bernard De Voto, Across the Wide Missouri
1949—Roy F. Nichols, The Disruption of American Democracy
1950—O. W. Larkin, Art and Life in America
1951—R. Carlyle Buley, The Old Northwest: Pioneer Period 1815-1840
1952—Oscar Handlin, The Uprooted
1953—George Dangerfield, The Era of Good Feelings
1954—Bruce Catton, A Stillness at Appomattox
1955—Paul Horgan, Great River: The Rio Grande in North American History
1956—Richard Hofstadter, The Age of Reform
1957—George F. Kennan, Russia Leaves the War
1958—Bray Hammond, Banks and Politics in America—From the Revolution to the Civil War
1959—Leonard D. White and Jean Schneider, The Republican Era; 1869-1901
1960—Margaret Leech, In the Days of McKinley
1961—Herbert Feis, Between War and Peace: The Potsdam Conference
1962—Lawrence H. Gibson, The Triumphant Empire: Thunderclouds Gather in the West
1963—Constance McLaughlin Green, Washington: Village and Capital, 1800-1878
1964—Sumner Chilton Powell, Puritan Village: The Formation of a New England Town
1965—Irwin Unger, The Greenback Era
1966—Perry Miller, Life of the Mind in America
1967—William H. Goetzmann, Exploration and Empire: The Explorer and Scientist in the Winning of the American West
1968—Bernard Bailyn, The Ideological Origins of the American Revolution
1969—Leonard W. Levy, Origin of the Fifth Amendment
1970—Dean Acheson, Present at the Creation: My Years in the State Department
1971—James McGregor Burns, Roosevelt: The Soldier of Freedom
1972—Carl N. Degler, Neither Black nor White
1973—Michael Kammen, People of Paradox: An Inquiry Concerning the Origins of American Civilization
1974—Daniel J. Boorstin, The Americans: The Democratic Experience
1975—Dumas Malone, Jefferson and His Time
1976—Paul Horgan, Lamy of Santa Fe
1977—David M. Potter, The Impending Crisis
1978—Alfred D. Chandler Jr., The Visible Hand: The Managerial Revolution in American Business
1979—Don E. Fehrenbacher, The Dred Scott Case: Its Significance in American Law and Politics
1980—Leon F. Litwack, Been in the Storm So Long
1981—Lawrence A. Cremin, American Education: The National Experience, 1783-1876
1982—C. Vann Woodward, ed., Mary Chestnut's Civil War
1983—Rhys L. Issac, The Transformation of Virginia, 1740-1790
1985—Thomas K. McCraw, Prophets of Regulation
1986—Walter A. McDougall, ... The Heavens and the Earth
1987—Bernard Bailyn, Voyagers to the West
1988—Robert V. Bruce, The Launching of Modern American Science 1846-1876
1989—Taylor Branch, Parting the Waters: America in the King Years, 1954-63; and James M. McPherson, Battle Cry of Freedom: The Civil War Era
1990—Stanley Karnow, In Our Image: America's Empire in the Philippines
1991—Laurel Thatcher Ulrich, A Midwife's Tale: The Life of Martha Ballard, based on her diary, 1785-1812
1992—Mark E. Neely Jr., The Fate of Liberty: Abraham Lincoln and Civil Liberties
1993—Gordon S. Wood, The Radicalism of the American Revolution

Biography or Autobiography

For a distinguished biography or autobiography by an American author.
1917—Laura E. Richards and Maude Howe Elliott, assisted by Florence Howe Hall, Julia Ward Howe
1918—William Cabell Bruce, Benjamin Franklin, Self-Revealed
1919—Henry Adams, The Education of Henry Adams
1920—Albert J. Beveridge, The Life of John Marshall
1921—Edward Bok, The Americanization of Edward Bok
1922—Hamlin Garland, A Daughter of the Middle Border
1923—Burton J. Hendrick, The Life and Letters of Walter H. Page
1924—Michael Pupin, From Immigrant to Inventor
1925—M. A. DeWolfe Howe, Barrett Wendell and His Letters
1926—Harvey Cushing, Life of Sir William Osler
1927—Emory Holloway, Whitman: An Interpretation in Narrative
1928—Charles Edward Russell, The American Orchestra and Theodore Thomas
1929—Burton J. Hendrick, The Training of an American: The Earlier Life and Letters of Walter H. Page
1930—Marquis James, The Raven (Sam Houston)
1931—Henry James, Charles W. Eliot
1932—Henry F. Pringle, Theodore Roosevelt
1933—Allan Nevins, Grover Cleveland
1934—Tyler Dennett, John Hay
1935—Douglas Southall Freeman, R. E. Lee
1936—Ralph Barton Perry, The Thought and Character of William James
1937—Allan Nevins, Hamilton Fish: The Inner History of the Grant Administration
1938—Divided between Odell Shepard, Pedlar's Progress; Marquis James, Andrew Jackson
1939—Carl Van Doren, Benjamin Franklin
1940—Ray Stannard Baker, Woodrow Wilson, Life and Letters
1941—Ola Elizabeth Winslow, Jonathan Edwards
1942—Forrest Wilson, Crusader in Crinoline
1943—Samuel Eliot Morison, Admiral of the Ocean Sea (Columbus)
1944—Carleton Mabee, The American Leonardo: The Life of Samuel F. B. Morse
1945—Russell Blaine Nye, George Bancroft; Brahmin Rebel.
1946—Linny Marsh Wolfe, Son of the Wilderness
1947—William Allen White, The Autobiography of William Allen White
1948—Margaret Clapp, Forgotten First Citizen: John Bigelow
1949—Robert E. Sherwood, Roosevelt and Hopkins
1950—Samuel Flag Bemis, John Quincy Adams and the Foundations of American Foreign Policy
1951—Margaret Louise Colt, John C. Calhoun: American Portrait
1952—Merlo J. Pusey, Charles Evans Hughes
1953—David J. Mays, Edmund Pendleton, 1721-1803
1954—Charles A. Lindbergh, The Spirit of St. Louis
1955—William S. White, The Taft Story
1956—Talbot F. Hamlin, Benjamin Henry Latrobe
1957—John F. Kennedy, Profiles in Courage
1958—Douglas Southall Freeman (decd. 1953), George Washington, Vols. I-VI; John Alexander Carroll and Mary Wells Ashworth, Vol. VII
1959—Arthur Walworth, Woodrow Wilson: American Prophet
1960—Samuel Eliot Morison, John Paul Jones
1961—David Donald, Charles Sumner and the Coming of the Civil War
1963—Leon Edel, Henry James: Vol. II, The Conquest of London, 1870-1881; Vol. III, The Middle Years, 1881-1895
1964—Walter Jackson Bate, John Keats
1965—Ernest Samuels, Henry Adams
1966—Arthur M. Schlesinger Jr., A Thousand Days
1967—Justin Kaplan, Mr. Clemens and Mark Twain
1968—George F. Kennan, Memoirs (1925-1950)
1969—B. L. Reid, The Man From New York: John Quinn and His Friends
1970—T. Harry Williams, Huey Long
1971—Lawrence Thompson, Robert Frost: The Years of Triumph, 1915-1938
1972—Joseph P. Lash, Eleanor and Franklin
1973—W. A. Swanberg, Luce and His Empire
1974—Louis Sheaffer, O'Neill, Son and Artist
1975—Robert A. Caro, The Power Broker: Robert Moses and the Fall of New York
1976—R.W.B. Lewis, Edith Wharton: A Biography
1977—John E. Mack, A Prince of Our Disorder: The Life of T.E. Lawrence
1978—Walter Jackson Bate, Samuel Johnson

1979—Leonard Baker, Days of Sorrow and Pain: Leo Baeck and the Berlin Jews
1980—Edmund Morris, The Rise of Theodore Roosevelt
1981—Robert K. Massie, Peter the Great: His Life and World
1982—William S. McFeely, Grant: A Biography
1983—Russell Baker, Growing Up
1984—Louis R. Harlan, Booker T. Washington
1985—Kenneth Silverman, The Life and Times of Cotton Mather
1986—Elizabeth Frank, Louise Bogan: A Portrait
1987—David J. Garrow, Bearing the Cross: Martin Luther King Jr. and the Southern Christian Leadership Conference
1988—David Herbert Donald, Look Homeward: A Life of Thomas Wolfe
1989—Richard Ellmann, Oscar Wilde
1990—Sebastian de Grazia, Machiavelli in Hell
1991—Steven Naifeh and Gregory White Smith, Jackson Pollock: An American Saga
1992—Lewis B. Puller Jr., Fortunate Son: The Healing of a Vietnam Vet
1993—David McCullough, Truman
1994—David Levering Lewis, W.E.B. DuBois: Biography of a Race, 1868-1919

American Poetry

Before this prize was established in 1922, awards were made from gifts provided by the Poetry Society: **1918**—Love Songs, by Sara Teasdale. **1919**—Old Road to Paradise, by Margaret Widemer; Corn Huskers, by Carl Sandburg.

1922—Edwin Arlington Robinson, Collected Poems
1923—Edna St. Vincent Millay, The Ballad of the Harp-Weaver; A Few Figs From Thistles; Eight Sonnets in American Poetry, 1922; A Miscellany
1924—Robert Frost, New Hampshire: A Poem With Notes and Grace Notes
1925—Edwin Arlington Robinson, The Man Who Died Twice
1926—Amy Lowell, What's O'Clock
1927—Leonora Speyer, Fiddler's Farewell
1928—Edwin Arlington Robinson, Tristram
1929—Stephen Vincent Benet, John Brown's Body
1930—Conrad Aiken, Selected Poems
1931—Robert Frost, Collected Poems
1932—George Dillon, The Flowering Stone
1933—Archibald MacLeish, Conquistador
1934—Robert Hillyer, Collected Verse
1935—Audrey Wurdemann, Bright Ambush
1936—Robert P. Tristram Coffin, Strange Holiness
1937—Robert Frost, A Further Range
1938—Marya Zaturenska, Cold Morning Sky
1939—John Gould Fletcher, Selected Poems
1940—Mark Van Doren, Collected Poems
1941—Leonard Bacon, Sunderland Capture
1942—William Rose Benet, The Dust Which Is God
1943—Robert Frost, A Witness Tree
1944—Stephen Vincent Benet, Western Star
1945—Karl Shapiro, V-Letter and Other Poems
1947—Robert Lowell, Lord Weary's Castle
1948—W. H. Auden, The Age of Anxiety
1949—Peter Viereck, Terror and Decorum
1950—Gwendolyn Brooks, Annie Allen
1951—Carl Sandburg, Complete Poems
1952—Marianne Moore, Collected Poems
1953—Archibald MacLeish, Collected Poems
1954—Theodore Roethke, The Waking
1955—Wallace Stevens, Collected Poems
1956—Elizabeth Bishop, Poems, North and South
1957—Richard Wilbur, Things of This World
1958—Robert Penn Warren, Promises: Poems 1954-1956
1959—Stanley Kunitz, Selected Poems 1928-1958
1960—W. D. Snodgrass, Heart's Needle
1961—Phyllis McGinley, Times Three: Selected Verse from Three Decades
1962—Alan Dugan, Poems
1963—William Carlos Williams, Pictures From Breughel
1964—Louis Simpson, At the End of the Open Road
1965—John Berryman, 77 Dream Songs
1966—Richard Eberhart, Selected Poems
1967—Anne Sexton, Live or Die
1968—Anthony Hecht, The Hard Hours
1969—George Oppen, Of Being Numerous
1970—Richard Howard, Untitled Subjects
1971—William S. Merwin, The Carrier of Ladders
1972—James Wright, Collected Poems
1973—Maxine Winokur Kumin, Up Country
1975—Gary Snyder, Turtle Island
1976—John Ashbery, Self-Portrait in a Convex Mirror
1977—James Merrill, Divine Comedies
1978—Howard Nemerov, Collected Poems
1979—Robert Penn Warren, Now and Then: Poems 1976-1978
1980—Donald Justice, Selected Poems
1981—James Schuyler, The Morning of the Poem
1982—Sylvia Plath, The Collected Poems
1983—Galway Kinnell, Selected Poems
1984—Mary Oliver, American Primitive
1985—Carolyn Kizer, Yin
1986—Henry Taylor, The Flying Change
1987—Rita Dove, Thomas and Beulah
1988—William Meredith, Partial Accounts: New and Selected Poems
1989—Richard Wilbur, New and Collected Poems
1990—Charles Simic, The World Doesn't End
1991—Mona Van Duyn, Near Changes
1992—James Tate, Selected Poems
1993—Louise Glück, The Wild Iris
1994—Yusef Komunyakaa, Neon Vernacular

General Nonfiction

1962—Theodore H. White, The Making of the President 1960
1963—Barbara W. Tuchman, The Guns of August
1964—Richard Hofstadter, Anti-Intellectualism in American Life
1965—Howard Mumford Jones, O Strange New World
1966—Edwin Way Teale, Wandering Through Winter
1967—David Brion Davis, The Problem of Slavery in Western Culture
1968—Will and Ariel Durant, Rousseau and Revolution
1969—Norman Mailer, The Armies of the Night; Rene Jules Dubos, So Human an Animal: How We Are Shaped by Surroundings and Events
1970—Eric H. Erikson, Gandhi's Truth
1971—John Toland, The Rising Sun
1972—Barbara W. Tuchman, Stilwell and the American Experience in China, 1911-1945
1973—Frances FitzGerald, Fire in the Lake: The Vietnamese and the Americans in Vietnam; Robert Coles, Children of Crisis, Volumes II & III
1974—Ernest Becker, The Denial of Death
1975—Annie Dillard, Pilgrim at Tinker Creek
1976—Robert N. Butler, Why Survive? Being Old in America
1977—William W. Warner, Beautiful Swimmers
1978—Carl Sagan, The Dragons of Eden
1979—Edward O. Wilson, On Human Nature
1980—Douglas R. Hofstadter, Gödel, Escher, Bach: An Eternal Golden Braid
1981 —Carl E. Schorske, Fin-de-Siecle Vienna: Politics and Culture
1982—Tracy Kidder, The Soul of a New Machine
1983—Susan Sheehan, Is There No Place on Earth for Me?
1984—Paul Starr, Social Transformation of American Medicine
1985—Studs Terkel, The Good War
1986—Joseph Lelyveld, Move Your Shadow; J. Anthony Lukas, Common Ground
1987—David K. Shipler, Arab and Jew
1988—Richard Rhodes, The Making of the Atomic Bomb
1989—Neil Sheehan, A Bright Shining Lie: John Paul Vann and America in Vietnam
1990—Dale Maharidge and Michael Williamson, And Their Children After Them
1991—Bert Holldobler and Edward O. Wilson, The Ants
1992—Daniel Yergin, The Prize: The Epic Quest for Oil
1993—Garry Wills, Lincoln at Gettysburg
1994—David Remnick, Lenin's Tomb: The Last Days of the Soviet Empire

Music

For composition by an American (before 1977, by a composer resident in the U.S.), in the larger forms of chamber, orchestra, or choral music or for an operatic work including ballet. A special posthumous award was granted in 1976 to Scott Joplin.

1943—William Schuman, Secular Cantata No. 2, A Free Song
1944—Howard Hanson, Symphony No. 4, Op. 34
1945—Aaron Copland, Appalachian Spring
1946—Leo Sowerby, The Canticle of the Sun
1947—Charles E. Ives, Symphony No. 3
1948—Walter Piston, Symphony No. 3
1949—Virgil Thomson, Louisiana Story
1950—Gian-Carlo Menotti, The Consul
1951—Douglas Moore, Giants in the Earth
1952—Gail Kubik, Symphony Concertante
1954—Quincy Porter, Concerto for Two Pianos and Orchestra

1955—Gian-Carlo Menotti, The Saint of Bleecker Street
1956—Ernest Toch, Symphony No. 3
1957—Norman Dello Joio, Meditations on Ecclesiastes
1958—Samuel Barber, Vanessa
1959—John La Montaine, Concerto for Piano and Orchestra
1960—Elliott Carter, Second String Quartet
1961—Walter Piston, Symphony No. 7
1962—Robert Ward, The Crucible
1963—Samuel Barber, Piano Concerto No. 1
1966—Leslie Bassett, Variations for Orchestra
1967—Leon Kirchner, Quartet No. 3
1968—George Crumb, Echoes of Time and The River
1969—Karel Husa, String Quartet No. 3
1970—Charles W. Wuorinen, Time's Encomium
1971—Mario Davidovsky, Synchronisms No. 6
1972—Jacob Druckman, Windows
1973—Elliott Carter, String Quartet No. 3
1974—Donald Martino, Notturno. (Special Citation) Roger Sessions
1975—Dominick Argento, From the Diary of Virginia Woolf
1976—Ned Rorem, Air Music
1977—Richard Wernick, Visions of Terror and Wonder
1978—Michael Colgrass, Deja Vu for Percussion and Orchestra
1979—Joseph Schwantner, Aftertones of Infinity
1980—David Del Tredici, In Memory of a Summer Day
1982—Roger Sessions, Concerto for Orchestra (Special Citation) Milton Babbitt
1983—Ellen T. Zwilich, Three Movements for Orchestra
1984—Bernard Rands, Canti del Sole
1985—Stephen Albert, Symphony, RiverRun
1986—George Perle, Wind Quintet IV
1987—John Harbison, The Flight Into Egypt
1988—William Bolcom, 12 New Etudes for Piano
1989—Roger Reynolds, Whispers Out of Time
1990—Mel Powell, Duplicates: A Concerto for Two Pianos and Orchestra
1991—Shulamit Ran, Symphony
1992—Wayne Peterson, The Face of the Night, The Heart of the Dark
1993—Christopher Rouse, Trombone Concerto
1994—Gunther Schuller, Of Reminiscences and Reflections

Special Awards

Awarded in 1993 or 1994

Books

Academy of American Poets Awards, Fellowship for Distinguished Poetic Achievement, $20,000: Gerald Stern; Lamont Poetry Selection, $1,000 and purchase of 2,000 copies of book: Rosanna Warren, *Stained Glass*; Lavan Younger Poet Awards, $1,000 each: Thomas Bolt, David Clewell, and Christopher Merrill; Walt Whitman Award, $1,000 and the purchase of 2,000 copies of the book: Alison Hawthorne Deming, *Science and Other Poems*; Landon Translation Award, $1,000: Charles Simic, *The Horse Has Six Legs: An Anthology of Serbian Poetry*

Han Christian Anderson Awards, every 2 years for important contribution to children's literature: author: Michio Mado, Japan; illustrator: Jörg Müller, Switzerland

Booker Prize, British award for fiction: Roddy Doyle, *Paddy Clarke Ha Ha Ha*

Curtis Benjamin Award, for creative publishing: Margaret K. McElderry

Caldecott Medal, by American Library Assn., for most distinguished American picture book: Allen Say, *Grandfather's Journey*

Christopher Awards, by The Christophers, for expression of highest values of human spirit, bronze medallion each: Luis Alberto Urrea, *Across the Wire*; Helen Prejean, C.S.J., *Dead Man Walking*; Ronald Takaki, *A Different Mirror*; Brian Keenan, *An Evil Cradling*; Gilbert M. Gaul, *Giant Steps*; Sarah and A. Elizabeth Delany with Amy Hill, *Having Our Say*; Doris Donnelly, *Spiritual Fitness*; Kay Mills, *This Little Light of Mine*; Gerda Marie Scheidl, *The Crystal Ball*; Phillip Hoose, *It's Our World, Too!*; Ruud van der Rol and Rian Verhoeven, *Anne Frank: Beyond the Diary*

Golden Kite Awards, by Society of Children's Book Writiers and Illustrators: fiction: Virginia Euwer Wolff, *Make Lemonade*; nonfiction: Russell Freedman, *Eleanor Roosevelt*; picture-illustration: Kevin Hawkes, *By the Light of the Halloween Moon*

Society of American Historians, Francis Parkman Prize: David Levering Lewis, *W.E.B. DuBois: Biography of a Race, 1868-1919*; Bruce Catton Prize for Lifetime Achievement: John Hope Franklin; Allan Nevins Dissertation Prize: Dean David Grodzins

Kingsley Tufts Poetry Prize, by Claremont Graduate School, $50,000: Yusef Komunyakaa, *Neon Vernacular*

Ruth Lilly Poetry Prize, by Modern Poetry Assn. and American Council for the Arts, $25,000: Donald Hall

Lincoln Prize, by Lincoln Soldiers Institute at Gettysburg College, for lifetime contribution to Civil War studies, $40,000 and a bronze bust of Lincoln: *Free at Last: A Documentary History of Slavery, Freedom, and the Civil War*, edited by Ira Berlin, Barbara J. Fields, Steven Miller, Joseph P. Reidy, and Leslie Rowland

National Book Awards, by National Book Foundation, $10,000 each: nonfiction: Gore Vidal, *United States: Essays 1952-1992*; poetry: S. R. Ammons, *Garbage*; fiction: E. Annie Proulx, *The Shipping News*; Medal for Distinguished Contribution to American Letters: Clifton Fadiman

National Book Critics Circle Awards, fiction: Ernest J. Gaines, *A Lesson Before Dying*; nonfiction: Alan Lomax, *The Land Where the Blues Began*; criticism: John Dizikes, *Opera in America: A Cultural History*; biography, autobiography: Edmund White, *Genet*; poetry: Mark Doty, *My Alexandria*

Newbery Award, by American Library Assn., for most distinguished contribution to American literature for children: Lois Lowry, *The Giver*

PEN/Faulkner Award for Fiction, $15,000: Philip Roth, *Operation Shylock*

Rea Award for the Short Story, by Dugannon Foundation, for lifetime achievement, $25,000: Tillie Olsen, *Tell Me a Riddle*

Whiting Writers Awards, by Whiting Foundation, for achievement and promise alike, $30,000 each: Jeffrey Eugenides, Dagoberto Gilb, Kevin King, Mark Levine, Nathaniel Mackey, Dionisio D. Martinez, Sigrid Nunez, Janet Peery, Kathleen Peirce, Lisa Shea

Journalism

Helen B. Bernstein Award, by New York Public Library, $15,000: David Remnick, *Lenin's Tomb: The Last Days of the Soviet Empire*

National Journalism Awards, by Scripps Howard Foundation, for print journalism: Charles E. Scripps Award, for newspaper's service to literacy, $2,500: *Columbus* (GA) *Ledger-Enquirer*; Pyle Award, for human interest writing, $2,500: John Woestendiek, *The Philadelphia Inquirer*; Walker Stone Award for editorial writing, $2,000: Richard L. Aregood, *Philadelphia Daily News*; Meemam Award, for environmental reporting, $2,000 each: *Mobile* (AL) *Register* and *The Dallas Morning News*; Howard Award, for public service reporting, $2,500 each: *Chicago Tribune* and *The Albuquerque* (NM) *Tribune*; E. W. Scripps Award, for service to First Amendment, $2,500: *Tribune Chronicle*, Warren, OH

National Magazine Awards, by American society of Magazine Editors and Columbia Univ. Graduate School of Journalism: general excellence, circulation over 1 million: *Business Week*; under 1 million: *Health*, *Wired*, *Print*; single topic issue: *Health*, "For Our Parents"; feature writing: *Harper's Bazaar*, "The Last Shot," Darcy Frey; fiction: *Harper's Bazaar*, "The Practical Heart," Allan Gurganus, "The Prophet From Jupiter," Tony Earley, "The 400-Pound C.E.O.," George Saunders; design: *Allure*; photography: *Martha Stewart Living*; reporting: *The New Yorker*,

"Remembering Satan," Lawrence Wright; personal service: *Fortune*; public interest: *Philadelphia*; essays and criticism: *Harper's Bazaar*, "Mirrorings," Lucy Grealy, "A Woman's Work," Louise Erdrich, "The Crash of Blue-Sky California," David Beers.

George Polk Awards, by Long Island Univ., for excellence in journalism: national: Eileen Welsome, *The Albuquerque Tribune*; regional: Isabel Wilkerson, *The New York Times*; foreign: Keith Richburg, *The Washington Post*; local: Ying Chan, *The New York Daily News*; medical: Larry Keller and Fred Schulte, *The Ft. Lauderdale* (FL) *Sun-Sentinel* magazine: Oliver Sacks, *The New Yorker*; business: Paul Nyden, *The Charleston Gazette*; political: *The Springfield* (IL) *State Journal-Register;* financial: Scot J. Paltrow, *The Los Angeles Times*; radio commentary, Daniel Schorr, National Public Radio; book: David Remnick, *Lenin's Tomb: The Last Days of the Soviet Empire*; television: Christine Amanpour, CNN; career: Richard Dudman, *The St. Louis Post-Dispatch*

Reuben Awards, by National Cartoonists Society: best cartoonist of 1993: Jim Borgman; editorial cartoons: Bill Schorr; advertising illustration: Edward Sorel; greeting cards: W. B. Park; comic books: Mark Chiarello; newspaper panels: Bill Rechin; gag cartoons: George Booth; sports cartoons: Drew Little; animation: Tim Burton; newspaper comic strip: Bud Grace; magazine and book illustration: Hal Mayforth

Science in Society Print Journalism Awards, by National Assn. of Science Writers, $1,000 each: newspapers: Justin Catanoso, Taft Wireback, *Greensboro* (NC) *News & Record*; magazines: John Horgan, *Scientific American*; broadcast: Miles O'Brien, Kate King, CNN

John Peter Zenger Award, by the University of Arizona for distinguished service in behalf of freedom of the press: Jane Kirtley, executive director of the Reporters Committee for Freedom of the Press

Entertainment

Christopher Awards, by The Christophers: movies: *In the Name of the Father, Rudy, Schindler's List, Shadowlands*; television: *The American Experience: Eisenhower, I'll Fly Away: Then and Now, Silent Cries, Something Within Me, There Are No Children Here, Travels: For the Sake of the Children*; The James Keller Youth Award: Chris Burke; Special Christopher Award: The Hallmark Hall of Fame

Directors Guild of America, movie director: Steven Spielberg, *Schindler's List*

Drama Desk Awards, by New York theater critics writing for non-New York publications: play: *Angels in America: Perestroika*; musical: *Passion*; actor: Boyd Gaines, *She Loves Me*; actress: Donna Murphy, *Passion*; musical revival: *She Loves Me*; score: *Passion*

Emmy Awards, Daytime, by Academy of Television Arts and Sciences: actor: Michael Zaslow, *Guiding Light*, CBS; actress: Hillary B. Smith, *One Life to Live*, ABC; drama series: *All My Children*, ABC; directing team: *Guiding Light,* CBS; writing team: *One Life to Live,* ABC; supporting actor: Justin Deas, *Guiding Light*, CBS; supporting actress: Susan Haskell, *One Life to Live*, ABC; talk show host: Oprah Winfrey; animated children's program: *Rugrats,* Nickelodeon; children's series: *Sesame Street*; talk show: *The Oprah Winfrey Show*; game show: *Jeopardy!;* game show host: Bob Barker, *The Price is Right*

Emmy Awards, Prime-Time, by Academy of Television Arts and Sciences, 1993-94: drama series: *Picket Fences,* CBS; actor, drama series: Dennis Franz, *N.Y.P.D. Blue,* ABC; actress, drama series: Sela Ward, *Sisters*, NBC; supporting actor, drama series: Fyvush Finkel, *Picket Fences*, CBS; supporting actress, drama series: Leigh Taylor-Young, *Picket Fences,* CBS; writing, drama series: *N.Y.P.D. Blue*, "Steroid Boy," ABC; director, drama series: Daniel Sackheim, *N.Y.P.D. Blue*, "Tempest in a C-Cup," ABC; comedy series: *Frasier*, NBC; actor, comedy series: Kelsey Grammer, *Frasier*, NBC; actress, comedy series: Candice Bergen, *Murphy Brown*, CBS; supporting actor, comedy series: Michael Richards, *Seinfeld*, NBC; supporting actress, comedy series: Laurie Metcalf, *Roseanne,* ABC; writing, comedy series: *Frasier,* "The Good Son," NBC; director, comedy series: James Burrows, *Frasier*, "The Good Son," NBC; miniseries: *Mystery, Prime Suspect 3*, PBS; actor, miniseries: Hume Cronyn, *Hallmark Hall of Fame: To Dance With the White Dog*, CBS; actress, miniseries: Kirstie Alley, *David's Mother*, CBS; supporting actor, miniseries: Michael Goorjian, *David's Mother*, CBS; supporting actress, miniseries: Cicely Tyson, *Oldest Living Confederate Widow Tells All*, CBS; director, miniseries: John Frankenheimer, *Against the Wall*, HBO; writing, miniseries: *David's Mother*, CBS; made for television movie: *And the Band Played On*, HBO; variety, music, or comedy series: *Late Show With David Letterman,* CBS; variety, music, or comedy special: *The Kennedy Center Honors*, CBS; director, variety or music program: Walter C. Miller, *The Tony Awards*, CBS; writing, variety or music show: *Dennis Miller Live*, HBO; individual performance, variety or music show: Tracey Ullman, *Tracey Ullman Takes on New York*, HBO

National Society of Film Critics: film: *Schindler's List*; actor: David Thewlis, *Naked*; actress: Holly Hunter, *The Piano*; director: Steven Spielberg, *Schindler's List*; supporting actor: Ralph Fiennes, *Schindler's List*; cinematography: Janusz Kaminski, *Schindler's List*; screen writer: Jane Campion, *The Piano*; supporting actress: Madeleine Stowe, *Short Cuts*; foreign language film: *The Story of Qiu Ju*; documentary: *Visions of Light*

Rock-and-Roll Hall of Fame, 1994 inductees: Grateful Dead, Elton John, Rod Stewart, John Lennon, Bob Marley, Duane Eddy, the Animals, the Band, Willie Dixon, Johnny Otis

Tony (Antoinette Perry) Awards: play: *Angels in America: Perestroika*, Tony Kushner; musical: *Passion*; play revival: *An Inspector Calls*; musical revival: *Carousel*; actor, play: Stephen Spinella, *Angels in America: Perestroika*; actress, play: Diana Rigg, *Medea*; actor, musical: Boyd Gaines, *She Loves Me*; actress, musical: Donna Murphy, *Passion*; featured actor, play: Jeffrey Wright, *Angels in America: Perestroika*; featured actress, play: Jane Adams, *An Inspector Calls*; featured actor, musical: Jarrod Emick, *Damn Yankees*; featured actress, musical: Audra Ann McDonald, *Carousel*; director, play: Stephen Daldry, *An Inspector Calls*; director, musical: Nicholas Hytner, *Carousel*; book, musical: James Lapine, *Passion*; original score: Stephen Sondheim, *Passion*; scenic design: Bob Crowley, *Carousel*; costume design: Ann Hould-Ward, *Beauty and the Beast*; lighting design: Rick Fisher, *An Inspector Calls*; choreography: Sir Kenneth MacMillan, *Carousel*; life achievement: Jessica Tandy and Hume Cronyn; regional theater: McCarter Theater, Princeton, NJ

Miscellaneous Awards

American Institute of Architects Gold Medal: Sir Norman Foster

James Beard Awards: chef of the year: Daniel Boulud; restaurant of the year: Spago, West Hollywood, CA; pastry chef: Jacques Torres, Le Cirque; outstanding service: Joseph Baum, Rainbow Room; lifetime achievement: Robert Mondavi; rising star: Sarah Stegner, Ritz-Carlton, Chicago

Charles Frankel Prizes, by National Endowment for the Humanities, for those who have increased public awareness of the humanities, $5,000 each: Richard E. Alegria, John Hope Franklin, Hanna Holborn Gray, Andrew Heiskell, Laurel T. Ulrich

National Inventor of the Year Awards, by Intellectual Property Owners, recognizing most outstanding inventors: Pak-Wing S. Chum, George W. Knight, John R. Wilson, Shih-Yaw Lai, James C. Stevens; Spirit of American Ingenuity Award: Harvey M. Severson

John F. Kennedy Center for the Performing Arts Awards, for contribution to U.S. cultural life: Johnny Carson, Stephen Sondheim, Arthur Mitchell, Sir Georg Solti, Marion Williams

Library of the Year Award, by Gale Research, Inc., and *Library Journal*, $10,000 grant: Brown County Library, Green Bay, WI

McGraw-Hill Prize in Education, for distinguished contribution to the advancement of education, $25,000 each: Sr. Mary Costello, R.S.M., Sharon Darling, Booth Gardner

National Medal of Arts, by White House, for outstanding contributions to cultural life in the U.S.: Walter and Leonore Annenberg, Bess Lomax Hawes, Stanley Kunitz, Robert Rauschenberg, William Styron, Paul Taylor, Billy Wilder, Arthur Miller, Ray Charles, Cab Calloway, Robert Merrill, Lloyd Richards

Pritzker Architecture Prize, by the Hyatt Foundation, $100,000: Christian de Portzamparc, France

Franklin Delano Roosevelt Freedom Medal, by the Franklin and Eleanor Roosevelt Institute: Dalai Lama

Samuel H. Scripps American Dance Festival Award, for lifetime achievement in dance, $25,000: Trisha Brown

1994 Teacher of the Year, by the Council of Chief State School Officers and Encyclopædia Britannica: Sandra McBrayer

Templeton Prize for Progress in Religion, by Templeton Foundation, about $1 million: Michael Novak

Westinghouse Talent Search: 1st prize, $40,000 scholarship, Forrest Newell Anderson, Helena High School, Helena, MT

The Spingarn Medal

The Spingarn Medal has been awarded annually since 1914 by the National Association for the Advancement of Colored People for the highest achievement by a black American.

1946	Dr. Percy L. Julian
1947	Channing H. Tobias
1948	Ralph J. Bunche
1949	Charles Hamilton Houston
1950	Mabel Keaton Staupers
1951	Harry T. Moore
1952	Paul R. Williams
1953	Theodore K. Lawless
1954	Carl Murphy
1955	Jack Roosevelt Robinson
1956	Martin Luther King Jr.
1957	Mrs. Daisy Bates and the Little Rock Nine
1958	Edward Kennedy (Duke) Ellington
1959	Langston Hughes
1960	Kenneth B. Clark
1961	Robert C. Weaver
1962	Medgar Wiley Evers
1963	Roy Wilkins
1964	Leontyne Price
1965	John H. Johnson
1966	Edward W. Brooke
1967	Sammy Davis Jr.
1968	Clarence M. Mitchell Jr.
1969	Jacob Lawrence
1970	Leon Howard Sullivan
1971	Gordon Parks
1972	Wilson C. Riles
1973	Damon Keith
1974	Henry (Hank) Aaron
1975	Alvin Ailey
1976	Alex Haley
1977	Andrew Young
1978	Mrs. Rosa L. Parks
1979	Dr. Rayford W. Logan
1980	Coleman Young
1981	Dr. Benjamin Elijah Mays
1982	Lena Horne
1983	Thomas Bradley
1984	Bill Cosby
1985	Dr. Benjamin L. Hooks
1986	Percy E. Sutton
1987	Frederick Douglass Patterson
1988	Jesse Jackson
1989	L. Douglas Wilder
1990	Gen. Colin L. Powell
1991	Barbara Jordan
1992	Dorothy I. Height
1993	Maya Angelou

Miss America Winners

1921	Margaret Gorman, Washington, D.C.
1922-23	Mary Campbell, Columbus, Ohio
1924	Ruth Malcolmson, Philadelphia, Pennsylvania
1925	Fay Lamphier, Oakland, California
1926	Norma Smallwood, Tulsa, Oklahoma
1927	Lois Delaner, Joliet, Illinois
1933	Marion Bergeron, West Haven, Connecticut
1935	Henrietta Leaver, Pittsburgh, Pennsylvania
1936	Rose Coyle, Philadelphia, Pennsylvania
1937	Bette Cooper, Bertrand Island, New Jersey
1938	Marilyn Meseke, Marion, Ohio
1939	Patricia Donnelly, Detroit, Michigan
1940	Frances Marie Burke, Philadelphia, Pennsylvania
1941	Rosemary LaPlanche, Los Angeles, California
1942	Jo-Caroll Dennison, Tyler, Texas
1943	Jean Bartel, Los Angeles, California
1944	Venus Ramey, Washington, D.C.
1945	Bess Myerson, New York City, New York
1946	Marilyn Buferd, Los Angeles, California
1947	Barbara Walker, Memphis, Tennessee
1948	BeBe Shopp, Hopkins, Minnesota
1949	Jacque Mercer, Litchfield, Arizona
1951	Yolande Betbeze, Mobile, Alabama
1952	Coleen Kay Hutchins, Salt Lake City, Utah
1953	Neva Jane Langley, Macon, Georgia
1954	Evelyn Margaret Ay, Ephrata, Pennsylvania
1955	Lee Meriwether, San Francisco, California
1956	Sharon Ritchie, Denver, Colorado
1957	Marian McKnight, Manning, South Carolina
1958	Marilyn Van Derbur, Denver, Colorado
1959	Mary Ann Mobley, Brandon, Mississippi
1960	Lynda Lee Mead, Natchez, Mississippi
1961	Nancy Fleming, Montague, Michigan
1962	Maria Fletcher, Asheville, North Carolina
1963	Jacquelyn Mayer, Sandusky, Ohio
1964	Donna Axum, El Dorado, Arkansas
1965	Vonda Kay Van Dyke, Phoenix, Arizona
1966	Deborah Irene Bryant, Overland Park, Kansas
1967	Jane Anne Jayroe, Laverne, Oklahoma
1968	Debra Dene Barnes, Moran, Kansas
1969	Judith Anne Ford, Belvidere, Illinois
1970	Pamela Anne Eldred, Birmingham, Michigan
1971	Phyllis Ann George, Denton, Texas
1972	Laurie Lea Schaefer, Columbus, Ohio
1973	Terry Anne Meeuwsen, DePere, Wisconsin
1974	Rebecca Ann King, Denver, Colorado
1975	Shirley Cothran, Fort Worth, Texas
1976	Tawney Elaine Godin, Yonkers, New York
1977	Dorothy Kathleen Benham, Edina, Minnesota
1978	Susan Perkins, Columbus, Ohio
1979	Kylene Barker, Galax, Virginia
1980	Cheryl Prewitt, Ackerman, Mississippi
1981	Susan Powell, Elk City, Oklahoma
1982	Elizabeth Ward, Russellville, Arkansas
1983	Debra Maffett, Anaheim, California
1984	Vanessa Williams, Milwood, New York*
	Suzette Charles, Mays Landing, New Jersey
1985	Sharlene Wells, Salt Lake City, Utah
1986	Susan Akin, Meridian, Mississippi
1987	Kellye Cash, Memphis, Tennessee
1988	Kaye Lani Rae Rafko, Monroe, Michigan
1989	Gretchen Carlson, Anoka, Minnesota
1990	Debbye Turner, Columbia, Missouri
1991	Marjorie Vincent, Oak Park, Illinois
1992	Carolyn Suzanne Sapp, Honolulu, Hawaii
1993	Leanza Cornett, Jacksonville, Florida
1994	Kimberly Aiken, Columbia, South Carolina
1995	Heather Whitestone, Birmingham, Alabama

* Resigned July 23, 1984.

Academy Awards (Oscars)

1927-28

Picture: *Wings,* Paramount
Actor: Emil Jannings, *The Way of All Flesh*
Actress: Janet Gaynor, *Seventh Heaven*
Director: Frank Borzage, *Seventh Heaven;* Lewis Milestone, *Two Arabian Knights*

1928-29

Picture: *Broadway Melody,* MGM
Actor: Warner Baxter, *In Old Arizona*
Actress: Mary Pickford, *Coquette*
Director: Frank Lloyd, *The Divine Lady*

1929-30

Picture: *All Quiet on the Western Front,* University
Actor: George Arliss, *Disraeli*
Actress: Norma Shearer, *The Divorcee*
Director: Lewis Milestone, *All Quiet on the Western Front*

1930-31

Picture: *Cimarron,* RKO
Actor: Lionel Barrymore, *Free Soul*
Actress: Marie Dressler, *Min and Bill*
Director: Norman Taurog, *Skippy*

1931-32

Picture: *Grand Hotel,* MGM
Actor: Fredric March, *Dr. Jekyll and Mr. Hyde;* Wallace Beery, *The Champ* (tie)
Actress: Helen Hayes, *The Sin of Madelon Claudet*
Director: Frank Borzage, *Bad Girl*
Special: Walt Disney, *Mickey Mouse*

1932-33

Picture: *Cavalcade,* Fox
Actor: Charles Laughton, *The Private Life of Henry VIII*
Actress: Katharine Hepburn, *Morning Glory*
Director: Frank Lloyd, *Cavalcade*

1934

Picture: *It Happened One Night,* Columbia
Actor: Clark Gable, *It Happened One Night*
Actress: Claudette Colbert, *It Happened One Night*
Director: Frank Capra, *It Happened One Night*

1935

Picture: *Mutiny on the Bounty,* MGM
Actor: Victor McLaglen, *The Informer*
Actress: Bette Davis, *Dangerous*
Director: John Ford, *The Informer*

1936

Picture: *The Great Ziegfeld,* MGM
Actor: Paul Muni, *Story of Louis Pasteur*
Actress: Luise Rainer, *The Great Ziegfeld*
Sup. Actor: Walter Brennan, *Come and Get It*
Sup. Actress: Gale Sondergaard, *Anthony Adverse*
Director: Frank Capra, *Mr. Deeds Goes to Town*

1937

Picture: *Life of Emile Zola,* Warner
Actor: Spencer Tracy, *Captains Courageous*
Actress: Luise Rainer, *The Good Earth*
Sup. Actor: Joseph Schildkraut, *Life of Emile Zola*
Sup. Actress: Alice Brady, *In Old Chicago*
Director: Leo McCarey, *The Awful Truth*

1938

Picture: *You Can't Take It With You,* Columbia
Actor: Spencer Tracy, *Boys Town*
Actress: Bette Davis, *Jezebel*
Sup. Actor: Walter Brennan, *Kentucky*
Sup. Actress: Fay Bainter, *Jezebel*
Director: Frank Capra, *You Can't Take It With You*

1939

Picture: *Gone With the Wind,* Selznick International
Actor: Robert Donat, *Goodbye, Mr. Chips*
Actress: Vivien Leigh, *Gone With the Wind*
Sup. Actor: Thomas Mitchell, *Stage Coach*
Sup. Actress: Hattie McDaniel, *Gone With the Wind*
Director: Victor Fleming, *Gone With the Wind*

1940

Picture: *Rebecca,* Selznick International
Actor: James Stewart, *The Philadelphia Story*
Actress: Ginger Rogers, *Kitty Foyle*
Sup. Actor: Walter Brennan, *The Westerner*
Sup. Actress: Jane Darwell, *The Grapes of Wrath*
Director: John Ford, *The Grapes of Wrath*

1941

Picture: *How Green Was My Valley,* 20th Cent.-Fox
Actor: Gary Cooper, *Sergeant York*
Actress: Joan Fontaine, *Suspicion*
Sup. Actor: Donald Crisp, *How Green Was My Valley*
Sup. Actress: Mary Astor, *The Great Lie*
Director: John Ford, *How Green Was My Valley*

1942

Picture: *Mrs. Miniver,* MGM
Actor: James Cagney, *Yankee Doodle Dandy*
Actress: Greer Garson, *Mrs. Miniver*
Sup. Actor: Van Heflin, *Johnny Eager*
Sup. Actress: Teresa Wright, *Mrs. Miniver*
Director: William Wyler, *Mrs. Miniver*

1943

Picture: *Casablanca,* Warner
Actor: Paul Lukas, *Watch on the Rhine*
Actress: Jennifer Jones, *The Song of Bernadette*
Sup. Actor: Charles Coburn, *The More the Merrier*
Sup. Actress: Katina Paxinou, *For Whom the Bell Tolls*
Director: Michael Curtiz, *Casablanca*

1944

Picture: *Going My Way,* Paramount
Actor: Bing Crosby, *Going My Way*
Actress: Ingrid Bergman, *Gaslight*
Sup. Actor: Barry Fitzgerald, *Going My Way*
Sup. Actress: Ethel Barrymore, *None But the Lonely Heart*
Director: Leo McCarey, *Going My Way*

1945

Picture: *The Lost Weekend,* Paramount
Actor: Ray Milland, *The Lost Weekend*
Actress: Joan Crawford, *Mildred Pierce*
Sup. Actor: James Dunn, *A Tree Grows in Brooklyn*
Sup. Actress: Anne Revere, *National Velvet*
Director: Billy Wilder, *The Lost Weekend*

1946

Picture: *The Best Years of Our Lives,* Goldwyn, RKO
Actor: Fredric March, *The Best Years of Our Lives*
Actress: Olivia de Havilland, *To Each His Own*
Sup. Actor: Harold Russell, *The Best Years of Our Lives*
Sup. Actress: Anne Baxter, *The Razor's Edge*
Director: William Wyler, *The Best Years of Our Lives*

1947

Picture: *Gentleman's Agreement,* 20th Cent.-Fox
Actor: Ronald Colman, *A Double Life*
Actress: Loretta Young, *The Farmer's Daughter*
Sup. Actor: Edmund Gwenn, *Miracle on 34th Street*
Sup. Actress: Celeste Holm, *Gentleman's Agreement*
Director: Elia Kazan, *Gentleman's Agreement*

1948

Picture: *Hamlet,* Two Cities Film, Universal International
Actor: Laurence Olivier, *Hamlet*
Actress: Jane Wyman, *Johnny Belinda*
Sup. Actor: Walter Huston, *Treasure of Sierra Madre*
Sup. Actress: Claire Trevor, *Key Largo*
Director: John Huston, *Treasure of Sierra Madre*

1949

Picture: *All the King's Men,* Columbia
Actor: Broderick Crawford, *All the King's Men*
Actress: Olivia de Havilland, *The Heiress*
Sup. Actor: Dean Jagger, *Twelve O'Clock High*
Sup. Actress: Mercedes McCambridge, *All the King's Men*
Director: Joseph L. Mankiewicz, *Letter to Three Wives*

1950

Picture: *All About Eve,* 20th Century-Fox
Actor: Jose Ferrer, *Cyrano de Bergerac*
Actress: Judy Holliday, *Born Yesterday*
Sup. Actor: George Sanders, *All About Eve*
Sup. Actress: Josephine Hull, *Harvey*
Director: Joseph L. Mankiewicz, *All About Eve*

1951

Picture: *An American in Paris,* MGM
Actor: Humphrey Bogart, *The African Queen*
Actress: Vivien Leigh, *A Streetcar Named Desire*
Sup. Actor: Karl Malden, *A Streetcar Named Desire*
Sup. Actress: Kim Hunter, *A Streetcar Named Desire*
Director: George Stevens, *A Place in the Sun*

1952

Picture: *The Greatest Show on Earth,* C.B. DeMille, Paramount
Actor: Gary Cooper, *High Noon*
Actress: Shirley Booth, *Come Back, Little Sheba*
Sup. Actor: Anthony Quinn, *Viva Zapata!*
Sup. Actress: Gloria Grahame, *The Bad and the Beautiful*
Director: John Ford, *The Quiet Man*

1953

Picture: *From Here to Eternity,* Columbia
Actor: William Holden, *Stalag 17*
Actress: Audrey Hepburn, *Roman Holiday*
Sup. Actor: Frank Sinatra, *From Here to Eternity*
Sup. Actress: Donna Reed, *From Here to Eternity*
Director: Fred Zinnemann, *From Here to Eternity*

1954

Picture: *On the Waterfront,* Horizon-American, Columbia
Actor: Marlon Brando, *On the Waterfront*
Actress: Grace Kelly, *The Country Girl*
Sup. Actor: Edmond O'Brien, *The Barefoot Contessa*

Sup. Actress: Eva Marie Saint, *On the Waterfront*
Director: Elia Kazan, *On the Waterfront*

1955

Picture: *Marty,* Hecht and Lancaster's Steven Prods., U.A.
Actor: Ernest Borgnine, *Marty*
Actress: Anna Magnani, *The Rose Tattoo*
Sup. Actor: Jack Lemmon, *Mister Roberts*
Sup. Actress: Jo Van Fleet, *East of Eden*
Director: Delbert Mann, *Marty*

1956

Picture: *Around the World in 80 Days,* Michael Todd, U.A.
Actor: Yul Brynner, *The King and I*
Actress: Ingrid Bergman, *Anastasia*
Sup. Actor: Anthony Quinn, *Lust for Life*
Sup. Actress: Dorothy Malone, *Written on the Wind*
Director: George Stevens, *Giant*

1957

Picture: *The Bridge on the River Kwai,* Columbia
Actor: Alec Guinness, *The Bridge on the River Kwai*
Actress: Joanne Woodward, *The Three Faces of Eve*
Sup. Actor: Red Buttons, *Sayonara*
Sup. Actress: Miyoshi Umeki, *Sayonara*
Director: David Lean, *The Bridge on the River Kwai*

1958

Picture: *Gigi,* Arthur Freed Production, MGM
Actor: David Niven, *Separate Tables*
Actress: Susan Hayward, *I Want to Live*
Sup. Actor: Burl Ives, *The Big Country*
Sup. Actress: Wendy Hiller, *Separate Tables*
Director: Vincente Minnelli, *Gigi*

1959

Picture: *Ben-Hur,* MGM
Actor: Charlton Heston, *Ben-Hur*
Actress: Simone Signoret, *Room at the Top*
Sup. Actor: Hugh Griffith, *Ben-Hur*
Sup. Actress: Shelley Winters, *Diary of Anne Frank*
Director: William Wyler, *Ben-Hur*

1960

Picture: *The Apartment,* Mirisch Co., U.A.
Actor: Burt Lancaster, *Elmer Gantry*
Actress: Elizabeth Taylor, *Butterfield 8*
Sup. Actor: Peter Ustinov, *Spartacus*
Sup. Actress: Shirley Jones, *Elmer Gantry*
Director: Billy Wilder, *The Apartment*

1961

Picture: *West Side Story,* United Artists
Actor: Maximilian Schell, *Judgment at Nuremberg*
Actress: Sophia Loren, *Two Women*
Sup. Actor: George Chakiris, *West Side Story*
Sup. Actress: Rita Moreno, *West Side Story*
Director: Jerome Robbins, Robert Wise, *West Side Story*

1962

Picture: *Lawrence of Arabia,* Columbia
Actor: Gregory Peck, *To Kill a Mockingbird*
Actress: Anne Bancroft, *The Miracle Worker*
Sup. Actor: Ed Begley, *Sweet Bird of Youth*
Sup. Actress: Patty Duke, *The Miracle Worker*
Director: David Lean, *Lawrence of Arabia*

1963

Picture: *Tom Jones,* Woodfall Prod., U.A.-Lopert Pictures
Actor: Sidney Poitier, *Lilies of the Field*
Actress: Patricia Neal, *Hud*
Sup. Actor: Melvyn Douglas, *Hud*
Sup. Actress: Margaret Rutherford, *The V.I.P.s*
Director: Tony Richardson, *Tom Jones*

1964

Picture: *My Fair Lady,* Warner Bros.
Actor: Rex Harrison, *My Fair Lady*
Actress: Julie Andrews, *Mary Poppins*
Sup. Actor: Peter Ustinov, *Topkapi*
Sup. Actress: Lila Kedrova, *Zorba the Greek*
Director: George Cukor, *My Fair Lady*

1965

Picture: *The Sound of Music,* 20th Century-Fox
Actor: Lee Marvin, *Cat Ballou*
Actress: Julie Christie, *Darling*
Sup. Actor: Martin Balsam, *A Thousand Clowns*
Sup. Actress: Shelley Winters, *A Patch of Blue*
Director: Robert Wise, *The Sound of Music*

1966

Picture: *A Man for All Seasons,* Columbia
Actor: Paul Scofield, *A Man for All Seasons*
Actress: Elizabeth Taylor, *Who's Afraid of Virginia Woolf?*
Sup. Actor: Walter Matthau, *The Fortune Cookie*
Sup. Actress: Sandy Dennis, *Who's Afraid of Virginia Woolf?*
Director: Fred Zinnemann, *A Man for All Seasons*

1967

Picture: *In the Heat of the Night*
Actor: Rod Steiger, *In the Heat of the Night*
Actress: Katharine Hepburn, *Guess Who's Coming to Dinner*
Sup. Actor: George Kennedy, *Cool Hand Luke*
Sup. Actress: Estelle Parsons, *Bonnie and Clyde*
Director: Mike Nichols, *The Graduate*

1968

Picture: *Oliver!*
Actor: Cliff Robertson, *Charly*
Actress: Katharine Hepburn, *The Lion in Winter;* Barbra Streisand, *Funny Girl* (tie)
Sup. Actor: Jack Albertson, *The Subject Was Roses*
Sup. Actress: Ruth Gordon, *Rosemary's Baby*
Director: Sir Carol Reed, *Oliver!*

1969

Picture: *Midnight Cowboy*
Actor: John Wayne, *True Grit*
Actress: Maggie Smith, *The Prime of Miss Jean Brodie*
Sup. Actor: Gig Young, *They Shoot Horses, Don't They?*
Sup. Actress: Goldie Hawn, *Cactus Flower*
Director: John Schlesinger, *Midnight Cowboy*

1970

Picture: *Patton*
Actor: George C. Scott, *Patton* (refused)
Actress: Glenda Jackson, *Women in Love*
Sup. Actor: John Mills, *Ryan's Daughter*
Sup. Actress: Helen Hayes, *Airport*
Director: Franklin Schaffner, *Patton*

1971

Picture: *The French Connection*
Actor: Gene Hackman, *The French Connection*
Actress: Jane Fonda, *Klute*
Sup. Actor: Ben Johnson, *The Last Picture Show*
Sup. Actress: Cloris Leachman, *The Last Picture Show*
Director: William Friedkin, *The French Connection*

1972

Picture: *The Godfather*
Actor: Marlon Brando, *The Godfather* (refused)
Actress: Liza Minnelli, *Cabaret*
Sup. Actor: Joel Grey, *Cabaret*
Sup. Actress: Eileen Heckart, *Butterflies Are Free*
Director: Bob Fosse, *Cabaret*

1973

Picture: *The Sting*
Actor: Jack Lemmon, *Save the Tiger*
Actress: Glenda Jackson, *A Touch of Class*
Sup. Actor: John Houseman, *The Paper Chase*
Sup. Actress: Tatum O'Neal, *Paper Moon*
Director: George Roy Hill, *The Sting*

1974

Picture: *The Godfather, Part II*
Actor: Art Carney, *Harry and Tonto*
Actress: Ellen Burstyn, *Alice Doesn't Live Here Anymore*
Sup. Actor: Robert DeNiro, *The Godfather, Part II*
Sup. Actress: Ingrid Bergman, *Murder on the Orient Express*
Director: Francis Ford Coppola, *The Godfather, Part II*

1975

Picture: *One Flew Over the Cuckoo's Nest*
Actor: Jack Nicholson, *One Flew Over the Cuckoo's Nest*
Actress: Louise Fletcher, *One Flew Over the Cuckoo's Nest*
Sup. Actor: George Burns, *The Sunshine Boys*
Sup. Actress: Lee Grant, *Shampoo*
Director: Milos Forman, *One Flew Over the Cuckoo's Nest*

1976

Picture: *Rocky*
Actor: Peter Finch, *Network*
Actress: Faye Dunaway, *Network*
Sup. Actor: Jason Robards, *All the President's Men*
Sup. Actress: Beatrice Straight, *Network*
Director: John G. Avildsen, *Rocky*

1977

Picture: *Annie Hall*
Actor: Richard Dreyfuss, *The Goodbye Girl*
Actress: Diane Keaton, *Annie Hall*
Sup. Actor: Jason Robards, *Julia*
Sup. Actress: Vanessa Redgrave, *Julia*
Director: Woody Allen, *Annie Hall*

1978

Picture: *The Deer Hunter*
Actor: Jon Voight, *Coming Home*
Actress: Jane Fonda, *Coming Home*
Sup. Actor: Christopher Walken, *The Deer Hunter*
Sup. Actress: Maggie Smith, *California Suite*
Director: Michael Cimino, *The Deer Hunter*

1979

Picture: *Kramer vs. Kramer*
Actor: Dustin Hoffman, *Kramer vs. Kramer*
Actress: Sally Field, *Norma Rae*
Sup. Actor: Melvyn Douglas, *Being There*
Sup. Actress: Meryl Streep, *Kramer vs. Kramer*
Director: Robert Benton, *Kramer vs. Kramer*

1980

Picture: *Ordinary People*
Actor: Robert DeNiro, *Raging Bull*

Actress: Sissy Spacek, *Coal Miner's Daughter*
Sup. Actor: Timothy Hutton, *Ordinary People*
Sup. Actress: Mary Steenburgen, *Melvin & Howard*
Director: Robert Redford, *Ordinary People*

1981

Picture: *Chariots of Fire*
Actor: Henry Fonda, *On Golden Pond*
Actress: Katharine Hepburn, *On Golden Pond*
Sup. Actor: John Gielgud, *Arthur*
Sup. Actress: Maureen Stapleton, *Reds*
Director: Warren Beatty, *Reds*

1982

Picture: *Gandhi*
Actor: Ben Kingsley, *Gandhi*
Actress: Meryl Streep, *Sophie's Choice*
Sup. Actor: Louis Gossett, Jr., *An Officer and a Gentleman*
Sup. Actress: Jessica Lange, *Tootsie*
Director: Richard Attenborough, *Gandhi*

1983

Picture: *Terms of Endearment*
Actor: Robert Duvall, *Tender Mercies*
Actress: Shirley MacLaine, *Terms of Endearment*
Supporting Actor: Jack Nicholson, *Terms of Endearment*
Supporting Actress: Linda Hunt, *The Year of Living Dangerously*
Director: James L. Brooks, *Terms of Endearment*

1984

Picture: *Amadeus*
Actor: F. Murray Abraham, *Amadeus*
Actress: Sally Field, *Places in the Heart*
Supporting Actor: Haing S. Ngor, *The Killing Fields*
Supporting Actress: Peggy Ashcroft, *A Passage to India*
Director: Milos Forman, *Amadeus*

1985

Picture: *Out of Africa*
Actor: William Hurt, *Kiss of the Spider Woman*
Actress: Geraldine Page, *The Trip to Bountiful*
Supporting Actor: Don Ameche, *Cocoon*
Supporting Actress: Anjelica Huston, *Prizzi's Honor*
Director: Sydney Pollack, *Out of Africa*

1986

Picture: *Platoon*
Actor: Paul Newman, *The Color of Money*
Actress: Marlee Matlin, *Children of a Lesser God*
Supporting Actor: Michael Caine, *Hannah and Her Sisters*
Supporting Actress: Dianne Wiest, *Hannah and Her Sisters*
Director: Oliver Stone, *Platoon*

1987

Picture: *The Last Emperor*
Actor: Michael Douglas, *Wall Street*
Actress: Cher, *Moonstruck*
Supporting Actor: Sean Connery, *The Untouchables*
Supporting Actress: Olympia Dukakis, *Moonstruck*
Director: Bernardo Bertolucci, *The Last Emperor*

1988

Picture: *Rain Man*
Actor: Dustin Hoffman, *Rain Man*
Actress: Jodie Foster, *The Accused*
Supporting Actor: Kevin Kline, *A Fish Called Wanda*
Supporting Actress: Geena Davis, *The Accidental Tourist*
Director: Barry Levinson, *Rain Man*

1989

Picture: *Driving Miss Daisy*
Actor: Daniel Day-Lewis, *My Left Foot*
Actress: Jessica Tandy, *Driving Miss Daisy*
Supporting Actor: Denzel Washington, *Glory*
Supporting Actress: Brenda Fricker, *My Left Foot*
Director: Oliver Stone, *Born on the Fourth of July*

1990

Picture: *Dances With Wolves*
Actor: Jeremy Irons, *Reversal of Fortune*
Actress: Kathy Bates, *Misery*
Supporting Actor: Joe Pesci, *Goodfellas*
Supporting Actress: Whoopi Goldberg, *Ghost*
Director: Kevin Costner, *Dances With Wolves*

1991

Picture: *The Silence of the Lambs*
Actor: Anthony Hopkins, *The Silence of the Lambs*
Actress: Jodie Foster, *The Silence of the Lambs*
Supporting Actor: Jack Palance, *City Slickers*
Supporting Actress: Mercedes Ruehl, *The Fisher King*
Director: Jonathan Demme, *The Silence of the Lambs*

1992

Picture: *Unforgiven*
Actor: Al Pacino, *Scent of a Woman*
Actress: Emma Thompson, *Howards End*
Supporting Actor: Gene Hackman, *Unforgiven*
Supporting Actress: Marisa Tomei, *My Cousin Vinny*
Director: Clint Eastwood, *Unforgiven*

1993

Picture: *Schindler's List*
Actor: Tom Hanks, *Philadelphia*
Actress: Holly Hunter, *The Piano*
Supporting Actor: Tommy Lee Jones, *The Fugitive*
Supporting Actress: Anna Paquin, *The Piano*
Director: Steven Spielberg, *Schindler's List*
Foreign Film: *Belle Époque*, Spain
Original Screenplay: Jane Campion, *The Piano*
Adapted Screenplay: Steven Zaillian, *Schindler's List*
Cinematography: Janusz Kaminski, *Schindler's List*
Editing: Michael Kahn, *Schindler's List*
Original Score: John Williams, *Schindler's List*
Original Song: Bruce Springsteen, "Streets of Philadelphia," from *Philadelphia*
Art Direction: Allan Starski, Ewa Braun, *Schindler's List*
Costume: Gabriella Pescucci, *The Age of Innocence*
Makeup: Greg Cannom, Ve Neill, Yolanda Toussieng, *Mrs. Doubtfire*
Visual Effects: Dennis Muren, Stan Winston, Phil Tippett, Michael Lantieri, *Jurassic Park*
Sound: Gary Summers, Gary Rydstrom, Shawn Murphy, Ron Judkins, *Jurassic Park*
Documentary Feature: *I Am a Promise: The Children of Stanton Elementary School*
Documentary Short Subject: *Defending Our Lives*
Short Film, Live: *Black Rider*
Short Film, Animated: *The Wrong Trousers*
Honorary Award: Deborah Kerr
Jean Hersholt Humanitarian Award: Paul Newman
Gordon E. Sawyer Technical Award: Petro Vlahos
Technical Award of Merit: Panavision, Inc.; Manfred G. Michelson

Grammy Awards, 1958-92

Source: National Academy of Recording Arts & Sciences; first Grammys awarded for records released in 1958

Record	Year	Album
Domenico Modugno, Nel Blu Dipinto Di Blu (Volare)	1958	Henry Mancini, The Music From Peter Gunn
Bobby Darin, Mack the Knife	1959	Frank Sinatra, Come Dance With Me
Percy Faith, Theme From a Summer Place	1960	Bob Newhart, Button Down Mind
Henry Mancini, Moon River	1961	Judy Garland, Judy at Carnegie Hall
Tony Bennett, I Left My Heart in San Francisco	1962	Vaughn Meader, The First Family
Henry Mancini, The Days of Wine and Roses	1963	The Barbra Streisand Album
Stan Getz, Astrud Gilberto, The Girl From Ipanema	1964	Stan Getz, Astrud Gilberto, Getz/Gilberto
Herb Alpert, A Taste of Honey	1965	Frank Sinatra, September of My Years
Frank Sinatra, Strangers in the Night	1966	Frank Sinatra, A Man and His Music
5th Dimension, Up, Up and Away	1967	The Beatles, Sgt. Pepper's Lonely Hearts Club Band
Simon & Garfunkel, Mrs. Robinson	1968	Glen Campbell, By the Time I Get to Phoenix
5th Dimension, Aquarius/Let the Sunshine In	1969	Blood, Sweat and Tears
Simon & Garfunkel, Bridge Over Troubled Water	1970	Simon & Garfunkel, Bridge Over Troubled Water
Carole King, It's Too Late	1971	Carole King, Tapestry
Roberta Flack, The First Time Ever I Saw Your Face	1972	The Concert for Bangla Desh
Roberta Flack, Killing Me Softly With His Song	1973	Stevie Wonder, Innervisions
Olivia Newton-John, I Honestly Love You	1974	Stevie Wonder, Fulfillingness' First Finale

(continued)

Record	Year	Album
Captain & Tennille, Love Will Keep Us Together	1975	Paul Simon, Still Crazy After All These Years
George Benson, This Masquerade	1976	Stevie Wonder, Songs in the Key of Life
Eagles, Hotel California	1977	Fleetwood Mac, Rumours
Billy Joel, Just the Way You Are	1978	Bee Gees, Saturday Night Fever
The Doobie Brothers, What a Fool Believes	1979	Billy Joel, 52nd Street
Christopher Cross, Sailing	1980	Christopher Cross, Christopher Cross
Kim Carnes, Bette Davis Eyes	1981	John Lennon, Yoko Ono, Double Fantasy
Toto, Rosanna	1982	Toto, Toto IV
Michael Jackson, Beat It	1983	Michael Jackson, Thriller
Tina Turner, What's Love Got to Do With It	1984	Lionel Richie, Can't Slow Down
USA for Africa, We Are the World	1985	Phil Collins, No Jacket Required
Steve Winwood, Higher Love	1986	Paul Simon, Graceland
Paul Simon, Graceland	1987	U2, The Joshua Tree
Bobby McFerrin, Don't Worry, Be Happy	1988	George Michael, Faith
Bette Midler, Wind Beneath My Wings	1989	Bonnie Raitt, Nick of Time
Phil Collins, Another Day in Paradise	1990	Quincy Jones, Back on the Block
Natalie Cole, with Nat "King" Cole, Unforgettable	1991	Natalie Cole, with Nat "King" Cole, Unforgettable
Eric Clapton, Tears in Heaven	1992	Eric Clapton, Unplugged

1993 Grammy Awards

Record: Whitney Houston, I Will Always Love You
Album: Whitney Houston, The Bodyguard
Song: A Whole New World (Aladdin's Theme)
New Artist: Toni Braxton
Female Pop Vocalist: Whitney Houston, I Will Always Love You
Male Pop Vocalist: Sting, If I Ever Lose My Faith in You
Duo or Group Pop Vocal: Peabo Bryson and Regina Belle, A Whole New World (Aladdin's Theme)
Traditional Pop Vocalist: Tony Bennett, Steppin' Out
Pop Instrumental Performance: Bruce Hornsby and Branford Marsalis, Barcelona Mona
Solo Rock Vocalist: Meatloaf, I'd Do Anything for Love
Hard Rock With Vocal: Stone Temple Pilots, Plush
Rock Song: David Pirner, Runaway Train
Alternative Album: U2, Zooropa
R & B Song: Janet Jackson, James Harris 3d, Terry Lewis, That's the Way Love Goes
Rap Duo or Group: Digable Planets, Rebirth of Slick
Jazz Vocalist: Natalie Cole, Take a Look
Traditional Blues Album: B.B. King, Blues Summit
Country Vocalist, Female: Mary-Chapin Carpenter, Passionate Kisses
Country Vocalist, Male: Dwight Yoakam, Ain't That Lonely Yet
Country Song: Lucinda Williams, Passionate Kisses

Newbery Medal Books

The Newbery Medal is awarded annually by the Association for Library Service to Children, a division of the American Library Association, to the author of the most distinguished contribution to American literature for children.

Year Awarded	Book, Author
1922	*The Story of Mankind,* Hendrik Willem van Loon
1923	*The Voyages of Dr. Dolittle,* Hugh Lofting
1924	*The Dark Frigate,* Charles Boardman Hawes
1925	*Tales From Silver Lands,* Charles Joseph Finger
1926	*Shen of the Sea,* Arthur Bowie Chrisman
1927	*Smoky, the Cowhorse,* Will James
1928	*Gay-Neck,* Dhan Gopal Mukerji
1929	*The Trumpeter of Krakow,* Eric P. Kelly
1930	*Hitty, Her First Hundred Years,* Rachel Field
1931	*The Cat Who Went to Heaven,* Elizabeth Coatsworth
1932	*Waterless Mountain,* Laura Adams Armer
1933	*Young Fu of the Upper Yangtze,* Elizabeth Foreman Lewis
1934	*Invincible Louisa,* Cornelia Lynde Meigs
1935	*Dobry,* Monica Shannon
1936	*Caddie Woodlawn,* Carol Ryrie Brink
1937	*Roller Skates,* Ruth Sawyer
1938	*The White Stag,* Kate Seredy
1939	*Thimble Summer,* Elizabeth Enright
1940	*Daniel Boone,* James Daugherty
1941	*Call It Courage,* Armstrong Sperry
1942	*The Matchlock Gun,* Walter D. Edmonds
1943	*Adam of the Road,* Elizabeth Janet Gray
1944	*Johnny Tremain,* Esther Forbes
1945	*Rabbit Hill,* Robert Lawson
1946	*Strawberry Girl,* Lois Lenski
1947	*Miss Hickory,* Carolyn S. Bailey
1948	*Twenty-One Balloons,* William Pène Du Bois
1949	*King of the Wind,* Marguerite Henry
1950	*The Door in the Wall,* Marguerite de Angeli
1951	*Amos Fortune, Free Man,* Elizabeth Yates
1952	*Ginger Pye,* Eleanor Estes
1953	*Secret of the Andes,* Ann Nolan Clark
1954	*... And Now Miguel,* Joseph Krumgold
1955	*The Wheel on the School,* Meindert DeJong
1956	*Carry On, Mr. Bowditch,* Jean Lee Latham
1957	*Miracles on Maple Hill,* Virginia Sorensen
1958	*Rifles for Watie,* Harold Keith
1959	*The Witch of Blackbird Pond,* Elizabeth George Speare
1960	*Onion John,* Joseph Krumgold
1961	*Island of the Blue Dolphins,* Scott O'Dell
1962	*The Bronze Bow,* Elizabeth George Speare
1963	*A Wrinkle in Time,* Madeleine L'Engle
1964	*It's Like This, Cat,* Emily Cheney Neville
1965	*Shadow of a Bull,* Maja Wojciechowska
1966	*I, Juan de Pareja,* Elizabeth Borton de Trevino
1967	*Up a Road Slowly,* Irene Hunt
1968	*From the Mixed-Up Files of Mrs. Basil E. Frankweiler,* E. L. Konigsburg
1969	*The High King,* Lloyd Alexander
1970	*Sounder,* William H. Armstrong
1971	*The Summer of the Swans,* Betsy Byars
1972	*Mrs. Frisby and the Rats of NIMH,* Robert C. O'Brien
1973	*Julie of the Wolves,* Jean George
1974	*The Slave Dancer,* Paula Fox
1975	*M. C. Higgins the Great,* Virginia Hamilton
1976	*Grey King,* Susan Cooper
1977	*Roll of Thunder, Hear My Cry,* Mildred D. Taylor
1978	*Bridge to Terabithia,* Katherine Paterson
1979	*The Westing Game,* Ellen Raskin
1980	*A Gathering of Days,* Joan Blos
1981	*Jacob Have I Loved,* Katherine Paterson
1982	*A Visit to William Blake's Inn: Poems for Innocent and Experienced Travelers,* Nancy Willard
1983	*Dicey's Song,* Cynthia Voigt
1984	*Dear Mr. Henshaw,* Beverly Cleary
1985	*The Hero and the Crown,* Robin McKinley
1986	*Sarah, Plain and Tall,* Patricia MacLachlan
1987	*The Whipping Boy,* Sid Fleischman
1988	*Lincoln: A Photobiography,* Russell Freedman
1989	*Joyful Noise: Poems for Two Voices,* Paul Fleischman
1990	*Number the Stars,* Lois Lowry
1991	*Maniac Magee,* Jerry Spinelli
1992	*Shiloh,* Phyllis Reynolds Naylor
1993	*Missing May,* Cynthia Ryland
1994	*The Giver,* Lois Lowry

NOTED PERSONALITIES

Widely Known Americans of the Present

Statesmen, journalists, authors of nonfiction, and other prominent persons not listed in other categories; as of mid-1994.

Name (Birthplace)	Birthdate
Adler, Mortimer (New York, NY)	12/2/02
Ailes, Roger (Knoxville, TN)	7/3/40
Albright, Madeleine (Prague, Czech.)	5/15/37
Ambrose, Stephen E. (Decatur, IL)	1/10/36
Anderson, Jack (Long Beach, CA)	10/19/22
Annenberg, Walter H. (Milwaukee, WI)	3/13/08
Arledge, Roone (Forest Hills, NY)	7/8/31
Armstrong, Neil (Wapakoneta, OH)	8/5/30
Aspin, Les (Milwaukee, WI)	7/21/38
Babbitt, Bruce (Los Angeles, CA)	6/27/38
Baker, James A. (Houston, TX)	4/28/30
Baker, Russell (Loudoun Co., VA)	8/14/25
Barry, Dave (Armonk, NY)	7/3/47
Barthelmy, Sidney K. (New Orleans, LA)	3/17/42
Bartley, Robert (Marshall, MN)	10/12/37
Bennett, William J. (Salem, OH)	5/4/44
Bentsen, Lloyd (Mission, TX)	2/11/21
Biden, Joseph R., Jr. (Scranton, PA)	11/20/42
Blackmun, Harry (Nashville, IL)	11/12/08
Bloom, Harold (New York, NY)	7/11/30
Bombeck, Erma (Dayton, OH)	2/21/27
Boorstin, Daniel (Atlanta, GA)	10/1/14
Boxer, Barbara (Brooklyn, NY)	11/11/40
Bradlee, Ben (Boston, MA)	8/26/21
Bradley, Bill (Crystal City, MO)	7/28/43
Bradley, Ed (Philadelphia, PA)	6/22/41
Bradley, Thomas (Calvert, TX)	12/29/17
Brennan, William J. (Newark, NJ)	4/25/06
Breslin, Jimmy (Jamaica, NY)	10/17/30
Breyer, Stephen (San Francisco, CA)	8/15/38
Brinkley, David (Wilmington, NC)	7/10/20
Broder, David (Chicago Heights, IL)	9/11/29
Brody, Jane (Brooklyn, NY)	5/19/41
Brokaw, Tom (Webster, SD)	2/6/40
Brothers, Joyce (New York, NY)	9/20/28
Brown, Helen Gurley (Green Forest, AR)	2/18/22
Brown, Jerry (San Francisco, CA)	4/7/38
Brown, Ron (Washington, DC)	8/1/41
Buchanan, Pat (Washington, DC)	11/2/38
Buchwald, Art (Mt. Vernon, NY)	10/20/25
Buckley, William F. (New York, NY)	11/24/25
Buffet, Warren (Omaha, NE)	8/30/30
Bumpers, Dale (Charleston, AR)	8/12/25
Buscaglia, Leo (Los Angeles, CA)	3/31/24
Bush, Barbara (Rye, NY)	6/8/25
Bush, George Herbert Walker (Milton, MA)	6/12/24
Byrd, Robert (N. Wilkesboro, NC)	11/20/17
Canby, Vincent (Chicago, IL)	7/27/24
Carter, Jimmy (Plains, GA)	10/1/24
Carter, Rosalynn (Plains, GA)	8/18/27
Chancellor, John (Chicago, IL)	7/14/27
Child, Julia (Pasadena, CA)	8/15/12
Chisholm, Shirley (Brooklyn, NY)	11/30/24
Christopher, Warren (Scranton, PA)	10/27/25
Chung, Connie (Washington, DC)	8/20/46
Cisneros, Henry (San Antonio, TX)	6/11/47
Claiborne, Liz (Brussels, Belg.)	3/31/29
Clinton, Bill (Hope, AR)	8/19/46
Clinton, Chelsea (Little Rock, AR)	2/27/80
Clinton, Hillary Rodham (Chicago, IL)	10/26/47
Collins, Martha (Shelby Co., KY)	12/7/36
Commager, Henry Steele (Pittsburgh, PA)	10/25/02
Cooney, Joan Ganz (Phoenix, AZ)	10/30/29
Cosell, Howard (Winston-Salem, NC)	3/25/20
Couric, Katie (Washington, DC)	1/7/57
Cronkite, Walter (St. Joseph, MO)	11/4/16
Cuomo, Mario (Queens, NY)	6/15/32
Daley, Richard M. (Chicago, IL)	4/24/42
D'Amato, Alfonse M. (Brooklyn, NY)	8/1/37
Deford, Frank (Baltimore, MD)	12/16/38
Dellums, Ronald (Oakland, CA)	11/24/35
Dershowitz, Alan (Brooklyn, NY)	9/1/38
Diller, Barry (San Francisco, CA)	2/2/42
Dingell, John D., Jr. (Colorado Springs, CO)	7/8/26
Dixon, Sharon Pratt (Washington, DC)	1/31/44
Dodd, Christopher (Willimantic, CT)	5/27/44
Dole, Elizabeth (Salisbury, NC)	7/29/36
Dole, Robert (Russell, KS)	7/22/23
Domenici, Pete (Albuquerque, NM)	5/7/32
Donaldson, Sam (El Paso, TX)	3/11/34
Drew, Elizabeth (Cincinnati, OH)	11/16/35
Dukakis, Michael S. (Boston, MA)	11/3/33

Name (Birthplace)	Birthdate
Edelman, Marian Wright (Bennetsville, SC)	6/6/39
Eisner, Michael (New York, NY)	3/7/42
Ephron, Nora (New York, NY)	5/19/41
Evangelista, Linda (St. Catherine's,Onatrio)	5/10/65
Falwell, Jerry (Lynchburg, VA)	8/11/33
Feinstein, Dianne (San Francisco, CA)	6/22/33
Ferraro, Geraldine (Newburgh, NY)	8/26/35
Florio, James J. (New York, NY)	8/29/37
Foley, Thomas S. (Spokane, WA)	3/6/29
Foote, Shelby (Greenville, MS)	11/17/16
Ford, Betty (Chicago, IL)	4/8/18
Ford, Gerald R. (Omaha, NE)	7/14/13
Frankel, Max (Gera, Germany)	4/3/30
Friedan, Betty (Peoria, IL)	2/4/21
Friedman, Milton (Brooklyn, NY)	7/31/12
Galbraith, John Kenneth (Iona Station, Ontario)	10/15/08
Gates, Bill (Seattle, WA)	10/28/55
Gephardt, Richard (St. Louis, MO)	1/31/41
Gergen, David R. (Durham, NC)	5/9/42
Gibson, Charles (Evanston, IL)	3/9/43
Gingrich, Newt (Harrisburg, PA)	6/17/43
Ginsberg, Allen (Paterson, NJ)	6/3/21
Ginsburg, Ruth Bader (Brooklyn, NY)	3/15/33
Giuliani, Rudolph (New York, NY)	5/28/44
Glenn, John (Cambridge, OH)	7/18/21
Goldwater, Barry M. (Phoenix, AZ)	1/1/09
Goodman, Ellen (Newton, MA)	4/11/41
Gore, Al (Washington, DC)	3/31/48
Gore, Tipper (Washington, DC)	8/19/48
Gottlieb, Robert A. (New York, NY)	4/29/31
Gould, Stephen Jay (New York, NY)	9/10/41
Graham, Billy (Charlotte, NC)	11/7/18
Graham, Donald (Baltimore, MD)	4/22/45
Graham, Katharine (New York, NY)	6/16/17
Gramm, Phil (Ft. Benning, GA)	7/8/42
Gray, William H., 3d (Baton Rouge, LA)	8/20/41
Greene, Bob (Columbus, OH)	5/10/47
Greenfield, Meg (Seattle, WA)	12/27/30
Greenspan, Alan (New York, NY)	3/6/26
Gumbel, Bryant (New Orleans, LA)	9/29/48
Halberstam, David (New York, NY)	4/10/34
Hamilton, Lee (Daytona Beach, FL)	4/20/31
Harkin, Tom (Cumming, IA)	11/19/39
Harvey, Paul (Tulsa, OK)	9/4/18
Heflin, Howell (Poulan, GA)	6/19/21
Helms, Jesse (Monroe, NC)	10/18/21
Helmsley, Leona (New York, NY)	c1920
Heloise (Waco, TX)	4/15/51
Hollings, Ernest (Charleston, SC)	1/1/22
Hutchison, Kay Bailey (Galveston, TX)	7/22/43
Iacocca, Lee A. (Allentown, PA)	10/15/24
Inouye, Daniel K. (Honolulu, HI)	9/7/24
Ireland, Patricia (Oak Park, IL)	10/19/45
Jackson, Jesse (Greenville, SC)	10/8/41
Jennings, Peter (Toronto, Ontario)	8/29/38
Johnson, Lady Bird (Karnack, TX)	12/22/12
Jordan, Barbara (Houston, TX)	2/21/36
Kael, Pauline (Petaluma, CA)	6/19/19
Kantor, Mickey (Nashville, TN)	8/7/39
Karan, Donna (Forest Hills, NY)	10/2/48
Kassebaum, Nancy (Topeka, KS)	7/29/32
Kemp, Jack (Los Angeles, CA)	7/13/35
Kennedy, Anthony (Sacramento, CA)	7/23/36
Kennedy, Edward M. (Brookline, MA)	2/22/32
Kennedy, Rose (Boston, MA)	7/22/1890
Kerr, Walter (Evanston, IL)	7/8/13
King, Coretta Scott (Marion, AL)	4/27/27
King, Larry (Brooklyn, NY)	11/19/34
Kinsley, Michael (Detroit, MI)	3/9/51
Kirkland, Lane (Camden, SC)	3/12/22
Kirkpatrick, Jeane (Duncan, OK)	11/19/26
Kissinger, Henry (Fuerth, Germany)	5/27/23
Klein, Calvin (New York, NY)	11/19/42
Koch, Edward I. (New York, NY)	12/12/24
Koop, C. Everett (Brooklyn, NY)	10/14/16
Koppel, Ted (Lancashire, England)	2/8/40
Kuhn, Maggie (Buffalo, NY)	1905
Kunstler, William (New York, NY)	7/7/19
Kuralt, Charles (Wilmington, NC)	9/10/34
Landers, Ann (Sioux City, IA)	7/4/18
Lansing, Sherry Lee (Chicago, IL)	7/31/44
Lauder, Estee (New York, NY)	9/1/08

Name (Birthplace)	Birthdate
Lauren, Ralph (Bronx, NY)	10/14/39
Leahy, Patrick (Montpelier, VT)	3/31/40
Lear, Frances (Hudson, NY)	7/14/23
Lear, Norman (New Haven, CT)	7/27/22
Lehrer, Jim (Wichita, KS)	5/19/34
Lelyveld, Joseph (Cincinnati, OH)	4/5/37
Lewis, Anthony (New York, NY)	3/27/27
Limbaugh, Rush (Cape Girardeau, MO)	1/12/51
Lindbergh, Anne Morrow (Englewood, NJ)	1906
Lorenzo, Frank (New York, NY)	5/19/40
Lott, Trent (Grenada, MS)	10/9/41
Lugar, Richard G. (Indianapolis, IN)	4/4/32
Lukas, J. Anthony (New York, NY)	4/25/33
Lunden, Joan (Sacramento, CA)	9/19/50
MacNeil, Robert (Montreal, Quebec)	1/19/31
Manchester, William (Attleboro, MA)	4/1/22
Martin, Lynn (Evanston, IL)	12/26/39
Maslin, Janet (New York, NY)	8/12/49
McClendon, Sarah (Tyler, TX)	7/8/10
McGovern, George (Avon, SD)	7/19/22
McNamara, Robert (San Francisco, CA)	6/9/16
Metzenbaum, Howard (Cleveland, OH)	6/4/17
Michel, Robert H. (Peoria, IL)	3/2/23
Mikulski, Barbara (Baltimore, MD)	7/20/36
Mitchell, George (Waterville, ME)	8/20/33
Mondale, Walter (Ceylon, MN)	1/5/28
Moseley-Braun, Carol (Chicago, IL)	8/16/47
Moyers, Bill (Hugo, OK)	6/5/34
Moynihan, Daniel P. (Tulsa, OK)	3/16/27
Mudd, Roger (Washington, DC)	2/9/28
Murray, Patty (Seattle, WA)	10/11/50
Myers, Dee Dee (Quonset Point, RI)	9/1/61
Nader, Ralph (Winsted, CT)	2/27/34
North, Oliver (San Antonio, TX)	10/7/43
Norton, Eleanor Holmes (Washington, DC)	6/13/37
Novak, Robert (Joliet, IL)	2/26/31
Novello, Antonia (Fajardo, PR)	8/23/44
Nunn, Sam (Perry, GA)	9/8/38
O'Connor, Cardinal John (Phila., PA)	1/15/20
O'Connor, Sandra Day (nr. Duncan, AZ)	3/26/30
Osgood, Charles (New York, NY)	1/8/33
Packwood, Bob (Portland, OR)	9/11/32
Paglia, Camille (Endicott, NY)	—
Panetta, Leon F. (Monterey, CA)	6/28/38
Pauley, Jane (Indianapolis, IN)	10/31/50
Perot, H. Ross (Texarkana, TX)	6/27/30
Phillips, Kevin (New York, NY)	11/30/40
Pickens, T. Boone (Holdenville, OK)	5/22/28
Pickering, Thomas (Orange, NJ)	11/5/31
Plimpton, George (New York, NY)	3/18/27
Podhoretz, Norman (New York, NY)	1/16/30
Poussaint, Alvin F. (New York, NY)	5/15/34
Powell, Colin (New York, NY)	4/5/37
Quayle, Dan (Indianapolis, IN)	2/4/47
Quindlen, Anna (Phildelphia, PA)	7/8/53
Quinn, Jane Bryant (Niagara Falls, NY)	2/5/39
Rangel, Charles (New York, NY)	6/11/30
Rather, Dan (Wharton, TX)	10/31/31
Redstone, Sumner M. (Boston, MA)	5/27/23
Reagan, Nancy (New York, NY)	7/6/23
Reagan, Ronald (Tampico, IL)	2/6/11
Rehnquist, William (Milwaukee, WI)	10/1/24
Reich, Robert B. (Scranton, PA)	6/24/46
Reno, Janet (Miami, FL)	7/21/38
Rich, Frank (Washington, DC)	6/2/49
Richards, Ann (Waco, TX)	9/3/33
Ride, Sally K. (Encino, CA)	5/26/51
Riley, Richard (Greenville, SC)	1/2/33
Roberts, Oral (nr. Ada, OK)	1/24/18
Robertson, Pat (Lexington, VA)	3/22/30
Rockefeller, David (New York, NY)	6/12/15
Rockefeller, John D., 4th, "Jay" (New York, NY)	6/18/37
Rockefeller, Laurance S. (New York, NY)	5/26/10
Rooney, Andy (Albany, NY)	1/14/19
Rostenkowski, Dan (Chicago, IL)	1/2/28
Rukeyser, Louis (New York, NY)	1/30/33
Safer, Morley (Toronto, Ontario)	11/8/31
Safire, William (New York, NY)	12/17/29
Sagan, Carl (New York, NY)	11/9/34
Salk, Jonas (New York, NY)	10/28/14
Sawyer, Diane (Glasgow, KY)	12/22/45
Scalia, Antonin (Trenton, NJ)	3/11/36
Schlesinger, Arthur, Jr. (Columbus, OH)	10/15/17
Schroeder, Patricia (Portland, OR)	7/30/40
Schuller, Robert (Alton, IA)	9/16/26
Schwarzkopf, H. Norman (Trenton, NJ)	8/22/34
Scott, Willard (Alexandria, VA)	3/7/34
Scowcroft, Brent (Ogden, UT)	3/19/25
Seaborg, Glenn T. (Ishpeming, MI)	4/19/12
Shalala, Donna E. (Cleveland, OH)	2/14/41
Shalikashvili, John (Warsaw, Poland)	6/27/36
Shanker, Albert (New York, NY)	9/14/28
Shaw, Bernard (Chicago, IL)	1940
Shriver, Maria (Chicago, IL)	11/6/55
Shultz, George P. (New York, NY)	12/13/20
Silver, Joan Micklin (Omaha, NE)	5/25/35
Simon, Paul (Eugene, OR)	11/29/28
Simpson, Alan K. (Cody, WY)	9/2/31
Skinner, Samuel (Chicago, IL)	6/10/38
Smith, Harry (Lansing, IL)	8/21/51
Smith, Hedrick (Kilmacolm, Scotland)	7/9/33
Smith, Liz (Ft. Worth, TX)	2/2/23
Souter, David H. (Melrose, MA)	9/17/39
Specter, J. Arlen (Wichita, KS)	2/12/30
Spock, Benjamin (New Haven, CT)	5/2/03
Stahl, Lesley (Lynn, MA)	12/16/41
Steinbrenner, George (Rocky River, OH)	7/4/30
Steinem, Gloria (Toledo, OH)	3/25/34
Stephanopolous, George (Fall River, MA)	2/10/61
Stern, David J. (New York, NY)	9/22/42
Stevens, John Paul (Chicago, IL)	4/20/20
Sulzberger, Arthur Ochs, Sr. (New York, NY)	2/5/26
Sulzberger, Arthur Ochs, Jr. (Mt. Kisco, NY)	9/22/51
Sununu, John H. (Havana, Cuba)	7/2/39
Tagliabue, Paul (Jersey City, NJ)	11/24/40
Tartikoff, Brandon (Long Island, NY)	1/13/49
Terkel, Studs (New York, NY)	5/16/12
Thomas, Clarence (Savannah, GA)	6/23/48
Thurmond, J. Strom (Edgefield, SC)	12/5/02
Tisch, Laurence (New York, NY)	3/15/23
Toland, John (LaCrosse, WI)	6/29/12
Trillin, Calvin (Kansas City, MO)	12/5/35
Truman, Margaret (Independence, MO)	2/17/24
Trump, Donald (New York, NY)	1946
Turner, Ted (Cincinnati, OH)	11/19/38
Udall, Morris K. (St. Johns, AZ)	6/15/22
Ueberroth, Peter (Chicago, IL)	9/2/37
Valenti, Jack (Houston, TX)	9/5/21
Van Buren, Abigail (Sioux City, IA)	7/4/18
Wallace, George (Clio, AL)	8/25/19
Wallace, Mike (Brookline, MA)	5/9/18
Walters, Barbara (Boston, MA)	9/25/31
Wattleton, Faye (St. Louis, MO)	7/8/43
Weicker, Lowell (Paris, France)	5/16/31
Wenner, Jann (New York, NY)	1/7/46
Westheimer, Ruth (Frankfurt, Germany)	1928
White, Bill (Lakewood, FL)	1/28/34
White, Byron (Ft. Collins, CO)	6/8/17
Wicker, Tom (Hamlet, NC)	6/18/26
Wiesel, Elie (Sighet, Romania)	9/30/28
Wilder, L. Douglas (Richmond, VA)	1/17/31
Will, George (Champaign, IL)	5/4/41
Wilson, Pete (Lake Forest, IL)	8/23/33
Yard, Molly (Shanghai, China)	c1910
Young, Coleman (Tuscaloosa, AL)	5/24/18
Zahn, Paula (Omaha, NE)	2/24/56
Zuckerman, Mortimer (Montreal, Quebec)	6/4/37

Noted Black Americans

Names of black athletes and entertainers are not included here as they are listed elsewhere in *The World Almanac*.

Rev. Dr. Ralph David Abernathy, 1926-90, organizer, 1957, and president, 1968, of the Southern Christian Leadership Conference.

Maya Angelou, b 1928, author, read her poem "On the Pulse of Morning" at Pres. Bill Clinton's inauguration.

Crispus Attucks, c 1723-70, agitator who led group that precipitated the "Boston Massacre," Mar. 5, 1770.

James Baldwin, 1924-87, author, playwright; *The Fire Next Time, Blues for Mister Charlie, Just Above My Head.*

Benjamin Banneker, 1731-1806, inventor, astronomer, mathematician, and gazetteer; served on commission that surveyed and laid out Washington, DC.

Imamu Amiri Baraka, b LeRoi Jones, 1934, poet, playwright.

James P. Beckwourth, 1798-c 1867, western fur trader, scout, after whom Beckwourth Pass in northern California is named.

Dr. Mary McCleod Bethune, 1875-1955, adviser to presidents Franklin Roosevelt and Harry Truman; division administrator, Natl. Youth Administration, 1935; founder, president, Bethune-Cookman College.

Henry Blair, 19th century, obtained patents (believed among first issued to a black) for a corn-planter, 1834, and for a cotton-planter, 1836.

Guion S. Bluford, Jr., b 1942, astronaut, first black American to go into space, 1983.

Julian Bond, b 1940, civil rights leader, first elected to the Georgia state legislature, 1965; helped found Student Nonviolent Coordinating Committee.

Edward Bouchet, 1852-1918, first black to earn a Ph.D. at a U.S. university (Yale, 1876); first black elected to Phi Beta Kappa.

Thomas Bradley, b 1917, mayor of Los Angeles, 1973-93.

Andrew F. Brimmer, b 1926, first black member, 1966, Federal Reserve Board.

Edward W. Brooke, b 1919, attorney general of Massachusetts, 1962, first black elected to U. S. Senate, 1967, since Reconstruction.

Gwendolyn Brooks, b 1917, poet, novelist; first black to win a Pulitzer Prize, 1950, *Annie Allen.*

Sterling A. Brown, 1901-89, poet, literature professor; helped establish African-American literary criticism.

William Wells Brown, 1815-84, novelist, dramatist; first American black to publish a novel.

Dr. Ralph Bunche, 1904-71, first black to win the Nobel Peace Prize, 1950; undersecretary of the UN, 1950.

Sherian Grace Cadoria, b 1940, brigadier general; retired in 1990 as the highest-ranking black woman in U.S. armed forces.

Alexa Canady, b 1950, first black woman neurosurgeon in U.S.

George E. Carruthers, b 1940, physicist; developed the *Apollo 16* lunar surface ultraviolet camera/spectograph.

George Washington Carver, 1861-1943, botanist, chemurgist, and educator; his extensive experiments in soil building and plant diseases revolutionized the economy of the South.

Charles Waddell Chestnutt, 1858-1932, author known primarily for his short stories, including *The Conjure Woman.*

Shirley Chisholm, b 1924, first black woman elected to U.S. House of Representatives, Brooklyn, NY, 1968.

Rev. James Cleveland, 1931-91, first black gospel artist to appear in Carnegie Hall, composer, musician.

Bishop Philip R. Cousin, b 1933, President, Natl. Council of Churches of Christ in the USA, 1985-87.

Countee Cullen, 1903-46, poet, played a prominent role in the Harlem Renaissance of the 1920s; "Heritage," *The Black Christ.*

Lt. Gen. Benjamin O. Davis, Jr., b 1912, West Point, 1936, first black Air Force general, 1954.

Brig. Gen. Benjamin O. Davis, Sr., 1877-1970, first black general, 1940, in U. S. Army.

William L. Dawson, 1886-1970, Illinois congressman, first black chairman of a major U.S. House of Representatives committee.

David Dinkins, b 1927, first black mayor of New York City, 1990-93.

Sharon Pratt Dixon, b 1944, mayor of Washington, DC, 1990-

Aaron Douglas, 1900-79, painter; called father of black American art.

Frederick Douglass, 1817-95, author, editor, orator, diplomat; edited the abolitionist weekly, *The North Star,* in Rochester, NY; U.S. minister and consul general to Haiti.

St. Clair Drake, 1911-90, black studies pioneer, *Black Metropolis* (1945, with Horace R. Cayton); first permanent director, African and African American Studies, Stanford Univ.

Dr. Charles Richard Drew, 1904-50, pioneer in development of blood banks; director of American Red Cross blood donor project in World War II.

William Edward Burghardt (W.E.B.) Du Bois, 1868-1963, historian, sociologist; a founder of the National Association for the Advancement of Colored People (NAACP), 1909, and founder of its magazine *The Crisis*; author, *The Souls of Black Folk.*

Paul Laurence Dunbar, 1872-1906, poet, novelist; won fame with *Lyrics of Lowly Life,* 1896.

Jean Baptiste Point du Sable, c 1750-1818, pioneer trader and first settler of Chicago, 1779.

Marian Wright Edelman, b 1939, founder, president of Children's Defense Fund.

Joycelyn Elders, b 1933, first black U.S. Surgeon General, confirmed 1993.

Ralph Ellison, 1914-94, novelist, essayist, *Invisible Man.*

Michael Espy, b 1953, first black secretary of agriculture.

James Farmer, b 1920, a founder of the Congress of Racial Equality, 1942; asst. secretary, Dept. of HEW, 1969.

Henry O. Flipper, 1856-1940, first black to graduate, 1877, from West Point.

Charles Fuller, b 1939, Pulitzer Prize-winning playwright; *A Soldier's Play.*

Mary Hatwood Futrell, b 1940, president, Natl. Education Assn., 1983-89.

Henry Louis Gates, Jr., b 1950, noted author, scholar, chair Department of African-American studies, Harvard University,1991-

Marcus Garvey, 1887-1940, founded Universal Negro Improvement Assn., 1911.

Kenneth Gibson, b 1932, Newark, NJ, mayor, 1970-86.

Charles Gordone, b 1925, won 1970 Pulitzer Prize in Drama, with *No Place to Be Somebody.*

Vice Adm. Samuel L. Gravely, Jr. b 1922, first black admiral, 1971, served in World War II, Korea, and Vietnam; commander, Third Fleet.

William H. Gray, 3d, b 1941, U.S. representative from PA, 1979-91; chairman, Budget Committee, 1985-88; chairman, House Democratic Caucus, 1988-89; majority whip, 1989-91; president, United Negro College fund, 1991-

Ewart Guinier, 1911-90, trade unionist, first chairman of Harvard Univ.'s Department of African American Studies.

Jupiter Hammon, c 1720-1800, poet; the first black American to have his works published, 1761.

Lorraine Hansberry, 1930-65, playwright; won New York Drama Critics Circle Award, 1959; *A Raisin in the Sun.*

Barbara Harris, b 1931, first woman Episcopal bishop.

Patricia Roberts Harris, 1924-85, U.S. ambassador to Luxembourg, 1965-67; secretary, Dept. of HUD, 1977-79, Dept. of HHS, 1979-81.

William H. Hastie, 1904-76, first black federal judge, appointed 1937; governor of Virgin Islands, 1946-49; judge, U.S. Circuit Court of Appeals, 1949.

Matthew A. Henson, 1866-1955, member of Peary's 1909 expedition to the North Pole; placed U.S. flag at the pole.

Chester Himes, 1909-84, novelist, *Cotton Comes to Harlem.*

Dr. William A. Hinton, 1883-1959, developed the Hinton and Davies-Hinton tests for detection of syphilis; first black professor, 1949, at Harvard Medical School.

Benjamin L. Hooks, b 1925, first black member, 1972-79, Federal Communications Comm.; executive dir., NAACP, 1977-93.

Charles Hamilton Houston, 1895-50, lawyer, Howard University instructor, and champion of minority rights,

Nathan I. Huggins, 1927-89, historian, scholar; Harvard professor from 1980, director of that university's Institute for African-American Research from 1981.

Langston Hughes, 1902-67, poet; story, song lyric author, a major influence in the Harlem Renaissance of the 1920s; *The Weary Blues, Montage of a Dream Deferred.*

Charlayne Hunter-Gault, b 1942, first black woman admitted to University of Georgia, 1961; ran *New York Times* Harlem Bureau, 1968-77; broadcast journalist, 1978-

Rev. Jesse Jackson, b 1941, national director, Operation Bread Basket; campaigned for Democratic presidential nomination, 1984, 1988; pres., founder, Rainbow Coalition; "shadow senator" for District of Columbia, 1991-

Maynard Jackson, b 1938, mayor of Atlanta, 1973-81; 1989-93.

Gen. Daniel James, Jr., 1920-78, first black 4-star general, 1975; Commander, North American Air Defense Command.

Mae C. Jemison, M.D., b 1956, astronaut, first black woman launched into space, 1992.

Pvt. Henry Johnson, 1897-1929, the first American decorated by France in World War I with the Croix de Guerre.

James Weldon Johnson, 1871-1938, poet, novelist; 1st black admitted to FL bar; U.S. consul in Venezuela and Nicaragua.

John H. Johnson, b 1918, publisher, editor of *Ebony, Jet, Ebony Jr.* magazines, 1942- .

Barbara Jordan, b 1936, former congresswoman from Texas; member, House Judiciary Committee.

Vernon E. Jordan, b 1935, executive director, National Urban League, 1972-81.

Ernest Everett Just, 1883-1941, marine biologist, studied egg development; author, *Biology of Cell Surfaces,* 1941.

Leontine T. C. Kelly, b 1920, United Methodist bishop; first black woman bishop of a major American denomination, 1989.

Rev. Dr. Martin Luther King, Jr., 1929-68, led 382-day Montgomery, AL, boycott that brought 1956 U.S. Supreme Court decision holding segregation on buses unconstitutional; founder, president, Southern Christian Leadership Conference, 1957; won Nobel Peace Prize, 1964.

Lewis H. Latimer, 1848-1928, associate of Edison; supervised installation of first electric street lighting in NYC.

Mickey Leland, 1944-89, U.S. representative from Texas, 1978 until death; chairman of Congressional Black Caucus, House Select Committee on Hunger.

Malcolm X, 1925-65, Black Muslim leader and black nationalist whose ideas and oratory contributed to the black pride and black power movements in the 1960s.

Thurgood Marshall, 1908-93, first black U.S. solicitor general, 1965; first black justice of the U.S. Supreme Court, 1967-91; as a lawyer led the legal battery that won the Supreme Court decision declaring racial segregation of public schools unconstitutional, 1954.

Jan Matzeliger, 1852-89, invented lasting machine, patented 1883, which revolutionized the shoe industry.
Benjamin Mays, 1895-1984, educator, civil rights leader; headed Morehouse College, 1940-67.
Wade H. McCree, Jr., 1920-87, U.S. solicitor general, 1977-81.
Donald E. McHenry, b 1936, U.S. ambassador to the United Nations, 1979-81.
Ronald McNair, 1950-86, physicist, astronaut; killed in *Challenger* explosion.
Dorie Miller, 1919-43, Navy hero of Pearl Harbor attack; awarded the Navy Cross.
Ernest N. Morial, b 1929, elected first black mayor of New Orleans, 1977.
Toni Morrison, b 1931, novelist; *Song of Solomon, Sula, Tar Baby;* 1988 Pulitzer Prize for *Beloved;* first African-American woman to win the Nobel Prize for literature, 1993.
Carol Moseley-Braun, b 1947, first black woman elected to the U.S. Senate, 1992.
Willard Motley, 1912-65, novelist; *Knock on Any Door.*
Elijah Muhammad, 1897-1975, founded Black Muslims, 1931.
Pedro Alonzo Niño, navigator of the Niña, one of Columbus's 3 ships on his first voyage of discovery to the New World, 1492.
Rosa Parks, b 1913, Montgomery, AL, citizen arrested for refusing to move to the back of the bus, Dec. 1, 1955, bringing a 382-day bus boycott led by Martin Luther King, Jr.
Frederick D. Patterson, 1901-88, founder of United Negro College Fund, 1944; Tuskegee Institute's third president, 1935-53.
Harold R. Perry, 1916-91, first black American made a Roman Catholic bishop in the 20th century, 1966; first black clergyman to deliver the opening prayer in the U.S. Congress, 1964.
Adam Clayton Powell, 1908-72, early civil rights leader, congressman, 1945-69; chairman, House Committee on Education and Labor, 1960-67.
Colin Powell, b 1937, first black Natl. Security Advisor, 1987-88; first black chairman of Joint Chiefs of Staff, 1989-93.
Joseph H. Rainey, 1832-87, first black elected to U.S. House of Representatives, 1869, from South Carolina.
A. Philip Randolph, 1889-1979, organized the Brotherhood of Sleeping Car Porters, 1925; organizer of 1941 and 1963 March on Washington movements; vice president, AFL-CIO.
Charles Rangel, b 1930, congressman from NYC, 1970- ; member, Ways and Means Committee; chairman, Select Committee on Narcotics Abuse & Control.
Hiram R. Revels, 1822-1901, first black U.S. senator, elected in Mississippi, served 1870-71.
Lloyd Richards, b 1922(?), first black to direct a Broadway play, 1959; dean, Yale Univ. School of Drama, 1979-91; artistic director of Yale Repertory Theatre, 1979-91.
Wilson C. Riles, b 1917, elected, 1970, California State Superintendent of Public Instruction.
Norbert Rillieux, 1806-94; invented a vacuum pan evaporator, 1846, revolutionizing the sugar-refining industry.
Paul Robeson, 1898-1976, actor, concert singer, graduated 1st in class at Rutgers, 1918, Phi Beta Kappa; grad. Columbia Univ. law school, 1923; associated with communist causes.
Max Robinson, 1939-88, TV journalist, first black to anchor network news, 1978.
Carl T. Rowan, b 1925, prize-winning journalist; director of the U.S. Information Agency, 1964-65, the first black to sit on the National Security Council; U.S. ambassador to Finland, 1963-64.
John B Russwurm, 1799-1851, with **Samuel E. Cornish,** 1793-1858, founded, 1827, the nation's first black newspaper, *Freedom's Journal,* in NYC.
Bayard Rustin, 1910-87, organizer of the 1963 March on Washington; executive director, A. Philip Randolph Institute.
Peter Salem, at the Battle of Bunker Hill, June 17, 1775, shot and killed British commander Maj. John Pitcairn.
Ntozake Shange, b 1948, writer, *For Colored Girls Who Have Considered Suicide/When the Rainbow is Enuf.*
Bishop Stephen Spottswood, 1897-1974, board chairman of NAACP, 1961-1974.
Rev. Leon H. Sullivan, b 1922, economic development planner, first black on General Motors Board of Directors.
Willard Townsend, 1895-1957, organized the United Transport Service Employees, 1935 (redcaps, etc.); vice pres. AFL-CIO.
Sojourner Truth, 1797-1883, born Isabella Baumfree; preacher, abolitonist; raised funds for Union in Civil War; worked for black educational opportunities.
Harriet Tubman, 1823-1913, Underground Railroad conductor, served as nurse and spy for Union Army in the Civil War.
Nat Turner, 1800-31, led the most significant of more than 200 slave revolts in U.S., in Southampton, VA; hanged.
Alice Walker, b 1944, novelist, essayist; Pulitzer Prize for fiction, 1983, *The Color Purple.*
Booker T. Washington, 1856-1915, founder, 1881, and first president of Tuskegee Institute; author, *Up From Slavery.*
Harold Washington, 1922-87, first black mayor of Chicago, from 1983 until death.
Dr. Robert C. Weaver, b 1907, first black member of the U.S. Cabinet, secretary, Department of HUD, 1966-68.
Ida B. Wells (Barnett), 1862-1931, journalist who waged anti-lynching crusade.
Clifton R. Wharton, Jr., b 1926, first black pres. of major U.S. university, Michigan State, 1970-78; chancellor, SUNY system 1978-87; chairman & CEO, country's largest pension fund, 1987-93, Deputy Sec. of State, U.S. State Department 1993- .
Phillis Wheatley, c 1753-84, poet; 2d American woman and 1st black woman to have her works published, 1770.
Bill White, b 1934, first black baseball league president; National League president, 1989- .
Walter White, 1893-1955, exec. secretary, NAACP, 1931-55.
L. Douglas Wilder, b 1931, first black elected governor, became Virginia chief executive in 1989.
Roy Wilkins, 1901-81, exec. director, NAACP, 1955-77.
Dr. Daniel Hale Williams, 1858-1931, performed one of first 2 open-heart operations, 1893; founded Provident, Chicago's first Negro hospital; first black elected a fellow of the American College of Surgeons.
August Wilson, b 1945, playwright, 1987 Pulitzer Prize, *Fences,* 1990 Pulitzer, *The Piano Lesson.*
Granville T. Woods, 1856-1910, invented the third-rail system now used in subways, a complex railway telegraph device that helped reduce train accidents, and an automatic air brake.
Dr. Carter G. Woodson, 1875-1950, historian; founded Assn. for the Study of Negro Life and History, 1915, and *Journal of Negro History,* 1916.
Richard Wright, 1908-60, novelist; *Native Son, Black Boy.*
Frank Yerby, 1916-91, first best-selling American black novelist; *The Foxes of Harrow, Vixen.*
Andrew Young, b 1932, civil rights leader, congressman from Georgia, U.S. ambassador to the United Nations, 1977-79; mayor of Atlanta, 1982-89.
Whitney M. Young, Jr., 1921-71, exec. director, National Urban League, 1961; author, lecturer, newspaper columnist.

About 5,000 blacks served in the Continental Army during the **American Revolution,** mostly in integrated units, some in all-black combat units. Some 200,000 blacks served in the Union Army during the **Civil War;** 38,000 gave their lives; 22 won the Medal of Honor, the nation's highest award. Of 367,000 blacks in the armed forces during **World War I,** 100,000 served in France. More than 1,000,000 blacks served in the armed forces during **World War II;** all-black fighter and bomber AAF units and infantry divisions gave distinguished service. In 1954 the policy of all-black units was finally abolished. Of 274,937 blacks who served in the armed forces during the **Vietnam War** (1965-74), 5,681 were killed in combat. During the **Persian Gulf War** (1990-91), 104,000 blacks served in the Kuwaiti theater—20.0% of U.S. soldiers, compared with 8.7% during World War II and 9.8% in Vietnam.

As of Jan. 1993, there were 356 black mayors, 2 black governors, 388 state representatives, 135 state senators, 38 U.S. representatives, and 1 U.S. senator. There were then 8,015 blacks holding elected office in the U.S. and Virgin Islands, an increase of 6.1% over the previous year, according to a survey by the Joint Center for Political Studies, Washington, DC. The number of black women elected to local, county, state, and congressional offices rose to 2,332, up by 211, or 10.0%, from the Jan. 1992 figure. From 1989 to Jan. 1993, the number of male black elected officials increased by 271; the number of female black elected officials increased by 518.

Notable Living American Writers

Name (Birthplace)	Birthdate	Name (Birthplace)	Birthdate
Adams, Alice (Fredericksburg, VA)	8/14/26	Beattie, Ann (Washington, DC)	9/7/47
Albee, Edward (Washington, DC)	3/12/28	Bellow, Saul (Lachine, Quebec)	7/10/15
Auchincloss, Louis (Lawrence, NY)	9/27/17	Benchley, Peter (New York, NY)	5/8/40
		Berger, Thomas (Cincinnati, OH)	7/20/24
Barth, John (Cambridge, MD)	5/27/30	Blume, Judy (Elizabeth, NJ)	2/12/38

Name (Birthplace)	Birthdate
Bradbury, Ray (Waukegan, IL)	8/22/20
Brooks, Gwendolyn (Topeka, KS)	6/7/17
Calisher, Hortense (New York, NY)	12/20/11
Clancy, Tom (Baltimore, MD)	1947
Clark, Mary Higgins (New York, NY)	12/24/31
Clavell, James (Sydney, Australia)	10/10/24
Cleary, Beverly (McMinnville, OR)	1916
Connell, Evan S. (Kansas City, MO)	8/17/24
Conroy, Pat (Atlanta, GA)	10/26/45
Crews, Harry (Alma, GA)	6/6/35
Crichton, Michael (Chicago, IL)	10/23/42
Dailey, Janet (Storm Lake, IA)	5/21/44
De Vries, Peter (Chicago, IL)	2/27/10
Didion, Joan (Sacramento, CA)	12/5/34
Doctorow, E. L. (New York, NY)	1/6/31
Dove, Rita (Akron, OH)	8/28/52
Dunne, John Gregory (Hartford, CT)	5/25/32
Elkin, Stanley (New York, NY)	5/11/30
Fast, Howard (New York, NY)	11/11/14
Fox, Paula (New York, NY)	4/22/23
French, Marilyn (New York, NY)	11/21/29
Fuller, Charles (Philadelphia, PA)	3/5/39
Gaddis, William (New York, NY)	1922
Gilroy, Frank (New York, NY)	10/13/25
Godwin, Gail (Birmingham, AL)	6/18/37
Goldman, William (Chicago, IL)	8/12/31
Gordon, Mary (Long Island, NY)	12/8/49
Grau, Shirley Ann (New Orleans, LA)	7/8/29
Grisham, John (Jonesboro, AR)	2/8/55
Guare, John (New York, NY)	2/5/38
Hailey, Arthur (Luton, England)	4/5/20
Hawkes, John (Stamford, CT)	8/17/25
Heller, Joseph (Brooklyn, NY)	5/1/23
Helprin, Mark (New York, NY)	6/28/47
Hinton, S. E. (Tulsa, OK)	1948
Irving, John (Exeter, NH)	3/2/42
Jakes, John (Chicago, IL)	3/31/32
Jong, Erica (New York, NY)	3/26/42
Keillor, Garrison (Anoka, MN)	8/7/42
Kennedy, William (Albany, NY)	1/16/28
Kerr, Jean (Scranton, PA)	7/10/23
King, Stephen (Portland, ME)	9/21/47
Kingston, Maxine Hong (Stockton, CA)	10/27/40
Knowles, John (Fairmont, WV)	9/16/26
Krantz, Judith (New York, NY)	1/9/28
Kumin, Maxine (Philadelphia, PA)	6/6/25
Kushner, Tony	—
LeGuin, Ursula (Berkeley, CA)	10/21/29
L'Engle, Madeleine (New York, NY)	11/29/18
Leonard, Elmore (New Orleans, LA)	10/11/25
Levin, Ira (New York, NY)	8/27/29
Ludlum, Robert (New York, NY)	5/25/27
Lurie, Alison (Chicago, IL)	9/3/26

Name (Birthplace)	Birthdate
Mailer, Norman (Long Branch, NJ)	1/31/23
Mamet, David (Chicago, IL)	11/30/47
McCarthy, Cormac (Providence, RI)	7/20/33
McGuane, Thomas (Wyandotte, MI)	12/11/39
McMurtry, Larry (Wichita Falls, TX)	6/3/36
Michener, James A. (New York, NY)	2/3/07
Miller, Arthur (New York, NY)	10/17/15
Morris, Wright (Central City, NE)	1/6/10
Morrison, Toni (Lorain, OH)	2/18/31
Oates, Joyce Carol (Lockport, NY)	6/16/38
Ozick, Cynthia (New York, NY)	4/17/28
Paley, Grace (New York, NY)	12/11/22
Piercy, Marge (Detroit, MI)	3/31/36
Potok, Chaim (New York, NY)	2/17/29
Price, Reynolds (Macon, NC)	2/1/33
Proulx, E. Annie (Norwich, CT)	8/22/35
Puzo, Mario (New York, NY)	10/15/20
Pynchon, Thomas (Glen Cove, NY)	5/8/37
Rabe, David (Dubuque, IA)	3/10/40
Reed, Ishmael (Chattanooga, TN)	2/22/38
Rice, Anne (New Orleans, LA)	10/14/41
Roth, Henry (Austria-Hungary)	2/8/06
Roth, Philip (Newark, NJ)	3/19/33
Salinger, J. D. (New York, NY)	1/1/19
Sanders, Lawrence (New York, NY)	1920
Sendak, Maurice (New York, NY)	6/10/28
Shepard, Sam (Ft. Sheridan, IL)	11/5/43
Silverstein, Shel (Chicago, IL)	1932
Simon, Neil (New York, NY)	7/4/27
Spillane, Mickey (Brooklyn, NY)	3/9/18
Stern, Richard (New York, NY)	2/25/28
Stone, Robert (Brooklyn, NY)	8/21/37
Styron, William (Newport News, VA)	6/11/25
Tan, Amy (Oakland, CA)	2/19/52
Taylor, Peter (Trenton, TN)	1/8/17
Theroux, Paul (Medford, MA)	4/10/41
Turow, Scott F. (Chicago, IL)	4/12/49
Tyler, Anne (Minneapolis, MN)	10/25/41
Updike, John (Shillington, PA)	3/18/32
Uris, Leon (Baltimore, MD)	8/3/24
Vidal, Gore (West Point, NY)	10/3/25
Vonnegut, Kurt, Jr. (Indianapolis, IN)	11/11/22
Walker, Alice (Eatonton, GA)	2/9/44
Wambaugh, Joseph (East Pittsburgh, PA)	1/22/37
Wasserstein, Wendy (New York, NY)	—
Welty, Eudora (Jackson, MS)	4/13/09
Wideman, John Edgar (Pittsburgh, PA)	6/14/41
Wilson, August (Pittsburgh, PA)	4/27/45
Wilson, Lanford (Lebanon, MO)	4/13/37
Wolfe, Tom (Richmond, VA)	3/2/31
Wolff, Tobias (Birmingham, AL)	6/19/45
Wouk, Herman (New York, NY)	5/27/15

American Architects and Some of Their Achievements

Max Abramovitz, b 1908, Avery Fisher Hall, Lincoln Center, NYC.

Henry Bacon, 1866-1924, Lincoln Memorial, Washington, DC.

Pietro Belluschi, 1899-1994, Juilliard School of Music, Lincoln Center, Pan Am Building (now MetLife Bldg.) (with Walter Gropius), NYC.

Marcel Breuer, 1902-81, with Hamilton Smith, Whitney Museum of American Art, NYC.

Charles Bulfinch, 1763-1844, State House, Boston; Capitol (part), Washington, DC.

Gordon Bunshaft, 1909-90, Lever House, Park Ave, NYC; Hirshhorn Museum, Washington, DC.

Daniel H. Burnham, 1846-1912, Union Station, Washington DC; Flatiron Bldg., NYC.

Irwin Chanin, 1892-1988, theaters, skyscrapers, NYC.

Ralph Adams Cram, 1863-1942, Cathedral of St. John the Divine, NYC; U.S. Military Academy (part), West Point, NY.

R. Buckminster Fuller, 1895-1983, U.S. Pavilion (geodesic domes), Expo 67, Montreal.

Cass Gilbert, 1859-1934, Custom House, Woolworth Bldg., NYC; Supreme Court Bldg., Washington, DC.

Bertram G. Goodhue, 1869-1924, Capitol, Lincoln, NE; St. Thomas's Church, St. Bartholomew's Church, NYC.

Walter Gropius, 1883-1969, Pan Am Building (now MetLife Bldg.) (with Pietro Belluschi), NYC.

Peter Harrison, 1716-75, Touro Synagogue, Redwood Library, Newport, RI.

Wallace K. Harrison, 1895-1981, Metropolitan Opera House, Lincoln Center, NYC.

Thomas Hastings, 1860-1929, NY Public Library with John Carrère, Frick Mansion, NYC.

James Hoban, 1762-1831, The White House, Washington, DC.

Raymond Hood, 1881-1934, Rockefeller Center (part), Daily News, NYC; Tribune, Chicago.

Richard M. Hunt, 1827-95, Metropolitan Museum (part), NYC; National Observatory, Washington, DC.

William Le Baron Jenney, 1832-1907, Home Insurance (demolished 1931), Chicago.

Philip C. Johnson, b 1906, NY State Theater, Lincoln Center, NYC.

Albert Kahn, 1869-1942, General Motors Bldg., Detroit.

Louis Kahn, 1901-74, Salk Laboratory, La Jolla, CA; Yale Art Gallery, New Haven, CT.

Christopher Grant LaFarge, 1862-1938, Roman Catholic Chapel, West Point, NY.

Benjamin H. Latrobe, 1764-1820, Capitol (part), Washington, DC.

William Lescaze, 1896-1969, Philadelphia Savings Fund Society; Borg-Warner Bldg., Chicago.

Maya Lin, b 1959, Vietnam Veterans Memorial, Washington, DC.

Bernard R. Maybeck, 1862-1957, Hearst Hall, Chick House, Univ. of CA, First Church of Christ Scientist, Berkeley, CA.

Charles F. McKim, 1847-1909, Public Library, Boston; Columbia Univ. (part), NYC.

Charles M. McKim, b 1920, KUHT-TV Transmitter Building, Lutheran Church of the Redeemer, Houston, TX.

Ludwig Mies van der Rohe, 1886-1969, Seagram Building, (with Philip C. Johnson), NYC; National Gallery, Berlin.

Robert Mills, 1781-1855, Washington Monument, Washington, DC.

Charles Moore, 1925-93, Sea Ranch, near San Francisco; Faculty Club, Santa Barbara, CA; Piazza d'Italia, New Orleans, LA.

Richard J. Neutra, 1892-1970, Mathematics Park, Princeton, NJ; Orange Co. Courthouse, Santa Ana, CA.

Gyo Obata, b 1923, Natl. Air & Space Museum, Smithsonian Institution, Washington, DC; Dallas-Ft. Worth Airport.

Frederick L. Olmsted, 1822-1903, Central Park, NYC; Fairmount Park, Philadelphia.

I(eoh) **M**(ing) **Pei,** b 1917, National Center for Atmospheric Research, Boulder, CO; East Wing, Natl. Gallery of Art, Washington, DC; Pyramid, The Louvre, Paris.

William Pereira, 1909-85, Cape Canaveral; Transamerica Bldg., San Francisco.

John Russell Pope, 1874-1937, National Gallery, Washington, DC.

John Portman, b 1924, Peachtree Center, Atlanta.

George Browne Post, 1837-1913, New York Stock Exchange, NYC; Capitol, Madison, WI.

James Renwick, Jr., 1818-95, Grace Church, St. Patrick's Cathedral, NYC; Smithsonian Institution, Corcoran Galleries, Washington, DC.

Henry H. Richardson, 1838-86, Trinity Church, Boston.

Kevin Roche, b 1922, Oakland Museum, Oakland, CA; Fine Arts Center, University of Massachusetts, Amherst.

James Gamble Rogers, 1867-1947, Columbia-Presbyterian Medical Center, NYC; Northwestern Univ., Evanston, IL.

John Wellborn Root, 1887-1963, Palmolive Building, Chicago; Hotel Statler, Washington, DC; Hotel Tamanaco, Caracas, Venezuela.

Paul Rudolph, b 1918, Jewitt Art Center, Wellesley College, Wellesley, MA; Art & Architecture Bldg., Yale, New Haven, CT.

Eero Saarinen, 1910-61, Gateway to the West Arch, St. Louis; Trans World Flight Center, NYC.

Louis Skidmore, 1897-1962, Atomic Energy Commission town site, Oak Ridge, TN; Terrace Plaza Hotel, Cincinnati, OH.

Clarence S. Stein, 1882-1975, Temple Emanu-El, NYC.

Edward Durell Stone, 1902-78, U.S. Embassy, New Delhi, India; (H. Hartford) Gallery of Modern Art, NYC.

Louis H. Sullivan, 1856-1924, Auditorium Building, Chicago.

Richard Upjohn, 1802-78, Trinity Church, NYC.

Ralph T. Walker, 1889-1973, N.Y. Telephone Bldg. (now NYNEX), NYC; IBM Research Lab, Poughkeepsie, NY.

Roland A. Wank, 1898-1970, Cincinnati Union Terminal, Cincinnati, OH; head architect (1933-44), Tennessee Valley Authority.

Stanford White, 1853-1906, Washington Arch in Washington Square Park, first Madison Square Garden, NYC.

Frank Lloyd Wright, 1867 (or 1869)-1959, Imperial Hotel, Tokyo; Guggenheim Museum, NYC; Unity Church, Oak Park, IL; Robie House, Chicago; Taliesin, WI.

William Wurster, 1895-1973, Ghirardelli Sq., San Francisco; Cowell College, UC, Berkeley, CA.

Minoru Yamasaki, 1912-86, World Trade Center, NYC.

Noted American Cartoonists

Charles Addams, 1912-88, macabre cartoons.

Brad Anderson, b 1924, Marmaduke.

Peter Arno, 1904-68, *New Yorker* urban characterizations.

Tex Avery, 1908-80, **Friz Freleng,** b 1905?, **Chuck Jones,** b 1912, animators of Bugs Bunny, Porky Pig, Daffy Duck.

George Baker, 1915-75, The Sad Sack.

C. C. Beck, 1910-89, Captain Marvel.

Jim Berry, b 1932, Berry's World.

Herb Block (Herblock), b 1909, leading political cartoonist.

George Booth, b 1926, *New Yorker* cartoonist.

Berke Breathed, b 1957, Bloom County.

Clare Briggs, 1875-1930, Mr. & Mrs.

Dik Browne, 1917-89, Hi & Lois, Hagar the Horrible.

Marjorie Buell, 1904-93, Little Lulu.

Ernie Bushmiller, 1905-82, Nancy.

Milton Caniff, 1907-88, Terry & the Pirates; Steve Canyon.

Al Capp, 1909-79, Li'l Abner.

Roz Chast, b 1954, *New Yorker* "bonfire of the banalities" cartoons.

Paul Conrad, 1924, political cartoonist.

Roy Crane, 1901-77, Captain Easy; Buz Sawyer.

Robert Crumb, b 1943, "Underground" cartoonist.

Jay N. Darling (Ding), 1876-1962, political cartoonist.

Jack Davis, b 1926, *Mad* magazine.

Jim Davis, b 1945, Garfield.

Billy DeBeck, 1890-1942, Barney Google.

Rudolph Dirks, 1877-1968, The Katzenjammer Kids.

Walt Disney, 1901-66, producer of animated cartoons; created Mickey Mouse and Donald Duck.

Steve Ditko, b 1927, Spider-Man.

Mort Drucker, b 1929, *Mad* magazine.

Jules Feiffer, b 1929, satirical *Village Voice* cartoonist.

Bud Fisher, 1884-1954, Mutt & Jeff.

Ham Fisher, 1900-55, Joe Palooka.

James Montgomery Flagg, 1877-1960, illustrator; created the famous Uncle Sam recruiting poster during WWI.

Max Fleischer, 1883-1972, creator of Betty Boop, Popeye cartoons.

Hal Foster, 1892-1982, Tarzan; Prince Valiant.

Fontaine Fox, 1884-1964, Toonerville Folks.

Rube Goldberg, 1883-1970, Boob McNutt.

Chester Gould, 1900-85, Dick Tracy.

Harold Gray, 1894-1968, Little Orphan Annie.

Matt Groening, b 1954, Life Is Hell, The Simpsons.

Cathy Guisewite, b 1950, Cathy.

Bill Hanna, b 1910, & **Joe Barbera,** b 1911, animators of Tom & Jerry, Huckleberry Hound, Yogi Bear, Flintstones.

Johnny Hart, b 1931, BC, Wizard of Id.

Jimmy Hatlo, 1898-1963, Little Iodine.

John Held, Jr., 1889-1958, "Jazz Age" cartoonist.

George Herriman, 1881-1944, Krazy Kat.

Harry Hershfield, 1885-1974, Abie the Agent.

Al Hirschfeld, b 1903, *N.Y. Times* theater caricaturist.

Burne Hogarth, b 1911, Tarzan.

Helen Hokinson, 1900-49, satirized clubwomen.

Nicole Hollander, b 1939, Sylvia.

Lynn Johnston, b 1947, For Better or For Worse.

Bob Kane, b 1916, Batman.

Bil Keane, b 1922, The Family Circus.

Walt Kelly, 1913-73, Pogo.

Hank Ketcham, b 1920, Dennis the Menace.

Ted Key, b 1912, Hazel.

Frank King, 1883-1969, Gasoline Alley.

Jack Kirby, 1917-94, Fantastic Four.

Rollin Kirby, 1875-1952, political cartoonist.

B(ernard) Kliban, 1935-91, cat books.

Edward Koren, b 1935, *New Yorker* woolly characters.

Harvey Kurtzman, 1921-93, *Mad* magazine.

Walter Lantz, b 1900-94, Woody Woodpecker.

Gary Larson, b 1950, The Far Side.

Mell Lazarus, b 1929, Momma, Miss Peach.

Stan Lee, b 1922, Marvel Comics.

David Levine, b 1926, *N.Y. Review of Books* caricatures.

Doug Marlette, b 1949, editorial cartoonist; Kudzu.

Don Martin, b 1931, *Mad* magazine.

Bill Mauldin, b 1921, depicted squalid life of the G.I. in WWII.

Jeff MacNelly, b 1947, political cartoonist, and strip Shoe.

Winsor McCay, 1872-1934, Little Nemo.

John T. McCutcheon, 1870-1949, midwestern rural life.

George McManus, 1884-1954, Bringing Up Father.

Dale Messick, b 1906, Brenda Starr.

Norman Mingo, 1896-1980, Alfred E. Neuman.

Bob Montana, 1920-75, Archie.

Dick Moores, 1909-86, Gasoline Alley.

Willard Mullin, 1902-78, sports cartoonist; created Dodgers "Bum" and Mets "Kid".

Russell Myers, b 1938, Broom Hilda.

Thomas Nast, 1840-1902, political cartoonist; created the Democratic donkey and Republican elephant.

Pat Oliphant, b 1935, political cartoonist.

Frederick Burr Opper, 1857-1937, Happy Hooligan.

Richard Outcault, 1863-1928, Yellow Kid; Buster Brown.

Mike Peters, b 1943, editorial cartoons; Mother Goose & Grimm.

George Price, b 1901, *New Yorker* lower-class life.

Alex Raymond, 1909-56, Flash Gordon; Jungle Jim.

Art Sansom, 1920-91, The Born Loser.

Charles Schulz, b 1922, Peanuts.

Elzie C. Segar, 1894-1938, Popeye.

Jerry Siegel, b 1914, & **Joe Shuster,** 1914-92, Superman.

Sydney Smith, 1887-1935, The Gumps.

Otto Soglow, 1900-75, Little King; Canyon Kiddies.

Art Spiegelman, b 1948, Raw; Maus.

William Steig, b 1907, *New Yorker* cartoonist.

James Swinnerton, 1875-1974, Little Jimmy.

Paul Terry, 1887-1971, animator of Mighty Mouse.

Bob Thaves, b 1924, Frank and Ernest.

James Thurber, 1894-61, *New Yorker* cartoonist.

Garry Trudeau, b 1948, Doonesbury.

Mort Walker, b 1923, Beetle Bailey.

Bill Watterson, b 1958, Calvin and Hobbes.

Russ Westover, 1887-1966, Tillie the Toiler.

Frank Willard, 1893-1958, Moon Mullins.

J. R. Williams, 1888-1957, The Willets Family; Out Our Way.

Gahan Wilson, b 1930, cartoonist of the macabre.

Tom Wilson, b 1931, Ziggy.

Art Young, 1866-1943, political radical and satirist.

Chic Young, 1901-73, Blondie.

Noted Political Leaders of the Past

(U.S. presidents and vice presidents, Supreme Court justices, signers of Declaration of Independence listed elsewhere.)

Abu Bakr, 573-634, Mohammedan leader, first caliph, chosen successor to Muhammad.

Dean Acheson, 1893-1971, (U.S.) secretary of state, chief architect of cold war foreign policy.

Samuel Adams, 1722-1803, (U.S.) patriot, Boston Tea Party firebrand.

Konrad Adenauer, 1876-1967, (Ger.) West German chancellor.

Emilio Aguinaldo, 1869-1964, (Philip.) revolutionary, fought against Spain and the U.S.

Akbar, 1542-1605, greatest Mogul emperor of India.

Salvador Allende Gossens, 1908-1973, (Chilean) president, advocate of democratic socialism.

Herbert H. Asquith, 1852-1928, (British) liberal prime minister, instituted an advanced program of social reform.

Atahualpa, ?-1533, Inca (ruling chief) of Peru.

Kemal Atatürk, 1881-1938, (Turk.) founded modern Turkey.

Clement Attlee, 1883-1967, (British) Labour party leader, prime minister, enacted national health, nationalized many industries.

Stephen F. Austin, 1793-1836, (U.S.) led Texas colonization.

Mikhail Bakunin, 1814-76, (Russ.) revolutionary, leading exponent of anarchism.

Arthur J. Balfour, 1848-1930, (British) as foreign secretary under Lloyd George issued Balfour Declaration expressing official British approval of Zionism.

Bernard M. Baruch, 1870-1965, (U.S.) financier, gvt. adviser.

Fulgencio Batista y Zaldívar, 1901-73, (Cuban) ruler overthrown by Castro.

Lord Beaverbrook, 1879-1964, (British) financier, statesman, newspaper owner.

Menachem Begin, 1913-92, (Isr.) Israeli prime minister, won 1978 Nobel Peace Prize.

Eduard Benes, 1884-1948, (Czech.) president during interwar and post-WW II eras.

David Ben-Gurion, 1886-1973, (Isr.) first prime minister of Israel.

Thomas Hart Benton, 1782-1858, (U.S.) Missouri senator, championed agrarian interests and westward expansion.

Lavrenti Beria, 1899-1953, (USSR) Communist leader prominent in political purges under Stalin.

Aneurin Bevan, 1897-1960, (British) Labour party leader.

Ernest Bevin, 1881-1951, (British) Labour party leader, foreign minister, helped lay foundation for NATO.

Otto von Bismarck, 1815-98, (Ger.) statesman known as the Iron Chancellor, uniter of Germany, 1870.

James G. Blaine, 1830-93, (U.S.) Republican politician, diplomat, influential in launching Pan-American movement.

Léon Blum, 1872-1950, (Fr.) socialist leader, writer, headed first Popular Front government.

Simón Bolívar, 1783-1830, (Venez.) South American revolutionary who liberated much of the continent from Spanish rule.

William E. Borah, 1865-1940, (U.S.) isolationist senator, instrumental in blocking U.S. membership in League of Nations and the World Court.

Cesare Borgia, 1476-1507, (Ital.) soldier, politician, an outstanding figure of the Italian Renaissance.

Leonid Brezhnev, 1906-82, (USSR) leader of the Soviet Union, 1964-82.

Aristide Briand, 1862-1932, (Fr.) foreign minister, chief architect of Locarno Pact and anti-war Kellogg-Briand Pact.

William Jennings Bryan, 1860-1925, (U.S.) Democratic, populist leader, orator, 3 times lost race for presidency.

Nikolai Bukharin, 1888-1938, (USSR) communist leader.

William C. Bullitt, 1891-1967, (U.S.) diplomat, first ambassador to USSR, ambassador to France.

Ralph Bunche, 1904-71, (U.S.) a founder and key diplomat of United Nations for more than 20 years.

John C. Calhoun, 1782-1850, (U.S.) political leader, champion of states' rights and a symbol of the Old South.

Robert Castlereagh, 1769-1822, (British) foreign secretary, guided Grand Alliance against Napoleon.

Camillo Benso Cavour, 1810-61, (Ital.) statesman, largely responsible for uniting Italy under the House of Savoy.

Nicolae Ceausescu, 1918-89, (Romanian) Communist leader, head of state 1967-89.

Austen Chamberlain, 1863-1937, (British) Conservative party leader, largely responsible for Locarno Pact of 1925.

Neville Chamberlain, 1869-1940, (British) Conservative prime minister whose appeasement of Hitler led to Munich Pact.

Salmon P. Chase, 1808-73, (U.S.) public official, abolitionist, jurist, 6th chief justice of the U.S.

Chiang Kai-shek, 1887-1975, (Chin.) Nationalist Chinese president whose government was driven from mainland to Taiwan.

Winston Churchill, 1874-1965, (British) prime minister, soldier, author, guided Britain through WW II.

Galeazzo Ciano, 1903-44, (Ital.) fascist foreign minister, helped create Rome-Berlin Axis, executed by Mussolini.

Henry Clay, 1777-1852, (U.S.) "The Great Compromiser," one of most influential pre-Civil War political leaders.

Georges Clemenceau, 1841-1929, (Fr.) twice premier, Wilson's chief antagonist at Paris Peace Conference after WW I.

DeWitt Clinton, 1769-1828, (U.S.) political leader, responsible for promoting idea of the Erie Canal.

Robert Clive, 1725-74, (British) first administrator of Bengal, laid foundation for British Empire in India.

Jean Baptiste Colbert, 1619-83, (Fr.) statesman, influential under Louis XIV, created the French navy.

Oliver Cromwell, 1599-1658, (British) Lord Protector of England, led parliamentary forces during Civil War.

Curzon of Kedleston, 1859-1925, (British) viceroy of India, foreign secretary, major force in dealing with post-WW I problems in Europe and Far East.

Édouard Daladier, 1884-1970, (Fr.) radical socialist politician, arrested by Vichy, interned by Germans until liberation in 1945.

Georges Danton, 1759-94, (Fr.) a leading figure in the French Revolution.

Jefferson Davis, 1808-89, (U.S.) president of the Confederate States of America.

Charles G. Dawes, 1865-1951, (U.S.) statesman, banker, advanced Dawes Plan to stabilize post-WW I German finances.

Alcide De Gasperi, 1881-1954, (Ital.) prime minister, founder of the Christian Democratic party.

Charles DeGaulle, 1890-1970, (Fr.) general, statesman, and first president of the Fifth Republic.

Eamon De Valera, 1882-1975, (Irish-U.S.) statesman, led fight for Irish independence.

Thomas E. Dewey, 1902-71, (U.S.) New York governor, twice loser in try for presidency.

Ngo Dinh Diem, 1901-63, (Viet.) South Vietnamese president, assassinated in government take-over.

Everett M. Dirksen, 1896-1969, (U.S.) Senate Republican minority leader, orator.

Benjamin Disraeli, 1804-81, (British) prime minister, considered founder of modern Conservative party.

Engelbert Dollfuss, 1892-1934, (Austrian) chancellor, assassinated by Austrian Nazis.

Andrea Doria, 1466-1560, (Ital.) Genoese admiral, statesman, called "Father of Peace" and "Liberator of Genoa."

Stephen A. Douglas, 1813-61, (U.S.) Democratic leader, orator, opposed Lincoln for the presidency.

Alexander Dubcek, 1921-92, (Czech.) statesman whose attempted liberalization was crushed, 1968.

John Foster Dulles, 1888-1959, (U.S.) secretary of state under Eisenhower, cold war policy maker.

Friedrich Ebert, 1871-1925, (Ger.) Social Democratic movement leader, instrumental in bringing about Weimar constitution.

Sir Anthony Eden, 1897-1977, (British) foreign secretary, prime minister during Suez invasion of 1956.

Ludwig Erhard, 1897-1977, (Ger.) economist, West German chancellor, led nation's economic rise after WW II.

Hamilton Fish, 1808-93, (U.S.) secretary of state, successfully mediated disputes with Great Britain, Latin America.

James V. Forrestal, 1892-1949, (U.S.) secretary of navy, first secretary of defense.

Francisco Franco, 1892-1975, (Sp.) leader of rebel forces during Spanish Civil War and dictator of Spain.

Benjamin Franklin, 1706-90, (U.S.) printer, publisher, author, inventor, scientist, diplomat.

Louis de Frontenac, 1620-98, (Fr.) governor of New France (Canada); encouraged explorations, fought Iroquois.

Hugh Gaitskell, 1906-63, (British) Labour party leader, major force in reversing its stand for unilateral disarmament.

Albert Gallatin, 1761-1849, (U.S.) secretary of treasury who was instrumental in negotiating end of War of 1812.

Léon Gambetta, 1838-82, (Fr.) statesman, politician, one of the founders of the Third Republic.

Indira Gandhi, 1917-84, (In.) daughter of Jawaharlal Nehru; became prime minister when Lal Bahadur Shastri died in 1966.

Mohandas K. Gandhi, 1869-1948, (In.) political leader, ascetic, led nationalist movement against British rule.

Giuseppe Garibaldi, 1807-82, (Ital.) patriot, soldier, a leading figure in the Risorgimento, the Italian unification movement.

Genghis Khan, c 1167-1227, Mongol conqueror, ruler of vast Asian empire.

William E. Gladstone, 1809-98, (British) prime minister 4 times, dominant force of Liberal party from 1868 to 1894.

Paul Joseph Goebbels, 1897-1945, (Ger.) Nazi propagandist, master of mass psychology.

Klement Gottwald, 1896-1953, (Czech.) communist leader ushered communism into his country.

Che (Ernesto) Guevara, 1928-67, (Arg.) guerrilla leader, prominent in Cuban revolution, killed in Bolivia.

Haile Selassie, 1891-1975, (Eth.) emperor, maintained monarchy through invasion, occupation, internal resistance.

Alexander Hamilton, 1755-1804, (U.S.) first treasury secretary, champion of strong central government.

Dag Hammarskjold, 1905-61, (Swed.) statesman, UN secretary-general.

John Hancock, 1737-93, (U.S.) revolutionary leader, first signer of Declaration of Independence.

John Hay, 1838-1905, (U.S.) secretary of state, primarily associated with Open Door Policy toward China.

Patrick Henry, 1736-99, (U.S.) major revolutionary figure, remarkable orator.

Édouard Herriot, 1872-1957, (Fr.) Radical Socialist leader, twice premier, president of National Assembly.

Theodor Herzl, 1860-1904, (Austrian) founder of modern Zionism.

Heinrich Himmler, 1900-45, (Ger.) notorious head of Nazi SS and Gestapo.

Paul von Hindenburg, 1847-1934, (Ger.) field marshal, president.

Hirohito, 1902-89 (Jap.); emperor of Japan from 1926.

Adolf Hitler, 1889-1945, (Ger.) dictator, founder of National Socialism; wrote *Mein Kampf,* strategy for world domination.

Ho Chi Minh, 1890-1969, (Viet.) North Vietnamese president, Vietnamese Communist leader, national hero.

Harry L. Hopkins, 1890-1946, (U.S.) New Deal administrator, closest adviser to FDR during WW II.

Edward M. House, 1858-1938, (U.S.) diplomat, confidential adviser to Woodrow Wilson.

Samuel Houston, 1793-1863, (U.S.) leader of struggle to win control of Texas from Mexico.

Cordell Hull, 1871-1955, (U.S.) secretary of state, initiated reciprocal trade to lower tariffs, helped organize UN.

Hubert H. Humphrey, 1911-78, (U.S.) Minnesota Democrat, senator, vice president, spent 32 years in public service.

Ibn Saud, c 1888-1953, (Saudi Arabian) founder of Saudi Arabia and its first king.

Jacob Javits, 1904-86 (U.S.) U.S. senator from New York for 24 years.

Jinnah, Muhammed Ali, 1876-1948, (Pak.) founder, first governor-general of Pakistan.

Benito Juarez, 1806-72, (Mex.) rallied his country against foreign threats, sought to create democratic, federal republic.

Kamehameha I, c 1758-1819, (Hawaiian) founder, first monarch of unified Hawaii.

Frank B. Kellogg, 1856-1937, (U.S.) secretary of state, negotiated Kellogg-Briand Pact to outlaw war.

Robert F. Kennedy, 1925-68, (U.S.) attorney general, senator, assassinated while seeking presidential nomination.

Aleksandr Kerensky, 1881-1970, (Russ.) revolutionary, served as prime minister after Feb. 1917 revolution until Bolshevik overthrow.

Ruhollah Khomeini, 1900-89, (Iranian), religious leader with Islamic title "ayatollah," directed overthrow of shah, 1979, became source of political authority in succeeding governments.

Nikita Khrushchev, 1894-1971, (USSR) premier, first secretary of Communist party, initiated de-Stalinization.

Kim Il Sung, 1912-94, (Korean) leader of North Korea from 1948 until his death.

Lajos Kossuth, 1802-94, (Hung.) principal figure in 1848 Hungarian revolution.

Pyotr Kropotkin, 1842-1921, (Russ.) anarchist, championed the peasants but opposed Bolshevism.

Kublai Khan, c 1215-94, Mongol emperor, founder of Yüan dynasty in China.

Béla Kun, 1886-c1939, (Hung.) communist, member of 3d International, tried to foment worldwide revolution.

Robert M. LaFollette, 1855-1925, (U.S.) Wisconsin public official, leader of progressive movement.

Pierre Laval, 1883-1945, (Fr.) politician, Vichy foreign minister, executed for treason.

Andrew Bonar Law, 1858-1923, (British) Conservative party politician, led opposition to Irish home rule.

Vladimir Ilyich Lenin (Ulyanov), 1870-1924, (Russ.) revolutionary, founder of Bolshevism, Soviet leader 1917-24.

Ferdinand de Lesseps, 1805-94, (Fr.) diplomat, engineer, conceived idea of Suez Canal.

Rene Levesque, 1922-87, (Can.) premier of Quebec, 1976-85; led unsuccessful fight to separate from Canada.

Maxim Litvinov, 1876-1951, (Pol.-Russ.) revolutionary, commissar of foreign affairs, favored cooperation with Western powers.

Liu Shaoqi, c 1898-1974, (Chin.) communist leader, fell from grace during "cultural revolution."

David Lloyd George, 1863-1945, (British) Liberal party prime minister, laid foundations for modern welfare state.

Henry Cabot Lodge, 1850-1924, (U.S.) Republican senator, led opposition to participation in League of Nations.

Huey P. Long, 1893-1935, (U.S.) Louisiana political demagogue, governor, assassinated.

Rosa Luxemburg, 1871-1919, (Ger.) revolutionary, leader of the German Social Democratic party and Spartacus party.

J. Ramsay MacDonald, 1866-1937, (British) first Labour party prime minister of Great Britain.

Harold Macmillan, 1895-1987 (British) prime minister of Great Britain, 1957-63.

Joseph R. McCarthy, 1908-57, (U.S.) senator notorious for his witch hunt for communists in the government.

Makarios III, 1913-77, (Cypr.) Greek Orthodox archbishop, first president of Cyprus.

Malcolm X (Malcolm Little), 1925-65, (U.S.) black separatist leader, assassinated.

Mao Zedong, 1893-1976, (Chin.) chief Chinese Marxist theorist, soldier, led Chinese revolution establishing his nation as an important communist state.

Jean Paul Marat, 1743-93, (Fr.) revolutionary, politician, identified with radical Jacobins, assassinated.

José Martí, 1853-95, (Cub.) patriot, poet, leader of Cuban struggle for independence.

Jan Masaryk, 1886-1948, (Czech.) foreign minister, died by mysterious suicide following communist coup.

Thomas G. Masaryk, 1850-1937, (Czech.) statesman, philosopher, first president of Czechoslovak Republic.

Jules Mazarin, 1602-61, (Fr.) cardinal, statesman, prime minister under Louis XIII and queen regent Anne of Austria.

Giuseppe Mazzini, 1805-72, (Ital.), reformer dedicated to the Risorgimento, 19th-century movement for the political and social renewal of Italy.

Tom Mboya, 1930-69, (Kenyan) political leader, instrumental in securing independence for Kenya.

Cosimo I de' Medici, 1519-74, (Ital.) Duke of Florence, grand duke of Tuscany.

Lorenzo de' Medici, the Magnificent, 1449-92, (Ital.) merchant prince, a towering figure in Italian Renaissance.

Catherine de Medicis, 1519-89, (Fr.) queen consort of Henry II, regent of France, influential in Catholic-Huguenot wars.

Golda Meir, 1898-1979, (Isr.) a founder of the state of Israel and prime minister, 1969-74.

Klemens W. N. L. Metternich, 1773-1859, (Austrian) statesman, arbiter of post-Napoleonic Europe.

Anastas Mikoyan, 1895-1978, (USSR) prominent Soviet leader from 1917; president of the Presidium of the Supreme Soviet of the USSR, 1964-65.

Guy Mollet, 1905-75, (Fr.) social politician, resistance leader.

Henry Morgenthau, Jr., 1891-1967, (U.S.) secretary of treasury, raised funds to finance New Deal and U.S. WW II activities.

Gouverneur Morris, 1752-1816, (U.S.) statesman, diplomat, financial expert who helped plan decimal coinage system.

Muhammad Ali, 1769?-1849, (Egypt), pasha, founder of dynasty that encouraged emergence of modern Egyptian state.

Benito Mussolini, 1883-1945, (Ital.) dictator and leader of the Italian fascist state.

Imre Nagy, c 1896-1958, (Hung.) communist premier, assassinated after Soviets crushed 1956 uprising.

Gamal Abdel Nasser, 1918-70, (Egypt.) leader of Arab unification, second Egyptian president.

Jawaharlal Nehru, 1889-1964, (Indian) prime minister, guided India through its early years of independence.

Kwame Nkrumah, 1909-72, (Ghan.) 1st prime minister, 1957-60, and president, 1960-66, of Ghana.

Frederick North, 1732-92, (British) prime minister, his inept policies led to loss of American colonies.

Daniel O'Connell, 1775-1847, (Irish) political leader, known as The Liberator.

Omar, c 581-644, Muslim leader, 2d caliph, led Islam to become an imperial power.

Thomas P. O'Neill, Jr., 1912-94, (U.S.) U.S. congressman, Speaker of the House, 1977-86.

Ignace Paderewski, 1860-1941, (Pol.) statesman, pianist, composer, briefly prime minister, an ardent patriot.

Viscount Palmerston, 1784-1865, (British) Whig-Liberal prime minister, foreign minister, embodied British nationalism.

Georgios Papandreou, 1888-1968, (Gk.) Republican politician, served three times as prime minister.

Franz von Papen, 1879-1969, (Ger.) politician, played major role in overthrow of Weimar Republic and rise of Hitler.

Charles Stewart Parnell, 1846-1891, (Irish) nationalist leader, "uncrowned king of Ireland."

Lester Pearson, 1897-1972, (Can.) diplomat, Liberal party leader, prime minister.

Robert Peel, 1788-1850, (British) reformist prime minister, founder of Conservative party.

Juan Perón, 1895-1974, (Arg.) president, dictator of Argentina.

Joseph Pilsudski, 1867-1935, (Pol.) statesman, instrumental in reestablishing Polish state in the 20th century.

Charles Pinckney, 1757-1824, (U.S.) founding father, his Pinckney plan was largely incorporated into constitution.

William Pitt, the Elder, 1708-78, (British) statesman, called the "Great Commoner," transformed Britain into imperial power.

William Pitt, the Younger, 1759-1806, (British) prime minister during French Revolutionary wars.

Georgi Plekhanov, 1857-1918, (Russ.) revolutionary, social philosopher, called "father of Russian Marxism."

Raymond Poincaré, 1860-1934, (Fr.) 9th president of the Republic, advocated harsh punishment of Germany after WW I.

Georges Pompidou, 1911-74, (Fr.) Gaullist political leader, president from 1969-74.

Grigori Potemkin, 1739-91, (Russ.) field marshal, favorite of Catherine II.

Edmund Randolph, 1753-1813, (U.S.) attorney, prominent in drafting, ratification of constitution.

John Randolph, 1773-1833, (U.S.) southern planter, strong advocate of states' rights.

Jeannette Rankin, 1880-1973, (U.S.) pacifist, first woman member of U.S. Congress.

Walter Rathenau, 1867-1922, (Ger.) industrialist, social theorist, statesman.

Sam Rayburn, 1882-1961, (U.S.) Democratic leader, representative for 47 years, House speaker for 17.

Paul Reynaud, 1878-1966, (Fr.) statesman, premier in 1940 at the time of France's defeat by Germany.

Syngman Rhee, 1875-1965, (Korean) first president of the Republic of Korea.

Cecil Rhodes, 1853-1902, (British) imperialist, industrial magnate, established Rhodes scholarships in his will

Cardinal de Richelieu, 1585-1642, (Fr.) statesman, known as "red eminence," chief minister to Louis XIII.

Maximilien Robespierre, 1758-94, (Fr.) leading figure of French Revolution, responsible for much of Reign of Terror.

Nelson Rockefeller, 1908-79, (U.S.) Republican gov. of NY, 1959-73; U.S. vice president, 1974-77.

Eleanor Roosevelt, 1884-1962, (U.S.) humanitarian, United Nations diplomat.

Elihu Root, 1845-1937, (U.S.) lawyer, statesman, diplomat, leading Republican supporter of the League of Nations.

John Russell, 1792-1878, (British) Liberal prime minister during the Irish potato famine.

Anwar al-Sadat, 1918-81, (Egypt.) president, 1970-1981, promoted peace with Israel; assassinated.

António de O. Salazar, 1889-1970, (Port.) statesman, long-time dictator.

José de San Martin, 1778-1850, South American revolutionary, protector of Peru.

Eisaku Sato, 1901-75, (Jap.) prime minister, presided over Japan's post-WW II emergence as major world power.

Philipp Scheidemann, 1865-1939, (Ger.) Social Democratic leader, first chancellor of the German republic.

Robert Schuman, 1886-1963, (Fr.) statesman, founded European Coal and Steel Community.

Carl Schurz, 1829-1906, (U.S.) German-American political leader, journalist, orator, dedicated reformer.

Kurt Schuschnigg, 1897-1977, (Austrian) chancellor, unsuccessful in stopping his country's annexation by Germany.

William H. Seward, 1801-72, (U.S.) anti-slavery activist, as U.S. secretary of state purchased Alaska.

Carlo Sforza, 1872-1952, (Ital.) foreign minister, anti-fascist.

Sitting Bull, c 1831-90, (Native American) Sioux leader in Battle of Little Bighorn over George A. Custer, 1876; fostered Ghost Dance religion.

Alfred E. Smith, 1873-1944, (U.S.) New York Democratic governor, first Roman Catholic to run for presidency.

Jan C. Smuts, 1870-1950, (S. African) statesman, philosopher, soldier, prime minister.

Paul Henri Spaak, 1899-1972, (Belg.) statesman, socialist leader.

Joseph Stalin, 1879-1953, (USSR) Soviet dictator, 1924-53.

Edwin M. Stanton, 1814-69, (U.S.) Lincoln's secretary of war during the Civil War.

Edward R. Stettinius, Jr., 1900-49, (U.S.) industrialist, secretary of state who coordinated aid to WW II allies.

Adlai E. Stevenson, 1900-65, (U.S.) Democratic leader, diplomat, Illinois governor, presidential candidate.

Henry L. Stimson, 1867-1950, (U.S.) statesman, served in 5 administrations, influenced foreign policy in 1930s and 1940s.

Gustav Stresemann, 1878-1929, (Ger.) chancellor, foreign minister, dedicated to regaining friendship for post-WW I Germany.

Sukarno, 1901-70, (Indon.) dictatorial first president of the Indonesian republic.

Sun Yat-sen, 1866-1925, (Chin.) revolutionary, leader of Kuomintang, regarded as the father of modern China.

Robert A. Taft, 1889-1953, (U.S.) conservative Senate leader, called "Mr. Republican."

Charles de Talleyrand, 1754-1838, (Fr.) statesman, diplomat, the major force of the Congress of Vienna of 1814-15.

U Thant, 1909-74 (Bur.) statesman, UN secretary-general.

Norman M. Thomas, 1884-1968, (U.S.) social reformer, 6 times unsuccessful Socialist party presidential candidate.

Josip Broz Tito, 1892-1980, (Yug.) president of Yugoslavia from 1953, World War II guerrilla chief, postwar rival of Stalin, leader of 3d world movement.

Palmiro Togliatti, 1893-1964, (Ital.) major leader of Italian Communist party.

Hideki Tojo, 1885-1948, (Jap.) statesman, soldier, prime minister during most of WW II.

François Toussaint L'Ouverture, c 1744-1803, (Hait.) patriot, martyr, thwarted French colonial aims.

Leon Trotsky, 1879-1940, (Russ.) revolutionary, founded Red Army, expelled from party in conflict with Stalin.

Rafael L. Trujillo Molina, 1891-1961, (Dom.) absolute dictator, assassinated.

Moise K. Tshombe, 1919-69, (Cong.) politician, president of secessionist Katanga, premier of Republic of Congo (Zaire).

William M. Tweed, 1823-78, (U.S.) politician, absolute leader of Tammany Hall, NYC's Democratic political machine.

Walter Ulbricht, 1893-1973, (Ger.) communist leader of German Democratic Republic.

Arthur H. Vandenberg, 1884-1951, (U.S.) senator, proponent of anti-communist bipartisan foreign policy after WW II.

Eleutherios Venizelos, 1864-1936, (Gk.) most prominent Greek statesman in early 20th century; expanded territory.

Hendrik F. Verwoerd, 1901-66, (S. African) prime minister, rigorously applied apartheid policy despite protest.

Robert Walpole, 1676-1745, (British) statesman, generally considered Britain's first prime minister.

Daniel Webster, 1782-1852, (U.S.) orator, politician, advocate of business interests during Jacksonian agrarianism.

Chaim Weizmann, 1874-1952, Zionist leader, scientist, first Israeli president.

Wendell L. Willkie, 1892-1944, (U.S.) Republican who tried to unseat FDR when he ran for his 3d term.

Emiliano Zapata, c 1879-1919, (Mex.) revolutionary, major influence on modern Mexico.

Zhou Enlai, 1898-1976, (Chin.) diplomat, prime minister, a leading figure of the Chinese Communist party.

Notable Military and Naval Leaders of the Past

Creighton Abrams, 1914-74, (U.S.) commanded forces in Vietnam, 1968-72.

Harold Alexander, 1891-1969, (British) led Allied invasion of Italy, 1943, WW2.

Ethan Allen, 1738-89, (U.S.) headed Green Mountain Boys; captured Ft. Ticonderoga, 1775, American Revolution.

Edmund Allenby, 1861-1936, (British) in Boer War, WW1; led Egyptian expeditionary force, 1917-18.

Benedict Arnold, 1741-1801, (U.S.) victorious at Saratoga; tried to betray West Point to British, American Revolution.

Henry "Hap" Arnold, 1886-1950, (U.S.) commanded Army Air Force in WW2.

John Barry, 1745-1803, (U.S.) won numerous sea battles during American Revolution.

Pierre Beauregard, 1818-93, (U.S.) Confederate general, ordered bombardment of Ft. Sumter that began the Civil War.

Gebhard von Blücher, 1742-1819, (Ger.) helped defeat Napoleon at Waterloo.

Napoleon Bonaparte, 1769-1821, (Fr.) defeated Russia and Austria at Austerlitz, 1805; invaded Russia, 1812; defeated at Waterloo, 1815.

Edward Braddock, 1695-1755, (British) commanded forces in French and Indian War.

Omar N. Bradley, 1893-1981, (U.S.) headed U.S. ground troops in Normandy invasion, 1944, WW2.

John Burgoyne, 1722-92, (British) defeated at Saratoga, American Revolution.

Claire Chennault, 1890-1958, (U.S.) headed Flying Tigers in WW2.

Mark Clark, 1896-1984, (U.S.) led forces in WW2 and Korean War.

Karl von Clausewitz, 1780-1831, (Prussian) wrote books on military theory.

Lucius D. Clay, 1897-1978, (U.S.) led Berlin airlift, 1948-49.

Henry Clinton, 1738-95, (British) commander of forces in American Revolution, 1778-81.

Cochise, c 1815-74, (Native American) chief of Chiricahua band of Apache Indians in Southwest.

Charles Cornwallis, 1738-1805, (British) victorious at Brandywine, 1777; surrendered at Yorktown, American Revolution.

Crazy Horse, 1849-77, (Native American) Sioux war chief victorious at Little Big Horn.

George A. Custer, 1839-76, (U.S.) defeated and killed at Little Big Horn.

Moshe Dayan, 1915-81, (Isr.) directed campaigns in the 1967, 1973 Arab-Israeli wars.

Stephen Decatur, 1779-1820, (U.S.) naval hero of Barbary wars, War of 1812.

Anton Denikin, 1872-1947, (Russ.) led White forces in Russian civil war.

George Dewey, 1837-1917, (U.S.) destroyed Spanish fleet at Manila, 1898, Spanish-American War.

Hugh C. Dowding, 1883-1970, (British) headed RAF, 1936-40, WW2.

Jubal Early, 1816-94, (U.S.) Confederate general led raid on Washington, 1864, Civil War.

Dwight D. Eisenhower, 1890-1969, (U.S.) commanded Allied forces in Europe, WW2.

David Farragut, 1801-70, (U.S.) Union admiral, captured New Orleans, Mobile Bay, Civil War.

Ferdinand Foch, 1851-1929, (Fr.) headed victorious Allied armies, 1918, WW1.

Nathan Bedford Forrest, 1821-77, (U.S.) Confederate general led cavalry raids against Union supply lines, Civil War.

Frederick the Great, 1712-86, (Prussian) led Prussia in The Seven Years War.

Horatio Gates, 1728-1806, (U.S.) commanded army at Saratoga, American Revolution.

Geronimo, 1829-1909 (Native American) leader of Chiricahua band of Apache Indians.

Charles G. Gordon, 1833-85, (British) led forces in China, Crimean War; killed at Khartoum.

Ulysses S. Grant, 1822-85, (U.S.) headed Union army, Civil War, 1864-65; forced Lee's surrender, 1865.

Nathanael Greene, 1742-86, (U.S.) defeated British in Southern campaign, 1780-81.

Heinz Guderian, 1888-1953, (Ger.) tank theorist, led panzer forces in Poland, France, Russia, WW2.

Douglas Haig, 1861-1928, (British) led British armies in France, 1915-18, WW1.

William F. Halsey, 1882-1959, (U.S.) defeated Japanese fleet at Leyte Gulf, 1944, WW2.

Sir Arthur Travers Harris, 1895-1984, (British) led Britain's WW2 bomber command.

Richard Howe, 1726-99, (British) commanded navy in American Revolution, 1776-78; June 1 victory against French, 1794.

William Howe, 1729-1814, (British) commanded forces in American Revolution, 1776-78.

Isaac Hull, 1773-1843, (U.S.) sunk British frigate *Guerriere,* War of 1812.

Thomas (Stonewall) Jackson, 1824-63, (U.S.) Confederate general led Shenandoah Valley campaign, Civil War.

Joseph Joffre, 1852-1931, (Fr.) headed Allied armies, won Battle of the Marne, 1914, WW1.

John Paul Jones, 1747-92, (U.S.) commanded *Bonhomme Richard* in victory over Serapis, American Revolution, 1779.

Stephen Kearny, 1794-1848, (U.S.) headed Army of the West in Mexican War.

Ernest J. King, 1878-1956, (U.S.) chief naval strategist in WW2.

Horatio H. Kitchener, 1850-1916, (British) led forces in Boer War; victorious at Khartoum; organized army in WW1.

Lavrenti Kornilov, 1870-1918, (Russ.) commander-in-chief, 1917; led counter-revolutionary march on Petrograd.

Thaddeus Kosciusko, 1746-1817, (Pol.) aided American cause in American Revolution.

Mikhail Kutuzov, 1745-1813, (Russ.) fought French at Borodino, Napoleonic Wars, 1812; abandoned Moscow; forced French retreat.

Marquis de Lafayette, 1757-1834, (Fr.) aided American cause in American Revolution.

T(homas) E. Lawrence (of Arabia), 1888-1935, (British) organized revolt of Arabs against Turks in WW1.

Henry (Light-Horse Harry) Lee, 1756-1818, (U.S.) cavalry officer in American Revolution.

Robert E. Lee, 1807-70, (U.S.) Confederate general defeated at Gettysburg, Civil War; surrendered to Grant, 1865.

Lyman Lemnitzer, 1899-1988, (U.S.) WW2 hero, later general, chairman of Joint Chiefs of Staff.

James Longstreet, 1821-1904, (U.S.) aided Lee at Gettysburg, Civil War.

Douglas MacArthur, 1880-1964, (U.S.) commanded forces in SW Pacific in WW2; headed occupation forces in Japan, 1945-51; UN commander in Korean War.

Francis Marion, 1733-95, (U.S.) led guerrilla actions in South Carolina during American Revolution.

Duke of Marlborough, 1650-1722, (British) led forces against Louis XIV in War of the Spanish Succession.

George C. Marshall, 1880-1959, (U.S.) chief of staff in WW2; authored Marshall Plan.

George B. McClellan, 1826-85, (U.S.) Union general, commanded Army of the Potomac, 1861-62, Civil War.

George Meade, 1815-72; (U.S.) commanded Union forces at Gettysburg, Civil War.

Billy Mitchell, 1879-1936, (U.S.) WW1 air-power advocate; court-martialed for insubordination, later vindicated.

Helmuth von Moltke, 1800-91; (Ger.) victorious in Austro-Prussian, Franco-Prussian wars.

Louis de Montcalm, 1712-59, (Fr.) headed troops in Canada, French and Indian War; defeated at Quebec, 1759.

Bernard Law Montgomery, 1887-1976, (British) stopped German offensive at Alamein, 1942, WW2; helped plan Normandy invasion.

Daniel Morgan, 1736-1802, (U.S.) victorious at Cowpens, 1781, American Revolution.

Louis Mountbatten, 1900-79, (British) Supreme Allied Commander of SE Asia, 1943-46, WW2.

Joachim Murat, 1767-1815, (Fr.) leader of cavalry at Marengo, 1800; Austerlitz, 1805; and Jena, 1806, Napoleonic Wars.

Horatio Nelson, 1758-1805, (British) naval commander destroyed French fleet at Trafalgar.

Michel Ney, 1769-1815, (Fr.) commanded forces in Switzerland, Austria, Russia, Napoleonic Wars; defeated at Waterloo.

Chester Nimitz, 1885-1966, (U.S.) commander of naval forces in Pacific in WW2.

George S. Patton, 1885-1945, (U.S.) led assault on Sicily, 1943, Third Army invasion of German-occupied Europe, WW2.

Oliver Perry, 1785-1819, (U.S.) won Battle of Lake Erie in War of 1812.

John Pershing, 1860-1948, (U.S.) commanded Mexican border campaign, 1916; American expeditionary forces in WW1.

Henri Philippe Pétain, 1856-1951, (Fr.) defended Verdun, 1916; headed Vichy government in WW2.

George E. Pickett, 1825-75, (U.S.) Confederate general famed for "charge" at Gettysburg, Civil War.

Hyman Rickover, 1900-86 (U.S.) father of nuclear navy.

Erwin Rommel, 1891-1944, (Ger.) headed Afrika Korps, WWII.

Karl von Rundstedt, 1875-1953, (Ger.) supreme commander in West, 1942-45, WW1.

Aleksandr Samsonov, 1859-1914, (Russ.) led invasion of E. Prussia, WW1, defeated at Tannenberg, 1914.

Winfield Scott, 1786-1866, (U.S.) hero of War of 1812; headed forces in Mexican war, took Mexico City.

Philip Sheridan, 1831-88, (U.S.) Union cavalry officer, headed Army of the Shenandoah, 1864-65, Civil War.

William T. Sherman, 1820-91, (U.S.) Union general, sacked Atlanta during "march to the sea," 1864, Civil War.

Carl Spaatz, 1891-1974, (U.S.) directed strategic bombing against Germany, later Japan, in WW2.

Raymond Spruance, 1886-1969, (U.S.) victorious at Midway Island, 1942, WW2.

Joseph W. Stilwell, 1883-1946, (U.S.) headed forces in the China, Burma, India theater in WW2.

J.E.B. Stuart, 1833-64, (U.S.) Confederate cavalry commander, Civil War.

George H. Thomas, 1816-70, (U.S.) saved Union army at Chattanooga, 1863; victorious at Nashville, 1864, Civil War.

Semyon Timoshenko, 1895-1970, (USSR) defended Moscow, Stalingrad, WW2; led winter offensive, 1942-43.

Alfred von Tirpitz, 1849-1930, (Ger.) responsible for submarine blockade in WW1.

Jonathan M. Wainwright, 1883-1953, (U.S.) forced to surrender on Corregidor, 1942, WW2.

George Washington, 1732-99, (U.S.) led Continental army, 1775-83, American Revolution.

Archibald Wavell, 1883-1950, (British) commanded forces in N. and E. Africa, and SE Asia in WW2.

Anthony Wayne, 1745-96, (U.S.) captured Stony Point, 1779, American Revolution; defeated Indians at Fallen Timbers, 1794.

Duke of Wellington, 1769-1852, (British) defeated Napoleon at Waterloo.

James Wolfe, 1727-59, (British) captured Quebec from French, 1759, French and Indian War.

Georgi Zhukov, 1895-1974, (Russ.) defended Moscow, 1941, led assault on Berlin, 1945, WW2.

Poets Laureate of England

There is no authentic record of the origin of the office of Poet Laureate of England. According to Warton, there was a Versificator Regis, or King's Poet, in the reign of Henry III (1216-72), and he was paid 100 shillings a year. Geoffrey Chaucer (1340-1400) assumed the title of Poet Laureate and in 1389 got a royal grant of a yearly allowance of wine. In the reign of Edward IV (1461-83), John Kay held the post. Under Henry VII (1485-1509), Andrew Bernard was the Poet Laureate and was succeeded under Henry VIII (1509-47) by John Skelton. Next came Edmund Spenser, who died in 1599; then Samuel Daniel, appointed 1599, and then Ben Jonson, 1619. Sir William D'Avenant was appointed in 1637. He was a godson of William Shakespeare.

Others were: John Dryden, 1670; Thomas Shadwell, 1688; Nahum Tate, 1692; Nicholas Rowe, 1715; the Rev. Laurence Eusden, 1718; Colley Cibber, 1730; William Whitehead, 1757, on the refusal of Thomas Gray; Rev. Thomas Warton, 1785, on the refusal of William Mason; Henry J. Pye, 1790; Robert Southey, 1813, on the refusal of Sir Walter Scott; William Wordsworth, 1843; Alfred, Lord Tennyson, 1850; Alfred Austin, 1896; Robert Bridges, 1913; John Masefield, 1930; Cecil Day Lewis, 1967; Sir John Betjeman, 1972; Ted Hughes, 1984.

U.S. Poets Laureate

Robert Penn Warren—the poet, novelist, and essayist—was named the country's first official Poet Laureate on Feb. 26, 1986. The only writer to have won the Pulitzer Prize for fiction and poetry (twice), Warren was chosen by Daniel J. Boorstin, the Librarian of Congress. The appointment began in Sept. 1986. Other appointments, all beginning in Sept., are: 1987, Richard Wilbur; 1988, Howard Nemerov; 1990, Mark Strand; 1991, Joseph Brodsky; 1992, Mona Van Duyn, the first female poet laureate; 1993, Rita Dove, the first black poet laureate.

Noted Writers of the Past

George Ade, 1866-1944, (U.S.) humorist. *Fables in Slang.*

Conrad Aiken, 1889-1973, (U.S.) poet, critic. *Ushant.*

Louisa May Alcott, 1832-88, (U.S.) novelist. *Little Women.*

Sholom Aleichem, 1859-1916, (R.) Yiddish writer. *Tevye's Daughter, Adventures of Mottel, The Old Country.*

Vicente Aleixandre, 1898-1984, (Sp.) poet. *La destrucción o el amor, Dialogolos del conocimiento.*

Horatio Alger, 1832-1899, (U.S.) "rags-to-riches" books.

Hans Christian Andersen, 1805-75, (Dan.) author of fairy tales. *The Princess and the Pea, The Ugly Duckling.*

Maxwell Anderson, 1888-1959, (U.S.) playwright. *What Price Glory?, High Tor, Winterset, Key Largo.*

Sherwood Anderson, 1876-1941, (U.S.) short-story writer. "Death in the Woods"; *Winesburg, Ohio* (collection).

Matthew Arnold, 1822-88, (Br.) poet, critic. "Thrysis," "Dover Beach," "The Gypsy Scholar"; "Culture and Anarchy."

Isaac Asimov, 1920-92, (U.S.) science fiction writer. *I Robot.*

Jane Austen, 1775-1817, (Br.) novelist. *Pride and Prejudice, Sense and Sensibility, Emma, Mansfield Park.*

Isaac Babel, 1894-1941, (R.) short-story writer, playwright. *Odessa Tales, Red Cavalry.*

Honoré de Balzac, 1799-1850, (F.) novelist. *Le Père Goriot, Cousine Bette, Eugénie Grandet, The Human Comedy.*

James M. Barrie, 1860-1937, (Br.) playwright, novelist. *Peter Pan, Dear Brutus, What Every Woman Knows.*

Charles Baudelaire, 1821-67, (F.) symbolist poet. *Les Fleurs du Mal.*

L. Frank Baum, 1856-1919, (U.S.) writer. Wizard of Oz series of children's books.

Simone de Beauvoir, 1908-86, (F.) novelist, essayist. *The Second Sex, Memoirs of a Dutiful Daughter.*

Samuel Beckett, 1906-89, (Ir.) novelist, playwright, in French and English. *Waiting for Godot, Endgame* (plays); *Murphy, Watt, Molloy* (novels).

Brendan Behan, 1923-64, (Ir.) playwright. *The Quare Fellow, The Hostage, Borstal Boy.*

Robert Benchley, 1889-1945, (U.S.) humorist. *From Bed to Worse, My Ten Years in a Quandary.*

Stephen Vincent Benét, 1898-1943, (U.S.) poet, novelist. *John Brown's Body.*

John Berryman, 1914-72, (U.S.) poet. *Homage to Mistress Bradstreet.*

Ambrose Bierce, 1842-1914, (U.S.) short-story writer, journalist. *In the Midst of Life, The Devil's Dictionary.*

William Blake, 1757-1827, (Br.) poet, artist. *Songs of Innocence, Songs of Experience, The Marriage of Heaven and Hell.*

Giovanni Boccaccio, 1313-75, (It.) poet, storyteller. *Decameron, Filostrato.*

Jorge Luis Borges, 1900-86 (Arg.) short-story writer, poet, essayist. *Labyrinths.*

James Boswell, 1740-95, (Sc.) biographer. *The Life of Samuel Johnson, A Journal of a Tour of the Hebrides.*

Pierre Boulle, (1913-94) (F.) author. *The Bridge Over the River Kwai, Planet of the Apes.*

Anne Bradstreet, c 1612-72, (U.S.) poet. *The Tenth Muse Lately Sprung Up in America.*

Bertolt Brecht, 1898-1956, (G.) dramatist, poet. *The Threepenny Opera, Mother Courage and Her Children.*

Charlotte Brontë, 1816-55, (Br.) novelist. *Jane Eyre.*

Emily Brontë, 1818-48, (Br.) novelist. *Wuthering Heights.*

Elizabeth Barrett Browning, 1806-61, (Br.) poet. *Sonnets From the Portuguese, Aurora Leigh.*

Robert Browning, 1812-89, (Br.) poet. "My Last Duchess," "Fra Lippo Lippi," *The Ring and The Book.*

Pearl Buck, 1892-1973, (U.S.) novelist. *The Good Earth.*

Mikhail Bulgakov, 1891-1940, (R.) novelist, playwright. *The Heart of a Dog, The Master and Margarita.*

John Bunyan, 1628-88, (Br.) writer. *Pilgrim's Progress.*

Anthony Burgess, 1917-93, (Br.) author. *A Clockwork Orange.*

Robert Burns, 1759-96, (Sc.) poet. "Flow Gently, Sweet Afton," "My Heart's in the Highlands," "Auld Lang Syne."

Edgar Rice Burroughs, 1875-1950, (U.S.) novelist. *Tarzan of the Apes.*

George Gordon Byron, Lord Byron, 1788-1824, (Br.) poet. *Don Juan, Childe Harold, Manfred, Cain.*

Italo Calvino, 1923-85 (It.) novelist, short-story writer. *If on a Winter's Night a Traveler*

Albert Camus, 1913-60, (F.) writer. *The Stranger.*

Karel Capek, 1890-1938, (Czech.) playwright, novelist, essayist. *R.U.R. (Rossum's Universal Robots).*

Lewis Carroll, 1832-98, (Br.) writer, mathematician. *Alice's Adventures in Wonderland, Through the Looking Glass.*

Giacomo Casanova, 1725-98, (It.) adventurer, memoirist.

Willa Cather, 1873-1947, (U.S.) novelist, essayist. *O Pioneers! My Antonia, Death Comes for the Archbishop.*

Miguel de Cervantes Saavedra, 1547-1616, (Sp.) novelist, dramatist, poet. *Don Quixote de la Mancha.*

Raymond Chandler, 1888-1959, (U.S.) writer of detective fiction. Philip Marlowe series.

Geoffrey Chaucer, c 1340-1400, (Br.) poet. *The Canterbury Tales, Troilus and Criseyde.*

John Cheever, 1912-82, (U.S.) short-story writer, novelist. *The Wapshot Scandal,* "The Country Husband."

Anton Chekhov, 1860-1904, (R.) short-story writer, dramatist. *Uncle Vanya, The Cherry Orchard, The Three Sisters.*

G. K. Chesterton, 1874-1936, (Br.) critic, novelist. Father Brown series of mysteries.

Kate Chopin, 1851-1904, (U.S.) writer. *The Awakening.*

Agatha Christie, 1890-1976, (Br.) mystery writer. *And Then There Were None, Murder on the Orient Express.*

Jean Cocteau, 1889-1963, (F.) writer, visual artist, filmmaker. *The Beauty and the Beast, Les Enfants Terribles.*

Samuel Taylor Coleridge, 1772-1834, (Br.) poet, critic. "Kubla Khan," "The Rime of the Ancient Mariner," "Christabel."

(Sidonie) Colette, 1873-1954, (F.) novelist. *Claudine, Gigi.*

Joseph Conrad, 1857-1924, (Br.) novelist. *Lord Jim, Heart of Darkness, The Nigger of the Narcissus, Nostromo.*

James Fenimore Cooper, 1789-1851, (U.S.) novelist. Leatherstocking Tales.

Pierre Corneille, 1606-84, (F.) dramatist. *Medeé, Le Cid, Horace, Cinna, Polyeucte.*

Hart Crane, 1899-1932, (U.S.) poet. "The Bridge."

Stephen Crane, 1871-1900, (U.S.) novelist, short-story writer. *The Red Badge of Courage,* "The Open Boat."

e.e. cummings, 1894-1962, (U.S.) poet. *Tulips and Chimneys.*

Roald Dahl, 1916-90, (Br.-U.S.) writer. *Charlie and the Chocolate Factory.*

Gabriele D'Annunzio, 1863-1938, (It.) poet, novelist, dramatist. *The Child of Pleasure, The Intruder, The Victim.*

Dante Alighieri, 1265-1321, (It.) poet. *The Divine Comedy.*
Daniel Defoe, 1660-1731, (Br.) writer. *Robinson Crusoe, Moll Flanders, Journal of the Plague Year.*
Charles Dickens, 1812-70, (Br.) novelist. *David Copperfield, Oliver Twist, Great Expectations, The Pickwick Papers.*
Emily Dickinson, 1830-86, (U.S.) poet.
Isak Dinesen (Karen Blixen), 1885-1962, (Dan.) author. *Out of Africa, Seven Gothic Tales, Winter's Tales.*
John Donne, 1573-1631, (Br.) poet. *Songs and Sonnets.*
John Dos Passos, 1896-1970, (U.S.) novelist. *U.S.A.*
Fyodor Dostoyevsky, 1821-81, (R.) novelist. *Crime and Punishment, The Brothers Karamazov, The Possessed.*
Arthur Conan Doyle, 1859-1930, (Br.) novelist. Sherlock Holmes mystery series.
Theodore Dreiser, 1871-1945, (U.S.) novelist. *An American Tragedy, Sister Carrie.*
John Dryden, 1631-1700, (Br.) poet, dramatist, critic. *All for Love, Mac Flecknoe, Absalom and Achitopel.*
Alexandre Dumas, 1802-70, (F.) novelist, dramatist. *The Three Musketeers, The Count of Monte Cristo.*
Alexandre Dumas (fils), 1824-95, (F.) dramatist, novelist. *La Dame aux Camélias, Le Demi-Monde.*
Ilya G. Ehrenburg, 1891-1967, (R.) writer. *The Thaw.*
George Eliot (Mary Ann Evans or Marian Evans), 1819-80, (Br.) novelist. *Middlemarch, The Mill on the Floss.*
T. S. Eliot, 1888-1965, (Br.) poet, critic. *The Waste Land,* "The Love Song of J. Alfred Prufrock," *Four Quartets.*
Ralph Ellison, 1914-94, (U.S.), writer. *Invisible Man.*
Ralph Waldo Emerson, 1803-82, (U.S.) poet, essayist. "Brahma," "Nature," "The Over-Soul," "Self-Reliance."
James T. Farrell, 1904-79, (U.S.) novelist. *Studs Lonigan.*
William Faulkner, 1897-1962, (U.S.) novelist. *Sanctuary, Light in August, The Sound and the Fury, Absalom, Absalom!*
Henry Fielding, 1707-54, (Br.) novelist. *Tom Jones.*
F. Scott Fitzgerald, 1896-1940, (U.S.) short-story writer, novelist. *The Great Gatsby, Tender Is the Night.*
Gustave Flaubert, 1821-80, (F.) novelist. *Madame Bovary.*
C. S. Forester, 1899-1966, (Br.) writer. Horatio Hornblower.
E. M. Forster, 1879-1970, (Br.) novelist. *A Passage to India.*
Anatole France, 1844-1924, (F.) writer. *Penguin Island, My Friend's Book, The Crime of Sylvestre Bonnard.*
Robert Frost, 1874-1963, (U.S.) poet. "Birches," "Fire and Ice," "Stopping by Woods on a Snowy Evening."
John Galsworthy, 1867-1933, (Br.) novelist, dramatist. *The Forsyte Saga, A Modern Comedy.*
Erle Stanley Gardner, 1889-1970, (U.S.) novelist. Perry Mason series of mysteries.
Jean Genet, 1911-86, (F.) playwright, novelist. *The Blacks, The Maids, The Balcony.*
André Gide, 1869-1951, (F.) writer. *The Immoralist, The Pastoral Symphony, Strait Is the Gate.*
Jean Giraudoux, 1882-1944, (F.) novelist, dramatist. *Electra, The Madwoman of Chaillot, Ondine, Tiger at the Gate.*
Johann Wolfgang von Goethe, 1749-1832, (G.) poet, dramatist, novelist. *Faust, The Sorrows of Young Werther.*
Nikolai Gogol, 1809-52, (R.) short-story writer, dramatist, novelist. *Dead Souls, The Inspector General.*
William Golding, 1911-93, (Br.) writer. *Lord of the Flies.*
Oliver Goldsmith, 1730?-74, (Br.-Ir.) writer. *The Vicar of Wakefield, She Stoops to Conquer.*
Maxim Gorky, 1868-1936, (R.) writer. *The Lower Depths.*
Robert Graves, 1895-1985, (Br.) poet, classical scholar, novelist. *I, Claudius; The White Goddess.*
Thomas Gray, 1716-71, (Br.) poet. "Elegy Written in a Country Churchyard," "The Progress of Poesy."
Graham Greene, 1904-91, (Br.) novelist. *The Power and the Glory, The Heart of the Matter, The Ministry of Fear.*
Zane Grey, 1872-1939, (U.S.) writer of western stories.
Jakob Grimm, 1785-1863, (G.) philologist, folklorist. *German Methodology, Grimm's Fairy Tales.*
Wilhelm Grimm, 1786-1859, (G.) philologist, folklorist. *Grimm's Fairy Tales.*
Alex Haley, 1921-92, (U.S.) author. *Roots, The Autobiography of Malcolm X.*
Dashiell Hammett, 1894-1961, (U.S.) writer of detective fiction, created Sam Spade.
Knute Hamsun, 1859-1952 (Nor.) novelist. *Hunger.*
Thomas Hardy, 1840-1928, (Br.) novelist, poet. *The Return of the Native, Tess of the D'Urbervilles, Jude the Obscure.*
Joel Chandler Harris, 1848-1908, (U.S.) short-story writer. Uncle Remus series.
Moss Hart, 1904-61, (U.S.) playwright. *Once in a Lifetime, You Can't Take It With You, The Man Who Came to Dinner.*
Bret Harte, 1836-1902, (U.S.) short-story writer, poet. *The Luck of Roaring Camp.*
Jaroslav Hasek, 1883-1923, (Czech.) writer. *The Good Soldier Schweik.*
Nathaniel Hawthorne, 1804-64, (U.S.) novelist, short-story writer. *The Scarlet Letter,* "The Artist of the Beautiful."
Heinrich Heine, 1797-1856, (G.) poet. *Book of Songs.*
Lillian Hellman, 1905-84, (U.S.) playwright, author of memoirs. "The Little Foxes," *An Unfinished Woman, Pentimento.*
Ernest Hemingway, 1899-1961, (U.S.) novelist, short-story writer. *A Farewell to Arms, For Whom the Bell Tolls.*
O. Henry (W. S. Porter), 1862-1910, (U.S.) short-story writer. "The Gift of the Magi."
John Hersey, 1914-93, (U.S.) novelist, journalist. *Hiroshima, A Bell for Adano.*
Hermann Hesse, 1877-1962, (G.) novelist, poet. *Death and the Lover, Steppenwolf, Siddhartha.*
Oliver Wendell Holmes, 1809-94, (U.S.) poet, novelist. *The Autocrat of the Breakfast-Table.*
Alfred E. Housman, 1859-1936, (Br.) poet. *A Shropshire Lad.*
William Dean Howells, 1837-1920, (U.S.) novelist, critic. *The Rise of Silas Lapham.*
Langston Hughes, 1902-67, (U.S.) poet, playwright. *The Weary Blues, One-Way Ticket, Shakespeare in Harlem.*
Victor Hugo, 1802-85, (F.) poet, dramatist, novelist. *Notre Dame de Paris, Les Misérables.*
Nora Zeale Hurston, 1903-60, (U.S.) novelist, folklorist. *Their Eyes Were Watching God, Mules and Men.*
Aldous Huxley 1894-1963, (Br.) writer. *Brave New World.*
Henrik Ibsen, 1828-1906, (Nor.) dramatist, poet. *A Doll's House, Ghosts, The Wild Duck, Hedda Gabler.*
Eugene Ionesco, 1910-94, (F.) surrealist writer. *The Bald Soprano, The Chairs.*
Washington Irving, 1783-1859, (U.S.) writer. "Rip Van Winkle," "The Legend of Sleepy Hollow."
Shirley Jackson, 1919-65, (U.S.) writer. "The Lottery."
Henry James, 1843-1916, (U.S.) novelist, short-story writer, critic. *The Portrait of a Lady, The American, Daisy Miller.*
Robinson Jeffers, 1887-1962, (U.S.) poet, dramatist. *Tamar and Other Poems, Medea.*
Samuel Johnson, 1709-84, (Br.) author, scholar, critic. *Dictionary of the English Language.*
Ben Jonson, 1572-1637, (Br.) dramatist, poet. *Volpone.*
James Joyce, 1882-1941, (Ir.) writer. *Ulysses, Dubliners, A Portrait of the Artist As a Young Man, Finnegans Wake.*
Franz Kafka, 1883-1924, (G.) novelist, short-story writer. *The Trial, Amerika, The Castle, The Metamorphosis.*
George S. Kaufman, 1889-1961, (U.S.) playwright. *The Man Who Came to Dinner, You Can't Take It With You, Stage Door.*
Nikos Kazantzakis, 1883?-1957, (Gk.) novelist. *Zorba the Greek, A Greek Passion.*
John Keats, 1795-1821, (Br.) poet. "Ode on a Grecian Urn," "Ode to a Nightingale," "La Belle Dame Sans Merci."
Joyce Kilmer, 1886-1918, (U.S.) poet, "Trees."
Rudyard Kipling, 1865-1936, (Br.) author, poet. "The White Man's Burden," "Gunga Din," *The Jungle Book.*
Jean de la Fontaine, 1621-95, (F.) poet. *Fables choisies.*
Pär Lagerkvist, 1891-1974, (Swed.) poet, dramatist, novelist. *Barabbas, The Sybil.*
Selma Lagerlöf, 1858-1940, (Swed.) novelist. *Jerusalem, The Ring of the Lowenskolds.*
Alphonse de Lamartine, 1790-1869, (F.) poet, novelist, statesman. *Méditations poétiques.*
Charles Lamb, 1775-1834, (Br.) essayist. *Specimens of English Dramatic Poets, Essays of Elia.*
Giuseppe di Lampedusa, 1896-1957, (It.) novelist. *The Leopard.*
Ring Lardner, 1885-1933, (U.S.) short-story writer, humorist. *You Know Me, Al.*
D. H. Lawrence, 1885-1930, (Br.) novelist. *Sons and Lovers, Women in Love, Lady Chatterley's Lover.*
Mikhail Lermontov, 1814-41, (R.) novelist, poet. "Demon," *Hero of Our Time.*
Alain-René Lesage, 1668-1747, (F.) novelist. *Gil Blas de Santillane.*
Gotthold Lessing, 1729-81, (G.) dramatist, philosopher, critic. *Miss Sara Sampson, Minna von Barnhelm.*
Sinclair Lewis, 1885-1951, (U.S.) novelist. *Babbitt, Arrowsmith, Dodsworth, Main Street.*
Vachel Lindsay, 1879-1931, (U.S.) poet. *General William Booth Enters into Heaven, The Congo.*
Hugh Lofting, 1886-1947, (Br.) writer. Dr. Doolittle series.
Jack London, 1876-1916, (U.S.) novelist, journalist. *Call of the Wild, The Sea-Wolf.*
Henry Wadsworth Longfellow, 1807-82, (U.S.) poet. *Evangeline, The Song of Hiawatha.*
Amy Lowell, 1874-1925, (U.S.) poet, critic. "Lilacs."
James Russell Lowell, 1819-91, (U.S.) poet, editor. *Poems, The Biglow Papers.*
Robert Lowell, 1917-77, (U.S.) poet. "Lord Weary's Castle".
Niccolò Machiavelli, 1469-1527, (It.) writer, statesman. *The Prince, Discourses on Livy.*
Bernard Malamud, 1914-86, (U.S.) short-story writer, novelist. "The Magic Barrel," *The Assistant, The Fixer.*
Stéphane Mallarmé, 1842-98, (F.) poet. *Poésies.*

Thomas Malory, ?-1471, (Br.) writer. *Morte d'Arthur.*
Andre Malraux, 1901-76, (F.) novelist. *Man's Fate.*
Osip Mandelstam, 1891-1938, (R.) poet. *Stone, Tristia.*
Thomas Mann, 1875-1955, (G.) novelist, essayist. *Buddenbrooks, Death in Venice, The Magic Mountain.*
Katherine Mansfield, 1888-1923, (Br.) writer. "Bliss."
Christopher Marlowe, 1564-93, (Br.) dramatist, poet. *Tamburlaine the Great, Dr. Faustus, The Jew of Malta.*
John Masefield, 1878-1967, (Br.) poet. "Sea Fever," "Cargoes," *Salt Water Ballads.*
Edgar Lee Masters, 1869-1950, (U.S.) poet, biographer. *Spoon River Anthology.*
W. Somerset Maugham, 1874-1965, (Br.) author. *Of Human Bondage, The Razor's Edge, The Moon and Sixpence.*
Guy de Maupassant, 1850-93, (F.) novelist, short-story writer. "A Life," "Bel-Ami," "The Necklace."
François Mauriac, 1885-1970, (F.) novelist, dramatist. *Viper's Tangle, The Kiss to the Leper.*
Vladimir Mayakovsky, 1893-1930, (R.) poet, dramatist. *The Cloud in Trousers.*
Mary McCarthy, 1912-89, (U.S.) critic, novelist. *Memories of a Catholic Girlhood.*
Carson McCullers, 1917-67, (U.S.) novelist. *The Heart Is a Lonely Hunter, Member of the Wedding.*
Herman Melville, 1819-91, (U.S.) novelist, poet. *Moby Dick, Typee, Billy Budd, Omoo.*
H. L. Mencken, 1880-1956, (U.S.) author, critic, editor. *Prejudices, The American Language.*
George Meredith, 1828-1909, (Br.) novelist, poet. *The Ordeal of Richard Feverel, The Egoist.*
Prosper Mérimée, 1803-70, (F.) author. *Carmen.*
Edna St. Vincent Millay, 1892-1950, (U.S.) poet. *The Harp Weaver and Other Poems, A Few Figs from Thistles.*
Henry Miller, 1891-1980, (U.S.), writer. *Tropic of Cancer*
A. A. Milne, 1882-1956, (Br.) author. *Winnie-the-Pooh.*
John Milton, 1608-74, (Br.) poet. *Paradise Lost.*
Mishima Yukio (Hiraoka Kimitake), 1925-70, (Jap.) writer. *Confessions of a Mask.*
Gabriela Mistral, 1889-1957, (Chil.) poet. *Sonnets of Death.*
Margaret Mitchell, 1900-49, (U.S.) author. *Gone With the Wind.*
Jean Baptiste Molière, 1622-73, (F.) dramatist. *Le Tartuffe, Le Misanthrope, Le Bourgeois Gentilhomme.*
Ferenc Molnár, 1878-1952, (Hung.) dramatist, novelist. *Liliom, The Guardsman, The Swan.*
Michel de Montaigne, 1533-92, (F.) essayist. *Essais.*
Eugenio Montale, 1896-1981, (It.) poet.
Clement C. Moore, 1779-1863, (U.S.) poet, educator. "A Visit From Saint Nicholas."
Marianne Moore, 1887-1972, (U.S.) poet. *Collected Poems.*
Thomas More, 1478-1535, (Br.) writer. *Utopia.*
H. H. Munro (Saki), 1870-1916, (Br.) writer. *Reginald, The Chronicles of Clovis, Beasts and Super-Beasts.*
Murasaki Shikibu, c 978-1031?, (Jap.) novelist. *The Tale of Genji.*
Alfred de Musset, 1810-57, (F.) poet, dramatist. *La Confession d'un Enfant du Siècle.*
Vladimir Nabokov, 1899-1977, (R.-U.S.) novelist. *Lolita.*
Ogden Nash, 1902-71, (U.S.) poet. *Hard Lines, I'm a Stranger Here Myself, The Private Dining Room.*
Pablo Neruda, 1904-73, (Chil.) poet. *Twenty Love Poems and One Song of Despair, Toward the Splendid City.*
Sean O'Casey, 1884-1964, (Ir.) dramatist. *Juno and the Paycock, The Plough and the Stars.*
Flannery O'Connor, 1925-64, (U.S.) novelist, short-story writer. *Wise Blood,* "A Good Man Is Hard to Find."
Clifford Odets, 1906-63, (U.S.) playwright. *Waiting for Lefty, Awake and Sing, Golden Boy, The Country Girl.*
John O'Hara, 1905-70, (U.S.) novelist, short-story writer. *From the Terrace, Appointment in Samarra, Pal Joey.*
Omar Khayyam, c 1028-1122, (Per.) poet. *Rubaiyat.*
Eugene O'Neill, 1888-1953, (U.S.) playwright. *Emperor Jones, Anna Christie, Long Day's Journey into Night.*
George Orwell, 1903-50, (Br.) novelist, essayist. *Animal Farm, Nineteen Eighty-Four.*
Thomas (Tom) Paine, 1737-1809, (U.S.) writer, political theorist. *Common Sense.*
Dorothy Parker, 1893-1967, (U.S.) poet, short-story writer. *Enough Rope, Laments for the Living.*
Boris Pasternak, 1890-1960, (R.) poet, novelist. *Doctor Zhivago, My Sister, Life.*
Samuel Pepys, 1633-1703, (Br.) public official, diarist.
S. J. Perelman, 1904-79, (U.S.) humorist. *The Road to Miltown, Under the Spreading Atrophy.*
Francesco Petrarca, 1304-74, (It.) poet. *Africa, Trionfi, Canzoniere, On Solitude.*
Luigi Pirandello, 1867-1936, (It.) novelist, dramatist. *Six Characters in Search of an Author.*
Sylvia Plath, 1932-63, (U.S.) author, poet. *The Bell Jar.*
Edgar Allan Poe, 1809-49, (U.S.) poet, short-story writer, critic. "Annabel Lee," "The Raven," "The Purloined Letter."
Alexander Pope, 1688-1744, (Br.) poet. *The Rape of the Lock, An Essay on Man.*
Katherine Anne Porter, 1890-1980, (U.S.) novelist, short-story writer. *Ship of Fools.*
Ezra Pound, 1885-1972, (U.S.) poet. *Cantos.*
Marcel Proust, 1871-1922, (F.) novelist. *Remembrance of Things Past.*
Aleksandr Pushkin, 1799-1837, (R.) poet, prose writer. *Boris Godunov, Eugene Onegin, The Bronze Horseman.*
François Rabelais, 1495-1553, (F.) writer. *Gargantua.*
Jean Racine, 1639-99, (F.) dramatist. *Andromaque, Phèdre, Bérénice, Britannicus.*
Ayn Rand, 1905-82 (R.-U.S.) novelist, philosopher. *The Fountainhead, Atlas Shrugged.*
Erich Maria Remarque, 1898-1970, (G.-U.S.) novelist. *All Quiet on the Western Front.*
Samuel Richardson, 1689-1761, (Br.) novelist. *Clarissa Harlowe, Pamela; or Virtue Rewarded.*
Rainer Maria Rilke, 1875-1926, (G.) poet. *Life and Songs, Duino Elegies, Poems from the Book of Hours.*
Arthur Rimbaud, 1854-91, (F.) poet. *A Season in Hell.*
Edwin Arlington Robinson, 1869-1935, (U.S.) poet. "Richard Cory," "Miniver Cheevy."
Theodore Roethke, 1908-63, (U.S.) poet. *Open House, The Waking, The Far Field.*
Romain Rolland, 1866-1944, (F.) novelist, biographer. *Jean-Christophe.*
Pierre de Ronsard, 1524-85, (F.) poet. *Sonnets pour Hélène, La Franciade.*
Edmond Rostand, 1868-1918, (F.) poet, dramatist. *Cyrano de Bergerac.*
Damon Runyon, 1880-1946, (U.S.) short-story writer, journalist. *Guys and Dolls, Blue Plate Special.*
John Ruskin, 1819-1900, (Br.) critic, social theorist. *Modern Painters, The Seven Lamps of Architecture.*
Antoine de Saint-Exupéry, 1900-44, (F.) writer. *Wind, Sand and Stars, The Little Prince.*
George Sand (Amandine Aurore Lucile), 1804-76, (F.) novelist. *Consuelo, The Haunted Pool, The Master Bell-Ringer.*
Carl Sandburg, 1878-1967, (U.S.) poet. *The People, Yes; Chicago Poems, Smoke and Steel, Harvest Poems.*
George Santayana, 1863-1952, (U.S.) poet, essayist, philosopher. *The Sense of Beauty, The Realms of Being.*
William Saroyan, 1908-81, (U.S.) playwright, novelist. *The Time of Your Life, The Human Comedy.*
Jean-Paul Sartre, 1905-80, (F.) philosopher, novelist, playwright. *Nausea, No Exit, Being and Nothingness.*
Richard Scarry, 1920-94, (U.S.) author of children's books. *Richard Scarry's Best Story Book Ever.*
Friedrich von Schiller, 1759-1805, (G.) dramatist, poet, historian. *Don Carlos, Maria Stuart, Wilhelm Tell.*
Sir Walter Scott, 1771-1832, (Sc.) novelist, poet. *Ivanhoe.*
Jaroslav Seifert, 1902-86, (Czech.) poet.
Dr. Seuss (Theodor Seuss Geisel), 1904-91, (U.S.) children's book author and illustrator. *The Cat in the Hat.*
William Shakespeare, 1564-1616, (Br.) dramatist, poet. *Romeo and Juliet, Hamlet, King Lear, Julius Caesar, The Merchant of Venice, Othello, Macbeth, The Tempest;* sonnets.
George Bernard Shaw, 1856-1950, (Ir.-Br.) playwright, critic. *St. Joan, Pygmalion, Major Barbara, Man and Superman.*
Mary Wollstonecraft Shelley, 1797-1851, (Br.) novelist, feminist. *Frankenstein, The Last Man.*
Percy Bysshe Shelley, 1792-1822, (Br.) poet. *Prometheus Unbound, Adonais,* "Ode to the West Wind," "To a Skylark."
Richard B. Sheridan, 1751-1816, (Br.) dramatist. *The Rivals, School for Scandal.*
William I. Shirer, 1904-93, (U.S.) author. *The Rise and Fall of the Third Reich.*
Mikhail Sholokhov, 1906-84, (R.) writer. *The Silent Don.*
Upton Sinclair, 1878-1968, (U.S.) novelist. *The Jungle.*
Isaac Bashevis Singer, 1904-91, (Pol.-U.S.) novelist, short story writer, in Yiddish. *The Magician of Lubin.*
Edmund Spenser, 1552-99, (Br.) poet. *The Faerie Queen.*
Christina Stead, 1903-83, (Austral.) novelist, short-story writer. *The Man Who Loved Children.*
Richard Steele, 1672-1729, (Br.) essayist, playwright, began the *Tatler* and *Spectator. The Conscious Lovers.*
Lincoln Steffens, 1866-1936, (U.S.) editor, writer. *The Shame of the Cities.*
Gertrude Stein, 1874-1946, (U.S.) writer. *Three Lives.*
John Steinbeck, 1902-68, (U.S.) novelist. *The Grapes of Wrath, Of Mice and Men, The Winter of Our Discontent.*
Stendhal (Marie Henri Beyle), 1783-1842, (F.) novelist. *The Red and the Black, The Charterhouse of Parma.*
Laurence Sterne, 1713-68, (Br.) novelist. *Tristram Shandy.*
Wallace Stevens, 1879-1955, (U.S.) poet. *Harmonium, The Man With the Blue Guitar, Notes Toward a Supreme Fiction.*

Robert Louis Stevenson, 1850-94, (Br.) novelist, poet, essayist. *Treasure Island, A Child's Garden of Verses.*

Rex Stout, 1886-1975, (U.S.) novelist, created Nero Wolfe.

Harriet Beecher Stowe, 1811-96, (U.S.) novelist. *Uncle Tom's Cabin.*

Lytton Strachey, 1880-1932, (Br.) biographer, critic. *Eminent Victorians, Queen Victoria, Elizabeth and Essex.*

August Strindberg, 1849-1912, (Swed.) dramatist, novelist. *The Father, Miss Julie, The Creditors.*

Jonathan Swift, 1667-1745, (Br.) writer. *Gulliver's Travels.*

Algernon C. Swinburne, 1837-1909, (Br.) writer. *Atalanta in Calydon.*

John M. Synge, 1871-1909, (Ir.) poet, dramatist. *Riders to the Sea, The Playboy of the Western World.*

Rabindranath Tagore, 1861-1941, (Ind.) author, poet. *Sadhana, The Realization of Life, Gitanjali.*

Booth Tarkington, 1869-1946, (U.S.) novelist. *Seventeen, Alice Adams, Penrod.*

Sara Teasdale, 1884-1933, (U.S.) poet. *Helen of Troy and Other Poems, Rivers to the Sea, Flame and Shadow.*

Tennyson, Alfred, Lord, 1809-92, (Br.) poet. *Idylls of the King, In Memoriam,* "The Charge of the Light Brigade."

William Makepeace Thackeray, 1811-63, (Br.) novelist. *Vanity Fair, Henry Esmond, Pendennis.*

Dylan Thomas, 1914-53, (Welsh) poet. *Under Milk Wood, A Child's Christmas in Wales.*

Henry David Thoreau, 1817-62, (U.S.) author. *Walden.*

James Thurber, 1894-1961, (U.S.) humorist, cartoonist. "The Secret Life of Walter Mitty," *My Life and Hard Times.*

J. R. R. Tolkien, 1892-1973, (Br.) writer. *Lord of the Rings.*

Leo Tolstoy, 1828-1910, (R.) novelist, short-story writer. *War and Peace, Anna Karenina,* "The Death of Ivan Ilyich."

Anthony Trollope, 1815-82, (Br.) novelist. *The Warden, Barchester Towers,* The Palliser novels.

Ivan Turgenev, 1818-83, (R.) novelist, short-story writer. *Fathers and Sons, First Love, A Month in the Country.*

Mark Twain (Samuel Clemens), 1835-1910, (U.S.) novelist, humorist. *The Adventures of Huckleberry Finn, Tom Sawyer.*

Sigrid Undset, 1881-1949, (Nor.) novelist, poet. *Kristin Lavransdatter.*

Paul Valéry, 1871-1945, (F.) poet, critic. *La Jeune Parque, The Graveyard by the Sea.*

Jules Verne, 1828-1905, (F.) novelist. *Twenty Thousand Leagues Under the Sea.*

François Villon, 1431-63?, (F.) poet. *The Lays, The Grand Testament.*

Evelyn Waugh, 1903-66, (Br.) novelist. *The Loved One.*

H. G. Wells, 1866-1946, (Br.) novelist. *The Time Machine, The Invisible Man, The War of the Worlds.*

Rebecca West, 1893-1983, (Br.) critic. *Black Lamb and Grey Falcon.*

Edith Wharton, 1862-1937, (U.S.) novelist. *The Age of Innocence, The House of Mirth, Ethan Frome.*

E. B. White, 1899-1985, (U.S.), essayist, novelist. *Here Is New York, Charlotte's Web, Stuart Little.*

T. H. White, 1906-64, (Br.) author. *The Once and Future King, A Book of Beasts.*

Walt Whitman, 1819-92, (U.S.) poet. *Leaves of Grass.*

John Greenleaf Whittier, 1807-92, (U.S.) poet, journalist. *Snow-Bound.*

Oscar Wilde, 1854-1900, (Ir.) playwright, story-writer. *The Picture of Dorian Gray, The Importance of Being Earnest.*

Laura Ingalls Wilder, 1867-1957, (U.S.) novelist. Little House on the Prairie series of children's books.

Thornton Wilder, 1897-1975, (U.S.) playwright. *Our Town, The Skin of Our Teeth, The Matchmaker.*

Tennessee Williams, 1911-83, (U.S.) playwright. *A Streetcar Named Desire, Cat on a Hot Tin Roof, The Glass Menagerie.*

William Carlos Williams, 1883-1963, (U.S.) poet. *Tempers, Al Que Quiere! Paterson.*

Edmund Wilson, 1895-1972, (U.S.) critic, novelist. *Axel's Castle, To the Finland Station.*

P. G. Wodehouse, 1881-1975, (Br.-U.S.) humorist. The "Jeeves" novels, *Anything Goes.*

Thomas Wolfe, 1900-38, (U.S.) novelist. *Look Homeward, Angel, You Can't Go Home Again, Of Time and the River.*

Virginia Woolf, 1882-1941, (Br.) novelist, essayist. *Mrs. Dalloway, To the Lighthouse, The Waves, A Room of One's Own.*

William Wordsworth, 1770-1850, (Br.) poet. "Tintern Abbey," "Ode: Intimations of Immortality," *The Prelude.*

William Butler Yeats, 1865-1939, (Ir.) poet, playwright. *The Wild Swans at Coole, The Tower, Last Poems.*

Émile Zola, 1840-1902, (F.) novelist. *Nana, The Dram Shop.*

Noted Artists, Photographers, and Sculptors of the Past

Artists are painters unless otherwise indicated.

Berenice Abbot, 1898-1991, (U.S.) photographer. Documentary of New York City, *Changing New York* (1939).

Ansel Easton Adams, 1902-84, (U.S.) photographer. Landscapes of the American Southwest.

Washington Allston, 1779-1843, (U.S.) landscapist. *Belshazzar's Feast.*

Albrecht Altdorfer, 1480-1538, (G.) landscapist. Battle of Alexander.

Andrea del Sarto, 1486-1530, (It.) frescoes. *Madonna of the Harpies.*

Fra Angelico, c 1400-55, (It.) Renaissance muralist. *Madonna of the Linen Drapers' Guild.*

Diane Arbus, 1923-71, (U.S.) photographer. Photographs of disturbing images on bizarre individuals.

Alexsandr Archipenko, 1887-1964, (U.S.) sculptor. *Boxing Match, Medranos.*

Eugène Atget, 1856-1927, (Fr.) photographer. Series on Parisian life.

John James Audubon, 1785-1851, (U.S.) *Birds of America.*

Hans Baldung-Grien, 1484-1545, (G.) *Todentanz.*

Ernst Barlach, 1870-1938, (G.) Expressionist sculptor. *Man Drawing a Sword.*

Frederic-Auguste Bartholdi, 1834-1904, (F.) *Liberty Enlightening the World, Lion of Belfort.*

Fra Bartolommeo, 1472-1517, (It.) *Vision of St. Bernard.*

Aubrey Beardsley, 1872-98, (Br.) illustrator. *Salome, Lysistrata.*

Max Beckmann, 1884-1950, (G.) Expressionist. *The Descent from the Cross.*

Gentile Bellini, 1426-1507, (It.) Renaissance. *Procession in St. Mark's Square.*

Giovanni Bellini, 1428-1516, (It.) *St. Francis in Ecstasy.*

Jacopo Bellini, 1400-70, (It.) *Crucifixion.*

George Wesley Bellows, 1882-1925, (U.S.) sports artist. *Stag at Sharkey's.*

Thomas Hart Benton, 1889-1975, (U.S.) American regionalist. *Threshing Wheat, Arts of the West.*

Gianlorenzo Bernini, 1598-1680, (It.) Baroque sculpture. *The Assumption.*

Albert Bierstadt, 1830-1902, (U.S.) landscapist. *The Rocky Mountains, Mount Corcoran.*

George Caleb Bingham, 1811-79, (U.S.) *Fur Traders Descending the Missouri.*

William Blake, 1752-1827, (Br.) engraver. *Book of Job, Songs of Innocence, Songs of Experience.*

Rosa Bonheur, 1822-99, (F.) *The Horse Fair.*

Pierre Bonnard, 1867-1947, (F.) Intimist. *The Breakfast Room.*

Gutzon Borglum, 1871-1941, (U.S.) sculptor. Mt. Rushmore Memorial.

Hieronymus Bosch, 1450-1516, (Flem.) religious allegories. *The Crowning with Thorns.*

Sandro Botticelli, 1444-1510, (It.) Renaissance. *Birth of Venus.*

Margaret Bourke-White, 1906-71, (U.S.) photographer, photojournalist. *USSR, A Portfolio of Photographs,* WWII, rural South during the Depression.

Mathew Brady, c 1823-96, (U.S.) photographer. Official photographer of the Civil War.

Constantin Brancusi, 1876-1957, (Rom.) Nonobjective sculptor. *Flying Turtle, The Kiss.*

Georges Braque, 1882-1963, (F.) Cubist. *Violin and Palette.*

Pieter Bruegel the Elder, c 1525-69, (Flem.) *The Peasant Dance.*

Pieter Bruegel the Younger, 1564-1638, (Flem.) *Village Fair, The Crucifixion.*

Edward Burne-Jones, 1833-98, (Br.) Pre-Raphaelite artist-craftsman. *The Mirror of Venus.*

Alexander Calder, 1898-1976, (U.S.) sculptor. *Lobster Trap and Fish Tail.*

Julia Cameron, 1815-79, (Br.) photographer. Considered one of the most important portraitists of the 19th cent.

Robert Capa (Andrei Friedmann), 1913-54, (Hung.-U.S.) photographer. War photojournalist; invasion of Normandy.

Michelangelo Merisi da Caravaggio, 1573-1610, (It.) Baroque. *The Supper at Emmaus.*

Emily Carr, 1871-1945, (Can.) landscapist. *Blunden Harbour, Big Raven.*

Carlo Carrà, 1881-1966, (It.) Metaphysical school. *Lot's Daughters.*

Mary Cassatt, 1845-1926, (U.S.) Impressionist. *Woman Bathing.*

George Catlin, 1796-1872, (U.S.) American Indian life. *Gallery of Indians.*

Benvenuto Cellini, 1500-71, (It.) Mannerist sculptor, goldsmith. *Perseus.*

Paul Cézanne, 1839-1906, (F.) *Card Players, Mont-Sainte-Victoire with Large Pine Trees.*

Marc Chagall, 1887-1985, (Rus.) Jewish life and folklore. *I and the Village.*

Jean Simeon Chardin, 1699-1779, (F.) still lifes. *The Kiss, The Grace.*

Frederick Church, 1826-1900, (U.S.) Hudson River school. *Niagara, Andes of Ecuador.*

Giovanni Cimabue, 1240-1302, (It.) Byzantine mosaicist. *Madonna Enthroned with St. Francis.*

Claude Lorrain, 1600-82, (F.) ideal-landscapist. *The Enchanted Castle.*

Thomas Cole, 1801-48, (U.S.) Hudson River school. *The Ox-Bow.*

John Constable, 1776-1837, (Br.) landscapist. *Salisbury Cathedral from the Bishop's Grounds.*

John Singleton Copley, 1738-1815, (U.S.) portraitist. *Samuel Adams, Watson and the Shark.*

Lovis Corinth, 1858-1925, (G.) Expressionist. *Apocalypse.*

Jean-Baptiste-Camille Corot, 1796-1875, (F.) landscapist. *Souvenir de Mortefontaine, Pastorale.*

Correggio, 1494-1534, (It.) Renaissance muralist. *Mystic Marriages of St. Catherine.*

Gustave Courbet, 1819-77, (F.) Realist. *The Artist's Studio.*

Lucas Cranach the Elder, 1472-1553, (G.) Protestant Reformation portraitist. *Luther.*

Imogen Cunningham, 1883-1976, (U.S.) photographer. Portraitist; plant photography.

Nathaniel Currier, 1813-88, and **James M. Ives,** 1824-95, (both U.S.) lithographers. *A Midnight Race on the Mississippi.*

John Steuart Curry, 1897-1946, (U.S.) Americana, murals. *Baptism in Kansas.*

Salvador Dalí, 1904-89, (Sp.) Surrealist. *Persistence of Memory.*

Honoré Daumier, 1808-79, (F.) caricaturist. *The Third-Class Carriage.*

Jacques-Louis David, 1748-1825, (F.) Neoclassicist. *The Oath of the Horatii.*

Arthur Davies, 1862-1928, (U.S.) Romantic landscapist. *Unicorns.*

Edgar Degas, 1834-1917, (F.) *The Ballet Class.*

Eugène Delacroix, 1798-1863, (F.) Romantic. *Massacre at Chios.*

Paul Delaroche, 1797-1856, (F.) historical themes. *Children of Edward IV.*

Luca Della Robbia, 1400-82, (It.) Renaissance terracotta artist. *Cantoria* (singing gallery), Florence cathedral.

Donatello, 1386-1466, (It.) Renaissance sculptor. *David, Gattamelata.*

Jean Dubuffet, 1902-85, (F.) painter, sculptor, printmaker. *Group of Four Trees.*

Marcel Duchamp, 1887-1968, (F.) *Nude Descending a Staircase.*

Raoul Dufy, 1877-1953, (F.) Fauvist. *Chateau and Horses.*

Asher Brown Durand, 1796-1886, (U.S.) Hudson River school. *Kindred Spirits.*

Albrecht Dürer, 1471-1528, (G.) Renaissance engraver, woodcuts. *St. Jerome in His Study, Melancholia I, Apocalypse.*

Anthony van Dyck, 1599-1641, (Flem.) Baroque portraitist. *Portrait of Charles I Hunting.*

Thomas Eakins, 1844-1916, (U.S.) Realist. *The Gross Clinic.*

Peter Henry Emerson, 1856-1936, (Br.) photographer. Photography as an independent art form.

Jacob Epstein, 1880-1959, (Br.) religious and allegorical sculptor. *Genesis, Ecce Homo.*

Jan van Eyck, c 1390-1441, (Flem.) naturalistic panels. *Adoration of the Lamb.*

Roger Fenton, 1819-68, (Br.) photographer. Crimean War photographer.

Anselm Feuerbach, 1829-80, (G.) Romantic Classicist. *Judgment of Paris, Iphigenia.*

John Bernard Flannagan, 1895-1942, (U.S.) animal sculptor. *Triumph of the Egg.*

Jean-Honore Fragonard, 1732-1806, (F.) Rococo. *The Swing.*

Daniel Chester French, 1850-1931, (U.S.) *The Minute Man of Concord,* seated *Lincoln,* Lincoln Memorial, Washington, D.C.

Caspar David Friedrich, 1774-1840, (G.) Romantic landscapes. *Man and Woman Gazing at the Moon.*

Thomas Gainsborough, 1727-88, (Br.) portraitist. *The Blue Boy.*

Alexander Gardner, 1821-82, (U.S.) photographer. Civil War; railroad construction; Great Plains Indians.

Paul Gauguin, 1848-1903, (F.) Post-impressionist. *The Tahitians.*

Lorenzo Ghiberti, 1378-1455, (It.) Renaissance sculptor. Gates of Paradise baptistery doors, Florence.

Alberto Giacometti, 1901-66, (Swiss) attenuated sculptures of solitary figures. *Man Pointing.*

Giorgione, c 1477-1510, (It.) Renaissance. *The Tempest.*

Giotto di Bondone, 1267-1337, (It.) Renaissance. *Presentation of Christ in the Temple.*

François Girardon, 1628-1715, (F.) Baroque sculptor of classical themes. *Apollo Tended by the Nymphs.*

Vincent van Gogh, 1853-90, (Dutch) *The Starry Night, L'Arlesienne.*

Arshile Gorky, 1905-48, (U.S.) Surrealist. *The Liver Is the Cock's Comb.*

Francisco de Goya y Lucientes, 1746-1828, (Sp.) *The Naked Maja, The Disasters of War* (etchings).

El Greco, 1541-1614, (Sp.) *View of Toledo.*

Horatio Greenough, 1805-52, (U.S.) Neo-classical sculptor. *George Washington.*

Matthias Grünewald, 1480-1528, (G.) mystical religious themes. *The Resurrection.*

Frans Hals, c 1580-1666, (Dutch) portraitist. *Laughing Cavalier, Gypsy Girl.*

Childe Hassam, 1859-1935, (U.S.) Impressionist. *Southwest Wind.*

Edward Hicks, 1780-1849, (U.S.) folk painter. *The Peaceable Kingdom.*

Lewis Wickes Hine, 1874-1940, (U.S.) photographer. Studies of immigrants, children in industry, construction of the Empire State Building.

Hans Hofmann, 1880-1966, (U.S.) early Abstract Expressionist. *Spring, The Gate.*

William Hogarth, 1697-1764, (Br.) caricaturist. *The Rake's Progress.*

Katsushika Hokusai, 1760-1849, (Jap.) printmaker. *Crabs.*

Hans Holbein the Elder, 1460-1524, (G.) late Gothic. *Presentation of Christ in the Temple.*

Hans Holbein the Younger, 1497-1543, (G.) portraitist. *Henry VIII.*

Winslow Homer, 1836-1910, (U.S.) marine themes. *Marine Coast, High Cliff.*

Edward Hopper, 1882-1967, (U.S.) realistic urban scenes. *Sunlight in a Cafeteria.*

Jean-Auguste-Dominique Ingres, 1780-1867, (F.) Classicist. *Valpincon Bather.*

George Inness, 1825-94, (U.S.) luminous landscapist. *Delaware Water Gap.*

William Henry Jackson, 1843-1942, (U.S.) photographer. American West, Native Americans, Yellowstone, building of Union Pacific Railroad.

Donald Judd, 1928-94, (U.S.) sculptor, major figure in Minimal Art, sleek cubic art characterized by lush metals and translucent or opaque plexiglass.

Vasily Kandinsky, 1866-1944, (Rus.) Abstractionist. *Capricious Forms.*

Paul Klee, 1879-1940, (Swiss) Abstractionist. *Twittering Machine.*

Oscar Kokoschka, 1886-1980, (Austrian) Expressionist. *View of Prague.*

Kathe Kollwitz, 1867-1945, (G.) printmaker, social justice themes. *The Peasant War.*

Gaston Lachaise, 1882-1935, (U.S.) figurative sculptor. *Standing Woman.*

John La Farge, 1835-1910, (U.S.) muralist. *Red and White Peonies.*

Dorothea Lange, 1895-1965, (U.S.), photographer. Depression photographs, migrant farm workers.

Fernand Léger, 1881-1955, (F.) machine art. *The Cyclists.*

Leonardo da Vinci, 1452-1519, (It.) *Mona Lisa, Last Supper, The Annunciation.*

Emanuel Leutze, 1816-68, (U.S.) historical themes. *Washington Crossing the Delaware.*

Jacques Lipchitz, 1891-1973, (F.) Cubist sculptor. *Harpist.*

Filippino Lippi, 1457-1504, (It.) Renaissance. *The Vision of St. Bernard.*

Fra Filippo Lippi, 1406-69, (It.) Renaissance. *Coronation of the Virgin.*

Morris Louis, 1912-62, (U.S.) Abstract Expressionist. *Signa, Stripes.*

Aristide Maillol, 1861-1944, (F.) sculptor. *L'Harmonie.*

Édouard Manet, 1832-83, (F.) forerunner of Impressionism. *Luncheon on the Grass, Olympia.*

Andrea Mantegna, 1431-1506, (It.) Renaissance frescoes. *Triumph of Caesar.*

Franz Marc, 1880-1916, (G.) Expressionist. *Blue Horses.*

John Marin, 1870-1953, (U.S.) expressionist seascapes. *Maine Island.*

Reginald Marsh, 1898-1954, (U.S.) satirical artist. *Tattoo and Haircut.*

Masaccio, 1401-28, (It.) Renaissance. *The Tribute Money.*

Henri Matisse, 1869-1954, (F.) Fauvist. *Woman with the Hat.*
Michelangelo Buonarroti, 1475-1564, (It.) *Pieta, David, Moses, The Last Judgment,* Sistine ceiling.
Jean-Francois Millet, 1814-75, (F.) painter of peasant subjects. *The Gleaners, The Man with a Hoe.*
Joan Miró, 1893-1983, (Sp.) Exuberant colors, playful images. Catalan landscape, *Dutch Interior.*
Amedeo Modigliani, 1884-1920, (It.) *Reclining Nude.*
Piet Mondrian, 1872-1944, (Dutch) Abstractionist. *Composition.*
Claude Monet, 1840-1926, (F.) Impressionist. *The Bridge at Argenteuil, Haystacks.*
Henry Moore, 1898-1986, (Br.) sculptor of large-scale, abstract works. *Reclining Figure* (several).
Gustave Moreau, 1826-98, (F.) Symbolist. *The Apparition, Dance of Salome.*
James Wilson Morrice, 1865-1924, (Can.) landscapist. *The Ferry, Quebec, Venice, Looking Over the Lagoon.*
Grandma Moses, 1860-1961, (U.S.) folk painter. *Out for the Christmas Trees.*
Edvard Munch, 1863-1944, (Nor.) Expressionist. *The Cry.*
Bartolome Murillo, 1618-82, (Sp.) Baroque religious artist. *Vision of St. Anthony, The Two Trinities.*
Eadweard Muybridge, 1830-1904, (Br.-U.S.) photographer. Studies of motion, *Animal Locomotion.*
Barnett Newman, 1905-70, (U.S.) Abstract Expressionist. *Stations of the Cross.*
Isamu Noguchi, 1904-88, (U.S.) trad. Japanese art, modern techniques.
Georgia O'Keeffe, 1887-1986, (U.S.) Southwest motifs. *Cow's Skull: Red, White, and Blue, The Shelton with Sunspots.*
José Clemente Orozco, 1883-1949, (Mex.) frescoes. *House of Tears.*
Timothy H. O'Sullivan, 1840-82, (U.S.) photographer of the Civil War.
Charles Willson Peale, 1741-1827, (U.S.) American Revolutionary portraitist. Washington, Franklin, Jefferson, John Adams.
Rembrandt Peale, 1778-1860, (U.S.) portraitist. Thomas Jefferson.
Pietro Perugino, 1446-1523, (It.) Renaissance. *Delivery of the Keys to St. Peter.*
Pablo Picasso, 1881-1973, (Sp.) *Guernica, Dove, Head of a Woman.*
Piero della Francesca, c 1415-92, (It.) Renaissance. *Duke of Urbino, Flagellation of Christ.*
Camille Pissarro, 1830-1903, (F.) Impressionist. *Morning Sunlight.*
Jackson Pollock, 1912-56, (U.S.) Abstract Expressionist. *Autumn Rhythm.*
Nicolas Poussin, 1594-1665, (F.) Baroque pictorial classicism. *St. John on Patmos.*
Maurice B. Prendergast, c 1860-1924, (U.S.) Post-impressionist water colorist. *Umbrellas in the Rain.*
Pierre-Paul Prud'hon, 1758-1823, (F.) Romanticist. *Crime Pursued by Vengeance and Justice.*
Pierre Cecile Puvis de Chavannes, 1824-98, (F.) muralist. *The Poor Fisherman.*
Raphael Sanzio, 1483-1520, (It.) Renaissance. *Disputa, School of Athens, Sistine Madonna.*
Man Ray, 1890-1976, (U.S.) Dadaist. *Observing Time, The Lovers.*
Odilon Redon, 1840-1916, (F.) Symbolist lithographer. *In the Dream.*
Rembrandt van Rijn, 1606-69, (Dutch) *The Bridal Couple, The Night Watch.*
Frederic Remington, 1861-1909, (U.S.) painter, sculptor, portrayer of the American West. *Bronco Buster.*
Pierre-Auguste Renoir, 1841-1919, (F.) Impressionist. *The Luncheon of the Boating Party, Dance in the Country.*
Joshua Reynolds, 1723-92, (Br.) portraitist. *Mrs. Siddons As the Tragic Muse.*
Diego Rivera, 1886-1957, (Mex.) frescoes. *The Fecund Earth.*
Henry Peach Robinson, 1830-1901 (Br.) photographer. A leader of "high art" photography.
Norman Rockwell, 1894-1978, (U.S.) illustrator. *Saturday Evening Post* covers.
Auguste Rodin, 1840-1917, (F.) sculptor. *The Thinker, The Burghers of Calais.*
Mark Rothko, 1903-70, (U.S.) Abstract Expressionist. *Light, Earth and Blue.*
Georges Rouault, 1871-1958, (F.) Expressionist.
Henri Rousseau, 1844-1910, (F.) primitive exotic themes. *The Snake Charmer.*
Theodore Rousseau, 1812-67, (Swiss-F.) landscapist. *Under the Birches, Evening.*
Peter Paul Rubens, 1577-1640, (Flem.) Baroque. *Mystic Marriage of St. Catherine.*
Jacob van Ruisdael, c 1628-82, (Dutch) landscapist. *Jewish Cemetery.*
Charles M. Russell, 1866-1926, (U.S.) Western life.
Salomon van Ruysdael, c 1600-70, (Dutch) landscapist. *River with Ferry-Boat.*
Albert Pinkham Ryder, 1847-1917, (U.S.) seascapes and allegories. *Toilers of the Sea.*
Augustus Saint-Gaudens, 1848-1907, (U.S.) memorial statues. *Farragut, Mrs. Henry Adams (Grief).*
Andrea Sansovino, 1460-1529, (It.) Renaissance sculptor. *Baptism of Christ.*
Jacopo Sansovino, 1486-1570, (It.) Renaissance sculptor. *St. John the Baptist.*
John Singer Sargent, 1856-1925, (U.S.) Edwardian society portraitist. The Wyndham Sisters, Madam X.
Georges Seurat, 1859-91, (F.) Pointillist. *Sunday Afternoon on the Island of Grande Jatte.*
Gino Severini, 1883-1966, (It.) Futurist and Cubist. *Dynamic Hieroglyph of the Bal Tabarin.*
Ben Shahn, 1898-1969, (U.S.) social and political themes. Sacco and Vanzetti series, *Seurat's Lunch, Handball.*
Charles Sheeler, 1883-1965, (U.S.) Abstractionist.
David Alfaro Siqueiros, 1896-1974, (Mex.) political muralist. *March of Humanity.*
John F. Sloan, 1871-1951, (U.S.) depictions of New York City. *Wake of the Ferry.*
David Smith, 1906-65, (U.S.) welded metal sculpture. *Hudson River Landscape, Zig, Cubi* series.
Edward Steichen, 1879-1973, (U.S.) photographer. Credited with the transformation of photography into an art form.
Alfred Stieglitz, 1864-1946, (U.S.) photographer.
Paul Strand, 1890-1976, (U.S.), photographer. Landscapes, nature.
Gilbert Stuart, 1755-1828, (U.S.) portraitist.
Thomas Sully, 1783-1872, (U.S.) portraitist. *Col. Thomas Handasyd Perkins, The Passage of the Delaware.*
William Henry Fox Talbot, 1800-77, (Br.) photographer. *Pencil of Nature,* one of the first photographically illustrated books.
George Tames, 1919-94, (U.S.) photographer, chronicled presidents, political leaders.
Yves Tanguy, 1900-55, (F.) Surrealist. *Rose of the Four Winds.*
Giovanni Battista Tiepolo, 1696-1770, (It.) Rococo frescoes. *The Crucifixion.*
Jacopo Tintoretto, 1518-94, (It.) Mannerist. *The Last Supper.*
Titian, c 1485-1576, (It.) Renaissance. *Venus and the Lute Player, The Bacchanal.*
Jose Rey Toledo, 1916-94, (U.S.) Native American artist, captured the essence of tribal dances on canvas.
Henri de Toulouse-Lautrec, 1864-1901, (F.) *At the Moulin Rouge.*
John Trumbull, 1756-1843, (U.S.) historical themes. *The Declaration of Independence.*
J(oseph) M(allord) W(illiam) Turner, 1775-1851, (Br.) Romantic landscapist. *Snow Storm.*
Paolo Uccello, 1397-1475, (It.) Gothic-Renaissance. *The Rout of San Romano.*
Maurice Utrillo, 1883-1955, (F.) Impressionist. *Sacre-Coeur de Montmartre.*
John Vanderlyn, 1775-1852, (U.S.) Neo-classicist. *Ariadne Asleep on the Island of Naxos.*
Diego Velázquez, 1599-1660, (Sp.) Baroque. *Las Meninas, Portrait of Juan de Pareja.*
Jan Vermeer, 1632-75, (Dutch) interior genre subjects. *Young Woman with a Water Jug.*
Paolo Veronese, 1528-88, (It.) devotional themes, vastly peopled canvases. *The Temptation of St. Anthony.*
Andrea del Verrocchio, 1435-88, (It.) Florentine sculptor. *Colleoni.*
Maurice de Vlaminck, 1876-1958, (F.) Fauvist landscapist.
Andy Warhol, 1928-87, (U.S.) Pop Art. *Campbell's Soup Cans.*
Antoine Watteau, 1684-1721, (F.) Rococo painter of "scenes of gallantry". *The Embarkation for Cythera.*
George Frederic Watts, 1817-1904, (Br.) painter and sculptor of grandiose allegorical themes. *Hope.*
Benjamin West, 1738-1820, (U.S.) realistic historical themes. *Death of General Wolfe.*
Edward Weston, 1886-1958, (U.S.) photographer. Landscapes of American West.
James Abbott McNeill Whistler, 1834-1903, (U.S.) *Arrangement in Grey and Black, No. 1: The Artist's Mother.*
Archibald M. Willard, 1836-1918, (U.S.) *The Spirit of '76.*
Grant Wood, 1891-1942, (U.S.) Midwestern regionalist. *American Gothic, Daughters of Revolution.*
Ossip Zadkine, 1890-1967, (Rus.) School of Paris sculptor. *The Destroyed City, Musicians, Christ.*

Noted Philosophers and Religionists of the Past

Lyman Abbott, 1835-1922, (U.S.) clergyman, reformer; advocate of Christian Socialism.

Pierre Abelard, 1079-1142, (F.) philosopher, theologian, and teacher, used dialectic method to support Christian dogma.

Felix Adler, 1851-1933, (U.S.) German-born founder of the Ethical Culture Society.

Aristotle, 384-322 BC, (Gr.) philosopher, emphasized direct observation of nature.

St. Augustine, 354-430, Latin bishop considered the founder of formalized Christian theology.

Averroes, 1126-98, (Sp.) Islamic philosopher.

Roger Bacon, c 1214-94, (Eng.) philosopher and scientist.

Bahaullah (Mirza Husayn Ali), 1817-92, (Pers.) founder of Bahai faith.

Karl Barth, 1886-1968, (Sw.) theologian, a leading force in 20th-century Protestantism.

St. Benedict, c 480-547, (It.) founded the Benedictines.

Jeremy Bentham, 1748-1832, (Br.) philosopher, reformer, founder of Utilitarianism.

Henri Bergson, 1859-1941, (F.) philosopher of evolution.

George Berkeley, 1685-1753, (Ir.) philosopher, churchman.

John Biddle, 1615-62, (Eng.) founder of English Unitarianism.

Jakob Boehme, 1575-1624, (G.) theosophist and mystic.

William Brewster, 1567-1644, (Eng.) headed Pilgrims.

Emil Brunner, 1889-1966, (Sw.) Protestant theologian.

Giordano Bruno, 1548-1600, (It.) philosopher, first to state the cosmic theory.

Martin Buber, 1878-1965, (G.) Jewish philosopher, theologian, wrote *I and Thou.*

Buddha (Siddhartha Gautama), c 563-c 483 BC, (Ind.) philosopher, founded Buddhism.

Kenneth Burke, 1897-1993 (U.S.), one of the founders of New Criticism literary philosophy, *A Grammar of Motives.*

John Calvin, 1509-64, (F.) theologian, a key figure in the Protestant Reformation.

Rudolph Carnap, 1891-1970, (U.S.) German-born philosopher, a founder of logical positivism.

William Ellery Channing, 1780-1842, (U.S.) clergyman, early spokesman for Unitarianism.

Auguste Comte, 1798-1857, (F.) philosopher, the founder of positivism.

Confucius, 551-479 BC, (Chin.) founder of Confucianism.

John Cotton, 1584-1652, (Eng.) Puritan theologian.

Thomas Cranmer, 1489-1556, (Eng.) churchman, wrote much of *Book of Common Prayer.*

René Descartes, 1596-1650, (F.) philosopher, mathematician, "father of modern philosophy."

John Dewey, 1859-1952, (U.S.) philosopher, educator; helped inaugurate the progressive education movement.

Denis Diderot, 1713-84, (F.) philosopher, encyclopedist.

Mary Baker Eddy, 1821-1910, (U.S.) founder of Christian Science, wrote *Science and Health.*

Jonathan Edwards, 1703-58, (U.S.) preacher, theologian.

(Desiderius) Erasmus, c 1466-1536, (Du.) Renaissance humanist, wrote *On the Freedom of the Will.*

Johann Fichte, 1762-1814, (G.) philosopher, the first of the Transcendental Idealists.

George Fox, 1624-91, (Br.) founder of Society of Friends.

St. Francis of Assisi, 1182-1226, (It.) founded Franciscans.

al-Ghazali, 1058-1111, Islamic philosopher.

Georg W. Hegel, 1770-1831, (G.) Idealist philosopher.

Martin Heidegger, 1889-1976, (G.) existentialist philosopher, affected fields ranging from physics to literary criticism.

Johann G. Herder, 1744-1803, (G.) philosopher, cultural historian; a founder of German Romanticism.

David Hume, 1711-76, (Sc.) philosopher, historian.

Jan Hus, 1369-1415, (Czech.) religious reformer.

Edmund Husserl, 1859-1938, (G.) philosopher, founded the Phenomenological movement.

Thomas Huxley, 1825-95, (Br.) philosopher, educator.

Ignatius of Loyola, 1491-1556, (Sp.) founder of the Jesuits.

William Inge, 1860-1954, (Br.) theologian, explored the mystic aspects of Christianity.

William James, 1842-1910, (U.S.) philosopher, psychologist; advanced theory of the pragmatic nature of truth.

Karl Jaspers, 1883-1969, (G.) existentialist philosopher.

Immanuel Kant, 1724-1804, (G.) metaphysician, preeminent founder of modern critical philosophy; *Critique of Pure Reason.*

Soren Kierkegaard, 1813-55, (Dan.) philosopher, considered the father of Existentialism.

Russell Kirk, 1918-94, (U.S.), social philosopher, *The Conservative Mind.*

John Knox, 1505-72, (Sc.) leader of the Protestant Reformation in Scotland.

Lao-Tzu, 604-531 BC, (Chin.) philosopher, considered the founder of the Taoist religion.

Gottfried von Leibniz, 1646-1716, (G.) philosopher, mathematician, influenced German Enlightenment.

Martin Luther, 1483-1546, (G.) leader of the Protestant Reformation, founded Lutheran church.

Maimonides, 1135-1204, (Sp.) Jewish philosopher.

Jacques Maritain, 1882-1973, (F.) Neo-Thomist philosopher.

Cotton Mather, 1663-1728, (U.S.) defender of orthodox Puritanism; founded Yale, 1701.

Philipp Melanchthon, 1497-1560, (G.) theologian, humanist; an important voice in the Reformation.

Thomas Merton, 1915-68, (U.S.) Trappist monk, spiritual writer; *The Seven Storey Mountain.*

John Stuart Mill, 1806-73, (Br.) philosopher, economist.

Muhammad, c 570-632, (Arab) the prophet of Islam.

Dwight Moody, 1837-99, (U.S.) evangelist.

George E. Moore, 1873-1958, (Br.) ethical theorist.

Elijah Muhammad, 1897-1975, (U.S.) leader of the Black Muslim sect.

Heinrich Muhlenberg, 1711-87, (G.) organized the Lutheran Church in America.

John H. Newman, 1801-90, (Br.) Roman Catholic cardinal, led Oxford Movement; *Apologia pro Vita Sua.*

Reinhold Niebuhr, 1892-1971, (U.S.) Protestant theologian, social and political critic.

Friedrich Nietzsche, 1844-1900, (G.) moral philosopher; *The Birth of Tragedy, Thus Spake Zarathustra.*

Blaise Pascal, 1623-62, (F.) philosopher, mathematician.

St. Patrick, c 389-c 461, brought Christianity to Ireland.

St. Paul, ?-c 67, a founder of Christianity; his epistles are first Christian theological writing.

Norman Vincent Peale, 1898-1993, (U.S.) religious leader, author, *The Power of Positive Thinking.*

Charles S. Peirce, 1839-1914, (U.S.) philosopher, logician; originated concept of Pragmatism, 1878.

Plato, c 428-347 BC, (Gr.) philosopher, argued for independent reality of ideas; *Republic.*

Josiah Royce 1855-1916, (U.S.) Idealist philosopher.

Charles T. Russell, 1852-1916, (U.S.) founder of Jehovah's Witnesses.

Fredrich von Schelling, 1775-1854, (G.) philosopher of romantic movement.

Friedrich Schleiermacher, 1768-1834, (G.) theologian, a founder of modern Protestant theology.

Arthur Schopenhauer, 1788-1860, (G.) philosopher.

Joseph Smith, 1805-44, (U.S.) founded Latter Day Saints (Mormon) movement, 1830.

Socrates, 469-399 BC, (Gr.) philosopher.

Herbert Spencer, 1820-1903, (Br.) philosopher of evolution.

Baruch Spinoza, 1632-77, (Du.) rationalist philosopher.

Billy Sunday, 1862-1935, (U.S.) evangelist.

Daisetz Teitaro Suzuki, 1870-1966, (Jap.) Buddhist scholar.

Emanuel Swedenborg, 1688-1772, (Swed.) philosopher, mystic.

Thomas à Becket, 1118-70, (Eng.) archbishop of Canterbury, opposed Henry II.

Thomas à Kempis, c 1380-1471, (G.) theologian, probably wrote *Imitation of Christ.*

Thomas Aquinas, 1225-74, (It.) Roman Catholic saint, wrote *Summa Theologica.*

Paul Tillich, 1886-1965, (U.S.) German-born philosopher and theologian; brought depth psychology to Protestantism.

John Wesley, 1703-91, (Br.) theologian, evangelist; founded Methodism.

Alfred North Whitehead, 1861-1947, (Br.) philosopher, mathematician; *Principia Mathematica* (with Bertrand Russell).

William of Occam, c 1285-c 1349 (Eng.) medieval scholastic philosopher.

Roger Williams, c 1603-83, (U.S.) clergyman, championed religious freedom and separation of church and state.

Ludwig Wittgenstein, 1889-1951, (Austrian) philosopher, influenced language philosophy.

John Wycliffe, 1320-84, (Eng.) theologian, reformer.

Brigham Young, 1801-77, (U.S.) Mormon leader after Smith's assassination, colonized Utah.

Huldrych Zwingli, 1484-1531, (Sw.) theologian, led Swiss Protestant Reformation.

Noted Social Reformers and Educators of the Past

Jane Addams, 1860-1935, (U.S.) co-founder of Hull House; won Nobel Peace Prize, 1931.

Susan B. Anthony, 1820-1906, (U.S.) a leader in temperance, anti-slavery, and woman suffrage movements.

Henry Barnard, 1811-1900, (U.S.) public school reformer.
Thomas Barnardo, 1845-1905, (Br.) social reformer, pioneered in the care of destitute children.
Clara Barton, 1821-1912, (U.S.) organizer of the American Red Cross.
Henry Ward Beecher, 1813-87, (U.S.) clergyman, abolitionist.
Sarah G. Blanding, 1899-1985, (U.S.) head of Vassar College, 1946-64.
Amelia Bloomer, 1818-94, (U.S.) social reformer.
William Booth, 1829-1912, (Br.) founded the Salvation Army.
John Brown, 1800-59, (U.S.) abolitionist who led murder of 5 pro-slavery men, was hanged.
Nicholas Murray Butler, 1862-1947, (U.S.) educator, headed Columbia Univ., 1902-45; Nobel Peace Prize, 1931.
Frances X. (Mother) Cabrini, 1850-1917, (U.S.) Italian-born nun, founded charitable institutions; first American canonized.
Carrie Chapman Catt, 1859-1947, (U.S.) suffragette, helped win passage of the 19th amendment.
Cesar Chavez, 1927-93, (U.S.) labor leader who organized migrant farm workers, helped establish United Farm Workers of America.
Clarence Darrow, 1857-1938, (U.S.) lawyer, defender of "underdog," opponent of capital punishment.
Dorothy Day, 1897-1980, (U.S.) founder of Catholic Worker Movement.
Eugene V. Debs, 1855-1926, (U.S.) labor leader, led Pullman strike, 1894; 4-time Socialist presidential candidate.
Melvil Dewey, 1851-1931, (U.S.) devised decimal system of library-book classification.
Dorothea Dix, 1802-87, (U.S.) crusader for the mentally ill.
Frederick Douglass, 1817-95, (U.S.) abolitionist.
William Lloyd Garrison, 1805-79, (U.S.) abolitionist.
Giovanni Gentile, 1875-1944, (It.) philosopher, educator; reformed Italian educational system.
Emma Goldman, 1869-1940, (Rus.-U.S.) published anarchist *Mother Earth,* birth-control advocate.
Samuel Gompers, 1850-1924, (U.S.) labor leader; a founder and president of AFL.
William Green, 1873-1952, (U.S.) president of AFL, 1924-52.
Michael Harrington, 1928-89, (U.S.) revealed poverty in affluent U.S. in *The Other America,* 1963.
Sidney Hillman, 1887-1946, (U.S.) labor leader, helped organize CIO.
John Holt, 1924-85, (U.S.) educator and author.
Samuel G. Howe, 1801-76, (U.S.) social reformer, changed public attitudes toward the handicapped.
Helen Keller, 1880-1968, (U.S.) crusader for better treatment for the handicapped.
Martin Luther King, Jr., 1929-68, (U.S.) civil rights leader; won Nobel Peace Prize, 1964.
John L. Lewis, 1880-1969, (U.S.) labor leader, headed United Mine Workers, 1920-60.
Horace Mann, 1796-1859, (U.S.) pioneered modern public school system.
William H. McGuffey, 1800-73, (U.S.) author of *Reader,* the mainstay of 19th-century U.S. public education.
Alexander Meiklejohn, 1872-1964, (U.S.) Br.-born educator, championed academic freedom and experimental curricula.
Karl Menninger, 1893-1991, (U.S.) with brother William made Menninger Clinic, and Menninger Foundation in Topeka, Kansas, the center of U.S. psychiatry.
Maria Montessori, 1870-1952, (It.) educator and physician, originated Montessori method of student self-motivation.
Lucretia Mott, 1793-1880, (U.S.) reformer, pioneer feminist.
Philip Murray, 1886-1952, (U.S.) Scotch-born labor leader.
Florence Nightingale, 1820-1910, (Br.) founder of modern nursing.
Emmeline Pankhurst, 1858-1928, (Br.) woman suffragist.
Elizabeth P. Peabody, 1804-94, (U.S.) education pioneer, founded 1st kindergarten in U.S., 1860.
Walter Reuther, 1907-70, (U.S.) labor leader, headed UAW.
Jacob Riis, 1849-1914, (U.S.) crusader for urban reforms.
Margaret Sanger, 1883-1966, (U.S.) social reformer, pioneered the birth-control movement.
Elizabeth Seton, 1774-1821, (U.S.) established parochial school education in U.S.
Earl of Shaftesbury (A. A. Cooper), 1801-85, (Br.) social reformer.
Elizabeth Cady Stanton, 1815-1902, (U.S.) woman suffrage pioneer.
Lucy Stone, 1818-93, (U.S.) feminist, abolitionist.
Harriet Tubman, c 1820-1913, (U.S.) abolitionist, ran Underground Railroad.
Philip Vera Cruz, 1905-94, (Filipino-U.S.) helped to found the United Farm Workers Union.
Booker T. Washington, 1856-1915, (U.S.) educator, reformer; championed vocational training for blacks.
Walter F. White, 1893-1955, (U.S.) headed NAACP, 1931-55.
William Wilberforce, 1759-1833, (Br.) social reformer, prominent in struggle to abolish the slave trade.
Emma Hart Willard, 1787-1870, (U.S.) pioneered higher education for women.
Frances E. Willard, 1839-98, (U.S.) temperance, women's rights leader.
Mary Wollstonecraft, 1759-97, (Br.) wrote *Vindication of the Rights of Women.*
Whitney M. Young, Jr., 1921-71, (U.S.) civil rights leader, headed National Urban League, 1961-71.

Noted Historians, Economists, and Social Scientists of the Past

Brooks Adams, 1848-1927, (U.S.) historian, political theoretician; *The Law of Civilization and Decay.*
Henry Adams, 1838-1918, (U.S.) historian; *History of the United States of America, The Education of Henry Adams.*
Francis Bacon, 1561-1626, (Eng.) philosopher, essayist, and statesman; applied scientific induction to philosophy.
George Bancroft, 1800-91, (U.S.) historian, wrote 10-volume *History of the United States.*
Jack Barbash, 1911-94, (U.S.) labor economist who helped create the AFL-CIO.
Charles A. Beard, 1874-1948, (U.S.) historian; *The Economic Basis of Politics;* helped found New School for Social Research.
Bede (the Venerable), c 673-735, (Eng.) scholar historian whose writings virtually constitute the learning of his time.
Ruth Benedict, 1887-1948, (U.S.) anthropologist, studied Indian tribes of the Southwest.
Bruno Bettleheim, 1903-90, (Aust.-U.S.) psychoanalyst specializing in autistic children; *The Uses of Enchantment.*
Louis Blanc, 1811-82, (F.) Socialist leader and historian whose ideas were a link between utopian and Marxist socialism.
Leonard Bloomfield, 1887-1949, (U.S.) linguist; *Language.*
Franz Boas, 1858-1942, (U.S.) German-born anthropologist, studied American Indians.
Van Wyck Brooks, 1886-1963, (U.S.) historian, critic of New England culture, especially literature.
Edmund Burke, 1729-97, (Ir.) Br. parliamentarian and political philosopher; influenced many Federalists.
Joseph Campbell, 1904-87, (U.S.) wrote books on mythology, folklore.
Thomas Carlyle, 1795-1881, (Sc.) historian, critic; *Sartor Resartus, Past and Present, The French Revolution.*
Edward Channing, 1856-1931, (U.S.) historian, wrote 6-volume *History of the United States.*
John R. Commons, 1862-1945, (U.S.) economist, labor historian; *Legal Foundations of Capitalism.*
Benedetto Croce, 1866-1952, (It.) philosopher, statesman, and historian; *Philosophy of the Spirit.*
Bernard A. De Voto, 1897-1955, (U.S.) historian; wrote trilogy on American West; edited Mark Twain manuscripts.
Ariel Durant, 1898-1981, (U.S.) historian, collaborated with husband on 11-volume *Story of Civilization.*
Will Durant, 1885-1981, (U.S.) historian; *The Story of Civilization, The Story of Philosophy.*
Emile Durkheim, 1858-1917, (F.) a founder of modern sociology; *The Rules of Sociological Method.*
Friedrich Engels, 1820-95, (G.) political writer; with Marx wrote the *Communist Manifesto.*
Erik Erikson, 1902-94, (U.S.) psychoanalyst, author, theory of developmental stages of life, *Childhood and Society.*
Irving Fisher, 1867-1947, (U.S.) economist, contributed to the development of modern monetary theory.
John Fiske, 1842-1901, (U.S.) historian and lecturer, popularized Darwinian theory of evolution.
Charles Fourier, 1772-1837, (F.) utopian socialist.
Henry George, 1839-97, (U.S.) economist, reformer, led single-tax movement.
Edward Gibbon, 1737-94, (Br.) historian, wrote *The History of the Decline and Fall of the Roman Empire.*
Francesco Guicciardini, 1483-1540, (It.) historian, wrote *Storia d'Italia,* principal historical work of the 16th cent.
Thomas Hobbes, 1588-1679, (Eng.) political philosopher; *Leviathan.*
Richard Hofstadter, 1916-70, (U.S.) historian; *The Age of Reform.*
John Maynard Keynes, 1883-1946, (Br.) economist, principal advocate of deficit spending.
Alfred L. Kroeber, 1876-1960, (U.S.) cultural anthropologist, studied Indians of North and South America.
Christopher Lasch, 1932-94, (U.S.) social critic, historian; *The Culture of Narcissism.*
James L. Laughlin, 1850-1933, (U.S.) economist, helped establish Federal Reserve System.
Lucien Lévy-Bruhl, 1857-1939, (F.) philosopher, studied the psychology of primitive societies; *Primitive Mentality.*

Kurt Lewin, 1890-1947, (U.S.) German-born psychologist, studied human motivation and group dynamics.

John Locke, 1632-1704, (Eng.) philosopher; *Essay Concerning Human Understanding.*

Konrad Lorenz, 1904-89, (Austrian) ethologist, pioneer in study of animal behavior.

Thomas B. Macauley, 1800-59, (Br.) historian, statesman.

Bronislaw Malinowski, 1884-1942, (Pol.) considered the father of social anthropology.

Thomas R. Malthus, 1766-1834, (Br.) economist, famed for *Essay on the Principle of Population.*

Karl Mannheim, 1893-1947, (Hung.) sociologist, historian; *Ideology and Utopia.*

Karl Marx, 1818-83, (G.) political philosopher, proponent of modern communism; *Communist Manifesto, Das Kapital.*

Giuseppe Mazzini, 1805-72, (It.) political philosopher.

George H. Mead, 1863-1931, (U.S.) philosopher, social psychologist.

Margaret Mead, 1901-78, (U.S.) cultural anthropologist, popularized field; *Coming of Age in Samoa.*

James Mill, 1773-1836, (Sc.) philosopher, historian, economist; a proponent of Utilitarianism.

Perry G. Miller, 1905-63, (U.S.) historian, interpreted 17th-century New England.

Theodor Mommsen, 1817-1903, (G.) historian; *The History of Rome.*

Charles-Louis Montesquieu, 1689-1755, (F.) social philosopher; *The Spirit of Laws.*

Samuel Eliot Morison, 1887-1976, (U.S.) historian, chronicled voyages of early explorers.

Lewis Mumford, 1895-1990, (U.S.) sociologist, critic; *The Culture of Cities.*

Gunnar Myrdal, 1898-1987, (Swed.) economist, social scientist.

Allan Nevins, 1890-1971, (U.S.) historian, biographer; *The Ordeal of the Union.*

José Ortega y Gasset, 1883-1955, (Sp.) philosopher, advocated control by elite; *The Revolt of the Masses.*

Robert Owen, 1771-1858, (Br.) political philosopher, reformer; pioneer in cooperative movement.

Vilfredo Pareto, 1848-1923, (It.) economist, sociologist.

Francis Parkman, 1823-93, (U.S.) historian; *France and England in North America, 1851-92.*

Marco Polo, c 1254-1324, (It.) narrated an account of his travels to China.

William Prescott, 1796-1859, (U.S.) early American historian; *The Conquest of Peru.*

Pierre Joseph Proudhon, 1809-65, (F.) social theorist, the father of anarchism; *The Philosophy of Property.*

François Quesnay, 1694-1774, (F.) economic theorist, demonstrated circular flow of economic activity through society.

David Ricardo, 1772-1823, (Br.) economic theorist, advocated free international trade.

James H. Robinson, 1863-1936, (U.S.) historian, educator.

Carl Rogers, 1902-87, (U.S.) psychotherapist, author.

Jean-Jacques Rousseau, 1712-78, (F.) social philosopher, the father of romantic sensibility; *Confessions.*

Edward Sapir, 1884-1939, (G.-U.S.) anthropologist, studied ethnology and linguistics of some U.S. Indian groups.

Ferdinand de Saussure, 1857-1913, (Swiss) a founder of modern linguistics.

Hjalmar Schacht, 1877-1970, (G.) economist.

Joseph Schumpeter, 1883-1950, (Czech.-U.S.) economist, championed big business, capitalism.

Albert Schweitzer, 1875-1965, (Alsatian) organist, social philosopher, theologian, medical missionary.

George Simmel, 1858-1918, (G.) sociologist, philosopher; helped establish German sociology.

B. F. Skinner, 1904-89, (U.S.) psychologist, behaviorism.

Adam Smith, 1723-90, (Br.) economist, advocated laissez-faire economy and free trade.

Jared Sparks, 1789-1866, (U.S.) historian, educator, editor; *The Library of American Biography.*

Oswald Spengler, 1880-1936, (G.) philosopher and historian; *The Decline of the West.*

William G. Sumner, 1840-1910, (U.S.) social scientist, economist; laissez-faire economy, Social Darwinism.

Hippolyte Taine, 1828-93, (F.) historian, basis of naturalistic school; *The Origins of Contemporary France.*

Frank W. Taussig, 1859-1940, (U.S.) economist, educator.

A(lan) J(ohn) P(ercivale) Taylor, 1906-89, (Br.) historian; *The Origins of the Second World War.*

Nikolaas Tinbergen, 1907-88, (Dutch-Br.) ethologist, pioneer in study of animal behavior.

Alexis de Tocqueville, 1805-59, (F.) political scientist, historian; *Democracy in America.*

Francis E. Townsend, 1867-1960, (U.S.) led old-age pension movement, 1933.

Arnold Toynbee, 1889-1975, (Br.) historian.

Heinrich von Treitschke, 1834-96, (G.) historian, political writer; *A History of Germany in the 19th Century.*

George Trevelyan, 1838-1928, (Br.) historian, statesman; favored "literary" over "scientific" history; *History of England.*

Barbara Tuchman, 1912-89, (U.S.) author of popular history books, *The Guns of August, The March of Folly.*

Frederick J. Turner, 1861-1932, (U.S.) historian, educator; *The Frontier in American History.*

Thorstein B. Veblen, 1857-1929, (U.S.) economist, social philosopher; *The Theory of the Leisure Class.*

Giovanni Vico, 1668-1744, (It.) historian, philosopher; regarded by many as first modern historian; *New Science.*

Voltaire (F.M. Arouet), 1694-1778, (F.) philosopher, historian, writer of "philosophical romances"; *Candide.*

Izaak Walton, 1593-1683, (Eng.) wrote biographies, political-philosophical study of fishing, *The Compleat Angler.*

Sidney J., 1859-1947, and wife **Beatrice,** 1858-1943, **Webb,** (Br.) leading figures in Fabian Society and Br. Labour Party.

Walter P. Webb, 1888-1963, (U.S.) historian of the West.

Max Weber, 1864-1920, (G.) sociologist; *The Protestant Ethic and the Spirit of Capitalism.*

Noted Scientists of the Past

Howard H. Aiken, 1900-73, (U.S.) mathematician, credited with designing forerunner of digital computer.

Albertus Magnus, 1193-1280, (G.) theologian, philosopher, established medieval Christian study of natural science.

Andre-Marie Ampère, 1775-1836, (F.) scientist known for contributions to electrodynamics.

Amedeo Avogadro, 1776-1856, (It.) chemist, physicist, advanced important theories on properties of gases.

John Bardeen, 1908-91, (U.S.) co-inventor of the transistor that led to modern electronics.

A. C. Becquerel, 1788-1878, (F.) physicist, pioneer in electrochemical science.

A. H. Becquerel, 1852-1908, (F.) physicist, discovered radioactivity in uranium.

Alexander Graham Bell, 1847-1922, (U.S.) inventor, first to patent and commercially exploit the telephone, 1876.

Daniel Bernoulli, 1700-82, (Swiss) mathematician, advanced kinetic theory of gases and fluids.

Jöns Jakob Berzelius, 1779-1848, (Swed.) chemist, developed modern chemical symbols and formulas.

Henry Bessemer, 1813-98, (Br.) engineer, invented Bessemer steel-making process.

Louis Blériot, 1872-1936, (F.) engineer, pioneer aviator, invented and constructed monoplanes.

Niels Bohr, 1885-1962, (Dan.) physicist, leading figure in the development of quantum theory.

Max Born, 1882-1970, (G.) physicist known for research in quantum mechanics.

Satyendranath Bose, 1894-1974, (In.) physicist, chemist, mathematician, forerunner of modern quantum theory.

Walter Brattain, 1902-87, (U.S.) inventor, worked on invention of transistor.

Louis de Broglie, 1893-1987, (F.) physicist, best known for wave theory.

Robert Bunsen, 1811-99, (G.) chemist, invented Bunsen burner.

Luther Burbank, 1849-1926, (U.S.) plant breeder whose work developed plant breeding into a modern science.

Vannevar Bush, 1890-1974, (U.S.) electrical engineer, developed differential analyzer, first electronic analogue computer.

Alexis Carrel, 1873-1944, (F.) surgeon, biologist, developed methods of suturing blood vessels and transplanting organs.

George Washington Carver, 1860?-1943, (U.S.) agricultural chemist at Tuskegee Institute, discovered hundreds of uses for peanut, sweet potato, soybean.

Henry Cavendish, 1731-1810, (Br.) chemist, physicist, discovered hydrogen.

James Chadwick, 1891-1974, (Br.) physicist, discovered the neutron.

Jean M. Charcot, 1825-93, (F.) neurologist known for work on hysteria, hypnotism, sclerosis.

Albert Claude, 1899-1983, (Belg.) a founder of modern cell biology.

John D. Cockcroft, 1897-1967, (Br.) nuclear physicist, constructed first atomic particle accelerator with E.T. S. Walton.

Nicholas Copernicus, 1473-1543, (Pol.) astronomer who first described solar system, with earth as one of planets revolving around sun.

William Crookes, 1832-1919, (Br.) physicist, chemist, discovered thallium, invented a cathode-ray tube, radiometer.

Marie Curie, 1867-1934, (Pol.-F.) physical chemist known for work on radium and its compounds.

Pierre Curie, 1859-1906, (F.) physical chemist known for work with his wife on radioactivity.

Gottlieb Daimler, 1834-1900, (G.) engineer, inventor, pioneer automobile manufacturer.

John Dalton, 1766-1844, (Br.) chemist, physicist, formulated atomic theory, made first table of atomic weights.

Charles Darwin, 1809-82, (Br.) naturalist, established theory of organic evolution; *Origin of Species.*

Humphry Davy, 1778-1829, (Br.) chemist, research in electrochemistry led to isolation of potassium, sodium, calcium, barium, boron, magnesium, and strontium.

Lee De Forest, 1873-1961, (U.S.) inventor, pioneer in development of wireless telegraphy, sound pictures, television.

Max Delbruck, 1907-81, (U.S.) pioneer in modern molecular genetics.

Rudolf Diesel, 1858-1913, (G.) mechanical engineer, patented Diesel engine.

Thomas Dooley, 1927-61, (U.S.) "jungle doctor," noted for efforts to supply medical aid to developing countries.

Christian Doppler, 1803-53, (Austrian) physicist, demonstrated Doppler effect (change in energy wavelengths caused by motion).

Thomas A. Edison, 1847-1931, (U.S.) inventor, held more than 1,000 patents, including incandescent electric lamp.

Paul Ehrlich, 1854-1915, (G.) bacteriologist, pioneer in modern immunology and bacteriology.

Albert Einstein, 1879-1955, (G.-U.S.) theoretical physicist, known for formulation of relativity theory.

John F. Enders, 1897-1985, (U.S.) virologist who helped discover vaccines against polio, measles, and mumps.

Leonhard Euler, 1707-83, (Swiss) mathematician, physicist, authored first calculus book.

Gabriel Fahrenheit, 1686-1736, (G.) physicist, introduced Fahrenheit scale for thermometers.

Michael Faraday, 1791-1867, (Br.) chemist, physicist, known for work in field of electricity.

Pierre de Fermat, 1601-65, (F.) mathematician, founded modern theory of numbers and calculus of probabilities.

Enrico Fermi, 1901-54, (It.-U.S.) physicist, one of primary architects of the nuclear age.

Galileo Ferraris, 1847-97, (It.) physicist, electrical engineer, discovered principle of rotary magnetic field.

Richard Feynman, 1918-88, (U.S.) a leading theoretical physicist of the postwar generation.

Camille Flammarion, 1842-1925, (F.) astronomer, popularized study of astronomy.

Alexander Fleming, 1881-1955, (Scot.) bacteriologist, discovered penicillin.

Jean B. J. Fourier, 1768-1830, (F.) mathematician, discovered theorem governing periodic oscillation.

James Franck, 1882-1964, (G.) physicist, proved value of quantum theory.

Sigmund Freud, 1856-1939, (Austrian) psychiatrist, founder of psychoanalysis.

Galileo Galilei, 1564-1642, (It.) astronomer, physicist, a founder of the experimental method.

Luigi Galvani, 1737-98, (It.) physician, physicist, known as founder of galvanism.

Carl Friedrich Gauss, 1777-1855, (G.) mathematician, astronomer, physicist, made important contributions to almost every field of physical science, founded a number of new fields.

Joseph Gay-Lussac, 1778-1850, (F.) chemist, physicist, investigated behavior of gases, discovered law of combining volumes.

Josiah W. Gibbs, 1839-1903, (U.S.) theoretical physicist, chemist, founded chemical thermodynamics.

Robert H. Goddard, 1882-1945, (U.S.) physicist, father of modern rocketry.

George W. Goethals, 1858-1928, (U.S.) army engineer, built the Panama Canal.

William C. Gorgas, 1854-1920, (U.S.) sanitarian, U.S. army surgeon-general, his work to prevent yellow fever, malaria helped ensure construction of Panama Canal.

Ernest Haeckel, 1834-1919, (G.) zoologist, evolutionist, a strong proponent of Darwin.

Otto Hahn, 1879-1968, (G.) chemist, worked on atomic fission.

J. B. S. Haldane, 1892-1964, (Sc.) scientist, known for work as geneticist and application of mathematics to science.

James Hall, 1761-1832, (Br.) geologist, chemist, founded experimental geology, geochemistry.

Edmund Halley, 1656-1742, (Br.) astronomer, calculated the orbits of many planets.

William Harvey, 1578-1657, (Eng.) physician, anatomist, discovered circulation of the blood.

Hermann von Helmholtz, 1821-94, (G.) physicist, anatomist, physiologist, made fundamental contributions to physiology, optics, electrodynamics, mathematics, meteorology.

William Herschel, 1738-1822, (Br.) astronomer, discovered Uranus.

Heinrich Hertz, 1857-94, (G.) physicist, his discoveries led to wireless telegraphy.

David Hilbert, 1862-1943, (G.) mathematician, formulated first satisfactory set of axioms for modern Euclidean geometry.

Edwin P. Hubble, 1889-1953, (U.S.) astronomer, produced first observational evidence of expanding universe.

Alexander von Humboldt, 1769-1859, (G.) explorer, naturalist, earth scientist, originated ecology, geophysics.

Julian Huxley, 1887-1975, (Br.) biologist, a gifted exponent and philosopher of science.

Edward Jenner, 1749-1823, (Br.) physician, discovered vaccination.

William Jenner, 1815-98, (Br.) physician, pathological anatomist.

Frederic Joliot-Curie, 1900-58, (F.) physicist, with his wife continued work of Curies on radioactivity.

Irene Joliot-Curie, 1897-1956, (F.) physicist, continued work of Curies in radioactivity.

James P. Joule, 1818-89, (Br.) physicist, determined relationship between heat and mechanical energy (conservation of energy).

Carl Jung, 1875-1961, (Sw.) psychiatrist, founder of analytical psychology.

Wm. Thomson Kelvin, 1824-1907, (Br.) mathematician, physicist, known for work on heat and electricity.

Sister Elizabeth Kenny, 1886-1952, (Austral.) nurse, developed method of treatment for polio.

Johannes Kepler, 1571-1630, (G.) astronomer, discovered important laws of planetary motion.

Joseph Lagrange, 1736-1813, (F.) geometer, astronomer, number theorist, analytical and celestial mechanics.

Jean B. Lamarck, 1744-1829, (F.) naturalist, forerunner of Darwin in evolutionary theory.

Edwin Land, 1910-91, (U.S.) invented Polaroid camera.

Irving Langmuir, 1881-1957, (U.S.) physical chemist, colloid research and biochemistry.

Pierre S. Laplace, 1749-1827, (F.) astronomer, physicist, put forth nebular hypothesis of origin of solar system.

Antoine Lavoisier, 1743-94, (F.) chemist, founder of modern chemistry.

Ernest O. Lawrence, 1901-58, (U.S.) physicist, invented the cyclotron.

Jerome Lejeune, 1927-94, (F.) geneticist, discovered the cause of Down's syndrome.

Louis Leakey, 1903-72, (Br.) anthropologist, discovered important fossils, remains of early hominids.

Anton van Leeuwenhoek, 1632-1723, (Du.) microscopist, father of microbiology.

Gottfried Wilhelm Leibniz, 1646-1716, (G.) mathematician, developed theories of differential and integral calculus.

Justus von Liebig, 1803-73, (G.) chemist, established quantitative organic chemical analysis.

Joseph Lister, 1827-1912, (Br.) pioneered antiseptic surgery.

Percival Lowell, 1855-1916, (U.S.) astronomer, predicted the existence of Pluto.

Louis, 1864-1984, and **Auguste Lumière,** 1862-1954, (F.) invented cinematograph.

Guglielmo Marconi, 1874-1937, (It.) physicist, known for his development of wireless telegraphy.

James Clerk Maxwell, 1831-79, (Sc.) physicist, known especially for his work in electricity and magnetism.

Maria Goeppert Mayer, 1906-72, (G.-U.S.) physicist, independently developed theory of structure of atomic nuclei.

Lise Meitner, 1878-1968, (Austrian) physicist whose work contributed to the development of the atomic bomb.

Gregor J. Mendel, 1822-84, (Austrian) botanist, known for his experimental work on heredity.

Franz Mesmer, 1734-1815, (G.) physician, developed theory of animal magnetism.

Albert A. Michelson, 1852-1931, (U.S.) physicist, established speed of light as a fundamental constant.

Robert A. Millikan, 1868-1953, (U.S.) physicist, noted for study of elementary electronic charge and photoelectric effect.

Thomas Hunt Morgan, 1866-1945, (U.S.) geneticist, embryologist, established chromosome theory of heredity.

Isaac Newton, 1642-1727, (Eng.) natural philosopher, mathematician, discovered law of gravitation, laws of motion.

Robert N. Noyce, 1927-89, (U.S.) inventor of the microchip, which revolutionized the electronics industry.

J. Robert Oppenheimer, 1904-67, (U.S.) physicist, director of Los Alamos during development of the atomic bomb.

Wilhelm Ostwald, 1853-1932, (G.) physical chemist, philosopher, primary founder of physical chemistry.

Robert Morris Page, 1903-92, (U.S.) physicist, research director of U.S. Naval Research Laboratory, a leading figure in development of radar technology.

Louis Pasteur, 1822-95, (F.) chemist, originated process of pasteurization.

Linus C. Pauling, 1901-94, (U.S.) chemist, specializing in chemical bonds, and political activist.

Max Planck, 1858-1947, (G.) physicist, originated and developed quantum theory.

Roy J. Plunkett, 1922-94, (U.S.) chemist, created Teflon ™.

Henri Poincaré, 1854-1912, (F.) mathematician, physicist, influenced cosmology, relativity, and topology.

Joseph Priestley, 1733-1804, (Br.) chemist, one of the discoverers of oxygen.

Isidor Isaac Rabi, 1899-1988, (U.S.) physicist, pioneered atom exploration.

Walter S. Reed, 1851-1902, (U.S.) army pathologist, bacteriologist, proved mosquitoes transmit yellow fever.

Bernhard Riemann, 1826-66, (G.) mathematician, contributed to development of calculus and mathematical physics.

Wilhelm Roentgen, 1845-1923, (G.) physicist, discovered X ray.

Bertrand Russell, 1872-1970, (Br.) logician, philosopher, one of the founders of modern logic.

Ernest Rutherford, 1871-1937, (Br.) physicist, discovered the atomic nucleus.

Albert B. Sabin, 1906-93, (Rus.-U.S.) In 1954, developed oral polio vaccine, which was licensed in 1961.

Giovanni Schiaparelli, 1835-1910, (It.) astronomer, hypothesized canals on the surface of Mars.

Angelo Secchi, 1818-78, (It.) astronomer, pioneer in classifying stars by their spectra.

Harlow Shapley, 1885-1972, (U.S.) astronomer, noted for his studies of the galaxy.

Roger Sperry, 1913-94, (U.S.) brain expert, studied relationship between the right and left sides of the brain.

Charles P. Steinmetz, 1865-1923, (G.-U.S.) electrical engineer, developed basic ideas on alternating current systems.

Frederick Stewart, 1904-93, (Br.) botanist, cell biologist, studies considered foundations of molecular biology.

Leo Szilard, 1898-1964, (Hung.-U.S.) physicist, helped create first sustained nuclear reaction.

Nikola Tesla, 1856-1943, (Croatia-U.S.) electrical engineer, contributed to most developments in electronics.

Rudolf Virchow, 1821-1902, (G.) pathologist, a founder of cellular pathology.

Alessandro Volta, 1745-1827, (It.) physicist, pioneer in electricity.

Werner von Braun, 1912-77, (G.-U.S.) pioneered development of rockets for warfare and space exploration.

Alfred Russell Wallace, 1823-1913, (Br.) naturalist, proposed concept of evolution similar to Darwin.

August von Wasserman, 1866-1925, (G.) bacteriologist, discovered reaction used as test for syphilis.

James E. Watt, 1736-1819, (Sc.) mechanical engineer, inventor, invented modern steam-condensing engine.

Alfred L. Wegener, 1880-1930, (G.) meteorologist, geophysicist, postulated theory of continental drift.

Norbert Wiener, 1894-1964, (U.S.) mathematician, founder of the science of cybernetics.

Sewall Wright, 1889-1988, (U.S.) evolutionary theorist.

Ferdinand von Zeppelin, 1838-1917, (G.) soldier, aeronaut, airship designer.

Noted Business Leaders, Industrialists, and Philanthropists of the Past

Elizabeth Arden (F. N. Graham), 1884-1966, (U.S.) Canadian-born founder of cosmetics empire.

Philip D. Armour, 1832-1901, (U.S.) industrialist, streamlined meatpacking.

John Jacob Astor, 1763-1848, (U.S.) German-born fur trader, banker, real estate magnate; at death, richest in U.S.

Francis W. Ayer, 1848-1923, (U.S.) ad industry pioneer.

August Belmont, 1816-90, (U.S.) German-born financier.

James B. (Diamond Jim) Brady, 1856-1917, (U.S.) financier, philanthropist, legendary bon vivant.

Adolphus Busch, 1839-1913, (U.S.) German-born businessman, established brewery empire.

Asa Candler, 1851-1929, (U.S.) founded Coca-Cola Co.

Andrew Carnegie, 1835-1919, (U.S.) Scottish-born industrialist, founded U.S. Steel; financed more than 2,800 libraries.

Tom Carvel, 1908-89, (Gr.-U.S.) founded ice cream chain.

William Colgate, 1783-1857, (U.S.) Br.-born businessman, philanthropist; founded soap-making empire.

Jay Cooke, 1821-1905, (U.S.) financier, sold $1 billion in Union bonds during Civil War.

Peter Cooper, 1791-1883, (U.S.) industrialist, inventor, philanthropist.

Ezra Cornell, 1807-74, (U.S.) businessman, philanthropist; headed Western Union, established university.

Erastus Corning, 1794-1872, (U.S.) financier, headed N.Y. Central.

Charles Crocker, 1822-88, (U.S.) railroad builder, financier.

Samuel Cunard, 1787-1865, (Can.) pioneered trans-Atlantic steam navigation.

Marcus Daly, 1841-1900, (U.S.) Ir.-born copper magnate.

George T. Delacorte, 1893-1991, (U.S.) publisher; Central Park donations included Alice in Wonderland statue.

W. Edwards Deming, 1900-93, (U.S.) quality-control expert who revolutionized Japanese manufacturing.

Walt Disney, 1901-66, (U.S.) pioneer in cinema animation, built entertainment empire.

Herbert H. Dow, 1866-1930, (U.S.) founder of chemical co.

James Duke, 1856-1925, (U.S.) founded American Tobacco, Duke Univ.

Eleuthere I. du Pont, 1771-1834, (F.-U.S.) gunpowder manufacturer; founded one of world's largest business empires.

Thomas C. Durant, 1820-85, (U.S.) railroad official, financier.

William C. Durant, 1861-1947, (U.S.) industrialist, formed General Motors.

George Eastman, 1854-1932, (U.S.) inventor, manufacturer of photographic equipment.

Marshall Field, 1834-1906, (U.S.) merchant, founded Chicago's largest department store.

Harvey Firestone, 1868-1938, (U.S.) founded tire company.

Avery Fisher, 1906-94, (U.S.) industrialist, philanthropist, founded Fisher electronics.

Henry M. Flagler, 1830-1913, (U.S.) financier, helped form Standard Oil; developed Florida as resort state.

Malcolm Forbes, 1919-90, (U.S.) magazine publisher.

Henry Ford, 1863-1947, (U.S.) auto maker, developed first popular low-priced car.

Henry Ford 2d, 1917-87, (U.S.) headed auto company founded by grandfather.

Henry C. Frick, 1849-1919, (U.S.) industrialist, helped organize U.S. Steel.

Jakob Fugger (Jakob the Rich), 1459-1525, (G.) headed leading banking, trading house, in 16th-century Europe.

Alfred C. Fuller, 1885-1973, (U.S.) Canadian-born businessman, founded brush co.

Elbert H. Gary, 1846-1927, (U.S.) headed U.S. Steel, 1903-27.

Jean Paul Getty, 1892-1976, (U.S.) founded oil empire.

Amadeo P. Giannini, 1870-1949, (U.S.) founded Bank of America.

Stephen Girard, 1750-1831, (U.S.) French-born financier, philanthropist; richest man in U.S. at his death.

Jay Gould, 1836-92, (U.S.) railroad magnate, financier, speculator.

Hetty Green, 1834-1916, (U.S.) financier, the "witch of Wall St."; richest woman in U.S. in her day.

William Gregg, 1800-67, (U.S.) launched textile industry in the South.

Meyer Guggenheim, 1828-1905, (U.S.) Swiss-born merchant, philanthropist; built merchandising, mining empires.

Armand Hammer, 1898-1990, (U.S.) headed Occidental Petroleum; promoted U.S.-Soviet ties.

Edward H. Harriman, 1848-1909, (U.S.) railroad financier, administrator; headed Union Pacific.

William Randolph Hearst, 1863-1951, (U.S.) a dominant figure in American journalism; built vast publishing empire.

Henry J. Heinz, 1844-1919, (U.S.) founded food empire.

James J. Hill, 1838-1916, (U.S.) Canadian-born railroad magnate, financier; founded Great Northern Railway.

Conrad N. Hilton, 1888-1979, (U.S.) hotel chain founder.

Howard Hughes, 1905-76, (U.S.) industrialist, financier, movie maker.

H. L. Hunt, 1889-1974, (U.S.) oil magnate.

Collis P. Huntington, 1821-1900, (U.S.) railroad magnate.

Henry E. Huntington, 1850-1927, (U.S.) railroad builder, philanthropist.

Walter L. Jacobs, 1898-1985, (U.S.) founder of the first rental car agency, which later became Hertz.

Howard Johnson, 1896-1972, (U.S.) founded restaurants.

Henry J. Kaiser, 1882-1967, (U.S.) industrialist, built empire in steel, aluminum.

Minor C. Keith, 1848-1929, (U.S.) railroad magnate; founded United Fruit Co.

Will K. Kellogg, 1860-1951, (U.S.) businessman, philanthropist, founded breakfast food co.

Richard King, 1825-85, (U.S.) cattleman, founded half-million acre King Ranch in Texas.

William S. Knudsen, 1879-1948, (U.S.) Danish-born auto industry executive.

Samuel H. Kress, 1863-1955, (U.S.) businessman, art collector, philanthropist; founded "dime store" chain.

Ray A. Kroc, 1902-84, (U.S.) builder of McDonald's fast food empire.

Alfred Krupp, 1812-87, (G.) armaments magnate.

Albert Lasker, 1880-1952, (U.S.) businessman.

Mary W. Lasker, 1901-94, (U.S.) philanthropist.

William Levitt, 1907-94, (U.S.) industrialist, "suburb maker".

Thomas Lipton, 1850-1931, (Scot.) merchant, tea empire.

James McGill, 1744-1813, (Scot.-Can.) founded university.

Andrew W. Mellon, 1855-1937, (U.S.) financier, industrialist; benefactor of National Gallery of Art.

Charles E. Merrill, 1885-1956, (U.S.) financier, developed firm of Merrill Lynch.

John Pierpont Morgan, 1837-1913, (U.S.) most powerful figure in finance and industry at the turn of the century.

Malcolm Muir, 1885-1979, (U.S.) created *Business Week* magazine; headed *Newsweek,* 1937-61.

Samuel Newhouse, 1895-1979, (U.S.) publishing and broadcasting magnate, built communications empire.

Aristotle Onassis, 1900-75, (Gr.) shipping magnate.

William S. Paley, 1901-89, (U.S.) built CBS communications empire.

George Peabody, 1795-1869, (U.S.) merchant, financier, philanthropist.

James C. Penney, 1875-1971, (U.S.) businessman, developed department store chain.

William C. Procter, 1862-1934, (U.S.) headed soap co.

John D. Rockefeller, 1839-1937, (U.S.) industrialist, established Standard Oil; became world's wealthiest person.

John D. Rockefeller, Jr., 1874-1960, (U.S.) philanthropist, established foundation; provided land for United Nations.

Meyer A. Rothschild, 1743-1812, (G.) founded international banking house.

Thomas Fortune Ryan, 1851-1928, (U.S.) financier, a founder of American Tobacco.

Russell Sage, 1816-1906, (U.S.) financier.

David Sarnoff, 1891-1971, (U.S.) broadcasting pioneer, established first radio network, NBC.

Richard Sears, 1863-1914, (U.S.) founded mail-order co.

(Ernst) Werner von Siemens, 1816-92, (G.) industrialist, inventor.

Alfred P. Sloan, 1875-1966, (U.S.) industrialist, philanthropist; headed General Motors.

A. Leland Stanford, 1824-93, (U.S.) railroad official, philanthropist; founded university.

Nathan Straus, 1848-1931, (U.S.) German-born merchant, philanthropist; headed Macy's.

Levi Strauss, c 1829-1902, (U.S.) pants manufacturer.

Clement Studebaker, 1831-1901, (U.S.) wagon, carriage manufacturer.

Gustavus Swift, 1839-1903, (U.S.) pioneer meatpacker; promoted refrigerated railroad cars.

Gerard Swope, 1872-1957, (U.S.) industrialist, economist; headed General Electric.

James Walter Thompson, 1847-1928, (U.S.) ad executive.

Alice Tully, 1902-93, (U.S.) philanthropist, arts patron.

Theodore N. Vail, 1845-1920, (U.S.) organized Bell Telephone system, headed AT&T.

Cornelius Vanderbilt, 1794-1877, (U.S.) financier, established steamship, railroad empires.

Henry Villard, 1835-1900, (U.S.) German-born railroad executive, financier.

George Westinghouse, 1846-1914, (U.S) inventor, manufacturer, organized Westinghouse Electric Co., 1886.

Charles R. Walgreen, 1873-1939, (U.S.) founded drugstore chain.

DeWitt Wallace, 1890-1981, (U.S.) and **Lila Wallace,** 1890-1984, (U.S.) co-founders of *Reader's Digest* magazine.

Sam Walton, 1918-92, (U.S.) founder of Wal-Mart stores.

John Wanamaker, 1838-1922, (U.S.) pioneered department-store merchandising.

Aaron Montgomery Ward, 1843-1913, (U.S.) established first mail-order firm.

Thomas J. Watson, 1874-1956, (U.S.) IBM head, 1924-49.

John Hay Whitney, 1905-82, (U.S.) publisher, sportsman, philanthropist.

Charles E. Wilson, 1890-1961, (U.S.) auto industry executive; public official.

Frank W. Woolworth, 1852-1919, (U.S.) created 5 & 10 chain.

William Wrigley, Jr., 1861-1932, (U.S.) founded chewing gum company.

Composers of the Western World

Carl Philipp Emanuel Bach, 1714-88, (Ger.) Cantatas, passions, numerous keyboard and instrumental works.

Johann Christian Bach, 1735-82, (Ger.) Concertos, operas, sonatas.

Johann Sebastian Bach, 1685-1750, (Ger.) St. Matthew Passion, The Well-Tempered Clavier.

Samuel Barber, 1910-81, (U.S.) Adagio for Strings, Vanessa.

Béla Bartók, 1881-1945, (Hung.) Concerto for Orchestra, The Miraculous Mandarin.

Ludwig van Beethoven, 1770-1827, (Ger.) Concertos (Emperor), sonatas (Moonlight, Pathetique), 9 symphonies.

Vincenzo Bellini, 1801-35, (Ital.) I Puritani, La Sonnambula, Norma.

Alban Berg, 1885-1935, (Austrian) Wozzeck, Lulu.

Hector Berlioz, 1803-69, (Fr.) Damnation of Faust, Symphonie Fantastique, Requiem.

Leonard Bernstein, 1918-90, (U.S.) Chichester Psalms, Jeremiah Symphony, Mass.

Georges Bizet, 1838-75, (Fr.) Carmen, Pearl Fishers.

Ernest Bloch, 1880-1959, (Swiss-U.S.) Macbeth (opera), Schelomo, Voice in the Wilderness.

Luigi Boccherini, 1743-1805, (Ital.) Chamber music and guitar pieces.

Alexander Borodin, 1833-87, (Russ.) Prince Igor, In the Steppes of Central Asia, Polovtzian Dances.

Johannes Brahms, 1833-97, (Ger.) Liebeslieder Waltzes, Academic Festival Overture, chamber music, 4 symphonies.

Benjamin Britten, 1913-76, (British) Peter Grimes, Turn of the Screw, A Ceremony of Carols, War Requiem.

Anton Bruckner, 1824-96, (Ausrian) 9 symphonies.

Ferruccio Busoni, 1866-1924, (Ital.) Doctor Faust.

Dietrich Buxtehude, 1637-1707, (Dan.) Organ works, vocal music.

William Byrd, 1543-1623, (British) Masses, motets.

Emmanuel Chabrier, 1841-94, (Fr.) Le Roi Malgré Lui, Espana.

Gustave Charpentier, 1860-1956, (Fr.) Louise.

Frédéric Chopin, 1810-49, (Pol.) Mazurkas, waltzes, etudes, nocturnes, polonaises (Polonaise No. 6 in A flat major [Heroic]), sonatas.

Aaron Copland, 1900-90, (U.S.) Appalachian Spring, Fanfare for the Common Man, Lincoln Portrait.

Claude Debussy, 1862-1918, (Fr.) Pelleas et Melisande, La Mer, Prelude to the Afternoon of a Faun.

Leo Delibes, 1836-91, (Fr.) Lakme, Coppelia, Sylvia.

Norman Dello Joio, b 1913, (U.S.) The Triumph of St. Joan.

Gaetano Donizetti, 1797-1848, (Ital.) Elixir of Love, Lucia di Lammermoor, Daughter of the Regiment.

Paul Dukas, 1865-1935, (Fr.) Sorcerer's Apprentice.

Antonin Dvorak, 1841-1904, (Czech.) Cello Concerto in B Minor, Songs My Mother Taught Me, Symphony in E Minor (From the New World).

Edward Elgar, 1857-1934, (British) Enigma Variations, Pomp and Circumstance.

Manuel de Falla, 1876-1946, (Sp.) El Amor Brujo, La Vida Breve, The Three-Cornered Hat.

Gabriel Faurè, 1845-1924, (Fr.) Requiem, Elègie for Cello and Piano.

Friedrich von Flotow, 1812-83, (Ger.) Martha.

Cesar Franck, 1822-90, (Belg.) Symphony in D minor , Violin Sonata.

George Gershwin, 1898-1937, (U.S.) Rhapsody in Blue, An American in Paris, Porgy and Bess.

Umberto Giordano, 1867-1948, (Ital.) Andrea Chènier.

Alexander K. Glazunoff, 1865-1936, (Russ.) Raymonda, Violin Concerto.

Mikhail Glinka, 1804-57, (Russ.) A Life for the Tsar, Ruslan and Ludmilla.

Christoph W. Gluck, 1714-87, (Ger.) Alceste, Iphigènie en Tauride.

Charles Gounod, 1818-93, (Fr.) Faust, Romeo and Juliet.

Edvard Grieg, 1843-1907, (Nor.) Peer Gynt Suite, Concerto in A minor for piano.

George Frideric Handel, 1685-1759, (Ger.-British) Messiah, Water Music.

Howard Hanson, 1896-1981, (U.S.) Symphonies No. 1 (Nordic) and No. 2 (Romantic).

Roy Harris, 1898-1979, (U.S.) Symphonies.

Joseph Haydn, 1732-1809, (Austrian) Symphonies (Clock, London Toy), chamber music, oratorios.

Paul Hindemith, 1895-1963, (U.S.) Mathis der Maler.

Gustav Holst, 1874-1934, (British) The Planets.

Arthur Honegger, 1892-1955, (Fr.) Judith, Le Roi David, Pacific 231.

Alan Hovhaness, b 1911, (U.S.) Symphonies, Magnificat.

Engelbert Humperdinck, 1854-1921, (Ger.) Hansel and Gretel.

Charles Ives, 1874-1954, (U.S.) Concord Sonata, 4 symphonies.

Aram Khachaturian, 1903-78, (Russ.) Ballets, piano pieces, Sabre Dance.

Zoltán Kodaly, 1882-1967, (Hung.) Háry János, Psalmus Hungaricus.

Fritz Kreisler, 1875-1962, (Austrian) Caprice Viennois, Tambourin Chinois.

Rodolphe Kreutzer, 1766-1831, (Fr.) 40 Etudes for violin.

Edouard Lalo, 1823-92, (Fr.) Symphonie Espagnole.

Ruggero Leoncavallo, 1857-1919, (Ital.) Pagliacci.

Franz Liszt, 1811-86, (Hung.) 20 Hungarian rhapsodies, symphonic poems.

Witold Lutoslawski, 1913-94, (Pol.), Orchestral and chamber works, Concerto for Orchestra, Funeral Music.

Edward MacDowell, 1861-1908, (U.S.) To a Wild Rose.

Gustav Mahler, 1860-1911, (Austrian) Das Lied von der Erde.

Pietro Mascagni, 1863-1945, (Ital.) Cavalleria Rusticana.

Jules Massenet, 1842-1912, (Fr.) Manon, Le Cid, Thaïs.

Felix Mendelssohn, 1809-47, (Ger.) A Midsummer Night's Dream, Songs Without Words, violin concerto.

Gian-Carlo Menotti, b 1911, (Ital.-U.S.) The Medium, The Consul, Amahl and the Night Visitors.

Giacomo Meyerbeer, 1791-1864, (Ger.) Les Huguenots.

Claudio Monteverdi, 1567-1643, (Ital.) Opera, masses, madrigals.

Modest Moussorgsky, 1839-81, (Russ.) Boris Godunov, Pictures at an Exhibition.

Wolfgang Amadeus Mozart, 1756-91, (Austrian) Chamber music, concertos, operas (Magic Flute, Marriage of Figaro), 41 symphonies.

Jacques Offenbach, 1819-80, (Fr.) Tales of Hoffmann.

Carl Orff, 1895-1982, (Ger.) Carmina Burana.

Johann Pachelbel, 1653-1706, (Ger.) Canon and Gigue in D major.

Ignacy Paderewski, 1860-1941, (Pol.) Minuet in G.

Niccolò Paganini, 1782-1840, (Ital.) Caprices for violin solo.

Palestrina, c 1525-94, (Ital.) Masses, madrigals.

Amilcare Ponchielli, 1834-86, (Ital.) La Gioconda.

Francis Poulenc, 1899-1963, (Fr.) Dialogues des Carmèlites.

Sergei Prokofiev, 1891-1953, (Russ.) Classical Symphony, Love for Three Oranges, Peter and the Wolf.

Giacomo Puccini, 1858-1924, (Ital.) La Boheme, Manon Lescaut, Tosca, Madama Butterfly.

Henry Purcell, 1659-95, (Eng.) Dido and Aeneas.

Sergei Rachmaninov, 1873-1943, (Russ.) Concertos, preludes (Prelude in C sharp minor), symphonies.

Maurice Ravel, 1875-1937, (Fr.) Bolèro, Daphnis et Chloè, Piano Concerto in D for Left Hand Alone.

Nikolai Rimsky-Korsakov, 1844-1908, (Russ.) Golden Cockerel, Capriccio Espagnol, Scheherazade, Russian Easter Overture, Flight of the Bumblebee.

Gioacchino Rossini, 1792-1868, (Ital.) Barber of Seville, Othello, William Tell.

Camille Saint-Saëns, 1835-1921, (Fr.) Carnival of Animals (The Swan), Samson and Delilah, Danse Macabre.

Alessandro Scarlatti, 1660-1725, (Ital.) Cantatas, oratorios, operas.

Domenico Scarlatti, 1685-1757, (Ital.) Harpsichord works.

Arnold Schoenberg, 1874-1951, (Austrian) Pelleas and Melisande, Pierrot Lunaire, Verklärte Nacht.

Franz Schubert, 1797-1828, (Austrian) Chamber music (Trout Quintet), lieder, symphonies (Unfinished).

William Schuman, 1910-92, (U.S.) Credendum, New England Triptych.

Robert Schumann, 1810-56, (Ger.) Die Frauenliebe und Leben, Traümeri.

Aleksandr Scriabin, 1872-1915, (Russ.) Prometheus.

Dimitri Shostakovich, 1906-75, (Russ.) Symphonies, Lady Macbeth of the District Mzensk.

Jean Sibelius, 1865-1957, (Finn.) Finlandia.

Bedrich Smetana, 1824-84, (Czech.) The Bartered Bride.

Karlheinz Stockhausen, b 1928, (Ger.) KontraPunkte, Kontakte for Electronic Instruments.

Richard Strauss, 1864-1949, (Ger.) Salome, Elektra, Der Rosenkavalier, Thus Spake Zarathustra.

Igor Stravinsky, 1882-1971, (Russ.) Noah and the Flood, The Rake's Progress, The Rite of Spring.

Peter I. Tchaikovsky, 1840-93, (Russ.) Nutcracker, Swan Lake, The Sleeping Beauty.

Virgil Thomson, 1896-1989, (U.S.) Opera, film music, Four Saints in Three Acts.

Ralph Vaughan Williams, 1872-1958, (Eng.) Fantasiz on a Theme by Thomas Tallis, symphonies, vocal music.

Giuseppe Verdi, 1813-1901, (Ital.) Aida, Rigoletto, Don Carlo, Il Trovatore, La Traviata, Falstaff, Macbeth.

Heitor Villa-Lobos, 1887-1959, (Brazil) Bachianas Brasileiras.

Antonio Vivaldi, 1678-1741, (Ital.) Concerto grossos (The Four Seasons).

Richard Wagner, 1813-83, (Ger.) Rienzi, Tannhäuser, Lohengrin, Tristan und Isolde.

Carl Maria von Weber, 1786-1826, (Ger.) Der Freischutz.

Composers of Operettas, Musicals, and Popular Music

Richard Adler, b 1921, (U.S.) *Pajama Game; Damn Yankees.*

Milton Ager, 1893-1979, (U.S.) I Wonder What's Become of Sally; Hard Hearted Hannah; Ain't She Sweet?

Arthur Altman, 1910-94, (U.S.) *All or Nothing at All.*

Leroy Anderson, 1908-75, (U.S.) Syncopated Clock.

Paul Anka, b 1941, (Can.) My Way; She's a Lady; *Tonight Show* theme.

Harold Arlen, 1905-86, (U.S.) Stormy Weather; Over the Rainbow; Blues in the Night; That Old Black Magic.

Burt Bacharach, b 1928, (U.S.) Raindrops Keep Fallin' on My Head; Walk on By; What the World Needs Now Is Love.

Ernest Ball, 1878-1927, (U.S.) Mother Machree; When Irish Eyes Are Smiling.

Irving Berlin, 1888-1989, (U.S.) *Annie Get Your Gun; Call Me Madam;* God Bless America; White Christmas.

Leonard Bernstein, 1918-90, (U.S.) *On the Town; Wonderful Town; Candide; West Side Story.*

Eubie Blake, 1883-1983, (U.S.) *Shuffle Along;* I'm Just Wild about Harry.

Jerry Bock, b 1928, (U.S.) *Mr. Wonderful; Fiorello; Fiddler on the Roof; The Rothschilds.*

Carrie Jacobs Bond, 1862-1946, (U.S.) I Love You Truly.

Nacio Herb Brown, 1896-1964, (U.S.) Singing in the Rain; You Were Meant for Me; All I Do Is Dream of You.

Hoagy Carmichael, 1899-1981, (U.S.) Stardust; Georgia on My Mind; Old Buttermilk Sky.

George M. Cohan, 1878-1942, (U.S.) Give My Regards to Broadway; You're A Grand Old Flag; Over There.

Cy Coleman, b 1929, (U.S.) *Sweet Charity;* Witchcraft.

Noel Coward, 1899-1973, (British) *Bitter Sweet;* Mad Dogs and Englishmen; Mad About the Boy.

Neil Diamond, b 1941, (U.S.) I'm a Believer; Sweet Caroline.

Walter Donaldson, 1893-1947, (U.S.) My Buddy; Carolina in the Morning; You're Driving Me Crazy; Makin' Whoopee.

Vernon Duke, 1903-69, (U.S.) April in Paris.

Bob Dylan, b 1941, (U.S.) Blowin' in the Wind.

Gus Edwards, 1879-1945, (U.S.) School Days; By the Light of the Silvery Moon; In My Merry Oldsmobile.

Sherman Edwards, 1919-81, (U.S.) See You in September; Wonderful! Wonderful!

Duke Ellington, 1899-1974, (U.S.) Sophisticated Lady; Satin Doll; It Don't Mean a Thing; Solitude.

Sammy Fain, 1902-89, (U.S.) I'll Be Seeing You; Love Is a Many-Splendored Thing.

Fred Fisher, 1875-1942, (U.S.) Peg O' My Heart; Chicago.

Stephen Collins Foster, 1826-64, (U.S.) My Old Kentucky Home; Old Folks at Home.

Rudolf Friml, 1879-1972, (naturalized U.S.) *The Firefly; Rose Marie; Vagabond King; Bird of Paradise.*

John Gay, 1685-1732, (British) *The Beggar's Opera.*

George Gershwin, 1898-1937, (U.S.) Someone to Watch Over Me; I've Got a Crush on You; Embraceable You.

Ferde Grofe, 1892-1972, (U.S.) Grand Canyon Suite.

Marvin Hamlisch, b 1944, (U.S.) The Way We Were, Nobody Does It Better, *A Chorus Line.*

W. C. Handy, 1873-1958, (U.S.) St. Louis Blues.

Ray Henderson, 1896-1970, (U.S.) *George White's Scandals;* That Old Gang of Mine; Five Foot Two, Eyes of Blue.

Victor Herbert, 1859-1924, (Ir.-U.S.) *Mlle. Modiste; Babes in Toyland; The Red Mill; Naughty Marietta; Sweethearts.*

Jerry Herman, b 1932, (U.S.) *Hello Dolly; Mame.*

Brian Holland, b 1941, **Lamont Dozier,** b 1941, **Eddie Holland,** b 1939, (all U.S.) Heat Wave; Stop! In the Name of Love; Baby, I Need Your Loving.

Billy (William Martin) Joel, b 1949, (U.S.) *Just the Way You Are, Honesty,* Piano Man.

Scott Joplin, 1868-1917, (U.S.) *Treemonisha.*

John Kander, b 1927, (U.S.) *Cabaret; Chicago; Funny Lady.*

Jerome Kern, 1885-1945, (U.S.) *Sally; Sunny; Show Boat.*

Carole King, b 1942, (U.S.) Will You Love Me Tomorrow?; Natural Woman; One Fine Day; Up on the Roof.

Burton Lane, b 1912, (U.S.) *Finian's Rainbow.*

Franz Lehar, 1870-1948, (Hung.) *Merry Widow.*

Jerry Leiber, & **Mike Stoller,** both b 1933, (both U.S.) Hound Dog; Searchin'; Yakety Yak; Love Me Tender.

Mitch Leigh, b 1928, (U.S.) *Man of La Mancha.*

John Lennon, 1940-80, & **Paul McCartney,** b 1942, (both British) I Want to Hold Your Hand; She Loves You; Hard Day's Night; Can't Buy Me Love; And I Love Her.

Frank Loesser, 1910-69, (U.S.) *Guys and Dolls; Where's Charley?; The Most Happy Fella; How to Succeed ....*

Frederick Loewe, 1901-88, (Aust.-U.S.) *The Day Before Spring; Brigadoon; Paint Your Wagon; My Fair Lady; Camelot.*

Henry Mancini, 1924-94, (U.S.) Moon River; Days of Wine and Roses; Pink Panther Theme.

Barry Mann, b 1939, & **Cynthia Weil,** b 1937, (both U.S.) You've Lost That Loving Feeling, Saturday Night at the Movies.

Jimmy McHugh, 1894-1969, (U.S.) Don't Blame Me; I'm in the Mood for Love; I Feel a Song Coming On.

Alan Menken, b 1950, (U.S.) *Little Shop of Horrors.*
Joseph Meyer, 1894-1987, (U.S.) If You Knew Susie; California, Here I Come; Crazy Rhythm.
Chauncey Olcott, 1860-1932, (U.S.) Mother Machree.
Jerome "Doc" Pomus, 1925-91, (U.S.) Save the Last Dance for Me, A Teenager in Love.
Cole Porter, 1893-1964, (U.S.) *Anything Goes; Kiss Me Kate; Can Can; Silk Stockings.*
Smokey Robinson, b 1940, (U.S.) Shop Around; My Guy; My Girl; Get Ready.
Richard Rodgers, 1902-79, (U.S.) *Oklahoma!; Carousel; South Pacific; The King and I; The Sound of Music.*
Sigmund Romberg, 1887-1951, (Hung.) *Maytime; The Student Prince; Desert Song; Blossom Time.*
Harold Rome, b 1908, (U.S.) *Pins and Needles; Call Me Mister; Wish You Were Here; Fanny; Destry Rides Again.*
Vincent Rose, b 1880-1944, (U.S.) Avalon; Whispering; Blueberry Hill.
Harry Ruby, 1895-1974, (U.S.) Three Little Words; Who's Sorry Now?
Arthur Schwartz, 1900-84, (U.S.) *The Band Wagon;* Dancing in the Dark; By Myself; That's Entertainment.
Neil Sedaka, b 1939, (U.S.) Breaking Up Is Hard to Do.
Paul Simon, b 1942, (U.S.) Sounds of Silence; I Am a Rock; Mrs. Robinson; Bridge Over Troubled Waters.
Stephen Sondheim, b 1930, (U.S.) *A Little Night Music; Company; Sweeney Todd; Sunday in the Park with George.*
John Philip Sousa, 1854-1932, (U.S.) *El Capitan;* Stars and Stripes Forever.
Oskar Straus, 1870-1954, (Austrian) *Chocolate Soldier.*
Johann Strauss, 1825-99, (Austrian) *Gypsy Baron; Die Fledermaus;* waltzes: Blue Danube, Artist's Life.
Charles Strouse, b 1928, (U.S.) *Bye Bye, Birdie; Annie.*
Jule Styne, 1905-94, (Br.-U.S.) *Gentlemen Prefer Blondes; Bells Are Ringing; Gypsy; Funny Girl.*
Arthur S. Sullivan, 1842-1900, (British) *H.M.S. Pinafore, Pirates of Penzance; The Mikado.*
Deems Taylor, 1885-1966, (U.S.) *Peter Ibbetson.*
Egbert van Alstyne, 1882-1951, (U.S.) In the Shade of the Old Apple Tree; Memories; Pretty Baby.
Jimmy Van Heusen, 1913-90, (U.S.) Moonlight Becomes You; Swinging on a Star; All the Way; Love and Marriage.
Albert von Tilzer, 1878-1956, (U.S.) I'll Be With You in Apple Blossom Time; Take Me Out to the Ball Game.
Harry von Tilzer, 1872-1946, (U.S.) Only a Bird in a Gilded Cage; On a Sunday Afternoon.
Fats Waller, 1904-43, (U.S.) Honeysuckle Rose; Ain't Misbehavin'.
Harry Warren, 1893-1981, (U.S.) You're My Everything; We're in the Money; I Only Have Eyes for You.
Jimmy Webb, b 1946, (U.S.) Up, Up and Away; By the Time I Get to Phoenix; Didn't We?; Wichita Lineman.
Andrew Lloyd Webber, b 1948, (British) *Jesus Christ Superstar, Evita, Cats, The Phantom of the Opera.*
Kurt Weill, 1900-50, (Ger.-U.S.) *Threepenny Opera; Lady in the Dark; Knickerbocker Holiday; One Touch of Venus.*
Percy Wenrich, 1887-1952, (U.S.) When You Wore a Tulip; Moonlight Bay; Put On Your Old Gray Bonnet.
Richard A. Whiting, 1891-1938, (U.S.) Till We Meet Again; Sleepytime Gal; Beyond the Blue Horizon; My Ideal.
John Williams, b 1932, (U.S.) *Jaws, E.T., Star Wars* series, *Raiders of the Lost Ark* series.
Meredith Willson, 1902-84, (U.S.) *The Music Man.*
Stevie Wonder, b 1950, (U.S.) You Are the Sunshine of My Life; Signed, Sealed, Delivered, I'm Yours.
Vincent Youmans, 1898-1946, (U.S.) *Two Little Girls in Blue; Wildflower; No, No, Nanette; Hit the Deck; Rainbow; Smiles.*

Lyricists

Howard Ashman, 1950-91, (U.S.) *Little Shop of Horrors, The Little Mermaid.*
Johnny Burke, 1908-84, (U.S.) What's New?; Misty; Imagination; Polka Dots and Moonbeams.
Sammy Cahn, 1913-93, (U.S.) High Hopes; Love and Marriage; The Second Time Around; It's Magic.
Betty Comden, b 1919, (U.S.) and **Adolph Green,** b 1915, (U.S.) The Party's Over; Just in Time; New York, New York.
Hal David, b 1921, (U.S.) What the World Needs Now Is Love; Close to You.
Buddy De Sylva, 1895-1950, (U.S.) When Day Is Done; Look for the Silver Lining; April Showers.
Howard Dietz, 1896-1983, (U.S.) Dancing in the Dark; You and the Night and the Music; That's Entertainment.
Al Dubin, 1891-1945, (U.S.) Tiptoe Through the Tulips; Anniversary Waltz; Lullaby of Broadway.
Fred Ebb, b 1936, (U.S.) *Cabaret, Zorba, Woman of the Year.*
Dorothy Fields, 1905-74, (U.S.) On the Sunny Side of the Street; Don't Blame Me; The Way You Look Tonight.
Ira Gershwin, 1896-1983, (U.S.) The Man I Love; Fascinating Rhythm; S'Wonderful; Embraceable You.
William S. Gilbert, 1836-1911, (British) *The Mikado; H.M.S. Pinafore, Pirates of Penzance.*
Gerry Goffin, b 1939, (U.S.) Will You Love Me Tomorrow, Take Good Care of My Baby, Up on the Roof, One Fine Day.
Mack Gordon, 1905-59, (Pol.-U.S.) You'll Never Know; The More I See You; Chattanooga Choo-Choo.
Oscar Hammerstein II, 1895-1960, (U.S.) Ol' Man River; *Oklahoma; Carousel.*
E. Y. (Yip) Harburg, 1898-1981, (U.S.) Brother, Can You Spare a Dime; April in Paris; Over the Rainbow.
Lorenz Hart, 1895-1943, (U.S.) Isn't It Romantic; Blue Moon; Lover; Manhattan; My Funny Valentine.
DuBose Heyward, 1885-1940, (U.S.) Summertime; A Woman Is a Sometime Thing.
Gus Kahn, 1886-1941, (U.S.) Memories; Ain't We Got Fun.
Alan J. Lerner, 1918-86, (U.S.) *Brigadoon; My Fair Lady; Camelot; Gigi; On a Clear Day You Can See Forever.*
Johnny Mercer, 1909-76, (U.S.) Blues in the Night; Come Rain or Come Shine; Laura; That Old Black Magic.
Bob Merrill, b 1921, (U.S.) People; Don't Rain on My Parade.
Jack Norworth, 1879-1959, (U.S.) Take Me Out to the Ball Game; Shine On Harvest Moon.
Mitchell Parish, 1901-93, (U.S.) Stairway to the Stars; Stardust.
Andy Razaf, 1895-1973, (U.S.) Honeysuckle Rose, Ain't Misbehavin', S'posin'.
Leo Robin, 1900-84, (U.S.) Thanks for the Memory; Hooray for Love; Diamonds Are a Girl's Best Friend.
Paul Francis Webster, 1907-84, (U.S.) I Got It Bad and That Ain't Good, Secret Love, The Shadow of Your Smile, Love Is a Many-Splendored Thing.
Jack Yellen, 1892-1991, (U.S.) Down by the O-Hi-O; Ain't She Sweet; Happy Days Are Here Again.

Noted Jazz Artists

Jazz has been called America's only completely unique contribution to Western culture. The following individuals have made major contributions in this field.

Julian "Cannonball" Adderley, 1928-75: alto sax.
Louis "Satchmo" Armstrong, 1900-71: trumpet, singer; originated the "scat" vocal.
Mildred Bailey, 1907-51: blues singer.
Chet Baker, 1929-88: trumpet.
Count Basie, 1904-84: orchestra leader, piano.
Sidney Bechet, 1897-1959: early innovator, soprano sax.
Bix Beiderbecke, 1903-31: cornet, piano, composer.
Tommy Benford, 1906-94: drummer.
George Benson, b 1943: guitarist, composer.
Bunny Berigan, 1909-42: trumpet, singer.
Barney Bigard, 1906-80: clarinet.
Art Blakey, 1919-90: drums, leader.
Jimmy Blanton, 1921-42: bass.
Charles "Buddy" Bolden, 1868-1931: cornet; formed the first jazz band in the 1890s.
Big Bill Broonzy, 1893-1958: blues singer, guitar.
Clifford Brown, 1930-56: trumpet.
Ray Brown, b 1926: bass.
Dave Brubeck, b 1920: piano, combo leader.
Don Byas, 1912-72: tenor sax.
Harry Carney, 1910-74: baritone sax.
Benny Carter, b 1907: alto sax, trumpet, clarinet.
Ron Carter, b 1937: bass, cello.
Sidney Catlett, 1910-51: drums.
Charlie Christian, 1919-42: guitar.
Kenny Clarke, 1914-85: pioneer of modern drums.
Buck Clayton, 1911-91: trumpet, arranger.
Al Cohn, 1925-88: tenor sax, composer.
Cozy Cole, 1909-81: drums.
Ornette Coleman, b 1930: saxophone; unorthodox style.
John Coltrane, 1926-67: tenor sax innovator.
Eddie Condon, 1904-73: guitar, band leader; promoter of Dixieland.

Chick Corea, b 1941: pianist, composer.
Tadd Dameron, 1917-65: piano, composer.
Eddie "Lockjaw" Davis, 1921-86: tenor sax.
Miles Davis, 1926-91: trumpet; pioneer of cool jazz.
Wild Bill Davison, 1906-89: cornet, leader; prominent in early Chicago jazz.
Buddy De Franco, b 1933: clarinet.
Paul Desmond, 1924-77: alto sax.
Vic Dickenson, 1906-84: trombone, composer.
Warren "Baby" Dodds, 1898-1959: Dixieland drummer.
Johnny Dodds, 1892-1940: clarinet.
Eric Dolphy, 1928-64: alto sax, composer.
Jimmy Dorsey, 1904-57: clarinet, alto sax; band leader.
Tommy Dorsey, 1905-56: trombone; band leader.
Roy Eldridge, 1911-89: trumpet, drums, singer.
Duke Ellington, 1899-1974: piano, band leader, composer.
Bill Evans, 1929-80: piano.
Gil Evans, 1912-88: composer, arranger, piano.
Ella Fitzgerald, b 1918: singer.
"Red" Garland, 1923-84; piano.
Erroll Garner, 1921-77: piano, composer, "Misty."
Stan Getz, 1927-91: tenor sax.
Dizzy Gillespie, 1917-93: trumpet, composer; bop developer.
Benny Goodman, 1909-86: clarinet, band and combo leader.
Dexter Gordon, 1923-90: tenor sax; bop-derived style.
Stephane Grappelli, b 1908: violin.
Bobby Hackett, 1915-76: trumpet, cornet.
Lionel Hampton, b 1913: vibes, drums, piano, combo leader.
Herbie Hancock, b 1940: piano, composer.
W. C. Handy, 1873-1958: composer, "St. Louis Blues."
Coleman Hawkins, 1904-69: tenor sax; 1939 recording of "Body and Soul" a classic.
Roy Haynes, b 1926: drums.
Fletcher Henderson, 1898-1952: orchestra leader, arranger, pioneered jazz and dance bands of the 30s.
Woody Herman, 1913-87: clarinet, alto sax, band leader.
Jay C. Higginbotham, 1906-73: trombone.
Earl "Fatha" Hines, 1905-83: piano, songwriter.
Johnny Hodges, 1906-70: alto sax.
Billie Holiday, 1915-59: blues singer, "Strange Fruit."
Sam "Lightnin' " Hopkins, 1912-82: blues singer, guitar.
Mahalia Jackson, 1911-72: gospel singer.
Milt Jackson, b 1923: vibes, piano, guitar.
Illinois Jacquet, b 1922: tenor sax.
Keith Jarrett, b 1945: technically phenomenal pianist.
Blind Lemon Jefferson, 1897-1930: blues singer, guitar.
Bunk Johnson, 1879-1949: cornet, trumpet.
James P. Johnson, 1891-1955: piano, composer.
J. J. Johnson, b 1924: trombone, composer.
Elvin Jones, b 1927: drums.
Jo Jones, 1911-85: drums.
Philly Joe Jones, 1923-85: drums.
Quincy Jones, b 1933: arranger.
Thad Jones, 1923-86: trumpet, cornet.
Scott Joplin, 1868-1917: composer, "Maple Leaf Rag."
Stan Kenton, 1912-79: orchestra leader, composer, piano.
Barney Kessel, b 1923: guitar.
Lee Konitz, b 1927: alto sax.
Gene Krupa, 1909-73: drums, band and combo leader.
Scott LaFaro, 1936-61: bass.
Huddie Ledbetter (Leadbelly), 1888-1949: blues singer, guitar.
John Lewis, b 1920: composer, piano, combo leader.
Mel Lewis, 1929-90: drummer, orchestra leader.
Jimmie Lunceford, 1902-47: band leader, sax.
Herbie Mann, b 1930: flute.
Wynton Marsalis, b 1961: trumpet.
Jimmy McPartland, 1907-91: trumpet.
Marian McPartland, b 1920: piano.
Glenn Miller, 1904-44: trombone, dance band leader.
Charles Mingus, 1922-79: bass, composer, combo leader.
Thelonious Monk, 1920-82: piano, composer, combo leader; a developer of bop.
Wes Montgomery, 1925-68: guitar.
"Jelly Roll" Morton, 1885-1941: composer, piano, singer.
Bennie Moten, 1894-1935: piano; an early organizer of large jazz orchestras.
Gerry Mulligan, b 1927: baritone sax, arranger, leader.
Turk Murphy, 1915-87: trombone, band leader.
Theodore "Fats" Navarro, 1923-50: trumpet.
Red Nichols, 1905-65: cornet, combo leader.
Red Norvo, b 1908: vibes, band leader.
Anita O'Day, b 1919: singer.
King Oliver, 1885-1938: cornet, band leader; teacher of Louis Armstrong.
Sy Oliver, 1910-88: Swing Era arranger, composer, conductor.
Kid Ory, 1886-1973: trombone, "Muskrat Ramble".
Charlie "Bird" Parker, 1920-55: alto sax, composer; rated by many as the greatest jazz improviser.
Joe Pass, 1929-94: guitarist.
Art Pepper, 1925-82: alto sax.
Oscar Peterson, b 1925: piano, composer, combo leader.
Oscar Pettiford, 1922-60: a leading bassist in the bop era.
Bud Powell, 1924-66: piano; modern jazz pioneer.
Tito Puente, b 1923: band leader.
Sun Ra, 1915?-93: big band leader, pianist, composer.
Gertrude "Ma" Rainey, 1886-1939: blues singer.
Don Redman, 1900-64: composer, arranger; pioneer in the evolution of the large orchestra.
Django Reinhardt, 1910-53: guitar; Belgian gypsy, first European to influence American jazz.
Buddy Rich, 1917-87: drums, band leader.
Max Roach, b 1925: drums.
Red Rodney, 1928-94: trumpeter.
Sonny Rollins, b 1929: tenor sax.
Frank Rosollino, 1926-78: trombone.
Jimmy Rushing, 1903-72: blues singer.
George Russell, b 1923: composer, piano.
Pee Wee Russell, 1906-69: clarinet.
Artie Shaw, b 1910: clarinet, combo leader.
George Shearing, b 1919: piano, composer.
Horace Silver, b 1928: piano, combo leader.
Zoot Sims, 1925-85: tenor, alto sax; clarinet.
Zutty Singleton, 1898-1975: Dixieland drummer.
Bessie Smith, 1894-1937: blues singer.
Clarence "Pinetop" Smith, 1904-29: piano, singer; pioneer of boogie woogie.
Willie "The Lion" Smith, 1897-1973: stride style pianist.
Muggsy Spanier, 1906-67: cornet, band leader.
Billy Strayhorn, 1915-67: composer, piano.
Sonny Stitt, 1924-82: alto, tenor sax.
Art Tatum, 1910-56: piano; technical virtuoso.
Billy Taylor, b 1921: piano, composer.
Cecil Taylor, b 1933: piano, composer.
Jack Teagarden, 1905-64: trombone, singer.
Mel Torme, b 1925: singer.
Dave Tough, 1908-48: drums.
Lennie Tristano, 1919-78: piano, composer.
Joe Turner, 1911-85: blues singer.
McCoy Tyner, b 1938: piano, composer.
Sarah Vaughan, 1924-90: singer.
Joe Venuti, 1904-78: first great jazz violinist.
Thomas "Fats" Waller, 1904-43: piano, singer, composer, "Ain't Misbehavin'".
Dinah Washington, 1924-63: singer.
Chick Webb, 1902-39: band leader, drums.
Ben Webster, 1909-73: tenor sax.
Paul Whiteman, 1890-1967: orchestra leader; a major figure in the introduction of jazz to a large audience.
Charles "Cootie" Williams, 1908-85: trumpet, band leader.
Mary Lou Williams, 1914-81: piano, composer.
Teddy Wilson, 1912-86: piano, composer.
Kai Winding, 1922-83: trombone, composer.
Jimmy Yancey, 1894-1951: piano.
Lester "Pres" Young, 1909-59: tenor sax, composer: a bop pioneer.

Rock & Roll Notables

For more than a quarter-century, rock & roll has been an important force in American popular culture. The following individuals or groups have made a significant impact. Next to each is an associated single record or record album.

Paula Abdul: "Forever Your Girl"
Aerosmith: "Sweet Emotion"
The Allman Brothers Band: "Ramblin' Man"
The Animals: "House of the Rising Sun"
Paul Anka: "Lonely Boy"
The Association: "Cherish"
Frankie Avalon: "Venus"

The Band: "The Weight"
The Beach Boys: "Good Vibrations"
The Beatles: *Sergeant Pepper's Lonely-Hearts Club Band*
The Bee Gees: "Stayin' Alive"
Pat Benatar: "Hit Me With Your Best Shot"
Chuck Berry: "Johnny B. Goode"
The Big Bopper: "Chantilly Lace"
Black Sabbath: "Paranoid"
Blind Faith: "Can't Find My Way Home"
Blondie: "Heart of Glass"
Blood, Sweat and Tears: "Spinning Wheel"
Bon Jovi: *Slippery When Wet*

Gary "U.S." Bonds: "Quarter to Three"
Booker T. and the MGs: "Green Onions"
Earl Bostic: "Flamingo"
David Bowie: "Let's Dance"
James Brown: "Papa's Got a Brand New Bag"
Jackson Browne: "Doctor My Eyes"
Buffalo Springfield: "For What It's Worth"
The Byrds: "Turn! Turn! Turn!"

Canned Heat: "Going Up the Country"
The Cars: "Shake It Up"
Tracy Chapman: "Fast Car"
Ray Charles: "Georgia on My Mind"
Chubby Checker: "The Twist"
Chicago: "Saturday in the Park"
Eric Clapton: "Layla"
The Coasters: "Yakety Yak"
Eddie Cochran: "Summertime Blues"
Phil Collins: "Another Day in Paradise"
Sam Cooke: "You Send Me"
Alice Cooper: "School's Out"
Elvis Costello: "Alison"
Cream: "Sunshine of Your Love"
Creedence Clearwater Revival: "Proud Mary"
Crosby, Stills, Nash and Young: "Suite: Judy Blue Eyes"
The Crystals: "Da Doo Ron Ron"

DJ Jazzy Jeff & the Fresh Prince: "Summertime"
Danny and the Juniors: "At the Hop"
Bobby Darin: "Splish Splash"
Spencer Davis Group: "Gimme Some Lovin'"
Bo Diddley: "Who Do You Love?"
Dion and the Belmonts: "A Teenager in Love"
Dire Straits: *Brothers in Arms*
Fats Domino: "Blueberry Hill"
The Doobie Brothers: "What a Fool Believes"
The Doors: "Light My Fire"
The Drifters: "Save the Last Dance for Me"
Bob Dylan: "Like a Rolling Stone"

The Eagles: "Hotel California"
Earth, Wind and Fire: "Shining Star"
Emerson, Lake and Palmer: "From the Beginning"
The Eurythmics: "Sweet Dreams (Are Made of This)"
Everly Brothers: "Wake Up Little Susie"

The Five Satins: "In the Still of the Night"
Fleetwood Mac: *Rumours*
The Four Seasons: "Sherry"
The Four Tops: "I Can't Help Myself"
Aretha Franklin: "Respect"

Marvin Gaye: "I Heard It Through the Grapevine"
Grand Funk Railroad: "We're an American Band"
The Grateful Dead: "Truckin' "
Guns N' Roses: *Appetite for Destruction*

Bill Haley and the Comets: "Rock Around the Clock"
M. C. Hammer: "U Can't Touch This"
Jimi Hendrix: *Are You Experienced?*
Buddy Holly and the Crickets: "That'll Be the Day"
Whitney Houston: "The Greatest Love"

The Isley Brothers: "It's Your Thing"

The Jackson 5/The Jacksons: "ABC"
Janet Jackson: *Rhythm Nation*
Michael Jackson: *Thriller*
Tommy James & The Shondells: "Crimson and Clover"
Jay and the Americans: "This Magic Moment"
The Jefferson Airplane/Jefferson Starship: "White Rabbit"
Jethro Tull: *Aqualung*
Joan Jett: "I Love Rock' n' Roll"
Billy Joel: "Piano Man"
Elton John: "Sad Songs"
Janis Joplin: "Me and Bobby McGee"

Chaka Khan: "I Feel for You"
B. B. King: "The Thrill Is Gone"
Carole King: *Tapestry*
The Kinks: "You Really Got Me"
Kiss: "Rock' n' Roll All Night"
Gladys Knight and the Pips: "Midnight Train to Georgia"
L. L. Cool J: "Mama Said Knock You Out"
Led Zeppelin: "Stairway to Heaven"
Brenda Lee: "I'm Sorry"
John Lennon: "Imagine"
Jerry Lee Lewis: "Whole Lotta Shakin' Going On"
Little Anthony and the Imperials: "Tears on My Pillow"
Little Richard: "Tutti Frutti"
Lovin Spoonful: "Do You Believe in Magic?"
Frankie Lymon: "Why Do Fools Fall in Love?"
Lynyrd Skynyrd: "Freebird"

Madonna: "Material Girl"
The Mamas and the Papas: "Monday, Monday"
Bob Marley: "Jamming"
Martha and the Vandellas: "Dancin' in the Streets"
The Marvelettes: "Please Mr. Postman"
Paul McCartney: *Band on the Run*
Clyde McPhatter: "Money Honey"
John Mellencamp: "Hurt So Good"
George Michael: *Faith*
Joni Mitchell: "Big Yellow Taxi"
The Monkees: "I'm a Believer"
Moody Blues: "Nights in White Satin"

Rick Nelson: "Hello Mary Lou"
Nirvana: *Nevermind*

Roy Orbison: "Oh Pretty Woman"

Pearl Jam: *Ten*
Carl Perkins: "Blue Suede Shoes"
Tom Petty and the Heartbreakers: "Refugee"
Pink Floyd: *The Wall*
Poco: *Deliverin'*
The Police: "Every Breath You Take"
Iggy Pop: "Lust for Life"
Elvis Presley: "Love Me Tender"
The Pretenders: *Learning to Crawl*
Lloyd Price: "Stagger Lee"
Prince: "Purple Rain"
Procol Harum: "A Whiter Shade of Pale"
Public Enemy: "Fight the Power"

Queen: "Bohemian Rhapsody"

R.E.M.: "Losing My Religion"
The Rascals: "Good Lovin' "
Otis Redding: "The Dock of the Bay"
Lou Reed: "Walk on the Wild Side"
Righteous Brothers: "You've Lost that Lovin' Feeling"
Johnny Rivers: "Poor Side of Town"
Smokey Robinson and the Miracles: "Ooh Baby Baby"
The Rolling Stones: "Satisfaction"
The Ronettes: "Be My Baby"
Linda Ronstadt: "You're No Good"
Run D.M.C.: "Raisin' Hell"

Sam and Dave: "Soul Man"
Santana: "Black Magic Woman"
Neil Sedaka: "Breaking Up Is Hard to Do"
Del Shannon: "Runaway"
The Shirelles: "Soldier Boy"
Simon and Garfunkel: "Bridge Over Troubled Water"
Carly Simon: "You're So Vain"
Paul Simon: *Graceland*
Sly and the Family Stone: "Everyday People"
Patti Smith: "Because the Night"
Southside Johnny and the Asbury Jukes: *This Time*
Dusty Springfield: "You Don't Have to Say You Love Me"
Bruce Springsteen: "Born in the U.S.A."
Steely Dan: "Rikki Don't Lose That Number"
Steppenwolf: "Born to Be Wild"
Rod Stewart: "Maggie Mae"
Sting: "If You Love Somebody, Set Them Free"
Donna Summer: "She Works Hard for the Money"
The Supremes: "Stop! In the Name of Love"

Talking Heads: "Once in a Lifetime"
James Taylor: "You've Got a Friend"
The Temptations: "My Girl"
Three Dog Night: "Joy to the World"
Traffic: "Feelin' Alright"
Big Joe Turner: "Shake, Rattle & Roll"
Tina Turner: "What's Love Got to Do with It?"

U2: *Joshua Tree*

Van Halen: "Jump"

Dionne Warwick: "I'll Never Fall in Love Again"
Muddy Waters: "Rollin' Stone"
Mary Wells: "My Guy"
The Who: "My Generation"
Jackie Wilson: "That's Why"
Stevie Wonder: "You Are the Sunshine of My Life"

The Yardbirds: "For Your Love"
Yes: "Yours Is No Disgrace"
Frank Zappa/Mothers of Invention: *Sheik Yerbouti*

Entertainment Personalities — Where and When Born

Actors, Actresses, Dancers, Musicians, Producers, Directors, Radio-TV Performers, Singers
(As of mid-1994)

Name	Birthplace	Birthdate
Abbado, Claudio	Milan, Italy	6/26/33
Abbott, George	Forestville, NY	6/25/1887
Abdul, Paula	San Fernando, CA	6/19/62
Abraham, F. Murray	Pittsburgh, PA	10/24/39
Adams, Bryan	Kingston, Ontario.	11/5/59
Adams, Don	New York, NY	4/19/26
Adams, Edie	Kingston, PA	4/16/29
Adams, Joey	New York, NY	1/6/11
Adams, Mason	New York, NY	2/26/19
Adjani, Isabelle	W Germany	6/27/55
Agutter, Jenny	London, England	12/20/52
Aiello, Danny	New York, NY	6/20/33
Aimee, Anouk	Paris, France	4/27/32
Albanese, Licia	Bari, Italy	7/22/13
Alberghetti, Anna Maria	Pesaro, Italy	5/15/36
Albert, Eddie	Rock Island, IL	4/22/08
Albert, Marv	New York, NY	6/12/43
Alda, Alan	New York, NY	1/28/36
Alexander, Jane	Boston, MA	10/28/39
Alexander, Jason	Newark, NJ	9/23/59
Allen, Debbie	Houston, TX	1/16/50
Allen, Joan	Rochelle, IL	8/20/56
Allen, Karen	Carrollton, IL	10/5/51
Allen, Mel	Birmingham, AL	2/14/13
Allen, Nancy	New York, NY	6/24/49
Allen, Steve	New York, NY	12/26/21
Allen, Tim	Denver, CO	6/13/--
Allen, Woody	Brooklyn, NY	12/1/35
Alley, Kirstie	Wichita, KS	1/12/55
Allman, Gregg	Nashville, TN	12/7/47
Allyson, June	New York, NY	10/7/17
Alonso, Maria Conchita	Cuba	1957
Alpert, Herb	Los Angeles, CA	3/31/35
Altman, Robert	Kansas City, MO	2/20/25
Ames, Ed	Boston, MA	7/9/27
Amos, John	Newark, NJ	12/27/42
Amsterdam, Morey	Chicago, IL	12/14/14
Anderson, Harry	Newport, RI	10/14/49
Anderson, Ian	Dunfermline, Scotland	8/10/47
Anderson, Kevin	Illinois	1/13/60
Anderson, Loni	St. Paul, MN	8/5/46
Anderson, Lynn	Grand Forks, ND	9/26/47
Anderson, Melissa Sue	Berkeley, CA	9/26/62
Anderson, Richard	Long Branch, NJ	8/8/26
Anderson, Richard Dean	Minneapolis, MN	1/23/50
Andersson, Bibi	Stockholm, Sweden	11/11/35
Andress, Ursula	Bern, Switzerland	3/19/36
Andrews, Anthony	London, England	1/12/48
Andrews, Julie	Walton, England	10/1/35
Andrews, Maxene	Minneapolis, MN	1/3/18
Andrews, Patty	Minneapolis, MN	2/16/20
Anka, Paul	Ottawa, Ontario	7/30/41
Ann-Margret	Stockholm, Sweden	4/28/41
Anton, Susan	Oak Glen, CA	10/12/50
Applegate, Christina	Los Angeles, CA	11/25/72
Archer, Anne	Los Angeles, CA	8/25/50
Arkin, Alan	New York, NY	3/26/34
Arnaz, Desi Jr.	Los Angeles, CA	1/19/53
Arnaz, Lucie	Hollywood, CA	7/17/51
Arness, James	Minneapolis, MN	5/26/23
Arnold, Eddy	Henderson, TN	5/15/18
Arquette, Rosanna	New York, NY	8/10/59
Arroyo, Martina	New York, NY	2/2/37
Arthur, Beatrice	New York, NY	5/13/26
Ashley, Elizabeth	Ocala, FL	8/30/41
Asner, Ed	Kansas City, MO	11/15/29
Assante, Armand	New York, NY	10/4/49
Astin, John	Baltimore, MD	3/30/30
Atherton, William	New Haven, CT	7/30/47
Atkins, Chet	Luttrell, TN	6/20/24
Attenborough, Richard	Cambridge, England	8/29/23
Auberjonois, Rene	New York, NY	6/1/40
Aumont, Jean-Pierre	Paris, France	1/5/09
Austin, Patti	New York, NY	8/10/48
Autry, Alan	Shreveport, LA	7/31/52
Autry, Gene	Tioga, TX	9/29/07
Avalon, Frankie	Philadelphia, PA	9/18/39
Ax, Emmanuel	Lvov, Ukraine	6/8/49

Name	Birthplace	Birthdate
Axton, Hoyt	Duncan, OK	3/25/38
Aykroyd, Dan	Ottawa, Ontario	7/1/52
Ayres, Lew	Minneapolis, MN	12/28/08
Aznavour, Charles	Paris, France	5/22/24
Bacall, Lauren	New York, NY	9/16/24
Bacon, Kevin	Philadelphia, PA	7/8/58
Baez, Joan	Staten Island, NY	1/9/41
Bain, Conrad	Lethbridge, Alberta	2/4/23
Baio, Scott	Brooklyn, NY	9/22/61
Baker, Anita	Toledo, OH	1/26/58
Baker, Carroll	Johnstown, PA	5/28/31
Baker, Joe Don	Groesbeck, TX	2/12/36
Bakula, Scott	St. Louis, MO	10/9/--
Baldwin, Alec	Massapequa, N.Y.	4/3/58
Baldwin, William	Massapequa, NY	1963
Ballard, Kaye	Cleveland, OH	11/20/26
Balsam, Martin	New York, NY	11/4/19
Bancroft, Anne	New York, NY	9/17/31
Banks, Jonathan	Washington, DC	1/31/47
Bannon, Jack	Los Angeles, CA	6/14/40
Barbeau, Adrienne	Sacramento, CA	6/11/45
Bardot, Brigitte	Paris, France	9/28/34
Barker, Bob	Darrington, WA	12/12/23
Barkin, Ellen	New York, NY	4/16/55
Barrault, Jean-Louis	Vesinet, France	9/8/10
Barrie, Barbara	Chicago, IL	5/23/31
Barry, Gene	New York, NY	6/14/19
Barty, Billy	Millsboro, PA	10/25/24
Barrymore, Drew	Los Angeles, CA	2/22/75
Baryshnikov, Mikhail	Riga, Latvia	1/28/48
Basinger, Kim	Athens, GA	12/8/53
Bassey, Shirley	Cardiff, Wales	1/8/37
Bateman, Jason	Rye, NY	1/14/69
Bateman, Justine	Rye, NY	2/19/66
Bates, Alan	Allestree, England	2/17/34
Bates, Kathy	Memphis, TN	6/28/48
Battle, Kathleen	Portsmouth, OH	8/13/48
Baxter, Meredith	Los Angeles, CA	6/21/47
Beal, John	Joplin, MO	8/13/09
Beasley, Allyce	New York, NY	7/6/54
Beatty, Ned	Louisville, KY	7/6/37
Beatty, Warren	Richmond, VA	3/30/37
Beck, John	Chicago, IL	1/28/43
Bedelia, Bonnie	New York, NY	3/25/48
Beery, Noah Jr.	New York, NY	8/10/13
Begley, Ed Jr.	Los Angeles, CA	9/16/49
Belafonte, Harry	New York, NY	3/1/27
Bel Geddes, Barbara	New York, NY	10/31/22
Belmondo, Jean-Paul	Neuilly-sur-Seine, France	4/9/33
Belushi, Jim	Chicago, IL	6/15/54
Benatar, Pat	Brooklyn, NY	1/10/53
Benedict, Dirk	Helena, MT	3/1/45
Bening, Annette	Topeka, KS	1958
Benjamin, Richard	New York, NY	5/22/38
Bennett, Tony	New York, NY	8/3/26
Benson, George	Pittsburgh, PA	3/22/43
Benson, Robby	Dallas, TX	1/21/55
Beradino, John	Los Angeles, CA	5/1/17
Berenger, Tom	Chicago, IL	5/31/50
Bergen, Candice	Beverly Hills, CA	5/9/46
Bergen, Polly	Knoxville, TN	7/14/30
Bergerac, Jacques	Biarritz, France	5/26/27
Bergman, Ingmar	Uppsala, Sweden	7/14/18
Berle, Milton	New York, NY	7/12/08
Berlinger, Warren	Brooklyn, NY	8/31/37
Berman, Lazar	Leningrad, Russia	2/26/30
Berman, Shelley	Chicago, IL	2/3/26
Bernard, Crystal	Dallas, TX	9/30/64
Bernhard, Sandra	Flint, MI	6/6/55
Bernsen, Corbin	N. Hollywood, CA	9/7/55
Berry, Chuck	St. Louis, MO	10/18/26
Berry, Halle	Cleveland, OH	1969
Berry, Ken	Moline, IL	11/3/33
Bertinelli, Valerie	Wilmington, DE	4/23/60
Bialik, Mayim	San Diego, CA	12/12/75
Bikel, Theodore	Vienna, Austria	5/2/24
Birney, David	Washington, DC	4/23/39
Bishop, Joey	Bronx, NY	2/3/18
Bisoglio, Val	New York, NY	5/7/26
Bisset, Jacqueline	Weybridge, England	9/13/44
Black, Clint	Katy, TX	1962

Name	Birthplace	Birthdate
Black, Karen	Park Ridge, IL	7/1/42
Blackstone Jr., Harry	Three Rivers, MI	6/30/34
Blades, Ruben	Panama City, Panama	7/16/48
Blaine, Vivian	Newark, NJ	11/21/21
Blair, Linda	St. Louis, MO	1/22/59
Blake, Robert	Nutley, NJ	9/18/33
Bledsoe, Tempestt	Chicago, IL	8/1/73
Bloom, Claire	London, England	2/15/31
Blyth, Ann	Mt. Kisco, NY	8/16/28
Bochco, Steven	New York, NY	12/16/43
Bogarde, Dirk	London, England	3/28/20
Bogosian, Eric	Boston, MA	4/24/53
Bogdanovich, Peter	Kingston, NY	7/30/39
Bolton, Michael	New Haven, CT	—
Bonham-Carter, Helena	London, England	5/26/66
Bon Jovi, Jon	Sayreville, NJ	3/2/62
Bono, Sonny	Detroit, MI	2/16/35
Boone, Debby	Hackensack, NJ	9/22/56
Boone, Pat	Jacksonville, FL	6/1/34
Borge, Victor	Copenhagen, Denmark	1/3/09
Borgnine, Ernest	Hamden, CT	1/24/17
Bosco, Philip	Jersey City, NJ	9/26/30
Bosley, Tom	Chicago, IL	10/1/27
Bostwick, Barry	San Mateo, CA	2/24/46
Bottoms, Timothy	Santa Barbara, CA	8/30/51
Bowie, David	London, England	1/8/47
Boxleitner, Bruce	Elgin, IL	5/12/50
Boy George	London, England	6/14/61
Boyle, Peter	Philadelphia, PA	10/18/33
Bracco, Lorraine	New York, NY	1955
Bracken, Eddie	New York, NY	2/7/20
Branagh, Kenneth	Belfast, No. Ireland	12/10/60
Brando, Marlon	Omaha, NE	4/3/24
Brazzi, Rossano	Bologna, Italy	9/18/16
Brennan, Eileen	Los Angeles, CA	9/3/35
Brenner, David	Philadelphia, PA	2/4/45
Brewer, Teresa	Toledo, OH	5/7/31
Bridges, Beau	Hollywood, CA	12/9/41
Bridges, Jeff	Los Angeles, CA	12/4/49
Bridges, Lloyd	San Leandro, CA	1/15/13
Brimley, Wilford	Salt Lake City, UT	9/27/34
Broderick, Matthew	New York, NY	3/21/62
Brolin, James	Los Angeles, CA	7/18/40
Bronson, Charles	Ehrenfeld, PA	11/3/22
Brooks, Albert	Beverly Hills, CA	7/22/47
Brooks, Avery	Evansville, IN	10/2/48
Brooks, Garth	Tulsa, OK	2/7/62
Brooks, Mel	New York, NY	6/28/26
Brosnan, Pierce	Co. Meath, Ireland	5/15/53
Brown, Blair	Washington, DC	1948
Brown, Bryan	Sydney, Australia	1947
Brown, James	Pulaski, TN	6/17/28
Brown, Jim	St. Simons Island, GA	2/17/36
Brown, Les	Reinerton, PA	3/14/12
Brown, Ray	Pittsburgh, PA	10/13/26
Browne, Roscoe Lee	Woodbury, NJ	5/2/25
Buckley, Betty	Ft. Worth, TX	7/3/47
Bujold, Genevieve	Montreal, Quebec	7/1/42
Bumbry, Grace	St. Louis, MO	1/4/37
Burghoff, Gary	Bristol, CT	5/24/40
Burke, Delta	Orlando, FL	7/30/56
Burnett, Carol	San Antonio, TX	4/26/33
Burns, George	New York, NY	1/20/1896
Burrows, Darren E.	Winfield, KS	9/12/66
Burstyn, Ellen	Detroit, MI	12/7/32
Burton, LeVar	Landstuhl, W Germany	2/16/57
Busey, Gary	Goose Creek, TX	6/29/44
Busfield, Timothy	Lansing, MI	6/12/57
Butkus, Dick	Chicago, IL	12/9/42
Buttons, Red	New York, NY	2/5/19
Buzzi, Ruth	Westerly, RI	7/24/36
Byrne, David	Dumbarton, Scotland	5/14/52
Caan, James	New York, NY	3/26/39
Caballe, Montserrat	Barcelona, Spain	4/12/33
Caesar, Sid	Yonkers, NY	9/8/22
Cage, Nicolas	Long Beach, CA	1/7/64
Caine, Michael	London, England	3/14/33
Caldwell, Sarah	Maryville, MO	3/6/24
Caldwell, Zoe	Melbourne, Australia	9/14/33
Calhoun, Rory	Los Angeles, CA	8/8/23
Calloway, Cab	Rochester, NY	12/25/07
Cameron, Kirk	Panorama City, CA	10/12/70
Camp, Hamilton	London, England	10/30/34
Campanella, Joseph	New York, NY	11/21/27
Campbell, Glen	Billstown, AK	4/22/36
Cannell, Stephen J.	Los Angeles, CA	2/5/42
Cannon, Dyan	Tacoma, WA	1/4/37
Cantrell, Lana	Sydney, Australia	8/7/43
Cara, Irene	New York, NY	3/18/59
Carey, Mariah	Huntington, NY	1970
Cariou, Len	Winnipeg, Canada	9/30/39
Carlin, George	New York, NY	5/12/37
Carlisle, Kitty	New Orleans, LA	9/3/15
Carmen, Eric	Cleveland, OH	8/11/49
Carmichael, Ian	Hull, England	6/18/20
Carney, Art	Mt. Vernon, NY	11/4/18
Caron, Leslie	Boulogne, France	7/1/31
Carr, Vikki	El Paso, TX	7/19/41
Carradine, David	Hollywood, CA	10/8/36
Carradine, Keith	San Mateo, CA	8/8/49
Carreras, Jose	Barcelona, Spain	12/5/47
Carroll, Diahann	Bronx, NY	7/17/35
Carroll, Pat	Shreveport, LA	5/5/27
Carrey, Jim	Newmarket, Ontario	1963
Carson, Johnny	Corning, IA	10/23/25
Carter, Dixie	McLemoresville, TN	5/25/39
Carter, Jack	New York, NY	6/24/23
Carter, June	Maces Spring, VA	6/23/29
Carter, Lynda	Phoenix, AZ	7/24/51
Carter, Nell	Birmingham, AL	9/13/48
Caruso, David	Forest Hills, NY	1/17/56
Carvey, Dana	Missoula, MT	6/6/55
Casadesus, Gaby	Marseilles, France	8/9/01
Cash, Johnny	Kingsland, AK	2/26/32
Cash, Rosanne	Memphis, TN	5/24/55
Cass, Peggy	Boston, MA	5/21/24
Cassidy, David	New York, NY	4/12/50
Cavett, Dick	Gibbon, NE	11/19/36
Chamberlain, Richard	Beverly Hills, CA	3/31/35
Channing, Carol	Seattle, WA	1/31/23
Channing, Stockard	New York, NY	2/13/44
Chaplin, Geraldine	Santa Monica, CA	7/31/44
Chapman, Tracy	Cleveland, OH	1964
Charisse, Cyd	Amarillo, TX	3/8/21
Charles, Ray	Albany, GA	9/23/30
Charo	Murcia, Spain	1/15/51
Chase, Chevy	New York, NY	10/8/43
Checker, Chubby	Philadelphia, PA	10/3/41
Cher	El Centro, CA	5/20/46
Chiklis, Michael	Lowell, MA	8/30/63
Chong, Rae Dawn	California	1962
Chong, Thomas	Edmonton, Alberta	5/24/38
Christie, Julie	Assam, India	4/14/40
Christopher, William	Evanston, IL	10/20/32
Church, Thomas Hayden	El Paso, TX	6/17/-
Clapton, Eric	Surrey, England	3/30/45
Clark, Dane	New York, NY	2/18/13
Clark, Dick	Mt. Vernon, NY	11/30/29
Clark, Petula	Ewell, Surrey, England	11/15/32
Clark, Roy	Meherrin, VA	4/15/33
Clark, Susan	Sarnia, Ontario	3/8/40
Clary, Robert	Paris, France	3/1/26
Clayburgh, Jill	New York, NY	4/30/44
Cleese, John	England	10/27/39
Cliburn, Van	Shreveport, LA	7/12/34
Clooney, Rosemary	Maysville, KY	5/23/28
Close, Glenn	Greenwich, CT	3/19/47
Coburn, James	Laurel, NE	8/31/28
Coca, Imogene	Philadelphia, PA	11/18/08
Colbert, Claudette	Paris, France	9/13/03
Cole, Gary	Park Ridge, IL	9/20/57
Cole, Natalie	Los Angeles, CA	2/6/50
Cole, Olivia	Memphis, TN	11/26/42
Coleman, Dabney	Austin, TX	1/3/32
Coleman, Gary	Zion, IL	2/8/68
Collins, Joan	London, England	5/23/33
Collins, Judy	Seattle, WA	5/1/39
Collins, Pauline	Exmouth, England	9/3/40
Collins, Phil	London, England	1/30/51
Comden, Betty	Brooklyn, NY	5/3/19
Como, Perry	Canonsburg, PA	5/18/12
Conner, Nadine	Compton, CA	2/20/13
Connery, Sean	Edinburgh, Scotland	8/25/30
Connick Jr., Harry	New Orleans, LA	9/11/67
Conniff, Ray	Attleboro, MA	11/6/16
Connors, Mike	Fresno, CA	8/15/25
Conrad, Robert	Chicago, IL	3/1/35
Constantine, Michael	Reading, PA	5/22/27
Conti, Tom	Paisley, Scotland	11/22/41
Conway, Tim	Willoughby, OH	12/15/33
Cook, Barbara	Atlanta, GA	10/25/27
Cook, Peter	Torquay, England	11/17/37
Cooke, Alistair	Manchester, England	11/20/08
Coolidge, Rita	Nashville, TN	5/1/45

Name	Birthplace	Birthdate
Cooper, Alice	Detroit, MI	2/4/48
Cooper, Jackie	Los Angeles, CA	9/15/21
Copperfield, David	Metuchen, NJ	9/16/56
Coppola, Francis	Detroit, MI	4/7/39
Corbin, Barry	Lamesa, TX	10/16/40
Corby, Ellen	Racine, WI	6/3/13
Cord, Alex	New York, NY	8/3/31
Corea, Chick	Chelsea, MA	6/12/41
Corelli, Franco	Ancona, Italy	4/8/23
Corey, Jeff	New York, NY	8/10/14
Cosby, Bill	Philadelphia, PA	7/12/37
Costas, Bob	New York, NY	3/22/52
Costello, Elvis	London, England	8/25/54
Costner, Kevin	Compton, CA	1/18/55
Cougar, John	Seymour, IN	10/7/51
Courtenay, Tom	Hull, England	2/25/37
Cox, Ronny	Cloudcroft, NM	8/23/38
Craddock, Crash	Greensboro, NC	6/16/40
Crain, Jeanne	Barstow, CA	5/25/25
Crawford, Michael	Salisbury, England	1/19/42
Crenna, Richard	Los Angeles, CA	11/30/26
Crespin, Regine	Marseilles, France	2/23/26
Cronyn, Hume	London, Ontario	7/18/11
Crosby, David	Los Angeles, CA	8/14/41
Cross, Ben	London, England	12/16/47
Crouse, Lindsay	New York, NY	5/12/48
Crowell, Rodney	Houston, TX	8/17/50
Cruise, Tom	Syracuse, NY	7/3/62
Crystal, Billy	Long Beach, NY	3/14/47
Culkin, Macaulay	New York, NY	8/26/80
Cullum, John	Knoxville, TN	3/2/30
Culp, Robert	Oakland, CA	8/16/30
Cummings, Constance	Seattle, WA	5/15/10
Curry, Tim	Cheshire, England	4/19/46
Curtin, Jane	Cambridge, MA	9/6/47
Curtis, Jamie Lee	Los Angeles, CA	11/22/58
Curtis, Keene	Salt Lake City, UT	2/15/23
Curtis, Tony	New York, NY	6/3/25
Cusack, Cyril	Durban, S Africa	11/26/10
Cusack, Joan	Evanston, IL	10/11/62
Cusack, John	Evanston, IL	6/28/66
Cyrus, Billy Ray	Flatwoods, KY	1961
Dafoe, Willem	Appleton, WI	7/22/55
Dahl, Arlene	Minneapolis, MN	8/11/28
Dale, Jim	Rothwell, England	8/15/35
Dalton, Abby	Las Vegas, NV	8/15/32
Dalton, Timothy	Wales	3/21/44
Daltrey, Roger	London, England	3/1/44
Daly, Timothy	Suffern, NY	3/1/58
Daly, Tyne	Madison, WI	2/21/47
Damone, Vic	Brooklyn, NY	6/12/28
D'Angelo, Beverly	Columbus, OH	11/15/54
Dangerfield, Rodney	Babylon, NY	11/22/22
Daniels, Charlie	Wilmington, NC	10/28/36
Daniels, Jeff	Georgia	2/19/55
Daniels, William	Brooklyn, NY	3/31/27
Danner, Blythe	Philadelphia, PA	2/3/44
Danson, Ted	San Diego, CA	12/29/47
Danza, Tony	New York, NY	4/21/50
Darby, Kim	Hollywood, CA	7/8/48
D'Arby, Terence Trent	New York, NY	3/15/62
Davidson, John	Pittsburgh, PA	12/13/41
Davis, Ann B.	Schenectady, NY	5/5/26
Davis, Clifton	Chicago, IL	10/4/45
Davis, Geena	Wareham, MA	1/21/57
Davis, Judy	Perth, Australia	1956
Davis, Mac	Lubbock, TX	1/21/42
Davis, Ossie	Cogdell, GA	12/18/17
Dawber, Pam	Farmington Hills, MI	10/18/51
Dawson, Richard	Hampshire, England	11/20/32
Day, Doris	Cincinnati, OH	4/3/24
Day-Lewis, Daniel	London, England	4/29/57
Dean, Jimmy	Plainview, TX	8/10/28
De Camp, Rosemary	Prescott, AZ	11/14/10
DeCarlo, Yvonne	Vancouver, B.C.	9/1/22
Dee, Frances	Los Angeles, CA	11/26/07
Dee, Ruby	Cleveland, OH	10/27/23
Dee, Sandra	Bayonne, NJ	4/23/42
DeHaven, Gloria	Los Angeles, CA	7/23/25
De Havilland, Olivia	Tokyo, Japan	7/1/16
Delany, Dana	New York, NY	3/13/57
Della Chiesa, Vivienne	Chicago, IL	10/9/20
Delon, Alain	Sceaux, France	11/8/35
DeLuise, Dom	Brooklyn, NY	8/1/33
Demme, Jonathan	Rockville Centre, NY	2/22/44
De Mornay, Rebecca	Santa Rosa, CA	11/29/61
Deneuve, Catherine	Paris, France	10/22/43
De Niro, Robert	New York, NY	8/17/43
Dennehy, Brian	Bridgeport, CT	7/9/38
Denver, Bob	New Rochelle, NY	1/9/35
Denver, John	Roswell, NM	12/31/43
DePalma, Brian	Newark, NJ	9/11/40
Depardieu, Gerard	Chateauroux, France	12/27/48
Depp, Johnny	Owensboro, KY	6/9/63
Derek, Bo	Long Beach, CA	11/20/56
Derek, John	Hollywood, CA	8/12/26
Dern, Bruce	Chicago, IL	6/4/36
Dern, Laura	Santa Monica, CA	2/1/67
Devane, William	Albany, NY	9/5/37
DeVito, Danny	Neptune, NJ	11/17/44
DeWitt, Joyce	Wheeling, WV	4/23/49
Dey, Susan	Pekin, IL	12/10/52
Diamond, Neil	Brooklyn, NY	1/24/41
Dickinson, Angie	Kulm, ND	9/30/31
Diddley, Bo	McComb, MS	12/20/28
Diller, Phyllis	Lima, OH	7/17/17
Dillman, Bradford	San Francisco, CA	4/14/30
Dillon, Matt	New Rochelle, NY	2/18/64
Dobson, Kevin	New York, NY	3/18/44
Doherty, Shannen	Memphis, TN	4/21/71
Domingo, Placido	Madrid, Spain	1/21/41
Domino, Fats	New Orleans, LA	2/26/28
Donahue, Phil	Cleveland, OH	12/21/35
Donahue, Troy	New York, NY	1/27/36
Dotrice, Roy	Guernsey, England	5/26/23
Douglas, Kirk	Amsterdam, NY	12/9/18
Douglas, Michael	New Brunswick, NJ	9/25/44
Down, Leslie-Ann	London, England	3/17/54
Downey, Robert Jr.	New York, NY	4/4/65
Downs, Hugh	Akron, OH	2/14/21
Drake, Larry	Tulsa, OK	2/21/--
Draper, Polly	Gary, IN	6/15/--
Drew, Ellen	Kansas City, MO	11/23/15
Dryer, Fred	Hawthorne, CA	7/6/46
Dreyfuss, Richard	Brooklyn, NY	10/29/47
Dru, Joanne	Logan, WV	1/31/23
Duffy, Julia	Minneapolis, MN	6/27/51
Duffy, Patrick	Townsend, MT	3/17/49
Dufour, Val	New Orleans, LA	2/5/27
Dukakis, Olympia	Lowell, MA	6/20/31
Duke, Patty	New York, NY	12/14/46
Dukes, David	San Francisco, CA	6/6/45
Dullea, Keir	Cleveland, OH	5/30/36
Dunaway, Faye	Bascom, FL	1/14/41
Duncan, Sandy	Henderson, TX	2/20/46
Dunham, Katherine	Joliet, IL	6/22/10
Dunne, Griffin	New York, NY	6/8/55
Durbin, Deanna	Winnipeg, Manitoba	12/4/21
Durning, Charles	Highland Falls, NY	2/28/23
Dussault, Nancy	Pensacola, FL	6/30/36
Dutton, Charles S.	Baltimore, MD	1/30/51
Duvall, Robert	San Diego, CA	1/5/31
Duvall, Shelley	Houston, TX	7/7/49
Dylan, Bob	Duluth, MN	5/24/41
Dysart, Richard	Augusta, ME	3/30/29
Dzundza, George	Rosenheim, Germany	7/19/45
Eastwood, Clint	San Francisco, CA	5/31/30
Ebert, Roger	Urbana, IL	6/18/42
Ebsen, Buddy	Belleville, IL	4/2/08
Edelman, Herb	Brooklyn, NY	11/5/33
Eden, Barbara	Tucson, AZ	8/23/34
Edwards, Anthony	Santa Barbara, CA	1/19/62
Edwards, Blake	Tulsa, OK	7/26/22
Edwards, Ralph	Merino, CO	6/13/13
Eichhorn, Lisa	Reading, PA	2/4/52
Eikenberry, Jill	New Haven, CT	1/21/47
Ekberg, Anita	Malmo, Sweden	9/29/31
Ekland, Britt	Stockholm, Sweden	10/6/42
Elam, Jack	Miami, AZ	11/13/16
Elizondo, Hector	New York, NY	12/22/36
Elliott, Bob	Boston, MA	3/26/23
Elliott, Sam	Sacramento, CA	8/9/44
Englund, Robert	Hollywood, CA	6/6/48
Elvira (Cassandra Peterson)	Manhattan, KS	9/17/51
Estefan, Gloria	Havana, Cuba	9/1/58
Estevez, Emilio	New York, NY	5/12/62
Estrada, Erik	New York, NY	3/16/49
Evans, Dale	Uvalde, TX	10/31/12
Evans, Linda	Hartford, CT	11/18/42
Evans, Robert	New York, NY	6/29/30
Everett, Chad	South Bend, IN	6/11/36
Everly, Don	Brownie, KY	2/1/37
Everly, Phil	Chicago, IL	1/19/38
Evigan, Greg	S. Amboy, NJ	10/14/53

Name	Birthplace	Birthdate
Fabares, Shelley	Santa Monica, CA	1/19/42
Fabian (Forte)	Philadelphia, PA.	2/6/43
Fabray, Nanette	San Diego, CA.	10/27/20
Fairbanks, Douglas Jr.	New York, NY	12/9/09
Fairchild, Morgan	Dallas, TX.	2/3/50
Falana, Lola	Philadelphia, PA.	9/11/46
Falk, Peter	New York, NY	9/16/27
Farentino, James	Brooklyn, NY	2/24/38
Fargo, Donna	Mt. Airy, NC	11/10/45
Farr, Jamie	Toledo, OH	7/1/34
Farrell, Eileen	Willimantic, CT.	2/13/20
Farrell, Mike	St. Paul, MN	2/6/39
Farrow, Mia	Los Angeles, CA	2/9/45
Faustino, David	California	3/3/74
Fawcett, Farrah	Corpus Christi, TX	2/2/47
Faye, Alice	New York, NY	5/5/12
Feinstein, Michael	Columbus, OH	9/7/56
Feld, Fritz	Berlin, Germany	10/15/00
Feldon, Barbara	Pittsburgh, PA	3/12/41
Feliciano, Jose	Lares, Puerto Rico	9/10/45
Fell, Norman	Philadelphia, PA.	3/24/24
Fenn, Sherilyn	Detroit, MI.	1965
Ferrell, Conchata	Charleston, WV	3/28/43
Ferrer, Mel	Elberon, NJ.	8/25/17
Fiedler, John	Platville, WI.	2/3/25
Field, Sally	Pasadena, CA.	11/6/46
Finney, Albert	Salford, England	5/9/36
Firkusny, Rudolf	Napajedla, Czechoslovakia	2/11/12
Firth, Peter	Yorkshire, England	10/27/53
Fischer-Dieskau, Dietrich	Berlin, Germany	5/28/25
Fishburne, Larry	Augusta, GA	7/30/61
Fisher, Carrie	Beverly Hills, CA	10/21/56
Fisher, Eddie	Philadelphia, PA.	8/10/28
Fitzgerald, Ella	Newport News, VA	4/25/18
Fitzgerald, Geraldine	Dublin, Ireland	11/24/13
Flack, Roberta	Black Mountain, NC	2/10/39
Flanagan, Fionnula	Dublin, Ireland	12/10/41
Flanders, Ed	Minneapolis, MN	12/29/34
Fleming, Rhonda	Hollywood, CA.	8/10/23
Fletcher, Louise	Birmingham, AL	7/22/34
Foch, Nina	Leyden, Netherlands	4/20/24
Fogelberg, Dan	Peoria, IL	8/13/51
Fonda, Bridget	Los Angeles, CA	1964
Fonda, Jane	New York, NY	12/21/37
Fonda, Peter	New York, NY	2/23/39
Fontaine, Joan	Tokyo, Japan.	10/22/17
Ford, Faith	Alexandria, LA.	9/14/--
Ford, Glenn	Quebec, Canada	5/1/16
Ford, Harrison	Chicago, IL	7/13/42
Forrest, Steve	Huntsville, TX	9/29/24
Forsythe, John	Penns Grove, NJ	1/29/18
Foster, Jodie	New York, NY	11/19/62
Fox, James	London, England	5/19/39
Fox, Michael J.	Edmonton, Alberta	6/9/61
Foxworth, Robert	Houston, TX	11/1/41
Frampton, Peter	Kent, England	4/22/50
Franciosa, Anthony	New York, NY	10/25/28
Francis, Anne	Ossining, NY.	9/16/30
Francis, Arlene	Boston, MA.	10/20/08
Francis, Connie	Newark, NJ.	12/12/38
Frankenheimer, John	Malba, NY.	2/19/30
Franklin, Aretha	Memphis, TN.	3/25/42
Franklin, Bonnie	Santa Monica, CA	1/6/44
Franklin, Joe	New York, NY	1929
Frann, Mary	St. Louis, MO	2/27/43
Franz, Dennis	Maywood, IL	10/28/44
Freeman Jr., Al	San Antonio, TX.	3/21/34
Freeman, Morgan	Memphis, TN.	6/1/37
Friedkin, William	Chicago, IL	8/29/39
Frost, David	Tenterden, England	4/7/39
Funicello, Annette	Utica, NY	10/22/42
Funt, Allen	New York, NY	9/16/14
Gabor, Eva	Hungary	1921
Gabor, Zsa Zsa	Hungary	2/6/17
Gabriel, John	Niagara Falls, NY	5/25/31
Gabriel, Peter	London, England	2/13/50
Gail, Max	Detroit, MI.	4/5/43
Galway, James	Belfast, Ireland.	12/8/39
Garagiola, Joe	St. Louis, MO	2/12/26
Garcia, Andy	Havana, Cuba	4/12/56
Garfunkel, Art	New York, NY	11/5/41
Garland, Beverly	Santa Cruz, CA	10/17/26
Garner, James	Norman, OK	4/7/28
Garr, Teri	Lakewood, OH.	12/11/45
Garrett, Betty	St. Joseph, MO	5/23/19
Garson, Greer	Co. Down, N Ireland	9/29/08
Garth, Jennie	Champaign, IL	4/3/--
Gatlin, Larry	Seminole, TX.	5/2/48
Gayle, Crystal	Paintsville, KY	1/9/51
Gaynor, Mitzi	Chicago, IL	9/4/30
Gazzara, Ben	New York, NY	8/28/30
Gedda, Nicolai	Stockholm, Sweden	7/11/25
Gere, Richard	Philadelphia, PA.	8/31/49
Getty, Estelle	New York, NY	7/25/24
Ghostley, Alice	Eve, MO.	8/14/26
Giannini, Giancarlo	Spezia, Italy	8/1/42
Gibbs, Marla	Chicago, IL	6/14/31
Gibson, Debbie	New York, NY	8/31/70
Gibson, Henry	Germantown, PA	9/21/35
Gibson, Mel	Peekskill, NY.	1/3/56
Gielgud, John	London, England	4/14/04
Gifford, Frank	Santa Monica, CA	8/16/30
Gifford, Kathy Lee	Paris, France	8/16/53
Gilbert, Melissa	Los Angeles, CA	5/8/64
Gilberto, Astrud	Salvador, Brazil	3/30/40
Gillette, Anita	Baltimore, MD	8/16/38
Gilley, Mickey	Natchez, MS	3/9/36
Gilpin, Peri	Waco, TX	5/27/--
Ginty, Robert	New York, NY	11/14/48
Givens, Robin	New York, NY	11/27/64
Glaser, Paul Michael	Cambridge, MA	3/25/42
Glenn, Scott	Pittsburgh, PA	1/26/42
Gless, Sharon	Los Angeles, CA	5/31/43
Glover, Danny	San Francisco, CA	7/22/47
Godard, Jean Luc	Paris, France.	12/3/30
Godunov, Alexander	Sakhalin Is., Russia	11/28/49
Goldberg, Whoopi	New York, NY	11/13/49
Goldblum, Jeff	Pittsburgh, PA	10/22/52
Goldsboro, Bobby	Marianna, FL.	1/18/42
Goldthwait, Bob	Syracuse, NY	1962
Goodman, John	St. Louis, MO	6/20/53
Gordon, Gale	New York, NY	2/2/06
Gorme, Eydie	Bronx, NY.	8/16/32
Gorshin, Frank	Pittsburgh, PA	4/5/34
Gossett Jr., Louis	Brooklyn, NY.	5/27/36
Gould, Elliott	Brooklyn, NY.	8/29/38
Gould, Harold	Schenectady, NY	12/10/23
Gould, Morton	Richmond Hill, NY	12/10/13
Goulet, Robert	Lawrence, MA	11/26/33
Gowdy, Curt	Green River, WY	7/31/19
Graham, Virginia	Chicago, IL	7/4/12
Grammer, Kelsey	Virgin Islands.	2/20/--
Granger, Farley	San Jose, CA	7/1/25
Grant, Amy	Augusta, GA	12/25/60
Grant, Lee	New York, NY	10/31/29
Graves, Peter	Minneapolis, MN	3/18/26
Gray, Linda	Santa Monica, CA	9/12/40
Grayson, Kathryn	Winston-Salem, NC	2/9/22
Greco, Jose	Abruzzi, Italy	12/23/18
Green, Adolph	New York, NY	12/2/15
Green, Al	Forest City, AK	4/13/46
Greene, Michele	Las Vegas, NV.	2/3/--
Greene, Shecky	Chicago, IL	4/8/26
Gregory, Cynthia	Los Angeles, CA	7/8/46
Gregory, Dick	St. Louis, MO	10/12/32
Gregory, James	Bronx, NY.	12/23/11
Grey, Jennifer	New York, NY	3/22/60
Grey, Joel	Cleveland, OH.	4/11/32
Grier, David Alan	Detroit, MI.	6/30/55
Griffin, Merv	San Mateo, CA	7/6/25
Griffith, Andy	Mount Airy, NC	6/1/26
Griffith, Melanie	New York, NY	8/9/57
Grimes, Tammy	Lynn, MA	1/30/34
Grizzard, George	Roanoke Rapids, NC	4/1/28
Grodin, Charles	Pittsburgh, PA	4/21/35
Groh, David	New York, NY	5/21/41
Grosbard, Ulu	Antwerp, Belgium	1/19/29
Gross, Michael	Chicago, IL	6/21/47
Guardino, Harry	New York, NY	12/23/25
Guillaume, Robert	St. Louis, MO	11/30/37
Guinness, Alec	London, England	4/2/14
Gumbel, Greg	New Orleans, LA	5/3/46
Guthrie, Arlo	New York, NY	7/10/47
Guttenberg, Steve	New York, NY	8/24/58
Guy, Jasmine	Boston, MA.	3/10/64
Hackett, Buddy	Brooklyn, NY.	8/31/24
Hackman, Gene	San Bernardino, CA	1/30/30
Hagen, Uta	Gottingen, Germany	6/12/19
Haggard, Merle	Bakersfield, CA	4/6/37
Hagman, Larry	Weatherford, TX	9/21/31
Haid, Charles	San Francisco, CA	6/2/44
Hale, Barbara	DeKalb, IL.	4/18/22
Hall, Arsenio	Cleveland, OH.	2/12/55
Hall, Daryl	Pottstown, PA	10/11/48
Hall, Deidre	Milwaukee, WI	10/31/48

Name	Birthplace	Birthdate
Hall, Huntz	New York, NY	8/15/19
Hall, Monty	Winnipeg, Manitoba	8/25/25
Hall, Tom T.	Olive Hill, KY	5/25/36
Hamel, Veronica	Philadelphia, PA.	11/20/43
Hamill, Mark	Oakland, CA	9/25/51
Hamilton, George	Memphis, TN.	8/12/39
Hamilton, Linda	Salisbury, MD	9/26/56
Hamlin, Harry	Pasadena, CA	10/30/51
Hammer	Oakland, CA	1962
Hampton, Lionel	Birmingham, AL	4/12/13
Hancock, Herbie	Chicago, IL	4/12/40
Hanks, Tom	Oakland, CA	7/9/56
Hannah, Daryl	Chicago, IL	1961
Hardison, Kadeem	New York, NY	7/24/--
Harewood, Dorian	Dayton, OH	8/6/51
Harmon, Mark	Burbank, CA	9/2/51
Harper, Jessica	Chicago, IL	10/10/49
Harper, Tess	Mammoth Springs, AK	8/15/50
Harper, Valerie	Suffern, NY	8/22/40
Harrelson, Woody	Midland, TX.	7/23/61
Harrington, Pat	New York, NY	8/13/29
Harris, Barbara	Evanston, IL	7/25/35
Harris, Ed	Englewood, NJ	11/28/50
Harris, Emmylou	Birmingham, AL	4/2/47
Harris, Julie	Grosse Pte. Park, MI.	12/2/25
Harris, Neil Patrick	Albuquerque, NM	6/15/73
Harris, Phil	Linton, IN	6/24/04
Harris, Richard	Co. Limerick, Ireland	10/1/33
Harris, Rosemary	Ashby, England	9/19/30
Harrison, George	Liverpool, England	2/25/43
Harrison, Gregory	Avalon, CA	5/31/50
Harry, Deborah	Miami, FL	7/1/45
Hart, Mary	Madison, SD	11/8/51
Hartley, Mariette	New York, NY	6/21/40
Hartman, David	Pawtucket, RI	5/19/35
Hartman, Lisa	Houston, TX	6/1/56
Hartman, Phil	Ontario, Canada	9/24/48
Hasselhoff, David	Baltimore, MD	7/17/52
Hasso, Signe	Stockholm, Sweden	8/15/10
Hauer, Rutger	Netherlands	1/23/44
Haver, June	Rock Island, IL.	6/10/26
Havoc, June	Seattle, WA	11/8/16
Hawn, Goldie	Washington, DC	11/21/45
Hayden, Melissa	Toronto, Ontario	4/25/23
Hayes, Isaac	Covington, TN	8/20/42
Hays, Robert	Bethesda, MD	7/24/47
Heard, John	Washington, DC	3/7/45
Hearn, George	Memphis, TN	1935
Heckart, Eileen	Columbus, OH	3/29/19
Helmond, Katherine	Galveston, TX	7/5/34
Hemingway, Margaux	Portland, OR	2/19/55
Hemingway, Mariel	Mill Valley, CA	11/21/61
Hemmings, David	Guildford, England	11/18/41
Hemsley, Sherman	Philadelphia, PA	2/1/38
Henderson, Florence	Dale, IN	2/14/34
Henderson, Skitch	Halstad, MN	1/27/18
Henley, Don	Gilmer, TX	7/22/47
Henner, Marilu	Chicago, IL	4/6/52
Henning, Doug	Ft. Garry, Manitoba	5/3/47
Hepburn, Katharine	Hartford, CT	5/12/07
Herman, Pee-wee	Peekskill, NY	8/27/52
Herrmann, Edward	Washington, DC	7/21/43
Hershey, Barbara	Los Angeles, CA	2/5/48
Hesseman, Howard	Lebanon, OR	2/27/40
Heston, Charlton	Evanston, IL	10/4/24
Hewett, Christopher	Sussex, England	4/5/--
Hildegarde	Adell, WI	2/1/06
Hill, Arthur	Melfort, Sask.	8/1/22
Hill, Steven	Seattle, WA	2/24/22
Hill, George Roy	Minneapolis, MN	12/20/22
Hiller, Wendy	Stockport, England	8/15/12
Hillerman, John	Denison, TX	12/30/32
Hines, Gregory	New York, NY	2/14/46
Hines, Jerome	Hollywood, CA	11/8/21
Hingle, Pat	Miami, FL	7/19/24
Hirsch, Judd	New York, NY	3/15/35
Hirt, Al	New Orleans, LA	11/7/22
Ho, Don	Kakaako, Oahu, HI.	8/13/30
Hoffman, Dustin	Los Angeles, CA	8/8/37
Hogan, Paul	New South Wales, Australia	10/8/39
Holbrook, Hal	Cleveland, OH	2/17/25
Holder, Geoffrey	Trinidad	8/1/30
Holliman, Earl	Delhi, LA.	9/11/28
Holliday, Polly	Jasper, AL	8/2/37
Holm, Celeste	New York, NY	4/29/19
Hooks, Jan	Decatur, GA	4/23/57
Hooks, Robert	Washington, DC	4/18/37
Hope, Bob	London, England	5/29/03
Hopkins, Anthony	Wales	12/31/37
Hopkins, Telma	Louisville, KY	10/28/48
Hopper, Dennis	Dodge City, KS	5/17/36
Horne, Lena	Brooklyn, NY	6/30/17
Horne, Marilyn	Bradford, PA	1/16/34
Horsley, Lee	Muleshoe, TX	5/15/55
Hoskins, Bob	Suffolk, England	10/26/42
Houston, Whitney	E Orange, NJ	8/9/63
Howard, Ken	El Centro, CA	3/28/44
Howard, Ron	Duncan, OK	3/1/53
Howell, C. Thomas	Los Angeles, CA	12/7/66
Howes, Sally Ann	London, England	7/20/30
Hughes, Barnard	Bedford Hills, NY	7/16/15
Hulce, Tom	Whitewater, WI	12/6/53
Humperdinck, Engelbert	Madras, India	5/3/36
Hunt, Helen	Los Angeles, CA	6/15/63
Hunt, Linda	Morristown, NJ	4/2/45
Hunter, Holly	Conyers, GA	3/20/58
Hunter, Kim	Detroit, MI	11/12/22
Hunter, Ross	Cleveland, OH	5/6/21
Hunter, Tab	New York, NY	7/11/31
Hurt, John	Chesterfield, England	1/22/40
Hurt, Mary Beth	Marshalltown, IA	9/26/46
Hurt, William	Washington, DC	3/20/50
Hussey, Ruth	Providence, RI	10/30/14
Huston, Anjelica	Ireland	7/8/51
Hutton, Betty	Battle Creek, MI	2/26/21
Hutton, Timothy	Malibu, CA	8/16/60
Hyman, Earle	Rocky Mount, NC	10/11/26
Ian, Janis	New York, NY	4/7/51
Idol, Billy	London, England	11/30/55
Iglesias, Julio	Madrid, Spain	9/23/43
Ingram, James	Akron, OH	2/16/56
Irons, Jeremy	Cowes, England	9/19/48
Irving, Amy	Palo Alto, CA	9/10/53
Irving, George S.	Springfield, MA	11/1/22
Ives, Burl	Hunt Township, IL	6/14/09
Ivey, Judith	El Paso, TX	9/4/51
Ivory, James	Berkeley, CA	6/7/28
Jackee	Winston-Salem, NC	8/14/57
Jackson, Anne	Allegheny, PA	9/3/25
Jackson, Glenda	Liverpool, England	5/9/36
Jackson, Janet	Gary, IN	5/16/66
Jackson, Jermaine	Gary, IN	12/11/54
Jackson, La Toya	Gary, IN	5/29/56
Jackson, Kate	Birmingham, AL	10/29/48
Jackson, Michael	Gary, IN	8/29/58
Jacobi, Derek	London, England	10/22/38
Jaeckel, Richard	Long Beach, NY	10/10/26
Jagger, Mick	Dartford, England	7/26/43
James, Dennis	Jersey City, NJ	8/24/17
Janis, Conrad	New York, NY	2/11/28
Jarreau, Al	Milwaukee, WI	3/12/40
Jeffreys, Anne	Goldsboro, NC	1/26/23
Jennings, Waylon	Littlefield, TX	6/15/37
Jeter, Michael	Lawrenceburg, TN	8/20/52
Jett, Joan	Philadelphia, PA	9/22/60
Jewison, Norman	Toronto, Ontario	7/21/26
Jillian, Ann	Cambridge, MA	1/29/50
Joel, Billy	Bronx, NY	5/9/49
John, Elton	Middlesex, England	3/25/47
Johns, Glynis	Durban, S Africa	10/5/23
Johnson, Anne-Marie	Los Angeles, CA	7/18/--
Johnson, Arte	Benton Harbor, MI	1/20/29
Johnson, Ben	Foraker, OK	6/13/18
Johnson, Don	Flatt Creek, MO	12/15/49
Johnson, Van	Newport, RI	8/25/16
Jones, Charlie	Ft. Smith, AK	11/9/30
Jones, Dean	Morgan City, AL	1/25/35
Jones, George	Saratoga, TX	9/12/31
Jones, Grace	Spanishtown, Jamaica	5/19/52
Jones, Grandpa	Niagara, KY	10/20/13
Jones, Henry	Philadelphia, PA	8/1/12
Jones, Jack	Hollywood, CA	1/14/38
Jones, James Earl	Tate Co., MS	1/17/31
Jones, Jennifer	Tulsa, OK	3/2/19
Jones, Shirley	Smithton, PA	3/31/34
Jones, Tom	Pontypridd, Wales	6/7/40
Jones, Tommy Lee	San Saba, TX	9/15/46
Jordan, Richard	New York, NY	7/19/38
Jourdan, Louis	Marseilles, France	6/19/19
Judd, Naomi	Ashland, KY	1/11/46
Judd, Wynonna	Ashland, KY	5/3/64
Julia, Raul	San Juan, P.R.	3/9/40
Jump, Gordon	Dayton, OH	4/1/32

Name	Birthplace	Birthdate
Kahn, Madeline	Boston, MA	9/29/42
Kanaly, Steve	Burbank, CA	3/14/46
Kane, Carol	Cleveland, OH	6/18/52
Karlen, John	New York, NY	5/28/33
Karras, Alex	Gary, IN	7/15/35
Kasem, Casey	Detroit, MI	1933
Kavner, Julie	Los Angeles, CA	9/7/51
Kazan, Elia	Istanbul, Turkey	9/7/09
Kazan, Lainie	New York, NY	5/15/42
Keach, Stacy	Savannah, GA	6/2/41
Keaton, Diane	Santa Ana, CA	1/5/46
Keaton, Michael	Pittsburgh, PA	9/9/51
Keel, Howard	Gillespie, IL	4/13/17
Keeshan, Bob	Lynbrook, NY	6/27/27
Keitel, Harvey	Brooklyn, NY	—
Keith, Brian	Bayonne, NJ	11/14/21
Keith, David	Knoxville, TN	5/8/54
Kellerman, Sally	Long Beach, CA	6/2/37
Kelley, DeForest	Atlanta, GA	1/20/20
Kelly, Gene	Pittsburgh, PA	8/23/12
Kennedy, George	New York, NY	2/18/25
Kennedy, Jayne	Washington, DC	11/27/51
Kent, Allegra	Los Angeles, CA	8/11/37
Kercheval, Ken	Wolcottville, IN	7/15/35
Kerns, Joanna	San Francisco, CA	2/12/53
Kerr, Deborah	Helensburgh, Scotland	9/30/21
Khan, Chaka	Great Lakes, IL	3/23/53
Kidder, Margot	Yellowknife, N.W.T.	10/17/48
Kidman, Nicole	Hawaii	1967
Kiley, Richard	Chicago, IL	3/31/22
Kilmer, Val	Los Angeles, CA	12/31/59
Kimbrough, Charles	St. Paul, MN	5/23/--
King, Alan	Brooklyn, NY	12/26/27
King, B. B.	Itta Bena, MS	9/16/25
King, Carole	Brooklyn, NY	2/9/42
King, Larry	New York, NY	11/19/33
King, Perry	Alliance, OH	4/30/48
Kingsley, Ben	Yorkshire, England	12/31/43
Kinski, Nastassja	Berlin, W Germany	1/24/60
Kirby, Bruno	New York, NY	1949
Kirby, Durward	Covington, KY	8/24/12
Kirkland, Gelsey	Bethlehem, PA	12/29/53
Kitt, Eartha	North, SC	1/26/28
Klein, Robert	New York, NY	2/8/42
Klemperer, Werner	Cologne, Germany	3/22/19
Kline, Kevin	St. Louis, MO	10/24/47
Klugman, Jack	Philadelphia, PA	4/27/22
Knight, Gladys	Atlanta, GA	5/28/44
Knotts, Don	Morgantown, WV	7/21/24
Kopell, Bernie	New York, NY	6/21/33
Korman, Harvey	Chicago, IL	2/15/27
Kotto, Yaphet	New York, NY	11/15/37
Kramer, Stanley	New York, NY	9/29/13
Kristofferson, Kris	Brownsville, TX	6/22/36
Kubelik, Rafael	Bychori, Czechoslovakia	6/29/14
Kubrick, Stanley	Bronx, NY	7/26/28
Kurtz, Swoosie	Omaha, NE	9/6/44
LaBelle, Patti	Philadelphia, PA	10/4/44
Ladd, Cheryl	Huron, SD	7/12/51
Ladd, Diane	Meridian, MS	11/29/32
Lahti, Christine	Detroit, MI	4/5/50
Laine, Cleo	Middlesex, England	10/28/27
Laine, Frankie	Chicago, IL	3/30/13
Lamarr, Hedy	Vienna, Austria	11/9/13
Lamas, Lorenzo	Santa Monica, CA	1/20/58
Lamb, Gil	Minneapolis, MN	6/14/06
Lamour, Dorothy	New Orleans, LA	12/10/14
Lancaster, Burt	New York, NY	11/2/13
Landau, Martin	New York, NY	6/20/34
Landis, John	Chicago, IL	8/3/50
Lane, Diane	New York, NY	1/22/63
Lane, Priscilla	Indianola, IA	6/12/17
lang, k.d.	Consort, Alberta	11/2/61
Lang, Stephen	New York, NY	7/11/52
Lange, Hope	Redding Ridge, CT	11/28/31
Lange, Jessica	Cloquet, MN	4/20/49
Langella, Frank	Bayonne, NJ	1/1/40
Langford, Frances	Lakeland, FL	4/4/13
Lansbury, Angela	London, England	10/16/25
Lansing, Robert	San Diego, CA	6/5/28
Laredo, Ruth	Detroit, MI	11/20/37
Larroquette, John	New Orleans, LA	11/25/47
Lasser, Louise	New York, NY	4/11/39
Lauper, Cyndi	New York, NY	6/20/53
Laurie, Piper	Detroit, MI	1/22/32
Lauter, Ed	Long Beach, NY	10/30/40
Lavin, Linda	Portland, ME	10/15/37

Name	Birthplace	Birthdate
Lawrence, Carol	Melrose Park, IL	9/5/34
Lawrence, Steve	Brooklyn, NY	7/8/35
Lawrence, Vicki	Inglewood, CA	3/26/49
Leach, Robin	London, England	8/29/41
Leachman, Cloris	Des Moines, IA	4/4/26
Lear, Norman	New Haven, CT	7/27/22
Learned, Michael	Washington, DC	4/9/39
LeBon, Simon	Bushey, England	10/27/58
Lee, Brenda	Atlanta, GA	12/11/44
Lee, Christopher	London, England	5/27/22
Lee, Michele	Los Angeles, CA	6/24/42
Lee, Peggy	Jamestown, ND	5/26/20
Lee, Spike	Atlanta, GA	3/20/57
Leeves, Jane	London, England	4/13/--
Legrand, Michel	Paris, France	2/24/32
Leibman, Ron	New York, NY	10/11/37
Leifer, Carol	E. Williston, NY	1956
Leigh, Janet	Merced, CA	7/6/27
Leigh, Jennifer Jason	Los Angeles, CA	2/5/62
Leinsdorf, Erich	Vienna, Austria	2/4/12
Leisure, David	San Diego, CA	11/16/--
Lemmon, Jack	Boston, MA	2/8/25
Leno, Jay	New Rochelle, NY	4/28/50
Leonard, Sheldon	New York, NY	2/22/07
Leontovich, Eugenie	Moscow, Russia	3/21/00
Leslie, Joan	Detroit, MI	1/26/25
Letterman, David	Indianapolis, IN	4/12/47
Levine, James	Cincinnati, OH	6/23/43
Levinson, Barry	Baltimore, MD	6/2/32
Lewis, Dawnn	New York, NY	8/13/60
Lewis, Huey	New York, NY	7/5/51
Lewis, Jerry	Newark, NJ	3/16/26
Lewis, Jerry Lee	Ferriday, LA	9/29/35
Lewis, Richard	New York, NY	6/29/47
Lewis, Shari	New York, NY	1/17/34
Light, Judith	Trenton, NJ	2/9/50
Lightfoot, Gordon	Orillia, Ontario	11/17/38
Linden, Hal	New York, NY	3/20/31
Lindfors, Viveca	Uppsala, Sweden	12/29/20
Linkletter, Art	Saskatchewan, Canada	7/17/12
Linn-Baker, Mark	St. Louis, MO	6/17/53
Liotta, Ray	Newark, NJ	12/18/55
Lithgow, John	Rochester, NY	10/19/45
Little, Rich	Ottawa, Ontario	11/26/38
Little Richard	Macon, GA	12/5/32
Lloyd, Christopher	Stamford, CT	10/22/38
Lloyd, Emily	England	9/29/70
Locke, Sondra	Shelbyville, TN	5/28/47
Lockhart, June	New York, NY	6/25/25
Locklear, Heather	Los Angeles, CA	9/25/61
Loggia, Robert	New York, NY	1/3/30
Loggins, Kenny	Everett, WA	1/17/47
Lollobrigida, Gina	Subiaco, Italy	7/4/27
Lom, Herbert	Prague, Czechoslovakia	1/9/17
Long, Shelley	Ft. Wayne, IN	8/23/49
Lord, Jack	New York, NY	12/30/22
Loren, Sophia	Rome, Italy	9/20/34
Loring, Gloria	New York, NY	12/10/46
Loudon, Dorothy	Boston, MA	9/17/33
Louis-Dreyfus, Julia	New York, NY	1/13/62
Lovitz, Jon	Tarzana, CA	7/21/57
Lowe, Rob	Charlottesville, VA	3/17/64
Lucas, George	Modesto, CA	5/14/44
Lucci, Susan	Scarsdale, NY	12/23/50
Luckinbill, Laurence	Ft. Smith, AK	11/21/34
Ludwig, Christa	Berlin, Germany	3/16/28
Lumet, Sidney	Philadelphia, PA	6/25/24
Lupino, Ida	London, England	2/4/14
LuPone, Patti	Northport, NY	4/21/49
Lynch, David	Missoula, MT	1/20/46
Lynn, Jeffrey	Auburn, MA	2/16/09
Lynn, Loretta	Butcher Hollow, KY	4/14/35
Maazel, Lorin	Paris, France	3/6/30
MacArthur, James	Los Angeles, CA	12/8/37
MacCorkindale, Simon	Cambridge, England	2/12/52
MacDowell, Andie	Gaffney, SC	4/21/58
MacGraw, Ali	Pound Ridge, NY	4/1/38
Mac Lachlan, Kyle	Yakima, WA	2/22/59
MacLaine, Shirley	Richmond, VA	4/24/34
MacLeod, Gavin	Mt. Kisco, NY	2/28/30
MacNee, Patrick	London, England	2/6/22
MacNeil, Cornell	Minneapolis, MN	9/24/22
Macchio, Ralph	Long Island, NY	11/4/62
Macy, Bill	Revere, MA	5/18/22
Madden, John	Austin, MN	4/10/36
Madigan, Amy	Chicago, IL	9/11/51
Madonna (Ciccone)	Bay City, MI	8/16/58
Mahoney, John	Manchester, England	6/20/--

Name	Birthplace	Birthdate
Majors, Lee	Wyandotte, MI	4/23/40
Malbin, Elaine	New York, NY	5/24/32
Malden, Karl	Chicago, IL	3/22/13
Malkovich, John	Christopher, IL	12/9/53
Malle, Louis	Thumeries, France	10/30/32
Malone, Dorothy	Chicago, IL	1/30/25
Manchester, Melissa	Bronx, NY	2/15/51
Mancini, Henry	Cleveland, OH	4/16/24
Mandel, Howie	Toronto, Ontario	11/29/55
Mandrell, Barbara	Houston, TX	12/25/48
Mangione, Chuck	Rochester, NY	11/29/40
Manilow, Barry	New York, NY	6/17/46
Mann, Herbie	New York, NY	4/16/30
Manoff, Dinah	New York, NY	1/25/58
Mantegna, Joe	Chicago, IL	11/13/47
Marceau, Marcel	Strasbourg, France	3/22/23
Marchand, Nancy	Buffalo, NY	6/19/28
Margolin, Janet	New York, NY	7/25/43
Marin, Cheech	Los Angeles, CA	7/13/46
Markova, Alicia	London, England	12/1/10
Marriner, Neville	Lincoln, England	4/15/24
Marsalis, Branford	New Orleans, LA	8/26/60
Marsalis, Wynton	New Orleans, LA	10/18/61
Marsh, Jean	London, England	7/1/34
Marshall, E. G.	Owatonna, MN	6/18/10
Marshall, Penny	New York, NY	10/15/43
Marshall, Peter	Huntington, WV	3/30/27
Martin, Dean	Steubenville, OH	6/17/17
Martin, Dick	Detroit, MI	1/30/23
Martin, Steve	Waco, TX	4/14/45
Martin, Tony	San Francisco, CA	12/25/13
Martins, Peter	Copenhagen, Denmark	10/27/46
Mason, Jackie	Sheboygan, WI	6/9/31
Mason, Marsha	St. Louis, MO	4/3/42
Masterson, Mary Stuart	Los Angeles, CA	6/28/66
Mastrantonio, Mary Eliz.	Lombard, IL	11/17/58
Mastroianni, Marcello	Rome, Italy	9/28/23
Masur, Kurt	Brieg, Germany	7/18/27
Matheson, Tim	Glendale, CA	12/31/47
Mathis, Johnny	San Francisco, CA	9/30/35
Matlin, Marlee	Morton Grove, IL	8/24/65
Mattea, Kathy	Cross Lanes, W. VA	—
Matthau, Walter	New York, NY	10/1/20
Mature, Victor	Louisville, KY	1/29/16
May, Elaine	Philadelphia, PA	4/21/32
Mayfield, Curtis	Chicago, IL	6/3/42
Mayo, Virginia	St. Louis, MO	11/30/20
Mazursky, Paul	Brooklyn, NY	4/25/30
McArdle, Andrea	Philadelphia, PA	11/5/63
McBride, Patricia	Teaneck, NJ	8/23/42
McCallum, David	Glasgow, Scotland	9/19/33
McCambridge, Mercedes	Joliet, IL	3/17/18
McCarthy, Andrew	New York, NY	1962
McCarthy, Kevin	Seattle, WA	2/15/14
McCartney, Paul	Liverpool, England	6/18/42
McCarver, Tim	Memphis, TN	10/16/41
McClanahan, Rue	Healdton, OK	2/21/36
McClure, Doug	Glendale, CA	5/11/35
McClurg, Edie	Kansas City, MO	7/23/51
McCoo, Marilyn	Jersey City, NJ	9/30/43
McDonnell, Mary	Ithaca, NY	1953
McDowall, Roddy	London, England	9/28/28
McDowell, Malcolm	Leeds, England	6/13/43
McEntire, Reba	McAlester, OK	3/28/54
McFerrin, Bobby	New York, NY	3/11/50
McGavin, Darren	Spokane, WA	5/7/22
McGoohan, Patrick	New York, NY	3/19/28
McGovern, Elizabeth	Evanston, IL	7/18/61
McGovern, Maureen	Youngstown, OH	7/27/49
McGuire, Al	New York, NY	9/7/31
McGuire, Dorothy	Omaha, NE	6/14/19
McKechnie, Donna	Pontiac, MI	11/16/42
McKee, Lonette	Detroit, MI	1954
McKellen, Ian	Burnley, England	5/25/39
McLerie, Allyn	Grand Mere, Quebec	12/1/26
McMahon, Ed	Detroit, MI	3/6/23
McNichol, Kristy	Los Angeles, CA	9/11/62
McQueen, Butterfly	Tampa, FL	1/7/11
McRaney, Gerald	Collins, MS	8/19/48
Meadows, Audrey	Wu Chang, China	2/8/24
Meadows, Jayne	Wu Chang, China	9/27/20
Meara, Anne	New York, NY	9/20/29
Mehta, Zubin	Bombay, India	4/29/36
Mendes, Sergio	Niteroi, Brazil	2/11/41
Menuhin, Yehudi	New York, NY	4/22/16
Mercer, Marian	Akron, OH	11/26/35
Meredith, Burgess	Cleveland, OH	11/16/09
Merrick, David	St. Louis, MO	11/27/12

Name	Birthplace	Birthdate
Merrill, Dina	New York, NY	12/9/25
Merrill, Robert	Brooklyn, NY	6/4/19
Messina, Jim	Maywood, CA	12/5/47
Metcalf, Laurie	Carbondale, IL	6/16/55
Meyers, Ari	San Juan, Puerto Rico	4/6/69
Michael, George	Watford, England	6/26/63
Michaels, Al	New York, NY	11/12/44
Midler, Bette	Paterson, NJ	12/1/45
Milano, Alyssa	New York, NY	12/19/72
Miles, Sarah	Ingatestone, England	12/31/41
Miles, Vera	near Boise City, OK	8/23/29
Miller, Ann	Houston, TX	4/12/19
Miller, Dennis	Pittsburgh, PA	11/3/53
Miller, Mitch	Rochester, NY	7/4/11
Miller, Penelope Ann	Log Angeles, CA	1/13/64
Mills, Donna	Chicago, IL	12/11/42
Mills, John	Suffolk, England	2/22/08
Milner, Martin	Detroit, MI	12/28/27
Milnes, Sherrill	Downers Grove, IL	1/10/35
Milsap, Ronnie	Robinsville, NC	1/16/44
Minnelli, Liza	Los Angeles, CA	3/12/46
Mitchell, James	Sacramento, CA	2/29/20
Mitchell, Joni	McLeod, Alberta	11/7/43
Mitchum, Robert	Bridgeport, CT	8/6/17
Modine, Matthew	Loma Linda, CA	3/22/59
Moffat, Donald	Plymouth, England	12/26/30
Moffo, Anna	Wayne, PA	6/27/27
Molinaro, Al	Kenosha, WI	6/24/19
Moll, Richard	Pasadena, CA	1/13/43
Montalban, Ricardo	Mexico City, Mexico	11/25/20
Montgomery, Elizabeth	Hollywood, CA	4/15/33
Moody, Ron	London, England	1/8/24
Moore, Clayton	Chicago, IL	9/14/08
Moore, Demi	Roswell, NM	11/11/62
Moore, Dudley	London, England	4/19/35
Moore, Mary Tyler	Brooklyn, NY	12/29/37
Moore, Melba	New York, NY	10/29/45
Moore, Roger	London, England	10/14/27
Moore, Terry	Los Angeles, CA	1/1/29
Moranis, Rick	Toronto, Ontario	4/18/53
Moreno, Rita	Humacao, P.R.	12/11/31
Morgan, Harry	Detroit, MI	4/10/15
Moriarty, Michael	Detroit, MI	4/5/41
Morita, Pat	Isleton, CA	6/28/32
Morris, Howard	New York, NY	9/4/25
Morrow, Rob	New Rochelle, NY	9/21/62
Morse, Robert	Newton, MA	5/18/31
Morton, Joe	New York, NY	10/18/47
Moses, William	Los Angeles, CA	11/17/59
Muldaur, Diana	New York, NY	8/19/38
Mulgrew, Kate	Dubuque, IA	4/29/55
Mulhare, Edward	Ireland	4/8/23
Mull, Martin	Chicago, IL	8/18/43
Mulligan, Richard	New York, NY	11/13/32
Munsel, Patrice	Spokane, WA	5/14/25
Murphy, Ben	Jonesboro, AK	3/6/42
Murphy, Eddie	Brooklyn, NY	4/3/61
Murphy, Michael	Los Angeles, CA	5/5/38
Murray, Anne	Springhill, Nova Scotia	6/20/45
Murray, Bill	Evanston, IL	9/21/50
Murray, Don	Hollywood, CA	7/31/29
Musante, Tony	Bridgeport, CT	6/30/36
Musburger, Brent	Portland, OR	5/26/39
Muti, Riccardo	Naples, Italy	7/28/41
Myers, Mike	Toronto, Ontario	1962
Nabors, Jim	Sylacauga, AL	6/12/33
Nash, Graham	Blackpool, England	2/2/42
Natwick, Mildred	Baltimore, MD	6/19/08
Naughton, James	Middletown, CT	7/6/46
Neal, Patricia	Packard, KY	1/20/26
Nealon, Kevin	Bridgeport, CT	11/18/53
Neeson, Liam	N. Ireland	6/7/52
Neill, Sam	New Zealand	1948
Nelligan, Kate	London, Ontario	3/16/51
Nelson, Craig T.	Spokane, WA	4/4/46
Nelson, Ed	New Orleans, LA	12/21/28
Nelson, Harriet (Hilliard)	Des Moines, IA	7/18/14
Nelson, Judd	Portland, ME	11/28/59
Nelson, Tracy	Santa Monica, CA	10/25/63
Nelson, Willie	Abbott, TX	4/30/33
Nero, Peter	New York, NY	5/22/34
Neuwirth, Bebe	Newark, NJ	12/31/--
Newhart, Bob	Oak Park, IL	9/29/29
Newley, Anthony	Hackney, England	9/24/31
Newman, Paul	Cleveland, OH	1/26/25
Newman, Randy	Los Angeles, CA	11/28/43

Name	Birthplace	Birthdate
Newton, Wayne	Norfolk, VA	4/3/42
Newton-John, Olivia	Cambridge, England	9/26/47
Nicholas, Denise	Detroit, MI	7/12/44
Nicholas, Fayard	Philadelphia, PA	10/20/14
Nicholas, Harold	Philadelphia, PA	3/27/24
Nichols, Mike	Berlin, Germany	11/6/31
Nicholson, Jack	Neptune, NJ	4/28/37
Nicks, Stevie	Phoenix, AZ	5/26/48
Nielsen, Leslie	Regina, Sask.	2/11/26
Nilsson, Birgit	Karup, Sweden	5/17/18
Nimoy, Leonard	Boston, MA	3/26/31
Nolte, Nick	Omaha, NE	2/8/40
Norman, Jessye	Augusta, GA	9/15/45
Norris, Chuck	Ryan, OK	3/10/40
North, Sheree	Los Angeles, CA	1/17/33
Noth, Christopher	Madison, WI	11/13/--
Novak, Kim	Chicago, IL	2/13/33
Oates, John	New York, NY	4/7/48
O'Brian, Hugh	Rochester, NY	4/19/25
O'Brien, Conan	Brookline, MA	1963
O'Brien, Margaret	San Diego, CA	1/15/37
Ocean, Billy	Trinidad	1/21/50
O'Connor, Carroll	New York, NY	8/2/24
O'Connor, Donald	Chicago, IL	8/28/25
O'Connor, Sinead	Dublin, Ireland	12/8/67
Odetta	Birmingham, AL	12/31/30
O'Donnell, Chris	Winnetka, IL	1970
O'Hara, Maureen	Dublin, Ireland	8/17/20
O'Herlihy, Dan	Wexford, Ireland	5/1/19
Oldman, Gary	London, England	3/21/58
Olin, Ken	Chicago, IL	7/30/54
Olin, Lena	Sweden	3/22/55
Olmos, Edward James	E. Los Angeles, CA	2/24/47
Olsen, Merlin	Logan, UT	9/15/40
O'Neal, Ryan	Los Angeles, CA	4/20/41
O'Neal, Tatum	Los Angeles, CA	11/5/63
O'Neill, Ed	Youngstown, OH	1946
Ontkean, Michael	Vancouver, B.C.	1/24/46
Orbach, Jerry	New York, NY	10/20/35
Orlando, Tony	New York, NY	4/3/44
Osbourne, Ozzy	Birmingham, England	12/3/46
O'Shea, Milo	Dublin, Ireland	6/2/26
Oslin, K.T.	Crossit, AK	1942
Osmond, Donny	Ogden, UT	12/9/57
Osmond, Marie	Ogden, UT	10/13/59
O'Sullivan, Maureen	Boyle, Ireland	5/17/11
O'Toole, Annette	Houston, TX	4/1/53
O'Toole, Peter	Connemara, Ireland	8/2/32
Owens, Buck	Sherman, TX	8/12/29
Oz, Frank	Herford, England	5/25/44
Ozawa, Seiji	Shenyang, China	9/1/35
Paar, Jack	Canton, OH	5/1/18
Pacino, Al	New York, NY	4/25/40
Packer, Billy	Wellsville, NY	2/25/40
Page, Patti	Claremore, OK	11/8/27
Paige, Janis	Tacoma, WA	9/16/22
Palance, Jack	Lattimer, PA	2/18/20
Palin, Michael	England	5/5/43
Palmer, Betsy	East Chicago, IN	11/1/29
Papas, Irene	Greece	3/9/26
Parker, Alan	London, England	2/14/44
Parker, Eleanor	Cedarville, OH	6/26/22
Parker, Fess	Ft. Worth, TX	8/16/25
Parker, Jameson	Baltimore, MD	11/18/47
Parker, Jean	Deer Lodge, MT	8/11/12
Parker, Sarah Jessica	Nelsonville, OH	3/25/65
Parsons, Estelle	Lynn, MA	11/20/27
Parton, Dolly	Sevierville, TN	1/19/46
Patinkin, Mandy	Chicago, IL	11/30/52
Pavarotti, Luciano	Modena, Italy	10/12/35
Paycheck, Johnny	Greenfield, OH	5/31/41
Pearl, Minnie	Centerville, TN	10/25/12
Peck, Gregory	La Jolla, CA	4/5/16
Pendergrass, Teddy	Philadelphia, PA	3/26/50
Penn, Arthur	Philadelphia, PA	9/27/22
Penn, Sean	Burbank, CA	8/17/60
Penny, Joe	London, England	9/14/56
Perkins, Elizabeth	New York, NY	11/18/60
Perlman, Itzhak	Tel Aviv, Israel	8/31/45
Perlman, Rhea	Brooklyn, NY	3/31/48
Perlman, Ron	New York, NY	4/13/50
Perrine, Valerie	Galveston, TX	9/3/43
Perry, Luke	Fredericktown, OH	10/11/--
Persoff, Nehemiah	Jerusalem	8/14/20
Pesci, Joe	Newark, NJ	2/9/43
Peters, Bernadette	New York, NY	2/28/48
Peters, Brock	New York, NY	7/2/27

Name	Birthplace	Birthdate
Peters, Roberta	New York, NY	5/4/30
Petty, Tom	Gainesville, FL	10/20/53
Pfeiffer, Michelle	Santa Ana, CA	4/29/57
Philbin, Regis	New York, NY	—
Phillips, Lou Diamond	Philippines	2/17/62
Phillips, Michelle	Long Beach, CA	6/4/44
Pickett, Cindy	Norman, OK	4/18/47
Pierce, David Hyde	Sarasota Springs, NY	4/3/--
Pinchot, Bronson	New York, NY	5/20/59
Piscopo, Joe	Passaic, NJ	6/17/51
Pitt, Brad	Missouri	12/18/65
Pleasence, Donald	Worksop, England	10/5/19
Pleshette, Suzanne	New York, NY	1/31/37
Plowright, Joan	Brigg, England	10/28/29
Plummer, Amanda	New York, NY	3/23/57
Plummer, Christopher	Toronto, Ontario	12/13/27
Poitier, Sidney	Miami, FL	2/20/27
Polanski, Roman	Paris, France	8/18/33
Pollack, Sydney	Lafayette, IN	7/1/34
Ponti, Carlo	Milan, Italy	12/11/13
Post, Markie	Palo Alto, CA	11/4/50
Poston, Tom	Columbus, OH	10/17/27
Potts, Annie	Nashville, TN	10/28/52
Povich, Maury	Washington, DC	1/17/39
Powell, Jane	Portland, OR	4/1/28
Powers, Stefanie	Hollywood, CA	11/2/42
Prentiss, Paula	San Antonio, TX	3/4/39
Presley, Priscilla	New York, NY	5/24/46
Preston, Billy	Houston, TX	9/9/46
Previn, Andre	Berlin, Germany	4/6/29
Price, Leontyne	Laurel, MS	2/10/27
Price, Ray	Perryville, TX	1/12/26
Pride, Charlie	Sledge, MS	3/18/39
Priestley, Jason	Vancouver, British Columbia	8/28/69
Prince	Minneapolis, MN	6/7/58
Principal, Victoria	Japan	—
Prosky, Robert	Philadelphia, PA	12/13/30
Pryce, Jonathan	Wales	6/1/47
Pryor, Richard	Peoria, IL	12/1/40
Pulliam, Keshia Knight	Newark, NJ	4/9/79
Pyle, Denver	Bethune, CO	5/11/20
Quaid, Dennis	Houston, TX	4/9/54
Quaid, Randy	Houston, TX	10/1/50
Quinn, Aidan	Chicago, IL	3/8/59
Quinn, Anthony	Chihuahua, Mexico	4/21/15
Quinn, Martha	Albany, NY	5/11/59
Rabb, Ellis	Memphis, TN	6/20/30
Rabbitt, Eddie	Brooklyn, NY	11/27/41
Rachins, Alan	Cambridge, MA	10/10/47
Rae, Charlotte	Milwaukee, WI	4/22/26
Rainer, Luise	Vienna, Austria	1/12/09
Raitt, Bonnie	Burbank, CA	11/8/49
Ramey, Samuel	Colby, KS	3/28/42
Rampal, Jean-Pierre	Marseilles, France	1/7/22
Randall, Tony	Tulsa, OK	2/26/20
Randolph, John	New York, NY	6/1/15
Randolph, Joyce	Detroit, MI	10/21/25
Raphael, Sally Jessy	Easton, PA	2/25/43
Rashad, Phylicia	Houston, TX	6/17/48
Ratzenberger, John	Bridgeport, CT	4/6/47
Rawls, Lou	Chicago, IL	12/1/36
Raye, Martha	Butte, MT	8/27/16
Raymond, Gene	New York, NY	8/13/08
Reddy, Helen	Melbourne, Australia	10/25/41
Redford, Robert	Santa Monica, CA	8/18/37
Redgrave, Lynn	London, England	3/8/43
Redgrave, Vanessa	London, England	1/30/37
Reed, Jerry	Atlanta, GA	3/20/37
Reed, Oliver	London, England	2/13/38
Reed, Rex	Ft. Worth, TX	10/2/38
Reed, Shanna	Kansas City, KS	10/30/--
Reese, Della	Detroit, MI	7/6/31
Reeve, Christopher	New York, NY	9/25/52
Reeves, Keanu	Beirut, Lebanon	9/2/64
Regalbuto, Joe	New York, NY	8/24/--
Reid, Tim	Norfolk, VA	12/19/44
Reilly, Charles Nelson	New York, NY	1/13/31
Reiner, Carl	Bronx, NY	3/20/22
Reiner, Rob	Bronx, NY	3/6/45
Reinhold, Judge	Wilmington, DE	5/21/56
Reinking, Ann	Seattle, WA	11/10/50
Reiser, Paul	New York, NY	3/30/57
Resnik, Regina	New York, NY	8/30/24
Reynolds, Burt	Waycross, GA	2/11/36
Reynolds, Debbie	El Paso, TX	4/1/32
Rhue, Madlyn	Washington, DC	10/3/34
Rich, Charlie	Forest City, AK	12/14/32

Name	Birthplace	Birthdate
Richards, Keith	Kent, England	12/18/43
Richards, Michael	Los Angeles, CA	—
Richardson, Miranda	Lancashire, England	1958
Richardson, Natasha	London, England	5/11/63
Richie, Lionel	Tuskegee, AL	6/20/50
Rickles, Don	New York, NY	5/8/26
Rickman, Alan	London, England	1946
Riegert, Peter	New York, NY	4/11/47
Rigg, Diana	Doncaster, England	7/20/38
Ringwald, Molly	Rosewood, CA	2/14/68
Ritter, John	Burbank, CA	9/17/48
Rivera, Chita	Washington, DC	1/23/33
Rivera, Geraldo	New York, NY	7/4/43
Rivers, Joan	Brooklyn, NY	6/8/37
Robards, Jason Jr.	Chicago, IL	7/26/22
Robbins, Jerome	New York, NY	10/11/18
Robbins, Tim	W. Covina, CA	10/16/58
Roberts, Doris	St. Louis, MO	11/4/29
Roberts, Eric	Biloxi, MS	4/18/56
Roberts, Julia	Smyrna, GA	10/25/67
Roberts, Pernell	Waycross, GA	5/18/30
Roberts, Tony	New York, NY	10/22/39
Robertson, Cliff	La Jolla, CA	9/9/25
Robertson, Dale	Harrah, OK	7/14/23
Robinson, Charles	Houston, TX	11/9/--
Robinson, Smokey	Detroit, MI	2/19/40
Roche, Eugene	Boston, MA	9/22/28
Rodgers, Jimmy	Camas, WA	9/18/33
Rodrigues, Percy	Montreal, Quebec	6/13/24
Rodriquez, Johnny	Sabinal, TX	12/10/51
Rogers, Fred	Latrobe, PA	3/20/28
Rogers, Ginger	Independence, MO	7/16/11
Rogers, Kenny	Houston, TX	8/21/38
Rogers, Mimi	Coral Gables, FL	1/27/56
Rogers, Roy	Cincinnati, OH	11/5/12
Rogers, Wayne	Birmingham, AL	4/7/33
Rolle, Esther	Pompano Beach, FL	11/8/33
Rollins, Howard	Baltimore, MD	10/17/50
Ronstadt, Linda	Tucson, AZ	7/15/46
Rooney, Mickey	Brooklyn, NY	9/23/20
Rose, Axl	Lafayette, IN	2/6/66
Rose Marie	New York, NY	8/15/25
Roseanne	Salt Lake City, UT	11/3/52
Ross, Diana	Detroit, MI	3/26/44
Ross, Katharine	Hollywood, CA	1/29/42
Ross, Marion	Albert Lea, MN	10/25/28
Rossellini, Isabella	Rome, Italy	6/18/52
Rostropovich, Mstislav	Baku, Azerbaijan	3/12/27
Roth, David Lee	Bloomington, IN	10/10/55
Rourke, Mickey	Miami, FL	1953
Rowlands, Gena	Cambria, WI	6/19/34
Ruehl, Mercedes	New York, NY	—
Rush, Barbara	Denver, CO	1/4/30
Russell, Jane	Bemidji, MN	6/21/21
Russell, Ken	Southampton, England	7/3/27
Russell, Kurt	Springfield, MA	3/17/51
Russell, Mark	Buffalo, NY	8/23/32
Russell, Nipsey	Atlanta, GA	10/13/24
Russell, Theresa	San Diego, CA	3/20/57
Rutherford, Ann	Toronto, Ontario	11/2/20
Ruttan, Susan	Oregon City, OR	9/16/50
Ryan, Meg	Fairfield, CT	11/19/63
Ryan, Peggy	Long Beach, CA	8/28/24
Ryan, Roz	Detroit, MI	7/7/51
Rydell, Bobby	Philadelphia, PA	4/26/42
Ryder, Winona	Winona, MN	10/29/71
Saget, Bob	Philadelphia, PA	5/17/56
Sahl, Mort	Montreal, Quebec	5/11/27
Saint, Eva Marie	Newark, NJ	7/4/24
St. James, Susan	Los Angeles, CA	8/14/46
St. John, Jill	Los Angeles, CA	8/19/40
Sajak, Pat	Chicago, IL	10/26/47
Saks, Gene	New York, NY	11/8/21
Sales, Soupy	Franklinton, NC	1/8/26
Samms, Emma	London, England	8/28/60
Sanderson, William	Memphis, TN	1/10/48
Sandy, Gary	Dayton, OH	12/25/45
Sanford, Isabel	New York, NY	8/29/17
Sarandon, Susan	New York, NY	10/4/46
Sarnoff, Dorothy	New York, NY	5/25/17
Savage, Fred	Highland Park, IL	7/9/76
Saxon, John	Brooklyn, NY	8/5/35
Sayles, John	Schenectady, NY	9/28/50
Scaggs, Boz	Dallas, TX	6/8/44
Schallert, William	Los Angeles, CA	7/6/22
Scheider, Roy	Orange, NJ	11/10/32
Schell, Maria	Vienna, Austria	1/15/26
Schell, Maximilian	Vienna, Austria	12/8/30

Name	Birthplace	Birthdate
Schenkel, Chris	Bippus, IN	8/21/23
Schnabel, Stefan	Berlin, Germany	2/2/12
Schneider, John	Mt. Kisco, NY	4/8/54
Schroder, Rick	Staten Island, NY	4/3/70
Schwarzenegger, Arnold	Graz, Austria	7/30/47
Schwarzkopf, Elisabeth	Jarotschin, Poland	12/9/15
Sciorra, Annabella	New York, NY	1964
Scofield, Paul	Hurst, Pierpont, England	1/21/22
Scolari, Peter	New Rochelle, IL	9/12/54
Scorsese, Martin	New York, NY	11/17/42
Scott, George C.	Wise, VA	10/18/27
Scott, Lizabeth	Scranton, PA	9/29/22
Scott, Martha	Jamesport, MO	9/22/14
Scotto, Renata	Savona, Italy	2/24/35
Scully, Vin	New York, NY	11/29/27
Seagal, Steven	Lansing, MI	4/10/51
Sedaka, Neil	New York, NY	3/13/39
Seeger, Pete	New York, NY	5/3/19
Segal, George	Great Neck, NY	2/13/34
Seidelman, Susan	Philadelphia, PA	12/11/52
Seinfeld, Jerry	New York, NY	1954
Sellecca, Connie	New York, NY	5/25/55
Selleck, Tom	Detroit, MI	1/29/45
Severinsen, Doc	Arlington, OR	7/7/27
Seymour, Jane	Middlesex, England	2/15/51
Shackelford, Ted	Oklahoma City, OK	6/23/46
Shaffer, Paul	Thunder Bay, Ontario	11/28/49
Shandling, Garry	Tucson, AZ	11/29/49
Shankar, Ravi	India	4/7/20
Sharif, Omar	Alexandria, Egypt	4/10/32
Shatner, William	Montreal, Quebec	3/22/31
Shea, John	N. Conway, NH	4/14/49
Shearer, Moira	Scotland	1/17/26
Sheedy, Ally	New York, NY	6/12/62
Sheen, Charlie	New York, NY	9/3/65
Sheen, Martin	Dayton, OH	8/3/40
Shelley, Carole	London, England	8/16/39
Shepard, Sam	Ft. Sheridan, IL	11/5/43
Shepherd, Cybill	Memphis, TN	2/18/49
Shields, Brooke	New York, NY	5/31/65
Shire, Talia	New York, NY	4/25/46
Short, Bobby	Danville, IL	9/15/24
Short, Martin	Hamilton, Ontario	3/26/50
Shull, Richard B.	Evanston, IL	2/24/29
Sidney, Sylvia	New York, NY	8/8/10
Siepi, Cesare	Milan, Italy	2/10/23
Sikking, James B.	Los Angeles, CA	3/5/34
Sills, Beverly	Brooklyn, NY	5/25/29
Silver, Ron	New York, NY	7/2/46
Simmons, Gene	Haifa, Israel	8/25/49
Simmons, Jean	London, England	1/31/29
Simmons, Richard	New Orleans, LA	7/12/48
Simon, Carly	New York, NY	6/25/45
Simon, Paul	Newark, NJ	10/13/41
Simone, Nina	Tyron, NC	2/21/33
Sinatra, Frank	Hoboken, NJ	12/12/15
Sinbad	Benton Harbor, MI	11/10/--
Sinclair, Madge	Kingston, Jamaica	4/28/38
Siskel, Gene	Chicago, IL	1/26/46
Skelton, Red (Richard)	Vincennes, IN	7/18/13
Skerritt, Tom	Detroit, MI	8/25/33
Slater, Christian	New York, NY	8/19/69
Slater, Helen	Massapequa, NY	12/14/63
Slezak, Erika	Hollywood, CA	8/5/46
Slick, Grace	Chicago, IL	10/30/39
Smirnoff, Yakov	Odessa, Russia	1/24/51
Smith, Allison	New York, NY	12/9/69
Smith, Buffalo Bob	Buffalo, NY	11/27/17
Smith, Jaclyn	Houston, TX	10/26/47
Smith, Keely	Norfolk, VA	3/9/35
Smith, Maggie	Ilford, England	12/28/34
Smith, Will	Philadelphia, PA	9/25/69
Smits, Jimmy	New York, NY	7/9/55
Smothers, Dick	New York, NY	11/20/39
Smothers, Tom	New York, NY	2/2/37
Snipes, Wesley	Orlando, FL	7/31/63
Snow, Hank	Nova Scotia, Canada	5/9/14
Solti, Georg	Budapest, Hungary	10/21/12
Somers, Suzanne	San Bruno, CA	10/16/46
Sommer, Elke	Berlin, Germany	11/5/41
Sorvino, Paul	New York, NY	1939
Sothern, Ann	Valley City, ND	1/22/09
Soul, David	Chicago, IL	8/28/43
Spacek, Sissy	Quitman, TX	12/25/49
Spacey, Kevin	S. Orange, NJ	7/26/59
Spader, James	Boston, MA	2/7/60

Name	Birthplace	Birthdate
Spelling, Aaron	Dallas, TX	4/22/28
Spencer, John	New Jersey	1946
Spielberg, Steven	Cincinnati, OH	12/18/47
Springfield, Dusty	London, England	4/16/39
Springfield, Rick	Sydney, Australia	8/23/49
Springsteen, Bruce	Freehold, NJ	9/23/49
Stack, Robert	Los Angeles, CA	1/13/19
Stafford, Jo	Coalinga, CA	11/12/18
Stahl, Richard	Detroit, MI	1/4/32
Stallone, Sylvester	New York, NY	7/6/46
Stamos, John	Cypress, CA	8/19/63
Stamp, Terence	Stepney, England	7/22/39
Stander, Lionel	New York, NY	1/11/08
Stang, Arnold	New York, NY	9/28/25
Stanley, Kim	Tularosa, NM	2/11/25
Stanton, Harry Dean	Kentucky	7/14/26
Stapleton, Jean	New York, NY	1/19/23
Stapleton, Maureen	Troy, NY	6/21/25
Starr, Ringo	Liverpool, England	7/7/40
Steenburgen, Mary	Newport, AZ	2/8/53
Steiger, Rod	W. Hampton, NY	4/14/25
Stephens, James	Mt. Kisco, NY	5/18/51
Stern, Daniel	Stamford, CT	5/28/57
Stern, Howard	New York, NY	1/12/54
Stern, Isaac	Kreminiecz, Russia	7/21/20
Sternhagen, Frances	Washington, DC	1/13/30
Stevens, Andrew	Memphis, TN	6/10/55
Stevens, Cat	London, England	7/21/48
Stevens, Connie	Brooklyn, NY	8/8/38
Stevens, Rise	New York, NY	6/11/13
Stevens, Stella	Yazoo City, MS	10/1/36
Stevenson, McLean	Normal, IL	11/14/29
Stevenson, Parker	Philadelphia, PA	6/4/52
Stewart, James	Indiana, PA	5/20/08
Stewart, Patrick	Mirfield, England	7/13/40
Stewart, Rod	London, England	1/10/45
Stickney, Dorothy	Dickinson, ND	6/21/00
Stiers, David Ogden	Peoria, IL	10/31/42
Stiller, Jerry	New York, NY	6/8/29
Stills, Stephen	Dallas, TX	1/3/45
Sting (G. Sumner)	Newcastle, England	10/2/51
Stockwell, Dean	Hollywood, CA	3/5/36
Stoltz, Eric	American Samoa	1961
Stone, Oliver	New York, NY	9/15/46
Stone, Sharon	Meadville, PA	1958
Stookey, Paul	Baltimore, MD	12/30/37
Storch, Larry	New York, NY	1/8/23
Storm, Gale	Bloomington, TX	4/5/22
Stowe, Madeleine	Los Angeles, CA	8/18/58
Straight, Beatrice	Old Westbury, NY	8/2/18
Strait, George	Pearsall, TX	5/1/52
Strasser, Robin	New York, NY	5/7/45
Stratas, Teresa	Toronto, Ontario	5/26/38
Strauss, Peter	New York, NY	2/20/47
Streep, Meryl	Summit, NJ	6/22/49
Streisand, Barbra	Brooklyn, NY	4/24/42
Stritch, Elaine	Detroit, MI	2/2/26
Struthers, Sally	Portland, OR	7/28/48
Stuarti, Enzo	Rome, Italy	3/3/25
Sullivan, Susan	New York, NY	11/18/44
Sumac, Yma	Ichocan, Peru	9/10/27
Summer, Donna	Boston, MA	12/31/48
Sutherland, Donald	St. John, New Brunswick	7/17/34
Sutherland, Joan	Sydney, Australia	11/7/26
Sutherland, Kiefer	London, England	12/20/66
Swayze, Patrick	Houston, TX	8/18/54
Swit, Loretta	Passaic, NJ	11/4/37
Mr. T (Lawrence Tero)	Chicago, IL	5/21/52
Tallchief, Maria	Fairfax, OK	1/24/25
Tarkenton, Fran	Richmond, VA	2/3/40
Taylor, Elizabeth	London, England	2/27/32
Taylor, James	Boston, MA	3/12/48
Taylor, Rip	Washington, DC	1/13/30
Taylor, Rod	Sydney, Australia	1/11/29
Te Kanawa, Kiri	Gisborne, New Zealand	3/6/44
Tebaldi, Renata	Pesaro, Italy	2/1/22
Temple, Shirley	Santa Monica, CA	4/23/28
Tennant, Victoria	London, England	9/30/50
Tennille, Toni	Montgomery, AL	5/8/43
Tharp, Twyla	Portland, IN	7/1/41
Thicke, Alan	Kirkland Lake, Ontario	3/1/47
Thomas, Jay	New Orleans, LA	7/12/48
Thomas, Marlo	Detroit, MI	11/21/43
Thomas, Philip Michael	Columbus, OH	5/26/49
Thomas, Richard	New York, NY	6/13/51
Thompson, Emma	London, England	4/15/59
Thompson, Jack	Sydney, Australia	8/31/40
Thompson, Lea	Rochester, MN	5/31/61
Thompson, Sada	Des Moines, IA	9/27/29
Thulin, Ingrid	Sweden	1/27/29
Tiegs, Cheryl	Minnesota	9/27/47
Tiffany	Norwalk, CA	10/2/71
Tillis, Mel	Tampa, FL	8/8/32
Tiny Tim	New York, NY	4/12/23
Todd, Richard	Dublin, Ireland	6/11/19
Tomei, Marisa	New York, NY	12/4/64
Tomlin, Lily	Detroit, MI	9/1/39
Tomlinson, David	Scotland	5/7/17
Torme, Mel	Chicago, IL	9/13/25
Torn, Rip	Temple, TX	2/6/31
Townsend, Robert	Chicago, IL	2/6/57
Travanti, Daniel J.	Kenosha, WI	3/7/40
Travers, Mary	Louisville, KY	11/9/36
Travis, Nancy	New York, NY	9/21/61
Travis, Randy	Marshville, NC	5/4/59
Travolta, John	Englewood, NJ	2/18/54
Trebek, Alex	Sudbury, Ontario	7/22/40
Trevor, Claire	New York, NY	3/8/09
Troyanos, Tatiana	New York, NY	9/12/38
Tucker, Michael	Baltimore, MD	2/6/44
Tucker, Tanya	Seminole, TX	10/10/58
Tune, Tommy	Wichita Falls, TX	2/28/39
Turner, Janine	Lincoln, NE	12/6/62
Turner, Kathleen	Springfield, MO	6/19/54
Turner, Lana	Wallace, ID	2/8/20
Turner, Tina	Nutbush, TN	11/26/38
Turturro, John	New York, NY	2/28/57
Turturro, Nicholas	Queens, NY	—
Twiggy (Leslie Hornby)	London, England	9/19/46
Tyson, Cicely	New York, NY	12/19/33
Uecker, Bob	Milwaukee, WI	1/26/35
Uggams, Leslie	New York, NY	5/25/43
Ullman, Tracey	Slough, England	12/30/59
Ullmann, Liv	Tokyo, Japan	12/16/38
Underwood, Blair	Tacoma, WA	8/25/64
Urich, Robert	Toronto, Ontario	12/19/46
Ustinov, Peter	London, England	4/16/21
Vaccaro, Brenda	Brooklyn, NY	11/18/39
Vale, Jerry	New York, NY	7/8/31
Valente, Caterina	Paris, France	1/14/31
Valli, Frankie	Newark, NJ	5/3/37
Van Ark, Joan	New York, NY	6/16/43
Vandross, Luther	New York, NY	4/20/51
Van Dyke, Dick	West Plains, MO	12/13/25
Van Dyke, Jerry	Danville, IL	7/27/31
Van Fleet, Jo	Oakland, CA	12/30/22
Van Halen, Eddie	Nijmegen, Netherlands	1/26/57
Van Pallandt, Nina	Copenhagen, Denmark	7/15/32
Van Patten, Dick	New York, NY	12/9/28
Van Peebles, Mario	Mexico	1/15/57
Vaughn, Robert	New York, NY	11/22/32
Vedder, Eddie	Evanston, IL	12/23/66
Venuta, Benay	San Francisco, CA	1/27/11
Verdon, Gwen	Los Angeles, CA	1/13/25
Vereen, Ben	Miami, FL	10/10/46
Verrett, Shirley	New Orleans, LA	5/31/31
Vickers, Jon	Prince Albert, Sask.	10/26/26
Vigoda, Abe	New York, NY	2/24/21
Vincent, Jan-Michael	Denver, CO	7/15/44
Vinson, Helen	Beaumont, TX	9/17/07
Vinton, Bobby	Canonsburg, PA	4/16/35
Vitale, Dick	E Rutherford, NJ	6/9/40
Voight, Jon	Yonkers, NY	12/29/38
Von Stade, Frederica	Somerville, NJ	6/1/45
Von Sydow, Max	Lund, Sweden	4/10/29
Wagner, Lindsay	Los Angeles, CA	6/22/49
Wagner, Robert	Detroit, MI	2/10/30
Wagoner, Porter	West Plains, MO	8/12/27
Wahl, Ken	Chicago, IL	2/14/56
Wain, Bea	Bronx, NY	4/30/17
Waite, Ralph	White Plains, NY	6/22/29
Walden, Robert	New York, NY	9/25/43
Walken, Christopher	New York, NY	3/31/43
Wallach, Eli	Brooklyn, NY	12/7/15
Walston, Ray	Laurel, MS	11/2/24
Walter, Jessica	New York, NY	1/31/44
Wanamaker, Sam	Chicago, IL	6/14/19
Ward, Fred	San Diego, CA	1943
Ward, Sela	Merisian, MS	8/11/--
Ward, Simon	London, England	10/19/41
Warden, Jack	Newark, NJ	9/18/20
Warfield, William	W Helena, AK	1/22/20

Name	Birthplace	Birthdate
Warner, Malcolm-Jamal	Jersey City, NJ	8/18/70
Warren, Lesley Ann	New York, NY	8/16/46
Warrick, Ruth	St. Joseph, MO	6/29/16
Warwick, Dionne	E Orange, NJ	12/12/41
Washington, Denzel	Mt. Vernon, NY	12/28/54
Waterston, Sam	Cambridge, MA	11/15/40
Watkins, Carlene	Hartford, CT	6/4/52
Watts, Andre	Nuremberg, Germany	6/20/46
Wayans, Damon	New York, NY	1960
Wayans, Keenan Ivory	New York, NY	6/8/58
Wayne, David	Traverse City, MI	1/30/14
Waxman, Al	Toronto, Ontario	3/2/35
Weaver, Dennis	Joplin, MO	6/4/24
Weaver, Fritz	Pittsburgh, PA	1/19/26
Weaver, Sigourney	New York, NY	10/8/49
Weber, Steven	New York, NY	3/4/--
Weir, Peter	Sydney, Australia	8/8/44
Weitz, Bruce	Norwalk, CT	5/27/43
Welch, Raquel	Chicago, IL	9/5/40
Weld, Tuesday	New York, NY	8/27/43
Wells, Kitty	Nashville, TN	8/30/19
Wendt, George	Chicago, IL	10/17/48
Weston, Jack	Cleveland, OH	8/21/24
Wheaton, Wil	Burbank, CA	7/29/72
Whitaker, Forest	Longview, TX	7/15/61
White, Barry	Galveston, TX	9/12/44
White, Betty	Oak Park, IL	1/17/22
White, Jesse	Buffalo, NY	1/3/19
White, Vanna	N Myrtle Beach, SC	2/18/57
Whiting, Margaret	Detroit, MI	7/22/24
Whitmore, James	White Plains, NY	10/1/21
Widmark, Richard	Sunrise, MN	12/26/14
Wiest, Dianne	Kansas City, MO	3/28/48
Wilder, Billy	Vienna, Austria	6/22/06
Wilder, Gene	Milwaukee, WI	6/11/35
Williams, Andy	Wall Lake, IA	12/3/30
Williams, Billy Dee	New York, NY	4/6/37
Williams, Cindy	Van Nuys, CA	8/22/47
Williams, Esther	Los Angeles, CA	8/8/23
Williams, Hal	Columbus, OH	12/14/38
Williams Jr., Hank	Shreveport, LA	5/26/49
Williams, Joe	Cordele, GA	12/12/18
Williams, JoBeth	Houston, TX	1953
Williams, Paul	Omaha, NE	9/19/40
Williams, Robin	Chicago, IL	7/21/52
Williams, Treat	Rowayton, CT	12/1/51
Williams, Vanessa	New York, NY	3/18/63
Williamson, Nicol	Hamilton, Scotland	9/14/38
Willis, Bruce	W Germany	3/19/55
Wilson, Demond	Valdosta, GA	10/13/46
Wilson, Elizabeth	Grand Rapids, MI	4/4/25
Wilson, Flip	Jersey City, NJ	12/8/33
Wilson, Nancy	Chillicothe, OH	2/20/37
Windom, William	New York, NY	9/28/23
Winfield, Paul	Los Angeles, CA	5/22/41
Winfrey, Oprah	Kosciusko, MS	1/29/54
Winger, Debra	Cleveland, OH	5/16/55
Winkler, Henry	New York, NY	10/30/45
Winningham, Mare	Phoenix, AZ	5/6/59
Winters, Jonathan	Dayton, OH	11/11/25
Winters, Shelley	St. Louis, MO	8/18/22
Winwood, Steve	Birmingham, England	5/12/48
Wiseman, Joseph	Montreal, Quebec	5/15/18
Withers, Jane	Atlanta, GA	4/12/26
Wonder, Stevie	Saginaw, MI	5/13/50
Woodard, Alfre	Tulsa, OK	11/2/53
Woods, James	Vernal, NJ	4/18/47
Woodward, Edward	Croyden, England	6/1/30
Woodward, Joanne	Thomasville, GA	2/27/30
Woolery, Chuck	Ashland, KY	3/16/--
Worth, Irene	Nebraska	6/23/16
Wray, Fay	Alberta, Canada	9/10/07
Wright, Martha	Seattle, WA	3/23/26
Wright, Max	Detroit, MI	8/2/--
Wright, Steven	New York, NY	12/6/55
Wright, Teresa	New York, NY	10/27/18
Wyatt, Jane	Campgaw, NJ	8/10/11
Wyman, Jane	St. Joseph, MO	1/4/14
Wynette, Tammy	Red Bay, AL	5/5/42
Yarborough, Glenn	Milwaukee, WI	1/12/30
Yarrow, Peter	New York, NY	5/31/38
York, Michael	Fulmer, England	3/27/42
York, Susannah	London, England	1/9/42
Young, Alan	Northumberland, England	11/19/19
Young, Burt	New York, NY	4/30/40
Young, Loretta	Salt Lake City, UT	1/6/13
Young, Neil	Toronto, Ontario	11/12/45
Young, Robert	Chicago, IL	2/22/07
Young, Sean	Louisville, KY	11/20/59
Youngman, Henny	Liverpool, England	1/12/06
Zeffirelli, Franco	Florence, Italy	2/12/23
Zerbe, Anthony	Long Beach, CA	5/20/36
Zimbalist, Efrem Jr.	New York, NY	11/30/23
Zukerman, Pinchas	Tel Aviv, Israel	7/16/48

Entertainment Personalities of the Past

(As of mid-1994)

Born	Died	Name
1895	1974	Abbott, Bud
1903	1992	Acuff, Roy
1872	1953	Adams, Maude
1855	1926	Adler, Jacob P.
1903	1984	Adler, Luther
1898	1933	Adoree, Renee
1902	1986	Aherne, Brian
1931	1989	Ailey, Alvin
1918	1994	Akins, Claude
1909	1964	Albertson, Frank
1907	1981	Albertson, Jack
1894	1956	Allen, Fred
1906	1964	Allen, Gracie
1883	1950	Allgood, Sara
1908	1993	Ameche, Don
1903	1993	Ames, Leon
1902	1993	Anderson, Marian
1909	1992	Andrews, Dana
1913	1967	Andrews, Laverne
1887	1933	Arbuckle, Fatty (Roscoe)
1908	1990	Arden, Eve
1900	1976	Arlen, Richard
1868	1946	Arliss, George
1888	1945	Armetta, Henry
1900	1971	Armstrong, Louis
1917	1986	Arnaz, Desi
1890	1956	Arnold, Edward
1905	1974	Arquette, Cliff
1900	1991	Arthur, Jean
1899	1987	Astaire, Fred
1906	1987	Astor, Mary
1885	1946	Atwill, Lionel
1905	1967	Auer, Mischa
1900	1972	Austin, Gene
1913	1989	Backus, Jim
1918	1990	Bailey, Pearl
1892	1968	Bainter, Fay
1906	1975	Baker, Josephine
1904	1983	Balanchine, George
1911	1989	Ball, Lucille
1882	1956	Bancroft, George
1902	1968	Bankhead, Tallulah
1890	1952	Banks, Leslie
1890	1955	Bara, Theda
1810	1891	Barnum, Phineas T.
1879	1959	Barrymore, Ethel
1882	1942	Barrymore, John
1878	1954	Barrymore, Lionel
1848	1905	Barrymore, Maurice
1897	1963	Barthelmess, Richard
1914	1984	Basehart, Richard
1904	1984	Basie, Count
1923	1985	Baxter, Anne
1889	1951	Baxter, Warner
1904	1965	Beatty, Clyde
1902	1962	Beavers, Louise
1884	1946	Beery, Noah
1889	1949	Beery, Wallace
1901	1970	Begley, Ed
1904	1991	Bellamy, Ralph
1949	1982	Belushi, John
1906	1968	Benaderet, Bea
1906	1964	Bendix, William
1904	1965	Bennett, Constance
1910	1990	Bennett, Joan
1943	1987	Bennett, Michael
1894	1974	Benny, Jack
1924	1970	Benzell, Mimi
1899	1966	Berg, Gertrude
1903	1978	Bergen, Edgar
1915	1982	Bergman, Ingrid
1895	1976	Berkeley, Busby
1923	1986	Bernardi, Herschel
1844	1923	Bernhardt, Sarah
1893	1943	Bernie, Ben
1889	1967	Bickford, Charles
1934	1993	Bixby, Bill
1911	1960	Bjoerling, Jussi
1895	1973	Blackmer, Sidney
1908	1989	Blanc, Mel
1928	1972	Blocker, Dan
1909	1979	Blondell, Joan
1888	1959	Blore, Eric
1901	1975	Blue, Ben
1899	1957	Bogart, Humphrey
1880	1965	Boland, Mary
1895	1969	Boles, John
1904	1987	Bolger, Ray
1903	1960	Bond, Ward
1892	1981	Bondi, Beulah
1917	1981	Boone, Richard
1833	1893	Booth, Edwin
1796	1852	Booth, Junius Brutus
1898	1992	Booth, Shirley
1905	1965	Bow, Clara
1874	1946	Bowes, Maj. Edward
1928	1977	Boyd, Stephen
1898	1972	Boyd, William
1899	1978	Boyer, Charles
1893	1939	Brady, Alice
1894	1974	Brennan, Walter

Born	Died	Name
1904	1979	Brent, George
1891	1951	Brice, Fanny
1891	1959	Broderick, Helen
1892	1973	Brown, Joe E.
1926	1966	Bruce, Lenny
1895	1953	Bruce, Nigel
1910	1982	Bruce, Virginia
1915	1985	Brynner, Yul
1903	1979	Buchanan, Edgar
1938	1982	Buono, Victor
1885	1970	Burke, Billie
1911	1967	Burnette, Smiley
1917	1993	Burr, Raymond
1925	1984	Burton, Richard
1897	1946	Busch, Mae
1883	1966	Bushman, Francis X.
1896	1946	Butterworth, Charles
1893	1971	Byington, Spring
1904	1972	Cabot, Bruce
1918	1977	Cabot, Sebastian
1899	1986	Cagney, James
1895	1956	Calhern, Louis
1923	1977	Callas, Maria
1933	1976	Cambridge, Godfrey
1865	1940	Campbell, Mrs. Patrick
1950	1994	Candy, John
1892	1964	Cantor, Eddie
1897	1991	Capra, Frank
1878	1947	Carey, Harry
1913	1994	Carey, Macdonald
1950	1983	Carpenter, Karen
1906	1988	Carradine, John
1880	1961	Carrillo, Leo
1892	1972	Carroll, Leo G.
1905	1965	Carroll, Nancy
1910	1963	Carson, Jack
1873	1921	Caruso, Enrico
1876	1973	Casals, Pablo
1929	1989	Cassavetes, John
1893	1969	Castle, Irene
1887	1918	Castle, Vernon
1873	1938	Chaliapin, Feodor
1919	1980	Champion, Gower
1918	1961	Chandler, Jeff
1883	1930	Chaney, Lon
1905	1973	Chaney Jr., Lon
1942	1981	Chapin, Harry
1889	1977	Chaplin, Charles
1893	1961	Chatterton, Ruth
1888	1972	Chevalier, Maurice
1888	1960	Clark, Bobby
1914	1968	Clark, Fred
1920	1966	Clift, Montgomery
1932	1963	Cline, Patsy
1892	1967	Clyde, Andy
1911	1976	Cobb, Lee J.
1877	1961	Coburn, Charles
1878	1942	Cohan, George M.
1902	1986	Cohen, Myron
1919	1965	Cole, Nat (King)
1890	1965	Collins, Ray
1891	1958	Colman, Ronald
1908	1934	Columbo, Russ
1920	1994	Conrad, William
1917	1982	Conried, Hans
1911	1975	Conte, Richard
1914	1984	Coogan, Jackie
1935	1964	Cooke, Sam
1901	1961	Cooper, Gary
1888	1971	Cooper, Gladys
1896	1973	Cooper, Melville
1914	1968	Corey, Wendell
1893	1974	Cornell, Katherine
1890	1972	Correll, Charles (Andy)
1905	1979	Costello, Dolores
1906	1959	Costello, Lou
1905	1994	Cotton, Joseph
1899	1973	Coward, Noel
1924	1973	Cox, Wally
1908	1983	Crabbe, Buster
1928	1978	Crane, Bob
1911	1986	Crawford, Broderick
1908	1977	Crawford, Joan
1880	1942	Crews, Laura Hope
1880	1974	Crisp, Donald
1942	1973	Croce, Jim
1903	1977	Crosby, Bing
1910	1986	Crothers, Scatman
1908	1990	Cummings, Robert
1878	1968	Currie, Finlay
1914	1978	Dailey, Dan
1923	1965	Dandridge, Dorothy
1894	1963	Daniell, Henry
1901	1971	Daniels, Bebe
1936	1973	Darin, Bobby
1921	1965	Darnell, Linda
1879	1967	Darwell, Jane
1909	1986	Da Silva, Howard
1866	1949	Davenport, Harry
1908	1989	Davis, Bette
1907	1961	Davis, Joan
1925	1990	Davis Jr., Sammy
1931	1955	Dean, James
1917	1993	Defore, Don
1905	1968	Dekker, Albert
1908	1983	Del Rio, Dolores
1892	1983	Demarest, William
1905	1993	DeMille, Agnes
1881	1959	DeMille, Cecil B.
1891	1967	Denny, Reginald
1901	1974	DeSica, Vittorio
1905	1977	Devine, Andy
1924	1991	Dewhurst, Colleen
1942	1972	De Wilde, Brandon
1907	1974	De Wolfe, Billy
1920	1985	Diamond, Selma
1901	1992	Dietrich, Marlene
1879	1947	Digges, Dudley
1901	1966	Disney, Walt
1894	1949	Dix, Richard
1905	1958	Donat, Robert
1889	1972	Donlevy, Brian
1901	1981	Douglas, Melvyn
1907	1959	Douglas, Paul
1889	1956	Draper, Ruth
1881	1965	Dresser, Louise
1869	1934	Dressler, Marie
1820	1897	Drew, Mrs. John
1909	1951	Duchin, Eddy
1890	1974	Dumbrille, Douglass
1889	1965	Dumont, Margaret
1878	1927	Duncan, Isadora
1905	1967	Dunn, James
1898	1990	Dunne, Irene
1893	1980	Durante, Jimmy
1907	1968	Duryea, Dan
1858	1924	Duse, Eleanora
1894	1929	Eagels, Jeanne
1914	1993	Eckstine, Billy
1901	1967	Eddy, Nelson
1897	1971	Edwards, Cliff
1879	1945	Edwards, Gus
1899	1974	Ellington, Duke
1941	1974	Elliot, Cass
1891	1967	Elman, Mischa
1881	1951	Errol, Leon
1888	1976	Evans, Edith
1901	1989	Evans, Maurice
1909	1994	Ewell, Tom
1883	1939	Fairbanks, Douglas
1914	1970	Farmer, Frances
1870	1929	Farnum, Dustin
1876	1953	Farnum, William
1882	1967	Farrar, Geraldine
1904	1971	Farrell, Glenda
1897	1961	Fay, Frank
1895	1962	Fazenda, Louise
1933	1982	Feldman, Marty
1920	1993	Fellini, Fedrico
1912	1992	Ferrer, Jose
1898	1985	Fetchit, Stepin
1894	1979	Fiedler, Arthur
1918	1973	Field, Betty
1898	1979	Fields, Gracie
1879	1946	Fields, W.C.
1931	1978	Fields, Totie
1916	1977	Finch, Peter
1902	1975	Fine, Larry
1865	1932	Fiske, Minnie Maddern
1888	1961	Fitzgerald, Barry
1895	1962	Flagstad, Kirsten
1900	1971	Flippen, Jay C.
1909	1959	Flynn, Errol
1925	1974	Flynn, Joe
1910	1968	Foley, Red
1905	1982	Fonda, Henry
1920	1978	Fontaine, Frank
1887	1983	Fontanne, Lynn
1919	1991	Fonteyn, Margot
1895	1973	Ford, John
1901	1976	Ford, Paul
1919	1991	Ford, Tennessee Ernie
1899	1966	Ford, Wallace
1927	1987	Fosse, Bob
1901	1970	Foster, Preston
1922	1991	Foxx, Redd
1857	1928	Foy, Eddie
1903	1968	Francis, Kay
1887	1966	Frawley, William
1870	1955	Friganza, Trixie
1890	1958	Frisco, Joe
1901	1960	Gable, Clark
1905	1990	Garbo, Greta
1922	1990	Gardner, Ava
1913	1952	Garfield, John
1922	1969	Garland, Judy
1939	1984	Gaye, Marvin
1906	1984	Gaynor, Janet
1902	1978	Geer, Will
1900	1954	George, Gladys
1892	1962	Gibson, Hoot
1894	1971	Gilbert, Billy
1895	1936	Gilbert, John
1855	1937	Gillette, William
1897	1987	Gingold, Hermione
1898	1968	Gish, Dorothy
1893	1993	Gish, Lillian
1916	1987	Gleason, Jackie
1886	1959	Gleason, James
1884	1938	Gluck, Alma
1905	1990	Goddard, Paulette
1903	1983	Godfrey, Arthur
1882	1974	Goldwyn, Samuel
1909	1986	Goodman, Benny
1915	1969	Gorcey, Leo
1896	1985	Gordon, Ruth
1899	1982	Gosden, Freeman (Amos)
1869	1944	Gottschalk, Ferdinand
1829	1869	Gottschalk, Louis
1916	1973	Grable, Betty
1894	1991	Graham, Martha
1925	1981	Grahame, Gloria
1913	1993	Granger, Stewart
1904	1986	Grant, Cary
1915	1987	Greene, Lorne
1879	1954	Greenstreet, Sydney
1874	1948	Griffith, David Wark
1912	1980	Griffith, Hugh
1912	1967	Guthrie, Woody
1875	1959	Gwenn, Edmund
1926	1993	Gwynne, Fred
1892	1950	Hale, Alan
1925	1981	Haley, Bill
1899	1979	Haley, Jack
1902	1985	Hamilton, Margaret
1847	1919	Hammerstein, Oscar
1893	1964	Hardwicke, Cedric
1892	1957	Hardy, Oliver
1911	1937	Harlow, Jean
1908	1990	Harrison, Rex
1870	1946	Hart, William S.
1928	1973	Harvey, Laurence
1910	1973	Hawkins, Jack
1890	1973	Hayakawa, Sessue
1885	1969	Hayes, Gabby
1900	1993	Hayes, Helen
1902	1971	Hayward, Leland
1917	1975	Hayward, Susan
1918	1987	Hayworth, Rita
1896	1937	Healy, Ted
1910	1971	Heflin, Van
1901	1987	Heifetz, Jascha
1873	1918	Held, Anna
1942	1970	Hendrix, Jimi
1912	1969	Henie, Sonja
1908	1992	Henreid, Paul
1936	1990	Henson, Jim
1929	1993	Hepburn, Audrey
1886	1956	Hersholt, Jean
1899	1980	Hitchcock, Alfred
1914	1955	Hodiak, John
1894	1973	Holden, Fay
1918	1981	Holden, William
1922	1965	Holliday, Judy

Born	Died	Name
1936	1959	Holly, Buddy
1888	1951	Holt, Jack
1918	1973	Holt, Tim
1898	1978	Homolka, Oscar
1902	1972	Hopkins, Miriam
1858	1935	Hopper, DeWolf
1915	1970	Hopper, William
1904	1989	Horowitz, Vladimir
1886	1970	Horton, Edward Everett
1874	1926	Houdini, Harry
1902	1988	Houseman, John
1906	1952	Howard, Curly
1881	1965	Howard, Eugene
1867	1961	Howard, Joe
1890	1943	Howard, Leslie
1897	1975	Howard, Moe
1891	1955	Howard, Shemp
1885	1955	Howard, Tom
1916	1988	Howard, Trevor
1885	1949	Howard, Willie
1925	1985	Hudson, Rock
1890	1977	Hull, Henry
1886	1957	Hull, Josephine
1895	1958	Humphrey, Doris
1925	1969	Hunter, Jeffrey
1901	1962	Husing, Ted
1906	1987	Huston, John
1884	1950	Huston, Walter
1895	1969	Ingram, Rex
1895	1980	Iturbi, Jose
1936	1990	Ireland, Jill
1915	1992	Ireland, John
1838	1905	Irving, Henry
1875	1942	Jackson, Joe
1911	1972	Jackson, Mahalia
1891	1984	Jaffe, Sam
1903	1991	Jagger, Dean
1916	1983	James, Harry
1889	1956	Janis, Elsie
1886	1950	Jannings, Emil
1930	1980	Janssen, David
1900	1974	Jenkins, Allen
1898	1981	Jessel, George
1892	1962	Johnson, Chic
1886	1950	Jolson, Al
1889	1942	Jones, Buck
1933	1983	Jones, Carolyn
1911	1965	Jones, Spike
1943	1970	Joplin, Janis
1902	1982	Jory, Victor
1905	1981	Joslyn, Allyn
1910	1966	Kane, Helen
1887	1969	Karloff, Boris
1893	1970	Karns, Roscoe
1913	1987	Kaye, Danny
1811	1868	Kean, Charles
1806	1880	Kean, Mrs. Charles
1787	1833	Kean, Edmund
1895	1966	Keaton, Buster
1910	1993	Keeler, Ruby
1894	1973	Kellaway, Cecil
1898	1979	Kelly, Emmett
1928	1982	Kelly, Grace
1910	1981	Kelly, Patsy
1907	1968	Kelton, Pert
1926	1959	Kendall, Kay
1914	1990	Kennedy, Arthur
1890	1948	Kennedy, Edgar
1886	1956	Kibbee, Guy
1888	1964	Kilbride, Percy
1923	1986	Knight, Ted
1901	1980	Kostelanetz, Andre
1919	1962	Kovacs, Ernie
1885	1974	Kruger, Otto
1921	1991	Kulp, Nancy
1913	1964	Ladd, Alan
1895	1967	Lahr, Bert
1919	1973	Lake, Veronica
1915	1982	Lamas, Fernando
1902	1986	Lanchester, Elsa
1919	1948	Landis, Carole
1904	1972	Landis, Jessie Royce
1936	1991	Landon, Michael
1884	1944	Langdon, Harry
1853	1929	Langtry, Lillie

Born	Died	Name
1921	1959	Lanza, Mario
1870	1950	Lauder, Harry
1899	1962	Laughton, Charles
1890	1965	Laurel, Stan
1923	1984	Lawford, Peter
1898	1952	Lawrence, Gertrude
1908	1991	Lean, David
1940	1973	Lee, Bruce
1907	1952	Lee, Canada
1914	1970	Lee, Gypsy Rose
1888	1976	Lehmann, Lotte
1913	1967	Leigh, Vivien
1922	1976	Leighton, Margaret
1940	1980	Lennon, John
1898	1981	Lenya, Lotte
1870	1941	Leonard, Eddie
1900	1987	LeRoy, Mervyn
1906	1972	Levant, Oscar
1905	1980	Levene, Sam
1902	1971	Lewis, Joe E.
1892	1971	Lewis, Ted
1919	1987	Liberace
1820	1887	Lind, Jenny
1894	1989	Lillie, Beatrice
1893	1971	Lloyd, Harold
1870	1922	Lloyd, Marie
1891	1957	Lockhart, Gene
1913	1969	Logan, Ella
1909	1942	Lombard, Carole
1902	1977	Lombardo, Guy
1927	1974	Long, Richard
1895	1975	Lopez, Vincent
1888	1968	Lorne, Marion
1904	1964	Lorre, Peter
1912	1962	Lovejoy, Frank
1890	1971	Lowe, Edmund
1905	1993	Loy, Myrna
1892	1947	Lubitsch, Ernst
1882	1956	Lugosi, Bela
1894	1971	Lukas, Paul
1892	1977	Lunt, Alfred
1926	1982	Lynde, Paul
1926	1971	Lynn, Diana
1903	1965	MacDonald, Jeanette
1902	1969	MacLane, Barton
1908	1991	MacMurray, Fred
1921	1986	MacRae, Gordon
1909	1973	Macready, George
1908	1973	Magnani, Anna
1890	1975	Main, Marjorie
1932	1967	Mansfield, Jayne
1905	1980	Mantovani, Annunzio
1897	1975	March, Fredric
1945	1981	Marley, Bob
1890	1966	Marshall, Herbert
1913	1990	Martin, Mary
1920	1981	Martin, Ross
1924	1987	Marvin, Lee
1888	1964	Marx, Arthur (Harpo)
1901	1979	Marx, Herbert (Zeppo)
1890	1977	Marx, Julius (Groucho)
1886	1961	Marx, Leonard (Chico)
1893	1977	Marx, Milton (Gummo)
1909	1984	Mason, James
1896	1983	Massey, Raymond
1885	1957	Mayer, Louis B.
1895	1973	Maynard, Ken
1884	1945	McCormack, John
1905	1990	McCrea, Joel
1895	1952	McDaniel, Hattie
1899	1981	McHugh, Frank
1907	1991	McIntire, John
1883	1959	McLaglen, Victor
1907	1971	McMahon, Horace
1930	1980	McQueen, Steve
1920	1980	Medford, Kay
1880	1946	Meek, Donald
1861	1931	Melba, Nellie
1890	1973	Melchior, Lauritz
1890	1963	Menjou, Adolphe
1902	1966	Menken, Helen
1925	1994	Mercouri, Melina
1908	1984	Merman, Ethel
1905	1986	Milland, Ray
1904	1944	Miller, Glenn
1898	1936	Miller, Marilyn

Born	Died	Name
1903	1955	Minnevitch, Borrah
1913	1955	Miranda, Carmen
1918	1994	Mitchell, Cameron
1892	1962	Mitchell, Thomas
1880	1940	Mix, Tom
1926	1962	Monroe, Marilyn
1911	1973	Monroe, Vaughn
1917	1951	Montez, Maria
1904	1981	Montgomery, Robert
1901	1947	Moore, Grace
1914	1993	Moore, Garry
1876	1962	Moore, Victor
1906	1974	Moorehead, Agnes
1910	1994	Morgan, Dennis
1890	1949	Morgan, Frank
1900	1941	Morgan, Helen
1915	1994	Morgan, Henry
1901	1970	Morris, Chester
1914	1959	Morris, Wayne
1943	1971	Morrison, Jim
1932	1982	Morrow, Vic
1915	1977	Mostel, Zero
1897	1969	Mowbray, Alan
1895	1967	Muni, Paul
1915	1970	Munshin, Jules
1924	1971	Murphy, Audie
1902	1992	Murphy, George
1885	1965	Murray, Mae
1896	1970	Nagel, Conrad
1900	1973	Naish, J. Carroll
1898	1961	Naldi, Nita
1906	1975	Nelson, Ozzie
1940	1985	Nelson, Rick
1885	1967	Nesbit, Evelyn
1909	1983	Niven, David
1890	1950	Nijinsky, Vaslav
1893	1974	Nilsson, Anna Q.
1902	1985	Nolan, Lloyd
1894	1930	Normand, Mabel
1899	1968	Novarro, Ramon
1938	1993	Nureyev, Rudolf
1903	1978	Oakie, Jack
1860	1926	Oakley, Annie
1928	1982	Oates, Warren
1911	1979	Oberon, Merle
1915	1985	O'Brien, Edmond
1899	1983	O'Brien, Pat
1908	1981	O'Connell, Arthur
1921	1993	O'Connell, Helen
1880	1959	O'Connor, Una
1908	1968	O'Keefe, Dennis
1880	1938	Oland, Warner
1860	1932	Olcott, Chauncey
1883	1942	Oliver, Edna May
1907	1989	Olivier, Laurence
1892	1963	Olsen, Ole
1927	1994	O'Neal, Patrick
1849	1920	O'Neill, James
1936	1988	Orbison, Roy
1899	1985	Ormandy, Eugene
1876	1949	Ouspenskaya, Maria
1887	1972	Owen, Reginald
1860	1941	Paderewski, Ignace
1924	1987	Page, Geraldine
1889	1954	Pallette, Eugene
1914	1986	Palmer, Lilli
1894	1958	Pangborn, Franklin
1914	1992	Parks, Bert
1914	1975	Parks, Larry
1881	1940	Pasternack, Josef A.
1837	1908	Pastor, Tony
1843	1919	Patti, Adelina
1840	1889	Patti, Carlotta
1885	1931	Pavlova, Anna
1912	1989	Payne, John
1904	1984	Peerce, Jan
1899	1967	Pendleton, Nat
1905	1941	Penner, Joe
1928	1994	Peppard, George
1932	1992	Perkins, Anthony
1915	1963	Piaf, Edith
1893	1979	Pickford, Mary
1897	1984	Pidgeon, Walter
1892	1957	Pinza, Ezio
1898	1963	Pitts, Zasu
1904	1976	Pons, Lily

Born	Died	Name
1897	1981	Ponselle, Rosa
1904	1963	Powell, Dick
1912	1982	Powell, Eleanor
1892	1984	Powell, William
1913	1958	Power, Tyrone
1905	1986	Preminger, Otto
1935	1977	Presley, Elvis
1918	1987	Preston, Robert
1911	1993	Price, Vincent
1911	1978	Prima, Louis
1954	1977	Prinze, Freddie
1946	1989	Radner, Gilda
1895	1980	Raft, George
1890	1967	Rains, Claude
1902	1994	Ralson, Esther
1892	1967	Rathbone, Basil
1897	1960	Ratoff, Gregory
1941	1967	Redding, Otis
1908	1985	Redgrave, Michael
1921	1986	Reed, Donna
1932	1992	Reed, Robert
1914	1959	Reeves, George
1873	1943	Reinhardt, Max
1935	1991	Remick, Lee
1909	1971	Rennie, Michael
1902	1983	Richardson, Ralph
1921	1985	Riddle, Nelson
1898	1977	Ritchard, Cyril
1907	1974	Ritter, Tex
1905	1969	Ritter, Thelma
1901	1965	Ritz, Al
1906	1986	Ritz, Harry
1903	1985	Ritz, Jimmy
1925	1982	Robbins, Marty
1898	1976	Robeson, Paul
1878	1949	Robinson, Bill
1893	1973	Robinson, Edward G.
1905	1977	Rochester (E. Anderson)
1897	1933	Rodgers, Jimmie
1879	1935	Rogers, Will
1905	1994	Roland, Gilbert
1907	1994	Romero, Cesar
1880	1962	Rooney, Pat
1899	1966	Rose, Billy
1922	1987	Rowan, Dan
1887	1982	Rubinstein, Artur
1886	1970	Ruggles, Charles
1924	1961	Russell, Gail
1861	1922	Russell, Lillian
1911	1976	Russell, Rosalind
1892	1972	Rutherford, Margaret
1903	1973	Ryan, Irene
1909	1973	Ryan, Robert
1877	1968	St. Denis, Ruth
1884	1955	Sakall, S.Z.
1885	1936	Sale (Chic), Charles
1906	1972	Sanders, George
1924	1994	Savalas, Telly
1895	1964	Schildkraut, Joseph
1889	1965	Schipa, Tito

Born	Died	Name
1882	1951	Schnabel, Artur
1920	1981	Scott, Hazel
1898	1987	Scott, Randolph
1914	1965	Scott, Zachary
1843	1896	Scott-Siddons, Mrs.
1938	1979	Seberg, Jean
1892	1974	Seeley, Blossom
1893	1987	Segovia, Andres
1925	1980	Sellers, Peter
1902	1965	Selznick, David O.
1884	1960	Sennett, Mack
1927	1978	Shaw, Robert
1891	1972	Shawn, Ted
1868	1949	Shean, Al
1902	1983	Shearer, Norma
1915	1967	Sheridan, Ann
1917	1994	Shore, Dinah
1875	1953	Shubert, Lee
1755	1831	Siddons, Mrs. Sarah
1921	1985	Signoret, Simone
1912	1985	Silvers, Phil
1900	1976	Sim, Alastair
1858	1942	Skinner, Otis
1863	1948	Smith, C. Aubrey
1907	1986	Smith, Kate
1854	1932	Sousa, John Philip
1884	1957	Sparks, Ned
1907	1990	Stanwyck, Barbara
1934	1970	Stevens, Inger
1882	1977	Stokowski, Leopold
1879	1953	Stone, Lewis
1904	1980	Stone, Milburn
1898	1959	Sturges, Preston
1911	1960	Sullavan, Margaret
1912	1994	Sullivan, Barry
1902	1974	Sullivan, Ed
1903	1956	Sullivan, Francis L.
1892	1946	Summerville, Slim
1899	1983	Swanson, Gloria
1904	1969	Swarthout, Gladys
1893	1957	Talmadge, Norma
1899	1972	Tamiroff, Akim
1909	1994	Tandy, Jessica
1878	1947	Tanguay, Eva
1885	1966	Taylor, Deems
1899	1958	Taylor, Estelle
1887	1946	Taylor, Laurette
1911	1969	Taylor, Robert
1847	1928	Terry, Ellen
1899	1936	Thalberg, Irving
1912	1991	Thomas, Danny
1882	1976	Thorndike, Sybil
1896	1960	Tibbett, Lawrence
1920	1991	Tierney, Gene
1909	1958	Todd, Michael
1903	1968	Tone, Franchot
1867	1957	Toscanini, Arturo
1898	1968	Tracy, Lee
1900	1967	Tracy, Spencer
1903	1972	Traubel, Helen
1894	1975	Treacher, Arthur
1853	1917	Tree, Herbert Beerbohm

Born	Died	Name
1890	1973	Truex, Ernest
1932	1984	Truffaut, Francois
1919	1986	Tucker, Forrest
1915	1975	Tucker, Richard
1884	1966	Tucker, Sophie
1874	1940	Turpin, Ben
1908	1959	Twelvetrees, Helen
1933	1993	Twitty, Conway
1895	1926	Valentino, Rudolph
1901	1986	Vallee, Rudy
1911	1979	Vance, Vivian
1924	1990	Vaughan, Sarah
1893	1943	Veidt, Conrad
1926	1981	Vera-Ellen
1885	1957	Von Stroheim, Erich
1906	1981	Von Zell, Harry
1922	1992	Walker, Nancy
1914	1951	Walker, Robert
1887	1980	Walsh, Raoul
1876	1962	Walter, Bruno
1876	1958	Warner, H. B.
1924	1963	Washington, Dinah
1900	1977	Waters, Ethel
1907	1979	Wayne, John
1891	1966	Webb, Clifton
1920	1982	Webb, Jack
1903	1992	Welk, Lawrence
1915	1985	Welles, Orson
1896	1975	Wellman, William
1892	1980	West, Mae
1895	1968	Wheeler, Bert
1889	1938	White, Pearl
1891	1967	Whiteman, Paul
1865	1948	Whitty, May
1912	1979	Wilding, Michael
1877	1922	Williams, Bert
1923	1953	Williams, Hank
1905	1975	Wills, Bob
1903	1978	Wills, Chill
1917	1972	Wilson, Marie
1884	1969	Winninger, Charles
1904	1959	Withers, Grant
1907	1961	Wong, Anna May
1938	1981	Wood, Natalie
1892	1978	Wood, Peggy
1888	1963	Woolley, Monty
1902	1981	Wyler, William
1886	1966	Wynn, Ed
1916	1986	Wynn, Keenan
1890	1960	Young, Clara Kimball
1913	1978	Young, Gig
1887	1953	Young, Roland
1902	1979	Zanuck, Darryl F.
1940	1993	Zappa, Frank
1869	1932	Ziegfeld, Florenz
1873	1976	Zukor, Adolph

Original Names of Selected Entertainers

Edie Adams: Elizabeth Edith Enke
Eddie Albert: Edward Albert Heimberger
Alan Alda: Alphonso D'Abruzzo
Jane Alexander: Jane Quigley
Fred Allen: John Sullivan
Woody Allen: Allen Konigsberg
Julie Andrews: Julia Wells
Eve Arden: Eunice Quedens
Beatrice Arthur: Bernice Frankel
Jean Arthur: Gladys Greene
Fred Astaire: Frederick Austerlitz
Alan Autry: Carlos Brown
Lauren Bacall: Betty Joan Perske
Anne Bancroft: Anna Maria Italiano
Brigitte Bardot: Camille Javal
Gene Barry: Eugene Klass
Orson Bean: Dallas Burrows
Bonnie Bedelia: Bonnie Culkin
Pat Benatar: Patricia Andrejewski
Robbie Benson: Robert Segal
Tony Bennett: Anthony Benedetto
Busby Berkeley: William Berkeley Enos
Jack Benny: Benjamin Kubelsky
Joey Bishop: Joseph Gottlieb
Robert Blake: Michael Gubitosi
Victor Borge: Borge Rosenbaum
David Bowie: David Robert Jones
Boy George: George Alan O'Dowd
Fanny Brice: Fanny Borach
Charles Bronson: Charles Buchinski
Albert Brooks: Albert Einstein
Mel Brooks: Melvin Kaminsky
George Burns: Nathan Birnbaum
Ellen Burstyn: Edna Gilhooley
Richard Burton: Richard Jenkins
Red Buttons: Aaron Chwatt
Nicolas Cage: Nicholas Coppola
Michael Caine: Maurice Micklewhite
Maria Callas: Maria Kalogeropoulos
Vikki Carr: Florencia Casillas
Diahann Carroll: Carol Diahann Johnson
Cyd Charisse: Tula Finklea
Ray Charles: Ray Charles Robinson
Cher: Cherilyn Sarkisian
Patsy Cline: Virginia Patterson Hensley
Lee J. Cobb: Leo Jacoby

Claudette Colbert: Lily Chauchoin
Michael Connors: Kreker Ohanian
Robert Conrad: Conrad Robert Falk
Alice Cooper: Vincent Furnier
David Copperfield: David Kotkin
Howard Cosell: Howard Cohen
Elvis Costello: Declan Patrick McManus
Lou Costello: Louis Cristillo
Joan Crawford: Lucille Le Sueur
Michael Crawford: Michael Dumbell-Smith
Tom Cruise: Thomas Mapother
Tony Curtis: Bernard Schwartz
Vic Damone: Vito Farinola
Rodney Dangerfield: Jacob Cohen
Bobby Darin: Walden Robert Cassotto
Doris Day: Doris von Kappelhoff
Yvonne De Carlo: Peggy Middleton
Sandra Dee: Alexandra Zuck
John Denver: Henry John Deutschendorf Jr.
Bo Derek: Cathleen Collins
John Derek: Derek Harris
Danny DeVito: Daniel Michaeli
Susan Dey: Susan Smith
Angie Dickinson: Angeline Brown
Bo Diddley: Elias Bates
Phyllis Diller: Phyllis Driver
Diana Dors: Diana Fluck
Kirk Douglas: Issur Danielovitch
Melvyn Douglas: Melvyn Hesselberg
Bob Dylan: Robert Zimmerman
Sheena Easton: Sheena Shirley Orr
Barbara Eden: Barbara Huffman
Ron Ely: Ronald Pierce
Chad Everett: Raymond Cramton
Tom Ewell: S. Yewell Tompkins
Douglas Fairbanks: Douglas Ullman
Morgan Fairchild: Patsy McClenny
Alice Faye: Ann Leppert
Stepin Fetchit: Lincoln Perry
Sally Field: Sally Mahoney
W.C. Fields: William Claude Dukenfield
Peter Finch: William Mitchell
Barry Fitzgerald: William Joseph Shields
Joan Fontaine: Joan de Havilland
John Ford: Sean O'Fearna
John Forsythe: John Freund
Redd Foxx : John Sanford
Anthony Franciosa: Anthony Papaleo
Arlene Francis: Arlene Kazanjian
Connie Francis: Concetta Franconero
Greta Garbo: Greta Gustafsson
Vincent Gardenia: Vincent Scognamiglio
John Garfield: Julius Garfinkle
Judy Garland: Frances Gumm
James Garner: James Bumgarner
Crystal Gayle: Brenda Gayle Webb
Paulette Goddard: Marion Levy
Whoopi Goldberg: Caryn Johnson
Eydie Gorme: Edith Gormezano
Stewart Granger: James Stewart
Cary Grant: Archibald Leach
Lee Grant: Lyova Rosenthal
Joel Grey: Joe Katz
Robert Guillaume: Robert Williams
Buddy Hackett: Leonard Hacker
Hammer: Stanley Kirk Burrell
Jean Harlow: Harlean Carpentier
Rex Harrison: Reginald Carey
Laurence Harvey: Larushka Skikne
Helen Hayes: Helen Brown
Susan Hayward: Edythe Marriner
Rita Hayworth: Margarita Cansino
Pee-Wee Herman: Paul Rubenfeld
Barbara Hershey: Barbara Herzstine
William Holden: William Beedle
Judy Holliday: Judith Tuvim
Harry Houdini: Ehrich Weiss
Leslie Howard: Leslie Stainer
Moe Howard: Moses Horowitz
Rock Hudson: Roy Scherer Jr. (later Fitzgerald)
Engelbert Humperdinck: Arnold Dorsey
Kim Hunter: Janet Cole
Mary Beth Hurt: Mary Supinger
Betty Hutton: Betty Thornberg
David Janssen: David Meyer
Elton John: Reginald Dwight
Don Johnson: Donald Wayne
Jennifer Jones: Phyllis Isley
Tom Jones: Thomas Woodward
Louis Jourdan: Louis Gendre
Boris Karloff: William Henry Pratt
Danny Kaye: David Kaminsky
Diane Keaton: Diane Hall
Michael Keaton: Michael Douglas
Howard Keel: Harold Leek
Chaka Khan: Yvette Stevens
Carole King: Carole Klein
Larry King: Larry Zeigler
Ben Kingsley: Krishna Banji
Nastassja Kinski: Nastassja Naksyznyski
Ted Knight: Tadeus Wladyslaw Konopka
Cheryl Ladd: Cheryl Stoppelmoor
Veronica Lake: Constance Ockleman
Dorothy Lamour: Mary Kaumeyer
Michael Landon: Eugene Orowitz
Mario Lanza: Alfredo Cocozza
Stan Laurel: Arthur Jefferson
Steve Lawrence: Sidney Leibowitz
Brenda Lee: Brenda Mae Tarpley
Bruce Lee: Lee Yuen Kam
Gypsy Rose Lee: Rose Louise Hovick
Michelle Lee: Michelle Dusiak
Peggy Lee: Norma Egstrom
Janet Leigh: Jeanette Morrison
Vivien Leigh: Vivien Hartley
Huey Lewis: Hugh Cregg
Jerry Lewis: Joseph Levitch
Hal Linden: Harold Lipshitz
Carole Lombard: Jane Peters
Jack Lord: John Joseph Ryan
Sophia Loren: Sophia Scicoloni
Peter Lorre: Laszio Lowenstein
Myrna Loy: Myrna Williams
Bela Lugosi: Bela Ferenc Blasko
Moms Mabley: Loretta Mary Aitken
Shirley MacLaine: Shirley Beaty
Madonna: Madonna Louise Ciccone
Lee Majors: Harvey Lee Yeary 2d
Karl Malden: Malden Sekulovich
Jayne Mansfield: Vera Jane Palmer
Fredric March: Frederick Bickel
Peter Marshall: Pierre LaCock
Dean Martin: Dino Crocetti
Ethel Merman: Ethel Zimmerman
George Michael: Georgios Panayiotou
Ray Milland: Reginald Truscott-Jones
Ann Miller: Lucille Collier
Joni Mitchell: Roberta Joan Anderson
Marilyn Monroe: Norma Jean Mortenson, (later) Baker
Yves Montand: Ivo Levi
Ron Moody: Ronald Moodnick
Demi Moore: Demi Guynes
Garry Moore: Thomas Garrison Morfit
Rita Moreno: Rosita Alverio
Harry Morgan: Harry Bratsburg
Paul Muni: Muni Weisenfreund
Mike Nichols: Michael Igor Peschowsky
Chuck Norris: Carlos Ray
Sheree North: Dawn Bethel
Hugh O'Brian: Hugh Krampke
Maureen O'Hara: Maureen Fitzsimmons
Patti Page: Clara Ann Fowler
Jack Palance: Walter Palanuik
Bert Parks: Bert Jacobson
Minnie Pearl: Sarah Ophelia Cannon
Bernadette Peters: Bernadette Lazzaro
Edith Piaf: Edith Gassion
Slim Pickens: Louis Lindley
Mary Pickford: Gladys Smith
Stephanie Powers: Stefania Federkiewicz
Paula Prentiss: Paula Ragusa
Robert Preston: Robert Preston Meservey
Prince: Prince Rogers Nelson
Tony Randall: Leonard Rosenberg
Martha Raye: Margaret O'Reed
Donna Reed: Donna Belle Mullenger
Della Reese: Delloreese Patricia Early
Joan Rivers: Joan Sandra Molinsky
Edward G. Robinson: Emmanuel Goldenberg
Ginger Rogers: Virginia McMath
Roy Rogers: Leonard Slye
Mickey Rooney: Joe Yule Jr.
Lillian Russell: Helen Leonard
Theresa Russell: Theresa Paup
Winona Ryder: Winona Horowitz
Susan St. James: Susan Miller
Soupy Sales: Milton Hines
Susan Sarandon: Susan Tomaling

Randolph Scott: George Randolph Crane
Jane Seymour: Joyce Frankenberg
Omar Sharif: Michael Shalhoub
Martin Sheen: Ramon Estevez
Beverly Sills: Belle Silverman
Talia Shire: Talia Coppola
Phil Silvers: Philip Silversmith
Suzanne Somers: Suzanne Mahoney
Ann Sothern: Harriette Lake
Robert Stack: Robert Modini
Barbara Stanwyck: Ruby Stevens
Jean Stapleton: Jeanne Murray
Ringo Starr: Richard Starkey
Connie Stevens: Concetta Ingolia
Sting: Gordon Sumner
Donna Summer: La Donna Gaines
Rip Taylor: Charles Elmer Jr.
Robert Taylor: Spangler Arlington Brugh
Danny Thomas: Muzyad Yakhoob, later Amos Jacobs
Randy Travis: Randy Traywick
Sophie Tucker: Sophia Kalish
Tina Turner: Annie Mae Bullock
Conway Twitty: Harold Lloyd Jenkins
Rudolph Valentino: Rudolpho D'Antonguolla
Frankie Valli: Frank Castelluccio
David Wayne: Wayne McMeekan
John Wayne: Marion Morrison
Clifton Webb: Webb Parmalee Hollenbeck
Raquel Welch: Raquel Tejada
Gene Wilder: Jerome Silberman
Shelley Winters: Shirley Schrift
Stevie Wonder: Stevland Morris
Natalie Wood: Natasha Gurdin
Jane Wyman: Sarah Jane Fulks
Gig Young: Byron Barr

Selected International Figures of the Present

(Excluding most heads of state, entertainers, and athletes; for heads of state, see individual nations)

Name (Birthplace)	Birthdate
Chinua Achebe (Ogidi, Nigeria)	11/16/30
Jorge Amado (Bahia, Brazil)	8/1/12
Martin Amis (Oxford, England)	8/25/49
Yasir Arafat (Jerusalem, Palestine)	1929
Moshe Arens (Kaumas, Lithuania)	12/27/25
Oscar Arias Sanchez (Heredia, Costa Rica)	9/13/41
Margaret Atwood (Ottawa, Ontario)	11/18/39
Aung San Suu Kyi (Yangon, Myanmar)	6/19/45
Benazir Bhutto (Karachi, Pakistan)	6/21/53
Boutros Boutros-Ghali (Cairo, Egypt)	11/14/22
British Royal Family	
Queen Elizabeth II (London, England)	4/21/26
Prince Philip (Corfu, Greece)	6/1/21
Prince Charles (London, England)	11/14/48
Princess Diana (Sandringham, England)	7/1/61
Prince William (London, England)	6/21/82
Prince Henry (London, England)	9/15/84
Princess Anne (London, England)	8/15/50
Prince Andrew (London, England)	2/19/60
Sarah Ferguson (London, England)	10/15/59
Princess Beatrice (London, England)	8/8/88
Princess Eugenie (London, England)	3/23/90
Prince Edward (London, England)	3/1/64
Princess Margaret (Glamis, Scotland)	8/21/30
Gro Harlem Bruntland (Oslo, Norway)	4/2/39
Elias Canetti (Ruschuk, Bulgaria)	7/25/05
Camilo Jose Cela (Ira Flavia, Spain)	5/11/16
Jacques Cousteau (St. Andre-de-Cubzae, France)	6/11/10
Dalai Lama: Tenzin Gyatso (Kokonor, Tibet)	6/6/35
Robertson Davies (Thamesville, Ontario)	8/28/13
Frederik DeKlerk (Johannesburg, S Africa)	3/18/36
Jacques Derrida (El Biar, Algeria)	7/15/30
Takako Doi (Hyogo, Japan)	11/30/28
Margaret Drabble (Sheffield, England)	6/5/39
Valery Giscard d'Estaing (Koblenz, Germany)	2/2/26
Carlos Fuentes (Mexico City, Mexico)	11/11/28
Athol Fugard (Kanroo, South Africa)	1932
Gabriel Garcia Marquez (Aracata, Colombia)	3/6/28
Mikhail Gorbachev (Privalnaye, Stavropol, Russia)	3/21/31
Nadine Gordimer (Springs, South Africa)	11/2/23

Name (Birthplace)	Birthdate
Günter Grass, (Danzig, Germany)	10/16/27
Germaine Greer (Melbourne, Australia)	1/29/39
Stephen Hawking (Oxford, England)	1/8/42
Michael Heseltine (Swansea, Wales)	3/21/33
Ted Hughes (Mytholmroyd, England)	8/17/30
P.D. James (Oxford, England)	8/3/20
John Paul II, His Holiness Pope (Wadowice, Pol.)	5/18/20
Milan Kundera (Brno, Czechoslovakia)	4/1/29
John le Carré (Poole, England)	10/19/31
Doris Lessing (Kermanshah, Persia)	10/22/19
Naguib Mahfouz (Cairo, Egypt)	12/11/11
Crown Princess Masako (Tokyo, Japan)	12/9/63
Czeslaw Milosz (Sateinial, Lithuania)	6/3/11
Monaco Royal Family	
Prince Ranier III (Monaco)	5/31/23
Prince Albert (Monte Carlo, Monaco)	3/14/58
Princess Caroline (Monte Carlo, Monaco)	1/23/57
Princess Stephanie (Monaco-Ville, Monaco)	2/1/65
Winnie Mandela (Transkei,S Africa)	1934
Alice Munro (Wingham, Ontario)	7/10/31
Iris Murdoch (Dublin, Ireland)	7/15/19
Rupert Murdoch (Melbourne, Australia)	3/11/31
Crown Prince Naruhito (Tokyo, Japan)	2/23/60
Edna O'Brien (Tuamgraney, Ireland)	12/15/31
Amoz Oz (Jerusalem, Palestine)	5/4/39
Andreas Papandreou (Chios, Greece)	2/5/19
Octavio Paz (Mexico City, Mexico)	3/31/14
Shimon Perez (Wolozyn, Poland)	8/16/23
Yitzak Rabin (Jerusalem, Palestine)	3/1/22
Mordecai Richler (Montreal, Quebec)	1/27/31
Mary Robinson (Ballina, Ireland)	5/21/44
Salman Rushdie (Bombay, India)	6/19/47
Yitzak Shamir (Kuzinoy, Poland)	11/3/14
Wole Soyinka (Abeokuta, Nigeria)	7/13/34
Muriel Spark (Edinburgh, Scotland)	2/1/18
Hanna Suchocka (Pleszewa, Poland)	4/3/46
Mother Teresa (Skopje, Macedonia)	8/27/10
Margaret Thatcher (Grantham, England)	10/13/25
Bishop Desmond Tutu (Klerksdorp, South Africa)	10/7/31
Vladimir Zhirinovsky (Kazakhstan)	4/26/46

National Women's Hall of Fame, 1994 Inductees

Source: The National Women's Hall of Fame, Seneca Falls, NY

The National Women's Hall of Fame is the only national membership organization that honors and celebrates the achievements of extraordinary American women. Founded in 1969 in Seneca Falls, NY, where in 1848 the first Women's Rights Convention was held, the Hall inducts distinguished women and offers programs and exhibits in Seneca Falls, Washington, DC, and elsewhere. The Hall's last induction was Sept. 24, 1994.

Bella Abzug
Ella Baker
Myra Bradwell
Annie Jump Cannon
Jane Cunningham Croly
Catherine East
Geraldine Ferraro
Charlotte Perkins Gilman
Grace Hopper
Helen Hunt
Zora Neale Hurston
Anne Hutchinson
Frances Wisemart Jacobs
Susette La Flesche
Louise McManus
Maria Mitchell
Antonia Novello
Linda Richards
Wilma Rudolph
Betty Bone Schiess
Muriel Siebert
Nettie Stevens
Oprah Winfrey
Sarah Winnemucca
Fanny Wright

UNITED STATES POPULATION

A Typical American as Seen Through the Eyes of the Census Bureau, 1994

by
Dr. Harry A. Scarr
Deputy Director, Bureau of the Census
U.S. Department of Commerce

I am often asked to describe a typical American: What do we do? Where do we live? How much money do we make? According to Census Bureau data, typical America is a patchwork of cultures, lifestyles, and economic groups. Let's look at that typical American and at some not-so-typical Americans.

Who We Are

Typical America is composed of many racial and ethnic groups. On April 1, 1994, almost 26 million of us (9.9%) were of Hispanic origin, and more than 9 million of us (3.5%) identified ourselves as Asian-Pacific Islanders. Blacks numbered 32.5 million, or 12.5% of the population, and the American Indian/Eskimo/Aleut populations made up about 2.2 million (0.8%). An estimated 192.5 million people (74.1%) considered themselves to be white non-Hispanic.

According to the 1990 Census, nearly 20 million of us were not born in America, but call it home. In 1993, about 33% of our population growth came from net international migration.

America speaks many **languages:** More than 31 million of us speak a language other than English at home; more than half this number speaks Spanish.

We are also aging: since 1980 our **median age** has risen from 30.0 to 34.0 in 1994 (the median for blacks is 28.9, and the median for whites is 35.0). More than 26% of us are under 18 years of age, and more than 12.7% are 65 and older.

Females outnumber males in America by 6.1 million; 51% of the total population was female, as of April 1, 1994.

There were 96.4 million **households** in our nation in March 1993; 70% of them contained families. Of all households, 55% are maintained by married couples, and 74% of all households with children under 18 include a married couple. In about one-fourth of all households, one person lives alone.

What We Do

About 66% of Americans 16 years and older were in the labor force in 1993: almost 76% of men and nearly 58% of women. The unemployment rate was 6.7%.

Our top three **occupations** are administrative support, including clerical; professional specialty; and executive, administrative, and managerial. There are 20.2 million persons employed in the retail sales industry.

More than 8 million working-age Americans are prevented from working because of a disability, but 16 million persons with a disability work at a job or business.

Of the more than 115.1 million employed workers, 73.2% drive to work alone, and 13.4% are in car pools. About 76.1% of us work in the county in which we live, and our **commuting time** averages about 22.4 minutes (one way).

Where We Live

At least half of our population (56.4%), lives in the South and West regions of the country. Between 1980 and 1990, the West grew by 22.3%, and the South grew by 13.4%, well above the U.S. average of 9.8%. From 1990 to 1993, the trend continued (West, 6.2%; South, 4.7%; U.S. 3.7%).

Since 1990, we have been increasing by about 2.8 million persons a year. Our 5 most populous states are California (31.2 million), New York (18.2 million), Texas (18.0 million), Florida (13.7 million), and Pennsylvania (12 million). The 5 states at the other end of the spectrum are Delaware (700,000), North Dakota (635,000), Alaska (599,000), Vermont (576,000), and Wyoming (470,000).

Most of us—79.5%—live in **metropolitan areas,** and more than half of us (53.7%) live in one of the 41 metropolitan areas with populations of at least 1 million.

Our 5 largest metropolitan areas are scattered across the map: New York/Northern New Jersey/Long Island (19.7 million), Los Angeles/Riverside/Orange County (15.0 million), Chicago/Gary/Kenosha Counties (8.4 million), Washington/Baltimore (6.9 million), and San Francisco/Oakland/San Jose (6.4 million). Although the New York area remains in first position, the Los Angeles area is growing at a much faster rate (3.6 versus 0.6% since 1990).

How We Live

Typical Americans live in a household with others. The average number of people living in a household in the U.S. was 2.63 in 1993.

We have a total of about 105 million **housing units** nationwide; nearly 93 million of them are occupied. The vast majority of housing units have public water and sewer service, and our top 2 house heating fuel sources are utility gas (51 million units) and electricity (27 million units). About 3 million units lack complete plumbing facilities, and 4 million lack complete kitchen facilities.

Almost two-thirds (64%) of us are **homeowners.** Of the 60 million owner units, nearly 35 million have mortgages. The median monthly costs for all owner units is $455. The median for mortgage units is $761, and the median for non-mortgage units is $222. The median value of owner homes is $80,000.

If you live in one of the 33 million **renter-occupied housing units,** your housing costs are $462 per month.

Quality of Life

Education: Typical America has more high school graduates than at any other time in U.S. history: more than 80.2% of all Americans age 25 and older. About 21.9% of this same group have a bachelor's degree or higher.

Educational attainment has a direct impact on many aspects of life, but most directly on earnings. Average annual earnings for persons without a high school diploma are $14,391; with a diploma, $20,036; with a bachelor's degree, $34,096; with a doctorate, $54,982; and with a professional degree, $74,725. We spend an average of $4,700 annually per student in our public elementary and secondary schools.

Health insurance: Nearly 85% of us have health insurance. Those most likely to be insured are the elderly, the employed, and those with at least a high school diploma.

Poverty: In 1992, 36.9 million persons had income below the official government poverty level, up from 35.7 million in 1991 and 31.5 million in 1989. The 1992 poverty rate was 14.5%—not statistically different from the 1991 poverty rate of 14.2%, but different from the 1989 rate of 12.8%.

Child care: Families with working mothers and preschool children spend about 7% of their family income on child care for their children. Most care for preschoolers takes place in a home environment, such as with relatives or neighbors (67%); about 23% of child care for preschoolers is in organized facilities, such as nursery schools and day-care centers; 9% are cared for by the mother while she works; and 1% are in a school-based activity.

Child support: Of the 5.7 million women awarded child support, 5.0 million were supposed to receive payments in 1989. Of the women due payments, about half received the full amount they were due. The average amount of child support received in 1989 was $2,995. The aggregate amount of child support received in 1989 was $11.2 billion, 69% of $16.3 billion due.

The 1995 Census Test

Source: Bureau of the Census, U.S. Dept. of Commerce

On Mar. 4, 1995, the Bureau of the Census will begin the 1995 Census Test in preparation for the 22d decennial census that will be taken in the year 2000. Unlike a decennial census, which counts all persons residing in the U.S. and on military vessels, the Census Test is a sample survey conducted in only 4 sites, 3 urban and 1 rural. The urban sites are New Haven, CT, Oakland, CA, and Paterson, NJ. The rural site comprises the 6 parishes that form northwestern Louisiana: Bienville, De Soto, Jackson, Natchitoches, Red River, and Winn.

Although the 1995 Census Test design is not necessarily the design of the 2000 decennial census, it will contribute significantly toward specifying the types of questions that will be asked and the procedures that will be followed to collect data in the 2000 decennial census.

In the 1995 Census Test, 13 methods aimed at either reducing the number of persons not counted by the census and/or reducing the cost of the enumeration will be tested. Methods that proved successful in the 1990 decennial census will be incorporated into both the 1995 Census Test and the 2000 decennial census.

The basic data collection method will not change from 1990. In urban areas, households will receive a letter announcing the census test. A few days later, the household will receive a questionnaire to complete and return by mail. A reminder card will arrive after a few days. Three weeks later a replacement questionnaire will be mailed to those who do not return a questionnaire.

In rural areas, households will receive a letter by mail announcing the 1995 Census Test, and then enumerators will deliver the questionnaire and request that it be returned by mail. This basic procedure was used in the 1990 decennial census.

To improve coverage, other methods will be tested. The Census Bureau will observe the success of leaving questionnaires in places where historically undercounted populations reside and frequent, and a toll-free number for respondents to call for assistance in filling out their forms will also be provided.

Another new strategy is greater use of sampling and statistical estimation. Because one of the most costly parts of the 1990 decennial census was sending enumerators to follow up on all housing units that did not return a questionnaire, the Census Bureau hopes that sampling and estimating can provide accurate results that will lessen the need for numerous and costly follow-up visits.

Last, the Census Bureau will test new technologies in automated matching, data collecting, and electronic imaging.

After the data are collected, the Census Bureau will use the analyzed results, along with other research, policy decisions, and public reaction, to arrive at a design for the 2000 decennial census. The initial design must be presented to the U.S. Congress by Apr. 1, 1998.

Estimated Population of American Colonies, 1630-1780

Source: Bureau of the Census, U.S. Dept. of Commerce
(in thousands)

Colony	1780	1770	1750	1740	1720	1700	1690	1670	1650	1630
Total	**2,780.4**	**2,148.1**	**1,170.8**	**905.6**	**466.2**	**250.9**	**210.4**	**111.9**	**50.4**	**4.6**
Maine (counties)[1]	49.1	31.3	...	...	...	...	...	...	1.0	0.4
New Hampshire[2]	87.8	62.4	27.5	23.3	9.4	5.0	4.2	1.8	1.3	0.5
Vermont[3]	47.6	10.0	...	...	...	...	...	...	...	...
Plymouth and Massachusetts[1,2,4]	268.6	235.3	188.0	151.6	91.0	55.9	56.9	35.3	15.6	0.9
Rhode Island[2]	52.9	58.2	33.2	25.3	11.7	5.9	4.2	2.2	0.8	...
Connecticut[2]	206.7	183.9	111.3	89.6	58.8	26.0	21.6	12.6	4.1	...
New York[2]	210.5	162.9	76.7	63.7	36.9	19.1	13.9	5.8	4.1	0.4
New Jersey[2]	139.6	117.4	71.4	51.4	29.8	14.0	8.0	1.0	...	...
Pennsylvania[2]	327.3	240.1	119.7	85.6	31.0	18.0	11.4	...	...	...
Delaware[2]	45.4	35.5	28.7	19.9	5.4	2.5	1.5	0.7	0.2	...
Maryland[2]	245.5	202.6	141.1	116.1	66.1	29.6	24.0	13.2	4.5	...
Virginia[2]	538.0	447.0	231.0	180.4	87.8	58.6	53.0	35.3	18.7	2.5
North Carolina[2]	270.1	197.2	73.0	51.8	21.3	10.7	7.6	3.8	...	...
South Carolina[2]	180.0	124.2	64.0	45.0	17.0	5.7	3.9	0.2	...	...
Georgia[2]	56.1	23.4	5.2	2.0	...	...	...	...	...	...
Kentucky[5]	45.0	15.7	...	...	...	...	...	...	...	...
Tennessee[6]	10.0	1.0	...	...	...	...	...	...	...	...

(1) For 1660-1750, Maine counties included with Massachusetts. Maine was part of Massachusetts until it became a separate state in 1820. (2) One of the original 13 states. (3) Admitted to statehood in 1791. (4) Plymouth became a part of the Province of Massachusetts in 1691. (5) Admitted to statehood in 1792. (6) Admitted to statehood in 1796.

Race and Hispanic Origin for the U.S., 1990 and 1980

Source: Bureau of the Census, U.S. Dept. of Commerce

	1990 Census		1980 Census		Percentage change
	Number	Percent	Number	Percent	1980-1990
Race					
All persons	**248,709,873**	**100.0**	**226,545,805**	**100.0**	**9.8**
White	199,686,070	80.3	188,371,622	83.1	6.0
Black	29,986,060	12.1	26,495,025	11.7	13.2
American Indian, Eskimo, or Aleut	1,959,234	0.8	1,420,400	0.6	37.9
American Indian	1,878,285	0.8	1,364,033	0.6	37.7
Eskimo	57,152	0.0	42,162	0.0	35.6
Aleut	23,797	0.0	14,205	0.0	67.5
Asian-Pacific Islander	7,273,662	2.9	3,500,439[1]	1.5	107.8
Chinese	1,645,472	0.7	806,040	0.4	104.1
Filipino	1,406,770	0.6	774,652	0.3	81.6
Japanese	847,562	0.3	700,974	0.3	20.9
Asian Indian	815,447	0.3	361,531	0.2	125.6
Korean	798,849	0.3	354,593	0.2	125.3
Vietnamese	614,547	0.2	261,729	0.1	134.8
Hawaiian	211,014	0.1	166,814	0.1	26.5
Samoan	62,964	0.0	41,948	0.0	50.1
Guamanian	49,345	0.0	32,158	0.0	53.4
Other Asian-Pacific Islander	821,692	0.3	(NA)	(NA)	(NA)
Other race	9,804,847	3.9	6,758,319	3.0	45.1
Hispanic origin					
Hispanic origin[2]	22,354,059	9.0	14,608,673	6.4	53.0
Mexican	13,495,938	5.4	8,740,439	3.9	54.4
Puerto Rican	2,727,754	1.1	2,013,945	0.9	35.4
Cuban	1,043,932	0.4	803,226	0.4	30.0
Other Hispanic	5,086,435	2.0	3,051,063	1.3	66.7
Not of Hispanic origin	226,355,814	91.0	211,937,132	93.6	6.8

(NA) Not available from 1980 100% tabulations. (1) The 1980 numbers for Asian-Pacific Islanders in this table are not entirely comparable with 1990 counts. The 1980 count of 3,500,439 Asian-Pacific Islanders based on 100% tabulations includes only the 9 specific Asian-Pacific Islander groups listed separately in the 1980 race item. The 1980 total Asian-Pacific Islander population of 3,726,440 from sample tabulations is comparable to the 1990 count; these figures include groups not listed separately in the race item on the 1980 census form. (2) Persons of Hispanic origin may be of any race.

Definitions of Race and Hispanic Origin Groups

Source: Bureau of the Census, U.S. Dept. of Commerce

Race

The concept of race as used by the Census Bureau reflects self-identification. It does not denote any clear-cut scientific definition of biological stock. The data for race represent self-classification by people according to the race with which they most closely identify.

Persons identified their race by classifying themselves in one of the categories listed, i.e., white, black, American Indian, Eskimo, Aleut, Chinese, Filipino, Japanese, Asian Indian, Korean, Vietnamese, Hawaiian, Samoan, Guamanian, Other API, or Other race. If persons did not identify with any of the given race categories, they were directed to identify as "Other API" (API means Asian- Pacific Islander) or "Other race" and to write in the name of their race in the space provided. Thus, data for the Asian- Pacific Islander groups not listed on the census questionnaire but contained in Census Bureau tables—Cambodian, Hmong, Laotian, Thai, Bangladeshi, Burmese, Indonesian, Malayan, Okinawan, Pakistani, Sri Lankan, Tongan, Tahitian, Northern Mariana Islander, Palauan, and Fijian—were tabulated from write-in responses.

The "Other race" category includes persons not included in the race categories described above. Persons reporting in the "Other race" category and providing write-in entries such as a Spanish/Hispanic origin group (i.e., Mexican, Cuban, Puerto Rican) are included here.

Spanish/Hispanic Origin

Persons of Spanish/Hispanic origin or descent are those who classify themselves in one of the specific Hispanic origin categories listed on the census questionnaire—for example, Mexican, Puerto Rican, or Cuban—as well as those who indicated that they were of other Spanish/Hispanic origin.

Persons reporting "Other Spanish/Hispanic" are those whose origins are from other Spanish-speaking countries of the Caribbean, of Central or South America, or from Spain or were persons identifying themselves generally as Spanish, Spanish-American, Hispano, Hispanic, Latino, etc.

Spanish origin and race are distinct; thus, persons of Spanish/Hispanic origin may be of any race.

The Census

On April 1, 1990, the Bureau of the Census began to take the 21st decennial census of the United States. The Census Bureau took the first census in 1790, when it counted 3.9 million people, and has conducted a census every 10 years over the past 200 years, as mandated by the U.S. Constitution, Article 1, Section 2. The primary purpose of the census was, and is, to provide population counts needed to apportion seats in the U.S. House of Representatives, and to subsequently determine state legislative district boundaries. In addition, the findings of the 1990 census are critical to many other federal, state, and local programs, including federal programs that determine compliances with the Voting Rights Act and amendments; allocate funds from federal grant programs; identify areas needing bilingual education; assess the need for equal employment opportunity programs; allocate funds and analyze programs for American Indians and Alaska Natives; identify areas needing energy assistance; develop programs to reduce unemployment; identify areas needing programs to stimulate economic growth; establish fair lending practices; assess the need for developing or expanding low-income housing programs; and identify areas requiring child assistance programs.

For state and local government programs, the census results help develop social services programs, including programs for the elderly and handicapped; assess transportation systems and improve commuting patterns; identify areas for low-cost housing programs; establish occupational and vocational education programs; plan school district boundaries and school construction programs; and assess the need for state housing bonds for below-market interest rates on mortgages.

U.S. Population by Official

State	1790[1]	1800[1]	1810[1]	1820	1830	1840	1850	1860	1870	1880	1890
AL	....	1	9	127,901	309,527	590,756	771,623	964,201	996,992	1,262,505	1,513,401
AK	....	....	....	....	....	....	....	....	....	33,426	32,052
AZ	....	....	....	....	....	....	....	....	9,658	40,440	88,243
AR	....	....	1	14,273	30,388	97,574	209,897	435,450	484,471	802,525	1,128,211
CA	....	....	....	....	....	....	92,597	379,994	560,247	864,694	1,213,398
CO	....	....	....	....	....	....	....	34,277	39,864	194,327	413,249
CT	238	251	262	275,248	297,675	309,978	370,792	460,147	537,454	622,700	746,258
DE	59	64	73	72,749	76,748	78,085	91,532	112,216	125,015	146,608	168,493
DC	....	8	16	23,336	30,261	33,745	51,687	75,080	131,700	177,624	230,392
FL	....	....	....	....	34,730	54,477	87,445	140,424	187,748	269,493	391,422
GA	83	163	252	340,989	516,823	691,392	906,185	1,057,286	1,184,109	1,542,180	1,837,353
HI	....	....	....	....	....	....	....	....	....	....	....
ID	....	....	....	....	....	....	....	....	14,999	32,610	88,548
IL	....	....	12	55,211	157,445	476,183	851,470	1,711,951	2,539,891	3,077,871	3,826,352
IN	....	6	25	147,178	343,031	685,866	988,416	1,350,428	1,680,637	1,978,301	2,192,404
IA	....	....	....	....	....	43,112	192,214	674,913	1,194,020	1,624,615	1,912,297
KS	....	....	....	....	....	....	....	107,206	364,399	996,096	1,428,108
KY	74	221	407	564,317	687,917	779,828	982,405	1,155,684	1,321,011	1,648,690	1,858,635
LA	....	....	77	153,407	215,739	352,411	517,762	708,002	726,915	939,946	1,118,588
ME	97	152	229	298,335	399,455	501,793	583,169	628,279	626,915	648,936	661,086
MD	320	342	381	407,350	447,040	470,019	583,034	687,049	780,894	934,943	1,042,390
MA	379	423	472	523,287	610,408	737,699	994,514	1,231,066	1,457,351	1,783,085	2,238,947
MI	....	....	5	8,896	31,639	212,267	397,654	749,113	1,184,059	1,636,937	2,093,890
MN	....	....	....	....	....	....	6,077	172,023	439,706	780,773	1,310,283
MS	....	8	31	75,448	136,621	375,651	606,526	791,305	827,922	1,131,597	1,289,600
MO	....	....	20	66,586	140,455	383,702	682,044	1,182,012	1,721,295	2,168,380	2,679,185
MT	....	....	....	....	....	....	....	....	20,595	39,159	142,924
NE	....	....	....	....	....	....	....	28,841	122,993	452,402	1,062,656
NV	....	....	....	....	....	....	....	6,857	42,491	62,266	47,355
NH	142	184	214	244,161	269,328	284,574	317,976	326,073	318,300	346,991	376,530
NJ	184	211	246	277,575	320,823	373,306	489,555	672,035	906,096	1,131,116	1,444,933
NM	....	....	....	....	....	....	61,547	93,516	91,874	119,565	160,282
NY	340	589	959	1,372,812	1,918,608	2,428,921	3,097,394	3,880,735	4,382,759	5,082,871	6,003,174
NC	394	478	556	638,829	737,987	753,419	869,039	992,622	1,071,361	1,399,750	1,617,949
ND	....	....	....	....	....	....	....	....	2,405[2]	36,909	190,983
OH	....	45	231	581,434	937,903	1,519,467	1,980,329	2,339,511	2,665,260	3,198,062	3,672,329
OK	....	....	....	....	....	....	....	....	....	....	258,657
OR	....	....	....	....	....	....	12,093	52,465	90,923	174,768	317,704
PA	434	602	810	1,049,458	1,348,233	1,724,033	2,311,786	2,906,215	3,521,951	4,282,891	5,258,113
RI	69	69	77	83,059	97,199	108,830	147,545	174,620	217,353	276,531	345,506
SC	249	346	415	502,741	581,185	594,398	668,507	703,708	705,606	995,577	1,151,149
SD	....	....	....	....	....	....	....	4,837[2]	11,776[2]	98,268	348,600
TN	36	106	262	422,823	681,904	829,210	1,002,717	1,109,801	1,258,520	1,542,359	1,767,518
TX	....	....	....	....	....	....	212,592	604,215	818,579	1,591,749	2,235,527
UT	....	....	....	....	....	....	11,380	40,273	86,786	143,963	210,779
VT	85	154	218	235,981	280,652	291,948	314,120	315,098	330,551	332,286	332,422
VA	692	808	878	938,261	1,044,054	1,025,227	1,119,348	1,219,630	1,225,163	1,512,565	1,655,980
WA	....	....	....	....	....	....	1,201	11,594	23,955	75,116	357,232
WV	56	79	105	136,808	176,924	224,537	302,313	376,688	442,014	618,457	762,794
WI	....	....	....	....	....	30,945	305,391	775,881	1,054,670	1,315,497	1,693,330
WY	....	....	....	....	....	....	....	....	9,118	20,789	62,555
U.S.	**3,929**	**5,308**	**7,240**	**9,638,453**	**12,860,702**	**17,063,353[3]**	**23,191,876**	**31,443,321[3]**	**38,558,371**	**50,189,209**	**62,979,766**

Note: Where possible, population shown is that of 1990 area of state. Members of the Armed Forces overseas or other U.S. nationals are not included. (1) Totals for 1790, 1800, and 1810 are in thousands. (2) 1860 figure is for Dakota Territory; 1870 figures are for parts of Dakota Territory. (3) U.S. total includes persons (5,318 in 1830 and 6,100 in 1840) on public ships in the service of the U.S. not credited to any region, division, or state.

Congressional Apportionment

Source: Bureau of the Census, U.S. Dept. of Commerce

State	1990	1980
AL	7	7
AK	1	1
AZ	6	5
AR	4	4
CA	52	45
CO	6	6
CT	6	6
DE	1	1
FL	23	19
GA	11	10
HI	2	2
ID	2	2
IL	20	22
IN	10	10
IA	5	6
KS	4	5
KY	6	7
LA	7	8
ME	2	2
MD	8	8
MA	10	11
MI	16	18
MN	8	8
MS	5	5
MO	9	9
MT	1	2
NE	3	3
NV	2	2
NH	2	2
NJ	13	14
NM	3	3
NY	31	34
NC	12	11
ND	1	1
OH	19	21
OK	6	6
OR	5	5
PA	21	23
RI	2	2
SC	6	6
SD	1	1
TN	9	9
TX	30	27
UT	3	3
VT	1	1
VA	11	10
WA	9	8
WV	3	4
WI	9	9
WY	1	1
Totals	**435**	**435**

The Constitution, in Article 1, Section 2, provided for a census of the population every 10 years to establish a basis for apportionment of representatives among the states. This apportionment largely determines the number of electoral votes allotted to each state.

The number of representatives of each state in Congress is determined by the state's population, but each state is entitled to one representative regardless of population. A congressional apportionment has been made after each decennial census except that of 1920.

Under provisions of a law that became effective Nov. 15, 1941, representatives are apportioned by the method of equal proportions. In the application of this method, the apportionment is made so that the average population per representative has the least possible variation between one state and any other. The first House of Representatives, in 1789, had 65 members, as provided by the Constitution. As the population grew, the number of representatives was increased, but the total membership has been fixed at 435 since the apportionment based on the 1910 census.

Census, 1790 - 1990

1900	1910	1920	1930	1940	1950	1960	1970	1980	1990
1,828,697	2,138,093	2,348,174	2,646,248	2,832,961	3,061,743	3,266,740	3,444,354	3,894,025	4,040,587
63,592	64,356	55,036	59,278	72,524	128,643	226,167	302,583	401,851	550,043
122,931	204,354	334,162	435,573	499,261	749,587	1,302,161	1,775,399	2,716,546	3,665,228
1,311,564	1,574,449	1,752,204	1,854,482	1,949,387	1,909,511	1,786,272	1,923,322	2,286,357	2,350,725
1,485,053	2,377,549	3,426,861	5,677,251	6,907,387	10,586,223	15,717,204	19,971,069	23,667,764	29,760,021
539,700	799,024	939,629	1,035,791	1,123,296	1,325,089	1,753,947	2,209,596	2,889,735	3,294,394
908,420	1,114,756	1,380,631	1,606,903	1,709,242	2,007,280	2,535,234	3,032,217	3,107,564	3,287,116
184,735	202,322	223,003	238,380	266,505	318,085	446,292	548,104	594,338	666,168
278,718	331,069	437,571	486,869	663,091	802,178	763,956	756,668	638,432	606,900
528,542	752,619	968,470	1,468,211	1,897,414	2,771,305	4,951,560	6,791,418	9,746,961	12,937,926
2,216,331	2,609,121	2,895,832	2,908,506	3,123,723	3,444,578	3,943,116	4,587,930	5,462,982	6,478,216
154,001	191,874	255,881	368,300	422,770	499,794	632,772	769,913	964,691	1,108,229
161,772	325,594	431,866	445,032	524,873	588,637	667,191	713,015	944,127	1,006,749
4,821,550	5,638,591	6,485,280	7,630,654	7,897,241	8,712,176	10,081,158	11,110,285	11,427,409	11,430,602
2,516,462	2,700,876	2,930,390	3,238,503	3,427,796	3,934,224	4,662,498	5,195,392	5,490,214	5,544,159
2,231,853	2,224,771	2,404,021	2,470,939	2,538,268	2,621,073	2,757,537	2,825,368	2,913,808	2,776,755
1,470,495	1,690,949	1,769,257	1,880,999	1,801,028	1,905,299	2,178,611	2,249,071	2,364,236	2,477,574
2,147,174	2,289,905	2,416,630	2,614,589	2,845,627	2,944,806	3,038,156	3,220,711	3,660,324	3,685,296
1,381,625	1,656,388	1,798,509	2,101,593	2,363,880	2,683,516	3,257,022	3,644,637	4,206,116	4,219,973
694,466	742,371	768,014	797,423	847,226	913,774	969,265	993,722	1,125,043	1,227,928
1,188,044	1,295,346	1,449,661	1,631,526	1,821,244	2,343,001	3,100,689	3,923,897	4,216,933	4,781,468
2,805,346	3,366,416	3,852,356	4,249,614	4,316,721	4,690,514	5,148,578	5,689,170	5,737,093	6,016,425
2,420,982	2,810,173	3,668,412	4,842,325	5,256,106	6,371,766	7,823,194	8,881,826	9,262,044	9,295,297
1,751,394	2,075,708	2,387,125	2,563,953	2,792,300	2,982,483	3,413,864	3,806,103	4,075,970	4,375,099
1,551,270	1,797,114	1,790,618	2,009,821	2,183,796	2,178,914	2,178,141	2,216,994	2,520,770	2,573,216
3,106,665	3,293,335	3,404,055	3,629,367	3,784,664	3,954,653	4,319,813	4,677,623	4,916,766	5,117,073
243,329	376,053	548,889	537,606	559,456	591,024	674,767	694,409	786,690	799,065
1,066,300	1,192,214	1,296,372	1,377,963	1,315,834	1,325,510	1,411,330	1,485,333	1,569,825	1,578,385
42,335	81,875	77,407	91,058	110,247	160,083	285,278	488,738	800,508	1,201,833
411,588	430,572	443,083	465,293	491,524	533,242	606,921	737,681	920,610	1,109,252
1,883,669	2,537,167	3,155,900	4,041,334	4,160,165	4,835,329	6,066,782	7,171,112	7,365,011	7,730,188
195,310	327,301	360,350	423,317	531,818	681,187	951,023	1,017,055	1,303,302	1,515,069
7,268,894	9,113,614	10,385,227	12,588,066	13,479,142	14,830,192	16,782,304	18,241,391	17,558,165	17,990,455
1,893,810	2,206,287	2,559,123	3,170,276	3,571,623	4,061,929	4,556,155	5,084,411	5,880,095	6,628,637
319,146	577,056	646,872	680,845	641,935	619,636	632,446	617,792	652,717	638,800
4,157,545	4,767,121	5,759,394	6,646,697	6,907,612	7,946,627	9,706,397	10,657,423	10,797,603	10,847,115
790,391	1,657,155	2,028,283	2,396,040	2,336,434	2,233,351	2,328,284	2,559,463	3,025,487	3,145,585
413,536	672,765	783,389	953,786	1,089,684	1,521,341	1,768,687	2,091,533	2,633,156	2,842,321
6,302,115	7,665,111	8,720,017	9,631,350	9,900,180	10,498,012	11,319,366	11,800,766	11,864,720	11,881,643
428,556	542,610	604,397	687,497	713,346	791,896	859,488	949,723	947,154	1,003,464
1,340,316	1,515,400	1,683,724	1,738,765	1,899,804	2,117,027	2,382,594	2,590,713	3,120,729	3,486,703
401,570	583,888	636,547	692,849	642,961	652,740	680,514	666,257	690,768	696,004
2,020,616	2,184,789	2,337,885	2,616,556	2,915,841	3,291,718	3,567,089	3,926,018	4,591,023	4,877,185
3,048,710	3,896,542	4,663,228	5,824,715	6,414,824	7,711,194	9,579,677	11,198,655	14,225,513	16,986,510
276,749	373,351	449,396	507,847	550,310	688,862	890,627	1,059,273	1,461,037	1,722,850
343,641	355,956	352,428	359,611	359,231	377,747	389,881	444,732	511,456	562,758
1,854,184	2,061,612	2,309,187	2,421,851	2,677,773	3,318,680	3,966,949	4,651,448	5,346,797	6,187,358
518,103	1,141,990	1,356,621	1,563,396	1,736,191	2,378,963	2,853,214	3,413,244	4,132,353	4,866,692
958,800	1,221,119	1,463,701	1,729,205	1,901,974	2,005,552	1,860,421	1,744,237	1,950,186	1,793,477
2,069,042	2,333,860	2,632,067	2,939,006	3,137,587	3,434,575	3,951,777	4,417,821	4,705,642	4,891,769
92,531	145,965	194,402	225,565	250,742	290,529	330,066	332,416	469,557	453,588
76,212,168	**92,228,496**	**106,021,537**	**123,202,624**	**132,164,569**	**151,325,798**	**179,323,175**	**203,302,031**	**226,542,203**	**248,709,873**

U.S. Center of Population, 1790-1990

Source: Bureau of the Census, U.S. Dept. of Commerce

Center of Population is that point which may be considered as center of population gravity of the U.S. or that point upon which the U.S. would balance if it were a rigid plane without weight and the population distributed thereon with each individual being assumed to have equal weight and to exert an influence on a central point proportional to his or her distance from that point. The 1990 center is 818.6 miles from the 1790 center of population and is 39.5 miles SW of the 1980 center.

Year	N Lat °	'	"	W Long °	'	"	Approximate location
1790	39	16	30	76	11	12	23 miles east of Baltimore, Md.
1800	39	16	6	76	56	30	18 miles west of Baltimore, Md.
1810	39	11	30	77	37	12	40 miles northwest by west of Washington, D.C. (in Va.)
1820	39	5	42	78	33	0	16 miles east of Moorefield, W. Va.[1]
1830	38	57	54	79	16	54	19 miles west-southwest of Moorefield, W. Va.[1]
1840	39	2	0	80	18	0	16 miles south of Clarksburg, W. Va.[1]
1850	38	59	0	81	19	0	23 miles southeast of Parkersburg, W. Va.[1]
1860	39	0	24	82	48	48	20 miles south by east of Chillicothe, Oh.
1870	39	12	0	83	35	42	48 miles east by north of Cincinnati, Oh.
1880	39	4	8	84	39	40	8 miles west by south of Cincinnati, Oh. (in Ky.)
1890	39	11	56	85	32	53	20 miles east of Columbus, Ind.
1900	39	9	36	85	48	54	6 miles southeast of Columbus, Ind.
1910	39	10	12	86	32	20	In the city of Bloomington, Ind.
1920	39	10	21	86	43	15	8 miles south-southeast of Spencer, Owen County, Ind.
1930	39	3	45	87	8	6	3 miles northeast of Linton, Greene County, Ind.
1940	38	56	54	87	22	35	2 miles southeast by east of Carlisle, Haddon township, Sullivan Co., Ind.
1950 (Inc. Alaska & Hawaii)	38	48	15	88	22	8	3 miles northeast of Louisville, Clay County, Ill.
1960	38	35	58	89	12	35	6 1/2 miles northwest of Centralia, Clinton Co., Ill.
1970	38	27	47	89	42	22	5 miles east southeast of Mascoutah, St. Clair County, Ill.
1980	38	8	13	90	34	26	1/4 mile west of De Soto, Jefferson Co., Mo.
1990	37	52	20	91	12	55	9.7 miles northwest of Steelville, Mo.

(1) West Virginia was set off from Virginia on Dec. 31, 1862, and was admitted as a state on June 20, 1863.

U.S. Population, by Age, Sex, and Household, 1990

Source: Bureau of the Census, U.S. Dept. of Commerce; 1990 Census

Total population	**248,709,873**
Sex	
Male	121,239,418
Female	127,470,455
Age	
Under 5 years	18,354,443
5 to 17 years	45,249,989
18 to 20 years	11,726,868
21 to 24 years	15,010,898
25 to 44 years	80,754,835
45 to 54 years	25,223,086
55 to 59 years	10,531,756
60 to 64 years	10,616,167
65 to 74 years	18,106,558
75 to 84 years	10,055,108
85 years and over	3,080,165
Median age	32.9
Under 18 years	63,604,432
Percentage of total population	25.6
65 years and over	31,241,831
Percentage of total population	12.6

Households by type	
Total households	**91,947,410**
Family households (families)	64,517,947
Married-couple families	50,708,322
Percentage of total households	55.1
Other family, male householder	3,143,582
Other family, female householder	10,666,043
Nonfamily households	27,429,463
Percentage of total households	29.8
Householder living alone	22,580,420
Householder 65 years and over	8,824,845
Persons living in households	242,012,129
Persons per household	2.63
Group quarters	
Persons living in group quarters	6,697,744
Institutionalized persons	3,334,018
Other persons in group quarters	3,363,726

U.S. Asian and Pacific Islander Population, Social and Economic Characteristics, 1991

Source: Bureau of the Census

(Figures are estimates from March 1, 1991, Sample Survey)

Characteristics	Total (in thousands)[1]	Percent Distribution[1]
Total persons	**7,023**	**100.0**
Under 5 years old	606	8.6
5 to 14 years old	1,170	16.7
15 to 44 years old	3,494	49.8
45 to 64 years old	1,240	17.6
65 years old and over	514	7.3
YEARS OF SCHOOL COMPLETED		
Characteristics		
Persons 25 years old and over	**4,158**	**100.0**
Elementary: 0 to 8 years	515	12.4
High School: 1 to 3 years	243	5.8
4 years	1,186	28.5
College: 1 to 3 years	591	14.2
4 years or more	1,623	39.0
LABOR FORCE STATUS		
Characteristics		
Civilians 16 years old and over	**5,121**	**100.0**
Civilian labor force	3,261	63.7
Employed	3,054	59.6
Unemployed	207	4.0
Unemployment rate[2]	6.3	(NA)
Not in labor force	1,860	36.3
FAMILY TYPE AND INCOME IN 1990		
Characteristics		
Total families	**1,536**	**100.0**
Married couple	1,230	80.1
Female householder, no spouse present	194	12.7
Male householder, no spouse present	112	7.3
Less than $5,000	60	3.9
$5,000 to $9,999	70	4.6
$10,000 to $14,999	88	5.7
$15,000 to $24,999	193	12.5
$25,000 to $34,999	197	12.8
$35,000 to $49,999	303	19.7
$50,000 and over	626	40.7
Median income ($)	42,245[3]	(NA)
POVERTY		
Characteristics		
Families below poverty level	169	11.0
Persons below poverty level	858	12.2
HOUSING TENURE		
Characteristics		
Total occupied units	**1,958**	**100.0**
Owner-occupied	995	50.8
Renter-occupied	947	48.4
No cash rent	15	0.8

(NA) = not applicable. (1) Due to rounding, figures may not equal totals. (2) Total unemployment as percent of civilian labor force. (3) Number not in thousands.

Counties with 1990 Population over 1 Million

Source: **Bureau of the Census**

County	April 1, 1990 census	April 1, 1980 census	Percent change 1980-90
Los Angeles, CA	8,863,052	7,477,238	18.5
Cook, IL	5,105,067	5,253,628	–2.8
Harris, TX	2,818,199	2,409,547	17.0
San Diego, CA	2,498,016	1,861,846	34.2
Orange, CA	2,410,668	1,932,921	24.7
Kings, NY	2,300,664	2,231,028	3.1
Maricopa, AZ	2,122,101	1,509,175	40.6
Wayne, MI	2,111,687	2,337,843	–9.7
Queens, NY	1,951,598	1,891,325	3.2
Dade, FL	1,937,194	1,625,509	19.2
Dallas, TX	1,852,810	1,556,419	19.0
Philadelphia, PA	1,585,577	1,688,210	–6.1
King, WA	1,507,305	1,269,898	18.7
Santa Clara, CA	1,497,577	1,295,071	15.6
New York, NY	1,487,536	1,428,285	4.1
San Bernardino, CA	1,418,380	895,016	58.5
Cuyahoga, OH	1,412,140	1,498,400	–5.8
Middlesex, MA	1,398,468	1,367,034	2.3
Allegheny, PA	1,336,449	1,450,195	–7.8
Suffolk, NY	1,321,768	1,284,231	2.9
Nassau, NY	1,287,444	1,321,582	–2.6
Alameda, CA	1,279,702	1,105,379	15.8
Broward, FL	1,255,518	1,018,257	23.3
Bronx, NY	1,203,789	1,168,972	3.0
Bexar, TX	1,185,394	988,971	19.9
Riverside, CA	1,170,413	663,199	76.5
Tarrant, TX	1,170,103	860,880	35.9
Oakland, MI	1,083,592	1,011,793	7.1
Sacramento, CA	1,041,219	783,381	32.9
Hennepin, MN	1,032,431	941,411	9.7

Los Angeles County, the nation's largest, also had the largest numeric increase, 1.4 million, followed by San Diego and Maricopa (Phoenix), each with over 600,000, and San Bernardino and Riverside, each with more than 500,000. New York City encompasses 5 counties, 4 of which exceed a million population. The largest is Kings (Brooklyn), with 2.3 million, followed by Queens, New York (Manhattan), and Bronx. For the first time since 1950, the population of all five counties increased.

Density of Population by State

Source: Bureau of the Census, U.S. Dept. of Commerce

(per square mile, land area only)

State	1920	1960	1980	1990	State	1920	1960	1980	1990	State	1920	1960	1980	1990
AL	45.8	64.2	76.6	79.6	LA	39.6	72.2	94.5	96.9	OK	29.2	33.8	44.1	45.8
AK*	0.1	0.4	0.7	1.0	ME	25.7	31.3	36.3	39.8	OR	8.2	18.4	27.4	29.6
AZ	2.9	11.5	23.9	32.3	MD	145.8	313.5	428.7	489.2	PA	194.5	251.4	264.3	265.1
AR	33.4	34.2	43.9	45.1	MA	479.2	657.3	733.3	767.6	RI	566.4	819.3	897.8	960.3
CA	22.0	100.4	151.4	190.8	MI	63.8	137.7	162.6	163.6	SC	55.2	78.7	103.4	115.8
CO	9.1	16.9	27.9	31.8	MN	29.5	43.1	51.2	55.0	SD	8.3	9.0	9.1	9.2
CT	286.4	520.6	637.8	678.4	MS	38.6	46.0	53.4	54.9	TN	56.1	86.2	111.6	118.3
DE	113.5	225.2	307.6	340.8	MO	49.5	62.6	71.3	74.3	TX	17.8	36.4	54.3	64.9
DC	7,292.9	12,523.9	10,132.3	9,882.8	MT	3.8	4.6	5.4	5.5	UT	5.5	10.8	17.8	21.0
FL	17.7	91.5	180.0	239.6	NE	16.9	18.4	20.5	20.5	VT	38.6	42.0	55.2	60.8
GA	49.3	67.8	94.1	111.9	NV	0.7	2.6	7.3	10.9	VA	57.4	99.6	134.7	156.3
HI*	39.9	98.5	150.1	172.5	NH	49.1	67.2	102.4	123.7	WA	20.3	42.8	62.1	73.1
ID	5.2	8.1	11.5	12.2	NJ	420.0	805.5	986.2	1,042.0	WV	60.9	77.2	80.8	74.5
IL	115.7	180.4	205.3	205.6	NM	2.9	7.8	10.7	12.5	WI	47.6	72.6	86.5	90.1
IN	81.3	128.8	152.8	154.6	NY	217.9	350.6	370.6	381.0	WY	2.0	3.4	4.9	4.7
IA	43.2	49.2	52.1	49.7	NC	52.5	93.2	120.4	136.1					
KS	21.6	26.6	28.9	30.3	ND	9.2	9.1	9.4	9.3	**U.S.**	***29.9**	**50.6**	**64.0**	**70.3**
KY	60.1	76.2	92.3	92.8	OH	141.4	236.6	263.3	264.9					

* For purposes of comparison, Alaska and Hawaii are included in above tabulation for 1920, even though not states then.

Population by State, 1990-93

Source: Bureau of the Census, U.S. Dept. of Commerce

State	1993 population	1990 population	Percentage change 1990-93	State	1993 population	1990 population	Percentage change 1990-93
U.S.	**257,907,937**	**248,709,873**	**3.7**	CO	3,565,959	3,294,394	8.2
CA	31,210,750	29,760,021	4.9	CT	3,277,316	3,287,116	-0.3
NY	18,197,154	17,990,455	1.1	OK	3,231,464	3,145,585	2.7
TX	18,031,484	16,986,510	6.2	OR	3,031,867	2,842,321	6.7
FL	13,678,914	12,937,926	5.7	IA	2,814,064	2,776,755	1.3
PA	12,048,271	11,881,643	1.4	MS	2,642,748	2,573,216	2.7
IL	11,697,336	11,430,602	2.3	KS	2,530,746	2,477,574	2.1
OH	11,091,301	10,847,115	2.3	AR	2,424,418	2,350,725	3.1
MI	9,477,545	9,295,297	2.0	UT	1,859,582	1,722,850	7.9
NJ	7,879,164	7,730,188	1.9	WV	1,820,137	1,793,477	1.5
NC	6,945,180	6,628,637	4.8	NM	1,616,483	1,515,069	6.7
GA	6,917,140	6,478,216	6.8	NE	1,607,199	1,578,385	1.8
VA	6,490,634	6,187,358	4.9	NV	1,388,910	1,201,833	15.6
MA	6,012,268	6,016,425	-0.1	ME	1,239,448	1,227,928	0.9
IN	5,712,779	5,544,159	3.0	HI	1,171,592	1,108,229	5.7
WA	5,255,276	4,866,692	8.0	NH	1,125,310	1,109,252	1.4
MO	5,233,849	5,117,073	2.3	ID	1,099,096	1,006,749	9.2
TN	5,098,798	4,877,185	4.5	RI	1,000,012	1,003,464	-0.3
WI	5,037,928	4,891,769	3.0	MT	839,422	799,065	5.1
MD	4,964,898	4,781,468	3.8	SD	715,392	696,004	2.8
MN	4,517,416	4,375,099	3.3	DE	700,269	666,168	5.1
LA	4,295,477	4,219,973	1.9	ND	634,935	638,800	-0.6
AL	4,186,806	4,040,587	3.6	AK	599,151	550,043	8.9
AZ	3,936,142	3,665,228	7.4	DC	578,448	606,900	-4.7
KY	3,788,808	3,685,296	2.8	VT	575,691	562,758	2.3
SC	3,642,718	3,486,703	4.5	WY	470,242	453,588	3.7

25 Counties With the Highest Growth Rate, 1980-92

Source: Bureau of the Census, U.S. Dept. of Commerce

County	Growth Rate	County	Growth Rate	County	Growth Rate
Flager, FL	207.7	Elko, NV	116.3	Cherokee, GA	97.4
Douglas, CO	191.4	Nye, NV	115.6	Manassas, VA*	95.4
Camden, GA	181.7	Washington, UT	112.3	Fort Bend, TX	95.3
Matanuka-Susitna, AK	152.2	Denton, TX	105.9	Riverside, CA	94.3
Hernando, FL	148.5	Charlotte, FL	104.0	Spotsylvania, VA	92.0
Osceola, FL	141.9	Collin, TX	101.2	Collier, FL	91.6
Fayette, GA	140.0	Williamson, TX	100.1	Mohave, AZ	89.8
Gwinnett, GA	134.9	Sandoval, NM	99.9		
Dawson, GA	116.5	Rockwall, TX	99.5	**United States**	**12.6**

*Independent city.

25 Counties With the Largest Population Decline, 1980-92

Source: Bureau of the Census, U.S. Dept. of Commerce

County	Number	County	Number	County	Number
Wayne, MI	-241,664	Washington, DC	-53,211	Westmoreland, PA	-17,884
Philadelphia, PA	-135,638	Erie, NY	-43,183	Richmond, VA*	-16,951
Alleghany, PA	-115,799	Lake, IN	-41,099	Genesee, MI	-16,941
Cook, IL	-114,287	Mahoning, OH	-23,880	Peoria, IL	-16,912
Cuyahoga, OH	-87,191	St. Louis, MO	-23,727	Rock Island, IL	-16,885
Essex, NJ	-77,884	Kanawha, WV	-23,645	McDowell, WV	-15,788
St. Louis, MO*	-69,068	Cambria, PA	-21,167	Beaver, PA	-15,782
Orleans, LA	-68,332	Nassau, NY	-19,515	Saginaw, MI	-15,582
Baltimore, MD*	-60,645				

*Independent city.

25 Largest Counties, by Population, 1980 and 1992

Source: Bureau of the Census, U.S. Dept. of Commerce

County	1992 population	1980 population	Percentage change 1980-92
Los Angeles, CA	9,053,645	7,477,238	21.1
Cook, IL	5,139,341	5,253,628	-2.2
Harris, TX	2,971,765	2,409,547	23.3
San Diego, CA	2,801,055	1,861,846	50.4
Orange, CA	2,484,789	1,932,921	28.6
Kings, NY	2,266,167	2,231,028	1.6
Maricopa, AZ	2,209,567	1,509,175	46.4
Wayne, MI	2,096,179	2,337,843	-10.3
Dade, FL	2,007,972	1,891,325	6.2
Queens, NY	1,951,034	1,556,419	25.4
Dallas, TX	1,913,395	1,625,509	17.7
King, WA	1,557,537	1,269,898	22.7
Philadelphia, PA	1,552,572	1,688,210	-8.0
San Bernardino, CA	1,534,343	895,016	71.4
Santa Clara, CA	1,526,527	1,295,071	17.9
New York, NY	1,489,066	1,428,285	4.3
Cuyahoga, OH	1,411,209	1,498,400	-5.8
Middlesex, MA	1,394,408	1,367,034	2.0
Suffolk, NY	1,338,204	1,284,231	4.2
Allegheny, PA	1,334,396	1,450,195	-8.0
Alameda, CA	1,307,572	1,105,379	18.3
Nassau, NY	1,302,067	1,321,582	-1.5
Broward, FL	1,301,274	1,018,257	27.8
Riverside, CA	1,288,435	663,199	94.3
Bexar, TX	1,233,096	988,971	24.7

Population Density, by Counties, 1992

Source: Bureau of the Census, U.S. Dept. of Commerce

25 Counties With the Most People per Square Mile

County	Number
New York, NY	52,431.9
Kings, NY	32,427.9
Bronx, NY	28,443.2
Queens, NY	17,833.9
San Francisco, CA	15,608.6
Hudson, NJ	11,883.3
Philadelphia, PA	11,492.0
Suffolk, MA	10,926.4
Washington, DC	9,531.3
Baltimore, MD*	8,986.3
Alexandria, VA*	7,394.4
Richmond, NY	6,673.8
Arlington, VA	6,624.8
St. Louis, MO*	6,199.2
Essex, NJ	6,123.7
Cook, IL	5,434.4
Union, NJ	4,755.8
Norkfolk, VA*	4,716.9
Falls Church, VA*	4,622.0
Nassau, NY	4,504.0
Milwaukee, WI	3,939.9
Charlottesville, VA*	3,937.7
Manassas Park, VA*	3,914.4
Bergen, NJ	3,565.3
Wayne, MI	3,413.4

25 Counties With the Fewest People per Square Mile

County	Number
Lake and Peninsula, AK	0.1
North Slope, AK	0.1
Yukon-Koyukuk, AK	0.1
Dillingham, AK	0.2
Northwest Arctic, AK	0.2
Southeast Fairbanks, AK	0.2
Loving,TX	0.2
Bethel, AK	0.3
Skagway-Yakutat-Angoon, AK	0.3
Valdez-Cordova, AK	0.3
Garfield, MT	0.3
Petroleum, MT	0.3
Kenedy, TX	0.3
Aleutians East, AK	0.4
Nome, AK	0.4
Wade Hampton, AK	0.4
Hinsdale, CO	0.4
Carter, MT	0.4
Esmeralda, NV	0.4
Eureka, NV	0.4
Lincoln, NV	0.4
Catron, NM	0.4
King, TX	0.4
Clark, ID	0.5
Harding, NM	0.5

*Independent city. **Note:** Rankings based on all counties or equivalent areas in state with the exception of Kalawao, HI, and Yellowstone National Park, MT.

Population of 100 Largest U.S. Cities

Source: Bureau of the Census, U.S. Dept. of Commerce (100 most populous cities ranked by April 1990 census; revised April 1994)

Rank	City	1990	1980	1970	1960	1950	1900	1850
1	New York, NY	7,322,564	7,071,639	7,895,563	7,781,984	7,891,957	3,437,202	696,115
2	Los Angeles, CA	3,485,557	2,966,850	2,811,801	2,479,015	1,970,358	102,479	1,610
3	Chicago, IL	2,783,726	3,005,072	3,369,357	3,550,404	3,620,962	1,698,575	29,963
4	Houston, TX	1,629,902	1,595,138	1,233,535	938,219	596,163	44,633	2,396
5	Philadelphia, PA	1,585,577	1,688,210	1,949,996	2,002,512	2,071,605	1,293,697	121,376
6	San Diego, CA	1,110,623	875,538	697,471	573,224	334,387	17,700	...
7	Detroit, MI	1,027,974	1,203,368	1,514,063	1,670,144	1,849,568	285,704	21,019
8	Dallas, TX	1,007,618	904,078	844,401	679,684	434,462	42,638	...
9	Phoenix, AZ	983,403	789,704	584,303	439,170	106,818	5,544	...
10	San Antonio, TX	935,393	785,880	654,153	587,718	408,442	53,321	3,488
11	San Jose, CA	782,224	629,442	459,913	204,196	95,280	21,500	...
12	Indianapolis, IN	741,952	700,807	736,856	476,258	427,173	169,164	8,091
13	Baltimore, MD	736,014	786,741	905,787	939,024	949,708	508,957	169,054
14	San Francisco, CA	723,959	678,974	715,674	740,316	775,357	342,782	34,776
15	Jacksonville, FL	672,971	540,920	504,265	201,030	204,517	28,429	1,045
16	Columbus, OH	632,945	564,871	540,025	471,316	375,901	125,560	17,882
17	Milwaukee, WI	628,088	636,212	717,372	741,324	637,392	285,315	20,061
18	Memphis, TN	610,337	646,170	623,988	497,524	396,000	102,320	8,841
19	Washington, DC	606,900	638,432	756,668	763,956	802,178	278,718	40,001
20	Boston, MA	574,283	562,994	641,071	697,197	801,444	560,892	136,881
21	Seattle, WA	516,259	493,846	530,831	557,087	467,591	80,671	...
22	El Paso, TX	515,342	425,259	322,261	276,687	130,485	15,906	...
23	Nashville-Davidson, TN	510,784	455,651	426,029	170,874	174,307	80,865	10,165
24	Cleveland, OH	505,616	573,822	750,879	876,050	914,808	381,768	17,034
25	New Orleans, LA	496,938	557,927	593,471	627,525	570,445	287,104	116,375
26	Denver, CO	467,610	492,694	514,678	493,887	415,786	133,859	...
27	Austin, TX	465,648	345,496	253,539	186,545	132,459	22,258	629
28	Fort Worth, TX	447,619	385,164	393,455	356,268	278,778	26,688	...
29	Oklahoma City, OK	444,724	403,213	368,164	324,253	243,504	10,037	...
30	Portland, OR	438,802	366,383	379,967	372,676	373,628	90,426	...
31	Kansas City, MO	434,829	448,159	507,330	475,539	456,622	163,752	...
32	Long Beach, CA	429,321	361,334	358,879	344,168	250,767	2,252	...
33	Tucson, AZ	405,323	330,537	262,933	212,892	45,454	7,531	...

Rank	City	1990	1980	1970	1960	1950	1900	1850
34	St. Louis, MO	396,685	452,801	622,236	750,026	856,796	575,238	77,860
35	Charlotte, NC	395,925	314,447	241,420	201,564	134,042	18,091	1,065
36	Atlanta, GA	393,929	425,022	495,039	487,455	331,314	89,872	2,572
37	Virginia Beach, VA	393,089	262,199	172,106	8,091	5,390	...	...
38	Albuquerque, NM	384,619	331,767	244,501	201,189	96,815	6,238	...
39	Oakland, CA	372,242	339,337	361,561	367,548	384,575	66,960	...
40	Pittsburgh, PA	369,879	423,960	520,089	604,332	676,806	321,616	46,601
41	Sacramento, CA	369,365	275,741	257,105	191,667	137,572	29,282	6,820
42	Minneapolis, MN	368,383	370,951	434,400	482,872	521,718	202,718	...
43	Tulsa, OK	367,302	360,919	330,350	261,685	182,740	1,390	...
44	Honolulu, HI	365,272	365,048	324,871	294,194	248,034	39,306	...
45	Cincinnati, OH	364,114	385,410	453,514	502,550	503,998	325,902	115,435
46	Miami, FL	358,648	346,865	334,859	291,688	249,276	1,681	...
47	Fresno, CA	354,091	218,202	165,655	133,929	91,669	12,470	...
48	Omaha, NE	335,719	314,255	346,929	301,598	251,117	102,555	...
49	Toledo, OH	332,943	354,635	383,062	318,003	303,616	131,822	3,829
50	Buffalo, NY	328,175	357,870	462,768	532,759	580,132	352,387	42,261
51	Wichita, KS	304,017	279,272	276,554	254,698	168,279	24,671	...
52	Santa Ana, CA	293,827	203,713	155,710	100,350	45,533	4,933	...
53	Mesa, AZ	288,104	152,453	63,049	33,772	16,790	722	...
54	Colorado Springs, CO	280,430	215,150	135,517	70,194	45,472	21,085	...
55	Tampa, FL	280,015	271,523	277,714	274,970	124,681	15,839	...
56	Newark, NJ	275,221	329,248	381,930	405,220	438,776	246,070	38,894
57	St. Paul, MN	272,235	270,230	309,866	313,411	311,349	163,065	1,112
58	Louisville, KY	269,555	298,694	361,706	390,639	369,129	204,731	43,194
59	Anaheim, CA	266,406	219,311	166,408	104,184	14,556	1,456	...
60	Birmingham, AL	265,347	288,297	300,910	340,887	326,037	38,415	...
61	Arlington, TX	261,721	160,113	90,229	44,775	7,692	1,079	...
62	Norfolk, VA	261,229	266,979	307,951	304,869	213,513	46,624	14,326
63	Las Vegas, NV	258,204	164,674	125,787	64,405	24,624	...	...
64	Corpus Christi, TX	257,428	231,999	204,525	167,690	108,287	4,703	...
65	St. Petersburg, FL	240,318	238,647	216,159	181,298	96,738	1,575	...
66	Rochester, NY	230,356	241,741	295,011	318,611	332,488	162,608	36,403
67	Jersey City, NJ	228,517	223,532	260,350	276,101	299,017	206,433	6,856
68	Riverside, CA	226,546	170,876	140,089	84,332	46,764	7,973	...
69	Anchorage, AK	226,338	174,431	48,081	44,237	11,254	...	...
70	Lexington-Fayette, KY	225,366	204,165	108,137	62,810	55,534	26,369	8,159
71	Akron, OH	223,019	237,590	275,425	290,351	274,605	42,728	3,266
72	Aurora, CO	222,103	158,588	74,974	48,548	11,421	202	...
73	Baton Rouge, LA	219,531	220,394	165,921	152,419	125,629	11,269	3,905
74	Raleigh, NC	212,050	150,255	122,830	93,931	65,679	13,643	4,518
75	Stockton, CA	210,943	149,779	109,963	86,321	70,853	17,506	...
76	Richmond, VA	202,798	219,214	249,332	219,958	230,310	85,050	27,570
77	Shreveport, LA	198,518	205,820	182,064	164,372	127,206	16,013	1,728
78	Jackson, MS	196,637	202,895	153,968	144,422	98,271	7,816	1,881
79	Mobile, AL	196,263	200,452	190,026	194,856	129,009	38,469	20,515
80	Des Moines, IA	193,189	191,003	201,404	208,982	177,965	62,139	...
81	Lincoln, NE	191,972	171,932	149,518	128,521	98,884	40,169	...
82	Madison, WI	190,766	170,616	171,809	126,706	96,056	19,164	1,525
83	Grand Rapids, MI	189,126	181,843	197,649	177,313	176,515	87,565	2,686
84	Yonkers, NY	188,082	195,351	204,297	190,634	152,798	47,931	...
85	Hialeah, FL	188,008	145,254	102,452	66,972	19,676	...	...
86	Montgomery, AL	187,543	177,857	133,386	134,393	106,525	30,346	8,728
87	Lubbock, TX	186,206	173,979	149,101	126,691	71,747	...	...
88	Greensboro, NC	183,894	170,279	144,076	119,574	74,389	10,035	...
89	Dayton, OH	182,005	193,549	243,023	262,332	243,872	85,333	10,977
90	Huntington Beach, CA	181,519	170,505	115,960	11,492	5,237	...	...
91	Garland, TX	180,635	138,857	81,437	38,501	10,571	819	...
92	Glendale, CA	180,038	139,060	133,000	119,000	96,000	...	...
93	Columbus, GA	178,681	169,441	155,028	116,779	79,611	17,614	9,621
94	Spokane, WA	177,165	171,300	170,516	181,608	161,721	36,848	...
95	Tacoma, WA	176,664	158,501	154,407	147,979	143,673	37,714	...
96	Little Rock, AR	175,727	158,461	132,483	107,813	102,213	38,307	2,167
97	Bakersfield, CA	174,978	105,611	69,515	56,848	...	...	...
98	Fremont, CA	173,339	131,945	100,869	43,790	...	...	...
99	Fort Wayne, IN	172,971	172,196	178,269	161,776	133,607	45,115	4,282
100	Newport News, VA	171,439	144,903	138,000	114,000	42,000	...	...

Cities With Largest Percentage Loss in Population, 1980-90

Source: Bureau of the Census, U.S. Dept. of Commerce; 1990 Census

	City	1990	1980	Change
1.	Gary, IN	116,646	151,968	-23.2%
2.	Newark	275,221	329,248	-16.4
3.	Detroit	1,027,974	1,203,368	-14.6
4.	Pittsburgh	369,879	423,960	-12.8
5.	St. Louis	396,685	452,801	-12.4
6.	Cleveland	505,616	573,822	-11.9
7.	Flint, MI	140,761	159,611	-11.8
8.	New Orleans	496,938	557,927	-10.9
9.	Warren, MI	144,864	161,134	-10.1
10.	Chattanooga, TN	152,494	169,514	-10.0
11.	Louisville, KY	269,555	298,694	-9.8
12.	Peoria, IL	113,504	124,160	-8.9
13.	Erie, PA	108,718	119,123	-8.7
14.	Buffalo	328,175	357,870	-8.3
15.	Macon, GA	107,365	116,896	-8.2
16.	Birmingham, AL	265,965	288,297	-7.7
17.	Richmond	202,798	219,214	-7.5
18.	Chicago	2,783,726	3,005,072	-7.4
19.	Atlanta	394,017	425,022	-7.3
20.	Kansas City, KS	149,800	161,148	-7.0
21.	Baltimore	736,014	786,741	-6.4
22.	Akron, OH	223,019	237,590	-6.1
23.	Toledo, OH	332,943	354,635	-6.1
24.	Philadelphia	1,585,577	1,688,210	-6.1
25.	Dayton, OH	182,055	193,549	-5.9

Projections of Total Population, by Race, 1995-2050

Source: Bureau of the Census, U.S. Dept. of Commerce

Year	Total population (1,000) Lowest series	Middle series	Highest series	Zero migration	By race (middle series) (1,000) White	Black	American Indian[1]	Asian-Pacific Islander	Percentage distribution White	Black	American Indian[1]	Asian-Pacific Islander
1995 . .	262,051	263,434	264,715	260,713	218,334	33,117	2,226	9,756	82.9	12.6	0.8	3.7
1996 . .	263,905	266,096	268,138	262,414	220,023	33,597	2,257	10,219	NA	NA	NA	NA
2000 . .	270,259	276,241	281,957	268,459	226,267	35,469	2,380	12,125	81.9	12.8	0.9	4.4
2005 . .	276,316	288,286	299,941	274,872	233,343	37,793	2,543	14,608	80.9	13.1	0.9	5.1
2010 . .	281,180	300,431	319,536	280,935	240,297	40,224	2,719	17,191	80.0	13.4	0.9	5.7
2015 . .	285,680	313,116	340,794	287,170	247,542	42,797	2,904	19,873	NA	NA	NA	NA
2020 . .	289,553	325,942	363,213	293,166	254,791	45,409	3,309	22,653	78.2	13.9	0.9	8.1
2030 . .	292,902	349,993	410,991	302,280	267,457	50,596	3,473	28,467	76.4	14.5	1.0	9.3
2040 . .	290,351	371,505	463,579	307,356	277,232	55,917	3,894	34,461	74.6	15.1	1.0	10.3
2050 . .	285,502	392,031	522,098	310,418	285,591	61,586	4,346	40,508	72.8	15.7	1.1	11.3

NA = Not available. **Note:** For the series shown, different assumptions were made regarding fertility rates (lifetime births per woman), life expectancy, and immigration in the coming decades. Assumptions were based on a July 1992 estimate of U.S. population consistent with the 1990 decennial census. Yearly net immigration was assumed to be 350,000 for the lowest series, 880,000 for the middle series, and 1,370,000 for the highest series. Immigration is not a factor in the zero migration series. All figures shown are for July 1 of the given year. Resident population only. Percentage distribution may not equal 100 due to rounding. (1) American Indian refers to American Indian, Eskimo, and Aleut.

Projections of Total Population, by Age, 1995-2050

Source: Bureau of the Census, U.S. Dept. of Commerce

(in thousands)

Age	1995 Population	Percentage distribution	2000 Population	Percentage distribution	2010 Population	Percentage distribution	2050 Population	Percentage distribution
Total . .	263,434	100.0	276,241	100.0	300,431	100.0	392,031	100.0
Under 5 years	20,181	7.7	19,431	7.0	20,017	6.7	25,382	6.5
5-13 years	34,262	13.0	36,547	13.2	36,213	12.1	45,742	11.7
14-17 years	14,591	5.5	15,811	5.7	17,388	6.5	20,630	5.3
18-24 years	25,465	9.7	25,911	9.4	30,220	10.1	35,710	9.1
25-34 years	41,670	15.8	38,237	13.8	38,179	12.7	49,462	12.6
35-44 years	42,150	16.0	45,123	16.3	39,659	13.2	47,739	12.2
45-64 years	51,465	19.5	59,860	21.7	78,651	26.2	87,257	22.3
65 years and over	33,649	12.8	35,322	12.8	40,104	13.3	80,109	20.4
85 years and over	3,598	1.4	4,333	1.6	5,969	2.0	18,893	4.8
100 years and over	52	0.0	75	0.0	170	0.1	1,208	0.3

Note: Figures are for the middle series. Assumptions, based on a July 1992 population estimate consistent with the 1990 decennial census, were made regarding fertility rates (lifetime births per woman), life expectancy, and immigration in the coming decades. Yearly net immigration was assumed to be 880,000. All figures are for July 1 of the given year. Resident population only.

Persons With Disabilities, by Race and Hispanic Origin, 1991-92

Source: Bureau of the Census, U.S. Dept. of Commerce

(in thousands)

Characteristic	White Number	Percentage distribution	Black Number	Percentage distribution	Hispanic origin Number	Percentage Distribution
All ages						
Total	210,873	100.0	31,420	100.0	21,905	100.0
With a disability	41,521	19.7	6,277	20.0	3,343	15.3
Severe	19,736	9.4	3,836	12.2	1,838	8.4
Not severe	21,785	10.3	2,441	7.8	1,505	6.9
Persons 0-14 years						
Total	44,704	100.0	8,868	100.0	6,506	100.0
With a disability	2,403	5.4	428	4.8	202	3.1
Severe	451	1.0	59	0.7	26	0.4
Not severe	1,952	4.4	369	4.2	228	3.5
Persons 15 years and over						
Total	166,169	100.0	22,551	100.0	15,399	100.0
With a disability	39,118	23.5	5,849	25.9	3,141	20.4
Severe	19,285	11.6	3,776	16.8	1,812	11.8
Not Severe	19,833	11.9	2,073	9.2	1,329	8.6
Persons 16-67 years						
Total	141,612	100.0	19,858	100.0	14,027	100.0
With a work disability	16,276	11.5	2,722	13.7	1,559	11.1
Prevented from working	6,664	4.7	1,713	8.6	853	6.1
Persons 16 years and over						
Total	163,542	100.0	21,982	100.0	14,975	100.0
With a housework disability	15,233	9.3	2,497	11.4	1,266	8.5
Unable to do housework	2,935	1.8	567	2.6	258	1.7

Poverty Rate

Source: Bureau of the Census, U.S. Dept. of Commerce

The poverty rate is the proportion of the population whose income falls below the government's official poverty level, which is adjusted each year for inflation. The national poverty rate of 14.5% in 1992 was lower than the recent peak of 15.2% reached in 1983, but remained well above the levels reached in any year from 1969 through 1980. Nationwide, children living in poverty increased 22% in the 1980s. Children remain overrepresented among the poor, with a poverty rate of 21.9%. As a group the elderly are slightly underrepresented. Poverty rates for children under 18 years and persons 18 to 44 years increased between 1990 and 1992.

Poverty, by Family Status, Sex, and Race, 1978-92

Source: Bureau of the Census, U.S. Dept. of Commerce; in thousands

	1992		1990		1986		1978	
	No.[1]	%[2]	No.[1]	%[2]	No.[1]	%[2]	No.[1]	%[2]
Total poor	**36,880**	**14.5**	**33,585**	**13.5**	**32,370**	**13.6**	**24,497**	**11.4**
In families	27,947	13.0	25,232	12.0	24,754	12.0	19,062	10.0
Head of household	7,960	11.7	7,098	10.7	7,023	10.9	5,280	9.1
Related children	13,876	21.1	12,715	19.9	12,257	19.8	9,722	15.7
Unrelated individuals	**7,991**	**21.8**	**7,446**	**20.7**	**6,846**	**21.6**	**5,435**	**22.1**
In families with a female householder, no husband present	13,716	38.5	12,578	37.2	11,944	38.3	9,269	35.6
Head of household	4,171	34.9	3,768	33.4	3,613	34.6	2,654	31.4
Related children	8,032	54.3	7,363	53.4	6,943	54.4	5,687	50.6
Unrelated female individuals	**4,888**	**25.1**	**4,589**	**24.0**	**4,311**	**25.1**	**3,611**	**26.0**
All other	**14,231**	**7.9**	**12,654**	**7.1**	**12,811**	**7.3**	**9,793**	**5.9**
Head of household	3,789	6.7	3,330	6.0	3,410	6.3	2,626	5.3
Related children	5,844	11.5	5,352	10.7	5,313	10.8	4,035	7.9
Unrelated male individuals	**3,103**	**18.0**	**2,857**	**16.9**	**2,536**	**17.5**	**1,824**	**17.1**
Total white poor	**24,523**	**11.6**	**22,326**	**10.7**	**22,183**	**11.0**	**16,259**	**8.7**
In families	17,645	9.8	15,916	9.0	16,393	9.4	12,050	7.3
Head of household	5,160	8.9	4,622	8.1	4,811	8.6	3,523	6.9
Female	**2,202**	**28.1**	**2,010**	**26.8**	**2,041**	**28.2**	**1,391**	**23.5**
Related children	8,333	16.0	7,696	15.1	7,714	15.3	5,674	11.0
Unrelated individuals	**6,087**	**19.5**	**5,739**	**18.6**	**5,198**	**19.2**	**4,209**	**19.8**
Total black poor	**10,613**	**33.3**	**9,837**	**31.9**	**8,983**	**31.1**	**7,625**	**30.6**
In families	8,908	32.7	8,160	31.0	7,410	29.7	6,493	29.5
Head of household	2,435	30.9	2,193	29.3	1,987	28.0	1,622	27.5
Female	1,835	49.8	1,648	48.1	1,488	50.1	1,208	50.6
Related children	4,850	46.3	4,412	44.2	4,039	42.7	3,781	41.2
Unrelated individuals	**1,584**	**35.8**	**1,491**	**35.1**	**1,431**	**38.5**	**1,132**	**38.6**

(1) Beginning in 1980, total includes members of unrelated subfamilies not shown separately. For earlier years, unrelated subfamily members are included in the "in family" category. (2) Percentage of total population in that general category who fell below poverty level. For example, of all black female heads of households in 1992, 49.8% were poor.

Poverty Level by Family Size, 1991-92

Source: Bureau of the Census, U.S. Dept. of Commerce

	1991	1992
1 person	$ 6,932	$ 7,143
Under 65 years	7,086	7,299
65 years and over	6,532	6,729
2 persons	8,865	9,137
Householder under 65 years	9,165	9,443
Householder 65 years and over	8,241	8,487
3 persons	$10,860	$ 11,186
4 persons	13,924	14,335
5 persons	16,456	16,952
6 persons	18,587	19,137
7 persons	21,058	21,594
8 persons	23,605	24,053
9 persons or more	27,942	28,745

Persons Below Poverty Level, 1960-92

Source: Bureau of the Census, U.S. Dept. of Commerce

	Number below poverty level (mil)				Percentage below poverty level				Avg. income cutoffs for nonfarm family of 4 at poverty level[3]
Year	All races[1]	White	Black	Hispanic origin[2]	All races[1]	White	Black	Hispanic origin[2]	
1960	39.9	28.3	NA	NA	22.2	17.8	NA	NA	$3,022
1965	33.2	22.5	NA	NA	17.3	13.3	NA	NA	3,223
1970	25.4	17.5	7.5	NA	12.6	9.9	33.5	NA	3,968
1975	25.9	17.8	7.5	3.0	12.3	9.7	31.3	26.9	5,500
1980[4]	29.3	19.7	8.6	3.5	13.0	10.2	32.5	25.7	8,414
1989	31.5	20.8	9.3	5.4	12.8	10.0	30.7	26.2	12,674
1990	33.6	22.3	9.8	6.0	13.5	10.7	31.9	28.1	13,359
1991	35.7	23.7	10.2	6.3	14.2	11.3	32.7	28.7	13,924
1992	36.9	24.5	10.6	6.7	14.5	11.6	33.3	29.3	14,343

NA = Not available. (1) Includes other races not shown separately. (2) Persons of Hispanic origin may be of any race. (3) Beginning in 1981, income cutoffs for nonfarm families are applied to both farm and nonfarm families. (4) Data based on revised poverty definition.

Income Distribution by Population Fifths

Source: Bureau of the Census, U.S. Dept. of Commerce

Families, 1992	Upper limit of each fifth[1]					Percentage distribution of total income					
Race	Lowest	Second	Third	Fourth	Top 5%[2]	Lowest fifth	Second fifth	Third fifth	Fourth fifth	Highest fifth	Top 5%
Total	$16,960	$30,000	$44,200	$64,300	$106,509	4.4	10.5	16.5	24.0	44.6	17.6
White	19,000	32,000	46,250	66,252	109,900	4.9	10.9	16.7	23.7	43.8	17.3
Black	7,531	15,609	26,800	44,200	75,619	3.0	8.2	15.0	25.0	48.8	18.5

(1) The highest fifth does not have an upper limit. (2) Lower limit for top 5%.

Median Net Worth, by Type of Household and Age, 1991 and 1988

Source: Bureau of the Census, U.S. Dept. of Commerce

Type of household, by age of householder	1991 Number of households[1]	1991 Median net worth[2] Total	1991 Median net worth[2] Excluding home equity	1988 (in 1991 dollars) Number of households[1]	1988 Median net worth[2] Total	1988 Median net worth[2] Excluding home equity
Married-couple households	**52,216**	**$60,065**	**$18,606**	**51,697**	**$66,275**	**$18,900**
Under 35 years	12,247	12,036	5,235	13,357	13,968	5,458
35-54 years	23,080	60,505	18,689	21,437	70,309	19,630
55-64 years	7,849	128,782	44,827	8,186	139,383	49,575
65 years and over	9,040	147,904	56,080	8,736	144,326	53,232
Male householders	**15,297**	**$11,986**	**$5,661**	**14,383**	**$15,141**	**$6,327**
Under 35 years	5,746	5,014	3,507	5,592	5,752	3,038
35-54 years	5,409	17,740	7,101	4,857	19,784	7,075
55-64 years	1,514	30,857	5,860	1,586	40,278	12,391
65 years and over	2,627	64,381	17,322	2,346	56,704	18,460
Female householders	**27,179**	**$14,762**	**$3,596**	**25,437**	**$15,742**	**$4,214**
Under 35 years	7,038	1,360	930	6,430	1,598	1,314
35-54 years	7,959	10,684	3,224	7,236	12,696	3,406
55-64 year s	3,211	39,591	6,048	3,336	47,323	8,125
65 years and over	8,972	59,521	12,689	8,471	54,790	12,404

(1) In thousands. Excludes individuals living in group quarters, such as rooming and boarding houses. The householder is the person in whose name the home is owned or rented. A household includes the related family members and all unrelated persons, if any, such as lodgers, foster children, wards, or employees who share the housing unit. A person living alone in a housing unit or a group of unrelated persons sharing a housing unit as partners is also counted as a household. (2) Net worth is defined as the value of assets less any debts.

Aid to Families With Dependent Children

Source: Admin. for Children and Families, Office of Family Assistance, U.S. Dept. of Health and Human Services

FY 1993 State	Total assistance payments[1]	Average monthly caseload	Average monthly recipients	Average monthly children	Average monthly payment per Family	Average monthly payment per Person
Alabama	$95,852	51,559	139,752	100,115	$154.92	$57.16
Alaska	110,707	12,129	36,388	23,049	760.65	253.54
Arizona	269,610	70,047	196,680	134,054	320.75	114.23
Arkansas	59,524	26,565	72,714	51,815	186.73	68.22
California	5,897,367	859,284	2,462,489	1,704,516	571.93	199.57
Colorado	163,952	42,543	123,244	82,700	321.15	110.86
Connecticut	386,254	57,315	161,506	108,248	561.59	199.30
Delaware	39,730	11,397	27,676	18,662	290.49	119.63
Dist. of Columbia	110,730	24,784	66,706	45,863	372.32	138.33
Florida	830,374	254,006	694,535	477,127	272.43	99.63
Georgia	433,929	141,279	398,329	276,356	255.95	90.78
Hawaii	143,929	18,339	55,876	37,197	651.90	213.96
Idaho	28,539	7,938	21,295	14,222	299.61	111.68
Illinois	899,510	231,262	688,864	472,425	324.13	108.82
Indiana	221,179	73,013	212,280	140,252	252.44	86.83
Iowa	163,402	36,672	101,079	66,157	371.32	134.72
Kansas	125,876	30,179	88,072	59,205	347.58	119.10
Kentucky	210,540	82,799	224,833	144,653	211.90	78.04
Louisiana	177,466	90,019	262,703	188,492	164.28	56.29
Maine	117,144	23,854	677,447	41,941	409.24	144.74
Maryland	316,544	80,199	221,190	149,676	328.91	119.26
Massachusetts	750,500	114,441	325,431	208,651	546.35	192.13
Michigan	1,192,105	229,585	688,127	449,909	432.70	144.37
Minnesota	385,800	64,145	191,466	125,843	501.20	167.91
Mississippi	87,163	60,079	171,745	124,148	120.90	42.29
Missouri	286,137	89,906	261,463	171,302	265.22	91.20
Montana	47,014	11,738	34,596	22,463	333.79	113.24
Nebraska	65,855	16,746	48,247	32,700	327.71	113.75
Nevada	44,015	13,006	35,223	24,501	282.02	104.13
New Hampshire	56,045	11,021	29,483	18,755	423.76	158.41
New Jersey	533,594	125,930	349,388	238,277	353.10	127.27
New Mexico	118,521	31,279	95,392	61,785	315.77	103.54
New York	2,837,446	432,788	1,196,589	782,094	546.35	197.61
North Carolina	356,960	130,736	334,761	223,434	227.53	88.86
North Dakota	28,074	6,494	18,518	11,970	360.26	126.34
Ohio	980,774	257,983	718,701	473,064	316.91	113.72
Oklahoma	172,577	48,483	138,059	94,346	296.63	104.17
Oregon	202,577	42,591	117,697	77,749	396.36	143.45
Pennsylvania	916,260	205,435	607,870	407,979	371.67	125.61
Rhode Island	134,955	22,191	61,727	40,458	506.79	182.19
South Carolina	117,966	53,314	146,626	105,722	184.39	67.05
South Dakota	25,041	7,203	20,104	14,214	289.69	103.79
Tennessee	220,553	107,865	310,872	216,844	170.39	59.12
Texas	533,764	278,657	781,622	545,516	159.62	56.91
Utah	77,959	18,443	52,613	34,804	352.25	123.48
Vermont	65,878	10,009	28,547	17,529	548.50	192.31
Virginia	231,731	73,650	194,326	133,435	262.20	99.37
Washington	602,392	101,310	288,076	184,918	495.50	174.26
West Virginia	122,181	41,383	118,995	73,964	246.04	85.56
Wisconsin	441,615	79,989	236,860	137,079	460.08	155.37
Wyoming	26,466	6,509	18,238	12,249	338.84	120.93
U.S. Total[2]	**$22,553,082**	**4,981,301**	**14,144,315**	**9,538,576**	**$377.30**	**$132.87**

(1) Numbers are in thousands. Total assistance payments include AFDC-Basic, AFDC-Unemployed Parent, Title IV-A Payments under JOBS, Home Repair, and payments to Indian tribes. (2) U.S. total includes outlying areas, not shown.

Immigrants Admitted, by Type and Selected Class of Admission

Source: Immigration and Naturalization Service, U.S. Dept. of Justice

Type and class of admission	Fiscal Year 1991	Fiscal Year 1992	Fiscal Year 1993
Total, all immigrants	**1,827,167**	**973,977**	**904,292**
New arrivals	443,107	511,769	536,294
Adjustments	1,384,060	462,208	367,998
Total, IRCA legislation	**1,123,162**	**163,342**	**24,278**
Residents since 1982	214,003	46,962	18,717
Special agricultural workers	909,159	116,380	5,561
Total, nonlegalization	**704,005**	**810,635**	**880,014**
Preference immigrants	**275,613**	**329,321**	**373,788**
Family sponsored	**216,088**	**213,123**	**226,776**
Unmarried sons/daughters of U.S. citizens[1]	15,385	12,486	12,819
Spouses of alien residents[1]	110,126	118,247	128,308
Married sons/daughters of U.S. citizens[2]	27,115	22,195	23,385
Siblings of U.S. citizens[2,3]	63,462	60,195	62,264
Employment-based immigrants[2]	**59,525**	**116,198**	**147,012**
Priority workers	NA	5,456	21,114
Professionals with advanced degrees or aliens with exceptional ability	NA	58,401	29,468
Skilled workers	NA	47,568	87,689
Special immigrants	4,576	4,063	8,158
Employment creation	NA	59	583
Pre-1992	54,949	651	NA
Immediate relatives of U.S. citizens	**237,103**	**235,484**	**255,059**
Spouses	125,397	128,396	145,843
Children[4]	48,130	42,324	46,788
Orphans	9,008	6,536	7,348
Parents	63,576	64,764	62,428
Refugees and asylees	**139,079**	**117,037**	**127,343**
Refugee adjustments	116,415	106,379	115,539
Asylee adjustments	22,664	10,658	11,804
Other immigrants	**52,210**	**128,793**	**123,824**
Amerasians (P.L. 100-2021)	16,010	17,253	11,116
Children born abroad to alien residents	2,224	2,116	2,030
Cuban/Haitan entrants (P.L. 99-603)	213	99	62
Diversity transition	NA	33,911	33,468
Legalization dependents	NA	52,272	55,344
Nationals of adversely affected countries (P.L. 99-603)	12,268	1,557	10
Natives of underrepresented countries (P.L. 100-658)	9,802	880	2
Parolees, Soviet Union or Indochina (P.L. 101-267)	4,998	13,661	15,772
Registered nurses and their families (P.L. 101-238)	3,069	3,572	2,178
Registry, entered prior to 1/1/72	2,282	1,293	938
Suspension of deportation	782	1,013	1,468
Other	562	1,166	1,436

Note: For further information on laws regarding the entrance of immigrants to the U.S., see "U.S. Immigration Law" in the Nations section. NA=Not applicable. (1) Includes children. (2) Includes spouses and children. (3) Includes immigrants issued third preference, sixth preference, and special immigrant visas prior to fiscal year 1992. (4) Includes orphans.

Immigrants Admitted for Top 30 Metropolitan Areas of Intended Residence, 1993

Source: Immigration and Naturalization Service, U.S. Dept. of Justice

Metropolitan statistical area of intended residence	Total Number	Total Percentage
Total[1]	**904,292**	**100.0**
1. New York, NY	128,434	14.2
2. Los Angeles-Long Beach, CA	106,703	11.8
3. Chicago, IL	44,121	4.9
4. Miami-Hialeah, FL	30,464	3.4
5. Washington, DC-MD-VA	27,427	3.0
6. Orange County, CA	24,921	2.8
7. Houston, TX	22,634	2.5
8. San Francisco, CA	21,054	2.3
9. Boston-Lawrence-Lowell-Brockton, MA	20,414	2.3
10. San Jose, CA	19,473	2.2
11. San Diego, CA	16,931	1.9
12. Oakland, CA	16,087	1.8
13. Newark, NJ	13,551	1.5
14. Bergen-Passaic, NJ	12,931	1.4
15. Philadelphia, PA-NJ	12,842	1.4
16. Nassau-Suffolk, NY	11,601	1.3
17. Seattle-Bellevue-Everett, WA	11,509	1.3
18. Riverside-San Bernadino, CA	11,187	1.2
19. Dallas, TX	10,959	1.2
20. Detroit, MI	9,816	1.1
21. Jersey City, NJ	8,754	1.0
22. Ft. Lauderdale, FL	8,124	0.9
23. Atlanta, GA	8,031	0.9
24. Middlesex-Sommerset-Hunterdon, NJ	7,371	0.8
25. Honolulu, HI	6,880	0.8
26. Fresno, CA	6,780	0.7
27. Sacramento, CA	6,746	0.7
28. Minneapolis-St. Paul, MN-WI	6,349	0.7
29. Phoenix-Mesa, AZ	5,918	0.7
30. Portland-Vancouver, OR-WA	5,800	0.6

(1) Includes metropolitan areas not listed.

Immigration to U.S. From Selected Countries, by State of Intended Residence, 1993

Source: Immigration and Naturalization Service, U.S. Dept. of Justice; fiscal year 1993

Countries listed were selected by individual immigrants as nation of their birth. Countries listed in the table were the top five sources of immigrants. Other countries supplying large numbers of immigrants (with number of immigrants in fiscal year 1993) are, in descending order: Dominican Republic (45,420), India (40,121), El Salvador (26,818), United Kingdom (18,783), Korea (18,026), Jamaica (17,241), Canada (17,156), Taiwan (14,329), Cuba (13,666), and Ireland (13,590).

State	All countries	Mexico	China, Mainland	Philippines	Vietnam	Soviet Union
Total U.S.	**904,292**	**126,561**	**65,578**	**63,457**	**59,614**	**58,571**
AL	2,298	67	378	88	226	64
AK	1,286	48	56	411	16	76
AZ	9,778	4,719	416	345	808	269
AR	1,312	115	150	95	129	25
CA	260,090	63,221	13,700	27,614	25,429	16,886
CO	6,650	1,688	638	239	651	594
CT	10,966	136	763	286	454	744
DE	1,132	53	152	64	13	37
DC	3,608	33	239	123	453	57
FL	61,423	1,832	1,572	1,930	1,384	1,113
GA	10,213	606	937	369	1,599	515
HI	8,528	39	745	4,672	481	20
ID	1,270	494	132	50	73	81
IL	46,744	8,911	3,170	2,842	923	2,381
IN	4,539	486	929	200	182	248
IA	2,626	186	495	95	661	110
KA	3,225	560	452	117	616	187
KY	2,182	73	334	127	245	164
LA	3,725	116	411	165	846	60
ME	838	7	85	53	97	57
MD	16,899	187	1,730	1,007	666	933
MA	25,011	99	3,002	425	1,915	2,691
MI	14,913	400	1,574	497	729	1,195
MN	7,438	192	911	201	812	942
MS	906	31	184	94	90	7
MO	4,644	182	792	274	810	497
MT	509	12	75	41	7	47
NE	1,980	225	252	65	615	157
NV	4,045	1,049	164	723	121	36
NH	1,263	19	150	49	90	76
NJ	50,285	482	2,548	4,637	937	1,875
NM	3,409	2,010	167	88	229	39
NY	151,209	1,911	13,958	4,905	1,759	14,345
NC	6,892	341	849	290	749	261
ND	601	13	59	21	105	106
OH	10,703	151	1,846	414	481	1,866
OK	2,942	574	317	140	575	23
OR	7,250	901	676	341	1,070	1,527
PA	16,964	220	1,877	549	1,637	2,920
RI	3,168	23	227	86	17	343
SC	2,195	66	276	186	136	70
SD	543	7	35	38	44	95
TN	4,287	125	473	177	457	217
TX	67,380	31,773	3,606	2,031	5,173	808
UT	3,266	297	546	82	395	255
VT	709	6	83	9	157	45
VA	16,451	278	1,133	1,390	1,300	525
WA	17,147	1,108	1,313	1,834	3,080	2,678
WV	689	19	113	60	41	8
WI	5,168	356	691	172	116	290
WY	263	36	53	13	0	
U.S. territories and possessions						
GU	3,072	3	70	2,430	14	0
MP	158	0	10	136	0	0
PR	7,614	60	62	6	0	0
VI	1,610	1	2	4	0	0
Armed Service posts	236	2	0	157	1	0

U.S. Places of 5,000 or More Population—With ZIP and Area Codes

Source: U.S. Bureau of the Census, Dept. of Commerce

The following is a list of places of 5,000 or more inhabitants recognized by the Bureau of the Census, U.S. Dept. of Commerce. This list includes places that are incorporated under the laws of their respective states as cities, boroughs, towns, and villages, with the following exceptions: boroughs in Alaska and towns in the six New England states (Connecticut, Maine, Massachusetts, New Hampshire, Rhode Island, and Vermont), New York, and Wisconsin. Unincorporated places that the Census Bureau designates as "census designated places (CDP's)" are also included. These communities, marked (u), are statistically compatible with incorporated communities because of their population density. CDP boundaries can change from one census to another. Hawaii is the only state that has no incorporated places recognized by the Census Bureau; all places shown for Hawaii are CDP's.

This list also includes, in *italics*, minor civil divisions (MCD's) for the following states: Connecticut, Maine, Massachusetts, New Hampshire, New Jersey, Rhode Island, Vermont, and Wisconsin. MCD's are areas that are not incorporated under the laws of the state and that are not recognized by the Census Bureau as a CDP but are often the primary political or administrative divisions of a county. These areas may also serve as general-purpose local governments.

The geographical boundaries for places marked with a dagger (†) changed from the 1980 census to the 1990 census.

An asterisk (*) denotes that the ZIP code given is for general delivery; named streets and/or post office boxes within the community may differ. Consult the local postmaster for the correct ZIP code for specific addresses within the community.

Area codes refer only to home and business numbers. Overlay area codes for celluar phone customers are excluded.

Alabama

Area code (334) will go into effect on Jan. 15, 1995. Until then, use (205).

ZIP code	Place		1990	1980
35007	Alabaster	(205)	14,619	7,079
35950	Albertville	(205)	14,507	12,039
35010	Alexander City	(205)	14,917	13,807
36420	Andalusia	(334)	9,269	10,415
*36201	Anniston	(205)	26,638	29,135
35016	Arab	(205)	6,321	6,053
35611	Athens	(205)	16,901	14,558
*36502	Atmore	(334)	8,046	8,789
35954	Attalla	(205)	6,859	7,737
*36830	Auburn	(334)	33,830	28,471
36507	Bay Minette	(334)	7,168	7,455
*35020	Bessemer	(205)	33,581	31,729
*35203	Birmingham	(205)	265,347	284,413
35957	Boaz	(205)	6,928	7,151
*36426	Brewton	(334)	5,885	6,680
35215	Center Point(u)	(205)	22,658	23,317
36611	Chickasaw	(205)	6,649	7,402
35045	Clanton	(205)	7,669	5,832
*35055	Cullman	(205)	13,367	13,084
36322	Daleville	(334)	5,117	4,250
36526	Daphne	(205)	11,291	3,406
*35601	Decatur	(205)	48,778	42,002
36732	Demopolis	(334)	7,512	7,678
*36301	Dothan	(334)	53,721	48,750
*36330	Enterprise	(334)	20,119	18,033
*36027	Eufaula	(334)	13,220	12,097
35064	Fairfield	(205)	12,200	13,242
36532	Fairhope	(334)	8,490	7,286
*35630	Florence	(205)	36,426	37,029
35214	Forestdale(u)	(205)	10,395	10,814
35967	Fort Payne	(205)	11,838	11,485
36362	Fort Rucker(u)	(205)	7,593	8,932
35068	Fultondale	(205)	6,400	6,217
*35901	Gadsden	(205)	42,523	47,565
35071	Gardendale	(205)	9,251	8,005
36037	Greenville	(334)	7,494	7,807
35976	Guntersville	(205)	7,038	7,041
35570	Hamilton	(205)	5,787	5,093
35640	Hartselle	(205)	10,867	8,858
35209	Homewood	(205)	23,644	21,412
35236	Hoover	(205)	40,000	18,996
35023	Hueytown	(205)	15,280	13,452
*35801	Huntsville	(205)	159,880	142,513
35210	Irondale	(205)	9,458	6,510
36545	Jackson	(334)	5,819	6,073
36265	Jacksonville	(205)	10,283	9,735
*35501	Jasper	(205)	13,553	11,894
36863	Lanett	(205)	8,985	8,922
35094	Leeds	(205)	10,009	8,638
35758	Madison	(205)	14,792	4,057
35228	Midfield	(205)	5,559	6,182
36054	Millbrook	(205)	6,046	3,101
*36601	Mobile	(334)	196,263	200,452
*36460	Monroeville	(334)	6,993	5,674
*36104	Montgomery	(334)	187,543	177,857
35223	Mountain Brook	(205)	19,810	19,718
35667	Muscle Shoals	(205)	9,611	8,911
35476	Northport	(205)	17,297	14,291
*36801	Opelika	(334)	22,122	21,896
36467	Opp	(334)	7,011	7,204
36203	Oxford	(205)	9,537	8,939
*36360	Ozark	(334)	13,030	13,188
35124	Pelham	(205)	9,356	6,759
35125	Pell City	(205)	7,945	6,616
36867	Phenix City	(334)	25,311	26,928
36272	Piedmont	(205)	5,347	5,544
35126	Pinson-Clay-Chalkville(u)	(205)	10,987	....
35127	Pleasant Grove	(205)	8,458	7,102
*36067	Prattville	(334)	19,816	18,647
36610	Prichard	(205)	34,320	39,541
35906	Rainbow City	(205)	7,667	6,299
36274	Roanoke	(334)	6,362	5,809
35653	Russellville	(205)	7,812	8,195
36201	Saks(u)	(205)	11,138	11,118
36571	Saraland	(205)	11,760	9,833
36572	Satsuma	(205)	5,194	3,822
35768	Scottsboro	(205)	13,786	14,758
*36701	Selma	(334)	23,755	26,684
35660	Sheffield	(205)	10,380	11,903
35901	Southside	(205)	5,580	5,141
35150	Sylacauga	(205)	12,520	12,708
35160	Talladega	(205)	18,175	19,128
36045	Tallassee	(334)	5,112	4,763
35217	Tarrant City	(205)	8,046	8,148
*36582	Theodore(u)	(205)	6,509	6,392
36619	Tillman's Corner(u)	(205)	17,988	15,941
36081	Troy	(334)	13,051	13,124
35173	Trussville	(205)	8,283	3,507
*35401	Tuscaloosa	(205)	77,866	75,211
35674	Tuscumbia	(205)	8,413	9,137
36083	Tuskegee	(334)	12,257	13,327
*36854	Valley†	(205)	8,215	8,946
35216	Vestavia Hills	(205)	19,550	15,722

Alaska (907)

ZIP code	Place	1990	1980
*99501	Anchorage	226,338	174,431
*99708	College(u)	11,249	4,043
99702	Eielson AFB(u)	5,251	5,232
*99701	Fairbanks	30,843	22,645
*99801	Juneau	26,751	19,528
99611	Kenai	6,327	4,324
*99901	Ketchikan	8,263	7,198
*99615	Kodiak	6,365	4,756
99639	Ninilchik(u)	10,523	341
99835	Sitka	8,588	7,803

Arizona

Area code (520) will go into effect on Mar. 19, 1995. Until then, use (602).

ZIP code	Place		1990	1980
*85220	Apache Junction	(602)	18,092	9,935
85323	Avondale	(602)	16,182	8,168
85603	Bisbee	(520)	6,288	7,154
85326	Buckeye	(602)	4,436	3,434
*86430	Bullhead City†	(520)	21,951	10,719
86322	Camp Verde†	(520)	6,243	3,824
*85222	Casa Grande	(520)	19,076	14,971
*85225	Chandler	(602)	89,862	29,673
86503	Chinle(u)	(520)	5,059	2,815
85228	Coolidge	(520)	6,934	6,851
86326	Cottonwood	(520)	5,918	4,550
.....	Cottonwood-Verde Village(u)	(520)	7,037	....
*85607	Douglas	(520)	13,137	13,058
85335	El Mirage	(602)	5,001	4,307
85231	Eloy	(520)	7,211	6,240
*86004	Flagstaff	(520)	45,857	34,743
85232	Florence	(520)	7,321	3,391
85726	Flowing Wells(u)	(520)	14,013	....
.....	Fortuna Foothills(u)	(520)	7,737	....
*85266	Fountain Hills†	(602)	10,030	2,771
*85234	Gilbert	(602)	29,122	5,717
*85301	Glendale	(602)	147,864	97,172
*85501	Globe	(520)	6,062	6,886

ZIP code	Place		1990	1980
85338	Goodyear	(602)	6,258	2,747
*85622	Green Valley(u)	(520)	13,231	7,999
85283	Guadalupe	(602)	5,458	4,506
86401	Kingman	(520)	12,722	9,257
*86403	Lake Havasu City	(520)	24,363	15,909
*85201	Mesa	(602)	288,104	152,404
86440	Mohave Valley(u)	(520)	6,962	....
.....	New Kingman-Butler(u)	(520)	11,627	....
*85621	Nogales	(520)	19,489	15,683
85737	Oro Valley	(520)	6,670	1,489
86040	Page	(520)	6,598	4,907
85253	Paradise Valley	(602)	11,773	11,085
*85541	Payson	(520)	8,377	5,068
*85345	Peoria	(602)	50,675	12,171
*85026	Phoenix	(602)	983,403	789,704
*86301	Prescott	(520)	26,592	19,865
*86314	Prescott Valley	(520)	8,904	2,284
*85546	Safford	(520)	7,359	7,010
*85251	Scottsdale	(602)	130,075	88,622
*86336	Sedona†	(520)	7,720	5,319
85901	Show Low	(520)	5,020	4,298
*85635	Sierra Vista	(520)	32,983	24,937
85635	Sierra Vista Southeast(u)	(520)	9,237	....
85350	Somerton	(520)	5,282	3,969
85713	South Tucson	(520)	5,171	6,554
*85351	Sun City(u)	(602)	38,126	40,505
85375	Sun City West(u)	(602)	15,997	3,772
85248	Sun Lakes(u)	(602)	6,578	1,925
85374	Surprise	(602)	7,122	3,723
*85282	Tempe	(602)	141,993	106,919
86045	Tuba City(u)	(520)	7,323	5,045
*85726	Tucson	(520)	405,323	330,537
86047	Winslow	(520)	9,279	7,921
*85364	Yuma	(520)	54,923	42,481

Arkansas (501)

ZIP code	Place	1990	1980
71923	Arkadelphia	10,014	10,005
71822	Ashdown	5,150	4,218
*72501	Batesville	9,187	8,447
72714	Bella Vista(u)	9,083	2,589
*72015	Benton	18,177	17,717
72712	Bentonville	11,257	8,756
72315	Blytheville	22,523	23,844
72022	Bryant	5,269	2,682
72023	Cabot	8,319	4,806
71701	Camden	14,701	15,356
72830	Clarksville	5,833	5,237
*72032	Conway	26,481	20,375
71635	Crossett	6,282	6,706
71639	Dumas	5,520	6,091
*71730	El Dorado	23,146	25,270
*72701	Fayetteville	42,247	36,608
72335	Forrest City	13,364	13,803
*72901	Fort Smith	72,798	71,626
*72601	Harrison	9,936	9,567
72543	Heber Springs	5,628	4,589
72342	Helena	7,491	9,598
71801	Hope	9,768	10,290
*71901	Hot Springs	32,462	35,781
71909	Hot Springs Village(u)	6,361	2,083
*72076	Jacksonville	29,101	27,589
72401	Jonesboro	46,535	31,530
*72201	Little Rock	175,727	159,151
71753	Magnolia	11,151	11,909
72104	Malvern	9,236	10,163
72360	Marianna	6,033	6,220
72113	Maumelle†	6,714	1,368
71953	Mena	5,475	5,154
71655	Monticello	8,119	8,259
72110	Morrilton	6,551	7,355
72653	Mountain Home	9,027	8,066
72112	Newport	7,459	8,339
*72114	North Little Rock	61,829	64,388
72370	Osceola	8,930	8,881
72450	Paragould	18,540	15,248
*71601	Pine Bluff	57,140	56,636
72455	Pocahontas	6,151	5,995
*72756	Rogers	24,692	17,429
72801	Russellville	21,260	14,518
72143	Searcy	15,180	13,612
72120	Sherwood	18,878	10,423
72761	Siloam Springs	8,151	7,940
*72764	Springdale	29,945	23,458
72160	Stuttgart	10,420	10,941
75502	Texarkana	22,631	21,459
72472	Trumann	6,346	6,395
72956	Van Buren	14,899	12,020
71671	Warren	6,455	7,646
72390	West Helena	10,137	11,367
*72301	West Memphis	28,259	28,138
72396	Wynne	8,817	7,927

California

ZIP code	Place		1990	1980
94301	Adelanto		6,791	2,164
91301	Agoura Hills†	(818)	20,391	11,399
*94501	Alameda	(510)	73,979	63,852
94507	Alamo(u)	(510)	12,277	8,505
94706	Albany	(510)	16,327	15,130
*91802	Alhambra	(818)	82,087	64,767
92656	Aliso Viejo(u)		7,612	....
90249	Alondra Park(u)	(310)	12,215	12,189
*91901	Alpine(u)	(619)	9,695	5,368
*91001	Altadena(u)	(818)	42,658	40,983
95945	Alta Sierra(u)		5,709	2,168
94589	American Canyon(u)	(707)	7,706	5,712
*92803	Anaheim	(714)	266,406	219,494
96007	Anderson	(916)	8,299	7,381
*94509	Antioch	(510)	62,195	42,683
*92307	Apple Valley†	(619)	46,079	16,748
*95003	Aptos(u)	(408)	9,061	7,039
*91006	Arcadia	(818)	48,284	45,993
95521	Arcata	(707)	15,211	12,849
95825	Arden-Arcade(u)	(916)	92,040	87,570
*93420	Arroyo Grande	(805)	14,432	11,290
*90701	Artesia	(310)	15,464	14,301
93203	Arvin	(805)	9,286	6,863
94577	Ashland(u)	(510)	16,590	13,893
93422	Atascadero	(805)	23,138	16,232
94025	Atherton	(415)	7,163	7,797
95301	Atwater	(209)	22,282	17,530
*95603	Auburn	(916)	10,653	7,540
92505	August(u)	(714)	6,376	6,350
93204	Avenal		9,770	4,137
91746	Avocado Heights(u)	(818)	14,232	11,733
91702	Azusa	(818)	41,203	29,380
*93302	Bakersfield	(805)	174,978	105,611
91706	Baldwin Park	(818)	69,330	50,554
92220	Banning	(714)	20,572	14,020
*92312	Barstow	(619)	21,472	17,690
93402	Baywood-Los Osos(u)	(805)	14,377	10,933
95903	Beale AFB(u)	(916)	6,912	6,329
92223	Beaumont	(714)	9,685	6,818
90201	Bell	(213)	34,365	25,450
*90706	Bellflower	(310)	61,815	53,441
90201	Bell Gardens	(213)	42,315	34,117
94002	Belmont	(415)	24,165	24,505
94510	Benicia	(707)	24,437	15,376
95005	Ben Lomond(u)	(408)	7,884	7,238
*94704	Berkeley	(510)	102,724	103,328
*90210	Beverly Hills	(310)	31,971	32,646
92314	Big Bear Lake†	(714)	5,351	4,896
94506	Black Hawk(u)		6,199	....
92316	Bloomington(u)	(714)	15,116	12,781
*92226	Blythe	(619)	8,448	6,805
.....	Bonadella Ranchos-Madera Ranchos(u)		5,705	3,272
91902	Bonita(u)	(619)	12,542	6,257
92021	Bostonia(u)		13,670	....
95006	Boulder Creek(u)	(408)	6,725	5,662
95416	Boyes Hot Springs(u)		5,973	4,177
92227	Brawley	(619)	18,923	14,946
92622	Brea	(714)	32,873	27,913
94513	Brentwood	(510)	7,563	4,434
*90622	Buena Park	(714)	68,784	64,165
*91505	Burbank	(818)	93,649	84,625
*94010	Burlingame	(415)	26,666	26,173
*92232	Calexico	(619)	18,633	14,412
*93505	California City		5,955	2,743
*93010	Camarillo	(805)	52,297	37,797
93428	Cambria(u)		5,382	3,061
95682	Cameron Park(u)	(916)	11,897	5,607
95008	Campbell	(408)	36,048	26,843
92055	Camp Pendleton North(u)	(714)	10,373	2,065
92055	Camp Pendleton South(u)	(714)	11,299	7,952
92587	Canyon Lake(u)		7,938	2,039
95010	Capitola	(408)	10,171	9,095
*92008	Carlsbad	(619)	63,292	35,490
95608	Carmichael(u)	(916)	48,702	43,108
93013	Carpinteria	(805)	13,747	10,835
90745	Carson	(310)	83,995	81,221
92077	Casa de Oro-Mt. Helix(u)	(619)	30,727	19,651
*94546	Castro Valley(u)	(510)	48,619	43,810
95012	Castroville	(408)	5,272	4,396
*92235	Cathedral City†	(619)	30,085	11,096
95307	Ceres	(209)	26,413	13,281
90703	Cerritos	(310)	53,244	53,020
91724	Charter Oak(u)	(818)	8,858	6,840
94541	Cherryland(u)	(415)	11,088	9,425
92223	Cherry Valley(u)	(714)	5,945	5,012
*95926	Chico	(916)	39,970	26,716
*91708	Chino	(714)	59,682	40,165
91709	Chino Hills(u)		27,608	....
93610	Chowchilla	(209)	5,930	5,122
*91910	Chula Vista	(619)	135,160	83,927
95610	Citrus(u)	(916)	9,481	12,450
*95621	Citrus Heights(u)	(916)	107,439	85,911
91711	Claremont	(714)	32,610	31,028
94517	Clayton		7,317	4,325
95422	Clearlake†		11,804	8,343
*93612	Clovis	(209)	50,323	33,021
92236	Coachella	(619)	16,896	9,129
93210	Coalinga	(209)	8,212	6,593
92324	Colton	(714)	40,213	21,310
90022	Commerce	(310)	12,135	10,509

ZIP code	Place		1990	1980
*90221	Compton	(310)	90,454	81,350
*94520	Concord	(510)	111,308	103,763
93212	Corcoran	(209)	13,360	6,454
96021	Corning	(916)	5,870	4,745
91718	Corona	(714)	75,943	37,791
*92118	Coronado	(619)	26,540	18,790
*94925	Corte Madera	(415)	8,272	8,074
*92628	Costa Mesa	(714)	96,357	82,562
94931	Cotati	(707)	5,714	3,346
94556	Country Club(u)	(209)	9,325	9,585
*91722	Covina	(818)	43,332	32,746
92325	Crestline(u)	(714)	8,594	6,715
90201	Cudahy	(213)	22,817	18,275
*90230	Culver City	(310)	38,793	38,139
*95014	Cupertino	(408)	39,967	34,297
90630	Cypress	(714)	42,655	40,738
*94015	Daly City	(415)	92,088	78,519
92629	Dana Point	(714)	31,896	21,271†
*94526	Danville	(510)	31,306	26,143†
95616	Davis	(916)	46,322	36,640
90250	Del Aire(u)	(310)	8,040	8,487
*93215	Delano	(805)	22,762	16,491
.....	Del Monte Forest(u)		5,069	....
*92240	Desert Hot Springs	(619)	11,668	5,941
*91765	Diamond Bar	(714)	53,672	....
93618	Dinuba	(209)	12,743	9,907
94514	Discovery Bay(u)		5,351	1,326
95620	Dixon	(916)	10,417	7,541
*90241	Downey	(310)	91,444	82,602
*91010	Duarte	(818)	20,716	16,766
94568	Dublin†	(510)	23,229	13,496
93219	Earlimart(u)	(805)	5,881	4,578
90220	East Compton(u)	(310)	7,967	6,435
.....	East Foothills(u)		14,898	16,890
92343	East Hemet(u)	(714)	17,611	14,712
90638	East La Mirada(u)	(310)	9,367	9,688
90022	East Los Angeles(u)	(310)	126,379	110,017
94303	East Palo Alto†	(415)	23,451	18,106
91117	East Pasadena(u)		5,910	....
93257	East Porterville(u)	(209)	5,790	5,218
.....	East San Gabriel(u)		12,736	....
*93523	Edwards AFB(u)	(805)	7,423	8,554
*92020	El Cajon	(619)	88,693	73,892
92244	El Centro	(619)	31,405	23,996
94530	El Cerrito	(510)	22,869	22,731
95762	El Dorado Hills(u)		6,395	3,453
95624	Elk Grove(u)	(916)	17,483	10,959
*91734	El Monte	(818)	106,162	79,494
*93446	El Paso de Robles	(310)	18,583	9,163
93030	El Rio(u)	(805)	6,419	5,674
90245	El Segundo	(310)	15,223	13,752
94802	El Sobrante(u)	(510)	9,852	10,535
92630	El Toro(u)	(714)	62,685	38,153
92709	El Toro Station(u)	(714)	6,869	7,632
*94608	Emeryville	(510)	5,740	3,714
*92024	Encinitas†	(619)	55,406	36,550
*92025	Escondido	(619)	108,648	64,355
*95501	Eureka	(707)	27,025	24,153
93221	Exeter	(209)	7,276	5,606
*94930	Fairfax	(415)	6,931	7,391
94533	Fairfield	(707)	78,650	58,099
95628	Fair Oaks(u)	(916)	26,867	22,602
93238	Fairview(u)		9,045	....
*92028	Fallbrook(u)	(619)	22,095	14,041
93223	Farmersville	(209)	6,235	5,544
95018	Felton(u)	(408)	5,350	4,564
*93015	Fillmore	(805)	11,992	9,602
90001	Florence-Graham(u)	(213)	57,147	48,662
95828	Florin(u)	(916)	24,330	16,523
95630	Folsom	(916)	29,802	11,003
*92335	Fontana	(714)	87,535	36,804
95841	Foothill Farms(u)	(916)	17,135	13,700
95437	Fort Bragg	(707)	6,078	5,019
95540	Fortuna	(707)	8,788	7,591
94404	Foster City	(415)	28,176	23,287
92728	Fountain Valley	(714)	53,691	55,080
95019	Freedom(u)	(408)	8,361	6,416
*94537	Fremont	(510)	173,339	131,945
*93706	Fresno	(209)	354,091	217,491
*92634	Fullerton	(714)	114,144	102,246
95632	Galt	(209)	8,889	5,514
*90247	Gardena	(310)	49,841	45,165
95205	Garden Acres(u)	(213)	8,547	7,361
*92642	Garden Grove	(714)	143,965	123,307
92394	George AFB(u)	(619)	5,085	7,061
95020	Gilroy	(408)	31,487	21,641
92509	Glen Avon(u)	(714)	12,663	8,444
*91205	Glendale	(818)	180,038	139,060
91740	Glendora	(818)	47,832	38,500
93561	Golden Hills(u)		5,423	....
92324	Grand Terrace	(714)	10,946	8,498
*95945	Grass Valley	(916)	9,048	6,697
93308	Greenacres(u)	(805)	7,379	5,381
93927	Greenfield	(805)	7,464	4,181
93433	Grover City	(805)	11,602	8,827
93434	Guadalupe		5,479	3,629
91745	Hacienda Heights(u)	(818)	52,354	49,422
94019	Half Moon Bay	(415)	8,886	7,282
93230	Hanford	(209)	30,463	20,958
90716	Hawaiian Gardens	(213)	13,639	10,548
*90250	Hawthorne	(310)	71,349	56,437
*94544	Hayward	(510)	111,343	93,585
95448	Healdsburg	(707)	9,469	7,217
92546	Hemet	(714)	36,094	22,531
94547	Hercules	(415)	16,829	5,963
90254	Hermosa Beach	(310)	18,219	18,070
*92340	Hesperia†	(619)	50,418	20,612
92346	Highland†	(714)	34,439	21,720
94010	Hillsborough	(415)	10,667	10,372
*95023	Hollister	(408)	19,318	11,488
91720	Home Gardens(u)	(714)	7,780	5,783
*92647	Huntington Beach	(714)	181,519	170,505
90255	Huntington Park	(213)	56,129	45,932
*91932	Imperial Beach	(619)	26,512	22,689
*92202	Indio	(619)	36,850	21,611
*90301	Inglewood	(310)	109,602	94,162
.....	Interlaken(u)		6,404	....
95640	Ione		6,516	2,207
*92716	Irvine	(714)	110,330	62,134
93117	Isla Vista(u)	(805)	20,395	....
94904	Kentfield(u)	(415)	6,030	....
93630	Kerman	(209)	5,448	4,002
93930	King City	(408)	7,634	5,495
93631	Kingsburg	(209)	7,245	5,115
*91011	La Canada Flintridge	(818)	19,378	20,153
91214	La Crescenta-Montrose(u)	(818)	16,968	16,531
90045	Ladera Heights(u)	(310)	6,316	6,647
94549	Lafayette	(510)	23,366	20,837
.....	Laguna(u)		9,828	....
*92607	Laguna Beach	(714)	23,170	17,858
*92607	Laguna Hills(u)	(714)	46,731	33,600
92607	Laguna Niguel†	(714)	44,723	12,237
*90631	La Habra	(310)	51,263	45,232
.....	La Habra Heights	(310)	6,226	4,786
92352	Lake Arrowhead(u)	(714)	6,539	6,272
*92331	Lake Elsinore†	(714)	18,316	5,982
92530	Lakeland Village(u)		5,159	2,796
93535	Lake Los Angeles(u)		7,977	....
92040	Lakeside(u)	(619)	39,412	23,921
*90714	Lakewood	(310)	73,553	74,511
*91941	La Mesa	(619)	52,911	50,308
*90638	La Mirada	(714)	40,452	40,986
93241	Lamont(u)	(805)	11,517	9,616
93534	Lancaster	(805)	97,300	48,027
90623	La Palma	(714)	15,392	15,399
91747	La Puente	(818)	36,955	30,882
92253	La Quinta†		11,215	4,027
.....	La Riviera(u)	(916)	10,986	10,906
95403	Larkfield-Wikiup(u)		6,779	....
*94939	Larkspur	(415)	11,068	11,064
95330	Lathrop†		6,841	4,112
91750	La Verne	(714)	30,843	23,508
90260	Lawndale	(310)	27,331	23,460
91945	Lemon Grove	(619)	23,984	20,780
93245	Lemoore	(209)	13,622	8,832
90304	Lennox(u)	(310)	22,757	18,445
95648	Lincoln	(916)	7,248	4,132
95901	Linda(u)	(916)	13,033	10,225
93247	Lindsay	(209)	8,338	6,936
95953	Live Oak(u)	(916)	15,212	11,482
*94550	Livermore	(510)	56,741	48,349
95334	Livingston	(209)	7,317	5,326
*95240	Lodi	(209)	51,874	35,221
92354	Loma Linda	(714)	18,470	10,694
90717	Lomita	(213)	19,442	18,807
*93436	Lompoc	(805)	37,649	26,267
*90801	Long Beach	(310)	429,321	361,498
95650	Loomis†		5,705	3,663
*90720	Los Alamitos	(310)	11,788	11,529
*94022	Los Altos	(415)	26,599	25,769
94022	Los Altos Hills	(415)	7,514	7,421
*90086	Los Angeles	(213)	3,485,557	2,968,528
93635	Los Banos	(209)	14,519	10,341
*95030	Los Gatos	(408)	27,357	26,906
91709	Los Serranos(u)		7,099	....
94903	Lucas Valley-Marinwood(u)	(415)	5,982	6,409
90262	Lynwood	(310)	61,945	48,289
93250	Mc Farland	(805)	7,005	5,151
95521	McKinleyville(u)	(707)	10,749	7,772
*93638	Madera	(209)	29,282	21,732
.....	Madera Acres(u)		5,245	2,173
95954	Magalia(u)		8,987	....
90266	Manhattan Beach	(310)	32,063	31,542
95336	Manteca	(209)	40,773	24,925
92518	March AFB(u)	(714)	5,523	3,607
93933	Marina	(408)	26,512	20,647
*90292	Marina Del Rey(u)	(310)	7,431	6,336
94553	Martinez	(510)	31,808	22,582
95901	Marysville	(916)	12,324	9,898
90270	Maywood	(213)	27,893	21,810
93640	Mendota	(209)	6,821	5,038
*94025	Menlo Park	(415)	28,403	26,438
92359	Mentone(u)	(714)	5,675	....
*95340	Merced	(209)	56,155	36,423
94030	Millbrae	(415)	20,414	20,058
*94941	Mill Valley	(415)	13,038	12,967
*95035	Milpitas	(408)	50,690	37,820
91752	Mira Loma(u)	(714)	15,786	7,394

ZIP code	Place	Area code	1990	1980
93641	Mira Monte(u)		7,744	....
*92690	Mission Viejo†	(714)	72,820	48,503
*95350	Modesto	(209)	164,746	106,963
*91016	Monrovia	(818)	35,733	30,531
91763	Montclair	(714)	28,434	22,628
90640	Montebello	(213)	59,564	52,929
93940	Monterey	(408)	31,954	27,558
91754	Monterey Park	(818)	60,738	54,338
*93021	Moorpark†	(805)	25,494	7,798
94556	Moraga	(510)	15,987	15,014
*92552	Moreno Valley†	(714)	118,779	28,139
*95037	Morgan Hill	(408)	23,928	17,060
*93442	Morro Bay	(805)	9,664	9,064
*94041	Mountain View	(415)	67,365	58,655
92405	Muscoy(u)	(714)	7,541	6,188
*94558	Napa	(707)	61,865	50,879
*91950	National City	(619)	54,249	48,772
92363	Needles	(619)	5,191	4,120
94560	Newark	(510)	37,861	32,126
*92658	Newport Beach	(714)	66,643	62,556
93444	Nipomo(u)	(805)	7,109	5,247
91760	Norco	(714)	23,302	19,732
95603	North Auburn(u)	(916)	10,301	7,619
94025	North Fair Oaks(u)	(415)	13,912	10,308
95660	North Highlands(u)	(916)	42,105	37,825
90650	Norwalk	(310)	94,279	84,901
*94947	Novato	(415)	47,585	43,916
95361	Oakdale	(209)	11,978	8,474
*94617	Oakland	(510)	372,242	339,337
94561	Oakley(u)		18,374	2,816
93445	Oceano(u)		6,169	4,478
*92054	Oceanside	(619)	128,090	76,698
93308	Oildale(u)	(805)	26,553	23,382
93023	Ojai	(805)	7,613	6,816
95961	Olivehurst(u)	(916)	9,738	8,929
*91761	Ontario	(714)	133,179	88,820
95060	Opal Cliffs(u)	(408)	5,940	5,041
*92613	Orange	(714)	110,658	91,450
93646	Orange Cove	(209)	5,604	4,026
95662	Orangevale(u)	(916)	26,266	20,585
94563	Orinda†	(510)	16,642	17,030
95963	Orland	(916)	5,052	4,031
93647	Orosi(u)		5,486	4,076
95965	Oroville	(916)	11,885	8,683
.....	Oroville East(u)		8,462	....
*93030	Oxnard	(805)	142,560	108,195
94044	Pacifica	(415)	37,670	36,866
93950	Pacific Grove	(408)	16,117	15,755
95968	Palermo(u)		5,260	2,572
93550	Palmdale	(805)	68,946	12,277
92261	Palm Desert	(619)	23,252	11,801
.....	Palm Desert Country(u)		5,626	....
92263	Palm Springs	(619)	40,144	32,359
*94303	Palo Alto	(415)	55,900	55,225
90274	Palos Verdes Estates	(310)	13,512	14,376
*95969	Paradise	(916)	25,401	22,571
90723	Paramount	(310)	47,669	36,407
95823	Parkway-So. Sacramento(u)	(916)	31,903	26,815
93648	Parlier	(209)	7,938	2,902
*91109	Pasadena	(818)	131,586	118,072
95363	Patterson	(209)	8,626	3,908
92509	Pedley(u)		8,869	....
*92572	Perris	(714)	21,500	6,827
*94952	Petaluma	(707)	43,166	33,834
*90660	Pico Rivera	(310)	59,177	53,387
*94611	Piedmont	(510)	10,602	10,498
94564	Pinole	(510)	17,460	14,253
*93449	Pismo Beach	(805)	7,669	5,364
94565	Pittsburg	(510)	47,607	33,465
92670	Placentia	(714)	41,259	35,041
95667	Placerville	(916)	8,286	6,739
94523	Pleasant Hill	(510)	31,583	25,547
*94566	Pleasanton	(510)	50,570	35,160
*91769	Pomona	(714)	131,700	92,742
93257	Porterville	(209)	29,521	19707
93044	Port Hueneme	(805)	20,322	17,803
92064	Poway†	(619)	43,396	33,439
93907	Prunedale(u)		7,393	....
*93551	Quartz Hill(u)	(805)	9,626	7,421
92065	Ramona(u)	(619)	13,040	8,173
95670	Rancho Cordova(u)	(916)	48,731	42,881
91730	Rancho Cucamonga	(714)	101,409	55,250
92270	Rancho Mirage	(619)	9,778	6,281
*90274	Rancho Palos Verdes	(310)	41,667	36,577
.....	Rancho San Diego(u)		6,977	....
92688	Rancho Santa Margarita(u)		11,390	....
96080	Red Bluff	(916)	12,363	9,490
*96049	Redding	(916)	66,462	42,103
*92373	Redlands	(714)	60,395	43,619
*90277	Redondo Beach	(310)	60,167	57,102
*94063	Redwood City	(415)	66,072	54,951
93654	Reedley	(209)	15,791	11,071
*92377	Rialto	(714)	72,395	37,862
*94802	Richmond	(510)	86,019	74,676
*93555	Ridgecrest	(619)	28,295	15,929
95003	Rio Del Mar(u)	(408)	8,919	7,067
95673	Rio Linda(u)	(916)	9,481	7,359
95366	Ripon	(209)	7,455	3,509
95367	Riverbank	(209)	8,591	5,695
*92502	Riverside	(714)	226,546	170,591
*95677	Rocklin	(916)	18,806	7,344
94572	Rodeo(u)	(415)	7,589	8,286
*94928	Rohnert Park	(707)	36,326	22,965
90274	Rolling Hills Estates	(310)	7,789	7,701
93560	Rosamond(u)	(805)	7,430	2,869
95401	Roseland(u)	(707)	8,779	7,915
91770	Rosemead	(818)	51,638	42,604
95826	Rosemont(u)	(916)	22,851	18,888
*95678	Roseville	(916)	44,685	24,347
90720	Rossmoor(u)	(310)	9,893	10,457
91748	Rowland Heights(u)	(818)	42,647	28,258
92509	Rubidoux(u)	(714)	24,367	17,048
*95814	Sacramento	(916)	369,365	275,741
*93907	Salinas	(408)	108,777	80,479
*94960	San Anselmo	(415)	11,735	12,067
*92401	San Bernardino	(714)	164,676	118,794
94066	San Bruno	(415)	38,961	35,417
*93001	San Buenaventura (Ventura)	(805)	92,557	73,774
94070	San Carlos	(415)	26,382	24,710
92674	San Clemente	(714)	41,100	27,325
*92138	San Diego	(619)	1,110,554	875,538
.....	San Diego Country Estates(u)		6,874	....
91773	San Dimas	(714)	32,398	24,014
*91340	San Fernando	(818)	22,580	17,731
*94142	San Francisco	(415)	723,959	678,974
*91778	San Gabriel	(818)	37,120	30,072
93657	Sanger	(209)	16,839	12,542
*92581	San Jacinto	(714)	16,210	7,098
*95113	San Jose	(408)	782,248	629,400
*92690	San Juan Capistrano	(714)	26,183	18,959
*94577	San Leandro	(510)	68,223	63,952
94580	San Lorenzo(u)	(510)	19,987	20,545
*93401	San Luis Obispo	(805)	41,958	34,252
*92069	San Marcos	(619)	38,974	17,479
*91108	San Marino	(818)	12,959	13,307
*94402	San Mateo	(415)	85,619	77,640
94806	San Pablo	(510)	25,158	19,750
*94915	San Rafael	(415)	48,410	44,700
94583	San Ramon†	(510)	35,303	20,511
*92711	Santa Ana	(714)	293,827	204,023
*93102	Santa Barbara	(805)	85,571	74,414
*95050	Santa Clara	(408)	93,613	87,700
*91354	Santa Clarita†	(805)	110,690	66,730
*95060	Santa Cruz	(408)	49,711	41,483
90670	Santa Fe Springs	(310)	15,520	14,520
93454	Santa Maria	(805)	61,552	39,685
*90401	Santa Monica	(310)	86,905	88,314
93060	Santa Paula	(805)	25,062	20,658
*95402	Santa Rosa	(707)	113,261	82,658
92071	Santee†	(619)	52,902	40,298
95070	Saratoga	(408)	28,061	29,261
94965	Sausalito	(415)	7,152	7,338
95066	Scotts Valley	(408)	8,667	6,891
90740	Seal Beach	(310)	25,098	25,975
93955	Seaside	(408)	38,826	36,567
*95472	Sebastopol	(707)	7,008	5,595
93662	Selma	(209)	14,757	10,942
93263	Shafter	(805)	8,409	7,010
*91024	Sierra Madre	(818)	10,762	10,837
90806	Signal Hill	(310)	8,371	5,734
*93065	Simi Valley	(805)	100,218	77,500
92075	Solana Beach†	(619)	12,956	12,250
93960	Soledad	(408)	7,161	5,928
95476	Sonoma	(707)	8,168	6,054
95073	Soquel(u)	(408)	9,188	6,212
91733	South El Monte	(213)	20,850	16,623
90280	South Gate	(213)	86,284	66,784
*91030	South Lake Tahoe	(916)	21,586	20,681
95965	South Oroville(u)	(916)	7,463	7,246
91030	South Pasadena	(818)	23,936	22,681
94080	South San Francisco	(415)	54,312	49,393
91770	South San Gabriel(u)	(213)	7,700	5,421
91744	South San Jose Hills(u)	(408)	17,814	16,076
90605	South Whittier(u)	(310)	49,514	43,815
95991	South Yuba(u)	(916)	8,816	7,530
*91979	Spring Valley(u)	(619)	55,331	40,191
94305	Stanford(u)	(415)	18,097	11,045
90680	Stanton	(714)	30,491	23,723
*95208	Stockton	(209)	210,943	148,283
94585	Suisun City	(707)	22,704	11,087
*92386	Sun City(u)	(714)	14,930	8,460
*94086	Sunnyvale	(408)	117,324	106,618
96130	Susanville	(916)	7,279	6,520
93268	Taft	(805)	5,902	5,316
94941	Tamalpais-Homestead Valley(u)	(415)	9,601	8,511
*93561	Tehachapi	(805)	6,182	4,126
*92589	Temecula†	(909)	27,177	4,289
91780	Temple City	(818)	31,153	28,972
95965	Thermalito(u)		5,646	4,961
*91359	Thousand Oaks	(805)	104,381	77,072
94920	Tiburon	(415)	7,554	6,685
*90503	Torrance	(310)	133,107	129,881
95396	Tracy	(209)	33,558	18,428
*93274	Tulare	(209)	33,249	22,530
*95380	Turlock	(209)	42,224	26,287
92681	Tustin	(714)	50,689	32,248
92705	Tustin Foothills(u)	(714)	24,358	26,174

ZIP code	Place		1990	1980
*92277	Twentynine Palms†	(619)	11,821	8,802
92278	Twentynine Palms Base(u)	(619)	10,606	7,079
.....	Twin Lakes(u)		5,379	4,502
95482	Ukiah	(707)	14,632	12,035
94587	Union City	(510)	53,762	39,406
*91785	Upland	(714)	63,374	47,647
*95687	Vacaville	(707)	71,476	43,367
91744	Valinda(u)	(818)	18,735	18,712
*94590	Vallejo	(707)	109,199	80,303
92343	Valle Vista(u)	(714)	8,751	5,474
93437	Vandenberg AFB(u)	(805)	9,846	8,136
93436	Vandenberg Village(u)	(805)	5,971	5,839
*92393	Victorville	(619)	40,674	14,220
90043	View Park-Windsor Hills(u)	(310)	11,769	12,101
92667	Villa Park	(714)	6,299	7,137
.....	Vincent(u)		13,713	....
93277	Visalia	(209)	75,659	49,729
*92083	Vista	(619)	71,865	35,834
*91788	Walnut	(714)	29,105	12,478
*94596	Walnut Creek	(510)	60,569	54,033
90255	Walnut Park(u)	(310)	14,722	11,811
93280	Wasco	(805)	12,412	9,613
95076	Watsonville	(408)	31,099	23,662
90044	West Athens(u)	(310)	8,859	8,531
90502	West Carson(u)	(213)	20,143	17,997
90247	West Compton(u)	(310)	5,451	5,907
*91790	West Covina	(818)	96,226	80,292
90069	West Hollywood†	(310)	36,118	35,754
91359	Westlake Village†		7,455	6,130
92684	Westminster	(714)	78,293	71,133
90047	Westmont(u)	(213)	31,044	27,916
94565	West Pittsburg(u)	(510)	17,453	10,244
91746	West Puente Valley(u)	(818)	20,254	20,445
95691	West Sacramento†	(916)	28,898	24,482
*90606	West Whittier-Los Nietos(u)	(310)	24,164	21,001
*90605	Whittier	(310)	77,671	68,558
92595	Wildomar(u)		10,411	....
95490	Willits	(707)	5,027	4,008
90222	Willowbrook(u)	(213)	32,772	30,962
95988	Willows	(916)	5,988	4,777
95492	Windsor(u)		13,371	....
95388	Winton(u)		7,559	4,995
92502	Woodcrest(u)		7,796	....
93286	Woodlake	(209)	5,678	4,343
*95695	Woodland	(916)	40,230	30,235
94062	Woodside	(415)	5,034	5,291
*92686	Yorba Linda	(714)	52,422	28,254
96097	Yreka City	(916)	6,948	5,916
*95991	Yuba City	(916)	27,385	18,736
92399	Yucaipa†	(714)	32,824	27,654
*92284	Yucca Valley(u)	(619)	13,701	8,294

Colorado

ZIP code	Place		1990	1980
*80840	Air Force Academy	(719)	9,062	8,655
81101	Alamosa	(719)	7,579	6,830
80401	Applewood(u)	(303)	11,069	12,040
*80004	Arvada	(303)	89,218	84,576
*81611	Aspen	(303)	5,049	3,678
*80017	Aurora	(303)	222,103	158,588
.....	Black Forest(u)	(719)	8,143	3,372
*80302	Boulder	(303)	83,295	76,685
80601	Brighton	(303)	14,203	12,773
*80020	Broomfield	(303)	24,638	20,730
*81212	Canon City	(719)	12,687	13,037
80104	Castle Rock	(303)	8,710	3,921
.....	Castlewood(u)	(303)	24,392	16,413
80110	Cherry Hills Village	(303)	5,245	5,127
81220	Cimarron Hills(u)	(719)	11,160	6,597
81520	Clifton(u)	(303)	12,671	5,223
*80903	Colorado Springs	(719)	280,430	215,105
80120	Columbine(u)	(303)	23,969	23,523
*80022	Commerce City	(303)	16,466	16,234
81321	Cortez	(303)	7,284	7,095
*81625	Craig	(303)	8,091	8,133
*80202	Denver	(303)	467,610	492,686
80022	Derby(u)	(303)	6,043	8,578
*81301	Durango	(303)	12,439	11,649
*80110	Englewood	(303)	29,396	30,021
80620	Evans	(303)	5,876	5,063
80439	Evergreen(u)	(303)	7,582	6,376
80221	Federal Heights	(303)	9,342	7,838
80913	Fort Carson(u)	(719)	11,309	13,219
*80525	Fort Collins	(303)	87,491	65,092
80621	Fort Lupton	(303)	5,159	4,251
80701	Fort Morgan	(303)	9,068	8,768
80817	Fountain	(719)	10,175	8,324
81504	Fruitvale(u)		5,222	....
81522	Gateway(u)	(303)	7,510	....
81601	Glenwood Springs	(303)	6,561	4,637
*80401	Golden	(303)	13,127	12,237
*81501	Grand Junction	(303)	29,255	27,956
*80631	Greeley	(303)	60,454	53,006
*80111	Greenwood Village	(303)	7,589	5,729
80501	Gunbarrel(u)	(303)	9,388	5,172
80126	Highlands Ranch(u)		10,181	....
.....	Ken Caryl(u)	(303)	24,391	10,661
80026	Lafayette	(303)	14,708	8,985
81050	La Junta	(719)	7,678	8,338
80215	Lakewood	(303)	126,475	113,808
81052	Lamar	(719)	8,343	7,713
*80120	Littleton	(303)	33,711	28,631
*80501	Longmont	(303)	51,529	42,942
80027	Louisville	(303)	12,363	5,593
*80538	Loveland	(303)	37,357	30,215
*81401	Montrose	(303)	8,854	8,722
80233	Northglenn	(303)	27,195	29,847
80649	Orchard Mesa(u)		5,977	4,876
80134	Parker†	(303)	5,450	290
*81003	Pueblo	(719)	98,640	101,686
.....	Redlands(u)		9,355	....
80911	Security-Widefield(u)	(719)	23,822	18,768
80221	Sherrelwood(u)	(303)	16,636	17,629
80122	Southglenn(u)	(303)	43,087	37,787
*80477	Steamboat Springs	(303)	6,695	5,098
80751	Sterling	(303)	10,362	11,385
80906	Stratmoor(u)	(719)	5,854	5,519
80229	Thornton	(303)	55,031	42,054
81082	Trinidad	(719)	8,580	9,663
80229	Welby(u)	(303)	10,218	9,668
80030	Westminster	(303)	74,619	50,211
80221	Westminster East(u)	(303)	5,197	6,002
*80033	Wheat Ridge	(303)	29,419	30,293
80550	Windsor	(303)	5,062	4,277

Connecticut (203)

See note on page 387

ZIP code	Place	1990	1980
06401	Ansonia	18,403	19,039
06001	*Avon*	13,937	11,201
06403	*Beacon Falls*	5,083	3,995
06037	*Berlin*	16,787	15,121
06801	*Bethel*	17,541	16,004
06002	*Bloomfield*	19,483	18,608
06405	*Branford*	27,603	23,363
*06602	Bridgeport	141,686	142,546
*06010	Bristol	60,640	57,370
06804	*Brookfield*	14,113	12,872
06234	*Brooklyn*	6,681	5,691
06013	*Burlington*	7,026	5,660
06019	*Canton*	8,268	7,635
06040	Central Manchester(u)	30,934	31,058
06410	*Cheshire*	25,684	21,788
06413	*Clinton*	12,767	11,195
06415	*Colchester*	10,980	7,761
06340	Conning Towers-Nautilus Park(u)	10,013	9,665
06238	*Coventry*	10,063	8,895
06416	*Cromwell*	12,286	10,265
*06810	Danbury	65,585	60,470
06820	Darien	18,130	18,892
06418	Derby	12,199	12,346
06422	*Durham*	5,732	5,143
06423	*East Haddam*	6,676	5,621
06424	*East Hampton*	10,428	8,572
*06101	East Hartford(u)	50,452	52,563
06512	East Haven(u)	26,144	25,036
06333	*East Lyme*	15,340	13,870
06016	*East Windsor*	10,081	8,925
06425	*Easton*	6,303	5,962
06029	*Ellington*	11,197	9,711
*06082	*Enfield*	45,532	42,695
06426	*Essex*	5,904	5,078
06430	*Fairfield*	53,418	54,849
*06032	*Farmington*	20,608	16,407
06033	Glastonbury Center(u)	7,082	7,049
06035	*Granby*	9,369	7,956
*06830	*Greenwich*	58,441	59,565
06351	*Griswold*	10,384	8,967
06340	*Groton*	45,144	41,062
06340	Groton Borough	9,837	10,086
06437	*Guilford*	19,848	17,375
06438	*Haddam*	6,769	6,383
*06514	*Hamden*	52,434	51,071
*06101	Hartford	139,739	136,392
06791	*Harwinton*	5,228	4,889
06082	Hazardville(u)	5,179	5,436
06248	Hebron	7,079	5,453
06037	Kensington(u)	8,306	7,502
06239	*Killingly*	15,889	14,519
06249	Lebanon	6,041	4,762
06339	*Ledyard*	14,913	13,735
06759	*Litchfield*	8,365	7,605
06443	*Madison*	15,485	14,031
06040	*Manchester*	51,618	49,761
06250	*Mansfield*	21,103	20,634
06447	*Marlborough*	5,535	4,746
*06450	Meriden	59,479	57,118
06762	*Middlebury*	6,145	5,995
06457	Middletown	42,762	39,040
06460	Milford	49,938	48,168
06468	*Monroe*	16,896	14,010
06353	*Montville*	16,673	16,455
06770	Naugatuck	30,625	26,456
*06050	New Britain	75,491	73,840
06840	*New Canaan*	17,864	17,931
06810	*New Fairfield*	12,911	11,260

ZIP code	Place	1990	1980
06057	*New Hartford*	5,769	4,884
*06510	New Haven	130,474	126,089
*06111	Newington(u)	29,208	28,841
06320	New London	28,540	28,842
06776	*New Milford*	23,629	19,420
06470	*Newtown*	20,779	19,107
06471	*North Branford*	12,996	11,554
06473	North Haven(u)	22,249	22,080
*06856	Norwalk	78,331	77,767
06360	Norwich	37,391	38,074
06779	Oakville(u)	8,741	8,737
06371	*Old Lyme*	6,535	6,159
06475	*Old Saybrook*	9,552	9,287
06477	*Orange*	12,830	13,237
06483	*Oxford*	8,685	6,634
02891	Pawcatuck(u)	5,289	5,216
06374	*Plainfield*	14,363	12,774
06062	*Plainville*	17,392	16,401
06782	*Plymouth*	11,822	10,732
06480	*Portland*	8,418	8,383
06360	*Preston*	5,006	4,644
06712	*Prospect*	7,775	6,807
06260	Putnam	6,835	6,855
.....	*Putnam*†	9,031	8,580
06875	*Redding*	7,927	7,272
06877	Ridgefield Center(u)	6,363	6,066
06877	*Ridgefield*	20,919	20,120
06067	*Rocky Hill*	16,554	14,559
06483	*Seymour*	14,288	13,434
06484	Shelton	35,418	31,314
06082	Sherwood Manor(u)	6,357	6,303
06070	*Simsbury*	22,023	21,161
06071	*Somers*	9,108	8,473
06488	*Southbury*	15,818	14,156
06489	*Southington*	38,518	36,879
06074	*South Windsor*	22,090	17,198
06082	Southwood Acres(u)	8,963	9,779
06075	*Stafford*	11,091	9,268
*06904	Stamford	108,056	102,466
06378	*Stonington*	16,919	16,220
06268	Storrs(u)	12,198	11,394
06497	Stratford(u)	49,389	50,541
06078	*Suffield*	11,427	9,294
06786	Terryville(u)	5,426	5,234
06787	*Thomaston*	6,947	6,272
06277	*Thompson*	8,668	8,141
06082	Thompsonville(u)	8,458	8,151
06084	*Tolland*	11,001	9,694
06790	Torrington	33,687	30,987
06611	Trumbull(u)	32,000	32,989
06066	*Vernon*	29,841	27,974
06492	*Wallingford*	40,822	37,274
*06701	Waterbury	108,961	103,266
06385	*Waterford*	17,930	17,843
06795	*Watertown*	20,456	19,489
06107	West Hartford(u)	60,110	61,301
06516	West Haven	54,021	53,184
06498	*Westbrook*	5,414	5,216
06883	*Weston*	8,648	8,284
*06880	Westport(u)	24,407	25,290
06109	Wethersfield(u)	25,651	26,013
06226	Willimantic(u)†	14,746	14,652
06279	*Willington*	5,979	4,694
06897	*Wilton*	15,989	15,351
06094	*Winchester*	11,524	10,841
06280	*Windham*	22,039	21,062
06095	*Windsor*	27,817	25,204
06096	Windsor Locks(u)	12,358	12,190
06098	Winsted	8,254	8,092
06716	*Wolcott*	13,700	13,008
06525	*Woodbridge*	7,924	7,761
06798	*Woodbury*	8,131	6,942
06281	*Woodstock*	6,008	5,117

Delaware (302)

ZIP code	Place	1990	1980
19713	Brookside(u)	15,307	15,255
19703	Claymont(u)	9,800	10,022
*19901	Dover	27,630	23,507
19809	Edgemoor(u)	5,853	7,397
19805	Elsmere	5,935	6,493
19963	Milford	6,032	5,366
*19711	Newark	26,463	25,247
19800	Pike Creek(u)	10,163	....
19973	Seaford	5,689	5,256
19977	Smyrna	5,231	4,750
19804	Stanton(u)	5,028	5,495
19803	Talleyville(u)	6,346	6,880
*19899	Wilmington	71,529	70,195
19720	Wilmington Manor	8,568	9,233

District of Columbia (202)

ZIP code	Place	1990	1980
*20090	Washington	606,900	638,432

Florida

ZIP code	Place	Area code	1990	1980
*32714	Altamonte Springs	(407)	35,167	21,105
.....	Andover(u)		6,251	....
33572	Apollo Beach(u)		6,025	4,014
*32712	Apopka	(407)	13,611	6,019
33821	Arcadia	(813)	6,488	6,002
32233	Atlantic Beach	(904)	11,636	7,847
33823	Auburndale	(813)	8,846	6,501
33280	Aventura(u)	(305)	14,914	9,698
33825	Avon Park	(813)	8,078	8,026
32857	Azalea Park(u)	(407)	8,926	8,301
33830	Bartow	(813)	14,716	14,780
.....	Bay Hill(u)		5,346	....
34667	Bayonet Point(u)	(813)	21,860	16,455
33505	Bayshore Gardens(u)	(813)	17,062	14,945
33589	Beacon Square(u)	(813)	6,265	6,513
.....	Bee Ridge		6,406	3,313
32073	Bellair-Meadowbrook Terrace(u)	(813)	15,606	12,144
33430	Belle Glade	(407)	16,177	16,535
.....	Belle Isle		5,272	2,848
32526	Belleview(u)	(904)	19,386	15,439
34464	Beverly Hills(u)	(904)	6,163	5,024
.....	Bloomingdale(u)		13,912	....
.....	Boca Del Mar(u)		17,754	....
*33431	Boca Raton	(407)	61,486	49,447
*33923	Bonita Springs(u)	(813)	13,600	5,435
*33436	Boynton Beach	(407)	46,284	35,624
*34206	Bradenton	(813)	43,769	30,228
*33509	Brandon(u)	(813)	57,985	41,826
32503	Brent(u)	(904)	21,624	21,872
33317	Broadview Park(u)	(305)	6,109	6,022
33313	Broadview-Pompano Park(u)	(305)	5,230	5,223
*34601	Brooksville	(904)	7,589	5,582
33311	Browardale(u)	(305)	6,257	7,409
33142	Brownsville(u)	(813)	15,607	18,058
34743	Buena Ventura Lakes(u)		14,148	....
32404	Callaway	(904)	12,253	7,154
32920	Cape Canaveral	(407)	8,014	5,733
*33990	Cape Coral	(813)	74,991	32,103
33055	Carol City(u)	(305)	53,331	47,349
33688	Carrollwood(u)	(813)	7,195	....
.....	Carrollwood Village(u)		15,051	....
*32707	Casselberry	(407)	18,849	15,037
33401	Century Village(u)	(305)	8,363	10,619
*34618	Clearwater	(813)	98,746	85,170
*32711	Clermont	(904)	6,910	5,461
33440	Clewiston	(813)	6,085	5,219
32923	Cocoa	(407)	17,710	16,096
*32931	Cocoa Beach	(407)	12,123	10,926
32922	Cocoa West(u)	(407)	6,160	6,432
33063	Coconut Creek	(305)	27,269	6,288
33064	Collier Manor-Cresthaven(u)	(305)	7,322	7,045
33801	Combee Settlement(u)	(813)	5,463	5,400
32809	Conway(u)	(407)	13,159	24,027
33328	Cooper City	(305)	21,335	10,140
33114	Coral Gables	(305)	40,091	43,241
33077	Coral Springs	(305)	78,864	37,349
.....	Coral Terrace(u)	(305)	23,255	22,702
32536	Crestview	(904)	9,886	7,617
33803	Crystal Lake(u)	(813)	5,300	6,827
33157	Cutler(u)	(305)	16,201	15,608
33157	Cutler Ridge(u)	(305)	21,268	20,886
33884	Cypress Gardens(u)	(813)	9,188	8,043
.....	Cypress Lake(u)	(813)	10,491	8,721
*33525	Dade City	(904)	5,633	4,923
33004	Dania	(305)	13,183	11,796
33314	Davie	(305)	47,143	20,500
*32114	Daytona Beach	(904)	61,991	54,176
32713	De Bary	(407)	7,176	4,980
*33441	Deerfield Beach	(305)	46,997	39,193
32433	DeFuniak Springs	(904)	5,200	5,563
*32720	De Land	(904)	16,622	15,354
*33444	Delray Beach	(407)	47,184	34,329
33617	Del Rio(u)	(813)	8,248	7,409
*32725	Deltona(u)	(407)	50,828	15,710
*32541	Destin†	(904)	8,090	3,913
.....	Doctor Phillips(u)		7,963	....
*34698	Dunedin	(813)	34,427	30,203
33610	East Lake-Orient Park(u)	(813)	6,171	5,612
33940	East Naples(u)	(813)	22,951	12,127
*32132	Edgewater	(904)	15,351	6,726
32542	Eglin AFB(u)	(904)	8,347	7,574
33614	Egypt Lake(u)	(813)	14,580	11,932
34680	Elfers(u)	(813)	12,356	11,396
*34223	Englewood(u)	(813)	15,025	10,229
32534	Ensley(u)	(904)	16,362	14,422
*32726	Eustis	(904)	12,856	9,453
32804	Fairview Shores(u)	(305)	13,192	10,174
*32034	Fernandina Beach	(904)	8,765	7,224
32730	Fern Park(u)	(407)	8,294	8,904
32514	Ferry Pass(u)	(904)	26,301	16,910
33034	Florida City	(305)	5,978	6,174
.....	Florida Ridge(u)		12,218	4,988
32714	Forest City(u)	(407)	10,638	6,819
.....	Forest Island Park(u)		5,988	....
*33310	Fort Lauderdale	(305)	149,238	153,279
*33902	Fort Myers	(813)	44,947	36,638
*33931	Fort Myers Beach(u)	(813)	9,284	5,753
.....	Fort Myers Shores(u)		5,460	4,426
*34981	Fort Pierce	(407)	36,830	33,802
33452	Fort Pierce North(u)	(407)	5,833	5,929

ZIP code	Place	Area code	1990	1980
.....	Fort Pierce South(u)	(407)	5,320	3,324
*32548	Fort Walton Beach	(904)	21,407	20,829
.....	Fruit Cove(u)		5,904	3,906
.....	Fruitville(u)	(813)	9,808	2,551
*32602	Gainesville	(904)	85,075	81,371
33801	Gibsonia(u)	(813)	5,168	5,011
33534	Gibsonton(u)	(813)	7,706	....
32960	Gifford(u)	(407)	6,278	6,240
.....	Gladeview(u)	(305)	15,637	18,919
33143	Glenvar Heights(u)	(305)	14,823	13,216
33999	Golden Gate(u)		14,148	4,327
33055	Golden Glades(u)	(305)	25,474	23,154
32733	Goldenrod(u)	(407)	12,362	13,677
32560	Gonzalez(u)	(904)	7,669	6,084
33170	Goulds(u)	(305)	7,284	7,078
.....	Greater Northdale(u)		16,318	....
33463	Greenacres City	(407)	18,683	8,870
*32561	Gulf Breeze	(904)	5,530	5,478
33581	Gulf Gate Estates(u)	(813)	11,622	9,248
33707	Gulfport	(813)	11,709	11,180
33844	Haines City	(813)	11,683	10,799
*33009	Hallandale	(305)	30,997	36,517
.....	Hammocks(u)		10,897	....
.....	Hamptons at Boca Raton(u)		11,686	....
*33010	Hialeah	(305)	188,008	145,254
33016	Hialeah Gardens		7,727	2,700
.....	Highpoint		13,818	....
*33455	Hobe Sound(u)	(407)	11,507	6,822
*34690	Holiday(u)	(813)	19,360	18,392
32117	Holly Hill	(904)	11,141	9,953
*33022	Hollywood	(305)	121,720	121,323
*33030	Homestead	(305)	26,694	20,668
33039	Homestead AFB(u)	(305)	5,153	7,594
34447	Homosassa Springs(u)†	(904)	6,271	1,426
*34667	Hudson(u)	(813)	7,344	5,799
33934	Immokalee(u)	(813)	14,120	11,038
32937	Indian Harbour Beach	(407)	6,933	5,967
*34450	Inverness	(904)	5,797	4,095
33880	Inwood(u)	(813)	6,824	6,668
.....	Iona(u)		9,565	....
33162	Ives Estates(u)	(305)	13,531	10,613
32250	Jacksonville Beach	(904)	17,839	15,462
*32203	Jacksonville	(904)	635,230	540,920
.....	Jan Phyl Village(u)		5,308	2,785
33568	Jasmine Estates(u)	(813)	17,136	11,995
*34957	Jensen Beach(u)	(407)	9,884	6,642
*33458	Jupiter	(407)	24,907	9,868
33183	Kendale Lakes(u)	(305)	48,524	32,769
33256	Kendall(u)	(305)	87,271	73,758
.....	Kendall Lakes West(u)	(305)	6,038	....
33149	Key Biscayne(u)	(305)	8,854	6,313
33037	Key Largo(u)	(305)	11,336	7,447
*33040	Key West	(305)	24,832	24,382
.....	Kings Point(u)	(305)	12,422	8,724
*34744	Kissimmee	(407)	30,337	15,487
*32159	Lady Lake		8,071	1,193
*32055	Lake City	(904)	9,626	9,257
*33804	Lakeland	(813)	70,576	47,406
33801	Lakeland Highlands(u)	(813)	9,972	10,426
.....	Lake Lorraine(u)	(904)	6,779	5,427
33054	Lake Lucerne(u)	(305)	9,478	9,762
33612	Lake Magdalene(u)	(813)	15,973	13,256
*32746	Lake Mary	(407)	5,929	2,853
33403	Lake Park	(407)	6,704	6,909
.....	Lakes by the Bay(u)		5,615	....
....	Lakeside(u)	(904)	29,137	10,534
*33853	Lake Wales	(813)	9,670	8,466
.....	Lakewood Park(u)		7,211	3,411
*33461	Lake Worth	(407)	28,564	27,048
34639	Land O'Lakes(u)	(813)	7,892	4,515
33462	Lantana	(407)	8,392	8,048
*34640	Largo	(813)	65,910	57,958
33313	Lauderdale Lakes	(305)	27,341	25,426
33313	Lauderhill	(305)	49,015	37,271
34272	Laurel(u)	(813)	8,245	6,368
33714	Lealman(u)	(813)	21,748	19,873
*34748	Leesburg	(904)	14,783	13,191
*33936	Lehigh Acres(u)	(813)	13,611	9,604
33033	Leisure City(u)	(305)	19,379	17,905
33074	Lighthouse Point	(305)	10,378	11,488
.....	Lindgren Acres(u)	(305)	22,290	11,986
32060	Live Oak	(904)	6,332	6,732
32860	Lockhart(u)	(407)	11,636	10,569
34228	Longboat Key	(813)	5,937	4,843
*32750	Longwood	(407)	13,316	10,029
33549	Lutz(u)	(813)	10,552	5,555
32444	Lynn Haven	(904)	9,270	6,239
.....	McGregor(u)		6,504	....
*32751	Maitland	(407)	8,932	8,763
33550	Mango(u) †	(813)	8,700	6,493
33050	Marathon(u)	(305)	8,857	7,568
33937	Marco(u)		9,493	4,694
33063	Margate	(305)	42,985	35,900
*32446	Marianna	(904)	6,292	7,006
*32901	Melbourne	(407)	60,034	46,536
32666	Melrose Park(u)	(904)	6,477	5,672
33561	Memphis(u)	(813)	6,760	5,501
*32953	Merritt Island(u)	(407)	32,886	30,708
*33101	Miami	(305)	358,648	346,681
33109	Miami Beach	(305)	92,639	96,298
33023	Miami Gardens —Utopia-Carver(u)	(305)	7,448	8,482
33014	Miami Lakes(u)	(305)	12,750	9,809
33153	Miami Shores	(305)	10,084	9,244
33166	Miami Springs	(305)	13,268	12,350
.....	Micco(u)		8,757	3,585
32068	Middleburg(u)		6,223	....
32570	Milton	(904)	7,216	7,206
32754	Mims(u)	(407)	9,412	7,583
33023	Miramar	(305)	40,663	32,813
32757	Mount Dora	(904)	7,316	5,883
32526	Myrtle Grove(u)	(904)	17,402	14,238
*33940	Naples	(813)	19,505	17,581
33940	Naples Park(u)	(813)	8,002	5,438
33092	Naranja(u) †	(305)	5,790	10,381
32266	Neptune Beach	(904)	6,816	5,248
*34653	New Port Richey	(813)	14,044	11,196
33552	New Port Richey East(u)	(813)	9,683	6,147
32168	New Smyrna Beach	(904)	16,549	13,557
*32578	Niceville	(904)	10,509	8,543
33269	Norland(u)	(305)	22,109	19,471
33308	North Andrews Gardens(u)	(305)	9,002	8,994
33141	North Bay Village		5,383	4,920
33918	North Fort Myers(u)	(813)	30,027	22,808
33068	North Lauderdale	(305)	26,473	18,653
33961	North Miami	(305)	50,001	42,566
33160	North Miami Beach	(305)	35,361	36,553
33940	North Naples(u)	(813)	13,422	7,950
33408	North Palm Beach	(407)	11,284	11,344
34287	North Port	(813)	11,973	6,205
.....	North Sarasota(u)		6,702	4,997
33334	Oakland Park	(305)	26,326	22,944
33860	Oak Ridge(u)	(813)	15,388	15,477
*34478	Ocala	(904)	42,045	37,170
32548	Ocean City(u)	(904)	5,422	5,582
32761	Ocoee	(407)	12,778	7,803
33163	Ojus(u)	(305)	15,519	17,344
34677	Oldsmar	(813)	8,361	2,608
33265	Olympia Heights(u)	(305)	37,792	33,112
*33054	Opa-Locka	(305)	15,283	14,460
33054	Opa-Locka North(u)	(305)	6,568	5,721
*32763	Orange City		5,347	2,795
*32073	Orange Park	(904)	9,488	8,766
*32802	Orlando	(407)	164,674	128,291
32861	Orlo Vista(u)	(407)	5,990	6,474
*32174	Ormond Beach	(904)	29,721	21,436
32074	Ormond By-The-Sea(u)	(904)	8,157	7,665
*32765	Oviedo	(407)	11,114	3,074
32571	Pace(u)	(904)	6,277	5,006
.....	Page Park-Pine Manor(u)		5,116	....
33476	Pahokee	(407)	6,822	6,346
*32177	Palatka	(904)	10,447	10,175
*32906	Palm Bay	(407)	62,543	18,560
33480	Palm Beach	(407)	9,814	9,729
33403	Palm Beach Gardens	(407)	22,990	14,407
32135	Palm Coast(u)		14,287	2,837
*34221	Palmetto	(813)	9,268	8,637
33157	Palmetto Estates(u)	(305)	12,293	11,116
*34683	Palm Harbor(u)	(813)	50,256	5,215
33619	Palm River-Clair Mel(u)	(813)	13,691	14,447
33460	Palm Springs	(407)	9,763	8,166
33012	Palm Springs North(u)	(407)	5,300	5,838
.....	Palm Valley		9,960	....
*32401	Panama City	(904)	34,396	33,346
33029	Pembroke Pines	(305)	65,566	35,776
*32502	Pensacola	(904)	59,198	57,619
33257	Perrine(u)	(305)	15,576	16,129
32347	Perry	(904)	7,151	8,254
32859	Pine Castle(u)	(407)	8,276	9,992
32858	Pine Hills(u)	(407)	35,322	31,029
.....	Pine Island Ridge		5,244	....
*34665	Pinellas Park	(813)	43,571	32,811
33168	Pinewood(u)	(305)	15,518	14,346
33318	Plantation	(305)	66,814	48,653
*33566	Plant City	(813)	22,754	17,064
*33060	Pompano Beach	(305)	72,411	52,618
33064	Pompano Beach Highlands(u)	(305)	17,915	16,154
33952	Port Charlotte(u)	(813)	41,535	25,770
32124	Port Orange	(904)	35,399	18,756
32927	Port St. John(u)		8,933	1,837
34985	Port St. Lucie	(407)	55,761	14,690
34992	Port Salerno(u)		7,786	4,511
33032	Princeton(u)	(305)	7,073	....
*33950	Punta Gorda	(813)	10,637	6,797
*32351	Quincy	(904)	7,452	8,591
33156	Richmond Heights(u)	(305)	8,583	8,577
33312	Riverland(u)	(305)	5,376	5,919
33569	Riverview(u)	(813)	6,478	....
33419	Riviera Beach	(407)	27,646	26,489
*32955	Rockledge	(407)	16,023	11,877
.....	Royal Palm Beach	(407)	15,532	3,423
*33570	Ruskin(u)	(813)	6,046	5,117
34695	Safety Harbor	(813)	15,120	6,461
*32084	Saint Augustine	(904)	11,695	11,985
*34769	Saint Cloud	(407)	12,684	7,840
*33733	Saint Petersburg	(813)	240,318	238,647
33736	Saint Petersburg Beach	(813)	9,200	9,354
.....	San Carlos Park(u)		11,785	3,590

ZIP code	Place		1990	1980
33432	Sandalfoot Cove(u)	(305)	14,214	5,299
*32771	Sanford	(407)	32,387	23,176
33957	Sanibel		5,468	3,363
*34236	Sarasota	(813)	50,897	48,868
33577	Sarasota Springs(u)	(813)	16,088	13,860
32937	Satellite Beach	(407)	9,889	9,163
.....	Scott Lake(u)	(305)	14,588	14,154
*32958	Sebastian	(407)	10,248	2,831
*33871	Sebring	(813)	8,841	8,736
33584	Seffner(u)		5,371	....
*34642	Seminole	(813)	9,251	4,856
33578	Siesta Key(u)	(813)	7,772	7,010
34472	Silver Springs Shores(u)		6,421	3,983
32809	Sky Lake(u)	(407)	6,202	6,692
32703	South Apopka(u)	(407)	6,360	5,687
33505	South Bradenton(u)	(813)	20,398	14,297
32121	South Daytona	(904)	12,488	11,252
34277	Southgate(u)	(813)	7,324	7,322
.....	South Gate Ridge(u)		5,924	4,259
33243	South Miami	(305)	10,404	10,895
33157	South Miami Heights(u)	(305)	30,030	23,559
33707	South Pasadena	(813)	5,644	4,188
32937	South Patrick Shores(u)	(407)	10,249	9,816
.....	South Sarasota(u)		5,298	4,267
33595	South Venice(u)	(813)	11,951	8,075
32401	Springfield	(904)	8,719	7,220
*34606	Spring Hill(u)	(904)	31,117	6,468
32091	Starke	(904)	5,226	5,306
*34994	Stuart	(407)	11,936	9,467
33573	Sun City Center(u)	(813)	8,326	5,605
33160	Sunny Isles(u)	(305)	11,772	12,564
*33322	Sunrise	(305)	65,683	39,681
33283	Sunset(u)	(305)	15,810	13,531
33144	Sweetwater	(305)	13,909	8,067
*32301	Tallahassee	(904)	124,773	81,548
33320	Tamarac	(305)	44,822	29,376
33144	Tamiami(u)	(305)	33,845	17,607
*33602	Tampa	(813)	280,015	271,577
*34689	Tarpon Springs	(813)	17,874	13,251
32778	Tavares	(904)	7,383	4,398
33687	Temple Terrace	(813)	16,444	11,097
*32780	Titusville	(407)	39,394	31,910
32505	Town 'n' Country(u)	(813)	60,946	37,834
33706	Treasure Island	(813)	7,266	6,316
32867	Union Park(u)	(407)	6,890	19,175
33620	University West(u)†	(904)	23,760	24,514
.....	Upper Grand Lagoon(u)		7,855	3,314
32580	Valparaiso	(904)	6,316	6,142
*34285	Venice	(813)	17,052	12,153
33595	Venice Gardens(u)	(813)	7,701	6,568
*32960	Vero Beach	(407)	17,350	16,176
32960	Vero Beach South(u)	(407)	16,973	12,636
.....	Villages of Oriole(u)		5,698	....
33901	Villas(u)	(813)	9,898	8,724
32507	Warrington(u)	(904)	16,040	15,792
33314	Washington Park(u)	(305)	6,930	7,240
32703	Wekiva Springs(u)	(407)	23,026	13,386
.....	Wellington(u)		20,670	4,622
33155	Westchester(u)	(305)	29,883	29,272
.....	Westgate-Belvedere Homes(u)		6,880	....
33138	West Little River(u)	(305)	33,575	32,492
32904	West Melbourne	(407)	8,398	5,078
33144	West Miami	(305)	5,727	6,076
*33406	West Palm Beach	(407)	67,764	63,305
.....	West Park(u)		10,347	9,003
32505	West Pensacola(u)	(904)	22,107	24,371
33168	Westview(u)	(305)	9,668	9,102
33165	Westwood Lakes(u)	(305)	11,522	11,478
.....	Whiskey Creek(u)		5,061	....
33305	Wilton Manors	(305)	11,804	12,742
33803	Winston(u)	(813)	9,118	9,315
*34787	Winter Garden	(407)	9,863	6,789
*33880	Winter Haven	(813)	24,725	21,119
*32789	Winter Park	(407)	22,623	22,339
*32708	Winter Springs	(407)	22,151	10,475
32547	Wright(u)	(904)	18,945	13,011
32097	Yulee(u)		6,915	3,168
33540	Zephyrhills	(813)	8,220	5,742

Georgia

ZIP code	Place		1990	1980
31620	Adel	(912)	5,093	5,592
*31706	Albany	(912)	78,804	74,425
*30201	Alpharetta		13,002	3,128
31709	Americus	(912)	16,516	16,120
*30603	Athens	(706)	45,734	42,549
*30301	Atlanta	(404)	393,929	425,022
*30903	Augusta	(706)	44,707	47,532
31717	Bainbridge	(912)	10,803	10,553
30032	Belvedere Park(u)	(404)	18,089	17,766
31723	Blakely	(912)	5,595	5,880
*31520	Brunswick	(912)	16,433	17,605
30518	Buford	(404)	8,771	6,578
31728	Cairo	(912)	9,035	8,777
*30701	Calhoun	(706)	7,135	5,563
31730	Camilla	(912)	5,124	5,414
30032	Candler-McAfee(u)	(404)	29,491	27,306
*30117	Carrollton	(404)	16,029	14,078
30120	Cartersville	(404)	12,037	9,247
30125	Cedartown	(404)	7,976	8,619
30366	Chamblee	(404)	7,668	7,137
30021	Clarkston		5,385	4,539
30337	College Park	(404)	20,645	24,632
*31908	Columbus	(706)	178,681	169,441
30027	Conley(u)	(404)	5,528	6,033
*30208	Conyers	(404)	7,380	6,567
31015	Cordele	(912)	10,833	11,184
.....	Country Club Estates(u)		7,500	....
30209	Covington	(404)	9,860	10,586
*30720	Dalton	(706)	22,218	20,581
31742	Dawson	(912)	5,295	5,699
*30030	Decatur	(404)	17,304	18,404
31520	Dock Junction(u)	(912)	7,094	6,189
30362	Doraville	(404)	7,626	7,414
31533	Douglas	(912)	10,464	10,980
*30134	Douglasville	(404)	11,635	7,641
30333	Druid Hills(u)	(404)	12,174	12,700
*31021	Dublin	(912)	16,312	16,083
30136	Duluth		9,821	2,956
30356	Dunwoody(u)	(404)	26,302	17,768
31023	Eastman	(912)	5,241	5,330
30364	East Point	(404)	34,595	37,486
30635	Elberton	(706)	4,973	5,686
30809	Evans(u)	(404)	13,713	....
30060	Fair Oaks(u)	(404)	6,996	8,486
30535	Fairview(u)	(404)	6,444	6,558
30214	Fayetteville		5,827	2,715
31750	Fitzgerald	(912)	8,901	10,187
*30050	Forest Park	(404)	16,958	18,782
31905	Fort Benning South(u)	(404)	14,617	15,074
30905	Fort Gordon(u)	(404)	9,140	14,069
30742	Fort Oglethorpe	(404)	5,880	5,443
31314	Fort Stewart(u)	(912)	13,774	15,031
31030	Fort Valley	(912)	8,198	9,000
.....	Gaines School(u)		11,354	....
*30501	Gainesville	(404)	17,885	15,280
31408	Garden City	(912)	7,410	6,895
31754	Georgetown(u)	(912)	5,554	2,785
30316	Gresham Park(u)	(404)	9,000	6,232
*30223	Griffin	(404)	21,325	20,728
30354	Hapeville	(404)	5,483	6,166
31313	Hinesville	(912)	21,596	11,309
31545	Jesup	(912)	8,958	9,418
30144	Kennesaw	(404)	8,936	5,095
31548	Kingsland	(912)	5,474	2,008
30728	La Fayette	(706)	6,313	6,517
*30240	La Grange	(706)	25,574	24,204
.....	Lakeview(u)		5,237	5,403
*30245	Lawrenceville	(404)	17,250	8,928
*30247	Lilburn		9,295	3,765
30057	Lithia Springs(u)	(404)	11,403	9,145
30059	Mableton(u)	(404)	25,725	25,111
*31201	Macon	(912)	107,365	116,896
*30060	Marietta	(404)	44,129	30,821
30917	Martinez(u)	(404)	33,731	16,472
31061	Milledgeville	(912)	17,727	12,176
30655	Monroe	(404)	9,759	8,854
*30287	Morrow		5,168	3,791
*31768	Moultrie	(912)	14,865	15,105
30087	Mountain Park(u)	(404)	11,025	9,425
*30263	Newnan	(404)	12,497	11,449
*30071	Norcross	(404)	5,947	3,363
30319	North Atlanta(u)	(404)	27,812	30,521
30033	North Decatur(u)	(404)	13,936	11,830
30033	North Druid Hills(u)	(404)	14,170	12,438
30032	Panthersville(u)	(404)	9,874	11,366
30269	Peachtree City	(404)	19,027	6,429
31069	Perry	(912)	9,452	9,453
30073	Powder Springs		6,862	3,381
31643	Quitman	(912)	5,292	5,188
30074	Redan(u)		24,376	....
*30274	Riverdale	(404)	9,455	7,121
*30161	Rome	(706)	30,325	28,915
*30077	Roswell	(404)	47,986	23,337
31558	Saint Marys		8,204	3,596
31522	Saint Simons Island(u)	(912)	12,026	6,566
31082	Sandersville	(912)	6,290	6,137
30358	Sandy Springs(u)	(404)	67,842	46,877
*31402	Savannah	(912)	137,812	141,654
30079	Scottdale(u)	(404)	8,636	8,770
*30080	Smyrna	(404)	30,981	20,312
30278	Snellville	(404)	12,084	8,514
30901	South Augusta(u)	(404)	55,998	51,072
*30458	Statesboro	(912)	15,854	14,866
*30086	Stone Mountain		6,544	4,867
30747	Summerville	(706)	5,025	4,878
30401	Swainsboro	(912)	7,361	7,602
31791	Sylvester	(912)	6,023	5,860
30286	Thomaston	(706)	9,127	9,682
*31792	Thomasville	(912)	17,554	18,463
30824	Thomson	(706)	6,862	7,001
*31794	Tifton	(912)	14,215	13,749
30577	Toccoa	(706)	8,720	8,869
*30084	Tucker(u)	(404)	25,781	25,399
30291	Union City	(404)	8,887	4,780

ZIP code	Place		1990	1980
*31603	Valdosta	(912)	40,038	37,596
30474	Vidalia	(912)	11,118	10,393
30180	Villa Rica		6,542	3,420
.....	Vinings(u)		7,417	....
*31088	Warner Robins	(912)	43,861	39,893
*31501	Waycross	(912)	16,410	19,371
30830	Waynesboro	(706)	5,669	5,760
30901	West Augusta(u)	(404)	27,637	24,242
31410	Wilmington Island(u)	(912)	11,230	7,546
30680	Winder	(404)	7,373	6,705

Hawaii (808)

See note on page 387

ZIP code	Place		1990	1980
96706	Aiea(u)		8,906	32,879
.....	Aliamanu(u)		8,835	....
96706	Ewa Beach(u)		14,315	14,369
.....	Halawa(u)		13,408	....
.....	Heeia(u)		5,010	5,432
.....	Hickman Housing(u)		6,553	4,425
96720	Hilo(u)		37,808	35,269
*96815	Honolulu(u)		365,272	365,048
96732	Kahului(u)		16,889	12,978
96734	Kailua(u)		9,126	4,751
96863	Kailua(u)		36,818	35,812
96744	Kaneohe(u)		35,448	29,919
.....	Kaneohe Station(u)		11,662	11,615
96746	Kapaa(u)		8,149	4,467
96753	Kihei(u)		11,107	5,644
96761	Lahaina(u)		9,073	6,095
96762	Laie(u)		5,577	4,643
96766	Lihue(u)		5,536	4,000
.....	Maili(u)		6,059	5,026
.....	Makaha(u)		7,990	6,582
.....	Makakilo(u)		9,828	7,691
96768	Makawao(u)		5,405	2,900
96789	Mililani Town(u)		29,359	21,365
96792	Nanakuli(u)		9,575	8,185
96782	Pearl City(u)		30,993	42,575
96788	Pukalani(u)		5,879	3,950
.....	Schofield Barracks(u)		19,597	18,851
.....	Village Park(u)		7,407	....
96786	Wahiawa(u)		17,386	16,911
96792	Waianae(u)		8,758	7,941
96793	Wailuku(u)		10,688	10,260
.....	Waimalu(u)		29,967	....
96796	Waimea(u)		5,972	1,179
96797	Waipahu(u)		31,435	29,139
.....	Waipio(u)		11,812	....
.....	Waipio Acres(u)		5,304	4,091

Idaho (208)

ZIP code	Place		1990	1980
83401	Ammon		5,002	4,669
83221	Blackfoot		9,646	10,065
*83707	Boise City		125,551	102,249
83318	Burley		8,702	8,761
*83605	Caldwell		18,400	17,699
83202	Chubbuck		7,794	7,052
*83814	Coeur D'Alene		24,561	19,913
83714	Garden City		6,369	4,571
*83402	Idaho Falls		43,973	39,739
83338	Jerome		6,529	6,891
83501	Lewiston		28,082	27,986
*83642	Meridian		9,596	6,658
83843	Moscow		18,398	16,513
83647	Mountain Home		7,913	7,540
83648	Mountain Home AFB(u)		5,936	6,403
*83651	Nampa		28,365	25,112
83661	Payette		5,672	5,448
*83201	Pocatello		46,117	46,340
83854	Post Falls		7,349	5,736
83440	Rexburg		14,298	11,559
83350	Rupert		5,455	5,476
83864	Sandpoint		5,203	4,460
*83301	Twin Falls		27,634	26,209

Illinois

ZIP code	Place		1990	1980
60101	Addison	(708)	32,053	29,826
60102	Algonquin	(708)	11,693	5,834
60658	Alsip	(708)	18,227	17,134
62002	Alton	(618)	33,064	34,171
60002	Antioch	(708)	6,105	4,419
*60005	Arlington Heights	(708)	75,463	66,116
*60505	Aurora	(708)	99,556	81,293
*60010	Barrington	(708)	9,538	9,029
60103	Bartlett	(708)	19,395	13,254
61607	Bartonville	(309)	5,671	6,137
60510	Batavia	(708)	17,076	12,574
.....	Beach Park†	(708)	9,492	8,468
62618	Beardstown	(217)	5,270	6,338
*62220	Belleville	(618)	42,806	41,580
60104	Bellwood	(708)	20,241	19,811
61008	Belvidere	(815)	15,962	15,176
60106	Bensenville	(708)	17,767	16,106
62812	Benton	(618)	7,216	7,778
60163	Berkeley	(708)	5,137	5,467
60402	Berwyn	(708)	45,426	46,849
62010	Bethalto	(618)	9,507	8,630
60108	Bloomingdale	(708)	16,614	12,656
*61701	Bloomington	(309)	51,889	44,189
60406	Blue Island	(708)	21,203	21,855
60440	Bolingbrook	(708)	40,843	37,261
60538	Boulder Hill(u)	(708)	8,894	9,333
60914	Bourbonnais	(815)	13,929	13,280
60915	Bradley	(815)	10,918	11,015
60455	Bridgeview	(708)	14,402	14,155
60153	Broadview	(708)	8,538	8,618
60513	Brookfield	(708)	18,876	19,395
60089	Buffalo Grove	(708)	36,417	22,230
60459	Burbank	(708)	27,600	28,462
60521	Burr Ridge	(708)	7,684	3,838
62206	Cahokia	(618)	17,550	18,904
60409	Calumet City	(708)	37,840	39,697
60643	Calumet Park	(708)	8,418	8,788
61520	Canton	(309)	13,959	14,626
*62901	Carbondale	(618)	27,033	26,414
62626	Carlinville	(217)	5,416	5,439
62821	Carmi	(618)	5,626	6,107
*60188	Carol Stream	(708)	31,759	15,472
60110	Carpentersville	(708)	23,049	23,272
60013	Cary	(708)	10,043	6,640
62801	Centralia	(618)	14,274	15,126
62206	Centreville	(618)	7,489	9,747
*61821	Champaign	(217)	63,502	58,267
61920	Charleston	(217)	20,398	19,355
62629	Chatham	(217)	6,074	5,597
62233	Chester	(618)	8,204	8,401
*60607	Chicago	(312)	2,783,726	3,005,072
60411	Chicago Heights	(708)	32,966	37,026
60415	Chicago Ridge	(708)	13,643	13,473
61523	Chillicothe	(309)	5,959	6,176
60650	Cicero	(708)	67,436	61,232
60514	Clarendon Hills	(708)	6,994	6,870
61727	Clinton	(217)	7,437	8,014
62234	Collinsville	(618)	22,424	19,475
62236	Columbia	(618)	5,524	4,269
60478	Country Club Hills	(708)	15,431	14,676
60525	Countryside	(708)	5,961	6,242
60435	Crest Hill	(815)	10,999	9,252
60445	Crestwood	(708)	10,823	10,852
60417	Crete	(708)	6,773	5,417
61611	Creve Coeur	(309)	5,938	6,851
*60014	Crystal Lake	(815)	24,696	18,590
*61832	Danville	(217)	33,828	38,985
60561	Darien	(708)	18,148	14,956
*62525	Decatur	(217)	83,900	93,939
60015	Deerfield	(708)	17,327	17,432
60115	De Kalb	(815)	35,076	33,157
*60018	Des Plaines	(708)	53,414	53,568
61021	Dixon	(815)	15,134	15,710
60419	Dolton	(708)	23,956	24,766
60515	Downers Grove	(708)	46,845	42,259
62832	Du Quoin	(618)	6,697	6,594
62024	East Alton	(618)	7,063	7,096
61244	East Moline	(309)	20,147	20,907
61611	East Peoria	(309)	21,378	22,385
*62201	East St. Louis	(618)	40,944	55,200
62025	Edwardsville	(618)	14,582	12,480
62401	Effingham	(217)	11,927	11,270
*60120	Elgin	(708)	77,010	63,668
*60009	Elk Grove Village	(708)	33,429	28,679
60126	Elmhurst	(708)	42,029	44,276
60635	Elmwood Park	(708)	23,206	24,016
*60201	Evanston	(708)	73,233	73,706
60642	Evergreen Park	(708)	20,874	22,260
62837	Fairfield	(618)	5,442	5,944
62208	Fairview Heights	(618)	14,351	12,111
62839	Flora	(618)	5,093	5,379
60422	Flossmoor	(708)	8,651	8,423
60130	Forest Park	(708)	14,918	15,177
60020	Fox Lake	(708)	7,539	6,831
60423	Frankfort		7,180	4,357
.....	Frankfort Square(u)		6,227	....
60131	Franklin Park	(708)	18,485	17,507
61032	Freeport	(815)	25,840	26,266
60030	Gages Lake(u)	(708)	8,349	3,814
*61401	Galesburg	(309)	33,530	35,305
61254	Geneseo	(309)	5,990	6,373
60134	Geneva	(708)	12,625	9,881
62034	Glen Carbon	(618)	7,774	5,197
60022	Glencoe	(708)	8,499	9,200
60139	Glendale Heights	(708)	27,915	23,251
*60137	Glen Ellyn	(708)	24,919	23,691
60025	Glenview	(708)	37,052	32,060
60425	Glenwood	(708)	9,289	10,538
62035	Godfrey(u)	(618)	5,436	....
.....	Goodings Grove(u)		14,054	....
62040	Granite City	(618)	32,766	36,815
60030	Grayslake	(708)	7,388	5,260
62246	Greenville	(618)	5,108	5,271
60031	Gurnee	(708)	13,715	7,179
60103	Hanover Park	(708)	32,918	28,719
62946	Harrisburg	(618)	9,318	10,410
60033	Harvard	(815)	5,975	5,126

ZIP code	Place		1990	1980
60426	Harvey	(708)	29,771	35,810
60656	Harwood Heights	(312)	7,680	8,228
60429	Hazel Crest	(708)	13,334	13,973
62948	Herrin	(618)	10,857	10,708
60457	Hickory Hills	(708)	13,021	13,778
62249	Highland	(618)	7,546	7,122
60035	Highland Park	(708)	30,575	30,599
60040	Highwood	(708)	5,331	5,455
60162	Hillside	(708)	7,672	8,279
*60521	Hinsdale	(708)	16,029	16,726
60195	Hoffman Estates	(708)	46,363	37,272
60430	Homewood	(708)	19,278	19,724
60942	Hoopeston	(217)	5,871	6,411
60067	Inverness	(708)	6,516	4,046
60143	Itasca	(708)	6,947	7,129
*62650	Jacksonville	(217)	19,327	20,284
62052	Jerseyville	(618)	7,382	7,506
*60436	Joliet	(815)	77,217	77,956
60458	Justice	(708)	11,137	10,552
60901	Kankakee	(815)	27,541	29,633
61443	Kewanee	(309)	12,969	14,508
60525	La Grange	(708)	15,362	15,693
60525	La Grange Park	(708)	12,861	13,359
60044	Lake Bluff	(708)	5,486	4,434
60045	Lake Forest	(708)	17,836	15,245
60102	Lake in the Hills	(708)	5,900	5,651
60047	Lake Zurich	(708)	14,927	8,225
60438	Lansing	(708)	28,131	29,039
61301	La Salle	(815)	9,717	10,347
60439	Lemont	(708)	7,359	5,640
*60048	Libertyville	(708)	19,174	16,520
62656	Lincoln	(217)	15,418	16,327
60645	Lincolnwood	(708)	11,365	11,921
60046	Lindenhurst	(708)	8,044	6,220
60532	Lisle	(708)	19,584	13,638
62056	Litchfield	(217)	6,883	7,204
60441	Lockport	(815)	9,401	9,192
60148	Lombard	(708)	39,408	36,879
61130	Loves Park	(815)	15,457	13,192
60411	Lynwood	(708)	6,535	4,195
60534	Lyons	(708)	9,828	9,925
*60050	McHenry	(815)	16,343	10,737
61115	Machesney Park†	(815)	19,042	19,514
61455	Macomb	(309)	19,952	19,863
62959	Marion	(618)	14,545	14,031
60426	Markham	(708)	13,136	15,172
62258	Mascoutah	(618)	5,511	4,962
60443	Matteson	(708)	11,378	10,223
61938	Mattoon	(217)	18,441	19,293
60153	Maywood	(708)	27,139	27,998
*60160	Melrose Park	(708)	20,859	20,735
61342	Mendota	(815)	7,017	7,134
62960	Metropolis	(618)	6,734	7,171
60445	Midlothian	(708)	14,372	14,274
61264	Milan	(309)	5,753	6,371
60448	Mokena		6,128	4,578
*61265	Moline	(309)	43,080	46,407
61462	Monmouth	(309)	9,489	10,706
60450	Morris	(815)	10,274	8,833
61550	Morton	(309)	13,799	14,178
60053	Morton Grove	(708)	22,373	23,747
62863	Mount Carmel	(618)	8,287	8,908
60056	Mount Prospect	(708)	53,168	52,634
62864	Mount Vernon	(618)	17,082	17,193
60060	Mundelein	(708)	21,224	17,053
62966	Murphysboro	(618)	9,176	9,866
*60540	Naperville	(708)	85,806	42,601
60451	New Lenox	(815)	9,698	5,792
60714	Niles	(708)	28,375	30,363
61761	Normal	(309)	40,023	35,672
60634	Norridge	(708)	14,459	16,483
60542	North Aurora	(708)	6,010	5,205
*60062	Northbrook	(708)	32,572	30,778
60064	North Chicago	(708)	34,978	38,774
60164	Northlake	(708)	12,505	12,166
60546	North Riverside	(708)	6,180	6,764
60521	Oak Brook	(708)	9,087	6,676
60452	Oak Forest	(708)	26,202	25,040
*60455	Oak Lawn	(708)	56,182	60,590
*60303	Oak Park	(708)	53,648	54,887
62269	O'Fallon	(618)	16,064	12,173
62450	Olney	(618)	8,661	9,026
60477	Orland Hills		5,510	2,784
60462	Orland Park	(708)	35,720	23,045
61350	Ottawa	(815)	17,528	18,166
*60067	Palatine	(708)	38,894	32,171
60463	Palos Heights	(708)	11,478	11,096
60465	Palos Hills	(708)	17,803	16,654
62557	Pana	(217)	5,796	6,040
61944	Paris	(217)	9,016	9,885
60466	Park Forest	(708)	24,656	26,222
60068	Park Ridge	(708)	36,175	38,704
*61554	Pekin	(309)	32,254	33,967
*61601	Peoria	(309)	113,504	124,160
61614	Peoria Heights	(309)	6,930	7,453
61354	Peru	(815)	9,302	10,886
60545	Plano	(708)	5,104	4,875
61764	Pontiac	(815)	11,428	11,227
61356	Princeton	(815)	7,197	7,342
60070	Prospect Heights	(708)	15,236	11,823
*62301	Quincy	(217)	39,682	42,554
61866	Rantoul	(217)	17,212	20,161
60471	Richton Park	(708)	10,523	9,403
60627	Riverdale	(708)	13,671	13,233
60305	River Forest	(708)	11,669	12,392
60171	River Grove	(708)	9,961	10,368
60546	Riverside	(708)	8,774	9,236
60472	Robbins	(708)	7,498	8,853
62454	Robinson	(618)	6,740	7,285
61068	Rochelle	(815)	8,769	8,982
61071	Rock Falls	(815)	9,669	10,633
*61125	Rockford	(815)	139,704	139,712
*61201	Rock Island	(309)	40,630	46,821
60008	Rolling Meadows	(708)	22,598	20,167
60441	Romeoville	(815)	14,101	15,519
60172	Roselle	(708)	20,803	17,034
60073	Round Lake Beach	(708)	16,406	12,921
*60174	Saint Charles	(708)	22,620	17,492
62881	Salem	(618)	7,470	7,813
60548	Sandwich	(815)	5,607	5,356
60411	Sauk Village	(708)	9,926	10,906
*60194	Schaumburg	(708)	68,586	53,355
60176	Schiller Park	(708)	11,189	11,458
62225	Scott AFB(u)	(618)	7,245	8,648
60436	Shorewood	(815)	6,264	4,714
61282	Silvis	(309)	6,926	7,130
*60077	Skokie	(708)	59,432	60,278
60177	South Elgin	(708)	7,474	5,970
60473	South Holland	(708)	22,105	24,977
*62703	Springfield	(217)	105,417	100,054
61362	Spring Valley	(815)	5,246	5,822
60475	Steger	(708)	8,592	9,269
61081	Sterling	(815)	15,142	16,281
60402	Stickney	(708)	5,678	5,893
60107	Streamwood	(708)	31,197	23,456
61364	Streator	(815)	14,121	14,795
60501	Summit	(708)	9,971	10,110
62221	Swansea	(618)	8,201	5,529
60178	Sycamore	(815)	9,896	9,219
62568	Taylorville	(217)	11,133	11,386
60477	Tinley Park	(708)	37,115	26,178
62294	Troy	(618)	6,019	3,772
60466	University Park	(708)	6,204	6,245
61801	Urbana	(217)	36,383	35,978
62471	Vandalia	(618)	6,114	5,338
60061	Vernon Hills	(708)	15,319	9,827
60181	Villa Park	(708)	22,279	23,155
60555	Warrenville	(708)	11,389	7,519
61571	Washington	(309)	10,136	10,364
62204	Washington Park	(618)	7,431	8,223
62298	Waterloo	(618)	5,030	4,646
60970	Watseka	(815)	5,424	5,543
60084	Wauconda	(708)	6,294	5,688
*60085	Waukegan	(708)	69,481	67,653
60154	Westchester	(708)	17,301	17,730
*60185	West Chicago	(708)	14,808	12,550
60558	Western Springs	(708)	11,956	12,876
62896	West Frankfort	(618)	8,526	9,437
60559	Westmont	(708)	21,402	17,353
61604	West Peoria(u)	(309)	5,314	5,219
*60187	Wheaton	(708)	51,441	43,043
60090	Wheeling	(708)	29,911	23,266
60514	Willowbrook	(708)	8,701	4,953
60091	Wilmette	(708)	26,694	28,221
60190	Winfield	(708)	7,096	4,422
60093	Winnetka	(708)	12,210	12,772
60096	Winthrop Harbor	(708)	6,240	5,427
60097	Wonder Lake(u)	(815)	6,664	5,917
60191	Wood Dale	(708)	12,394	11,251
60517	Woodridge	(708)	26,359	21,763
62095	Wood River	(618)	11,490	12,446
60098	Woodstock	(815)	14,368	11,725
60482	Worth	(708)	11,208	11,592
60099	Zion	(708)	19,783	17,865

Indiana

ZIP code	Place		1990	1980
46001	Alexandria	(317)	5,709	6,028
*46011	Anderson	(317)	59,459	64,695
46703	Angola	(219)	5,851	5,486
46706	Auburn	(219)	9,386	8,122
47421	Bedford	(812)	13,817	14,410
46107	Beech Grove	(317)	13,383	13,196
*47408	Bloomington	(812)	60,633	52,663
46714	Bluffton	(219)	9,104	8,705
47601	Boonville	(812)	6,686	6,300
47834	Brazil	(812)	7,640	7,852
46112	Brownsburg	(317)	7,628	6,242
*46032	Carmel	(317)	25,380	18,272
46303	Cedar Lake	(219)	8,885	8,754
47111	Charlestown	(812)	5,889	5,596
46304	Chesterton	(219)	9,118	8,531
47129	Clarksville	(812)	19,838	15,164
47842	Clinton	(317)	5,040	5,267
46725	Columbia City	(219)	5,700	5,091

ZIP code	Place		1990	1980
*47201	Columbus	(812)	31,802	30,614
47331	Connersville	(317)	15,550	17,023
47933	Crawfordsville	(317)	13,584	13,325
46307	Crown Point	(219)	17,728	16,455
46733	Decatur	(219)	8,642	8,649
46514	Dunlap(u)	(219)	5,705	5,397
46311	Dyer	(219)	10,923	9,555
46312	East Chicago	(219)	33,892	39,786
*46513	Elkhart	(219)	43,627	41,305
46036	Elwood	(317)	9,494	10,867
*47708	Evansville	(812)	126,272	130,496
46038	Fishers		7,189	2,008
*46802	Fort Wayne	(219)	172,971	172,391
46041	Frankfort	(317)	14,754	15,168
46131	Franklin	(317)	12,932	11,563
46738	Garrett	(219)	5,349	4,751
*46401	Gary	(219)	116,646	151,968
46933	Gas City	(317)	6,296	6,370
*46526	Goshen	(219)	23,794	19,665
46530	Granger(u)		20,241	....
46135	Greencastle	(317)	8,984	8,403
46140	Greenfield	(317)	11,657	11,288
47240	Greensburg	(812)	9,286	9,254
*46142	Greenwood	(317)	26,507	19,327
46319	Griffith	(219)	17,914	17,026
*46320	Hammond	(219)	84,236	93,714
47348	Hartford City	(317)	6,960	7,622
46322	Highland	(219)	23,696	25,935
46342	Hobart	(219)	21,822	22,987
47542	Huntingburg	(812)	5,236	5,376
46750	Huntington	(219)	16,389	16,202
*46206	Indianapolis	(317)	731,327	700,807
47546	Jasper	(812)	10,030	9,097
*47130	Jeffersonville	(812)	21,968	21,220
46755	Kendallville	(219)	7,773	7,299
*46902	Kokomo	(317)	44,996	47,808
*47901	Lafayette	(317)	43,758	43,011
.....	Lakes of the Four Seasons(u)		6,556	....
46405	Lake Station	(219)	13,899	15,087
46350	La Porte	(219)	21,507	21,796
46226	Lawrence	(317)	26,779	25,591
46052	Lebanon	(317)	12,059	11,456
47441	Linton	(812)	5,814	6,315
46947	Logansport	(219)	16,865	17,731
*46356	Lowell	(219)	6,430	5,827
47250	Madison	(812)	12,006	12,472
*46952	Marion	(317)	32,607	35,874
46151	Martinsville	(317)	11,677	11,311
46410	Merrillville	(219)	27,257	27,677
46360	Michigan City	(219)	33,822	36,850
*46544	Mishawaka	(219)	42,635	40,201
47960	Monticello	(219)	5,237	5,162
46158	Mooresville	(317)	5,541	5,349
47620	Mount Vernon	(812)	7,217	7,656
*47302	Muncie	(317)	71,170	77,216
46321	Munster	(219)	19,949	20,671
46550	Nappanee		5,474	4,694
*47150	New Albany	(812)	36,322	37,103
47362	New Castle	(317)	17,753	20,056
46774	New Haven	(219)	9,338	6,714
46060	Noblesville	(317)	17,655	12,253
46962	North Manchester	(219)	6,383	5,998
47265	North Vernon	(812)	5,129	5,768
47130	Oak Park(u)	(812)	5,630	5,871
46970	Peru	(317)	12,843	13,764
46168	Plainfield	(317)	10,438	9,191
46563	Plymouth	(219)	8,291	7,693
46368	Portage	(219)	29,062	27,409
47371	Portland	(219)	6,483	7,074
47670	Princeton	(812)	8,127	8,976
47978	Rensselaer	(219)	5,045	4,944
*47374	Richmond	(317)	38,705	41,349
46975	Rochester	(219)	5,969	5,050
46173	Rushville	(317)	5,533	6,113
47167	Salem	(812)	5,619	5,290
46375	Schererville	(219)	20,155	13,209
47170	Scottsburg	(812)	5,334	5,068
47172	Sellersburg	(812)	5,914	3,211
47274	Seymour	(812)	15,579	15,050
46176	Shelbyville	(317)	15,347	14,989
*46624	South Bend	(219)	105,511	109,727
46383	South Haven(u)	(219)	6,112	6,679
46224	Speedway	(317)	13,092	12,641
47586	Tell City	(812)	8,088	8,704
*47808	Terre Haute	(812)	55,430	61,125
46383	Valparaiso	(219)	24,414	22,247
47591	Vincennes	(812)	19,867	20,857
46992	Wabash	(219)	12,127	12,985
*46580	Warsaw	(219)	10,968	10,647
47501	Washington	(812)	10,864	11,325
47906	West Lafayette	(317)	26,144	21,247
46391	Westville		5,255	2,887
46394	Whiting	(219)	5,155	5,630
47394	Winchester	(317)	5,095	5,659
46077	Zionsville		5,281	3,948

Iowa

ZIP code	Place		1990	1980
50511	Algona	(515)	6,015	6,289
50009	Altoona	(515)	7,242	5,764
*50010	Ames	(515)	47,198	45,775
52205	Anamosa	(319)	5,100	4,958
50021	Ankeny	(515)	18,482	15,429
50022	Atlantic	(712)	7,432	7,789
52722	Bettendorf	(319)	28,139	27,381
50036	Boone	(515)	12,392	12,602
52601	Burlington	(319)	27,208	29,529
51401	Carroll	(712)	9,579	9,705
50613	Cedar Falls	(319)	34,298	36,322
*52401	Cedar Rapids	(319)	108,772	110,243
52544	Centerville	(515)	5,936	6,558
50616	Charles City	(515)	7,878	8,778
51012	Cherokee	(712)	6,026	7,004
51632	Clarinda	(712)	5,104	5,458
50428	Clear Lake	(515)	8,183	7,458
*52732	Clinton	(319)	29,201	32,828
50053	Clive	(515)	7,462	6,064
52241	Coralville	(319)	10,347	7,687
*51501	Council Bluffs	(712)	54,315	56,449
50801	Creston	(515)	7,911	8,429
*52802	Davenport	(319)	95,333	103,264
52101	Decorah	(319)	8,063	7,991
51442	Denison	(712)	6,604	6,675
*50318	Des Moines	(515)	193,189	191,003
52001	Dubuque	(319)	57,538	62,374
51334	Estherville	(712)	6,720	7,518
52556	Fairfield	(515)	9,768	9,428
50501	Fort Dodge	(515)	25,894	29,423
52627	Fort Madison	(319)	11,614	13,520
50112	Grinnell	(515)	8,902	8,868
51537	Harlan	(712)	5,148	5,357
50644	Independence	(319)	5,972	6,392
50125	Indianola	(515)	11,340	10,843
52240	Iowa City	(319)	59,735	50,508
50126	Iowa Falls	(515)	5,435	6,174
52632	Keokuk	(319)	12,451	13,536
50138	Knoxville	(515)	8,232	8,143
51031	Le Mars	(712)	8,454	8,276
52057	Manchester	(319)	5,137	4,942
52060	Maquoketa	(319)	6,130	6,313
52302	Marion	(319)	20,442	19,474
50158	Marshalltown	(515)	25,178	26,938
50401	Mason City	(515)	29,040	30,144
52641	Mount Pleasant	(319)	7,959	7,322
52761	Muscatine	(319)	22,881	23,467
50201	Nevada	(515)	6,009	5,912
50208	Newton	(515)	14,799	15,292
50211	Norwalk		5,726	2,676
50662	Oelwein	(319)	6,493	7,564
52577	Oskaloosa	(515)	10,600	10,989
52501	Ottumwa	(515)	24,488	27,381
50219	Pella	(515)	9,270	8,349
50220	Perry	(515)	6,652	7,053
51566	Red Oak	(712)	6,264	6,810
51601	Shenandoah	(712)	5,572	6,274
51250	Sioux Center	(712)	5,074	4,588
*51101	Sioux City	(712)	80,505	82,003
51301	Spencer	(712)	11,066	11,726
50588	Storm Lake	(712)	8,769	8,814
50322	Urbandale	(515)	23,500	17,869
52349	Vinton	(319)	5,103	5,040
52353	Washington	(319)	7,074	6,584
*50701	Waterloo	(319)	66,467	75,985
50677	Waverly	(319)	8,539	8,444
50595	Webster City	(515)	7,894	8,572
*50265	West Des Moines	(515)	31,702	21,894
50311	Windsor Heights	(515)	5,190	5,474

Kansas

ZIP code	Place		1990	1980
67410	Abilene	(913)	6,242	6,572
67005	Arkansas City	(316)	12,762	13,201
66002	Atchison	(913)	10,656	11,407
67010	Augusta	(316)	7,848	6,968
66012	Bonner Springs	(913)	6,413	6,266
66720	Chanute	(316)	9,488	10,506
67337	Coffeyville	(316)	12,917	15,185
67701	Colby	(913)	5,510	5,544
66901	Concordia	(913)	6,152	6,847
67037	Derby	(316)	14,691	9,786
67801	Dodge City	(316)	21,129	18,001
67042	El Dorado	(316)	11,495	11,551
66801	Emporia	(316)	25,512	25,287
66442	Fort Riley North(u)	(913)	12,848	16,086
66701	Fort Scott	(316)	8,362	8,893
67846	Garden City	(316)	24,097	18,256
67530	Great Bend	(316)	15,427	16,608
67601	Hays	(913)	17,814	16,301
67060	Haysville	(316)	8,364	8,006
*67501	Hutchinson	(316)	39,308	40,284
67301	Independence	(316)	10,030	10,598
66749	Iola	(316)	6,351	6,938
66441	Junction City	(913)	20,642	19,305
*66102	Kansas City	(913)	149,800	161,148
66043	Lansing	(913)	7,120	5,307
*66044	Lawrence	(913)	65,603	52,738
66048	Leavenworth	(913)	38,495	33,656
66209	Leawood	(913)	19,693	13,360
66210	Lenexa	(913)	34,110	18,639

ZIP code	Place		1990	1980
*67901	Liberal	(316)	16,573	14,911
67460	Mc Pherson	(316)	12,422	11,753
66502	Manhattan	(913)	37,737	32,644
66202	Merriam	(913)	11,819	10,794
66202	Mission	(913)	9,504	8,643
67114	Newton	(316)	16,700	16,332
*66061	Olathe	(913)	63,402	37,258
66067	Ottawa	(913)	10,667	11,016
66202	Overland Park	(913)	111,790	81,784
67219	Park City†		5,054	4,056
67357	Parsons	(316)	11,919	12,898
66762	Pittsburg	(316)	17,789	18,770
66202	Prairie Village	(913)	23,186	24,657
67124	Pratt	(316)	6,687	6,885
66202	Roeland Park	(913)	7,706	7,962
*67401	Salina	(913)	42,299	41,843
66203	Shawnee	(913)	37,962	29,653
*66601	Topeka	(913)	119,883	118,690
67880	Ulysses	(316)	5,474	4,653
67152	Wellington	(316)	8,517	8,212
*67209	Wichita	(316)	304,017	279,838
67156	Winfield	(316)	11,931	10,736

Kentucky

ZIP code	Place		1990	1980
41001	Alexandria		5,592	4,735
*41101	Ashland	(606)	23,622	27,064
40004	Bardstown	(502)	6,712	6,155
41073	Bellevue	(606)	6,997	7,678
40403	Berea	(606)	9,129	8,226
*42102	Bowling Green	(502)	41,688	40,450
40261	Buechel(u)	(502)	7,081	6,855
41005	Burlington(u)		6,070	....
*42718	Campbellsville	(502)	9,592	8,715
42330	Central City		5,015	5,214
*40701	Corbin	(606)	7,644	8,075
*41011	Covington	(606)	43,646	49,585
41031	Cynthiana	(606)	6,497	5,881
*40422	Danville	(606)	12,559	12,942
41074	Dayton	(606)	6,576	6,979
.....	Douglass Hills	(502)	5,431	4,384
41017	Edgewood	(606)	8,143	7,243
*42701	Elizabethtown	(502)	18,167	15,380
41018	Elsmere	(606)	6,847	7,203
41018	Erlanger	(606)	15,979	14,466
40118	Fairdale(u)	(502)	6,563	7,315
40291	Fern Creek(u)	(502)	16,406	16,866
41139	Flatwoods	(606)	7,799	8,354
*41042	Florence	(606)	18,586	15,586
42223	Fort Campbell North(u)	(502)	18,861	17,211
40121	Fort Knox(u)	(502)	21,495	31,055
41017	Fort Mitchell	(606)	7,438	7,294
41075	Fort Thomas	(606)	16,032	16,012
41011	Fort Wright		6,404	4,481
*40601	Frankfort	(502)	26,535	25,973
*42134	Franklin	(502)	7,607	7,738
40324	Georgetown	(502)	11,414	10,972
*42141	Glasgow	(502)	12,351	12,958
40330	Harrodsburg	(606)	7,335	7,265
*41701	Hazard	(606)	5,416	5,371
42420	Henderson	(502)	25,945	24,834
40228	Highview(u)	(502)	14,814	13,286
40229	Hillview	(502)	6,119	5,196
*42240	Hopkinsville	(502)	29,809	27,318
41051	Independence	(606)	10,444	7,998
40269	Jeffersontown	(502)	23,223	15,795
40342	Lawrenceburg	(502)	5,911	5,167
40033	Lebanon	(502)	5,695	6,590
*40507	Lexington	(606)	225,366	204,165
*40741	London	(606)	5,757	4,002
*40232	Louisville	(502)	269,555	298,694
40252	Lyndon		8,037	1,553
42431	Madisonville	(502)	16,203	16,979
42066	Mayfield	(502)	9,935	10,705
41056	Maysville	(606)	7,169	7,983
40965	Middlesboro	(606)	11,328	12,251
40253	Middletown		5,016	414
42633	Monticello	(606)	5,357	5,677
40351	Morehead	(606)	8,357	7,789
40353	Mount Sterling	(606)	5,362	5,820
40047	Mount Washington	(502)	5,256	3,997
42071	Murray	(502)	14,442	14,248
40218	Newburg(u)	(502)	21,647	24,612
*41071	Newport	(606)	18,871	21,587
*40356	Nicholasville	(606)	13,603	10,400
40259	Okolona(u)	(502)	18,902	20,039
42303	Owensboro	(502)	53,577	54,450
*42003	Paducah	(502)	27,256	29,315
*40361	Paris	(606)	8,730	7,935
41501	Pikeville	(606)	6,324	4,756
40268	Pleasure Ridge Park(u)	(502)	25,131	27,332
42445	Princeton	(502)	6,940	7,073
*40160	Radcliff	(502)	19,778	14,656
*40475	Richmond	(606)	21,183	21,705
42276	Russellville	(502)	7,454	7,520
.....	Saint Dennis(u)		10,326	....
40206	Saint Matthews	(502)	15,691	13,519
*40066	Shelbyville	(502)	6,155	5,329
40256	Shively	(502)	15,535	16,645
*42501	Somerset	(606)	10,735	10,649
.....	Taylor Mill		5,530	4,509
40272	Valley Station(u)	(502)	22,840	24,474
40383	Versailles	(606)	7,269	6,427
.....	Villa Hills	(606)	7,370	4,384
41101	Westwoods(u)	(606)	5,300	5,973
40769	Williamsburg	(606)	5,493	5,560
*40391	Winchester	(606)	15,799	15,216

Louisiana

ZIP code	Place		1990	1980
*70510	Abbeville	(318)	11,184	12,391
*71301	Alexandria	(318)	49,049	51,648
70032	Arabi(u)	(504)	8,787	10,248
70094	Avondale(u)	(504)	5,813	6,699
*70714	Baker	(504)	13,087	12,865
*71220	Bastrop	(318)	13,916	15,527
*70821	Baton Rouge	(504)	219,531	220,394
70360	Bayou Cane(u)	(504)	15,876	15,723
70037	Belle Chasse(u)	(504)	8,512	5,412
*70427	Bogalusa	(504)	14,280	16,976
*71111	Bossier City	(318)	52,721	50,817
70517	Breaux Bridge	(318)	6,694	5,922
70094	Bridge City(u)		8,327	....
70811	Brownfields(u)		5,229	....
71291	Brownsville-Bawcomville(u)	(318)	7,397	7,252
71322	Bunkie	(318)	5,044	5,364
70520	Carencro		5,518	3,712
*70043	Chalmette(u) †	(504)	31,860	33,847
71291	Claiborne(u)	(318)	8,300	6,278
*70433	Covington	(504)	7,691	7,892
*70526	Crowley	(318)	13,983	16,036
70345	Cut Off(u)	(504)	5,325	5,049
*70726	Denham Springs	(504)	8,381	8,563
70634	De Ridder	(318)	9,868	10,337
70047	Destrehan	(504)	8,031	2,382
70346	Donaldsonville	(504)	7,949	7,901
70072	Estelle(u)	(504)	14,091	12,724
70535	Eunice	(318)	11,162	12,479
71459	Fort Polk South	(318)	10,911	12,498
70538	Franklin	(318)	9,004	9,584
70820	Gardere		7,209	....
*70737	Gonzales	(504)	7,208	7,287
71245	Grambling		5,512	4,226
*70053	Gretna	(504)	17,208	20,615
*70401	Hammond	(504)	15,871	15,226
70123	Harahan	(504)	9,927	11,384
*70058	Harvey(u)	(504)	21,222	22,709
*70360	Houma	(504)	30,495	32,602
70544	Jeanerette	(318)	6,205	6,511
70502	Jefferson(u)	(504)	14,521	15,550
70546	Jennings	(318)	11,305	12,401
*70062	Kenner	(504)	72,033	66,382
70445	Lacombe(u)	(504)	6,523	5,146
*70501	Lafayette	(318)	94,438	80,584
*70601	Lake Charles	(318)	70,580	75,226
71254	Lake Providence	(318)	5,380	6,361
*70068	La Place(u)	(504)	24,194	16,112
70373	Larose(u)	(504)	5,772	5,234
*71446	Leesville	(318)	7,638	9,054
*70448	Mandeville	(504)	7,474	6,076
71052	Mansfield	(318)	5,389	6,485
71351	Marksville	(318)	5,526	5,113
*70072	Marrero(u)	(504)	36,671	36,548
70075	Meraux(u)	(504)	8,849	....
70812	Merrydale(u)		10,395	....
*70009	Metairie(u)	(504)	149,428	164,160
*71055	Minden	(318)	13,661	15,084
*71203	Monroe	(318)	54,909	57,597
*70380	Morgan City	(504)	14,531	16,114
70612	Moss Bluff(u)	(318)	8,039	7,004
*71457	Natchitoches	(318)	16,609	16,664
*70560	New Iberia	(318)	31,828	32,766
*70140	New Orleans	(504)	496,938	557,927
70760	New Roads		5,303	3,924
71463	Oakdale	(318)	6,837	7,155
70810	Oak Hills Place		5,479	....
*70570	Opelousas	(318)	19,091	18,903
70392	Patterson	(504)	5,166	4,693
*71360	Pineville	(318)	12,255	12,034
*70764	Plaquemine	(504)	7,101	7,521
70454	Ponchatoula	(504)	5,425	5,469
70767	Port Allen	(504)	6,277	6,114
70601	Prien(u)	(318)	6,448	6,224
70394	Raceland(u)	(504)	5,564	6,302
70578	Rayne	(318)	8,502	9,066
.....	Red Chute(u)		5,431	....
70084	Reserve(u)	(504)	8,847	7,288
70123	River Ridge(u)	(504)	14,800	17,146
*71270	Ruston	(318)	20,071	20,585
70582	Saint Martinville	(318)	7,226	7,965
70087	Saint Rose(u)	(504)	6,259	....
70817	Shenandoah(u)		13,429	....
*71103	Shreveport	(318)	198,518	206,989
*70458	Slidell	(504)	24,124	26,718
71075	Springhill	(318)	5,668	6,516
*70663	Sulphur	(318)	20,125	19,709

ZIP code	Place		1990	1980
*71282	Tallulah	(318)	8,526	11,341
70056	Terrytown(u)	(504)	23,787	23,548
*70301	Thibodaux	(504)	14,125	15,810
70053	Timberlane(u)	(504)	12,614	11,579
70809	Village Saint George(u)		6,242	....
70586	Ville Platte	(318)	9,037	9,201
70092	Violet(u)	(504)	8,574	11,678
70094	Waggaman(u)	(504)	9,405	9,004
70669	Westlake	(318)	5,007	5,246
71291	West Monroe	(318)	14,096	14,993
*70094	Westwego	(504)	11,218	12,663
71483	Winnfield	(318)	6,138	7,311
71295	Winnsboro	(318)	5,755	5,921
70791	Zachary	(504)	9,036	7,297

Maine (207)

See note on page 387

ZIP code	Place	1990	1980
*04210	Auburn	24,309	23,128
*04330	Augusta	21,325	21,819
*04401	Bangor	33,181	31,643
04530	Bath	9,799	10,246
04915	Belfast	6,355	6,243
03901	*Berwick*	5,995	4,149
*04005	Biddeford	20,710	19,638
04412	Brewer	9,021	9,017
04011	Brunswick Center(u)	14,683	10,990
04011	*Brunswick*	20,906	17,366
04093	*Buxton*	6,494	5,775
04843	*Camden*	5,060	4,584
04107	*Cape Elizabeth*	8,854	7,838
04736	Caribou	9,415	9,916
04021	*Cumberland*	5,836	5,284
03903	*Eliot*	5,329	4,948
04605	Ellsworth	5,975	5,179
04937	*Fairfield*	6,718	6,113
04105	*Falmouth*	7,610	6,853
04938	*Farmington*	7,436	6,730
04032	*Freeport*	6,905	5,863
04345	Gardiner	6,746	6,485
04038	*Gorham*	11,856	10,101
04039	Gray	5,904	4,344
04444	*Hampden*	5,974	5,250
.....	*Harpswell*	5,012	3,796
04730	Houlton Center(u)	5,627	5,730
04730	*Houlton*	6,613	6,766
04239	*Jay*	5,080	5,080
04043	*Kennebunk*	8,004	6,621
03904	Kittery Center(u)	5,151	5,465
03904	*Kittery*	9,372	9,314
*04240	Lewiston	39,757	40,481
04750	*Limestone*	9,922	8,719
04457	*Lincoln*	5,587	5,066
04250	*Lisbon*	9,457	8,769
04750	Loring AFB(u)	7,829	6,572
04462	Millinocket Center(u)	6,922	7,567
04462	*Millinocket*	6,956	7,567
04963	*Oakland*	5,595	5,162
04064	Old Orchard Beach Ctr.(u)	7,789	6,023
04064	*Old Orchard Beach*	7,789	6,291
04468	Old Town	8,317	8,422
04473	Orono Center(u)	9,789	9,891
04473	*Orono*	10,573	10,578
*04101	Portland	64,358	61,572
04769	Presque Isle	10,550	11,172
04841	Rockland	7,972	7,919
04276	Rumford Compact(u)	5,419	6,256
04276	*Rumford*	7,078	8,240
04072	Saco	15,181	12,921
04073	Sanford Center(u)	10,296	10,268
04073	*Sanford*	20,463	18,020
*04074	*Scarborough*	12,518	11,347
04976	Skowhegan Center(u)	6,990	6,517
04976	*Skowhegan*	8,725	8,098
03908	*South Berwick*	5877	4,046
04106	South Portland	23,163	22,712
04084	*Standish*	7,678	5,946
04086	*Topsham*	8,746	6,431
*04901	Waterville	17,173	17,779
04090	*Wells*	7,778	8,211
*04092	Westbrook	16,121	14,976
04082	*Windham*	13,020	11,282
04901	Winslow Center(u)	5,436	5,903
04901	*Winslow*	7,997	8,057
04364	*Winthrop*	5,986	5,889
04096	*Yarmouth*	7,862	6,585
03909	*York*	9,818	8,465

Maryland

ZIP code	Place		1990	1980
21001	Aberdeen	(410)	13,087	11,533
21005	Aberdeen Proving Ground(u)		5,267	5,722
20783	Adelphi(u)	(301)	13,524	12,530
20331	Andrews AFB(u)	(410)	10,228	10,064
*21401	Annapolis	(410)	33,195	31,740
21227	Arbutus(u)	(410)	19,750	20,163
21012	Arnold(u)	(410)	20,261	12,285
20916	Aspen Hill(u)	(301)	45,494	47,455
.....	Ballenger Creek†		5,546	2,659
*21203	Baltimore	(410)	736,014	786,741
21014	Bel Air	(410)	8,942	7,814
21050	Bel Air North(u)	(410)	14,880	5,043
21014	Bel Air South(u)	(410)	26,421	9,140
*20705	Beltsville(u)	(301)	14,476	12,760
*20814	Bethesda(u)	(301)	62,936	63,022
20710	Bladensburg	(301)	8,064	7,691
*20715	Bowie	(301)	37,642	33,695
.....	Bowleys Quarters(u)		5,595	....
21225	Brooklyn Park(u)	(410)	10,987	11,508
21716	Brunswick		5,117	4,572
20866	Burtonsville(u)		5,853	2,046
20818	Cabin John(u)		5,341	5,135
20619	California(u)	(410)	7,626	5,770
.....	Calverton(u)	(301)	12,046	7,649
21613	Cambridge	(410)	11,514	11,703
20748	Camp Springs(u)	(301)	16,392	16,118
21401	Cape St. Clair(u)	(410)	7,878	6,022
21234	Carney(u)	(410)	25,578	21,488
21228	Catonsville(u)	(410)	35,233	33,208
.....	Chesapeake Ranch Estates(u)		5,423	....
20784	Cheverly	(301)	6,023	5,751
*20825	Chevy Chase(u)	(301)	8,559	12,232
20783	Chillum(u)	(301)	31,309	32,775
20735	Clinton(u)	(301)	19,987	16,438
20904	Cloverly(u)	(301)	7,904	5,153
21030	Cockeysville(u)	(410)	18,668	17,013
20914	Colesville(u)	(301)	18,819	14,359
*20740	College Park	(301)	23,714	23,614
*21045	Columbia(u)	(301)	75,883	52,518
20743	Coral Hills(u)	(410)	11,032	11,602
21114	Crofton(u)	(410)	12,781	12,009
*21502	Cumberland	(301)	23,712	25,933
20872	Damascus(u)	(301)	9,817	4,129
20747	District Heights	(301)	6,711	6,799
21222	Dundalk(u)	(410)	65,800	71,293
21601	Easton	(410)	9,372	7,536
20737	East Riverdale(u)	(301)	14,187	14,104
21219	Edgemere(u)	(410)	9,226	9,078
21040	Edgewood(u)	(410)	23,903	19,455
21784	Eldersburg(u)		9,720	4,959
.....	Elkridge(u)		12,953	....
*21921	Elkton	(410)	9,073	6,468
*21043	Ellicott City(u)	(410)	41,396	21,784
21221	Essex(u)	(410)	40,872	39,614
20904	Fairland(u)	(301)	19,828	5,154
21047	Fallston(u)	(410)	5,730	5,572
21061	Ferndale(u)	(410)	16,355	14,314
20747	Forestville(u)	(301)	16,731	16,401
20755	Fort Meade(u)	(301)	12,509	14,083
20744	Fort Washington(u)		24,032	....
*21701	Frederick	(301)	40,186	28,086
.....	Friendly(u)	(301)	9,028	8,848
21532	Frostburg	(301)	8,069	7,715
*20877	Gaithersburg	(301)	39,676	26,424
21055	Garrison(u)		5,045	....
*20874	Germantown(u)	(301)	41,145	9,721
20706	Glenarden		5,025	4,993
*21061	Glen Burnie(u)	(410)	37,305	37,263
20769	Glenn Dale(u)	(301)	9,689	4,829
20772	Greater Upper Marlboro		11,528	....
*20770	Greenbelt	(301)	20,561	17,332
21122	Green Haven(u)	(410)	14,416	6,577
.....	Green Valley(u)		9,424	4,504
*21740	Hagerstown	(301)	35,306	34,132
21740	Halfway(u)	(301)	8,873	8,659
21078	Havre De Grace	(410)	8,952	8,763
20903	Hillandale(u)		10,318	9,686
20748	Hillcrest Heights(u)	(301)	17,136	17,021
*20780	Hyattsville	(301)	13,864	12,709
20794	Jessup(u)		6,537	4,288
21085	Joppatowne(u)	(410)	11,084	11,348
20785	Kentland(u)	(301)	7,967	8,596
20772	Kettering(u)		9,901	6,972
21122	Lake Shore(u)	(410)	13,269	10,181
20785	Landover(u)	(301)	5,052	5,374
20787	Langley Park(u)	(301)	17,474	14,038
20706	Lanham-Seabrook(u)	(301)	16,792	15,814
21227	Lansdowne-Baltimore Highlands(u)		15,509	16,759
20646	La Plata	(301)	5,841	2,484
20772	Largo(u)	(301)	9,475	5,557
*20707	Laurel	(301)	19,086	12,103
20653	Lexington Pk.(u)	(410)	9,943	10,361
21090	Linthicum(u)	(410)	7,547	7,457
21207	Lochearn(u)	(410)	25,240	26,908
21037	Londontowne(u)	(410)	6,992	6,052
.....	Long Meadow(u)†		5,594	1,203
*21093	Lutherville-Timonium(u)		16,442	16,871
20748	Marlow Heights(u)	(301)	5,885	5,824
.....	Marlton		5,523	....
20707	Maryland City(u)		6,813	6,949
.....	Mays Chapel(u)		10,132	5,213
21220	Middle River(u)	(410)	24,616	26,756
.....	Milford Mill(u)		22,547	20,354
20717	Mitchellville		12,593	....
20886	Montgomery Village(u)	(301)	32,315	18,725
20712	Mount Rainier	(301)	7,954	7,361
21402	Naval Academy(u)	(410)	5,420	5,367

ZIP code	Place		1990	1980
20784	New Carrollton	(301)	12,002	12,632
20815	North Bethesda(u)	(301)	29,656	22,671
20895	North Kensington(u)	(301)	8,607	9,039
20707	North Laurel(u)	(301)	15,008	6,093
20878	North Potomac(u)	(301)	18,456	....
21842	Ocean City	(410)	5,146	4,946
21113	Odenton(u)	(410)	12,833	13,270
*20832	Olney(u)	(301)	23,019	13,026
21206	Overlea(u)	(410)	12,137	12,965
21117	Owings Mills(u)	(410)	9,474	9,526
20745	Oxon Hill-Glassmanor(u)†	(301)	35,794	36,267
20785	Palmer Park(u)	(301)	7,019	7,986
21234	Parkville(u)	(410)	31,617	35,159
21401	Parole(u)		10,054	3,377
21122	Pasadena(u)	(410)	10,012	7,439
21128	Perry Hall(u)	(410)	22,723	13,455
21208	Pikesville(u)	(410)	24,815	22,555
*20854	Potomac(u)	(301)	45,634	40,313
21227	Pumphrey(u)		5,483	5,666
21133	Randallstown(u)	(410)	26,277	25,927
.....	Redland(u)	(301)	16,145	10,528
21136	Reisterstown(u)	(410)	19,314	19,385
*20737	Riverdale		4,843	4,761
21122	Riviera Beach(u)	(410)	11,376	8,812
*20850	Rockville	(301)	44,830	43,811
.....	Rosaryville(u)		8,976	....
21237	Rosedale(u)	(410)	18,703	19,956
.....	Rossmoor(u)		6,182	....
21221	Rossville(u)		9,492	8,646
20602	Saint Charles(u)	(301)	28,717	13,921
*21801	Salisbury	(410)	20,592	16,429
20763	Savage-Guilford(u)		9,669	2,928
20743	Seat Pleasant	(301)	5,359	5,217
21144	Severn(u)	(410)	24,499	20,147
21146	Severna Park(u)	(410)	25,879	21,253
*20907	Silver Spring(u)	(301)	76,046	72,893
21061	South Gate(u)	(410)	27,564	24,185
20895	South Kensington(u)	(301)	8,777	9,344
20707	South Laurel(u)		18,591	18,034
20746	Suitland-Silver Hills(u)	(301)	35,111	32,164
*20912	Takoma Park	(301)	16,724	16,231
*20748	Temple Hills(u)	(301)	6,865	6,630
21285	Towson(u)	(410)	49,445	51,083
*20602	Waldorf(u)	(301)	15,058	9,782
20743	Walker Mill(u)	(301)	10,920	10,651
*21157	Westminster	(410)	13,060	8,808
20902	Wheaton Glenmont(u)	(301)	53,720	48,598
21162	White Marsh(u)		8,183	....
20903	White Oak(u)	(301)	18,671	13,700
21207	Woodlawn(u)	(410)	32,907	29,453
21207	Woodlawn(u)		5,329	5,306

Massachusetts

See note on page 387

ZIP code	Place		1990	1980
02351	Abington(u)	(617)	13,817	13,887
01720	*Acton*	(508)	17,872	17,544
02743	*Acushnet*	(508)	9,554	8,704
01220	Adams Center(u)	(413)	6,356	6,857
01220	*Adams*	(413)	9,445	10,381
01001	*Agawam*	(413)	27,323	26,271
01913	Amesbury Center(u)	(508)	12,109	12,236
01913	*Amesbury*	(508)	14,997	13,971
01002	Amherst Center(u)	(413)	17,824	17,773
*01002	*Amherst*	(413)	35,228	33,229
01810	Andover(u)	(508)	8,242	8,445
01810	*Andover*	(508)	29,151	26,370
02174	Arlington(u)	(617)	44,630	48,219
01430	*Ashburnham*	(508)	5,433	4,075
01721	*Ashland*	(508)	12,066	9,165
01331	Athol Center(u)	(508)	8,732	8,708
01331	*Athol*	(508)	11,451	10,634
02703	Attleboro	(508)	38,383	34,196
01501	*Auburn*	(508)	15,005	14,845
*01432	*Ayer*	(508)	6,871	6,993
02630	*Barnstable*	(508)	40,949	30,898
01730	*Bedford*	(617)	12,996	13,067
01007	*Belchertown*	(413)	10,579	8,339
02019	*Bellingham*	(508)	14,877	14,300
02178	Belmont(u)	(617)	24,720	26,100
01915	Beverly	(508)	38,195	37,655
*01821	*Billerica*	(508)	37,609	36,727
01504	*Blackstone*	(508)	8,023	6,570
*02109	Boston	(617)	574,283	562,994
02532	*Bourne*	(508)	16,064	13,874
01921	*Boxford*	(508)	6,266	5,374
*02184	Braintree(u)	(617)	33,836	36,337
02631	*Brewster*	(508)	8,440	5,226
02324	*Bridgewater*	(508)	21,249	17,202
*02403	Brockton	(508)	92,788	95,172
02146	Brookline(u)	(617)	54,718	55,062
01803	*Burlington*	(617)	23,302	23,486
*02139	Cambridge	(617)	95,802	95,322
02021	*Canton*	(617)	18,530	18,182
02330	*Carver*	(508)	10,590	6,988
02632	Centerville	(508)	9,190	3,640
01507	*Charlton*	(508)	9,576	6,719
02633	*Chatham*	(508)	6,579	6,071
01824	Chelmsford(u)	(508)	32,383	31,174
02150	Chelsea	(617)	28,710	25,431
*01020	Chicopee	(413)	56,632	55,112
01510	*Clinton*	(508)	13,222	12,771
01778	Cochituate(u)	(508)	6,046	6,126
02025	*Cohasset*	(617)	7,075	7,174
01742	*Concord*	(508)	17,076	16,293
*01226	*Dalton*	(413)	7,155	6,797
01923	Danvers(u)	(508)	24,174	24,100
02714	*Dartmouth*	(508)	27,244	23,966
02026	Dedham(u)	(617)	23,782	25,298
01342	*Deerfield*	(413)	5,018	4,517
02638	*Dennis*	(508)	13,864	12,360
02715	*Dighton*	(508)	5,631	5,352
.....	*Douglas*	(508)	5,438	3,730
01826	*Dracut*	(508)	25,594	21,249
01570	*Dudley*	(508)	9,540	8,717
*02332	*Duxbury*	(617)	13,895	11,807
02333	*East Bridgewater*	(508)	11,104	9,945
02536	East Falmouth(u)	(508)	5,577	5,181
01027	*Easthampton*	(413)	15,537	15,580
01028	*East Longmeadow*	(413)	13,367	12,905
02334	*Easton*	(508)	19,807	16,623
02149	Everett	(617)	35,701	37,195
02719	*Fairhaven*	(508)	16,132	15,759
*02722	Fall River	(508)	92,703	92,574
*02540	*Falmouth*	(508)	27,960	23,640
01420	Fitchburg	(508)	41,194	39,580
01433	Fort Devens(u)	(508)	8,973	9,546
02035	Foxborough(u)	(508)	5,706	5,697
01701	*Framingham*	(508)	64,989	65,113
02038	Franklin Center(u)	(508)	9,965	9,296
02038	*Franklin*	(508)	22,095	18,217
02702	*Freetown*	(508)	8,522	7,058
01440	Gardner	(508)	20,125	17,900
01833	*Georgetown*	(508)	6,384	5,687
*01930	Gloucester	(508)	28,716	27,768
01519	*Grafton*	(508)	13,035	11,238
01033	*Granby*	(413)	5,565	5,380
01230	*Great Barrington*	(413)	7,725	7,405
*01301	Greenfield Center(u)	(413)	14,016	14,198
01302	*Greenfield*	(413)	18,666	18,436
01450	*Groton*	(508)	7,511	6,154
01834	*Groveland*	(508)	5,214	5,040
02338	*Halifax*	(617)	6,526	5,513
01936	*Hamilton*	(508)	7,280	6,960
02339	*Hanover*	(617)	11,912	11,358
02341	*Hanson*	(617)	9,028	8,617
01451	*Harvard*	(508)	12,329	12,170
02645	*Harwich*	(508)	10,275	8,971
*01830	Haverhill	(508)	51,418	46,865
02043	*Hingham*	(617)	19,821	20,339
02343	Holbrook(u)	(617)	11,041	11,140
01520	*Holden*	(508)	14,628	13,336
01746	*Holliston*	(508)	12,926	12,622
*01040	Holyoke	(413)	43,704	44,678
01747	*Hopedale*	(508)	5,666	3,905
01748	*Hopkinton*	(508)	9,191	7,114
01749	Hudson Center(u)	(508)	14,267	14,156
01749	*Hudson*	(508)	17,233	16,408
02045	Hull(u)	(617)	10,466	9,714
02601	Hyannis(u)	(508)	14,120	9,118
01938	*Ipswich*	(508)	11,873	11,158
02364	*Kingston*	(617)	9,045	7,362
02346	*Lakeville*	(617)	7,785	5,931
01523	*Lancaster*	(508)	6,661	6,334
*01842	Lawrence	(508)	70,207	63,175
01238	*Lee*	(413)	5,849	6,247
01524	*Leicester*	(508)	10,191	9,446
01240	*Lenox*	(413)	5,069	6,523
01453	Leominster	(508)	38,145	34,508
02173	Lexington(u)	(617)	28,974	29,479
01773	*Lincoln*	(617)	7,666	7,098
01460	*Littleton*	(508)	7,051	6,970
01106	Longmeadow(u)	(413)	15,467	16,301
*01853	Lowell	(508)	103,439	92,418
01056	*Ludlow*	(413)	18,820	18,150
01462	*Lunenburg*	(508)	9,117	8,405
*01901	Lynn	(617)	81,245	78,471
01940	Lynnfield(u)	(617)	11,274	11,267
02148	Malden	(617)	53,884	53,386
01944	*Manchester*	(508)	5,286	5,424
02048	*Mansfield*	(508)	16,568	13,453
01945	Marblehead(u)	(617)	19,971	20,126
01752	Marlborough	(508)	31,813	30,617
02050	*Marshfield*	(617)	21,531	20,916
02648	Marstons Mills(u)		8,017	....
02649	*Mashpee*	(508)	7,884	3,700
02739	*Mattapoisett*	(508)	5,850	5,597
01754	Maynard(u)	(508)	10,325	9,590
02052	*Medfield*	(508)	10,531	10,220
02155	Medford	(617)	57,407	58,076
02053	*Medway*	(508)	9,931	8,447
02176	Melrose	(617)	28,150	30,055
01860	Merrimac	(508)	5,166	4,451
01844	*Methuen*	(508)	39,990	36,701
02346	Middleborough Center(u)	(617)	6,837	7,012
02346	*Middleborough*	(617)	17,867	16,404
01757	Milford Center(u)	(508)	23,339	21,730
01757	*Milford*	(508)	25,355	23,390

ZIP code	Place		1990	1980
01527	*Millbury*	(508)	12,228	11,808
02054	*Millis*	(508)	7,613	6,908
02186	Milton(u)	(617)	25,725	25,860
01057	*Monson*	(413)	7,776	7,315
01351	*Montague*	(413)	8,316	8,011
02554	*Nantucket*	(508)	6,012	5,087
01760	*Natick*	(508)	30,510	29,461
*02192	Needham(u)	(617)	27,557	27,901
*02740	New Bedford	(508)	99,922	98,478
01951	*Newbury*	(508)	5,623	4,529
01950	Newburyport	(508)	16,317	15,900
*02205	Newton	(617)	82,585	83,622
02056	*Norfolk*	(508)	9,270	6,363
01247	North Adams	(413)	16,797	18,063
01002	North Amherst(u)	(413)	6,239	5,616
01060	Northampton	(413)	29,289	29,286
01845	*North Andover*	(508)	22,792	20,129
*02760	*North Attleborough*	(508)	25,038	21,095
01532	*Northborough*	(508)	11,929	10,568
01534	*Northbridge*	(508)	13,371	12,246
01864	*North Reading*	(508)	12,002	11,455
02766	*Norton*	(508)	14,265	12,690
02061	*Norwell*	(617)	9,279	9,182
02062	Norwood(u)	(617)	28,700	29,711
01364	*Orange*	(508)	7,312	6,844
02653	*Orleans*	(508)	5,838	5,306
01540	Oxford Center(u)	(508)	5,969	6,369
01540	*Oxford*	(508)	12,588	11,680
01069	*Palmer*	(413)	12,054	11,389
01960	Peabody	(508)	47,264	45,976
02359	*Pembroke*	(617)	14,544	13,487
01463	*Pepperell*	(508)	10,098	8,061
01866	Pinehurst(u)	(508)	6,614	6,588
01201	Pittsfield	(413)	48,622	51,974
02762	*Plainville*	(508)	6,871	5,857
*02360	Plymouth Center(u)	(508)	7,258	7,232
02360	*Plymouth*	(508)	45,608	35,913
02169	Quincy	(617)	84,985	84,743
02368	Randolph(u)	(617)	30,093	28,218
02767	*Raynham*	(508)	9,867	9,085
01867	Reading(u)	(617)	22,539	22,678
02769	*Rehoboth*	(508)	8,656	7,570
02151	Revere	(617)	42,786	42,423
02370	*Rockland*	(617)	16,123	15,695
01966	*Rockport*	(508)	7,482	6,345
01970	Salem	(508)	38,091	38,276
01950	*Salisbury*	(508)	6,882	5,973
02563	*Sandwich*	(508)	15,489	8,727
01906	Saugus(u)	(617)	25,549	24,746
02066	*Scituate*	(617)	16,786	17,317
02771	*Seekonk*	(508)	13,046	12,269
02067	*Sharon*	(617)	15,517	13,601
01464	*Shirley*	(508)	6,118	5,124
01545	*Shrewsbury*	(508)	24,146	22,674
*02725	Somerset(u)	(508)	17,655	18,813
*02205	Somerville(u)	(617)	76,210	77,372
01002	South Amherst	(413)	5,053	4,861
01772	*Southborough*	(508)	6,628	6,193
01550	Southbridge Center(u)	(508)	13,631	12,882
01550	*Southbridge*	(508)	17,816	16,665
01075	*South Hadley*	(413)	16,685	16,399
01077	*Southwick*	(413)	7,667	7,382
02664	South Yarmouth(u)	(508)	10,358	7,525
01562	Spencer Center(u)	(508)	6,306	6,350
01562	*Spencer*	(508)	11,645	10,774
*01101	Springfield	(413)	156,983	152,319
01564	*Sterling*	(508)	6,481	5,440
02180	*Stoneham*	(617)	22,203	21,424
02072	*Stoughton*	(617)	26,777	26,710
01775	*Stow*	(508)	5,328	5,144
01566	*Sturbridge*	(508)	7,775	5,976
01776	*Sudbury*	(508)	14,358	14,027
01527	*Sutton*	(508)	6,824	5,855
01907	Swampscott(u)	(617)	13,650	13,837
02777	*Swansea*	(508)	15,411	15,461
02780	Taunton	(508)	49,832	45,001
01468	*Templeton*	(508)	6,438	6,070
01876	*Tewksbury*	(508)	27,266	24,635
01983	*Topsfield*	(508)	5,754	5,709
01469	*Townsend*	(508)	8,496	7,201
01879	*Tyngsborough*	(508)	8,642	5,683
01569	*Uxbridge*	(508)	10,415	8,374
01880	Wakefield(u)	(617)	24,825	24,895
02081	*Walpole*	(508)	20,223	18,859
02154	Waltham	(617)	57,878	58,200
01082	Ware Center(u)	(413)	6,533	6,806
01082	*Ware*	(413)	9,808	8,953
02571	*Wareham*	(508)	19,232	18,457
02205	Watertown(u)	(617)	33,284	34,384
01778	*Wayland*	(508)	11,874	12,170
01570	Webster Center(u)	(508)	11,849	11,175
01570	*Webster*	(508)	16,196	14,480
02181	*Wellesley*	(617)	26,615	27,209
01581	*Westborough*	(508)	14,133	13,619
01583	*West Boylston*	(508)	6,611	6,204
02379	*West Bridgewater*	(508)	6,389	6,359
01742	West Concord(u)	(508)	5,761	5,331
01085	Westfield	(413)	38,372	36,465
01886	*Westford*	(508)	16,392	13,434
01473	*Westminster*	(508)	6,191	5,139
02193	*Weston*	(617)	10,200	11,169
02790	*Westport*	(508)	13,852	13,763
01089	West Springfield(u)	(413)	27,537	27,042
02090	*Westwood*	(617)	12,557	13,212
02673	West Yarmouth	(508)	5,409	3,852
*02205	Weymouth(u)	(617)	54,063	55,601
01588	Whitinsville(u)	(508)	5,639	5,379
02382	*Whitman*	(617)	13,240	13,534
01095	*Wilbraham*	(413)	12,635	12,053
01267	*Williamstown*	(413)	8,220	8,741
01887	Wilmington(u)	(508)	17,651	17,471
01475	*Winchendon*	(508)	8,805	7,019
01890	Winchester(u)	(617)	20,267	20,701
02152	Winthrop(u)	(617)	18,127	19,294
01801	Woburn	(617)	35,943	36,626
*01613	Worcester	(508)	169,759	161,799
02093	*Wrentham*	(508)	9,006	7,580
02675	*Yarmouth*	(508)	21,174	18,449

Michigan

ZIP code	Place		1990	1980
49221	Adrian	(517)	22,097	21,276
49224	Albion	(517)	10,066	11,059
49401	Allendale(u)		6,950	....
48101	Allen Park	(313)	31,092	34,196
48801	Alma	(517)	9,034	9,652
49707	Alpena	(517)	11,354	12,214
*48107	Ann Arbor	(313)	109,608	107,969
48321	Auburn Hills†	(313)	17,076	15,388
*49016	Battle Creek	(616)	53,516	35,724
*48707	Bay City	(517)	38,936	41,593
48505	Beecher(u)	(313)	14,465	17,178
48809	Belding	(616)	5,969	5,634
*49022	Benton Harbor	(616)	12,818	14,707
49022	Benton Heights(u)	(616)	5,465	6,787
48072	Berkley	(313)	16,960	18,637
48025	Beverly Hills	(313)	10,610	11,598
49307	Big Rapids	(616)	12,603	14,361
*48012	Birmingham	(810)	19,997	21,689
48301	Bloomfield(u)	(313)	42,137	42,876
48722	Bridgeport(u)	(517)	8,569	....
48116	Brighton	(810)	5,686	4,268
48601	Buena Vista(u)		8,196	....
*48509	Burton	(810)	27,437	29,976
49601	Cadillac	(616)	10,104	10,199
48187	Canton(u)	(313)	57,047	....
48724	Carrollton(u)	(517)	6,521	7,482
48015	Center Line	(810)	9,026	9,293
48813	Charlotte	(517)	8,083	8,251
48017	Clawson	(313)	13,874	15,103
49236	Clinton(u)	(517)	85,866	72,400
49036	Coldwater	(517)	9,607	9,461
49321	Comstock Park(u)	(616)	6,530	5,506
49508	Cutlerville(u)	(616)	11,228	8,256
48423	Davison	(810)	5,693	6,087
*48120	Dearborn	(313)	89,286	90,660
48127	Dearborn Heights	(313)	60,838	67,706
*48231	Detroit	(313)	1,027,974	1,203,368
49047	Dowagiac	(616)	6,418	6,307
49506	East Grand Rapids	(616)	10,807	10,914
48826	East Lansing	(517)	50,677	51,392
48021	Eastpointe	(810)	35,283	38,280
49001	Eastwood(u)	(616)	6,340	7,186
48229	Ecorse	(313)	12,180	14,447
49829	Escanaba	(906)	13,659	14,355
49022	Fair Plain(u)	(616)	8,051	8,289
*48333	Farmington	(810)	10,170	11,022
48333	Farmington Hills	(810)	74,614	58,056
48430	Fenton	(313)	8,434	8,098
48220	Ferndale	(313)	25,084	26,227
48134	Flat Rock	(313)	7,290	6,853
*48501	Flint	(810)	140,925	140,925
48433	Flushing	(810)	8,542	8,624
49506	Forest Hills(u)		16,690	....
48026	Fraser	(810)	13,899	14,560
*48135	Garden City	(313)	31,846	35,640
48439	Grand Blanc	(810)	7,760	6,848
49417	Grand Haven	(616)	11,951	11,763
48837	Grand Ledge	(517)	7,562	6,920
*49501	Grand Rapids	(616)	189,126	181,843
*49418	Grandville	(616)	15,624	12,412
48838	Greenville	(616)	8,101	8,019
48138	Grosse Ile(u)	(313)	9,781	9,320
48236	Grosse Pointe	(313)	5,681	5,901
48230	Grosse Pointe Farms	(313)	10,092	10,551
48230	Grosse Pointe Park	(313)	12,857	13,562
48230	Grosse Pointe Woods	(313)	17,715	18,886
48212	Hamtramck	(313)	18,372	21,300
48225	Harper Woods	(313)	14,903	16,361
48625	Harrison(u)	(517)	24,685	23,649
48840	Haslett(u)	(517)	10,230	7,025
49058	Hastings	(616)	6,549	6,418
48030	Hazel Park	(810)	20,051	20,914
48203	Highland Park	(313)	20,121	27,909
49242	Hillsdale	(517)	8,175	7,432
*49423	Holland	(616)	30,745	26,281
48442	Holly	(810)	5,595	4,874
48842	Holt(u)	(517)	11,744	10,097

ZIP code	Place		1990	1980
49931	Houghton	(906)	7,498	7,512
*48843	Howell	(517)	8,147	6,976
49426	Hudsonville		6,170	4,844
48070	Huntington Woods	(313)	6,419	6,937
48141	Inkster	(313)	30,772	35,190
48846	Ionia	(616)	5,990	5,920
49801	Iron Mountain	(906)	8,525	8,341
49938	Ironwood	(906)	6,849	7,741
49849	Ishpeming	(906)	7,200	7,538
*49204	Jackson	(517)	37,425	39,739
*49428	Jenison(u)	(616)	17,882	16,330
*49001	Kalamazoo	(616)	80,277	79,722
49518	Kentwood	(616)	37,826	30,438
49801	Kingsford	(906)	5,480	5,290
49843	K.I. Sawyer AFB(u)	(906)	6,577	7,345
48144	Lambertville(u)	(313)	7,860	6,341
*48901	Lansing	(517)	127,321	130,414
48446	Lapeer	(810)	7,759	6,198
48146	Lincoln Park	(313)	41,832	45,105
*48150	Livonia	(313)	100,850	104,814
49431	Ludington	(616)	8,507	8,937
48071	Madison Heights	(313)	32,196	35,375
49660	Manistee	(616)	6,734	7,665
49855	Marquette	(906)	21,977	23,288
49068	Marshall	(616)	6,941	7,201
48040	Marysville	(810)	8,515	7,345
48854	Mason	(517)	6,768	6,019
48122	Melvindale	(313)	11,216	12,322
49858	Menominee	(906)	9,398	10,099
*48640	Midland	(517)	38,053	37,269
48381	Milford	(810)	5,500	5,041
48161	Monroe	(313)	22,902	23,531
48046	Mount Clemens	(810)	18,405	18,991
*48804	Mount Pleasant	(517)	23,299	23,746
*49440	Muskegon	(616)	39,809	40,823
49444	Muskegon Heights	(616)	13,176	14,611
48047	New Baltimore	(810)	5,798	5,439
49120	Niles	(616)	12,458	13,115
.....	Northview(u)		13,712	11,662
48167	Northville	(313)	6,226	5,698
49441	Norton Shores	(616)	21,755	22,025
48376	Novi	(810)	32,998	22,525
48237	Oak Park	(313)	30,468	31,537
48805	Okemos(u)	(517)	20,216	8,882
48867	Owosso	(517)	16,322	16,455
49770	Petoskey	(616)	6,056	6,097
48170	Plymouth	(313)	9,560	9,986
48170	Plymouth Township(u)	(313)	23,646	....
*48343	Pontiac	(810)	71,136	76,715
49081	Portage	(616)	41,042	38,157
48061	Port Huron	(810)	33,694	33,981
48239	Redford(u)	(313)	54,387	58,441
48218	River Rouge	(313)	11,314	12,912
48192	Riverview	(313)	13,894	14,569
*48308	Rochester	(810)	7,130	7,203
48306	Rochester Hills†		61,766	40,704
48174	Romulus	(313)	22,897	24,857
48066	Roseville	(313)	51,412	54,311
*48068	Royal Oak	(810)	65,410	70,893
*48605	Saginaw	(517)	69,512	77,508
48604	Saginaw Township North(u)	(517)	23,018	....
48603	Saginaw Township South(u)	(517)	13,987	....
48079	Saint Clair	(810)	5,116	4,780
*48080	Saint Clair Shores	(810)	68,107	76,210
48879	Saint Johns	(517)	7,392	7,376
49085	Saint Joseph	(616)	9,214	9,622
48176	Saline	(313)	6,663	6,483
49783	Sault Sainte Marie	(906)	14,689	14,448
49455	Shelby(u)		48,655	....
48609	Shields(u)		6,634	....
*48037	Southfield	(810)	75,727	75,568
48195	Southgate	(313)	30,771	32,058
49090	South Haven	(616)	5,563	5,943
48178	South Lyon	(810)	6,479	5,214
48161	South Monroe(u)		5,266	4,232
49015	Springfield	(616)	5,582	5,917
*48311	Sterling Heights	(313)	117,810	108,999
49091	Sturgis	(616)	10,130	9,468
48180	Taylor	(313)	70,811	77,568
49286	Tecumseh	(517)	7,462	7,320
48182	Temperance(u)	(313)	6,542	....
49093	Three Rivers	(616)	7,464	7,015
*49684	Traverse City	(616)	15,155	15,516
48183	Trenton	(313)	20,586	22,762
*48099	Troy	(810)	72,884	67,102
48318	Utica	(810)	5,081	5,282
49504	Walker	(616)	17,279	15,088
48390	Walled Lake		6,278	4,748
*48390	Warren	(313)	144,864	161,134
48329	Waterford(u)	(313)	66,692	64,250
48917	Waverly(u)		15,614	....
48184	Wayne	(313)	19,899	21,159
*48325	West Bloomfield(u)	(313)	54,843	41,962
48185	Westland	(313)	84,724	84,603
49019	Westwood(u)	(616)	8,957	8,519
48393	Wixom	(313)	8,550	6,705
48183	Woodhaven	(313)	11,631	10,902
48753	Wurtsmith AFB(u)	(517)	5,080	5,166
*48192	Wyandotte	(313)	30,938	34,006
49509	Wyoming	(616)	63,891	59,616

ZIP code	Place		1990	1980
48197	Ypsilanti	(313)	24,846	24,031
49464	Zeeland	(616)	5,417	4,764

Minnesota

ZIP code	Place		1990	1980
56007	Albert Lea	(507)	18,310	19,200
56308	Alexandria	(612)	8,029	7,608
55303	Andover	(612)	15,216	9,387
55303	Anoka	(612)	17,192	15,634
55124	Apple Valley	(612)	34,598	21,818
55112	Arden Hills	(612)	9,199	8,012
55912	Austin	(507)	21,926	23,020
*56601	Bemidji	(218)	11,165	10,949
55449	Blaine	(612)	38,975	28,558
*55420	Bloomington	(612)	86,335	81,831
56401	Brainerd	(218)	12,353	11,489
55429	Brooklyn Center	(612)	28,887	31,230
55443	Brooklyn Park	(612)	56,381	43,332
55313	Buffalo	(612)	6,856	4,560
55337	Burnsville	(612)	51,288	35,674
55008	Cambridge		5,094	3,287
55316	Champlin	(612)	16,849	9,006
55317	Chanhassen	(612)	11,732	6,359
55318	Chaska	(612)	11,339	8,346
55719	Chisholm	(218)	5,290	5,930
55720	Cloquet	(218)	10,885	11,142
55421	Columbia Heights	(612)	18,910	20,029
55433	Coon Rapids	(612)	52,978	35,826
.....	Corcoran	(612)	5,199	4,252
55016	Cottage Grove	(612)	22,935	18,994
56716	Crookston	(218)	8,119	8,628
55428	Crystal	(612)	23,788	25,543
*56501	Detroit Lakes	(218)	6,635	7,106
*55806	Duluth	(218)	85,493	92,811
55121	Eagan	(612)	47,409	20,700
55005	East Bethel	(612)	8,050	6,626
56721	East Grand Forks	(218)	8,658	8,537
*55344	Eden Prairie	(612)	39,311	16,263
55424	Edina	(612)	46,075	46,073
55330	Elk River	(612)	11,143	6,785
56031	Fairmont	(507)	11,265	11,506
55113	Falcon Heights	(612)	5,380	5,291
55021	Faribault	(507)	17,085	16,241
55024	Farmington	(612)	5,940	4,370
*56537	Fergus Falls	(218)	12,362	12,519
55025	Forest Lake	(612)	5,833	4,596
55432	Fridley	(612)	28,335	30,228
55427	Golden Valley	(612)	20,971	22,775
*55744	Grand Rapids	(218)	7,976	7,934
*55304	Ham Lake	(612)	8,924	7,832
55033	Hastings	(612)	15,478	12,827
55810	Hermantown	(218)	6,761	6,759
*55746	Hibbing	(218)	18,046	21,193
55343	Hopkins	(612)	16,529	15,336
55350	Hutchinson	(612)	11,459	9,244
56649	International Falls	(218)	8,301	5,611
55076	Inver Grove Heights	(612)	22,477	17,171
55042	Lake Elmo	(612)	5,900	5,296
55044	Lakeville	(612)	24,854	14,790
.....	Lino Lakes	(612)	8,807	4,966
55355	Litchfield	(612)	6,041	5,904
55117	Little Canada	(612)	8,971	7,102
56345	Little Falls	(612)	7,371	7,250
55115	Mahtomedi		5,633	3,851
*56001	Mankato	(507)	31,405	28,646
55311	Maple Grove	(612)	38,736	20,525
55109	Maplewood	(612)	30,954	26,990
56258	Marshall	(507)	12,023	11,161
55118	Mendota Heights	(612)	9,388	7,288
*55440	Minneapolis	(612)	368,383	370,951
55345	Minnetonka	(612)	48,370	38,683
56265	Montevideo	(612)	5,499	5,845
*55362	Monticello	(612)	5,045	4,693
*56560	Moorhead	(218)	32,295	29,998
56267	Morris	(612)	5,613	5,367
55364	Mound	(612)	9,634	9,280
55112	Mounds View	(612)	12,541	12,593
55112	New Brighton	(612)	22,207	23,269
54427	New Hope	(612)	21,853	23,087
56073	New Ulm	(507)	13,132	13,755
55057	Northfield	(507)	14,684	12,562
56001	North Mankato	(507)	10,662	9,145
55109	North Saint Paul	(612)	12,376	11,921
55119	Oakdale	(612)	18,377	12,123
55323	Orono	(612)	7,285	6,845
55060	Owatonna	(507)	19,386	18,632
55421	Plymouth	(612)	50,889	31,615
55372	Prior Lake	(612)	11,482	7,284
55303	Ramsey	(612)	12,408	10,093
55066	Red Wing	(612)	15,134	13,736
55423	Richfield	(612)	35,710	37,851
55422	Robbinsdale	(612)	14,396	14,422
*55901	Rochester	(507)	70,729	57,906
55068	Rosemount	(612)	8,622	5,083
55113	Roseville	(612)	33,485	35,820
55418	Saint Anthony	(612)	7,727	7,981
*56301	Saint Cloud	(612)	48,812	42,566
55426	Saint Louis Park	(612)	43,787	42,931
*55101	Saint Paul	(612)	272,235	270,230

ZIP code	Place	Area code	1990	1980
56082	Saint Peter	(507)	9,481	9,056
56377	Sartell	(612)	5,409	3,427
56379	Sauk Rapids	(612)	7,823	5,793
56378	Savage	(612)	9,906	3,954
55379	Shakopee	(612)	11,739	9,941
55126	Shoreview	(612)	24,587	17,300
55331	Shorewood		5,917	4,646
55075	South Saint Paul	(612)	20,197	21,235
55432	Spring Lake Park	(612)	6,532	6,477
*55082	Stillwater	(612)	13,882	12,290
56701	Thief River Falls	(218)	8,010	9,105
55127	Vadnais Heights	(612)	11,041	5,111
*55792	Virginia	(218)	9,410	11,056
56387	Waite Park		5,020	3,496
56093	Waseca	(507)	8,385	8,219
55118	West Saint Paul	(612)	19,248	18,527
55110	White Bear Lake	(612)	24,622	22,538
56201	Willmar	(612)	17,531	15,895
55987	Winona	(507)	25,435	25,075
55125	Woodbury	(612)	20,075	10,297
56187	Worthington	(507)	9,977	10,243

Mississippi (601)

ZIP code	Place	1990	1980
39730	Aberdeen	6,837	7,184
38821	Amory	7,093	7,307
38606	Batesville	6,403	5,162
*39520	Bay Saint Louis	8,063	7,850
*39530	Biloxi	46,319	49,311
38829	Booneville	7,955	6,199
*39042	Brandon	11,077	9,626
39601	Brookhaven	10,243	10,800
39046	Canton	10,062	11,116
38614	Clarksdale	19,717	21,137
38732	Cleveland	15,384	14,524
*39056	Clinton	21,847	14,660
39429	Columbia	6,815	7,733
*39701	Columbus	23,799	27,503
38834	Corinth	11,820	13,180
39059	Crystal Springs	5,643	4,902
39532	D'Iberville†	6,566	6,236
39074	Forest	5,062	5,229
39553	Gautier†	10,088	10,392
*38701	Greenville	45,226	40,613
*38930	Greenwood	18,906	20,115
*38901	Grenada	10,864	11,508
.....	Gulf Hills(u)	5,004	4,512
*39501	Gulfport	40,775	39,676
*39401	Hattiesburg	41,906	40,829
*38635	Holly Springs	7,261	7,285
38637	Horn Lake	9,069	4,326
38751	Indianola	11,809	8,050
*39205	Jackson	196,637	202,895
39090	Kosciusko	6,986	7,415
*39440	Laurel	18,827	21,897
38756	Leland	6,366	6,667
39560	Long Beach	15,804	14,199
39339	Louisville	7,165	7,323
39648	McComb	11,797	12,331
*39110	Madison	7,471	2,241
*39302	Meridian	41,036	46,577
*39563	Moss Point	17,837	18,998
*39120	Natchez	19,460	22,209
38652	New Albany	6,775	7,072
*39564	Ocean Springs	14,673	14,504
39567	Orange Grove(u)	15,676	13,476
38655	Oxford	10,026	9,882
*39567	Pascagoula	25,899	29,318
39571	Pass Christian	5,557	5,014
39288	Pearl	19,588	18,602
39465	Petal	7,883	8,476
39350	Philadelphia	6,758	6,434
39466	Picayune	10,633	10,361
*39157	Ridgeland	11,714	5,461
38663	Ripley	5,371	4,271
.....	Saint Martin(u)	6,349	....
38671	Southaven†	17,949	16,441
39759	Starkville	18,458	16,139
*38801	Tupelo	30,685	23,905
*39180	Vicksburg	20,909	25,434
39576	Waveland	5,369	4,186
39367	Waynesboro	5,143	5,349
.....	West Hattiesburg(u)	5,450	....
39773	West Point	8,489	8,811
38967	Winona	5,724	6,177
39194	Yazoo City	12,427	12,092

Missouri

ZIP code	Place	Area code	1990	1980
63123	Affton(u)	(314)	21,106	23,181
63010	Arnold	(314)	18,828	19,141
65605	Aurora	(417)	6,459	6,437
*63011	Ballwin	(314)	21,406	12,656
63137	Bellefontaine Neighbors	(314)	10,918	12,082
64012	Belton	(816)	18,145	12,708
63134	Berkeley	(314)	12,250	15,922
63031	Black Jack	(314)	6,131	5,293
*64015	Blue Springs	(816)	40,103	25,936
65613	Bolivar	(417)	6,845	5,919
65233	Boonville	(816)	7,095	6,959
63114	Breckenridge Hills	(314)	5,181	5,666
63144	Brentwood	(314)	8,150	8,209
63044	Bridgeton	(314)	17,732	18,445
*63701	Cape Girardeau	(314)	34,475	34,361
64836	Carthage	(417)	10,747	11,104
63830	Caruthersville	(314)	7,389	7,958
63834	Charleston	(314)	5,085	5,230
63017	Chesterfield†	(314)	38,630	28,384
64601	Chillicothe	(816)	8,799	9,089
63105	Clayton	(314)	13,926	14,306
64735	Clinton	(816)	8,703	8,366
*65201	Columbia	(314)	69,133	62,061
63128	Concord(u)	(314)	19,859	20,896
63126	Crestwood	(314)	11,229	12,815
63141	Creve Coeur	(314)	12,289	11,743
63136	Dellwood	(314)	5,245	6,200
63020	De Soto	(314)	5,993	5,993
63131	Des Peres	(314)	8,388	7,953
63841	Dexter	(314)	7,506	7,043
63011	Ellisville	(314)	7,183	6,233
64024	Excelsior Springs	(816)	10,373	10,424
63640	Farmington	(314)	11,596	8,270
63135	Ferguson	(314)	22,290	24,549
63028	Festus	(314)	8,105	7,574
*63033	Florissant	(314)	51,038	55,721
65473	Fort Leonard Wood(u)	(314)	15,863	21,262
65251	Fulton	(314)	10,033	11,046
64118	Gladstone	(816)	26,243	24,990
65254	Glasgow Village(u)	(314)	5,199	....
63122	Glendale	(314)	5,945	6,035
64030	Grandview	(816)	24,973	24,561
63401	Hannibal	(314)	18,004	18,811
64701	Harrisonville	(816)	7,696	6,372
*63042	Hazelwood	(314)	15,512	13,098
*64050	Independence	(816)	112,301	111,797
63755	Jackson	(314)	9,256	7,827
*65101	Jefferson City	(314)	35,517	33,619
63136	Jennings	(314)	15,841	16,934
*64801	Joplin	(417)	40,866	39,126
*64108	Kansas City	(816)	434,829	448,028
63857	Kennett	(314)	10,941	10,145
63501	Kirksville	(816)	17,152	17,167
63122	Kirkwood	(314)	27,291	27,739
63124	Ladue	(314)	8,795	9,369
63367	Lake Saint Louis		7,536	3,843
65536	Lebanon	(417)	9,983	9,507
*64063	Lee's Summit	(816)	46,418	28,741
63125	Lemay(u)	(314)	18,005	35,424
64068	Liberty	(816)	20,459	16,251
63552	Macon	(816)	5,571	5,680
63863	Malden	(314)	5,123	6,096
63011	Manchester	(314)	6,537	6,351
63143	Maplewood	(314)	9,962	10,960
65340	Marshall	(816)	12,711	12,781
63043	Maryland Heights†	(314)	25,440	26,413
64468	Maryville	(816)	10,663	9,558
.....	Mehlville(u)		27,557	....
65265	Mexico	(314)	11,290	12,276
65270	Moberly	(816)	12,839	13,418
65708	Monett	(417)	6,529	6,148
63026	Murphy(u)	(314)	9,342	8,121
64850	Neosho	(417)	9,254	9,493
64772	Nevada	(417)	8,597	9,044
63121	Normandy	(314)	5,063	5,174
63121	Northwoods	(314)	5,106	5,831
.....	Oakville(u)		31,750	....
63366	O'Fallon	(314)	17,427	8,677
63132	Olivette	(314)	7,573	7,952
63114	Overland	(314)	17,987	19,620
63775	Perryville	(314)	6,933	7,343
63120	Pine Lawn	(314)	5,083	6,570
63901	Poplar Bluff	(314)	16,841	17,139
64083	Raymore	(816)	5,592	3,154
64133	Raytown	(816)	30,601	31,831
65738	Republic		6,290	4,485
64085	Richmond	(816)	5,738	5,499
63117	Richmond Heights	(314)	10,448	11,516
63124	Rock Hill	(314)	5,217	5,702
65401	Rolla	(314)	14,090	13,303
63074	Saint Ann	(314)	14,449	15,523
*63301	Saint Charles	(314)	50,634	37,379
63114	Saint John	(314)	7,502	7,854
*64501	Saint Joseph	(816)	71,852	76,691
*63166	Saint Louis	(314)	396,685	452,801
63376	Saint Peters	(314)	40,660	15,700
63126	Sappington(u)	(314)	10,917	11,388
*65301	Sedalia	(816)	19,800	20,927
63119	Shrewsbury	(314)	6,416	5,077
63801	Sikeston	(314)	17,641	17,431
63138	Spanish Lake(u)	(314)	20,322	20,632
*65801	Springfield	(417)	140,494	133,116
63080	Sullivan	(314)	5,661	5,461
63006	Town and Country		9,503	3,187
64683	Trenton	(816)	6,129	6,811
63084	Union	(314)	6,048	5,506
63130	University City	(314)	40,087	42,690
64093	Warrensburg	(816)	15,244	13,807
63090	Washington	(314)	10,704	9,251

ZIP code	Place	1990	1980
64870	Webb City (417)	7,449	7,309
63119	Webster Groves (314)	22,992	23,097
63385	Wentzville (314)	4,640	3,193
65775	West Plains (417)	8,913	7,741

Montana (406)

ZIP code	Place	1990	1980
59711	Anaconda	10,356	12,518
*59106	Billings	81,125	66,818
*59715	Bozeman	22,660	21,645
*59701	Butte	33,336	37,205
*59401	Great Falls	55,125	56,884
59501	Havre	10,201	10,891
*59601	Helena	24,609	23,938
.....	Helena Valley West Central(u)	6,327	....
*59901	Kalispell	11,917	10,689
59044	Laurel	5,686	5,481
59457	Lewistown	6,097	7,104
59047	Livingston	6,701	6,994
59402	Malmstrom AFB(u)	5,938	6,675
59301	Miles City	8,461	9,602
*59801	Missoula	42,918	33,351
59801	Orchard Homes(u)	10,317	10,837
59270	Sidney	5,217	5,726

Nebraska

ZIP code	Place	1990	1980
69301	Alliance (308)	9,765	9,920
68310	Beatrice (402)	12,352	12,891
68005	Bellevue (402)	30,948	21,813
68008	Blair (402)	6,860	6,418
69337	Chadron (308)	5,588	5,933
.....	Chalco(u)	7,337	....
*68601	Columbus (402)	19,480	17,328
68025	Fremont (402)	23,680	23,979
69341	Gering (308)	7,946	7,760
*68802	Grand Island (308)	39,487	33,180
*68901	Hastings (402)	22,837	23,045
68949	Holdrege (308)	5,671	5,624
*68847	Kearney (308)	24,396	21,158
68128	La Vista (402)	9,840	9,588
68850	Lexington (308)	6,600	7,040
*68501	Lincoln (402)	191,972	171,932
69001	McCook (308)	8,112	8,404
68410	Nebraska City (402)	6,547	7,127
*68701	Norfolk (402)	21,476	19,449
69101	North Platte (308)	22,605	24,509
68113	Offutt AFB West(u) (402)	10,883	8,787
69153	Ogallala (308)	5,095	5,638
*68108	Omaha (402)	335,719	313,939
68046	Papillion (402)	10,378	6,399
68048	Plattsmouth (402)	6,415	6,295
68127	Ralston (402)	6,236	5,143
*69361	Scottsbluff (308)	13,711	14,156
68434	Seward (402)	5,641	5,713
69162	Sidney (308)	5,959	6,010
68776	South Sioux City (402)	9,677	9,339
68787	Wayne (402)	5,142	5,240
68467	York (402)	7,940	7,723

Nevada (702)

ZIP code	Place	1990	1980
*89005	Boulder City	12,567	9,590
*89701	Carson City	40,443	32,022
89112	East Las Vegas(u)	11,087	6,449
*89801	Elko	14,836	8,758
.....	Enterprise(u)	6,412	....
*89406	Fallon	6,430	4,262
89408	Fernley(u)	5,164	....
89410	Gardnerville Ranchos(u)	7,455	3,542
*89015	Henderson	64,948	24,363
*89450	Incline Village-Crystal Bay(u)	7,119	6,225
*89125	Las Vegas	258,204	164,674
89191	Nellis AFB(u)	8,377	7,476
*89030	North Las Vegas	47,849	42,739
89041	Pahrump(u)	7,424	....
89109	Paradise(u)	124,682	84,818
*89501	Reno	133,850	100,756
*89431	Sparks	53,367	40,780
.....	Spring Creek(u) †	5,866	4,155
.....	Spring Valley(u)	51,726	....
89110	Sunrise Manor(u)	95,362	44,155
89433	Sun Valley(u)	11,391	8,822
89101	Winchester(u)	23,365	19,728
*89445	Winnemucca	6,102	4,140

New Hampshire (603)

See note on page 387

ZIP code	Place	1990	1980
03031	*Amherst*	9,068	8,243
03811	*Atkinson*	5,188	4,397
03825	*Barrington*	6,164	4,404
03102	*Bedford*	12,563	9,481
03220	*Belmont*	5,796	4,026
03570	Berlin	11,824	13,084
03304	*Bow*	5,500	4,015
03743	Claremont	13,902	14,557
*03301	Concord	36,006	30,400
03818	*Conway*	7,940	7,158
03038	Derry Compact(u)	20,446	12,248
03038	*Derry*	29,603	18,875
03820	Dover	25,042	22,377
03824	Durham Compact(u)	9,236	8,448
03824	*Durham*	11,818	10,652
03042	*Epping*	5,162	3,460
03833	Exeter Compact(u)	9,556	8,947
03833	*Exeter*	12,481	11,024
03835	*Farmington*	5,739	4,630
03235	Franklin	8,304	7,901
03246	*Gilford*	5,867	4,841
03045	*Goffstown*	14,621	11,315
03841	*Hampstead*	6,732	3,785
03842	Hampton Compact(u)	7,989	6,779
03842	*Hampton*	12,278	10,493
03755	Hanover Compact(u)	6,538	6,861
03756	*Hanover*	9,212	9,119
03049	*Hollis*	5,705	4,679
03106	*Hooksett*	9,002	7,303
03051	*Hudson*	19,530	14,022
03452	*Jaffrey*	5,361	4,349
03431	Keene	22,430	21,449
03848	*Kingston*	5,591	4,111
*03246	Laconia	15,743	15,575
*03766	Lebanon	12,183	11,134
.....	*Litchfield*	5,516	4,150
03561	*Littleton*	5,827	5,558
03053	Londonderry Compact(u)	10,114	....
03053	*Londonderry*	19,781	13,598
*03103	Manchester	99,332	90,936
03054	*Merrimack*	22,156	15,406
03055	Milford Compact(u)	8,015	6,269
03055	*Milford*	11,795	8,685
*03060	Nashua	79,662	67,865
03857	*Newmarket*	7,157	4,290
03773	*Newport*	6,110	6,229
03076	*Pelham*	9,408	8,090
03275	*Pembroke*	6,561	6,561
03458	*Peterborough*	5,239	4,895
03865	*Plaistow*	7,316	5,609
03264	*Plymouth*	5,811	5,094
*03801	Portsmouth	25,925	26,254
03077	*Raymond*	8,713	5,453
*03867	Rochester	26,630	21,560
03079	*Salem*	25,746	24,124
03874	*Seabrook*	6,503	5,917
03878	Somersworth	11,249	10,350
03275	Suncook(u)	5,214	4,698
.....	*Swanzey*	6,236	5,183
03281	*Weare*	6,193	3,232
03087	*Windham*	9,000	5,664

New Jersey

See note on page 387

ZIP code	Place	1990	1980
08201	Absecon (609)	7,298	6,859
07401	Allendale (201)	5,900	5,901
07712	Asbury Park (908)	16,799	17,015
*08401	Atlantic City (609)	37,986	40,199
08106	Audubon (609)	9,205	9,533
07001	Avenel(u) (908)	15,504	....
08007	Barrington (609)	6,792	7,418
07002	Bayonne (201)	61,464	65,047
08722	Beachwood (908)	9,324	7,687
07109	Belleville(u)† (201)	34,213	35,367
*08031	Bellmawr (609)	12,603	13,721
07719	Belmar (908)	5,877	6,771
07621	Bergenfield (201)	24,458	25,568
07922	Berkeley Heights Twp.(u) (908)	11,980	12,549
08009	Berlin (609)	5,672	5,786
07924	Bernardsville (908)	6,597	6,715
08012	Blackwood(u) (609)	5,120	5,219
07003	Bloomfield(u)† (201)	45,061	47,792
07403	Bloomingdale (201)	7,530	7,867
07603	Bogota (201)	7,824	8,344
07005	Boonton (201)	8,343	8,620
08805	Bound Brook (908)	9,487	9,710
*08724	Brick Twp.(u) (201)	66,473	53,629
08302	Bridgeton (609)	18,942	18,795
08807	Bridgewater Twp.(u) (908)	32,509	29,175
08203	Brigantine (609)	11,354	8,318
08015	Browns Mills(u) (609)	11,429	10,568
07828	Budd Lake(u) (201)	7,272	6,523
08016	Burlington (609)	9,835	10,246
07405	Butler (201)	7,392	7,616
*07006	Caldwell(u)† (201)	7,549	7,624
*08101	Camden (609)	87,492	84,910
07072	Carlstadt (201)	5,510	6,166
08069	Carney's Point Twp. (u) (609)	8,443	8,396
07008	Carteret (908)	19,025	20,598
07009	Cedar Grove Twp.(u) (201)	12,053	12,600
07928	Chatham (201)	8,007	8,537
*08034	Cherry Hill Twp.(u) (609)	69,319	68,785

ZIP code	Place		1990	1980
08077	Cinnaminson Twp.(u)	(609)	14,583	16,072
07066	Clark Twp.(u)	(908)	14,629	16,699
08312	Clayton	(609)	6,155	6,013
08021	Clementon	(609)	5,601	5,764
07010	Cliffside Park	(201)	20,393	21,464
*07015	Clifton	(201)	71,984	74,388
07624	Closter	(201)	8,094	8,164
08108	Collingswood	(609)	15,289	15,838
07067	Colonia(u)	(908)	18,238	....
07016	Cranford Twp.(u)	(908)	22,633	24,573
07626	Cresskill	(201)	7,558	7,609
.....	Crestwood Village(u)	(201)	8,030	7,965
*07801	Dover	(201)	15,115	14,681
07628	Dumont	(201)	17,187	18,334
08812	Dunellen	(908)	6,528	6,593
08816	East Brunswick Twp.(u)	(908)	43,548	37,711
07936	East Hanover Twp.(u)	(201)	9,926	9,319
*07019	East Orange	(201)	73,552	77,878
07073	East Rutherford	(201)	7,902	7,849
07724	Eatontown	(908)	13,800	12,703
07020	Edgewater	(201)	5,001	4,628
08010	Edgewater Park Twp.(u)	(609)	8,388	9,273
*08818	Edison Twp.(u)	(908)	88,680	70,193
*07207	Elizabeth	(908)	110,002	106,201
07407	Elmwood Park	(201)	17,623	18,377
07630	Emerson	(201)	6,930	7,793
*07631	Englewood	(201)	24,850	23,701
07632	Englewood Cliffs	(201)	5,634	5,698
08618	Ewing Twp.(u)	(609)	34,185	34,842
07006	Fairfield(u)	(201)	7,615	7,987
07701	Fair Haven	(908)	5,270	5,679
07410	Fair Lawn	(201)	30,548	32,229
07022	Fairview	(201)	10,733	10,519
07023	Fanwood	(908)	7,115	7,767
08518	Florence-Roebling(u)	(609)	8,564	7,677
07932	Florham Park	(201)	8,521	9,359
08863	Fords(u)	(908)	14,392	....
08640	Fort Dix(u)	(609)	10,205	14,297
07024	Fort Lee	(201)	31,997	32,449
07417	Franklin Lakes	(201)	9,873	8,769
.....	Franklin Twp. (Somerset)(u)	(201)	42,780	31,358
07728	Freehold	(908)	10,742	10,020
07026	Garfield	(201)	26,727	26,803
08753	Gilford Park(u)	(908)	8,668	6,528
08028	Glassboro	(609)	15,614	14,574
08029	Glendora(u)	(609)	5,201	5,632
07028	Glen Ridge(u)†	(201)	7,076	7,855
07452	Glen Rock	(201)	10,883	11,497
08030	Gloucester City	(609)	12,649	13,121
07093	Guttenberg	(201)	8,268	7,340
*07602	Hackensack	(201)	37,049	36,039
07840	Hackettstown	(908)	8,120	8,850
08033	Haddonfield	(609)	11,633	12,337
08035	Haddon Heights	(609)	7,860	8,361
*07508	Haledon	(201)	6,951	6,607
*08609	Hamilton Twp. (Mercer)(u)	(609)	86,553	82,811
08037	Hammonton	(609)	12,208	12,298
07981	Hanover Twp.(u)	(201)	11,538	11,846
07029	Harrison	(201)	13,425	12,242
07604	Hasbrouck Heights	(201)	11,488	12,166
*07506	Hawthorne	(201)	17,084	18,200
07730	Hazlet Twp.(u)	(908)	21,976	23,013
08904	Highland Park	(201)	13,279	13,396
08520	Hightstown	(609)	5,126	4,581
07642	Hillsdale	(201)	9,750	10,495
07205	Hillside Twp.(u)	(908)	21,044	21,440
07030	Hoboken	(201)	33,397	42,460
08753	Holiday City-Berkeley(u)	(908)	14,293	9,019
.....	Holiday City South(u)	(908)	5,452	....
07843	Hopatcong	(201)	15,586	15,531
*08560	Hopewell Twp. (Mercer)(u)	(609)	10,893	11,590
07111	Irvington(u)†	(201)	59,774	61,473
08830	Iselin(u)	(908)	16,141	....
*08527	Jackson Twp.(u)	(908)	33,283	25,644
08831	Jamesburg		5,294	4,114
*07303	Jersey City	(201)	228,517	223,532
07734	Keansburg	(908)	11,069	10,613
07032	Kearny	(201)	34,874	35,735
08824	Kendall Park(u)	(908)	7,127	7,419
07033	Kenilworth	(908)	7,574	8,221
07735	Keyport	(908)	7,586	7,413
07405	Kinnelon	(201)	8,470	7,770
07871	Lake Mohawk(u)	(201)	8,930	8,498
08701	Lakewood(u)	(908)	26,095	22,863
08879	Laurence Harbor(u)	(908)	6,361	6,737
08648	Lawrenceville(u)		6,446	....
.....	Leisure Village West-Pine Lake Park(u)		10,139	....
07605	Leonia	(201)	8,365	8,027
07035	Lincoln Park	(201)	10,978	8,806
07738	Lincroft(u)		6,193	....
07036	Linden	(908)	36,701	37,836
08021	Lindenwold	(609)	18,734	18,196
08221	Linwood	(609)	6,866	6,144
07424	Little Falls Twp.(u)	(201)	11,294	11,496
07643	Little Ferry	(201)	9,989	9,399
07739	Little Silver	(908)	5,721	5,548
07039	Livingston Twp.(u)	(201)	26,609	28,040
07644	Lodi	(201)	22,355	23,956
07740	Long Branch	(908)	28,658	29,819
*07946	Long Hill Twp.(u)	(908)	7,826	7,275
07071	Lyndhurst Twp.(u)	(201)	18,262	20,326
08641	McGuire AFB(u)	(609)	7,580	7,853
07940	Madison	(201)	15,850	15,357
08859	Madison Park(u)	(201)	7,490	7,447
*07430	Mahwah Twp.(u)	(201)	17,905	12,127
08736	Manasquan	(908)	5,369	5,354
08835	Manville	(908)	10,567	11,278
08052	Maple Shade Twp.(u)	(609)	19,211	20,525
07040	Maplewood Twp.(u)	(201)	21,756	22,950
08402	Margate City	(609)	8,431	9,179
07746	Marlboro Twp.(u)	(908)	27,974	17,560
08053	Marlton(u)	(609)	10,228	9,411
07747	Matawan	(908)	9,239	8,837
07607	Maywood	(201)	9,536	9,895
08619	Mercerville-Hamilton Sq.(u)	(609)	26,873	25,446
08840	Metuchen	(908)	12,804	13,762
08846	Middlesex	(908)	13,055	13,480
07748	Middletown Twp.(u)	(908)	68,183	62,574
07432	Midland Park	(201)	7,047	7,381
07041	Millburn Twp.(u)	(201)	18,630	19,543
08850	Milltown	(908)	6,968	7,136
08332	Millville	(609)	25,992	24,815
08094	Monroe Twp. (Gloucester)(u)	(609)	26,703	21,639
*07042	Montclair(u)	(201)	37,729	38,321
07645	Montvale	(201)	6,946	7,318
07045	Montville Twp.(u)	(201)	15,600	14,290
08057	Moorestown-Lenola(u)	(609)	13,242	13,695
07950	Morris Plains	(201)	5,219	5,305
07960	Morristown	(201)	16,189	16,614
07092	Mountainside	(908)	6,657	7,118
08060	Mount Holly Twp.(u)	(609)	10,639	10,818
08087	Mystic Island(u)		7,400	4,929
*07753	Neptune Twp.(u)	(908)	28,148	28,366
*07102	Newark	(201)	275,221	329,248
*08901	New Brunswick	(908)	41,711	41,442
07646	New Milford	(201)	15,990	16,876
07974	New Providence	(908)	11,439	12,426
07860	Newton	(201)	7,521	7,748
07032	North Arlington	(201)	13,790	16,587
07047	North Bergen Twp.(u)	(201)	48,414	47,019
08902	North Brunswick Twp.(u)†	(908)	31,287	22,220
07006	North Caldwell(u)†	(201)	6,706	5,832
08225	Northfield	(609)	7,305	7,795
07508	North Haledon	(201)	7,987	8,177
07060	North Plainfield	(908)	18,820	19,108
08260	North Wildwood		5,017	4,714
07110	Nutley(u)†	(201)	27,099	28,998
07436	Oakland	(201)	11,997	13,443
*08758	Ocean Twp. (Ocean)(u)	(908)	5,416	3,731
.....	Ocean Acres(u)		5,587	4,850
08226	Ocean City	(609)	15,512	13,949
07757	Oceanport	(908)	6,146	5,888
08857	Old Bridge(u)	(908)	22,151	21,815
08857	Old Bridge Twp.(u)	(908)	56,493	51,515
07649	Oradell	(201)	8,024	8,658
*07050	Orange(u)†	(201)	29,925	31,136
07650	Palisades Park	(201)	14,536	13,732
08065	Palmyra	(609)	7,056	7,085
07652	Paramus	(201)	25,004	26,474
07656	Park Ridge	(201)	8,102	8,515
07054	Parsippany-Troy Hills Twp.(u)	(201)	48,478	49,868
*07055	Passaic	(201)	58,041	52,463
*07510	Paterson	(201)	140,891	137,970
08066	Paulsboro	(609)	6,577	6,944
08110	Pennsauken Twp.(u)	(609)	34,738	33,775
08069	Penns Grove	(609)	5,228	5,760
08070	Pennsville Center(u)	(609)	12,218	12,467
07440	Pequannock Twp.(u)	(201)	12,844	13,776
*08861	Perth Amboy	(908)	41,967	38,951
08865	Phillipsburg	(908)	15,757	16,647
08021	Pine Hill	(609)	9,854	8,684
*08854	Piscataway Twp.(u)	(908)	47,089	42,223
08071	Pitman	(609)	9,365	9,7447
*07061	Plainfield	(908)	46,577	45,555
08232	Pleasantville	(609)	16,027	13,435
08742	Point Pleasant	(908)	18,177	17,747
08742	Point Pleasant Beach	(908)	5,112	5,415
07442	Pompton Lakes	(201)	10,539	10,660
*08540	Princeton	(609)	12,016	12,035
07508	Prospect Park	(201)	5,053	5,142
07065	Rahway	(908)	25,325	26,723
08057	Ramblewood(u)	(609)	6,181	6,475
07446	Ramsey	(201)	13,228	12,899
07869	Randolph Twp.(u)	(201)	19,974	17,828
08869	Raritan	(908)	5,798	6,128
07701	Red Bank	(908)	10,636	12,031
07657	Ridgefield	(201)	9,996	10,294
07660	Ridgefield Park	(201)	12,454	12,738
*07451	Ridgewood	(201)	24,152	25,208
07456	Ringwood	(201)	12,623	12,625
07661	River Edge	(201)	10,603	11,111
08075	Riverside Twp.(u)	(609)	7,974	7,941
07675	River Vale(u)	(201)	9,410	9,489
07726	Robertsville(u)	(908)	9,841	8,461
07662	Rochelle Park Twp.	(201)	5,587	5,603
07866	Rockaway	(201)	6,243	6,852

ZIP code	Place	1990	1980
07203	Roselle . . . . (908)	20,314	20,641
07204	Roselle Park. . . . . (201)	12,805	13,377
07760	Rumson. . . . . (908)	6,701	7,623
08078	Runnemede . . . . (609)	9,042	9,461
*07070	Rutherford . . . . (201)	17,790	19,068
07662	Saddle Brook Twp.(u). . . . (201)	13,296	14,084
08079	Salem . . . . (609)	6,883	6,959
08872	Sayreville. . . . . (908)	34,998	29,969
07076	Scotch Plains Twp.(u). . . . (908)	21,150	20,774
07094	Secaucus. . . . . (201)	14,061	13,719
08753	Silverton . . . . (908)	9,175	7,236
08083	Somerdale . . . . (609)	5,440	5,900
*08873	Somerset(u). . . . . (908)	22,070	21,731
08244	Somers Point . . . . (609)	11,216	10,330
08876	Somerville . . . . (908)	11,632	11,973
08879	South Amboy . . . . (908)	7,851	8,322
07079	South Orange Twp.(u) . . . (201)	16,390	15,864
07080	South Plainfield. . . . . . . (908)	20,489	20,521
08882	South River . . . . (908)	13,692	14,361
07871	Sparta Twp.(u) . . . . (201)	15,157	13,333
08884	Spotswood . . . . (908)	7,983	7,840
07081	Springfield Twp.(u). . . . . (201)	13,420	13,955
07762	Spring Lake Heights. . . . . (908)	5,341	5,424
08084	Stratford. . . . . (609)	7,614	8,005
07747	Strathmore(u) . . . . (201)	7,060	....
07876	Succasunna-Kenvil(u) . . . (201)	11,781	10,931
07901	Summit . . . . (908)	19,757	21,071
07666	Teaneck Twp.(u) . . . . . . (201)	37,825	39,007
07670	Tenafly . . . . (201)	13,326	13,552
07724	Tinton Falls. . . . . (908)	12,361	7,740
*08753	Toms River(u). . . . . (908)	7,524	7,465
07512	Totowa . . . . (201)	10,177	11,448
*08650	Trenton . . . . (609)	88,675	92,124
08520	Twin Rivers(u). . . . . (609)	7,715	7,742
07083	Union Twp. (Union)(u) . . . (908)	50,024	50,184
07735	Union Beach. . . . . (908)	6,156	6,354
07087	Union City . . . . (201)	58,012	55,593
07458	Upper Saddle River . . . . . (201)	7,198	7,958
08406	Ventnor City . . . . (609)	11,005	11,704
07044	Verona(u)† . . . . (201)	13,597	14,166
08251	Villas(u) . . . . (609)	8,136	5,909
08360	Vineland . . . . (609)	54,780	53,753
07463	Waldwick . . . . (201)	9,757	10,802
07057	Wallington . . . . (201)	10,828	10,741
07465	Wanaque . . . . (201)	9,711	10,025
07882	Washington . . . . (908)	6,474	6,429
07675	Washington Twp. (Bergen)(u)(201)	9,245	9,550
07060	Watchung. . . . . (908)	5,110	5,290
*07470	Wayne Twp.(u) . . . . (201)	47,025	46,474
07087	Weehawken Twp.(u) . . . . (201)	12,385	13,168
07006	West Caldwell(u)† . . . . . . (201)	10,422	11,407
*07091	Westfield . . . . (908)	28,870	30,447
07728	West Freehold(u). . . . . . . (908)	11,166	9,929
07764	West Long Branch . . . . . . (908)	7,690	7,380
07480	West Milford Twp.(u)† . . . (201)	25,430	22,750
07093	West New York . . . . (201)	38,125	39,194
07052	West Orange(u)†. . . . . . . (201)	39,103	39,510
07424	West Paterson . . . . (201)	10,982	11,293
07675	Westwood . . . . (201)	10,446	10,714
07885	Wharton. . . . . (201)	5,405	5,485
08610	White Horse(u) . . . . (609)	9,397	10,098
07886	White Meadow Lake(u). . . (201)	8,002	8,429
08094	Williamstown . . . . (609)	10,891	5,768
08046	Willingboro Twp.(u) . . . . (609)	36,291	39,912
08095	Winslow Twp.(u) . . . . . . (609)	30,087	20,034
07095	Woodbridge(u) . . . . (908)	17,434	....
*07095	Woodbridge Twp.(u). . . . . (908)	93,092	90,074
08096	Woodbury . . . . (609)	10,904	10,353
07675	Woodcliff Lake . . . . (201)	5,303	5,644
07075	Wood-Ridge . . . . (201)	7,506	7,929
07481	Wyckoff Twp.(u) . . . . . . (201)	15,372	15,500
08620	Yardville-Groveville(u) . . . (609)	9,248	9,414
.....	Yorketown(u) . . . . (609)	6,313	5,330

New Mexico (505)

ZIP code	Place	1990	1980
*88310	Alamogordo	27,596	24,024
*87101	Albuquerque.	384,619	332,920
88021	Anthony(u)	5,160	3,285
88210	Artesia.	10,610	10,385
87410	Aztec.	5,480	5,512
87002	Belen	6,547	5,617
87004	Bernalillo	5,960	2,988
87413	Bloomfield	5,214	4,881
*88220	Carlsbad	24,952	25,496
*88101	Clovis	30,954	31,194
87048	Corrales.	5,453	2,791
*88030	Deming	10,970	9,964
87532	Espanola	8,389	6,803
*87401	Farmington.	33,997	31,222
*87301	Gallup	19,157	18,167
87020	Grants	8,626	11,439
*88240	Hobbs	29,121	29,153
88330	Holloman AFB(u).	5,891	7,245
*88001	Las Cruces.	62,360	45,086
87701	Las Vegas	14,753	14,322
87544	Los Alamos(u).	11,455	11,039
87031	Los Lunas	6,013	3,525
88260	Lovington.	9,322	9,727
87107	North Valley(u)	12,507	12,984
87114	Paradise Hills(u)	5,513	5,096
88130	Portales.	10,690	9,940
87740	Raton	7,372	8,225
87124	Rio Rancho†.	32,512	9,985
*88201	Roswell	44,260	39,676
87115	Sandia(u).	6,742	5,288
*87501	Santa Fe	56,537	49,160
87420	Shiprock(u)	7,687	7,237
*88061	Silver City	10,683	9,887
87801	Socorro	8,159	7,173
87105	South Valley(u)	35,701	38,898
88063	Sunland Park†	8,179	4,313
87901	Truth or Consequences	6,221	5,219
88401	Tucumcari	6,827	6,765
87544	White Rock(u).	6,192	6,560
87327	Zuni Pueblo(u)	5,857	5,551

New York

See note on page 387

ZIP code	Place	1990	1980
10901	Airmont(u)	7,835	....
*12201	Albany. . . . . (518)	100,031	101,727
11507	Albertson(u) . . . . (516)	5,166	5,561
14411	Albion . . . . (716)	5,863	4,897
11701	Amityville . . . . (516)	9,286	9,076
12010	Amsterdam. . . . . (518)	20,714	21,872
12603	Arlington(u) . . . . (914)	11,948	11,305
13021	Auburn . . . . (315)	31,258	32,548
*11702	Babylon. . . . . (516)	12,249	12,388
11510	Baldwin(u) . . . . (516)	22,719	31,630
11510	Baldwin Harbor(u)	7,899	....
13027	Baldwinsville. . . . . (315)	6,591	6,446
12020	Ballston Spa. . . . . (518)	5,194	4,711
14020	Batavia . . . . (716)	16,310	16,703
14810	Bath . . . . (607)	5,801	6,042
11705	Bayport(u) . . . . (516)	7,702	9,282
11706	Bay Shore(u) . . . . (516)	21,279	10,784
11709	Bayville . . . . (516)	7,193	7,034
.....	Baywood(u)	7,351	....
12508	Beacon . . . . (914)	13,243	12,937
11710	Bellmore(u) . . . . (516)	16,438	18,106
11714	Bethpage(u) . . . . (516)	15,761	16,840
*13902	Binghamton . . . . (607)	53,008	55,860
11716	Bohemia(u) . . . . (516)	9,556	9,308
11717	Brentwood(u) . . . . (516)	45,218	44,321
10510	Briarcliff Manor . . . . (914)	7,070	7,115
14610	Brighton (u) . . . . (716)	34,455	35,776
14420	Brockport. . . . . (716)	8,749	9,776
10708	Bronxville. . . . . (914)	6,028	6,267
*14240	Buffalo. . . . . (716)	328,175	357,870
*14424	Canandaigua . . . . (716)	10,725	10,419
13617	Canton . . . . (315)	6,379	7,055
11514	Carle Place(u). . . . . (516)	5,107	5,470
11516	Cedarhurst. . . . . (516)	5,716	6,162
11720	Centereach(u). . . . . (516)	26,720	30,136
11934	Center Moriches(u) . . . . . (516)	5,987	5,703
11721	Centerport(u) . . . . (516)	5,333	6,576
11722	Central Islip(u) . . . . (516)	26,028	19,734
*14225	Cheektowaga(u) . . . . (716)	84,387	92,145
10977	Chestnut Ridge†	7,517	8,217
12043	Cobleskill. . . . . (518)	5,268	5,272
12047	Cohoes . . . . (518)	16,825	18,144
12205	Colonie . . . . (518)	8,019	8,869
11725	Commack(u). . . . . (516)	36,124	34,719
10920	Congers(u). . . . . (914)	8,003	7,123
11726	Copiague(u) . . . . (516)	20,769	20,132
11727	Coram(u) . . . . (516)	30,111	24,752
14830	Corning . . . . (607)	11,938	12,953
13045	Cortland. . . . . (607)	19,801	20,138
10520	Croton-on-Hudson . . . . . . (914)	7,018	6,889
14437	Dansville . . . . (716)	5,002	4,979
11729	Deer Park(u). . . . . (516)	28,840	30,394
12054	Delmar(u). . . . . (518)	8,360	8,423
14043	Depew. . . . . (716)	17,673	19,819
13214	DeWitt(u) . . . . (315)	8,244	9,024
11746	Dix Hills(u) . . . . (516)	25,849	26,693
10522	Dobbs Ferry . . . . (914)	9,940	10,053
14048	Dunkirk . . . . (716)	13,989	15,310
14052	East Aurora . . . . (716)	6,647	6,803
10709	Eastchester(u) . . . . (914)	18,537	20,305
12302	East Glenville(u) . . . . (518)	6,518	6,537
11576	East Hills . . . . (516)	6,746	7,160
11730	East Islip(u) . . . . (516)	14,325	13,852
11758	East Massapequa(u) . . . . (516)	19,550	13,987
11554	East Meadow(u) . . . . (516)	36,909	39,317
11731	East Northport(u). . . . . . . (516)	20,411	20,187
11772	East Patchogue(u). . . . . . (516)	20,195	18,139
14445	East Rochester . . . . (716)	6,932	7,596
11518	East Rockaway . . . . (516)	10,152	10,917
11786	East Shoreham(u)	5,461	....
*14901	Elmira . . . . (607)	33,724	35,327
11003	Elmont(u) . . . . (516)	28,612	27,592
11731	Elwood(u) . . . . (516)	10,916	11,847
*13760	Endicott . . . . (607)	13,531	14,457
13760	Endwell(u) . . . . (607)	12,602	13,745
13219	Fairmount(u). . . . . (315)	12,266	13,415
14450	Fairport . . . . (716)	5,943	5,970
11735	Farmingdale . . . . (516)	8,022	7,946

ZIP code	Place	1990	1980
11738	Farmingville(u) (516)	14,842	13,398
*11001	Floral Park (516)	15,947	16,805
13603	Fort Drum(u)	11,578	....
11768	Fort Salonga(u) (516)	9,176	9,550
11010	Franklin Square(u) (516)	28,205	29,051
14063	Fredonia (716)	10,436	11,126
11520	Freeport (516)	39,894	38,272
13069	Fulton (315)	12,929	13,312
11530	Garden City (516)	21,675	22,927
11040	Garden City Park(u) (516)	7,437	7,712
14624	Gates-North Gates(u) (716)	14,995	15,244
14454	Geneseo (716)	7,187	6,746
14456	Geneva (315)	14,143	15,133
11542	Glen Cove (516)	24,149	24,618
12801	Glens Falls (518)	15,023	15,897
12801	Glens Falls North(u) (518)	7,978	6,956
12078	Gloversville (518)	16,656	17,836
10924	Goshen (914)	5,255	4,874
*11021	Great Neck (516)	8,745	9,168
11020	Great Neck Plaza (516)	5,897	5,604
14616	Greece(u) (716)	15,632	16,177
11740	Greenlawn(u) (516)	13,208	13,869
*12771	Greenville(u) (914)	9,528	8,706
14075	Hamburg (716)	10,442	10,582
11946	Hampton Bays(u) (516)	7,893	7,256
10528	Harrison (914)	23,308	23,046
10530	Hartsdale(u) (914)	9,587	10,216
10706	Hastings-on-Hudson (914)	8,000	8,573
11787	Hauppauge(u) (516)	19,750	20,960
10927	Haverstraw (914)	9,438	8,800
*11551	Hempstead (516)	47,982	40,404
13350	Herkimer (315)	7,945	8,383
11557	Hewlett(u) (516)	6,620	6,986
*11802	Hicksville(u) (516)	40,174	43,245
10977	Hillcrest(u) (914)	6,447	5,733
14468	Hilton	5,216	4,151
11741	Holbrook(u) (516)	25,273	24,382
11742	Holtsville(u) (516)	14,972	13,515
14843	Hornell (607)	9,877	10,234
*14845	Horseheads (607)	6,802	7,348
12534	Hudson (518)	8,034	7,986
12839	Hudson Falls (518)	7,651	7,419
11743	Huntington(u) (516)	18,243	21,727
11746	Huntington Station(u) (516)	28,247	28,769
13357	Ilion (315)	8,888	9,450
11696	Inwood(u) (516)	7,767	8,228
14617	Irondequoit(u) (716)	52,322	57,648
10533	Irvington (914)	6,348	5,774
11751	Islip(u) (516)	18,924	13,438
11752	Islip Terrace(u) (516)	5,530	5,588
*14850	Ithaca (607)	29,541	28,732
*14702	Jamestown (716)	34,681	35,775
10535	Jefferson Valley-Yorktown(u) (914)	14,118	13,380
11753	Jericho(u) (516)	13,141	12,739
13790	Johnson City (607)	16,578	17,126
12095	Johnstown (518)	9,058	9,360
14217	Kenmore (716)	17,180	18,474
11754	Kings Park(u) (516)	17,773	16,131
12401	Kingston (914)	23,095	24,481
.....	Kiryas Joel	7,437	2,088
14218	Lackawanna (716)	20,585	22,701
10512	Lake Carmel(u) (914)	8,489	7,295
11755	Lake Grove (516)	9,612	9,692
11779	Lake Ronkonkoma(u) (516)	18,997	38,336
11552	Lakeview(u) (516)	5,476	5,276
14086	Lancaster (716)	11,940	13,056
10538	Larchmont (914)	6,181	6,308
12110	Latham(u) (518)	10,131	11,182
11559	Lawrence (516)	6,513	6,175
11756	Levittown(u) (516)	53,286	57,045
11757	Lindenhurst (516)	26,879	26,919
13365	Little Falls (315)	5,829	6,156
14094	Lockport (716)	24,426	24,844
11561	Long Beach (516)	33,510	34,073
12211	Loudonville(u) (518)	10,822	11,480
11563	Lynbrook (516)	19,208	20,424
10541	Mahopac(u) (914)	7,755	7,681
12953	Malone (518)	6,777	7,668
11565	Malverne (516)	9,054	9,262
10543	Mamaroneck (914)	17,325	17,616
11030	Manhasset(u) (516)	7,718	8,485
11050	Manorhaven (516)	5,672	5,384
11949	Manorville(u) (516)	6,198	....
11758	Massapequa(u) (516)	22,018	24,454
11762	Massapequa Park (516)	18,044	19,779
13662	Massena (315)	11,716	12,851
11950	Mastic(u) (516)	13,778	10,413
11951	Mastic Beach(u) (516)	10,293	8,318
13211	Mattydale(u) (315)	6,418	7,511
12118	Mechanicville (518)	5,249	5,500
11763	Medford(u) (516)	21,274	20,418
14103	Medina (716)	6,686	6,392
11746	Melville(u) (516)	12,586	8,139
11566	Merrick(u) (516)	23,042	24,478
11953	Middle Island(u) (516)	7,848	5,703
10940	Middletown (914)	24,160	21,454
11764	Miller Place(u) (516)	9,315	7,877
11501	Mineola (516)	19,005	20,757
10950	Monroe (914)	6,672	5,996
10952	Monsey(u) (914)	13,986	12,380
12701	Monticello (914)	6,597	6,306
10970	Mount Ivy(u)	6,013	....
10549	Mount Kisco (914)	9,108	8,025
11766	Mount Sinai(u) (516)	8,023	6,591
*10551	Mount Vernon (914)	67,153	66,713
12590	Myers Corner(u) (914)	5,599	5,180
10954	Nanuet(u) (914)	14,065	12,578
11767	Nesconset(u) (516)	10,712	10,706
14513	Newark (315)	9,849	10,017
*12550	Newburgh (914)	26,454	23,438
11590	New Cassel(u) (516)	10,257	9,635
10956	New City(u) (914)	33,673	35,859
11040	New Hyde Park (516)	9,728	9,801
12561	New Paltz (914)	5,470	4,938
*10802	New Rochelle (914)	67,265	70,794
*12550	New Windsor Center(u) (914)	8,898	7,812
*10001	New York (212)/(718)	7,322,564	7,071,639
*14302	Niagara Falls (716)	61,840	71,384
11701	North Amityville(u) (516)	13,849	13,140
11703	North Babylon(u) (516)	18,081	19,019
11706	North Bay Shore(u) (516)	12,799	35,020
11710	North Bellmore(u) (516)	19,707	20,630
11713	North Bellport(u) (516)	8,182	7,432
11757	North Lindenhurst(u) (516)	10,563	11,511
11758	North Massapequa(u) (516)	19,365	21,385
11566	North Merrick(u) (516)	12,113	12,848
11040	North New Hyde Park(u) (516)	14,359	15,114
11772	North Patchogue(u) (516)	7,374	7,126
11768	Northport (516)	7,572	7,651
13212	North Syracuse (315)	7,363	7,970
10591	North Tarrytown (914)	8,152	7,994
14120	North Tonawanda (716)	34,989	35,760
11580	North Valley Stream(u) (516)	14,574	14,530
11793	North Wantagh(u) (516)	12,276	12,677
13815	Norwich (607)	7,613	8,082
10960	Nyack (914)	6,558	6,428
11769	Oakdale(u) (516)	7,875	8,090
11572	Oceanside(u) (516)	32,423	33,639
13669	Ogdensburg (315)	13,521	12,375
11804	Old Bethpage(u) (516)	5,610	6,215
14760	Olean (716)	16,946	18,207
13421	Oneida (315)	10,850	10,810
13820	Oneonta (607)	13,954	14,933
12550	Orange Lake(u) (914)	5,196	5,120
10562	Ossining (914)	22,582	20,196
13126	Oswego (315)	19,195	19,793
11771	Oyster Bay(u) (516)	6,687	6,497
11772	Patchogue (516)	11,060	11,291
10965	Pearl River(u) (914)	15,314	15,893
10566	Peekskill (914)	19,536	18,236
10803	Pelham (914)	6,413	6,848
10803	Pelham Manor (914)	5,443	6,130
14527	Penn Yan (315)	5,257	5,242
11714	Plainedge(u) (516)	8,739	9,629
11803	Plainview(u) (516)	26,207	28,037
12901	Plattsburgh (518)	21,255	21,057
12903	Plattsburgh AFB(u) (518)	5,483	5,905
10570	Pleasantville (914)	6,592	6,749
10573	Port Chester (914)	24,728	23,565
11777	Port Jefferson (516)	7,455	6,731
11776	Port Jefferson Station(u) (516)	7,232	17,009
12771	Port Jervis (914)	9,060	8,699
11050	Port Washington(u) (516)	15,387	14,521
13676	Potsdam (315)	10,251	10,635
*12601	Poughkeepsie (914)	28,844	29,757
12144	Rensselaer (518)	8,255	9,047
11961	Ridge(u) (516)	11,734	8,977
11901	Riverhead(u) (516)	8,814	6,339
*14692	Rochester (716)	230,356	241,741
*11571	Rockville Centre (516)	24,727	25,412
11778	Rocky Point(u) (516)	8,596	7,012
12205	Roessleville(u) (518)	10,753	11,685
13440	Rome (315)	44,350	43,826
11779	Ronkonkoma(u) (516)	20,391	....
11575	Roosevelt(u) (516)	15,030	14,109
11577	Roslyn Heights(u) (516)	6,405	6,546
12303	Rotterdam(u) (518)	21,228	22,933
10580	Rye (914)	14,936	15,083
10573	Rye Brook†	7,765	7,996
11780	Saint James(u) (516)	12,703	12,122
14779	Salamanca (716)	6,566	6,890
13454	Salisbury(u)	12,226	9,732
12983	Saranac Lake (518)	5,377	5,578
12866	Saratoga Springs (518)	25,001	23,906
11782	Sayville(u) (516)	16,550	12,013
10583	Scarsdale (914)	16,987	17,650
*12301	Schenectady (518)	65,566	67,972
10940	Scotchtown(u) (914)	8,765	7,352
12302	Scotia (518)	7,359	7,280
11579	Sea Cliff (516)	5,054	5,364
11783	Seaford(u) (516)	15,597	16,117
11507	Searingtown(u)	5,020	....
11784	Selden(u) (516)	20,608	17,259
13148	Seneca Falls (315)	7,370	7,466
11733	Setauket-East Setauket(u) (516)	13,634	10,176
11967	Shirley(u) (516)	22,936	18,072
11787	Smithtown(u) (516)	25,638	30,906
13209	Solvay (315)	6,717	7,140
11789	Sound Beach(u) (516)	9,102	8,071

ZIP code	Place		1990	1980
11735	South Farmingdale(u)	(516)	15,377	16,439
14850	South Hill(u)	(607)	5,423	5,276
11746	South Huntington(u)	(516)	9,624	14,854
14094	South Lockport(u)		7,112	3,366
11971	Southold(u)		5,192	4,770
14904	Southport(u)	(607)	7,753	8,329
11581	South Valley Stream(u)	(516)	5,328	5,462
10977	Spring Valley	(914)	21,802	20,537
11790	Stony Brook(u)	(516)	13,726	16,155
10980	Stony Point(u)	(315)	10,587	8,686
10901	Suffern	(914)	11,055	10,794
11791	Syosset(u)	(516)	18,967	9,818
*13220	Syracuse	(315)	163,860	170,105
10983	Tappan(u)	(914)	6,867	8,267
10591	Tarrytown	(914)	10,739	10,648
11776	Terryville		10,275	....
10984	Thiells		5,204	....
10594	Thornwood(u)	(914)	7,025	7,197
14150	Tonawanda	(716)	17,284	18,693
14151	Tonawanda(u)	(716)	65,284	72,795
*12180	Troy	(518)	54,269	56,638
10707	Tuckahoe	(914)	6,302	6,076
11553	Uniondale(u)	(516)	20,328	20,016
*13504	Utica	(315)	68,637	75,632
10989	Valley Cottage(u)	(914)	9,007	8,214
*11580	Valley Stream	(516)	33,946	35,769
11792	Wading River(u)	(516)	5,317	....
12586	Walden	(914)	5,836	5,659
11793	Wantagh(u)	(516)	18,567	19,817
10990	Warwick		5,984	4,320
13165	Waterloo	(315)	5,116	5,303
*13601	Watertown	(315)	29,429	27,861
12189	Watervliet	(518)	11,061	11,354
14580	Webster	(716)	5,464	5,499
14895	Wellsville	(716)	5,241	5,769
11704	West Babylon(u)	(516)	42,410	41,699
11590	Westbury	(516)	13,060	13,871
14905	West Elmira(u)	(607)	5,218	5,485
12801	West Glens Falls(u)	(518)	5,964	5,331
10993	West Haverstraw	(914)	9,183	9,181
11552	West Hempstead(u)	(516)	17,689	18,536
11743	West Hills(u)	(516)	5,849	6,071
11795	West Islip(u)	(516)	28,419	29,533
12203	Westmere(u)	(518)	6,750	6,881
10996	West Point(u)	(914)	8,024	8,105
14224	West Seneca(u)	(716)	47,866	51,210
13219	Westvale(u)	(315)	5,952	6,169
11798	Wheatley Heights(u)		5,027	....
*10602	White Plains	(914)	48,718	46,999
14221	Williamsville	(716)	5,583	6,017
11596	Williston Park	(516)	7,516	8,216
11797	Woodbury(u)	(516)	8,008	7,043
11598	Woodmere(u)	(516)	15,578	17,205
11792	Wyandach(u)	(516)	8,950	13,215
*10702	Yonkers	(914)	188,082	195,351
10598	Yorktown Heights(u)	(914)	7,690	7,696

North Carolina

ZIP code	Place		1990	1980
*28001	Albemarle	(704)	14,940	15,110
27263	Archdale	(919)	6,975	5,326
*27203	Asheboro	(910)	16,362	15,252
*28801	Asheville	(704)	61,855	54,022
28012	Belmont	(704)	8,434	4,607
28711	Black Mountain		5,533	4,083
28607	Boone	(704)	12,949	10,191
28712	Brevard	(704)	5,388	5,323
*27215	Burlington	(910)	39,498	37,266
28547	Camp Le Jeune(u)	(919)	36,716	30,764
27510	Carrboro	(919)	12,134	7,336
*27511	Cary	(919)	44,397	21,763
*27514	Chapel Hill	(919)	38,711	32,421
*28204	Charlotte	(704)	395,925	315,474
27012	Clemmons†	(919)	5,982	4,842
28328	Clinton	(910)	8,385	7,552
*28025	Concord	(704)	27,601	16,942
28613	Conover	(704)	5,311	4,245
*28334	Dunn	(910)	8,556	8,962
*27701	Durham	(919)	136,612	101,149
*27288	Eden	(910)	15,238	15,672
27932	Edenton	(919)	5,268	5,357
*27909	Elizabeth City	(919)	14,292	14,004
*28302	Fayetteville	(910)	75,850	59,507
28043	Forest City	(704)	7,475	7,688
28307	Fort Bragg(u)	(919)	34,744	37,834
27529	Garner	(919)	14,716	10,073
*28052	Gastonia	(704)	54,725	47,218
*27530	Goldsboro	(919)	40,709	31,871
27253	Graham	(919)	10,368	8,674
*27420	Greensboro	(919)	183,894	155,642
*27834	Greenville	(919)	46,305	35,740
.....	Half Moon(u)		6,306	3,592
28345	Hamlet	(919)	6,324	4,720
28532	Havelock	(919)	20,300	17,718
27536	Henderson	(919)	15,655	13,522
*28739	Hendersonville	(704)	7,284	6,862
28603	Hickory	(704)	28,474	20,757
*27260	High Point	(910)	69,428	63,479
28348	Hope Mills	(919)	8,272	5,412
*28540	Jacksonville	(910)	30,398	18,237
*28081	Kannapolis†	(704)	29,709	30,303
*27284	Kernersville	(910)	10,899	5,875
28086	Kings Mountain	(704)	8,768	9,080
*28501	Kinston	(919)	25,295	25,234
28352	Laurenburg	(919)	11,643	11,480
28645	Lenoir	(704)	14,223	13,748
*27292	Lexington	(704)	16,583	15,711
*28092	Lincolnton	(704)	6,955	4,879
*28358	Lumberton	(910)	18,656	18,241
.....	Masonboro(u)		7,010	3,729
*28105	Matthews	(704)	13,651	1,648
28212	Mint Hill	(704)	11,615	7,915
*28110	Monroe	(704)	16,385	12,639
28115	Mooresville	(704)	9,317	8,575
28557	Morehead	(919)	6,046	4,359
*28655	Morganton	(704)	15,085	13,763
27030	Mount Airy	(910)	7,156	6,862
28120	Mount Holly	(704)	7,710	4,530
*28562	New Bern	(919)	17,363	14,557
27604	New Hope (Wake)(u)	(704)	5,694	6,745
28540	New River Station(u)	(919)	9,732	5,401
28658	Newton	(704)	9,077	7,624
27565	Oxford	(919)	7,965	7,709
28374	Pinehurst†	(919)	5,091	1,746
28399	Piney Green(u)	(919)	8,999	6,058
*27611	Raleigh	(919)	212,092	150,255
*27320	Reidsville	(910)	12,183	12,492
27870	Roanoke Rapids	(919)	15,722	14,702
28379	Rockingham	(910)	9,399	8,300
*27801	Rocky Mount	(919)	49,438	41,526
27573	Roxboro	(910)	7,332	7,532
28601	Saint Stephens(u)	(704)	8,734	10,797
*28144	Salisbury	(704)	23,626	22,677
*27330	Sanford	(919)	14,755	14,773
.....	Seagate(u)		5,444	3,421
*28150	Shelby	(704)	14,669	15,310
.....	Smith Creek(u)		7,461	6,562
27577	Smithfield	(919)	7,540	7,288
*28387	Southern Pines	(910)	9,213	8,620
.....	South Gastonia(u)		5,487	4,767
28390	Spring Lake	(919)	7,552	6,273
*28677	Statesville	(704)	17,567	18,622
27886	Tarboro	(919)	11,037	8,741
*27360	Thomasville	(910)	15,915	14,144
27370	Trinity(u)	(919)	5,469	6,887
*27587	Wake Forest	(919)	5,832	3,780
27889	Washington	(919)	9,160	8,418
28786	Waynesville	(704)	6,760	6,765
28472	Whiteville	(910)	5,078	5,565
27892	Williamston	(919)	5,503	6,159
*28402	Wilmington	(910)	55,530	44,000
*27893	Wilson	(919)	36,930	34,424
*27102	Winston-Salem	(910)	143,532	131,885

North Dakota (701)

ZIP code	Place	1990	1980
*58501	Bismarck	49,272	44,485
58301	Devils Lake	7,782	7,442
*58601	Dickinson	16,097	15,924
*58102	Fargo	74,084	61,383
*58201	Grand Forks	49,417	43,765
58204	Grand Forks AFB(u)	9,343	9,390
*58401	Jamestown	15,571	16,280
58554	Mandan	15,177	15,513
*58701	Minot	34,544	32,843
*58704	Minot AFB(u)	9,095	9,880
58072	Valley City	7,163	7,774
*58075	Wahpeton	8,751	9,064
58078	West Fargo	12,287	10,099
*58801	Williston	13,136	13,336

Ohio

ZIP code	Place		1990	1980
45810	Ada	(419)	5,428	5,669
*44309	Akron	(216)	223,019	237,177
44601	Alliance	(216)	23,376	24,315
44001	Amherst	(216)	10,332	10,638
44805	Ashland	(419)	20,079	20,326
44004	Ashtabula	(216)	21,633	23,449
45701	Athens	(614)	21,265	19,743
44202	Aurora	(216)	9,192	8,177
44515	Austintown(u)	(216)	32,371	33,636
44011	Avon	(216)	7,337	7,241
44012	Avon Lake	(216)	15,066	13,222
44203	Barberton	(216)	27,623	29,751
44140	Bay Village	(216)	17,000	17,846
44122	Beachwood	(216)	10,644	9,983
45434	Beavercreek	(513)	33,626	31,589
44146	Bedford	(216)	14,822	15,056
44146	Bedford Heights	(216)	12,131	13,214
43906	Bellaire	(614)	6,028	8,241
45305	Bellbrook	(513)	6,511	5,174
43311	Bellefontaine	(513)	12,126	11,888
44811	Bellevue	(419)	8,157	8,187
45714	Belpre	(614)	6,796	7,193

ZIP code	Place		1990	1980
44017	Berea	(216)	19,051	19,567
43209	Bexley	(614)	13,088	13,405
43004	Blacklick Estates(u)	(614)	10,080	11,223
45242	Blue Ash	(513)	11,923	9,510
44513	Boardman(u)	(216)	38,596	39,086
43402	Bowling Green	(419)	28,303	25,728
44141	Brecksville	(216)	11,818	10,132
45211	Bridgetown North(u)	(513)	11,748	11,460
44147	Broadview Heights	(216)	12,219	10,920
44144	Brooklyn	(216)	11,706	12,342
44142	Brookpark	(216)	22,865	26,195
44212	Brunswick	(216)	28,218	28,104
43506	Bryan	(419)	8,348	7,879
44820	Bucyrus	(419)	13,496	13,433
43725	Cambridge	(614)	11,748	13,573
44405	Campbell	(216)	10,038	11,619
44406	Canfield	(216)	5,409	5,535
*44711	Canton	(216)	84,161	93,077
45822	Celina	(419)	9,923	9,137
45459	Centerville	(513)	21,082	18,886
45211	Cheviot	(513)	9,616	9,888
45601	Chillicothe	(614)	21,923	23,420
*45202	Cincinnati	(513)	364,114	385,409
43113	Circleville	(614)	11,666	11,700
*44101	Cleveland	(216)	505,616	573,822
44118	Cleveland Heights	(216)	54,052	56,438
43410	Clyde	(419)	5,776	5,489
*43216	Columbus	(614)	632,945	565,021
44030	Conneaut	(216)	13,241	13,835
44410	Cortland	(216)	5,652	5,011
43812	Coshocton	(614)	12,193	13,405
45238	Covedale(u)	(513)	6,669	5,830
*44222	Cuyahoga Falls	(216)	48,950	43,890
*45401	Dayton	(513)	182,005	193,536
45236	Deer Park	(513)	6,181	6,745
43512	Defiance	(419)	16,787	16,810
43015	Delaware	(614)	19,966	18,780
45833	Delphos	(419)	7,093	7,314
45247	Dent(u)		6,416	....
44622	Dover	(216)	11,329	11,782
45427	Drexel(u)		5,143	....
.....	Dry Run(u)		5,389	....
43016	Dublin	(614)	16,366	3,855
44112	East Cleveland	(216)	33,096	36,957
44094	Eastlake	(216)	21,161	22,104
43920	East Liverpool	(216)	13,654	16,687
44413	East Palestine	(216)	5,168	5,306
45320	Eaton	(513)	7,396	6,839
44004	Edgewood(u)		5,189	3,099
*44035	Elyria	(216)	56,746	57,538
45322	Englewood	(513)	11,402	11,329
44117	Euclid	(216)	54,875	59,999
45324	Fairborn	(513)	31,300	29,702
45014	Fairfield	(513)	39,709	30,777
44313	Fairlawn	(216)	5,779	6,100
44126	Fairview Park	(216)	18,028	19,311
45839	Findlay	(419)	35,703	35,594
45224	Finneytown(u)		13,096	....
45405	Forest Park	(513)	18,621	18,566
45230	Forestville(u)		9,185	....
45426	Fort McKinley(u)	(513)	9,740	10,161
44830	Fostoria	(419)	14,971	15,743
45005	Franklin	(513)	11,026	10,711
43420	Fremont	(419)	17,619	17,834
43230	Gahanna	(614)	23,898	18,001
44833	Galion	(419)	11,859	12,391
44125	Garfield Heights	(216)	31,739	34,938
44041	Geneva	(216)	6,597	6,655
44420	Girard	(216)	11,304	12,517
43212	Grandview Heights	(614)	7,010	7,420
45123	Greenfield	(513)	5,172	5,150
45331	Greenville	(513)	12,863	12,999
45239	Groesbeck(u)	(513)	6,684	9,594
43123	Grove City	(614)	19,661	16,816
*45011	Hamilton	(513)	61,436	63,189
45030	Harrison	(513)	7,520	5,855
43056	Heath	(614)	7,231	6,969
44124	Highland Heights	(216)	6,249	5,739
43026	Hilliard	(614)	11,794	8,131
45133	Hillsboro	(513)	6,235	6,356
44484	Howland Center(u)	(216)	6,732	7,441
44425	Hubbard	(216)	8,248	9,245
45424	Huber Heights	(513)	38,696	35,480
43081	Huber Ridge(u)	(614)	5,255	5,835
44236	Hudson	(216)	5,159	4,615
44839	Huron	(419)	7,067	7,123
44131	Independence	(216)	6,500	6,607
45638	Ironton	(614)	12,751	14,290
45640	Jackson	(614)	6,167	6,675
44240	Kent	(216)	28,835	26,164
43326	Kenton	(419)	8,356	8,605
43606	Kenwood(u)	(513)	7,469	9,943
45429	Kettering	(513)	60,569	61,186
44094	Kirtland	(216)	5,881	5,969
44107	Lakewood	(216)	59,718	61,963
43130	Lancaster	(614)	34,507	34,953
45039	Landen(u)		9,263	2,870
45036	Lebanon	(513)	10,461	9,636
*45802	Lima	(419)	45,553	47,827
43228	Lincoln Village(u)	(614)	9,958	10,548
43138	Logan	(614)	6,725	6,557
43140	London	(614)	7,807	6,958
*44052	Lorain	(216)	71,245	75,416
44641	Louisville	(216)	8,087	7,996
45140	Loveland	(513)	10,122	9,106
44124	Lyndhurst	(216)	15,982	18,092
44056	Macedonia	(216)	7,509	6,571
.....	Mack South(u)		5,767	....
45243	Madeira	(513)	9,141	9,341
*44901	Mansfield	(419)	50,627	53,927
44137	Maple Heights	(216)	27,089	29,735
45750	Marietta	(614)	15,026	16,467
*43302	Marion	(614)	34,075	37,040
43935	Martins Ferry	(614)	8,003	9,331
43040	Marysville	(513)	9,656	7,414
45040	Mason	(513)	11,450	8,692
*44646	Massillon	(216)	30,969	30,557
43537	Maumee	(419)	15,561	15,747
44124	Mayfield Heights	(216)	19,847	21,550
44256	Medina	(216)	19,231	15,268
*44060	Mentor	(216)	47,491	42,065
44060	Mentor-on-the-Lake	(216)	8,271	7,919
*45342	Miamisburg	(513)	17,834	15,304
44130	Middleburg Heights	(216)	14,702	16,218
*45042	Middletown	(513)	46,022	43,719
45150	Milford	(513)	5,660	5,232
45242	Montgomery	(513)	9,733	10,084
45439	Moraine	(513)	5,989	5,325
45231	Mount Healthy	(513)	7,580	7,562
43050	Mount Vernon	(614)	14,550	14,323
44262	Munroe Falls	(216)	5,359	4,731
43545	Napoleon	(419)	8,884	8,614
*43055	Newark	(614)	44,396	41,200
45344	New Carlisle	(513)	6,049	6,498
43764	New Lexington	(614)	5,117	5,179
44663	New Philadelphia	(216)	15,698	16,883
44446	Niles	(216)	21,128	23,088
45239	Northbrook(u)	(513)	11,471	8,357
44720	North Canton	(216)	14,904	14,228
45239	North College Hill	(513)	11,002	11,114
.....	Northgate(u)		7,864	....
44057	North Madison(u)	(216)	8,699	8,741
44070	North Olmsted	(216)	34,204	36,486
45502	Northridge(u)	(513)	5,939	5,559
45414	Northridge(u)	(513)	9,448	9,720
44039	North Ridgeville	(216)	21,564	21,522
44133	North Royalton	(216)	23,197	17,671
.....	Northview(u)	(513)	10,337	9,973
43619	Northwood	(419)	5,506	5,495
44203	Norton	(216)	11,477	12,242
44857	Norwalk	(419)	14,731	14,358
45212	Norwood	(513)	23,674	26,342
45873	Oakwood	(419)	8,957	9,372
44074	Oberlin	(216)	8,191	8,660
44138	Olmsted Falls	(216)	6,741	5,868
43616	Oregon	(419)	18,334	18,675
44667	Orrville	(216)	7,712	7,511
45431	Overlook-Page Manor(u)	(513)	13,242	14,825
45056	Oxford	(513)	18,937	17,655
44077	Painesville	(216)	15,769	16,391
44129	Parma	(216)	87,876	92,548
44130	Parma Heights	(216)	21,448	23,112
44124	Pepper Pike	(216)	6,185	6,177
44646	Perry Heights(u)	(216)	9,055	9,206
*43551	Perrysburg	(419)	12,551	10,215
43147	Pickerington		5,668	3,917
45356	Piqua	(513)	20,612	20,480
44319	Portage Lakes(u)	(216)	13,373	11,310
43452	Port Clinton	(419)	7,106	7,223
45662	Portsmouth	(614)	22,676	25,943
44266	Ravenna	(216)	12,069	11,987
45215	Reading	(513)	12,038	12,843
43068	Reynoldsburg	(614)	25,748	20,661
44143	Richmond Heights	(216)	9,611	10,095
44270	Rittman	(216)	6,147	6,063
44116	Rocky River	(216)	20,410	21,084
43460	Rossford	(419)	5,861	5,978
45217	Saint Bernard	(513)	5,344	5,396
43950	Saint Clairsville	(614)	5,136	5,452
45885	Saint Marys	(419)	8,441	8,414
44460	Salem	(216)	12,233	12,869
*44870	Sandusky	(419)	29,764	31,360
44870	Sandusky South(u)	(419)	6,336	6,548
44131	Seven Hills	(216)	12,339	13,650
44120	Shaker Heights	(216)	30,867	32,487
45241	Sharonville	(513)	13,121	10,108
44054	Sheffield Lake	(216)	9,825	10,484
44875	Shelby	(419)	9,610	9,703
44878	Shiloh(u)	(419)	11,607	11,735
45365	Sidney	(513)	18,710	17,657
45236	Silverton	(513)	5,859	6,172
44139	Solon	(216)	18,548	14,341
44121	South Euclid	(216)	23,866	25,713
45066	Springboro	(513)	6,574	4,962
45246	Springdale	(216)	10,621	10,111

ZIP code	Place		1990	1980
*45501	Springfield	(513)	70,487	72,563
43952	Steubenville	(614)	22,125	26,400
44224	Stow	(216)	27,998	25,303
44241	Streetsboro	(216)	9,932	9,055
44136	Strongsville	(216)	35,308	28,577
44471	Struthers	(216)	12,284	13,624
43560	Sylvania	(419)	17,489	15,527
44278	Tallmadge	(216)	14,870	15,269
45243	The Village of Indian Hill	(513)	5,383	5,521
44883	Tiffin	(419)	18,604	19,549
45371	Tipp City	(513)	6,027	5,595
*43601	Toledo	(419)	332,943	354,635
43964	Toronto	(614)	6,127	6,934
45067	Trenton	(513)	6,189	6,401
45426	Trotwood	(513)	8,816	7,802
45373	Troy	(513)	19,478	19,086
44087	Twinsburg	(216)	9,606	7,632
44683	Uhrichsville	(614)	5,604	6,130
45322	Union	(513)	5,531	5,219
44118	University Heights	(216)	14,787	15,401
43221	Upper Arlington	(614)	34,128	35,648
43351	Upper Sandusky	(419)	5,906	5,967
43078	Urbana	(513)	11,353	10,762
45377	Vandalia	(513)	13,872	13,161
45891	Van Wert	(419)	10,922	11,035
44089	Vermilion	(216)	11,127	11,012
44281	Wadsworth	(216)	15,718	15,166
45895	Wapakoneta	(419)	9,214	8,402
*44481	Warren	(216)	50,793	56,629
44122	Warrensville Heights	(216)	15,745	16,565
43160	Washington C.H.	(614)	13,080	12,682
43567	Wauseon	(419)	6,322	6,173
45692	Wellston	(614)	6,049	6,016
45449	West Carrollton City	(513)	14,403	13,148
43081	Westerville	(614)	30,269	23,414
44145	Westlake	(216)	27,018	19,483
45694	Wheelersburg(u)		5,113	4,796
43213	Whitehall	(614)	20,572	21,299
45239	White Oak(u)	(513)	12,430	9,563
44092	Wickliffe	(216)	14,558	16,790
44890	Willard	(419)	6,210	5,720
*44094	Willoughby	(216)	20,510	19,329
44094	Willoughby Hills	(216)	8,427	8,612
44095	Willowick	(216)	15,269	17,834
45177	Wilmington	(513)	11,199	10,431
45459	Woodbourne-Hyde Park(u)	(513)	7,837	8,826
44691	Wooster	(216)	22,427	19,289
43085	Worthington	(614)	14,869	15,016
45433	Wright-Patterson AFB(u)	(513)	8,579	9,155
45215	Wyoming	(513)	8,128	8,282
45385	Xenia	(513)	24,836	24,653
*44501	Youngstown	(216)	95,732	115,511
43701	Zanesville	(614)	26,778	28,655

Oklahoma

ZIP code	Place		1990	1980
*74820	Ada	(405)	15,765	15,902
*73521	Altus	(405)	21,910	23,101
73717	Alva	(405)	5,495	6,416
73005	Anadarko	(405)	6,586	6,378
*73401	Ardmore	(405)	23,079	23,689
*74003	Bartlesville	(918)	34,256	34,568
73008	Bethany	(405)	20,075	22,038
74008	Bixby	(918)	9,502	6,969
74631	Blackwell	(405)	7,538	8,400
*74012	Broken Arrow	(918)	58,082	35,761
73018	Chickasha	(405)	14,988	15,828
*73020	Choctaw	(405)	8,545	7,520
*74017	Claremore	(918)	13,280	12,085
73601	Clinton	(405)	9,298	8,796
74429	Coweta		6,159	4,554
74023	Cushing	(918)	7,218	7,720
73115	Del City	(405)	23,928	28,523
*73533	Duncan	(405)	21,732	22,517
*74701	Durant	(405)	12,929	11,972
*73034	Edmond	(405)	52,310	34,637
*73644	Elk City	(405)	10,428	9,579
73036	El Reno	(405)	15,414	15,486
*73701	Enid	(405)	45,309	50,363
73503	Fort Sill(u)	(405)	12,107	15,924
73542	Frederick	(405)	5,221	6,153
74033	Glenpool	(918)	6,688	2,706
73044	Guthrie	(405)	10,440	10,312
73942	Guymon	(405)	7,803	8,492
74437	Henryetta	(918)	5,872	6,432
74743	Hugo	(405)	5,978	7,172
74745	Idabel	(405)	6,957	7,622
74037	Jenks	(918)	7,484	5,876
*73501	Lawton	(405)	80,561	80,054
*74501	McAlester	(918)	16,370	17,255
*74354	Miami	(918)	13,142	14,237
73140	Midwest City	(405)	52,267	49,559
73153	Moore	(405)	40,318	35,063
*74401	Muskogee	(918)	37,708	40,011
73064	Mustang	(405)	10,434	7,496
*73069	Norman	(405)	80,071	68,020
*73125	Oklahoma City	(405)	444,724	404,014
74447	Okmulgee	(918)	13,441	16,263
74055	Owasso	(918)	11,151	6,149
73075	Pauls Valley	(405)	6,150	5,664
74601	Ponca City	(405)	26,359	26,238
74953	Poteau	(918)	7,210	7,089
74361	Pryor Creek	(918)	8,327	8,483
74955	Sallisaw	(918)	7,122	6,403
74063	Sand Springs	(918)	15,339	13,121
*74066	Sapulpa	(918)	18,074	15,853
*74868	Seminole	(405)	7,071	8,590
*74801	Shawnee	(405)	26,017	26,506
*74074	Stillwater	(405)	36,676	38,268
*74464	Tahlequah	(918)	10,586	9,708
74873	Tecumseh	(405)	5,570	5,123
*74103	Tulsa	(918)	367,302	360,919
73156	The Village	(405)	10,353	11,114
74301	Vinita	(918)	5,804	6,740
*74467	Wagoner	(918)	6,894	6,191
73132	Warr Acres	(405)	9,288	9,940
73096	Weatherford	(405)	10,124	9,640
*73801	Woodward	(405)	12,340	13,781
*73099	Yukon	(405)	20,935	17,112

Oregon (503)

ZIP code	Place	1990	1980
97321	Albany	29,540	26,511
97006	Aloha(u)	34,284	28,353
97601	Altamont(u)	18,591	19,805
97520	Ashland	16,252	14,943
97103	Astoria	10,069	9,998
97814	Baker City	9,140	9,471
*97005	Beaverton	53,307	31,962
*97701	Bend	20,447	17,263
97013	Canby	8,990	7,659
97225	Cedar Hills(u)	9,294	9,619
97291	Cedar Mill(u)†	9,697	22,118
97502	Central Point	7,512	6,357
97058	City of the Dalles	11,021	10,820
97420	Coos Bay	15,076	14,424
97113	Cornelius	6,148	4,462
*97333	Corvallis	44,757	40,960
97424	Cottage Grove	7,403	7,148
97338	Dallas	9,422	8,530
*97401	Eugene	112,773	105,664
97439	Florence	5,171	4,411
97116	Forest Grove	13,559	11,499
97301	Four Corners(u)	12,156	11,316
97223	Garden Home-Whitford(u)	6,652	6,911
97027	Gladstone	10,152	9,500
*97526	Grants Pass	17,503	15,032
.....	Green(u)	5,076	3,897
97030	Gresham	68,249	33,005
97303	Hayesville(u)	14,318	9,413
97230	Hazelwood(u)	11,480	25,541
97838	Hermiston	10,047	9,408
97123	Hillsboro	37,598	27,664
.....	Jennings Lodge(u)	6,530	....
97303	Keizer†	21,884	19,785
*97601	Klamath Falls	17,737	16,661
97850	La Grande	11,766	11,354
*97034	Lake Oswego	30,576	22,527
97355	Lebanon	10,950	10,413
97367	Lincoln City	5,903	5,469
97128	McMinnville	17,894	14,080
*97501	Medford	47,021	39,746
97862	Milton-Freewater	5,533	5,086
97222	Milwaukie	18,670	17,931
97361	Monmouth	6,288	5,594
97132	Newberg	13,086	10,394
97365	Newport	8,437	7,519
97459	North Bend	9,614	9,779
.....	North Springfield(u)	5,451	6,140
97268	Oak Grove(u)	12,576	11,640
.....	Oak Hills(u)	6,450	....
.....	Oatfield(u)	15,348	....
97914	Ontario	9,394	8,814
97045	Oregon City	14,698	14,673
97801	Pendleton	15,142	14,521
*97208	Portland	438,802	368,148
97236	Powellhurst-Centennial(u)	28,756	20,122
97754	Prineville	5,355	5,276
97225	Raleigh Hills(u)	6,066	6,517
97756	Redmond	7,165	6,452
97404	River Road(u)	9,443	10,370
.....	Rockcreek(u)	8,282	....
97470	Roseburg	17,069	16,644
97470	Roseburg North(u)	6,831	....
97051	Saint Helens	7,535	7,064
*97301	Salem	107,793	89,091
97401	Santa Clara(u)	12,834	14,288
97138	Seaside	5,359	5,193
97381	Silverton	5,635	5,168
*97477	Springfield	44,664	41,621
97383	Stayton	5,011	4,396
97479	Sutherlin	5,020	4,560

ZIP code	Place		1990	1980
97386	Sweet Home		6,850	6,921
97223	Tigard		29,435	14,799
97060	Troutdale		7,852	5,908
97062	Tualatin		14,664	7,483
.....	West Haven-Sylvan(u)		6,009	....
97068	West Linn		16,389	11,358
97225	West Slope(u)		7,959	5,364
97503	White City(u)		5,891	5,445
97070	Wilsonville		7,106	2,920
97071	Woodburn		13,404	11,196

Pennsylvania

Communities with area codes marked with a double dagger (‡) are split between area codes (215) and (610); consult local operators. Please also see note on page 387.

ZIP code	Place	Area code	1990	1980
15001	Aliquippa	(412)	13,374	17,094
*18105	Allentown	(610)	105,301	103,758
*16603	Altoona	(814)	51,881	57,078
19002	Ambler	(215)‡	6,609	6,628
15003	Ambridge	(412)	8,133	9,575
18403	Archbald	(717)	6,291	6,295
19003	Ardmore(u)	(610)	12,646	....
15068	Arnold	(412)	6,113	6,853
19407	Audubon(u)†		6,328	6,853
15202	Avalon	(412)	5,784	6,240
15005	Baden	(412)	5,074	5,318
15234	Baldwin	(412)	21,923	24,714
18013	Bangor	(610)	5,383	5,006
15009	Beaver	(412)	5,028	5,441
15010	Beaver Falls	(412)	10,687	12,525
16823	Bellefonte	(814)	6,358	6,300
15202	Bellevue	(412)	9,126	10,128
18603	Berwick	(717)	10,976	11,850
15102	Bethel Park	(412)	33,823	34,755
*18016	Bethlehem	(610)	71,427	70,419
18447	Blakely	(717)	7,222	7,438
17815	Bloomsburg	(717)	12,439	11,717
19422	Blue Bell(u)		6,091	....
19061	Boothwyn(u)		5,069	....
16701	Bradford	(814)	9,625	11,211
15227	Brentwood	(412)	10,823	11,859
15017	Bridgeville	(412)	5,445	6,154
19007	Bristol	(215)	10,405	10,867
19015	Brookhaven	(610)	8,567	7,912
19008	Broomall(u)	(610)	10,930	....
*16001	Butler	(412)	15,714	17,026
15419	California	(412)	5,748	5,703
*17011	Camp Hill	(717)	7,831	8,422
15317	Canonsburg	(412)	9,200	10,459
18407	Carbondale	(717)	10,664	11,255
17013	Carlisle	(717)	18,419	18,314
15106	Carnegie	(412)	9,278	10,099
15108	Carnot-Moon(u)	(412)	10,187	11,102
15234	Castle Shannon	(412)	9,135	10,164
18032	Catasauqua	(610)	6,662	6,711
17201	Chambersburg	(717)	16,647	16,174
15022	Charleroi	(412)	5,014	5,717
*19013	Chester	(610)	41,856	45,794
19013	Chester Twp.(u)	(610)	5,399	5,687
15025	Clairton	(412)	9,656	12,188
16214	Clarion	(814)	6,457	6,198
18411	Clarks Summit	(717)	5,433	5,272
16830	Clearfield	(814)	6,633	7,580
19018	Clifton Heights	(610)	7,111	7,320
19320	Coatesville	(610)	11,038	10,698
19023	Collingdale	(610)	9,175	9,539
.....	Colonial Park(u)		13,777	....
17512	Columbia	(717)	10,701	10,466
15425	Connellsville	(412)	9,229	10,319
19428	Conshohocken	(215)‡	8,064	8,591
15108	Coraopolis	(412)	6,747	7,308
16407	Corry	(814)	7,216	7,149
15205	Crafton	(412)	7,188	7,623
19020	Croydon(u)	(215)	9,967	....
17821	Danville	(717)	5,165	5,239
19023	Darby	(610)	11,140	11,513
19036	Darby Twp.(u)	(610)	10,955	12,264
19333	Devon-Berwyn(u)	(610)	5,019	5,246
18519	Dickson City	(717)	6,276	6,699
15033	Donora	(412)	5,928	7,524
15216	Dormont	(412)	9,772	11,275
19335	Downingtown	(610)	7,749	7,650
18901	Doylestown	(215)	8,575	8,717
19026	Drexel Hill(u)	(610)	29,744	....
15801	Du Bois	(814)	8,286	9,290
18512	Dunmore	(717)	15,403	16,781
15110	Duquesne	(412)	8,525	10,094
19401	East Norriton(u)	(215)‡	13,324	12,711
*18042	Easton	(610)	26,276	26,027
18301	East Stroudsburg	(717)	8,781	8,039
17405	East York(u)	(717)	8,487	....
15005	Economy	(412)	9,305	9,538
16412	Edinboro	(814)	7,736	6,324
18704	Edwardsville	(717)	5,399	5,729
17022	Elizabethtown	(717)	9,952	8,233
16117	Ellwood City	(412)	8,894	9,998
18049	Emmaus	(610)	11,157	11,001
17025	Enola(u)		5,961	....
17522	Ephrata	(717)	12,133	11,095
*16501	Erie	(814)	108,718	119,123
18643	Exeter	(717)	5,691	5,493
19030	Fairless Hills(u)	(215)	9,026	....
16121	Farrell	(412)	6,835	8,645
19047	Feasterville-Trevose(u)	(215)	6,696	....
.....	Fernway(u)		9,072	3,843
19032	Folcroft	(610)	7,506	8,231
.....	Folsom(u)		8,173	....
15221	Forest Hills	(412)	8,173	8,198
18704	Forty Fort	(717)	5,049	5,590
15238	Fox Chapel	(412)	5,319	5,049
16323	Franklin	(814)	7,329	8,146
15143	Franklin Park	(412)	10,109	6,135
18052	Fullerton(u)	(610)	13,127	8,055
17325	Gettysburg	(717)	7,025	7,194
15045	Glassport	(412)	5,582	6,242
19036	Glenolden	(610)	7,260	7,633
19038	Glenside(u)	(215)	8,704	....
15601	Greensburg	(412)	16,318	17,558
16125	Greenville	(412)	6,734	7,730
16127	Grove City	(412)	8,240	8,162
.....	Hampton Twp.(u)		15,568	....
17331	Hanover	(717)	14,399	14,890
19438	Harleysville(u)	(215)‡	7,405	3,673
*17105	Harrisburg	(717)	52,376	53,264
15636	Harrison Twp.(u)		11,763	....
19040	Hatboro	(215)	7,382	7,579
18201	Hazleton	(717)	24,730	27,318
18055	Hellertown	(610)	5,662	6,025
16148	Hermitage†	(412)	15,260	16,365
17033	Hershey(u)	(717)	11,860	13,249
16648	Hollidaysburg	(814)	5,624	5, 892
16001	Homeacre-Lyndora(u)	(412)	7,511	8,333
19044	Horsham(u)	(215)	15,051	9,900
16652	Huntingdon	(814)	6,843	7,042
15701	Indiana	(412)	15,174	16,051
15644	Jeannette	(412)	11,221	13,106
15344	Jefferson	(412)	9,533	8,643
18229	Jim Thorpe	(717)	5,048	5,263
*15907	Johnstown	(814)	28,124	35,496
15108	Kennedy Twp.(u)	(412)	7,152	7,159
19348	Kennett Square	(610)	5,218	4,715
19406	King of Prussia(u)	(215)‡	18,406	....
18704	Kingston	(717)	14,507	15,681
16201	Kittanning	(412)	5,120	5,432
19443	Kulpsville(u)		5,183	....
*17604	Lancaster	(717)	55,551	54,725
19446	Lansdale	(215)	16,362	16,526
19050	Lansdowne	(610)	11,712	11,891
15650	Latrobe	(412)	9,265	10,799
17540	Leacock-Leola-Bareville(u)		5,685	....
17042	Lebanon	(717)	24,800	25,711
18235	Lehighton	(610)	5,914	5,826
19055	Levittown(u)	(215)	55,362	....
17837	Lewisburg	(717)	5,785	5,407
17044	Lewistown	(717)	9,341	9,830
17112	Linglestown(u)		5,862	....
19353	Lionville-Marchwood(u)	(610)	6,468	....
17543	Lititz	(717)	8,280	7,590
17745	Lock Haven	(717)	9,230	9,617
.....	Lower Allen(u)		6,329	....
15068	Lower Burrell	(412)	12,251	13,200
15237	McCandless Twp.(u)	(412)	28,781	26,191
*15134	McKeesport	(412)	26,016	31,012
15136	McKees Rocks	(412)	7,691	8,742
17948	Mahanoy City	(717)	5,209	6,167
17545	Manheim	(717)	5,011	5,015
19002	Maple Glen(u)		5,881	....
16335	Meadville	(814)	14,318	15,544
17055	Mechanicsburg	(717)	9,452	9,487
*19063	Media	(610)	5,957	6,119
17057	Middletown (Dauphin)	(717)	9,254	10,122
18017	Middletown (Northampton)(u)	(610)	6,866	5,801
17551	Millersville	(717)	8,099	7,668
17847	Milton	(717)	6,746	6,730
15061	Monaca	(412)	6,739	7,661
15062	Monessen	(412)	9,901	11,928
18936	Montgomeryville(u)	(215)	9,114	....
18507	Moosic	(717)	5,397	6,068
19067	Morrisville	(215)	9,765	9,845
17851	Mount Carmel	(717)	7,196	8,190
17552	Mount Joy	(717)	6,398	5,680
15228	Mount Lebanon(u)	(412)	33,362	34,414
15120	Munhall	(412)	13,158	14,535
15146	Municipality of Monroeville	(412)	29,169	30,977
15668	Municipality of Murrysville	(412)	17,240	16,036
18634	Nanticoke	(717)	12,267	13,044
18064	Nazareth	(610)	5,713	5,443
.....	Nether Providence Twp.(u)	(610)	13,229	12,730
15066	New Brighton	(412)	6,854	7,364
*16108	New Castle	(412)	28,334	33,621
17070	New Cumberland	(717)	7,665	8,051
15068	New Kensington	(412)	15,894	17,660
*19401	Norristown	(610)	30,754	34,684
18067	Northampton	(610)	8,717	8,240

ZIP code	Place	1990	1980
15104	North Braddock (412)	7,036	8,711
15137	North Versailles(u) (412)	12,302	13,294
16421	Northwest Harborcreek(u) (814)	6,662	7,485
19074	Norwood (610)	6,162	6,647
15139	Oakmont (412)	6,961	7,039
.....	O'Hara(u)	9,096	....
16301	Oil City (814)	11,949	13,881
18518	Old Forge (717)	8,834	9,304
18447	Olyphant (717)	5,222	5,204
19075	Oreland(u)	5,695	....
18071	Palmerton (610)	5,394	5,455
17078	Palmyra (717)	6,910	7,228
19301	Paoli(u) (610)	5,603	5,277
.....	Park Forest Village(u)	6,703	....
17331	Parkville(u) (717)	6,014	5,009
15235	Penn Hills(u) (717)	51,430	57,632
.....	Penn Wynne(u)	5,807	....
18944	Perkasie (215)	7,787	5,241
*19104	Philadelphia (215)	1,585,577	1,688,210
19460	Phoenixville (610)	15,066	14,165
*15233	Pittsburgh (412)	369,879	423,959
*18640	Pittston (717)	9,389	9,903
15236	Pleasant Hills (412)	8,884	9,604
15239	Plum (412)	25,609	25,309
18651	Plymouth (717)	7,134	7,605
19462	Plymouth Meeting(u) (215)‡	6,241	....
19464	Pottstown (610)	21,831	22,729
17901	Pottsville (717)	16,603	18,195
.....	Progress(u)	9,654	....
19076	Prospect Park (610)	6,764	6,593
15767	Punxsutawney (814)	6,782	7,479
18951	Quakertown (215)	8,982	8,867
19087	Radnor Twp.(u) (610)	28,705	27,676
*19612	Reading (610)	78,380	78,686
17356	Red Lion (717)	6,130	5,824
18954	Richboro(u) (215)	5,332	5,141
19078	Ridley Park (610)	7,592	7,889
15949	Robinson(u)	10,830	....
15237	Ross Twp.(u) (412)	33,482	35,102
15857	Saint Marys (814)	5,511	6,417
19464	Sanatoga(u)	5,534	3,723
18840	Sayre (717)	5,791	6,951
17972	Schuylkill Haven (717)	5,610	5,977
15683	Scottdale (412)	5,184	5,833
15106	Scott Twp.(u) (412)	17,118	20,413
*18505	Scranton (717)	81,805	88,117
17870	Selinsgrove (717)	5,384	5,227
15116	Shaler Twp.(u) (412)	30,533	33,694
17872	Shamokin (717)	9,184	10,357
16146	Sharon (412)	17,533	19,057
19079	Sharon Hill (610)	5,771	6,221
17976	Shenandoah (717)	6,221	7,589
19607	Shillington (610)	5,062	5,601
17404	Shiloh(u) (717)	8,245	5,315
17257	Shippensburg (717)	5,331	5,261
15501	Somerset (814)	6,454	6,474
18964	Souderton (215)	5,957	6,657
.....	South Park Twp.(u)	14,292	....
17701	South Williamsport (717)	6,496	6,581
19064	Springfield(u) (717)	24,160	25,326
16804	State College (814)	38,981	36,130
17113	Steelton (717)	5,152	6,484
15136	Stowe Twp.(u) (412)	7,681	9,202
18360	Stroudsburg (717)	5,312	5,148
16323	Sugar Creek (717)	5,532	5,954
17801	Sunbury (717)	11,591	12,292
19081	Swarthmore (610)	6,157	5,950
15218	Swissvale (412)	10,637	11,345
18704	Swoyersville (717)	5,630	5,795
18252	Tamaqua (717)	7,943	8,843
15084	Tarentum (412)	5,674	6,419
18517	Taylor (717)	6,941	7,246
16354	Titusville (814)	6,434	6,884
19401	Trooper(u) (610)	5,137	7,370
15145	Turtle Creek (412)	6,556	6,959
16686	Tyrone (814)	5,743	6,346
15401	Uniontown (412)	12,034	14,510
19063	Upper Providence Twp.(u) (610)	9,727	9,477
15241	Upper Saint Clair(u) (412)	19,692	19,023
15690	Vandergrift (412)	5,904	6,823
.....	Village Green-Green Ridge(u)	9,026	....
16365	Warren (814)	11,122	12,146
15301	Washington (412)	15,864	18,363
17268	Waynesboro (717)	9,578	9,726
.....	Weigelstown(u) (717)	8,665	5,213
*19380	West Chester (610)	18,041	17,435
19380	West Goshen(u) (610)	8,948	7,998
15122	West Mifflin (412)	23,644	26,322
15905	Westmont (814)	5,789	6,113
19401	West Norriton(u) (610)	15,209	14,034
18643	West Pittston (717)	5,590	5,980
15229	West View (412)	7,734	7,648
18052	Whitehall (610)	14,451	15,143
15131	White Oak (717)	8,761	9,480
*18703	Wilkes-Barre (717)	47,523	51,551
15221	Wilkinsburg (412)	21,080	23,669
15145	Wilkins Twp.(u) (412)	7,487	8,472
17701	Williamsport (717)	31,933	33,401
19090	Willow Grove(u) (610)	16,325	....
17584	Willow Street(u)	5,817	....
15025	Wilson (412)	7,830	7,564
19094	Woodlyn(u) (610)	10,151	....
19118	Wyndmoor(u) (215)	5,682	....
19610	Wyomissing (610)	7,332	6,551
19050	Yeadon (610)	11,980	11,727
*17405	York (717)	42,192	44,619

Rhode Island (401)

See note on page 387

ZIP code	Place	1990	1980
02806	Barrington(u)	15,849	16,174
02809	Bristol(u)	21,625	20,128
02830	*Burrillville*	16,230	13,164
02863	Central Falls	17,638	16,995
02813	*Charlestown*	6,478	4,800
02816	*Coventry*	31,083	27,065
02910	Cranston	76,060	71,992
02864	*Cumberland*	29,038	27,069
02864	Cumberland Hill(u)	6,379	5,421
02818	*East Greenwich*	11,865	10,211
02914	East Providence	50,380	50,980
02822	*Exeter*	5,461	4,453
02814	*Glocester*	9,227	7,550
02828	Greenville(u)	8,303	7,576
02833	*Hopkinton*	6,873	6,406
02919	*Johnston*	26,542	24,907
02881	Kingston(u)	6,504	5,479
02865	*Lincoln*	18,045	16,949
02840	*Middletown*	19,460	17,216
02882	*Narragansett*	15,004	12,088
02840	Newport	28,227	29,259
02843	Newport East(u)	11,080	11,030
02852	*North Kingstown*	23,786	21,938
02908	North Providence(u)	32,090	29,188
02876	*North Smithfield*	10,497	9,972
02859	Pascoag(u)	5,011	3,807
*02860	Pawtucket	72,644	71,204
02871	*Portsmouth*	16,857	14,257
*02904	Providence	160,728	156,804
.....	Richmond	5,351	4,018
02857	*Scituate*	9,796	8,405
02917	*Smithfield*	19,163	16,886
02879	*South Kingstown*	24,631	20,414
.....	Tiverton(u)	7,259	7,653
02878	*Tiverton*	14,312	13,526
02864	Valley Falls(u)	11,175	10,892
*02880	Wakefield-Peacedale(u)	7,134	6,474
02885	*Warren*	11,385	10,640
*02887	Warwick	85,427	87,123
02891	*Westerly*	21,605	18,580
02891	Westerly Center(u)	16,477	14,093
02893	West Warwick (u)	29,268	27,026
02895	Woonsocket	43,877	45,914

South Carolina (803)

ZIP code	Place	1990	1980
29620	Abbeville	5,778	5,833
*29801	Aiken	20,386	14,978
*29621	Anderson	26,385	27,546
29812	Barnwell	5,255	5,572
*29902	Beaufort	9,576	8,634
29841	Belvedere(u)	6,133	6,859
29512	Bennettsville	10,095	8,774
29611	Berea(u)	13,535	13,164
.....	Brookdale(u)	5,339	6,123
29902	Burton(u)	6,917	3,619
29020	Camden	6,696	7,462
29033	Cayce	10,824	11,701
*29402	Charleston	79,925	69,779
29520	Cheraw	5,553	5,654
29706	Chester	7,158	6,820
*29631	Clemson	11,145	8,118
29325	Clinton	9,603	8,596
*29201	Columbia	103,477	101,229
*29526	Conway	9,819	10,240
29532	Darlington	7,310	7,989
29204	Dentsville(u)	11,839	13,579
29536	Dillon	6,829	7,060
*29640	Easley	15,179	14,264
*29501	Florence	29,913	29,842
29206	Forest Acres	7,181	6,062
*29341	Gaffney	13,149	13,453
29605	Gantt(u)	13,891	13,719
.....	Garden City(u)	6,305	....
*29440	Georgetown	9,517	10,144
29445	Goose Creek	24,692	17,811
*29602	Greenville	58,256	58,242
*29646	Greenwood	20,807	21,613
*29650	Greer	10,322	10,525
29410	Hanahan	13,176	13,224
*29550	Hartsville	8,372	7,631
*29928	Hilton Head Island†	23,694	11,239
29621	Homeland Park(u)	6,569	6,720
29063	Irmo	11,277	3,957
29456	Ladson(u)	13,540	13,246
29560	Lake City	7,153	6,731
*29720	Lancaster	8,914	9,703

ZIP code	Place	1990	1980
29360	Laurens	9,694	10,587
29571	Marion	7,658	7,700
29662	Mauldin	11,662	8,143
29461	Moncks Corner	5,599	4,179
*29464	Mount Pleasant	30,108	14,464
29574	Mullins	5,910	6,068
*29577	Myrtle Beach	24,848	18,446
29108	Newberry	10,543	9,866
29841	North Augusta	15,684	13,593
29410	North Charleston	70,304	62,479
*29582	North Myrtle Beach	8,731	3,960
29565	Oak Grove(u)	7,173	7,092
29115	Orangeburg	13,772	14,933
.....	Parker(u)	11,072	....
29905	Parris Island(u)	7,172	7,752
.....	Red Bank(u)	5,950	....
.....	Red Hill(u)	6,112	....
*29730	Rock Hill	41,610	35,327
29417	Saint Andrews(u)	25,692	20,245
29609	Sans Souci(u)	7,612	8,393
*29678	Seneca	7,726	7,436
.....	Seven Oaks(u)	15,722	16,604
29681	Simpsonville	11,744	9,037
29577	Socastee(u)	10,426	1,082
*29306	Spartanburg	43,479	43,826
*29483	Summerville	22,519	6,492
*29150	Sumter	40,977	24,921
29687	Taylors(u)	19,619	15,801
29379	Union	9,840	10,523
29607	Wade Hampton(u)	20,014	20,180
29488	Walterboro	5,595	6,209
29611	Welcome(u)	6,560	6,922
*29169	West Columbia	10,944	10,409
29206	Woodfield(u)	8,862	9,588
29745	York	6,709	6,412

South Dakota (605)

ZIP code	Place	1990	1980
*57401	Aberdeen	24,995	25,851
57006	Brookings	16,270	14,951
57706	Ellsworth AFB(u)	7,017	4,766
57350	Huron	12,448	13,000
57042	Madison	6,257	6,210
57301	Mitchell	13,798	13,916
57501	Pierre	12,906	11,973
*57701	Rapid City	54,523	46,492
.....	Rapid Valley(u)	5,968	3,265
*57101	Sioux Falls	100,836	81,343
57783	Spearfish Canyon	6,966	5,251
57785	Sturgis	5,330	5,184
57069	Vermillion	10,034	10,136
57201	Watertown	17,632	15,649
57078	Yankton	12,703	12,011

Tennessee

ZIP code	Place	Area code	1990	1980
37701	Alcoa	(615)	6,400	6,870
*37303	Athens	(615)	12,054	12,080
38134	Bartlett	(901)	26,989	17,170
37660	Bloomingdale(u)	(615)	10,953	12,088
38008	Bolivar	(901)	5,969	6,597
*37027	Brentwood	(615)	16,392	9,431
*37621	Bristol	(615)	23,421	23,986
38012	Brownsville	(901)	10,017	9,307
*37401	Chattanooga	(615)	152,393	169,514
*37040	Clarksville	(615)	75,542	54,777
*37311	Cleveland	(615)	30,354	26,415
*37716	Clinton	(615)	8,960	5,245
37315	Collegedale	(615)	5,048	4,607
*38017	Collierville	(901)	14,501	7,839
37663	Colonial Heights(u)	(615)	6,716	6,744
*38401	Columbia	(615)	28,583	26,571
*38501	Cookeville	(615)	21,744	20,535
38019	Covington	(901)	7,487	6,065
*38555	Crossville	(615)	6,930	6,394
37321	Dayton	(615)	5,671	5,233
37055	Dickson	(615)	8,783	7,040
*38024	Dyersburg	(901)	16,321	15,856
37801	Eagleton Village(u)	(615)	5,169	5,331
37411	East Brainerd(u)		11,594	....
37412	East Ridge	(615)	21,101	21,236
*37643	Elizabethton	(615)	11,931	12,431
37650	Erwin	(615)	5,017	4,739
37922	Farragut†	(615)	12,802	5,992
37334	Fayetteville	(615)	7,158	7,559
*37064	Franklin	(615)	20,098	12,407
37066	Gallatin	(615)	18,794	17,191
38138	Germantown	(901)	33,016	21,467
*37072	Goodlettsville	(615)	11,219	8,327
*37743	Greeneville	(615)	13,532	14,097
37215	Green Hills(u)		6,763	....
38040	Halls(u)	(901)	6,450	10,363
37748	Harriman	(615)	7,119	8,303
37341	Harrison(u)	(615)	7,191	6,206
*37075	Hendersonville	(615)	32,188	26,561
38343	Humboldt	(901)	9,651	10,209
*38301	Jackson	(901)	49,145	49,258
37760	Jefferson City	(615)	5,522	5,612
*37601	Johnson City	(615)	49,479	39,753
*37662	Kingsport	(615)	36,353	32,027
*37950	Knoxville	(615)	165,039	175,045
37766	La Follette	(615)	7,201	8,198
37086	LaVergne	(615)	7,499	5,495
38464	Lawrenceburg	(615)	10,397	10,184
*37087	Lebanon	(615)	15,208	11,872
37771	Lenoir City	(615)	6,147	5,180
37091	Lewisburg	(615)	9,879	8,760
38351	Lexington	(901)	5,810	5,934
38201	McKenzie	(901)	5,168	5,405
37110	McMinnville	(615)	11,194	10,683
37355	Manchester	(615)	7,709	7,250
38237	Martin	(901)	8,588	8,898
*37804	Maryville	(615)	19,208	17,480
*38101	Memphis	(901)	610,337	646,174
37343	Middle Valley(u)	(615)	12,255	11,420
38358	Milan	(901)	7,512	8,083
*38053	Millington	(901)	17,866	20,236
*37813	Morristown	(615)	21,316	19,570
37122	Mount Juliet		5,389	2,879
*37130	Murfreesboro	(615)	44,922	32,845
*37202	Nashville	(615)	488,374	455,651
37821	Newport	(615)	7,123	7,580
*37830	Oak Ridge	(615)	27,310	27,662
38242	Paris	(901)	9,332	10,728
37148	Portland	(615)	5,165	4,030
37849	Powell(u)	(615)	7,534	7,220
38478	Pulaski	(615)	7,916	7,184
37415	Red Bank	(615)	12,320	13,129
38063	Ripley	(901)	6,188	6,366
37854	Rockwood	(615)	5,348	5,687
38372	Savannah	(901)	6,547	6,992
*37862	Sevierville	(615)	7,178	4,556
37865	Seymour(u)		7,026	....
37160	Shelbyville	(615)	14,042	13,530
37377	Signal Mountain	(615)	7,034	5,818
37167	Smyrna	(615)	13,647	8,839
37379	Soddy-Daisy	(615)	8,240	8,388
.....	South Cleveland(u)		5,372	4,360
37172	Springfield	(615)	11,227	10,814
37874	Sweetwater	(615)	5,066	4,725
37388	Tullahoma	(615)	16,761	15,800
38261	Union City	(901)	10,513	10,436
37398	Winchester	(615)	6,305	5,821

Texas

ZIP code	Place	Area code	1990	1980
*79604	Abilene	(915)	106,707	98,315
75001	Addison	(214)	8,783	5,553
78516	Alamo	(210)	8,352	5,831
78209	Alamo Heights	(210)	6,502	6,252
77039	Aldine(u)	(713)	11,133	12,623
*78332	Alice	(512)	19,788	20,961
75002	Allen	(214)	19,315	8,314
*79830	Alpine	(915)	5,622	5,465
*77511	Alvin	(713)	19,220	16,515
*79105	Amarillo	(806)	157,571	149,230
78750	Anderson Mill(u)		9,468	....
79714	Andrews	(915)	10,678	11,061
*77515	Angleton	(409)	17,140	13,929
*78336	Aransas Pass	(512)	7,180	7,173
*76004	Arlington	(817)	261,717	160,113
75751	Athens	(903)	10,982	10,197
75551	Atlanta	(214)	6,118	6,272
*78767	Austin	(512)	465,648	345,890
*76020	Azle	(817)	8,868	5,822
77518	Bacliff(u)		5,549	4,851
75180	Balch Springs	(214)	17,406	13,746
*77414	Bay City	(409)	18,170	17,837
*77520	Baytown	(713)	63,843	56,923
*77707	Beaumont	(409)	114,323	118,102
*76021	Bedford	(817)	43,762	20,821
*78102	Beeville	(512)	13,547	14,574
*77401	Bellaire	(713)	13,844	14,950
76704	Bellmead	(817)	8,336	7,569
76513	Belton	(817)	12,463	10,660
76126	Benbrook	(817)	19,564	13,579
*79720	Big Spring	(915)	23,093	24,804
75418	Bonham	(903)	6,688	7,338
*79007	Borger	(806)	15,675	15,837
76825	Brady	(915)	5,946	5,969
76424	Breckenridge	(817)	5,665	6,921
*77833	Brenham	(409)	11,952	10,966
77611	Bridge City	(409)	8,010	7,667
79316	Brownfield	(806)	9,560	10,387
*78520	Brownsville	(210)	98,962	84,997
*76801	Brownwood	(915)	18,387	19,396
78717	Brushy Creek(u)		5,833	....
*77801	Bryan	(409)	55,002	44,337
76354	Burkburnett	(817)	10,145	10,668
*76028	Burleson	(817)	16,113	11,734
76520	Cameron	(817)	5,635	5,721
79015	Canyon	(806)	11,365	10,724
78132	Canyon Lake(u)		9,975	....
78834	Carrizo Springs	(210)	5,745	6,886
*75006	Carrolton	(214)	82,169	40,595
75633	Carthage	(903)	6,496	6,447
75104	Cedar Hill	(214)	19,988	6,849
*78613	Cedar Park		5,121	3,474

ZIP code	Place	1990	1980
77530	Channelview(u) (713)	25,564	17,471
79201	Childress (817)	5,055	5,817
*76031	Cleburne (817)	22,205	19,218
*77327	Cleveland (713)	7,124	5,977
77015	Cloverleaf(u) (713)	18,230	17,317
77531	Clute (409)	9,467	9,577
76834	Coleman (915)	5,410	5,960
*77840	College Station (409)	52,443	37,272
76034	Colleyville (817)	12,724	6,700
*75428	Commerce (903)	6,825	8,136
77301	Conroe (409)	27,675	18,034
78109	Converse (512)	8,887	5,150
75019	Coppell	16,881	3,826
76522	Copperas Cove (817)	24,079	19,469
*78469	Corpus Christi (512)	257,428	232,134
75110	Corsicana (903)	22,911	21,712
75835	Crockett (409)	7,024	7,405
76036	Crowley (817)	6,974	5,852
78839	Crystal City (512)	8,263	8,334
77954	Cuero (512)	6,700	7,124
79022	Dalhart (806)	6,246	6,854
*75221	Dallas (214)	1,007,618	904,599
77535	Dayton (409)	5,042	4,908
77536	Deer Park (713)	27,424	22,648
*78840	Del Rio (210)	30,705	30,034
*75020	Denison (903)	21,505	23,884
*76201	Denton (817)	66,270	48,063
79323	Denver City	5,156	4,704
75115	De Soto (214)	30,544	15,538
77539	Dickinson (713)	9,497	7,505
78537	Donna (210)	12,652	9,952
79029	Dumas (806)	12,871	12,194
75138	Duncanville (214)	35,008	27,781
76135	Eagle Mountain(u)	5,847	....
*78852	Eagle Pass (210)	20,651	21,407
78539	Edinburg (210)	29,885	24,075
77957	Edna (512)	5,343	5,650
77437	El Campo (409)	10,511	10,462
*79910	El Paso (915)	515,342	425,259
78543	Elsa (210)	5,242	5,061
75119	Ennis (214)	13,869	12,110
76039	Euless (817)	38,149	24,002
76140	Everman (817)	5,672	5,387
79838	Fabens(u)	5,599	4,285
78355	Falfurrias (512)	5,788	6,103
75234	Farmers Branch (214)	24,250	24,863
.....	First Colony(u)	18,327	....
78114	Floresville	5,247	4,381
75028	Flower Mound	15,527	4,402
76119	Forest Hill (817)	11,482	11,684
79906	Fort Bliss(u) (915)	13,915	12,687
76544	Fort Hood(u) (817)	35,580	31,250
79735	Fort Stockton (915)	8,524	8,688
*76161	Fort Worth (817)	447,619	385,164
78624	Fredericksburg (210)	6,934	6,412
77541	Freeport (409)	11,389	13,444
77546	Friendswood (713)	22,814	10,719
75034	Frisco	6,138	3,499
76240	Gainesville (817)	14,256	14,081
77547	Galena Park (713)	10,033	9,879
77550	Galveston (409)	59,067	61,902
*75040	Garland (214)	180,635	138,857
76528	Gatesville (817)	11,492	6,078
*78626	Georgetown (512)	14,840	9,468
75647	Gladewater (903)	6,027	6,548
78629	Gonzales (210)	6,527	7,152
76450	Graham (817)	8,986	9,170
*75051	Grand Prairie (214)	99,606	71,462
*76051	Grapevine (817)	29,198	11,801
*75401	Greenville (903)	23,071	22,161
77619	Groves (409)	16,744	17,090
76117	Haltom City (817)	32,856	29,014
76543	Harker Heights (817)	12,932	7,345
*78550	Harlingen (210)	48,746	43,543
77859	Hearne (409)	5,132	5,418
*75652	Henderson (903)	11,139	11,473
79045	Hereford (806)	14,745	15,853
76643	Hewitt (817)	8,983	5,247
75205	Highland Park (214)	8,739	8,909
77562	Highlands(u) (713)	6,632	6,467
75067	Highland Village	7,027	3,246
76645	Hillsboro (817)	7,072	7,397
77563	Hitchcock (409)	5,868	6,103
78861	Hondo (210)	6,018	6,057
*77052	Houston (713)	1,629,902	1,595,138
*77338	Humble (713)	12,060	6,729
*77340	Huntsville (409)	27,925	23,936
76053	Hurst (817)	33,574	31,420
78362	Ingleside (512)	5,696	5,436
76367	Iowa Park (817)	6,072	6,184
*75015	Irving (214)	155,037	109,943
77029	Jacinto City (713)	9,343	8,953
75766	Jacksonville (214)	12,765	12,264
75951	Jasper (409)	7,160	6,959
78729	Jollyville(u)	15,206	....
77449	Katy (713)	8,004	5,660
75142	Kaufman (214)	5,251	4,658
*76248	Keller (817)	13,683	4,156
79745	Kermit (915)	6,875	8,015
*78028	Kerrville (210)	17,384	15,276
75662	Kilgore (903)	11,066	11,331
*76540	Killeen (817)	63,535	46,296
*78363	Kingsville (512)	25,276	28,808
77325	Kingwood(u) (713)	37,397	16,261
78219	Kirby (210)	8,326	6,435
78236	Lackland AFB(u) (210)	9,352	14,459
77566	Lake Jackson (409)	22,771	19,102
77568	La Marque (409)	14,120	15,372
79331	Lamesa (806)	10,809	11,790
76550	Lampasas (512)	6,382	6,165
75146	Lancaster (214)	22,117	14,807
*77571	La Porte (713)	27,910	14,062
*78041	Laredo (210)	122,893	91,449
*77573	League City (713)	30,159	16,578
78268	Leon Valley (210)	9,581	9,088
*79336	Levelland (806)	13,986	13,809
*75067	Lewisville (214)	46,521	24,273
77575	Liberty (713)	7,690	7,945
79339	Littlefield (806)	6,489	7,409
78233	Live Oak (210)	10,023	8,183
77351	Livingston (409)	5,019	4,928
78644	Lockhart (512)	9,205	7,953
*75606	Longview (903)	70,311	62,762
*79408	Lubbock (806)	186,206	174,361
*75901	Lufkin (409)	30,210	28,562
77711	Lumberton	6,640	2,480
*78501	McAllen (210)	84,021	66,281
75070	McKinney (214)	21,283	16,256
76063	Mansfield (817)	15,615	8,102
76661	Marlin (817)	6,386	7,099
*75670	Marshall (903)	23,682	24,921
78368	Mathis (512)	5,423	5,667
78570	Mercedes (210)	12,694	11,851
*75149	Mesquite (214)	101,484	67,053
76667	Mexia (817)	6,933	7,094
*79701	Midland (915)	89,343	70,525
76065	Midlothian (214)	5,040	3,219
*76067	Mineral Wells (817)	14,935	14,468
*78572	Mission (210)	28,653	22,653
.....	Mission Bend(u)	24,945	....
77489	Missouri City (713)	36,178	24,423
79756	Monahans (915)	8,101	8,397
75455	Mount Pleasant (903)	12,291	11,003
*75961	Nacogdoches (409)	30,872	27,149
77868	Navasota (409)	6,296	5,971
77627	Nederland (409)	16,192	16,855
75570	New Boston	5,057	4,628
*78130	New Braunfels (210)	27,334	22,402
76118	North Richland Hills (817)	45,895	30,592
*79761	Odessa (915)	89,699	90,027
*77630	Orange (409)	19,370	23,628
*75801	Palestine (903)	18,042	15,948
*79065	Pampa (806)	19,959	21,396
*75460	Paris (903)	24,799	25,498
*77501	Pasadena (713)	119,604	112,560
*77581	Pearland (713)	18,927	13,248
78061	Pearsall (210)	6,924	7,383
78721	Pecan Grove(u)	9,502	....
79772	Pecos (915)	12,069	12,855
79070	Perryton (806)	7,619	7,991
78577	Pharr (210)	32,921	21,381
*79072	Plainview (806)	21,698	22,187
*75074	Plano (214)	127,885	72,331
78064	Pleasanton (210)	7,678	6,346
*77640	Port Arthur (409)	58,551	61,251
78374	Portland (512)	12,224	12,023
77979	Port Lavaca (512)	10,886	10,911
77651	Port Neches (409)	12,908	13,944
78580	Raymondville (210)	8,880	9,493
76028	Rendon(u)	7,658	....
*75080	Richardson (214)	74,840	72,496
76118	Richland Hills (817)	7,978	7,977
*77469	Richmond (713)	10,042	9,692
78582	Rio Grande City(u) (210)	9,891	8,930
77019	River Oaks (817)	6,580	6,890
76701	Robinson (817)	7,111	6,074
78380	Robstown (512)	12,849	12,100
76567	Rockdale (512)	5,235	5,611
75087	Rockwall (214)	10,486	5,939
78584	Roma	8,059	3,384
77471	Rosenberg (713)	20,183	17,840
*78681	Round Rock (512)	30,923	12,740
*75088	Rowlett (214)	23,260	7,522
75048	Sachse	5,346	1,640
76179	Saginaw (817)	8,551	5,736
*76902	San Angelo (915)	84,462	73,240
*78265	San Antonio (210)	935,393	785,940
78586	San Benito (210)	20,125	17,988
78589	San Juan (210)	10,815	7,608
*78666	San Marcos (512)	28,738	23,420
*77510	Santa Fe (713)	8,429	6,172
78154	Schertz (210)	10,597	7,262
77586	Seabrook (713)	6,685	4,670
75159	Seagoville (214)	8,969	7,304
*78155	Seguin (210)	18,692	17,854
79360	Seminole (915)	6,342	6,080

ZIP code	Place		1990	1980
*75090	Sherman	(903)	31,584	30,413
77656	Silsbee	(409)	6,368	7,684
78387	Sinton	(512)	5,549	6,044
79364	Slaton	(806)	6,078	6,804
*79549	Snyder	(915)	12,195	12,705
79910	Socorro		22,995	12,341†
77587	South Houston	(713)	14,207	13,293
76092	Southlake		7,082	2,808
*77373	Spring(u)	(713)	33,111	....
*77477	Stafford	(713)	8,395	4,755
76401	Stephenville	(817)	13,502	11,881
*77478	Sugar Land	(713)	24,549	8,826
*75482	Sulphur Springs	(903)	14,062	12,804
79556	Sweetwater	(915)	11,967	12,242
76574	Taylor	(512)	11,472	10,619
*76501	Temple	(817)	46,150	42,354
75160	Terrell	(214)	12,490	13,269
*75501	Texarkana	(903)	31,658	31,271
*77590	Texas City	(409)	40,822	41,201
75056	The Colony	(214)	22,113	11,586
77387	The Woodlands(u)	(713)	29,205	8,443
*77335	Tomball	(713)	6,370	3,996
.....	Town West(u)		6,166	....
*75702	Tyler	(903)	75,450	70,508
78148	Universal City	(512)	13,057	10,720
76308	University Park	(214)	22,259	22,254
*78801	Uvalde	(210)	14,729	14,178
*76384	Vernon	(817)	12,001	12,695
*77901	Victoria	(512)	55,076	50,695
*77662	Vidor	(409)	10,935	11,834
*76702	Waco	(817)	103,590	101,261
76148	Watauga	(817)	20,009	10,284
75165	Waxahachie	(214)	17,984	14,624
*76086	Weatherford	(817)	14,804	12,049
78728	Wells Branch(u)		7,094	....
*78596	Weslaco	(210)	21,877	19,331
79764	West Odessa(u)		16,568	....
77005	West University Place	(713)	12,920	12,010
77488	Wharton	(409)	9,011	9,033
75693	White Oak		5,136	4,415
76108	White Settlement	(817)	15,472	13,508
*76307	Wichita Falls	(817)	96,259	94,201
78239	Windcrest	(210)	5,331	5,332
76712	Woodway	(817)	8,695	7,091
75098	Wylie		8,716	3,152
77995	Yoakum	(512)	5,611	6,148
78076	Zapata(u)	(512)	7,119	3,831

Utah (801)

ZIP code	Place	1990	1980
84003	American Fork	15,722	12,564
*84010	Bountiful	36,147	32,877
84302	Brigham City	15,644	15,596
84109	Canyon Rim(u)	10,527	....
*84720	Cedar City	13,443	10,972
84014	Centerville	11,500	8,069
*84015	Clearfield	21,435	17,982
84015	Clinton	7,945	5,777
84121	Cottonwood Heights(u)	28,766	22,665
.....	Cottonwood West(u)	17,476	11,117
84020	Draper	7,143	5,521
84109	East Millcreek(u)	21,184	24,150
84025	Farmington	9,049	4,691
84004	Highland	5,007	2,435
84117	Holladay-Cottonwood(u)†	14,095	22,189
84037	Kaysville	13,961	9,811
84118	Kearns(u)	28,374	21,353
*84041	Layton	41,784	22,862
84043	Lehi	8,475	6,848
.....	Little Cottonwood Creek Valley(u)	5,042	....
*84321	Logan	32,771	26,844
84044	Magna(u)	17,829	13,138
84047	Midvale	11,886	10,146
84109	Millcreek(u)	32,230	....
84117	Mount Olympus(u)	7,413	6,068
84107	Murray	31,274	25,750
84404	North Ogden	11,593	9,309
84054	North Salt Lake	6,464	5,548
*84401	Ogden	63,943	64,407
.....	Oquirrh(u)	7,593	....
*84057	Orem	67,561	52,399
84651	Payson	9,510	8,246
84062	Pleasant Grove	13,476	10,833
84501	Price	8,712	9,086
*84601	Provo	86,835	74,111
84701	Richfield	5,593	5,482
84403	Riverdale	6,419	6,031
84065	Riverton	11,261	7,032
84067	Roy	24,595	19,694
*84770	Saint George	28,572	11,350
*84101	Salt Lake City	159,928	163,034
*84070	Sandy	75,240	52,210
84335	Smithfield	5,566	4,993
84095	South Jordan	12,215	7,492
84403	South Ogden	12,105	11,366
84115	South Salt Lake	10,129	10,413
84660	Spanish Fork	11,272	9,825
84663	Springville	13,950	12,101
84015	Sunset	5,128	5,733
84107	Taylorsville-Bennion(u)†	52,351	17,448
84074	Tooele	13,887	14,335
84047	Union(u)	13,684	9,665
*84078	Vernal	6,640	6,600
84403	Washington Terrace	8,189	8,212
84084	West Jordan	42,915	27,325
*84119	West Valley City†	86,969	72,509
84070	White City(u)	6,506	7,267
84087	Woods Cross	5,384	4,263

Vermont (802)

See note on page 387

ZIP code	Place	1990	1980
05641	Barre	9,482	9,824
05641	*Barre*	7,411	7,090
05201	*Bennington*	16,451	15,815
05201	Bennington(u)	9,532	9,349
05301	Brattleboro Center(u)	8,612	8,596
*05301	*Brattleboro*	12,241	11,886
*05401	Burlington	39,127	37,712
*05446	*Colchester*	14,731	12,629
05451	*Essex*	16,498	14,392
*05452	Essex Junction	8,396	7,033
05047	*Hartford*	9,404	7,963
05849	*Lyndon*	5,371	5,371
05753	Middlebury	8,034	7,574
05468	*Milton*	8,404	6,829
*05446	Montpelier	8,247	8,241
05663	*Northfield*	5,610	5,435
.....	*Rockingham*	5,484	5,538
*05701	Rutland	18,230	18,436
05478	Saint Albans	7,339	7,308
05819	Saint Johnsbury(u)	7,608	6,424
05482	*Shelburne*	5,871	5,000
*05401	South Burlington	12,809	10,679
05156	*Springfield*	9,579	10,190
05488	Swanton	5,636	5,141
05404	Winooski	6,649	6,318

Virginia

ZIP code	Place		1990	1980
24210	Abingdon	(703)	7,003	4,318
*22313	Alexandria	(703)	111,182	103,217
22003	Annandale(u)	(703)	50,975	49,524
.....	Aquia Harbour(u)		6,308	2,870
*22210	Arlington(u)	(703)	170,936	152,599
23005	Ashland	(804)	5,864	4,640
22041	Bailey's Crossroads(u)	(703)	19,507	12,564
24523	Bedford	(703)	6,073	5,991
22306	Belle Haven(u)	(804)	6,427	6,520
23234	Bellwood(u)	(804)	6,178	6,439
23234	Bensley(u)	(804)	5,093	5,299
*24060	Blacksburg	(703)	34,590	30,638
24605	Bluefield	(703)	5,363	5,946
23235	Bon Air(u)	(804)	16,413	16,224
*24203	Bristol	(703)	18,426	19,042
24416	Buena Vista	(703)	6,406	6,717
.....	Bull Run(u)		5,525	....
*22015	Burke(u)	(703)	57,734	33,835
24018	Cave Spring(u)	(703)	24,053	21,682
22020	Centreville(u)	(703)	26,585	7,473
*22021	Chantilly(u)	(703)	29,337	12,259
*22906	Charlottesville	(804)	40,475	39,916
*23320	Chesapeake	(804)	151,982	114,486
23831	Chester(u)	(804)	14,986	11,728
*24073	Christiansburg	(703)	15,004	10,345
24078	Collinsville(u)	(703)	7,280	7,517
23834	Colonial Heights	(804)	16,064	16,509
.....	Commonwealth(u)		5,538	3,505
.....	Countryside(u)		8,349	....
24426	Covington	(703)	6,991	9,063
22701	Culpeper	(703)	8,581	6,621
22191	Dale City(u)	(703)	47,170	33,127
*24541	Danville	(804)	53,056	45,642
23228	Dumbarton(u)	(804)	8,526	8,149
22027	Dunn Loring(u)	(703)	6,509	6,077
23222	East Highland Park(u)	(804)	11,850	11,797
23847	Emporia	(804)	5,479	4,840
23803	Ettrick(u)		5,290	4,890
*22030	Fairfax	(703)	19,629	19,390
*22046	Falls Church	(703)	9,522	9,515
23901	Farmville	(804)	6,046	6,067
24551	Forest(u)	(804)	5,624	....
22060	Fort Belvoir(u)	(703)	8,590	7,726
22308	Fort Hunt(u)	(703)	12,989	14,294
23801	Fort Lee(u)	(804)	6,895	9,784
22310	Franconia(u)	(703)	19,882	8,476
23851	Franklin	(804)	7,864	7,308
*22404	Fredericksburg	(703)	19,027	15,322
22630	Front Royal	(703)	11,880	11,126
24333	Galax	(703)	6,670	6,524
*23060	Glen Allen(u)	(804)	9,010	6,202
23062	Gloucester Point(u)	(804)	8,509	5,841
22066	Great Falls(u)		6,945	2,419
22306	Groveton(u)	(703)	19,997	18,860
*23670	Hampton	(804)	133,811	122,617
22801	Harrisonburg	(703)	30,707	19,671
*22070	Herndon	(703)	16,139	11,449
23075	Highland Springs(u)	(804)	13,823	12,146

ZIP code	Place	1990	1980
24019	Hollins(u) . . . . (703)	13,305	12,295
23860	Hopewell . . . . (804)	23,101	23,397
22303	Huntington(u) . . . . (703)	7,489	5,813
22306	Hybla Valley(u) . . . . (703)	15,491	15,533
22043	Idylwood(u). . . . . (703)	14,710	11,982
22042	Jefferson(u) . . . . (804)	25,782	24,342
22041	Lake Barcroft(u) . . . . (703)	8,686	8,725
22191	Lake Ridge(u) . . . . (703)	23,862	11,072
23228	Lakeside(u) . . . . (804)	12,081	12,289
23060	Laurel(u) . . . . (804)	13,011	10,569
22075	Leesburg . . . . (703)	16,202	8,357
24450	Lexington . . . . (703)	6,959	7,292
22312	Lincolnia(u). . . . . (703)	13,041	10,350
*22079	Lorton(u) . . . . (703)	15,385	5,813
*24506	Lynchburg . . . . (804)	66,049	66,743
*22101	McLean(u) . . . . (703)	38,168	35,664
24572	Madison Heights(u) . . . . . (804)	11,700	14,146
*22110	Manassas . . . . (703)	27,957	15,438
22110	Manassas Park . . . . (703)	6,734	6,524
22030	Mantua(u) . . . . (703)	6,804	6,523
24354	Marion . . . . (703)	6,630	7,287
*24112	Martinsville . . . . (703)	16,162	18,149
23111	Mechanicsville(u). . . . . . . (804)	22,027	9,269
22081	Merrifield(u) . . . . (703)	8,399	7,525
.....	Montclair(u)	11,399	4,098
23231	Montrose(u) . . . . (804)	6,405	5,349
22121	Mount Vernon(u) . . . . (703)	27,485	24,058
22122	Newington(u) . . . . (703)	17,965	8,313
*23607	Newport News . . . . (804)	171,439	144,903
*23503	Norfolk. . . . . (804)	261,250	266,979
22151	North Springfield(u) . . . . . (703)	8,996	9,538
22124	Oakton(u). . . . . (703)	24,610	19,150
*23804	Petersburg . . . . (804)	37,027	41,055
22043	Pimmit Hills(u). . . . . (703)	6,019	6,658
23662	Poquoson. . . . . (804)	11,005	8,726
*23705	Portsmouth. . . . . (804)	103,910	104,577
24301	Pulaski . . . . (703)	9,985	10,106
22134	Quantico Station(u) . . . . . (703)	7,425	7,121
*24141	Radford . . . . (703)	15,940	13,225
*22090	Reston(u). . . . . (703)	48,556	36,407
*23232	Richmond. . . . . (804)	202,798	219,214
.....	Rio	5,133	2,851
*24022	Roanoke . . . . (703)	96,509	100,220
24281	Rose Hill(u) . . . . (703)	12,675	11,926
24153	Salem . . . . (703)	23,797	23,958
22044	Seven Corners(u) . . . . . . (703)	7,280	6,058
24592	South Boston . . . . (804)	6,997	7,093
*22150	Springfield(u) . . . . (703)	23,706	21,435
*24401	Staunton . . . . (703)	24,461	21,857
20164	Sterling(u) . . . . (703)	20,512	16,080
24477	Stuarts Draft(u)	5,087	1,776
23162	Sudley(u)	7,321	4,674
*23434	Suffolk. . . . . (804)	52,143	47,621
22170	Sugarland Run(u) . . . . . . (703)	9,357	6,258
24502	Timberlake(u) . . . . (804)	10,314	9,697
23229	Tuckahoe(u) . . . . (804)	42,629	39,868
22101	Tysons Corner(u) . . . . . . (703)	13,124	10,065
.....	University Heights(u)	6,900	6,736
*22180	Vienna. . . . . (703)	14,852	15,469
24179	Vinton . . . . (703)	7,643	8,027
*23458	Virginia Beach. . . . . (804)	393,089	262,199
22980	Waynesboro . . . . (703)	18,549	15,329
22110	West Gate(u) . . . . (703)	6,565	7,119
22152	West Springfield(u) . . . . . (703)	28,126	25,012
*23185	Williamsburg. . . . . (804)	11,409	9,870
*22601	Winchester. . . . . (703)	21,947	20,217
24592	Wolf Trap(u) . . . . (804)	13,133	9,875
22191	Woodbridge(u) . . . . (703)	26,401	24,004
24382	Wytheville . . . . (703)	8,036	7,135
.....	Yorkshire(u)	5,699	4,940

Washington

Area code (360) will go into effect on Jan. 15, 1995. Prior to that date use (206). Please also see note on page 387.

ZIP code	Place	1990	1980
98520	Aberdeen . . . . (360)	16,565	18,739
98036	Alderwood Manor-Bothell North(u). . . . . (206)	22,945	16,524
98221	Anacortes. . . . . (360)	11,451	9,013
98335	Artondale(u)	7,141	....
*98002	Auburn. . . . . (206)	33,650	26,417
*98009	Bellevue. . . . . (206)	86,872	73,903
*98225	Bellingham . . . . (360)	52,179	45,794
98390	Bonney Lake. . . . . (206)	7,494	5,328
*98011	Bothell. . . . . (206)	12,345	7,943
*98310	Bremerton . . . . (206)	38,142	36,208
98036	Brier	5,633	2,915
98178	Bryn Mawr-Skyway(u) . . . (206)	12,514	11,754
98166	Burien(u) . . . . (206)	25,089	23,189
98607	Camas. . . . . (360)	6,442	5,681
98055	Cascade-Fairwood(u) . . . . (206)	30,107	16,939
98684	Cascade Park East(u)	6,996	....
98684	Cascade Park West(u)	6,656	....
98531	Centralia . . . . (360)	12,101	11,555
98532	Chehalis . . . . (360)	6,527	6,100
99004	Cheney . . . . (509)	7,723	7,630
99403	Clarkston . . . . (509)	6,753	6,903
99324	College Place . . . . (509)	6,308	5,771
.....	Country Homes(u)	5,126	....
98042	Covington-Sawyer-Wilderness(u)	24,321	....
98198	Des Moines . . . . (206)	17,283	7,378
99213	Dishman(u) . . . . (509)	9,671	10,169
.....	East Hill-Meridian(u)	42,696	....
98366	East Port Orchard(u)	5,409	4,631
98056	East Renton Highlands(u) . (206)	13,218	11,695
98801	East Wenatchee Bench(u) (509)	12,539	11,410
.....	Edgewood-North Hill(u)	9,120	....
*98020	Edmonds . . . . (206)	30,743	27,679
98387	Elk Plain(u)	12,197	....
98926	Ellensburg . . . . (509)	12,360	11,752
.....	Ellsworth North(u)	5,796	....
98022	Enumclaw . . . . (360)	7,227	5,427
98823	Ephrata . . . . (509)	5,349	5,359
99210	Esperance(u) . . . . (509)	11,236	11,120
*98201	Everett . . . . (360)	69,974	54,413
98411	Evergreen(u)	11,249	....
98055	Fairwood(u) . . . . (206)	5,807	5,337
*98063	Federal Way. . . . . (206)	67,554	....
98248	Ferndale . . . . (360)	5,398	3,855
98466	Fircrest . . . . (206)	5,258	5,477
98597	Five Corners(u).	6,776	....
98433	Fort Lewis(u) . . . . (206)	22,224	23,761
98930	Grandview . . . . (509)	7,169	5,615
.....	Harbour Pointe(u)	9,107	....
98660	Hazel Dell North(u)† . . . . (206)	6,924	15,386
98665	Hazel Dell South(u) . . . . . (206)	5,796	....
98550	Hoquiam . . . . (206)	8,972	9,719
98011	Inglewood-Finn Hill(u)†. . . (206)	29,132	12,467
98027	Issaquah . . . . (206)	7,786	5,536
98626	Kelso. . . . . (360)	11,767	11,129
98028	Kenmore(u) . . . . (206)	8,917	7,281
*99336	Kennewick . . . . (509)	42,148	34,397
*98031	Kent . . . . (206)	37,960	22,961
98033	Kingsgate(u). . . . . (206)	14,259	12,652
*98033	Kirkland. . . . . (206)	40,059	18,785
98503	Lacey . . . . (360)	19,279	13,940
98155	Lake Forest North(u) . . . . (206)	8,002	7,995
.....	Lakeland North(u) . . . . . . (206)	14,402	11,648
.....	Lakeland South(u) . . . . . . (206)	9,027	5,225
98036	Lake Serene-North Lynnwood(u)	14,290	....
.....	Lake Shore(u).	6,268	....
98259	Lakewood(u). . . . . (206)	58,412	54,533
.....	Lea Hill(u)	6,876	....
98632	Longview . . . . (360)	31,499	31,052
98264	Lynden . . . . (360)	5,709	4,022
*98036	Lynnwood . . . . (206)	28,637	22,641
.....	Martha Lake(u) . . . . (206)	10,155	7,022
98270	Marysville . . . . (360)	10,328	5,080
98040	Mercer Island . . . . (206)	20,816	21,522
.....	Midland(u)	5,587	....
98012	Mill Creek†	7,180	1,803
.....	Minnehaha(u)	9,661	....
98837	Moses Lake . . . . (509)	11,235	10,629
98043	Mountlake Terrace. . . . . . (206)	19,320	16,534
98273	Mount Vernon. . . . . (360)	17,647	13,009
98275	Mukilteo. . . . . (206)	6,982	1,426
98006	Newport Hills(u) . . . . (206)	14,736	12,245
98166	Normandy Park. . . . . (206)	6,709	4,268
98155	North City-Ridgecrest(u) . . (206)	13,832	13,551
.....	North Creek-Canyon Park(u) . .	23,236	....
.....	North Hill(u) . . . . (206)	5,706	10,170
98270	North Marysville(u) . . . . . (206)	18,711	15,159
98277	Oak Harbor . . . . (360)	17,176	12,271
*98501	Olympia. . . . . (360)	33,729	27,447
99214	Opportunity(u). . . . . (509)	22,326	21,241
98662	Orchards North(u)† . . . . . (360)	6,479	8,828
98662	Orchards South(u). . . . . . (360)	12,956	....
99027	Otis Orchards-East Farms(u) (360)	5,811	4,597
.....	Paine Field-Lake Stickney(u) . .	18,670	....
98444	Parkland(u) . . . . (206)	20,882	23,355
98366	Parkwood(u).	6,853	4,599
99302	PASCO . . . . (509)	20,337	18,428
98027	Pine Lake(u).	13,940	....
98362	Port Angeles. . . . . (360)	17,710	17,311
98368	Port Townsend . . . . (360)	7,001	6,067
98390	Prairie Ridge(u).	8,278	....
99163	Pullman . . . . (509)	23,478	23,579
*98371	Puyallup . . . . (206)	23,878	18,251
*98052	Redmond . . . . (206)	35,800	23,318
*98058	Renton . . . . (206)	41,688	31,031
99352	Richland . . . . (509)	32,315	33,578
98160	Richmond Beach-Innis Arden(u) (206)	7,242	6,700
98113	Richmond Highlands(u) . . (206)	26,037	24,463
98188	Riverton-Boulevard Park(u)† . . (206)	15,337	14,182
.....	Sahalee(u)	13,951	....
98686	Salmon Creek(u)	11,989	....
*98148	Seatac. . . . . (206)	22,694	....
*98101	Seattle. . . . . (206)	516,259	493,846
98284	Sedro Woolley . . . . (360)	6,333	6,110
98942	Selah . . . . (509)	5,113	4,500
98584	Shelton . . . . (360)	7,241	7,629
98155	Sheridan Beach(u). . . . . . (206)	6,518	6,873
98383	Silverdale(u). . . . . (360)	7,660	....
98201	Silver Lake-Fircrest(u) . . . (360)	24,474	10,299
*98290	Snohomish. . . . . (360)	6,499	5,294
98373	South Hill(u)	12,963	....
98387	Spanaway(u) . . . . (206)	15,001	8,868
*99210	Spokane . . . . (509)	177,165	171,300

ZIP code	Place	1990	1980
98303	Steilacoom (206)	5,728	4,886
98371	Summit(u)	6,312	....
98390	Sumner (206)	6,459	4,936
98944	Sunnyside (509)	11,238	9,225
*98402	Tacoma (206)	176,664	158,501
98501	Tanglewilde-Thompson Place(u)	6,061	5,910
98948	Toppenish (509)	7,419	6,517
98138	Tukwila (206)	11,874	3,578
98502	Tumwater (360)	9,976	6,705
98464	University Place(u) (206)	27,701	20,381
*98661	Vancouver (360)	46,380	42,834
98662	Vancouver Mall(u) (360)	6,938	....
99037	Veradale(u) (509)	7,836	7,256
99362	Walla Walla (509)	26,482	25,618
.....	Waller(u)	6,415	....
*98801	Wenatchee (509)	21,746	17,257
.....	West Lake Sammamish(u)	6,087	....
98258	West Lake Stevens(u) (206)	12,453	....
99301	West Pasco(u) (509)	7,312	5,726
99181	West Valley(u)	6,594	....
98166	White Center-Shorewood(u) (206)	20,531	19,362
98072	Woodinville(u)	23,654	....
98032	Woodmont Beach(u)	7,493	....
*98903	Yakima (509)	54,843	49,826

West Virginia (304)

ZIP code	Place	1990	1980
*25801	Beckley	18,274	20,492
24701	Bluefield	12,756	16,060
26330	Bridgeport	6,695	6,604
26201	Buckhannon	5,909	6,820
*25301	Charleston	57,287	63,968
*26301	Clarksburg	17,970	22,371
25301	Cross Lanes(u)	10,878	....
25064	Dunbar	8,697	9,285
26241	Elkins	7,494	8,536
*26554	Fairmont	20,210	23,863
26354	Grafton	5,524	6,845
*25704	Huntington	54,844	63,684
26726	Keyser	5,870	6,569
25401	Martinsburg	14,073	13,063
*26505	Morgantown	25,879	27,605
26041	Moundsville	10,753	12,419
26155	New Martinsville	6,705	7,109
25143	Nitro	6,851	8,074
25901	Oak Hill	6,812	7,120
26101	Parkersburg	33,862	39,946
.....	Pea Ridge(u)	6,535	....
*24740	Princeton	7,043	7,538
25177	Saint Albans	11,257	12,402
25303	South Charleston	13,645	15,968
25569	Teays Valley(u)	8,436	....
26105	Vienna	10,862	11,618
26062	Weirton	22,124	25,371
26003	Wheeling	34,882	43,070

Wisconsin

See note on page 387

ZIP code	Place	1990	1980
54301	Allouez† (414)	14,431	14,882
54720	Altoona	5,889	4,393
54409	Antigo (715)	8,284	8,653
59411	Appleton (414)	65,695	58,913
54806	Ashland (715)	8,695	9,115
54304	Ashwaubenon (414)	16,376	14,486
53913	Baraboo (608)	9,203	8,081
53916	Beaver Dam (414)	14,196	14,149
.....	Bellevue Town(u)	7,541	....
*53511	Beloit (608)	35,571	35,207
54923	Berlin (414)	5,371	5,478
53045	Brookfield (414)	35,184	34,035
53209	Brown Deer (414)	12,236	12,921
53105	Burlington (414)	8,855	8,385
53012	Cedarburg (414)	10,086	9,005
54729	Chippewa Falls (715)	12,727	12,270
53110	Cudahy (414)	18,659	19,547
53018	Delafield	5,347	4,083
53115	Delavan (414)	6,073	5,684
54115	De Pere (414)	16,569	14,892
54703	Eau Claire (715)	56,806	51,509
53121	Elkhorn (414)	5,337	4,605
53122	Elm Grove (414)	6,261	6,735
53714	Fitchburg† (608)	15,648	11,965
*54935	Fond Du Lac (414)	37,757	35,863
53538	Fort Atkinson (414)	10,213	9,785
53217	Fox Point (414)	7,238	7,649
53132	Franklin (414)	21,855	16,871
53022	Germantown (414)	13,658	10,729
53209	Glendale (414)	14,088	13,882
53024	Grafton (414)	9,340	8,381
*54303	Green Bay (414)	96,466	87,899
53129	Greendale (414)	15,128	16,928
53220	Greenfield (414)	33,403	31,353
53130	Hales Corners (414)	7,623	7,110
53027	Hartford (414)	8,188	7,159
53029	Hartland (414)	6,906	5,559
54303	Howard (414)	9,874	8,240
54016	Hudson (715)	6,378	5,434
*53545	Janesville (608)	52,210	51,071
53549	Jefferson (414)	6,078	5,647
54130	Kaukauna (414)	11,982	11,310
*53140	Kenosha (414)	80,426	77,685
54136	Kimberly (414)	5,406	5,881
*54601	La Crosse (608)	51,120	48,347
53147	Lake Geneva (414)	5,979	5,612
54140	Little Chute (414)	9,207	7,907
53558	McFarland (608)	5,232	3,783
*53714	Madison (608)	190,766	170,616
*54220	Manitowoc (414)	32,521	32,547
54143	Marinette (715)	11,843	11,965
54449	Marshfield (715)	19,291	18,290
54952	Menasha (414)	14,711	14,728
*53051	Menomonee Falls (414)	26,840	27,845
54751	Menomonie (715)	13,547	12,769
53092	Mequon (414)	18,885	16,193
54452	Merrill (715)	9,860	9,578
53562	Middleton (608)	13,785	11,851
*53201	Milwaukee (414)	628,088	636,297
53716	Monona (608)	8,637	8,809
53566	Monroe (608)	10,241	10,027
53150	Muskego (414)	16,813	15,277
*54956	Neenah (414)	23,219	22,432
53151	New Berlin (414)	33,592	30,529
54961	New London (414)	6,658	6,210
54017	New Richmond (715)	5,106	4,306
53154	Oak Creek (414)	19,513	16,932
53066	Oconomowoc (414)	10,993	9,909
54650	Onalaska (608)	11,414	9,249
*54901	Oshkosh (414)	55,006	49,620
53072	Pewaukee	5,287	4,637
53818	Platteville (608)	9,862	9,580
53158	Pleasant Prairie† (414)	12,037	12,176
54467	Plover (715)	8,176	5,310
53073	Plymouth (414)	6,769	6,027
53901	Portage (608)	8,640	7,896
53074	Port Washington (414)	9,338	8,612
53821	Prairie du Chien (608)	5,657	5,859
*53401	Racine (414)	84,298	85,725
53959	Reedsburg (608)	5,834	5,038
54501	Rhinelander (715)	7,382	7,873
54868	Rice Lake (715)	7,998	7,691
53581	Richland Center (608)	5,018	4,997
54971	Ripon (414)	7,241	7,111
54022	River Falls (715)	10,610	9,019
53207	Saint Francis (414)	9,245	10,095
54166	Shawano (715)	7,598	7,013
*53081	Sheboygan (414)	49,587	48,085
53085	Sheboygan Falls (414)	5,823	5,253
53211	Shorewood (414)	14,116	14,327
53172	South Milwaukee (414)	20,958	21,069
54656	Sparta (608)	7,788	6,934
54481	Stevens Point (715)	23,006	22,970
53589	Stoughton (608)	8,786	7,589
54235	Sturgeon Bay (414)	9,176	8,847
53590	Sun Prairie (608)	15,333	12,931
54880	Superior (715)	27,134	29,571
53089	Sussex	5,039	3,482
54660	Tomah (608)	7,570	7,204
54241	Two Rivers (414)	13,030	13,354
53593	Verona	5,374	3,336
*53094	Watertown (414)	19,142	18,113
*53186	Waukesha (414)	56,958	50,365
53597	Waunakee	5,897	3,866
53963	Waupun (414)	8,844	8,132
*54403	Wausau (715)	37,060	32,426
53213	Wauwatosa (414)	49,366	51,308
53214	West Allis (414)	63,221	63,982
53095	West Bend (414)	24,470	21,484
54476	Weston(u) (715)	9,714	8,775
53217	Whitefish Bay (414)	14,272	14,930
53190	Whitewater (414)	12,636	11,520
*54494	Wisconsin Rapids (715)	18,245	17,995

Wyoming (307)

ZIP code	Place	1990	1980
*82601	Casper	46,765	51,016
*82001	Cheyenne	50,008	47,283
82414	Cody	7,897	6,599
82633	Douglas	5,076	6,030
*82930	Evanston	10,904	6,265
*82716	Gillette	17,545	12,134
82935	Green River	12,711	12,807
82520	Lander	7,023	7,867
*82071	Laramie	26,687	24,410
82435	Powell	5,292	5,310
82301	Rawlins	9,380	11,547
82501	Riverton	9,202	9,562
*82901	Rock Springs	19,050	19,458
82801	Sheridan	13,904	15,146
82240	Torrington	5,651	5,441
82401	Worland	5,742	6,391

Census and Areas of Counties and States

Source: U.S. Bureau of the Census, Dept. of Commerce; World Almanac research

Population figures listed below are final counts in the 1990 census, conducted on Apr. 1, 1990; updated as of Apr. 1994.

Alabama

(67 counties, 50,750 sq mi land; pop. 4,040,587)

County	Pop.	County Seat or court house	Land area sq mi
Autauga	34,222	Prattville	596
Baldwin	98,280	Bay Minette	1,596
Barbour	25,417	Clayton	885
Bibb	16,576	Centreville	622
Blount	39,248	Oneonta	645
Bullock	11,042	Union Springs	625
Butler	21,892	Greenville	776
Calhoun	116,032	Anniston	608
Chambers	36,876	Lafayette	597
Cherokee	19,543	Centre	553
Chilton	32,458	Clanton	694
Choctaw	16,018	Butler	913
Clarke	27,240	Grove Hill	1,238
Clay	13,252	Ashland	605
Cleburne	12,730	Heflin	560
Coffee	40,240	Elba	679
Colbert	51,666	Tuscumbia	594
Conecuh	14,054	Evergreen	850
Coosa	11,063	Rockford	652
Covington	36,478	Andalusia	1,034
Crenshaw	13,635	Luverne	609
Cullman	67,613	Cullman	738
Dale	49,633	Ozark	561
Dallas	48,130	Selma	980
De Kalb	54,651	Fort Payne	777
Elmore	49,210	Wetumpka	621
Escambia	35,518	Brewton	947
Etowah	99,840	Gadsden	534
Fayette	17,962	Fayette	627
Franklin	27,814	Russellville	635
Geneva	23,647	Geneva	576
Greene	10,153	Eutaw	645
Hale	15,498	Greensboro	643
Henry	15,374	Abbeville	561
Houston	81,331	Dothan	580
Jackson	47,796	Scottsboro	1,078
Jefferson	651,520	Birmingham	1,112
Lamar	15,715	Vernon	604
Lauderdale	79,661	Florence	669
Lawrence	31,513	Moulton	693
Lee	87,146	Opelika	608
Limestone	46,005	Athens	568
Lowndes	12,658	Hayneville	718
Macon	24,928	Tuskegee	610
Madison	238,912	Huntsville	804
Marengo	23,084	Linden	977
Marion	29,830	Hamilton	741
Marshall	70,832	Guntersville	567
Mobile	378,643	Mobile	1,233
Monroe	23,968	Monroeville	1,025
Montgomery	209,085	Montgomery	789
Morgan	100,043	Decatur	599
Perry	12,759	Marion	719
Pickens	20,699	Carrollton	881
Pike	27,595	Troy	671
Randolph	19,881	Wedowee	581
Russell	46,860	Phenix City	641
Saint Clair	49,811	Ashville & Pell City	633
Shelby	99,363	Columbiana	794
Sumter	16,174	Livingston	904
Talladega	74,109	Talladega	739
Tallapoosa	38,826	Dadeville	718
Tuscaloosa	150,522	Tuscaloosa	1,325
Walker	67,670	Jasper	794
Washington	16,694	Chatom	1,080
Wilcox	13,568	Camden	888
Winston	22,053	Double Springs	614

Alaska

(25 divisions, 570,374 sq mi land; pop. 550,043)

Census Division	Pop.	Land area sq mi
Aleutian East Borough	2,464	6,985
Aleutians West Census Area	9,478	4,402
Anchorage Borough	226,338	1,732
Bethel Census Area	13,656	36,104
Bristol Bay Borough	1,410	531
Dillingham Census Area	4,012	46,042
Fairbanks North Star Borough	77,720	7,404
Haines Borough	2,117	2,374
Juneau Borough	26,751	2,626
Kenai Peninsula Borough	40,802	16,056
Ketchikan Gateway Borough	13,828	1,242
Kodiak Island Borough	13,309	4,796
Lake and Peninsula Borough	1,668	....
Matanuska-Susitna Borough	39,683	24,502
Nome Census Area	8,288	23,871
North Slope Borough	5,979	90,955
Northwest Arctic Borough	6,113	....
Prince of Wales-Outer Ketchikan Census Area	6,278	7,660
Sitka Borough	8,588	2,938
Skagway-Yakutat-Angoon Census Area	4,385	13,239
Southeast Fairbanks Census Area	5,913	24,169
Valdez-Cordova Census Area	9,952	39,229
Wade Hampton Census Area	5,791	17,816
Wrangell-Petersburg Census Area	7,042	6,167
Yukon-Koyukuk Census Area	8,478	159,099

Arizona

(15 counties, 113,642 sq mi land; pop. 3,665,228)

County	Pop.	County Seat or court house	Land area sq mi
Apache	61,591	Saint Johns	11,211
Cochise	97,624	Bisbee	6,218
Coconino	96,591	Flagstaff	18,608
Gila	40,216	Globe	4,752
Graham	26,554	Safford	4,630
Greenlee	8,008	Clifton	1,837
La Paz	13,844	Parker	4,430
Maricopa	2,122,101	Phoenix	9,127
Mohave	93,497	Kingman	13,285
Navajo	77,674	Holbrook	9,955
Pima	666,957	Tucson	9,187
Pinal	116,379	Florence	5,343
Santa Cruz	29,676	Nogales	1,238
Yavapai	107,714	Prescott	8,123
Yuma	106,895	Yuma	5,564

Arkansas

(75 counties, 52,075 sq mi land; pop. 2,350,725)

County	Pop.	County Seat or court house	Land area sq mi
Arkansas	21,653	DeWitt & Stuttgart	1,033
Ashley	24,319	Hamburg	939
Baxter	31,186	Mountain Home	586
Benton	97,499	Bentonville	876
Boone	28,297	Harrison	601
Bradley	11,793	Warren	654
Calhoun	5,826	Hampton	632
Carroll	18,654	Berryville & Eureka Sp.	642
Chicot	15,713	Lake Village	690
Clark	21,437	Arkadelphia	882
Clay	18,107	Corning & Piggott	641
Cleburne	19,411	Heber Springs	591
Cleveland	7,781	Rison	598
Columbia	25,691	Magnolia	766
Conway	19,151	Morrilton	566
Craighead	68,956	Jonesboro & Lake City	713
Crawford	42,493	Van Buren	604
Crittenden	49,939	Marion	636
Cross	19,225	Wynne	622
Dallas	9,614	Fordyce	668
Desha	16,798	Arkansas City	819
Drew	17,369	Monticello	835
Faulkner	60,006	Conway	664
Franklin	14,897	Charleston & Ozark	919
Fulton	10,037	Salem	620
Garland	73,397	Hot Springs	734
Grant	13,948	Sheridan	633
Greene	31,804	Paragould	579
Hempstead	21,621	Hope	741
Hot Spring	26,115	Malvern	622
Howard	13,569	Nashville	595
Independence	31,192	Batesville	771
Izard	11,364	Melbourne	584
Jackson	18,944	Newport	641
Jefferson	85,487	Pine Bluff	913
Johnson	18,221	Clarksville	682
Lafayette	9,643	Lewisville	545
Lawrence	17,455	Walnut Ridge	592
Lee	13,053	Marianna	619
Lincoln	13,690	Star City	572
Little River	13,966	Ashdown	564
Logan	20,557	Booneville & Paris	731
Lonoke	39,268	Lonoke	802
Madison	11,618	Huntsville	837
Marion	12,001	Yellville	640
Miller	38,467	Texarkana	637
Mississippi	57,525	Blytheville & Osceola	919
Monroe	11,333	Clarendon	621
Montgomery	7,841	Mount Ida	800

County	Pop.	County Seat or court house	Land area sq mi
Nevada	10,101	Prescott	620
Newton	7,666	Jasper	823
Ouachita	30,574	Camden	739
Perry	7,969	Perryville	560
Phillips	28,836	Helena	727
Pike	10,086	Murfreesboro	613
Poinsett	24,664	Harrisburg	763
Polk	17,347	Mena	862
Pope	45,883	Russellville	830
Prairie	9,518	Des Arc & De Valls Bluff	675
Pulaski	349,569	Little Rock	807
Randolph	16,558	Pocahontas	656
Saint Francis	28,497	Forrest City	642
Saline	64,183	Benton	730
Scott	10,205	Waldron	898
Searcy	7,841	Marshall	668
Sebastian	99,590	Fort Smith & Greenwood	546
Sevier	13,637	De Queen	581
Sharp	14,109	Ash Flat	606
Stone	9,775	Mountain View	609
Union	46,719	El Dorado	1,055
Van Buren	14,008	Clinton	724
Washington	113,409	Fayetteville	956
White	54,676	Searcy	1,042
Woodruff	9,520	Augusta	594
Yell	17,759	Danville & Dardanelle	948

California

(58 counties, 155,973 sq mi land; pop. 29,760,021)

County	Pop.	County Seat or court house	Land area sq mi
Alameda	1,276,702	Oakland	736
Alpine	1,113	Markleeville	738
Amador	30,039	Jackson	589
Butte	182,120	Oroville	1,646
Calaveras	31,998	San Andreas	1,021
Colusa	16,275	Colusa	1,152
Contra Costa	803,732	Martinez	730
Del Norte	23,460	Crescent City	1,007
El Dorado	125,995	Placerville	1,715
Fresno	667,490	Fresno	5,978
Glenn	24,798	Willows	1,319
Humboldt	119,118	Eureka	3,579
Imperial	109,303	El Centro	4,173
Inyo	18,281	Independence	10,223
Kern	543,981	Bakersfield	8,130
Kings	101,469	Hanford	1,392
Lake	50,631	Lakeport	1,262
Lassen	27,598	Susanville	4,553
Los Angeles	8,863,052	Los Angeles	4,070
Madera	88,090	Madera	2,145
Marin	230,096	San Rafael	523
Mariposa	14,302	Mariposa	1,456
Mendocino	80,345	Ukiah	3,512
Merced	178,403	Merced	1,944
Modoc	9,678	Alturas	4,064
Mono	9,956	Bridgeport	3,018
Monterey	355,660	Salinas	3,303
Napa	110,765	Napa	744
Nevada	78,510	Nevada City	960
Orange	2,410,668	Santa Ana	798
Placer	172,796	Auburn	1,416
Plumas	19,739	Quincy	2,573
Riverside	1,170,413	Riverside	7,214
Sacramento	1,041,219	Sacramento	971
San Benito	36,697	Hollister	1,388
San Bernardino	1,418,380	San Bernardino	20,064
San Diego	2,498,016	San Diego	4,212
San Francisco	723,959	San Francisco	46
San Joaquin	480,628	Stockton	1,415
San Luis Obispo	217,162	San Luis Obispo	3,308
San Mateo	649,623	Redwood City	447
Santa Barbara	369,608	Santa Barbara	2,748
Santa Clara	1,497,577	San Jose	1,293
Santa Cruz	229,734	Santa Cruz	446
Shasta	147,036	Redding	3,786
Sierra	3,318	Downieville	959
Siskiyou	43,531	Yreka	6,281
Solano	339,471	Fairfield	834
Sonoma	388,222	Santa Rosa	1,604
Stanislaus	370,522	Modesto	1,506
Sutter	64,415	Yuba City	602
Tehama	49,625	Red Bluff	2,953
Trinity	13,063	Weaverville	3,190
Tulare	311,921	Visalia	4,808
Tuolumne	48,456	Sonora	2,234
Ventura	669,016	Ventura	1,862
Yolo	141,210	Woodland	1,014
Yuba	58,228	Marysville	640

Colorado

(63 counties, 103,973 sq mi land; pop. 3,294,394)

County	Pop.	County Seat or court house	Land area sq mi
Adams	265,038	Brighton	1,235
Alamosa	13,617	Alamosa	719
Arapahoe	391,511	Littleton	800
Archuleta	5,345	Pagosa Springs	1,353
Baca	4,556	Springfield	2,554
Bent	5,048	Las Animas	1,517
Boulder	225,339	Boulder	742
Chaffee	12,684	Salida	1,008
Cheyenne	2,397	Cheyenne Wells	1,783
Clear Creek	7,619	Georgetown	396
Conejos	7,453	Conejos	1,284
Costilla	3,190	San Luis	1,227
Crowley	3,946	Ordway	790
Custer	1,926	Westcliffe	740
Delta	20,980	Delta	1,141
Denver	467,610	Denver	111
Dolores	1,504	Dove Creek	1,064
Douglas	60,391	Castle Rock	841
Eagle	21,928	Eagle	1,690
Elbert	9,646	Kiowa	1,851
El Paso	397,014	Colorado Springs	2,129
Fremont	32,273	Canon City	1,538
Garfield	29,974	Glenwood Springs	2,952
Gilpin	3,070	Central City	149
Grand	7,966	Hot Sulphur Springs	1,854
Gunnison	10,273	Gunnison	3,238
Hinsdale	467	Lake City	1,115
Huerfano	6,009	Walsenburg	1,584
Jackson	1,605	Walden	1,614
Jefferson	438,430	Golden	768
Kiowa	1,688	Eads	1,758
Kit Carson	7,140	Burlington	2,160
Lake	6,007	Leadville	379
La Plata	32,284	Durango	1,692
Larimer	186,136	Fort Collins	2,604
Las Animas	13,765	Trinidad	4,771
Lincoln	4,529	Hugo	2,586
Logan	17,567	Sterling	1,818
Mesa	93,145	Grand Junction	3,309
Mineral	558	Creede	877
Moffat	11,357	Craig	4,732
Montezuma	18,672	Cortez	2,038
Montrose	24,423	Montrose	2,240
Morgan	21,939	Fort Morgan	1,276
Otero	20,185	La Junta	1,247
Ouray	2,295	Ouray	542
Park	7,174	Fairplay	2,192
Phillips	4,189	Holyoke	688
Pitkin	12,661	Aspen	968
Prowers	13,347	Lamar	1,629
Pueblo	123,051	Pueblo	2,377
Rio Blanco	6,051	Meeker	3,222
Rio Grande	10,770	Del Norte	913
Routt	14,088	Steamboat Springs	2,367
Saguache	4,619	Saguache	3,167
San Juan	745	Silverton	388
San Miguel	3,653	Telluride	1,287
Sedgwick	2,690	Julesburg	540
Summit	12,881	Breckenridge	607
Teller	12,468	Cripple Creek	559
Washington	4,812	Akron	2,520
Weld	131,821	Greeley	3,990
Yuma	8,954	Wray	2,365

Connecticut

(8 counties, 4,845 sq mi land; pop. 3,287,116)

County	Pop.	County Seat or court house	Land area sq mi
Fairfield	827,645	Bridgeport	632
Hartford	851,783	Hartford	739
Litchfield	174,092	Litchfield	921
Middlesex	143,196	Middletown	373
New Haven	804,219	New Haven	610
New London	254,957	Norwich	669
Tolland	128,699	Rockville	412
Windham	102,525	Putnam	515

Delaware

(3 counties, 1,955 sq mi land; pop. 666,168)

County	Pop.	County Seat or court house	Land area sq mi
Kent	110,993	Dover	595
New Castle	441,946	Wilmington	396
Sussex	113,229	Georgetown	942

District of Columbia

(68 sq mi land; pop. 606,900)

Florida

(67 counties, 53,937 sq mi land; pop. 12,937,926)

County	Pop.	County Seat or court house	Land area sq mi
Alachua	181,596	Gainesville	901
Baker	18,486	Macclenny	585
Bay	126,994	Panama City	758
Bradford	22,515	Starke	293
Brevard	398,978	Titusville	995
Broward	1,255,531	Fort Lauderdale	1,211
Calhoun	11,011	Blountstown	568
Charlotte	110,975	Punta Gorda	690
Citrus	93,513	Inverness	629
Clay	105,986	Green Cove Springs	592
Collier	152,099	Naples	1,994
Columbia	42,613	Lake City	796
Dade	1,937,194	Miami	1,955
De Soto	23,865	Arcadia	636
Dixie	10,585	Cross City	701
Duval	672,971	Jacksonville	776
Escambia	262,798	Pensacola	660
Flagler	28,701	Bunnell	491
Franklin	8,967	Apalachicola	545
Gadsden	41,116	Quincy	518
Gilchrist	9,667	Trenton	354
Glades	7,591	Moore Haven	763
Gulf	11,504	Port Saint Joe	559
Hamilton	10,930	Jasper	517
Hardee	19,499	Wauchula	637
Hendry	25,773	La Belle	1,163
Hernando	101,115	Brooksville	477
Highlands	68,432	Sebring	1,029
Hillsborough	834,054	Tampa	1,053
Holmes	15,778	Bonifay	488
Indian River	90,208	Vero Beach	497
Jackson	41,375	Marianna	942
Jefferson	11,296	Monticello	609
Lafayette	5,578	Mayo	545
Lake	152,104	Tavares	954
Lee	335,113	Fort Myers	803
Leon	192,493	Tallahassee	676
Levy	25,912	Bronson	1,100
Liberty	5,569	Bristol	837
Madison	16,569	Madison	710
Manatee	211,707	Bradenton	747
Marion	194,835	Ocala	1,610
Martin	100,900	Stuart	555
Monroe	78,024	Key West	1,034
Nassau	43,941	Fernandina Beach	649
Okaloosa	143,777	Crestview	936
Okeechobee	29,627	Okeechobee	770
Orange	677,491	Orlando	910
Osceola	107,728	Kissimmee	1,350
Palm Beach	863,503	West Palm Beach	1,993
Pasco	281,131	New Port Richey	738
Pinellas	851,659	Clearwater	280
Polk	405,382	Bartow	1,823
Putnam	65,070	Palatka	733
Saint Johns	83,829	Saint Augustine	617
Saint Lucie	150,171	Fort Pierce	581
Santa Rosa	81,608	Milton	1,024
Sarasota	277,776	Sarasota	573
Seminole	287,521	Sanford	298
Sumter	31,577	Bushnell	561
Suwannee	26,780	Live Oak	690
Taylor	17,111	Perry	1,058
Union	10,252	Lake Butler	246
Volusia	370,737	De Land	1,113
Wakulla	14,202	Crawfordville	601
Walton	27,759	De Funiak Springs	1,066
Washington	16,919	Chipley	590

Georgia

(159 counties, 57,919 sq mi land; pop. 6,478,216)

County	Pop.	County Seat or court house	Land area sq mi
Appling	15,744	Baxley	510
Atkinson	6,213	Pearson	344
Bacon	9,566	Alma	286
Baker	3,615	Newton	347
Baldwin	39,530	Milledgeville	257
Banks	10,308	Homer	234
Barrow	29,721	Winder	163
Bartow	55,915	Cartersville	456
Ben Hill	16,245	Fitzgerald	254
Berrien	14,153	Nashville	456
Bibb	150,137	Macon	253
Bleckley	10,430	Cochran	219
Brantley	11,077	Nahunta	445
Brooks	15,398	Quitman	491
Bryan	15,438	Pembroke	441
Bulloch	43,125	Statesboro	678
Burke	20,579	Waynesboro	833
Butts	15,326	Jackson	187
Calhoun	5,013	Morgan	284
Camden	30,167	Woodbine	649
Candler	7,744	Metter	248
Carroll	71,422	Carrollton	501
Catoosa	42,464	Ringgold	162
Charlton	8,496	Folkston	780
Chatham	216,774	Savannah	443
Chattahoochee	16,934	Cusseta	250
Chattooga	22,242	Summerville	313
Cherokee	90,204	Canton	424
Clarke	87,594	Athens	122
Clay	3,364	Fort Gaines	196
Clayton	181,436	Jonesboro	148
Clinch	6,160	Homerville	821
Cobb	447,745	Marietta	343
Coffee	29,592	Douglas	602
Colquitt	36,645	Moultrie	557
Columbia	66,031	Appling	290
Cook	13,456	Adel	233
Coweta	53,853	Newnan	444
Crawford	8,991	Knoxville	328
Crisp	20,011	Cordele	275
Dade	13,147	Trenton	176
Dawson	9,429	Dawsonville	210
Decatur	25,517	Bainbridge	586
De Kalb	546,171	Decatur	270
Dodge	17,607	Eastman	504
Dooly	9,901	Vienna	397
Dougherty	96,321	Albany	330
Douglas	71,120	Douglasville	203
Early	11,854	Blakely	516
Echols	2,334	Statenville	421
Effingham	25,687	Springfield	482
Elbert	18,949	Elberton	367
Emanuel	20,546	Swainsboro	688
Evans	8,724	Claxton	186
Fannin	15,992	Blue Ridge	384
Fayette	62,415	Fayetteville	199
Floyd	81,251	Rome	519
Forsyth	44,083	Cumming	226
Franklin	16,650	Carnesville	264
Fulton	648,779	Atlanta	534
Gilmer	13,368	Ellijay	427
Glascock	2,357	Gibson	144
Glynn	62,496	Brunswick	412
Gordon	35,067	Calhoun	355
Grady	20,279	Cairo	459
Greene	11,793	Greensboro	389
Gwinnett	352,910	Lawrenceville	435
Habersham	27,622	Clarkesville	278
Hall	95,434	Gainesville	379
Hancock	8,908	Sparta	470
Haralson	21,966	Buchanan	283
Harris	17,788	Hamilton	464
Hart	19,712	Hartwell	230
Heard	8,628	Franklin	292
Henry	58,741	McDonough	321
Houston	89,208	Perry	380
Irwin	8,649	Ocilla	362
Jackson	30,005	Jefferson	342
Jasper	8,453	Monticello	371
Jeff Davis	12,032	Hazlehurst	335
Jefferson	17,408	Louisville	529
Jenkins	8,247	Millen	353
Johnson	8,329	Wrightsville	306
Jones	20,739	Gray	394
Lamar	13,038	Barnesville	186
Lanier	5,531	Lakeland	194
Laurens	39,988	Dublin	816
Lee	16,250	Leesburg	358
Liberty	52,745	Hinesville	517
Lincoln	7,442	Lincolnton	196
Long	6,202	Ludowici	402
Lowndes	75,981	Valdosta	507
Lumpkin	14,573	Dahlonega	287
McDuffie	20,119	Thomson	256
McIntosh	8,634	Darien	425
Macon	13,114	Oglethorpe	404
Madison	21,050	Danielsville	285
Marion	5,590	Buena Vista	366
Meriwether	22,411	Greenville	506
Miller	6,280	Colquitt	284
Mitchell	20,275	Camilla	512
Monroe	17,113	Forsyth	397
Montgomery	7,379	Mount Vernon	244
Morgan	12,883	Madison	349
Murray	26,147	Chatsworth	345
Muscogee	179,278	Columbus	218
Newton	41,808	Covington	277
Oconee	17,618	Watkinsville	186

County	Pop.	County Seat or court house	Land area sq mi
Oglethorpe	9,763	Lexington	442
Paulding	41,611	Dallas	312
Peach	21,189	Fort Valley	152
Pickens	14,432	Jasper	232
Pierce	13,328	Blackshear	344
Pike	10,224	Zebulon	219
Polk	33,815	Cedartown	311
Pulaski	8,108	Hawkinsville	249
Putnam	14,137	Eatonton	344
Quitman	2,210	Georgetown	146
Rabun	11,648	Clayton	370
Randolph	8,023	Cuthbert	431
Richmond	189,719	Augusta	326
Rockdale	54,091	Conyers	132
Schley	3,590	Ellaville	169
Screven	13,842	Sylvania	655
Seminole	9,010	Donalsonville	225
Spalding	54,457	Griffin	199
Stephens	23,436	Toccoa	177
Stewart	5,654	Lumpkin	452
Sumter	30,232	Americus	489
Talbot	6,524	Talbotton	395
Taliaferro	1,915	Crawfordville	196
Tattnall	17,722	Reidsville	484
Taylor	7,642	Butler	382
Telfair	11,000	MacRae	444
Terrell	10,653	Dawson	337
Thomas	38,943	Thomasville	551
Tift	34,998	Tifton	268
Toombs	24,072	Lyons	371
Towns	6,754	Hiawassee	165
Treutlen	5,994	Soperton	202
Troup	55,532	La Grange	414
Turner	8,703	Ashburn	289
Twiggs	9,806	Jeffersonville	362
Union	11,993	Blairsville	320
Upson	26,300	Thomaston	326
Walker	58,340	La Fayette	446
Walton	38,586	Monroe	330
Ware	35,471	Waycross	907
Warren	6,078	Warrenton	286
Washington	19,112	Sandersville	684
Wayne	22,356	Jesup	647
Webster	2,263	Preston	210
Wheeler	4,903	Alamo	299
White	13,006	Cleveland	242
Whitfield	72,462	Dalton	291
Wilcox	7,008	Abbeville	382
Wilkes	10,597	Washington	470
Wilkinson	10,228	Irwinton	451
Worth	19,744	Sylvester	575

Hawaii

(4 counties, 6,423 sq mi land; pop. 1,108,229)

County	Pop.	County Seat or court house	Land area sq mi
Hawaii	120,317	Hilo	4,034
Honolulu	836,231	Honolulu	596
Kauai	51,177	Lihue	620
Maui	100,374	Wailuku	1,175

Idaho

(44 counties, 82,751 sq mi land; pop. 1,006,749)

County	Pop.	County Seat or court house	Land area sq mi
Ada	205,775	Boise	1,052
Adams	3,254	Council	1,362
Bannock	66,026	Pocatello	1,112
Bear Lake	6,084	Paris	990
Benewah	7,937	Saint Maries	784
Bingham	37,583	Blackfoot	2,096
Blaine	13,552	Hailey	2,634
Boise	3,509	Idaho City	1,901
Bonner	26,622	Sandpoint	1,726
Bonneville	72,207	Idaho Falls	1,840
Boundary	8,332	Bonners Ferry	1,268
Butte	2,918	Arco	2,236
Camas	727	Fairfield	1,071
Canyon	90,076	Caldwell	584
Caribou	6,963	Soda Springs	1,763
Cassia	19,532	Burley	2,560
Clark	762	Dubois	1,763
Clearwater	8,505	Orofino	2,460
Custer	4,133	Challis	4,927
Elmore	21,205	Mountain Home	3,071
Franklin	9,232	Preston	664
Fremont	10,937	Saint Anthony	1,852
Gem	11,844	Emmett	558
Gooding	11,633	Gooding	728
Idaho	13,768	Grangeville	8,497
Jefferson	16,543	Rigby	1,093
Jerome	15,138	Jerome	601
Kootenai	69,795	Coeur d'Alene	1,240

County	Pop.	County Seat or court house	Land area sq mi
Latah	30,617	Moscow	1,077
Lemhi	6,899	Salmon	4,564
Lewis	3,516	Nezperce	478
Lincoln	3,308	Shoshone	1,205
Madison	23,674	Rexberg	468
Minidoka	19,361	Rupert	757
Nez Perce	33,754	Lewiston	845
Oneida	3,492	Malad City	1,200
Owyhee	8,392	Murphy	7,643
Payette	16,434	Payette	405
Power	7,086	American Falls	1,403
Shoshone	13,931	Wallace	2,641
Teton	3,439	Driggs	448
Twin Falls	53,580	Twin Falls	1,944
Valley	6,109	Cascade	3,670
Washington	8,550	Weiser	1,454

Illinois

(102 counties, 55,593 sq mi land; pop. 11,430,602)

County	Pop.	County Seat or court house	Land area sq mi
Adams	66,090	Quincy	862
Alexander	10,626	Cairo	229
Bond	14,991	Greenville	378
Boone	30,806	Belvidere	283
Brown	5,836	Mount Sterling	306
Bureau	35,688	Princeton	866
Calhoun	5,322	Hardin	247
Carroll	16,805	Mount Carroll	456
Cass	13,437	Virginia	371
Champaign	173,025	Urbana	1,000
Christian	34,418	Taylorville	709
Clark	15,921	Marshall	505
Clay	14,460	Louisville	464
Clinton	33,944	Carlyle	434
Coles	51,644	Charleston	506
Cook	5,105,044	Chicago	954
Crawford	19,464	Robinson	443
Cumberland	10,670	Toledo	347
DeKalb	77,932	Sycamore	636
De Witt	16,516	Clinton	399
Douglas	19,464	Tuscola	420
Du Page	781,689	Wheaton	337
Edgar	19,595	Paris	628
Edwards	7,440	Albion	225
Effingham	31,704	Effingham	481
Fayette	20,893	Vandalia	703
Ford	14,275	Paxton	488
Franklin	40,319	Benton	434
Fulton	38,080	Lewiston	877
Gallatin	6,909	Shawneetown	328
Greene	15,317	Carrollton	543
Grundy	32,337	Morris	432
Hamilton	8,499	McLeansboro	435
Hancock	21,373	Carthage	797
Hardin	5,189	Elizabethtown	183
Henderson	8,096	Oquawka	376
Henry	51,159	Cambridge	826
Iroquois	30,787	Watseka	1,122
Jackson	61,067	Murphysboro	605
Jasper	10,609	Newton	495
Jefferson	37,020	Mount Vernon	573
Jersey	20,539	Jerseyville	376
Jo Daviess	21,821	Galena	606
Johnson	11,347	Vienna	345
Kane	317,471	Geneva	520
Kankakee	96,255	Kankakee	678
Kendall	39,413	Yorkville	320
Knox	56,393	Galesburg	728
Lake	516,418	Waukegan	457
La Salle	106,913	Ottawa	1,150
Lawrence	15,972	Lawrenceville	374
Lee	34,392	Dixon	728
Livingston	39,301	Pontiac	1,043
Logan	30,798	Lincoln	622
McDonough	35,244	Macomb	582
McHenry	183,241	Woodstock	610
McLean	129,180	Bloomington	1,173
Macon	117,206	Decatur	578
Macoupin	47,679	Carlinville	872
Madison	249,238	Edwardsville	733
Marion	41,561	Salem	579
Marshall	12,846	Lacon	391
Mason	16,269	Havana	541
Massac	14,752	Metropolis	245
Menard	11,164	Petersburg	312
Mercer	17,290	Aledo	556
Monroe	22,422	Waterloo	382
Montgomery	30,728	Hillsboro	705
Morgan	36,397	Jacksonville	561
Moultrie	13,930	Sullivan	326
Ogle	45,957	Oregon	758
Peoria	182,827	Peoria	623
Perry	21,412	Pinckneyville	439

County	Pop.	County Seat or court house	Land area sq mi
Piatt	15,548	Monticello	437
Pike	17,577	Pittsfield	828
Pope	4,373	Golconda	381
Pulaski	7,523	Mound City	204
Putnam	5,730	Hennepin	160
Randolph	34,583	Chester	594
Richland	16,545	Olney	364
Rock Island	148,723	Rock Island	424
Saint Clair	262,852	Belleville	673
Saline	26,551	Harrisburg	383
Sangamon	178,386	Springfield	879
Schuyler	7,498	Rushville	434
Scott	5,644	Winchester	251
Shelby	22,261	Shelbyville	752
Stark	6,534	Toulon	291
Stephenson	48,052	Freeport	568
Tazewell	123,692	Pekin	652
Union	17,619	Jonesboro	416
Vermilion	88,257	Danville	899
Wabash	13,111	Mount Carmel	222
Warren	19,181	Monmouth	541
Washington	14,965	Nashville	564
Wayne	17,241	Fairfield	715
White	16,522	Carmi	502
Whiteside	60,186	Morrison	687
Will	357,313	Joliet	847
Williamson	57,733	Marion	429
Winnebago	252,913	Rockford	519
Woodford	32,653	Eureka	528

Indiana

(92 counties, 35,870 sq mi land; pop. 5,544,159)

County	Pop.	County Seat or court house	Land area sq mi
Adams	31,095	Decatur	339
Allen	300,836	Fort Wayne	657
Bartholomew	63,657	Columbus	407
Benton	9,441	Fowler	406
Blackford	14,067	Hartford City	165
Boone	38,147	Lebanon	423
Brown	14,080	Nashville	312
Carroll	18,809	Delphi	372
Cass	38,413	Logansport	413
Clark	87,774	Jeffersonville	375
Clay	24,705	Brazil	358
Clinton	30,974	Frankfort	405
Crawford	9,914	English	306
Daviess	27,533	Washington	431
Dearborn	38,835	Lawrenceburg	305
Decatur	23,645	Greensburg	373
DeKalb	35,324	Auburn	363
Delaware	119,659	Muncie	393
Dubois	36,616	Jasper	430
Elkhart	156,198	Goshen	464
Fayette	26,015	Connersville	215
Floyd	64,404	New Albany	148
Fountain	17,808	Covington	396
Franklin	19,580	Brookville	386
Fulton	18,840	Rochester	369
Gibson	31,913	Princeton	489
Grant	74,169	Marion	414
Greene	30,410	Bloomfield	542
Hamilton	108,936	Noblesville	398
Hancock	45,527	Greenfield	306
Harrison	29,890	Corydon	485
Hendricks	75,717	Danville	408
Henry	48,139	New Castle	393
Howard	80,827	Kokomo	293
Huntington	35,427	Huntington	383
Jackson	37,730	Brownstown	509
Jasper	24,960	Rensselaer	560
Jay	21,512	Portland	384
Jefferson	29,797	Madison	361
Jennings	23,661	Vernon	377
Johnson	88,109	Franklin	320
Knox	39,884	Vincennes	516
Kosciusko	65,294	Warsaw	538
Lagrange	29,477	Lagrange	380
Lake	475,594	Crown Point	497
La Porte	107,066	La Porte	598
Lawrence	42,836	Bedford	449
Madison	130,669	Anderson	452
Marion	797,159	Indianapolis	396
Marshall	42,182	Plymouth	444
Martin	10,369	Shoals	336
Miami	36,897	Peru	376
Monroe	108,978	Bloomington	394
Montgomery	34,436	Crawfordsville	505
Morgan	55,920	Martinsville	407
Newton	13,551	Kentland	402
Noble	37,877	Albion	411
Ohio	5,315	Rising Sun	87
Orange	18,409	Paoli	400
Owen	17,281	Spencer	385
Parke	15,410	Rockville	445
Perry	19,107	Cannelton	381
Pike	12,509	Petersburg	336
Porter	128,932	Valparaiso	418
Posey	25,968	Mount Vernon	409
Pulaski	12,643	Winamac	434
Putnam	30,315	Greencastle	480
Randolph	27,148	Winchester	453
Ripley	24,616	Versailles	446
Rush	18,129	Rushville	408
Saint Joseph	247,052	South Bend	457
Scott	20,991	Scottsburg	190
Shelby	40,307	Shelbyville	413
Spencer	19,490	Rockport	399
Starke	22,747	Knox	309
Steuben	27,446	Angola	309
Sullivan	18,993	Sullivan	447
Switzerland	7,738	Vevay	221
Tippecanoe	130,598	Lafayette	500
Tipton	16,119	Tipton	260
Union	6,976	Liberty	162
Vanderburgh	165,058	Evansville	235
Vermillion	16,773	Newport	257
Vigo	106,107	Terre Haute	403
Wabash	35,069	Wabash	413
Warren	8,176	Williamsport	365
Warrick	44,920	Boonville	384
Washington	23,717	Salem	515
Wayne	71,951	Richmond	404
Wells	25,948	Bluffton	370
White	23,265	Monticello	505
Whitley	27,651	Columbia City	336

Iowa

(99 counties, 55,875 sq mi land; pop. 2,776,755)

County	Pop.	County Seat or court house	Land area sq mi
Adair	8,409	Greenfield	570
Adams	4,866	Corning	426
Allamakee	13,855	Waukon	660
Appanoose	13,743	Centerville	515
Audubon	7,334	Audubon	444
Benton	22,429	Vinton	718
Black Hawk	123,798	Waterloo	573
Boone	25,186	Boone	574
Bremer	22,813	Waverly	439
Buchanan	20,844	Independence	573
Buena Vista	19,965	Storm Lake	580
Butler	15,731	Allison	582
Calhoun	11,508	Rockwell City	573
Carroll	21,423	Carroll	570
Cass	15,128	Atlantic	565
Cedar	17,444	Tipton	582
Cerro Gordo	46,733	Mason City	575
Cherokee	14,098	Cherokee	577
Chickasaw	13,295	New Hampton	505
Clarke	8,287	Osceola	431
Clay	17,585	Spencer	573
Clayton	19,054	Elkader	795
Clinton	51,040	Clinton	710
Crawford	16,775	Denison	714
Dallas	29,755	Adel	591
Davis	8,312	Bloomfield	505
Decatur	8,338	Leon	535
Delaware	18,035	Manchester	579
Des Moines	42,614	Burlington	429
Dickinson	14,909	Spirit Lake	404
Dubuque	86,403	Dubuque	616
Emmet	11,569	Estherville	402
Fayette	21,843	West Union	731
Floyd	17,058	Charles City	501
Franklin	11,364	Hampton	583
Fremont	8,226	Sidney	517
Greene	10,045	Jefferson	572
Grundy	12,029	Grundy Center	501
Guthrie	10,935	Guthrie Center	594
Hamilton	16,071	Webster City	577
Hancock	12,638	Garner	573
Hardin	19,094	Eldora	569
Harrison	14,730	Logan	701
Henry	19,226	Mount Pleasant	436
Howard	9,809	Cresco	473
Humboldt	10,756	Dakota City	436
Ida	8,365	Ida Grove	432
Iowa	14,630	Marengo	588
Jackson	19,950	Maquoketa	650
Jasper	34,795	Newton	732
Jefferson	16,310	Fairfield	440
Johnson	96,119	Iowa City	623
Jones	19,444	Anamosa	576
Keokuk	11,624	Sigourney	580
Kossuth	18,591	Algona	976
Lee	38,687	Fort Madison and Keokuk	540
Linn	168,767	Cedar Rapids	724
Louisa	11,592	Wapello	417

County	Pop.	County Seat or court house	Land area sq mi
Lucas	9,070	Chariton	435
Lyon	11,952	Rock Rapids	588
Madison	12,483	Winterset	563
Mahaska	21,532	Oskaloosa	572
Marion	30,001	Knoxville	575
Marshall	38,276	Marshalltown	573
Mills	13,202	Glenwood	441
Mitchell	10,928	Osage	470
Monona	10,034	Onawa	699
Monroe	8,114	Albia	434
Montgomery	12,076	Red Oak	424
Muscatine	39,907	Muscatine	449
O'Brien	15,444	Primghar	574
Osceola	7,267	Sibley	399
Page	16,870	Clarinda	535
Palo Alto	10,669	Emmetsburg	568
Plymouth	23,388	Le Mars	864
Pocahontas	9,525	Pocahontas	578
Polk	327,140	Des Moines	592
Pottawattamie	82,628	Council Bluffs	959
Poweshiek	19,033	Montezuma	586
Ringgold	5,420	Mount Ayr	536
Sac	12,324	Sac City	578
Scott	150,973	Davenport	469
Shelby	13,230	Harlan	591
Sioux	29,903	Orange City	769
Story	74,252	Nevada	574
Tama	17,419	Toledo	722
Taylor	7,114	Bedford	537
Union	12,750	Creston	427
Van Buren	7,676	Keosauqua	489
Wapello	35,696	Ottumwa	436
Warren	36,033	Indianola	573
Washington	19,612	Washington	571
Wayne	7,067	Corydon	527
Webster	40,342	Fort Dodge	718
Winnebago	12,122	Forest City	402
Winneshiek	20,847	Decorah	690
Woodbury	98,276	Sioux City	877
Worth	7,991	Northwood	402
Wright	14,269	Clarion	582

Kansas

(105 counties, 81,823 sq mi land; pop. 2,477,574)

County	Pop.	County Seat or court house	Land area sq mi
Allen	14,638	Iola	505
Anderson	7,803	Garnett	584
Atchison	16,932	Atchison	431
Barber	5,874	Medicine Lodge	1,136
Barton	29,382	Great Bend	895
Bourbon	14,966	Fort Scott	638
Brown	11,128	Hiawatha	572
Butler	50,580	El Dorado	1,443
Chase	3,021	Cottonwood Falls	777
Chautauqua	4,407	Sedan	644
Cherokee	21,374	Columbus	590
Cheyenne	3,243	Saint Francis	1,021
Clark	2,418	Ashland	975
Clay	9,158	Clay Center	632
Cloud	11,023	Concordia	718
Coffey	8,404	Burlington	615
Comanche	2,313	Coldwater	789
Cowley	36,915	Winfield	1,128
Crawford	35,582	Girard	595
Decatur	4,021	Oberlin	894
Dickinson	18,958	Abilene	852
Doniphan	8,134	Troy	388
Douglas	81,798	Lawrence	461
Edwards	3,787	Kinsley	620
Elk	3,327	Howard	650
Ellis	26,004	Hays	900
Ellsworth	6,586	Ellsworth	717
Finney	33,070	Garden City	1,302
Ford	27,463	Dodge City	1,099
Franklin	21,994	Ottawa	577
Geary	30,453	Junction City	377
Gove	3,231	Gove	1,072
Graham	3,543	Hill City	898
Grant	7,159	Ulysses	575
Gray	5,396	Cimarron	868
Greeley	1,774	Tribune	778
Greenwood	7,847	Eureka	1,135
Hamilton	2,388	Syracuse	998
Harper	7,124	Anthony	802
Harvey	31,028	Newton	540
Haskell	3,886	Sublette	578
Hodgeman	2,177	Jetmore	860
Jackson	11,525	Holton	658
Jefferson	15,905	Oskaloosa	535
Jewell	4,251	Mankato	910
Johnson	355,021	Olathe	478
Kearny	4,027	Lakin	868
Kingman	8,292	Kingman	865
Kiowa	3,660	Greensburg	723
Labette	23,693	Oswego	653
Lane	2,375	Dighton	717
Leavenworth	64,371	Leavenworth	463
Lincoln	3,653	Lincoln	720
Linn	8,254	Mound City	601
Logan	3,081	Oakley	1,073
Lyon	34,732	Emporia	844
McPherson	27,268	McPherson	900
Marion	12,888	Marion	944
Marshall	11,705	Marysville	878
Meade	4,247	Meade	979
Miami	23,466	Paola	590
Mitchell	7,203	Beloit	717
Montgomery	38,816	Independence	646
Morris	6,198	Council Grove	693
Morton	3,480	Elkhart	731
Nemaha	10,446	Seneca	719
Neosho	17,035	Erie	576
Ness	4,033	Ness City	1,074
Norton	5,947	Norton	873
Osage	15,248	Lyndon	695
Osborne	4,867	Osborne	882
Ottawa	5,634	Minneapolis	721
Pawnee	7,555	Larned	755
Phillips	6,590	Phillipsburg	887
Pottawatomie	16,128	Westmoreland	828
Pratt	9,702	Pratt	735
Rawlins	3,404	Atwood	1,069
Reno	62,389	Hutchinson	1,259
Republic	6,482	Belleville	719
Rice	10,610	Lyons	728
Riley	67,139	Manhattan	593
Rooks	6,039	Stockton	888
Rush	3,842	LaCrosse	718
Russell	7,835	Russell	869
Saline	49,301	Salina	721
Scott	5,289	Scott City	718
Sedgwick	403,662	Wichita	1,007
Seward	18,743	Liberal	640
Shawnee	160,976	Topeka	549
Sheridan	3,043	Hoxie	896
Sherman	6,926	Goodland	1,057
Smith	5,078	Smith Center	897
Stafford	5,365	Saint John	788
Stanton	2,333	Johnson	681
Stevens	5,048	Hugoton	727
Sumner	25,841	Wellington	1,183
Thomas	8,258	Colby	1,075
Trego	3,694	WaKeeney	890
Wabaunsee	6,603	Alma	797
Wallace	1,821	Sharon Springs	914
Washington	7,073	Washington	898
Wichita	2,758	Leoti	719
Wilson	10,289	Fredonia	575
Woodson	4,116	Yates Center	498
Wyandotte	162,026	Kansas City	149

Kentucky

(120 counties, 39,732 sq mi land; pop. 3,685,296)

County	Pop.	County Seat or court house	Land area sq mi
Adair	15,360	Columbia	407
Allen	14,628	Scottsville	346
Anderson	14,571	Lawrenceburg	203
Ballard	7,902	Wickliffe	251
Barren	34,001	Glasgow	491
Bath	9,692	Owingsville	279
Bell	31,506	Pineville	361
Boone	57,589	Burlington	246
Bourbon	19,236	Paris	291
Boyd	51,150	Catlettsburg	160
Boyle	25,641	Danville	182
Bracken	7,766	Brooksville	203
Breathitt	15,703	Jackson	495
Breckinridge	16,312	Hardinsburg	572
Bullitt	47,567	Shepherdsville	299
Butler	11,245	Morgantown	428
Caldwell	13,232	Princeton	347
Calloway	30,735	Murray	386
Campbell	83,866	Newport	152
Carlisle	5,238	Bardwell	193
Carroll	9,292	Carrollton	130
Carter	24,340	Grayson	411
Casey	14,211	Liberty	446
Christian	68,941	Hopkinsville	721
Clark	29,496	Winchester	254
Clay	21,746	Manchester	471
Clinton	9,135	Albany	198
Crittenden	9,196	Marion	362
Cumberland	6,784	Burkesville	306
Daviess	87,189	Owensboro	462

County	Pop.	County Seat or court house	Land area sq mi
Edmonson	10,357	Brownsville	303
Elliott	6,455	Sandy Hook	234
Estill	14,614	Irvine	254
Fayette	225,366	Lexington	286
Fleming	12,292	Flemingsburg	351
Floyd	43,586	Prestonsburg	394
Franklin	44,143	Frankfort	211
Fulton	8,271	Hickman	209
Gallatin	5,393	Warsaw	99
Garrard	11,579	Lancaster	231
Grant	15,737	Williamstown	260
Graves	33,550	Mayfield	556
Grayson	21,050	Leitchfield	504
Green	10,371	Greensburg	289
Greenup	36,742	Greenup	346
Hancock	7,864	Hawesville	189
Hardin	89,240	Elizabethtown	628
Harlan	36,574	Harlan	467
Harrison	16,248	Cynthiana	310
Hart	14,890	Munfordville	416
Henderson	43,044	Henderson	440
Henry	12,823	New Castle	289
Hickman	5,566	Clinton	245
Hopkins	46,126	Madisonville	551
Jackson	11,955	McKee	346
Jefferson	665,123	Louisville	385
Jessamine	30,508	Nicholasville	173
Johnson	23,248	Paintsville	262
Kenton	142,031	Covington	163
Knott	17,906	Hindman	352
Knox	29,676	Barbourville	388
Larue	11,679	Hodgenville	263
Laurel	43,438	London	436
Lawrence	13,998	Louisa	419
Lee	7,422	Beattyville	210
Leslie	13,642	Hyden	404
Letcher	27,000	Whitesburg	339
Lewis	13,029	Vanceburg	485
Lincoln	20,045	Stanford	337
Livingston	9,062	Smithland	316
Logan	24,416	Russellville	556
Lyon	6,624	Eddyville	216
McCracken	62,879	Paducah	251
McCreary	15,603	Whitley City	428
McLean	9,628	Calhoun	254
Madison	57,508	Richmond	441
Magoffin	13,077	Salyersville	310
Marion	16,499	Lebanon	347
Marshall	27,205	Benton	305
Martin	12,526	Inez	231
Mason	16,666	Maysville	241
Meade	24,170	Brandenburg	309
Menifee	5,092	Frenchburg	204
Mercer	19,148	Harrodsburg	251
Metcalfe	8,963	Edmonton	291
Monroe	11,401	Tompkinsville	331
Montgomery	19,561	Mount Sterling	199
Morgan	11,648	West Liberty	381
Muhlenberg	31,318	Greenville	475
Nelson	29,710	Bardstown	423
Nicholas	6,725	Carlisle	197
Ohio	21,105	Hartford	594
Oldham	33,263	La Grange	189
Owen	9,035	Owenton	352
Owsley	5,036	Booneville	198
Pendleton	12,036	Falmouth	280
Perry	30,283	Hazard	342
Pike	72,583	Pikeville	788
Powell	11,686	Stanton	180
Pulaski	49,489	Somerset	662
Robertson	2,124	Mount Olivet	100
Rockcastle	14,803	Mount Vernon	318
Rowan	20,353	Morehead	281
Russell	14,716	Jamestown	254
Scott	23,867	Georgetown	285
Shelby	24,824	Shelbyville	384
Simpson	15,145	Franklin	236
Spencer	6,801	Taylorsville	186
Taylor	21,146	Campbellsville	270
Todd	10,940	Elkton	376
Trigg	10,361	Cadiz	443
Trimble	6,090	Bedford	149
Union	16,557	Morganfield	345
Warren	77,720	Bowling Green	545
Washington	10,441	Springfield	301
Wayne	17,468	Monticello	459
Webster	13,955	Dixon	335
Whitley	33,326	Williamsburg	440
Wolfe	6,503	Campton	223
Woodford	19,955	Versailles	191

Louisiana

(64 parishes, 43,566 sq mi land; pop. 4,219,973)

County	Pop.	County Seat or court house	Land area sq mi
Acadia	55,882	Crowley	657
Allen	21,226	Oberlin	765
Ascension	58,214	Donaldsonville	296
Assumption	22,753	Napoleonville	342
Avoyelles	39,159	Marksville	846
Beauregard	30,083	De Ridder	1,163
Bienville	15,979	Arcadia	816
Bossier	86,088	Benton	845
Caddo	248,253	Shreveport	894
Calcasieu	168,134	Lake Charles	1,082
Caldwell	9,806	Columbia	541
Cameron	9,260	Cameron	1,417
Catahoula	11,065	Harrisonburg	732
Claiborne	17,405	Homer	765
Concordia	20,828	Vidalia	717
De Soto	25,346	Mansfield	880
East Baton Rouge	380,105	Baton Rouge	458
East Carroll	9,709	Lake Providence	426
East Feliciana	19,211	Clinton	455
Evangeline	33,274	Ville Platte	667
Franklin	22,387	Winnsboro	635
Grant	17,526	Colfax	653
Iberia	68,297	New Iberia	589
Iberville	31,049	Plaquemine	638
Jackson	15,705	Jonesboro	579
Jefferson	448,306	Gretna	348
Jefferson Davis	30,722	Jennings	655
Lafayette	164,762	Lafayette	270
Lafourche	85,860	Thibodaux	1,141
La Salle	13,662	Jena	638
Lincoln	41,745	Ruston	472
Livingston	70,523	Livingston	661
Madison	12,463	Tallulah	631
Morehouse	31,938	Bastrop	807
Natchitoches	36,689	Natchitoches	1,264
Orleans	496,938	New Orleans	199
Ouachita	142,191	Monroe	627
Plaquemines	25,575	Pointe a la Hache	1,035
Pointe Coupee	22,540	New Roads	566
Rapides	131,556	Alexandria	1,341
Red River	9,387	Coushatta	394
Richland	20,629	Rayville	563
Sabine	22,646	Many	855
Saint Bernard	66,631	Chalmette	486
Saint Charles	42,437	Hahnville	286
Saint Helena	9,874	Greensburg	409
Saint James	20,879	Convent	248
Saint John The Baptist	39,996	Edgard	213
Saint Landry	80,312	Opelousas	936
Saint Martin	44,097	Saint Martinville	749
Saint Mary	58,086	Franklin	613
Saint Tammany	144,500	Covington	873
Tangipahoa	85,709	Amite	783
Tensas	7,103	Saint Joseph	623
Terrebonne	96,982	Houma	1,367
Union	20,796	Farmerville	884
Vermilion	50,055	Abbeville	1,205
Vernon	61,961	Leesville	1,332
Washington	43,185	Franklinton	676
Webster	41,989	Minden	602
West Baton Rouge	19,419	Port Allen	194
West Carroll	12,093	Oak Grove	360
West Feliciana	12,915	Saint Francisville	406
Winn	16,269	Winnfield	953

Maine

(16 counties, 30,865 sq mi land; pop. 1,227,928)

County	Pop.	County Seat or court house	Land area sq mi
Androscoggin	105,259	Auburn	477
Aroostook	86,936	Houlton	6,721
Cumberland	243,135	Portland	876
Franklin	29,008	Farmington	1,699
Hancock	46,948	Ellsworth	1,537
Kennebec	115,904	Augusta	876
Knox	36,310	Rockland	370
Lincoln	30,357	Wiscasset	458
Oxford	52,602	South Paris	2,053
Penobscot	146,601	Bangor	3,430
Piscataquis	18,653	Dover-Foxcroft	3,986
Sagadahoc	33,535	Bath	257
Somerset	49,767	Skowhegan	3,930
Waldo	33,018	Belfast	730
Washington	35,308	Machias	2,586
York	164,587	Alfred	1,008

Maryland

(23 cos., 1 ind. city, 9,775 sq mi land; pop. 4,781,468)

County	Pop.	County Seat or court house	Land area sq mi
Allegany	74,946	Cumberland	421
Anne Arundel	427,239	Annapolis	418
Baltimore	692,134	Towson	598
Calvert	51,372	Prince Frederick	213
Caroline	27,035	Denton	321
Carroll	123,372	Westminster	452
Cecil	71,347	Elkton	360

County	Pop.	County Seat or court house	Land area sq mi
Charles	101,154	La Plata	452
Dorchester	30,236	Cambridge	593
Frederick	150,208	Frederick	663
Garrett	28,138	Oakland	657
Harford	182,132	Bel Air	448
Howard	187,328	Ellicott City	251
Kent	17,842	Chestertown	278
Montgomery	757,027	Rockville	495
Prince Georges	728,553	Upper Marlboro	487
Queen Annes	33,953	Centreville	372
Saint Mary's	75,974	Leonardtown	373
Somerset	23,440	Princess Anne	338
Talbot	30,549	Easton	259
Washington	121,393	Hagerstown	455
Wicomico	74,339	Salisbury	379
Worcester	35,028	Snow Hill	475
Independent City			
Baltimore	736,014		80

Massachusetts

(14 counties, 7,838 sq mi land; pop. 6,016,425)

County	Pop.	County Seat or court house	Land area sq mi
Barnstable	186,605	Barnstable	400
Berkshire	139,352	Pittsfield	929
Bristol	506,325	Taunton	557
Dukes	11,639	Edgartown	102
Essex	670,080	Salem	495
Franklin	70,092	Greenfield	702
Hampden	456,310	Springfield	618
Hampshire	146,568	Northampton	528
Middlesex	1,398,468	East Cambridge	822
Nantucket	6,012	Nantucket	47
Norfolk	616,087	Dedham	400
Plymouth	435,276	Plymouth	655
Suffolk	663,906	Boston	57
Worcester	709,705	Worcester	1,513

Michigan

(83 counties, 56,809 sq mi land; pop. 9,295,297)

County	Pop.	County Seat or court house	Land area sq mi
Alcona	10,145	Harrisville	679
Alger	8,972	Munising	912
Allegan	90,509	Allegan	832
Alpena	30,605	Alpena	567
Antrim	18,185	Bellaire	480
Arenac	14,906	Standish	367
Baraga	7,954	L'Anse	901
Barry	50,057	Hastings	560
Bay	111,723	Bay City	447
Benzie	12,200	Beulah	322
Berrien	161,378	Saint Joseph	576
Branch	41,502	Coldwater	508
Calhoun	135,982	Marshall	712
Cass	49,477	Cassopolis	496
Charlevoix	21,468	Charlevoix	421
Cheboygan	21,398	Cheboygan	720
Chippewa	34,604	Sault Sainte Marie	1,590
Clare	24,952	Harrison	570
Clinton	57,883	Saint Johns	573
Crawford	12,260	Grayling	559
Delta	37,780	Escanaba	1,173
Dickinson	26,831	Iron Mountain	770
Eaton	92,879	Charlotte	579
Emmet	25,040	Petoskey	468
Genesee	430,459	Flint	642
Gladwin	21,896	Gladwin	505
Gogebic	18,052	Bessemer	1,105
Grand Traverse	64,273	Traverse City	466
Gratiot	38,982	Ithaca	570
Hillsdale	43,431	Hillsdale	603
Houghton	35,446	Houghton	1,014
Huron	34,951	Bad Axe	830
Ingham	281,912	Mason	560
Ionia	57,024	Ionia	577
Iosco	30,209	Tawas City	546
Iron	13,175	Crystal Falls	1,163
Isabella	54,624	Mount Pleasant	577
Jackson	149,756	Jackson	705
Kalamazoo	223,411	Kalamazoo	562
Kalkaska	13,497	Kalkaska	563
Kent	500,631	Grand Rapids	862
Keweenaw	1,701	Eagle River	543
Lake	8,583	Baldwin	568
Lapeer	74,768	Lapeer	658
Leelanau	16,527	Leland	341
Lenawee	91,476	Adrian	753
Livingston	115,645	Howell	574
Luce	5,763	Newberry	904
Mackinac	10,674	Saint Ignace	1,025
Macomb	717,400	Mount Clemens	482
Manistee	21,265	Manistee	543
Marquette	70,887	Marquette	1,821
Mason	25,537	Ludington	494
Mecosta	37,308	Big Rapids	560
Menominee	24,920	Menominee	1,045
Midland	75,651	Midland	525
Missaukee	12,147	Lake City	565
Monroe	133,600	Monroe	557
Montcalm	53,059	Stanton	713
Montmorency	8,936	Atlanta	550
Muskegon	158,983	Muskegon	507
Newaygo	38,206	White Cloud	847
Oakland	1,083,592	Pontiac	875
Oceana	22,455	Hart	541
Ogemaw	18,681	West Branch	570
Ontonagon	8,854	Ontonagon	1,311
Osceola	20,146	Reed City	569
Oscoda	7,842	Mio	568
Otsego	17,957	Gaylord	516
Ottawa	187,768	Grand Haven	567
Presque Isle	13,743	Rogers City	656
Roscommon	19,776	Roscommon	528
Saginaw	211,946	Saginaw	815
Saint Clair	145,607	Port Huron	734
Saint Joseph	58,913	Centreville	503
Sanilac	39,928	Sandusky	964
Schoolcraft	8,302	Manistique	1,173
Shiawassee	69,770	Corunna	540
Tuscola	55,498	Caro	812
Van Buren	70,060	Paw Paw	611
Washtenaw	282,937	Ann Arbor	710
Wayne	2,111,687	Detroit	615
Wexford	26,360	Cadillac	566

Minnesota

(87 counties, 79,617 sq mi land; pop. 4,375,099)

County	Pop.	County Seat or court house	Land area sq mi
Aitkin	12,425	Aitkin	1,834
Anoka	243,641	Anoka	430
Becker	27,881	Detroit Lakes	1,312
Beltrami	34,384	Bemidji	2,507
Benton	30,185	Foley	408
Big Stone	6,285	Ortonville	497
Blue Earth	54,044	Mankato	749
Brown	26,984	New Ulm	610
Carlton	29,259	Carlton	864
Carver	47,915	Chaska	351
Cass	21,791	Walker	2,033
Chippewa	13,228	Montevideo	584
Chisago	30,521	Center City	417
Clay	50,422	Moorhead	1,049
Clearwater	8,309	Bagley	999
Cook	3,868	Grand Marais	1,412
Cottonwood	12,694	Windom	640
Crow Wing	44,249	Brainerd	1,008
Dakota	275,189	Hastings	574
Dodge	15,731	Mantorville	439
Douglas	28,674	Alexandria	643
Faribault	16,937	Blue Earth	714
Fillmore	20,777	Preston	862
Freeborn	33,060	Albert Lea	705
Goodhue	40,690	Red Wing	763
Grant	6,246	Elbow Lake	547
Hennepin	1,032,431	Minneapolis	541
Houston	18,497	Caledonia	564
Hubbard	14,939	Park Rapids	936
Isanti	25,921	Cambridge	440
Itasca	40,863	Grand Rapids	2,661
Jackson	11,677	Jackson	699
Kanabec	12,802	Mora	527
Kandiyohi	38,761	Willmar	784
Kittson	5,767	Hallock	1,104
Koochiching	16,299	International Falls	3,108
Lac qui Parle	8,924	Madison	772
Lake	10,415	Two Harbors	2,053
Lake of the Woods	4,076	Baudette	1,296
Le Sueur	23,239	Le Center	446
Lincoln	6,890	Ivanhoe	538
Lyon	24,789	Marshall	714
McLeod	32,030	Glencoe	489
Mahnomen	5,044	Mahnomen	559
Marshall	10,993	Warren	1,760
Martin	22,914	Fairmont	706
Meeker	20,846	Litchfield	624
Mille Lacs	18,670	Milaca	578
Morrison	29,604	Little Falls	1,124
Mower	37,385	Austin	711
Murray	9,660	Slayton	702
Nicollet	28,076	Saint Peter	440
Nobles	20,098	Worthington	714
Norman	7,975	Ada	877
Olmsted	106,470	Rochester	655
Otter Tail	50,714	Fergus Falls	1,973

County	Pop.	County Seat or court house	Land area sq mi
Pennington	13,306	Thief River Falls	618
Pine	21,264	Pine City	1,421
Pipestone	10,491	Pipestone	466
Polk	32,589	Crookston	1,982
Pope	10,745	Glenwood	668
Ramsey	485,783	Saint Paul	154
Red Lake	4,525	Red Lake Falls	433
Redwood	17,254	Redwood Falls	882
Renville	17,673	Olivia	984
Rice	49,183	Faribault	501
Rock	9,806	Luverne	483
Roseau	15,026	Roseau	1,677
Saint Louis	198,213	Duluth	6,125
Scott	57,846	Shakopee	357
Sherburne	41,945	Elk River	435
Sibley	14,366	Gaylord	593
Stearns	119,324	Saint Cloud	1,338
Steele	30,729	Owatonna	431
Stevens	10,634	Morris	560
Swift	10,724	Benson	743
Todd	23,363	Long Prairie	941
Traverse	4,463	Wheaton	575
Wabasha	19,744	Wabasha	537
Wadena	13,154	Wadena	538
Waseca	18,079	Waseca	422
Washington	145,858	Stillwater	390
Watonwan	11,682	Saint James	435
Wilkin	7,516	Breckenridge	751
Winona	47,828	Winona	630
Wright	68,710	Buffalo	672
Yellow Medicine	11,684	Granite Falls	758

Mississippi

(82 counties, 46,914 sq mi land; pop. 2,573,216)

County	Pop.	County Seat or court house	Land area sq mi
Alcorn	31,722	Corinth	401
Amite	13,328	Liberty	732
Attala	18,481	Kosciusko	737
Benton	8,046	Ashland	407
Bolivar	41,875	Cleveland & Rosedale	892
Calhoun	14,908	Pittsboro	573
Carroll	9,237	Carrollton & Vaiden	634
Chickasaw	18,085	Houston & Okolona	503
Choctaw	9,071	Ackerman	420
Claiborne	11,370	Port Gibson	494
Clarke	17,313	Quitman	692
Clay	21,120	West Point	415
Coahoma	31,665	Clarksdale	559
Copiah	27,592	Hazlehurst	779
Covington	16,527	Collins	416
De Soto	67,910	Hernando	483
Forrest	68,314	Hattiesburg	469
Franklin	8,377	Meadville	566
George	16,673	Lucedale	483
Greene	10,220	Leakesville	718
Grenada	21,555	Grenada	421
Hancock	31,760	Bay Saint Louis	478
Harrison	165,365	Gulfport	581
Hinds	254,441	Jackson & Raymond	875
Holmes	21,604	Lexington	759
Humphreys	12,134	Belzoni	430
Issaquena	1,909	Mayersville	406
Itawamba	20,017	Fulton	541
Jackson	115,243	Pascagoula	731
Jasper	17,114	Bay Springs & Paulding	678
Jefferson	8,653	Fayette	523
Jefferson Davis	14,051	Prentiss	409
Jones	62,031	Ellisville & Laurel	695
Kemper	10,356	De Kalb	766
Lafayette	31,826	Oxford	669
Lamar	30,424	Purvis	499
Lauderdale	75,555	Meridian	705
Lawrence	12,458	Monticello	435
Leake	18,436	Carthage	584
Lee	65,579	Tupelo	451
Leflore	37,341	Greenwood	605
Lincoln	30,278	Brookhaven	586
Lowndes	59,308	Columbus	517
Madison	53,794	Canton	717
Marion	25,544	Columbia	548
Marshall	30,361	Holly Springs	709
Monroe	36,582	Aberdeen	772
Montgomery	12,387	Winona	408
Neshoba	24,800	Philadelphia	571
Newton	20,291	Decatur	580
Noxubee	12,604	Macon	698
Oktibbeha	38,375	Starkville	459
Panola	29,996	Batesville & Sardis	695
Pearl River	38,714	Poplarville	819
Perry	10,865	New Augusta	651
Pike	36,882	Magnolia	410
Pontotoc	22,237	Pontotoc	499
Prentiss	23,278	Booneville	417
Quitman	10,490	Marks	406
Rankin	87,161	Brandon	782
Scott	24,137	Forest	610
Sharkey	7,066	Rolling Fork	435
Simpson	23,953	Mendenhall	591
Smith	14,798	Raleigh	635
Stone	10,750	Wiggins	446
Sunflower	35,129	Indianola	707
Tallahatchie	15,210	Charleston & Sumner	651
Tate	21,432	Senatobia	406
Tippah	19,523	Ripley	458
Tishomingo	17,683	Iuka	434
Tunica	8,164	Tunica	460
Union	22,085	New Albany	417
Walthall	14,352	Tylertown	404
Warren	47,880	Vicksburg	597
Washington	67,935	Greenville	733
Wayne	19,517	Waynesboro	813
Webster	10,222	Walthall	424
Wilkinson	9,678	Woodville	678
Winston	19,433	Louisville	610
Yalobusha	12,033	Coffeeville & Water Valley	478
Yazoo	25,506	Yazoo City	933

Missouri

(114 cos., 1 ind. city, 68,898 sq mi land; pop. 5,117,073)

County	Pop.	County Seat or court house	Land area sq mi
Andrew	14,632	Savannah	435
Atchison	7,457	Rockport	542
Audrain	23,599	Mexico	697
Barry	27,547	Cassville	773
Barton	11,312	Lamar	596
Bates	15,025	Butler	849
Benton	13,859	Warsaw	729
Bollinger	10,619	Marble Hill	621
Boone	112,379	Columbia	687
Buchanan	83,083	Saint Joseph	409
Butler	38,765	Poplar Buff	698
Caldwell	8,380	Kingston	430
Callaway	32,809	Fulton	842
Camden	27,495	Camdenton	641
Cape Girardeau	61,633	Jackson	577
Carroll	10,748	Carrollton	695
Carter	5,515	Van Buren	509
Cass	63,808	Harrisonville	701
Cedar	12,093	Stockton	470
Chariton	9,202	Keytesville	758
Christian	32,644	Ozark	564
Clark	7,547	Kahoka	507
Clay	153,411	Liberty	403
Clinton	16,595	Plattsburg	423
Cole	63,579	Jefferson City	392
Cooper	14,835	Boonville	567
Crawford	19,173	Steelville	744
Dade	7,449	Greenfield	491
Dallas	12,646	Buffalo	543
Daviess	7,865	Gallatin	568
De Kalb	9,967	Maysville	425
Dent	13,702	Salem	755
Douglas	11,876	Ava	814
Dunklin	33,112	Kennett	547
Franklin	80,603	Union	922
Gasconade	14,006	Hermann	521
Gentry	6,854	Albany	493
Greene	207,949	Springfield	677
Grundy	10,536	Trenton	437
Harrison	8,469	Bethany	725
Henry	20,044	Clinton	729
Hickory	7,335	Hermitage	379
Holt	6,034	Oregon	457
Howard	9,631	Fayette	465
Howell	31,447	West Plains	928
Iron	10,726	Ironton	552
Jackson	633,234	Kansas City	611
Jasper	90,465	Carthage	641
Jefferson	171,380	Hillsboro	661
Johnson	42,514	Warrensburg	834
Knox	4,482	Edina	507
Laclede	27,158	Lebanon	768
Lafayette	31,107	Lexington	632
Lawrence	30,236	Mount Vernon	613
Lewis	10,233	Monticello	509
Lincoln	28,892	Troy	627
Linn	13,885	Linneus	620
Livingston	14,592	Chillicothe	537
McDonald	16,938	Pineville	540
Macon	15,345	Macon	797
Madison	11,127	Fredericktown	497
Maries	7,976	Vienna	528
Marion	27,682	Palmyra	438
Mercer	3,723	Princeton	454
Miller	20,700	Tuscumbia	593
Mississippi	14,442	Charleston	410

County	Pop.	County Seat or court house	Land area sq mi
Moniteau	12,298	California	417
Monroe	9,104	Paris	670
Montgomery	11,355	Montgomery City	540
Morgan	15,574	Versailles	594
New Madrid	20,928	New Madrid	658
Newton	44,445	Neosho	627
Nodaway	21,709	Maryville	875
Oregon	9,470	Alton	792
Osage	12,018	Linn	606
Ozark	8,598	Gainesville	731
Pemiscot	21,921	Caruthersville	517
Perry	16,648	Perryville	473
Pettis	35,437	Sedalia	686
Phelps	35,248	Rolla	674
Pike	15,969	Bowling Green	673
Platte	57,867	Platte City	421
Polk	21,826	Bolivar	636
Pulaski	41,307	Waynesville	550
Putnam	5,079	Unionville	520
Ralls	8,476	New London	482
Randolph	24,370	Huntsville	477
Ray	21,968	Richmond	568
Reynolds	6,661	Centerville	809
Ripley	12,303	Doniphan	631
Saint Charles	212,751	Saint Charles	558
Saint Clair	8,457	Osceola	699
Saint Francois	48,904	Farmington	451
Saint Louis	993,508	Clayton	506
Sainte Genevieve	16,037	Sainte Genevieve	504
Saline	23,523	Marshall	755
Schuyler	4,236	Lancaster	309
Scotland	4,822	Memphis	438
Scott	39,376	Benton	423
Shannon	7,613	Eminence	1,004
Shelby	6,942	Shelbyville	501
Stoddard	28,895	Bloomfield	815
Stone	19,078	Galena	451
Sullivan	6,326	Milan	651
Taney	25,561	Forsyth	608
Texas	21,476	Houston	1,180
Vernon	19,041	Nevada	837
Warren	19,534	Warrenton	429
Washington	20,380	Potosi	762
Wayne	11,543	Greenville	762
Webster	23,753	Marshfield	594
Worth	2,440	Grant City	266
Wright	16,758	Hartville	682
Independent City			
Saint Louis	396,685		61

Montana

(56 counties, 145,556 sq mi land; pop. 799,065)

County	Pop.	County Seat or court house	Land area sq mi
Beaverhead	8,424	Dillon	5,542
Big Horn	11,337	Hardin	4,995
Blaine	6,728	Chinook	4,226
Broadwater	3,318	Townsend	1,191
Carbon	8,080	Red Lodge	2,048
Carter	1,503	Ekalaka	3,340
Cascade	77,691	Great Falls	2,698
Chouteau	5,452	Fort Benton	3,973
Custer	11,697	Miles City	3,783
Daniels	2,266	Scobey	1,426
Dawson	9,505	Glendive	2,373
Deer Lodge	10,278	Anaconda	737
Fallon	3,103	Baker	1,620
Fergus	12,083	Lewistown	4,339
Flathead	59,218	Kalispell	5,099
Gallatin	50,463	Bozeman	2,507
Garfield	1,589	Jordan	4,668
Glacier	12,121	Cut Bank	2,995
Golden Valley	912	Ryegete	1,175
Granite	2,548	Philipsburg	1,728
Hill	17,654	Havre	2,896
Jefferson	7,939	Boulder	1,657
Judith Basin	2,282	Stanford	1,870
Lake	21,041	Polson	1,494
Lewis & Clark	47,495	Helena	3,461
Liberty	2,295	Chester	1,430
Lincoln	17,481	Libby	3,613
McCone	2,276	Circle	2,643
Madison	5,989	Virginia City	3,587
Meagher	1,819	White Sulphur Springs	2,392
Mineral	3,315	Superior	1,220
Missoula	78,687	Missoula	2,598
Musselshell	4,106	Roundup	1,867
Park	14,484	Livingston	2,656
Petroleum	519	Winnett	1,654
Phillips	5,163	Malta	5,140
Pondera	6,433	Conrad	1,625
Powder River	2,090	Broadus	3,297
Powell	6,620	Deer Lodge	2,326
Prairie	1,383	Terry	1,737
Ravalli	25,010	Hamilton	2,394
Richland	10,716	Sidney	2,084
Roosevelt	10,999	Wolf Point	2,356
Rosebud	10,505	Forsyth	5,012
Sanders	8,669	Thompson Falls	2,762
Sheridan	4,732	Plentywood	1,677
Silver Bow	33,941	Butte	718
Stillwater	6,536	Columbus	1,795
Sweet Grass	3,154	Big Timber	1,855
Teton	6,271	Choteau	2,273
Toole	5,046	Shelby	1,911
Treasure	874	Hysham	979
Valley	8,239	Glasgow	4,921
Wheatland	2,246	Harlowton	1,423
Wibaux	1,191	Wibaux	889
Yellowstone	113,419	Billings	2,635

Nebraska

(93 counties, 76,878 sq mi land; pop. 1,578,385)

County	Pop.	County Seat or court house	Land area sq mi
Adams	29,625	Hastings	564
Antelope	7,965	Neligh	859
Arthur	462	Arthur	711
Banner	852	Harrisburg	747
Blaine	675	Brewster	714
Boone	6,667	Albion	687
Box Butte	13,130	Alliance	1,077
Boyd	2,835	Butte	532
Brown	3,657	Ainsworth	1,214
Buffalo	37,447	Kearney	945
Burt	7,868	Tekamah	486
Butler	8,601	David City	584
Cass	21,318	Plattsmouth	557
Cedar	10,131	Hartington	740
Chase	4,381	Imperial	894
Cherry	6,307	Valentine	5,961
Cheyenne	9,494	Sidney	1,196
Clay	7,123	Clay Center	574
Colfax	9,139	Schuyler	410
Cuming	10,117	West Point	575
Custer	12,270	Broken Bow	2,571
Dakota	16,742	Dakota City	258
Dawes	9,021	Chadron	1,397
Dawson	19,940	Lexington	982
Deuel	2,237	Chappell	437
Dixon	6,143	Ponca	474
Dodge	34,500	Fremont	534
Douglas	416,444	Omaha	333
Dundy	2,582	Benkelman	920
Fillmore	7,103	Geneva	576
Franklin	3,938	Franklin	576
Frontier	3,101	Stockville	976
Furnas	5,553	Beaver City	721
Gage	22,794	Beatrice	858
Garden	2,460	Oshkosh	1,680
Garfield	2,141	Burwell	570
Gosper	1,928	Elwood	461
Grant	769	Hyannis	775
Greeley	3,006	Greeley	570
Hall	48,925	Grand Island	537
Hamilton	8,862	Aurora	543
Harlan	3,810	Alma	555
Hayes	1,222	Hayes Center	713
Hitchcock	3,750	Trenton	709
Holt	12,599	O'Neill	2,406
Hooker	793	Mullen	721
Howard	6,057	Saint Paul	564
Jefferson	8,759	Fairbury	575
Johnson	4,673	Tecumseh	377
Kearney	6,629	Minden	519
Keith	8,584	Ogallala	1,039
Keya Paha	1,029	Springview	769
Kimball	4,108	Kimball	952
Knox	9,564	Center	1,105
Lancaster	213,641	Lincoln	839
Lincoln	32,508	North Platte	2,525
Logan	878	Stapleton	571
Loup	683	Taylor	574
McPherson	546	Tryon	859
Madison	32,655	Madison	575
Merrick	8,049	Central City	478
Morrill	5,423	Bridgeport	1,405
Nance	4,275	Fullerton	439
Nemaha	7,980	Auburn	409
Nuckolls	5,786	Nelson	576
Otoe	14,252	Nebraska City	615
Pawnee	3,317	Pawnee City	433
Perkins	3,367	Grant	885
Phelps	9,715	Holdrege	540
Pierce	7,827	Pierce	575
Platte	29,820	Columbus	669
Polk	5,668	Osceola	437
Red Willow	11,705	McCook	718
Richardson	9,937	Falls City	553
Rock	2,019	Bassett	1,003

County	Pop.	County Seat or court house	Land area sq mi
Saline	12,715	Wilber	575
Sarpy	102,583	Papillion	238
Saunders	18,285	Wahoo	753
Scotts Bluff	36,025	Gering	725
Seward	15,450	Seward	575
Sheridan	6,750	Rushville	2,453
Sherman	3,718	Loup City	564
Sioux	1,549	Harrison	2,070
Stanton	6,244	Stanton	431
Thayer	6,635	Hebron	575
Thomas	851	Thedford	713
Thurston	6,936	Pender	391
Valley	5,169	Ord	567
Washington	16,607	Blair	386
Wayne	9,364	Wayne	443
Webster	4,279	Red Cloud	575
Wheeler	948	Bartlett	575
York	14,428	York	576

Nevada

(16 cos., 1 ind. city, 109,806 sq mi land; pop. 1,201,833)

County	Pop.	County Seat or court house	Land area sq mi
Churchill	17,938	Fallon	4,913
Clark	741,368	Las Vegas	8,084
Douglas	27,637	Minden	751
Elko	33,463	Elko	17,181
Esmeralda	1,344	Goldfield	3,570
Eureka	1,547	Eureka	4,182
Humboldt	12,844	Winnemucca	9,704
Lander	6,266	Battle Mountain	5,621
Lincoln	3,775	Pioche	10,650
Lyon	20,001	Yerington	2,024
Mineral	6,475	Hawthorne	3,837
Nye	17,781	Tonopah	18,064
Pershing	4,336	Lovelock	6,031
Storey	2,526	Virginia City	262
Washoe	254,667	Reno	6,608
White Pine	9,264	Ely	8,905
Independent City			
Carson City	40,443	Carson City	153

New Hampshire

(10 counties, 8,969 sq mi land; pop. 1,109,252)

County	Pop.	County Seat or court house	Land area sq mi
Belknap	49,216	Laconia	404
Carroll	35,410	Ossipee	933
Cheshire	70,121	Keene	711
Coos	34,828	Lancaster	1,804
Grafton	74,929	Woodsville	1,719
Hillsborough	335,838	Nashua	876
Merrimack	120,240	Concord	936
Rockingham	245,845	Exeter	699
Strafford	104,233	Dover	370
Sullivan	38,592	Newport	540

New Jersey

(21 counties, 7,419 sq mi land; pop. 7,730,188)

County	Pop.	County Seat or court house	Land area sq mi
Atlantic	224,327	Mays Landing	568
Bergen	825,380	Hackensack	237
Burlington	395,066	Mount Holly	808
Camden	502,824	Camden	223
Cape May	95,089	Cape May Court House	263
Cumberland	138,053	Bridgeton	498
Essex	778,964	Newark	127
Gloucester	230,082	Woodbury	327
Hudson	553,099	Jersey City	46
Hunterdon	107,802	Flemington	426
Mercer	325,824	Trenton	227
Middlesex	671,811	New Brunswick	316
Monmouth	553,093	Freehold	472
Morris	421,361	Morristown	470
Ocean	433,203	Toms River	641
Passaic	453,302	Paterson	187
Salem	65,294	Salem	338
Somerset	240,245	Somerville	305
Sussex	130,943	Newton	526
Union	493,819	Elizabeth	103
Warren	91,607	Belvidere	359

New Mexico

(33 counties, 121,364 sq mi land; pop. 1,515,069)

County	Pop.	County Seat or court house	Land area sq mi
Bernalillo	480,577	Albuquerque	1,169
Catron	2,563	Reserve	6,929
Chaves	57,849	Roswell	6,066
Cibola	23,794	Grants	4,468
Colfax	12,925	Raton	3,762
Curry	42,207	Clovis	1,408
De Baca	2,252	Fort Sumner	2,323
Dona Ana	135,510	Las Cruces	3,819
Eddy	48,605	Carlsbad	4,184
Grant	27,676	Silver City	3,969
Guadalupe	4,156	Santa Rosa	3,032
Harding	987	Mosquero	2,122
Hidalgo	5,958	Lordsburg	3,445
Lea	55,765	Lovington	4,390
Lincoln	12,219	Carrizozo	4,832
Los Alamos	18,115	Los Alamos	109
Luna	18,110	Deming	2,965
McKinley	60,686	Gallup	5,442
Mora	4,264	Mora	1,930
Otero	51,928	Alamogordo	6,626
Quay	10,823	Tucumcari	2,874
Rio Arriba	34,365	Tierra Amarilla	5,856
Roosevelt	16,702	Portales	2,453
Sandoval	63,319	Bernalillo	3,707
San Juan	91,605	Aztec	5,522
San Miguel	25,743	Las Vegas	4,709
Santa Fe	98,928	Santa Fe	1,905
Sierra	9,912	Truth or Consequences	4,178
Socorro	14,764	Socorro	6,625
Taos	23,118	Taos	2,204
Torrance	10,285	Estancia	3,335
Union	4,124	Clayton	3,830
Valencia	45,235	Los Lunas	1,068

New York

(62 counties, 47,224 sq mi land; pop. 17,990,455)

County	Pop.	County Seat or court house	Land area sq mi
Albany	292,793	Albany	524
Allegany	50,470	Belmont	1,031
Bronx	1,203,789	Bronx	42
Broome	212,160	Binghamton	707
Cattaraugus	84,234	Little Valley	1,310
Cayuga	82,313	Auburn	693
Chautauqua	141,895	Mayville	1,062
Chemung	95,195	Elmira	408
Chenango	51,768	Norwich	894
Clinton	85,969	Plattsburgh	1,039
Columbia	62,982	Hudson	636
Cortland	48,963	Cortland	500
Delaware	47,225	Delhi	1,446
Dutchess	259,462	Poughkeepsie	802
Erie	968,584	Buffalo	1,045
Essex	37,152	Elizabethtown	1,797
Franklin	46,540	Malone	1,632
Fulton	54,191	Johnstown	496
Genesee	60,060	Batavia	494
Greene	44,739	Catskill	648
Hamilton	5,279	Lake Pleasant	1,721
Herkimer	65,809	Herkimer	1,412
Jefferson	110,943	Watertown	1,272
Kings	2,300,664	Brooklyn	71
Lewis	26,796	Lowville	1,276
Livingston	62,372	Geneseo	632
Madison	69,166	Wampsville	656
Monroe	713,968	Rochester	659
Montgomery	51,981	Fonda	405
Nassau	1,287,444	Mineola	287
New York	1,487,536	New York	28
Niagara	220,756	Lockport	523
Oneida	250,836	Utica	1,213
Onondaga	468,973	Syracuse	780
Ontario	95,101	Canandaigua	644
Orange	307,647	Goshen	816
Orleans	41,846	Albion	391
Oswego	121,785	Oswego	953
Otsego	60,517	Cooperstown	1,003
Putnam	83,941	Carmel	232
Queens	1,951,598	Jamaica	109
Rensselaer	154,429	Troy	654
Richmond	378,977	Saint George	59
Rockland	265,475	New City	174
Saint Lawrence	111,974	Canton	2,686
Saratoga	181,276	Ballston Spa	812
Schenectady	149,285	Schenectady	206
Schoharie	31,859	Schoharie	622
Schuyler	18,662	Watkins Glen	329

County	Pop.	County Seat or court house	Land area sq mi
Seneca	33,683	Ovid & Waterloo	325
Steuben	99,088	Bath	1,393
Suffolk	1,321,768	Riverhead	911
Sullivan	69,277	Monticello	970
Tioga	52,337	Owego	519
Tompkins	94,097	Ithaca	476
Ulster	165,304	Kingston	1,127
Warren	59,209	Queensbury	870
Washington	59,330	Hudson Falls	836
Wayne	89,123	Lyons	604
Westchester	874,866	White Plains	433
Wyoming	42,507	Warsaw	593
Yates	22,810	Penn Yan	338

North Carolina

(100 counties, 48,718 sq mi land; pop. 6,628,637)

County	Pop.	County Seat or court house	Land area sq mi
Alamance	108,213	Graham	433
Alexander	27,544	Taylorsville	259
Alleghany	9,590	Sparta	235
Anson	23,474	Wadesboro	533
Ashe	22,209	Jefferson	426
Avery	14,867	Newland	247
Beaufort	42,283	Washington	826
Bertie	20,388	Windsor	701
Bladen	28,663	Elizabethtown	879
Brunswick	50,985	Bolivia	860
Buncombe	174,819	Asheville	659
Burke	75,744	Morganton	504
Cabarrus	98,935	Concord	364
Caldwell	70,709	Lenoir	471
Camden	5,904	Camden	240
Carteret	52,553	Beaufort	526
Caswell	20,693	Yanceyville	428
Catawba	118,412	Newton	396
Chatham	38,759	Pittsboro	708
Cherokee	20,170	Murphy	452
Chowan	13,506	Edenton	182
Clay	7,155	Hayesville	214
Cleveland	84,713	Shelby	468
Columbus	49,587	Whiteville	938
Craven	81,613	New Bern	701
Cumberland	274,713	Fayetteville	657
Currituck	13,736	Currituck	256
Dare	22,746	Manteo	391
Davidson	126,677	Lexington	548
Davie	27,859	Mocksville	267
Duplin	39,995	Kenansville	819
Durham	181,854	Durham	298
Edgecombe	56,692	Tarboro	506
Forsyth	265,878	Winston-Salem	412
Franklin	36,414	Louisburg	494
Gaston	175,093	Gastonia	357
Gates	9,305	Gatesville	338
Graham	7,196	Robbinsville	289
Granville	38,341	Oxford	534
Greene	15,384	Snow Hill	266
Guilford	347,420	Greensboro	651
Halifax	55,516	Halifax	724
Harnett	67,833	Lillington	601
Haywood	46,942	Waynesville	555
Henderson	69,285	Hendersonville	374
Hertford	22,523	Winton	356
Hoke	22,856	Raeford	391
Hyde	5,411	Swan Quarter	624
Iredell	92,935	Statesville	574
Jackson	26,846	Sylva	491
Johnston	81,306	Smithfield	795
Jones	9,414	Trenton	470
Lee	41,370	Sanford	259
Lenoir	57,274	Kinston	402
Lincoln	50,319	Lincolnton	298
McDowell	35,681	Marion	437
Macon	23,499	Franklin	517
Madison	16,953	Marshall	451
Martin	25,078	Williamston	461
Mecklenburg	511,481	Charlotte	528
Mitchell	14,433	Bakersville	222
Montgomery	23,352	Troy	490
Moore	59,000	Carthage	701
Nash	76,677	Nashville	540
New Hanover	120,284	Wilmington	185
Northampton	20,798	Jackson	538
Onslow	149,838	Jacksonville	763
Orange	93,851	Hillsborough	400
Pamlico	11,368	Bayboro	341
Pasquotank	31,298	Elizabeth City	228
Pender	28,885	Burgaw	875
Perquimans	10,447	Hertford	246
Person	30,180	Roxboro	398
Pitt	108,480	Greenville	657
Polk	14,416	Columbus	238
Randolph	106,546	Asheboro	789
Richmond	44,518	Rockingham	477
Robeson	105,170	Lumberton	949
Rockingham	86,064	Wentworth	569
Rowan	110,605	Salisbury	519
Rutherford	56,919	Rutherfordton	568
Sampson	47,297	Clinton	947
Scotland	33,763	Laurinburg	319
Stanly	51,765	Albemarle	396
Stokes	37,223	Danbury	452
Surry	61,704	Dobson	539
Swain	11,268	Bryson City	526
Transylvania	25,520	Brevard	378
Tyrrell	3,856	Columbia	407
Union	84,210	Monroe	639
Vance	38,892	Henderson	249
Wake	426,301	Raleigh	854
Warren	17,265	Warrenton	427
Washington	13,997	Plymouth	332
Watauga	36,952	Boone	314
Wayne	104,666	Goldsboro	554
Wilkes	59,393	Wilkesboro	752
Wilson	66,061	Wilson	374
Yadkin	30,488	Yadkinville	336
Yancey	15,419	Burnsville	314

North Dakota

(53 counties, 68,994 sq mi land; pop. 638,800)

County	Pop.	County Seat or court house	Land area sq mi
Adams	3,174	Hettinger	988
Barnes	12,545	Valley City	1,498
Benson	7,198	Minnewaukan	1,412
Billings	1,108	Medora	1,152
Bottineau	8,011	Bottineau	1,668
Bowman	3,596	Bowman	1,162
Burke	3,002	Bowbells	1,118
Burleigh	60,131	Bismarck	1,618
Cass	102,874	Fargo	1,767
Cavalier	6,064	Langdon	1,507
Dickey	6,107	Ellendale	1,139
Divide	2,899	Crosby	1,288
Dunn	4,005	Manning	1,993
Eddy	2,951	New Rockford	634
Emmons	4,830	Linton	1,499
Foster	3,983	Carrington	640
Golden Valley	2,108	Beach	1,003
Grand Forks	70,683	Grand Forks	1,440
Grant	3,549	Carson	1,660
Griggs	3,303	Cooperstown	708
Hettinger	3,445	Mott	1,133
Kidder	3,332	Steele	1,362
La Moure	5,383	La Moure	1,150
Logan	2,847	Napoleon	1,000
McHenry	6,528	Towner	1,887
McIntosh	4,021	Ashley	984
McKenzie	6,383	Watford City	2,754
McLean	10,457	Washburn	2,065
Mercer	9,808	Stanton	1,044
Morton	23,700	Mandan	1,921
Mountrail	7,021	Stanley	1,837
Nelson	4,410	Lakota	991
Oliver	2,381	Center	723
Pembina	9,238	Cavalier	1,120
Pierce	5,052	Rugby	1,037
Ramsey	12,681	Devils Lake	1,241
Ransom	5,921	Lisbon	862
Renville	3,160	Mohall	874
Richland	18,148	Wahpeton	1,436
Rolette	12,772	Rolla	914
Sargent	4,549	Forman	857
Sheridan	2,148	McClusky	989
Sioux	3,761	Fort Yates	1,099
Slope	907	Amidon	1,219
Stark	22,832	Dickinson	1,338
Steele	2,420	Finley	713
Stutsman	22,241	Jamestown	2,263
Towner	3,627	Cando	1,035
Traill	8,752	Hillsboro	861
Walsh	13,840	Grafton	1,290
Ward	57,921	Minot	2,041
Wells	5,864	Fessenden	1,288
Williams	21,129	Williston	2,074

Ohio

(88 counties, 40,953 sq mi land; pop. 10,847,115)

County	Pop.	County Seat or court house	Land area sq mi
Adams	25,371	West Union	586
Allen	109,755	Lima	405
Ashland	47,507	Ashland	424
Ashtabula	99,821	Jefferson	703
Athens	59,549	Athens	508
Auglaize	44,585	Wapakoneta	398
Belmont	71,074	Saint Clairsville	537

County	Pop.	County Seat or court house	Land area sq mi
Brown	34,966	Georgetown	493
Butler	291,479	Hamilton	470
Carroll	26,521	Carrollton	393
Champaign	36,019	Urbana	429
Clark	147,548	Springfield	398
Clermont	150,167	Batavia	456
Clinton	35,417	Wilmington	410
Columbiana	108,276	Lisbon	534
Coshocton	35,427	Coshocton	566
Crawford	47,870	Bucyrus	403
Cuyahoga	1,412,140	Cleveland	459
Darke	53,619	Greenville	600
Defiance	39,350	Defiance	414
Delaware	66,929	Delaware	443
Erie	76,779	Sandusky	264
Fairfield	103,472	Lancaster	506
Fayette	27,466	Washington Court House	405
Franklin	961,437	Columbus	543
Fulton	38,498	Wauseon	407
Gallia	30,954	Gallipolis	471
Geauga	81,129	Chardon	408
Greene	136,731	Xenia	416
Guernsey	39,024	Cambridge	522
Hamilton	866,228	Cincinnati	412
Hancock	65,536	Findlay	532
Hardin	31,111	Kenton	471
Harrison	16,085	Cadiz	400
Henry	29,108	Napoleon	415
Highland	35,728	Hillsboro	553
Hocking	25,533	Logan	423
Holmes	32,849	Millersburg	424
Huron	56,240	Norwalk	494
Jackson	30,230	Jackson	420
Jefferson	80,298	Steubenville	410
Knox	47,473	Mount Vernon	529
Lake	215,499	Painesville	231
Lawrence	61,834	Ironton	457
Licking	128,300	Newark	686
Logan	42,310	Bellefontaine	458
Lorain	271,126	Elyria	495
Lucas	462,361	Toledo	341
Madison	37,068	London	467
Mahoning	264,806	Youngstown	417
Marion	64,274	Marion	403
Medina	122,354	Medina	422
Meigs	22,987	Pomeroy	432
Mercer	39,443	Celina	457
Miami	93,182	Troy	410
Monroe	15,497	Woodsfield	457
Montgomery	573,809	Dayton	458
Morgan	14,194	McConnelsville	420
Morrow	27,749	Mount Gilead	406
Muskingum	82,068	Zanesville	654
Noble	11,336	Caldwell	399
Ottawa	40,029	Port Clinton	253
Paulding	20,488	Paulding	419
Perry	31,557	New Lexington	412
Pickaway	48,244	Circleville	503
Pike	24,249	Waverly	443
Portage	142,585	Ravenna	493
Preble	40,113	Eaton	426
Putnam	33,819	Ottawa	484
Richland	126,137	Mansfield	497
Ross	69,330	Chillicothe	692
Sandusky	61,963	Fremont	409
Scioto	80,327	Portsmouth	613
Seneca	59,733	Tiffin	553
Shelby	44,915	Sidney	409
Stark	367,585	Canton	574
Summit	514,990	Akron	412
Trumbull	227,813	Warren	612
Tuscarawas	84,090	New Philadelphia	570
Union	31,969	Marysville	437
Van Wert	30,464	Van Wert	410
Vinton	11,098	McArthur	414
Warren	113,927	Lebanon	403
Washington	62,254	Marietta	640
Wayne	101,461	Wooster	557
Williams	36,956	Bryan	422
Wood	113,269	Bowling Green	619
Wyandot	22,254	Upper Sandusky	406

Oklahoma

(77 counties, 68,679 sq mi land; pop. 3,145,585)

County	Pop.	County Seat or court house	Land area sq mi
Adair	18,421	Stillwell	577
Alfalfa	6,416	Cherokee	864
Atoka	12,778	Atoka	980
Beaver	6,023	Beaver	1,808
Beckham	18,812	Sayre	904
Blaine	11,470	Watonga	920
Bryan	32,089	Durant	902
Caddo	29,550	Anadarko	1,286
Canadian	74,409	El Reno	901
Carter	42,919	Ardmore	828
Cherokee	34,049	Tahlequah	748
Choctaw	15,302	Hugo	762
Cimarron	3,301	Boise City	1,842
Cleveland	174,253	Norman	529
Coal	5,780	Coalgate	520
Comanche	111,486	Lawton	1,076
Cotton	6,651	Walters	656
Craig	14,104	Vinita	763
Creek	60,915	Sapulpa	930
Custer	26,897	Arapaho	981
Delaware	28,070	Jay	720
Dewey	5,551	Taloga	1,007
Ellis	4,497	Arnett	1,232
Garfield	56,735	Enid	1,060
Garvin	26,605	Pauls Valley	813
Grady	41,747	Chickasha	1,106
Grant	5,689	Medford	1,004
Greer	6,559	Mangum	638
Harmon	3,793	Hollis	537
Harper	4,063	Buffalo	1,039
Haskell	10,940	Stigler	570
Hughes	13,014	Holdenville	806
Jackson	28,764	Altus	817
Jefferson	7,010	Waurika	769
Johnston	10,032	Tishomingo	639
Kay	48,056	Newkirk	921
Kingfisher	13,212	Kingfisher	906
Kiowa	11,347	Hobart	1,019
Latimer	10,333	Wilburton	728
Le Flore	43,270	Poteau	1,585
Lincoln	29,216	Chandler	964
Logan	29,011	Guthrie	748
Love	8,157	Marietta	519
McClain	22,795	Purcell	582
McCurtain	33,433	Idabel	1,826
McIntosh	16,779	Eufaula	599
Major	8,055	Fairview	958
Marshall	10,829	Madill	372
Mayes	33,366	Pryor	644
Murray	12,042	Sulphur	420
Muskogee	68,078	Muskogee	815
Noble	11,045	Perry	736
Nowata	9,992	Nowata	540
Okfuskee	11,551	Okemah	628
Oklahoma	599,611	Oklahoma City	708
Okmulgee	36,490	Okmulgee	698
Osage	41,645	Pawhuska	2,265
Ottawa	30,561	Miami	465
Pawnee	15,575	Pawnee	551
Payne	61,507	Stillwater	691
Pittsburg	40,581	McAlester	1,251
Pontotoc	34,119	Ada	717
Pottawatomie	58,760	Shawnee	783
Pushmataha	10,997	Antlers	1,417
Roger Mills	4,147	Cheyenne	1,146
Rogers	55,170	Claremore	683
Seminole	25,412	Wewoka	639
Sequoyah	33,828	Sallisaw	678
Stephens	42,299	Duncan	884
Texas	16,419	Guymon	2,040
Tillman	10,384	Frederick	904
Tulsa	503,341	Tulsa	572
Wagoner	47,883	Wagoner	559
Washington	48,066	Bartlesville	423
Washita	11,441	Cordell	1,006
Woods	9,103	Alva	1,291
Woodward	18,976	Woodward	1,242

Oregon

(36 counties, 96,002 sq mi land; pop. 2,842,321)

County	Pop.	County Seat or court house	Land area sq mi
Baker	15,317	Baker City	3,089
Benton	70,811	Corvallis	679
Clackamas	278,850	Oregon City	1,870
Clatsop	33,301	Astoria	873
Columbia	37,557	Saint Helens	687
Coos	60,273	Coquille	1,629
Crook	14,111	Prineville	2,991
Curry	19,327	Gold Beach	1,648
Deschutes	74,976	Bend	3,055
Douglas	94,649	Roseburg	5,071
Gilliam	1,717	Condon	1,223
Grant	7,853	Canyon City	4,525
Harney	7,060	Burns	10,228
Hood River	16,903	Hood River	533
Jackson	146,387	Medford	2,801
Jefferson	13,676	Madras	1,791
Josephine	62,649	Grants Pass	1,640
Klamath	57,702	Klamath Falls	6,135
Lake	7,186	Lakeview	8,359
Lane	282,912	Eugene	4,620
Lincoln	38,889	Newport	992
Linn	91,227	Albany	2,296

County	Pop.	County Seat or court house	Land area sq mi
Malheur	26,038	Vale	9,926
Marion	228,483	Salem	1,194
Morrow	7,625	Heppner	2,094
Multnomah	583,887	Portland	465
Polk	49,541	Dallas	741
Sherman	1,918	Moro	831
Tillamook	21,570	Tillamook	1,125
Umatilla	59,249	Pendleton	3,218
Union	23,598	La Grande	2,038
Wallowa	6,911	Enterprise	3,150
Wasco	21,683	The Dalles	2,396
Washington	311,554	Hillsboro	727
Wheeler	1,396	Fossil	1,713
Yamhill	65,551	McMinnville	718

Pennsylvania

(67 counties, 44,820 sq mi land; pop. 11,881,643)

County	Pop.	County Seat or court house	Land area sq mi
Adams	78,274	Gettysburg	521
Allegheny	1,336,449	Pittsburgh	727
Armstrong	73,478	Kittanning	646
Beaver	186,093	Beaver	436
Bedford	47,919	Bedford	1,017
Berks	336,523	Reading	861
Blair	130,542	Hollidaysburg	527
Bradford	60,967	Towanda	1,152
Bucks	541,174	Doylestown	610
Butler	152,013	Butler	789
Cambria	163,029	Ebensburg	691
Cameron	5,913	Emporium	398
Carbon	56,973	Jim Thorpe	384
Centre	124,812	Bellefonte	1,106
Chester	376,396	West Chester	758
Clarion	41,699	Clarion	607
Clearfield	78,097	Clearfield	1,149
Clinton	37,182	Lock Haven	891
Columbia	63,202	Bloomsburg	486
Crawford	86,170	Meadville	1,011
Cumberland	195,257	Carlisle	547
Dauphin	237,813	Harrisburg	528
Delaware	547,651	Media	184
Elk	34,878	Ridgway	830
Erie	275,572	Erie	804
Fayette	145,351	Uniontown	794
Forest	4,802	Tionesta	428
Franklin	121,082	Chambersburg	774
Fulton	13,837	McConnellsburg	438
Greene	39,550	Waynesburg	577
Huntingdon	44,164	Huntingdon	877
Indiana	89,994	Indiana	829
Jefferson	46,083	Brookville	657
Juniata	20,625	Mifflintown	392
Lackawanna	219,097	Scranton	461
Lancaster	422,822	Lancaster	952
Lawrence	96,246	New Castle	363
Lebanon	113,744	Lebanon	363
Lehigh	291,130	Allentown	348
Luzerne	328,149	Wilkes-Barre	891
Lycoming	118,710	Williamsport	1,237
McKean	47,131	Smethport	979
Mercer	121,003	Mercer	672
Mifflin	46,197	Lewistown	413
Monroe	95,582	Stroudsburg	609
Montgomery	678,111	Norristown	486
Montour	17,735	Danville	131
Northampton	247,105	Easton	376
Northumberland	96,771	Sunbury	461
Perry	41,172	New Bloomfield	557
Philadelphia	1,585,577	Philadelphia	136
Pike	27,966	Milford	550
Potter	16,717	Coudersport	1,081
Schuylkill	152,585	Pottsville	782
Snyder	36,680	Middleburg	329
Somerset	78,218	Somerset	1,073
Sullivan	6,104	Laporte	451
Susquehanna	40,380	Montrose	826
Tioga	41,126	Wellsboro	1,131
Union	36,176	Lewisburg	317
Venango	59,381	Franklin	679
Warren	45,049	Warren	885
Washington	204,584	Washington	958
Wayne	39,944	Honesdale	731
Westmoreland	370,321	Greensburg	1,033
Wyoming	28,076	Tunkhannock	399
York	339,574	York	906

Rhode Island

(5 counties, 1,045 sq mi land; pop. 1,003,464)

County	Pop.	County Seat or court house	Land area sq mi
Bristol	48,859	Bristol	26
Kent	161,135	East Greenwich	172
Newport	87,194	Newport	107
Providence	596,270	Providence	416
Washington	110,006	West Kingston	333

South Carolina

(46 counties, 30,111 sq mi land; pop. 3,486,703)

County	Pop.	County Seat or court house	Land area sq mi
Abbeville	23,862	Abbeville	508
Aiken	120,991	Aiken	1,092
Allendale	11,722	Allendale	413
Anderson	145,177	Anderson	718
Bamberg	16,902	Bamberg	395
Barnwell	20,293	Barnwell	558
Beaufort	86,425	Beaufort	579
Berkeley	128,776	Moncks Corner	1,108
Calhoun	12,753	Saint Matthews	380
Charleston	295,041	Charleston	938
Cherokee	44,506	Gaffney	396
Chester	32,170	Chester	580
Chesterfield	38,575	Chesterfield	802
Clarendon	28,450	Manning	602
Colleton	34,377	Walterboro	1,052
Darlington	61,851	Darlington	563
Dillon	29,114	Dillon	406
Dorchester	83,060	Saint George	575
Edgefield	18,360	Edgefield	490
Fairfield	22,295	Winnsboro	685
Florence	114,344	Florence	804
Georgetown	46,302	Georgetown	822
Greenville	320,167	Greenville	795
Greenwood	59,567	Greenwood	451
Hampton	18,191	Hampton	561
Horry	144,053	Conway	1,143
Jasper	15,487	Ridgeland	655
Kershaw	43,599	Camden	723
Lancaster	54,516	Lancaster	552
Laurens	58,092	Laurens	712
Lee	18,437	Bishopville	411
Lexington	167,611	Lexington	707
McCormick	8,868	McCormick	350
Marion	33,899	Marion	493
Marlboro	29,716	Bennettsville	483
Newberry	33,172	Newberry	634
Oconee	57,494	Walhalla	629
Orangeburg	84,803	Orangeburg	1,111
Pickens	93,896	Pickens	499
Richland	286,321	Columbia	762
Saluda	16,357	Saluda	456
Spartanburg	226,793	Spartanburg	814
Sumter	102,637	Sumter	665
Union	30,337	Union	515
Williamsburg	36,815	Kingstree	934
York	131,497	York	685

South Dakota

(67 counties, 75,896 sq mi land; pop. 696,004)

County	Pop.	County Seat or court house	Land area sq mi
Aurora	3,135	Plankinton	707
Beadle	18,253	Huron	1,259
Bennett	3,206	Martin	1,182
Bon Homme	7,089	Tyndall	552
Brookings	25,207	Brookings	795
Brown	35,580	Aberdeen	1,722
Brule	5,485	Chamberlain	815
Buffalo	1,759	Gannvalley	475
Butte	7,914	Belle Fourche	2,251
Campbell	1,965	Mound City	732
Charles Mix	9,131	Lake Andes	1,090
Clark	4,403	Clark	953
Clay	13,186	Vermillion	409
Codington	22,698	Watertown	694
Corson	4,195	McIntosh	2,467
Custer	6,179	Custer	1,559
Davison	17,503	Mitchell	436
Day	6,978	Webster	1,022
Deuel	4,522	Clear Lake	631
Dewey	5,523	Timber Lake	2,310
Douglas	3,746	Armour	434
Edmunds	4,356	Ipswich	1,149
Fall River	7,353	Hot Springs	4,742
Faulk	2,744	Faulkton	1,004
Grant	8,372	Milbank	681
Gregory	5,359	Burke	1,013
Haakon	2,624	Philip	1,822
Hamlin	4,974	Hayti	512
Hand	4,272	Miller	1,437
Hanson	2,994	Alexandria	433
Harding	1,669	Buffalo	2,678
Hughes	14,817	Pierre	757
Hutchinson	8,262	Olivet	816
Hyde	1,696	Highmore	860

County	Pop.	County Seat or court house	Land area sq mi
Jackson	2,811	Kadoka	1,872
Jerauld	2,425	Wessington Springs	530
Jones	1,324	Murdo	971
Kingsbury	5,925	De Smet	824
Lake	10,550	Madison	560
Lawrence	20,655	Deadwood	800
Lincoln	15,427	Canton	578
Lyman	3,638	Kennebec	1,679
McCook	5,688	Salem	576
McPherson	3,228	Leola	1,148
Marshall	4,844	Britton	848
Meade	21,878	Sturgis	3,481
Mellette	2,137	White River	1,311
Miner	3,272	Howard	570
Minnehaha	123,809	Sioux Falls	810
Moody	6,507	Flandreau	520
Pennington	81,343	Rapid City	2,783
Perkins	3,932	Bison	2,884
Potter	3,190	Gettysburg	869
Roberts	9,914	Sisseton	1,102
Sanborn	2,833	Woonsocket	569
Shannon	9,902	(Attached to Fall River)	2,094
Spink	7,981	Redfield	1,505
Stanley	2,453	Fort Pierre	1,431
Sully	1,589	Onida	972
Todd	8,352	(Attached to Tripp)	1,388
Tripp	6,924	Winner	1,618
Turner	8,576	Parker	617
Union	10,189	Elk Point	453
Walworth	6,087	Selby	707
Yankton	19,252	Yankton	518
Ziebach	2,220	Dupree	1,969

Tennessee

(95 counties, 41,219 sq mi land; pop. 4,877,185)

County	Pop.	County Seat or court house	Land area sq mi
Anderson	68,250	Clinton	339
Bedford	30,411	Shelbyville	475
Benton	14,524	Camden	392
Bledsoe	9,669	Pikeville	407
Blount	85,969	Maryville	558
Bradley	73,712	Cleveland	327
Campbell	35,079	Jacksboro	479
Cannon	10,467	Woodbury	266
Carroll	27,514	Huntingdon	600
Carter	51,505	Elizabethton	341
Cheatham	27,140	Ashland City	304
Chester	12,819	Henderson	289
Claiborne	26,137	Tazewell	432
Clay	7,238	Celina	227
Cocke	29,141	Newport	432
Coffee	40,339	Manchester	428
Crockett	13,378	Alamo	266
Cumberland	34,736	Crossville	682
Davidson	510,784	Nashville	501
Decatur	10,472	Decaturville	330
De Kalb	14,360	Smithville	291
Dickson	35,061	Charlotte	491
Dyer	34,854	Dyersburg	520
Fayette	25,559	Somerville	705
Fentress	14,669	Jamestown	498
Franklin	34,725	Winchester	543
Gibson	46,315	Trenton	602
Giles	25,741	Pulaski	610
Grainger	17,095	Rutledge	273
Greene	55,853	Greeneville	619
Grundy	13,362	Altamont	361
Hamblen	50,480	Morristown	156
Hamilton	285,536	Chattanooga	539
Hancock	6,739	Sneedville	223
Hardeman	23,377	Bolivar	670
Hardin	22,633	Savannah	578
Hawkins	44,565	Rogersville	486
Haywood	19,437	Brownsville	534
Henderson	21,844	Lexington	520
Henry	27,888	Paris	560
Hickman	16,754	Centerville	610
Houston	7,018	Erin	200
Humphreys	15,813	Waverly	528
Jackson	9,297	Gainesboro	308
Jefferson	33,016	Dandridge	265
Johnson	13,766	Mountain City	297
Knox	335,749	Knoxville	506
Lake	7,129	Tiptonville	169
Lauderdale	23,491	Ripley	474
Lawrence	35,303	Lawrenceburg	617
Lewis	9,247	Hohenwald	282
Lincoln	28,157	Fayetteville	571
Loudon	31,255	Loudon	235
McMinn	42,383	Athens	429
McNairy	22,422	Selmer	562
Macon	15,906	Lafayette	307
Madison	77,982	Jackson	558
Marion	24,860	Jasper	512
Marshall	21,539	Lewisburg	376
Maury	54,812	Columbia	616
Meigs	8,033	Decatur	189
Monroe	30,541	Madisonville	648
Montgomery	100,498	Clarksville	539
Moore	4,721	Lynchburg	129
Morgan	17,300	Wartburg	523
Obion	31,717	Union City	550
Overton	17,636	Livingston	433
Perry	6,612	Linden	412
Pickett	4,548	Byrdstown	159
Polk	13,643	Benton	438
Putnam	51,373	Cookeville	399
Rhea	24,344	Dayton	309
Roane	47,227	Kingston	357
Robertson	41,492	Springfield	476
Rutherford	118,570	Murfreesboro	606
Scott	18,358	Huntsville	528
Sequatchie	8,863	Dunlap	266
Sevier	51,043	Sevierville	590
Shelby	826,330	Memphis	772
Smith	14,143	Carthage	313
Stewart	9,479	Dover	454
Sullivan	143,596	Blountville	415
Sumner	103,281	Gallatin	529
Tipton	37,568	Covington	454
Trousdale	5,920	Hartsville	114
Unicoi	16,549	Erwin	186
Union	13,694	Maynardville	218
Van Buren	4,846	Spencer	273
Warren	32,992	McMinnville	431
Washington	92,315	Jonesboro	326
Wayne	13,935	Waynesboro	734
Weakley	31,972	Dresden	581
White	20,090	Sparta	373
Williamson	81,021	Franklin	584
Wilson	67,675	Lebanon	570

Texas

(254 counties, 261,914 sq mi land; pop. 16,986,510)

County	Pop.	County Seat or court house	Land area sq mi
Anderson	48,024	Palestine	1,077
Andrews	14,338	Andrews	1,501
Angelina	69,884	Lufkin	807
Aransas	17,892	Rockport	280
Archer	7,973	Archer City	907
Armstrong	2,021	Claude	909
Atascosa	30,533	Jourdanton	1,218
Austin	19,832	Bellville	656
Bailey	7,064	Muleshoe	826
Bandera	10,562	Bandera	793
Bastrop	38,263	Bastrop	895
Baylor	4,385	Seymour	862
Bee	25,135	Beeville	880
Bell	191,073	Belton	1,055
Bexar	1,185,394	San Antonio	1,248
Blanco	5,972	Johnson City	714
Borden	799	Gail	900
Bosque	15,125	Meridian	989
Bowie	81,665	Boston	891
Brazoria	191,707	Angleton	1,407
Brazos	121,862	Bryan	589
Brewster	8,653	Alpine	6,169
Briscoe	1,971	Silverton	887
Brooks	8,204	Falfurrias	942
Brown	34,371	Brownwood	936
Burleson	13,625	Caldwell	669
Burnet	22,677	Burnet	994
Caldwell	26,392	Lockhart	546
Calhoun	19,053	Port Lavaca	540
Callahan	11,859	Baird	899
Cameron	260,120	Brownsville	906
Camp	9,904	Pittsburg	203
Carson	6,576	Panhandle	924
Cass	29,982	Linden	937
Castro	9,070	Dimmitt	899
Chambers	20,088	Anahuac	616
Cherokee	41,049	Rusk	1,052
Childress	5,953	Childress	707
Clay	10,024	Henrietta	1,086
Cochran	4,377	Morton	775
Coke	3,424	Robert Lee	908
Coleman	9,710	Coleman	1,277
Collin	264,036	McKinney	851
Collingsworth	3,573	Wellington	909
Colorado	18,383	Columbus	965
Comal	51,832	New Braunfels	555
Comanche	13,381	Comanche	930

County	Pop.	County Seat or court house	Land area sq mi
Concho	3,044	Paint Rock	992
Cooke	30,777	Gainesville	893
Coryell	64,226	Gatesville	1,057
Cottle	2,247	Paducah	895
Crane	4,652	Crane	782
Crockett	4,078	Ozona	2,806
Crosby	7,304	Crosbyton	899
Culberson	3,407	Van Horn	3,815
Dallam	5,461	Dalhart	1,505
Dallas	1,852,810	Dallas	880
Dawson	14,349	Lamesa	903
Deaf Smith	19,153	Hereford	1,497
Delta	4,857	Cooper	278
Denton	273,525	Denton	911
Dewitt	18,840	Cuero	910
Dickens	2,571	Dickens	907
Dimmit	10,433	Carrizo Springs	1,307
Donley	3,696	Clarendon	929
Duval	12,918	San Diego	1,795
Eastland	18,488	Eastland	924
Ector	118,934	Odessa	903
Edwards	2,266	Rocksprings	2,121
Ellis	85,167	Waxahachie	939
El Paso	591,610	El Paso	1,014
Erath	27,991	Stephenville	1,080
Falls	17,712	Marlin	770
Fannin	24,804	Bonham	895
Fayette	20,095	La Grange	950
Fisher	4,842	Roby	897
Floyd	8,497	Floydada	992
Foard	1,794	Crowell	703
Fort Bend	225,421	Richmond	876
Franklin	7,802	Mount Vernon	294
Freestone	15,818	Fairfield	888
Frio	13,472	Pearsall	1,133
Gaines	14,123	Seminole	1,504
Galveston	217,396	Galveston	399
Garza	5,143	Post	895
Gillespie	17,204	Fredericksburg	1,061
Glasscock	1,447	Garden City	900
Goliad	5,980	Goliad	859
Gonzales	17,205	Gonzales	1,068
Gray	23,967	Pampa	921
Grayson	95,019	Sherman	934
Gregg	104,948	Longview	273
Grimes	18,828	Anderson	799
Guadalupe	64,873	Seguin	713
Hale	34,671	Plainview	1,005
Hall	3,905	Memphis	877
Hamilton	7,733	Hamilton	836
Hansford	5,848	Spearman	921
Hardeman	5,283	Quanah	688
Hardin	41,320	Kountze	898
Harris	2,818,101	Houston	1,734
Harrison	57,483	Marshall	908
Hartley	3,634	Channing	1,462
Haskell	6,820	Haskell	901
Hays	65,614	San Marcos	678
Hemphill	3,720	Canadian	903
Henderson	58,543	Athens	888
Hidalgo	383,545	Edinburg	1,569
Hill	27,146	Hillsboro	968
Hockley	24,199	Levelland	908
Hood	28,981	Granbury	425
Hopkins	28,833	Sulphur Springs	789
Houston	21,375	Crockett	1,234
Howard	32,343	Big Spring	901
Hudspeth	2,915	Sierra Blanca	4,567
Hunt	64,343	Greenville	840
Hutchinson	25,689	Stinnett	872
Irion	1,629	Mertzon	1,052
Jack	6,981	Jacksboro	920
Jackson	13,039	Edna	844
Jasper	31,102	Jasper	921
Jeff Davis	1,946	Fort Davis	2,257
Jefferson	239,389	Beaumont	937
Jim Hogg	5,109	Hebbronville	1,136
Jim Wells	37,679	Alice	867
Johnson	97,165	Cleburne	730
Jones	16,490	Anson	931
Karnes	12,455	Karnes City	753
Kaufman	52,220	Kaufman	788
Kendall	14,589	Boerne	663
Kenedy	460	Sarita	1,389
Kent	1,010	Jayton	878
Kerr	36,304	Kerrville	1,107
Kimble	4,122	Junction	1,250
King	354	Guthrie	914
Kinney	3,119	Brackettville	1,359
Kleberg	30,274	Kingsville	853
Knox	4,837	Benjamin	845
Lamar	43,949	Paris	919
Lamb	15,072	Littlefield	1,013
Lampasas	13,521	Lampasas	714
La Salle	5,254	Cotulla	1,517
Lavaca	18,690	Hallettsville	971
Lee	12,854	Giddings	631
Leon	12,665	Centerville	1,079

County	Pop.	County Seat or court house	Land area sq mi
Liberty	52,726	Liberty	1,174
Limestone	20,946	Groesbeck	930
Lipscomb	3,143	Lipscomb	933
Live Oak	9,556	George West	1,057
Llano	11,631	Llano	939
Loving	107	Mentone	670
Lubbock	222,636	Lubbock	900
Lynn	6,758	Tahoka	888
McCulloch	8,778	Brady	1,071
McLennan	189,123	Waco	1,031
McMullen	817	Tilden	1,163
Madison	10,931	Madisonville	472
Marion	9,984	Jefferson	385
Martin	4,956	Stanton	914
Mason	3,423	Mason	934
Matagorda	36,928	Bay City	1,127
Maverick	36,378	Eagle Pass	1,287
Medina	27,312	Hondo	1,331
Menard	2,252	Menard	902
Midland	106,611	Midland	902
Milam	22,946	Cameron	1,019
Mills	4,531	Goldthwaite	748
Mitchell	8,016	Colorado City	912
Montague	17,274	Montague	928
Montgomery	182,201	Conroe	1,047
Moore	17,865	Dumas	905
Morris	13,200	Daingerfield	256
Motley	1,532	Matador	959
Nacogdoches	54,753	Nacogdoches	939
Navarro	39,926	Corsicana	1,068
Newton	13,569	Newton	935
Nolan	16,594	Sweetwater	915
Nueces	291,145	Corpus Christi	847
Ochiltree	9,128	Perryton	919
Oldham	2,278	Vega	1,485
Orange	80,509	Orange	362
Palo Pinto	25,055	Palo Pinto	949
Panola	22,035	Carthage	812
Parker	64,785	Weatherford	902
Parmer	9,863	Farwell	885
Pecos	14,675	Fort Stockton	4,777
Polk	30,687	Livingston	1,061
Potter	97,841	Amarillo	902
Presidio	6,637	Marfa	3,857
Rains	6,715	Emory	243
Randall	89,673	Canyon	917
Reagan	4,514	Big Lake	1,173
Real	2,412	Leakey	697
Red River	14,317	Clarksville	1,054
Reeves	15,852	Pecos	2,626
Refugio	7,976	Refugio	771
Roberts	1,025	Miami	915
Robertson	15,511	Franklin	864
Rockwall	25,604	Rockwall	128
Runnels	11,294	Ballinger	1,056
Rusk	43,735	Henderson	932
Sabine	9,586	Hemphill	486
San Augustine	7,999	San Augustine	524
San Jacinto	16,372	Coldspring	572
San Patricio	58,749	Sinton	693
San Saba	5,401	San Saba	1,136
Schleicher	2,990	Eldorado	1,309
Scurry	18,634	Snyder	900
Shackelford	3,316	Albany	915
Shelby	22,034	Center	791
Sherman	2,858	Stratford	923
Smith	151,309	Tyler	932
Somervell	5,360	Glen Rose	188
Starr	40,518	Rio Grande City	1,226
Stephens	9,010	Breckenridge	894
Sterling	1,438	Sterling City	923
Stonewall	2,013	Aspermont	925
Sutton	4,135	Sonora	1,455
Swisher	8,133	Tulia	902
Tarrant	1,170,103	Fort Worth	868
Taylor	119,655	Abilene	917
Terrell	1,410	Sanderson	2,357
Terry	13,218	Brownfield	887
Throckmorton	1,880	Throckmorton	912
Titus	24,009	Mount Pleasant	412
Tom Green	98,458	San Angelo	1,515
Travis	576,407	Austin	989
Trinity	11,445	Groveton	692
Tyler	16,646	Woodville	922
Upshur	31,370	Gilmer	587
Upton	4,447	Rankin	1,243
Uvalde	23,340	Uvalde	1,564
Val Verde	38,721	Del Rio	3,150
Van Zandt	37,944	Canton	855
Victoria	74,361	Victoria	887
Walker	50,917	Huntsville	786
Waller	23,389	Hempstead	514
Ward	13,115	Monahans	836
Washington	26,154	Brenham	610
Webb	133,239	Laredo	3,362
Wharton	39,955	Wharton	1,086
Wheeler	5,879	Wheeler	904
Wichita	122,378	Wichita Falls	606
Wilbarger	15,121	Vernon	947

County	Pop.	County Seat or court house	Land area sq mi
Willacy	17,705	Raymondville	589
Williamson	139,551	Georgetown	1,137
Wilson	22,650	Floresville	807
Winkler	8,626	Kermit	840
Wise	34,679	Decatur	902
Wood	29,380	Quitman	689
Yoakum	8,786	Plains	800
Young	18,126	Graham	919
Zapata	9,279	Zapata	999
Zavala	12,162	Crystal City	1,298

Utah

(29 counties, 82,168 sq mi land; pop. 1,722,850)

County	Pop.	County Seat or court house	Land area sq mi
Beaver	4,765	Beaver	2,590
Box Elder	36,485	Brigham City	5,724
Cache	70,183	Logan	1,165
Carbon	20,228	Price	1,479
Daggett	690	Manila	698
Davis	187,941	Farmington	305
Duchesne	12,645	Duchesne	3,238
Emery	10,332	Castle Dale	4,452
Garfield	3,980	Panguitch	5,175
Grand	6,620	Moab	3,682
Iron	20,789	Parowan	3,299
Juab	5,817	Nephi	3,392
Kane	5,169	Kanab	3,992
Millard	11,333	Fillmore	6,590
Morgan	5,528	Morgan	609
Piute	1,277	Junction	758
Rich	1,725	Randolph	1,029
Salt Lake	725,956	Salt Lake City	737
San Juan	12,621	Monticello	7,821
Sanpete	16,259	Manti	1,588
Sevier	15,431	Richfield	1,910
Summit	15,518	Coalville	1,871
Tooele	26,601	Tooele	6,946
Uintah	22,211	Vernal	4,477
Utah	263,590	Provo	1,998
Wasatch	10,089	Heber City	1,181
Washington	48,560	Saint George	2,427
Wayne	2,177	Loa	2,461
Weber	158,330	Ogden	576

Vermont

(14 counties, 9,249 sq mi land; pop. 562,758)

County	Pop.	County Seat or court house	Land area sq mi
Addison	32,953	Middlebury	773
Bennington	35,845	Bennington	676
Caledonia	27,846	Saint Johnsbury	651
Chittenden	131,761	Burlington	540
Essex	6,405	Guildhall	666
Franklin	39,980	Saint Albans	649
Grand Isle	5,318	North Hero	89
Lamoille	19,735	Hyde Park	461
Orange	26,149	Chelsea	690
Orleans	24,053	Newport	697
Rutland	62,142	Rutland	932
Washington	54,928	Montpelier	690
Windham	41,588	Newfane	786
Windsor	54,055	Woodstock	972

Virginia

(95 cos., 41 ind. cities, 39,598 sq mi land; pop. 6,187,358)

County	Pop.	County Seat or court house	Land area sq mi
Accomack	31,703	Accomac	476
Albemarle	68,172	Charlottesville	740
Alleghany	13,176	Covington	444
Amelia	8,787	Amelia Court House	366
Amherst	28,578	Amherst	470
Appomattox	12,298	Appomattox	345
Arlington	170,897	Arlington	26
Augusta	54,677	Staunton	968
Bath	4,799	Warm Springs	540
Bedford	45,656	Bedford	771
Bland	6,514	Bland	369
Botetourt	24,992	Fincastle	549
Brunswick	15,987	Lawrenceville	579
Buchanan	31,333	Grundy	508
Buckingham	12,873	Buckingham	582
Campbell	47,572	Rustburg	511
Caroline	19,217	Bowling Green	549
Carroll	26,594	Hillsville	494
Charles City	6,282	Charles City	208
Charlotte	11,688	Charlotte Court House	471
Chesterfield	209,564	Chesterfield	446
Clarke	12,101	Berryville	174
Craig	4,372	New Castle	336
Culpeper	27,791	Culpeper	389
Cumberland	7,825	Cumberland	292
Dickenson	17,620	Clintwood	335
Dinwiddie	22,319	Dinwiddie	502
Essex	8,689	Tappahannock	264
Fairfax	818,623	Fairfax	399
Fauquier	48,860	Warrenton	660
Floyd	11,965	Floyd	383
Fluvanna	12,429	Palmyra	282
Franklin	39,549	Rocky Mount	721
Frederick	45,723	Winchester	432
Giles	16,366	Pearisburg	369
Gloucester	30,131	Gloucester	257
Goochland	14,163	Goochland	289
Grayson	16,278	Independence	494
Greene	10,297	Stanardsville	153
Greensville	8,630	Emporia	301
Halifax	29,033	Halifax	806
Hanover	63,306	Hanover	436
Henrico	217,849	Henrico	244
Henry	56,942	Martinsville	385
Highland	2,635	Monterey	416
Isle of Wight	25,053	Isle of Wight	319
James City	34,970	Williamsburg	144
King and Queen	6,289	King and Queen Court House	327
King George	13,527	King George	183
King William	10,913	King William	286
Lancaster	10,896	Lancaster	153
Lee	24,496	Jonesville	438
Loudoun	86,129	Leesburg	517
Louisa	20,325	Louisa	514
Lunenburg	11,419	Lunenburg	443
Madison	11,949	Madison	327
Mathews	8,348	Mathews	87
Mecklenburg	29,241	Boydton	675
Middlesex	8,653	Saluda	138
Montgomery	73,913	Christiansburg	395
Nelson	12,778	Lovingston	471
New Kent	10,445	New Kent	221
Northampton	13,061	Eastville	209
Northumberland	10,524	Heathsville	223
Nottoway	14,993	Nottoway	308
Orange	21,421	Orange	355
Page	21,690	Luray	310
Patrick	17,473	Stuart	467
Pittsylvania	55,672	Chatham	985
Powhatan	15,328	Powhatan	272
Prince Edward	17,320	Farmville	357
Prince George	27,394	Prince George	276
Prince William	215,677	Manassas	345
Pulaski	34,496	Pulaski	335
Rappahannock	6,622	Washington	267
Richmond	7,273	Warsaw	203
Roanoke	79,294	Salem	248
Rockbridge	18,350	Lexington	604
Rockingham	57,482	Harrisonburg	865
Russell	28,667	Lebanon	483
Scott	23,204	Gate City	539
Shenandoah	31,636	Woodstock	507
Smyth	32,370	Marion	435
Southampton	17,550	Courtland	599
Spotsylvania	57,403	Spotsylvania	409
Stafford	61,236	Stafford	277
Surry	6,145	Surry	306
Sussex	10,248	Sussex	496
Tazewell	45,960	Tazewell	522
Warren	26,142	Front Royal	219
Washington	45,887	Abingdon	578
Westmoreland	15,480	Montross	250
Wise	39,573	Wise	405
Wythe	25,471	Wytheville	460
York	42,434	Yorktown	122
Independent Cities			
Alexandria	111,183		16
Bedford	6,073		7
Bristol	18,426		12
Buena Vista	6,406		7
Charlottesville	40,341		10
Chesapeake	151,976		353
Clifton Forge	4,679		3
Colonial Heights	16,064		8
Covington	6,991		5
Danville	53,056		44
Emporia	5,306		7
Fairfax	19,622		6
Falls Church	9,578		2
Franklin	7,864		8
Fredericksburg	19,027		10
Galax	6,670		8
Hampton	133,793		57
Harrisonburg	30,707		17
Hopewell	23,101		11
Lexington	6,959		2
Lynchburg	66,049		50
Manassas	27,957		11
Manassas Park	6,734		3

County	Pop.	County Seat or court house	Land area sq mi
Martinsville	16,162		11
Newport News	170,045		69
Norfolk	261,229		66
Norton	4,247		7
Petersburg	38,386		23
Poquoson	11,005		10
Portsmouth	103,907		30
Radford	15,940		9
Richmond	203,056		63
Roanoke	96,397		43
Salem	23,756		14
South Boston	6,997		5
Staunton	24,461		20
Suffolk	52,141		430
Virginia Beach	393,069		310
Waynesboro	18,549		14
Williamsburg	11,530		9
Winchester	21,947		9

Washington

(39 counties, 66,581 sq mi land; pop. 4,866,692)

County	Pop.	County Seat or court house	Land area sq mi
Adams	13,603	Ritzville	1,921
Asotin	17,605	Asotin	635
Benton	112,560	Prosser	1,715
Chelan	52,250	Wenatchee	2,916
Clallam	56,210	Port Angeles	1,753
Clark	238,053	Vancouver	627
Columbia	4,024	Dayton	865
Cowlitz	82,119	Kelso	1,140
Douglas	26,205	Waterville	1,817
Ferry	6,295	Republic	2,200
Franklin	37,473	Pasco	1,243
Garfield	2,248	Pomeroy	706
Grant	54,798	Ephrata	2,660
Grays Harbor	64,175	Montesano	1,918
Island	60,195	Coupeville	212
Jefferson	20,406	Port Townsend	1,805
King	1,507,305	Seattle	2,128
Kitsap	189,731	Port Orchard	393
Kittitas	26,725	Ellensburg	2,308
Klickitat	16,616	Goldendale	1,880
Lewis	59,358	Chehalis	2,409
Lincoln	8,864	Davenport	2,310
Mason	38,341	Shelton	961
Okanogan	33,350	Okanogan	5,281
Pacific	18,882	South Bend	908
Pend Oreille	8,915	Newport	1,400
Pierce	586,203	Tacoma	1,675
San Juan	10,035	Friday Harbor	179
Skagit	79,545	Mount Vernon	1,735
Skamania	8,289	Stevenson	1,672
Snohomish	465,628	Everett	2,098
Spokane	361,333	Spokane	1,762
Stevens	30,948	Colville	2,470
Thurston	161,238	Olympia	727
Wahkiakum	3,327	Cathlamet	261
Walla Walla	48,439	Walla Walla	1,261
Whatcom	127,780	Bellingham	2,125
Whitman	38,775	Colfax	2,151
Yakima	188,823	Yakima	4,287

West Virginia

(55 counties, 24,087 sq mi land; pop. 1,793,477)

County	Pop.	County Seat or court house	Land area sq mi
Barbour	15,699	Philippi	343
Berkeley	59,253	Martinsburg	321
Boone	25,870	Madison	503
Braxton	12,998	Sutton	513
Brooke	26,992	Wellsburg	90
Cabell	96,827	Huntington	282
Calhoun	7,885	Grantsville	280
Clay	9,983	Clay	346
Doddridge	6,994	West Union	321
Fayette	47,952	Fayetteville	667
Gilmer	7,669	Glenville	340
Grant	10,428	Petersburg	480
Greenbrier	34,693	Lewisburg	1,025
Hampshire	16,498	Romney	644
Hancock	35,233	New Cumberland	84
Hardy	10,977	Moorefield	585
Harrison	69,371	Clarksburg	417
Jackson	25,938	Ripley	464
Jefferson	35,926	Charles Town	209
Kanawha	207,619	Charleston	901
Lewis	17,223	Weston	389
Lincoln	21,382	Hamlin	439
Logan	43,032	Logan	456
McDowell	35,233	Welch	535
Marion	57,249	Fairmont	312
Marshall	37,356	Moundsville	305
Mason	25,178	Point Pleasant	433
Mercer	64,980	Princeton	420
Mineral	26,697	Keyser	329
Mingo	33,739	Williamson	424
Monongalia	75,509	Morgantown	363
Monroe	12,406	Union	473
Morgan	12,128	Berkeley Springs	230
Nicholas	26,775	Summersville	650
Ohio	50,871	Wheeling	106
Pendleton	8,054	Franklin	698
Pleasants	7,546	St. Marys	131
Pocahontas	9,008	Marlinton	942
Preston	29,037	Kingwood	651
Putnam	42,835	Winfield	346
Raleigh	76,819	Beckley	608
Randolph	27,803	Elkins	1,040
Ritchie	10,233	Harrisville	454
Roane	15,120	Spencer	484
Summers	14,204	Hinton	353
Taylor	15,144	Grafton	174
Tucker	7,728	Parsons	421
Tyler	9,796	Middlebourne	258
Upshur	22,867	Buckhannon	355
Wayne	41,636	Wayne	508
Webster	10,729	Webster Springs	556
Wetzel	19,258	New Martinsville	359
Wirt	5,192	Elizabeth	235
Wood	86,915	Parkersburg	367
Wyoming	28,990	Pineville	502

Wisconsin

(72 counties, 54,314 sq mi land; pop. 4,891,769)

County	Pop.	County Seat or court house	Land area sq mi
Adams	15,682	Friendship	648
Ashland	16,307	Ashland	1,048
Barron	40,750	Barron	865
Bayfield	14,008	Washburn	1,462
Brown	194,594	Green Bay	524
Buffalo	13,584	Alma	699
Burnett	13,084	Meenon	818
Calumet	34,291	Chilton	326
Chippewa	52,360	Chippewa Falls	1,017
Clark	31,647	Neillsville	1,218
Columbia	45,088	Portage	771
Crawford	15,940	Prairie du Chien	566
Dane	367,085	Madison	1,205
Dodge	76,559	Juneau	887
Door	25,690	Sturgeon Bay	492
Douglas	41,758	Superior	1,305
Dunn	35,909	Menomonie	853
Eau Claire	85,183	Eau Claire	638
Florence	4,590	Florence	486
Fond du Lac	90,083	Fond du Lac	725
Forest	8,776	Crandon	1,011
Grant	49,266	Lancaster	1,144
Green	30,339	Monroe	583
Green Lake	18,651	Green Lake	357
Iowa	20,150	Dodgeville	760
Iron	6,153	Hurley	751
Jackson	16,588	Black River Falls	998
Jefferson	67,783	Jefferson	562
Juneau	21,650	Mauston	774
Kenosha	128,181	Kenosha	273
Kewaunee	18,878	Kewaunee	343
La Crosse	97,904	La Crosse	457
Lafayette	16,074	Darlington	634
Langlade	19,505	Antigo	873
Lincoln	26,993	Merrill	886
Manitowoc	80,421	Manitowoc	594
Marathon	115,400	Wausau	1,559
Marinette	40,548	Marinette	1,395
Marquette	12,321	Montello	455
Menominee	3,890	Keshena	359
Milwaukee	959,275	Milwaukee	241
Monroe	36,633	Sparta	904
Oconto	30,226	Oconto	1,002
Oneida	31,679	Rhinelander	1,130
Outagamie	140,510	Appleton	642
Ozaukee	72,831	Port Washington	235
Pepin	7,107	Durand	231
Pierce	32,765	Ellsworth	576
Polk	34,773	Balsam Lake	919
Portage	61,405	Stevens Point	810
Price	15,600	Phillips	1,256
Racine	175,034	Racine	334
Richland	17,521	Richland Center	585
Rock	139,510	Janesville	724
Rusk	15,079	Ladysmith	913
Saint Croix	50,251	Hudson	723
Sauk	46,975	Baraboo	838
Sawyer	14,181	Hayward	1,255
Shawano	37,157	Shawano	897
Sheboygan	103,877	Sheboygan	515
Taylor	18,901	Medford	975
Trempealeau	25,263	Whitehall	736

County	Pop.	County Seat or court house	Land area sq mi
Vernon	25,617	Viroqua	808
Vilas	17,707	Eagle River	867
Walworth	75,000	Elkhorn	556
Washburn	13,772	Shell Lake	815
Washington	95,328	West Bend	431
Waukesha	304,715	Waukesha	554
Waupaca	46,104	Waupaca	754
Waushara	19,385	Wautoma	628
Winnebago	140,320	Oshkosh	449
Wood	73,605	Wisconsin Rapids	801

Wyoming

(23 counties, 97,105 sq mi land; pop. 453,588)

County	Pop.	County Seat or court house	Land area sq mi
Albany	30,797	Laramie	4,268
Big Horn	10,525	Basin	3,139
Campbell	29,370	Gillette	4,796
Carbon	16,659	Rawlins	7,877
Converse	11,128	Douglas	4,271
Crook	5,294	Sundance	2,855
Fremont	33,662	Lander	9,181
Goshen	12,373	Torrington	2,186
Hot Springs	4,809	Thermopolis	2,005
Johnson	6,145	Buffalo	4,166
Laramie	73,142	Cheyenne	2,684
Lincoln	12,625	Kemmerer	4,070
Natrona	61,226	Casper	5,347
Niobrara	2,499	Lusk	2,684
Park	23,178	Cody	6,936
Platte	8,145	Wheatland	2,023
Sheridan	23,562	Sheridan	2,532
Sublette	4,843	Pinedale	4,872
Sweetwater	38,823	Green River	10,352
Teton	11,173	Jackson	4,011
Unita	18,705	Evanston	2,085
Washakie	8,388	Worland	2,243
Weston	6,518	Newcastle	2,402

Population of Outlying Areas

Source: Bureau of the Census, U.S. Dept. of Commerce; World Almanac research

Final population counts and land area figures from the U.S. census conducted on Apr. 1, 1990. Because only selected cities are shown, the population and land area figures may not equal the total reported. ZIP codes with an asterisk (*) are general delivery ZIP codes. Consult the local postmaster for more specific delivery information. Wake Atoll, Johnson Atoll, and Midway Atoll receive mail through APO and FPO addresses. U.S. outlying areas that are not listed in this table do not receive U.S. mail delivery.

Commonwealth of Puerto Rico

Zip code	Municipios	Pop.	Land area sq mi
00601	Adjuntas	19,451	67
00602	Aguada	35,911	31
*00605	Aguadilla	59,335	37
00703	Aguas Buenas	25,424	31
00705	Aibonito	24,971	31
00610	Anasco	25,234	39
*00006	Arecibo	93,385	126
00714	Arroyo	18,910	15
00617	Barceloneta	20,947	23
00794	Barranquitas	25,605	34
*00958	Bayamon	220,262	44
00623	Cabo Rojo	38,521	70
*00726	Caguas	133,447	59
00627	Camuy	28,917	46
00729	Canovanas	36,816	33
*00984	Carolina	177,806	45
*00962	Catano	34,587	5
*00007	Cayey	46,553	52
00735	Ceiba	17,145	29
00638	Ciales	18,084	67
00739	Cidra	35,601	36
00769	Coamo	33,837	78
00782	Comerio	20,265	28
00783	Corozal	33,095	43
00775	Culebra	1,542	12
00646	Dorado	30,759	23
00738	Fajardo	36,882	30
00650	Florida	8,689	10
00653	Guanica	19,984	37
00784	Guayama	41,588	65
00656	Guayanilla	21,581	42
*00970	Guaynabo	92,886	27
00778	Gurabo	28,737	28
00659	Hatillo	32,703	42
00660	Hormigueros	15,212	11
*00792	Humacao	55,203	45
00662	Isabela	39,147	55
00664	Jayuya	15,527	45
00795	Juana Diaz	45,198	60
00777	Juncos	30,612	27
00667	Lajas	23,271	60
00669	Lares	29,015	62
00670	Las Marias	9,306	46
00771	Las Piedras	27,896	34
00772	Loiza	29,307	19
00773	Luquillo	18,100	26
00674	Manati	38,692	45
00606	Maricao	6,206	37
00707	Maunabo	12,347	21
*00681	Mayagüez	100,371	78
00676	Moca	32,926	50
00687	Morovis	25,288	39
00718	Naguabo	22,620	52
00719	Naranjito	27,914	27
00720	Orocovis	21,158	64
00723	Patillas	19,633	47
00624	Penuelas	22,515	45
*00732	Ponce	187,749	116
00678	Quebradillas	21,425	23
00677	Rincon	12,213	14
00721	Rio Grande	45,648	61
00637	Sabana Grande	22,843	36
00751	Salinas	28,335	69
00683	San German	34,962	55
*00936	San Juan	437,745	48
00754	San Lorenzo	35,163	53
00685	San Sebastian	38,799	70
00757	Santa Isabel	19,318	34
*00953	Toa Alta	44,101	27
*00949	Toa Baja	89,454	23
*00976	Trujillo Alto	61,120	21
00641	Utuado	34,980	114
00692	Vega Alta	34,559	28
*00693	Vega Baja	55,997	46
00765	Vieques	8,602	51
00766	Villalba	23,559	36
00767	Yabucoa	36,483	55
00698	Yauco	42,058	68
Total		**3,522,037**	**3,427**

Commonwealth of the Northern Mariana Islands

Zip code	Municipality	Pop.	Land area sq mi
96950	Northern Islands	36	60
96951	Rota	2,295	33
96950	Saipan	38,896	47
96952	Tinian	2,118	39
Total		**43,345**	**179**

U.S. External Territories

Zip code	Area	Pop.	Land area sq mi
	American Samoa		
96799	American Samoa	46,773	77
	Guam		
*96910	Agaña	1,139	1
.....	Agaña Hts.	3,646	1
*96915	Agat	4,960	10
.....	Asan	2,070	6
*96913	Barrigada	8,846	9
.....	Chalan-Pago-Ordot	4,451	6
96912	Dededo	31,728	30
96916	Inarajan	2,469	19
.....	Mangilao	10,483	10
96916	Merizo	1,742	6
.....	Mongmong-Toto-Maite	5,845	2
.....	Piti	1,827	7
96915	Santa Rita	11,857	17
.....	Sinajana	2,658	1
.....	Talofofo	2,310	17
96911	Tamuning	16,673	6
96918	Umatac	897	6
96921	Yigo	14,213	35
96914	Yona	5,338	20
Total		**133,152**	**210**
	Virgin Islands		
.....	Saint Croix	50,139	83
.....	Saint John	3,504	20
.....	Saint Thomas	48,166	31
00801	Charlotte Amalie	12,331	
*00820	Christiansted	2,555	
*00840	Frederiksted	1,064	
Total		**101,809**	**134**
	Trust Territory		
96940	Palau (Belau), Republic of	15,122	179

U.S. Area and Population: 1790 to 1990

Source: Bureau of the Census, U.S. Dept. of Commerce

Census date	Area (sq mi) Gross	Land	Water	Population Number	per sq mi of land	Increase over preceding census Number	%
1990 (Apr. 1)	3,787,428	3,536,344	251,084[1]	248,709,873	70.3	22,164,068	9.8
1980 (Apr. 1)	3,618,770	3,539,289	79,481	226,542,203	64.0	23,240,172	11.4
1970 (Apr. 1)	3,618,770	3,536,855	81,915	203,302,031	57.5	23,978,856	13.4
1960 (Apr. 1)	3,618,770	3,540,911	77,859	179,323,175	50.6	27,997,377	18.5
1950 (Apr. 1)	3,618,770	3,552,206	66,564	151,325,798	42.6	19,161,229	14.5
1940 (Apr. 1)	3,618,770	3,554,608	64,162	132,164,569	37.2	8,961,945	7.3
1930 (Apr. 1)	3,618,770	3,551,608	67,162	123,202,624	34.7	17,181,087	16.2
1920 (Jan. 1)	3,618,770	3,546,931	71,839	106,021,537	29.9	13,793,041	15.0
1910 (Apr. 15)	3,618,770	3,547,045	71,725	92,228,496	26.0	16,016,328	21.0
1900 (June 1)	3,618,770	3,547,314	71,456	76,212,168	21.5	13,232,402	21.0
1890 (June 1)	3,612,299	3,540,705	71,594	62,979,766	17.8	12,790,557	25.5
1880 (June 1)	3,612,299	3,540,705	71,594	50,189,209	14.2	11,630,838	30.2
1870 (June 1)	3,612,299	3,540,705	71,594	38,558,371	10.9	7,115,050	22.6
1860 (June 1)	3,021,295	2,969,640	51,655	31,443,321	10.6	8,251,445	35.6
1850 (June 1)	2,991,655	2,940,042	51,613	23,191,876	7.9	6,122,423	35.9
1840 (June 1)	1,792,552	1,749,462	43,090	17,069,453	9.8	4,203,433	32.7
1830 (June 1)	1,792,552	1,749,462	43,090	12,866,020	7.4	3,227,567	33.5
1820 (June 1)	1,792,552	1,749,462	43,090	9,638,453	5.5	2,398,572	33.1
1810 (Aug. 6)	1,722,685	1,681,828	40,857	7,239,881	4.3	1,931,398	36.4
1800 (Aug. 4)	891,364	864,746	26,618	5,308,483	6.1	1,379,269	35.1
1790 (Aug. 2)	891,364	864,746	26,618	3,929,214	4.5	—	—

(1) Comprises inland, coastal, Great Lakes, and territorial water. Data for prior years cover inland water only.

Note: Percent changes are computed on basis of change in population since preceding census date, and period covered therefore is not always exactly 10 years.

Population density figures given for various years represent the area within the boundaries of the U.S. that was under the jurisdiction on date in question, including in some cases considerable areas not organized or settled and not covered by the census. In 1870, for example, Alaska was not covered by the census.

Revised figure of 39,818,449 for the 1870 population includes adjustments for undernumeration in the southern states. On the basis of the revised figure, the population increased by 8,375,128, or 26.6%, between 1860 and 1870, and by 10,370,760, or 26.1%, between 1870 and 1880.

Resident Population, by Sex, Race, Residence, and Median Age, 1790 to 1990

Source: Bureau of the Census, U.S. Dept. of Commerce (in thousands, except as indicated)

Date	Sex		Race				Residence		Median Age (years)		
				Black							
	Male	Female	White	Number	Percent	Other	Urban	Rural	All races	White	Black
Conterminous U.S.[1]											
1790 (Aug. 2)	NA	NA	3,172	757	19.3	NA	202	3,728	NA	NA	NA
1810 (Aug. 6)	NA	NA	5,862	1,378	19.0	NA	525	6,714	NA	16.0	NA
1820 (Aug. 7)	4,897	4,742	7,867	1,772	18.4	NA	693	8,945	16.7	16.5	17.2
1840 (June 1)	8,689	8,381	14,196	2,874	16.8	NA	1,845	15,224	17.8	17.9	17.3
1860 (June 1)	16,085	15,358	26,923	4,442	14.1	79	6,217	25,227	19.4	19.7	17.7
1870 (June 1)	19,494	19,065	33,589	4,880	12.7	89	9,902	28,656	20.2	20.4	18.5
1880 (June 1)	25,519	24,637	43,403	6,581	13.1	172	14,130	36,026	20.9	21.4	18.0
1890 (June 1)	32,237	30,711	55,101	7,489	11.9	358	22,106	40,841	22.0	22.5	17.8
1900 (June 1)	38,816	37,178	66,809	8,834	11.6	351	30,160	45,835	22.9	23.4	19.4
1920 (Jan. 1)	53,900	51,810	94,821	10,463	9.9	427	54,158	51,553	25.3	25.6	22.3
1930 (Apr. 1)	62,137	60,638	110,287	11,891	9.7	597	68,955	53,820	26.4	26.9	23.5
1940 (Apr. 1)	66,062	65,608	118,215	12,866	9.8	589	74,424	57,246	29.0	29.5	25.3
United States											
1950 (Apr. 1)	75,187	76,139	135,150	15,045	9.9	1,131	96,847	54,479	30.2	30.7	26.2
1960 (Apr. 1)	88,331	90,992	158,832	18,872	10.5	1,620	125,269	54,054	29.5	30.3	23.5
1970 (Apr. 1)[2]	98,926	104,309	178,098	22,581	11.1	2,557	149,325	53,887	28.0	28.9	22.4
1980 (Apr. 1)[3]	110,053	116,493	194,713	26,683	11.8	5,150	167,051	59,495	30.0	30.9	24.9
1983 (July 1, est)	113,119	120,365	199,849	28,056	12.0	6,379	NA	NA	30.8	31.7	25.9
1985 (July 1, est)	116,160	122,576	202,769	28,870	12.1	7,097	NA	NA	31.4	32.3	26.6
1990 (Apr. 1)	121,239	127,470	199,686	29,986	12.1	9,805	187,053	61,656	32.9	34.4	28.1

NA=Not available. (1) Excludes Alaska and Hawaii. (2) The revised 1970 resident population count is 203,302,031, which incorporates changes due to errors found after tabulations were completed. The race and sex data shown here reflect the official 1970 census count; the residence data come from the tabulated count. (3) The race data shown for Apr. 1, 1980, have been modified.

UNITED STATES HISTORY

1492

Christopher Columbus and crew sighted land **Oct. 12** in the present-day Bahamas.

1497

John Cabot explored northeast coast to Delaware.

1513

Juan Ponce de León explored Florida coast.

1524

Giovanni da Verrazano led French expedition along coast from Carolina north to Nova Scotia; entered New York harbor.

1539

Hernando de Soto landed in Florida **May 28;** crossed Mississippi River, **1541.**

1540

Francisco Vásquez de Coronado explored Southwest north of Rio Grande. Hernando de Alarcón reached Colorado River, Don Garcia Lopez de Cardenas reached Grand Canyon. Others explored California coast.

1565

St. Augustine, Fla. founded by Pedro Menéndez. Razed by Francis Drake **1586.**

1579

Francis Drake entered San Francisco Bay and claimed region for Britain.

1607

Capt. John Smith and 105 cavaliers in 3 ships landed on Virginia coast, started first permanent English settlement in New World at **Jamestown** in May.

1609

Henry Hudson, English explorer of Northwest Passage, employed by Dutch, sailed into New York harbor in **Sept.,** and up Hudson to Albany. The same year, **Samuel de Champlain** explored Lake Champlain just to the north.

Spaniards settled **Santa Fe, N.M.**

1619

House of Burgesses, first representative assembly in New World, elected **July 30** at Jamestown, Va.

First black laborers — indentured servants — in English N. American colonies, landed by Dutch at Jamestown in **Aug.** Chattel slavery legally recognized, **1650.**

1620

Plymouth Pilgrims, Puritan separatists from Church of England, some living in Holland, left Plymouth, England **Sept. 16** on Mayflower. Original destination Virginia, they reached Cape Cod **Nov. 19,** explored coast; 103 passengers landed **Dec. 26** at Plymouth. Mayflower Compact was agreement to form a government and abide by its laws. Half of colony died during harsh winter.

1624

Dutch colonies started in Albany and in New York area, where New Netherland was established in May.

1626

Peter Minuit bought Manhattan for Dutch from Man-a-hat-a Indians during summer for goods valued at $24; named island New Amsterdam.

1630

Settlement of **Boston** established by Mass. colonists led by John Winthrop.

1634

Maryland founded as Catholic colony with religious tolerance.

1636

Roger Williams founded Providence, R.I., **June,** as a democratically ruled colony with separation of church and state. Charter was granted, **1644.**

Harvard College founded **Oct. 28,** now oldest in U.S.; Grammar school, compulsory education established at Boston.

1660

British Parliament passed **Navigation Act,** regulating colonial commerce to suit English needs.

1664

Three hundred **British troops Sept. 8 seized New Netherland** from Dutch, who yield peacefully. Charles II granted province of New Netherland and city of New Amsterdam to brother, Duke of York; both renamed New York. The Dutch recaptured the colony **Aug. 9, 1673,** but ceded it to Britain **Nov. 10, 1674.**

1676

Nathaniel Bacon led planters against autocratic British Gov. Berkeley, burned Jamestown, Va. Bacon died, 23 followers executed.

Bloody **Indian war** in New England ended **Aug. 12.** King Philip, Wampanoag chief, and many Narragansett Indians killed.

1682

Robert Cavelier, Sieur de La Salle, claimed lower Mississippi River country for France, called it Louisiana **Apr. 9.** Had French outposts built in Illinois and Texas, **1684.** Killed during mutiny **Mar. 19, 1687.**

1683

William Penn signed treaty with Delaware Indians and made payment for Pennsylvania lands.

1692

Witchcraft delusion at Salem, Mass.; 20 executed by special court.

1696

Capt. William Kidd, who was born in Scotland and settled in America, was hired by British to fight pirates and take booty, but himself became a pirate. Arrested and sent to England, he was hanged **1701.**

1699

French settlements made in Mississippi, Louisiana.

1704

Indians attacked Deerfield, Mass. **Feb. 28-29,** killed 40, carried off 100.

Boston News Letter, first regular newspaper, started by John Campbell, postmaster. (*Publick Occurences* was suppressed after one issue **1690.**)

1709

British-Colonial troops captured French fort, Port Royal, Nova Scotia, in **Queen Anne's War 1701-13.** France yielded Nova Scotia by treaty **1713.**

1712

Slaves revolted in New York **Apr. 6.** Six committed suicide, 21 were executed. Second rising, **1741;** 13 slaves hanged, 13 burned, 71 deported.

1716

First theater in colonies opened in Williamsburg, Va.

1732

Benjamin Franklin published first *Poor Richard's Almanac;* published annually to 1757.

1735

Freedom of the press recognized in New York by acquittal of John Peter Zenger, editor of *Weekly Journal,* on charge of libeling British Gov. Cosby by criticizing his conduct in office.

1740-41

Capt. Vitus Bering, Dane employed by Russians, reached Alaska.

1744

King George's War pitted British and colonials vs. French. Colonials captured Louisburg, Cape Breton Is. **June 17, 1745.** Returned to France **1748** by Treaty of Aix-la-Chapelle.

1752

Benjamin Franklin, flying kite in thunderstorm, proved lightning is electricity **June 15;** invented lightning rod.

1754

French and Indian War (in Europe called 7 Years War, started 1756) began when French occupied Ft. Duquesne (Pittsburgh). British moved Acadian French from Nova Scotia to Louisiana **Oct. 8, 1755.** British captured Québec **Sept. 18, 1759** in battles in which French Gen. Montcalm and British Gen. Wolfe were killed. Peace signed **Feb. 10, 1763.** French lost Canada and American Midwest. British tightened colonial administration in North America.

1764

Sugar Act placed duties on lumber, foodstuffs, molasses and rum in colonies, to pay French and Indian War debts.

1765

Stamp Act required revenue stamps to help defray cost of royal troops. Nine colonies, led by New York and Massachusetts at Stamp Act Congress in New York **Oct. 7-25, 1765,** adopted Declaration of Rights opposing taxation without representation in Parliament and trial without jury by admiralty courts. Stamp Act **repealed Mar. 17, 1766.**

1767

Townshend Acts levied taxes on glass, painter's lead, paper, and tea. In **1770** all duties except on tea were repealed.

1770

British troops fired **Mar. 5** into Boston mob, killed 5 including **Crispus Attucks,** a black man, reportedly leader of group; later called **Boston Massacre.**

1773

East India Co. tea ships turned back at Boston, New York, Philadelphia in **May.** Cargo ship burned at Annapolis **Oct. 14,** cargo thrown overboard at **Boston Tea Party Dec. 16,** to protest the tea tax.

1774

"Intolerable Acts" of Parliament curtailed Massachusetts self-rule; barred use of Boston harbor till tea was paid for.

First Continental Congress held in Philadelphia **Sept. 5-Oct. 26;** protested British measures, called for civil disobedience.

Rhode Island abolished slavery.

1775

Patrick Henry addressed Virginia convention, **Mar. 23,** said "Give me liberty or give me death."

Paul Revere and William Dawes on night of **Apr. 18** rode to alert patriots that British were on way to Concord to destroy arms. At Lexington, Mass. **Apr. 19** Minutemen lost 8. On return from Concord British took 273 casualties.

Col. Ethan Allen (joined by Col. Benedict Arnold) captured Ft. **Ticonderoga, N.Y. May 10;** also Crown Point. Colonials headed for **Bunker Hill,** fortified Breed's Hill, Charlestown, Mass., repulsed British under Gen. William Howe twice before retreating **June 17;** British casualties 1,000; called Battle of Bunker Hill. Continental Congress **June 15** named **George Washington** commander-in-chief.

1776

France and Spain each agreed **May 2** to provide one million livres in arms to Americans.

In Continental Congress **June 7,** Richard Henry Lee (Va.) moved "that these united colonies are and of right ought to be free and independent states." Resolution adopted July 2. **Declaration of Independence** approved **July 4.**

Col. Moultrie's batteries at **Charleston, S.C.** repulsed British sea attack **June 28.**

Washington, with 10,000 men, lost **Battle of Long Island Aug. 27,** evacuated New York.

Nathan Hale executed as spy by British **Sept. 22.**

Brig. Gen. Arnold's **Lake Champlain** fleet was defeated at Valcour **Oct. 11,** but British returned to Canada. Howe failed to destroy Washington's army at **White Plains Oct. 28.** Hessians captured Ft. Washington, Manhattan, and 3,000 men **Nov. 16;** Ft. Lee, N.J. **Nov. 18.**

Washington in Pennsylvania, recrossed **Delaware River Dec. 25-26,** defeated 1,400 Hessians at Trenton, N.J. **Dec. 26.**

1777

Washington defeated Lord Cornwallis at **Princeton Jan. 3.** Continental Congress adopted Stars and Stripes.

Maj. Gen. John Burgoyne with 8,000 from Canada captured **Ft. Ticonderoga July 6.** Americans beat back Burgoyne at Bemis Heights **Oct. 7** and cut off British escape route. Burgoyne surrendered 5,000 men at **Saratoga, N.Y. Oct. 17.**

Marquis de Lafayette, aged 20, made major general.

Articles of Confederation and Perpetual Union adopted by Continental Congress **Nov. 15.**

France recognized independence of 13 colonies **Dec. 17.**

1778

France signed treaty of aid with U.S. **Feb. 6.** Sent fleet; British evacuated Philadelphia in consequence **June 18.**

1779

John Paul Jones on the *Bonhomme Richard* defeated *Serapis* in British North Sea waters **Sept. 23.**

1780

Charleston, S.C. fell to the British **May 12,** but a British force was defeated near **Kings Mountain, N.C. Oct. 7** by militiamen.

Benedict Arnold found to be a traitor **Sept. 23.** Arnold escaped, made brigadier general in British army.

1781

Bank of North America incorporated in Philadelphia **May 26.**

Cornwallis, sapped by patriot victories, retired to **Yorktown, Va.** Adm. De Grasse landed 3,000 French and stopped British fleet in Hampton Roads. Washington and Rochambeau joined forces, arrived near Williamsburg **Sept. 26.** When siege of Cornwallis began **Oct. 6,** British had 6,000, Americans 8,846, French 7,800. **Cornwallis surrendered Oct. 19.**

1782

New **British** cabinet agreed **in March** to **recognize U.S.** independence. Preliminary agreement signed in Paris **Nov. 30.**

1783

Massachusetts Supreme Court **outlawed slavery** in that state, noting the words in the state Bill of Rights "all men are born free and equal."

Britain, U.S. signed **peace treaty Sept. 3** (Congress ratified it **Jan. 14, 1784).**

Washington ordered army disbanded Nov. 3, bade farewell to his officers at Fraunces Tavern, N.Y. City **Dec. 4.**

Noah Webster published *American Spelling Book,* great best-seller.

1784

Jefferson's proposal to **ban slavery** in new territory after 1802 is narrowly defeated **Mar. 1.**

First successful daily newspaper, **Pennsylvania Packet & General Advertiser,** published **Sept. 21.**

1786

Delegates from 5 states at **Annapolis, Md. Sept. 11-14** asked Congress to call convention in Philadelphia to write practical constitution for the 13 states.

1787

Shays's Rebellion, of debt-ridden farmers in Massachusetts, failed **Jan. 25.**

Northwest Ordinance adopted **July 13** by Continental Congress. Determined government of Northwest Territory north of Ohio River, west of New York; 60,000 inhabitants could get statehood. Guaranteed freedom of religion, support for schools, no slavery.

Constitutional convention opened at Philadelphia **May 25** with George Washington presiding. Constitution adopted by delegates **Sept. 17;** ratification by 9th state, New Hampshire, **June 21, 1788,** meant adoption; declared in effect **Mar. 4, 1789.**

1789

George Washington chosen president by all electors voting (73 eligible, 69 voting, 4 absent); John Adams, vice president, 34 votes. **Feb. 4.** First Congress met at Federal Hall, N.Y. City; regular sessions began **Apr. 6.** Washington inaugurated there **Apr. 30.** Supreme Court created by Federal Judiciary Act **Sept. 24.** Congress submitted Bill of Rights to states **Sept. 25.**

1790

Congress passed **Census Act Mar. 1; Naturalization Act** (2-year residency) **Mar. 26.**

Congress met in Phila. **Dec. 6,** new temporary Capital.

1791

Bill of Rights went into effect **Dec. 15.**

1792

Coinage Act established **U.S. Mint** in Philadelphia **Apr. 2.**

Gen. **"Mad" Anthony Wayne** made commander in Ohio-Indiana area, trained "American Legion", established string of forts. Routed Indians at Fallen Timbers on Maumee River **Aug. 20, 1794,** checked British at Fort Miami, Ohio.

White House cornerstone laid **Oct. 13.**

1793

Eli Whitney invented **cotton gin,** reviving southern slavery.

1794

Whiskey Rebellion, west Pennsylvania farmers protesting liquor tax of **1791,** was suppressed by 15,000 militiamen **Sept. 1794.** Alexander Hamilton used incident to establish authority of the new federal government in enforcing its laws.

1795

U.S. bought peace from **Algerian pirates** by paying $1 mln. ransom for 115 seamen **Sept. 5,** followed by annual tributes.

Gen. Wayne signed peace with Indians at Fort Greenville.

Univ. of North Carolina became first operating state university.

1796

Washington's Farewell Address as president delivered **Sept. 19.** Gave strong warnings against permanent alliances with foreign powers, big public debt, large military establishment and devices of "small, artful, enterprising minority" to control or change government.

1797

U.S. **frigate United States** launched at Philadelphia **July 10;** Constellation at Baltimore **Sept. 7;** Constitution (Old Ironsides) at Boston **Sept. 20.**

1798

Alien & Sedition Acts passed by Federalists **June-July;** intended to silence political opposition.

War with France threatened over French raids on U.S. shipping and rejection of U.S. diplomats. Congress voided all treaties with France, ordered Navy to capture French armed ships. Navy (45 ships) and 365 privateers captured 84 French ships. USS Constellation took French warship Insurgente **1799.** Napoleon stopped French raids after becoming First Consul.

1800

Federal gvt. moves from Philadelphia to **Washington, D.C.**

1801

Tripoli declared war June 10 against U.S., which refused added tribute to commerce-raiding Arab corsairs. Land and naval campaigns forced Tripoli to negotiate **peace June 4, 1805.**

1803

Supreme Court, in **Marbury v. Madison** case, for the first time overturned a U.S. law **Feb. 24.**

Napoleon, who had recovered Louisiana from Spain by secret treaty, sold all of **Louisiana,** stretching to Canadian border, to U.S., for $11,250,000 in bonds, plus $3,750,000 indemnities to American citizens with claims against France. U.S. took title **Dec. 20.** Purchases doubled U.S. area.

1804

Lewis and Clark expedition ordered by Pres. Jefferson to explore what is now northwest U.S. Started from St. Louis **May 14;** ended **Sept. 23, 1806.** Sacagawea, an Indian woman, served as guide.

Vice Pres. **Aaron Burr,** after long political rivalry, **shot Alexander Hamilton** in a duel **July 11** in Weehawken, N.J.; Hamilton died the next day.

1807

Robert Fulton made first practical steamboat trip; left N.Y. City **Aug. 17,** reached Albany, 150 mi., in 32 hrs.

Embargo Act bans all trade with foreign countries, forbids ships to set sail for foreign ports **Dec. 22.**

1808

Slave importation outlawed. Some 250,000 slaves were illegally imported **1808-1860.**

1811

William Henry Harrison, governor of Indiana, defeated Indians under the Prophet, in battle of Tippecanoe **Nov. 7.**

Cumberland Road begun at Cumberland, Md.; became important route to West.

1812

War of 1812 had 3 main causes: Britain seized U.S. ships trading with France; Britain seized 4,000 naturalized U.S. sailors by **1810;** Britain armed Indians who raided western border. U.S. stopped trade with Europe **1807** and **1809.** Trade with Britain only was stopped, **1810.**

Unaware that Britain had raised the blockade against France 2 days before, **Congress declared war June 18** by a small majority. The West favored war, New England opposed it. The British were handicapped by war with France.

U.S. naval victories in **1812** included: USS Essex captured Alert **Aug. 13;** USS Constitution destroyed Guerriere **Aug. 19;** USS Wasp took Frolic **Oct. 18;** USS United States defeated Macedonian off Azores **Oct. 25;** Constitution beat Java **Dec. 29.** British captured Detroit **Aug. 16.**

1813

Oliver H. Perry defeated British fleet at Battle of Lake Erie, **Sept. 10.** U.S. victory at Battle of the Thames, Ont., **Oct. 5,** broke Indian allies of Britain, and made Detroit frontier safe for U.S. But Americans failed in Canadian invasion attempts. York (Toronto) and Buffalo were burned.

1814

British landed in Maryland in August, defeated U.S. force **Aug. 24, burned Capitol** and White House. Maryland militia stopped British advance **Sept. 12.** Bombardment of Ft. McHenry, Baltimore, for 25 hours, **Sept. 13-14,** by British fleet failed; Francis Scott Key wrote words to **Star Spangled Banner.**

U.S. won naval Battle of **Lake Champlain Sept. 11.** Peace treaty signed at Ghent **Dec. 24.**

1815

Some 5,300 British, unaware of peace treaty, attacked U.S. entrenchments near **New Orleans, Jan. 8.** British had over 2,000 casualties, Americans lost 71.

U.S. flotilla finally ended piracy by **Algiers, Tunis, Tripoli** by **Aug. 6.**

1816

Second **Bank of the U.S.** chartered.

1817

Rush-Bagot treaty signed **Apr. 28-29;** limited U.S., British armaments on the Great Lakes.

1819

Spain cedes **Florida** to U.S. **Feb. 22.**

American steamship Savannah made first part steam-powered, part sail-powered crossing of Atlantic, Savannah, Ga. to Liverpool, Eng., 29 days.

1820

First organized **immigration of blacks to Africa** from U.S. began with 86 free blacks sailing **Feb.** to Sierra Leone, Brit. Colony.

Henry Clay's **Missouri Compromise** bill passed by Congress **March 3.** Slavery was allowed in Missouri, but not elsewhere west of the Mississippi River north of 36° 30′ latitude (the southern line of Missouri). Repealed **1854.**

1821

Emma Willard founded Troy Female Seminary, first U.S. women's college.

1823

Monroe Doctrine enunciated **Dec. 2,** opposing European intervention in the Americas.

1824

Pawtucket, R.I. **weavers strike** in first such action by women.

1825

Erie Canal opened; first boat left Buffalo **Oct. 26,** reached NYC **Nov. 4.** Canal cost $7 million but opened Great Lakes area, made NYC chief Atlantic port.

John Stevens, of Hoboken, N.J., built and operated first experimental **steam locomotive** in U.S.

1828

South Carolina **Dec. 19** declared the right of state **nullification of federal laws,** opposing the "Tariff of Abominations."

Noah Webster published his *American Dictionary of the English Language.*

Baltimore & Ohio, 1st U.S. passenger RR, was begun **July 4.**

1830

Mormon church organized by Joseph Smith in Fayette, N.Y. **Apr. 6.**

1831

William Lloyd Garrison began abolitionist newspaper *The Liberator* **Jan. 1.**

Nat Turner, black slave in Virginia, led local slave rebellion, killed 57 whites in **Aug.** Troops called in, 100 slaves killed, Turner captured, tried, and hanged.

1832

Black Hawk War (Ill.-Wis.) **Apr.-Sept.** pushed Sauk and Fox Indians west across Mississippi.

South Carolina convention passed **Ordinance of Nullification in Nov.** against permanent tariff, threatening to withdraw from the Union. Congress **Feb. 1833** passed a compromise tariff act, whereupon South Carolina repealed its act.

1833

Oberlin College, first in U.S. to adopt coeducation; refused to bar students on account of race, **1835.**

1835

Seminole Indians in Florida under Osceola began attacks **Nov. 1,** protesting forced removal. The unpopular 8-year war ended **Aug. 14, 1842;** Indians were sent to Oklahoma. War cost the U.S. 1,500 soldiers.

Texas proclaimed right to secede from Mexico; Sam Houston put in command of Texas army, **Nov. 2-4.**

Gold discovered on **Cherokee land** in Georgia. Indians forced to cede lands **Dec. 20** and to cross Mississippi.

1836

Texans besieged in Alamo in San Antonio by Mexicans under Santa Anna **Feb. 23-Mar. 6;** entire garrison killed. Texas independence declared, **Mar. 2.** At San Jacinto **Apr. 21** Sam Houston and Texans defeated Mexicans.

Marcus Whitman, H.H. Spaulding and wives reached Fort Walla Walla on Columbia River, Oregon. **First white women to cross plains.**

1838

Cherokee Indians made "**Trail of Tears,**" removed from Georgia to Oklahoma starting **Oct.**

1841

First emigrant **wagon train for California,** 47 persons, left Independence, Mo. **May 1,** reached Cal. **Nov. 4.**

Brook Farm commune set up by New England Transcendentalist intellectuals. Lasts to **1846.**

1842

Webster-Ashburton Treaty signed **Aug. 9,** fixing the U.S.-Canada border in Maine and Minnesota.

First use of **anesthetic** (sulphuric ether gas).

Settlement of Oregon begins via **Oregon Trail.**

1843

More than 1,000 settlers left Independence, Mo. for Oregon **May 22,** arrived **Oct.**

1844

First message over first **telegraph line** sent **May 24** by inventor Samuel F.B. Morse from Washington to Baltimore: "What hath God wrought!"

1845

Texas Congress **voted for annexation** by U.S. **July 4.** U.S. Congress admits Texas to Union **Dec. 29.**

1846

Mexican War. Pres. James K. Polk ordered Gen. Zachary Taylor to seize disputed Texan land settled by Mexicans. After border clash, U.S. declared war **May 13;** Mexico **May 23.** Northern Whigs opposed war, southerners backed it.

Bear flag of Republic of California raised by American settlers at Sonoma **June 14.**

About 12,000 U.S. troops took Vera Cruz Mar. 27, 1847, Mexico City Sept. 14, 1847. By **treaty, Feb. 1848,** Mexico ceded claims to Texas, California, Arizona, New Mexico, Nevada, Utah, part of Colorado. U.S. assumed $3 million American claims and paid Mexico $15 million.

Treaty with Great Britain **June 15** set **boundary in Oregon** territory at 49th parallel (extension of existing line). Expansionists had used slogan "54° 40′ or fight."

Mormons, after violent clashes with settlers over polygamy, left Nauvoo, Ill. for West under Brigham Young, settled **July 1847 at Salt Lake City, Utah.**

Elias Howe invented **sewing machine.**

1847

First **adhesive U.S. postage stamps** on sale **July 1;** Benjamin Franklin 5¢, Washington 10¢.

Ralph Waldo Emerson published first book of poems; **Henry Wadsworth Longfellow** published *Evangeline.*

1848

Gold discovered Jan. 24 in California; 80,000 prospectors emigrate in **1849.**

Lucretia Mott and Elizabeth Cady Stanton lead **Seneca Falls, N.Y. Women's Rights Convention July 19-20.**

1850

Sen. Henry Clay's **Compromise of 1850** admitted California as 31st state **Sept. 9,** slavery forbidden; made Utah and New Mexico territories without decision on slavery; made Fugitive Slave Law more harsh; ended District of Columbia slave trade.

1851

Herman Melville's *Moby Dick,* **Nathaniel Hawthorne's** *House of the Seven Gables* published.

1852

Uncle Tom's Cabin, by **Harriet Beecher Stowe,** published.

1853

Commodore Matthew C. Perry, U.S.N., received by Lord of Toda, Japan **July 14; negotiated treaty to open Japan** to U.S. ships.

1854

Republican Party formed at Ripon, Wis. **Feb. 28.** Opposed Kansas-Nebraska Act (became law **May 30**), which left issue of slavery to vote of settlers.

Henry David Thoreau published *Walden.*

1855

Walt Whitman published *Leaves of Grass.*

First railroad train crossed Mississippi on the river's first bridge, Rock Island, Ill.-Davenport, Ia. **Apr. 21.**

1856

Republican Party's first nominee for president, **John C. Fremont,** defeated. Abraham Lincoln made 50 speeches for him.

Lawrence, Kan. sacked **May 21** by pro-slavery group; abolitionist **John Brown** led anti-slavery men against Missourians at **Osawatomie, Kan. Aug. 30.**

1857

Dred Scott decision by U.S. Supreme Court **Mar. 6** held, 6-3, that a slave did not become free when taken into a free state, Congress could not bar slavery from a territory, and blacks could not be citizens.

1858

First **Atlantic cable** completed by Cyrus W. Field **Aug. 5;** cable failed **Sept. 1.**

Lincoln-Douglas debates in Illinois **Aug. 21-Oct. 15.**

1859

First commercially productive **oil well,** drilled near Titusville, Pa., by Edwin L. Drake **Aug. 27.**

Abolitionist **John Brown** with 21 men seized U.S. Armory at **Harpers Ferry (then Va.) Oct. 16.** U.S. Marines captured raiders, killing several. Brown was hanged for treason by Virginia **Dec. 2.**

1860

Approximately 20,000 **New England shoe workers** strike **Feb. 22** and win higher wages.

Abraham Lincoln, Republican, elected president in 4-way race.

First **Pony Express** between Sacramento, Cal. and St. Joseph, Mo. started **Apr. 3;** service ended **Oct. 24, 1861** when first transcontinental telegraph line was completed.

1861

Seven southern states set up **Confederate States of America Feb. 8,** with Jefferson Davis as president, captured Federal arsenals and forts. **Civil War** began as Confederates fired on **Ft. Sumter** in Charleston, S.C. **Apr. 12;** they captured it **Apr. 14.**

President **Lincoln called for 75,000 volunteers Apr. 15.** By **May,** 11 states had seceded. Lincoln blockaded southern ports **Apr. 19,** cutting off vital exports, aid.

Confederates repelled Union forces at first **Battle of Bull Run July 21.**

First **transcontinental telegraph** was put in operation.

1862

Homestead Act was approved **May 20;** it granted free family farms to settlers.

Land Grant Act approved **July 7,** providing for public land sale to benefit agricultural education; eventually led to establishment of state university systems.

Union forces were victorious in western campaigns, took **New Orleans.** Battles in East were inconclusive.

1863

Lincoln issued **Emancipation Proclamation Jan. 1,** freeing "all slaves in areas still in rebellion."

The entire **Mississippi River** was in Union hands by **July 4.** Union forces won a major victory at **Gettysburg, Pa. July 1-July 3.** Lincoln read his **Gettysburg Address Nov. 19.**

In **draft riots** in N.Y. City about 1,000 were killed or wounded; some blacks were hanged by mobs **July 13-16.** Rioters protested provision allowing money payment in place of service. Such payments were ended 1864.

1864

Gen. Sherman marched through Georgia, taking Atlanta **Sept. 1,** Savannah **Dec. 22.**

Sand Creek massacre of Cheyenne and Arapaho Indians **Nov. 29.** Cavalry attacked Indians who were awaiting surrender terms.

1865

Robert E. Lee surrendered 27,800 Confederate troops to Grant at Appomattox Court House, Va. **Apr. 9.** J.E. Johnston surrendered 31,200 to Sherman at Durham Station, N.C. **Apr. 18.** Last rebel troops surrendered **May 26.**

President **Lincoln was shot Apr. 14** by John Wilkes Booth in Ford's Theater, Washington; died the following morning. Booth was reported dead **Apr. 26.** Four co-conspirators were hanged **July 7.**

Thirteenth Amendment, abolishing slavery, was ratified **Dec. 6.**

1866

Ku Klux Klan formed secretly in South to terrorize blacks who voted. Disbanded **1869-71.** A second Klan was organized **1915.**

Congress took control of southern Reconstruction, backed freedmen's rights.

1867

Alaska sold to U.S. by Russia for $7.2 million **Mar. 30** through efforts of Sec. of State William H. Seward.

Horatio Alger published first book, *Ragged Dick.*

The **Grange** was organized **Dec. 4,** to protect farmer interests.

1868

The World Almanac, a publication of the *New York World,* appeared for the first time.

Pres. **Andrew Johnson** tried to remove Edwin M. Stanton, secretary of war; was impeached by House **Feb. 24** for violation of Tenure of Office Act; acquitted by Senate **March-May.** Stanton resigned.

1869

Financial **"Black Friday"** in New York **Sept. 24;** caused by attempt to "corner" gold.

Transcontinental railroad completed; golden spike driven at Promontory, Utah **May 10** marking the junction of Central Pacific and Union Pacific.

Knights of Labor formed in Philadelphia. By **1886,** it had 700,000 members nationally.

Woman suffrage law passed in Territory of Wyoming on **Dec. 10.**

1871

Great fire destroyed Chicago Oct. 8-11; loss est. at $196 million.

1872

Amnesty Act restored civil rights to citizens of the South **May 22** except for 500 Confederate leaders.

Congress founded first national park—**Yellowstone** in Wyoming.

1873

First U.S. **postal card** issued **May 1.**

Banks failed, panic began in **Sept.** Depression lasted 5 years.

"Boss" William Tweed of N.Y. City convicted of stealing public funds. He died in jail in **1878.**

Bellevue Hospital in N.Y. City started the first **school of nursing.**

1875

Congress passed **Civil Rights Act Mar. 1** giving equal rights to blacks in public accommodations and jury duty. Act invalidated in **1883** by Supreme Court.

First **Kentucky Derby** held **May 17** at Churchill Downs, Louisville, Ky.

1876

Samuel J. Tilden, Democrat, received majority of popular votes for president over **Rutherford B. Hayes,** Republican, but 22 electoral votes were in dispute; issue left to Congress. Hayes given presidency **in Feb. 1877** after Republicans agree to end Reconstruction of South.

Col. **George A. Custer** and 264 soldiers of the 7th Cavalry killed **June 25** in "last stand," Battle of the Little Big Horn, Mont., in Sioux Indian War.

Mark Twain published *Tom Sawyer.*

1877

Molly Maguires, Irish terrorist society in Scranton, Pa. mining areas, broken up by hanging of 11 leaders for murders of mine officials and police.

Pres. Hayes sent troops in violent national **railroad strike.**

1878

First commercial **telephone** exchange opened, New Haven, Conn. **Jan. 28.**

Thomas A. Edison founded **Edison Electric Light Co.** on **Oct. 15.**

1879

F.W. Woolworth opened his first five-and-ten store in Utica, N.Y. **Feb. 22.**

Henry George published *Progress & Poverty,* advocating single tax on land.

1881

Pres. **James A. Garfield shot** in Washington, D.C. **July 2;** died **Sept. 19.**

Booker T. Washington founded Tuskegee Institute for blacks.

Helen Hunt Jackson published *A Century of Dishonor* about mistreatment of Indians.

1883

Pendleton Act, passed **Jan. 16,** reformed federal civil service.

Brooklyn Bridge opened **May 24.**

1886

Haymarket riot and bombing, evening of **May 4,** followed bitter labor battles for 8-hour day in Chicago; 7 police and 4 workers died, 66 wounded. Eight anarchists found guilty. Gov. John P. Altgeld denounced trial as unfair.

Geronimo, Apache Indian, finally surrendered **Sept. 4.**

The **Statue of Liberty** was dedicated **Oct. 28.**

American Federation of Labor (AFL) formed **Dec. 8** by 25 craft unions.

1888

Great blizzard in eastern U.S. **Mar. 11-14;** 400 deaths.

1889

U.S. declared Oklahoma open to white settlement **Apr. 22;** within 24 hours **claims for 2 mln. acres** were staked by 50,000 settlers.

Johnstown, Pa. flood May 31; 2,200 lives lost.

1890

First execution by **electrocution:** William Kemmler **Aug. 6** at Auburn Prison, Auburn, N.Y., for murder.

Battle of **Wounded Knee, S.D. Dec. 29,** the last major conflict between Indians and U.S. troops. About 200 Indian men, women, and children, and 29 soldiers were killed.

Sherman Antitrust Act begins federal effort to curb monopolies.

Jacob Riis published *How the Other Half Lives,* about city slums.

1891

Forest Reserve Act Mar. 3 let Pres. close public forest land to settlement for establishment of national parks.

1892

Homestead, Pa., strike at Carnegie steel mills; 7 guards and 11 strikers and spectators shot to death **July 6;** setback for unions. **Ellis Island** opened as N.Y. immigration depot.

1893

Financial panic began, led to 4-year depression.

1894

Thomas A. **Edison's kinetoscope** (motion pictures) (invented **1887**) given first public showing **Apr. 14.**

Jacob S. Coxey led 500 unemployed from the Midwest into Washington, D.C. **Apr. 30.** Coxey was arrested for trespassing on Capitol grounds.

1896

William Jennings Bryan delivered "Cross of Gold" speech **July 7**; wins Democratic Party nomination.

Supreme Court, in **Plessy v. Ferguson,** approved racial segregation under the "separate but equal" doctrine.

1898

U.S. **battleship Maine** blown up **Feb. 15** at Havana, 260 killed.

U.S. blockaded Cuba Apr. 22 in aid of independence forces. U.S. declared war on Spain, **Apr. 24,** destroyed Spanish fleet in Philippines **May 1,** took Guam **June 20.**

Puerto Rico taken by U.S. **July 25-Aug. 12.** Spain agreed **Dec. 10** to cede Philippines, Puerto Rico, and Guam, and approved independence for Cuba.

U.S. annexed independent republic of **Hawaii.**

1899

Filipino insurgents, unable to get recognition of independence from U.S., started guerrilla war **Feb. 4.** Crushed with capture **May 23, 1901** of leader, Emilio Aguinaldo.

U.S. declared **Open Door Policy** to make China an open international market and to preserve its integrity as a nation.

John Dewey published *School and Society,* backing progressive education.

1900

Carry Nation, Kansas anti-saloon agitator, began raiding with hatchet.

U.S. helped suppress **"Boxers"** in Beijing.

International Ladies' Garment Workers Union was founded in NYC in **Nov.**

1901

Texas had its first significant **oil strike**, near Beaumont **Jan. 10.**

Pres. William **McKinley was shot Sept. 6** by an anarchist, Leon Czolgosz; died **Sept. 14.**

1903

Treaty between U.S. and Colombia to have U.S. dig **Panama Canal** signed **Jan. 22,** rejected by Colombia. Panama declared independence with U.S. support **Nov. 3;** recognized by Pres. Theodore Roosevelt **Nov. 6.** U.S., Panama signed canal treaty **Nov. 18.**

Wisconsin set first **direct primary** voting system **May 23.**

First **automobile trip** across U.S. from San Francisco to New York **May 23-Aug. 1.**

First successful flight in heavier-than-air mechanically propelled airplane by **Orville Wright Dec. 17** near Kitty Hawk, N.C., 120 ft. in 12 seconds. Fourth flight same day by **Wilbur Wright,** 852 ft. in 59 seconds. Improved plane patented **May 22, 1906.**

Jack London published *Call of the Wild.*

Great Train Robbery, pioneering film, produced.

1904

Ida Tarbell published muckraking *History of Standard Oil.*

1905

First **Rotary Club** founded in Chicago **Dec.**

1906

San Francisco earthquake and fire **Apr. 18-19** left 503 dead, $350 million damages.

Pure Food and Drug Act and Meat Inspection Act both passed **June 30.**

1907

Financial panic and depression started **Mar. 13.**

First round-world cruise of U.S. **"Great White Fleet";** 16 battleships, 12,000 men.

1908

Henry Ford introduced **Model T** car, priced at $850 **Oct. 1.**

1909

Adm. Robert E. Peary reached **North Pole Apr. 6** on 6th attempt, accompanied by Matthew Henson, a black man, and 4 Eskimos.

National Conference on the Negro convened **May 30,** leading to founding of the National Association for the Advancement of Colored People.

1910

Boy Scouts of America founded **Feb. 8.**

1911

Supreme Court dissolved **Standard Oil Co. May 15.**

Building holding NYC's **Triangle Shirtwaist Co.** sweatshop caught fire **Mar. 25;** 146 died, mostly young women; some trapped and killed, others jumped to their deaths.

First **transcontinental airplane flight** (with numerous stops) by C.P. Rodgers, New York to Pasadena, **Sept. 17-Nov. 5;** time in air 82 hrs., 4 min.

1912

Amer. Girl Guides founded **Mar. 12;** name changed in 1913 to **Girl Scouts.**

U.S. sent marines **Aug. 14** to **Nicaragua,** which was in default of loans to U.S. and Europe.

1913

N.Y. Armory Show brought modern art to U.S. **Feb. 17.**

U.S. blockaded Mexico in support of revolutionaries.

Charles Beard published his *Economic Interpretation of the Constitution.*

Federal Reserve System was authorized **Dec. 23,** in a major reform of U.S. banking and finance.

1914

Ford Motor Co. raised basic wage rates from $2.40 for 9-hr. day to $5 for 8-hr. day **Jan. 5.**

When U.S. sailors were arrested at Tampico, Mexico, **Apr. 9,** Atlantic fleet was sent to **Veracruz,** occupied city.

Pres. Wilson proclaimed **U.S. neutrality** in the European war **Aug. 4.**

Panama Canal was officially opened **Aug. 15.**

The **Clayton Antitrust Act** was passed **Oct. 15,** strengthening federal anti-monopoly powers.

1915

First **telephone talk,** New York to San Francisco, **Jan. 25** by Alexander Graham Bell and Thomas A. Watson.

British ship **Lusitania** sunk **May 7** by German submarine; 128 American passengers lost (Germany had warned passengers in advance). As a result of U.S. campaign, Germany issued apology and promise of payments **Oct. 5.** Pres. Wilson asked for a military fund increase **Dec. 7.**

U.S. troops landed in **Haiti July 28.** Haiti became a virtual U.S. protectorate under **Sept. 16** treaty.

1916

Gen. John J. **Pershing entered Mexico** to pursue Francisco (Pancho) Villa, who had raided U.S. border areas. Forces withdrawn **Feb. 5, 1917.**

Rural Credits Act passed **July 17,** followed by Warehouse Act **Aug. 11;** both provided financial aid to farmers.

Bomb exploded during **San Francisco** Preparedness Day parade **July 22,** killed 10. Thomas J. Mooney, labor organizer, and Warren K. Billings, shoe worker, were convicted; both pardoned in **1939.**

U.S. bought **Virgin Islands** from Denmark **Aug. 4.**

Jeannette Rankin, 1st U.S. Congresswoman (R-Montana) elected.

U.S. established military government in the **Dominican Republic Nov. 29.**

Trade and loans to **European Allies** soared during the year.

John Dewey published *Democracy and Education.*

Carl Sandburg published *Chicago Poems.*

1917

Germany, suffering from British blockade, declared almost unrestricted **submarine warfare Jan. 31.** U.S. cut diplomatic ties with Germany **Feb. 3,** and formally declared war **Apr. 6.**

Conscription law was passed **May 18.** First U.S. troops arrived in Europe **June 26.**

The 18th **(Prohibition)** Amendment to the Constitution was submitted to the states by Congress **Dec. 18.** On **Jan. 16, 1919,** the 36th state (Nevada) ratified it. Franklin D. Roosevelt, as 1932 presidential candidate, endorsed repeal; 21st Amendment repealed 18th; ratification completed **Dec. 5, 1933.**

1918

Pres. Wilson set out his **14 Points** as basis for peace **Jan. 8.**

Over one million **American troops** were in Europe by **July.** War ended **Nov. 11.**

Influenza epidemic killed an estimated 20 million worldwide, 548,000 in U.S.

1919

First **transatlantic flight,** by U.S. Navy seaplane, left Rockaway, N.Y. **May 8,** stopped at Newfoundland, Azores, Lisbon **May 27.**

Boston police strike Sept. 9; National Guard breaks strike.

Sherwood Anderson published *Winesburg, Ohio.*

About 250 **alien radicals** were deported **Dec. 22.**

1920

In national **Red Scare,** some 2,700 Communists, anarchists, and other radicals were arrested **Jan.-May.**

Senate refused **Mar. 19** to ratify the **League of Nations Covenant.**

Nicola Sacco, 29, shoe factory employee and radical agitator, and **Bartolomeo Vanzetti,** 32, fish peddler and anarchist, accused of killing 2 men in Mass. payroll holdup **Apr. 15.** Found guilty **1921.** A 6-year worldwide campaign for release on grounds of want of conclusive evidence and prejudice failed. Both were executed **Aug. 23, 1927.** Vindicated July 19, 1977 by proclamation of Mass. Gov. Dukakis.

First regular licensed **radio broadcasting** begun **Aug. 20.**

19th Amendment ratified **Aug. 18,** giving women right to vote.

League of Women Voters founded.

Wall St., N.Y. City, **bomb** explosion killed 30, injured 100, did $2 million damage **Sept. 16.**

Sinclair Lewis's *Main Street,* **F. Scott Fitzgerald's** *This Side of Paradise* published.

1921

Congress sharply curbed **immigration,** set national quota system **May 19.**

Joint Congressional resolution declaring **peace with Germany, Austria, and Hungary** signed **July 2** by Pres. Harding; treaties were signed in **Aug.**

Limitation of Armaments Conference met in Washington **Nov. 12 to Feb. 6, 1922.** Major powers agreed to curtail naval construction, outlaw poison gas, restrict submarine attacks on merchant vessels, respect integrity of China.

Ku Klux Klan began revival with violence against Catholics in North, South, and Midwest.

1922

Violence during **coal-mine strike** at Herrin, Ill., **June 22-23** cost 36 lives, 21 of them non-union miners.

Reader's Digest founded.

1923

First **sound-on-film motion picture,** "Phonofilm" was shown by Lee de Forest at Rivoli Theater, N.Y. City, beginning in **April.**

1924

Law approved by Congress **June 15** making all **Indians citizens.**

Nellie Tayloe Ross elected governor of Wyoming **Nov. 9** after death of her husband **Oct. 2; installed Jan. 5, 1925,** first woman governor. **Miriam (Ma) Ferguson** was elected governor of Texas **Nov. 9; installed Jan. 20, 1925.**

George Gershwin wrote *Rhapsody in Blue.*

1925

John T. Scopes found guilty of having taught evolution in Dayton, Tenn. high school, fined $100 and costs **July 24.**

1926

Dr. Robert H. Goddard demonstrated practicality of **rockets Mar. 16** at Auburn, Mass. with first liquid fuel rocket; rocket traveled 184 ft. in 2.5 secs.

Congress established **Army Air Corps July 2.**

Air Commerce Act passed **Nov. 2**, providing federal aid for airlines and airports.

1927

About 1,000 **marines landed in China Mar. 5** to protect property in civil war.

Capt. **Charles A. Lindbergh** left Roosevelt Field, N.Y. **May 20** alone in plane Spirit of St. Louis on first New York-Paris nonstop flight. Reached Le Bourget airfield **May 21,** 3,610 miles in 33 ½ hours.

The Jazz Singer, with **Al Jolson,** demonstrated part-talking pictures in N.Y. City **Oct. 6.**

Show Boat opened in New York **Dec. 27.**

O. E. Rolvaag published *Giants in the Earth.*

1928

Herbert Hoover elected president against **Alfred E. Smith,** the Catholic governor of New York.

Amelia Earhart became first woman to fly the Atlantic **June 17.**

1929

"St. Valentine's Day massacre" in Chicago **Feb. 14;** gangsters killed 7 rivals.

Farm price stability aided by **Agricultural Marketing Act,** passed **June 15.**

Albert B. Fall, former sec. of the interior, was convicted of accepting a bribe of $100,000 in the leasing of the **Elk Hills (Teapot Dome)** naval oil reserve; sentenced **Nov. 1** to $100,000 fine and year in prison.

Stock Market crash Oct. 29 marked end of postwar prosperity as stock prices plummeted. Stock losses for 1929-31 estimated at $50 billion; worst American depression began.

Thomas Wolfe published *Look Homeward, Angel.* **William Faulkner** published *The Sound and the Fury.*

1930

London **Naval Reduction Treaty** signed by U.S., Britain, Italy, France, and Japan **Apr. 22;** in effect **Jan. 1, 1931;** expired **Dec. 31, 1936.**

Hawley-Smoot Tariff signed; rate hikes slash world trade.

1931

Empire State Building opened in N.Y. City **May 1.**

Al Capone was convicted of tax evasion **Oct. 17.**

Pearl Buck published *The Good Earth.*

1932

Reconstruction Finance Corp. established **Jan. 22** to stimulate banking and business. Unemployment at 12 million.

Charles Lindbergh Jr. kidnapped Mar. 1, found dead **May 12.**

Bonus March on Washington **May 29** by World War I veterans demanding Congress pay their bonus in full.

1933

FDR named **Frances Perkins** U.S. Secy of Labor; 1st woman in U.S. Cabinet.

All **banks in the U.S. were ordered closed** by Pres. Roosevelt **Mar. 6.**

In the "100 days" special session, **Mar. 9-June 16,** Congress passed **New Deal** social and economic measures.

Gold standard dropped by U.S.; announced by Pres. Roosevelt **Apr. 19,** ratified by Congress **June 5.**

Prohibition ended in the U.S. as 36th state ratified 21st Amendment **Dec. 5.**

U.S. foreswore armed intervention in **Western Hemisphere** nations **Dec. 26.**

1934

U.S. troops pull out of **Haiti Aug. 6.**

1935

Comedian **Will Rogers** and aviator Wiley Post **killed Aug. 15** in Alaska plane crash.

Social Security Act passed by Congress **Aug. 14.**

Huey Long, Senator from Louisiana and national political leader, was **assassinated Sept. 8.**

Porgy and Bess, **George Gershwin** opera on American theme, opened **Oct. 10** in N.Y. City.

Committee for Industrial Organization (CIO; later Congress of Industrial Organizations) formed to expand industrial unionism **Nov. 9.**

1936

Boulder Dam completed.

Margaret Mitchell published *Gone With the Wind.*

1937

Joe Louis knocked out James J. Braddock, became world heavyweight champ **June 22.**

Amelia Earhart, aviator, and co-pilot Fred Noonan lost **July 2** near Howland Is. in the Pacific.

Pres. Roosevelt asked for 6 additional Supreme Court justices; **"packing" plan** defeated.

Auto, steel labor unions won first big contracts.

1938

Naval Expansion Act passed **May 17.**

National minimum wage enacted **June 25.**

Orson Welles radio dramatization of *War of the Worlds* caused nationwide scare **Oct. 30.**

1939

Pres. Roosevelt asked for **defense budget hike Jan. 5, 12.**

N.Y. World's Fair opened **Apr. 30,** closed **Oct. 31;** reopened **May 11, 1940,** and finally closed **Oct. 21.**

Einstein alerts FDR to **A-bomb** opportunity in **Aug. 2** letter.

U.S. declares its neutrality in European war **Sept. 5.**

Roosevelt proclaimed a limited **national emergency Sept. 8,** an unlimited emergency **May 27, 1941.** Both ended by Pres. Truman **Apr. 28, 1952.**

John Steinbeck published *Grapes of Wrath.*

1940

U.S. okayed sale of **surplus war material** to Britain **June 3;** announced transfer of 50 overaged destroyers **Sept. 3.**

First **peacetime draft** approved **Sept. 14.**

Richard Wright published *Native Son.*

1941

The **Four Freedoms** termed essential by Pres. Roosevelt in speech to Congress **Jan. 6:** freedom of speech and religion, freedom from want and fear.

Lend-Lease Act signed **Mar. 11,** providing $7 billion in military credits for Britain. Lend-Lease for USSR approved in **Nov.**

U.S. occupied **Iceland July 7.**

The **Atlantic Charter,** 8-point declaration of principles, issued by Roosevelt and Winston Churchill **Aug. 14.**

Japan attacked **Pearl Harbor,** Hawaii, 7:55 a.m. Hawaiian time, **Dec. 7,** 19 ships sunk or damaged, 2,300 dead. U.S. declared war on Japan **Dec. 8,** on Germany and Italy **Dec. 11** after those countries declared war.

1942

Federal government forcibly moved 110,000 **Japanese-Americans** (including 75,000 U.S. citizens) from West Coast to detention camps. Exclusion lasted 3 years.

Battle of **Midway June 4-7** was Japan's first major defeat.

Marines landed on **Guadalcanal Aug. 7;** last Japanese not expelled until **Feb. 9, 1943.**

U.S., Britain invaded North Africa **Nov. 8.**

First **nuclear chain reaction** (fission of uranium isotope U-235) produced at Univ. of Chicago, under physicists Arthur Compton, Enrico Fermi, others **Dec. 2.**

1943

All war contractors barred from **racial discrimination** on **May 27.**

Pres. Roosevelt signed **June 10** the pay-as-you-go income tax bill. Starting **July 1** wage and salary earners were subject to a **paycheck withholding** tax.

Race riot in Detroit June 21; 34 dead, 700 injured. Riot in Harlem section of N.Y. City; 6 killed.

U.S. troops invaded Italy **Sept. 9.**

Marines advanced in **Gilbert Is. in Nov.**

1944

U.S., Allied forces invaded Europe at **Normandy June 6.**

G.I. Bill of Rights signed **June 22,** providing veterans benefits.

U.S. forces landed on **Leyte,** Philippines **Oct. 20.**

1945

Yalta Conference met in the Crimea, USSR, **Feb. 3-11.** Roosevelt, Churchill, and Stalin agreed Russia would enter war against Japan.

Marines landed on **Iwo Jima Feb. 19;** U.S. forces invaded **Okinawa Apr. 1.**

Pres. Roosevelt, 63, died of cerebral hemorrhage in Warm Springs, Ga. **Apr. 12;** V.P. **Harry S. Truman** became pres.

Germany surrendered May 7.

First **atomic bomb,** produced at Los Alamos, N.M., exploded at Alamogordo, N.M. **July 16.** Bomb dropped on **Hiroshima Aug. 6,** on **Nagasaki Aug. 9.** Japan surrendered **Aug. 14.**

U.S. forces entered **Korea** south of 38th parallel to displace Japanese **Sept. 8.**

Gen. Douglas MacArthur took over supervision of Japan **Sept. 9.**

1946

Strike by 400,000 **mine workers** began **Apr. 1;** other industries followed.

Philippines given independence by U.S. **July 4.**

1947

Truman Doctrine: Pres. Truman asked Congress to aid Greece and Turkey to combat Communist terrorism **Mar. 12.** Approved **May 15.**

United Nations Security Council voted unanimously **Apr. 2** to place under **U.S. trusteeship** the Pacific islands formerly mandated to Japan.

Jackie Robinson on Brooklyn Dodgers **Apr. 11,** broke the color barrier in major league baseball.

Taft-Hartley Labor Act curbing strikes was vetoed by Truman **June 20;** Congress overrode the veto.

Proposals later known as the **Marshall Plan,** under which the U.S. would extend aid to European countries, were made by Sec. of State George C. Marshall **June 5.** Congress authorized some $12 billion in next 4 years.

1948

USSR began a land **blockade of Berlin's** Allied sectors **Apr. 1.** This blockade and Western counter-blockade were lifted **Sept. 30, 1949,** after British and U.S. planes had lifted 2,343,315 tons of food and coal into the city.

Organization of American States founded **Apr. 30.**

Alger Hiss, former State Dept. official, indicted Dec. 15 for perjury, after denying he had passed secret documents to Whittaker Chambers for transmission to a communist spy ring. His second trial ended in conviction **Jan. 21, 1950,** and a sentence of 5 years in prison.

Kinsey Report on Sexuality in the Human Male published.

1949

U.S. troops withdrawn from **Korea June 29.**

North Atlantic Treaty Organization **(NATO)** established **Aug. 24** by U.S., Canada, and 10 West European nations, agreeing that an armed attack against one or more of them would be considered an attack against all.

Mrs. I. Toguri D'Aquino **(Tokyo Rose** of Japanese wartime broadcasts) was sentenced **Oct. 7** to 10 years in prison for treason. Paroled **1956,** pardoned **1977.**

Eleven leaders of **U.S. Communist party** convicted **Oct. 14,** after 9-month trial in N.Y. City, of advocating violent overthrow of U.S. government. Ten defendants sentenced to 5 years in prison each and the 11th to 3 years. Supreme Court upheld the convictions **June 4, 1951.**

1950

U.S. **Jan. 14** recalled all consular officials from **China** after the latter seized the American consulate general in Peking.

Masked bandits robbed **Brink's Inc.,** Boston express office, **Jan. 17** of $2.8 million, of which $1.2 million was in cash. Case solved **1956,** 8 sentenced to life.

Pres. Truman authorized production of **H-bomb Jan. 31.**

United Nations asked for troops to restore Korea peace **June 25.**

Truman ordered Air Force and Navy to Korea **June 27** after North Korea invaded South. Truman approved ground forces, air strikes against North **June 30.**

U.S. sent 35 military advisers to **South Vietnam June 27,** and agreed to provide military and economic aid to anti-Communist government.

Army seized all railroads Aug. 27 on Truman's order to prevent a general strike; roads returned to owners in **1952.**

U.S. forces landed at Inchon Sept. 15; UN force took Pyongyang **Oct. 20,** reached China border **Nov. 20,** China sent troops across border **Nov. 26.**

Two members of a **Puerto Rican nationalist** movement tried to kill Pres. Truman **Nov. 1.**

U.S. **Dec. 8** banned shipments to **Communist China** and to Asiatic ports trading with it.

1951

Sen. **Estes Kefauver** led Senate investigation into organized crime. Preliminary report **Feb. 28** said gambling take was over $20 billion a year.

Julius Rosenberg, his wife, Ethel, and Morton Sobell, all U.S. citizens, were found guilty **Mar. 29** of conspiracy to commit wartime espionage. Rosenbergs sentenced to death, Sobell to 30 years. Rosenbergs **executed June 19, 1953.** Sobell released **Jan. 14, 1969.**

Gen. Douglas MacArthur was removed from his Korea command **Apr. 11** for unauthorized policy statements.

Korea cease-fire talks began in July; lasted 2 years. **Fighting ended July 27, 1953.**

Tariff concessions by the U.S. to the Soviet Union, Communist China, and all communist-dominated lands were suspended **Aug. 1.**

The U.S., **Australia,** and **New Zealand** signed a mutual security pact **Sept. 1.**

Transcontinental television inaugurated **Sept. 4** with Pres. Truman's address at the Japanese Peace Treaty Conference in San Francisco.

Japanese Peace Treaty signed in San Francisco **Sept. 8** by U.S., Japan, and 47 other nations.

J.D. Salinger published *Catcher in the Rye.*

1952

U.S. **seizure of nation's steel mills** was ordered by Pres. Truman **Apr. 8** to avert a strike. Ruled illegal by Supreme Court **June 2.**

Peace contract between West Germany, U.S., Great Britain, and France was signed **May 26.**

The last racial and ethnic barriers to naturalization were removed, **June 26-27,** with the passage of the **Immigration and Naturalization Act of 1952.**

First **hydrogen device** explosion **Nov. 1** at Eniwetok Atoll in Pacific.

1953

Pres. Eisenhower announced **May 8** that U.S. had given France $60 million for **Indochina War.** More aid was announced in **Sept.** In **1954** it was reported that three fourths of the war's costs were met by U.S.

1954

Nautilus, first atomic-powered submarine, was launched at Groton, Conn. **Jan. 21.**

Five members of Congress were wounded in the House **Mar. 1** by 4 **Puerto Rican independence supporters** who fired at random from a spectators' gallery.

Sen. Joseph McCarthy led televised hearings **Apr. 22-June 17** into alleged Communist influence in the Army.

Racial segregation in public schools was unanimously ruled unconstitutional by the Supreme Court **May 17,** as a violation of the 14th Amendment clause guaranteeing equal protection of the laws.

Southeast Asia Treaty Organization **(SEATO)** formed by collective defense pact signed in Manila **Sept. 8** by the U.S., Britain, France, Australia, New Zealand, Philippines, Pakistan, and Thailand.

Condemnation of **Sen. Joseph R. McCarthy** (R., Wis.) voted by Senate, 67-22 **Dec. 2** for contempt of a Senate elections subcommittee, for abuse of its members, and for insults to the Senate during his Army investigation hearings.

1955

U.S. agreed **Feb. 12** to help train **South Vietnamese** army.

Supreme Court ordered **"all deliberate speed"** in integration of public schools **May 31.**

A **summit meeting** of leaders of U.S., Britain, France, and USSR took place **July 18-23** in Geneva, Switzerland.

Rosa Parks refused **Dec. 1** to give her seat to a white man on a bus in Montgomery, Ala. Bus segregation ordinance declared unconstitutional by a federal court following boycott and NAACP protest.

Merger of America's 2 largest labor organizations was effected **Dec. 5** under the name American Federation of Labor and Congress of Industrial Organizations. The merged **AFL-CIO** had a membership estimated at 15 million.

1956

Massive resistance to Supreme Court desegregation rulings was called for **Mar. 12** by 101 Southern congressmen.

Federal-Aid **Highway Act** signed **June 29,** inaugurating interstate highway system.

First transatlantic **telephone cable** went into operation **Sept. 25.**

1957

Congress approved first **civil rights bill** for blacks since Reconstruction **Apr. 29,** to protect voting rights.

National Guardsmen, called out by Arkansas Gov. Orval Faubus **Sept. 4,** barred 9 black students from entering previously all-white Central High School in **Little Rock.** Faubus complied **Sept. 21** with a federal court order to remove the National Guardsmen. The blacks entered school **Sept. 23** but were ordered to withdraw by local authorities because of fear of mob violence. Pres. Eisenhower sent federal troops **Sept. 24** to enforce the court's order.

Jack Kerouac published *On the Road.*

1958

First U.S. earth satellite to go into orbit, **Explorer I,** launched by Army **Jan. 31** at Cape Canaveral, Fla.; discovered Van Allen radiation belt.

Five thousand U.S. Marines sent to **Lebanon** to protect elected government from threatened overthrow **July-Oct.**

First domestic **jet airline** passenger service in U.S. opened by National Airlines **Dec. 10** between N.Y. and Miami.

1959

Alaska admitted as 49th state **Jan. 3; Hawaii** admitted **Aug. 21.**

St. Lawrence Seaway opened **Apr. 25.**

Soviet Premier **Khrushchev** paid unprecedented visit to U.S. **Sept. 15-27,** made transcontinental tour.

1960

Sit-ins began **Feb. 1** when 4 black college students in Greensboro, N.C. refused to move from a Woolworth lunch counter when denied service. By **Sept. 1961** more than 70,000 students, whites and blacks, had participated in sit-ins.

Congress approved a strong **voting rights act Apr. 21.**

A **U-2 reconnaisance plane** of the U.S. was shot down in the Soviet Union **May 1.** The incident led to cancellation of an imminent Paris summit conference.

U.S. announced **Dec. 15** it backed rightist group in **Laos,** which took power the next day.

1961

The U.S. severed diplomatic and consular relations with **Cuba Jan. 3,** after disputes over nationalizations of U.S. firms, U.S. military presence at Guantanamo base, etc.

Invasion of Cuba's **"Bay of Pigs" Apr. 17** by Cuban exiles trained, armed, and directed by the U.S., attempting to overthrow the regime of Premier Fidel Castro, failed.

Commander Alan B. Shepard Jr. was rocketed from Cape Canaveral, Fla., 116.5 mi. above the earth in a Mercury capsule **May 5** in the first U.S. manned sub-orbital space flight.

1962

Lt. Col. John H. Glenn Jr. became the first American in orbit **Feb. 20** when he circled the earth 3 times in the Mercury capsule **Friendship 7.**

Pres. Kennedy said **Feb. 14** U.S. military advisers in Vietnam would fire if fired upon.

Supreme Court **Mar. 26** backed **one-man one-vote** apportionment of seats in state legislatures.

First U.S. **communications satellite** launched in **July.**

James Meredith became first black student at Univ. of Mississippi **Oct. 1** after 3,000 troops put down riots.

A Soviet **offensive missile buildup in Cuba** was revealed **Oct. 22** by Pres. Kennedy, who ordered a naval and air quarantine on shipment of offensive military equipment to the island. Kennedy and Soviet Premier Khrushchev reached agreement **Oct. 28** on a formula to end the crisis. Kennedy announced **Nov. 2** that Soviet missile bases in Cuba were being dismantled.

Rachel Carson's *Silent Spring* launched environmentalist movement.

1963

Supreme Court ruled **Mar. 18** that all **criminal defendants** must have counsel and that illegally acquired evidence was not admissible in state as well as federal courts.

Supreme Court ruled, 8-1, **June 17** that laws requiring **recitation of the Lord's Prayer** or Bible verses in public schools were unconstitutional.

A limited **nuclear test-ban treaty** was agreed upon **July 25** by the U.S., Soviet Union, and Britain barring all nuclear tests except underground.

Washington demonstration by 200,000 persons **Aug. 28** in support of **black demands** for equal rights. Highlight was speech in which Dr. Martin Luther King said: "I have a dream that this nation will rise up and live out the true meaning of its creed, 'We hold these truths to be self-evident: that all men are created equal.' "

South Vietnam Pres. **Ngo Dinh Diem assassinated Nov. 2;** U.S. had earlier withdrawn support.

Pres. John F. Kennedy was shot and fatally wounded by an assassin **Nov. 22** as he rode in a motorcade through downtown Dallas, Tex. Vice Pres. Lyndon B. Johnson was sworn in as president shortly after in Dallas. Lee Harvey Oswald was arrested and charged with the murder. Oswald was shot and fatally wounded **Nov. 24** by Jack Ruby, 52, a Dallas nightclub owner, who was convicted of murder **Mar. 14, 1964** and sentenced to death. Ruby died of natural causes **Jan. 3, 1967** while awaiting retrial.

U.S. troops in **Vietnam** totalled over 15,000 by year-end; aid to South Vietnam was over $500 million in **1963.**

Betty Friedan's *The Feminine Mystique* ignites the women's movement.

1964

Panama suspended relations with U.S. **Jan. 9** after riots. U.S. offered **Dec. 18** to negotiate a new canal treaty.

Supreme Court ordered **Feb. 17** that **congressional districts** have equal populations.

U.S. reported **May 27** it was sending military planes to **Laos.**

Omnibus **civil rights bill** passed **June 29** banning discrimination in voting, jobs, public accommodations, etc.

Three **civil rights workers** were reported missing in Mississippi **June 22;** found buried **Aug. 4.** Twenty-one white men were arrested. On **Oct. 20, 1967,** an all-white federal jury convicted 7 of conspiracy in the slayings.

U.S. Congress **Aug. 7** passed **Tonkin Resolution,** authorizing presidential action in Vietnam, after North Vietnam boats reportedly attacked 2 U.S. destroyers **Aug. 2.**

Congress approved War on Poverty bill **Aug. 11.**

The **Warren Commission** released **Sept. 27** a report concluding that Lee Harvey Oswald was solely responsible for the Kennedy assassination.

1965

Pres. Johnson in **Feb.** ordered continuous **bombing of North Vietnam** below 20th parallel.

Some 14,000 U.S. troops sent to **Dominican Republic** during civil war **Apr. 28.** All troops withdrawn by next year.

New **Voting Rights Act** signed **Aug. 6.**

Los Angeles riot by blacks living in **Watts** area resulted in death of 34 persons and property damage est. at $200 million **Aug. 11-16.**

National origins quota system of **immigration** abolished **Oct. 3.**

Electric power failure blacked out most of northeastern U.S., parts of 2 Canadian provinces the night of **Nov. 9-10.**

U.S. forces in **S. Vietnam** reached 184,300 by year-end.

1966

U.S. forces began firing into **Cambodia May 1.**

Bombing of Hanoi area of North Vietnam by U.S. planes began **June 29.** By **Dec. 31,** 385,300 U.S. troops were stationed in South Vietnam, plus 60,000 offshore and 33,000 in Thailand.

Medicare, government program to pay part of the medical expenses of citizens over 65, began **July 1.**

Edward Brooke (R, Mass.) elected **Nov. 8** as first black U.S. senator in 85 years.

1967

Black representative **Adam Clayton Powell** (D, N.Y.) was denied **Mar. 1** his seat in Congress because of charges he misused gvt. funds. Reelected in 1968, he was seated, but fined $25,000 and stripped of his 22 years' seniority.

Pres. Johnson and Soviet Premier Aleksei Kosygin met **June 23 and 25** at **Glassboro State College** in N.J.; agreed not to let any crisis push them into war.

Riots by blacks in **Newark, N.J. July 12-17** killed 26, injured 1,500; over 1,000 arrested. In Detroit, Mich., **July 23-30** at least 40 died; 2,000 injured, 5,000 left homeless by rioting, looting, burning in city's black ghetto. Quelled by 4,700 federal paratroopers and 8,000 National Guardsmen.

Thurgood Marshall sworn in **Oct. 2** as first black U.S. Supreme Court Justice. Carl B. Stokes (D, Cleveland) and Richard G. Hatcher (D, Gary, Ind.) were elected first black mayors of major U.S. cities **Nov. 7.**

By **December** 475,000 U.S. troops were in **South Vietnam.**

1968

USS Pueblo and 83-man crew seized in Sea of Japan **Jan. 23** by North Koreans; 82 men released **Dec. 22.**

"Tet offensive": Communist troops attacked Saigon, 30 province capitals **Jan. 30,** suffer heavy casualties.

Pres. Johnson **curbed bombing** of North Vietnam **Mar. 31.** Peace talks began in Paris **May 10.** All bombing of North halted **Oct. 31.**

Martin Luther King Jr., 39, assassinated Apr. 4 in Memphis, Tenn. James Earl Ray, an escaped convict, pleaded guilty to the slaying, was sentenced to 99 years.

Sen. Robert F. Kennedy (D, N.Y.), 42, **shot June 5** in Hotel Ambassador, Los Angeles, after celebrating presidential primary victories. Died **June 6.** Sirhan Bishara Sirhan, Jordanian, convicted of murder.

Rep. Shirley Chisholm (D, N.Y.) became the first black woman elected to Congress.

1969

Expanded four-party **Vietnam peace talks** began **Jan. 18.** U.S. force peaked at 543,400 in April. Withdrawal started **July 8.** Pres. Nixon set Vietnamization policy **Nov. 3.**

U.S. astronaut **Neil A. Armstrong,** 38, commander of the Apollo 11 mission, became the first man to **set foot on the moon July 20.**

Woodstock music festival near Bethel, N.Y., drew 300,000-500,000 people, **Aug. 15-17.**

Anti-Vietnam War **demonstrations reached peak** in U.S.; some 250,000 marched in Washington, D.C. **Nov. 15.**

Massacre of hundreds of civilians at **Mylai, South Vietnam** in 1968 incident was reported **Nov. 16.**

1970

United Mine Workers official **Joseph A. Yablonski,** his wife, and their daughter were found shot **Jan. 5** in their Clarksville, Pa. home. UMW chief W. A. (Tony) Boyle was later convicted of the killing.

A federal jury **Feb. 18** found the **"Chicago 7"** innocent of conspiring to incite riots during the 1968 Democratic National Convention. However, 5 were convicted of crossing state lines with intent to incite riots.

Millions of Americans participated in anti-pollution demonstrations **Apr. 22** to mark the first **Earth Day.**

U.S. and South Vietnamese forces crossed **Cambodian** borders **Apr. 30** to get at enemy bases. Four students were killed **May 4** at **Kent St.** Univ. in Ohio by National Guardsmen during a protest against the war.

Two **women generals,** the first in U.S. history, were named by Pres. Nixon **May 15.**

A **postal reform** measure was signed **Aug. 12,** creating an independent U.S. Postal Service, thus relinquishing governmental control of the U.S. mails after almost 2 centuries.

1971

Charles Manson, 36, and 3 of his followers were found guilty **Jan. 26** of first-degree murder in the 1969 slaying of actress Sharon Tate and 6 others.

A Constitutional Amendment lowering the **voting age to 18** in all elections was approved in the Senate by a vote of 94-0 **Mar. 10.** The proposed 26th Amendment got House approval by a 400-19 vote **Mar. 23.** It was ratified July 1.

A court-martial jury Mar. 29, convicted **Lt. William L. Calley Jr.** of premeditated murder of 22 South Vietnamese at Mylai on **Mar. 16, 1968.** He was sentenced to life imprisonment **Mar. 31.** Sentence was reduced to 20 years **Aug. 20.**

Publication of classified **Pentagon papers** on the U.S. involvement in Vietnam was begun **June 13** by the *New York Times.* In a 6-3 vote, the U.S. Supreme Court **June 30** upheld the right of the *Times* and the *Washington Post* to publish the documents under the protection of the First Amendment.

U.S. bombers struck massively in North Vietnam for 5 days starting **Dec. 26,** in retaliation for alleged violations of agreements reached prior to the 1968 bombing halt. U.S. forces at year-end were down to 140,000.

1972

Pres. Nixon arrived in **Beijing Feb. 21** for an 8-day visit to China, which he called a "journey for peace." The unprecedented visit ended with a joint communique pledging that both powers would work for "a normalization of relations."

By a vote of 84 to 8, the Senate approved **Mar. 22** a Constitutional Amendment banning **discrimination against women** because of their sex and sent the measure to the states for ratification.

North Vietnamese forces launched the biggest attacks in 4 years across the demilitarized zone **Mar. 30.** The U.S. responded **Apr. 15** by resumption of bombing of Hanoi and Haiphong after a 4-year lull.

Nixon announced **May 8** the mining of **North Vietnam ports.** Last U.S. combat troops left **Aug. 11.**

Alabama Gov. George C. Wallace, campaigning for the presidency at a Laurel, Md. shopping center **May 15, was shot** and seriously wounded. Arthur H. Bremer, 21, was sentenced to 63 years for shooting Wallace and 3 bystanders.

In the first visit of a U.S. president to Moscow, Nixon arrived **May 22** for a week of summit talks with Kremlin leaders that culminated in a landmark **strategic arms pact.**

Five men were arrested **June 17** for breaking into the offices of the Democratic National Committee in the **Watergate** office complex in Washington, D.C.

Full-scale bombing of North Vietnam resumed after Paris peace negotiations reached an impasse **Dec. 18.**

1973

Five of seven defendants in the **Watergate** break-in trial pleaded guilty **Jan. 11 and 15,** and the other 2 were convicted **Jan. 30.**

In **Roe v. Wade,** the Supreme Court ruled 7-2, **Jan. 22,** that a state may not prevent a woman from having an **abortion** during the **first 3 months of pregnancy,** and could regulate but not prohibit abortion during the second trimester; decision in effect overturned anti-abortion laws in 46 states.

Four-party **Vietnam peace pacts** were signed in Paris **Jan. 27,** and North Vietnam released some 590 U.S. prisoners by **Apr. 1.** Last U.S. troops left **Mar. 29.**

The **end of the military draft** was announced **Jan. 27.**

Top **Nixon aides** H.R. Haldeman, John D. Ehrlichman, and John W. Dean, and Attorney General Richard Kleindienst **resigned Apr. 30** amid charges of White House efforts to obstruct justice in the Watergate case.

John Dean, former Nixon counsel, told Senate hearings **June 25** that Nixon, his staff and campaign aides, and the Justice Department all had conspired to cover up Watergate facts. Nixon refused July 23 to release **tapes** of relevant White House conversations. Some tapes were turned over to the court **Nov. 26.**

The U.S. officially ceased bombing in **Cambodia** at midnight **Aug. 14** in accord with a June Congressional action.

Vice Pres. Spiro T. Agnew Oct. 10 resigned and pleaded "nolo contendere" (no contest) to charges of tax evasion on payments made to him by Maryland contractors when he was governor of that state. Gerald Rudolph Ford **Oct. 12** became first appointed vice president under the 25th Amendment; sworn in **Dec. 6.**

A total ban on **oil exports** to the U.S. was imposed by Arab oil-producing nations **Oct. 19-21** after the outbreak of an Arab-Israeli war. The ban was lifted **Mar. 18, 1974.**

Atty. Gen. Elliot Richardson resigned, and his deputy William D. Ruckelshaus and Watergate Special Prosecutor Archibald Cox were fired by Pres. Nixon **Oct. 20** when Cox threatened to secure a judicial ruling that Nixon was violating a court order to turn tapes over to Watergate case Judge John Sirica.

Leon Jaworski, conservative Texas Democrat, was named **Nov. 1** by the Nixon administration to be special prosecutor to succeed Archibald Cox.

Congress overrode **Nov. 7** Nixon's veto of the **war powers** bill, which curbed the president's power to commit armed forces to hostilities abroad without Congressional approval.

1974

Impeachment hearings were opened **May 9** against Nixon by the House Judiciary Committee.

John D. Ehrlichman and 3 **White House "plumbers"** were found guilty **July 12** of conspiring to violate the civil rights of Dr. Lewis Fielding, formerly psychiatrist to Pentagon Papers leaker Daniel Ellsberg, by breaking into his Beverly Hills, Cal. office.

The U.S. Supreme Court ruled, 8-0, **July 24** that Nixon had to turn over **64 tapes** of White House conversations sought by Watergate Special Prosecutor Leon Jaworski.

The House Judiciary Committee, in televised hearings **July 24-30,** recommended 3 **articles of impeachment** against Nixon. The first, voted 27-11 **July 27,** charged Nixon with taking part in a criminal conspiracy to obstruct justice in the Watergate cover-up. The second, voted 28-10 **July 29,** charged he "repeatedly" failed to carry out his constitutional oath in a series of alleged abuses of power. The third, voted 21-17 **July 30,** accused him of unconstitutional defiance of committee subpoenas. The House of Representatives voted without debate **Aug. 20,** by 412-3, to accept the committee report, which included the recommended impeachment articles.

Nixon resigned Aug. 9. Vice President Gerald R. Ford was sworn in as the 38th U.S. president on **Aug. 9.**

An **unconditional pardon** to ex-Pres. Nixon for all federal crimes that he "committed or may have committed" while president was issued by Pres. Gerald Ford **Sept. 8.**

1975

Found guilty of **Watergate** cover-up charges **Jan. 1** were ex-Atty. Gen. John N. Mitchell, ex-presidential advisers H.R. Haldeman and John D. Ehrlichman.

U.S. civilians were evacuated from **Saigon Apr. 29** as communist forces completed takeover of South Vietnam.

U.S. merchant ship **Mayaguez** and crew of 39 seized by Cambodian forces in Gulf of Siam **May 12.** In rescue operation, U.S. Marines attacked Tang Is., planes bombed air base; Cambodia surrendered ship and crew.

Congress voted $405 million for South **Vietnam refugees May 16;** 140,000 were flown to the U.S.

Illegal **CIA operations,** including records on 300,000 persons and groups, and infiltration of agents into black, anti-war and political movements, were described by a "blue-ribbon" panel headed by Vice Pres. Rockefeller **June 10.**

FBI agents captured **Patricia (Patty) Hearst,** kidnapped **Feb. 4, 1974,** in San Francisco **Sept. 18** with others. She was indicted for bank robbery; a San Francisco jury convicted her **Mar. 20, 1976.**

1976

The U.S. celebrated its **Bicentennial July 4,** marking the 200th anniversary of its independence with festivals, parades, and N.Y. City's Operation Sail, a gathering of tall ships from around the world viewed by 6 million persons.

A mystery ailment **"legionnaire's disease"** killed 29 persons who attended an American Legion convention **July 21-24** in Philadelphia. The cause was found to be a bacterium, it was reported **June 18, 1977.**

The Viking II set down on **Mars'** Utopia Plains **Sept. 3,** following the successful landing by Viking I **July 20.**

1977

Pres. Jimmy Carter **Jan. 21** pardoned most Vietnam War **draft evaders,** who numbered some 10,000.

Convicted murderer **Gary Gilmore** was executed by a Utah firing squad **Jan. 17,** in the first exercise of capital punishment anywhere in the U.S. since **1967.** Gilmore had opposed all attempts to delay the execution.

Carter signed an act **Aug. 4** creating a new Cabinet-level **Energy Department.**

1978

U.S. Senate voted **Apr. 18** to turn over the **Panama Canal** to Panama on Dec. 31, 1999; **Mar. 16** vote had given approval to a treaty guaranteeing the area's neutrality after the year 2000.

1979

A major accident occurred, **Mar. 28,** at a nuclear reactor on **Three Mile Island** near Middletown, Pa.

The federal government announced, **Nov. 1,** a $1.5 billion loan-guarantee plan to aid the nation's 3d largest automaker, **Chrysler Corp.,** which had reported a loss of $460.6 million for the 3d quarter of 1979.

Some 90 people, including 63 Americans, were taken hostage, **Nov. 4,** at the **American embassy in Teheran,** Iran, by militant student followers of Ayatollah Khomeini who demanded the return of former Shah Mohammad Reza Pahlavi, who was undergoing medical treatment in New York City.

1980

Pres. Carter announced, **Jan. 4, punitive measures against the USSR,** including an embargo on the sale of grain and high technology, in retaliation for the Soviet invasion of Afghanistan. At Carter's request, the **U.S. Olympic Committee** voted, **Apr. 12,** not to attend the Moscow Summer Olympics.

Eight Americans were killed and 5 wounded, **Apr. 24,** in an ill-fated attempt to **rescue the hostages** held by Iranian **militants** at the U.S. Embassy in Teheran.

In Washington, **Mt. St. Helens erupted, May 18,** in a violent blast estimated to be 500 times as powerful as the Hiroshima atomic bomb. The blast, followed by others on **May 25** and **June 12,** left about 60 dead, and economic losses estimated at nearly $3 billion.

In a sweeping victory, **Nov. 4, Ronald Wilson Reagan** was elected 40th President of the United States, defeating incumbent Jimmy Carter. The stunning GOP victory extended to the U.S. Congress where Republicans gained control of the Senate and wrested 33 House seats from the Democrats.

Former Beatle **John Lennon** was shot and killed, **Dec. 8,** outside his apartment building in New York City.

1981

Minutes after the **inauguration of Pres. Ronald Reagan, Jan. 20,** the **52 Americans** who had been held **hostage in Iran** for 444 days were flown to freedom following an agreement in which the U.S. agreed to return to Iran $8 billion in frozen assets.

President Reagan was **shot in the chest** by a would-be assassin, **Mar. 30,** in Washington, D.C., as he walked to his limousine following an address.

The world's first reusable spacecraft, the **Space Shuttle** *Columbia,* was sent into space, **Apr. 12,** and completed its successful mission 2 days later.

Both houses of Congress passed, **July 29,** President Reagan's **tax-cut legislation.** The largest tax cut in the nation's history was expected to reduce taxes by $37.6 bln. in fiscal 1982, and to save taxpayers $750 bln. over the next 5 years.

Federal air traffic controllers, Aug. 3, began an **illegal nationwide strike** after their union rejected the government's final offer for a new contract. Most of the 13,000 striking controllers defied the back-to-work order and were dismissed by President Reagan **Aug. 5.**

In a 99-0 vote, the Senate confirmed, **Sept. 21,** the appointment of **Sandra Day O'Connor** as an **associate justice of the U.S. Supreme Court.** She was the first woman appointed to that body.

1982

The 13-year-old lawsuit against **AT&T** by the **Justice Dept.** was settled **Jan. 8.** AT&T agreed to give up the 22 Bell System companies but in return was allowed to expand into previously prohibited areas including data processing, telephone and computer equipment sales, and computer communication devices.

The Equal Rights Amendment was defeated after a 10-year struggle for ratification.

In Dec., the **unemployment rate** rose to 10.8%, the highest since 1940.

Lech Walesa, former leader of **Solidarity,** the Polish labor union, was freed **Nov. 13,** after 11 months of internment following the imposition of martial law and the outlawing of Solidarity. Pres. Reagan lifted the **U.S. embargo on sales of oil and gas equipment to the Soviet Union.**

The **Space Shuttle** *Columbia* completed its first operational flight **Nov. 16.**

A retired dentist, **Dr. Barney B. Clark,** 61, became the first recipient of a **permanent artificial heart** during a 7½ hour operation in Salt Lake City **Dec. 2.** The heart was designed by **Dr. Robert Jarvik,** also on the surgical team.

1983

On **Apr. 20, Pres. Reagan** signed a compromise, bipartisan bill designed to rescue the **Social Security System** from bankruptcy.

In an 8-1 decision, **the U.S. Supreme Court** held, **May 24,** that the **Internal Revenue Service** could deny **tax exemptions** to **private schools** that practiced **racial discrimination.**

Sally Ride became the first American **woman** to travel in **space, June 18,** when the **space shuttle** *Challenger* was launched from Cape Canaveral, Fla.

On **Oct. 23,** 241 **U.S. Marines and sailors,** members of the multinational **peacekeeping force** in **Lebanon,** were killed when a TNT-laden suicide **terrorist** blew up Marine headquarters at **Beirut** Intl. Airport. Almost simultaneously, a second truck bomb blew up a **French paratroop** barracks two miles away, killing more than 40.

U.S. Marines and Rangers and a small force from 6 **Caribbean** nations invaded the island of **Grenada** on **Oct. 25,** in response to a request from the **Organization of Eastern Caribbean States.** After a few days, Grenadian militia and Cuban "construction workers" were overcome, hundreds of U.S. citizens evacuated safely, and the Marxist regime deposed. The U.S. Congress applied the War Powers Resolution, requiring U.S. troops to leave Grenada by **Dec. 24.**

1984

The space shuttle *Challenger* was launched on its 4th trip into space, **Feb. 3.** On **Feb. 7,** Navy Capt. Bruce McCandless, followed by Army Lt. Colonel Robert Stewart, **became the first humans to fly free of a spacecraft.**

During **March,** the U.S. Senate rejected 2 Constitutional amendments that would have permitted **prayer in the public schools.**

On **May 7,** American **Vietnam war** veterans reached an **out-of-court settlement with 7 chemical companies** in their class-action suit regarding the herbicide **Agent Orange.**

On **June 6,** former vice president **Walter Mondale** won the **Democratic presidental nomination.** In a historic move, **July 12, Mondale chose a woman, Rep. Geraldine Ferraro (N.Y.)** as candidate for **vice president.**

Ronald Reagan was reelected U.S. President **Nov. 6** in the greatest Republican **landslide** in history, carrying 49 states against Walter F. Mondale.

1985

E. F. Hutton, one of the nation's largest brokerage companies, **pleaded guilty, May 2,** to 2,000 **federal charges** related to the manipulation of its checking accounts. The company agreed to pay $2 million in fines and to pay back up to $8 million to banks it had defrauded.

"Live Aid," a 17-hour rock concert broadcast **July 13** on radio and TV from London and Phila. to 152 countries, raised $70 million for the starving peoples of Africa.

On **Oct. 7, 4 hijackers seized an Italian cruise ship, the *Achille Lauro,*** in the open sea as it approached Port Said, Egypt. More than 400 passengers and crew were aboard, including American Leon Klinghoffer, who was killed. The hijackers, members of the Palestine Liberation Front, a faction that had broken away from the PLO, demanded the release of 50 Palestinians held by Israel.

In November, for the first time in 6 years, the leaders of the U.S. and the Soviet Union met at a **summit conference.** In Geneva, Switzerland, **Pres. Reagan** and **Mikhail Gorbachev,** the general secretary of the Soviet Communist Party, talked privately for 5 hours, **Nov. 19 and 20.**

1986

On **Jan. 20,** for the 1st time, the U.S. officially observed **Martin Luther King Day.**

Moments after liftoff, **Jan. 28,** the **space shuttle *Challenger* exploded, killing 6 astronauts and Christa McAuliffe, a New Hampshire teacher.** Subsequent investigations found that NASA had abandoned "good judgment and common sense" regarding safety problems that caused the explosion.

U.S. warplanes struck targets in Tripoli and Benghazi, Libya, Apr. 14—retaliation against the Libyan bombing of a W. Berlin disco that killed 3, injured 200, Apr. 5.

U.S. officials said, **June 12, that AIDS cases and deaths would increase tenfold in the next 5 years.** At that time, the government had recorded 21,517 cases, 11,713 deaths. An anti-viral drug, azidothymidine (AZT) was found to improve the health of some AIDS patient, but was not a cure.

The U.S., **via Congress's Sept. override of Pres. Reagan's veto,** joined other nations in imposing **economic sanctions on So. Africa,** pressuring the Botha gvt. to end apartheid.

The U.S. Senate confirmed, **Sept. 17,** Pres. Reagan's nomination of **William Rehnquist as chief justice, Antonin Scalia as associate justice of the Supreme Court.**

Congress passed, in late **Sept.,** the comprehensive **Tax Reform Law.** In effect in 1987, it simplified the system, drastically changing tax brackets, deductions, and more.

One day before the 1986 Congressional elections, it was reported that the U.S. had sent spare parts and ammunition to Iran. Over the next months it was revealed that **additional arms sales had been made to Iran,** and **profits diverted to a fund for Nicaraguan contras.**

In the **Congressional races, Nov. 4, Democrats won a 55-45 Senate majority,** after 6 yrs. of a Republican majority, and **enlarged their House majority by 5, to 258-177.**

The most scandalous year in Wall Street history ended with **Ivan Boesky's agreeing, Nov. 14,** to **plead guilty to an unspecified criminal count, pay a $100 million fine, and return profits;** he was barred for life from trading securities.

1987

Pres. Reagan produced the nation's first **trillion-dollar budget, Jan. 5.**

The stock market continued its phenomenal rise. The **Dow closed at 2002.25, Jan. 8,** its first finish above 2000.

The **Tower Commission Report, Feb. 27,** found **Pres. Reagan confused and uninformed** in Iran-contra dealings, and further faulted White House Chief of Staff Donald Regan; former Natl. Security Adviser Robert McFarlane; his successor Adm. John Poindexter; and CIA Director William Casey.

An **Iraqi warplane missile killed 37 sailors** on the frigate U.S.S. *Stark* in the Persian Gulf, **May 17.** Iraq called it an accident. The Stark's officers were found negligent, June 14. The U.S. escorted Kuwaiti oil tankers to the Gulf, reflagging them for the U.S.

Public hearings by the Senate and House committees investigating the **Iran-contra affair** went on from **May-Aug.** Lt. Col. Oliver North said he had believed all his activities were authorized by his superiors. Pres. Reagan, Aug. 12, again denied knowing of the funds' diversion to the contras.

Wall Street crashed, Oct. 19, the Dow plummeting a record 508 points—22.6 percent—after a record high of 2722.42, Aug. 25.

Pres. Reagan and **Soviet leader Gorbachev** met in Wash., **Dec. 8,** and signed **an unprecedented agreement** calling for the **dismantling of all 1,752 U.S. and 859 Soviet missiles with a 300- to 3,400-mile range.**

1988

Federal grand juries in Miami and Tampa returned **indictments, Feb. 4,** against **Gen. Manuel Noriega,** ruler of Panama, charging that he had protected and otherwise assisted the Medellín drug cartel.

Nearly **1.4 million illegal aliens** met the **May 4** deadline for applying for **amnesty** under a U.S. Immigration and Naturalization Service policy. An estimated 50+ percent of applications were in Calif.; nationwide, about 71 percent of the aliens had entered the U.S. from Mexico.

Much of the U.S. suffered the worst **drought** in more than 50 years. By June 23, half of the nation's agricultural counties had been designated disaster areas.

A missile, fired from the **U.S. Navy warship *Vincennes,*** in the Persian Gulf, **struck and destroyed a commercial Iranian airliner, July 3, killing all 290 persons** on the plane. Navy personnel had mistaken the airliner for an Iranian F-14 jet fighter.

George Bush, vice president under Ronald Reagan, **was elected 41st U.S. president, Nov. 8.** Bush defeated the Democratic nominee, Gov. Michael Dukakis (Mass.).

Drexel Burnham Lambert agreed, **Dec. 21, to plead guilty to 6 violations of federal law,** including insider trading, stock manipulation, and falsified records; and **to pay penalties of $650 million,** by far the largest such settlement.

1989

The Labor Dept. reported, **Jan. 6,** that **unemployment was 5.3%** in Dec. 1988, the lowest since July 1974.

The **largest oil spill in U.S. history** occurred after the *Exxon Valdez* struck Bligh Reef in **Alaska's Prince William Sound, Mar. 24.** Initially estimated at 240,000 barrels, as of Mar. 29, the spill extended 45 miles.

Former Natl. Security Council staff member **Oliver North** became the first person, **May 4, convicted in a jury trial** in connection with the **Iran-contra** scandal. North received, **July 6,** a 3-year suspended prison sentence, 2 years' probation, a $150,000 fine, and an order to perform 1,200 hours of community service.

The **U.S. Supreme Court** announced, **July 3,** its 5-4 decision to put new **restraints** on a **woman's right to have an abortion,** although it did not overturn Roe v. Wade.

Legislation passed by Congress to **rescue the savings and loan industry** was signed into law, **Aug. 9,** by Pres. George Bush. The bill provided $166 billion over 10 years to close or merge insolvent S&Ls. The total cost was put at $400 billion over 30 years, most to be paid by taxpayers.

Army Gen. Colin Powell was nominated by Pres. Bush, **Aug. 10,** to serve as **chairman of the Joint Chiefs of Staff;** he became the first black to hold the post.

Minutes before the start of the 3d game of the 1989 World Series between the San Francisco Giants and the Oakland

Athletics, **Oct. 17**, an **earthquake struck the San Francisco Bay area,** causing at least 59 deaths and massive property damage.

Democrats won most of the **top offices** at stake and **black candidates scored major breakthroughs** in off-year elections, **Nov. 7.** Lt. Gov. L. Douglas Wilder, a Democrat, was elected governor of Virginia, the nation's first black governor since Reconstruction. Manhattan Borough Pres. David Dinkins, also a Democrat, became the first black elected mayor of New York City.

Pres. Bush signed into law, **Nov. 19**, an increase in the **minimum wage.** Currently $3.35 an hour, the wage would rise to $4.25 an hour by 1991, with a training wage of $3.35 for 16- to 19-year-olds in their first 3 months on a job.

Pennsylvania became the first state, **Nov. 18,** to **restrict abortions,** after the U.S. Supreme Court gave states the right to do so in July.

U.S. troops invaded Panama, Dec. 20, overthrowing the government of Manuel Noriega, who eluded capture, took refuge in the Vatican mission, then surrendered to the U.S. Jan. 3, 1990.

1990

The Dow Jones Industrial average pushed to an all-time high, **July 16 and 17**, finishing at 2,999.75.

Pres. Bush signed a bill that would bar **discrimination** against people with **physical or mental disabilities, July 26.**

Justice William Brennan announced, **July 20,** his immediate resignation from the U.S. Supreme Court, due to illness; Pres. Bush nominated **Judge David Souter** of the U.S. Court of Appeals for the First Circuit in Boston, **July 23**, and the Senate voted to confirm him, **Sept. 27.**

Operation Desert Shield forces left for **Saudi Arabia, Aug. 7,** to defend that country following the **invasion** of its neighbor **Kuwait by Iraq,** Aug. 2.

Pres. Bush **vetoed, Oct. 22,** a **civil rights bill** that sought in effect to reverse 6 recent Supreme Court decisions that civil rights organizations contended had weakened anti-discrimination laws on hiring and promoting.

Pres. Bush signed, **Nov. 15,** a bill designed to **reduce budget deficits** by nearly $500 billion over 5 years. The top personal income tax rate would rise from 28 to 31 percent and exemptions for upper-income Americans would be phased out; gas, cigarette, liquor taxes would increase; a luxury tax would be imposed on some planes, cars, boats, furs, and jewelry.

1991

The **U.S. and its allies defeated Iraq** in **Jan.** and **Feb. 1991** and liberated Kuwait, which Iraq had overrun in Aug. 1990. After Iraq's invasion, for nearly 6 months, diplomats of many nations had sought to persuade Pres. Saddam Hussein to pull his occupying forces out of the oil-rich sheikhdom. Finally, in **Jan.,** the allies launched an **attack on Iraq from the air** that sharply reduced its offensive and defensive military capacity. In a **ground war in Feb.** that lasted just 100 hours, the U.S.-led attackers killed or captured many thousands of Iraqi soldiers and sent the rest into retreat before Pres. George Bush ordered a cease-fire.

The **Dow Jones Industrial Average** finished above 3000 for the first time, **Apr. 17,** closing at 3004.46.

Justice Thurgood Marshall, the first black ever to serve on the U.S. Supreme Court, announced, **June 27,** that he would retire when a successor was approved.

Pres. Bush approved, **July 10,** the recommendations of the **Defense Base Closure and Realignment Commission,** which had proposed that 34 domestic military installations be closed and 48 others realigned, due to the federal budget crunch and the end of the cold war.

The **case against Oliver North was "terminated,"** with all charges dropped, **Sept. 16.** In 1989, North, a leading figure in the Iran-contra affair, had been convicted of obstructing a congressional investigation, destroying documents, and accepting an illegal gratuity. In 1990, a federal appeals court had overturned one conviction and sent the others back to the federal district court.

The General Accounting Office revealed that in a recent 12-month period, **8,331 checks** had been written against **insufficient funds** in a bank that operated at the Capitol with only House members for depositors. On **Oct. 3,** House Speaker Tom Foley said the bank would be closed at the end of 1991 and that the House Ethics Committee would investigate.

The **U.S. Senate approved the nomination of Clarence Thomas** to serve as an **associate justice of the Supreme Court,** after investigating an allegation of sexual harassment that had been leveled against him. Thomas and his accusor, **Anita Hill, a law professor at the Univ. of Oklahoma,** testified before the Senate Judiciary Committee, **Oct. 11-12,** while a huge TV audience watched. The Senate confirmed Thomas, 52-48.

Charles Keating was convicted of 17 counts of securities fraud, Dec. 4. The prosecution asserted that as chairman of the Lincoln Savings & Loan Assn. in Cal., Keating had induced some 17,000 investors to buy $250 million in bonds that were not insured.

1992

In the annual **State of the Union address, Jan. 28,** Pres. George Bush announced proposals to **reduce nuclear arsenals** and to deal with the U.S. **economic recession.** To speed economic growth, Bush said he had instructed federal departments and agencies to impose a 3-month moratorium on new government regulations and had told the IRS to reduce the amount withheld from employees' paychecks.

R. H. Macy & Co. and **Trans World Airlines** both filed for bankruptcy in Jan. The **"Big 3" U.S. automakers–** Chrysler, Ford, and General Motors–announced **huge losses in Feb.** However, the **Dow Jones Industrial Average** closed, **Feb. 24,** at **3283.32,** an **all-time high.**

Rioting, looting, and arson swept **South-Central Los Angeles** in **late April and early May** after a jury that included no blacks acquitted 4 policemen on all but one count in the beating of a black man, Rodney King. The attack on King had been videotaped and shown on TV newcasts across the country. The death toll in the L.A. violence was put at 52; damage was said to run as high as $1 billion.

A **27th Amendment, regarding congressional pay raises,** became part of the **U.S. Constitution** in **May**. Proposed by James Madison, it had been approved by Congress in 1798 and submitted to the states for ratification. Approval of three-fourths of the states, 38 at the present time, was required for the amendment to become part of the Constitution. On **May 7, 1992,** the Michigan legislature became the 38th to approve it.

The **Democratic Party** nominated **Gov. Bill Clinton (Ark.)** as its **candidate for president, July 15,** and **Sen. Al Gore Jr. (Tenn.)** as its **candidate for vice president, July 16,** in New York City. **Texan H. Ross Perot,** who had mounted an independent campaign, announced, **July 16,** that he would **not seek the presidency** both because the Democratic Party had "revitalized itself" and because his candidacy would cause the election to be thrown into the House for resolution, disrupting the country.

The **Republican Party** renominated **Pres. George Bush** and **Vice Pres. Dan Quayle** at the convention in Houston, Tex. in **early August,** while a Gallup Poll reported, Aug. 4, that Bush's public-approval rating had fallen to 29%, a new low.

Pres. Bush and **Gov. Bill Clinton** participated in **3 TV debates in Oct.** They were joined by independent candidate **H. Ross Perot** who, on **Oct. 1**, 33 days before the election, had **re-declared his candidacy.**

Gov. Bill Clinton of Arkansas was **elected 42d president of the U.S.** on **Nov. 3,** and his running mate on the **Democratic** ticket, **Sen. Al Gore Jr. of Tennessee,** was **elected vice president.** They carried **32 states** and the **District of Columbia,** winning **370 electoral votes.** Republican presidential candidate, Pres. George Bush, and his running mate, Vice Pres. Dan Quayle, won 18 states and 188 electoral votes. In the nationwide popular vote, the official tally gave Clinton 44,908,254 (43 percent), Bush 39,102,343 (38 percent), and independent candidate H. Ross Perot 19,741,065 (19 percent). The **Democrats** retained control of both houses of Congress. There would be **110 new House members,** the biggest turnover since 1948, and the new House would include **record numbers of women** (47), **blacks** (38), and **Hispanics** (17). The new **Senate** also would have a **record number of women** (6); two women Democrats won Senate elections in Calif., and **Carol Moseley Braun of Illinois** became the **first black woman** to serve in the **Senate.** The **Democrats** also picked up 2 **governorships,** for a **30-18** margin over the Republicans.

A **UN-sanctioned military force,** led by **American troops,** arrived in **Somalia** beginning **Dec. 9** to ensure the delivery of food by "all necessary means to starving people in the war-torn nation."

1993

Bill Clinton was inaugurated **Jan. 20** as the 42d president of the U.S.

IBM, Jan. 19, announced that it had lost $4.97 billion in 1992, the largest one-year loss ever for any U.S. corporation. McDonnell Douglas, the largest U.S. defense contractor, announced, **Jan. 25**, that it would cut 8,700 jobs. Sears, Roebuck & Co., the nation's 3d largest retailer, said, **Jan. 25**, that it would eliminate 50,000 jobs, close 113 stores, and cease publication of its catalog, a part of American life since 1896.

By executive order, **Jan. 22, Pres. Clinton overturned restrictions on abortion** imposed during the Reagan and Bush administrations.

Pres. Clinton, **Jan. 25**, appointed **Hillary Rodham Clinton head of the Task Force on National Health Care Reform.**

Pres. Clinton claimed his first legislative victory, **Feb. 4**, when the Senate and House both passed the **Family and Medical Leave Act**, which Clinton then signed into law on **Feb. 5.**

A powerful bomb exploded in an underground parking garage beneath the World Trade Center in New York City, **Feb. 26**, killing 6 people. The explosion left a crater 200 ft wide and several stories deep within the garage. More than 1,000 people suffered injuries. Five men were arrested in March in connection with the bombing. A 6th man was indicted, **Mar. 31**, but remained at large. A 7th suspect was charged **May 6**.

Four federal agents were killed, Feb. 28, during an unsuccessful raid on the **Branch Davidian compound in Waco, Tex.** Agents of the U.S. Bureau of Alcohol, Tobacco, and Firearms, carrying warrants, attempted to search the premises for illegal guns and explosives and to arrest cult leader David Koresh. This led to a 51-day siege of the compound by ATF agents and hundreds of officers from federal, state, and local agencies. The confrontation ended **Apr. 19**, when, by order of the FBI, armored vehicles pumped tear gas into the compound at 6 AM. The FBI said those inside responded with gunfire. Shortly after 12 noon, flames appeared at a window; the compound was leveled by fire in 30 minutes, leaving 72 cult members, including 17 children, dead. The U.S. Treasury Dept. issued a report, **Sept. 30**, that sharply criticized top ATF officials for their handling of the raid.

Janet Reno, a Florida state attorney, became the first woman to serve as attorney general of the U.S. when she took the oath of office **Mar. 12**.

A gay-rights march and rally in Washington, D.C., Apr. 25, drew 300,000 to 1 million demonstrators. Participants called for an end to the ban on gays in the military, more money to fight AIDS, and a civil-rights bill for gays.

A federal jury, **Apr. 17, found 2 Los Angeles police officers, Sgt. Stacey Koon and Officer Laurence Powell, guilty** and 2 officers not guilty of violating the civil rights of Rodney King, a black motorist whom they had arrested and beaten in 1991. The two officers convicted were sentenced, **Aug. 4**, to 2½ years in prison.

Defense Sec. Les Aspin, **Apr. 28**, removed restrictions on aerial combat roles by women in the armed forces.

The **"motor-voter" bill** was signed by Pres. Clinton, **May 20**. Under the bill, citizens in any state can register to vote when applying for a driver's license. They can also register at welfare and disability benefits offices, at military recruitment stations, and by mail.

Pres. Clinton, **July 2**, approved recommendations that **33 major military installations be closed.** Nearly 100 smaller bases would also be closed, and 45 others would be reduced in scale. An estimated 120,000 jobs would be lost.

A flood that was worse than anyone in the Midwest could remember surged down the Mississippi River and its tributaries in the summer of 1993. **"The Great Flood of 1993"** inundated 8 million acres of land and left 12 million acres too wet to cultivate. The floods left 50 people dead and some 70,000 homeless. By **July 26**, disaster areas had been declared in Illinois, Iowa, Kansas, Minnesota, Missouri, Nebraska, North Dakota, South Dakota, and Wisconsin. State and federal officials put total damage estimates at $12 billion, with nearly $8 billion of this suffered by farmers. Pres. Clinton signed a $6.2 billion flood relief bill **Aug. 12.**

Robert Rota, former postmaster for the U.S. House of Representatives, pleaded guilty, July 19, to one count of conspiring to embezzle public funds and to 2 counts of helping embezzlement by House members. Rota did not profit personally.

Pres. Clinton, **July 19**, announced circumstances under which homosexual men and women could serve in the U.S. military. An approach of "don't ask, don't tell, don't pursue" was endorsed.

Vincent Foster, the deputy White House counsel and long-time friend of Bill and Hillary Clinton, was found shot to death in a park in northern Virginia **July 20.** An autopsy indicated that he had committed suicide.

Judge Ruth Bader Ginsburg was sworn in, Aug. 10, as the 107th justice of the U.S. Supreme Court, replacing Associate Justice Byron White who announced his retirement, Mar. 19.

After a long and acrimonious debate, **Congress narrowly approved a bill designed to reduce federal budget deficits by $496 billion over 5 years.** The bill raised taxes on taxable incomes above $115,000 and increased the federal tax on all transportation fuels by 4.3 cents per gallon. All salary income would be subject to a 2.9% Medicare tax. For individuals earning more than $34,000 (couples, $44,000), the portion of Social Security benefits subject to income tax would rise from 50% to 85%. Total discretionary federal spending would be frozen at 1993 levels. The House approved the bill, **Aug. 5**, by a bare 218-216 margin, and the Senate, divided 50-50, passed the bill, **Aug. 6**, with the tie-breaking vote of Vice Pres. Al Gore. Pres. Bill Clinton signed the bill **Aug. 10**.

Sheikh Omar Abdel Rahman was indicted, Aug. 25, on conspiracy charges of leading a terrorist group responsible for the World Trade Center bombing, a plot to bomb the United Nations and other New York City targets, and the 1990 assassination of Rabbi Meir Kahane.

Pres. Clinton revealed his health-care reform package, **Sept. 22**, before a joint session of Congress. Under the concept of "managed competition," the **American Health Security Act of 1993** would guarantee health-care coverage for all American citizens and legal immigrants. Projected to cost $350 billion over 7 years, the plan would be funded largely out of savings from Medicare, Medicaid, and other health programs and by a tax on tobacco.

The trial of 4 of the 7 suspects in the World Trade Center bombing opened, **Oct. 4,** in U.S. District Court in New York City.

In a plebiscite, **Nov. 14**, Puerto Ricans voted to continue their commonwealth status with the U.S. The statehood option was defeated by a slim margin of 48% to 46%.

After extensive debate, the House, **Nov. 17**, approved the North American Free Trade Agreement, 234-200. The Senate endorsed the treaty **Nov. 20**, by a vote of 61-38. **NAFTA** was to go into effect Jan. 1, 1994.

The **"Brady Bill,"** which provides for a 5-day waiting period and establishes a national computer network as a means to check the backgrounds of gun buyers, became law when it was signed by Pres. Clinton **Nov. 30**.

The space shuttle *Endeavour* with a crew of 7 was launched **Dec. 2.** The mission to repair the Hubble telescope was successful.

Sec. of Energy Hazel O'Leary said, **Dec. 7**, that 204 underground nuclear tests had been conducted in Nevada from 1963 to 1990 without any notice to the public. Additionally, the Dept. of Energy said, **Dec. 28**, that some 800 people had been exposed to radiation in government experiments from the 1940s to the 1960s.

Late in the year, federal investigators initiated a probe into the dealings of the Madison Guaranty Savings and Loan, an Arkansas thrift that failed in 1989. Madison's owner James B. McDougal was a partner with Bill and Hillary Rodham Clinton in the **Whitewater** Development Co., a real estate firm. Investigators were examining whether federally insured deposits from Madison were illegally diverted to Bill Clinton's gubernatorial campaign and the Whitewater Development Co. White House Counsel Bernard Nussbaum removed files relating to the Clintons' holdings in Whitewater from the office of Vincent Foster after Foster committed suicide in July. On **Dec. 23**, the Clintons had instructed their attorneys to provide federal investigators with all their legal documents and financial records relating to Whitewater.

The Mayflower Compact

The threat of James I to "harry them out of the land" sent a little band of religious dissenters from England to Holland in 1608. They were known as "Separatists" because they wished to cut all ties with the Established Church. In 1620, some of them, known now as the Pilgrims, joined with a larger group in England to set sail on the *Mayflower* for the New World. A joint stock company financed their venture.

In November, they sighted Cape Cod and decided to land an exploring party at Plymouth Harbor. However, a rebellious group picked up at Southampton and London troubled the Pilgrim leaders, and to control their actions forty-one of the Pilgrims drew up the "Mayflower Compact," which was signed before going ashore. The voluntary agreement to govern themselves was America's first written constitution.

In the name of God, Amen. We, whose names are underwritten, the Loyal Subjects of our dread Sovereign Lord, King *James,* by the Grace of God, of *Great Britain, France and Ireland,* King, *Defender of the Faith,* etc.

Having undertaken for the Glory of God, and Advancement of the Christian Faith, and the Honour of our King and Country, a voyage to plant the first colony in the northern Parts of Virginia; do by these Presents, solemnly and mutually in the Presence of God and one of another, convenant and combine ourselves together into a civil Body Politick, for our better Ordering and Preservation, and Furtherance of the Ends aforesaid; And by Virtue hereof to enact, constitute, and frame, such just and equal Laws, Ordinances, Acts, Constitutions and Offices, from time to time, as shall be thought most meet and convenient for the General good of the Colony; unto which we promise all due Submission and Obedience.

In Witness whereof we have hereunto subscribed our names at *Cape Cod* the eleventh of *November,* in the Reign of our Sovereign Lord, King *James* of *England, France* and *Ireland,* the eighteenth, and of *Scotland* the fifty-fourth. *Anno Domini, 1620.*

The Continental Congress: Meetings, Presidents

Meeting places	Dates of meetings	Congress presidents	Date elected
Philadelphia	Sept. 5 to Oct. 26, 1774	Peyton Randolph, Va. (1)	Sept. 5, 1774
"	"	Henry Middleton, S.C.	Oct. 22, 1774
Philadelphia	May 10, 1775 to Dec. 12, 1776	Peyton Randolph, Va.	May 10, 1775
"	"	John Hancock, Mass.	May 24, 1775
Baltimore	Dec. 20, 1776 to Mar. 4, 1777	"	
Philadelphia	Mar. 5 to Sept. 18, 1777	"	
Lancaster, Pa.	Sept. 27, 1777 (one day)	"	
York, Pa.	Sept. 30, 1777 to June 27, 1778	Henry Laurens, S.C.	Nov. 1, 1777(4)
Philadelphia	July 2, 1778 to June 21, 1783	John Jay, N.Y.	Dec. 10, 1778
"	"	Samuel Huntington, Conn.	Sept. 28, 1779
"	"	Thomas McKean, Del.	July 10, 1781
"	"	John Hanson, Md. (2)	Nov. 5, 1781
"	"	Elias Boudinot, N.J.	Nov. 4, 1782
Princeton, N.J.	June 30 to Nov. 4, 1783	Thomas Mifflin, Pa.	Nov. 3, 1783
Annapolis, Md.	Nov. 26, 1783 to June 3, 1784	"	
Trenton, N.J.	Nov. 1 to Dec. 24, 1784	Richard Henry Lee, Va.	Nov. 30, 1784
New York City	Jan. 11 to Nov. 4, 1785	"	
"	Nov. 7, 1785 to Nov. 3, 1786	John Hancock, Mass. (3)	Nov. 23, 1785
"	"	Nathaniel Gorham, Mass.	June 6, 1786
"	Nov. 6, 1786 to Oct. 30, 1787	Arthur St. Clair, Pa.	Feb. 2, 1787
"	Nov. 5, 1787 to Oct. 21, 1788	Cyrus Griffin, Va.	Jan. 22, 1788
"	Nov. 3, 1788 to Mar. 2, 1789	"	

(1) Resigned Oct. 22, 1774. (2) Titled "President of the United States in Congress Assembled," John Hanson is considered by some to be the first U.S. President as he was the first to serve under the Articles of Confederation. He was, however, little more than presiding officer of the Congress, which retained full executive power. He could be considered the head of government, but not head of state. (3) Resigned May 29, 1786, without serving, because of illness. (4) Articles of Confederation agreed upon, Nov. 15, 1777; last ratification from Maryland, Mar. 1, 1781.

Patrick Henry's Speech to the Virginia Convention

The following is an excerpt from Patrick Henry's speech to the Virginia Convention on Mar. 23, 1775:

Gentlemen may cry, peace, peace—but there is no peace. The war is actually begun! The next gale that sweeps from the north will bring to our ears the clash of resounding arms! Our brethren are already in the field! Why stand we here idle? What is it that gentlemen wish? What would they have? Is life so dear, or peace so sweet, as to be purchased at the price of chains and slavery? Forbid it, Almighty God! I know not what course others may take; but as for me, give me liberty, or give me death!

Common Sense

The following is an excerpt from Thomas Paine's *Common Sense.* Paine adopted the doctrine of separation from Britain after the battles of Lexington and Concord, and published his pamphlet in Jan. 1776.

The cause of America is in great measure the cause of all mankind. Many circumstances hath, and will arise, which are not local, but universal, and through which principles of all Lovers of Mankind are affected, and in the Event of which, their Affections are interested. The laying a Country desolate with Fire and Sword, declaring war against natural rights of all Mankind, and extirpating the Defenders thereof from the Face of the Earth, is the Concern of every Man to whom Nature hath given the Power of feeling; . . . It is repugnant to reason, to the universal order of things, to all examples from former ages, to suppose, that this continent can longer remain subject to any external power . . .

The last cord is now broken, the people of England are presenting addresses against us. There are injuries which nature cannot forgive; she would cease to be nature if she did . . .

O ye that love mankind! Ye that dare oppose, not only the tyranny, but the tyrant, stand forth! Every spot of the old world is overrun with oppression. Freedom hath been hunted round the globe. Asia, and Africa, have long expelled her—Europe regards her like a stranger, and England hath given her warning to depart. O! Receive the fugitive, and prepare in time an asylum for mankind.

How the Declaration of Independence Was Adopted

On June 7, 1776, Richard Henry Lee, who had issued the first call for a congress of the colonies, introduced in the Continental Congress at Philadelphia a resolution declaring "that these United Colonies are, and of right ought to be, free and independent states, that they are absolved from all allegiance to the British Crown, and that all political connection between them and the state of Great Britain is, and ought to be, totally dissolved."

The resolution, seconded by John Adams on behalf of the Massachusetts delegation, came up again June 10 when a committee of 5, headed by Thomas Jefferson, was appointed to express the purpose of the resolution in a declaration of independence. The others on the committee were John Adams, Benjamin Franklin, Robert R. Livingston, and Roger Sherman.

Drafting the Declaration was assigned to Jefferson, who worked on a portable desk of his own construction in a room at Market and 7th Sts. The committee reported the result June 28, 1776. The members of the Congress suggested a number of changes, which Jefferson called "deplorable." They didn't approve Jefferson's arraignment of the British people and King George III for encouraging and fostering the slave trade, which Jefferson called "an execrable commerce." They made 86 changes, eliminating 480 words and leaving 1,337. In the final form capitalization was erratic. Jefferson had written that men were endowed with "inalienable" rights; in the final copy it came out as "unalienable" and has been thus ever since.

The Lee-Adams resolution of independence was adopted by 12 yeas July 2 — the actual date of the act of independence. The Declaration, which explains the act, was adopted July 4, in the evening.

After the Declaration was adopted, July 4, 1776, it was turned over to John Dunlap, printer, to be printed on broadsides. The original copy was lost and one of his broadsides was attached to a page in the journal of the Congress. It was read aloud July 8 in Philadelphia, Easton, Pa., and Trenton, N.J. On July 9 at 6 p.m. it was read by order of Gen. George Washington to the troops assembled on the Common in New York City (City Hall Park).

The Continental Congress of July 19, 1776, adopted the following resolution:

"Resolved, That the Declaration passed on the 4th, be fairly engrossed on parchment with the title and stile of 'The Unanimous Declaration of the thirteen United States of America' and that the same, when engrossed, be signed by every member of Congress."

Not all delegates who signed the engrossed Declaration were present on July 4. Robert Morris (Pa.), William Williams (Conn.) and Samuel Chase (Md.) signed on Aug. 2, Oliver Wolcott (Conn.), George Wythe (Va.), Richard Henry Lee (Va.) and Elbridge Gerry (Mass.) signed in August and September, Matthew Thornton (N. H.) joined the Congress Nov. 4 and signed later. Thomas McKean (Del.) rejoined Washington's army before signing and said later that he signed in 1781.

Charles Carroll of Carrollton was appointed a delegate by Maryland on July 4, 1776, presented his credentials July 18, and signed the engrossed Declaration Aug. 2. Born Sept. 19, 1737, he was 95 years old and the last surviving signer when he died Nov. 14, 1832.

Two Pennsylvania delegates who did not support the Declaration on July 4 were replaced.

The 4 New York delegates did not have authority from their state to vote on July 4. On July 9 the New York state convention authorized its delegates to approve the Declaration and the Congress was so notified on July 15, 1776. The 4 signed the Declaration on Aug. 2.

The original engrossed Declaration is preserved in the National Archives Building in Washington.

Declaration of Independence

The Declaration of Independence was adopted by the Continental Congress in Philadelphia, on July 4, 1776. John Hancock was president of the Congress and Charles Thomson was secretary. A copy of the Declaration, engrossed on parchment, was signed by members of Congress on and after Aug. 2, 1776. On Jan. 18, 1777, Congress ordered that "an authenticated copy, with the names of the members of Congress subscribing the same, be sent to each of the United States, and that they be desired to have the same put upon record." Authenticated copies were printed in broadside form in Baltimore, where the Continental Congress was then in session. The following text is that of the original printed by John Dunlap at Philadelphia for the Continental Congress.

IN CONGRESS, July 4, 1776.

A DECLARATION

By the REPRESENTATIVES of the

UNITED STATES OF AMERICA,

In GENERAL CONGRESS assembled

When in the Course of human Events, it becomes necessary for one People to dissolve the Political Bands which have connected them with another, and to assume among the Powers of the Earth, the separate and equal Station to which the Laws of Nature and of Nature's God entitle them, a decent Respect to the Opinions of Mankind requires that they should declare the causes which impel them to the Separation.

We hold these Truths to be self-evident, that all Men are created equal, that they are endowed by their Creator with certain unalienable Rights, that among these are Life, Liberty, and the Pursuit of Happiness—That to secure these Rights, Governments are instituted among Men, deriving their just Powers from the Consent of the Governed, that whenever any Form of Government becomes destructive of these Ends, it is the Right of the People to alter or to abolish it, and to institute new Government, laying its Foundation on such Principles, and organizing its Powers in such Form, as to them shall seem most likely to effect their Safety and Happiness. Prudence, indeed, will dictate that Governments long established should not be changed for light and transient Causes; and accordingly all Experience hath shewn, that Mankind are more disposed to suffer, while Evils are sufferable, than to right themselves by abolishing the Forms to which they are accustomed. But when a long Train of Abuses and Usurpations, pursuing invariably the same Object, evinces a Design to reduce them under absolute Despotism, it is their Right, it is their Duty, to throw off such Government, and to provide new Guards for their future Security. Such has been the patient Sufferance of these Colonies; and such is now the Necessity which constrains them to alter their former Systems of Government. The History of the present King of Great-Britain is a History of repeated Injuries and Usurpations, all having in direct Object the Establishment of an absolute Tyranny over these States. To prove this, let Facts be submitted to a candid World.

He has refused his Assent to Laws, the most wholesome and necessary for the public Good.

He has forbidden his Governors to pass Laws of immediate and pressing Importance, unless suspended in their Operation till his Assent should be obtained; and when so suspended, he has utterly neglected to attend to them.

He has refused to pass other Laws for the Accommodation of large Districts of People, unless those People would relinquish the Right of Representation in the Legislature, a Right inestimable to them, and formidable to Tyrants only.

He has called together Legislative Bodies at Places unusual, uncomfortable, and distant from the Depository of their Public Records, for the sole Purpose of fatiguing them into Compliance with his Measures.

He has dissolved Representative Houses repeatedly, for opposing with manly Firmness his Invasions on the Rights of the People.

He has refused for a long Time, after such Dissolutions, to cause others to be elected; whereby the Legislative Powers, incapable of Annihilation, have returned to the People at large for their exercise; the State remaining in the mean time exposed to all the Dangers of Invasion from without, and Convulsions within.

He has endeavoured to prevent the Population of these States; for that Purpose obstructing the Laws for Naturalization of Foreigners; refusing to pass others to encourage their Migrations hither, and raising the Conditions of new Appropriations of Lands.

He has obstructed the Administration of Justice, by refusing his Assent to Laws for establishing Judiciary Powers.

He has made Judges dependent on his Will alone, for the Tenure of their Offices, and the Amount and payment of their Salaries.

He has erected a Multitude of new Offices, and sent hither Swarms of Officers to harrass our People, and eat out their Substance.

He has kept among us, in Times of Peace, Standing Armies, without the consent of our Legislatures.

He has affected to render the Military independent of, and superior to the Civil Power.

He has combined with others to subject us to a Jurisdiction foreign to our Constitution, and unacknowledged by our Laws; giving his Assent to their Acts of pretended Legislation:

For quartering large Bodies of Armed Troops among us:

For protecting them, by a mock Trial, from Punishment for any Murders which they should commit on the Inhabitants of these States:

For cutting off our Trade with all Parts of the World:

For imposing Taxes on us without our Consent:

For depriving us, in many Cases, of the Benefits of Trial by Jury:

For transporting us beyond Seas to be tried for pretended Offences:

For abolishing the free System of English Laws in a neighbouring Province, establishing therein an arbitrary Government, and enlarging its Boundaries, so as to render it at once an Example and fit Instrument for introducing the same absolute Rule into these Colonies:

For taking away our Charters, abolishing our most valuable Laws, and altering fundamentally the Forms of our Governments:

For suspending our own Legislatures, and declaring themselves invested with Power to legislate for us in all Cases whatsoever.

He has abdicated Government here, by declaring us out of his Protection and waging War against us.

He has plundered our Seas, ravaged our Coasts, burnt our towns, and destroyed the Lives of our People.

He is, at this Time, transporting large Armies of foreign Mercenaries to complete the works of Death, Desolation, and Tyranny, already begun with circumstances of Cruelty and Perfidy, scarcely paralleled in the most barbarous Ages, and totally unworthy the Head of a civilized Nation.

He has constrained our fellow Citizens taken Captive on the high Seas to bear Arms against their Country, to become the Executioners of their Friends and Brethren, or to fall themselves by their Hands.

He has excited domestic Insurrections amongst us, and has endeavoured to bring on the Inhabitants of our Frontiers, the merciless Indian Savages, whose known Rule of Warfare, is an undistinguished Destruction, of all Ages, Sexes and Conditions.

In every stage of these Oppressions we have Petitioned for Redress in the most humble Terms: Our repeated Petitions have been answered only by repeated Injury. A Prince, whose Character is thus marked by every act which may define a Tyrant, is unfit to be the Ruler of a free People.

Nor have we been wanting in Attentions to our British Brethren. We have warned them from Time to Time of Attempts by their Legislature to extend an unwarrantable Jurisdiction over us. We have reminded them of the Circumstances of our Emigration and Settlement here. We have appealed to their native Justice and Magnanimity, and we have conjured them by the Ties of our common Kindred to disavow these Usurpations, which, would inevitably interrupt our Connections and Correspondence. They too have been deaf to the Voice of Justice and of Consanguinity. We must, therefore, acquiesce in the Necessity, which denounces our Separation, and hold them, as we hold the rest of Mankind, Enemies in War, in Peace, Friends.

We, therefore, the Representatives of the UNITED STATES OF AMERICA, in General Congress, Assembled, appealing to the Supreme Judge of the World for the Rectitude of our Intentions, do, in the Name, and by Authority of the good People of these Colonies, solemnly Publish and Declare, That these United Colonies are, and of Right ought to be, Free and Independent States; that they are absolved from all Allegiance to the British Crown, and that all political Connection between them and the State of Great-Britain, is and ought to be totally dissolved; and that as Free and Independent States, they have full Power to levy War, conclude Peace, contract Alliances, establish Commerce, and to do all other Acts and Things which Independent States may of right do. And for the support of this declaration, with a firm Reliance on the Protection of divine Providence, we mutually pledge to each other our lives, our Fortunes, and our sacred Honor.

JOHN HANCOCK, President

Attest.
CHARLES THOMSON, Secretary.

Signers of the Declaration of Independence

Delegate (state)	Vocation	Birthplace	Born	Died
Adams, John (Mass.)	Lawyer	Braintree (Quincy), Mass.	Oct. 30, 1735	July 4, 1826
Adams, Samuel (Mass.)	Political leader	Boston, Mass.	Sept. 27, 1722	Oct. 2, 1803
Bartlett, Josiah (N.H.)	Physician, judge	Amesbury, Mass.	Nov. 21, 1729	May 19, 1795
Braxton, Carter (Va.)	Farmer	Newington Plantation, Va.	Sept. 10, 1736	Oct. 10, 1797
Carroll, Chas. of Carrollton (Md.)	Lawyer	Annapolis, Md.	Sept. 19, 1737	Nov. 14, 1832
Chase, Samuel (Md.)	Judge	Princess Anne, Md.	Apr. 17, 1741	June 19, 1811
Clark, Abraham (N.J.)	Surveyor	Roselle, N.J.	Feb. 15, 1726	Sept. 15, 1794
Clymer, George (Pa.)	Merchant	Philadelphia, Pa.	Mar. 16, 1739	Jan. 23, 1813
Ellery, William (R.I.)	Lawyer	Newport, R.I.	Dec. 22, 1727	Feb. 15, 1820
Floyd, William (N.Y.)	Soldier	Brookhaven, N.Y.	Dec. 17, 1734	Aug. 4, 1821
Franklin, Benjamin (Pa.)	Printer, publisher	Boston, Mass.	Jan. 17, 1706	Apr. 17, 1790
Gerry, Elbridge (Mass.)	Merchant	Marblehead, Mass.	July 17, 1744	Nov. 23, 1814
Gwinnett, Button (Ga.)	Merchant	Down Hatherly, England	c. 1735	May 19, 1777
Hall, Lyman (Ga.)	Physician	Wallingford, Conn.	Apr. 12, 1724	Oct. 19, 1790
Hancock, John (Mass.)	Merchant	Braintree (Quincy), Mass.	Jan. 12, 1737	Oct. 8, 1793

Delegate (state)	Vocation	Birthplace	Born	Died
Harrison, Benjamin (Va.)	Farmer	Berkeley, Va.	Apr. 5, 1726	Apr. 24, 1791
Hart, John (N.J.)	Farmer	Stonington, Conn.	c. 1711	May 11, 1779
Hewes, Joseph (N.C.)	Merchant	Princeton, N.J.	Jan. 23, 1730	Nov. 10, 1779
Heyward, Thos. Jr. (S.C.)	Lawyer, farmer	St. Luke's Parish, S.C.	July 28, 1746	Mar. 6, 1809
Hooper, William (N.C.)	Lawyer	Boston, Mass.	June 28, 1742	Oct. 14, 1790
Hopkins, Stephen (R.I.)	Judge, educator	Providence, R.I.	Mar. 7, 1707	July 13, 1785
Hopkinson, Francis (N.J.)	Judge, author	Philadelphia, Pa.	Sept. 21, 1737	May 9, 1791
Huntington, Samuel (Conn.)	Judge	Windham County, Conn.	July 3, 1731	Jan. 5, 1796
Jefferson, Thomas (Va.)	Lawyer	Shadwell, Va.	Apr. 13, 1743	July 4, 1826
Lee, Francis Lightfoot (Va.)	Farmer	Westmoreland County, Va.	Oct. 14, 1734	Jan. 11, 1797
Lee, Richard Henry (Va.)	Farmer	Westmoreland County, Va.	Jan. 20, 1732	June 19, 1794
Lewis, Francis (N.Y.)	Merchant	Llandaff, Wales	Mar., 1713	Dec. 31, 1802
Livingston, Philip (N.Y.)	Merchant	Albany, N.Y.	Jan. 15, 1716	June 12, 1778
Lynch, Thomas Jr. (S.C.)	Farmer	Winyah, S.C.	Aug. 5, 1749	(at sea) 1779
McKean, Thomas (Del.)	Lawyer	New London, Pa.	Mar. 19, 1734	June 24, 1817
Middleton, Arthur (S.C.)	Farmer	Charleston, S.C.	June 26, 1742	Jan. 1, 1787
Morris, Lewis (N.Y.)	Farmer	Morrisania (Bronx County), N.Y.	Apr. 8, 1726	Jan. 22, 1798
Morris, Robert (Pa.)	Merchant	Liverpool, England	Jan. 20, 1734	May 9, 1806
Morton, John (Pa.)	Judge	Ridley, Pa.	1724	Apr., 1777
Nelson, Thos. Jr. (Va.)	Farmer	Yorktown, Va.	Dec. 26, 1738	Jan. 4, 1789
Paca, William (Md.)	Judge	Abingdon, Md.	Oct. 31, 1740	Oct. 23, 1799
Paine, Robert Treat (Mass.)	Judge	Boston, Mass.	Mar. 11, 1731	May 12, 1814
Penn, John (N.C.)	Lawyer	Near Port Royal, Va.	May 17, 1741	Sept. 14, 1788
Read, George (Del.)	Judge	Near North East, Md.	Sept. 18, 1733	Sept. 21, 1798
Rodney, Caesar (Del.)	Judge	Dover, Del.	Oct. 7, 1728	June 29, 1784
Ross, George (Pa.)	Judge	New Castle, Del.	May 10, 1730	July 14, 1779
Rush, Benjamin (Pa.)	Physician	Byberry, Pa. (Philadelphia)	Dec. 24, 1745	Apr. 19, 1813
Rutledge, Edward (S.C.)	Lawyer	Charleston, S.C.	Nov. 23, 1749	Jan. 23, 1800
Sherman, Roger (Conn.)	Lawyer	Newton, Mass.	Apr. 19, 1721	July 23, 1793
Smith, James (Pa.)	Lawyer	Dublin, Ireland	c. 1719	July 11, 1806
Stockton, Richard (N.J.)	Lawyer	Near Princeton, N.J.	Oct. 1, 1730	Feb. 28, 1781
Stone, Thomas (Md.)	Lawyer	Charles County, Md.	1743	Oct. 5, 1787
Taylor, George (Pa.)	Ironmaster	Ireland	1716	Feb. 23, 1781
Thornton, Matthew (N.H.)	Physician	Ireland	1714	June 24, 1803
Walton, George (Ga.)	Judge	Prince Edward County, Va.	1741	Feb. 2, 1804
Whipple, William (N.H.)	Merchant, judge	Kittery, Me.	Jan. 14, 1730	Nov. 28, 1785
Williams, William (Conn.)	Merchant	Lebanon, Conn.	Apr. 23, 1731	Aug. 2, 1811
Wilson, James (Pa.)	Judge	Carskerdo, Scotland	Sept. 14, 1742	Aug. 28, 1798
Witherspoon, John (N.J.)	Clergyman, educator	Gifford, Scotland	Feb. 5, 1723	Nov. 15, 1794
Wolcott, Oliver (Conn.)	Judge	Windsor, Conn.	Dec. 1, 1726	Dec. 1, 1797
Wythe, George (Va.)	Lawyer	Elizabeth City Co. (Hampton), Va.	1726	June 8, 1806

Origin of the Constitution

The War of Independence was conducted by delegates from the original 13 states, called the Congress of the United States of America and known as the Continental Congress. In 1777 the Congress submitted to the legislatures of the states the Articles of Confederation and Perpetual Union, which were ratified by New Hampshire, Massachusetts, Rhode Island, Connecticut, New York, New Jersey, Pennsylvania, Delaware, Virginia, North Carolina, South Carolina, and Georgia, and finally, in 1781, by Maryland.

The first article of the instrument read: "The stile of this confederacy shall be the United States of America." This did not signify a sovereign nation, because the states delegated only those powers they could not handle individually. Taxes for the payment of such debts were levied by the individual states. The president under the Articles signed himself "President of the United States in Congress assembled," but here the United States were considered in the plural, a cooperating group. Canada was invited to join the union on equal terms but did not act.

When the war was won, it became evident that a stronger federal union was needed. The Congress left the initiative to the legislatures. Virginia in Jan. 1786 appointed commissioners to meet with representatives of other states; delegates from Virginia, Delaware, New York, New Jersey, and Pennsylvania met at Annapolis. Alexander Hamilton prepared for their call by asking delegates from all states to meet in Philadelphia in May 1787 "to render the Constitution of the Federal government adequate to the exigencies of the union." Congress endorsed the plan Feb. 21, 1787. Delegates were appointed by all states except Rhode Island.

The convention met May 14, 1787. George Washington was chosen president (presiding officer). The states certified 65 delegates, but 10 did not attend. The work was done by 55, not all of whom were present at all sessions. Of the 55 attending delegates, 16 failed to sign, and 39 actually signed Sept. 17, 1787, some with reservations. Some historians have said 74 delegates (9 more than the 65 actually certified) were named and 19 failed to attend. These 9 additional persons refused the appointment, were never delegates, and never counted as absentees. Washington sent the Constitution to Congress, and that body, Sept. 28, 1787, ordered it sent to the legislatures, "in order to be submitted to a convention of delegates chosen in each state by the people thereof."

The Constitution was ratified by votes of state conventions as follows: Delaware, Dec. 7, 1787, unanimous; Pennsylvania, Dec. 12, 1787, 43 to 23; New Jersey, Dec. 18, 1787, unanimous; Georgia, Jan. 2, 1788, unanimous; Connecticut, Jan. 9, 1788, 128 to 40; Massachusetts, Feb. 6, 1788, 187 to 168; Maryland, Apr. 28, 1788, 63 to 11; South Carolina, May 23, 1788, 149 to 73; New Hampshire, June 21, 1788, 57 to 46; Virginia, June 25, 1788, 89 to 79; New York, July 26, 1788, 30 to 27. Nine states were needed to establish the operation of the Constitution "between the states so ratifying the same," and New Hampshire was the 9th state. The government did not declare the Constitution in effect until the first Wednesday in Mar. 1789, which was Mar. 4. After that, North Carolina ratified it Nov. 21, 1789, 194 to 77; and Rhode Island, May 29, 1790, 34 to 32. Vermont in convention ratified it Jan. 10, 1791, and by act of Congress approved Feb. 18, 1791, was admitted into the Union as the 14th state, Mar. 4, 1791.

Constitution of the United States
The Original 7 Articles

The text below (with the exception of Amendment XXVII) is taken from the pocket-size edition of the Constitution published by the U.S. Government Printing Office as a result of a U.S. House and Senate resolution to print the Constitution in its original form as amended through July 5, 1971. Text in **boldface** summarizes an article or amendment and was added by *The World Almanac*. Text in *italic* indicates that an item has been superseded or amended, or provides background information on amendments.

PREAMBLE

We, the People of the United States, in Order to form a more perfect Union, establish Justice, insure domestic Tranquility, provide for the common defence, promote the general Welfare, and secure the Blessings of Liberty to ourselves and our Posterity, do ordain and establish this Constitution for the United States of America.

ARTICLE I.

Section 1—Legislative powers; in whom vested:

All legislative Powers herein granted shall be vested in a Congress of the United States, which shall consist of a Senate and House of Representatives.

Section 2—House of Representatives, how and by whom chosen. Qualifications of a Representative. Representatives and direct taxes, how apportioned. Enumeration. Vacancies to be filled. Power of choosing officers, and of impeachment.

The House of Representatives shall be composed of Members chosen every second Year by the People of the several States, and the Electors in each State shall have the Qualifications requisite for Electors of the most numerous Branch of the State Legislature.

No person shall be a Representative who shall not have attained to the Age of twenty-five Years, and been seven Years a Citizen of the United States, and who shall not, when elected, be an Inhabitant of that State in which he shall be chosen.

(Representatives and direct taxes shall be apportioned among the several States which may be included within this Union, according to their respective Numbers, which shall be determined by adding to the whole Number of free Persons, including those bound to Service for a Term of Years, and excluding Indians not taxed, three-fifths of all other persons.) (The previous sentence was superseded by Amendment XIV, section 2.) The actual Enumeration shall be made within three Years after the first Meeting of the Congress of the United States, and within every subsequent Term of ten Years, in such Manner as they shall by Law direct. The Number of Representatives shall not exceed one for every thirty Thousand, but each State shall have at Least one Representative; and until such enumeration shall be made, the State of New Hampshire shall be entitled to chuse three, Massachusetts eight, Rhode-Island and Providence Plantations one, Connecticut five, New-York six, New Jersey four, Pennsylvania eight, Delaware one, Maryland six, Virginia ten, North Carolina five, South Carolina five, and Georgia three.

When vacancies happen in the Representation from any State, the Executive Authority thereof shall issue Writs of Election to fill such Vacancies.

The House of Representatives shall chuse their Speaker and other Officers; and shall have the sole Power of Impeachment.

Section 3—Senators, how and by whom chosen. How classified. Qualifications of a Senator. President of the Senate, his right to vote. President pro tem., and other officers of the Senate, how chosen. Power to try impeachments. When President is tried, Chief Justice to preside. Sentence.

The Senate of the United States shall be composed of two Senators from each State, *(chosen by the Legislature thereof), (The preceding five words were superseded by Amendment XVII, section 1.)* for six Years; and each Senator shall have one Vote.

Immediately after they shall be assembled in Consequence of the first Election, they shall be divided as equally as may be into three Classes. The Seats of the Senators of the first Class shall be vacated at the Expiration of the second Year, of the second Class at the Expiration of the fourth Year, and of the third Class at the Expiration of the Sixth year, so that one-third may be chosen every second Year; *(and if Vacancies happen by Resignation, or otherwise, during the Recess of the Legislature of any State, the Executive thereof may make temporary Appointments until the next Meeting of the Legislature, which shall then fill such Vacancies.) (The words in parentheses were superseded by Amendment XVII, section 2.)*

No person shall be a Senator who shall not have attained to the Age of thirty Years, and been nine Years a Citizen of the United States, and who shall not, when elected, be an Inhabitant of that State for which he shall be chosen.

The Vice President of the United States shall be President of the Senate, but shall have no Vote, unless they be equally divided.

The Senate shall chuse their other Officers, and also a President pro tempore, in the absence of the Vice President, or when he shall exercise the Office of President of the United States.

The Senate shall have the sole Power to try all Impeachments. When sitting for that Purpose, they shall be on Oath or Affirmation. When the President of the United States is tried, the Chief Justice shall preside: And no Person shall be convicted without the Concurrence of two thirds of the Members present.

Judgment in Cases of Impeachment shall not extend further than to removal from Office, and disqualification to hold and enjoy any Office of honor, Trust or Profit under the United States: but the Party convicted shall nevertheless be liable and subject to Indictment, Trial, Judgment and Punishment, according to Law.

Section 4—Times, etc., of holding elections, how prescribed. One session each year.

The Times, Places and Manner of holding Elections for Senators and Representatives, shall be prescribed in each State by the Legislature thereof; but the Congress may at any time by Law make or alter such Regulations, except as to the Place of Chusing Senators.

The Congress shall assemble at least once in every Year, and such Meeting shall *(be on the first Monday in December,) (The words in parentheses were superseded by Amendment XX, section 2.)* unless they shall by Law appoint a different Day.

Section 5—Membership, quorum, adjournments, rules. Power to punish or expel. Journal. Time of adjournments, how limited, etc.

Each House shall be the Judge of the Elections, Returns and Qualifications of its own Members, and a Majority of each shall constitute a Quorum to do Business; but a smaller number may adjourn from day to day, and may be authorized to compel the Attendance of absent Members, in such manner, and under such Penalties as each House may provide.

Each House may determine the Rules of its Proceedings, punish its members for disorderly Behavior, and, with the Concurrence of two thirds, expel a Member.

Each House shall keep a Journal of its Proceedings, and from time to time publish the same, excepting such Parts as may in their Judgment require Secrecy; and the Yeas and Nays of the Members of either House on any question shall, at the Desire of one fifth of those Present, be entered on the Journal.

Neither House, during the Session of Congress, shall, without the Consent of the other, adjourn for more than three days, nor to any other Place than that in which the two Houses shall be sitting.

Section 6—Compensation, privileges, disqualifications in certain cases.

The Senators and Representatives shall receive a Compensation for their Services, to be ascertained by Law, and paid out of the Treasury of the United States. They shall in all Cases, except Treason, Felony and Breach of the Peace, be privileged from Arrest during their Attendance at the Session of their respective Houses, and in going to and returning from the same; and for any Speech or Debate in either House, they shall not be questioned in any other Place.

No Senator or Representative shall, during the Time for which he was elected, be appointed to any civil Office under the Authority of the United States, which shall have been created, or the Emoluments whereof shall have been encreased during such time; and no Person holding any Office under the United States, shall be a Member of either House during his Continuance in Office.

Section 7—House to originate all revenue bills. Veto. Bill may be passed by two-thirds of each House, notwithstanding, etc. Bill, not returned in ten days, to become a law. Provisions as to orders, concurrent resolutions, etc.

All bills for raising Revenue shall originate in the House of Representatives; but the Senate may propose or concur with Amendments as on other Bills.

Every Bill which shall have passed the House of Representatives and the Senate, shall, before it become a Law, be presented to the President of the United States; If he approve he shall sign it, but if not he shall return it, with his Objections to that House in which it shall have originated, who shall enter the Objections at large on their Journal, and proceed to reconsider it. If after such Reconsideration two thirds of that House shall agree to pass the Bill, it shall be sent, together with the Objections, to the other House, by which it shall likewise be reconsidered, and if approved by two thirds of that House, it shall become a Law. But in all such Cases the Votes of both Houses shall be determined by Yeas and Nays, and the Names of the Persons voting for and against the Bill shall be entered on the Journal of each House respectively. If any Bill shall not be returned by the President within ten Days (Sundays excepted) after it shall have been presented to him, the Same shall be a Law, in like Manner as if he had signed it, unless the Congress by their Adjournment prevent its Return, in which Case it shall not be a Law.

Every order, Resolution, or Vote to which the Concurrence of the Senate and House of Representatives may be necessary (except on a question of Adjournment) shall be presented to the President of the United States; and before the Same shall take Effect, shall be approved by him, or being disapproved by him, shall be repassed by two thirds of the Senate and House of Representatives, according to the Rules and Limitations prescribed in the Case of a Bill.

Section 8—Powers of Congress.

The Congress shall have Power To lay and collect Taxes, Duties, Imposts and Excises, to pay the Debts and provide for the common Defence and general Welfare of the United States; but all Duties, Imposts and Excises shall be uniform throughout the United States;

To borrow money on the credit of the United States;

To regulate Commerce with foreign Nations, and among the several States, and with the Indian Tribes;

To establish an uniform Rule of Naturalization, and uniform Laws on the subject of Bankruptcies throughout the United States;

To coin Money, regulate the Value thereof, and of foreign Coin, and fix the Standard of Weights and Measures;

To provide for the Punishment of counterfeiting the Securities and current Coin of the United States;

To establish Post Offices and post Roads;

To promote the Progress of Science and useful Arts, by securing for limited Times to Authors and Inventors the exclusive Right to their respective Writings and Discoveries;

To constitute Tribunals inferior to the supreme Court;

To define and punish Piracies and Felonies committed on the high Seas, and Offenses against the Law of Nations;

To declare War, grant Letters of Marque and Reprisal, and make Rules concerning Captures on Land and Water;

To raise and support Armies, but no Appropriation of Money to that Use shall be for a longer Term than two Years;

To provide and maintain a Navy;

To make Rules for the Government and Regulation of the land and naval Forces;

To provide for calling forth the Militia to execute the Laws of the Union, suppress Insurrections and repel Invasions;

To provide for organizing, arming, and disciplining the Militia, and for governing such Part of them as may be employed in the Service of the United States, reserving to the States respectively, the Appointment of the Officers, and the Authority of training the Militia according to the discipline prescribed by Congress;

To exercise exclusive Legislation in all Cases whatsoever, over such District (not exceeding ten Miles square) as may, by Cession of particular States, and the acceptance of Congress, become the Seat of the Government of the United States, and to exercise like Authority over all Places purchased by the Consent of the Legislature of the State in which the Same shall be, for the Erection of Forts, Magazines, Arsenals, dock-Yards, and other needful Buildings;—And

To make all Laws which shall be necessary and proper for carrying into Execution the foregoing Powers, and all other Powers vested by this Constitution in the Government of the United States, or in any Department or Officer thereof.

Section 9—Provision as to migration or importation of certain persons. Habeas corpus, bills of attainder, etc. Taxes, how apportioned. No export duty. No commercial preference. Money, how drawn from Treasury, etc. No titular nobility. Officers not to receive presents, etc.

The Migration or Importation of such Persons as any of the States now existing shall think proper to admit, shall not be prohibited by the Congress prior to the Year one thousand eight hundred and eight, but a tax or duty may be imposed on such Importation, not exceeding ten dollars for each Person.

The privilege of the Writ of Habeas Corpus shall not be suspended, unless when in Cases of Rebellion or Invasion the public Safety may require it.

No Bill of Attainder or ex post facto Law shall be passed.

No capitation, or other direct, Tax shall be laid, unless in Proportion to the Census or Enumeration herein before directed to be taken. *(Modified by Amendment XVI.)*

No Tax or Duty shall be laid on Articles exported from any State.

No Preference shall be given by any Regulation of Commerce or Revenue to the Ports of one State over those of another: nor shall Vessels bound to, or from, one State, be obliged to enter, clear, or pay Duties in another.

No Money shall be drawn from the Treasury, but in Consequence of Appropriations made by Law; and a regular Statement and Account of the Receipts and Expenditures of all public Money shall be published from time to time.

No Title of Nobility shall be granted by the United States: and no Person holding any Office of Profit or Trust under them, shall, without the Consent of the Congress, accept of any present, Emolument, Office, or Title, of any kind whatever, from any King, Prince, or foreign State.

Section 10—States prohibited from the exercise of certain powers.

No State shall enter into any Treaty, Alliance, or Confederation; grant Letters of Marque and Reprisal; coin Money; emit Bills of Credit; make any Thing but gold and silver Coin a Tender in Payment of Debts; pass any Bill of Attainder, ex post facto Law, or Law impairing the Obligation of Contracts, or grant any Title of Nobility.

No State shall, without the Consent of the Congress, lay any Imposts or Duties on Imports or Exports, except what may be absolutely necessary for executing its inspection Laws: and the net Produce of all Duties and Imposts, laid by any State on Imports or Exports, shall be for the Use of the Treasury of the United States; and all such Laws shall be subject to the Revision and Control of the Congress.

No State shall, without the Consent of Congress, lay any duty of Tonnage, keep Troops, or Ships of War in time of Peace, enter into any Agreement or Compact with another State, or with a foreign Power, or engage in War, unless actually invaded, or in such imminent Danger as will not admit of delay.

ARTICLE II.

Section 1—President: his term of office. Electors of President; number and how appointed. Electors to vote on same day. Qualification of President. On whom his duties devolve in case of his removal, death, etc. President's compensation. His oath of office.

The executive Power shall be vested in a President of the United States of America. He shall hold his Office during the Term of four Years, and, together with the Vice President, chosen for the same Term, be elected, as follows.

Each State shall appoint, in such Manner as the Legislature thereof may direct, a Number of Electors, equal to the whole Number of Senators and Representatives to which the State may be entitled in the Congress: but no Senator or Representative, or Person holding an Office of Trust or Profit under the United States, shall be appointed an Elector.

(The Electors shall meet in their respective States, and vote by Ballot for two persons, of whom one at least shall not be an Inhabitant of the same State with themselves. And they shall make a List of all the Persons voted for, and of the Number of Votes for each; which List they shall sign and certify, and transmit sealed to the Seat of the Government of the United States, directed to the President of the Senate. The President of the Senate shall, in the Presence of the Senate and House of Representatives, open all the Certificates, and the Votes shall then be counted. The Person having the greatest Number of Votes shall be the President, if such Number be a Majority of the whole Number of Electors appointed; and if there be more than one who have such Majority, and have an equal Number of Votes, then the House of Representatives shall immediately chuse by Ballot one of them for President; and if no Person have a Majority, then from the five highest on the List the said House shall in like Manner chuse the President. But in chusing the President, the Votes shall be taken by States, the Representation from each State having one Vote; a quorum for this Purpose shall consist of a Member or Members from two thirds of the States, and a Majority of all the States shall be necessary to a Choice. In every Case, after the Choice of the President, the Person having the greatest Number of Votes of the Electors shall be the Vice President. But if there should remain two or more who have equal Votes, the Senate shall chuse from them by Ballot the Vice-President.)

(This clause was superseded by Amendment XII.)

The Congress may detemine the Time of chusing the Electors, and the Day on which they shall give their Votes; which Day shall be the same throughout the United States.

No person except a natural born Citizen, or a Citizen of the United States, at the time of the Adoption of this Constitution, shall be eligible to the Office of President; neither shall any Person be eligible to that Office who shall not have attained to the Age of thirty-five Years, and been fourteen Years a Resident within the United States.

(For qualification of the Vice President, see Amendment XII.)

In Case of the Removal of the President from Office, or of his Death, Resignation, or Inability to discharge the Powers and Duties of the said Office, the same shall devolve on the Vice President, and the Congress may by Law, provide for the Case of Removal, Death, Resignation or Inability, both of the President and Vice President, declaring what Officer shall then act as President, and such Officer shall act accordingly, until the Disability be removed, or a President shall be elected.

(This clause has been modified by Amendments XX and XXV.)

The President shall, at stated Times, receive for his Services, a Compensation, which shall neither be encreased nor diminished during the Period for which he shall have been elected, and he shall not receive within that Period any other Emolument from the United States, or any of them.

Before he enter on the Execution of his Office, he shall take the following Oath or Affirmation:–"I do solemnly swear (or affirm) that I will faithfully execute the Office of President of the United States, and will to the best of my Ability, preserve, protect and defend the Constitution of the United States."

Section 2—President to be Commander-in-Chief. He may require opinions of cabinet officers, etc., may pardon. Treaty-making power. Nomination of certain officers. When President may fill vacancies.

The President shall be Commander in Chief of the Army and Navy of the United States, and of the Militia of the several States, when called into the actual Service of the United States; he may require the Opinion in writing, of the principal Officer in each of the executive Departments, upon any subject relating to the Duties of their respective Offices, and he shall have Power to Grant Reprieves and Pardons for Offenses against the United States, except in Cases of Impeachment.

He shall have Power, by and with the Advice and Consent of the Senate, to make Treaties, provided two-thirds of the Senators present concur; and he shall nominate, and by and with the Advice and Consent of the Senate, shall appoint Ambassadors, other public Ministers and Consuls, Judges of the supreme Court, and all other Officers of the United States, whose Appointments are not herein otherwise provided for, and which shall be established by Law: but the Congress may by Law vest the Appointment of such inferior Officers, as they think proper, in the President alone, in the Courts of Law, or in the Heads of Departments.

The President shall have Power to fill up all Vacancies that may happen during the Recess of the Senate, by granting Commissions which shall expire at the End of their next Session.

Section 3—President shall communicate to Congress. He may convene and adjourn Congress, in case of disagreement, etc. Shall receive ambassadors, execute laws, and commission officers.

He shall from time to time give to the Congress Information of the State of the Union, and recommend to their Consideration such Measures as he shall judge necessary and expedient; he may, on extraordinary Occasions, convene both Houses, or either of them, and in Case of Disagreement between them, with Respect to the Time of Adjournment, he may adjourn them to such Time as he shall think proper; he shall receive Ambassadors and other public Ministers; he shall take Care that the Laws be faithfully executed, and shall Commission all the Officers of the United States.

Section 4—All civil offices forfeited for certain crimes.

The President, Vice President and all civil Officers of the United States, shall be removed from Office on Impeachment for, and Conviction of, Treason, Bribery, or other high Crimes and Misdemeanors.

ARTICLE III.

Section 1—Judicial powers, Tenure. Compensation.

The judicial Power of the United States, shall be vested in one supreme Court, and in such inferior Courts as the Congress may from time to time ordain and establish. The Judges, both of the supreme and inferior Courts, shall hold their Offices during good Behaviour, and shall, at stated Times, receive for their Services, a Compensation, which shall not be diminished during their Continuance in Office.

Section 2—Judicial power; to what cases it extends. Original jurisdiction of Supreme Court; appellate jurisdiction. Trial by jury, etc. Trial, where.

The judicial Power shall extend to all Cases, in Law and Equity, arising under this Constitution, the Laws of the United States, and Treaties made, or which shall be made, under their Authority;–to all Cases affecting Ambassadors, other public Ministers and Consuls;–to all Cases cf admiralty and maritime Jurisdiction;–to Controversies to which the United States shall be a Party;–to Controversies between two or more States;–between a State and Citizens of another State;–between Citizens of different States;–between Citizens of the same State claiming Lands under Grants of different States, and between a State, or the Citizens thereof, and foreign States, Citizens or Subjects.

(This section is modified by Amendment XI.)

In all Cases affecting Ambassadors, other public Ministers and Consuls, and those in which a State shall be Party, the supreme Court shall have original Jurisdiction. In all the other Cases before mentioned, the supreme Court shall have appellate Jurisdiction, both as to Law and Fact, with such Exceptions, and under such Regulations as the Congress shall make.

The trial of all Crimes, except in Cases of Impeachment, shall be by Jury; and such Trial shall be held in the State where the said Crimes shall have been committed; but when not committed within any State, the Trial shall be at such Place or Places as the Congress may by Law have directed.

Section 3—Treason Defined, Proof of, Punishment of.

Treason against the United States, shall consist only in levying War against them, or in adhering to their Enemies, giving them Aid and Comfort. No Person shall be convicted of Treason unless on the Testimony of two Witnesses to the same overt Act, or on Confession in open Court.

The Congress shall have Power to declare the Punishment of Treason, but no Attainder of Treason shall work Corruption of Blood, or Forfeiture except during the Life of the Person attainted.

ARTICLE IV.

Section 1—Each State to give credit to the public acts, etc., of every other State.

Full Faith and Credit shall be given in each State to the public Acts, Records, and judicial Proceedings of every other State. And the Congress may by general Laws prescribe the Manner in which such Acts, Records and Proceedings shall be proved, and the Effect thereof.

Section 2—Privileges of citizens of each State. Fugitives from justice to be delivered up. Persons held to service having escaped, to be delivered up.

The Citizens of each State shall be entitled to all Privileges and Immunities of Citizens in the several States.

A Person charged in any State with Treason, Felony, or other Crime, who shall flee from Justice, and be found in another State, shall on demand of the executive Authority of the State from which he fled, be delivered up, to be removed to the State having Jurisdiction of the Crime.

(No Person held to Service or Labour in one State, under the Laws thereof, escaping into another, shall, in Consequence of any Law or Regulation therein, be discharged from such Service or Labour, but shall be delivered up on Claim of the Party to whom such Service or Labour may be due.) (This clause was superseded by Amendment XIII.)

Section 3—Admission of new States. Power of Congress over territory and other property.

New States may be admitted by the Congress into this Union; but no new State shall be formed or erected within the Jurisdiction of any other State; nor any State be formed by the Junction of two or more States, or parts of States, without the Consent of the Legislatures of the States concerned as well as of the Congress.

The Congress shall have Power to dispose of and make all needful Rules and Regulations respecting the Territory or other Property belonging to the United States; and nothing in this Constitution shall be so construed as to Prejudice any Claims of the United States, or of any particular State.

Section 4—Republican form of government guaranteed. Each state to be protected.

The United States shall guarantee to every State in this Union a Republican Form of Government, and shall protect each of them against Invasion; and on Application of the Legislature, or of the Executive (when the Legislature cannot be convened) against domestic Violence.

ARTICLE V.

Constitution: how amended; proviso.

The Congress, whenever two-thirds of both Houses shall deem it necessary, shall propose Amendments to this Constitution, or, on the Application of the Legislatures of two-thirds of the several States, shall call a Convention for proposing Amendments, which, in either Case, shall be valid to all Intents and Purposes, as part of this Constitution, when ratified by the Legislatures of three-fourths of the several States, or by Conventions in three-fourths thereof, as the one or the other Mode of Ratification may be proposed by the Congress: Provided that no Amendment which may be made prior to the Year One thousand eight hundred and eight shall in any Manner affect the first and fourth Clauses in the Ninth Section of the first Article; and that no State, without its Consent, shall be deprived of its equal Suffrage in the Senate.

ARTICLE VI.

Certain debts, etc., declared valid. Supremacy of Constitution, treaties, and laws of the United States. Oath to support Constitution, by whom taken. No religious test.

All Debts contracted and Engagements entered into, before the Adoption of this Constitution, shall be as valid against the United States under this Constitution, as under the Confederation.

This Constitution, and the Laws of the United States which shall be made in Pursuance thereof; and all Treaties made, or which shall be made, under the Authority of the United States, shall be the supreme Law of the Land; and the Judges in every State shall be bound thereby, any Thing in the Constitution or Laws of any State to the Contrary notwithstanding.

The Senators and Representatives before mentioned, and the Members of the several State Legislatures, and all executive and judicial Officers, both of the United States and of the several States, shall be bound by Oath or Affirmation, to support this Constitution; but no religious Test shall ever be required as a Qualification to any Office or public Trust under the United States.

ARTICLE VII.

What ratification shall establish Constitution.

The Ratification of the Conventions of nine States shall be sufficient for the Establishment of this Constitution between the States so ratifying the Same.

Done in Convention by the Unanimous Consent of the States present the Seventeenth Day of September in the Year of our Lord one thousand seven hundred and Eighty seven and of the Independence of the United States of America the Twelfth.

In Witness whereof We have hereunto subscribed our Names.

Go WASHINGTON, Presidt and deputy from Virginia

New Hampshire—John Langdon, Nicholas Gilman

Massachusetts—Nathaniel Gorham, Rufus King

Connecticut—Wm Saml Johnson, Roger Sherman

New York—Alexander Hamilton

New Jersey—Wil: Livingston, David Brearley, Wm Paterson, Jona: Dayton

Pennsylvania—B Franklin, Thomas Mifflin, Robt. Morris, Geo. Clymer, Thos. FitzSimons, Jared Ingersoll, James Wilson, Gouv Morris

Delaware—Geo: Read, Gunning Bedford jun, John Dickinson, Richard Bassett, Jaco: Broom

Maryland—James McHenry, Dan: of St Thos Jenifer, Danl Carrol

Virginia—John Blair, James Madison Jr.

North Carolina—Wm Blount, Richd. Dobbs Spaight, Hu Williamson

South Carolina—J. Rutledge, Charles Cotesworth Pinckney, Charles Pinckney, Pierce Butler

Georgia—William Few, Abr Baldwin

Attest: William Jackson, Secretary.

Ten Original Amendments: The Bill of Rights

In force Dec. 15, 1791

(The First Congress, at its first session in the City of New York, Sept. 25, 1789, submitted to the states 12 amendments to clarify certain individual and state rights not named in the Constitution. They are generally called the Bill of Rights.

(Influential in framing these amendments was the Declaration of Rights of Virginia, written by George Mason (1725-1792) in 1776. Mason, a Virginia delegate to the Constitutional Convention, did not sign the Constitution and opposed its ratification on the ground that it did not sufficiently oppose slavery or safeguard individual rights.

(In the preamble to the resolution offering the proposed amendments, Congress said: "The conventions of a number of the States having at the time of their adopting the Constitution, expressed a desire, in order to prevent misconstruction or abuse of its powers, that further declaratory and restrictive clauses should be added, and as extending the ground of public confidence in the government will best insure the beneficent ends of its institution, be it resolved," etc.

(Ten of these amendments now commonly known as one to 10 inclusive, but originally 3 to 12 inclusive, were ratified by the states as follows: New Jersey, Nov. 20, 1789; Maryland, Dec. 19, 1789; North Carolina, Dec. 22, 1789; South Carolina, Jan. 19, 1790; New Hampshire, Jan. 25, 1790; Delaware, Jan. 28, 1790; New York, Feb. 27, 1790; Pennsylvania, Mar. 10, 1790; Rhode Island, June 7, 1790; Vermont, Nov. 3, 1791; Virginia, Dec. 15, 1791; Massachusetts, Mar. 2, 1939; Georgia, Mar. 18, 1939; Connecticut, Apr. 19, 1939. These original 10 ratified amendments follow as Amendments I to X inclusive.

(Of the two original proposed amendments that were not ratified promptly by the necessary number of states, the first related to apportionment of Representatives; the second, relating to compensation of members of Congress, was ratified in 1992 and became Amendment 27.)

AMENDMENT I.

Religious establishment prohibited. Freedom of speech, of the press, and right to petition.

Congress shall make no law respecting an establishment of religion, or prohibiting the free exercise thereof; or abridging the freedom of speech, or of the press; or the right of the people peaceably to assemble, and to petition the Government for a redress of grievances.

AMENDMENT II.

Right to keep and bear arms.

A well regulated Militia, being necessary to the security of a free State, the right of the people to keep and bear Arms, shall not be infringed.

AMENDMENT III.

Conditions for quarters for soldiers.

No Soldier shall, in time of peace be quartered in any house, without the consent of the Owner, nor in time of war, but in a manner to be prescribed by law.

AMENDMENT IV.

Right of search and seizure regulated.

The right of the people to be secure in their persons, houses, papers, and effects, against unreasonable searches and seizures, shall not be violated, and no Warrants shall issue, but upon probable cause, supported by Oath or affirmation, and particularly describing the place to be searched, and the persons or things to be seized.

AMENDMENT V.

Provisions concerning prosecution. Trial and punishment—private property not to be taken for public use without compensation.

No person shall be held to answer for a capital, or otherwise infamous crime, unless on a presentment or indictment of a Grand Jury, except in cases arising in the land or naval forces, or in the Militia, when in actual service in time of War or public danger; nor shall any person be subject for the same offence to be twice put in jeopardy of life or limb; nor shall be compelled in any criminal case to be a witness against himself, nor be deprived of life, liberty, or property, without due process of law; nor shall private property be taken for public use, without just compensation.

AMENDMENT VI.

Right to speedy trial, witnesses, etc.

In all criminal prosecutions, the accused shall enjoy the right to a speedy and public trial, by an impartial jury of the State and district wherein the crime shall have been committed, which district shall have been previously ascertained by law, and to be informed of the nature and cause of the accusation; to be confronted with the witnesses against him; to have compulsory process for obtaining witnesses in his favor, and to have the Assistance of Counsel for his defence.

AMENDMENT VII.

Right of trial by jury.

In suits at common law, where the value in controversy shall exceed twenty dollars, the right of trial by jury shall be preserved, and no fact tried by a jury, shall be otherwise reexamined in any Court of the United States, than according to the rules of the common law.

AMENDMENT VIII.

Excessive bail or fines and cruel punishment prohibited.

Excessive bail shall not be required, nor excessive fines imposed, nor cruel and unusual punishments inflicted.

AMENDMENT IX.

Rule of construction of Constitution.

The enumeration in the Constitution, of certain rights, shall not be construed to deny or disparage others retained by the people.

AMENDMENT X.

Rights of States under Constitution.

The powers not delegated to the United States by the Constitution, nor prohibited by it to the States, are reserved to the States respectively, or to the people.

Amendments Since the Bill of Rights

AMENDMENT XI.

Judicial powers construed.

The Judicial power of the United States shall not be construed to extend to any suit in law or equity, commenced or prosecuted against one of the United States by Citizens of another State, or by Citizens or Subjects of any Foreign State.

(This amendment was proposed to the Legislatures of the several States by the Third Congress on March 4, 1794, and was declared to have been ratified in a message from the President to Congress, dated Jan. 8, 1798.

(It was on Jan. 5, 1798, that Secretary of State Pickering received from 12 of the States authenticated ratifications, and informed President John Adams of that fact.

(As a result of later research in the Department of State, it is now established that Amendment XI became part of the Constitution on Feb. 7, 1795, for on that date it had been ratified by 12 States as follows:

(1. New York, Mar. 27, 1794. 2. Rhode Island, Mar. 31, 1794. 3. Connecticut, May 8, 1794. 4. New Hampshire, June 16, 1794. 5. Massachusetts, June 26, 1794. 6. Vermont, between Oct. 9, 1794, and Nov. 9, 1794. 7. Virginia, Nov. 18, 1794. 8. Georgia, Nov. 29, 1794. 9. Kentucky, Dec. 7, 1794.

10. Maryland, Dec. 26, 1794. 11. Delaware, Jan. 23, 1795. 12. North Carolina, Feb. 7, 1795.

(On June 1, 1796, more than a year after Amendment XI had become a part of the Constitution—but before anyone was officially aware of this—Tennessee had been admitted as a State; but not until Oct. 16, 1797, was a certified copy of the resolution of Congress proposing the amendment sent to the Governor of Tennessee, John Sevier, by Secretary of State Pickering, whose office was then at Trenton, New Jersey, because of the epidemic of yellow fever at Philadelphia; it seems, however, that the Legislature of Tennessee took no action on Amendment XI, owing doubtless to the fact that public announcement of its adoption was made soon thereafter.

(Besides the necessary 12 States, one other, South Carolina, ratified Amendment XI, but this action was not taken until Dec. 4, 1797; the two remaining States, New Jersey and Pennsylvania, failed to ratify.)

AMENDMENT XII.

Manner of choosing President and Vice-President.

(Proposed by Congress Dec. 9, 1803; ratified June 15, 1804.)

The Electors shall meet in their respective states and vote by ballot for President and Vice-President, one of whom, at least, shall not be an inhabitant of the same state with themselves; they shall name in their ballots the person voted for as President, and in distinct ballots the person voted for as Vice-President, and they shall make distinct lists of all persons voted for as President, and of all persons voted for as Vice-President, and of the number of votes for each, which lists they shall sign and certify, and transmit sealed to the seat of the government of the United States, directed to the President of the Senate;–The President of the Senate shall, in presence of the Senate and House of Representatives, open all the certificates and the votes shall then be counted;—The person having the greatest number of votes for President, shall be the President, if such number be a majority of the whole number of Electors appointed; and if no person have such majority, then from the persons having the highest numbers not exceeding three on the list of those voted for as President, the House of Representatives shall choose immediately, by ballot, the President. But in choosing the President, the votes shall be taken by states, the representation from each state having one vote; a quorum for this purpose shall consist of a member or members from two-thirds of the states, and a majority of all the states shall be necessary to a choice. *(And if the House of Representatives shall not choose a President whenever the right of choice shall devolve upon them, before the fourth day of March next following, then the Vice-President shall act as President, as in the case of the death or other constitutional disability of the President.) (The words in parentheses were superseded by Amendment XX, section 3.)* The person having the greatest number of votes as Vice-President, shall be the Vice-President, if such number be a majority of the whole number of Electors appointed, and if no person have a majority, then from the two highest numbers on the list, the Senate shall choose the Vice-President; a quorum for the purpose shall consist of two-thirds of the whole number of Senators, and a majority of the whole number shall be necessary to a choice. But no person constitutionally ineligible to the office of President shall be eligible to that of Vice-President of the United States.

THE RECONSTRUCTION AMENDMENTS

(Amendments XIII, XIV, and XV are commonly known as the Reconstruction Amendments, inasmuch as they followed the Civil War, and were drafted by Republicans who were bent on imposing their own policy of reconstruction on the South. Post-bellum legislatures there—Mississippi, South Carolina, Georgia, for example—had set up laws which, it was charged, were contrived to perpetuate Negro slavery under other names.)

AMENDMENT XIII.

Slavery abolished.

(Proposed by Congress Jan. 31, 1865; ratified Dec. 6, 1865. The amendment, when first proposed by a resolution in Congress, was passed by the Senate, 38 to 6, on Apr. 8, 1864, but was defeated in the House, 95 to 66 on June 15, 1864. On reconsideration by the House, on Jan. 31, 1865, the resolution passed, 119 to 56. It was approved by President Lincoln on Feb. 1, 1865, although the Supreme Court had decided in 1798 that the President has nothing to do with the proposing of amendments to the Constitution, or their adoption.)

1. Neither slavery nor involuntary servitude, except as a punishment for crime whereof the party shall have been duly convicted, shall exist within the United States, or any place subject to their jurisdiction.

2. Congress shall have power to enforce this article by appropriate legislation.

AMENDMENT XIV.

Citizenship rights not to be abridged.

(The following amendment was proposed to the Legislatures of the several states by the 39th Congress, June 13, 1866, ratified July 9, 1868, and declared to have been ratified in a proclamation by the Secretary of State, July 28, 1868.

(The 14th amendment was adopted only by virtue of ratification subsequent to earlier rejections. Newly constituted legislatures in both North Carolina and South Carolina (respectively July 4 and 9, 1868), ratified the proposed amendment, although earlier legislatures had rejected the proposal. The Secretary of State issued a proclamation, which, though doubtful as to the effect of attempted withdrawals by Ohio and New Jersey, entertained no doubt as to the validity of the ratification by North and South Carolina. The following day (July 21, 1868), Congress passed a resolution which declared the 14th Amendment to be a part of the Constitution and directed the Secretary of State so to promulgate it. The Secretary waited, however, until the newly constituted Legislature of Georgia had ratified the amendment, subsequent to an earlier rejection, before the promulgation of the ratification of the new amendment.)

1. All persons born or naturalized in the United States, and subject to the jurisdiction thereof, are citizens of the United States and of the State wherein they reside. No State shall make or enforce any law which shall abridge the privileges or immunities of citizens of the United States; nor shall any State deprive any person of life, liberty, or property, without due process of law; nor deny to any person within its jurisdiction the equal protection of the laws.

2. Representatives shall be apportioned among the several States according to their respective numbers, counting the whole number of persons in each State, excluding Indians not taxed. But when the right to vote at any election for the choice of electors for President and Vice-President of the United States, Representatives in Congress, the Executive and Judicial officers of a State, or the members of the Legislature thereof, is denied to any of the male inhabitants of such State, being twenty-one years of age, and citizens of the United States, or in any way abridged, except for participation in rebellion, or other crime, the basis of representation therein shall be reduced in the proportion which the number of such male citizens shall bear to the whole number of male citizens twenty-one years of age in such State.

3. No person shall be a Senator or Representative in Congress, or elector of President and Vice-President, or hold any office, civil or military, under the United States, or under any State, who, having previously taken an oath, as a member of Congress, or as an officer of the United States, or as a member of any State legislature, or as an executive or judicial officer of any State, to support the Constitution of the United States, shall have engaged in insurrection or rebellion against the same, or given aid or comfort to the enemies thereof. But Congress may by a vote of two-thirds of each House, remove such disability.

4. The validity of the public debt of the United States, authorized by law, including debts incurred for payment of pensions and bounties for services in suppressing insurrection or rebellion, shall not be questioned. But neither the United States nor any State shall assume or pay any debt or

obligation incurred in aid of insurrection or rebellion against the United States, or any claim for the loss or emancipation of any slave; but all such debts, obligations and claims shall be held illegal and void.

The Congress shall have power to enforce, by appropriate legislation, the provisions of this article.

AMENDMENT XV.

Race no bar to voting rights.

(The following amendment was proposed to the legislatures of the several States by the 40th Congress, Feb. 26, 1869, and ratified Feb. 8, 1870.)

1. The right of citizens of the United States to vote shall not be denied or abridged by the United States or by any State on account of race, color, or previous condition of servitude–

2. The Congress shall have power to enforce this article by appropriate legislation.

AMENDMENT XVI.

Income taxes authorized.

(Proposed by Congress July 12, 1909; ratified Feb. 3, 1913.)

The Congress shall have power to lay and collect taxes on incomes, from whatever source derived, without apportionment among the several States, and without regard to any census or enumeration.

AMENDMENT XVII.

United States Senators to be elected by direct popular vote.

(Proposed by Congress May 13, 1912; ratified Apr. 8, 1913.)

The Senate of the United States shall be composed of two Senators from each State, elected by the people thereof, for six years; and each Senator shall have one vote. The electors in each State shall have the qualifications requisite for electors of the most numerous branch of the State legislatures.

When vacancies happen in the representation of any State in the Senate, the executive authority of such State shall issue writs of election to fill such vacancies: *Provided*, That the legislature of any State may empower the executive thereof to make temporary appointments until the people fill the vacancies by election as the legislature may direct.

This amendment shall not be so construed as to affect the election or term of any Senator chosen before it becomes valid as part of the Constitution.

AMENDMENT XVIII.

Liquor prohibition amendment.

(Proposed by Congress Dec. 18, 1917; ratified Jan. 16, 1919. Repealed by Amendment XXI, effective Dec. 5, 1933.)

1. After one year from the ratification of this article the manufacture, sale, or transportation of intoxicating liquors within, the importation thereof into, or the exportation thereof from the United States and all territory subject to the jurisdiction thereof for beverage purposes is hereby prohibited.

2. The Congress and the several States shall have concurrent power to enforce this article by appropriate legislation.

3. This article shall be inoperative unless it shall have been ratified as an amendment to the Constitution by the legislatures of the several States as provided in the Constitution, within seven years from the date of the submission hereof to the States by the Congress.

(The total vote in the Senates of the various States was 1,310 for, 237 against—84.6% dry. In the lower houses of the States the vote was 3,782 for, 1,035 against—78.5% dry.

(The amendment ultimately was adopted by all the States except Connecticut and Rhode Island.)

AMENDMENT XIX.

Giving nationwide suffrage to women.

(Proposed by Congress June 4, 1919; ratified Aug. 18, 1920.)

The right of citizens of the United States to vote shall not be denied or abridged by the United States or by any State on account of sex.

Congress shall have power to enforce this Article by appropriate legislation.

AMENDMENT XX.

Terms of President and Vice President to begin on Jan. 20; those of Senators, Representatives, Jan. 3.

(Proposed by Congress Mar. 2, 1932; ratified Jan. 23, 1933.)

1. The terms of the President and Vice President shall end at noon on the 20th day of January, and the terms of Senators and Representatives at noon on the 3d day of January, of the years in which such terms would have ended if this article had not been ratified; and the terms of their successors shall then begin.

2. The Congress shall assemble at least once in every year, and such meeting shall begin at noon on the 3d day of January, unless they shall by law appoint a different day.

3. If, at the time fixed for the beginning of the term of the President, the President elect shall have died, the Vice President elect shall become President. If a President shall not have been chosen before the time fixed for the beginning of his term, or if the President elect shall have failed to qualify, then the Vice President elect shall act as President until a President shall have qualified; and the Congress may by law provide for the case wherein neither a President elect nor a Vice President elect shall have qualified, declaring who shall then act as President, or the manner in which one who is to act shall be selected, and such person shall act accordingly until a President or Vice President shall have qualified.

4. The Congress may by law provide for the case of the death of any of the persons from whom the House of Representatives may choose a President whenever the right of choice shall have devolved upon them, and for the case of the death of any of the persons from whom the Senate may choose a Vice President whenever the right of choice shall have devolved upon them.

5. Sections 1 and 2 shall take effect on the 15th day of October following the ratification of this article (Oct. 1933).

6. This article shall be inoperative unless it shall have been ratified as an amendment to the Constitution by the legislatures of three-fourths of the several States within seven years from the date of its submission.

AMENDMENT XXI.

Repeal of Amendment XVIII.

(Proposed by Congress Feb. 20, 1933; ratified Dec. 5, 1933.)

1. The eighteenth article of amendment to the Constitution of the United States is hereby repealed.

2. The transportation or importation into any State, Territory, or possession of the United States for delivery or use therein of intoxicating liquors, in violation of the laws thereof, is hereby prohibited.

3. This article shall be inoperative unless it shall have been ratified as an amendment to the Constitution by conventions in the several States, as provided in the Constitution, within seven years from the date of the submission hereof to the States by the Congress.

AMENDMENT XXII.

Limiting Presidential terms of office.

(Proposed by Congress Mar. 24, 1947; ratified Feb. 27, 1951.)

1. No person shall be elected to the office of the President more than twice, and no person who has held the office of President, or acted as President, for more than two years of a term to which some other person was elected President shall be elected to the office of the President

more than once. But this Article shall not apply to any person holding the office of President when this Article was proposed by the Congress, and shall not prevent any person who may be holding the office of President, or acting as President, during the term within which this Article becomes operative from holding the office of President or acting as President during the remainder of such term.

2. This article shall be inoperative unless it shall have been ratified as an amendment to the Constitution by the legislatures of three-fourths of the several States within seven years from the date of its submission to the States by the Congress.

AMENDMENT XXIII.

Presidential vote for District of Columbia.

(Proposed by Congress June 16, 1960; ratified Mar. 29, 1961.)

1. The District constituting the seat of Government of the United States shall appoint in such manner as the Congress may direct:

A number of electors of President and Vice President equal to the whole number of Senators and Representatives in Congress to which the District would be entitled if it were a State, but in no event more than the least populous State; they shall be in addition to those appointed by the States, but they shall be considered, for the purposes of the election of President and Vice President, to be electors appointed by a State; and they shall meet in the District and perform such duties as provided by the twelfth article of amendment.

2. The Congress shall have power to enforce this article by appropriate legislation.

AMENDMENT XXIV.

Barring poll tax in federal elections.

(Proposed by Congress Aug. 27, 1962; ratified Jan. 23, 1964.)

1. The right of citizens of the United States to vote in any primary or other election for President or Vice President, for electors for President or Vice President, or for Senator or Representative in Congress, shall not be denied or abridged by the United States or any State by reason of failure to pay any poll tax or other tax.

2. The Congress shall have power to enforce this article by appropriate legislation.

AMENDMENT XXV.

Presidential disability and succession.

(Proposed by Congress July 6, 1965; ratified Feb. 10, 1967.)

1. In case of the removal of the President from office or of his death or resignation, the Vice President shall become President.

2. Whenever there is a vacancy in the office of the Vice President, the President shall nominate a Vice President who shall take office upon confirmation by a majority vote of both houses of Congress.

3. Whenever the President transmits to the President pro tempore of the Senate and the Speaker of the House of Representatives his written declaration that he is unable to discharge the powers and duties of his office, and until he transmits to them a written declaration to the contrary, such powers and duties shall be discharged by the Vice President as Acting President.

4. Whenever the Vice President and a majority of either the principal officers of the executive departments or of such other body as Congress may by law provide, transmit to the President pro tempore of the Senate and the Speaker of the House of Representatives their written declaration that the President is unable to discharge the powers and duties of his office, the Vice President shall immediately assume the powers and duties of the office as Acting President.

Thereafter, when the President transmits to the President pro tempore of the Senate and the Speaker of the House of Representatives his written declaration that no inability exists, he shall resume the powers and duties of his office unless the Vice President and a majority of either the principal officers of the executive department or of such other body as Congress may by law provide, transmit within four days to the President pro tempore of the Senate and the Speaker of the House of Representatives their written declaration that the President is unable to discharge the powers and duties of his office. Thereupon Congress shall decide the issue, assembling within forty-eight hours for that purpose if not in session. If the Congress, within twenty-one days after receipt of the latter written declaration, or, if Congress is not in session, within twenty-one days after Congress is required to assemble, determines by two-thirds vote of both Houses that the President is unable to discharge the powers and duties of his office, the Vice President shall continue to discharge the same as Acting President; otherwise, the President shall resume the powers and duties of his office.

AMENDMENT XXVI.

Lowering voting age to 18 years.

(Proposed by Congress Mar. 23, 1971; ratified July 1, 1971.)

1. The right of citizens of the United States, who are eighteen years of age or older, to vote shall not be denied or abridged by the United States or by any State on account of age.

2. The Congress shall have the power to enforce this article by appropriate legislation.

AMENDMENT XXVII.

Congressional pay.

(Proposed by Congress Sept. 25, 1789; ratified May 7, 1992.)

No law, varying the compensation for the services of the Senators and Representatives, shall take effect, until an election of Representatives shall have intervened.

How a Bill Becomes a Law

1. A Senator or Representative introduces a bill by sending it to the clerk of the House or Senate, who assigns it a number and title. This procedure is termed the *first reading*. The clerk then refers the bill to the appropriate Senate or House committee.
2. If the committee opposes the bill, it will *table,* or kill, it. Otherwise, the committee holds hearings to listen to opinions and facts offered by members and other interested people. The committee then debates the bill and possibly offers amendments. A vote is taken, and if favorable, the bill is sent back to the clerk of the House or Senate.
3. The clerk reads the bill to the house. This is termed the *second reading*. Members may then debate the bill and suggest amendments.
4. After debate and possibly amendment, the bill is given a *third reading,* simply of the title, and put to a voice or roll-call vote.
5. If passed, the bill goes to the other house, where it may be defeated, or passed with or without amendments. If defeated, the bill dies. If passed with amendments, a conference committee made up of members of both houses works out the differences and arrives at a compromise.
6. After passage of the final version by both houses, the bill is sent to the President. If he signs it, the bill becomes a law. However, he may *veto* the bill by refusing to sign it and sending it back to the house where it originated, with his reasons for the veto.
7. The President's objections are then read and debated and a roll-call vote taken. If the bill receives less than a two-thirds vote, it is defeated. If it receives at least two-thirds, it is sent to the other house. If that house also passes it by at least a two-thirds majority, the veto is *overridden*, and the bill becomes a law.
8. If the President neither signs nor vetoes the bill within 10 days–not including Sundays–it automatically becomes a law even without his signature. However, if Congress has adjourned within those 10 days, the bill is automatically killed; this indirect rejection is termed a *pocket veto.*

Confederate States and Secession

The American Civil War, 1861-65, grew out of sectional disputes over the continued existence of slavery in the South and the contention of Southern legislators that the states retained many sovereign rights, including the right to secede from the Union.

The war was not fought by state against state but by one federal regime against another, the Confederate government in Richmond assuming control over the economic, political, and military life of the South, under protest from Georgia and South Carolina.

South Carolina voted an ordinance of secession from the Union, repealing its 1788 ratification of the U.S. Constitution on Dec. 20, 1860, to take effect Dec. 24. Other states seceded in 1861. Their votes in conventions were:

Mississippi, Jan. 9, 84-15; Florida, Jan. 10, 62-7; Alabama, Jan. 11, 61-39; Georgia, Jan. 19, 208-89; Louisiana, Jan. 26, 113-17; Texas, Feb. 1, 166-7, ratified by popular vote Feb. 23 (for 34,794, against 11,325); Virginia, Apr. 17, 88-55, ratified by popular vote May 23 (for 128,884; against 32,134); Arkansas, May 6, 69-1; Tennessee, May 7, ratified by popular vote June 8 (for 104,019, against 47,238); North Carolina, May 21.

Missouri Unionists stopped secession in conventions Feb. 28 and Mar. 9. The legislature condemned secession Mar. 7. Under the protection of Confederate troops, secessionist members of the legislature adopted a resolution of secession at Neosho, Oct. 31. The Confederate Congress seated the secessionists' representatives.

Kentucky did not secede and its government remained Unionist. In a part occupied by Confederate troops, Kentuckians approved secession and the Confederate Congress admitted their representatives.

The Maryland legislature voted against secession Apr. 27, 53-13. Delaware did not secede. Western Virginia held conventions at Wheeling, named a pro-Union governor June 11, 1861; admitted to Union as West Virginia June 20, 1863; its constitution provided for gradual abolition of slavery.

Confederate Government

Forty-two delegates from South Carolina, Georgia, Alabama, Mississippi, Louisiana, and Florida met in convention at Montgomery, Ala., Feb. 4, 1861. They adopted a provisional constitution of the Confederate States of America, and elected Jefferson Davis (Miss.) provisional president, and Alexander H. Stephens (Ga.) provisional vice president.

A permanent constitution was adopted Mar. 11; it abolished the African slave trade. The Congress moved to Richmond, Va., July 20. Davis was elected president in October and was inaugurated Feb. 22, 1862.

The Congress adopted a flag, consisting of a red field with a white stripe, and a blue jack with a circle of white stars. Later the more popular flag was the red field with blue diagonal cross bars that held 13 white stars. The stars represented the 11 states actually in the Confederacy plus Kentucky and Missouri.

Lincoln's Address at Gettysburg, 1863

Fourscore and seven years ago our fathers brought forth on this continent a new nation, conceived in liberty and dedicated to the proposition that all men are created equal.

Now we are engaged in a great civil war, testing whether that nation or any nation so conceived and so dedicated can long endure. We are met on a great battle field of that war. We have come to dedicate a portion of that field, as a final resting-place for those who here gave their lives that that nation might live. It is altogether fitting and proper that we should do this.

But, in a larger sense, we can not dedicate — we can not consecrate — we can not hallow — this ground. The brave men, living and dead, who struggled here, have consecrated it, far above our poor power to add or detract. The world will little note, nor long remember, what we say here, but it can never forget what they did here. It is for us the living, rather, to be dedicated here to the unfinished work which they who fought here have thus far so nobly advanced. It is rather for us to be here dedicated to the great task remaining before us — that from these honored dead we take increased devotion to that cause for which they gave the last full measure of devotion — that we here highly resolve that these dead shall not have died in vain — that this nation, under God, shall have a new birth of freedom — and that government of the people, by the people, for the people, shall not perish from the earth.

Selected Landmark Decisions of the U.S. Supreme Court

1803: Marbury v. Madison. The Court ruled that Congress exceeded its power in the Judiciary Act of 1789; thus, the Court established its power to review acts of Congress and declare invalid those it found in conflict with the Constitution.

1819: McCulloch v. Maryland. The Court ruled that Congress had the authority to charter a national bank, under the Constitution's granting of the power to enact all laws "necessary and proper" to exact the responsibilities of government. The Court also held that the national bank was immune to state taxation.

1819: Trustees of Dartmouth College v. Woodward. The Court ruled that a state could not arbitrarily alter the terms of a college's contract. (In later years the Court widened the implications by using the same principle to limit the states' ability to interfere with business contracts.)

1857: Dred Scott v. Sanford. The Court declared unconstitutional the already-repealed Missouri Compromise of 1820 because it deprived a person of his property—a slave—without due process of law. The Court also ruled that slaves were not citizens of any state nor of the U.S. (The latter part of the decision was overturned by ratification of the 14th Amendment in 1868.)

1896: Plessy v. Ferguson. The Court ruled that a state law requiring federal railroad trains to provide separate but equal facilities for black and white passengers neither infringed upon federal authority to regulate interstate commerce nor violated the 13th and 14th Amendments. (The "separate but equal" doctrine remained effective until the 1954 Brown v. Board of Education decision.)

1904: Northern Securities Co. v. U.S. The Court ruled that a holding company formed solely to eliminate competition between two railroad lines was a combination in restraint of trade, thus a violation of the federal antitrust act.

1908: Muller v. Oregon. The Court ruled to uphold a state law limiting the maximum working hours of women. (Instead of presenting legal arguments, Louis D. Brandeis, counsel for the state, brought forth evidence from social workers, physicians, and factory inspectors that the number of hours women worked affected their health and morals.)

1911: Standard Oil Co. of New Jersey et al. v. U.S. The Court ruled that the Standard Oil Trust must be dissolved because of its unreasonable restraint of trade, not because of its size.

1919: Schenck v. U.S. In its first decision regarding the extent of protection afforded by the First Amendment, the Court sustained the Espionage Act of 1917, maintaining that freedom of speech and press could be constrained if "the words used are in such circumstances and are of such a nature as to create a clear and present danger. . ."

1925: Gitlow v. New York. The Court ruled that the First Amendment prohibition against government abridgement of the freedom of speech applied to the states as well as to the federal government. The decision was the first of a number of rulings holding that the 14th Amendment extended the guarantees of the Bill of Rights to state action.

1935: Schechter Poultry Corp. v. U.S. The Court ruled that Congress exceeded its authority to delegate legislative powers and to regulate interstate commerce when it enacted the National Industrial Recovery Act, which afforded the U.S. president too much discretionary power.

1951: Dennis et al. v. U.S. The Court upheld convictions under the Smith Act of 1940 for speaking about communist theory that advocated the forcible overthrow of the government. (In the 1957 Yates v. U.S. decision, the Court moderated this ruling by allowing such advocacy in the abstract, if not connected to action to achieve the goal.)

1954: Brown v. Board of Education of Topeka. The Court ruled that separate public schools for black and white students were inherently unequal, thus state-sanctioned segregation in public schools violated the equal protection guarantee of the 14th Amendment. And in **Bolling v. Sharpe** the Court ruled that the congressionally-mandated segregated public school system in the District of Columbia violated the Fifth Amendment's due process guarantee of personal liberty. (The Brown ruling also led to the abolition of state-sponsored segregation in other public facilities.)

1957: Roth v. U.S., Alberts v. California. The Court ruled that obscene material was not protected by the First Amendment guarantees of freedom of speech and press, defining obscene as "utterly without redeeming social value" and appealing to "prurient interests" in the view of the average person. (This definition, the first offered by the Court, was modified in several subsequent decisions, and the "average person" standard was replaced by the "local community" standard in the **1973 Miller v. California** case.)

1961: Mapp v. Ohio. The Court ruled that evidence obtained in violation of the 4th Amendment guarantee against unreasonable search and seizure must be excluded from use at state as well as federal trials.

1962: Engel v. Vitale. The Court ruled that public school officials could not require pupils to recite a state-composed prayer at the start of each school day, even if the prayer was non-denominational and pupils who so desired could be excused from reciting it, because such official state sanction of religious utterances was an unconstitutional attempt to establish religion.

1962: Baker v. Carr. The Court held that the constitutional challenges to the unequal distribution of voters among legislative districts could be resolved by federal courts, rejecting the doctrine set out in **Colegrove v. Green** in 1946 that such apportionment challenges were "political questions."

1963: Gideon v. Wainwright. The Court ruled that the due process clause of the 14th Amendment extended to state as well as federal defendants, thus all persons charged with serious crimes must be provided with an attorney, and states were required to appoint counsel for defendants unable to pay their own attorneys' fees.

1964: New York Times Co. v. Sullivan. The Court ruled that the First Amendment guarantee of freedom of the press protected the press from libel suits for defamatory reports on public officials unless the officials proved that the reports were made from actual malice. The Court defined malice as "with knowledge that (the defamatory statement) was false or with reckless disregard of whether it was false or not."

1965: Griswold v. Conn. The Court ruled that a state unconstitutionally interfered with personal privacy in the marriage relationship when it prohibited anyone, including married couples, from using contraceptives.

1966: Miranda v. Arizona. The Court ruled that the guarantee of due process required that before any questioning of suspects in police custody, the suspects must be informed of their right to remain silent, that anything they say may be used against them, and that they have the right to counsel.

1973: Roe v. Wade, Doe v. Bolton. The Court ruled that the right to privacy inherent in the 14th Amendment's due process guarantee of personal liberty protected a woman's decision whether or not to bear a child, and was impermissibly abridged by state laws that made abortion a crime. During the first trimester of pregnancy, the Court maintained, the decision to have an abortion should be left entirely to a woman and her physician.

1974: U.S. v. Nixon. The Court ruled that neither the separation of powers nor the need to preserve the confidentiality of presidential communications could alone justify an absolute executive privilege of immunity from judicial demands for evidence to be used in a criminal trial.

1976: Gregg v. Georgia, Profitt v. Fla., Jurek v. Texas. The Court held that death, as a punishment for persons convicted of first degree murder, was not in and of itself cruel and unusual punishment in violation of the 8th Amendment. The Court also ruled that the Amendment required the sentencing judge and jury to consider the individual character of the offender and the circumstances of the particular crime before deciding whether or not to impose the death sentence. In the associated **Woodson v. N.C., Roberts v. La.,** the Court ruled that states could not make death the mandatory penalty for first-degree murder, since that would fail to meet the constitutional requirement for the consideration of the individual offender and offense.

1978: Regents of Univ. of Calif. v. Bakke. The Court ruled that a special admissions program for a state medical school under which a set number of places were set aside for minority group members, with white applicants denied the opportunity to compete for those seats, violated Title XIV of the 1964 Civil Rights Act, which forbids the exclusion of anyone, because of race, from participation in a federally-funded program. The Court also ruled that admissions programs that considered race as one of a complex of factors involved in the decision to admit or reject an applicant were not unconstitutional.

1979: United Steelworkers of America v. Weber, Kaiser Aluminum v. Weber, U.S. v. Weber. The Court ruled that Title VII of the 1964 Civil Rights Act, which forbids racial discrimination in employment, did not forbid employers to adopt voluntarily race-conscious affirmative action programs to encourage minority participation in areas in which they traditionally were underrepresented.

1986: Bowers v. Hardwick. The Court refused to extend the right of privacy inherent in the Constitution to homosexual activity, upholding a Georgia law that made sodomy a crime. (Although the Georgia law covered heterosexual sodomy as well as homosexual sodomy, enforcement in Georgia and most other states had been confined to homosexual activity.)

1990: Cruzan v. Missouri. The Court ruled that a person had the right to refuse life-sustaining medical treatment. However, the Court also ruled that, in the case of a comatose patient, a state could require "clear and convincing evidence" that the patient would not have wanted to live under those conditions before such treatment could be withheld.

Presidential Oath of Office

The Constitution (Article II) directs that the President shall take the following oath or affirmation: "I do solemnly swear (affirm) that I will faithfully execute the office of President of the United States, and will, to the best of my ability, preserve, protect, and defend the Constitution of the United States." (Custom decrees the use of the words "So help me God" at the end of the oath when taken by the President-elect, his/her left hand on the Bible for the duration of the oath, with his/her right hand slightly raised.)

Law on Succession to the Presidency

If by reason of death, resignation, removal from office, inability, or failure to qualify there is neither a president nor vice president to discharge the powers and duties of the office of president, then the speaker of the House of Representatives shall upon his resignation as speaker and as representative, act as president. The same rule shall apply in the case of the death, resignation, removal from office, or inability of an individual acting as president.

If at the time when a speaker is to begin the discharge of the powers and duties of the office of president there is no speaker, or the speaker fails to qualify as acting president, then the president pro tempore of the Senate, upon his resignation as president pro tempore and as senator, shall act as president.

An individual acting as president shall continue to act until the expiration of the then current presidential term, except that (1) if his discharge of the powers and duties of the office is founded in whole or in part in the failure of both the president-elect and the vice president-elect to qualify, then he shall act only until a president or vice president qualifies, and (2) if his discharge of the powers and duties of the office is founded in whole or in part on the inability of the president or vice president, then he shall act only until the removal of the disability of one of such individuals.

If, by reason of death, resignation, removal from office, or failure to qualify, there is no president pro tempore to act as president, then the officer of the United States who is highest on the following list, and who is not under any disability to discharge the powers and duties of president shall act as president; the secretaries of state, treasury, defense, attorney general; secretaries of interior, agriculture, commerce, labor, health and human services, housing and urban development, transportation, energy, education, veterans affairs.

(Legislation approved July 18, 1947; amended Sept. 9, 1965, Oct. 15, 1966, Aug. 4, 1977, and Sept. 27, 1979. See also Constitutional Amendment XXV.)

Origin of the United States National Motto

In God We Trust, designated as the U.S. National Motto by Congress in 1956, originated during the Civil War as an inscription for U. S. coins, although it was used by Francis Scott Key in a slightly different form when he wrote The Star Spangled Banner in 1814. On Nov. 13, 1861, when Union morale had been shaken by battlefield defeats, the Rev. M. R. Watkinson, of Ridleyville, Pa., wrote to Secy. of the Treasury Salmon P. Chase. "From my heart I have felt our national shame in disowning God as not the least of our present national disasters," the minister wrote, suggesting "recognition of the Almighty God in some form on our coins." Secy. Chase ordered designs prepared with the inscription *In God We Trust* and backed coinage legislation that authorized use of this slogan. It first appeared on some U.S. coins in 1864, disappeared and reappeared on various coins until 1955, when Congress ordered it placed on all paper money and all coins.

The Great Seal of the U.S.

On July 4, 1776, the Continental Congress appointed a committee consisting of Benjamin Franklin, John Adams, and Thomas Jefferson "to bring in a device for a seal of the United States of America." The designs submitted by this and a subsequent committee were considered unacceptable. After many delays, a third committee, appointed early in 1782, presented a design prepared by William Barton. Charles Thomson, the secretary of Congress, suggested certain changes, and Congress finally approved the design on June 20, 1782. The obverse side of the seal shows an American bald eagle. In its mouth is a ribbon bearing the motto *e pluribus unum* (one out of many). In the eagle's talons are the arrows of war and an olive branch of peace. The reverse side shows an unfinished pyramid with an eye (the eye of Providence) above it.

The American's Creed

William Tyler Page, Clerk of the U.S. House of Representatives, wrote "The American's Creed" in 1917. It was accepted by the House on behalf of the American people on April 3, 1918.

"I believe in the United States of America as a government of the people, by the people, for the people; whose just powers are derived from the consent of the governed; a democracy in a republic; a sovereign Nation of many sovereign States; a perfect union, one and inseparable; established upon those principles of freedom, equality, justice, and humanity for which American patriots sacrificed their lives and fortunes.

"I therefore believe it is my duty to my country to love it, to support its Constitution, to obey its laws, to respect its flag, and to defend it against all enemies."

The Flag of the U.S.—The Stars and Stripes

The 50-star flag of the United States was raised for the first time officially at 12:01 a.m. on July 4, 1960, at Fort McHenry National Monument in Baltimore, Md. The 50th star had been added for Hawaii; a year earlier the 49th, for Alaska. Before that, no star had been added since 1912, when N.M. and Ariz. were admitted to the Union.

The true history of the Stars and Stripes has become so cluttered by a volume of myth and tradition that the facts are difficult, and in some cases impossible, to establish. For example, it is not certain who designed the Stars and Stripes, who made the first such flag, or even whether it ever flew in any sea fight or land battle of the American Revolution.

One thing all agree on is that the Stars and Stripes originated as the result of a resolution offered by the Marine Committee of the Second Continental Congress at Philadelphia and adopted June 14, 1777. It read:

Resolved: that the flag of the United States be thirteen stripes, alternate red and white; that the union be thirteen stars, white in a blue field, representing a new constellation.

Congress gave no hint as to the designer of the flag, no instructions as to the arrangement of the stars, and no information on its appropriate uses. Historians have been unable to find the original flag law.

The resolution establishing the flag was not even published until Sept. 2, 1777. Despite repeated requests, Washington did not get the flags until 1783, after the Revolutionary War was over. And there is no certainty that they were the Stars and Stripes.

Early Flags

Although it was never officially adopted by the Continental Congress, many historians consider the first flag of the U.S. to have been the Grand Union (sometimes called Great Union) flag. This was a modification of the British Meteor flag, which had the red cross of St. George and the white cross of St. Andrew combined in the blue canton. For the Grand Union flag, 6 horizontal stripes were imposed on the red field, dividing it into 13 alternate red and white stripes. On Jan. 1, 1776, when the Continental Army came into formal existence, this flag was unfurled on Prospect Hill, Somerville, Mass. Washington wrote that "we hoisted the Union Flag in compliment to the United Colonies."

One of several flags about which controversy has raged for years is at Easton, Pa. Containing the devices of the national flag in reversed order, this has been in the public library at Easton for over 150 years. Some contend that this flag was actually the first Stars and Stripes, first displayed on July 8, 1776. This flag has 13 red and white stripes in the canton, 13 white stars centered in a blue field.

A flag was hastily improvised from garments by the defenders of Fort Schuyler at Rome, N.Y., Aug. 3-22, 1777. Historians believe it was the Grand Union Flag.

The Sons of Liberty had a flag of 9 red and white stripes, to signify 9 colonies, when they met in New York in 1765 to oppose the Stamp Tax. By 1775, the flag had grown to 13 red and white stripes, with a rattlesnake on it.

At Concord, Apr. 19, 1775, the minute men from Bedford, Mass., are said to have carried a flag having a silver arm with sword on a red field.

At Cambridge, Mass., the Sons of Liberty used a plain red flag with a green pine tree on it.

In June 1775, Washington went from Philadelphia to Boston to take command of the army, escorted to New York by the Philadelphia Light Horse Troop. It carried a yellow flag which had an elaborate coat of arms — the shield charged with 13 knots, the motto "For These We Strive" — and a canton of 13 blue and silver stripes.

In Feb., 1776, Col. Christopher Gadsden, member of the Continental Congress, gave the S. Carolina Provincial Congress a flag "such as is to be used by the commander-in-chief of the American Navy." It had a yellow field, with a rattlesnake about to strike and the words "Don't Tread on Me."

At the battle of Bennington, Aug. 16, 1777, patriots used a flag of 7 white and 6 red stripes with a blue canton extending down 9 stripes and showing an arch of 11 white stars over the figure 76 and a star in each of the upper corners. The stars are seven-pointed. This flag is preserved in the Historical Museum at Bennington, Vt.

At the Battle of Cowpens, Jan. 17, 1781, the 3d Maryland Regt. is said to have carried a flag of 13 red and white stripes, with a blue canton containing 12 stars in a circle around one star.

Who Designed the Flag? No one knows for certain. Francis Hopkinson, designer of a naval flag, declared he also had designed the flag and in 1781 asked Congress to reimburse him for his services. Congress did not do so. Dumas Malone of Columbia Univ. wrote: "This talented man … designed the American flag."

Who Called the Flag Old Glory? — The flag is said to have been named Old Glory by William Driver, a sea captain of Salem, Mass. One legend has it that when he raised the flag on his brig, the Charles Doggett, in 1824, he said: "I name thee Old Glory." But his daughter, who presented the flag to the Smithsonian Institution, said he named it at his 21st birthday celebration Mar. 17, 1824, when his mother presented the homemade flag to him.

The Betsy Ross Legend — The widely publicized legend that Mrs. Betsy Ross made the first Stars and Stripes in June 1776, at the request of a committee composed of George Washington, Robert Morris, and George Ross, an uncle, was first made public in 1870, by a grandson of Mrs. Ross. Historians have been unable to find a historical record of such a meeting or committee.

Adding New Stars

The flag of 1777 was used until 1795. Then, on the admission of Vermont and Kentucky to the Union, Congress passed and Pres. Washington signed an act that after May 1, 1795, the flag should have 15 stripes, alternate red and white, and 15 white stars on a blue field in the union.

When new states were admitted it became evident that the flag would become burdened with stripes. Congress thereupon ordered that after July 4, 1818, the flag should have 13 stripes, symbolizing the 13 original states; that the union have 20 stars, and that whenever a new state was admitted a new star should be added on the July 4 following admission. No law designates the permanent arrangement of the stars. However, since 1912 when a new state has been admitted, the new design has been announced by executive order. No star is specifically identified with any state.

Code of Etiquette for Display and Use of the U.S. Flag

Although the Stars and Stripes originated in 1777, it was not until 146 years later that there was a serious attempt to establish a uniform code of etiquette for the U.S. flag. The War Department issued Feb. 15, 1923, a circular on the rules of flag usage. These were adopted almost in their entirety June 14, 1923, by a conference of 68 patriotic organizations in Washington. Finally, on June 22, 1942, a joint resolution of Congress, amended by Public Law 94-344 July 7, 1976, codified "existing rules and customs pertaining to the display and use of the flag…"

When to Display the Flag—The flag should be displayed on all days, especially on legal holidays and other special occasions, on official buildings when in use, in or near polling places on election days, and in or near schools when in session. Citizens may fly the flag at any time they wish. It is customary to display the flag only from sunrise to sunset on buildings and on stationary flagstaffs in the open. However, it may be displayed at night on special occasions, preferably lighted. In Washington, the flag now flies over the White House both day and night. It flies over the Senate wing of the Capitol when the Senate is in session and over the House wing when that body is in session. It flies day and night over the east and west fronts of the Capitol, without floodlights at night but receiving light from the illuminated Capitol Dome. It flies 24 hours a day at several other places, including the Fort McHenry Nat'l Monument in Baltimore, where it inspired Francis Scott Key to write The Star Spangled Banner. The flag also flies 24 hours a day, properly illuminated, at U.S. Customs ports of entry.

How to Fly the Flag—The flag should be hoisted briskly and lowered ceremoniously, and should never be allowed to touch the ground or the floor. When hung over a sidewalk from a rope extending from a building to a pole, the union should be away from the building. When hung over the center of a street it should have the union to the north in an east-west street and to the east in a north-south street. No other flag may be flown above or, if on the same level, to the right of the U.S. flag, except that at the United Nations Headquarters the UN flag may be placed above flags of all member nations and other national flags may be flown with equal prominence or honor with the flag of the U.S. At services by Navy chaplains at sea, the church pennant may be flown above the flag.

When two flags are placed against a wall with crossed staffs, the U.S. flag should be at right—its own right, and its staff should be in front of the staff of the other flag; when a number of flags are grouped and displayed from staffs, it should be at the center and highest point of the group.

Church and Platform Use—In an auditorium, the flag may be displayed flat, above and behind the speaker. When displayed from a staff in a church or public auditorium, the flag should hold the position of superior prominence, in advance of the audience, and in the position of honor at the clergyman's or speaker's right as he faces the audience. Any other flag so displayed should be placed on the left of the clergyman or speaker or to the right of the audience.

When the flag is displayed horizontally or vertically against a wall, the stars should be uppermost and at the observer's left.

How to Dispose of Worn Flags—The flag, when it is in such condition that it is no longer a fitting emblem for display, should be destroyed in a dignified way, preferably by burning.

When to Salute the Flag—All persons present should face the flag, stand at attention and salute on the following occasions: (1) When the flag is passing in a parade or in a review, (2) During the ceremony of hoisting or lowering, (3) When the National Anthem is played, and (4) During the Pledge of Allegiance. Those present in uniform should render the military salute. Those not in uniform should place the right hand over the heart. A man wearing a hat should remove it with his right hand and hold it to his left shoulder during the salute.

On Memorial Day, the flag should fly at half-staff until noon, then be raised to the peak.

As provided by Presidential proclamation the flag should fly at half-staff for 30 days from the day of death of a president or former president; for 10 days from the day of death of a vice president, chief justice or retired chief justice of the U.S., or speaker of the House of Representatives; from day of death until burial of an associate justice of the Supreme Court, cabinet member, former vice president, or Senate president pro tempore, majority or minority Senate leader, or majority or minority House leader; for a U.S. senator, representative, territorial delegate, or the resident commissioner of Puerto Rico, on day of death and the following day within the metropolitan area of the District of Columbia and from day of death until burial within the decedent's state, congressional district, territory or commonwealth; and for the death of the governor of a state, territory, or possession of the U.S., from day of death until burial within that state, territory, or possession.

When used to cover a casket, the flag should be placed so that the union is at the head and over the left shoulder. It should not be lowered into the grave nor touch the ground.

Prohibited Uses of the Flag—The flag should not be dipped to any person or thing. (An exception—customarily, ships salute by dipping their colors.) It should never be displayed with the union down save as a distress signal. It should never be carried flat or horizontally, but always aloft and free.

It should not be displayed on a float, motor car or boat except from a staff.

It should never be used as a covering for a ceiling, nor have placed upon it any word, design, or drawing. It should never be used as a receptacle for carrying anything. It should not be used to cover a statue or a monument.

The flag should never be used for advertising purposes, nor be embroidered on such articles as cushions or hankerchiefs, printed or otherwise impressed on boxes or anything that is designed for temporary use and discard; or used as a costume or athletic uniform. Advertising signs should not be fastened to its staff or halyard.

The flag should never be used as drapery of any sort, never festooned, drawn back, nor up, in folds, but always allowed to fall free. Bunting of blue, white and red always arranged with the blue above and the white in the middle, should be used for covering a speaker's desk, draping the front of a platform, and for decoration in general.

An Act of Congress approved Feb. 8, 1917, provided certain penalties for the desecration, mutilation or improper use of the flag within the District of Columbia. A 1968 federal law provided penalties of up to a year's imprisonment or a $1,000 fine or both, for publicly burning or otherwise desecrating any flag of the United States. In addition, many states have laws against flag desecration. In 1989, the Supreme Court ruled that no laws could prohibit political protesters from burning the flag. The decision had the effect of declaring unconstitutional the flag desecration laws of 48 states, as well as a similar Federal statute, in cases of peaceful political expression.

The Supreme Court, June 1990, declared that a new Federal law making it a crime to burn or deface the American flag violates the free-speech guarantee of the First Amendment. The 5-4 decision led to renewed calls in Congress for a constitutional amendment to make it possible to prosecute flag burning.

Pledge of Allegiance to the Flag

I pledge allegiance to the flag of the United States of America and to the republic for which it stands, one nation under God, indivisible, with liberty and justice for all.

This, the current official version of the Pledge of Allegiance, has developed from the original pledge, which was first published in the Sept. 8, 1892, issue of the Youth's Companion, a weekly magazine then published in Boston. The original pledge contained the phrase "my flag," which was changed more than 30 years later to "flag of the United States of America." An act of Congress in 1954 added the words "under God."

The authorship of the pledge had been in dispute for many years. The Youth's Companion stated in 1917 that the original draft was written by James B. Upham, an executive of the magazine who died in 1910. A leaflet circulated by the magazine later named Upham as the originator of the draft "afterwards condensed and perfected by him and his associates of the Companion force."

Francis Bellamy, a former member of the Youth's Companion editorial staff, publicly claimed authorship of the pledge in 1923. The United States Flag Assn., acting on the advice of a committee named to study the controversy, upheld in 1939 the claim of Bellamy, who had died 8 years earlier. The Library of Congress issued in 1957 a report attributing the authorship to Bellamy.

The History of the National Anthem

The Star-Spangled Banner was ordered played by the military and naval services by President Woodrow Wilson in 1916. It was designated the National Anthem by Act of Congress, Mar. 3, 1931. It was written by Francis Scott Key, of Georgetown, D.C., during the bombardment of Fort McHenry, Baltimore, Md., Sept. 13-14, 1814. Key was a lawyer, a graduate of St. John's College, Annapolis, and a volunteer in a light artillery company. When a friend, Dr. Beanes, a physician of Upper Marlborough, Md., was taken aboard Admiral Cockburn's British squadron for interfering with ground troops, Key and J. S. Skinner, carrying a note from President Madison, went to the fleet under a flag of truce on a cartel ship to ask Beanes' release. Admiral Cockburn consented, but as the fleet was about to sail up the Patapsco to bombard Fort McHenry he detained them, first on H. M. S. Surprise, and then on a supply ship.

Key witnessed the bombardment from his own vessel. It began at 7 a.m., Sept. 13, 1814, and lasted, with intermissions, for 25 hours. The British fired over 1,500 shells, each weighing as much as 220 lbs. They were unable to approach closely because the Americans had sunk 22 vessels in the channel. Only four Americans were killed and 24 wounded. A British bomb-ship was disabled.

During the bombardment Key wrote a stanza on the back of an envelope. Next day at Indian Queen Inn, Baltimore, he wrote out the poem and gave it to his brother-in-law, Judge J. H. Nicholson. Nicholson suggested the tune, Anacreon in Heaven, and had the poem printed on broadsides, of which two survive. On Sept. 20 it appeared in the "Baltimore American." Later Key made 3 copies; one is in the Library of Congress and one in the Pennsylvania Historical Society.

The copy that Key wrote in his hotel Sept. 14, 1814, remained in the Nicholson family for 93 years. In 1907 it was sold to Henry Walters of Baltimore. In 1934 it was bought at auction in New York from the Walters estate by the Walters Art Gallery, Baltimore, for $26,400. The Walters Gallery in 1953 sold the manuscript to the Maryland Historical Society for the same price.

The flag that Key saw during the bombardment is preserved in the Smithsonian Institution, Washington. It is 30 by 42 ft., and has 15 alternate red and white stripes and 15 stars, for the original 13 states plus Kentucky and Vermont. It was made by Mary Young Pickersgill. The Baltimore Flag House, a museum, occupies her premises, which were restored in 1953.

The Star-Spangled Banner

I

Oh, say can you see by the dawn's early light
What so proudly we hailed at the twilight's last gleaming?
Whose broad stripes and bright stars thru the perilous fight,
O'er the ramparts we watched were so gallantly streaming?
And the rocket's red glare, the bombs bursting in air,
Gave proof through the night that our flag was still there.
Oh, say does that star-spangled banner yet wave
O'er the land of the free and the home of the brave?

II

On the shore, dimly seen through the mists of the deep,
Where the foe's haughty host in dread silence reposes,
What is that which the breeze, o'er the towering steep,
As it fitfully blows, half conceals, half discloses?
Now it catches the gleam of the morning's first beam,
In full glory reflected now shines in the stream:
'Tis the star-spangled banner! Oh long may it wave
O'er the land of the free and the home of the brave!

III

And where is that band who so vauntingly swore
That the havoc of war and the battle's confusion,
A home and a country should leave us no more!
Their blood has washed out their foul footsteps' pollution.
No refuge could save the hireling and slave
From the terror of flight, or the gloom of the grave:
And the star-spangled banner in triumph doth wave
O'er the land of the free and the home of the brave!

IV

Oh! thus be it ever, when freemen shall stand
Between their loved home and the war's desolation!
Blest with victory and peace, may the heav'n rescued land
Praise the Power that hath made and preserved us a nation.
Then conquer we must, when our cause it is just,
And this be our motto: "In God is our trust."
And the star-spangled banner in triumph shall wave
O'er the land of the free and the home of the brave!

America
(My Country 'Tis of Thee)

First sung in public on July 4, 1831, at a service in the Park Street Church, Boston, the words were written by Rev. Samuel Francis Smith, a Baptist clergyman, who set them to a melody he found in a German songbook, unaware that it was the tune for the British anthem, "God Save the King/Queen."

My country, 'tis of thee,
Sweet land of liberty, Of thee I sing.
Land where my fathers died!
Land of the Pilgrims' pride!
From ev'ry mountainside,
Let freedom ring!

My native country, thee,
Land of the noble free,
Thy name I love.
I love thy rocks and rills,
Thy woods and templed hills;
My heart with rapture thrills
Like that above.

Let music swell the breeze,
And ring from all the trees
Sweet freedom's song.
Let mortal tongues awake;
Let all that breathe partake;
Let rocks their silence break,
The sound prolong.

Our fathers' God, to Thee,
Author of liberty,
To Thee we sing.
Long may our land be bright
With freedom's holy light;
Protect us by Thy might,
Great God, our King!

America, the Beautiful

Composed by Katherine Lee Bates, a Massachusetts educator and author, in 1893. It was inspired by the view Bates experienced atop Pikes Peak. Its final form was established in 1911 and is set to the music of Samuel A. Ward's "Materna."

O beautiful for spacious skies,
For amber waves of grain,
For purple mountain majesties
Above the fruited plain.
America! America!
God shed His grace on thee,
And crown thy good with brotherhood
From sea to shining sea.
O beautiful for pilgrim feet
Whose stern impassion'd stress
A thorough-fare for freedom beat
Across the wilderness.
America! America!
God mend thine ev'ry flaw,
Confirm thy soul in self control,
Thy liberty in law.

O beautiful for heroes prov'd
In liberating strife,
Who more than self their country lov'd
And mercy more than life.
America! America!
May God thy gold refine
Till all success be nobleness,
And ev'ry gain divine.
O beautiful for patriot dream
That sees beyond the years,
Thine alabaster cities gleam,
Undimmed by human tears.
America! America!
God shed His grace on thee,
And crown thy good with brotherhood
From sea to shining sea.

The Liberty Bell: Its History and Significance

The Liberty Bell, in Independence Hall, Philadelphia, is an object of great reverence to Americans because of its association with the historic events of the War of Independence.

The original Province bell, ordered to commemorate the 50th anniversary of the Commonwealth of Pennsylvania, was cast by Thomas Lister, Whitechapel, London, and reached Philadelphia in Aug. 1752. It bore an inscription from Leviticus XXV, 10: "Proclaim liberty throughout all the land unto all the inhabitants thereof."

The bell was cracked by a stroke of its clapper in Sept. 1752 while it hung on a truss in the State House yard for testing. Pass & Stow, Philadelphia founders, recast the bell, adding 1½ ounces of copper to a pound of the original metal to reduce brittleness. It was found that the bell contained too much copper, injuring its tone, so Pass & Stow recast it again, this time successfully.

In June 1753 the bell was hung in the wooden steeple of the State House, erected on top of the brick tower. In use while the Continental Congress was in session in the State House, it rang out in defiance of British tax and trade restrictions, and proclaimed the Boston Tea Party and the first public reading of the Declaration of Independence.

On Sept. 18, 1777, when the British Army was about to occupy Philadelphia, the bell was moved in a baggage train of the American Army to Allentown, Pa., where it was hidden in the Zion Reformed Church until June 27, 1778. It was moved back to Philadelphia after the British left.

In July 1781 the wooden steeple became insecure and had to be taken down. The bell was lowered into the brick section of the tower. Because of its association with the War of Independence it was not recast but remained mute in this location until 1846, the year of the Mexican War, when it was placed on exhibition in the Declaration Chamber of Independence Hall.

In 1876, when many thousands of Americans visited Philadelphia for the Centennial Exposition, it was placed in its old walnut frame in the tower hallway. In 1877 it was hung from the ceiling of the tower by a chain of 13 links. It was returned again to the Declaration Chamber and in 1896 taken back to the tower hall, where it occupied a glass case. In 1915 the case was removed so that the public might touch it. On Jan. 1, 1976, just after midnight to mark the opening of the Bicentennial Year, the bell was moved to a new glass and steel pavilion behind Independence Hall for easier viewing by the larger number of visitors expected during the year.

The measurements of the bell follow: circumference around the lip, 12 ft.; circumference around the crown, 7 ft. 6 in.; lip to the crown, 3 ft.; height over the crown, 2 ft. 3 in.; thickness at lip, 3 in.; thickness at crown, 1¼ in.; weight, 2080 lbs.; length of clapper, 3 ft. 2 in.; cost, £60 14s 5d.

The specific source of the crack in the bell is unknown.

Statue of Liberty National Monument

Since 1886, the Statue of Liberty Enlightening the World has stood as a symbol of freedom in New York harbor. It also commemorates French-American friendship, for it was given by the people of France and designed by French sculptor Frederic Auguste Bartholdi (1834-1904).

Edouard de Laboulaye, French historian and admirer of American political institutions, suggested that the French present a monument to the United States, the latter to provide pedestal and site. Bartholdi visualized a colossal statue at the entrance of New York harbor, welcoming the peoples of the world with the torch of liberty.

On Washington's Birthday, Feb. 22, 1877, Congress approved the use of a site on Bedloe's Island suggested by Bartholdi. This island of 12 acres had been owned in the 17th century by a Walloon named Isaac Bedloe. It was called Bedloe's until Aug. 3, 1956, when Pres. Eisenhower approved a resolution of Congress changing the name to Liberty Island.

The statue was finished May 21, 1884, and formally presented to the U.S. minister to France, Levi Parsons Morton, July 4, 1884, by Ferdinand de Lesseps, head of the Franco-American Union, promoter of the Panama Canal, and builder of the Suez Canal.

On Aug. 5, 1884, the Americans laid the cornerstone for the pedestal. This was to be built on the foundations of Fort Wood, which had been erected by the government in 1811. The American committee had raised $125,000, but this was found to be inadequate. Joseph Pulitzer, owner of the *New York World,* appealed on Mar. 16, 1885, for general donations. By Aug. 11, 1885, he had raised $100,000.

The statue arrived dismantled, in 214 packing cases, from Rouen, France, in June 1885. The last rivet of the statue was driven Oct. 28, 1886, when Pres. Grover Cleveland dedicated the monument.

The statue weighs 450,000 lbs., or 225 tons. The copper sheeting weighs 200,000 lbs. There are 167 steps from the land level to the top of the pedestal, 168 steps inside the statue to the head, and 54 rungs on the ladder leading to the arm that holds the torch.

A $2.5 million building housing the American Museum of Immigration was opened by Pres. Richard Nixon Sept. 26, 1972, at the base of the statue. It houses a permanent exhibition of photos, posters, and artifacts tracing the history of American immigration. The Statue of Liberty National Monument is administered by the National Park Service.

Two years of restoration work was completed before the statue's centennial celebration on July 4, 1986. Among other repairs, the multimillion dollar project included replacing the 1,600 wrought iron bands that hold the statue's copper skin to its frame, replacing its torch, and installing an elevator.

A four-day extravaganza of concerts, tall ships, ethnic festivals, and fireworks celebrated the 100th anniversary. The festivities included Chief Justice Warren E. Burger's swearing-in of 5,000 new citizens on Ellis Island, while 20,000 others across the country were simultaneously sworn in through a satellite telecast.

The ceremonies were followed by others on Oct. 28, 1986, the statue's 100th birthday.

Ellis Island was the gateway to America for more than 12 million immigrants between 1892 and 1924. In the late 18th century, Samuel Ellis, a New York City merchant purchased the island and gave it his name. From Ellis, it passed to New York State, and the U.S. government bought it in 1808. In 1892 the government opened an immigration center on the island. The 27½-acre site eventually supported more than 35 buildings, including the Main Building with its Great Hall, in which up to 5,000 people a day were processed during peak periods. Closed as an immigration station in 1954, Ellis Island was proclaimed part of the National Monument in 1965 by Pres. Lyndon B. Johnson. After an 8-year privately funded $156 million restoration project, Ellis Island was reopened as a museum in 1990. Artifacts, historic photographs and documents, oral histories, and ethnic music depicting 400 years of American immigration are housed in the museum. The museum also includes the American Immigrant Wall of Honor, inscribed with some 420,000 names.

Emma Lazarus' Famous Poem

A poem by Emma Lazarus is graven on a tablet within the pedestal on which the statue stands.

The New Colossus

Not like the brazen giant of Greek fame,
With conquering limbs astride from land to land;
Here at our sea-washed, sunset gates shall stand
A mighty woman with a torch, whose flame
Is the imprisoned lightning, and her name
Mother of Exiles. From her beacon-hand
Glows world-wide welcome; her mild eyes command
The air-bridged harbor that twin cities frame.
"Keep ancient lands, your storied pomp!" cries she
With silent lips. "Give me your tired, your poor,
Your huddled masses yearning to breathe free,
The wretched refuse of your teeming shore.
Send these, the homeless, tempest-tost to me,
I lift my lamp beside the golden door!"

Dimensions of the Statue	Ft.	In.
Height from base to torch (45.3 meters)	151	1
Foundation of pedestal to torch (91.5 meters)	305	1
Heel to top of head	111	1
Length of hand	16	5
Index finger	8	0
Circumference at second joint	3	6
Size of finger nail	13x10 in.	
Head from chin to cranium	17	3
Head thickness from ear to ear	10	0
Distance across the eye	2	6
Length of nose	4	6
Right arm, length	42	0
Right arm, greatest thickness	12	0
Thickness of waist	35	0
Width of mouth	3	0
Tablet, length	23	7
Tablet, width	13	7
Tablet, thickness	2	0

BIOGRAPHIES OF U.S. PRESIDENTS

George Washington (1789-1797)

George Washington, first president, was born Feb. 22, 1732 (Feb. 11, 1732, old style), the son of Augustine Washington and Mary Ball, at Wakefield on Pope's Creek, Westmoreland Co., Va. His early childhood was spent on a farm, near Fredericksburg. His father died when George was 11. He studied mathematics and surveying and when 16 went to live with his half brother Lawrence, who built and named Mount Vernon. George surveyed the lands of William Fairfax in the Shenandoah Valley, keeping a diary. He accompanied Lawrence to Barbados, West Indies, contracted small pox, and was deeply scarred. Lawrence died in 1752 and George acquired his property by inheritance. He valued land and when he died owned 70,000 acres in Virginia and 40,000 acres in what is now West Virginia.

Washington's military service began in 1753 when Gov. Dinwiddie of Virginia sent him on missions deep into Ohio country. He clashed with the French and had to surrender Fort Necessity July 3, 1754. He was an aide to Braddock and at his side when the army was ambushed and defeated on a march to Ft. Duquesne, July 9, 1755. He helped take Fort Duquesne from the French in 1758.

After his marriage to Martha Dandridge Custis, a widow, in 1759, Washington managed his family estate at Mount Vernon. Although not at first for independence, he opposed British exactions and took charge of the Virginia troops before war broke out. He was made commander-in-chief by the Continental Congress June 15, 1775.

The successful issue of a war filled with hardships was due to his leadership. He was resourceful, a stern disciplinarian, and the one strong, dependable force for unity. He favored a federal government and became chairman of the Constitutional Convention of 1787. He helped get the Constitution ratified and was unanimously elected president by the electoral college and inaugurated, Apr. 30, 1789, on the balcony of New York's Federal Hall.

He was reelected 1792, but refused to consider a 3d term and retired to Mount Vernon. He suffered acute laryngitis after a ride in snow and rain around his estate, was bled profusely, and died Dec. 14, 1799.

John Adams (1797-1801)

John Adams, 2d president, Federalist, was born in Braintree (Quincy), Mass., Oct. 30, 1735 (Oct. 19, o. s.), the son of John Adams, a farmer, and Susanna Boylston. He was a great-grandson of Henry Adams, who came from England in 1636. He graduated from Harvard, 1755, taught school, studied law. In 1765 he argued against taxation without representation before the royal governor. In 1770 he defended in court the British soldiers who fired on civilians in the "Boston Massacre." He was a delegate to the first Continental Congress, and signed the Declaration of Independence. He was a commissioner to France, 1778, with Benjamin Franklin and Arthur Lee; won recognition of the U.S. by The Hague, 1782; was first American minister to England, 1785-1788, and was elected vice president, 1788 and 1792.

In 1796 Adams was chosen president by the electors. Intense antagonism to America by France caused agitation for war, led by Alexander Hamilton. Adams, breaking with Hamilton, opposed war.

To fight alien influence and muzzle criticism Adams supported the Alien and Sedition laws of 1798, which led to his defeat for reelection. He died July 4, 1826, on the same day as Jefferson (the 50th anniversary of the Declaration of Independence).

Thomas Jefferson (1801-1809)

Thomas Jefferson, 3d president, was born Apr. 13, 1743 (Apr. 2, o. s.), at Shadwell, Va., the son of Peter Jefferson, a civil engineer of Welsh descent who raised tobacco, and Jane Randolph. His father died when he was 14, leaving him 2,750 acres and his slaves. Jefferson attended the College of William and Mary, 1760-1762, read classics in Greek and Latin and played the violin. In 1769 he was elected to the House of Burgesses. In 1770 he began building Monticello, near Charlottesville. He was a member of the Virginia Committee of Correspondence and the Continental Congress. Named a member of the committee to draw up a Declaration of Independence, he wrote the basic draft. He was a member of the Virginia House of Delegates, 1776-79, elected governor to succeed Patrick Henry, 1779, reelected 1780, resigned June 1781, amid charges of ineffectual military preparation. During his term he wrote the statute on religious freedom. In the Continental Congress, 1783, he drew up an ordinance for the Northwest Territory forbidding slavery after 1800; its terms were put into the Ordinance of 1787. He was sent to Paris with Benjamin Franklin and John Adams to negotiate commercial treaties, 1784; made minister to France, 1785.

Washington appointed him secretary of state, 1789. Jefferson's strong faith in the consent of the governed, as opposed to executive control favored by Hamilton, secretary of the treasury, often led to conflict: Dec. 31, 1793, he resigned. He was the Democrat Republican candidate for president in 1796; beaten by John Adams, he became vice president. In 1800, Jefferson and Aaron Burr received equal electoral college votes for president. The House of Representatives elected Jefferson. Major events of his administration were the Louisiana Purchase, 1803, and the Lewis and Clark Expedition. He established the Univ. of Virginia and designed its buildings. He died July 4, 1826, on the same day as John Adams.

James Madison (1809-1817)

James Madison, 4th president, Democrat Republican, was born Mar. 16, 1751 (Mar. 5, o. s.), at Port Conway, King George Co., Va., eldest son of James Madison and Eleanor Rose Conway. Madison was graduated from Princeton, 1771; studied theology, 1772; sat in the Virginia Constitutional Convention, 1776. He was a member of the Continental Congress. He was chief recorder at the Constitutional Convention in 1787, and supported ratification in the Federalist Papers, written with Alexander Hamilton and John Jay. He was elected to the House of Representatives in 1789, helped frame the Bill of Rights and fought the Alien and Sedition Acts. He became Jefferson's secretary of state, 1801.

Elected president in 1808, Madison was a "strict constructionist," opposed to the free interpretation of the Constitution by the Federalists. He was reelected in 1812 by the votes of the agrarian South and recently admitted western states. Caught between British and French maritime restrictions, the U.S. drifted into war, declared June 18, 1812. The war ended in a stalemate. He retired in 1817 to his estate, Montpelier. There he edited his famous papers on the Constitutional Convention. He became rector of the Univ. of Virginia, 1826. He died June 28, 1836.

James Monroe (1817-1825)

James Monroe, 5th president, Democrat Republican, was born Apr. 28, 1758, in Westmoreland Co., Va., the son of Spence Monroe and Eliza Jones, who were of Scottish and Welsh descent, respectively. He attended the College of William and Mary, fought in the 3d Virginia Regiment at White Plains, Brandywine, Monmouth, and was wounded at Trenton. He studied law with Thomas Jefferson, 1780, was a member of the Virginia House of Delegates and of Congress, 1783-86. He opposed ratification of the Constitution because it lacked a bill of rights; was U.S. senator, 1790; minister to France, 1794-96; governor of Virginia, 1799-1802, and 1811. Jefferson sent him to France as minister, 1803. He helped Robert Livingston negotiate the Louisiana Purchase, 1803. He ran against Madison for president in 1808. He was elected to the Virginia Assembly, 1810-1811; was secretary of state under Madison, 1811-1817.

In 1816 Monroe was elected president; in 1820 reelected with all but one electoral college vote. Monroe's administration became the "Era of Good Feeling." He obtained Florida from Spain; settled boundaries with Canada, and eliminated border forts. He supported the anti-slavery position that led to the Missouri Compromise. His most significant contribution was the "Monroe Doctrine," which became a cornerstone of U.S. foreign policy. Monroe retired to Oak Hill, Va. Financial problems forced him to sell his property. He moved to New York City to live with a daughter. He died there July 4, 1831.

John Quincy Adams (1825-1829)

John Quincy Adams, 6th president, independent Federalist, later Democrat Republican, was born July 11, 1767, at Braintree (Quincy), Mass., the son of John and Abigail Adams. His father was the 2d president. He was educated in Paris, Leyden, and Harvard, graduating in 1787. He served as American minister in various European capitals, and helped draft the War of 1812 peace treaty. He was U.S. Senator, 1803-08. President Monroe made him secretary of state, 1817, and he negotiated the cession of the Floridas from Spain, supported exclusion of slavery in the Missouri Compromise, and helped formulate the Monroe Doctrine. In 1824 he was elected president by the House after he failed to win an electoral college majority. His expansion of executive powers was strongly opposed and he was beaten in 1828 by Jackson. In 1831 he entered Congress and served 17 years with distinction. He opposed slavery, the annexation of Texas, and the Mexican War. He helped establish the Smithsonian Institution. He had a stroke in the House and died in the Speaker's Room, Feb. 23, 1848.

Andrew Jackson (1829-1837)

Andrew Jackson, 7th president, was a Jeffersonian-Republican, later a Democrat. He was born in the Waxhaws district, New Lancaster Co., S.C., Mar. 15, 1767, the posthumous son of Andrew Jackson and Elizabeth Hutchinson, who were Irish immigrants. At 13, he joined the militia in the Revolution and was captured.

He read law in Salisbury, N.C., moved to Nashville, Tenn., speculated in land, married, and practiced law. In 1796 he helped draft the constitution of Tennessee and for a year occupied its one seat in Congress. He was in the Senate in 1797, and again in 1823. He defeated the Creek Indians at Horseshoe Bend, Ala., 1814. With 6,000 backwoods fighters he defeated Pakenham's 12,000 British troops at the Chalmette, outside New Orleans, Jan. 8, 1815. In 1818 he briefly invaded Spanish Florida to quell Seminoles and outlaws who harassed frontier settlements. In 1824 he ran for president against John Quincy Adams and had the most popular and electoral votes but not a majority; the election was decided by the House, which chose Adams. In 1828 he defeated Adams, carrying the West and South. He was a noisy debater and a duelist and introduced rotation in office called the "spoils system." Suspicious of privilege, he ruined the Bank of the United States by depositing federal funds with state banks. Though "Let the people rule" was his slogan, he at times supported strict constructionist policies against the expansionist West. He killed the congressional caucus for nominating presidential candidates and substituted the national convention, 1832. When South Carolina refused to collect imports under his protective tariff he ordered army and naval forces to Charleston. Jackson recognized the Republic of Texas, 1836. He died at the Hermitage, June 8, 1845.

Martin Van Buren (1837-1841)

Martin Van Buren, 8th president, Democrat, was born Dec. 5, 1782, at Kinderhook, N.Y., the son of Abraham Van Buren, a Dutch farmer, and Mary Hoes. He was surrogate of Columbia County, N.Y., state senator and attorney general. He was U.S. senator 1821, reelected, 1827, elected governor of New York, 1828. He helped swing eastern support to Jackson in 1828 and was his secretary of state 1829-31. In 1832 he was elected vice president. He was a consummate politician, known as "the little magician," and influenced Jackson's policies. In 1836 he defeated William Henry Harrison for president and took office as the Panic of 1837 initiated a 5-year nationwide depression. He inaugurated the independent treasury system. His refusal to spend land revenues led to his defeat by Harrison in 1840. He lost the Democratic nomination in 1844 to Polk. In 1848 he ran for president on the Free Soil ticket and lost. He died July 24, 1862, at Kinderhook.

William Henry Harrison (1841)

William Henry Harrison, 9th president, Whig, who served only 31 days, was born in Berkeley, Charles City Co., Va., Feb. 9, 1773, the 3d son of Benjamin Harrison, signer of the Declaration of Independence. He attended Hampden Sydney College. He was secretary of the Northwest Territory, 1798; its delegate in Congress, 1799; first governor of Indiana Territory, 1800; and superintendent of Indian affairs. With 900 men he routed Tecumseh's Indians at Tippecanoe, Nov. 7, 1811. A major general, he defeated British and Indians at Battle of the Thames, Oct. 5, 1813. He served in Congress, 1816-19; Senate, 1825-28. In 1840, he was elected president with a "log cabin and hard cider" slogan. He caught pneumonia during the inauguration and died Apr. 4, 1841.

John Tyler (1841-1845)

John Tyler, 10th president, independent Whig, was born Mar. 29, 1790, in Greenway, Charles City Co., Va., son of John Tyler and Mary Armistead. His father was governor of Virginia, 1808-11. Tyler was graduated from William and Mary, 1807; member of the House of Delegates, 1811; in Congress, 1816-21; in Virginia legislature, 1823-25; governor of Virginia, 1825-26; U.S. senator, 1827-36. In 1840 he was elected vice president and, on Harrison's death, succeeded him. He favored pre-emption, allowing settlers to get government land; rejected a national bank bill and thus alienated most Whig supporters; refused to honor the spoils system. He signed the resolution annexing Texas, Mar. 1, 1845. He accepted renomination, 1844, but withdrew before election. In 1861, he chaired an unsuccessful Washington conference called to avert civil war. After its failure he supported secession, sat in the provisional Confederate Congress, became a member of the Confederate House, but died in Richmond, Jan. 18, 1862, before it met.

James Knox Polk (1845-1849)

James Knox Polk, 11th president, Democrat, was born in Mecklenburg Co., N.C., Nov. 2, 1795, the son of Samuel Polk, farmer and surveyor of Scotch-Irish descent, and Jane Knox. He graduated from the Univ. of North Carolina, 1818; member of the Tennessee state legislature, 1823-25. He served in Congress 1825-39 and as speaker 1835-39. He was governor of Tennessee 1839-41, but was defeated 1841 and 1843. In 1844, when both Clay and Van Buren announced opposition to annexing Texas, the Democrats made Polk the first dark horse nominee because he demanded control of all Oregon and annexation of Texas. Polk re-established the independent treasury system originated by Van Buren. His expansionist policy was opposed by Clay, Webster, Calhoun; he sent troops under Zachary Taylor to the Mexican border and, when Mexicans attacked, declared war existed. The Mexican war ended with the annexation of California and much of the Southwest as part of America's "manifest destiny." He compromised on the Oregon boundary ("54-40 or fight!") by accepting the 49th parallel and giving Vancouver to the British. Polk died in Nashville, June 15, 1849.

Zachary Taylor (1849-1850)

Zachary Taylor, 12th president, Whig, who served only 16 months, was born Nov. 24, 1784, in Orange Co., Va., the son of Richard Taylor, later collector of the port of Louisville, Ky., and Sarah Strother. Taylor was commissioned first lieutenant, 1808; fought in the War of 1812; the Black Hawk War, 1832; and the second Seminole War, 1837. He was called Old Rough and Ready. He settled on a plantation near Baton Rouge, La. In 1845 Polk sent him with an army to the Rio Grande. When the Mexicans attacked him, Polk declared war. Taylor was successful at Palo Alto and Resaca de la Palma, 1846; occupied Monterrey. Polk made him major general but sent many of his troops to Gen. Winfield Scott. Outnumbered 4-1, he defeated Santa Anna at Buena Vista, 1847. A national hero, he received the Whig nomination in 1848, and was elected president. He resumed the spoils system and though once a slave-holder worked to have California admitted as a free state. He died in office July 9, 1850.

Millard Fillmore (1850-1853)

Millard Fillmore, 13th president, Whig, was born Jan. 7, 1800, in Cayuga Co., N.Y., the son of Nathaniel Fillmore and Phoebe Millard. He taught school and studied law; admitted to the bar, 1823. He was a member of the state assembly, 1829-32; in Congress, 1833-35 and again 1837-43. He opposed the entrance of Texas as slave territory and voted for a protective tariff. In 1844 he was defeated for governor of New York. In 1848 he was elected vice president and succeeded as president July 10, 1850, after Taylor's death. Fillmore favored the Compromise of 1850 and signed the Fugitive Slave Law. His policies pleased neither expansionists nor slave-holders and he was not renominated in 1852. In 1856 he was nominated by the American (Know-Nothing) party and accepted by the Whigs, but defeated by Buchanan. He died in Buffalo, Mar. 8, 1874.

Franklin Pierce (1853-1857)

Franklin Pierce, 14th president, Democrat, was born in Hillsboro, N. H., Nov. 23, 1804, the son of Benjamin Pierce, veteran of the Revolution and governor of New Hampshire, 1827. He graduated from Bowdoin, 1824. A lawyer, he served in the state legislature 1829-33; in Congress, supporting Jackson, 1833-37; U.S. senator, 1837-42. He enlisted in the Mexican War, became brigadier general under Gen. Winfield Scott. In 1852 Pierce was nominated on the 49th ballot over Lewis Cass, Stephen A. Douglas, and James Buchanan, and defeated Gen. Scott, Whig. Though against slavery, Pierce was influenced by pro-slavery Southerners. He approved the Kansas-Nebraska Act, leaving slavery to popular vote ("squatter sovereignty"), 1854. He signed a reciprocity treaty with Canada and approved the Gadsden Purchase from Mexico, 1853. Denied renomination by the Democrats, he spent most of his remaining years in Concord, N.H., where he died Oct. 8, 1869.

James Buchanan (1857-1861)

James Buchanan, 15th president, Federalist, later Democrat, was born of Scottish descent near Mercersburg, Pa., Apr. 23, 1791, the son of James Buchanan, merchant, and Elizabeth Speer. He graduated from Dickinson, 1809; was a volunteer in the War of 1812; member, Pennsylvania legislature, 1814-16, Congress, 1820-31; Jackson's minister to Russia, 1831-33; U.S. senator, 1834-45. As Polk's secretary of state, 1845-49, he ended the Oregon dispute with Britain, supported the Mexican War and annexation of Texas. As minister to Britain, 1853, he signed the Ostend Manifesto. Nominated by Democrats, he was elected, 1856, over John C. Fremont (Republican) and Millard Fillmore (American Know-Nothing and Whig tickets). On slavery he favored popular sovereignty and choice by state constitutions; he accepted the pro-slavery Dred Scott decision as binding. He denied the right of states to secede. A strict constructionist, he desired to keep peace and found no authority for using force. He died at Wheatland, near Lancaster, Pa., June 1, 1868.

Abraham Lincoln (1861-1865)

Abraham Lincoln, 16th president, Republican, was born Feb. 12, 1809, in a log cabin on a farm then in Hardin Co., Ky., now in Larue. He was the son of Thomas Lincoln, a carpenter, and Nancy Hanks.

The Lincolns moved to Spencer Co., Ind., near Gentryville, when Abe was 7. When his mother died his father married Mrs. Sarah Bush Johnston, 1819; she had a favorable influence on Abe. In 1830 the family moved to Macon Co., Ill. Lincoln lost election to the Illinois General Assembly, 1832, but later won 4 times, beginning in 1834. He enlisted in the militia for the Black Hawk War, 1832. In New Salem he ran a store, surveyed land, and was postmaster.

In 1837 Lincoln was admitted to the bar and became partner in a Springfield, Ill., law office. He was elected to Congress, 1847-49. He opposed the Mexican War. He supported Zachary Taylor, 1848. He opposed the Kansas-Nebraska Act and extension of slavery, 1854. He failed in his bid for the Senate, 1855. He supported John C. Fremont, 1856.

In 1858 Lincoln had Republican support in the Illinois legislature for the Senate but was defeated by Stephen A. Douglas, Dem., who had sponsored the Kansas-Nebraska Act.

Lincoln was nominated for president by the Republican party on an anti-slavery platform, 1860. He ran against Douglas, a northern Democrat; John C. Breckinridge, southern pro-slavery Democrat; John Bell, Constitutional Union party. When he won the election, South Carolina seceded from the Union Dec. 20, 1860, followed in 1861 by 10 Southern states.

The Civil War erupted when Fort Sumter was attacked Apr. 12, 1861. On Sept. 22, 1862, 5 days after the battle of Antietam, he announced that slaves in territory then in rebellion would be free Jan. 1, 1863, date of the Emancipation Proclamation. His speeches, including his Gettysburg and Inaugural addresses, are remembered for their eloquence.

Lincoln was reelected, 1864, over Gen. George B. McClellan, Democrat. Lee surrendered Apr. 9, 1865. On Apr. 14, Lincoln was shot by actor John Wilkes Booth in Ford's Theatre, Washington. He died the next day.

Andrew Johnson (1865-1869)

Andrew Johnson, 17th president, Democrat, was born in Raleigh, N.C., Dec. 29, 1808, the son of Jacob Johnson, porter at an inn and church sexton, and Mary McDonough. He was apprenticed to a tailor but ran away and eventually settled in Greeneville, Tenn. He became an alderman, 1828; mayor, 1830; state representative and senator, 1835-43; member of Congress, 1843-53; governor of Tennessee, 1853-57; U.S. senator, 1857-62. He supported John C. Breckinridge against Lincoln in 1860. He had held slaves, but opposed secession and tried to prevent his home state, Tennessee, from seceding. In Mar. 1862, Lincoln appointed him military governor of occupied Tennessee. In 1864 he was nominated for vice president with Lincoln on the National Union ticket to win Democratic support. He succeeded Lincoln as president Apr. 15, 1865. In a controversy with Congress over the president's power over the South, he proclaimed, May 26, 1865, an amnesty to all Confederates except certain leaders if they would ratify the 13th Amendment abolishing slavery. States doing so added anti-Negro provisions that enraged Congress, which restored military control over the South. When Johnson removed Edwin M. Stanton, secretary of war, without notifying the Senate, thus repudiating the Tenure of Office Act, the House impeached him for this and other reasons. He was tried by the Senate, and acquitted by only one vote, May 26, 1868. He returned to the Senate in 1875. Johnson died July 31, 1875.

Ulysses Simpson Grant (1869-1877)

Ulysses S. Grant, 18th president, Republican, was born at Point Pleasant, Oh., Apr. 27, 1822, son of Jesse R. Grant, a tanner, and Hannah Simpson. The next year the family moved to Georgetown, Oh. Grant was named Hiram Ulysses, but on entering West Point, 1839, his name was entered as Ulysses Simpson and he adopted it. He was graduated in 1843; served under Gens. Taylor and Scott in the Mexican War; resigned, 1854; worked in St. Louis until 1860, then went to Galena, Ill. With the start of the Civil War, he was named colonel of the 21st Illinois Vols., 1861, then brigadier general; took Forts Henry and Donelson; fought at Shiloh, took Vicksburg. After his victory at Chattanooga, Lincoln placed him in command of the Union Armies. He accepted Lee's surrender at Appomattox, Apr., 1865. President Johnson appointed Grant secretary of war when he suspended Stanton, but Grant was not confirmed. He was nominated for president by the Republicans in 1868 and elected over Horatio Seymour, Democrat. The 15th Amendment, amnesty bill, and civil service reform were events of his administration. The Liberal Republicans and Democrats opposed him with Horace Greeley, 1872, but he was reelected. An attempt by the Stalwarts (Old Guard) to nominate him in 1880 failed. In 1884 the collapse of Grant & Ward, investment house, left him penniless. He wrote his personal memoirs while ill with cancer and completed them 4 days before his death at Mt. McGregor, N.Y., July 23, 1885. The book realized over $450,000.

Rutherford Birchard Hayes (1877-1881)

Rutherford B. Hayes, 19th president, Republican, was born in Delaware, Oh., Oct. 4, 1822, the posthumous son of Rutherford Hayes, a farmer, and Sophia Birchard. He was raised by his uncle Sardis Birchard. He graduated from Kenyon College, 1842, and Harvard Law School, 1845. He practiced law in Lower Sandusky, Oh., now Fremont; was city solicitor of Cincinnati, 1858-61. In the Civil War, he was major of the 23d Ohio Vols., was wounded several times, and rose to the rank of brevet major general, 1864. He served in Congress 1864-67, supporting Reconstruction and Johnson's impeachment. He was elected governor of Ohio, 1867 and 1869; beaten in the race for Congress, 1872; reelected governor, 1875. In 1876 he was nominated for president and believed he had lost the election to Samuel J. Tilden, Democrat. But a few Southern states submitted 2 different sets of electoral votes and the result was in dispute. An electoral commission, appointed by Congress, 8 Republicans and 7 Democrats, awarded all disputed votes to Hayes allowing him to become president by one electoral vote. Hayes, keeping a promise to southerners, withdrew troops from areas still occupied in the South, ending the era of Reconstruction. He proceeded to reform the civil service, alienating political spoilsmen. He advocated repeal of the Tenure of Office Act. He supported sound money and specie payments. Hayes died in Fremont, Oh., Jan. 17, 1893.

James Abram Garfield (1881)

James A. Garfield, 20th president, Republican, was born Nov. 19, 1831, in Orange, Cuyahoga Co., Oh., the son of Abram Garfield and Eliza Ballou. His father died in 1833. He worked as a canal bargeman, farmer, and carpenter; attended Western Reserve Eclectic, later Hiram College, and was graduated from Williams in 1856. He taught at Hiram, and later became principal. He was in the Ohio senate in 1859. Anti-slavery and anti-secession, he volunteered for the war, became colonel of the 42d Ohio Infantry and brigadier in 1862. He fought at Shiloh, was chief of staff for Rosecrans and was made major general for gallantry at Chickamauga. He entered Congress as a radical Republican in 1863; supported specie payment as against paper money (greenbacks). On the electoral commission in 1877 he voted for Hayes against Tilden on strict party lines. He was senator-elect in 1880 when he became the Republican nominee for president. He was chosen as a compromise over Gen. Grant, James G. Blaine, and John Sherman. This alienated the Grant following but Garfield was elected. On July 2, 1881, Garfield was shot by mentally disturbed office-seeker, Charles J. Guiteau, while entering a railroad station in Washington. He died Sept. 19, 1881, at Elberon, N.J.

Chester Alan Arthur (1881-1885)

Chester A. Arthur, 21st president, Republican, was born at Fairfield, Vt., Oct. 5, 1830, the son of the Rev. William Arthur, from County Antrim, Ireland, and Malvina Stone. He graduated from Union College, 1848, taught school at Pownall, Vt., studied law in New York. In 1853 he argued in a fugitive slave case that slaves transported through N.Y. State were thereby freed. He was made collector of the Port of New York, 1871. President Hayes, reforming the civil service, forced Arthur to resign, 1879. This made the

New York machine stalwarts enemies of Hayes. Arthur and the stalwarts tried to nominate Grant for a 3d term in 1880. When Garfield was nominated, Arthur received 2d place in the interests of harmony. When Garfield died, Arthur became president. He supported civil service reform and the tariff of 1883. He was defeated for renomination by James G. Blaine. He died in New York City, Nov. 18, 1886.

Grover Cleveland (1885-1889) (1893-1897)

(According to a ruling of the State Dept., Grover Cleveland is both the 22d and the 24th president, because his 2 terms were not consecutive. By individuals, he is only the 22d.)

Grover Cleveland, 22d and 24th president, Democrat, was born in Caldwell, N.J., Mar. 18, 1837, the son of Richard F. Cleveland, a Presbyterian minister, and Ann Neale. He was named Stephen Grover, but dropped the Stephen. He clerked in Clinton and Buffalo, N.Y.; taught at the N.Y. City Institution for the Blind; was admitted to the bar in Buffalo, 1859; became assistant district attorney, 1863; sheriff, 1871; mayor, 1881; governor of New York, 1882. He was an independent, honest administrator who hated corruption. He was nominated for president over Tammany Hall opposition, 1884, and defeated Republican James G. Blaine. He enlarged the civil service, vetoed many pension raids on the Treasury. In 1888 he was defeated by Benjamin Harrison, although his popular vote was larger. Reelected over Harrison in 1892, he faced a money crisis brought about by lowering of the gold reserve, circulation of paper and exorbitant silver purchases under the Sherman Act; obtained a repeal of the latter and a reduced tariff. A severe depression and labor troubles racked his administration but he refused to interfere in business matters and rejected Jacob Coxey's demand for unemployment relief. He broke the Pullman strike, 1894. In 1896, the Democrats repudiated his administration and chose silverite William Jennings Bryan as their candidate. Cleveland died in Princeton, N.J., June 24, 1908.

Benjamin Harrison (1889-1893)

Benjamin Harrison, 23d president, Republican, was born at North Bend, Oh., Aug. 20, 1833. His great-grandfather, Benjamin Harrison, was a signer of the Declaration of Independence; his grandfather, William Henry Harrison, was 9th President; his father, John Scott Harrison, was a member of Congress. His mother was Elizabeth F. Irwin. He attended school on his father's farm; graduated from Miami Univ. at Oxford, Oh., 1852; admitted to the bar, 1853, and practiced in Indianapolis. In the Civil War, he rose to the rank of brevet brigadier general, fought at Kennesaw Mountain, Peachtree Creek, Nashville, and in the Atlanta campaign. He failed to be elected governor of Indiana, 1876; but became senator, 1881. In 1888 he defeated Cleveland for president despite having fewer popular votes. He expanded the pension list, signed the McKinley high tariff bill, the Sherman Antitrust Act, and the Sherman Silver Purchase Act. During his administration, 6 states were admitted to the union. He was defeated for reelection, 1892. He represented Venezuela in a boundary arbitration with Great Britain in Paris, 1899. He died in Indianapolis, Mar. 13, 1901.

William McKinley (1897-1901)

William McKinley, 25th president, Republican, was born in Niles, Oh., Jan. 29, 1843, the son of William McKinley, an ironmaker, and Nancy Allison. McKinley attended school in Poland, Oh., and Allegheny College, Meadville, Pa., and enlisted for the Civil War at 18 in the 23d Ohio, in which Rutherford B. Hayes was a major. He rose to captain and in 1865 was made brevet major. He studied law in the Albany, N.Y., law school; opened an office in Canton, Oh., in 1867, and campaigned for Grant and Hayes. He served in the House of Representatives, 1877-83, 1885-91, and led the fight for passage of the McKinley Tariff, 1890. Defeated for reelection on the tariff issue in 1890, he was governor of Ohio, 1892-96. He had support for president in the convention that nominated Benjamin Harrison in 1892. In 1896 he was elected president on a protective tariff, sound money (gold standard) platform over William Jennings Bryan, Democratic proponent of free silver. McKinley was reluctant to intervene in Cuba but the loss of the battleship *Maine* at Havana crystallized opinion. He demanded Spain's withdrawal from Cuba; Spain made some concessions but Congress announced state of war as of Apr. 21. He was reelected in the 1900 campaign, defeating Bryan's anti-imperialist arguments with the promise of a "full dinner pail." McKinley was respected for his conciliatory nature, but conservative on business issues. On Sept. 6, 1901, while welcoming citizens at the Pan-American Exposition, Buffalo, N.Y., he was shot by Leon Czolgosz, an anarchist. He died Sept. 14.

Theodore Roosevelt (1901-1909)

Theodore Roosevelt, 26th president, Republican, was born in N.Y. City, Oct. 27, 1858, the son of Theodore Roosevelt, a glass importer, and Martha Bulloch. He was a 5th cousin of Franklin D. Roosevelt and an uncle of Eleanor Roosevelt. Roosevelt graduated from Harvard, 1880; attended Columbia Law School briefly; sat in the N.Y. State Assembly, 1882-84; ranched in North Dakota, 1884-86; failed election as mayor of N.Y. City, 1886; member of U.S. Civil Service Commission, 1889; president, N.Y. Police Board, 1895, supporting the merit system; assistant secretary of the Navy under McKinley, 1897-98. In the war with Spain, he organized the 1st U.S. Volunteer Cavalry (Rough Riders) as lieutenant colonel; led the charge up Kettle Hill at San Juan. Elected New York governor, 1898-1900, he fought the spoils system and achieved taxation of corporation franchises. Nominated for vice president, 1900, he became nation's youngest president when McKinley died. He was reelected in 1904. As president he fought corruption of politics by big business; dissolved Northern Securities Co. and others for violating anti-trust laws; intervened in coal strike on behalf of the public, 1902; obtained Elkins Law forbidding rebates to favored corporations, 1903; Hepburn Law regulating railroad rates, 1906; Pure Food and Drugs Act, 1906, Reclamation Act and employers' liability laws. He organized conservation, mediated the peace between Japan and Russia, 1905; won the Nobel Peace Prize. He was the first to use the Hague Court of International Arbitration. By recognizing the new Republic of Panama he made Panama Canal possible.

In 1908 he obtained the nomination of William H. Taft, who was elected. Feeling that Taft had abandoned his policies, Roosevelt unsuccessfully sought the nomination in 1912. He bolted the party and ran on the Progressive "Bull Moose" ticket against Taft and Woodrow Wilson, splitting the Republicans and insuring Wilson's election. He was shot during the campaign but recovered. In 1916 he supported Charles E. Hughes, Republican. A strong friend of Britain, he fought American isolation in World War I. He wrote some 40 books on many topics; his *Winning of the West* is best known. He died Jan. 6, 1919, at Sagamore Hill, Oyster Bay, N.Y.

William Howard Taft (1909-1913)

William Howard Taft, 27th president, Republican, was born in Cincinnati, Oh., Sept. 15, 1857, the son of Alphonso Taft and Louisa Maria Torrey. His father was secretary of war and attorney general in Grant's cabinet; minister to Austria and Russia under Arthur. Taft was graduated from Yale, 1878; Cincinnati Law School, 1880; became law reporter for Cincinnati newspapers; was assistant prosecuting attorney, 1881-83; assistant county solicitor, 1885; judge, superior court, 1887; U.S. solicitor-general, 1890; federal circuit judge, 1892. In 1900 he became head of the U.S. Philippines Commission and was first civil governor of the Philippines, 1901-04; secretary of war, 1904; provisional governor of Cuba, 1906. He was groomed for president by Roosevelt and elected over Bryan, 1908. His administration dissolved Standard Oil and tobacco trusts; instituted Dept. of Labor; drafted direct election of senators and income tax amendments. His tariff and conservation policies angered progressives; though renominated he was opposed by Roosevelt; the result was Democrat Woodrow Wilson's election. Taft, with some reservations, supported the League of Nations. He was professor of constitutional law, Yale, 1913-21; chief justice of the U.S. Supreme Court, 1921-30; illness forced him to resign. He died in Washington, Mar. 8, 1930.

Woodrow Wilson (1913-1921)

Woodrow Wilson, 28th president, Democrat, was born at Staunton, Va., Dec. 28, 1856, as Thomas Woodrow Wilson, son of a Presbyterian minister, the Rev. Joseph Ruggles Wilson and Janet (Jessie) Woodrow. In his youth Wilson lived in Augusta, Ga., Columbia, S.C., and Wilmington, N.C. He attended Davidson College, 1873-74; was graduated from Princeton, A.B., 1879; A.M., 1882; read law at the Univ. of Virginia, 1881; practiced law, Atlanta, 1882-83; Ph.D., Johns Hopkins, 1886. He taught at Bryn Mawr, 1885-88; at Wesleyan, 1888-90; was professor of jurisprudence and political economy at Princeton, 1890-1910; president of Princeton, 1902-1910; governor of New Jersey, 1911-13. In 1912 he was nominated for president with the aid of William Jennings Bryan, who sought to block James "Champ" Clark and Tammany Hall. Wilson won the election because the Republican vote for Taft was split by the Progressives under Roosevelt.

Wilson protected American interests in revolutionary Mexico and fought for American rights on the high seas. His sharp warnings to Germany led to the resignation of his secretary of state, Bryan, a pacifist. In 1916 he was reelected by a slim margin with the slogan, "He kept us out of war." Wilson's attempts to mediate in the war failed. After 4 American ships had been sunk by the Germans, he secured a declaration of war against Germany on Apr. 6, 1917.

Wilson proposed peace Jan. 8, 1918, on the basis of his "Fourteen Points," a state paper with worldwide influence. His doctrine of self-determination continues to play a major role in territorial disputes. The Germans accepted his terms and an armistice, Nov. 11.

Wilson went to Paris to help negotiate the peace treaty, the crux of which he considered the League of Nations. The Senate demanded reservations that would not make the U.S. subordinate to the votes of other nations in case of war. Wilson refused to consider any reservations and toured the country to get support. He suffered a stroke, Oct., 1919. An invalid for months, he clung to his executive powers while his wife and doctor sought to shield him from affairs which would tire him.

He was awarded the 1919 Nobel Peace Prize, but the treaty embodying the League of Nations was rejected by the Senate, 1920. He died in Washington, Feb. 3, 1924.

Warren Gamaliel Harding (1921-1923)

Warren Gamaliel Harding, 29th president, Republican, was born near Corsica, now Blooming Grove, Oh., Nov. 2, 1865, the son of Dr. George Tyron Harding, a physician, and Phoebe Elizabeth Dickerson. He attended Ohio Central College. He was state senator, 1900-04; lieutenant governor, 1904-06; defeated for governor, 1910; chosen U.S. senator, 1915. He supported Taft, opposed federal control of food and fuel; voted for anti-strike legislation, woman's suffrage, and the Volstead prohibition enforcement act over President Wilson's veto; and opposed the League of Nations. In 1920 he was nominated for president and defeated James M. Cox in the election. The Republicans capitalized on war weariness and fear that Wilson's League of Nations would curtail U.S. sovereignty. Harding stressed a return to "normalcy"; worked for tariff revision and repeal of excess profits law and high income taxes. Two Harding appointees, Albert B. Fall (interior) and Harry Daugherty (attorney general), became involved in the Teapot Dome scandal that embittered Harding's last days. He called the International Conference on Limitation of Armaments, 1921-22. Returning from a trip to Alaska he became ill and died in San Francisco, Aug. 2, 1923.

Calvin Coolidge (1923-1929)

Calvin Coolidge, 30th president, Republican, was born in Plymouth, Vt., July 4, 1872, the son of John Calvin Coolidge, a storekeeper, and Victoria J. Moor, and named John Calvin Coolidge. Coolidge graduated from Amherst in 1895. He entered Republican state politics and served as mayor of Northampton, Mass., state senator, lieutenant governor, and, in 1919, governor. In Sept., 1919, Coolidge attained national prominence by calling out the state guard in the Boston police strike. He declared: "There is no right to strike against the public safety by anybody, anywhere, anytime." This brought his name before the Republican convention of 1920, where he was nominated for vice president. He succeeded to the presidency on Harding's death. He opposed the League of Nations; approved the World Court; vetoed the soldiers' bonus bill, which was passed over his veto. In 1924 he was elected by a huge majority. He reduced the national debt by $2 billion in 3 years. He twice vetoed the McNary-Haugen farm bill, which would have provided relief to financially hard-pressed farmers. With Republicans eager to renominate him he announced, Aug. 2, 1927: "I do not choose to run for president in 1928." He died in Northampton, Jan. 5, 1933.

Herbert Clark Hoover (1929-1933)

Herbert C. Hoover, 31st president, Republican, was born at West Branch, Ia., Aug. 10, 1874, son of Jesse Clark Hoover, a blacksmith, and Hulda Randall Minthorn. Hoover grew up in Indian Territory (now Oklahoma) and Oregon; won his A.B. in engineering at Stanford, 1891. He worked briefly with U.S. Geological Survey and western mines; then was a mining engineer in Australia, Asia, Europe, Africa, U.S. While chief engineer, imperial mines, China, he directed food relief for victims of Boxer Rebellion, 1900. He directed American Relief Committee, London, 1914-15; U.S. Comm. for Relief in Belgium, 1915-1919; was U.S. Food Administrator, 1917-1919; American Relief Administrator, 1918-1923, feeding children in defeated nations; Russian Relief, 1918-

1923. He was secy. of commerce, 1921-28. He was elected president over Alfred E. Smith, 1928. In 1929 the stock market crashed and the economy collapsed. During the depression, Hoover inaugurated government assistance programs but opposed direct federal aid to the unemployed. He was defeated in the 1932 election by Franklin D. Roosevelt. President Truman made him coordinator of European Food Program, 1947, chairman of the Commission for Reorganization of the Executive Branch, 1947-49. He died in N.Y. City, Oct. 20, 1964.

Franklin Delano Roosevelt (1933-1945)

Franklin D. Roosevelt, 32d president, Democrat, was born near Hyde Park, N.Y., Jan. 30, 1882, the son of James Roosevelt and Sara Delano. He graduated from Harvard, 1904; attended Columbia Law School; was admitted to the bar. He went to the N.Y. Senate, 1910 and 1913. In 1913 President Wilson made him assistant secretary of the navy.

Roosevelt ran for vice president, 1920, with James Cox and was defeated. From 1920 to 1928 he was a N.Y. lawyer and vice president of Fidelity & Deposit Co. In Aug., 1921, polio paralyzed his legs. He learned to walk with leg braces and a cane.

Roosevelt was elected governor of New York, 1928 and 1930. In 1932, W. G. McAdoo, pledged to John N. Garner, threw his votes to Roosevelt, who was nominated for president. The depression and the promise to repeal prohibition ensured his election. He asked for emergency powers, proclaimed the New Deal, and put into effect a vast number of administrative changes. Foremost was the use of public funds for relief and public works, resulting in deficit financing. He greatly expanded the federal government's regulation of business and by an excess profits tax and progressive income taxes produced a redistribution of earnings on an unprecedented scale. The Wagner Act gave labor many advantages in organizing and collective bargaining. He was the last president inaugurated on Mar. 4 (1933) and the first inaugurated on Jan. 20 (1937).

Roosevelt was the first president to use radio for "fireside chats." When the Supreme Court nullified some New Deal laws, he sought power to "pack" the court with additional justices, but Congress refused to give him the authority. He was the first president to break the "no 3d term" tradition (1940) and was elected to a 4th term, 1944, despite failing health. He was openly hostile to fascist governments before World War II and launched a lend-lease program on behalf of the Allies. He wrote the principles of fair dealing into the Atlantic Charter, Aug. 14, 1941 (with Winston Churchill), and urged the Four Freedoms (freedom of speech, of worship, from want, from fear) Jan. 6, 1941. When Japan attacked Pearl Harbor, Dec. 7, 1941, the U.S. entered the war. He conferred with allied heads of state at Casablanca, Jan., 1943; Quebec, Aug., 1943; Teheran, Nov.-Dec., 1943; Cairo, Dec., 1943; Yalta, Feb., 1945. He died at Warm Springs, Ga., Apr. 12, 1945.

Harry S. Truman (1945-1953)

Harry S. Truman, 33d president, Democrat, was born at Lamar, Mo., May 8, 1884, the son of John Anderson Truman and Martha Ellen Young. A family disagreement on whether his middle name was Shippe or Solomon, after names of 2 grandfathers, resulted in his using only the middle initial S. He attended public schools in Independence, Mo., worked for the *Kansas City Star*, 1901, and as railroad timekeeper, and helper in Kansas City banks up to 1905. He ran his family's farm, 1906-17. He was commissioned a first lieutenant and took part in the Vosges, Meuse-Argonne, and St. Mihiel actions in World War I. After the war he ran a haberdashery; was a judge on the Jackson Co. Court, 1922-24; attended Kansas City School of Law, 1923-25.

Truman was elected U.S. senator in 1934; reelected 1940. In 1944 with Roosevelt's backing he was nominated for vice president and elected. On Roosevelt's death Truman became president. In 1948 he was elected president.

Truman authorized the first uses of the atomic bomb (Hiroshima and Nagasaki, Aug. 6 and 9, 1945), bringing World War II to a rapid end. He was responsible for creating NATO, the Marshall Plan, and what came to be called the Truman Doctrine (to aid nations such as Greece and Turkey, threatened by communist takeover). He broke a Soviet blockade of West Berlin with a massive airlift, 1948-49. When communist North Korea invaded South Korea, June 1950, he won UN approval for a "police action" and sent in forces under Gen. Douglas MacArthur. When MacArthur opposed his policy of limited objectives, Truman removed him from command.

Truman was responsible for higher minimum-wage, increased social-security, and aid-for-housing laws. Truman died Dec. 26, 1972, in Kansas City, Mo.

Dwight David Eisenhower (1953-1961)

Dwight D. Eisenhower, 34th president, Republican, was born Oct. 14, 1890, in Denison, Tex., the son of David Jacob Eisenhower and Ida Elizabeth Stover. He graduated from West Point, 1915. He was on the staff of Gen. Douglas MacArthur in the Philippines from 1935 to 1939. He was made commander of Allied forces landing in North Africa, 1942, full general, 1943. He became supreme Allied commander in Europe, 1943, and as such led the Normandy invasion June 6, 1944. He was given the rank of general of the army Dec. 20, 1944, made permanent in 1946. On May 7, 1945, he received the surrender of the Germans at Rheims. He returned to the U.S. to serve as chief of staff, 1945-48. In 1948, Eisenhower published *Crusade in Europe,* his war memoirs, which quickly became a best-seller. From 1948 to 1953, he was president of Columbia Univ., but took leave of absence in 1950 to command NATO forces.

Eisenhower resigned from the army and was nominated for president by the Republicans, 1952. He defeated Adlai E. Stevenson in the 1952 election and then again in 1956. He called himself a moderate; favored "free market system" vs. government price and wage controls; kept government out of labor disputes; reorganized defense establishment; promoted missile programs. He continued foreign aid; sped end of Korean fighting; endorsed Taiwan and SE Asia defense treaties; backed UN in condemning Anglo-French raid on Egypt; advocated "open skies" policy of mutual inspection to USSR. He sent U.S. troops into Little Rock, Ark., Sept. 1957, during the segregation crisis.

Eisenhower died Mar. 28, 1969, in Washington, D.C.

John Fitzgerald Kennedy (1961-1963)

John F. Kennedy, 35th president, Democrat, was born May 29, 1917, in Brookline, Mass., the son of Joseph P. Kennedy, financier, who later became ambassador to Great Britain, and Rose Fitzgerald. He received a B.S. from Harvard, 1940. He served in the navy, 1941-45, commanded a PT boat in the Solomons, and won the Navy and Marine Corps Medal. He wrote *Profiles in Courage,* which won a Pulitzer prize. He served as representative in Congress, 1947-53; was elected to the Senate in 1952, reelected 1958.

In 1960, Kennedy won the Democratic nomination for president and defeated Richard M. Nixon, Republican. He was the first Roman Catholic president.

In Apr. 1961, Kennedy's new administration suffered a severe setback when an invasion force of anti-Castro Cubans, trained and directed by the U.S. Central Intelligence Agency, failed to establish a beachhead at the Bay of Pigs in Cuba.

Kennedy's most important act was his successful demand Oct. 22, 1962, that the Soviet Union dismantle its missile bases in Cuba. He established a quarantine of arms shipments to Cuba and continued surveillance by air. He defied Soviet attempts to force the Allies out of Berlin. He backed civil rights and expanded medical care for the aged. Space exploration was greatly developed during his administration.

On Nov. 22, 1963, Kennedy was assassinated in Dallas, Tex.

Lyndon Baines Johnson (1963-1969)

Lyndon B. Johnson, 36th president, Democrat, was born near Stonewall, Tex., Aug. 27, 1908, son of Sam Ealy Johnson and Rebekah Baines. He graduated from Southwest Texas State Teachers College, 1930, and attended Georgetown Univ. Law School, 1935. He taught public speaking in Houston, 1930-32; served as secretary to Rep. R. M. Kleberg, 1932-35. In 1937 Johnson won an election to fill the vacancy caused by the death of a representative and in 1938 was elected to the full term, after which he returned for 4 terms. He was elected U.S. senator in 1948 and reelected in 1954. He became Democratic leader, 1953. Johnson had strong support for the Democratic presidential nomination at the 1960 convention, where the nominee, John F. Kennedy, asked him to run for vice president. His campaigning helped overcome religious bias against Kennedy in the South.

Johnson became president when Kennedy was assassinated. He was elected to a full term, 1964. Johnson won passage of major civil rights, anti-poverty, aid to education, and health care (Medicare, Medicaid) legislation—the "Great Society" program. However, his escalation of the war in Vietnam came to overshadow other developments during his administration.

In face of increasing division in the nation and in his own party over his handling of the war, Johnson did not seek another term.

He died Jan. 22, 1973, in San Antonio, Tex.

Richard Milhous Nixon (1969-1974)

Richard M. Nixon, 37th president, Republican, was the only president to resign. He was born in Yorba Linda, Cal., Jan. 9, 1913, the son of Francis Anthony Nixon and Hannah Milhous. Nixon graduated from Whittier College, 1934; Duke Univ. Law School, 1937. After practicing law in Whittier and serving briefly in the Office of Price Administration in 1942, he entered the navy and served in the South Pacific.

Nixon was elected to the House of Representatives in 1946 and 1948. He achieved prominence as the House Un-American Activities Committee member who forced the showdown that resulted in the Alger Hiss perjury conviction. In 1950 Nixon was elected to the Senate.

He was elected vice president in the Eisenhower landslides of 1952 and 1956. Nixon won the Republican nomination in 1960. He was defeated by Democrat John F. Kennedy, returned to California, and was defeated in his race for governor, 1962.

In 1968, he won the presidential nomination and went on to defeat Democrat Hubert H. Humphrey.

Nixon was the first U.S. president to visit China (1972). He and his foreign affairs adviser, Henry A. Kissinger, achieved a détente with the Soviet Union. Nixon appointed 4 Supreme Court justices, including the chief justice, thus altering the court's balance in favor of a more conservative view.

Reelected 1972, Nixon secured a cease-fire agreement in Vietnam.

Nixon's 2d term was cut short by a series of scandals beginning with the burglary of Democratic Party national headquarters in the Watergate office complex on June 17, 1972. On July 16, 1973, a White House aide, under questioning by a Senate committee, revealed that most of Nixon's office conversations and phone calls had been recorded. Nixon claimed executive privilege to keep the tapes secret, and the courts and Congress sought the tapes for criminal proceedings against former White House aides and for a House inquiry into possible impeachment.

On July 24, 1974, the Supreme Court ruled that Nixon's claim of executive privilege must fall before the special prosecutor's subpoenas of tapes relevant to criminal trial proceedings. That same day, the House Judiciary Committee opened debate on impeachment. On July 30, the committee recommended House adoption of 3 articles of impeachment charging Nixon with obstruction of justice, abuse of power, and contempt of Congress.

On Aug. 5, Nixon released transcripts of conversations held 6 days after the Watergate break-in showing that Nixon had known of, approved, and directed Watergate cover-up activities. Nixon resigned from office Aug. 9.

In later years, Nixon emerged as an elder statesman. He died Apr. 22, 1994, in New York City.

Gerald Rudolph Ford (1974-1977)

Gerald R. Ford, 38th president, Republican, was born July 14, 1913, in Omaha, Neb., son of Leslie King and Dorothy Gardner, and was named Leslie Jr. When he was 2, his parents were divorced, and his mother moved with the boy to Grand Rapids, Mich. There she met and married Gerald R. Ford, who formally adopted the boy and gave him his own name.

Ford graduated from the Univ. of Michigan, 1935, and Yale Law School, 1941.

He began practicing law in Grand Rapids, but in 1942 joined the navy and served in the Pacific, leaving the service in 1946 as a lieutenant commander.

He entered Congress in 1949 and spent 25 years in the House, 8 of them as Republican leader.

On Oct. 12, 1973, after Vice President Spiro T. Agnew resigned, Ford was nominated by President Nixon to replace him. It was the first use of the procedures set out in the 25th Amendment.

When Nixon resigned Aug. 9, 1974, Ford became president, the first to serve without being elected vice president in a national election. On Sept. 8 he pardoned Nixon for any federal crimes he might have committed as president. Ford vetoed 48 bills in his first 21 months in office, saying most would prove too costly. He visited China. He was defeated in the 1976 election by Democrat Jimmy Carter.

Jimmy (James Earl) Carter (1977-1981)

Jimmy (James Earl) Carter, 39th president, Democrat, was the first president from the Deep South since before the Civil War. He was born Oct. 1, 1924, in Plains, Ga., the son of James and Lillian Gordy Carter.

He graduated from the U.S. Naval Academy, 1946. He entered the navy's nuclear submarine program as an aide to Adm. Hyman Rickover and studied nuclear physics at Union College.

His father died in 1953, and Carter left the navy to take over the family businesses. He was elected to the Georgia state senate, was defeated for governor, 1966, but elected in 1970. In 1976, Carter won the Democratic nomination and defeated President Gerald R. Ford.

On his first full day in office, Carter pardoned all Vietnam draft evaders. He played a major role in the peace negotiations between Israel and Egypt.

However, Carter was widely criticized for the poor state of the economy and high inflation. He was also viewed as weak in his handling of foreign policy. In Nov. 1979, Iranian student militants attacked the U.S. embassy in Teheran and held members of the embassy staff hostage. His failure to obtain the release of the remaining 52 hostages plagued Carter to the end of his term. He reacted to the Soviet invasion of Afghanistan by imposing a grain embargo and boycotting the Moscow Olympic games. He was defeated by Ronald Reagan in the 1980 election. Carter administration efforts finally resulted in the release of the hostages on Inauguration Day, 1981, just after Reagan officially became president.

Ronald Wilson Reagan (1981-1989)

Ronald Wilson Reagan, 40th president, Republican, was born Feb. 6, 1911, in Tampico, Ill., the son of John Edward Reagan and Nellie Wilson. Reagan graduated from Eureka (Ill.) College in 1932, after which he worked as a sports announcer in Des Moines, Ia.

Reagan began a successful career as a film actor in 1937, starring in numerous movies, and later television, until the 1960s. He was a captain in the Army Air Force during World War II.

He served as president of the Screen Actors Guild from 1947 to 1952, and in 1959.

Reagan was elected governor of California in 1966, and reelected in 1970. In 1980, he gained the Republican nomination and won a landslide victory over Jimmy Carter. He was easily reelected in 1984.

Reagan successfully forged a bipartisan coalition in Congress, which led to enactment of an economic program that included the largest budget and tax cuts in U.S. history and a Social Security reform bill designed to ensure the long-term solvency of the system. In 1986, he signed into law a revolutionary tax-reform bill. He was shot in an assassination attempt in 1981.

In 1983, Reagan sent a task force to lead the invasion of Grenada, and joined 3 European nations in maintaining a peacekeeping force in Beirut, Lebanon. His opposition to international terrorism led to the U.S. bombing of Libyan military installations in 1986. He strongly supported El Salvador, the Nicaraguan contras, and other anti-communist governments and forces throughout the world.

Reagan held 4 summit meetings with Soviet leader Mikhail Gorbachev. At the 1987 meeting in Washington, D.C., an historic treaty eliminating short- and medium-range missiles from Europe was signed.

Reagan faced a major crisis in 1986-87, when it was revealed that the U.S. had sold weapons to Iran in exchange for the release of U.S. hostages being held in Lebanon and that subsequently some of the money was diverted to the Nicaraguan contras (Congress had barred aid to the contras). The scandal led to the resignation of leading White House aides.

As Reagan left office, the nation was experiencing its 6th consecutive year of economic prosperity. Along with the strong economy, the nation enjoyed low unemployment, energy costs, and inflation. Reagan, however, was unable to control the high budget deficits that plagued him throughout his administration.

George Herbert Walker Bush (1989-1993)

George Herbert Walker Bush, 41st president, Republican, was born June 12, 1924, in Milton, Mass., the son of Prescott Bush, U.S. senator from Connecticut, and Dorothy Walker. He served as a U.S. Navy pilot in World War II. After graduating from Yale Univ. (1948), he settled in Texas where, in 1953, he helped found an oil company.

After losing a bid for a U.S. Senate seat in Texas, 1964, he was elected to the House of Representatives in 1966 and 1968. He lost a 2d U.S. Senate race in 1970. He served as U.S. ambassador to the United Nations, 1971-73, headed the U.S. Liaison Office in Beijing, 1974-75, and was director of the Central Intelligence Agency, 1976-77.

Following an unsuccessful bid for the 1980 Republican presidential nomination, Bush was chosen by Ronald Reagan as his vice presidential running mate. He served as U.S. vice president, 1981-89.

In 1988, he gained the Republican presidential nomination and defeated Democrat Michael Dukakis. Bush took office faced with the ongoing U.S. budget and trade deficits as well as the rescue of insolvent U.S. savings and loan institutions.

Bush annually faced a severe budget deficit, struggled with military cutbacks in light of reduced "cold war" tensions, and vetoed congressional actions favorable to freedom of choice on abortion, a minimum-wage law, and an anti-discrimination bill that didn't reflect his own views.

Bush supported Soviet reforms and Eastern Europe democratization. He was criticized, however, for not supporting strongly enough the independence effort of the Baltic republics, for keeping U.S. policy tied for too long to Mikhail Gorbachev as the Soviet leader lost power and his nation broke apart, and for his soft reaction to the Chinese government's violent repression of a pro-democracy movement.

In Dec. 1989, Bush sent military forces to Panama which overthrew the government and captured military strongman Gen. Manuel Noriega.

Bush reacted to Iraq's Aug. 1990 invasion of Kuwait by sending U.S. forces to the Persian Gulf area and assembling a U.N.-backed coalition including NATO and Arab League members. After a month-long air war, in Feb. 1991, Allied forces retook Kuwait in a 4-day ground assault. The quick victory gave Bush one of the highest presidential approval ratings in history. His popularity plummeted by the end of 1991 as the economy struggled through a prolonged recession and he was perceived as being indifferent to the nation's domestic problems. He was defeated by Bill Clinton in the 1992 election.

Bill (William Jefferson) Clinton (1993-)

Bill Clinton, 42d president, Democrat, was born William Jefferson Blythe 3d on Aug. 19, 1946, in Hope, Ark., the son of William Blythe and Virginia Cassidy. Blythe, a traveling salesman, died in an auto accident before his son was born. His mother married Roger Clinton and several years later, at age 16, Bill Blythe changed his name to Bill Clinton. Clinton attended Georgetown Univ., Oxford Univ. in England as a Rhodes scholar, and Yale Law School.

Clinton worked on George McGovern's 1972 presidential campaign. He taught at the Univ. of Arkansas, 1973-76. He was elected Arkansas State Attorney General in 1976.

In 1978, he was elected governor of Arkansas, becoming the nation's youngest governor, but he was defeated for reelection in 1980. He successfully ran for governor again in 1982, 1984, 1986, and 1990. He married Hillary Rodham in 1975.

Despite personal attacks on his character, he won the majority of the 1992 presidential primaries while moving the Democratic Party toward the center, trying to appeal to middle-class suburbanites who had deserted the party during the Reagan era. He defeated Pres. George Bush in the presidential election.

In August 1993, Clinton narrowly won congressional passage of some $500 billion in taxes and spending cuts to reduce the federal budget deficits. Later in the year he sent Congress major health-care reform legislation.

Wives and Children of the Presidents

Listed in order of presidential administrations.

Name (Born–died, married)	State	Sons/ daughters
Martha Dandridge Custis Washington (1732-1802, 1759)	Va.	None
Abigail Smith Adams (1744-1818, 1764)	Mass.	3/2
Martha Wayles Skelton Jefferson (1748-1782, 1772)	Va.	1/5
Dorothea "Dolley" Payne Todd Madison (1768-1849, 1794)	N.C.	None
Elizabeth Kortright Monroe (1768-1830, 1786)	N.Y.	. . ./2 (A)
Louisa Catherine Johnson Adams (1775-1852, 1797)	Md. (B)	3/1
Rachel Donelson Robards Jackson (1767-1828, 1791)	Va.	None
Hannah Hoes Van Buren (1783-1819, 1807)	N.Y.	4/. . .
Anna Symmes Harrison (1775-1864, 1795)	N.J.	6/4
Letitia Christian Tyler (1790-1842, 1813)	Va.	3/5
Julia Gardiner Tyler (1820-1889, 1844)	N.Y.	5/2
Sarah Childress Polk (1803-1891, 1824)	Tenn.	None
Margaret Smith Taylor (1788-1852, 1810)	Md.	1/5
Abigail Powers Fillmore (1798-1853, 1826)	N.Y.	1/1
Caroline Carmichael McIntosh Fillmore (1813-1881, 1858)	N.J.	None
Jane Means Appleton Pierce (1806-1863, 1834)	N.H.	3/. . .
Mary Todd Lincoln (1818-1882, 1842)	Ky.	4/. . .
Eliza McCardle Johnson (1810-1876, 1827)	Tenn.	3/2
Julia Dent Grant (1826-1902, 1848)	Mo.	3/1
Lucy Ware Webb Hayes (1831-1889, 1852)	Oh.	7/1
Lucretia Rudolph Garfield (1832-1918, 1858)	Oh.	4/1
Ellen Lewis Herndon Arthur (1837-1880, 1859)	Va.	2/1
Frances Folsom Cleveland (1864-1947, 1886)	N.Y.	2/3
Caroline Lavinia Scott Harrison (1832-1892, 1853)	Oh.	1/1
Mary Scott Lord Dimmick Harrison (1858-1948, 1896)	Pa.	. . ./1
Ida Saxton McKinley (1847-1907, 1871)	Oh.	. . ./2
Alice Hathaway Lee Roosevelt (1861-1884, 1880)	Mass.	. . ./1
Edith Kermit Carow Roosevelt (1861-1948, 1886)	Conn.	4/1
Helen Herron Taft (1861-1943, 1886)	Oh.	2/1
Ellen Louise Axson Wilson (1860-1914, 1885)	Ga.	. . ./3
Edith Bolling Galt Wilson (1872-1961, 1915)	Va.	None
Florence Kling De Wolfe Harding (1860-1924, 1891)	Oh.	None
Grace Anna Goodhue Coolidge (1879-1957, 1905)	Vt.	2/. . .
Lou Henry Hoover (1875-1944, 1899)	Ia.	2/. . .
Anna Eleanor Roosevelt Roosevelt (1884-1962, 1905)	N.Y.	4/1 (A)
Bess Wallace Truman (1885-1982, 1919)	Mo.	. . ./1
Mamie Geneva Doud Eisenhower (1896-1979, 1916)	Ia.	1/. . . (A)
Jacqueline Lee Bouvier Kennedy (1929-94, 1953)	N.Y.	1/1 (A)
Claudia "Lady Bird" Alta Taylor Johnson (b. 1912, 1934)	Tex.	. . ./2
Thelma Catherine Patricia Ryan Nixon (1912-1993, 1940)	Nev.	. . ./2
Elizabeth Bloomer Warren Ford (b. 1918, 1948)	Ill.	3/1
Rosalynn Smith Carter (b. 1927, 1946)	Ga.	3/1
Anne Frances "Nancy" Robbins Davis Reagan (b. 1921, 1952)	N.Y.	1/1 (C)
Barbara Pierce Bush (b. 1925, 1945)	N.Y.	4/2
Hillary Rodham Clinton (b. 1947, 1975)	Ill.	. . ./1

James Buchanan, 15th president, was unmarried. (A) plus one infant, deceased. (B) Born London, father a Md. citizen. (C) President Reagan married and divorced Jane Wyman. They had a son and a daughter.

First Lady: Hillary Rodham Clinton

The first lady was born in Chicago, Ill., Oct. 26, 1947, the daughter of Hugh and Dorothy Rodham. She graduated from Wellesley College and Yale Law School. She married Bill Clinton in 1975. Their daughter, Chelsea, was born in 1980.

She has been active in the areas of children's rights and education reform. From 1979 to 1992, she was a partner in a Little Rock law firm and, in 1988 and 1991, was voted one of the "100 Most Influential Lawyers in America" by the National Law Journal.

After Bill Clinton became president, she played a leading role in drafting and promoting sweeping legislation to reform the U.S. health-care system.

Burial Places of the Presidents

Washington	Mt. Vernon, Va.
J. Adams	Quincy, Mass.
Jefferson	Charlottesville, Va.
Madison	Montpelier Station, Va.
Monroe	Richmond, Va.
J.Q. Adams	Quincy, Mass.
Jackson	Nashville, Tenn.
Van Buren	Kinderhook, N.Y.
W.H. Harrison	North Bend, Oh.
Tyler	Richmond, Va.
Polk	Nashville, Tenn.
Taylor	Louisville, Ky.
Fillmore	Buffalo, N.Y.
Pierce	Concord, N.H.
Buchanan	Lancaster, Pa.
Lincoln	Springfield, Ill.
A. Johnson	Greeneville, Tenn.
Grant	New York City
Hayes	Fremont, Oh.
Garfield	Cleveland, Oh.
Arthur	Albany, N.Y.
Cleveland	Princeton, N.J.
B. Harrison	Indianapolis, Ind.
McKinley	Canton, Oh.
T. Roosevelt	Oyster Bay, N.Y.
Taft	Arlington Nat'l. Cem'y.
Wilson	Washington Cathedral
Harding	Marion, Oh.
Coolidge	Plymouth, Vt.
Hoover	West Branch, Ia.
F.D. Roosevelt	Hyde Park, N.Y.
Truman	Independence, Mo.
Eisenhower	Abilene, Kan.
Kennedy	Arlington Nat'l. Cem'y.
L.B. Johnson	Stonewall, Tex.
Nixon	Yorba Linda, Cal.

AFGHANISTAN
ALBANIA
ALGERIA
ANDORRA
ANGOLA
ANTIGUA AND BARBUDA
ARGENTINA
ARMENIA
AUSTRALIA
AUSTRIA
AZERBAIJAN
THE BAHAMAS
BAHRAIN
BANGLADESH
BARBADOS
BELARUS
BELGIUM
BELIZE
BENIN
BHUTAN
BOLIVIA
BOSNIA AND HERZEGOVINA
BOTSWANA
BRAZIL
BRUNEI DARUSSALAM
BULGARIA
BURKINA FASO
BURUNDI
CAMBODIA
CAMEROON
CANADA
CAPE VERDE
CENTRAL AFRICAN REPUBLIC
CHAD
CHILE
CHINA
COLOMBIA
COMOROS
CONGO
COSTA RICA
COTE D'IVOIRE
CROATIA
CUBA
CYPRUS
CZECH REPUBLIC
DENMARK
DJIBOUTI
DOMINICA
DOMINICAN REPUBLIC
ECUADOR
EGYPT
EL SALVADOR
EQUATORIAL GUINEA
ERITREA
ESTONIA

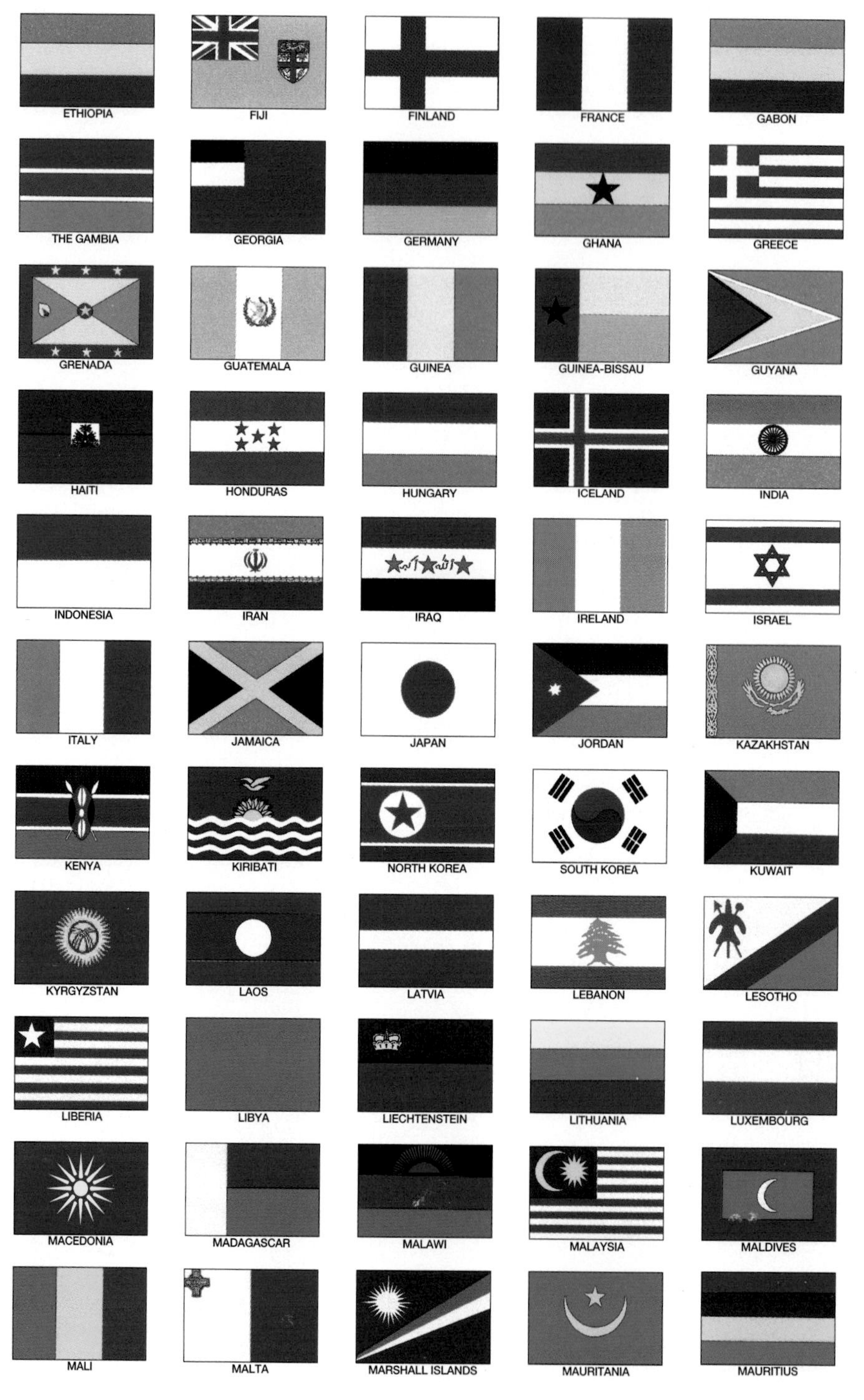
ETHIOPIA
FIJI
FINLAND
FRANCE
GABON
THE GAMBIA
GEORGIA
GERMANY
GHANA
GREECE
GRENADA
GUATEMALA
GUINEA
GUINEA-BISSAU
GUYANA
HAITI
HONDURAS
HUNGARY
ICELAND
INDIA
INDONESIA
IRAN
IRAQ
IRELAND
ISRAEL
ITALY
JAMAICA
JAPAN
JORDAN
KAZAKHSTAN
KENYA
KIRIBATI
NORTH KOREA
SOUTH KOREA
KUWAIT
KYRGYZSTAN
LAOS
LATVIA
LEBANON
LESOTHO
LIBERIA
LIBYA
LIECHTENSTEIN
LITHUANIA
LUXEMBOURG
MACEDONIA
MADAGASCAR
MALAWI
MALAYSIA
MALDIVES
MALI
MALTA
MARSHALL ISLANDS
MAURITANIA
MAURITIUS

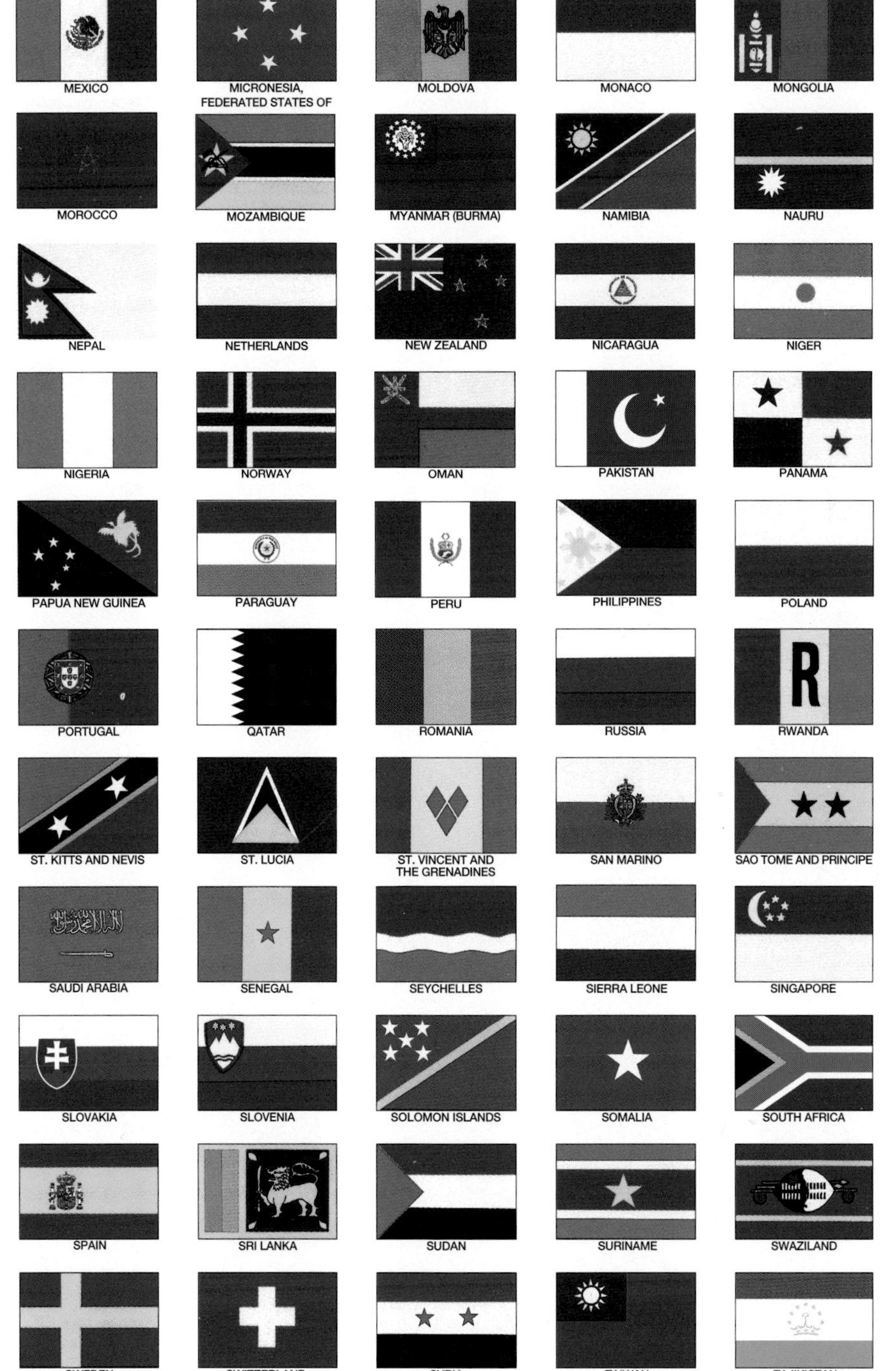
MEXICO
MICRONESIA, FEDERATED STATES OF
MOLDOVA
MONACO
MONGOLIA
MOROCCO
MOZAMBIQUE
MYANMAR (BURMA)
NAMIBIA
NAURU
NEPAL
NETHERLANDS
NEW ZEALAND
NICARAGUA
NIGER
NIGERIA
NORWAY
OMAN
PAKISTAN
PANAMA
PAPUA NEW GUINEA
PARAGUAY
PERU
PHILIPPINES
POLAND
PORTUGAL
QATAR
ROMANIA
RUSSIA
RWANDA
R
ST. KITTS AND NEVIS
ST. LUCIA
ST. VINCENT AND THE GRENADINES
SAN MARINO
SAO TOME AND PRINCIPE
SAUDI ARABIA
SENEGAL
SEYCHELLES
SIERRA LEONE
SINGAPORE
SLOVAKIA
SLOVENIA
SOLOMON ISLANDS
SOMALIA
SOUTH AFRICA
SPAIN
SRI LANKA
SUDAN
SURINAME
SWAZILAND
SWEDEN
SWITZERLAND
SYRIA
TAIWAN
TAJIKISTAN

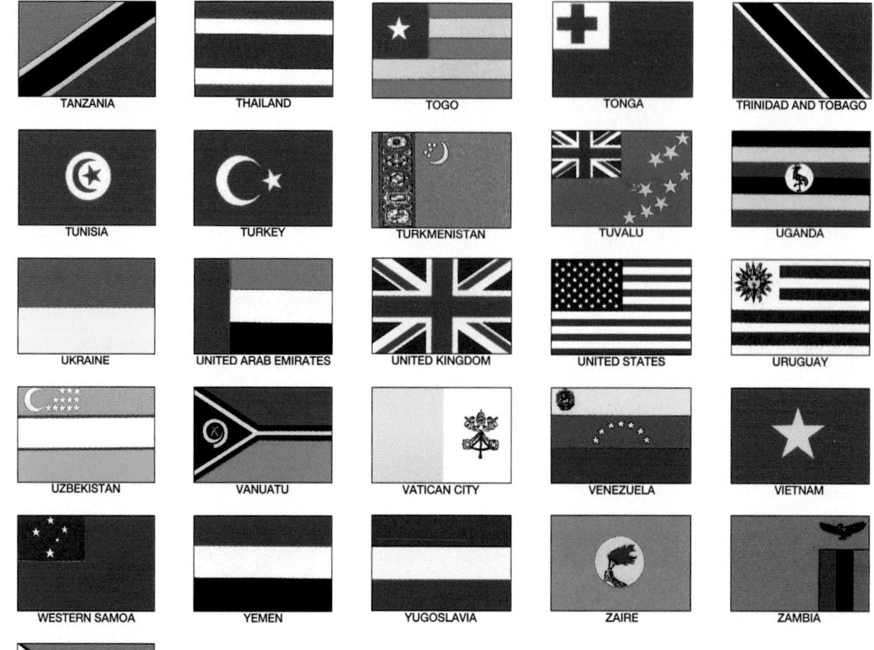

INTERNATIONAL TIME ZONES

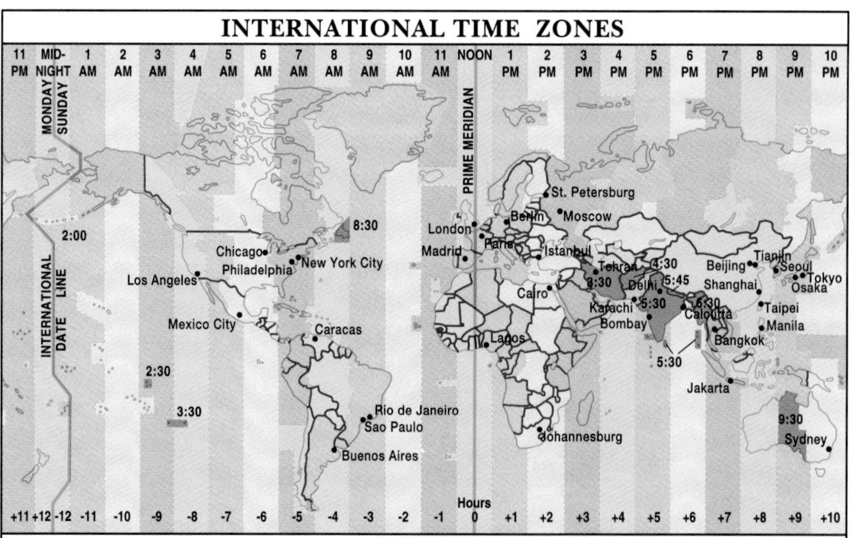

The world is divided into 24 time zones, each 15° longitude wide. The longitudinal meridian passing through Greenwich, England, is the starting point, and is called the *prime meridian.* The 12th zone is divided by the 180th meridian (International Date Line). When the line is crossed going west, the date is advanced one day; when crossed going east, the date becomes a day earlier.

© The World Almanac and Book of Facts 1995

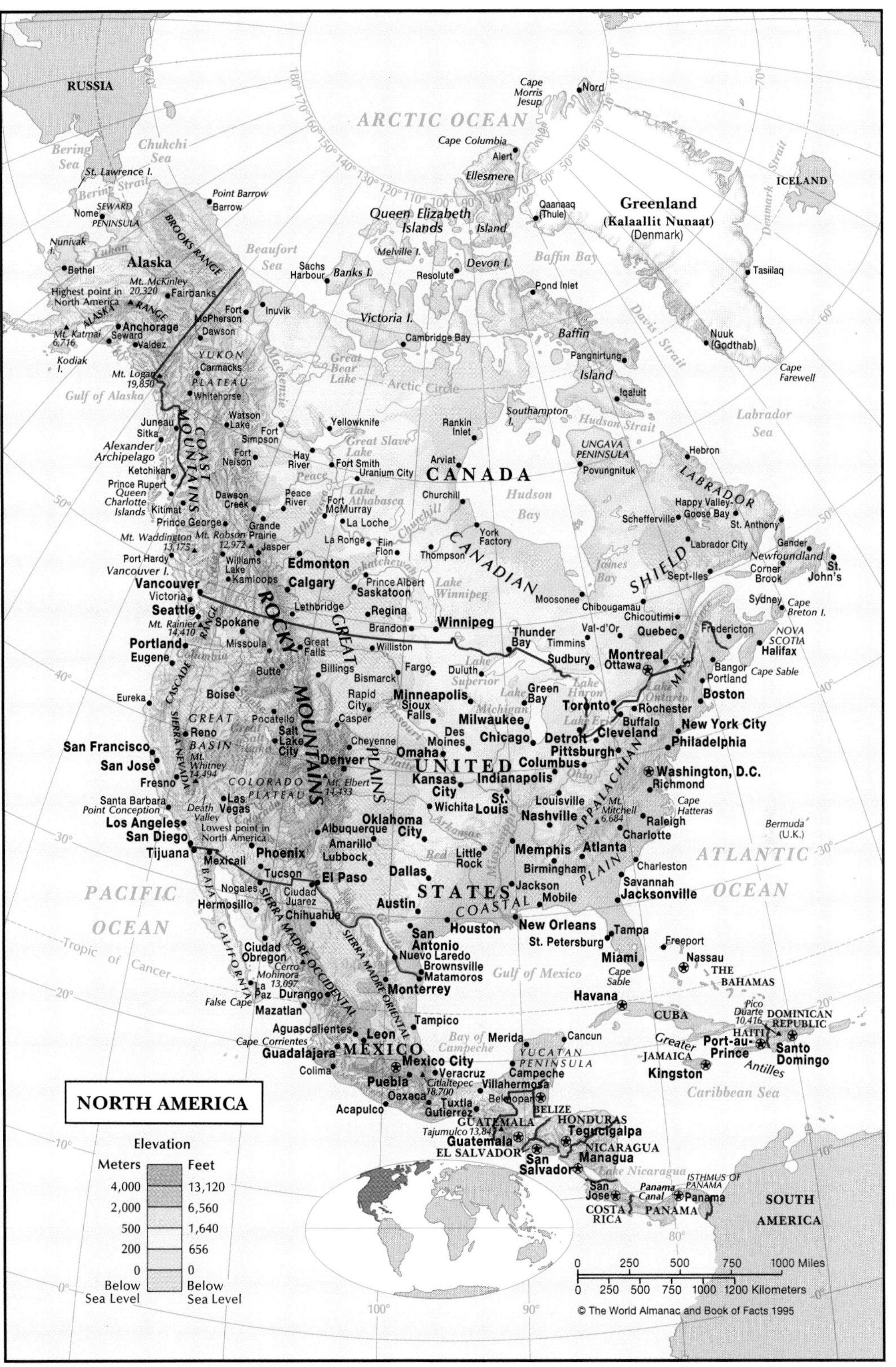
NORTH AMERICA
Elevation
Meters
Feet
4,000
13,120
2,000
6,560
500
1,640
200
656
0
0
Below Sea Level
Below Sea Level
0 250 500 750 1000 Miles
0 250 500 750 1000 1200 Kilometers
© The World Almanac and Book of Facts 1995
RUSSIA
ARCTIC OCEAN
Cape Morris Jesup
Nord
Cape Columbia
Alert
Ellesmere Island
Qaanaaq (Thule)
Greenland
(Kalaallit Nunaat)
(Denmark)
ICELAND
Denmark Strait
Tasiilaq
Nuuk (Godthab)
Cape Farewell
Davis Strait
Baffin Bay
Pond Inlet
Baffin Island
Pangnirtung
Iqaluit
Labrador Sea
Hudson Strait
Queen Elizabeth Islands
Melville I.
Devon I.
Resolute
Sachs Harbour
Banks I.
Victoria I.
Cambridge Bay
Beaufort Sea
Bering Sea
Chukchi Sea
St. Lawrence I.
Bering Strait
Point Barrow
Barrow
BROOKS RANGE
Nome
SEWARD PENINSULA
Nunivak I.
Yukon
Alaska
Bethel
Mt. McKinley 20,320
Highest point in North America
Fairbanks
ALASKA RANGE
Anchorage
Seward
Valdez
Mt. Katmai 6,716
Kodiak I.
Fort McPherson
Inuvik
Dawson
YUKON PLATEAU
Carmacks
Mt. Logan 19,850
Whitehorse
Gulf of Alaska
Mackenzie
Great Bear Lake
Arctic Circle
Watson Lake
Fort Simpson
Yellowknife
Rankin Inlet
Southampton I.
Juneau
Sitka
COAST MOUNTAINS
Alexander Archipelago
Ketchikan
Prince Rupert
Queen Charlotte Islands
Kitimat
Great Slave Lake
Hay River
Fort Smith
Uranium City
Fort Nelson
Arviat
CANADA
UNGAVA PENINSULA
Povungnituk
Hebron
LABRADOR
Peace
Peace River
Dawson Creek
Lake Athabasca
Fort McMurray
Churchill
Hudson Bay
Happy Valley-Goose Bay
Schefferville
St. Anthony
Prince George
Grande Prairie
Athabasca
La Loche
Mt. Waddington 13,175
Mt. Robson 12,972
Jasper
La Ronge
Flin Flon
York Factory
CANADIAN SHIELD
Labrador City
Gander
Newfoundland
St. John's
Port Hardy
Vancouver I.
Williams Lake
Kamloops
Edmonton
Thompson
Corner Brook
Sept-Iles
James Bay
Vancouver
Victoria
Calgary
Saskatchewan
Prince Albert
Saskatoon
Lake Winnipeg
Moosonee
Sydney
Cape Breton I.
Seattle
Mt. Rainier 14,410
ROCKY
Lethbridge
Regina
Chibougamau
Chicoutimi
Spokane
GREAT
Brandon
Winnipeg
Thunder Bay
Val-d'Or
Quebec
Fredericton
NOVA SCOTIA
Halifax
Portland
Eugene
Columbia
CASCADE RANGE
Missoula
Great Falls
Williston
Timmins
Sudbury
Montreal
Ottawa
Butte
Billings
Bismarck
Fargo
Duluth
Lake Superior
Lake Huron
Bangor
Portland
Cape Sable
Eureka
Boise
MOUNTAINS
Rapid City
Minneapolis
Sioux Falls
Lake Michigan
Green Bay
Toronto
Lake Ontario
Rochester
Boston
Snake
GREAT BASIN
SIERRA NEVADA
Pocatello
Reno
Salt Lake City
Great Salt Lake
Casper
Milwaukee
Buffalo
Lake Erie
Detroit
Cleveland
New York City
San Francisco
San Jose
Mt. Whitney 14,494
Cheyenne
Des Moines
Chicago
Pittsburgh
Philadelphia
Omaha
Denver
PLAINS
UNITED
Columbus
Ohio
Washington, D.C.
Fresno
COLORADO PLATEAU
Mt. Elbert 14,433
Kansas City
Indianapolis
Richmond
APPALACHIAN MTS.
Santa Barbara
Point Conception
Las Vegas
Death Valley
Lowest point in North America
Wichita
St. Louis
Louisville
Mt. Mitchell 6,684
Cape Hatteras
Los Angeles
San Diego
Tijuana
Albuquerque
Oklahoma City
Arkansas
Nashville
Raleigh
Bermuda (U.K.)
Phoenix
Amarillo
Red
Little Rock
Memphis
Atlanta
Charlotte
Mexicali
Tucson
Lubbock
Mississippi
Birmingham
PLAIN
Charleston
ATLANTIC OCEAN
PACIFIC OCEAN
BAJA CALIFORNIA
Nogales
Ciudad Juarez
El Paso
Dallas
STATES
Jackson
COASTAL
Savannah
Jacksonville
Hermosillo
Chihuahua
Austin
Mobile
SIERRA MADRE OCCIDENTAL
San Antonio
Houston
New Orleans
Tampa
Tropic of Cancer
Ciudad Obregon
Cerro Mohinora 13,097
Nuevo Laredo
Brownsville
Matamoros
Grande
St. Petersburg
Freeport
Miami
Nassau
THE BAHAMAS
Cape Sable
Gulf of Mexico
La Paz
Durango
SIERRA MADRE ORIENTAL
Monterrey
False Cape
Mazatlan
Havana
CUBA
Pico Duarte 10,416
DOMINICAN REPUBLIC
Tampico
Aguascalientes
Leon
Bay of Campeche
Merida
Cancun
HAITI
Cape Corrientes
Guadalajara
MEXICO
YUCATAN PENINSULA
Greater Antilles
Port-au-Prince
Santo Domingo
Mexico City
JAMAICA
Kingston
Colima
Veracruz
Campeche
Puebla
Citlaltepec 18,700
Villahermosa
Caribbean Sea
Oaxaca
Belmopan
Acapulco
Tuxtla Gutierrez
BELIZE
GUATEMALA
HONDURAS
Tajumulco 13,845
Tegucigalpa
Guatemala
NICARAGUA
EL SALVADOR
San Salvador
Managua
Lake Nicaragua
ISTHMUS OF PANAMA
San Jose
Panama Canal
Panama
COSTA RICA
PANAMA
SOUTH AMERICA
100°
90°
80°

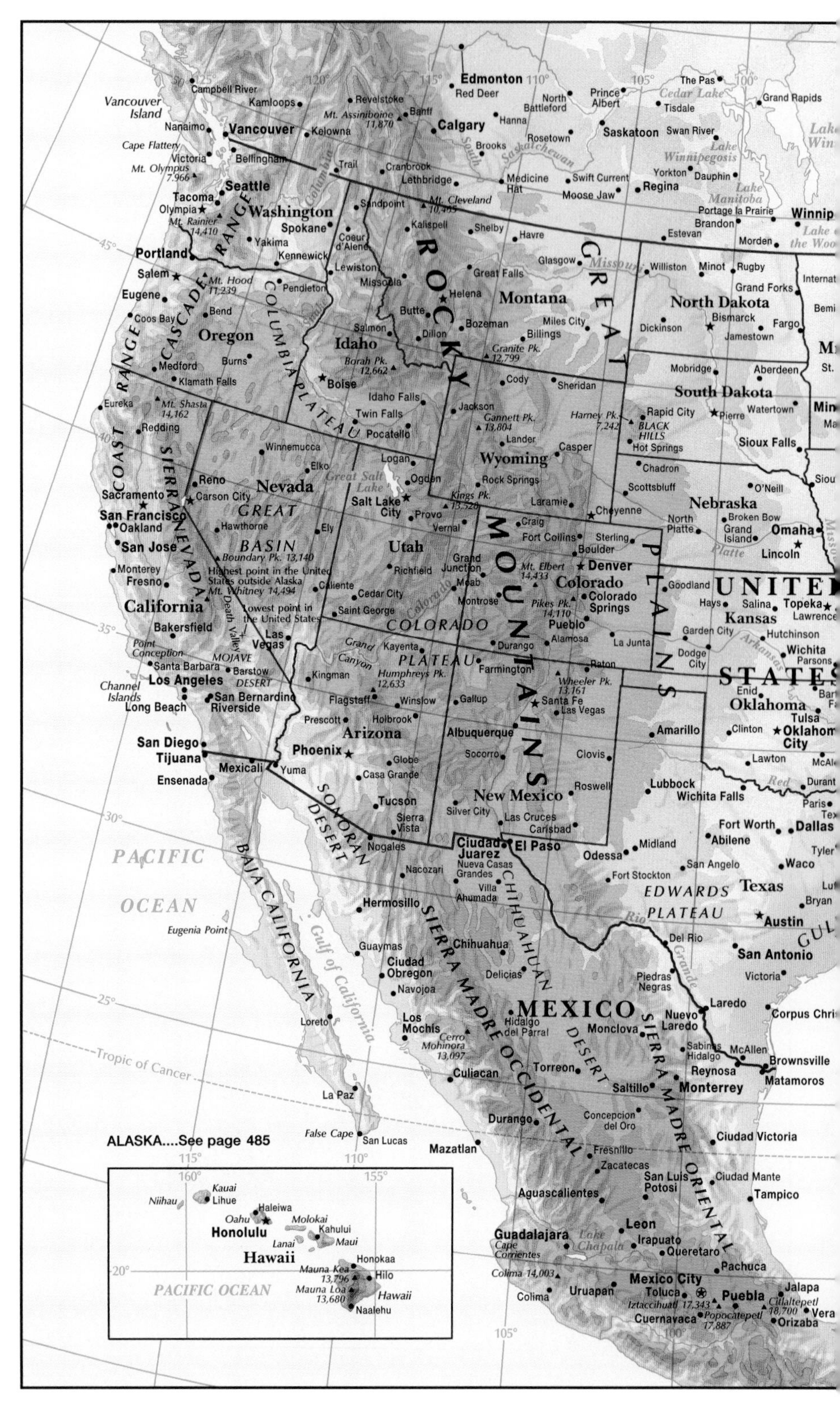
Edmonton
Red Deer
The Pas
Cedar Lake
Grand Rapids
Campbell River
Kamloops
Revelstoke
Mt. Assiniboine 11,870
Banff
North Battleford
Prince Albert
Tisdale
Vancouver Island
Nanaimo
Vancouver
Kelowna
Calgary
Hanna
Rosetown
Saskatoon
Swan River
Lake Winnipegosis
Cape Flattery
Victoria
Mt. Olympus 7,966
Bellingham
Trail
Cranbrook
Brooks
South Saskatchewan
Lethbridge
Medicine Hat
Swift Current
Moose Jaw
Regina
Yorkton
Dauphin
Lake Manitoba
Tacoma
Seattle
Olympia
Mt. Rainier 14,410
Washington
Spokane
Yakima
Sandpoint
Mt. Cleveland 10,466
Kalispell
Shelby
Havre
Columbia
Portage la Prairie
Brandon
Winnip
Estevan
Morden
Lake of the Woo
Portland
Kennewick
Coeur d'Alene
Glasgow
Missouri
Williston
Minot
Rugby
Salem
Mt. Hood 11,239
Pendleton
Lewiston
Missoula
Great Falls
Helena
Montana
Grand Forks
North Dakota
Eugene
Bend
Coos Bay
Oregon
Butte
Salmon
Bozeman
Miles City
Billings
Dickinson
Bismarck
Jamestown
Fargo
Idaho
Dillon
Granite Pk. 12,799
Burns
Borah Pk. 12,662
Medford
Klamath Falls
Boise
Cody
Sheridan
Mobridge
Aberdeen
South Dakota
Eureka
Mt. Shasta 14,162
Redding
Idaho Falls
Twin Falls
Pocatello
Jackson
Gannett Pk. 13,804
Lander
Harney Pk. 7,242
Rapid City
BLACK HILLS
Hot Springs
Pierre
Watertown
Sioux Falls
Winnemucca
Elko
Logan
Wyoming
Casper
Chadron
Reno
Carson City
Nevada
Great Salt Lake
Ogden
Rock Springs
Scottsbluff
O'Neill
Sacramento
San Francisco
Oakland
Salt Lake City
Provo
Kings Pk. 13,528
Vernal
Laramie
Cheyenne
Nebraska
Broken Bow
Hawthorne
GREAT BASIN
Ely
Craig
Fort Collins
Sterling
North Platte
Grand Island
Omaha
San Jose
Boundary Pk. 13,140
Utah
Boulder
Platte
Lincoln
Monterey
Fresno
Highest point in the United States outside Alaska Mt. Whitney 14,494
Richfield
Grand Junction
Mt. Elbert 14,433
Denver
Colorado
Goodland
UNITED
California
Death Valley
Caliente
Cedar City
Moab
Montrose
Pikes Pk. 14,110
Colorado Springs
Hays
Salina
Topeka
Lawrence
Lowest point in the United States
Saint George
Pueblo
Kansas
Bakersfield
Las Vegas
COLORADO
Garden City
Hutchinson
Point Conception
MOJAVE DESERT
Kayenta
Durango
Alamosa
La Junta
Arkansas
Dodge City
Wichita
Parsons
Santa Barbara
Barstow
Grand Canyon
PLATEAU
Farmington
Raton
STATES
Channel Islands
Los Angeles
San Bernardino
Riverside
Long Beach
Kingman
Humphreys Pk. 12,633
Wheeler Pk. 13,161
Enid
Flagstaff
Winslow
Gallup
Santa Fe
Las Vegas
Oklahoma
Tulsa
Prescott
Holbrook
Albuquerque
Amarillo
Clinton
Oklahoma City
San Diego
Tijuana
Arizona
Phoenix
Socorro
Clovis
Lawton
Ensenada
Mexicali
Yuma
Globe
Casa Grande
Red
Roswell
Lubbock
Wichita Falls
Tucson
New Mexico
Silver City
Las Cruces
Carlsbad
Paris
Sierra Vista
Fort Worth
Dallas
Abilene
PACIFIC OCEAN
SONORAN DESERT
Nogales
Ciudad Juarez
El Paso
Midland
Odessa
Tyler
Nacozari
Nueva Casas Grandes
Fort Stockton
San Angelo
Waco
Villa Ahumada
EDWARDS PLATEAU
Texas
Bryan
Hermosillo
Rio Grande
Austin
Eugenia Point
BAJA CALIFORNIA
Del Rio
Guaymas
Chihuahua
San Antonio
Ciudad Obregon
Navojoa
CHIHUAHUAN
Delicias
Victoria
Gulf of California
Piedras Negras
Laredo
Corpus Chri
Loreto
Los Mochis
Cerro Mohinora 13,097
MEXICO
Hidalgo del Parral
Monclova
Nuevo Laredo
DESERT
Sabinas Hidalgo
McAllen
Brownsville
Tropic of Cancer
Culiacan
Torreon
Reynosa
Matamoros
SIERRA MADRE OCCIDENTAL
Saltillo
Monterrey
La Paz
Durango
Concepcion del Oro
SIERRA MADRE ORIENTAL
False Cape
San Lucas
Ciudad Victoria
ALASKA....See page 485
Mazatlan
Fresnillo
Zacatecas
San Luis Potosi
Ciudad Mante
Tampico
Aguascalientes
Kauai
Lihue
Niihau
Haleiwa
Oahu
Honolulu
Molokai
Kahului
Maui
Lanai
Hawaii
Honokaa
Mauna Kea 13,796
Hilo
Mauna Loa 13,680
Naalehu
PACIFIC OCEAN
Guadalajara
Lake Chapala
Cape Corrientes
Leon
Irapuato
Queretaro
Pachuca
Colima 14,003
Colima
Uruapan
Mexico City
Toluca
Iztaccihuatl 17,343
Puebla
Popocatepetl 17,887
Cuernavaca
Citlaltepetl 18,700
Jalapa
Orizaba
Vera
SIERRA NEVADA
COAST RANGES
CASCADE RANGE
COLUMBIA PLATEAU
ROCKY MOUNTAINS
GREAT PLAINS
Snake
Sevier
45°
40°
35°
30°
25°
20°
50°
125°
120°
115°
110°
105°
100°
160°
155°

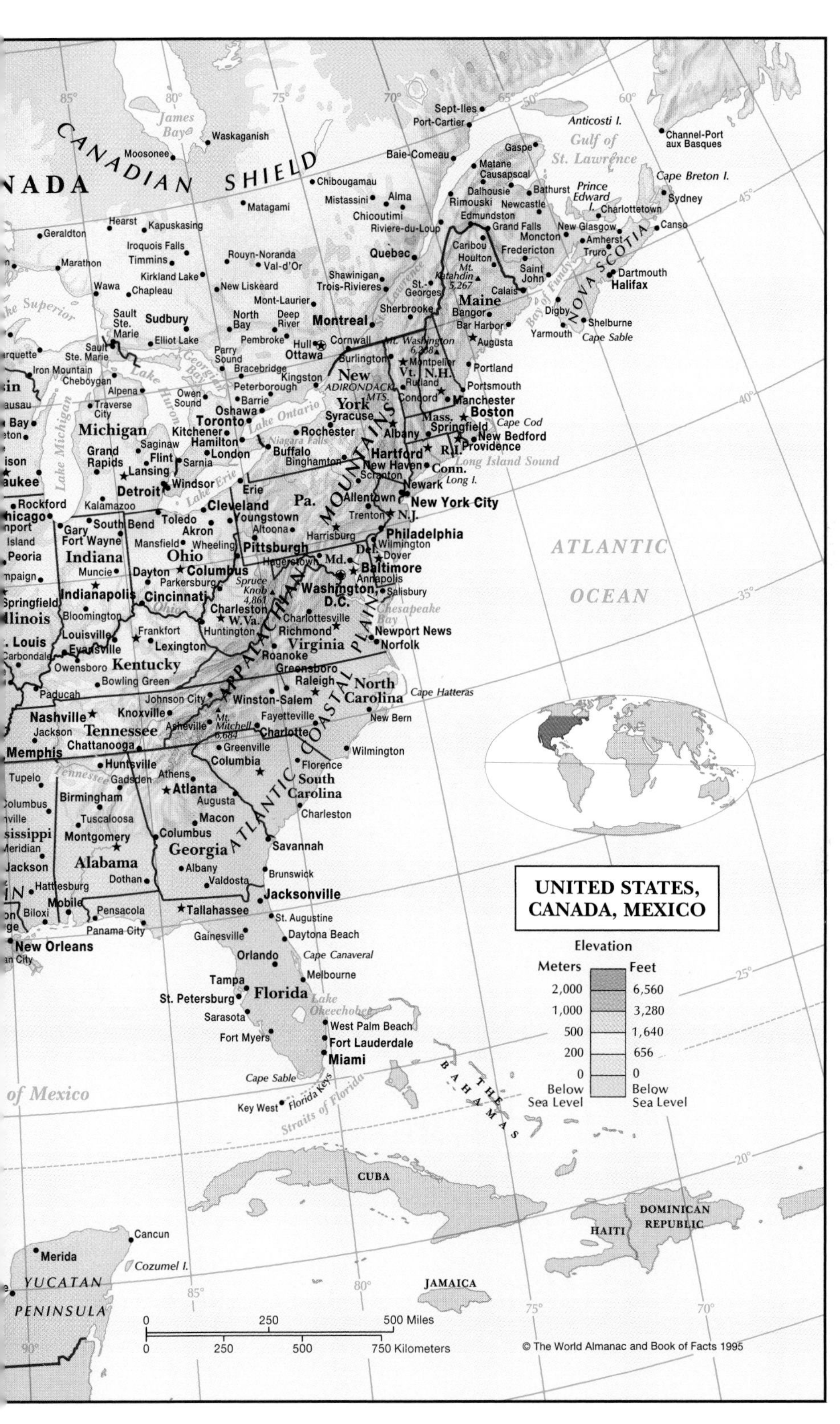

UNITED STATES, CANADA, MEXICO
Elevation
Meters
Feet
2,000
6,560
1,000
3,280
500
1,640
200
656
0
0
Below Sea Level
Below Sea Level
0
250
500 Miles
0
250
500
750 Kilometers
© The World Almanac and Book of Facts 1995
CANADIAN SHIELD
NADA
James Bay
Waskaganish
Moosonee
Chibougamau
Matagami
Mistassini
Alma
Chicoutimi
Sept-Iles
Port-Cartier
Baie-Comeau
Anticosti I.
Gulf of St. Lawrence
Channel-Port aux Basques
Gaspe
Matane
Causapscal
Dalhousie
Bathurst
Rimouski
Newcastle
Prince Edward I.
Charlottetown
Cape Breton I.
Sydney
Canso
Edmundston
Riviere-du-Loup
Grand Falls
New Glasgow
Amherst
Truro
NOVA SCOTIA
Dartmouth
Halifax
Moncton
Fredericton
Caribou
Houlton
Mt. Katahdin 5,267
Saint John
Calais
Bay of Fundy
Digby
Yarmouth
Shelburne
Cape Sable
Quebec
Shawinigan
Trois-Rivieres
St. Lawrence
St.-Georges
Sherbrooke
Maine
Bangor
Bar Harbor
Augusta
Geraldton
Hearst
Kapuskasing
Iroquois Falls
Timmins
Marathon
Kirkland Lake
Rouyn-Noranda
Val-d'Or
Wawa
Chapleau
New Liskeard
Mont-Laurier
Lake Superior
Sault Ste. Marie
Sudbury
North Bay
Deep River
Montreal
Elliot Lake
Pembroke
Hull
Ottawa
Cornwall
Mt. Washington 6,288
Parry Sound
Bracebridge
Burlington
Montpelier
Portland
Georgian Bay
Kingston
New York
Vt.
N.H.
Portsmouth
Marquette
Iron Mountain
Cheboygan
Alpena
Lake Huron
Owen Sound
Peterborough
Barrie
ADIRONDACK MTS.
Rutland
Concord
Manchester
Traverse City
Oshawa
Toronto
Lake Ontario
Syracuse
Mass.
Boston
Cape Cod
Michigan
Lake Michigan
Kitchener
Hamilton
Rochester
Albany
Springfield
New Bedford
Providence
R.I.
Saginaw
Niagara Falls
Buffalo
London
Grand Rapids
Flint
Sarnia
Binghamton
Hartford
New Haven
Conn.
Long Island Sound
Lansing
Detroit
Windsor
Lake Erie
Erie
Scranton
Newark
Long I.
Rockford
Chicago
Kalamazoo
Cleveland
Pa.
Allentown
New York City
Gary
South Bend
Toledo
Youngstown
Trenton
N.J.
Fort Wayne
Akron
Altoona
Harrisburg
Philadelphia
Peoria
Indiana
Mansfield
Wheeling
Pittsburgh
Wilmington
Del.
Dover
Ohio
Hagerstown
Md.
Baltimore
Muncie
Dayton
Columbus
Annapolis
Indianapolis
Parkersburg
Spruce Knob 4,861
Washington, D.C.
Salisbury
Springfield
Illinois
Cincinnati
Charleston
W. Va.
Chesapeake Bay
Bloomington
Ohio
Huntington
Charlottesville
St. Louis
Louisville
Frankfort
Richmond
Newport News
Carbondale
Evansville
Lexington
Virginia
Norfolk
Owensboro
Kentucky
Roanoke
Bowling Green
Greensboro
Raleigh
North Carolina
Cape Hatteras
Paducah
Johnson City
Winston-Salem
APPALACHIAN MOUNTAINS
ATLANTIC COASTAL PLAIN
Nashville
Knoxville
Fayetteville
New Bern
Jackson
Tennessee
Asheville
Mt. Mitchell 6,684
Charlotte
Memphis
Chattanooga
Greenville
Wilmington
Columbia
Florence
Huntsville
Tupelo
Tennessee
Gadsden
Athens
South Carolina
Atlanta
Columbus
Birmingham
Augusta
Charleston
Tuscaloosa
Macon
Mississippi
Montgomery
Columbus
Meridian
Alabama
Georgia
Savannah
Jackson
Albany
Dothan
Valdosta
Brunswick
Hattiesburg
Mobile
Jacksonville
Biloxi
Pensacola
Tallahassee
St. Augustine
Panama City
Gainesville
Daytona Beach
New Orleans
Orlando
Cape Canaveral
Melbourne
Tampa
St. Petersburg
Florida
Lake Okeechobee
Sarasota
West Palm Beach
Fort Myers
Fort Lauderdale
Miami
Cape Sable
THE BAHAMAS
Gulf of Mexico
Key West
Florida Keys
Straits of Florida
ATLANTIC OCEAN
CUBA
HAITI
DOMINICAN REPUBLIC
JAMAICA
Cancun
Merida
Cozumel I.
YUCATAN PENINSULA
85°
80°
75°
70°
65°
60°
50°
45°
40°
35°
25°
20°
90°

ATLANTIC
OCEAN
Caribbean
Sea
Tropic of Cancer
Equator
MEXICO
Volcan Tajumulco 13,845
BELIZE
Belize City
Belmopan
Gulf of Honduras
GUATEMALA
Guatemala
EL SALVADOR
San Salvador
Santa Ana
Escuintla
HONDURAS
Tegucigalpa
San Pedro Sula
La Ceiba
Cerro Las Minas 9,347
NICARAGUA
Managua
Leon
Granada
Lake Nicaragua
MOSQUITO COAST
COSTA RICA
San Jose
Puntarenas
Limon
Volcan Irazu 11,260
PANAMA
Panama
Colon
David
Volcan Baru 11,401
Gulf of Panama
ISTHMUS OF PANAMA
CUBA
Havana
Santa Clara
Camaguey
Holguin
Santiago de Cuba
Guantanamo
Isle of Youth
Cayman Is. (U.K.)
JAMAICA
Kingston
Montego Bay
THE BAHAMAS
Turks & Caicos Is. (U.K.)
HAITI
Port-au-Prince
Cap-Haitien
DOMINICAN REPUBLIC
Santiago
Santo Domingo
Pico Duarte 10,417
Puerto Rico (U.S.)
San Juan
Ponce
Virgin Islands (U.S., U.K.)
Anguilla (U.K.)
ST. KITTS & NEVIS
ANTIGUA & BARBUDA
Montserrat (U.K.)
Guadeloupe (Fr.)
DOMINICA
Martinique (Fr.)
SAINT LUCIA
BARBADOS
ST. VINCENT & THE GRENADINES
GRENADA
TRINIDAD & TOBAGO
Port-of-Spain
Aruba (Neth.)
Curacao (Neth.)
Bonaire (Neth.)
Margarita Island
VENEZUELA
Caracas
Maracaibo
Lake Maracaibo
Maracay
Valencia
Barquisimeto
Barcelona
Cumana
Maturin
Ciudad Guayana
Ciudad Bolivar
El Tigre
Coro
Cabimas
Valera
Merida
San Cristobal
San Fernando de Apure
Puerto Ayacucho
Pico Bolivar 16,427
Angel Falls
Orinoco
LLANOS
COLOMBIA
Bogota
Medellin
Cali
Barranquilla
Cartagena
Santa Marta
Valledupar
Cucuta
Bucaramanga
Barrancabermeja
Sincelejo
Monteria
Tunja
Villavicencio
Ibague
Manizales
Pereira
Armenia
Palmira
Neiva
Popayan
Pasto
Buenaventura
Nevada del Huila 18,865
Pico Cristobal Colon 18,947
GUYANA
Georgetown
New Amsterdam
SURINAME
Paramaribo
French Guiana (Fr.)
Cayenne
Kourou
Mt. Roraima 9,094
GUIANA HIGHLANDS
Boa Vista
ECUADOR
Quito
Guayaquil
Esmeraldas
Portoviejo
Ambato
Cuenca
Machala
Cotopaxi 19,347
Chimborazo 20,561
Galapagos Islands (Ecuador)
ANDES
PERU
Callao
Trujillo
Chiclayo
Chimbote
Piura
Sullana
Talara
Tumbes
Aguja Point
Cajamarca
Huanuco
Cerro de Pasco
Huancayo
Ayacucho
Pucallpa
Yurimaguas
Iquitos
Puerto Maldonado
Nev. Huascaran 22,205
Nev. Yerupaja 21,709
LA MONTANA
Marañon
Putumayo
BRAZIL
Manaus
Belem
Macapa
Marajo Island
Santarem
Sao Luis
Parnaiba
Fortaleza
Teresina
Natal
Joao Pessoa
Recife
Campina Grande
Maceio
Aracaju
Feira de Santana
Juazeiro do Norte
Imperatriz
Gurupi
Porto Velho
Guajara-Mirim
Riberalta
Rio Branco
Cobija
Cruzeiro do Sul
Benjamin Constant
SELVAS
Amazon
Negro
Madeira
Tapajos
Xingu
Tocantins
Purus
Jurua
PACIFIC

SOUTH AMERICA
CENTRAL AMERICA
& THE CARIBBEAN
Elevation
Meters Feet
4,000 13,120
2,000 6,560
500 1,640
200 656
0 0
Below Sea Level Below Sea Level
0 250 500 750 Miles
0 250 500 750 1,000 Kilometers
© The World Almanac and Book of Facts 1995
Tropic of Capricorn
ANDES
ATACAMA DESERT
GRAN CHACO
PAMPAS
CAMPOS
PATAGONIA
CHILE
ARGENTINA
PARAGUAY
URUGUAY
Iquique
Calama
Antofagasta
Tarija
San Salvador de Jujuy
Salta
San Miguel de Tucuman
Cerro Ojos del Salado 22,572
San Felix Island (Chile)
San Ambrosio Island (Chile)
Copiapo
Cerro Bonete
Catamarca
Santiago del Estero
La Rioja
La Serena
Highest point in South America
Cerro Aconcagua
Vina del Mar
Valparaiso
Santiago
San Bernardo
Rancagua
Cerro Tupungato 22,310
Juan Fernandez Islands (Chile)
Talca
Chillan
Talcahuano
Concepcion
Temuco
Valdivia
Osorno
Puerto Montt
Chiloe Island
Chonos Archipelago
Taitao Peninsula
Punta Arenas
Cordoba
San Juan
Mendoza
Rio Cuarto
San Rafael
Santa Fe
Concordia
Parana
Rosario
Junin
Buenos Aires
Avellaneda
La Plata
Santa Rosa
Bahia Blanca
Punta Alta
Mar del Plata
Neuquen
San Carlos de Bariloche
Esquel
Viedma
San Matias Gulf
Valdes Peninsula
Lowest point in South America
Trelew
Rawson
Comodoro Rivadavia
Gulf of San Jorge
Cape Tres Puntas
Bahia Grande
Rio Gallegos
Str. of Magellan
Tierra del Fuego
Ushuaia
Cape Horn
Stanley
Falkland Islands (U.K.) (Islas Malvinas)
South Georgia (U.K.)
Concepcion
Asuncion
Formosa
Coronel Oviedo
Iguazu Falls
Encarnacion
Resistencia
Corrientes
Posadas
Santo Tome
Curuzu Cuatia
Salto
Paysandu
Rivera
Pelotas
Melo
Minas
Montevideo
Rio de la Plata
Campo Grande
Rio Preto
Presidente Prudente
Bauru
Ribeirao Preto
Pico da Bandeira 9,482
Vitoria
Londrina
Campinas
Jundiai
Sorocaba
Sao Paulo
Santos
Juiz de Fora
Volta Redonda
Niteroi
Rio de Janeiro
Ponta Grossa
Curitiba
Joinvile
Florianopolis
Passo Fundo
Caxias do Sul
Santa Maria
Porto Alegre

EUROPE
Elevation
Meters
Feet
4,000
13,120
2,000
6,560
500
1,640
200
656
0
0
Below Sea Level
Below Sea Level
Greenland (Den.)
Arctic Circle
North Cape
Hammerfest
Tromso
Ivalo
LAPLAND
Murmansk
Keflavik
Reykjavik
Akureyri
ICELAND
Hekla 4,892
Norwegian Sea
Bodo
Kiruna
Rovaniemi
Arkhangelsk
Lulea
Oulu
Belomorsk
NORWAY
Umea
FINLAND
Faeroe Is. (Den.)
Trondheim
Ostersund
Kuopio
Alesund
Vaasa
Lake Onega
SWEDEN
Petrozavodsk
Shetland Is. (U.K.)
Glittertind 8,113
Tampere
Lake Ladoga
Bergen
Gavle
Aland Is. (Fin.)
Turku
Helsinki
Gulf of Bothnia
Gulf of Finland
Orkney Is.
St. Petersburg
Oslo
Uppsala
Tallinn
ATLANTIC OCEAN
Hebrides
Inverness
Stavanger
Skien
Stockholm
ESTONIA
Novgorod
Aberdeen
Kristiansand
Linkoping
Tartu
RUSSIA
Glasgow
Dundee
Jonkoping
Edinburgh
Goteborg
Gotland (Swe.)
Riga
LATVIA
Belfast
UNITED KINGDOM
North Sea
Alborg
Jutland
Arhus
Baltic Sea
Daugavpils
IRELAND
Newcastle
Helsingborg
Dublin
Copenhagen
Malmo
Klaipeda
LITHUANIA
Smolensk
Liverpool
Leeds
DENMARK
Odense
Kaunas
Vitsyebsk
Cork
Limerick
Manchester
Sheffield
Bornholm (Den.)
(RUSSIA)
Vilnius
Kaliningrad
Birmingham
Hamburg
Rostock
Gdansk
Minsk
Mahilyow
Bryansk
Cardiff
NETHERLANDS
Bremen
Szczecin
Bialystok
BELARUS
London
Amsterdam
Hannover
Berlin
POLAND
Bristol
Land's End
Plymouth
Portsmouth
Hague
Rotterdam
Poznan
Warsaw
Brest
Homyel
English Channel
Antwerp
Essen
Magdeburg
Channel Is. (U.K.)
Brussels
Cologne
Leipzig
Lodz
Le Havre
Rouen
BELGIUM
Bonn
GERMANY
Dresden
Wroclaw
Lublin
Kiev
Brest
Luxembourg
Frankfurt
Prague
Katowice
UKRAINE
Paris
LUX.
Nurnberg
CZECH REP.
Ostrava
Krakow
Lviv
Nantes
Orleans
Mannheim
Brno
CARPATHIAN MOUNTAINS
Vynnytsya
Strasbourg
Stuttgart
Dniester
Tours
Dijon
Munich
Danube
SLOVAKIA
Kosice
Bay of Biscay
FRANCE
Basel
Linz
Miskolc
MOLDOVA
Zurich
Salzburg
Vienna
Bratislava
Debrecen
Iasi
Chisinau
Limoges
Bern
SWITZ.
LIECH.
AUSTRIA
Budapest
Odesa
La Coruna
Geneva
Graz
HUNGARY
Cluj-Napoca
Bordeaux
Lyon
Mt. Blanc
Matterhorn 14,690
SLOVENIA
Ljubljana
ROMANIA
Gijon
Grenoble
Milan
Trieste
Pecs
Brasov
Vigo
Bilbao
CROATIA
Timisoara
Oporto
San Sebastian
Toulouse
Turin
Verona
Venice
Zagreb
Belgrade
Constanta
Valladolid
PYRENEES
Genoa
Bucharest
Coimbra
Pico de Aneto 11,168
Marseille
Nice
Bologna
BOS. & HERZ.
SERBIA
Danube
Black Sea
MONACO
SAN MARINO
Sarajevo
Ruse
PORTUGAL
IBERIAN PENINSULA
ANDORRA
Florence
Split
YUGO.
BALKAN
Varna
Burgas
Madrid
Zaragoza
Corsica (Fr.)
Elba
Adriatic Sea
Dubrovnik
MONT.
BULGARIA
Lisbon
SPAIN
Barcelona
Ajaccio
Skopje
Sofia
Plovdiv
Cape St. Vincent
Rome
ITALY
Tirana
MACE.
Cordoba
Valencia
Naples
Bari
ALBANIA
Thessaloniki
Palma
Vesuvius 4,202
Vlore
Olympus 9,570
Seville
Balearic Is. (Sp.)
Sardinia (It.)
Cagliari
Tyrrhenian Sea
Corfu
Larisa
Volos
TURKEY
Cadiz
Granada
Alicante
GREECE
Strait of Gibraltar
Malaga
Gibraltar (U.K.)
Mediterranean Sea
Palermo
Messina
Ionian Sea
Aegean Sea
Athens
Etna 11,053
Catania
Patras
Peloponnesus
Sicily
Rhodes
MALTA
Iraklion
AFRICA
Crete
0
250
500 Miles
0
250
500
750 Kilometers
© The World Almanac and Book of Facts 1995

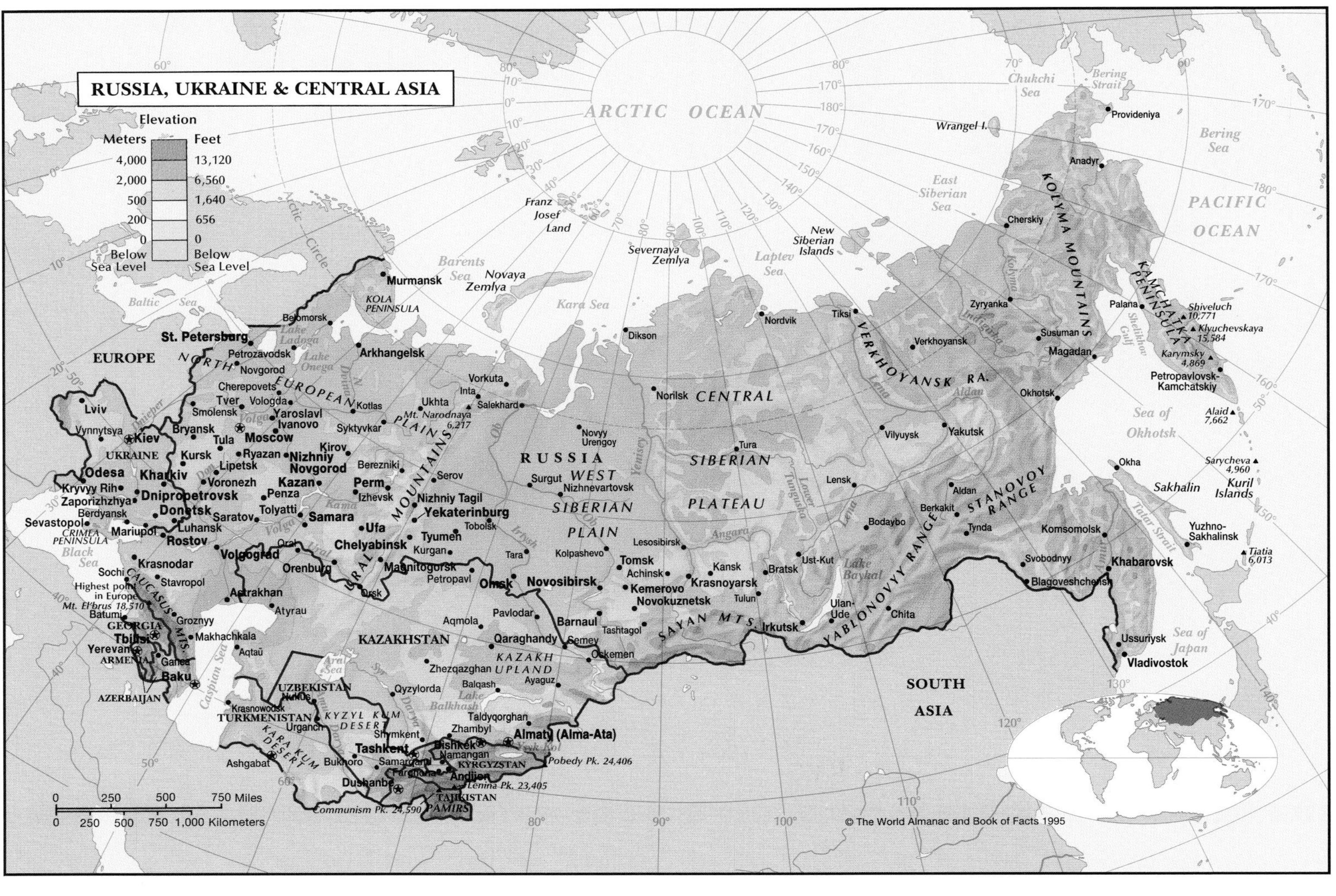

RUSSIA, UKRAINE & CENTRAL ASIA
Elevation
Meters
Feet
4,000
13,120
2,000
6,560
500
1,640
200
656
0
0
Below Sea Level
Below Sea Level
0 250 500 750 Miles
0 250 500 750 1,000 Kilometers
© The World Almanac and Book of Facts 1995
ARCTIC OCEAN
PACIFIC OCEAN
EUROPE
SOUTH ASIA
RUSSIA
KAZAKHSTAN
UKRAINE
GEORGIA
ARMENIA
AZERBAIJAN
UZBEKISTAN
TURKMENISTAN
KYRGYZSTAN
TAJIKISTAN
NORTH EUROPEAN PLAIN
WEST SIBERIAN PLAIN
CENTRAL SIBERIAN PLATEAU
URAL MOUNTAINS
KOLYMA MOUNTAINS
VERKHOYANSK RA.
STANOVOY RANGE
YABLONOVYY RANGE
SAYAN MTS.
CAUCASUS MTS.
KAZAKH UPLAND
KYZYL KUM DESERT
KARA KUM DESERT
PAMIRS
KAMCHATKA PENINSULA
KOLA PENINSULA
CRIMEA PENINSULA
Barents Sea
Kara Sea
Laptev Sea
East Siberian Sea
Chukchi Sea
Bering Sea
Bering Strait
Sea of Okhotsk
Shelikhov Gulf
Sea of Japan
Tatar Strait
Baltic Sea
Black Sea
Caspian Sea
Aral Sea
Lake Balkhash
Lake Baikal
Lake Ladoga
Lake Onega
Arctic Circle
Novaya Zemlya
Franz Josef Land
Severnaya Zemlya
New Siberian Islands
Wrangel I.
Sakhalin
Kuril Islands
Moscow
St. Petersburg
Kiev
Odesa
Kharkiv
Dnipropetrovsk
Donetsk
Lviv
Vynnytsya
Kryvyy Rih
Zaporizhzhya
Berdyansk
Mariupol
Sevastopol
Luhansk
Rostov
Krasnodar
Stavropol
Sochi
Batumi
Tbilisi
Yerevan
Baku
Ganca
Groznyy
Makhachkala
Astrakhan
Volgograd
Saratov
Voronezh
Lipetsk
Kursk
Bryansk
Smolensk
Tula
Ryazan
Tver
Novgorod
Petrozavodsk
Cherepovets
Vologda
Yaroslavl
Ivanovo
Nizhniy Novgorod
Kazan
Penza
Tolyatti
Samara
Kirov
Perm
Izhevsk
Ufa
Orenburg
Orsk
Chelyabinsk
Magnitogorsk
Yekaterinburg
Nizhniy Tagil
Serov
Tyumen
Kurgan
Tobolsk
Omsk
Tara
Petropavl
Aqmola
Pavlodar
Qaraghandy
Zhezqazghan
Balqash
Taldyqorghan
Almaty (Alma-Ata)
Semey
Oskemen
Barnaul
Novosibirsk
Tomsk
Kemerovo
Novokuznetsk
Tashtagol
Achinsk
Krasnoyarsk
Kansk
Tulun
Bratsk
Ust-Kut
Irkutsk
Ulan-Ude
Chita
Lesosibirsk
Kolpashevo
Surgut
Nizhnevartovsk
Novyy Urengoy
Salekhard
Vorkuta
Inta
Ukhta
Syktyvkar
Kotlas
Berezniki
Arkhangelsk
Belomorsk
Murmansk
Dikson
Norilsk
Tura
Nordvik
Tiksi
Lensk
Bodaybo
Vilyuysk
Verkhoyansk
Yakutsk
Aldan
Berkakit
Tynda
Svobodnyy
Blagoveshchensk
Komsomolsk
Khabarovsk
Ussuriysk
Vladivostok
Okha
Yuzhno-Sakhalinsk
Okhotsk
Magadan
Susuman
Zyryanka
Cherskiy
Anadyr
Provideniya
Palana
Petropavlovsk-Kamchatskiy
Aqtau
Atyrau
Krasnowodsk
Ashgabat
Nukus
Urganch
Bukhoro
Samarqand
Tashkent
Shymkent
Qyzylorda
Zhambyl
Bishkek
Namangan
Andijon
Farghona
Dushanbe
Mt. Narodnaya 6,217
Mt. Elbrus 18,510
Highest point in Europe
Communism Pk. 24,590
Lenina Pk. 23,405
Pobedy Pk. 24,406
Shiveluch 10,771
Klyuchevskaya 15,584
Karymsky 4,869
Alaid 7,662
Sarycheva 4,960
Tiatia 6,013
Volga
Don
Dnieper
N. Dvina
Kama
Ural
Ob
Irtysh
Yenisey
Lower Tunguska
Angara
Lena
Aldan
Indigirka
Kolyma
Amur
Syr Darya
Amu Darya

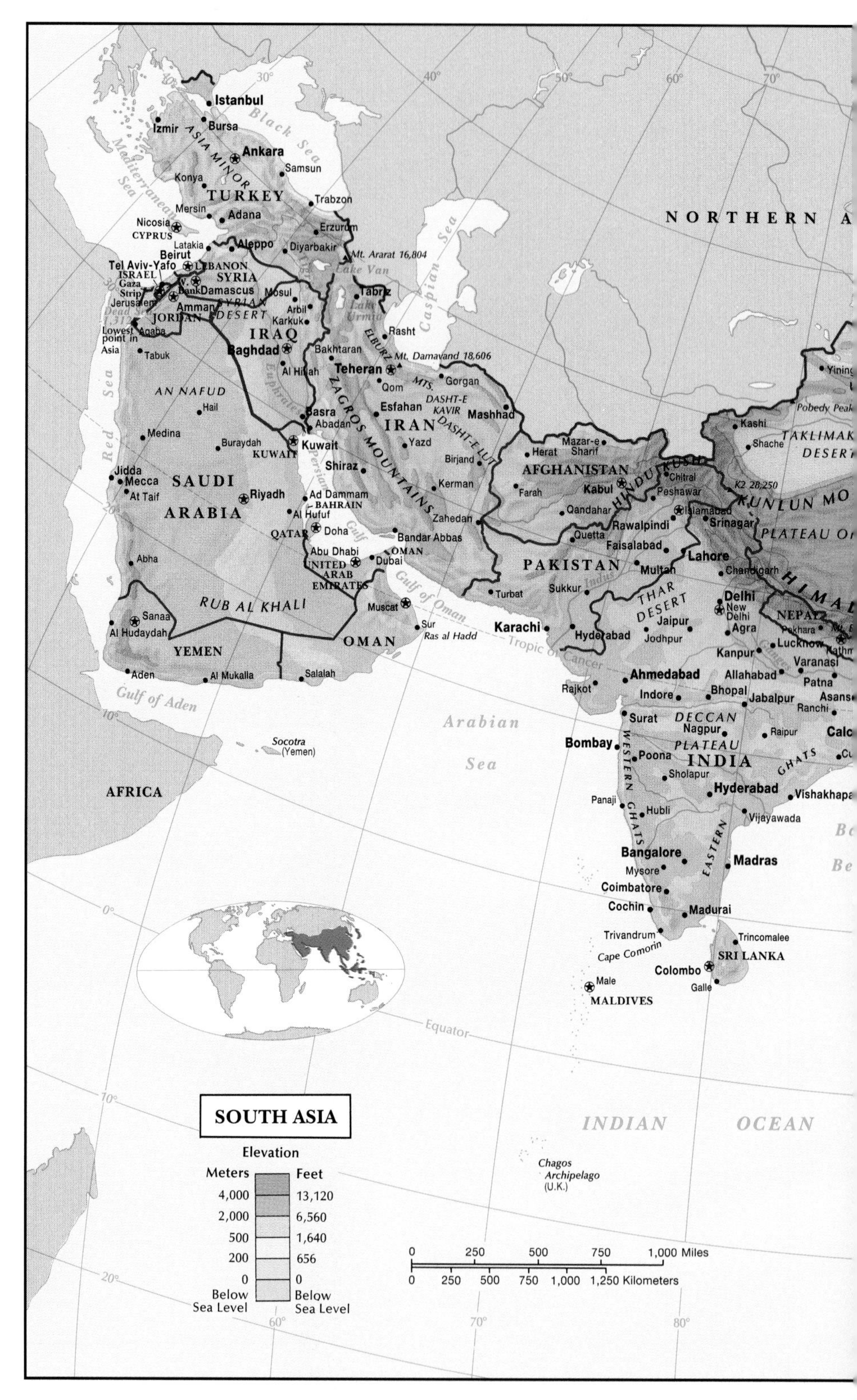
SOUTH ASIA
Elevation
Meters
Feet
4,000
13,120
2,000
6,560
500
1,640
200
656
0
0
Below Sea Level
Below Sea Level
0 250 500 750 1,000 Miles
0 250 500 750 1,000 1,250 Kilometers
Istanbul
Izmir
Bursa
Ankara
Samsun
Konya
TURKEY
ASIA MINOR
Black Sea
Mediterranean Sea
Trabzon
Mersin
Adana
Nicosia
CYPRUS
Erzurum
Latakia
Aleppo
Diyarbakir
Mt. Ararat 16,804
Lake Van
Beirut
LEBANON
Tel Aviv-Yafo
ISRAEL
SYRIA
Damascus
Jerusalem
Amman
JORDAN
SYRIAN DESERT
Mosul
Arbil
Karkuk
IRAQ
Baghdad
Tabriz
Rasht
Caspian Sea
Lowest point in Asia
Aqaba
Tabuk
Bakhtaran
Al Hillah
Teheran
Mt. Damavand 18,606
Gorgan
Qom
Esfahan
ELBURZ MTS.
DASHT-E KAVIR
Mashhad
IRAN
ZAGROS MOUNTAINS
DASHT-E LUT
AN NAFUD
Hail
Basra
Abadan
Red Sea
Medina
Buraydah
Kuwait
KUWAIT
Yazd
Birjand
Shiraz
Jidda
Mecca
At Taif
SAUDI ARABIA
Riyadh
Ad Dammam
BAHRAIN
Al Hufuf
Doha
QATAR
Kerman
Zahedan
Bandar Abbas
Abu Dhabi
UNITED ARAB EMIRATES
Dubai
OMAN
Abha
RUB AL KHALI
Muscat
Gulf of Oman
Sanaa
Al Hudaydah
YEMEN
Sur
Ras al Hadd
OMAN
Aden
Al Mukalla
Salalah
Gulf of Aden
Socotra (Yemen)
Arabian Sea
AFRICA
NORTHERN A
Herat
Mazar-e Sharif
AFGHANISTAN
HINDU KUSH
Farah
Kabul
Chitral
Peshawar
Qandahar
Islamabad
Rawalpindi
Quetta
Faisalabad
Srinagar
K2 28,250
KUNLUN MO
PLATEAU O
Lahore
PAKISTAN
Multan
Chandigarh
Turbat
Sukkur
Indus
THAR DESERT
Delhi
New Delhi
Jaipur
Agra
Karachi
Hyderabad
Jodhpur
Tropic of Cancer
Kanpur
Lucknow
NEPAL
Pokhara
Allahabad
Varanasi
Patna
Rajkot
Ahmedabad
Indore
Bhopal
Jabalpur
Ranchi
Surat
DECCAN
Nagpur
PLATEAU
Raipur
Bombay
Poona
INDIA
WESTERN GHATS
Sholapur
EASTERN GHATS
Hyderabad
Vishakhapa
Panaji
Hubli
Vijayawada
Bangalore
Madras
Mysore
Coimbatore
Cochin
Madurai
Trivandrum
Cape Comorin
Trincomalee
SRI LANKA
Colombo
Galle
Male
MALDIVES
Yining
Pobedy Peak
Kashi
Shache
TAKLIMAK DESERT
Equator
INDIAN OCEAN
Chagos Archipelago (U.K.)

MONGOLIA
CHINA
JAPAN
N. KOREA
S. KOREA
TAIWAN
PHILIPPINES
LAOS
THAILAND
CAMBODIA
VIETNAM
MALAYSIA
BRUNEI
SINGAPORE
INDONESIA
AUSTRALIA
PACIFIC OCEAN
Sea of Japan
Yellow Sea
East China Sea
South China Sea
Philippine Sea
Celebes Sea
Banda Sea
Java Sea
Timor Sea
Gulf of Tonkin
Gulf of Thailand
Andaman Sea
Tropic of Cancer
Equator
Beijing
Tianjin
Shanghai
Tokyo
Seoul
Pyongyang
Manila
Hanoi
Bangkok
Jakarta
Singapore
Kuala Lumpur
Hong Kong (U.K.)
Macau (Port.)
Canton (Guangzhou)
Ho Chi Minh City
Ulaanbaatar
Taipei
Hokkaido
Honshu
Shikoku
Kyushu
Luzon
Mindanao
Borneo
Sumatra
Java
Celebes
New Guinea
Hainan (China)
Iwo Jima (Japan)
GOBI DESERT
GREATER KHINGAN RANGE
MONGOLIAN PLATEAU
Fuji-san 12,388
© The World Almanac and Book of Facts 1995

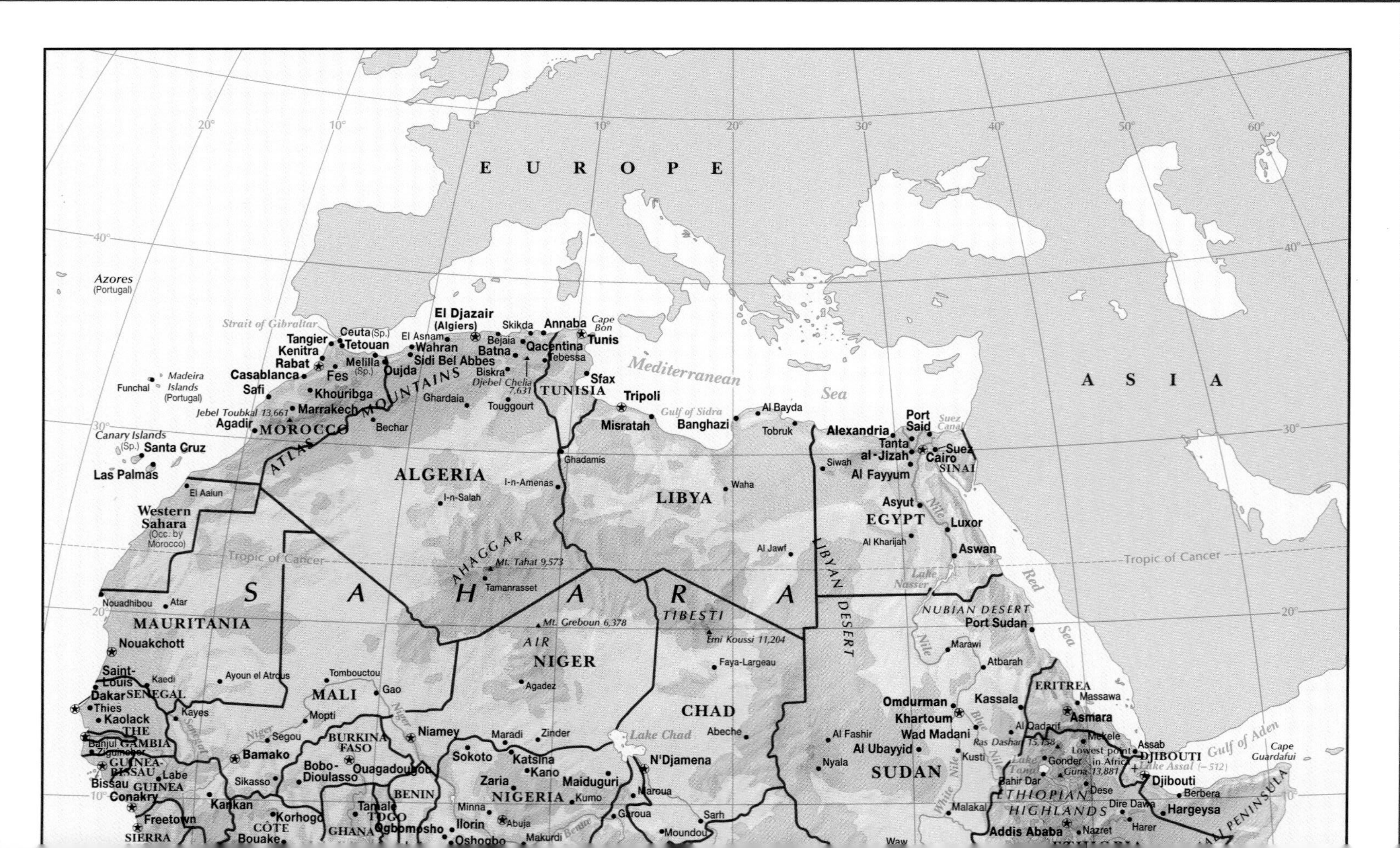

EUROPE
ASIA
Azores (Portugal)
Strait of Gibraltar
Madeira Islands (Portugal)
Funchal
Canary Islands (Sp.)
Santa Cruz
Las Palmas
Tangier
Ceuta (Sp.)
Tetouan
Kenitra
Rabat
Melilla (Sp.)
Casablanca
Fes
Oujda
Safi
Khouribga
Jebel Toubkal 13,661
Marrakech
Agadir
MOROCCO
ATLAS MOUNTAINS
Bechar
El Djazair (Algiers)
El Asnam
Wahran
Sidi Bel Abbes
Skikda
Bejaia
Annaba
Cape Bon
Tunis
Batna
Qacentina
Tebessa
Biskra
Djebel Chelia 7,631
Ghardaia
Touggourt
TUNISIA
Sfax
Mediterranean Sea
Tripoli
Misratah
Gulf of Sidra
Banghazi
Al Bayda
Tobruk
Alexandria
Port Said
Suez Canal
Tanta
al-Jizah
Cairo
Suez
SINAI
Siwah
Al Fayyum
ALGERIA
I-n-Amenas
Ghadamis
I-n-Salah
LIBYA
Waha
El Aaiun
Western Sahara (Occ. by Morocco)
AHAGGAR
Mt. Tahat 9,573
Tamanrasset
Tropic of Cancer
Al Jawf
LIBYAN DESERT
Asyut
EGYPT
Nile
Luxor
Al Kharijah
Aswan
Lake Nasser
Red Sea
SAHARA
Nouadhibou
Atar
MAURITANIA
Mt. Greboun 6,378
TIBESTI
Emi Koussi 11,204
AIR
NIGER
Agadez
NUBIAN DESERT
Port Sudan
Marawi
Atbarah
Nouakchott
Faya-Largeau
Saint-Louis
Kaedi
Ayoun el Atrous
Tombouctou
Dakar
SENEGAL
Thies
Kaolack
Kayes
MALI
Gao
Mopti
CHAD
THE GAMBIA
Banjul
Ziguinchor
GUINEA-BISSAU
Bissau
Labe
GUINEA
Conakry
Segou
Bamako
Sikasso
BURKINA FASO
Bobo-Dioulasso
Ouagadougou
Niamey
Maradi
Zinder
Lake Chad
Abeche
Sokoto
Katsina
Kano
Zaria
Maiduguri
NIGERIA
Kumo
Minna
Abuja
Ilorin
Oshogbo
Ogbomosho
Makurdi
Benue
N'Djamena
Maroua
Garoua
Moundou
Sarh
BENIN
TOGO
Tamale
GHANA
Kankan
Korhogo
CÔTE
Bouake
Freetown
SIERRA
Omdurman
Khartoum
Wad Madani
Kassala
Al Fashir
Al Ubayyid
Nyala
SUDAN
Kusti
Blue Nile
White Nile
Malakal
Waw
ERITREA
Massawa
Asmara
Al Qadarif
Mekele
Ras Dashan 15,158
Lake Tana
Bahir Dar
Gonder
Lowest point in Africa
Guna 13,881
Dese
ETHIOPIAN HIGHLANDS
Dire Dawa
Harer
Nazret
Addis Ababa
Assab
DJIBOUTI
Lake Assal (−512)
Djibouti
Gulf of Aden
Cape Guardafui
Berbera
Hargeysa
SOMALI PENINSULA
20°
10°
0°
30°
40°
50°
60°

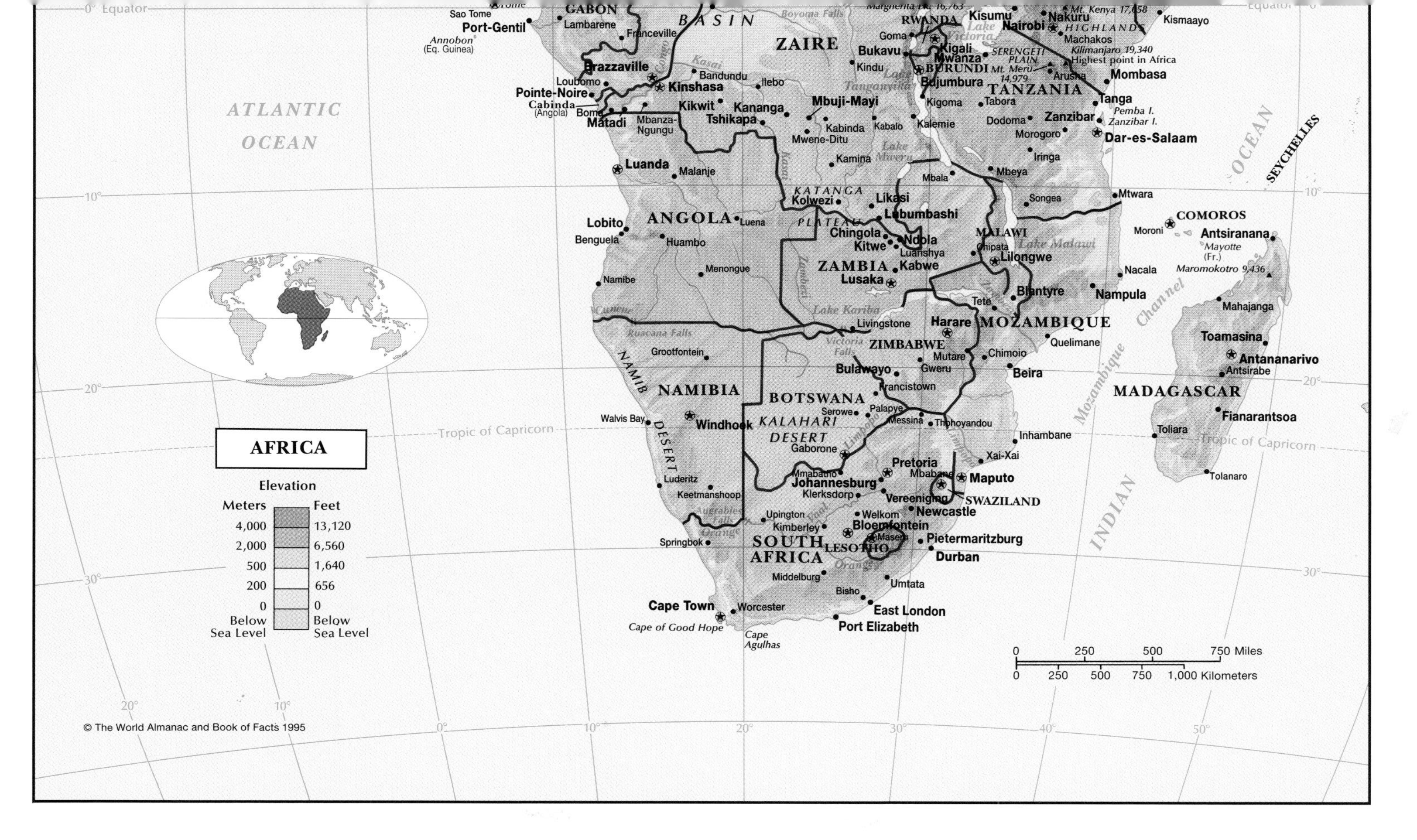
AFRICA
Elevation
Meters Feet
4,000 13,120
2,000 6,560
500 1,640
200 656
0 0
Below Sea Level Below Sea Level
ATLANTIC OCEAN
INDIAN OCEAN
ZAIRE
ANGOLA
ZAMBIA
NAMIBIA
BOTSWANA
ZIMBABWE
MOZAMBIQUE
TANZANIA
MALAWI
SOUTH AFRICA
LESOTHO
SWAZILAND
MADAGASCAR
COMOROS
SEYCHELLES
0 250 500 750 Miles
0 250 500 750 1,000 Kilometers
© The World Almanac and Book of Facts 1995

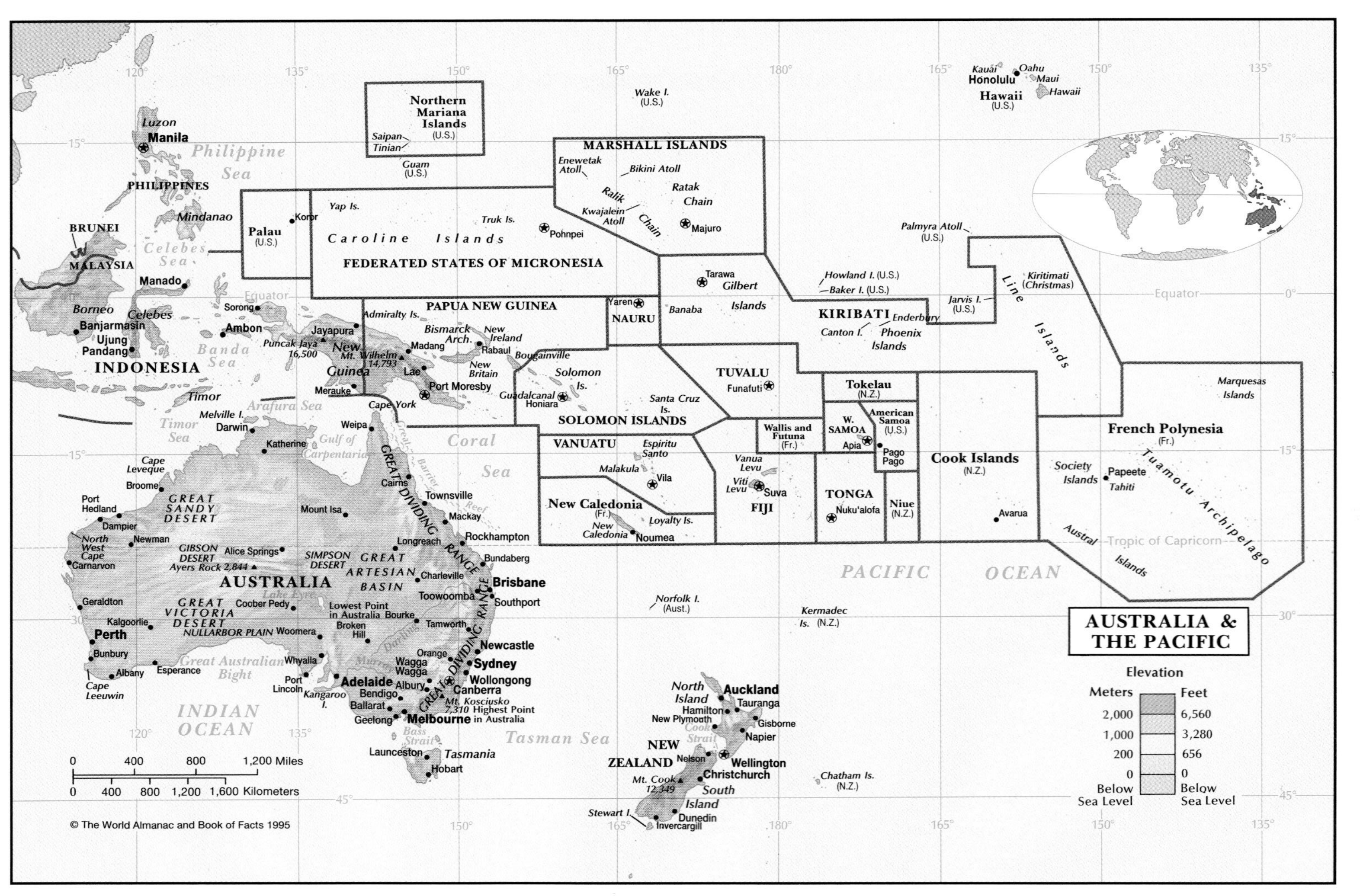
AUSTRALIA &
THE PACIFIC
Elevation
Meters
2,000
1,000
200
0
Below Sea Level
Feet
6,560
3,280
656
0
Below Sea Level
0 400 800 1,200 Miles
0 400 800 1,200 1,600 Kilometers
© The World Almanac and Book of Facts 1995
Luzon
Manila
Philippine Sea
PHILIPPINES
Mindanao
BRUNEI
MALAYSIA
Celebes Sea
Manado
Borneo
Celebes
Banjarmasin
Ujung Pandang
INDONESIA
Sorong
Ambon
Banda Sea
Timor
Timor Sea
Arafura Sea
Equator
Jayapura
Puncak Jaya 16,500
New Guinea
Mt. Wilhelm 14,793
Merauke
Madang
Lae
Port Moresby
Admiralty Is.
Bismarck Arch.
New Ireland
Rabaul
New Britain
Bougainville
PAPUA NEW GUINEA
Northern Mariana Islands (U.S.)
Saipan
Tinian
Guam (U.S.)
Palau (U.S.)
Koror
Yap Is.
Truk Is.
Pohnpei
Caroline Islands
FEDERATED STATES OF MICRONESIA
MARSHALL ISLANDS
Enewetak Atoll
Bikini Atoll
Ralik Chain
Kwajalein Atoll
Ratak Chain
Majuro
Wake I. (U.S.)
Kauai
Oahu
Honolulu
Maui
Hawaii
Hawaii (U.S.)
Palmyra Atoll (U.S.)
Howland I. (U.S.)
Baker I. (U.S.)
Jarvis I. (U.S.)
Kiritimati (Christmas)
Line Islands
Tarawa
Gilbert Islands
Banaba
Yaren
NAURU
KIRIBATI
Enderbury
Canton I.
Phoenix Islands
Solomon Is.
Guadalcanal
Honiara
Santa Cruz Is.
SOLOMON ISLANDS
TUVALU
Funafuti
Tokelau (N.Z.)
W. SAMOA
Apia
American Samoa (U.S.)
Pago Pago
Wallis and Futuna (Fr.)
Cook Islands (N.Z.)
Avarua
Marquesas Islands
French Polynesia (Fr.)
Society Islands
Papeete
Tahiti
Tuamotu Archipelago
Austral Islands
Tropic of Capricorn
VANUATU
Espiritu Santo
Malakula
Vila
Vanua Levu
Viti Levu
Suva
FIJI
TONGA
Nuku'alofa
Niue (N.Z.)
New Caledonia (Fr.)
New Caledonia
Loyalty Is.
Noumea
Coral Sea
PACIFIC OCEAN
Norfolk I. (Aust.)
Kermadec Is. (N.Z.)
Chatham Is. (N.Z.)
Melville I.
Darwin
Katherine
Gulf of Carpentaria
Weipa
Cape York
Great Barrier Reef
Cairns
Townsville
Mackay
Rockhampton
Bundaberg
Brisbane
Southport
Cape Leveque
Broome
Port Hedland
Dampier
North West Cape
Carnarvon
Newman
GREAT SANDY DESERT
GIBSON DESERT
Alice Springs
Ayers Rock 2,844
Mount Isa
SIMPSON DESERT
GREAT ARTESIAN BASIN
Longreach
Charleville
Toowoomba
GREAT DIVIDING RANGE
AUSTRALIA
Lake Eyre
Coober Pedy
Lowest Point in Australia
Bourke
Broken Hill
Darling
Tamworth
Newcastle
Geraldton
Kalgoorlie
Perth
Bunbury
Albany
Cape Leeuwin
Esperance
GREAT VICTORIA DESERT
NULLARBOR PLAIN
Woomera
Great Australian Bight
Whyalla
Port Lincoln
Kangaroo I.
Adelaide
Murray
Orange
Wagga Wagga
Albury
Sydney
Wollongong
Canberra
Mt. Kosciusko 7,310 Highest Point in Australia
Bendigo
Ballarat
Geelong
Melbourne
Bass Strait
Launceston
Tasmania
Hobart
INDIAN OCEAN
Tasman Sea
North Island
Auckland
Tauranga
Hamilton
New Plymouth
Gisborne
Napier
Cook Strait
NEW ZEALAND
Nelson
Wellington
Christchurch
Mt. Cook 12,349
South Island
Dunedin
Invercargill
Stewart I.
120°
135°
150°
165°
180°
15°
0°
30°
45°

UNITED STATES FACTS

Superlative U.S. Statistics

Source: U.S. Geological Survey, Dept. of the Interior; U.S. Bureau of the Census, Dept. of Commerce; World Almanac research

Area for 50 states and Washington, DC	Total Land 3,536,278 sq. mi.— Water 251,041 sq. mi.	3,787,319 sq. mi.
Largest state	Alaska	656,424 sq. mi.
Smallest state	Rhode Island	1,545 sq. mi.
Largest county (excludes Alaska)	San Bernardino County, California	20,064 sq. mi.
Smallest county	Kalawo, Hawaii	14 sq. mi.
Northernmost city	Barrow, Alaska	71°17′ N.
Northernmost point	Point Barrow, Alaska	71°23′ N.
Southernmost city	Hilo, Hawaii	19°43′ N.
Southernmost settlement	Naalehu, Hawaii	19°03′ N.
Southernmost point	Ka Lae (South Cape), Island of Hawaii	18°55′ N. (155°41′ W.)
Easternmost city	Eastport, Maine	66°59′ 02″ W.
[1]Easternmost settlement	Amchitka I., Alaska	179°15′ E.
[1]Easternmost point	Semisopochnoi I., Alaska	179°52′ E.
Westernmost city	Atka, Alaska	174°20′ W.
Westernmost settlement	Adak Station, Alaska	176°39′ W.
Westernmost point	Amatignak I., Alaska	179°06′ W.
Highest settlement	Climax, Colorado	11,560 ft.
Lowest settlement	Calipatria, California	–185 ft.
Highest point on Atlantic coast	Cadillac Mountain, Mount Desert I., Maine	1,530 ft.
Oldest national park	Yellowstone National Park (1872), Wyoming, Montana, Idaho	3,468 sq. mi.
Largest national park	Wrangell-St. Elias, Alaska	13,018 sq. mi.
Largest national monument	Death Valley, California, Nevada	3,231 sq. mi.
Highest waterfall	Yosemite Falls—Total in three sections	2,425 ft.
	Upper Yosemite Fall	1,430 ft.
	Cascades in middle section	675 ft.
	Lower Yosemite Fall	320 ft.
Longest river	Mississippi-Missouri	3,710 mi.
Highest mountain	Mount McKinley, Alaska	20,320 ft.
Lowest point	Death Valley, California	–282 ft.
Deepest lake	Crater Lake, Oregon	1,932 ft.
Rainiest spot	Mt. Waialeale, Hawaii	Annual aver. rainfall 460 inches
Largest gorge	Grand Canyon, Colorado River, Arizona	277 miles long, 600 ft. to 18 miles wide, 1 mile deep
Deepest gorge	Hells Canyon, Snake River, Oregon-Idaho	7,900 ft.
Strongest surface wind	Mount Washington, New Hampshire recorded 1934	231 mph
Largest dam	New Cornelia Tailings, Ten Mile Wash, Arizona[2]	274,026,000 cu. yds. material used
Tallest building	Sears Tower, Chicago, Illinois	1,454 ft.
Largest building	Boeing 747 Manufacturing Plant, Everett, Washington	205,600,000 cu. ft.; covers 47 acres.
Tallest structure	TV tower, Blanchard, North Dakota	2,063 ft.
Longest bridge span	Verrazano-Narrows, New York	4,260 ft.
Highest bridge	Royal Gorge, Colorado	1,053 ft. above water
Deepest well	Gas well, Washita County, Oklahoma	31,441 ft.

The 48 Contiguous States

Area for 48 states and Washington, DC	Total Land 2,959,481 sq. mi.— Water 160,483 sq. mi.	3,119,963 sq. mi.
Largest state	Texas	266,807 sq. mi.
Northernmost city	Bellingham, Washington	48°46′ N.
Northernmost settlement	Angle Inlet, Minnesota	49°21′ N.
Northernmost point	Northwest Angle, Minnesota	49°23′ N.
Southernmost city	Key West, Florida	24°33′ N.
Southernmost mainland city	Florida City, Florida	25°27′ N.
Southernmost point	Key West, Florida	24°33′ N.
Easternmost settlement	Lubec, Maine	66°58′49″ W.
Easternmost point	West Quoddy Head, Maine	66°57′ W.
Westernmost town	La Push, Washington	124°38′ W.
Westernmost point	Cape Alava, Washington	124°44′ W.
Highest mountain	Mount Whitney, California	14,494 ft.

(1) Alaska's Aleutian Islands extend into the eastern hemisphere and therefore technically contain the easternmost point and settlement in the U.S. (2) The New Cornelia Tailings Dam is a privately owned industrial dam composed of tailings, which are remnants of a mining process that once occurred on this site.

Geodetic Datum of North America

In July 1986, the National Oceanic and Atmospheric Administration's National Geodetic Survey (NGS), in cooperation with Canada and Mexico, completed the readjustment and redefinition of the system of latitudes and longitudes. Known as the North American Datum of 1983 (NAD 83), it replaces the North American Datum of 1927, as well as local reference systems for the Hawaiian Islands (the Old Hawaiian Datum) and Puerto Rico and the Virgin Islands (the Puerto Rico Datum). The change was prompted by an increased need for accurate coordinate information. To facilitate the use of satellite surveying and navigation systems, such as the Global Positioning System (GPS), the new datum was redefined using the Geodetic Reference System 1980 as the reference ellipsoid because this model more closely approximates the true size and shape of the earth. In addition, the origin of the coordinate system is referenced to the mass center of the earth to coincide with the orbital orientation of the GPS satellites. Positional changes resulting from the datum redefinition can be as much as 330 ft in the continental U.S., Can., and Mex. Changes that exceed 660 ft can be expected in AK, PR, and the Virgin Islands. Hawaii's coordinates changed approximately 1,300 ft.

Statistical Information About the U.S.

In the *Statistical Abstract of the United States,* the Bureau of the Census, U.S. Dept. of Commerce, annually publishes a summary of social, political, and economic information. A book of more than 1,000 pages is prepared under the direction of Glenn W. King, Chief, Statistical Compendia Staff, Bureau of the Census. Information concerning these and other publications may be obtained from the Supt. of Documents, Government Printing Office, Washington, DC 20402, or from the U.S. Bureau of the Census, Data User Services Division, Washington, DC 20233.

Highest and Lowest Altitudes in the U.S. and Territories

Source: U.S. Geological Survey, Dept. of the Interior
(Minus sign means below sea level.)

State	Highest Point Name	Highest Point County	Elev. (ft.)	Lowest Point Name	Lowest Point County	Elev. (ft.)
Alabama	Cheaha Mountain	Cleburne	2,405	Gulf of Mexico		Sea level
Alaska	Mount McKinley		20,320	Pacific Ocean		Sea level
Arizona	Humphreys Peak	Coconino	12,633	Colorado R	Yuma	70
Arkansas	Magazine Mountain	Logan	2,753	Ouachita R	Ashley-Union	55
California	Mount Whitney	Inyo-Tulare	14,494	Death Valley	Inyo	–282
Colorado	Mount Elbert	Lake	14,433	Arkansas R	Prowers	3,350
Connecticut	Mount Frissell	Litchfield	2,380	Long Island Sound		Sea level
Delaware	On Ebright Road	New Castle	442	Atlantic Ocean		Sea level
Dist. of Col.	Tenleytown	N. W. part	410	Potomac R		1
Florida	Sec. 30, T6N, R20W	Walton	345	Atlantic Ocean		Sea level
Georgia	Brasstown Bald	Towns-Union	4,784	Atlantic Ocean		Sea level
Guam	Mount Lamlam	Agat District	1,332	Pacific Ocean		Sea level
Hawaii	Mauna Kea	Hawaii	13,796	Pacific Ocean		Sea level
Idaho	Borah Peak	Custer	12,662	Snake R	Nez Perce	710
Illinois	Charles Mound	Jo Daviess	1,235	Mississippi R	Alexander	279
Indiana	Franklin Township	Wayne	1,257	Ohio R	Posey	320
Iowa	Sec. 29, T100N, R41W	Osceola	1,670	Mississippi R	Lee	480
Kansas	Mount Sunflower	Wallace	4,039	Verdigris R	Montgomery	679
Kentucky	Black Mountain	Harlan	4,139	Mississippi R	Fulton	257
Louisiana	Driskill Mountain	Bienville	535	New Orleans	Orleans	–8
Maine	Mount Katahdin	Piscataquis	5,267	Atlantic Ocean		Sea level
Maryland	Backbone Mountain	Garrett	3,360	Atlantic Ocean		Sea level
Massachusetts	Mount Greylock	Berkshire	3,487	Atlantic Ocean		Sea level
Michigan	Mount Arvon	Baraga	1,979	Lake Erie	Monroe	571
Minnesota	Eagle Mountain	Cook	2,301	Lake Superior		600
Mississippi	Woodall Mountain	Tishomingo	806	Gulf of Mexico		Sea level
Missouri	Taum Sauk Mt.	Iron	1,772	St. Francis R	Dunklin	230
Montana	Granite Peak	Park	12,799	Kootenai R	Lincoln	1,800
Nebraska	Johnson Township	Kimball	5,426	Missouri R.	Richardson	840
Nevada	Boundary Peak	Esmeralda	13,140	Mount Manchester	Clark	479
New Hamp.	Mt. Washington	Coos	6,288	Atlantic Ocean	Rockingham	Sea level
New Jersey	High Point	Sussex	1,803	Atlantic Ocean		Sea level
New Mexico	Wheeler Peak	Taos	13,161	Red Bluff Res.	Eddy	2,842
New York	Mount Marcy	Essex	5,344	Atlantic Ocean		Sea level
North Carolina	Mount Mitchell	Yancey	6,684	Atlantic Ocean		Sea level
North Dakota	White Butte	Slope	3,506	Red R	Pembina	750
Ohio	Campbell Hill	Logan	1,549	Ohio R	Hamilton	455
Oklahoma	Black Mesa	Cimarron	4,973	Little R	McCurtain	289
Oregon	Mount Hood	Clackamas-Hood R.	11,239	Pacific Ocean		Sea level
Pennsylvania	Mt. Davis	Somerset	3,213	Delaware R.	Delaware	Sea level
Puerto Rico	Cerro de Punta	Ponce District	4,390	Atlantic Ocean		Sea level
Rhode Island	Jerimoth Hill	Providence	812	Atlantic Ocean		Sea level
Samoa	Lata Mountain	Tau Island	3,160	Pacific Ocean		Sea level
South Carolina	Sassafras Mountain	Pickens	3,560	Atlantic Ocean		Sea level
South Dakota	Harney Peak	Pennington	7,242	Big Stone Lake	Roberts	966
Tennessee	Clingmans Dome	Sevier	6,643	Mississippi R	Shelby	178
Texas	Guadalupe Peak	Culberson	8,749	Gulf of Mexico		Sea level
Utah	Kings Peak	Duchesne	13,528	Beaverdam Wash.	Washington	2,000
Vermont	Mount Mansfield	Lamoille	4,393	Lake Champlain		95
Virginia	Mount Rogers	Grayson-Smyth	5,729	Atlantic Ocean		Sea level
Virgin Islands	Crown Mountain	St. Thomas Island	1,556	Atlantic Ocean		Sea level
Washington	Mount Rainier	Pierce	14,410	Pacific Ocean		Sea level
West Virginia	Spruce Knob	Pendleton	4,861	Potomac R	Jefferson	240
Wisconsin	Timms Hill	Price	1,951	Lake Michigan		579
Wyoming	Gannett Peak	Fremont	13,804	Belle Fourche R	Crook	3,099

Sec=section; T=township; R=range; N=north; W=west.

U.S. Coastline by States

Source: NOAA, U.S. Dept. of Commerce
(statute miles)

State	Coastline[1]	Shoreline[2]
Atlantic coast	**2,069**	**28,673**
Connecticut	0	618
Delaware	28	381
Florida	580	3,331
Georgia	100	2,344
Maine	228	3,478
Maryland	31	3,190
Massachusetts	192	1,519
New Hampshire	13	131
New Jersey	130	1,792
New York	127	1,850
North Carolina	301	3,375
Pennsylvania	0	89
Rhode Island	40	384
South Carolina	187	2,876
Virginia	112	3,315
Gulf coast	**1,631**	**17,141**
Alabama	53	607
Florida	770	5,095
Louisiana	397	7,721
Mississippi	44	359
Texas	367	3,359
Pacific coast	**7,623**	**40,298**
Alaska	5,580	31,383
California	840	3,427
Hawaii	750	1,052
Oregon	296	1,410
Washington	157	3,026
Arctic coast, Alaska	**1,060**	**2,521**
United States	**12,383**	**88,633**

(1) Figures are lengths of general outline of seacoast. Measurements were made with a unit measure of 30 minutes of latitude on charts as near the scale of 1:1,200,000 as possible. Coastline of sounds and bays is included to a point where they narrow to width of unit measure, and includes the distance across at such point. (2) Figures obtained in 1939-40 with a recording instrument on the largest-scale charts and maps then available. Shoreline of outer coast, offshore islands, sounds, bays, rivers, and creeks is included to the head of tidewater or to a point where tidal waters narrow to a width of 100 feet.

States: Settled, Capitals, Entry into Union, Area, Rank

The 13 colonies that seceded from Great Britain and fought the War of Independence (American Revolution) became the 13 original states. They were (in the order in which they ratified the Constitution): Delaware, Pennsylvania, New Jersey, Georgia, Connecticut, Massachusetts, Maryland, South Carolina, New Hampshire, Virginia, New York, North Carolina, and Rhode Island.

State	Settled[1]	Capital	Entered Union: Date	Entered Union: Order	Extent in miles (approx. mean): Long	Extent in miles (approx. mean): Wide	Area in square miles: Land	Area in square miles: Inland Water	Area in square miles: Total	Rank in area[2]
AL	1702	Montgomery	Dec. 14, 1819	22	330	190	50,750	1,673	52,423	30
AK	1784	Juneau	Jan. 3, 1959	49	1,480[3]	810[3]	570,374	86,050	656,424	1
AZ	1776	Phoenix	Feb. 14, 1912	48	400	310	113,642	364	114,006	6
AR	1686	Little Rock	June 15, 1836	25	260	240	52,075	1,107	53,182	29
CA	1769	Sacramento	Sept. 9, 1850	31	770	250	155,973	7,734	163,707	3
CO	1858	Denver	Aug. 1, 1876	38	380	280	103,729	371	104,100	8
CT	1634	Hartford	Jan. 9, 1788	5	110	70	4,845	698	5,544	48
DE	1638	Dover	Dec. 7, 1787	1	100	30	1,955	535	2,489	49
DC	NA	Washington	NA	NA	...	...	61	7	68	51
FL	1565	Tallahassee	Mar. 3, 1845	27	500	160	53,937	11, 821	65,756	22
GA	1733	Atlanta	Jan. 2, 1788	4	300	230	57,919	1,522	59,441	24
HI	1820	Honolulu	Aug. 21, 1959	50	...	...	6,423	4,508	10,932	43
ID	1842	Boise	July 3, 1890	43	570	300	82,751	823	83,574	14
IL	1720	Springfield	Dec. 3, 1818	21	390	210	55,593	2,325	57,918	25
IN	1733	Indianapolis	Dec. 11, 1816	19	270	140	35,870	550	36,420	38
IA	1788	Des Moines	Dec. 28, 1846	29	310	200	55,875	401	56,276	26
KS	1727	Topeka	Jan. 29, 1861	34	400	210	81,823	459	82,282	15
KY	1774	Frankfort	June 1, 1792	15	380	140	39,732	679	40,411	37
LA	1699	Baton Rouge	Apr. 30, 1812	18	380	130	43,566	8,277	51,843	31
ME	1624	Augusta	Mar. 15, 1820	23	320	190	30,865	4,523	35,387	39
MD	1634	Annapolis	Apr. 28, 1788	7	250	90	9,775	2,632	12,407	42
MA	1620	Boston	Feb. 6, 1788	6	190	50	7,838	2,717	10,555	44
MI	1668	Lansing	Jan. 26, 1837	26	490	240	56,809	39,896	96,705	11
MN	1805	St. Paul	May 11, 1858	32	400	250	79,617	7,326	86,943	12
MS	1699	Jackson	Dec. 10, 1817	20	340	170	46,914	1,520	48,434	32
MO	1735	Jefferson City	Aug. 10, 1821	24	300	240	68,898	811	69,709	21
MT	1809	Helena	Nov. 8, 1889	41	630	280	145,556	1,490	147,046	4
NE	1823	Lincoln	Mar. 1, 1867	37	430	210	76,878	481	77,358	16
NV	1849	Carson City	Oct. 31, 1864	36	490	320	109,806	761	110,567	7
NH	1623	Concord	June 21, 1788	9	190	70	8,969	382	9,351	46
NJ	1660	Trenton	Dec. 18, 1787	3	150	70	7,419	1,303	8,722	47
NM	1610	Santa Fe	Jan. 6, 1912	47	370	343	121,364	234	121,598	5
NY	1614	Albany	July 26, 1788	11	330	283	47,224	7,247	54,471	27
NC	1660	Raleigh	Nov. 21, 1789	12	500	150	48,718	5,103	53,821	28
ND	1812	Bismarck	Nov. 2, 1889	39	340	211	68,994	1,710	70,704	19
OH	1788	Columbus	Mar. 1, 1803	17	220	220	40,953	3,875	44,828	34
OK	1889	Oklahoma City	Nov. 16, 1907	46	400	220	68,679	1,224	69,903	20
OR	1811	Salem	Feb. 14, 1859	33	360	261	96,002	2,383	98,386	9
PA	1682	Harrisburg	Dec. 12, 1787	2	283	160	44,820	1,239	46,058	33
RI	1636	Providence	May 29, 1790	13	40	30	1,045	500	1,545	50
SC	1670	Columbia	May 23, 1788	8	260	200	30,111	1,897	32,008	40
SD	1859	Pierre	Nov. 2, 1889	40	380	210	75,896	1,225	77,121	17
TN	1769	Nashville	June 1, 1796	16	440	120	41,219	926	42,146	36
TX	1682	Austin	Dec. 29, 1845	28	790	660	261,914	6,687	268,601	2
UT	1847	Salt Lake City	Jan. 4, 1896	45	350	270	82,168	2,736	84,904	13
VT	1724	Montpelier	Mar. 4, 1791	14	160	80	9,249	366	9,615	45
VA	1607	Richmond	June 25, 1788	10	430	200	39,598	3,179	42,777	35
WA	1811	Olympia	Nov. 11, 1889	42	360	240	66,581	4,721	71,302	18
WV	1727	Charleston	June 20, 1863	35	240	130	24,087	145	24,231	41
WI	1766	Madison	May 29, 1848	30	310	260	54,314	11,186	65,499	23
WY	1834	Cheyenne	July 10, 1890	44	360	280	97,105	714	97,818	10

NA=not applicable. (1) First European permanent settlement. (2) Rank is based on total area, including inland water. (3) Aleutian Islands and Alexander Archipelago are not considered in these lengths.

The Continental Divide of the U.S.

The Continental Divide of the U.S., also known as the Great Divide, is located at the watershed that is created by the mountain ranges, or tablelands, of the Rocky Mountains. This watershed separates the waters that drain easterly into the Atlantic Ocean and its marginal seas, such as the Gulf of Mexico, from those waters that drain westerly into the Pacific Ocean. The majority of easterly flowing water drains into the Gulf of Mexico before reaching the Atlantic Ocean. The majority of westerly flowing water, before reaching the Pacific Ocean, either drains through the Columbia R. or through the Colorado R., which flows into the Gulf of California before reaching the Pacific Ocean.

The location and route of the Continental Divide across the U.S. can briefly be described as follows:

Beginning at point of crossing the U.S.-Mexican boundary, near long 108°45′ W, the Divide, in a northerly direction, crosses New Mexico along the western edge of the Rio Grande drainage basin, entering Colorado near long 106°41′ W.

Thence, by a very irregular route northerly across Colorado along the W summits of the Rio Grande and of the Arkansas, the South Platte, and the North Platte river basins, and across Rocky Mountain National Park, entering Wyoming near long 106°52′ W.

Thence, in a northwesterly direction, forming the W rims of the North Platte, the Big Horn, and the Yellowstone river basins, crossing the SW portion of Yellowstone National Park.

Thence, in a westerly and then a northerly direction forming the common boundary of Idaho and Montana, to a point on said boundary near long 114°00′ W.

Thence, northeasterly and northwesterly through Montana and the Glacier National Park, entering Canada near long 114°04′ W.

Chronological List of Territories and State Admission to Union

Source: National Archives and Records Service

Name of territory	Date of Organic Act	Organic Act effective	Admission as state	Yrs. terr.
Northwest Territory(a)	July 13, 1787	No fixed date	Mar. 1, 1803(b)	16
Territory southwest of River Ohio	May 26, 1790	No fixed date	June 1, 1796(c)	6
Mississippi	Apr. 7, 1798	When president acted	Dec. 10, 1817	19
Indiana	May 7, 1800	July 4, 1800	Dec. 11, 1816	16
Orleans	Mar. 26, 1804	Oct. 1, 1804	Apr. 30, 1812(d)	7
Michigan	Jan. 11, 1805	June 30, 1805	Jan. 26, 1837	31
Louisiana-Missouri(e)	Mar. 3, 1805	July 4, 1805	Aug. 10, 1821	16
Illinois	Feb. 3, 1809	Mar. 1, 1809	Dec. 3, 1818	9
Alabama	Mar. 3, 1817	When Miss. became a state	Dec. 14, 1819	2
Arkansas	Mar. 2, 1819	July 4, 1819	June 15, 1836	17
Florida	Mar. 30, 1822	No fixed date	Mar. 3, 1845	23
Wisconsin	Apr. 20, 1836	July 3, 1836	May 29, 1848	12
Iowa	June 12, 1838	July 3, 1838	Dec. 28, 1846	8
Oregon	Aug. 14, 1848	Date of act	Feb. 14, 1859	10
Minnesota	Mar. 3, 1849	Date of act	May 11, 1858	9
New Mexico	Sept. 9, 1850	On president's proclamation	Jan. 6, 1912	61
Utah	Sept. 9, 1850	Date of act	Jan. 4, 1896	46
Washington	Mar. 2, 1853	Date of act	Nov. 11, 1889	36
Nebraska	May 30, 1854	Date of act	Mar. 1, 1867	12
Kansas	May 30, 1854	Date of act	Jan. 29, 1861	6
Colorado	Feb. 28, 1861	Date of act	Aug. 1, 1876	15
Nevada	Mar. 2, 1861	Date of act	Oct. 31, 1864	3
Dakota	Mar. 2, 1861	Date of act	Nov. 2, 1889	28
Arizona	Feb. 24, 1863	Date of act	Feb. 14, 1912	49
Idaho	Mar. 3, 1863	Date of act	July 3, 1890	27
Montana	May 26, 1864	Date of act	Nov. 8, 1889	25
Wyoming	July 25, 1868	When officers were qualified	July 10, 1890	22
Alaska(f)	May 17, 1884	No fixed date	Jan. 3, 1959	75
Oklahoma	May 2, 1890	Date of act	Nov. 16, 1907	17
Hawaii	Apr. 30, 1900	June 14, 1900	Aug. 21, 1959	59

(a) Included Ohio, Indiana, Illinois, Michigan, Wisconsin, eastern Minnesota; (b) as the state of Ohio; (c) as the state of Tennessee; (d) as the state of Louisiana; (e) organic act for Missouri Territory of June 4, 1812, became effective Dec. 7, 1812; (f) Although the May 17, 1884 act actually constituted Alaska as a district, it was often referred to as a territory, and unofficially administered as such. The Territory of Alaska was legally and formally organized by an act of Aug. 24, 1912.

Geographic Centers, U.S. and Each State

Source: U.S. Geological Survey, Dept. of the Interior

There is no generally accepted definition of geographic center, and there is no satisfactory method for determining it. The geographic center of an area may be defined as the center of gravity of the surface or as that point on which the surface of the area would balance if it were a plane of uniform thickness.

No marked or monumented point has been established by any government agency as the geographic center of either the 50 states, the contiguous U.S., or the North American continent. A monument was erected in Lebanon, KS, contiguous U.S. center, by a group of citizens. A cairn in Rugby, ND marks the center of the North American continent.

United States, including Alaska and Hawaii — South Dakota; Butte County, W of Castle Rock, Approx. lat. 44°58′N. long. 103°46′W.
Contiguous U. S. (48 states) — Near Lebanon, Smith Co., Kansas, lat. 39°50′N. long. 98°35′W.
North American continent — The geographic center is in Pierce County, North Dakota, 6 miles W of Balta, latitude 48°10′, longitude 100°10′W.

State—county, locality

Alabama—Chilton, 12 miles SW of Clanton.
Alaska—lat. 63°50′N. long. 152°W. Approx. 60 mi. NW of Mt. McKinley.
Arizona—Yavapai, 55 miles ESE of Prescott.
Arkansas—Pulaski, 12 miles NW of Little Rock.
California—Madera, 38 miles E of Madera.
Colorado—Park, 30 miles NW of Pikes Peak.
Connecticut—Hartford, at East Berlin.
Delaware—Kent, 11 miles S of Dover.
District of Columbia—Near 4th and L Sts., NW.
Florida—Hernando, 12 miles NNW of Brooksville.
Georgia—Twiggs, 18 miles SE of Macon.
Hawaii—Hawaii, 20°15′N, 156°20′W, off Maui Island.
Idaho—Custer, at Custer, SW of Challis.
Illinois—Logan, 28 miles NE of Springfield.
Indiana—Boone, 14 miles NNW of Indianapolis.
Iowa—Story, 5 miles NE of Ames.
Kansas—Barton, 15 miles NE of Great Bend.
Kentucky—Marion, 3 miles NNW of Lebanon.
Louisiana—Avoyelles, 3 miles SE of Marksville.
Maine—Piscataquis, 18 miles north of Dover.
Maryland—Prince Georges, 4.5 miles NW of Davidsonville.
Massachusetts—Worcester, north part of city.
Michigan—Wexford, 5 miles NNW of Cadillac.
Minnesota—Crow Wing, 10 miles SW of Brainerd.
Mississippi—Leake, 9 miles WNW of Carthage.
Missouri—Miller, 20 miles SW of Jefferson City.
Montana—Fergus, 11 miles west of Lewistown.
Nebraska—Custer, 10 miles NW of Broken Bow.
Nevada—Lander, 26 miles SE of Austin.
New Hampshire—Belknap, 3 miles E of Ashland.
New Jersey—Mercer, 5 miles SE of Trenton.
New Mexico—Torrance, 12 miles SSW of Willard.
New York—Madison, 12 miles S of Oneida and 26 miles SW of Utica.
North Carolina—Chatham, 10 miles NW of Sanford.
North Dakota—Sheridan, 5 miles SW of McClusky.
Ohio—Delaware, 25 miles NNE of Columbus.
Oklahoma—Oklahoma, 8 miles N of Oklahoma City.
Oregon—Crook, 25 miles SSE of Prineville.
Pennsylvania—Centre, 2.5 miles SW of Bellefonte.
Rhode Island—Kent, 1 mile SSW of Crompton.
South Carolina—Richland, 13 miles SE of Columbia.
South Dakota—Hughes, 8 miles NE of Pierre.
Tennessee—Rutherford, 5 miles NE of Murfreesboro.
Texas—McCulloch, 15 miles NE of Brady.
Utah—Sanpete, 3 miles N of Manti.
Vermont—Washington, 3 miles E of Roxbury.
Virginia—Buckingham, 5 miles SW of Buckingham.
Washington—Chelan, 10 miles WSW of Wenatchee.
West Virginia—Braxton, 4 miles E of Sutton.
Wisconsin—Wood, 9 miles SE of Marshfield.
Wyoming—Fremont, 58 miles ENE of Lander.

International Boundary Lines of the U.S.

The length of the N boundary of the contiguous U.S.—the U.S.-Canadian border, excluding Alaska—is 3,987 mi according to the U.S. Geological Survey, Dept. of the Interior. The length of the Alaskan-Canadian border is 1,538 mi. The length of the U.S.-Mexican border, from the Gulf of Mexico to the Pacific Ocean, is approximately 1,933 mi (1963 boundary agreement).

Origin of the Names of U.S. States

Source: State officials, the Smithsonian Institution, and the Topographic Division, U.S. Geological Survey, Dept. of the Interior

Alabama—Indian for tribal town, later a tribe (Alabamas or Alibamons) of the Creek confederacy.

Alaska—Russian version of Aleutian (Eskimo) word, alakshak, for "peninsula," "great lands," or "land that is not an island."

Arizona—Spanish version of Pima Indian word for "little spring place," or Aztec arizuma, meaning "silver-bearing."

Arkansas—French variant of Quapaw ("downstream people"), a Siouan people.

California—Bestowed by the Spanish conquistadors (possibly by Cortez). It was the name of an imaginary island, an earthly paradise, in "Las Serges de Esplandian," a Spanish romance written by Montalvo in 1510. Baja California (Lower California, in Mexico) was first visited by Spanish in 1533. The present U.S. state was called Alta (Upper) California.

Colorado—Spanish, red, first applied to Colorado River.

Connecticut—From Mohican and other Algonquin words meaning "long river place."

Delaware—Named for Lord De La Warr, early governor of Virginia; first applied to river, then to Indian tribe (Lenni-Lenape), and the state.

District of Columbia—For Columbus, 1791.

Florida—Named by Ponce de Leon on Pascua Florida, "Flowery Easter," on Easter Sunday, 1513.

Georgia—For King George II of England by James Oglethorpe, colonial administrator, 1732.

Hawaii—Possibly derived from native word for homeland, Hawaiki or Owhyhee.

Idaho—A coined name with an invented Indian meaning: "gem of the mountains;" originally suggested for the Pikes Peak mining territory (Colorado), then applied to the new mining territory of the Pacific Northwest. Another theory suggests Idaho may be a Kiowa Apache term for the Comanche.

Illinois—French for Illini or land of Illini, Algonquin word meaning men or warriors.

Indiana—Means "land of the Indians."

Iowa—Indian word variously translated as "one who puts to sleep" or "beautiful land."

Kansas—Sioux word for "south wind people."

Kentucky—Indian word variously translated as "dark and bloody ground," "meadow land," and "land of tomorrow."

Louisiana—Part of territory called Louisiana by Sieur de La Salle for French King Louis XIV.

Maine—From Maine, ancient French province. Also: descriptive, referring to the mainland as distinct from the many coastal islands.

Maryland—For Queen Henrietta Maria, wife of Charles I of England.

Massachusetts—From Indian tribe named after "large hill place" identified by Capt. John Smith as being near Milton, Mass.

Michigan—From Chippewa words mici gama meaning "great water," after the lake of the same name.

Minnesota—From Dakota Sioux word meaning "cloudy water" or "sky-tinted water" of the Minnesota River.

Mississippi—Probably Chippewa; mici zibi, "great river" or "gathering-in of all the waters." Also: Algonquin word, "Messipi."

Missouri—An Algonquin Indian term meaning "river of the big canoes."

Montana—Latin or Spanish for "mountainous."

Nebraska—From Omaha or Otos Indian word meaning "broad water" or "flat river," describing the Platte River.

Nevada—Spanish, meaning snow-clad.

New Hampshire—Named 1629 by Capt. John Mason of Plymouth Council for his home county in England.

New Jersey—The Duke of York, 1664, gave a patent to John Berkeley and Sir George Carteret to be called Nova Caesaria, or New Jersey, after England's Isle of Jersey.

New Mexico—Spaniards in Mexico applied term to land north and west of Rio Grande in the 16th century.

New York—For Duke of York and Albany who received patent to New Netherland from his brother Charles II and sent an expedition to capture it, 1664.

North Carolina—In 1619 Charles I gave a large patent to Sir Robert Heath to be called Province of Carolana, from Carolus, Latin name for Charles. A new patent was granted by Charles II to Earl of Clarendon and others. Divided into North and South Carolina, 1710.

North Dakota—Dakota is Sioux for friend or ally.

Ohio—Iroquois word for "fine or good river."

Oklahoma—Choctaw-coined word meaning red man, proposed by Rev. Allen Wright, Choctaw-speaking Indian.

Oregon—Origin unknown. One theory holds that the name may have been derived from that of the Wisconsin River shown on a 1715 French map as "Ouaricon-sint."

Pennsylvania—William Penn, the Quaker, who was made full proprietor by King Charles II in 1681, suggested Sylvania, or woodland, for his tract. The king's government owed Penn's father, Admiral William Penn, £16,000, and the land was granted as partial settlement. Charles II added the Penn to Sylvania, against the desires of the modest proprietor, in honor of the admiral.

Puerto Rico—Spanish for Rich Port.

Rhode Island—Exact origin is unknown. One theory notes that Giovanni de Verrazano recorded an island about the size of Rhodes in the Mediterranean in 1524, but others believe the state was named Roode Eylandt by Adriaen Block, Dutch explorer, because of its red clay.

South Carolina—See North Carolina.

South Dakota—See North Dakota.

Tennessee—Tanasi was the name of Cherokee villages on the Little Tennessee River. From 1784 to 1788 this was the State of Franklin, or Frankland.

Texas—Variant of word used by Caddo and other Indians meaning friends or allies, and applied to them by the Spanish in eastern Texas. Also written texias, tejas, teysas.

Utah—From a Navajo word meaning upper, or higher up, as applied to a Shoshone tribe called Ute. Spanish form is Yutta, English Uta or Utah. Proposed name Deseret, "land of honeybees," from Book of Mormon, was rejected by Congress.

Vermont—From French words vert (green) and mont (mountain). The Green Mountains were said to have been named by Samuel de Champlain. When the state was formed, 1777, Dr. Thomas Young suggested combining vert and mont into Vermont.

Virginia—Named by Sir Walter Raleigh, who fitted out the expedition of 1584, in honor of Queen Elizabeth, the Virgin Queen of England.

Washington—Named after George Washington. When the bill creating the Territory of Columbia was introduced in the 32d Congress, the name was changed to Washington because of the existence of the District of Columbia.

West Virginia—So named when western counties of Virginia refused to secede from the United States, 1863.

Wisconsin—An Indian name, spelled Ouisconsin and Mesconsing by early chroniclers. Believed to mean "grassy place" in Chippewa. Congress made it Wisconsin.

Wyoming—The word was taken from Wyoming Valley, Pa., which was the site of an Indian massacre and became widely known by Campbell's poem, "Gertrude of Wyoming." In Algonquin it means "large prairie place."

Territorial Sea of the U.S.

According to a Dec. 27, 1988, proclamation by Pres. Ronald Reagan: "The territorial sea of the United States henceforth extends to 12 nautical miles from the baselines of the United States determined in accordance with international law. In accordance with international law, as reflected in the applicable provisions of the 1982 United Nations Convention on the Law of the Sea, within the territorial sea of the United States, the ships of all countries enjoy the right of innocent passage and the ships and aircraft of all countries enjoy the right of transit passage through international straits."

Accession of Territory by the U.S.

Source: U.S. Geological Survey, Dept. of the Interior

	Acquisition date	Total area (sq mi)[1]
Total U.S.	**NA**	**3,540,558**
United States	NA	3,536,338
Territory in 1790[2]	NA	895,415
Louisiana Purchase	1803	909,380
Purchase of Florida	1819	58,666
Texas	1845	388,687
Oregon Territory	1846	286,541
Mexican Cession	1848	529,189
Gadsden Purchase	1853	29,670
Alaska	1867	570,374
Hawaii	1898	6,423
Other areas:		
Puerto Rico[3]	1898	3,427
Guam[4]	1898	210
American Samoa[5]	1899	77
U.S. Virgin Islands	1917	134
Republic of Palau[6]	1947	179
N. Mariana Islands[7]	1947	177
All other[8]	NA	16

NA=not applicable. (1) Area figures from the Bureau of the Census, Apr. 1, 1990. As a result of independent rounding, the sum of these figures do not equal the total. (2) Includes that part of a drainage basin of Red River of the North, S of 49th parallel, sometimes considered part of Louisiana Purchase. (3) Ceded by Spain in 1898, ratified in 1899, and became the Commonwealth of Puerto Rico by Act of Congress on July 25, 1952. (4) Acquired 1898; ratified 1899. (5) Acquired 1899; ratified 1900. (6) Reflects the remaining portion of the United Nations Trust Territory of the Pacific Islands (TTPI), under UN trusteeship since 1947. The TTPI formerly included the Marshall Islands and Micronesia, both officially recognized as independent nations in 1991, and the Northern Mariana Islands, which became a U.S. commonwealth in 1986. (7) Attained commonwealth status in 1986, separate from the TTPI, of which it had been a part since 1947. (8) Comprises the following islands with gross areas as indicated in sq mi: Midway (2), Wake (3), Palmyra (4), Navassa (2), Baker, Howland, and Jarvis (combined area, 3), Johnson Atoll (combined area, less than 0.5), and Kingman Reef (less than 0.5).

Public Lands of the U.S.

Source: Bureau of Land Management, U.S. Dept. of the Interior

Disposition of Public Lands 1781 to 1992

Disposition by methods not elsewhere classified[1]	Acres
Disposition by methods not elsewhere classified[1]	303,500,000
Granted or sold to homesteaders	287,500,000
Granted to railroad corporations	94,400,000
Granted to veterans as military bounties	61,000,000
Confirmed as private land claims[2]	34,000,000
Sold under timber and stone law[3]	13,900,000
Granted or sold under timber culture law[4]	10,900,000
Sold under desert land law[5]	10,700,000

Granted to states for:	Acres
Support of common schools	77,630,000
Reclamation of swampland	64,920,000
Construction of railroads	37,130,000
Support of misc. institutions[6]	21,700,000
Purposes not elsewhere classified[7]	117,600,000
Canals and rivers	6,100,000
Construction of wagon roads	3,400,000
Total granted to states	**328,480,000**

(1) Chiefly public, private, and preemption sales, but includes mineral entries, scrip locations, sales of townsites and townlots. (2) The Government has confirmed title to lands claimed under valid grants made by foreign governments prior to the acquisition of the public domain by the United States. (3) The law provided for the sale of lands valuable for timber or stone and unfit for cultivation. (4) The law provided for the granting of public lands to settlers on condition that they plant and cultivate trees on the lands granted. (5) The law provided for the sale of arid agricultural public lands to settlers who irrigate them and bring them under cultivation. (6) Universities, hospitals, asylums, etc. (7) For construction of various public improvements (individual items not specified in the granting act) reclamation of desert lands, construction of water reservoirs, etc.

Public Lands Administered by Federal Agencies

Agency (Acres, Sept. 30, 1992)	Public domain	Acquired	Total
Forest Service	161,038,854.3	28,341,223.5	189,380,077.8
Bureau of Land Management	269,710,529	2,318,889	272,029,418
Bureau of Reclamation	3,533,817.5	1,969,275.9	5,503,093.4
Fish and Wildlife Service	81,321,344	10,097,347	91,318,691
National Park Service	64,325,741.0	8,517,114.8	72,842,855.8
Bureau of Indian Affairs	2,554,358.7	193,079.6	2,747,438.3
Tennessee Valley Authority	0	1,040,231.3	1,040,231.3
Corps of Engineers	604,971.2	4,869,200.0	5,474,171.2
U.S. Army	3,187,901.0	6,495,173.0	9,683,074.0
U.S. Navy	618,005.6	1,743,750.2	2,361,755.8
U.S. Air Force	6,858,510.0	1,255,022.0	8,113,532.0
Department of Energy	1,465,862.4	700,478.8	2,166,341.2
Total, all agencies (incl. those not shown)	**660,976,655.8**	**63,089,515.1**	**724,066,170.9**

National Recreation Areas Administered by the U.S. Forest Service

Source: U.S. Forest Service, Dept. of Agriculture, 1994

Area Name	Location	Estab.	Acres
Allegheny	PA	1984	23,063
Arapaho	CO	1978	34,928
Ed Jenkins	GA	1991	23,330
Flaming Gorge	WY-UT	1968	201,114
Grand Island	MI	1990	12,957
Hells Canyon	ID-OR	1975	541,336
Jemez	NM	1993	57,000
Mount Baker	WA	1984	8,473
Mount Rogers	VA	1966	154,816
Oregon Dunes	OR	1972	31,566
Pine Ridge	NE	1986	6,600
Rattlesnake	MT	1980	61,000
Sawtooth	ID	1972	756,019
Smith River	CA	1990	331,229
Spring Mts.	NV	1993	316,000
Spruce Knob-Seneca Rocks	WV	1965	100,000
Whiskeytown Shasta-Trinity	CA	1965	203,587
White Rocks	VT	1984	36,400
Winding Stair Mt.	OK	1988	26,445

National Parks, Other Areas Administered by National Park Service

Figures given are date area initially protected by Congress or presidential proclamation, date given current designation, and gross area in acres as of 6/31/94.

National Parks

Acadia, Me. (1916/1929) 41,972. Includes Mount Desert Island, half of Isle au Haut, Schoodic Peninsula on mainland. Highest elevation on Eastern seaboard.

American Samoa. American Samoa (1988) 9,000. Features a paleotropical rain forest.

Arches, Ut. (1929/1971) 73,379. Contains giant red sandstone arches and other products of erosion.

Badlands, S.D. (1929/1978) 242,756; prairie with bison, bighorn, and antelope. Contains animal fossils from 26-37 million years ago.

Big Bend, Tex. (1935) 801,163. Rio Grande, Chisos Mts.

Biscayne, Fla. (1968/1980) 172,924. Aquatic park encompasses chain of islands south of Miami.

Bryce Canyon, Ut. (1923/1928) 35,835. Spectacularly colorful and unusual display of erosion effects.

Canyonlands, Ut. (1964) 337,570. At junction of Colorado and Green rivers, extensive evidence of prehistoric Indians.

Capitol Reef, Ut. (1937/1971) 241,904. A 70-mile uplift of sandstone cliffs dissected by high-walled gorges.

Carlsbad Caverns, N.M. (1923/1930) 46,766. Largest known caverns; not yet fully explored.

Channel Islands, Cal. (1938/1980) 249,354. Sea lion breeding place, nesting sea birds, unique plants.

Crater Lake, Ore. (1902) 183,224. Extraordinary blue lake in crater of extinct volcano encircled by lava walls 500 to 2,000 feet high.

Denali, Alas. (1917/1980) 4,741,910. Name changed from Mt. McKinley NP. Contains highest mountain in U.S.; wildlife.

Dry Tortugas, Fla. (1935/1992) 64,700. Formerly Ft. Jefferson National Monument.

Everglades, Fla. (1934) 1,506,499. Largest remaining subtropical wilderness in continental U.S.

Gates of the Arctic, Alas. (1978/1980) 7,523,888. Vast wilderness in north central region.

Glacier, Mon. (1910) 1,013,572. Superb Rocky Mt. scenery, numerous glaciers and glacial lakes. Part of Waterton-Glacier Intl. Peace Park established by U.S. and Canada in 1932.

Glacier Bay, Alas. (1925/1980) 3,225,284. Great tidewater glaciers that move down mountain sides and break up into the sea; much wildlife.

Grand Canyon, Ariz. (1908/1919) 1,217,158. Most spectacular part of Colorado River's greatest canyon.

Grand Teton, Wy. (1929) 309,992. Most impressive part of the Teton Mountains, winter feeding ground of largest American elk herd.

Great Basin, Nev. (1922/1986) 77,180. Includes Wheeler Pk., Lexington Arch, and Lehman Caves.

Great Smoky Mountains, N.C.-Tenn. (1926) 520,269. Largest eastern mountain range, magnificent forests.

Guadalupe Mountains, Tex. (1966) 86,416. Extensive Permian limestone fossil reef; tremendous earth fault.

Haleakala, Ha. (1916/1960) 28,099. Dormant volcano on Maui with large colorful craters.

Hawaii Volcanoes, Ha. (1916/1961) 229,177. Contains Kilauea and Mauna Loa, active volcanoes.

Hot Springs, Ark. (1832/1921) 5,543. Bathhouses are furnished with thermal waters from the park's 47 hot springs; these waters are used for bathing and drinking.

Isle Royale, Mich. (1931) 571,790. Largest island in Lake Superior, noted for its wilderness area and wildlife.

Katmai, Alas. (1918/1980) 3,716,000. Valley of Ten Thousand Smokes, scene of 1912 volcanic eruption.

Kenai Fjords, Alas. (1978/1980) 669,541. Abundant marine mammals, birdlife; the Harding Icefield, one of the major icecaps in U.S.

Kings Canyon, Cal. (1890/1940) 461,901. Mountain wilderness, dominated by Kings River Canyons and High Sierra; contains giant sequoias.

Kobuk Valley, Alas. (1978/1980) 1,750,736. Contains geological and recreational sites and wildlife.

Lake Clark, Alas. (1978/1980) 2,636,839. Across Cook Inlet from Anchorage. A scenic wilderness rich in fish and wildlife.

Lassen Volcanic, Cal. (1907/1916) 106,372. Contains Lassen Peak, recently active volcano, and other volcanic phenomena.

Mammoth Cave, Ky. (1926/1941) 52,419. 144 miles of surveyed underground passages, beautiful natural formations, river 300 feet below surface.

Mesa Verde, Col. (1906) 52,122. Most notable and best preserved prehistoric cliff dwellings in the United States.

Mount Rainier, Wash. (1899) 235,612. Greatest single-peak glacial system in the lower 48 states.

North Cascades, Wash. (1968) 504,781. Spectacular mountainous region with many glaciers, lakes.

Olympic, Wash. (1909/1938) 922,651. Mountain wilderness containing finest remnant of Pacific Northwest rain forest, active glaciers, Pacific shoreline, rare elk.

Petrified Forest, Ariz. (1906/1962) 93,533. Extensive petrified wood and Indian artifacts. Contains part of Painted Desert.

Redwood, Cal. (1968) 110,232. Forty miles of Pacific coastline, groves of ancient redwoods and world's tallest trees.

Rocky Mountain, Col. (1915) 265,727. On the continental divide, includes peaks over 14,000 feet.

Sequoia, Cal. (1890) 402,482. Groves of giant sequoias, highest mountain in contiguous United States—Mount Whitney (14,494 feet). World's largest tree.

Shenandoah, Va. (1926) 196,466. Portion of the Blue Ridge Mountains; overlooks Shenandoah Valley; Skyline Drive.

Theodore Roosevelt, N.D. (1947/1978) 70,447. Contains part of T.R.'s ranch and scenic badlands.

Virgin Islands, V.I. (1956) 14,689. Covers 75% of St. John Island, lush growth, lovely beaches, Indian petroglyphs, evidence of colonial Danes.

Voyageurs, Minn. (1971) 218,035. Abundant lakes, forests, wildlife, canoeing, boating.

Wind Cave, S.D. (1903) 28,295. Limestone caverns in Black Hills. Extensive wildlife includes a herd of bison.

Wrangell-St. Elias, Alas. (1978/1980) 4,852,773. Largest area in park system, most peaks over 16,000 feet, abundant wildlife; day's drive east of Anchorage.

Yellowstone, Ida., Mon., Wy., (1872) 2,219,791. World's first national park. World's greatest geyser area has about 3,000 geysers and hot springs; spectacular falls and impressive canyons of the Yellowstone River; grizzly bear, moose, and bison.

Yosemite, Cal. (1890) 761,236. Yosemite Valley, the nation's highest waterfall, 1 grove of sequoias, and mountains.

Zion, Ut. (1909/1919) 146,598. Unusual shapes and landscapes have resulted from erosion and faulting; Zion Canyon, with sheer walls ranging up to 2,640 feet, is readily accessible.

National Historical Parks

Appomattox Court House, Va. (1930/1954) 1,594. Where Lee surrendered to Grant.

Boston, Mass. (1974) 41. Includes Faneuil Hall, Old North Church, Bunker Hill, Paul Revere House.

Chaco Culture, N.M. (1907/1980) 33,974. Ruins of pueblos built by prehistoric Indians.

Chesapeake and Ohio Canal, Md.-W.Va.-D.C. (1938/1971) 19,236. 184-mile historic canal; D.C. to Cumberland, Md.

George Rogers Clark, Vincennes, Ind. (1966) 26. Commemorates American defeat of British in west during Revolution.

Colonial, Va. (1930/1936) 9,330. Includes most of Jamestown Island, site of first successful English colony; Yorktown, site of Cornwallis' surrender to George Washington; and the Colonial Parkway.

Cumberland Gap, Ky.-Tenn.-Va. (1940) 20,445. Mountain pass of the Wilderness Road, which carried the first great migration of pioneers into America's interior.

Dayton Aviation, Oh. (1992). Commemorates the area's aviation heritage.

Harpers Ferry, Md., W.Va. (1944/1963) 2,287. At the confluence of the Shenandoah and Potomac rivers, the site of John Brown's 1859 raid on the Army arsenal.

Hopewell Culture, Oh. (1923/1992) 1,032. Formerly Mound City Group National Monument.

Independence, Pa. (1948) 45. Contains several properties in Philadelphia associated with the Revolutionary War and the founding of the U.S. Includes Independence Hall.

Kalaupapa, Ha. (1980) 10,779. Molokai's former leper colony site and other historic areas.

Kaloko-Honokohau, Ha. (1978) 1,161. Preserves the native culture of Hawaii.

Keweenaw, Mich. (1992). Site of first significant Copper Mine in U.S.

Klondike Gold Rush, Alas.-Wash. (1976) 13,191. Alaskan Trails in 1898 Gold Rush. Museum in Seattle.

Jean Laffite (and preserve), La. (1939/1978) 20,020. Includes Chalmette, site of 1815 Battle of New Orleans; French Quarter.

Lowell, Mass. (1978) 137. Textile mills, canal, 19th C. structures; park shows planned city of Industrial Revolution.

Lyndon B. Johnson, Tex. (1969/1980) 1,571. President's birthplace, boyhood home, ranch.

Marsh-Billings, Vt. (1992) 643. Boyhood home of George Perkins Marsh.

Minute Man, Mass. (1959) 789. Where the colonial Minute Men battled the British, April 19, 1775. Also contains Nathaniel Hawthorne's home.

Morristown, N.J. (1933) 1,683. Sites of important military encampments during the Revolutionary War; Washington's headquarters 1777, 1779-80.

Natchez, Miss. (1988) 108. Mansions, townhouses, and villas concerning history of Natchez, Miss.

Nez Perce, Ida. (1965) 2,109. Illustrates the history and culture of the Nez Perce Indian country; with more than 20 separate sites.

Pecos, N.M. (1965/1990) 6,570. Ruins of ancient Pueblo of Pecos, archaeological sites, and 2 associated Spanish colonial missions from the 17th and 18th centuries.

Pu'uhonua o Honaunau, Ha. (1955/1978) 182. Until 1819, a sanctuary for Hawaiians vanquished in battle, and those guilty of crimes or breaking taboos.

Salt River Bay, St. Croix, V.I. (1992) 912. The only site known where, 500 years ago, members of a Columbus party landed on what is now territory of the U.S.

San Antonio Missions, Tex. (1978) 819. Four of finest Spanish missions in U.S., 18th C. irrigation system.

San Francisco Maritime, Cal. (1988) 50. Artifacts, photographs, and historic vessels related to the development of the Pacific Coast.

San Juan Island, Wash. (1966) 1,752. Commemorates peaceful relations of the U.S., Canada, and Great Britain since the 1872 boundary disputes.

Saratoga, N.Y. (1938) 3,393. Scene of a major battle that became a turning point in the War of Independence.

Sitka, Alas. (1910/1972) 107. Scene of last major resistance of the Tlingit Indians to the Russians, 1804.

Tumacacori, Ariz. (1908/1990) 46. Historic Spanish Catholic mission building stands near the site first visited by Jesuit Father Kino in 1691.

Valley Forge, Pa. (1976) 3,468. Continental Army campsite in 1777-78 winter.

War in the Pacific, Guam (1978) 1,960. Seven distinct units illustrating the Pacific theater of WWII.

Women's Rights, N.Y. (1980) 6. Seneca Falls site where Susan B. Anthony, Elizabeth Cady Stanton began rights movement in 1848.

Zuni-Cibola, N. Mex. (1988) 800. Historical, archaeological, and cultural site associated with the Zuni tribe over its 1,700-year cultural continuum.

National Battlefields

Antietam, Md. (1890/1978) 3,255. Battle ended first Confederate invasion of North, Sept. 17, 1862.

Big Hole, Mon. (1910/1963) 656. Site of major battle with Nez Perce Indians.

Cowpens, S.C. (1929/1972) 842. Revolutionary War battlefield.

Fort Donelson, Tenn. (1928/1985) 551. Site of first major Union victory.

Fort Necessity, Pa. (1931/1961) 903. First battle of French and Indian War.

Monocacy, Md. (1934/1976) 1,647. Civil War battle in defense of Wash., D.C., July 9, 1864.

Moores Creek, N.C. (1926/1980) 87. 1776 battle between Patriots and Loyalists commemorated here.

Petersburg, Va. (1926/1962) 2,744. Scene of 10-month Union campaign 1864-65.

Stones River, Tenn. (1927/1960) 709. Scene of battle that began federal offensive to trisect the Confederacy.

Tupelo, Miss. (1929/1961) 1. Crucial battle over Sherman's supply line.

Wilson's Creek, Mo. (1960/1970) 1,750. Civil War battle for control of Missouri.

National Battlefield Parks

Kennesaw Mountain, Ga. (1917/1935) 2,885. Two major battles of Atlanta campaign in Civil War.

Manassas, Va. (1940) 5,072. Two battles in Civil War, 1861 and 1862.

Richmond, Va. (1936) 771. Site of battles defending Confederate capital.

National Battlefield Site

Brices Cross Roads, Miss. (1929) 1. Civil War battlefield.

National Military Parks

Chickamauga and Chattanooga, Ga.-Tenn. (1890) 8,106. Site of major Confederate victory, 1863.

Fredericksburg and Spotsylvania County, Va. (1927) 7,788. Sites of several major Civil War battles and campaigns.

Gettysburg, Pa. (1895) 5,895. Site of decisive Confederate defeat in North. Gettysburg Address.

Guilford Courthouse, N.C. (1917) 220. Revolutionary War battle site.

Horseshoe Bend, Ala. (1956) 2,040. On Tallapoosa River, where Gen. Andrew Jackson broke the power of the Creek Indian Confederacy.

Kings Mountain, S.C. (1931) 3,945. Revolutionary War battle.

Pea Ridge, Ark. (1956) 4,300. Civil War battle.

Shiloh, Tenn. (1894) 3,972. Major Civil War battle; site includes some well-preserved Indian burial mounds.

Vicksburg, Miss. (1899) 1,736. Union victory gave North control of the Mississippi and split the Confederacy in two.

National Memorials

Arkansas Post, Ark. (1960) 389. First permanent French settlement in the lower Mississippi River valley.

Arlington House, the Robert E. Lee Memorial, Va. (1925/1972) 28. Lee's home overlooking the Potomac.

Chamizal, El Paso, Tex. (1966/1974) 55. Commemorates 1963 settlement of 99-year border dispute with Mexico.

Coronado, Ariz. (1941/1952) 4,750. Commemorates first European exploration of the Southwest.

DeSoto, Fla. (1948) 27. Commemorates 16th-century Spanish explorations.

Federal Hall, N.Y. (1939/1955) 0.45. First seat of U.S. government under the Constitution.

Fort Caroline, Fla. (1950) 138. On St. Johns River, overlooks site of a French Huguenot colony.

Fort Clatsop, Ore. (1958) 125. Lewis and Clark encampment 1805-06.

General Grant, N.Y. (1958) 0.76. Tombs of Pres. and wife.

Hamilton Grange, N.Y. (1962) 0.11. Home of Alexander Hamilton.

John F. Kennedy Center for the Performing Arts, D.C. (1958/1964) 18. Presents plays, concerts, films, operas, and ballet.

Johnstown Flood, Pa. (1964) 164. Commemorates tragic flood of 1889.

Lincoln Boyhood, Ind. (1962) 200. Lincoln grew up here.

Lincoln Memorial, D.C. (1911) 110. Marble statue of the 16th U.S. president.

Lyndon B. Johnson Grove on the Potomac, D.C. (1973) 17. Overlooks the Potomac R vista of the Capital.

Mount Rushmore, S.D. (1925) 1,278. World famous sculpture of 4 presidents.

Perry's Victory and International Peace Memorial, Put-in-Bay, Oh. (1936/1972) 25. The world's most massive Doric column, constructed 1912-15, inculcates the lessons of international peace by arbitration and disarmament.

Roger Williams, R.I. (1965) 5. Memorial to founder of Rhode Island.

Thaddeus Kosciuszko, Pa. (1972) 0.02. Memorial to Polish hero of American Revolution.

Theodore Roosevelt Island, D.C. (1932) 89. Statue of Roosevelt in wooded island sanctuary.

Thomas Jefferson Memorial, D.C. (1934) 18. Statue of Jefferson in an inscribed circular, colonnaded structure.

USS Arizona, Ha. (1980). 00. Memorializes American losses at Pearl Harbor.

Vietnam Veterans, D.C. (1980) 2. Black granite wall inscribed with names of those killed in action and missing in the Vietnam War.

Washington Monument, D.C. (1848) 106. Obelisk honoring the first U.S. president.

Wright Brothers, N.C. (1927/1953) 431. Site of first powered flight.

National Historic Sites

Abraham Lincoln Birthplace, Hodgenville, Ky. (1916/1959) 117. Early 17th-cent. cabin.

Adams, Quincy, Mass. (1946/1952) 10. Home of Presidents John Adams, John Quincy Adams, and celebrated descendants.

Allegheny Portage Railroad, Pa. (1964) 1,247. Linked the Pennsylvania Canal system and the West.

Andersonville, Andersonville, Ga. (1970) 495. Noted Civil War prisoner-of-war camp.

Andrew Johnson, Greeneville, Tenn. (1935/1963) 17. Two homes and the tailor shop of the 17th U.S. president.

Bent's Old Fort, Col. (1960) 800. Reconstruction of S Plains outpost.

Boston African American (1980) Pre-Civil War black history structures.

Brown v. Board of Education, Kan. (1992). Commemorates the landmark 1954 U.S. Supreme Court Decision.

Carl Sandburg Home, N.C. (1968) 263. Poet's home.

Charles Pinckney, S.C. (1988) 28. Statesman's farm.

Christiansted, St. Croix, V.I. (1952/1961) 27. Commemorates Danish colony.

Clara Barton, Md. (1974) 9. Home of founder of American Red Cross.

Edgar Allan Poe, Pa. (1978/1980). U.S. writer's home.

Edison, West Orange, N.J. (1955/1962) 21. Inventor's home and laboratory.

Eisenhower, Gettysburg, Pa. (1967) 690. Home of 34th president.

Eleanor Roosevelt, Hyde Park, N.Y. (1977) 181. Personal retreat.

Eugene O'Neill, Danville, Cal. (1976) 13. Playwright's home.

Ford's Theatre, D.C. (1866/1970) 0.29. Includes theater, now restored, where Lincoln was assassinated, house where he died, and Lincoln Museum.

Fort Bowie, Ariz. (1964) 1,000. Focal point of operations against Geronimo and the Apaches.

Fort Davis, Tex. (1961) 460. Key frontier outpost in West Texas.

Fort Laramie, Wy. (1938/1960) 833. Military post on Oregon Trail.

Fort Larned, Kan. (1964/1966) 718. Military post on Santa Fe Trail.

Fort Point, San Francisco, Cal. (1970) 29. West Coast fortification.

Fort Raleigh, N.C. (1941) 513. First attempted English settlement in N Amer.

Fort Scott, Kan. (1965/1978) 17. Commemorates U.S. frontier of 1840s and '50s.

Fort Smith, Ark. (1961) 75. Active post from 1817 to 1890.

Fort Union Trading Post, Mon., N.D. (1966) 442. Principal fur-trading post on upper Missouri, 1829-1867.

Fort Vancouver, Wash. (1948/1961) 209. Hdqts. for Hudson's Bay Company in 1825. Early political seat.

Frederick Douglass Home, D.C. (1962/1988) 9. Home of nation's leading black spokesman.

Frederick Law Olmsted, Mass. (1979) 2. Home of famous city planner.

Friendship Hill, Pa. (1978) 675. Home of Albert Gallatin, Jefferson's and Madison's Secretary of Treasury.

Golden Spike, Utah (1957) 2,735. Commemorates completion of first transcontinental railroad in 1869.

Grant-Kohrs Ranch, Mon. (1972) 1,498. Ranch house and part of 19th-century ranch.

Hampton, Md. (1948) 62. 18th-century Georgian mansion.

Harry S. Truman, Mo. (1983) 1. Home of Pres. Truman after 1919.

Herbert Hoover, West Branch, Ia. (1965) 187. Birthplace and boyhood home of 31st president.

Home of Franklin D. Roosevelt, Hyde Park, N.Y. (1944) 290. Birthplace, home, and "Summer White House".

Hopewell Furnace, Pa. (1938/1985) 848. 19th-century iron-making village.

Hubbell Trading Post, Ariz. (1965) 160. Still-active trading post.

James A. Garfield, Mentor, Oh. (1980) 8. President's home.

Jefferson National Expansion Memorial, St. Louis, Mo. (1935/1969) 91. Commemorates westward expansion.

Jimmy Carter, Ga. (1987) 70. Birthplace and home of 39th president.

John Fitzgerald Kennedy, Brookline, Mass. (1967) 0.09. Birthplace and childhood home of the President.

John Muir, Martinez, Cal. (1964) 340. Home of early conservationist and writer.

Knife River Indian Villages, N.D. (1974) 1,758. Remnants of villages last occupied by Hidatsa and Mandan Indians.

Lincoln Home, Springfield, Ill. (1971) 12. Lincoln's residence at the time he was elected President, 1860.

Longfellow, Cambridge, Mass. (1972) 2. Longfellow's home, 1837-82, and Washington's hqts. during Boston Siege, 1775-76.

Maggie L. Walker, Va. (1978) 1. Richmond home of black leader and bank president; daughter of an ex-slave.

Manzanar, Lone Pine, Cal. (1992) 500. Commemorates Manzanar War Relocation Ctr., a Japanese-American internment camp during WWII.

Martin Luther King, Jr., Atlanta, Ga. (1980) 23. Birthplace, grave, and church of the civil rights leader.

Martin Van Buren, N.Y. (1974) 40. Lindenwald, home of 8th president, near Kinderhook.

Mary McLeod Bethune Council House, D.C. (1991). Commemorates Bethune's leadership in the black women's movement.

Ninety Six, S.C. (1976) 989. Colonial trading village.

Palo Alto Battlefield, Tex. (1978) 50. First battle of the Mexican War.

Pennsylvania Avenue, D.C. (1965) NA. Includes area between Capitol and White House, Ford's Theatre.

Puukohola Heiau, Ha. (1972) 80. Ruins of temple built by King Kamehameha.

Sagamore Hill, Oyster Bay, N.Y. (1962) 83. Home of President Theodore Roosevelt from 1885 until his death in 1919.

Saint-Gaudens, Cornish, N.H. (1964) 148. Home, studio, and gardens of American sculptor Augustus Saint-Gaudens.

Saint Paul's Church, N.Y. (1943) 6. 18th-century site associated with John Peter Zenger's "freedom of press" trial.

Salem Maritime, Mass. (1938) 9. Only port never seized from the patriots by the British. Major fishing and whaling port.

San Juan, P.R. (1949) 75. 16th-century Spanish fortifications.

Saugus Iron Works, Mass. (1968) 9. Reconstructed 17th-century colonial ironworks.

Springfield Armory, Mass. (1974) 55. Small arms manufacturing center for nearly 200 years.

Steamtown, Pa. (1986) 62. Railyard, roadhouse, and repair shops of former Delaware, Lackawanna, and Western Railroad.

Theodore Roosevelt Birthplace, N.Y., N.Y. (1962) 0.11. Reconstructed brownstone.

Theodore Roosevelt Inaugural, Buffalo, N.Y. (1966) 1. Wilcox House where he took oath of office, 1901.

Thomas Stone, Md. (1978) 328. Home of signer of Declaration of Independence, built in 1771.

Tuskegee Institute, Ala. (1974) 57. College founded by Booker T. Washington in 1881 for blacks.

Ulysses S. Grant, St. Louis Co., Mo. (1989) 10. Home of Grant during pre-Civil War years.

Vanderbilt Mansion, Hyde Park, N.Y. (1940) 212. Mansion of 19th-century financier.

Weir Farm, Witon, Conn. (1990) 58. Home and studio of American Impressionist painter J. Alden Weir.

Whitman Mission, Wash. (1936/1963) 98. Site where Dr. and Mrs. Marcus Whitman ministered to the Indians until slain by them in 1847.

William Howard Taft, Cincinnati, Oh. (1969) 3. Birthplace and early home of the 27th president.

National Monuments

Name	State	Year	Acreage
Agate Fossil Beds	Neb.	1965	3,055
Alibates Flint Quarries	N.M.-Tex.	1965	1,371
Aniakchak	Alas.	1978	17
Aztec Ruins	N.M.	1923	319
Bandelier	N.M.	1916	32,737
Black Canyon of the Gunnison	Col.	1933	20,766
Booker T. Washington	Va.	1956	224
Buck Island Reef	V.I.	1961	880
Cabrillo	Cal.	1913	137
Canyon de Chelly	Ariz.	1931	83,840
Cape Krusenstern	Alas.	1978	659,807
Capulin Volcano	N.M.	1916	793
Casa Grande Ruins	Ariz.	1892	473
Castillo de San Marcos	Fla.	1924	20
Castle Clinton	N.Y.	1946	1
Cedar Breaks	Ut.	1933	6,155
Chiricahua	Ariz.	1924	11,985
Colorado	Col.	1911	20,454
Congaree Swamp	S.C.	1976	22,200
Craters of the Moon	Ida.	1924	53,545
Death Valley	Cal.-Nev.	1933	2,067,628
Devils Postpile	Cal.	1911	798
Devils Tower	Wy.	1906	1,347
Dinosaur	Col.-Ut.	1915	210,844
Effigy Mounds	Ia.	1949	1,481
El Malpais	N.M.	1987	114,335
El Morro	N.M.	1906	1,279
Florissant Fossil Beds**	Col.	1969	5,998
Fort Frederica	Ga.	1936	216
Fort Matanzas	Fla.	1924	228
Fort McHenry National Monument and Historic Shrine	Md.	1925	43
Fort Pulaski	Ga.	1924	5,623
Fort Stanwix	N.Y.	1935	16
Fort Sumter	S.C.	1948	194
Fort Union	N.M.	1954	721
Fossil Butte	Wy.	1972	8,198
G. Washington Birthplace	Va.	1930	533
George Washington Carver	Mo.	1943	210
Gila Cliff Dwellings	N.M.	1907	533
Grand Portage	Minn.	1951	710
Great Sand Dunes	Col.	1932	38,662
Hagerman Fossil Beds	Ida.	1988	4,280
Hohokam Pima*	Ariz.	1972	1,690
Homestead Nat'l. Monument of America	Neb.	1936	195
Hovenweep	Col.-Ut.	1923	785
Jewel Cave	S.D.	1908	1,274
John Day Fossil Beds	Ore.	1974	14,014
Joshua Tree	Cal.	1936	559,955
Lava Beds	Cal.	1925	46,560
Little Big Horn Battlefield	Mon.	1879	765
Montezuma Castle	Ariz.	1906	858
Muir Woods	Cal.	1908	554
Natural Bridges	Ut.	1908	7,636
Navajo	Ariz.	1909	360
Ocmulgee	Ga.	1934	683
Oregon Caves	Ore.	1909	488
Organ Pipe Cactus	Ariz.	1937	330,689
Petroglyph	N.M.	1990	5,207
Pinnacles	Cal.	1908	16,265
Pipe Spring	Ariz.	1923	40
Pipestone	Minn.	1937	282
Poverty Point	La.	1988	911
Rainbow Bridge	Ut.	1910	160
Russell Cave	Ala.	1961	310
Saguaro	Ariz.	1933	87,691

(continued)

Name	State	Year	Acreage
Salinas	N.M.	1901	1,101
Scotts Bluff	Neb.	1919	3,003
Statue of Liberty	N.J.-N.Y	1924	58
Sunset Crater	Ariz.	1930	3,040
Timpanogos Cave	Ut.	1922	250
Tonto	Ariz.	1907	1,120
Tuzigoot	Ariz.	1939	801
Walnut Canyon	Ariz.	1915	2,249
White Sands	N.M.	1933	143,733
Wupatki	Ariz.	1924	35,253
Yucca House*	Col.	1919	10

National Preserves

Name	State	Year	Acreage
Aniakchak	Alas	1978	465,603
Bering Land Bridge	Alas	1978	2,784,960
Big Cypress	Fla	1974	716,000
Big Thicket	Tex	1974	96,563
Denali	Alas	1917	1,334,618
Gates of the Arctic	Alas	1978	948,629
Glacier Bay	Alas	1925	57,884
Katmai	Alas	1918	374,000
Lake Clark	Alas	1978	1,407,293
Little River Canyon	Ala	1992	NA
Noatak	Alas	1978	6,574,481
Timucuan Ecological & Historic Preserve	Fla	1988	46,000
Wrangell-St. Elias	Alas.	1978	4,856,721
Yukon-Charley Rivers	Alas	1978	2,523,509

National Seashores

Name	State	Year	Acreage
Assateague Island	Md.-Va	1965	39,733
Canaveral	Fla.	1975	57,662
Cape Cod	Mass.	1961	43,569
Cape Hatteras	N.C.	1937	30,319
Cape Lookout**	N.C.	1966	28,243
Cumberland Island	Ga.	1972	36,415
Fire Island	N.Y.	1964	19,579
Gulf Islands	Fla.-Miss.	1971	135,625
Padre Island	Tex.	1962	130,434
Point Reyes	Cal.	1962	71,049

National Parkways

Name	State	Year	Acreage
Blue Ridge	Va.-N.C.	1933	88,157
George Washington Memorial	Va.-Md.	1930	7,248
John D. Rockefeller Jr. Mem.	Wy.	1972	23,777
Natchez Trace	Ala.-Miss.-Tenn.	1938	51,748

National Lakeshores

Name	State	Year	Acreage
Apostle Islands	Wis.	1970	69,372
Indiana Dunes	Ind.	1966	14,981
Pictured Rocks	Mich.	1966	73,174
Sleeping Bear Dunes	Mich.	1970	71,189

National Reserves

Name	State	Year	Acreage
City of Rocks	Ida.	1988	14,407
Ebeys Landing	Wash.	1992	8,000

National Rivers

Name	State	Year	Acreage
Big South Fork Natl. R. and Recreation	Tenn.-Ky.	1976	125,000
Buffalo	Ark.	1972	94,219
New River Gorge	W.Va.	1978	62,144
Ozark	Mo.	1964	80,791
Mississippi Natl. R. and Recreation	Minn.	1988	53,775
Niobrara/Missouri	Neb.-S.D.	1991	NA

National Wild and Scenic Rivers

Name	State	Year	Acreage
Alagnak Wild	Alas.	1980	24,038
Bluestone	W.Va.	1978	4,268
Delaware	N.Y.-N.J.-Pa.	1978	1,973
Great Egg Harbor	N.J.	1992	NA
Obed Wild	Tenn.	1976	5,067
Rio Grande	Tex.	1978	9,600
Saint Croix	Minn.-Wis.	1968	67,457
Upper Delaware	N.Y.-N.J.	1978	75,000

Parks (no other classification)

Name	State	Year	Acreage
Catoctin Mountain	Md	1954	5,770
Constitution Gardens	D.C.	1978	52
Fort Washington	Md.	1930	341
Greenbelt	Md.	1950	1,176
National Capital	D.C.	1993	6,525
Piscataway	Md.	1961	4,263
Prince William Forest	Va.	1948	18,572
Rock Creek	D.C.	1890	1,754
White House	D.C.	1933	18
Wolf Trap Farm Park for the Performing Arts	Va.	1966	130

National Recreation Areas

Name	State	Year	Acreage
Amistad	Tex.	1965	57,292
Bighorn Canyon	Mon.-Wy.	1966	120,296
Chattahoochee R.	Ga.	1978	9,260
Chickasaw	Okla.	1902	9,930
Coulee Dam	Wash.	1946	100,390
Curecanti	Col.	1965	42,114
Cuyahoga Valley	Oh.	1974	32,525
Delaware Water Gap	N.J.-Pa.	1965	67,205
Gateway	N.Y.-N.J.	1972	26,311
Gauley R.	W.Va.	1988	10,300
Glen Canyon	Ariz.-Ut.	1958	1,236,880
Golden Gate	Cal.	1972	73,180
Lake Chelan	Wash.	1968	61,887
Lake Mead	Ariz.-Nev.	1936	1,495,666
Lake Meredith	Tex.	1965	44,978
Ross Lake	Wash.	1968	117,575
Santa Monica Mts.	Cal.	1978	150,050
Whiskeytown	Cal.	1965	42,503

Name	State	Year	Acreage
National Mall	D.C	1933	146

National Scenic Trails

Name	State	Year	Acreage
Appalachian	Me. to Ga.	1968	169,995
Natchez Trace	Ala.-Miss.-Tenn.	1983	10,995
Potomac Heritage	Md.-D.C.-Va.-Pa	1983	***

International Historic Sites

Name	State	Year	Acreage
Saint Croix Island	Me.	1949	35

*Not open to the public. **No federal facilities. ***Undetermined. NA=Not available.

Most Visited Sites in the National Park System, 1993

Source: National Park Service

Attendance at all areas administered by the National Park Service in 1993 was 273,120,925 recreation visits.

Site (Location)	Recreation Visits
Blue Ridge Parkway (NC, VA)	17,889,335
Golden Gate National Recreation Area (CA)	14,695,711
Great Smoky Mountains National Park (TN, NC)	9,283,848
Lake Mead National Recreation Area (AZ, NV)	8,941,226
Gateway National Recreation Area (NY, NJ)	5,898,453
Natchez Trace Parkway (MS, AL, TN)	5,752,880
George Washington Memorial Parkway (VA, MD)	5,491,037
Gulf Islands National Seashore (FL, MS)	5,458,294
Cape Cod National Seashore (MA)	5,154,810
Grand Canyon National Park (AZ)	4,575,602
Delaware Water Gap National Recreation Area (PA, NJ)	4,187,638
Statue of Liberty National Monument (NY, NJ)	4,112,003
Yosemite National Park (CA)	3,839,645
Chesapeake and Ohio Canal National Historical Park (MD, WV, DC)	3,661,497
San Francisco Maritime National Historical Park (CA)	3,549,325
Glen Canyon National Recreation Area (AZ, UT)	3,584,158
Castle Clinton National Monument (NY)	3,319,237
Independence National Historical Park (PA)	3,188,317
Yellowstone National Park (WY, MT, ID)	2,912,193
Chattahoochee River National Recreation Area (GA)	2,844,674
Rocky Mountain National Park (CO)	2,780,342
Olympic National Park (WA)	2,679,698
Acadia National Park (ME)	2,658,034
Grand Teton National Park (WY)	2,588,589
Point Reyes National Seashore (CA)	2,581,234

Federal Indian Reservations and Trust Lands[1]

Source: Tiller Research, Inc., Albuquerque, NM

State	No. of reser.	Tribally owned acreage[2]	Individually owned acreage[2]	No. of persons[3]	Major tribes and/or nations
Alabama	1	230	0	16,506	Poarch Creek
Alaska	1[4]	86,773	1,265,432	85,698	Aleut, Eskimo, Athapascan,[5] Haida, Tlingit, Tsimpshian
Arizona	23	19,775,959	311,579	203,527	Navajo, Apache, Papago, Hopi, Yavapai, Pima
California	96	520,049	66,769	242,164	Hoopa, Paiute, Yurok, Karok, Cherokee
Colorado	2	764,120	2,805	27,776	Ute
Connecticut	1	1,638	0	6,654	Mashantucket Pequot
Florida	4	153,874	0	36,335	Seminole, Miccosukee, Cherokee
Idaho	4	609,622	327,301	13,780	Shoshone, Bannock, Nez Perce
Iowa	1	3,550	0	7,349	Sac and Fox
Kansas	4	7,219	23,763	21,965	Potawatomi, Kickapoo, Iowa
Louisiana	3	415	0	18,541	Chitimacha, Coushatta, Tunica-Biloxi
Maine	3	191,511	0	5,998	Passamaquoddy, Penobscot, Maliseet
Massachusetts	1	157	0	12,241	Wampanoag
Michigan	8	14,411	9,276	55,638	Chippewa, Potawatomi, Ottawa, Cherokee
Minnesota	14	779,138	50,338	49,909	Chippewa, Sioux
Mississippi	1	20,486	0	8,525	Choctaw
Montana	7	2,663,385	2,911,450	47,679	Blackfeet, Crow, Sioux, Assiniboine, Cheyenne
Nebraska	3	23,792	43,208	12,410	Omaha, Winnebago, Santee Sioux
Nevada	19	1,147,088	78,529	19,637	Paiute, Shoshone, Washoe
New Mexico	25	7,252,326	630,293	134,355	Apache, Navajo, Pueblo
New York	8	118,199	0	62,651	Seneca, Mohawk, Onondaga, Oneida
North Carolina	1	56,509	0	80,155	Cherokee, Lumbee
North Dakota	3	214,006	627,289	25,917	Sioux, Chippewa, Mandan, Arikara, Hidatsa
Oklahoma	36[6]	96,839	1,000,165	252,420	Cherokee, Creek, Choctaw, Chickasaw, Osage, Cheyenne, Arapahoe, Kiowa, Comanche
Oregon	7	660,367	135,053	38,496	Warm Springs, Wasco, Paiute, Umatilla, Siletz
Rhode Island	1	1,800	0	4,071	Narragansett
South Carolina	1	639	0	8,246	Catawba
South Dakota	9	2,399,531	2,121,188	50,575	Sioux
Texas	3	4,726	0	65,877	Alabama-Coushatta, Tiwa, Kickapoo
Utah	4	2,286,448	32,838	24,283	Ute, Goshute, Southern Paiute, Navajo
Washington	27	2,250,731	467,785	81,483	Yakama, Lummi, Quinault
Wisconsin	11	338,097	80,345	39,387	Chippewa, Oneida, Winnebago
Wyoming	1	1,958,095	101,537	9,479	Shoshone, Arapahoe

(1) In Oct. 1993, the Bureau of Indian Affairs of the U.S. Dept. of the Interior published in the *Federal Register* (vol. 58, no. 202, pp. 54364-69) a comprehensive listing of 552 "Indian Entities Recognized and Eligible To Receive Services From the United States Bureau of Indian Affairs" (328 in the contiguous 48 states, 224 in Alaska). The term *Indian entities* includes Indian tribes, bands, villages, groups, and pueblos; also included are Eskimo and Aleut villages and tribes. All such entities have a government-to-government relationship with the U.S. Some reservation boundaries transcend state boundaries (e.g., Navajo, which is in Arizona, New Mexico, and Utah). For the purpose of "Number of Reservations," such reservations are counted in the state where their population is predominant and/or tribal headquarters are located. (2) Information provided by the Bureau of Indian Affairs; data current as of 1990. Acreages refer only to lands that are either owned by the tribes and individual members or that are held in trust by the U.S. government. Many of these parcels are located off reservations. Not all lands within reservation boundaries are necessarily trust lands. Many are privately owned by tribes, tribal members, or non-Indians others are the property of various governmental agencies. (3) Total Native American (Indian, Eskimo, or Aleut) population in each state with reservation/trust lands, including those persons living outside the Bureau of Indian Affairs service area. (4) The only federally recognized reservation in Alaska is the Annette Island Reserve. In all other cases, the U.S. government's relationship to Native Americans in Alaska is set out by the Alaska Native Claims Settlement Act of 1971. The act provided for the establishment of regional and village corporations to conduct business for profit and nonprofit purposes; these corporations are also landowners. There are 12 regional corporations, each with organized village corporations, plus one regional corporation for Alaska Natives outside the state. (5) Aleuts and Eskimos are racially and linguistically related. Athapascans are related to the Navajo and Apache Indians. (6) There are 36 tribal entities in Oklahoma, each of which owns land in the state. Because of the way in which the state of Oklahoma was formed out of the Oklahoma and Indian territories, the reservation status of land in the state is frequently disputed in both civil and criminal proceedings.

American Indian Population

Source: Bureau of the Census, U.S. Dept. of Commerce, 1990 Census

The Bureau of the Census figures reflect personal self-identification and therefore do not necessarily reflect any designation of a federally or state-recognized tribe.

State	Total	State	Total	State	Total	State	Total	State	Total	State	Total
AL	16,312	GA	12,926	ME	5,945	NV	19,377	OR	37,443	VA	14,893
AK	31,245	HI	4,738	MD	12,601	NH	2,075	PA	14,210	WA	77,627
AZ	203,009	ID	13,594	MA	11,857	NJ	14,500	RI	3,987	WV	2,365
AR	12,641	IL	20,970	MI	56,131	NM	134,097	SC	8,049	WI	38,986
CA	236,078	IN	12,453	MN	49,392	NY	60,855	SD	50,501	WY	9,426
CO	27,271	IA	7,217	MS	8,435	NC	79,825	TN	9,859		
CT	6,472	KS	21,767	MO	19,508	ND	25,870	TX	64,349	**Total**	
DE	1,982	KY	5,614	MT	47,524	OH	19,859	UT	24,093	**U.S.**	1,878,285
FL	35,461	LA	18,361	NE	12,344	OK	252,069	VT	1,650		

WORLD HISTORY

Prehistory: Our Ancestors Take Over

Homo sapiens. The precise origins of *Homo sapiens,* the species to which all humans belong, are subject to broad speculation based on a small number of fossils, on genetic and anatomical studies, and on the geological record. Most scientists agree, however, that humans evolved from apelike primate ancestors in a process that began millions of years ago.

Current theories trace the first hominid (humanlike primate) to Africa, where 2 lines of hominids appeared 5 to 7 million years ago. One was *Australopithecus,* a social animal, who lived from perhaps 4 to 3 million years ago, and then apparently became extinct. The other was a human line, *Homo habilis,* a large-brained specimen that walked upright and had a dextrous hand. *Homo habilis* appeared some 2.5 million years ago, lived in semipermanent camps, and had a food-gathering and sharing economy.

Homo erectus, our nearest ancestor, appeared in Africa perhaps 1.75 million years ago and began spreading into Asia and Europe soon after. It had a fairly large brain and a skeletal structure similar to ours. *Homo erectus* learned to control fire and probably had primitive language skills. The final brain development to *Homo sapiens* and then to our subspecies *Homo sapiens sapiens* occurred between 500,000 and 50,000 years ago, either in one place—probably Africa—or virtually simultaneously and independently in different places in Africa, Europe, and Asia. All modern races are unquestionably members of the subspecies *Homo sapiens sapiens.*

The spread of humankind into the remaining habitable continents probably took place near the end of the last Ice Age: from Asia to the Americas, across a land bridge, and to Australia, across the **Timor Straits.**

Earliest cultures. A variety of cultural modes—in toolmaking, diet, shelter, and possibly social arrangements and spiritual expression—arose as early humankind adapted to different geographic and climatic zones.

Archeologists recognize 3 basic toolmaking traditions as arising and often coexisting from one million years ago to the near past: the *chopper tradition,* found largely in E Asia, producing crude chopping tools and simple flake tools; the *flake tradition,* found in Africa and W Europe, producing a variety of small cutting and flaking tools; and the *biface* tradition, found in all of Africa, W and S Europe, and S Asia, producing pointed hand axes chipped on both faces. Later biface sites yield more refined axes and a variety of other tools, weapons, and ornaments using bone, antler, and wood as well as stone.

Only sketchy evidence remains for the stages in increasing human control over the environment. Traces of 400,000-year-old covered wood shelters have been found at Nice, France. Scraping tools at Neanderthal sites (200,000-30,000 BC in Europe, N Africa, the Middle East, and Central Asia) suggest the treatment of skins for clothing. Sites from all parts of the world show seasonal migration patterns and exploitation of a wide range of plant and animal food sources.

Painting and decoration, for which there is evidence at the Nice site, flourished, along with stone and ivory sculpture, from 25,000 years ago: more than 200 caves in Europe, mainly in S France (Lascaux) and N Spain (Altamira), show remarkable examples of wall painting. Other examples have been found in Africa. Proto-religious rites are suggested by these works, by evidence of ritual cannibalism by Peking Man (500,000 BC), and by evidence of ritual burial with medicinal plants and flowers by Neanderthals at Shanidar in Iraq.

The Neolithic Revolution. Some time after 10,000 BC, among widely separated human communities, a series of dramatic technological and social changes occurred that are summed up as the Neolithic Revolution. The cultivation of previously wild plants encouraged the growth of permanent settlements. Animals were domesticated as a work force and a food source. The manufacture of pottery and cloth began. These techniques permitted a huge increase in world population and in human control over the earth.

No region can safely claim priority as the "inventor" of these techniques. Dispersed sites in Cen. and S America, SE Europe, and the Middle East show roughly contemporaneous (10,000-8000 BC) evidence of one or another "neolithic" trait. Dates near 6000-3000 BC have been given for E and S Asian, W European, and sub-Saharan African neolithic remains. The variety of crops —field grains, rice, maize, and roots—and the varying mix of other traits suggest that the revolution occurred independently in all these regions.

History Begins: 4000-1000 BC

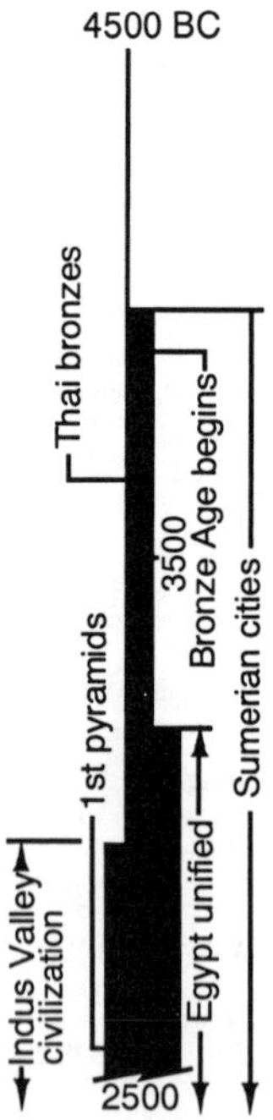

Near Eastern cradle. If history began with writing, the first chapter opened in Mesopotamia, the Tigris-Euphrates river valley. The Sumerians used clay tablets with pictographs to keep records after 4000 BC. A cuneiform (wedge-shaped) script evolved by 3000 BC as a full syllabic alphabet. Neighboring peoples adapted the script to their own language.

Sumerian life centered, from 4000 BC, on large cities (Eridu, Ur, Uruk, Nippur, Kish, and Lagash) organized around temples and priestly bureaucracies, with the surrounding plains watered by vast irrigation works and worked with traction plows. Sailboats, wheeled vehicles, potter's wheels, and kilns were used. Copper was smelted and tempered in Sumeria from c 4000 BC, and bronze was produced not long after. Ores, as well as precious stones and metals, were obtained through long-distance ship and caravan trade. Iron was used from c 2000 BC. Improved ironworking, developed partly by the Hittites, became widespread by 1200 BC.

Sumerian political primacy passed among cities and their kingly dynasties. Semitic-speaking peoples, with cultures derived from the Sumerian, founded a succession of dynasties that ruled in Mesopotamia and neighboring areas for most of 1800 years; among them were the **Akkadians** (first under Sargon I c 2350 BC), the Amorites (whose laws, codified by **Hammurabi,** c 1792-1750 BC, have biblical parallels), and the Assyrians, with interludes of rule by the Hittites, Kassites, and Mitanni, all possibly Indo-Europeans. The political and cultural center of gravity shifted NW with each successive empire.

Mesopotamian learning, maintained by scribes and preserved by successive rulers in vast libraries, was not abstract or theoretical. Algebraic and geometric problems could be solved on a practical basis in construction, commerce, and administration. Systematic lists of astronomical phenomena, plants, animals, and stones were kept; medical texts listed ailments and their herbal cures.

The Sumerians worshiped anthropomorphic gods representing natural forces: Anu, god of heaven, and Enlil (Ea), god of water. Epic poetry related these and other gods in a hierarchy. Sacrifices were made at **ziggurats** —huge stepped temples. Gods were thought to control all events, which could be foretold using oracular materials. This religious pattern persisted into the 1st millennium BC.

The Syria-Palestine area, site of some of the earliest urban remains (Jericho, 7000 BC), and of the recently uncovered **Ebla** civilization (fl 2500 BC), experienced Egyptian cultural and political influence along with Mesopotamian. The **Phoenician** coast was an active commercial center. A phonetic alphabet was invented here before 1600 BC. It became the ancestor of all European, Middle Eastern, Indian, SE Asian, Ethiopian, and many other alphabets.

Egypt. Agricultural villages along the Nile were united by 3300 BC into 2 kingdoms, Upper and Lower Egypt, unified (c 3100 BC) under the Pharaoh Menes. A national bureaucracy supervised construction of canals and monuments (**pyramids** starting 2700 BC). Control over Nubia to the S was asserted beginning 2600 BC.

Brilliant Old Kingdom Period achievements in architecture, sculpture, and painting, which reached their height during the 3d and 4th Dynasties, set the standards and forms for all subsequent Egyptian civilization and are still admired. **Hieroglyphic writing** appeared by 3200 BC, recording a sophisticated literature that included religious writings, philosophies, history, and science.

An ordered hierarchy of gods, including totemistic animal elements, was served by a powerful priesthood in Memphis. The pharaoh was identified with the falcon god Horus. Other trends were the belief in an afterlife and the short-lived quasimonotheistic reforms of the pharaoh **Akhenaton** (c 1379-1362 BC).

After a period of dominance by Semitic Hyksos from Asia (c 1700-1550 BC), the New Kingdom established an empire in Syria. Egypt became increasingly embroiled in Asiatic wars and diplomacy. Conquered by Persia in 525 BC, it eventually faded away as an independent culture.

India. An urban civilization with a so-far-undeciphered writing system stretched across the Indus Valley and along the Arabian Sea c 3000-1500 BC. Major sites are Harappa and **Mohenjo-Daro** in Pakistan, well-planned geometric cities with underground sewers and vast granaries. The entire region (600,000 sq mi) may have been ruled as a single state. Bronze was used, and arts and crafts were highly developed. Religious life apparently took the form of fertility cults.

Indus civilization was probably in decline when it was destroyed by **Aryan invaders** from the NW, speaking an Indo-European language from which most of the languages of Pakistan, N India, and Bangladesh descend. Led by a warrior aristocracy whose legendary deeds are in the **Rig Veda**, the Aryans spread E and S, bringing their pantheon of sky gods, elaborate priestly (Brahman) ritual, and the beginnings of the caste system; local customs and beliefs were assimilated by the conquerors.

Europe. On Crete, the Bronze Age **Minoan civilization** emerged c 2500 BC. A prosperous economy and richly decorative art was supported by seaborne commerce. Mycenae and other cities in mainland Greece and in Asia Minor (e.g., **Troy**) preserved elements of the culture until c 1200 BC. Cretan Linear A script (c 2000-1700 BC) remains undeciphered; Linear B script (c 1300-1200 BC) records an early Greek dialect.

Unclear is the possible connection between Mycenaean monumental stonework and the great megalithic monuments and tombs of W Europe, Iberia, and Malta (c 4000-1500 BC).

China. Proto-Chinese neolithic cultures had long covered N and SE China when the first large political state was organized in the north by the **Shang dynasty** (c 1523 BC). Shang kings called themselves Sons of Heaven, and they presided over a cult of human and animal sacrifice to ancestors and nature gods. The Chou dynasty, starting c 1027 BC, expanded the area of the Son of Heaven's dominion, but feudal states exercised most temporal power.

A writing system with 2,000 characters was already in use under the Shang, with **pictographs** later supplemented by phonetic characters. Many of its principles and symbols, despite changes in spoken Chinese, were preserved in later writing systems.

Technical advances allowed urban specialists to create fine ceramic and jade products, and bronze casting after 1500 BC was the most advanced in the world. Bronze artifacts have recently been discovered in northern Thailand dating from 3600 BC, hundreds of years before similar Middle Eastern finds.

Americas. Olmecs settled (1500 BC) on the Gulf coast of Mexico and soon developed the first civilization in the western hemisphere. Temple cities and huge stone sculpture date from 1200 BC. A rudimentary calendar and writing system existed. Olmec religion, centering on a jaguar god, and art forms influenced all later Meso-American cultures.

Classical Era of Old World Civilizations

Greece. After a period of decline during the Dorian Greek invasions (1200-1000 BC), Greece and the Aegean area developed a unique civilization. Drawing upon Mycenaean traditions, Mesopotamian learning (weights and measures, lunisolar calendar, astronomy, musical scales), the Phoenician alphabet (modified for Greek), and Egyptian art, the revived **Greek city-states** saw a rich elaboration of intellectual life. Homer's epics the *Iliad* and the *Odyssey* were written in the 8th cent. BC. Long-range commerce was aided by metal coinage (introduced by the Lydians in Asia Minor before 700 BC); colonies were founded around the Mediterranean (Cumae in Italy in 760 BC; Massalia in France c 600 BC) and Black Sea shores.

Philosophy, starting with Ionian speculation on the nature of matter and the universe (Thales, c 634-546 BC) and including mathematical speculation (Pythagoras, c 580-c 500 BC), culminated in Athens in the rationalist idealism of **Plato** (c 428-347 BC), a disciple of **Socrates** (c 469-399 BC); the latter was sentenced to death for alleged impiety. **Aristotle** (384-322 BC) united all fields of study in his system. The arts were highly valued. Architecture culminated in the **Parthenon** (438 BC) in Athens by Phidias (fl 490-430 BC) with his sculpture of Athena; poetry and drama (Aeschylus, 525-456 BC) thrived. Male beauty and strength, a chief artistic theme, were enhanced at the gymnasium and celebrated at the national games at Olympia. Ruled by local tyrants or oligarchies, the Greeks were never politically united, but they managed to resist inclusion in the Persian Empire (Darius defeated at Marathon 490 BC, Xerxes at Salamis, Plataea 479 BC). Local warfare was common; the **Peloponnesian Wars** (431-404 BC) ended in Sparta's victory over Athens. Greek political power waned, but classical Greek cultural forms spread throughout the ancient world from the Atlantic to India.

Hebrews. Nomadic Hebrew tribes entered Canaan before 1200 BC, settling among other Semitic peoples speaking the same language. They brought from the desert a **monotheistic** faith said to have been revealed to Abraham in Canaan c 1800 BC and to Moses at Mt. Sinai c 1250 BC, after the Hebrews' escape from bondage in Egypt. David (ruled 1000-961 BC) and Solomon (ruled 961-922 BC) united the Hebrews in a kingdom that briefly dominated the area. Phoenicians to the N established colonies around the E and W Mediterranean (Carthage, c 814 BC) and sailed into the Atlantic.

(continues on p. 511)

2500 BC
Ebla civilization
Bronze-age Minoan civilization emerges on Crete
Egyptian literature begins
Peruvian neolithic ceremonial centers
Phonetic alphabet invented before 1600
Hammurabi
1750
Aryans invade India
Chinese Shang dynasty
Mt. Sinai revelations to Moses
Mexican Olmec civilization established
1000 BC

Paleontology: The History of Life

All dates are approximate, and are subject to change based on new fossil finds or new dating techniques; but the sequence of events is generally accepted. Dates are in years before the present.

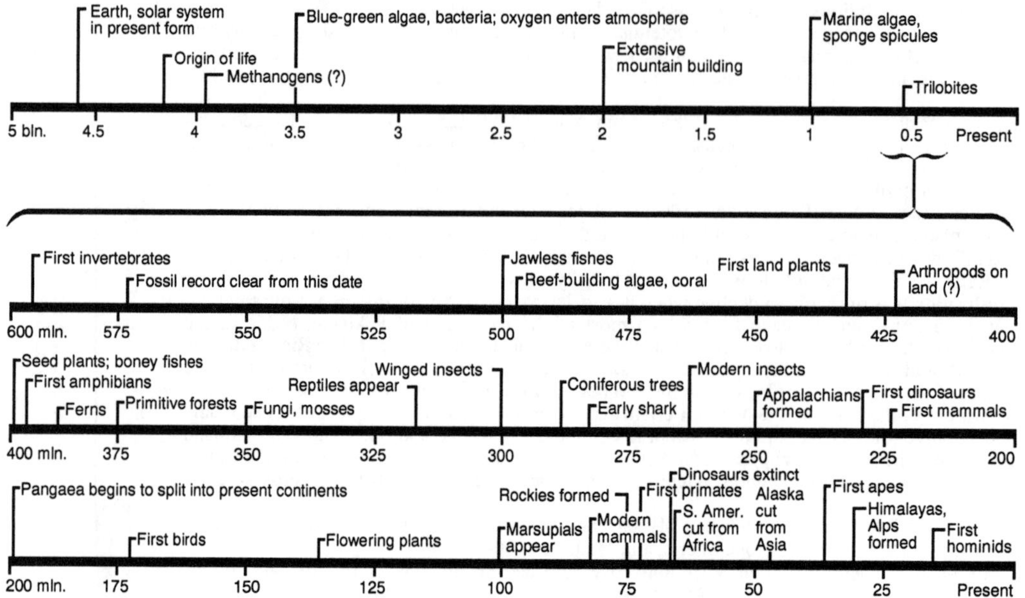

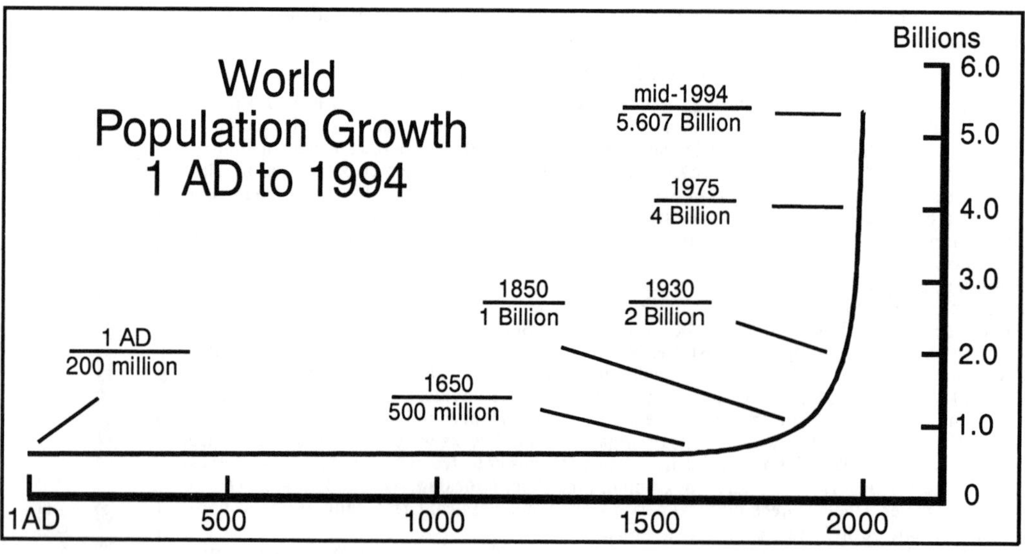

A temple in Jerusalem became the national religious center, with sacrifices performed by a hereditary priesthood. Polytheistic influences, especially of the fertility cult of Baal, were opposed by **prophets** (Elijah, Amos, Isaiah).

Divided into **two kingdoms** after Solomon, the Hebrews were unable to resist the revived Assyrian empire, which conquered Israel, the N kingdom in 722 BC. Judah, the S kingdom, was conquered in 586 BC by the Babylonians under Nebuchadnezzar II. But with the fixing of most of the biblical canon by the mid-4th cent. BC and the emergence of rabbis, Judaism successfully survived the loss of Hebrew autonomy. A Jewish kingdom was revived under the Hasmoneans (168-42 BC).

China. During the **Eastern Chou** dynasty (770-256 BC), Chinese culture spread E to the sea and S to the Yangtze R. Large feudal states on the periphery of the empire contended for preeminence, but continued to recognize the Son of Heaven (king), who retained a purely ritual role enriched with courtly music and dance. In the Age of Warring States (403-221 BC), when the first sections of the **Great Wall** were built, the Ch'in state in the W gained supremacy and finally united all of China.

Iron tools entered China c 500 BC, and casting techniques were advanced, aiding agriculture. Peasants owned their land and owed civil and military service to nobles. Cities grew in number and size, although barter remained the chief trade medium.

Intellectual ferment among noble scribes and officials produced the Classical Age of Chinese literature and philosophy. **Confucius** (551-479 BC) urged a restoration of a supposedly harmonious social order of the past through proper conduct in accordance with one's station and through filial and ceremonial piety. The *Analects* attributed to him are revered throughout E Asia. **Mencius** (d 289 BC) added the view that the Mandate of Heaven can be removed from an unjust dynasty. The Legalists sought to curb the supposed natural wickedness of people through new institutions and harsh laws; they aided the Ch'in rise to power. The Naturalists emphasized the balance of opposites—yin, yang—in the world. **Taoists** sought mystical knowledge through meditation and disengagement.

India. The political and cultural center of India shifted from the Indus to the Ganges River Valley. Buddhism, Jainism, and mystical revisions of orthodox Vedism all developed c 500-300 BC. The *Upanishads,* last part of the *Veda,* urged escape from the physical world. Vedism remained the preserve of the Brahman caste. In contrast, **Buddhism**, founded by Siddarta Gautama (c 563-c 483 BC)—Buddha ("Enlightened One")—appealed to merchants in the urban centers and took hold at first (and most lastingly) on the geographic fringes of Indian civilization. The classic Indian epics were composed in this era: the **Ramayana** perhaps c 300 BC, the **Mahabharata** over a period starting 400 BC.

Northern India was divided into a large number of monarchies and aristocratic republics, probably derived from tribal groupings, when the Magadha kingdom was formed in Bihar c 542 BC. It soon became the dominant power. The **Maurya dynasty**, founded by Chandragupta c 321 BC, expanded the kingdom, uniting most of N India in a centralized bureaucratic empire. The third Mauryan king, **Asoka** (ruled c 274-236 BC), conquered most of the subcontinent: He converted to Buddhism and inscribed its tenets on pillars throughout India. He downplayed the caste system and tried to end expensive sacrificial rites.

Before its final decline in India, Buddhism developed into a popular worship of heavenly Bodhisattvas ("enlightened beings"); and produced a refined architecture (the Great Stupa [shrine] at Sanchi, 100 AD) and sculpture (Gandhara reliefs 1-400 AD).

Persia. Aryan peoples (Persians, Medes) dominated the area of present Iran by the beginning of the 1st millennium BC. The prophet **Zoroaster** (born c 628 BC) introduced a dualistic religion in which the forces of good (Ahura Mazda, "Lord of Wisdom") and evil (Ahriam) battle for dominance; individuals are judged by their actions and earn damnation or salvation. Zoroaster's hymns (*Gathas*) are included in the *Avesta*, the Zoroastrian scriptures. A version of this faith became the established religion of the Persian Empire and probably influenced later monotheistic religions.

Africa. Nubia, periodically occupied by Egypt since about 2600 BC, ruled Egypt c 750-661 BC and survived as an independent Egyptianized kingdom (**Kush;** capital Meroe) for 1,000 years. The Iron Age Nok culture flourished c 500 BC-200 AD on the Benue Plateau of **Nigeria**.

Americas. The Chavin culture controlled N Peru from 900 BC to 200 BC. Its ceremonial centers, featuring the jaguar god, survived long after. Chavin architecture, ceramics, and textiles influenced other Peruvian cultures.

Mayan civilization began to develop in Central America as early as 1500 BC.

Great Empires Unite the Civilized World: 400 BC - 400 AD

Persia and Alexander the Great. **Cyrus,** ruler of a small kingdom in Persia from 559 BC, united the Persians and Medes within 10 years and conquered Asia Minor and Babylonia in another 10. His son Cambyses followed by **Darius** (ruled 522-486 BC) added vast lands to the E and N as far as the Indus Valley and Central Asia, as well as Egypt and Thrace. The whole empire was ruled by an international bureaucracy and army, with Persians holding the chief positions. The resources and styles of all the subject civilizations were exploited to create a rich syncretic art.

The kingdom of Macedon, which under Phillip II dominated the Greek world and Egypt, passed to his son **Alexander** in 336 BC. Within 13 years, Alexander conquered all the Persian dominions. Imbued by his tutor Aristotle with Greek ideals, Alexander encouraged Greek colonization, and Greek-style cities were founded. After his death in 323 BC, wars of succession divided the empire into 3 parts—**Macedon,** Egypt (ruled by the **Ptolemies**), and the **Seleucid** Empire.

In the ensuing 300 years (the **Hellenistic Era**), a cosmopolitan Greek-oriented culture permeated the ancient world from W Europe to the borders of India, absorbing native elites everywhere.

Hellenistic philosophy stressed the private individual's search for happiness. The Cynics followed Diogenes (c 372-287 BC), who stressed self-sufficiency and restriction of desires and expressed contempt for luxury and social convention. Zeno (c 335-c 263 BC) and the Stoics exalted reason, identified it with virtue, and counseled an ascetic disregard for misfortune. The Epicureans tried to build lives of moderate pleasure without political or emotional involvement. Hellenistic arts imitated life realistically, especially in sculpture and literature (comedies of Menander, 342-292 BC).

(continues on p. 513)

1000 BC
Hebrew kingdom divided
Chavin dynasty begins in Peru
Carthage established
Chou dynasty begins in China
800
Metal coins in Asia Minor
Isaiah d.
Nubia begins rule of Egypt
Zoroaster b.
Pythagoras b.
600
Indian Buddhism, Jainism begin
Confucius b.
Siddarta b.
Aeschylus b.
Socrates b.
Plato b.
Parthenon
Peloponnesian Wars
400 BC

The Seven Wonders of the Ancient World

These ancient works of art and architecture were considered awe-inspiring in splendor and/or size by the Greek and Roman world of the Alexandrian epoch. Later Classical writers disagreed as to which works made up the list of Wonders, but the following were usually included.

The Pyramids of Egypt: The only surviving Wonder, these monumental structures of masonry located at Giza on the W bank of the Nile R above Cairo were built from c 2700 to 2500 BC as royal tombs. Three—Khufu (Cheops), Khafra (Chephren), and Menkaura (Mycerimus)—were often grouped as the first Wonder of the World. The largest, **The Great Pyramid of Khufu**, is a solid mass of limestone blocks covering 13 acres. It is estimated to contain 2.3 million blocks of stone, the stones themselves averaging 2½ tons and some weighing 30 tons. Its construction reputedly took 100,000 laborers 20 years.

The Hanging Gardens of Babylon: These gardens were laid out on a brick terrace about 400 ft square and 75 ft above the ground. To irrigate the trees, shrubs, and flowers, screws were turned to lift water from the Euphrates R. The gardens were probably built by King Nebuchadnezzar II about 600 BC. **The Walls of Babylon**, long, thick, and made of colorfully glazed brick, were considered by some among the Seven Wonders.

The Statue of Zeus (Jupiter) at Olympia: This statue of the king of the gods showed him seated on a throne. His flesh was made of ivory, his robe and ornaments of gold. Reputedly 40 ft high, the statue was made by Phidias and was placed in the great temple of Zeus in the sacred grove of Olympia about 457 BC.

The Colossus of Rhodes: A bronze statue of the sun god Helios, the Colossus was worked on for 12 years in the third century BC by the sculptor Chares. It was probably 120 ft high. A symbol of the city of Rhodes at its height, the statue stood on a promontory overlooking the harbor.

The Temple of Artemis (Diana) at Ephesus: This largest and most complex temple of ancient times was built about 550 BC and was made of marble except for its tile-covered wooden roof. It was begun in honor of a non-Hellenic goddess who later became identified with the Greek goddess of the same name. Ephesus was one of the greatest of the Ionian cities.

The Mausoleum at Halicarnassus: The source of our word *mausoleum*, this marble tomb was built in what is now SE Turkey by Artemisia for her husband Mausolus, king of Caria in Asia Minor, who died in 353 BC. About 135 ft high, the tomb was adorned with the works of 4 sculptors.

The Pharos (Lighthouse) of Alexandria: This structure was designed about 270 BC, during the reign of King Ptolemy II, by the Greek architect Sostratos. Estimates of its height range from 200 to 600 ft.

The Seven Wonders of the Middle Ages

These sites and structures were considered significant by the people of the Middle Ages (from c 5th cent. to c 15th cent.).

The Colosseum of Rome: Erected by the Roman emperor Vespasian, this amphitheater was dedicated by his son and successor Titus in AD 80. It could seat about 50,000 persons and was used for Roman spectacles and contests. It is now in ruins.

The Catacombs of Alexandria, Egypt: This network of subterranean chambers and galleries was used for burial purposes by peoples of the ancient world and as refuge for early Christians.

The Great Wall of China: Begun c 221 BC and completed c 204 BC, this fortification finally reached a length of about 1500 mi. It is built of earth and stone and is faced with brick in the E parts. On average, it is about 20 ft thick at the base and tapers to some 12 ft at the top. The height averages 25 ft, exclusive of the crenellated parapets. Several hundred miles of the Great Wall remain intact in the E reaches.

Stonehenge: This prehistoric ritual monument is situated on Salisbury Plain, N of Salisbury, England, and dates from the late Stone and early Bronze ages (c. 3000-1000 BC). The monument itself consists of 4 concentric ranges of stones. Grouped around the main structure are a number of barrows, some of which contain chips of a blue stone similar to that found in the concentric ranges. In 1964, an American astronomer Gerald S. Hawkins concluded that Stonehenge functioned as a means of predicting the positions of the sun and moon relative to the earth, and thereby the seasons, and perhaps also as a simple daily calendar.

The Leaning Tower of Pisa: Construction on this bell tower began in 1174 but was suspended when the builders became aware that the shallow foundation would be inadequate in the soft soil. The structure was nevertheless complete by the second half of the 14th cent. The Leaning Tower is cylindrical in shape, with 8 arcaded stories, and today slants more than 14 ft from the perpendicular.

The Porcelain Tower of Nanking: This tower in China was built to a height of 260 ft during the 15th cent. and was destroyed in 1853.

The Mosque of Hagia Sophia: Built in the 6th cent., this imposing structure was originally a church (Holy Wisdom). It was converted to a mosque in the 15th cent. and is now a museum.

The Seven Natural Wonders of the World

This list names areas of geological significance and was compiled by world travelers during recent centuries.

Mt. Everest: The highest peak in the world, Mt. Everest is in S central Asia, in the Himalaya range, on the frontier of Nepal and Tibet. Controversy surrounds its actual elevation. A 1954 Indian government survey placed it at 29,028 ft above sea level; however, more recent surveys cast some doubt on this figure. The summit was first scaled in 1953.

Victoria Falls: This 400 ft waterfall is on the Zambezi R in S central Africa on the border between Zimbabwe and Zambia. The river here is about 1 mi wide. A railroad bridge, completed in 1905, spans the gorge below the falls.

The Grand Canyon: This exceptionally deep (more than 1 mi) and extremely beautiful steep-walled chasm in NW Arizona is about 217 mi long and 4 to 18 mi wide. Excavated by the Colorado R, it is of relatively recent origin; apparently erosion began a little more than a million years ago. The canyon contains towering buttes, mesas, and valleys within its main gorge.

The Great Barrier Reef: This chain of coral reefs is in the Coral Sea, off the E coast of Queensland, Australia. It is the largest known deposit of coral and extends in a NW direction more than 1200 mi. The reef serves as a barrier to disturbances in the Coral Sea, thus affording a sheltered passage for ships.

The Northern Lights: Also known as aurora borealis, the northen lights consists of rapidly shifting patches and dancing columns of light of various hues. The aurora assumes an endless variety of forms, including the arch, the band, filaments and streamers at right angles to the arch or band, the corona, clouds, the glow, and curtains, fans, flames, or streamers of various shapes.

Paricutin: This volcano is one of the world's youngest. It was discovered in 1943 west of Mexico City.

The Harbor at Rio de Janeiro, Brazil (as seen from the sea): One of the world's most beautiful natural harbors, the harbor at Rio is surrounded by low mountain ranges whose spurs extend almost to the waterside, and thus divide the city.

The sciences thrived, especially at Alexandria, where the Ptolemies financed a great library and museum. Fields of study included mathematics (**Euclid's** geometry, c 300 BC; Menelaus non-Euclidean geometry, c 100 AD); astronomy (heliocentric theory of Aristarchus, 310-230 BC; Julian calendar, 45 BC; Ptolemy's *Almagest*, c 150 AD); geography (world map of Eratosthenes, 276-194 BC); hydraulics (**Archimedes,** 287-212 BC); medicine (Galen, 130-200 AD); and chemistry. Inventors refined uses for siphons, valves, gears, springs, screws, levers, cams, and pulleys.

A restored Persian empire under the **Parthians** (N Iranian tribesmen) controlled the eastern Hellenistic world from 250 BC to 229 AD. The Parthians and the succeeding Sassanian dynasty (c 224-651 AD) fought with Rome periodically. The **Sassanians** revived Zoroastrianism as a state religion and patronized a nationalistic artistic and scholarly renaissance.

Rome. The city of Rome was founded, according to legend, by Romulus in 753 BC. Through military expansion and colonization, and by granting citizenship to conquered tribes, the city annexed all of Italy south of the Po in the 100-year period before 268 BC. The Latin and other Italic tribes were annexed first, followed by the Etruscans (founders of a great civilization, N of Rome) and the Greek colonies in the S. With a large standing army and reserve forces of several hundred thousand, Rome was able to defeat Carthage in the 3 **Punic Wars** (264-241, 218-201, 149-146 BC), despite the invasion of Italy (218 BC) by Hannibal, thus gaining Sicily and territory in Spain and North Africa.

New provinces were added in the E, as Rome exploited local disputes to conquer Greece and Asia Minor in the 2d century BC, and Egypt in the 1st (after the defeat and suicide of **Antony and Cleopatra**, 30 BC). All the Mediterranean civilized world up to the disputed Parthian border was now Roman and remained so for 500 years. Less civilized regions were added to the Empire: Gaul (conquered by Julius Caesar, 58-51 BC), Britain (43 AD), and Dacia NE of the Danube (107 AD).

The original aristocratic republican government, with democratic features added in the 5th and 4th centuries BC, deteriorated under the pressures of empire and class conflict (**Gracchus** brothers, social reformers, murdered in 133 BC and 121 BC; slave revolts in 135 BC and 73 BC). After a series of civil wars (Marius vs. Sulla 88-82 BC, Caesar vs. Pompey 49-45 BC, triumvirate vs. Caesar's assassins 44-43 BC, Antony vs. Octavian 32-30 BC), the empire came under the rule of a deified monarch (first emperor, **Augustus**, 27 BC-14 AD). Provincials (nearly all granted citizenship by Caracalla, 212 AD) came to dominate the army and civil service. Traditional Roman law, systematized and interpreted by independent jurists, and local self-rule in provincial cities were supplanted by a vast tax-collecting bureaucracy in the 3d and 4th centuries. The legal rights of women, children, and slaves were strengthened.

Roman innovations in **civil engineering** included water mills, windmills, and rotary mills and the use of cement that hardened under water. Monumental architecture (baths, theaters, temples) relied on the arch and the dome. The network of roads (some still standing) stretched 53,000 mi, passing through mountain tunnels as long as 3.5 mi. Aqueducts brought water to cities; underground sewers removed waste.

Unlike architecture, Roman art and literature were derivative of Greek models. Innovations were made in sculpture (naturalistic busts and equestrian statues), decorative wall painting (as at Pompeii), satire (Juvenal, 60-127 AD), history (Tacitus, 56-120 AD), prose romance (Petronius, d 66 AD). Gladiatorial contests dominated mass public amusements, which were supported by the state.

India. The **Gupta** monarchs reunited N India c 320 AD. Their peaceful and prosperous reign saw a revival of Hindu religious thought and Brahman power. The old Vedic traditions were combined with devotion to a plethora of indigenous deities (who were seen as manifestations of Vedic gods). **Caste lines** were reinforced, and Buddhism gradually disappeared. The art (often erotic), architecture, and literature of the period, patronized by the Gupta court, are considered among India's finest achievements (Kalidasa, poet and dramatist, fl. c 400 AD). Mathematical innovations included the use of the zero and decimal numbers. Invasions by White Huns from the NW destroyed the empire c 550.

Rich cultures also developed in S India in this era. Emotional Tamil religious poetry aided the Hindu revival. The Pallava kingdom controlled much of S India c 350-880 and helped spread Indian civilization to SE Asia.

China. The Ch'in ruler Shih Huang Ti (ruled 221-210 BC), known as the First Emperor, centralized political authority in China, standardized the written language, laws, weights, measures, and coinage, and conducted a census, but tried to destroy most philosophical texts. The **Han dynasty** (202 BC-220 AD) instituted the Mandarin bureaucracy, which lasted for 2,000 years. Local officials were selected by examination in the Confucian classics and trained at the imperial university and at provincial schools. The invention of **paper** facilitated this bureaucratic system. Agriculture was promoted, but the peasants bore most of the tax burden. Irrigation was improved; water clocks and sundials were used; astronomy and mathematics thrived; and landscape painting was perfected.

With the expansion S and W (to nearly the present borders of today's China), trade was opened with India, SE Asia, and the Middle East, over sea and caravan routes. Indian missionaries brought Mahayana Buddhism to China by the 1st century AD and spawned a variety of sects. Taoism was revived and merged with popular superstitions. Taoist and Buddhist monasteries and convents multiplied in the turbulent centuries after the collapse of the Han dynasty.

Monotheism Emerges: 1-750 AD

Christianity. In the Roman Empire polytheism was practiced, and religions indigenous to particular Middle Eastern nations became international in the first 3 centuries of the Roman Empire. Roman citizens worshiped **Isis** of Egypt, **Mithras** of Persia, **Demeter** of Greece, and the great mother **Cybele** of Phrygia. Their cults centered on mysteries (secret ceremonies) and the promise of an afterlife, symbolized by the death and rebirth of the god. The Jews living in the empire preserved their monotheistic religion—Judaism, the world's oldest (c 1200 BC) continuous religion. Its teachings are contained in the Bible (the Old Testament). First-century Judaism embraced several sects, including the **Sadducees**, mostly drawn from the Temple priesthood, who were culturally Hellenized; the **Pharisees**, who upheld the full range of traditional customs and practices as of equal weight to literal scriptural law and elaborated synagogue worship; and the **Essenes**, an ascetic, millennarian sect. Messianic fervor led to repeated,

400 BC
Chinese Age of Warring States
Alexander becomes king
Aristotle b.
Mahabharata begun
Euclid's geometry
Great Wall of China begun
200 BC
Hannibal invades Italy
1st Roman slave revolt
Punic Wars end
Hellenistic Era
Julius Caesar b.
Antony, Cleopatra defeated
Julian calendar
1 AD
Jesus d.
Mayan civilization begins in Guatemala
Roman Empire
Nero's persecution
200 AD

200 AD
Constantinople founded
African Axum kingdom expands
1st Christian monastery
Augustine b.
350
Japan united
Ghana begins rule
Huns in Europe
W. Roman Empire ends
Gupta Empire in India
Patrick converts Ireland
Justinian code
Benedict founds monastery
Clovis unites Franks
500
Sui dynasty begins
Mohammed's life
Tang dynasty
Talmud completed
650 AD

unsuccessful rebellions against Rome (66-70, 135). As a result, the Temple in Jerusalem was destroyed and the population decimated; this event marked the beginning of the Diaspora (living in exile).

To avoid the dissolution of the faith, a program of codification of law was begun at the academy of Yavneh. The work continued for some 500 years in Palestine and in Babylonia, ending in the final redaction (c 600) of the **Talmud**, a huge collection of legal and moral debates, rulings, liturgy, biblical exegesis, and legendary materials.

Christianity, which emerged as a distinct sect in the second half of the 1st cent. AD, is based on the teachings of **Jesus**, whom believers considered the Savior (Messiah or Christ), and the son of God. The missionary activities of the Apostles and such early leaders as **Paul of Tarsus** spread the faith. Intermittent persecution, as in Rome under Nero in 64 AD, on grounds of suspected disloyalty, failed to disrupt the Christian communities. Each congregation, generally urban and of plebeian character, was tightly organized under a leader (bishop), elders (presbyters or priests), and assistants (deacons). The Gospels (the New Testament), containing the teachings of Jesus, and the Acts of the Apostles were written down in the late 1st and early 2d centuries and circulated along with letters of Paul. An authoritative canon of these writings was not fixed until the 4th century.

A school for priests was established at Alexandria in the 2d century. Its teachers (**Origen** c 182-251) helped define Christian doctrine and promote the faith in Greek-style philosophical works. Pagan Neoplatonism was given Christian coloration in the works of Church Fathers such as Augustine (354-430). Christian hermits, often drawn from the lower classes, began to associate in monasteries, first in Egypt (St. Pachomius c 290-345), then in other E lands, then in the W (**St. Benedict's rule**, 529). Popular devotion to saints, especially Mary, mother of Jesus, spread.

Under **Constantine** (ruled 306-37), Christianity became in effect the established religion of the Empire. Pagan temples were expropriated, state funds were used to build huge churches and support the hierarchy, and laws were adjusted in accordance with Christian notions. Pagan worship was banned by the end of the 4th century, and severe restrictions were placed on Judaism.

The newly established church was rocked by doctrinal disputes, often exacerbated by regional rivalries both within and outside the Empire. Chief heresies (as defined by church councils backed by imperial authority) were **Arianism**, which denied the divinity of Jesus; **Donatism**, which rejected the convergence of church and state and denied the validity of sacraments performed by sinful clergy; and the **Monophysite** position denying the dual nature of Christ.

Islam. The earliest Arab civilization emerged by the end of the 2d millennium BC in the watered highlands of Yemen. Seaborne and caravan trade in frankincense and myrrh connected the area with the Nile and the Fertile Crescent. The Minaean, Sabean (Sheba), and Himyarite states successively held sway. By Mohammed's time (7th cent. AD), the region was a province of Sassanian Persia. In the N, the **Nabataean kingdom** at Petra and the kingdom of Palmyra were first Aramaicized, then Romanized, and finally absorbed, as neighboring Judea had been, into the Roman Empire. Nomads shared the central region with a few trading towns and oases. Wars between tribes and raids on settled communities were common and were celebrated in a poetic tradition that by the 6th century helped establish a classic literary Arabic.

In 611 **Mohammed**, a 40-year-old Arab of Mecca, announced a revelation from the one true God, calling on him to repudiate pagan idolatry. Drawing on elements of Judaism and Christianity, and eventually incorporating some Arab pagan traditions (such as reverence for the black stone at the Kaaba shrine in Mecca), Mohammed's teachings, recorded in the **Koran**, forged a new religion, Islam (submission to Allah). Opposed by the leaders of Mecca, Mohammed made a *hejira* (migration) to Medina to the N in 622, the beginning of the Muslim lunar calendar. He and his followers defeated the Meccans in 624 in the first *jihad* (holy war), and by his death (632) nearly all the Arabian peninsula accepted his religious and secular leadership.

Under the first two **caliphs** (successors), Abu Bakr (632-34) and Omar (634-44), Muslim rule over Arabia was confirmed. Raiding parties into Byzantine and Persian border areas developed into campaigns of conquest against the 2 empires, which had been weakened by wars and by disaffection among subject peoples (including Coptic and Syriac Christians opposed to the Byzantine Orthodox church). Syria, Palestine, Egypt, Iraq, and Persia all fell to the Arab armies. The Arabs at first remained a distinct minority, using non-Muslims in the new administrative system and tolerating Christians, Jews, and Zoroastrians as self-governing "Peoples of the Book," whose taxes supported the empire.

Disputes over the succession, and puritan reaction to the wealth and refinement that empire brought to the ruling strata, led to the growth of schismatic movements. The followers of Mohammed's son-in-law Ali (assassinated 661) and his descendants became the founders of the more mystical **Shi'ite** sect, still the largest non-orthodox Muslim sect. The Karijites, puritanical, militant, and egalitarian, persist as a minor sect to the present.

Under the **Omayyad** caliphs (661-750), the boundaries of Islam were extended across N Africa and into Spain (711). Arab armies in the W were stopped at Tours (France) in 732 by the Frankish King **Charles Martel**. Asia Minor, the Indus Valley, and Transoxiana were conquered in the E. The vast majority of the subject population gradually converted to Islam, encouraged by tax and career privileges. The Arab language supplanted the local tongues in the central and W areas, but Arab soldiers and rulers in the E eventually became assimilated to the indigenous languages.

New Peoples Enter World History: 400-900

Barbarian invasions. Germanic tribes infiltrated S and E from their Baltic homeland during the 1st millennium BC, reaching S Germany by 100 BC and the Black Sea by 214 AD. Organized into large federated tribes under elected kings, most resisted Roman domination and raided the empire in time of civil war (Goths took Dacia in 214 and raided Thrace in 251-69). Germanic troops and commanders came to dominate the Roman armies by the end of the 4th century. **Huns**, invaders from Asia, entered Europe in 372, driving more Germans into the W empire. Emperor Valens allowed Visigoths to cross the Danube in 376. Huns under Attila (d 453) raided Gaul, Italy, and the Balkans. The W empire, weakened by overtaxation and social stagnation, was overrun in the 5th cent. Gaul was effectively lost in 406-7, Spain in 409, Britain in 410, and Africa in 429-39. Rome was sacked in 410 by Visigoths under

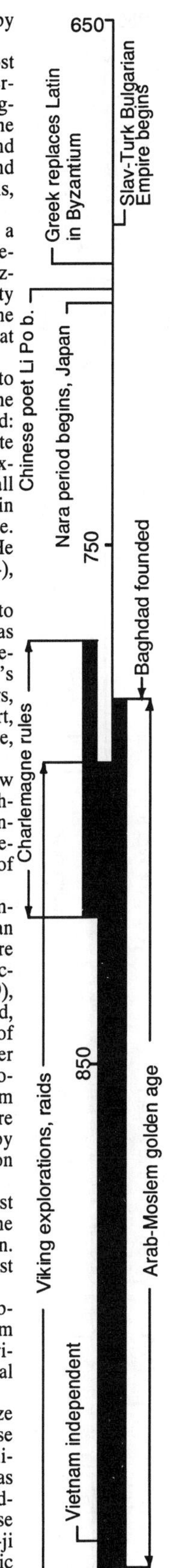

Alaric and in 455 by Vandals. The last western emperor, Romulus Augustulus, was deposed in 476 by the Germanic chief Odovacar.

Celts. Celtic cultures, which in pre-Roman times covered most of W Europe, were confined almost entirely to the British Isles after the Germanic invasions. **St. Patrick** completed (c 457-92) the conversion of Ireland. A strong monastic tradition took hold. Irish monastic missionaries in Scotland, England, and the continent (Columba c 521-97; Columban c 543-615) helped restore Christianity after the Germanic invasions. The monasteries became renowned centers of classic and Christian learning and presided over the recording of a Christianized Celtic mythology, elaborated by secular writers and bards. An intricate decorative art style developed, especially in book illumination (Lindisfarne Gospels, c 700; Book of Kells, 8th cent.).

Successor states. The Visigothic kingdom in Spain (from 419) and much of France (to 507) saw a continuation of much Roman administration, language, and law (Breviary of Alaric, 506) until its destruction by the Muslims in 711. The Vandal kingdom in Africa, from 429, was conquered by the Byzantines in 533. Italy was ruled in succession by an Ostrogothic kingdom under Byzantine suzerainty (489-554), direct Byzantine government, and the German Lombards (568-774). The latter divided the peninsula with the Byzantines and the papacy under the dynamic reformer Pope Gregory the Great (590-604) and his successors.

King Clovis (ruled 481-511) united the Franks on both sides of the Rhine and, after his conversion to Christianity, defeated the Arian heretics, the Burgundians (after 500), and the Visigoths (507) with the support of the native clergy and the papacy. Under the **Merovingian** kings, a feudal system emerged: Power was fragmented among hierarchies of military landowners. Social stratification, which in late Roman times had acquired legal, hereditary sanction, was reinforced. The Carolingians (747-987) expanded the kingdom and restored central power. **Charlemagne** (ruled 768-814) conquered nearly all the Germanic lands, including Lombard Italy, and was crowned Emperor by Pope Leo III in Rome in 800. A centuries-long decline in commerce and the arts was reversed under Charlemagne's patronage. He welcomed Jews to his kingdom, which became a center of Jewish learning (Rashi, 1040-1105). He sponsored the Carolingian Renaissance of learning under the Anglo-Latin scholar Alcuin (c 732-804), who reformed church liturgy.

Byzantine Empire. Under Diocletian (ruled 284-305) the empire had been divided into 2 parts to facilitate administration and defense. Constantine founded (330) **Constantinople** (at old Byzantium) as a fully Christian city. Commerce and taxation financed a sumptuous, orientalized court, a class of hereditary bureaucratic families, and magnificent urban construction (Hagia Sophia, 532-37). The city's fortifications and naval innovations (Greek fire) repelled assaults by Goths, Huns, Slavs, Bulgars, Avars, Arabs, and Scandinavians. Greek replaced Latin as the official language by c 700. Byzantine art, a solemn, sacral, and stylized variation of late classical styles (mosaics at the Church of San Vitale, Ravenna, Italy 526-48), was a starting point for medieval art in E and W Europe.

Justinian (ruled 527-65) reconquered parts of Spain, N Africa, and Italy, codified Roman law (Codex Justinianus [529] was medieval Europe's chief legal text), closed the Platonic Academy at Athens, and ordered all pagans to convert. Lombards in Italy and Arabs in Africa retook most of his conquests. The Isaurian dynasty from Anatolia (from 717) and the Macedonian dynasty (867-1054) restored military and commercial power. The Iconoclast controversy (726-843) over the permissibility of images helped alienate the Eastern Church from the papacy.

Arab Empire. Baghdad (est 762) became the seat of the **Abbasid** Caliphate (est 750), while Ummayads continued to rule in Spain. A brilliant cosmopolitan civilization emerged, inaugurating an Arab-Muslim golden age. Arab lyric poetry revived; Greek, Syriac, Persian, and Sanskrit books were translated into Arabic, often by Syriac Christians and Jews, whose theology and Talmudic law, respectively, influenced Islam. The arts and music flourished at the court of **Harun al-Rashid** (786-809), celebrated in *The Arabian Nights*. The sciences, medicine, and mathematics were pursued at Baghdad, Cordova, and Cairo (est 969). Science and Aristotelian philosophy culminated in the systems of Avicenna (980-1037), Averroes (1126-98), and Maimonides (1135-1204), a Jew; all influenced later Christian scholarship and theology. The Islamic ban on images encouraged a sinuous, geometric decorative tradition, applied to architecture and illumination. A gradual loss of Arab control in Persia (from 874) led to the capture (945) of Baghdad by Persians. By the next century, Spain and N Africa were ruled by Berbers, while Turks prevailed in Asia Minor and the Levant. The loss of political power by the caliphs allowed for the growth of nonorthodox trends, especially the mystical **Sufi** tradition (theologian Ghazali, 1058-1111).

Africa. Immigrants from Saba in S Arabia helped set up the **Axum** kingdom in Ethiopia in the 1st century (their language, Ge'ez, is preserved by the Ethiopian Church). In the 3d century, when the kingdom became Christianized, it defeated Kushite Meroe and expanded its influence into Yemen. Axum was the center of a vast ivory trade and controlled the Red Sea coast until c 1100. Arab conquest in Egypt cut Axum's political and economic ties with Byzantium.

The Iron Age entered W Africa by the end of the 1st millennium BC. **Ghana**, the first known sub-Saharan state, ruled in the upper Senegal-Niger region c 400-1240, controlling the trade of gold from mines in the S to trans-Sahara caravan routes to the N. The **Bantu** peoples, probably of W African origin, began to spread E and S perhaps 2,000 years ago, displacing the Pygmies and Bushmen of central and S Africa during a 1,500-year period.

Japan. The advanced Neolithic Yayoi period, when irrigation, rice farming, and iron and bronze casting techniques were introduced from China or Korea, persisted to c 400 AD. The myriad Japanese states were then united by the **Yamato** clan, under an emperor who acted as the chief priest of the animistic Shinto cult. Japanese political and military intervention by the 6th century in Korea, which was then under strong Chinese influence, quickened a Chinese cultural invasion of Japan, bringing Buddhism, the Chinese language (which long remained a literary and governmental medium), Chinese ideographs, and Buddhist styles in painting, sculpture, literature, and architecture (7th century, Horyu-ji temple at Nara). The Taika Reforms (646) tried to centralize Japan according to Chinese bureaucratic and Buddhist philosophical values, but failed to curb traditional Japanese decentralization. A nativist reaction against the Buddhist **Nara period** (710-94) ushered in the **Heian period** (794-1185) centered

950
Cairo founded
Otto I emperor
Leif Eriksson reaches Amer.
Poland begins eastern conquest
Kiev Christian under Vladimir
Tale of Genji in Japan
Choir of St. Denis
E, W Church split
Jewish scholar Rashi b.
1050
Christians capture Toledo
Seljuk Turks take Baghdad
Sufi mystic Ghazali b.
Angkor Wat temple built
Univ. Bologna founded
Maimonides b.
Crusades
1150
German Frederick II b.
Zen comes to Japan
Ghengis Khan b.
Sultanate of Delhi founded
Magna Carta
Aquinas b.
Dominicans, Franciscans founded
Mali replaces Ghana
1250

at the new capital, Kyoto. Japanese elegance and simplicity modified Chinese styles in architecture, scroll painting, and literature; the writing system was also simplified. The courtly novel *Tale of Genji* (1010-20) testifies to the enhanced role of women.

Southeast Asia. The historic peoples of Southeast Asia began arriving some 2,500 years ago from China and Tibet, displacing scattered aborigines. Their agriculture relied on rice and tubers (yams), which they may have introduced to Africa. Indian cultural influences were strongest; literacy and Hindu and Buddhist ideas followed the southern India-China trade route. From the southern tip of Indochina, the kingdom of **Funan** (1st-7th century) traded as far W as Persia. It was absorbed by Chenla, itself conquered by the **Khmer Empire** (600-1300). The Khmers, under Hindu god-kings (Suryavarman II, 1113-c 1150) built the monumental Angkor Wat temple center for the royal phallic cult. The **Nam-Viet** kingdom in Annam, dominated by China and Chinese culture for 1,000 years, emerged in the 10th century, growing at the expense of the Khmers, who also lost ground in the NW to the new, highly organized **Thai** kingdom. On Sumatra, the **Srivijaya** Empire at Palembang controlled vital sea lanes (7th to 10th century). A Buddhist dynasty, the Sailendras, ruled central **Java** (8th-9th century), building at Borobudur one of the largest stupas in the world.

China. The short-lived Sui dynasty (581-618) ushered in a period of commercial, artistic, and scientific achievement in China, continuing under the **Tang** dynasty (618-906). Such inventions as the magnetic compass, gunpowder, the abacus, and printing were introduced or perfected. Medical innovations included cataract surgery. The state, from the cosmopolitan capital, Chang-an, supervised foreign trade, which exchanged Chinese silks, porcelains, and artworks for spices, ivory, etc. over Central Asian caravan routes and sea routes reaching Africa. A golden age of poetry bequeathed tens of thousands of works to later generations (Tu Fu, 712-70; Li Po, 701-62). Landscape painting flourished. Commercial and industrial expansion continued under the **Northern Sung** dynasty (960-1126), facilitated by paper money and credit notes. But commerce never achieved respectability; government monopolies expropriated successful merchants. The population, long stable at 50 million, doubled in 200 years with the introduction of early-ripening rice and the double harvest. In art, native Chinese styles were revived.

Americas. From 300 to 600 a Native American empire stretched from the Valley of Mexico to Guatemala, centering on the huge city **Teotihuacán** (founded 100 BC). To the S, in Guatemala, a high **Mayan** civilization developed (150-900) around hundreds of rural ceremonial centers. The Mayans improved on Olmec writing and the calendar and pursued astronomy and mathematics (using the idea of zero). In South America, a widespread pre-Inca culture grew from **Tiahuanacu,** Bolivia, near Lake Titicaca (Gateway of the Sun, c 700).

Christian Europe Regroups and Expands: 900-1300

Scandinavians. Pagan Danish and Norse (Viking) adventurers, traders, and pirates raided the coasts of the British Isles (Dublin, founded c 831), France, and even the Mediterranean for more than 200 years beginning in the late 8th century. Inland settlement in the W was limited to Great Britain (King Canute, 994-1035) and Normandy, settled (911) under Rollo, as a fief of France. Other Vikings reached Iceland (874), Greenland (c 986), and North America (Leif Eriksson, c 1000). Norse traders (**Varangians**) developed Russian river commerce from the 8th to the 11th century and helped set up a state at Kiev in the late 9th century. Conversion to Christianity occurred during the 10th century, reaching Sweden 100 years later. Eleventh-century Norman bands conquered S Italy and Sicily. Duke **William of Normandy** conquered (1066) England, bringing continental feudalism and the French language, essential elements in later English civilization.

Central and East Europe. Slavs began to expand from about 150 AD in all directions in Europe, and by the 7th cent. they reached as far S as the Adriatic and Aegean seas. In the Balkan Peninsula they dislocated Romanized local populations or assimilated newcomers (Bulgarians, a Turkic people). The first Slavic states were Moravia (628) in Central Europe and the Bulgarian state (680) in the Balkans. Missions of St. Methodius and Cyril (whose Greek-based cyrillic alphabet is still used by some S and E Slavs) converted (863) Moravia. The Eastern Slavs, part-civilized under the overlordship of the Turkish-Jewish **Khazar** trading empire (7th-10th century), gravitated toward Constantinople by the 9th century. The **Kievan state** adopted (989) Eastern Christianity under Prince Vladimir. King Boleslav I (992-1025) began **Poland's** long history of eastern conquest. The Magyars (**Hungarians**), in present-day Hungary since 896, accepted (1001) Latin Christianity.

Germany. The German kingdom that emerged after the breakup of Charlemagne's W Empire remained a confederation of largely autonomous states. Otto I, a Saxon who was king from 936, established the **Holy Roman Empire**—a union of Germany and N Italy—in alliance with Pope John XII, who crowned (962) him emperor; he defeated (955) the Magyars. Imperial power was greatest under the **Hohenstaufens** (1138-1254), despite the growing opposition of the papacy, which ruled central Italy, and the Lombard League cities. Frederick II (1194-1250) improved administration and patronized the arts; after his death, German influence was removed from Italy.

Christian Spain. From its N mountain redoubts, Christian rule slowly migrated S through the 11th century, when Muslim unity collapsed. After the capture (1085) of **Toledo**, the kingdoms of Portugal, Castile, and Aragon undertook repeated crusades of reconquest, finally completed in 1492. Elements of Islamic civilization persisted in recaptured areas, influencing all Western Europe.

Crusades. Pope Urban II called (1095) for a crusade to restore Asia Minor to Byzantium and to regain the Holy Land from the Turks. Some 10 crusades (to 1291) succeeded only in founding 4 temporary Frankish states in the Levant. The 4th crusade sacked (1204) Constantinople. In Rhineland (1096), England (1290), and France (1306), Jews were massacred or expelled, and wars were launched against Christian heretics (**Albigensian** crusade in France, 1229). Trade in eastern luxuries expanded, led by the Venetian naval empire.

Economy. The agricultural base of European life benefited from improvements in **plow design** (c 1000) and by draining of lowlands and clearing of forests, leading to a rural population increase. Towns grew in N Italy, Flanders, and N Germany (Hanseatic League). Improvements in **loom design** permitted factory textile production. **Guilds** dominated urban trades from the 12th century. Banking (centered in Italy, 12th-15th century) facilitated long-distance trade.

The Church. The split between the Eastern and Western churches was formalized in 1054. Western and Central Europe was divided into 500 bishoprics under one united hierarchy, but conflicts between secular and church authorities were frequent (German **Investiture Controversy**, 1075-1122). Clerical power was first strengthened through the international monastic reform begun at Cluny in 910. Popular religious enthusiasm often expressed itself in heretical movements (Waldensians from 1173), but was channelled by the **Dominican** (1215) and **Franciscan** (1223) friars into the religious mainstream.

Arts. Romanesque architecture (11th-12th century) expanded on late Roman models, using the rounded arch and massed stone to support enlarged basilicas. Painting and sculpture followed Byzantine models. The literature of **chivalry** was exemplified by the epic (Chanson de Roland, c 1100) and by courtly love poems of the troubadours of Provence and minnesingers of Germany. **Gothic** architecture emerged in France (choir of St. Denis, c 1040) and spread as French cultural influence predominated in Europe. Rib vaulting and pointed arches were used to combine soaring heights with delicacy, and they freed walls for display of stained glass. Exteriors were covered with painted relief sculpture and elaborate architectural detail.

Learning. Law, medicine, and philosophy were advanced at independent **universities** (Bologna, late 11th century), originally corporations of students and masters. Twelfth-century translations of Greek classics, especially Aristotle, encouraged an analytic approach. Scholastic philosophy, from Anselm (1033-1109) to Aquinas (1225-74) attempted to reconcile reason and revelation.

Apogee of Central Asian Power; Islam Grows: 1250-1500

Turks. Turkic peoples, of Central Asian ancestry, were a military threat to the Byzantine and Persian Empires from the 6th century. After several waves of invasions, during which most of the Turks adopted Islam, the **Seljuk Turks** took (1055) Baghdad. They ruled Persia, Iraq and, after 1071, Asia Minor, where massive numbers of Turks settled. The empire was divided in the 12th century into smaller states ruled by Seljuks, Kurds (**Saladin,** c 1137-93), and Mamelukes (a military caste of former Turk, Kurd, and Circassian slaves), which governed Egypt and the Middle East until the Ottoman era (c 1290-1922).

Osman I (ruled c 1290-1326) and succeeding sultans united Anatolian Turkish warriors in a militaristic state that waged holy war against Byzantium and Balkan Christians. Most of the Balkans had been subdued, and Anatolia united, when Constantinople fell (1453). By the mid-16th century, Hungary, the Middle East, and North Africa had been conquered. The Turkish advance was stopped at Vienna (1529) and at the naval battle of Lepanto (1571) by Spain, Venice, and the papacy.

The Ottoman state was governed in accordance with orthodox Muslim law. Greek, Armenian, and Jewish communities were segregated and were ruled by religious leaders responsible for taxation; they dominated trade. State offices and most army ranks were filled by slaves through a system of child conscription among Christians.

India. Mahmud of Ghazni (971-1030) led repeated Turkish raids into N India. Turkish power was consolidated in 1206 with the start of the **Sultanate at Delhi**. Centralization of state power under the early Delhi sultans went far beyond traditional Indian practice. Muslim rule of most of the subcontinent lasted until the British conquest some 600 years later.

Mongols. Genghis Khan (c 1167-1227) first united the feuding Mongol tribes, and built their armies into an effective offensive force around a core of highly mobile cavalry. He and his immediate successors created the largest land empire in history; by 1279 it stretched from the E coast of Asia to the Danube, from the Siberian steppes to the Arabian Sea. East-West trade and contacts were facilitated (Marco Polo, c 1254-1324). The W Mongols were Islamized by 1295; successor states soon lost their Mongol character by assimilation. They were briefly reunited under the Turk Tamerlane (1336-1405).

Kublai Khan ruled China from his new capital Beijing (est 1264). Naval campaigns against Japan (1274, 1281) and Java (1293) were defeated, the latter by the Hindu-Buddhist maritime kingdom of Majapahit. The **Yuan** dynasty used Mongols and other foreigners (including Europeans) in official posts and tolerated the return of Nestorian Christianity (suppressed 841-45) and the spread of Islam in the S and W. A native reaction expelled the Mongols in 1367-68.

Russia. The Kievan state in Russia, weakened by the decline of Byzantium and the rise of the Catholic Polish-Lithuanian state, was overrun (1238-40) by the Mongols. Only the N trading republic of Novgorod remained independent. The grand dukes of Moscow emerged as leaders of a coalition of princes that eventually (by 1481) defeated the Mongols. With the fall of Constantinople, the **Tsars** (Caesars) at Moscow (from Ivan III, r 1462-1505) set up an independent Russian Orthodox Church. Commerce failed to revive. The isolated Russian state remained agrarian, with the peasant class falling into serfdom.

Persia. A revival of Persian literature, using the Arab alphabet and literary forms, began in the 10th cent. (epic of Firdausi, 935-1020). An art revival, influenced by Chinese styles introduced after the Mongols came to power in Iran, began in the 13th. Persian cultural and political forms, and often the Persian language, were used for centuries by Turkish and Mongol elites from the Balkans to India. Persian mystics from Rumi (1207-73) to Jami (1414-92) promoted **Sufism** in their poetry.

Africa. Two militant Islamic Berber dynasties emerged from the Sahara to carve out empires from the Sahel to central Spain—the **Almoravids** (c 1050-1140) and the fanatical **Almohads** (c 1125-1269). The Ghanaian empire was replaced in the upper Niger by Mali (c 1230-c 1340), whose Muslim rulers imported Egyptians to help make **Timbuktu** a center of commerce (in gold, leather, and slaves) and learning. The Songhay empire (to 1590) replaced Mali. To the S, forest kingdoms produced refined artworks (Ife terra cotta, **Benin** bronzes). Other Muslim states in Nigeria (Hausas) and Chad originated in the 11th cent. and continued in some form until the 19th-cent. European conquest. Less-developed Bantu kingdoms existed across central Africa.

Some 40 Muslim Arab-Persian trading colonies and city-states were established all along the E African coast from the 10th cent. (Kilwa, Mogadishu). The interchange with Bantu peoples produced the **Swahili** language and culture. Gold, palm oil, and slaves were brought from the interior, stimulating the growth of the Monamatapa kingdom of the Zambezi (15th cent.). The Christian Ethiopian empire (from 13th cent.) continued the traditions of Axum.

1250

Giotto b. Dante b.
Philip IV rules France
Ciompi revolt, Florence
Hundred Years War
Constantinople falls
Columbus in Amer.

Marco Polo's journeys
Petrarch b.
1375 Mongols expelled from China
Persian poet Jami b.
Michelangelo b.
Inca empire begins

Beijing founded
Tamerlane b.
Chaucer b.
Medicis begin rule
Masaccio b.
Portugese explorations begin
Ivan III rules Russia

Hapsburgs in Austria
Western Mongols Islamized
Wycliffe b.
Bubonic plague in Europe
Jacquerie in Fr.
Van Eyck b.
Gutenberg b.
Joan of Arc executed
Leonardo b.
Copernicus b.
Rifle invented

1500

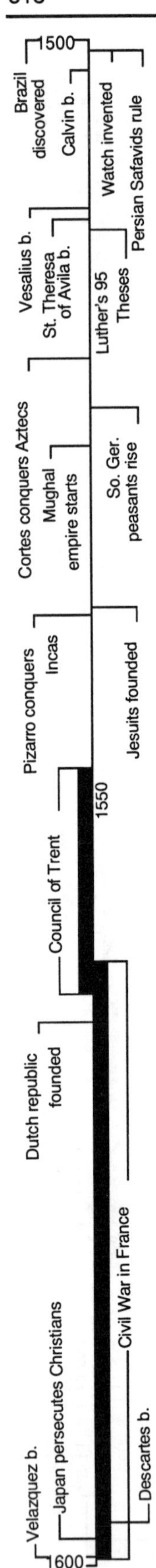

Southeast Asia. Islam was introduced into Malaya and the Indonesian islands by Arab, Persian, and Indian traders. Coastal Muslim cities and states (starting before 1300), enriched by trade, soon dominated the interior. Chief among these was the **Malacca** state (c 1400-1511), on the Malay peninsula.

Arts and Statecraft Thrive in Europe: 1350-1600

Italian Renaissance & Humanism. Distinctive Italian achievements in the arts in the late Middle Ages (Dante, 1265-1321; Giotto, 1276-1337) led to the vigorous new styles of the Renaissance (14th-16th century). Patronized by the rulers of the quarreling petty states of Italy (Medicis in Florence and the papacy, c 1400-1737), the plastic arts perfected realistic techniques, including **perspective** (Masaccio, 1401-28, Leonardo, 1452-1519). Classical motifs were used in architecture, and increased talent and expense were put into secular buildings. The Florentine dialect was refined as a national literary language (Petrarch, 1304-74). Greek refugees from the E strengthened the respect of humanist scholars for the classic sources (Bruni, 1370-1444). Soon an international movement aided by the spread of **printing** (Gutenberg, c 1400-68), **humanism** was optimistic about the power of human reason (Erasmus of Rotterdam, 1466-1536, Thomas More's *Utopia*, 1516) and valued individual effort in the arts and in politics (Machiavelli, 1469-1527).

France. The French monarchy, strengthened in its repeated struggles with powerful nobles (Burgundy, Flanders, Aquitaine) by alliances with the growing commercial towns, consolidated bureaucratic control under Philip IV (r 1285-1314) and extended French influence into Germany and Italy (popes at Avignon, France, 1309-1417). The **Hundred Years War** (1337-1453) ended English dynastic claims in France (battles of Crécy, 1346, and Poitiers, 1356; Joan of Arc executed, 1431). A French Renaissance, dating from royal invasions (1494, 1499) of Italy, was encouraged at the court of Francis I (r 1515-47), who centralized taxation and law. French vernacular literature consciously asserted its independence (La Pléiade, 1549).

England. The evolution of England's unique political institutions began with the Magna Carta (1215), by which King John guaranteed the privileges of nobles and church against the monarchy and assured jury trial. After the Wars of the Roses (1455-85), the **Tudor dynasty** reasserted royal prerogatives (Henry VIII, r 1509-47), but the trend toward independent departments and ministerial government also continued. English trade (wool exports from c 1340) was protected by the nation's growing maritime power (**Spanish Armada** destroyed, 1588).

English replaced French and Latin in the late 14th cent. in law and literature (Chaucer, c 1340-1400) and English translation of the Bible began (Wycliffe, 1380s). Elizabeth I (r 1558-1603) presided over a confident flowering of poetry (Spenser, 1552-99), drama (**Shakespeare**, 1564-1616), and music.

German Empire. From among a welter of minor feudal states, church lands, and independent cities, the **Hapsburgs** assembled a far-flung territorial domain, based in Austria from 1276. The family held the title Holy Roman Emperor from 1438 to the Empire's dissolution in 1806, but failed to centralize its domains, leaving Germany disunited for centuries. Resistance to Turkish expansion brought Hungary under Austrian control from the 16th cent. The Netherlands, Luxembourg, and Burgundy were added in 1477, curbing French expansion.

The Flemish painting tradition of naturalism, technical proficiency, and bourgeois subject matter began in the 15th cent. (Jan Van Eyck, c 1390-1441), the earliest northern manifestation of the Renaissance. **Dürer** (1471-1528) typified the merging of late Gothic and Italian trends in 16th-cent. German art. Imposing civic architecture flourished in the prosperous commercial cities.

Spain. Despite the unification of Castile and Aragon in 1479, the 2 countries retained separate governments, and the nobility, especially in Aragon and Catalonia, retained many privileges. Spanish lands in Italy (Naples, Sicily) and the Netherlands entangled the country in European wars through the mid-17th cent., while explorers, traders, and conquerors built up a Spanish empire in the Americas and the Philippines.

From the late 15th century, a **golden age** of literature and art produced works of social satire (plays of Lope de Vega, 1562-1635; Cervantes, 1547-1616), as well as spiritual intensity (El Greco, 1541-1614; Velazquez, 1599-1660).

Black Death. The bubonic plague reached Europe from the E in 1348, killing as much as half the population by 1350. Labor scarcity forced a rise in wages and brought greater freedom to the peasantry, making possible **peasant uprisings** (Jacquerie in France, 1358; Wat Tyler's rebellion in England, 1381). In the *ciompi* revolt (1378), Florentine wage earners demanded a say in economic and political power.

Explorations. Organized European maritime exploration began, seeking to evade the Venice-Ottoman monopoly of E trade and to promote Christianity. Beginning in 1418, expeditions from Portugal explored the W coast of Africa, until **Vasco da Gama** rounded the Cape of Good Hope in 1497 and reached India. A Portuguese trading empire was consolidated by the seizure of Goa (1510) and Malacca (1551). Japan was reached in 1542. The voyages of **Columbus** (1492-1504) uncovered a new world, which Spain hastened to subdue. Navigation schools in Spain and Portugal, the development of large sailing ships (carracks), and the invention (c 1475) of the rifle aided European penetration.

Mughals and Safavids. East of the Ottoman Empire, 2 Muslim dynasties ruled unchallenged in the 16th and 17th centuries. The Mughal dynasty of India, founded by Persianized Turkish invaders from the NW under Babur, dates from their 1526 conquest of the Delhi Sultanate. The dynasty ruled most of India for more than 200 years, surviving nominally until 1857. **Akbar** (r 1556-1605) consolidated administration at his glorious court, where the Urdu language (Persian-influenced Hindi) developed. Trade relations with Europe increased. Under Shah Jahan (1629-58), a secularized art fusing Hindu and Muslim element flourished in miniature painting and in architecture (Taj Mahal). Sikhism (founded c 1519) combined elements of both faiths. Suppression of Hindus and Shi'ite Muslims in S India in the late 17th cent. weakened the empire.

Fanatical devotion to the Shi'ite sect characterized the Safavids (1502-1736) of Persia and led to hostilities with the Sunni Ottomans for more than a century. The prosperity and the strength of the empire are evidenced by the mosques at its capital, **Isfahan**. The Safavids enhanced Iranian national consciousness.

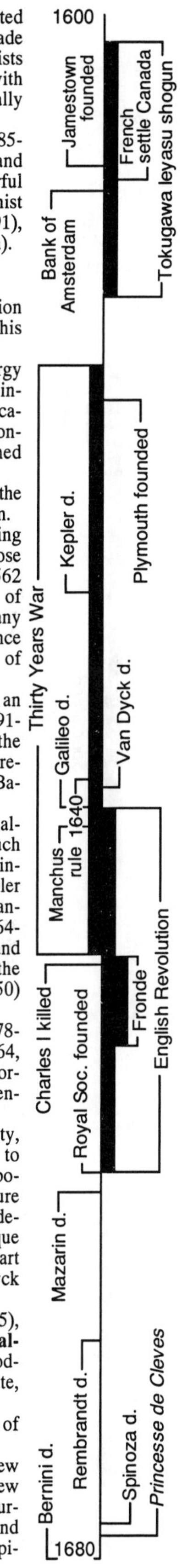

China. The Ming emperors (1368-1644), the last native dynasty in China, wielded unprecedented personal power, while the Confucian bureaucracy began to suffer from inertia. European trade (Portuguese monopoly through **Macao** from 1557) was strictly controlled. Jesuit scholars and scientists (Matteo Ricci, 1552-1610) introduced some Western science; their writings familiarized the West with China. Chinese technological inventiveness declined from this era, but the arts thrived, especially painting and ceramics.

Japan. After the decline of the first hereditary shogunate (chief generalship) at **Kamakura** (1185-1333), fragmentation of power accelerated, as did the consequent social mobility. Under Kamakura and the Ashikaga shogunate (1338-1573), the daimyos (lords) and samurai (warriors) grew more powerful and promoted a martial ideology. Japanese pirates and traders plied the China coast. Popular Buddhist movements included the nationalist Nichiren sect (from c 1250) and **Zen** (brought from China, 1191), which stressed meditation and a disciplined esthetic (tea ceremony, gardening, martial arts, No drama).

Reformed Europe Expands Overseas: 1500-1700

Reformation begun. Theological debate and protests against real and perceived clerical corruption existed in the medieval Christian world, expressed by such dissenters as Wycliffe (c 1320-84) and his followers, the Lollards, in England, and **Huss** (burned as a heretic, 1415) in Bohemia.

Luther (1483-1546) preached that only faith could lead to salvation, without the mediation of clergy or good works. He attacked the authority of the pope, rejected priestly celibacy, and recommended individual study of the Bible (which he translated c 1525). His 95 Theses (1517) led to his excommunication (1521). **Calvin** (1509-64) said that God's elect were predestined for salvation and that good conduct and success were signs of election. Calvin in Geneva and Knox (1505-72) in Scotland established theocratic states.

Henry VIII asserted English national authority and secular power by breaking away (1534) from the Catholic Church. Monastic property was confiscated, and some Protestant doctrines given official sanction.

Religious wars. A century and a half of religious wars began with a South German peasant uprising (1524), repressed with Luther's support. Radical sects—democratic, pacifist, millennarian—arose (Anabaptists ruled Münster in 1534-35) and were suppressed violently. Civil war in France from 1562 between **Huguenots** (Protestant nobles and merchants) and Catholics ended with the 1598 Edict of Nantes tolerating Protestants (revoked 1685). Hapsburg attempts to restore Catholicism in Germany were resisted in 25 years of fighting; the 1555 Peace of Augsburg guarantee of religious independence to local princes and cities was confirmed only after the **Thirty Years War** (1618-48), when much of Germany was devastated by local and foreign armies (Sweden, France).

A Catholic Reformation, or **Counter Reformation**, met the Protestant challenge, clearly defining an official theology at the Council of Trent (1545-63). The **Jesuit** order, founded in 1534 by Loyola (1491-1556), helped reconvert large areas of Poland, Hungary, and S Germany and sent missionaries to the New World, India, and China, while the Inquisition helped suppress heresy in Catholic countries. A revival of piety appeared in the devotional literature (Theresa of Avila, 1515-82) and the grandiose Baroque art (Bernini, 1598-1680) of Roman Catholic countries.

Scientific Revolution. The late nominalist thinkers (Ockham, c 1300-49) of Paris and Oxford challenged Aristotelian orthodoxy, allowing for a freer scientific approach. But metaphysical values, such as the Neoplatonic faith in an orderly, mathematical cosmos, still motivated and directed subsequent inquiry. **Copernicus** (1473-1543) promoted the heliocentric theory, which was confirmed when Kepler (1571-1630) discovered the mathematical laws describing the orbits of the planets. The Christian-Aristotelian belief that heavens and earth were fundamentally different collapsed when **Galileo** (1564-1642) discovered moving sunspots, irregular moon topography, and moons around Jupiter. He and **Newton** (1642-1727) developed a mechanics that unified cosmic and earthly phenomena. To meet the needs of the new physics, Newton and Leibnitz (1646-1716) invented calculus, Descartes (1596-1650) invented analytic geometry.

An explosion of observational science included the discovery of blood circulation (Harvey, 1578-1657) and microscopic life (Leeuwenhoek, 1632-1723) and advances in anatomy (Vesalius, 1514-64, dissected corpses) and chemistry (Boyle, 1627-91). Scientific research institutes were founded: Florence (1657), London (**Royal Society**, 1660), Paris (1666). Inventions proliferated (Savery's steam engine, 1696).

Arts. Mannerist trends of the High Renaissance (**Michelangelo**, 1475-1564) exploited virtuosity, grace, novelty, and exotic subjects and poses. The notion of artistic genius was promoted, in contrast to the anonymous medieval artisan. Private connoisseurs entered the art market. These trends were elaborated in the 17th cent. **Baroque** era on a grander scale. Dynamic movement in painting and sculpture was emphasized by sharp lighting effects, use of rich materials (colored marble, gilt), and realistic details. Curved facades, broken lines, rich, deep-cut detail, and ceiling decoration characterized Baroque architecture, especially in Germany. Monarchs, princes, and prelates, usually Catholic, used Baroque art to enhance and embellish their authority, as in royal portraits by Velazquez (1599-1660) and Van Dyck (1599-1641).

National styles emerged. In France, a taste for rectilinear order and serenity (Poussin, 1594-1665), linked to the new rational philosophy, was expressed in classical forms. The influence of **classical values** in French literature (tragedies of Racine, 1639-99) gave rise to the "battle of the Ancients and Moderns." New forms included the essay (Montaigne, 1533-92) and novel (*Princesse de Cleves*, La Fayette, 1678).

Dutch painting of the 17th cent. was unique in its wide social distribution. The Flemish tradition of undemonstrative realism reached its peak in **Rembrandt** (1606-69) and Vermeer (1632-75).

Economy. European economic expansion was stimulated by the new trade with the East, by New World gold and silver, and by a doubling of population (50 million in 1450, 100 million in 1600). New business and financial techniques were developed and refined, such as joint-stock companies, insurance, and letters of credit and exchange. The Bank of Amsterdam (1609) and the Bank of England (1694) broke the old monopoly of private banking families. The rise of a business mentality was typi-

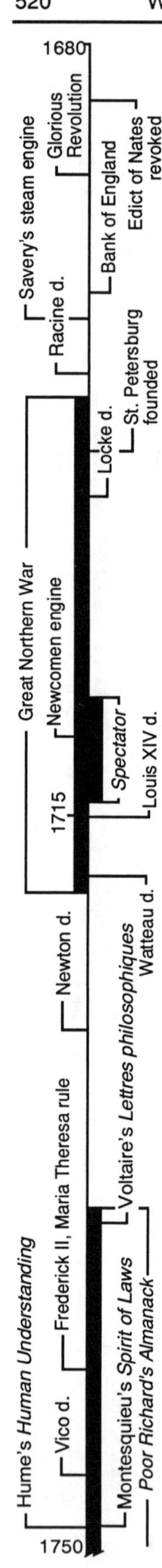

fied by the spread of clock towers in cities in the 14th cent. By the mid-15th cent., portable clocks were available; the first watch was invented in 1502.

By 1650, most governments had adopted the **mercantile system**, in which they sought to amass metallic wealth by protecting their merchants' foreign and colonial trade monopolies. The rise in prices and the new coin-based economy undermined the craft guild and feudal manorial systems. Expanding industries, such as clothweaving and mining, benefited from technical advances. Coal replaced disappearing wood as the chief fuel; it was used to fuel new 16th-cent. blast furnaces making cast iron.

New World. The **Aztecs** united much of the Meso-American culture area in a militarist empire by 1519, from their capital, Tenochtitlán (pop. 300,000), which was the center of a cult requiring enormous levels of ritual human sacrifice. Most of the civilized areas of South America were ruled by the centralized Inca Empire (1476-1534), stretching 2,000 mi from Ecuador to NW Argentina. Lavish and sophisticated traditions in pottery, weaving, sculpture, and architecture were maintained in both regions.

These empires, beset by revolts, fell in 2 short campaigns to gold-seeking Spanish forces based in the Antilles and Panama. **Cortes** took Mexico (1519-21); **Pizarro,** Peru (1532-35). From these centers, land and sea expeditions claimed most of North and South America for Spain. The Indian high cultures did not survive the impact of Christian missionaries and the new upper class of whites and mestizos. In turn, New World silver and such Indian products as potatoes, tobacco, corn, peanuts, chocolate, and rubber exercised a major economic influence on Europe. Although the Spanish administration intermittently concerned itself with the welfare of Indians, the population remained impoverished at most levels, despite the growth of a distinct South American civilization. European diseases reduced the native population.

Brazil, which the Portuguese reached in 1500 and settled after 1530, and the Caribbean colonies of several European nations developed a plantation economy where sugarcane, tobacco, cotton, coffee, rice, indigo, and lumber were grown commercially by slaves. From the early 16th to the late 19th century, some 10 million Africans were transported to **slavery** in the New World.

Netherlands. The urban, Calvinist N provinces of the Netherlands rebelled (1568) against Hapsburg Spain and founded an oligarchic mercantile republic. Their strategic control of the Baltic grain market enabled them to exploit Mediterranean food shortages. Religious refugees—French and Belgian Protestants, Iberian Jews—added to the cosmopolitan commercial talent pool. After Spain absorbed Portugal in 1580, the Dutch seized Portuguese possessions and created a vast, though generally short-lived commercial empire in Brazil, the Antilles, Africa, India, Ceylon, Malacca, Indonesia, and Taiwan and challenged or supplanted Portuguese traders in China and Japan. Revolution in 1640 restored Portuguese independence.

England. Anglicanism became firmly established under Elizabeth I after a brief Catholic interlude under "Bloody Mary" (1553-58). But religious and political conflicts led to a rebellion (1642) by Parliament. Roundheads (Puritans) defeated Cavaliers (Royalists); Charles I was beheaded (1649). The new **Commonwealth** was ruled as a military dictatorship by Cromwell, who also brutally crushed (1649-51) an Irish rebellion. Conflicts within the Puritan camp (democratic Levelers defeated 1649) aided the Stuart restoration (1660), but Parliament was permanently strengthened and the peaceful **"Glorious Revolution"** (1688) advanced political and religious liberties (writings of Locke, 1632-1704). British privateers (Drake, 1540-96) challenged Spanish control of the New World and penetrated Asian trade routes (Madras taken, 1639). North American colonies (Jamestown, 1607; Plymouth, 1620) provided an outlet for religious dissenters from Europe.

France. Emerging from the religious civil wars in 1628, France regained military and commercial great power status under the ministries of **Richelieu** (1624-42), Mazarin (1643-61), and Colbert (1662-83). Under Louis XIV (r 1643-1715) royal absolutism triumphed over nobles and local *parlements* (defeat of Fronde, 1648-53). Permanent colonies were founded in Canada (1608), the Caribbean (1626), and India (1674).

Sweden. Sweden seceded from the Scandinavian Union in 1523. The thinly populated agrarian state (with copper, iron, and timber exports) was united by the Vasa kings, whose conquests by the mid-17th cent. made Sweden the dominant Baltic power. The empire collapsed in the Great Northern War (1700-21).

Poland. After the union with Lithuania in 1447, Poland ruled vast territories from the Baltic to the Black Sea, resisting German and Turkish incursions. Catholic nobles failed to gain the loyalty of their Orthodox Christian subjects in the E; commerce and trades were practiced by German and Jewish immigrants. The bloody 1648-49 Cossack uprising began the kingdom's dismemberment.

China. A new dynasty, the Manchus, invaded from the NE, seized power in 1644, and expanded Chinese control to its greatest extent in Central and Southeast Asia. Trade and diplomatic contact with Europe grew, carefully controlled by China. New crops (sweet potato, maize, peanut) allowed an economic and population growth (pop. 300 million, in 1800). Traditional arts and literature were pursued with increased sophistication (*Dream of the Red Chamber*, novel, mid-18th cent.).

Japan. Tokugawa Ieyasu, shogun from 1603, finally unified and pacified feudal Japan. Hereditary daimyos and samurai monopolized government office and the professions. An urban merchant class grew, literacy spread, and a cultural renaissance occurred (haiku, a verse innovation of the poet Basho, 1644-94). Fear of European domination led to persecution of Christian converts from 1597 and to stringent isolation from outside contact from 1640.

Philosophy, Industry, and Revolution: 1700-1800

Science and Reason. Faith in human reason and science as the source of truth and a means to improve the physical and social environment, espoused since the Renaissance (Francis Bacon, 1561-1626), was bolstered by scientific discoveries in spite of theological opposition (Galileo's forced retraction, 1633). Descartes applied the logical method of mathematics to discover "self-evident" scientific and philosophical truths, and Newton emphasized induction from experimental observation.

The challenge of reason to traditional religious and political values and institutions began with **Spinoza** (1632-77), who interpreted the Bible historically and called for political and intellectual freedom.

French philosophers assumed leadership of the **Enlightenment** in the 18th cent. Montesquieu (1689-1755) used British history to support his notions of limited government. Voltaire's (1694-1778) diaries

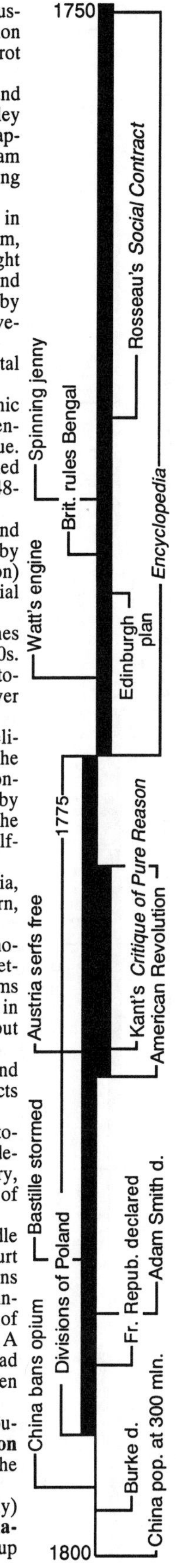

and novels of exotic travel illustrated the intellectual trends toward secular ethics and relativism. Rousseau's (1712-1778) radical concepts of the **social contract** and of the inherent goodness of the common man gave impetus to antimonarchical republicanism. The *Encyclopedia* (1751-72), edited by Diderot and d'Alembert and designed as a monument to reason, was largely devoted to practical technology.

In England, ideals of political and religious liberty were connected with empiricist philosophy and science in the followers of Locke. But the extreme **empiricism of Hume** (1711-76) and Berkeley (1685-1753) posed limits to the identification of reason with absolute truth, as did the evolutionary approach to law and politics of Burke (1729-97) and the utilitarianism of Bentham (1748-1832). Adam Smith (1723-90) and other **physiocrats** called for a rationalization of economic activity by removing artificial barriers to a supposedly natural free exchange of goods.

Despite the political disunity and backwardness of most of Germany, German writers participated in the new philosophical trends popularized by Wolff (1679-1754). **Kant's** (1724-1804) idealism, unifying an empirical epistemology with a priori moral and logical concepts, directed German thought away from skepticism. Italian contributions included work on electricity by Galvani (1737-98) and Volta (1745-1827), the pioneer **historiography of Vico** (1668-1744), and writings on penal reform by Beccaria (1738-94). Benjamin Franklin (1706-90) was celebrated in Europe for his varied achievements.

The growth of the **press** (*Spectator*, 1711-12) and the wide distribution of realistic but sentimental **novels** attested to the increase of a large bourgeois public.

Arts. Rococo art, characterized by extravagant decorative effects, asymmetries copied from organic models, and artificial pastoral subjects, was favored by the continental aristocracy for most of the century (Watteau, 1684-1721) and had musical analogies in the ornamentalized polyphony of late Baroque. The **Neoclassical** art after 1750, associated with the new scientific archeology, was more streamlined and was infused with the supposed moral and geometric rectitude of the Roman Republic (David, 1748-1825). In England, **town planning** on a grand scale began.

Industrial Revolution in England. Agricultural improvements, such as the sowing drill (1701) and livestock breeding, were implemented on the large fields provided by enclosure of common lands by private owners. Profits from agriculture and from colonial and foreign trade (1800 volume, £54 million) were channeled through hundreds of banks and the **Stock Exchange** (est 1773) into new industrial processes.

The Newcomen steam pump (1712) aided coal mining. Coal fueled the new efficient steam engines patented by Watt in 1769, and coke-smelting produced cheap, sturdy iron for machinery by the 1730s. The **flying shuttle** (1733) and **spinning jenny** (c 1764) were used in the large new cotton textile factories, where women and children were much of the work force. Goods were transported cheaply over **canals** (2,000 mi built 1760-1800).

American Revolution. The British colonies in North America attracted a mass immigration of religious dissenters and poor people throughout the 17th and 18th centuries, coming from all parts of the British Isles, Germany, the Netherlands, and other countries. The population reached 3 million nonnatives by the 1770s. The small native population was greatly reduced by European diseases and by wars with and between the various colonies. British attempts to control colonial trade and to tax the colonists to pay for the costs of colonial administration and defense clashed with traditions of local self-government and eventually provoked the colonies to rebellion.

Central and East Europe. The monarchs of the three states that dominated E Europe—Austria, Prussia, and Russia—accepted the advice and legitimation of philosophes in creating more modern, centralized institutions in their kingdoms, enlarged by the division (1772-95) of Poland.

Under **Frederick II** (r 1740-86) Prussia, with its efficient modern army, doubled in size. State monopolies and tariff protection fostered industry, and some legal reforms were introduced. Austria's heterogeneous realms were unified under **Maria Theresa** (r 1740-80) and **Joseph II** (r 1780-90). Reforms in education, law, and religion were enacted, and the Austrian serfs were freed (1781). With its defeat in the Seven Years' War in 1763, Austria failed to regain Silesia and ceased its active role in Germany, but was compensated by expansion to the E and S (Hungary, Slavonia, 1699; Galicia, 1772).

Russia, whose borders continued to expand in all directions, adopted some Western bureaucratic and economic policies under **Peter I** (r 1682-1725) and Catherine II (r 1762-96). Trade and cultural contacts with the West multiplied from the new Baltic Sea capital, **St. Petersburg** (est 1703).

French Revolution. The growing French middle class lacked political power and resented aristocratic tax privileges, especially in light of the successful American Revolution. Peasants lacked adequate land and were burdened with feudal obligations to nobles. Wars with Britain drained the treasury, finally forcing the king to call the **Estates-General** in 1789 (first time since 1614), in an atmosphere of food riots (poor crop in 1788).

Aristocratic resistance to absolutism was soon overshadowed by the reformist Third Estate (middle class), which proclaimed itself the **National Constituent Assembly** June 17 and took the "Tennis Court oath" on June 20 to secure a constitution. The storming of the **Bastille** on July 14 by Parisian artisans was followed by looting and seizure of aristocratic property throughout France. Assembly reforms included abolition of class and regional privileges, a Declaration of Rights, suffrage by taxpayers (75% of males), and the **Civil Constitution of the Clergy** providing for election and loyalty oaths for priests. A republic was declared Sept. 22, 1792, in spite of royalist pressure from Austria and Prussia, which had declared war in April (joined by Britain the next year). Louis XVI was beheaded Jan. 21, 1793, Queen Marie Antoinette was beheaded Oct. 16, 1793.

Royalist uprisings in La Vendée and military reverses led to a **reign of terror** in which tens of thousands of opponents of the Revolution and criminals were executed. Radical reforms in the **Convention** period (Sept. 1793-Oct. 1795) included the abolition of colonial slavery, economic measures to aid the poor, support of public education, and a short-lived de-Christianization.

Division among radicals (execution of Hebert, March 1794; Danton, April; and Robespierre, July) aided the ascendance of a moderate **Directory**, which consolidated military victories. **Napoleon Bonaparte** (1769-1821), a popular young general, exploited political divisions and participated in a coup Nov. 9, 1799, making himself first consul (dictator).

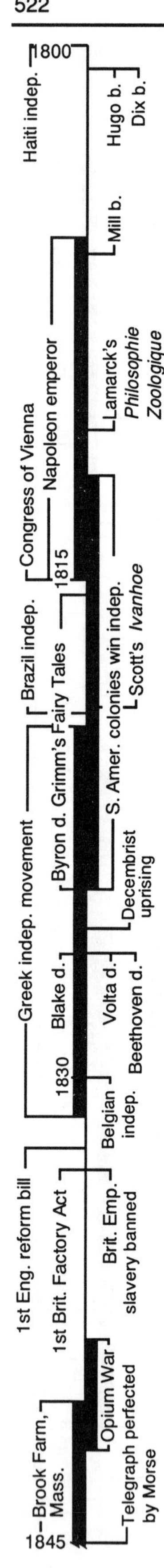

India. Sikh and Hindu rebels (Rajputs, Marathas) and Afghans destroyed the power of the Mughals during the 18th cent. After France's defeat (1763) in the Seven Years' War, Britain was the primary European trade power in India. Its control of inland **Bengal and Bihar** was recognized (1765) by the Mughal shah, who granted the **British East India Co**. (under Clive, 1725-74) the right to collect land revenue there. Despite objections from Parliament (1784 India Act), the company's involvement in local wars and politics led to repeated acquisitions of new territory. The company exported Indian textiles, sugar, and indigo.

Change Gathers Steam: 1800-40

French ideals and empire spread. Inspired by the ideals of the French Revolution, and supported by the expanding French armies, new republican regimes arose near France: the **Batavian** Republic in the Netherlands (1795-1806), the **Helvetic** Republic in Switzerland (1798-1803), the **Cisalpine** Republic in N Italy (1797-1805), the **Ligurian** Republic in Genoa (1797-1805), and the **Parthenopean** Republic in S Italy (1799). A Roman Republic existed briefly in 1798 after Pope Pius VI was arrested by French troops. In Italy and Germany, new nationalist sentiments were stimulated both in imitation of and in reaction to France (anti-French and anti-Jacobin peasant uprisings in Italy, 1796-99).

From 1804, when Napoleon declared himself emperor, to 1812, a succession of military victories (Austerlitz, 1805; Jena, 1806) extended his control over most of Europe, through puppet states (**Confederation of the Rhine** united W German states for the first time and **Grand Duchy of Warsaw** revived Polish national hopes), expansion of the empire, and alliances.

Among the lasting reforms initiated under Napoleon's absolutist reign were: establishment of the Bank of France, centralization of tax collection, codification of law along Roman models (Code Napoléon), and reform and extension of secondary and university education. In an 1801 concordat, the papacy recognized the effective autonomy of the French Catholic Church. Some 400,000 French soldiers were killed in the Napoleonic Wars, along with 600,000 foreign troops.

Last gasp of old regime. France's coastal blockade of Europe (**Continental System**) failed to neutralize Britain. The disastrous 1812 invasion of Russia exposed Napoleon's overextension. After Napoleon's 1814 exile at Elba, his armies were defeated (1815) at **Waterloo**, by British and Prussian troops.

At the **Congress of Vienna**, the monarchs and princes of Europe redrew their boundaries, to the advantage of Prussia (in Saxony and the Ruhr), Austria (in Illyria and Venetia), and Russia (in Poland and Finland). British conquest of Dutch and French colonies (S Africa, Ceylon, Mauritius) was recognized, and France, under the restored Bourbons, retained its expanded 1792 borders. The settlement brought 50 years of international peace to Europe.

But the Congress was unable to check the advance of liberal ideals and of nationalism among the smaller European nations. The 1825 **Decembrist uprising** by liberal officers in Russia was easily suppressed. But an independence movement in **Greece**, stirred by commercial prosperity and a cultural revival, succeeded in expelling Ottoman rule by 1831, with the aid of Britain, France, and Russia.

A constitutional monarchy was secured in France by the **1830 Revolution**; Louis Philippe became king. The revolutionary contagion spread to **Belgium**, which gained its independence (1830) from the Dutch monarchy, to **Poland**, whose rebellion was defeated (1830-31) by Russia, and to Germany.

Romanticism. A new style in intellectual and artistic life began to replace Neoclassicism and Rococo after the mid-18th cent. By the early 19th cent., this style, Romanticism, had prevailed in the European world.

Rousseau had begun the reaction against excessive rationalism and skepticism; in education (*Émile*, 1762) he stressed subjective spontaneity over regularized instruction. In Germany, Lessing (1729-81) and Herder (1744-1803) favorably compared the German folk song to classical forms and began a cult of Shakespeare, whose passion and "natural" wisdom was a model for the romantic *Sturm und Drang* (Storm and Stress) movement. **Goethe's** *Sorrows of Young Werther* (1774) set the model for the tragic, passionate genius.

A new interest in **Gothic architecture** in England after 1760 (Walpole, 1717-97) spread through Europe, associated with an aesthetic Christian and mystic revival (Blake, 1757-1827). Celtic, Norse, and German mythology and folk tales were revived or imitated (Macpherson's Ossian translation, 1762; Grimm's Fairy Tales, 1812-22). The medieval revival (Scott's *Ivanhoe*, 1819) led to a new interest in history, stressing national differences and organic growth (Carlyle, 1795-1881; Michelet, 1798-1874), corresponding to theories of natural evolution (Lamarck's *Philosophie Zoologique*, 1809; Lyell's *Geology*, 1830-33).

Revolution and war fed an obsession with freedom and conflict, expressed by poets (**Byron**, 1788-1824; **Hugo**, 1802-85) and philosophers (**Hegel**, 1770-1831).

Wild gardens replaced the formal French variety, and painters favored rural, stormy, and mountainous landscapes (**Turner**, 1775-1851; **Constable**, 1776-1837). Clothing became freer, with wigs, hoops, and ruffles discarded. Originality and genius were expected in the life as well as the work of inspired artists (Murger's *Scenes from Bohemian Life*, 1847-49). Exotic locales and themes (as in Gothic horror stories) were used in art and literature (Delacroix, 1798-1863; **Poe**, 1809-49).

Music exhibited the new dramatic style and a breakdown of classical forms (Beethoven, 1770-1827). The use of folk melodies and modes aided the growth of distinct national traditions (Glinka in Russia, 1804-57).

Latin America. Haiti, under the former slave **Toussaint L'Ouverture**, was the first Latin American independent state (1804). All the mainland Spanish colonies won their independence (1810-24), under such leaders as **Bolivar** (1783-1830). Brazil became an independent empire (1822) under the Portuguese prince regent. A new class of military officers divided power with large landholders and the church.

United States. Heavy immigration and exploitation of ample natural resources fueled rapid economic growth. The spread of the franchise, public education, and antislavery sentiment were signs of a widespread democratic ethic.

China. Failure to keep pace with Western arms technology exposed China to greater European influence and hampered efforts to bar imports of opium, which had damaged Chinese society and drained wealth overseas. In the **Opium War** (1839-42), Britain forced China to expand trade opportunities and to cede Hong Kong.

Triumph of Progress: 1840-80

Idea of Progress. As a result of the cumulative scientific, economic, and political changes of the preceding eras, the idea took hold among literate people in the West that continuing growth and improvement was the usual state of human and natural life.

Darwin's statement of the **theory of evolution** and survival of the fittest (*Origin of Species*, 1859), defended by intellectuals and scientists against theological objections, was taken as confirmation that progress was the natural direction of life. The controversy helped define popular ideas of the dedicated scientist and ever-expanding human knowledge of and control over the world (Foucault's demonstration of earth's rotation, 1851; Pasteur's germ theory, 1861).

Liberals following Ricardo (1772-1823) in their faith that unrestrained competition would bring continuous economic expansion sought to adjust political life to the new social realities and believed that unregulated competition of ideas would yield truth (Mill, 1806-73). In England, successive reform bills (1832, 1867, 1884) gave representation to the new industrial towns and extended the franchise to the middle and lower classes and to Catholics, Dissenters, and Jews. On both sides of the Atlantic, reformists tried to improve conditions for the mentally ill (Dix, 1802-87), women (Anthony, 1820-1906), and prisoners. Slavery was barred in the British Empire (1833); the U.S. (1865); and Brazil (1888).

Socialist theories based on ideas of human perfectibility or historical progress were widely disseminated. Utopian socialists such as Saint-Simon (1760-1825) envisaged an orderly, just society directed by a technocratic elite. A model factory town, New Lanark, Scotland, was set up by utopian Robert Owen (1771-1858), and utopian communal experiments were tried in the U.S. (Brook Farm, Mass., 1841-47). Bakunin's (1814-76) anarchism represented the opposite utopian extreme of total freedom. Marx (1818-83) posited the inevitable triumph of socialism in the industrial countries through a historical process of class conflict.

Spread of industry. The technical processes and managerial innovations of the English industrial revolution spread to Europe (especially Germany) and the U.S., causing an explosion of industrial production, demand for raw materials, and competition for markets. Inventors, both trained and self-educated, provided the means for larger-scale production (Bessemer steel, 1856; sewing machine, 1846). Many inventions were shown at the 1851 London Great Exhibition at the Crystal Palace, the theme of which was universal prosperity.

Local specialization and long-distance trade were aided by a revolution in transportation and communication. Railroads were first introduced in the 1820s in England and the U.S. More than 150,000 mi of track had been laid worldwide by 1880, with another 100,000 mi laid in the next decade. Steamships were improved (*Savannah* crossed Atlantic, 1819). The telegraph, perfected by 1844 (Morse), connected the Old and New Worlds by cable in 1866 and quickened the pace of international commerce and politics. The first commercial telephone exchange went into operation in the U.S. in 1878.

The new class of industrial workers, uprooted from their rural homes, lacked job security and suffered from dangerous overcrowded conditions at work and at home. Many responded by organizing trade unions (legalized in England, 1824; France, 1884). The U.S. Knights of Labor had 700,000 members by 1886. The First International (1864-76) tried to unite workers internationally around a Marxist program. The quasi-Socialist Paris Commune uprising (1871) was violently suppressed. Factory Acts to reduce child labor and regulate conditions were passed (1833-50 in England). Social security measures were introduced by the Bismarck regime (1883-89) in Germany.

Revolutions of 1848. Among the causes of the continent-wide revolutions were an international collapse of credit and resulting unemployment, bad harvests in 1845-47, and a cholera epidemic. The new urban proletariat and expanding bourgeoisie demanded a greater political role. Republics were proclaimed in France, Rome, and Venice. Nationalist feelings reached fever pitch in the Hapsburg empire, as Hungary declared independence under Kossuth, as a Slav Congress demanded equality, and as Piedmont tried to drive Austria from Lombardy. A national liberal assembly at Frankfurt called for German unification.

But riots fueled bourgeois fears of socialism (Marx and Engels, *Communist Manifesto*, 1848), and peasants remained conservative. The old establishment—The Papacy, the Hapsburgs with the help of the Czarist Russian army —was able to rout the revolutionaries by 1849. The French Republic succumbed to a renewed monarchy by 1852 (Emperor Napoleon III).

Great nations unified. Using the "blood and iron" tactics of Bismarck from 1862, Prussia controlled N Germany by 1867 (war with Denmark, 1864; Austria, 1866). After defeating France in 1870 (annexation of Alsace-Lorraine), it won the allegiance of S German states. A new **German Empire** was proclaimed (1871). **Italy**, inspired by Mazzini (1805-72) and Garibaldi (1807-82), was unified by the reformed Piedmont kingdom through uprisings, plebiscites, and war.

The **U.S.**, its area expanded after the 1846-48 Mexican War, defeated (1861-65) a secession attempt by slave states. The Canadian provinces were united in an autonomous **Dominion of Canada** (1867). Control in **India** was removed from the East India Co. and centralized under British administration after the 1857-58 Sepoy rebellion, laying the groundwork for the modern Indian State. Queen Victoria was named Empress of India (1876).

Europe dominates Asia. The Ottoman Empire began to collapse in the face of Balkan nationalisms and European imperial incursions in N Africa (Suez Canal, 1869). The Turks had lost control of most of both regions by 1882. Russia completed its expansion S by 1884 (despite the temporary setback of the Crimean War with Turkey, Britain, and France, 1853-56), taking Turkestan, all the Caucasus, and Chinese areas in the E and sponsoring Balkan Slavs against the Turks. A succession of reformist and reactionary regimes presided over a slow modernization (serfs freed, 1861). Persian independence suffered as Russia and British India competed for influence.

China was forced to sign a series of unequal treaties with European powers and Japan. Overpopulation and an inefficient dynasty brought misery and caused rebellions (Taiping, Muslims) leaving tens of millions dead. Japan was forced by the U.S. (Commodore Perry's visits, 1853-54) and Europe to end its

1845
Communist Manifesto
Sewing machine
Mexican War begins
Perry in Japan
Freud b.
Bessemer steel
1860
Sepoy rebellion
Second Empire in France
U.S. Civil War
Overseas cable
Canada united
Marxist 1st International
1870
Paris commune
German empire founded
Mazzini d.
1st telephone
1880

1880 — Dostoyevsky d. — Marx d. — Indian Natl. Cong. — 1885 — Brazil bans slavery — Kipling's *Barrack Room Ballads* — Europe conquers Africa — Rimbaud d. — Sino-Jap. War — radio — Span.-Am. War — 1895 — Russ. Soc. Dem. Party — Dreyfus case — Gorky's *Lower Depths* — Boxer rebellion — Wilde d. — Ford Motor Co. — Panama Canal — Australia united — 1904

isolation. The Meiji restoration (1868) gave power to a Westernizing oligarchy. Intensified empire-building gave Burma to Britain (1824-85) and Indochina to France (1862-95). Christian missionary activity followed imperial and trade expansion in Asia.

Respectability. The fine arts were expected to reflect and encourage the progress of morals and manners among the Victorians. Prudery, exaggerated delicacy, and familial piety were heralded by **Bowdler's** expurgated edition (1818) of Shakespeare. Government-supported mass education inculcated a work ethic as a means to escape poverty (Horatio Alger, 1832-99).

The official **Beaux Arts** school in Paris set an international style of imposing public buildings (Paris Opera, 1861-74; Vienna Opera, 1861-69) and uplifting statues (Bartholdi's *Statue of Liberty*, 1884). Realist painting, influenced by photography (Daguerre, 1837), appealed to a new mass audience with social or historical narrative (Wilkie, 1785-1841; Poynter, 1836-1919) or with serious religious, moral, or social messages (pre-Raphaelites, Millet's *Angelus*, 1858) often drawn from ordinary life. The **Impressionists** (Monet, 1840-1926; Pissarro, 1830-1903; Renoir, 1841-1919) rejected the formalism, sentimentality, and precise techniques of academic art in favor of a spontaneous, undetailed rendering of the world through careful representation of the effect of natural light on objects.

Realistic **novelists** presented the full panorama of social classes and personalities, but retained sentimentality and moral judgment (Dickens, 1812-70; Eliot, 1819-80; Tolstoy, 1828-1910; Balzac, 1799-1850).

Veneer of Stability: 1880-1900

Imperialism triumphant. The vast **African** interior, visited by European explorers (Barth, 1821-65; Livingstone, 1813-73), was conquered by the European powers in rapid, competitive thrusts from their coastal bases after 1880, mostly for domestic political and international strategic reasons. W African Muslim kingdoms (Fulani), Arab slave traders (Zanzibar), and Bantu military confederations (Zulu) were alike subdued. Only Christian Ethiopia (defeat of Italy, 1896) and Liberia resisted successfully. France (W Africa) and Britain ("Cape to Cairo," Boer War, 1899-1902) were the major beneficiaries. The ideology of "the white man's burden" (Kipling, *Barrack Room Ballads*, 1892) or of a "civilizing mission" (France) justified the conquests.

W European foreign capital investment soared to nearly $40 billion by 1914, but most was in E Europe (France, Germany), the Americas (Britain), and the Europeans' colonies. The foundation of the modern interdependent world economy was laid, with cartels dominating raw material trade.

An industrious world. Industrial and technological proficiency characterized the 2 new great powers—Germany and the **U.S.** Coal and iron deposits enabled Germany to reach 2d or 3d place status in iron, steel, and shipbuilding by the 1900s. German electrical and chemical industries were world leaders. The U.S. post-Civil War boom (interrupted by "panics"—1884, 1893, 1896) was shaped by massive immigration from S and E Europe from 1880, government subsidy of railroads, and huge private monopolies (Standard Oil, 1870; U.S. Steel, 1901). The **Spanish-American War**, 1898 (Philippine rebellion, 1899-1901), and the Open Door policy in China (1899) made the U.S. a world power.

England led in **urbanization** (72% by 1890), with **London** the world capital of finance, insurance, and shipping. Sewer systems (Paris, 1850s), electric subways (London, 1890), parks, and bargain department stores helped improve living standards for most of the urban population of the industrial world.

Westernization of Asia. Asian reaction to European economic, military, and religious incursions took the form of imitation of Western techniques and adoption of Western ideas of progress and freedom. The Chinese "self-strengthening" movement of the 1860s and '70s included rail, port, and arsenal improvements and metal and textile mills. Reformers such as **K'ang Yu-wei** (1858-1927) won liberalizing reforms in 1898, right after the European and Japanese "scramble for concessions."

A universal education system in Japan and importation of foreign industrial, scientific, and military experts aided Japan's unprecedented rapid modernization after 1868, under the authoritarian Meiji regime. Japan's victory in the **Sino-Japanese War** (1894-95) put Formosa and Korea in its power.

In India, the British alliance with the remaining princely states masked reform sentiment among the Westernized urban elite; higher education had been conducted largely in English for 50 years. The **Indian National Congress**, founded in 1885, demanded a larger government role for Indians.

***Fin-de-siècle* sophistication**. **Naturalist** writers pushed realism to its extreme limits, adopting a quasi-scientific attitude and writing about formerly taboo subjects such as sex, crime, extreme poverty, and corruption (Flaubert, 1821-80; Zola, 1840-1902; Hardy, 1840-1928). Unseen or repressed psychological motivations were explored in the clinical and theoretical works of **Freud** (1856-1939) and in the fiction of Dostoyevsky (1821-81), James (1843-1916), Schnitzler (1862-1931), and others.

A contempt for bourgeois life or a desire to shock a complacent audience was shared by the French **symbolist** poets (Verlaine, 1844-96; Rimbaud, 1854-91), by neopagan English writers (Swinburne, 1837-1909), by continental dramatists (Ibsen, 1828-1906) and by satirists (Wilde, 1854-1900). **Nietzsche** (1844-1900) was influential in his elitism and pessimism.

Postimpressionist art neglected long-cherished conventions of representation (Cezanne, 1839-1906) and showed a willingness to learn from primitive and non-European art (Gauguin, 1848-1903; Japanese prints).

Racism. Gobineau (1816-82) gave a pseudobiological foundation to modern racist theories, which spread in the latter 19th cent., along with **Social Darwinism**, the belief that societies are and should be organized as a struggle for survival of the fittest. The medieval period was interpreted as an era of natural Germanic rule (Chamberlain, 1855-1927), and notions of superiority were associated with German national aspirations (Treitschke, 1834-96). **Anti-Semitism**, with a new racist rationale, became a significant political force in Germany (Anti-Semitic Petition, 1880), Austria (Lueger, 1844-1910), and France (Dreyfus case, 1894-1906).

Last Respite: 1900-9

Alliances. While the peace of Europe (and its dependencies) continued to hold (1907 **Hague Conference** extended the rules of war and international arbitration procedures), imperial rivalries, protectionist trade practices (in Germany and France), and the escalating arms race (British *Dreadnought* battleship launched; Germany widens Kiel canal, 1906) exacerbated minor disputes (German-French Moroccan "crises," 1905, 1911).

Security was sought through alliances: **Triple Alliance** (Germany, Austria-Hungary, Italy; renewed in 1902 and 1907); Anglo-Japanese Alliance (1902), Franco-Russian Alliance (1899), **Entente Cordiale** (Britain, France, 1904), Anglo-Russian Treaty (1907), German-Ottoman friendship.

Ottomans decline. The inefficient, corrupt Ottoman government was unable to resist further loss of territory. Nearly all European lands were lost in 1912 to Serbia, Greece, Montenegro, and Bulgaria. Italy took Libya and the Dodecanese islands the same year, and Britain took Kuwait (1899) and the Sinai (1906). The **Young Turk** revolution in 1908 forced the sultan to restore a constitution, and it introduced some social reform, industrialization, and secularization.

British Empire. British trade and cultural influence remained dominant in the empire, but constitutional reforms presaged its eventual dissolution: The colonies of **Australia** were united in 1901 under a self-governing commonwealth. **New Zealand** acquired dominion status in 1907. The old Boer republics joined Cape Colony and Natal in the self-governing **Union of South Africa** in 1910.

The 1909 Indian Councils Act enhanced the role of elected province legislatures in **India**. The Muslim League (founded 1906) sought separate communal representation.

East Asia. Japan exploited its growing industrial power to expand its empire. Victory in the 1904-5 war against Russia (naval battle of Tsushima, 1905) assured Japan's domination of **Korea** (annexed 1910) and Manchuria (Port Arthur taken, 1905).

In China, central authority began to crumble (empress died, 1908). Reforms (Confucian exam system ended 1905, modernization of the army, building of railroads) were inadequate, and secret societies of reformers and nationalists, inspired by the Westernized **Sun Yat-sen** (1866-1925) fomented periodic uprisings in the S.

Siam, whose independence had been guaranteed by Britain and France in 1896, was split into spheres of influence by those countries in 1907.

Russia. The population of the Russian Empire approached 150 million in 1900. Reforms in education, in law, and in local institutions (*zemstvos*) and an industrial boom starting in the 1880s (oil, railroads) created the beginnings of a modern state, despite the autocratic tsarist regime. Liberals (1903 Union of Liberation), Socialists (Social Democrats founded 1898, Bolsheviks split off 1903), and populists (Social Revolutionaries founded 1901) were periodically repressed, and national minorities were persecuted (anti-Jewish pogroms, 1903, 1905-6).

An industrial crisis after 1900 and harvest failures aggravated poverty among urban workers, and the 1904-5 defeat by Japan (which checked Russia's Asian expansion) sparked the Revolution of 1905-6. A **Duma** (parliament) was created, and an agricultural reform (under Stolypin, prime minister 1906-11) created a large class of landowning peasants (kulaks).

The world shrinks. Developments in transportation and communication and mass population movements helped create an awareness of an interdependent world. Early **automobiles** (Daimler, Benz, 1885) were experimental or were designed as luxuries. Assembly-line mass production (Ford Motor Co., 1903) made the invention practicable, and by 1910 nearly 500,000 motor vehicles were registered in the U.S. alone. **Heavier-than-air flights** began in 1903 in the U.S. (Wright brothers), preceded by glider, balloon, and model plane advances in several countries. Trade was advanced by improvements in **ship design** (gyrocompass, 1910), speed (*Lusitania* crossed Atlantic in 5 days, 1907), and reach (Panama Canal begun, 1904).

The first transatlantic **radio** telegraphic transmission occurred in 1901, 6 years after Marconi discovered radio. Radio transmission of human speech had been made in 1900. Telegraphic transmission of photos was achieved in 1904, lending immediacy to news reports. **Phonographs**, popularized by Caruso's recordings (starting 1902), made for quick international spread of musical styles (ragtime). **Motion pictures**, perfected in the 1890s (Dickson, Lumière brothers), became a popular and artistic medium after 1900; newsreels appeared in 1909.

Emigration from crowded European centers soared in the decade: 9 million migrated to the U.S., and millions more went to Siberia, Canada, Argentina, Australia, South Africa, and Algeria. Some 70 million Europeans emigrated in the century before 1914. Several million Chinese, Indians, and Japanese migrated to Southeast Asia, where their urban skills often enabled them to take a predominant economic role.

Social reform. The social and economic problems of the poor were kept in the public eye by realist fiction writers (Dreiser's *Sister Carrie*, 1900; Gorky's *Lower Depths*, 1902; Sinclair's *Jungle*, 1906), journalists (U.S. **muckrakers**—Steffens, Tarbell) and artists (Ashcan school). Frequent labor strikes and occasional assassinations by anarchists or radicals (Empress Elizabeth of Austria, 1898; King Umberto I of Italy, 1900; U.S. Pres. McKinley, 1901; Russian Interior Minister Plehve, 1904; Portugal's King Carlos, 1908) added to social tension and fear of revolution.

But democratic reformism prevailed. In Germany, Bernstein's (1850-1932) **revisionist Marxism**, downgrading revolution, was accepted by the powerful Social Democrats and trade unions. The British Fabian Society (the Webbs, Shaw) and the Labour Party (founded 1906) worked for reforms such as Social Security and union rights (1906), while woman suffragists grew more militant. U.S. **progressives** fought big business (Pure Food and Drug Act, 1906). In France, the 10-hour work day (1904) and separation of church and state (1905) were reform victories, as was universal suffrage in Austria (1907).

Arts. An unprecedented period of experimentation, centered in France, produced several new **painting** styles: Fauvism exploited bold color areas (Matisse, *Woman with Hat*, 1905); expressionism reflected powerful inner emotions (the Brücke group, 1905); cubism combined several views of an object on one flat surface (Picasso's *Demoiselles*, 1906-7); futurism tried to depict speed and motion (Italian Futurist Manifesto, 1910). **Architects** explored new uses of steel structures, with facades either neoclassical (Adler and Sullivan in U.S.); curvilinear Art Nouveau (Gaudi's Casa Mila, 1905-10); or functionally streamlined (Wright's Robie House, 1909).

Music and Dance shared the experimental spirit. Ruth St. Denis (1877-1968) and Isadora Duncan (1878-1927) pioneered modern dance, while Diaghilev in Paris revitalized classic ballet from 1909.

1904
Russo-Jap. War
Rev. in Russia
Pure Food & Drug Act
Labour Party
Ibsen d.
Dreadnought launched
Hague Conf.
Young Turks rev.
Robie House
Mex. rev. starts
Portugal rev. starts 1910
Futurist Manifesto
Japan annexes Korea
2d Morocco crisis
Diaz Mex. rule ends
Chinese repub.
Ottomans lose Europe
Theory of Relativity
Maugham's *Of Human Bondage*
World War I
1916

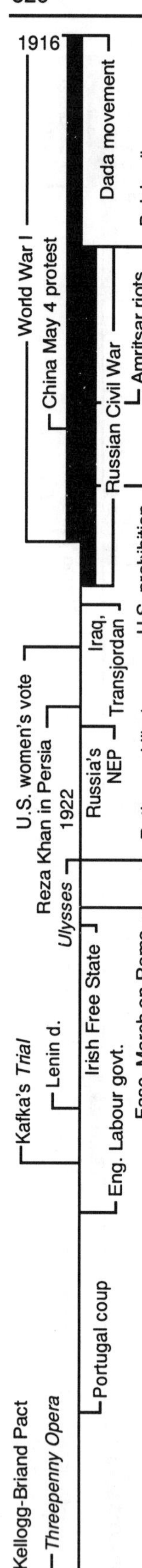

Composers explored atonal music (Debussy, 1862-1918) and dissonance (Schoenberg, 1874-1951) or revolutionized classical forms (Stravinsky, 1882-1971), often showing jazz or folk music influences.

War and Revolution: 1910-19

War threatens. Germany under Wilhelm II sought a political and imperial role consonant with its industrial strength, challenging Britain's world supremacy and threatening France, which was still resenting the loss (1871) of Alsace-Lorraine. Austria wanted to curb an expanded Serbia (after 1912) and the threat it posed to its own Slav lands. Russia feared Austrian and German political and economic aims in the Balkans and Turkey. An accelerated arms race resulted: The German standing army rose to more than 2 million men by 1914. Russia and France had more than a million each, and Austria and the British Empire nearly a million each. Dozens of enormous battleships were built by the powers after 1906.

The **assassination of Austrian Archduke Franz Ferdinand** by a Serbian, June 28, 1914, was the pretext for war. The system of alliances made the conflict Europe-wide; Germany's invasion of Belgium to outflank France forced Britain to enter the war. Patriotic fervor was nearly unanimous among all classes in most countries.

World War I. German forces were stopped in France in one month. The rival armies dug **trench networks**. Artillery and improved machine guns prevented either side from any lasting advance despite repeated assaults (600,000 dead at **Verdun**, Feb.-July 1916). Poison gas, used by Germany in 1915, proved ineffective. More than 1 million U.S. troops tipped the balance after mid-1917, forcing Germany to sue for peace the next year. The formal armistice was signed at 5 AM, Nov. 11, 1918.

In the E, the Russian armies were thrown back (battle of **Tannenberg**, Aug. 20, 1914), and the war grew unpopular in Russia. An allied attempt to relieve Russia through Turkey failed (**Gallipoli**, 1915). The **Russian Revolution** (1917) abolished the monarchy. The new Bolshevik regime signed the capitulatory Brest-Litovsk peace in March 1918. Italy entered the war on the allied side in May 1915 but was pushed back by Oct. 1917. A renewed offensive with Allied aid in Oct.-Nov. 1918 forced Austria to surrender.

The British Navy successfully blockaded Germany, which responded with submarine U-boat attacks; **unrestricted submarine warfare** against neutrals after Jan. 1917 helped bring the U.S. into the war. Other battlefields included Palestine and Mesopotamia, both of which Britain wrested from the Turks in 1917, and the African and Pacific colonies of Germany, most of which fell to Britain, France, Australia, Japan, and South Africa.

From 1916, the civilian populations and economies of both sides were mobilized to an unprecedented degree. Hardships intensified among fighting nations in 1917 (French mutiny crushed in May). More than 10 million soldiers died in the war.

Settlement. At the **Paris Peace Conference** (Jan.-June 1919), concluded by the **Treaty of Versailles**, and in subsequent negotiations and local wars (Russian-Polish War, 1920), the map of Europe was redrawn with a nod to U.S. Pres. Wilson's principle of self-determination. Austria and Hungary were separated, and much of their land was given to Yugoslavia (formerly Serbia), Romania, Italy, and the newly independent Poland and Czechoslovakia. Germany lost territory in the W, N, and E, while Finland and the Baltic states were detached from Russia. Turkey lost nearly all its Arab lands to British-sponsored Arab states or to direct French and British rule. Belgium's sovereignty was recognized.

A huge **reparations** burden and partial demilitarization were imposed on Germany. Pres. Wilson obtained approval for a League of Nations, but the U.S. Senate refused to allow the U.S. to join.

Russian revolution. Military defeats and high casualties caused a contagious lack of confidence in Tsar Nicholas, who was forced to abdicate Mar. 1917. A liberal provisional government failed to end the war, and massive desertions, riots, and fighting between factions followed. A moderate socialist government under Kerensky was overthrown in a violent coup by the **Bolsheviks** in Petrograd under Lenin, who disbanded the elected Constituent Assembly in Nov. 1917.

The Bolsheviks brutally suppressed all opposition and ended the war with Germany in Mar. 1918. **Civil war** broke out in the summer between the Red Army, including the Bolsheviks and their supporters, and monarchists, anarchists, nationalities (Ukrainians, Georgians, Poles), and others. Small U.S., British, French, and Japanese units also opposed the Bolsheviks (1918-19; Japan in Vladivostok to 1922). The civil war, anarchy, and pogroms devastated the country until the 1920 Red Army victory. The wartime total monopoly of political, economic, and police power by the Communist Party leadership was retained.

Other European revolutions. An unpopular monarchy in **Portugal** was overthrown in 1910. The new republic took severe anticlerical measures in 1911.

After a century of Home Rule agitation, during which **Ireland** was devastated by famine (1 million dead, 1846-47) and emigration, republican militants staged an unsuccessful uprising in Dublin during Easter 1916. The execution of the leaders and mass arrests by the British won popular support for the rebels. The Irish Free State, comprising all but the 6 N counties, achieved dominion status in 1922.

In the aftermath of the world war, radical revolutions were attempted in Germany (**Spartacist** uprising, Jan. 1919), **Hungary** (Kun regime, 1919), and elsewhere. All were suppressed or failed for lack of support.

Chinese revolution. The Manchu Dynasty was overthrown and a republic proclaimed in Oct. 1911. First president Sun Yat-sen resigned in favor of strongman Yuan Shih-k'ai. Sun organized the parliamentarian **Kuomintang** party.

Students launched protests on May 4, 1919, against League of Nations concessions in China to Japan. Nationalist, liberal, and socialist ideas and political groups spread. The **Communist Party** was founded in 1921. A communist regime took power in Mongolia with Soviet support in 1921.

India restive. Indian objections to British rule erupted in nationalist riots as well as in the nonviolent tactics of Gandhi (1869-1948). Nearly 400 unarmed demonstrators were shot at **Amritsar** in Apr. 1919. Britain approved limited self-rule that year.

Mexican revolution. Under the long Diaz dictatorship (1877-1911) the economy advanced, but Indian and mestizo lands were confiscated, and concessions to foreigners (mostly U.S.) damaged the

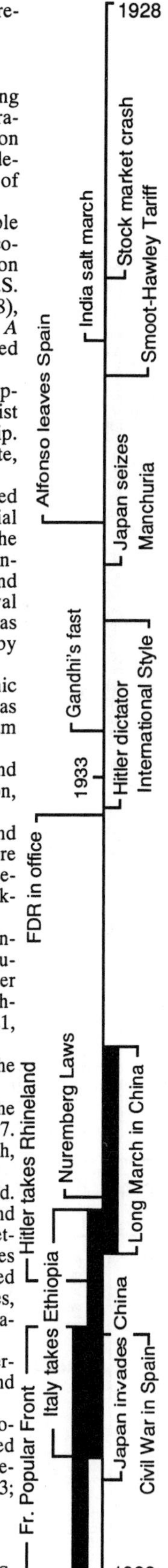

middle class. A **revolution in 1910** led to civil wars and U.S. intervention (1914, 1916-17). Land reform and a more democratic constitution (1917) were achieved.

The Aftermath of War: 1920-29

U.S. Easy credit, technological ingenuity, and war-related industrial decline in Europe caused a long economic boom, in which ownership of the new products—autos, phones, radios—became democratized. Prosperity, an increase in women workers, woman suffrage (1920), and drastic change in fashion (flappers, mannish bob for women, clean-shaven men) created a wide perception of social change, despite prohibition of alcoholic beverages (1919-33). Union membership and strikes increased. Fear of radicals led to Palmer raids (1919-20) and the Sacco/Vanzetti case (1921-27).

Europe sorts itself out. Germany's liberal **Weimar constitution** (1919) could not guarantee a stable government in the face of rightist violence (Rathenau assassinated, 1922) and Communist refusal to cooperate with Socialists. Reparations and Allied occupation of the Rhineland caused staggering inflation that destroyed middle-class savings, but economic expansion resumed after mid-decade, aided by U.S. loans. A sophisticated, innovative culture developed in architecture and design (Bauhaus, 1919-28), film (Lang, *M*, 1931), painting (Grosz), music (Weill, *Threepenny Opera*, 1928), theater (Brecht, *A Man's a Man*, 1926), criticism (Benjamin), philosophy (Jung), and fashion. This culture was considered decadent and socially disruptive by rightists.

England elected its first labor governments (Jan. 1924, June 1929). A 10-day general strike in support of coal miners failed in May 1926. In **Italy**, strikes, political chaos, and violence by small Fascist bands culminated in the Oct. 1922 Fascist March on Rome, which established Mussolini's dictatorship. Strikes were outlawed (1926), and Italian influence was pressed in the Balkans (Albania a protectorate, 1926). A conservative dictatorship was also established in **Portugal** in a 1926 military coup.

Czechoslovakia, the only stable democracy to emerge from the war in Central or East Europe, faced opposition from Germans (in the Sudetenland), Ruthenians, and some Slovaks. As the industrial heartland of the old Hapsburg empire, it remained fairly prosperous. With French backing, it formed the Little Entente with Yugoslavia (1920) and **Romania** (1921) to block Austrian or Hungarian irredentism. Hungary remained dominated by the landholding classes and expansionist feeling. Croats and Slovenes in **Yugoslavia** demanded a federal state until King Alexander I proclaimed (1929) a royal dictatorship. Poland faced nationality problems as well (Germans, Ukrainians, Jews); Pilsudski ruled as dictator from 1926. The Baltic states were threatened by traditionally dominant ethnic Germans and by Soviet-supported communists.

An economic collapse and famine in **Russia** (1921-22) claimed 5 million lives. The New Economic Policy (1921) allowed landownership by peasants and some private commerce and industry. Stalin was absolute ruler within 4 years of Lenin's death (1924). He inaugurated a brutal collectivization program (1929-32) and used foreign communist parties for Soviet state advantage.

Internationalism. Revulsion against World War I led to pacifist agitation, to the Kellogg-Briand Pact renouncing aggressive war (1928), and to **naval disarmament** pacts (Washington, 1922; London, 1930). But the League of Nations was able to arbitrate only minor disputes (Greece-Bulgaria, 1925).

Middle East. Mustafa Kemal (Ataturk) led **Turkish** nationalists in resisting Italian, French, and Greek military advances (1919-23). The sultanate was abolished (1922), and elaborate reforms were passed, including secularization of law and adoption of the Latin alphabet. Ethnic conflict led to persecution of **Armenians** (more than 1 million dead in 1915, 1 million expelled), Greeks (forced Greek-Turk population exchange, 1923), and Kurds (1925 uprising).

With evacuation of the Turks from **Arab** lands, the puritanical Wahabi dynasty of E Arabia conquered (1919-25) what is now Saudi Arabia. British, French, and Arab dynastic and nationalist maneuvering resulted in the creation of 2 more Arab monarchies in 1921—Iraq and Transjordan (both under British control)—and 2 French mandates—Syria and Lebanon. Jewish immigration into British-mandated **Palestine**, inspired by the Zionist movement, was resisted by Arabs, at times violently (1921, 1929 massacres).

Reza Khan ruled **Persia** after his 1921 coup (shah from 1925), centralized control, and created the trappings of a modern state.

China. The Kuomintang under **Chiang Kai-shek** (1887-1975) subdued the warlords by 1928. The Communists were brutally suppressed after their alliance with the Kuomintang was broken in 1927. Relative peace thereafter allowed for industrial and financial improvements, with some Russian, British, and U.S. cooperation.

Arts. Nearly all bounds of subject matter, style, and attitude were broken in the arts of the period. **Abstract** art first took inspiration from natural forms or narrative themes (Kandinsky from 1911) and then worked free of any representational aims (Malevich's suprematism, 1915-19; Mondrian's geometric style from 1917). The **Dada** movement (from 1916) mocked artistic pretension with absurd collages and constructions (Arp, Tzara, from 1916). Paradox, illusion, and psychological taboos were exploited by **surrealists** by the latter 1920s (Dali, Magritte). Architectural schools celebrated industrial values, whether vigorous abstract constructivism (Tatlin, *Monument to 3rd International*, 1919) or the machined, streamlined **Bauhaus** style, which was extended to many design fields (Helvetica typeface).

Prose writers explored revolutionary narrative modes related to dreams (Kafka's *Trial*, 1925), internal monologue (Joyce's **Ulysses**, 1922), and word play (Stein's *Making of Americans*, 1925). Poets and novelists wrote of modern alienation (Eliot's *Waste Land*, 1922) and aimlessness (Lost Generation).

Sciences. Scientific specialization prevailed by the 20th cent. Advances in knowledge and technological aptitude increased with the geometric rise in the number of practitioners. Physicists challenged common-sense views of causality, observation, and a mechanistic universe, putting science further beyond popular grasp (Einstein's general theory of relativity, 1915; Bohr's quantum mechanics, 1913; Heisenberg's uncertainty principle, 1927).

Rise of Totalitarians: 1930-39

Depression. A worldwide financial panic and economic depression began with the Oct. 1929 U.S. stock market crash and the May 1931 failure of the Austrian Credit-Anstalt. A credit crunch caused in-

1938
Munich pact
Germany attacks Poland
Nazi-Soviet pact
Germans win Balkans
Russia seizes E. Poland
Dunkirk
Russia takes Baltic
Axis in Russia
Stranger
Midway
World War II
Being & Nothingness
Stalingrad
Abstract Expressionism starts
Allies in Germany
Germany surrenders
A-bombs on Japan
UN charter
Japan surrenders
Jap. constitution
Nuremberg convictions
Cominform
Truman Doctrine
1948

ternational bankruptcies and **unemployment**: 12 million jobless by 1932 in the U.S., 5.6 million in Germany, 2.7 million in England. Governments responded with **tariff restrictions** (Smoot-Hawley Act, 1930; Ottawa Imperial Conference, 1932), which dried up world trade. Government public works programs were vitiated by deflationary budget balancing.

Germany. Years of agitation by violent extremists were brought to a head by the Depression. Nazi leader **Hitler** was named chancellor by Pres. Hindenburg in Jan. 1933 and given dictatorial power by the Reichstag in March. Opposition parties were disbanded, strikes banned, and all aspects of economic, cultural, and religious life were brought under central government and Nazi party control and manipulated by sophisticated propaganda. Severe persecution of Jews began (**Nuremberg Laws,** Sept. 1935). Many Jews, political opponents, and others were sent to concentration camps (Dachau, 1933), where thousands died or were killed. Public works, renewed conscription (1935), arms production, and a 4-year plan (1936) all but ended unemployment.

Hitler's expansionism started with reincorporation of the Saar (1935), occupation of the **Rhineland** (Mar. 1936), and annexation of Austria (Mar. 1938). At **Munich** (Sept. 1938) an indecisive Britain and France sanctioned German dismemberment of Czechoslovakia.

Russia. Urbanization and education advanced. Rapid industrialization was achieved through successive **5-year-plans** starting in 1928, using severe labor discipline and mass forced labor. Industry was financed by a decline in living standards and exploitation of agriculture, which was almost totally collectivized by the early 1930s (*kolkhoz*, collective farm; *sovkhoz*, state farm, often in newly worked lands). Successive **purges** increased the role of professionals and management at the expense of workers. Millions perished in a series of manufactured disasters: elimination (1929-34) of kulaks (peasant landowners), severe famine (1932-33), party purges (Great Purge, 1936-38), suppression of nationalities; and poor conditions in labor camps.

Spain. An industrial revolution during World War I created an urban proletariat, which was attracted to socialism and anarchism; Catalan nationalists challenged central authority. The 5 years after King Alfonso left Spain in Apr. 1931 were dominated by tension between intermittent leftist and anticlerical governments and clericals, monarchists, and other rightists. Anarchist and communist rebellions were crushed, but a July 1936 extreme right rebellion led by Gen. Francisco Franco and aided by Nazi Germany and Fascist Italy succeeded, after a 3-year **civil war** (more than 1 million dead in battles and atrocities). The war polarized international public opinion.

Italy. Despite propaganda for the ideal of the Corporate State, few domestic reforms were attempted. An entente with Hungary and Austria (Mar. 1934), a pact with Germany and Japan (Nov. 1937), and intervention by 50,000-75,000 troops in Spain (1936-39) sealed Italy's identification with the fascist bloc (anti-Semitic laws after Mar. 1938). Ethiopia was conquered (1935-36), and **Albania** annexed (Jan. 1939) in conscious imitation of ancient Rome.

East Europe. Repressive regimes fought for power against an active opposition (liberals, socialists, communists, peasants, Nazis). Minority groups and Jews were restricted within national boundaries that did not coincide with ethnic population patterns. In the destruction of **Czechoslovakia**, **Hungary** occupied S Slovakia (Nov. 1938) and Ruthenia (Mar. 1939), and a pro-Nazi regime took power in the rest of Slovakia. Other boundary disputes (e.g., Poland-Lithuania, Yugoslavia-Bulgaria, Romania-Hungary) doomed attempts to build joint fronts against Germany or Russia. Economic depression was severe.

East Asia. After a period of liberalism in **Japan**, nativist militarists dominated the government with peasant support. Manchuria was seized (Sept. 1931-Feb. 1932), and a puppet state was set up (Manchukuo). Adjacent Jehol (Inner Mongolia) was occupied in 1933. China proper was invaded in July 1937; large areas were conquered by Oct. 1938.

In **China** Communist forces left Kuomintang-besieged strongholds in the S in a Long March (1934-35) to the N. The Kuomintang-Communist civil war was suspended in Jan. 1937 in the face of threatening Japan.

The democracies. The Roosevelt Administration, in office Mar. 1933, embarked on an extensive program of social reform and economic stimulation, including protection for labor unions (heavy industries organized), Social Security, public works, wage-and-hour laws, and assistance to farmers. Isolationist sentiment (1937 Neutrality Act) prevented U.S. intervention in Europe, but military expenditures were increased in 1939.

French political instability and polarization prevented resolution of economic and international security questions. The **Popular Front** government under Blum (June 1936-Apr. 1938) passed social reforms (40-hour week) and raised arms spending. National coalition governments, which ruled Britain from Aug. 1931, brought some economic recovery but failed to define a consistent international policy until Chamberlain's government (from May 1937), which practiced deliberate **appeasement** of Germany and Italy.

India. Twenty years of agitation for autonomy and then for independence (Gandhi's **salt march,** 1930) achieved some constitutional reform (extended provincial powers, 1935) despite Muslim-Hindu strife. Social issues assumed prominence with peasant uprisings (1921), strikes (1928), Gandhi's efforts for untouchables (1932 "fast unto death"), and social and agrarian reform by the provinces after 1937.

Arts. The streamlined, geometric design motifs of Art Deco (from 1925) prevailed through the 1930s. Abstract art flourished (Moore sculptures from 1931) alongside a new realism related to social and political concerns (**Socialist Realism,** the official Soviet style from 1934; Mexican muralist Rivera, 1886-1957; and Orozco, 1883-1949), which were also expressed in fiction and poetry (Steinbeck's *Grapes of Wrath*, 1939; Sandburg's *The People, Yes*, 1936). Modern architecture (International Style, 1932) was unchallenged in its use of artificial materials (concrete, glass), lack of decoration, and monumentality (Rockefeller Center, 1929-40). U.S.-made films captured a worldwide audience with their larger-than-life fantasies *(Gone with the Wind*, 1939).

War, Hot and Cold: 1940-49

War in Europe. The Nazi-Soviet nonaggression pact (Aug. 1939) freed Germany to attack Poland (Sept.). Britain and France, who had guaranteed Polish independence, declared war on Germany. Russia

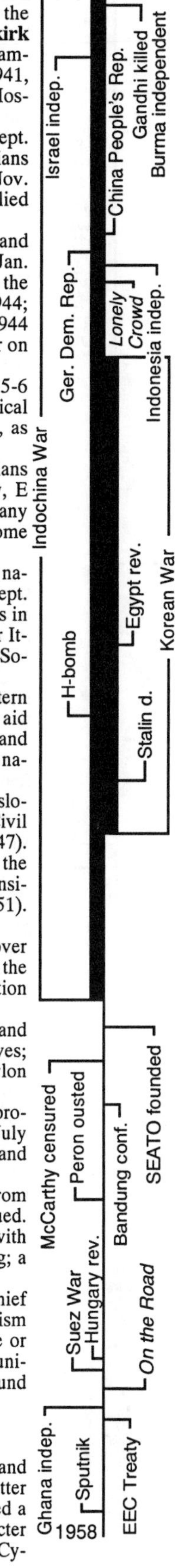

seized E Poland (Sept.), attacked Finland (Nov.), and took the Baltic states (July 1940). Mobile German forces staged *blitzkrieg* attacks during Apr.-June 1940, conquering neutral Denmark, Norway, and the Low Countries and defeating France; 350,000 British and French troops were evacuated at **Dunkirk** (May). The Battle of Britain (June-Dec. 1940) denied Germany air superiority. German-Italian campaigns won the Balkans by Apr. 1941. Three million Axis troops **invaded Russia** in June 1941, marching through Ukraine to the Caucasus, and through White Russia and the Baltic republics to Moscow and Leningrad.

Russian winter counterthrusts (1941-42 and 1942-43) stopped the German advance (Stalingrad, Sept. 1942-Feb. 1943). With British and U.S. Lend-Lease aid and sustaining great casualties, the Russians drove the Axis from all E Europe and the Balkans in the next 2 years. Invasions of N Africa (Nov. 1942), Italy (Sept. 1943), and Normandy (June 1944) brought U.S., British, Free French, and allied troops to Germany by spring 1945. Germany surrendered May 7, 1945.

War in Asia-Pacific. Japan occupied Indochina in Sept. 1940, dominated Thailand in Dec. 1941, and attacked Hawaii, the Philippines, Hong Kong, Malaya on Dec. 7, 1941. Indonesia was attacked in Jan. 1942, and Burma was conquered in Mar. 1942. The Battle of **Midway** (June 1942) turned back the Japanese advance. "Island-hopping" battles (Guadalcanal, Aug. 1942-Jan. 1943; **Leyte Gulf,** Oct. 1944; Iwo Jima, Feb.-Mar. 1945; Okinawa, Apr. 1945) and massive bombing raids on Japan from June 1944 wore out Japanese defenses. Two U.S. atom bombs, dropped Aug. 6 and 9, forced Japan to surrender on Aug. 14, 1945.

Atrocities. The war brought 20th-cent. cruelty to its peak. The Nazi regime systematically killed 5-6 million Jews, including some 3 million who died in death camps (e.g., Auschwitz). Gypsies, political opponents, sick and retarded people, and others deemed undesirable were murdered by the Nazis, as were vast numbers of Slavs, especially leaders.

Civilian deaths. German bombs killed 70,000 British civilians. Some 100,000 Chinese civilians were killed by Japanese forces in the capture of Nanking. Severe retaliation by the Soviet army, E European partisans, Free French, and others took a heavy toll. U.S. and British bombing of Germany killed hundreds of thousands, as did U.S. bombing of Japan (80,000-200,000 at Hiroshima alone). Some 45 million people lost their lives in the war.

Settlement. The United Nations charter was signed in San Francisco on June 26, 1945, by 50 nations. The International Tribunal at Nuremberg convicted 22 German leaders for war crimes in Sept. 1946; 23 Japanese leaders were convicted in Nov. 1948. Postwar border changes included large gains in territory for the USSR, losses for Germany, a shift westward in Polish borders, and minor losses for Italy. Communist regimes, supported by Soviet troops, took power in most of E Europe, including Soviet-occupied Germany (GDR proclaimed Oct. 1949). Japan lost all overseas lands.

Recovery. Basic political and social changes were imposed on Japan and W Germany by the western allies (Japan constitution adopted, Nov. 1946; W German basic law, May 1949). U.S. Marshall Plan aid ($12 billion, 1947-51) spurred W European economic recovery after a period of severe inflation and strikes in Europe and the U.S. The British Labour Party introduced a national health service and nationalized basic industries in 1946.

Cold War. Western fears of further Soviet advances (Cominform formed in Oct. 1947; Czechoslovakia coup, Feb. 1948; Berlin blockade, Apr. 1948-Sept. 1949) led to the formation of NATO. Civil War in Greece and Soviet pressure on Turkey led to U.S. aid under the Truman Doctrine (Mar. 1947). Other anti-Communist security pacts were the Organization of American States (Apr. 1948) and the Southeast Asia Treaty Organization (Sept. 1954). A new wave of Soviet purges and repression intensified in the last years of Stalin's rule, extending to E Europe (Slansky trial in Czechoslovakia, 1951). Only Yugoslavia resisted Soviet control (expelled by Cominform, June 1948; U.S. aid, June 1949).

China, Korea. Communist forces emerged from World War II strengthened by the Soviet takeover of industrial Manchuria. In 4 years of fighting, the Kuomintang was driven from the mainland; the People's Republic was proclaimed Oct. 1, 1949. Korea was divided by USSR and U.S. occupation forces. Separate republics were proclaimed in the 2 zones in Aug.-Sept. 1948.

India. India and Pakistan became independent dominions on Aug. 15, 1947. Millions of Hindu and Muslim refugees were created by the partition; riots (1946-47) took hundreds of thousands of lives; Gandhi was assassinated in Jan. 1948. Burma became completely independent in Jan. 1948; Ceylon took dominion status in Feb.

Middle East. The UN approved partition of Palestine into Jewish and Arab states. Israel was proclaimed on May 14, 1948. Arabs rejected partition, but failed to defeat Israel in war (May 1948-July 1949). Immigration from Europe and the Middle East swelled Israel's Jewish population. British and French forces left Lebanon and Syria in 1946. Transjordan occupied most of Arab Palestine.

Southeast Asia. Communists and others fought against restoration of French rule in Indochina from 1946; a non-Communist government was recognized by France in Mar. 1949, but fighting continued. Both Indonesia and the Philippines became independent; the former in 1949 after 4 years of war with Netherlands, the latter in 1946. Philippine economic and military ties with the U.S. remained strong; a Communist-led peasant rising was checked in 1948.

Arts. New York became the center of the world art market; abstract expressionism was the chief mode (Pollock from 1943, de Kooning from 1947). Literature and philosophy explored existentialism (Camus's *Stranger*, 1942; Sartre's *Being and Nothingness*, 1943). Non-Western attempts to revive or create regional styles (Senghor's Négritude, Mishima's novels) only confirmed the emergence of a universal culture. Radio and phonograph records spread American popular music (swing, bebop) around the world.

The American Decade: 1950-59

Polite decolonization. The peaceful decline of European political and military power in Asia and Africa accelerated in the 1950s. Nearly all of **N Africa** was freed by 1956, but France fought a bitter war to retain Algeria, with its large European minority, until 1962. **Ghana**, independent in 1957, led a parade of new black African nations (more than 2 dozen by 1962), which altered the political character of the UN. Ethnic disputes often exploded in the new nations after decolonization (UN troops in Cy-

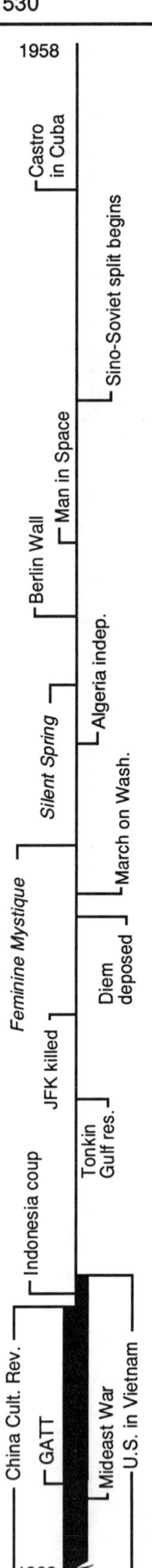

prus, 1964; **Nigeria** civil war, 1967-70). Leaders of the new states, mostly sharing socialist ideologies, tried to create an Afro-Asian bloc (Bandung Conference, 1955), but Western economic influence and U.S. political ties remained strong (Baghdad Pact, 1955).

Trade. World trade volume soared, in an atmosphere of monetary stability assured by international accords (**Bretton Woods,** 1944). In Europe, economic integration advanced (**European Economic Community,** 1957; European Free Trade Association, 1960). Comecon (1949) coordinated the economies of Soviet-bloc countries.

U.S. Economic growth produced an abundance of consumer goods (9.3 million motor vehicles sold, 1955). Suburban housing tracts changed life patterns for middle and working classes (Levittown, 1946-51). **Eisenhower's** landslide election victories (1952, 1956) reflected consensus politics. Censure of McCarthy (Dec. 1954) curbed the political abuse of anti-Communism. A system of alliances and military bases bolstered U.S. influence on all continents. Trade and payments surpluses were balanced by overseas investments and foreign aid ($50 billion, 1950-59).

USSR. In the "thaw" after Stalin's death in 1953, relations with the West improved (evacuation of Vienna, Geneva summit conference, both 1955). Repression of scientific and cultural life eased, and many prisoners were freed or rehabilitated culminating in **de-Stalinization** (1956). Khrushchev's leadership aimed at consumer sector growth, but farm production lagged, despite the virgin lands program (from 1954). The 1956 Hungarian revolution, the 1960 U-2 spy plane episode, and other incidents renewed East-West tension and domestic curbs.

East Europe. Resentment of Russian domination and Stalinist repression combined with nationalist, economic, and religious factors to produce periodic violence. East Berlin workers rioted (1953), Polish workers rioted in Poznan (June 1956), and a broad-based revolution broke out in Hungary (Oct. 1956). All were suppressed by Soviet force or threats (at least 7,000 dead in Hungary). But Poland was allowed to restore private ownership of farms, and a degree of personal and economic freedom returned to Hungary. Yugoslavia experimented with worker self-management and a market economy.

Korea. The 1945 division of Korea left industry in the N, which was organized into a militant regime and armed by the USSR. The S was politically disunited. More than 60,000 North Korean troops invaded the S on June 25, 1950. The U.S., backed by the UN Security Council, sent troops. UN troops reached the Chinese border in Nov. Some 200,000 Chinese troops crossed the Yalu R. and drove back UN forces. A cease-fire in July 1951 found the opposing forces near the original 38th parallel border. After 2 years of sporadic fighting, an armistice was signed on July 27, 1953. U.S. troops remained in the S, and U.S. economic and military aid continued. The war stimulated rapid economic recovery in Japan.

China. Starting in 1952, industry, agriculture, and social institutions were forcibly collectivized. As many as several million people were executed as Kuomintang supporters or as class and political enemies. The Great Leap Forward (1958-60) unsuccessfully tried to force the pace of development by substituting labor for investment.

Indochina. Ho Chi Minh's forces, aided by the USSR and the new Chinese Communist government, fought French and pro-French Vietnamese forces to a standstill and captured the strategic Dienbienphu camp in May 1954. The Geneva Agreements divided Vietnam in half pending elections (never held) and recognized Laos and Cambodia as independent. The U.S. aided the anti-Communist Republic of Vietnam in the S.

Middle East. Arab revolutions placed leftist, militantly nationalist regimes in power in Egypt (1952) and Iraq (1958). But Arab unity attempts failed (United Arab Republic joined Egypt, Syria, Yemen, 1958-61). Arab refusal to recognize Israel (Arab League economic blockade began Sept. 1951) led to a permanent state of war, with repeated incidents (Gaza, 1955). Israel occupied Sinai, and Britain and France took (Oct. 1956) the Suez Canal, but were replaced by the UN Emergency Force. The Mossadegh government in Iran nationalized (May 1951) the British-owned oil industry May, but was overthrown (Aug. 1953) in a U.S.-aided coup.

Latin America. Argentinian Dictator Juan Peron, in office 1946, enforced land reform, some nationalization, welfare state measures, and curbs on the Roman Catholic Church, but crushed opposition. A Sept. 1955 coup deposed Peron. The 1952 revolution in Bolivia brought land reform, nationalization of tin mines, and improvement in the status of Indians, who nevertheless remained poor. The Batista regime in Cuba was overthrown (Jan. 1959) by Fidel Castro, who imposed a Communist dictatorship, aligned Cuba with the USSR, and improved education and health care. A U.S.-backed anti-Castro invasion (Bay of Pigs, Apr. 1961) was crushed. Self-government advanced in the British Caribbean.

Technology. Large outlays on research and development in the U.S. and the USSR focused on military applications (H-bomb in U.S., 1952; USSR, 1953; Britain, 1957; intercontinental missiles, late 1950s). Soviet launching of the Sputnik satellite (Oct. 1957) spurred increases in U.S. science education funds (National Defense Education Act).

Literature and film. Alienation from social and literary conventions reached an extreme in the theater of the absurd (Beckett's *Waiting for Godot,* 1952), the "new novel" (Robbe-Grillet's *Voyeur,* 1955), and avant-garde film (Antonioni's *L'Avventura,* 1960). U.S. Beatniks (Kerouac's *On the Road,* 1957) and others rejected the supposed conformism of Americans (Riesman's *The Lonely Crowd,* 1950).

Rising Expectations: 1960-69

Economic boom. The longest sustained economic boom on record spanned almost the entire decade in the capitalist world; the closely watched GNP figure doubled (1960-70) in the U.S., fueled by Vietnam War-related budget deficits. The **General Agreement on Tariffs and Trade** (1967) stimulated W European prosperity, which spread to peripheral areas (Spain, Italy, E Germany). Japan became a top economic power ($20 billion exports in 1970). Foreign investment aided the industrialization of Brazil. Soviet 1965 economic reform attempts (decentralization, material incentives) were limited, but growth continued.

Reform and radicalization. Pres. John F. Kennedy, inaugurated 1961, emphasized youthful idealism and vigor; he was assassinated Nov. 22, 1963. A series of political and social reform movements took root in the U.S., later spreading to other countries. Blacks demonstrated nonviolently and with partial success against segregation and poverty (1963 March on Washington; 1964 **Civil Rights Act**), but some urban ghettos erupted in extensive riots (Watts, 1965; Detroit, 1967; King assassination, Apr. 4, 1968). New concern for the poor (Harrington's *Other America*, 1963) led to Pres. Johnson's **"Great Society"** programs (Medicare, Water Quality Act, Higher Education Act, all 1965). Concern with the **environment** surged (Carson's *Silent Spring*, 1962). **Feminism** revived as a cultural and political movement (Friedan's *Feminine Mystique*, 1963; National Organization for Women founded 1966) and a movement for homosexual rights emerged (Stonewall riot in NYC, 1969). Pope John XXIII called Vatican II (1962-65), which liberalized Roman Catholic liturgy.

Opposition to U.S. involvement in Vietnam, especially among university students (**Moratorium** protest, Nov. 1969), turned violent (Weatherman Chicago riots, Oct. 1969). New Left and Marxist theories became popular, and membership in radical groups swelled (Students for a Democratic Society, Black Panthers). Maoist groups, especially in Europe, called for total transformation of society. In France, students sparked a nationwide strike affecting 10 million workers in May-June 1968, but an electoral reaction barred revolutionary change.

Arts and styles. The boundary between fine and popular arts was blurred in the 1960s by Pop Art (Warhol) and rock musicals (*Hair*, 1968). Informality and exaggeration prevailed in fashion (beards, miniskirts). A nonpolitical "counterculture" developed, rejecting traditional bourgeois life goals and personal habits, and use of marijuana and hallucinogens spread (Woodstock festival, Aug. 1969). Indian influence was felt in religion (Ram Dass) and fashion and The Beatles, who brought unprecedented sophistication to rock music, became for many a symbol of the decade.

Science. Achievements in space (men on moon, July 1969) and electronics (lasers, integrated circuits) encouraged a faith in scientific solutions to problems in agriculture ("green revolution"), medicine (heart transplants, 1967), and other areas. The harmful effects of science, it was believed, could be controlled (1963 nuclear weapon test ban treaty, 1968 nonproliferation treaty).

China. Mao's revolutionary militance caused disputes with the USSR under "revisionist" Khrushchev, starting in 1960. The 2 powers exchanged fire in 1969 border disputes. China used force to capture (1962) areas disputed with India. The "Great Proletarian Cultural Revolution" tried to impose a utopian egalitarian program in China and spread revolution abroad; political struggle, often violent, convulsed China in 1965-68.

Indochina. Communist-led guerrillas aided by N Vietnam fought from 1960 against the S Vietnam government of Ngo Dinh Diem (killed 1963). The U.S. military role increased after the 1964 Tonkin Gulf incident. U.S. forces peaked at 543,400 in Apr. 1969. Massive numbers of N Vietnamese troops also fought. Laotian and Cambodian neutrality were threatened by Communist insurgencies, with N Vietnamese aid, and U.S. intrigues.

Third World. A bloc of authoritarian leftist regimes among the newly independent nations emerged in political opposition to the U.S.-led Western alliance and came to dominate the conference of non-aligned nations (Belgrade, 1961; Cairo, 1964; Lusaka, 1970). Soviet political ties and military bases were established in Cuba, Egypt, Algeria, Guinea, and other countries, whose leaders were regarded as revolutionary heroes by opposition groups in pro-Western or colonial countries. Some leaders were ousted in coups by pro-Western groups—Zaire's Lumumba (killed 1961), Ghana's Nkrumah (exiled 1966), and Indonesia's Sukarno (effectively ousted in 1965 after a Communist coup failed).

Middle East. Arab-Israeli tension erupted into a brief war June 1967. Israel emerged as a major regional power. Military shipments before and after the war brought much of the Arab world into the Soviet political sphere. Most Arab states broke U.S. diplomatic ties, while Communist countries cut their ties to Israel. Intra-Arab disputes continued: Egypt and Saudi Arabia supported rival factions in a bloody Yemen civil war 1962-70; Lebanese troops fought Palestinian commandos 1969.

East Europe. To stop the large-scale exodus of citizens, E German authorities built (Aug. 1961) a fortified wall across Berlin. Soviet sway in the Balkans was weakened by Albania's support of China (USSR broke ties in Dec. 1961) and Romania's assertion (1964) of industrial and foreign policy autonomy. Liberalization (spring 1968) in Czechoslovakia was crushed by troops of 5 Warsaw Pact countries. W German treaties (1970) with the USSR and Poland facilitated the transfer of German technology and confirmed postwar boundaries.

Disillusionment: 1970-79

U.S.: Caution and neoconservatism. A relatively sluggish economy, energy and resource shortages (natural gas crunch, 1975; gasoline shortage, 1979), and environmental problems contributed to a **"limits of growth"** philosophy. Suspicion of science and technology killed or delayed major projects (supersonic transport dropped, 1971; Seabrook nuclear power plant protests, 1977-78) and was fed by the Three Mile Island nuclear reactor accident (Mar. 1979).

Mistrust of big government weakened support for government reform plans among liberals. School busing and racial quotas were opposed (Bakke decision, June 1978); the Equal Rights Amendment for women languished; civil rights for homosexuals were opposed (Dade County referendum, June 1977).

Completion of communist forces' takeover of **S Vietnam** (evacuation of U.S. civilians, Apr. 1975), revelations of Central Intelligence Agency misdeeds (Rockefeller Commission report, June 1975), and **Watergate** scandals (Nixon resigned in Aug. 1974) reduced faith in U.S. moral and material capacity to influence world affairs. Revelations of Soviet crimes (Solzhenitsyn's *Gulag Archipelago,* 1974) and Russian intervention in Africa aided a revival of anti-Communist sentiment.

Economy sluggish. The 1960s boom faltered in the 1970s; a severe recession in the U.S. and Europe (1974-75) followed a huge oil price hike (Dec. 1973). Monetary instability (U.S. cut ties to gold in Aug. 1971), the decline of the dollar, and **protectionist** moves by industrial countries (1977-78) threatened trade. Business investment and spending for research declined. Severe inflation plagued many countries (25% in Britain, 1975; 18% in U.S., 1979).

China picks up pieces. After the 1976 deaths of Mao and Zhou, a power struggle for the leadership succession was won by pragmatists. A nationwide purge of orthodox Maoists was carried out, and the **Gang of Four** led by Mao's widow, Chiang Ching, was arrested.

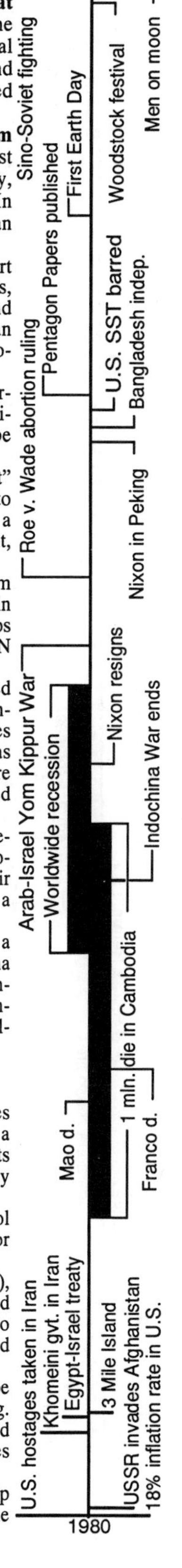

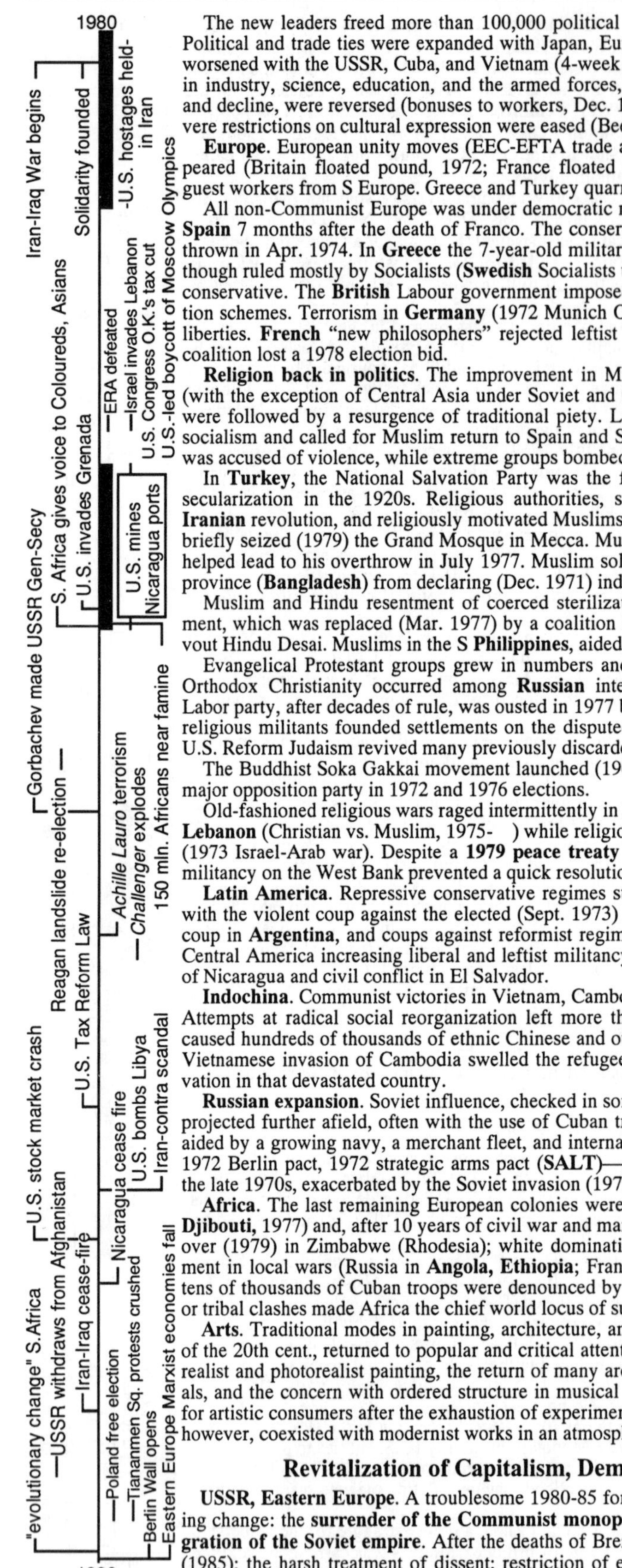

The new leaders freed more than 100,000 political prisoners and reduced public adulation of Mao. Political and trade ties were expanded with Japan, Europe, and the U.S. in the late 1970s, as relations worsened with the USSR, Cuba, and Vietnam (4-week invasion by China, 1979). Ideological guidelines in industry, science, education, and the armed forces, which the ruling faction said had caused chaos and decline, were reversed (bonuses to workers, Dec. 1977; exams for college entrance, Oct. 1977). Severe restrictions on cultural expression were eased (Beethoven ban lifted, Mar. 1977).

Europe. European unity moves (EEC-EFTA trade accord, 1972) faltered as economic problems appeared (Britain floated pound, 1972; France floated franc, 1974). Germany and Switzerland curbed guest workers from S Europe. Greece and Turkey quarreled over Cyprus and Aegean oil rights.

All non-Communist Europe was under democratic rule after free elections were held (June 1976) in **Spain** 7 months after the death of Franco. The conservative, colonialist regime in **Portugal** was overthrown in Apr. 1974. In **Greece** the 7-year-old military dictatorship yielded power in 1974. N Europe, though ruled mostly by Socialists (**Swedish** Socialists unseated in 1976 after 44 years in power), turned conservative. The **British** Labour government imposed (1975) wage curbs and suspended nationalization schemes. Terrorism in **Germany** (1972 Munich Olympics killings) led to laws curbing some civil liberties. **French** "new philosophers" rejected leftist ideologies, and the shaky Socialist-Communist coalition lost a 1978 election bid.

Religion back in politics. The improvement in Muslim countries' political fortunes by the 1950s (with the exception of Central Asia under Soviet and Chinese rule) and the growth of Arab oil wealth were followed by a resurgence of traditional piety. Libyan dictator Qaddafi mixed Islamic laws with socialism and called for Muslim return to Spain and Sicily. The illegal Muslim Brotherhood in **Egypt** was accused of violence, while extreme groups bombed (1977) theaters to protest secular values.

In **Turkey**, the National Salvation Party was the first Islamic group to share (1974) power since secularization in the 1920s. Religious authorities, such as Ayatollah Ruhollah Khomeini, led the **Iranian** revolution, and religiously motivated Muslims took part in the insurrection in Saudi Arabia that briefly seized (1979) the Grand Mosque in Mecca. Muslim puritan opposition to **Pakistan** Pres. Bhutto helped lead to his overthrow in July 1977. Muslim solidarity, however, could not prevent Pakistan's E province (**Bangladesh**) from declaring (Dec. 1971) independence after a bloody civil war.

Muslim and Hindu resentment of coerced sterilization in **India** helped defeat the Gandhi government, which was replaced (Mar. 1977) by a coalition including religious Hindu parties and led by devout Hindu Desai. Muslims in the **S Philippines**, aided by Libya, rebelled against central rule from 1973.

Evangelical Protestant groups grew in numbers and prosperity in the U.S. A revival of interest in Orthodox Christianity occurred among **Russian** intellectuals (Solzhenitsyn). The secularist **Israeli** Labor party, after decades of rule, was ousted in 1977 by conservatives led by Begin, an observant Jew; religious militants founded settlements on the disputed West Bank, part of biblically promised Israel. U.S. Reform Judaism revived many previously discarded traditional practices.

The Buddhist Soka Gakkai movement launched (1964) the Komeito party in Japan, which became a major opposition party in 1972 and 1976 elections.

Old-fashioned religious wars raged intermittently in **N Ireland** (Catholic vs. Protestant, 1969-) and **Lebanon** (Christian vs. Muslim, 1975-) while religious militancy complicated the Israel-Arab dispute (1973 Israel-Arab war). Despite a **1979 peace treaty between Egypt and Israel,** increased religious militancy on the West Bank prevented a quick resolution.

Latin America. Repressive conservative regimes strengthened their hold on most of the continent, with the violent coup against the elected (Sept. 1973) Allende government in **Chile**, the 1976 military coup in **Argentina**, and coups against reformist regimes in **Bolivia** (1971, 1979) and **Peru** (1976). In Central America increasing liberal and leftist militancy led to the ouster (1979) of the Somoza regime of Nicaragua and civil conflict in El Salvador.

Indochina. Communist victories in Vietnam, Cambodia, and Laos by May 1975 did not bring peace. Attempts at radical social reorganization left more than 1 million dead (1975-78) in Cambodia and caused hundreds of thousands of ethnic Chinese and others to flee Vietnam ("boat people," 1979). The Vietnamese invasion of Cambodia swelled the refugee population and contributed to widespread starvation in that devastated country.

Russian expansion. Soviet influence, checked in some countries (troops ousted by Egypt, 1972) was projected further afield, often with the use of Cuban troops (Angola, 1975-89; Ethiopia, 1977-88) and aided by a growing navy, a merchant fleet, and international banking ability. Détente with the West — 1972 Berlin pact, 1972 strategic arms pact (**SALT**)—gave way to a more antagonistic relationship in the late 1970s, exacerbated by the Soviet invasion (1979) of Afghanistan.

Africa. The last remaining European colonies were granted independence (**Spanish Sahara**, 1976; **Djibouti,** 1977) and, after 10 years of civil war and many negotiation sessions, a black government took over (1979) in Zimbabwe (Rhodesia); white domination remained in **S Africa**. Great power involvement in local wars (Russia in **Angola, Ethiopia**; France in **Chad, Zaire, Mauritania**) and the use of tens of thousands of Cuban troops were denounced by some African leaders as neocolonialism. Ethnic or tribal clashes made Africa the chief world locus of sustained warfare in the late 1970s.

Arts. Traditional modes in painting, architecture, and music, pursued in relative obscurity for much of the 20th cent., returned to popular and critical attention in the 1970s. The pictorial emphasis in neorealist and photorealist painting, the return of many architects to detail, decoration, and natural materials, and the concern with ordered structure in musical composition were, ironically, novel experiences for artistic consumers after the exhaustion of experimental possibilities. These more conservative styles, however, coexisted with modernist works in an atmosphere of variety and tolerance.

Revitalization of Capitalism, Demand for Democracy: 1980-89

USSR, Eastern Europe. A troublesome 1980-85 for the USSR was followed by 5 years of astonishing change: the **surrender of the Communist monopoly, remaking of the Soviet state, and disintegration of the Soviet empire**. After the deaths of Brezhnev (1982), Andropov (1984), and Chernenko (1985); the harsh treatment of dissent; restriction of emigration; and the invasion (Dec. 1979) of Afghanistan; Gen. Secy. **Mikhail Gorbachev** (in office 1985-1991) promoted **glasnost** and **pere-**

stroika—economic, political, and social reform. Supported by the Communist Party (July 1988), he signed (Dec. 1987) the **INF treaty**. Gorbachev pledged (1988) to cut the military budget; military withdrawal from Afghanistan was completed in Feb.1989; democratization was not hindered in Poland and Hungary; the Soviet people chose (Mar. 1989) part of the new Congress from competing candidates. At decade's end, Gorbachev was widely considered responsible for the **1989 ending of the Cold War**.

Poland. Solidarity, the labor union founded (1980) by **Lech Walesa**, was outlawed in 1982 and then legalized in 1988, after years of unrest. Poland's first free election since the Communist takeover brought Solidarity victory (June 1989); Tadeusz Mazowiecki, a Walesa adviser, became (Aug. 1989) prime minister in a government with the Communists.

In the fall of 1989 the failure of Marxist economies in **Hungary, E Germany, Czechoslovakia, Bulgaria, and Romania** brought the fall of the Communist monopoly and the demand for democracy. The **Berlin Wall** was opened in Nov. 1989.

U.S. "The Reagan Years" (1981-88) brought the **longest economic boom** in U.S. history via budget and tax cuts, deregulation, "junk bond" financing, leveraged buyouts, and mergers and takeovers, as well as a **strong anti-Communist stance**, via increased defense spending, aid to anti-Communists in Central America, the invasion of Cuba-threatened Grenada, and a championing of the MX missile system and "Star Wars." Four Reagan-Gorbachev summits (1985-88) climaxed in the INF treaty (1987). Financial scandals mounted (E. F. Hutton, 1985; Ivan Boesky, 1986), the stock market crashed (Oct.1987), the trade imbalance grew (especially with Japan), the budget deficit soared ($3.2 trillion in 1988); and homelessness and drug abuse (esp. "crack") grew. The Iran-contra affair (North's TV testimony, July 1987) was the low point, but Vice Pres. Bush was elected president in 1988.

Middle East. This area remained militarily unstable, with sharp divisions on economic, political, racial, and religious lines. In **Iran**, the revolution (1979-80) and violent political upheavals after, brought a strong anti-U.S. stance. In Sept. 1980, **Iraq** repudiated its border agreement with Iran and began major hostilities that led to an 8-year war in which millions were killed.

Libya's support for international terrorism caused the U.S. to close (May 1981) the diplomatic mission and embargo (Mar. 1982) oil. U.S. accused Muammar al-Qaddafi of aiding (Dec. 1985) terrorists in Rome and of Vienna airport attacks and retaliated by bombing (Apr. 1986) Libya.

Israel affirmed (July 1980) all Jerusalem as its capital, destroyed (1981) an Iraqi atomic reactor, and invaded (1982) Lebanon, forcing the PLO to agree to withdraw. A **Palestinian uprising**, including women and children hurling rocks and bottles at troops, began (Dec.1987) in Israeli-occupied Gaza and spread to the West Bank; troops responded with force, killing 300 by the end of 1988, with 6,000 more in detention camps.

Israeli withdrawal from **Lebanon** began in Feb. 1985 and ended in June 1985, as Lebanon continued torn by military and political conflict. Premier Karami was assassinated in June 1987. Artillery duels (Mar.-Apr. 1989) between Christian East Beirut and Muslim West Beirut left 200 dead and 700 wounded. At decade's end, violence still dominated.

Central America. In **Nicaragua**, the leftist Sandinista National Liberation Front, in power after the 1979 civil war, faced problems as a result of Nicaragua's military aid to leftist guerrillas in El Salvador and U.S. backing of antigovernment contras. The U.S. CIA admitted (1984) directing the mining of Nicaraguan ports, and the U.S. sent humanitarian (1985) and military (1986) aid. Profits from secret arms sales to Iran were found (1987) diverted to contras. Cease-fire talks between the Sandinista government and contras came in 1988, and elections were held in Feb. 1990.

In **El Salvador**, a military coup (Oct. 1979) failed to halt extreme right-wing violence and left-wing activity. Archbishop Oscar Romero was assassinated in Mar. 1980; from Jan. to June some 4,000 civilians reportedly were killed. In 1984, newly elected Pres. Duarte decreased rights abuses. Leftist guerrillas continued their offensive in 1989.

Africa. 1980-85 marked the rapid decline of the economies of virtually all African countries, the result of accelerating desertification, the world economic recession, heavy indebtedness to overseas creditors, rapid population growth, and political instability. Some 60 million Africans faced prolonged hunger in 1981; much of Africa had one of the worst droughts ever in 1983, and by year's end **150 million faced near-famine**. "Live Aid," a marathon rock concert, was presented in July 1985, and the U.S. and Western nations sent aid in Sept. 1985. Economic hardship fueled political unrest and coups. Wars in Ethiopia and Sudan and military strife in 6 other nations continued through 1989. AIDS took a heavy toll.

South Africa. Antiapartheid sentiment gathered force; demonstrations and violent police response grew. South African white voters approved (Nov. 1983) the first constitution to give Coloureds and Asians a voice, while still excluding blacks—70% of the population. The U.S. imposed economic sanctions in Aug. 1985, and 11 Western nations followed in Sept. **P. W. Botha**, 1980s president, was succeeded by **F. W. de Klerk**, in Sept. 1989, on a platform of "evolutionary" change via negotiation with the black population.

China. From 1980 through mid-1989 the Communist Party, under **Chairman Deng Xiaoping**, pursued **far-reaching changes** in political and economic institutions, expanding commercial and technical ties to the industrialized world and increasing the role of market forces in stimulating urban economic development. But Apr. 1989 brought the demand for more changes: students camped out in Tiananmen Sq., Beijing; some 100,000 students and workers marched, and at least 20 other cities saw protests. Martial law was imposed; army troops crushed protests in Tiananmen Sq. on June 3-4, with death toll estimates at 500-7,000, as many as 10,000 injured, as many as 10,000 dissidents arrested, and 31 tried and executed. The conciliatory Communist Party chief was ousted; the Politburo adopted (July) reforms against official corruption.

Japan. Relations with other nations, especially the U.S., were dominated (1980-89) by **trade imbalances favoring Japan**. In 1985 the U.S. trade deficit with Japan was $49.7 billion, one-third of the total U.S. trade deficit. After Japan was found (Apr. 1986) to sell semiconductors and computer memory chips below cost, the U.S. was assured a "fair share" of the market, but charged (Mar. 1987) Japan with failing to live up to the agreement. The **Omnibus Trade Bill** (Aug. 1988) provided for retaliation; Pres. Bush called Japan's practices "unjustifiable," and the law gave Japan 18 months to stop or face trade restrictions.

European Community. With the addition of Greece, Portugal, and Spain, the EC became a **common market of more than 300 million people**, the West's largest trading entity. **Margaret Thatcher** became the first British prime minister in this century to win 3 consecutive terms (1987). France elected (1981) its first socialist president, **François Mitterrand**, who was reelected in 1988. Italy elected (1983) its first socialist premier, **Bettino Craxi**.

International Terrorism. With the 1979 overthrow of the Shah of Iran, terrorism became a prominent political tactic that increased through the '80s, but with fewer high profile attacks after 1985. In 1979-81, Iranian militants held 52 Americans hostage in Iran for 444 days; in 1983 a TNT-laden suicide terrorist blew up U.S. Marine headquarters in Beirut, killing 241 Americans, and a truck bomb blew up a French paratroop barracks, killing 58. The *Achille Lauro* was hijacked (1985), an American passenger killed, and the U.S. subsequently intercepted the Egyptian plane flying the terrorists to safety. Incidents rose to 700 in 1985, and to 1,000 in 1988. The Pentagon reported (Jan. 1989) 52 terrorist groups.

Assassinations included Egypt's Pres. **Anwar al-Sadat** (1981), India's Prime Minister **Indira Gandhi** (1984), Lebanese Premier **Rashid Karami** (1987), and Pakistan's Pres. **Mohammed Zia ul-Haq** (1988).

HISTORICAL FIGURES

Ancient Greeks and Latins

Greeks

Aeschines, orator, 389-314BC.
Aeschylus, dramatist, 525-456BC.
Aesop, fableist, c620-c560BC.
Alcibiades, politician, 450-404BC.
Anacreon, poet, c582-c485BC.
Anaxagoras, philosopher, c500-428BC.
Anaximander, philosopher, 611-546BC.
Antiphon, speechwriter, c480-411BC.
Apollonius, mathematician, c265-170BC.
Archimedes, math. 287-212BC.
Aristophanes, dramatist, c448-380BC.
Aristotle, philosopher, 384-322BC.
Athenaeus, scholar, fl.c200.
Callicrates, architect, fl.5th cent.BC.
Callimachus, poet, c305-240BC.
Cratinus, comic dramatist, 520-421BC.
Democritus, philosopher, c460-370BC.
Demosthenes, orator, 384-322BC.
Diodorus, historian, fl.20BC.
Diogenes, philosopher, 372-c287BC.
Dionysius, historian, d.c7BC.
Empedocles, philosopher, c490-430BC.
Epicharmus, dramatist, c530-440BC.
Epictetus, philosopher, c55-c135.
Epicurus, philosopher, 341-270BC.
Eratosthenes, scientist, 276-194BC.
Euclid, mathematician, fl.c300BC.
Euripides, dramatist, c484-406BC.
Galen, physician, 130-200.
Heraclitus, philosopher, c535-c475BC.
Herodotus, historian, c484-420BC.
Hesiod, poet, 8th cent. BC.
Hippocrates, physician, c460-377BC.
Homer, poet, believed lived c850BC.
Isocrates, orator, 436-338BC.
Menander, dramatist, 342-292BC.
Phidias, sculptor, c500-435BC.
Pindar, poet, c518-c438BC.
Plato, philosopher, c428-347BC.
Plutarch, biographer, c46-120.
Polybius, historian, c200-c118BC.
Praxiteles, sculptor, 400-330BC.
Pythagoras, phil., math., c580-c500BC.
Sappho, poet, c610-c580BC.
Simonides, poet, 556-c468BC.
Socrates, philosopher, 469-399BC.
Solon, statesman, 640-560BC.
Sophocles, dramatist, c496-406BC.
Strabo, geographer, c63BC-AD24.
Thales, philosopher, c634-546BC.
Themistocles, politician, c524-c460BC.
Theocritus, poet, c310-250BC.
Theophrastus, phil., c372-c287BC.
Thucydides, historian, fl.5th cent.BC.
Timon, philosopher, c320-c230BC.
Xenophon, historian, c434-c355BC.
Zeno, philosopher, c495-c430BC.

Latins

Ammianus, historian, c330-395.
Apuleius, satirist, c124-c170.
Boethius, scholar, c480-524.
Caesar, Julius, leader, 100-44BC.
Catilina, politician, c108-62BC.
Cato (Elder), statesman, 234-149BC.
Catullus, poet, c84-54BC.
Cicero, orator, 106-43BC.
Claudian, poet, c370-c404.
Ennius, poet, 239-170BC.
Gellius, author, c130-c165.
Horace, poet, 65-8BC.
Juvenal, satirist, 60-127.
Livy, historian, 59BC-AD17.
Lucan, poet, 39-65.
Lucilius, poet, c180-c102BC.
Lucretius, poet, c99-c55BC.
Martial, epigrammatist, c38-c103.
Nepos, historian, c100-c25BC.
Ovid, poet, 43BC-AD17.
Persius, satirist, 34-62.
Plautus, dramatist, c254-c184BC.
Pliny, scholar, 23-79.
Pliny (Younger), author, 62-113.
Quintilian, rhetorician, c35-c97.
Sallust, historian, 86-34BC.
Seneca, philosopher, 4BC-AD65.
Silius, poet, c25-101.
Statius, poet, c45-c96.
Suetonius, biographer, c69-c122.
Tacitus, historian, 56-120.
Terence, dramatist, 185-c159BC.
Tibullus, poet, c55-c19BC.
Virgil, poet, 70-19BC.
Vitruvius, architect, fl.1st cent.BC.

Rulers of England and Great Britain

Name	England	Began	Died	Age	Rgd
	Saxons and Danes				
Egbert	King of Wessex, won allegiance of all English	**829**	**839**	—	10
Ethelwulf	Son, King of Wessex, Sussex, Kent, Essex	**839**	**858**	—	19
Ethelbald	Son of Ethelwulf, displaced father in Wessex	**858**	**860**	—	2
Ethelbert	2d son of Ethelwulf, united Kent and Wessex	**860**	**866**	—	6
Ethelred I	3d son, King of Wessex, fought Danes	**866**	**871**	—	5
Alfred	The Great, 4th son, defeated Danes, fortified London	**871**	**899**	52	28
Edward	The Elder, Alfred's son, united English, claimed Scotland	**899**	**924**	55	25
Athelstan	The Glorious, Edward's son, King of Mercia, Wessex	**924**	**940**	45	16
Edmund	3d son of Edward, King of Wessex, Mercia	**940**	**946**	25	6
Edred	4th son of Edward	**946**	**955**	32	9
Edwy	The Fair, eldest son of Edmund, King of Wessex	**955**	**959**	18	3
Edgar	The Peaceful, 2d son of Edmund, ruled all English	**959**	**975**	32	17
Edward	The Martyr, eldest son of Edgar, murdered by stepmother	**975**	**978**	17	4
Ethelred II	The Unready, 2d son of Edgar, married Emma of Normandy	**978**	**1016**	48	37
Edmund II	Ironside, son of Ethelred II, King of London	**1016**	**1016**	27	0
Canute	The Dane, gave Wessex to Edmund, married Emma	**1016**	**1035**	40	19
Harold I	Harefoot, natural son of Canute	**1035**	**1040**	—	5
Hardecanute	Son of Canute by Emma, Danish King	**1040**	**1042**	24	2
Edward	The Confessor, son of Ethelred II (Canonized 1161)	**1042**	**1066**	62	24
Harold II	Edward's brother-in-law, last Saxon King	**1066**	**1066**	44	0
	House of Normandy				
William I	The Conqueror, defeated Harold at Hastings	**1066**	**1087**	60	21
William II	Rufus, 3d son of William I, killed by arrow	**1087**	**1100**	43	13
Henry I	Beauclerc, youngest son of William I	**1100**	**1135**	67	35
	House of Blois				
Stephen	Son of Adela, daughter of William I, and Count of Blois	**1135**	**1154**	50	19
	House of Plantagenet				
Henry II	Son of Geoffrey Plantagenet (Angevin) by Matilda, dau. of Henry I	**1154**	**1189**	56	35
Richard I	Coeur de Lion, son of Henry II, crusader	**1189**	**1199**	42	10
John	Lackland, son of Henry II, signed Magna Carta, 1215	**1199**	**1216**	50	17
Henry III	Son of John, acceded at 9, under regency until 1227	**1216**	**1272**	65	56
Edward I	Longshanks, son of Henry III	**1272**	**1307**	68	35
Edward II	Son of Edward I, deposed by Parliament, 1327	**1307**	**1327**	43	20
Edward III	Of Windsor, son of Edward II	**1327**	**1377**	65	50
Richard II	Grandson of Edw. III, minor until 1389, deposed 1399	**1377**	**1400**	33	22
	House of Lancaster				
Henry IV	Son of John of Gaunt, Duke of Lancaster, son of Edw. III	**1399**	**1413**	47	13
Henry V	Son of Henry IV, victor of Agincourt	**1413**	**1422**	34	9
Henry VI	Son of Henry V, deposed 1461, died in Tower	**1422**	**1471**	49	39

Name		Began	Died	Age	Rgd
	House of York				
Edward IV	Great-great-grandson of Edward III, son of Duke of York	**1461**	**1483**	41	22
Edward V	Son of Edward IV, murdered in Tower of London	**1483**	**1483**	13	0
Richard III	Crookback, bro. of Edward IV, fell at Bosworth Field	**1483**	**1485**	35	2
	House of Tudor				
Henry VII	Son of Edmund Tudor, Earl of Richmond, whose father had married the widow of Henry V; descended from Edward III through his mother, Margaret Beaufort via John of Gaunt. By marriage with dau. of Edward IV he united Lancaster and York	**1485**	**1509**	53	24
Henry VIII	Son of Henry VII by Elizabeth, dau. of Edward IV	**1509**	**1547**	56	38
Edward VI	Son of Henry VIII, by Jane Seymour, his 3d queen. Ruled under regents. Was forced to name Lady Jane Grey his successor. Council of State proclaimed her queen July 10, 1553. Mary Tudor won Council, was proclaimed queen July 19, 1553. Mary had Lady Jane Grey beheaded for treason, Feb., 1554	**1547**	**1553**	16	6
Mary I	Daughter of Henry VIII, by Catherine of Aragon	**1553**	**1558**	43	5
Elizabeth I	Daughter of Henry VIII, by Anne Boleyn	**1558**	**1603**	69	44

Great Britain

Name		Began	Died	Age	Rgd
	House of Stuart				
James I	James VI of Scotland, son of Mary, Queen of Scots. *First to call himself King of Great Britain. This became official with the Act of Union, 1707.*	**1603**	**1625**	59	22
Charles I	Only surviving son of James I; beheaded Jan. 30, 1649	**1625**	**1649**	48	24
	Commonwealth, 1649-1660				
	Council of State, 1649; Protectorate, 1653				
The Cromwells	Oliver Cromwell, Lord Protector	**1653**	**1658**	59	—
	Richard Cromwell, son, Lord Protector, resigned May 25, 1659	**1658**	**1712**	86	—
	House of Stuart (Restored)				
Charles II	Eldest son of Charles I, died without issue	**1660**	**1685**	55	25
James II	2d son of Charles I. Deposed 1688. Interregnum Dec. 11, 1688, to Feb. 13, 1689	**1685**	**1701**	68	3
William III	Son of William, Prince of Orange, by Mary, dau. of Charles I	**1689**	**1702**	51	13
and Mary II	Eldest daughter of James II and wife of William III		**1694**	33	6
Anne	2d daughter of James II	**1702**	**1714**	49	12
	House of Hanover				
George I	Son of Elector of Hanover, by Sophia, grand-dau. of James I	**1714**	**1727**	67	13
George II	Only son of George I, married Caroline of Brandenburg	**1727**	**1760**	77	33
George III	Grandson of George II, married Charlotte of Mecklenburg	**1760**	**1820**	81	59
George IV	Eldest son of George III, Prince Regent, from Feb., 1811	**1820**	**1830**	67	10
William IV	3d son of George III, married Adelaide of Saxe-Meiningen	**1830**	**1837**	71	7
Victoria	Dau. of Edward, 4th son of George III; married (1840) Prince Albert of Saxe-Coburg and Gotha, who became Prince Consort	**1837**	**1901**	81	63
	House of Saxe-Coburg and Gotha				
Edward VII	Eldest son of Victoria, married Alexandra, Princess of Denmark	**1901**	**1910**	68	9
	House of Windsor				
	Name Adopted July 17, 1917				
George V	2d son of Edward VII, married Princess Mary of Teck	**1910**	**1936**	70	25
Edward VIII	Eldest son of George V; acceded Jan. 20, 1936, abdicated Dec. 11	**1936**	**1972**	77	1
George VI	2d son of George V; married Lady Elizabeth Bowes-Lyon	**1936**	**1952**	56	15
Elizabeth II	Elder daughter of George VI, acceded Feb. 6, 1952	**1952**	**—**	—	—

Rulers of Scotland

Kenneth I MacAlpin was the first Scot to rule both Scots and Picts, 846 AD.

Duncan I was the first general ruler, 1034. Macbeth seized the kingdom 1040, was slain by Duncan's son, Malcolm III MacDuncan (Canmore), 1057.

Malcolm married Margaret, Saxon princess who had fled from the Normans. Queen Margaret introduced English language and English monastic customs. She was canonized, 1250. Her son Edgar, 1097, moved the court to Edinburgh. His brothers Alexander I and David I succeeded. Malcolm IV, the Maiden, 1153, grandson of David I, was followed by his brother, William the Lion, 1165, whose son was Alexander II, 1214. The latter's son, Alexander III, 1249, defeated the Norse and regained the Hebrides. When he died, 1286, his granddaughter, Margaret, child of Eric of Norway and grandniece of Edward I of England, known as the Maid of Norway, was chosen ruler, but died 1290, aged 8.

John Baliol, 1292-1296. (Interregnum, 10 years).

Robert Bruce (The Bruce), 1306-1329, victor at Bannockburn, 1314.

David II, only son of Robert Bruce, ruled 1329-1371.

Robert II, 1371-1390, grandson of Robert Bruce, son of Walter, the Steward of Scotland, was called The Steward, first of the so-called Stuart line.

Robert III, son of Robert II, 1390-1406.

James I, son of Robert III, 1406-1437.

James II, son of James I, 1437-1460.

James III, eldest son of James II, 1460-1488.

James IV, eldest son of James III, 1488-1513.

James V, eldest son of James IV, 1513-1542.

Mary, daughter of James V, born 1542, became queen when one week old; was crowned 1543. Married, 1558, Francis, son of Henry II of France, who became king 1559, died 1560. Mary ruled Scots 1561 until abdication, 1567. She also married (2) Henry Stewart, Lord Darnley, and (3) James, Earl of Bothwell. Imprisoned by Elizabeth I, Mary was beheaded 1587.

James VI, 1566-1625, son of Mary and Lord Darnley, became King of England on death of Elizabeth in 1603. Although the thrones were thus united, the legislative union of Scotland and England was not effected until the Act of Union, May 1, 1707.

Prime Ministers of Great Britain

(W=Whig; T=Tory; Cl=Coalition; P=Peelite; L=Liberal; C=Conservative; La=Labour)

Sir Robert Walpole (W)	1721-1742
Earl of Wilmington (W)	1742-1743
Henry Pelham (W)	1743-1754
Duke of Newcastle (W)	1754-1756
Duke of Devonshire (W)	1756-1757
Duke of Newcastle (W)	1757-1762
Earl of Bute (T)	1762-1763
George Grenville (W)	1763-1765
Marquess of Rockingham (W)	1765-1766
William Pitt the Elder (Earl of Chatham) (W)	1766-1768
Duke of Grafton (W)	1768-1770
Frederick North (Lord North) (T)	1770-1782
Marquess of Rockingham (W)	1782
Earl of Shelburne (W)	1782-1783
Duke of Portland (Cl)	1783
William Pitt the Younger (T)	1783-1801
Henry Addington (T)	1801-1804
William Pitt the Younger (T)	1804-1806
William Wyndham Grenville, Baron Grenville (W)	1806-1807
Duke of Portland (T)	1807-1809
Spencer Perceval (T)	1809-1812
Earl of Liverpool (T)	1812-1827
George Canning (T)	1827
Viscount Goderich (T)	1827-1828
Duke of Wellington (T)	1828-1830
Earl Grey (W)	1830-1834
Viscount Melbourne (W)	1834
Sir Robert Peel (T)	1834-1835
Viscount Melbourne (W)	1835-1841
Sir Robert Peel (T)	1841-1846
Lord John Russell (later Earl) (W)	1846-1852
Earl of Derby (T)	1852
Earl of Aberdeen (P)	1852-1855
Viscount Palmerston (L)	1855-1858
Earl of Derby (C)	1858-1859
Viscount Palmerston (L)	1859-1865
Earl Russell (L)	1865-1866
Earl of Derby (C)	1866-1868
Benjamin Disraeli (C)	1868
William E. Gladstone (L)	1868-1874
Benjamin Disraeli (C)	1874-1880
William E. Gladstone (L)	1880-1885
Marquess of Salisbury(C)	1885-1886
William E. Gladstone (L)	1886
Marquess of Salisbury(C)	1886-1892
William E. Gladstone (L)	1892-1894
Earl of Rosebery (L)	1894-1895
Marquess of Salisbury(C)	1895-1902
Arthur J. Balfour (C)	1902-1905
Sir Henry Campbell-Bannerman (L)	1905-1908
Herbert H. Asquith (L)	1908-1915
Herbert H. Asquith (Cl)	1915-1916
David Lloyd George (Cl)	1916-1922
Andrew Bonar Law (C)	1922-1923
Stanley Baldwin (C)	1923-1924
James Ramsay MacDonald (La)	1924
Stanley Baldwin (C)	1924-1929
James Ramsay MacDonald (La)	1929-1931
James Ramsay MacDonald (Cl)	1931-1935
Stanley Baldwin (Cl)	1935-1937
Neville Chamberlain (Cl)	1937-1940
Winston Churchill (Cl)	1940-1945
Winston Churchill (C)	1945
Clement Attlee (La)	1945-1951
Sir Winston Churchill (C)	1951-1955
Sir Anthony Eden (C)	1955-1957
Harold Macmillan (C)	1957-1963
Sir Alec Douglas-Home (C)	1963-1964
Harold Wilson (La)	1964-1970
Edward Heath (C)	1970-1974
Harold Wilson (La)	1974-1976
James Callaghan (La)	1976-1979
Margaret Thatcher (C)	1979-1990
John Major (C)	1990-

Historical Periods of Japan

Yamato	c.300-592	Conquest of Yamato plain c. 300 AD.
Asuka	592-710	Accession of Empress Suiko, 592.
Nara	710-794	Completion of Heijo (Nara), 710; capital moves to Nagaoka, 784.
Heian	794-1185	Completion of Heian (Kyoto), 794.
Fujiwara	858-1160	Fujiwara-no-Yoshifusa becomes regent, 858.
Taira	1160-1185	Taira-no-Kiyomori assumes control, 1160; Minamoto-no-Yoritomo victor over Taira, 1185.
Kamakura	1192-1333	Yoritomo becomes shogun, 1192.
Namboku	1334-1392	Restoration of Emperor Godaigo, 1334; Southern Court established by Godaigo at Yoshino, 1336.
Ashikaga	1338-1573	Ashikaga Takauji becomes shogun, 1338.
Muromachi	1392-1573	Unification of Southern and Northern Courts, 1392.
Sengoku	1467-1600	Beginning of the Onin war, 1467.
Momoyama	1573-1603	Oda Nobunaga enters Kyoto, 1568; Nobunaga deposes last Ashikaga shogun, 1573; Tokugawa Ieyasu victor at Sekigahara, 1600.
Edo	1603-1867	Ieyasu becomes shogun, 1603.
Meiji	1868-1912	Enthronement of Emperor Mutsuhito (Meiji), 1867; Meiji Restoration and Charter Oath, 1868.
Taisho	1912-1926	Accession of Emperor Yoshihito, 1912.
Showa	1926-1989	Accession of Emperor Hirohito, 1926.
Heisei	1989-	Accession of Emperor Akihito, 1989.

Rulers of France: Kings, Queens, Presidents

Caesar to Charlemagne

Julius Caesar subdued the Gauls, native tribes of Gaul (France) 58 to 51 BC. The Romans ruled 500 years. The Franks, a Teutonic tribe, reached the Somme from the East ca. 250 AD. By the 5th century the Merovingian Franks ousted the Romans. In 451 AD, with the help of Visigoths, Burgundians and others, they defeated Attila and the Huns at Chalons-sur-Marne.

Childeric I became leader of the Merovingians 458 AD. His son Clovis I (Chlodwig, Ludwig, Louis), crowned 481, founded the dynasty. After defeating the Alemanni (Germans) 496, he was baptized a Christian and made Paris his capital. His line ruled until Childeric III was deposed, 751.

The West Merovingians were called Neustrians, the eastern Austrasians. Pepin of Herstal (687-714), major domus, or head of the palace, of Austrasia, took over Neustria as dux (leader) of the Franks. Pepin's son, Charles, called Martel (the Hammer), defeated the Saracens at Tours-Poitiers, 732; was succeeded by his son, Pepin the Short, 741, who deposed Childeric III and ruled as king until 768.

His son, Charlemagne, or Charles the Great (742-814) became king of the Franks, 768, with his brother Carloman, who died 771. He ruled France, Germany, parts of Italy, Spain, Austria, and enforced Christianity. Crowned Emperor of the Romans by Pope Leo III in St. Peter's, Rome, Dec. 25, 800 AD. Succeeded by son, Louis I the Pious, 814. At death, 840, Louis left empire to sons, Lothair (Roman emperor); Pepin I (king of Aquitaine); Louis II (of Germany); Charles the Bald (France). They quarreled and by the peace of Verdun, 843, divided the empire.

Date in bold is year of accession.

The Carolingians

843 Charles I (the Bald); Roman Emperor, 875
877 Louis II (the Stammerer), son
879 Louis III (died 882) and Carloman, brothers
885 Charles II (the Fat); Roman Emperor, 881
888 Eudes (Odo), elected by nobles
898 Charles III (the Simple), son of Louis II, defeated by
922 Robert, brother of Eudes, killed in war
923 Rudolph (Raoul), Duke of Burgundy
936 Louis IV, son of Charles III
954 Lothair, son, aged 13, defeated by Capet
986 Louis V (the Sluggard), left no heirs

The Capets

987 Hugh Capet, son of Hugh the Great
996 Robert II (the Wise), his son
1031 Henry I, his son
1060 Philip I (the Fair), son
1108 Louis VI (the Fat), son
1137 Louis VII (the Younger), son
1180 Philip II (Augustus), son, crowned at Reims
1223 Louis VIII (the Lion), son
1226 Louis IX, son, crusader; Louis IX (1214-1270) reigned 44 years, arbitrated disputes with English King Henry III; led crusades, 1248 (captured in Egypt 1250) and 1270, when he died of plague in Tunis. Canonized 1297 as St. Louis.
1270 Philip III (the Hardy), son
1285 Philip IV (the Fair), son, king at 17
1314 Louis X (the Headstrong), son. His posthumous son, John I, lived only 7 days
1316 Philip V (the Tall), brother of Louis X
1322 Charles IV (the Fair), brother of Louis X

House of Valois

1328 Philip VI (of Valois), grandson of Philip III
1350 John II (the Good), his son, retired to England
1364 Charles V (the Wise), son
1380 Charles VI (the Beloved), son
1422 Charles VII (the Victorious), son. In 1429 Joan of Arc (Jeanne d'Arc) promised Charles to oust the English, who occupied northern France. Joan won at Orleans and Patay and had Charles crowned at Reims July 17, 1429. Joan was captured May 24, 1430, and executed May 30, 1431, at Rouen for heresy. Charles ordered her rehabilitation, effected 1455.
1461 Louis XI (the Cruel), son, civil reformer
1483 Charles VIII (the Affable), son
1498 Louis XII, great-grandson of Charles V
1515 Francis I, of Angouleme, nephew, son-in-law. Francis I (1494-1547) reigned 32 years, fought 4 big wars, was patron of the arts, aided Cellini, del Sarto, Leonardo da Vinci, Rabelais, embellished Fontainebleau.
1547 Henry II, son, killed at a joust in a tournament. He was the husband of Catherine de Medicis (1519-1589) and the lover of Diane de Poitiers (1499-1566). Catherine was born in Florence, daughter of Lorenzo de Medici. By her marriage to Henry II she became the mother of Francis II, Charles IX, Henry III and Queen Margaret (Reine Margot), wife of Henry IV. She persuaded Charles IX to order the massacre of Huguenots on the Feast of St. Bartholomew, Aug. 24, 1572, the day her daughter was married to Henry of Navarre.
1559 Francis II, son. In 1548, Mary, Queen of Scots since infancy, was betrothed when 6 to Francis, aged 4. They were married 1558. Francis died 1560, aged 16; Mary ruled Scotland, abdicated 1567.
1560 Charles IX, brother
1574 Henry III, brother, assassinated

House of Bourbon

1589 Henry IV, of Navarre, assassinated. Henry IV made enemies when he gave tolerance to Protestants by Edict of Nantes, 1598. He was grandson of Queen Margaret of Navarre, literary patron. He married Margaret of Valois, daughter of Henry II and Catherine de Medicis; was divorced; in 1600 married Marie de Medicis, who became Regent of France, 1610-17, for her son, Louis XIII, but was exiled by Richelieu, 1631.
1610 Louis XIII (the Just), son. Louis XIII (1601-1643) married Anne of Austria. His ministers were Cardinals Richelieu and Mazarin.
1643 Louis XIV (The Grand Monarch), son. Louis XIV was king 72 years. He exhausted a prosperous country in wars for thrones and territory. By revoking the Edict of Nantes (1685) he caused the emigration of the Huguenots. He said: "I am the state."
1715 Louis XV, great-grandson. Louis XV married a Polish princess; lost Canada to the English. His favorites, Mme. Pompadour and Mme. Du Barry, influenced policies. Noted for saying "After me, the deluge".
1774 Louis XVI, grandson; married Marie Antoinette, daughter of Empress Maria Therese of Austria. King and queen beheaded by Revolution, 1793. Their son, called Louis XVII, died in prison, never ruled.

First Republic

1792 National Convention of the French Revolution
1795 Directory, under Barras and others
1799 Consulate, Napoleon Bonaparte, first consul. Elected consul for life, 1802.

First Empire

1804 Napoleon I, emperor. Josephine (de Beauharnais), empress, 1804-09; Marie Louise, empress, 1810-1814. Her son, Francois (1811-1832), titular King of Rome, later Duke de Reichstadt and "Napoleon II," never ruled. Napoleon abdicated 1814, died 1821.

Bourbons Restored

1814 Louis XVIII king; brother of Louis XVI
1824 Charles X, brother; reactionary; deposed by the July Revolution, 1830

House of Orleans

1830 Louis-Philippe, the "citizen king"

Second Republic

1848 Louis Napoleon Bonaparte, president, nephew of Napoleon I. He became:

Second Empire

1852 Napoleon III, emperor; Eugenie (de Montijo), empress. Lost Franco-Prussian war, deposed 1870. Son, Prince Imperial (1856-79), died in Zulu War. Eugenie died 1920.

Third Republic—Presidents

1871 Thiers, Louis Adolphe (1797-1877)
1873 MacMahon, Marshal Patrice M. de (1808-1893)
1879 Grevy, Paul J. (1807-1891)
1887 Sadi-Carnot, M. (1837-1894), assassinated
1894 Casimir-Perier, Jean P. P. (1847-1907)
1895 Faure, François Felix (1841-1899)
1899 Loubet, Emile (1838-1929)
1906 Fallieres, C. Armand (1841-1931)
1913 Poincare, Raymond (1860-1934)
1920 Deschanel, Paul (1856-1922)
1920 Millerand, Alexandre (1859-1943)
1924 Doumergue, Gaston (1863-1937)
1931 Doumer, Paul (1857-1932), assassinated
1932 Lebrun, Albert (1871-1950), resigned 1940
1940 **Vichy govt.** under German armistice: Henri Philippe Petain (1856-1951), Chief of State, 1940-1944.
Provisional govt. after liberation: Charles de Gaulle (1890-1970) Oct. 1944-Jan. 21, 1946; Felix Gouin (1884-1977) Jan. 23, 1946; Georges Bidault (1899-1983) June 24, 1946.

Fourth Republic—Presidents

1947 Auriol, Vincent (1884-1966)
1954 Coty, Rene (1882-1962)

Fifth Republic—Presidents

1959 de Gaulle, Charles Andre J. M. (1890-1970)
1969 Pompidou, Georges (1911-1974)
1974 Giscard d'Estaing, Valery (1926-)
1981 Mitterrand, François (1916-)

Rulers of Middle Europe; Rise and Fall of Dynasties

Carolingian Dynasty

Charles the Great, or Charlemagne, ruled France, Italy, and Middle Europe; established Ostmark (later Austria); crowned Roman emperor by pope in Rome, 800 AD; died 814.

Louis I (Ludwig) the Pious, son; crowned by Charlemagne 814; died 840.

Louis II, the German, son; succeeded to East Francia (Germany) 843-876.

Charles the Fat, son; inherited East Francia and West Francia (France) 876, reunited empire, crowned emperor by pope, 881, deposed 887.

Arnulf, nephew, 887-899. Partition of empire.

Louis the Child, 899-911, last direct descendant of Charlemagne.

Conrad I, duke of Franconia, first elected German king, 911-918, founded House of Franconia.

Saxon Dynasty; First Reich

Henry I, the Fowler, duke of Saxony, 919-936.

Otto I, the Great, 936-973, son; crowned Holy Roman Emperor by pope, 962.

Otto II, 973-983, son; failed to oust Greeks and Arabs from Sicily.

Otto III, 983-1002, son; crowned emperor at 16.

Henry II, the Saint, duke of Bavaria, 1002-1024, great-grandson of Otto the Great.

House of Franconia

Conrad II, 1024-1039, elected king of Germany.

Henry III, the Black, 1039-1056, son; deposed 3 popes; annexed Burgundy.

Henry IV, 1056-1106, son; regency by his mother, Agnes of Poitou. Banned by Pope Gregory VII, he did penance at Canossa.

Henry V, 1106-1125, son; last of Salic House.

Lothair, duke of Saxony, 1125-1137. Crowned emperor in Rome, 1134.

House of Hohenstaufen

Conrad III, duke of Swabia, 1138-1152. In 2d Crusade.

Frederick I, Barbarossa, 1152-1190; Conrad's nephew.

Henry VI, 1190-1196, took lower Italy from Normans. Son became king of Sicily.

Philip of Swabia, 1197-1208, brother.

Otto IV, of House of Welf, 1198-1215; deposed.

Frederick II, 1215-1250, son of Henry VI; king of Sicily; crowned king of Jerusalem in 5th Crusade.

Conrad IV, 1250-1254, son; lost lower Italy to Charles of Anjou.

Conradin, 1252-1268, son, king of Jerusalem and Sicily, beheaded. Last Hohenstaufen.

Interregnum, 1254-1273, Rise of the Electors.

Transition

Rudolph I of Hapsburg, 1273-1291, defeated King Ottocar II of Bohemia. Bequeathed duchy of Austria to eldest son, Albert.

Adolph of Nassau, 1292-1298, killed in war with Albert of Austria.

Albert I, king of Germany, 1298-1308, son of Rudolph.

Henry VII, of Luxemburg, 1308-1313, crowned emperor in Rome. Seized Bohemia, 1310.

Louis IV of Bavaria (Wittelsbach), 1314-1347. Also elected was Frederick of Austria, 1314-1330 (Hapsburg). Abolition of papal sanction for election of Holy Roman Emperor.

Charles IV, of Luxemburg, 1347-1378, grandson of Henry VII, German emperor and king of Bohemia, Lombardy, Burgundy; took Mark of Brandenburg.

Wenceslaus, 1378-1400, deposed.

Rupert, Duke of Palatine, 1400-1410.

Sigismund, 1411-1437.

Hungary

Stephen I, house of Arpad, 997-1038. Crowned king 1000; converted Magyars; canonized 1083. After several centuries of feuds Charles Robert of Anjou became Charles I, 1308-1342.

Louis I, the Great, son, 1342-1382; joint ruler of Poland with Casimir III, 1370. Defeated Turks.

Mary, daughter, 1382-1395, ruled with husband. Sigismund of Luxemburg, 1387-1437, also king of Bohemia. As bro. of Wenceslaus he succeeded Rupert as Holy Roman Emperor, 1410.

Albert, 1438-1439, son-in-law of Sigismund; also Roman emperor as Albert II. *(see under Hapsburg)*

Ulaszlo I of Poland, 1440-1444.

Ladislaus V, posthumous son of Albert II, 1444-1457. John Hunyadi (Hunyadi Janos), governor (1446-1452), fought Turks, Czechs; died 1456.

Matthias I (Corvinus), son of Hunyadi, 1458-1490. Shared rule of Bohemia, captured Vienna, 1485, annexed Austria, Styria, Carinthia.

Ulaszlo II (king of Bohemia), 1490-1516.

Louis II, son, aged 10, 1516-1526. Wars with Suleiman, Turk. In 1527 Hungary was split between Ferdinand I, Archduke of Austria, bro.-in-law of Louis II, and John Zapolya of Transylvania. After Turkish invasion, 1547, Hungary was split between Ferdinand, Prince John Sigismund (Transylvania) and the Turks.

House of Hapsburg

Albert V of Austria, Hapsburg, crowned king of Hungary, Jan. 1438, Roman emperor, March 1438, as Albert II; died 1439.

Frederick III, cousin, 1440-1493. Fought Turks.

Maximilian I, son, 1493-1519. Assumed title of Holy Roman Emperor (German), 1493.

Charles V, grandson, 1519-1556. King of Spain with mother co-regent; crowned Roman emperor at Aix, 1520. Confronted Luther at Worms; attempted church reform and religious conciliation; abdicated 1556.

Ferdinand I, king of Bohemia, 1526, of Hungary, 1527; disputed. German king, 1531. Crowned Roman emperor on abdication of brother Charles V, 1556.

Maximilian II, son, 1564-1576.

Rudolph II, son, 1576-1612.

Matthias, brother, 1612-1619, king of Bohemia and Hungary.

Ferdinand II of Styria, king of Bohemia, 1617, of Hungary, 1618, Roman emperor, 1619. Bohemian Protestants deposed him, elected Frederick V of Palatine, starting Thirty Years War.

Ferdinand III, son, king of Hungary, 1625, Bohemia, 1627, Roman emperor, 1637. Peace of Westphalia, 1648, ended war. Leopold I, 1658-1705; Joseph I, 1705-1711; Charles VI, 1711-1740.

Maria Theresa, daughter, 1740-1780, Archduchess of Austria, queen of Hungary; ousted pretender, Charles VII, crowned 1742; in 1745 obtained election of her husband Francis I as Roman emperor and co-regent (d. 1765). Fought Seven Years' War with Frederick II (the Great) of Prussia. Mother of Marie Antoinette, Queen of France.

Joseph II, son, 1765-1790, Roman emperor, reformer; powers restricted by Empress Maria Theresa until her death, 1780. First partition of Poland. Leopold II, 1790-1792.

Francis II, son, 1792-1835. Fought Napoleon. Proclaimed first hereditary emperor of Austria, 1804. Forced to abdicate as Roman emperor, 1806; last use of title. Ferdinand I, son, 1835-1848, abdicated during revolution.

Austro-Hungarian Monarchy

Francis Joseph I, nephew, 1848-1916, emperor of Austria, king of Hungary. Dual monarchy of Austria-Hungary formed, 1867. After assassination of heir, Archduke Francis Ferdinand, June 28, 1914, Austrian diplomacy precipitated World War I.

Charles I, grand-nephew, 1916-1918, last emperor of Austria and king of Hungary. Abdicated Nov. 11-13, 1918, died 1922.

Rulers of Prussia

Nucleus of Prussia was the Mark of Brandenburg. First margrave was Albert the Bear (Albrecht), 1134-1170. First Hohenzollern margrave was Frederick, burgrave of Nuremberg, 1417-1440.

Frederick William, 1640-1688, the Great Elector. Son, Frederick III, 1688-1713, was crowned King Frederick of Prussia, 1701.

Frederick William I, son, 1713-1740.

Frederick II, the Great, son, 1740-1786, annexed Silesia, part of Austria.

Frederick William II, nephew, 1786-1797.

Frederick William III, son, 1797-1840. Napoleonic wars.

Frederick William IV, son, 1840-1861. Uprising of 1848 and first parliament and constitution.

Second and Third Reich

William I, 1861-1888, brother. Annexation of Schleswig and Hanover; Franco-Prussian war, 1870-71, proclamation of German Reich, Jan. 18, 1871, at Versailles; William, German emperor (Deutscher Kaiser), Bismarck, chancellor.

Frederick III, son, 1888.

William II, son, 1888-1918. Led Germany in World War I, abdicated as German emperor and king of Prussia, Nov. 9, 1918. Died in exile in Netherlands June 4, 1941. Minor rulers of Bavaria, Saxony, Wurttemberg also abdicated.

Germany proclaimed republic at Weimar, July 1, 1919. Presidents: Frederick Ebert, 1919-1925; Paul von Hindenburg-Beneckendorff, 1925, reelected 1932, d. Aug. 2, 1934. Adolf Hitler, chancellor, chosen successor as Leader-Chancellor (Fuehrer-Reichskanzler) of Third Reich. Annexed Austria, March, 1938. Precipitated World War II, 1939-1945. Suicide April 30, 1945.

Rulers of Poland

House of Piasts

Miesko I, 962?-992; Poland Christianized 966. Expansion under 3 Boleslavs: I, 992-1025, son, crowned king 1024; II, 1058-1079, great-grandson, exiled after killing bishop Stanislav who became chief patron saint of Poland; III, 1106-1138, nephew, divided Poland among 4 sons, eldest suzerain.

1138-1306, feudal division. 1226 founding in Prussia of military order Teutonic Knights. 1226 invasion by Tartars/Mongols.

Vladislav I, 1306-1333, reunited most Polish territories, crowned king 1320. Casimir III the Great, 1333-1370, son, developed economic, cultural life, foreign policy.

House of Anjou

Louis I, 1370-1382, nephew/identical with Louis I of Hungary.

Jadwiga, 1384-1399, daughter, married 1386 Jagiello, Grand Duke of Lituania.

House of Jagelloneans

Vladislav II, 1386-1434, Christianized Lituania, founded personal union between Poland & Lituania. Defeated 1410 Teutonic Knights at Grunwald.

Vladislav III, 1434-1444, son, simultaneously king of Hungary. Fought Turks, killed 1444 in battle of Varna.

Casimir IV, 1446-1492, brother, competed with Hapsburgs, put son Vladislav on throne of Bohemia, later also of Hungary.

Sigismund I, 1506-1548, brother, patronized science & arts, his & son's reign "Golden Age."

Sigismund II, 1548-1572, son, established 1569 real union of Poland and Lituania (lasted until 1795).

Elective kings

Polish nobles proclaimed 1572 Poland a Republic headed by king to be elected by whole nobility.

Stephen Batory, 1576-1586, duke of Transylvania, married Ann, sister of Sigismund II August. Fought Russians.

Sigismund III Vasa, 1587-1632, nephew of Sigismund II. 1592-1598 also king of Sweden. His generals fought Russians, Turks.

Vladislav II Vasa, 1632-1648, son. Fought Russians.

John II Casimir Vasa, 1648-1668, brother. Fought Cossacks, Swedes, Russians, Turks, Tartars (the "Deluge"). Abdicated 1668.

John III Sobieski, 1674-1696. Won Vienna from besieging Turks, 1683.

Stanislav II, 1764-1795, last king. Encouraged reforms; 1791 1st modern Constitution in Europe. 1772, 1793, 1795 Poland partitioned among Russia, Prussia, Austria. Unsuccessful insurrection against foreign invasion 1794 under Kosciuszko, Amer.-Polish gen.

1795-1918 Poland under foreign rule

1807-1815 Grand Duchy of Warsaw created by Napoleon I, Frederick August of Saxony grand duke.

1815 Congress of Vienna proclaimed part of Poland "Kingdom" in personal union with Russia.

Polish uprisings: 1830 against Russia, 1846, 1848 against Austria, 1863 against Russia—all repressed.

1918-1939 Second Republic

1918-1922 Head of State Jozef Pilsudski. Presidents: Gabriel Narutowicz 1922, assassinated. Stanislav Wojciechowski 1922-1926, had to abdicate after Pilsudski's coup d'état. Ignacy Moscicki, 1926-1939, ruled with Pilsudski as (until 1935) virtual dictator.

1939-1945 Poland under foreign occupation

Nazi aggression Sept. 1939. Polish govt.-in-exile, first in France, then in England. Vladislav Raczkiewicz pres., Gen. Vladislav Sikorski, then Stanislav Mikolajczyk, prime ministers. Polish Committee of Natl. Liberation proclaimed at Lublin July 1944, transformed into govt. Jan. 1, 1945.

Rulers of Denmark, Sweden, Norway

Denmark

Earliest rulers invaded Britain; King Canute, who ruled in London 1016-1035, was most famous. The Valdemars furnished kings until the 15th century. In 1282 the Danes won the first national assembly, Danehof, from King Erik V.

Most redoubtable medieval character was Margaret, daughter of Valdemar IV, born 1353, married at 10 to King Haakon VI of Norway. In 1376 she had her first infant son Olaf made king of Denmark. After his death, 1387, she was regent of Denmark and Norway. In 1388 Sweden accepted her as sovereign. In 1389 she made her grand-nephew, Duke Erik of Pomerania, titular king of Denmark, Sweden, and Norway, with herself as regent. In 1397 she effected the Union of Kalmar of the three kingdoms and had Erik VII crowned. In 1439 the three kingdoms deposed him and elected, 1440, Christopher of Bavaria king (Christopher III). On his death, 1448, the union broke up.

Succeeding rulers were unable to enforce their claims as rulers of Sweden until 1520, when Christian II conquered Sweden. He was thrown out 1522, and in 1523 Gustavus Vasa united Sweden. Denmark continued to dominate Norway until the Napoleonic wars, when Frederick VI, 1808-1839, joined the Napoleonic cause after Britain had destroyed the Danish fleet, 1807. In 1814 he was forced to cede Norway to Sweden and Helgoland to Britain, receiving Lauenburg. Successors Christian VIII, 1839; Frederick VII, 1848; Christian IX, 1863; Frederick VIII, 1906; Christian X, 1912; Frederick IX, 1947; Margrethe II, 1972.

Sweden

Early kings ruled at Uppsala, but did not dominate the country. Sverker, c1130-c1156, united the Swedes and Goths. In 1435 Sweden obtained the Riksdag, or parliament. After the Union of Kalmar, 1397, the Danes either ruled or harried the country until Christian II of Denmark conquered it anew, 1520. This led to a rising under Gustavus Vasa, who ruled Sweden 1523-1560, and established an independent kingdom. Charles IX, 1599-1611, crowned 1604, conquered Moscow. Gustavus II Adolphus, 1611-1632, was called the Lion of the North. Later rulers: Christina, 1632; Charles X Gustavus 1654; Charles XI, 1660; Charles XII (invader of Russia and Poland, defeated at Poltava, June 28, 1709), 1697; Ulrika Eleanora, sister, elected queen 1718; Frederick I (of Hesse), her husband, 1720; Adolphus Frederick, 1751; Gustavus III, 1771; Gustavus IV Adolphus, 1792; Charles XIII, 1809. (Union with Norway began 1814.) Charles XIV John, 1818. He was Jean Bernadotte, Napoleon's Prince of Ponte Corvo, elected 1810 to succeed Charles XIII. He founded the present dynasty: Oscar I, 1844; Charles XV, 1859; Oscar II, 1872; Gustavus V, 1907; Gustav VI Adolf, 1950; Carl XVI Gustaf, 1973.

Norway

Overcoming many rivals, Harald Haarfager, 872-930, conquered Norway, Orkneys, and Shetlands; Olaf I, great-grandson, 995-1000, brought Christianity into Norway, Iceland, and Greenland. In 1035 Magnus the Good also became king of Denmark. Haakon V, 1299-1319, had married his daughter to Erik of Sweden. Their son, Magnus, became ruler of Norway and Sweden at 6. His son, Haakon VI, married Margaret of Denmark; their son Olaf IV became king of Norway and Denmark, followed by Margaret's regency and the Union of Kalmar, 1397.

In 1450 Norway became subservient to Denmark. Christian IV, 1588-1648, founded Christiania, now Oslo. After Napoleonic wars, when Denmark ceded Norway to Sweden, a strong nationalist movement forced recognition of Norway as an independent kingdom united with Sweden under the Swedish kings, 1814-1905. In 1905 the union was dissolved and Prince Charles of Denmark became Haakon VII. He died Sept. 21, 1957; succeeded by son, Olav V. Olav V died January 17, 1991; succeeded by son, Harald V.

Rulers of the Netherlands and Belgium

The Netherlands (Holland)

William Frederick, Prince of Orange, led a revolt against French rule, 1813, and was crowned King of the Netherlands, 1815. Belgium seceded Oct. 4, 1830, after a revolt. The secession was ratified by the two kingdoms by treaty Apr. 19, 1839.

Succession: William II, son, 1840; William III, son, 1849; Wilhelmina, daughter of William III and his 2d wife Princess Emma of Waldeck, 1890; Wilhelmina abdicated, Sept. 4, 1948, in favor of daughter, Juliana. Juliana abdicated Apr. 30, 1980, in favor of daughter, Beatrix.

Belgium

A national congress elected Prince Leopold of Saxe-Coburg King; he took the throne July 21, 1831, as Leopold I. Succession: Leopold II, son 1865; Albert I, nephew of Leopold II, 1909; Leopold III, son of Albert, 1934; Prince Charles, Regent 1944; Leopold returned 1950, yielded powers to son Baudouin, Prince Royal, Aug. 6, 1950, abdicated July 16, 1951. Baudouin I took throne July 17, 1951; died July 31, 1993; succeeded by brother, Albert II.

Roman Rulers

From Romulus to the end of the Empire in the West. Rulers of the Roman Empire in the East sat in Constantinople and for a brief period in Nicaea, until the capture of Constantinople by the Turks in 1453, when Byzantium was succeeded by the Ottoman Empire.

BC	Name
	The Kingdom
753	Romulus (Quirinus)
716	Numa Pompilius
673	Tullus Hostilius
640	Ancus Marcius
616	L. Tarquinius Priscus
578	Servius Tullius
534	L. Tarquinius Superbus
	The Republic
509	Consulate established
509	Quaestorship instituted
498	Dictatorship introduced
494	Plebeian Tribunate created
494	Plebeian Aedileship created
444	Consular Tribunate organized
435	Censorship instituted
366	Praetorship established
366	Curule Aedileship created
362	Military Tribunate elected
326	Proconsulate introduced
311	Naval Duumvirate elected
217	Dictatorship of Fabius Maximus
133	Tribunate of Tiberius Gracchus
123	Tribunate of Gaius Gracchus
82	Dictatorship of Sulla
60	First Triumvirate formed (Caesar, Pompeius, Crassus)
46	Dictatorship of Caesar
43	Second Triumvirate formed (Octavianus, Antonius, Lepidus)
	The Empire
27	Augustus (Gaius Julius Caesar Octavianus)
AD	
14	Tiberius I
37	Gaius Caesar (Caligula)
41	Claudius I
54	Nero
68	Galba
69	Galba; Otho, Vitellius
69	Vespasianus
79	Titus
81	Domitianus
96	Nerva

AD	Name
98	Trajanus
117	Hadrianus
138	Antoninus Pius
161	Marcus Aurelius and Lucius Verus
169	Marcus Aurelius (alone)
180	Commodus
193	Pertinax; Julianus I
193	Septimius Severus
211	Caracalla and Geta
212	Caracalla (alone)
217	Macrinus
218	Elagabalus (Heliogabalus)
222	Alexander Severus
235	Maximinus I (the Thracian)
238	Gordianus I and Gordianus II; Pupienus and Balbinus
238	Gordianus III
244	Philippus (the Arabian)
249	Decius
251	Gallus and Volusianus
253	Aemilianus
253	Valerianus and Gallienus
258	Gallienus (alone)
268	Claudius Gothicus
270	Quintillus
270	Aurelianus
275	Tacitus
276	Florianus
276	Probus
282	Carus
283	Carinus and Numerianus
284	Diocletianus
286	Diocletianus and Maximianus
305	Galerius and Constantius I
306	Galerius, Maximinus II, Severus I
307	Galerius, Maximinus II, Constantinus I, Licinius, Maxentius
311	Maximinus II, Constantinus I, Licinius, Maxentius
314	Maximinus II, Constantinus I, Licinius
314	Constantinus I and Licinius
324	Constantinus I (the Great)

AD	Name
337	Constantinus II, Constans I, Constantius II
340	Constantius II and Constans I
350	Constantius II
361	Julianus II (the Apostate)
363	Jovianus
	West (Rome) and East (Constantinople)
364	Valentinianus I (West) and Valens (East)
367	Valentinianus I with Gratianus (West) and Valens (East)
375	Gratianus with Valentinianus II (West) and Valens (East)
378	Gratianus with Valentinianus II (West), Theodosius I (East)
383	Valentinianus II (West) and Theodosius I (East)
394	Theodosius I (the Great)
395	Honorius (West) and Arcadius (East)
408	Honorius (West) and Theodosius II (East)
423	Valentinianus III (West) and Theodosius II (East)
450	Valentinianus III (West) and Marcianus (East)
455	Maximus (West), Avitus (West); Marcianus (East)
456	Avitus (West), Marcianus (East)
457	Majorianus (West), Leo I (East)
461	Severus II (West), Leo I (East)
467	Anthemius (West), Leo I (East)
472	Olybrius (West), Leo I (East)
473	Glycerius (West), Leo I (East)
474	Julius Nepos (West), Leo II (East)
475	Romulus Augustulus (West) and Zeno (East)
476	End of Empire in West; Odovacar, King, drops title of Emperor; murdered by King Theodoric of Ostrogoths 493 AD

Rulers of Modern Italy

After the fall of Napoleon in 1814, the Congress of Vienna, 1815, restored Italy as a political patchwork, comprising the Kingdom of Naples and Sicily, the Papal States, and smaller units. Piedmont and Genoa were awarded to Sardinia, ruled by King Victor Emmanuel I of Savoy.

United Italy emerged under the leadership of Camillo, Count di Cavour (1810-1861), Sardinian prime minister. Agitation was led by Giuseppe Mazzini (1805-1872) and Giuseppe Garibaldi (1807-1882), soldier; Victor Emmanuel I abdicated 1821. After a brief regency for a brother, Charles Albert was King 1831-1849, abdicating when defeated by the Austrians at Novara. Succeeded by Victor Emmanuel II, 1849-1861.

In 1859 France forced Austria to cede Lombardy to Sardinia, which gave rights to Savoy and Nice to France. In 1860 Garibaldi led 1,000 volunteers in a spectacular campaign, took Sicily and expelled the King of Naples. In 1860 the House of Savoy annexed Tuscany, Parma,

Modena, Romagna, the Two Sicilies, the Marches, and Umbria. Victor Emmanuel assumed the title of King of Italy at Turin Mar. 17, 1861. In 1866 he allied with Prussia in the Austro-Prussian War, with Prussia's victory received Venetia. On Sept. 20, 1870, his troops under Gen. Raffaele entered Rome and took over the Papal States, ending the temporal power of the Roman Catholic Church.

Succession: Umberto I, 1878, assassinated 1900; Victor Emmanuel III, 1900, abdicated 1946, died 1947; Humbert II, 1946, ruled a month. In 1921 Benito Mussolini (1883-1945) formed the Fascist party and became prime minister Oct. 31, 1922. He entered World War II as an ally of Hitler. He was deposed July 25, 1943.

At a plebiscite June 2, 1946, Italy voted for a republic; Premier Alcide de Gasperi became chief of state June 13, 1946. On June 28, 1946, the Constituent Assembly elected Enrico de Nicola, Liberal, provisional president. Successive presidents: Luigi Einaudi, elected May 11, 1948; Giovanni Gronchi, Apr. 29, 1955; Antonio Segni, May 6, 1962; Giuseppe Saragat, Dec. 28, 1964; Giovanni Leone, Dec. 29, 1971; Alessandro Pertini, July 9, 1978; Francesco Cossiga, July 9, 1985; Oscar Luigi Scalfaro, May 25, 1992.

Rulers of Spain

From 8th to 11th centuries Spain was dominated by the Moors (Arabs and Berbers). The Christian reconquest established small kingdoms (Asturias, Aragon, Castile, Catalonia, Leon, Navarre, and Valencia). In 1474 Isabella, b. 1451, became Queen of Castile & Leon. Her husband, Ferdinand, b. 1452, inherited Aragon 1479, with Catalonia, Valencia, and the Balearic Islands, became Ferdinand V of Castile. By Isabella's request Pope Sixtus IV established the Inquisition, 1478. Last Moorish kingdom, Granada, fell 1492. Columbus opened New World of colonies, 1492. Isabella died 1504, succeeded by her daughter, Juana "the Mad," but Ferdinand ruled until his death 1516.

Charles I, b. 1500, son of Juana and grandson of Ferdinand and Isabella, and of Maximilian I of Hapsburg; succeeded later as Holy Roman Emperor, Charles V, 1520; abdicated 1556. Philip II, son, 1556-1598, inherited only Spanish throne; conquered Portugal, fought Turks, persecuted non-Catholics, sent Armada against England. Was married to Mary I of England, 1554-1558. Succession: Philip III, 1598-1621; Philip IV, 1621-1665; Charles II, 1665-1700, left Spain to Philip of Anjou, grandson of Louis XIV, who as Philip V, 1700-1746, founded Bourbon dynasty; Ferdinand VI, 1746-1759; Charles III, 1759-1788; Charles IV, 1788-1808, abdicated.

Napoleon now dominated politics and made his brother Joseph King of Spain 1808, but the Spanish ousted him in 1813. Ferdinand VII, 1808, 1814-1833, lost American colonies; succeeded by daughter Isabella II, aged 3, with wife Maria Christina of Naples regent until 1843. Isabella deposed by revolution 1868. Elected king by the Cortes, Amadeo of Savoy, 1870; abdicated 1873. First republic, 1873-74. Alphonso XII, son of Isabella, 1875-85. His posthumous son was Alphonso XIII, with his mother, Queen Maria Christina regent; Spanish-American war, Spain lost Cuba, gave up Puerto Rico, Philippines, Sulu Is., Marianas. Alphonso took throne 1902, aged 16, married British Princess Victoria Eugenia of Battenberg. The dictatorship of Primo de Rivera, 1923-30, precipitated the revolution of 1931. Alphonso agreed to leave without formal abdication. The monarchy was abolished and the second republic established, with socialist backing. Presidents were Niceto Alcala Zamora, to 1936, when Manuel Azaña was chosen.

In July, 1936, the army in Morocco revolted against the government and General Francisco Franco led the troops into Spain. The revolution succeeded by Feb. 1939, when Azaña resigned. Franco became chief of state, with provisions that if he was incapacitated the Regency Council by two-thirds vote may propose a king to the Cortes, which must have a two-thirds majority to elect him.

Alphonso XIII died in Rome Feb. 28, 1941, aged 54. His property and citizenship had been restored.

A succession law restoring the monarchy was approved in a 1947 referendum. Prince Juan Carlos, son of the pretender to the throne, was designated by Franco and the Cortes in 1969 as the future king and chief of state. Upon Franco's death, Nov. 20, 1975, Juan Carlos was proclaimed king, Nov. 22, 1975.

Leaders in the South American Wars of Liberation

Simon Bolivar (1783-1830), Jose Francisco de San Martin (1778-1850), and Francisco Antonio Gabriel Miranda (1750-1816), are among the heroes of the early 19th century struggles of South American nations to free themselves from Spain. All three, and their contemporaries, operated in periods of factional strife, during which soldiers and civilians suffered.

Miranda, a Venezuelan, who had served with the French in the American Revolution and commanded parts of the French Revolutionary armies in the Netherlands, attempted to start a revolt in Venezuela in 1806 and failed. In 1810, with British and American backing, he returned and was briefly a dictator, until the British withdrew their support. In 1812 he was overcome by the royalists in Venezuela and taken prisoner, dying in a Spanish prison in 1816.

San Martin was born in Argentina and during 1789-1811 served in campaigns of the Spanish armies in Europe and Africa. He first joined the independence movement in Argentina in 1812 and in 1817 invaded Chile with 4,000 men over the mountain passes. Here he and Gen. Bernardo O'Higgins (1778-1842) defeated the Spaniards at Chacabuco, 1817, and O'Higgins was named Liberator and became first director of Chile, 1817-23. In 1821 San Martin occupied Lima and Callao, Peru, and became protector of Peru.

Bolivar, the greatest leader of South American liberation from Spain, was born in Venezuela, the son of an aristocratic family. He first served under Miranda in 1812 and in 1813 captured Caracas, where he was named Liberator. Forced out next year by civil strife, he led a campaign that captured Bogota in 1814. In 1817 he was again in control of Venezuela and was named dictator. He organized Nueva Granada with the help of General Francisco de Paula Santander (1792-1840). By joining Nueva Granada, Venezuela, and the present terrain of Panama and Ecuador, the republic of Colombia was formed with Bolivar president. After numerous setbacks he decisively defeated the Spaniards in the second battle of Carabobo, Venezuela, June 24, 1821.

In May, 1822, Gen. Antonio Jose de Sucre, Bolivar's lieutenant, took Quito. Bolivar went to Guayaquil to confer with San Martin, who resigned as protector of Peru and withdrew from politics. With a new army of Colombians and Peruvians Bolivar defeated the Spaniards in a battle at Junín in 1824 and cleared Peru.

De Sucre organized Charcas (Upper Peru) as Republica Bolivar (now Bolivia) and acted as president in place of Bolivar, who wrote its constitution. De Sucre defeated the Spanish faction of Peru at Ayacucho, Dec. 19, 1824.

Continued civil strife finally caused the Colombian federation to break apart. Santander turned against Bolivar, but the latter defeated him and banished him. In 1828 Bolivar gave up the presidency he had held precariously for 14 years. He became ill from tuberculosis and died Dec. 17, 1830. He is buried in the national pantheon in Caracas.

Rulers of Russia; Leaders of the USSR

First ruler to consolidate Slavic tribes was Rurik, leader of the Russians who established himself at Novgorod, 862 AD. He and his immediate successors had Scandinavian affiliations. They moved to Kiev after 972 AD and ruled as Dukes of Kiev. In 988 Vladimir was converted and adopted the Byzantine Greek Orthodox service, later modified by Slav influences. Important as organizer and lawgiver was Yaroslav, 1019-1054, whose daughters married kings of Norway, Hungary, and France. His grandson, Vladimir II (Monomakh), 1113-1125, was progenitor of several rulers, but in 1169 Andrew Bogolubski overthrew Kiev and began the line known as Grand Dukes of Vladimir.

Of the Grand Dukes of Vladimir, Alexander Nevsky, 1246-1263, had a son, Daniel, first to be called Duke of Muscovy (Moscow), who ruled 1294-1303. His successors became Grand Dukes of Muscovy. After Dmitri III Donskoi defeated the Tartars in 1380, they also became Grand Dukes of all Russia. Independence of the Tartars and considerable territorial expansion were achieved under Ivan III, 1462-1505.

Tsars of Muscovy—Ivan III was referred to in church ritual as Tsar. He married Sofia, niece of the last Byzantine emperor. His successor, Basil III, died in 1533 when Basil's son Ivan was only 3. He became Ivan IV, "the Terrible"; crowned 1547 as Tsar of all the Russias, ruled till 1584. Under the weak rule of his son, Feodor I, 1584-1598, Boris Godunov had control. The dynasty died, and after years of tribal strife and intervention by Polish and Swedish armies, the Russians united under 17-year-old Michael Romanov, distantly related to the first wife of Ivan IV. He ruled 1613-1645 and established the Romanov line. Fourth ruler after Michael was Peter I.

Tsars, or Emperors of Russia (Romanovs)—Peter I, 1682-1725, known as Peter the Great, took title of Emperor in 1721. His successors and dates of accession were: Catherine, his widow, 1725; Peter II, his grandson, 1727; Anne, Duchess of Courland, 1730, daughter of Peter the Great's brother, Tsar Ivan V; Ivan VI, 1740, great-grandson of Ivan V, child, kept in prison and murdered 1764; Elizabeth, daughter of Peter I, 1741; Peter III, grandson of Peter I, 1761, deposed 1762 for his consort, Catherine II, former princess of Anhalt Zerbst (Germany) who is known as Catherine the Great; Paul I, her son, 1796, killed 1801; Alexander I, son of Paul, 1801, defeated Napoleon; Nicholas I, his brother, 1825; Alexander II, son of Nicholas, 1855, assassinated 1881 by terrorists; Alexander III, son, 1881.

Nicholas II, son, 1894-1917, last Tsar of Russia, was forced to abdicate by the Revolution that followed losses to Germany in WWI. The Tsar, the Empress, the Tsesarevich (Crown Prince) and the Tsar's 4 daughters were murdered by the Bolsheviks in Ekaterinburg, July 16, 1918.

Provisional Government—Prince Georgi Lvov and Alexander Kerensky, premiers, 1917.

Union of Soviet Socialist Republics

Bolshevik Revolution, Nov. 7, 1917, displaced Kerensky; council of People's Commissars formed, Lenin (Vladimir Ilyich Ulyanov), premier. Lenin died Jan. 21, 1924. Aleksei Rykov (executed 1938) and V. M. Molotov held the office, but actual ruler was Joseph Stalin (Joseph Vissarionovich Djugashvili), general secretary of the Central Committee of the Communist Party. Stalin became president of the Council of Ministers (premier) May 7, 1941, died Mar. 5, 1953. Succeeded by Georgi M. Malenkov, as head of the Council and premier and Nikita S. Khrushchev, first secretary of the Central Committee. Malenkov resigned Feb. 8, 1955, became deputy premier, was dropped July 3, 1957. Marshal Nikolai A. Bulganin became premier Feb. 8, 1955; was demoted and Khrushchev became premier Mar. 27, 1958. Khrushchev was ousted Oct. 14-15, 1964, replaced by Leonid I. Brezhnev as first secretary of the party and by Aleksei N. Kosygin as premier. On June 16, 1977, Brezhnev took office as president. Brezhnev died Nov. 10, 1982; 2 days later the Central Committee unanimously elected former KGB head Yuri V. Andropov president. Andropov died Feb. 9, 1984; on Feb. 13, Konstantin U. Chernenko was chosen by Central Committee as its general secretary. Chernenko died Mar. 10, 1985. On Mar. 11, he was succeeded as general secretary by Mikhail Gorbachev, who replaced Andrei Gromyko as president on Oct. 1, 1988. Gorbachev resigned Dec. 25, 1991, and the Soviet Union officially disbanded the next day. A loose Commonwealth of Independent States, made up of most of the 15 former Soviet constituent republics, was created.

Post-Soviet Russia

After adopting a degree of sovereignty, the Russian Republic held elections in June 1991. The winner, Boris Yeltsin, was sworn in, July 10, 1991, as Russia's first elected president. With the December 1991 dissolution of the Soviet Union, Russia (renamed Russian Federation) became a founding member of the Commonwealth of Independent States.

Governments of China

(Until 221 BC and frequently thereafter, China was not a unified state. Where dynastic dates overlap, the rulers or events referred to appeared in different areas of China.)

Government	From	To
Hsia	c1994 BC	c1523 BC
Shang	c1523	c1028
Western Chou	c1027	770
Eastern Chou	770	256
Warring States	403	222
Ch'in (first unified empire)	221	206
Han	202 BC	220 AD
Western Han (expanded Chinese state beyond the Yellow and Yangtze River valleys)	202 BC	9 AD
Hsin (Wang Mang, usurper)	9 AD	23 AD
Eastern Han (expanded Chinese state into Indo-China and Turkestan)	25	220
Three Kingdoms (Wei, Shu, Wu)	220	265
Chin (western)	265	317
(eastern)	317	420
Northern Dynasties (followed several short-lived governments by Turks, Mongols, etc.)	386	581
Southern Dynasties (capital: Nanking)	420	589
Sui (reunified China)	581	618
Tang (a golden age of Chinese culture; capital: Sian)	618	906
Five Dynasties (Yellow River basin)	902	960
Ten Kingdoms (southern China)	907	979
Liao (Khitan Mongols; capital: Peking)	947	1125
Sung	960	1279
Northern Sung (reunified central and southern China)	960	1126
Western Hsai (non-Chinese rulers in northwest)	990	1227
Chin (Tartars; drove Sung out of central China)	1115	1234
Yuan (Mongols; Kublai Khan made Peking his capital in 1267)	1271	1368
Ming (China reunified under Chinese rule; capital: Nanking, then Peking in 1420)	1368	1644
Ch'ing (Manchus, descendents of Tartars)	1644	1911
Republic (disunity; provincial rulers, warlords)	1912	1949
People's Republic of China	1949	—

Leaders Since 1949

Mao Zedong	Chairman, Central People's Administrative Council, Communist Party (CPC), 1949-76
Zhou Enlai	Premier, foreign minister, 1949-76
Deng Xiaoping	Vice Premier, 1949-76; 1977-87
Liu Shaoqi	President, 1959-69
Hua Guofeng	Premier, 1976-80; CPC Chairman, 1976-81
Zhao Ziyang	Premier, 1980-88; CPC Chairman, 1987-89
Hu Yaobang	CPC Chairman, 1981-87
Li Xiannian	President, 1983-88
Yong Shang-Kun	President, 1988-93
Li Peng	Premier, 1988-
Jiang Zemin	CPC General Secretary, 1989- ; President, 1993-

WORLD EXPLORATION AND GEOGRAPHY

Early Explorers of the Western Hemisphere

The first people to discover the New World or Western Hemisphere are believed to have walked across a "land bridge" from Siberia to Alaska, an isthmus since broken by the Bering Strait. From Alaska, these ancestors of the Native Americans spread through North, Central, and South America. Anthropologists have placed these crossings at between 18,000 and 14,000 BC, but evidence found in 1967 near Puebla, Mex., indicates people may have reached there as early as 35,000-40,000 years ago.

At first, these people were hunters using flint weapons and tools. In Mexico, about 7000-6000 BC, they founded farming cultures, developing corn, squash, etc. Eventually, they created complex civilizations — Olmec, Toltec, Aztec, and Maya and, in South America, Inca. Carbon-14 tests show humans lived about 8000 BC near what are now Front Royal, VA, Kanawha, WV, and Dutchess Quarry, NY. The Hopewell Culture, based on farming, flourished about 1000 BC; remains of it are seen today in large mounds in Ohio and other states.

Norsemen (Norwegian Vikings sailing out of Iceland and Greenland) are credited by most scholars with being the first Europeans to discover America, with at least 5 voyages about AD 1000 to areas they called Helluland, Markland, Vinland—possibly what are known today as Labrador, Nova Scotia or Newfoundland, and New England.

Christopher Columbus, the most famous explorer, was born Cristoforo Colombo in or near Genoa, Italy, probably in 1451, but made his voyages of exploration for the Spanish rulers Ferdinand and Isabella. Dates of his voyages, places he reached, and other information follow:

1492—First voyage. Left Palos, Spain, Aug. 3 with 88 (est.) men. His fleet consisted of 3 vessels—the *Niña,* the *Pinta,* and the *Santa María.* Landed San Salvador, (Guanahani or Watling Is., Bahamas) Oct. 12. Also Cuba, Hispaniola (Haiti-Dominican Republic); built Fort La Navidad on latter.

1493—Second voyage, first part. Left Sept. 25, with 17 ships, 1,500 men. Dominica (Lesser Antilles) Nov. 3; Guadeloupe, Montserrat, Antigua, San Martin, Santa Cruz, Puerto Rico, Virgin Islands. Settled Isabela on Hispaniola. **Second part.** (Columbus having remained in Western Hemisphere) Jamaica, Isle of Pines, La Mona Is.

1498—Third voyage. Left Spain, May 30, 1498, 6 ships. Landed Trinidad. Saw South American continent, Aug. 1, 1498, but called it Isla Sancta (Holy Island). Entered Gulf of Paria and landed, first time on continental soil. At mouth of Orinoco, Aug. 14, he decided this was the mainland.

1502—Fourth voyage. 4 caravels, 150 men. St. Lucia, Guanaja off Honduras; Cape Gracias a Dios, Honduras; San Juan River, Costa Rica; Almirante, Portobelo, and Laguna de Chiriquí, Panama.

Year	Explorer	Nationality and employer	Area reached or explored
1497	John Cabot	Italian-English	Newfoundland or Nova Scotia
1498	John and Sebastian Cabot	Italian-English	Labrador to Hatteras
1499	Alonso de Ojeda	Spanish	N South American coast, Venezuela
1500, Feb.	Vicente Yáñez Pinzón	Spanish	South American coast, Amazon R.
1500, Apr.	Pedro Alvarez Cabral	Portuguese	Brazil (for Portugal)
1500-02	Gaspar Corte-Real	Portuguese	Labrador
1501	Rodrigo de Bastidas	Spanish	Central America
1513	Vasco Núñez de Balboa	Spanish	Panama, Pacific Ocean
1513	Juan Ponce de León	Spanish	Florida
1515	Juan de Solis	Spanish	Río de la Plata
1519	Alonso de Pineda	Spanish	Mouth of Mississippi R.
1519	Hernando Cortés	Spanish	Mexico
1520	Ferdinand Magellan	Portuguese-Spanish	Straits of Magellan, Tierra del Fuego
1524	Giovanni da Verrazano	Italian-French	Atlantic coast, inc. New York harbor
1528	Cabeza de Vaca	Spanish	Texas coast and interior
1532	Francisco Pizarro	Spanish	Peru
1534	Jacques Cartier	French	Canada, Gulf of St. Lawrence
1536	Pedro de Mendoza	Spanish	Buenos Aires
1539	Francisco de Ulloa	Spanish	California coast
1539-41	Hernando de Soto	Spanish	Mississippi R. near Memphis
1539	Marcos de Niza	Italian-Spanish	SW U.S.
1540	Francisco de Coronado	Spanish	SW U.S.
1540	Hernando Alarcón	Spanish	Colorado R.
1540	Garcia de L. Cardenas	Spanish	Colorado, Grand Canyon
1541	Francisco de Orellana	Spanish	Amazon R.
1542	Juan Rodriguez Cabrillo	Portuguese-Spanish	W Mexico, San Diego harbor
1565	Pedro Menéndez de Aviles	Spanish	St. Augustine, FL
1576	Sir Martin Frobisher	English	Frobisher's Bay, Canada
1577-80	Sir Francis Drake	English	California coast
1582	Antonio de Espejo	Spanish	SW U.S. (named New Mexico)
1584	Amadas & Barlow (for Raleigh)	English	Virginia
1585-87	Sir Walter Raleigh's men	English	Roanoke Is., NC
1595	Sir Walter Raleigh	English	Orinoco R.
1603-09	Samuel de Champlain	French	Canadian interior, Lake Champlain
1607	Capt. John Smith	English	Atlantic coast
1609-10	Henry Hudson	English-Dutch	Hudson R., Hudson Bay
1634	Jean Nicolet	French	Lake Michigan, Wisconsin
1673	Jacques Marquette, Louis Jolliet	French	Mississippi R. S to Arkansas
1682	Robert Cavelier, sieur de La Salle	French	Mississippi R. S to Gulf of Mexico
1789	Sir Alexander Mackenzie	Canadian	NW Canada

Arctic Exploration

Early Explorers

1587 — John Davis (Eng.). Davis Strait to Sanderson's Hope, 72° 12′ N.

1596 — Willem Barents and Jacob van Heemskerck (Holland). Discovered Bear Isl., touched NW tip of Spitsbergen, 79° 49′ N, rounded Novaya Zemlya, wintered at Ice Haven.

(continued)

1607 — Henry Hudson (Eng.). North along Greenland's E coast to Cape Hold-with-Hope, 73° 30′, then N of Spitsbergen to 80° 23′. Returning he explored Hudson's Touches (Jan Mayen).

1616 — William Baffin and Robert Bylot (Eng.). Baffin Bay to Smith Sound.

1728 — Vitus Bering (Russ.). Proved Asia and America were separated by sailing through strait now bearing his name.

1733-40 — Great Northern Expedition (Russ.). Surveyed Siberian Arctic coast.

1741 — Vitus Bering (Russ.). Sighted Alaska from sea, named Mount St. Elias. His lieutenant, Chirikof, explored coast.

1771 — Samuel Hearne (Hudson's Bay Co.). Overland from Prince of Wales Fort (Churchill) on Hudson Bay to mouth of Coppermine R.

1778 — James Cook (Brit.). Through Bering Strait to Icy Cape, Alaska, and North Cape, Siberia.

1789 — Alexander Mackenzie (North West Co., Brit.). Montreal to mouth of Mackenzie River.

1806 — William Scoresby (Brit.). N of Spitsbergen to 81° 30′.

1820-23 — Ferdinand von Wrangel (Russ.). Completed a survey of Siberian Arctic coast. His exploration joined that of James Cook at North Cape, confirming separation of the continents.

1845 — Sir John Franklin (Brit.) was one of many to seek the Northwest Passage—an ocean route connecting the Atlantic and Pacific via the Arctic. His ships, the *Erebus* and *Terror* were last seen entering Lancaster Sound July 26.

1881 — The U.S. steamer *Jeannette* on an expedition led by Lt. Cmdr. George W. DeLong was trapped in ice and crushed, June 1881. DeLong and 11 others died; 12 survived.

1888 — Fridtjof Nansen (Nor.) crossed Greenland's icecap.

1893-96 — Nansen in *Fram* drifted from New Siberian Isls. to Spitsbergen; tried polar dash in 1895, reached Franz Josef Land, 86° 14′ N.

1897 — Salomon A. Andrée (Sw.) and 2 others started in balloon from Spitsbergen, July 11, to drift across pole to U.S., and disappeared. More than 33 yrs. later, Aug. 6, 1930, their frozen bodies were found on White Isl., 82° 57′ N, 29° 52′ E.

1903-6 — Roald Amundsen (Nor.) first sailed Northwest Passage.

North Pole Exploration

Robert E. Peary explored Greenland's coast, 1891-92; tried for North Pole, 1893. In 1900 he reached N limit of Greenland and 83° 50′ N; in 1902 he reached 84° 06′ N; in 1906 he went from Ellesmere Isl. to 87° 06′ N. He sailed in the *Roosevelt,* July 1908, to winter off Cape Sheridan, Grant Land. The dash for the North Pole began Mar. 1 from Cape Columbia, Ellesmere Isl. Peary reached the pole, 90° N, Apr. 6, 1909.

Peary had several supporting groups carrying supplies until the last group turned back at 87° 47′ N. Peary, Matthew Henson, and 4 Eskimos proceeded with dog teams and sleds. They crossed the pole several times, finally built an igloo at 90°, remained 36 hours. Started south, Apr. 7 at 4 PM, for Cape Columbia. The Eskimos were Coqueeh, Ootah, Eginwah, and Seegloo.

1914 — Donald MacMillan (U.S.). Northwest, 200 miles, from Axel Heiberg Island to seek Peary's Crocker Land.

1915-17 — Vihjalmur Stefansson (Can.). Discovered Borden, Brock, Meighen, and Lougheed Isls.

1918-20 — Roald Amundsen sailed Northeast Passage.

1925 — Amundsen and Lincoln Ellsworth (U.S.) reached 87° 44′ N in attempt to fly to North Pole from Spitsbergen.

1926 — Richard E. Byrd and Floyd Bennett (U.S.) first over North Pole by air, May 9.

1926 — Amundsen, Ellsworth, and Umberto Nobile (It.) flew from Spitsbergen over North Pole May 12, to Teller, Alaska, in dirigible *Norge.*

1928 — Nobile crossed North Pole in airship, May 24, crashed, May 25. Amundsen died attempting a rescue.

North Pole Exploration Records

On Aug. 3, 1958, the *Nautilus,* under Comdr. William R. Anderson, became the first ship to cross the North Pole beneath the Arctic ice.

The nuclear-powered U.S. submarine *Seadragon,* Comdr. George P. Steele 2d, made the first E-W underwater transit through the Northwest Passage during August 1960. It sailed from Portsmouth, NH, headed between Greenland and Labrador through Baffin Bay, then W through Lancaster Sound and McClure Strait to the Beaufort Sea. Traveling submerged for the most part, the submarine made 850 mi from Baffin Bay to the Beaufort Sea in 6 days.

On Aug. 16, 1977, the Soviet nuclear icebreaker *Arktika* reached the North Pole and became the first surface ship to break through the Arctic ice pack to the top of the world.

On April 30, 1978, Naomi Uemura, a Jap. explorer, became the first man to reach the North Pole alone by dog sled. During the 54-day, 600-mi trek over the frozen Arctic, Uemura survived attacks by a marauding polar bear.

In April 1982, Sir Ranulph Fiennes and Charles Burton, Brits. explorers, reached the North Pole and became the first to circle the earth from pole to pole. They had reached the South Pole 16 months earlier. The 52,000-mi trek took 3 years, involved 23 people, and cost an estimated $18 mln. The expedition was also the first to travel down the Scott Glacier and the first to journey up the Yukon and through the Northwest Passage in a single season.

On May 2, 1986, 6 Amer. and Can. explorers reached the North Pole assisted only by dogs. They became the first to reach the pole without mechanical assistance since Robert E. Peary planted a flag there in 1909. The explorers, Amer. Will Steger, Paul Schurke, Anne Bancroft, and Geoff Carroll, and Can. Brent Boddy and Richard Weber, completed the 500-mi journey in 56 days.

Antarctic Exploration

Early History

Antarctica has been approached since 1773-75, when Capt. James Cook (Brit.) reached 71° 10′ S. Many sea and landmarks bear names of early explorers. Fabian von Bellingshausen (Russ.) discovered Peter I and Alexander I Islands, 1819-21. Nathaniel Palmer (U.S.) traveled throughout Palmer Peninsula, 60° W, 1820, without realizing that this was a continent. Capt. John Davis (U.S.) made the first known landing on the continent in 1821. Later, in 1823, James Weddell (Brit.) found Weddell Sea, 74° 15′ S, the southernmost point that had been reached.

First to announce existence of the continent of Antarctica was Charles Wilkes (U.S.), who followed the coast for 1,500 mi, 1840. Adelie Coast, 140° E, was found by Dumont d'Urville (Fr.), 1840. Ross Ice Shelf was found by James Clark Ross (Brit.), 1841-42.

1895 — Leonard Kristensen (Nor.) landed a party on the coast of Victoria Land. They were the first ashore on the main continental mass. C. E. Borchgrevink, a member of that party, returned in 1899 with a Brit. expedition, first to winter on Antarctica.

1902-4 — Robert F. Scott (Brit.) explored Edward VII Peninsula. He reached 82° 17′ S, 146° 33′ E from McMurdo Sound.

1908-9 — Ernest Shackleton (Brit.) introduced the use of Manchurian ponies in Antarctic sledging. He reached 88° 23′ S, discovering a route on to the plateau by way of the Beardmore Glacier and pioneering the way to the pole.

South Pole Exploration

1911 — Roald Amundsen (Nor.) with 4 men and dog teams reached the pole, Dec. 14.

1912 — Scott reached the pole from Ross Isl., Jan. 18, with 4 companions. None of Scott's party survived. Their bodies and expedition notes were found, Nov. 12.

1928 — First man to use an airplane over Antarctica was Sir George Hubert Wilkins (Austral.).

1929 — Richard E. Byrd (U.S.) established Little America on Bay of Whales. On 1,600-mi airplane flight begun Nov. 28, he crossed South Pole, Nov. 29, with 3 others.

1934-35 — Byrd led 2d expedition to Little America, explored 450,000 sq mi, wintered alone at weather station, 80° 08′ S.

1934-37 — John Rymill led British Graham Land expedition; discovered that Palmer Penin. is part of Antarctic mainland.

1935 — Lincoln Ellsworth (U.S.) flew S along Palmer Penin.'s E coast, then crossed continent to Little America, making 4 landings on unprepared terrain in bad weather.

1939-41 — U.S. Antarctic Service Expedition built West Base on Ross Ice Shelf under Paul Siple, and East Base on Palmer Peninsula under Richard Black. U.S. Navy plane flights discovered about 150,000 sq mi of new land.

1940 — Byrd charted most of coast between Ross Sea and Palmer Penin.

1946-47 — U.S. Navy undertook Operation Highjump, commanded by Byrd, included 13 ships and 4,000 men. Airplanes photomapped coastline and penetrated beyond pole.

1946-48 — Ronne Antarctic Research Expedition, Comdr. Finn Ronne, USNR, determined the Antarctic to be only one continent with no strait between Weddell Sea and Ross Sea; explored 250,000 sq mi of land by flights to 79° S, and made 14,000 aerial photographs over 450,000 sq mi of land. Mrs. Ronne and Mrs. H. Darlington were the first women to winter on Antarctica.

1955-57 — U.S. Navy's Operation Deep Freeze led by Adm. Byrd. Supporting U.S. scientific efforts for the International Geophysical Year (IGY), the operation was commanded by Rear Adm. George Dufek. It established 5 coastal stations fronting the Indian, Pacific, and Atlantic oceans and also 3 interior stations; explored more than 1,000,000 sq mi in Wilkes Land.

1957-58 — During the IGY, July 1957 through Dec. 1958, scientists from 12 countries conducted ambitious programs of Antarctic research. A network of some 60 stations on the continent and sub-Arctic islands studied oceanography, glaciology, meteorology, seismology, geomagnetism, the ionosphere, cosmic rays, aurora, and airglow.

Dr. Vivian E. Fuchs led a 12-man Trans-Antarctic Expedition on the first land-crossing of Antarctica. Starting from the Weddell Sea, they reached Scott Station, Mar. 2, 1958, after traveling 2,158 mi in 98 days.

1958 — A group of 5 U.S. scientists led by Edward C. Thiel, seismologist, moving by tractor from Ellsworth Station on Weddell Sea, identified a huge mountain range, 5,000 ft above the ice sheet and 9,000 ft above sea level. The range, originally seen by a Navy plane, was named the Dufek Massif, for Rear Adm. George Dufek.

1959 — Twelve nations — Argentina, Australia, Belgium, Chile, France, Japan, New Zealand, Norway, South Africa, the Soviet Union, the United Kingdom, and the U.S. — signed a treaty suspending any territorial claims for 30 yrs. and reserving the continent, S of 60° S, for research.

1961-62 — Scientists discovered the Bentley Trench, running from Ross Ice Shelf into Marie Byrd Land, near the end of the Ellsworth Mts., toward the Weddell Sea.

1962 — First nuclear power plant began operation at McMurdo Sound.

1963 — On Feb. 22 a U.S. plane made the longest nonstop flight ever made in the S Pole area, covering 3,600 mi in 10 hr. The flight was from McMurdo Station S past the geographical S Pole to Shackleton Mts., SE to the "Area of Inaccessibility" and back to McMurdo Station.

1964 — A Brit. survey team was landed by helicopter on Cook Island, the first recorded visit since 1775.

1964 — New Zealanders mapped the mountain area from Cape Adare W some 400 mi to Pennell Glacier.

1985 — Igor A. Zotikov, a Moscow Institute of Geography researcher, discovered sediments in the Ross Ice Shelf that seem to support the continental drift theory. Research by the Ocean Drilling Project off the Queen Maud Land coast indicated the ice sheets of E Antartica are 37 million yrs. old.

1989 — Victoria Murden and Shirley Metz both became the first women and the first Americans to reach the South Pole overland when they arrived with 9 others on Jan. 17, 1989. The 51-day trek on skis covered 740 mi.

1991 — Twenty-four nations approved a protocol to the 1959 Antarctia Treaty, Oct. 4. Amendments called for various conservation provisions, including banning oil and other mineral exploration for 50 yrs.

Volcanoes

Source: Global Volcanism Network, Smithsonian Institution; as of Apr. 1994

More than 75 percent of the world's 850 active volcanoes lie within the Ring of Fire, a zone running along the W coast of the Americas from Chile to Alaska and down the E coast of Asia from Siberia to New Zealand. Twenty % of these volcanoes are in Indonesia. Other prominent groupings are in Japan, the Aleutian Islands, and Central America. Almost all active regions are at the boundaries of the large moving plates that constitute the earth's surface. The Ring of Fire marks the boundary between the plates underlying the Pacific Ocean and those underlying the surrounding continents. Other active regions, such as the Mediterranean Sea and Iceland, are on plate boundaries.

Major Historical Eruptions

Approximately 7,000 years ago, Mazama, a 9,900-ft volcano in S Oregon, erupted violently, ejecting ash and lava. The ash spread over the entire northwestern U.S. and as far away as Saskatchewan, Can. During the eruption, the top of the mountain collapsed, leaving a caldera 6 mi across and about a half mile deep, which filled with rainwater to form what is now called Crater Lake.

In AD 79, Vesuvio, or Vesuvius, a 4,190-ft volcano overlooking Naples Bay became active after several centuries of quiescence. On Aug. 24 of that year, a heated mud and ash flow swept down the mountain, engulfing the cities of Pompeii, Herculaneum, and Stabiae with debris more than 60 feet deep. About 10 % of the population of the 3 towns was killed.

The largest eruptions in recent centuries have been in Indonesia. In 1883, an eruption similar to the Mazama eruption occurred on the island of Krakatau. On Aug. 27, the 2,640-ft peak of the volcano collapsed to 1,000 feet below sea level, leaving only a small portion of the island standing above the sea. Ash from the eruption colored sunsets around the world for 2 years. A tsunami (tidal wave) generated by the collapse killed 36,000 people in nearby Java and Sumatra and eventually reached England. A similar, but even more powerful, eruption had taken place 68 years earlier at Tambora volcano on the Indonesian island of Sumbawa.

Notable Active Volcanoes

Name (latest eruption)	Location	Height (ft)
Africa		
Cameroon (1982)	Cameroon	13,354
Nyirangongo (1977)	Zaire	11,400
Nyamuragira (1991)	Zaire	10,028
Karthala (1977)	Comoro Isls.	8,000
Piton de la Fournaise (1991)	Reunion Isl.	5,981
Erta-Ale (1992)	Ethiopia	1,650
Antarctica		
Erebus (1991)	Ross Isl.	12,450
Deception Island (1970)	S. Shetland Isls.	1,890

(continued)

Name (latest eruption)	Location	Height (ft)
Asia-Oceania		
Kliuchevskoi (1993)	Russia	15,584
Kerinci (1987)	Sumatra	12,467
Semeru (1994)	Java	12,060
Slamet (1988)	Java	11,247
Raung (1991)	Java	10,932
On-Take (1991)	Japan	10,049
Mayon (1993)	Philippines	9,991
Merapi (1994)	Java	9,551
Marapi (1988)	Sumatra	9,485
Ruapehu (1994)	New Zealand	9,175
Asama (1991)	Japan	8,300
Niigata Yakeyama (1989)	Japan	8,111
Canlaon (1991)	Philippines	8,070
Alaid (1972)	Kuril Isl.	7,662
Ulawun (1992)	New Britain	7,532
Ngauruhoe (1975)	New Zealand	7,515
Chokai (1974)	Japan	7,300
Galunggung (1982)	Java	7,113
Azuma (1978)	Japan	6,700
Pinatubo (1992)	Philippines	5,770
Sangeang Api (1988)	Indonesia	6,351
Nasu (1977)	Japan	6,210
Tiatia (1973)	Kuril Isl.	6,013
Manam (1994)	Papua New Guinea	6,000
Soputan (1989)	Indonesia	5,994
Siau (1976)	Indonesia	5,853
Kelud (1990)	Java	5,679
Kirisima (1982)	Japan	5,577
Bagana (1992)	Papua New Guinea	6,558
Akita Komaga take (1970)	Japan	5,449
Gamkonora (1981)	Indonesia	5,364
Aso (1993)	Japan	5,223
Lokon-Empung (1991)	Indonesia	5,187
Bulusan (1988)	Philippines	5,115
Sarycheva (1976)	Kuril Isl.	4,960
Karkar (1981)	Papua New Guinea	4,920
Lopevi (1982)	Vanuatu	4,755
Unzen (1994)	Japan	4,462
Ambrym (1991)	Vanuatu	4,376
Awu (1992)	Indonesia	4,350
Sakura-jima (1994)	Japan	3,668
Langila (1994)	New Britain	3,586
Suwanose-jima (1993)	Japan	2,640
Oshima (1990)	Japan	2,550
Usu (1978)	Japan	2,400
Pagan (1993)	N. Mariana Isls.	1,870
White Island (1994)	New Zealand	1,075
Taal (1988)	Philippines	984
Central America—Caribbean		
Acatenango (1972)	Guatemala	12,992
Fuego (1991)	Guatemala	12,582
Tacana (1988)	Guatemala	12,400
Santiaguito (Santa María) (1993)	Guatemala	12,362
Irazú (1992)	Costa Rica	11,260
Turrialba (1992)	Costa Rica	10,650
Póas (1994)	Costa Rica	8,930
Pacaya (1993)	Guatemala	8,346
San Miguel (1986)	El Salvador	6,994
Rincón de la Vieja (1993)	Costa Rica	6,234
El Viejo (San Cristobal) (1991)	Nicaragua	5,840
Ometepe (Concepción) (1986)	Nicaragua	5,106
Arenal (1994)	Costa Rica	5,092
Momotombo (1982)	Nicaragua	4,199
Soufriere (1979)	St. Vincent	4,048
Telica (1987)	Nicaragua	3,409
South America		
Guallatiri (1987)	Chile	19,882
Láscar (1994)	Chile	19,652
Cotopaxi (1975)	Ecuador	19,347
Tupungatito (1986)	Chile	18,504
Ruiz (1992)	Colombia	17,716
Sangay (1988)	Ecuador	17,159
Guagua Pichincha (1988)	Ecuador	15,696
Purace (1977)	Colombia	15,601
Galeras (1993)	Colombia	13,996
Llaima (1994)	Chile	10,239
Villarrica (1992)	Chile	9,318
Hudson (1991)	Chile	8,580
Alcedo (1970)	Galapagos Isl.	3,599
Mid-Pacific		
Mauna Loa (1987)	Hawaii	13,680
Kilauea (1994)	Hawaii	4,077
Mid-Atlantic Ridge		
Beerenberg (1985)	Jan Mayen Isl.	7,470
Hekla (1991)	Iceland	4,892
Leirhnukur (1975)	Iceland	2,145
Krafla (1984)	Iceland	2,145
Europe		
Etna (1994)	Italy	11,053
Stromboli (1994)	Italy	3,038
North America		
Colima (1994)	Mexico	14,003
Redoubt (1991)	Alaska	10,197
Iliamna (1978)	Alaska	10,016
Shishaldin (1987)	Aleutian Isl.	9,387
Mt. St. Helens (1991)	Washington	8,300+
Pavlof (1988)	Aleutian Isl.	8,261
Veniaminof (1994)	Alaska	8,225
El Chichon (1983)	Mexico	7,300
Katmai (1974)	Alaska	6,715
Makushin (1987)	Aleutian Isl.	6,680
Great Sitkin (1974)	Aleutian Isl.	5,710
Cleveland (1987)	Aleutian Isl.	5,675
Gareloi (1982)	Aleutian Isl.	5,334
Korovin (1987)	Aleutian Isl.	4,852
Akutan (1992)	Aleutian Isl.	4,275
Kiska (1990)	Aleutian Isl.	4,275
Augustine (1988)	Alaska	3,999
Okmok (1988)	Aleutian Isl.	3,519
Seguam (1993)	Alaska	3,458

Notable Volcanic Eruptions

Date	Volcano	Estimated Deaths
AD 79	Mt. Vesuvius, Italy	16,000
1169	Mt. Etna, Sicily	15,000
1631	Mt. Vesuvius, Italy	4,000
1669	Mt. Etna, Sicily	20,000
1772	Mt. Papandayan, Java	3,000
1792	Mt. Unzen-Dake, Japan	10,400
1815	Tamboro, Java	12,000
Aug. 26-28, 1883	Krakatau, Indonesia	35,000
Apr. 8, 1902	Santa María, Guatemala	1,000
May 8, 1902	Mt. Pelée, Martinique	30,000
1911	Mt. Taal, Philippines	1,400
1919	Mt. Kelud, Java	5,000
Jan. 18-21, 1951	Mt. Lamington, New Guinea	3,000
Apr. 26, 1966	Mt. Kelud, Java	1,000
May 18, 1980	Mt. St. Helens, U.S.	60
Nov. 13, 1985	Nevado del Ruiz, Colombia	22,940
Aug. 24, 1986	NW Cameroon	1,700

Mountains

Height of Mount Everest

Mt. Everest was considered 29,002 ft when Edmund Hillary and Tenzing Norgay scaled it in 1953. This triangulation figure had been accepted since 1850. In 1954 the Surveyor General of the Republic of India set the height at 29,028 ft., plus or minus 10 ft because of snow. The National Geographic Society accepts the new figure, but many mountaineering groups still use 29,002 ft.

In 1987, new calculations based on satellite measurements indicate that the Himalayan peak K-2 rose 29,064 ft above sea level and that Mt. Everest is 800 ft higher. The National Geographic Society has not accepted the revised figure.

United States, Canada, Mexico

Name	Place	Height (ft)
McKinley	AK	20,320
Logan	Yukon	19,850
Citlaltepec (Orizaba)	Mexico	18,700
St. Elias	AK-Yukon	18,008
Popocatepetl	Mexico	17,887
Foraker	AK	17,400
Iztaccihuatl	Mexico	17,343
Lucania	Yukon	17,147
King	Yukon	16,971
Steele	Yukon	16,644
Bona	AK	16,550
Blackburn	AK	16,390
Kennedy	AK	16,286
Sanford	AK	16,237
South Buttress	AK	15,885
Wood	Yukon	15,885
Vancouver	AK-Yukon	15,700
Churchill	AK	15,638
Fairweather	AK-Yukon	15,300
Zinantecatl (Toluca)	Mexico	15,016
Hubbard	AK-Yukon	15,015
Bear	AK	14,831
Walsh	Yukon	14,780
East Buttress	AK	14,730
Matlalcueyetl	Mexico	14,636
Hunter	AK	14,573
Alverstone	AK-Yukon	14,565
Browne Tower	AK	14,530
Whitney	CA	14,494
Elbert	CO	14,433
Massive	CO	14,421
Harvard	CO	14,420
Rainier	WA	14,410
Williamson	CA	14,375
Blanca Peak	CO	14,345
La Plata	CO	14,336
Uncompahgre	CO	14,309
Crestone	CO	14,294
Lincoln	CO	14,286
Grays Peak	CO	14,270
Antero	CO	14,269
Torreys	CO	14,267
Castle	CO	14,265
Quandary	CO	14,265
Evans	CO	14,264
Longs Peak	CO	14,256
McArthur	Yukon	14,253
Wilson	CO	14,246
White	CA	14,246
North Palisade	CA	14,242
Shavano	CO	14,229
Belford	CO	14,197
Princeton	CO	14,197
Crestone Needle	CO	14,197
Yale	CO	14,196
Bross	CO	14,172
Kit Carson	CO	14,165
Wrangell	AK	14,163
Shasta	CA	14,162
Sill	CA	14,162
El Diente	CO	14,159
Maroon	CO	14,156
Tabeguache	CO	14,155
Oxford	CO	14,153
Sneffels	CO	14,150
Point Success	WA	14,150
Democrat	CO	14,148
Capitol	CO	14,130
Liberty Cap	WA	14,112
Pikes Peak	CO	14,110
Snowmass	CO	14,092
Windom	CO	14,087
Russell	CA	14,086
Eolus	CO	14,084
Columbia	CO	14,073
Augusta	AK-Yukon	14,070
Missouri	CO	14,067
Humboldt	CO	14,064

South America

Peak, country	Height (ft)
Aconcagua, Argentina	22,834
Ojos del Salado, Arg.-Chile	22,572
Bonete, Argentina	22,546
Tupungato, Argentina-Chile	22,310
Pissis, Argentina	22,241
Mercedario, Argentina	22,211
Huascaran, Peru	22,205
Llullaillaco, Argentina-Chile	22,057
El Libertador, Argentina	22,047
Cachi, Argentina	22,047
Yerupaja, Peru	21,709
Galan, Argentina	21,654
El Muerto, Argentina-Chile	21,457
Sajama, Bolivia	21,391
Nacimiento, Argentina	21,302
Illimani, Bolivia	21,201
Coropuna, Peru	21,083
Laudo, Argentina	20,997
Ancohuma, Bolivia	20,958
Ausangate, Peru	20,945
Toro, Argentina-Chile	20,932
Illampu, Bolivia	20,873
Tres Cruces, Argentina-Chile	20,853
Huandoy, Peru	20,852
Parinacota, Bolivia-Chile	20,768
Tortolas, Argentina-Chile	20,745
Ampato, Peru	20,702
Condor, Argentina	20,669
Salcantay, Peru	20,574
Chimborazo, Ecuador	20,561
Huancarhuas, Peru	20,531
Famatina, Argentina	20,505
Pumasillo, Peru	20,492
Solo, Argentina	20,492
Polleras, Argentina	20,456
Pular, Chile	20,423
Chani, Argentina	20,341
Aucanquilcha, Chile	20,295
Juncal, Argentina-Chile	20,276
Negro, Argentina	20,184
Quela, Argentina	20,128
Condoriri, Bolivia	20,095
Palermo, Argentina	20,079
Solimana, Peru	20,068
San Juan, Argentina-Chile	20,049
Sierra Nevada, Arg.-Chile	20,023
Antofalla, Argentina	20,013
Marmolejo, Argentina-Chile	20,013
Chachani, Peru	19,931
Licancabur, Argentina-Chile	19,425

The highest point in the West Indies is in the Dominican Republic, Pico Duarte (10,417 ft).

Africa, Southeast Asian Islands, Australia, New Zealand

Peak, country/island	Height (ft)
Kilimanjaro, Tanzania	19,340
Kenya, Kenya	17,058
Margherita Pk., Uganda-Zaire	16,763
Jaja, New Guinea	16,500
Trikora, New Guinea	15,585
Mandala, New Guinea	15,420
Ras Dashan, Ethiopia	15,158
Meru, Tanzania	14,979
Wilhelm, New Guinea	14,793
Karisimbi, Zaire-Rwanda	14,787
Elgon, Kenya-Uganda	14,178
Batu, Ethiopia	14,131
Guna, Ethiopia	13,881
Gughe, Ethiopia	13,780
Toubkal, Morocco	13,661
Kinabalu, Malaysia	13,455
Cameroon, Cameroon	13,353
Kerinci, Sumatra	12,467
Cook, New Zealand	12,349
Teide, Canary Islands	12,198
Semeru, Java	12,060
Kosciusko, Australia	7,310

Europe

Peak, country	Height (ft)
Alps	
Mont Blanc, Fr.-It.	15,771
Monte Rosa (highest peak of group), Switz.	15,203
Dom, Switz.	14,911
Liskamm, It., Switz.	14,852
Weisshom, Switz.	14,780
Taschhorn, Switz.	14,733
Matterhorn, It., Switz.	14,690
Dent Blanche, Switz.	14,293
Nadelhorn, Switz.	14,196
Grand Combin, Switz.	14,154
Lenzpitze, Switz.	14,088
Finsteraarhorn, Switz.	14,022
Castor, Switz.	13,865
Zinalrothorn, Switz.	13,849
Hohberghom, Switz.	13,842
Alphubel, Switz.	13,799
Rimpfischhom, Switz.	13,776
Aletschorn, Switz.	13,763
Strahlhorn, Switz.	13,747
Dent D'Herens, Switz.	13,686
Breithorn, It., Switz.	13,665
Bishorn, Switz.	13,645
Jungfrau, Switz.	13,642
Ecrins, Fr.	13,461
Monch, Switz.	13,448
Pollux, Switz.	13,422
Schreckhorn, Switz.	13,379
Ober Gabelhorn, Switz.	13,330
Gran Paradiso, It.	13,323

(continued)

Peak, country	Height (ft)
Bernina, It., Switz.	13,284
Fiescherhorn, Switz.	13,283
Grunhorn, Switz.	13,266
Lauteraarhorn, Switz.	13,261
Durrenhorn, Switz.	13,238
Allalinhorn, Switz.	13,213
Weissmies, Switz.	13,199
Lagginhorn, Switz.	13,156
Zupo, Switz.	13,120
Fletschhorn, Switz.	13,110
Adlerhorn, Switz.	13,081
Gletscherhorn, Switz.	13,068
Schalihorn, Switz.	13,040
Scerscen, Switz.	13,028
Eiger, Switz.	13,025
Jagerhorn, Switz.	13,024
Rottalhorn, Switz.	13,022

Pyrenees

Peak, country	Height (ft)
Aneto, Sp.	11,168
Posets, Sp.	11,073
Perdido, Sp.	11,007
Vignemale, Fr.-Sp.	10,820
Long, Sp.	10,479
Estats, Sp.	10,304
Montcalm, Sp.	10,105

Caucasus (Europe-Asia)

Peak, country	Height (ft)
El'brus, Russia	18,510
Shkara, Russia	17,064
Dykh Tau, Russia	17,054
Kashtan Tau, Russia	16,877
Dzhangi Tau, Russia	16,565
Kazbek, Russia	16,558

Asia (Mainland)

Peak	Place	Height (ft)
Everest	Nepal-Tibet	29,028
K2 (Godwin Austen)	Kashmir	28,250
Kanchenjunga	India-Nepal	28,208
Lhotse I (Everest)	Nepal-Tibet	27,923
Makalu I	Nepal-Tibet	27,824
Lhotse II (Everest)	Nepal-Tibet	27,560
Dhaulagiri	Nepal	26,810
Manaslu I	Nepal	26,760
Cho Oyu	Nepal-Tibet	26,750
Nanga Parbat	Kashmir	26,660
Annapurna I	Nepal	26,504
Gasherbrum	Kashmir	26,470
Broad	Kashmir	26,400
Gosainthan	Tibet	26,287
Annapurna II	Nepal	26,041
Gyachung Kang	Nepal-Tibet	25,910
Disteghil Sar	Kashmir	25,868
Himalchuli	Nepal	25,801
Nuptse (Everest)	Nepal-Tibet	25,726
Masherbrum	Kashmir	25,660
Nanda Devi	India	25,645
Rakaposhi	Kashmir	25,550
Kamet	India-Tibet	25,447
Namcha Barwa	Tibet	25,445
Gurla Mandhata	Tibet	25,355
Ulugh Muz Tagh	Xinjiang-Tibet	25,340
Kungur	Xinjiang	25,325
Tirich Mir	Pakistan	25,230
Makalu II	Nepal-Tibet	25,120
Minya Konka	China	24,900
Kula Gangri	Bhutan-Tibet	24,784
Changtzu (Everest)	Nepal-Tibet	24,780
Muz Tagh Ata	Xinjiang	24,757
Skyang Kangri	Kashmir	24,750
Communism Peak	Tajikistan	24,590
Jongsang Peak	India-Nepal	24,472
Pobedy Peak	Xinjiang-Kyrgyzstan	24,406
Sia Kangri	Kashmir	24,350
Haramosh Peak	Pakistan	24,270
Istoro Nal	Pakistan	24,240
Tent Peak	India-Nepal	24,165
Chomo Lhari	Bhutan-Tibet	24,040
Chamlang	Nepal	24,012
Kabru	India-Nepal	24,002
Alung Gangri	Tibet	24,000
Baltoro Kangri	Kashmir	23,990
Mussu Shan	Xinjiang	23,890
Mana	India	23,860
Baruntse	Nepal	23,688
Nepal Peak	India-Nepal	23,500
Amne Machin	China	23,490
Gauri Sankar	Nepal-Tibet	23,440
Badrinath	India	23,420
Nunkun	Kashmir	23,410
Lenin Peak	Tajikistan	23,405
Pyramid	India-Nepal	23,400
Api	Nepal	23,399
Pauhunri	India-Tibet	23,385
Trisul	India	23,360
Kangto	India-Tibet	23,260
Nyenchhe Thanglha	Tibet	23,255
Trisuli	India	23,210
Pumori	Nepal-Tibet	23,190
Dunagiri	India	23,184
Lombo Kangra	Tibet	23,165
Saipal	Nepal	23,100
Macha Pucchare	Nepal	22,958
Numbar	Nepal	22,817
Kanjiroba	Nepal	22,580
Ama Dablam	Nepal	22,350
Cho Polu	Nepal	22,093
Lingtren	Nepal-Tibet	21,972
Khumbutse	Nepal-Tibet	21,785
Hlako Gangri	Tibet	21,266
Mt. Grosvenor	China	21,190
Thagchhab Gangri	Tibet	20,970
Damavand	Iran	18,606
Ararat	Turkey	16,804

Antarctica

Peak	Height (ft)
Vinson Massif	16,864
Tyree	16,290
Shinn	15,750
Gardner	15,375
Epperly	15,100
Kirkpatrick	14,855
Elizabeth	14,698
Markham	14,290
Bell	14,117
Mackellar	14,098
Anderson	13,957
Bentley	13,934
Kaplan	13,878
Andrew Jackson	13,750
Sidley	13,720
Ostenso	13,710
Minto	13,668
Miller	13,650
Long Gables	13,620
Dickerson	13,517
Giovinetto	13,412
Wade	13,400
Fisher	13,386
Fridtjof Nansen	13,350
Wexler	13,202
Lister	13,200
Shear	13,100
Odishaw	13,008
Donaldson	12,894
Ray	12,808
Sellery	12,779
Waterman	12,730
Anne	12,703
Press	12,566
Falla	12,549
Rucker	12,520
Goldthwait	12,510
Morris	12,500
Erebus	12,450
Campbell	12,434
Don Pedro Christophersen	12,355
Lysaght	12,326
Huggins	12,247
Sabine	12,200
Astor	12,175
Mohl	12,172
Frankes	12,064
Jones	12,040
Gjelsvik	12,008
Coman	12,000

Some Notable U.S. Mountains

Name	Place	Height (ft)
Gannett Peak	WY	13,804
Grand Teton	WY	13,766
Kings	UT	13,528
Cloud	WY	13,175
Boundary	NV	13,140
Wheeler	NM	13,065
Granite	MT	12,799
Borah	ID	12,662
Humphreys	AZ	12,633
Adams	WA	12,307
San Gorgonio	CA	11,502
Hood	OR	11,235
Lassen	CA	10,457
Granite	CA	10,321
Guadalupe	TX	8,751
Olympus	WA	7,965
Harney	SD	7,242
Mitchell	NC	6,684
Clingmans Dome	NC-TN	6,643
Washington	NH	6,288
Rogers	VA	5,927
Marcy	NY	5,344
Katahdin	ME	5,268
Spruce Knob	WV	4,862
Mansfield	VT	4,393
Black Mountain	KY	4,145

Important Islands and Their Areas

Source: Bureau of the Census, U.S. Dept. of Commerce; National Atlas Information Services, Natural Resources Canada; World Almanac research

Figure in parentheses shows rank among the world's 10 largest islands. Because some islands have not been surveyed accurately, estimated areas are shown. Figures are for total land area.

Location-Ownership

Area in square miles

Arctic Ocean

Canadian

Island	Area
Axel Heiberg	16,671
Baffin (5)	195,928
Banks	27,038
Bathurst	6,194
Devon	21,331
Ellesmere (9)	75,767
Melville	16,274
Prince of Wales	12,872
Somerset	9,570
Southampton	15,913
Victoria (10)	83,897

Norwegian

Island	Area
Svalbard	23,940
Nordaustlandet	5,410
Spitsbergen	15,060

Russian

Island	Area
Franz Josef Land	8,000
Novaya Zemlya (two is.)	31,730
Wrangel	2,800

Atlantic Ocean

Island	Area
Anticosti, Canada	3,066
Ascension, UK	34
Azores, Portugal	888
Faial	67
Sao Miguel	291
Bahamas	5,386
Bermuda Is., UK	20
Bioko Is., Equatorial Guinea	785
Block, Rhode Island	10
Canary Is., Spain	2,808
Fuerteventura	668
Gran Canaria	592
Tenerife	795
Cape Breton, Canada	3,981
Cape Verde Is.	1,557
Faeroe Is., Denmark	540
Falkland Is., UK	4,700
Fernando de Noronha Archipelago, Brazil	7
Greenland, Denmark (1)	840,000
Iceland	39,769
Long Island, N.Y.	1,320
Madeira Is., Portugal	307
Marajo, Brazil	15,444
Martha's Vineyard, Mass.	89
Mount Desert, Me.	104
Nantucket, Mass.	45
Newfoundland, Canada	42,031
Prince Edward, Canada	2,170
St. Helena, UK	47
South Georgia, UK	1,450
Tierra del Fuego, Chile and Argentina	18,800
Tristan da Cunha, UK	40

British Isles

Island	Area
Great Britain, mainland (8)	84,200
Channel Islands	75
Guernsey	24
Jersey	45
Sark	2
Hebrides	2,744
Ireland	32,599
Irish Republic	27,136
Northern Ireland	5,463
Man	227
Orkney Is.	390
Scilly Is.	6
Shetland Is.	567
Skye	670
Wight	147

Baltic Sea

Island	Area
Aland Is., Finland	581
Bornholm, Denmark	227
Gotland, Sweden	1,159

Caribbean Sea

Island	Area
Antigua	108
Aruba, Netherlands	75
Barbados	166
Cuba	44,218
Isle of Youth	1,182
Curacao, Netherlands	171
Dominica	290
Guadeloupe, France	687
Hispaniola, Haiti and Dominican Republic	29,371
Jamaica	4,244
Martinique, France	425
Puerto Rico, U.S.	3,339
Tobago	116
Trinidad	1,864
Virgin Is., UK	59
Virgin Is., U.S.	134

Indian Ocean

Island	Area
Andaman Is., India	2,500
Madagascar (4)	226,658
Mauritius	720
Pemba, Tanzania	380
Reunion, France	969
Seychelles	171
Sri Lanka	25,332
Zanzibar, Tanzania	640

Persian Gulf

Island	Area
Bahrain	255

Mediterranean Sea

Island	Area
Balearic Is., Spain	1,936
Corfu, Greece	229
Corsica, France	3,369
Crete, Greece	3,189
Cyprus	3,572
Elba, Italy	86
Euboea, Greece	1,411
Malta	95
Rhodes, Greece	540
Sardinia, Italy	9,262
Sicily, Italy	9,822

Pacific Ocean

Island	Area
Aleutian Is., U.S.	6,912
Adak	275
Amchitka	116
Attu	350
Kanaga	142
Kiska	106
Tanaga	195
Umnak	686
Unalaska	1,051
Unimak	1,571
Canton, Kiribati*	4
Caroline Is.	472
Christmas, Kiribati*	94
Clipperton, France	2
Diomede, Big, Russia	11
Diomede, Little, U.S.	3
Easter, Chile	69
Fiji	7,056
Vanua Levu	2,242
Viti Levu	4,109
Funafuti, Tuvalu*	2
Galapagos Is., Ecuador	3,043
Guadalcanal	2,180
Guam	210
Hainan, China	13,000
Hawaiian Is., U.S.	6,423
Hawaii	4,028
Oahu	600
Hong Kong	29
Japan	145,809
Hokkaido	30,144
Honshu (7)	87,805
Iwo Jima	8
Kyushu	14,114
Okinawa	459
Shikoku	7,049
Kodiak, U.S.	3,465
Marquesas Is., France	492
Marshall Is.	70
Bikini*	2
Nauru	8
New Caledonia, France	6,530
New Guinea (2)	306,000
New Zealand	103,883
Chatham	372
North	44,035
South	58,305
Stewart	674
Northern Mariana Is.	179
Philippines	115,831
Leyte	2,787
Luzon	40,880
Mindanao	36,775
Mindoro	3,790
Negros	4,907
Palawan	4,554
Panay	4,446
Samar	5,050
Quemoy	56
Sakhalin, Russia	29,500
Samoa Is.	1,177
American Samoa	77
Tutuila	55
Samoa (Western)	1,133
Savaii	670
Upolu	429
Santa Catalina, U.S.	75
Tahiti, France	402
Taiwan	13,823
Tasmania, Australia	26,178
Tonga Is.	270
Vancouver, Canada	12,079
Vanuatu	5,700

East Indies

Island	Area
Bali, Indonesia	2,171
Borneo, Indonesia-Malaysia-Brunei (3)	280,100
Celebes, Indonesia	69,000
Java, Indonesia	48,900
Madura, Indonesia	2,113
Moluccas, Indonesia	32,307
New Britain, Papua New Guinea	14,093
New Ireland, Papua New Guinea	3,707
Sumatra, Indonesia (6)	165,000
Timor	13,094

* **Atolls:** Bikini (lagoon area 230 sq mi, land area 2 sq mi); Canton (lagoon 20 sq mi, land 4 sq mi), Kiribati; Christmas (lagoon 140 sq mi, land 94 sq mi), Kiribati; Funafuti (lagoon 84 sq mi, land 2 sq mi), Tuvalu. **Australia,** often called an island, is a continent.

Islands in minor waters: Manhattan (22 sq mi), Staten (59 sq mi), and Governors (173 acres), all in New York Harbor, U.S.; Isle Royale (209 sq mi), Lake Superior, U.S.; Manitoulin (1,068 sq mi), Lake Huron, Canada; Pinang (110 sq mi), Strait of Malacca, Malaysia; Singapore (239 sq mi), Singapore Strait, Singapore.

Latitude, Longitude, and Altitude of U.S. and Canadian Cities

Source: U.S. geographic positions were provided by National Oceanic Atmospheric Administration, U.S. Dept. of Commerce. U.S. altitudes were provided by Geological Survey, U.S. Dept. of the Interior. Canadian geographic positions were provided by the Geodetic Survey of Canada, Natural Resources Canada. Canadian altitudes were provided by National Atlas Information Service, Natural Resources Canada.

Altitudes are measured in feet at the downtown business areas of U.S. cities or at the city hall of Canadian cities, except where (a) indicates measurements were made at the tower of a major airport located within the city.

City	Lat. N °	'	"	Long. W °	'	"	Alt. (ft)
Abilene, Tex.	32	27	05	99	43	51	1,710
Akron, Oh.	41	05	00	81	30	44	874
Albany, N.Y.	42	39	01	73	45	01	20
Albuquerque, N.M.	35	05	01	106	39	05	4,945
Alert, N.W.T.	82	29	50	62	21	15	95
Allentown, Pa.	40	36	11	75	28	06	255
Amarillo, Tex.	35	12	27	101	50	04	3,685
Anchorage, Alas.	61	10	00	149	59	00	118
Ann Arbor, Mich.	42	16	59	83	44	52	880
Asheville, N.C.	35	35	42	82	33	26	1,985
Ashland, Ky.	38	28	36	82	38	23	536
Atlanta, Ga.	33	45	10	84	23	37	1,050
Atlantic City, N.J.	39	21	32	74	25	53	10
Augusta, Ga.	33	28	20	81	58	00	143
Augusta, Me.	44	18	53	69	46	29	45
Austin, Tex.	30	16	09	97	44	37	505
Bakersfield, Cal.	35	22	31	119	01	18	400
Baltimore, Md.	39	17	26	76	36	45	20
Bangor, Me.	44	48	13	68	46	18	20
Baton Rouge, La.	30	26	58	91	11	00	57
Battle Creek, Mich.	42	18	58	85	10	48	820
Bay City, Mich.	43	36	04	83	53	15	595
Beaumont, Tex.	30	05	20	94	06	09	20
Belleville, Ont.	44	09	42	77	23	11	257
Bellingham, Wash.	48	45	34	122	28	36	60
Berkeley, Cal.	37	52	10	122	16	17	40
Billings, Mon.	45	47	00	108	30	04	3,120
Biloxi, Miss.	30	23	48	88	53	00	20
Binghamton, N.Y.	42	06	03	75	54	47	865
Birmingham, Ala.	33	31	01	86	48	36	600
Bismarck, N.D.	46	48	23	100	47	17	1,674
Bloomington, Ill.	40	28	58	88	59	36	800
Boise, Ida.	43	37	07	116	11	58	2,704
Boston, Mass.	42	21	24	71	03	25	21
Bowling Green, Ky.	36	59	41	86	26	33	510
Brandon, Man.	49	51	00	99	57	00	1,343(a)
Brantford, Ont.	43	08	34	80	15	39	705(a)
Brattleboro, Vt.	42	51	06	72	33	48	300
Bridgeport, Conn.	41	10	49	73	11	22	10
Brockton, Mass.	42	05	02	71	01	25	130
Buffalo, N.Y.	42	52	52	78	52	21	585
Burlington, Ont.	43	19	33	79	47	57	284
Burlington, Vt.	44	28	34	73	12	46	110
Butte, Mon.	46	01	06	112	32	11	5,765
Calgary, Alta.	51	02	46	114	03	24	3,427
Cambridge, Mass.	42	22	01	71	06	22	20
Canton, Oh.	40	47	50	81	22	37	1,030
Carson City, Nev.	39	10	00	119	46	00	4,680
Cedar Rapids, Ia.	41	58	01	91	39	53	730
Central Islip, N.Y.	40	47	24	73	12	00	80
Champaign, Ill.	40	07	05	88	14	48	740
Charleston, S.C.	32	46	35	79	55	53	9
Charleston, W.Va.	38	21	01	81	37	52	601
Charlotte, N.C.	35	13	44	80	50	45	720
Charlottetown, P.E.I.	46	14	07	63	07	49	31
Chattanooga, Tenn.	35	02	41	85	18	32	675
Cheyenne, Wy.	41	08	09	104	49	07	6,100
Chicago, Ill.	41	52	28	87	38	22	595
Churchill, Man.	58	45	15	94	10	00	94(a)
Cincinnati, Oh.	39	06	07	84	30	35	550
Cleveland, Oh.	41	29	51	81	41	50	660
Colorado Springs, Col.	38	50	07	104	49	16	5,980
Columbia, Mo.	38	57	03	92	19	46	730
Columbia, S.C.	34	00	02	81	02	00	190
Columbus, Ga.	32	28	07	84	59	24	265
Columbus, Oh.	39	57	47	83	00	17	780
Concord, N.H.	43	12	22	71	32	25	290
Corpus Christi, Tex.	27	47	51	97	23	45	35
Dallas, Tex.	32	47	09	96	47	37	435
Dartmouth, N.S.	44	39	50	63	34	08	24
Dawson, Yukon	64	03	30	139	26	00	1,050
Dayton, Oh.	39	45	32	84	11	43	574
Daytona Beach, Fla.	29	12	44	81	01	10	7
Decatur, Ill.	39	50	42	88	56	47	682
Denver, Col.	39	44	58	104	59	22	5,280
Des Moines, Ia.	41	35	14	93	37	00	803
Detroit, Mich.	42	19	48	83	02	57	585
Dodge City, Kan.	37	45	17	100	01	09	2,480
Dubuque, Ia.	42	29	55	90	40	08	620
Duluth, Minn.	46	46	56	92	06	24	610
Durham, N.C.	36	00	00	78	54	45	405
Eau Claire, Wis.	44	48	31	91	29	49	790
Edmonton, Alta.	53	32	43	113	29	21	2,186
Elizabeth, N.J.	40	39	43	74	12	59	21
El Paso, Tex.	31	45	36	106	29	11	3,695
Enid, Okla.	36	23	40	97	52	35	1,240
Erie, Pa.	42	07	15	80	04	57	685
Eugene, Ore.	44	03	16	123	05	30	422
Eureka, Cal.	40	48	08	124	09	46	45
Evansville, Ind.	37	58	20	87	34	21	385
Fairbanks, Alas.	64	48	00	147	51	00	448
Fall River, Mass.	41	42	06	71	09	18	40
Fargo, N.D.	46	52	30	96	47	18	900
Flagstaff, Ariz.	35	11	36	111	39	06	6,900
Flint, Mich.	43	00	50	83	41	33	750
Ft. Smith, Ark.	35	23	10	94	25	36	440
Ft. Wayne, Ind.	41	04	21	85	08	26	790
Ft. Worth, Tex.	32	44	55	97	19	44	670
Fredericton, N.B.	45	57	47	66	38	38	29
Fresno, Cal.	36	44	12	119	47	11	285
Gadsden, Ala.	34	00	57	86	00	41	555
Gainesville, Fla.	29	38	56	82	19	19	175
Gallup, N.M.	35	31	30	108	44	30	6,540
Galveston, Tex.	29	18	10	94	47	43	5
Gary, Ind.	41	36	12	87	20	19	590
Grand Junction, Col.	39	04	06	108	33	54	4,590
Grand Rapids, Mich.	42	58	03	85	40	13	610
Great Falls, Mon.	47	29	33	111	18	23	3,340
Green Bay, Wis.	44	30	48	88	00	50	590
Greensboro, N.C.	36	04	17	79	47	25	839
Greenville, S.C.	34	50	50	82	24	01	966
Guelph, Ont.	43	32	35	80	14	54	1,065
Gulfport, Miss.	30	22	04	89	05	36	20
Halifax, N.S.	44	38	54	63	34	30	60
Hamilton, Oh.	39	23	59	84	33	47	600
Hamilton, Ont.	43	15	20	79	52	30	329
Harrisburg, Pa.	40	15	43	76	52	59	365
Hartford, Conn.	41	46	12	72	40	49	40
Helena, Mon.	46	35	33	112	02	24	4,155
Hilo, Ha.	19	43	30	155	05	24	40
Honolulu, Ha.	21	18	22	157	51	35	21
Houston, Tex.	29	45	26	95	21	37	40
Hull, Que.	45	25	42	75	42	41	185
Huntsville, Ala.	34	44	18	86	35	19	640
Indianapolis, Ind.	39	46	07	86	09	46	710
Iowa City, Ia.	41	39	37	91	31	53	685
Jackson, Mich.	42	14	43	84	24	22	940
Jackson, Miss.	32	17	56	90	11	06	298
Jacksonville, Fla.	30	19	44	81	39	42	20
Jersey City, N.J.	40	43	50	74	03	56	20
Johnstown, Pa.	40	19	35	78	55	03	1,185
Joplin, Mo.	37	05	26	94	30	00	990
Juneau, Alas.	58	18	12	134	24	30	50
Kalamazoo, Mich.	42	17	29	85	35	14	755
Kansas City, Kan.	39	07	04	94	38	24	750
Kansas City, Mo.	39	04	56	94	35	20	750
Kenosha, Wis.	42	35	43	87	50	11	610
Key West, Fla.	24	33	30	81	48	12	5
Kingston, Ont.	44	13	53	76	28	48	264
Kitchener, Ont.	43	26	58	80	29	12	1,100
Knoxville, Tenn.	35	57	39	83	55	07	890
Lafayette, Ind.	40	25	11	86	53	39	550
Lancaster, Pa.	40	02	25	76	18	29	355
Lansing, Mich.	42	44	01	84	33	15	830
Laredo, Tex.	27	30	22	99	30	30	440
La Salle, Que.	45	25	30	73	39	30	110
Las Vegas, Nev.	36	10	20	115	08	37	2,030
Laval, Que.	45	33	05	73	44	42	142
Lawrence, Mass.	42	42	16	71	10	08	65
Lethbridge, Alta.	49	41	38	112	49	58	2,985
Lexington, Ky.	38	02	50	84	29	46	955
Lihue, Ha.	21	58	48	159	22	30	210

City	Lat. N °	′	″	Long. W °	′	″	Alt. (ft)
Lima, Oh.	40	44	35	84	06	20	865
Lincoln, Neb.	40	48	59	96	42	15	1,150
Little Rock, Ark.	34	44	42	92	16	37	286
London, Ont.	42	59	17	81	14	03	822
Los Angeles, Cal.	34	03	15	118	14	28	340
Louisville, Ky.	38	14	47	85	45	49	450
Lowell, Mass.	42	38	25	71	19	14	100
Lubbock, Tex.	33	35	05	101	50	33	3,195
Macon, Ga.	32	50	12	83	37	36	335
Madison, Wis.	43	04	23	89	22	55	860
Manchester, N.H.	42	59	28	71	27	41	175
Marshall, Tex.	32	33	00	94	23	00	410
Memphis, Tenn.	35	08	46	90	03	13	275
Meriden, Conn.	41	32	06	72	47	30	190
Miami, Fla.	25	46	37	80	11	32	10
Milwaukee, Wis.	43	02	19	87	54	15	635
Minneapolis, Minn.	44	58	57	93	15	43	815
Minot, N.D.	48	14	09	101	17	38	1,550
Mississauga, Ont.	43	33	00	79	35	00	510
Mobile, Ala.	30	41	36	88	02	33	5
Moncton, N.B.	46	05	18	64	46	41	38
Montgomery, Ala.	32	22	33	86	18	31	160
Montpelier, Vt.	44	15	36	72	34	41	485
Montréal, Que.	45	30	33	73	33	14	90
Moose Jaw, Sask.	50	23	34	105	32	04	1,784
Muncie, Ind.	40	11	28	85	23	16	950
Nashville, Tenn.	36	09	33	86	46	55	450
Natchez, Miss.	31	33	48	91	23	30	210
Newark, N.J.	40	44	14	74	10	19	55
New Britain, Conn.	41	40	08	72	46	59	200
New Haven, Conn.	41	18	25	72	55	30	40
New Orleans, La.	29	56	53	90	04	10	5
New York, N.Y.	40	45	06	73	59	39	55
Niagara Falls, Ont.	43	06	22	79	03	51	590
Nome, Alas.	64	30	00	165	25	00	25
Norfolk, Va.	36	51	10	76	17	21	10
North Bay, Ont.	46	18	35	79	27	45	670
Oakland, Cal.	37	48	03	122	15	54	25
Ogden, Ut.	41	13	31	111	58	21	4,295
Oklahoma City, Okla.	35	28	26	97	31	04	1,195
Omaha, Neb.	41	15	42	95	56	14	1,040
Orlando, Fla.	28	32	42	81	22	38	70
Ottawa, Ont.	45	26	24	75	41	42	185
Paducah, Ky.	37	05	13	88	35	56	345
Pasadena, Cal.	34	08	44	118	08	41	830
Paterson, N.J.	40	55	01	74	10	21	100
Pensacola, Fla.	30	24	51	87	12	56	15
Peoria, Ill.	40	41	42	89	35	33	470
Peterborough, Ont.	44	18	32	78	19	13	673
Philadelphia, Pa.	39	56	58	75	09	21	100
Phoenix, Ariz.	33	27	12	112	04	28	1,090
Pierre, S.D.	44	22	18	100	20	54	1,480
Pittsburgh, Pa.	40	26	19	80	00	00	745
Pittsfield, Mass.	42	26	53	73	15	14	1,015
Pocatello, Ida.	42	51	38	112	27	01	4,460
Pt. Arthur, Tex.	29	52	30	93	56	15	10
Portland, Me.	43	39	33	70	15	19	25
Portland, Ore.	45	31	06	122	40	35	77
Portsmouth, N.H.	43	04	30	70	45	24	20
Portsmouth, Va.	36	50	07	76	18	14	10
Prince Rupert, B.C.	54	19	00	130	19	00	125(a)
Providence, R.I.	41	49	32	71	24	41	80
Provo, Ut.	40	14	06	111	39	24	4,550
Pueblo, Col.	38	16	17	104	36	33	4,690
Québec City, Que.	46	48	51	71	12	30	163
Racine, Wis.	42	43	49	87	47	12	630
Raleigh, N.C.	35	46	38	78	38	21	365
Rapid City, S.D.	44	04	52	103	13	11	3,230
Reading, Pa.	40	20	09	75	55	40	265
Regina, Sask.	50	26	55	104	36	50	1,894(a)
Reno, Nev.	39	31	27	119	48	40	4,490
Richmond, Va.	37	32	15	77	26	09	160
Roanoke, Va.	37	16	13	79	56	44	905
Rochester, Minn.	44	01	21	92	28	03	990
Rochester, N.Y.	43	09	41	77	36	21	515
Rockford, Ill.	42	16	07	89	05	48	715
Sacramento, Cal.	38	34	57	121	29	41	30
Saginaw, Mich.	43	25	52	83	56	05	595
St. Catharines, Ont.	43	09	33	79	14	50	362(a)
St. Cloud, Minn.	45	34	00	94	10	24	1,040
St. John, N.B.	45	16	22	66	03	48	27
St. John's, Nfld.	47	33	42	52	42	48	200(a)

City	Lat. N °	′	″	Long. W °	′	″	Alt. (ft)
St. Joseph, Mo.	39	45	57	94	51	02	850
St. Louis, Mo.	38	37	45	90	12	22	455
St. Paul, Minn.	44	57	19	93	06	07	780
St. Petersburg, Fla.	27	46	18	82	38	19	20
Salem, Ore.	44	56	24	123	01	59	155
Salina, Kan.	38	50	36	97	36	46	1,229
Salt Lake City, Ut.	40	45	23	111	53	26	4,390
San Antonio, Tex.	29	25	37	98	29	06	650
San Bernardino, Cal.	34	06	30	117	17	28	1,080
San Diego, Cal.	32	42	53	117	09	21	20
San Francisco, Cal.	37	46	39	122	24	40	65
San Jose, Cal.	37	20	16	121	53	24	90
San Juan, P.R.	18	27	00	66	04	15	35
Santa Barbara, Cal.	34	25	18	119	41	55	100
Santa Cruz, Cal.	36	58	18	122	01	18	20
Santa Fe, N.M.	35	41	11	105	56	10	6,950
Sarasota, Fla.	27	20	05	82	32	30	20
Saskatoon, Sask.	52	07	49	106	39	35	1,587
Sault Ste. Marie, Ont.	46	30	24	84	20	04	589
Savannah, Ga.	32	04	42	81	05	37	20
Schenectady, N.Y.	42	48	42	73	55	42	245
Seattle, Wash.	47	36	32	122	20	12	10
Sheboygan, Wis.	43	45	03	87	42	52	630
Sherbrooke, Que.	45	24	27	71	51	07	627
Sheridan, Wy.	44	47	55	106	57	10	3,740
Shreveport, La.	32	30	46	93	44	58	204
Sioux City, Ia.	42	29	46	96	24	30	1,110
Sioux Falls, S.D.	43	32	35	96	43	35	1,395
South Bend, Ind.	41	40	33	86	15	01	710
Spartanburg, S.C.	34	57	03	81	56	06	875
Spokane, Wash.	47	39	32	117	25	33	1,890
Springfield, Ill.	39	47	58	89	38	51	610
Springfield, Mass.	42	06	21	72	35	32	85
Springfield, Mo.	37	13	03	93	17	32	1,300
Springfield, Oh.	39	55	38	83	48	29	980
Stamford, Conn.	41	03	09	73	32	24	35
Steubenville, Oh.	40	21	42	80	36	53	660
Stockton, Cal.	37	57	30	121	17	16	20
Sudbury, Ont.	46	29	24	80	59	24	879
Superior, Wis.	46	43	14	92	06	07	630
Sydney, N.S.	46	08	15	60	11	48	25
Syracuse, N.Y.	43	03	04	76	09	14	400
Tacoma, Wash.	47	14	59	122	26	15	110
Tallahassee, Fla.	30	26	30	84	16	56	150
Tampa, Fla.	27	56	58	82	27	25	15
Terre Haute, Ind.	39	28	03	87	24	26	496
Texarkana, Tex.	33	25	48	94	02	30	324
Thunder Bay, Ont.	48	22	54	89	14	42	616
Toledo, Oh.	41	39	14	83	32	39	585
Topeka, Kan.	39	03	16	95	40	23	930
Toronto, Ont.	43	39	10	79	23	00	300
Trenton, N.J.	40	13	14	74	46	13	35
Trois-Rivières, Que.	46	20	36	72	32	37	115(a)
Troy, N.Y.	42	43	45	73	40	58	35
Tucson, Ariz.	32	13	15	110	58	08	2,390
Tulsa, Okla.	36	09	12	95	59	34	804
Urbana, Ill.	40	06	42	88	12	06	725
Utica, N.Y.	43	06	12	75	13	33	415
Vancouver, B.C.	49	18	56	123	04	44	141
Victoria, B.C.	48	25	43	123	21	49	57
Waco, Tex.	31	33	12	97	08	00	405
Walla Walla, Wash.	46	04	08	118	20	24	936
Washington, D.C.	38	53	51	77	00	33	25
Waterloo, Ia.	42	29	40	92	20	20	850
West Palm Beach, Fla.	26	42	36	80	03	07	15
Wheeling, W.Va.	40	04	03	80	43	20	650
Whitehorse, Yukon	60	43	17	135	03	03	2,050
White Plains, N.Y.	41	02	00	73	45	48	220
Wichita, Kan.	37	41	30	97	20	16	1,290
Wilkes-Barre, Pa.	41	14	32	75	53	17	640
Wilmington, Del.	39	44	46	75	32	51	135
Wilmington, N.C.	34	14	14	77	56	58	35
Windsor, Ont.	42	18	56	83	02	10	603
Winnipeg, Man.	49	53	56	97	08	23	762
Winston-Salem, N.C.	36	05	52	80	14	42	860
Worcester, Mass.	42	15	37	71	48	17	475
Yakima, Wash.	46	36	09	120	30	39	1,060
Yellowknife, N.W.T.	62	27	16	114	22	33	674
Youngstown, Oh.	41	05	57	80	39	02	840
Yuma, Ariz.	32	42	54	114	37	24	160
Zanesville, Oh.	39	56	18	82	00	30	720

World Cities

Source: Defense Mapping Agency, Hydrographic/Topographic Center, U.S. Dept. of Defense

City	Lat. °	Lat. ′	Long. °	Long. ′	Alt. (ft)	City	Lat. °	Lat. ′	Long. °	Long. ′	Alt. (ft)
Athens, Greece	37	59 N	23	44 E	300	Mexico City, Mexico	19	24 N	99	09 W	7,347
Bangkok, Thailand	13	45 N	100	31 E	0	Moscow, Russia	55	45 N	37	35 E	394
Beijing, China	39	56 N	116	24 E	600	New Delhi, India	28	36 N	77	12 E	770
Berlin, Germany	52	31 N	13	25 E	110	Panama City, Panama	08	58 N	79	32 W	0
Bogotá, Colombia	04	36 N	74	05 W	11,490	Paris, France	48	52 N	02	20 E	300
Bombay, India	18	58 N	72	50 E	27	Quito, Ecuador	00	13 S	78	30 W	9,222
Buenos Aires, Argentina	34	36 S	58	28 W	0	Rio de Janeiro, Brazil	22	43 S	43	13 W	30
Cairo, Egypt	30	03 N	31	15 E	381	Rome, Italy	41	53 N	12	30 E	95
Jakarta, Indonesia	06	10 S	106	48 E	26	Santiago, Chile	33	27 S	70	40 W	4,921
Jerusalem, Israel	31	46 N	35	14 E	2,500	Seoul, South Korea	37	34 N	127	00 E	34
Johannesburg, So. Afr.	26	12 S	28	05 E	5,740	Sydney, Australia	33	53 S	151	12 E	25
Kathmandu, Nepal	27	43 S	85	19 E	4,500	Tehran, Iran	35	40 N	51	26 E	3,937
Kiev, Ukraine	50	26 N	30	31 E	0	Tokyo, Japan	35	42 S	139	46 E	30
London, UK (Greenwich)	51	30 N	00	00	245	Tripoli, Libya	32	54 N	13	11 E	0
Manila, Philippines	14	35 N	120	00 E	0	Warsaw, Poland	52	15 N	21	00 E	360
Mecca, Saudi Arabia	21	27 N	39	49 E	6,562	Wellington, New Zealand	41	18 S	174	47 E	0

Ocean Areas and Average Depths

Geographers and mapmakers recognize four major bodies of water: the Pacific, the Atlantic, the Indian, and the Arctic oceans. The Atlantic and Pacific oceans are considered divided at the equator into the N and S Atlantic and the N and S Pacific. The Arctic Ocean is the name for waters N of the continental landmasses in the region of the Arctic Circle.

	Area (sq mi)	Avg. depth (ft)		Area (sq mi)	Avg. depth (ft)
Pacific Ocean	64,186,300	12,925	Hudson Bay	281,900	305
Atlantic Ocean	33,420,000	11,730	East China Sea	256,600	620
Indian Ocean	28,350,500	12,598	Andaman Sea	218,100	3,667
Arctic Ocean	5,105,700	3,407	Black Sea	196,100	3,906
South China Sea	1,148,500	4,802	Red Sea	174,900	1,764
Caribbean Sea	971,400	8,448	North Sea	164,900	308
Mediterranean Sea	969,100	4,926	Baltic Sea	147,500	180
Bering Sea	873,000	4,893	Yellow Sea	113,500	121
Gulf of Mexico	582,100	5,297	Persian Gulf	88,800	328
Sea of Okhotsk	537,500	3,192	Gulf of California	59,100	2,375
Sea of Japan	391,100	5,468			

Principal Ocean Depths

Source: Defense Mapping Agency, Hydrographic/Topographic Center, U.S. Dept. of Defense

Name of area	Location (lat.)	Location (long.)	Depth (meters)	Depth (fathoms)	Depth (ft)
Pacific Ocean					
Mariana Trench	11°22′N	142°36′E	10,924	5,973	35,840
Tonga Trench	23°16′S	174°44′W	10,800	5,906	35,433
Philippine Trench	10°38′N	126°36′E	10,057	5,499	32,995
Kermadec Trench	31°53′S	177°21′W	10,047	5,494	32,963
Bonin Trench	24°30′N	143°24′E	9,994	5,464	32,788
Kuril Trench	44°15′N	150°34′E	9,750	5,331	31,988
Izu Trench	31°05′N	142°10′E	9,695	5,301	31,808
New Britain Trench	06°19′S	153°45′E	8,940	4,888	29,331
Yap Trench	08°33′N	138°02′E	8,527	4,663	27,976
Japan Trench	36°08′N	142°43′E	8,412	4,600	27,599
Peru-Chile Trench	23°18′S	71°14′W	8,064	4,409	26,457
Palau Trench	07°52′N	134°56′E	8,054	4,404	26,424
Aleutian Trench	50°51′N	177°11′E	7,679	4,199	25,194
New Hebrides Trench	20°36′S	168°37′E	7,570	4,139	24,836
North Ryukyu Trench	24°00′N	126°48′E	7,181	3,927	23,560
Mid. America Trench	14°02′N	93°39′W	6,662	3,643	21,857
Atlantic Ocean					
Puerto Rico Trench	19°55′N	65°27′W	8,605	4,705	28,232
S Sandwich Trench	55°42′S	25°56′E	8,325	4,552	27,313
Romanche Gap	0°13′S	18°26′W	7,728	4,226	25,354
Cayman Trench	19°12′N	80°00′W	7,535	4,120	24,721
Brazil Basin	09°10′S	23°02′W	6,119	3,346	20,076
Indian Ocean					
Java Trench	10°19′S	109°58′E	7,125	3,896	23,376
Ob' Trench	09°45′S	67°18′E	6,874	3,759	22,553
Diamantina Trench	35°50′S	105°14′E	6,602	3,610	21,660
Vema Trench	09°08′S	67°15′E	6,402	3,501	21,004
Agulhas Basin	45°20′S	26°50′E	6,195	3,387	20,325
Arctic Ocean					
Eurasia Basin	82°23′N	19°31′E	5,450	2,980	17,881
Mediterranean Sea					
Ionian Basin	36°32′N	21°06′E	5,150	2,816	16,896

Note: Deeper depths have been reported in some of the above areas. They are not official, however, unless confirmed by research vessels.

Principal World Rivers

Source: Geological Survey, U.S. Dept. of the Interior

River	Outflow	Length (mi)
Albany	James Bay	610
Amazon	Atlantic Ocean	4,000
Amu	Aral Sea	1,578
Amur	Tatar Strait	2,744
Angara	Yenisey River	1,151
Arkansas	Mississippi	1,459
Back	Arctic Ocean	605
Brahmaputra	Bay of Bengal	1,800
Bug, Southern	Dnieper River	532
Bug, Western	Wisla River	481
Canadian	Arkansas River	906
Chang Jiang	E. China Sea	3,964
Churchill, Man.	Hudson Bay	1,000
Churchill, Que.	Atlantic Ocean	532
Colorado	Gulf of Calif.	1,450
Columbia	Pacific Ocean	1,243
Congo	Atlantic Ocean	2,718
Danube	Black Sea	1,776
Dnieper	Black Sea	1,420
Dniester	Black Sea	877
Don	Sea of Azov	1,224
Drava	Danube River	447
Dvina, North	White Sea	824
Dvina, West	Gulf of Riga	634
Ebro	Mediterranean	565
Elbe	North Sea	724
Euphrates	Shatt al-Arab	1,700
Fraser	Str. of Georgia	850
Gambia	Atlantic Ocean	700
Ganges	Bay of Bengal	1,560
Garonne	Bay of Biscay	357
Huang	Yellow Sea	3,395
Indus	Arabian Sea	1,800
Irrawaddy	Bay of Bengal	1,337
Japura	Amazon River	1,750
Jordan	Dead Sea	200
Kootenay	Columbia River	485
Lena	Laptev Sea	2,734
Loire	Bay of Biscay	634
Mackenz ie	Arctic Ocean	2,635
Madeira	Amazon River	2,013
Magdalena	Caribbean Sea	956
Marne	Seine River	326
Mekong	S. China Sea	2,600
Meuse	North Sea	580
Mississippi	Gulf of Mexico	2,340
Missouri	Mississippi	2,315
Murray-Darling	Indian Ocean	2,310
Negro	Amazon	1,400
Nelson	Hudson Bay	410
Niger	Gulf of Guinea	2,590
Nile	Mediterranean	4,160
Ob-Irtysh	Gulf of Ob	3,362
Oder	Baltic Sea	567
Ohio	Mississippi	981
Orange	Atlantic Ocean	1,300
Orinoco	Atantic Ocean	1,600
Ottawa	St. Lawrence R.	790
Paraguay	Parana River	1,584
Parana	Rio de la Plata	2,485
Peace	Slave River	1,210
Pilcomayo	Paraguay River	1,000
Po	Adriatic Sea	405
Purus	Amazon River	2,100
Red	Mississippi	1,290
Red River of N.	Lake Winnipeg	545
Rhine	North Sea	820
Rhone	Gulf of Lions	505
Rio de la Plata	Atlantic Ocean	150
Rio Grande	Gulf of Mexico	1,900
Rio Roosevelt	Aripuana	400
Saguenay	St. Lawrence R.	434
St. John	Bay of Fundy	418
St. Lawrence	Gulf of St. Law.	800
Salween	Andaman Sea	1,500
Sao Francisco	Atlantic Ocean	1,988
Saskatchewan	Lake Winnipeg	1,205
Seine	English Chan.	496
Shannon	Atlantic Ocean	230
Snake	Columbia River	1,038
Songhua	Amur River	1,150
Syr	Aral Sea	1,370
Tajo, Tagus	Atlantic Ocean	626
Tennessee	Ohio River	652
Thames	North Sea	236
Tiber	Tyrrhenian Sea	252
Tigris	Shatt al-Arab	1,180
Tisza	Danube River	600
Tocantins	Para River	1,677
Ural	Caspian Sea	1,575
Uruguay	Rio de la Plata	1,000
Volga	Caspian Sea	2,290
Weser	North Sea	454
Wisla	Bay of Danzig	675
Xi	S. China Sea	1,200
Yellow (See Huang)		
Yenisey	Kara Sea	2,543
Yukon	Bering Sea	1,979
Zambezi	Indian Ocean	1,700

Major Rivers in North America

Source: Geological Survey, U.S. Dept. of the Interior

River	Source or Upper Limit of Length	Outflow	Length (mi)
Alabama	Gilmer County, Ga.	Mobile River	729
Albany	Lake St. Joseph, Ontario	James Bay	610
Allegheny	Potter County, Pa.	Ohio River	325
Altamaha-Ocmulgee	Junction of Yellow and South Rivers, Newton County, Ga.	Atlantic Ocean	392
Apalachicola-Chattahoochee	Towns County, Ga.	Gulf of Mexico	524
Arkansas	Lake County, Col.	Mississippi River	1,459
Assiniboine	Eastern Saskatchewan	Red River	450
Attawapiskat	Attawapiskat, Ontario	James Bay	465
Back (N.W.T.)	Contwoyto Lake	Chantrey Inlet	605
Big Black (Miss.)	Webster County, Miss.	Mississippi River	330
Brazos	Junction of Salt and Double Mountain Forks, Stonewall County, Tex.	Gulf of Mexico	923
Canadian	Las Animas County, Col.	Arkansas River	906
Cedar (Iowa)	Dodge County, Minn.	Iowa River	329
Cheyenne	Junction of Antelope Creek and Dry Fork, Converse County, Wyo.	Missouri River	290
Churchill	Methy Lake, Saskatchewan	Hudson Bay	1,000
Cimarron	Colfax County, N.M.	Arkansas River	600
Colorado (Ariz.)	Rocky Mountain National Park, Col. (90 miles in Mexico)	Gulf of Cal.	1,450
Colorado (Texas)	West Texas	Matagorda Bay	862
Columbia	Columbia Lake, British Columbia	Pacific Ocean, bet. Ore. and Wash.	1,243
Columbia, Upper	Columbia Lake, British Columbia	To mouth of Snake River	890
Connecticut	Third Connecticut Lake, N.H.	L.I. Sound, Conn.	407
Coppermine (N.W.T.)	Lac de Gras	Coronation Gulf (Arctic Ocean)	525
Cumberland	Letcher County, Ky.	Ohio River	720
Delaware	Schoharie County, N.Y.	Liston Point, Delaware Bay	390
Fraser	Near Mount Robson (on Continental Divide)	Strait of Georgia	850
Gila	Catron County, N.M.	Colorado River	649
Green (Ut.-Wyo.)	Junction of Wells and Trail Creeks, Sublette County, Wyo.	Colorado River	730
Hamilton (Lab.)	Lake Ashuanipi	Atlantic Ocean	532
Hudson	Henderson Lake, Essex County, N.Y.	Upper N.Y. Bay	306
Illinois	St. Joseph County, Ind.	Mississippi River	420
James (N.D.-S.D.)	Wells County, N.D.	Missouri River	710
James (Va.)	Junction of Jackson and Cowpasture Rivers, Botetourt County, Va.	Hampton Roads	340
Kanawha-New	Junction of North and South Forks of New River, N.C.	Ohio River	352

(continued)

River	Source or Upper Limit of Length	Outflow	Length (mi)
Kentucky	Junction of North and Middle Forks, Lee County, Ky.	Ohio River	259
Klamath	Lake Ewauna, Klamath Falls, Ore.	Pacific Ocean	250
Koyukuk	Endicott Mountains, Alaska	Yukon River	470
Kuskokwim	Alaska Range	Kuskokwim Bay	724
Liard	Southern Yukon, Alaska	Mackenzie River	693
Little Missouri	Crook County, Wyo.	Missouri River	560
Mackenzie	Great Slave Lake, N.W.T.	Arctic Ocean	2,635
Milk	Junction of North and South Forks, Alberta	Missouri River	625
Minnesota	Big Stone Lake, Minn.	Mississippi River	332
Mississippi	Lake Itasca, Minn.	Mouth of Southwest Pass	2,340
Mississippi, Upper	Lake Itasca, Minn.	To mouth of Missouri River	1,171
Mississippi-Missouri-Red Rock	Source of Red Rock, Beaverhead Co., Mon.	Mouth of Southwest Pass	3,710
Missouri	Junction of Jefferson, Madison, and Gallatin rivers, Madison County, Mon.	Mississippi River	2,315
Missouri-Red Rock	Source of Red Rock, Beaverhead Co., Mon.	Mississippi River	2,540
Mobile-Alabama-Coosa	Gilmer County, Ga.	Mobile Bay	774
Nelson (Manitoba)	Lake Winnipeg	Hudson Bay	410
Neosho	Morris County, Kan.	Arkansas River, Okla.	460
Niobrara	Niobrara County, Wyo.	Missouri River, Neb.	431
North Canadian	Union County, N.M.	Canadian River, Okla.	800
North Platte	Junction of Grizzly and Little Grizzly creeks, Jackson County, Col.	Platte River, Neb.	618
Ohio	Junction of Allegheny and Monongahela rivers, Pittsburgh, Pa.	Mississippi River	981
Ohio-Allegheny	Potter County, Pa.	Mississippi River	1,310
Osage	East-central Kansas	Missouri River	500
Ottawa	Lake Capimitchigama	St. Lawrence River	790
Ouachita	Polk County, Ark.	Red River	605
Peace	Stikine Mountains, B.C.	Slave River	1,210
Pearl	Neshoba County, Miss.	Gulf of Mexico	411
Pecos	Mora County, N.M.	Rio Grande	926
Pee Dee-Yadkin	Watauga County, N.C.	Winyah Bay	435
Pend Oreille-Clark Fork	Near Butte, Mon.	Columbia River	531
Platte	Junction of North and South Platte Rivers, Neb.	Missouri River	310
Porcupine	Ogilvie Mountains, Alaska	Yukon River, Alaska	569
Potomac	Garrett County, Md.	Chesapeake Bay	383
Powder	Junction of South and Middle Forks, Wyo.	Yellowstone River	375
Red (Okla.-Tex.-La.)	Curry County, N.M.	Mississippi River	1,290
Red River of the North	Junction of Otter Tail and Bois de Sioux Rivers, Wilkin County, Minn.	Lake Winnipeg	545
Republican	Junction of North Fork and Arikaree River, Neb.	Kansas River	445
Rio Grande	San Juan County, Col.	Gulf of Mexico	1,900
Roanoke	Junction of North and South Forks, Montgomery County, Va.	Albemarle Sound	380
Rock (Ill.-Wis.)	Dodge County, Wis.	Mississippi River	300
Sabine	Junction of South and Caddo Forks, Hunt County, Tex.	Sabine Lake	380
Sacramento	Siskiyou County, Cal.	Suisun Bay	377
St. Francis	Iron County, Mo.	Mississippi River	425
St. Lawrence	Lake Ontario	Gulf of St. Lawrence (Atlantic Ocean)	800
Salmon (Idaho)	Custer County, Ida.	Snake River	420
San Joaquin	Junction of South and Middle Forks, Madera County, Cal.	Suisun Bay	350
San Juan	Silver Lake, Archuleta County, Col.	Colorado River	360
Santee-Wateree-Catawba	McDowell County, N.C.	Atlantic Ocean	538
Saskatchewan, North	Rocky Mountains	Saskatchewan R.	800
Saskatchewan, South	Rocky Mountains	Saskatchewan R.	865
Savannah	Junction of Seneca and Tugaloo rivers, Anderson County, S.C.	Atlantic Ocean, Ga.-S.C.	314
Severn (Ontario)	Sandy Lake	Hudson Bay	610
Smoky Hill	Cheyenne County, Col.	Kansas River, Kan.	540
Snake	Teton County, Wyo.	Columbia River, Wash.	1,038
South Platte	Junction of South and Middle Forks, Park County, Col.	Platte River	424
Susitna	Alaska Range	Cook Inlet	313
Susquehanna	Huyden Creek, Otsego County, N.Y.	Chesapeake Bay	447
Tallahatchie	Tippah County, Miss.	Yazoo River	301
Tanana	Wrangell Mountains, Alaska	Yukon River	659
Tennessee	Junction of French Broad and Holston Rivers	Ohio River	652
Tennessee-French Broad	Courthouse Creek, Transylvania County, N.C.	Ohio River	886
Tombigbee	Prentiss County, Miss.	Mobile River	525
Trinity	North of Dallas, Tex.	Galveston Bay	360
Wabash	Darke County, Oh.	Ohio River	512
Washita	Hemphill County, Tex.	Red River, Okla.	500
White (Ark.-Mo.)	Madison County, Ark.	Mississippi River	722
Willamette	Douglas County, Ore.	Columbia River	309
Wind-Bighorn	Junction of Wind and Little Wind Rivers, Fremont Co., Wyo. (Source of Wind R. is Togwotee Pass, Teton Co., Wyo.)	Yellowstone River	336
Wisconsin	Lac Vieux Desert, Vilas County, Wis.	Mississippi River	430
Yellowstone	Park County, Wyo.	Missouri River	692
Yukon	McNeil R., Yukon Territory	Bering Sea	1,979

Lakes of the World

Source: Geological Survey, U.S. Dept. of the Interior

A lake is a body of water surrounded by land. Although some lakes are called seas (such as the Caspian Sea and the Aral Sea), they are lakes by definition.

Name	Continent	Area (sq mi)	Length (mi)	Depth (ft)	Elevation (ft)
Caspian Sea	Asia-Europe	143,244	760	3,363	–92
Superior	North America	31,700	350	1,330	600
Victoria	Africa	26,828	250	270	3,720
Aral Sea	Asia	24,904(A)	280	220	174
Huron	North America	23,000	206	750	579
Michigan	North America	22,300	307	923	579
Tanganyika	Africa	12,700	420	4,823	2,534
Baykal	Asia	12,162	395	5,315	1,493
Great Bear	North America	12,096	192	1,463	512
Nyasa	Africa	11,150	360	2,280	1,550
Great Slave	North America	11,031	298	2,015	513
Erie	North America	9,910	241	210	570
Winnipeg	North America	9,417	266	60	713
Ontario	North America	7,340	193	802	245
Balkhash	Asia	7,115	376	85	1,115
Ladoga	Europe	6,835	124	738	13
Chad	Africa	6,300	175	24	787
Maracaibo	South America	5,217	133	115	Sea level
Onega	Europe	3,710	145	328	108
Eyre	Australia	3,600	90	4	–52
Volta	Africa	3,276	250	....	....
Titicaca	South America	3,200	122	922	12,500
Nicaragua	North America	3,100	102	230	102
Athabasca	North America	3,064	208	407	700
Reindeer	North America	2,568	143	720	1,106
Rudolf	Africa	2,473	154	240	1,230
Issyk Kul	Asia	2,355	115	2,303	5,279
Torrens	Australia	2,230	130	....	92
Vanern	Europe	2,156	91	328	144
Nettilling	North America	2,140	67	....	95
Winnipegosis	North America	2,075	141	38	830
Albert	Africa	2,075	100	168	2,030
Kariba	Africa	2,050	175	390	1,590
Nipigon	North America	1,872	72	540	1,050
Gairdner	Australia	1,840	90	....	112
Urmia	Asia	1,815	90	49	4,180
Manitoba	North America	1,799	140	12	813

(A) Probably less because of the diversion of feeder rivers.

The Great Lakes

Source: National Ocean Service, U.S. Dept. of Commerce

The Great Lakes form the largest body of fresh water in the world and with their connecting waterways are the largest inland water transportation unit. Draining the great North Central basin of the U.S., they enable shipping to reach the Atlantic via their outlet, the St. Lawrence R., and also the Gulf of Mexico via the Illinois Waterway, from Lake Michigan to the Mississippi R. A third outlet connects with the Hudson R. and thence the Atlantic via the N.Y. State Barge Canal System. Traffic on the Illinois Waterway and the N.Y. State Barge Canal System is limited to recreational boating and small shipping vessels.

Only one of the lakes, Lake Michigan, is wholly in the U.S.; the others are shared with Canada. Ships move from the shores of Lake Superior to Whitefish Bay at the E end of the lake, thence through the Soo (Sault Ste. Marie) locks, through the St. Mary's R. and into Lake Huron. To reach Gary and the Port of Indiana and South Chicago, Ill., ships move W from Lake Huron to Lake Michigan through the Straits of Mackinac.

Lake Superior is 600 ft above mean water level at Point-au-Pere, Quebec, on the International Great Lakes Datum (1955). From Duluth, Minn., to the E end of Lake Ontario is 1,156 mi.

	Superior	Michigan	Huron	Erie	Ontario
Length in mi	350	307	206	241	193
Breadth in mi	160	118	183	57	53
Deepest soundings in ft	1,330	923	750	210	802
Volume of water in cubic mi	2,900	1,180	850	116	393
Area (sq mi) water surface—U.S.	20,600	22,300	9,100	4,980	3,560
Canada	11,100	.....	13,900	4,930	3,990
Area (sq mi) entire drainage basin—U.S.	16,900	45,600	16,200	18,000	15,200
Canada	32,400	.....	35,500	4,720	12,100
Total Area (sq mi) U.S. and Canada	**81,000**	**67,900**	**74,700**	**32,630**	**34,850**
Mean surface above mean water level at Point-auPere, Quebec, aver. level in ft (1900-1988)	600.61	578.34	578.34	570.53	244.74
Latitude, North	46° 25′	41° 37′	43° 00′	41° 23′	43° 11′
	49° 00′	46° 06′	46° 17′	42° 52′	44° 15′
Longitude, West	84° 22′	84° 45′	79° 43′	78° 51′	76° 03′
	92° 06′	88° 02′	84° 45′	83° 29′	79° 53′
National boundary line in mi	282.8	None	260.8	251.5	174.6
United States shoreline (mainland only) mi	863	1,400	580	431	300

Highest and Lowest Continental Altitudes

Source: National Geographic Society

Continent	Highest point	Elevation (ft)	Lowest point	Elevation (ft) below sea level
Asia	Mount Everest, Nepal-Tibet	29,028	Dead Sea, Israel-Jordan	1,312
South America	Mount Aconcagua, Argentina	22,834	Valdes Peninsula, Argentina	131

(continued)

Continent	Highest point	Elevation (ft)	Lowest point	Elevation (ft) below sea level
North America	Mount McKinley, Alaska	20,320	Death Valley, California	282
Africa	Kilimanjaro, Tanzania	19,340	Lake Assal, Djibouti	512
Europe	Mount El'brus, Russia	18,510	Caspian Sea, Russia, Azerbaijan	92
Antarctica	Vinson Massif	16,864	Unknown	...
Australia	Mount Kosciusko, New South Wales	7,310	Lake Eyre, South Australia	52

Famous Waterfalls

Source: National Geographic Society

The earth has thousands of waterfalls, some of considerable magnitude. Their importance is determined not only by height but by volume of flow, steadiness of flow, crest width, whether the water drops sheerly or over a sloping surface, and in one leap or a succession of leaps. A series of low falls flowing over a considerable distance is known as a cascade.

Estimated mean annual flow, in cubic feet per second, of major waterfalls are: Niagara, 212,200; Paulo Afonso, 100,000; Urubupunga, 97,000; Iguazu, 61,000; Patos-Maribondo, 53,000; Victoria, 35,400; and Kaieteur, 23,400.

Height = total drop in feet in one or more leaps. †= falls of more than one leap; *= falls that diminish greatly seasonally; **= falls that reduce to a trickle or are dry for part of each year. If river names not shown, they are same as the falls. R. = river; L. = lake; (C) = cascade type.

Name and location	Elevation (ft)
Africa	
Angola	
Ruacana, Cuene R.	406
Ethiopia	
Fincha	508
Lesotho	
*Maletsunyane	630
Zimbabwe-Zambia	
*Victoria, Zambezi R.	343
South Africa	
*Augrabies, Orange R.	480
† Tugela	2,014
Tanzania-Zambia	
*Kalambo	726
Asia	
India—*Cauvery	330
*Jog (Gersoppa), Sharavathi R.	830
Japan	
*Kegon, Daiya R.	330
Australasia	
Australia	
New South Wales	
Wentworth	614
Wollomombi	1,100
Queensland	
Tully	885
† Wallaman, Stony Cr.	1,137
New Zealand	
Helena	890
† Sutherland, Arthur R.	1,904
Europe	
Austria—† Gastein	492
† Krimml	1,312
France—*Gavarnie	1,385
Great Britain	
Scotland	
Glomach	370
Wales	
Rhaiadr	240
Italy—Frua, Toce R. (C)	470
Norway	
Mardalsfossen (Northern)	1,535
† Mardalsfossen (Southern)	2,149
† **Skjeggedal, Nybuai R.	1,378
**Skykje	984
Vetti, Morka-Koldedola R.	900
Sweden	
† Handol	427
Switzerland	
Giessbach (C)	984
† Reichenbach	656
† Simmen	459
Staubbach	984
† Trummelbach	1,312
North America	
Canada	
Alberta	
Panther, Nigel Cr.	600
British Columbia	
† Della	1,443
† Takakkaw, Daly Glacier	1,200
Quebec	
Montmorency	274
Canada—United States	
Niagara: American	182
Horseshoe	173
United States	
California	
*Feather, Fall R.	640
Yosemite National Park	
*Bridalveil	620
*Illilouette	370
*Nevada, Merced R.	594
**Ribbon	1,612
**Silver Strand, Meadow Br.	1,170
*Vernal, Merced R.	317
† **Yosemite	2,425
Colorado	
† Seven, South Cheyenne Cr.	300
Hawaii	
Akaka, Kolekole Str.	442
Idaho	
**Shoshone, Snake R.	212
Kentucky	
Cumberland	68
Maryland	
*Great, Potomac R. (C)	71
Minnesota	
**Minnehaha	53
New Jersey	
Passaic	70
New York	
*Taughannock	215
Oregon	
† Multnomah	620
Tennessee	
Fall Creek	256
Washington	
Mt. Rainier Natl. Park	
Sluiskin, Paradise R.	300
**Snoqualmie	268
Wisconsin	
*Big Manitou, Black R. (C)	165
Wyoming	
Yellowstone Natl. Pk. Tower	132
*Yellowstone (upper)	109
*Yellowstone (lower)	308
Mexico	
El Salto	218
South America	
Argentina-Brazil	
Iguazu	230
Brazil	
Glass	1,325
Patos-Maribondo, Grande R.	115
Paulo Afonso, Sao Francisco R.	275
Colombia	
Catarata de Candelas, Cusiana R.	984
*Tequendama, Bogota R.	427
Ecuador	
*Agoyan, Pastaza R.	200
Guyana	
Kaieteur, Potaro R.	741
Great, Kamarang R.	1,600
† Marina, Ipobe R.	500
Venezuela	
† *Angel	3,212
Cuquenan	2,000

Notable Deserts of the World

Arabian (Eastern), 70,000 sq mi in Egypt between the Nile river and Red Sea, extending southward into Sudan.

Atacama, 600 mi. long area rich in nitrate and copper deposits in N. Chile.

Chihuahuan, 140,000 sq mi in Tex., N.M., Ariz., and Mexico.

Death Valley, 3,300 sq mi in E. Cal. and SW Nev. Contains lowest point below sea level (282 ft.) in Western Hemisphere.

Gibson, 120,000 sq mi in the interior of W. Australia.

Gobi, 500,000 sq mi in Mongolia and China.

Great Sandy, 150,000 sq mi in W. Australia.

Great Victoria, 150,000 sq mi in W. and S. Australia.

Kalahari, 225,000 sq mi in southern Africa.

Kara-Kum, 120,000 sq mi in Turkmenistan.

Kyzyl Kum, 100,000 sq mi in Kazakhstan & Uzbekistan.

Libyan, 450,000 sq mi in the Sahara extending from Libya through SW Egypt into Sudan.

Lut (Dasht-e Lut), 20,000 sq mi in E. Iran.

Mojave, 15,000 sq mi in S. Cal.

Namib, long narrow area extending 800 miles along SW coast of Africa.

Nubian, 100,000 sq mi in the Sahara in NE Sudan.

Painted Desert, section of high plateau in N. Ariz. extending 150 mi.

Rub al Khali (Empty Quarter), 250,000 sq mi in the south Arabian Peninsula.

Sahara, 3,500,000 sq mi in N. Africa extending westward to the Atlantic. Largest desert in the world.

Sonoran, 70,000 sq mi in SW Ariz. and SE Cal. extending into Mexico.

Syrian, 100,000 sq mi arid wasteland extending over much of N. Saudi Arabia, E. Jordan, S. Syria, and W. Iraq.

Taklimakan, 140,000 sq mi in Xinjiang Province, China.

Thar (Great Indian), 100,000 sq mi arid area extending 400 mi. along India-Pakistan border.

WEIGHTS AND MEASURES

Source: National Institute of Standards and Technology, U.S. Dept. of Commerce

The International System of Units

Two systems of weights and measures exist in the U.S. today: the U.S. Customary System and the International System of Units (SI, after the initials of Système International). SI, commonly referred to as the metric system, is actually a more complete, coherent version of it. Throughout U.S. history, the Customary System (inherited from, but now different from, the British Imperial System) has been customarily used; a plethora of federal and state legislation has given it, through implication, standing as the primary weights and measures system. The metric system, however, is the only system that Congress has ever specifically sanctioned. An 1866 law reads:

> It shall be lawful throughout the United States of America to employ the weights and measures of the metric system; and no contract or dealing, or pleading in any court, shall be deemed invalid or liable to objection because the weights or measures expressed or referred to therein are weights or measures of the metric system.

Since that time, use of the metric system in the U.S. has slowly and steadily increased, particularly in the scientific community, in the pharmaceutical industry, and in the manufacturing sector—the last motivated by international commerce, in which the metric system is now predominantly used.

On Feb. 10, 1964, the National Bureau of Standards (now known as the National Institute of Standards and Technology) issued the following bulletin:

> Henceforth it shall be the policy of the National Bureau of Standards to use the units of the International System (SI), as adopted by the 11th General Conference on Weights and Measures (October 1960), except when the use of these units would obviously impair communication or reduce the usefulness of a report.

On Dec. 23, 1975, Pres. Gerald R. Ford signed the Metric Conversion Act of 1975. It defines the metric system as being the International System of Units as interpreted in the U.S. by the secretary of commerce.

The Trade Act of 1988 and other legislation declare the metric system the preferred system of weights and measures for U.S. trade and commerce, call for the federal government to adopt metric specifications, and mandate the Commerce Dept. to oversee the program. The conversion process is currently underway; however, the metric system has not become the system of choice for most Americans' daily use.

The following seven units serve as the base for the International System: **length**—meter; **mass**—kilogram; **time**—second; **electric current**—ampere; **thermodynamic temperature**—kelvin; **amount of substance**—mole; and **luminous intensity**—candela.

Prefixes

The following prefixes, in combination with the basic unit names, provide the multiples and submultiples in the International System. For example, the unit name *meter*, with the prefix *kilo* added, produces *kilometer*, meaning "1,000 meters."

Prefix	Symbol	Multiples	Equivalent	Prefix	Symbol	Submultiples	Equivalent
yotta	Y	10^{24}	sextillionfold	deci	d	10^{-1}	tenth part
zetta	Z	10^{21}	septillionfold	centi	c	10^{-2}	hundredth part
exa	E	10^{18}	quintillionfold	milli	m	10^{-3}	thousandth part
peta	P	10^{15}	quadrillionfold	micro	µ	10^{-6}	millionth part
tera	T	10^{12}	trillionfold	nano	n	10^{-9}	billionth part
giga	G	10^{9}	billionfold	pico	p	10^{-12}	trillionth part
mega	M	10^{6}	millionfold	femto	f	10^{-15}	quadrillionth part
kilo	k	10^{3}	thousandfold	atto	a	10^{-18}	quintillionth part
hecto	h	10^{2}	hundredfold	zepto	z	10^{-21}	sextillionth part
deka	da	10	tenfold	yocto	y	10^{-24}	septillionth part

Tables of Metric Weights and Measures

Linear Measure

10 millimeters (mm)	= 1 centimeter (cm)
10 centimeters	= 1 decimeter (dm) = 100 millimeters
10 decimeters	= 1 meter (m) = 1,000 millimeters
10 meters	= 1 dekameter (dam)
10 dekameters	= 1 hectometer (hm) = 100 meters
10 hectometers	= 1 kilometer (km) = 1,000 meters

Area Measure

100 square millimeters (mm^2)	= 1 square centimeter (cm^2)
10,000 square centimeters	= 1 square meter (m^2) = 1,000,000 square millimeters
100 square meters	= 1 are (a)
100 ares	= 1 hectare (ha) = 10,000 square meters
100 hectares	= 1 square kilometer (km^2) = 1,000,000 square meters

Fluid Volume Measure

10 milliliters (mL)	= 1 centiliter (cL)
10 centiliters	= 1 deciliter (dL) = 100 milliliters
10 deciliters	= 1 liter (L) = 1,000 milliliters
10 liters	= 1 dekaliter (daL)
10 dekaliters	= 1 hectoliter (hL) = 100 liters
10 hectoliters	= 1 kiloliter (kL) = 1,000 liters

Cubic Measure

1,000 cubic millimeters (mm^3)	= 1 cubic centimeter (cm^3)
1,000 cubic centimeters	= 1 cubic decimeter (dm^3) = 1,000,000 cubic millimeters
1,000 cubic decimeters	= 1 cubic meter (m^3) = 1 stere = 1,000,000 cubic centimeters = 1,000,000,000 cubic millimeters

Weight

10 milligrams (mg)	= 1 centigram (cg)
10 centigrams	= 1 decigram (dg) = 100 milligrams
10 decigrams	= 1 gram (g) = 1,000 milligrams
10 grams	= 1 dekagram (dag)
10 dekagrams	= 1 hectogram (hg) = 100 grams
10 hectograms	= 1 kilogram (kg) = 1,000 grams
1,000 kilograms	= 1 metric ton (t)

Table of U.S. Customary Weights and Measures

Linear Measure

12 inches (in)	= 1 foot (ft)
3 feet	= 1 yard (yd)
5 ½ yards	= 1 rod (rd), pole, or perch (16 ½ feet)
40 rods	= 1 furlong (fur)=220 yards= 660 feet
8 furlongs	= 1 statute mile (mi) = 1,760 yards = 5,280 feet
3 miles	= 1 league = 5,280 yards = 15,840 feet
6076.11549 feet	= 1 International Nautical Mile

Liquid Measure

When necessary to distinguish the liquid pint or quart from the dry pint or quart, the word *liquid* or the abbreviation *liq* should be used in combination with the name or abbreviation of the liquid unit.

4 gills	= 1 pint (pt) = 28.875 cubic inches
2 pints	= 1 quart (qt) = 57.75 cubic inches
4 quarts	= 1 gallon (gal) = 231 cubic inches = 8 pints = 32 gills

Area Measure

Squares and cubes of units are sometimes abbreviated by using superscripts. For example, ft^2 means square foot, and ft^3 means cubic foot.

144 square inches	= 1 square foot (ft^2)
9 square feet	= 1 square yard (yd^2) = 1,296 square inches
30 ¼ square yards	= 1 square rod (rd^2) = 272 ¼ square feet
160 square rods	= 1 acre = 4,840 square yards = 43,560 square feet
640 acres	= 1 square mile (mi^2)
1 mile square	= 1 section (of land)
6 miles square	= 1 township = 36 sections = 36 square miles

Cubic Measure

1 cubic foot (ft^3)	= 1,728 cubic inches (in^3)
27 cubic feet	= 1 cubic yard (yd^3)

Gunter's, or Surveyor's, Chain Measure

7.92 inches (in)	= 1 link
100 links	= 1 chain (ch) = 4 rods = 66 feet
80 chains	= 1 survey mile (mi) = 320 rods = 5,280 feet

Troy Weight

24 grains	= 1 pennyweight (dwt)
20 pennyweights	= 1 ounce troy (oz t) = 480 grains
12 ounces troy	= 1 pound troy (lb t) = 240 pennyweights = 5,760 grains

Dry Measure

When necessary to distinguish the dry pint or quart from the liquid pint or quart, the word *dry* is used in combination with the name or abbreviation of the dry unit.

2 pints (pt)	= 1 quart (qt) = 67.2006 cubic inches
8 quarts	= 1 peck (pk) = 537.605 cubic inches = 16 pints
4 pecks	= 1 bushel (bu) = 2,150.42 cubic inches = 32 quarts

Avoirdupois Weight

When necessary to distinguish the avoirdupois ounce or pound from the troy ounce or pound, the word *avoirdupois* or the abbreviation *avdp* is used in combination with the name or abbreviation of the avoirdupois unit. The *grain* is the same in avoirdupois and troy weight.

27 11/32 grains	= 1 dram (dr)
16 drams	= 1 ounce (oz) = 437 ½ grains
16 ounces	= 1 pound (lb) = 256 drams = 7,000 grains
100 pounds	= 1 hundredweight (cwt)°
20 hundredweights	= 1 ton = 2,000 pounds°

In *gross* or *long* measure, the following values are recognized.

112 pounds	= 1 gross or long hundredweight°
20 gross or long hundredweights	= 1 gross or long ton = 2,240 pounds°

°When the terms *hundredweight* and *ton* are used unmodified, they are commonly understood to mean the 100-pound hundredweight and the 2,000-pound ton, respectively: these units may be designated *net* or *short* when necessary to distinguish them from the corresponding units in gross or long measure.

Tables of Equivalents

In this table it is necessary to distinguish between the *international* and the *survey* foot. The international foot, defined in 1959 as exactly equal to 0.3048 meter, is shorter than the old survey foot by exactly 2 parts in one million. The survey foot is still used in data expressed in feet in geodetic surveys within the U.S. In this table the survey foot is italicized.

When the name of a unit is enclosed in brackets thus, [1 hand], either (1) the unit is not in general current use in the U.S. or (2) the unit is believed to be based on custom and usage rather than on formal definition.

Equivalents involving decimals are, in most instances, rounded to the third decimal place; exact equivalents are so designated.

Lengths

1 angstrom (A)	0.1 nanometer (exactly) 0.000 1 micrometer (exactly) 0.000 000 1 millimeter (exactly) 0.000 000 004 inch
1 cable's length	120 fathoms (exactly) 720 *feet* (exactly) 219 meters
1 centimeter (cm)	0.3937 inch
1 chain (ch) (Gunter's or surveyor's)	66 *feet* (exactly) 20.1168 meters
1 chain (engineers)	100 feet 30.48 meters (exactly)
1 decimeter (dm)	3.937 inches
1 degree (geographical)	364,566.929 feet 69,047 miles (avg.) 111.123 kilometers (avg.)
-of latitude	68.708 miles at equator 69.403 miles at poles
-of longitude	69,171 miles at equator
1 dekameter (dam)	32.808 feet
1 fathom	6 *feet* (exactly) 1.8288 meters (exactly)
1 foot (ft)	0.3048 meters (exactly)
1 furlong (fur)	10 chains (surveyors) (exactly) 660 *feet* (exactly) 1/8 statute mile (exactly) 201.168 meters
[1 hand] (height measure for horses from ground to top of shoulders)	4 inches
1 inch (in)	2.54 centimeters (exactly)
1 kilometer (km)	0.621 mile 3,281.5 feet
1 league (land)	3 survey miles (exactly) 4.828 kilometers
1 link (Gunter's or surveyor's)	7.92 inches (exactly) 0.201 meter
1 link engineers	1 foot 0.305 meter
1 meter (m)	39.37 inches 1.094 yards
1 micrometer (μm) [the Greek letter mu]	0.001 millimeter (exactly) 0.000 039 37 inch
1 mil	0.001 inch (exactly) 0.025 4 millimeter (exactly)
1 mile (mi) (statute or land)	5,280 feet (exactly) 1.609 kilometers
1 international nautical mile (nmi)	1.852 kilometers (exactly) 1.150779 survey miles 6,076.11549 feet
1 millimeter (mm)	0.039 37 inch
1 nanometer (nm)	0.001 micrometer (exactly) 0.000 000 039 37 inch
1 pica (typography)	12 points
1 point (typography)	0.013 837 inch (exactly) 0.351 millimeter
1 rod (rd), pole, or perch	16 ½ *feet* (exactly) 5.029 meters
1 yard (yd)	0.9144 meter (exactly)

Areas or Surfaces

1 acre	43,560 square *feet* (exactly) 4,840 square yards 0.405 hectare
1 are (a)	119.599 square yards 0.025 acre

1 bolt (cloth measure):	
length	100 yards (on modern looms)
width	45 or 60 inches
1 hectare (ha)	2.471 acres
[1 square (building)]	100 square feet
1 square centimeter (cm^2)	0.155 square inch
1 square decimeter (dm^2)	15.500 square inches
1 square foot (ft^2)	929.030 square centimeters
1 square inch (in^2)	6.4516 square centimeters (exactly)
1 square kilometer (km^2)	247.104 acres 0.386 square mile
1 square meter (m^2)	1.196 square yards 10.764 square feet
1 square mile (mi^2)	258.999 hectares
1 square millimeter (mm^2)	0.002 square inch
1 square rod (rd^2), sq. pole, or sq. perch	25.293 square meters
1 square yard (yd^2)	0.836 square meter

Capacities or Volumes

1 barrel (bbl) liquid	31 to 42 gallons°

°There are a variety of "barrels," established by law or usage. For example: federal taxes on fermented liquors are based on a barrel of 31 gallons: many state laws fix the "barrel for liquids" as 31½ gallons; one state fixes a 36-gallon barrel for cistern measurement; federal law recognizes a 40-gallon barrel for "proof spirits"; by custom, 42 gallons constitute a barrel of crude oil or petroleum products for statistical purposes, and this equivalent is recognized "for liquids" by 4 states.

1 barrel (bbl), standard, for fruits, vegetables, and other dry commodities except dry cranberries	7,056 cubic inches 105 dry quarts 3.281 bushels, struck measure
1 barrel (bbl), standard, cranberry	5,826 cubic inches 86 45/64 dry quarts 2.709 bushels, struck measure
1 board foot (lumber measure)	a foot-square board 1 inch thick
1 bushel (bu) (U.S.) (struck measure)	2,150.42 cubic inches (exactly) 35.239 liters
[1 bushel, heaped (U.S.)]	2,747.715 cubic inches 1.278 bushels, struck measure°

°Frequently recognized as 1¼ bushels, struck measure.

[1 bushel (bu) (British Imperial) (struck measure)]	1.032 U.S. bushels struck measure 2,219.36 cubic inches
1 cord (cd) firewood	128 cubic feet (exactly)
1 cubic centimeter (cm^3)	0.061 cubic inch
1 cubic decimeter (dm^3)	61.024 cubic inches
1 cubic inch (in^3)	0.554 fluid ounce 4.433 fluid drams 16.387 cubic centimeters
1 cubic foot (ft^3)	7.481 gallons 28.317 cubic decimeters
1 cubic meter (m^3)	1.308 cubic yards
1 cubic yard (yd^3)	0.765 cubic meter
1 cup, measuring	8 fluid ounces (exactly) ½ liquid pint (exactly)
[1 dram, fluid (fl dr) (British)]	0.961 U.S. fluid dram 0.217 cubic inch 3.552 milliliters
1 dekaliter (daL)	2.642 gallons 1.135 pecks
1 gallon (gal) (U.S.)	231 cubic inches (exactly) 3.785 liters 0.833 British gallon 128 U.S. fluid ounces (exactly)
[1 gallon (gal) British Imperial]	277.42 cubic inches 1.201 U.S. gallons 4.546 liters 160 British fluid ounces (exactly)
1 gill (gi)	7.219 cubic inches 4 fluid ounces (exactly) 0.118 liter
1 hectoliter (hL)	26.418 gallons 2.838 bushels
1 liter (L) (1 cubic decimeter exactly)	1.057 liquid quarts 0.908 dry quart 61.025 cubic inches
1 milliliter (mL) (1 cu cm exactly)	0.271 fluid dram 16.231 minims 0.061 cubic inch
1 ounce, liquid (U.S.)	1.805 cubic inches 29.573 milliliters 1.041 British fluid ounces
[1 ounce, fluid (fl oz) (British)]	0.961 U.S. fluid ounce 1.734 cubic inches 28.412 milliliters
1 peck (pk)	8.810 liters
1 pint (pt), dry	33.600 cubic inches 0.551 liter
1 pint (pt), liquid	28.875 cubic inches (exactly) 0.473 liter
1 quart (qt) dry (U.S.)	67.201 cubic inches 1.01 liters 0.969 British quart
1 quart (qt) liquid (U.S.)	57.75 cubic in (exactly) 0.946 liter 0.833 British quart
[1 quart (qt) (British)]	69.354 cubic inches 1.032 U.S. dry quarts 1.201 U.S. liquid quarts
1 tablespoon	3 teaspoons°(exactly) 4 fluid drams ½ fluid ounce (exactly)
1 teaspoon	⅓ tablespoon°(exactly) 1⅓ fluid drams°

°The equivalent "1 teaspoon=1⅓ fluid drams" has been found by the bureau to correspond more closely with the actual capacities of "measuring" and silver teaspoons than the equivalent "1 teaspoon=1 fluid dram" which is given by many dictionaries.

Weights or Masses

1 assay ton°° (AT)	29.167 grams

°°Used in assaying. The assay ton bears the same relation to the milligram that a ton of 2,000 pounds avoirdupois bears to the ounce troy; hence, the weight in milligrams of precious metal obtained from one assay ton of ore gives directly the number of troy ounces to the net ton.

1 bale (cotton measure)	500 pounds in U.S. 750 pounds in Egypt
1 carat (c)	200 milligrams (exactly) 3.086 grains
1 dram avoirdupois (dr avdp)	27 11/32 (=27.344) grains 1.772 grams
1 gamma (γ)	1 microgram (exactly), see below
1 grain	64.799 milligrams
1 gram	15.432 grains 0.035 ounce, avoirdupois
1 hundredweight, gross or long°°° (gross cwt)	112 pounds (exactly) 50.802 kilograms
1 hundredweight, net or short (cwt or net cwt)	100 pounds (exactly) 45.359 kilograms
1 kilogram (kg)	2.205 pounds
1 microgram (µg [The Greek letter mu in combination with the letter g])	0.000001 gram (exactly)
1 milligram (mg)	0.015 grain
1 ounce, avoirdupois (oz avdp)	437.5 grains (exactly) 0.911 troy ounce 28.350 grams
1 ounce, troy (oz t)	480 grains (exactly) 1.097 avoirdupois ounces 31.103 grams
1 pennyweight (dwt)	1.555 grams
1 pound, avoirdupois (lb avdp)	7,000 grains (exactly) 1.215 troy pounds 453.592 37 grams (exactly)
1 pound, troy (lb t)	5,760 grains (exactly) 0.823 avoirdupois pound 373.242 grams
1 ton, gross or long°°° (gross ton)	2,240 pounds (exactly) 1.12 net tons (exactly) 1.016 metric tons

°°°The gross or long ton and hundredweight are used commercially in the United States to only a limited extent, usually in restricted industrial fields. These units are the same as British ton and hundredweight.

1 ton, metric (t)	2,204.623 pounds 0.984 gross ton 1.102 net tons
1 ton, net or short (sh ton)	2,000 pounds (exactly) 0.893 gross ton 0.907 metric ton

Tables of Interrelation of Units of Measurement

Units of length and area of the international and survey measures are included in the following tables. Units unique to the survey measure are *italicized.* See Tables of Equivalents, 1st paragraph.

1 international foot	= 0.999 998 survey foot (exactly)
1 survey foot	= 1200/3937 meter (exactly)
1 international foot	= 12 × 0.0254 meter (exactly)

Bold face type indicates exact values

Units of Length

Units	Inches	*Links*	Feet	Yards	*Rods*	*Chains*	Miles	cm	Meters
1 inch=	**1**	0.126 263	0.083 333	0.027 778	0.005 051	0.001 263	0.000 016	**2.54**	**0.025 4**
1 *link*=	**7.92**	**1**	**0.66**	**0.22**	**0.04**	**0.01**	**0.000 125**	20.117	0.201 168
1 foot=	**12**	1.515 152	**1**	0.333 333	0.060 606	0.015 152	0.000 189	**30.48**	**0.304 8**
1 yard=	**36**	4.545 45	**3**	**1**	0.181 818	0.045 455	0.000 568	**91.44**	**0.914 4**
1 *rod*=	**198**	**25**	**16.5**	**5.5**	**1**	**0.25**	**0.003 125**	502.92	5.029 2
1 *chain*=	**792**	**100**	**66**	**22**	**4**	**1**	**0.012 5**	2011.68	20.116 8
1 mile=	**63 360**	**8000**	**5280**	**1760**	**320**	**80**	**1**	**160 934.4**	**1609.344**
1 cm=	0.3937	0.049 710	0.032 808	0.010 936	0.001 988	0.000 497	0.000 006	**1**	**0.01**
1 meter=	39.37	4.970 960	3.280 840	1.093 613	0.198 838	0.049 710	0.000 621	**100**	**1**

Units of Area

Units	Sq. inches	*Sq. links*	Sq. feet	Sq. yards	*Sq. rods*	*Sq. chains*
1 sq. inch=	**1**	0.015 942 3	0.006 944	0.000 771 605	0.000 025 5	0.000 001 594
1 sq. *link*=	62.726 4	**1**	**0.435 6**	**0.0484**	**0.0016**	**0.000 1**
1 sq. foot=	**144**	2.295 684	**1**	0.111 111 1	0.003 673 09	0.000 229 568
1 sq. yard=	**1296**	20.661 16	**9**	**1**	0.033 057 85	0.002 066 12
1 sq. *rod*=	**39 204**	**625**	**272.25**	**30.25**	**1**	**0.062 5**
1 sq. *chain*=	**627 264**	**10 000**	**4 356**	**484**	**16**	**1**
1 *acre*=	**6 272 640**	**100 000**	**43 560**	**4 840**	**160**	**10**
1 sq. mile=	**4 014 489 600**	**64 000 000**	**27 878 400**	**3 097 600**	**102 400**	**6400**
1 sq. cm=	0.155 000 3	0.002 471 05	0.001 076	0.000 119 599	0.000 003 954	0.000 000 247
1 sq. meter=	1550.003	24.710 44	10.763 91	1.195 990	0.039 536 70	0.002 471 044
1 *hectare*=	15 500 031	247 104	107 639.1	11 959.90	395.367 0	24.710 44

Units	*Acres*	Sq. miles	Sq. cm	Sq. meters	*Hectares*
1 sq. inch=	0.000 000 159 423	0.000 000 000 249 10	**6.451 6**	**0.000 645 16**	0.000 000 065
1 sq. *link*=	**0.000 01**	**0.000 000 015 625**	404.685 642 24	0.040 468 56	0.000 004 047
1 sq. foot=	0.000 022 956 84	0.000 000 035 870 06	929.034 1	0.092 903 41	0.000 009 290
1 sq. yard=	0.000 206 611 6	0.000 000 322 830 6	**8 361.273 6**	**0.836 127 36**	0.000 083 613
1 sq. *rod*=	**0.006 25**	**0.000 009 765 625**	252 929.5	25.292 95	0.002 529 295
1 sq. *chain*=	**0.1**	**0.000 156 25**	4 046 873	404.687 3	0.040 468 73
1 *acre*=	**1**	**0.001 562 5**	40 468 730	4 046.873	0.404 687 3
1 sq. mile=	**640**	**1**	25 899 881 103	2 589 988.11	258.998 811 034
1 sq. cm=	0.000 000 024 711	0.000 000 000 038 610	**1**	**0.000 1**	**0.000 000 01**
1 sq. meter=	0.000 247 104 4	0.000 000 386 102 2	**10 000**	**1**	**0.0001**
1 *hectare*=	2.471 044	0.003 861 006	**100 000 000**	**10 000**	**1**

Units of Mass Not Greater Than Pounds and Kilograms

Units	Grains	Pennyweights	Avdp drams	Avdp ounces
1 grain=	**1**	0.041 666 67	0.036 571 43	0.002 285 71
1 pennyweight=	**24**	**1**	0.877 714 3	0.054 857 14
1 dram avdp=	**27.343 75**	1.139 323	**1**	**0.062 5**
1 ounce avdp=	**437.5**	18.229 17	**16**	**1**
1 ounce troy=	**480**	**20**	17.554 29	1.097 143
1 pound troy=	**5760**	**240**	210.651 4	13.165 71
1 pound avdp=	**7000**	291.666 7	**256**	**16**
1 milligram=	0.015 432	0.000 643 015	0.000 564 383	0.000 035 274
1 gram=	15.432 36	0.643 014 9	0.564 383 4	0.035 273 96
1 kilogram=	15 432.36	643.014 9	564.383 4	35.273 96

Units	Troy ounces	Troy pounds	Avdp pounds	Milligrams	Grams	Kilograms
1 grain=	0.002 083 33	0.000 173 611	0.000 142 857	**64.798 91**	**0.064 798 91**	0.000 064 799
1 pennywt.=	**0.05**	0.004 166 667	0.003 428 571	**1555.173 84**	**1.555 173 84**	0.001 555 174
1 dram avdp=	0.056 966 15	0.004 747 179	0.003 906 25	1771.845 195	1.771 845 195	0.001 771 845
1 oz avdp=	0.911 458 3	0.075 954 86	**0.062 5**	**28 349.523 125**	**28.349 523 125**	0.028 349 52
1 oz troy=	**1**	0.083 333 333	0.068 571 43	**31 103.476 8**	**31.103 476 8**	0.031 103 48
1 lb troy=	**12**	**1**	0.822 857 1	**373 241.721 6**	**373.241 721 6**	0.373 241 722
1 lb avdp=	14.583 33	1.215 278	**1**	**453 592.37**	**453.592 37**	**0.453 592 37**
1 milligram=	0.000 032 151	0.000 002 679	0.000 002 205	**1**	**0.001**	**0.000 001**
1 gram=	0.032 150 75	0.002 679 229	0.002 204 623	**1000**	**1**	**0.001**
1 kilogram=	32.150 75	2.679 229	2.204 623	**1 000 000**	**1000**	**1**

Units of Mass Not Less Than Avoirdupois Ounces

Units	Avdp oz	Avdp lb	Short cwt	Short tons	Long tons	Kilograms	Metric tons
1 oz av=	**1**	**0.0625**	**0.000 625**	**0.000 031 25**	0.000 027 902	0.028 349 523	0.000 028 350
1 lb av=	**16**	**1**	**0.01**	**0.000 5**	0.000 446 429	**0.453 592 37**	0.000 453 592
1 sh cwt=	**1 600**	**100**	**1**	**0.05**	0.044 642 86	**45.359 237**	**0.045 359 237**
1 sh ton=	**32 000**	**2000**	**20**	**1**	0.892 857 1	**907.184 74**	**0.907 184 74**
1 long ton=	**35 840**	**2240**	**22.4**	**1.12**	**1**	**1 016.046 908 8**	1.016 046 909
1 kg=	35.273 96	2.204 623	0.022 046 23	0.001 102 311	0.000 984 207	**1**	**0.001**
1 metric ton=	35 273.96	2 204.623	22.046 23	1.102 311	0.984 206 5	**1000**	**1**

Units of Volume

Units	Cubic inches	Cubic feet	Cubic yards	Cubic cm	Cubic dm	Cubic meters
1 cubic inch=	1	0.000 578 704	0.000 021 433	16.387 064	0.016 387	0.000 016 387
1 cubic foot=	1728	1	0.037 037 04	28 316.846 592	28.316 847	0.028 316 847
1 cubic yard=	46 656	27	1	764 554.857 984	764.554 858	0.764 554 858
1 cubic cm=	0.061 023 74	0.000 035 315	0.000 001 308	1	0.001	0.000 001
1 cubic dm=	61.023 74	0.035 314 67	0.001 307 951	1 000	1	0.001
1 cubic meter=	61 023.74	35.314 67	1.307 951	1 000 000	1000	1

Units of Capacity (Liquid Measure)

Units	Minims	Fluid drams	Fluid ounces	Gills	Liquid pt
1 minim=	1	0.016 666 7	0.002 083 33	0.000 520 833	0.000 130 208
1 fluid dram=	60	1	0.125	0.031 25	0.007 812 5
1 fluid ounce=	480	8	1	0.25	0.062 5
1 gill=	1920	32	4	1	0.25
1 liquid pint=	7680	128	16	4	1
1 liquid quart=	15 360	256	32	8	2
1 gallon=	61 440	1024	128	32	8
1 cubic inch=	265.974	4.432 900	0.554 112 6	0.138 528 1	0.034 632 03
1 cubic foot=	459 603.1	7 660.052	957.506 5	239.376 6	59.844 16
1 milliliter=	16.230 73	0.270 512 18	0.033 814 02	0.008 453 506	0.002 113 376
1 liter=	16 230.73	270.512 18	33.814 02	8.453 506	2.113 376

Units	Liquid quarts	Gallons	Cubic inches	Cubic feet	Liters
1 minim=	0.000 065 104 17	0.000 016 276 04	0.003 759 766	0.000 002 175 790	0.000 061 611 52
1 flu. dram=	0.003 906 25	0.000 976 562 5	0.225 585 9	0.000 130 547 4	0.003 696 691
1 fluid oz=	0.031 25	0.007 812 5	1.804 687 5	0.001 044 379	0.029 573 53
1 gill=	0.125	0.031 25	7.218 75	0.004 177 517	0.118 294 118
1 liquid pt=	0.5	0.125	28.875	0.016 710 07	0.473 176 473
1 liquid qt=	1	0.25	57.75	0.033 420 14	0.946 352 946
1 gallon=	4	1	231	0.133 680 6	3.785 411 784
1 cubic inch=	0.017 316 02	0.004 329 004	1	0.000 578 703 7	0.016 387 064
1 cubic foot=	29.922 08	7.480 519	1728	1	28.316 846 592
1 liter=	1.056 688	0.264 172 05	61.023 74	0.035 314 67	1

Units of Capacity (Dry Measure)

Units	Dry pints	Dry quarts	Pecks	Bushels	Cubic in.	Liters
1 dry pint=	1	0.5	0.062 5	0.015 625	33.600 312 5	0.550 610 47
1 dry quart=	2	1	0.125	0.031 25	67.200 625	1.101 220 9
1 peck=	16	8	1	0.25	537.605	8.809 767 5
1 bushel=	64	32	4	1	2 150.42	35.239 07
1 cubic inch=	0.029 761 6	0.014 880 8	0.001 860 10	0.000 465 025	1	0.016 387 06
1 liter=	1.816 166	0.908 083	0.113 510 37	0.028 377 59	61.023 74	1

Miscellaneous Measures

Caliber—the diameter of a gun bore. In the U.S., caliber is traditionally expressed in hundredths of inches, eg. .22 or .30. In Britain, caliber is often expressed in thousandths of inches, eg. .270 or .465. Now, it is commonly expressed in millimeters, eg. the 5.56 mm. M16 rifle. Heavier weapons' caliber has long been expressed in millimeters, eg. the 81 mm. mortar, the 105 mm. howitzer (light), the 155 mm. howitzer (medium or heavy).

Naval guns' caliber refers to the barrel length as a multiple of the bore diameter. A 5-inch, 50-caliber naval gun has a 5-inch bore and a barrel length of 250 inches.

Carat—a measure of the amount of alloy per 24 parts in gold. Thus 24-carat gold is pure; 18-carat gold is one-fourth alloy.

Decibel (dB)—a measure of the relative loudness or intensity of sound. A 20-decibel sound is 10 times louder than a 10-decibel sound; 30 decibels is 100 times louder; 40 decibels is 1,000 times louder, etc. One decibel is the smallest difference between sounds detectable by the human ear. A 120-decibel sound is painful.

10 decibels	– a light whisper
20	– quiet conversation
30	– normal conversation
40	– light traffic
50	– typewriter, loud conversation
60	– noisy office
70	– normal traffic, quiet train
80	– rock music, subway
90	– heavy traffic, thunder
100	– jet plane at takeoff

Em—a printer's measure designating the square width of any given type size. Thus, an em of 10-point type is 10 points. An en is half an em.

Gauge—a measure of shotgun bore diameter. Gauge numbers originally referred to the number of lead balls of the gun barrel diameter in a pound. Thus, a 16-gauge shotgun's bore was smaller than a 12-gauge shotgun's. Today, an international agreement assigns millimeter measures to each gauge, eg.:

Gauge	Bore diameter in mm
6	23.34
10	19.67
12	18.52
14	17.60
16	16.81
20	15.90

Horsepower—the power needed to lift 550 pounds one foot in one second, or to lift 33,000 pounds one foot in one minute. Equivalent to 746 watts or 2,546.0756 Btu/h.

Quire—25 sheets of paper

Ream—500 sheets of paper

Knot—a measure of the speed of ships. A knot equals 1 nautical mile per hour.

Electrical Units

The **watt** is the unit of power (electrical, mechanical, thermal, etc.). Electrical power is given by the product of the voltage and the current.

Energy is sold by the **joule,** but in common practice the billing of electrical energy is expressed in terms of the **kilowatt-hour,** which is 3,600,000 joules or 3.6 megajoules.

The **horsepower** is a non-metric unit sometimes used in mechanics. It is equal to 746 watts.

The **ohm** is the unit of electrical resistance and represents the physical property of a conductor that offers a resistance to the flow of electricity, permitting just 1 ampere to flow at 1 volt of pressure.

Compound Interest

Compounded Annually

Principal	Period	4%	5%	6%	7%	8%	9%	10%	12%	14%	16%
$100	1 day	0.011	0.014	0.016	0.019	0.022	0.025	0.027	0.033	0.038	0.044
	1 week	0.077	0.096	0.115	0.134	0.153	0.173	0.192	0.230	0.268	0.307
	6 mos.	2.00	2.50	3.00	3.50	4.00	4.50	5.00	6.00	7.00	8.00
	1 year	4.00	5.00	6.00	7.00	8.00	9.00	10.00	12.00	14.00	16.00
	2 years	8.16	10.25	12.36	14.49	16.64	18.81	21.00	25.44	29.96	34.56
	3 years	12.49	15.76	19.10	22.50	25.97	29.50	33.10	40.49	48.15	56.09
	4 years	16.99	21.55	26.25	31.08	36.05	41.16	46.41	57.35	68.90	81.06
	5 years	21.67	27.63	33.82	40.26	46.93	53.86	61.05	76.23	92.54	110.03
	6 years	26.53	34.01	41.85	50.07	58.69	67.71	77.16	97.38	119.50	143.64
	7 years	31.59	40.71	50.36	60.58	71.38	82.80	94.87	121.07	150.23	182.62
	8 years	36.86	47.75	59.38	71.82	85.09	99.26	114.36	147.60	185.26	227.84
	9 years	42.33	55.13	68.95	83.85	99.90	117.19	135.79	177.31	225.19	280.30
	10 years	48.02	62.89	79.08	96.72	115.89	136.74	159.37	210.58	270.72	341.14
	12 years	60.10	79.59	101.22	125.22	151.82	181.27	213.84	289.60	381.79	493.60
	15 years	80.09	107.89	139.66	175.90	217.22	264.25	317.72	847.36	613.79	826.55
	20 years	119.11	165.33	220.71	286.97	366.10	460.44	572.75	864.63	1,274.35	1,846.08

Ancient Measures

Biblical

Cubit	=	21.8 inches
Omer	=	0.45 peck 3.964 liters
Ephah	=	10 omers
Shekel	=	0.497 ounce 14.1 grams

Greek

Cubit	=	18.3 inches
Stadion	=	607.2 or 622 feet
Obolos	=	715.38 milligrams
Drachma	=	4.2923 grams
Mina	=	0.9463 pound
Talent	=	60 mina

Roman

Cubit	=	17.5 inches
Stadium	=	202 yards
As, libra, pondus	=	325.971 grams, 0.71864 pound

Weight of Water

at 20°C

1	cubic inch	.0360 pound
12	cubic inches	.433 pound
1	cubic foot	62.4 pounds
1	cubic foot	7.48052 U.S. gal
1.8	cubic feet	112.0 pounds
35.96	cubic feet	2240.0 pounds
1	U.S. gallon	8.33 pounds
13.45	U.S. gallons	112.0 pounds
269.0	U.S. gallons	2240.0 pounds

metric weights, at 4°C (maximum denstiy):

1	cubic centimeter	1 gram
1	liter	1 kilogram
1	cubic meter	1 metric ton

Density of Gases and Vapors

at 0°C and 760 mmHg; kilograms per cubic meter

Gas	Wt.	Gas	Wt.	Gas	Wt.
Acetylene	1.171	Ethylene	1.260	Methyl fluoride	1.545
Air	1.293	Fluorin	1.696	Mono methylamine	1.38
Ammonia	.759	Helium	.178	Neon	.900
Argon	1.784	Hydrogen	.090	Nitric oxide	1.341
Arsine	3.48	Hydrogen bromide	3.50	Nitrogen	1.250
Butane-iso	2.60	Hydrogen chloride	1.639	Nitrosyl chloride	2.99
Butane-n	2.519	Hydrogen iodide	5.724	Nitrous oxide	1.997
Carbon dioxide	1.977	Hydrogen selenide	3.66	Oxygen	1.429
Carbon monoxide	1.250	Hydrogen sulfide	1.539	Phosphine	1.48
Carbon oxysulfide	2.72	Krypton	3.745	Propane	2.020
Chlorine	3.214	Methane	.717	Silicon tetrafluoride	4.67
Chlorine monoxide	3.89	Methyl chloride	2.25	Sulfur dioxide	2.927
Ethane	1.356	Methyl ether	2.091	Xenon	5.897

Temperature Conversion Table

The numbers in **bold face type** refer to the temperature either in degrees Celsius or Fahrenheit that are to be converted. If converting from degrees Fahrenheit to Celsius, the equivalent is in the column on the left; if converting from degrees Celsius to Fahrenheit, the answer is in the column on the right.

For temperatures not shown. To convert Fahrenheit to Celsius, subtract 32 degrees and divide by 1.8; to convert Celsius to Fahrenheit, multiply by 1.8 and add 32 degrees.

Note: Although "Centigrade" is still frequently used, the International Committee on Weights and Measures and the National Institute of Standards and Technology have recommended since 1948 that this scale be called "Celsius."

Celsius		Fahrenheit	Celsius		Fahrenheit	Celsius		Fahrenheit
-273.2	**-459.7**	......	-17.8	**0**	32	35.0	**95**	203
-184	**-300**	......	-12.2	**10**	50	36.7	**98**	208.4
-169	**-273**	-459.4	- 6.67	**20**	68	37.8	**100**	212
-157	**-250**	-418	- 1.11	**30**	86	43	**110**	230
-129	**-200**	-328	4.44	**40**	104	49	**120**	248
-101	**-150**	-238	10.0	**50**	122	54	**130**	266
-73.3	**-100**	-148	15.6	**60**	140	60	**140**	284
-45.6	**-50**	- 58	21.1	**70**	158	66	**150**	302
-40.0	**-40**	- 40	23.9	**75**	167	93	**200**	392
-34.4	**-30**	- 22	26.7	**80**	176	121	**250**	482
-28.9	**-20**	- 4	29.4	**85**	185	149	**300**	572
-23.3	**-10**	14	32.2	**90**	194			

Boiling and Freezing Points of Water

Water boils at 212°F at sea level. For every 550 feet above sea level, boiling point of water is lower by about 1°F. Methyl alcohol boils at 148°F. Average human oral temperature, 98.6°F. Water freezes at 32°F.

Breaking the Sound Barrier; Speed of Sound

The prefix Mach is used to describe supersonic speed. It was named for Ernst Mach (1838-1916), a Czech-born Austrian physicist, who contributed to the study of sound. When a plane moves at the speed of sound, it is Mach 1. When twice the speed of sound, it is Mach 2. When it is near but below the speed of sound, its speed can be designated at less than Mach 1, for example, Mach .90. Mach is defined as "the ratio of the velocity of a rocket or a jet to the velocity of sound in the medium being considered."

When a plane passes the sound barrier—flying faster than sound travels—listeners in the area hear thunderclaps, but the pilot of the plane does not hear them.

Sound is produced by vibrations of an object and is transmitted by alternate increase and decrease in pressures that radiate outward through a material media of molecules —somewhat like waves spreading out on a pond after a rock has been tossed into it.

The frequency of sound is determined by the number of times the vibrating waves undulate per second and is measured in cycles per second. The slower the cycle of waves, the lower the frequency. As frequencies increase, the sound is higher in pitch.

Sound is audible to human beings only if the frequency falls within a certain range. The human ear is usually not sensitive to frequencies of fewer than 20 vibrations per second, or more than about 20,000 vibrations per second—although this range varies among individuals. Anything at a pitch higher than the human ear can hear is termed ultrasonic.

Intensity, or loudness, is the strength of the pressure of these radiating waves and is measured in decibels. The human ear responds to intensity in a range from zero to 120 decibels. Any sound with pressure over 120 decibels is painful to the human ear.

The speed of sound is generally placed at 1,088 feet per second at sea level at 32°F. It varies in other temperatures and in different media. Sound travels faster in water than in air, and even faster in iron and steel. It travels a mile in 5 seconds in air, it does a mile under water in 1 second, and it travels through iron in 1/3 second. It travels through ice cold vapor at approximately 4,708 feet per second; ice-cold water, 4,938; granite, 12,960; hardwood, 12,620; brick, 11,960; glass, 16,410 to 19,690; silver, 8,658; gold, 5,717.

Colors of the Spectrum

Color, an electromagnetic wave phenomenon, is a sensation produced through the excitation of the retina of the eye by rays of light. The colors of the spectrum may be produced by viewing a light beam refracted by passage through a prism, which breaks the light into its wavelengths.

Customarily, the primary colors of the spectrum are those 6 monochromatic colors that occupy relatively large areas of the spectrum: red, orange, yellow, green, blue, and violet. However, Sir Isaac Newton named a 7th, indigo, situated between blue and violet on the spectrum. Aubert estimated (1865) the solar spectrum to contain approximately 1,000 distinguishable hues of which according to Rood (1881) 2 million tints and shades can be distinguished; Luckiesh stated (1915) that 55 distinctly different hues have been seen in a single spectrum.

Many physicists recognize only 3 primary colors: red, yellow, and blue (Mayer, 1775); red, green, and violet (Thomas Young, 1801); red, green, and blue (Clerk Maxwell, 1860).

The color sensation of black is due to complete lack of stimulation of the retina, that of white to complete stimulation. The infrared and ultraviolet rays, below the red (long) end of the spectrum and above the violet (short) end respectively, are invisible to the naked eye. Heat is the principal effect of the infrared rays, and chemical action that of the ultraviolet rays.

Common Fractions Reduced to Decimals

8ths	16ths	32ds	64ths	8ths	16ths	32ds	64ths	8ths	16ths	32ds	64ths
			1 .015625				23 .359375				45 .703125
		1	2 .03125	3	6	12	24 .375			23	46 .71875
			3 .046875				25 .390625				47 .734375
	1	2	4 .0625			13	26 .40625	6	12	24	48 .75
			5 .078125				27 .421875				49 .765625
		3	6 .09375		7	14	28 .4375			25	50 .78125
			7 .109375				29 .453125				51 .796875
1	2	4	8 .125			15	30 .46875		13	26	52 .8125
			9 .140625				31 .484375				53 .828125
		5	10 .15625	4	8	16	32 .5			27	54 .84375
			11 .171875				33 .515625				55 .859375
	3	6	12 .1875			17	34 .53125	7	14	28	56 .875
			13 .203125				35 .546875				57 .890625
		7	14 .21875			18	36 .5625			29	58 .90625
			15 .234375				37 .578125				59 .921875
2	4	8	16 .25			19	38 .59375		15	30	60 .9375
			17 .265625				39 .609375				61 .953125
		9	18 .28125	5	10	20	40 .625			31	62 .96875
			19 .296875				41 .640625				63 .984375
	5	10	20 .3125			21	42 .65625	8	16	32	64 1.
			21 .328125				43 .671875				
		11	22 .34375		11	22	44 .6875				

Spirits Measures

- Pony .... 0.5 jigger
- Shot .... 0.666 jigger; 1.0 ounce
- Jigger .... 1.5 shot
- Pint .... 16 shots; 0.625 fifth
- Fifth .... 25.6 shots; 1.6 pints; 0.8 quart; 0.75706 liter
- Quart .... 32 shots; 1.25 fifth
- Magnum .... 2 quarts; 2.49797 bottles (wine)

For champagne and brandy only:

- Jeroboam .... 6.4 pints; 1.6 magnum; 0.8 gallon

For champagne only:

- Rehoboam .... 3 magnums
- Methuselah .... 4 magnums
- Salmanazar .... 6 magnums
- Balthazar ..... 8 magnums
- Nebuchadnezzar. 10 magnums

Wine bottle (standard): .... 0.800633 quart; 0.7576778 liter

Mathematical Formulas

To find the CIRCUMFERENCE of a:

Circle — Multiply the diameter by 3.14159265 (usually 3.1416).

To find the AREA of a:

Circle — Multiply the square of the diameter by .785398 (usually .7854).
Rectangle — Multiply the length of the base by the height.
Sphere (surface) — Multiply the square of the radius by 3.1416 and multiply by 4.
Square — Square the length of one side.
Trapezoid — Add the two parallel sides, multiply by the height, and divide by 2.
Triangle — Multiply the base by the height and divide by 2.

To find the VOLUME of a:

Cone — Multiply the square of the radius of the base by 3.1416, multiply by the height, and divide by 3.

Cube — Cube the length of one edge.

Cylinder— Multiply the square of the radius of the base by 3.1416 and multiply by the height.

Pyramid — Multiply the area of the base by the height and divide by 3.
Rectangular Prism — Multiply the length by the width by the height.
Sphere —Multiply the cube of the radius by 3.1416, multiply by 4, and divide by 3.

Playing Cards and Dice Chances

Poker Hands

Hand	Number possible	Odds against
Royal flush	4	649,739 to 1
Other straight flush	36	72,192 to 1
Flush	5,108	508 to 1
Straight	10,200	254 to 1
Three of a kind	54,912	46 to 1
Two pairs	123,552	20 to 1
One pair	1,098,240	4 to 3(1.37 to 1)
Nothing	1,302,540	1 to 1
Total	**2,598,960**	

Dice
(probabilities on 2 dice)

Total	Odds against (Single toss)	Total	Odds against (Single toss)
2	35 to 1	8	31 to 5
3	17 to 1	9	8 to 1
4	11 to 1	10	11 to 1
5	8 to 1	11	17 to 1
6	31 to 5	12	35 to 1
7	5 to 1		

Dice
(Probabilities of consecutive winning plays)

No. consecutive wins	By 7,11, or point	No. consecutive wins	By 7, 11, or point
1	244 in 495	6	1 in 70
2	6 in 25	7	1 in 141
3	3 in 25	8	1 in 287
4	1 in 17	9	1 in 582
5	1 in 34		

Pinochle Auction
(Odds against finding in "widow" of 3 cards)

Open places	Odds against	Open places	Odds against
1	5 to 1	4	3 to 2 for
2	2 to 1	5	2 to 1 for
3	Even		

Bridge

The odds—against suit distribution in a hand of 4-4-3-2 are about 4 to 1, against 5-4-2-2 about 8 to 1, against 6-4-2-1 about 20 to 1, against 7-4-1-1 about 254 to 1, against 8-4-1-0 about 2,211 to 1, and against 13-0-0-0 about 158,753,389,899 to 1.

Measures of Force and Pressure

Dyne = force necessary to accelerate a 1-gram mass 1 centimeter per second squared = 0.000072 poundal
Poundal = force necessary to accelerate a 1-pound mass 1 foot per second squared = 13,825.5 dynes = 0.138255 newtons
Newton = force needed to accelerate a 1-kilogram mass 1 meter per second squared
Pascal (pressure) = 1 newton per square meter = 0.020885 pound per square foot
Atmosphere (air pressure at sea level) = 2,116.102 pounds per square foot = 14.6952 pounds per square inch = 1.0332 kilograms per square centimeter = 101,323 newtons per square meter.

Large Numbers

U.S.	Number of zeros	French British, German	U.S.	Number of zeros	French British, German
million	6	million	sextillion	21	1,000 trillion
billion	9	milliard	septillion	24	quadrillion
trillion	12	billion	octillion	27	1,000 quadrillion
quadrillion	15	1,000 billion	nonillion	30	quintillion
quintillion	18	trillion	decillion	33	1,000 quintillion

Roman Numerals

I	1	VI	6	XI	11	L	50	CD	400	$\overline{X}$	10,000
II	2	VII	7	XIX	19	LX	60	D	500	$\overline{L}$	50,000
III	3	VIII	8	XX	20	XC	90	CM	900	$\overline{C}$	100,000
IV	4	IX	9	XXX	30	C	100	M	1,000	$\overline{D}$	500,000
V	5	X	10	XL	40	CC	200	$\overline{V}$	5,000	$\overline{M}$	1,000,000

DISASTERS

Disasters are reported as of mid-1994.

Some Notable Shipwrecks Since 1850

(Figures indicate estimated lives lost)

1854, Mar.—City of Glasgow; British steamer missing in N Atlantic; 480.

1854, Sept. 27—Arctic; U.S. (Collins Line) steamer sunk in collision with French steamer Vesta near Cape Race; 285-351.

1856, Jan. 23—Pacific; U.S. (Collins Line) steamer missing in N Atlantic; 186-286.

1858, Sept. 23—Austria; German steamer destroyed by fire in N Atlantic; 471.

1863, Apr. 27—Anglo-Saxon; British steamer wrecked at Cape Race; 238.

1865, Apr. 27—Sultana; a Mississippi River steamer blew up near Memphis, Tenn.; 1,450.

1869, Oct. 27—Stonewall; steamer burned on Mississippi River below Cairo, Ill.; 200.

1870, Jan. 25—City of Boston; British (Inman Line) steamer vanished between New York and Liverpool; 177.

1870, Oct. 19—Cambria; British steamer wrecked off N Ireland; 196.

1872, Nov. 7—Mary Celeste; U.S. half-brig sailed from New York for Genoa; found abandoned in Atlantic 4 weeks later in mystery of sea; crew never heard from; loss of life unknown.

1873, Jan. 22—Northfleet; British steamer foundered off Dungeness, England; 300.

1873, Apr. 1—Atlantic; British (White Star) steamer wrecked off Nova Scotia; 585.

1873, Nov. 23—Ville du Havre; French steamer, sunk after collision with British sailing ship Loch Earn; 226.

1875, May 7—Schiller; German steamer wrecked off Scilly Isles; 312.

1875, Nov. 4—Pacific; U.S. steamer sunk after collision off Cape Flattery; 236.

1878, Sept. 3—Princess Alice; British steamer sank after collision in Thames River; 700.

1878, Dec. 18—Byzantin; French steamer sank after Dardanelles collision; 210.

1881, May 24—Victoria; steamer capsized in Thames River, Canada; 200.

1883, Jan. 19—Cimbria; German steamer sunk in collision with British steamer Sultan in North Sea; 389.

1887, Nov. 15—Wah Yeung; British steamer burned at sea; 400.

1890, Feb. 17—Duburg; British steamer wrecked, China Sea; 400.

1890, Sept. 19—Ertogrul; Turkish frigate foundered off Japan; 540.

1891, Mar. 17—Utopia; British steamer sank in collision with British ironclad Anson off Gibraltar; 562.

1895, Jan. 30—Elbe; German steamer sank in collision with British steamer Craithie in North Sea; 332.

1895, Mar. 11—Reina Regenta; Spanish cruiser foundered near Gibraltar; 400.

1898, Feb. 15—Maine; U.S. battleship blown up in Havana Harbor; 260.

1898, July 4—La Bourgogne; French steamer sunk in collision with British sailing ship Cromartyshire off Nova Scotia; 549.

1898, Nov. 26—Portland; U.S. steamer wrecked off Cape Cod; 157.

1904, June 15—General Slocum; excursion steamer burned in East River, New York City; 1,030.

1904, June 28—Norge; Danish steamer wrecked on Rockall Island, Scotland; 620.

1906, Aug. 4—Sirio; Italian steamer wrecked off Cape Palos, Spain; 350.

1908, Mar. 23—Matsu Maru; Japanese steamer sank in collision near Hakodate, Japan; 300.

1909, Aug. 1—Waratah; British steamer, Sydney to London, vanished; 300.

1910, Feb. 9—General Chanzy; French steamer wrecked off Minorca, Spain; 200.

1911, Sept. 25—Liberté; French battleship exploded at Toulon; 285.

1912, Mar. 5—Principe de Asturias; Spanish steamer wrecked off Spain; 500.

1912, Apr. 14-15—Titanic; British (White Star) steamer hit iceberg in N Atlantic; 1,503.

1912, Sept. 28—Kichemaru; Japanese steamer sank off Japanese coast; 1,000.

1914, May 29—Empress of Ireland; British (Canadian Pacific) steamer sunk in collision with Norwegian collier in St. Lawrence River; 1,014.

1915, May 7—Lusitania; British (Cunard Line) steamer torpedoed and sunk by German submarine off Ireland; 1,198.

1915, July 24—Eastland; excursion steamer capsized in Chicago River; 812.

1916, Feb. 26—Provence; French cruiser sank in Mediterranean; 3,100.

1916, Mar. 3—Principe de Asturias; Spanish steamer wrecked near Santos, Brazil; 558.

1916, Aug. 29—Hsin Yu; Chinese steamer sank off Chinese coast; 1,000.

1917, Dec. 6—Mont Blanc, Imo; French ammunition ship and Belgian steamer collided in Halifax Harbor; 1,600.

1918, Apr. 25—Kiang-Kwan; Chinese steamer sank in collision off Hankow; 500.

1918, July 12—Kawachi; Japanese battleship blew up in Tokayama Bay; 500.

1918, Oct. 25—Princess Sophia; Canadian steamer sank off Alaskan coast; 398.

1919, Jan. 17—Chaonia; French steamer lost in Straits of Messina, Italy; 460.

1919, Sept. 9—Valbanera; Spanish steamer lost off Florida coast; 500.

1921, Mar. 18—Hong Kong; steamer wrecked in South China Sea; 1,000.

1922, Aug. 26—Niitaka; Japanese cruiser sank in storm off Kamchatka, USSR; 300.

1927, Oct. 25—Principessa Mafalda; Italian steamer blew up, sank off Porto Seguro, Brazil; 314.

1928, Nov. 12—Vestris; British steamer sank in gale off Virginia; 113.

1934, Sept. 8—Morro Castle; U.S. steamer, Havana to New York, burned off Asbury Park, N.J.; 134.

1939, May 23—Squalus; U.S. submarine sank off Portsmouth, N.H.; 26.

1939, June 1—Thetis; British submarine, sank in Liverpool Bay; 99.

1942, Feb. 18—Truxtun and Pollux; U.S. destroyer and cargo ship ran aground, sank off Newfoundland; 204.

1942, Oct. 2—Curacao; British cruiser sank after collision with liner Queen Mary; 338.

1944, Dec. 17-18—3 U.S. Third Fleet destroyers sank during typhoon in Philippine Sea; 790.

1947, Jan. 19—Himera; Greek steamer hit a mine off Athens; 392.

1947, Apr. 16—Grandcamp; French freighter exploded in Texas City, Tex., Harbor, starting fires; 510.

1948, Nov.—Chinese army evacuation ship exploded and sunk off S Manchuria; 6,000.

1948, Dec. 3—Kiangya; Chinese refugee ship wrecked in explosion S of Shanghai; 1,100+.

1949, Sept. 17—Noronic; Canadian Great Lakes Cruiser burned at Toronto dock; 130.

1952, Apr. 26—Hobson and Wasp; U.S. destroyer and aircraft carrier collided in Atlantic; 176.

1954, Sept. 26—Toya Maru; Japanese ferry sank in Tsugaru Strait, Japan; 1,172.

1956, July 26—Andrea Doria and Stockholm; Italian liner and Swedish liner collided off Nantucket; 51.

1957, July 14—Eshghabad; Soviet ship ran aground in Caspian Sea; 270.

1961, July 8—Save; Portuguese ship ran aground off Mozambique; 259.

1962, Apr. 8—Dara; British liner exploded and sunk in Persian Gulf; 236.

1963, Apr. 10—Thresher; U.S. Navy atomic submarine sank in N Atlantic; 129.

1964, Feb. 10—Voyager, Melbourne; Australian destroyer sank after collision with Australian aircraft carrier Melbourne off New South Wales; 82.

1965, Nov. 13—Yarmouth Castle; Panamanian registered cruise ship burned and sank off Nassau; 90.

1967, July 29—Forrestal; U.S. aircraft carrier caught fire off N Vietnam; 134.

1968, Jan. 25—Dakar; Israeli submarine vanished in Mediterranean Sea; 69.

1968, Jan. 27—Minerve; French submarine vanished in Mediterranean; 52.

1968, late May—Scorpion; U.S. nuclear submarine sank in Atlantic near Azores; 99 (located Oct. 31).

1969, June 2—Evans; U.S. destroyer cut in half by Australian carrier Melbourne, S China Sea; 74.

1970, Mar. 4—Eurydice; French submarine sank in Mediterranean near Toulon; 57.

1970, Dec. 15—Namyong-Ho; South Korean ferry sank in Korea Strait; 308.

1974, May 1— Motor launch capsized off Bangladesh; 250.

1974, Sept. 26— Soviet destroyer burned and sank in Black Sea; 200+.

(continued)

Some Notable Shipwrecks Since 1850 *(continued)*

1976, Oct. 20—George Prince and Frosta; ferryboat and Norwegian tanker collided on Mississippi R. at Luling, La.; 77.

1976, Dec. 25—Patria; Egyptian liner caught fire and sank in the Red Sea; c. 100.

1979, Aug. 14—23 yachts competing in Fastnet yacht race sunk or abandoned during storm in S Irish Sea; 18.

1981, Jan. 27—Tamponas II; Indonesian passenger ship caught fire and sank in Java Sea; 580.

1981, May 26—Nimitz; U.S. Marine combat jet crashed on deck of U.S. aircraft carrier; 14.

1983, Feb. 12—Marine Electric; coal freighter sank during storm off Chincoteague, Va.; 33.

1983, May 25—10th of Ramadan; Nile steamer caught fire and sank in L. Nassar; 357.

1986, Aug. 31—Soviet passenger ship **Admiral Nakhimov** and Soviet freighter **Pyotr Vasev** collided in Black Sea; 398.

1987, Mar. 6—British ferry capsized off Zeebrugge, Belgium; 188.

1987, Dec. 20—Philippine ferry **Dona Paz** and oil tanker **Victor** collided in Tablas Strait; 3,000+.

1988, Aug. 6—Indian ferry capsized on Ganges R.; 400+.

1989, Apr. 7—Soviet submarine sank off Norway; 42.

1989, Apr. 19—USS Iowa; U.S. battleship; explosion in gun turret; 47.

1989, Aug. 20—British barge **Bowbelle** struck British pleasure cruiser **Marchioness** on Thames R. in central London; 56.

1989, Sept. 10—Romanian pleasure boat and Bulgarian barge collided on Danube R.; 161.

1991, Apr. 10—Auto ferry and oil tanker collided outside Livorno Harbor, Italy; 140.

1991, Dec. 14—Salem Express; ferry rammed coral reef nr. Safaga, Egypt; 462.

1993, Feb. 17—Neptune; ferry capsized off Port-au-Prince, Haiti; 500+.

1993, Oct. 10—West Sea Ferry; capsized in Yellow Sea near W South Korea during storm; 285.

1994, Sept. 28—Estonia; ferry sank in Baltic Sea when water entered through bow door; 900+.

Some Notable Aircraft Disasters Since 1937

Date			Aircraft	Site of accident	Deaths
1937	May	6	German zeppelin Hindenburg	Burned at mooring, Lakehurst, N.J.	36
1944	Aug.	23	U.S. Air Force B-24	Hit school, Freckelton, England	76[1]
1945	July	28	U.S. Army B-25	Hit Empire State Building, N.Y.C.	14[1]
1952	Dec.	20	U.S. Air Force C-124	Fell, burned, Moses Lake, Wash.	87
1953	Mar.	3	Canadian Pacific Comet Jet	Karachi, Pakistan	11[2]
1953	June	18	U.S. Air Force C-124	Crashed, burned near Tokyo	129
1955	Nov.	1	United Air Lines DC-6B	Exploded, crashed near Longmont, Col.	44[3]
1956	June	20	Venezuelan Super-Constellation	Crashed in Atlantic off Asbury Park, N.J.	74
1956	June	30	TWA Super-Const., United DC-7	Collided over Grand Canyon, Arizona	128
1960	Dec.	16	United DC-8 jet, TWA Super-Const.	Collided over N.Y. City	134[4]
1962	Mar.	16	Flying Tiger Super-Const.	Vanished in W Pacific	107
1962	June	3	Air France Boeing 707 jet	Crashed on takeoff from Paris	130
1962	June	22	Air France Boeing 707 jet	Crashed in storm, Guadeloupe, W.I.	113
1963	June	3	Chartered Northw. Airlines DC-7	Crashed in Pacific off British Columbia	101
1963	Nov.	29	Trans-Canada Airlines DC-8F	Crashed after takeoff from Montreal	118
1965	May	20	Pakistani Boeing 720-B	Crashed at Cairo, Egypt, airport	121
1966	Jan.	24	Air India Boeing 707 jetliner	Crashed on Mont Blanc, France-Italy	117
1966	Feb.	4	All-Nippon Boeing 727	Plunged into Tokyo Bay	133
1966	Mar.	5	BOAC Boeing 707 jetliner	Crashed on Mount Fuji, Japan	124
1966	Dec.	24	U.S. military-chartered CL-44	Crashed into village in South Vietnam	129[1]
1967	Apr.	20	Swiss Britannia turboprop	Crashed at Nicosia, Cyprus	126
1967	July	19	Piedmont Boeing 727, Cessna 310	Collided in air, Hendersonville, N.C.	82
1968	Apr.	20	S. African Airways Boeing 707	Crashed on takeoff, Windhoek, SW Africa	122
1968	May	3	Braniff International Electra	Crashed in storm near Dawson, Tex.	85
1969	Mar.	16	Venezuelan DC-9	Crashed after takeoff from Maracaibo, Venezuela	155[5]
1969	Dec.	8	Olympia Airways DC-6B	Crashed near Athens in storm	93
1970	Feb.	15	Dominican DC-9	Crashed into sea on takeoff from Santo Domingo	102
1970	July	3	British chartered jetliner	Crashed near Barcelona, Spain	112
1970	July	5	Air Canada DC-8	Crashed near Toronto International Airport	108
1970	Aug.	9	Peruvian turbojet	Crashed after takeoff from Cuzco, Peru	101[1]
1970	Nov.	14	Southern Airways DC-9	Crashed in mountains near Huntington, W.Va.	75[6]
1971	July	30	All-Nippon Boeing 727 and Japanese Air Force F-86	Collided over Morioka, Japan	162[7]
1971	Sept.	4	Alaska Airlines Boeing 727	Crashed into mountain near Juneau, Alaska	111
1972	Aug.	14	E German Ilyushin-62	Crashed on take-off East Berlin	156
1972	Oct.	13	Aeroflot Ilyushin-62	E German airline crashed near Moscow	176
1972	Dec.	3	Chartered Spanish airliner	Crashed on take-off, Canary Islands	155
1972	Dec.	29	Eastern Airlines Lockheed Tristar	Crashed on approach to Miami Int'l. Airport	101
1973	Jan.	22	Chartered Boeing 707	Burst into flames during landing, Kano Airport, Nigeria	176
1973	Feb.	21	Libyan jetliner	Shot down by Israeli fighter planes over Sinai	108
1973	Apr.	10	British Vanguard turboprop	Crashed during snowstorm at Basel, Switzerland	104
1973	June	3	Soviet Supersonic TU-144	Crashed near Goussainville, France	14[8]
1973	July	11	Brazilian Boeing 707	Crashed on approach to Orly Airport, Paris	122
1973	July	31	Delta Airlines jetliner	Crashed, landing in fog at Logan Airport, Boston	89
1973	Dec.	23	French Caravelle jet	Crashed in Morocco	106
1974	Mar.	3	Turkish DC-10 jet	Crashed at Ermenonville near Paris	346
1974	Apr.	23	Pan American 707 jet	Crashed in Bali, Indonesia	107
1974	Dec.	1	TWA-727	Crashed in storm, Upperville, Va.	92
1974	Dec.	4	Dutch-chartered DC-8	Crashed in storm near Colombo, Sri Lanka	191
1975	Apr.	4	Air Force Galaxy C-5B	Crashed near Saigon, South Vietnam, after takeoff with load of orphans	172
1975	June	24	Eastern Airlines 727 jet	Crashed in storm, JFK Airport, N.Y. City	113
1975	Aug.	3	Chartered 707	Hit mountainside, Agadir, Morocco	188
1976	Sept.	10	British Airways Trident, Yugoslav DC-9	Collided near Zagreb, Yugoslavia	176
1976	Sept.	19	Turkish 727	Hit mountain, S Turkey	155
1976	Oct.	13	Bolivian 707 cargo jet	Crashed in Santa Cruz, Bolivia	100[9]
1977	Mar.	27	KLM 747, Pan American 747	Collided on runway, Tenerife, Canary Islands	582
1977	Nov.	19	TAP Boeing 727	Crashed on Madeira	130
1977	Dec.	4	Malaysian Boeing 737	Hijacked, then exploded in mid-air over Straits of Johore	100
1977	Dec.	13	U.S. DC-3	Crashed after takeoff at Evansville, Ind.	29[10]
1978	Jan.	1	Air India 747	Exploded, crashed into sea off Bombay	213
1978	Sept.	25	Boeing 727, Cessna 172	Collided in air, San Diego, Cal.	150

Date			Aircraft	Site of accident	Deaths
1978	Nov.	15	Chartered DC-8	Crashed near Colombo, Sri Lanka	183
1979	May	25	American Airlines DC-10	Crashed after takeoff at O'Hare Intl. Airport, Chicago	275[11]
1979	Aug.	17	Two Soviet Aeroflot jetliners	Collided over Ukraine	173
1979	Nov.	26	Pakistani Boeing 707	Crashed near Jidda, Saudi Arabia	156
1979	Nov.	28	New Zealand DC-10	Crashed into mountain in Antarctica	257
1980	Mar.	14	Polish Ilyushin 62	Crashed making emergency landing, Warsaw	87[12]
1980	Aug.	19	Saudi Arabian Tristar	Burned after emergency landing, Riyadh	301
1981	Dec.	1	Yugoslavian DC-9	Crashed into mountain in Corsica	174
1982	Jan.	13	Air Florida Boeing 737	Crashed into Potomac River after takeoff	78
1982	July	9	Pan-Am Boeing 727	Crashed after takeoff in Kenner, La.	153[13]
1982	Sept.	11	U.S. Army CH-47 Chinook helicopter	Crashed during air show in Mannheim, W Germany	46
1983	Sept.	1	S. Korean Boeing 747	Shot down after violating Soviet airspace	269
1983	Nov.	27	Colombian Boeing 747	Crashed near Barajas Airport, Madrid	183
1985	Feb.	19	Spanish Boeing 727	Crashed into Mt. Oiz, Spain	148
1985	June	23	Air-India Boeing 747	Crashed into Atlantic Ocean S of Ireland	329
1985	Aug.	2	Delta Air Lines jumbo jet	Crashed at Dallas-Ft. Worth Intl. Airport	133
1985	Aug.	12	Japan Air Lines Boeing 747	Crashed into Mt. Ogura, Japan	520[14]
1985	Dec.	12	Arrow Air DC-8	Crashed after takeoff in Gander, Newfoundland	256[15]
1986	Mar.	31	Mexican Boeing 727	Crashed NW of Mexico City	166
1986	Aug.	31	Aeromexico DC-9	Collided with Piper PA-28 over Cerritos, Cal.	82[16]
1987	May	9	Ilyushin 62M	Crashed after takeoff in Warsaw, Poland	183
1987	Aug.	16	Northwest Airlines MD-82	Crashed after takeoff in Romulus, Mich.	156
1988	July	3	Iranian A300 Airbus	Shot down by U.S. Navy warship *Vincennes* over Persian Gulf	290
1988	Dec.	21	Pan Am Boeing 747	Exploded and crashed in Lockerbie, Scotland	270[17]
1989	Feb.	8	Boeing 707	Crashed into mountain in Azores Islands off Portugual	144
1989	June	7	Suriname DC-8	Crashed near Paramaribo Airport, Suriname	168
1989	July	19	United Airlines DC-10	Crashed while landing with a disabled hydraulic system, Sioux City, Ia.	111
1989	Sept.	19	French DC-10	Exploded in air over Niger	171
1991	May	26	Lauda Air Boeing 767-300	Exploded over rural Thailand	223
1991	July	11	Nigerian DC-8	Crashed while landing at Jidda, Saudi Arabia	261
1994	Jan.	3	Aeroflot TU-154	Crashed and exploded after takeoff in Irkhutsk, Russia	125[18]
1994	Apr.	26	China Airlines Airbus A-300-600R	Crashed at Japan's Nagoya Airport	264
1994	June	16	China Northwest Airlines TU-154	Crashed 10 min. after takeoff	160
1994	Sept.	8	USAir Boeing 737-300	Crashed in Aliquippa, PA, near Pittsburgh Intl. Airport	132

(1) Including those on the ground and in buildings. (2) First fatal crash of commercial jet plane. (3) Caused by bomb planted by John G. Graham in insurance plot to kill his mother, a passenger. (4) Including all 128 aboard the planes and 6 on ground. (5) Killed 84 on plane and 71 on ground. (6) Including 43 Marshall U. football players and coaches. (7) Airliner-fighter crash, pilot of fighter parachuted to safety, was arrested for negligence. (8) First supersonic plane crash killed 6 crewmen and 8 on the ground; there were no passengers. (9) Crew of 3 killed; 97, mostly children, killed on ground. (10) Including U. of Evansville basketball team. (11) Highest death toll in U.S. aviation history. (12) Including 22 members of U.S. boxing team. (13) Including 8 on ground. (14) Worst single-plane disaster. (15) Incl. 248 members of U.S. 101st Airborne Division. (16) Incl. 15 on the ground. (17) Incl. 11 on the ground. (18) Incl. 1 on the ground.

Notable Railroad Disasters

Date			Location	Deaths
1876	Dec.	29	Ashtabula, Oh.	92
1880	Aug.	11	Mays Landing, N. J.	40
1887	Aug.	10	Chatsworth, Ill.	81
1888	Oct.	10	Mud Run, Pa.	55
1891	June	14	Nr. Basel, Switzerland	100
1896	July	30	Atlantic City, N. J.	60
1903	Dec.	23	Laurel Run, Pa.	53
1904	Aug.	7	Eden, Col.	96
1904	Sept.	24	New Market, Tenn.	56
1906	Mar.	16	Florence, Col.	35
1906	Oct.	28	Atlantic City, N. J.	40
1906	Dec.	30	Washington, D. C.	53
1907	Jan.	2	Volland, Kan.	33
1907	Jan.	19	Fowler, Ind.	29
1907	Feb.	16	New York, N.Y.	22
1907	Feb.	23	Colton, Cal.	26
1907	May	11	Lompoc, Cal.	36
1907	July	20	Salem, Mich.	33
1910	Mar.	1	Wellington, Wash.	96
1910	Mar.	21	Green Mountain, Ia.	55
1911	Aug.	25	Manchester, N. Y.	29
1912	July	4	East Corning, N. Y.	39
1912	July	5	Ligonier, Pa.	23
1914	Aug.	5	Tipton Ford, Mo.	43
1914	Sept.	15	Lebanon, Mo.	28
1915	May	22	Nr. Gretna, Scotland	227
1916	Mar.	29	Amherst, Oh.	27
1917	Sept.	28	Kellyville, Okla.	23
1917	Dec.	12	Modane, France	543[1]
1917	Dec.	20	Shepherdsville, Ky.	46
1918	June	22	Ivanhoe, Ind.	68
1918	July	9	Nashville, Tenn.	101
1918	Nov.	1	Brooklyn, N. Y.	97
1919	Jan.	12	South Byron, N. Y.	22
1919	Dec.	20	Onawa, Maine	23
1921	Feb.	27	Porter, Ind.	37
1921	Dec.	5	Woodmont, Pa.	27
1922	Aug.	5	Sulphur Spring, Mo.	34
1922	Dec.	13	Humble, Tex.	22
1923	Sept.	27	Lockett, Wy.	31
1925	June	16	Hackettstown, N. J.	50
1925	Oct.	27	Victoria, Miss.	21
1926	Sept.	5	Waco, Col.	30
1928	Aug.	24	I.R.T. subway, Times Sq., N. Y.	18
1937	July	16	Nr. Patna, India	107
1938	June	19	Saugus, Mont.	47
1939	Aug.	12	Harney, Nev.	24
1939	Dec.	22	Nr. Magdeburg, Germany	132
1939	Dec.	22	Nr. Friedrichshafen, Germany	99
1940	Apr.	19	Little Falls, N. Y.	31
1940	July	31	Cuyahoga Falls, Oh.	43
1943	Aug.	29	Wayland, N. Y.	27
1943	Sept.	6	Frankford Junction, Philadelphia, Pa.	79
1943	Dec.	16	Between Rennert and Buie, N. C.	72
1944	Jan.	16	Leon Province, Spain	500
1944	Mar.	2	Salerno, Italy	521
1944	July	6	High Bluff, Tenn.	35
1944	Aug.	4	Near Stockton, Ga.	47
1944	Sept.	14	Dewey, Ind.	29
1944	Dec.	31	Bagley, Utah	50
1945	Aug.	9	Michigan, N. D.	34
1946	Mar.	20	Aracaju, Mexico	185
1946	Apr.	25	Naperville, Ill.	45
1947	Feb.	18	Gallitzin, Pa.	24
1949	Oct.	22	Nr. Dwor, Poland	200+
1950	Feb.	17	Rockville Centre, N. Y.	31
1950	Sept.	11	Coshocton, Oh.	33
1950	Nov.	22	Richmond Hill, N. Y.	79
1951	Feb.	6	Woodbridge, N. J.	84
1951	Nov.	12	Wyuta, Wyo.	17
1951	Nov.	25	Woodstock, Ala.	17
1952	Mar.	4	Nr. Rio de Janeiro, Brazil	119
1952	July	9	Rzepin, Poland	160
1952	Oct.	8	Harrow, England	112
1953	Mar.	27	Conneaut, Oh.	21
1955	Apr.	3	Guadalajara, Mexico	300
1956	Jan.	22	Los Angeles, Cal.	30
1956	Feb.	28	Swampscott, Mass.	13
1956	Sept.	5	Springer, N. M.	20
1957	June	11	Vroman, Col.	12
1957	Sept.	1	Kendal, Jamaica	178
1957	Sept.	29	Montgomery, W Pakistan	250
1957	Dec.	4	London, England	90
1958	May	8	Rio de Janeiro, Brazil	128
1958	Sept.	15	Elizabethport, N. J.	48
1960	Mar.	14	Bakersfield, Cal.	14

(continued)

Notable Railroad Disasters *(continued)*

Date			Location	Deaths
1960	Nov.	14	Pardubice, Czech.	110
1962	Jan.	8	Woerden, Netherlands	91
1962	May	3	Tokyo, Japan	163
1962	July	28	Steelton, Pa.	19
1964	July	26	Oporto, Portugal	94
1966	Dec.	28	Everett, Mass.	13
1970	Feb.	1	Buenos Aires, Argentina	236
1971	June	10	Salem, Ill.	11
1972	June	16	Vierzy, France	107
1972	July	21	Seville, Spain	76
1972	Oct.	6	Saltillo, Mexico	208
1972	Oct.	30	Chicago, Ill.	45
1974	Aug.	30	Zagreb, Yugoslavia	153
1977	Jan.	18	Granville, Australia	82
1977	Feb.	4	Chicago, Ill., elevated train	11
1981	June	6	Bihar, India	500+
1982	Jan.	27	El Asnam, Algeria	130
1982	July	11	Tepic, Mexico	120
1983	Feb.	19	Empalme, Mexico	100
1987	Jan.	4	Essex, Md.	16
1988	Dec.	12	London, England	115
1989	Jan.	15	Maizdi Khan, Bangladesh	110+
1990	Jan.	4	Sindh Province, Pakistan	210+
1991	May	14	Shigaraki, Japan	42
1991	July	31	Camden, S.C.	7
1991	Aug.	28	N.Y. City subway	5
1993	Jan.	18	Gary, Ind.	7
1993	Sept.	22	Big Bayou Conot, Ala.	47
1994	Mar.	8	Nr. Durban, South Africa	63

(1) World's worst train wreck; passenger train derailed.

Principal U.S. Mine Disasters Since 1900

Source: Bureau of Mines, U.S. Dept. of the Interior; Mine Safety and Health Admin., U.S. Dept. of Labor

Note: Prior to 1968, only disasters with losses of 65 or more lives are listed; since 1968, all disasters in which 5 or more people were killed are listed. Only fatalities to mining company employees are included. All bituminous-coal mines unless otherwise noted.

Date		Location	Deaths
1900	May 1	Scofield, Ut.	200
1902	May 19	Coal Creek, Tenn.	184
1902	July 10	Johnstown, Pa.	112
1903	June 30	Hanna, Wy.	169
1904	Jan. 25	Cheswick, Pa.	179
1905	Feb. 20	Virginia City, Ala.	112
1907	Jan. 29	Stuart W. Va.	84
1907	Dec. 6	Monongah, W. Va.	361
1907	Dec. 19	Jacobs Creek, Pa.	239
1908	Nov. 28	Marianna, Pa.	154
1909	Jan. 12	Switchback, W. Va.	67
1909	Nov. 13	Cherry, Ill.	259
1910	Jan. 31	Primero, Col.	75
1910	May 5	Palos, Ala.	90
1910	Nov.8	Delagua, Col.	79
1911[1]	Apr. 7	Throop, Pa.	72
1911	Apr. 8	Littleton, Ala.	128
1911	Dec.9	Briceville, Tenn.	84
1912	Mar. 20	McCurtain, Okla.	73
1912	Mar. 26	Jed, W. Va.	83
1913	Apr. 23	Finleyville, Pa.	96
1913	Oct. 22	Dawson, N.M.	263
1914	Apr. 28	Eccles, W. Va.	181
1915	Mar. 2	Layland, W. Va.	112
1917	Apr. 27	Hastings, Col.	121
1917[2]	June 8	Butte, Mon.	163
1919[1]	June 5	Wilkes-Barre, Pa.	92
1922	Nov. 6	Spangler, Pa.	77
1922	Nov. 22	Dolomite, Ala.	90
1923	Feb. 8	Dawson, N.M.	120
1923	Aug. 14	Kemmerer, Wy.	99
1924	Mar. 8	Castle Gate, Ut.	171
1924	Apr. 28	Benwood, W. Va.	119
1926	Jan. 13	Wilburton, Okla.	91
1927	Apr. 30	Everettville, W. Va.	97
1928	May 19	Mather, Pa.	195
1930	Nov. 5	Millfield, Oh.	79
1940	Jan. 10	Bartley, W. Va.	91
1940	Mar. 16	St. Clairsville, Oh.	72
1943	Feb. 27	Washoe, Mon.	74
1944	July 5	Belmont, Oh.	66
1947	Mar. 25	Centralia, Ill.	111
1951	Dec. 21	West Frankfort, Ill.	119
1968[3]	Mar. 6	Calumet, La.	21
1968	Nov. 20	Farmington, W. Va.	78
1970	Dec. 30	Hyden, Ky.	38
1972[2]	May 2	Kellogg, Ida.	91
1976	Mar. 9, 11	Oven Fork, Ky.	23
1977	Mar. 1	Tower City, Pa.	9
1980	Nov. 7	Clothier, W. Va.	5
1981	Apr. 15	Redstone, Col.	15
1981	Dec. 7	Topmost, Ky.	8
1981	Dec. 8	Whitwell, Tenn.	13
1982	Jan. 20	Floyd County, Ky.	7
1983	June 21	Dante, Va	7
1984	Dec. 19	Huntington, Ut.	27
1986	Feb. 6	Fairmont, W. Va.	5
1989	Sept. 13	Sturgis, Ky.	10
1992	Dec. 7	Norton, Va.	8

(1) Anthracite mine. (2) Metal mine. (3) Nonmetal mine.
World's worst mine disaster killed 1,549 workers in Honkeiko Colliery in Manchuria Apr. 25, 1942.

Some Notable U.S. Tornadoes Since 1925

Date			Location	Deaths
1925	Mar.	18	Mo., Ill., Ind.	689
1927	Apr.	12	Rock Springs, Tex.	74
1927	May	9	Arkansas, Poplar Bluff, Mo.	92
1927	Sept.	29	St. Louis, Mo.	90
1930	May	6	Hill, Navarro, Ellis Co., Tex.	41
1932	Mar.	21	Ala. (series of tornadoes)	268
1936	Apr.	5	Miss., Ga.	455
1936	Apr.	6	Gainesville, Ga.	203
1938	Sept.	29	Charleston, S.C.	32
1942	Mar.	16	Central to NE Miss.	75
1942	Apr.	27	Rogers & Mayes Co., Okla.	52
1944	June	23	Oh., Pa., W. Va., Md.	150
1945	Apr.	12	Okla.-Ark.	102
1947	Apr.	9	Tex., Okla. & Kan.	169
1948	Mar.	19	Bunker Hill & Gillespie, Ill.	33
1949	Jan.	3	La. & Ark.	58
1952	Mar.	21	Ark., Mo., Tenn. (series)	208
1953	May	11	Waco, Tex.	114
1953	June	8	Mich., Oh.	142
1953	June	9	Worcester and vicinity, Mass.	90
1953	Dec.	5	Vicksburg, Miss.	38
1955	May	25	Kan., Mo., Okla., Tex.	115
1957	May	20	Kan., Mo.	48
1958	June	4	NW Wisconsin	30
1959	Feb.	10	St. Louis, Mo.	21
1960	May	5, 6	SE Oklahoma, Arkansas	30
1965	Apr.	11	Ind., Ill., Oh., Mich., Wis.	271
1966	Mar.	3	Jackson, Miss.	57
1966	Mar.	3	Mississippi, Alabama	61
1967	Apr.	21	Ill., Mich.	33
1968	May	15	Midwest	71
1969	Jan.	23	Mississippi	32
1971	Feb.	21	Mississippi delta	110
1973	May	26-27	South, Midwest (series)	47
1974	Apr.	3-4	Ala., Ga., Tenn., Ky., Oh.	315
1977	Apr.	4	Ala., Miss., Ga.	22
1979	Apr.	10	Tex., Okla.	60
1980	June	3	Grand Island, Neb. (series)	4
1982	Mar.	2-4	South, Midwest (series)	17
1982	May	29	S Ill.	10
1983	May	18-22	Tex.	12
1984	Mar.	28	N. Carolina, S. Carolina	57
1984	Apr.	21-22	Mississippi	15
1984	Apr.	26	Okla. to Minn. (series)	17
1985	May	31	N.Y., Pa., Oh., Ont. (series)	75
1987	May	22	Saragosa, Tex.	29
1989	Nov.	15	Huntsville, Ala.	18
1989	Nov.	16	Newburgh, N.Y.	9
1990	June	2-3	Midwest, Great Lakes	13
1990	Aug.	28	N Ill.	25
1991	Apr.	26	Kan., Okla.	23
1992	Nov.	21-23	South, Midwest	26
1993	Aug.	6	Petersburg, Va.	4
1994	Mar.	27-28	Ala., Tenn., Ga., N.C., S.C. (series)	52
1994	Apr.	26	Cen. Tex.	4

Some Notable Hurricanes, Typhoons, Blizzards, Other Storms

Names of hurricanes and typhoons in italics: H.—hurricane; T.—typhoon

Date		Location	Deaths
1888	Mar. 11-14	Blizzard, E U.S.	400
1900	Aug.-Sept.	H., Galveston, Tex.	6,000
1906	Sept. 19-24	H., La., Miss.	350
1906	Sept. 18	Typhoon, Hong Kong	10,000
1926	Sept. 11-22	H., Fla., Ala.	243
1926	Oct. 20	H., Cuba	600
1928	Sept. 6-20	H., S Fla.	1,836
1930	Sept. 3	H., Dominican Rep.	2,000
1938	Sept. 21	H., Long Island, N.Y., New England	600
1940	Nov. 11-12	Blizzard, U.S. NE, Midwest	144
1942	Oct. 15-16	H., Bengal, India.	40,000
1944	Sept. 9-16	H., N.C. to New Eng.	46
1947	Dec. 26	Blizzard, N.Y. City, N Atlantic states	55
1952	Oct. 22	Typhoon, Philippines	440
1954	Aug. 30	H. *Carol,* NE U.S.	68
1954	Oct. 5-18	H. *Hazel,* E U.S., Haiti	347
1955	Aug. 12-13	H. *Connie,* Carolinas, Va., Md.	43
1955	Aug. 7-21	H. *Diane,* E U.S.	400
1955	Sept. 19	H. *Hilda,* Mexico	200
1955	Sept. 22-28	H. *Janet,* Caribbean	500
1956	Feb. 1-29	Blizzard, W Europe	1,000
1957	June 25-30	H. *Audrey,* Tex. to Ala.	390
1958	Feb. 15-16	Blizzard, NE U.S.	171
1959	Sept. 17-19	T. *Sarah,* Japan, S. Korea	2,000
1959	Sept. 26-27	T. *Vera,* Honshu, Japan	4,466
1960	Sept. 4-12	H. *Donna,* Caribbean, E U.S.	148
1961	Sept. 11-14	H. *Carla,* Tex.	46
1961	Oct. 31	H. *Hattie,* Br. Honduras	400
1963	May 28-29	Windstorm, Bangladesh	22,000
1963	Oct. 4-8	H. *Flora,* Caribbean	6,000
1964	Oct. 4-7	H. *Hilda,* La., Miss., Ga.	38
1964	June 30	T. *Winnie,* N Philippines	107
1964	Sept. 5	T. *Ruby,* Hong Kong and China	735
1965	May 11-12	Windstorm, Bangladesh	17,000
1965	June 1-2	Windstorm, Bangladesh	30,000
1965	Sept. 7-12	H. *Betsy,* Fla., Miss., La.	74
1965	Dec. 15	Windstorm, Bangladesh	10,000
1966	June 4-10	H. *Alma,* Honduras, SE U.S.	51
1966	Sept. 24-30	H. *Inez,* Carib., Fla., Mex.	293
1967	July 9	T. *Billie,* SW Japan	347
1967	Sept. 5-23	H. *Beulah,* Carib., Mex., Tex.	54
1967	Dec. 12-20	Blizzard, SW, U.S.	51
1968	Nov. 18-28	T. *Nina,* Philippines	63
1969	Aug. 17-18	H. *Camille,* Miss., La.	256
1970	July 30-Aug. 5	H. *Celia,* Cuba, Fla., Tex.	31
1970	Aug. 20-21	H. *Dorothy,* Martinique	42
1970	Sept. 15	T. *Georgia,* Philippines	300
1970	Oct. 14	T. *Sening,* Philippines	583
1970	Oct. 15	T. *Titang,* Philippines	526
1970	Nov. 13	Cyclone, Bangladesh	300,000
1971	Aug. 1	T. *Rose,* Hong Kong	130
1972	June 19-29	H. *Agnes,* Fla. to N.Y.	118
1972	Dec. 3	T. *Theresa,* Philippines	169
1973	June-Aug.	Monsoon rains in India	1,217
1974	June 11	Storm Dinah, Luzon Is., Philip.	71
1974	July 11	T. *Gilda,* Japan, S. Korea	108
1974	Sept. 19-20	H. *Fifi,* Honduras	2,000
1974	Dec. 25	Cyclone leveled Darwin, Aus.	50
1975	Sept. 13-27	H. *Eloise,* Caribbean, NE U.S.	71
1976	May 20	T. *Olga,* floods, Philippines	215
1977	July 25, 31	T. *Thelma,* T. *Vera,* Taiwan	39
1978	Oct. 27	T. *Rita,* Philippines	c. 400
1979	Aug. 30-Sept. 7	H. *David,* Caribbean, E. U.S.	1,100
1980	Aug. 4-11	H. *Allen,* Caribbean, Texas	272
1981	Nov. 25	T. *Irma,* Luzon Is., Philippines	176
1983	June	Monsoon rains in India	900
1983	Aug. 18	H. *Alicia,* S Texas	17
1984	Sept. 2	T. *Ike,* S Philippines	1,363
1985	May 25	Cyclone, Bangladesh	10,000
1985	Oct. 26-Nov. 6	H. *Juan,* SE U.S.	97
1987	Nov. 25	T. *Nina,* Philippines	650
1988	Sept. 10-17	H. *Gilbert,* Caribbean, G. of Mexico	260
1989	Sept. 16-22	H. *Hugo,* Caribbean, SE U.S.	504
1990	May 6-11	Cyclones, SE India	450
1991	Apr. 30	Cyclone, Bangladesh	139,000
1992	Aug. 24-26	H. *Andrew,* S Fla., La.	14
1993	Mar. 13-14	Blizzard, E U.S.	200
1993	June	Monsoon rains in Bangladesh	2,000

Some Notable Floods, Tidal Waves

Date		Location	Deaths
1228	....	Holland	100,000
1642	....	China	300,000
1883	Aug. 27	Indonesia	36,000
1887	....	Huang He River, China	900,000
1889	May 31	Johnstown, Pa.	2,200
1900	Sept. 8	Galveston, Tex.	5,000
1903	June 15	Heppner, Ore.	325
1911	....	Chang Jiang River, China	100,000
1913	Mar. 25-27	Ohio, Indiana	732
1915	Aug. 17	Galveston, Tex.	275
1928	Mar. 13	Collapse of St. Francis Dam, Saugus, Cal.	450
1928	Sept. 13	Lake Okeechobee, Fla.	2,000
1931	Aug.	Huang He River, China	3,700,000
1937	Jan. 22	Ohio, Miss. Valleys	250
1939	....	N China	200,000
1946	Apr. 1	Hawaii, Alaska	159
1947	Sept. 20	Honshu Island, Japan	1,900
1951	Aug.	Manchuria	1,800
1953	Jan. 31	W Europe	2,000
1954	Aug. 17	Farahzad, Iran	2,000
1955	Oct. 7-12	India, Pakistan	1,700
1959	Nov. 1	W Mexico	2,000
1959	Dec. 2	Frejus, France	412
1960	Oct. 10	Bangladesh	6,000
1960	Oct. 31	Bangladesh	4,000
1962	Feb. 17	German North Sea coast	343
1962	Sept. 27	Barcelona, Spain	445
1963	Oct. 9	Dam collapse, Vaiont, Italy	1,800
1966	Nov. 3-4	Florence, Venice, Italy	113
1967	Jan. 18-24	E Brazil	894
1967	Mar. 19	Rio de Janeiro, Brazil	436
1967	Nov. 26	Lisbon, Portugal	464
1968	Aug. 7-14	Gujarat State, India	1,000
1968	Oct. 7	NE India	780
1969	Jan. 18-26	S Cal.	100
1969	Mar. 17	Mundau Valley, Alagoas, Brazil	218
1969	Aug. 20-22	W Virginia	189
1969	Sept. 15	South Korea	250
1969	Oct. 1-8	Tunisia	500
1970	May 20	Central Romania	160
1970	July 22	Himalayas, India	500
1971	Feb. 26	Rio de Janeiro, Brazil	130
1972	Feb. 26	Buffalo Creek, W. Va.	118
1972	June 9	Rapid City, S.D.	236
1972	Aug. 7	Luzon Is., Philippines	454
1972	Aug. 19-31	Pakistan	1,500
1974	Mar. 29	Tubaro, Brazil	1,000
1974	Aug. 12	Monty-Long, Bangladesh	2,500
1976	June 5	Teton Dam collapse, Ida.	11
1976	July 31	Big Thompson Canyon, Col.	139
1976	Nov. 17	East Java, Indonesia	136
1977	July 19-20	Johnstown, Pa.	68
1978	June-Sept.	N India	1,200
1979	Jan.-Feb.	Brazil	204
1979	July 17	Lomblem Is., Indonesia	539
1979	Aug. 11	Morvi, India	15,000
1980	Feb. 13-22	S Cal., Ariz.	26
1981	Apr.	N China	550
1981	July	Sichuan, Hubei Prov., China	1,300
1982	Jan. 23	Nr. Lima, Peru	600
1982	May 12	Guangdong, China	430
1982	June 6	S Conn.	12
1982	Sept. 17-21	El Salvador, Guatemala	1,300+
1982	Dec. 2-9	Ill., Mo., Ark.	22
1983	Feb.-Mar.	Cal. coast	13
1983	Apr. 6-12	Ala., La., Miss., Tenn.	15
1984	May 27	Tulsa, Okla.	13
1984	Aug-Sept.	S. Korea	200+
1985	July 19	N Italy, dam burst	361
1987	Aug.-Sept.	N Bangladesh	1,000+
1988	Sept.	N India	1,000+
1990	June 14	Shadyside, Oh.	23
1991	Dec. 18-26	Texas	18
1992	Feb. 9-15	S Cal.	13
1992	Apr. 13	Downtown Chicago	0
1993	July-Aug.	Midwest	48
1994	July	Georgia, Alabama	32

Some Notable Fires

Date			Location	Deaths
1835	Dec.	16	New York City, 500 bldgs. destroyed	—
1845	May		Canton, China, theater	1,670
1871	Oct.	8	Chicago, $196 million loss	250
1871	Oct.	8	Peshtigo, Wis., forest fire	1,182
1872	Nov.	9	Boston, 800 bldgs. destroyed	—
1876	Dec.	5	Brooklyn (N.Y.), theater	295
1877	June	20	St. John, N. B., Canada	100
1881	Dec.	8	Ring Theater, Vienna	850
1887	May	25	Opera Comique, Paris	200
1887	Sept.	4	Exeter, England, theater	200
1894	Sept.	1	Minn., forest fire	413
1897	May	4	Paris, charity bazaar	150
1900	June	30	Hoboken, N. J., docks	326
1902	Sept.	20	Birmingham, Ala., church	115
1903	Dec.	30	Iroquois Theater, Chicago	602
1908	Jan.	13	Rhoads Theater, Boyertown, Pa.	170
1908	Mar.	4	Collinwood, Oh., school	176
1911	Mar.	25	Triangle Shirtwaist factory, N.Y. City	146
1913	Oct.	14	Mid Glamorgan, Wales, colliery	439
1918	Apr.	13	Norman Okla., state hospital	38
1918	Oct.	12	Cloquet, Minn., forest fire	400
1919	June	20	Mayaguez Theater, San Juan	150
1923	May	17	Camden, S. C., school	76
1924	Dec.	24	Babb's Switch, Okla., school	35
1929	May	15	Cleveland, Oh., clinic	125
1930	Apr.	21	Columbus, Oh., penitentiary	320
1931	July	24	Pittsburgh, Pa., home for aged	48
1934	Dec.	11	Hotel Kerns, Lansing, Mich.	34
1938	May	16	Atlanta, Ga., Terminal Hotel	35
1940	Apr.	23	Natchez, Miss., dance hall	198
1942	Nov.	28	Cocoanut Grove, Boston	491
1942			St. John's, Newfoundland, hostel	100
1943	Sept.	7	Gulf Hotel, Houston	55
1944	July	6	Ringling Circus, Hartford	168
1946	June	5	LaSalle Hotel, Chicago	61
1946	Dec.	7	Winecoff Hotel, Atlanta	119
1946	Dec.	12	New York, ice plant, tenement	37
1949	Apr.	5	Effingham, Ill., hospital	77
1950	Jan.	7	Davenport, Ia., Mercy Hospital	41
1953	Mar.	29	Largo, Fla., nursing home	35
1953	Apr.	16	Chicago, metalworking plant	35
1957	Feb.	17	Warrenton, Mo., home for aged	72
1958	Mar.	19	New York City, loft building	24
1958	Dec.	1	Chicago, parochial school	95
1958	Dec.	16	Bogota, Colombia, store	83
1959	June	23	Stalheim, Norway, resort hotel	34
1960	Mar.	12	Pusan, Korea, chemical plant	68
1960	July	14	Guatemala City, mental hospital	225
1960	Nov.	13	Amude, Syria, movie theater	152
1961	Jan.	6	Thomas Hotel, San Francisco	20
1961	Dec.	8	Hartford, Conn., hospital	16
1961	Dec.	17	Niteroi, Brazil, circus	323
1963	May	4	Diourbel, Senegal, theater	64
1963	Nov.	18	Surfside Hotel, Atlantic City, N.J.	25
1963	Nov.	23	Fitchville, Oh., rest home	63
1963	Dec.	29	Roosevelt Hotel, Jacksonville, Fla.	22
1964	May	8	Manila, apartment bldg.	30
1964	Dec.	18	Fountaintown, Ind., nursing home	20
1965	Mar.	1	LaSalle, Canada, apartment	28
1965	Aug.	11-16	Watts riot fires, Cal.	30+
1966	Mar.	11	Numata, Japan, 2 ski resorts	31
1966	Aug.	13	Melbourne, Australia, hotel	29
1966	Sept.	12	Anchorage, Alaska, hotel	14
1966	Oct.	17	N. Y. City bldg. (firefighters)	12
1966	Dec.	7	Erzurum, Turkey, barracks	68
1967	Feb.	7	Montgomery, Ala., restaurant	25
1967	May	22	Brussels, Belgium, store	322
1967	July	16	Jay, Fla., state prison	37
1968	Feb.	26	Shrewsbury, England, hospital	22
1968	May	11	Vijayawada, India, wedding hall	58
1968	Nov.	18	Glasgow, Scotland, factory	24
1969	Dec.	2	Notre Dame, Can., nursing home	54
1970	Jan.	9	Marietta, Oh., nursing home	27
1970	Mar.	20	Seattle, Wash., hotel	19
1970	Nov.	1	Grenoble, France, dance hall	145
1970	Dec.	20	Tucson, Arizona, hotel	28
1971	Mar.	6	Burghoezli, Switzerland, psychiatric clinic	28
1971	Apr.	20	Bangkok, Thailand, hotel	24
1971	Dec.	25	Seoul, South Korea, hotel	162
1972	May	13	Osaka, Japan, nightclub	116
1972	July	5	Sherborne, England, hospital	30
1973	Feb.	6	Paris, France, school	21
1973	Nov.	6	Fukui, Japan, train	28
1973	Nov.	29	Kumamoto, Japan, department store	107
1973	Dec.	2	Seoul, South Korea, theater	50
1974	Feb.	1	Sao Paulo, Brazil, bank building	189
1974	June	30	Port Chester, N. Y., discotheque	24
1974	Nov.	3	Seoul, South Korea, hotel discotheque	88
1975	Dec.	12	Mina, Saudi Arabia, tent city	138
1976	Oct.	24	Bronx, N.Y., social club	25
1977	Feb.	25	Moscow, Rossiya hotel	45
1977	May	28	Southgate, Ky., nightclub	164
1977	June	9	Abidjan, Ivory Coast, nightclub	41
1977	June	26	Columbia, Tenn., jail	42
1977	Nov.	14	Manila, Philippines, hotel	47
1978	Jan.	28	Kansas City, Coates House Hotel	16
1979	July	14	Saragossa, Spain, hotel	80
1979	Dec.	31	Chapais, Quebec, social club	42
1980	May	20	Kingston, Jamaica, nursing home	157
1980	Nov.	21	MGM Grand Hotel, Las Vegas	84
1980	Dec.	4	Stouffer Inn, Harrison, N.Y.	26
1981	Jan.	9	Keansburg, N.J., boarding home	30
1981	Feb.	10	Las Vegas Hilton	8
1981	Feb.	14	Dublin, Ireland, discotheque	44
1982	Sept.	4	Los Angeles, apartment house	24
1982	Nov.	8	Biloxi, Miss., county jail	29
1983	Feb.	13	Turin, Italy, movie theater	64
1983	Dec.	17	Madrid, Spain, discotheque	83
1984	May	11	Great Adventure Amusement Park, N.J.	8
1985	Apr.	21	Tabaco, Philippines, movie theater	44
1985	Apr.	26	Buenos Aires, Argentina hospital	79
1985	May	11	Bradford, England, soccer stadium	53
1986	Dec.	31	Puerto Rico, Dupont Plaza Hotel	96
1987	May 6-June 2		N China, forest fire	193
1987	Nov.	17	London, England subway	30
1990	Mar.	25	N.Y. City, social club	87
1991	Sept.	3	Hamlet, N.C., chicken-processing plant	25
1991	Oct.	20-21	Oakland, Berkeley, Cal., wildfire	24
1992	Nov.	20	Windsor Castle, England	0
1993	Apr.	19	Waco, Tex., cult compound	72
1993	Nov.	2	Malibu, Cal., wildfire	3
1994	May	10	Bangkok, Thailand, toy factory	213
1994	July	4-10	Glenwood Springs, Co. (firefighters)	14

Some Notable Explosions

Date			Location	Deaths
1910	Oct.	1	Los Angeles Times Bldg.	21
1913	Mar.	7	Dynamite, Baltimore harbor	55
1915	Sept.	27	Gasoline tank car, Ardmore, Okla.	47
1917	Apr.	10	Munitions plant, Eddystone, Pa.	133
1917	Dec.	6	Halifax Harbor, Canada	1,654
1918	May	18	Chemical plant, Oakdale, Pa.	193
1918	July	2	Explosives, Split Rock, N.Y.	50
1918	Oct.	4	Shell plant, Morgan Station, N.J.	64
1919	May	22	Food plant, Cedar Rapids, Ia.	44
1920	Sept.	16	Wall Street, New York, bomb	30
1921	Sept.	21	Chemical storage facility, Oppau, Ger.	561
1924	Jan.	3	Food plant, Pekin, Ill.	42
1928	April	13	Dance hall, West Plains, Mo.	40
1937	Mar.	18	New London, Tex., school	413
1940	Sept.	12	Hercules Powder, Kenvil, N.J.	55
1942	June	5	Ordnance plant, Elwood, Ill.	49
1944	Apr.	14	Bombay, India, harbor	700
1944	July	17	Port Chicago, Cal., pier	322
1944	Oct.	21	Liquid gas tank, Cleveland	135
1947	Apr.	16	Texas City, Tex., pier	561
1948	July	28	Farben works, Ludwigshafen, Ger.	184
1950	May	19	Munitions barges, S. Amboy, N. J.	30
1956	Aug.	7	Dynamite trucks, Cali, Colombia	1,100
1958	Apr.	18	Sunken munitions ship, Okinawa	40
1958	May	22	Nike missiles, Leonardo, N.J.	10
1959	Apr.	10	World War II bomb, Philippines	38
1959	June	28	Rail tank cars, Meldrin, Ga.	25
1959	Aug.	7	Dynamite truck, Roseburg, Ore.	13

Date			Location	Deaths
1959	Nov.	2	Jamuri Bazar, India, explosives	46
1959	Dec.	13	Dortmund, Ger., 2 apt. bldgs.	26
1960	Mar.	4	Belgian munitions ship, Havana	100
1960	Oct.	25	Gas, Windsor, Ont., store	11
1962	Jan.	16	Gas pipeline, Edson, Alberta, Canada	8
1962	Oct.	3	Telephone Co. office, N. Y. City	23
1963	Jan.	2	Packing plant, Terre Haute, Ind.	16
1963	Mar.	9	Dynamite plant, S. Africa	45
1963	Aug.	13	Explosives dump, Gauhiti, India	32
1963	Oct.	31	State Fair Coliseum, Indianapolis	73
1964	July	23	Bone, Algeria, harbor munitions	100
1965	Mar.	4	Gas pipeline, Natchitoches, La.	17
1965	Aug.	9	Missile silo, Searcy, Ark.	53
1965	Oct.	21	Bridge, Tila Bund, Pakistan	80
1965	Oct.	30	Cartagena, Colombia	48
1965	Nov.	24	Armory, Keokuk, Ia.	20
1966	Oct.	13	Chemical plant, La Salle, Que.	11
1967	Feb.	17	Chemical plant, Hawthorne, N.J.	11
1967	Dec.	25	Apartment bldg., Moscow	20
1968	Apr.	6	Sports store, Richmond, Ind.	43
1970	Apr.	8	Subway construction, Osaka, Japan	73
1971	June	24	Tunnel, Sylmar, Cal.	17
1971	June	28	School, fireworks, Pueblo, Mex.	13
1971	Oct.	21	Shopping center, Glasgow, Scot.	20
1973	Feb.	10	Liquefied gas tank, Staten Is., N.Y.	40
1975	Dec.	27	Chasnala, India, mine	431
1976	Apr.	13	Lapua, Finland, munitions works	40
1977	Nov.	11	Freight train, Iri, South Korea	57
1977	Dec.	22	Grain elevator, Westwego, La.	35
1978	Feb.	24	Derailed tank car, Waverly, Tenn.	12
1978	July	11	Propylene tank truck, Spanish coastal campsite	150
1980	Oct.	23	School, Ortuella, Spain	64
1981	Feb.	13	Sewer system, Louisville, Ky	0
1982	Apr.	7	Tanker truck, tunnel, Oakland, Cal.	7
1982	Apr.	25	Antiques exhibition, Todi, Italy	33
1982	Nov.	2	Salang Tunnel, Afghanistan	1,000-3,000
1984	Feb.	25	Oil pipeline, Cubatao, Brazil	508
1984	June	21	Naval supply depot, Severomorsk, USSR	200+
1984	Nov.	19	Gas storage area, NE Mexico City	334
1984	Dec.	3	Chemical plant, Bhopal, cen. India	2,500
1984	Dec.	5	Coal mine, Taipei, Taiwan	94
1985	June	25	Fireworks factory, Hallett, Okla.	21
1988	July	6	Oil rig, North Sea	167
1989	June	3	Gas pipeline, between Ufa, Asha, USSR	650+
1992	Mar.	3	Coal mine, Kozlu, Turkey	270+
1992	Apr.	22	Guadalajara, Mexico sewer	190
1992	May	9	Coal mine, Plymouth, Nova Scotia	26
1993	Feb.	26	World Trade Center, N.Y. City	6
1994	Jul.	18	Jewish community center, Buenos Aires	100

Notable Nuclear Accidents

Oct. 7, 1957 — A fire in the Windscale plutonium production reactor N of Liverpool, England, spread radioactive material throughout the countryside. In 1983, the British government said that 39 people probably died of cancer as a result.

1957 — A chemical explosion in Kasli, USSR (now in Russia), in tanks containing nuclear waste, spread radioactive material and forced a major evacuation.

Jan. 3, 1961 — An experimental reactor at a federal installation near Idaho Falls, Id., killed three workers—the only deaths in U.S. reactor operations. The plant had high radiation levels but damage was contained.

Oct. 5, 1966 — A sodium cooling system malfunction caused a partial core meltdown at the Enrico Fermi demonstration breeder reactor near Detroit, Mich. Radiation was contained.

Jan. 21, 1969 — A coolant malfunction from an experimental underground reactor at Lucens Vad, Switzerland, resulted in the release of a large amount of radiation into a cavern, which was then sealed.

Mar. 22, 1975 — A technician checking for air leaks with a lighted candle caused a $100 million fire at the Brown's Ferry reactor in Decatur, Ala. The fire burned out electrical controls, lowering the cooling water to dangerous levels.

Mar. 28, 1979 — The worst commercial nuclear accident in the U.S. occurred as equipment failures and human mistakes led to a loss of coolant and partial core meltdown at the Three Mile Island reactor in Middletown, Pa.

Feb. 11, 1981 — Eight workers were contaminated when over 100,000 gallons of radioactive coolant leaked into the containment building of the TVA's Sequoyah 1 plant in Tennessee.

Apr. 25, 1981 — Some 100 workers were exposed to radioactive material during repairs of a nuclear plant at Tsuruga, Japan.

Jan. 6, 1986 — A cylinder of nuclear material burst after being improperly heated at a Kerr-McGee plant at Gore, Okla. One worker died and 100 were hospitalized.

Apr. 26, 1986 — In the worst accident in the history of the nuclear power industry, fires and explosions resulting from an unauthorized experiment at the Chernobyl nuclear power plant near Kiev, USSR (now in Ukraine), left at least 31 people dead in the immediate aftermath of the disaster and spread significant quantities of radioactive material over much of Europe. An estimated 135,000 people were evacuated from areas around Chernobyl, some of which were rendered uninhabitable for years. As a result of the radiation released into the atmosphere, tens of thousands of excess cancer deaths (as well as increased rates of birth defects) were expected in succeeding decades.

Record Oil Spills

As a rule, the number of tons can be multiplied by 7 to estimate the number of barrels spilled; the exact number of barrels in a ton varies with the type of oil. Each barrel contains 42 gallons.

Name, place	Date	Cause	Tons
Ixtoc I oil well, S Gulf of Mexico	June 3, 1979	Blowout	600,000
Nowruz oil field, Persian Gulf	Feb. 1983	Blowout	600,000 (est.)
Atlantic Empress & Aegean Captain, off Trinidad & Tobago	July 19, 1979	Collision	300,000
Castillo de Bellver, off Cape Town, South Africa	Aug. 6, 1983	Fire	250,000
Amoco Cadiz, near Portsall, France	March 16, 1978	Grounding	223,000
Torrey Canyon, off Land's End, England	March 18, 1967	Grounding	119,000
Sea Star, Gulf of Oman	Dec. 19, 1972	Collision	115,000
Urquiola, La Coruna, Spain	May 12, 1976	Grounding	100,000
Hawaiian Patriot, N Pacific	Feb. 25, 1977	Fire	99,000
Othello, Tralhavet Bay, Sweden	March 20, 1970	Collision	60,000-100,000

Other Notable Oil Spills

Name, place	Date	Cause	Gallons
Persian Gulf	Jan. 23, 1991 (began)	Spillage by Iraq	130,000,000*
Braer, off Shetland Islands	Jan. 5, 1993	Grounding	26,000,000
Aegean Sea, off N Spain	Dec. 3, 1992	Unknown	21,500,000
World Glory, off South Africa	June 13, 1968	Hull failure	13,524,000
Burmah Agate, Galveston Bay, Tex.	Nov. 1, 1979	Collision	10,700,000
Exxon Valdez, Prince William Sound, Alas.	Mar. 24, 1989	Grounding	10,080,000
Keo, off Massachusetts	Nov. 5, 1969	Hull failure	8,820,000
Storage tank, Sewaren, N.J.	Nov. 4, 1969	Tank rupture	8,400,000

* Estimated by Saudi Arabia. Some estimates are as low as 25,000,000 gallons.

(continued)

Other Notable Oil Spills *(continued)*

Name, place	Date	Cause	Gallons
Ekofisk oil field, North Sea	Apr. 22, 1977	Well blowout	8,200,000
Argo Merchant, Nantucket, Mass.	Dec. 15, 1976	Grounding	7,700,000
Pipeline, West Delta, La.	Oct. 15, 1967	Dragging anchor	6,720,000
Tanker off Japan	Nov. 30, 1971	Ship broke in half	6,258,000
Storage tank, Monongahela River	Jan. 2, 1988	Tank rupture	3,800,000

Major Earthquakes

Source: Global Volcanism Network, Smithsonian Institution; U.S. Geological Survey, Dept. of the Interior; World Almanac research

Magnitude of earthquakes (Mag.), distinct from deaths or damage caused, is measured on the Richter scale, on which each higher number represents a tenfold increase in energy measured in ground motion. Adopted in 1935, the scale has been applied in the following table to earthquakes as far back as reliable seismograms are available.

Date		Location	Deaths	Mag.
526	May 20	Syria, Antioch	250,000	NA
856	....	Greece, Corinth	45,000	"
1057	....	China, Chihli	25,000	"
1268	....	Asia Minor, Cilicia	60,000	"
1290	Sept. 27	China, Chihli	100,000	"
1293	May 20	Japan, Kamakura	30,000	"
1531	Jan. 26	Portugal, Lisbon	30,000	"
1556	Jan. 24	China, Shaanxi	830,000	"
1667	Nov.	Caucasia, Shemaka	80,000	"
1693	Jan. 11	Italy, Catania	60,000	"
1730	Dec. 30	Japan, Hokkaido	137,000	"
1737	Oct. 11	India, Calcutta	300,000	"
1755	June 7	N Persia	40,000	"
1755	Nov. 1	Portugal, Lisbon	60,000	8.75*
1783	Feb. 4	Italy, Calabria	30,000	NA
1797	Feb. 4	Ecuador, Quito	41,000	"
1811-12		New Madrid, Mo. (series)	NA	8.7*
1822	Sept. 5	Asia Minor, Aleppo	22,000	NA
1828	Dec. 28	Japan, Echigo	30,000	"
1868	Aug. 13-15	Peru and Ecuador	40,000	"
1875	May 16	Venezuela, Colombia	16,000	"
1886	Aug. 31	Charleston, S.C.	60	6.6
1896	June 15	Japan, sea wave	27,120	NA
1906	Apr. 18-19	San Francisco, Cal.	503[1]	8.3
1906	Aug. 16	Chile, Valparaiso	20,000	8.6
1908	Dec. 28	Italy, Messina	83,000	7.5
1915	Jan. 13	Italy, Avezzano	29,980	7.5
1918	Oct. 11	Mona Passage, P.R.	116	7.5
1920	Dec. 16	China, Gansu	100,000	8.6
1923	Sept. 1	Japan, Yokohama	200,000	8.3
1927	May 22	China, Nan-Shan	200,000	8.3
1932	Dec. 26	China, Gansu	70,000	7.6
1933	Mar. 2	Japan	2,990	8.9
1933	Mar. 10	Long Beach, Cal.	115	6.2
1934	Jan. 15	India, Bihar-Nepal	10,700	8.4
1935	May 31	India, Quetta	50,000	7.5
1939	Jan. 24	Chile, Chillan	28,000	8.3
1939	Dec. 26	Turkey, Erzincan	30,000	7.9
1946	Dec. 21	Japan, Honshu	2,000	8.4
1948	June 28	Japan, Fukui	5,131	7.3
1949	Aug. 5	Ecuador, Pelileo	6,000	6.8
1950	Aug. 15	India, Assam	1,530	8.7
1953	Mar. 18	NW Turkey	1,200	7.2
1956	June 10-17	N Afghanistan	2,000	7.7
1957	July 2	N Iran	2,500	7.4
1957	Dec. 13	W Iran	2,000	7.1
1960	Feb. 29	Morocco, Agadir	12,000	5.8
1960	May 21-30	S Chile	5,000	8.3
1962	Sept. 1	NW Iran	12,230	7.1
1963	July 26	Yugoslavia, Skopje	1,100	6.0
1964	Mar. 27	Alaska	131	8.4
1966	Aug. 19	E Turkey	2,520	6.9
1968	Aug. 31	NE Iran	12,000	7.4
1970	Jan. 5	Yunnan Province, China	10,000	7.7
1970	Mar. 28	W Turkey	1,086	7.4
1970	May 31	N Peru	66,794	7.7
1971	Feb. 9	San Fernando Valley, Cal.	65	6.6
1972	Apr. 10	S Iran	5,057	6.9
1972	Dec. 23	Nicaragua	5,000	6.2
1974	Dec. 28	Pakistan (9 towns)	5,200	6.3
1975	Sept. 6	Turkey (Lice, etc.)	2,312	6.8
1976	Feb. 4	Guatemala	22,778	7.5
1976	May 6	NE Italy	946	6.5
1976	June 26	New Guinea, Irian Jaya	443	7.1
1976	July 28	China, Tangshan	242,000	8.2
1976	Aug. 17	Philippines, Mindanao	8,000	7.8
1976	Nov. 24	E Turkey	4,000	7.9
1977	Mar. 4	Romania	1,541	7.5
1977	Aug. 19	Indonesia	200	8.0
1977	Nov. 23	NW Argentina	100	8.2
1978	Sept. 16	NE Iran	25,000	7.7
1979	Sept. 12	Indonesia	100	8.1
1979	Dec. 12	Colombia, Ecuador	800	7.9
1980	Oct. 10	NW Algeria	4,500	7.3
1980	Nov. 23	S Italy	4,800	7.2
1982	Dec. 13	N Yemen	2,800	6.0
1983	May 26	N Honshu, Japan	81	7.7
1983	Oct. 30	E Turkey	1,300	7.1
1985	Mar. 3	Chile	146	7.8
1985	Sept. 19, 21	Mexico City	4,200+	8.1
1987	Mar. 5-6	NE Ecuador	4,000+	7.3
1988	Aug. 20	India/Nepal border	1,000+	6.5
1988	Nov. 6	China/Burma border	1,000	7.3
1988	Dec. 7	NW Armenia	55,000+	6.8
1989	Oct. 17	San Francisco Bay area	62	6.9
1990	May 30	N Peru	115	6.3
1990	June 21	NW Iran	40,000+	7.7
1990	July 16	Luzon, Philippines	1,621	7.7
1991	Feb. 1	Pakistan, Afghanistan border	1,200	6.8
1992	Mar. 13, 15	E Turkey	4,000	6.2/6.0
1992	June 28	S Cal.	1	7.5/6.6
1992	Dec. 12	Flores Isl., Indonesia	2,500	7.5
1993	July 12	off Hokkaido, Japan	200+	7.7
1993	Sept. 29	Maharashtra, S India	9,748[2]	6.4
1994	Jan. 17	Northridge, Cal.	61	6.8
1994	Feb. 15	S Sumatra, Indonesia	215	7.0
1994	June 6	Cauca, SW Colombia	1,000	6.8

(*) estimated from earthquake intensity. NA=not available. (1) With subsequent fires, death toll rose to 700. (2) Official death toll released by Indian govt. Other sources reported 30,000 deaths.

Some Recent Earthquakes

Source: Global Volcanism Network, Smithsonian Institution

Date	Location	Magnitude
June 9, 1994	La Paz, Bolivia	8.2
June 6	Cauca, SW Colombia	6.8
Mar. 14	Mex.-Guatemala border	6.8
Feb. 12	SW Vanuatu	7.2
Feb. 15	S Sumatra, Indonesia	7.0
Jan. 21	Halmahera, Indonesia	7.3
Jan. 19	Irian Jaya, Indonesia	6.9
Jan. 17	Northridge, Cal.	6.8
Nov. 13, 1993	off coast of Kamchatka	7.1
Oct. 25	Papua New Guinea	7.0
Oct. 24	near Acapulo, Mexico	6.6
Oct. 13	Papua New Guinea	6.8
Oct. 13	E Papua New Guinea	7.2
Oct. 11	off Tokyo coast	6.5
Sept. 29	Maharashtra, S India	6.4
Sept. 20	near Klamath Falls, Or.	5.8
Sept. 10	Chiapas, Mexico	7.2
Aug. 10	SW S Isl., New Zealand	7.1
Aug. 8	Agaña, Guam	8.0
July 12	off Hokkaido, Japan	7.7
Mar. 12	Fiji	6.5
Mar. 6	Solomon Islands	6.5
Mar. 6	Fiji	6.7
Mar. 6	Santa Cruz Islands	7.1
Jan. 15	Kushiro, Japan	7.0

Historic Assassinations Since 1865

1865—Apr. 14. U.S. Pres. Abraham Lincoln, shot by John Wilkes Booth in Washington, D.C.; died Apr. 15.

1881—Mar. 13. Alexander II, of Russia.—July 2. U.S. Pres. James A. Garfield, shot by Charles J. Guiteau, Washington D.C.; died Sept. 19.

1900—July 29. Umberto I, king of Italy.

1901—Sept. 6. U.S. Pres. William McKinley in Buffalo, N.Y., died Sept. 14. Leon Czolgosz executed for the crime Oct. 29.

1913—Feb. 23. Mexican Pres. Francisco I. Madero and Vice Pres. Jose Pino Suarez.—Mar. 18. George, king of Greece.

1914—June 28. Archduke Francis Ferdinand of Austria-Hungary and his wife in Sarajevo, Bosnia (later part of Bosnia and Herzegovina), by Gavrilo Princip.

1916—Dec. 30. Grigori Rasputin, politically powerful Russian monk.

1918—July 12. Grand Duke Michael of Russia, at Perm.—July 16. Nicholas II, abdicated as czar of Russia; his wife, the Czarina Alexandra; their son, Czarevitch Alexis; their daughters, Grand Duchesses Olga, Tatiana, Marie, Anastasia; and 4 members of their household were executed by Bolsheviks at Ekaterinburg.

1920—May 20. Mexican Pres. Gen. Venustiano Carranza in Tlaxcalantongo.

1922—Aug. 22. Michael Collins, Irish revolutionary.—Dec. 16. Polish President Gabriel Narutowicz in Warsaw by an anarchist.

1923—July 20. Gen. Francisco "Pancho" Villa, ex-rebel leader, in Parral, Mexico.

1928—July 17. Gen. Alvaro Obregon, president-elect of Mexico, in San Angel, Mexico.

1934—July 25. In Vienna, Austrian Chancellor Engelbert Dollfuss by Nazis.

1935—Sept. 8. U.S. Sen. Huey P. Long, shot in Baton Rouge, La., by Dr. Carl Austin Weiss, who was slain by Long's bodyguards; Long died Sept. 10.

1940—Aug. 20. Leon Trotsky (Lev Bronstein), 63, exiled Russian war minister, near Mexico City. Killer identified as Ramon Mercador del Rio, a Spaniard, served 20 years in Mexican prison.

1948—Jan. 30. Mohandas K. Gandhi, 78, shot in New Delhi, India, by Nathuram Vinayak Godse.— Sept. 17. Count Folke Bernadotte, UN mediator for Palestine, ambushed in Jerusalem.

1951—July 20. King Abdullah ibn Hussein of Jordan. — Oct. 16. Prime Min. Liaquat Ali Khan of Pakistan shot in Rawalpindi.

1956—Sept. 21. Pres. Anastasio Somoza of Nicaragua, in Leon; died Sept. 29.

1957—July 26. Pres. Carlos Castillo Armas of Guatemala, in Guatemala City by one of his own guards.

1958—July 14. King Faisal of Iraq; his uncle, Crown Prince Abdullah; and July 15, Premier Nuri as-Said, by rebels in Baghdad.

1959—Sept. 25. Prime Minister Solomon Bandaranaike of Ceylon, by Buddhist monk in Colombo.

1961—Jan. 17. Ex-Premier Patrice Lumumba of the Congo, in Katanga Province—May 30. Dominican dictator Rafael Leonidas Trujillo Molina shot to death by assassins near Ciudad Trujillo.

1963—June 12. Medgar W. Evers, NAACP's Mississippi field secretary, in Jackson, Miss.—Nov. 2. Pres. Ngo Dinh Diem of South Vietnam and his brother, Ngo Dinh Nhu, in a military coup.—Nov. 22. U.S. Pres. John F. Kennedy fatally shot in Dallas, Tex.; accused Lee Harvey Oswald murdered by Jack Ruby while awaiting trial.

1965—Jan. 21. Iranian premier Hassan Ali Mansour fatally wounded by assassin in Teheran; 4 executed.—Feb. 21. Malcolm X, black nationalist, fatally shot in N.Y. City.

1966—Sept. 6. Prime Minister Hendrik F. Verwoerd of South Africa stabbed to death in parliament at Cape Town.

1968—Apr. 4. Rev. Dr. Martin Luther King Jr. fatally shot in Memphis, Tenn. by James Earl Ray.—June 5. Sen. Robert F. Kennedy (D-N.Y.) fatally shot in Los Angeles; Sirhan Sirhan, resident alien, convicted of murder.

1971—Nov. 28. Prime Minister Wasfi Tal of Jordan, in Cairo, by Palestinian guerrillas.

1973—Mar. 2. U.S. Ambassador Cleo A. Noel Jr., U.S. Charge d'Affaires George C. Moore and Belgian Charge d'Affaires Guy Eid killed by Palestinian guerrillas in Khartoum, Sudan.

1974—Aug. 19. U.S. Ambassador to Cyprus, Rodger P. Davies, killed by sniper's bullet in Nicosia.

1975—Feb. 11. Pres. Richard Ratsimandrava, of Madagascar, shot in Tananarive.—Mar. 25. King Faisal of Saudi Arabia shot by nephew Prince Musad Abdel Aziz, in royal palace, Riyadh.— Aug. 15. Bangladesh Pres. Sheik Mujibur Rahman killed in coup.

1976—Feb. 13. Nigerian head of state, Gen. Murtala Ramat Mohammed, slain by self-styled "young revolutionaries."

1977—Mar. 16. Kamal Jumblat, Lebanese Druse chieftain, was shot near Beirut.— Mar. 18. Congo Pres. Marien Ngouabi shot in Brazzaville.

1978—July 9. Former Iraqi Premier Abdul Razak Al-Naif shot in London.

1979—Feb. 14. U.S. Ambassador Adolph Dubs shot and killed by Afghan Muslim extremists in Kabul.— Aug. 27. Lord Mountbatten, World War II hero, and 2 others were killed when a bomb exploded on his fishing boat off the coast of Co. Sligo, Ire. The IRA claimed responsibility. — Oct. 26. South Korean President Park Chung Hee and 6 bodyguards fatally shot by Kim Jae Kyu, head of South Korean CIA, and 5 aides in Seoul.

1980—Apr. 12. Liberian President William R. Tolbert slain in military coup.—Sept. 17. Former Nicaraguan President Anastasio Somoza Debayle shot in Paraguay.

1981— Oct. 6. Egyptian President Anwar al-Sadat fatally shot by a band of commandos while reviewing a military parade in Cairo.

1982—Sept. 14. Lebanese President-elect Bashir Gemayel killed by bomb in east Beirut.

1983— Aug. 21. Philippine opposition political leader Benigno Aquino Jr. fatally shot by a gunman at Manila International Airport.

1984—Oct. 31. Indian Prime Minister Indira Gandhi shot and killed by 2 of her bodyguards, who were members of the minority Sikh sect, in New Delhi.

1986—Feb. 28. Swedish Premier Olaf Palme shot and killed by a gunman in Stockholm.

1987—June 1. Lebanese Premier Rashid Karami killed when a bomb exploded aboard a helicopter in which he was traveling.

1988—Apr. 16. PLO military chief Khalil Wazir (Abu Jihad) was gunned down by Israeli commandos in Tunisia.

1989—Aug. 18. Colombian Liberal Party presidential candidate Luis Carlos Galan was killed by Medellín cartel drug traffickers at a campaign rally in Bogotá.—Nov. 22. Lebanese President Rene Moawad was killed when a bomb exploded next to his motorcade.

1990—Mar. 22. Colombian Patriotic Union presidential candidate Bernando Jamamillo Ossa was shot by a gunman at an airport in Bogotá.

1991—May 21. Rajiv Gandhi, former prime minister of India, was killed when a bomb exploded during an election rally in Madras.

1992—June 29. Mohammed Boudiaf, president of Algeria, was shot by a gunman in Annaba.

1993—May 1. Ranasinghe Premadasa, president of Sri Lanka, killed by bomb in Colombo.

1994—Mar. 16. Luis Donaldo Colosio, Mexican presidential candidate, was shot by a gunman.—Apr. 6. Burundian President Cyprien Ntaryamira and Rwandan President Juvenal Habyarimana were killed, with 8 others, when their plane was apparently shot down.

Assassination Attempts

1910—Aug. 6. N.Y. City Mayor William J. Gaynor shot and seriously wounded by discharged city employee.

1912—Oct. 14. Former U.S. President Theodore Roosevelt shot and seriously wounded by demented man in Milwaukee, Wis.

1933—Feb. 15. In Miami, Fla., Joseph Zangara, anarchist, shot at Pres.-elect Franklin D. Roosevelt, but a woman seized his arm, and the bullet fatally wounded Mayor Anton J. Cermak, of Chicago, who died Mar. 6. Zangara was electrocuted on Mar. 20, 1933.

1950—Nov. 1. In an attempt to assassinate President Truman, 2 members of a Puerto Rican nationalist movement—Griselio Torresola and Oscar Collazo—tried to shoot their way into Blair House. Torresola was killed, and a guard, Pvt. Leslie Coffelt, was fatally shot. Collazo was convicted, Mar. 7, 1951, for the murder of Coffelt.

1970—Nov. 27. Pope Paul VI unharmed by knife-wielding assailant who attempted to attack him in Manila airport.

1972—May 15. Alabama Gov. George Wallace shot in Laurel, Md., by Arthur Bremer; seriously crippled.

1972—Dec. 7. Imelda Marcos, wife of Philippine President Ferdinand Marcos, was stabbed and seriously injured in Pasay City, Philippines.

1975—Sept. 5. Pres. Gerald R. Ford was unharmed when a Secret Service agent grabbed a pistol aimed at him by Lynette (Squeaky) Fromme, a Charles Manson follower, in Sacramento.

1975—Sept. 22. Pres. Ford escaped unharmed when Sara Jane Moore, a political activist, fired a revolver at him.

1980—May 29. Civil rights leader Vernon E. Jordan Jr. shot and wounded in Ft. Wayne, Ind.

1981—Jan. 16. Irish political activist Bernadette Devlin McAliskey and her husband were shot and seriously wounded by 3 members of a Protestant paramilitary group in Co. Tyrone, Ire.

1981—Mar. 30. Pres. Ronald Reagan, Press Sec. James Brady, Secret Service agent Timothy J. McCarthy, and Washington, D.C., policeman Thomas Delahanty were shot and seriously wounded by John W. Hinckley Jr. in Washington, D.C.

1981—May 13. Pope John Paul II and 2 bystanders were shot and wounded by Mehmet Ali Agca, an escaped Turkish murderer, in St. Peter's Square, Rome.

1982—May 12. Pope John Paul II was unharmed when a man with a knife was overpowered by guards, in Fatima, Portugal.

1984—Oct. 12. British Prime Minister Margaret Thatcher narrowly escaped injury when a bomb, said to be planted by the Irish Republican Army, exploded at the Grand Hotel in Brighton, England, during the annual Conservative Party conference. Four died, including a Conservative member of Parliament.

1986—Sept. 7. Chilean President Gen. Augusto Pinochet Ugarte escaped unharmed when his motorcade was attacked by rebels using rockets, bazookas, grenades, and rifles.

Notable U.S. Kidnappings Since 1924

Robert Franks, 13, in Chicago, **May 22, 1924,** by 2 youths, Richard Loeb and Nathan Leopold, who killed boy. Demand for $10,000 ignored. Loeb died in prison, Leopold paroled 1958.

Charles A. Lindbergh Jr., 20 mos. old, in Hopewell, N.J., **Mar. 1, 1932;** found dead May 12. Ransom of $50,000 was paid to man identified as Bruno Richard Hauptmann, 35, paroled German convict who entered U.S. illegally. Hauptmann was convicted after spectacular trial at Flemington, and electrocuted in Trenton, N.J., prison, Apr. 3. 1936.

William A. Hamm Jr., 39, in St. Paul, **June 15, 1933.** $100,000 paid. Alvin Karpis given life, paroled in 1969.

Charles F. Urschel, in Oklahoma City, **July 22, 1933.** Released July 31 after $200,000 paid. George (Machine Gun) Kelly and 5 others given life.

Brooke L. Hart, 22, in San Jose, Cal. Thomas Thurmond and John Holmes arrested after demanding $40,000 ransom. When Hart's body was found in San Francisco Bay, **Nov. 26, 1933,** a mob attacked the jail at San Jose and lynched the 2 kidnappers.

George Weyerhaeuser, 9, in Tacoma, Wash., **May 24, 1935.** Returned home June 1 after $200,000 paid. Kidnappers given 20 to 60 years.

Charles Mattson, 10, in Tacoma, Wash., **Dec. 27, 1936.** Found dead Jan. 11, 1937. Kidnapper asked $28,000, failed to contact.

Arthur Fried, in White Plains, N.Y., **Dec. 4, 1937.** Body not found. Two kidnappers executed.

Robert C. Greenlease, 6, taken from Kansas City, Mo., school **Sept. 28, 1953,** and held for $600,000. Body found Oct. 7. Bonnie Brown Heady and Carl A. Hall pleaded guilty and were executed.

Peter Weinberger, 32 days old, Westbury, N.Y., **July 4, 1956,** for $2,000 ransom, not paid. Child found dead. Angelo John LaMarca, 31, convicted, executed.

Lee Crary, 8, in Everett, Wash., **Sept. 22, 1957;** $10,000 ransom, not paid. He escaped after 3 days, led police to George E. Collins, who was convicted.

Frank Sinatra Jr., 19, from hotel room in Lake Tahoe, Cal., **Dec. 8, 1963.** Released **Dec. 11** after his father paid $240,000 ransom. Three men sentenced to prison.

Barbara Jane Mackle, 20, abducted **Dec. 17, 1968,** from Atlanta, Ga., motel, was found unharmed 3 days later, buried in a coffin-like wooden box 18 inches underground, after her father had paid $500,000 ransom; Gary Steven Krist sentenced to life, Ruth Eisenmann-Schier to 7 years.

Mrs. Roy Fuchs, 35, and 3 children held hostage 2 hours, **May 14, 1969,** in Long Island, N.Y., released after her husband, a bank manager, paid kidnappers $129,000 in bank funds; 4 men arrested, ransom recovered.

Virginia Piper, 49, abducted **July 27, 1972,** from her home in suburban Minneapolis; found unharmed near Duluth 2 days later after her husband paid $1 million ransom.

Patricia (Patty) Hearst, 19, taken from her Berkeley, Cal., apartment **Feb. 4, 1974.** Symbionese Liberation Army demanded her father, Randolph A. Hearst, publisher, give millions to poor. She was identified by FBI as taking part in a San Francisco bank holdup, **Apr. 15.** FBI, **Sept. 18, 1975,** captured her and others in San Francisco; they were indicted on various charges. Patricia Hearst convicted of bank robbery, **Mar. 20, 1976.** She was released from prison under executive clemency, **Feb. 1, 1979.** In 1978, William and Emily Harris were sentenced to 10 years to life for the Hearst kidnapping. Both were paroled in 1983.

J. Reginald Murphy, 40, an editor of *Atlanta* (Ga.) *Constitution,* kidnapped **Feb. 20, 1974;** freed **Feb. 22** after payment of $700,000 ransom by the newspaper. Police arrested William A. H. Williams, a contractor; most of the money was recovered.

E. B. Reville, Hepzibah, Ga., banker, and wife, Jean, kidnapped **Sept. 30, 1974.** Ransom of $30,000 paid. He was found alive; Jean Reville was found dead **Oct. 2.**

Jack Teich, Kings Point, N.Y., steel executive, seized **Nov. 12, 1974;** released **Nov. 19** after payment of $750,000.

Sidney J. Reso, oil co. executive, seized **Apr. 29, 1992;** died May 3; Arthur D. Seale and wife, Irene, arrested **June 19.** Arthur Seale pleaded guilty and was sentenced to life in prison; Irene Seale was sentenced to a 20-year prison term.

Katie Beers, 9, Long Island, N.Y., disappeared **Dec. 28, 1992,** found unharmed **Jan. 13, 1993,** in an underground bunker in the home of a family friend. John Esposito pleaded guilty; he was sentenced, **July 26, 1994,** to 15 years to life in prison.

Polly Klaas, 12, Petaluma, Cal., abducted at knife-point, **Oct. 1, 1993,** during a slumber party at her home; found dead **Dec. 4** in wooded area of Cloverdale, Cal. Police arrested Richard Allen Davis on **Nov. 30.** Davis pleaded not guilty, **Dec. 21.**

ASSOCIATIONS AND SOCIETIES

Source: World Almanac questionnaire

Arranged according to **key words** in titles. Founding year of organization in parentheses; last figure after ZIP code indicates membership.

AFS Intercultural Programs (1917), 220 E. 42d St., N.Y., NY 10017; 475,000.

ASM International (1913), 9639 Kinsman Rd., Materials Park, OH 44073-0002; 48,625.

Aaron Burr Assn. (1946), 4520 King Edward Ct., Annandle, VA 22003; 600.

Abortion Federation, Natl. (1977), 1436 U St. NW, Ste. 103, Wash., DC 20009; 300 organizations.

Accountants, Amer. Institute of Certified Public (1887), 1211 Ave. of the Americas, N.Y., NY 10036; 318,000.

Accountants, Institute of Management (1919), 10 Paragon Dr., Box 433, Montvale, NJ 07645-1760; 85,000.

Accountants for Cooperatives, Natl. Soc. of (1936), 6320 Augusta Dr., Ste. 800, Springfield, VA 22150; 2,000.

Acoustical Society of America (1929), 500 Sunnyside Blvd., Woodbury, NY 11797; 7,000.

Actors' Equity Assn. (1913), 165 W. 46 St., N.Y., NY 10036.

Actuaries, Society of (1949), 475 N. Martingale Rd., Ste. 800, Schaumburg, IL 60173-2226; 13,830.

Advertisers, Assn. of Natl. (1910), 155 E. 44th St., N.Y., NY 10017; 245 companies.

Advertising Agencies, Amer. Assn. of (1917), 666 Third Ave., N.Y., NY 10017; 700 agencies.

Aeronautic Assn., Natl. (1905), 1815 N. Fort Myer Dr., Ste. 700, Arlington, VA 22209.

Aerospace Industries Assn. of America (1919), 1250 Eye St. NW, Wash., DC 20005; 53 companies.

Aerospace Medical Assn. (1929), 320 S. Henry St., Alexandria, VA 22314-3579; 4,500.

Afro-American Life and History, Assn. for the Study of (1915), 1407 14th St. NW, Wash., DC 20005; 4,000.

Aging Assn., Amer. (1970), 2129 Providence Ave., Chester, PA 19013-5506; 500.

Agricultural Chemicals Assn., Natl. (1933), 1155 15th St. NW, Wash., DC 20005; 83 companies.

Agricultural Economics Assn., Amer. (1910), 80 Heady Hall, Iowa State Univ., Ames, IA 50011; 3,188.

Agricultural History Society (1919), Room 932, 1301 New York Ave. NW, Wash., DC 20005; 1,100.

Agronomy, Amer. Society of (1907), 677 S. Segoe Rd., Madison, WI 53711; 12,600.

Aircraft Assn., Experimental (1953), EAA Aviation Center, Oshkosh, WI 54903-3086; 140,000.

Aircraft Owners and Pilots Assn. (1939), 421 Aviation Way, Frederick, MD 21701; 320,000.

Air Force Assn. (1946), 1501 Lee Hwy., Arlington, VA 22209.

Air Force Gunners Assn. (1986), 3644 Elk Grove Ct., Land O'Lakes, FL 34639; 1,407.

Air Line Pilots Assn. (1931), 1625 Massachusetts Ave. NW, Wash., DC 20036; 41,000.

Airmen, Assn. of Independent (1989), 1625 Massachusetts Ave. NW, Wash., DC 20036; 3,000.

Air Transport Assn. of America (1936), 1709 New York Ave. NW, Wash., DC 20006; 19 airlines.

Air & Waste Management Assn. (1907), PO Box 2861, Pittsburgh, PA 15230; 14,057.

Al-Anon Family Groups (1950), PO Box 862, Midtown Sta., N.Y., NY 10018; 500,000 worldwide.

Alcohol Problems, Amer. Council on (1895), 3426 Bridgeland Dr., Bridgeton, MO 63044; 36 state affiliates.

Alcoholics Anonymous (1935), PO Box 459, Grand Central Station, N.Y., NY 10163; more than 2 mil.

Alcoholism and Drug Dependence, Natl. Council on (1944), 12 W. 21st St., N.Y., NY 10010; 185 affiliates.

Allergy and Immunology, Amer. Academy of (1943), 611 E. Wells St., Milwaukee, WI 53202; 4,900.

Alpine Club, Amer. (1902), 710 Tenth St., Ste. 100, Golden, CO 80401; 2,000+.

Alzheimer's Assn. (1980), 919 Michigan Ave., Chicago, IL 60611.

Amer. Indian Affairs, Assn. on (1922), 245 Fifth Ave., Ste. 1801, N.Y., NY, 10016-8728; 40,000.

American Legion, The (1919), 700 N. Pennsylvania St., Indianapolis, IN 46204; 3.1 mil. **American Legion Auxiliary** (1919), 777 N. Meridian St., Indianapolis, IN 46204; 1 mil.

Amer. Veterans (AMVETS) (1947); **AMVETS Auxiliary** (1946), 4647 Forbes Blvd., Lanham, MD 20706-9961; 200,000.

Americares Foundation (1982), 161 Cherry St., New Canaan, CT 06840.

Amideast (Amer. Mideast Educational & Training Services) (1951), 1100 17th St. NW, Ste. 300, Wash., DC 20036-4601.

Amnesty Intl. USA (1961), 322 Eighth Ave., N.Y., NY 10001.

Amputation Foundation, Natl. (1919), 73 Church St., Malverne, NY 11565; 2,200.

Anachronism, Society for Creative (1966), PO Box 360743, Milpitas, CA 95036-0743; 23,000.

Animal Protection Institute of America (1968), 2831 Fruitridge Rd., Sacramento, CA 95822; 150,000.

Animal Welfare Institute (1951), PO Box 3650, Wash., DC 20007; 8,500.

Animals, Amer. Society for Prevention of Cruelty to (ASPCA) (1866), 424 E. 92d St., N.Y., NY 10128; 350,000.

Animals, People for the Ethical Treatment of (1980), PO Box 42516, Wash., DC 20015; 400,000.

Anthropological Assn., Amer. (1902), 4350 N. Fairfax Dr., Ste. 640, Arlington, VA 22203; 11,000.

Antiquarian Society, Amer. (1812), 185 Salisbury St., Worcester, MA 01609-1634; 558.

Anti-Vivisection Society, New England (1895), 333 Washington St., Boston, MA 02108-5100; 10,000.

Appalachian Mountain Club (1876), 5 Joy St., Boston, MA 02108; 54,952.

Appalachian Trail Conference (1925), Washington & Jackson Sts., Harpers Ferry, WV 25425; 23,000.

Appraisers, Amer. Society of (1936), 535 Herndon Pkwy., #150, Herndon, VA 22070; 6,500.

Arab Americans, Natl. Assn. of (1972), 2033 M St. NW, Wash., DC 20036.

Arbitration Assn., Amer. (1926), 140 W. 51st St., N.Y., NY 10020-1203; 6,523.

Arc, The (1950), 500 E. Border St., Ste. 300, Arlington, TX 76010; 140,000.

Archaeological Institute of America (1879), 675 Commonwealth Ave., Boston, MA 02215; 11,500.

Archaeology, Institute of Nautical (1976), PO Drawer HG, College Station, TX 77841-5137; 1,100.

Archery Assn., Natl. (1879), One Olympic Plaza, Colorado Springs, CO 80909; 3,800.

Architects, Amer. Institute of (1857), 1735 New York Ave. NW, Wash., DC 20006; 55,000.

Architectural Historians, Society of (1940), 1232 Pine Street, Philadelphia, PA 19107-5944; 4,000.

Armed Forces Communications and Electronics Assn. (1946), 4400 Fair Lakes Ct., Fairfax, VA 22033; 40,000.

Army, Assn. of the United States (1950), 2425 Wilson Blvd., Arlington, VA 22201-3385; 119,000.

Arthritis Foundation (1948), 1314 Spring St. NW, Atlanta, GA 30309; 300,000.

Arts, Amer. Council for the (1960), One E. 53d Street, N.Y., NY 10022-4201; 1,500.

Arts, Amer. Federation of (1909), 41 E. 65th St., N.Y., NY 10021.

Arts and Letters, Natl. Society of (1944), 655 15th St. NW, Wash., DC 20005; 1,600.

Arts & Sciences, Amer. Academy of (1780), Norton's Woods, 136 Irving St., Cambridge, MA 02138; 4,000.

Association Executives, Amer. Society of (1920), 1575 Eye St. NW, Wash., DC 20005; 18,000.

Association Publications, Society of Natl. (1963), 3299 K St. NW, Ste. 700, Wash., DC 20007; 210 publications.

Astrologers, Amer. Federation of (1938), 6535 S. Rural Rd., Tempe, AZ 85283; 4,500.

Astronautical Society, Amer. (1954), 6352 Rolling Mill Pl., Ste. 102, Springfield, VA 22152; 1,500.

Astronomical Society, Amer. (1899), 2000 Florida Ave. NW, Ste. 300, Wash., DC 20009; 5,700.

Ataxia Foundation, Natl. (1957), 750 Twelve Oaks Ctr., 15500 Wayzata Blvd., Wayzata MN 55391; 7,500.

Atheists, Amer. (1963), PO Box 140195, Austin, TX 78714.

Athletic Assn., Natl. Jr. College (1938), 1825 Austin Bluffs Pkwy., Ste. 100, Colorado Springs, CO 80918; 518.

Athletic Associations, Natl. Federation of State H. S. (1920), 11724 Plaza Circle, Box 20626, Kansas City, MO 64195.

Athletic Union of the U.S. Amateur (1888), 3600 W. 86th St., Indianapolis, IN 46268; 300,000.

Auctioneers Assn., Natl. (1949), 8880 Ballentine, Overland Park, KS 66214; 5,900.

Audubon Society, Natl. (1905), 700 Broadway, N.Y., NY 10003; 500,000.

Authors Guild, Inc., The (1921), 330 W. 42d St., N.Y., NY 10036; 6,500.

Authors League of America (1912), 234 W. 44th St., N.Y., NY 10036; 15,000.

Autism Society of America (1965), 7910 Woodmont Ave., Ste. 650, Bethesda, MD 20814; 14,000.

Autograph Collectors Club, Universal (1965), PO Box 6181, Wash., DC 20044-6181; 2,000.

Automobile Assn., Amer. (1902), 1000 AAA Dr., Heathrow, FL 32746: 34 mil.

Automobile Club of America, Antique (1935), 501 W. Governor Rd., Hershey, PA 17033; 53,000.

Automobile Dealers Assn., Natl. (1917), 8400 Westpark Dr., McLean, VA 22102; 19,000.

Automobile License Plate Collectors' Assn. (1954), PO Box 77, Horner, WV 26372; 2,600.

Automotive Hall of Fame (1939), 3225 Cook Rd., PO Box 1727, Midland, MI 48641-1727; 1,865.

Badminton Assn., U.S. (1936), One Olympic Plaza, Colorado Springs, CO 80909; 2,600.

Baker Street Irregulars (1934), 34 Pierson Ave., Norwood, NJ 07648; 275.

Bald-Headed Men of America (1973), 102 Bald Dr., Morehead City, NC 28557; 26,000.

Ball Players of Amer., Assn. of Professional (1924), 12062 Valley View St., #211, Garden Grove, CA 92645; 58,000.

Band & Choral Directors Hall of Fame, Natl. (1985), 519 N. Halifax Ave., Daytona Beach, FL 32118.

Bankers Assn., Amer. (1875), 1120 Connecticut Ave. NW, Wash., DC 20036.

Bankers Assn. of America, Independent (1930), One Thomas Circle NW, Ste. 950, Wash. DC 20005; 5,800 banks.

Bar Assn., Federal (1920), 1815 H St. NW, Wash., DC 20006; 14,600.

Barbershop Quartet Singing in Amer., Soc. for Preservation & Encouragement of (1938), 6315 Third Ave., Kenosha, WI 53140-5199; 34,000.

Baseball Congress, Amer. Amateur (1935), 118-19 Redfield Plaza, Marshall, MI 49068; 12,000 teams.

Baseball Congress, Natl. (1931), PO Box 1420, Wichita, KS 67201.

Baseball Research, Society for Amer. (1971), PO Box 93183, Cleveland, OH 44101; 6,500+.

Basketball Assn., Natl. (1946), 645 Fifth Ave., N.Y., NY 10022.

Battleship Assn., Amer. (1964), PO Box 711247, San Diego, CA 92171; 1,508.

Beer Can Collectors of America (1970), 747 Merus Ct., Fenton, MO 63026-2092; 4,100.

Beta Gamma Sigma (1913), 11701 Borman Dr., Ste. 320, St. Louis, MO 63146-4194; 340,000.

Beta Sigma Phi (1931), 1800 W. 91st Pl., Kansas City, MO 64114; 250,000.

Bible Society, Amer. (1816), 1865 Broadway, N.Y., NY 10023; 300,000.

Biblical Literature, Society of (1880), 1549 Clairmont Rd., Ste. 204, Decatur, GA 30033-4635; 5,500.

Bibliographical Society of America (1904), PO Box 397, Grand Central Sta., N.Y., NY 10163; 1,250.

Big Brothers/Big Sisters of America (1902), 230 N. 13th St., Philadelphia, PA 19107; 494 agencies.

Biochemistry and Molecular Biology, Amer. Society for (1906), 9650 Rockville Pike, Bethesda, MD 20814-3996; 9,000.

Biological Sciences, American Institute of (1947), 730 11th St. NW, Wash., DC 20001-4521; 6,000.

Bison Assn., Amer. (1976), PO Box 16660, Denver, CO 80216.

Black History Honors & Awards, Contemporary & (1990), 6514 Georgia Rd., Birmingham, AL 35212; 152.

Blind, Amer. Council of the (1961), 1155 15th St. NW, Wash., DC 20005; 40,000.

Blind, Natl. Federation of the (1940), 1800 Johnson St., Baltimore, MD 21230; 30,000+.

Blindness, Natl. Society to Prevent (1908), 500 E. Remington Rd., Schaumburg, IL 60173; 26 affiliates.

Blue Angels Assn. (1982), 4600 Twin Oaks Dr., Apt. 702, Pensacola, FL 32506; 250.

Blue Cross and Blue Shield Assn. (1946), 676 St. Clair, Chicago, IL 60611; 74 plans.

Blueberry Council, North Amer. (1965), PO Box 166, Marmora, NJ 08223.

B'nai B'rith Intl. (1853), 1640 Rhode Island Ave. NW, Wash., DC 20036; 150,000.

Boat Club, Chris Craft Antique (1973), 217 S. Adams St., Tallahassee, FL 32301; 2,000.

Boat Owners Assn. of the U.S. (1966), 880 S. Pickett St., Alexandria, VA 22304; 500,000.

Bodybuilders Assn., Amer. (1981), 6991 Simson St., Oakland, CA 94605-2226; 854.

Bookplate Collectors and Designers, Amer. Soc. of (1922), 605 N. Stoneman Ave., #F, Alhambra, CA 91801; 200.

Booksellers Assn., Amer. (1900), 122 E. 42d St., N.Y., NY 10168; 8,500+.

Bottle Collectors, Federation of Historical (1969), 4098 Faxon Ave., Memphis, TN 38122; 600.

Bowling Congress, Amer. (1895), 5301 S. 76th St., Greendale, WI 53129; 2,576,809.

Boys' Clubs of America (1906), 771 First Ave., N.Y., NY 10017; 1.2 mil.

Boy Scouts of America (1910), 1325 Walnut Hill Lane, Irving, TX 75015-2079; 3.8 mil.

Bridge, Tunnel and Turnpike Assn., Intl. (1932), 2120 L St. NW, Ste. 305, Wash., DC 20037; 250 organizations.

Brith Sholom, Natl. (1905), 3939 Conshohocken Ave., Philadelphia, PA 19131; 4,500.

Broadcasters, Natl. Assn. of (1922), 1771 N. St. NW, Wash., DC 20036.

Burroughs Bibliophiles, The (1960), 454 Elaine Dr., Pittsburgh, PA 15236-2417; 534.

Business Bureaus, Council of Better (1970), 4200 Wilson Blvd., Arlington, VA 22203; 180 bureaus.

Business Clubs, Natl. Assn. of Amer. (1922), 3315 N. Main St., High Point, NC 27262; 7,000.

Business Communicators, Intl. Assn. of (1970), One Hallidie Pl., Ste. 600, San Francisco, CA 94102.

Business Education Assn., Natl. (1946), 1906 Association Dr., Reston, VA 22091; 18,000.

Button Society, Natl. (1938), 2733 Juno Pl., Akron, OH 44313-4137; 3,785.

Byron Society, The (1971 England, 1973 in U.S.), 259 New Jersey Ave., Collingswood, NJ 08108; 300.

CLU & CHFC, Amer. Soc. of (1928), 270 S. Bryn Mawr Ave., Bryn Mawr, PA 19010; 35,000.

CPCU, The Society of (1944), 720 Providence Rd., Malvern, PA 19355-0709; 24,000.

Camp Fire Boys & Girls (1910), 4601 Madison Ave., Kansas City, MO 64112; 700,000.

Campers and RVers, Family (1954), 4804 Transit Rd., Bldg. 2, Depew, NY 14043; 20,000 families.

Camping Assn., Amer. (1910), 5000 State Rd. 67 N., Martinsville, IN 46131; 5,500.

Cancer Society, Amer. (1913), 90 Park Ave., N.Y., NY 10017.

Carillonneurs in North America, Guild of (1936), 3718 Settle Rd., Cincinnati, OH 45227; 507.

Carnegie Hero Fund Commission (1904), 2307 Oliver Bldg., Pittsburgh, PA 15222; 21 members.

Cartoonists Society, Natl. (1946), 157 W. 57th St., Ste. 904, N.Y., NY 10019; 500.

Cat Fanciers' Assn. (1906), 1805 Atlantic Ave., Manasquan, NJ 08736-1005; 650 clubs.

Catholic Bishops, Natl. Conference of/U.S. Cath. Conference (1966), 3211 4th St. NE, Wash., DC 20015.

Catholic Church Extension Society of the U.S.A. (1905), 35 E. Wacker Dr., #400, Chicago, IL 60601; 220,000.

Catholic Daughters of the Americas (1903), 10 W. 71st St., N.Y., NY 10023; 135,000.

Catholic Educational Assn., Natl. (1904), 1077-30th St. NW, Ste. 100, Wash., DC 20007; 18,353.

Catholic Historical Soc., Amer. (1884), 263 S. Fourth St., PO Box 84, Philadelphia, PA 19106-3819; 800.

Catholic Library Assn. (1921), 461 W. Lancaster Ave., Haverford, PA 19041; 1,518.

Catholic Rural Life Conference, Natl. (1923), 4625 Beaver Ave., Des Moines, IA 50310-2199; 3,200.

Catholic War Veterans of the U.S.A. (1935), 419 North Lee St., Alexandria, VA 22314; 30,000.

Cemetery Assn., Amer. (1889), 5201 Leesburg Pike, Falls Church, VA 22041; 1,600.

Ceramic Society, Amer. (1898), 735 Ceramic Pl., Westerville, OH 43081; 13,000.

Cerebral Palsy Assns., United (1948), 1522 K St. NW, Ste. 1112, Wash., DC 20005; 155 affiliates.

Chamber Music Players, Amateur (1948), 1123 Broadway, Rm. 304, N.Y., NY 10010-2007; 4,000.

Chamber of Commerce of the U.S.A. (1912), 1615 H St. NW, Wash., DC 20062.

Chaplain's Intl. Assn. (1960), Adjutant General Office, 5045 N. Robberson, Springfield, MO 65803; 1,035.

Checker Federation, Amer. (1948), 220 Lynn Ray Rd., PO Box 365, Petal, MS 39465; 1,000.

Chemical Manufacturers Assn. (1872), 2501 M St. NW, Wash., DC 20037; 171 companies.

Chemical Society, Amer. (1876), 1155 16th St. NW, Wash., DC 20036; 149,261.

Chemists, Amer. Assn. of Cereal (1915), 3340 Pilot Knob Rd., St. Paul, MN 55121; 3,891.

Chemists, Amer. Society of Brewing (1934), 3340 Pilot Knob Rd., St. Paul MN 55121; 730.

Chess Federation, U.S. (1939), 186 Rte. 9W, New Windsor, NY 12553; 75,000.

Chess League of Amer., Correspondence (1897), PO Box 3481, Barrington, IL 60011-3481; 1,200.

Child Welfare League of America (1920), 440 First St. NW, Wash., DC 20001-2085; 730 agencies.

Childhood Education, Intl. Assn. for (1892), 11501 Georgia Ave., Ste. 315, Wheaton, MD 20902; 11,000.

Children, Natl. Center for Missing and Exploited (1984), 2101 Wilson Blvd., Arlington, VA 22201.

Children of the Amer. Revolution, Natl. Society of the (1895), 1776 D St. NW, Wash., DC 20006.

Children's Aid Society (1853), 105 E. 22d St., N.Y., NY 10010; 1,207.

Children's Book Council (1945), 568 Broadway, Ste. 404, N.Y., NY 10012; 75 publishing houses.

Chiropractic Assn., Amer. (1930), 1916 Wilson Blvd., Arlington, VA 22201; 20,000.

Christian Endeavor, Intl. (1885), 3575 Valley Rd., PO Box 820, Liberty Corner, NJ 07938-0820.

Christian Laity Counseling Board (1970), 5901 Plainfield Dr., Charlotte, NC 28215; 38 mil.

Christians and Jews, Natl. Conference of (1927), 71 Fifth Ave., Ste. 1100, N.Y., NY 10003.

Church Federation, Ecumenical (1982), 13014-270 N. Dalemabry, Tampa, FL 33618-2808.

Churches, U.S. Conference for the World Council of (1948), 475 Riverside Dr., N.Y., NY 10115; 317 denominations.

Church Women United (1941), 475 Riverside Dr., Rm. 812, N.Y., NY 10115.

Cincinnati, Society of the (1783), 2118 Massachusetts Ave. NW, Wash., DC 20008; 3,300.

Circulation Managers Assn., Intl. (1889), 11600 Sunrise Valley Dr., Reston, VA 22091; 1,705.

Cities, Natl. League of (1924), 1301 Pennsylvania Ave. NW, Wash., DC 20004; 1,450 cities.

City/County Management Assn., Intl. (1914), 777 N. Capitol St. NE, Ste. 500, Wash., DC 20002; 8,000.

Civic League, Natl. (1894), 55 W. 44th St., N.Y., NY 10036; 3,000.

Civil Air Patrol (1941), HQ CAP-USAF, Maxwell AFB, AL 36112-5572; 63,000.

Civil Engineers, Amer. Society of (1852), 345 E. 47th St., N.Y., NY 10017; 104,000.

Civil Liberties Union, Amer. (1920), 132 W. 43d St., N.Y. NY 10036; 250,000.

Civitan Internatl. (1920), One Civitan Pl., Birmingham, AL 35213-1983; 58,000.

Classical League, Amer. (1919), Hall, Miami Univ., Oxford, OH 45056; 3,604.

Clinical Pathologists, Amer. Society of (1922), 2100 W. Harrison St., Chicago, IL 60612; 58,757.

Coal Association, Natl. (1917), 1130 17th St. NW, Wash., DC 20036; 150 corporate members.

Coast Guard Combat Veterans Assn. (1985), 17728 Striley Dr., Ashton, MD 20861-9763; 1,576.

Coaster Enthusiasts, American (1978), PO Box 8226, Chicago, IL 60680; 4,700+.

Co-Dependents Anonymous (1986), PO Box 33577, Phoenix, AZ 85067-3577.

College Board, The (1900), 45 Columbus Ave., N.Y., NY 10023; 2,900 institutions.

College Music Society (1958), 202 W. Spruce St., Missoula, MT 59802; 4,000.

College Placement Council (1956), 62 Highland Ave., Bethlehem, PA 18017; 3,063 institutes.

Colleges, Amer. Assn. of Community and Jr. (1921), One Dupont Circle NW, Ste. 410, Wash., DC 20036.

Colleges, Assn. of Amer. (1915), 1818 R St. NW, Wash., DC 20009; 640 institutions.

Colleges and Universities, Assn. of Intl. (1973), 1301 S. Noland Rd., Independence, MO 64055; 9,790.

Collegiate Athletic Assn., Natl. (1906), 6201 College Blvd., Overland Park, KS 66211-2422; 828 institutions.

Collegiate Schools of Business, Amer. Assembly of (1916), 605 Old Ballas Rd., St. Louis, MO 63141-7077.

Colonial Dames XVII Century, Natl. Society (1915), 1300 New Hampshire Ave. NW, Wash., DC 20036-1595; 14,000.

Colonial Wars, General Society of (1892), 840 Woodbine Ave., Glendale, OH 45246; 4,300.

Commerce, U.S. Junior Chamber of (1915), 4 W. 21st St., Tulsa, OK 74114-1116; 200,000.

Commercial Collectors Assn., Amer. (1970), 4040 W. 70th St., Minneapolis, MN 55435; 3,225.

Commercial Law League of America (1895), 175 W. Jackson, #1541, Chicago, IL 60604; 5,100.

Commercial Travelers of America, Order of United (1888), 632 N. Park St., Columbus, OH 43215; 186,000.

Common Cause (1970), 2030 M St. NW, Wash., DC 20036.

Communication, Intl. Training in (1938), 2519 Woodland Dr., Anaheim, CA 92801; 15,000.

Communities, Federation of Egalitarian (1976), E. Wind, Rte. 3, Box 6B2, Tecumseh, MO 65760; 250+.

Community Cultural Center Assoc., Amer. (1978), 19 Foothills Dr., Pompton Plains, NJ 07444.

Composers/USA, Natl. Assn. of (1932), PO Box 49652, Barrington Sta., Los Angeles, CA 90049; 600.

Composers, Authors & Publishers, Amer. Society of (ASCAP) (1914), One Lincoln Plaza, N.Y., NY 10023; 24,000.

Computer Professionals, Inst. for Certification of (1973), 2200 E. Devon Ave., Ste. 268, Des Plaines, IL 60018-4503; 47,000.

Computing Machinery, Assn. for (1947), 1515 Broadway, N.Y., NY 10036; 55,000.

Concrete Institute, Amer. (1904), 22400 W. Seven Mile Rd., Detroit, MI 48219-1849.

Conscientious Objectors, Central Committee for (1948), 2208 South St., Philadelphia, PA 19146.

Conservation Engineers, Assn. of (1961), Alabama Dept. of Conservation, 64 N. Union St., Montgomery, AL 36104; 298.

Constantian Society, The (1970), 123 Orr Rd., Pittsburgh, PA 15241; 600.

Construction Industry Manufacturers Assn. (1911), 111 E. Wisconsin Ave., Milwaukee, WI 53202; 150 companies.

Construction Specifications Institute (1948), 601 Madison St., Alexandria, VA 22314-1791; 19,200.

Consulting Organizations, Council of (1989), 521 5th Ave., N.Y., NY 10175.

Consumer Credit Assn., Intl. (1912), 243 N. Lindbergh, St. Louis, MO 63141; 20,000.

Consumer Federation of America (1968), 1424 16th St. NW, #604, Wash., DC 20036; 240 organizations.

Consumer Interests, Amer. Council on (1953), 240 Stanley Hall, Univ. of Missouri, Columbia, MO 65211; 1,400.

Consumer Protection Institute (1970), 5901 Plainfield Dr., Charlotte, NC 28215.

Consumers Union of the U.S. (1936), 101 Truman Ave., Yonkers, NY 10703; 405,990.

Contract Bridge League, Amer. (1937), 2990 Airways Blvd., Memphis, TN 38116-3847; 200,000+.

Contractors of Amer., General (1919), 1957 E St. NW, Wash., DC 20006; 32,000.

Cooperative Business Assn., Natl. (1916), 1401 New York Ave. NW, #1100, Wash., DC 20005; 540.

Cooperative League of the U.S.A. (1916), 1401 New York Ave. NW, Ste. 1100, Wash., DC 20005; 285 co-ops.

Correctional Assn., Amer. (1870), 8025 Laurel Lakes Court, Laurel, MD 20707; 20,000+.

Correctional Officers, Intl. Assn. of (1977), 8600 Glenarden Pkwy., Glenarden, MD 20706-1599.

Cosmetology Assn., Natl. (1921), 3510 Olive St., St. Louis, MO 63103; 47,000.

Cotton Council of America, Natl. (1938), 1918 N. Parkway, Memphis, TN 38112; 297 delegates.

Counseling and Development, Amer. Assn. for (1953), 5999 Stevenson Ave., Alexandria, VA 22304; 58,065.

Country Music Assn. (1958), One Music Circle S, Nashville, TN 37203; 6,588.

Creative Children and Adults, Natl. Assn. for (1974), 8080 Springvalley Dr., Cincinnati, OH 45236-1395; 6,000.

Credit Assn., International (1912), 243 N. Lindberg, St. Louis, MO 63141; 10,000.

Credit Union Natl. Assn. (1934), 5710 Mineral Point Rd., Madison, WI 53705; 52 state credit union leagues.

Cribbage Congress, American (1978), PO Box 10486, Napa, CA 94581; 7,500+.

Crime and Delinquency, Natl. Council on (1907), 685 Market St., Ste. 620, San Francisco, CA 94105; 500.

Criminology, Amer. Society of (1941), 1314 Kinnear Rd., Ste. 212, Columbus, OH 43212; 2,600.

Crop Science Society of America (1955), 677 S. Segoe Rd., Madison, WI 53711; 5,200.

Cryogenic Soc. of Amer. (1964), 1033 South Blvd., #13, Oak Park, IL 60302.

Customs Brokers & Forwarders Assn. of Am., Natl. (1897), One World Trade Center, Ste. 1153, N.Y., NY 10048.

Cystic Fibrosis Foundation (1955), 6931 Arlington Rd., Bethesda, MD 20814.

Dairy Council, Natl. (1915), 6300 N. River Rd., Rosemont, IL 60018.

Dairy and Food Industries Supply Assn. (1917), 6245 Executive Blvd., Rockville, MD 20852; 800 companies.

Dairy Goat Assn., American (1904), 209 W. Main St., Spindale, NC 28160; 13,000.

Danish Brotherhood in America (1882), 3717 Harney St., Omaha, NE 68131; 8,600.

Daughters of the American Revolution, Natl. Society (1890), 1776 D St. NW, Wash., DC 20006-5392; 200,000.

Daughters of the British Empire in the U.S.A. (1909), 839 Elm Way, Edrondo, WA 98020; 5,206.

Daughters of the Confederacy, United (1894), 328 N. Blvd., Richmond, VA 23220-4057; 25,000.

Daughters of the Republic of Texas (1891), 510 E. Anderson Ln., Austin, TX 78752; 6,450+.

Daughters of Union Veterans of the Civil War (1885), 503 S. Walnut St., Springfield, IL 62704; 4,100+.

Deaf, Alexander Graham Bell Assn. for the (1890), 3417 Volta Pl. NW, Wash., DC 20007.

Deaf, Natl. Assn. of the (1880), 814 Thayer Ave., Silver Spring, MD 20910; 22,000.

Defense Preparedness Assn., Amer. (1919), 2101 Wilson Blvd., Ste. 400, Arlington, VA 22201-3061; 29,000.

Delta Kappa Gamma Society Intl. (1929), 416 W. 12th St., Austin, TX 78701; 165,000.

Deltiologists of America (1960), PO Box 8, Norwood, PA 19074; 980.

Democratic Natl. Committee (1792), 430 S. Capitol St. SE, Wash., DC 20003.

DeMolay, Intl. Supreme Council, Order of (1919), 10200 N. Executive Hills Blvd., Kansas City, MO 64153-1367; 30,000.

Dental Assn., Amer. (1859), 211 E. Chicago Ave., Chicago, IL 60611; 140,000.

Descendants of the Colonial Clergy, Society of the (1933), 30 Leewood Rd., Wellesley, MA 02181; 1,024.

Descendants of the Signers of the Declaration of Independence (1907), William Penn Annex, PO Box 54145, 9th & Chestnut Sts., Philadelphia, PA 19105; 1,024.

Descendants of Washington's Army at Valley Forge, Society of (1976), PO Box 915, Valley Forge, PA 19482-0915.

Desert Protective Council (1954), PO Box 2312, Valley Center, CA 92082; 305.

Diabetes Assn., Amer. (1940), 1660 Duke St., Alexandria, VA 22314; 280,000.

Dialect Society, Amer. (1889), c/o Allan Metcalf, English Dept., MacMurray College, Jacksonville, IL 62650; 550.

Direct Marketing Assn. (1917), W. 42d St., N.Y., NY 10036-8096; 3,600.

Directors Guild of America (1936), 7920 Sunset Blvd., Los Angeles, CA 90046; 9,700.

Disabled Amer. Veterans (1923), PO Box 14301, Cincinnati, OH 45250-0301; 1.2 mil.

Disabled Collectors' Correspondence Club (1991), PO Box 3113, Fremont, CA 94539.

Dogs Intl., Therapy (1980), 260 Fox Chase Rd., Chester, NJ 07930; 2,500+.

Dogs on Stamp Study Unit (1979), 3208 Hana Rd., Edison, NJ 08817-2552; 400.

Dollhouse Museum of the Southwest (1988), 2208 Routh St., Dallas, TX 75201; 256.

Dozenal Society of America (1944), Math Dept., Nassau Community College, Garden City, NY 11530; 144.

Dracula Society, Count (1962), 334 W. 54th St., Los Angeles, CA 90037; 500.

Drug, Chemical and Allied Trades Assn. (1890), 2 Roosevelt Ave., Syosset, NY 11791; 2,018.

Ducks Unlimited (1937), One Waterfowl Way, Memphis, TN 38120; 500,000+.

Dutch Settlers Soc. of Albany (1924), RD#2, Box 313, Altamont, NY 12009-9531; 250.

Eaglehunters (1994), PO Box 1539, Hernando, FL 34442; 1,000.

Eagles, Fraternal Order of (1898), 12660 W. Capitol Dr., Brookfield, WI 53055; 1.1 mil.

Easter Seal Society, Natl. (1919), 230 W. Monroe, Chicago, IL 60606.

Eastern Star, General Grand Chapter, Order of the (1876), 1618 New Hampshire Ave. NW, Wash., DC 20009; 1.5 mil.

Economic Assn., Amer. (1885), 2014 Broadway, Ste. 305, Nashville, TN 37203; 20,000.

Edsel Club, Intl. (1969), PO Box 371, Sully, IA 50251; 1,076.

Education, Amer. Council on (1918), One Dupont Circle NW, #800, Wash., DC 20036; 1,700.

Education, Amer. Soc. for Engineering (1893), 11 Dupont Circle NW, Ste. 200, Wash., DC 20036; 10,000+.

Education, Council for Advancement & Support of (1974), 11 Dupont Circle NW, Wash., DC 20036; 2,950 schools.

Education, Institute of Intl. (1919), 809 United Nations Plaza, N.Y., NY 10017; 700 U.S colleges, univ.

Education, Natl. Assn. for Family and Community (1936), 5963 Jefferson St., Burlington, KY 41005-9596; 341,651.

Education Assn., Natl. (1857), 1201 16th St. NW, Wash., DC 20036; 2 mil.

Education of Young Children, Natl. Assn. for the (1926), 1509 16th St. NW, Wash., DC 20036; 82,000.

Educational Exchange, Council on Intl. (1947), 205 E. 42d St., N.Y., NY 10017; 240 organizations.

Educational Research Assn., Amer. (1916), 1230 17th St. NW, Wash., DC 20036; 17,000.

Educators for World Peace, International Assn. of (1969), PO Box 3282, Mastin Lake Station, Huntsville, AL 35810-0282; 22,000.

8th Air Force Historical Society (1975), 711 S. Smith Ave., St. Paul, MN 55107; 18,400.

82nd Airborne Division Assn., Inc. (1944), NFCS, PO Box 9308, Fayetteville, NC 28311-7694; 23,000.

88th Infantry Division Assn., Inc. (1948), PO Box 925, Havertown, PA 19083; 5,152.

Electrical and Electronics Engineers, Institute of (1884), 445 Hoes Lane, PO Box 1331, Piscataway, NJ 08855-1331; 300,000.

Electrical Manufacturers Assn., Natl. (1926), 2101 L St. NW, Wash., DC 20037; 560 companies.

Electrochemical Society (1902), 10 S. Main St., Pennington, NJ 08534-2896; 6,000.

Electronic Circuits, The Institute for Interconnecting & Packaging (1957), 7380 N. Lincoln, Lincolnwood, IL 60646-1705; 1900 companies.

Electronic Industries Assn. (1924), 2001 Pennsylvania Ave., Wash., DC 20006-1813; 1,058 companies.

Electronics Technicians, Intl. Society of Certified (1970), 2708 W. Berry, Ft. Worth, TX 76109; 2,000.

Electroplaters' and Surface Finishers' Society, Amer. (1909), 12644 Research Pkwy., Orlando, FL 32826; 8,500.

Elks of the U.S.A., Benevolent and Protective Order of (1868), 2750 N. Lakeview Ave., Chicago, IL 60614; 1.5 mil.

Elvis Burning Love Fan Club (1983), 1904 Williamsburg Dr., Streamwood, IL 60107; 1,100.

Elvis Presley Fan Club of Ceylon (1964), 113/1, Pirivena Rd., Mt. Lavania, Sri Lanka; 2,000.

Energy Research Institute, Clean (1974), Univ. of Miami, Coral Gables, FL, 33124.

Engineering, Natl. Academy of (1964), 2101 Constitution Ave. NW, Wash., DC 20418; 1,700.

Engineering, Soc. for the Advancement of Material & Process (1944), 1161 Parkview Dr., Covina, CA 91724; 7,683.

Engineering Society of N. America, Illuminating (1906), 120 Wall St., 17th Floor, N.Y., NY 10005; 9,500.

Engineers, Amer. Inst. of Chemical (1908), 345 E. 47th St., N.Y., NY 10017; 53,622.

Engineers, Amer. Institute of Mining, Metallurgical and Petroleum (1871), 345 E. 47th St., N.Y., NY 10017.

Engineers, Amer. Soc. of Agricultural (1907), 2950 Niles Rd., St. Joseph, MI 49085-9659; 8,000.

Engineers, Amer. Soc. of Civil (1852), 345 E. 47th St., N.Y., NY 10017; 111,112.

Engineers, American Soc. of Mechanical (1881), 345 E. 47th St., N.Y., NY 10017; 120,000.

Engineers, Amer. Soc. of Naval (1888), 1452 Duke St., Alexandria, VA 22314; 7,200.

Engineers, Amer. Soc. of Safety (1911), 1800 E. Oakton St., Des Plaines, IL 60018-2187; 28,000.

Engineers, Assn. of Energy (1977), 4025 Pleasantdale Rd., Ste. 420, Atlanta, GA 30340; 8,600.

Engineers, Inst. of Industrial (1948), 25 Technology Park, Atlanta, GA 30092; 43,000.

Engineers, Inst. of Transportation (1930), 525 School St. NW, Ste. 410, Wash., DC 20024; 7,700.

Engineers, Natl. Society of Professional (1934), 1420 King St., Alexandria, VA 22314; 72,615.

Engineers, Soc. of Fire Protection (1950), One Liberty Sq., Boston, MA 02109; 4,050.

Engineers, Soc. of Logistics (1966), 8100 Professional Pl., Ste. 211, New Carrollton, MD 20785; 7,000.

Engineers, Soc. of Manufacturing (1932), One SME Drive, PO Box 930, Dearborn, MI 48121; 70,000.

Engineers, Society of Mining (1871), 8307 Shaffer Pkwy., Littleton, CO 80127; 23,058.

Engineers, Society of Plastics (1942), 14 Fairfield Dr., Brookfield Ctr., CT 06805; 25,000.

English, U.S. (1983), 818 Connecticut Ave. NW, Ste. 200, Wash., DC 20006; 565,000.

English Assn., Inc., The College (1939), English Dept., Winthrop Univ., Rock Hill, SC 29732; 1,350.

Entomological Society of America (1897), 9301 Annapolis Rd., Lanham, MD 20706-3115; 8,500.

Environmental Health Assn., Natl. (1937), 720 S. Colorado Blvd., Ste. 970, Denver, CO 80222; 5,500.

Environmental Information Assn. (1983), 1777 N.E. Expressway, Ste. 150, Atlanta, GA 30329; 2,000.

Environmental Medicine, American Academy of (1965), PO Box 16106, Denver, CO 80216; 450.

Epigraphic Society, Inc., The (1974), 6625 Bamburgh Dr., San Diego, CA 92117; 800.

Esperanto League for North America (1952), PO Box 1129, El Cerrito, CA 94530; 1,000.

Evangelism Crusades, Intl. (1959), 14617 Victory Blvd., Van Nuys, CA 91411; 1,500.

Exchange Club, Natl. (1911), 3050 Central Ave., Toledo, OH 43606-1700; 36,679.

Fairs & Expositions, Intl. Assn. of (1919), PO Box 985, Springfield, MO 65801; 2,400.

Family Relations, Natl. Council on (1938), 3989 Central Ave. NE, Ste. 550, Minneapolis, MN 55421; 3,800.

Family Service America (1911), 11700 W. Lake Park Dr., Milwaukee, WI 53224; 270 agencies.
Farm Bureau Federation, Amer. (1919), 225 Touhy Ave., Park Ridge, IL 60068; 4 mil.
Farmers Union, Natl. (1902), Denver, CO 80251; 250,000.
Farmers' Educational and Co-Operative Union of America (1902), 10065 E. Harvard Ave., Denver, CO 80231; 250,000.
Fat Acceptance, Natl. Assn. to Advance (NAAFA) (1969), PO Box 188620, Sacramento, CA 95818; 4,000.
Federal Employees, Natl. Assn. of Retired (1921), 1533 New Hampshire Ave. NW, Wash., DC 20036-1279.
Federal Employees, Natl. Fed. of (1917), 1016 16th St. NW, Wash., DC 20036.
Feminists for Life of America (1972), 733 15th St. NW, Wash., DC 20005; 5,000.
Financial Analysts Federation (1945), #5 Boar's Head Lane, Charlottesville, VA 22903; 22,700.
Financial Executives Institute (1931), 10 Madison Ave., PO Box 1938, Morristown, NJ 07962-1938; 14,000.
Financiers, Intl. Soc. of (1979), PO Box 18508, Asheville, NC 28814; 300.
Fire Chiefs, Intl. Assn. of (1873), 4025 Fair Ridge Dr., Fairfax, VA 22033-2868.
Fire Protection Assn., Natl. (1896), Batterymarch Park, Quincy, MA 02269; 38,000.
First Amendment Studies, Institute for (1984), 187 Main St., Great Barrington, MA 01230; 27,000.
Fish Assn., Intl. Game (1939), 1301 E. Atlantic Blvd., Pompano Beach, FL 33060; 20,000.
Fisheries Soc., American (1870), 5410 Grosvenor Lane, Ste. 110, Bethesda, MD 20814; 8,500.
Fishes, Soc. for the Protection of Old (1967), School of Fisheries, WH-10, Univ. of Washington, Seattle, WA 98195; 275.
Fishing Tackle Manufacturers Assn., Amer. (1933), 1250 Grove Ave., Barrington, IL 60010; 500 companies.
Flag Research Center, The (1962), Box 580, Winchester, MA 01890; 1,300.
Flight Attendants, Assn. of (1973), 1625 Massachusetts Ave. NW, Wash., DC 20036; 28,000.
Fly Fishers, Fed. of (1965), 502 S. 19th, Ste. 1, Bozeman, MT 59715; 11,600.
Flying Disc Fed., World (1985), Gnejsvägen 24, 85357, Sundsvall, Sweden; 15,000.
Food Brokers Assn., Natl. (1904), 1010 Massachusetts Ave. NW, Wash., DC 20001; 1,800 companies.
Food Institute, Amer. Frozen (1942), 1764 Old Meadow Ln., Ste. 350, McLean, VA 22102; 550 firms.
Footwear Industries Assn., Amer. (1869), 1420 K St. NW, Wash. DC 20005; 150.
Foreign Student Affairs, Natl. Assn. for (1948), 1860 19th St. NW, Wash., DC 20009; 5,500.
Foreign Study, Amer. Institute for (1964), 102 Greenwich Ave., Greenwich, CT 06830; 300,000.
Foreign Trade Council, Inc., Natl. (1914), 1625 K St. NW, Wash., DC 20006; 500 companies.
Forensic Sciences, Amer. Academy of (1948), 410 N. 21st St., Ste. 203, Colorado Springs, CO 80904; 3,435.
Forest & Paper Assn., Amer. (1993), 1111 19th St. NW, Wash., DC 20036.
Forest Council (1932), 1250 Connecticut Ave. NW, Ste. 320, Wash., DC 20036.
Forest History Society (1946), 701 Vickers Ave., Durham, NC 27701; 1,500.
Forest Products Research Society (1947), 2801 Marshall Ct., Madison, WI 53705; 2,362.
Foresters, Society of Amer. (1900), 5400 Grosvenor La., Bethesda, MD 20814; 17,000.
Forestry Assn., Amer. (1875), 1516 P St. NW, Wash., DC 20005; 150,000.
Forests, Amer. (1875), 1516 P St. NW, Wash., DC 20005; 115,000.
Fortean Organization, Intl. (1966), PO Box 367, Arlington, VA 22210-0367; 1,045.
Founders and Patriots of Amer., The Order of the (1896), 3813 Acapulco Ct., Irving, TX 75062; 1,250.
Foundrymen's Society, Amer. (1896), 505 State St., Des Plaines, IL 60016-8399; 13,389.
4-H Clubs (1901-1905), Extension Service, U.S. Dept of Agriculture, Wash., DC 20250; 5.8 mil.
Frederick A. Cook Soc., The (1957), Sullivan County Historical Museum, PO Box 247, Hurleyville, NY 12747-0247; 200.
Freedom of Information Center (1958), 20 Walter Williams Hall, Univ. of Missouri, Columbia, MO 65211.
Freedoms Foundation at Valley Forge (1949), Valley Forge, PA 19481; 4,800.
French Institute/Alliance Francaise (1971), 22 E. 60th St., N.Y., NY 10022-1077; 8,500.
Friendship and Good Will, Intl. Soc. of (1978), 9538 Summerville St., Spring Valley, San Diego County, CA 91977; 4,643.
Funeral and Memorial Societies, Continental Assn. of (1963), 2001 S St. NW, Ste. 530, Wash., DC 20009.
Future Farmers of Amer. Org., Natl. (1928), 5632 Mt. Vernon Memorial Hwy., Alexandria, VA 22309-0160; 401,574.

Gamblers Anonymous (1957), PO Box 17173, Los Angeles, CA 90017.
Garden Club of Amer. (1913), 598 Madison Ave., N.Y., NY 10022; 15,000.
Garden Clubs, Natl. Council of State (1929), 4401 Magnolia Ave., St. Louis, MO 63110; 308,623.
Garden Clubs of America, Men's (1932), 5560 Merle Hay Rd., Johnston, IA 50131; 9,500.
Gas Appliance Manufacturers Assn. (1935), 1901 N. Moore St., Arlington, VA 22209; 205 companies.
Gas Assn., Amer. (1918), 1515 Wilson Blvd., Arlington, VA 22209; 229 companies; 3,000 individuals.
Gay and Lesbian Task Force, Natl. (1973), 1734 14th St. NW, Wash., DC 20009; 20,000.
Genealogical Society, Natl. (1903), 4527 17th St. N, Arlington, VA 22207; 12,000.
Genetic Assn., Amer. (1903), PO Box 39, Buckeystown, MD 21717; 850.
Geographers, Assn. of Amer. (1904), 1710 16th St. NW, Wash., DC 20009-3198; 7,000.
Geographic Education, Natl. Council for (1915), 16A Leonard Hall, IUPA, Indiana, PA 15705; 2,000.
Geographic Society, Natl. (1888), 1145 17th St. NW, Wash., DC 20036; 9.7 mil.
Geographical Society, Amer. (1851), 156 Fifth Ave., Ste. 600, N.Y., NY 10010-7002; 1,500.
Geological Society of America (1888), 3300 Penrose Pl., PO Box 9140, Boulder, CO 80301; 17,000.
Geologists, Amer. Assn. of Petroleum (1917), 1444 S. Boulder, Tulsa, OK 74119; 32,700.
Geophysicists, Society of Exploration (1930), PO Box 702740, Tulsa, OK 74170; 14,500.
Geriatrics Society, Amer. (1942), 770 Lexington Ave., Ste. 300, N.Y., NY 10021; 6,500.
Gideons Intl. (1899), 2900 Lebanon Rd., Nashville, TN 37214; 104,000.
Gifted Children, Natl. Assn. for (1957), 1155 15th St. NW, Ste. 1002, Wash., DC 20005; 6,500.
Girl Scouts of the U.S.A. (1912), 830 Third Ave., N.Y., NY 10022; 3.2 mil.
Girls Incorporated (1945), 30 E. 33d St., N.Y., NY 10016; 250,000.
Glenn Miller Birthplace Soc. (1976), PO Box 61, Clarinda, IA 51632; 1,200.
Gold Star Mothers, Amer. (1928), 2128 Leroy Pl. NW, Wash., DC 20008; 3,000.
Golf Association, U.S. (1894), Golf House, Far Hills, NJ 07931; 8,000 clubs.
Gospel Music Assn. (1964), 7 Music Circle N, Nashville, TN 37203; 2,900.
Government Finance Officers Assn. (1906), 180 N. Michigan Ave., Ste. 800, Chicago, IL 60601; 12,500.
Graduate Schools in the U.S., Council of (1961), One Dupont Circle NW, Wash., DC 20036; 413 institutions.
Grandmothers Clubs of America, Natl. Federation of (1934), 203 N. Wabash Ave., Chicago, IL 60601; 10,000.
Grange, Natl. (1867), 1616 H St. NW, Wash., DC 20006.
Graphic Arts, Amer. Institute of (1914), 1059 Third Ave., N.Y., NY 10021; 6,000.
Gray Panthers (1970), 2025 Pennsylvania Ave. NW, Ste. 821, Wash., DC 20006; 15,000.
Green Mountain Club, The (1910), RR1, Box 650, Waterbury Ctr., VT 05677; 5,200.
Grocers, Natl. Assn. of (1893), 1825 Samuel Morse Dr., Reston, VA 22090.
Grocery Manufacturers of America (1908), 1010 Wisconsin Ave., Ste. 800, Wash., DC 20007; 140 companies.
Guide Dog Foundation for the Blind (1946), 371 E. Jericho Tnpk., Smithtown, NY 11787-2976.
Gyro Intl. (1912), 1096 Mentor Ave., Painesville, OH 44077.

HIAS (Hebrew Immigrant Aid Society) (1880), 333 7th Ave., 17th Floor, N.Y., NY 10001-5004.
Hadassah, the Women's Zionist Organization of America (1912), 50 W. 58th St., N.Y., NY 10019; 385,000.
Hairdressers and Cosmetologists Assn., Natl. (1921), 3510 Olive St., St. Louis, MO 63103; 50,406.
Handball Assn., U.S. (1951), 2333 N. Tucson Blvd., Tucson, AZ 85716; 8,200.
Handicapped, Federation of the (1935), 211 W. 14th St., N.Y., NY 10011; 650.
Handicapped, Natl. Assn. of the Physically (1958), Bethesda Scarlet Oaks, #117, 440 Lafayette Ave., Cincinnati, OH 45220-1000; 700.

Handicapped Sports, Natl. (1967), 451 Hungerford Dr., Ste. 100, Rockville, MD 20850; 60,000.
Health Council, Natl. (1920), 1730 M St. NW, Ste. 500, Wash., DC 20036.
Health Info. Management Assoc., American (1928), 919 N. Michigan Ave., #1400, Chicago, IL 60611-1683; 35,000.
Health, Physical Education, Recreation and Dance, Amer. Alliance for (1885), 1900 Association Dr., Reston, VA 22091.
Health Professions, Assn. of Schools of Allied (1967), 1101 Connecticut Ave. NW, Ste. 700, Wash., DC 20036-4387.
Hearing Society, Intl. (1951), 20361 Middlebelt Rd., Livonia, MI 48152; 2,981.
Hearing and Speech Action, Natl. Assn. for (1910), 10801 Rockville Pike, Rockville, MD 20852.
Heart Assn., Amer. (1924), 7272 Greenville Ave., Dallas, TX 75231.
Hearts, Mended (1951), 7320 Greenville Ave., Dallas, TX 75231; 20,000.
Heating, Refrigerating & Air Conditioning Engineers, Amer. Soc. of (1894), 1791 Tullie Circle NE, Atlanta, GA 30329.
Helicopter Assn. Intl. (1948), 1619 Duke St., Alexandria, VA 22314; 1,800.
Helicopter Society, Amer. (1943), 217 N. Washington St., Alexandria, VA 22314; 6,140.
Hemispheric Affairs, Council on (1975), 724 9th St. NW, Wash., DC 20001; 1,750.
High School Assns., Natl. Federation of State (1920), PO Box 20626, Kansas City, MO 64195.
High Twelve Internatl. (1921), 11155-B2 South Towne Square, St. Louis, MO 63123-7823; 22,000.
Highpointers Club (1987), Box 327, Mtn. Home, AR 72653; 823.
Hiking Society, Amer. (1977), PO Box 20160, Wash., DC 20041-2160; 5,000.
Historians, Organization of Amer. (1907), 112 N. Bryan St., Bloomington, IN 47408; 12,000.
Historical Assn., Amer. (1884), 400 A St. SE, Wash., DC 20003; 15,200.
Historic Preservation, Natl. Trust for (1949), 1785 Massachusetts Ave. NW, Wash., DC 20036; 250,000.
Hockey, U.S.A. (1937), 4965 N. 30th St., Colorado Springs, CO 80919; 300,000.
Home Builders, Natl. Assn. of (1942), 1201 15th St. NW, Wash., DC 20005; 157,000.
Home Economics Assn., Amer. (1909), 1555 King St., Alexandria, VA 22314; 20,000.
Homemakers of America, Future (1945), 1910 Association Dr., Reston, VA 22091; 281,000+.
Honor Society, Natl. (1921), 1904 Association Dr., Reston, VA 22091; 21,000.
Horatio Alger Soc. (1961), 4907 Allison Dr., Lansing, MI 48910; 300.
Horse Council, American (1969), 1700 K St. NW, #300, Wash., DC 20006; 2,500.
Horse Protection Assn., Amer. (1966), 1000 29th St. NW, Ste. T-100, Wash., DC 20007; 8,000.
Horse Shows Assn., Amer. (1917), 220 E. 42d St., N.Y., NY 10017-5806; 60,000.
Hospital Association, Amer. (1899), 840 N. Lake Shore Dr., Chicago, IL 60611; 40,000.
Hospital Marketing and Public Relations, Amer. Society for (1964), 840 N. Lake Shore Dr., Chicago, IL 60611; 3,167.
Hot Rod Assn., Natl. (1951), 2035 Financial Way, Glendora, CA 91740; 80,000.
Hotel & Motel Assn., Amer. (1910), 1201 New York Ave. NW, Wash., DC 20005-3917.
Humanism, Council for Democratic and Secular (1980), Box 664, Buffalo, NY 14226; 4,000.
Human Resource Management, Society for (1948), 606 N. Washington St., Alexandria, VA 22314; 57,000.
Humane Society of the U.S. (1954), 2100 L St. NW, Wash., DC 20037; 650,000.
Hydrogen Energy, Intl. Assn. for (1975), PO Box 248266, Coral Gables, FL 33124; 2,500.

Idaho, U.S.S. (BB-42) Assn. (1957), PO Box 711247, San Diego, CA 92171; 615.
Identification, Intl. Assn. for (1916), PO Box 2423, Alameda, CA 94501; 3,300.
Illustrators, Society of (1901), 128 E. 63d St., N.Y., NY 10021; 932.
Impotence Inst. of Amer. (1983), 2020 Pennsylvania Ave. NW, Ste. 292, Wash., DC 20006.
Industrial Designers Society of America (1965), 1142-E Walker Rd., Great Falls, VA 22066; 2,300.
Industrial Engineers, Amer. Institute of (1948), 25 Technology Park, Norcross, GA 30092; 40,000.
Industrial Health Foundation (1935), 34 Penn Circle W, Pittsburgh, PA 15206; 170 companies.
Industrial Security, Amer. Soc. for (1955), 1655 N. Ft. Myer Dr., Ste. 1200, Arlington, VA 22209; 24,000.
Information and Image Management, Assn. for (1943), 1100 Wayne Ave., Ste. 1100, Silver Spring, MD 20910; 11,000.
Information Industry Assn. (1969), 555 New Jersey Ave. NW, Ste. 800, Wash., DC 20001; 500 companies.
Inner Network, The (1991), 300 Darby Hill Rd., RD #1, Delanson, NY 12053; 452.
Insurance Assn., Amer. (1964), 1130 Connecticut Ave. NW, Ste. 1000, Wash., DC 20036; 250+ companies.
Insurance Society, Inc., Intl. (1965), Univ. of Alabama, Rm. 445, Alston Hall, Tuscaloosa, AL 35487; 1,200.
Intellectual Property Owners (1972), 1255 23d St. NW, Wash., DC 20037; 300.
Intelligence Officers, Assn. of Former (1975), 6723 Whittier Ave., Ste. 303A, McLean, VA 22101; 2,700.
Intercollegiate Athletics, Natl. Assn. of (1940), Two Warren Pl., 6120 S. Yale Ave., Ste. 1450, Tulsa, OK 74136; 412 schools.
Interior Designers, Amer. Society of (1931), 608 Massachusetts Ave. NE, Wash., DC 20002; 33,000.
International Interculture Programs, AFS (1947), 313 E. 43d St., N.Y., NY 10017; 100,000.
Inventors, Amer. Assn. of (1891), 2020 Pennsylvania Ave. NW, Wash., DC 20006; 5,727.
Investment Clubs, Natl. Assn. of (1951), 1515 E. Eleven Mile Rd., Royal Oak, MI 48067; 140,000.
Investors Corp., Natl. Assn. of (1951), 711 Thirteen Mile Rd., Madison Heights, MI 48071; 257,000.
Irish-American Cultural Inst. (1962), 2115 Summit Ave., #5026, Univ. of St. Thomas, St. Paul, MN 55105; 5,000.
Irish Historical Society, American- (1897), 991 5th Ave., N.Y., NY 10028; 600.
Iron Castings Society (1897), 455 State St., Des Plaines, IL 60016; 200 firms.
Iron and Steel Engineers, Assn. of (1907), Three Gateway Center, Ste. 2350, Pittsburgh, PA 15222; 10,000.
Iron and Steel Institute, Amer. (1855), 1101 17th St. NW, Ste. 1300, Wash., DC 20036; 1,100.
Italian Historical Society of America (1949), 111 Columbia Heights, Brooklyn, NY 11201.
Izaak Walton League of America, The (1922), 1401 Wilson Blvd., Level B, Arlington, VA 22209; 53,000.

Jamestowne Society (1936), PO Box 14523, Richmond, VA 23221; 3,000.
Jane Austen Society of North Amer. (1979), 207 Pinecroft Dr., Raleigh, NC 27609; 2,700+.
Japanese Amer. Citizens League (1929), 1765 Sutter St., San Francisco, CA 94115; 24,000.
Jewish Book Council (1943), 15 E. 26th St., N.Y., NY 10010.
Jewish Committee, Amer. (1906), 165 E. 56th St., N.Y., NY 10022; 50,000.
Jewish Community Centers Assn. (1917), 15 E. 26th St., N.Y., NY 10010.
Jewish Congress, Amer. (1918), 15 E. 84th St., N.Y., NY 10028; 50,000.
Jewish Federations, Council of (1932), 730 Broadway, N.Y., NY 10003; 200 agencies.
Jewish Historical Society, Amer. (1892), 2 Thornton Rd., Waltham, MA 02154; 2,500.
Jewish War Veterans of the U.S.A. (1896), 1811 R St. NW, Wash., DC 20009; 100,000.
Jewish Women, Natl. Council of (1893), 53 W. 23d St., N.Y., NY 10010; 100,000.
Job's Daughters, Internatl. Order of (1920), 233 W. 6th St., Papillion, NE 68046; 21,000.
Jockey Club (1894), 380 Madison Ave., N.Y., NY 10017; 90.
John Birch Society (1958), PO Box 8040, Appleton, WI 54913.
Joseph Diseases Foundation, Intl. (1977), PO Box 2550, Livermore, CA 94550; 3,789.
Journalists, Society of Professional (1909), PO Box 77, Greencastle, IN 46135; 16,000.
Journalists and Authors, Amer. Society of (1948), 1501 Broadway, Ste. 302, N.Y., NY 10036; 900.
Judaism, Amer. Council for (1943), PO Box 9009, Alexandria, VA 22304.
Judicature Society, Amer. (1913), 25 E. Washington, Chicago, IL 60602; 20,000.
Juggler's Assn., Intl. (1947), PO Box 218, Montague, MA 01351; 3,100.
Junior Achievement (1919), One Education Way, Colorado Springs, CO 80906; 300,000.
Junior Auxiliaries, Natl. Assn. of (1941), 845 S. Main, Greenville, MS 38701; 10,200.
Junior Leagues, Assn. of (1921), 660 First Ave., N.Y., NY 10016; 190,000.

Kennel Club, Amer. (1884), 51 Madison Ave., N.Y., NY 10010; 500+ clubs.
Kidney Fund, Amer. (1971), 6110 Executive Blvd., #1010, Rockville, MD 20852.
Kiwanis Intl. (1915), 3636 Woodview Trace, Indianapolis, IN 46268-3196; 325,000.
Knights of Columbus (1882), One Columbus Plaza, New Haven, CT 06510; 1,540,324.
Knights of Pythias (1864), 2785 E. Desert Inn Rd., #150, Las Vegas, NV 89121; 78,000.
Knights Templar U.S.A., Grand Encampment (1816), 5097 N. Elston, Ste. 101, Chicago, IL 60630.
Krishna Consciousness, Intl. Soc. for (ISKON) (1966), 3764 Watseka Ave., Los Angeles, CA 92109; 1 mil.

LCI National Assn., U.S.S. (1991), 134 Lancaster Ave., Columbia, PA 17512; 1,972.
La Leche League Intl. (1956), 9616 Minneapolis Ave., PO Box 1209, Franklin Park, IL 60131; 48,000.
Lambs, The (1874), 3 W. 51st St., N.Y., NY 10019; 120.
Landscape Architects, Amer. Society of (1899), 4401 Connecticut Ave. NW, Wash., DC 20008-2302; 10,000.
Law, Amer. Society of International (1906), 2223 Massachusetts Ave. NW, Wash., DC 20008; 4,300.
Law Enforcement Officers Assn., Amer. (1966), 1000 Connecticut Ave. NW, Ste. 9, Wash., DC 20036; 50,000.
Law Libraries, Amer. Assn. of (1906), 53 W. Jackson Blvd., Chicago, IL 60604; 4,630.
Learned Societies, Amer. Council of (1919), 228 E. 45th St., N.Y., NY 10017; 45 societies.
Lefthanders Intl. (1975), PO Box 8249, Topeka, KS 66608.
Legal Administrators, Assn. of (1971), 175 E. Hawthorn Pkwy., #325, Vernon Hills, IL 60061-1428; 8,000.
Legion of Valor of the U.S.A. (1890), 92 Oak Leaf Lane, Chapel Hill, NC 27516; 821.
Leif Ericson Society (1926), 3 Toft Woods Way, Media, PA 19063; 999.
Leprosy Missions, Amer. (1906), One Alm Way, Greenville, SC 29601.
Leukemia Society of America (1949), 733 Third Ave., N.Y., NY 10017; 57 chapters.
Lewis and Clark Trail Heritage Foundation, Inc. (1969), PO Box 3434, Great Falls, MT 59403; 1,506.
Lewis Carroll Society of N. America (1974), 617 Rockford Rd., Silver Spring, MD 20902; 400.
Libertarian Party, The (1971), 1528 Pennsylvania Ave. SE, Wash., DC 20003-3116; 100,000+.
Liberty Lobby (1955), 300 Independence Ave. SE, Wash., DC 20003; 20,000.
Libraries Assn., Special (1909), 1700 18th St. NW, Wash., DC 20009; 14,200.
Library Assn., Amer. (1876), 50 E. Huron St., Chicago, IL 60611; 57,000.
Library Assn., Am. Theological (1947), 820 Church St., Ste. 300, Evanston, IL 60201; 188 libraries.
Library Assn., Medical (1861), 6 N. Michigan Ave., Ste. 300, Chicago, IL 60602; 5,000+.
Life, Americans United for (1971), 343 S. Dearborn St., Ste. 1804, Chicago, IL 60604.
Life Insurance, Amer. Council of (1976), 1001 Pennsylvania Ave. NW, Wash., DC 20004; 616 firms.
Life Underwriters, Amer. Soc. of Certified (1929), 270 Bryn Mawr Ave., Byrn Mawr, PA 19010; 28,000.
Life Underwriters, Natl. Assn. of (1890), 1922 F St. NW, Wash., DC 20006; 143,000.
Lighter Than Air Society (1952), 1436 Triplett Blvd., Akron, OH 44306; 1,200.
Lions Clubs, Intl. Assn. of (1917), 300 22d St., Oak Brook, IL 60521-8842; 1.4 mil.
Liquid Crystal Soc., Intl. (1990), Liquid Crystal Institute, Kent State Univ., Kent, OH 44242-0001; 700.
Litchfield Institute, The (1984), 2121 W. Oakland Park Blvd., #333, Ft. Lauderdale, FL 33311-1507; 51.
Literacy Volunteers of America (1962), 5795 Widewaters Pkwy., Syracuse, NY 13214.
Little League Baseball (1939), Rte. 15, S. Williamsport, PA 17701; 2.75 mil. players.
Little People of America (1957), PO Box 9897, Wash., DC 20016; 4,000.
London Club (1975), Rte. 1, Lecompton, KS 66050; 100+.
Lung Assn., Amer. (1904), 1740 Broadway, N.Y., NY 10019.
Lutheran Education Assn. (1942), 7400 Augusta St., River Forest, IL 60305; 3,800.

Magazine Photographers, Am. Soc. of (1944), 419 Park Ave. South, N.Y., NY 10016; 5,000+.
Magazine Publishers of America (1919), 919 Third Ave., N.Y., NY 10022; 1,200 titles.
Magicians, Intl. Brotherhood of (1926), PO Box 192090, Saint Louis, MO 63119-9998; 13,500.
Magicians, Society of Amer. (1902), 1333 Cory St., Yellow Springs, OH 45387; 5,500.
Management Assn., Amer. (1923), 135 W. 50th St., N.Y., NY 10020; 70,000.
Management Consultants, Institute of (1968), 521 5th Ave., 35th Floor, N.Y., NY 10175-3598; 2,201.
Manufacturers, Natl. Assn. of (1895), 1331 Penna. Ave. NW, Ste. 1500N, Wash., DC 20004-1703; 12,000 companies.
Manufacturers' Agents Natl. Assn. (1947), 23016 Mill Creek Rd., PO Box 3467, Laguna Hills, CA 92654; 10,000.
March of Dimes Birth Defects Foundation (1938), 1275 Mamaroneck Ave., White Plains, NY 10605; 2 mil.+.
Marine Corps League (1923), PO Box 3070, Merrifield, VA 22116-3070; 38,000.
Marine Manufacturers Assn., Natl. (1904), 401 N. Michigan Ave., Chicago, IL 60611; 1,650 companies.
Marketing Assn., Amer. (1934), 250 S. Wacker Dr., Chicago, IL 60606; 40,000.
Masonic Relief Assn. of U.S. and Canada (1895), 3827 Canal St., New Orleans, LA 70119.
Masons, Ancient and Accepted Scottish Rite, Southern Jurisdiction, Supreme Council 33° (1801), 1733 16th St. NW, Wash., DC 20009; 493,278.
Masons, Royal Arch, General Grand Chapter (1797), PO Box 489, 111 S. 4th St., Danville, KY 40423-0489; 250,000.
Masons, Supreme Council 33°, Ancient and Accepted Scottish Rite, Northern Masonic Jurisdiction (1813), 33 Marrett Rd., Lexington, MA 02173; 372,215.
Mathematical Society, Amer. (1888), 201 Charles St., Providence, RI 02904; 30,000.
Mathematical Statistics, Institute of (1935), 3401 Investment Blvd., Ste. 7, Hayward, CA 94545; 4,000.
Mathematics, Society for Industrial and Applied (1952), 3600 University City Science Ctr., Philadelphia, PA 19104-2688; 9,076.
Mayflower Descendants, General Society of (1897), 4 Winslow St., PO Box 3297, Plymouth, MA 02361; 25,000.
Mayors, U.S. Conference of (1932), 1620 Eye St. NW, Wash., DC 20006.
Mechanics, Amer. Academy of (1969), Dept. of Civil Engineering, Northwestern Univ., Evanston, IL 60201; 1,200.
Medical Assn., Amer. (1847), 535 N. Dearborn St., Chicago, IL 60610; 290,000.
Medical Assn., Natl. (1895), 1012 Tenth St. NW, Wash., DC 20001; 16,000.
Medical Record Assn., Amer. (1928), 919 N. Michigan Ave., Chicago, IL 60611; 31,000.
Medieval Academy of America (1926), 1430 Massachusetts Ave., Cambridge, MA 02138; 4,616.
Men, Natl. Coalition of Free (1977), PO Box 129, Manhasset, NY 11030; 2,000.
Mensa, Amer. (1960), 2626 E. 14th St., Brooklyn, NY 11235.
Mental Health Assn., Natl. (1909), 1021 Prince St., Alexandria, VA 22314; 326 affiliates.
Mental Health Program Directors, Natl. Assn. of State (1959), 66 Canal Ctr. Plaza, Ste. 302, Alexandria, VA 22314; 55.
Mentally Ill, Natl. Alliance for the (1979), 2101 Wilson Blvd., Ste. 302, Arlington, VA 22201; 140,000.
Merchant Marine Library Assn., Amer. (1921), One World Trade Center, Ste. 2161, N.Y., NY 10048.
Merchant Marine Veterans of WWII, U.S. (1945), PO Box 629, San Pedro, CA 90733; 7,612.
Merchants Assn., Natl. Retail (1911), 100 W. 31st St., N.Y., NY 10001; 45,000.
Merrill's Marauders Assn. (1947), 11244 N. 33rd St., Phoenix, AZ 85028-2723; 1,437.
Metallurgy Institute, Amer. Powder (1959), 105 College Rd. East, Princeton, NJ 08540; 2,700.
Metal Powder Industries Federation (1943), 105 College Rd. East, Princeton, NJ 08540; 225 cos.
Metals, Amer. Society for (ASM Internatl.) (1913), Metals Park, OH 44073; 53,000.
Meteorological Society, Amer. (1919), 45 Beacon St., Boston, MA 02108; 10,200.
Metric Assn., U.S. (1966), 10245 Andasol Ave., Northridge, CA 91325; 1,500.
Microbiology, Amer. Society for (1899), 1325 Massachusetts Ave. NW, Wash. DC 20005; 40,000.
Military Order of the Loyal Legion of the U.S.A. (1865), 1805 Pine St., Philadelphia, PA 19103; 900.
Military Order of the Purple Heart of the USA (1932), 5413-B Backlick Rd., Springfield, VA 22151; 30,000.
Military Order of the World Wars (1919), 435 N. Lee St., Alexandria, VA 22314; 14,000.
Military Service, Veterans of Underage (1991), 3444 Walker Dr., Ellicott City, MD 21042; 532.

Miniatures Industry Association of America (MIAA) (1979), 1100-H Brandywine Blvd., PO Box 2188, Zanesville, OH 43702-2108; 369.

Mining, Metallurgy and Exploration, Inc., Society for (1871), 8307 Shaffer Pkwy., Littleton, CO 80127; 18,000.

Ministerial Assn., Amer. (1929), 2210 Wilshire Blvd., Ste. 582, Santa Monica, CA 90403; 1,000+.

Model Railroad Assn., Natl. (1935), 4121 Cromwell Rd., Chattanooga, TN 37421; 25,000.

Modern Language Assn. of America (1883), 10 Astor Pl., N.Y., NY 10003; 32,000.

Modern Language Teachers Assns., Natl. Federation of (1916), Gannon Univ., Erie, PA 16541; 7,200.

Moose Intl., Inc. (1988), Mooseheart, IL 60539; 1.8 mil.

Mothers, American (1935), 301 Park Ave., N.Y., NY 10022; 3,000.

Mothers of Twins Clubs, Natl. Organization of (1960), PO Box 23188, Albuquerque, NM 87192-1188; 14,000.

Motion Picture Arts & Sciences, Academy of (1927), 8949 Wilshire Blvd., Beverly Hills, CA 90211; 5,300.

Motion Picture & Television Engineers, Society of (1916), 595 West Hartsdale Ave., White Plains, NY 10607; 9,000.

Motion Pictures, Natl. Board of Review of (1909), PO Box 589, Lenox Hill Sta., N.Y., NY 10021.

Motor Fire Apparatus in Amer., Soc. for the Preservation & Appreciation of Antique (1958), PO Box 2005, Syracuse, NY 13220-2005; 3,000.

Motor Vehicle Manufacturers Assn. (1903), 7430 2d Ave., Ste. 300, Detroit, MI 48202; 7 companies.

Motorcyclist Assn., American (1924), 33 Collegeview Rd., Westerville, OH 43081-6114; 200,000.

Multiple Sclerosis Society, Natl. (1946), 733 Third Ave., N.Y., NY 10017; 400,000.

Muscular Dystrophy Assn. (1950), 3300 E. Sunrise Dr., Tucson, AZ 85718.

Museums, Amer. Assn. of (1906), 1225 Eye St. NW, Ste. 200, Wash., DC 20005; 12,000.

Music Center, Amer. (1939), 30 W. 26th St., N.Y., NY 10010.

Music Council, Natl. (1940), 40 W. 37th St., N.Y., NY 10018; 50 organizations.

Music Educators Natl. Conference (1907), 1902 Association Dr., Reston, VA 22090; 60,000.

Music Scholarship Assn., Amer. (1956), 1826 Carew Tower, Cincinnati, OH 45202; 15,000.

Music Teachers Natl. Assn. (1876), The Carew Tower, 441 Vine St., #505, Cincinnati, OH 44502-2814; 25,000.

Musicological Society, Amer. (1934), 201 S. 34th St., Philadelphia, PA 19104; 3,600.

Muzzle Loading Rifle Assn., Natl. (1933), PO Box 67, Friendship, IN 47021; 26,000.

Myasthenia Gravis Foundation, The (1952), 222 S. Riverside Plaza, Ste. 1540, Chicago, IL 60606; 25,000.

NAACP (Natl. Assn. for the Advancement of Colored People) (1909), 4805 Mt. Hope Dr., Baltimore, MD 21215.

Na'amat USA (1925), 200 Madison Ave., N.Y., NY 10016.

Narcotics Anonymous (1953), PO Box 9999, Van Nuys, CA 91409; 1 mil.

National Guard Assn. of the U.S. (1878), One Massachusetts Ave. NW, Wash., DC 20001; 54,000.

Nature Conservancy (1951), 1815 N. Lynn St., Arlington, VA 22209; 692,000.

Naturist Society, The (1980), PO Box 132, Oshkosh, WI 54902; 20,000.

Naval Architects & Marine Engineers, The Society of (1893), 601 Pavonia Ave., Ste. 400, Jersey City, NJ 07306.

Naval Institute, U.S. (1873), 118 Maryland Ave., Annapolis, MD 21402; 100,000.

Naval Reserve Assn. (1954), 1619 King St., Alexandria, VA 22314; 24,000+.

Navigation, Institute of (1945), 1800 Diagonal Rd., Ste. 480, Alexandria, VA 22314; 2,700.

Navy League of the U.S. (1902), 2300 Wilson Blvd., Arlington, VA 22201; 69,000.

Needlework Guild of America (1885), 1007-B Street Rd., Southampton, PA 18966; 100,000.

Negro College Fund, United (1944), 500 E. 62d St., N.Y., NY 10021; 41 institutions.

Neurofibromatosis Foundation, Natl. (1978), 141 Fifth Ave., Ste. 7-S, N.Y., NY 10010; 7,000.

New Age Walkers (1982), 3301 Bellaire Dr., Altadena, CA 91001; 4,700.

Newspaper Assn. of Amer. (1992), NAA, The Newspaper Center, 11600 Sunrise Valley Dr., Reston, VA 22091.

Newspaper Editors, Amer. Society of (1922), PO Box 17004, Wash., DC 20041.

Newspaper Marketing Assn., Intl. (1930), 11600 Sunrise Valley Dr., Reston, VA 22091; 1,300+.

Newswomen's Club of N.Y. (1922), 15 Gramercy Park S., N.Y., NY 10003; 200.

Nikola Tesla Walkers (1982), 10799 Sherman Grove Ave., #18, Sunland, CA 91040; 4,900.

Ninety-Nines (Intl. Organization of Women Pilots) (1929), Box 965, 7100 Terminal Dr., Oklahoma City, OK 72159.

Nobel Committee, Amer. (1942), 1 Morningside Dr. N., Westport, CT 06880.

Non-Commissioned Officers Assn. (1960), 10635 IH 35 North, San Antonio, TX 78233; 160,000.

Northern Cross Society (1986), Route One, Big Springs, KS 66050; 100+.

Notaries, Amer. Society of (1965), 918 16th St. NW, Wash., DC 20006; 20,044.

Nuclear Society, Amer. (1954), 555 N. Kensington Ave., La Grange Park, IL 60525; 16,000.

Numismatic Assn., Amer. (1891), 818 N. Cascade Ave., Colorado Springs, CO 80903-3279; 29,000.

Numismatic Society, Amer. (1858), Broadway at 155th St., N.Y., NY 10032; 2,185.

Nurses' Assn., Amer. (1896), 600 Maryland Ave. SW, Ste. 100 W, Wash., DC 20024; 207,000.

Nursing, Natl. League for (1952), 350 Hudson St., N.Y., NY 10014; 16,000.

Nutrition, Amer. Institute of (1928), 9650 Rockville Pike, Bethesda, MD 20814; 3,300.

ORT Federation, Amer. (Org. for Rehabilitation through Training) (1924), 817 Broadway, N.Y., NY 10019; 20,000.

Odd Fellows, Independent Order of (1819), 422 N. Trade St., Winston-Salem, NC 27101-2830; 360,000.

Old Crows, Assn. of (1964), 1000 N. Payne St., Alexandria, VA 22314-1696; 25,000.

Olympic Committee, U.S. (1921), 1750 E. Boulder St., Colorado Springs, CO 80909; 70 organizations.

Opthalmology, Amer. Academy of (1979), 655 Beach St., San Francisco, CA 94109; 21,000.

Optical Society of America (1916), 2010 Massachusetts Ave. NW, Wash., DC 20036; 12,200.

Optimist Intl. (1919), 4494 Lindell Blvd., St. Louis, MO 63108.

Optometric Assn., Amer. (1898), 243 N. Lindbergh Blvd., St. Louis, MO 63141; 30,395.

Organists, Amer. Guild of (1896), 475 Riverside Dr., Ste. 1260, N.Y., NY 10115; 20,200.

Oriental Society, Amer. (1842), 329 Sterling Memorial Library, Yale Sta., New Haven, CT 06520; 1,500.

Ornithologists' Union, Amer. (1883), c/o National Museum of Natural History, Smithsonian, Wash., DC 20560; 5,000.

Osteopathic Assn., Amer. (1887), 212 E. Ohio St., Chicago, IL 60611; 23,292.

Ostomy Assn., United (1963), 36 Executive Park, Ste. 120, Irving, CA 92714, 41,009.

Outlaw and Lawman History, Natl. Organization for (1974), 1201 Holly Ct., Harker Heights, TX 76543; 450.

Overeaters Anonymous (1960), World Service Office, 383 Van Ness Ave., #1601, Torrance, CA 90501; 152,000.

PTA (Natl. Congress of Parents and Teachers), Natl. (1897), 330 N. Wabash, Chicago, IL 60611; 7 mil.

Paper Industry, Technical Assn. of the Pulp and (1915), 15 Technology Pkwy. S., Norcross, GA 30092; 33,000.

Paralyzed Veterans of America (1947), 801 18th St. NW, Wash., DC 20006; 16,000.

Parametric Analysts, Intl. Soc. of (1979), PO Box 1056, Germantown, MD 20878; 600.

Parents Without Partners (1957), 8807 Colesville Rd., Silver Spring, MD 20910; 100,000.

Parkinson's Disease Foundation (1957), 710 W. 168th St., N.Y., NY 10032; 90,000.

Parliamentarians, Natl. Assn. of (1930), 6601 Winchester, Kansas City, MO 64133-4600; 4,400.

Parliamentary Law, Intl. Organization of Professionals in (1975), 3611 Victoria Ave., Los Angeles, CA 90016; 250.

Pasta Assn., Natl. (1904), 2101 Wilson Blvd., Ste. 920, Arlington, VA 22201.

Pathologists, Amer. Assn. of (1976), 9650 Rockville Pike, Bethesda, MD 20814; 2,000.

Pathology, Amer. Soc. for Investigative (1900), 9650 Rockville Pike, Bethesda, MD 20814-3993; 2,300.

Patton Historical Soc., George S. Jr. (1970), 3116 Thorn St., San Diego, CA 92104-4618.

Pearl Harbor History Associates (1983), PO Box 205, Sperryville, VA 22740-0205; 498.

PEN Amer. Center (1922), 568 Broadway, N.Y., NY 10012; 2,600.

Pen Friends, Intl. (1967), PO Box 290065, Brooklyn, NY 11229; 300,000.

PEN Women, Natl. League of Amer. (1897), 1300 17th St. NW, Wash., DC 20036-1973; 5,000.

P.E.O. (Philanthropic Educational Organization) Sisterhood (1869), 3700 Grand Ave., Des Moines, IA 50312; 242,000.

Personnel Administration, Amer. Society for (1948), 606 N. Washington St., Alexandria, VA 22314; 40,000.

Petroleum Equipment Inst. (1951), 6514 E. 69 St., Tulsa, OK 74133; 1,500 member companies.

Petroleum Institute, Amer. (1919), 1220 L St. NW, Wash., DC 20005; 250 corporations.

Pharmaceutical Assn., Amer. (1852), 2215 Constitution Ave. NW, Wash., DC 20037; 44,000.

Phi Delta Kappa (1906), 408 N. Union, PO Box 789, Bloomington, IN 47402-0789; 172,000.

Philatelic Pages & Panels, Amer. Soc. for (1984), 4116 Kilmer Ave., Allentown, PA 18104; 950.

Philatelic Society, Amer. (1886), 100 Oakwood Ave., PO Box 8000, State College, PA 16803; 57,500.

Philological Assn., Amer. (1869), Dept. of Classics, College of the Holy Cross, Worcester, MA 01610-2395; 2,500.

Philosophical Assn., Amer. (1900), Univ. of Delaware, Newark, DE 19716; 8,500.

Philosophical Enquiry, Intl. Soc. For (1974), 277 Washington Blvd., Hudson, NY 12534-1322; 590.

Philosophical Society, Amer. (1743), 104 S. 5th St., Philadelphia, PA 19106; 690.

Photogrammetry and Remote Sensing, Amer. Society of (1934), 5410 Grosvenor Ln., Ste. 210, Bethesda, MD 20814.

Photographers of America, Professional (1880), 57 Forsyth St. NW, Ste. 1600, Atlanta, GA 30303; 14,000.

Photographic Society of Amer. (1934), 3000 United Founders Blvd., #103, Oklahoma City, OK 73112.

Physical Therapy Assn., Amer. (1921), 1111 N. Fairfax St., Alexandria, VA 22314; 16,020.

Physicians, Amer. Academy of Family (1947), 8880 Ward Pkwy., Kansas City, MO 64114; 79,000.

Physics, Amer. Inst. of (1931), One Physics Ellipse, College Park, MD 20740-3843.

Physiological Society, Amer. (1887), 9650 Rockville Pike, Bethesda, MD 20814; 7,000.

Pilgrim Society (1820), 75 Court St., Plymouth, MA 02360-3891; 1,105.

Pilot Intl. (1921), PO Box 4844, 244 College St., Macon, GA 31213-0599; 19,000.

Planetary Society (1980), 65 N. Catalina Ave., Pasadena, CA 91106; 100,000.

Planned Parenthood Federation of America (1916), 810 Seventh Ave., N.Y., NY 10019; 187 affiliates.

Plastic Modelers Society, Intl. (1963), PO Box 6138, Warner Robins, GA 31095-6138; 3,875.

Plastics Industry, Society of (1937), 1275 K St. NW, Ste. 400, Wash., DC 20005.

Platform Assn., Intl. (1831), Box 250, Winnetka, IL 60093.

Poetry Day Committee, Natl. (1947), 1110 N. Venetian Dr., Miami, FL 33139-1019; 17,500.

Poetry Society of America (1910), 15 Gramercy Park, N.Y., NY 10003; 1,700.

Poets, Academy of Amer. (1934), 584 Broadway, N.Y., NY 10024; 2,220.

Police, Internatl. Assn. of Chiefs of (1893), 515 N. Washington St., #400, Alexandria, VA 22314-2340; 13,500.

Polish Army Veterans Assn. of America (1921), 155 Noble St., Brooklyn, NY 11222; 3,500.

Polish Cultural Society of America (1940), PO Box 31, Wall Street, N.Y., NY 10005; 104,693.

Political Items Collectors, Amer. (1945), PO Box 340339, San Antonio, TX 78234; 3,200.

Political Science, Academy of (1880), 475 Riverside Dr., Ste. 1274, N.Y., NY 10115-0012; 8,500.

Political Science Assn., Amer. (1903), 1527 New Hampshire Ave. NW, Wash., DC 20036; 16,200.

Political & Social Science, Amer. Academy of (1889), 3937 Chestnut St., Philadelphia, PA 19104; 4,000.

Polo Assn., U.S. (1890), 4059 Iron Works Pike, Lexington, KY, 40511; 3,000.

Population Assn. of America (1931), 1722 N St. NW, Wash., DC 20036; 2,700.

Portuguese-American Federation, Inc. (1965), PO Box 694, Bristol, RI 02809; 235.

Portuguese Continental Union of the U.S.A. (1925), 899 Boylston St., Boston, MA 02115.

Postmasters of the U.S., Natl. Assn. of (1898), 8 Herbert St., Arlington, VA 22305; 43,000.

Postmasters of the U.S., Natl. League of (1904), 1023 N. Royal St., Alexandria, VA 22314; 21,874.

Poultry Science Assn. (1921), 309 W. Clark St., Champaign, IL 61820.

Power Boat Assn., Amer. (1903), 17640 E. Nine Mile Rd., PO Box 377, Eastpointe, MI 48021; 6,815.

Precancel Collectors, Natl. Assn. of (1951), 5121 Park Blvd., Wildwood, NJ 08260-0121; 7,600.

Press, Associated (1848), 50 Rockefeller Plaza, N.Y., NY 10020; 1,554 newspapers & 6,000 broadcast stations.

Press Club, Natl. (1908), 529 14th St. NW, Wash., DC 20045.

Press Intl., United (1907), 1400 I St. NW, Wash., DC 20005.

Press and Radio Club (1948), PO Box 70023, Montgomery, AL 36107; 750.

Printing Industries of America (1887), 100 Dangerfield Rd., Alexandria, VA 22314; 14,000.

Prisoners of War, Amer. Ex- (1942), 3201 E. Pioneer Pkwy., #40, Arlington, TX 76010-5396; 33,000.

Procrastinators Club of America (1956), Box 712, Bryn Athyn, PA 19009; 10,000.

Production and Inventory Control Soc., American, 500 W. Annandale Rd., Falls Church, VA 22046-4274; 69,114.

Psoriasis Foundation, Natl. (1968), 6443 S.W. Beaverton Hwy., #210, Portland, OR 97221; 24,000.

Psychiatric Assn., Amer. (1844), 1400 K St. NW, Wash., DC 20005; 37,380.

Psychical Research, Amer. Society for (1907), 5 W. 73d St., N.Y., NY 10023; 2,000.

Psychoanalytic Assn., Amer. (1911), 309 E. 49th St., N.Y., NY 10017; 3,000.

Psychological Assn., Amer. (1892), 750 1st St. NE, Wash., DC 20002-4242; 119,000.

Psychological Assn. for Psychoanalysis, Natl. (1948), 150 W. 13th St., N.Y., NY 10011-7891; 355.

Psychological Minorities, Society for the Aid of (1953), 42-25 Hampton St., Elmhurst, NY 11373; 530.

Public Administration, Amer. Soc. for (1939), 1120 G St. NW, Wash., DC 20005; 14,800.

Public Health Assn., World Fed. of (1967), 1015 15th St. NW, Wash., DC 20005; 48 natl. assn.

Public Relations Soc. of Amer. (1947), 33 Irving Pl., N.Y., NY 10003-2376; 15,462.

Publishers, Assn. of Amer. (1970), 220 E. 23d St., N.Y., NY 10010; 230 companies.

Puppeteers of Amer. (1937), 5 Cricklewood Path, Pasadena, CA 91107; 2,010.

Puzzle Buffs Intl. (1978), 1772 State Rd., Cuyahoga Falls, OH 44223; 39,000.

Quality Control, Amer. Society for (1946), 611 E. Wisconsin Ave., Milwaukee, WI 53201-3005; 120,000.

Quota International, Inc. (1919), 1420 21st St. NW, Wash., DC 20036; 11,000+.

Rabbis, Central Conference of Amer. (1889), 192 Lexington Ave., N.Y., NY 10016; 1,540.

Racial Equality, Congress of (CORE) (1942), 1457 Flatbush Ave., Brooklyn, NY 11210; 100,000.

Radio, Natl. Assn. of Business and Educational (1965), 1501 Duke St., Alexandria, VA 22314; 2,400.

Radio Union, Intl. Amateur (1925), PO Box AAA, Newington, CT 06111; 126 societies.

Radio and TV Society, Intl. (1939), 420 Lexington Ave., Ste. 1714, N.Y., NY 10170; 1,750.

Radio Relay League, Amer. (1914), 225 Main St., Newington, CT 06111; 160,000.

Railsplitter Society, 84th Infantry Division (1945), 1100 S. Cliff Ave., Sioux Falls, SD 57105; 3,304.

Railway Historical Society, Natl. (1935), PO Box 58153, Philadelphia, PA 19102-8153; 21,000+.

Railway Progress Institute (1908), 700 N. Fairfax St., Ste. 601, Alexandria, VA 22314-2098; 103 companies.

Range Management, Society for (1948), 1839 York St., Denver, CO 80206; 5,300.

Reading Assn., Intl. (1956), PO Box 8139, 800 Barksdale Rd., Newark, DE 19714-8139; 93,000.

Real Estate Institute, Intl. (1975), 8383 E. Evans Rd., Scottsdale, AZ 85260-3614; 4,500.

Rebekah Assemblies, Intl. Assn. of (1916), 422 N. Trade, Winston-Salem, NC 27101; 171,276.

Reconciliation, Fellowship of (1915), 523 N. Broadway, Nyack, NY 10960; 10,000.

Records Managers & Administrators, Assn. of (1975), 4200 Somerset Dr., Ste. 215, Prairie Village, KS 66208; 10,600.

Recreation and Park Assn., Natl. (1965), 2775 S. Quincy St., Ste. 300, Arlington, VA 22206-2204; 22,000+.

Recycling Coalition, Natl., 1101 30th St. NW, Ste. 305, Wash., DC 20007.

Red Cross, American (1881), 17th & D Sts. NW, Wash., DC 20006; 1.5 mil. volunteers.

Red Men, Improved Order of (1765), 4521 Speight Ave., Waco, TX 76711-1708; 28,000.

Redwoods League, Save-the- (1918), 114 Sansome St., Rm. 605, San Francisco, CA 94104; 45,000.

Rehabilitation Assn., Natl. (1925), 1910 Association Dr., Ste. 205, Reston, VA 22091.

Religion, Amer. Academy of (1909), 501 Hall of Languages, Syracuse Univ., Syracuse, NY 13244-1170; 5,600.

Religion Foundation, Freedom from (1978), PO Box 750, Madison, WI 53701; 3,200.

Renaissance Society of America (1954), 24 W. 12th St., N.Y., NY 10011; 3,500.

Republican National Committee (1856), 310 1st St. SE, Wash., DC 20003-1801.

Reserve Officers Assn. of the U.S. (1922), One Constitution Ave. NE, Wash., DC 20002; 123,000.

Restaurant Assn., Natl. (1919), 1200 17th St. NW, Wash., DC 20036; 20,000.

Retail Federation, Natl. (1918), 100 W. 31st St., N.Y., NY 10001; 50,000.

Retired Credit Union People, Natl. Assn. for (1978), PO Box 391, 5910 Mineral Pt. Rd., Madison, WI 53705; 81,180.

Retired Federal Employees, Natl. Assn. of (1921), 1533 New Hampshire Ave. NW, Wash., DC 20036; 500,000.

Retired Officers Assn. (1929), 201 N. Washington St., Alexandria, VA 22314-2529; 380,000.

Retired Persons, Amer. Assn. of (1958), 1909 K St. NW, Wash., DC 20049; 32 mil.

Retired Teachers Assn., Natl. (1947), 1909 K St. NW, Wash., DC 20049; 540,000.

Revolver Assn., U.S. (1900), 40 Larchmont Ave., Taunton, MA 02780; 1,400.

Reye's Syndrome Foundation, Natl. (1974), 426 N. Lewis, Bryan, OH 43506; 10,000+.

Richard III Society (1969), PO Box 13786, New Orleans, LA 70185; 700.

Rifle Assn., Natl. (1871), 11250 Waples Mill Rd., Fairfax, VA 22030; 3.4 mil.

Road & Transportation Builders' Assn., Amer. (1902), 1010 Massachusetts Ave. NW, Wash., DC 20001; 4,000.

Rocky Horror Picture Show Preservation Soc. of Terra (1993), One Caddo Ct., Kenner, LA 70065-3920.

Rodeo Cowboys Assn., Professional (1936), 101 Pro Rodeo Dr., Colorado Springs, CO 80919; 8,648.

Roller Skating, U.S. Amateur Confederation of (1937), 4730 South St., PO Box 6579, Lincoln, NE 68506; 20,000.

Rose Society, Amer. (1892), 8877 Jefferson Paige Rd., Shreveport, LA 71119; 38,000.

Rotary Intl. (1905), 1560 Sherman Ave., Evanston, IL 60201; 2.2 mil.

Running and Fitness Assn., Amer. (1968), 4405 East West Hwy., Ste. 405, Bethesda, MD 20814; 12,000.

Ruritan Natl. (1928), Ruritan Natl. Rd., Dublin, VA 24084.

Safety and Fairness Everywhere, Natl. Organization Taunting (1980), PO Box 5743WA, Montecito, CA 93150; 677.

Safety Council, Natl. (1913), 1121 Spring Lake Dr., Itasca, IL 60143; 12,500.

Sailors, Tin Can (1976), PO Box 100, Somerset, MA 02726; 17,000.

Sailors Assn., Destroyer-Escort (1975), 352 W. Story Rd., Ocoee, FL 34761; 12,000.

St. Andrew, The Brotherhood of (1883), 1109 Merchant St., PO Box 632, Ambridge, PA 15003; 5,000.

St. Paul, Natl. Guild of (1937), 601 Hill 'n Dale, Lexington, KY 40503; 13,652.

Salespersons, Natl. Assn. of Professional (1970), PO Box 76461, Atlanta, GA 30358; 35,000.

Salt Institute (1914), 700 N. Fairfax St., Ste. 600, Alexandria, VA, 22314-2040; 23 companies.

Sand Castle Builders, Intl. Society of (1988), 172 N. Pershing Ave., Akron, OH 44313; 150.

School Administrators, Amer. Assn. of (1865), 1801 N. Moore St., Arlington, VA 22209; 16,409.

School Boards Assn., Natl. (1940), 1680 Duke St., Alexandria, VA 22314.

School Counselor Assn., Amer. (1953), 5999 Stevenson Ave., Alexandria, VA 22304; 13,000.

Schools of Art, Natl. Assn. of (also: School of Art and Design; School of Dance, Music, and Theater) (1944), 11250 Roger Bacon Dr., Reston, VA 22090; 553 institutions.

Schools & Colleges, Amer. Council on (1927), 13014 Dale Mabry Hwy., Ste. 270-B, Tampa, FL 33180-2808; 317.

Science, Amer. Assn. for the Advancement of (1848), 1333 H St. NW, Wash., DC 20005; 141,000.

Science Fiction Society, World (1939), PO Box 1270, Kendall Sq. Sta., Cambridge, MA 02142; 5,000.

Science Service (1921), 1719 N St. NW, Wash., DC 20036.

Science Teachers Assn., Natl. (1949), 1840 Wilson Blvd., Arlington, VA 22201; 49,000.

Science Writers, Natl. Assn. of (1934), PO Box 294, Greenlawn, NY 11740; 1,835.

Sciences, Natl. Academy of (1863), 2101 Constitution Ave. NW, Wash., DC 20418; 1,936.

Scrabble Assn., Natl. (1973), 120 Front St. Garden, Greenport, NY 11944; 10,000.

Screen Actors Guild (1933), 7065 Hollywood Blvd., Hollywood, CA 90028; 78,000.

Screen Printing Assn. Intl. (1948), 10015 Main St., Fairfax, VA 22031; 3,000+.

Sculpture Soc., Natl. (1893), 1177 Ave. of the Americas, N.Y., NY 10036; 3,600.

2d Air Division Assn. (1947), 06-410 Delaire Landing Rd., Philadelphia, PA 19114; 7,852.

Secondary School Principals, Natl. Assn. of (1916), 1904 Association Dr., Reston, VA 22091; 42,000.

Secretaries Intl., Professional (1942), 10502 N.W. Ambassador Dr., Kansas City, MO 64153; 40,000.

Secretaries, Natl. Assn. of Legal (1920), 2250 E. 73d, Ste. 550, Tulsa, OK 74136-6864; 16,000.

Securities Industry Assn. (1972), 120 Broadway, N.Y., NY 10271; 600 firms.

Separation of Church & State, Americans United for (1947), 8120 Fenton St., Silver Spring, MD 20910; 50,000.

Sertoma Internatl. (1912), 1912 E. Meyer Blvd., Kansas City, MO 64132; 30,000.

Sex Information & Education Council of the U.S. (SIECUS) (1964), 130 W. 42d St., Ste. 2500, N.Y., NY 10036; 2,500+.

Sharkhunters Intl. (1983), PO Box 1539, Hernanado, FL 32642; 4,000+.

Shipbuilders Council of America (1921), 1110 Vermont Ave. NW, Wash., DC 20005; 50 organizations.

Ships-in-Bottles Assn. of Amer. (1983), PO Box 180550, Coronado, CA 92178; 395.

Shore & Beach Preservation Assn., Amer. (1926), PO Box 279, Middletown, CA 95461; 900.

Shrine, Ancient Arabic Order of the Nobles of the Mystic (1872), 2900 Rocky Pt. Dr., Tampa, FL 33607; 799,000.

Sierra Club (1892), 730 Polk St., San Francisco, CA 94109.

Skeet Shooting Assn., Natl. (1946), PO Box 680007, San Antonio, TX 78268; 15,800.

Ski Assn., U.S. (1904), PO Box 100, Park City, UT 84060.

Small Business United, Natl. (1986), 1155 15th St. NW, Ste. 710, Wash., DC 20005; 65,000.

Smokers' Pollution, Inc., Group Against (GASP) (1971), PO Box 632, College Park, MD 20741-0632; 10,000+.

Smoking & Health, Natl. Clearinghouse for (1965), Center for Disease Control, 1600 Clifton Rd. NE, Atlanta, GA 30333.

Soccer Federation, U.S. (1913), 1801-1811 S. Prairie Ave., Chicago, IL 60616; 2 mil.

Social Sciences, Natl. Institute of (1865), 444 Madison Ave., Ste. 2901, N.Y., NY 10022; 300.

Social Work Education, Council on (1952), 1600 Duke St., Alexandria, VA 22314; 2,500.

Sociological Assn., Amer. (1905), 1722 N St. NW, Wash., DC 20036; 13,000.

Softball Association, Amateur (1933), 2801 N.E. 50th St., Oklahoma City, OK 73111; 4.5 mil.

Soft Drink Assn., Natl. (1921), 1101 16th St. NW, Wash., DC 20036; 1,700.

Soil & Water Conservation Society of America (1945), 7515 N.E. Ankeny Rd., Ankeny, IA 50021-9764; 11,000.

Soil Science Society of America (1936), 677 S. Segoe Rd., Madison, WI 53711; 6,100.

Soldier's, Sailor's and Airmen's Club (1919), 283 Lexington Ave., N.Y., NY 10016.

Songwriters Guild of America, The (1931), 276 Fifth Ave., Ste. 306, N.Y., NY 10001; 3,500.

Sons of the Amer. Legion (1932), Box 1055, Indianapolis, IN 46206; 161,376.

Sons of the American Revolution, Natl. Society of (1889), 1000 S. 4th, Louisville, KY 40203; 26,000.

Sons of Confederate Veterans (1896), Southern Station, Box 5164, Hattiesburg, MS 39406-5164; 13,000.

Sons of the Desert (1965), PO Box 8341, Universal City, CA 91608; 15,000.

Sons of Italy in America, Order (1905), 219 E St. NE, Wash. DC 20002; 500,000.

Sons of Norway (1895), 1455 W. Lake St., Minneapolis, MN 55408; 74,428.

Sons of Poland, Assn. of the (1903), 591 Summit Ave., Rm. 702, Jersey City, NJ 07306; 10,000.

Sons of the Republic of Texas, The (1922), 5942 Abrams Rd., #222, Dallas, TX 75231; 2,400.

Sons of St. Patrick, Society of the Friendly (1784), 80 Wall St., N.Y., NY 10005; 1,500.

Sons of Sherman's March to the Sea (1965), 1725 Farmer, Tempe, AZ 85281-6533; 750.

Sons of Union Veterans of the Civil War (1881), 411 Bartlett St., Lansing, MI 48915; 2,700.

Soroptimist Intl. of the Americas (1921), 1616 Walnut St., Philadelphia, PA 19103; 47,000.

Southern Christian Leadership Conference (1957), 334 Auburn Ave. NE, Atlanta, GA 30303; 1 mil.

Space Education Assoc., U.S. (1973), PO Box 249, Rheems, PA 17570-0249; 1,250.

Special Olympics Intl. (1968), 1350 New York Ave. NW, Ste. 500, Wash., DC 20005.

Speech Communication Assn. (1914), 5105 Backlick Rd., Annandale, VA 22003; 6,800.

Speech-Language-Hearing Assn., Amer. (1925), 10801 Rockville Pike, Rockville, MD 20852.

Speedskating Union of the U.S., Amateur (1927), 1033 Shady Lane, Glen Ellyn, IL 60137; 3,000.

Speleological Society, Natl. (1941), 2813 Cave Ave., Huntsville, AL 35810; 11,500.

Spiritual Awareness, Assn. for (1984), PO Box 41, Clifton Hill, MO 65244; 1,500.

Sports Car Club of America (1944), 9033 E. Eastern Pl., Englewood, CO 80112; 50,000+.

Sports Club, Indoor (1930), 1145 Highland St., Napoleon, OH 43545; 950.

Sportscasters Assn., Amer. (1980), 5 Beekman St., N.Y., NY 10038; 500+.

State Governments, Council of (1933), PO Box 11910, Lexington, KY 40517; 50 states, 4 territories.

State & Local History, Amer. Assn. for (1940), 530 Church St., Ste. 600, Nashville, TN 37219; 6,000.

Statistical Assn., Amer. (1839), 1429 Duke St., Alexandria, VA 22314-3402; 19,000.

Steamship Historical Society of America (1940), 300 Ray Dr., Ste. 4, Providence, RI 02906; 3,400.

Steel Construction, Amer. Institute of (1921), 1 E. Wacker Dr., Ste. 3100, Chicago, IL 60601-2001; 2,770.

Stock Car Auto Racing, Natl. Assn. for (NASCAR) (1947), PO Box 2875, Daytona Beach, FL 32120-2875; 47,000.

Stock Exchange (1790), 1900 Market St., Philadelphia, PA 19103; 505.

Stock Exchange, Amer. (1911), 86 Trinity Pl., N.Y., NY 10006; 871.

Stock Exchange, N.Y. (1792), 11 Wall St., N.Y., NY 10005.

Student Councils, Natl. Assn. of (1931), 1904 Association Dr., Reston, VA 22091; 9,000 schools.

Stuttering Project, Natl. (1977), 2151 Irving St., Ste. 208, San Francisco, CA 94122-1609; 4,300.

Sudden Infant Death Syndrome Alliance, Natl. (1987), 10500 Little Patuxent Pkwy., Ste. 420, Columbia, MD 21044.

Sugar Brokers Assn., Natl. (1903), 1 World Trade Center, N.Y., NY 10047; 100.

Sunbathing Assn., Amer. (1931), 1703 N. Main St., Kissimmee, FL 34744; 44,000.

Surfing Committee, U.S. (1960), Box 545921, Surfhouse, Surfside, FL 33154-5492; 6,007,803.

Surgeons, Amer. College of (1913), 55 E. Erie St., Chicago, IL 60611-2797; 57,158.

Surgeons of the U.S., Assn. of Military (1891), 9320 Old Georgetown Rd., Bethesda, MD 20814; 14,500.

Surveying & Mapping, Amer. Congress on (1941), 5410 Grosvenor Ln., Bethesda, MD 20814-2122; 9,500.

Symphony Orchestra League, Amer. (1942), 777 14th St. NW, Ste. 500, Wash., DC 20005; 860 orchestras.

Systems Management, Assn. for (1947), PO Box 38370, Cleveland, OH 44138; 5,100.

Table Tennis Assn., U.S. (1933), One Olympic Plaza, Colorado Springs, CO 80909; 7,000.

Tailhook Assn., The (1957), 9696 Business Park Ave., PO Box 26700, San Diego, CA 92131.

Tax Accountants, Natl. Assn. of Enrolled Federal (1960), PO Box 59-009, Chicago, IL 60659-0009; 450.

Tax Administrators, Federation of (1937), 444 N. Capitol St. NW, Wash., DC 20001.

Tax Foundation, Inc. (1937), 1250 H St. NW, Ste. 750, Wash., DC 20005.

Taxpayers Union, Natl. (1969), 325 Pennsylvania Ave. SE, Wash., DC 20003; 250,000.

Tea Assn. of the U.S.A. (1899), 230 Park Ave., N.Y., NY 10169; 100 firms.

Teachers of English, Natl. Council of (1911), 1111 Kenyon Rd., Urbana, IL 61801; 125,000.

Teachers of English to Speakers of Other Languages (1969), 1600 Cameron St., Ste. 300, Alexandria, VA 22314.

Teachers of French, Amer. Assn. of (1927), 57 E. Armory Ave., Champaign, IL 61820; 11,000.

Teachers of Mathematics, Natl. Council of (1920), 1906 Association Dr., Reston, VA 22091; 112,763.

Teachers of Singing, Natl. Assn. of (1944), 2800 Univ. Blvd. N., J.U. Sta., Jacksonville, FL 32211; 5,000.

Teachers of Spanish & Portuguese, Amer. Assn. of (1917), Gunter Hall, Rm. 106, Univ. of Colorado, Greeley, CO 80939.

Technicians Assn., Market (1973), 71 Broadway, 2d Fl., N.Y., NY 10006; 600.

Telephone Pioneers of Amer. (1911), 930 15th St., 12th Fl., Denver, CO 80202; 850,000.

Television, Inc., Viewers for Quality (1984), PO Box 195, Fairfax Station, VA 22039; 2,500.

Television Arts & Sciences, Natl. Academy of (1947), 111 W. 57th St., Ste. 1020, N.Y., NY 10019; 12,000.

Television Bureau of Advertising (1954), 477 Madison Ave., N.Y., NY 10022.

Television & Radio Artists, Amer. Federation of (1937), 1350 Ave. of the Americas, N.Y., NY 10019; 66,000.

Telluride Assn. (1911), 217 West Ave., Ithaca, NY 14850.

Tennis Assn., U.S. (1881), 1212 Ave. of the Americas, N.Y., NY 10036.

Terraplane Club, Hudson-Essex (1959), 100 E. Cross St., Ypsilanti, MI 48198; 3,200.

Tesla Memorial Soc., Inc. (1979), 453 Martin Rd., Buffalo, NY 14218; 1,700.

Testing & Materials, Amer. Society for (1898), 1916 Race St., Philadelphia, PA 19103; 35,000.

Textile Manufacturers Institute, Amer. (1949), 1801 K St. NW, Ste. 900, Wash., DC 20006.

Theodore Roosevelt Assn. (1919), PO Box 719, Oyster Bay, NY 11771; 2,000.

Theological Schools in the U.S. and Canada, Assn. of (1918), 10 Summit Park Dr., Pittsburgh, PA 15275-1103.

Theosophical Society in America, The (1886), 1926 N. Main St., Wheaton, IL 60189-0270; 4,600.

Thoreau Society (1941), 156 Belknap St., Concord, MA 01742; 1,500.

Thoroughbred Racing Assns. (1942), 420 Fair Hill Dr., Ste. 1, Elkton, MD 21921; 49 racing associations.

Tin Can Soldiers, Inc. (1976), 1231 County, PO Box 100, Somerset, MA 02726; 15,000.

Titanic Historical Society (1963), 208 Main St., Indian Orchard, MA 01151-0053; 5,223.

Toastmasters Intl. (1924), PO Box 9052, Mission Viejo, CA 92690-7052.

Topical Assn., Amer. (1949), PO Box 630, Johnstown, PA 15907; 7,000.

Toy Manufacturers of America (1916), 200 Fifth Ave., N.Y., NY 10010; 265.

Track & Field, USA (1979), One Hoosier Dome, Indianapolis, IN 46225; 100,000+.

Trail Assn., North Country (1981), PO Box 311, White Cloud, MI 49349; 700+.

Transit Assn., Amer. Public (1974), 1201 New York Ave. NW, Wash., DC 20005; 11,000 organizations.

Translators Assn., Amer. (1960), 1735 Jefferson Davis Hwy., #903, Arlington, VA 22202-3413; 5,000.

Trapshooting Assn., Amateur (1923), 601 W. National Rd., Vandalia, OH 45377; 96,351.

Travel Agents, Amer. Society of (1931), 1101 King St., Alexandria, VA 22314; 23,000.

Travelers Protective Assn. of America (1890), 3755 Lindell Blvd., St. Louis, MO 63108; 164,000.

Trilateral Commission, The (1973), 345 E. 46th St., N.Y., NY 10017; 325.

Truck Historical Soc., Amer. (1971), 300 Office Park Dr., Ste. 120, Birmingham, AL 35223; 17,007.

Trucking Assn., Amer. (1933), 2200 Mill Rd., Alexandria, VA 22314-4677; 4,100 companies.

True Sisters, United Order (1846), 212 Fifth Ave., N.Y., NY 10010; 7,000.

T. S. Eliot Soc. (1980), 5007 Waterman Blvd., St. Louis, MO 63108; 200.

Tuberous Sclerosis Assn. of Amer. (1970), 8000 Corporate Dr., Ste. 120, Landover, MD 20785; 3,000+.

UFOs, Natl. Investigation Committee on (1967), 14617 Victory Blvd., Ste. 4, Van Nuys, CA 91411; 750.

UNICEF, U.S. Committee for (1947), 333 E. 38th St., N.Y., NY 10016.

USO (United Service Organizations) (1941), 601 Indiana Ave. NW, Wash., DC 20004.

Underwriters, Amer. Soc. of Chartered Life (1927), 270 Bryn Mawr Ave., Bryn Mawr, PA 19010; 30,000.

Underwriters, Soc. of Chartered Property and Casualty (1944), Kahler Hall, 720 Providence Rd., Malvern, PA 19355.

United Nations Assn. of the U.S.A. (1923, as League of Nations Assn.), 485 Fifth Ave., N.Y., NY 10017; 30,000.

United Way of America (1918), 801 N. Fairfax St., Alexandria, VA 22309; 1,200.

Universities, Assn. of Amer. (1914), One Dupont Circle, Ste. 730, Wash., DC 20036; 59 institutions.

Universities & Colleges, Assn. of Governing Bds. of (1921), One Dupont Circle NW, Ste. 400, Wash., DC 20036.

University Continuing Education Assn., Natl. (1915), One Dupont Circle, Ste. 615, Wash., DC 20036; 2,000.

University Extension Assn., Natl. (1915), One Dupont Circle NW, Ste. 400, Wash., DC 20036; 1,100.

University Foundation, Intl. (1973), 1301 S. Noland Rd., Independence, MO 64055; 63,911.

University Professors, Amer. Assn. of (1915), 1012 14th St. NW, Ste. 500, Wash., DC 20005; 41,000.

University Women, Amer. Assn. of (1881), 1111 16th St. NW, Wash., DC 20036.

Urban League, Natl. (1910), 500 E. 62d St., N.Y., NY 10020.

Useless Skills, Institute of Totally (1987), Box 181, Temple, NH 03084; 354.

Utility Commissioners, Natl. Assn. of Regulatory (1889), 1102 Interstate Commerce Commission Bldg., 12th & Constitution Ave. NW, Wash., DC 20044-0684; 400.

Vampire Research Center (1972), PO Box 252, Elmhurst, NY 11373; 1,075.

Variety Clubs Intl. (1928), 1560 Broadway, N.Y., NY 10036.

VASA Order of America (1896), 65 Bryant Rd., Cranston, RI 02910; 30,000.

Ventriloquists, North American Assn. of (1944), Box 420, Littleton, CO 80160; 1,700.

Veterans Assn., Blinded (1958), 477 H St. NW, Wash., DC 20001; 7,500.

Veterans of Foreign Wars of the U.S. (1899) **& Ladies Auxiliary** (1914), 406 W. 34th St., Kansas City, MO 64111.

Veterans of the Vietnam War (1980), 760 Jumper Rd., Wilkes-Barre, PA 18702-8033; 30,000.

Veterans of World War I (1958), PO Box 8027, Alexandria, VA 22306; 26,000.

Veterans of WWII, U.S. Submarine (1955), 3214 Averill Ave. N., Flint, MI 48506-2504; 8,000.

Veterinary Medical Assn., Amer. (1863), 1931 N. Meacham Rd., Schaumburg, IL 60173; 53,512.

Victorian Society in America (1965), 219 S. Sixth St., Philadelphia, PA 19106; 2,300.

Violet Soc. of Amer., African (1946), 2375 North, Beaumont, TX 77702; 12,000.

Virgil Fox Society, The (1977), 88 Chestnut St., Brooklyn, NY 11208; 450+.

Volleyball Assn., U.S. (1928), 3595 E. Fountain Blvd., Ste. I-2, Colorado Springs, CO 80910-1740; 95,000.

War Mothers, Amer. (1917), 2615 Woodley Pl. NW, Wash., DC 20008; 2,000.

Warrant and Warrant Officers' Assn., Chief, U.S. Coast Guard (1929), c/o Fort McNair Yacht Basin, 200 V St. SW, Wash., DC 20024; 3,346.

Watch & Clock Collectors, Natl. Assn. of (1943), 514 Poplar St., Columbia, PA 17512; 38,000.

Water Assn., Natl. Ground (1948), 6375 Riverside Dr., Dublin, OH 43017; 24,000.

Water Environment Federation (1928), 601 Wythe St., Alexandria, VA 22314; 40,000.

Water Pollution Control Admin., Assn. of State and Interstate (1961), 750 First St. NE, Ste. 910, Wash., DC 20001.

Water Pollution Control Federation (1928), 601 Wythe St., Alexandria, VA 22314-1994; 32,000.

Water Resources Assn., Amer. (1964), 5410 Grosvenor Ln., Ste. 220, Bethesda, MD 20814-2192; 4,000.

Water Ski Assn., Amer. (1939), 799 Overlook Dr. SE, Winter Haven, FL 33884; 30,000.

Water Works Assn., Amer. (1881), 6666 W. Quincy Ave., Denver, CO 80235; 55,000.

Watercolor Soc., American (1867), 47 Fifth Ave., N.Y., NY 10003; 506.

Welding Society, Amer. (1919), 550 N.W. LeJeune Rd., Miami, FL 33126; 41,000.

Wheelchair Sports, USA (1956), 3595 E. Fountain Blvd., Ste. L-1, Colorado Springs, CO 80918; 4,000.

Widows, Society of Military (1968), 5535 Hemstead Way, Springfield, VA 22151; 2,000.

Wilderness Society (1935), 900 17th St. NW, Wash., DC 20006; 300,000.

Wildflower Research Center, Natl. (1982), 2600 FM 973 N., Austin, TX 78725-4201; 16,000.

Wildlife, Defenders of (1947), 1244 19th St. NW, Wash., DC 20036; 80,000.

Wildlife Federation, Natl. (1936), 1400 16th St. NW, Wash., DC 20036-2266; 4.7 mil.

Wildlife Fund, World (1961), 1250 24th St. NW, Wash., DC 20037; 1.25 mil.

Wildlife Management Institute (1911), 1101 14th St. NW, Ste. 801, Wash., DC 20005.

William Penn Assn. (1886), 709 Brighton Rd., Pittsburgh, PA 15233; 90,000.

Wireless Pioneers, Society of (1968), PO Box 86, Geyserville, CA 95441; 3,500.

Wizard of Oz Club, Intl. (1957), Box 95, Kinderhook, IL 62345; 3,000.

Women, Natl. Assn. of Bank (1920), 500 N. Michigan Ave., Ste. 1400, Chicago, IL 60611; 30,000.

Women, Natl. Organization for (NOW) (1966), 1000 16th St. NW, Ste. 700, Wash., DC 20036; 250,000.

Women Artists, Natl. Assn. of (1889), 41 Union Sq., N.Y., NY 10003; 800.

Women Engineers, Society of (1950), 120 Wall St., 11th Fl., N.Y., NY 10005; 16,000.

Women for America, Concerned (1979), 370 L'Enfant Promenade SW, #800, Wash., DC 20024; 600,000.

Women in Communications (1908), 2101 Wilson Blvd., Ste. 417, Arlington, VA 22201; 11,000.

Women in Radio and TV, Inc. (1950), 1650 Tyson's Blvd., Ste. 200, McLean, VA 22102; 1,729.

Women Intl., Financial (1921), 500 N. Michigan Ave., Ste. 1400, Chicago, IL 60611; 35,000.

Women Strike for Peace (1961), 110 Maryland Ave. NE, Ste. 302, Wash., DC 20002; 10,000.

Women of the U.S., Inc., Natl. Council of (1888), 777 UN Plaza, N.Y., NY 10017; 7 mil.

Women Voters of the U.S., League of (1920), 1730 M St. NW, Wash., DC 20036; 120,000.

Women World War Veterans (1919), 237 Madison Ave., N.Y., NY 10016; 35,000.

Women's Army Corps Veterans Assn. (1947), Hwy. 21, Anniston, AL 36206; 3,500.

Women's Association, American Business (1949), 9100 Ward Pkwy., PO Box 8728, Kansas City, MO 64114; 90,000+.

Women's Christian Temperance Union, Natl. (1874), 1730 Chicago Ave., Evanston, IL 60201; 40,000.

Women's Clubs, General Federation of (1890), 1734 N St. NW, Wash., DC, 20036-2990; 300,000 U.S.

Women's Clubs, Natl. Federation of Business & Professional (1919), 2012 Massachusetts Ave. NW, Wash., DC 20036.

Women's Intl. League for Peace & Freedom (1915), 1213 Race St., Philadelphia, PA 19107; 50,000.

Women's Legal Defense Fund (1971), 1875 Connecticut Ave. NW, Ste. 710, Wash., DC 20009; 2,500.

Women's Overseas Service League (1921), PO Box 39058, Friendship Station, Wash., DC 20016; 1,164.

Woodmen of America, Modern (1883), 1701 1st Ave., Rock Island, IL 61201; 730,000.

Woodmen of the World Life Insurance Soc. (1890), 1700 Farnam St., Omaha, NE 68102; 980,000.

Workmen's Circle (1900), 45 E. 33d St., N.Y., NY 10016.

World Federalist Assn. (1975), 418 7th St. SE, Wash., DC 20003; 9,000.

World Future Society (1966), 7910 Woodmont Ave., Ste. 450, Bethesda, MD 20814; 30,000.

World Learning Inc. (1932), Kipling Rd., PO Box 676, Brattleboro, VT 05302-0676; 60,000.

World Peace, Intl Assn. of Educators for (1969), PO Box 3282, Mastin Lake Sta., Huntsville, AL 35810-0282; 22,000.

World's Fair Collectors Soc. (1968), PO Box 20806, Sarasota, FL 34276-3806; 500.

Writers Guild of America, West (1933), 8955 Beverly Blvd., W. Hollywood, CA 90048; 7,500+.

Yachting Assn., Southern California (1921), 1086 Peninsula St., Ventura, CA 93001; 20,000 families.

Young America's Foundation (1971), 110 Elden St., Herndon, VA 22070.

Young Men's Christian Assns. of the U.S.A. (1851), 101 N. Wacker Dr., Chicago, IL 60606; 13 mil.

YM-YWHAs of Greater New York, Associated (1957), 130 E. 59th St., N.Y., NY 10020; 55,100.

Young Women's Christian Assn. of the U.S.A. (1906), 726 Broadway, N.Y., NY 10003; 1.6 mil.

Youth Hostels, American (1934), 733 15th Street NW, Ste. 840, Wash., DC 20005; 137,000.

Zero Population Growth (1968), 1400 16th St. NW, Ste. 320, Wash., DC 20036; 50,000.

Zionist Organization of America (1897), 4 E. 34th St., N.Y., NY 10016; 110,000.

Zoo and Aquarium Assn., American (1924), 7970-D Old Georgetown Rd., Bethesda, MD 20814-2493; 6,300.

Zoologists, Amer. Society of (1902), 401 N. Michigan Ave., Chicago, IL 60611; 4,000.

POSTAL INFORMATION

U.S. Postal Service

The Postal Reorganization Act, creating a government-owned postal service under the executive branch and replacing the old Post Office Department, was signed into law by President Richard Nixon on Aug. 12, 1970. The service officially came into being on July 1, 1971.

The U.S. Postal Service is governed by an 11-person Board of Governors. Nine members are appointed to 9-year terms by the president with Senate approval. These 9, in turn, choose a postmaster general. The board and the postmaster general choose the 11th member, who serves as deputy postmaster general. An independent Postal Rate Commission of 5 members, appointed by the president, reviews and rules on proposed postal rate increases submitted by the Board of Governors. As of Sept. 30, 1993, there were 28,591 post offices throughout the U.S.

U.S. Domestic Rates

Postal rates and fees shown below were implemented on Feb. 3, 1991. Domestic rates apply to the U.S., its territories and possessions, and APOs and FPOs. On Mar. 7, 1994, the U.S. Postal Board of Governors approved a proposal from the U.S. Postal Service to increase postal rates. The proposal then went to the Postal Rate Commission, which had 10 months to rule on the increase.

First Class

Letters written, and matter sealed against inspection, 29¢ for 1st oz. or fraction, 23¢ for each additional oz. or fraction.

U.S. Postal Service cards, single 19¢, double 38¢; private postcards, same.

First class includes written matter, namely letters, postal cards, postcards (private mailing cards) and all other matter wholly or partly in writing, whether sealed or unsealed, except manuscripts for books, periodical articles and music, manuscript copy accompanying proofsheets or corrected proofsheets of the same and the writing authorized by law on matter of other classes. Also matter sealed or closed against inspection, bills and statements of accounts.

Express Mail

Express Mail Service is available for any mailable article up to 70 pounds, and guarantees delivery between major U.S. cities or your money back. Articles received by the acceptance time authorized by the postmaster at a postal facility offering Express Mail will be delivered by 3 p.m. the next day to some locations or will be delivered by noon the next day to other destinations. Or, if you prefer, your shipment can be picked up as early as 10 a.m. the next business day. Second day service is available to locations not on the Next Day Delivery Network. Rates include insurance, Shipment Receipt, and Record of Delivery at the destination post office.

Consult Postmaster for other Express Mail Services and rates. (The Postal Service will refund, upon application to originating office, the postage for any Express Mail shipments not meeting the service standard except for those delayed by strike or work stoppage, delay or cancellation of flights, or governmental action beyond the control of the Postal Service.)

Third Class

Third class (limit up to but not including 16 ounces): Mailable matter not in 1st and 2d classes.

Single mailing: Publications, small parcels, printed matter, booklets and catalogs, 29¢ the first ounce, 52¢ for over 1 to 2 ozs., 75¢ for over 2 to 3 ozs., 98¢ for over 3 to 4 ozs., $1.21 for over 4 to 6 ozs., $1.33 for over 6 to 8 ozs., $1.44 for over 8 to 10 ozs., $1.56 for over 10 to 12 ozs., $1.67 for over 12 to 14 ozs., $1.79 for over 14 but less than 16 ozs.

Bulk mailing: At least 200 pieces or 50 pounds of such items as solicitations, newsletters, advertising materials, books and cassettes, each item of which individually weighs less than 1 pound. Minimum rate per piece: Basic presort, $0.198 for pieces weighing 3.3067 ounces or less; for pieces weighing more than 3.3067 ounces, the rate is $0.109 per piece + $0.600 per pound. Contact your post office for the discounts offered for presorted, destination entry and automation compatible mail.

Separate rates for some nonprofit organizations. Bulk mailing fee, $75 per calendar year. Apply to postmaster for permit. One-time fee for permit imprint, $75.

Parcel Post—Fourth Class

Fourth class or parcel post (16 ounces and over): Merchandise, printed matter, etc., may be sealed, subject to inspection.

Priority Mail Flat Rate

First class mail of more than 11 ounces can be sent "Priority Mail" service. The most expeditious handling and transportation available will be used for fastest delivery.

The pickup service for Priority Mail costs $4.50 for each stop by the Postal Service. There is also a $2.90 flat Priority Mail rate for matter sent in the Special Postal Service-provided envelope.

Forwarding Addresses

The mailer, in order to obtain a forwarding address, must endorse the envelope or cover "Address Correction Requested." The destination post office then will determine whether a forwarding address has been left on file and provide it for a fee of 35¢ per manual correction and 20¢ per automated correction.

Priority Mail

Packages weighing up to 70 pounds and not exceeding 108 inches in length and girth combined, including written and other material of the first class, whether sealed or unsealed, fractions of a pound being charged as a full pound.

Rates according to zone apply between the U.S. and Puerto Rico and Virgin Islands. The mileage between the specific geographic locations of 3-digit ZIP codes determines the zone number to be used. The mileage range represented by the zone number is: Zone 1—up to 50 miles; 2—51 to 150 miles; 3—151 to 300 miles; 4—301 to 600 miles; 5—601 to 1,000 miles; 6—1,001 to 1,400 miles; 7—1,401 to 1,800 miles; 8—over 1,800 miles.

Parcels weighing less than 15 pounds, measuring over 84 inches but not exceeding 108 inches in length and girth combined are chargeable with a minimum rate equal to that for a 15 pound parcel for the zone to which addressed.

Zones	To 2 lbs	3 lbs	4 lbs	5 lbs*
1, 2, 3, 4, 5, 6, 7, 8	$2.90	$4.10	$4.65	$5.45

*Consult postmaster for rates for parcels over 5 lbs.

Special Handling

Third and fourth class parcels will be handled and delivered as expeditiously as practicable (but not special delivery) upon payment, in addition to the regular postage: up to 10 lbs., $1.80; over 10 lbs., $2.50. Such parcels must be endorsed, Special Handling.

Special Delivery

First class mail up to 2 lbs., $7.65; over 2 lbs. and up to 10 lbs., $7.95; over 10 lbs., $8.55. All other classes up to 2 lbs., $8.05; over 2 and up to 10 lbs., $8.65; over 10 lbs., $9.30.

Bound Printed Matter Rates

(Single Piece Zone Rate)

Fourth-Class Mail: Single-Piece Bound Printed Matter Rate

Weight		Zones						
lbs.	Local	1&2	3	4	5	6	7	8
1.5	$0.93	$1.27	$1.30	$1.36	$1.45	$1.54	$1.65	$1.75
2	0.94	1.30	1.34	1.42	1.53	1.66	1.81	1.93
2.5	0.96	1.33	1.38	1.48	1.62	1.78	1.97	2.12
3	0.98	1.35	1.42	1.54	1.71	1.90	2.12	2.31
3.5	0.99	1.38	1.46	1.60	1.80	2.02	2.28	2.50
4	1.01	1.41	1.50	1.66	1.89	2.14	2.44	2.69
4.5	1.02	1.44	1.54	1.72	1.98	2.26	2.59	2.88
5	1.04	1.47	1.58	1.78	2.07	2.38	2.75	3.07
6	1.07	1.53	1.66	1.89	2.24	2.61	3.06	3.44
7	1.10	1.59	1.74	2.01	2.42	2.85	3.38	3.82
8	1.14	1.64	1.82	2.13	2.60	3.09	3.69	4.20
9	1.17	1.70	1.90	2.25	2.77	3.33	4.01	4.57
10	1.20	1.76	1.98	2.37	2.95	3.57	4.32	4.95

(Includes both catalogs and similar bound printed matter.)

(Bound printed matter must weigh at least 1 pound and not more than 10 pounds. Bound printed matter includes catalogs, directories and books not eligible for special fourth-class rates.)

Domestic Mail Special Services

Registry — Only matter prepaid with postage at First-class postage rates may be registered. Stamps or meter stamps must be attached. The face of the article must be at least 5″ long, 3½″ high. The mailer is required to declare the value of mail presented for registration.

Registered Mail

Value	Insured	Uninsured
$0.00 to $100	$4.50	$4.40
$100.01 to $500	4.85	4.70
$500.01 to $1,000	5.25	5.05
$1,000.01 to $2,000	5.70	5.40
$2,000.01 to $3,000	6.15	5.75
$3,000.01 to $4,000	6.60	6.10
$4,000.01 to $5,000	7.05	6.45
$5,000.01 to $6,000	7.50	6.80
$6,000.01 to $7,000	7.95	7.15
$7,000.01 to $8,000	8.40	7.50
$8,000.01 to $9,000	8.85	7.85
$9,000.01 to $10,000	9.30	8.20

Consult postmaster for registry rates above $10,000.

C.O.D.: Unregistered — is applicable to first-, third-, fourth-class, and express mail matter. Such mail must be based on bona fide orders or be in conformity with agreements between senders and addressees. **Registered** — for details consult postmaster.

Insurance — is applicable to third and fourth class matter. Matter for sale addressed to prospective purchasers who have not ordered it or authorized its sending will not be insured.

Insured Mail

$0.01 to $50	$0.75
50.01 to $100	1.60
100.01 to $150	2.40
150.01 to $200	2.40
200.01 to $300	3.50
300.01 to $400	4.60
400.01 to $500	5.40
500.01 to $600	6.20

Liability for insured mail is limited to $600.

Certified mail — service is available for any matter having no intrinsic value on which 1st class or air mail postage is paid. Receipt is furnished at time of mailing and evidence of delivery obtained. The fee is $1.00 in addition to postage. Return receipt, restricted delivery, and special delivery are available upon payment of additional fees. No indemnity.

Special Fourth Class Rate

(limit 70 lbs.)

First pound or fraction, $1.05 (59¢ if 500 pieces or more of special rate matter are presorted to 5 digit ZIP code or 88¢ if 500 pieces or more are presorted to Bulk Mail Cntrs.); each additional pound or fraction through 7 pounds, 43¢; each additional pound, 25¢. Only the following specific articles: Books of at least 8 printed pages consisting wholly of reading matter or scholarly bibliography, or reading matter with incidental blank spaces for notations and containing no advertising matter other than incidental announcements of books; 16-millimeter or narrower width films in final form and catalogs of such films of 24 pages or more (at least 22 of which are printed) except films and film catalogs sent to or from commercial theaters; printed music in bound or sheet form; printed objective test materials; sound recordings, playscripts and manuscripts for books, periodicals, and music; printed educational reference charts; loose-leaf pages and binders thereof consisting of medical information for distribution to doctors, hospitals, medical schools, and medical students; computer-readable media containing prerecorded information and guides for use with such media. Package must be marked "Special 4th Class Rate" stating item contained.

Library Rate (limit 70 lbs.)

First pound 65¢, each additional pound through 7 pounds, 24¢; each additional pound, 12¢. Books when loaned or exchanged between and sent to or from schools, colleges, public libraries, and certain non-profit organizations; books, printed music, bound academic theses, periodicals, sound recordings, other library materials, museum materials (specimens, collections), scientific or mathematical kits, instruments or other devices; also catalogs, guides or scripts for some of these materials. Must be marked "Library Rate".

Also qualifying for library rate are: Books mailed from publishers or distributors to schools, libraries, colleges or universities or to bookstores owned, operated and controlled by schools, colleges or universities.

Parcel Post Rate Schedule

(Inter BMC/ASF Zip Codes Only, Machinable Parcels, No Discount, No Surcharge)

Weight up to but not exceeding—(pounds)	Zones 1 and 2	3	4	5	6	7	8
2	$2.19	$2.32	$2.46	$2.74	$2.85	$2.85	$2.85
3	2.29	2.49	2.70	3.12	3.54	4.00	4.05
4	2.39	2.65	2.94	3.50	4.06	4.35	4.60
5	2.49	2.81	3.17	3.88	4.58	5.20	5.40
6	2.59	2.98	3.41	4.26	5.10	6.33	8.55
7	2.68	3.14	3.65	4.64	5.62	7.06	9.60
8	2.78	3.31	3.89	5.02	6.14	7.78	10.65
9	2.88	3.47	4.12	5.40	6.67	8.51	11.70
10	2.98	3.63	4.36	5.78	7.19	9.24	12.75
11	3.08	3.80	4.60	6.16	7.71	9.97	13.75

Weight up to but not exceeding—(pounds)	Zones 1 and 2	3	4	5	6	7	8
12	3.18	3.96	4.83	6.54	8.23	10.69	14.80
13	3.25	4.08	4.99	6.79	8.57	11.17	15.85
14	3.32	4.19	5.16	7.04	8.92	11.65	16.90
15	3.38	4.28	5.27	7.23	9.17	11.99	17.95
16	3.43	4.36	5.39	7.40	9.40	12.31	19.00
17	3.48	4.44	5.49	7.56	9.62	12.61	19.91
18	3.53	4.51	5.60	7.72	9.83	12.90	20.38
19	3.58	4.59	5.69	7.87	10.03	13.17	20.83
20	3.63	4.65	5.79	8.01	10.22	13.43	21.26
21	3.68	4.72	5.88	8.15	10.40	13.68	21.66
22	3.72	4.79	5.97	8.28	10.57	13.91	22.05
23	3.77	4.85	6.05	8.40	10.74	14.14	22.43
24	3.81	4.91	6.13	8.52	10.90	14.36	22.78
25	3.85	4.97	6.21	8.64	11.05	14.57	23.13

Postal Union Mail Special Services

Registration — available to practically all countries. Fee $4.40. The maximum indemnity payable — generally only in case of complete loss (of both contents and wrapper) — is $32.35. To Canada only the fee is $4.50 providing indemnity for loss up to $100, $4.85 for loss up to $500, and $5.25 for loss up to $1,000.

Return receipt — showing to whom and date delivered, $1.00.

Special delivery — Available to most countries. Consult post office. Fees for International Special Delivery same for air or surface: for letters, letter packages and postcards not over 2 pounds, $7.65. If over 2 pounds, $7.95, for printed matter, matter for the blind, or small packets, $8.05 if not over 2 pounds; if over 2 pounds, $8.65.

Marking — an article intended for special delivery service must have affixed to the cover near the name of the country of destination "EXPRES" (special delivery) label, obtainable at the post office, or it may be marked on the cover boldly in red "EXPRES" (special delivery).

Special handling — entitles AO surface packages to priority handling between mailing point and U.S. point of dispatch. Fees: $1.80 for packages to 10 pounds, and $2.50 for packages over 10 pounds.

Airmail — there is daily air service to practically all countries.

Prepayment of replies from other countries — a mailer who wishes to prepay a reply by letter from another country may do so by sending his correspondent one or more international reply coupons, which may be purchased at United States post offices. One coupon should be accepted in any country in exchange for stamps to prepay an air mail letter of the first unit of weight to the U.S.

Additional international special services: Insurance: Available to many countries for loss of or damage to items paid at parcel post rate. Consult postmaster for indemnity limits for individual countries.

Limit of Indemnity Not Over	Fees Canada	All Other Countries
$50	$0.75	$1.60
100	1.60	2.40
200	2.40	3.50
300	3.50	4.60
400	4.60	5.40
500	5.40	6.20
600	6.20	6.60
700		6.90
800		7.20
900		7.50
1,000		7.80
1,100		8.10
1,200		8.40

Restricted Delivery: Available to many countries for registered mail, limits who may receive an item. Fee: $2.50.

Post Office-Authorized 2-Letter State Abbreviations

The abbreviations below are approved by the U.S. Postal Service for use in addresses. The official list follows, including the District of Columbia, Guam, Puerto Rico, the Canal Zone, and the Virgin Islands (all capital letters are used):

Alabama	AL	Hawaii	HI	Missouri	MO	Puerto Rico	PR
Alaska	AK	Idaho	ID	Montana	MT	Rhode Island	RI
American Samoa	AS	Illinois	IL	Nebraska	NE	South Carolina	SC
Arizona	AZ	Indiana	IN	Nevada	NV	South Dakota	SD
Arkansas	AR	Iowa	IA	New Hampshire	NH	Tennessee	TN
California	CA	Kansas	KS	New Jersey	NJ	Texas	TX
Colorado	CO	Kentucky	KY	New Mexico	NM	Utah	UT
Connecticut	CT	Louisiana	LA	New York	NY	Vermont	VT
Delaware	DE	Maine	ME	North Carolina	NC	Virginia	VA
Dist. of Col.	DC	Marshall Islands[1]	MH	North Dakota	ND	Virgin Islands	VI
Federated States of Micronesia[1]	FM	Maryland	MD	Northern Mariana Is.	MP	Washington	WA
Florida	FL	Massachusetts	MA	Ohio	OH	West Virginia	WV
Georgia	GA	Michigan	MI	Oklahoma	OK	Wisconsin	WI
Guam	GU	Minnesota	MN	Oregon	OR	Wyoming	WY
		Mississippi	MS	Pennsylvania	PA		

(1) Although an independent nation, this country is currently subject to domestic rates and fees.

Canadian Province and Territory Postal Codes

Alberta	AL	Northwest Territories	NT
British Columbia	BC	Ontario	ON
Manitoba	MB	Prince Edward Island	PE
New Brunswick	NB	Quebec	PQ
Newfoundland	NF	Saskatchewan	SK
Nova Scotia	NS	Yukon Territory	YT

International Air Mail

Aerogrammes — 45¢ each to all countries.
Air mail postcards (single) — 40¢ to all countries except Canada and Mexico (30¢ each)
International letters and letter packages: airmail to Canada and Mexico (there are no surface rates to these countries)—weight not over 0.5 ozs., 40¢ to Canada, 35¢ to Mexico; not over 1.0 ozs., 40¢ to Canada, 45¢ to Mexico; not over 2 ozs., 63¢ to Canada, 65¢ to Mexico; not over 3 ozs., 86¢ to Canada, 90¢ to Mexico.

Air Mail, Letter and Letter Package Rates, Countries Other Than Canada and Mexico

Weight not over	Rate	Weight not over	Rate	Weight not over	Rate	Weight not over	Rate
0.5 ozs.	$ 0.50	12.5 ozs.	$ 9.92	24.5 ozs.	$19.28	41 ozs.	$28.64
1.0	0.95	13.0	10.31	25.0	19.67	42	29.03
1.5	1.34	13.5	10.70	25.5	20.06	43	29.42
2.0	1.73	14.0	11.09	26.0	20.45	44	29.81
2.5	2.12	14.5	11.48	26.5	20.84	45	30.20
3.0	2.51	15.0	11.87	27.0	21.23	46	30.59
3.5	2.90	15.5	12.26	27.5	21.62	47	30.98
4.0	3.29	16.0	12.65	28.0	22.01	48	31.37
4.5	3.68	16.5	13.04	28.5	22.40	49	31.76
5.0	4.07	17.0	13.43	29.0	22.79	50	32.15
5.5	4.46	17.5	13.82	29.5	23.18	51	32.54
6.0	4.85	18.0	14.21	30.0	23.57	52	32.93
6.5	5.24	18.5	14.60	30.5	23.96	53	33.32
7.0	5.63	19.0	14.99	31.0	24.35	54	33.71
7.5	6.02	19.5	15.38	31.5	24.74	55	34.10
8.0	6.41	20.0	15.77	32.0	25.13	56	34.49
8.5	6.80	20.5	16.16	33	25.52	57	34.88
9.0	7.19	21.0	16.55	34	25.91	58	35.27
9.5	7.58	21.5	16.94	35	26.30	59	35.66
10.0	7.97	22.0	17.33	36	26.69	60	36.05
10.5	8.36	22.5	17.72	37	27.08	61	36.44
11.0	8.75	23.0	18.11	38	27.47	62	36.83
11.5	9.14	23.5	18.50	39	27.86	63	37.22
12.0	9.53	24.0	18.89	40	28.25	64	37.61

Weight limit: 64 oz. (4 lbs.)

Air Mail, Parcel Post Rates

Weight steps	Air Parcel Post Rate Groups A	B	C	D	E
First pound	$6.00	$7.75	$9.25	$10.70	$12.30
Each additional pound or fraction up to 5 pounds	3.00	4.25	5.00	6.00	7.00
Each additional pound or fraction over 5 pounds	2.00	3.00	4.00	5.00	6.00

Air Parcel Post Rate Groups (For further information, consult your local post office.)

Country	Rate group	Maximum weight limit
Afghanistan	D	44
Albania	C	44
Algeria	D	44
Andorra	B	44
Angola	E	22
Anguilla	A	22
Antigua & Barbuda	A	22
Argentina	D	44
Armenia	E	22
Aruba	A	44
Ascension	No Air Service	
Australia	D	44
Austria	B	44
Azerbaijan	E	22
Azores	C	44
Bahamas	A	22
Bahrain	D	22
Bangladesh	E	22
Barbados	B	44
Belarus	E	22
Belgium	D	44
Belize	A	44
Benin	C	44
Bermuda	A	44
Bhutan	E	44
Bolivia	B	44
Bosnia and Herzegovina	C	33
Botswana	E	22
Brazil	E	44
British Virgin Islands	A	44
Brunei	D	22
Bulgaria	D	44
Burkina Faso	D	44
Burma	See Myanmar	
Burundi	E	44
Cambodia	No Parcel Post Service	
Cameroon	D	44
Canada	Separate Rate Group	66
Cape Verde	D	22
Cayman Islands	A	44
Central African Rep.	E	44
Chad	D	44
Chile	D	44
China (People's Republic of)	D	44
Colombia	B	44
Comoros	E	44
Congo	D	44
Corsica	E	44
Costa Rica	A	44
Côte d'Ivoire	D	44
Croatia	C	44
Cuba	No Parcel Post Service	
Cyprus	C	44
Czech Republic	C	33
Denmark	C	66
Djibouti	D	44
Dominica	A	22
Dominican Rep.	A	44
East Timor	No Parcel Post Service	
Ecuador	C	44
Egypt	D	44
El Salvador	B	44
Equatorial Guinea	D	44
Eritrea	D	44

Country	Rate group	Maximum weight limit
Estonia	E	22
Ethiopia	D	44
Faeroe Islands	C	44
Falkland Islands	D	44
Fiji	B	44
Finland	D	44
France	E	44
French Guiana	C	44
French Polynesia	D	44
Gabon	D	44
Gambia	B	22
Georgia, Republic of	E	22
Germany	C	44
Ghana	D	22
Gibraltar	C	44
Great Britain and Northern Ireland	C	50
Greece	C	44
Greenland	D	44
Grenada	A	44
Guadeloupe	A	44
Guatemala	A	44
Guinea	B	44
Guinea-Bissau	B	22
Guyana	B	44
Haiti	A	44
Honduras	B	44
Hong Kong	C	44
Hungary	C	44
Iceland	C	44
India	D	44
Indonesia	E	44
Iran	D	44
Iraq	D	44
Ireland (Eire)	C	50
Israel	C	33
Italy (incl. San Marino)	C	44
Ivory Coast	See Côte d'Ivoire	
Jamaica	A	22
Japan	E	44
Jordan	C	44
Kazakhstan	E	22
Kenya	D	44
Kiribati	B	44
Korea, Democratic People's Rep. of (North)	No Parcel Post Service	
Korea, Republic of (South)	C	44
Kuwait	C	44
Kyrgyzstan	E	22
Laos	E	44
Latvia	E	44
Lebanon	C	11
Lesotho	E	44
Liberia	C	22
Libya	D	44
Liechtenstein	B	44
Lithuania	E	22
Luxembourg	B	44
Macao	C	44
Macedonia	C	33
Madagascar	E	44
Madeira Islands	B	44
Malawi	D	22
Malaysia	D	22
Maldives	D	22
Mali	C	44
Malta	C	22
Martinique	A	44
Mauritania	D	44
Mauritius	E	22
Mexico	A	44
Moldova	E	22
Monaco	E	44
Mongolia	No Parcel Post Service	
Montserrat	A	44
Morocco	C	44
Mozambique	E	22
Myanmar	D	22
Namibia	D	44
Nauru	C	44
Nepal	D	44
Netherlands	C	44
Netherlands Antilles	A	44
New Caledonia	D	44
New Zealand	D	44
Nicaragua	B	44
Niger	D	44
Nigeria	C	22
Norway	D	44
Oman	D	22
Pakistan	D	22
Panama	A	44
Papua New Guinea	D	44
Paraguay	D	44
Peru	B	44
Philippines	D	44
Pitcairn Islands	B	22
Poland	B	33
Portugal	C	22
Qatar	C	44
Reunion	E	44
Romania	C	44
Russia	E	22
Rwanda	D	44
Saint Helena	C	44
Saint Kitts & Nevis	A	44
Saint Lucia	A	44
Saint Pierre & Miguelon	A	44
Saint Vincent & the Grenadines	A	22
San Marino	C	44
Sao Tome & Principe	D	44
Saudi Arabia	D	22
Senegal	D	44
Seychelles	D	22
Sierre Leone	D	44
Singapore	D	44
Slovakia	E	22
Slovenia	C	44
Solomon Islands	C	44
Somalia	D	44
South Africa	D	44
Spain	C	44
Sri Lanka	D	44
Sudan	D	44
Suriname	B	44
Swaziland	D	44
Sweden	D	44
Switzerland	B	44
Syria	C	44
Taiwan	C	44
Tajikistan	E	22
Tanzania	E	22
Thailand	D	44
Togo	D	44
Tonga	B	22
Trinidad & Tobago	B	22
Tristan da Cunha	E	22
Tunisia	C	44
Turkey	C	44
Turkmenistan	E	22
Turks and Caicos Islands	A	22
Tuvalu	B	44
Uganda	D	22
Ukraine	E	22
United Arab Emirates	D	44
Uruguay	B	44
Uzbekistan	E	22
Vanuatu	B	44
Vatican City State	C	44
Venezuela	B	44
Vietnam	E	44
Wallis & Futuna Islands	D	44
Western Samoa	B	22
Yemen	E	44
Yugoslavia	C	33
Zaire	E	33
Zambia	E	44
Zimbabwe	E	44

International Post Cards, Surface Rates

Canada and Mexico: 30¢. All other countries: 35¢. Maximum size permitted, 6 × 4¼ inches; minimum size, 5½ × 3½ inches.

LANGUAGE

New Words in English

Source: Words and definitions from Merriam-Webster Inc., publisher of *Merriam-Webster's Collegiate Dictionary, Tenth Edition*

biodiversity biological diversity in an environment as indicated by numbers of different species of plants and animals.

buppie a college-educated black adult who is employed in a well-paying profession and who lives or works in or near a large city.

channeler a person who conveys thoughts or energy from a source believed to be outside the person's body or conscious mind; *specifically*: one who speaks for nonphysical beings or spirits.

codependency a psychological condition or a relationship in which a person is controlled or manipulated by another who is affected with a pathological condition (as an addiction to alcohol or heroin).

desktop publishing the production of printed matter by means of a desktop computer having a layout program that integrates text and graphics.

DNA fingerprinting a method of identification (as for forensic purposes) by determining the sequence of base pairs in the DNA especially of a person.

hypertext a database format in which information related to that on display can be accessed directly from the display.

intrapreneur a corporate executive who develops new enterprises within the corporation.

karaoke a device that plays instrumental accompaniments for a selection of songs to which the user sings along and that records the user's singing with the music.

letterboxed *of a video recording* formatted so as to display the full rectangular frame of a wide-screen motion picture.

liposuction surgical removal of local fat deposits (as in the thighs) especially for cosmetic purposes.

mommy track a career path that allows a mother flexible or reduced work hours but tends to slow or block advancement.

politically correct conforming to a belief that language and practices that could offend political sensibilities (as in matters of sex or race) should be eliminated.

smart card a card that functions as a credit or a debit card but also has a built-in microprocessor to store and process data and records (as of bank transactions)

spin doctor a person (as a political aide) responsible for ensuring that others interpret an event from a particular point of view.

stressed-out suffering from high levels of physical or especially psychological stress.

surimi a fish product made from inexpensive whitefish (as pollack) and often processed to resemble more expensive seafood (as crab meat or scallops).

telecommute to work at home by the use of an electronic linkup with a central office.

tiramisu a dessert made with ladyfingers, mascarpone, chocolate, and espresso.

vaporware a new computer-related product that has been widely advertised but is not yet available.

virtual reality an artificial environment that is experienced through sensory stimuli (as sights and sounds) provided by a computer and in which one's actions partially determine what happens in the environment.

wanna-be a person who wants or aspires to be someone or something else or who tries to look or act like someone else.

Eponyms

(words named for people)

Bloody Mary—a vodka and tomato juice drink; after the nickname of Mary I, Queen of England (1553-58), notorious for her persecution of Protestants.

bloomers—full, loose trousers gathered at the knee; after Amelia Bloomer, an American social reformer who advocated (1851) such clothing.

bobbies—in Great Britain, police officers; after Sir Robert Peel, the statesman who organized the London police force, 1850.

bowdlerize—to delete written matter considered indelicate; after Thomas Bowdler, English editor of an expurgated Shakespeare (1825).

boycott—to combine against in a policy of nonintercourse for economic or political reasons; after Charles C. Boycott, an English land agent in County Mayo, Ireland, ostracized in 1880 for refusing to reduce rents.

Braille—a system of writing for the blind; after Louis Braille, the French teacher of the blind who invented it (1853).

Casanova—a man who is a promiscuous and unscrupulous lover; after Giovanni Giacomo Casanova (1725-98), an Italian adventurer.

chauvinist—excessively patriotic; after Nicolas Chauvin, a character devoted to Napoleon in a 19th-cent. play.

derby—a stiff felt hat with a dome-shaped crown and rather narrow rolled brim; after Edward Stanley, 12th earl of Derby, who in 1780 founded the Derby horse race at Epsom Downs, England, to which these hats are worn.

diesel—a type of internal combustion engine or a vehicle driven by such an engine; after Rudolf Diesel (1858-1913), who built the first successful diesel engine.

gerrymander—to draw an election district in such a way as to favor a political party; after Elbridge Gerry, who created (1812) just such an election district (shaped like a salamander) during his governorship of MA.

guillotine—a machine for beheading; after Joseph Guillotin, a French physician who proposed its use in 1789 as more humane than hanging.

leotard—a close-fitting garment for the torso, worn by dancers, acrobats, and the like; after Julius Leotard, a 19th-century French aerial gymnast.

sandwich—2 or more slices of bread having a filling in between; after John Montagu, 4th earl of Sandwich (1718-92), who supposedly ate food in this form so that he would not have to leave the gaming table.

silhouette—an outline image; from Étienne de Silhouette (1709-67), a close-fisted French finance minister.

Foreign Words and Phrases

(L=Latin; F=French; Y=Yiddish; R=Russian; G=Greek; I=Italian; S=Spanish)

ad hoc (L; ad HOK): for the particular end or purpose at hand

ad infinitum (L; ad in-fi-NITE-um): endless

ad nauseam (L; ad NAWZ-ee-um): to a sickening degree

apropos (L; ap-ruh-POH): being relevant

bête noire (F; BET NWAHR): a thing or person viewed with particular dislike

bon appetit (F; BOH nap-uh-teet): good appetite

bona fide (L; BOH nuh-feyed): genuine

carte blanche (F; kahrt BLANNSH): full discretionary power

cause célèbre (F; kawz suh-LEB-ruh): a notorious incident

c'est la vie (F; se lah VEE): that's life

chutzpah (Y; KHOOT-spuh): amazing nerve bordering on arrogance

coup de grâce (F; kooh duh GRAHS): the final blow

coup d'état (F; kooh duh tah): forceful overthrow of a government

crème de la crème (F; KREM duh luh KREM): the best of the best

cum laude/magna cum laude/summa cum laude (L; KUHM loud-ay; MAHN-ya...; SOO-ma...): with praise or honor; with great praise or honor; with the highest praise or honor

de facto (L; di FAK-toh): in fact; generally agreed to without a formal decision

déjà vu (F; DAY-zhah VOOH): the sensation that something happening has happened before

de jure (L; dee JOOR-ee, day YOOR-ay): determined by law, as opposed to de facto

de rigueur (F; duh ree-GUR): necessary according to convention

détente (F; day-TAHNT): an easing or relaxation of strained relations

éminence grise (F; ay-meh-NAHNN-suh GREEZ): one who wields power behind the scenes

enfant terrible (F; ahnn-FAHNN te-REE-bluh): one whose unconventional behavior causes embarrassment

en masse (F; ahn MAHS): in a large body

ergo (L; ER-goh): therefore

esprit de corps (F; es-PREE duh KAWR): group spirit; feeling of camaraderie

eureka (G; YOOR-EE-kuh): I have found it

ex post facto (L; eks pohst FAK-toh): an explanation or regulation concocted after the event

fait accompli (F; fayt uh-kom-PLEE): an accomplished fact

faux pas (F; fowe PAH): a social blunder

hoi polloi (G; hoy puh-LOY): the masses

in loco parentis (L; in LOH-koh puh-REN-tis): in place of a parent

in memoriam (L; in muh-MAWR-ee-uhm): in memory of

in situ (L; in SEYE-tyooh): in the original arrangement

in toto (L; in TOH-toh): totally

je ne sais quoi (F; zhuh nuh say KWAH): I don't know what; the little something that eludes description

joie de vivre (F; zhwah duh VEEV-ruh): joy of living, love of life

mea culpa (L; MAY-uh CUL-puh): my fault

modus operandi (L; MOH-duhs op-uh-RAN-dee): method of operation

noblesse oblige (F; noh-BLES uh-BLEEZH): the obligation of nobility to help the less fortunate

non compos mentis (L; non KOM-puhs MEN-tis): out of control of the mind; insane

nouveau riche (F; nooh-voh REESH); pejorative for recent rich who spend money conspicuously

perestroika (R; PAIR-es TROY-kuh): restructuring

persona non grata (L; per-SOH-nah non GRAH-tah): unacceptable person

post-mortem (L; pohst-MORE-tuhm): after death; autopsy; analysis after event

prima donna (I; pree-muh DAH-nuh): temperamental person

pro tempore (L; proh TEM-puh-ree): for the time being

que sera sera (S; keh sair-ah sair-AH): what will be, will be

quid pro quo (L; kwid proh KWOH): something given or received for something else

raison d'être (F; RAY-zohnn DET-ruh): reason for being

savoir-faire (F; sav-wahr-FAIR): dexterity in social and practical affairs

semper fidelis (L; SEM-puhr fee-DAY-lis): always faithful

shlemiel (Y; shleh-MEEL): an unlucky bungling person

status quo (L; STAY-tus QWOH): existing order of things

terra firma (L; TER-uh FUR-muh): solid ground

tour de force (L; TOOR duh FAWRS): feat accomplished through great skill

verbatim (L; ver-BAY-tuhm): word for word

vis-à-vis (F; vee-ZUH-VEE): compared with

National Spelling Bee Champions

The Scripps Howard National Spelling Bee, conducted by Scripps Howard Newspapers and other leading newspapers since 1939, was instituted by the Louisville (Ky.) *Courier-Journal* in 1925. Children under 16 years of age and not beyond the 8th grade are eligible to compete for cash prizes at the finals, which are held annually in Washington, DC. The 1994 winners were: first prize, **Ned G. Andrews,** Knoxville, TN; second prize, **Brian Kane Lee,** Minot, ND; third prize (tie), **Anthony Chuang,** Ft. Worth, TX, **Willie Larkin,** El Paso, TX, and **Srinivas Ayyagari,** Memphis, TN.

Winning Words

These were the last words given in each of the years 1965-94 at the Scripps Howard National Spelling Bee. They were all correctly spelled, thereby determining the national champion.

1965 — eczema
1966 — ratoon
1967 — chihuahua
1968 — abalone
1969 — interlocutory
1970 — croissant
1971 — shalloon
1972 — macerate
1973 — vouchsafe
1974 — hydrophyte
1975 — incisor
1976 — narcolepsy
1977 — cambist
1978 — deification
1979 — maculature
1980 — elucubrate
1981 — sarcophagus
1982 — psoriasis
1983 — purim
1984 — luge
1985 — milieu
1986 — odontalgia
1987 — staphylococci
1988 — elegiacal
1989 — spoliator
1990 — fibranne
1991 — antipyretic
1992 — lyceum
1993 — kamikaze
1994 — antediluvian

Common Abbreviations

Usage of periods after abbreviations varies, but recently the tendency has been toward omission. Definitions preceding those in parentheses are in Latin unless otherwise noted.

AA=Alcoholics Anonymous
AAA=American Automobile Association
abbr.=abbreviation
AC=alternating current
AD=*anno Domini* (in the year of the Lord)
AFL=American Federation of Labor
AIDS=acquired immune deficiency syndrome
AM=*ante meridiem* (before noon)
AMA=American Medical Association
anon=anonymous
ASAP=as soon as possible
ASCAP=American Society of Composers, Authors, and Publishers
BA=Bachelor of Arts
bbl=barrel(s)
BC=before Christ
BS=Bachelor of Science
Btu=British thermal unit(s)
bu=bushel(s)
C= Celsius, centigrade
c=*circa* (about), copyright
CEO=chief executive officer
CIA=Central Intelligence Agency
cm=centimeter(s)
COD=Cash (or Collect) on Delivery
CPA=Certified Public Accountant
CPR=cardiopulmonary resuscitation
DA=district attorney
DAR=Daughters of the American Revolution
DC=direct current
DD=Doctor of Divinity
DDS=Doctor of Dental Science (or Surgery)
DNA=deoxyribonucleic acid
DOA=dead on arrival
DWI=driving while intoxicated
ed.=edited, edition, editor
e.g.=*exempli gratia* (for example)
ESP=extrasensory perception
esp.=especially
et al.=*et alii* (and others)
etc.=*et cetera* (and so forth)
F=Fahrenheit
FBI=Federal Bureau of Investigation
FOB=free on board
ft=foot, feet
FYI=for your information
gal=gallon(s)
GB=gigabyte(s)
GDP=gross domestic product
GIGO=garbage in, garbage out
GNP=gross national product
GOP=Grand Old Party (Republican Party)
Hon.=the Honorable
hr=hour(s)
ht=height
HVAC=heating, ventilating, and air-conditioning
i.e.=*id est* (that is)
in.=inch(es)
IQ=Intelligence Quotient
IRA=Individual Retirement Account, Irish Republican Army
IRS=Internal Revenue Service
ISBN=International Standard Book Number
JD=*Juris Doctor* (Doctor of Laws)
JP=Justice of the Peace
K=Kelvin
k=karat
KB=kilobyte(s)
kg=kilogram(s)
km=kilometer(s)
kW=kilowatt(s)
kWh=kilowatt-hour(s)
l=liter(s)
lb=*libra* (pound or pounds)
LLB=Bachelor of Laws
m=meter(s)
MA=Master of Arts
MB=megabyte(s)
MD=*Medicinae Doctor* (Doctor of Medicine)
mfg=manufacturing
mi=mile(s)
MIA=missing in action
min=minute(s)
ml=milliliter(s)
mm=millimeter(s)
mph=miles per hour
MS=Master of Science
MSG=monosodium glutamate
no=*numero* (number)
op=*opus* (work)
oz=ounce(s)
p., pp.=page, pages
PC=personal computer
Ph.D.=Doctor of Philosophy
PM=post meridiem (afternoon)
POW=prisoner of war
PS=*post scriptum* (postscript)
pt=part(s), pint(s), point(s)
qt=quart(s)
REM=rapid eye movement
Rev.=Reverend
RFD=rural free delivery
R.I.P.=*Requiescat in pace* (May he/she rest in peace)
RN=registered nurse
RNA=ribonucleic acid
ROTC=Reserve Officers' Training Corps
rpm=revolutions per minute
RR=railroad
RSVP=Répondez, s'il vous plait (Fr.) (Please reply)
SAD=seasonal affective disorder
SASE=self-addressed stamped envelope
sec=second(s)
SPCA=Society for the Prevention of Cruelty to Animals
SRO=standing room only
St.=saint, street
stat=*statim* (immediately)
t=ton(s)
TGIF=thank God it's Friday
UFO=unidentified flying object
UHF=ultrahigh frequency
USS=United States ship
v (or vs)=*versus* (against)
VCR=videocassette recorder
VHF=very high frequency
W=watt(s)
yd=yard(s)

A Collection of Animal Collectives

The English language boasts an abundance of names to describe groups of things, particularly pairs or aggregations of animals. Some of these words have fallen into comparative disuse, but many of them are still in service, helping to enrich the vocabularies of those who like their language to be precise, who tire of hearing a group referred to as "a bunch of," or who enjoy the sound of words that aren't overworked.

bale of turtles
band of gorillas
bed of clams, oysters
bevy of quail, swans
brace of ducks
brood of chicks
cast of hawks
cete of badgers
charm of goldfinches
cloud of gnats
clowder of cats
clutch of chicks
clutter of cats
colony of ants
congregation of plovers
covey of quail, partridge
crash of rhinoceri
cry of hounds
down of hares
drift of swine
drove of cattle, sheep
exaltation of larks
flight of birds
flock of sheep, geese
gaggle of geese
gam of whales
gang of elks
grist of bees
herd of elephants
horde of gnats
husk of hares
kindle or **kendle** of kittens
knot of toads
leap of leopards
leash of greyhounds, foxes
litter of pigs
mob of kangaroos
murder of crows
muster of peacocks
mute of hounds
nest of vipers
nest, nide of pheasants
pack of hounds, wolves
pair of horses
pod of whales, seals
pride of lions
school of fish
sedge or **siege** of cranes
shoal of fish, pilchards
skein of geese
skulk of foxes
sleuth of bears
sounder of boars, swine
span of mules
spring of teals
swarm of bees
team of ducks, horses
tribe or **trip** of goats
troop of kangaroos, monkeys
volery of birds
watch of nightingales
wing of plovers
yoke of oxen

Young of Animals Have Special Names

The young of many mammals, birds, and fish have come to be called by special names. A young eel, for example, is an elver. Many young animals, of course, are often referred to simply as infants, babies, younglets, or younglings

bunny: rabbit
calf: cattle, elephant, antelope, rhino, hippo, whale, others
cheeper: grouse, partridge, quail
chick, chicken: fowl
cockerel: rooster
codling, sprag: codfish
colt: horse (male)
cub: lion, bear, shark, fox, others
cygnet: swan
duckling: duck
eaglet: eagle
elver: eel
eyas: hawk, others
fawn: deer
filly: horse (female)
fingerling: fish generally
flapper: wild fowl
fledgling: birds generally
foal: horse, zebra, others
fry: fish generally
gosling: goose
heifer: cow
joey: kangaroo, others
kid: goat
kit: fox, beaver, rabbit, cat
kitten, kitty, catling: cats, other small mammals
lamb, lambkin, cosset, hog: sheep
leveret: hare
nestling: birds generally
owlet: owl
parr, smolt, grilse: salmon
piglet, shoat, farrow, suckling: pig
polliwog, tadpole: frog
poult: turkey
pullet: hen
pup: dog, seal, sea lion, fox
puss, pussy: cat
spike, blinker, tinker: mackerel
squab: pigeon
squeaker: pigeon, others
whelp: dog, tiger, beasts of prey
yearling: cattle, sheep, horse, others

Foreign Idioms

English	Italian
Naked as a jaybird	Naked as a worm (Nudo come un verme)
A bird in the hand is worth two in the bush.	Better a finch in hand than a thrush on a branch. (Meglio fringuello in man che tordo in frasca.)
To kill two birds with one stone	To catch two pigeons with one bean (Pigliare due piccioni con una fava)
To eat crow	To swallow the toad (Inghiottire il rospo)
To eat like a pig	To eat like a buffalo (Mangiare come un bufalo)
Don't bite off more than you can chew.	Don't take a step longer than your leg. (Non fare il passo piu lungo della gamba.)
Pride goes before a fall.	Pride rode out on horseback and came back on foot. (La superbia andò a cavallo e tornò a piedi.)
To go by fits and starts	To go by hiccups (Andare a singhiozzo)
There is honor among thieves.	A dog doesn't eat a dog. (Cane non mangia cane.)
Once in a blue moon	Every death of a pope (Ad oogni morte di papa)

English	French
Don't waste your breath!	Save your saliva! (Epargne ta salive!)
To turn up like a bad penny	To arrive like a hair in the soup. (Arriver comme un cheveu sur la soupe.)
To talk to yourself	To talk to angels (Parler aux anges)
Let's get back to the subject.	Let's get back to our sheep. (Revenons à nos moutons.)
To pull a long face	To make a funny nose (Faire un drôle de nez)
He laughs in your face.	He laughs in your nose. (Il vous rit au nez.)
By rule of thumb	From the view of the nose (A vue de nez)
To be knock-kneed	To have your legs in an X (Avoir les jambes en X)
Put that in your pipe and smoke it!	Put this in your pocket with your handkerchief on top! (Mets-le dans ta poche avec ton mouchoir dessus!)
It's Greek to me!	It's Chinese! (C'est du chinois!)

English	Spanish
To hit the ceiling	To scream at the sky (Poner el grito en el cielo)
Go fly a kite!	Go fry asparagus! (Véte a freír esparragos!)
There's always room for one more.	Where six can eat, seven can eat. (Donde comen seis, comen siete.)
To have the tables turned	To go out for wool and come home shorn (Ir por lana y volver esquilado)
To cut off your nose to spite your face	To throw stones at your own roof (Tirar piedras contra su propio tejado)
To slam the door in your face	To slam the door on your nostrils (Cerrarle la puerta en las narices)
Give him an inch, he'll take a mile.	Give him a hand and he takes a foot. (Le da la mano y se toma el pie.)
To be alive and kicking	To be alive and wagging your tail (Estar vivo y coleando)
You can't make a silk purse out of a sow's ear.	A monkey dressed in silk is still a monkey. (Aunque la mona se vista de seda, mona se queda.)
To swear a blue streak	To toss out toads and snakes (Echar sapos y culebras)

English	Yiddish
Go jump in the lake!	Go whistle in the ocean! (Gai feifen ahfenyam!)
You can only do one thing at a time.	You can't dance at two weddings at the same time. (Me ken nit tantzen auf tsvai chassenes mit ain mol.)
He's as slow as molasses.	He creeps like a bedbug. (Er kricht vi a vantz.)
He repeats himself.	He grinds ground flour. (Er molt gemolen mel.)
Where there's smoke, there's fire.	When bells ring, it's usually a holiday. (Az es klingt, iz misstomeh chogeh.)
Are you in a hurry?	Are you standing on one leg? (Bist ahf ain fus?)
Drop dead!	You should lie in the earth! (Zolst ligen in drerd!)
He makes a lot of trouble for me.	He makes my wedding black. (Er macht mir a shvartzeh chasseneh.)
Go fight City Hall.	Go fight with God. (Shlog zich mit Got arum.)
Thanks for nothing.	Many thanks in your belly button. (A shainem dank dir im pupik.)

Idioms: Their Meaning and Derivation

dyed in the wool: to have traits deeply ingrained; from the fact that if wool is dyed before being made into yarn, or while still raw wool, the color is more firmly fixed.

feet of clay: a blemish in the character of one previously held above reproach; from Daniel's interpretation of Nebuchadnezzar's dream in the Old Testament. The king dreamed of an image made of precious metals, except for feet made of clay and iron. Daniel said that the feet symbolized human vulnerability to weakness and destruction.

hands down: effortlessly; incontestably; from the way a jockey, sure of victory, drops his hands, loosening his grip on the reins.

in seventh heaven: in a state of bliss; especially in Islamic beliefs, the heaven of heavens, the home of God and the highest angels.

kiss of death: something that seems good but is in reality the instrument of one's downfall; from the earlier phrase "Judas kiss," betraying Jesus to the authorities.

mad as a hatter: crazy; from mercury's use in the making of felt hats, thus hatters often were afflicted with a violent twitching of the muscles as a result of its effects.

red herring: a false lead; a herring cured by smoke; from the persistent odor, hence the use, trailed over the ground, for training a dog to follow this scent over any other.

red-letter day: a memorable day; from the custom of using red or purple colors to mark holy days on the calendar.

to bark up the wrong tree: to pursue a false lead; an Americanism that comes from hunting, some say specifically nocturnal racoon hunting, in which dogs often lost track of their quarry.

to buckle down: to adopt an attitude of effort and determination; probably from the act of buckling on armor to prepare for battle.

to go at it with hammer and tongs: no holds barred; from the blacksmith who, with his tongs (long-handled pincers) took a piece of red-hot metal from the forge, laid it on the anvil, and beat it into shape with his hammer.

to hold water: to pass a test for soundness; from testing a pitcher by filling it with water.

to knuckle under: to submit to another; from the time when one knelt before a conquerer, putting the "knuckles" of one's knees (the rounded part of the bone where the joint is bent) on the ground.

to make hay while the sun shines: to seize the opportunity; from hay's composition of mown grass dried for fodder, with the sun as the cheapest and most available drying agent.

to strike while the iron is hot: to seize the opportunity; from the blacksmith's need to swing the hammer while the metal on the anvil is glowing, or he must start up the forge again and reheat the iron.

Names of the Days

English	Russian	Hebrew	French	Italian	Spanish	German	Japanese
Sunday	Voskresenje	Yom rishon	Dimanche	domenica	domingo	Sonntag	Nichiyōbi
Monday	Ponedeljnic	Yom sheni	Lundi	luned	lunes	Montag	Getsuyōbi
Tuesday	Vtornik	Yom shlishi	Mardi	marted	martes	Dienstag	Kayōbi
Wednesday	Sreda	Yom ravii	Mercredi	mercoled	miércoles	Mittwoch	Suiyōbi
Thursday	Chetverg	Yom hamishi	Jeudi	gioved	jueves	Donnerstag	Mokuyōbi
Friday	Pjatnitsa	Yom shishi	Vendredi	venerd	viernes	Freitag	Kin-yōbi
Saturday	Subbota	Shabbat	Samedi	sabato	sábado	Samstag	Doyōbi

Commonly Confused English Words

adverse: unfavorable
averse: opposed

affect: to influence
effect: to cause

aggravate: to make worse
annoy: to irritate

allusion: an indirect reference
illusion: an unreal impression

anxious: apprehensive
eager: avid

capital: the seat of government
capitol: the building in which a legislative body meets

complement: to make complete; something that completes
compliment: to praise; praise

denote: to mean
connote: to suggest beyond the explicit meaning

discreet: prudent
discrete: separate

disinterested: impartial
uninterested: without interest

elicit: to draw or bring out
illicit: illegal

emigrate: to leave for another place of residence
immigrate: to come to another place of residence

farther: more distant in space
further: an extension of time or degree

flaunt: to display ostentatiously
flout: to treat with contemptuous disregard

historic: an important occurrence
historical: any occurrence in the past

imminent: ready to take place
eminent: standing out

imply: to relay information but not explicitly
infer: to understand information that is not relayed explicitly

include: used when the items following are part of a whole
comprise: used when the items following are all of a whole

incredible: unbelievable
incredulous: skeptical

ingenious: clever
ingenuous: innocent

insidious: intended to trick
invidious: detrimental to reputation

literally: actually
figuratively: metaphorically

oral: spoken, as opposed to written
verbal: referring to skill with language, as opposed to other skills

pestilence: a contagious or infectious epidemic disease
petulance: rudeness

prevaricate: to lie
procrastinate: to put off

prostrate: stretched out flat, face down
prostate: of or relating to the prostate gland

qualitative: relating to quality
quantitative: relating to number

Commonly Misspelled English Words

accidentally
accommodate
acquainted
all right
already
amateur
appearance
appropriate
bureau
character
commitment
conscientious
conscious
convenience
deceive
describe
description
desirable
despair
desperate
eliminate
embarrass
fascinating
finally
fluorine
foreign
forty
government
grammar
harass
humorous
hurrying
incidentally
independent
inoculate
irresistible
laboratory
lightning
liquefy
maintenance
marriage
miniature
misspelled
mysterious
necessary
opportunity
optimistic
performance
permanent
rhythm
ridiculous
similar
sincerely
transferred

Forms of Address

Addressee	Address	Salutation
Government		
President of the U.S.	The President, The White House, Washington, DC 20500; also, The President and Mrs. ______ or The President and Mr. ______	Dear Sir or Madam; Mr. President or Madam President; Dear Mr. President or Dear Madam President [1]
Vice President of the U.S.	The Vice President, Old Executive Office Building, Washington, DC 20501; also, The Vice President and Mrs. ______ or The Vice President and Mr. ______	Dear Sir or Madam; Mr. Vice President or Madam Vice President; Dear Mr. Vice President or Dear Madam Vice President
Chief Justice	The Hon. *FirstName Surname*, Chief Justice of the U.S., The Supreme Court, Washington, DC 20543	Dear Sir or Madam; Dear Mr. or Madam Chief Justice
Associate Justice	Mr. Justice *Surname*, The Supreme Court, Washington, DC 20543	Dear Sir or Madam; Dear Justice *Surname*
Judge	The Hon. *FirstName Surname*, Associate Judge, U.S. District Court	Dear Judge *Surname*
Attorney General	The Hon. *FirstName Surname*, Attorney General, Dept. of Justice, Constitution Ave. & 10th St. NW, Washington, DC 20530	Dear Sir or Madam; Dear Mr. or Ms. Attorney General
Cabinet Officer	The Hon. *FirstName Surname*, Secretary of ______	Dear Mr. or Madam Secretary; or Dear Mr. or Ms. *Surname*
Senator	The Hon. or Sen. *FirstName Surname*, U.S. Senate, Washington, DC 20510	Dear Mr. or Madam Senator, or Dear Mr. or Ms. *Surname*
Representative	The Hon. or Rep. *FirstName Surname*, House of Representatives, Washington, DC 20515	Dear Mr. or Madam *Surname*
Speaker of the House	The Hon. Speaker of the House of Representatives, House of Representatives, Washington, DC 20515	Dear Mr. or Madam Speaker
Ambassador, U.S.	The Hon. *FirstName Surname*, American Ambassador[2]	Sir or Madam; Dear Mr. or Madam Ambassador
Ambassador, Foreign	His or Her Excellency *FirstName Surname*, Ambassador of ______	Excellency;[3] Dear Mr. or Madam Ambassador
Governor	The Hon. *FirstName Surname*, Governor of *State*; or in some states, His or Her Excellency, the Governor of *State*	Sir or Madam; Dear Governor *Surname*
Mayor	The Hon. *FirstName Surname*, Mayor of *City*	Sir or Madam; Dear Mayor *Surname*
Military Personnel		
All Titles	Full or abbreviated rank + full name + comma + abbreviation for branch of service. Example: Adm. John Smith, USN	Dear *Rank Surname*
Clerical and Religious Orders		
Clergy, Protestant	The Reverend *FirstName Surname*[4]	Dear Ms. or Mr. *Surname*
Pope	His Holiness Pope *Name* or His Holiness the Pope	Your Holiness or Most Holy Father
Priest	The Reverend *FirstName Surname* or The Reverend Father *Surname*	Reverend Father, Dear Father *Surname*, or Dear Father
Rabbi	Rabbi *FirstName Surname*	Dear Rabbi *Surname*
Royalty and Nobility		
King or Queen	His or Her Majesty, King or Queen of *Country*	Sir or Madam, or May it please Your Majesty

(1) The trend in the Clinton White House is toward first names; however, if you sign your letter formally, the president will address his reply formally, as he does in addressing the elderly and those in the military. (2) If in Canada or Latin America, The Ambassador of the United States of America. (3) An American ambassador is not to be addressed as His or Her Excellency. (4) Any member of the clergy who has a doctorate may be so addressed; for example, The Reverend *FirstName Surname*, DD, and Dear Dr. *Surname*.

Pen Names

Alain-Fournier (Henri Fournier)
Shalom Aleichem (Solomon J. Rabinowitz
Woody Allen (Allen Stewart Konigsberg)
Currer, Ellis, and Acton Bell (Charlotte, Emily, and Anne Brontë)
John le Carré (David John Moore Cornwell)
Lewis Carroll (Charles Lutwidge Dodgson)
Colette (Sidonie Gabrielle Colette)
Isak Dinesen (Karen Blixen)
Elia (Charles Lamb)
George Eliot (Mary Ann or Marian Evans)
Maksim Gorky (Aleksey Maksimovich Peshkov)
O. Henry (William Sydney Porter)
James Herriot (James Alfred Wight)
P. D. James (Phyllis Dorothy James White)
[John] Ross Macdonald (Kenneth Millar)
André Maurois (Émile Herzog)
Molière (Jean Baptiste Poquelin)
George Orwell (Eric Arthur Blair)
Ellery Queen (Frederic Dannay and Manfred B. Lee)
Mary Renault (Mary Challans)
Françoise Sagan (Françoise Quoirez)
Saki (Hector Hugh Munro)
George Sand (Amandine Lucie Aurore Dupine)
Dr. Seuss (Theodor Seuss Geisel)
Stendahl (Marie Henri Beyle)
Mark Twain (Samuel Clemens)
Voltaire (François Marie Arouet)
Artemus Ward (Charles Farrar Browne)
Tom Wolfe (Thomas Kennerly, Jr.)

The Principal Languages of the World

Source: S. Culbert, NI-25, University of Washington, Seattle, WA 98195; data as of mid-1993

Languages spoken by more than 100,000,000 people

	Speakers (millions)			Speakers (millions)			Speakers (millions)	
	Native	Total		Native	Total		Native	Total
Mandarin	836	952	Bengali	189	196	Japanese	125	126
Hindi	333	418	Arabic	186	219	German	98	121
Spanish	332	381	Russian	170	288	French	72	124
English	322	470	Portuguese	170	182	Malay-Indonesian	50	155

Total number of speakers (native plus non-native) of languages spoken by at least one million speakers. A native speaker is one for whom the language is his or her first language. Locations in parentheses are principal areas where language is spoken.

Achinese (N Sumatra, Indonesia) 3
Afghan (see Pashtu)
Afrikaans (S Africa) 10
Akan (or Twi-Fanti) (Ghana) 7
Albanian (Albania; Kosovo, Yugoslavia) 5
Amharic (Ethiopia) 20
Arabic (see above) 219
Armenian (Armenia) 5
Assamese[1] (India; Bangladesh) 22
Aymara (Bolivia; Peru) 2
Azeri (Azerbaijan) 15
Balinese (Bali, Indonesia) 3
Baluchi (Baluchistan, in SW Pakistan and SE Iran) 5
Bashkir (Bashkortostan, Russia) 1
Batak Toba (Indonesia) 4
Baule (Côte d'Ivoire) 2
Beja (Kassala, Sudan; Ethiopia) 1
Bemba (Zambia) 2
Bengali[1] (see above) 196
Berber[2]
Beti (Cameroon; Gabon; Eq. Guinea) 2
Bhili (India) 3
Bikol (SE Luzon, Philippines) 4
Brahvi (Pakistan) 2
Bugis (Indonesia; Malaysia) 4
Bulgarian (Bulgaria) 9
Burmese (Myanmar) 31
Buyi (S Guizhou, S China) 2
Byelorussian (Belarus) 10
Cantonese (China; Hong Kong) 66
Catalan (NE Spain; Balearic Is.; S France; Andorra) 9
Cebuano (Bohol Sea, Philippines) 13
Chagga (Kilimanjaro area, Tanzania) 1
Chiga (Uganda) 1
Chinese[3]
Chuvash (Chuvash, Russia) 2
Czech (Czech Republic) 12
Danish (Denmark) 5
Dimli (EC Turkey) 1
Dogri (Jammu-Kashmir, CE India) 1
Dong (SC China) 2
Dutch-Flemish (Netherlands; Belg.; NE France) 21
Dyerma (SW Niger) 2
Edo (Bendel, S Nigeria) 1
Efik (incl. Ibibio) (SE Nigeria) 6
English (see above) 470
Estonian (Estonia) 1
Ewe (SE Ghana; S Togo) 3
Fang-Bulu (Dialects of Beti, q. v.)
Farsi (see Persian)
Finnish (Finland; Sweden) 6
Fon (SC Benin; S Togo) 1
French (see above) 124
Fula (or Peulh) (Cameroon; Nigeria) 13
Fulakunda (Senegal; Gambia; Guinea-Bissau) 2
Futa Jalon (Guinea; Sierra Leone) 3
Galician (Galicia, NW Spain) 4
Galla (see Oromo)
Ganda (or Luganda) (S Uganda) 3
Georgian (Georgia) 4
German (see above) 121
Gilaki (Gilan, NW Iran) 2
Gogo (Riff Valley, Tanzania) 1
Gondi (Central India) 2
Greek (Greece) 12
Guarani (Paraguay) 4
Gujarati[1] (WC India; S Pakistan) 41
Gusii (Kisii District, Nyanza, Kenya) 2
Gypsy (see Romany)
Hadiyya (Arusi, Ethiopia) 2
Hakka (or Kejia) (SE China) 34
Hani (S China) 1
Hausa (N Nigeria; Niger; Cameroon) 38
Haya (Kagera, NW Tanzania) 1
Hebrew (Israel) 4
Hindi[1,4] (see above) 418
Ho (Bihar and Orissa States, India) 1
Hungarian (or Magyar) (Hungary) 14
Iban (Indonesia; Malaysia) 1
Ibibio (see Efik)
Igbo (or Ibo) (lower Niger, Nigeria) 17
Ijaw (Niger River delta, Nigeria) 2
Ilocano (NW Luzon, Philippines) 7
Indonesian (see Malay-Indonesian)
Italian (Italy) 63
Japanese (see above) 126
Javanese (Java, Indonesia) 64
Kabyle (W Kabylia, N Algeria) 3
Kamba (E Kenya) 3
Kannada[1] (S India) 44
Kanuri (Nigeria; Niger; Chad; Cameroon) 4
Karen (see Sgaw)
Karo-Dairi (N Sumatra, Indonesia) 2
Kashmiri[1] (N India; NE Pakistan) 4
Kazakh (Kazakhstan) 8
Kenuzi-Dongola (S Egypt; Sudan) 1
Khalka (see Mongolian)
Khmer (Cambodia; Vietnam; Thai.) 8
Khmer, Northern (Thailand) 1
Kikuyu (or Gekoyo) (WC Kenya) 5
Kituba (Bas-Zaire, Bandundu, Zaire) 4
Kongo (W Zaire; S Congo; NW Ang.) 3
Konkani (Maharashtra and SW India) 4
Korean (Korea; China; Japan) 75
Kurdish (Iran; Iraq; Turkey) 11
Kurukh (or Oraon) (C and E India) 2
Kyrgyz (Kyrgyzstan) 2
Lampung (Sumatra, Indonesia) 2
Lao[5] (Laos) 4
Latvian (Latvia) 2
Lingala (incl. Bangala) (Zaire) 7
Lithuanian (Lithuania) 3
Luba-Lulua (or Chiluba) (Zaire) 7
Luba-Shaba (Shaba, Zaire) 1
Lubu (E Sumatra, Indonesia) 1
Luhya (W Kenya) 1
Luo (Kenya; Nyanza, Tanzania) 4
Luri (SW Iran; Iraq) 4
Lwena (E Angola; W Zambia) 2
Macedonian (Macedonia) 2
Madurese (Madura, Indonesia) 10
Magindanaon (S Philippines) 1
Makassar (S Sulawesi, Indonesia) 2
Makua (S Tanzania; N Mozambique) 4
Malagasy (Madagascar) 12
Malay-Indonesian (see above) 155
Malay, Pattani (SE Thailand) 1
Malayalam[1] (Kerala, S India) 35
Malinke-Bambara-Dyula (W Africa) 9

Mandarin (see above)	952
Marathi[1] (Maharashtra, India)	70
Mazandarani (S Mazandaran, N Iran)	2
Mbundu (Benguela, Angola)	4
Mbundu (Luanda, Angola)	3
Meithei (NE India; Bangladesh)	1
Mende (Sierra Leone)	2
Meru (Eastern Province, C Tanzania)	1
Miao (or Hmong) (S China; SE Asia)	6
Mien (China; Viet.; Laos; Thailand)	2
Min (SE China; Taiwan; Malaysia)	50
Minangkabau (W Sumatra, Indon.)	6
Moldavian (included with Romanian)	
Mongolian (Mongolia; NE China)	6
Mordvin (Mordova, Russia)	1
Moré (central part of Burkina Faso)	4
Nepali (Nepal; NE India; Bhutan)	16
Ngulu (Mozambique; Malawi)	2
Nkole (Western Prov., Uganda)	1
Norwegian (Norway)	5
Nung (NE of Hanoi, Vietnam; China)	2
Nupe (Kwara, Niger States, Nigeria)	1
Nyamwezi-Sukuma (NW Tanzania)	5
Nyanja (Malawi; Zambia; Zimbabwe)	5
Oriya[1] (Central and E India)	32
Oromo (West Ethiopia; N Kenya)	10
Pampangan (NW of Manila, Philip.)	2
Panay-Hiligaynon (Philippines)	7
Pangasinan (Lingayen G., Philip.)	2
Pashtu (Pakistan; Afghanistan; Iran)	21
Pedi (see Sotho, Northern)	
Persian (Iran; Afghanistan)	34
Polish (Poland)	44
Portuguese (see above)	182
Provençal (S France)	4
Punjabi[1] (Punjab, Pakistan; India)	94
Pushto (see Pashtu)	
Quechua A (Peru; Boliv.; Ec.; Arg.)	8
Rejang (SW Sumatra, Indonesia)	1
Riff (N Morocco; Algerian coast)	1
Romanian (Romania; Moldova)	26
Romany[7]	2
Ruanda (Rwanda; Uganda; Zaire)	7
Rundi (Burundi)	6
Russian (see above)	288
Samar-Leyte (Central E Philippines)	3
Sango (Central African Republic)	4
Santali (E India; Nepal)	5
Sasak (Lombok, Alas Strait, Indon.)	2
Serbo-Croatian (Croatia; Serbia; and other former Yugoslav republics and autonomous regions)	20
Sgaw (SW Myanmar)	2
Shan (E Myanmar)	3
Shilha (W Algeria; S Morocco)	3
Shona (Zimbabwe)	8
Sidamo (Sidamo, S Ethiopia)	2
Sindhi[1] (SE Pakistan; W India)	18
Sinhalese (Sri Lanka)	13
Slovak (Slovakia)	5
Slovene (Slovenia)	2
Soga (Busoga, Uganda)	1
Somali (Som.; Eth.; Ken.; Djibouti)	5
Songye (Kasai Or., NW Shala, Zaire)	1
Soninke (Mali; countries to W S E)	1
Sotho, Northern (So. Africa)	3
Sotho, Southern (So. Afr.; Lesotho)	4
Spanish (see above)	381
Sundanese (Sunda Strait, Indonesia)	26
Swahili (Kenya; Tanz.; Zaire; Ug.)	48
Swati (Swaziland; S. Africa)	1
Swedish (Sweden; Finland)	9
Sylhetti (Bangladesh)	5
Tagalog (Philippines)	53
Tajiki (Tajikistan; Uzbek.; Kyrgyz.)	5
Tamazight (N Morocco; W Algeria)	3
Tamil[1] (Tamil Nadu, India; Sri Lanka)	69
Tatar (Tatarstan, Russia)	8
Tausug (Philippines; Malaysia)	1
Telugu[1] (Andhra Pradesh, SE India)	73
Temne (central Sierra Leone)	2
Thai[5] (Thailand)	50
Tho (N Vietnam; S China)	2
Thonga (Mozambique; So. Africa)	3
Tibetan (SW China; N India; Nepal)	5
Tigrinya (S Eritrea; Tigre, Ethiopia)	4
Tiv (SE Nigeria; Cameroon)	2
Tong (see Dong)	
Tonga (SW Zambia; NW Zimbabwe)	2
Tswana (Botswana; So. Africa)	4
Tudza (N Vietnam; S China)	1
Tulu (S India)	2
Tumbuka (N Malawi; NE Zambia)	2
Turkish (Turkey)	59
Turkmen (Turkmenistan; Afghanistan)	3
Twi-Fante (see Akan)	
Uighur (Xinjiang, NW China)	8
Ukrainian (Ukraine; Russia; Poland)	47
Urdu[1,4] (Pakistan; India)	100
Uzbek (Uzbekistan)	14
Vietnamese (Vietnam)	64
Wolaytta (SE Ethiopia)	2
Wolof (Senegal)	7
Wu (Shanghai region, China)	65
Xhosa (SW Cape Prov., So. Africa)	8
Yao (see Mien)	
Yao (Malawi; Tanzania; Mozambique)	1
Yi (S and SW China)	7
Yiddish[6]	
Yoruba (SW Nigeria; Zou, Benin)	20
Zande (NE Zaire; SW Sudan)	1
Zhuang (S China)	15
Zulu (N. Natal, So. Africa; Lesotho)	9

(1) One of the15 languages of the Constitution of India. (2) See Kabyle, Riff, Shilha, and Tamazight. (3) See Mandarin, Cantonese, Wu, Min, and Hakka. The "common speech" (Putonghua) or the "national language" (Guoyu) is a standardized form of Mandarin as spoken in the area of Beijing. (4) Hindi and Urdu are essentially the same language, Hindustani. As the official language of Pakistan, it is written in a modified Arabic script and called Urdu. As the official language of India, it is written in the Devanagari script and called Hindi. (5) The distinctions between some Thai dialects and Lao are political rather than linguistic. (6) Yiddish is usually considered a variant of German, although it has its own standard grammar and dictionaries, has a highly developed literature, and is written in Hebrew characters. (7) Mainly in central, E, and SE Europe and Turkey; some in the U.S.

Esperanto

Esperanto is the most commonly spoken of the international languages, invented languages intended to provide a universal means of communication to bridge the gap among speakers of the world's many natural languages. International languages are based on natural languages, with simplifications of grammar and spelling. Speakers of Esperanto number at most a few hundred thousand. Esperanto, invented in 1887 by the Polish physician and linguist Dr. Ludwik L. Zamenhof (1859-1917), is derived from a combination of Latin, the Romance languages, and the Germanic languages. Its name comes from the pseudonym ("Doktoro Esperanto") used by Zamenhof in his textbook describing the language. Because of its logical structure, phonemic spelling, and regular grammar, Esperanto can generally be learned more quickly than a typical natural language. An example of Esperanto:

Inteligenta persono lernas la lingvon Esperanto rapide kaj facile. Esperanto estas la moderna, kultura lingvo por la tuta mondo.

Non-English-Speaking Americans

Source: Bureau of the Census, U.S. Dept. of Commerce

According to data from the 1990 census, more than 31.8 million people (almost 14% of the U.S. population age 5 and over) spoke a language other than English in 1990, compared with 23.1 million (11%) in 1980, an increase of almost 38% during the decade. After English, Spanish was the most common language, spoken by more than half the non-English-speaking Americans. Spanish was 10 times more commonly used than the next choice, French, which was followed by German, Italian, and Chinese.

Top 25 Languages, Other Than English, Spoken at Home by Americans

Source: Bureau of the Census, U.S. Dept. of Commerce

	Language used at home	Total speakers over 5 years old 1990	Total speakers over 5 years old 1980	Percentage change*
1.	Spanish	17,339,000	11,549,000	50.1%
2.	French	1,703,000	1,572,000	8.3%
3.	German	1,547,000	1,607,000	-3.7%
4.	Italian	1,309,000	1,633,000	-19.9%
5.	Chinese	1,249,000	632,000	97.7%
6.	Tagalog	843,000	452,000	86.6%
7.	Polish	723,000	826,000	-12.4%
8.	Korean	626,000	276,000	127.2%
9.	Vietnamese	507,000	203,000	149.5%
10	Portuguese	430,000	361,000	19.0%
11	Japanese	428,000	342,000	25.0%
12	Greek	388,000	410,000	-5.4%
13	Arabic	355,000	227,000	57.4%
14.	Hindi, Urdu, related	331,000	130,000	155.1%
15.	Russian	242,000	175,000	38.5%
16.	Yiddish	213,000	320,000	-33.5%
17.	Thai	206,000	89,000	131.6%
18.	Persian	202,000	109,000	84.7%
19.	French Creole	188,000	25,000	654.1%
20.	Armenian	150,000	102,000	46.3%
21.	Navajo	149,000	123,000	20.6%
22.	Hungarian	148,000	180,000	-17.9%
23.	Hebrew	144,000	99,000	45.5%
24.	Dutch	143,000	146,000	-2.6%
25.	Mon-Khmer	127,000	16,000	676.3%

*Calculations are from numbers before rounding.

Language Spoken at Home by Persons Ages 5 Years and Older, by State, 1990

State	Population 5 years and older	Speaks only English	Total non-English	Percent non-English
United States	**230,445,777**	**196,600,798**	**31,844,979**	**13.8**
Alabama	3,759,802	3,651,936	107,866	2.9
Alaska	495,425	435,260	60,165	12.1
Arizona	3,374,806	2,674,519	700,287	20.8
Arkansas	2,186,665	2,125,884	60,781	2.8
California	27,383,547	18,764,213	8,619,334	31.5
Colorado	3,042,986	2,722,355	320,631	10.5
Connecticut	3,060,000	2,593,825	466,175	15.2
Delaware	617,720	575,393	42,327	6.9
Distr. of Columbia	570,284	498,936	71,348	12.5
Florida	12,095,284	9,996,969	2,098,315	17.3
Georgia	5,984,188	5,699,642	284,546	4.8
Hawaii	1,026,209	771,485	254,724	24.8
Idaho	926,703	867,708	58,995	6.4
Illinois	10,585,838	9,086,726	1,499,112	14.2
Indiana	5,146,160	4,900,334	245,826	4.8
Iowa	2,583,526	2,483,135	100,391	3.9
Kansas	2,289,615	2,158,011	131,604	5.7
Kentucky	3,434,955	3,348,473	86,482	2.5
Louisiana	3,886,353	3,494,359	391,994	10.1
Maine	1,142,122	1,036,681	105,441	9.2
Maryland	4,425,285	4,030,234	395,051	8.9
Massachusetts	5,605,751	4,753,523	852,228	15.2
Michigan	8,594,737	8,024,930	569,807	6.6
Minnesota	4,038,861	3,811,700	227,161	5.6
Mississippi	2,378,805	2,312,289	66,516	2.8
Missouri	4,748,704	4,570,494	178,210	3.8
Montana	740,218	703,198	37,020	5.0
Nebraska	1,458,904	1,389,032	69,872	4.8
Nevada	1,110,450	964,298	146,152	13.2
New Hampshire	1,024,621	935,825	88,796	8.7
New Jersey	7,200,696	5,794,548	1,406,148	19.5
New Mexico	1,390,048	896,049	493,999	35.5
New York	16,743,048	12,834,328	3,908,720	23.3
North Carolina	6,172,301	5,931,435	240,866	3.9
North Dakota	590,839	543,942	46,897	7.9
Ohio	10,063,212	9,517,064	546,148	5.4
Oklahoma	2,921,755	2,775,957	145,798	5.0
Oregon	2,640,482	2,448,772	191,710	7.3
Pennsylvania	11,085,170	10,278,294	806,876	7.3
Rhode Island	936,423	776,931	159,492	17.0
South Carolina	3,231,539	3,118,376	113,163	3.5
South Dakota	641,226	599,232	41,994	6.5
Tennessee	4,544,743	4,413,193	131,550	2.9
Texas	15,605,822	11,635,518	3,970,304	25.4
Utah	1,553,351	1,432,947	120,404	7.8
Vermont	521,521	491,112	30,409	5.8
Virginia	5,746,419	5,327,898	418,521	7.3
Washington	4,501,879	4,098,706	403,173	9.0
West Virginia	1,686,932	1,642,729	44,203	2.6
Wisconsin	4,531,134	4,267,496	263,638	5.8
Wyoming	418,713	394,904	23,809	5.7

PRESIDENTIAL ELECTIONS

Popular and Electoral Vote, 1988 and 1992

Source: Voter News Service; Federal Election Commission

	1992						1988			
	Electoral Vote			Democrat	Republican	Ind.	Electoral Vote		Democrat	Republican
States	Clinton	Bush	Perot	Clinton	Bush	Perot	Dukakis	Bush	Dukakis	Bush
Ala.	0	9	0	690,080	804,283	183,109	0	9	549,506	815,576
Alas.	0	3	0	78,294	102,000	73,481	0	3	72,584	119,251
Ariz.	0	8	0	543,050	572,086	353,741	0	7	454,029	702,541
Ark.	6	0	0	505,823	337,324	99,132	0	6	349,237	466,578
Cal.	54	0	0	5,121,325	3,630,574	2,296,006	0	47	4,702,233	5,054,917
Col.	8	0	0	629,681	562,850	366,010	0	8	621,453	728,177
Conn.	8	0	0	682,318	578,313	348,771	0	8	676,584	750,241
Del.	3	0	0	126,054	102,313	59,213	0	3	108,647	139,639
D.C.	3	0	0	192,619	20,698	9,681	3	0	159,407	27,590
Fla.	0	25	0	2,071,651	2,171,781	1,052,481	0	21	1,655,851	2,616,597
Ga.	13	0	0	1,008,966	995,252	309,657	0	12	714,792	1,081,331
Ha.	4	0	0	179,310	136,822	53,003	4	0	192,364	158,625
Ida.	0	4	0	137,013	202,645	130,395	0	4	147,272	253,881
Ill.	22	0	0	2,453,350	1,734,096	840,515	0	24	2,215,940	2,310,939
Ind.	0	12	0	848,420	989,375	455,934	0	12	860,643	1,297,763
Ia.	7	0	0	586,353	504,891	253,468	8	0	670,557	545,355
Kan.	0	6	0	390,434	449,951	312,358	0	7	422,636	554,049
Ky.	8	0	0	665,104	617,178	203,944	0	9	580,368	734,281
La.	9	0	0	815,971	733,386	211,478	0	10	717,460	883,702
Me.	4	0	0	263,420	206,504	206,820	0	4	243,569	307,131
Md.	10	0	0	988,571	707,094	281,414	0	10	826,304	876,167
Mass.	12	0	0	1,318,639	805,039	630,731	13	0	1,401,415	1,194,635
Mich.	18	0	0	1,871,182	1,554,940	824,813	0	20	1,675,783	1,965,486
Minn.	10	0	0	1,020,997	747,841	562,506	10	0	1,109,471	962,337
Miss.	0	7	0	400,258	487,793	85,626	0	7	363,921	557,890
Mo.	11	0	0	1,053,873	811,159	518,741	0	11	1,001,619	1,084,953
Mon.	3	0	0	154,507	144,207	107,225	0	4	168,936	190,412
Neb.	0	5	0	216,864	343,678	174,104	0	5	259,235	397,956
Nev.	4	0	0	189,148	175,828	132,580	0	4	132,738	206,040
N.H.	4	0	0	209,040	202,484	121,337	0	4	163,696	281,537
N.J.	15	0	0	1,436,206	1,356,865	521,829	0	16	1,317,541	1,740,604
N.M.	5	0	0	261,617	212,824	91,895	0	5	244,497	270,341
N.Y.	33	0	0	3,444,450	2,346,649	1,090,721	36	0	3,347,882	3,081,871
N.C.	0	14	0	1,114,042	1,134,661	357,864	0	13	890,167	1,237,258
N.D.	0	3	0	99,168	136,244	71,084	0	3	127,739	166,559
Oh.	21	0	0	1,984,942	1,894,310	1,036,426	0	23	1,939,629	2,416,549
Okla.	0	8	0	473,066	592,929	319,878	0	8	483,423	678,367
Ore.	7	0	0	621,314	475,757	354,091	7	0	616,206	560,126
Pa.	23	0	0	2,239,164	1,791,841	902,667	0	25	2,194,944	2,300,087
R.I.	4	0	0	213,299	131,601	105,045	4	0	225,123	177,761
S.C.	0	8	0	479,514	577,507	138,872	0	8	370,554	606,443
S.D.	0	3	0	124,888	136,718	73,295	0	3	145,560	165,415
Tenn.	11	0	0	933,521	841,300	199,968	0	11	679,794	947,233
Tex.	0	32	0	2,281,815	2,496,071	1,354,781	0	29	2,352,748	3,036,829
Ut.	0	5	0	183,429	322,632	203,400	0	5	207,352	428,442
Vt.	3	0	0	133,590	88,122	65,985	0	3	115,775	124,331
Va.	0	13	0	1,038,650	1,150,517	348,639	0	12	859,799	1,309,162
Wash.	11	0	0	993,037	731,234	541,780	10	0	933,516	903,835
W.Va.	5	0	0	331,001	241,974	108,829	5[1]	0	341,016	310,065
Wis.	11	0	0	1,041,066	930,855	544,479	11	0	1,126,794	1,047,499
Wyo.	0	3	0	68,160	79,347	51,263	0	3	67,113	106,867
Total	**370**	**168**	**0**	**44,908,254**	**39,102,343**	**19,741,065**	**111[1]**	**426**	**41,805,422**	**48,881,221**

(1) Lloyd Bentsen (D, TX) received 1 electoral vote from W.Va.

Presidential Election Returns by Counties

All 1992 results are official. Results for New England states are for selected cities or towns due to unavailability of county results. Totals are always statewide.

Source: Voter News Service; Federal Election Commission

Alabama

County	1992 Clinton (D)	1992 Bush (R)	1992 Perot (I)	1988 Dukakis (D)	1988 Bush (R)
Autauga	4,819	8,715	1,916	3,667	7,828
Baldwin	12,195	26,270	7,656	9,271	25,933
Barbour	4,836	4,475	1,020	3,836	4,958
Bibb	2,900	3,124	686	2,244	2,885
Blount	5,433	8,882	1,949	4,485	8,754
Bullock	3,259	1,253	266	3,122	1,421
Butler	4,021	3,494	867	3,465	3,923
Calhoun	16,453	20,623	4,717	12,451	19,806
Chambers	5,938	5,682	1,427	5,103	7,694
Cherokee	4,222	2,745	846	3,176	2,868
Chilton	4,946	8,126	1,363	3,820	8,761
Choctaw	3,941	3,069	489	3,491	3,629
Clarke	5,023	5,495	872	4,217	5,708
Clay	2,073	2,859	652	1,602	3,496
Cleburne	2,144	2,425	630	1,383	3,071
Coffee	5,776	7,591	2,021	4,319	8,890
Colbert	12,206	8,073	2,098	10,397	7,775
Conecuh	3,155	2,463	552	3,022	3,256
Coosa	2,330	1,973	476	1,860	2,405
Covington	5,004	6,840	1,880	3,845	8,130
Crenshaw	2,404	2,339	485	1,836	2,617
Cullman	10,451	14,411	4,113	8,517	14,351
Dale	5,098	8,123	2,423	3,476	9,266
Dallas	11,053	7,394	1,110	9,660	7,630
DeKalb	8,245	10,519	2,741	7,333	11,478
Elmore	6,223	11,356	2,765	4,501	10,852
Escambia	4,809	5,955	1,616	4,020	6,807
Etowah	20,558	17,467	4,277	17,762	17,828
Fayette	3,830	3,604	1,012	3,186	4,338
Franklin	5,953	4,794	1,075	4,961	5,146
Geneva	3,622	4,843	1,323	2,685	5,703
Greene	3,865	805	194	3,295	1,048
Hale	3,481	2,001	486	3,187	2,414
Henry	2,804	2,970	667	2,206	3,613
Houston	8,857	17,360	3,492	7,001	19,989
Jackson	10,628	5,711	2,462	7,418	6,090
Jefferson	125,889	149,832	22,191	107,766	148,879
Lamar	2,849	3,262	763	2,274	3,214
Lauderdale	15,936	13,728	4,009	12,862	12,942
Lawrence	6,364	3,576	1,624	4,646	3,616
Lee	13,770	16,885	4,572	9,078	17,180
Limestone	8,087	9,862	3,584	5,455	9,086
Lowndes	3,500	1,328	284	3,328	1,405
Macon	7,253	1,134	283	6,351	1,304
Madison	38,974	51,444	16,989	25,800	53,575
Marengo	5,632	4,470	919	4,402	4,241
Marion	6,167	5,692	1,389	4,505	5,955
Marshall	10,421	12,249	3,795	7,357	12,148
Mobile	54,962	72,935	15,105	45,524	72,203
Monroe	3,872	4,919	759	3,509	5,379
Montgomery	37,342	40,742	7,647	28,709	41,131
Morgan	15,091	21,073	7,683	10,594	18,679
Perry	3,712	1,829	213	3,574	2,107
Pickens	3,783	3,634	690	3,107	3,851
Pike	4,688	5,423	1,024	3,813	5,897
Randolph	3,318	3,813	919	2,462	4,625
Russell	8,647	5,587	1,360	6,589	6,333
St. Clair	6,517	12,447	2,614	4,335	10,604
Shelby	10,317	32,736	5,022	7,138	27,052
Sumter	4,810	1,807	388	4,390	2,212
Talladega	10,695	12,661	2,629	8,291	12,973
Tallapoosa	5,703	8,140	1,562	4,598	8,502
Tuscaloosa	23,495	27,454	7,011	18,166	27,396
Walker	14,831	11,301	3,344	11,338	11,011
Washington	4,046	3,270	829	3,402	3,741
Wilcox	3,439	1,671	174	3,369	1,739
Winston	3,415	5,550	1,110	2,954	6,235
Totals	**690,080**	**804,283**	**183,109**	**549,506**	**815,576**

Alabama Vote Since 1944

1944, Roosevelt, Dem., 198,918; Dewey, Rep., 44,540; Watson, Proh., 1,095; Thomas, Soc., 190.

1948, Thurmond, States' Rights, 171,443; Dewey, Rep., 40,930; Wallace, Prog., 1,522; Watson, Proh., 1,085.

1952, Eisenhower, Rep., 149,231; Stevenson, Dem., 275,075; Hamblen, Proh., 1,814.

1956, Stevenson, Dem., 290,844; Eisenhower, Rep. 195,694; Independent electors, 20,323.

1960, Kennedy, Dem., 324,050; Nixon, Rep., 237,981; Faubus, States' Rights, 4,367; Decker, Proh., 2,106; King, Afro-Americans, 1,485; scattering, 236.

1964, Dem. 209,848 (electors unpledged); Goldwater, Rep., 479,085; scattering, 105.

1968, Nixon, Rep., 146,923; Humphrey, Dem., 196,579; Wallace, 3d party, 691,425; Munn, Proh., 4,022.

1972, Nixon, Rep., 728,701; McGovern, Dem., 219,108 plus 37,815 Natl. Demo. Party of Alabama; Schmitz, Conservative, 11,918; Munn., Proh., 8,551.

1976, Carter, Dem., 659,170; Ford, Rep., 504,070; Maddox, Am. Ind., 9,198; Bubar, Proh., 6,669; Hall, Com., 1,954; MacBride, Libertarian, 1,481.

1980, Reagan, Rep., 654,192; Carter, Dem., 636,730; Anderson, Independent, 16,481; Rarick, Amer. Ind., 15,010; Clark, Libertarian, 13,318; Bubar, Statesman, 1,743; Hall, Com., 1,629; DeBerry, Soc. Work., 1,303; McReynolds, Socialist, 1,006; Commoner, Citizens, 517.

1984, Reagan, Rep., 872,849; Mondale, Dem., 551,899; Bergland, Libertarian, 9,504.

1988, Bush, Rep., 815,576; Dukakis, Dem., 549,506; Paul, Lib., 8,460; Fulani, Ind., 3,311.

1992, Bush, Rep., 804,283; Clinton, Dem., 690,080; Perot, Ind., 183,109; Marrou, Libertarian, 5,737; Fulani, New Alliance, 2,161.

Alaska

Election District	1992 Clinton (D)	1992 Bush (R)	1992 Perot (I)	1988 Dukakis (D)	1988 Bush (R)
No. 1	2,055	2,495	2,120		
No. 2	2,565	2,916	2,137		
No. 3	4,064	2,447	1,424		
No. 4	2,688	2,894	1,561		
No. 5	2,095	1,844	1,684		
No. 6	1,546	2,345	1,748		
No. 7	2,088	2,173	2,244		
No. 8	1,509	2,499	2,325		
No. 9	1,540	2,349	2,368		
No. 10	1,947	3,548	1,899		
No. 11	2,009	2,730	2,081		
No. 12	1,831	2,999	2,039		
No. 13	3,001	2,963	1,907		
No. 14	1,423	3,013	1,599		
No. 15	2,389	1,842	1,591		
No. 16	1,814	1,375	1,320		
No. 17	1,749	2,623	1,958		
No. 18	2,483	3,629	2,134		
No. 19	1,931	2,539	1,840		
No. 20	2,383	2,914	1,823		
No. 21	2,386	2,437	1,693		
No. 22	2,253	3,164	1,713		
No. 23	1,139	2,127	1,217		
No. 24	1,876	3,441	1,930		
No. 25	1,513	3,197	2,122		
No. 26	1,439	2,675	2,419		
No. 27	1,625	2,757	2,401		
No. 28	1,522	2,459	2,825		
No. 29	3,216	2,205	2,026		
No. 30	1,860	2,434	1,912		
No. 31	1,969	2,223	1,992		
No. 32	1,150	2,339	1,724		
No. 33	1,712	3,100	2,278		
No. 34	1,455	3,408	2,201		
No. 35	1,572	2,525	2,139		
No. 36	1,748	2,081	1,322		
No. 37	1,822	1,689	925		
No. 38	1,897	2,011	850		
No. 39	1,797	1,777	860		
No. 40	1,211	1,786	1,122		
Totals	**78,294**	**102,000**	**73,481**	**72,584**	**119,251**

Alaska Vote Since 1960

1960, Kennedy, Dem., 29,809; Nixon, Rep., 30,953.

1964, Johnson, Dem., 44,329; Goldwater, Rep., 22,930.

1968, Nixon, Rep., 37,600; Humphrey, Dem., 35,411; Wallace, 3d party, 10,024.

1972, Nixon, Rep., 55,349; McGovern, Dem., 32,967; Schmitz, American, 6,903.

1976, Carter, Dem., 44,058; Ford, Rep., 71,555; MacBride, Libertarian, 6,785.

1980, Reagan, Rep., 86,112; Carter, Dem., 41,842; Clark, Libertarian, 18,479; Anderson, Ind., 11,155; Write-in, 857.

1984, Reagan, Rep., 138,377; Mondale, Dem., 62,007; Bergland, Libertarian, 6,378.

1988, Bush, Rep., 119,251; Dukakis, Dem., 72,584; Paul, Lib., 5,484; Fulani, New Alliance, 1,024.

1992, Bush, Rep., 102,000; Clinton, Dem., 78,294; Perot, Ind., 73,481; Gritz, Populist/America First, 1,379; Marrou, Libertarian, 1,378.

Arizona

County	1992 Clinton (D)	1992 Bush (R)	1992 Perot (I)	1988 Dukakis (D)	1988 Bush (R)
Apache	11,218	4,588	1,979	8,944	5,347
Cochise	12,701	12,202	7,857	11,812	15,815
Coconino	18,888	13,769	9,363	14,660	16,649
Gila	7,571	5,781	4,694	7,147	7,861
Graham	3,391	4,169	1,860	3,407	5,120
Greenlee	1,695	1,451	794	1,733	1,526
La Paz	1,808	1,599	1,488	1,746	2,562
Maricopa	285,457	360,049	221,475	230,952	442,337
Mohave	13,255	13,684	12,706	10,197	17,651
Navajo	10,882	7,994	4,787	9,023	10,393
Pima	128,569	97,036	53,925	113,824	117,899
Pinal	15,468	11,669	9,231	13,850	14,966
Santa Cruz	3,512	3,024	1,447	3,268	3,320
Yavapai	18,268	23,419	16,409	14,514	27,842
Yuma	10,367	11,652	5,726	8,952	13,253
Totals	**543,050**	**572,086**	**353,741**	**454,029**	**702,541**

Arizona Vote Since 1944

1944, Roosevelt, Dem., 80,926; Dewey, Rep., 56,287; Watson, Proh., 421.

1948, Truman, Dem., 95,251; Dewey, Rep., 77,597; Wallace, Prog., 3,310; Watson, Proh., 786; Teichert, Soc. Labor, 121.

1952, Eisenhower, Rep., 152,042; Stevenson, Dem., 108,528.

1956, Eisenhower, Rep., 176,990; Stevenson, Dem., 112,880; Andrews, Ind. 303.

1960, Kennedy, Dem., 176,781; Nixon, Rep., 221,241; Hass, Soc. Labor, 469.

1964, Johnson, Dem., 237,753; Goldwater, Rep., 242,535; Hass, Soc. Labor, 482.

1968, Nixon, Rep., 266,721; Humphrey, Dem., 170,514; Wallace, 3d party, 46,573; McCarthy, New Party, 2,751; Halstead, Soc. Worker, 85; Cleaver, Peace and Freedom, 217; Blomen, Soc. Labor, 75.

1972, Nixon, Rep., 402,812; McGovern, Dem., 198,540; Schmitz, Amer., 21,208; Soc. Workers, 30,945. Due to ballot peculiarities in 3 counties (particularly Pima), thousands of voters cast ballots for the Socialist Workers Party *and* one of the major candidates. Court ordered both votes counted as official.

1976, Carter, Dem., 295,602; Ford, Rep., 418,642; McCarthy, Ind., 19,229; MacBride, Libertarian, 7,647; Camejo, Soc. Workers, 928; Anderson, Amer., 564; Maddox, Am. Ind., 85.

1980, Reagan, Rep., 529,688; Carter, Dem., 246,843; Anderson, Ind., 76,952; Clark, Libertarian, 18,784; De Berry, Soc. Workers, 1,100; Commoner, Citizens, 551; Hall, Com., 25; Griswold, Workers World, 2.

1984, Reagan, Rep., 681,416; Mondale, Dem., 333,854; Bergland, Libertarian, 10,585.

1988, Bush, Rep., 702,541; Dukakis, Dem., 454,029; Paul, Lib., 13,351; Fulani, New Alliance, 1,662.

1992, Bush, Rep., 572,086; Clinton, Dem., 543,050; Perot, Ind., 353,741; Gritz, Populist/America First, 8,141; Marrou, Libertarian, 6,759; Hagelin, Natural Law, 2,267.

Arkansas

County	1992 Clinton (D)	1992 Bush (R)	1992 Perot (I)	1988 Dukakis (D)	1988 Bush (R)
Arkansas	4,709	2,594	639	3,075	4,007
Ashley	5,876	2,686	931	4,466	4,111
Baxter	6,991	5,640	2,938	4,808	8,614
Benton	15,774	21,126	6,128	9,399	24,295
Boone	6,128	6,094	2,079	3,998	7,567
Bradley	2,954	1,482	391	2,167	2,089
Calhoun	1,389	1,047	257	1,024	1,316
Carroll	3,769	3,535	1,500	2,632	4,553
Chicot	3,504	1,242	347	2,426	1,901
Clark	5,767	2,403	714	4,675	3,389
Clay	4,848	1,647	568	3,442	2,766
Cleburne	5,090	3,580	1,263	3,404	4,932
Cleveland	1,893	1,127	337	1,404	1,462
Columbia	4,747	3,702	1,090	3,706	5,810
Conway	4,898	2,719	803	4,134	4,066
Craighead	13,931	9,104	2,274	9,083	11,887
Crawford	6,656	6,882	2,442	3,582	9,092
Crittenden	9,683	5,910	848	6,702	7,441
Cross	4,058	2,303	602	2,989	3,186
Dallas	2,107	1,458	345	1,990	1,947
Desha	3,815	1,279	392	2,859	2,334
Drew	3,748	1,938	596	2,578	2,995
Faulkner	13,000	9,491	2,437	7,302	10,678
Franklin	3,217	2,495	987	2,458	3,588
Fulton	2,827	1,258	631	2,018	1,918
Garland	18,811	12,886	3,475	11,406	19,281
Grant	3,190	2,272	702	2,142	2,717
Greene	7,541	3,510	1,213	5,065	5,161
Hempstead	5,476	2,387	1,022	3,841	3,938
Hot Spring	6,308	3,036	1,209	5,090	4,181
Howard	2,764	1,728	466	1,818	2,510
Independence	7,083	4,232	1,444	4,523	6,637
Izard	3,419	1,532	606	2,652	2,824
Jackson	4,944	1,864	673	4,199	3,049
Jefferson	21,819	7,525	2,067	16,664	12,520
Johnson	3,951	2,563	1,013	2,818	4,046
Lafayette	2,273	1,188	504	1,915	1,860
Lawrence	4,146	2,124	636	3,179	3,205
Lee	3,436	1,293	308	2,878	1,863
Lincoln	2,805	1,142	390	2,204	1,557
Little River	3,327	1,483	890	2,740	2,347
Logan	3,995	3,408	1,220	1,254	2,203
Lonoke	7,963	6,253	1,554	4,786	7,215
Madison	2,415	2,238	598	2,106	3,067
Marion	2,757	2,023	1,327	2,033	2,993
Miller	7,050	5,273	2,249	5,437	7,110
Mississippi	10,046	4,697	981	6,759	7,841
Monroe	2,578	1,324	355	2,052	1,862
Montgomery	1,904	1,205	576	1,362	1,752
Nevada	2,242	1,217	455	1,732	1,714
Newton	1,765	1,730	608	1,489	2,504
Ouachita	7,411	3,711	1,238	5,229	6,297
Perry	1,906	1,162	412	1,470	1,627
Phillips	6,456	2,695	634	5,580	3,892
Pike	2,168	1,577	472	1,681	2,105
Poinsett	5,341	2,425	761	3,873	3,644
Polk	3,162	2,757	1,225	2,390	4,099
Pope	7,704	8,056	1,989	4,941	10,084
Prairie	2,366	1,154	434	1,688	1,947
Pulaski	79,482	47,789	8,751	55,857	70,562
Randolph	3,921	1,766	578	2,781	2,560
St. Francis	6,548	3,289	766	4,656	4,298
Saline	12,671	10,105	2,751	8,436	12,353
Scott	2,228	1,695	610	1,707	2,507
Searcy	1,679	1,772	503	1,340	2,743
Sebastian	16,570	16,817	6,023	9,684	24,426
Sevier	2,558	1,592	643	2,037	2,254
Sharp	3,761	2,486	921	2,955	3,623
Stone	2,622	1,672	697	1,728	2,186
Union	8,786	7,305	1,919	5,931	10,581
Van Buren	3,819	2,612	888	2,607	3,562
Washington	22,029	20,292	5,304	12,557	23,601
White	10,494	8,538	2,366	6,957	11,094
Woodruff	2,589	676	227	1,924	1,097
Yell	4,165	2,506	940	2,763	3,535
Totals	**505,823**	**337,324**	**99,132**	**349,237**	**466,578**

Arkansas Vote Since 1944

1944, Roosevelt, Dem., 148,965; Dewey, Rep., 63,551; Thomas, Soc., 438.

1948, Truman, Dem., 149,659; Dewey, Rep., 50,959; Thurmond, States' Rights, 40,068; Thomas, Soc., 1,037; Wallace, Prog., 751; Watson, Proh., 1.

1952, Eisenhower, Rep., 177,155; Stevenson, Dem., 226,300; Hamblen, Proh., 886; MacArthur, Christian Nationalist, 458; Hass, Soc. Labor, 1.

1956, Stevenson, Dem., 213,277; Eisenhower, Rep., 186,287; Andrews, Ind., 7,008.

1960, Kennedy, Dem., 215,049; Nixon, Rep., 184,508; Nat'l. States' Rights, 28,952.

1964, Johnson, Dem., 314,197; Goldwater, Rep., 243,264; Kasper, Nat'l. States Rights, 2,965.

1968, Nixon, Rep., 189,062; Humphrey, Dem., 184,901; Wallace, 3d party, 235,627.

1972, Nixon, Rep., 445,751; McGovern, Dem., 198,899; Schmitz, Amer., 3,016.

1976, Carter, Dem., 498,604; Ford, Rep., 267,903; McCarthy, Ind., 639; Anderson, Amer., 389.

1980, Reagan, Rep., 403,164; Carter, Dem., 398,041; Anderson, Ind., 22,468; Clark, Libertarian, 8,970; Commoner, Citizens, 2,345; Bubar, Statesman, 1,350; Hall, Com., 1,244.

1984, Reagan, Rep., 534,774; Mondale, Dem., 338,646; Bergland, Libertarian, 2,220.

1988, Bush, Rep., 466,578; Dukakis, Dem., 349,237; Duke, Chr. Pop., 5,146; Paul, Lib., 3,297.

1992, Clinton, Dem., 505,823; Bush, Rep., 337,324; Perot, Ind., 99,132; Phillips, U.S. Taxpayers, 1,437; Marrou, Libertarian, 1,261; Fulani, New Alliance, 1,022.

California

County	1992 Clinton (D)	1992 Bush (R)	1992 Perot (I)	1988 Dukakis (D)	1988 Bush (R)
Alameda . . .	334,224	109,292	81,643	310,283	162,815
Alpine	215	222	186	230	306
Amador	5,286	5,477	4,553	5,197	6,893
Butte.	32,489	31,608	20,231	30,406	40,143
Calaveras . .	5,989	6,006	4,848	5,674	7,640
Colusa.	1,798	2,589	1,206	2,022	3,077
Contra Costa	194,960	112,965	72,518	169,411	158,652
Del Norte . . .	3,639	3,083	2,575	3,587	3,714
El Dorado. . .	21,012	25,906	17,503	19,801	30,021
Fresno.	92,418	89,137	36,299	92,635	94,835
Glenn	2,666	3,812	2,278	2,894	4,944
Humboldt . . .	28,854	18,299	12,340	29,781	21,460
Imperial	11,109	9,759	4,247	10,243	12,889
Inyo	2,695	3,689	1,999	2,653	5,042
Kern	60,510	80,762	36,891	55,083	90,550
Kings	9,982	10,673	4,899	9,142	12,118
Lake	10,548	6,678	5,797	9,828	9,366
Lassen	3,388	3,836	3,004	3,446	5,157
Los Angeles .	1,446,529	799,607	488,624	1,372,352	1,239,716
Madera	10,863	13,066	6,156	10,642	13,255
Marin	76,158	30,479	22,986	69,394	46,855
Mariposa . . .	3,023	2,982	2,211	2,998	3,768
Mendocino . .	18,344	7,958	9,753	17,152	12,979
Merced	20,133	17,981	10,914	20,105	21,717
Modoc.	1,489	1,803	1,269	1,416	2,518
Mono	1,489	1,570	1,248	1,284	2,177
Monterey . . .	54,861	36,461	24,472	48,998	50,022
Napa.	24,215	15,662	13,150	22,283	23,235
Nevada	15,433	17,343	11,072	14,980	21,383
Orange	306,930	426,613	232,394	269,013	586,230
Placer	30,783	38,298	21,741	27,516	42,096
Plumas	3,742	3,599	2,551	4,251	4,603
Riverside . . .	166,241	159,457	102,233	133,122	199,979
Sacramento .	197,540	160,366	91,412	188,557	201,832
San Benito . .	5,354	4,112	3,182	4,559	5,578
San Bernardino	183,634	176,563	109,183	151,118	235,167
San Diego . .	367,397	352,125	259,249	333,264	523,143
San Francisco	233,263	57,352	29,018	201,887	72,503
San Joaquin .	63,655	58,355	31,205	61,699	75,309
San Luis Obispo	40,136	36,384	27,314	35,667	46,613
San Mateo . .	149,232	75,080	50,465	141,859	109,261
Santa Barbara	69,215	57,375	35,105	63,586	77,524
Santa Clara .	296,265	170,870	128,895	277,810	254,442
Santa Cruz. .	66,183	24,916	21,615	63,133	37,728
Shasta.	21,605	28,190	17,990	21,171	32,402
Sierra	653	691	519	791	860
Siskiyou. . . .	8,254	6,660	5,567	8,365	9,056
Solano.	64,320	38,883	27,851	54,344	50,314
Sonoma. . . .	104,334	47,619	43,859	91,262	67,725
Stanislaus . .	52,415	47,275	27,651	44,685	51,648
Sutter	7,883	12,956	4,881	6,557	14,100
Tehama. . . .	7,508	7,419	5,884	7,213	9,854
Trinity	1,967	1,886	2,092	2,518	3,267
Tulare	31,188	40,482	16,430	30,711	46,891
Tuolumne. . .	9,216	8,525	6,294	8,717	10,646
Ventura	99,011	94,911	71,844	89,065	147,604
Yolo	33,297	17,574	11,073	30,429	22,358
Yuba.	5,785	7,333	3,637	5,444	8,937
Totals.	**5,121,325**	**3,630,574**	**2,296,006**	**4,702,233**	**5,054,917**

California Vote Since 1944

1944, Roosevelt, Dem., 1,988,564; Dewey, Rep., 1,512,965; Watson, Proh., 14,770; Thomas, Soc., 3,923; Teichert, Soc. Labor, 327.

1948, Truman, Dem., 1,913,134; Dewey, Rep., 1,895,269; Wallace, Prog., 190,381; Watson, Proh., 16,926; Thomas, Soc., 3,459; Thurmond, States' Rights, 1,228; Teichert, Soc. Labor, 195; Dobbs, Soc. Workers, 133.

1952, Eisenhower, Rep., 2,897,310; Stevenson, Dem., 2,197,548; Hallinan, Prog., 24,106; Hamblen, Proh., 15,653; MacArthur, (Tenny Ticket), 3,326; (Kellems Ticket) 178; Hass, Soc. Labor, 273; Hoopes, Soc., 206; scattered, 3,249.

1956, Eisenhower, Rep., 3,027,668; Stevenson, Dem., 2,420,136; Holtwick, Proh., 11,119; Andrews, Constitution, 6,087; Hass, Soc. Labor, 300; Hoopes, Soc., 123; Dobbs, Soc. Workers, 96; Smith, Christian Nat'l., 8.

1960, Kennedy, Dem., 3,224,099; Nixon, Rep., 3,259,722; Decker, Proh., 21,706; Hass, Soc. Labor, 1,051.

1964, Johnson, Dem., 4,171,877; Goldwater, Rep., 2,879,108; Hass, Soc. Labor, 489; DeBerry, Soc. Worker, 378; Munn, Proh., 305; Hensley, Universal, 19.

1968, Nixon, Rep., 3,467,664; Humphrey, Dem., 3,244,318; Wallace, 3d party, 487,270; Peace and Freedom party, 27,707; McCarthy, Alternative, 20,721; Gregory, write-in, 3,230; Mitchell, Com., 260; Munn, Proh., 59; Blomen, Soc. Labor, 341; Soeters, Defense, 17.

1972, Nixon, Rep., 4,602,096; McGovern, Dem., 3,475,847; Schmitz, Amer., 232,554; Spock, Peace and Freedom, 55,167; Hall, Com., 373; Hospers, Libertarian, 980; Munn, Proh., 53; Fisher, Soc. Labor, 197; Jenness, Soc. Workers, 574; Green, Universal, 21.

1976, Carter, Dem., 3,742,284; Ford, Rep., 3,882,244; MacBride, Libertarian, 56,388; Maddox, Am. Ind., 51,098; Wright, People's, 41,731; Camejo, Soc. Workers, 17,259; Hall, Com., 12,766; write-in, McCarthy, 58,412; other write-in, 4,935.

1980, Reagan, Rep. 4,524,858; Carter, Dem., 3,083,661; Anderson, Ind., 739,833; Clark, Libertarian, 148,434; Commoner, Ind., 61,063; Smith, Peace & Freedom, 18,116; Rarick, Amer. Ind., 9,856.

1984, Reagan, Rep. 5,305,410; Mondale, Dem., 3,815,947; Bergland, Libertarian, 48,400.

1988, Bush, Rep., 5,054,917; Dukakis, Dem., 4,702,233; Paul, Lib., 70,105; Fulani, Ind., 31,181.

1992, Clinton, Dem., 5,121,325; Bush, Rep., 3,630,575; Perot, Ind., 2,296,006; Marrou, Libertarian, 48,139; Daniels, Ind., 18,597; Phillips, U.S. Taxpayers, 12,711.

Colorado

County	1992 Clinton (D)	1992 Bush (R)	1992 Perot (I)	1988 Dukakis (D)	1988 Bush (R)
Adams	45,357	30,856	26,379	49,464	43,163
Alamosa	1,928	1,572	1,089	2,146	2,567
Arapahoe. . . .	66,607	72,221	44,363	61,113	95,926
Archuleta	819	1,242	741	795	1,440
Baca.	726	1,240	647	851	1,670
Bent	985	759	506	1,088	1,032
Boulder	64,567	33,553	27,762	57,265	48,174
Chaffee	2,284	2,419	1,549	2,548	3,080
Cheyenne	301	615	292	399	760
Clear Creek . .	1,744	1,356	1,308	1,698	1,820
Conejos.	1,705	1,160	578	1,976	1,445
Costilla	1,180	366	199	1,120	454
Crowley.	570	602	276	630	862
Custer.	343	651	368	310	753
Delta.	3,424	4,359	2,627	3,521	5,449
Denver	121,961	55,418	37,298	127,173	77,753
Dolores	242	315	285	230	488
Douglas.	9,991	18,592	11,329	6,931	17,035
Eagle	3,870	3,100	3,821	3,314	4,366
Elbert	1,237	2,205	1,567	1,566	2,805
El Paso	45,827	86,044	34,346	39,995	96,965
Fremont.	5,356	5,961	3,709	5,278	7,623
Garfield	5,082	4,404	4,408	4,620	6,358
Gilpin	726	462	545	804	728
Grand	1,678	1,763	1,454	1,451	2,306
Gunnison. . . .	2,389	1,662	1,671	1,897	2,520
Hinsdale	151	188	136	111	295
Huerfano	1,224	685	385	1,876	1,079
Jackson.	216	422	326	294	584
Jefferson	80,834	82,705	58,404	81,824	110,820
Kiowa	290	472	267	398	645
Kit Carson . . .	925	1,801	919	1,196	2,262
Lake	1,426	605	863	1,516	969
La Plata.	5,913	5,522	4,083	5,443	7,714
Larimer	38,232	35,995	24,879	35,703	45,967
Las Animas . .	3,847	1,739	953	4,075	2,162
Lincoln	640	1,079	581	874	1,356
Logan	2,718	3,420	2,184	3,382	4,485
Mesa.	15,162	18,169	10,474	14,372	22,150
Mineral	171	159	117	174	217
Moffat	1,386	1,809	1,875	1,634	2,757
Montezuma . .	2,270	3,124	2,205	2,233	4,208
Montrose	3,713	4,847	3,093	3,748	6,012
Morgan	2,985	3,724	2,175	3,728	4,795
Otero	3,485	3,120	1,590	3,910	4,265
Ouray	461	653	466	439	814
Park	1,307	1,530	1,396	1,343	1,909
Philips.	692	1,075	525	923	1,317
Pitkin	3,820	1,686	1,907	3,420	2,801
Prowers.	1,770	2,371	1,184	2,207	2,978
Pueblo.	30,261	16,120	9,841	32,788	20,119
Rio Blanco . . .	778	1,231	794	803	1,821
Rio Grande . .	1,541	1,927	1,043	1,545	2,626
Routt.	3,188	2,358	2,564	2,922	3,264
Saguache . . .	1,011	675	471	1,033	945
San Juan	147	118	183	192	210
San Miguel. . .	1,380	628	634	961	798
Sedgwick. . . .	397	447	295	611	921
Summit	3,344	2,256	2,715	2,595	2,893
Teller	1,873	3,050	1,927	1,656	3,760
Washington . .	660	1,266	671	958	1,707
Weld.	19,295	20,958	13,571	20,548	26,497
Yuma	1,269	2,019	1,197	1,835	2,513
Totals.	**629,681**	**52,850**	**366,010**	**621,453**	**728,177**

Colorado Vote Since 1944

1944, Roosevelt, Dem., 234,331; Dewey, Rep., 268,731; Thomas, Soc., 1,977.
1948, Truman, Dem., 267,288; Dewey, Rep., 239,714; Wallace, Prog., 6,115; Thomas, Soc., 1,678; Dobbs, Soc. Workers, 228; Teichert, Soc. Labor, 214.
1952, Eisenhower, Rep., 379,782; Stevenson, Dem., 245,504; MacArthur, Constitution, 2,181; Hallinan, Prog., 1,919; Hoopes, Soc., 365; Hass, Soc. Labor, 352.
1956, Eisenhower, Rep., 394,479; Stevenson, Dem., 263,997; Hass, Soc. Lab., 3,308; Andrews, Ind., 759; Hoopes, Soc., 531.
1960, Kennedy, Dem., 330,629; Nixon, Rep., 402,242; Hass, Soc. Labor, 2,803; Dobbs, Soc. Workers, 572.
1964, Johnson, Dem., 476,024; Goldwater, Rep., 296,767; Hass, Soc. Labor, 302; DeBerry, Soc. Worker, 2,537; Munn, Proh., 1,356.
1968, Nixon, Rep., 409,345; Humphrey, Dem., 335,174; Wallace, 3d party, 60,813; Blomen, Soc. Labor, 3,016; Gregory, New-party, 1,393; Munn, Proh., 275; Halstead, Soc. Worker, 235.
1972, Nixon, Rep., 597,189; McGovern, Dem., 329,980; Fisher, Soc. Labor, 4,361; Hospers, Libertarian, 1,111; Hall, Com., 432; Jenness, Soc. Workers, 555; Munn, Proh., 467; Schmitz, Amer., 17,269; Spock, Peoples, 2,403.
1976, Carter, Dem., 460,353; Ford, Rep., 584,367; McCarthy, Ind., 26,107; MacBride, Libertarian, 5,330; Bubar, Proh., 2,882.
1980, Reagan, Rep., 652,264; Carter, Dem., 367,973; Anderson, Ind., 130,633; Clark, Libertarian, 25,744; Commoner, Citizens, 5,614; Bubar, Statesman, 1,180; Pulley, Socialist, 520; Hall, Com., 487.
1984, Reagan, Rep., 821,817; Mondale, Dem., 454,975; Bergland, Libertarian, 11,257.
1988, Bush, Rep., 728,177; Dukakis, Dem., 621,453; Paul, Lib., 15,482; Dodge, Proh., 4,604.
1992, Clinton, Dem., 629,681; Bush, Rep., 562,850; Perot, Ind., 366,010; Marrou, Libertarian, 8,669; Fulani, New Alliance, 1,608.

Connecticut

City	1992 Clinton (D)	1992 Bush (R)	1992 Perot (I)	1988 Dukakis (D)	1988 Bush (R)
Bridgeport . . .	22,321	13,149	6,263	23,831	17,084
Hartford	26,971	6,180	3,390	27,295	8,100
New Britain. . .	14,159	7,040	4,983	15,843	9,569
New Haven. . .	29,774	8,931	4,130	31,951	11,616
Norwalk	16,488	14,743	6,046	14,518	18,618
Stamford	23,185	19,809	6,763	20,773	24,877
Waterbury . . .	16,366	16,155	9,188	18,202	20,018
West Hartford .	19,623	12,266	5,017	19,311	16,482
Other.	513,431	480,040	302,991	504,860	623,877
Totals	**682,318**	**578,313**	**348,771**	**676,584**	**750,241**

Connecticut Vote Since 1944

1944, Roosevelt, Dem., 435,146; Dewey, Rep., 390,527; Thomas, Soc., 5,097; Teichert, Soc. Labor, 1,220.
1948, Truman, Dem., 423,297; Dewey, Rep., 437,754; Wallace, Prog., 13,713; Thomas, Soc., 6,964; Teichert, Soc. Labor, 1,184; Dobbs, Soc. Workers, 606.
1952, Eisenhower, Rep., 611,012; Stevenson, Dem., 481,649; Hoopes, Soc., 2,244; Hallinan, Peoples, 1,466; Hass, Soc. Labor, 535; write-in, 5.
1956, Eisenhower, Rep., 711,837; Stevenson, Dem., 405,079; scattered, 205.
1960, Kennedy, Dem., 657,055; Nixon, Rep., 565,813.
1964, Johnson, Dem., 826,269; Goldwater, Rep., 390,996; scattered, 1,313.
1968, Nixon, Rep., 556,721; Humphrey, Dem., 621,561; Wallace, 3d party, 76,650; scattered, 1,300.
1972, Nixon, Rep., 810,763; McGovern, Dem., 555,498; Schmitz, Amer., 17,239; scattered, 777.
1976, Carter, Dem., 647,895; Ford, Rep., 719,261; Maddox, George Wallace Party, 7,101; LaRouche, U.S. Labor, 1,789.
1980, Reagan, Rep., 677,210; Carter, Dem., 541,732; Anderson, Ind., 171,807; Clark, Libertarian, 8,570; Commoner, Citizens, 6,130; scattered, 836.
1984, Reagan, Rep., 890,877; Mondale, Dem., 569,597.
1988, Bush, Rep., 750,241; Dukakis, Dem., 676,584; Paul, Lib., 14,071; Fulani, New Alliance, 2,491.
1992, Clinton, Dem., 682,318; Bush, Rep., 578,313; Perot, Ind., 348,771; Marrou, Libertarian, 5,391; Fulani, New Alliance, 1,363.

Delaware

County	1992 Clinton (D)	1992 Bush (R)	1992 Perot (I)	1988 Dukakis (D)	1988 Bush (R)
Kent.	15,364	15,562	8,916	12,996	19,923
New Castle . . .	91,516	66,311	37,581	79,147	92,587
Sussex.	19,174	20,440	12,716	16,504	27,129
Totals	**126,054**	**102,313**	**59,213**	**108,647**	**139,639**

Delaware Vote Since 1944

1944, Roosevelt, Dem., 68,166; Dewey, Rep., 56,747; Watson, Proh., 294; Thomas, Soc., 154.
1948, Truman, Dem., 67,813; Dewey, Rep., 69,688; Wallace, Prog., 1,050; Watson, Proh., 343; Thomas, Soc., 250; Teichert, Soc. Labor, 29.
1952, Eisenhower, Rep., 90,059; Stevenson, Dem., 83,315; Hass, Soc. Labor, 242; Hamblen, Proh., 234; Hallinan, Prog., 155; Hoopes, Soc., 20.
1956, Eisenhower, Rep., 98,057; Stevenson, Dem., 79,421; Oltwick, Proh., 400; Hass, Soc. Labor, 110.
1960, Kennedy, Dem., 99,590; Nixon, Rep., 96,373; Faubus, States' Rights, 354; Decker, Proh., 284; Hass, Soc. Labor, 82.
1964, Johnson, Dem., 122,704; Goldwater, Rep., 78,078; Hass, Soc. Labor, 113; Munn, Proh., 425.
1968, Nixon, Rep., 96,714; Humphrey, Dem., 89,194; Wallace, 3d party, 28,459.
1972, Nixon, Rep., 140,357; McGovern, Dem., 92,283; Schmitz, Amer., 2,638; Munn, Proh., 238.
1976, Carter, Dem., 122,596; Ford, Rep., 109,831; McCarthy, non-partisan, 2,437; Anderson, Amer., 645; LaRouche, U.S. Labor, 136; Bubar, Proh., 103; Levin, Soc. Labor, 86.
1980, Reagan, Rep., 111,252; Carter, Dem., 105,754; Anderson, Ind., 16,288; Clark, Libertarian, 1,974; Greaves, American, 400.
1984, Reagan, Rep., 152,190; Mondale, Dem., 101,656; Bergland, Libertarian, 268.
1988, Bush, Rep., 139,639; Dukakis, Dem., 108,647; Paul, Lib., 1,162; Fulani, New Alliance, 443.
1992, Clinton, Dem., 126,054; Bush, Rep., 102,313; Perot, Ind., 59,213; Fulani, New Alliance, 1,105.

District of Columbia

	1992 Clinton (D)	1992 Bush (R)	1992 Perot (I)	1988 Dukakis (D)	1988 Bush (R)
Totals	**192,619**	**20,698**	**9,681**	**159,407**	**27,590**

District of Columbia Vote Since 1964

1964, Johnson, Dem., 169,796; Goldwater, Rep., 28,801.
1968, Nixon, Rep., 31,012; Humphrey, Dem., 139, 566.
1972, Nixon, Rep., 35,226; McGovern, Dem., 127,627; Reed, Soc. Workers, 316; Hall, Com., 252.
1976, Carter, Dem., 137,818; Ford, Rep., 27,873; Camejo, Soc. Workers, 545; MacBride, Libertarian, 274; Hall, Com., 219; LaRouche, U.S. Labor, 157.
1980, Reagan, Rep., 23,313; Carter, Dem., 130,231; Anderson, Ind., 16,131; Commoner, Citizens, 1,826; Clark, Libertarian, 1,104; Hall, Com., 369; DeBerry, Soc. Work., 173; Griswold, Workers World, 52; write-ins, 690.
1984, Mondale, Dem., 180,408; Reagan, Rep., 29,009; Bergland, Libertarian, 279.
1988, Bush, Rep., 27,590; Dukakis, Dem., 159,407; Fulani, New Alliance, 2,901; Paul, Lib., 554.
1992, Clinton, Dem., 192,619; Bush, Rep., 20,698; Perot, Ind., 9,681; Fulani, New Alliance, 1,459; Daniels, Ind., 1,186.

Florida

County	1992 Clinton (D)	1992 Bush (R)	1992 Perot (I)	1988 Dukakis (D)	1988 Bush (R)
Alachua.	37,876	22,806	15,293	29,375	30,124
Baker	1,974	3,417	1,315	1,353	3,414
Bay.	12,830	22,820	9,702	11,582	31,712
Bradford	3,040	3,671	1,572	2,386	4,218
Brevard	61,070	84,545	49,491	42,967	104,721
Broward.	276,309	164,782	90,923	218,211	220,196

Calhoun	1,665	1,721	1,176	1,329	2,420
Charlotte	22,904	24,302	14,711	15,967	28,879
Citrus	15,935	16,402	12,310	12,177	21,052
Clay	10,597	26,313	8,414	7,766	25,882
Collier	18,794	38,447	14,514	12,768	38,910
Columbia	5,526	6,489	2,906	4,072	7,759
Dade	254,444	235,149	53,957	216,847	270,672
De Soto	2,646	3,070	1,687	2,181	4,237
Dixie	1,855	1,401	1,094	1,366	2,027
Duval	92,010	123,480	33,335	74,832	127,875
Escambia	32,018	52,775	19,868	29,934	64,774
Flagler	6,692	6,241	3,387	4,241	6,494
Franklin	1,534	1,660	1,143	1,283	1,911
Gadsden	8,478	3,975	1,871	6,368	5,987
Gilchrist	1,511	1,395	1,090	1,137	1,854
Glades	1,305	1,185	878	1,034	1,546
Gulf	1,938	2,650	1,245	1,687	3,040
Hamilton	1,622	1,402	695	1,314	2,062
Hardee	2,017	2,898	1,498	1,688	3,636
Hendry	2,690	3,279	2,032	2,036	3,962
Hernando	19,171	17,896	11,845	15,432	21,179
Highlands	11,234	14,497	6,592	8,087	16,713
Hillsborough	115,261	130,611	63,037	98,969	150,065
Holmes	1,877	3,196	1,426	1,639	4,221
Indian River	12,359	19,137	12,375	10,447	24,619
Jackson	5,481	6,720	2,447	5,002	8,392
Jefferson	2,270	1,506	894	2,055	2,326
Lafayette	866	1,037	612	722	1,450
Lake	23,199	30,818	15,606	16,762	37,314
Lee	53,656	73,423	38,446	40,709	87,247
Leon	47,770	31,964	17,207	33,446	36,032
Levy	4,330	3,796	2,784	3,433	5,250
Liberty	820	1,126	617	709	1,419
Madison	2,644	2,006	1,174	1,950	2,556
Manatee	33,826	42,708	23,282	26,618	51,160
Marion	30,823	35,438	20,524	20,679	41,488
Martin	14,778	24,768	13,433	11,486	31,270
Monroe	10,435	9,891	8,306	10,151	15,919
Nassau	5,497	9,364	3,251	4,138	8,366
Okaloosa	12,003	32,755	16,649	9,726	40,295
Okeechobee	3,418	3,298	2,645	3,007	4,733
Orange	82,656	108,738	44,827	53,991	117,141
Osceola	15,009	19,139	11,021	9,811	21,350
Palm Beach	187,840	140,317	76,223	144,143	181,408
Pasco	53,125	47,721	34,650	50,369	63,788
Pinellas	160,217	158,733	101,150	152,374	210,971
Polk	51,442	65,952	28,198	38,236	77,065
Putnam	10,707	8,909	5,975	8,569	11,621
St. Johns	12,284	20,173	7,397	7,999	19,164
St. Lucie	23,873	24,397	19,813	17,427	32,241
Santa Rosa	6,526	17,229	8,735	5,251	18,948
Sarasota	54,536	66,831	34,281	42,095	84,585
Seminole	35,649	57,085	24,477	22,627	60,328
Sumter	5,027	4,366	2,901	3,900	5,933
Suwannee	3,985	4,571	2,790	3,126	5,859
Taylor	2,568	2,693	1,929	1,762	4,054
Union	1,247	1,543	770	691	1,643
Volusia	65,213	59,155	30,813	55,437	74,116
Wakulla	2,319	2,586	1,790	1,605	3,157
Walton	3,886	5,719	3,886	3,231	7,481
Washington	2,544	3,694	1,596	2,139	4,366
Totals	**2,071,651**	**2,171,781**	**1,052,481**	**1,655,851**	**2,616,597**

Florida Vote Since 1944

1944, Roosevelt, Dem., 339,377; Dewey, Rep., 143,215.

1948, Truman, Dem., 281,988; Dewey, Rep., 194,280; Thurmond, States' Rights, 89,755; Wallace, Prog., 11,620.

1952, Eisenhower, Rep., 544,036; Stevenson, Dem., 444,950; scattered, 351.

1956, Eisenhower, Rep., 643,849; Stevenson, Dem., 480,371.

1960, Kennedy, Dem., 748,700; Nixon, Rep., 795,476.

1964, Johnson, Dem., 948,540; Goldwater, Rep., 905,941.

1968, Nixon, Rep., 886,804; Humphrey, Dem., 676,794; Wallace, 3d party, 624,207.

1972, Nixon, Rep., 1,857,759; McGovern, Dem., 718,117; scattered, 7,407.

1976, Carter, Dem., 1,636,000; Ford, Rep., 1,469,531; McCarthy, Ind., 23,643; Anderson, Amer., 21,325.

1980, Reagan, Rep., 2,046,951; Carter, Dem., 1,419,475; Anderson, Ind., 189,692; Clark, Libertarian, 30,524; write-ins, 285.

1984, Reagan, Rep., 2,728,775; Mondale, Dem., 1,448,344.

1988, Bush, Rep., 2,616,597; Dukakis, Dem., 1,655,851; Paul, Lib., 19,796, Fulani, New Alliance, 6,655.

1992, Bush, Rep., 2,171,781; Clinton, Dem., 2,071,651; Perot, Ind., 1,052,481; Marrou, Libertarian, 15,068.

Georgia

	1992			1988	
County	Clinton (D)	Bush (R)	Perot (I)	Dukakis (D)	Bush (R)
Appling	2,455	2,514	1,047	1,837	3,000
Atkinson	1,056	779	342	887	1,126
Bacon	1,423	1,301	604	780	1,407
Baker	864	391	210	707	629
Baldwin	5,813	4,262	1,679	4,008	5,852
Banks	1,530	1,551	583	984	1,590
Barrow	3,991	4,328	1,633	2,442	4,738
Bartow	6,675	7,742	2,500	4,884	8,039
Ben Hill	2,348	1,476	619	1,867	2,005
Berrien	2,103	1,637	796	1,381	2,030
Bibb	28,070	19,847	6,021	22,084	22,179
Bleckley	1,710	1,570	662	1,175	1,950
Brantley	1,883	1,541	840	1,450	1,539
Brooks	1,895	1,779	630	1,500	2,136
Bryan	2,031	2,789	1,095	1,423	2,802
Bulloch	4,903	5,690	2,020	3,417	6,354
Burke	3,647	2,390	807	2,861	2,988
Butts	2,448	1,768	619	1,730	2,184
Calhoun	1,301	464	248	901	644
Camden	2,952	3,517	1,077	2,090	2,913
Candler	1,192	1,014	541	877	1,261
Carroll	8,404	10,750	3,358	4,706	10,754
Catoosa	4,817	7,599	2,290	3,588	9,319
Charlton	1,127	1,333	427	943	1,327
Chatham	31,533	31,925	8,269	25,063	35,623
Chattahoochee	604	413	177	362	454
Chattooga	2,976	2,439	965	2,206	3,665
Cherokee	8,113	16,054	4,950	4,378	14,593
Clarke	15,403	10,459	2,987	11,154	11,150
Clay	778	264	155	595	398
Clayton	25,890	23,965	7,942	14,689	28,225
Clinch	759	790	286	594	863
Cobb	63,960	103,734	28,747	39,297	106,621
Coffee	3,275	3,778	1,256	2,777	4,019
Colquitt	3,891	4,680	1,682	2,998	5,653
Columbia	7,115	16,657	4,379	4,617	16,401
Cook	1,731	1,318	537	1,226	1,555
Coweta	7,093	9,814	3,587	4,212	9,668
Crawford	1,648	974	549	1,340	1,235
Crisp	2,610	2,253	823	1,690	2,916
Dade	1,782	2,191	823	1,120	2,539
Dawson	1,399	1,696	790	761	1,908
Decatur	3,198	3,142	1,068	2,348	3,866
DeKalb	124,559	70,282	19,741	92,521	90,179
Dodge	3,002	2,287	978	2,164	2,677
Dooly	1,993	1,034	350	1,613	1,386
Dougherty	15,236	12,455	3,178	12,579	15,520
Douglas	8,869	13,349	4,362	5,086	13,493
Early	1,970	1,457	652	1,359	1,918
Echols	312	361	238	245	422
Effingham	2,690	3,814	1,443	1,905	3,933
Elbert	3,025	2,372	757	2,118	2,796
Emanuel	2,951	2,662	755	2,387	3,530
Evans	1,230	1,244	480	1,023	1,707
Fannin	2,902	3,255	1,028	2,123	4,271
Fayette	8,430	17,576	5,598	4,593	16,443
Floyd	11,614	12,378	3,779	8,548	14,697
Forsyth	4,936	8,652	3,453	2,347	7,947
Franklin	2,505	2,391	1,014	1,842	2,615
Fulton	147,459	85,451	23,578	120,752	91,785
Gilmer	2,311	2,661	879	1,363	3,353
Glascock	316	516	180	210	580
Glynn	8,581	11,242	3,053	6,339	11,126
Gordon	4,103	5,265	1,818	2,369	6,051
Grady	2,520	2,370	1,126	1,883	2,989
Greene	2,259	1,307	483	1,818	1,432
Gwinnett	44,253	81,822	23,926	20,948	66,372
Habersham	3,098	4,569	1,444	2,114	4,871
Hall	11,214	16,108	5,043	7,782	17,415
Hancock	2,461	506	189	1,947	621
Haralson	3,281	3,142	1,167	2,404	4,529
Harris	2,679	3,316	954	1,905	3,414
Hart	3,614	2,607	1,376	2,476	3,044
Heard	1,456	1,190	617	874	1,551
Henry	7,817	12,634	3,769	4,348	10,882
Houston	12,270	14,119	6,263	8,664	15,748
Irwin	1,366	973	465	918	1,226
Jackson	3,792	3,976	1,381	2,607	4,407
Jasper	1,485	1,153	373	1,188	1,474
Jeff Davis	2,031	1,947	958	1,242	2,050
Jefferson	3,220	2,077	685	2,346	2,788
Jenkins	1,401	929	394	953	1,288
Johnson	1,473	1,314	502	927	1,567
Jones	3,338	2,770	1,159	2,662	3,618
Lamar	2,065	1,707	600	1,416	2,035
Lanier	811	600	298	698	725
Laurens	6,184	6,146	1,602	4,879	6,929
Lee	1,811	3,061	1,024	995	2,875
Liberty	3,853	2,832	1,176	2,906	3,100
Lincoln	1,327	1,149	479	893	1,417
Long	874	719	355	681	858
Lowndes	9,019	10,276	2,864	6,427	10,855
Lumpkin	2,010	1,972	1,035	1,286	2,688
McDuffie	2,640	2,955	860	1,704	3,231
McIntosh	1,925	1,027	550	1,527	1,273
Macon	2,491	944	363	2,268	1,412
Madison	2,393	3,351	1,129	1,639	3,724
Marion	1,145	711	198	844	804
Meriwether	4,002	2,364	942	2,934	3,101
Miller	934	826	455	515	1,105
Mitchell	3,052	1,917	818	2,260	2,590
Monroe	2,774	2,423	949	1,970	2,570
Montgomery	1,185	1,009	416	903	1,228

Morgan	2,057	1,797	596	1,508	2,108
Murray	2,764	3,256	1,186	1,679	3,996
Muscogee	25,476	21,386	4,327	18,772	23,058
Newton	5,811	5,804	1,998	3,111	5,809
Oconee	2,745	4,125	1,182	1,990	4,265
Oglethorpe	1,491	1,590	620	1,154	1,951
Paulding	5,212	7,180	2,654	2,717	7,329
Peach	3,677	2,327	947	2,972	2,782
Pickens	2,359	2,332	1,037	1,430	3,021
Pierce	1,852	1,899	708	1,558	1,947
Pike	1,651	1,822	623	1,176	2,074
Polk	4,872	4,158	1,598	2,977	5,454
Pulaski	1,756	1,075	614	1,476	1,400
Putnam	2,149	1,756	775	1,532	2,111
Quitman	523	284	113	436	296
Rabun	1,878	1,902	825	1,301	2,278
Randolph	1,756	887	315	1,369	1,319
Richmond	28,910	24,227	6,290	20,489	27,566
Rockdale	7,003	11,945	3,664	4,330	12,413
Schley	601	511	180	439	635
Screven	1,940	1,705	709	1,461	2,178
Seminole	1,193	850	468	1,171	1,469
Spalding	6,392	7,262	2,044	4,318	7,730
Stephens	2,976	4,047	1,448	2,185	4,329
Stewart	1,540	1,186	175	1,136	832
Sumter	4,489	3,616	1,046	3,332	4,289
Talbot	1,768	671	238	1,248	802
Taliaferro	755	269	80	469	306
Tattnall	2,360	2,566	996	1,694	3,172
Taylor	1,508	1,078	281	1,134	1,145
Telfair	2,238	1,324	613	1,765	1,805
Terrell	1,942	1,143	384	1,383	1,517
Thomas	4,841	5,500	1,591	3,530	6,572
Tift	3,930	4,485	1,139	2,446	4,760
Toombs	2,648	3,609	1,210	1,152	4,433
Towns	1,487	1,674	537	942	1,783
Treutlen	1,116	898	318	726	970
Troup	6,412	8,118	2,488	4,562	9,484
Turner	1,669	936	370	1,122	1,312
Twiggs	2,097	853	432	1,730	1,261
Union	2,304	2,533	804	1,258	2,396
Upson	3,740	4,053	1,186	2,666	4,614
Walker	6,217	8,489	2,748	4,753	10,487
Walton	4,821	5,619	1,923	3,091	5,974
Ware	4,573	4,573	1,263	4,292	4,819
Warren	1,239	751	180	1,091	897
Washington	3,508	2,384	820	2,615	2,752
Wayne	3,052	3,381	1,107	2,417	3,340
Webster	600	208	103	427	361
Wheeler	880	601	214	658	709
White	1,756	2,477	981	1,028	2,648
Whitfield	7,335	12,003	2,866	4,618	12,761
Wilcox	1,365	916	433	1,079	1,235
Wilkes	1,955	1,535	464	1,549	1,810
Wilkinson	2,286	1,232	520	1,831	1,546
Worth	2,578	2,344	905	1,311	2,668
Totals	**1,008,966**	**995,252**	**309,657**	**714,792**	**1,081,331**

Georgia Vote Since 1944

1944, Roosevelt, Dem., 268,187; Dewey, Rep., 56,506; Watson, Proh., 36.

1948, Truman, Dem., 254,646; Dewey, Rep., 76,691; Thurmond, States' Rights, 85,055; Wallace, Prog., 1,636; Watson, Proh., 732.

1952, Eisenhower, Rep., 198,979; Stevenson, Dem., 456,823; Liberty Party, 1.

1956, Stevenson, Dem., 444,388; Eisenhower, Rep., 222,778; Andrews, Ind., write-in, 1,754.

1960, Kennedy, Dem., 458,638; Nixon, Rep., 274,472; write-in, 239.

1964, Johnson, Dem., 522,557; Goldwater, Rep., 616,600.

1968, Nixon, Rep., 380,111; Humphrey, Dem., 334,440; Wallace, 3d party, 535,550; write-in, 162.

1972, Nixon, Rep., 881,496; McGovern, Dem., 289,529; Schmitz, Amer., 2,288; scattered.

1976, Carter, Dem., 979,409; Ford, Rep., 483,743; write-in, 4,306.

1980, Reagan, Rep., 654,168; Carter, Dem., 890,955; Anderson, Ind., 36,055; Clark, Libertarian, 15,627.

1984, Reagan, Rep., 1,068,722; Mondale, Dem., 706,628.

1988, Bush, Rep., 1,081,331; Dukakis, Dem., 714,792; Paul, Lib., 8,435; Fulani, New Alliance, 5,099.

1992, Clinton, Dem., 1,008,966; Bush, Rep., 995,252; Perot, Ind., 309,657; Marrou, Libertarian, 7,110.

Hawaii

	1992			1988	
County	Clinton (D)	Bush (R)	Perot (I)	Dukakis (D)	Bush (R)
Hawaii	25,725	15,460	8,889	24,091	17,125
Honolulu	123,908	103,937	35,728	138,971	120,258
Kauai	10,715	6,274	1,756	11,770	8,298
Maui	18,962	11,151	6,630	17,532	12,944
Totals	**179,310**	**136,822**	**53,003**	**192,364**	**158,625**

Hawaii Vote Since 1960

1960, Kennedy, Dem., 92,410; Nixon, Rep., 92,295.

1964, Johnson, Dem., 163,249; Goldwater, Rep., 44,022.

1968, Nixon, Rep., 91,425; Humphrey, Dem., 141,324; Wallace, 3d party, 3,469.

1972, Nixon, Rep., 168,865; McGovern, Dem., 101,409.

1976, Carter, Dem., 147,375; Ford, Rep., 140,003; MacBride, Libertarian, 3,923.

1980, Reagan, Rep., 130,112; Carter, Dem., 135,879; Anderson, Ind., 32,021; Clark, Libertarian, 3,269; Commoner, Citizens, 1,548; Hall, Com., 458.

1984, Reagan, Rep., 184,934; Mondale, Dem., 147,098; Bergland, Libertarian, 2,167.

1988, Bush, Rep., 158,625; Dukakis, Dem., 192,364; Paul, Lib., 1,999; Fulani, New Alliance, 1,003.

1992, Clinton, Dem., 179,310; Bush, Rep., 136,822; Perot, Ind., 53,003; Gritz, Populist/America First, 1,452; Marrou, Libertarian, 1,119.

Idaho

	1992			1988	
County	Clinton (D)	Bush (R)	Perot (I)	Dukakis (D)	Bush (R)
Ada	31,941	49,000	28,192	30,525	54,951
Adams	457	754	695	643	1,107
Bannock	11,091	12,016	8,116	13,074	14,986
Bear Lake	562	1,419	684	867	2,084
Benewah	1,270	1,223	1,165	1,518	1,650
Bingham	3,565	7,333	4,144	4,346	10,131
Blaine	2,865	2,243	2,831	2,498	3,130
Boise	623	912	754	620	1,044
Bonner	4,995	3,937	4,645	5,555	5,721
Bonneville	7,014	16,557	10,241	7,032	22,613
Boundary	1,095	1,479	1,136	1,336	1,800
Butte	433	602	392	521	899
Camas	134	202	145	136	288
Canyon	9,095	19,220	8,974	10,207	21,426
Caribou	562	1,350	1,088	867	2,239
Cassias	1,351	4,052	1,785	1,833	5,345
Clark	95	195	119	133	281
Clearwater	1,433	1,152	1,098	1,861	1,659
Custer	564	829	729	616	1,253
Elmore	1,858	3,087	1,867	2,078	3,756
Franklin	524	2,115	890	806	2,992
Fremont	903	2,333	1,349	1,178	3,401
Gem	1,609	2,455	1,555	2,064	2,926
Gooding	1,530	2,178	1,591	1,872	2,908
Idaho	1,974	2,709	1,900	2,198	3,541
Jefferson	978	3,471	2,164	1,198	5,295
Jerome	1,739	2,972	1,768	1,985	3,830
Kootenai	11,553	13,065	11,261	11,621	15,093
Latah	7,233	5,353	3,602	6,544	6,367
Lemhi	996	1,540	1,175	1,157	2,378
Lewis	674	593	491	807	786
Lincoln	514	656	441	574	918
Madison	741	4,591	1,920	1,009	6,197
Minidoka	1,815	3,304	1,875	2,290	4,623
Nez Perce	7,069	5,431	4,363	7,754	7,027
Oneida	351	713	590	508	1,269
Owyhee	686	1,469	862	848	1,707
Payette	1,656	2,895	2,055	1,900	3,786
Power	837	1,352	697	1,095	1,838
Shoshone	3,182	1,441	1,878	3,379	2,134
Teton	472	762	608	531	982
Twin Falls	6,593	10,335	6,043	7,078	13,243
Valley	1,259	1,548	1,313	1,251	1,897
Washington	1,122	1,802	1,204	1,359	2,380
Totals	**137,013**	**202,645**	**130,395**	**147,272**	**253,881**

Idaho Vote Since 1944

1944, Roosevelt, Dem., 107,399; Dewey, Rep., 100,137; Watson, Proh., 503; Thomas, Soc., 282.

1948, Truman, Dem., 107,370; Dewey, Rep., 101,514; Wallace, Prog., 4,972; Watson, Proh., 628; Thomas, Soc., 332.

1952, Eisenhower, Rep., 180,707; Stevenson Dem., 95,081; Hallinan, Prog., 443; write-in, 23.

1956, Eisenhower, Rep., 166,979; Stevenson, Dem., 105,868; Andrews, Ind., 126; write-in, 16.

1960, Kennedy, Dem., 138,853; Nixon, Rep., 161,597.

1964, Johnson, Dem., 148,920; Goldwater, Rep., 143,557.

1968, Nixon, Rep., 165,369; Humphrey, Dem., 89,273; Wallace, 3d party, 36,541.

1972, Nixon, Rep., 199,384; McGovern, Dem., 80,826; Schmitz, Amer., 28,869; Spock, Peoples, 903.

1976, Carter, Dem., 126,549; Ford, Rep., 204,151; Maddox, Amer., 5,935; MacBride, Libertarian, 3,558; LaRouche, U.S. Labor, 739.

1980, Reagan, Rep., 290,699; Carter, Dem., 110,192; Anderson, Ind., 27,058; Clark, Libertarian, 8,425; Rarick, Amer., 1,057.
1984, Reagan, Rep., 297,523; Mondale, Dem., 108,510; Bergland, Libertarian, 2,823.
1988, Bush, Rep., 253,881; Dukakis, Dem., 147,272; Paul, Lib., 5,313; Fulani, Ind., 2,502.
1992, Clinton, Dem., 137,013; Bush, Rep., 202,645; Perot, Ind., 130,395; Gritz, Populist/America First, 10,281; Marrou, Libertarian, 1,167.

Illinois

	1992			1988	
County	Clinton (D)	Bush (R)	Perot (I)	Dukakis (D)	Bush (R)
Adams	11,748	13,529	6,157	13,768	15,831
Alexander	2,566	1,301	474	2,693	1,954
Bond	3,428	2,715	1,373	3,459	3,608
Boone	5,114	5,589	2,880	4,234	6,923
Brown	1,146	1,029	504	1,267	1,373
Bureau	7,551	6,836	3,465	7,354	8,896
Calhoun	1,519	745	532	1,544	1,238
Carroll	2,854	3,297	1,502	2,990	4,464
Cass	3,200	2,162	1,072	3,316	2,916
Champaign	35,003	27,096	13,571	29,733	33,247
Christian	9,042	5,087	3,401	8,295	7,040
Clark	3,338	3,175	1,450	3,275	4,508
Clay	2,962	2,471	1,193	2,761	3,494
Clinton	6,686	5,771	3,315	5,935	7,681
Coles	9,402	8,098	4,707	8,327	11,043
Cook	1,249,533	605,300	281,999	1,129,973	878,582
Crawford	3,964	3,606	2,062	3,555	4,951
Cumberland	2,111	1,860	1,209	1,904	2,667
DeKalb	13,744	12,655	7,680	11,811	17,182
DeWitt	3,009	3,164	1,543	2,660	3,942
Douglas	3,341	3,309	1,600	3,184	4,378
DuPage	114,564	178,271	76,839	94,285	217,907
Edgar	4,014	3,790	1,930	3,880	5,538
Edwards	1,299	1,601	634	1,218	2,212
Effingham	5,221	6,329	3,354	4,553	8,431
Fayette	4,833	3,508	1,730	4,632	5,452
Ford	2,175	3,046	1,222	2,026	4,059
Franklin	12,744	5,504	3,180	11,023	7,677
Fulton	9,725	5,062	2,874	9,046	6,999
Gallatin	2,371	990	568	2,455	1,580
Greene	3,164	2,391	1,461	3,020	3,136
Grundy	6,122	6,346	3,724	5,525	8,743
Hamilton	2,582	1,521	862	2,618	2,622
Hancock	4,213	3,714	2,091	4,740	4,568
Hardin	1,665	985	515	1,308	1,504
Henderson	2,013	1,310	715	2,085	1,726
Henry	11,077	8,989	4,231	11,594	11,358
Iroquois	4,440	6,948	3,073	4,221	9,596
Jackson	13,373	6,899	3,995	11,334	9,687
Jasper	2,284	1,996	1,160	2,135	3,024
Jefferson	8,665	5,497	3,403	7,729	7,624
Jersey	4,749	2,933	2,363	4,376	4,343
JoDaviess	4,044	4,249	2,102	4,141	4,923
Johnson	2,299	2,124	944	1,872	2,797
Kane	44,568	55,684	27,179	36,366	66,283
Kankakee	17,229	15,411	7,264	15,147	20,316
Kendall	5,423	8,521	4,394	4,347	10,653
Knox	12,524	8,331	4,357	12,752	10,842
Lake	81,693	99,000	42,384	64,327	114,115
LaSalle	23,276	16,078	10,434	22,271	22,166
Lawrence	3,270	2,681	1,498	3,140	3,655
Lee	5,530	6,652	3,191	4,608	8,903
Livingston	6,007	8,004	3,029	5,009	10,324
Logan	5,169	6,567	2,420	4,727	8,490
McDonough	5,814	5,297	2,770	5,247	7,173
McHenry	24,783	41,356	21,817	18,919	46,135
McLean	23,090	25,726	10,282	18,659	30,572
Macon	27,449	18,684	9,236	25,364	23,862
Macoupin	12,050	6,518	5,018	12,195	9,362
Madison	58,484	32,167	23,110	54,175	44,907
Marion	9,669	5,764	3,407	8,592	8,695
Marshall	2,819	2,491	1,169	2,742	3,588
Mason	3,969	2,473	1,245	3,406	3,424
Massac	3,347	2,754	892	3,227	3,507
Menard	2,264	2,834	1,179	2,103	3,560
Mercer	3,990	2,983	1,535	4,204	3,683
Monroe	4,894	4,807	2,813	4,529	6,275
Montgomery	7,424	4,407	2,956	7,293	6,388
Morgan	6,351	6,566	3,317	6,032	8,808
Moultrie	3,056	2,065	1,322	3,013	3,167
Ogle	6,512	9,008	4,455	5,641	11,644
Peoria	38,099	30,718	12,195	35,253	37,605
Perry	6,009	3,105	1,955	5,167	4,576
Piatt	3,520	3,076	1,822	3,099	4,137
Pike	4,016	3,342	1,643	4,614	3,965
Pope	1,063	951	391	996	1,202
Pulaski	1,987	1,169	379	1,793	1,666
Putnam	1,574	969	752	1,601	1,516
Randolph	8,529	4,899	3,092	7,844	7,396
Richland	3,286	3,053	1,689	2,863	4,264
Rock Island	37,412	23,212	10,416	40,174	27,412
St. Clair	57,625	31,951	17,592	55,465	41,439
Saline	7,258	3,667	2,302	6,676	5,798
Sangamon	40,052	39,641	16,861	37,729	50,175
Schuyler	1,650	1,512	815	1,866	2,178
Scott	1,057	1,132	588	1,243	1,535
Shelby	5,101	3,631	2,401	4,650	5,370
Stark	1,336	1,384	625	1,274	1,841
Stephenson	7,899	9,005	4,677	7,460	11,342
Tazewell	26,428	23,469	9,927	24,603	28,861
Union	4,681	3,003	1,373	4,197	4,244
Vermilion	18,383	11,703	8,162	17,918	16,943
Wabash	2,436	2,485	1,302	2,241	3,453
Warren	3,661	3,325	1,436	3,617	4,584
Washington	2,986	3,003	1,542	2,689	4,127
Wayne	3,332	3,809	1,702	3,135	5,481
White	4,308	3,057	1,428	4,144	4,354
Whiteside	12,329	10,146	4,589	11,328	12,978
Will	59,633	58,337	32,788	49,816	73,129
Williamson	14,361	9,462	4,779	12,712	12,274
Winnebago	48,298	42,221	21,227	45,280	55,699
Woodford	5,490	8,032	2,733	4,604	9,474
Totals	**2,453,350**	**1,734,096**	**840,515**	**2,215,940**	**2,310,939**

Illinois Vote Since 1944

1944, Roosevelt, Dem., 2,079,479; Dewey, Rep., 1,939,314; Teichert, Soc. Labor, 9,677; Watson, Proh., 7,411; Thomas, Soc., 180.
1948, Truman, Dem., 1,994,715; Dewey, Rep., 1,961,103; Watson, Proh., 11,959; Thomas, Soc., 11,522; Teichert, Soc. Labor, 3,118.
1952, Eisenhower, Rep., 2,457,327; Stevenson, Dem., 2,013,920; Hass, Soc. Labor, 9,363; write-in, 448.
1956, Eisenhower, Rep., 2,623,327; Stevenson, Dem., 1,775,682; Hass, Soc. Labor, 8,342; write-in, 56.
1960, Kennedy, Dem., 2,377,846; Nixon, Rep., 2,368,988; Hass, Soc. Labor, 10,560; write-in, 15.
1964, Johnson, Dem., 2,796,833; Goldwater, Rep., 1,905,946; write-in, 62.
1968, Nixon, Rep., 2,174,774; Humphrey, Dem., 2,039,814; Wallace, 3d party, 390,958; Blomen, Soc. Labor, 13,878; write-in, 325.
1972, Nixon, Rep. 2,788,179; McGovern, Dem., 1,913,472; Fisher, Soc. Labor, 12,344; Schmitz, Amer., 2,471; Hall, Com., 4,541; others, 2,229.
1976, Carter, Dem., 2,271,295; Ford, Rep., 2,364,269; McCarthy, Ind., 55,939; Hall, Com., 9,250; MacBride, Libertarian, 8,057; Camejo, Soc. Workers, 3,615; Levin, Soc. Labor, 2,422; LaRouche, U.S. Labor, 2,018; write-in, 1,968.
1980, Reagan, Rep., 2,358,049; Carter, Dem., 1,981,413; Anderson, Ind., 346,754; Clark, Libertarian, 38,939; Commoner, Citizens, 10,692; Hall, Com., 9,711; Griswold, Workers World, 2,257; DeBerry, Socialist Workers, 1,302; write-ins, 604.
1984, Reagan, Rep., 2,707,103; Mondale, Dem., 2,086,499; Bergland, Libertarian, 10,086.
1988, Bush, Rep., 2,310,939; Dukakis, Dem., 2,215,940; Paul, Lib., 14,944; Fulani, Solid., 10,276.
1992, Clinton, Dem., 2,453,350; Bush, Rep., 1,734,096; Perot, Ind., 840,515; Marrou, Libertarian, 9,218; Fulani, New Alliance, 5,267; Gritz, Populist/America First, 3,577; Hagelin, Natural Law, 2,751; Warren, Socialist Workers, 1,361.

Indiana

	1992			1988	
County	Clinton (D)	Bush (R)	Perot (I)	Dukakis (D)	Bush (R)
Adams	3,708	6,078	2,865	3,811	8,137
Allen	39,629	55,003	25,809	39,238	74,638
Bartholomew	8,284	13,146	5,882	8,804	17,364
Benton	1,221	2,030	1,056	1,349	2,698
Blackford	2,088	2,347	1,319	2,253	3,336
Boone	3,982	9,485	3,826	4,168	11,608
Brown	2,029	2,633	1,635	2,115	3,348
Carroll	2,561	3,800	2,173	2,952	4,981
Cass	4,757	7,421	3,944	5,784	10,970
Clark	17,460	13,333	5,653	14,528	16,544
Clay	3,306	4,696	2,134	3,724	5,852
Clinton	3,490	6,141	2,535	4,412	8,570
Crawford	2,260	1,903	819	2,036	2,532
Daviess	3,201	5,591	1,695	3,483	6,768
Dearborn	5,116	6,974	3,384	5,066	8,195
Decatur	2,774	5,195	2,299	2,979	6,245
Dekalb	4,652	6,682	3,554	4,657	9,018
Delaware	19,556	20,473	10,453	20,548	27,348
Dubois	5,878	6,785	3,195	5,954	9,995
Elkhart	14,660	27,920	9,450	14,236	33,793
Fayette	3,969	4,376	2,299	4,118	5,949
Floyd	13,166	11,932	4,421	11,024	14,291

Fountain	2,829	3,391	2,162	3,279	5,113
Franklin	2,456	3,831	1,858	2,472	4,777
Fulton	2,552	3,982	1,963	2,788	5,234
Gibson	6,909	5,172	2,680	7,031	7,610
Grant	9,211	13,806	5,597	10,799	18,441
Greene	5,431	5,410	2,610	5,979	7,689
Hamilton	10,215	34,622	10,365	8,853	36,654
Hancock	4,752	11,072	4,752	5,355	13,374
Harrison.	5,768	5,403	2,469	4,933	6,702
Hendricks . . .	7,071	18,373	7,519	7,643	22,090
Henry	6,794	8,720	4,416	7,779	11,280
Howard	10,288	15,306	8,575	11,518	19,971
Huntington . . .	3,855	9,093	2,967	3,873	11,675
Jackson.	5,663	7,246	3,148	5,550	9,470
Jasper.	3,033	4,809	2,019	3,237	6,009
Jay	3,208	3,609	1,994	3,212	5,363
Jefferson	5,510	4,937	2,565	5,221	6,949
Jennings	3,471	4,392	2,370	3,667	5,636
Johnson.	8,712	20,353	8,246	9,001	24,654
Knox	6,718	6,683	3,719	7,006	9,813
Kosciusko . . .	5,307	14,179	5,115	5,321	17,761
LaGrange. . . .	2,093	3,584	1,736	2,029	4,495
Lake	102,778	53,867	28,635	105,026	79,929
LaPorte	17,717	14,962	9,641	17,585	20,537
Lawrence. . . .	5,557	7,712	3,452	5,787	10,742
Madison.	22,276	23,479	13,100	24,443	32,596
Marion.	122,234	141,369	57,878	128,627	184,519
Marshall.	4,912	8,048	3,522	5,488	10,490
Martin	2,018	2,523	883	2,132	3,066
Miami	3,967	6,416	3,428	4,613	8,533
Monroe	19,712	16,661	6,943	15,855	20,756
Montgomery . .	3,371	7,602	3,511	3,623	10,793
Morgan	4,690	10,939	5,375	5,375	14,284
Newton	1,757	2,295	1,274	1,744	3,274
Noble	4,411	5,883	3,328	4,143	7,889
Ohio	970	1,009	527	1,113	1,412
Orange	2,948	3,738	1,296	2,739	5,245
Owen	2,207	2,753	1,563	2,484	3,837
Parke	2,429	2,953	1,696	2,563	4,458
Perry.	4,829	2,973	1,560	4,804	4,720
Pike	2,960	2,156	1,238	3,037	3,294
Porter	21,022	22,644	13,096	19,390	29,790
Posey	4,632	4,435	2,357	4,468	5,987
Pulaski	1,950	2,712	1,214	2,213	3,677
Putnam	3,487	5,341	3,174	3,850	7,119
Randolph. . . .	3,870	4,937	2,939	3,990	6,856
Ripley	3,480	5,033	2,406	3,605	6,414
Rush	2,168	3,873	1,948	2,451	5,112
St. Joseph . . .	46,203	38,934	18,828	48,056	49,481
Scott	4,085	2,649	1,092	3,378	3,455
Shelby.	4,560	8,075	3,521	5,382	10,176
Spencer.	4,301	3,789	1,464	4,061	4,964
Starke	3,695	3,100	1,885	4,104	4,458
Steuben.	3,630	4,868	2,896	3,114	6,855
Sullivan	4,211	3,052	1,857	4,320	4,246
Switzerland . .	1,535	1,211	636	1,479	1,572
Tippecanoe . .	17,343	23,050	9,684	16,256	27,897
Tipton	2,125	3,906	1,816	2,485	5,148
Union	898	1,394	664	946	1,814
Vanderburgh .	33,799	30,271	12,513	31,270	38,928
Vermillion. . . .	3,652	2,360	1,794	4,044	3,674
Vigo	18,050	15,834	8,141	19,192	21,929
Wabash.	4,518	7,062	3,424	4,168	9,153
Warren	1,367	1,601	1,020	1,542	2,243
Warrick	8,612	8,087	3,862	7,999	10,504
Washington . .	4,092	4,043	1,846	3,370	4,998
Wayne.	9,960	12,221	5,095	10,209	16,388
Wells.	3,282	5,799	2,890	3,437	7,712
White	2,988	4,622	2,582	3,256	6,220
Whitley	3,569	5,217	3,195	3,642	7,679
Totals.	**848,420**	**989,375**	**455,934**	**860,643**	**1,297,763**

Indiana Vote Since 1944

1944, Roosevelt, Dem., 781,403; Dewey, Rep., 875,891; Watson, Proh., 12,574; Thomas, Soc., 2,223.

1948, Truman, Dem., 807,833; Dewey, Rep., 821,079; Watson, Proh., 14,711; Wallace, Prog., 9,649; Thomas, Soc., 2,179; Teichert, Soc. Labor, 763.

1952, Eisenhower, Rep., 1,136,259; Stevenson, Dem., 801,530; Hamblen, Proh., 15,335; Hallinan, Prog., 1,222; Hass, Soc. Labor, 979.

1956, Eisenhower, Rep., 1,182,811; Stevenson, Dem., 783,908; Holtwick, Proh., 6,554; Hass, Soc. Labor, 1,334.

1960, Kennedy, Dem., 952,358; Nixon, Rep., 1,175,120; Decker, Proh., 6,746; Hass, Soc. Labor, 1,136.

1964, Johnson, Dem. 1,170,848; Goldwater, Rep., 911,118; Munn, Proh., 8,266; Hass, Soc. Labor, 1,374.

1968, Nixon, Rep., 1,067,885; Humphrey, Dem., 806,659; Wallace, 3d party, 243,108; Munn, Proh., 4,616; Halstead, Soc. Worker, 1,293; Gregory, write-in, 36.

1972, Nixon, Rep., 1,405,154; McGovern, Dem., 708,568; Reed, Soc. Workers, 5,575; Fisher, Soc. Labor, 1,688; Spock, Peace & Freedom, 4,544.

1976, Carter, Dem., 1,014,714; Ford, Rep., 1,185,958; Anderson, Amer., 14,048; Camejo, Soc. Workers, 5,695; LaRouche, U.S. Labor, 1,947.

1980, Reagan, Rep., 1,255,656; Carter, Dem., 844,197; Anderson, Ind., 111,639; Clark, Libertarian, 19,627; Commoner, Citizens, 4,852; Greaves, American, 4,750; Hall, Com., 702; DeBerry, Soc., 610.

1984, Reagan, Rep., 1,377,230; Mondale, Dem., 841,481; Bergland, Libertarian, 6,741.

1988, Bush, Rep., 1,297,763; Dukakis, Dem., 860,643; Fulani, New Alliance, 10,215.

1992, Bush, Rep., 989,375; Clinton, Dem., 848,420; Perot, Ind., 455,934; Marrou, Libertarian, 7,936; Fulani, New Alliance, 2,583.

Iowa

		1992		1988	
County	Clinton (D)	Bush (R)	Perot (I)	Dukakis (D)	Bush (R)
Adair.	1,655	1,713	814	2,261	1,833
Adams	1,034	863	679	1,283	1,080
Allamakee . . .	2,362	2,627	1,543	2,768	3,186
Appanoose. . .	2,810	2,346	1,161	3,209	2,779
Audubon	1,589	1,373	887	1,863	1,478
Benton	4,467	3,469	2,454	5,873	4,011
Black Hawk . .	29,584	21,398	10,182	31,657	24,112
Boone	5,913	4,148	2,070	7,232	4,381
Bremer	4,774	4,482	2,338	4,961	5,079
Buchanan . . .	4,166	3,313	2,126	4,778	3,495
Buena Vista . .	3,374	3,863	1,955	4,580	4,170
Butler	2,548	3,209	1,333	2,593	3,523
Calhoun.	2,140	2,169	946	2,990	2,474
Carroll	3,800	3,439	2,192	5,437	3,701
Cass.	2,231	3,176	1,608	2,934	3,962
Cedar	3,296	2,965	1,945	4,032	3,373
Cerro Gordo . .	11,415	8,250	4,498	12,857	9,358
Cherokee. . . .	2,590	2,768	1,503	3,574	3,218
Chickasaw . . .	2,913	2,129	1,566	3,530	2,549
Clarke	1,921	1,417	899	2,262	1,631
Clay	3,346	3,011	1,964	4,173	3,641
Clayton	3,742	3,044	2,309	4,320	3,839
Clinton	11,683	8,746	4,414	12,549	10,243
Crawford	3,004	2,693	1,905	3,868	3,375
Dallas	6,554	5,587	2,665	7,501	4,858
Davis	1,962	1,344	718	2,246	1,563
Decatur	1,866	1,316	786	2,192	1,406
Delaware	3,093	3,195	2,144	3,947	3,425
Des Moines . .	11,309	6,378	3,386	11,593	7,652
Dickinson. . . .	3,106	3,196	1,974	3,342	3,678
Dubuque	20,539	14,007	8,208	23,797	14,530
Emmet	2,239	1,749	1,010	2,778	2,173
Fayette	4,412	3,879	2,493	5,304	4,921
Floyd.	3,688	2,404	1,611	4,377	3,266
Franklin	2,049	2,137	1,045	2,594	2,320
Fremont.	1,422	1,459	1,003	1,547	1,946
Greene	2,422	1,952	956	3,011	2,091
Grundy	1,895	3,160	1,069	2,211	3,433
Guthrie	2,234	1,962	1,216	2,910	2,005
Hamilton	3,262	3,031	1,348	4,156	3,277
Hancock	2,175	2,428	1,170	2,831	2,731
Hardin.	3,792	3,590	1,547	5,088	3,856
Harrison	2,349	2,763	1,691	2,883	3,108
Henry	3,544	3,435	1,522	3,754	3,951
Howard	2,099	1,516	1,193	2,330	1,970
Humboldt. . . .	1,765	2,299	1,093	2,713	2,594
Ida	1,449	1,714	1,061	1,787	1,951
Iowa	2,560	2,656	1,709	3,338	3,247
Jackson.	4,421	2,673	2,096	4,864	3,237
Jasper.	8,120	6,866	2,972	8,940	6,703
Jefferson	2,562	2,541	1,241	3,594	3,614
Johnson	28,656	14,041	8,625	28,759	15,453
Jones	3,508	3,071	2,306	4,641	3,496
Keokuk	2,329	1,981	1,238	2,899	2,278
Kossuth.	3,660	3,464	1,906	5,088	3,938
Lee.	9,366	4,777	2,920	10,911	6,228
Linn	38,567	30,215	19,643	42,993	33,129
Louisa.	2,091	1,691	1,044	2,268	2,060
Lucas	2,072	1,734	848	2,454	1,776
Lyon	1,331	3,272	1,068	1,706	3,517
Madison	2,525	2,421	1,168	3,421	2,410
Mahaska	3,714	4,953	1,508	4,451	4,798
Marion.	5,531	6,062	1,896	6,922	5,914
Marshall	8,303	6,784	3,100	9,760	7,657
Mills	1,798	2,699	1,638	2,092	3,212
Mitchell	2,177	1,933	1,199	2,870	2,338
Monona.	1,939	1,660	1,231	2,408	2,068
Monroe	1,829	1,323	612	2,338	1,313
Montgomery. .	1,599	2,404	1,341	1,898	3,166
Muscatine . . .	7,089	6,087	3,583	7,059	6,904
O'Brien	2,122	3,869	1,557	2,768	4,241
Osceola	990	1,756	813	1,277	1,951
Page.	1,951	3,670	1,669	2,185	4,583
Palo Alto	2,374	1,789	1,186	3,377	2,041
Plymouth	3,171	5,196	2,039	4,220	5,316
Pocahontas . .	1,919	1,743	942	2,722	1,871
Polk	78,585	63,708	24,155	84,476	57,854

Pottawattamie.	13,228	15,671	8,035	14,958	17,193
Poweshiek . . .	4,056	3,245	1,680	4,876	3,683
Ringgold	1,341	967	551	1,609	1,110
Sac.	1,896	2,138	1,157	2,613	2,411
Scott.	33,765	28,844	11,423	34,415	31,025
Shelby.	2,094	2,809	1,614	2,806	3,019
Sioux	2,226	10,637	1,771	2,923	10,270
Story.	17,118	12,702	6,275	19,051	13,782
Tama	3,573	2,948	1,748	4,584	3,362
Taylor	1,430	1,200	910	1,671	1,647
Union	2,565	2,224	1,280	3,236	2,751
Van Buren . . .	1,464	1,418	811	1,612	1,692
Wapello	8,670	4,852	2,513	10,177	5,350
Warren	8,612	7,242	3,217	9,627	6,424
Washington . .	3,384	3,576	1,994	3,776	3,741
Wayne.	1,632	1,299	642	1,988	1,467
Webster.	8,562	6,992	3,272	10,267	6,926
Winnebago. . .	2,322	2,407	1,329	2,804	2,863
Winneshiek . .	3,791	3,331	2,416	4,443	4,194
Woodbury . . .	17,398	18,148	7,182	20,153	18,790
Worth	2,009	1,382	1,044	2,440	1,488
Wright	2,776	2,708	1,151	3,353	2,658
Totals.	**586,353**	**504,891**	**253,468**	**670,557**	**545,355**

Iowa Vote Since 1944

1944, Roosevelt, Dem., 499,876; Dewey, Rep., 547,267; Watson, Proh., 3,752; Thomas, Soc., 1,511; Teichert, Soc. Labor, 193.

1948, Truman, Dem., 522,380; Dewey, Rep., 494,018; Wallace, Prog., 12,125; Teichert, Soc. Labor, 4,274; Watson, Proh., 3,382; Thomas, Soc., 1,829; Dobbs, Soc. Workers, 26.

1952, Eisenhower, Rep., 808,906; Stevenson, Dem., 451,513; Hallinan, Prog., 5,085; Hamblen, Proh., 2,882; Hoopes, Soc., 219; Hass, Soc. Labor, 139; scattering 29.

1956, Eisenhower, Rep., 729,187; Stevenson, Dem., 501,858; Andrews (A.C.P. of Iowa), 3,202; Hoopes, Soc., 192; Hass, Soc. Labor, 125.

1960, Kennedy, Dem., 550,565; Nixon, Rep., 722,381; Hass, Soc. Labor, 230; write-in, 634.

1964, Johnson, Dem., 733,030; Goldwater, Rep., 449,148; Hass, Soc. Labor, 182; DeBerry, Soc. Worker, 159; Munn, Proh., 1,902.

1968, Nixon, Rep., 619,106; Humphrey, Dem., 476,699; Wallace, 3d party, 66,422; Munn, Proh., 362; Halstead, Soc. Worker, 3,377; Cleaver, Peace and Freedom, 1,332; Blomen, Soc. Labor, 241.

1972, Nixon, Rep., 706,207; McGovern, Dem., 496,206; Schmitz, Amer., 22,056; Jenness, Soc. Workers, 488; Fisher, Soc. Labor, 195; Hall, Com. 272; Green, Universal, 199; scattered, 321.

1976, Carter, Dem., 619,931; Ford, Rep., 632,863; McCarthy, Ind., 20,051; Anderson, Amer., 3,040; MacBride, Libertarian, 1,452.

1980, Reagan, Rep., 676,026; Carter, Dem., 508,672; Anderson, Ind., 115,633; Clark, Libertarian, 13,123; Commoner, Citizens, 2,273; McReynolds, Socialist, 534; Hall, Com., 298; DeBerry, Soc. Work., 244; Greaves, American, 189; Bubar, Statesman, 150; scattering, 519.

1984, Reagan, Rep., 703,088; Mondale, Dem., 605,620; Bergland, Libertarian, 1,844.

1988, Bush, Rep., 545,355; Dukakis, Dem., 670,557; LaRouche, Ind., 3,526; Paul, Lib., 2,494.

1992, Clinton, Dem., 586,353; Bush, Rep., 504,891; Perot, Ind., 253,468; Hagelin, Natural Law, 3,079; Gritz, Populist/America First, 1,177; Marrou, Libertarian, 1,076.

Kansas

	1992			1988	
County	Clinton (D)	Bush (R)	Perot (I)	Dukakis (D)	Bush (R)
Allen	2,312	2,351	1,746	2,392	3,429
Anderson	1,178	1,218	1,282	1,466	1,781
Atchison	2,959	2,521	2,020	3,177	3,243
Barber	759	1,225	893	1,118	1,539
Barton.	3,846	5,113	4,574	5,024	7,741
Bourbon.	2,509	2,876	1,763	2,623	3,660
Brown	1,476	2,203	1,603	1,719	3,059
Butler	7,029	9,166	7,355	7,690	10,976
Chase	470	610	600	538	884
Chautauqua . .	598	853	607	661	1,247
Cherokee. . . .	4,083	3,589	2,067	4,069	4,281
Cheyenne . . .	407	863	477	594	1,105
Clark	293	676	341	409	876
Clay	947	2,198	1,434	1,112	2,997
Cloud	1,720	2,131	1,578	2,022	3,043
Coffey	1,021	1,824	1,443	1,246	2,581
Comanche . .	325	636	324	375	738
Cowley	5,405	5,422	4,911	6,186	7,778
Crawford	7,366	5,468	3,706	7,783	6,940
Decatur	576	940	565	793	1,291
Dickinson. . . .	2,518	3,851	2,833	2,870	5,121
Doniphan. . . .	1,177	1,579	1,200	1,312	2,162
Douglas	19,439	12,949	9,630	15,752	16,149
Edwards	567	769	584	792	993
Elk	485	748	503	608	1,075
Ellis	4,544	3,985	3,887	5,289	5,194
Ellsworth	1,010	1,197	1,020	1,219	1,711
Finney.	2,612	5,278	3,011	3,408	5,381
Ford	2,635	4,342	3,341	3,817	5,685
Franklin.	2,968	3,699	3,184	3,592	4,777
Geary	2,559	2,928	2,057	2,721	3,782
Gove.	379	792	532	663	966
Graham	554	752	603	702	1,139
Grant	619	1,561	835	907	1,654
Gray	443	1,039	686	696	1,180
Greeley	191	504	175	317	506
Greenwood . .	1,262	1,411	1,167	1,421	2,217
Hamilton	386	716	271	517	801
Harper	845	1,371	1,151	1,235	1,941
Harvey	5,047	6,259	3,653	5,503	6,893
Haskell	336	1,023	462	427	964
Hodgeman . .	258	625	343	439	732
Jackson.	1,639	1,970	1,927	2,261	2,759
Jefferson	2,538	2,569	2,642	2,810	3,605
Jewell	546	1,050	698	684	1,546
Johnson	59,573	85,418	49,136	55,183	95,591
Kearny	384	943	376	524	1,073
Kingman	1,100	1,680	1,370	1,420	2,205
Kiowa	355	1,057	475	485	1,276
Labette	4,196	3,368	2,577	4,433	5,125
Lane	265	674	356	450	768
Leavenworth. .	8,077	7,738	7,306	8,797	9,913
Lincoln	612	893	657	796	1,229
Linn	1,353	1,413	1,358	1,497	2,163
Logan	355	905	446	503	988
Lyon	4,811	5,090	4,717	5,314	6,820
McPherson. . .	3,645	5,745	3,561	4,354	6,563
Marion.	1,627	3,142	1,557	2,024	3,685
Marshall	2,022	2,030	1,786	2,560	3,140
Meade	430	1,135	592	664	1,322
Miami	3,835	3,528	3,701	4,427	4,807
Mitchell	938	1,601	1,098	1,145	2,257
Montgomery. .	5,453	6,848	3,570	5,429	9,067
Morris	957	1,071	1,071	1,165	1,682
Morton	398	915	350	569	1,074
Nemaha	1,580	2,220	1,804	2,261	2,849
Neosho	2,799	2,926	2,136	3,402	3,739
Ness	565	967	678	887	1,230
Norton	779	1,469	815	855	1,923
Osage.	2,297	2,561	2,532	2,840	3,496
Osborne	779	1,003	819	943	1,541
Ottawa	764	1,284	762	953	1,836
Pawnee.	1,118	1,357	1,097	1,474	1,825
Phillips	843	1,579	955	960	2,316
Pottawatomie .	2,099	3,106	2,759	2,544	3,897
Pratt	1,466	1,779	1,528	1,651	2,505
Rawlins	393	1,023	517	612	1,318
Reno.	9,257	11,377	7,636	11,545	12,753
Republic	939	1,767	1,084	1,069	2,346
Rice	1,555	2,158	1,543	2,033	2,503
Riley.	7,933	8,394	5,387	7,283	9,507
Rooks	771	1,249	1,063	1,012	1,938
Rush	689	756	665	1,020	1,045
Russell	1,178	1,434	1,395	1,448	2,403
Saline	7,890	8,565	7,108	7,998	11,371
Scott	480	1,426	621	717	1,590
Sedgwick. . . .	62,670	75,577	47,238	65,618	86,124
Seward	1,488	3,477	1,818	1,655	4,089
Shawnee	31,972	29,344	20,653	33,940	35,489
Sheridan	347	739	546	600	901
Sherman	810	1,630	828	1,082	1,929
Smith	789	1,236	816	1,004	1,951
Stafford	777	1,064	910	1,121	1,532
Stanton	224	556	214	310	592
Stevens	390	1,408	674	612	1,642
Summer	3,564	4,087	3,887	4,417	5,394
Thomas	932	1,849	1,129	1,408	2,342
Trego	608	727	574	795	979
Wabaunsee . .	851	1,254	1,258	1,166	1,737
Wallace	164	679	219	257	655
Washington . .	893	1,740	1,054	1,063	2,269
Wichita	241	681	303	399	721
Wilson.	1,331	1,925	1,365	1,545	2,743
Woodson . . .	590	662	604	761	1,062
Wyandotte . . .	34,397	12,872	13,620	38,678	19,097
Totals.	**390,434**	**449,951**	**312,358**	**422,636**	**554,049**

Kansas Vote Since 1944

1944, Roosevelt, Dem., 287,458; Dewey, Rep., 442,096; Watson, Proh., 2,609; Thomas, Soc., 1,613.

1948, Truman, Dem., 351,902; Dewey, Rep., 423,039; Watson, Proh., 6,468; Wallace, Prog., 4,603; Thomas, Soc., 2,807.

1952, Eisenhower, Rep., 616,302; Stevenson, Dem., 273,296; Hamblen, Proh., 6,038; Hoopes, Soc., 530.

1956, Eisenhower, Rep., 566,878; Stevenson. Dem., 296,317; Holtwick, Proh., 3,048.

1960, Kennedy, Dem., 363,213; Nixon, Rep., 561,474; Decker, Proh., 4,138.

1964, Johnson, Dem., 464,028; Goldwater, Rep., 386,579; Munn, Proh., 5,393; Hass, Soc. Labor, 1,901.

1968, Nixon, Rep., 478,674; Humphrey, Dem., 302,996; Wallace, 3d, 88,921; Munn, Proh., 2,192.

1972, Nixon, Rep., 619,812; McGovern, Dem., 270,287; Schmitz, Cons., 21,808; Munn, Proh., 4,188.

1976, Carter, Dem., 430,421; Ford, Rep., 502,752; McCarthy, Ind., 13,185; Anderson, Amer., 4,724; MacBride, Libertarian, 3,242; Maddox, Cons., 2,118; Bubar, Proh., 1,403.

1980, Reagan, Rep., 566,812; Carter, Dem., 326,150; Anderson, Ind., 68,231; Clark, Libertarian, 14,470; Shelton, American, 1,555; Hall, Com., 967; Bubar, Statesman, 821; Rarick, Conservative, 789.

1984, Reagan, Rep., 674,646; Mondale, Dem., 332,471; Bergland, Libertarian, 3,585.

1988, Bush, Rep., 554,049; Dukakis, Dem., 422,636; Paul, Ind., 12,553; Fulani, Ind., 3,806.

1992, Clinton, Dem., 390,434; Bush, Rep., 449,951; Perot, Ind., 312,358; Marrou, Libertarian, 4,314.

Kentucky

County	1992 Clinton (D)	Bush (R)	Perot (I)	1988 Dukakis (D)	Bush (R)
Adair	2,044	3,740	617	1,723	4,346
Allen	2,040	2,747	606	1,573	3,342
Anderson	2,491	2,731	1,219	2,176	3,225
Ballard	2,268	1,108	500	2,162	1,460
Barren	5,688	5,467	1,778	4,799	6,653
Bath	2,229	1,259	694	2,099	1,614
Bell	5,745	4,501	1,193	5,182	5,759
Boone	6,514	12,306	4,676	5,382	12,667
Bourbon	2,895	2,707	1,290	2,793	3,308
Boyd	10,496	7,387	3,195	9,552	9,379
Boyle	3,894	4,019	1,335	3,575	4,746
Bracken	1,259	1,162	500	1,176	1,630
Breathitt	3,496	1,303	515	3,387	2,149
Breckinridge	3,113	2,941	945	2,765	3,841
Bullitt	7,830	7,745	3,333	6,005	8,859
Butler	1,468	2,729	596	1,245	3,278
Caldwell	3,000	1,966	670	2,564	2,952
Calloway	6,181	4,654	1,853	5,287	6,225
Campbell	10,673	16,382	5,659	9,553	19,387
Carlisle	1,383	844	309	1,428	1,104
Carroll	2,119	1,046	566	1,913	1,702
Carter	4,224	3,305	989	4,570	4,325
Casey	1,409	3,317	542	1,216	3,857
Christian	6,709	7,737	1,789	5,704	9,250
Clark	4,892	4,625	1,955	4,252	5,329
Clay	2,012	4,747	648	1,709	4,156
Clinton	1,241	2,830	348	899	3,248
Crittenden	1,740	1,576	495	1,443	2,211
Cumberland	917	1,866	268	753	2,231
Daviess	16,592	14,936	5,112	14,815	17,356
Edmonson	1,653	2,486	438	1,243	2,555
Elliott	1,796	444	273	1,797	550
Estill	1,837	2,453	736	1,692	3,077
Fayette	38,306	41,908	14,215	32,554	48,065
Fleming	2,257	2,045	815	2,086	2,409
Floyd	13,351	3,540	1,723	12,327	5,296
Franklin	9,896	7,591	3,340	9,271	9,805
Fulton	1,813	1,073	306	1,531	1,474
Gallatin	1,171	699	445	1,060	881
Garrard	1,730	2,359	697	1,710	2,681
Grant	2,097	2,128	1,149	1,896	2,835
Graves	8,001	5,311	1,943	7,153	6,274
Grayson	2,909	4,533	993	2,575	5,186
Green	1,760	2,709	500	1,595	3,139
Greenup	7,214	4,975	2,188	6,956	6,559
Hancock	1,714	1,261	551	1,478	1,733
Hardin	9,417	12,299	4,026	7,262	13,240
Harlan	6,796	3,970	1,391	7,341	5,166
Harrison	2,795	2,148	1,225	2,748	2,983
Hart	2,852	2,401	579	2,519	2,927
Henderson	8,270	5,125	2,678	7,648	6,911
Henry	2,838	1,640	720	2,544	2,286
Hickman	1,296	861	294	1,158	1,142
Hopkins	8,881	6,032	2,565	7,453	7,979
Jackson	776	3,398	341	678	3,926
Jefferson	152,728	116,566	39,822	127,936	139,711
Jessamine	3,764	6,474	2,059	2,955	7,057
Johnson	3,669	3,614	1,118	3,538	4,619
Kenton	16,344	27,261	9,336	14,838	30,738
Knott	5,500	1,243	560	5,185	1,691
Knox	3,787	5,011	972	2,919	4,903
Larue	2,190	2,154	582	1,822	2,590
Laurel	4,560	8,583	1,859	3,620	9,296
Lawrence	2,400	2,084	557	2,198	2,294
Lee	1,170	1,617	356	984	1,588
Leslie	1,591	2,879	450	1,105	3,280
Letcher	5,817	3,011	1,206	4,697	3,601
Lewis	1,713	2,493	673	1,568	3,108
Lincoln	2,532	2,624	762	2,677	3,530
Livingston	2,386	1,339	578	2,052	1,834
Logan	4,064	3,710	1,043	3,379	4,295
Lyon	1,583	820	293	1,337	1,077
McCracken	13,341	10,657	3,077	12,208	12,160
McCreary	1,934	3,588	624	1,644	3,477
McLean	2,223	1,355	529	2,269	1,829
Madison	8,005	8,719	3,038	6,672	9,958
Magoffin	3,261	1,992	440	2,895	2,158
Marion	3,403	2,091	805	3,152	2,500
Marshall	6,576	4,368	1,773	5,888	5,256
Martin	1,715	1,961	393	1,581	2,587
Mason	2,657	2,432	916	2,721	3,158
Meade	3,387	2,641	1,298	3,079	3,441
Menifee	1,311	557	254	1,096	670
Mercer	3,010	3,211	1,298	2,832	3,904
Metcalfe	1,703	1,683	409	1,705	2,179
Monroe	1,515	3,776	480	1,025	4,214
Montgomery	3,686	2,590	1,308	3,082	3,435
Morgan	2,655	1,239	498	2,329	1,452
Muhlenberg	7,901	3,551	1,624	6,912	5,369
Nelson	5,437	4,495	1,638	4,788	5,283
Nicholas	1,341	894	513	1,242	1,271
Ohio	4,022	3,385	1,423	3,612	4,910
Oldham	5,457	8,263	2,855	4,025	8,716
Owen	1,830	1,108	613	1,823	1,468
Owsley	678	1,437	209	345	1,266
Pendleton	1,740	1,810	1,086	1,576	2,487
Perry	6,619	4,128	1,308	5,557	5,154
Pike	17,358	8,212	2,444	16,339	9,976
Powell	2,323	1,809	874	2,113	2,128
Pulaski	5,465	11,423	2,449	4,788	13,482
Robertson	439	329	170	515	511
Rockcastle	1,144	3,287	446	1,041	3,880
Rowan	3,558	2,469	1,212	2,968	3,093
Russell	1,950	4,641	673	1,455	4,292
Scott	3,639	3,810	1,800	3,380	4,482
Shelby	4,398	4,550	1,451	3,834	4,998
Simpson	2,834	2,280	708	2,138	2,699
Spencer	1,383	1,305	466	1,121	1,368
Taylor	3,518	4,319	1,044	2,879	5,362
Todd	1,858	1,691	612	1,632	2,282
Trigg	2,438	1,820	573	1,991	2,427
Trimble	1,413	789	413	1,342	1,083
Union	3,325	1,605	794	3,316	2,292
Warren	11,529	14,748	3,533	9,684	16,703
Washington	2,008	2,098	542	1,950	2,445
Wayne	2,516	3,412	560	2,057	3,672
Webster	3,380	1,408	854	3,019	2,159
Whitley	4,600	5,998	1,533	3,794	7,337
Wolfe	1,674	697	297	1,516	916
Woodford	3,161	3,992	1,535	2,653	4,512
Totals	**665,104**	**617,178**	**203,944**	**580,368**	**734,281**

Kentucky Vote Since 1944

1944, Roosevelt, Dem., 472,589; Dewey, Rep., 392,448; Watson, Proh., 2,023; Thomas, Soc., 535; Teichert, Soc. Labor, 326.

1948, Truman, Dem., 466,756; Dewey, Rep., 341,210; Thurmond, States' Rights, 10,411; Wallace, Prog., 1,567; Thomas, Soc., 1,284; Watson, Proh., 1,245; Teichert, Soc. Labor, 185.

1952, Eisenhower, Rep., 495,029; Stevenson, Dem., 495,729; Hamblen, Proh., 1,161; Hass, Soc. Labor, 893; Hallinan, Proh., 336.

1956, Eisenhower, Rep., 572,192; Stevenson, Dem., 476,453; Byrd, States' Rights, 2,657; Holtwick, Proh., 2,145; Hass, Soc. Labor, 358.

1960, Kennedy, Dem., 521,855; Nixon, Rep., 602,607.

1964, Johnson, Dem., 669,659; Goldwater, Rep., 372,977; Kasper, Nat'l. States Rights, 3,469.

1968, Nixon, Rep., 462,411; Humphrey, Dem., 397,547; Wallace, 3d p., 193,098; Halstead, Soc. Worker, 2,843.

1972, Nixon, Rep., 676,446; McGovern, Dem., 371,159; Schmitz, Amer., 17,627; Jenness, Soc. Workers, 685; Hall, Com., 464; Spock, Peoples, 1,118.

1976, Carter, Dem., 615,717; Ford, Rep., 531,852; Anderson, Amer., 8,308; McCarthy, Ind., 6,837; Maddox, Amer. Ind., 2,328; MacBride, Libertarian, 814.

1980, Reagan, Rep., 635,274; Carter, Dem., 616,417; Anderson, Ind., 31,127; Clark, Libertarian, 5,531; McCormack, Respect For Life, 4,233; Commoner, Citizens, 1,304; Pulley, Socialist, 393; Hall, Com., 348.

1984, Reagan, Rep., 815,345; Mondale, Dem., 536,756.

1988, Bush, Rep., 734,281; Dukakis, Dem., 580,368; Duke, Pop., 4,494; Paul, Lib., 2,118.

1992, Clinton, Dem., 665,104; Bush, Rep., 617,178; Perot, Ind., 203,944; Marrou, Libertarian, 4,513.

Louisiana

County	1992 Clinton (D)	1992 Bush (R)	1992 Perot (I)	1988 Dukakis (D)	1988 Bush (R)
Acadia	12,276	9,017	3,145	11,510	11,319
Allen	5,626	3,069	1,245	5,204	3,674
Ascension	13,036	10,275	4,295	12,147	10,726
Assumption	5,639	2,928	1,358	5,610	4,017
Avoyelles	8,696	4,851	2,139	7,353	7,659
Beauregard	5,037	5,119	2,103	4,704	6,466
Bienville	3,899	2,412	832	3,705	3,680
Bossier	11,313	15,628	4,863	9,035	20,807
Caddo	47,733	42,665	11,830	39,204	54,498
Calcasieu	33,570	24,847	10,980	33,932	29,649
Caldwell	2,061	1,752	653	1,423	2,997
Cameron	1,985	1,329	995	2,257	1,775
Catahoula	2,570	1,976	773	1,916	2,862
Claiborne	3,263	2,599	926	3,158	3,756
Concordia	4,283	3,223	1,317	3,461	5,037
DeSoto	5,671	3,643	1,358	5,366	5,022
E. Baton Rouge	68,622	81,072	16,102	59,270	86,791
East Carroll	1,835	1,142	283	1,809	1,536
East Feliciana	4,093	2,813	932	3,659	3,527
Evangeline	8,564	5,147	2,124	7,693	7,437
Franklin	4,127	3,889	1,311	3,043	5,520
Grant	3,122	3,214	1,174	2,628	4,402
Iberia	13,040	11,905	4,337	12,166	15,438
Iberville	8,218	5,211	1,543	8,678	5,855
Jackson	3,370	3,072	882	2,842	4,251
Jefferson	64,302	100,493	21,278	53,035	110,942
Jefferson Davis	7,022	4,513	2,221	6,799	5,851
Lafayette	28,583	32,406	9,124	24,133	36,648
Lafourche	16,182	12,744	5,077	15,013	16,152
LaSalle	2,389	3,068	993	1,622	4,559
Lincoln	7,205	7,220	1,751	5,427	8,853
Livingston	11,499	14,808	4,971	9,659	15,779
Madison	2,773	1,702	469	2,416	2,334
Morehouse	6,013	5,364	1,727	4,496	7,335
Natchitoches	6,974	5,694	1,606	6,151	7,224
Orleans	133,261	52,019	10,889	116,851	64,763
Ouachita	20,835	27,600	6,612	15,429	33,858
Plaquemines	4,467	5,018	1,729	3,997	6,084
Pointe Coupee	6,512	3,563	1,157	6,308	4,333
Rapides	20,873	22,783	6,599	17,928	29,977
Red River	2,360	1,649	566	2,254	2,266
Richland	3,706	3,808	1,054	2,833	5,226
Sabine	4,173	3,586	1,219	3,532	4,767
St. Bernard	12,305	16,131	4,308	11,406	19,609
St. Charles	8,810	9,158	2,593	7,973	9,685
St. Helena	3,416	1,515	589	3,013	2,006
St. James	6,609	3,339	993	6,707	3,799
St. John The Baptist	8,977	6,730	1,922	8,366	7,464
St. Landry	20,383	11,882	4,266	19,091	15,790
St. Martin	11,252	5,909	2,573	10,148	7,541
St. Mary	10,648	8,792	3,257	10,364	11,540
St. Tammany	19,735	37,839	9,005	15,638	38,334
Tangipahoa	15,194	14,128	4,612	13,527	16,669
Tensas	1,666	1,153	353	1,556	1,645
Terrebonne	13,325	14,662	5,505	12,686	18,745
Union	4,005	4,434	1,209	3,210	5,900
Vermilion	12,324	7,062	3,127	12,180	9,224
Vernon	6,005	5,912	2,313	4,998	7,453
Washington	9,095	7,227	2,303	8,369	9,374
Webster	8,380	6,640	2,629	7,434	10,204
W. Baton Rouge	5,131	3,522	1,249	4,686	3,972
West Carroll	2,068	2,082	771	1,607	3,077
West Feliciana	2,328	1,501	516	2,146	1,854
Winn	3,537	2,932	843	2,699	4,165
Totals	**815,971**	**733,386**	**211,478**	**717,460**	**883,702**

Louisiana Vote Since 1944

1944, Roosevelt, Dem., 281,564; Dewey, Rep., 67,750.

1948, Thurmond, States' Rights, 204,290; Truman, Dem., 136,344; Dewey, Rep., 72,657; Wallace, Prog., 3,035.

1952, Eisenhower, Rep., 306,925, Stevenson, Dem., 345,027.

1956, Eisenhower, Rep., 329,047; Stevenson, Dem., 243,977; Andrews, States' Rights, 44,520.

1960, Kennedy, Dem., 407,339; Nixon, Rep., 230,890; States' Rights (unpledged) 169,572.

1964, Johnson, Dem., 387,068; Goldwater, Rep., 509,225.

1968, Nixon, Rep., 257,535; Humphrey, Dem., 309,615; Wallace, 3d party, 530,300.

1972, Nixon, Rep., 686,852; McGovern, Dem., 298,142; Schmitz, Amer., 52,099; Jenness, Soc. Workers, 14,398.

1976, Carter, Dem., 661,365; Ford, Rep., 587,446; Maddox, Amer., 10,058; Hall, Com., 7,417; McCarthy, Ind., 6,588; MacBride, Libertarian, 3,325.

1980, Reagan, Rep., 792,853; Carter, Dem., 708,453; Anderson, Ind., 26,345; Rarick, Amer. Ind., 10,333; Clark, Libertarian, 8,240; Commoner, Citizens, 1,584; DeBerry, Soc. Work., 783.

1984, Reagan, Rep., 1,037,299; Mondale, Dem., 651,586; Bergland, Libertarian, 1,876.

1988, Bush, Rep., 883,702; Dukakis, Dem., 717,460; Duke, Pop., 18,612; Paul, Lib., 4,115.

1992, Clinton, Dem., 815,971; Bush, Rep., 733,386; Perot, Ind., 211,478; Gritz, Populist/America First, 18,545; Marrou, Libertarian, 3,155; Daniels, Ind., 1,663; Phillips, U.S. Taxpayers, 1,552; Fulani, New Alliance, 1,434; LaRouche, Ind., 1,136.

Maine

City	1992 Clinton (D)	1992 Bush (R)	1992 Perot (I)	1988 Dukakis (D)	1988 Bush (R)
Auburn	5,025	3,653	3,964	4,629	5,947
Augusta	4,657	3,003	3,002	4,576	5,182
Bangor	6,826	5,185	4,689	6,534	7,194
Bath	1,988	1,630	1,458	1,838	2,543
Bidderford	4,945	2,533	2,717	5,017	4,375
Brewer	1,788	1,907	1,625	1,784	2,908
Gardiner	1,391	1,054	1,115	1,395	1,609
Lewiston	9,265	4,372	6,180	9,225	7,265
Old Town	2,272	1,173	1,302	2,220	1,640
Portland	19,510	8,660	6,910	18,234	11,676
Rockland	1,192	1,081	1,059	1,198	1,850
Saco	4,000	2,769	2,303	3,169	3,852
Sanford	3,854	3,030	3,215	3,456	4,541
South Portland	5,933	3,999	2,734	5,820	5,744
Waterville	3,868	1,832	2,257	4,031	3,158
Westbrook	3,665	2,904	2,512	3,648	4,086
Other	183,241	157,719	159,778	166,795	233,561
Totals	**263,420**	**206,504**	**206,820**	**243,569**	**307,131**

Maine Vote Since 1944

1944, Roosevelt, Dem., 140,631; Dewey, Rep., 155,434; Teichert, Soc. Labor, 335.

1948, Truman, Dem., 111,916; Dewey, Rep., 150,234; Wallace, Prog., 1,884; Thomas, Soc., 547; Teichert, Soc. Labor, 206.

1952, Eisenhower, Rep., 232,353; Stevenson, Dem., 118,806; Hallinan, Prog., 332; Hass, Soc. Labor, 156; Hoopes, Soc., 138; scattered, 1.

1956, Eisenhower, Rep., 249,238; Stevenson, Dem., 102,468.

1960, Kennedy, Dem., 181,159; Nixon, Rep., 240,608.

1964, Johnson, Dem., 262,264; Goldwater, Rep., 118,701.

1968, Nixon, Rep., 169,254; Humphrey, Dem., 217,312; Wallace, 3d party, 6,370.

1972, Nixon, Rep., 256,458; McGovern, Dem., 160,584; scattered, 229.

1976, Carter, Dem., 232,279; Ford, Rep., 236,320; McCarthy, Ind., 10,874; Bubar, Proh., 3,495.

1980, Reagan, Rep., 238,522; Carter, Dem., 220,974; Anderson, Ind., 53,327; Clark, Libertarian, 5,119; Commoner, Citizens, 4,394; Hall, Com., 591; write-ins, 84.

1984, Reagan, Rep., 336,500; Mondale, Dem., 214,515.

1988, Bush, Rep., 307,131; Dukakis, Dem., 243,569; Paul, Lib., 2,700; Fulani, New Alliance, 1,405.

1992, Clinton, Dem., 263,420; Perot, Ind., 206,820; Bush, Rep., 206,504; Marrou, Libertarian, 1,681.

Maryland

County	1992 Clinton (D)	1992 Bush (R)	1992 Perot (I)	1988 Dukakis (D)	1988 Bush (R)
Allegany	11,501	13,862	5,081	11,844	17,462
Anne Arundel	68,629	81,467	35,191	55,440	98,540
Baltimore	143,498	126,728	51,757	121,570	163,881
Calvert	8,619	10,026	4,499	6,376	10,956
Caroline	2,822	3,856	1,729	2,440	4,661
Carroll	15,447	28,405	10,965	12,368	31,224
Cecil	10,232	10,784	6,115	7,807	13,224
Charles	14,498	17,293	6,501	11,823	20,828
Dorchester	3,933	4,934	2,010	3,709	6,343
Frederick	21,848	31,290	11,373	17,061	32,575
Garrett	2,856	5,714	1,987	2,557	6,665
Harford	27,164	36,350	17,002	19,803	38,493
Howard	44,763	38,594	16,182	34,007	44,153
Kent	3,093	3,094	1,411	2,925	3,761
Montgomery	199,757	119,705	41,971	165,187	154,191
Prince George's	168,691	62,955	23,355	133,816	86,545
Queen Anne's	4,668	6,829	2,958	3,857	7,803
St. Mary's	8,931	11,485	4,550	7,434	12,767
Somerset	3,210	3,450	1,230	2,911	4,222
Talbot	4,642	6,774	2,233	3,948	8,170
Washington	16,495	21,977	7,537	14,408	25,912
Wicomico	11,481	13,560	5,140	9,413	16,272
Worcester	6,040	7,237	3,256	4,787	8,430

City					
Baltimore	185,753	40,725	17,381	170,813	59,089
Totals	**988,571**	**707,094**	**281,414**	**826,304**	**876,167**

Maryland Vote Since 1944

1944, Roosevelt, Dem., 315,490; Dewey, Rep., 292,949.

1948, Truman, Dem., 286,521; Dewey, Rep., 294,814; Wallace, Prog., 9,983; Thomas, Soc., 2,941; Thurmond, States' Rights, 2,476; Wright, write-in, 2,294.

1952, Eisenhower, Rep., 499,424; Stevenson, Dem., 395,337; Hallinan, Prog., 7,313.

1956, Eisenhower, Rep., 559,738; Stevenson, Dem., 372,613.

1960, Kennedy, Dem., 565,800; Nixon, Rep., 489,538.

1964, Johnson, Dem., 730,912; Goldwater, Rep., 385,495; write-in, 50.

1968, Nixon, Rep., 517,995; Humphrey, Dem., 538,310; Wallace, 3d party, 178,734.

1972, Nixon, Rep., 829,305; McGovern, Dem., 505,781; Schmitz, Amer., 18,726.

1976, Carter, Dem., 759,612; Ford, Rep., 672,661.

1980, Reagan, Rep., 680,606; Carter, Dem., 726,161; Anderson, Ind., 119,537; Clark, Libertarian, 14,192.

1984, Reagan, Rep., 879,918; Mondale, Dem., 787,935; Bergland, Libertarian, 5,721.

1988, Bush, Rep., 876,167; Dukakis, Dem., 826,304; Paul, Lib., 6,748; Fulani, New Alliance, 5,115.

1992, Clinton, Dem., 988,571; Bush, Rep., 707,094; Perot, Ind., 281,414; Marrou, Libertarian, 4,715; Fulani, New Alliance, 2,786.

Massachusetts

	1992			1988	
City	Clinton (D)	Bush (R)	Perot (I)	Dukakis (D)	Bush (R)
Boston	114,260	41,868	25,189	122,349	62,202
Brockton	13,209	8,863	7,579	14,776	16,056
Cambridge	30,737	5,847	4,106	32,027	8,770
Fall River	18,652	5,456	6,922	20,184	8,394
Framingham	15,165	8,114	6,089	15,826	12,745
Lawrence	7,698	5,079	3,245	9,255	8,265
Lowell	14,492	8,467	8,893	16,391	13,998
Lynn	15,275	7,350	7,665	18,540	12,182
New Bedford	20,880	5,255	6,965	22,609	9,901
Newton	29,136	9,623	5,685	29,039	13,892
Quincy	18,891	12,306	9,068	20,911	18,403
Somerville	19,792	5,883	4,416	21,612	8,931
Springfield	27,302	12,200	10,361	30,113	16,244
Worcester	32,326	17,228	10,488	34,369	24,355
Other	940,824	651,500	514,060	993,414	960,297
Totals	**1,318,639**	**805,039**	**630,731**	**1,401,415**	**1,194,635**

Massachusetts Vote Since 1944

1944, Roosevelt, Dem., 1,035,296; Dewey, Rep., 921,350; Teichert, Soc. Labor, 2,780; Watson, Proh., 973.

1948, Truman, Dem., 1,151,788; Dewey, Rep., 909,370; Wallace, Prog., 38,157; Teichert, Soc. Labor, 5,535; Watson, Proh., 1,663.

1952, Eisenhower, Rep., 1,292,325; Stevenson, Dem., 1,083,525; Hallinan, Prog., 4,636; Hass, Soc. Labor, 1,957; Hamblen, Proh., 886; scattered, 69; blanks, 41,150.

1956, Eisenhower, Rep., 1,393,197; Stevenson, Dem., 948,190; Hass, Soc. Labor, 5,573; Holtwick, Proh., 1,205; others, 341.

1960, Kennedy, Dem., 1,487,174; Nixon, Rep., 976,750; Hass, Soc. Labor, 3,892; Decker, Proh., 1,633; others, 31; blank and void, 26,024.

1964, Johnson, Dem., 1,786,422; Goldwater, Rep., 549,727; Hass, Soc. Labor, 4,755; Munn, Proh., 3,735; scattered, 159; blank, 48,104.

1968, Nixon, Rep., 766,844; Humphrey, Dem., 1,469,218; Wallace, 3d party, 87,088; Blomen, Soc. Labor, 6,180; Munn, Proh., 2,369; scattered, 53; blanks, 25,394.

1972, Nixon, Rep., 1,112,078; McGovern, Dem., 1,332,540; Jenness, Soc. Workers, 10,600; Fisher, Soc. Labor, 129; Schmitz, Amer., 2,877; Spock, Peoples, 101; Hall, Com., 46; Hospers, Libertarian, 43; scattered, 342.

1976, Carter, Dem., 1,429,475; Ford, Rep., 1,030,276; McCarthy, Ind., 65,637; Camejo, Soc. Workers, 8,138; Anderson, Amer., 7,555; La Rouche, U.S. Labor, 4,922; MacBride, Libertarian, 135.

1980, Reagan, Rep., 1,057,631; Carter, Dem., 1,053,802; Anderson, Ind., 382,539; Clark, Libertarian, 22,038; DeBerry, Soc. Workers, 3,735; Commoner, Citizens, 2,056; McReynolds, Socialist, 62; Bubar, Statesman, 34; Griswold, Workers World, 19; scattered, 2,382.

1984, Reagan, Rep., 1,310,936; Mondale, Dem., 1,239,606.

1988, Bush, Rep., 1,194,635; Dukakis, Dem., 1,401,415; Paul, Lib., 24,251; Fulani, New Alliance, 9,561.

1992, Clinton, Dem., 1,318,639; Bush, Rep., 805,039; Perot, Ind., 630,731; Marrou, Libertarian, 9,021; Fulani, New Alliance, 3,172; Phillips, U.S. Taxpayers, 2,218; Hagelin, Natural Law, 1,812; LaRouche, Ind., 1,027.

Michigan

	1992			1988	
County	Clinton (D)	Bush (R)	Perot (I)	Dukakis (D)	Bush (R)
Alcona	2,383	2,247	1,117	1,918	2,966
Alger	2,144	1,471	941	2,210	1,830
Allegan	12,823	19,077	8,742	10,785	22,163
Alpena	6,894	4,878	3,236	6,341	6,664
Antrim	3,431	3,984	2,528	3,159	5,231
Arenac	3,244	2,330	1,608	3,211	3,064
Baraga	1,695	1,160	754	1,753	1,630
Barry	8,652	9,489	6,303	7,983	12,546
Bay	26,492	16,383	11,258	28,225	20,710
Benzie	2,715	2,438	1,657	2,437	3,240
Berrien	25,840	29,252	14,056	21,948	37,799
Branch	5,850	5,976	4,683	5,231	9,225
Calhoun	25,542	19,791	13,058	22,717	26,771
Cass	8,047	7,391	4,756	7,444	10,229
Charlevoix	4,063	4,017	3,360	3,875	5,802
Cheboygan	4,459	3,864	2,495	3,943	5,395
Chippewa	5,434	5,462	2,706	5,222	6,786
Clare	5,346	3,916	2,812	4,710	5,661
Clinton	10,116	12,216	7,877	9,225	15,497
Crawford	2,252	2,193	1,442	1,825	3,097
Delta	8,387	6,027	3,485	8,891	7,114
Dickinson	5,689	4,273	3,022	6,129	6,158
Eaton	16,752	18,669	12,208	15,322	24,193
Emmet	4,245	5,312	3,576	4,170	7,105
Genesee	105,156	47,834	46,259	104,880	70,922
Gladwin	4,457	3,616	2,649	4,164	4,746
Gogebic	4,792	2,838	1,543	5,151	3,509
Grand Traverse	11,148	13,629	9,495	10,098	17,191
Gratiot	5,678	6,280	3,866	5,719	8,447
Hillsdale	5,244	7,579	4,968	4,763	10,571
Houghton	6,558	5,575	2,945	6,510	7,098
Huron	6,023	6,491	4,064	5,714	9,419
Ingham	61,596	43,926	27,683	55,984	58,363
Ionia	8,370	9,135	6,211	8,160	12,028
Iosco	5,369	4,912	3,131	4,929	7,234
Iron	3,648	1,971	1,344	3,774	2,866
Isabella	8,784	7,706	5,434	7,960	10,362
Jackson	23,686	25,424	15,194	21,865	33,885
Kalamazoo	43,568	38,035	21,666	39,457	50,205
Kalkaska	2,297	2,173	1,915	2,092	3,369
Kent	82,305	115,285	43,707	73,467	131,910
Keweenaw	582	378	212	631	536
Lake	2,351	1,194	981	1,958	1,713
Lapeer	11,982	12,326	10,541	10,736	16,670
Leelanau	3,445	3,993	2,685	3,331	5,215
Lenawee	15,399	14,297	9,517	13,690	19,115
Livingston	17,851	27,539	15,971	13,749	31,331
Luce	972	958	660	864	1,528
Mackinac	2,293	2,278	1,379	2,093	3,127
Macomb	130,732	147,795	67,954	112,856	175,632
Manistee	5,193	3,491	2,923	4,765	5,368
Marquette	16,038	9,665	5,768	15,418	11,704
Mason	4,829	5,102	3,096	4,531	6,800
Mecosta	6,097	6,047	3,612	4,736	8,181
Menominee	4,559	3,995	2,487	4,918	5,440
Midland	13,382	16,149	8,945	13,452	19,994
Missaukee	1,893	2,829	1,306	1,621	3,566
Monroe	24,957	20,250	13,551	21,847	26,189
Montcalm	8,730	8,420	5,504	7,664	10,963
Montmorency	1,903	1,794	1,077	1,563	2,514
Muskegon	32,515	23,769	15,268	28,977	33,567
Newaygo	6,455	7,333	4,056	5,389	9,896
Oakland	214,733	242,160	94,911	174,745	283,359
Oceana	3,846	3,944	2,713	3,356	5,693
Ogemaw	4,016	2,936	2,122	4,012	4,091
Ontonagon	2,451	1,463	805	2,517	2,023
Osceola	3,529	3,606	2,199	2,860	5,218
Oscoda	1,471	1,583	755	1,170	1,972
Otsego	3,129	3,393	2,635	2,635	4,620
Ottawa	22,180	56,862	16,855	18,769	61,515
Presque Isle	3,308	2,398	1,612	3,025	3,614
Roscommon	5,243	4,170	2,551	4,394	5,866
Saginaw	43,819	32,103	20,523	45,616	42,401
St. Clair	23,385	24,508	18,523	20,909	32,336
St. Joseph	7,817	9,836	6,209	7,017	13,084
Sanilac	5,868	7,891	4,894	5,445	10,653
Schoolcraft	2,139	1,253	721	2,071	1,802
Shiawassee	12,629	10,930	8,632	13,056	15,506
Tuscola	9,138	8,636	6,765	9,060	12,093
Van Buren	12,466	10,357	7,255	10,668	14,522
Washtenaw	73,325	41,386	21,889	61,799	55,029
Wayne	508,464	227,002	102,074	450,222	291,996

Wexford.	4,894	4,696	2,923	4,287	6,043
Totals.	**1,871,182**	**1,554,940**	**824,813**	**1,675,783**	**1,965,486**

Michigan Vote Since 1944

1944, Roosevelt, Dem., 1,106,899; Dewey, Rep., 1,084,423; Watson, Proh., 6,503; Thomas, Soc., 4,598; Smith, America First, 1,530; Teichert, Soc. Labor, 1,264.

1948, Truman, Dem., 1,003,448; Dewey, Rep., 1,038,595; Wallace, Prog., 46,515; Watson, Proh., 13,052; Thomas, Soc. 6,063; Teichert, Soc. Labor, 1,263; Dobbs, Soc. Workers, 672.

1952, Eisenhower, Rep., 1,551,529; Stevenson, Dem., 1,230,657; Hamblen, Proh., 10,331; Hallinan, Prog., 3,922; Hass, Soc. Labor, 1,495; Dobbs, Soc. Workers, 655; scattered, 3.

1956, Eisenhower, Rep., 1,713,647; Stevenson, Dem., 1,359,898; Holtwick, Proh., 6,923.

1960, Kennedy, Dem., 1,687,269; Nixon, Rep., 1,620,428; Dobbs, Soc. Workers, 4,347; Decker, Proh., 2,029; Daly, Tax Cut, 1,767; Hass, Soc. Labor, 1,718; Ind. American, 539.

1964, Johnson, Dem., 2,136,615; Goldwater, Rep., 1,060,152; DeBerry, Soc. Workers, 3,817; Hass, Soc. Labor, 1,704; Proh. (no candidate listed), 699; scattering, 145.

1968, Nixon, Rep., 1,370,665; Humphrey, Dem., 1,593,082; Wallace, 3d party, 331,968; Halstead, Soc. Worker, 4,099; Blomen, Soc. Labor, 1,762; Cleaver, New Politics, 4,585; Munn, Proh., 60; scattering, 29.

1972, Nixon, Rep., 1,961,721; McGovern, Dem., 1,459,435; Schmitz, Amer., 63,321; Fisher, Soc. Labor, 2,437; Jenness, Soc. Workers, 1,603; Hall, Com., 1,210.

1976, Carter, Dem., 1,696,714; Ford, Rep., 1,893,742; McCarthy, Ind., 47,905; MacBride, Libertarian, 5,406; Wright, People's, 3,504, Camejo, Soc. Workers, 1,804; LaRouche, U.S. Labor, 1,366; Levin, Soc. Labor, 1,148; scattering, 2,160.

1980, Reagan, Rep., 1,915,225; Carter, Dem., 1,661,532; Anderson, Ind., 275,223; Clark, Libertarian, 41,597; Commoner, Citizens, 11,930; Hall, Com., 3,262; Griswold, Workers World, 30; Greaves, American, 21; Bubar, Statesman, 9.

1984, Reagan, Rep., 2,251,571; Mondale, Dem., 1,529,638; Bergland, Libertarian, 10,055.

1988, Bush, Rep., 1,965,486; Dukakis, Dem., 1,675,783; Paul, Lib., 18,336; Fulani, Ind., 2,513.

1992, Clinton, Dem., 1,871,182; Bush, Rep., 1,554,940; Perot, Ind., 824,813; Marrou, Libertarian, 10,175; Phillips, U.S. Taxpayers, 8,263; Hagelin, Natural Law, 2,954.

Minnesota

		1992		1988	
County	Clinton (D)	Bush (R)	Perot (I)	Dukakis (D)	Bush (R)
Aitkin.	3,400	2,151	1,951	3,863	3,011
Anoka	54,621	39,458	35,140	57,953	46,853
Becker.	4,958	5,430	3,238	5,787	6,738
Beltrami.	7,210	5,204	3,473	7,566	6,652
Benton	5,156	5,053	4,048	5,861	6,060
Big Stone. . . .	1,610	1,052	740	2,026	1,469
Blue Earth . . .	11,531	8,813	7,299	12,375	11,959
Brown	4,278	5,390	3,845	5,109	6,898
Carlton	7,736	3,922	3,005	8,790	4,626
Carver.	8,349	10,201	7,942	8,439	12,560
Cass	4,901	4,276	2,939	5,127	5,895
Chippewa. . . .	2,929	2,143	1,505	3,238	3,190
Chisago.	7,077	4,813	5,098	7,875	6,163
Clay	9,845	9,666	3,835	11,186	10,380
Clearwater . . .	1,587	1,315	841	1,769	1,763
Cook.	1,005	878	704	1,080	1,078
Cottonwood . .	2,382	2,481	1,749	3,095	3,390
Crow Wing . . .	8,896	9,112	6,367	9,674	11,017
Dakota	63,660	52,312	40,244	61,942	61,606
Dodge	2,620	3,049	2,231	2,925	3,848
Douglas.	5,252	6,356	4,138	5,803	7,898
Faribault	3,339	3,439	2,322	3,879	4,846
Fillmore	3,977	3,583	3,011	4,114	5,004
Freeborn	7,759	5,089	4,878	8,836	7,226
Goodhue	7,916	7,321	5,790	9,438	9,455
Grant	1,561	1,201	885	1,950	1,693
Hennepin. . . .	278,648	179,581	123,659	292,909	240,209
Houston.	3,744	3,853	2,697	3,936	4,777
Hubbard	3,362	3,227	1,949	3,306	4,365
Isanti.	5,386	3,988	3,898	6,075	5,246
Itasca	9,621	5,952	5,147	10,517	8,358
Jackson.	2,481	1,824	1,918	3,275	2,629
Kanabec	2,532	1,876	1,836	2,970	2,571
Kandiyohi. . . .	7,914	6,784	4,869	8,962	8,634
Kittson.	1,307	1,098	558	1,650	1,381
Koochiching . .	3,474	1,954	1,993	3,867	2,842
LacQuiParle . .	2,342	1,435	1,163	2,805	2,116
Lake	3,415	1,465	1,437	3,887	1,838
Lake O'Woods	794	762	629	798	984
Le Sueur	4,662	3,858	3,363	5,410	5,415
Lincoln	1,555	1,084	967	1,891	1,479
Lyon	4,481	4,591	3,180	5,657	5,969
McLeod	4,919	5,422	4,933	5,736	7,967
Mahnomen. . .	1,035	854	483	1,277	1,051
Marshall	2,309	2,136	1,306	3,001	2,752
Martin	4,019	4,438	3,089	4,922	5,724
Meeker	3,861	3,497	3,120	4,544	4,999
Mille Lacs . . .	3,648	2,814	2,615	4,327	3,862
Morrison	5,588	5,038	3,710	6,469	6,598
Mower.	9,935	5,147	5,001	11,893	6,969
Murray	1,993	1,609	1,588	2,840	2,316
Nicollet	6,055	5,091	3,799	6,786	6,878
Nobles	3,756	3,548	2,586	4,953	4,348
Norman	1,784	1,541	776	2,149	1,789
Olmsted.	19,039	23,404	13,806	19,423	27,683
Otter Tail	9,176	11,074	6,274	10,373	14,015
Pennington. . .	2,578	2,155	1,598	3,105	2,920
Pine	4,929	2,841	2,952	5,540	3,857
Pipestone . . .	1,773	1,953	1,429	2,382	2,760
Polk	5,850	5,817	3,176	7,523	7,032
Pope.	2,619	1,886	1,390	3,074	2,627
Ramsey.	130,932	68,206	50,757	143,767	88,736
Red Lake. . . .	1,020	691	472	1,229	918
Redwood	2,740	3,408	2,710	3,178	5,076
Renville.	3,414	2,852	2,598	4,454	4,356
Rice	10,908	7,015	6,057	11,570	9,460
Rock.	2,006	2,065	1,244	2,435	2,737
Roseau	2,346	2,785	2,099	2,630	3,500
St. Louis	61,813	24,579	21,714	70,344	31,799
Scott.	11,225	10,936	9,881	11,405	13,050
Sherburne . . .	7,843	7,339	6,534	7,959	8,360
Sibley	2,421	2,315	2,407	3,154	3,655
Stearns	21,451	22,502	14,834	23,798	27,529
Steele	5,152	5,964	4,542	5,496	7,981
Stevens.	2,466	2,229	1,086	2,721	2,679
Swift	2,980	1,603	1,359	3,579	2,156
Todd.	4,059	3,990	2,976	5,023	5,633
Traverse	1,053	841	582	1,399	1,061
Wabasha. . . .	3,736	3,397	3,012	4,442	4,681
Wadena.	2,340	2,492	1,535	2,484	3,733
Waseca.	3,146	3,118	2,621	3,721	4,471
Washington . .	35,820	26,568	22,585	34,952	30,850
Watonwan . . .	2,100	1,871	1,574	2,544	2,821
Wilkin	1,122	1,626	748	1,486	1,933
Winona	9,707	8,585	5,993	10,310	11,012
Wright.	12,465	11,650	10,829	14,177	14,987
Yellow Med . .	2,593	1,909	1,645	3,282	2,925
Totals.	**1,020,997**	**747,841**	**562,506**	**1,109,471**	**962,337**

Minnesota Vote Since 1944

1944, Roosevelt, Dem., 589,864; Dewey, Rep., 527,416; Thomas, Soc., 5,073; Teichert, Ind. Gov't., 3,176.

1948, Truman, Dem., 692,966; Dewey, Rep., 483,617; Wallace, Prog., 27,866; Thomas, Soc., 4,646; Teichert, Soc. Labor, 2,525; Dobbs, Soc. Workers, 606.

1952, Eisenhower, Rep., 763,211; Stevenson, Dem., 608,458; Hallinan, Prog., 2,666; Hass, Soc. Labor, 2,383; Hamblen, Proh., 2,147; Dobbs, Soc. Workers, 618.

1956, Eisenhower, Rep., 719,302; Stevenson, Dem., 617,525; Hass, Soc. Labor (Ind. Gov.), 2,080; Dobbs, Soc. Workers, 1,098.

1960, Kennedy, Dem., 779,933; Nixon, Rep., 757,915; Dobbs, Soc. Workers, 3,077; Industrial Gov., 962.

1964, Johnson, Dem., 991,117; Goldwater, Rep., 559,624; DeBerry, Soc. Workers, 1,177; Hass, Industrial Gov., 2,544.

1968, Nixon, Rep., 658,643; Humphrey, Dem., 857,738; Wallace, 3d party, 68,931; scattered, 2,443; Halstead, Soc. Worker, 808; Blomen, Ind. Gov't., 285; Mitchell, Com., 415; Cleaver, Peace, 935; McCarthy, write-in, 585; scattered, 170.

1972, Nixon, Rep., 898,269; McGovern, Dem., 802,346; Schmitz, Amer., 31,407; Spock, Peoples, 2,805; Fisher, Soc. Labor, 4,261; Jenness, Soc. Workers, 940; Hall, Com., 662; scattered, 962.

1976, Carter, Dem., 1,070,440; Ford, Rep., 819,395; McCarthy, Ind., 35,490; Anderson, Amer., 13,592; Camejo, Soc. Workers, 4,149; MacBride, Libertarian, 3,529; Hall, Com., 1,092.

1980, Reagan, Rep., 873,268; Carter, Dem., 954,173; Anderson, Ind., 174,997; Clark, Libertarian, 31,593; Commoner, Citizens, 8,406; Hall, Com., 1,117; DeBerry, Soc. Workers, 711; Griswold, Workers World, 698; McReynolds, Socialist, 536; write-ins, 281.

1984, Reagan, Rep., 1,032,603; Mondale, Dem., 1,036,364; Bergland, Libertarian, 2,996.

1988, Bush., 962,337; Dukakis, Dem., 1,109,471; McCarthy, Minn. Prog., 5,403; Paul, Lib., 5,109.

1992, Clinton, Dem., 1,020,997; Bush, Rep., 747,841; Perot, Ind., 526,506; Marrou, Libertarian, 3,373; Gritz, Populist/America First, 3,363; Hagelin, Natural Law, 1,406.

Mississippi

	1992			1988	
County	Clinton (D)	Bush (R)	Perot (I)	Dukakis (D)	Bush (R)
Adams	8,255	5,831	1,753	7,732	8,116
Alcorn	6,373	6,249	1,349	5,335	6,641
Amite	2,608	2,561	498	2,834	3,333
Attala	3,015	3,520	529	2,997	4,524
Benton	2,402	1,253	293	1,718	1,565
Bolivar	8,801	4,752	593	7,606	6,105
Calhoun	2,462	3,191	607	2,086	3,375
Carroll	1,182	1,695	200	1,560	2,628
Chickasaw	3,220	3,150	629	2,713	3,390
Choctaw	1,435	2,026	298	1,335	2,297
Claiborne	3,302	935	161	3,083	1,233
Clarke	2,259	4,207	450	2,576	4,522
Clay	4,620	3,297	626	3,849	3,645
Coahoma	6,409	4,120	518	6,139	4,939
Copiah	4,397	4,600	409	4,175	5,100
Covington	2,775	3,525	654	2,591	4,005
DeSoto	8,833	16,104	2,569	5,449	14,681
Forrest	8,333	12,432	1,909	6,953	14,249
Franklin	1,587	1,942	393	1,563	2,376
George	2,650	4,141	1,335	2,435	4,545
Greene	1,664	2,406	559	1,637	2,837
Grenada	4,203	4,721	609	3,683	5,352
Hancock	4,651	6,422	2,302	3,760	7,763
Harrison	15,268	25,049	6,855	14,439	32,892
Hinds	43,434	45,031	5,341	41,058	52,749
Holmes	4,092	1,694	203	5,350	2,737
Humphreys	2,696	1,721	258	2,644	2,018
Issaquena	550	298	79	511	424
Itawamba	3,635	4,142	918	3,143	4,535
Jackson	13,017	25,321	6,484	10,328	29,830
Jasper	3,059	2,789	568	3,184	3,368
Jefferson	2,796	562	156	2,693	702
Jefferson Davis	2,991	2,228	382	2,948	2,745
Jones	8,035	13,824	2,523	7,383	16,764
Kemper	2,243	1,830	278	2,069	2,128
Lafayette	5,224	5,251	861	3,967	5,841
Lamar	3,208	8,259	1,543	2,535	9,145
Lauderdale	8,489	17,098	1,659	7,967	18,302
Lawrence	2,582	2,689	765	2,517	3,682
Leake	3,333	3,943	497	2,787	4,168
Lee	7,710	12,231	2,041	6,604	13,767
Leflore	6,374	5,298	611	5,830	6,409
Lincoln	4,744	7,040	1,281	4,534	8,710
Lowndes	6,552	10,509	1,716	5,993	11,258
Madison	9,386	12,810	1,478	8,242	11,399
Marion	4,654	5,776	1,162	4,240	7,019
Marshall	7,913	3,847	689	6,982	4,668
Monroe	4,933	5,994	1,255	4,669	6,447
Montgomery	2,076	2,324	370	1,893	2,504
Neshoba	3,090	6,135	794	2,942	6,363
Newton	2,146	5,128	494	2,332	5,658
Noxubee	3,188	1,623	203	2,722	1,870
Oktibbeha	5,726	6,381	984	5,100	7,126
Panola	6,066	4,644	729	5,222	5,382
Pearl River	4,683	7,726	2,352	3,939	10,220
Perry	1,490	2,538	462	1,326	2,983
Pike	6,279	6,005	1,380	6,531	7,637
Pontotoc	2,965	4,595	777	2,772	4,939
Prentiss	3,385	4,317	781	3,429	4,348
Quitman	2,422	1,451	210	2,497	1,832
Rankin	8,155	24,537	3,454	6,201	22,937
Scott	3,349	5,268	691	2,939	5,522
Sharkey	1,526	1,008	145	1,609	1,277
Simpson	3,213	5,358	726	3,016	6,151
Smith	1,968	4,106	680	1,660	4,573
Stone	1,447	2,295	447	1,452	3,007
Sunflower	5,050	3,726	600	4,898	4,362
Tallahatchie	2,902	2,213	380	2,881	2,633
Tate	3,519	4,196	634	2,872	4,553
Tippah	3,475	4,444	802	2,958	4,593
Tishomingo	3,910	3,393	751	3,378	3,646
Tunica	1,451	693	96	1,510	896
Union	3,714	5,173	816	3,044	5,511
Walthall	2,476	2,728	711	2,354	3,103
Warren	8,175	10,209	2,146	7,437	12,507
Washington	10,588	7,598	795	10,222	10,229
Wayne	3,064	3,874	824	2,889	4,496
Webster	1,746	2,791	444	1,550	3,061
Wilkinson	3,210	1,399	307	2,678	1,528
Winston	3,953	4,311	688	3,851	5,317
Yalobusha	2,617	2,179	438	2,402	2,660
Yazoo	4,880	5,113	669	4,989	5,538
Totals	**400,258**	**487,793**	**85,626**	**363,921**	**557,890**

Mississippi Vote Since 1944

1944, Roosevelt, Dem., 158,515; Dewey, Rep., 3,742; Reg. Dem., 9,964; Ind. Rep., 7,859.

1948, Thurmond, States' Rights, 167,538; Truman, Dem., 19,384; Dewey, Rep., 5,043; Wallace, Prog., 225.

1952, Eisenhower, Ind. vote pledged to Rep. candidate, 112,966; Stevenson, Dem., 172,566.

1956, Eisenhower, Rep., 56,372; Stevenson, Dem., 144,498; Black and Tan Grand Old Party, 4,313; total, 60,685; Byrd, Ind., 42,966.

1960, Kennedy, Dem., 108,362; Democratic unpledged electors, 116,248; Nixon, Rep., 73,561. Mississippi's victorious slate of 8 unpledged Democratic electors cast their votes for Sen. Harry F. Byrd (D-Va.).

1964, Johnson, Dem., 52,618; Goldwater, Rep., 356,528.

1968, Nixon, Rep., 88,516; Humphrey, Dem., 150,644; Wallace, 3d party, 415,349.

1972, Nixon, Rep., 505,125; McGovern, Dem., 126,782; Schmitz, Amer., 11,598; Jenness, Soc. Workers, 2,458.

1976, Carter, Dem., 381,309; Ford, Rep., 366,846; Anderson, Amer., 6,678; McCarthy, Ind., 4,074; Maddox, Ind., 4,049; Camejo, Soc. Workers, 2,805; MacBride, Libertarian, 2,609.

1980, Reagan, Rep., 441,089; Carter, Dem., 429,281; Anderson, Ind., 12,036; Clark, Libertarian, 5,465; Griswold, Workers World, 2,402; Pulley, Soc. Worker, 2,347.

1984, Reagan, Rep., 582,377; Mondale, Dem., 352,192; Bergland, Libertarian, 2,336.

1988, Bush, Rep., 557,890; Dukakis, Dem., 363,921; Duke, Ind., 4,232; Paul, Lib., 3,329.

1992, Bush, Rep., 487,793; Clinton, Dem., 400,258; Perot, Ind., 85,626; Fulani, New Alliance, 2,625; Marrou, Libertarian, 2,154; Phillips, U.S. Taxpayers, 1,652; Hagelin, Natural Law, 1,140.

Missouri

	1992			1988	
County	Clinton (D)	Bush (R)	Perot (I)	Dukakis (D)	Bush (R)
Adair	4,232	4,141	2,224	3,571	5,721
Andrew	2,675	2,652	2,151	3,108	3,407
Atchison	1,208	1,140	840	1,468	1,761
Audrain	4,731	3,798	2,099	5,226	5,072
Barry	4,791	5,565	2,381	4,210	7,231
Barton	1,433	2,775	971	1,603	3,339
Bates	2,993	2,499	2,225	3,332	3,574
Benton	3,195	2,511	1,551	2,654	3,467
Bollinger	2,150	2,289	909	1,883	2,710
Boone	26,176	19,405	12,040	24,370	22,948
Buchanan	16,570	11,275	9,404	18,601	15,336
Butler	6,602	6,450	2,189	5,751	7,968
Caldwell	1,456	1,295	1,283	1,726	2,074
Callaway	5,799	4,880	3,266	5,209	6,687
Camden	5,140	5,554	3,891	3,930	7,773
Cape Girardeau	9,605	13,464	5,199	7,904	16,583
Carroll	2,100	1,774	1,495	2,330	2,811
Carter	1,169	1,101	405	1,087	1,429
Cass	10,246	10,349	9,216	10,092	12,799
Cedar	2,064	2,085	1,173	1,774	2,966
Chariton	2,141	1,378	1,067	2,347	2,193
Christian	6,242	7,422	3,422	4,724	7,670
Clark	1,815	1,039	725	1,925	1,493
Clay	30,565	23,798	20,951	29,620	30,293
Clinton	3,400	2,391	2,423	3,653	3,282
Cole	10,201	15,270	5,770	8,359	18,023
Cooper	2,709	2,867	1,735	2,510	3,737
Crawford	3,515	2,831	2,002	3,107	3,856
Dade	1,332	1,577	834	1,315	2,154
Dallas	2,533	2,116	1,392	2,293	2,898
Daviess	1,477	1,107	1,143	1,743	1,765
DeKalb	1,630	1,318	1,207	1,970	1,863
Dent	2,689	2,125	1,049	2,421	2,975
Douglas	2,126	2,569	1,081	1,735	3,225
Dunklin	6,277	4,024	1,166	5,281	5,026
Franklin	13,431	11,477	11,043	11,891	16,611
Gasconade	1,952	2,690	1,672	1,621	4,216
Gentry	1,519	1,272	921	1,872	1,554
Greene	41,137	46,457	17,770	35,475	52,211
Grundy	1,968	1,749	1,372	2,052	2,668
Harrison	1,590	1,563	1,059	1,776	2,271
Henry	4,232	2,681	2,807	4,135	4,167
Hickory	1,929	1,259	864	1,677	2,043
Holt	1,050	1,202	781	1,258	1,583
Howard	2,085	1,253	1,090	2,446	1,865
Howell	5,492	5,360	2,650	4,324	7,277
Iron	2,507	1,276	841	2,283	1,877
Jackson	145,999	78,611	66,142	147,964	107,810
Jasper	11,727	17,592	6,440	11,159	19,934
Jefferson	32,569	20,637	20,057	27,738	29,279

Johnson	5,546	5,032	4,578	5,373	7,512
Knox	1,010	724	523	1,255	1,212
Laclede	4,179	5,176	2,852	3,442	6,070
Lafayette	5,213	4,651	3,561	5,654	6,825
Lawrence	4,666	5,608	2,570	4,432	6,911
Lewis	2,196	1,461	892	2,460	1,803
Lincoln	5,453	3,718	3,572	4,605	5,305
Linn	2,916	1,967	1,524	3,150	3,061
Livingston	2,505	2,370	1,976	3,077	3,462
McDonald	2,281	3,010	1,551	2,299	3,812
Macon	3,194	2,256	1,697	3,215	3,406
Madison	2,501	1,673	899	2,167	2,528
Maries	1,732	1,356	915	1,552	1,919
Marion	5,156	4,762	1,841	5,617	5,034
Mercer	843	626	378	877	875
Miller	2,905	4,175	2,391	2,555	5,662
Missouri	3,226	1,675	776	2,814	2,218
Moniteau	2,018	2,566	1,499	1,936	3,502
Monroe	2,060	1,153	969	2,461	1,542
Montgomery	2,063	1,974	1,266	2,064	2,714
Morgan	2,906	2,819	2,028	2,604	3,958
New Madrid	4,883	2,431	962	3,812	3,387
Newton	5,987	8,804	3,567	5,798	10,617
Nodaway	3,723	3,147	2,484	4,240	4,103
Oregon	2,258	1,402	564	2,042	1,717
Osage	1,860	2,784	1,423	1,771	3,885
Ozark	1,581	1,772	906	1,329	2,404
Pemiscot	3,924	2,161	670	3,288	3,066
Perry	2,525	3,205	1,498	2,136	3,836
Pettis	5,314	6,823	4,278	5,486	9,648
Phelps	6,852	6,040	3,774	5,867	8,329
Pike	3,609	2,255	1,464	3,816	3,271
Platte	10,920	9,380	9,062	11,225	11,838
Polk	3,316	3,465	1,879	3,419	5,030
Pulaski	4,113	3,793	2,057	3,446	4,642
Putnam	838	1,143	522	803	1,365
Ralls	2,158	1,349	880	2,489	1,494
Randolph	4,951	3,025	2,212	5,291	4,384
Ray	4,457	2,563	2,567	4,879	3,763
Reynolds	2,014	776	532	1,864	1,162
Ripley	2,300	1,814	739	1,961	2,647
St. Charles	37,263	38,673	30,351	29,286	50,005
St. Clair	1,965	1,555	1,083	1,864	2,312
St. Francois	9,367	5,889	3,635	8,158	7,923
St. Louis	235,760	188,285	109,099	216,534	262,784
Ste. Genevieve	3,795	1,780	1,547	3,612	2,532
Saline	4,643	2,688	2,815	5,039	4,625
Schuyler	936	742	487	1,013	1,063
Scotland	1,070	798	617	1,117	1,248
Scott	7,452	6,265	2,763	5,914	8,013
Shannon	2,135	1,224	579	1,796	1,696
Shelby	1,435	1,169	786	1,818	1,586
Stoddard	5,720	4,608	1,977	4,701	5,822
Stone	3,256	4,035	1,884	2,889	5,080
Sullivan	1,510	1,326	596	1,562	1,897
Taney	4,682	6,081	2,395	3,888	7,043
Texas	4,597	3,470	1,900	3,887	4,584
Vernon	3,546	2,851	1,890	3,402	4,149
Warren	3,213	2,953	2,471	2,935	4,452
Washington	4,211	2,157	1,618	3,744	3,240
Wayne	3,073	2,101	837	2,456	2,648
Webster	4,149	4,361	2,108	3,890	5,123
Worth	599	483	328	732	677
Wright	2,814	3,427	1,425	2,232	4,151
City					
St. Louis	102,356	25,441	18,864	110,076	40,906
Totals	**1,053,873**	**811,159**	**518,741**	**1,001,619**	**1,084,953**

Missouri Vote Since 1944

1944, Roosevelt, Dem., 807,357; Dewey, Rep., 761,175; Thomas, Soc., 1,750; Watson, Proh., 1,175; Teichert, Soc. Labor, 221.

1948, Truman, Dem., 917,315; Dewey, Rep., 655,039; Wallace, Prog., 3,998; Thomas, Soc., 2,222.

1952, Eisenhower, Rep., 959,429; Stevenson, Dem., 929,830; Hallinan, Prog., 987; Hamblen, Proh., 885; MacArthur, Christian Nationalist, 302; America First, 233; Hoopes, Soc., 227; Hass, Soc. Labor, 169.

1956, Stevenson, Dem., 918,273; Eisenhower, Rep., 914,299.

1960, Kennedy, Dem., 972,201; Nixon, Rep., 962,221.

1964, Johnson, Dem., 1,164,344; Goldwater, Rep., 653,535.

1968, Nixon, Rep., 811,932; Humphrey, Dem., 791,444; Wallace, 3d party, 206,126.

1972, Nixon, Rep., 1,154,058; McGovern, Dem., 698,531.

1976, Carter, Dem., 999,163; Ford, Rep., 928,808; McCarthy, Ind., 24,329.

1980, Reagan, Rep., 1,074,181; Carter, Dem., 931,182; Anderson, Ind., 77,920; Clark, Libertarian, 14,422; DeBerry, Soc. Workers, 1,515; Commoner, Citizens, 573; write-ins, 31.

1984, Reagan, Rep., 1,274,188; Mondale, Dem., 848,583.

1988, Bush, Rep., 1,084,953; Dukakis, Dem., 1,001,619; Fulani, New Alliance, 6,656; Paul, write-in, 434.

1992, Clinton, Dem., 1,053,873; Bush, Rep., 811,159; Perot, Ind., 518,741; Marrou, Libertarian, 7,497.

Montana

	1992			1988	
County	Clinton (D)	Bush (R)	Perot (I)	Dukakis (D)	Bush (R)
Beaverhead	1,098	1,746	1,202	1,274	2,668
Big Horn	2,154	1,377	840	2,233	1,711
Blaine	1,355	971	699	1,460	1,402
Broadwater	491	830	505	592	1,054
Carbon	1,549	1,562	1,482	2,039	2,360
Carter	154	497	220	242	686
Cascade	14,719	12,494	9,151	15,718	15,946
Chouteau	959	1,380	870	1,166	1,980
Custer	1,968	2,105	1,505	2,343	3,007
Daniels	457	496	402	571	802
Dawson	1,785	1,679	1,370	2,120	2,658
Deer Lodge	3,174	832	1,207	3,185	1,168
Fallon	446	731	427	612	1,002
Fergus	1,615	2,736	1,934	2,052	3,948
Flathead	9,746	11,699	9,109	10,202	14,461
Gallatin	9,535	11,109	7,711	9,527	13,214
Garfield	125	403	281	196	631
Glacier	2,076	1,222	997	2,151	1,728
Golden Valley	142	192	157	203	335
Granite	358	556	386	511	789
Hill	3,618	2,408	2,017	4,219	3,467
Jefferson	1,415	1,541	1,172	1,746	2,007
Judith Basin	409	610	415	590	902
Lake	3,938	3,596	2,878	4,109	4,883
Lewis & Clark	11,117	9,351	5,560	11,932	10,946
Liberty	321	512	363	418	771
Lincoln	2,765	2,799	2,637	3,601	3,500
Madison	779	1,415	1,043	878	2,045
McCone	424	528	395	567	814
Meagher	260	422	310	337	656
Mineral	664	403	543	789	616
Missoula	20,347	12,898	9,735	19,178	15,965
Musselshell	648	876	691	898	1,280
Park	2,258	2,846	2,182	2,526	3,823
Petroleum	61	135	95	91	204
Phillips	634	1,026	949	905	1,462
Pondera	1,046	1,252	855	1,245	1,795
Powder River	258	547	340	395	815
Powell	989	1,058	872	1,174	1,574
Prairie	260	412	179	343	541
Ravalli	4,644	5,392	4,573	4,763	7,418
Richland	1,440	1,760	1,525	1,824	2,628
Roosevelt	1,827	1,212	1,089	2,083	1,957
Rosebud	1,669	1,130	1,099	1,869	1,822
Sanders	1,689	1,361	1,378	1,959	2,152
Sheridan	1,077	795	782	1,354	1,381
Silver Bow	9,960	3,491	4,570	11,422	5,043
Stillwater	1,178	1,390	1,056	1,407	1,920
Sweet Grass	395	880	507	462	1,242
Teton	1,043	1,364	969	1,303	1,876
Toole	854	943	903	1,070	1,505
Treasure	157	206	178	231	291
Valley	1,715	1,497	1,320	2,163	2,467
Wheatland	384	478	284	443	667
Wibaux	195	234	173	258	358
Yellowstone	20,163	22,822	13,133	21,987	28,069
Totals	**154,507**	**144,207**	**107,225**	**168,936**	**190,412**

Montana Vote Since 1944

1944, Roosevelt, Dem., 112,556; Dewey, Rep., 93,163; Thomas, Soc., 1,296; Watson, Proh., 340.

1948, Truman, Dem., 119,071; Dewey, Rep., 96,770; Wallace, Prog., 7,313; Thomas, Soc., 695; Watson, Proh., 429.

1952, Eisenhower, Rep., 157,394; Stevenson, Dem., 106,213; Hallinan, Prog., 723; Hamblen, Proh., 548; Hoopes, Soc., 159.

1956, Eisenhower, Rep., 154,933; Stevenson, Dem., 116,238.

1960, Kennedy, Dem., 134,891; Nixon, Rep., 141,841; Decker, Proh., 456; Dobbs, Soc. Workers, 391.

1964, Johnson, Dem., 164,246; Goldwater, Rep., 113,032; Kasper, Nat'l States Rights, 519; Munn, Proh., 499; DeBerry, Soc. Worker, 332.

1968, Nixon, Rep., 138,835; Humphrey, Dem., 114,117; Wallace, 3d party, 20,015; Halstead, Soc. Worker, 457; Munn, Proh., 510; Caton, New Reform, 470.

1972, Nixon, Rep., 183,976; McGovern, Dem., 120,197; Schmitz, Amer., 13,430.

1976, Carter, Dem., 149,259; Ford, Rep., 173,703; Anderson, Amer., 5,772.

1980, Reagan, Rep., 206,814; Carter, Dem., 118,032; Anderson, Ind., 29,281; Clark, Libertarian, 9,825.

1984, Reagan, Rep., 232,450; Mondale, Dem., 146,742; Bergland, Libertarian, 5,185.
1988, Bush, Rep., 190,412; Dukakis, Dem., 168,936; Paul, Lib., 5,047; Fulani, New Alliance, 1,279.
1992, Clinton, Dem., 154,507; Bush, Rep., 144,207; Perot, Ind., 107,225; Gritz, Populist/America First, 3,658.

Nebraska

	1992			1988	
County	Clinton (D)	Bush (R)	Perot (I)	Dukakis (D)	Bush (R)
Adams	3,445	6,346	3,273	4,145	8,063
Antelope	650	1,979	1,134	933	2,626
Arthur	18	148	97	58	210
Banner	68	284	128	112	361
Blaine	64	256	130	72	338
Boone	604	1,588	956	976	2,160
Box Butte	1,935	2,198	1,508	2,466	3,253
Boyd	353	744	468	480	967
Brown	311	999	525	435	1,335
Buffalo	3,742	9,708	4,083	4,700	9,980
Burt	1,224	1,667	1,009	1,458	2,050
Butler	1,087	1,881	1,157	1,715	2,083
Cass	2,949	4,314	2,657	3,674	4,658
Cedar	1,007	1,981	1,507	1,759	2,462
Chase	398	1,000	674	597	1,446
Cherry	563	1,707	730	642	2,240
Cheyenne	967	2,197	1,061	1,333	2,862
Clay	802	1,818	952	1,097	2,352
Colfax	1,011	1,915	1,197	1,542	2,329
Cuming	835	2,711	1,192	1,238	3,201
Custer	1,126	3,180	1,492	1,496	4,202
Dakota	2,322	2,771	1,307	2,941	2,744
Dawes	987	1,961	1,103	1,122	2,618
Dawson	1,739	4,710	2,305	2,184	5,529
Deuel	232	558	327	302	769
Dixon	830	1,484	726	1,166	1,802
Dodge	4,665	7,269	4,432	6,116	8,412
Douglas	67,003	93,421	38,641	76,444	99,806
Dundy	244	664	332	333	828
Fillmore	988	1,495	993	1,433	1,952
Franklin	477	967	527	768	1,294
Frontier	302	785	479	384	1,057
Furnas	624	1,365	804	791	1,830
Gage	3,309	3,995	2,726	4,008	5,114
Garden	212	697	385	366	986
Garfield	221	595	270	234	803
Gosper	254	492	297	331	694
Grant	75	247	124	89	301
Greeley	435	587	395	670	763
Hall	5,519	9,264	5,822	6,822	12,020
Hamilton	992	2,379	1,213	1,289	3,019
Harlan	488	991	623	725	1,403
Hayes	85	362	207	160	512
Hitchcock	359	824	540	480	1,132
Holt	835	3,131	1,714	1,327	4,081
Hooker	70	283	102	91	378
Howard	778	1,138	940	1,186	1,526
Jefferson	1,506	1,783	1,177	1,819	2,470
Johnson	822	885	642	1,162	1,182
Kearney	644	1,751	844	1,056	2,120
Keith	731	2,019	1,130	1,067	2,879
Keya Paha	105	368	158	145	446
Kimball	408	931	440	540	1,321
Knox	968	2,112	1,166	1,477	2,644
Lancaster	41,207	41,400	21,783	44,260	44,605
Lincoln	5,142	7,025	3,384	6,070	8,395
Logan	80	271	98	93	373
Loup	58	233	96	97	295
McPherson	49	217	62	60	229
Madison	2,352	7,851	3,486	2,779	9,135
Merrick	864	1,854	1,072	1,192	2,376
Morrill	577	1,184	752	753	1,554
Nance	559	851	569	794	1,185
Nemaha	1,110	1,696	1,020	1,457	2,293
Nuckolls	834	1,277	825	1,114	1,750
Otoe	2,038	2,960	1,800	2,616	3,724
Pawnee	566	670	565	767	975
Perkins	300	842	522	467	1,117
Phelps	829	2,748	1,298	1,047	3,316
Pierce	611	1,853	1,084	914	2,474
Platte	2,409	7,712	3,656	3,285	9,029
Polk	661	1,435	812	944	1,768
Red Willow	1,164	2,488	1,660	1,505	3,325
Richardson	1,513	2,050	1,356	1,926	2,702
Rock	162	588	233	198	756
Saline	2,425	1,740	1,576	3,119	2,352
Sarpy	10,720	20,482	9,270	10,936	20,179
Saunders	2,509	4,037	2,567	3,524	4,454
Scotts Bluff	4,173	7,213	3,514	4,454	8,594
Seward	2,118	3,044	1,722	2,682	3,467
Sheridan	535	1,698	751	612	2,251
Sherman	568	736	582	839	914
Sioux	148	445	206	194	568
Stanton	496	1,274	786	637	1,709
Thayer	923	1,387	1,077	1,322	1,981
Thomas	69	283	115	81	383
Thurston	865	898	487	1,225	1,105
Valley	716	1,173	693	873	1,603
Washington	2,108	4,035	2,148	2,552	4,567
Wayne	921	2,122	1,047	1,111	2,473
Webster	624	972	657	891	1,314
Wheeler	88	246	127	141	309
York	1,385	3,783	1,825	1,748	4,744
Totals	**216,864**	**343,678**	**174,104**	**259,235**	**397,956**

Nebraska Vote Since 1944

1944, Roosevelt, Dem., 233,246; Dewey, Rep., 329,880.
1948, Truman, Dem., 224,165; Dewey, Rep., 264,774.
1952, Eisenhower, Rep., 421,603; Stevenson Dem., 188,057.
1956, Eisenhower, Rep., 378,108; Stevenson, Dem., 199,029.
1960, Kennedy, Dem., 232,542; Nixon, Rep., 380,553.
1964, Johnson, Dem., 307,307; Goldwater, Rep., 276,847.
1968, Nixon, Rep., 321,163; Humphrey, Dem., 170,784; Wallace, 3d party, 44,904.
1972, Nixon, Rep., 406,298; McGovern, Dem., 169,991; scattered, 817.
1976, Carter, Dem., 233,287; Ford, Rep., 359,219; McCarthy, Ind., 9,383; Maddox, Amer. Ind., 3,378; MacBride, Libertarian, 1,476.
1980, Reagan, Rep., 419,214; Carter, Dem., 166,424; Anderson, Ind., 44,854; Clark, Libertarian, 9,041.
1984, Reagan, Rep., 459,135; Mondale, Dem., 187,475; Bergland, Libertarian, 2,075.
1988, Bush, Rep., 397,956; Dukakis, Dem., 259,235; Paul, Lib., 2,534; Fulani, New Alliance, 1,740.
1992, Bush, Rep., 343,678; Clinton, Dem., 216,864; Perot, Ind., 174,104; Marrou, Libertarian, 1,340.

Nevada

	1992			1988	
County	Clinton (D)	Bush (R)	Perot (I)	Dukakis (D)	Bush (R)
Churchill	1,770	3,789	1,964	1,481	4,578
Clark	124,586	97,403	75,364	78,359	108,110
Douglas	3,928	6,182	4,814	3,107	7,074
Elko	2,782	5,208	3,628	2,310	5,722
Esmeralda	118	221	220	143	380
Eureka	129	330	214	151	413
Humboldt	810	1,505	1,149	1,024	2,378
Lander	423	885	652	439	1,214
Lincoln	511	890	394	466	1,035
Lyon	2,777	3,509	2,716	2,301	4,390
Mineral	909	918	746	978	1,480
Nye	2,561	2,743	2,501	1,748	3,619
Pershing	467	643	429	458	867
Storey	488	458	550	432	651
Washoe	39,500	42,636	30,974	32,902	52,654
White Pine	1,354	1,206	1,070	1,351	1,774
City					
Carson City	6,035	7,302	5,195	5,088	9,701
Totals	**189,148**	**175,828**	**132,580**	**132,738**	**206,040**

Nevada Vote Since 1944

1944, Roosevelt, Dem., 29,623; Dewey, Rep., 24,611.
1948, Truman, Dem., 31,291; Dewey, Rep., 29,357; Wallace, Prog., 1,469.
1952, Eisenhower, Rep., 50,502; Stevenson, Dem., 31,688.
1956, Eisenhower, Rep., 56,049; Stevenson, Dem., 40,640.
1960, Kennedy, Dem., 54,880; Nixon, Rep., 52,387.
1964, Johnson, Dem., 79,339; Goldwater, Rep., 56,094.
1968, Nixon, Rep., 73,188; Humphrey, Dem., 60,598; Wallace, 3d party, 20,432.
1972, Nixon, Rep., 115,750; McGovern, Dem., 66,016.
1976, Carter, Dem., 92,479; Ford, Rep., 101,273; MacBride, Libertarian, 1,519; Maddox, Amer. Ind., 1,497; scattered, 5,108.
1980, Reagan, Rep., 155,017; Carter, Dem., 66,666; Anderson, Ind., 17,651; Clark, Libertarian, 4,358.
1984, Reagan, Rep., 188,770; Mondale, Dem., 91,655; Bergland, Libertarian, 2,292.
1988, Bush, Rep., 206,040; Dukakis, Dem., 132,738; Paul, Lib., 3,520; Fulani, New Alliance, 835.
1992, Clinton, Dem., 189,148; Bush, Rep., 175,828; Perot, Ind., 132,580; Gritz, Populist/America First, 2,892; Marrou, Libertarian, 1,835.

New Hampshire

	1992			1988	
City	Clinton (D)	Bush (R)	Perot (I)	Dukakis (D)	Bush (R)
Berlin City	2,680	1,272	1,162	2,271	2,529
Claremont	2,650	1,822	904	2,254	2,513

Concord.	8,325	5,651	2,843	6,698	7,439
Dover	5,449	4,197	2,246	4,803	5,357
Keene	5,210	3,257	1,736	4,466	4,535
Laconia	2,390	3,033	1,496	2,111	3,835
Manchester . .	16,627	16,298	7,441	12,567	23,893
Nashua	14,777	12,514	8,306	12,833	19,369
Portsmouth . .	6,132	3,563	2,088	5,377	4,827
Rochester . . .	4,588	4,272	2,541	3,591	5,368
Other	140,212	147,999	90,574	106,725	201,872
Totals.	**209,040**	**202,484**	**121,337**	**163,696**	**281,537**

New Hampshire Vote Since 1944

1944, Roosevelt, Dem., 119,663; Dewey, Rep., 109,916; Thomas, Soc., 46.

1948, Truman, Dem., 107,995; Dewey, Rep., 121,299; Wallace, Prog., 1,970; Thomas, Soc., 86; Teichert, Soc. Labor, 83; Thurmond, States' Rights, 7.

1952, Eisenhower, Rep., 166,287; Stevenson, Dem., 106,663.

1956, Eisenhower, Rep., 176,519; Stevenson, Dem., 90,364; Andrews, Const., 111.

1960, Kennedy, Dem., 137,772; Nixon, Rep., 157,989.

1964, Johnson, Dem., 182,065; Goldwater, Rep., 104,029.

1968, Nixon, Rep., 154,903; Humphrey, Dem., 130,589; Wallace, 3d party, 11,173; New Party, 421; Halstead, Soc. Worker, 104.

1972, Nixon, Rep., 213,724; McGovern, Dem., 116,435; Schmitz, Amer., 3,386; Jenness, Soc. Workers, 368; scattered, 142.

1976, Carter, Dem., 147,645; Ford, Rep., 185,935; McCarthy, Ind., 4,095; MacBride, Libertarian, 936; Reagan, write-in, 388; La Rouche, U.S. Labor, 186; Camejo, Soc. Workers, 161, Levin, Soc. Labor, 66; scattered, 215.

1980, Reagan, Rep., 221,705; Carter, Dem., 108,864; Anderson, Ind., 49,693; Clark, Libertarian, 2,067; Commoner, Citizens, 1,325; Hall, Com., 129; Griswold, Workers World, 76; DeBerry, Soc. Workers, 72; scattered, 68.

1984, Reagan, Rep., 267,051; Mondale, Dem., 120,377; Bergland, Libertarian, 735.

1988, Bush, Rep., 281,537; Dukakis, Dem., 163,696; Paul, Lib., 4,502; Fulani, New Alliance, 790.

1992, Clinton, Dem., 209,040; Bush, Rep., 202,484; Perot, Ind., 121,337; Marrou, Libertarian, 3,548.

New Jersey

	1992			1988	
County	**Clinton (D)**	**Bush (R)**	**Perot (I)**	**Dukakis (D)**	**Bush (R)**
Atlantic	39,633	34,279	15,890	34,047	44,748
Bergen	171,104	178,223	52,082	160,655	226,885
Burlington	72,845	63,709	35,322	61,140	87,416
Camden.	104,915	67,205	37,144	90,704	100,072
Cape May	17,324	21,502	9,798	15,105	28,738
Cumberland . . .	22,220	19,253	9,901	21,869	26,024
Essex	158,130	89,146	26,961	156,098	111,491
Gloucester	42,425	37,335	24,132	35,479	51,708
Hudson	99,799	66,505	14,569	95,696	81,807
Hunterdon	15,423	25,130	12,736	13,758	31,907
Mercer.	71,383	50,473	22,503	68,712	65,384
Middlesex	128,824	108,701	45,055	117,149	143,361
Monmouth	101,750	117,715	45,445	91,844	147,320
Morris	67,593	108,431	32,447	58,721	127,420
Ocean	75,431	95,984	41,668	64,474	124,587
Passaic	70,030	71,147	21,494	66,254	88,070
Salem	10,062	10,363	7,274	9,956	15,240
Somerset.	42,867	56,044	21,014	37,406	67,658
Sussex	14,775	29,510	12,537	13,676	36,086
Union	96,671	87,742	23,991	93,158	112,967
Warren	13,002	18,468	9,866	11,640	21,715
Totals.	**1,436,206**	**1,356,865**	**521,829**	**1,317,541**	**1,740,604**

New Jersey Vote Since 1944

1944, Roosevelt, Dem., 987,874; Dewey, Rep., 961,335; Teichert, Soc. Labor, 6,939; Watson, Nat'l. Proh., 4,255; Thomas, Soc., 3,385.

1948, Truman, Dem., 895,455; Dewey, Rep., 981,124; Wallace, Prog., 42,683; Watson, Proh., 10,593; Thomas, Soc., 10,521; Dobbs, Soc. Workers, 5,825; Teichert, Soc. Labor, 3,354.

1952, Eisenhower, Rep., 1,373,613; Stevenson, Dem., 1,015,902; Hoopes, Soc., 8,593; Hass, Soc. Labor, 5,815; Hallinan, Prog., 5,589; Krajewski, Poor Man's, 4,203; Dobbs, Soc. Workers, 3,850; Hamblen, Proh., 989.

1956, Eisenhower, Rep., 1,606,942; Stevenson Dem., 850,337; Holtwick, Proh., 9,147; Hass, Soc. Labor, 6,736; Andrews, Conservative, 5,317; Dobbs, Soc. Workers, 4,004; Krajewski, American Third Party, 1,829.

1960, Kennedy, Dem., 1,385,415; Nixon, Rep., 1,363,324; Dobbs, Soc. Workers, 11,402; Lee, Conservative, 8,708; Hass, Soc. Labor, 4,262.

1964, Johnson, Dem., 1,867,671; Goldwater, Rep., 963,843; DeBerry, Soc. Workers, 8,181; Hass, Soc. Labor, 7,075.

1968, Nixon, Rep., 1,325,467; Humphrey, Dem., 1,264,206; Wallace, 3d party, 262,187; Halstead, Soc. Worker, 8,667; Gregory, Peace Freedom, 8,084; Blomen, Soc. Labor, 6,784.

1972, Nixon, Rep., 1,845,502; McGovern, Dem., 1,102,211; Schmitz, Amer., 34,378; Spock, Peoples, 5,355; Fisher, Soc. Labor, 4,544; Jenness, Soc. Workers, 2,233; Mahalchik, Amer. First, 1,743; Hall, Com., 1,263.

1976, Carter, Dem., 1,444,653; Ford, Rep., 1,509,688; McCarthy, Ind., 32,717; MacBride, Libertarian, 9,449; Maddox, Amer., 7,716; Levin, Soc. Labor, 3,686; Hall, Com., 1,662; LaRouche, U.S. Labor, 1,650; Camejo, Soc. Workers, 1,184; Wright, People's, 1,044; Bubar, Proh., 554; Zeidler, Soc., 469.

1980, Reagan, Rep., 1,546,557; Carter, Dem., 1,147,364; Anderson, Ind., 234,632; Clark, Libertarian, 20,652; Commoner, Citizens, 8,203; McCormack, Right to Life, 3,927; Lynen, Middle Class, 3,694; Hall, Com., 2,555; Pulley, Soc. Workers, 2,198; McReynolds, Soc., 1,973; Gahres, Down With Lawyers, 1,718; Griswold, Workers World, 1,288; Wendelken, Ind., 923.

1984, Reagan, Rep., 1,933,630; Mondale, Dem., 1,261,323; Bergland, Libertarian, 6,416.

1988, Bush, Rep., 1,740,604; Dukakis, Dem., 1,317,541; Lewin, Peace & Freedom, 9,953; Paul, Lib., 8,421.

1992, Clinton, Dem., 1,436,206; Bush, Rep., 1,356,865; Perot, Ind., 521,829; Marrou, Libertarian, 6,822; Fulani, New Alliance, 3,513; Phillips, U.S. Taxpayers, 2,670; LaRouche, Ind., 2,095; Warren, Socialist Workers, 2,011; Daniels, Ind., 1,996; Gritz, Populist/America First, 1,867; Hagelin, Natural Law, 1,353.

New Mexico

	1992			1988	
County	**Clinton (D)**	**Bush (R)**	**Perot (I)**	**Dukakis (D)**	**Bush (R)**
Bernalillo	90,863	77,304	31,241	78,346	92,830
Catron.	465	771	289	490	925
Chaves	6,360	8,872	3,590	6,730	13,367
Cibola	3,334	2,051	847	3,458	2,640
Colfax	2,607	1,730	871	2,785	2,256
Curry	3,699	6,831	2,056	3,995	8,032
De Baca	451	526	204	480	643
Dona Ana . . .	19,894	16,308	7,682	19,608	21,582
Eddy.	7,409	7,313	3,430	8,544	9,805
Grant	5,603	2,917	1,685	5,443	4,196
Guadalupe . . .	1,225	691	173	1,243	861
Harding	268	312	98	291	377
Hidalgo	995	871	442	901	1,100
Lea.	5,047	7,921	3,233	5,879	11,309
Lincoln	1,730	2,669	1,431	1,690	3,511
Los Alamos . .	3,897	4,320	2,339	3,275	6,622
Luna	2,637	2,166	1,445	3,066	3,415
McKinley	9,405	4,720	1,304	9,595	5,694
Mora.	1,555	668	188	1,601	923
Otero	5,377	7,481	3,257	5,284	9,984
Quay.	1,758	1,759	755	1,901	2,454
Rio Arriba . . .	7,832	2,680	984	7,503	3,024
Roosevelt . . .	2,172	3,215	1,085	2,033	3,589
Sandoval	10,951	8,491	3,954	9,332	9,411
San Juan. . . .	11,302	13,415	5,351	11,094	16,202
San Miguel. . .	6,186	2,183	965	6,131	2,763
Santa Fe	27,189	9,684	5,656	23,581	12,891
Sierra	1,771	1,562	1,055	1,595	2,507
Socorro	2,908	2,186	918	2,960	3,114
Taos.	7,051	2,260	1,300	6,271	2,897
Torrance	1,662	1,667	810	1,618	2,252
Union	519	975	355	638	1,291
Valencia	7,495	6,305	2,902	7,136	7,874
Totals.	**261,617**	**212,824**	**91,895**	**244,497**	**270,341**

New Mexico Vote Since 1944

1944, Roosevelt, Dem., 81,389; Dewey, Rep., 70,688; Watson, Proh., 148.

1948, Truman, Dem., 105,464; Dewey, Rep., 80,303; Wallace, Prog., 1,037; Watson, Proh., 127; Thomas, Soc., 83; Teichert, Soc. Labor, 49.

1952, Eisenhower, Rep., 132,170; Stevenson, Dem., 105,661; Hamblen, Proh., 297; Hallinan, Ind. Prog., 225; MacArthur, Christian National, 220; Hass, Soc. Labor, 35.

1956, Eisenhower, Rep., 146,788; Stevenson, Dem., 106,098; Holtwick, Proh., 607; Andrews, Ind., 364; Hass, Soc. Labor, 69.

1960, Kennedy, Dem., 156,027; Nixon, Rep., 153,733; Decker, Proh., 777; Hass, Soc. Labor, 570.

1964, Johnson, Dem., 194,017; Goldwater, Rep., 131,838; Hass, Soc. Labor, 1,217; Munn, Proh., 543.

1968, Nixon, Rep., 169,692; Humphrey, Dem., 130,081; Wallace, 3d party, 25,737; Chavez, 1,519; Halstead, Soc. Worker, 252.

1972, Nixon, Rep., 235,606; McGovern, Dem., 141,084; Schmitz, Amer., 8,767; Jenness, Soc. Workers, 474.

1976, Carter, Dem., 201,148; Ford, Rep., 211,419; Camejo, Soc. Workers, 2,462; MacBride, Libertarian, 1,110; Zeidler, Soc., 240; Bubar, Proh., 211.

1980, Reagan, Rep., 250,779; Carter, Dem., 167,826; Anderson, Ind., 29,459; Clark, Libertarian, 4,365; Commoner, Citizens, 2,202; Bubar, Statesman, 1,281; Pulley, Soc. Worker, 325.

1984, Reagan, Rep., 307,101; Mondale, Dem., 201,769; Bergland, Libertarian, 4,459.

1988, Bush, Rep., 270,341; Dukakis, Dem., 244,497; Paul, Lib., 3,268; Fulani, New Alliance, 2,237.

1992, Clinton, Dem., 261,617; Bush, Rep., 212,824; Perot, Ind., 91,895; Marrou, Libertarian, 1,615.

New York

	1992			1988	
County	Clinton (D)	Bush (R)	Perot (I)	Dukakis (D)	Bush (R)
Albany	80,641	49,452	24,064	86,564	59,534
Allegany	4,848	8,976	4,703	5,614	11,880
Bronx	225,038	63,310	15,115	218,245	76,043
Broome	43,444	34,653	21,280	48,130	47,610
Cattaraugus	10,150	13,944	10,662	12,447	19,691
Cayuga	13,088	12,065	10,279	15,044	16,934
Chautauqua	22,645	21,222	18,455	25,814	31,642
Chemung	15,099	16,088	7,493	15,966	20,951
Chenango	8,017	8,114	5,356	8,021	11,727
Clinton	12,881	13,455	5,389	12,670	15,702
Columbia	11,368	11,568	5,829	11,585	15,111
Cortland	7,815	7,782	5,098	7,673	10,934
Delaware	7,152	8,829	4,404	7,463	11,391
Dutchess	41,655	46,709	26,320	38,968	62,165
Erie	196,233	129,444	123,358	238,779	188,796
Essex	6,717	8,278	3,784	6,623	10,350
Franklin	7,654	6,635	3,857	7,928	9,135
Fulton	8,400	9,137	5,120	9,012	11,757
Genesee	8,071	11,663	6,192	9,945	14,182
Greene	6,924	9,390	4,689	7,265	11,874
Hamilton	963	2,038	793	976	2,320
Herkimer	10,880	12,052	6,866	12,694	15,104
Jefferson	13,380	14,227	9,461	14,137	19,304
Kings	411,183	133,344	33,014	363,916	178,961
Lewis	3,676	4,101	3,164	4,252	5,787
Livingston	8,648	12,122	5,775	9,506	14,004
Madison	10,099	11,293	7,391	10,665	14,902
Monroe	141,502	134,021	63,229	153,650	155,271
Montgomery	9,509	8,802	5,020	11,371	11,128
Nassau	282,593	246,881	77,097	250,130	337,430
New York	416,142	84,501	27,689	385,675	115,927
Niagara	35,649	30,401	30,126	43,801	42,537
Oneida	40,966	43,806	22,717	47,665	55,039
Onondaga	90,645	77,642	45,175	94,751	104,080
Ontario	16,064	18,995	9,571	17,341	21,780
Orange	45,946	53,493	22,499	38,465	65,446
Orleans	4,927	7,468	4,275	5,913	9,028
Oswego	16,990	18,530	14,853	18,430	25,362
Otsego	10,471	10,141	5,841	11,069	13,021
Putnam	14,048	18,934	8,011	12,158	24,086
Queens	349,520	157,561	46,014	325,147	217,049
Rensselaer	29,793	28,937	15,198	33,066	35,412
Richmond	56,901	70,707	19,678	47,812	77,427
Rockland	56,759	49,608	15,026	47,634	63,825
St. Lawrence	18,197	13,901	9,758	18,921	20,290
Saratoga	33,011	36,917	19,091	31,684	43,498
Schenectady	32,335	26,258	14,838	36,483	33,364
Schoharie	4,997	5,678	3,327	5,389	7,008
Schuyler	2,859	3,226	2,051	2,900	4,291
Seneca	5,810	5,432	3,660	6,215	7,221
Steuben	12,043	19,761	9,378	12,824	25,359
Suffolk	220,811	229,467	112,973	199,215	311,242
Sullivan	13,717	11,396	6,336	11,635	15,713
Tioga	7,791	9,287	5,867	8,102	12,670
Tompkins	23,197	11,520	6,704	21,455	14,932
Ulster	32,886	29,223	17,952	30,744	41,173
Warren	9,820	12,260	6,401	8,580	15,860
Washington	8,429	10,305	6,143	8,201	14,103
Wayne	11,866	18,019	9,188	12,959	20,613
Westchester	184,300	151,990	39,933	169,860	197,956
Wyoming	4,045	7,324	4,837	5,228	9,451
Yates	3,242	4,366	2,354	3,507	5,488
Totals	**3,444,450**	**2,346,649**	**1,090,721**	**3,347,882**	**3,081,871**

New York Vote Since 1944

1944, Roosevelt, Dem., 2,478,598; American Lab., 496,405; Liberal, 329,325; total, 3,304,238; Dewey, Rep., 2,987,647; Teichert, Ind. Gov't., 14,352; Thomas, Soc., 10,553.

1948, Truman, Dem., 2,557,642; Liberal, 222,562; total, 2,780,204; Dewey, Rep., 2,841,163; Wallace, Amer. Lab., 509,559; Thomas, Soc., 40,879; Teichert, Ind. Gov't., 2,729; Dobbs, Soc. Workers, 2,675.

1952, Eisenhower, Rep., 3,952,815; Stevenson, Dem., 2,687,890; Liberal, 416,711; total, 3,104,601; Hallinan, American Lab., 64,211; Hoopes, Soc., 2,664; Dobbs, Soc. Workers, 2,212; Hass, Ind. Gov't., 1,560; scattering, 178; blank and void, 87,813.

1956, Eisenhower, Rep., 4,340,340; Stevenson, Dem., 2,458,212; Liberal, 292,557; total, 2,750,769; write-in votes for Andrews, 1,027; Werdel, 492; Hass, 150; Hoopes, 82; others, 476.

1960, Kennedy, Dem., 3,423,909; Liberal, 406,176; total, 3,830,085; Nixon, Rep., 3,446,419; Dobbs, Soc. Workers, 14,319; scattering, 256; blank and void, 88,896.

1964, Johnson, Dem., 4,913,156; Goldwater, Rep., 2,243,559; Hass, Soc. Labor, 6,085; DeBerry, Soc. Workers, 3,215; scattering, 188; blank and void, 151,383.

1968, Nixon, Rep., 3,007,932; Humphrey, Dem., 3,378,470; Wallace, 3d party, 358,864; Blomen, Soc. Labor, 8,432; Halstead, Soc. Worker, 11,851; Gregory, Freedom and Peace, 24,517; blank, void, and scattering, 171,624.

1972, Nixon, Rep., 3,824,642; Conservative, 368,136; McGovern, Dem., 2,767,956; Liberal, 183,128; Reed, Soc. Workers, 7,797; Fisher, Soc. Labor, 4,530; Hall, Com., 5,641; blank, void, or scattered, 161,641.

1976, Carter, Dem., 3,389,558; Ford, Rep., 3,100,791; MacBride, Libertarian, 12,197; Hall, Com., 10,270; Camejo, Soc. Workers, 6,996; LaRouche, U.S. Labor, 5,413; blank, void, or scattered, 143,037.

1980, Reagan, Rep., 2,893,831; Carter, Dem., 2,728,372; Anderson, Ind., 467,801; Clark, Libertarian, 52,648; McCormack, Right To Life, 24,159; Commoner, Citizens, 23,186; Hall, Com., 7,414; DeBerry, Soc. Workers, 2,068; Griswold, Workers World, 1,416; scattering, 1,064.

1984, Reagan, Rep., 3,664,763; Mondale, Dem., 3,119,609; Bergland, Libertarian, 11,949.

1988, Bush, Rep., 3,081,871; Dukakis, Dem., 3,347,882; Marra, Right to Life, 20,497; Fulani, New Alliance, 15,845.

1992, Clinton, Dem., 3,444,450; Bush, Rep., 2,346,649; Perot, Ind., 1,090,721; Warren, Socialist Workers, 15,472; Marrou, Libertarian, 13,451; Fulani, New Alliance, 11,318; Hagelin, Natural Law, 4,420.

North Carolina

	1992			1988	
County	Clinton (D)	Bush (R)	Perot (I)	Dukakis (D)	Bush (R)
Alamance	15,521	20,637	6,444	12,642	24,131
Alexander	4,849	6,764	2,002	4,148	7,968
Alleghany	2,271	1,853	600	2,087	2,174
Anson	5,269	2,334	921	4,831	2,782
Ashe	4,624	5,200	1,220	4,034	6,019
Avery	1,755	3,895	1,123	1,367	4,277
Beaufort	6,445	7,337	2,174	5,352	8,190
Bertie	4,382	1,756	600	3,762	2,145
Bladen	5,700	3,214	1,248	5,031	3,770
Brunswick	10,177	8,833	3,349	7,881	10,007
Buncombe	32,955	30,892	11,481	26,964	36,828
Burke	12,565	13,397	4,124	10,848	15,933
Cabarrus	13,513	21,281	6,251	10,686	22,524
Caldwell	9,033	12,543	3,965	7,862	15,176
Camden	1,153	1,039	479	1,081	1,144
Carteret	8,028	10,334	3,401	6,859	11,076
Caswell	4,725	2,793	827	4,189	3,299
Catawba	16,334	25,466	7,523	12,922	28,872
Chatham	9,520	6,568	2,425	7,600	6,999
Cherokee	3,686	4,021	1,040	2,567	4,557
Chowan	2,136	1,661	700	1,756	1,884
Clay	1,600	1,890	465	1,289	2,174
Cleveland	13,037	13,650	3,784	10,321	14,039
Columbus	11,469	5,462	1,963	9,172	6,659
Craven	9,998	11,575	3,679	7,313	12,057
Cumberland	30,291	27,139	6,792	23,789	27,057
Currituck	1,935	2,188	1,163	1,555	2,443
Dare	3,925	4,357	2,388	2,806	5,234

Davidson	16,462	24,869	8,324	13,215	28,374
Davie	3,675	6,796	1,903	3,166	7,988
Duplin	6,816	5,286	1,636	5,945	5,774
Durham	47,331	27,581	7,504	35,441	29,928
Edgecombe	11,174	6,275	2,175	9,044	6,831
Forsyth	49,006	52,787	14,262	39,726	57,688
Franklin	6,517	4,669	2,062	5,438	5,499
Gaston	19,121	34,714	7,490	14,582	34,775
Gates	2,206	1,158	466	2,024	1,451
Graham	1,551	1,919	403	1,313	2,091
Granville	6,178	4,538	1,321	5,280	4,880
Greene	2,768	2,180	780	2,729	2,498
Guilford	66,319	60,140	19,601	50,351	66,060
Halifax	9,960	5,769	2,047	8,726	7,462
Harnett	8,473	9,751	2,684	7,259	9,749
Haywood	10,385	7,292	3,303	9,010	8,957
Henderson	10,747	17,010	5,260	9,338	19,711
Hertford	4,609	2,208	846	4,943	2,977
Hoke	3,730	1,711	887	3,281	2,020
Hyde	1,206	740	340	1,316	940
Iredell	13,263	19,411	6,204	10,530	21,536
Jackson	5,753	4,275	1,516	4,933	5,166
Johnston	11,284	15,418	4,939	8,717	15,563
Jones	1,962	1,438	444	1,946	1,649
Lee	5,852	6,658	2,125	4,231	7,104
Lenoir	8,793	8,932	2,107	7,649	10,669
Lincoln	8,150	11,018	3,142	6,444	11,651
McDowell	5,309	6,090	1,881	4,449	6,526
Macon	4,624	4,797	1,829	3,773	6,026
Madison	3,980	3,121	857	3,033	3,453
Martin	4,069	2,958	981	3,598	3,149
Mecklenburg	97,065	99,496	31,283	71,907	106,236
Mitchell	1,727	4,405	877	1,377	4,620
Montgomery	4,422	3,543	1,185	3,995	4,504
Moore	9,649	12,448	4,448	7,642	14,543
Nash	10,809	14,446	4,544	8,740	15,906
New Hanover	20,291	24,338	7,401	15,401	23,807
Northampton	5,195	1,845	916	4,599	2,415
Onslow	8,045	11,842	4,387	7,162	12,253
Orange	28,595	13,009	5,535	22,326	14,503
Pamlico	2,229	1,929	809	2,188	2,297
Pasquotank	4,709	3,419	1,434	3,860	4,006
Pender	5,825	4,857	1,725	4,377	4,926
Perquimans	1,818	1,429	624	1,543	1,781
Person	4,323	4,460	1,431	3,777	4,832
Pitt	17,959	16,609	5,262	14,777	18,245
Polk	2,939	3,448	1,134	2,534	3,874
Randolph	11,274	20,697	6,870	8,641	23,881
Richmond	9,163	4,356	2,015	7,151	5,073
Robeson	19,378	7,777	3,277	16,988	9,908
Rockingham	13,880	12,678	4,671	11,551	14,591
Rowan	14,308	21,297	7,053	12,127	23,192
Rutherford	7,855	9,748	2,695	6,926	10,337
Sampson	8,698	8,007	1,852	8,009	8,524
Scotland	5,175	2,980	1,196	3,865	3,199
Stanly	7,735	11,030	2,855	6,627	11,885
Stokes	6,463	7,979	2,183	5,319	8,661
Surry	9,392	10,866	3,164	7,245	11,393
Swain	2,117	1,640	568	1,821	1,795
Transylvania	5,120	5,984	2,006	4,280	7,009
Tyrrell	928	553	189	785	637
Union	10,789	16,542	4,601	8,820	17,015
Vance	6,598	4,747	1,444	5,631	5,625
Wake	88,979	86,798	31,140	61,352	81,613
Warren	4,656	1,767	693	4,249	2,163
Washington	2,902	1,780	563	2,806	2,186
Watauga	8,262	7,899	3,007	6,048	8,662
Wayne	10,307	14,397	2,798	9,135	15,292
Wilkes	7,991	12,547	3,307	7,230	15,231
Wilson	10,105	10,176	2,630	8,214	10,997
Yadkin	3,913	7,311	1,725	3,195	7,918
Yancey	4,285	3,994	917	3,803	4,160
Totals	**1,114,042**	**1,134,661**	**357,864**	**890,167**	**1,237,258**

North Carolina Vote Since 1944

1944, Roosevelt, Dem., 527,399; Dewey, Rep., 263,155.

1948, Truman, Dem., 459,070; Dewey, Rep., 258,572; Thurmond, States' Rights, 69,652; Wallace, Prog., 3,915.

1952, Eisenhower, Rep., 558,107; Stevenson, Dem., 652,803.

1956, Eisenhower, Rep., 575,062; Stevenson, Dem., 590,530.

1960, Kennedy, Dem., 713,136; Nixon, Rep., 655,420.

1964, Johnson, Dem., 800,139; Goldwater Rep., 624,844.

1968, Nixon, Rep., 627,192; Humphrey, Dem., 464,113; Wallace, 3d party, 496,188.

1972, Nixon, Rep., 1,054,889; McGovern, Dem., 438,705; Schmitz, Amer., 25,018.

1976, Carter, Dem., 927,365; Ford, Rep., 741,960; Anderson, Amer., 5,607; MacBride, Libertarian, 2,219; LaRouche, U.S. Labor, 755.

1980, Reagan, Rep., 915,018; Carter, Dem., 875,635; Anderson, Ind., 52,800; Clark, Libertarian, 9,677; Commoner, Citizens, 2,287; DeBerry, Soc. Workers, 416.

1984, Reagan, Rep., 1,346,481; Mondale, Dem., 824,287; Bergland, Libertarian, 3,794.

1988, Bush, Rep., 1,237,258; Dukakis, Dem., 890,167; Fulani, New Alliance, 5,682; Paul, write-in, 1,263.

1992, Clinton, Dem., 1,114,042; Bush, Rep., 1,134,661; Perot, Ind., 357,864; Marrou, Libertarian, 5,171.

North Dakota

	1992			1988	
County	Clinton (D)	Bush (R)	Perot (I)	Dukakis (D)	Bush (R)
Adams	469	647	499	708	1,018
Barnes	2,124	2,728	1,568	2,858	3,631
Benson	1,126	874	610	1,691	1,316
Billings	123	279	270	211	437
Bottineau	1,266	1,787	1,036	1,684	2,530
Bowman	506	712	678	737	1,111
Burke	458	551	506	693	971
Burleigh	8,940	16,484	6,780	10,760	18,000
Cass	18,077	25,312	9,513	22,107	26,699
Cavalier	866	1,527	723	1,333	2,096
Dickey	918	1,514	616	1,249	2,064
Divide	634	515	456	875	869
Dunn	667	784	637	892	1,263
Eddy	575	591	432	748	891
Emmons	595	1,047	774	925	1,634
Foster	565	803	556	837	1,218
Golden Valley	255	503	352	388	781
Grand Forks	10,930	13,705	6,349	12,494	14,801
Grant	415	900	629	654	1,351
Griggs	647	773	330	846	1,020
Hettinger	465	854	500	698	1,395
Kidder	468	739	489	678	1,039
La Moure	797	1,270	679	1,223	1,642
Logan	383	703	390	540	1,111
McHenry	1,173	1,321	886	1,665	1,888
McIntosh	450	1,134	454	598	1,726
McKenzie	787	1,324	969	1,273	1,949
McLean	1,808	2,124	1,330	2,428	2,906
Mercer	1,323	2,274	1,378	1,843	3,013
Morton	3,594	5,042	2,787	4,708	5,588
Mountrail	1,393	1,017	861	1,977	1,443
Nelson	841	864	486	1,151	1,078
Oliver	306	503	407	526	696
Pembina	1,186	1,917	991	1,616	2,471
Pierce	761	1,099	554	1,008	1,422
Ramsey	2,008	2,516	1,507	2,665	3,103
Ransom	1,166	1,102	625	1,459	1,362
Renville	580	655	429	837	893
Richland	2,688	3,873	1,698	3,523	4,670
Rolette	2,002	895	660	2,426	1,126
Sargent	961	816	463	1,306	1,119
Sheridan	276	589	304	428	885
Sioux	463	264	244	701	325
Slope	145	226	162	202	315
Stark	3,003	4,491	3,123	3,678	6,137
Steele	598	503	267	895	690
Stutsman	3,313	4,039	2,580	4,214	5,375
Towner	748	600	402	970	946
Traill	1,638	2,019	875	1,940	2,562
Walsh	1,936	2,544	1,384	2,646	3,250
Ward	7,856	12,056	5,856	9,906	13,179
Wells	888	1,171	850	1,317	1,901
Williams	3,008	3,664	3,180	4,004	5,653
Totals	**99,168**	**136,244**	**71,084**	**127,739**	**166,559**

North Dakota Vote Since 1944

1944, Roosevelt, Dem., 100,144; Dewey, Rep., 118,535; Thomas, Soc., 943; Watson, Proh., 549.

1948, Truman, Dem., 95,812; Dewey, Rep., 115,139; Wallace, Prog., 8,391; Thomas, Soc., 1,000; Thurmond, States' Rights, 374.

1952, Eisenhower, Rep., 191,712; Stevenson, Dem., 76,694; MacArthur, Christian Nationalist, 1,075; Hallinan, Prog., 344; Hamblen, Proh., 302.

1956, Eisenhower, Rep., 156,766; Stevenson, Dem., 96,742; Andrews, Amer., 483.

1960, Kennedy, Dem., 123,963; Nixon, Rep., 154,310; Dobbs, Soc. Workers, 158.

1964, Johnson, Dem., 149,784; Goldwater, Rep., 108,207; DeBerry, Soc. Worker, 224; Munn, Proh., 174.

1968, Nixon, Rep., 138,669; Humphrey, Dem., 94,769; Wallace, 3d party, 14,244; Halstead, Soc. Worker, 128; Munn, Prohibition, 38; Troxell, Ind., 34.

1972, Nixon, Rep., 174,109; McGovern, Dem., 100,384; Jenness, Soc. Workers, 288; Hall, Com., 87; Schmitz, Amer., 5,646.

1976, Carter, Dem., 136,078; Ford, Rep., 153,470; Anderson, Amer., 3,698; McCarthy, Ind., 2,952; Maddox, Amer. Ind., 269; MacBride, Libertarian, 256; scattering, 371.

1980, Reagan, Rep., 193,695; Carter, Dem., 79,189; Anderson, Ind., 23,640; Clark, Libertarian, 3,743; Commoner,

Libertarian, 429; McLain, Nat'l People's League, 296; Greaves, American, 235; Hall, Com., 93; DeBerry, Soc. Workers, 89; McReynolds, Soc., 82; Bubar, Statesman, 54.

1984, Reagan, Rep., 200,336; Mondale, Dem., 104,429; Bergland, Libertarian, 703.

1988, Bush, Rep., 166,559; Dukakis, Dem., 127,739; Paul, Lib., 1,315; LaRouche, Natl. Econ. Recovery, 905.

1992, Clinton, Dem., 99,168; Bush, Rep., 136,244; Perot, Ind., 71,084.

Ohio

County	1992 Clinton (D)	1992 Bush (R)	1992 Perot (I)	1988 Dukakis (D)	1988 Bush (R)
Adams	3,998	4,722	1,993	3,740	5,916
Allen	13,777	25,322	8,131	13,727	31,021
Ashland	5,985	9,864	4,950	6,072	12,726
Ashtabula	18,843	13,254	10,765	20,536	17,654
Athens	13,423	7,184	5,074	10,795	9,314
Auglaize	4,960	10,455	4,840	4,756	13,562
Belmont	18,527	8,614	6,142	19,515	12,214
Brown	5,540	5,912	3,676	5,047	7,539
Butler	39,682	63,375	27,527	33,770	75,725
Carroll	4,731	4,224	3,434	4,667	6,179
Champaign	5,201	7,004	3,992	4,272	8,995
Clark	26,692	24,011	12,571	23,247	32,729
Clermont	17,558	32,065	14,279	15,352	37,417
Clinton	4,638	7,290	3,402	3,746	8,856
Columbiana	19,765	15,016	12,611	21,581	21,175
Coshocton	6,212	5,705	4,081	6,020	8,282
Crawford	6,351	8,618	5,764	6,018	12,472
Cuyahoga	337,548	187,186	112,352	353,401	242,439
Darke	7,016	11,098	6,217	6,851	14,914
Defiance	5,735	7,195	4,187	5,448	9,566
Delaware	9,263	18,225	9,244	7,590	20,693
Erie	14,531	12,459	8,720	15,097	16,670
Fairfield	14,249	24,125	12,246	12,504	29,208
Fayette	2,976	4,916	2,162	2,623	6,186
Franklin	176,656	186,324	79,049	147,585	226,265
Fulton	5,576	8,358	4,798	5,076	10,230
Gallia	5,350	5,776	2,549	4,834	7,399
Geauga	11,466	18,200	10,577	11,874	22,339
Greene	20,139	27,651	11,459	18,025	34,432
Guernsey	6,428	5,749	4,103	5,926	8,507
Hamilton	148,409	192,447	60,145	140,354	227,004
Hancock	7,944	16,821	7,002	7,435	19,896
Hardin	4,364	5,851	2,867	4,145	7,291
Harrison	3,830	2,289	1,679	3,881	3,298
Henry	3,933	6,196	3,178	3,764	8,618
Highland	4,866	7,020	3,315	4,278	8,776
Hocking	3,935	3,761	2,831	3,706	5,426
Holmes	1,969	5,079	1,945	2,179	5,064
Huron	7,930	9,480	6,751	7,794	12,633
Jackson	5,016	5,422	2,389	4,505	6,671
Jefferson	20,978	10,764	6,910	22,095	14,141
Knox	7,259	9,044	5,282	6,882	12,180
Lake	37,682	40,766	26,878	39,667	52,963
Lawrence	12,325	10,044	4,536	11,628	12,937
Licking	18,898	26,918	13,806	16,793	34,540
Logan	4,889	9,364	4,472	4,484	11,099
Lorain	50,962	36,803	30,425	55,600	50,410
Lucas	99,989	63,297	38,108	99,755	83,788
Madison	3,998	6,865	3,170	3,421	8,303
Mahoning	64,731	31,191	29,417	75,524	43,722
Marion	9,444	11,675	6,471	9,596	14,864
Medina	18,995	24,090	17,290	19,505	29,962
Meigs	4,226	3,916	2,098	3,699	5,486
Mercer	4,883	8,683	4,913	4,978	11,162
Miami	12,547	19,741	10,544	11,138	24,915
Monroe	4,235	1,823	1,505	4,269	2,557
Montgomery	108,017	104,751	47,854	95,737	131,596
Morgan	2,402	2,719	1,551	2,085	3,713
Morrow	3,907	5,208	3,623	3,515	7,130
Muskingum	11,670	14,168	8,731	11,691	19,736
Noble	2,201	2,223	1,429	2,079	3,155
Ottawa	8,128	6,782	4,832	8,038	9,352
Paulding	3,293	3,652	2,510	3,114	5,381
Perry	4,972	4,712	3,810	5,011	6,602
Pickaway	5,765	8,690	4,319	4,905	10,796
Pike	5,057	4,094	2,192	5,191	5,611
Portage	26,325	18,447	17,065	25,607	26,334
Preble	5,557	8,023	4,460	4,937	10,297
Putnam	3,962	9,338	3,648	4,004	11,183
Richland	19,606	23,532	13,370	19,617	30,047
Ross	10,452	10,825	5,616	9,271	14,563
Sandusky	9,878	10,772	6,682	9,709	14,203
Scioto	14,715	11,931	6,860	14,442	16,029
Seneca	9,280	9,763	6,967	9,504	13,704
Shelby	5,262	8,854	5,835	5,065	12,198
Stark	70,064	61,863	42,413	69,639	87,087
Summit	107,881	77,530	55,151	112,612	101,155
Trumbull	54,591	25,831	26,791	58,674	38,815
Tuscarawas	14,787	13,179	8,785	14,185	17,145
Union	3,465	7,818	3,433	3,130	8,846
Van Wert	3,822	7,227	3,102	3,848	9,410
Vinton	2,308	1,975	1,050	2,385	2,652
Warren	13,542	27,998	11,115	11,145	31,419
Washington	10,380	12,204	5,415	9,967	14,767
Wayne	13,953	18,350	9,482	13,571	22,320
Williams	4,862	7,614	4,902	4,666	10,782
Wood	20,754	20,579	11,682	18,579	26,013
Wyandot	3,031	4,411	2,929	2,936	6,178
Totals	**1,984,942**	**1,894,310**	**1,036,426**	**1,939,629**	**2,416,549**

Ohio Vote Since 1944

1944, Roosevelt, Dem., 1,570,763; Dewey, Rep., 1,582,293.

1948, Truman, Dem., 1,452,791; Dewey, Rep., 1,445,684; Wallace, Prog., 37,596.

1952, Eisenhower, Rep., 2,100,391; Stevenson, Dem., 1,600,367.

1956, Eisenhower, Rep., 2,262,610; Stevenson, Dem., 1,439,655.

1960, Kennedy, Dem., 1,944,248; Nixon, Rep., 2,217,611.

1964, Johnson, Dem., 2,498,331; Goldwater, Rep., 1,470,865.

1968, Nixon, Rep., 1,791,014; Humphrey, Dem., 1,700,586; Wallace, 3d party, 467,495; Gregory, 372; Munn, Proh., 19; Blomen, Soc. Labor, 120; Halstead, Soc. Worker, 69; Mitchell, Com., 23.

1972, Nixon, Rep., 2,441,827; McGovern, Dem., 1,558,889; Fisher, Soc. Labor, 7,107; Hall, Com., 6,437; Schmitz, Amer., 80,067; Wallace, Ind., 460.

1976, Carter, Dem., 2,011,621; Ford, Rep., 2,000,505; McCarthy, Ind., 58,258; Maddox, Amer. Ind., 15,529; MacBride, Libertarian, 8,961; Hall, Com., 7,817; Camejo, Soc. Workers, 4,717; LaRouche, U.S. Labor, 4,335; scattered, 130.

1980, Reagan, Rep., 2,206,545; Carter, Dem., 1,752,414; Anderson, Ind., 254,472; Clark, Libertarian, 49,033; Commoner, Citizens, 8,564; Hall, Com., 4,729; Congress, Ind. 4,029; Griswold, Workers World, 3,790; Bubar, Statesman, 27.

1984, Reagan, Rep., 2,678,559; Mondale, Dem., 1,825,440; Bergland, Libertarian, 5,886.

1988, Bush, Rep., 2,416,549; Dukakis, Dem., 1,939,629; Fulani, Ind., 12,017; Paul, Ind., 11,926.

1992, Clinton, Dem., 1,984,942; Bush, Rep., 1,894,310; Perot, Ind., 1,036,426; Marrou, Libertarian, 7,252; Fulani, New Alliance, 6,413; Gritz, Populist/America First, 4,699; Hagelin, Natural Law, 3,437; LaRouche, Ind., 2,446.

Oklahoma

County	1992 Clinton (D)	1992 Bush (R)	1992 Perot (I)	1988 Dukakis (D)	1988 Bush (R)
Adair	2,645	2,994	914	2,624	3,558
Alfalfa	741	1,567	722	1,117	1,960
Atoka	2,336	1,561	1,255	2,565	1,971
Beaver	580	1,699	565	777	2,013
Beckham	2,947	2,913	1,929	3,388	3,463
Blaine	1,564	2,209	1,258	1,775	2,889
Bryan	6,259	3,452	3,713	6,849	4,615
Caddo	4,861	3,664	2,911	5,387	4,689
Canadian	7,215	16,756	8,985	7,453	17,872
Carter	7,171	5,947	5,188	7,988	8,430
Cherokee	6,794	4,977	3,297	6,483	5,838
Choctaw	3,413	1,641	1,298	3,362	2,217
Cimarron	395	965	254	470	1,153
Cleveland	24,404	35,561	20,352	22,067	36,313
Coal	1,448	714	618	1,365	891
Comanche	12,237	15,704	7,463	11,441	17,464
Cotton	1,314	910	853	1,482	1,266
Craig	2,780	2,106	1,316	2,940	2,463
Creek	9,118	10,055	5,984	9,512	11,308
Custer	3,540	5,362	2,741	3,697	6,735
Delaware	4,842	4,840	2,689	4,889	5,248
Dewey	845	1,244	684	963	1,543
Ellis	594	1,072	632	786	1,422
Garfield	6,720	13,095	5,559	8,067	15,248
Garvin	4,811	3,983	3,014	5,438	5,109
Grady	6,177	6,997	4,528	6,689	7,994
Grant	864	1,311	871	1,249	1,690
Greer	1,162	964	640	1,256	1,225
Harmon	783	496	326	890	611
Harper	486	1,038	501	593	1,281
Haskell	3,069	1,461	995	2,963	1,822
Hughes	2,850	1,522	1,158	3,259	2,037
Jackson	3,273	3,893	2,227	3,542	4,423
Jefferson	1,580	671	758	1,767	1,063
Johnston	2,096	1,191	1,040	2,042	1,518
Kay	6,643	9,115	6,984	7,751	12,646
Kingfisher	1,379	3,479	1,534	1,777	4,011
Kiowa	2,143	1,635	1,114	2,296	2,030
Latimer	2,606	1,212	1,049	2,365	1,830

Le Flore	7,843	5,850	3,021	6,594	6,964
Lincoln	3,904	5,315	3,160	4,225	6,409
Logan	4,453	6,071	3,239	4,603	6,947
Love	1,708	922	1,033	1,889	1,361
McClain	3,378	4,377	2,996	3,594	4,771
McCurtain	5,082	3,519	2,852	4,928	4,920
McIntosh	4,184	2,225	1,469	4,041	2,665
Major	731	2,154	857	982	2,638
Marshall	2,519	1,478	1,486	2,730	1,911
Mayes	6,432	5,445	3,235	6,691	6,115
Murray	2,594	1,536	1,447	2,697	2,056
Muskogee	13,619	8,782	5,454	13,760	11,147
Noble	1,333	2,474	1,449	1,661	3,015
Nowata	1,912	1,531	1,063	2,203	2,000
Okfuskee	2,141	1,580	889	2,209	1,851
Oklahoma	76,271	126,788	56,139	75,812	135,376
Okmulgee	7,767	4,586	3,013	8,262	5,674
Osage	6,894	5,891	4,477	7,778	7,162
Ottawa	6,304	4,141	2,721	6,658	5,026
Pawnee	2,612	2,675	1,656	2,781	3,324
Payne	9,886	13,032	7,852	10,568	16,027
Pittsburg	8,523	5,659	4,594	8,623	7,594
Pontotoc	6,350	5,206	3,916	6,484	6,609
Pottawatomie	8,616	10,350	6,520	8,873	12,099
Pushmataha	2,553	1,319	1,000	2,430	1,841
Roger Mills	767	890	505	866	1,132
Rogers	8,257	12,455	7,101	8,771	12,940
Seminole	4,624	3,253	2,330	4,911	4,078
Sequoyah	6,092	4,925	2,486	4,951	5,710
Stephens	7,644	7,085	5,692	7,833	9,844
Texas	1,487	4,059	1,417	1,717	4,971
Tillman	1,749	1,377	1,039	2,148	1,754
Tulsa	71,165	117,465	49,760	69,044	127,512
Wagoner	7,041	9,053	5,381	7,378	10,219
Washington	6,593	11,342	5,664	6,971	14,613
Washita	1,929	1,912	1,468	2,290	2,402
Woods	1,361	2,225	1,167	1,735	2,835
Woodward	2,063	4,006	2,411	2,408	4,996
Totals	**473,066**	**592,929**	**319,878**	**483,423**	**678,367**

Oklahoma Vote Since 1944

1944, Roosevelt, Dem., 401,549; Dewey, Rep., 319,424; Watson, Proh., 1,663.
1948, Truman, Dem., 452,782; Dewey, Rep., 268,817.
1952, Eisenhower, Rep., 518,045; Stevenson, Dem., 430,939.
1956, Eisenhower, Rep., 473,769; Stevenson, Dem., 385,581.
1960, Kennedy, Dem., 370,111; Nixon, Rep., 533,039.
1964, Johnson, Dem., 519,834; Goldwater, Rep. 412,665.
1968, Nixon, Rep., 449,697; Humphrey, Dem., 301,658; Wallace, 3d party, 191,731.
1972, Nixon, Rep. 759,025; McGovern, Dem., 247,147; Schmitz, Amer., 23,728.
1976, Carter, Dem., 532,442; Ford, Rep., 545,708; McCarthy, Ind., 14,101.
1980, Reagan, Rep., 695,570; Carter, Dem., 402,026; Anderson, Ind., 38,284; Clark, Libertarian, 13,828.
1984, Reagan, Rep., 861,530; Mondale, Dem., 385,080; Bergland, Libertarian, 9,066.
1988, Bush, Rep., 678,367; Dukakis, Dem., 483,423; Paul, Lib., 6,261; Fulani, New Alliance, 2,985.
1992, Clinton, Dem., 473,066; Bush, Rep., 592,929; Perot, Ind., 319,878; Marrou, Libertarian, 4,486.

Oregon

	1992			1988	
County	Clinton (D)	Bush (R)	Perot (I)	Dukakis (D)	Bush (R)
Baker	2,395	2,862	2,191	2,896	3,696
Benton	17,966	11,550	8,103	16,930	14,004
Clackamas	60,310	53,724	39,776	59,799	61,381
Clatsop	7,700	4,683	4,316	8,074	5,956
Columbia	8,298	5,227	5,670	8,983	6,424
Coos	12,072	9,284	7,989	13,996	10,153
Crook	2,508	2,703	2,024	2,719	3,049
Curry	3,841	3,809	3,310	4,015	4,761
Deschutes	15,693	15,655	12,293	14,264	16,425
Douglas	14,137	19,011	12,377	17,255	20,120
Gilliam	374	377	283	417	470
Grant	1,135	1,496	1,302	1,437	2,264
Harney	973	1,350	1,024	1,379	1,833
Hood River	3,106	2,453	2,235	3,275	3,257
Jackson	29,146	28,704	18,633	28,028	32,516
Jefferson	2,161	1,962	1,741	2,346	2,509
Josephine	11,007	13,003	8,426	10,646	15,876
Klamath	7,918	11,864	6,636	8,429	13,484
Lake	1,019	1,791	980	1,237	2,161
Lane	74,083	41,789	34,906	69,883	47,563
Lincoln	9,603	5,716	6,127	9,598	7,364
Linn	15,399	16,461	13,256	17,007	18,312
Malheur	2,539	5,374	2,654	2,965	6,285
Marion	41,137	42,145	26,156	41,193	45,292
Morrow	1,174	1,187	1,089	1,375	1,529
Multnomah	165,081	72,326	58,236	161,361	95,561
Polk	9,551	10,082	5,818	9,626	10,553
Sherman	362	424	326	435	555
Tillamook	5,040	3,359	2,997	5,529	4,297
Umatilla	6,787	7,095	5,581	8,327	10,254
Union	3,990	4,223	3,305	4,682	5,061
Wallowa	1,203	1,630	1,209	1,425	1,993
Wasco	4,663	3,242	3,008	5,141	4,462
Washington	67,528	57,146	41,575	59,837	67,018
Wheeler	267	357	227	274	367
Yamhill	11,148	11,693	8,312	11,423	13,321
Totals	**621,314**	**475,757**	**354,091**	**616,206**	**560,126**

Oregon Vote Since 1944

1944, Roosevelt, Dem., 248,635; Dewey, Rep., 225,365; Thomas, Soc., 3,785; Watson, Proh., 2,362.
1948, Truman, Dem., 243,147; Dewey, Rep., 260,904; Wallace, Prog., 14,978; Thomas, Soc., 5,051.
1952, Eisenhower, Rep., 420,815; Stevenson, Dem., 270,579; Hallinan, Ind., 3,665.
1956, Eisenhower, Rep., 406,393; Stevenson, Dem., 329,204.
1960, Kennedy, Dem., 367,402; Nixon, Rep., 408,060.
1964, Johnson, Dem., 501,017; Goldwater, Rep., 282,779; write-in, 2,509.
1968, Nixon, Rep., 408,433; Humphrey, Dem., 358,866; Wallace, 3d party, 49,683; write-in, McCarthy, 1,496; N. Rockefeller, 69; others, 1,075.
1972, Nixon, Rep., 486,686; McGovern, Dem., 392,760; Schmitz, Amer., 46,211; write-in, 2,289.
1976, Carter, Dem., 490,407; Ford, Rep., 492,120; McCarthy, Ind., 40,207; write-in, 7,142.
1980, Reagan, Rep., 571,044; Carter, Dem., 456,890; Anderson, Ind., 112,389; Clark, Libertarian, 25,838; Commoner, Citizens, 13,642; scattered, 1,713.
1984, Reagan, Rep., 658,700; Mondale, Dem., 536,479.
1988, Bush, Rep., 560,126; Dukakis, Dem., 616,206; Paul, Lib., 14,811; Fulani, Ind., 6,487.
1992, Clinton, Dem., 621,314; Bush, Rep., 475,757; Perot, Ind., 354,091; Marrou, Libertarian, 4,277; Fulani, New Alliance, 3,030.

Pennsylvania

	1992			1988	
County	Clinton (D)	Bush (R)	Perot (I)	Dukakis (D)	Bush (R)
Adams	9,576	13,552	6,313	8,299	15,650
Allegheny	324,004	183,035	103,470	348,814	231,137
Armstrong	12,995	9,122	6,166	13,892	11,509
Beaver	44,877	21,361	15,954	50,327	25,764
Bedford	5,840	9,216	3,731	5,754	11,123
Berks	46,031	52,939	31,663	41,040	70,153
Blair	14,857	21,447	8,284	15,588	25,623
Bradford	6,903	10,221	5,452	6,635	13,568
Bucks	97,902	94,584	53,931	82,472	127,563
Butler	22,303	23,656	15,013	22,341	27,777
Cambria	34,334	20,770	11,070	38,517	25,626
Cameron	824	1,173	676	901	1,731
Carbon	9,072	7,243	5,222	9,104	10,232
Centre	21,177	20,478	9,356	18,357	23,875
Chester	59,643	74,002	34,536	44,853	93,522
Clarion	5,584	6,477	3,619	5,616	8,026
Clearfield	12,247	11,553	6,989	12,235	14,296
Clinton	5,397	4,471	2,654	5,759	5,735
Columbia	8,261	9,742	5,683	7,767	12,114
Crawford	12,813	14,112	7,392	13,021	17,249
Cumberland	26,635	43,447	14,344	24,613	47,292
Dauphin	36,990	45,479	16,063	35,079	48,917
Delaware	111,210	108,587	43,728	96,144	147,656
Elk	5,016	4,908	3,885	5,879	6,737
Erie	56,381	39,283	21,510	53,913	48,306
Fayette	30,577	12,820	10,162	33,098	16,915
Forest	890	801	448	895	1,159
Franklin	13,440	23,387	6,941	12,368	27,086
Fulton	1,588	2,558	869	1,532	3,086
Greene	8,438	3,482	3,186	9,126	4,879
Huntingdon	5,153	7,249	3,273	4,752	8,800
Indiana	15,194	10,966	7,089	16,514	14,983
Jefferson	5,998	7,271	4,403	6,235	9,743
Juniata	2,601	3,980	1,819	2,834	4,881
Lackawanna	45,054	33,443	15,667	45,591	42,083
Lancaster	44,255	88,447	26,807	38,982	96,979
Lawrence	20,830	12,359	7,950	21,884	15,829
Lebanon	12,350	21,512	9,005	11,912	24,415
Lehigh	46,711	42,631	24,853	42,801	56,363
Luzerne	56,623	49,285	21,007	58,553	59,059
Lycoming	13,315	20,536	9,170	13,528	24,792
McKean	5,331	6,965	4,019	5,300	9,323
Mercer	23,264	16,081	10,277	24,278	21,301
Mifflin	4,946	6,300	3,382	4,790	8,170
Monroe	13,468	14,557	9,257	9,859	17,185
Montgomery	136,572	125,704	53,738	109,834	170,294
Montour	2,150	3,096	1,373	2,031	3,617
Northampton	42,203	34,429	20,234	39,264	42,748

Northumberland	12,814	15,057	7,782	14,255	20,207
Perry.	4,086	7,871	3,334	3,910	8,545
Philadelphia . .	434,904	133,328	65,455	449,566	219,053
Pike	4,382	6,084	3,019	3,097	6,659
Potter	1,892	3,452	1,687	2,119	4,432
Schuylkill	23,679	25,780	13,398	24,797	32,666
Snyder	2,952	6,934	2,686	2,658	9,054
Somerset. . . .	12,493	13,858	6,333	13,815	16,809
Sullivan	1,030	1,340	731	1,091	1,808
Susquehanna .	5,368	7,356	3,946	4,871	9,077
Tioga	4,868	7,823	3,804	4,807	9,471
Union	3,623	6,362	2,255	3,163	7,912
Venango	8,230	8,545	4,695	8,624	11,468
Warren	6,972	6,585	4,795	6,790	8,991
Washington . .	46,143	21,977	16,083	47,527	28,651
Wayne.	4,817	8,184	3,727	3,775	9,926
Westmoreland	69,817	47,315	37,036	76,710	61,472
Wyoming	3,158	5,143	2,525	2,797	6,607
York	46,113	60,130	27,743	37,691	72,408
Totals.	**2,239,164**	**1,791,841**	**902,667**	**2,194,944**	**2,300,087**

Pennsylvania Vote Since 1944

1944, Roosevelt, Dem., 1,940,479; Dewey, Rep., 1,835,054; Thomas, Soc., 11,721; Watson, Proh., 5,750; Teichert, Ind. Gov., 1,789.

1948, Truman, Dem., 1,752,426; Dewey, Rep., 1,902,197; Wallace, Prog., 55,161; Thomas, Soc., 11,325; Watson, Proh., 10,338; Dobbs, Militant Workers, 2,133; Teichert, Ind. Gov., 1,461.

1952, Eisenhower, Rep., 2,415,789; Stevenson, Dem., 2,146,269; Hamblen, Proh., 8,771; Hallinan, Prog., 4,200; Hoopes, Soc., 2,684; Dobbs, Militant Workers, 1,502; Hass, Ind. Gov., 1,347; scattered, 155.

1956, Eisenhower, Rep., 2,585,252; Stevenson, Dem., 1,981,769; Hass, Soc. Labor, 7,447; Dobbs, Militant Workers, 2,035.

1960, Kennedy, Dem., 2,556,282; Nixon, Rep., 2,439,956; Hass, Soc. Labor, 7,185; Dobbs, Soc. Workers, 2,678; scattering, 440.

1964, Johnson, Dem., 3,130,954; Goldwater, Rep., 1,673,657; DeBerry, Soc. Workers, 10,456; Hass, Soc. Labor, 5,092; scattering, 2,531.

1968, Nixon, Rep., 2,090,017; Humphrey, Dem., 2,259,405; Wallace, 3d party, 378,582; Blomen, Soc. Labor, 4,977; Halstead, Soc. Workers, 4,862; Gregory, 7,821; others, 2,264.

1972, Nixon, Rep., 2,714,521; McGovern, Dem., 1,796,951; Schmitz, Amer., 70,593; Jenness, Soc. Workers, 4,639; Hall, Com., 2,686; others, 2,715.

1976, Carter, Dem., 2,328,677; Ford, Rep., 2,205,604; McCarthy, Ind., 50,584; Maddox, Constitution, 25,344; Camejo, Soc. Workers, 3,009; LaRouche, U.S. Labor, 2,744; Hall, Com., 1,891; others, 2,934.

1980, Reagan, Rep., 2,261,872; Carter, Dem., 1,937,540; Anderson, Ind., 292,921; Clark, Libertarian, 33,263; DeBerry, Soc. Workers, 20,291; Commoner, Consumer, 10,430; Hall, Com., 5,184.

1984, Reagan, Rep., 2,584,323; Mondale, Dem., 2,228,131; Bergland, Libertarian, 6,982.

1988, Bush, Rep., 2,300,087; Dukakis, Dem., 2,194,944; McCarthy, Consumer, 19,158; Paul, Lib., 12,051.

1992, Clinton, Dem., 2,239,164; Bush, Rep., 1,791,841; Perot, Ind., 902,667; Marrou, Libertarian, 21,477; Fulani, New Alliance, 4,661.

Rhode Island

City	1992 Clinton (D)	Bush (R)	Perot (I)	1988 Dukakis (D)	Bush (R)
Cranston	18,589	12,450	8,331	19,711	17,129
East Providence	11,701	5,843	4,661	11,948	8,181
Pawtucket . . .	14,177	6,322	6,244	15,985	9,359
Providence. . .	32,536	11,519	7,816	34,806	15,310
Warwick	20,504	13,348	10,526	21,662	18,052
Other	115,792	82,119	67,467	121,011	109,730
Totals.	**213,299**	**131,601**	**105,045**	**225,123**	**177,761**

Rhode Island Vote Since 1944

1944, Roosevelt, Dem., 175,356; Dewey, Rep., 123,487; Watson, Proh., 433.

1948, Truman, Dem., 188,736; Dewey, Rep., 135,787; Wallace, Prog., 2,619; Thomas, Soc., 429; Teichert, Soc. Labor, 131.

1952, Eisenhower, Rep., 210,935; Stevenson, Dem., 203,293; Hallinan, Prog., 187; Hass, Soc. Labor, 83.

1956, Eisenhower, Rep., 225,819; Stevenson, Dem., 161,790.

1960, Kennedy, Dem., 258,032; Nixon, Rep., 147,502.

1964, Johnson, Dem., 315,463; Goldwater, Rep., 74,615.

1968, Nixon, Rep., 122,359; Humphrey, Dem., 246,518; Wallace, 3d party, 15,678; Halstead, Soc. Worker, 383.

1972, Nixon, Rep., 220,383; McGovern, Dem., 194,645; Jenness, Soc. Workers, 729.

1976, Carter, Dem., 227,636; Ford, Rep., 181,249; MacBride, Libertarian, 715; Camejo, Soc. Workers, 462; Hall, Com., 334; Levin, Soc. Labor, 188.

1980, Reagan, Rep., 154,793; Carter, Dem., 198,342; Anderson, Ind., 59,819; Clark, Libertarian, 2,458; Hall, Com., 218; McReynolds, Socialist, 170; DeBerry, Soc. Worker, 90; Griswold, Workers World, 77.

1984, Reagan, Rep., 212,080; Mondale, Dem., 197,106; Bergland, Libertarian, 277.

1988, Bush, Rep., 177,761; Dukakis, Dem., 225,123; Paul, Lib., 825; Fulani, New Alliance, 280.

1992, Clinton, Dem., 213,299; Bush, Rep., 131,601; Perot, Ind., 105,045; Fulani, New Alliance, 1,878.

South Carolina

County	1992 Clinton (D)	Bush (R)	Perot (I)	1988 Dukakis (D)	Bush (R)
Abbeville	3,968	3,317	1,036	3,629	3,738
Aiken	14,802	25,731	6,056	10,598	27,665
Allendale	2,159	1,049	212	1,796	1,295
Anderson. . . .	16,072	24,793	6,966	12,281	25,939
Bamberg	3,426	1,906	360	2,830	2,403
Barnwell	3,344	4,026	752	2,564	4,467
Beaufort	11,466	14,735	4,966	8,691	16,184
Berkeley	12,533	18,048	4,632	9,312	16,779
Calhoun.	2,770	2,418	564	2,175	2,585
Charleston . . .	40,095	47,403	10,354	32,977	49,149
Cherokee. . . .	5,453	6,887	2,186	4,322	7,763
Chester	5,458	3,451	1,350	3,737	3,968
Chesterfield . .	5,691	4,183	1,315	4,699	4,999
Clarendon . . .	6,033	4,147	744	5,030	4,337
Colleton.	5,455	4,545	1,245	4,508	4,962
Darlington . . .	9,090	8,912	1,863	7,625	9,854
Dillon	4,953	3,575	831	3,251	3,793
Dorchester. . .	9,160	15,004	3,648	7,371	14,756
Edgefield	3,433	3,339	596	3,020	3,814
Fairfield	4,867	2,518	652	3,827	2,714
Florence	15,569	19,802	3,499	12,531	19,490
Georgetown . .	7,494	6,870	1,840	5,402	7,032
Greenville . . .	34,651	65,066	13,699	27,188	67,371
Greenwood . .	7,621	9,079	2,101	6,511	9,096
Hampton	4,332	2,402	564	3,435	2,826
Horry	18,896	23,489	8,472	13,316	24,843
Jasper.	3,453	1,725	549	2,894	2,004
Kershaw	6,585	8,499	2,150	4,494	8,877
Lancaster. . . .	8,307	7,757	2,563	6,181	9,152
Laurens.	6,638	8,347	2,157	5,930	9,731
Lee.	4,454	2,730	611	3,423	2,936
Lexington. . . .	18,312	41,759	8,652	11,366	41,467
McCormick. . .	1,846	899	295	1,722	1,172
Marion.	5,843	3,647	822	5,008	4,403
Marlboro	5,111	2,526	895	3,937	2,921
Newberry. . . .	4,896	5,980	1,393	3,825	6,427
Oconee	6,617	10,379	3,405	4,299	10,184
Orangeburg . .	18,440	11,328	2,383	14,655	13,281
Pickens	8,275	17,008	4,128	6,103	17,448
Richland	53,648	43,744	7,918	36,420	43,841
Saluda.	2,393	2,968	833	1,984	3,225
Spartanburg . .	25,488	37,707	8,900	22,964	40,801
Sumter	11,852	12,576	2,062	9,502	13,161
Union	4,644	4,647	1,371	4,420	6,019
Williamsburg .	8,077	5,289	864	7,343	5,914
York	15,844	21,297	6,418	11,458	21,657
Totals.	**479,514**	**577,507**	**138,872**	**370,554**	**606,443**

South Carolina Vote Since 1944

1944, Roosevelt, Dem., 90,601; Dewey, Rep., 4,547; Southern Democrats, 7,799; Watson, Proh., 365; Rep. Tolbert faction, 63.

1948, Thurmond, States' Rights, 102,607; Truman, Dem., 34,423; Dewey, Rep., 5,386; Wallace, Prog., 154; Thomas, Soc., 1.

1952, Eisenhower ran on two tickets. Under state law vote cast for two Eisenhower slates of electors could not be combined. Eisenhower, Ind., 158,289; Rep., 9,793; total, 168,082; Stevenson, Dem., 173,004; Hamblen, Proh., 1.

1956, Eisenhower, Rep., 75,700; Stevenson, Dem., 136,372; Byrd, Ind., 88,509; Andrews, Ind., 2.

1960, Kennedy, Dem., 198,129; Nixon, Rep., 188,558; write-in, 1.

1964, Johnson, Dem., 215,700; Goldwater, Rep., 309,048; write-ins: Nixon, 1, Wallace, 5; Powell, 1; Thurmond, 1.

1968, Nixon, Rep., 254,062; Humphrey, Dem., 197,486; Wallace, 3d party, 215,430.
1972, Nixon, Rep., 477,044; McGovern, Dem., 184,559; United Citizens, 2,265; Schmitz, Amer., 10,075; write-in, 17.
1976, Carter, Dem., 450,807; Ford, Rep., 346,149; Anderson, Amer., 2,996; Maddox, Amer. Ind., 1,950; write-in, 681.
1980, Reagan, Rep., 439,277; Carter, Dem., 428,220; Anderson, Ind., 13,868; Clark, Libertarian, 4,807; Rarick, Amer. Ind., 2,086.
1984, Reagan, Rep., 615,539; Mondale, Dem., 344,459; Bergland, Libertarian, 4,359.
1988, Bush, Rep., 606,443; Dukakis, Dem., 370,554; Paul, Lib., 4,935; Fulani, United Citizens, 4,077.
1992, Clinton, Dem., 479,514; Bush, Rep., 577,507; Perot, Ind., 138,872; Marrou, Libertarian, 2,719; Phillips, U.S. Taxpayers, 2,680; Fulani, New Alliance, 1,235.

South Dakota

County	1992 Clinton (D)	1992 Bush (R)	1992 Perot (I)	1988 Dukakis (D)	1988 Bush (R)
Aurora	680	594	435	987	856
Beadle	3,925	3,363	1,819	4,523	4,611
Bennett	413	556	221	579	663
Bon Homme	1,294	1,212	836	1,574	1,826
Brookings	4,645	4,698	2,614	4,860	5,394
Brown	7,521	6,665	3,812	8,673	8,537
Brule	1,060	908	687	991	971
Buffalo	282	137	72	334	151
Butte	973	1,674	1,039	1,256	2,291
Campbell	222	574	252	334	909
Chas. Mix	1,639	1,570	886	2,205	1,966
Clark	799	803	761	1,164	1,247
Clay	2,826	1,869	1,303	2,859	2,307
Codington	3,701	3,943	3,262	4,570	5,050
Corson	444	483	321	722	710
Custer	1,078	1,422	845	1,180	1,806
Davison	3,285	3,111	1,706	3,705	4,024
Day	1,578	1,161	973	2,137	1,616
Deuel	880	778	761	1,246	1,251
Dewey	766	642	340	1,007	765
Douglas	481	1,175	403	695	1,438
Edmunds	894	944	415	1,259	1,327
Fall River	1,416	1,533	792	1,380	2,002
Faulk	488	658	281	714	842
Grant	1,484	1,595	1,018	1,988	2,148
Gregory	879	1,027	688	1,138	1,566
Haakon	209	860	245	379	958
Hamlin	826	1,133	774	1,258	1,380
Hand	785	1,130	624	1,101	1,461
Hanson	566	522	341	776	786
Harding	139	515	225	259	633
Hughes	2,578	4,325	1,160	2,853	4,545
Hutchinson	1,211	2,002	920	1,594	2,700
Hyde	301	440	211	436	546
Jackson	351	627	184	450	671
Jerauld	600	518	346	751	777
Jones	166	454	154	261	521
Kingsbury	1,267	1,113	744	1,472	1,592
Lake	2,388	1,890	1,299	2,663	2,439
Lawrence	3,157	3,770	2,673	3,705	5,570
Lincoln	2,943	3,365	1,593	3,190	3,537
Lyman	486	669	311	631	843
McCook	1,167	1,177	617	1,492	1,501
McPherson	478	945	322	571	1,358
Marshall	1,056	810	427	1,372	1,142
Meade	2,694	4,724	2,611	3,212	5,189
Mellette	277	417	140	385	460
Miner	698	543	332	955	795
Minnehaha	27,016	25,081	11,496	29,135	26,765
Moody	1,473	898	715	1,715	1,161
Pennington	11,106	18,052	8,358	12,068	19,510
Perkins	566	872	541	851	1,326
Potter	493	901	375	701	1,175
Roberts	1,716	1,437	954	2,267	2,012
Sanborn	632	595	376	770	815
Shannon	1,267	225	137	1,206	256
Spink	1,732	1,527	839	2,071	1,969
Stanley	427	719	240	511	698
Sully	273	565	167	393	571
Todd	915	456	246	1,117	535
Tripp	1,046	1,459	848	1,219	2,113
Turner	1,507	1,906	867	1,780	2,436
Union	2,210	1,784	1,085	2,612	1,907
Walworth	829	1,439	628	1,094	1,940
Yankton	3,404	3,430	2,511	3,777	4,186
Ziebach	280	328	117	427	362
Totals	**124,888**	**136,718**	**73,295**	**145,560**	**165,415**

South Dakota Vote Since 1944

1944, Roosevelt, Dem., 96,711; Dewey, Rep., 135,365.
1948, Truman, Dem., 117,653; Dewey, Rep., 129,651; Wallace, Prog., 2,801.
1952, Eisenhower, Rep., 203,857; Stevenson, Dem., 90,426.
1956, Eisenhower, Rep., 171,569; Stevenson, Dem., 122,288.
1960, Kennedy, Dem., 128,070; Nixon, Rep., 178,417.
1964, Johnson, Dem., 163,010; Goldwater, Rep., 130,108.
1968, Nixon, Rep., 149,841; Humphrey, Dem., 118,023; Wallace, 3d party, 13,400.
1972, Nixon, Rep., 166,476; McGovern, Dem., 139,945; Jenness, Soc. Workers, 994.
1976, Carter, Dem., 147,068; Ford, Rep., 151,505; MacBride, Libertarian, 1,619; Hall, Com., 318; Camejo, Soc. Workers, 168.
1980, Reagan, Rep., 198,343; Carter, Dem., 103,855; Anderson, Ind., 21,431; Clark, Libertarian, 3,824; Pulley, Soc. Workers, 250.
1984, Reagan, Rep., 200,267; Mondale, Dem., 116,113.
1988, Bush, Rep., 165,415; Dukakis, Dem., 145,560; Paul, Lib., 1,060; Fulani, New Alliance, 730.
1992, Clinton, Dem., 124,888; Bush, Rep., 136,718; Perot, Ind., 73,295.

Tennessee

County	1992 Clinton (D)	1992 Bush (R)	1992 Perot (I)	1988 Dukakis (D)	1988 Bush (R)
Anderson	13,482	11,838	3,149	9,589	15,056
Bedford	5,978	3,836	1,541	4,046	4,856
Benton	3,896	1,625	559	2,826	2,167
Bledsoe	1,884	1,776	352	1,274	1,858
Blount	14,655	18,415	4,468	9,602	20,027
Bradley	9,889	16,528	3,212	6,122	15,829
Campbell	6,756	4,897	1,240	4,188	5,197
Cannon	2,593	1,229	495	1,726	1,604
Carroll	5,741	4,842	1,139	4,151	5,635
Carter	6,502	10,712	1,898	4,634	12,036
Cheatham	4,817	3,496	1,433	3,067	4,132
Chester	2,317	2,834	439	1,757	2,781
Claiborne	4,509	4,065	860	2,977	4,071
Clay	1,922	1,072	223	1,183	1,291
Cocke	3,495	5,298	1,124	2,115	5,430
Coffee	8,534	6,047	2,420	5,686	7,837
Crockett	2,657	2,180	507	1,742	2,214
Cumberland	6,393	7,116	2,200	3,964	7,557
Davidson	106,355	76,567	20,184	89,270	98,599
Decatur	2,633	1,667	351	1,880	2,286
De Kalb	4,382	1,714	608	2,452	2,098
Dickson	7,863	4,450	1,730	5,129	5,343
Dyer	5,845	5,668	1,241	3,690	6,508
Fayette	4,211	3,713	657	3,292	3,573
Fentress	2,730	2,391	606	1,856	3,103
Franklin	7,773	4,507	1,837	5,442	5,381
Gibson	9,555	7,161	1,536	7,542	8,415
Giles	5,601	2,827	1,309	3,918	3,518
Grainger	2,242	2,772	513	1,423	2,734
Greene	7,857	9,912	2,930	5,077	11,947
Grundy	2,997	1,004	366	2,415	1,429
Hamblen	7,114	8,898	1,760	5,061	10,418
Hamilton	46,770	53,476	14,400	40,990	68,111
Hancock	1,000	1,274	151	737	1,303
Hardeman	4,832	3,122	594	3,526	3,547
Hardin	3,922	3,875	734	2,808	4,252
Hawkins	6,623	7,758	1,847	5,212	9,356
Haywood	3,511	2,518	331	2,923	2,687
Henderson	3,502	4,719	785	2,296	5,418
Henry	6,797	3,661	1,588	5,138	4,784
Hickman	4,093	1,820	795	2,643	2,246
Houston	2,012	648	280	1,467	882
Humphreys	3,875	1,641	609	3,037	2,132
Jackson	3,208	708	332	1,962	1,168
Jefferson	4,740	6,184	1,385	3,168	6,832
Johnson	1,781	3,170	574	1,329	3,715
Knox	59,702	66,607	15,669	41,829	73,092
Lake	1,449	680	151	935	806
Lauderdale	4,452	2,928	561	3,296	3,308
Lawrence	6,816	5,608	1,403	4,903	6,273
Lewis	2,491	1,218	434	1,419	1,324
Lincoln	5,063	3,814	1,371	3,672	4,288
Loudon	5,414	6,444	1,602	3,480	7,122
McMinn	6,682	7,453	1,812	4,568	8,462
McNairy	4,691	4,093	774	3,510	4,625
Macon	2,961	2,299	443	1,538	2,962
Madison	13,629	14,869	2,634	11,001	16,952
Marion	5,589	3,262	1,186	4,175	4,407
Marshall	4,491	2,516	1,050	2,795	2,975
Maury	9,997	7,440	2,821	6,280	8,397
Meigs	1,673	1,355	453	1,048	1,507
Monroe	5,384	6,025	936	4,000	6,355
Montgomery	14,507	13,011	3,753	9,145	12,599
Moore	1,151	661	327	731	786
Morgan	3,190	2,306	658	1,941	2,576
Obion	6,497	4,812	1,494	4,785	6,037
Overton	4,489	1,657	468	2,511	1,873

Perry	1,889	708	317	1,208	854
Pickett	1,144	1,094	121	634	1,118
Polk	2,583	1,584	419	2,073	2,297
Putnam	10,858	7,998	2,473	6,606	9,547
Rhea	4,289	4,860	1,163	2,595	5,144
Roane	9,812	8,719	2,396	6,535	10,881
Robertson	8,498	5,271	1,978	5,884	5,714
Rutherford	21,084	18,877	7,005	12,245	20,397
Scott	2,730	3,011	643	1,611	2,562
Sequatchie	1,754	1,381	405	1,196	1,659
Sevier	6,719	11,714	2,760	3,643	11,920
Shelby	191,322	153,310	20,223	149,759	157,457
Smith	5,061	1,482	486	2,522	2,138
Stewart	2,779	1,046	487	1,979	1,302
Sullivan	20,935	28,801	6,730	17,396	32,996
Sumner	19,387	17,401	5,177	11,702	19,523
Tipton	5,652	6,757	1,279	3,824	6,052
Trousdale	1,846	565	243	1,193	969
Unicoi	2,375	3,344	709	1,794	3,664
Union	2,478	2,274	580	1,431	2,110
Van Buren	1,329	555	191	796	780
Warren	7,189	3,704	1,415	4,646	4,529
Washington	13,071	18,206	4,002	10,087	19,615
Wayne	1,868	2,955	424	1,516	3,405
Weakley	5,691	4,800	1,355	4,239	5,701
White	4,102	2,118	821	2,562	2,646
Williamson	13,053	22,015	5,026	7,864	20,847
Wilson	13,861	12,061	3,848	8,360	13,317
Totals	**933,521**	**841,300**	**199,968**	**679,794**	**947,233**

Tennessee Vote Since 1944

1944, Roosevelt, Dem., 308,707; Dewey, Rep., 200,311; Watson, Proh., 882; Thomas, Soc., 892.

1948, Truman, Dem., 270,402; Dewey, Rep., 202,914; Thurmond, States' Rights, 73,815; Wallace, Prog., 1,864; Thomas, Soc., 1,288.

1952, Eisenhower, Rep., 446,147; Stevenson, Dem., 443,710; Hamblen, Proh., 1,432; Hallinan, Prog., 885; MacArthur, Christian Nationalist, 379.

1956, Eisenhower, Rep., 462,288; Stevenson, Dem., 456,507; Andrews, Ind., 19,820; Holtwick, Proh., 789.

1960, Kennedy, Dem., 481,453; Nixon, Rep., 556,577; Faubus, States' Rights, 11,304; Decker, Proh., 2,458.

1964, Johnson, Dem. 635,047; Goldwater, Rep., 508,965; write-in, 34.

1968, Nixon, Rep., 472,592; Humphrey, Dem., 351,233; Wallace, 3d party, 424,792.

1972, Nixon, Rep., 813,147; McGovern, Dem., 357,293; Schmitz, Amer., 30,373; write-in, 369.

1976, Carter, Dem., 825,879; Ford, Rep., 633,969; Anderson, Amer., 5,769; McCarthy, Ind., 5,004; Maddox, Am. Ind., 2,303; MacBride, Libertarian, 1,375; Hall, Com., 547; LaRouche, U.S. Labor, 512; Bubar, Proh., 442; Miller, Ind., 316; write-in, 230.

1980, Reagan, Rep., 787,761; Carter, Dem., 783,051; Anderson, Ind., 35,991; Clark, Libertarian, 7,116; Commoner, Citizens, 1,112; Bubar, Statesman, 521; McReynolds, Socialist, 519; Hall, Com., 503; DeBerry, Soc. Worker, 490; Griswold, Workers World, 400; write-ins, 152.

1984, Reagan, Rep., 990,212; Mondale, Dem., 711,714; Bergland, Libertarian, 3,072.

1988, Bush, Rep., 947,233; Dukakis, Dem., 679,794; Paul, Ind., 2,041; Duke, Ind., 1,807.

1992, Clinton, Dem., 933,521; Bush, Rep., 841,300; Perot, Ind., 199,968; Marrou, Libertarian, 1,847.

Texas

	1992			1988	
County	Clinton (D)	Bush (R)	Perot (I)	Dukakis (D)	Bush (R)
Anderson	5,322	5,598	3,519	6,128	7,858
Andrews	1,081	2,266	875	1,122	3,052
Angelina	10,318	9,722	6,204	10,849	12,738
Aransas	2,246	2,826	1,676	2,305	3,858
Archer	1,284	1,560	1,106	1,627	2,010
Armstrong	278	561	187	314	720
Atascosa	3,766	3,806	2,035	4,657	4,777
Austin	2,278	4,015	1,585	2,593	4,524
Bailey	677	1,308	376	876	1,459
Bandera	1,059	2,674	1,537	1,251	3,435
Bastrop	6,252	4,980	3,240	8,004	5,991
Baylor	990	611	529	1,153	914
Bee	4,083	3,633	1,367	4,616	4,620
Bell	18,684	24,936	11,026	17,751	29,382
Bexar	172,513	168,816	72,110	174,036	193,192
Blanco	891	1,370	830	1,012	1,680
Borden	106	184	87	169	283
Bosque	2,173	2,300	1,999	2,670	3,458
Bowie	11,825	11,776	6,659	12,331	15,454
Brazoria	21,861	30,384	18,954	23,436	34,028
Brazos	14,819	23,943	10,372	14,885	29,369
Brewster	1,383	1,127	712	1,569	1,708
Briscoe	430	360	164	574	464
Brooks	2,856	585	318	2,859	608
Brown	4,264	5,313	3,034	4,763	6,810
Burleson	2,511	2,013	1,179	3,085	2,242
Burnet	3,638	4,272	2,865	4,343	5,120
Caldwell	3,794	2,749	1,776	4,649	3,553
Calhoun	2,550	2,640	1,579	3,314	3,183
Callahan	1,694	2,134	1,452	2,017	2,887
Cameron	29,435	20,123	9,286	30,972	24,263
Camp	1,938	1,219	821	2,121	1,908
Carson	825	1,647	578	1,034	2,100
Cass	5,476	3,999	2,168	5,941	5,305
Castro	1,113	1,307	485	1,436	1,604
Chambers	2,832	3,398	2,122	3,035	3,694
Cherokee	5,003	5,847	3,273	5,604	7,520
Childress	881	1,033	421	1,060	1,201
Clay	1,919	1,586	1,397	2,288	2,043
Cochran	454	750	255	681	771
Coke	580	640	393	674	863
Coleman	1,579	1,462	1,095	1,978	2,340
Collin	24,508	60,514	43,287	22,934	67,776
Collingsworth	635	697	265	809	872
Colorado	2,442	3,286	1,421	2,847	3,723
Comal	6,312	12,651	5,841	5,716	13,994
Comanche	2,296	1,666	1,281	2,622	2,120
Concho	489	414	329	643	617
Cooke	3,105	5,299	4,658	4,217	7,196
Coryell	4,157	6,144	3,974	4,026	7,461
Cottle	542	245	235	690	379
Crane	514	918	412	596	1,219
Crockett	653	623	368	881	932
Crosby	1,010	1,006	313	1,435	1,121
Culberson	424	251	171	557	417
Dallam	434	922	325	645	1,205
Dallas	231,412	256,007	170,571	243,198	347,094
Dawson	1,639	2,691	518	2,155	3,154
Deaf Smith	1,642	3,137	772	1,930	3,744
Delta	864	599	551	1,244	849
Denton	27,891	48,492	39,653	26,204	57,444
DeWitt	2,127	3,238	1,346	2,579	3,628
Dickens	536	373	250	696	435
Dimmit	3,172	844	361	2,735	900
Donley	578	893	260	661	1,043
Duval	4,006	698	326	4,177	907
Eastland	2,738	2,830	1,698	3,215	3,929
Ector	11,130	18,161	6,668	10,825	23,155
Edwards	254	460	171	368	556
Ellis	9,537	13,564	10,303	11,169	16,422
El Paso	67,715	47,224	19,738	62,622	55,573
Erath	3,531	3,835	3,046	4,113	5,427
Falls	2,761	1,826	1,185	2,877	2,344
Fannin	4,164	2,510	2,919	5,163	4,024
Fayette	2,923	3,789	2,088	3,390	4,551
Fisher	1,242	539	442	1,516	721
Floyd	947	1,676	385	1,391	1,741
Foard	435	207	152	513	306
Fort Bend	29,992	41,039	16,853	23,351	39,818
Franklin	1,338	1,058	942	1,453	1,439
Freestone	2,445	2,316	1,596	2,916	3,159
Frio	2,377	1,275	654	3,016	1,505
Gaines	1,095	2,138	696	1,310	2,265
Galveston	38,623	31,303	20,103	38,633	34,913
Garza	558	982	345	989	1,183
Gillespie	1,600	4,712	2,018	1,588	5,662
Glasscock	100	379	93	143	384
Goliad	1,069	1,236	521	1,358	1,427
Gonzales	2,006	2,502	1,018	2,897	2,983
Gray	2,426	6,105	1,810	2,460	7,259
Grayson	12,547	12,322	13,327	14,347	18,825
Gregg	12,797	20,542	8,437	12,486	26,465
Grimes	2,594	2,402	1,213	2,735	2,820
Guadalupe	6,567	10,818	5,618	7,111	13,265
Hale	2,761	6,098	1,357	3,502	6,284
Hall	819	631	263	1,029	714
Hamilton	1,100	1,232	921	1,355	1,718
Hansford	345	1,660	398	443	1,967
Hardeman	954	614	362	1,143	855
Hardin	6,753	5,885	4,129	8,245	6,897
Harris	360,171	406,778	172,922	342,919	464,217
Harrison	9,538	8,733	4,371	8,974	11,957
Hartley	406	1,081	308	505	1,229
Haskell	1,438	852	562	1,715	1,193
Hays	10,842	10,008	6,252	11,187	11,716
Hemphill	479	989	232	527	1,170
Henderson	9,105	8,368	6,746	9,819	11,005
Hidalgo	51,205	26,976	9,757	54,330	29,246
Hill	3,929	3,669	2,752	4,381	4,796
Hockley	2,301	4,261	1,291	2,850	4,368
Hood	4,359	5,313	4,457	4,255	7,400
Hopkins	4,085	3,398	3,147	4,984	5,133
Houston	3,250	3,067	1,690	3,846	3,882
Howard	3,735	5,129	1,984	4,445	6,024
Hudspeth	364	325	178	406	405
Hunt	7,452	9,739	7,387	8,820	12,331
Hutchinson	2,833	6,034	1,993	2,950	7,526
Irion	256	283	290	326	539
Jack	1,254	1,041	1,045	1,521	1,542
Jackson	1,722	2,451	976	2,141	2,954
Jasper	5,658	3,870	2,539	6,613	4,985
Jeff Davis	321	360	187	325	524
Jefferson	48,405	29,622	17,242	55,649	35,754

Jim Hogg	1,520	478	107	1,630	510
Jim Wells	7,812	3,311	1,413	8,495	4,335
Johnson	12,030	13,473	11,573	12,507	17,509
Jones	2,400	2,088	1,436	2,898	3,000
Karnes	1,897	1,990	802	2,529	2,383
Kaufman	6,498	6,578	5,913	7,358	8,466
Kendall	1,374	4,162	1,773	1,446	4,875
Kenedy	87	69	18	119	76
Kent	271	175	163	398	274
Kerr	3,707	8,787	3,790	3,587	11,207
Kimble	467	790	354	551	1,061
King	54	79	56	64	111
Kinney	598	634	299	669	771
Kleberg	5,109	3,897	1,470	5,367	4,443
Knox	854	521	438	1,013	765
Lamar	6,328	5,778	4,093	7,553	8,021
Lamb	1,737	2,998	709	2,230	3,064
Lampasas	1,508	2,233	1,432	1,954	3,000
LaSalle	1,522	586	211	1,651	693
Lavaca	2,700	3,362	1,696	3,531	4,377
Lee	1,847	2,108	1,088	2,527	2,513
Leon	2,042	2,212	1,251	2,316	2,778
Liberty	7,036	6,959	4,311	8,343	8,524
Limestone	3,188	2,358	1,505	3,476	3,257
Lipscomb	338	839	270	377	1,111
Live Oak	1,345	1,805	806	1,573	2,277
Llano	2,409	3,056	1,799	2,629	3,550
Loving	20	31	45	23	54
Lubbock	22,240	48,847	11,618	22,202	50,760
Lynn	902	1,233	291	1,086	1,279
McCulloch	1,393	1,108	986	1,665	1,618
McLennan	25,903	28,473	15,505	27,545	38,606
McMullen	78	274	89	94	302
Madison	1,553	1,544	778	1,835	1,896
Marion	2,156	1,245	882	2,255	1,857
Martin	641	986	356	632	1,017
Mason	570	776	364	671	975
Matagorda	4,759	5,328	3,045	5,675	6,787
Maverick	4,540	2,002	771	4,395	1,592
Medina	3,650	4,912	2,167	4,227	5,722
Menard	553	354	367	614	552
Midland	9,160	24,143	7,880	8,487	30,618
Milam	3,542	2,414	1,495	4,865	3,512
Mills	753	702	530	842	1,043
Mitchell	1,353	1,128	604	1,773	1,596
Montague	2,885	2,304	2,330	3,689	3,475
Montgomery	18,551	39,976	19,203	18,394	40,360
Moore	1,361	3,147	976	1,537	3,710
Morris	3,028	1,400	1,138	3,522	2,104
Motley	256	446	117	262	429
Nacogdoches	6,937	9,864	4,803	6,886	11,767
Navarro	6,006	4,897	3,800	6,749	6,445
Newton	3,249	1,212	1,032	3,640	1,659
Nolan	2,490	1,993	1,455	2,853	2,734
Nueces	46,317	36,781	17,374	49,209	46,337
Ochiltree	557	2,419	576	579	2,928
Oldham	225	583	177	303	691
Orange	15,305	9,793	7,321	17,834	11,959
Palo Pinto	3,392	2,852	3,010	3,930	4,649
Panola	3,950	3,473	1,906	4,123	4,642
Parker	7,934	10,321	9,148	8,517	14,090
Parmer	637	1,829	564	764	2,061
Pecos	1,778	1,836	895	1,960	2,483
Polk	5,942	5,390	2,884	5,943	5,831
Potter	9,527	13,510	4,655	9,563	16,400
Presidio	1,189	400	290	1,176	586
Rains	1,108	975	890	1,448	1,281
Randall	9,119	24,971	6,340	8,492	27,986
Reagan	337	651	259	418	935
Real	463	787	386	483	795
Red River	2,686	1,735	1,228	3,165	2,475
Reeves	2,569	1,244	734	2,812	1,724
Refugio	1,531	1,469	716	1,831	1,883
Roberts	126	391	99	135	441
Robertson	2,927	1,707	963	3,630	2,184
Rockwall	2,397	6,427	4,393	2,659	7,214
Runnels	1,401	1,653	1,279	1,720	2,417
Rusk	5,391	7,560	3,575	5,140	9,117
Sabine	2,288	1,490	894	2,053	1,925
San Augustine	1,737	1,243	667	2,118	1,946
San Jacinto	2,846	2,494	1,653	2,972	2,691
San Patricio	8,202	7,456	3,178	9,920	9,159
San Saba	716	723	660	1,165	1,099
Schleicher	420	452	355	494	653
Scurry	1,609	2,670	1,826	2,119	3,749
Shackelford	484	623	422	681	865
Shelby	3,986	3,217	1,487	4,261	3,999
Sherman	261	851	256	340	1,145
Smith	17,514	27,753	13,569	18,719	34,658
Somervell	782	872	903	983	1,304
Starr	7,668	1,209	345	6,958	1,218
Stephens	1,115	1,573	1,062	1,519	2,342
Sterling	127	322	182	188	464
Stonewall	561	242	322	724	421
Sutton	524	687	387	571	996
Swisher	1,413	989	541	1,893	1,271
Tarrant	156,230	183,387	129,998	151,310	242,660
Taylor	12,382	22,614	10,331	13,073	28,563
Terrell	325	176	128	390	296
Terry	1,461	2,309	619	1,941	2,645
Throckmorton	401	389	228	534	455
Titus	3,625	3,024	2,146	4,357	4,247
Tom Green	11,437	14,989	10,244	12,283	21,463
Travis	130,546	88,105	56,158	127,783	105,915
Trinity	2,784	1,988	1,133	2,657	2,448
Tyler	3,465	2,357	1,529	4,198	3,070
Upshur	4,776	4,511	2,896	5,242	5,991
Upton	489	908	313	544	1,189
Uvalde	3,482	3,635	1,387	3,684	4,266
Val Verde	4,748	4,102	2,093	5,044	5,109
Van Zandt	5,310	5,810	5,239	6,153	7,371
Victoria	7,604	13,086	5,136	8,923	15,056
Walker	5,619	6,662	3,619	5,826	8,473
Waller	4,270	3,065	1,692	3,957	3,607
Ward	1,695	1,769	948	1,858	2,709
Washington	3,283	5,817	1,738	2,960	6,041
Webb	14,509	7,789	2,517	16,227	7,528
Wharton	4,643	5,503	2,624	5,935	6,978
Wheeler	938	1,458	367	1,067	1,703
Wichita	17,021	17,956	11,478	17,956	23,324
Wilbarger	1,924	1,959	1,453	2,248	2,669
Willacy	3,359	1,490	652	3,165	1,750
Williamson	19,437	26,208	15,415	19,589	27,322
Wilson	3,711	3,766	2,105	3,953	4,436
Winkler	942	1,173	582	947	1,656
Wise	4,478	4,555	4,485	5,288	6,064
Wood	4,084	4,708	3,494	4,553	6,216
Yoakum	595	1,486	484	727	1,762
Young	2,464	2,894	2,302	3,007	4,156
Zapata	2,052	866	326	2,171	958
Zavala	3,058	571	237	3,338	628
Totals	**2,281,815**	**2,496,071**	**1,354,781**	**2,352,748**	**3,036,829**

Texas Vote Since 1944

1944, Roosevelt, Dem., 821,605; Dewey, Rep., 191,425; Texas Regulars, 135,439; Watson, Proh., 1,017; Thomas, Soc., 594; America First, 250.

1948, Truman, Dem., 750,700; Dewey, Rep., 282,240; Thurmond, States' Rights, 106,909; Wallace, Prog., 3,764; Watson, Proh., 2,758; Thomas, Soc., 874.

1952, Eisenhower, Rep., 1,102,878; Stevenson, Dem., 969,228; Hamblen, Proh., 1,983; MacArthur, Christian Nationalist, 833; MacArthur, Constitution, 730; Hallinan, Prog., 294.

1956, Eisenhower, Rep., 1,080,619; Stevenson, Dem., 859,958; Andrews, Ind., 14,591.

1960, Kennedy, Dem., 1,167,932; Nixon, Rep., 1,121,699; Sullivan, Constitution, 18,169; Decker, Proh., 3,870; write-in, 15.

1964, Johnson, Dem., 1,663,185; Goldwater, Rep., 958,566; Lightburn, Constitution, 5,060.

1968, Nixon, Rep., 1,227,844; Humphrey, Dem., 1,266,804; Wallace, 3d party, 584,269; write-in, 489.

1972, Nixon, Rep., 2,298,896; McGovern, Dem., 1,154,289; Schmitz, Amer., 6,039; Jenness, Soc. Workers, 8,664; others, 3,393.

1976, Carter, Dem., 2,082,319; Ford, Rep., 1,953,300; McCarthy, Ind., 20,118; Anderson, Amer., 11,442; Camejo, Soc. Workers, 1,723; write-in, 2,982.

1980, Reagan, Rep., 2,510,705; Carter, Dem., 1,881,147; Anderson, Ind., 111,613; Clark, Libertarian, 37,643; write-in, 528.

1984, Reagan, Rep., 3,433,428; Mondale, Dem., 1,949,276.

1988, Bush, Rep., 3,036,829; Dukakis, Dem., 2,352,748; Paul, Lib., 30,355; Fulani, New Alliance, 7,208.

1992, Clinton, Dem., 2,281,815; Bush, Rep., 2,496,071; Perot, Ind., 1,354,781; Marrou, Libertarian, 19,699.

Utah

County	1992 Clinton (D)	1992 Bush (R)	1992 Perot (I)	1988 Dukakis (D)	1988 Bush (R)
Beaver	668	1,040	330	816	1,286
Box Elder	2,186	7,712	4,507	2,736	12,585
Cache	4,973	15,971	8,032	5,871	21,766
Carbon	4,480	2,038	2,002	5,521	3,019
Daggett	122	172	117	132	272
Davis	14,924	39,087	24,105	16,868	50,469
Duchesne	772	1,983	1,229	1,227	3,118
Emery	1,349	1,643	1,138	1,788	2,322
Garfield	309	1,235	355	370	1,470
Grand	1,160	1,100	991	1,287	1,895
Iron	1,537	5,616	1,693	1,736	6,038
Juab	823	1,237	616	974	1,505
Kane	295	1,241	534	398	1,788
Millard	742	2,496	1,064	1,124	3,515
Morgan	520	1,339	851	647	1,889
Piute	169	429	146	206	476
Rich	154	525	187	234	621
Salt Lake	100,082	117,247	91,968	107,453	163,557
San Juan	1,639	2,004	576	1,407	2,377

Sanpete	1,302	2,995	1,742	1,822	4,579
Sevier	1,039	3,160	1,671	1,403	4,747
Summit	3,013	3,133	3,060	2,545	3,881
Tooele	3,270	3,676	3,011	4,166	5,539
Uintah	1,374	3,505	2,250	1,799	5,341
Utah	14,090	61,398	24,558	18,533	68,134
Wasatch	1,042	1,822	1,234	1,451	2,487
Washington	3,364	11,310	4,623	3,054	13,306
Wayne	236	706	251	353	784
Weber	17,795	26,812	20,559	21,431	39,676
Totals	**183,429**	**322,632**	**203,400**	**207,352**	**428,442**

Utah Vote Since 1944

1944, Roosevelt, Dem., 150,088; Dewey, Rep., 97,891; Thomas, Soc., 340.

1948, Truman, Dem., 149,151; Dewey, Rep., 124,402; Wallace, Prog., 2,679; Dobbs, Soc. Workers, 73.

1952, Eisenhower, Rep., 194,190; Stevenson, Dem., 135,364.

1956, Eisenhower, Rep., 215,631; Stevenson, Dem., 118,364.

1960, Kennedy, Dem., 169,248; Nixon, Rep., 205,361; Dobbs, Soc. Workers, 100.

1964, Johnson, Dem., 219,628; Goldwater, Rep., 181,785.

1968, Nixon, Rep., 238,728; Humphrey, Dem., 156,665; Wallace, 3d party, 26,906; Halstead, Soc. Worker, 89; Peace and Freedom, 180.

1972, Nixon, Rep., 323,643; McGovern, Dem., 126,284; Schmitz, Amer., 28,549.

1976, Carter, Dem., 182,110; Ford, Rep., 337,908; Anderson, Amer., 13,304; McCarthy, Ind., 3,907; MacBride, Libertarian, 2,438; Maddox, Am. Ind., 1,162; Camejo, Soc. Workers, 268; Hall, Com., 121.

1980, Reagan, Rep., 439,687; Carter, Dem., 124,266; Anderson, Ind., 30,284; Clark, Libertarian, 7,226; Commoner, Citizens, 1,009; Greaves, American, 965; Rarick, Amer. Ind., 522; Hall, Com., 139; DeBerry, Soc. Worker, 124.

1984, Reagan, Rep., 469,105; Mondale, Dem., 155,369; Bergland, Libertarian, 2,447.

1988, Bush, Rep., 428,442; Dukakis, Dem., 207,352; Paul, Lib., 7,473; Dennis, American, 2,158.

1992, Clinton, Dem., 183,429; Bush, Rep., 322,632; Perot, Ind., 203,400; Gritz, Populist/America First, 28,602; Marrou, Libertarian, 1,900; Hagelin, Natural Law, 1,319; LaRouche, Ind., 1,089.

Vermont

City	1992 Clinton (D)	1992 Bush (R)	1992 Perot (I)	1988 Dukakis (D)	1988 Bush (R)
Barre City	1,807	1,508	1,035	2,132	2,100
Bennington	3,646	2,151	1,536	3,180	2,748
Brattleboro	3,519	1,447	847	3,136	2,044
Burlington	12,508	4,462	3,241	9,748	6,382
Montpelier	2,490	1,407	657	2,351	2,013
Rutland City	3,888	2,915	1,722	3,590	3,631
St. Albans City	1,455	887	744	1,441	1,295
St. Johnsbury	1,249	1,243	836	1,188	1,974
South Burlington	3,730	2,131	1,359	3,373	3,136
Winooski	1,462	733	646	1,426	1,014
Other	97,836	69,238	53,362	84,210	97,994
Totals	**133,590**	**88,122**	**65,985**	**115,775**	**124,331**

Vermont Vote Since 1944

1944, Roosevelt, Dem., 53,820; Dewey, Rep., 71,527.

1948, Truman, Dem., 45,557; Dewey, Rep., 75,926; Wallace, Prog., 1,279; Thomas, Soc., 585.

1952, Eisenhower, Rep., 109,717; Stevenson, Dem., 43,355; Hallinan, Prog., 282; Hoopes, Soc., 185.

1956, Eisenhower, Rep., 110,390; Stevenson, Dem., 42,549; scattered, 39.

1960, Kennedy, Dem., 69,186; Nixon, Rep., 98,131.

1964, Johnson, Dem., 107,674; Goldwater, Rep., 54,868.

1968, Nixon, Rep., 85,142; Humphrey, Dem., 70,255; Wallace, 3d party, 5,104; Halstead, Soc. Worker, 295; Gregory, New Party, 579.

1972, Nixon, Rep., 117,149; McGovern, Dem., 68,174; Spock, Liberty Union, 1,010; Jenness, Soc. Workers, 296; scattered, 318.

1976, Carter, Dem., 77,798; Carter, Ind. Vermonter, 991; Ford, Rep., 100,387; McCarthy, Ind., 4,001; Camejo, Soc. Workers, 430; LaRouche, U.S. Labor, 196; scattered, 99.

1980, Reagan, Rep., 94,598; Carter, Dem., 81,891; Anderson, Ind., 31,760; Commoner, Citizens, 2,316; Clark, Libertarian, 1,900; McReynolds, Liberty Union, 136; Hall, Com., 118; DeBerry, Soc. Worker, 75; scattering, 413.

1984, Reagan, Rep., 135,865; Mondale, Dem., 95,730; Bergland, Libertarian, 1,002.

1988, Bush, Rep., 124,331; Dukakis, Dem., 115,775; Paul, Lib., 1,000; LaRouche, Ind., 275.

1992, Clinton, Dem., 133,590; Bush, Rep., 88,122; Perot, Ind., 65,985.

Virginia

County	1992 Clinton (D)	1992 Bush (R)	1992 Perot (I)	1988 Dukakis (D)	1988 Bush (R)
Accomack	4,950	5,666	2,304	4,443	6,926
Albemarle	13,886	13,894	3,855	10,363	15,117
Alleghany	2,396	2,294	926	2,316	2,555
Amelia	1,534	2,062	574	1,359	2,187
Amherst	4,101	5,482	1,268	3,567	6,507
Appomattox	1,919	2,830	801	1,740	3,205
Arlington	47,756	26,376	7,992	40,314	34,191
Augusta	5,190	12,896	3,397	4,170	13,251
Bath	855	1,075	354	881	1,273
Bedford	6,792	10,496	3,251	5,406	10,702
Bland	1,001	1,368	408	937	1,556
Botetourt	4,349	5,904	1,819	3,763	5,687
Brunswick	3,687	2,480	479	3,070	2,742
Buchanan	7,405	3,297	815	6,935	3,912
Buckingham	2,193	2,368	459	1,941	2,481
Campbell	5,999	10,931	2,553	4,574	12,713
Caroline	3,770	2,947	965	3,186	3,065
Carroll	3,790	5,664	1,388	3,190	6,377
Charles City	2,010	729	251	1,839	826
Charlotte	2,098	2,293	640	1,923	2,699
Chesterfield	28,028	56,626	16,898	18,723	58,828
Clarke	1,811	1,994	802	1,478	2,502
Craig	965	1,008	304	864	1,112
Culpeper	3,444	5,226	1,640	2,555	5,896
Cumberland	1,284	1,643	372	1,132	1,978
Dickenson	4,839	2,574	660	4,461	3,091
Dinwiddie	3,624	3,648	1,198	3,405	4,165
Essex	1,583	1,897	382	1,294	2,038
Fairfax	160,186	170,488	53,012	125,711	200,631
Fauquier	6,600	10,497	3,464	4,837	11,733
Floyd	2,026	2,575	672	1,727	2,921
Fluvanna	2,134	2,811	871	1,562	2,447
Franklin	6,590	6,724	2,232	5,734	7,391
Frederick	4,942	9,425	2,981	3,707	9,921
Giles	3,346	3,023	1,142	3,042	3,490
Gloucester	4,058	6,461	2,640	3,372	7,646
Goochland	2,589	3,834	994	2,209	3,765
Grayson	2,615	3,378	860	2,441	3,968
Greene	1,353	2,265	627	899	2,234
Greensville	2,237	1,335	360	2,083	1,610
Halifax	4,752	5,199	1,140	4,282	5,671
Hanover	8,021	20,336	5,674	5,985	20,570
Henrico	36,807	56,910	14,720	26,980	62,284
Henry	9,296	9,005	3,212	7,536	10,871
Highland	494	686	212	456	807
Isle of Wight	4,380	5,370	1,536	3,747	5,779
James City	6,536	8,781	2,675	4,642	8,945
King George	1,363	1,206	323	1,519	2,587
King and Queen	1,811	2,570	918	1,309	1,376
King William	1,822	2,591	758	1,561	2,735
Lancaster	1,812	2,841	739	1,551	3,380
Lee	5,215	3,504	1,002	4,906	4,080
Loudoun	14,462	19,290	7,391	10,101	20,448
Louisa	3,399	3,461	1,381	2,789	3,831
Lunenburg	2,082	2,227	505	1,870	2,530
Madison	1,700	2,341	653	1,427	2,501
Mathews	1,402	2,179	884	1,235	2,752
Mecklenburg	4,273	5,401	1,128	3,275	5,887
Middlesex	1,597	2,224	768	1,361	2,571
Montgomery	10,658	10,606	3,449	8,909	12,326
Nelson	2,586	2,159	748	2,272	2,502
New Kent	1,738	2,708	1,017	1,427	2,917
Northampton	2,568	2,088	844	2,242	2,562
Northumberland	1,862	2,667	729	1,506	2,984
Nottoway	2,411	2,610	606	2,217	3,161
Orange	3,348	4,092	1,425	2,592	4,319
Page	3,010	4,203	1,163	2,499	5,013
Patrick	2,465	3,521	1,026	2,093	3,990
Pittsylvania	7,675	11,467	2,296	6,612	12,229
Powhatan	1,950	3,832	1,232	1,467	4,040
Prince Edward	2,775	2,858	635	2,434	3,147
Prince George	3,087	4,799	1,459	2,469	4,982
Prince William	26,486	35,432	13,190	19,198	39,654
Pulaski	5,633	6,148	2,066	4,686	6,844
Rappahannock	1,273	1,410	487	1,003	1,657
Richmond	1,034	1,609	366	924	1,862
Roanoke	14,704	20,667	5,477	12,938	22,011
Rockbridge	2,908	3,228	1,254	2,412	3,541
Rockingham	5,407	13,016	2,839	4,716	13,241
Russell	6,480	3,891	958	6,222	4,374
Scott	3,979	4,515	957	3,616	4,986
Shenandoah	3,956	7,746	2,063	3,276	8,612
Smyth	4,924	6,128	1,618	3,989	7,446

Southampton	3,199	2,844	754	3,000	3,439
Spotsylvania	8,133	11,829	3,918	5,486	10,978
Stafford	7,718	12,528	4,481	5,380	12,234
Surry	1,823	1,046	364	1,602	1,246
Sussex	2,193	1,527	446	1,958	1,822
Tazewell	8,586	6,375	1,872	8,098	7,165
Warren	3,554	4,319	1,650	2,769	4,700
Washington	7,269	9,150	2,288	5,819	10,722
Westmoreland	2,758	2,554	818	2,311	2,974
Wise	7,681	5,144	1,835	7,017	6,189
Wythe	3,616	5,121	1,557	3,201	5,827
York	6,218	10,197	3,426	4,639	11,103
City					
Alexandria	30,784	16,700	4,934	24,358	20,913
Bedford	963	1,091	313	960	1,322
Bristol	2,948	3,616	851	2,446	4,407
Buena Vista	1,023	849	291	828	1,121
Charlottesville	8,685	4,705	1,397	7,671	5,817
Chesapeake	23,495	28,909	9,237	18,828	29,738
Clifton Forge	958	632	251	961	759
Colonial Heights	1,721	5,298	1,312	1,581	6,001
Covington	1,442	995	402	1,567	1,274
Danville	8,134	9,584	1,679	7,353	12,221
Emporia	1,048	1,094	157	977	1,289
Fairfax	3,884	4,333	1,439	3,430	5,576
Falls Church	2,864	1,912	599	2,484	2,470
Franklin	1,696	1,347	272	1,630	1,557
Fredericksburg	3,266	2,819	738	2,683	3,401
Galax	957	1,087	276	907	1,278
Hampton	23,395	19,219	6,581	19,106	24,034
Harrisonburg	3,414	4,935	1,162	2,799	5,376
Hopewell	2,863	3,818	1,227	2,566	4,672
Lexington	1,128	894	228	997	994
Lynchburg	9,587	12,518	2,545	8,279	15,323
Manassas	3,647	5,453	1,971	2,658	5,980
Manassas Park	567	792	356	434	993
Martinsville	3,073	2,690	748	2,794	3,360
Newport News	25,743	26,779	8,217	21,413	32,570
Norfolk	37,602	22,362	8,732	37,778	30,538
Norton	871	472	182	795	608
Petersburg	8,671	3,125	834	8,177	4,231
Poquoson	1,086	3,354	960	877	3,840
Portsmouth	20,416	12,575	4,360	19,698	16,087
Radford	2,183	1,996	582	1,855	2,481
Richmond	47,642	24,341	6,992	42,155	31,586
Roanoke	17,724	13,443	3,753	17,185	15,389
Salem	4,028	5,143	1,430	3,760	5,694
South Boston	1,051	1,435	252	936	1,694
Staunton	2,851	4,989	1,146	2,457	5,775
Suffolk	9,196	8,697	2,150	8,080	9,742
Virginia Beach	44,294	68,936	24,087	33,780	76,481
Waynesboro	2,302	3,758	961	2,038	4,672
Williamsburg	1,856	1,349	445	1,534	1,648
Winchester	2,768	3,833	1,048	2,300	4,497
Totals	**1,038,650**	**1,150,517**	**348,639**	**859,799**	**1,309,162**

Virginia Vote Since 1944

1944, Roosevelt, Dem., 242,276; Dewey, Rep., 145,243; Watson, Proh., 459; Thomas, Soc., 417; Teichert, Soc. Labor, 90.

1948, Truman, Dem., 200,786; Dewey, Rep., 172,070; Thurmond, States' Rights, 43,393; Wallace, Prog., 2,047; Thomas, Soc., 726; Teichert, Soc. Labor, 234.

1952, Eisenhower, Rep., 349,037; Stevenson, Dem., 268,677; Hass, Soc. Labor, 1,160; Hoopes, Social Dem., 504; Hallinan, Prog., 311.

1956, Eisenhower, Rep., 386,459; Stevenson, Dem., 267,760; Andrews, States' Rights, 42,964; Hoopes, Soc. Dem., 444; Hass, Soc. Labor, 351.

1960, Kennedy, Dem., 362,327; Nixon, Rep., 404,521; Coiner, Conservative, 4,204; Hass, Soc. Labor, 397.

1964, Johnson, Dem., 558,038; Goldwater, Rep., 481,334; Hass, Soc. Labor, 2,895.

1968, Nixon, Rep., 590,319; Humphrey, Dem., 442,387; Wallace, 3d party, *320,272; Blomen, Soc. Labor, 4,671; Munn, Proh., 601; Gregory, Peace and Freedom, 1,680.

*10,561 votes for Wallace were omitted in the count.

1972, Nixon, Rep., 988,493; McGovern, Dem., 438,887; Schmitz, Amer., 19,721; Fisher, Soc. Labor, 9,918.

1976, Carter, Dem., 813,896; Ford, Rep., 836,554; Camejo, Soc. Workers, 17,802; Anderson, Amer., 16,686; LaRouche, U.S. Labor, 7,508; MacBride, Libertarian, 4,648.

1980, Reagan, Rep., 989,609; Carter, Dem., 752,174; Anderson, Ind., 95,418; Commoner, Citizens, 14,024; Clark, Libertarian, 12,821; DeBerry, Soc. Worker, 1,986.

1984, Reagan, Rep., 1,337,078; Mondale, Dem., 796,250.

1988, Bush, Rep., 1,309,162; Dukakis, Dem., 859,799; Fulani, Ind., 14,312; Paul, Lib., 8,336.

1992, Clinton, Dem., 1,038,650; Bush, Rep., 1,150,517; Perot, Ind., 348,639; LaRouche, Ind., 11,937; Marrou, Libertarian, 5,730; Fulani, New Alliance, 3,192.

Washington

	1992			1988	
County	**Clinton (D)**	**Bush (R)**	**Perot (I)**	**Dukakis (D)**	**Bush (R)**
Adams	1,449	2,087	1,010	1,612	2,612
Asotin	3,239	2,425	1,849	3,422	2,874
Benton	16,459	22,883	12,878	14,817	28,688
Chelan	7,860	10,716	4,606	8,183	11,601
Clallam	10,820	9,765	7,775	11,123	11,200
Clark	42,648	36,906	26,163	40,021	37,285
Columbia	668	761	466	730	1,172
Cowlitz	15,052	10,000	9,246	16,090	12,009
Douglas	3,731	4,920	2,315	3,760	5,378
Ferry	963	773	762	972	972
Franklin	3,743	4,486	2,597	4,772	6,488
Garfield	473	620	222	593	714
Grant	7,278	9,503	4,898	7,564	10,859
Grays Harbor	12,599	6,904	7,460	14,097	8,860
Island	9,555	9,526	7,889	8,510	12,552
Jefferson	6,148	3,467	3,168	5,270	4,184
King	391,050	212,986	167,216	349,663	290,574
Kitsap	34,442	29,340	23,873	33,748	34,743
Kittitas	5,432	4,078	2,778	5,318	5,048
Klickitat	2,758	2,085	1,938	2,991	2,920
Lewis	7,810	12,316	6,684	8,629	14,184
Lincoln	1,653	2,152	1,098	1,884	2,689
Mason	8,076	5,776	5,577	7,826	7,426
Okanogan	5,015	4,265	3,541	5,630	5,856
Pacific	4,587	2,243	2,351	5,017	3,073
Pend Oreille	1,798	1,528	1,340	1,925	1,802
Pierce	102,243	77,410	59,523	96,688	94,167
San Juan	3,353	1,901	1,776	3,008	2,660
Skagit	15,936	13,388	10,973	15,159	16,550
Skamania	1,474	1,102	1,050	1,748	1,356
Snohomish	88,643	69,137	65,838	80,694	84,158
Spokane	69,526	59,984	38,251	68,520	68,787
Stevens	4,960	5,706	3,769	5,068	6,576
Thurston	38,293	25,643	19,551	33,860	31,980
Wahkiakum	696	488	584	961	629
Walla Walla	7,325	7,894	4,507	7,448	9,683
Whatcom	26,619	23,801	12,455	25,571	23,820
Whitman	7,637	6,428	3,220	7,403	7,680
Yakima	21,026	25,841	10,583	23,221	30,026
Totals	**993,037**	**731,234**	**541,780**	**933,516**	**903,835**

Washington Vote Since 1944

1944, Roosevelt, Dem., 486,774; Dewey, Rep., 361,689; Thomas, Soc., 3,824; Watson, Proh., 2,396; Teichert, Soc. Labor, 1,645.

1948, Truman, Dem., 476,165; Dewey, Rep., 386,315; Wallace, Prog., 31,692; Watson, Proh., 6,117; Thomas, Soc., 3,534; Teichert, Soc. Labor, 1,133; Dobbs, Soc. Workers, 103.

1952, Eisenhower, Rep., 599,107; Stevenson, Dem., 492,845; MacArthur, Christian Nationalist, 7,290; Hallinan, Prog., 2,460; Hass, Soc. Labor, 633; Hoopes, Soc., 254; Dobbs, Soc. Workers, 119.

1956, Eisenhower, Rep., 620,430; Stevenson, Dem., 523,002; Hass, Soc. Labor, 7,457.

1960, Kennedy, Dem., 599,298; Nixon, Rep., 629,273; Hass, Soc. Labor, 10,895; Curtis, Constitution, 1,401; Dobbs, Soc. Workers, 705.

1964, Johnson, Dem., 779,699; Goldwater, Rep., 470,366; Hass, Soc. Labor, 7,772; DeBerry, Freedom Soc., 537.

1968, Nixon, Rep., 588,510; Humphrey, Dem., 616,037; Wallace, 3d party, 96,990; Blomen, Soc. Labor, 488; Cleaver, Peace and Freedom, 1,609; Halstead, Soc. Worker, 270; Mitchell, Free Ballot, 377.

1972, Nixon, Rep., 837,135; McGovern, Dem., 568,334; Schmitz, Amer., 58,906; Spock, Ind., 2,644; Fisher, Soc. Labor, 1,102; Jenness, Soc. Worker, 623; Hall, Com., 566; Hospers, Libertarian, 1,537.

1976, Carter, Dem., 717,323; Ford, Rep., 777,732; McCarthy, Ind., 36,986; Maddox, Amer. Ind., 8,585; Anderson, Amer., 5,046; MacBride, Libertarian, 5,042; Wright, People's, 1,124; Camejo, Soc. Workers, 905; LaRouche, U.S. Labor, 903; Hall, Com., 817; Levin, Soc. Labor, 713; Zeidler, Soc., 358.

1980, Reagan, Rep., 865,244; Carter, Dem., 650,193; Anderson, Ind., 185,073; Clark, Libertarian, 29,213; Commoner, Citizens, 9,403; DeBerry, Soc. Worker, 1,137; McReynolds, Socialist, 956; Hall, Com., 834; Griswold, Workers World, 341.

1984, Reagan, Rep., 1,051,670; Mondale, Dem., 798,352; Bergland, Libertarian, 8,844.
1988, Bush, Rep., 903,835; Dukakis, Dem., 933,516; Paul, Lib., 17,240; LaRouche, Ind., 4,412.
1992, Clinton, Dem., 993,037; Bush, Rep., 731,234; Perot, Ind., 541,780; Marrou, Libertarian, 7,533; Gritz, Populist/America First, 4,854; Hagelin, Natural Law, 2,456; Phillips, U.S. Taxpayers, 2,354; Fulani, New Alliance, 1,776; Daniels, Ind., 1,171.

West Virginia

	1992			1988	
County	Clinton (D)	Bush (R)	Perot (I)	Dukakis (D)	Bush (R)
Barbour	3,467	2,322	1,153	3,221	3,023
Berkeley	7,159	9,134	3,645	6,313	10,761
Boone	6,576	2,021	1,037	6,539	2,786
Braxton	3,396	1,535	823	3,377	2,024
Brooke	5,693	2,582	2,103	6,258	4,006
Cabell	15,111	13,203	5,311	15,368	17,197
Calhoun	1,627	1,095	537	1,644	1,395
Clay	1,928	1,255	462	2,263	1,536
Doddridge	968	1,500	515	955	1,880
Fayette	9,574	3,991	2,002	11,009	5,143
Gilmer	1,576	1,085	484	1,661	1,387
Grant	1,011	2,762	519	893	3,215
Greenbrier	5,784	4,442	1,898	6,091	5,395
Hampshire	2,365	2,767	1,022	2,085	3,253
Hancock	7,830	3,897	3,267	8,338	5,882
Hardy	1,917	2,144	602	1,689	2,581
Harrison	15,480	9,687	5,131	17,005	13,364
Jackson	5,102	4,192	1,908	4,573	5,696
Jefferson	5,363	4,656	2,114	4,334	5,349
Kanawha	38,315	31,358	11,778	41,144	38,140
Lewis	2,931	2,413	1,197	3,272	3,602
Lincoln	4,502	2,637	787	5,049	3,457
Logan	11,095	3,336	1,835	11,317	4,244
McDowell	7,019	1,941	803	7,204	2,463
Marion	14,042	6,380	4,736	14,441	9,229
Marshall	7,298	4,463	3,402	7,903	6,793
Mason	5,331	3,808	2,045	5,468	5,332
Mercer	9,511	7,888	2,817	10,152	10,221
Mineral	3,992	4,837	1,884	4,059	6,015
Mingo	7,342	2,584	915	7,429	2,896
Monongalia	14,142	9,831	4,576	14,178	12,091
Monroe	2,418	2,311	685	2,427	2,719
Morgan	1,854	2,585	886	1,545	3,002
Nicholas	5,042	2,959	1,495	5,173	3,731
Ohio	9,522	7,421	3,632	10,121	10,341
Pendleton	1,626	1,589	362	1,595	1,901
Pleasants	1,387	1,248	731	1,421	1,761
Pocahontas	1,741	1,401	627	1,958	1,876
Preston	3,933	4,429	2,109	4,357	5,804
Putnam	6,817	7,653	2,910	6,640	8,163
Raleigh	13,171	8,700	3,247	14,302	10,395
Randolph	5,097	3,496	1,582	5,233	4,746
Ritchie	1,474	2,184	745	1,446	2,874
Roane	2,607	2,207	1,009	2,447	2,861
Summers	2,650	1,652	565	3,072	2,231
Taylor	2,843	2,022	1,242	2,852	2,816
Tucker	1,805	1,261	550	1,869	1,699
Tyler	1,587	1,593	1,013	1,501	2,365
Upshur	3,161	3,505	1,558	3,065	4,813
Wayne	8,392	5,729	2,199	8,621	7,123
Webster	2,320	811	436	2,185	1,016
Wetzel	3,753	2,271	1,550	3,928	3,381
Wirt	1,043	939	394	929	1,125
Wood	13,529	15,441	6,998	12,959	19,450
Wyoming	5,782	2,821	996	6,138	3,516
Totals	**331,001**	**241,974**	**108,829**	**341,016**	**310,065**

West Virginia Vote Since 1944

1944, Roosevelt, Dem., 392,777; Dewey, Rep., 322,819.
1948, Truman, Dem., 429,188; Dewey, Rep., 316,251; Wallace, Prog., 3,311.
1952, Eisenhower, Rep., 419,970; Stevenson, Dem., 453,578.
1956, Eisenhower, Rep., 449,297; Stevenson, Dem., 381,534.
1960, Kennedy, Dem., 441,786; Nixon, Rep., 395,995.
1964, Johnson, Dem., 538,087; Goldwater, Rep., 253,953.
1968, Nixon, Rep., 307,555; Humphrey, Dem., 374,091; Wallace, 3d party, 72,560.
1972, Nixon, Rep., 484,964; McGovern, Dem., 277,435.
1976, Carter, Dem., 435,864; Ford, Rep., 314,726.
1980, Reagan, Rep., 334,206; Carter, Dem., 367,462; Anderson, Ind., 31,691; Clark, Libertarian, 4,356.
1984, Reagan, Rep., 405,483; Mondale, Dem., 328,125.
1988, Bush, Rep., 310,065; Dukakis, Dem., 341,016; Fulani, New Alliance, 2,230.
1992, Clinton, Dem., 331,001; Bush, Rep., 241,974; Perot, Ind., 108,829; Marrou, Libertarian, 1,873.

Wisconsin

	1992			1988	
County	Clinton (D)	Bush (R)	Perot (I)	Dukakis (D)	Bush (R)
Adams	3,539	2,465	2,003	3,598	3,258
Ashland	4,213	2,372	1,746	4,526	2,926
Barron	8,063	6,572	5,479	8,951	8,527
Bayfield	3,873	2,393	1,786	4,323	3,095
Brown	37,513	42,352	22,395	41,788	43,625
Buffalo	2,996	2,029	1,889	3,481	2,783
Burnet	3,172	2,340	1,855	3,537	2,884
Calumet	5,701	7,541	5,055	6,481	8,107
Chippewa	10,487	8,215	6,408	11,447	9,757
Clark	5,540	4,977	4,284	6,642	6,296
Columbia	9,348	9,099	5,439	9,132	10,475
Crawford	3,540	2,390	1,797	3,608	3,238
Dane	114,724	61,957	31,874	105,414	69,143
Dodge	11,438	14,971	9,136	12,663	17,003
Door	4,735	5,468	3,506	5,425	6,907
Douglas	12,319	5,679	4,150	13,907	6,440
Dunn	7,965	5,283	4,809	9,205	7,273
Eau Claire	21,221	15,915	9,783	21,150	17,664
Florence	978	942	719	1,018	1,106
Fond du Lac	13,757	19,785	10,660	15,887	21,985
Forest	1,904	1,393	1,062	2,142	1,845
Grant	8,914	7,678	6,405	9,421	10,049
Green	5,467	4,887	3,735	5,153	6,636
Green Lake	2,772	3,897	2,827	3,033	5,205
Iowa	4,467	3,288	2,341	4,268	4,240
Iron	1,762	1,273	835	2,090	1,599
Jackson	3,681	2,644	2,040	3,924	3,555
Jefferson	11,593	13,072	7,960	11,816	14,309
Juneau	4,177	4,051	2,670	3,734	4,869
Kenosha	27,341	19,854	14,232	30,089	21,661
Kewaunee	4,050	3,570	2,700	4,786	4,330
La Crosse	22,838	18,891	10,224	22,204	21,548
La Fayette	3,143	2,582	2,079	3,521	3,665
Langlade	3,630	3,890	2,444	4,254	4,884
Lincoln	5,297	4,321	3,605	5,819	5,257
Manitowoc	15,903	14,008	11,179	19,680	16,020
Marathon	21,482	20,948	14,600	24,658	24,482
Marinette	7,626	7,984	5,412	8,030	9,637
Marquette	2,533	2,322	1,818	2,463	3,059
Menominee	691	244	221	1,028	381
Milwaukee	235,521	151,314	76,039	268,287	168,363
Monroe	6,427	6,118	4,183	6,437	7,073
Oconto	5,898	5,720	4,405	6,549	7,084
Oneida	7,160	6,725	4,782	7,414	8,130
Outagamie	23,735	30,370	18,479	27,771	33,113
Ozaukee	11,879	22,805	8,002	12,661	22,899
Pepin	1,673	1,098	781	1,906	1,311
Pierce	7,824	4,844	4,492	8,659	6,045
Polk	7,746	5,446	4,753	8,981	6,866
Portage	15,553	10,914	7,083	16,317	12,057
Price	3,575	2,654	2,286	3,987	3,450
Racine	34,875	32,310	20,227	39,631	36,342
Richland	3,458	3,144	1,899	3,643	4,026
Rock	31,154	21,942	15,700	29,576	28,178
Rusk	3,376	2,430	2,085	3,888	3,063
St. Croix	10,281	8,114	7,125	11,392	9,960
Sauk	9,128	8,886	5,280	8,324	10,225
Sawyer	2,796	2,658	1,861	3,231	3,260
Shawano	6,062	7,253	4,540	6,587	8,362
Sheboygan	20,568	22,526	11,295	23,429	23,471
Taylor	3,305	3,415	2,590	3,785	4,254
Trempealeau	6,218	3,577	3,160	6,212	4,902
Vernon	5,673	4,072	2,890	5,754	5,226
Vilas	3,764	4,616	2,827	3,781	5,842
Walworth	11,825	15,727	9,029	12,203	18,259
Washburn	3,080	2,586	1,978	3,393	3,074
Washington	13,339	22,739	13,045	15,907	24,328
Waukesha	50,270	91,461	36,622	57,598	90,467
Waupaca	6,666	10,252	6,088	7,078	11,559
Waushara	3,402	4,045	2,829	3,535	4,953
Winnebago	27,234	33,709	16,140	28,508	35,085
Wood	13,208	13,843	8,822	16,074	16,549
Totals	**1,041,066**	**930,855**	**544,479**	**1,126,794**	**1,047,499**

Wisconsin Vote Since 1944

1944, Roosevelt, Dem., 650,413; Dewey, Rep., 674,532; Thomas, Soc., 13,205; Teichert, Soc. Labor, 1,002.
1948, Truman, Dem., 647,310; Dewey, Rep., 590,959; Wallace, Prog., 25,282; Thomas, Soc., 12,547; Teichert, Soc. Labor, 399; Dobbs, Soc. Workers, 303.
1952, Eisenhower, Rep., 979,744; Stevenson, Dem., 622,175; Hallinan, Ind., 2,174; Dobbs, Ind., 1,350; Hoopes, Ind., 1,157; Hass, Ind., 770.
1956, Eisenhower, Rep., 954,844; Stevenson, Dem., 586,768; Andrews, Ind., 6,918; Hoopes, Soc., 754; Hass, Soc. Labor, 710; Dobbs, Soc. Workers, 564.
1960, Kennedy, Dem., 830,805; Nixon, Rep., 895,175; Dobbs, Soc. Workers, 1,792; Hass, Soc. Labor, 1,310.
1964, Johnson, Dem., 1,050,424; Goldwater, Rep., 638,495; DeBerry, Soc. Worker, 1,692; Hass, Soc. Labor, 1,204.

1968, Nixon, Rep., 809,997; Humphrey, Dem., 748,804; Wallace, 3d party, 127,835; Blomen, Soc. Labor, 1,338; Halstead, Soc. Worker, 1,222; scattered, 2,342.
1972 Nixon, Rep., 989,430; McGovern, Dem., 810,174; Schmitz, Amer., 47,525; Spock, Ind., 2,701; Fisher, Soc. Labor, 998; Hall, Com., 663; Reed, Ind., 506; scattered, 893.
1976, Carter, Dem., 1,040,232; Ford, Rep., 1,004,987; McCarthy, Ind., 34,943; Maddox, Amer. Ind., 8,552; Zeidler, Soc., 4,298; MacBride, Libertarian, 3,814; Camejo, Soc. Workers, 1,691; Wright, People's, 943; Hall, Com., 749; LaRouche, U.S. Lab., 738; Levin, Soc. Labor, 389; scattered, 2,839.
1980, Reagan, Rep., 1,088,845; Carter, Dem., 981,584; Anderson, Ind., 160,657; Clark, Libertarian, 29,135; Commoner, Citizens, 7,767; Rarick, Constitution, 1,519; McReynolds, Socialist, 808; Hall, Com., 772; Griswold, Workers World, 414; DeBerry, Soc. Workers, 383; scattering, 1,337.
1984, Reagan, Rep., 1,198,584; Mondale, Dem., 995,740; Bergland, Libertarian, 4,883.
1988, Bush, Rep., 1,047,499; Dukakis, Dem., 1,126,794; Paul, Lib., 5,157; Duke, Pop., 3,056.
1992, Clinton, Dem., 1,041,066; Bush, Rep., 930,855; Perot, Ind., 544,479; Marrou, Libertarian, 2,877; Gritz, Populist/America First, 2,311; Daniels, Ind., 1,883; Phillips, U.S. Taxpayers, 1,772; Hagelin, Natural Law, 1,070.

Wyoming

	1992			1988	
County	Clinton (D)	Bush (R)	Perot (I)	Dukakis (D)	Bush (R)
Albany	5,713	4,176	2,862	5,486	5,653
Big Horn	1,216	2,216	1,236	1,469	3,258
Campbell	2,709	5,315	3,133	2,288	6,702
Carbon	2,737	2,320	1,579	2,555	3,336
Converse	1,307	2,159	1,260	1,301	2,885
Crook	568	1,377	718	553	1,939
Fremont	4,765	5,387	3,594	5,020	7,681
Goshen	1,754	2,395	1,144	1,875	3,075
Hot Springs	740	978	652	800	1,490
Johnson	656	1,614	844	707	2,081
Laramie	12,177	12,890	6,607	11,851	15,561
Lincoln	1,430	2,595	1,495	1,592	3,237
Natrona	9,817	9,717	7,647	9,148	14,005
Niobrara	298	635	355	354	825
Park	2,771	5,218	3,145	2,646	6,884
Platte	1,398	1,668	956	1,482	2,253
Sheridan	4,139	4,303	3,035	4,655	5,980
Sublette	536	1,168	828	576	1,636
Sweetwater	6,417	4,476	3,879	6,720	6,780
Teton	3,120	2,854	2,340	2,217	3,616
Uinta	2,047	2,701	2,041	1,922	3,464
Washakie	1,118	1,720	1,084	1,197	2,538
Weston	727	1,465	829	699	1,988
Totals	**68,160**	**79,347**	**51,263**	**67,113**	**106,867**

Wyoming Vote Since 1944

1944, Roosevelt, Dem., 49,419; Dewey, Rep., 51,921.
1948, Truman, Dem., 52,354; Dewey, Rep., 47,947; Wallace, Prog., 931; Thomas, Soc., 137; Teichert, Soc. Labor, 56.
1952, Eisenhower, Rep., 81,047; Stevenson, Dem., 47,934; Hamblen, Proh., 194; Hoopes, Soc., 40; Haas, Soc. Labor, 36.
1956, Eisenhower, Rep., 74,573; Stevenson, Dem., 49,554.
1960, Kennedy, Dem., 63,331; Nixon, Rep., 77,451.
1964, Johnson, Dem., 80,718; Goldwater, Rep., 61,998.
1968, Nixon, Rep., 70,927; Humphrey, Dem., 45,173; Wallace, 3d party, 11,105.
1972, Nixon, Rep., 100,464; McGovern, Dem., 44,358; Schmitz, Amer., 748.
1976, Carter, Dem., 62,239; Ford, Rep., 92,717; McCarthy, Ind., 624; Reagan, Ind., 307; Anderson, Amer., 290; MacBride, Libertarian, 89; Brown, Ind., 47; Maddox, Amer. Ind., 30.
1980, Reagan, Rep., 110,700; Carter, Dem., 49,427; Anderson, Ind., 12,072; Clark, Libertarian, 4,514.
1984, Reagan, Rep., 133,241; Mondale, Dem., 53,370; Bergland, Libertarian, 2,357.
1988, Bush, Rep., 106,867; Dukakis, Dem., 67,113; Paul, Lib., 2,026; Fulani, New Alliance, 545.
1992, Clinton, Dem., 68,160; Bush, Rep., 79,347; Perot, Ind., 51,263.

Electoral Votes for President

(based on 1990 Census)

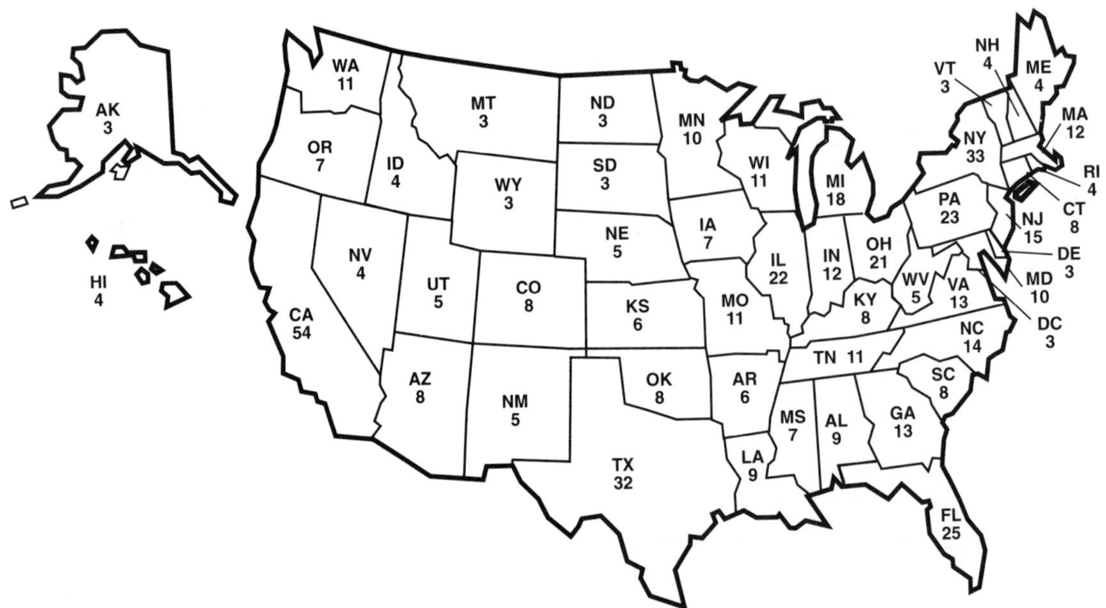

1992 Official Presidential General Election Results

Source: State Elections Offices; Voter News Service

Candidate (Party)	Popular Vote	Percent of Popular Vote
Bill Clinton (Democrat)	44,908,254	42.95
George Bush (Republican)	39,102,343	37.40
Ross Perot (Independent)	19,741,065	18.86
Andre Marrou (Libertarian)	291,612	.28
James "Bo" Gritz (Populist/ America First)	98,918	.09
Lenora Fulani (New Alliance)	73,248	.07
Howard Phillips (U.S. Taxpayers)	42,960	.04
John Hagelin (Natural Law)	37,137	.04
Ron Daniels (Independent)	27,396	.03
Lyndon LaRouche (Independent)	25,863	.02
James Mac Warren (Socialist Workers)	22,883	.02
Drew Bradford (Independent)	4,749	.00
Jack Herer (Grassroots)	3,875	.00
Helen Halyard (Workers League)	3,050	.00
John Quinn Brisben (Socialist)	2,909	.00
John Yiamouyiannis (Independent)	2,199	.00
Delbert Ehlers (Independent)	1,149	.00
Jim Boren (Apathy)	956	.00
Earl Dodge (Prohibition)	935	.00
Eugene Hem (Third Party)	405	.00
Isabelle Masters (Looking Back Group)	327	.00
Robert J. Smith (American)	292	.00
Gloria Estella La Riva (Workers World)	181	.00
Write-In	177,207	.17
None of the Above (Nevada)	2,537	.00
Total	**104,552,736**	**100**

Note: Party designations may vary from one state to another.

Voting for President

Source: Federal Election Commission; Commission for Study of American Electorate

	Candidates	Voter Participation (% of voting-age population)
1932	Roosevelt-Hoover	52.4
1936	Roosevelt-Landon	56.0
1940	Roosevelt-Willkie	58.9
1944	Roosevelt-Dewey	56.0
1948	Truman-Dewey	51.1
1952	Stevenson-Eisenhower	61.6
1956	Stevenson-Eisenhower	59.3
1960	Kennedy-Nixon	62.8
1964	Johnson-Goldwater	61.9
1968	Humphrey-Nixon	60.9
1972	McGovern-Nixon	55.2(a)
1976	Carter-Ford	53.5
1980	Carter-Reagan	54.0
1984	Mondale-Reagan	53.1
1988	Dukakis-Bush	50.2
1992	Clinton-Bush-Perot	55.9

(a) The sharp drop in 1972 reflects the expansion of eligibility with the enfranchisement of 18- to 21-year-olds.

U.S. Reported Voting and Registration, by Age, Nov. 1992

Source: Bureau of the Census, Dept. of Commerce
In thousands.

	All persons	Reported registered		Reported voted[1]		Reported that they did not vote[2]		
		Number	Percent	Number	Percent	Total	Registered	Not registered[3]
Total, 18 years and over	185,684	126,578	68.2	113,866	61.3	71,818	12,712	59,106
18 and 19 years	6,584	3,092	47.0	2,494	37.9	4,090	598	3,492
20 to 24 years	17,788	9,695	54.5	7,948	44.7	9,840	1,747	8,093
25 to 29 years	19,480	11,234	57.7	9,716	49.9	9,764	1,519	8,246
30 to 34 years	22,123	13,988	63.2	12,404	56.1	9,719	1,584	8,135
35 to 44 years	39,716	27,503	69.2	25,269	63.6	14,447	2,234	12,213
45 to 54 years	28,058	20,785	74.1	19,292	68.8	8,766	1,493	7,273
55 to 64 years	21,089	16,231	77.0	15,107	71.6	5,982	1,124	4,858
65 to 74 years	18,445	14,685	79.6	13,607	73.8	4,839	1,078	3,760
75 to 84 years	9,810	7,658	78.1	6,677	68.1	3,133	981	2,152
85 years and over	2,591	1,706	65.9	1,353	52.2	1,238	353	885

(1) Total reporting voting compares with 55.9 percent of population actually voting for president, as reported by Voter News Service. Differences between data may be the result of a variety of factors, including sample size (the total population was not surveyed and, therefore, estimates were made), differences in the respondents' interpretation of the questions, and the respondents' inability or unwillingness to provide correct information or recall correct information. (2) Includes persons who reported "did not vote" or "do not know" and persons who did not report an answer on voting. (3) Includes those who were not citizens.

Characteristics of the U.S. Voting-Age Population Reported Registered or Voting, Nov. 1988 and 1992

Source: Bureau of the Census, Dept. of Commerce
(In thousands. Civilian noninstitutionalized population.)

Characteristic	1992			1988		
	Number	Percent registered	Percent voted[1]	Number	Percent registered	Percent voted[1]
Total, 18 years and over	**185,684**	**68.2**	**61.3**	**178,098**	**66.6**	**57.4**
Region:						
Northeast	38,329	67.0	61.2	37,874	64.8	57.4
Midwest	44,410	74.6	67.2	43,309	72.5	62.9
South	63,659	67.2	59.0	60,725	65.6	54.5
West	39,286	63.6	58.5	36,190	63.0	55.6
Years of school completed:						
Less than 8th grade	15,391	43.9	35.1	19,145	47.5	36.7
Some high school, no diploma	20,970	50.4	41.2	21,052	52.8	41.3
High school graduate	65,281	64.9	57.5	70,003	64.6	54.7
Some college, including associate degree	46,691	75.4	68.7	34,264	73.5	64.5
Bachelor or higher degree	37,351	84.8	81.0	33,604	83.1	77.6
Labor force status:						
In civilian labor force	124,553	68.8	62.6	119,645	66.3	57.5
Employed	116,290	69.9	63.8	113,836	67.1	58.4

(continued)

Characteristic	1992 Number	1992 Percent registered	1992 Percent voted[1]	1988 Number	1988 Percent registered	1988 Percent voted[1]
Unemployed	8,263	53.7	46.2	5,809	50.4	38.6
Not in labor force	61,131	66.8	58.7	58,453	67.2	57.3
Tenure[2]:						
Owner occupied	128,545	75.4	69.1	47,540	78.1	70.0
Renter occupied	54,323	51.8	43.6	17,352	49.7	39.8

(1) Totals reporting voting compare with 55.9 percent of population actually voting for president in 1992 and 50.2 percent in 1988, as reported by Voter News Service. Differences between data may be the result of a variety of factors, including sample size (the total population was not surveyed and, therefore, estimates were made), differences in the respondents' interpretation of the questions, and the respondents' inability or unwillingness to provide correct information or recall correct information. (2) Restricted to family householders in 1988.

The Electoral College

The president and the vice president of the United States are the only elective federal officials not elected by direct vote of the people. They are elected by the members of the Electoral College. The House decided the outcome of the 1800 and 1824 presidential elections. The Senate chose the vice president following the 1836 election.

On presidential election day, the first Tuesday after the first Monday in November of every 4th year, each state chooses as many electors as it has senators and representatives in Congress. In 1964, for the first time, as provided by the 23d Amendment to the Constitution, the District of Columbia voted for 3 electors. Thus, with 100 senators and 435 representatives, there are 538 members of the Electoral College, with a majority of 270 electoral votes needed to elect the president and vice president.

Political parties customarily nominate their lists of electors at their respective state conventions. An elector cannot be a member of Congress or hold federal office.

Some states print the names of the candidates for president and vice president at the top of the November ballot; others list only the names of the electors. In either case, the electors of the party receiving the highest vote are elected. The electors meet on the first Monday after the 2d Wednesday in December in their respective state capitals or in some other place prescribed by state legislatures. By long-established custom they vote for their party nominees, although the Constitution does not require them to do so. The only constitutional requirement is that at least one of the persons each elector votes for shall not be an inhabitant of that elector's home state.

Certified and sealed lists of the votes of the electors in each state are sent to the president of the U.S. Senate, who then opens them in the presence of the members of the Senate and House of Representatives in a joint session held on Jan. 6 (the next day if that falls on a Sunday), and the electoral votes of all the states are then counted. If no candidate for president has a majority, the House of Representatives chooses a president from among the 3 highest candidates, with all representatives from each state combining to cast one vote for that state. If no candidate for vice president has a majority, the Senate chooses from the top 2, with the senators voting as individuals. In the elections of 1824, 1876, and 1888 the presidential candidate receiving the largest popular vote failed to win a majority of the electoral votes.

National Political Convention Sites: 1856-1992[1]

Year	Democrats	Republicans	Year	Democrats	Republicans	Year	Democrats	Republicans
1856	Cincinnati	Philadelphia	1904	St. Louis	Chicago	1952	Chicago	Chicago
1860	Baltimore[2]	Chicago	1908	Denver	Chicago	1956	Chicago	San Francisco
1864	Chicago	Baltimore	1912	Baltimore	Chicago	1960	Los Angeles	Chicago
1868	New York City	Chicago	1916	St. Louis	Chicago	1964	Atlantic City	San Francisco
1872	Baltimore	Philadelphia	1920	San Francisco	Chicago	1968	Chicago	Miami Beach
1876	St. Louis	Cincinnati	1924	New York City	Cleveland	1972	Miami Beach	Miami Beach
1880	Cincinnati	Chicago	1928	Houston	Kansas City	1976	New York City	Kansas City, Mo.
1884	Chicago	Chicago	1932	Chicago	Chicago	1980	New York City	Detroit
1888	St. Louis	Chicago	1936	Philadelphia	Cleveland	1984	San Francisco	Dallas
1892	Chicago	Minneapolis	1940	Chicago	Philadelphia	1988	Atlanta	New Orleans
1896	Chicago	St. Louis	1944	Chicago	Chicago	1992	New York City	Houston
1900	Kansas City, Mo.	Philadelphia	1948	Philadelphia	Philadelphia			

(1) The first Democratic National Convention was held in 1832. All conventions prior to 1856 were held in Baltimore. The first Republican National Convention was held in 1856. Chicago has hosted more conventions (24) than any other city. (2) An earlier convention, held in Charleston, S.C., had resulted in a split in the party. The official nomination was made at the Baltimore convention.

Party Nominees for President and Vice President

Asterisk (*) denotes winning ticket

Year	Democratic President	Democratic Vice President	Republican President	Republican Vice President
1856	James Buchanan*	John Breckinridge	John Fremont	William Dayton
1860	Stephen A. Douglas[1]	Herschel V. Johnson	Abraham Lincoln*	Hannibal Hamlin
1864	George McClellan	G.H. Pendleton	Abraham Lincoln*	Andrew Johnson
1868	Horatio Seymour	Francis Blair	Ulysses S. Grant*	Schuyler Colfax
1872	Horace Greeley	B. Gratz Brown	Ulysses S. Grant*	Henry Wilson
1876	Samuel J. Tilden	Thomas Hendricks	Rutherford B. Hayes*	William Wheeler
1880	Winfield Hancock	William English	James A. Garfield*	Chester A. Arthur
1884	Grover Cleveland*	Thomas Hendricks	James Blaine	John Logan
1888	Grover Cleveland	A.G. Thurman	Benjamin Harrison*	Levi Morton
1892	Grover Cleveland*	Adlai Stevenson	Benjamin Harrison	Whitelaw Reid
1896	William J. Bryan	Arthur Sewall	William McKinley*	Garret Hobart
1900	William J. Bryan	Adlai Stevenson	William McKinley*	Theodore Roosevelt
1904	Alton Parker	Henry Davis	Theodore Roosevelt*	Charles Fairbanks
1908	William J. Bryan	John Kern	William H. Taft*	James Sherman
1912	Woodrow Wilson*	Thomas Marshall	William H. Taft	James Sherman[2]
1916	Woodrow Wilson*	Thomas Marshall	Charles Hughes	Charles Fairbanks
1920	James M. Cox	Franklin D. Roosevelt	Warren G. Harding*	Calvin Coolidge
1924	John W. Davis	Charles W. Bryan	Calvin Coolidge*	Charles G. Dawes
1928	Alfred E. Smith	Joseph T. Robinson	Herbert Hoover*	Charles Curtis
1932	Franklin D. Roosevelt*	John N. Garner	Herbert Hoover	Charles Curtis
1936	Franklin D. Roosevelt*	John N. Garner	Alfred M. Landon	Frank Knox
1940	Franklin D. Roosevelt*	Henry A. Wallace	Wendell L. Willkie	Charles McNary
1944	Franklin D. Roosevelt*	Harry S. Truman	Thomas E. Dewey	John W. Bricker
1948	Harry S. Truman*	Alben W. Barkley	Thomas E. Dewey	Earl Warren
1952	Adlai E. Stevenson	John J. Sparkman	Dwight D. Eisenhower*	Richard M. Nixon
1956	Adlai E. Stevenson	Estes Kefauver	Dwight D. Eisenhower*	Richard M. Nixon
1960	John F. Kennedy*	Lyndon B. Johnson	Richard M. Nixon	Henry Cabot Lodge

1964	Lyndon B. Johnson*	Hubert H. Humphrey	Barry M. Goldwater	William E. Miller
1968	Hubert H. Humphrey	Edmund S. Muskie	Richard M. Nixon*	Spiro T. Agnew
1972	George S. McGovern	R. Sargent Shriver Jr.	Richard M. Nixon*	Spiro T. Agnew
1976	Jimmy Carter*	Walter F. Mondale	Gerald R. Ford	Robert J. Dole
1980	Jimmy Carter	Walter F. Mondale	Ronald Reagan*	George Bush
1984	Walter F. Mondale	Geraldine Ferraro	Ronald Reagan*	George Bush
1988	Michael S. Dukakis	Lloyd Bentsen	George Bush*	Dan Quayle
1992	Bill Clinton*	Al Gore	George Bush	Dan Quayle

(1) Douglas and Johnson were nominated at the Baltimore convention. An earlier convention, which had failed to reach a consensus, had nominated John Breckinridge for president and Joseph Lane for vice president. (2) Died Oct. 30; replaced on ballot by Nicholas Butler.

Major Parties' Popular and Electoral Vote for President

(F) Federalist; (D) Democrat; (R) Republican; (DR) Democratic Republican; (NR) National Republican; (W) Whig; (P) People's; (PR) Progressive; (SR) States' Rights; (LR) Liberal Republican; Asterisk (*)—See notes.

Year	President elected	Popular	Elec.	Losing candidate	Popular	Elec.
1789	George Washington (F)	Unknown	69	No opposition	—	—
1792	George Washington (F)	Unknown	132	No opposition	—	—
1796	John Adams (F)	Unknown	71	Thomas Jefferson (DR)	Unknown	68
1800*	Thomas Jefferson (DR)	Unknown	73	Aaron Burr (DR)	Unknown	73
1804	Thomas Jefferson (DR)	Unknown	162	Charles Pinckney (F)	Unknown	14
1808	James Madison (DR)	Unknown	122	Charles Pinckney (F)	Unknown	47
1812	James Madison (DR)	Unknown	128	DeWitt Clinton (F)	Unknown	89
1816	James Monroe (DR)	Unknown	183	Rufus King (F)	Unknown	34
1820	James Monroe (DR)	Unknown	231	John Quincy Adams (DR)	Unknown	1
1824*	John Quincy Adams (DR)	105,321	84	Andrew Jackson (DR)	155,872	99
				Henry Clay (DR)	46,587	37
				William H. Crawford (DR)	44,282	41
1828	Andrew Jackson (D)	647,231	178	John Quincy Adams (NR)	509,097	83
1832	Andrew Jackson (D)	687,502	219	Henry Clay (NR)	530,189	49
1836	Martin Van Buren (D)	762,678	170	William H. Harrison (W)	548,007	73
1840	William H. Harrison (W)	1,275,017	234	Martin Van Buren (D)	1,128,702	60
1844	James K. Polk (D)	1,337,243	170	Henry Clay (W)	1,299,068	105
1848	Zachary Taylor (W)	1,360,101	163	Lewis Cass (D)	1,220,544	127
1852	Franklin Pierce (D)	1,601,474	254	Winfield Scott (W)	1,386,578	42
1856	James Buchanan (D)	1,927,995	174	John C. Fremont (R)	1,391,555	114
1860	Abraham Lincoln (R)	1,866,352	180	Stephen A. Douglas (D)	1,375,157	12
				John C. Breckinridge (D)	845,763	72
				John Bell (Const. Union)	589,581	39
1864	Abraham Lincoln (R)	2,216,067	212	George McClellan (D)	1,808,725	21
1868	Ulysses S. Grant (R)	3,015,071	214	Horatio Seymour (D)	2,709,615	80
1872*	Ulysses S. Grant (R)	3,597,070	286	Horace Greeley (D-LR)	2,834,079	—
1876*	Rutherford B. Hayes (R)	4,033,950	185	Samuel J. Tilden (D)	4,284,757	184
1880	James A. Garfield (R)	4,449,053	214	Winfield S. Hancock (D)	4,442,030	155
1884	Grover Cleveland (D)	4,911,017	219	James G. Blaine (R)	4,848,334	182
1888*	Benjamin Harrison (R)	5,444,337	233	Grover Cleveland (D)	5,540,050	168
1892	Grover Cleveland (D)	5,554,414	277	Benjamin Harrison (R)	5,190,802	145
				James Weaver (P)	1,027,329	22
1896	William McKinley (R)	7,035,638	271	William J. Bryan (D-P)	6,467,946	176
1900	William McKinley (R)	7,219,530	292	William J. Bryan (D)	6,358,071	155
1904	Theodore Roosevelt (R)	7,628,834	336	Alton B. Parker (D)	5,084,491	140
1908	William H. Taft (R)	7,679,006	321	William J. Bryan (D)	6,409,106	162
1912	Woodrow Wilson (D)	6,286,214	435	Theodore Roosevelt (PR)	4,216,020	88
				William H. Taft (R)	3,483,922	8
1916	Woodrow Wilson (D)	9,129,606	277	Charles E. Hughes (R)	8,538,221	254
1920	Warren G. Harding (R)	16,152,200	404	James M. Cox (D)	9,147,353	127
1924	Calvin Coolidge (R)	15,725,016	382	John W. Davis (D)	8,385,586	136
				Robert M. LaFollette (PR)	4,822,856	13
1928	Herbert Hoover (R)	21,392,190	444	Alfred E. Smith (D)	15,016,443	87
1932	Franklin D. Roosevelt (D)	22,821,857	472	Herbert Hoover (R)	15,761,841	59
				Norman Thomas (Socialist)	884,781	—
1936	Franklin D. Roosevelt (D)	27,751,597	523	Alfred Landon (R)	16,679,583	8
1940	Franklin D. Roosevelt (D)	27,243,466	449	Wendell Willkie (R)	22,304,755	82
1944	Franklin D. Roosevelt (D)	25,602,505	432	Thomas E. Dewey (R)	22,006,278	99
1948	Harry S. Truman (D)	24,105,812	303	Thomas E. Dewey (R)	21,970,065	189
				J. Strom Thurmond (SR)	1,169,021	39
				Henry A. Wallace (PR)	1,157,172	—
1952	Dwight D. Eisenhower (R)	33,936,252	442	Adlai E. Stevenson (D)	27,314,992	89
1956*	Dwight D. Eisenhower (R)	35,585,316	457	Adlai E. Stevenson (D)	26,031,322	73
1960*	John F. Kennedy (D)	34,227,096	303	Richard M. Nixon (R)	34,108,546	219
1964	Lyndon B. Johnson (D)	43,126,506	486	Barry M. Goldwater (R)	27,176,799	52
1968	Richard M. Nixon (R)	31,785,480	301	Hubert H. Humphrey (D)	31,275,166	191
				George C. Wallace (3d party)	9,906,473	46
1972*	Richard M. Nixon (R)	47,165,234	520	George S. McGovern (D)	29,170,774	17
1976*	Jimmy Carter (D)	40,828,929	297	Gerald R. Ford (R)	39,148,940	240
1980	Ronald Reagan (R)	43,899,248	489	Jimmy Carter (D)	35,481,435	49
				John B. Anderson (independent)	5,719,437	—
1984	Ronald Reagan (R)	54,281,858	525	Walter F. Mondale (D)	37,457,215	13
1988*	George Bush (R)	48,881,221	426	Michael S. Dukakis (D)	41,805,422	111
1992	Bill Clinton (D)	44,908,254	370	George Bush (R)	39,102,343	168
				H. Ross Perot (independent)	19,741,065	—

1800—Elected by House of Representatives because of tied electoral vote. **1824**—Elected by House of Representatives. No candidate polled a majority. In 1824, the Democratic Republicans had become a loose coalition of competing political groups. By 1828, the supporters of Jackson were known as Democrats, and the John Q. Adams and Henry Clay supporters as National Republicans. **1872**—Greeley died Nov. 29, 1872. His electoral votes were split among 4 individuals. **1876**—Fla., La., Ore., and S.C. election returns were disputed. Congress in joint session (Mar. 2, 1877) declared Hayes and Wheeler elected President and Vice President. **1888**—Cleveland had more votes than Harrison but the 233 electoral votes cast for Harrison against the 168 for Cleveland elected Harrison president. **1956**—Democrats elected 74 electors but one from Alabama refused to vote for Stevenson. **1960**—Sen. Harry F. Byrd (D-Va.) received 15 electoral votes. **1972**—John Hospers of Cal. and Theodora Nathan of Ore. received one vote from an elector of Virginia. **1976**—Ronald Reagan of Cal. received one vote from an elector of Washington. **1988**—Sen. Lloyd Bentsen (D.-Tex.) received 1 electoral vote.

Presidents of the U.S.

No.	Name	Politics	Born	in	Inaug.	at age	Died	at age
1	George Washington	Fed.	1732, Feb. 22	Va.	1789	57	1799, Dec. 14	67
2	John Adams	Fed.	1735, Oct. 30	Mass.	1797	61	1826, July 4	90
3	Thomas Jefferson	Dem.-Rep.	1743, Apr. 13	Va.	1801	57	1826, July 4	83
4	James Madison	Dem.-Rep.	1751, Mar. 16	Va.	1809	57	1836, June 28	85
5	James Monroe	Dem.-Rep.	1758, Apr. 28	Va.	1817	58	1831, July 4	73
6	John Quincy Adams	Dem.-Rep.	1767, July 11	Mass.	1825	57	1848, Feb. 23	80
7	Andrew Jackson	Dem.	1767, Mar. 15	S.C.	1829	61	1845, June 8	78
8	Martin Van Buren	Dem.	1782, Dec. 5	N.Y.	1837	54	1862, July 24	79
9	William Henry Harrison	Whig	1773, Feb. 9	Va.	1841	68	1841, Apr. 4	68
10	John Tyler	Whig	1790, Mar. 29	Va.	1841	51	1862, Jan. 18	71
11	James Knox Polk	Dem.	1795, Nov. 2	N.C.	1845	49	1849, June 15	53
12	Zachary Taylor	Whig	1784, Nov. 24	Va.	1849	64	1850, July 9	65
13	Millard Fillmore	Whig	1800, Jan. 7	N.Y.	1850	50	1874, Mar. 8	74
14	Franklin Pierce	Dem.	1804, Nov. 23	N.H.	1853	48	1869, Oct. 8	64
15	James Buchanan	Dem.	1791, Apr. 23	Pa.	1857	65	1868, June 1	77
16	Abraham Lincoln	Rep.	1809, Feb. 12	Ky.	1861	52	1865, Apr. 15	56
17	Andrew Johnson	(1)	1808, Dec. 29	N.C.	1865	56	1875, July 31	66
18	Ulysses Simpson Grant	Rep.	1822, Apr. 27	Oh.	1869	46	1885, July 23	63
19	Rutherford Birchard Hayes	Rep.	1822, Oct. 4	Oh.	1877	54	1893, Jan. 17	70
20	James Abram Garfield	Rep.	1831, Nov. 19	Oh.	1881	49	1881, Sept. 19	49
21	Chester Alan Arthur	Rep.	1830, Oct. 5	Vt.	1881	50	1886, Nov. 18	56
22	Grover Cleveland	Dem.	1837, Mar. 18	N.J.	1885	47	1908, June 24	71
23	Benjamin Harrison	Rep.	1833, Aug. 20	Oh.	1889	55	1901, Mar. 13	67
24	Grover Cleveland	Dem.	1837, Mar. 18	N.J.	1893	55	1908, June 24	71
25	William McKinley	Rep.	1843, Jan. 29	Oh.	1897	54	1901, Sept. 14	58
26	Theodore Roosevelt	Rep.	1858, Oct. 27	N.Y.	1901	42	1919, Jan. 6	60
27	William Howard Taft	Rep.	1857, Sept. 15	Oh.	1909	51	1930, Mar. 8	72
28	Woodrow Wilson	Dem.	1856, Dec. 28	Va.	1913	56	1924, Feb. 3	67
29	Warren Gamaliel Harding	Rep.	1865, Nov. 2	Oh.	1921	55	1923, Aug. 2	57
30	Calvin Coolidge	Rep.	1872, July 4	Vt.	1923	51	1933, Jan. 5	60
31	Herbert Clark Hoover	Rep.	1874, Aug. 10	Ia.	1929	54	1964, Oct. 20	90
32	Franklin Delano Roosevelt	Dem.	1882, Jan. 30	N.Y.	1933	51	1945, Apr. 12	63
33	Harry S. Truman	Dem.	1884, May 8	Mo.	1945	60	1972, Dec. 26	88
34	Dwight David Eisenhower	Rep.	1890, Oct. 14	Tex.	1953	62	1969, Mar. 28	78
35	John Fitzgerald Kennedy	Dem.	1917, May 29	Mass.	1961	43	1963, Nov. 22	46
36	Lyndon Baines Johnson	Dem.	1908, Aug. 27	Tex.	1963	55	1973, Jan. 22	64
37	Richard Milhous Nixon (2)	Rep.	1913, Jan. 9	Cal.	1969	56	1994, Apr. 22	81
38	Gerald Rudolph Ford	Rep.	1913, July 14	Nebr.	1974	61		
39	Jimmy (James Earl) Carter	Dem.	1924, Oct. 1	Ga.	1977	52		
40	Ronald Reagan	Rep.	1911, Feb. 6	Ill.	1981	69		
41	George Bush	Rep.	1924, June 12	Mass.	1989	64		
42	Bill Clinton	Dem.	1946, Aug. 19	Ar.	1993	46		

(1) Andrew Johnson — a Democrat, nominated vice president by Republicans and elected with Lincoln on National Union ticket. (2) Resigned Aug. 9, 1974.

Presidents, Vice Presidents, Congresses

	President	Service		Vice President	Congress
1	George Washington	Apr. 30, 1789—Mar. 3, 1797	1	John Adams	1, 2, 3, 4
2	John Adams	Mar. 4, 1797—Mar. 3, 1801	2	Thomas Jefferson	5, 6
3	Thomas Jefferson	Mar. 4, 1801—Mar. 3, 1805	3	Aaron Burr	7, 8
	"	Mar. 4, 1805—Mar. 3, 1809	4	George Clinton	9, 10
4	James Madison	Mar. 4, 1809—Mar. 3, 1813		"(1)	11, 12
	"	Mar. 4, 1813—Mar. 3, 1817	5	Elbridge Gerry (2)	13, 14
5	James Monroe	Mar. 4, 1817—Mar. 3, 1825	6	Daniel D. Tompkins	15, 16, 17, 18
6	John Quincy Adams	Mar. 4, 1825—Mar. 3, 1829	7	John C. Calhoun	19, 20
7	Andrew Jackson	Mar. 4, 1829—Mar. 3, 1833		"(3)	21, 22
	"	Mar. 4, 1833—Mar. 3, 1837	8	Martin Van Buren	23, 24
8	Martin Van Buren	Mar. 4, 1837—Mar. 3, 1841	9	Richard M. Johnson	25, 26
9	William Henry Harrison (4)	Mar. 4, 1841—Apr. 4, 1841	10	John Tyler	27
10	John Tyler	Apr. 6, 1841—Mar. 3, 1845			27, 28
11	James K. Polk	Mar. 4, 1845—Mar. 3, 1849	11	George M. Dallas	29, 30
12	Zachary Taylor (4)	Mar. 5, 1849—July 9, 1850	12	Millard Fillmore	31
13	Millard Fillmore	July 10, 1850—Mar. 3, 1853			31, 32
14	Franklin Pierce	Mar. 4, 1853—Mar. 3, 1857	13	William R. King (5)	33, 34
15	James Buchanan	Mar. 4, 1857—Mar. 3, 1861	14	John C. Breckinridge	35, 36
16	Abraham Lincoln	Mar. 4, 1861—Mar. 3, 1865	15	Hannibal Hamlin	37, 38
	"(4)	Mar. 4, 1865—Apr. 15, 1865	16	Andrew Johnson	39
17	Andrew Johnson	Apr. 15, 1865—Mar. 3, 1869			39, 40
18	Ulysses S. Grant	Mar. 4, 1869—Mar. 3, 1873	17	Schuyler Colfax	41, 42
	"	Mar. 4, 1873—Mar. 3, 1877	18	Henry Wilson (6)	43, 44
19	Rutherford B. Hayes	Mar. 4, 1877—Mar. 3, 1881	19	William A. Wheeler	45, 46
20	James A. Garfield (4)	Mar. 4, 1881—Sept. 19, 1881	20	Chester A. Arthur	47
21	Chester A. Arthur	Sept. 20, 1881—Mar. 3, 1885			47, 48
22	Grover Cleveland (7)	Mar. 4, 1885—Mar. 3, 1889	21	Thomas A. Hendricks (8)	49, 50
23	Benjamin Harrison	Mar. 4, 1889—Mar. 3, 1893	22	Levi P. Morton	51, 52
24	Grover Cleveland (7)	Mar. 4, 1893—Mar. 3, 1897	23	Adlai E. Stevenson	53, 54
25	William McKinley	Mar. 4, 1897—Mar. 3, 1901	24	Garret A. Hobart (9)	55, 56
	"(4)	Mar. 4, 1901—Sept. 14, 1901	25	Theodore Roosevelt	57
26	Theodore Roosevelt	Sept. 14, 1901—Mar. 3, 1905			57, 58
	"	Mar. 4, 1905—Mar. 3, 1909	26	Charles W. Fairbanks	59, 60
27	William H. Taft	Mar. 4, 1909—Mar. 3, 1913	27	James S. Sherman (10)	61, 62
28	Woodrow Wilson	Mar. 4, 1913—Mar. 3, 1921	28	Thomas R. Marshall	63, 64, 65, 66

	President	Service		Vice President	Congress
29	Warren G. Harding (4)	Mar. 4, 1921—Aug. 2, 1923	29	Calvin Coolidge	67
30	Calvin Coolidge	Aug. 3, 1923—Mar. 3, 1925			68
	"	Mar. 4, 1925—Mar. 3, 1929	30	Charles G. Dawes	69, 70
31	Herbert C. Hoover	Mar. 4, 1929—Mar. 3, 1933	31	Charles Curtis	71, 72
32	Franklin D. Roosevelt (16)	Mar. 4, 1933—Jan. 20, 1941	32	John N. Garner	73, 74, 75, 76
	"	Jan. 20, 1941—Jan. 20, 1945	33	Henry A. Wallace	77, 78
	"(4)	Jan. 20, 1945—Apr. 12, 1945	34	Harry S. Truman	79
33	Harry S. Truman	Apr. 12, 1945—Jan. 20, 1949			79, 80
	"	Jan. 20, 1949—Jan. 20, 1953	35	Alben W. Barkley	81, 82
34	Dwight D. Eisenhower	Jan. 20, 1953—Jan. 20, 1961	36	Richard M. Nixon	83, 84, 85, 86
35	John F. Kennedy (4)	Jan. 20, 1961—Nov. 22, 1963	37	Lyndon B. Johnson	87, 88
36	Lyndon B. Johnson	Nov. 22, 1963—Jan. 20, 1965			88
	"	Jan. 20, 1965—Jan. 20, 1969	38	Hubert H. Humphrey	89, 90
37	Richard M. Nixon	Jan. 20, 1969—Jan. 20, 1973	39	Spiro T. Agnew (11)	91, 92, 93
	"(12)	Jan. 20, 1973—Aug. 9, 1974	40	Gerald R. Ford (13)	93
38	Gerald R. Ford (14)	Aug. 9, 1974—Jan. 20, 1977	41	Nelson A. Rockefeller (15)	93, 94
39	Jimmy (James Earl) Carter	Jan. 20, 1977—Jan. 20, 1981	42	Walter F. Mondale	95, 96
40	Ronald Reagan	Jan. 20, 1981—Jan. 20, 1989	43	George Bush	97, 98, 99, 100
41	George Bush	Jan. 20, 1989—Jan. 20, 1993	44	Dan Quayle	101, 102
42	Bill Clinton	Jan. 20, 1993—	45	Al Gore	103

(1) Died Apr. 20, 1812. (2) Died Nov. 23, 1814. (3) Resigned Dec. 28, 1832, to become U.S. Senator. (4) Died in office. (5) Died Apr. 18, 1853. (6) Died Nov. 22, 1875. (7) Terms not consecutive. (8) Died Nov. 25, 1885. (9) Died Nov. 21, 1899. (10) Died Oct. 30, 1912. (11) Resigned Oct. 10, 1973. (12) Resigned Aug. 9, 1974. (13) First non-elected vice president, chosen under 25th Amendment procedure. (14) First non-elected president. (15) 2d non-elected vice president. (16) First president to be inaugurated under 20th Amendment, Jan. 20, 1937.

Vice Presidents of the U.S.

The numerals given vice presidents do not coincide with those given presidents, because some presidents had none and some had more than one.

	Name	Birthplace	Year	Home	Inaug.	Politics	Place of death	Year	Age
1	John Adams	Quincy, Mass.	1735	Mass.	1789	Fed.	Quincy, Mass.	1826	90
2	Thomas Jefferson	Shadwell, Va.	1743	Va.	1797	Dem.-Rep.	Monticello, Va.	1826	83
3	Aaron Burr	Newark, N.J.	1756	N.Y.	1801	Dem.-Rep.	Staten Island, N.Y.	1836	80
4	George Clinton	Ulster Co., N.Y.	1739	N.Y.	1805	Dem.-Rep.	Washington, D.C.	1812	73
5	Elbridge Gerry	Marblehead, Mass.	1744	Mass.	1813	Dem.-Rep.	Washington, D.C.	1814	70
6	Daniel D. Tompkins	Scarsdale, N.Y.	1774	N.Y.	1817	Dem.-Rep.	Staten Island, N.Y.	1825	51
7	John C. Calhoun(1)	Abbeville, S.C.	1782	S.C.	1825	Dem.-Rep.	Washington, D.C.	1850	68
8	Martin Van Buren	Kinderhook, N.Y.	1782	N.Y.	1833	Dem.	Kinderhook, N.Y.	1862	79
9	Richard M. Johnson	Louisville, Ky.	1780	Ky.	1837	Dem.	Frankfort, Ky.	1850	70
10	John Tyler	Greenway, Va.	1790	Va.	1841	Whig	Richmond, Va.	1862	71
11	George M. Dallas	Philadelphia, Pa.	1792	Pa.	1845	Dem.	Philadelphia, Pa.	1864	72
12	Millard Fillmore	Summerhill, N.Y.	1800	N.Y.	1849	Whig	Buffalo, N.Y.	1874	74
13	William R. King	Sampson Co., N.C.	1786	Ala.	1853	Dem.	Dallas Co., Ala.	1853	67
14	John C. Breckinridge	Lexington, Ky.	1821	Ky.	1857	Dem.	Lexington, Ky.	1875	54
15	Hannibal Hamlin	Paris, Me.	1809	Me.	1861	Rep.	Bangor, Me.	1891	81
16	Andrew Johnson	Raleigh, N.C.	1808	Tenn.	1865	(2)	Carter Co., Tenn.	1875	66
17	Schuyler Colfax	New York, N.Y.	1823	Ind.	1869	Rep.	Mankato, Minn.	1885	62
18	Henry Wilson	Farmington, N.H.	1812	Mass.	1873	Rep.	Washington, D.C.	1875	63
19	William A. Wheeler	Malone, N.Y.	1819	N.Y.	1877	Rep.	Malone, N.Y.	1887	68
20	Chester A. Arthur	Fairfield, Vt.	1829	N.Y.	1881	Rep.	New York, N.Y.	1886	57
21	Thomas A. Hendricks	Muskingum Co., Oh.	1819	Ind.	1885	Dem.	Indianapolis, Ind.	1885	66
22	Levi P. Morton	Shoreham, Vt.	1824	N.Y.	1889	Rep.	Rhinebeck, N.Y.	1920	96
23	Adlai E. Stevenson(3)	Christian Co., Ky.	1835	Ill.	1893	Dem.	Chicago, Ill.	1914	78
24	Garret A. Hobart	Long Branch, N.J.	1844	N.J.	1897	Rep.	Paterson, N.J.	1899	55
25	Theodore Roosevelt	New York, N.Y.	1858	N.Y.	1901	Rep.	Oyster Bay, N.Y.	1919	60
26	Charles W. Fairbanks	Unionville Centre, Oh.	1852	Ind.	1905	Rep.	Indianapolis, Ind.	1918	66
27	James S. Sherman	Utica, N.Y.	1855	N.Y.	1909	Rep.	Utica, N.Y.	1912	57
28	Thomas R. Marshall	N. Manchester, Ind.	1854	Ind.	1913	Dem.	Washington, D.C.	1925	71
29	Calvin Coolidge	Plymouth, Vt.	1872	Mass.	1921	Rep.	Northampton, Mass.	1933	60
30	Charles G. Dawes	Marietta, Oh.	1865	Ill.	1925	Rep.	Evanston, Ill.	1951	85
31	Charles Curtis	Topeka, Kan.	1860	Kan.	1929	Rep.	Washington, D.C.	1936	76
32	John Nance Garner	Red River Co., Tex.	1868	Tex.	1933	Dem.	Uvalde, Tex.	1967	98
33	Henry Agard Wallace	Adair County, Ia.	1888	Iowa	1941	Dem.	Danbury, Conn.	1965	77
34	Harry S. Truman	Lamar, Mo.	1884	Mo.	1945	Dem.	Kansas City, Mo.	1972	88
35	Alben W. Barkley	Graves County, Ky.	1877	Ky.	1949	Dem.	Lexington, Va.	1956	78
36	Richard M. Nixon	Yorba Linda, Cal.	1913	Cal.	1953	Rep.	New York, N.Y.	1994	81
37	Lyndon B. Johnson	Johnson City, Tex.	1908	Tex.	1961	Dem.	San Antonio, Tex.	1973	64
38	Hubert H. Humphrey	Wallace, S.D.	1911	Minn.	1965	Dem.	Waverly, Minn.	1978	66
39	Spiro T. Agnew (4)	Baltimore, Md.	1918	Md.	1969	Rep.			
40	Gerald R. Ford	Omaha, Neb.	1913	Mich.	1973	Rep.			
41	Nelson A. Rockefeller	Bar Harbor, Me.	1908	N.Y.	1974	Rep.	New York, N.Y.	1979	70
42	Walter F. Mondale	Ceylon, Minn.	1928	Minn.	1977	Dem.			
43	George Bush	Milton, Mass.	1924	Tex.	1981	Rep.			
44	Dan Quayle	Indianapolis, Ind.	1947	Ind.	1989	Rep.			
45	Al Gore	Washington, D.C.	1948	Tenn.	1993	Dem.			

(1) John C. Calhoun resigned Dec. 28, 1832, having been elected to the Senate to fill a vacancy. (2) Andrew Johnson — a Democrat nominated by Republicans and elected with Lincoln on the National Union Ticket. (3) Adlai E. Stevenson, 23d vice president, was grandfather of Democratic candidate for president, 1952 and 1956. (4) Resigned Oct. 10, 1973.

TAXES

Federal Income Tax

Source: George W. Smith III, CPA, Nationally Syndicated Tax Author and Columnist

During the past decade, the U.S. Congress enacted some of the most dramatic changes in American tax law. The Tax Reform Act of 1986 was the most extensive overhaul of the tax code since 1954. More recently, the Omnibus Budget Reconciliation Act of 1993 enacted further tax changes, many of which took effect starting in 1994.

New Tax Provisions Taking Effect in 1994

Social Security Benefits. Effective Jan. 1, 1994, retirees whose incomes, including half their Social Security benefits, exceed $34,000 for single individuals or $44,000 for married couples filing jointly will pay income tax on a maximum of 85% of their Social Security benefits. Prior law, taxing up to 50% of these benefits, will continue to apply for retirees whose incomes, including half their Social Security benefits, exceed $25,000 for singles or $32,000 for married taxpayers filing jointly.

Moving Expense Deductions. Beginning in 1994, moving expense deductions associated with a new job are much more restricted. Meals while traveling, living expenses in temporary quarters, pre-move house-hunting trips, and expenses pertaining to the sale, purchase, or rental of an individual's residence are no longer deductible. However, a taxpayer will no longer need to itemize deductions to take a qualified moving expense deduction.

Business Meals and Entertainment. Congress reduced the deduction for qualified business meals and entertainment expenses in 1994 from 80% to 50%.

Club Dues. Beginning in 1994, Congress eliminated the entire business expense deduction for dues in business, social, athletic, luncheon, sporting, and country clubs, including airport and hotel clubs.

Lobbying Expenses. The business deduction for lobbying Congress and federal, state, and local government agencies has been eliminated.

Medicare Tax. Congress repealed the $135,000 ceiling on earned income subject to the payroll tax for Medicare. Effective Jan. 1, 1994, all wages are subject to the Medicare tax of 1.45% (paid by both the employer and the employee). Individuals will pay a 2.9% Medicare tax on all net self-employment income.

Child Care Credit. For 1994, the Young Child Care Credit and the Supplemental Health Insurance Credit were repealed.

Rental Passive Losses. Effective Jan. 1, 1994, certain real estate professionals will now be able to use losses from rental real estate to offset other nonpassive income such as wages and self-employment profits.

Charitable Contributions. Taxpayers deducting individual charitable contributions of $250 or more now must obtain written substantiation from the charity before filing a tax return. If a contribution of more than $75 is partly for goods and partly for services, the written statement must show the breakdown.

Retirement Plans. The maximum allowable compensation limit for a tax-qualified retirement plan participant was reduced from $235,840 to $150,000 for 1994. This includes all Profit Sharing, 401(k), Money Purchase Pension, Simplified Employee Pension (SEP), and Defined Benefit plans.

Estimated Taxes. If a taxpayer expects to owe $500 or more of taxes, he or she is now required to file estimated ncome tax payments unless current income tax withholding and credits are 100% of the tax owed on the prior year's return. The percentage increases to 110% of the previous year's tax if adjusted gross income for the year is more than $150,000 ($75,000 if married filing separately). Different rules apply for farmers and people engaged in commercial fishing.

Travel Expenses for Another Individual. Taxpayers can no longer deduct travel expenses paid for another individual who accompanies them on a business trip unless the individual:

(1) Is their employee;
(2) Has a bona fide business purpose for travel;
(3) Would otherwise be allowed to deduct the travel expense.

Other Recent Tax Law Changes and Tax Developments

As in 1993, there are currently 5 individual tax rates: 15%, 28%, 31%, 36%, and 39.6%. Both the 1994 Income Tax Tables and the 1994 Tax Rate Schedules are adjusted so that inflation will not increase an individual's tax.

The maximum income tax rate on net long-term capital gains for individuals, estates, and trusts remains at 28%.

Married couples filing jointly and single individuals can file Form 1040EZ, if they had no dependents, were not 65 or older or blind, had taxable income of less than $50,000, and had only wages, salaries, tips, and not more than $400 of interest income.

Effective Jan. 1, 1994, the annual limit on elective deferrals to 401(k) plans increased to $9,240 from $8,994 for 1993.

In 1994 an individual may not claim an exemption for a dependent child who qualifies as a full-time student and is over age 23 at the end of the year unless the child's gross income is less than $2,450.

Interest earned on Series EE bonds issued in 1990 or later may be exempt from federal income tax if used to pay tuition and fees for a taxpayer, spouse, or dependent to attend a college, university, or qualified technical school during the year the bonds are redeemed.

A person who buys a new vehicle powered primarily by an electric motor and with 4 wheels may be eligible for an income tax credit of 10% of the cost of the vehicle if the vehicle is placed in service between July 1, 1993, and Dec. 31, 2004. The maximum credit is $4,000 per qualified electric vehicle.

Individuals must file a tax return if they have net earnings of $400 or more from self-employment.

Parents may elect to include on their income tax return the unearned income of a dependent child under age 14 whose income is more than $500 but less than $5,000. The income must consist solely of interest and dividends. Form 8814, Parent's Election to Report Child's Interest and Dividends, is required to report this income. If a parent is able to elect to include the child's income on the parent's tax return, the child is not required to file a return. This election is not available, however, if estimated tax payments were made in the child's name.

For individuals age 55 or over, the 3-out-of-5-year home-use rule for the sale of a principal residence has been expanded. Certain incapacitated individuals who reside in state-licensed facilities may exclude from gross income up to $125,000 of gain resulting from the sale of their home if the house was used as their principal residence for at least one year out of the past 5 years. This is a once-in-a-lifetime exclusion.

The IRS provides videotaped instructions in English and in Spanish for completing and assisting in the preparation of tax returns. These tapes are available at participating libraries. Individuals can also call their local IRS office for assistance.

Various federal tax forms and tax instructions are now printed in Spanish.

The Unemployment Compensation Amendment Act of 1992 made 3 important changes to the treatment of distributions from qualified pension plans and annuities:

(1) Made most pension plan distributions eligible for rollovers;
(2) Required plans to permit direct rollovers;
(3) Imposed a mandatory federal withholding of 20% on distributions that are not directly rolled over into another retirement plan.

A taxpayer must list the Social Security number of any dependent claimed on his or her income tax return who is at least 1 year old by the end of the tax year. The penalty for noncompliance can be $50 per omitted number; the IRS also may deny exemption.

If a dependent child with taxable income cannot file an income tax return, a parent, guardian, or other legally responsible person must file the return for the child. The parent or guardian may be held liable for the unpaid income tax on the child's taxable income.

A business deduction is not allowed for the base rate charged on the first telephone line into a personal residence. This disallowance does not affect the deductibility of long distance calls or optional services such as call waiting, call forwarding,

3-way calling, or extra directory listings, as long as they are business related.

For 1994, the wage base for Social Security tax was increased to $60,600. The Social Security tax rate is 6.2%, paid by both employer and employee. (The combined Social Security and Medicare tax rate is 7.65%.)

Jury-duty pay returned by an employee to an employer in exchange for his or her normal salary can be deducted by the employee as an adjustment to income.

The business use of a cellular phone must be for the convenience of the employer and a condition of employment to be an allowable business deduction for employees.

Self-employed persons are entitled to an income tax deduction of one-half of their total Social Security self-employment tax liability.

Mar. 28, 1994, the IRS declared that "seller-paid points" on the purchase of a principal residence can be deducted by the buyer. Individuals who have purchased a home since 1991 should file amended tax returns for a possible refund.

A sole proprietor claiming a home office deduction on Schedule C, Profit or Loss From Business, must file Form 8829, Expenses for Business Use of Your Home, with his or her income tax return.

For 1994, the standard mileage rate for business use of an automobile was increased to 29 cents per mile for all business miles driven. U.S. Postal Service employees who collect or deliver mail on a rural route can use a special standard mileage rate of 43.5 cents per mile.

A maximum of $155 per month for employer-provided parking is tax free to an employee. An employee may exclude up to $60 a month for mass-transit passes.

Congress did not repeal the luxury automobile excise tax. For 1994, a passenger car costing more than $32,000 is subject to this tax.

Travel expenses that are reimbursed to employees and that include an additional Saturday night's lodging and meals in order to take advantage of lower air fares for roundtrip tickets can be deducted by the company and excluded from employees' gross income. These reimbursements are not subject to employment and withholding taxes.

The maximum earned income that retirees under the age of 65 can receive in 1994 without losing all or part of their Social Security benefits increased to $8,040. For individuals age 65 through age 69, the maximum amount for 1994 is $11,160. Individuals receiving Social Security benefits who are age 70 or over can receive full benefits regardless of earnings.

Owners of new diesel-powered highway automobiles not purchased for resale may be entitled to a tax credit of $102; the credit is $198 for the purchase of a diesel-powered light van or truck.

Certain itemized deductions may be limited if the taxpayer's adjusted gross income for 1994 is more than $111,800, or more than $55,900 if married filing separately.

The IRS telephone service for hearing-impaired persons is available for taxpayers who have access to TDD equipment. The toll-free number is 1-800-829-4059.

Individuals filing returns electronically can have their refund deposited directly into their checking or savings account.

Expenses paid for assignments away from home that last for more than one year in a single location are no longer considered "temporary" and are no longer deductible.

Capital gains can now be included in investment income when figuring the limit on the investment interest deduction. However, the taxpayer may have to reduce the amount of net long-term capital gain that is eligible for the maximum 28% capital gains tax rate in order to offset the additional investment interest deduction.

The "Section 179 Expense" deduction election to expense each year certain depreciable business assets increased to $17,500.

Goodwill, patents, copyrights, client lists, and certain other intangible assets now can be amortized over a 15-year period.

1994 Individual Tax Rates

There are 5 tax rates for 1994: 15%, 28%, 31%, 36%, and 39.6%. The dollar bracket amounts are adjusted each year for inflation.

Single

Tax Rate	Taxable Income
15%	$0 to $22,750
28%	$22,751 to $55,100
31%	$55,101 to $115,000
36%	$115,001 to $250,000
39.6%	More than $250,000

Married Filing Jointly or Qualifying Widow(er)

Tax Rate	Taxable Income
15%	$0 to $38,000
28%	$38,001 to $91,850
31%	$91,851 to $140,000
36%	$140,001 to $250,000
39.6%	More than $250,000

Married Filing Separately

Tax Rate	Taxable Income
15%	$0 to $19,000
28%	$19,001 to $45,925
31%	$45,926 to $70,000
36%	$70,001 to $125,000
39.6%	More than $125,000

Head of Household

Tax Rate	Taxable Income
15%	$0 to $30,500
28%	$30,501 to $78,700
31%	$78,701 to $127,500
36%	$127,501 to $250,000
39.6%	More than $250,000

The maximum tax rate on net long-term capital gains for an individual, estate, or trust is 28%.

The alternative minimum tax rate for noncorporate taxpayers is 26% for alternative minimum taxable income less the exemption amount up to $175,000 ($87,500 for married individuals filing separately). Above that dollar level, a 28% rate applies.

Standard Deduction

The standard deduction is a flat dollar amount that is subtracted from the adjusted gross income of taxpayers who do not itemize their deductions. The amount of the basic standard deduction depends on the taxpayer's filing status and is adjusted annually for inflation. Standard deductions for 1994 are:

1994 Basic Standard Deduction

Single	$3,800
Married filing jointly or qualifying widow(er)	$6,350
Married filing separately	$3,175
Head of household	$5,600

Taxpayers with itemized deductions such as medical expenses, property taxes, investment and home mortgage interest, charitable contributions, and gambling losses totaling more than the standard deduction amount should not use the standard deduction but should itemize their deductions.

An individual claimed as a dependent on another person's income tax return may claim on his or her own tax return only the larger of $600 or the amount of earned income up to the amount of the basic standard deduction that the taxpayer would normally be allowed. Earned income includes wages, salaries, commissions, and tips. It also includes net profit from self-employment received as compensation for personal services rendered. Any part of a scholarship or fellowship grant that must be included in gross income is also earned income.

Example 1: During 1994, a dependent parent, age 60, had unearned income (interest and dividends) of $1,700. She had no earned income. Her basic standard deduction would be $600. She would have taxable income of $1,100. A dependent cannot claim his or her own personal exemption.

Example 2: A dependent son had $10,000 of unearned income and $100 of earned income. He is entitled to a $600 standard deduction. He is limited to this amount because he is a dependent and his earned income is less than $600. The taxpayer would, therefore, have $9,500 in taxable income.

Example 3: A dependent daughter with $4,000 of earned income and $600 of unearned income would claim a maximum $3,800 standard deduction because her earned income of $4,000 is greater than the standard deduction. She would have taxable income of $800.

Additional Standard Deduction for Age and Blindness

Elderly or blind taxpayers may claim an additional standard deduction in addition to the basic standard deduction. Taxpayers who are age 65 or over or are blind at the end of 1994 qualify. Individuals who claim the additional standard deduction because of blindness must attach a doctor's statement to that effect to their income tax return.

1994 Additional Standard Deduction

Single or head of household, age 65 or over OR blind	$ 950
Single or head of household, age 65 or over AND blind	$1,900
Married filing jointly or qualifying widow(er), age 65 or over OR blind (per person)	$ 750
Married filing jointly or qualifying widow(er), age 65 or over AND blind (per person)	$1,500
Married filing separately, age 65 or over OR blind	$ 750
Married filing separately, age 65 or over AND blind	$1,500

Example 1: A single, 65-year-old individual would have a standard deduction of $4,750 computed as follows:

Basic standard deduction for a single person	$3,800
Additional standard deduction for age	950
Total	$4,750

Example 2: A 70-year-old husband and a 58-year-old blind wife filing jointly would be entitled to a standard deduction totaling $7,850 computed as follows:

Basic standard deduction for married filing jointly	$6,350
Additional standard deduction for (husband's) age	750
Additional standard deduction for (wife's) blindness	750
Total	$7,850

Taxpayers who itemize their deductions cannot claim the additional or basic standard deductions.

Dependent and Personal Exemptions

The exemption amount for 1994 has been increased to $2,450. This amount is adjusted each year for inflation.

The deduction for exemptions is phased out for certain higher income taxpayers. The exemption amount is reduced by 2% for each $2,500 ($1,250 for married filing separately) or a fraction thereof by which the adjusted gross income for 1994 exceeds the following threshold amount:

Married filing jointly	$167,700
Qualifying widow(er)	$167,700
Head of household	$139,750
Single	$111,800
Married filing separately	$ 83,850

The exemption amount is fully phased out when adjusted gross income is more than $122,500 ($61,250 for married filing separately) over the threshold amount.

Adjustments to Income

Individual Retirement Accounts (IRAs)

Taxpayers who are not covered by a qualified employer retirement plan may take an IRA deduction up to the lesser of $2,000 or the amount of their earned income, regardless of their total income. Income earned from IRAs will remain tax-free until the taxpayer withdraws it.

Taxpayers may still make contributions to their IRAs even if they are covered by an employer-sponsored qualified retirement plan. However, the amount that can be deducted on their income tax return is limited if they are covered by a qualified retirement plan. If either husband or wife participates in a qualified plan, *both* spouses are subject to these limitations.

For 1994, married taxpayers filing jointly with adjusted gross income of $40,000 or less may take an IRA deduction whether or not either one is an active participant in a qualified retirement plan. Single taxpayers in a qualified retirement plan may also deduct IRA contributions if their adjusted gross income is $25,000 or less.

The IRA deduction is phased out over the next $10,000 of adjusted gross income if taxpayers are active participants in a qualified retirement plan. Consequently, married couples filing jointly with adjusted gross income of $50,000 or more, or single filers with adjusted gross income of $35,000 or more, may not deduct any contributions to their IRAs.

A qualified retirement plan generally includes: (1) a qualified pension, profit-sharing, or stock bonus plan; (2) a qualified annuity plan; (3) a simplified employee pension plan; or (4) a plan established for its employees by federal, state, or local government or by an agency of these entities.

Moving Expenses

Taxpayers who change jobs during the year usually can deduct part of their moving expenses. These expenses include the cost of moving household goods and traveling to their new home. To qualify, the move must be for changing job locations or starting a new job and must also meet the distance and time tests.

Starting Jan. 1, 1994, expenses for moving household goods and traveling to a new home have some new limitations. The tax law was modified in 4 ways:

(1) The distance test is extended form 35 to 50 miles.

(2) Pre-move house-hunting trips, temporary living expenses, and any expenses that pertain to the sale, purchase, or rental of an individual's residence are no longer deductible. Meals while traveling to the new location also are no longer deductible.

(3) Qualified moving expenses paid or reimbursed by the taxpayer's employer are excludable from gross income.

(4) Moving expenses are deductible as an adjustment to income and not as an itemized deduction on Schedule A.

Any reimbursements, directly or indirectly, that are not qualified moving expenses must be included in gross income as compensation for services and are fully taxable. Moves within the U.S. are reported on Form 3903, Moving Expenses.

Itemized Deductions

- Many elective cosmetic surgeries, including hair transplants and other similar procedures, are no longer deductible medical expenses. Only cosmetic surgery for congenital abnormality, personal injury resulting from an accident or trauma, or a disfiguring disease is allowed as a medical deduction. Only the amount of medical expenses that exceeds 7.5% of the taxpayer's adjusted gross income is deductible.
- Investment interest is deductible only to the extent of net investment income. Any excess is carried over to future years.
- Most mortgage interest on a taxpayer's first and second homes remains fully deductible; however, there are limitations.
- Interest on home equity loans is deductible, but only up to the first $100,000 in equity debt.
- State and local income taxes, real estate taxes, and personal property taxes remain fully deductible. Sales taxes are not deductible.
- Casualty and theft losses are deductible subject to the $100 limitation rule and the 10% of adjusted gross income provision.
- Miscellaneous items, such as union and professional dues, tax preparation fees, safe deposit box rental expense, and employee business expenses, are deductible, but only the amount that exceeds 2% of the taxpayer's adjusted gross income.
- An individual can deduct gambling losses such as the cost of lottery tickets, but only up to the amount of the winnings reported on page 1, Form 1040.

Employee Business Expenses

All employee business expenses, including travel, automobile, telephone, gifts, and entertainment, are deductible on Schedule A as miscellaneous itemized deductions. Only 50% of the cost of customer meals and entertainment is now deductible. These expenses are then subject to the 2% of the taxpayer's adjusted gross income limitation for miscellaneous deductions. Country club dues are no longer deductible.

Itemized Deduction Reduction

Many itemized deductions otherwise allowed are further reduced by the lesser of 3% of a taxpayer's adjusted gross income in excess of $111,800 ($55,900 for married taxpayers filing separately) or 80% of the amount of these itemized deductions otherwise allowable for the year. These amounts are adjusted each year for inflation.

This provision does not affect medical expenses, investment interest expense, casualty losses, or gambling losses to the extent of gambling gains.

Earned Income Credit

Low-income workers who have dependent children and maintain a household are eligible for a refundable earned income credit. The credit for 1994 is calculated on earned income such as wages and tips. The maximum credit for a taxpayer with one qualifying child is $2,038. However, the earned income credit is (fully) phased out once an individual's adjusted gross income reaches $23,753. For a taxpayer with 2 or more qualifying children, the maximum credit is $2,527 and is phased out once an individual's adjusted gross income reaches $25,293.

If an individual qualifies, this credit is refundable even if the taxpayer is not required to file an income tax return. However, a tax return must be filed to receive this credit. To assist individuals, the IRS publishes a chart showing the earned income credit at various levels of income. This chart is available free at any IRS office. The IRS will also assist individuals in preparing this form.

Starting in 1994, the earned income tax credit is extended to include persons who work and do not have a qualifying child. The maximum credit is $306. To qualify:

(1) Earned income and adjusted gross income must be less than $9,000;

(2) An individual or spouse must be at least 25 years old but less than 65;

(3) An individual cannot be claimed as a dependent on another's return.

Taxing Children's Income

A child who may be claimed as a dependent by another taxpayer may not claim his or her own personal exemption even if the exemption is not actually claimed on the other taxpayer's return. Children under age 14 with at least one living parent may use up to $600 of their standard deduction against unearned income. Unearned income includes dividend and interest income. If the child's unearned income is more than $1,200, that income will be taxed at the child's tax rate or at the parent's rate, whichever is higher.

Parents have the option of including a child's unearned income on their tax return. However, when this income is included on the parents' tax return, all the income over $1,000 is subject to the higher tax rate. Therefore, if the child includes the unearned income on his or her tax return, the child could receive the benefit of a lower tax rate on an additional $200 of unearned income.

When to File

U.S. individual income tax returns for 1994 are required to be filed with the IRS no later than Monday, Apr. 17, 1995.

What if an individual can't file on time? File Form 4868, Application for Automatic Extension of Time to File U.S. Individual Income Tax Return. This gives the taxpayer an automatic 4-month extension of time to file, until Tuesday, Aug. 15, 1995. However, this is not an extension of time to pay the tax. Any federal income tax owed must be paid to the IRS by midnight April 17, 1995; otherwise, penalties and interest may be assessed for any income tax balance not paid.

Who Must File

Whether a U.S. citizen or resident alien living in the U.S. must file an income tax return depends on the person's gross income, filing status, and age.

Generally, a U.S. citizen or resident alien will have to file a return if the person's gross income for the year is at least as much as the amount shown in the following table.

Filing Status	1994 Gross Income
Single	
• Under 65	$ 6,250
• 65 or older	7,200
Married filing jointly	
• Both spouses under 65	11,250
• One spouse 65 or older	12,000
• Both spouses 65 or older	12,750
Married filing separately	2,450
Head of Household	
• Under 65	8,050
• 65 or older	9,000
Qualifying widow(er)	
• Under 65	8,800
• 65 or older	9,550

Example: John and Mary Smith intend to file a joint return for 1994. John's income is entirely from wages. Mary receives no income subject to tax. Neither John nor Mary is blind. John is 67 years old, but Mary will not be 65 until next year. For 1994, their combined gross income subject to tax will be $12,200. They will have to file a tax return because their gross income will be at least $12,000.

If Mary were age 65, they would not have to file a 1994 tax return because their gross income would be less than $12,750 as shown in the table.

Some Exceptions to Filing Requirements. A tax return must be filed if:

- Net earnings from self-employment for the year are $400 or more.
- Advance earned income credit payments were received during the year from an employer.
- A taxpayer wants to receive the earned income credit.
- A taxpayer expects an income tax refund.
- Gross income is less than the filing requirement amount, but additional taxes are owed for:
  - Social Security tax on unreported tips.
  - Alternative minimum tax.
  - Recapture of investment credit.
  - Tax attributable to qualified retirement distributions (including IRAs), annuities, and modified endowment contracts.

Which Form to File

Use either Form 1040EZ or Form 1040A unless the filing of Form 1040 lets you pay a lower tax or unless the rules say you must file Form 1040. The 1040EZ and 1040A are generally shorter and easier to complete than the longer Form 1040.

You may be able to use Form 1040EZ if:

- You are single or married filing jointly and do not claim any dependents.
- You are not 65 or older or blind.
- You have income only from wages, salaries, tips, or taxable scholarships or fellowships and not more than $400 of interest income.
- Your taxable income is less than $50,000.
- You do not itemize deductions, claim any adjustments to income, or have tax credits.
- You did not receive any advanced earned income credit payments.
- You did not make estimated tax payments.
- You file on or before Monday, Apr. 17, 1995. You cannot use Form 1040EZ after Apr. 17 even if you have filed for an extension.

You may be able to use Form 1040A if:

- You have income from wages, salaries, tips, taxable scholarships or fellowships, interest, and dividends.

(continued)

- You have income from IRA distributions, pensions, annuities, unemployment compensation, and Social Security or railroad retirement benefits.
- Your taxable income is less than $50,000.
- You do not itemize deductions.
- You claim a deduction for qualified contributions to an IRA.
- You claim a credit for child and dependent care expenses, credit for the elderly or the disabled, or the earned income credit.
- You take the education exclusion for interest income earned from Series EE U.S. Savings Bonds.
- You have made estimated tax payments.
- You filed for an extension of time to file.

Even if you do meet the above tests, you will have to file the longer Form 1040 if any of the following situations apply:

- Your taxable income is $50,000 or more.
- You itemize deductions.
- You receive any nontaxable dividends or capital gain distributions.
- You have foreign bank accounts and/or foreign trusts.
- You have taxable refunds of state or local income taxes.
- You have business, farm, or rental income.
- You sold or exchanged capital assets or business property.
- You have additional miscellaneous income not allowed on Form 1040EZ or 1040A such as alimony or lottery winnings.
- You have additional adjustments to income such as alimony paid.
- You can claim a foreign tax credit or certain other credits to which you are entitled.
- You have other taxes such as self-employment tax or the alternative minimum tax.
- You file any additional required forms, such as:

Form 2555, Foreign Earned Income

Form 3903, Moving Expenses

Form 4972, Tax on Lump-Sum Distributions

Form 5329, Return for Additional Taxes Attributable to Qualified Retirement Plans (including IRAs), Annuities, and Modified Endowment Contracts

Form 8814, Parent's Election to Report Child's Interest and Dividends

Internal Revenue Service Audit

Although fewer than one out of every 100 individual tax returns will probably be audited this year, the IRS is good at selecting returns for audit that will yield additional income taxes.

If your return is audited and you feel you are not being treated fairly or that proper attention is not being paid to your statements, you have a right to ask for a hearing at the IRS appellate level. If you are still dissatisfied, you can take your case to the U.S. Tax Court. If the total amount in question is less than $10,000, your case can be handled under the Small Tax Case procedures. If you are still dissatisfied, your next move would be the U.S. Circuit Court of Appeals.

Your Rights As a Taxpayer

Congress, responding to complaints that taxpayers were not being treated fairly by the IRS, passed a comprehensive law to force the IRS to explain, in easy-to-understand language, the actions it proposes to take against a taxpayer and to relax some of its audit and collection procedures. This law is called "The Taxpayer Bill of Rights." You can learn more about this law by obtaining a free copy of IRS Publication 1, *Your Rights as a Taxpayer*. Call 1-800-TAX-FORM for a copy.

Federal Gift and Estate Taxes

A federal gift tax return generally must be filed by an individual for gifts made to a person other than a spouse if the total annual gift exceeds $10,000 or if it is a gift of a future interest. Gifts made to any one person not exceeding the annual exclusion of $10,000 (or $20,000 if gifted by a married couple) are not subject to a gift tax. Recipients do not pay federal income tax on gifts when they are transferred to them.

Gifts are reported on Form 709, U.S. Gift (and Generation-Skipping Transfer) Tax Return. Gift tax rates are the same as those for estates.

The federal estate tax is a transfer tax on property "transferred" at the time of the decedent's death. The tax applies to taxable estates of more than $600,000 after taking into acoount taxable gifts and allowable deductions such as charitable bequests. This $600,000 exemption is equivalent to $192,800 in federal gift and estate taxes and is called a unified credit. By virtue of a "marital deduction," there is no federal estate tax on gifts or bequests to an individual's spouse who is a U.S. citizen.

An "estate" includes (but is not limited to) the decedent's cash, securities, personal property, residence, and other real estate holdings. The estate also could include insurance, interest in various trusts, jointly held property, and foreign bank and security accounts.

Form 706, U.S. Estate (and Generation-Skipping Transfer) Tax Return, must be filed by the executor for the estate of every citizen or resident of the U.S. whose gross estate, including taxable gifts and specific exemption, exceeds $600,000. The unified tax rate schedule that applies to gifts also applies to a decedent's estate.

Federal Unified Transfer Tax Rates for Gifts and Estates*

Base Over	But not over	Tentative Tax Amount +	This percent	Of amount over
$ 0	$ 10,000	$ 0	18	$ 0
10,000	20,000	1,800	20	10,000
20,000	40,000	3,800	22	20,000
40,000	60,000	8,200	24	40,000
60,000	80,000	13,000	26	60,000
80,000	100,000	18,200	28	80,000
100,000	150,000	23,800	30	100,000
150,000	250,000	38,800	32	150,000
250,000	500,000	70,800	34	250,000
500,000	750,000	155,800	37	500,000
$ 750,000	1,000,000	$ 248,300	39	$ 750,000
1,000,000	1,250,000	345,800	41	1,000,000
1,250,000	1,500,000	448,300	43	1,250,000
1,500,000	2,000,000	555,800	45	1,500,000
2,000,000	2,500,000	780,800	49	2,000,000
2,500,000	3,000,000	1,025,800	53	2,500,000
3,000,000		1,290,000	55	3,000,000

* Amount of tax due can be reduced by a maximum of $192,800 (the unified credit).

The Omnibus Budget Reconciliation Act of 1993 increased the maximum estate tax rate to 53% for taxable estates in excess of $2.5 million and to 55% for taxable estates in excess of $3 million. A 5% surtax applies to the estate's base amounts between $10 million and $21,040,000.

State Death Tax

Many states impose no death taxes. Some have individual inheritance taxes. And others may take only the amount of the credit computed on the federal estate tax return, Form 706. Some state tax may be due even if there is no federal tax.

In determining the federal estate tax, an individual may take a credit on Form 706 for any inheritance, estate, legacy, or succession taxes paid to any state or to the District of Columbia as the result of the decedent's death.

Because state taxes vary widely, the credit may be less than the total state taxes paid.

Maximum State Death Tax Credit for Estate Tax

Adjusted taxable estate*		Credit is		
At least	But less than	Credit	+	Percent of excess over amount in column 1
$ 0	$ 40,000	$ 0		none
40,000	90,000	0		0.8
90,000	140,000	400		1.6
140,000	240,000	1,200		2.4
240,000	440,000	3,600		3.2
440,000	640,000	10,000		4.0
640,000	840,000	18,000		4.8
840,000	1,040,000	27,600		5.6
1,040,000	1,540,000	38,800		6.4
1,540,000	2,040,000	70,800		7.2
2,040,000	2,540,000	106,800		8.0
$2,540,111	$3,040,000	$ 146,800		8.8
3,040,000	3,540,000	190,800		9.6
3,540,000	4,040,000	238,800		10.4
4,040,000	5,040,000	290,800		11.2
5,040,000	6,040,000	402,800		12.0
6,040,000	7,040,000	522,800		12.8
7,040,000	8,040,000	650,900		13.6
8,040,000	9,040,000	786,800		14.4
9,040,000	10,040,000	930,800		15.2
10,040,000		1,082,800		16.0

*The adjusted taxable estate is the taxable estate reduced $60,000.

Example: If a Florida resident dies with a taxable estate of $3,500,000, the Florida death tax is $229,200. This amount is computed by subtracting $60,000 from $3,500,000 and then using the above chart. The federal estate tax is $1,565,800 minus $192,800 (the federal unified credit), less $229,200 (state death credit), for a balance of $1,143,800.

State Government Individual Income Taxes

Source: U.S. Advisory Commission on Intergovernmental Relations

As of November 1993. Only basic rates, brackets, and exemptions are shown. Local income tax rates, even those mandated by the state, are not included. Taxable income rates and brackets listed below apply to single taxpayers and married taxpayers filing "combined separate" returns in states where this is permitted.

		Taxable Income Brackets		Personal Exemptions			Standard Deduction[a]			
State	Tax Rates (range in percent)	Lowest: Amount Under	Highest: Amount Over	Single	Married-Joint Return	Dependents	Percent	Single	Married-Joint Return	Federal Income Tax Deductible[b]
AL[+]*	2.0-5.0%	$500	$3,000	$1,500	$3,000	$300	20%	$2,000	$4,000	yes
AK				No state income tax						
AZ[c]	3.8-7.0	10,000	150,000	2,100	4,200	2,300	NA	3,500	7,000	no
AR*	1.0-7.0	3,000	25,000	20[d]	40[d]	20[d]	10	1,000	1,000	no
CA[c]*	1.0-11.0	4,666	212,380	64[d]	128[d]	64[d]	NA	2,402	4,804	no
CO				5% of modified taxable income						
CT*	4.5	Flat rate		12,000	24,000	0	NA	NA	NA	NA
DE*[']	3.2-7.7	2,000	40,000	1,250	2,500	1,250	NA	1,300	1,600	no
DC	6.0-9.5	10,000	20,000	1,370	2,740	1,370	NA	2,000	2,000	no
FL				No state income tax						no
GA	1.0-6.0	750	7,000	1,500	3,000	1,500	NA	2,300	3,000	no
HI*	2.0-10.0	1,500	20,500	1,040	2,080	1,040	NA	1,500	1,900	no
ID*	2.0-8.2	1,000	20,000			Same as federal				no
IL*	3.0	Flat rate		1,000	2,000	1,000	NA	NA	NA	no
IN[+]*	3.4	Flat rate		1,000	2,000	1,000	NA	NA	NA	no
IA[c]*	0.4-9.98	1,060	47,700	20[d]	40[d]	15[d]	NA	1,330	3,270	yes
KS*	4.4-7.75	20,000	30,000	2,000	4,000	2,000	NA	3,000	5,000	no
KY[+]*	2.0-6.0	3,000	8,000	20[d]	40[d]	20[d]	NA	650	650	no
LA	2.0-6.0	10,000	50,000	4,500	9,000	1,000	Combined w/Exemptions			yes
ME[c]	2.0-8.5	4,150	16,500	2,100	4,200	2,100	NA	3,700	6,200	no
MD[+]*	2.0-6.0	1,000	100,000	1,200	2,400	1,200	15	2,000	4,000	no
MA*	5.95-12.0	Flat rate		2,200	4,400	1,000	NA	NA	NA	no
MI[+]*	4.6	Flat rate		2,100	4,200	2,100	NA	NA	NA	no
MN	6.0-8.5	14,780	48,550			Same as federal				no
MS	3.0-5.0	5,000	10,000	6,000	9,500	1,500	NA	2,300	3,400	no
MO[+]*	1.5-6.0	1,000	9,000	1,200	2,400	400	NA	Same as federal		yes
MT[c]*	2.0-11.0	1,700	61,100	1,400	2,800	1,360	20	2,620	5,240	yes
NE[c]*	2.62-6.99	2,000	46,750	65[d]	130[d]	65[d]	NA	Same as federal		no
NV				No state income tax						
NH*				Limited income tax						
NJ*	2.0-7.0	20,000	75,000	1,000	2,000	1,500	NA	NA	NA	no
NM	1.8-8.5	5,200	41,600		Same as federal		NA	Same as federal		no
NY[+]*	4.0-7.875	5,500	13,000	0	0	1,000	NA	6,000	9,500	no
NC*	6.0-7.75	12,750	60,000	2,000	4,000	2,000	NA	3,000	5,000	no
ND*				14% of federal income tax liability						yes
OH[+]*	0.743-7.5	5,000	200,000	650	1,300	650	NA	NA	NA	no
OK*	0.5-7.0	1,000	9,950	1,000	2,000	1,000	15	2,000	2,000	yes
OR[c]*	5.0-9.0	2,000	5,000	109	218	109	NA	1,800	3,000	yes
PA[+]*	2.8	Flat rate		NA	NA	NA	NA	NA	NA	no
RI*				27.5% of federal income tax liability						no
SC[c]	2.5-7.0	2,160	10,800	2,350	4,700	2,350	Same as federal			no
SD				No state income tax						
TN*				Limited income tax						
TX				No state income tax						
UT*	2.55-7.2	750	3,750	1,725	3,450	1,725	Same as federal			50%
VT*				28-34% of federal income tax liability						no
VA	2.0-5.75	3,000	17,000	800	1,600	800	NA	3,000	5,000	no
WA				No state income tax						
WV	3.0-6.5	10,000	60,000	2,000	4,000	2,000	NA	NA	NA	no
WI*	4.9-6.93	7,500	15,000	0	0	50[d]	NA	5,200	8,900	no
WY				No state income tax						

(continued)

Notes: (NA) = not applicable. (+) = states in which one or more local governments levy a local income tax. (a) The lesser of (1) the percentage indicated, multiplied by adjusted gross income (AGI), or (2) the dollar value listed. In some states, when a standard deduction computed using a percentage of AGI is less than the fixed amount shown above, a minimum dollar deduction is allowed. Maryland and Utah have a minimum deduction as well. (b) A state provision that allows the taxpayer to deduct fully the federal income tax reduces the effective marginal tax rate for persons in the highest state and federal tax brackets by approximately 30% of the nominal tax rate—the deduction is of a lesser benefit to other taxpayers with lower federal and state top tax brackets. (c) Indexed by an inflation factor. Iowa indexes the standard deduction and income brackets. California, Maine, and South Carolina index personal exemptions and income brackets. Arizona, Nebraska, and Oregon index personal exemptions only. Montana indexes personal exemptions, income brackets, and standard deductions. (d) Exemption is a tax credit.

***State Notes:**

Alabama: Social Security taxes are included in itemized deductions. Taxable income brackets for married filing joint over $6,000, taxed at highest rate.

Arkansas: Tax credit per dependent. Taxpayers 65 or older, or blind or deaf receive an additional $20 credit. No tax is imposed on (1) a single taxpayer whose gross income is less than $5,500; (2) a married couple with gross income less than $10,000; and (3) head of household with gross income less than $7,150.

California: Taxpayers 65 and older receive additional $64 credit.

Connecticut: Personal exemption amount is reduced by $1,000 for each $1,000, or fraction thereof, by which the taxpayer's Connecticut AGI exceeds $24,000 (single, married filing separately), $38,000 (head of household), $48,000 (married filing jointly).

Delaware: Lowest personal income tax rate (3.2%) applies to income in the $2,000-$5,000 bracket. Taxable income under $2,000 is not subject to tax and is referred to as the "zero bracket" amount.

Hawaii: A refundable food/excise tax credit of at least $55 per exemption is granted; a refundable medical services excise tax credit of 4% of qualified medical expenses, subject to limitation, is granted.

Idaho: Idaho allows a refundable $15 per exemption credit.

Illinois: Effective 1/1/90, an additional $1,000 exemption for taxpayer or spouse 65 years of age or older. An additional $1,000 exemption for taxpayer or spouse who is blind.

Indiana: Additional $1,000 exemption if taxpayer or spouse is over 65 or blind.

Iowa: Tax may not reduce after-tax income of taxpayer below $9,000 (single) or $13,500 (married filing jointly, head of household, surviving spouse). Only limitation for the standard deduction is that the deduction otherwise allowable of $1,330 or $3,270 may not exceed the amount of income remaining after the federal tax deduction. Additional $20 personal credit is allowed for taxpayers that are legally blind or age 65 years and older. Voters within a school district may approve a school district income surtax, which is computed as a percentage of regular state tax liability before refundable credits.

Kansas: A child care credit equal to 25% of the federal child care credit is allowed to taxpayers claiming the federal credit.

Kentucky: Tax credit per dependent. Taxpayers 65 or older receive a $60 credit, as do taxpayers who are blind.

Maryland: For tax years 1992-94 only, the state income tax rate is 6% for taxable income $100,000 or over for single, married filing separately, and dependent taxpayers, $150,000 for all others. All counties have a local income tax surcharge of at least 20% of the state tax liability; most counties have a surcharge of 50%. The maximum local income tax rate is 60% (50% for income taxed at the 6% state rate). Single taxpayers have a minimum standard deduction of $1,500; married taxpayers a minimum standard deduction of $3,000. Blind and elderly get an additional exemption of $1,000. An additional $1,200 exemption is allowed for elderly dependents.

Massachusetts: 12% (flat rate) imposed on net capital gains, interest, and dividends of residents, and Massachusetts business income of nonresidents. All other net income taxed at 5.95%. No tax is imposed on a single person whose gross income is $8,000 or less ($12,000 married). Social Security taxes are deducted from taxable income up to $2,000 per taxpayer.

Michigan: Persons who can be claimed as a dependent on someone else's return get an exemption of $1,000. If their AGI is $1,500 or less, they owe no tax.

Missouri: For taxpayers itemizing deductions, Social Security taxes are deductible.

Montana: Tax rates do not reflect a 4.7% surtax in effect for tax year 1993.

Nebraska: Taxable income brackets will vary by filing status. Married individuals filing separate returns: lowest amount under $2,000; highest amount over $23,375. Personal tax credit is phased out for married joint above $90,000 AGI, single above $54,000 AGI, and head of household above $75,000 AGI.

New Hampshire: There is a 5% tax on taxable interest and dividends in excess of $1,200 ($2,400 married). There is no filing requirement for an individual whose total interest and dividend income, after deducting all interest from U.S. obligations, New Hampshire and Vermont banks or credit unions, and dividends from New Hampshire nonholding company banks is less than $1,200 ($2,400 for joint filers) for a taxable period.

New Jersey: The highest taxable income bracket is double for married filing jointly. No taxpayer is subject to tax if gross income is $3,000 or less ($1,500 married, filing separately).

New York: A supplemental tax is imposed on taxpayers with New York adjusted gross income in excess of $100,000. Taxpayers must add back the benefit of the lower tax brackets (i.e., 4%, 5%, 6%, and 7%). Taxpayers with New York AGI in excess of $150,000 are taxed at a flat rate of 7.875%.

North Carolina: Breaking points for higher marginal tax rates vary according to filing status. Taxable income brackets shown are for single taxpayers. North Carolina taxable income reflects federal reductions of personal exemptions and itemized deductions for higher income brackets.

North Dakota: Information in table applies to the short-form method, which is used by 95% of taxpayers. As an alternative, taxpayers may use the long-form method with tax rates ranging from 2.67% to 12.0% applied to income brackets ranging from $3,000 to over $50,000.

Ohio: Taxpayers take a $20 tax credit per exemption.

Oklahoma: These rates and brackets apply to single persons not deducting federal income tax. For individuals deducting the tax, rates range from 0.5% of the first $1,000 to 10% on income over $16,000 (single rate).

Oregon: Federal tax deduction limited to $3,000 ($1,500 if married filing separately). Income brackets are double for married filing jointly.

Pennsylvania: There are eight classes of income: (1) compensation; (2) net profits; (3) interest; (4) dividends; (5) net gain from sale or exchange of property; (6) rents, royalties, patents, and copyrights; (7) income derived through estates or trusts; and (8) gambling and lottery winnings except PA lottery winnings on or after 2/21/83.

Rhode Island: For 1992, if a taxpayer's federal income tax liability is greater than $15,000, the effective tax rate is 29.75% of federal income tax liability in excess of $15,000. For 1993, the effective tax rate on federal income tax liability in excess of $15,000 is 32%. For the period 1/1/94 and after, the tax rate is equal to 27.5% of the taxpayer's federal income tax liability.

Tennessee: Interest and dividends taxed at 6%. Persons over 65 having total annual gross income derived from any and all sources of $9,000 or less are exempt. Blindness is a basis for total exemption.

Utah: In determining Utah taxable income, 25% of federal personal exemptions are added back. Exemptions reflect this add-back.

Vermont: Refundable state earned income tax credit (28% of federal credit, maximum $619). Three percent surtax of liability between $3,400 and $13,100 and 6% liability over $13,100 are reflected in rates.

Wisconsin: The standard deduction is gradually phased out as income increases; deduction is completely phased out at $50,830 of AGI for single filers and $55,000 of AGI for joint filers. Taxpayers age 65 and older receive an additional $25 credit.

STATES AND OTHER AREAS OF THE U.S.

Sources: Population: Commerce Dept., Bureau of the Census (July, 1993 est., inc. armed forces personnel in each state but excluding such personnel stationed overseas); area: Bureau of the Census, Geography Division; forested land: Agriculture Dept., Forest Service; lumber production: Bureau of the Census, Industry Division; mineral production: Interior Dept., Bureau of Mines; commercial fishing: Commerce Dept., Natl. Marine Fisheries Service; value of construction: McGraw-Hill Information Systems Co., F.W. Dodge Division; personal per capita income: Commerce Dept., Bureau of Economic Analysis; unemployment: Labor Dept., Bureau of Labor Statistics; finance: Federal Deposit Insurance Corp.; federal employees: Labor Dept., Office of Personnel Management; energy: Energy Dept., Energy Information Administration; education: Education Dept., National Education Assn. Other information from sources in individual states, usually Commerce Dept.

Alabama

Heart of Dixie, Camellia State

People. Population (1993): 4,186,806; **rank:** 22. **Pop. density:** 81.5 per sq. mi. **Racial/ethnic distrib.** (1990): 73.6% white; 25.3% black; 0.6% Hispanic. **Net change** (1990-93): 3.6%.

Geography. Total area: 52,423 sq. mi.; **rank:** 30. **Land area:** 50,750 sq. mi. **Acres forested land:** 21,974,000. **Location:** East South Central state extending N-S from Tenn. to the Gulf of Mexico; east of the Mississippi River. **Climate:** long, hot summers; mild winters; generally abundant rainfall. **Topography:** coastal plains inc. Prairie Black Belt give way to hills, broken terrain; highest elevation, 2,407 ft. **Capital:** Montgomery.

Economy. Principal industries: pulp and paper, chemicals, electronics, apparel, textiles, primary metals, lumber and wood prods., food processing, fabricated metals, automotive tires, oil and gas exploration. **Principal manufactured goods** (1991-1992): electronics, cast iron and plastic pipe, fabricated steel prods., ships, paper products, chemicals, steel, mobile homes, fabrics, poultry processing, soft drinks, furniture, tires. **Agriculture: Chief crops** (1991-92): peanuts, cotton, soybeans, cottonseed, catfish, hay, corn, wheat, potatoes, pecans, peaches, sweet potatoes. **Livestock** (1990): 1.8 mln. cattle; 400,000 hogs/pigs; 14.8 mln. poultry; 2.7 mln. foodsize catfish. **Timber/lumber** (1992): pine, hardwoods; 2.07 bln. bd. ft. **Nonfuel Minerals** (1993): $569.7 mln.; mostly stone, cement, lime, sand & gravel. **Commercial fishing** (1993): $34.2 mln. **Chief ports:** Mobile. **Value of construction** (1993): $3.7 bln. **Employment distribution** (1991): 20% mfg.; 35% trade; 16% serv. **Per capita personal income** (1993): $17,234. **Unemployment** (1993): 7.5%. **Tourism** (1991): tourists spent $3.4 bln. **Sales Tax** (1991): 4%.

Finance. FDIC-insured commercial banks & trust companies (1993): 214. **Deposits:** $37.4 bln. **FDIC-insured savings institutions** (1993): 21. **Assets:** $4.2 bln.

Federal government. No. federal civilian employees (Mar. 1993): 45,609. **Avg. salary:** $36,564. **Notable federal facilities:** George C. Marshall NASA Space Center, Huntsville; Gunter Annex & Maxwell AFB, Montgomery; Ft. Rucker, Ozark; Ft. McClellan, Anniston; Natl. Fertilizer Development Center, Muscle Shoals; Navy Station & U.S. Corps of Engineers, Mobile; Redstone Arsenal, Huntsville.

Energy. Electricity production (1993, kWh, by source): Coal: 66.8 bln.; Petroleum: 72 mln.; Gas: 438 mln.; Hydroelectric: 9 bln.; Nuclear: 17.8 bln.

Education. Student-teacher ratio (1992): 17.4. **Avg. salary, public school teachers** (1993-94): $28,705.

State data. Motto: We dare defend our rights. **Flower:** Camellia. **Bird:** Yellowhammer. **Tree:** Southern pine. **Song:** Alabama. **Entered union** Dec. 14, 1819; rank, 22d. **State fair** at: Birmingham; early Oct.

History. First Europeans were Spanish explorers in the early 1500s. The French made the first permanent settlement, on Mobile Bay, 1701-02; later, English settled in the northern areas. France ceded the entire region to England at the end of the French and Indian War, 1763, but Spanish Florida claimed the Mobile Bay area until U.S. troops took it, 1813. Gen. Andrew Jackson broke the power of the Creek Indians, 1814, and they were removed to Oklahoma. The Confederate States were organized Feb. 4, 1861, at Montgomery, the first capital.

Tourist attractions. Jefferson Davis's "first White House" of the Confederacy; Montgomery's Civil Rights Memorial; Ivy Green, Helen Keller's birthplace, Tuscumbia; statue of Vulcan, Birmingham; George Washington Carver Museum, Tuskegee Univ.; W.C. Handy Home & Museum, Florence; Alabama Space and Rocket Center, Huntsville; Alabama Shakespeare Festival, Montgomery; Moundville State Monument, Moundville; Pike Pioneer Museum, Troy; USS Alabama Memorial Park, Mobile; 28 hunting areas, 24 public lakes, 82 campgrounds, 21 state parks.

At Russell Cave National Monument, near Bridgeport: a detailed record of occupancy by humans from about 10,000 BC to 1650 AD.

Famous Alabamians. Hank Aaron, Tallulah Bankhead, Hugo L. Black, Paul "Bear" Bryant, George Washington Carver, Nat King Cole, William C. Handy, Bo Jackson, Helen Keller, Harper Lee, Joe Louis, Willie Mays, John Hunt Morgan, Jesse Owens, George Wallace, Booker T. Washington, Hank Williams.

Alabama Business Council (State Chamber of Commerce). 468 S. Perry St., P.O. Box 76, Montgomery, AL 36195.

Toll-free travel information. 1-800-392-8096; 1-800-ALABAMA out of state.

Alaska

The Last Frontier (unofficial)

People. Population (1993): 599,151; **rank:** 48. **Pop. density:** 1.03 per sq. mi. **Racial/ethnic distrib.** (1990): 75.5% white; 4.1% black; 15.6% Amer. Ind., Eskimo or Aleut; 3.6% Asian or Pacific Is.; 3.2% Hispanic. **Net change** (1990-93): 8.9%.

Geography. Total area: 656,424 sq. mi.; **rank:** 1. **Land area:** 570,374 sq. mi. **Acres forested land:** 129,131,000. **Location:** NW corner of North America, bordered on east by Canada. **Climate:** SE, SW, and central regions, moist and mild; far north extremely dry. Extended summer days, winter nights, throughout. **Topography:** includes Pacific and Arctic mountain systems, central plateau, and Arctic slope. Mt. McKinley, 20,320 ft., is the highest point in North America. **Capital:** Juneau.

Economy. Principal industries: oil, gas, tourism, commercial fishing, mining, forestry. **Principal manufactured goods:** fish products, lumber and pulp, furs. **Agriculture** (1994): Chief crops: barley, hay, greenhouse nursery prods., potatoes, lettuce. **Livestock** (1994): 8,100 cattle; 1,900 sheep; 4,000 poultry; 35,000 reindeer. **Timber/lumber:** spruce, yellow cedar, hemlock. **Nonfuel Minerals** (1993): $420.7 mln.; zinc, gold, sand & gravel. **Commercial fishing** (1993): $1.4 bln. **Chief ports:** Anchorage, Dutch Harbor, Kodiak, Seward, Skagway, Juneau, Sitka, Valdez, Wrangell. **International airports at:** Anchorage. **Value of construction** (1993): $922.1 mln. **Employment distribution** (1993): 29% gvt.; 21.9% serv.; 19.5% trade. **Per capita personal income** (1993): $22,846. **Unemployment** (1993): 7.6%. **Tourism** (1993): out-of-state visitors spend $863 mln.

Finance. FDIC-insured commercial banks & trust companies (1993): 8. **Deposits:** $3.8 bln. **FDIC-insured savings institutions** (1993): 2. **Assets:** $219 mln.

Federal government. No. federal civilian employees (Mar. 1993): 12,574. **Avg. salary:** $39,155.

Energy. Electricity production (1993, kWh, by source): Coal: 323 mln.; Petroleum: 458 mln.; Gas: 2.5 bln.; Hydroelectric: 1.3 bln.

Education. Student-teacher ratio (1992): 16.8. **Avg. salary, public school teachers** (1993-94): $46,581.

State data. Motto: North to the future. **Flower:** Forget-Me-Not. **Bird:** Willow ptarmigan. **Tree:** Sitka spruce. **Song:** Alaska's Flag. **Entered union** Jan. 3, 1959; rank, 49th. **State fair** at: Palmer; late Aug.—early Sept.

History. Vitus Bering, a Danish explorer working for Russia, was the first European to land in Alaska, 1741. Alexander Baranov, first governor of Russian America, set up headquarters at Archangel, near present Sitka, in 1799. Secretary of State William H. Seward in 1867 bought Alaska from Russia for $7.2 million, a bargain some called "Seward's Folly." In 1896 gold was discovered and the famed Gold Rush was on.

Tourist attractions. Inside Passage, Portage Glacier, Mendenhall Glacier, Ketchikan Totems, Glacier Bay National Park, Denali National Park, one of North America's great wildlife sanctuaries, surrounding Mt. McKinley, N. America's highest peak. Transalaska Pipeline, Pribilof Islands fur seal rookeries, restored St. Michael's Russian Orthodox Cathedral, Sitka, Katmai National Park & Preserve.

Famous Alaskans. Tom Bodett, Susan Butcher, Ernest Gruening, Sydney Laurence, Libby Riddles, Jefferson "Soapy" Smith.

Tourist information. Alaska Division of Tourism, P.O. Box 110801, Juneau, AK 99811-0801; (907) 465-2010.

Arizona

Grand Canyon State

People. Population (1993): 3,936,142; **rank:** 23. **Pop. density:** 33.7 per sq. mi. **Racial/ethnic distrib.** (1990): 80.8% white; 3.0% black; 5.6% American Indian; 18.8% Hispanic. **Net change** (1990-93): 7.4%.

Geography. Total area: 114,006 sq. mi.; **rank:** 6. **Land area:** 113,642 sq. mi. **Acres forested land:** 19,596,000. **Location:** in the southwestern U.S. **Climate:** clear and dry in the southern regions and northern plateau; high central areas have heavy winter snows. **Topography:** Colorado plateau in the N, containing the Grand Canyon; Mexican Highlands running diagonally NW to SE; Sonoran Desert in the SW. **Capital:** Phoenix.

Economy. Principal industries: manufacturing, tourism, mining, agriculture. **Principal manufactured goods:** electronics, printing and publishing, foods, primary and fabricated metals, aircraft and missiles, apparel. **Agriculture: Chief crops:** cotton, lettuce, cauliflower, broccoli, sorghum, barley, corn, wheat, sugar beets, citrus fruits. **Livestock** (1994): 870,000 cattle; 140,000 hogs/pigs; 200,000 sheep; 350,000 poultry. **Timber/lumber** (1992): pine, fir, spruce; 272 mln. bd. ft. **Nonfuel Minerals** (1993): $2.7 bln.; copper, sand and gravel, cement, gold, molybdenum, silver. **International airports at:** Phoenix, Tucson, Yuma. **Value of construction** (1993): $6.3 bln. **Employment distribution** (1993): 28.5% services; 24.5% trade; 18.2% gvt.; 11.1% mfg. **Per capita personal income** (1993): $18,121. **Unemployment** (1993): 6.2%. **Tourism** (1993): tourists spent $8.1 bln. **Sales tax:** 5.0% (Maricopa, Pinal Counties, 5.5%).

Finance. FDIC-insured commercial banks & trust companies (1993): 37. **Deposits**: $29.7 bln. **FDIC-insured savings institutions** (1993): 2. **Assets:** $218 mln.

Federal government. No. federal civilian employees (Mar. 1993): 29,193. **Avg. salary:** $33,744. **Notable federal facilities:** Luke, Davis-Monthan AF bases; Ft. Huachuca Army Base; Yuma Proving Grounds.

Energy. Electricity production (1993, kWh, by source): Coal: 37 bln.; Petroleum: 60 mln.; Gas: 1.8 bln.; Hydroelectric: 7.0 mln.; Nuclear: 25.6 bln.

Education. Student-teacher ratio (1992): 18.7. **Avg. salary, public school teachers** (1993-94): $31,680.

State data. Motto: Ditat Deus (God enriches). **Flower:** Blossom of the Saguaro cactus. **Bird:** Cactus wren. **Tree:** Paloverde. **Song:** Arizona. **Entered union** Feb. 14, 1912; rank, 48th. **State fair** at: Phoenix; late Oct.–early Nov.

History. Marcos de Niza, a Franciscan, and Estevan, a black slave, explored the area, 1539. Eusebio Francisco Kino, Jesuit missionary, taught Indians Christianity and farming, 1690-1711, left a chain of missions. Spain ceded Arizona to Mexico, 1821. The U.S. took over at the end of the Mexican War, 1848. The area below the Gila River was obtained from Mexico in the Gadsden Purchase, 1854. Long Apache wars did not end until 1886, with Geronimo's surrender.

Tourist attractions. The Grand Canyon of the Colorado, an immense, vari-colored fissure 217 mi. long, 4 to 13 mi. wide at the brim, 4,000 to 5,500 ft. deep; the Painted Desert, extending for 30 mi. along U.S. 66; the Petrified Forest; Canyon Diablo, 225 ft. deep and 500 ft. wide; Meteor Crater, 4,150 ft. across, 570 ft. deep, made by a prehistoric meteor. Also, London Bridge at Lake Havasu City.

Famous Arizonans. Bruce Babbitt, Cochise, Geronimo, Barry Goldwater, Zane Grey, Carl Hayden, George W. P. Hunt, Helen Jacobs, Percival Lowell, Sandra Day O'Connor, William H. Pickering, John J. Rhodes, Morris Udall, Stewart Udall, Frank Lloyd Wright.

Tourist information. Phoenix & Valley of the Sun Visitor and Convention Bureau, 1-602-254-6500.

Arkansas

Land of Opportunity

People. Population (1993): 2,424,418; **rank:** 33. **Pop. density:** 46.1 per sq. mi. **Racial/ethnic distrib.** (1990): 82.7% white; 15.9% black; 0.8% Hispanic. **Net change** (1990-93): 3.1%.

Geography. Total area: 53,182 sq. mi.; **rank:** 29. **Land area:** 52,075 sq. mi. **Acres forested land:** 17,864,000. **Location:** in the west south-central U.S. **Climate:** long, hot summers, mild winters; generally abundant rainfall. **Topography:** eastern delta and prairie, southern lowland forests, and the northwestern highlands, which include the Ozark Plateaus. **Capital:** Little Rock.

Economy. Principal industries: manufacturing, agriculture, tourism, forestry. **Principal manufactured goods:** food prods., chemicals, lumber, paper, electric motors, furniture, auto components, airplane parts, apparel, machinery, petroleum prods., steel. **Agriculture: Chief crops:** soybeans, rice, cotton, tomatoes, grapes, apples, commercial vegetables, peaches, wheat. **Livestock** (1992): 1.71 mln. cattle; 810,000 hogs/pigs; 1,022,550 mln. poultry. **Timber/lumber** (1992): oak, hickory, gum, cypress, pine; 1.85 bln. bd. ft. **Nonfuel Minerals** (1993): 364.9 mln.; crushed stone, bromine, cement, sand & gravel. **Chief ports:** Little Rock, Pine Bluff, Osceola, Helena, Fort Smith, Van Buren, Camden, Dardanelle, North Little Rock, West Memphis, Crossett, McGehee. **Value of construction** (1993): $2.2 bln. **Employment distribution** (1993): 24.58% mfg.; 22.18% trade; 22.18% serv.; 17.12% gvt. **Per capita personal income** (1993): $16,143. **Unemployment** (1993): 7.2%. **Tourism** (1993): travelers spent $2.75 bln.

Finance. FDIC-insured commercial banks & trust companies (1993): 257. **Deposits:** $22.8 bln. **FDIC-insured savings institutions** (1993): 19. **Assets:** $3.1 bln.

Federal government. No. federal civilian employees (Mar. 1993): 12,475. **Avg. salary:** $32,017. **Notable federal facilities:** Nat'l. Center for Toxicological Research, Jefferson; Pine Bluff Arsenal, Little Rock AFB.

Energy. Electricity production (1993, kWh, by source): Coal: 18 bln.; Petroleum: 66 mln.; Gas: 1.9 bln.; Hydroelectric: 4.5 bln.; Nuclear: 13.5 bln.

Education. Student-teacher ratio (1992): 17.0. **Avg. salary, public school teachers** (1993-94): $28,705.

State data. Motto: Regnat Populus (The people rule). **Flower:** Apple blossom. **Bird:** Mockingbird. **Tree:** Pine. **Song:** Arkansas. **Entered union** June 15, 1836; rank, 25th. **State fair** at: Little Rock; late Sept.–early Oct.

History. First European explorers were de Soto, 1541; Jolliet, 1673; La Salle, 1682. First settlement was by the French under Henri de Tonty, 1686, at Arkansas Post. In 1762 the area was ceded by France to Spain, then back again in 1800, and was part of the Louisiana Purchase by the U. S. in 1803. Arkansas seceded from the Union in 1861, only after the Civil War began, and more than 10,000 Arkansans fought on the Union side.

Tourist attractions. 5 natl. parks & 48 state parks, inc. Hot Springs National Park, water ranging from 95° to 147°F. Eureka Springs, resort since 1879; Blanchard Caverns, near Mountain View, are among the nation's largest; Crater of Diamonds, near Murfreesboro, only U.S. diamond mine; Buffalo Natl. River; Mid-America Museum, Ozark Folk Center.

Famous Arkansans. Daisy Bates, Dee Brown, Glen Campbell, Johnny Cash, Hattie Caraway, President Bill Clinton, "Dizzy" Dean, Orval Faubus, James W. Fulbright, Douglas MacArthur, John L. McClellan, James S. McDonnel, Dick Powell, Winthrop Rockefeller, Mary Steenburgen, Edward Durell Stone, Archibald Yell.

Chamber of Commerce. One Spring Bldg., Little Rock, AR 72201-2486.

Toll-free travel information. 1-800-NATURAL.

California

Golden State

People. Population (1993): 31,210,750; **rank:** 1. **Pop. density:** 197.9 per sq. mi. **Racial/ethnic distrib.** (1990): 69.0% white; 7.4% black; 9.6% Asian; 25.8% Hispanic. **Net change** (1990-93): 4.9%.

Geography. Total area: 163,707 sq. mi.; **rank:** 3. **Land area:** 155,973 sq. mi. **Acres forested land:** 37,263,000. **Location:** on western coast of the U.S. **Climate:** moderate temperatures and rainfall along the coast; extremes in the interior. **Topography:** long mountainous coastline; central valley; Sierra Nevada on the east; desert basins of the southern interior; rugged mountains of the north. **Capital:** Sacramento.

Economy. Principal industries: agriculture, manufacturing, services, trade. **Principal manufactured goods:** foods, printed material, primary and fabricated metals, machinery, electric and electronic equipment, transportation equipment, instruments. **Agriculture: Chief crops:** grapes, cotton, flowers, oranges, nursery products, hay, tomatoes, lettuce, strawberries, almonds, broccoli, walnuts, sugar beets, peaches, potatoes. **Livestock** (1993): 4.5 mln. cattle & calves; 250,000 hogs/pigs; 945,000 sheep and lambs; 31.5 mln. chickens exc. broilers. **Timber/lumber** (1992): fir, pine, redwood, oak; 3.9 bln. bd. ft. **Nonfuel Minerals:** (1993): $2.3 bln.; mostly construction sand & gravel, boron minerals, cement, diatomite, asbestos, calcined gypsum. **Commercial fishing** (1993): $119.7 mln. **Chief ports:** Long Beach, Los Angeles, San Diego, Oakland, San Francisco, Sacramento, Stockton. **International airports at:** Los Angeles, San Francisco, San Jose, San Diego. **Value of construction** (1993): $27.3 bln. **Employment distribution** (1993): 28.9% serv.; 23.2% trade; 15% mfg.; 17.3% gvt. **Per capita personal income** (1993): $21,821. **Unemployment** (1993): 9.2%. **Tourism** (1992): $52.8 bln. **Sales tax:** 7¼-8¾%.

Finance. FDIC-insured commercial banks & trust companies (1993): 425. **Deposits**: $267.0 bln. **FDIC-insured savings institutions** (1993): 96. **Assets:** $264.8 bln.

Federal government. No. federal civilian employees (Mar. 1993): 200,451. **Avg. salary:** $37,937. **Notable federal facilities:** Vandenberg, Beale, Travis, McClellan AF bases, San Francisco Mint.

Energy. Electricity production (1993, kWh, by source): Petroleum: 2 bln.; Gas: 46.4 bln.; Hydroelectric: 38.2 bln.; Nuclear: 35.2 bln.

Education. Student-teacher ratio (1992): 24.1. **Avg. salary, public school teachers** (1993-94): $40,289.

State data. Motto: Eureka (I have found it). **Flower:** Golden poppy. **Bird:** California valley quail. **Tree:** California redwood. **Song:** I Love You, California. **Entered union** Sept. 9, 1850; rank, 31st. **State fair** at: Sacramento; late Aug.—early Sept.

History. First European explorers were Cabrillo, 1542, and Drake, 1579. First settlement was the Spanish Alta California mission at San Diego, 1769, first in a string founded by Franciscan Father Junipero Serra. U.S. traders and settlers arrived in the 19th century and staged the abortive Bear Flag Revolt, 1846; later that year U.S. forces occupied California; at the end of the Mexican War, Mexico ceded the province to the U.S., 1848, the same year the Gold Rush began.

Tourist attractions. Scenic regions are Yosemite Valley; Lassen and Sequoia-Kings Canyon national parks; Lake Tahoe; the Mojave and Colorado deserts; San Francisco Bay; Napa Valley; and Monterey Peninsula. Oldest living things on earth are believed to be a stand of Bristlecone pines in the Inyo National Forest, est. to be 4,600 years old. The world's tallest tree, the Howard Libbey redwood, 362 ft. with a girth of 44 ft., stands on Redwood Creek, Humboldt County.

Also, RMS Queen Mary, Spruce Goose, both Long Beach; Palomar Observatory; Disneyland; J. Paul Getty Museum, Malibu; Tournament of Roses and Rose Bowl; Universal Studios, Hollywood; Los Angeles County Art Museum; San Diego Zoo.

Famous Californians. Luther Burbank, John C. Fremont, Bret Harte, Wm. R. Hearst, Jack London, Aimee Semple McPherson, John Muir, Richard M. Nixon, William Saroyan, Junipero Serra, Leland Stanford, John Steinbeck, Earl Warren.

Chamber of Commerce. 1201 K St., Sacramento, CA 95814.

Toll-free travel information. 1-800-862-2543, x T100.

Colorado

Centennial State

People. Population (1993): 3,565,959; **rank:** 26. **Pop. density:** 33.5 per sq. mi. **Racial/ethnic distrib.** (1990): 88.2% white; 4.0% black; 12.9% Hispanic. **Net change** (1990-93): 8.2%.

Geography. Total area: 104,100 sq. mi.; **rank:** 8. **Land area:** 103,729 sq. mi. **Acres forested land:** 21,338,000. **Location:** in west central U.S. **Climate:** low relative humidity, abundant sunshine, wide daily, seasonal temperatures ranges; alpine conditions in the high mountains. **Topography:** eastern dry high plains; hilly to mountainous central plateau; western Rocky Mountains of high ranges alternating with broad valleys and deep, narrow canyons. **Capital:** Denver.

Economy. Principal industries: manufacturing, government, tourism, agriculture, aerospace, electronics equipment. **Principal manufactured goods:** computer equipment, instruments, foods, machinery, aerospace products. **Agriculture: Chief crops:** corn, wheat, hay, sugar beets, barley, potatoes, apples, peaches, pears, dry edible beans, sorghum, onions, oats. **Livestock** (1989): 2.8 mln. cattle; 220,000 hogs/pigs; 825,000 sheep; 4.0 mln. poultry. **Timber/lumber** (1992): oak, ponderosa pine, Douglas fir; 123 mln. bd. ft. **Nonfuel Minerals** (1993): $432 mln.; construction sand & gravel, gold, lead, zinc, molybdenum, crushed stone. **International airports at:** Denver. **Value of construction** (1993): $6.0 bln. **Employment distribution** (1993): 28.1% serv.; 24.2% trade; 17.8% gvt.; 11.3% mfg. **Per capita personal income** (1993): $21,564. **Unemployment** (1993): 5.2%. **Tourism** (1989): $5.6 bln. **Sales Tax:** 3%.

Finance. FDIC-insured commercial banks & trust companies (1993): 322. **Deposits:** $30.0 bln. **FDIC-insured savings institutions** (1993): 16. **Assets:** $2.2 bln.

Federal government. No. federal civilian employees (Mar. 1993): 40,186. **Avg. salary:** $37,227. **Notable federal facilities:** U.S. Air Force Academy; U.S. Mint; Ft. Carson; National Renewable Energy Labs; U.S. Rail Transport. Test Center; N. Amer. Aerospace Defense Command; Consolidated Space Operations Center; U.S. Documents Center, Fitzsimons Army Medical Center, Federal Center.

Energy. Electricity production (1993, kWh, by source): Coal: 30.4 bln.; Petroleum: 9 mln.; Gas: 372 mln.; Hydroelectric: 2.0 bln.

Education. Student-teacher ratio (1992): 18.3. **Avg. salary, public school teachers** (1993-94): $33,826.

State data. Motto: Nil Sine Numine (Nothing without Providence). **Flower:** Rocky Mountain columbine. **Bird:**

Lark bunting. **Tree:** Colorado blue spruce. **Song:** Where the Columbines Grow. **Entered union** Aug. 1, 1876; rank 38th. **State fair** at: Pueblo; last week in Aug.

History. Early civilization centered around Mesa Verde 2,000 years ago. The U.S. acquired eastern Colorado in the Louisiana Purchase, 1803; Lt. Zebulon M. Pike explored the area, 1806, discovering the peak that bears his name. After the Mexican War, 1846-48, U.S. immigrants settled in the east, former Mexicans in the south.

Tourist attractions. 310 or more sunshine days per year; more than 1,000 peaks of 2 or more miles; Rocky Mountain National Park; Garden of the Gods; Great Sand Dunes, Dinosaur, Black Canyon of the Gunnison, and Colorado national monuments; Pikes Peak and Mt. Evans highways; Mesa Verde National Park (ancient Anasazi Indian cliff dwellings); 35 major ski areas; the Grand Mesa tableland comprises Grand Mesa Forest, 659,584 acres, with 200 lakes stocked with trout. Mining towns of Central City, Silverton, Cripple Creek; Burlington's Old Town; Bent's Fort, outside La Junta; Georgetown Loop Historic Mining Railroad Park, Cumbres & Toltec Scenic Railroad.

Famous Coloradans. Frederick Bonfils, Molly Brown, William N. Byers, M. Scott Carpenter, Jack Dempsey, Mamie Eisenhower, Douglas Fairbanks, Scott Hamilton, "Baby Doe" Tabor, Lowell Thomas, Byron R. White, Paul Whiteman.

Toll-free travel information. 1-800-433-2656.

Connecticut

Constitution State, Nutmeg State

People. Population (1993): 3,277,316; **rank:** 27. **Pop. density:** 677.2 per sq. mi. **Racial/ethnic distrib.** (1990): 87.0% white; 8.3% black; 6.5% Hispanic. **Net change** (1990-93): -0.3%.

Geography. Total area: 5,544 sq. mi.; **rank:** 48. **Land area:** 4,845 sq. mi. **Acres forested land:** 1,819,000. **Location:** New England state in the northeastern corner of the U.S. **Climate:** moderate; winters avg. slightly below freezing, warm, humid summers. **Topography:** western upland, the Berkshires, in the NW, highest elevations; narrow central lowland N-S; hilly eastern upland drained by rivers. **Capital:** Hartford.

Economy. Principal industries: manufacturing, retail trade, government, services, finances, insurance, real estate. **Principal manufactured goods:** aircraft engines and parts, submarines, helicopters, instruments, machinery & computer equipment, electronics & electrical equipment, medical instruments, pharmaceuticals. **Agriculture: Chief crops:** nursery stock, Christmas trees, mushrooms, vegetables, sweet corn, tobacco, apples. **Livestock** (1989): 73,000 cattle; 50,000 horses; 6,800 hogs/pigs; 8,400 sheep; 5.6 mln. poultry. **Timber/lumber:** oak, birch, beech, maple. **Nonfuel Minerals** (1993): $86.4 mln.; crushed stone, construction sand & gravel. **Commercial fishing** (1993): $50.9 mln. **Chief ports:** New Haven, Bridgeport, New London. **International airports at:** Windsor Locks. **Value of construction** (1993): $3.0 bln. **Employment distribution** (1993): 18.7% mfg.; 30% serv. **Per capita personal income** (1992): $28,110. **Unemployment** (1993): 6.2%. **Tourism** (1991): out-of-state visitors spent $3.7 bln. **Sales tax**: 6.0%.

Finance. FDIC-insured commercial banks & trust companies (1993): 46. **Deposits:** $23.6 bln. **FDIC-insured savings institutions** (1993): 68. **Assets**: $41.8 bln.

Federal Government. No. federal civilian employees (Mar. 1993): 10,149. **Avg. salary:** $39,013. **Notable federal facilities:** U.S. Coast Guard Academy; U.S. Navy Submarine Base.

Energy. Electricity production (1993, kWh, by source): Coal: 1.9 bln.; Petroleum: 4.2 bln.; Gas: 47 mln.; Hydroelectric: 345 mln.; Nuclear: 21.8 bln.

Education. Student-teacher ratio (1992): 14.3. **Avg. salary, public school teachers** (1993-94): $49,500.

State data. Motto: Qui Transtulit Sustinet (He who transplanted still sustains). **Flower:** Mountain laurel. **Bird:** American robin. **Tree:** White oak. **Song:** Yankee Doodle. **Fifth** of the 13 original states to ratify the Constitution, Jan. 9, 1788.

History. Adriaen Block, Dutch explorer, was the first European visitor, 1614. By 1634, settlers from Plymouth Bay started colonies along the Connecticut River and in 1637 defeated the Pequot Indians. In the Revolution, Connecticut men fought in most major campaigns and turned back British raids on Danbury and other towns, while Connecticut privateers captured British merchant ships.

Tourist attractions. Mark Twain House, Hartford; Yale University's Art Gallery, Peabody Museum, both in New Haven; Mystic Seaport; Mystic Marine Life Aquarium; P.T. Barnum Museum, Bridgeport; Gillette Castle, Hadlyme; U.S.S. Nautilus Memorial, Groton (1st nuclear-powered submarine); Foxwoods Casino, Ledyard .

Famous "Nutmeggers." Ethan Allen, Phineas T. Barnum, Samuel Colt, Jonathan Edwards, Nathan Hale, Katharine Hepburn, Isaac Hull, J. Pierpont Morgan, Israel Putnam, Harriet Beecher Stowe, Mark Twain, Noah Webster, Eli Whitney.

Tourist information. State Dept. of Economic Development, 865 Brook St., Rocky Hill, CT 06067.

Toll-free travel information. 1-800-CT-BOUND (282-6863).

Delaware

First State, Diamond State

People. Population (1993): 700,269; **rank:** 46. **Pop. density:** 352.5 per sq. mi. **Racial/ethnic distrib.** (1990): 80.3% white; 16.9% black; 2.4% Hispanic. **Net change** (1990-93): 5.1%.

Geography. Total area: 2,489 sq. mi.; **rank:** 49. **Land area:** 1,955 sq. mi. **Acres forested land:** 398,000. **Location:** occupies the Delmarva Peninsula on the Atlantic coastal plain. **Climate:** moderate. **Topography:** Piedmont plateau to the N, sloping to a near sea-level plain. **Capital:** Dover.

Economy. Principal industries: chemistry, agriculture, finance, poultry, shellfish, tourism, auto assembly, food processing, transportation equipment. **Principal manufactured goods:** nylon, apparel, luggage, foods, autos, processed meats and vegetables, railroad and aircraft equipment. **Agriculture: Chief crops:** soybeans, potatoes, corn, mushrooms, lima beans, green peas, barley, cucumbers, snap beans, watermelons, apples, wheat, sweet corn. **Livestock** (1993): 15,000 cattle, 6,600 hogs, 251.4 mln. broilers. **Nonfuel Minerals** (1993): $11.2 mln; construction sand & gravel. **Commercial fishing** (1993): $4.6 mln. **Chief ports:** Wilmington. **International airports at:** Philadelphia/Wilmington. **Value of construction** (1993): $699.4 mln. **Employment distribution** (1993): 81% non-manufacturing; 19% mfg. **Per capita personal income** (1993): $21,481. **Unemployment** (1993): 5.3%. **Tourism** (1993): domestic travelers spent $806 mln.

Finance. FDIC-insured commercial banks & trust companies (1993): 36. **Deposits:** $34.9 bln. **FDIC-insured savings institutions** (1993): 5. **Assets:** $2.6 bln.

Federal government. No. federal civilian employees (Mar. 1993): 2,922. **Avg. salary:** $33,246. **Notable federal facilities:** Dover Air Force Base, Federal Wildlife Refuge, Bombay Hook.

Energy. Electricity production (1993, kWh, by source): Coal: 5.2 bln.; Petroleum: 2.1 bln.; Gas: 1.1 bln.

Education. Student-teacher ratio (1992): 16.7. **Avg. salary, public school teachers** (1993-94): $37,469.

State data. Motto: Liberty and independence. **Flower:** Peach blossom. **Bird:** Blue hen chicken. **Tree:** American holly. **Song:** Our Delaware. **First** of original 13 states to ratify the Constitution, Dec. 7, 1787. **State fair** at: Harrington; end of July.

History. The Dutch first settled in Delaware near present Lewes, 1631, but were wiped out by Indians. Swedes settled at present Wilmington, 1638; Dutch settled anew, 1651, near New Castle and seized the Swedish settlement, 1655, only to lose all Delaware and New Netherland to the British, 1664.

Tourist attractions. Ft. Christina Monument, the site of founding of New Sweden; John Dickinson "Penman of the Revolution" home, Dover; Henry Francis du Pont Winterthur Museum; Hagley Museum, Wilmington; Rehoboth Beach, "nation's summer capitol," Rehoboth; Dover Downs Intl. Speedway, Dover; Old Swedes (Trinity Parish) Church, erected 1698, is the oldest Protestant church in the U.S. still in use.

Famous Delawareans. Thomas F. Bayard, Henry Seidel Canby, E. I. du Pont, John P. Marquand, Howard Pyle, Caesar Rodney.

Chamber of Commerce. One Commerce Center, Wilmington, DE 19801.

Toll-free travel information. 1-800-441-8846.

Florida

Sunshine State

People. Population (1993): 13,678,914; **rank:** 4. **Pop. density:** 249.8 per sq. mi. **Racial/ethnic distrib.** (1990): 83.1% white; 13.6% black; 12.2% Hispanic. **Net change** (1990-93): 5.7%.

Geography. Total area: 65,756 sq. mi.; **rank:** 22. **Land area:** 53,937 sq. mi. **Acres forested land:** 16,549,000. **Location:** peninsula jutting southward 500 mi. bet. the Atlantic and the Gulf of Mexico. **Climate:** subtropical N of Bradenton-Lake Okeechobee-Vero Beach line; tropical S of line. **Topography:** land is flat or rolling; highest point is 345 ft. in the NW. **Capital:** Tallahassee.

Economy. Principal industries: tourism, agriculture, gvt., manufacturing, services, international trade. **Principal manufactured goods:** electric & electronic equip., transp. equipment; food; printing & publishing; machinery. **Agriculture: Chief crops:** citrus fruits, greenhouse products, vegetables, potatoes, melons, strawberries, sugarcane. **Livestock** (1993): 2.0 mln. cattle; 56,798 hogs/pigs; 9.9 mln. poultry. **Timber/lumber** (1992): pine, cypress, cedar; 577 mln. bd. ft. **Nonfuel Minerals** (1993): $1.3 bln.; mostly phosphate, crushed stone, cement. **Commercial fishing** (1993): $208.8 mln. **Chief ports:** Pensacola, Tampa, Manatee, Miami, Port Everglades, Jacksonville, St. Petersburg, Canaveral. **International airports at:** Daytona Beach, Miami, Tampa, Jacksonville, Key West, Melbourne, Orlando, Ft. Lauderdale-Hollywood, Palm Beach, Ft. Meyers, St. Petersburg, Sarasota. **Value of construction** (1993): $18.6 bln. **Per capita personal income** (1993): $20,857. **Unemployment** (1993): 7.0% **Tourism** (1993): out-of-state visitors spent $32 bln. **Sales tax:** 6%.

Finance. FDIC-insured commercial banks & trust companies (1993): 375. **Deposits:** $123.4 bln. **FDIC-insured savings institutions** (1993): 79. **Assets:** $32.9 bln.

Federal government. No. federal civilian employees (Mar. 1993): 64,698. **Avg. salary:** $35,964. **Notable federal facilities:** John F. Kennedy Space Center, NASA-Kennedy Space Center's Spaceport USA; Eglin Air Force Base.

Energy. Electricity production (1993, kWh, by source): Coal: 61.9 bln.; Petroleum: 34.3 bln.; Gas: 17.8 bln.; Hydroelectric: 211 mln.; Nuclear: 25.9 bln.

Education. Student-teacher ratio (1992): 18.4. **Avg. salary, public school teachers** (1993-94): $32,020.

State data. Motto: In God we trust. **Flower:** Orange blossom. **Bird:** Mockingbird. **Tree:** Sabal palmetto palm. **Song:** Old Folks at Home. **Entered union** Mar. 3, 1845; rank, 27th. **State fair** at: Tampa; early to mid-Feb.

History. First European to see Florida was Ponce de León, 1513. France established a colony, Fort Caroline, on the St. Johns River, 1564; Spain settled St. Augustine, 1565, and Spanish troops massacred most of the French. Britain's Francis Drake burned St. Augustine, 1586. Britain held the area briefly, 1763-83, returning it to Spain. After Andrew Jackson led a U.S. invasion, 1818, Spain ceded Florida to the U.S., 1819. The Seminole War, 1835-42, resulted in removal of most Indians to Oklahoma. Florida seceded from the Union, 1861, was readmitted, 1868.

Tourist attractions. Miami, with a variety of luxury hotels at Miami Beach; St. Augustine, oldest city in U.S.; Walt Disney World's Magic Kingdom, EPCOT Center, and Disney-MGM Studios, near Orlando; Spaceport USA, the visitors' center at the Kennedy Space Center.

Everglades National Park preserves the beauty of the vast Everglades swamp. Castillo de San Marcos, St. Augustine, is a national monument. Also, the Ringling Museum of Art and the Ringling Museum of the Circus, both in Sarasota; Sea World, Orlando; Cypress Gardens, Winter Haven; Busch Gardens, Tampa; Universal Studios, near Orlando.

Famous Floridians. Henry M. Flagler, James Weldon Johnson, MacKinlay Kantor, Henry B. Plant, Marjorie Kinnan Rawlings, Joseph W. Stilwell, Charles P. Summerall.

Tourist information. Florida Division of Tourism, 126 Van Buren St., Tallahassee, FL 32399-2000, 1-904-487-1462.

Georgia

Empire State of the South, Peach State

People. Population (1993): 6,917,140; **rank:** 11. **Pop. density:** 116.6 per sq. mi. **Racial/ethnic distrib.** (1990): 71.0% white; 27.0% black; 1.7% Hispanic. **Net change** (1990-93): 6.8%.

Geography. Total area: 59,441 sq. mi.; **rank:** 24. **Land area:** 57,919 sq. mi. **Acres forested land:** 24,137,000. **Location:** South Atlantic state. **Climate:** maritime tropical air masses dominate in summer; continental polar air masses in winter; east central area drier. **Topography:** most southerly of the Blue Ridge Mtns. cover NE and N central; central Piedmont extends to the fall line of rivers; coastal plain levels to the coast flatlands. **Capital:** Atlanta.

Economy. Principal industries: services, manufacturing, gvt., retail trade. **Principal manufactured goods** (1994): textiles, food, and kindred prods., pulp and paper products. **Agriculture: Chief crops** (1994): peanuts, cotton, corn, tobacco, hay, soybeans. **Livestock** (1994): 26.3 mln. poultry, excl. broilers; 1.54 mln. cattle; 1.03 hogs/pigs. **Timber/lumber** (1992): pine, hardwood; 2.76 bln. bd. ft. **Nonfuel Minerals** (1993): $1.7 bln.; mostly kaolin and other clays, crushed stone. **Commercial fishing** (1993): $21.2 mln. **Chief ports:** Savannah, Brunswick. **International airports at:** Atlanta. **Value of construction** (1993): $9.4 bln. **Employment distribution** (1993): 23.7% services; 17.6% mfg.; 24.9% retail trade; 17.6% gvt. **Per capita personal income** (1993): $19,278. **Unemployment** (1993): 5.8%. **Tourism** (1993): tourists spent $11.2 bln. **Sales tax:** 4%.

Finance. FDIC-insured commercial banks & trust companies (1993): 399. **Deposits:** $63.3 bln. **FDIC-insured savings institutions** (1993): 39. **Assets:** $6.6 bln.

Federal government. No. federal civilian employees (Mar. 1993): 70,355. **Avg. salary:** $34,561. **Notable federal facilities:** Dobbins AFB; Fts. Benning, Gordon, McPherson; Fed. Law Enforcement Training Ctr., Glynco, Warner Robins AFB; Centers for Disease Control, Atlanta.

Energy. Electricity production (1993, kWh, by source): Coal: 63.3 bln.; Petroleum: 237 mln.; Gas: 218 mln.; Hydroelectric: 4.8 bln.; Nuclear: 27.2 bln.

Education. Student-teacher ratio (1992): 18.0. **Avg. salary, public school teachers** (1993-94): $30,456.

State data. Motto: Wisdom, justice and moderation. **Flower:** Cherokee rose. **Bird:** Brown thrasher. **Tree:** Live oak. **Song:** Georgia On My Mind. **Fourth** of the 13 original states to ratify the Constitution, Jan. 2, 1788.

History. Gen. James Oglethorpe established the first settlements, 1733, for poor and religiously-persecuted Englishmen. Oglethorpe defeated a Spanish army from Florida at Bloody Marsh, 1742. In the Revolution, Georgians seized the Savannah armory, 1775, and sent the munitions to the Continental Army; they fought seesaw campaigns with Cornwallis's British troops, twice liberating Augusta and forcing final evacuation by the British from Savannah, 1782.

Tourist attractions. Atlanta area: State Capitol, Stone Mt. Park, Six Flags over Georgia, Kennesaw Mt. Natl. Battlefield Park, Martin Luther King Center, Underground Atlanta, Jimmy Carter Lib. & Museum, Whitewater Park. NW: Chickamauga Battlefield Park, Chattahoochee Natl. Forest. NE: alpine village of Helen; Dahlonega, site of America's first gold rush; Brasstown Bald Mt., Lake Lanier. SW: Roosevelt's Little White House, Callaway Gardens, Andersonville Natl. Historic Site. SE: Okefenokee Swamp. Coastal: Jekyll Island, St. Simons Island, Cumberland Island Natl. Seashore, historic riverfront district in Savannah, Ft. Pulaski.

Famous Georgians. Griffin Bell, James Bowie, James Brown, Erskine Caldwell, Jimmy Carter, Ray Charles, Lucius D. Clay, Ty Cobb, John C. Fremont, Joel Chandler Harris, Martin Luther King Jr., Gladys Knight, Sidney Lanier, Juliette Gordon Low, Margaret Mitchell, Flannery O'Connor, Otis Redding, Jackie Robinson, Alice Walker, Joseph Wheeler.

Chamber of Commerce. 235 International Blvd., Atlanta, GA 30303; (404) 880-9000.

Toll-free travel information. 1-800-VISIT GA.

Hawai'i

The Aloha State

People. Population (1993): 1,171,592; **rank:** 40. **Pop. density:** 180.5 per sq. mi. **Racial/ethnic distrib.** (1990): 33.4% white; 2.5% black; 61.8% Asian or Pacific Is.; 7.3% Hispanic. **Net change** (1990-93): 5.7%.

Geography. Total area: 10,932 sq. mi.; **rank:** 43. **Land area:** 6,423 sq. mi. **Acres forested land:** 1,748,000. **Location:** Hawaiian Islands lie in the North Pacific, 2,397 mi. SW from San Francisco. **Climate:** subtropical, with wide variations in rainfall; Waialeale, on Kaua'i, wettest spot in U.S. (annual rainfall 444 in.) **Topography:** islands are tops of a chain of submerged volcanic mountains; active volcanoes: Mauna Loa, Kilauea. **Capital:** Honolulu.

Economy. Principal industries: tourism, defense and other government, sugar, pineapple and diversified agriculture, aquaculture, fishing, motion pictures. **Principal manufactured goods:** processed sugar, canned pineapple, clothing, foods, printing and publishing. **Agriculture: Chief crops:** sugar, pineapples, macadamia nuts, fruits, coffee, vegetables, melons, floriculture. **Livestock** (1990): 214,000 cattle and calves; 36,000 hogs/pigs; 1.18 mln. chickens. **Nonfuel Minerals** (1993): $134.6 mln.; mostly crushed stone, cement. **Commercial fishing** (1993): $69.1 mln. **Chief ports:** Honolulu, Nawiliwili, Barbers Point, Kahului, Hilo. **International airports at:** Honolulu. **Value of construction** (1993): $2.3 bln. **Employment distribution** (1991): 25.3% trade; 29.4% serv.; 20.2% gvt. **Per capita personal income** (1993): $23,354. **Unemployment** (1993): 4.2%. **Tourism** (1992): visitors spent $9.6 bln. **General excise tax:** 4%. **Sales tax:** 4%.

Finance. FDIC-insured commercial banks & trust companies (1993): 17. **Deposits:** $14.3 bln. **FDIC-insured savings institutions** (1993): 5. **Assets:** $4.9 bln.

Federal government. No. federal civilian employees (Mar. 1993): 21,010. **Avg. salary:** $36,218. **Notable federal facilities:** Pearl Harbor Naval Shipyard; Hickam AFB; Schofield Barracks; Ft. Shafter; Marine Corps Base-Kaneohe Bay.

Energy. Electricity production (1993, kWh, by source): Petroleum: 6.1 bln.; Hydroelectric: 14 mln.

Education. Student-teacher ratio (1992): 17.6. **Avg. salary, public school teachers** (1993-94): $36,564.

State data. Motto: The life of the land is perpetuated in righteousness. **Flower:** Yellow hibiscus. **Bird:** Hawaiian goose. **Tree:** Kukui (Candlenut). **Song:** Hawai'i Pono'i. **Entered union** Aug. 21, 1959; rank, 50th. **State fair** at: Honolulu; late May–mid-June.

History. Polynesians from islands 2,000 mi. to the south settled the Hawaiian Islands, probably between 300 A.D. and 600 A.D. First European visitor was British Capt. James Cook, 1778. Missionaries arrived, 1820, taught religion, reading and writing. King Kamehameha III and his chiefs created the first Constitution and a Legislature that set up a public school system. Sugar production began in 1835 and it became the dominant industry. In 1893, Queen Liliuokalani was deposed, followed, 1894, by a republic headed by Sanford B. Dole. Annexation by the U.S. came in 1898.

Tourist attractions. Hawaii Volcanoes, Haleakala National Parks; National Memorial Cemetary of the Pacific; U.S.S. *Arizona* Memorial; Hanauma Bay; Polynesian Cultural Center, Waikiki Beach, Nu'uanu Pali, Bishop Museum, Waimea Canyon, Wailua River State Park .

Famous Islanders. Bernice Pauahi Bishop, John A. Burns, Father Damien de Veuster, Daniel K. Inouye, Duke Kahanamoku, King Kamehameha the Great, Queen Ka'ahumanu, Queen Liliuokalani, Ellison Onizuka.

Chamber of Commerce of Hawaii. 1132 Bishop St., Suite 200, Honolulu, HI 96813.

Idaho

Gem State

People. Population (1993): 1,099,096; **rank:** 42. **Pop. density:** 12.9 per sq. mi. **Racial/ethnic distrib.** (1990): 94.4% white; 0.3% black; 5.3% Hispanic. **Net change** (1990-93): 9.2%.

Geography. Total area: 83,574 sq. mi.; **rank:** 14. **Land area:** 82,751 sq. mi. **Acres forested land:** 21,621,000. **Location:** northwestern Mountain state bordering on British Columbia. **Climate:** tempered by Pacific westerly winds; drier, colder, continental clime in SE; altitude an important factor. **Topography:** Snake R. plains in the S; central region of mountains, canyons, gorges (Hells Canyon, 7,900 ft., deepest in N.A.); subalpine northern region. **Capital:** Boise.

Economy. Principal industries: agriculture, manufacturing, tourism, lumber, mining, electronics. **Principal manufactured goods:** processed foods, lumber and wood products, chemical products, primary metals, fabricated metal products, machinery, electronic components, computer equip. **Agriculture: Chief crops:** potatoes, peas, sugar beets, alfalfa seed, wheat, hops, barley, plums and prunes, mint, onions, corn, cherries, apples, hay. **Livestock** (1993): 1.68 mln. cattle; 250,000 sheep; 60,000 hogs; 1.22 mln. poultry. **Timber/lumber** (1992): yellow, white pine; Douglas fir; white spruce; 1.8 bln. bd. ft. **Nonfuel Minerals** (1993): $282.6 mln.; phosphate rock, gold, sand & gravel, silver. **Chief ports:** Lewiston. **Value of construction** (1993) $1.7 bln. **Employment distribution** (1993): 24% trade; 21% serv., 15% mfg.; 6% agric.; 5% constr. **Per capita personal income** (1993): $17,546. **Unemployment** (1993): 6.1%. **Tourism** (1993): travelers spent $1.7 bln. **Sales tax:** 5%.

Finance. FDIC-insured commercial banks & trust companies (1993): 21. **Deposits:** $8.3 bln. **FDIC-insured savings institutions** (1993): 4. **Assets:** $498 mln.

Federal government. No. federal civilian employees (Mar. 1993): 8,066. **Avg. salary:** $34,953. **Notable federal facilities:** Ida. Nat'l. Engineering Lab, Idaho Falls; Mt. Home Air Force Base, Mt. Home.

Energy. Electricity production (1993, kWh, by source): Hydroelectric: 9 bln.

Education: Student-teacher ratio (1992): 19.6. **Avg. salary, public school teachers** (1993-94): $27,803.

State data. Motto: Esto Perpetua (It is perpetual). **Flower:** Syringa. **Bird:** Mountain bluebird. **Tree:** White pine. **Song:** Here We Have Idaho. **Entered union** July 3, 1890; rank, 43d. **State fair** at: Boise, late Aug.; and Blackfoot, early Sept.

History. Exploration of the Idaho area began with Lewis and Clark, 1805-6. Next came fur traders, setting up posts, 1809-34, and missionaries, establishing missions, 1830s-1850s. Mormons made their first permanent settlement at Franklin, 1860. Idaho's Gold Rush began that same year, and brought thousands of permanent settlers. Strangest of the Indian Wars was the

1,300-mi. trek in 1877 of Chief Joseph and the Nez Perce tribe, pursued by troops that caught them a few miles short of the Canadian border. In 1890, Idaho adopted a progressive Constitution and became a state.

Tourist attractions. Hells Canyon, deepest gorge in N.A.; World Center for Birds of Prey; Craters of the Moon; Sun Valley, year-round resort in the Sawtooth Mtns.; Crystal Falls Cave; Shoshone Falls; Lava Hot Springs; Lake Pend Oreille; Lake Coeur d'Alene; Sawtooth Natl. Recreation Area; River of No Return Wilderness Area.

Famous Idahoans. William E. Borah, Frank Church, Fred T. Dubois, Chief Joseph, Sacagawea.

Tourist information. Department of Commerce, 700 W. State St., Boise, ID 83720.

Toll-free travel information. 1-800-635-7820.

Illinois

The Prairie State

People. Population (1993): 11,697,336; **rank:** 6. **Pop. density:** 209.2 per sq. mi. **Racial/ethnic distrib.** (1990): 78.3% white; 14.8% black; 7.9% Hispanic. **Net change** (1990-93): 2.3%.

Geography. Total area: 57,918 sq. mi.; **rank:** 25. **Land area:** 55,593 sq. mi. **Acres forested land:** 4,266,000. **Location:** East North Central state; western, southern, and eastern boundaries formed by Mississippi, Ohio, and Wabash rivers, respectively. **Climate:** temperate; typically cold, snowy winters, hot summers. **Topography:** prairie and fertile plains throughout; open hills in the southern region. **Capital:** Springfield.

Economy. Principal industries: services, manufacturing, travel, wholesale and retail trade, finance, insurance, real estate, construction, health care, agriculture. **Principal manufactured goods:** machinery, electric and electronic equipment, primary and fabricated metals, chemical products, printing and publishing, food and kindred prods. **Agriculture: Chief crops:** corn, soybeans, wheat, sorghum, hay. **Livestock** (1993): 1.98 mln. cattle; 5.3 mln. hogs/pigs; 95,000 sheep; 3.6 mln. poultry. **Timber/lumber** (1992): oak, hickory, maple, cottonwood; 8 mln. bd. ft. **Nonfuel Minerals** (1993): $731.6 mln.; mostly crushed stone, cement, construction & industrial sand & gravel, lime. **Commercial fishing** (1993): $275,000. **Chief ports:** Chicago. **International airports at:** Chicago. **Value of construction** (1993): $11.2 bln. **Employment distribution** (1993): 19.9% serv.; 16.4% trade; 18.9% mfg. **Per capita personal income** (1993): $22,582. **Unemployment** (1993): 7.4%. **Tourism** (1993): out-of-state visitors spent $15 bln. **Sales tax**: 6.25%.

Finance. FDIC-insured commercial banks & trust companies (1993): 958. **Deposits:** $161.2 bln. **FDIC-insured savings institutions** (1993): 166. **Assets:** $43.4 bln.

Federal government. No. federal civilian employees (Mar. 1993): 52,460. **Avg. salary:** $37,266. **Notable federal facilities:** Fermi Nat'l. Accelerator Lab; Argonne Nat'l. Lab; Rock Island Arsenal; Great Lakes, Naval Training Station, Scott AFB.

Energy. Electricity production (1993, kWh, by source): Coal: 59.8 bln.; Petroleum: 719 mln.; Gas: 1.2 bln.; Hydroelectric: 40 mln.; Nuclear: 78.4 bln.

Education. Student-teacher ratio (1992): 16.8. **Avg. salary, public school teachers** (1993-94): $40,989.

State data. Motto: State sovereignty—national union. **Flower:** Native violet. **Bird:** Cardinal. **Tree:** White oak. **Song:** Illinois. **Entered union** Dec. 3, 1818; rank, 21st. **State fair** at: Springfield, mid-Aug.; DuQuoin, late Aug.

History. Fur traders were the first Europeans in Illinois, followed shortly, 1673, by Jolliet and Marquette, and, 1680, La Salle, who built a fort near present Peoria. First settlements were French, at Fort St. Louis on the Illinois River, 1692, and Kaskaskia, 1700. France ceded the area to Britain, 1763; Amer. Gen. George Rogers Clark, 1778, took Kaskaskia from the British without a shot. Defeat of Indian tribes in Black Hawk War, 1832, and railroads in 1850s, inspired change.

Tourist attractions: Chicago museums, parks; Lincoln shrines at Springfield, New Salem, Sangamon County; Cahokia Mounds, E. St. Louis; Starved Rock State Park; Crab Orchard Wildlife Refuge; Mormon settlement at Nauvoo; Fts. Kaskaskia, Chartres, Massac (parks); Shawnee Natl. Forest, Southern Illinois; Illinois State Museum, Springfield; Dickson Mounds Museum, btwn. Havana & Lewistown.

Famous Illinoisans. Jane Addams, Saul Bellow, Jack Benny, Ray Bradbury, Gwendolyn Brooks, William Jennings Bryan, St. Francis Xavier Cabrini, Hillary Rodham Clinton, Clarence Darrow, John Deere, Stephen A. Douglas, James T. Farrell, George W. Ferris, Marshall Field, Betty Friedan, Benny Goodman, Ulysses S. Grant, Ernest Hemingway, Wild Bill Hickok, Abraham Lincoln, Vachel Lindsay, Edgar Lee Masters, Oscar Mayer, Cyrus McCormick, Ronald Reagan, Carl Sandburg, Adlai Stevenson, Frank Lloyd Wright, Philip Wrigley.

Tourist information. Illinois Dept. of Commerce and Community Affairs, 620 E. Adams St., Springfield, IL 62701. **Toll-free literature:** 1-800-223-0121.

Indiana

Hoosier State

People. Population (1993): 5,712,799; **rank:** 14. **Pop. density:** 157.8 per sq. mi. **Racial/ethnic distrib.** (1990): 90.6% white; 7.8% black; 1.8% Hispanic. **Net change** (1990-93): 3%.

Geography. Total area: 36,420 sq. mi.; **rank:** 38. **Land area:** 35,870 sq. mi. **Acres forested land:** 4,439,000. **Location:** East North Central state; Lake Michigan on northern border. **Climate:** 4 distinct seasons with a temperate climate. **Topography:** hilly southern region; fertile rolling plains of central region; flat, heavily glaciated north; dunes along Lake Michigan shore. **Capital:** Indianapolis.

Economy: Principal industries: manufacturing, services, agriculture, government, wholsesale and retail trade, transportation and public utilities. **Principal manufactured goods:** primary metals, transportation equipment, motor vehicles and equipment, industrial machinery and equipment, electronic and electric equipment. **Agriculture: Chief crops** (1992): corn, wheat, soybeans, nursery and greenhouse products, vegetables, sweet corn, melons, hay. **Livestock** (1992): 1.1 mln. cattle; 4.6 mln. hogs/pigs; 72,386 sheep; 58.7 mln. chickens; 12.6 mln. turkeys. **Timber/lumber** (1992): oak, tulip, beech, sycamore; 192 mln. bd. ft. **Nonfuel Minerals** (1993): $501.2 mln.; mostly crushed stone, cement, construction sand & gravel. **Commercial fishing** (1993): $2.3 mln. **Chief ports:** Burns Harbor, Portage; Southwind Maritime, Mt. Vernon; Clark Maritime, Jeffersonville. **International airports at:** Indianapolis, Ft. Wayne. **Value of construction** (1993): $7.1 bln. **Employment distribution** (1989): 27.9% mfg.; 24.8% trade; 19.8% serv; 12.3% gvt. **Per capita personal income** (1993): $19,203. **Unemployment** (1993): 5.3%. **Tourism** (1992): tourists spent $4.4 bln. **Sales tax**: 5%, with exemptions.

Finance. FDIC-insured commercial banks & trust companies (1993): 237. **Deposits:** $49.5 bln. **FDIC-insured savings institutions** (1993): 85. **Assets:** $13.9 bln.

Federal government. No. federal civilian employees (Mar. 1993): 26,107. **Avg. salary:** $34,366. **Notable federal facilities:** Naval Air Warfare Ctr.; Ft. Benjamin Harrison; Grissom AFB; Naval Surface Warfare Ctr., Crane.

Energy. Electricity production (1993, kWh, by source): Coal: 98.8 bln.; Petroleum: 719 mln.; Gas: 529 mln.; Hydroelectric: 448 mln.

Education. Student-teacher ratio (1992): 17.6. **Avg. salary, public school teachers** (1993-94): $36,255.

State data. Motto: Crossroads of America. **Flower:** Peony. **Bird:** Cardinal. **Tree:** Tulip poplar. **Song:** On the Banks of the Wabash, Far Away. **Entered union** Dec. 11, 1816; rank, 19th. **State fair** at: Indianapolis; mid-Aug.

History. Pre-historic Indian Mound Builders of 1,000 years ago were the earliest known inhabitants. A French trading post was built, 1731-32, at Vincennes and La Salle visited the present South Bend area, 1679 and 1681. France ceded the area to Britain, 1763. During the Revolution, American Gen. George Rogers Clark captured Vincennes, 1778, and defeated British forces 1779; at war's end Britain ceded the area to the U.S. Miami Indians defeated U.S. troops twice, 1790, but were beaten, 1794, at Fallen Timbers by Gen. Anthony Wayne. At Tippecanoe, 1811, Gen. William H. Harrison defeated Tecumseh's Indian confederation.

Tourist attractions. Lincoln Boyhood, George Rogers Clark memorials; Wyandotte Cave; Vincennes, Tippecanoe sites; Indiana Dunes; Hoosier Nat'l. Forest; Benjamin Harrison Home; Basketball Hall of Fame, New Harmony; Dan Quayle Museum, Huntington; Indianapolis 500 race and museum.

Famous "Hoosiers." Larry Bird, Ambrose Burnside, Hoagy Carmichael, Jim Davis, James Dean, Eugene V. Debs, Theodore Dreiser, Paul Dresser, Gil Hodges, David Letterman, Jane Pauley, Cole Porter, Gene Stratton Porter, Ernie Pyle, James Whitcomb Riley, Oscar Robertson, Red Skelton, Booth Tarkington, Lew Wallace, Wendell L. Willkie, Wilbur Wright.

Chamber of Commerce. One North Capital, Suite 200, Indianapolis, IN 46204.

Toll-free travel information. 1-800-289-6646.

Iowa

Hawkeye State

People. Population (1993): 2,814,064; **rank:** 30. **Pop. density:** 50.3 per sq. mi. **Racial/ethnic distrib.** (1990): 96.6% white; 1.7% black; 1.2% Hispanic. **Net change** (1990-93): 1.3%.

Geography. Total area: 56,276 sq. mi.; **rank:** 26. **Land area:** 55,875 sq. mi. **Acres forested land:** 2,050,000. **Location:** West North Central state bordered by Mississippi R. on the E and Missouri R. on the W. **Climate:** humid, continental. **Topography:** Watershed from NW to SE; soil especially rich and land level in the N central counties. **Capital:** Des Moines.

Economy. Principal industries: agriculture, communications, construction, finance, insurance, trade, services, mfg. **Principal manufactured goods:** tires, farm machinery, electronic products, appliances, household furniture, chemicals, fertilizers, auto accessories. **Agriculture: Chief crops:** silage and grain corn, soybeans, oats, hay. **Livestock** (1993): 4.4 mln. cattle; 15.0 mln. swine; 320,000 sheep & lambs; 8.4 mln. turkeys. **Timber/lumber** (1992): red cedar; 37 mln. bd. ft. **Nonfuel Minerals** (1993): $343.6 mln.; mostly crushed stone, portland cement, construction sand & gravel. **Value of construction** (1993): 2.3 bln. **Employment distribution** (1993): 25.4% trade; 24.5% serv.; 18.4% mfg.; 17.7% gvt. **Per capita personal income** (1993): $18,315. **Unemployment** (1993): 4.0%. **Tourism** (1992): tourists spent $2.5 bln. **Sales tax:** 5%.

Finance. FDIC-insured commercial banks & trust companies (1993): 530. **Deposits:** $32.0 bln. **FDIC-insured savings institutions** (1993): 31. **Assets:** $4.7 bln.

Federal government. No. federal civilian employees (Mar. 1993): 7,993. **Avg. salary:** $33,948.

Energy. Electricity production (1993, kWh, by source): Coal: 26.6 bln.; Petroleum: 49 mln.; Gas: 305 mln.; Hydroelectric: 737 mln.; Nuclear: 3.2 bln.

Education. Student-teacher ratio (1992): 15.8. **Avg. salary, public school teachers** (1993-94): $30,760.

State data. Motto: Our liberties we prize and our rights we will maintain. **Flower:** Wild rose. **Bird:** Eastern goldfinch. **Tree:** Oak. **Rock:** Geode. **Entered union** Dec. 28, 1846; rank, 29th. **State fair** at: Des Moines; mid-Aug.

History. A thousand years ago several groups of prehistoric Indian Mound Builders dwelt on Iowa's fertile plains. Marquette and Jolliet gave France its claim to the area, 1673. It became U.S. territory through the 1803 Louisiana Purchase. Indian tribes were moved into the area from states further east, but by mid-19th century were forced to move on to Kansas. Before and during the Civil War, Iowans strongly supported Abraham Lincoln and became traditional Republicans.

Tourist attractions. Herbert Hoover birthplace and library, West Branch; Effigy Mounds Nat'l. Monument, Marquette, a pre-historic Indian burial site; Amana Colonies; Davenport Municipal Art Gallery's collection of Grant Wood's paintings and memorabilia; Living History Farms, Des Moines; Adventureland, Altoona; Boone & Scenic Valley Railroad, Boone; Greyhound Parks in Dubuque, Council Bluffs & Waterloo; Prairie Meadows horse racing, Altoona; riverboat cruises and casino gambling, Mississippi River; Iowa Great Lakes, Okoboji.

Famous Iowans. James A. Van Allen, Marquis Childs, Buffalo Bill Cody, Mamie Dowd Eisenhower, George Gallup, Susan Glaspell, James Norman Hall, Harry Hansen, Herbert Hoover, Glenn Miller, Billy Sunday, Carl Van Vechten, Henry Wallace, John Wayne, Meredith Willson, Grant Wood.

Tourist information. Division of Tourism, Iowa Dept. of Economic Development, 200 E. Grand Ave., Des Moines, IA 50309.

Toll-free travel information. 1-800-345-IOWA.

Kansas

Sunflower State

People. Population (1993): 2,530,746; **rank:** 32. **Pop. density:** 30.8 per sq. mi. **Racial/ethnic distrib.** (1990): 90.1% white; 5.8% black; 3.8% Hispanic. **Net change** (1990-93): 2.1%.

Geography. Total area: 82,282 sq. mi.; **rank:** 15. **Land area:** 81,823 sq. mi. **Acres forested land:** 1,359,000. **Location:** West North Central state, with Missouri R. on E. **Climate:** temperate but continental, with great extremes bet. summer and winter. **Topography:** hilly Osage Plains in the E; central region level prairie and hills; high plains in the W. **Capital:** Topeka.

Economy. Principal industries: manufacturing, finance, insurance, real estate, services. **Principal manufactured goods:** transportation equip., machinery and computer equipment, food and kindred products, printing and publishing. **Agriculture: Chief crops:** wheat, sorghum, corn, hay, soybeans. **Livestock** (1992): 5.65 mln. cattle; 1.44 mln. hogs/pigs; 179,000 sheep & lambs; 1.8 mln. poultry. **Timber/lumber:** oak, walnut. **Nonfuel Minerals** (1993): $383.9 mln.; salt, helium, cement, crushed stone. **Chief ports:** Kansas City. **International airports at:** Wichita. **Value of construction** (1993): $2.7 bln. **Employment distribution** (1993): 20.6% trade; 20.6% serv.; 17.3% gvt.; 13.6% mfg. **Per capita personal income** (1993): $20,139. **Unemployment** (1993): 5.0%. **Tourism** (1991): out-of-state visitors spent $2.1 bln. **Sales tax:** 6.9% maximum.

Finance. FDIC-insured commercial banks & trust companies (1993): 490. **Deposits:** $25.5 bln. **FDIC-insured savings institutions** (1993): 25. **Assets** : $7.3 bln.

Federal government. No. federal civilian employees (Mar. 1993): 16,757. **Avg. salary:** $33,991. **Notable federal facilities:** McConnell AFB; Fts. Riley, Leavenworth.

Energy. Electricity production (1993, kWh, by source): Coal: 26.8 bln.; Petroleum: 76 mln.; Gas: 1.7 bln.; Nuclear: 7.9 bln.

Education. Student-teacher ratio (1992): 15.2. **Avg. salary, public school teachers** (1993-94): $34,178.

State data. Motto: Ad Astra per Aspera (To the stars through difficulties). **Flower:** Native sunflower. **Bird:** Western meadowlark. **Tree:** Cottonwood. **Song:** Home on the Range. **Entered union** Jan. 29, 1861; rank, 34th. **State fair** at: Hutchinson; begins Friday after Labor Day.

History. Coronado marched through the Kansas area, 1541; French explorers came next. The U.S. took over in the Louisiana Purchase, 1803. In the pre-war North-South struggle over slavery, so much violence swept the area it was called Bleeding Kansas. Railroad construction after the war made Abilene and Dodge City terminals of large cattle drives from Texas.

Tourist attractions. Eisenhower Center and "Place of Meditation," Abilene; Agricultural Hall of Fame and National Ctr., Bonner Springs, displays farm equipment; Dodge City-Boot Hill & Frontier Town; Cowtown historic frontier town, Wichita; Ft. Scott & Ft. Larned, restored 1800s cavalry forts; Kansas Cosmosphere and Space Discovery Center, Hutchinson.

Famous Kansans. Thomas Hart Benton, John Brown, Walter P. Chrysler, John Steuart Curry, Amelia Earhart, Dwight D. Eisenhower, Ron Evans, Wild Bill Hickok, Cyrus Holliday, William Inge, Walter Johnson, Alf Landon, Carry Nation, Gordon Parks, Jim Ryun, William Allen White.

Tourist information. Kansas Dept. of Commerce & Housing, Travel and Tourism Div., 700 SW Harrison, Suite 1300, Topeka, KS 66603; 1-913-296-2009.

Toll-free travel information. 1-800-2KANSAS.

Kentucky

Bluegrass State

People. Population (1993): 3,788,808; **rank:** 24. **Pop. density:** 94.5 per sq. mi. **Racial/ethnic distrib.** (1990): 92.0% white; 7.1% black; 0.6% Hispanic. **Net change** (1990-93): 2.8%.

Geography. Total area: 40,411 sq. mi.; **rank:** 37. **Land area:** 39,732 sq. mi. **Acres forested land:** 12,714,000. **Location:** East South Central state, bordered on N by Illinois, Indiana, Ohio; on E by West Virginia and Virginia; on S by Tennessee; on W by Missouri. **Climate:** moderate, with plentiful rainfall. **Topography:** mountainous in E; rounded hills of the Knobs in the N; Bluegrass, heart of state; wooded rocky hillsides of the Pennyroyal; Western Coal Field; the fertile Purchase in the SW. **Capital:** Frankfort.

Economy. Principal industries: manufacturing, finance, insurance and real estate, services, retail trade. **Principal manufactured goods:** transportation equip., chemicals, food products, industrial machinery, primary metals. **Agriculture: Chief crops** (1991): tobacco, soybeans, corn. **Livestock** (1993): 2.6 mln. cattle; 870,000 hogs/pigs; 23,000 sheep; 3.1 mln. chickens; 1993 receipts for horse & mule sales, $433 mln. **Timber/lumber** (1992): hardwoods, pines; 559 mln. bd. ft. **Nonfuel Minerals** (1993): $415.8 mln.; mostly crushed stone. **Chief ports:** Paducah, Louisville, Covington, Owensboro, Ashland, Henderson County, Lyon County, Hickman-Fulton County. **International airports at:** Covington. **Value of construction** (1993): $4.3 bln. **Employment distribution** (1993): 22.9% serv.; 22.8% trade; 18.5% mfg.; 17.5% gvt. **Per capita personal income** (1993): $17,173. **Unemployment** (1993): 6.2%. **Tourism** (1993): tourists spent $6.8 bln. **Sales tax:** 6%.

Finance. FDIC-insured commercial banks & trust companies (1993): 309. **Deposits:** $35.1 bln. **FDIC-insured savings institutions** (1993): 55. **Assets:** $7.3 bln.

Federal government. No. federal civilian employees (Mar. 1993): 27,823. **Avg. salary:** $30,792. **Notable federal facilities:** U.S. Gold Bullion Depository, Fort Knox; Federal Correctional Institution, Lexington.

Energy. Electricity production (1993, kWh, by source): Coal: 81.7 bln.; Petroleum: 96 mln.; Gas: 24 mln.; Hydroelectric: 3.2 bln.

Education. Student-teacher ratio (1992): 17.3. **Avg. salary, public school teachers** (1993-94): $31,582.

State data. Motto: United we stand, divided we fall. **Flower:** Goldenrod. **Bird:** Cardinal. **Tree:** Kentucky coffee tree. **Song:** My Old Kentucky Home. **Entered union** June 1, 1792; rank, 15th. **State fair** at: Louisville.

History. Kentucky was the first area west of the Alleghenies settled by American pioneers; first permanent settlement, Harrodsburg, 1774. Daniel Boone blazed the Wilderness Trail through the Cumberland Gap and founded Fort Boonesborough, 1775. Indian attacks, spurred by the British, were unceasing until, during the Revolution, Gen. George Rogers Clark captured British forts in Indiana and Illinois, 1778. In 1792, after Virginia dropped its claims to the region, Kentucky became the 15th state.

Tourist attractions. Kentucky Derby and accompanying festivities, Louisville; Land Between the Lakes Nat'l. Recreation Area encompassing Kentucky Lake and Lake Barkley; Mammoth Cave National Park with 330 mi. of explored passageways, 200-ft. high rooms, blind fish, and Echo River, 360 ft. below ground; Lake Cumberland in south central Kentucky; Lincoln birthplace, Hodgenville; My Old Kentucky Home, Bardstown; Cumberland Gap Natl. Historical Park, Middlesboro; Kentucky Horse Park, Lexington; Shaker Village, Pleasant Hill.

Famous Kentuckians. Muhammad Ali (Cassius Marcellus Clay), John James Audubon, Alben Barkley, Daniel Boone, Louis D. Brandeis, John C. Breckinridge, Kit Carson, Albert B. "Happy" Chandler, Henry Clay, Jefferson Davis, "Casey" Jones, Abraham Lincoln, Mary Todd Lincoln, Thomas Hunt Morgan, Carry Nation, Col. Harland Sanders, Diane Sawyer, Jesse Stuart, Adlai Stevenson, Zachary Taylor, Robert Penn Warren, Whitney Young, Jr.

Chamber of Commerce. 452 Versailles Rd., P.O. Box 817, Frankfort, KY 40602.

Toll-free travel information. 1-800-225-TRIP, extension 67 in U.S., Ontario & Quebec, Canada.

Louisiana

Pelican State

People. Population (1993): 4,295,477; **rank:** 21. **Pop. density:** 98.4 per sq. mi. **Racial/ethnic distrib.** (1990): 67.3% white; 30.8% black; 2.2% Hispanic. **Net change** (1990-93): 1.9%.

Geography. Total area: 51,843 sq. mi.; **rank:** 31. **Land area:** 43,566 sq. mi. **Acres forested land:** 13,864,000. **Location:** West South Central state on the Gulf Coast. **Climate:** subtropical, affected by continental weather patterns. **Topography:** lowlands of marshes and Mississippi R. flood plain; Red R. Valley lowlands; upland hills in the Florida Parishes; average elevation, 100 ft. **Capital:** Baton Rouge.

Economy. Principal industries: wholesale and retail trade, tourism, government, manufacturing, construction, transportation, mining. **Principal manufactured goods** (1991): chemical products, foods, transportation equipment, electronic equipment, petroleum products, lumber, wood, and paper. **Agriculture: Chief crops** (1991): soybean, sugarcane, rice, corn, cotton, sweet potatoes, pecans, sorghum. **Livestock** (1991): 1.02 mln. cattle; 60,000 hogs/pigs; 16,000 sheep; 1.85 mln. poultry. **Timber/lumber** (1992): pines, hardwoods, oak; 896 mln. bd. ft. **Nonfuel Minerals** (1993): $256 mln., mostly salt, construction sand & gravel, sulfur. **Commercial fishing** (1993): $261.8 mln. **Chief ports:** New Orleans, Baton Rouge, Lake Charles, S. Louisiana Port Commission at La Place, Shreveport. **International airports at:** New Orleans. **Value of construction** (1993): $3.5 bln. **Employment distribution** (1991): 22.8% trade; 23.8% serv.; 21.2% gvt.; 11.4% mfg. **Per capita personal income** (1993): $16,667. **Unemployment** (1993): 7.4%. **Tourism** (1992): out-of-state visitors spent $5.2 bln. **Sales tax**: 4%.

Finance. FDIC-insured commercial banks & trust companies (1993): 217. **Deposits**: $34.0 bln. **FDIC-insured savings institutions** (1993): 39. **Assets:** $4.5 bln.

Federal government. No. federal civilian employees (Mar. 1993): 22,171. **Avg. salary:** $33,552. **Notable federal facilities:** Barksdale, Ft. Polk military bases; Strategic Petroleum Reserve, New Orleans; Michoud Assembly Plant, New Orleans; U.S. Public Service Hospital, Carville.

Energy. Electricity production (1993, kWh, by source): Coal: 19.4 bln.; Petroleum: 1.8 bln.; Gas: 23.7 bln.; Nuclear: 14.4 bln.

Education. Student-teacher ratio (1992): 16.6. **Avg. salary, public school teachers** (1993-94): $28,508.

State data. Motto: Union, justice and confidence. **Flower:** Magnolia. **Bird:** Eastern brown pelican. **Tree:** Cypress. **Song:** Give Me Louisiana. **Entered union** Apr. 30, 1812; rank, 18th. **State fair** at: Shreveport; Oct.

History. The area was first visited, 1530, by Cabeza de Vaca and Panfilo de Narvaez. The region was claimed for France by La Salle, 1682. First permanent settlement was by French at Biloxi, now in Mississippi, 1699. France ceded the region to Spain, 1762, took it back, 1800, and sold it to the U.S., 1803, in the Louisiana Purchase. During the Revolution, Spanish Louisiana aided the Americans. Admitted to statehood, 1812, Louisiana was the scene of the Battle of New Orleans, 1815.

Louisiana Creoles are descendants of early French and/or Spanish settlers. About 4,000 Acadians, French settlers in Nova Scotia, Canada, were forcibly transported by the British to Louisiana in 1755 (an event commemorated in Longfellow's *Evangeline*) and settled near Bayou Teche; their descendants became known as Cajuns. Another group, the Islenos, were descendants of Canary Islanders brought to Louisiana by a Spanish governor in 1770. Traces of Spanish and French survive in local dialects.

Tourist attractions. Mardi Gras, French Quarter, Superdome, Dixieland jazz, Aquarium of the Americas, all New Orleans; Battle of New Orleans site; Longfellow-Evangeline Memorial Park; Kent House Museum, Alexandria; Hodges Gardens, Natchitoches.

Famous Louisianans. Louis Armstrong, Pierre Beauregard, Judah P. Benjamin, Braxton Bragg, Grace King, Huey Long, Leonidas K. Polk, Henry Miller Shreve, Edward D. White Jr.

Tourist information. State Dept. of Culture, Recreation & Tourism, P.O. Box 94291, Baton Rouge, LA 70804-9291.

Toll-free travel information. 1-800-633-6970.

Maine

Pine Tree State

People. Population (1993): 1,239,448; **rank:** 39. **Pop. density:** 40.0 per sq. mi. **Racial/ethnic distrib.** (1990): 98.4% white; 0.4% black; 0.6% Hispanic. **Net change** (1990-93): 0.9%.

Geography. Total area: 35,387 sq. mi.; **rank:** 39. **Land area:** 30,865 sq. mi. **Acres forested land:** 17,533,000. **Location:** New England state at northeastern tip of U.S. **Climate:** Southern interior and coastal, influenced by air masses from the S and W; northern clime harsher, avg. + 100 in. snow in winter. **Topography:** Appalachian Mtns. extend through state; western borders have rugged terrain; long sand beaches on southern coast; northern coast mainly rocky promontories, peninsulas, fjords. **Capital:** Augusta.

Economy. Principal industries: manufacturing, agriculture, fishing, services, trade, government, finance, insurance, real estate, construction. **Principal manufactured goods:** paper and wood products, transportation equipment. **Agriculture: Chief crops:** potatoes, apples, hay, blueberries. **Livestock** (1993): 114,000 cattle; 9,000 hogs/pigs; 18,000 sheep; 5.8 mln. poultry. **Timber/lumber** (1992): pine, spruce, fir; 872 mln. bd. ft. **Nonfuel Minerals** (1993): $60.9 mln.; cement, construction sand & gravel, crushed stone. **Commercial fishing** (1993): $181.1 mln. **Chief ports:** Searsport, Portland, Eastport. **International airports at:** Portland, Bangor. **Value of construction** (1993): $960.5 mln. **Employment distribution** (1993): 25.8% serv.; 25.1% trade; 18.3% govt.; 17.6% mfg. **Per capita personal income** (1993): $18,895. **Unemployment** (1993): 7.9%. **Tourism** (1991): $2.75 bln. **Sales tax:** 6%.

Finance. FDIC-insured commercial banks & trust companies (1993): 20. **Deposits**: $6.8 bln. **FDIC-insured savings institutions** (1993): 31. **Assets**: $6.4 bln.

Federal government. No. federal civilian employees (Mar. 1993): 11,068. **Avg. salary:** $34,077. **Notable federal facilities:** Kittery Naval Shipyard; Brunswick Naval Air Station.

Energy. Electricity production (1993, kWh, by source): Petroleum: 760 mln.; Hydroelectric: 1.6 bln.; Nuclear: 5.7 bln.

Education. Student-teacher ratio (1992): 14.1. **Avg. salary, public school teachers** (1993-94): $30,996.

State data. Motto: Dirigo (I direct). **Flower:** White pine cone and tassel. **Bird:** Chickadee. **Tree:** Eastern white pine. **Song:** State of Maine Song. **Entered union** Mar. 15, 1820; rank, 23d.

History. Maine's rocky coast was explored by the Cabots, 1498-99. French settlers arrived, 1604, at the St. Croix River; English, 1607, on the Kennebec. In 1691, Maine was made part of Massachusetts. In the Revolution, a Maine regiment fought at Bunker Hill; a British fleet destroyed Falmouth (now Portland), 1775, but the British ship Margaretta was captured near Machiasport. In 1820, Maine broke off from Massachusetts, became a separate state.

Tourist attractions. Acadia Nat'l. Park, Bar Harbor, on Mt. Desert Is.; Old Orchard Beach; Portland's Old Port; Kennebunkport; Common Ground Country Fair; Portland Headlight; Baxter State Park; Freeport; Camden.

Famous "Down Easters." James G. Blaine, Cyrus H.K. Curtis, Hannibal Hamlin, Stephen King, Longfellow, Sir Hiram and Hudson Maxim, Edna St. Vincent Millay, Edmund Muskie, Kate Douglas Wiggin, Ben Ames Williams.

Chamber of Commerce and Industry. 126 Sewall St., Augusta, ME 04330.

Toll-free travel information. 1-800-533-9595, out of state only; 1-207-623-0363, in-state.

Toll-free business information. 1-800-541-5872, out of state only; 1-800-872-3838, in state.

Maryland

Old Line State, Free State

People. Population (1993): 4,964,898; **rank:** 19. **Pop. density:** 502.1 per sq. mi. **Racial/ethnic distrib.** (1990): 71.0% white; 24.9% black; 2.9% Asian; 2.6% Hispanic. **Net change** (1990-93): 3.8%.

Geography. Total area: 12,407 sq. mi.; **rank:** 42. **Land area:** 9,775 sq. mi. **Acres forested land:** 2,700,000. **Location:** South Atlantic state stretching from the Ocean to the Allegheny Mtns. **Climate:** continental in the west; humid subtropical in the east. **Topography:** Eastern Shore of coastal plain and Maryland Main of coastal plain, piedmont plateau, and the Blue Ridge, separated by the Chesapeake Bay. **Capital:** Annapolis.

Economy. Principal industries: manufacturing, biotechnology and information technology, services, tourism. **Principal manufactured goods:** electric and electronic equipment; food and kindred products; chemicals and allied products; printed materials. **Agriculture: Chief crops** (1993): greenhouse & nursery prods., soybeans, corn. **Livestock** (1993): 315,000 cattle; 170,000 hogs/pigs; 33,000 sheep; 3.27 mln. layers; 294.7 mln. broilers. **Timber/lumber:** hardwoods. **Nonfuel Minerals** (1993): $361 mln.; crushed stone, sand & gravel, lime, portland cement. **Commercial fishing** (1993): $53.4 mln. **Chief ports:** Baltimore. **International airports at:** Baltimore-Washington Intl. **Value of construction** (1993): $5.2 bln. **Employment distribution** (1992): 30.3% serv.; 24.2% trade; 19.9% gvt. **Per capita personal income** (1993): $24,044. **Unemployment** (1993): 6.2%. **Tourism** (1993): tourists spent $4.5 bln. **Sales tax:** 5.0%.

Finance. FDIC-insured commercial banks & trust companies (1993): 94. **Deposits:** $40.7 bln. **FDIC-insured savings institutions** (1993): 83. **Assets:** $16.7 bln.

Federal government. No. federal civilian employees (Mar. 1993): 108,781. **Avg. salary:** $42,015. **Notable federal facilities:** U.S. Naval Academy, Annapolis; Natl. Agric. Research Cen.; Ft. George G. Meade, Aberdeen Proving Ground; Goddard Space Flight Center; Natl. Institutes of Health; Natl. Institute of Standards & Technology; Food & Drug Administration; Bureau of the Census.

Energy. Electricity production (1993, kWh, by source): Coal: 24.9 bln.; Petroleum: 4.0 bln.; Gas: 685 mln.; Hydroelectric: 1.7 bln.; Nuclear: 12.3 bln.

Education. Student-teacher ratio (1992): 16.9 **Avg. salary, public school teachers** (1993-94): $39,937.

State data. Motto: Fatti Maschii, Parole Femine (Manly deeds, womanly words). **Flower:** Black-eyed susan. **Bird:** Baltimore oriole. **Tree:** White oak. **Song:** Maryland, My Maryland. **Seventh** of the original 13 states to ratify Constitution, Apr. 28, 1788. **State fair** at: Timonium; late Aug.-early Sept.

History. Capt. John Smith first explored Maryland, 1608. William Claiborne set up a trading post on Kent Is. in Chesapeake Bay, 1631. Britain granted land to Cecilius Calvert, Lord Baltimore, 1632; his brother led 200 settlers to St. Marys River, 1634. The bravery of Maryland troops in the Revolution, as at the Battle of Long Island, won the state its nickname The Old Line State. In the War of 1812, when a British fleet tried to take Fort McHenry, Marylander Francis Scott Key, 1814, wrote *The Star-Spangled Banner.*

Tourist attractions. Racing events include the Preakness and Maryland Million, both at Pimlico track, Baltimore, and the International at Laurel Race Course; Baltimore Orioles pro baseball at Oriole Park, Camden Yards. Also Annapolis yacht races; Ocean City beach resort; restored Ft. McHenry, Baltimore, near which Francis Scott Key wrote *The Star-Spangled Banner;* Antietam Battlefield, 1862, near Hagerstown; South Mountain Battlefield, 1862; Edgar Allan Poe house, Baltimore; National Aquarium, Baltimore Harborplace; The State House, Annapolis, 1772, the oldest still in use in the U.S.; Montgomery & Prince George's County, gateway to Washington, D.C.

Famous Marylanders. Benjamin Banneker, Francis Scott Key, H.L. Mencken, Charles Willson Peale, William Pinkney, Upton Sinclair, Roger B. Taney.

Maryland Dept. of Economic & Employment Development. 217 E. Redwood St., Baltimore, MD 21202; (410) 333-6970.

Toll-free travel information. 1-800-543-1036.

Massachusetts

Bay State, Old Colony

People. Population (1993): 6,012,268; **rank:** 13. **Pop. density:** 765.3 per sq. mi. **Racial/ethnic distrib.** (1990): 89.8% white; 5.0% black; 2.4% Asian; 4.8% Hispanic. **Net change** (1990-93): –0.1%.

Geography. Total area: 10,555 sq. mi.; **rank:** 44. **Land area:** 7,838 sq. mi. **Acres forested land:** 3,203,000. **Location:** New England state along Atlantic seaboard. **Climate:** temperate, with colder and drier clime in western region. **Topography:** jagged indented coast from Rhode Island around Cape Cod; flat land yields to stony upland pastures near central region and gentle hilly country in west; except in west, land is rocky, sandy, and not fertile. **Capital:** Boston.

Economy. Principal industries (1990): services, trade, manufacturing. **Principal manufactured goods** (1990): electric and electronic equipment, machinery, industrial machinery and equipment, printing and publishing, fabricated metal products. **Agriculture: Chief crops:** cranberries, greenhouse, nursery, vegetables. **Livestock** (1983): 120,000 cattle; 50,000 hogs/pigs; 8,000 sheep; 125,000 horses, ponies; 3.6 mln. poultry. **Timber/lumber** (1992): white pine, oak, other hard woods; 38 mln. bd. ft. **Nonfuel Minerals** (1993): $166.4 mln.; mostly crushed stone, construction sand & gravel. **Commercial fishing** (1993): $232.1 mln. **Chief ports:** Boston, Fall River, New Bedford, Salem, Gloucester, Plymouth. **International airports at:** Boston. **Value of construction** (1993): $6.3 bln. **Employment distribution** (1990): 30.8% trade; 23.5% serv.; 17.5% mfg. **Per capita personal income** (1993): $24,563. **Unemployment** (1993): 6.9%. **Tourism** (1987): out-of-state visitors spent $12.9 bln. **Sales tax**: 5%.

Finance. FDIC-insured commercial banks & trust companies (1993): 61. **Deposits:** $70.0 bln. **FDIC-insured savings institutions** (1993): 224. **Assets**: $53.0 bln.

Federal government. No. federal civilian employees (Mar. 1993): 32,505. **Avg. salary:** $37,068. **Notable federal facilities:** Ft. Devens; Thomas P. O'Neill Jr. Federal Bldg., J.W. McCormack Bldg., John Fitzgerald Kennedy Federal Bldg., Boston; Q.M. Laboratory, Natick.

Energy. Electricity production (1993, kWh, by source): Coal: 9.8 bln.; Petroleum: 11.1 bln.; Gas: 2.9 bln.; Nuclear: 4.3 bln.

Education. Student-teacher ratio (1992): 15.0. **Avg. salary, public school teachers** (1993-94): $39,370.

State data. Motto: Ense Petit Placidam Sub Libertate Quietem (By the sword we seek peace, but peace only under liberty). **Flower:** Mayflower. **Bird:** Chickadee. **Tree:** American elm. **Song:** All Hail to Massachusetts. **Sixth** of the original 13 states to ratify Constitution, Feb. 6, 1788.

History. Pilgrims settled in Plymouth, 1620; the following year they gave thanks for their survival with the first Thanksgiving Day. Indian opposition reached a high point in King Philip's War, 1675-76, won by the colonists. Demonstrations against British restrictions set off the "Boston Massacre," 1770, and Boston "tea party," 1773. First bloodshed of the Revolution was at Lexington, 1775.

Tourist attractions. Cape Cod; Plymouth—Plymouth Rock, Plymouth Plantation, Mayflower II; Provincetown artists colony; Boston—Freedom Trail, Museum of Fine Arts, Children's Museum, Museum of Science, New England Aquarium, JFK Library, Boston Ballet, Boston Pops, Boston Symphony Orchestra; Berkshires—Tanglewood, Jacob's Pillow Dance Festival, Hancock Shaker Village, Berkshire Scenic Railroad; Old Sturbridge Village; Deerfield Historic District; Walden Pond; Naismith Memorial Basketball Hall of Fame, Springfield; Salem.

Famous "Bay Staters." John Adams, John Quincy Adams, Samuel Adams, Louisa May Alcott, Horatio Alger, Susan B. Anthony, Crispus Attucks, Clara Barton, Alexander Graham Bell, Stephen Breyer, Emily Dickinson, Ralph Waldo Emerson, John Hancock, Nathaniel Hawthorne, Oliver W. Holmes, Winslow Homer, Elias Howe, John Fitzgerald Kennedy, Samuel F.B. Morse, Edgar Allan Poe, Paul Revere, Henry David Thoreau, James McNeil Whistler, John Greenleaf Whittier.

Tourist information. Massachusetts Office of Travel & Tourism, 100 Cambridge St., 13th Floor, Boston, MA 02202.

Toll-free travel information. 1-800-624-MASS.

Michigan

Great Lakes State, Wolverine State

People. Population (1993): 9,477,545; **rank:** 8. **Pop. density:** 166.1 per sq. mi. **Racial/ethnic distrib.** (1990): 83.4% white; 13.9% black; 2.2% Hispanic. **Net change** (1990-93): 2.0%.

Geography. Total area: 96,705 sq. mi.; **rank:** 11. **Land area:** 56,809 sq. mi. **Acres forested land:** 18,253,000. **Location:** East North Central state bordering on 4 of the 5 Great Lakes, divided into an Upper and Lower Peninsula by the Straits of Mackinac, which link lakes Michigan and Huron. **Climate:** well-defined seasons tempered by the Great Lakes. **Topography:** low rolling hills give way to northern tableland of hilly belts in Lower Peninsula; Upper Peninsula is level in the east, with swampy areas; western region is higher and more rugged. **Capital:** Lansing.

Economy. Principal industries: manufacturing, services, tourism, agriculture, mining. **Principal manufactured goods:** transportation equipment, machinery, fabricated metals, food prods., plastics, office furniture. **Agriculture: Chief crops:** corn, winter wheat, soybeans, dry beans, oats, hay, sugar beets, honey, asparagus, sweet corn, apples, cherries, grapes, peaches, blueberries, flowers. **Livestock** (1992): 1.2 mln. cattle; 1.3 mln. hogs/pigs; 103,000 sheep; 11.5 mln. poultry. **Timber/lumber** (1992): maple, oak, aspen; 329 mln. bd. ft. **Nonfuel Minerals** (1993): $1.4 bln.; iron ore, portland cement, sand & gravel, crushed stone. **Commercial fishing** (1993): $9.3 mln. **Chief ports:** Detroit, Saginaw River, Escanaba, Muskegon, Sault Ste. Marie, Port Huron, Marine City. **International airports at:** Detroit,

Grand Rapids, Flint, Kalamazoo, Lansing, Saginaw. **Value of construction** (1993): $7.9 bln. **Employment distribution** (1992): 23% mfg.; 24% serv. **Per capita personal income** (1993): $20,453. **Unemployment** (1993): 7.0%. **Tourism** (1990): travelers spent $16.5 bln. **Sales tax:** 6%.

Finance. FDIC-insured commercial banks & trust companies (1993): 208. **Deposits**: $81.6 bln. **FDIC-insured savings institutions** (1993): 33. **Assets:** $30.0 bln.

Federal government. No. federal civilian employees (Mar. 1993): 26,434. **Avg. salary:** $36,317. **Notable federal facilities:** Isle Royal, Sleeping Bear Dunes national parks.

Energy. Electricity production (1993, kWh, by source): Coal: 61.6 bln.; Petroleum: 616 mln.; Gas: 680 mln.; Hydroelectric: 866 mln.; Nuclear: 28.5 bln.

Education. Student-teacher ratio (1992): 19.5. **Avg. salary, public school teachers** (1993-94): $42,500.

State data. Motto: Si Quaeris Peninsulam Amoenam Circumspice (If you seek a pleasant peninsula, look about you). **Flower:** Apple blossom. **Bird:** Robin. **Tree:** White pine. **Song:** Michigan, My Michigan. **Entered union** Jan. 26, 1837; rank, 26th. **State fair** at: Detroit, late Aug.-early Sept.; Upper Peninsula (Escanaba), mid-Aug; Michigan Festival, mid.-Aug.

History. French fur traders and missionaries visited the region, 1616, set up a mission at Sault Ste. Marie, 1641, and a settlement there, 1668. The whole region went to Britain, 1763. Anthony Wayne defeated their Indian allies at Fallen Timbers, Ohio, 1794. The British returned, 1812, seized Ft. Mackinac and Detroit. Oliver H. Perry's Lake Erie victory and William H. Harrison's troops, who carried the war to the Thames River in Canada, 1813, freed Michigan once more.

Tourist attractions. Henry Ford Museum, Greenfield Village, reconstruction of a typical 19th cent. American village, both in Dearborn; Michigan Space Ctr., Jackson; Tahquamenon *(Hiawatha)* Falls; DeZwaan windmill and Tulip Festival, Holland; "Soo Locks," St. Marys Falls Ship Canal, Sault Ste. Marie.

Famous Michiganders. Ralph Bunche, Paul de Kruif, Thomas A. Edison, Gerald R. Ford, Edna Ferber, Henry Ford, Aretha Franklin, Edgar Guest, Lee Iacocca, Robert Ingersoll, Magic Johnson, Will Kellogg, Ring Lardner, Elmore Leonard, Charles Lindbergh, Joe Louis, Madonna, Pontiac, Diana Ross, Tom Selleck, Lily Tomlin, Stewart Edward White, Malcolm X.

Chamber of Commerce. 600 S. Walnut, Lansing, MI 48933.

Toll-free travel information. 1-800-543-2937.

Minnesota

North Star State, Gopher State

People. Population (1993): 4,517,416; **rank:** 20. **Pop. density:** 56.3 per sq. mi. **Racial/ethnic distrib.** (1990): 94.4% white; 2.2% black; 1.8% Asian; 1.2% Hispanic. **Net change** (1990-93): 3.3%.

Geography. Total area: 86,943 sq. mi.; **rank:** 12. **Land area:** 79,617 sq. mi. **Acres forested land:** 16,718,000. **Location:** West North Central state bounded on the E by Wisconsin and Lake Superior, on the N by Canada, on the W by the Dakotas, and on the S by Iowa. **Climate:** northern part of state lies in the moist Great Lakes storm belt; the western border lies at the edge of the semi-arid Great Plains. **Topography:** central hill and lake region covering approx. half the state; to the NE, rocky ridges and deep lakes; to the NW, flat plain; to the S, rolling plains and deep river valleys. **Capital:** St. Paul.

Economy. Principal industries: agribusiness, forest products, mining, manufacturing, tourism. **Principal manufactured goods:** food processing, non-electrical machinery, chemicals, paper, electric and electronic equipment, printing and publishing, instruments, fabricated metal products. **Agriculture: Chief crops:** corn, soybeans, wheat, sugar beets, sunflowers, barley. **Livestock** (1990): 2.95 mln. cattle; 4.25 mln. hogs/pigs; 285,000 sheep; 12.7 mln. poultry. **Timber/lumber** (1992): needle-leaves and hardwoods; 90 mln. bd. ft. **Nonfuel Minerals** (1993): $1.3 bln.; mostly iron ore, construction sand & gravel, crushed stone, industrial sand and gravel. **Commercial fishing** (1993): $138,000. **Chief ports:** Duluth, St. Paul, Minneapolis. **International airports at:** Minneapolis-St. Paul. **Value of construction** (1993): $5.3 bln. **Employment distribution** (1990): 24.4% trade; 26.0% serv.; 18.3% mfg.; 15.8% gvt. **Per capita personal income** (1993): $21,063. **Unemployment** (1993): 5.1%. **Tourism** (1987): out-of-state visitors spent $3.6 bln. **Sales tax:** 6½%.

Finance. FDIC-insured commercial banks & trust companies (1993): 573. **Deposits**: $47.9 bln. **FDIC-insured savings institutions** (1993): 24. **Assets**: $6.5 bln.

Federal government. No. federal civilian employees (Mar. 1993): 14,726. **Avg. salary:** $36,584.

Energy. Electricity production (1993, kWh, by source): Coal: 27.1 bln.; Petroleum: 630 mln.; Hydroelectric: 834 mln.; Nuclear: 12.0 bln.

Education. Student-teacher ratio (1992): 17.6. **Avg. salary, public school teachers** (1993-94): $36,146.

State data. Motto: L'Etoile du Nord (The star of the north). **Flower:** Pink and white lady's-slipper. **Bird:** Common loon. **Tree:** Red pine. **Song:** Hail! Minnesota. **Entered union** May 11, 1858; rank, 32d. **State fair** at: Saint Paul; late Aug. to early Sept.

History. Fur traders and missionaries from French Canada opened the region in the 17th century. Britain took the area east of the Mississippi, 1763. The U.S. took over that portion after the Revolution and in 1803 bought the western area as part of the Louisiana Purchase. The U.S. built present Ft. Snelling, 1820, bought lands from the Indians, 1837. Sioux Indians staged a bloody uprising, 1862, and were driven from the state.

Tourist attractions. Minnehaha Falls, Minneapolis, inspiration for Longfellow's *Hiawatha;* over 15,000 lakes; 66 state parks; 25 historical sites; Minneapolis Aquatennial; Ordway Theater, St. Paul; Guthrie Theater, Minneapolis; professional baseball, football, hockey. Voyageurs Nat'l. Park, a water wilderness along the Canadian border; Mayo Clinic, Rochester; St. Paul Winter Carnival; North Shore (of Lake Superior).

Famous Minnesotans. F. Scott Fitzgerald, Cass Gilbert, Hubert Humphrey, Sister Elizabeth Kenny, Sinclair Lewis, Paul Manship, E. G. Marshall, William and Charles Mayo, Walter F. Mondale, Charles Schulz, Harold Stassen, Thorstein Veblen.

Tourist information. Minnesota Office of Tourism, 375 Jackson St., 250 Skyway Level, St. Paul, MN 55101.

Toll-free travel information. 1-800-328-1461.

Mississippi

Magnolia State

People. Population (1993): 2,642,748; **rank:** 31. **Pop. density:** 55.7 per sq. mi. **Racial/ethnic distrib.** (1990): 63.5% white; 35.6% black; 0.6% Hispanic. **Net change** (1990-93): 2.7%.

Geography. Total area: 48,434 sq. mi.; **rank:** 32. **Land area:** 46,914 sq. mi. **Acres forested land:** 17,000,000. **Location:** East South Central state bordered on the W by the Mississippi R. and on the S by the Gulf of Mexico. **Climate:** semi-tropical, with abundant rainfall, long growing season, and extreme temperatures unusual. **Topography:** low, fertile delta bet. the Yazoo and Mississippi rivers; loess bluffs stretching around delta border; sandy Gulf coastal terraces followed by piney woods and prairie; rugged, high sandy hills in extreme NE followed by black prairie belt, Pontotoc Ridge, and flatwoods into the north central highlands. **Capital:** Jackson.

Economy. Principal industries: manufacturing, government, wholesale and retail trade. **Principal manufactured goods:** apparel, food & kindred prods., furniture, lumber and wood products, electrical machinery, transportation equip. **Agriculture: Chief crops** (1993): cotton, catfish, rice, soybeans. **Livestock** (1991): 1.3 mln. cattle; 149,000 hogs/pigs; 456.5 mln. broilers. **Timber/lumber** (1992): pine, oak, hardwoods; 2.47 bln. bd. ft. **Nonfuel Minerals** (1993): $138.6 mln., mostly construction sand & gravel. **Commercial fishing** (1993):

$29.4 mln. **Chief ports:** Pascagoula, Vicksburg, Gulfport, Natchez, Greenville. **Value of construction** (1993): $2.4 bln. **Employment distribution** (1993): 25.5% mfg.; 21% gvt.; 21% trade; 20% serv. **Per capita personal income** (1993): $14,894. **Unemployment** (1993): 6.3%. **Tourism** (1993): out-of-state visitors spent $3.3 bln. **Sales tax:** 7%.

Finance. FDIC-insured commercial banks & trust companies (1993): 118. **Deposits:** $20.5 bln. **FDIC-insured savings institutions** (1993): 18. **Assets:** $2.3 bln.

Federal government. No. federal civilian employees (Mar. 1993): 18,499. **Avg. salary:** $34,300. **Notable federal facilities:** Columbus, Keesler AF bases; Meridian Naval Air Station, John C. Stennis Space Center; U.S. Army Corps of Engineers Waterway Experiment Station.

Energy. Electricity production (1993, kWh, by source): Coal: 8.8 bln.; Petroleum: 3.6 bln.; Gas: 3.0 bln.; Nuclear: 7.9 bln.

Education. Student-teacher ratio (1992): 18.2. **Avg. salary, public school teachers** (1993-94): $25,235.

State data. Motto: Virtute et Armis (By valor and arms). **Flower:** Magnolia. **Bird:** Mockingbird. **Tree:** Magnolia. **Song:** Go, Mississippi! **Entered union** Dec. 10, 1817; rank, 20th. **State fair** at: Jackson; Fall.

History. De Soto explored the area, 1540, sighted the Mississippi River, 1541. La Salle traced the river from Illinois to its mouth and claimed the entire valley for France, 1682. First settlement was the French Ft. Maurepas, near Ocean Springs, 1699. The area was ceded to Britain, 1763; American settlers followed. During the Revolution, Spain seized part of the area and refused to leave even after the U.S. acquired title at the end of the Revolution, finally moving out, 1798. Mississippi seceded 1861. Union forces captured Corinth and Vicksburg and destroyed Jackson and much of Meridian.

Tourist attractions. Vicksburg National Military Park and Cemetery, other Civil War sites; Natchez Trace; Indian mounds; Antebellum Home; pilgrimages in Natchez and some 25 other cities; Jubilee Jam, May, Jackson; Mardi Gras and blessing of the shrimp fleet, June, both in Biloxi.

Famous Mississippians. Dana Andrews, Jimmy Buffet, Hodding Carter III, William Faulkner, Shelby Foote, John Grisham, Fannie Lou Hamer, Jim Henson, Robert Johnson, James Earl Jones, B.B. King, L.Q.C. Lamar, Willie Morris, Elvis Presley, Leontyne Price, Charlie Pride, Margaret Walker, Eudora Welty, Tennessee Williams, Oprah Winfrey, Richard Wright, Tammy Wynette.

Dept. of Economic & Community Development. P.O. Box 849, Jackson, MS 39205-0849.

Toll-free travel information. 1-800-WARMEST.

Missouri

Show Me State

People. Population (1993): 5,233,849; **rank:** 16. **Pop. density:** 75.4 per sq. mi. **Racial/ethnic distrib.** (1990): 87.7% white; 10.7% black; 1.2% Hispanic. **Net change** (1990-93): 2.3%.

Geography. Total area: 69,709 sq. mi.; **rank:** 21. **Land area:** 68,898 sq. mi. **Acres forested land:** 14,007,000. **Location:** West North Central state near the geographic center of the conterminous U.S.; bordered on the E by the Mississippi R., on the NW by the Missouri R. **Climate:** continental, susceptible to cold Canadian air, moist, warm Gulf air, and drier SW air. **Topography:** rolling hills, open, fertile plains, and well-watered prairie N of the Missouri R.; south of the river land is rough and hilly with deep, narrow valleys; alluvial plain in the SE; low elevation in the west. **Capital:** Jefferson City.

Economy. Principal industries: agriculture, manufacturing, aerospace, tourism. **Principal manufactured goods:** transportation equipment, food and related products, electrical and electronic equipment, chemicals. **Agriculture: Chief crops:** soybeans, corn, wheat, hay. **Livestock** (1992): 4.6 mln. cattle; 2.8 mln. hogs/pigs; 97,000 sheep; 7.241 mln. chickens and eggs, 20.5 mln. turkeys. **Timber/lumber** (1992): oak, hickory; 257 mln. bd. ft. **Nonfuel Minerals** (1993): $785.4 mln., mostly lead, portland cement, crushed stone. **Chief ports:** St. Louis, Kansas City. **International airports at:** St. Louis, Kansas City. **Value of construction** (1993): $5.1 bln. **Employment distribution** (1992): 25.9% services; 23.9% trade; 17.7% mfg.; 16.0% gvt. **Per capita personal income** (1993): $19,463. **Unemployment** (1993): 6.4%. **Tourism** (1990): total travelers spent $5 bln. **Sales tax:** 4.225%.

Finance. FDIC-insured commercial banks & trust companies (1993): 490. **Deposits:** $55.7 bln. **FDIC-insured savings institutions** (1993): 60. **Assets:** $16.4 bln.

Federal government. No. federal civilian employees (Mar. 1993): 43,974. **Avg. salary:** $34,618. **Notable federal facilities:** Federal Reserve banks, St. Louis, Kansas City; Ft. Leonard Wood, Rolla; Jefferson Barracks, St. Louis; Whiteman AFB, Knob Noster.

Energy. Electricity production (1993 kWh, by source): Coal: 40.7 bln.; Petroleum: 634 mln.; Gas: 386 mln.; Hydroelectric: 3.1 bln.; Nuclear: 8.4 bln.

Education. Student-teacher ratio (1992): 16.2. **Avg. salary, public school teachers** (1993-94): $30,227.

State data. Motto: Salus Populi Suprema Lex Esto (The welfare of the people shall be the supreme law). **Flower:** Hawthorn. **Bird:** Bluebird. **Tree:** Dogwood. **Song:** Missouri Waltz. **Entered union** Aug. 10, 1821; rank, 24th. **State fair** at: Sedalia; 3d week in Aug.

History. DeSoto visited the area, 1541. French hunters and lead miners made the first settlement, c. 1735, at Ste. Genevieve. The U.S. acquired Missouri as part of the Louisiana Purchase, 1803. The fur trade and the Santa Fe Trail provided prosperity; St. Louis became the "jump-off" point for pioneers on their way West. Pro- and anti-slavery forces battled each other there during the Civil War.

Tourist attractions. Branson with 32 indoor theaters, 3 theme parks, 3 outdoor amphitheaters; Mark Twain Area, Hannibal; Pony Express Museum, St. Joseph; Harry S. Truman Library, Independence; Gateway Arch, St. Louis; Silver Dollar City, Branson Worlds of Fun, Kansas City; Lake of the Ozarks, Churchill Memorial, Fulton; State Capitol, Jefferson City.

Famous Missourians. Josephine Baker, Thomas Hart Benton, George Caleb Bingham, Gen. Omar Bradley, Dale Carnegie, George Washington Carver, Walter Cronkite, Walt Disney, T.S. Eliot, Betty Grable, Jesse James, J. C. Penney, John J. Pershing, Joseph Pulitzer, Ginger Rogers, Bess Truman, Harry S. Truman, Mark Twain, Tennessee Williams.

Chamber of Commerce. 400 E. High St., P.O. Box 149, Jefferson City, MO 65101.

Toll-free travel information. 1-800-877-1234.

Montana

Treasure State

People. Population (1993): 839,422; **rank:** 44. **Pop. density:** 5.66 per sq. mi. **Racial/ethnic distrib.** (1990): 92.7% white; 0.3% black; 6.0% Amer. Indian; 1.5% Hispanic. **Net change** (1990-93): 5.1%.

Geography. Total area: 147,046 sq. mi.; **rank:** 4. **Land area:** 145,556 sq. mi. **Acres forested land:** 22,512,000. **Location:** Mountain state bounded on the E by the Dakotas, on the S by Wyoming, on the S/SW by Idaho, and on the N by Canada. **Climate:** colder, continental climate with low humidity. **Topography:** Rocky Mtns. in western third of the state; eastern two-thirds gently rolling northern Great Plains. **Capital:** Helena.

Economy. Principal industries: agriculture, timber, mining, tourism, oil & gas. **Principal manufactured goods:** food prods., wood & paper prods., primary metals, printing & publishing, petroleum & coal prods. **Agriculture: Chief crops:** wheat, barley, sugar beets, hay, oats. **Livestock** (1993): 2.5 mln. cattle; 215,000 hogs/pigs; 554,000 sheep; 710,000 poultry. **Timber/lumber** (1992): Douglas fir, pines, larch; 1.40 bln. bd. ft. **Nonfuel Minerals** (1993): $495.8 mln., mostly metallics. **International airports at:** Great Falls, Billings, Kalispell, Missoula. **Value of construction** (1993): $736.8 mln. **Employment distribution** (1992): 27.2% serv.; 22.9% trade; 18.3% govt.; 6.7% agric.; 5.9% mfg.

Per capita personal income (1993): $17,322. **Unemployment** (1993): 6.0%. **Tourism** (1992 est.): non-resident visitors spent $930 mln.

Finance. FDIC-insured commercial banks & trust companies (1993): 117. **Deposits**: $6.8 bln. **FDIC-insured savings institutions** (1993): 9. **Assets**: $1.4 bln.

Federal government. No. federal civilian employees (Mar. 1993): 8,799. **Avg. salary:** $34,170. **Notable federal facilities:** Malmstrom AFB; Ft. Peck, Hungry Horse, Libby, Yellowtail dams; numerous missile silos.

Energy. Electricity production (1993, kWh, by source): Coal: 13.8 bln.; Petroleum: 21 mln.; Gas: 24 mln.; Hydroelectric: 9.5 bln.

Education. Student-teacher ratio (1992): 15.8. **Avg. salary, public school teachers** (1993-94): $28,210.

State data. Motto: Oro y Plata (Gold and silver). **Flower:** Bitterroot. **Bird:** Western meadowlark. **Tree:** Ponderosa pine. **Song:** Montana. **Entered union** Nov. 8, 1889; rank, 41st. **State fair** at: Great Falls; late July to early Aug.

History. French explorers visited the region, 1742. The U.S. acquired the area partly through the Louisiana Purchase, 1803, and partly through the explorations of Lewis and Clark, 1805-06. Fur traders and missionaries established posts in the early 19th century. Indian uprisings reached their peak with the Battle of the Little Bighorn, 1876. Mining activity and the coming of the Northern Pacific Railway, 1883, brought population growth.

Tourist attractions. Glacier Natl. Park, on the Continental Divide, is a scenic and recreational wonderland, with 60 glaciers, 200 lakes, and many trout streams. Yellowstone Natl. Park has 3 of the 5 entrances in Montana, with 2,221,000 acres of scenic beauty, inc. geysers, mountains, canyons, streams, lakes, forests, waterfalls.

Also, Museum of the Plains Indian, Blackfeet Reservation near Browning; Little Bighorn Battlefield Natl. Monument & Custer Natl. Cemetery; Flathead Lake, in the NW; Lewis and Clark Caverns State Park, near Whitehall; 7 Indian reservations, covering over 5 million acres; state capitol and historical society, Helena.

Famous Montanans. Gary Cooper, Marcus Daly, Chet Huntley, Will James, Myrna Loy, Mike Mansfield, Brent Musberger, Jeannette Rankin, Charles M. Russell, Lester Thurow.

Chamber of Commerce. 2030 11th Ave., P.O. Box 1730, Helena, MT 59624.

Toll-free travel information. 1-800-VISIT MT.

Nebraska

Cornhusker State

People. Population (1993): 1,607,199; **rank:** 37. **Pop. density:** 20.9 per sq. mi. **Racial/ethnic distrib.** (1990): 93.8% white; 3.6% black; 2.3% Hispanic. **Net change** (1990-93): 1.8%.

Geography. Total area: 77,358 sq. mi.; **rank:** 16. **Land area:** 76,878 sq. mi. **Acres forested land:** 462,000. **Location:** West North Central state with the Missouri R. for a NE/E border. **Climate:** continental semi-arid. **Topography:** till plains of the central lowland in the eastern third rising to the Great Plains and hill country of the north central and NW. **Capital:** Lincoln.

Economy. Principal industries: agriculture, manufacturing. **Principal manufactured goods:** processed foods, industrial machinery, printed materials, electric and electronic equipment, primary and fabricated metal products, transportation equipment. **Agriculture: Chief crops:** corn, sorghum, soybeans, hay, wheat, beans, oats, potatoes, sugar beets. **Livestock** (1993): 6.1 mln. cattle; 4.2 mln. hogs/pigs; 92,000 sheep; 9.0 mln. chickens, 2.5 mln. turkeys. **Nonfuel Minerals** (1993): $118.4 mln.; mostly construction sand & gravel, portland cement, crushed stone. **Chief ports:** Omaha, Sioux City, Brownville, Blair, Plattsmouth, Nebraska City. **Value of construction** (1993): $1.6 bln. **Employment distribution** (1993): 25.2% trade; 24.6% serv.; 19.6% gvt.; 13.5% mfg. **Per capita personal income** (1993): $19,726. **Unemployment** (1993): 2.6%. **Tourism** (1993): traveler expenditures $1.9 bln. **Sales tax**: 5%, + some local sales taxes of 0.5-1.5%.

Finance. FDIC-insured commercial banks & trust companies (1993): 361. **Deposits**: $20.9 bln. **FDIC-insured savings institutions** (1993): 15. **Assets**: $7.6 bln.

Federal government. No. federal civilian employees (Mar. 1993): 8,940. **Avg. salary:** $34,484. **Notable federal facilities:** Offutt AFB, Bellevue.

Energy. Electricity production (1993, kWh, by source): Coal: 14.7 bln.; Petroleum: 19 mln.; Gas: 153 mln.; Hydroelectric: 1 mln.; Nuclear: 6.8 bln.

Education. Student-teacher ratio (1992): 14.6. **Avg. salary, public school teachers** (1993-94): $29,564.

State data. Motto: Equality before the law. **Flower:** Goldenrod. **Bird:** Western meadowlark. **Tree:** Cottonwood. **Song:** Beautiful Nebraska. **Entered union** Mar. 1, 1867; rank, 37th. **State fair** at: Lincoln; late Aug. to mid-Sept.

History. Spanish and French explorers and fur traders visited the area prior to the Louisiana Purchase, 1803. Lewis and Clark passed through, 1804-06. First permanent settlement was Bellevue, near Omaha, 1823. Many Civil War veterans settled under free land terms of the 1862 Homestead Act; struggles followed between homesteaders and ranchers.

Tourist attractions. Architecturally unique, 400′-tall state capitol, Lincoln; Stuhr Museum of the Prairie Pioneer, Grand Island; Museum of the Fur Trade, Chadron; State Museum (Elephant Hall), Lincoln; Joslyn Art Museum, Omaha; Strategic Air Command Museum, Bellevue; Boys Town, founded by Fr. Flanagan, west of Omaha; Arbor Lodge State Park, Nebraska City; Buffalo Bill Ranch State Historical Park, North Platte; Pioneer Village, Minden; Oregon Trail landmarks, Scotts Bluff National Monument, Chimney Rock Historic Site, Ft. Robinson; Hastings Museum, McDonald Planetarium, Hastings.

Famous Nebraskans. Fred Astaire, Charles W. and William Jennings Bryan, Johnny Carson, Willa Cather, William F. "Buffalo Bill" Cody, Loren Eiseley, Rev. Edward J. Flanagan, Henry Fonda, Gerald R. Ford, Rollin Kirby, Harold Lloyd, Wright Morris, J. Sterling Morton, John Neidhardt, George Norris, Gen. John J. Pershing, Roscoe Pound, Chief Red Cloud, Mari Sandoz, Malcolm X.

Division of Travel and Tourism. P.O. Box 98913, Lincoln, NE 68509-8913.

Toll-free travel information. 1-800-228-4307.

Nevada

Sagebrush State, Battle Born State, Silver State

People. Population (1993): 1,388,910; **rank:** 38. **Pop. density:** 12.1 per sq. mi. **Racial/ethnic distrib.** (1990): 84.3% white; 6.6% black; 3.2% Asian; 10.4% Hispanic. **Net change** (1990-93): 15.6%.

Geography. Total area: 110,567 sq. mi.; **rank:** 7. **Land area:** 109,806 sq. mi. **Acres forested land:** 8,938,000. **Location:** Mountain state bordered on N by Oregon and Idaho, on E by Utah and Arizona, on SE by Arizona, and on SW/W by California. **Climate:** semi-arid and arid. **Topography:** rugged N-S mountain ranges; highest elevation, Boundary Peak, 13,140 ft.; southern area is within the Mojave Desert; lowest elevation, Colorado River at southern tip of state, 479 ft. **Capital:** Carson City.

Economy. Principal industries: gaming, tourism, mining, manufacturing, government, agriculture, warehousing, trucking. **Principal manufactured goods:** gaming devices, chemicals, aerospace prods.; lawn & garden irrigation equip.; seismic & machinery-monitoring devices. **Agriculture: Chief crops:** hay, alfalfa seed, potatoes, onions, garlic, barley, wheat. **Livestock** (1993): 470,000 cattle; 9,000 hogs/pigs; 90,000 sheep; 9,000 poultry. **Timber/lumber:** piñon, juniper, other pines. **Nonfuel Minerals** (1993): $2.7 bln.; mostly gold, construction sand & gravel. **International airports at:** Las Vegas, Reno. **Value of construction** (1993): $3.8 bln. **Employment distribution** (1993): 43.2% serv.; 19.8% trade; 13.1% gvt. **Per capita personal income**

(1993): $22,729. **Unemployment** (1993): 7.2%. **Tourism** (1992): out-of-state travelers spent over $15.4 bln. **Sales tax:** 6.5-7%.

Finance. FDIC-insured commercial banks & trust companies (1993): 21. **Deposits**: $10.2 bln. **FDIC-insured savings institutions** (1993): 4. **Assets**: $3.3 bln.

Federal government. No. federal civilian employees (Mar. 1993): 7,485. **Avg. salary:** $36,721. **Notable federal facilities:** Nevada Test Site; Hawthorne Army Ammunition Plant, Nellis Air Force Base & Gunnery Range; Fallon Naval Air Station; Palomino Valley Wild Horse & Burro Placement Center.

Energy. Electricity production (1993, kWh, by source): Coal: 15.6 bln.; Petroleum: 247 mln.; Gas: 2.0 bln.; Hydroelectric: 2.0 bln.

Education. Student-teacher ratio (1992): 18.7. **Avg. salary, public school teachers** (1993-94): $33,955.

State data. Motto: All for our country. **Flower:** Sagebrush. **Bird:** Mountain bluebird. **Trees:** Single-leaf piñon and bristlecone pine. **Song:** Home Means Nevada. **Entered union** Oct. 31, 1864; rank, 36th. **State fair** at: Reno; early Sept.

History. Nevada was first explored by Spaniards in 1776. Hudson's Bay Co. trappers explored the north and central region, 1825; trader Jedediah Smith crossed the state, 1826 and 1827. The area was acquired by the U.S., in 1848, at the end of the Mexican War. First settlement, Mormon Station, now Genoa, was est. 1849. In the early 20th century, Nevada adopted progressive measures such as the initiative, referendum, recall, and woman suffrage.

Tourist attractions. Legalized casino gambling provided the impetus for the development of resort facilities at Lake Tahoe, Reno, Las Vegas, Laughlin, and elsewhere. Ghost towns, rodeos, mountain climbing, skiing, golfing, trout fishing, water sports and hunting important. Notable are Hoover Dam, Lake Mead Natl. Recreation Area, Lake Tahoe, Great Basin Natl. Park, Valley of Fire State Park & Virginia City. Annual events inc. Helldorado Days & Rodeo, Las Vegas; Reno Rodeo; National Basque Festival, Elko; Nevada Day, Carson City; Cowboy Poetry Gathering, Elko.

Famous Nevadans. Walter Van Tilburg Clark, Sarah Winnemucca Hopkins, Paul Laxalt, Dat So La Lee, John William Mackay, Pat McCarran, Key Pittman, William Morris Stewart.

Tourist information. Commission on Tourism, Capitol Complex, Carson City, NV 89710.

Toll-free travel information. 1-800-638-2328.

New Hampshire

Granite State

People. Population (1993): 1,125,310; **rank:** 41. **Pop. density:** 123.8 per sq. mi. **Racial/ethnic distrib.** (1990): 98.0% white; 0.6% black; 1.0% Hispanic. **Net change** (1990-93): 1.4%.

Geography. Total area: 9,351 sq. mi.; **rank:** 46. **Land area:** 8,969 sq. mi. **Acres forested land:** 4,981,000. **Location:** New England state bounded on S by Massachusetts, on W by Vermont, on N/NW by Canada, on E by Maine and the Atlantic O. **Climate:** highly varied, due to its nearness to high mountains and ocean. **Topography:** low, rolling coast followed by countless hills and mountains rising out of a central plateau. **Capital:** Concord.

Economy. Principal industries: tourism, manufacturing, agriculture, trade, mining. **Principal manufactured goods:** machinery, electrical & electronic products, plastics, fabricated metal products. **Agriculture: Chief crops:** dairy products, nursery and greenhouse products, hay, vegetables, fruit, maple syrup & sugar prods. **Livestock** (1993): 52,000 cattle; 9,500 hogs/pigs; 9,000 sheep; 15,500 horses; 214,000 poultry. **Timber/lumber** (1992): white pine, hemlock, oak, birch; 217 mln. bd. ft. **Nonfuel Minerals** (1993): $35.9 mln.; mostly construction sand & gravel, crushed & dimension stone. **Commercial fishing** (1993): $11.8 mln. **Chief ports:** Portsmouth, Hampton, Rye. **Value of construction** (1993): $939 mln. **Employment distribution** (1992): 20.0% mfg.; 25.4% trade; 26.6% serv.; 14.9% gvt. **Per capita personal income** (1993): $22,659. **Unemployment** (1993): 6.6%. **Tourism** (1993): out-of-state visitors spent $3.4 bln.

Finance. FDIC-insured commercial banks & trust companies (1993): 26. **Deposits:** $5.8 bln. **FDIC-insured savings institutions** (1993): 30. **Assets**: $10.3 bln.

Federal government. No. federal civilian employees (Mar. 1993): 3,706. **Avg. salary:** $39,319.

Energy. Electricity production (1993, kWh, by source): Coal: 3.3 bln.; Petroleum: 1.3 bln.; Gas: 12 mln.; Hydroelectric: 1.0 bln.; Nuclear: 9.0 bln.

Education. Student-teacher ratio (1992): 15.6. **Avg. salary, public school teachers** (1993-94): $36,372.

State data. Motto: Live free or die. **Flower:** Purple lilac. **Bird:** Purple finch. **Tree:** White birch. **Song:** Old New Hampshire. **Ninth** of the original 13 states to ratify the Constitution, June 21, 1788.

History. First explorers to visit the New Hampshire area were England's Martin Pring, 1603, and Champlain, 1605. First settlement was Odiorne's Point (now port of Rye), 1623. Indian raids were halted, 1759, by Robert Rogers' Rangers. Before the Revolution, New Hampshire men seized a British fort at Portsmouth, 1774, and drove the royal governor out, 1775. Three regiments served in the Continental Army and scores of privateers raided British shipping.

Tourist attractions. Mt. Washington, highest peak in Northeast, hub of network of trails; Lake Winnipesaukee; White Mt. Natl. Forest; Crawford, Franconia, Pinkham notches in White Mt. region—Franconia famous for the Old Man of the Mountain, described by Hawthorne as the Great Stone Face; the Flume, a spectacular gorge; the aerial tramway on Cannon Mt; Strawbery Banke, Portsmouth; Shaker Village, Canterbury; Saint-Gaudens, natl. historic site, Cornish; Mt. Monadnock.

Famous New Hampshirites. Salmon P. Chase, Ralph Adams Cram, Mary Baker Eddy, Daniel Chester French, Robert Frost, Horace Greeley, Sarah Buell Hale, Franklin Pierce, Augustus Saint-Gaudens, David H. Souter, Daniel Webster.

Tourist information. Department of Resources and Economic Development, Division of Travel & Tourism Development, P.O. Box 1856, Concord, NH 03302-1856; 603-271-2666.

New Jersey

Garden State

People. Population (1993): 7,879,164; **rank:** 9. **Pop. density:** 1,049.9 per sq. mi. **Racial/ethnic distrib.** (1990): 79.3% white; 13.4% black; 3.5% Asian; 9.6% Hispanic. **Net change** (1990-93): 1.9%.

Geography. Total area: 8,722 sq. mi.; **rank:** 47. **Land area:** 7,419 sq. mi. **Acres forested land:** 2,007,000. **Location:** Middle Atlantic state bounded on the N and E by New York and the Atlantic O., on the S and W by Delaware and Pennsylvania. **Climate:** moderate, with marked difference bet. NW and SE extremities. **Topography:** Appalachian Valley in the NW also has highest elevation, High Pt., 1,801 ft.; Appalachian Highlands, flat-topped NE-SW mountain ranges; Piedmont Plateau, low plains broken by high ridges (Palisades) rising 400-500 ft.; Coastal Plain, covering three-fifths of state in SE, gradually rises from sea level to gentle slopes. **Capital:** Trenton.

Economy. Principal industries: services, trade, manufacturing. **Principal manufactured goods:** chemicals, electronic and electrical equipment, non-electrical machinery, fabricated metals. **Agriculture: Chief crops:** hay, corn, soybeans, tomatoes, blueberries, peaches, cranberries. **Livestock** (1992): 77,000 cattle; 24,000 hogs/pigs; 13,000 sheep; 2.1 mln. poultry. **Timber/lumber** (1992): pine, cedar, mixed hardwoods; 5 mln. bd. ft. **Nonfuel Minerals** (1993): $251.7 mln.; mostly crushed stone, construction sand & gravel. **Commercial fishing** (1993): $96.3 mln. **Chief ports:** Newark, Elizabeth, Hoboken, Camden. **International airports at:** Newark. **Value of construction** (1993): $6.1 bln. **Employment distribution** (1993): 29.1% serv.;

23.3% trade; 14.8% mfg.; 16.2% gvt. **Per capita personal income** (1993): $26,967. **Unemployment** (1993): 7.4%. **Tourism** (1992): tourists spent $17.9 bln. **Sales tax**: 6%.

Finance. FDIC-insured commercial banks & trust companies (1993): 99. **Deposits**: $84.4 bln. **FDIC-insured savings institutions** (1993): 100. **Assets**: $38.9 bln.

Federal government. No. federal civilian employees (Mar. 1993): 37,831. **Avg. salary:** $40,515. **Notable federal facilities:** McGuire AFB; Fort Dix; Fort Monmouth; Picatinny Arsenal; Lakewood Naval Air Station, Lakehurst Naval Air Engineering Center; Naval Air Warfare Center, Ewing.

Energy. Electricity production (1993, kWh, by source): Coal: 5.5 bln.; Petroleum: 1.0 bln.; Gas: 3.0 bln.; Nuclear: 24.9 bln.

Education. Student-teacher ratio (1992): 13.6. **Avg. salary, public school teachers** (1993-94): $45,308.

State data. Motto: Liberty and prosperity. **Flower:** Purple violet. **Bird:** Eastern goldfinch. **Tree:** Red oak. **Third** of the original 13 states to ratify the Constitution, Dec. 18, 1787. **State fair:** usually Aug.

History. The Lenni-Lenape (Delaware) Indians had mostly peaceful relations with European colonists who arrived after the explorers Verrazano, 1524, and Hudson, 1609. The Dutch were first; when the British took New Netherland, 1664, the area between the Delaware and Hudson Rivers was given to Lord John Berkeley and Sir George Carteret. New Jersey was the scene of nearly 100 battles, large and small, during the Revolution, including Trenton, 1776, Princeton, 1777, Monmouth, 1778.

Tourist attractions. 127 miles of beaches; Miss America Pageant and hotel-casinos, Atlantic City; Grover Cleveland birthplace, Caldwell; Cape May Historic District; Edison Labs, W. Orange; Great Adventure amusement park; Liberty State Park; Meadowlands Sports Complex; Pine Barrens wilderness area; Princeton University; numerous Revolutionary War historical sites; State Aquarium, Camden.

Famous New Jerseyans. Count Basie, Judy Blume, Aaron Burr, Grover Cleveland, James Fenimore Cooper, Stephen Crane, Thomas Edison, Albert Einstein, Alexander Hamilton, Joyce Kilmer, Gen. George McClellan, Thomas Paine, Molly Pitcher, Paul Robeson, Philip Roth, Walter Schirra, Frank Sinatra, Bruce Springsteen, Walt Whitman, William Carlos Williams, Woodrow Wilson.

Chamber of Commerce. 50 W. State St., Trenton, NJ 08608.

Toll-free travel information. 1-800-JERSEY-7.

New Mexico

Land of Enchantment

People. Population (1993): 1,616,483; **rank:** 36. **Pop. density:** 13.0 per sq. mi. **Racial/ethnic distrib.** (1990): 75.6% white; 2.0% black; 8.9% Amer. Indian; 38.2% Hispanic. **Net change** (1990-93): 6.7%.

Geography. Total area: 121,598 sq. mi.; **rank:** 5. **Land area:** 121,364 sq. mi. **Acres forested land:** 15,296,000. **Location:** southwestern state bounded by Colorado on the N, Oklahoma, Texas, and Mexico on the E and S, and Arizona on the W. **Climate:** dry, with temperatures rising or falling 5° F with every 1,000 ft. elevation. **Topography:** eastern third, Great Plains; central third, Rocky Mtns. (85% of the state is over 4,000 ft. elevation); western third, high plateau. **Capital:** Santa Fe.

Economy. Principal industries: government, services, trade. **Principal manufactured goods:** foods, machinery, apparel, lumber, printing, transportation equipment. **Agriculture: Chief crops:** hay, onions, wheat, pecans, corn, cotton, sorghum. **Livestock** (1990): 1.34 mln. cattle; 27,000 hogs; 462,000 sheep; 1.43 mln. poultry. **Timber/lumber** (1992): ponderosa pine, Douglas fir; 110 mln. bd. ft. **Nonfuel Minerals** (1993): $787.7 mln.; copper, potash, construction sand & gravel. **International airports at:** Albuquerque. **Value of construction** (1993): $1.6 bln. **Employment distribution** (1990): 26% serv.; 2% agric.; 10% mfg.; 26.2% gvt. **Per capita personal income** (1993): $16,297. **Unemployment** (1992): 6.8%. **Tourism** (1990): out-of-state visitors spent $2.2 bln. **Sales tax:** 5-6.75%.

Finance. FDIC-insured commercial banks & trust companies (1993): 81. **Deposits**: $11.2 bln. **FDIC-insured savings institutions** (1993): 12. **Assets**: $1.3 bln.

Federal government. No. federal civilian employees (Mar. 1993): 23,602. **Avg. salary:** $34,951. **Notable federal facilities:** Kirtland, Cannon, Holloman AF bases; Los Alamos Scientific Laboratory; White Sands Missile Range; National Solar Observatory; National Radio Astronomy Observatory.

Energy. Electricity production (1993, kWh, by source): Coal: 25.5 bln.; Petroleum: 35 mln.; Gas: 2.5 bln.; Hydroelectric: 294 mln.

Education. Student-teacher ratio (1992): 17.6. **Avg. salary, public school teachers** (1993-94): $27,922.

State data. Motto: Crescit Eundo (It grows as it goes). **Flower:** Yucca. **Bird:** Roadrunner. **Tree:** Piñon. **Song:** O, Fair New Mexico; Asi Es Nuevo Mexico. **Entered union** Jan. 6, 1912; rank, 47th. **State fair** at: Albuquerque; mid-Sept.

History. Franciscan Marcos de Niza and a black slave Estevan explored the area, 1539, seeking gold. First settlements were at San Juan Pueblo, 1598, and Santa Fe, 1610. Settlers alternately traded and fought with the Apaches, Comanches, and Navajos. Trade on the Santa Fe Trail to Missouri started 1821. The Mexican War was declared May, 1846, Gen. Stephen Kearny took Santa Fe, August. In the 1870s, cattlemen staged the famed Lincoln County War in which Billy (the Kid) Bonney played a leading role. Pancho Villa raided Columbus, 1916.

Tourist attractions. Carlsbad Caverns, a national park, has caverns on 3 levels and the largest natural cave "room" in the world, 1,500 by 300 ft., 300 ft. high; White Sands Natl. Monument, the largest gypsum deposit in the world.

Pueblo ruins from 100 AD, Chaco Canyon; Acoma, the "sky city," built atop a 357-ft. mesa; 19 Pueblo, 4 Navajo, and 2 Apache reservations. Also, ghost towns, dude ranches, skiing, hunting, and fishing.

Famous New Mexicans. Billy (the Kid) Bonney, Kit Carson, Peter Hurd, Archbishop Jean Baptiste Lamy, Nancy Lopez, Bill Mauldin, Georgia O'Keeffe, Kim Stanley, Al Unser, Bobby Unser, Lew Wallace.

Tourist information. New Mexico Dept. of Tourism, P.O. Box 20003, Santa Fe, N.M. 87503.

Toll-free travel information. 1-800-545-2040.

New York

Empire State

People. Population (1993): 18,197,154; **rank:** 2. **Pop. density:** 383.7 per sq. mi. **Racial/ethnic distrib.** (1990): 74.4% white; 15.9% black; 3.9% Asian; 12.3% Hispanic. **Net change** (1990-93): 1.1%.

Geography. Total area: 54,471 sq. mi.; **rank:** 27. **Land area:** 47,224 sq. mi. **Acres forested land:** 18,713,000. **Location:** Middle Atlantic state, bordered by the New England states, Atlantic Ocean, New Jersey and Pennsylvania, Lakes Ontario and Erie, and Canada. **Climate:** variable; the SE region moderated by the ocean. **Topography:** highest and most rugged mountains in the NE Adirondack upland; St. Lawrence-Champlain lowlands extend from Lake Ontario NE along the Canadian border; Hudson-Mohawk lowland follows the flows of the rivers N and W, 10-30 mi. wide; Atlantic coastal plain in the SE; Appalachian Highlands, covering half the state westward from the Hudson Valley, include the Catskill Mtns., Finger Lakes; plateau of Erie-Ontario lowlands. **Capital:** Albany.

Economy. Principal industries: manufacturing, finance, communications, tourism, transportation, services. **Principal manufactured goods:** books and periodicals, clothing and apparel, pharmaceuticals, machinery, instruments, toys and sporting goods, electronic equipment, automotive and aircraft components. **Agriculture: Chief crops:** apples, cabbage, cauliflower, celery, cherries, grapes, corn, peas, snap beans, sweet corn. **Products:** milk, cheese, maple syrup, wine. **Livestock**

(1993): 1.6 mln. cattle; 105,000 hogs/pigs; 78,000 sheep; 7.5 mln. poultry. **Timber/lumber** (1992): saw log production; 428 mln. bd. ft. **Nonfuel Minerals** (1993): $844.6 mln.; mostly crushed stone, salt, construction sand & gravel, cement. **Commercial fishing** (1993): $54.2 mln. **Chief ports:** New York, Buffalo, Albany. **International airports at:** New York, Buffalo, Syracuse, Massena, Ogdensburg, Watertown, Niagara Falls, Newburgh, Sullivan county. **Value of construction** (1993): $13.9 bln. **Employment distribution** (1993): 31% serv.; 20% trade; 18% gvt.; 13% mfg. **Per capita personal income** (1993): $24,623. **Unemployment** (1993): 7.7%. **Tourism** (1991): tourists spent $19.0 bln. **Sales tax**: 8½%.

Finance. FDIC-insured commercial banks & trust companies (1993): 175. **Deposits:** $493.9 bln. **FDIC-insured savings institutions** (1993): 125. **Assets**: $117.4 bln.

Federal government. No. federal civilian employees (Mar. 1993): 69,335. **Avg. salary:** $37,511. **Notable federal facilities:** West Point Military Academy; Merchant Marine Academy; Ft. Drum; Griffiss, Plattsburgh AF bases; Watervliet Arsenal.

Energy. Electricity production (1993, kWh, by source): Coal: 21.7 bln.; Petroleum: 14.4 bln.; Gas: 16.2 bln.; Hydroelectric: 27.0 bln.; Nuclear: 26.9 bln.

Education. Student-teacher ratio (1992): 15.2. **Avg. salary, public school teachers** (1993-94): $46,800.

State data. Motto: Excelsior (Ever upward). **Flower:** Rose. **Bird:** Bluebird. **Tree:** Sugar maple. **Song:** I Love New York. **Eleventh** of the original 13 states to ratify the Constitution, July 26, 1788. **State fair** at: Syracuse; late Aug.-early Sept.

History. In 1609 Henry Hudson visited the river that bears his name and Champlain explored the lake, far upstate, that was named for him. Dutch built posts near present-day Albany and New York City in 1624; in 1626 they settled Manhattan. A British fleet seized New Netherland, 1664. Ninety-two of the 300 or more engagements of the Revolution were fought in New York, including the Battle of Bemis Heights-Saratoga, a turning point of the war.

Tourist attractions. New York City; Adirondack and Catskill mtns.; Finger Lakes, Great Lakes; Long Island beaches; Thousand Islands; Niagara Falls; Saratoga Springs racing and spas; Philipsburg Manor, Sunnyside, the restored home of Washington Irving, The Dutch Church of Sleepy Hollow, all in Tarrytown area; Corning Glass Center and Steuben factory, Corning; Fenimore House, National Baseball Hall of Fame and Museum, both in Cooperstown; Ft. Ticonderoga overlooking Lakes George and Champlain; Albany's Empire State Plaza; Lake Placid Olympic Village.

The Franklin D. Roosevelt National Historic Site, Hyde Park, includes the graves of Pres. and Mrs. Roosevelt, the family home since 1867, and the Roosevelt Library. Sagamore Hill, Oyster Bay, the Theodore Roosevelt estate, includes his home.

Famous New Yorkers. Susan B. Anthony, Peter Cooper, George Eastman, Millard Fillmore, George and Ira Gershwin, Ruth Bader Ginsberg, Julia Ward Howe, Charles Evans Hughes, Henry and William James, Herman Melville, Franklin Delano Roosevelt, Theodore Roosevelt, Alfred E. Smith, Elizabeth Cady Stanton, Martin Van Buren, Walt Whitman.

Tourist information. N.Y. State Dept. of Economic Development, 1 Commerce Plaza, Albany, NY 12245.

Toll-free travel information. 1-800-CALLNYS from 50 states & U.S. territories; 1-518-474-4116 from other areas and Canada.

North Carolina

Tar Heel State, Old North State

People. Population (1993): 6,945,180; **rank:** 10. **Pop. density:** 140.5 per sq. mi. **Racial/ethnic distrib.** (1990): 75.6% white; 22.0% black; 1.2% Amer. Indian; 1.2% Hispanic. **Net change** (1990-93): 4.8%.

Geography. Total area: 53,821 sq. mi.; **rank:** 28. **Land area:** 48,718 sq. mi. **Acres forested land:** 19,278,000. **Location:** South Atlantic state bounded by Virginia, South Carolina, Georgia, Tennessee, and the Atlantic O. **Climate:** sub-tropical in SE, medium-continental in mountain region; tempered by the Gulf Stream and the mountains in W. **Topography:** coastal plain and tidewater, two-fifths of state, extending to the fall line of the rivers; piedmont plateau, another two-fifths, 200 mi. wide of gentle to rugged hills; southern Appalachian Mtns. contains the Blue Ridge and Great Smoky mtns. **Capital:** Raleigh.

Economy. Principal industries: manufacturing, agriculture, tobacco, tourism. **Principal manufactured goods:** textiles, rubber/plastics products, electrical/electronic equip., chemicals, furniture, food products, non-electrical machinery. **Agriculture: Chief crops:** tobacco, soybeans, corn, cotton, peanuts, sweet potatoes, feed grains, vegetables, fruits. **Livestock** (1993): 1.1 mln. cattle; 4.5 mln. hogs/pigs; 19.3 mln. chickens, 61 mln. turkeys. **Timber/lumber** (1992): yellow pine, oak, hickory, poplar, maple; 1.69 bln. bd. ft. **Nonfuel Minerals** (1993): $544.9 mln.; mostly clay, sand & gravel, crushed stone. **Commercial fishing** (1993): $57.9 mln. **International airports at:** Charlotte/Douglas, Raleigh/Durham. **Chief ports:** Morehead City, Wilmington. **Value of construction** (1993): $8.9 bln. **Employment distribution** (1993): 26.4% mfg.; 22.7% trade; 20% serv.; 15.8% gvt. **Per capita personal income** (1993): $17,488. **Unemployment** (1993): 4.9%. **Tourism** (1993): out-of-state visitors spent $8.0 bln. **Sales tax:** 6%.

Finance. FDIC-insured commercial banks & trust companies (1993): 71. **Deposits**: $70.3 bln. **FDIC-insured savings institutions** (1993): 87. **Assets:** $11.8 bln.

Federal government. No. federal civilian employees (Mar. 1993): 30,775. **Avg. salary:** $32,819. **Notable federal facilities:** Ft. Bragg; Camp LeJeune Marine Base; U.S. EPA Research and Development Labs, Cherry Point Marine Corps Air Station; Natl. Humanities Center; Natl. Inst. of Environmental Health Science; Natl. Center for Health Statistics Lab, Research Triangle Park.

Energy. Electricity production (1993, kWh, by source): Coal: 59.4 bln.; Petroleum: 165 mln.; Gas: 240 mln.; Hydroelectric: 5.2 bln.; Nuclear: 23.8 bln.

Education. Student-teacher ratio (1992): 16.7. **Avg. salary, public school teachers** (1993-94): $29,680.

State data. Motto: Esse Quam Videri (To be rather than to seem). **Flower:** Dogwood. **Bird:** Cardinal. **Tree:** Pine. **Song:** The Old North State. **Twelfth** of the original 13 states to ratify the Constitution, Nov. 21, 1789. **State fair** at: Raleigh; mid-Oct.

History. The first English colony in America was the first of 2 established by Sir Walter Raleigh on Roanoke Is., 1585 and 1587. The first group returned to England; the second, the "Lost Colony," disappeared without a trace. Permanent settlers came from Virginia, c. 1660. Roused by British repressions, the colonists drove out the royal governor, 1775; the province's congress was the first to vote for independence; ten regiments were furnished to the Continental Army. Cornwallis' forces were defeated at Kings Mountain, 1780, and forced out after Guilford Courthouse, 1781.

Tourist attractions. Cape Hatteras and Cape Lookout national seashores; Great Smoky Mtns. (half in Tennessee); Guilford Courthouse and Moore's Creek parks, 66 Revolutionary battle sites; Bennett Place, NW of Durham, where Gen. Joseph Johnston surrendered the last Confederate army to Gen. Wm. Sherman; Ft. Raleigh, Roanoke Is., where Virginia Dare, first child of English parents in the New World, was born Aug. 18, 1587; Wright Brothers National Memorial, Kitty Hawk; U.S.S. *North Carolina* battleship, Wilmington; N.C. Zoo, Asheboro; N.C. Symphony, & N.C. Museum, Raleigh; Carl Sandburg Home, Hendersonville.

Famous North Carolinians. Richard J. Gatling, Billy Graham, Andy Griffith, Andrew Jackson, Andrew Johnson, Michael Jordan, Wm. Rufus King, Charles Kuralt, Dolley Madison, Edward R. Murrow, James K. Polk, Enos Slaughter, Thomas Wolfe.

Tourist information. Travel & Tourism Division, 430 No. Salisbury St., Raleigh, NC 27603.

Toll-free travel information. 1-800-VISITNC.

North Dakota

Peace Garden State

People. Population (1993): 634,935; **rank:** 47. **Pop. density:** 9.2 per sq. mi. **Racial/ethnic distrib.** (1990): 94.6% white; 0.6% black; 4.1% Amer. Indian; 0.7% Hispanic. **Net change** (1990-93): –0.6%.

Geography. Total area: 70,704 sq. mi.; **rank:** 19. **Land area:** 68,994 sq. mi. **Acres forested land:** 722,000. **Location:** West North Central state, situated exactly in the middle of North America, bounded on the N by Canada, on the E by Minnesota, on the S by South Dakota, on the W by Montana. **Climate:** continental, with a wide range of temperature and moderate rainfall. **Topography:** Central Lowland in the E comprises the flat Red River Valley and the Rolling Drift Prairie; Missouri Plateau of the Great Plains on the W. **Capital:** Bismarck.

Economy. Principal industries: agriculture, mining, tourism, manufacturing, telecommunications, energy. **Principal manufactured goods:** farm equipment, processed foods, fabricated metal, high-tech. electronics. **Agriculture: Chief crops:** spring wheat, durum, barley, rye, flaxseed, oats, potatoes, dried edible beans, honey, soybeans, sugar beets, sunflowers, hay. **Livestock** (1994): 1.9 mln. cattle; 320,000 hogs/pigs; 165,000 sheep; 255,000 poultry. **Nonfuel Minerals** (1993): $25 mln.; mostly construction sand & gravel, lime. **International airports at:** Fargo, Grand Forks, Bismarck, Minot, Pembina, Dunseith. **Value of construction** (1993): $648.6 mln. **Employment distribution** (1991): 28.5% trade; 26.2% serv.; 20.5% gvt.; 7.1% mfg. **Per capita personal income** (1993): $17,488. **Unemployment** (1993): 4.3%. **Tourism** (1992): $826 mln. **Sales tax:** 5%.

Finance. FDIC-insured commercial banks & trust companies (1993): 141. **Deposits:** $7.1 bln. **FDIC-insured savings institutions** (1993): 4. **Assets:** $7.6 bln.

Federal government. No. federal civilian employees (Mar. 1993): 5,504. **Avg. salary:** $32,285. **Notable federal facilities:** Strategic Air Command bases at Minot, Grand Forks; Northern Prairie Wildlife Research Center; Garrison Dam; Theodore Roosevelt Natl. Park; Grand Forks Energy Research Center; Ft. Union Natl. Historic Site.

Energy. Electricity production (1993, kWh, by source): Coal: 27.0 bln.; Petroleum: 36 bln.; Hydroelectric: 1.4 bln.

Education. Student-teacher ratio (1992): 15.2. **Avg. salary, public school teachers** (1993-94): $25,508.

State data. Motto: Liberty and union, now and forever, one and inseparable. **Flower:** Wild prairie rose. **Bird:** Western meadowlark. **Tree:** American elm. **Song:** North Dakota Hymn. **Entered union** Nov. 2, 1889; rank, 39th. **State fair** at: Minot; 3d week in July.

History. Pierre La Verendrye was the first French fur trader in the area, 1738, followed later by the English. The U.S. acquired half the territory in the Louisiana Purchase, 1803. Lewis and Clark built Ft. Mandan, spent the winter of 1804-05 there. In 1818, American ownership of the other half was confirmed by agreement with Britain. First permanent settlement was at Pembina, 1812. Missouri River steamboats reached the area, 1832; the first railroad, 1873, bringing many homesteaders. The state was first to hold a presidential primary, 1912.

Tourist attractions. North Dakota Heritage Center, State Capitol grounds; Bonanzaville, Fargo, restored pioneer town; Ft. Union Trading Post Natl. Historic Site; Lake Sakakawea, 180 miles of fishing, boating, 1,600 miles of shoreline. Interntl. Peace Garden, 2,200-acre tract extending across the border into Manitoba; 65,000-acre Theodore Roosevelt National Park, Badlands, contains the president's Elkhorn Ranch; Ft. Abraham Lincoln State Park and Museum, S of Mandan; Dakota Dinosaur Museum, Dickinson.

Famous North Dakotans. Maxwell Anderson, Angie Dickinson, John Bernard Flannagan, Louis L'Amour, Peggy Lee, Eric Sevareid, Vilhjalmur Stefansson, Lawrence Welk.

Chamber of Commerce. P.O. Box 2639, 2000 Schafer St., Bismarck, ND 58501.

Toll-free travel information. 1-800-HELLOND.

Ohio

Buckeye State

People. Population (1993): 11,091,301; **rank:** 7. **Pop. density:** 269.0 per sq. mi. **Racial/ethnic distrib.** (1990): 87.8% white; 10.6% black; 1.3% Hispanic. **Net change** (1990-93): 2.3%.

Geography. Total area: 44,828 sq. mi.; **rank:** 34. **Land area:** 40,953 sq. mi. **Acres forested land:** 7,863,000. **Location:** East North Central state bounded on the N by Michigan and Lake Erie; on the E and S by Pennsylvania, West Virginia, and Kentucky; on the W by Indiana. **Climate:** temperate but variable; weather subject to much precipitation. **Topography:** generally rolling plain; Allegheny plateau in E; Lake [Erie] plains extend southward; central plains in the W. **Capital:** Columbus.

Economy. Principal industries: manufacturing, trade, services. **Principal manufactured goods:** transportation equipment, machinery, primary and fabricated metal products. **Agriculture: Chief crops:** corn, hay, winter wheat, oats, soybeans. **Livestock** (1992): 1.6 mln. cattle; 1.9 mln. hogs/pigs; 24.9 mln. broilers, 5 mln. turkeys. **Timber/lumber** (1992): oak, ash, maple, walnut, beech; 288 mln. bd. ft. **Nonfuel Minerals** (1993): $813.6 mln.; mostly crushed stone, construction sand & gravel, salt, lime. **Commercial fishing** (1993): $1.7 mln. **Chief ports:** Toledo, Conneaut, Cleveland, Ashtabula. **International airports at:** Cleveland, Cincinnati, Columbus, Dayton. **Value of construction** (1993): $11.1 bln. **Employment distribution** (1992): 21.7% mfg.; 24.0% trade; 25.6% serv.; 15.2% gvt. **Per capita personal income** (1993): $17,488. **Unemployment** (1993): 6.5%. **Tourism** (1992): travelers spent $8.8 bln. **Sales tax:** 5%.

Finance. FDIC-insured commercial banks & trust companies (1993): 263. **Deposits:** $96.5 bln. **FDIC-insured savings institutions** (1993): 172. **Assets:** $36.6 bln.

Federal government. No. federal civilian employees (Mar. 1993): 54,245. **Avg. salary:** $37,535. **Notable federal facilities:** Wright Patterson AFB; Defense Construction Supply Center; Lewis Research Ctr.; Portsmouth Gaseous Diffusion Plant; EG&G Mound Applied Tech. Laboratory.

Energy. Electricity production (1993, kWh, by source): Coal: 123.0 bln.; Petroleum: 276 mln.; Gas: 177 mln.; Hydroelectric: 183 mln.; Nuclear: 10.0 mln.

Education. Student-teacher ratio (1992): 16.9. **Avg. salary, public school teachers** (1993-94): $35,700.

State data. Motto: With God, all things are possible. **Flower:** Scarlet carnation. **Bird:** Cardinal. **Tree:** Buckeye. **Song:** Beautiful Ohio. **Entered union** Mar. 1, 1803; rank, 17th. **State fair** at: Columbus; August.

History. LaSalle visited the Ohio area, 1669. American furtraders arrived, beginning 1685; the French and Indians sought to drive them out. During the Revolution, Virginians defeated the Indians, 1774, but hostilities were renewed, 1777. The region became U.S. territory after the Revolution. First organized settlement was at Marietta, 1788. Indian warfare ended with Anthony Wayne's victory at Fallen Timbers, 1794. In the War of 1812, Oliver Hazard Perry's victory on Lake Erie and William Henry Harrison's invasion of Canada, 1813, ended British incursions.

Tourist attractions. Mound City Group National Monuments, a group of 24 prehistoric Indian burial mounds; Neil Armstrong Air and Space Museum, Wapakoneta; Air Force Museum, Dayton; Pro Football Hall of Fame, Canton; King's Island amusement park, Mason; Cedar Point amusement park, Sandusky; birthplaces, homes of, and memorials to Ohio's 8 U.S. presidents: William Henry Harrison, Grant, Garfield, Hayes, McKinley, Harding, Taft, Benjamin Harrison; Lake Erie Islands, Sandusky; Amish Region, Tuscarawas/Holmes counties; German Village, Columbus; Sea World, Aurora; Jack Nicklaus Sports Center, Mason; Bob Evans Farm, Rio Grande.

Famous Ohioans. Sherwood Anderson, Neil Armstrong, George Bellows, Johnny Bench, Ambrose Bierce, Erma Bombeck, Clarence Darrow, Paul Laurence Dunbar, Thomas Edison, Clark Gable, John Glenn, Bob

Hope, Jack Nicklaus, Jesse Owens, Eddie Rickenbacker, John D. Rockefeller Sr. and Jr., Pete Rose, Gen. Wm. Sherman, Harriet Beecher Stowe, Charles Taft, Robert A. Taft, William H. Taft, James Thurber, Orville Wright.

Chamber of Commerce. 35 E. Gay St., Columbus, OH 43215-3181.

Toll-free travel information. 1-800-BUCKEYE.

Oklahoma

Sooner State

People. Population (1993): 3,231,464; **rank:** 28. **Pop. density:** 46.8 per sq. mi. **Racial/ethnic distrib.** (1990): 82.1% white; 7.4% black; 8.0% Amer. Indian; 2.7% Hispanic. **Net change** (1990-93): 2.7%.

Geography. Total area: 69,903 sq. mi.; **rank:** 20. **Land area:** 68,679 sq. mi. **Acres forested land:** 7,539,000. **Location:** West South Central state bounded on the N by Colorado and Kansas; on the E by Missouri and Arkansas; on the S and W by Texas and New Mexico. **Climate:** temperate; southern humid belt merging with colder northern continental; humid eastern and dry western zones. **Topography:** high plains predominate in the W, hills and small mountains in the E; the east central region is dominated by the Arkansas R. Basin, and the Red R. Plains, in the S. **Capital:** Oklahoma City.

Economy. Principal industries: manufacturing, mineral and energy exploration and production, agriculture, services. **Principal manufactured goods:** non-electrical machinery, transportation equip., food products, fabricated metal products. **Agriculture: Chief crops:** wheat, cotton, hay, peanuts, grain sorghum, soybeans, corn, pecans. **Livestock** (1992): 5.5 mln. cattle; 190,000 hogs/pigs; 145,000 sheep; 5.5 mln. poultry. **Timber/lumber** (1992): pine, oaks, hickory; 225 mln. bd. ft. **Nonfuel Minerals** (1993): $282.5 mln.; mostly crushed stone, portland cement, sand & gravel, iodine. **Chief ports:** Catoosa, Muskogee. **International airports at:** Oklahoma City, Tulsa. **Value of construction** (1993): $2.3 bln. **Employment distribution** (1992): 23.7% serv.; 23.4% trade; 22.3% gvt.; 13.4% mfg. **Per capita personal income** (1993): $17,020. **Unemployment** (1993): 6.0%. **Tourism** (1992): tourists spent $2.64 bln. **Sales tax:** 4.5%.

Finance. FDIC-insured commercial banks & trust companies (1993): 371. **Deposits:** $27.0 bln. **FDIC-insured savings institutions** (1993): 15. **Assets:** $5.1 bln.

Federal government. No. federal civilian employees (Mar. 1993): 33,579. **Avg. salary:** $33,987. **Notable federal facilities:** Federal Aviation Agency and Tinker AFB, both Oklahoma City; Ft. Sill, Lawton; Altus AFB, Altus; Vance AFB, Enid.

Energy. Electricity production (1993, kWh, by source): Coal: 29.0 bln.; Petroleum: 14 mln.; Gas: 15.5 bln.; Hydroelectric: 4.3 bln.

Education. Student-teacher ratio (1992): 15.5. **Avg. salary, public school teachers** (1993-94): $26,749.

State data. Motto: Labor Omnia Vincit (Labor conquers all things). **Flower:** Mistletoe. **Bird:** Scissor-tailed flycatcher. **Tree:** Redbud. **Song:** Oklahoma! **Entered union** Nov. 16, 1907; rank, 46th. **State fair** at: Oklahoma City; last week of Sept.

History. Part of the Louisiana Purchase, 1803, Oklahoma was known as Indian Territory (but was not given territorial government) after it became the home of the "Five Civilized Tribes"—Cherokee, Choctaw, Chickasaw, Creek, and Seminole—1828-1846. The land was also used by Comanche, Osage, and other Plains Indians. As white settlers pressed west, land was opened for homesteading by runs and lottery, the first run taking place Apr. 22, 1889. The most famous run was to the Cherokee Outlet, 1893.

Tourist attractions. State park system—camping, hiking, water sports; Cherokee Heritage Center, Tahlequah; White Water Bay and Frontier City theme pks., both Oklahoma City; Will Rogers Memorial, Claremore; National Cowboy Hall of Fame and Remington Park Race Track, both Oklahoma City; restored Ft. Gibson Stockade, near Muskogee, the Army's largest outpost in Indian lands; Indian pow-wows; rodeos; fishing; hunting; Ouachita National Forest; Enterprise Square, museum devoted to American economic system; Tulsa's art deco district; Wichita Mts. Wildlife Refuge, Lawton; Woolaroc Museum & Wildlife Preserve, Bartlesville.

Famous Oklahomans. Carl Albert, Garth Brooks, L. Gordon Cooper, Woody Guthrie, Anita Hill, Gen. Patrick J. Hurley, Karl Jansky, Mickey Mantle, Reba McEntire, Carry Nation, Wiley Post, Oral Roberts, Will Rogers, Maria Tallchief, Jim Thorpe.

Chamber of Commerce. 4020 N. Lincoln Blvd., Oklahoma City, OK 73105.

Tourism Dept. P.O. Box 60789, Oklahoma City, OK 73146-0789.

Toll-free travel information. 1-800-652-6552.

Oregon

Beaver State

People. Population (1993): 3,031,867; **rank:** 29. **Pop. density:** 31.0 per sq. mi. **Racial/ethnic distrib.** (1990): 92.8% white; 1.6% black; 4.0% Hispanic. **Net change** (1990-93): 6.7%.

Geography. Total area: 98,386 sq. mi.; **rank:** 9. **Land area:** 96,002 sq. mi. **Acres forested land:** 27,997,000. **Location:** Pacific state, bounded on N by Washington; on E by Idaho; on S by Nevada and California; on W by the Pacific. **Climate:** coastal mild and humid climate; continental dryness and extreme temperatures in the interior. **Topography:** Coast Range of rugged mountains; fertile Willamette R. Valley to E and S; Cascade Mtn. Range of volcanic peaks E of the valley; plateau E of Cascades, remaining two-thirds of state. **Capital:** Salem.

Economy. Principal industries: manufacturing, forestry, agriculture, tourism, high technology. **Principal manufactured goods:** lumber & wood products, foods, machinery, fabricated metals, paper, printing & publishing, primary metals. **Agriculture: Chief crops:** greenhouse/nursery prods., farm forest prods., hay, wheat, potatoes, onions, grass seed, pears. **Livestock** (1993): 1.4 mln. cattle; 70,000 hogs/pigs; 415,000 sheep; 3.3 mln. poultry. **Timber/lumber** (1992): Douglas fir, hemlock, ponderosa pine; 6.05 bln. bd. ft. **Nonfuel Minerals** (1993): $233.5 mln.; mostly crushed stone, construction sand & gravel, portland cement. **Commercial fishing** (1993): $61.3 mln. **Chief ports:** Portland, Astoria, Coos Bay. **International airports at:** Portland, Klamath Falls. **Value of construction** (1993): $3.6 bln. **Employment distribution** (1991): 25.7% trade; 23.2% serv.; 18.0% mfg.; 17.8% gvt. **Per capita personal income** (1993): $19,443. **Unemployment** (1993): 7.2%. **Tourism** (1992): travel expenditures, $3.13 bln.

Finance. FDIC-insured commercial banks & trust companies (1993): 45. **Deposits:** $21.4 bln. **FDIC-insured savings institutions** (1993): 9. **Assets:** $5.3 bln.

Federal government. No. federal civilian employees (Mar. 1993): 20,798. **Avg. salary:** $35,623. **Notable federal facilities:** Bonneville Power Administration.

Energy. Electricity production (1993, kWh, by source): Coal: 3.4 bln.; Petroleum: 33 mln.; Gas: 1.7 bln.; Hydroelectric: 35.5 bln.

Education. Student-teacher ratio (1992): 19.2. **Avg. salary, public school teachers** (1993-94): $37,130.

State data. Motto: She flies with her own wings. **Flower:** Oregon grape. **Bird:** Western meadowlark. **Tree:** Douglas fir. **Song:** Oregon, My Oregon. **Entered union** Feb. 14, 1859; rank, 33d. **State fair** at: Salem; 12 days ending with Labor Day.

History. American Capt. Robert Gray sighted and sailed into the Columbia River, 1792; Lewis and Clark, traveling overland, wintered at its mouth 1805-6; fur traders followed. Settlers arrived in the Willamette Valley, 1834. In 1843 the first large wave of settlers arrived via the Oregon Trail. Early in the 20th century, the "Oregon System"—political reforms that included the initiative, referendum, recall, direct primary, and woman suffrage—was adopted.

Tourist attractions. John Day Fossil Beds National Monument; Columbia River Gorge; Mt. Hood & Timberline Lodge; Crater Lake National Park; Oregon Dunes

National Recreation Area; Ft. Clatsop National Memorial; Oregon Caves National Monument; Oregon Museum of Science and Industry; Shakespearean Festival, Ashland; High Desert Museum, Bend. Also, skiing, fishing; Annual Albany Timber Carnival, Pendelton Round-Up, Portland Rose Festival.

Famous Oregonians. Ernest Bloch, Ernest Haycox, Chief Joseph, Edwin Markham, Tom McCall, Dr. John McLoughlin, Joaquin Miller, Linus Pauling, John Reed, Alberto Salazar, Mary Decker Slaney, William Simon U'Ren.

Tourist information. Economic Development Department, 775 Summer St. NE, Salem, OR 97310.

Toll-free travel information. 1-800-547-7842 .

Pennsylvania

Keystone State

People. Population (1993): 12,048,271; **rank:** 5. **Pop. density:** 267.9 per sq. mi. **Racial/ethnic distrib.** (1990): 88.5% white; 9.2% black; 2.0% Hispanic. **Net change** (1990-93): 1.4%.

Geography. Total area: 45,308 sq. mi.; **rank:** 33. **Land area:** 46,058 sq. mi. **Acres forested land:** 16,969,000. **Location:** Middle Atlantic state, bordered on the E by the Delaware R.; on the S by the Mason-Dixon Line; on the W by West Virginia and Ohio; on the N/NE by Lake Erie and New York. **Climate:** continental with wide fluctuations in seasonal temperatures. **Topography:** Allegheny Mtns. run SW to NE, with Piedmont and Coast Plain in the SE triangle; Allegheny Front a diagonal spine across the state's center; N and W rugged plateau falls to Lake Erie Lowland. **Capital:** Harrisburg.

Economy. Principal industries: steel, travel, health, apparel, machinery, food & agriculture. **Principal manufactured goods:** primary metals; foods; fabricated metal products; non-electrical machinery; electrical machinery; printing and publishing; stone, clay, and glass products. **Agriculture: Chief crops:** corn, hay, mushrooms, apples, potatoes, winter wheat, oats, vegetables, tobacco, grapes. **Livestock** (1994): 1.8 mln. cattle; 1.4 mln. hogs/pigs; 139,000 sheep; 21.8 mln. poultry. **Timber/lumber** (1992): pine, oak, maple; 676 mln. bd. ft. **Nonfuel Minerals** (1993): $893.4 mln.; mostly crushed stone, cement, lime, construction sand & gravel. **Commercial fishing** (1993): $171,000. **Chief ports:** Philadelphia, Pittsburgh, Erie. **International airports at:** Allentown, Erie, Harrisburg, Philadelphia, Pittsburgh, Wilkes-Barre/Scranton. **Value of construction** (1993): $10.2 bln. **Employment distribution** (1992): 28% serv.; 26% trade; 20% mfg.; 14% gvt. **Per capita personal income** (1993): $21,351. **Unemployment** (1993): 7.0%. **Tourism** (1992): out-of-state visitors spent $10.2 bln.

Finance. FDIC-insured commercial banks & trust companies (1993): 261. **Deposits:** $140.1 bln. **FDIC-insured savings institutions** (1993): 135. **Assets:** $37.6 bln.

Federal government. No. federal civilian employees (Mar. 1993): 83,745. **Avg. salary:** $33,934. **Notable federal facilities:** Army War College, Carlisle; Ships Control Ctr., Mechanicsburg; New Cumberland Army Depot; Philadelphia Navy Yard, Philadelphia.

Energy. Electricity production (1993, kWh, by source): Coal: 100.4 bln.; Petroleum: 4.6 bln.; Gas: 797 mln.; Hydroelectric: 1.1 bln.; Nuclear: 59.3 bln.

Education. Student-teacher ratio (1992): 17.0. **Avg. salary, public school teachers** (1993-94): $43,688.

State data. Motto: Virtue, liberty and independence. **Flower:** Mountain laurel. **Bird:** Ruffed grouse. **Tree:** Hemlock. **Second** of the original 13 states to ratify the Constitution, Dec. 12, 1787. **State fair** at: Harrisburg; 2d week in Jan.

History. First settlers were Swedish, 1643, on Tinicum Is. In 1655 the Dutch seized the settlement but lost it to the British, 1664. The region was given by Charles II to William Penn, 1681, Philadelphia (brotherly love) was the capital of the colonies during most of the Revolution, and of the U.S., 1790-1800. Philadelphia was taken by the British, 1777; Washington's troops encamped at Valley Forge in the bitter winter of 1777-78. The Declaration of Independence, 1776, and the Constitution, 1787, were signed in Philadelphia.

Tourist attractions. Independence Hall & Natl. Historic Park, Franklin Institute Science Museum, Philadelphia Museum of Art, all in Philadelphia; Valley Forge Natl. Historic Park; Gettysburg Natl. Military Park; Pennsylvania Dutch Country; Hershey; Duquesne Incline, Carnegie Institute, Heinz Hall, all in Pittsburgh; year-round outdoor sports in Pocono Mtns., Pine Creek River Gorge, Alleghenies, Laurel Highlands & Presque Isle State Park.

Famous Pennsylvanians. Marian Anderson, Maxwell Anderson, James Buchanan, Andrew Carnegie, Stephen Foster, Benjamin Franklin, George C. Marshall, Andrew W. Mellon, Robert E. Peary, Mary Roberts Rinehart, Betsy Ross.

Chamber of Business and Industry. 417 Walnut St., Harrisburg, PA 17120.

Toll-free travel information. 1-800-VISITPA.

Rhode Island

Little Rhody, Ocean State

People. Population (1993): 1,000,012; **rank:** 43. **Pop. density:** 961.8 per sq. mi. **Racial/ethnic distrib.** (1990): 91.4% white; 3.9% black; 4.6% Hispanic. **Net change** (1990-93): –0.3%.

Geography. Total area: 1,545 sq. mi.; **rank:** 50. **Land area:** 1,045 sq. mi. **Acres forested land:** 401,000. **Location:** New England state. **Climate:** invigorating and changeable. **Topography:** eastern lowlands of Narragansett Basin; western uplands of flat and rolling hills. **Capital:** Providence.

Economy. Principal industries: services, manufacturing. **Principal manufactured goods:** costume jewelry, toys, machinery, textiles, electronics. **Agriculture: Chief crops:** nursery prods., turf, potatoes, apples. **Timber/lumber:** oak. **Nonfuel Minerals** (1993): $26.9 mln.; construction sand & gravel, crushed stone. **Commercial fishing** (1993): $76.3 mln. **Chief ports:** Providence, Quonset Point, Newport. **Value of construction** (1993): $1.2 bln. **Employment distribution** (1993): 32% services; 20% mfg.; 22% trade. **Per capita personal income** (1993): $21,096. **Unemployment** (1993): 7.7%. **Tourism** (1993): visitors spent $1.4 bln. **Sales tax:** 7%.

Finance. FDIC-insured commercial banks & trust companies (1993): 10. **Deposits:** $10.0 bln. **FDIC-insured savings institutions** (1993): 5. **Assets:** $4.5 bln.

Federal government. No. federal civilian employees (Mar. 1993): 5,877. **Avg. salary:** $37,872. **Notable federal facilities:** Naval War College; Naval Underwater Warfare Center, National Marine Fisheries Laboratory, EPA Environmental Research Laboratory.

Energy. Electricity production (1993, kWh, by source): Petroleum: 29 mln.; Gas: 25 mln.

Education. Student-teacher ratio (1992): 14.3. **Avg. salary, public school teachers** (1993-94): $39,261.

State data. Motto: Hope. **Flower:** Violet. **Bird:** Rhode Island red. **Tree:** Red maple. **Song:** Rhode Island. **Thirteenth** of original 13 states to ratify the Constitution, May 29, 1790. **State fair** at: Richmond; mid-Aug.

History. Rhode Island is distinguished for its battle for freedom of conscience and action, begun by Roger Williams, founder of Providence, who was exiled from Massachusetts Bay Colony in 1636, and Anne Hutchinson, exiled in 1638. Rhode Island gave protection to Quakers in 1657 and to Jews from Holland in 1658.

The colonists broke the power of the Narragansett Indians in the Great Swamp Fight, 1675, the decisive battle in King Philip's War. British trade restrictions angered the colonists and they burned the British revenue cutter Gaspee, 1772. The colony declared its independence May 4, 1776. Gen. John Sullivan and Lafayette won a partial victory, 1778, but failed to oust the British.

Tourist attractions. Newport mansions; summer resorts, and water sports; various yachting races inc. Newport to Bermuda; Block Is.; Touro Synagogue, Newport, 1763; first Baptist Church in America, Providence, 1638; Slater Mill Historic Site, inc. early cottonmill, 1793;

Gilbert Stuart birthplace, Saunderstown; Narragansett Indian Fall Festival.

Famous Rhode Islanders. Ambrose Burnside, George M. Cohan, Nelson Eddy, Jabez Gorham, Nathanael Greene, Christopher and Oliver La Farge, Matthew C. and Oliver Hazard Perry, Gilbert Stuart.

Chamber of Commerce. 30 Exchange Terr., Providence, RI 02908.

Toll-free travel information. 1-800-556-2484.

South Carolina

Palmetto State

People. Population (1993): 3,642,718; **rank:** 25. **Pop. density:** 119.7 per sq. mi. **Racial/ethnic distrib.** (1990): 69.0% white; 29.8% black; 0.9% Hispanic. **Net change** (1990-93): 4.5%.

Geography. Total area: 32,008 sq. mi.; **rank:** 40. **Land area:** 30,111 sq. mi. **Acres forested land:** 12,257,000. **Location:** South Atlantic state, bordered by North Carolina on the N; Georgia on the SW and W; the Atlantic O. on the E, SE, and S. **Climate:** humid subtropical. **Topography:** Blue Ridge province in NW has highest peaks; piedmont lies between the mountains and the fall line; coastal plain covers two-thirds of the state. **Capital:** Columbia.

Economy. Principal industries: tourism, agriculture, manufacturing. **Principal manufactured goods:** textiles, chemicals and allied products, machinery & fabricated metal products, apparel and related products. **Agriculture: Chief crops:** tobacco, soybeans, corn, cotton, peaches, hay. **Livestock** (1992): 600,000 cattle; 385,000 hogs/pigs; 6.0 mln. chickens, excl. broilers. **Timber/lumber** (1992): pine, oak; 1.42 bln. bd. ft. **Nonfuel Minerals** (1993): $361.3 mln.; mostly cement, crushed stone, clay. **Commercial fishing** (1993): $25.8 mln. **Chief ports:** Charleston, Georgetown, Beaufort/Port Royal. **International airports at:** Charleston. **Value of construction** (1993): $4.3 bln. **Employment distribution** (1993): 23.8% mfg.; 21.2% serv.; 22.4% trade; 6.8% gvt. **Per capita personal income** (1993): $16,923. **Unemployment** (1993): 7.5%. **Tourism** (1992): $6.5 bln. **Sales tax:** 5%.

Finance. FDIC-insured commercial banks & trust companies (1993): 78. **Deposits:** $20.6 bln. **FDIC-insured savings institutions** (1993): 38. **Assets:** $9.5 bln.

Federal government. No. federal civilian employees (Mar. 1993): 23,309. **Avg. salary:** $33,017. **Notable federal facilities:** Polaris Submarine Base; Barnwell Nuclear Power Plant; Ft. Jackson; Parris Island; Savannah River Plant.

Energy. Electricity production (1993, kWh, by source): Coal: 26.5 bln.; Petroleum: 121 mln.; Gas: 2.7 bln.; Hydroelectric: 2.7 bln.; Nuclear: 46.2 bln.

Education. Student-teacher ratio (1992): 17.0. **Avg. salary, public school teachers** (1993-94): $30,190.

State data. Motto: Dum Spiro Spero (While I breathe, I hope). **Flower:** Yellow jessamine. **Bird:** Carolina wren. **Tree:** Palmetto. **Song:** Carolina. **Eighth** of the original 13 states to ratify the Constitution, May 23, 1788. **State fair** at: Columbia; mid-Oct.

History. The first English colonists settled, 1670, on the Ashley River, moved to the site of Charleston, 1680. The colonists seized the government, 1775, and the royal governor fled. The British took Charleston, 1780, but were defeated at Kings Mountain that year, and at Cowpens and Eutaw Springs, 1781. In the 1830s, South Carolinians, angered by federal protective tariffs, adopted the Nullification Doctrine, holding that a state can void an act of Congress. The state was the first to secede in 1861, and Confederate troops fired on and forced the surrender of U.S. troops at Ft. Sumter, in Charleston Harbor, launching the Civil War.

Tourist attractions. Restored historic Charleston Harbor area and Charleston gardens: Middleton Place, Magnolia, Cypress; other gardens at Brookgreen, Edisto, Glencairn; state parks; coastal islands; shore resorts such as Myrtle Beach and Hilton Head Island; fishing and quail hunting; Revolutionary War battle sites; Andrew Jackson State Park & Museum; Ft. Sumter National Monument, in Charleston Harbor; Charleston Museum, est. 1773, the oldest museum in the U.S.; South Carolina State Museum, one of largest museums in the South, Columbia; Riverbanks Zoo, Columbia.

Famous South Carolinians. Charles Bolden, James F. Byrnes, John C. Calhoun, DuBose Heyward, Ernest F. Hollings, Andrew Jackson, Jesse Jackson, James Longstreet, Francis Marion, Ronald McNair, Charles Pinckney, John Rutledge, Thomas Sumter, Strom Thurmond, John B. Watson.

Tourist information. Chamber of Commerce, 930 Richland St., P.O. Box 1360, Columbia, SC 29201; and So. Carolina Dept. of Parks, Recreation, & Tourism, (803) 734-0122; Greater Columbia Convention & Visitors' Bureau, 301 Gervais St., Columbia, SC 29201, (803) 254-0479.

Toll-free travel information. 1-800-346-3634.

South Dakota

Coyote State, Mount Rushmore State

People. Population (1993): 715,392; **rank:** 45. **Pop. density:** 9.37 per sq. mi. **Racial/ethnic distrib.** (1990): 91.6% white; 0.5% black; 7.3% Amer. Indian; 0.8% Hispanic. **Net change** (1990-93): 2.8%.

Geography. Total area: 77,121 sq. mi.; **rank:** 17. **Land area:** 75,896 sq. mi. **Acres forested land:** 1,690,000. **Location:** West North Central state bounded on the N by North Dakota; on the E by Minnesota and Iowa; on the S by Nebraska; on the W by Wyoming and Montana. **Climate:** characterized by extremes of temperature, persistent winds, low precipitation and humidity. **Topography:** Prairie Plains in the E; rolling hills of the Great Plains in the W; the Black Hills, rising 3,500 ft., in the SW corner. **Capital:** Pierre.

Economy. Principal industries: agriculture, services, manufacturing. **Principal manufactured goods** (1991): food & kindred prods., machinery, electric & electronic equipment. **Agriculture: Chief crops** (1993): corn, oats, wheat, sunflowers, soybeans, sorghum. **Livestock** (1993): 3.75 mln. cattle; 1.75 mln. hogs/pigs; 543,000 sheep. **Timber/lumber** (1992): ponderosa pine; 247 mln. bd. ft. **Nonfuel Minerals** (1993): $324.3 mln.; mostly gold, portland cement. **Value of construction** (1993): $756.7 mln. **Employment distribution** (1993): 26% serv.; 12.4% mfg. **Per capita personal income** (1993): $17,666. **Unemployment** (1993): 3.5%. **Tourism** (1992): travelers' impact $979 mln. **Sales tax:** 4%.

Finance. FDIC-insured commercial banks & trust companies (1993): 121. **Deposits:** $11.0 bln. **FDIC-insured savings institutions** (1993): 7. **Assets:** $788 mln.

Federal government. No. federal civilian employees (Mar. 1993): 7,235. **Avg. salary:** $31,700. **Notable federal facilities:** Bureau of Indian Affairs, Ellsworth AFB, Corp of Engineers, Nat'l Park Service.

Energy. Electricity production (1993, kWh, by source): Coal: 2.6 bln.; Petroleum: 14 mln.; Gas: 7 mln.; Hydroelectric: 2.6 bln.

Education. Student-teacher ratio (1992): 15.3. **Avg. salary, public school teachers** (1993-94): $25,199.

State data. Motto: Under God, the people rule. **Flower:** Pasqueflower. **Bird:** Chinese ring-necked pheasant. **Tree:** Black Hills spruce. **Song:** Hail, South Dakota. **Entered union** Nov. 2, 1889; rank, 40th. **State fair** at: Huron; late Aug.-early Sept.

History. The Verendrye brothers (Fr.) explored the region, 1742-43. Lewis and Clark passed through the area, 1804 and 1806. First white American settlement was at Fort Pierre, 1817. Gold was discovered, 1874, on the Great Sioux Reservation; miners rushed in. The U.S. first tried to stop them, then relaxed its opposition. The "Great Dakota Boom" began 1879. Conflicts between the Indian and white communities climaxed in 1890 with the massacre of Indian families at Wounded Knee.

Tourist attractions. Black Hills; Mt. Rushmore, with colossal likeness of the faces of U.S. Presidents Washington, Jefferson, Lincoln & T. Roosevelt carved by sculptor Gutzon Borglum; Needles Highway; Harney Peak, at 7,242 ft. the tallest peak east of the Rockies;

Deadwood, an 1876 Gold Rush town; Custer State Park's buffalo and burro herds; Jewel Cave, the 4th longest cave in the world; Badlands Natl. Park's "moonscape"; "Great Lakes of So. Dakota"; Ft. Sisseton, restored 1864 army frontier post; Great Plains Zoo & Museum in Sioux Falls; Corn Palace in Mitchell; Wind Cave; Mammoth Site, ongoing excavation of prehistoric mammoths; Crazy Horse, mountain carving in progress.

Famous South Dakotans. Sparky Anderson, Tom Brokaw, Crazy Horse, Myron Floren, Alvin H. Hansen, Mary Hart, Cheryl Ladd, Dr. Ernest O. Lawrence, George McGovern, Billy Mills, Allen Neuharth, Pat O'Brien, Sitting Bull.

Tourist information. South Dakota Tourism, 711 E. Wells Ave., Pierre, SD 57501-3369.

Toll-free travel information. 1-800-SDAKOTA (732-5682).

Tennessee

Volunteer State

People. Population (1993): 5,098,798; **rank:** 17. **Pop. density:** 121.9 per sq. mi. **Racial/ethnic distrib.** (1990): 83.0% white; 16.0% black; 0.7% Hispanic. **Net change** (1990-93): 4.5%.

Geography. Total area: 42,146 sq. mi.; **rank:** 36. **Land area:** 41,219 sq. mi. **Acres forested land:** 13,612,000. **Location:** East South Central state bounded on the N by Kentucky and Virginia; on the E by North Carolina; on the S by Georgia, Alabama, and Mississippi; on the W by Arkansas and Missouri. **Climate:** humid continental to the N; humid sub-tropical to the S. **Topography:** rugged country in the E; the Great Smoky Mtns. of the Unakas; low ridges of the Appalachian Valley; the flat Cumberland Plateau; slightly rolling terrain and knobs of the Interior Low Plateau, the largest region; Eastern Gulf Coastal Plain to the W, is laced with meandering streams; Mississippi Alluvial Plain, a narrow strip of swamp and flood plain in the extreme W. **Capital:** Nashville.

Economy. Principal industries: manufacturing, trade, services, finance, ins., real estate. **Principal manufactured goods:** chemicals, food, transportation equip., industrial machinery & equip., fabr. metal prods., rubber/plastic prods., paper & allied prods., printing and publishing. **Agriculture: Chief crops** (1992): tobacco, cotton, lint, soybeans, grain, corn. **Livestock** (1993): 2.3 mln. cattle; 0.6 mln. hogs/pigs; 1.24 mln. poultry. **Timber/lumber** (1992): red oak, white oak, yellow poplar, hickory; 531 mln. bd. ft. **Nonfuel Minerals** (1993): $538.3 mln.; mostly crushed stone, sand & gravel, zinc, cement. **Chief ports:** Memphis, Nashville, Chattanooga, Knoxville. **International airports at:** Memphis, Nashville. **Value of construction** (1993): $5.5 bln. **Employment distribution** (1992): 23.0% mfg.; 23.2% trade; 24% serv.; 16% gvt. **Per capita personal income** (1993): $17,666. **Unemployment** (1993): 5.7%. **Tourism** (1992): out-of-state visitors spent $5.25 bln. **Sales tax:** 6.0% state, up to 2.75% local.

Finance. FDIC-insured commercial banks & trust companies (1993): 250. **Deposit:** $46.6 bln. **FDIC-insured savings institutions** (1993): 32. **Assets:** $6.3 bln.

Federal government. No. federal civilian employees (Mar. 1993): 37,445. **Avg. salary:** $35,703. **Notable federal facilities:** Tennessee Valley Authority; Oak Ridge Nat'l. Laboratories; Arnold Engineering Development Center; Ft. Campbell Army Base; Millington Naval Station.

Energy. Electricity production (1993, kWh, by source): Coal: 59.6 bln.; Petroleum: 235 mln.; Gas: 121 mln.; Hydroelectric: 8.4 bln.; Nuclear: 3.3 bln.

Education. Student-teacher ratio (1992): 19.4. **Avg. salary, public school teachers** (1993-94): $30,037.

State data. Motto: Agriculture and commerce. **Flower:** Iris. **Bird:** Mockingbird. **Tree:** Tulip poplar. **Song:** The Tennessee Waltz. **Entered union** June 1, 1796; rank, 16th. **State fair** at: Nashville; mid-Sept.

History. Spanish explorers first visited the area, 1541. English traders crossed the Great Smokies from the east while France's Marquette and Jolliet sailed down the Mississippi on the west, 1673. First permanent settlement was by Virginians on the Watauga River, 1769. During the Revolution, the colonists helped win the Battle of Kings Mountain, N.C., 1780, and joined other eastern campaigns. The state seceded from the Union 1861, and saw many engagements of the Civil War, but 30,000 soldiers fought for the Union.

Tourist attractions. Natural wonders include Reelfoot Lake, the reservoir basin of the Mississippi R. formed by the 1811 earthquake; Lookout Mountain, Chattanooga; Fall Creek Falls, 256 ft. high; Great Smoky Mountains National Park; Lost Sea, Sweetwater; Cherokee Natl. Forest.

Also, the Hermitage, 13 mi. E of Nashville, home of Andrew Jackson; the homes of presidents Polk and Andrew Johnson; American Museum of Science, Oak Ridge; the Parthenon, Nashville, a replica of the Parthenon of Athens; the Grand Old Opry, Nashville; Opryland, USA, theme park, Nashville; Graceland, home of Elvis Presley, Memphis; Alex Haley Home & Museum, Henning; Casey Jones Home & Museum, Jackson.

Famous Tennesseans. Roy Acuff, Davy Crockett, David Farragut, William C. Handy, Sam Houston, Cordell Hull, Grace Moore, Minnie Pearl, Dinah Shore, Alvin York.

Tourist information. Dept. of Tourist Development, 5th Floor, Rachel Jackson Bldg., 320 6th Ave. N., Nashville, TN 37202.

Texas

Lone Star State

People. Population (1993): 18,031,484; **rank:** 3. **Pop. density:** 67.4 per sq. mi. **Racial/ethnic distrib.** (1990): 75.2% white; 11.9% black; 25.5% Hispanic. **Net change** (1990-93): 6.2%.

Geography. Total area: 268,601 sq. mi.; **rank:** 2. **Land area:** 261,914 sq. mi.; **Acres forested land:** 19,193,000. **Location:** Southwestern state, bounded on the SE by the Gulf of Mexico; on the SW by Mexico, separated by the Rio Grande; surrounding states are Louisiana, Arkansas, Oklahoma, New Mexico. **Climate:** extremely varied; driest region is the Trans-Pecos; wettest is the NE. **Topography:** Gulf Coast Plain in the S and SE; North Central Plains slope upward with some hills; the Great Plains extend over the Panhandle, are broken by low mountains; the Trans-Pecos is the southern extension of the Rockies. **Capital:** Austin.

Economy. Principal industries: trade, services, manufacturing. **Principal manufactured goods:** machinery, transportation equipment, foods, electrical and electronic equip., chemicals and allied prods., apparel. **Agriculture: Chief crops:** cotton, grain sorghum, grains, vegetables, citrus and other fruits, pecans, peanuts. **Livestock** (1991): 13.4 mln. cattle; 500,000 hogs/pigs; 2.0 mln. sheep; 17.2 mln. poultry. **Timber/lumber** (1992): pine, cypress; 1.09 bln. bd. ft. **Nonfuel Minerals** (1993): $1.4 bln.; mostly cement, stone, magnesium, sand & gravel. **Commercial fishing** (1993): $152.8 mln. **Chief ports:** Houston, Galveston, Brownsville, Beaumont, Port Arthur, Corpus Christi. **Major international airports at:** Houston, Dallas/Ft. Worth, San Antonio. **Value of construction** (1993): $19.0 bln. **Employment distribution** (1993): 24.1% trade; 25.7% serv.; 18.4% gvt.; 13.2% mfg. **Per capita personal income** (1993): $19,189. **Unemployment** (1993): 7.0%. **Tourism** (1992): out-of-state visitors spent $20.6 bln. **Sales tax:** 6.25%, + optional 1% local, 1% transit.

Finance. FDIC-insured commercial banks & trust companies (1993): 1,011. **Deposits:** $151.2 bln. **FDIC-insured savings institutions** (1993): 62. **Assets:** $43.0 bln.

Federal government. No. federal civilian employees (Mar. 1993): $121,055. **Avg. salary:** $34,105. **Notable federal facilities:** Fort Hood (Killeen); Kelly AFB and Ft. Sam Houston, both San Antonio.

Energy. Electricity production (1993, kWh, by source): Coal: 128.2 bln.; Petroleum: 453 mln.; Gas: 105.0 bln.; Hydroelectric: 1.8 bln.; Nuclear: 12.4 bln.

Education. Student-teacher ratio (1992): 15.7. **Avg. salary, public school teachers** (1993-94): $30,519.

State data. Motto: Friendship. **Flower:** Bluebonnet. **Bird:** Mockingbird. **Tree:** Pecan. **Song:** Texas, Our

Texas. **Entered union** Dec. 29, 1845; rank, 28th. **State fair** at: Dallas; mid-Oct.

History. Pineda sailed along the Texas coast, 1519; Cabeza de Vaca and Coronado visited the interior, 1541. Spaniards made the first settlement at Ysleta, near El Paso, 1682. Americans moved into the land early in the 19th century. Mexico, of which Texas was a part, won independence from Spain, 1821; Santa Anna became dictator, 1835. Texans rebelled; Santa Anna wiped out defenders of the Alamo, 1836. Sam Houston's Texans defeated Santa Anna at San Jacinto and independence was proclaimed the same year. In 1845, Texas was admitted to the Union.

Tourist attractions. Padre Island National Seashore; Big Bend, Guadalupe Mtns. national parks; The Alamo; Ft. Davis; Six Flags Amusement Park; Sea World and Fiesta Texas, both in San Antonio. Named for Pres. Lyndon B. Johnson are a state park, a natl. historic site marking his birthplace, boyhood home, and ranch, all near Johnson City, and a library in Austin.

Famous Texans. Stephen F. Austin, Lloyd Bentsen, James Bowie, Carol Burnett, J. Frank Dobie, Dwight D. Eisenhower, Sam Houston, Howard Hughes, Lyndon B. Johnson, Mary Martin, Chester Nimitz, Katharine Ann Porter, Sam Rayburn.

Chamber of Commerce. 900 Congress, Suite 501, Austin, TX 78701.

Toll-free travel information. 1-800-888-8TEX.

Utah

Beehive State

People. Population (1993): 1,859,582; **rank:** 34. **Pop. density:** 22.1 per sq. mi. **Racial/ethnic distrib.** (1990): 93.8% white; 0.7% black; 4.9% Hispanic. **Net change** (1990-93): 7.9%.

Geography. Total area: 84,904 sq. mi.; **rank:** 13. **Land area:** 82,168 sq. mi. **Acres forested land:** 16,234,000. **Location:** Middle Rocky Mountain state; its southeastern corner touches Colorado, New Mexico, and Arizona, and is the only spot in the U.S. where 4 states join. **Climate:** arid; ranging from warm desert in SW to alpine in NE. **Topography:** high Colorado plateau is cut by brilliantly colored canyons of the SE; broad, flat, desert-like Great Basin of the W; the Great Salt Lake and Bonneville Salt Flats to the NW; Middle Rockies in the NE run E-W; valleys and plateaus of the Wasatch Front. **Capital:** Salt Lake City.

Economy. Principal industries: services, trade, manufacturing, government, construction. **Principal manufactured goods:** guided missiles and parts, electronic components, food products, fabricated metals, steel, electrical equipment, automobile airbags. **Agriculture: Chief crops:** hay, wheat, apples, barley, alfalfa seed, corn, potatoes, cherries, onions. **Livestock:** 855,000 cattle; 34,000 hogs/pigs; 600,000 sheep; 3.8 mln. poultry. **Timber/lumber:** aspen, spruce, pine. **Nonfuel Minerals** (1993): $1.3 bln.; mostly copper, gold, magnesium. **International airports at:** Salt Lake City. **Value of construction** (1993): $3.0 bln. **Employment distribution** (1993): 26.2% serv.; 23.6% trade; 19.7% govt; 13.6% mfg. **Per capita personal income** (1993): $16,180. **Unemployment** (1993): 3.9%. **Tourism** (1986): travelers spent $2.0 bln. **Sales tax:** 6.25%.

Finance. FDIC-insured commercial banks & trust companies (1993): 48. **Deposits:** $11.2 bln. **FDIC-insured savings institutions** (1993): 4. **Assets:** $989 mln.

Federal government. No. federal civilian employees (Mar. 1993): 30,696. **Avg. salary:** $32,635. **Notable federal facilities:** Hill AFB; Tooele Army Depot; IRS Western Service Center.

Energy. Electricity production (1993, kWh, by source): Coal: 31.9 bln.; Petroleum: 32 mln.; Gas: 543 mln.; Hydroelectric: 818 mln.

Education. Student-teacher ratio (1992): 24.2. **Avg. salary, public school teachers** (1993-94): $28,210.

State data. Motto: Industry. **Flower:** Sego lily. **Bird:** Seagull. **Tree:** Blue spruce. **Song:** Utah, We Love Thee. **Entered union** Jan. 4, 1896; rank, 45th. **State fair** at: Salt Lake City; Sept.

History. Spanish Franciscans visited the area, 1776, the first white men to do so. American fur traders followed. Permanent settlement began with the arrival of the Mormons, 1847. They made the arid land bloom and created a prosperous economy, organized the State of Deseret, 1849, and asked admission to the Union. This was not achieved until 1896, after a long period of controversy over the Mormon Church's doctrine of polygamy, which it discontinued in 1890.

Tourist attractions. Temple Square, Mormon Church hdqtrs., Salt Lake City; Great Salt Lake; fishing streams, lakes and reservoirs, numerous winter sports; campgrounds. Natural wonders may be seen at Zion, Canyonlands, Bryce Canyon, Arches, and Capitol Reef national parks; Dinosaur, Rainbow Bridge, Timpanogos Cave, and Natural Bridges national monuments. Also Lake Powell and Flaming Gorge reservoirs.

Famous Utahans. Maude Adams, Ezra Taft Benson, John Moses Browning, Mariner Eccles, Philo Farnsworth, James Fletcher, David M. Kennedy, J. Willard Marriott, Merlin Olsen, Osmond family, Ivy Baker Priest, George Romney, Brigham Young, Loretta Young.

Tourist information. Utah Travel Council, Council Hall, Salt Lake City, UT 84114.

Vermont

Green Mountain State

People. Population (1993): 575,691; **rank:** 49. **Pop. density:** 61.6 per sq. mi. **Racial/ethnic distrib.** (1990): 98.6% white; 0.3% black; 0.6% Asian; 0.7% Hispanic. **Net change** (1990-93): 2.3%.

Geography. Total area: 9,615 sq. mi.; **rank:** 45. **Land area:** 9,249 sq. mi. **Acres forested land:** 4,538,000. **Location:** northern New England state. **Climate:** temperate, with considerable temperature extremes; heavy snowfall in mountains. **Topography:** Green Mtns. N-S backbone 20-36 mi. wide; avg. altitude 1,000 ft. **Capital:** Montpelier.

Economy. Principal industries: manufacturing, tourism, agriculture, trade; finance, insurance, real estate, government. **Principal manufactured goods:** machine tools, furniture, scales, books, computer components, fishing rods. **Agriculture: Chief crops:** dairy products, apples, maple syrup, silage corn, hay. **Livestock** (1989): 320,000 cattle; 5,100 hogs/pigs; 20,456 sheep; 406,000 poultry. **Timber/lumber** (1992): pine, spruce, fir, hemlock; 201 mln. bd. ft. **Nonfuel Minerals** (1993): $44.8 mln.; mostly dimension stone, crushed stone, construction sand & gravel. **International airports at:** Burlington. **Value of construction** (1993): $537.7 mln. **Employment distribution** (1993): 33% serv.; 29% trade; 21% mfg. **Per capita personal income** (1993): $19,467. **Unemployment** (1993): 5.2%. **Tourism** (1990): visitors spent $1.25 bln. **Sales tax:** 5%.

Finance. FDIC-insured commercial banks & trust companies (1993): 20. **Deposits:** $4.8 bln. **FDIC-insured savings institutions** (1993): 9. **Assets:** $2.3 bln.

Federal government. No. federal civilian employees (Mar. 1993): 2,884. **Avg. salary:** $32,886.

Energy. Electricity production (1993, kWh, by source): Petroleum: 5 mln.; Gas: 21 mln.; Hydroelectric: 839 mln.; Nuclear: 3.4 bln.

Education. Student-teacher ratio (1992): 14.0. **Avg. salary, public school teachers** (1993-94): $36,043.

State data. Motto: Freedom and unity. **Flower:** Red clover. **Bird:** Hermit thrush. **Tree:** Sugar maple. **Song:** Hail, Vermont. **Entered union** Mar. 4, 1791; rank, 14th. **State fair** at: Rutland; early Sept.

History. Champlain explored the lake that bears his name, 1609. First American settlement was Ft. Dummer, 1724, near Brattleboro. Ethan Allen and the Green Mountain Boys captured Ft. Ticonderoga (NY), 1775; John Stark defeated part of Burgoyne's forces near Bennington, 1777. In the War of 1812, Thomas MacDonough defeated a British fleet on Champlain off Plattsburgh (NY), 1814.

Tourist attractions. Year-round outdoor sports, esp. hiking, camping, and skiing; there are numerous alpine & cross-country ski areas in the state. Popular are the

Shelburne Museum; Rock of Ages Tourist Center, Graniteville; Vermont Marble Exhibit, Proctor; Bennington Battle Monument; Pres. Coolidge homestead, Plymouth; Maple Grove Maple Museum, St. Johnsbury.

Famous Vermonters. Ethan Allen, Chester A. Arthur, Calvin Coolidge, Adm. George Dewey, John Dewey, Stephen A. Douglas, Dorothy Canfield Fisher, James Fisk.

Tourist information. Vermont Dept. of Travel and Tourism, 134 State St., Montpelier, VT 05602; 802-828-3236 .

Virginia

Old Dominion

People. Population (1993): 6,490,634; **rank:** 12. **Pop. density:** 161.0 per sq. mi. **Racial/ethnic distrib.** (1990): 77.4% white; 18.8% black; 2.6% Asian; 2.6% Hispanic. **Net change** (1990-93): 4.4%.

Geography. Total area: 42,777 sq. mi.; **rank:** 35. **Land area:** 39,598 sq. mi. **Acres forested land:** 15,858,000. **Location:** South Atlantic state bounded by the Atlantic O. on the E and surrounded by North Carolina, Tennessee, Kentucky, West Virginia, and Maryland. **Climate:** mild and equable. **Topography:** mountain and valley region in the W, including the Blue Ridge Mtns.; rolling piedmont plateau; tidewater, or coastal plain, including the eastern shore. **Capital:** Richmond.

Economy. Principal industries: services, trade, government, manufacturing, tourism, agriculture. **Principal manufactured goods:** textiles, transportation equipment, electric & electronic equipment, food processing, chemicals, printing. **Agriculture: Chief crops** (1992): soybeans, tobacco, peanuts, corn, far grain, tomatoes, apples, summer & sweet potatoes. **Livestock** (1992): 1.78 mln. cattle; 390,000 hogs/pigs; 122,000 sheep; 2.38 mln. broilers, 19.3 mln. turkeys. **Timber/lumber** (1992): pine and hardwoods; 1.2 bln. bd. ft. **Nonfuel Minerals** (1993): $515.3 mln.; mostly crushed stone. **Commercial fishing** (1993): $108.1 mln. **Chief ports:** Hampton Roads, Richmond, Alexandria. **International airports at:** Norfolk, Dulles, Richmond, Newport News. **Value of construction** (1993): $7.5 bln. **Employment distribution** (1992): 26.6% serv.; 22.3% trade; 20.7% gvt.; 14.3% mfg. **Per capita personal income** (1993): $21,634. **Unemployment** (1993): 5%. **Tourism** (1992): domestic travelers spent $8.6 bln. **Sales tax:** 4.5%.

Finance. FDIC-insured commercial banks & trust companies (1993): 165. **Deposits:** $57.5 bln. **FDIC-insured savings institutions** (1993): 43. **Assets:** $14.4 bln.

Federal government. No. federal civilian employees (Mar. 1993): 141,133. **Avg. salary:** $40,168. **Notable federal facilities:** Pentagon; Naval Sta., Norfolk; Naval Air Sta., Norfolk, Virginia Beach; Naval Shipyard, Portsmouth; Marine Corps Base, Quantico; Langley AFB; NASA at Langley.

Energy. Electricity production (1993, kWh, by source): Coal: 24.7 bln.; Petroleum: 2.2 bln.; Gas: 21.2 bln.; Hydroelectric: 2.1 bln.; Nuclear: 22.7 bln.

Education. Student-teacher ratio (1992): 15.9. **Avg. salary, public school teachers** (1993-94): $33,128.

State data. Motto: Sic Semper Tyrannis (Thus always to tyrants). **Flower:** Dogwood. **Bird:** Cardinal. **Tree:** Dogwood. **Song:** Carry Me Back to Old Virginia. **Tenth** of the original 13 states to ratify the Constitution, June 25, 1788. **State fair** at: Richmond; late Sept.-early Oct.

History. English settlers founded Jamestown, 1607. Virginians took over much of the government from royal Gov. Dunmore in 1775, forcing him to flee. Virginians under George Rogers Clark freed the Ohio-Indiana-Illinois area of British forces. Benedict Arnold burned Richmond and Petersburg for the British, 1781. That same year, Britain's Cornwallis was trapped at Yorktown and surrendered.

Tourist attractions. Colonial Williamsburg; Busch Gardens, Williamsburg; Wolf Trap Farm, near Falls Church; Arlington National Cemetery; Mt. Vernon, home of George Washington; Jamestown Festival Park; Yorktown; Jefferson's Monticello, Charlottesville; Robert E. Lee's birthplace, Stratford Hall, and grave, at Lexington; Appomattox; Shenandoah National Park; Blue Ridge Parkway; Virginia Beach; King's Dominion, near Richmond.

Famous Virginians. Richard E. Byrd, James B. Cabell, William Henry Harrison, Patrick Henry, Thomas Jefferson, Joseph E. Johnston, Robert E. Lee, Meriwether Lewis and William Clark, James Madison, John Marshall, George Mason, James Monroe, Edgar Allan Poe, Walter Reed, Zachary Taylor, John Tyler, Maggie Walker, Booker T. Washington, George Washington, Woodrow Wilson.

Chamber of Commerce. 9 South Fifth St., Richmond, VA 23219.

Toll-free travel information. 1-800-VISITVA.

Washington

Evergreen State

People. Population (1993): 5,255,276; **rank:** 15. **Pop. density:** 77.1 per sq. mi. **Racial/ethnic distrib.** (1990): 88.5% white; 3.1% black; 4.3% Asian; 4.4% Hispanic. **Net change** (1990-93): 8.0%.

Geography. Total area: 71,302 sq. mi.; **rank:** 18. **Land area:** 66,581 sq. mi. **Acres forested land:** 20,483,000. **Location:** Pacific state bordered by Canada on the N; Idaho on the E; Oregon on the S; and the Pacific O. on the W. **Climate:** mild, dominated by the Pacific O. and protected by the Rockies. **Topography:** Olympic Mtns. on NW peninsula; open land along coast to Columbia R.; flat terrain of Puget Sound Lowland; Cascade Mtns. region's high peaks to the E; Columbia Basin in central portion; highlands to the NE; mountains to the SE. **Capital:** Olympia.

Economy. Principal industries: forest products, aerospace, food products, primary metals, agriculture. **Principal manufactured goods:** aircraft, pulp and paper, lumber and plywood, aluminum, processed fruits and vegetables. **Agriculture: Chief crops:** apples, potatoes, hay, nursery/greenhouse plants, pears, hops, sweet cherries. **Livestock** (1993): 1.4 mln. cattle; 46,000 hogs/pigs; 75,000 sheep; 5.6 mln. poultry, excl. broilers. **Timber/lumber** (1993): Douglas fir, hemlock, cedar, pine; 4.4 bln. bd. ft. **Nonfuel Minerals** (1993): $480.4 mln.; mostly construction sand & gravel, crushed stone. **Commercial fishing** (1993): $111.8 mln. **Chief ports:** Seattle, Tacoma, Vancouver, Kelso-Longview. **International airports at:** Seattle/Tacoma, Spokane, Boeing Field. **Value of construction** (1993): $6.9 bln. **Employment distribution** (1993): 24.2% trade; 25.7% serv.; 19.1% gvt.; 15.1% mfg. **Per capita personal income** (1993): $21,887. **Unemployment** (1993): 7.5%. **Tourism** (1990): $5.3 bln. **Sales tax:** 6.5%.

Finance. FDIC-insured commercial banks & trust companies (1993): 87. **Deposits:** $34.5 bln. **FDIC-insured savings institutions** (1993): 29. **Assets:** $31.5 bln.

Federal government. No. federal civilian employees (Mar. 1993): 50,358. **Avg. salary:** $36,476. **Notable federal facilities:** Bonneville Power Admin.; Ft. Lewis; McChord AFB; Hanford Nuclear Reservation; Bremerton Naval Shipyards.

Energy. Electricity production (1993, kWh, by source): Coal: 8.8 bln.; Petroleum: 32 mln.; Gas: 224 mln.; Hydroelectric: 67.0 bln.; Nuclear: 11.5 bln.

Education. Student-teacher ratio (1992): 20.2. **Avg. salary, public school teachers** (1993-94): $35,860.

State data. Motto: Alki (By and by). **Flower:** Western rhododendron. **Bird:** Willow goldfinch. **Tree:** Western hemlock. **Song:** Washington, My Home. **Entered union** Nov. 11, 1889; rank, 42d. **State fairs** at: many county fairs, mostly in Aug. or Sept.

History. Spain's Bruno Hezeta sailed the coast, 1775. American Capt. Robert Gray sailed up the Columbia River, 1792. Canadian fur traders set up Spokane House, 1810; Americans under John Jacob Astor established a post at Fort Okanogan, 1811. Missionary Marcus Whitman settled near Walla Walla, 1836. Final agreement on the border of Washington and Canada was made with Britain, 1846, and gold was discovered in the state's northeast, 1855, bringing new settlers.

Tourist attractions. Mt. Rainier, Olympic, and North Cascades national parks; Mt. St. Helens; Pacific beaches; Puget Sound; wineries; Indian cultures; year-round outdoor recreation: Seattle Waterfront, Seattle Center, Space Needle, San Juan Islands, Grand Coulee Dam, Columbia R. Gorge National Scenic Area, Spokane's Riverfront Park.

Famous Washingtonians. Bing Crosby, William O. Douglas, Henry M. Jackson, Gary Larson, Mary McCarthy, Edward R. Murrow, Theodore Roethke, Marcus Whitman, Minoru Yamasaki.

Tourist information. WA State Tourism Division, P.O. Box 2500, Dept. 199, Olympia, WA 98504-2500.

Toll-free travel information. 1-800-544-1800.

West Virginia

Mountain State

People. Population (1993): 1,820,137. **rank:** 35. **Pop. density:** 75.2 per sq. mi. **Racial/ethnic distrib.** (1990): 96.2% white; 3.1% black; 0.5% Hispanic. **Net change** (1990-93): 1.5%.

Geography. Total area: 24,231 sq. mi.; **rank:** 41. **Land area:** 24,087 sq. mi. **Acres forested land:** 12,128,000. **Location:** South Atlantic state bounded on the N by Ohio, Pennsylvania, Maryland; on the S and W by Virginia, Kentucky, Ohio; on the E by Maryland and Virginia. **Climate:** humid continental climate except for marine modification in the lower panhandle. **Topography:** ranging from hilly to mountainous; Allegheny Plateau in the W, covers two-thirds of the state; mountains here are the highest in the state, over 4,000 ft. **Capital:** Charleston.

Economy. Principal industries: manufacturing, services, mining, tourism. **Principal manufactured goods:** machinery, plastic and hardwood prods., fabricated metals, basic organic and inorganic chemicals, aluminum, steel. **Agriculture: Chief crops:** apples, peaches, hay, tobacco, corn, wheat, oats. **Chief products:** dairy prods., eggs. **Livestock** (1993): 500,000 cattle; 31,000 hogs/pigs; 62,000 sheep; 2.0 mln. chickens. **Timber/lumber** (1992): oak, yellow poplar, hickory, walnut, cherry; 403 mln. bd. ft. **Nonfuel Minerals** (1993): $111.4 mln.; mostly crushed stone, cement. **Chief port:** Huntington. **Value of construction** (1993): $1.2 bln. **Employment distribution** (1993): 23% trade; 20% gvt.; 26% serv.; 13% mfg. **Per capita personal income** (1993): $16,209. **Unemployment** (1993): 10.8%. **Tourism** (1992): travel-related expenditures were $2.6 bln. **Sales tax:** 6%.

Finance. FDIC-insured commercial banks & trust companies (1993): 148. **Deposits:** $16.6 bln. **FDIC-insured savings institutions** (1993): 11. **Assets:** $1.3 bln.

Federal government. No. federal civilian employees (Mar. 1993): 11,264. **Avg. salary:** $33,718. **Notable federal facilities:** National Radio Astronomy Observatory, Green Bank; Bureau of Public Debt Bldg., Parkersburg; Natl. Park, Harpers Ferry; Correctional Institution for Women, Alderson.

Energy. Electricity production (1993, kWh, by source): Coal: 70.5 bln.; Petroleum: 215 mln.; Gas: 386 mln.; Hydroelectric: 362 mln.

Education. Student-teacher ratio (1992): 15.2. **Avg. salary, public school teachers** (1993-94): $30,549.

State data. Motto: Montani Semper Liberi (Mountaineers are always free). **Flower:** Big rhododendron. **Bird:** Cardinal. **Tree:** Sugar maple. **Songs:** The West Virginia Hills; This Is My West Virginia; West Virginia, My Home, Sweet Home. **Entered union** June 20, 1863; rank, 35th. **State fair** at: Lewisburg (Fairlea); late Aug.

History. Early explorers included George Washington, 1753, and Daniel Boone. The area became part of Virginia and often objected to rule by the eastern part of the state. When Virginia seceded, 1861, the Wheeling Conventions repudiated the act and created a new state, Kanawha, subsequently changed to West Virginia. It was admitted to the Union as such, 1863.

Tourist attractions. Harpers Ferry National Historic Park has been restored to its condition in 1859, when John Brown seized the U.S. Armory.

Also Science and Cultural Center, Charleston; White Sulphur and Berkeley Springs mineral water spas; Monongahela Natl. Forest; state parks and forests; trout fishing; turkey, deer, and bear hunting; white water rafting; paddleboat tours; skiing; glass tours at Fenton Glass in Williamstown, Viking Glass in New Martinsville, Blenko Glass in Milton; Sternwheel Regatta, Charleston; Mountain State Forest Festival; Mountain State Arts & Crafts Fair, Ripley.

Famous West Virginians. Newton D. Baker, Pearl Buck, John W. Davis, Thomas "Stonewall" Jackson, Don Knotts, Dwight Whitney Morrow, Nick Nolte, Michael Owens, Cyrus Vance, Col. Charles "Chuck" Yeager.

Tourist information. Dept. of Commerce, State Capitol, Charleston WV 25305.

Toll-free travel information. 1-800-CALLW.VA.

Wisconsin

Badger State

People. Population (1993): 5,037,928; **rank:** 18. **Pop. density:** 92.2 per sq. mi. **Racial/ethnic distrib.** (1990): 92.2% white; 5.0% black; 1.9% Hispanic. **Net change** (1990-93): 3.0%.

Geography. Total area: 65,499 sq. mi.; **rank:** 23. **Land area:** 54,314 sq. mi. **Acres forested land:** 15,513,000. **Location:** East North Central state, bounded on the N by Lake Superior and Upper Michigan; on the E by Lake Michigan; on the S by Illinois; on the W by the St. Croix and Mississippi rivers. **Climate:** long, cold winters and short, warm summers tempered by the Great Lakes. **Topography:** narrow Lake Superior Lowland plain met by Northern Highland, which slopes gently to the sandy crescent Central Plain; Western Upland in the SW; 3 broad parallel limestone ridges running N-S are separated by wide and shallow lowlands in the SE. **Capital:** Madison.

Economy. Principal industries: services, manufacturing, trade, government, agriculture, tourism. **Principal manufactured goods:** industrial machinery, food products, fabricated metals, paper products, printing and publishing, electronic and electrical machinery. **Agriculture: Chief crops:** corn, beans, cherries, peas, hay, oats, cranberries. **Chief products:** milk, butter, cheese. **Livestock** (1991): 4.0 mln. cattle; 1.2 mln. hogs/pigs; 105,000 sheep; 4.2 mln. poultry. **Timber/lumber** (1992): maple, birch, oak, evergreens; 513 mln. bd. ft. **Nonfuel Minerals** (1993): $200.3 mln.; mostly crushed stone, construction & industrial sand & gravel, lime. **Commercial fishing** (1993): $5.1 mln. **Chief ports:** Superior, Ashland, Milwaukee, Green Bay, Kewaunee, Pt. Washington, Manitowoc, Sheboygan, Marinette, Kenosha. **International airports at:** Milwaukee. **Value of construction** (1993): $5.1 bln. **Employment distribution** (1993): 22.3% trade; 22.7% mfg.; 24.0% serv.; 15.8% gvt. **Per capita personal income** (1993): $19,811. **Unemployment** (1993): 4.7%. **Tourism** (1992): out-of-state visitors spent $6.0 bln. **Sales tax:** 5%.

Finance. FDIC-insured commercial banks & trust companies (1993): 436. **Deposits:** $44.4 bln. **FDIC-insured savings institutions** (1993): 58. **Assets:** $19.8 bln.

Federal government. No. federal civilian employees (Mar. 1993): 12,468. **Avg. salary:** $33,752. **Notable federal facilities:** Ft. McCoy.

Energy. Electricity production (1993, kWh, by source): Coal: 33.6 bln.; Petroleum: 105 mln.; Gas: 224 mln.; Hydroelectric: 2.2 bln.; Nuclear: 11.5 bln.

Education. Student-teacher ratio (1992): 15.5. **Avg. salary, public school teachers** (1993-94): $36,644.

State data. Motto: Forward. **Flower:** Wood violet. **Bird:** Robin. **Tree:** Sugar maple. **Song:** On, Wisconsin! **Entered union** May 29, 1848; rank, 30th. **State fair** at: West Allis; mid-Aug.

History. Jean Nicolet was the first European to see the Wisconsin area, arriving in Green Bay, 1634; French missionaries and fur traders followed. The British took over, 1763. The U.S. won the land after the Revolution but the British were not ousted until after the War of 1812. Lead miners came next, then farmers. Railroads were started in 1851, serving growing wheat harvests and iron mines.

Tourist attractions. Old Wade House and Carriage Museum, Greenbush; Villa Louis, Prairie du Chien; Circus World Museum, Baraboo; Wisconsin Dells; Old World Wisconsin, Eagle; Door County peninsula; Chequamegon and Nicolet national forests; Lake Winnebago; numerous lakes for water sports, ice boating and fishing; skiing and hunting.

Famous Wisconsinites. Edna Ferber, King Camp Gillette, Harry Houdini, Robert La Follette, Alfred Lunt, Georgia O'Keeffe, Donald K. "Deke" Slayton, Spencer Tracy, Thorstein Veblen, Orson Welles, Thornton Wilder, Frank Lloyd Wright.

Tourist information. Wisconsin Dept. of Development, Division of Tourism, 123 W. Washington Ave., Madison, WI 53702.

Toll-free travel information. 1-800-372-2737.

Wyoming

Equality State

People. Population (1993): 470,242; **rank:** 50. **Pop. density:** 4.8 per sq. mi. **Racial/ethnic distrib.** (1990): 94.2% white; 0.8% black; 2.1% Amer. Indian; 5.7% Hispanic. **Net change** (1990-93): 3.7%.

Geography. Total area: 97,818 sq. mi.; **rank:** 9. **Land area:** 97,105 sq. mi. **Acres forested land:** 9,966,000. **Location:** Mountain state lying in the high western plateaus of the Great Plains. **Climate:** semi-desert conditions throughout; true desert in the Big Horn and Great Divide basins. **Topography:** the eastern Great Plains rise to the foothills of the Rocky Mtns.; the Continental Divide crosses the state from the NW to the SE. **Capital:** Cheyenne.

Economy. Principal industries: mineral extraction, tourism and recreation, agriculture. **Principal manufactured goods:** refined petroleum products, foods, wood products, stone, clay and glass products. **Agriculture: Chief crops:** wheat, beans, barley, oats, sugar beets, hay. **Livestock** (1992): 1.3 mln. cattle; 24,000 hogs/pigs; 850,000 sheep. **Timber/lumber** (1992): ponderosa & lodgepole pine, Douglas fir, Engelmann spruce; 187 mln. bd. ft. **Nonfuel Minerals** (1993): $858 mln.; mostly soda ash, clays, portland cement. **International airports at:** Casper. **Value of construction** (1993): $672.3 mln. **Employment distribution** (1992): 23% trade; 20% services; 9% mining. **Per capita personal income** (1993): $19,539. **Unemployment** (1993): 5.4%. **Tourism** (1992): out-of-state visitors spent $1.5 bln. **State sales tax:** 4%.

Finance. FDIC-insured commercial banks & trust companies (1993): 55. **Deposits:** $4.5 bln. **FDIC-insured savings institutions** (1993): 6. **Assets:** $855 mln.

Federal government. No. federal civilian employees (Mar. 1993): 4,947. **Avg. salary:** $33,558. **Notable federal facilities:** Warren AFB.

Energy. Electricity production (1993, kWh, by source): Coal: 39.3 bln.; Petroleum: 57 mln.; Gas: 9 mln.; Hydroelectric: 787 mln.

Education. Student-teacher ratio (1992): 17.2. **Avg. salary, public school teachers** (1993-94): $30,310.

State data. Motto: Equal Rights. **Flower:** Indian paintbrush. **Bird:** Meadowlark. **Tree:** Cottonwood. **Song:** Wyoming. **Entered union** July 10, 1890; rank, 44th. **State fair** at: Douglas; late Aug.

History. Francés Francois and Louis La Verendrye were the first Europeans, 1743. John Colter, American, was first to traverse Yellowstone Park, 1807-08. Trappers and fur traders followed in the 1820s. Forts Laramie and Bridger became important stops on the pioneer trail to the West Coast. Indian wars followed massacres of army detachments in 1854 and 1866. Population grew after the Union Pacific crossed the state, 1869. Women won the vote, for the first time in the U.S., from the Territorial Legislature, 1869.

Tourist attractions. Yellowstone National Park, 3,472 sq. mi. in the NW corner of Wyoming and the adjoining edges of Montana and Idaho, the oldest U.S. national park, est. 1872, has some 10,000 geysers, hot springs, mud volcanoes, fossil forests, a volcanic glass (obsidian) mountain, the 1,000-ft.-deep canyon and 308-ft.-high waterfall of the Yellowstone River, and a wide variety of animals living free in their natural habitat.

Also, Grand Teton National Park, with mountains 13,000 ft. high; National Elk Refuge, covering 25,000 acres; Devils Tower, a columnar rock of igneous origin 1,280 ft. high; Fort Laramie and surrounding areas of pioneer trails; Buffalo Bill Museum, Cody; Cheyenne Frontier Days Celebration, last full week in July, the state's largest rodeo, and world's largest purse.

Famous Wyomingites. James Bridger, Buffalo Bill Cody, Nellie Tayloe Ross.

Tourist information. Travel Commission, Etchepare Circle, Cheyenne, WY 82002.

Toll-free travel information. 1-800-CALLWYO.

District of Columbia

Total area: 68 sq. mi. **Land area:** 61 sq. mi. **Population** (1993): 578,448. **Motto:** Justitia omnibus (Justice for all). **Flower:** American beauty rose. **Tree:** Scarlet oak. **Bird:** Wood thrush. The city of Washington is coextensive with the District of Columbia.

The District of Columbia is the seat of the federal government of the United States. It lies on the west central edge of Maryland on the Potomac River, opposite Virginia. Its area was originally 100 sq. mi. taken from the sovereignty of Maryland and Virginia. Virginia's portion south of the Potomac was given back to that state in 1846.

The 23d Amendment, ratified in 1961, granted residents the right to vote for president and vice president for the first time since 1800 and gave them 3 members in the Electoral College. The first such votes were cast in Nov. 1964.

Congress, which has legislative authority over the District under the Constitution, established in 1874 a government of 3 commissioners appointed by the president. The Reorganization Plan of 1967 substituted a single appointive commissioner (also called mayor), assistant, and 9-member City Council. Funds were still appropriated by Congress; residents had no vote in local government, except to elect school board members.

In Sept. 1970, Congress approved legislation giving the District one delegate to the House of Representatives. The delegate could vote in committee but not on the House floor. The first was elected 1971.

In May 1974 voters approved a congressionally drafted charter giving them the right to elect their own mayor and a 13-member city council; the first took office Jan. 2, 1975. The district won the right to levy its own taxes, but Congress retained power to veto council actions and approve the city's annual budget.

Proposals for a "federal town" for the deliberations of the Continental Congress were made in 1783, 4 years before the adoption of the Constitution. Rivalry between Northern and Southern delegates over the site appeared in the First Congress, 1789. John Adams, presiding officer of the Senate, cast the deciding vote of that body for Germantown, Pa. In 1790 Congress compromised by making Philadelphia the temporary capital for 10 years. The Virginia members of the House wanted a capital on the eastern bank of the Potomac; they were defeated by the Northerners, while the Southerners defeated the Northern attempt to have the nation assume the war debts of the 13 original states, the Assumption Bill fathered by Alexander Hamilton. Hamilton and Jefferson arranged a compromise: the Virginia men voted for the Assumption Bill, and the Northerners conceded the capital to the Potomac. President Washington chose the site in Oct. 1790 and persuaded landowners to sell their holdings to the government at £25, then about $66, an acre. The capital was named Washington.

Washington appointed Pierre Charles L'Enfant, a Frenchman, to plan the capital on an area not over 10 mi. square. The L'Enfant plan, for streets 100 to 110 feet wide and one avenue 400 feet wide and a mile long, seemed grandiose and foolhardy, but Washington endorsed it. When L'Enfant ordered a wealthy landowner to remove his new manor house because it obstructed a vista, and demolished it when the owner refused, Washington stepped in and dismissed the architect. Andrew Ellicott, who was working on surveying the area, finished the official map and design of the city. Ellicott was assisted by Benjamin Banneker, a distinguished black architect and astronomer.

On Sept. 18, 1793, Pres. Washington laid the cornerstone of the north wing of the Capitol. On June 3, 1800, Pres. John Adams moved to Washington and on June 10, Philadelphia ceased to be the temporary capital. The City of Washington was incorporated in 1802; the District of Columbia was created as a municipal corporation in 1874, embracing Washington, Georgetown, and Washington County.

OUTLYING U.S. AREAS

American Samoa

Capital: Pago Pago, Island of Tutuila. **Total area:** 84 sq. mi. **Population:** (1993) 52,860. **Motto:** Samoa Muamua le Atua (In Samoa, God Is First). **Song:** Amerika Samoa. **Flower:** Paogo (Ula-fala). **Plant:** Ava.

Education. Student-teacher ratio (1992): 19.3.

Blessed with spectacular scenery and delightful South Seas climate, American Samoa is the most southerly of all lands under U.S. sovereignty. It is an unincorporated territory consisting of 7 small islands of the Samoan group: **Tutuila, Aunu'u, Manu'a Group (Ta'u, Olosega and Ofu), Rose,** and **Swains Island.** The islands are 2,300 mi. SW of Honolulu.

A tripartite agreement between Great Britain, Germany, and the U.S. in 1899 gave the U.S. sovereignty over the eastern islands of the Samoan group; these islands became American Samoa. Local chiefs officially ceded Tutuila and Aunu'u to the U.S. in April 1900 and the Manu'a group and Rose in July 1904; Swains Island was annexed in 1925.

Samoa (Western), comprising the larger islands of the Samoan group, was a New Zealand mandate and UN Trusteeship until it became an independent nation Jan. 1, 1962.

Tutuila and Aunu'u have an area of 53 sq. mi. Ta'u has an area of 17 sq. mi., and the islets of Ofu and Olosega, 5 sq. mi. with a population of a few thousand. Swains Island has nearly 2 sq. mi. and a population of about 100.

About 70% of the land is bush and mountains. Chief products and exports are fish products. Taro, breadfruit, yams, coconuts, pineapples, oranges, and bananas are also produced.

From 1900 to 1951, American Samoa was under the jurisdiction of the U.S. Navy. Since 1951, it has been under the Interior Dept. On Jan. 3, 1978, the first popularly elected Samoan governor and lieutenant governor were inaugurated. Previously, the governor was appointed by the Secretary of the Interior. American Samoa has a bicameral legislature and elects a delegate to the House of Representatives, who has a voice but no vote, except in committees.

The American Samoans are of Polynesian origin. They are nationals of the U.S.; approximately 20,000 live in Hawaii, 65,000 in California and Washington.

Guam

Where America's Day Begins

People. Population (1990): 133,152, a 26% increase over the 1980 figure of 105,979. **Pop. density:** 631.6 per sq. mi. **Urban** (1980): 39.5%. **Ethnic distribution** (1990): Chamorro 43%, Filipino 28.6%, stateside immigrants 20%, remainder Micronesians. Native Guamanians, ethnically called Chamorros, are basically of Indonesian stock, with a mixture of Spanish and Filipino. In addition to the offical language, they speak the native Chamorro. **Migration** (1990): About 52% of population were born elsewhere; of these, 48% in Asia, 40% in U.S.

Geography. Total area: 210 sq. mi. land, 30 mi. long and 4 to 8.5 mi. wide. **Location:** largest and southernmost of the Mariana Islands in the West Pacific, 3,700 mi. W of Hawaii. **Climate:** tropical, with temperatures from 70° to 90° F; avg. annual rainfall, about 70 in. **Topography:** coralline limestone plateau in the N; southern chain of low volcanic mountains sloping gently to the W, more steeply to coastal cliffs on the E; general elevation, 500 ft.; highest pt., Mt. Lamlam, 1,334 ft. **Capital:** Agana.

Economy. Principal industries: tourism, defense, construction, banking. **Principal manufactured goods:** textiles, foods. **Agriculture: Chief crops:** cabbages, eggplants, cucumber, long beans, tomatoes, bananas, coconuts, watermelon, yams, canteloupe, papayas, maize, sweet potatoes. **Livestock** (1984): 2,000 cattle; 14,000 hogs/pigs. **Chief port:** Apra Harbor. **International airport at:** Tamuning. **Value of construction** (1980): $80.6 mln. **Employment distribution** (1987): 61.3% private sector; 38.7% gvt. **Per capita income** (1986): $7,116. **Median household income** (1989): $30,755; persons per household 3.97; persons per family 4.26. **Unemployment** (1990): 3.8%. **Tourism** (1990): visitors' receipts $550 mln.

Finance. Notable industries: insurance, real estate, finance. **FDIC-insured commercial banks & trust companies** (1993): 2. **Deposits:** $563 mln. **FDIC-insured savings institutions** (1993): 2. **Assets:** 207 mln.

Federal government. No. federal employees (1990): 7,200. **Notable federal facilities:** Anderson AFB; naval, air, and port bases.

Education. Student-teacher ratio (1992): 18.5.

Misc. data. Flower: Puti Tai Nobio (Bougainvillea). **Bird:** Toto (Fruit dove). **Tree:** Ifit (Intsiabijuga). **Song:** Stand Ye Guamanians.

History. Guam was probably settled by voyagers from the Indonesian-Philippine archipelago by at least the third century B.C. Pottery, rice cultivation, and megalithic technology show strong East Asian cultural influence. Centralized, village clan-based communities engaged in agriculture and offshore fishing. The est. population by the early 16th century was between 50,000 and 75,000 inhabitants. Magellan arrived in the Marianas Mar. 6, 1521. They were colonized in 1668 by Spanish missionaries who named them the Mariana Islands in honor of Maria Anna, queen of Spain. When Spain ceded Guam to the U.S., it sold the other Marianas to Germany. Japan obtained a League of Nations mandate over the German islands in 1919; in Dec. 1941 it seized Guam; the island was retaken by the U.S. in July 1944.

Guam is a self-governing organized unincorporated U.S. territory. The Organic Act of 1950 provides for a governor and a 21-member unicameral legislature, elected biennially by the residents who are American citizens.

In 1972 a U.S. law gave Guam one delegate to the U.S. House of Representatives who has a voice but no vote, except in committees.

Guam's quest to change its status to a U.S. Commonwealth began in the late 1970's. The Guam Commission on Self-Determination, created in 1984, developed a Draft Commonwealth Act, which was submitted to Congress. This bill was resubmitted to the 103d Congress in Mar. 1993.

General tourist attractions. Tropical climate, oceanic marine environment; annual mid-Aug. Merizo Water Festival; Tarzan Falls; beaches; water sports; duty-free port shopping.

Commonwealth of the Northern Mariana Islands

Located in the perpetually warm climes between Guam and the Tropic of Cancer, the 14 islands of the Northern Marianas form a 300-mile-long archipelago, comprising a total land area of 179 sq. miles. The native population, 1990, was 43,345, concentrated on the 3 largest of the 6 inhabited islands: **Saipan,** the seat of government and commerce (38,896), **Rota** (2,295), and **Tinian** (2,118).

The people of the Northern Marianas are predominantly of Chamorro cultural extraction, although numbers of Carolinians and immigrants from other areas of E. Asia and Micronesia have also settled in the islands.

English is among the several languages commonly spoken. Pursuant to the Covenant of 1976, which established the Northern Marianas as a commonwealth in political union with the U.S., most natives and many domiciliaries of these islands achieved U.S. citizenship on Nov. 3, 1986, when the U.S. terminated its administration of the UN trusteeship as it affected the Northern Marianas. From July 18, 1947, the U.S. had administered the Northern Marianas under a trusteeship agreement with the UN Security Council.

The Northern Mariana Islands has been self-governing since 1978, when both a constitution drafted and adopted by the people became effective and a bicameral legislature with offices of governor and lieutenant governor was inaugurated. Commercial activity has increased steadily in recent years. In 1990, more than 417,146 tourists visited.

Commonwealth of Puerto Rico

(Estado Libre Asociado de Puerto Rico)

People. Population (1993): 3,522,037 (and about 2.7 mln. more Puerto Ricans reside in the mainland U.S.). **Pop. density:** 1,035 per sq. mi. **Urban** (1990): 66.8%. **Ethnic distribution** (1990): 99.9% Hispanic. **Language:** On Jan. 28, 1993, the Gov. of Puerto Rico declared Spanish and English joint official languages.

Geography. Total area: 3,492 sq. mi. **Land area:** 3,427 sq. mi. **Location:** island lying between the Atlantic to the N and the Caribbean to the S; it is easternmost of the West Indies group called the Greater Antilles, of which Cuba, Hispaniola, and Jamaica are the larger islands. **Climate:** mild, with a mean temperature of 77° F. **Topography:** mountainous throughout three-fourths of its rectangular area, surrounded by a broken coastal plain; highest peak is Cerro Puntita, 4,389 ft. **Capital:** San Juan.

Economy. Principal industries: manufacturing. **Principal manufactured goods:** pharmaceuticals, chemicals, machinery and metals, electric machinery and equipment, food products, apparel, petroleum refining. **Agriculture: Chief crops:** coffee, plantains, pineapples, tomatoes, sugarcane, bananas, peppers, pumpkins, lettuce, tobacco, yams. **Livestock** (1990): 600,000 cattle; 206,000 pigs; 7.4 mln. poultry. **Nonfuel Minerals** (1991): $119.2 mln., mostly cement. **Commercial fishing** (1992): $6.2 mln. **Chief ports/river shipping:** San Juan, Ponce, Mayagüez. **Major airports at:** San Juan, Ponce, Mayagüez, Aguadilla. **Value of construction** (1992): $2.7 bln. **Employment distribution** (1992): 22.5% public admin., 19.8% trade, 16.8% mfg., 3.4% agric. **Per capita income** (1992): $6,360. **Unemployment** (1993): 12.8%. **Tourism** (1992): Visitors spent $1.51 bln.

Finance. FDIC-insured commercial banks & trust companies (1993): 12. **Deposits:** $15.8 bln. **FDIC-insured savings institutions** (1993): 8. **Assets:** $4.6 bln.

Federal government. No. federal civilian employees (1992): 10,000. **Notable federal facilities:** U.S. Naval Station at Roosevelt Roads, Ceiba; U.S. Army Training Area and Ft. Allen at Salinas; Sabana SECA Communications Center (U.S. Navy); Ft. Buchanan at Guaynabo.

Energy. Electicity production (1992): 16,458 mln. kWh.

Education. Student-teacher ratio (1993): 16.6. **Avg. salary, public school teachers** (1992): $1,000 monthly.

Misc. data. Motto: Joannes Est Nomen Eius (John is his name). **Flower:** Maga. **Bird:** Reinita. **Tree:** Ceiba. **National anthem:** La Borinqueña.

History. Puerto Rico (or Borinquen, after the original Arawak Indian name Boriquen) was visited by Columbus, on his second voyage, Nov. 19, 1493. In 1508 the Spanish arrived.

Sugarcane was introduced, 1515, and slaves were imported 3 years later. Gold mining petered out, 1570. Spaniards fought off a series of British and Dutch attacks; slavery was abolished, 1873. Under the treaty of Paris, Puerto Rico was ceded to the U.S. after the Spanish-American War, 1898. In 1952 the people voted in favor of Commonwealth status.

The Commonwealth of Puerto Rico is a self-governing part of the U.S. with a primary Hispanic culture. The current commonwealth political status of Puerto Rico gives the island's citizens virtually the same control over their internal affairs as the 50 states of the U.S. However, they do not vote in national elections, although they do vote in national primary elections.

Puerto Rico is represented in the U.S. House of Representatives by a delagate who has a voice but no vote, except in committees.

No federal income tax is collected from residents on income earned from local sources in Puerto Rico. Nevertheless, as part of the U.S. legal system, Puerto Rico is subject to the provisions of the U.S. Constitution; most federal laws apply as they do in the 50 states.

Puerto Rico's famous "Operation Bootstrap," begun in the late 1940s, succeeded in changing the island from "The Poorhouse of the Caribbean" to an area with the highest per capita income in Latin America. This pioneering program encouraged manufacturing and the development of the tourist trade by selective tax exemption, low-interest loans, and other incentives. Despite the marked success of Puerto Rico's development efforts over an extended period of time, per capita income in Puerto Rico is low in comparison to that of the U.S.

General tourist attractions. Ponce Museum of Art; forts El Morro and San Cristobal; Old Walled City of San Juan; Arecibo Observatory; Cordillera Central and state parks; El Yunque Rain Forest; San Juan Cathedral; Porta Coeli Chapel and Museum of Religious Art, Interamerican Univ., San Germán; Condado Convention Center; Casa Blanca, Ponce de León family home, Puerto Rican Family Museum of 16th and 17th centuries, and the Fine Arts Center in San Juan.

Cultural facilities, festivals, etc. Festival Casals classical music concerts, mid-June; Puerto Rico Symphony Orchestra at Music Conservatory; Botanical Garden and Museum of Anthropology, Art, and History at the University of Puerto Rico; Institute of Puerto Rican Culture, at the Dominican Convent; and many popular festivals throughout the island.

Famous Puerto Ricans. Miguel Hernández Agosto, José Celso Barbosa, Julia de Burgos, Pablo Casals, Orlando Cepeda, Roberto Clemente, Rafael Hernández Colón, José de Diego, José Feliciano, Luis A. Ferré, José Ferrer, Doña Felisa Rincón de Gautier, Commodore Diégo E. Hernández, Rafael Hernández (El Jibarito), Marta Casals Istomin, Raúl Julía, Luis Muñoz Marín, René Marqués, Luis Palés Matos, Concha Meléndez, Rita Moreno, Adm. Horacio Rivero.

Chamber of Commerce. 100 Tetuán, P.O. Box S-3789, San Juan, PR 00904; Ponce & South: El Señorial Bldg., Ponce, PR 00731.

Virgin Islands

St. John, St. Croix, St. Thomas

People. Population (1990): 101,809 (50,139, St. Croix; 48,166, St. Thomas; 3,504, St. John). **Pop. density:** 748.6 per sq. mi. **Urban** (1980): 39%. **Racial distribution:** (1980) 15% white; 85% black. **Major ethnic groups:** West Indian, French, Hispanic.

Geography. Total area: 151 sq. mi. **Land area:** 134 sq. mi. **Location:** 3 larger and 50 smaller islands and cays in the S and W of the V.I. group (British V.I. colony to the N and E), which is situated 70 mi. E of Puerto Rico, located W of the Anegada Passage, a major channel connecting the Atlantic O. and the Caribbean Sea. **Climate:** subtropical; the sun tempered by gentle trade winds; humidity is low; average temperature, 78° F. **Topography:** St. Thomas is mainly a ridge of hills running E and W, and has little tillable land; St. Croix rises abruptly in the N but slopes to the S to flatlands and lagoons; St. John has steep, lofty hills and valleys with little level tillable land. **Capital:** Charlotte Amalie, St. Thomas.

Economy. Principal industries: tourism, rum, alumina prod., petroleum refining, watch industry, textiles, electronics. **Principal manufactured goods:** rum, textiles, pharmaceuticals, perfumes. **Gross Domestic Product** (1987): $1.246 bln. **Agriculture: Chief crops:** truck garden produce. **Minerals:** sand, gravel. **Chief ports:** Cruz Bay, St. John; Frederiksted and Christiansted, St. Croix; Charlotte Amalie, St. Thomas. **International airports on:** St. Thomas, St. Croix. **Value of construction** (1987): $167.0 mln. **Per capita income** (1989): $11,052. **Unemployment** (1992): 2.8%. **Tourism** (1988): $662.8 mln. **No. banks** (1990): 8.

Finance. FDIC-insured savings institutions (1993): 1. **Assets:** 48 mln.

Education. Student-teacher ratio (1992): 14.3.

Misc. data. Flower: Yellow elder or yellow trumpet, local designation Ginger Thomas. **Bird:** Yellow breast. **Song:** Virgin Islands March.

History. The islands were visited by Columbus in 1493. Spanish forces, 1555, defeated the Caribes and claimed the territory; by 1596 the native population was annihilated. First permanent settlement in the U.S. territory, 1672, by the Danes; U.S. purchased the islands, 1917, for defense purposes.

The Virgin Islands has a republican form of government, headed by a governor and lieut. governor elected, since 1970, by popular vote for 4-year terms. There is a 15-member unicameral legislature, elected by popular vote. Residents of the V.I. have been U.S. citizens since 1927. Since 1973 they have elected a delegate to the U.S. House of Representatives, who has a voice but no vote, except in committees.

General tourist attractions. Magens Bay, St. Thomas; duty-free shopping; Virgin Islands National Park, 14,488 acres on St. John of lush growth, beaches, Indian relics, and evidence of colonial Danes.

Tourist information. Dept. of Economic Development & Agriculture: St. Thomas, P.O. Box 6400, St. Thomas, VI 00801; St. Croix, P.O. Box 4535, Christiansted, St. Croix 00820.

Other Islands

Navassa lies between Jamaica and Haiti, 100 miles south of Guantanamo Bay, Cuba, in the Caribbean; it covers about 3 sq. mi., is reserved by the U.S. for a lighthouse, and is uninhabited. It is administered by the U.S. Coast Guard.

Wake Atoll, and its neighboring atolls, **Wilkes** and **Peale,** lie in the Pacific Ocean on the direct route from Hawaii to Hong Kong, about 2,300 mi. W of Honolulu and 1,290 mi. E of Guam. The group is 4.5 mi. long, 1.5 mi. wide, and totals less than 3 sq. mi.

The U.S. flag was hoisted over Wake Atoll, July 4, 1898, formal possession taken Jan. 17, 1899; Wake was administered by the U.S. Air Force, 1972-94. The population consists of about 200 persons.

Midway Atoll, acquired in 1867, consist of 2 atolls, **Sand** and **Eastern,** in the North Pacific 1,150 mi. NW of Honolulu, with an area of about 3 sq. mi., administered by the U.S. Navy. There is no indigenous population; its population is about 450.

Johnston Atoll, 717 miles WSW of Honolulu, area 1 sq. mi., is operated by the Defense Nuclear Agency, and the Fish and Wildlife Service, U.S. Dept. of the Interior; its population is about 1,200. **Kingman Reef,** 920 miles S of Hawaii, is under Navy control.

Howland, Jarvis, and **Baker Islands,** 1,400-1,650 miles SW of Honolulu, uninhabited since World War II, are under the Interior Dept.

Palmyra is an atoll about 1,000 miles south of Hawaii, 2 sq. mi. Privately owned, it is under the Interior Dept.

Islands Under Trusteeship

The Trust Territory of the Pacific Islands was established in 1947, as the only strategic trusteeship of the 11 trusteeships established by the UN. For nearly 4 decades, the territory had a heterogeneous population of about 140,000 people scattered among more than 2,100 islands and atolls in 3 major archipelagos: the Carolines, the Marshalls, and the Marianas. The entire geographic area is sometimes referred to as "Micronesia," meaning "little islands." The area of the Trust Territory covered some 3 million sq. miles of the Pacific Ocean, slightly larger than the continental U.S. However, its islands constituted a land area of only 715.8 sq. miles—half the size of Rhode Island. It initially consisted of 7 districts and then was reduced to 4 political jurisdictions: The Commonwealth of the Northern Mariana Islands (CNMI), the Federated States of Micronesia (FSM), the Republic of the Marshall Islands (RMI), and Palau. As of Oct. 21, 1986, the RMI entered into free association with the U.S., as did the FSM effective Nov. 3, 1986. The CNMI became a commonwealth of the U.S., also effective Nov. 3, 1986. Palau then became the only territory remaining under trusteeship.

Republic of Palau

The Republic of Palau (or Belau) consists of more than 200 islands in 16 states in the Caroline chain, of which 8 are permanently inhabited. The capital of Palau, Koror, lies 3,997 miles SW of Honolulu and 813 miles S of Guam. Population of Palau is 15,122 (1990), 10,501 (1990) in Koror. Average year-round temperature is 80° F, average annual rainfall 150 inches.

Until 1979, a High Commissioner, appointed by the U.S. President, in turn appointed a district administrator for Palau to oversee programs and administration there. In support of the islands' evolving political status, the U.S. recognized the Constitution of Palau and the establishment of the government of Palau, consistent with U.S. responsibilities in Palau as the administering authority of the UN Trust Territory of the Pacific Islands (TTPI).

The Assistant Secretary of the Interior for Territorial and International Affairs has been delegated U.S. authority with respect to Palau and may suspend any newly enacted national law in Palau, as well as any newly enacted state law that involves finance or the expenditure of funds, if the law is inconsistent with the trusteeship agreement or U.S. laws or regulations applicable to the TTPI. The Constitution became effective in 1980. The President and Vice President are elected by popular vote. A Council of Chiefs advises the President on matters concerning traditional law and custom. Palau has a bicameral national legislature composed of a House of Delegates and a Senate.

On Nov. 9, 1993, 68.3% of the voting population voted in favor of a compact of free association that would begin the process of changing Palau's status from a trust territory to a freely associated state.

Washington, Capital of the U.S.

Bureau of Engraving and Printing

Bureau of Engraving and Printing, headquarters for the making of U.S. paper money. Twenty-minute self-guided tours Monday through Friday. Closed federal holidays and Dec. 24 through Jan. 3.

Capitol

The **United States Capitol** was originally designed by Dr. William Thornton, an amateur architect, who submitted a plan in the spring of 1793 that won him $500 and a city lot.

The south, or House, wing was completed in 1807 under the direction of Benjamin H. Latrobe.

The present Senate and House wings and the iron dome were designed and constructed by Thomas U. Walter, the 4th architect of the Capitol, between 1851 and 1863.

The present cast iron dome at its greatest exterior measures 135 ft. 5 in., and it is topped by the bronze Statue of Freedom that stands 19½ ft. and weighs 14,985 pounds. On its base are the words "E Pluribus Unum" (Out of Many One).

The Capitol is normally open from 9 AM to 4:30 PM; from June to Aug., to 10 PM. It is closed on Dec. 25. Tours through the Capitol, including the House and Senate galleries, are conducted from 9 AM to 3:45 PM; there is no charge.

To observe the debate in the House or Senate while Congress is in session, individuals living in the U.S. may obtain tickets to the visitor's galleries from their congressperson or senator. Visitors from other countries may obtain passes at the Capitol.

Federal Bureau of Investigation

The **Federal Bureau of Investigation** offers a tour of its headquarters, beginning with a videotape presentation. Visitors learn about the history of the FBI and see such things as the weapons confiscated from famous gangsters, photos of the most-wanted fugitives, the DNA laboratory, goods forfeited and seized in narcotics operations, and a sharpshooting demonstration.

Tours are conducted Mon. through Fri., 8:45 AM through 4:15 PM, except Jan. 1, Dec. 25, and other federal holidays. Tickets may be obtained at the FBI on the day of the tour or through a congressperson or senator. Admission is free.

Folger Shakespeare Library

The **Folger Shakespeare Library,** on Capitol Hill, is a research institution devoted to the advancement of learning in the background of Anglo-American civilization in the 16th and 17th centuries and in most aspects of the European Renaissance. It has the largest collection of Shakespeareana in the world, including 79 copies of the First Folio.

Exhibit areas may be visited Mon. through Fri. from 10 AM to 4 PM.

Holocaust Memorial Museum

The **U.S. Holocaust Memorial Museum** opened on April 21, 1993. It is located on 100 Raoul Wallenberg Place SW (formerly 15th St. SW), near Independence Ave., just off the Mall. The Museum documents, through the use of permanent and temporary displays, interactive videos, and special lectures, the events of the Holocaust beginning in 1933 and continuing until the end of WW II. The permanent exhibition is not recommended for children under the age of 11.

The museum is open daily from 10 AM to 5:30 PM, except Yom Kippur and Dec. 25. Although a limited number of free tickets are available on the day of visit, advance tickets may be ordered for a small fee.

Jefferson Memorial

Dedicated in 1943, the **Thomas Jefferson Memorial** stands on the south shore of the Tidal Basin in West Potomac Park. It is a circular stone structure, with Vermont marble on the exterior and Georgia white marble inside, and combines architectural elements of the dome of the Pantheon in Rome and the rotunda designed by Jefferson for the University of Virginia.

The memorial is open daily from 8 AM to midnight. An elevator and curb ramps for the handicapped are in service.

John F. Kennedy Center

The **John F. Kennedy Center for the Performing Arts,** designated by Congress as the National Cultural Center and the official memorial in Washington to President Kennedy, opened September 8, 1971. Tours are available daily between 10:00 AM and 1:00 PM.

Library of Congress

Established by and for Congress in 1800, the **Library of Congress** has extended its services over the years to other government agencies and other libraries, to scholars, and to the general public, and it now serves as the national library. It contains more than 80 million items in 470 languages.

The library's exhibit halls are open to the public, from 8:30 AM to 9:30 PM, Mon. and Wed.-Thu.; 8:30 AM - 5:00 PM, Tues. and Fri.-Sat.; 8:30 AM - 6:30 PM, Sun. Guided tours begin at 10 AM, 1 PM, and 3 PM, Mon. through Fri. The library is closed Jan. 1 and Dec. 25.

Lincoln Memorial

The **Lincoln Memorial** in West Potomac Park, on the axis of the Capitol and the Washington Monument, consists of a large marble hall enclosing a heroic statue of Abraham Lincoln in meditation sitting on a large armchair. It was dedicated on Memorial Day, May 30, 1922. The Memorial was designed by Henry Bacon. The statue was designed by Daniel Chester French and sculpted by French and the Piccirilli brothers. Murals and ornamentation on the bronze ceiling beams are by Jules Guerin.

The memorial is open daily from 8 AM to midnight. An elevator for the handicapped is in service.

National Archives

The Declaration of Independence, the Constitution of the United States, and the Bill of Rights are on permanent display in the **National Archives** Exhibition Hall. They are sealed in glass-and-bronze cases. The National Archives also holds the permanently valuable federal records of the United States government.

The Exhibition Hall is open 10 AM to 5 PM, Mon. through Sat., 11 AM to 6 PM, Sun., except Jan. 1 and Dec. 25. Admission is free.

National Gallery of Art

The **National Gallery of Art**, situated on the north side of the Mall facing Constitution Avenue, was established by Joint Resolution of Congress Mar. 24, 1937, and opened Mar. 17, 1941. The original West building was designed by John Russell Pope. The East building, opened in 1978, was designed by I. M. Pei. The National Gallery is separate from, but maintains a relationship with, the Smithsonian Institution.

Normally open daily from 10 AM to 6 PM; 11 AM to 6 PM Sunday. Closed Jan. 1 and Dec. 25.

Smithsonian Institution

The **Smithsonian Institution,** established in 1846, the world's largest museum complex, consists of 14 museums and the National Zoo. It holds some 100 million artifacts and specimens in its trust "for the increase and diffusion of knowledge among men." Nine museums are located on the National Mall between the Washington Monument and the Capitol; 5 other museums and the zoo are elsewhere in Washington (the Cooper-Hewitt Museum and the National Museum of the American Indian, administered by the Smithsonian, are located in New York City). Most visitors begin their trip with a visit to the **Smithsonian Information Center,** located in "the Castle" on the Mall. Also on the Mall are the **National Museum of American History,** the **National Museum of Natural History,** the **National Air and Space Museum,** the **Hirshhorn Museum and Sculpture Garden,** the **Arthur M. Sackler Gallery,** the **National Museum of African Art,** the **Freer Gallery of Art,** and the **Arts and Industries Building.** Near the Sackler Gallery is the **Enid A. Haupt Garden.** Located nearby are the **National Postal Museum,** the **National Museum of American Art,** the **National Portrait Gallery,** and the **Renwick Gallery.** Farther away, at 1901 Fort Place SE, is the **Anacostia Museum.**

Most museums are open daily, except Dec. 25, from 10 AM to 5:30 PM.

Vietnam Veterans Memorial

Originally dedicated on November 13, 1982, the **Vietnam Veterans Memorial** is a symbol of the nation's recognition of the men and women who served in the armed forces in the Vietnam War. On a V-shaped black-granite wall, designed by Maya Ying Lan, are inscribed the names of the more than 58,000 Americans who lost their lives or remain missing. Since 1982, two additions have been made to the Memorial. The first, dediciated on Nov. 11, 1984, was the Frederick Hart sculpture "Three Servicemen." On Nov. 11, 1993, the "Vietnam Women's Memorial Project," a sculpture by Glenna Goodacre, was dedicated to the women who served in Vietnam.

The memorial is open daily from 8 AM to midnight.

Washington Monument

The **Washington Monument,** dedicated in 1885, is a tapering shaft, or obelisk, of white marble, 555 ft., 5 1/8 inches in height and 55 ft., 1½ inches square at base. Eight small windows, 2 on each side, are located at the 500-ft. level, where points of interest are indicated.

Open daily except Dec. 25, 9 AM to 4:30 PM., 8 AM to midnight Apr.-Labor Day.

The White House

The **White House,** the president's residence, stands on 18 acres on the south side of Pennsylvania Avenue, between the Treasury and the old Executive Office Building. The walls are of sandstone, quarried at Aquia Creek, VA. The exterior walls were painted, causing the building to be termed the "White House." On Aug. 24, 1814, during Madison's administration, the house was burned by the British. James Hoban rebuilt it by Oct. 1817.

The White House is normally open for tours from 10 AM to 12 noon, Tues.-Sat., and from 10 AM to 2 PM in summer (the ticket booth opens at 8 AM). Only the public rooms on the ground floor and state floor may be visited.

OTHER NEARBY ATTRACTIONS

Arlington National Cemetery

Arlington National Cemetery, on the former Custis estate in Arlington, Virginia, is the site of the **Tomb of the Unknowns** and the final resting place of John Fitzgerald Kennedy, president of the United States, who was buried there Nov. 25, 1963. A torch burns day and night over his grave. The remains of his brother Sen. Robert F. Kennedy (NY) were interred on June 8, 1968, in an area adjacent. Many other famous Americans are also buried at Arlington, as well as 175,000 American soldiers from every major war.

North of the National Cemetery, approximately 350 yards, stands the **U.S. Marine Corps War Memorial**, also known as Iwo Jima. The memorial is a bronze statue of the raising of the United States flag on Mt. Suribachi during WWII, executed by Felix de Weldon from the photograph by Joe Rosenthal, and presented to the nation by members and friends of the U.S. Marine Corps.

Mount Vernon

Mount Vernon, George Washington's estate, is on the south bank of the Potomac R., 16 miles below Washington, DC, in northern Virginia.

The present house is an enlargement of one apparently built on the site by Augustine Washington, who lived there 1735-38. His son Lawrence came there in 1743, when he renamed the plantation Mount Vernon in honor of Admiral Vernon, under whom he had served in the West Indies. Lawrence Washington died in 1752 and was succeeded as proprietor of Mount Vernon by his half-brother, George Washington.

The Pentagon

The **Pentagon,** headquarters of the Department of Defense, is one of the world's largest office buildings. Situated in Arlington, VA, it houses more than 23,000 employees in offices that occupy 3,707,745 square feet.

Tours are available Monday through Friday (excluding federal holidays), from 9:30 AM to 3:30 PM.

CITIES OF THE U.S.

Sources: Bureau of the Census: population (1990 Census, updated as of April 1994); population growth (1980-90). Geography Division, Bureau of the Census: population density (1990); area (1990). Bureau of Labor Statistics: employment (1993 averages for city proper only). Bureau of Economic Analysis: per capita personal income (Metropolitan Statistical Area, 1992).

Based on 1990 Census, the 100 most populous cities (inc.=incorporated; est.=established).

Akron, Ohio

Population: 223,019; **Pop. density:** 4,055 per sq. mi.; **Pop. growth:** -6.0%. **Area:** 55 sq. mi. **Employment:** 100,530 employed, 8.2% unemployed; **Per capita income:** $19,056; % change 1990-92: 7.7.

History: settled 1825; inc. as city 1865; located on Ohio-Erie Canal and is a port of entrysince 1870 the rubber capital of the U.S.

Transportation: 1 airport; major trucking industry; Conrail; metro transit system. **Communications:** 4 TV, 7 radio stations. **Medical facilities:** 11 hospitals; specialized children's treatment center. **Educational facilities:** 13 universities and colleges; 68 public schools. **Further information:** Akron Regional Development Board or Akron-Summit Convention and Visitors Bureau, Cascade Plaza, Akron, OH 44308.

Albuquerque, New Mexico

Population: 384,619; **Pop. density:** 2,829 per sq. mi.; **Pop. growth:** 15.6%. **Area:** 136 sq. mi. **Employment:** 210,160 employed, 6.4% unemployed; **Per capita income:** $17,758; % change 1990-92: 9.1.

History: founded 1706 by the Spanish; inc. 1890.

Transportation: 1 international airport; 1 railroad; 2 bus lines. **Communications:** 8 TV, 31 radio stations. **Medical facilities:** 10 major hospitals. **Educational facilities:** 1 university, 2 colleges. **Further information:** Convention & Visitors Bureau, 121 Tijeras Ave. NE, Albuquerque, NM 87125.

Anaheim, California

Population: 266,406; **Pop. density:** 6,498 per sq. mi.; **Pop. growth:** 21.4%. **Area:** 41 sq. mi. **Employment:** 134,800 employed, 7.7% unemployed; **Per capita income:** $24,651; % change 1990-92: 1.5.

History: founded 1858; inc. 1876; now known as home of Disneyland (since 1955).

Transportation: 3 municipal airports; 4 railroads; Greyhound buses. **Communications:** 12 TV, 4 radio stations within city limits. **Medical facilities:** 6 general hospitals. **Educational facilities:** 3 colleges, 5 junior colleges; 62 elementary, 8 junior high, 8 high schools. **Further information:** Chamber of Commerce, 100 South Anaheim Blvd., Suite 300, Anaheim, CA 92805.

Anchorage, Alaska

Population: 226,338; **Pop. density:** 131 per sq. mi.; **Pop. growth:** 29.8%. **Area:** 1,732 sq. mi. **Employment:** 125,206 employed, 5.9% unemployed; **Per capita income:** $25,077; % change 1990-92: 4.0.

History: founded 1914 as a construction camp for railroad; HQ of Alaska Defense Command, WWII; severely damaged in earthquake 1964.

Transportation: 1 international airport, 3 other airports. **Communications:** 7 TV, 19 radio stations. **Medical facilities:** 3 hospitals. **Educational facilities:** 2 universities, 1 community college. **Further information:** Chamber of Commerce, 441 W. 5th Ave., Ste. 300, Anchorage, AK 99501-2309.

Arlington, Texas

Population: 261,717; **Pop. density:** 3,313 per sq. mi.; **Pop. growth:** 63.5%. **Area:** 79 sq. mi. **Employment:** 157,752 employed, 5.6% unemployed; **Per capita income:** $20,250; % change 1990-92: 8.5.

History: settled in 1840s between Dallas and Ft. Worth; inc. 1884.

Transportation: Dallas/Ft. Worth airport is 20 minutes away; 11 railway lines; intercity transport system in planning stage. **Communications:** 11 TV, 44 radio stations. **Medical facilities:** 2 hospitals. **Educational facilities:** 1 university; 51 public schools. **Further information:** The Arlington Chamber, 316 W. Main St., Arlington, TX 76010.

Atlanta, Georgia

Population: 393,929; **Pop. density:** 3,008 per sq. mi.; **Pop. growth:** -7.3%. **Area:** 131 sq. mi. **Employment:** 181,906 employed, 8.3% unemployed; **Per capita income:** $21,849; % change 1990-92: 6.9.

History: founded as "Terminus" 1837; renamed Atlanta 1845; inc. 1847; played major role in Civil War and burned during Gen. Sherman's "March to the Sea."

Transportation: 1 international airport; 2 railroad lines; MARTA bus and rapid rail service. **Communications:** 11 TV, 51 radio stations; 26 cable TV companies. **Medical facilities:** 55 hospitals; VA hospital; Natl. Centers for Disease Control and Prevention; Natl. Cancer Center. **Educational facilities:** 37 colleges, universities, seminaries, junior colleges. **Further information:** Chamber of Commerce, 235 International Blvd., Atlanta, GA 30303.

Aurora, Colorado

Population: 222,103; **Pop. density:** 1,645 per sq. mi.; **Pop. growth:** 40.1%. **Area:** 135 sq. mi. **Employment:** 131,813 employed, 4.5% unemployed; **Per capita income:** $22,930; % change 1990-92: 9.2.

History: located 5 miles east of Denver; early growth stimulated by presence of military bases; fast-growing trade center.

Transportation: adjacent to new Denver Intl. Airport; 1 airport; 4 railroads; bus system. **Further information:** Aurora Economic Development Council, 15701 E. 1st Ave., Ste. 206, Aurora, CO 80011.

Austin, Texas

Population: 465,648; **Pop. density:** 4,014 per sq. mi.; **Pop. growth:** 34.6%. **Area:** 116 sq. mi. **Employment:** 296,709 employed, 4.5% unemployed; **Per capita income:** $18,770; % change 1990-92: 10.0.

History: first permanent settlement 1835; capital of Rep. of Texas 1838; named after Stephen Austin; inc. 1840.

Transportation: 1 international airport; 4 railroads. **Communications:** 5 TV, 18 radio stations. **Medical facilities:** 15 hospitals. **Educational facilities:** 7 universities and colleges. **Further information:** Chamber of Commerce, P.O. Box 1967, Austin, TX 78767.

Bakersfield, California

Population: 174,978; **Pop. density:** 2,033 per sq. mi.; **Pop. growth:** 65.5%. **Area:** 86 sq. mi. **Employment:** 83,117 employed, 11.0% unemployed; **Per capita income:** $15,836; % change 1990-92: 1.0.

History: incorporated in 1898.

Transportation: 1 airport; 3 railroads; Greyhound buses; local bus system. **Medical facilities:** 6 major hospitals; 9 convalescent; 1 psychiatric; 3 physical rehab. centers; 3 clinics; 5 urgent care centers. **Educational facilities:** 1 university, 1 community college; 9 vocational schools; 1 adult school; 1 college of law; 56 public schools. **Further information:** Greater Bakersfield Chamber of Commerce, 1033 Truxtun Avenue, Bakersfield, CA 93301.

Baltimore, Maryland

Population: 736,014; **Pop. density:** 9,200 per sq. mi.; **Pop. growth:** -6.4%. **Area:** 80 sq. mi. **Employment:** 286,242 employed, 10.7% unemployed; **Per capita income:** $22,412; % change 1990-92: 5.5.

History: founded by Maryland legislature 1729; inc. 1797; bombing of its Ft. McHenry 1814 inspired Francis

Scott Key to write "Star-Spangled Banner;" rebuilt after fire 1904.

Transportation: 1 major airport; 3 railroads; bus system; subway system; 2 underwater tunnels. **Communications:** 6 TV, 33 radio stations. **Medical facilities:** 29 hospitals; 2 major medical centers. **Educational facilities:** over 30 universities and colleges; 177 public schools. **Further information:** Greater Baltimore Committee, 111 S. Calvert St., Baltimore, MD 21202.

Baton Rouge, Louisiana

Population: 219,531; **Pop. density:** 3,599 per sq. mi.; **Pop. growth:** -0.4%. **Area:** 61 sq. mi. **Employment:** 102,981 employed, 6.7% unemployed; **Per capita income:** $17,831; % change 1990-92: 11.9.

History: claimed by Spain at time of La. Purchase 1803; est. independence by rebellion 1810; inc. as town 1817; held by Union during most of Civil War.

Transportation: 1 airport, 5 airlines; 1 bus line; 3 railroad trunk lines. **Communications:** 5 TV, 19 radio stations. **Medical facilities:** 7 hospitals. **Educational facilities:** 2 universities; 101 public, 45 private schools. **Further information:** Chamber of Commerce, P.O. Box 3217, Baton Rouge, LA 70821.

Birmingham, Alabama

Population: 265,347; **Pop. density:** 2,687 per sq. mi.; **Pop. growth:** -6.5%. **Area:** 99 sq. mi. **Employment:** 114,223 employed, 8.4% unemployed; **Per capita income:** $19,428; % change 1990-92: 10.4.

History: settled due to discovery of elements needed for steel production; inc. 1871; named after Great Britain's steel-making center.

Transportation: 1 airport; 4 major rail freight lines, Amtrak; 1 bus line; 75 truck line terminals; 4 interstate highways. **Communications:** 4 TV, 22 radio stations; 1 educational TV, 1 educational radio station. **Medical facilities:** Univ. of Alabama at Birmingham Medical Center; VA hospital with organ transplant program; 15 other hospitals. **Educational facilities:** 1 university, 2 colleges, 2 junior colleges. **Further information:** Chamber of Commerce, 2027 First Ave. N., Birmingham, AL 35202.

Boston, Massachusetts

Population: 574,283; **Pop. density:** 12,484 per sq. mi.; **Pop. growth:** 2.0%. **Area:** 46 sq. mi. **Employment:** 270,011 employed, 6.5% unemployed; **Per capita income:** $24,109; % change 1990-92: 6.7.

History: settled 1630 by John Winthrop; capital of Mass. Bay Colony; figured strongly in Am. Revolution, earning distinction as the "Cradle of Liberty"; inc. 1822.

Transportation: 1 major airport; 2 railroads; city rail and subway system; 3 underwater tunnels; port. **Communications:** 20 TV, 51 radio stations. **Medical facilities:** 16 hospitals; 8 major medical research centers. **Educational facilities:** 19 universities and colleges. **Further information:** Greater Boston Chamber of Commerce, 1 Beacon St., 4th fl., Boston, MA 02108-3114.

Buffalo, New York

Population: 328,175; **Pop. density:** 7,812 per sq. mi.; **Pop. growth:** -8.3%. **Area:** 42 sq. mi. **Employment:** 130,148 employed, 10.7% unemployed; **Per capita income:** $19,467; % change 1990-92: 8.9.

History: founded 1790 by the Dutch; raided twice by British during War of 1812; as western terminus for Erie Canal became a center for trade and manufacturing; inc. 1832.

Transportation: 1 international airport; 6 major railroads; metro rail system; water service to Great Lakes-St. Lawrence seaways system, and Atlantic seaboard. **Communications:** 8 TV, 31 radio stations. **Medical facilities:** 16 hospitals. **Educational facilities:** 2 universities, 11 colleges; 70 public and private schools. **Further information:** Greater Buffalo Partnership, 300 Main Place Tower, Buffalo, NY 14202.

Charlotte, North Carolina

Population: 395,925; **Pop. density:** 2,869 per sq. mi.; **Pop. growth:** 25.5%. **Area:** 138 sq. mi. **Employment:** 227,458 employed, 4.7% unemployed; **Per capita income:** $19,884; % change 1990-92: 6.9.

History: settled by Scotch-Irish immigrants 1740s; inc. 1767 and named after Queen Charlotte, George III's wife; scene of first major U.S. gold discovery 1799.

Transportation: 1 airport; 2 major railway lines; 2 bus lines; 280 trucking firms. **Communications:** 6 TV, 20 radio stations. **Medical facilities:** 12 hospitals, 1 medical center. **Educational facilities:** 2 universities, 5 colleges. **Further information:** Chamber of Commerce, P.O. Box 32785, Charlotte, NC 28232.

Chicago, Illinois

Population: 2,783,726; **Pop. density:** 12,209 per sq. mi.; **Pop. growth:** -7.4%. **Area:** 228 sq. mi. **Employment:** 1,225,096 employed, 9.0% unemployed; **Per capita income:** $23,891; % change 1990-92: 7.8.

History: site acquired from Indians 1795; significant white settlement began with opening of Erie Canal 1825; chartered as city 1837; boomed with arrival of railroads from east and canal to Mississippi R.; about one-third of city destroyed by fire 1871; major grain & livestock market.

Transportation: 3 airports; major railroad system; major trucking industry. **Communications:** 9 TV, 31 radio stations. **Medical facilities:** over 123 hospitals. **Educational facilities:** 95 institutions of higher learning. **Further information:** Chicagoland Chamber of Commerce, 1 IBM Plaza, Ste. 2800, Chicago, IL 60611.

Cincinnati, Ohio

Population: 364,114; **Pop. density:** 4,667 per sq. mi.; **Pop. growth:** -5.5%. **Area:** 78 sq. mi. **Employment:** 163,155 employed, 7.8% unemployed; **Per capita income:** $20,517; % change 1990-92: 8.5.

History: founded 1788 and named after the Society of Cincinnati, an organization of Revolutionary War officers; chartered as village 1802; inc. as city 1819.

Transportation: 1 international airport; 3 railroads; 1 bus system. **Communications:** 6 TV, 27 radio stations. **Medical facilities:** 32 hospitals; Children's Hospital Medical Center; VA hospital. **Educational facilities:** 4 universities; 5 colleges, 8 technical & 2-year colleges. **Further information:** Chamber of Commerce, 300 Carew Tower, 441 Vine St., Cincinnati, OH 45202.

Cleveland, Ohio

Population: 505,616; **Pop. density:** 6,400 per sq. mi.; **Pop. growth:** -11.9%. **Area:** 79 sq. mi. **Employment:** 181,766 employed, 12.8% unemployed; **Per capita income:** $21,533; % change 1990-92: 8.2.

History: surveyed in 1796; inc. as village 1814, as city 1836; annexed Ohio City 1854.

Transportation: 1 international airport; rail service; major port; rapid transit system. **Communications:** 9 TV, 26 radio stations. **Medical facilities:** 24 hospitals; major medical research center. **Educational facilities:** 13 universities and colleges; 127 public schools. **Further information:** Greater Cleveland Growth Assn., 200 Tower City Center, Cleveland, OH 44113.

Colorado Springs, Colorado

Population: 280,430; **Pop. density:** 2,730 per sq. mi.; **Pop. growth:** 30.7%. **Area:** 103 sq. mi. **Employment:** 142,519 employed, 6.0% unemployed; **Per capita income:** $18,300; % change 1990-92: 9.4.

History: founded 1871 at the foot of Pikes Peak; inc. 1872.

Transportation: 1 municipal airport; 2 railroads; bus line. **Communications:** 7 TV, 25 radio stations. **Medical facilities:** 5 hospitals. **Educational facilities:** 5 universities, 9 colleges. **Further information:** Chamber of Commerce, P.O. Box B, Colorado Springs, CO 80901.

Columbus, Georgia

Population: 178,681; **Pop. density:** 822 per sq. mi.; **Pop. growth:** 5.4%. **Area:** 218 sq. mi. **Employment:** 72,011 employed, 6.5% unemployed; **Per capita income:** $16,115; % change 1990-92: 10.4.

History: settled and inc. 1828; a port city on Chattahoochee R.

Transportation: 1 airport; metro bus system; 2 bus lines; 2 railroads. **Communications:** 5 TV, 12 radio stations. **Medical facilities:** 5 hospitals. **Educational facilities:** 2 colleges; 53 public schools. **Further information:** Chamber of Commerce, P.O. Box 1200, Columbus, GA 31902.

Columbus, Ohio

Population: 632,945; **Pop. density:** 3,497 per sq. mi.; **Pop. growth:** 12.0%. **Area:** 181 sq. mi. **Employment:** 345,113 employed, 5.4% unemployed; **Per capita income:** $19,974; % change 1990-92: 9.4.

History: first settlement 1797; laid out as new capital 1812 with current name; became city 1834.

Transportation: 2 airports; 3 railroads; 4 intercity bus lines. **Communications:** 8 TV, 25 radio stations. **Medical facilities:** 18 hospitals. **Educational facilities:** 13 universities and colleges. **Further information:** Chamber of Commerce, 37 N. High St., Columbus, OH 43216.

Corpus Christi, Texas

Population: 257,428; **Pop. density:** 2,476 per sq. mi.; **Pop. growth:** 10.9%. **Area:** 104 sq. mi. **Employment:** 117,862 employed, 8.6% unemployed; **Per capita income:** $16,371; % change 1990-92: 11.8.

History: settled 1839 and inc. 1852.

Transportation: 1 international airport; 2 bus lines, metro bus system; 3 freight railroads. **Communications:** 6 TV, 17 radio stations. **Medical facilities:** 14 hospitals including a children's center. **Educational facilities:** 1 university, 1 college. **Further information:** Chamber of Commerce, PO Box 640, Corpus Christi, TX 78403.

Dallas, Texas

Population: 1,007,618; **Pop. density:** 3,024 per sq. mi.; **Pop. growth:** 11.3%. **Area:** 333 sq. mi. **Employment:** 554,960 employed, 7.7% unemployed; **Per capita income:** $22,424; % change 1990-92: 9.5.

History: first settled 1841; platted 1846; inc. 1871; developed as the financial and commercial center of Southwest; known for its oil industry and cotton market.

Transportation: 1 international airport, 1 regional airport; Amtrak; transit system. **Communications:** 10 TV, 49 radio stations. **Medical facilities:** 17 general hospitals; major medical center. **Educational facilities:** 8 universities, 4 colleges. **Further information:** Chamber of Commerce, 1201 Elm, Dallas, TX 75270.

Dayton, Ohio

Population: 182,005; **Pop. density:** 3,793 per sq. mi.; **Pop. growth:** -5.9%. **Area:** 48 sq. mi. **Employment:** 70,807 employed, 9.3% unemployed; **Per capita income:** $19,411; % change 1990-92: 9.4.

History: settled 1796; inc. 1805; disastrous flood 1913; site where Wright Bros. invented first airplane to sustain flight 1903.

Transportation: 1 international airport, 14 airlines; 3 railroads; 2 bus lines; countywide Dayton Regional Transit Authority. **Communications:** 5 TV, 17 radio stations. **Medical facilities:** 14 hospitals including VA facility. **Educational facilities:** 3 colleges and universities. **Further information:** Dayton Area Chamber of Commerce, 1 Chamber Plaza, Dayton, OH 45402-2400.

Denver, Colorado

Population: 467,610; **Pop. density:** 4,213 per sq. mi.; **Pop. growth:** -5.1%. **Area:** 111 sq. mi. **Employment:** 249,319 employed, 5.9% unemployed; **Per capita income:** $22,930; % change 1990-92: 9.2.

History: settled 1858 by gold prospectors and miners; inc. 1861; growth spurred by gold and silver boom; the financial and industrial center of Rocky Mt. region.

Transportation: 1 international airport; 5 major rail freight lines, Amtrak; 1 bus line. **Communications:** 9 TV, 25 radio stations. **Medical facilities:** 20 hospitals. **Educational facilities:** 5 universities, 6 colleges. **Further information:** Greater Denver Chamber of Commerce, 1445 Market St., Denver, CO 80202.

Des Moines, Iowa

Population: 193,189; **Pop. density:** 2,927 per sq. mi.; **Pop. growth:** 1.1%. **Area:** 66 sq. mi. **Employment:** 113,124 employed, 4.4% unemployed; **Per capita income:** $21,647; % change 1990-92: 9.8.

History: Fort Des Moines built 1843; settled and inc. 1851; chartered as city 1857.

Transportation: 1 international airport; 4 bus lines; 5 railroads; metro bus system. **Communications:** 5 TV, 15 radio stations. **Medical facilities:** 8 hospitals. **Educational facilities:** 2 universities, 5 colleges. **Further information:** Greater Des Moines Chamber of Commerce Federation, 601 Locust St., Ste. 100, Des Moines, IA 50309.

Detroit, Michigan

Population: 1,027,974; **Pop. density:** 7,559 per sq. mi.; **Pop. growth:** -14.6%. **Area:** 136 sq. mi. **Employment:** 337,771 employed, 13.2% unemployed; **Per capita income:** $21,796; % change 1990-92: 6.4.

History: founded by French 1701; controlled by British 1760; acquired by U.S. 1796; destroyed by fire 1805; capital of state 1837-47; inc. as city 1824; auto manufacturing began 1899.

Transportation: 1 international airport; 10 railroads; major international port; public transit system. **Communications:** 9 TV, 37 radio stations. **Medical facilities:** 28 hospitals, major medical center. **Educational facilities:** 13 universities and colleges. **Further information:** Greater Detroit Chamber of Commerce, 600 W. Lafayette Blvd., Detroit, MI 48226.

El Paso, Texas

Population: 515,342; **Pop. density:** 2,156 per sq. mi.; **Pop. growth:** 21.2%. **Area:** 239 sq. mi. **Employment:** 223,076 employed, 9.8% unemployed; **Per capita income:** $12,497; % change 1990-92: 8.6.

History: first settled 1827; inc. 1873; arrival of railroad 1881 boosted city's population and industries.

Transportation: 1 international airport; 5 major rail lines; 8 bus lines; 9 major highways; gateway to Mexico. **Communications:** 10 TV, 23 radio stations. **Medical facilities:** 18 hospitals; cancer treatment center. **Educational facilities:** 2 colleges and universities. **Further information:** Greater El Paso Chamber of Commerce, 10 Civic Center Plaza, El Paso, TX 79901.

Fort Wayne, Indiana

Population: 172,971; **Pop. density:** 3,328 per sq. mi.; **Pop. growth:** 0.4%. **Area:** 52 sq. mi. **Employment:** 89,045 employed, 6.5% unemployed; **Per capita income:** $19,360; % change 1990-92: 8.1.

History: French fort 1680; U.S. fort 1794; settled by 1832; inc. 1840 prior to Wabash-Erie canal completion 1843.

Transportation: 2 airports; 3 railroads; 8 bus lines. **Communications:** 5 TV, 13 radio stations. **Medical facilities:** 3 major hospitals; VA hospital. **Educational facilities:** 5 colleges; 82 public schools. **Further information:** Chamber of Commerce, 826 Ewing Street, Fort Wayne, IN 46802-2182.

Fort Worth, Texas

Population: 447,619; **Pop. density:** 1,549 per sq. mi.; **Pop. growth:** 16.2%. **Area:** 289 sq. mi. **Employment:** 223,126 employed, 8.4% unemployed; **Per capita income:** $20,250; % change 1990-92: 8.5.

History: est. as military post 1849; inc. 1873; oil discovered 1917.

Transportation: 1 international airport; 8 major railroads, Amtrak; local bus service; 2 transcontinental, 2 intrastate bus lines. **Communications:** 14 TV, 37 radio stations. **Medical facilities:** 35 hospitals; 2 children's hospitals; 4 government hospitals. **Educational facilities:** 8 universities and colleges. **Further information:** Chamber of Commerce, 777 Taylor St. #900, Fort Worth, TX 76102.

Fremont, California

Population: 173,339; **Pop. density:** 2,211 per sq. mi.; **Pop. growth:** 31.4%. **Area:** 78.4 sq. mi. **Employment:** 94,908 employed, 4.6% unemployed; **Per capita income:** $24,359; % change 1990-92: 4.4.

History: area first settled by Spanish 1769; inc. 1956 with the consolidation of 5 communities.

Transportation: intracity bus line; Bay Area Rapid Transit System (southern terminal). **Communications:** NA. **Medical facilities:** 2 hospitals. **Educational facilities:** 1 junior college; 43 public schools. **Further information:** Chamber of Commerce, 2201 Walnut Ave., Ste. 110, Fremont, CA 94538.

Fresno, California

Population: 354,091; **Pop. density:** 5,449 per sq. mi.; **Pop. growth:** 62.9%. **Area:** 65 sq. mi. **Employment:** 161,176 employed, 13.0% unemployed; **Per capita income:** $16,376; % change 1990-92: 2.6.

History: founded 1872; inc. as city 1885.

Transportation: municipal airport; Amtrak; 1 bus line; intracity bus system. **Communications:** 11 TV, 30 radio stations. **Medical facilities:** 6 general hospitals including a VA facility. **Educational facilities:** 9 universities and colleges; 90 public schools. **Further information:** Chamber of Commerce, 2331 Fresno St., Fresno, CA 93721.

Garland, Texas

Population: 180,635; **Pop. density:** 3,226 per sq. mi.; **Pop. growth:** 30.1%. **Area:** 56 sq. mi. **Employment:** 106,347 employed, 5.1% unemployed; **Per capita income:** $22,424; % change 1990-92: 9.5.

History: settled 1850s; inc. 1891.

Transportation: 45 miles from Dallas/Ft. Worth airport; 2 railroads. **Communications:** 3 TV stations (from Dallas). **Medical facilities:** total of 306 hospital beds. **Educational facilities:** 1 university, 2 community colleges; 53 public schools. **Further information:** Chamber of Commerce, 914 S. Garland Ave., Garland, TX 75040.

Glendale, California

Population: 180,038; **Pop. density:** 5,886 per sq. mi.; **Pop. growth:** 29.0%. **Area:** 30.59 sq. mi. **Employment:** 82,512 employed, 9.1% unemployed; **Per capita income:** $21,434; % change 1990-92: 3.3.

History: township in 1887, incorporated in 1906. Adjacent to Los Angeles.

Transportation: 1 airport; 1 railroad; in triangle surrounded by 3 freeways; Southern California Rapid Transit system; Glendale Beeline bus. **Communications:** 2 radio stations. **Medical facilities:** 1,100 beds in three hospitals. **Educational facilities:** 1 community college. **Further information:** Chamber of Commerce, 200 S. Louise, Glendale, CA 91205.

Grand Rapids, Michigan

Population: 189,126; **Pop. density:** 4,358 per sq. mi.; **Pop. growth:** 4.0%. **Area:** 43.4 sq. mi. **Employment:** 91,939 employed, 7.6% unemployed; **Per capita income:** $18,924; % change 1990-92: 9.3.

History: originally site of Ottawa Indian village; trading post 1826; became lumbering center and chartered as town 1850.

Transportation: 1 international airport; 4 railroads; 5 bus lines; transit bus system. **Communications:** 6 TV, 25 radio stations. **Medical facilities:** 10 hospitals. **Educational facilities:** 8 colleges; 64 public schools. **Further information:** Chamber of Commerce, 111 Pearl St., NW, Grand Rapids, MI 49503.

Greensboro, North Carolina

Population: 183,894; **Pop. density:** 3,059 per sq. mi.; **Pop. growth:** 17.9%. **Area:** 60 sq. mi. **Employment:** 103,279 employed, 4.7% unemployed; **Per capita income:** $19,940; % change 1990-92: 8.0.

History: settled 1749; site of Revolutionary War conflict 1781 between Nathanael Greene and Cornwallis; inc. 1807.

Transportation: 1 regional airport; 2 railroads; Trailways/Greyhound bus service. **Communications:** all cable TV stations; 11 radio stations. **Medical facilities:** 4 hospitals. **Educational facilities:** 2 universities, 3 colleges; 38 public schools. **Further information:** Chamber of Commerce, P.O. Box 3246, Greensboro, NC 27402.

Hialeah, Florida

Population: 188,008; **Pop. density:** 8,545 per sq. mi.; **Pop. growth:** 29.4%. **Area:** 22 sq. mi. **Employment:** 93,667 employed, 8.1% unemployed; **Per capita income:** $17,124; % change 1990-92: 2.9.

History: inc. 1925; residential suburb NW of Miami; Hialeah Park horse racing track.

Transportation: Miami Int'l. airport is 5 miles away; Amtrak; 2 rail freight lines. **Communications:** NA. **Medical facilities:** 4 hospitals. **Educational facilities:** 5 universities and colleges. **Further information:** Hialeah-Dade Development, Inc., 501 Palm Ave., Hialeah, FL 33010.

Honolulu, Hawaii

Population: 365,272; **Pop. density:** 613 per sq. mi.; **Pop. growth:** 0.1%. **Area:** 596 sq. mi. **Employment (MSA):** 411,708 employed, 3.2% unemployed; **Per capita income:** $23,864; % change 1990-92: 8.4.

History: harbor entered by Europeans 1794; declared capital of kingdom by King Kamehameha III 1850; Pearl Harbor naval base attacked by Japanese Dec. 7, 1941.

Transportation: 1 major airport; large, active port for passengers and cargo. **Communications:** 10 TV, 30 radio stations. **Medical facilities:** 39 hospitals. **Educational facilities:** 4 universities, 5 colleges; 165 public schools, 98 private schools. **Further information:** Visitors Bureau, 2270 Kalakaua Avenue, Honolulu, HI 96815.

Houston, Texas

Population: 1,629,902; **Pop. density:** 2,933 per sq. mi.; **Pop. growth:** 2.2%. **Area:** 556 sq. mi. **Employment:** 866,320 employed, 8.8% unemployed; **Per capita income:** $21,737; % change 1990-92: 10.1.

History: founded 1836; inc. 1837; capital of Republic of Texas 1837-39; developed rapidly after completion of canal to Gulf of Mexico 1914; important oil and natural gas center.

Transportation: 3 commercial airports; 4 mainline railroads; major bus transit system; major international port. **Communications:** 11 TV, 53 radio stations. **Medical facilities:** 66 hospitals; major medical center. **Educational facilities:** 26 universities and colleges. **Further information:** Greater Houston Partnership, 1200 Smith St., Houston, TX 77002-4309.

Huntington Beach, California

Population: 181,519; **Pop. density:** 6,723 per sq. **Pop. growth:** 6.5%. **Area:** 27 sq. mi. **Employment**. mi.;: 102,961 employed, 5.1% unemployed; **Per capita income:** $21,434; % change 1990-92: 3.3.

History: settled in early 1880s; inc. 1909; oil discovered 1920, led to city's development.

Transportation: 1 railroad; 2 bus lines. **Communications:** 1 TV station. **Medical facilities:** 2 hospitals. **Educational facilities:** 1 junior college; 45 public schools. **Further information:** Chamber of Commerce, Seacliff Office Park, 2100 Main #200, Huntington Beach, CA 92648.

Indianapolis, Indiana

Population: 731,327; **Pop. density:** 2,108 per sq. mi.; **Pop. growth:** 4.3%. **Area:** 352 sq. mi. **Employment:** 379,705 employed, 4.9% unemployed; **Per capita income:** $20,992; % change 1990-92: 9.1.

History: settled 1820; became capital 1825.

Transportation: 1 international airport; 5 railroads; 3 interstate bus lines. **Communications:** 10 TV, 27 radio stations. **Medical facilities:** 17 hospitals; 1 major medical and research center. **Educational facilities:** 8 universities and colleges; major public library system. **Further information:** Chamber of Commerce, 320 N. Meridian Street, Indianapolis, IN 46204.

Jackson, Mississippi

Population: 196,637; **Pop. density:** 1,852 per sq. mi.; **Pop. growth:** -3.1%. **Area:** 106.2 sq. mi. **Employment:** 94,230 employed, 5.8% unemployed; **Per capita income:** $16,945; % change 1990-92: 10.4.

History: originally known as Le Fleur's Bluff; selected as capital 1822 and named for Andrew Jackson; inc. 1823; scene of secession convention 1861; captured by Sherman 1863.

Transportation: 7 airlines; 2 bus lines; 3 railroads. **Communications:** 5 TV, 26 radio stations. **Medical facilities:** 14 hospitals including a VA facility. **Educational facilities:** 2 universities, 4 colleges; 7 public school districts. **Further information:** Metro Jackson Chamber of Commerce, P.O. Box 22548, Jackson, MS 39225-2548.

Jacksonville, Florida

Population: 635,230; **Pop. density:** 885 per sq. mi.; **Pop. growth:** 17.9%. **Area:** 760 sq. mi. **Employment:** 313,485 employed, 5.7% unemployed; **Per capita income:** $19,146; % change 1990-92: 6.3.

History: settled 1816 as Cowford; renamed after Andrew Jackson 1822; inc. 1832; rechartered 1851; scene of conflicts in Seminole and Civil wars.

Transportation: 1 international airport; 3 railroads; 2 interstate bus lines. **Communications:** 6 TV, 21 radio stations. **Medical facilities:** 14 hospitals. **Educational facilities:** 5 universities and colleges. **Further information:** Chamber of Commerce, 3 Independent Drive, P.O. Box 329, Jacksonville, FL 32201.

Jersey City, New Jersey

Population: 228,517; **Pop. density:** 17,313 per sq. mi.; **Pop. growth:** 2.2%. **Area:** 13.2 sq. mi. **Employment:** 97,252 employed, 12.1% unemployed; **Per capita income:** $21,359; % change 1990-92: 9.9.

History: site bought from Indians 1630; chartered as town by British 1668; scene of Revolutionary War conflict 1779; chartered under present name 1838; important station on Underground Railroad.

Transportation: bus and subway system. **Medical facilities:** 7 hospitals. **Educational facilities:** 3 colleges. **Further information:** Hudson County Chamber of Commerce, 574 Summit Ave., Ste. 404, Jersey City, NJ 07306.

Kansas City, Missouri

Population: 434,829; **Pop. density:** 1,377 per sq. mi.; **Pop. growth:** -2.9%. **Area:** 316 sq. mi. **Employment:** 219,625 employed, 7.0% unemployed; **Per capita income:** $20,948; % change 1990-92: 9.5.

History: settled by 1838 at confluence of the Missouri and Kansas rivers; inc. 1851.

Transportation: 1 international airport; a major rail center; 191 trunk lines; several barge companies. **Communications:** 7 TV, 29 radio stations. **Medical facilities:** 14 hospitals; VA facility. **Educational facilities:** 9 universities and colleges. **Further information:** Greater Kansas City Chamber of Commerce, 911 Main St., Ste. 2600, Kansas City, MO 64105.

Las Vegas, Nevada

Population: 258,204; **Pop. density:** 4,696 per sq. mi.; **Pop. growth:** 56.9%. **Area:** 55 sq. mi. **Employment:** 155,651 employed, 7.1% unemployed; **Per capita income:** $19,994; % change 1990-92: 5.6.

History: occupied by Mormons 1855-57; bought by railroad 1903; city of Las Vegas inc. 1911; gambling legalized 1931.

Transportation: 1 international airport; 2 railroads; bus system. **Communcations:** 7 TV, 33 radio stations. **Medical facilities:** 9 hospitals. **Educational facilities:** 1 university, 1 college; 181 public schools. **Further information:** Chamber of Commerce, 711 E. Desert Inn Rd., Las Vegas, NV 89109.

Lexington, Kentucky

Population: 225,366; **Pop. density:** 794 per sq. mi.; **Pop. growth:** 10.4%. **Area:** 284 sq. mi. **Employment:** 128,912 employed, 3.5% unemployed; **Per capita income:** $18,893; % change 1990-92: 8.9.

History: site was founded and named 1775 by hunters who heard of the Revolutionary War battle at Lexington, Mass.; settled 1779; inc. 1832.

Transportation: 8 airlines; 2 railroads; city buses. **Communications:** 5 TV, 9 radio stations. **Medical facilities:** 5 general, 5 specialized hospitals. **Educational facilities:** 2 universities, 2 colleges. **Further information:** Chamber of Commerce, 330 East Main, Lexington, KY 40507.

Lincoln, Nebraska

Population: 191,972; **Pop. density:** 3,200 per sq. mi.; **Pop. growth:** 11.7%. **Area:** 60 sq. mi. **Employment:** 114,222 employed, 2.4% unemployed; **Per capita income:** $18,995; % change 1990-92: 10.2.

History: originally called Lancaster; chosen state capital 1867 and renamed after Abraham Lincoln; inc. 1869.

Transportation: 1 airport; Greyhound; Amtrak, 2 railroads. **Communications:** 1 TV, 13 radio stations. **Medical facilities:** 4 hospitals including a VA facility. **Educational facilities:** 2 universities, 1 college; 46 public, 15 private schools. **Further information:** Chamber of Commerce, 1221 N St., Lincoln, NE 68508.

Little Rock, Arkansas

Population: 175,727; **Pop. density:** 2,225 per sq. mi.; **Pop. growth:** 10.5%. **Area:** 79 sq. mi. **Employment:** 94,784 employed, 4.6% unemployed; **Per capita income:** $18,650; % change 1990-92: 13.2.**History:** founded 1821; inc. as city 1835.

Transportation: 1 airport, 8 airlines; 3 railroads; 1 bus line. **Communications:** 7 TV, 36 radio stations. **Medical facilities:** 20 hospitals; veterans' medical center. **Educational facilities:** 8 universities and colleges, Univ. of Arkansas; 51 public schools. **Further information:** Chamber of Commerce, One Spring St., Little Rock, AR 72201.

Long Beach, California

Population: 429,321; **Pop. density:** 8,589 per sq. mi.; **Pop. growth:** 18.8%. **Area:** 50 sq. mi. **Employment:** 186,708 employed, 9.0% unemployed; **Per capita income:** $21,434; % change 1990-92: 3.3.

History: settled as early as 1769 by Spanish; by 1884 present site developed due to its harbor; inc. 1888; oil discovered 1921.

Transportation: 1 airport; 3 railroads; major international port; 6 bus lines, "lite" rail service. **Communications:** 4 radio stations. **Medical facilities:** 10 hospitals. **Educational facilities:** 1 university, 1 college; 78 public schools. **Further information:** Chamber of Commerce, One World Trade Center, Long Beach, CA 90831.

Los Angeles, California

Population: 3,485,557; **Pop. density:** 7,495 per sq. mi.; **Pop. growth:** 17.4%. **Area:** 465 sq. mi. **Employment:** 1,582,270 employed, 10.9% unemployed; **Per capita income:** $21,434; % change 1990-92: 3.3.

History: founded by Spanish 1781; captured by U.S. 1846; inc. 1850; Hollywood a district of L.A.

Transportation: 1 international airport; 4 railroads;

major freeway system; intracity transit system. **Communications:** 19 TV, 71 radio stations. **Medical facilities:** 822 hospitals and clinics in metropolitan area. **Educational facilities:** 11 universities and colleges; 1,642 public schools; 800 private schools. **Further information:** Chamber of Commerce, 404 S. Bixel St., P.O. Box 3696, Los Angeles, CA 90051.

Louisville, Kentucky

Population: 269,555; **Pop. density:** 4,484 per sq. mi.; **Pop. growth:** -9.9%. **Area:** 60 sq. mi. **Employment:** 122,038 employed, 5.8% unemployed; **Per capita income:** $20,211; % change 1990-92: 11.1.

History: settled 1778; named for Louis XVI of France; inc. 1828; base for Union forces in Civil War.

Transportation: 2 municipal airports; 1 terminal, 4 trunk-line railroads; 2 bus lines; 5 barge lines. **Communications:** 4 TV, 21 radio stations, 2 educational. **Medical facilities:** 21 hospitals. **Educational facilities:** 10 universities and colleges, 9 business colleges and technical schools. **Further information:** Louisville Area Chamber of Commerce, 600 W. Main, Louisville, KY 40202.

Lubbock, Texas

Population: 186,206; **Pop. density:** 2,069 per sq. mi.; **Pop. growth:** 6.8%. **Area:** 90 sq. mi. **Employment:** 94,297 employed, 5.2% unemployed; **Per capita income:** $17,185; % change 1990-92: 8.8.

History: settled 1879; inc. 1909 through merger of two towns.

Transportation: 1 international airport; 2 railroads, bus line. **Communications:** 5 TV, 18 radio stations. **Medical facilities:** 7 hospitals. **Educational facilities:** 2 universities, 1 college; 51 public schools. **Further information:** Chamber of Commerce, P.O. Box 561, Lubbock, TX 79408.

Madison, Wisconsin

Population: 190,766; **Pop. density:** 3,188 per sq. mi.; **Pop. growth:** 12.1%. **Area:** 60 sq. mi. **Employment:** 119,733 employed, 2.3% unemployed; **Per capita income:** $21,883; % change 1990-92: 10.3.

History: first white settlement 1832; named after James Madison who died in 1836; chartered 1856.

Transportation: 1 airport, 9 airlines; 2 railroads; intercity and intracity bus systems. **Communications:** 5 TV, 19 radio stations. **Medical facilities:** 5 hospitals. **Educational facilities:** 3 colleges and universities, Univ. of Wisconsin; 43 public schools. **Further information:** Chamber of Commerce, P.O. Box 71, Madison, WI 53701.

Memphis, Tennessee

Population: 610,337; **Pop. density:** 2,312 per sq. mi.; **Pop. growth:** -5.5%. **Area:** 264 sq. mi. **Employment:** 265,963 employed, 6.5% unemployed; **Per capita income:** $19,517; % change 1990-92: 9.5.

History: French, Spanish, and U.S. forts by 1797; settled by 1819; inc. as town 1826, as city 1840; surrendered charter to state 1879 after yellow fever epidemics; rechartered as city 1893.

Transportation: 1 international airport; 6 railroads; bus system. **Communications:** 6 TV, 29 radio stations. **Medical facilities:** 23 hospitals. **Educational facilities:** 12 universities and colleges; 205 public, 76 private schools. **Further information:** Memphis Area Chamber of Commerce, 22 N. Front St., Box 224, Memphis, TN 38101.

Mesa, Arizona

Population: 288,104; **Pop. density:** 4,237 per sq. mi.; **Pop. growth:** 89.0%. **Area:** 68 sq. mi. **Employment:** 143,234 employed, 4.3% unemployed; **Per capita income:** $19,018; % change 1990-92: 6.2.

History: founded by Mormons 1878; inc. 1883; 15 mi. from Phoenix; population boomed fivefold 1960-80.

Transportation: near Sky Harbor international airport in Phoenix; 2 railroads; trolley and bus lines. **Medical facilities:** 4 major hospitals. **Educational facilities:** 1 university, 1 college; 63 public schools. **Further information:** Convention and Visitor's Bureau, 120 N. Center, Mesa, AZ 85201.

Miami, Florida

Population: 358,648; **Pop. density:** 10,546 per sq. mi.; **Pop. growth:** 3.4%. **Area:** 34 sq. mi. **Employment:** 158,042 employed, 11.1% unemployed; **Per capita income:** $17,124; % change 1990-92: -2.9.

History: site of fort 1836; settlement began 1870; inc. 1896 and modern city developed into resort and recreation center; land speculation 1920s added to city's growth, as did Cuban, Central, and South American, and Haitian immigration since 1960.

Transportation: 1 international airport; Amtrak, transit rail system; 2 bus lines; 65 truck lines. **Communications:** 9 commercial, 2 educational TV stations; 41 radio stations. **Medical facilities:** 36 hospitals, VA Hospital. **Educational facilities:** 6 universities and colleges. **Further information:** Metro-Dade Planning Dept., Research Div., III NW 1st St., Ste. 1220, Miami, FL 33128.

Milwaukee, Wisconsin

Population: 628,088; **Pop. density:** 6,543 per sq. mi.; **Pop. growth:** -1.3%. **Area:** 96 sq. mi. **Employment:** 273,868 employed, 6.2% unemployed; **Per capita income:** $21,797; % change 1990-92: 9.4.

History: Indian trading post by 1674; settlement began 1835; inc. as city 1848; famous beer industry.

Transportation: 1 international airport; 2 railroads; major port; 4 bus lines. **Communications:** 12 TV, 34 radio stations. **Medical facilities:** 24 hospitals; major medical center. **Educational facilities:** 12 universities and colleges. **Further information:** Association of Commerce, 756 N. Milwaukee Street, Milwaukee, WI 53202.

Minneapolis, Minnesota

Population: 368,383; **Pop. density:** 6,698 per sq. mi.; **Pop. growth:** -0.7%. **Area:** 55 sq. mi. **Employment:** 194,268 employed, 4.8% unemployed; **Per capita income:** $23,284; % change 1990-92: 8.7.

History: site visited by Hennepin 1680; included in area of military reservations 1819; inc. 1867.

Transportation: 1 international airport; 6 railroads; mass transit systems; 5 major barge lines. **Communicaions:** 6 TV, 39 radio stations. **Medical facilities:** 36 hospitals, including leading heart hospital at Univ. of Minnesota. **Educational facilities:** 13 universities and colleges; 48 public school districts. **Further information:** Greater Minneapolis Chamber of Commerce, 81 S. 9th St., Ste. 200, Minneapolis, MN 55402.

Mobile, Alabama

Population: 196,263; **Pop. density:** 1,596 per sq. mi.; **Pop. growth:** -2.1%. **Area:** 123 sq. mi. **Employment:** 90,665 employed, 8.9% unemployed; **Per capita income:** $15,806; % change 1990-92: 11.8.

History: settled by French 1711; later occupied by U.S. 1813; inc. as town 1814, as city 1819; only seaport of Alabama.

Transportation: 4 rail freight lines, Amtrak; 6 airlines; 65 truck lines; leading river system. **Communications:** 8 TV, 22 radio stations. **Medical facilities:** 7 hospitals. **Educational facilities:** 1 university, 3 colleges. **Further information:** Chamber of Commerce, P.O. Box 2187, Mobile, AL 36652.

Montgomery, Alabama

Population: 187,543; **Pop. density:** 1,462 per sq. mi.; **Pop. growth:** 5.2%. **Area:** 128 sq. mi. **Employment:** 87,742 employed, 6.4% unemployed; **Per capita income:** $17,931; % change 1990-92: 9.2.

History: inc. as town 1819, as city 1837; first capital of Confederacy 1861.

Transportation: 5 airlines; 2 railroads; 4 bus lines; Alabama River is navigable to Gulf of Mexico. **Communications:** 7 TV, 16 radio stations. **Medical facilities:** 10

hospitals; VA and 32 clinics. **Educational facilities:** 5 universities; 49 public, 31 private schools. **Further information:** Chamber of Commerce, P.O. Box 79, Montgomery, AL 36101.

Nashville, Tennessee

Population: 516,880; **Pop. density:** 984 per sq. mi.; **Pop. growth:** 6.9%. **Area:** 525 sq. mi. **Employment:** 262,162 employed, 4.0% unemployed; **Per capita income:** $20,569; % change 1990-92: 12.2.

History: settled 1779; first chartered 1806; home of the Grand Ole Opry.

Transportation: 1 airport; 1 railroad; bus line; transit system of buses and trolleys. **Communications:** 7 TV, 30 radio stations. **Medical facilities:** 14 hospitals; VA Hospital, speech-hearing center. **Educational facilities:** 16 universities and colleges. **Further information:** Chamber of Commerce, 161 4th Ave., Nashville, TN 37219.

Newark, New Jersey

Population: 275,221; **Pop. density:** 11,468 per sq. mi.; **Pop. growth:** -16.4%. **Area:** 24 sq. mi. **Employment:** 99,414 employed, 14.9% unemployed; **Per capita income:** $27,039; % change 1990-92: 9.6.

History: settled by Puritans 1666; used as supply base by Washington 1776; inc. as town 1833, as city 1836.

Transportation: 1 international airport; 2 railroads; bus system; 2 subways. **Communications:** 3 TV, 5 radio stations within city limits. **Medical facilities:** 6 hospitals. **Educational facilities:** 5 universities and colleges; 71 public schools. **Further information:** Regional Business Partnership, 1 Newark Center, Newark, NJ 07102-5265.

New Orleans, Louisiana

Population: 496,938; **Pop. density:** 2,497 per sq. mi.; **Pop. growth:** -10.9%. **Area:** 199 sq. mi. **Employment:** 184,586 employed, 7.2% unemployed; **Per capita income:** $18,087; % change 1990-92: 10.4.

History: founded by French 1718; became major seaport on Mississippi R.; acquired by U.S. as part of La. Purchase 1803; inc. as city 1805; Battle of New Orleans was last battle of War of 1812.

Transportation: 2 airports; major railroad center; major international port. **Communications:** 7 TV, 18 radio stations. **Medical facilities:** numerous hospitals; major medical research center. **Educational facilities:** 13 universities and colleges. **Further information:** Chamber of Commerce, 301 Camp Street, New Orleans, LA 70130.

Newport News, Virginia

Population: 171,439; **Pop. density:** 2,464 per sq. mi.; **Pop. growth:** 17.4%. **Area:** 69 sq. mi. **Employment:** 77,851 employed, 6.1% unemployed; **Per capita income:** $18,077; % change 1990-92: 8.0.

History: the cities of Warwick and Newport News consolidated in 1958 into the larger city of Newport News; one of the world's major shipbuilding centers.

Transportation: 1 international airport; 2 railroads; Greyhound buses; local bus system. **Communications:** 7 TV, 20 radio stations received in area. **Medical facilities:** 3 hospitals; adolescent psychiatry hospital. **Educational facilities:** 33 public schools. **Further information:** Virginia Peninsula Chamber of Commerce, Six Manhattan Sq., P.O. Box 7269, Hampton, VA 23666.

New York City, New York

Population: 7,322,564; **Pop. density:** 24,327 per sq. mi.; **Pop. growth:** 3.5%. **Area:** 301 sq. mi. **Employment:** 2,936,000 employed, 10.2% unemployed; **Per capita income:** $27,039; % change 1990-92: 9.6.

History: trading post established by H. Hudson 1609; British took control from Dutch 1664 and named New York; briefly capital of U.S.; Washington inaugurated as president 1789; composed of 5 boroughs: The Bronx, Brooklyn, Manhattan, Queens, Staten Island.

Transportation: 2 airports; 2 rail terminals; major subway network; ferry system; 4 underwater tunnels. **Communications:** 13 TV, 117 radio stations. **Medical facilities:** 100 hospitals; 5 medical research centers. **Educational facilities:** 94 universities and colleges; 976 public schools, 914 private schools. **Further information:** Convention and Visitors Bureau, 2 Columbus Circle, New York, NY 10019.

Norfolk, Virginia

Population: 261,250; **Pop. density:** 4,929 per sq. mi.; **Pop. growth:** -2.2%. **Area:** 53 sq. mi. **Employment:** 88,212 employed, 6.3% unemployed; **Per capita income:** $18,077; % change 1990-92: 8.0.

History: founded 1682; burned by patriots to prevent capture by British during Revolutionary War; rebuilt and inc. as town 1805, as city 1845; location of world's largest naval base.

Transportation: 1 international airport; Amtrak; bus system. **Communications:** 7 TV, 42 radio stations. **Medical facilities:** 11 hospitals. **Educational facilities:** 2 universities, 1 college, 1 medical school; 58 public schools. **Further information:** Hampton Roads Chamber of Commerce, 420 Bank St., P.O. Box 327, Norfolk, VA 23501.

Oakland, California

Population: 372,242; **Pop. density:** 6,893 per sq. mi.; **Pop. growth:** 9.7%. **Area:** 54 sq. mi. **Employment:** 160,202 employed, 10.4% unemployed; **Per capita income:** $24,359; % change 1990-92: 4.4.

History: area settled by Spanish 1820; inc. as city under present name 1854.

Transportation: 1 international airport; western terminus for 3 railroads; underground, underwater 75-mile subway. **Communications:** 1 TV, 3 radio stations within city limits. **Medical facilities:** 7 hospitals, including Children's Hospital Medical Center, VA hospital. **Educational facilities:** 8 "eastbay" colleges and universities; 94 public schools. **Further information:** Chamber of Commerce, 475 14th St., Oakland, CA 94612-1903.

Oklahoma City, Oklahoma

Population: 444,724; **Pop. density:** 736 per sq. mi.; **Pop. growth:** 10.1%. **Area.** 604 sq. mi. **Employment:** 218,322 employed, 5.7% unemployed; **Per capita income:** $17,645; % change 1990-92: 7.9.

History: settled during landrush in Midwest 1889; inc. 1890; oil discovered 1928.

Transportation: 1 international airport; 3 railroads; public transit system; 5 major bus lines. **Communications:** 8 TV, 24 radio stations. **Medical facilities:** 12 hospitals, VA hospital. **Educational facilities:** 17 universities and colleges; 83 public schools, 37 private schools. **Further information:** Chamber of Commerce, Economic Development Division, 123 Park Ave., Oklahoma City, OK 73102.

Omaha, Nebraska

Population: 335,719; **Pop. density:** 3,690 per sq. mi.; **Pop. growth:** 7.0%. **Area:** 91 sq. mi. **Employment:** 177,600 employed, 3.1% unemployed; **Per capita income:** $20,242; % change 1990-92: 9.6.

History: founded 1854; inc. 1857; large food-processing and telecommunications center; home for U.S. Strategic Air Command.

Transportation: 8 major airlines; 4 major railroads; intercity bus line. **Communications:** 8 TV, 22 radio stations. **Medical facilities:** 16 hospitals; institute for cancer research. **Educational facilities:** 3 universities, 6 colleges; 216 public, 82 private schools. **Further information:** Chamber of Commerce, 1301 Harney St., Omaha, NE 68102.

Philadelphia, Pennsylvania

Population: 1,585,577; **Pop. density:** 11,659 per sq. mi.; **Pop. growth:** -6.1%. **Area:** 136 sq. mi. **Employment:** 621,418 employed, 8.9% unemployed; **Per capita income:** $23,397; % change 1990-92: 8.8.

History: first settled by Swedes 1636; by English 1681; named Philadelphia 1682; chartered 1701; Continental Congresses convened 1774, 1775; Dec. of Independence signed 1776; national capital 1790-1800; cap. of Penn. 1683-1799.

Transportation: 1 major airport; 3 railroads; major freshwater port; subway, el, rail commuter, bus, and streetcar system. **Communications:** 6 TV, 53 radio stations. **Medical facilities:** 124 hospitals. **Educational facilities:** 88 degree-granting institutions. **Further information:** Office of City Representative, 1650 Arch St., 19th fl., Philadelphia, PA 19103.

Phoenix, Arizona

Population: 983,403; **Pop. density:** 3,035 per sq. mi.; **Pop. growth:** 24.5%. **Area:** 324 sq. mi. **Employment:** 508,280 employed, 5.6% unemployed; **Per capita income:** $19,018; % change 1990-92: 6.2.

History: settled 1870; inc. as city 1881.

Transportation: 1 international airport; 2 railroads; 2 transcontinental bus lines; public transit system. **Communications:** 11 TV, 40 radio stations. **Medical facilities:** 42 hospitals, 1 medical research center. **Educational facilities:** 12 institutions of higher learning; 161 public schools. **Further information:** Chamber of Commerce, 201 N. Central Ave. #2700, Phoenix, AZ 85004.

Pittsburgh, Pennsylvania

Population: 369,879; **Pop. density:** 6,725 per sq. mi.; **Pop. growth:** -12.8%. **Area:** 55 sq. mi. **Employment:** 156,891 employed, 6.7% unemployed; **Per capita income:** $21,175; % change 1990-92: 11.6.

History: settled around Ft. Pitt 1758; inc. as city 1816; has one of largest inland ports; by Civil War, already a center for iron production.

ransportation: 1 international airport; 20 railroads; 2 bus lines; trolley/subway system. **Communications:** 6 TV, 25 radio stations. **Medical facilities:** 32 hospitals; VA installation. **Educational facilities:** 3 universities, 6 colleges; 86 public schools. **Further information:** Chamber of Commerce, 3 Gateway Ctr., Pittsburgh, PA 15222.

Portland, Oregon

Population: 438,802; **Pop. density:** 4,246 per sq. mi.; **Pop. growth:** 18.8%. **Area:** 103 sq. mi. **Employment:** 240,033 employed, 6.9% unemployed; **Per capita income:** $20,681; % change 1990-92: 7.8.

History: settled by pioneers 1845; developed as trading center, aided by California Gold Rush 1849; chartered as city 1851.

Transportation: 1 international airport; 3 major rail freight lines, Amtrak; 2 intercity bus lines; 27-mi. frontage freshwater port; mass transit bus and rail system. **Communications:** 6 TV, 32 radio stations. **Medical facilities:** 20 hospitals; VA hospital. **Educational facilities:** 40 universities and colleges, 3 community colleges. **Further information:** Portland Metropolitan Chamber of Commerce, 221 N.W. 2nd Ave., Portland, OR 97209-3999.

Raleigh, North Carolina

Population: 212,092; **Pop. density:** 3,851 per sq. mi.; **Pop. growth:** 38.4%. **Area:** 54 sq. mi. **Employment:** 136,402 employed, 3.8% unemployed; **Per capita income:** $21,086; % change 1990-92: 8.6.

History: named after Sir Walter Raleigh; site chosen for capital 1788; laid out 1792; inc. 1795; occupied by Gen. Sherman 1865.

Transportation: 1 internatl. airport, 6 airlines; 3 railroads; 1 bus line. **Communications:** 6 TV, 20 radio stations. **Medical facilities:** 11 hospitals. **Educational facilities:** 4 universities and colleges, 4 junior colleges; 82 public schools. **Further information:** Chamber of Commerce, 800 S. Salisbury St., P.O. Box 2978, Raleigh, NC 27602.

Richmond, Virginia

Population: 202,798; **Pop. density:** 3,384 per sq. mi.; **Pop. growth:** -7.4%. **Area:** 60 sq. mi. **Employment:** 97,423 employed, 6.3% unemployed; **Per capita income:** $22,303; % change 1990-92: 4.6.

History: first settled 1607; attacked by British under Benedict Arnold 1781; inc. as city 1782; capital of Confederate States of America, 1861-65.

Transportation: 1 international airport; 4 railroads; 3 intracity bus lines; deepwater terminal accessible to oceangoing ships. **Communications:** 6 TV, 26 radio stations. **Medical facilities:** Medical Coll. of Virginia renowned for heart and kidney transplants; 19 other hospitals including VA facility. **Educational facilities:** 9 universities and colleges; 173 public, 45 private schools. **Further information:** Chamber of Commerce, P.O. Box 12324, Richmond, VA 23241.

Riverside, California

Population: 226,546; **Pop. density:** 3,190 per sq. mi.; **Pop. growth:** 32.8%. **Area:** 71 sq. mi. **Employment:** 108,222 employed, 11.6% unemployed; **Per capita income:** $17,021; % change 1990-92: 0.7.

History: founded 1870; inc. 1886; known for its citrus industry.

Communications: 11 TV, 13 radio stations. **Educational facilities:** 3 universities, 1 community college. **Further information:** Chamber of Commerce, 3685 Main St., Ste. 350, Riverside, CA 92501.

Rochester, New York

Population: 230,356; **Pop. density:** 6,813 per sq. mi.; **Pop. growth:** -4.2%. **Area:** 34 sq. mi. **Employment:** 105,538 employed, 7.8% unemployed; **Per capita income:** $21,217; % change 1990-92: 6.3.

History: first permanent white settlement 1812; inc. as village 1817, as city 1834; developed as Erie Canal town.

Transportation: 1 airport; Amtrak; 3 bus lines; intracity transit service; Port of Rochester. **Communications:** 5 TV, 18 radio stations. **Medical facilities:** 8 general hospitals. **Educational facilities:** 10 colleges, 3 community colleges. **Further information:** Chamber of Commerce, 55 St. Paul St., Rochester, NY 14604.

Sacramento, California

Population: 369,365; **Pop. density:** 3,848 per sq. mi.; **Pop. growth:** 34.0%. **Area:** 96 sq. mi. **Employment:** 160,712 employed, 10.1% unemployed; **Per capita income:** $20,398; % change 1990-92: 5.2.

History: settled 1839; important trading center during California Gold Rush 1840s.

Transportation: metropolitan airport; 2 mainline transcontinental rail carriers; bus and light rail system; Port of Sacramento. **Communications:** 7 TV, 25 radio stations. **Medical facilities:** 8 hospitals. **Educational facilities:** 2 universities, 4 community colleges. **Further information:** Chamber of Commerce, 917 7th St., P.O. Box 1017, Sacramento, CA 95812-1017.

St. Louis, Missouri

Population: 396,685; **Pop. density:** 6,503 per sq. mi.; **Pop. growth:** -12.4%. **Area:** 61 sq. mi. **Employment:** 156,097 employed, 9.3% unemployed; **Per capita income:** $21,700; % change 1990-92: 7.9.

History: founded 1764 as a fur trading post by French; acquired by U.S. 1803; chartered as city 1822; lies on Mississippi R., near confluence with Missouri R.

Transportation: 1 international airport; major rail center, 17 trunk-line railroads; major inland port; 14 bus lines; 14 barge lines. **Communications:** 7 TV, 35 radio stations. **Medical facilities:** 65 hospitals. **Educational facilities:** 6 universities, 25 colleges and seminaries. **Further information:** City Office, St. Louis Community Development Council, 330 N. 15th St., St. Louis, MO 63103.

St. Paul, Minnesota

Population: 272,235; **Pop. density:** 5,235 per sq. mi.; **Pop. growth:** 0.7%. **Area:** 52 sq. mi. **Employment:** 134,720 employed, 4.8% unemployed; **Per capita income:** $23,284; % change 1990-92: 8.7.

History: founded in early 1840s as "Pig's Eye Landing"; became capital of the Minnesota territory 1849 and chartered as St. Paul.

Transportation: 1 international airport; 6 major rail lines; 3 interstate bus lines; public transit system. **Communications:** 6 TV, 35 radio stations. **Medical facilities:** 7 hospitals. **Educational facilities:** 2 universities, 5 colleges. **Further information:** Chamber of Commerce, 55 E. 5th St., Norwest Ctr., Ste. 101, St. Paul, MN 55101.

St. Petersburg, Florida

Population: 240,318; **Pop. density:** 4,056 per sq. mi.; **Pop. growth:** 0.0%. **Area:** 59 sq. mi. **Employment:** 112,832 employed, 7.0% unemployed; **Per capita income:** $19,400; % change 1990-92: 8.0.

History: settled 1888; inc. 1892.

Transportation: 1 international airport; bus system; 1 full-service port. **Communications:** 12 TV, 22 radio stations. **Medical facilities:** 9 hospitals. **Educational facilities:** 6 colleges; 120 public schools. **Further information:** Chamber of Commerce, P.O. Box 1371, St. Petersburg, FL 33731.

San Antonio, Texas

Population: 935,393; **Pop. density:** 2,681 per sq. mi.; **Pop. growth:** 19.1%. **Area:** 349 sq. mi. **Employment:** 448,185 employed, 6.3% unemployed; **Per capita income:** $17,282; % change 1990-92: 10.9.

History: first Spanish garrison 1718; Battle at the Alamo fought here 1836; city subsequently captured by Texans; inc. 1837.

Transportation: 1 international airport; 4 railroads; 4 bus lines; public transit system. **Communications:** 8 TV, 33 radio stations. **Medical facilities:** 34 hospitals; major medical center. **Educational facilities:** 15 universities and colleges. **Further information:** Chamber of Commerce, 602 E. Commerce, P.O. Box 1628, San Antonio, TX 78296.

San Diego, California

Population: 1,110,554; **Pop. density:** 3,470 per sq. mi.; **Pop. growth:** 26.8%. **Area:** 320 sq. mi. **Employment:** 510,815 employed, 7.9% unemployed; **Per capita income:** $20,384; % change 1990-92: 3.3.

History: claimed by the Spanish 1542; first mission est. 1769; scene of conflict during Mexican-American War 1846; inc. 1850.

Transportation: 1 major airport; 1 railroad; major freeway system; bus system; trolley system. **Communications:** 8 TV, 22 radio stations. **Medical facilities:** 28 hospitals. **Educational facilities:** 5 universities, 7 colleges. **Further information:** Greater SD Chamber of Commerce, 402 W. Broadway, Suite 1000, San Diego, CA 92101-3585.

San Francisco, California

Population: 723,959; **Pop. density:** 15,403 per sq. mi.; **Pop. growth:** 6.6%. **Area:** 47 sq. mi. **Employment:** 374,711 employed, 7.2% unemployed; **Per capita income:** $31,262; % change 1990-92: 5.4.

History: nearby Farallon Islands sighted by Spanish 1542; city settled by 1776; claimed by U.S. 1846; became a major city during California Gold Rush 1849; inc. as city 1850; earthquake devastated city 1906.

Transportation: 1 major airport; intracity railway system; 2 railway transit systems; bus and railroad service; ferry system; 1 underwater tunnel. **Communications:** 14 TV and cable stations; 69 radio stations. **Medical facilities:** 23 hospitals; 1 major medical center. **Educational facilities:** 4 universities and colleges. **Further information:** Chamber of Commerce, 465 California Street, San Francisco, CA 94104.

San Jose, California

Population: 782,248; **Pop. density:** 4,951 per sq. mi.; **Pop. growth:** 24.3%. **Area:** 158 sq. mi. **Employment:** 395,320 employed, 7.9% unemployed; **Per capita income:** $25,924; % change 1990-92: 5.6.

History: founded by the Spanish 1777 between San Francisco and Monterey; briefly capital of Calif. 1849-51; inc. 1850.

Transportation: 1 international airport; 2 railroads; bus system. **Communications:** 4 TV, 14 radio stations. **Medical facilities:** 6 hospitals. **Educational facilities:** 3 universities and colleges. **Further information:** Chamber of Commerce, 180 S. Market St., San Jose, CA 95113.

Santa Ana, California

Population: 293,827; **Pop. density:** 10,879 per sq. mi.; **Pop. growth:** 44.0%. **Area:** 27 sq. mi. **Employment:** 133,722 employed, 11.7% unemployed; **Per capita income:** $24,651; % change 1990-92: 1.5.

History: founded 1869; inc. as city 1886.

Transportation: 1 airport; 5 major freeways including main Los Angeles-San Diego artery; Amtrak. **Communications:** NA. **Medical facilities:** 4 hospitals. **Educational facilities:** 1 community college. **Further information:** Chamber of Commerce, 801 Civic Center Dr. W., Ste. 110, Santa Ana, CA 92701.

Seattle, Washington

Population: 516,259; **Pop. density:** 6,146 per sq. mi.; **Pop. growth:** 4.5%. **Area:** 84 sq. mi. **Employment:** 292,604 employed, 7.4% unemployed; **Per capita income:** $25,769; % change 1990-92: 12.2.

History: settled 1851; inc. 1869; suffered severe fire 1889; played prominent role during Alaska Gold Rush 1897; growth followed opening of Panama Canal 1914; center of aircraft industry WWII.

Transportation: 1 international airport; 2 railroads; ferries serve Puget Sound, Alaska, Canada. **Communications:** 7 TV, 39 radio stations. **Medical facilities:** 40 hospitals. **Educational facilities:** 7 universities, 6 colleges, 11 community colleges. **Further information:** Greater Seattle Chamber of Commerce, 600 University St., Ste. 1200, Seattle, WA 98101-3186.

Shreveport, Louisiana

Population: 198,518; **Pop. density:** 2,482 per sq. mi.; **Pop. growth:** -4.1%. **Area:** 80 sq. mi. **Employment:** 83,431 employed, 6.9% unemployed; **Per capita income:** $17,061; % change 1990-92: 13.9.

History: founded 1833 near site of a 160-mile log jam cleared by Capt. Henry Shreve; inc. 1839; oil discovered 1906.

Transportation: 2 airports; 2 bus lines. **Communications:** 5 TV, 16 radio stations. **Medical facilities:** 13 hospitals. **Educational facilities:** 4 universities, 3 colleges. **Further information:** Chamber of Commerce, P.O. Box 20074, Shreveport, LA 71120.

Spokane, Washington

Population: 177,165; **Pop. density:** 3,408 per sq. mi.; **Pop. growth:** 3.4%. **Area:** 52 sq. mi. **Employment:** 82,943 employed, 7.2% unemployed; **Per capita income:** $18,069; % change 1990-92: 10.7.

History: settled 1872; inc. as village of Spokane Falls 1881 but destroyed in fire 1889; reinc. as city of Spokane 1891.

Transportation: 1 international airport; 2 railroads; bus system. **Communications:** 5 TV, 25 radio stations. **Medical facilities:** 6 major hospitals. **Educational facilities:** 8 universities and colleges; 14 public school districts, 11 high schools. **Further information:** Chamber of Commerce, W. 1020 Riverside Ave., P.O. Box 2147, Spokane, WA 99210.

Stockton, California

Population: 210,943; **Pop. density:** 5,274 per sq. mi.; **Pop. growth:** 42.3%. **Area:** 40 sq. mi. **Employment:** 84,523 employed, 15.5% unemployed; **Per capita income:** $16,942; % change 1990-92: 4.7.

History: site purchased 1842; settled 1847; inc. 1850; chief distributing point for agricultural products of San Joaquin Valley.

Transportation: 1 airport, 7 railroads; 2 bus lines, city bus system. **Communications:** 5 TV stations. **Medical facilities:** 4 hospitals; regional burn, cancer, and heart centers. **Educational facilities:** 6 universities and colleges; 45 public schools. **Further information:** Chamber of Commerce, 445 W. Weber Ave., Suite 220, Stockton, CA 95203.

Tacoma, Washington

Population: 176,664; **Pop. density:** 3,696 per sq. mi.; **Pop. growth:** 11.5%. **Area:** 47.8 sq. mi. **Employment:** 79,889 employed, 8.6% unemployed; **Per capita income:** $18,361; % change 1990-92: 8.0.

History: area explored 1792 by the British; first permanent settlement 1864; terminus for the Northern Pacific Railroad; inc. 1884.

Transportation: 1 internatl. airport; 2 railroads; transit system; Port of Tacoma. **Communications:** 6 TV stations. **Medical facilities:** 7 hospitals, Army Medical Center, VA facility. **Educational facilities:** 3 universities, 2 colleges. **Further information:** Chamber of Commerce, P.O. Box 1933, Tacoma, WA 98401-1933.

Tampa, Florida

Population: 280,015; **Pop. density:** 3,334 per sq. mi.; **Pop. growth:** 3.1%. **Area:** 84 sq. mi. **Employment:** 137,068 employed, 8.0% unemployed; **Per capita income:** $19,400; % change 1990-92: 8.0.

History: U.S. army fort on site 1824; inc. 1855.

Transportation: 1 international airport; Port of Tampa; bus system. **Communications:** 7 TV, 27 radio stations. **Medical facilities:** 17 hospitals. **Educational facilities:** 4 universities and colleges; 183 public schools. **Further information:** Chamber of Commerce, 801 E. Kennedy Blvd., P.O. Box 420, Tampa, FL 33601.

Toledo, Ohio

Population: 332,943; **Pop. density:** 3,964 per sq. mi.; **Pop. growth:** -6.1%. **Area:** 84 sq. mi. **Employment:** 143,808 employed, 8.0% unemployed; **Per capita income:** $19,166; % change 1990-92: 9.0.

History: site of Ft. Industry, 1794; settled 1817; figured in "Toledo War" 1835-36 between Ohio and Michigan over their borders; inc. 1837.

Transportation: 4 major airlines; 5 railroads; 100 motor freight lines; 2 interstate bus lines. **Communications:** 6 TV, 20 radio stations. **Medical facilities:** 9 major hospital complexes. **Educational facilities:** 6 universities and colleges. **Further information:** Greater Toledo Convention and Visitors Bureau, 401 Jefferson Ave., Toledo, OH 43604.

Tucson, Arizona

Population: 405,323; **Pop. density:** 4,095 per sq. mi.; **Pop. growth:** 22.6%. **Area:** 99 sq. mi. **Employment:** 196,967 employed, 4.8% unemployed; **Per capita income:** $16,651; % change 1990-92: 8.9.

History: settled 1775 by Spanish as a presidio; acquired by U.S. in Gadsden Purchase 1853; inc. 1877.

Transportation: 1 international airport; 3 railroads; bus system. **Communications:** 10 TV, 27 radio stations. **Medical facilities:** 13 hospitals. **Educational facilities:** 2 universities, 1 college; 165 public schools. **Further information:** Chamber of Commerce, P.O. Box 991, Tucson, AZ 85702.

Tulsa, Oklahoma

Population: 367,302; **Pop. density:** 1,979 per sq. mi.; **Pop. growth:** 1.8%. **Area:** 185.6 sq. mi. **Employment:** 189,878 employed, 6.5% unemployed; **Per capita income:** $18,681; % change 1990-92: 7.4.

History: settled in 1830s by Creek Indians; modern town founded 1882 and inc. 1898; oil discovered early 20th century.

Transportation: 1 international airport; 5 rail lines; 2 bus lines; transit bus system. **Communications:** 7 TV, 23 radio stations. **Medical facilities:** 9 hospitals. **Educational facilities:** 6 universities and colleges; 74 public, 25 private schools. **Further information:** Chamber of Commerce, 616 S. Boston Ave., Ste. 100, Tulsa, OK 74119-1298.

Virginia Beach, Virginia

Population: 393,089; **Pop. density:** 1,541 per sq. mi.; **Pop. growth:** 49.9%. **Area:** 255 sq. mi. **Employment:** 190,366 employed, 4.4% unemployed; **Per capita income:** $18,077; % change 1990-92: 8.0.

History: area founded by Capt. John Smith 1607; formed by merger with Princess Anne Co. 1963.

Transportation: 1 airport; 2 railroads; 2 bus lines; public transit system. **Communications:** 6 TV, 41 radio stations. **Medical facilities:** 2 hospitals. **Educational facilities:** 1 university, 2 colleges; 74 public schools. **Further information:** Virginia Beach Dept. of Economic Development, 780 Lynnhaven Parkway, Ste. 350, Virginia Beach, VA 23452.

Washington, District of Columbia

Population: 606,900; **Pop. density:** 9,633 per sq. mi.; **Pop. growth:** -4.9%. **Area:** 61 sq. mi. **Employment:** 280,000 employed, 8.5% unemployed; **Per capita income:** $26,817; % change 1990-92: 6.7.

History: capital of the U.S.; site at Potomac R. chosen by George Washington 1790 on land ceded from Va. and Md. (portion south of Potomac returned to Va. 1846); Congress first met 1800; inc. 1802; sacked by British, War of 1812.

Transportation: 3 airports; rail transit system; extensive local bus service; 1 bus, 2 rail lines. **Communications:** 5 TV, 61 radio stations. **Medical facilities:** 43 hospitals; major medical research center. **Educational facilities:** 10 universities and colleges. **Further information:** Convention and Visitors Association, 1301 Pennsylvania Ave. NW, Suite 309, Washington, DC 20004.

Wichita, Kansas

Population: 304,017; **Pop. density:** 3,010 per sq. mi.; **Pop. growth:** 8.6%. **Area:** 101 sq. mi. **Employment:** 160,492 employed, 6.0% unemployed; **Per capita income:** $20,589; % change 1990-92: 10.9.

History: founded 1864; inc. 1871.

Transportation: 2 airports; 3 major rail freight lines; 2 bus lines. **Communications:** 5 TV, 26 radio stations. **Medical facilities:** 7 hospitals, 2 psychiatric rehab. centers. **Educational facilities:** 2 universities, 2 colleges; 96 public schools. **Further information:** Chamber of Commerce, 350 W. Douglas, Wichita, KS 67202.

Yonkers, New York

Population: 188,082; **Pop. density:** 10,449 per sq. mi.; **Pop. growth:** -3.7%. **Area:** 18 sq. mi. **Employment:** 84,040 employed, 7.3% unemployed; **Per capita income:** $27,039; % change 1990-92: 9.6.

History: founded 1641 by the Dutch; inc. as town 1855; chartered as city 1872; borders NYC to the South.

Transportation: intracity bus system; rail service. **Communications:** see New York City. **Medical facilities:** 3 hospitals. **Educational facilities:** 1 college; 32 public schools. **Further information:** Chamber of Commerce, 540 Nepperhan Ave., Ste. 200, Yonkers, NY 10701.

BUILDINGS, BRIDGES, TUNNELS, AND DAMS

Notable Tall Buildings in North American Cities

Height from sidewalk to roof, including penthouse and tower if enclosed as integral part of structure; actual number of stories beginning at street level. Asterisk (*) denotes building still under construction. Year is date of completion.

Building	Ht. ft.	Stories
Albany, NY		
Erastus Corning II Tower	**589**	44
State Office Building	**388**	34
Atlanta, GA		
Nation's Bank Tower (1992)	**1,050**	57
One Peachtree Center (1992)	**880**	63
Atlantic Center/IBM (1988)	**828**	52
191 Peachtree (1990)	**770**	54
Westin Peachtree Plaza (1973)	**723**	71
Georgia Pacific Tower (1981)	**697**	51
Promenade II/AT&T (1989)	**691**	40
Southern Bell Telephone (1980)	**677**	47
GLG Grand/Occidental Hotel (1992)	**629**	53
Concourse Tower #5 (1988)	**570**	32
State of Georgia Tower (1968)	**556**	44
Marriott Marquis (1985)	**554**	52
Concourse Tower #6 (1991)	**553**	32
Equitable Building, 100 Peachtree (1967)	**453**	34
101 Marietta Tower, 101 Marietta (1975)	**446**	36
Ravinia #3 (1991)	**444**	34
AT&T Long Line Bldg. (1975)	**433**	...
Bell South Enterprises (1990)	**428**	28
Atlanta Plaza I (1986)	**425**	32
Park Place, 2660 Peachtree (1986)	**420**	40
Club Towers Apts. (1989)	**410**	38
34 Peachtree Bldg. (1961)	**409**	32
Peachtree Summit/Federal Bldg. (1975)	**406**	31
North Avenue Tower (1979)	**403**	26
Tower Place, 3361 Piedmont Rd. (1974)	**401**	29
First Union Bank (1987)	**396**	30
Richard B. Russell, Federal Bldg. (1978)	**383**	26
Atlanta Hilton Hotel (1974)	**383**	32
Peachtree Center, Harris Bldg. (1975)	**382**	31
*Hewlett-Packard Bldg. (1995)	**381**	27
Marquis One (1985)	**378**	30
Marquis Two (1987)	**378**	30
Trust Company Bank (1968)	**377**	28
260 Peachtree (1971)	**377**	27
Peachtree Center Cain Building (1972)	**376**	30
Peachtree Center Building (1966)	**374**	31
One Georgia Center (1966)	**371**	29
Mayfair Apts. Tower (1990)	**370**	34
The Campanile, 1145 Peachtree (1987)	**367**	25
Riverwood Tower(1989)	**362**	26
Austin, TX		
One American Center (1982)	**395**	32
One Congress Plaza (1987)	**391**	30
NCNB Tower (1975)	**328**	26
Baltimore, MD		
U.S. Fidelity & Guaranty Co.	**529**	40
Maryland National Bank Bldg.	**509**	34
6 St. Paul Place	**493**	37
World Trade Center Bldg.	**395**	32
Tremont Plaza Hotel	**395**	37
250 W Pratt St.	**360**	26
Harbor Court	**356**	28
Blaustein Bldg.	**342**	30
Union Trust Tower	**335**	24
Central Savings Bank Bldg.	**330**	28
Charles Center South	**330**	26
Baton Rouge, LA		
State Capitol (1932)	**460**	34
Hancock Bank Bldg. (1974)	**315**	24
Birmingham, AL		
Southtrust Tower (1986)	**454**	34
AmSouth/Harbert Plaza (1989)	**390**	30
AmSouth/Sonat Tower (1972)	**390**	30
South Central Bell HQ. Bldg.	**390**	30
City Federal Bldg. (1913)	**325**	27
Boston, MA		
John Hancock Tower	**790**	60
Prudential Center	**750**	52
Boston County Bldg., Court St.	**605**	41
Federal Reserve Bldg.	**604**	32
One International Place, 100 Oliver St.	**600**	46
First National Bank of Boston	**591**	37
One Financial Center	**590**	46
Two International Place	**538**	35
Shawmut Bank Bldg.	**520**	38
Exchange Place, 53 State St.	**510**	39
Sixty State St.	**509**	38
One Post Office Sq.	**507**	40
One Beacon St.	**507**	40
New England Merch. Bank Bldg.	**500**	40
U.S. Custom House	**496**	32
John Hancock Bldg.	**495**	26
State St. Bank Bldg.	**477**	34
125 High St. (1990)	**455**	30
One Hundred Summer St.	**450**	33
McCormack Bldg.	**401**	22
Keystone Custodian Funds	**400**	32
Saltonstall Office Bldg.	**396**	22
Devonshire, 250 Wash. St.	**396**	40
Harbor Towers (2 bldgs.)	**396**	40
Westin Hotel, Copley Place	**395**	36
Federal Center (1988)	**393**	28
75 State St. (1988)	**390**	31
John F. Kennedy Bldg.	**387**	24
Marriott Hotel, Copley Place	**383**	39
101 Federal St. (1988)	**382**	31
Longfellow Towers (2 bldgs.)	**380**	38
Buffalo, NY		
Marine Midland Center (1970)	**524**	38
Rand Bldg., incl. 40-ft. beacon (1929)	**351**	29
City Hall (1931)	**325**	30
Calgary, Alberta		
Petro-Canada Centre, W Tower (1984)	**689**	52
Bankers Hall (1989)	**645**	50
Calgary Tower (1988)	**626**	...
Canterra Tower (1988)	**580**	46
First Canadian Centre (1983)	**547**	44
Western Canadian Place - North Tower	**538**	41
Calgary Eatons Centre	**530**	40
Scotia Centre (1976)	**504**	38
Nova Bldg., 801 7th Ave. SW	**500**	37
Petro-Canada Centre, E Tower (1984)	**469**	33
Two Bow Valley Square (1974)	**468**	39
Fifth & Fifth Bldg.	**460**	35
Home Oil Tower	**463**	34
Canada Trust Tower (1991)	**462**	40
Shell Tower	**460**	34
Dome Oil Tower	**449**	33
Four Bow Valley Square (1982)	**441**	37
Esso Plaza (twin towers)	**435**	34
Oxford Square	**421**	33
Western Canadian Place - South Tower	**420**	32
Sovereign Life Bldg.	**410**	33
Pan Canadian Bldg., 150 9th Ave. SW.	**410**	28
Norcen Tower	**408**	33
Alberta Stock Exchange Bldg.	**407**	33
Suncor Building	**396**	32
Amoco Centre (1988)	**396**	30
Western Centre	**385**	40
Calgary Place	**385**	30
Three Bow Valley Square	**382**	33
Charlotte, NC		
NationsBank Corp. Center (1992)	**871**	60
One First Union Center (1988)	**580**	42
Nations Bank Plaza (1974)	**503**	40
Interstate Tower (1990)	**462**	32
Two First Union Center (1971)	**433**	32
Wachovia Center (1974)	**420**	32
Carillon (1991)	**394**	24
Charlotte Plaza (1982)	**388**	27
Chicago, IL		
Sears Tower (world's tallest) (1974)	**1,454**	110
Amoco (1973)	**1,136**	82
John Hancock Center (1969)	**1,127**	100
311 S. Wacker (1990)	**959**	70
Prudential Bldg., 130 E Randolph (1955) (including 311-ft. antenna tower)	**912**	41
Two Prudential Plaza (1990)	**901**	64
900 N Michigan (1989)	**871**	66
AT&T Corporate Center (1988)	**869**	60

Building	Ht. ft.	Stories
Water Tower Place (1976)	859	74
First Natl. Bank (1969)	850	60
Three First National Plaza (1981)	775	57
Olympia Centre (1986)	727	63
Leo Burnett Bldg. (1989)	700	46
IBM Plaza (1991)	695	52
One Magnificent Mile (1983)	673	58
Paine Webber Bldg., 181 W Madison	644	50
Daley Center (1965)	662	31
1,000 Lake Shore Plaza (1964)	648	55
Lake Point Tower (1968)	645	70
Board of Trade, incl. 81-ft. statue (1930)	605	44
CNA Plaza (1972)	600	44
Huron Apts.	599	56
Marina City Apts., 2 buildings	588	61
Mid Continental Plaza (1972)	580	50
Associates Center (1983)	575	41
Pittsfield, 55 E Washington St. (1927)	572	38
Onterie Center (1985)	570	58
Civic Opera Bldg. (1929)	555	45
Lincoln Tower, 75 E Wacker Dr. (1928)	554	42
Newberry Plaza, State & Oak (1974)	553	56
One South Wacker Dr. (1983)	550	40
Harbor Point (1975)	550	54
Madison Plaza (1982)	551	45
190 S LaSalle (1986)	550	40
LaSalle Natl. Bank (1934)	535	44
One N LaSalle Street (1930)	530	49
111 E Chestnut St. (1972)	529	56
Chicago Mercantile Exchange (2 bldgs)	525	40
River Plaza, Rush & Hubbard (1988)	524	56
35 E Wacker Drive (1926)	523	40
United Ins. Bldg., 1 E Wacker Dr. (1962)	522	41
Quaker Tower (1987)	518	35
Carbide & Carbon, 230 N Mich. (1929)	503	37
Walton Colonnade (1972)	500	44
Xerox Center (1980)	500	40
One Financial Place (1985)	498	40
LaSalle-Wacker, 221 N LaSalle St.	491	41
Amer. Nat'l. Bank, 33 N LaSalle St.	479	40
Bankers, 105 W Adams St. (1927)	476	41
Brunswick Bldg. (1965)	475	37
310 Center (1924)	475	37

Cincinnati, OH

Building	Ht. ft.	Stories
Carew Tower (1931)	568	49
PNC Center (1979)	504	33
312 Walnut St.	500	35
Dubois Tower, 5th & Walnut (1969)	423	32
Cincinnati Commerce Center (1984)	418	29
Chemed Center	411	31
Chiquita Center	391	29
Star Bank Center (1981)	351	26

Cleveland, OH

Building	Ht. ft.	Stories
Society Center (1991)	888	57
Terminal Tower (1930)	708	52
BP America (1985)	658	46
Plaza Tower at Erieview (1964)	529	40
One Cleveland Center (1983)	450	31
Bank One Center (1991)	446	28
Justice Center, 1250 Ontario (1976)	420	26
Federal Bldg. (1967)	419	32
National City Center (1980)	410	35
900 Euclid (1971)	383	29
Ohio-Bell (1927)	365	22
Cleveland St. J. A. Rhodes Tower (1971)	363	23
Eaton Center (1983)	360	28

Columbus, OH

Building	Ht. ft.	Stories
James A. Rhodes (State Office Tower)	629	41
LeVeque Tower, 50 W Broad	555	47
Ohio Bureau of Worker's Compensation & Ind. Comm. (1990)	530	33
Huntington Center, 41 S High St.	512	37
Verne-Riffe State Office Tower	503	33
One Nationwide Plaza	482	40
Franklin County Courthouse	464	27
One Riverside Plaza	456	31
Borden Bldg., 180 E Broad	438	34
Three Nationwide Plaza (1989)	408	27
One Columbus	366	26
Columbus Center, 100 E Broad	357	24

Dallas, TX

Building	Ht. ft.	Stories
National Bank Plaza (1985)	939	72
Bank One Center (1987)	787	60
Texas Commerce Tower (1987)	738	55
First Interstate Bank Tower (1986)	721	60
Renaissance Tower (1987)	710	56
Trammell Crow Center (1984)	686	50
First City Center (1984)	655	50
Thanksgiving Tower (1982)	645	50
First National Bank	625	52
Republic Bank Tower	598	50
SW Bell Admin. Tower	580	37
Lincoln Plaza (1984)	579	45
Olympia York Tower (1982)	562	36
Cityplace Center East (1988)	560	50
Southland Center Tower (1959)	550	42
Maxus Energy (1980)	550	34
2001 Bryan St. (1973)	512	40
San Jacinto Tower (1982)	456	33
NationsBank Center Tower 1 (1954)	452	36
Stouffer Hotel	451	29
Skyway Tower (1981)	448	31
One Main Place (1968)	445	34
1600 Pacific Bldg. (1964)	434	32
Magnolia Bldg. (1923)	430	27
Mart Hotel	400	29
Complex Union Tower	400	33

Dayton, OH

Building	Ht. ft.	Stories
Kettering Tower, 2d & Main (1970)	405	30
Mead World Hqtrs, 10 W 2d St. (1976)	385	28

Denver, CO

Building	Ht. ft.	Stories
Republic Plaza	714	56
Mountain Bell Center	709	54
United Bank of Denver	698	52
1999 Broadway	544	43
Arco Tower	527	41
Anaconda Tower	507	40
Amoco Bldg., 17th Ave. & Broadway	448	36
17th Street Plaza	438	35
Stellar Plaza	437	31
First Interstate Tower North	434	32
One Denver Place	428	34
Brooks Towers, 1020 15th St.	420	42
Tabor Center, #1	408	32
Manville Plaza	404	29
Colorado Nat'l. Bank, 17th & Curtis	389	26
First Interstate Tower South	385	28
1616 Glenarm Bldg.	384	33
Mellon Financial Center	374	31
Dominion Plaza	368	30
Lincoln Center	366	30
Denver Natl. Bank Plaza	363	29
Bank Western	357	27
Colorado State Bank	352	26

Des Moines, IA

Building	Ht. ft.	Stories
Principal Financial Group Bldg. (1990)	630	44
Ruan Center (1974)	457	35
Financial Center, 7th & Walnut (1973)	345	25
Marriott Hotel, 700 Grand Ave. (1981)	340	33
Plaza, 3d & Walnut (1984)	340	25

Detroit, MI

Building	Ht. ft.	Stories
Westin Hotel	720	71
One Detroit Center	620	45
Penobscot Bldg.	557	47
Guardian	485	40
Renaissance Center (4 bldgs.)	479	39
Book Tower	472	35
150 W Jefferson Bldg.	470	29
Prudential 3000 Town Center	448	32
Cadillac Tower	437	40
David Stott	436	38
ANR Bldg.	430	32
Fisher	420	28
J. L. Hudson Bldg.	397	28
McNamara Federal Office Bldg.	393	27
2000 Prudential Town Ctr.	392	28
American Center	374	27
Top of Troy Bldg.	374	27
Comerica Bldg., 211 N Fort	370	28
Edison Plaza	365	25
David Broderick Tower	358	34
1st National Bldg.	350	25

Edmonton, Alberta

Building	Ht. ft.	Stories
Manulife Place (1983)	479	36
AGT Tower (1971)	441	33
Canada Trust Tower (1982)	440	31
Commerce Place (1990)	409	30
Metropolitan Place (1980)	397	31
Oxford Tower (1978)	390	27

Building	Ht. ft.	Stories
TD Tower (1975)	**386**	27
Scotia Place (1983)	**366**	28
CN Tower (1966)	**365**	27
Phipps McKinnon (1977)	**359**	20

Fort Wayne, IN

Building	Ht. ft.	Stories
One Summit Square (1981)	**442**	26
Ft. Wayne Natl. Bank (1970)	**339**	26

Fort Worth, TX

Building	Ht. ft.	Stories
City Center Tower II (1984)	**546**	38
Burnett Plaza (1983)	**538**	40
Continental Plaza (1982)	**520**	40
Texas Commerce Tower(1982)	**475**	33
Bank One Tower (1974)	**457**	37
Texas Bldg. (1955)	**420**	31

Hartford, CT

Building	Ht. ft.	Stories
City Place (1983)	**535**	38
Travelers Ins. Co. Bldg. (1919)	**527**	34
Goodwin Square (1990)	**522**	30
Hartford Plaza (1967)	**420**	22
Shawmut Bank (1960)	**360**	26
One Commercial Plaza (1984)	**349**	28
Bushnell Tower (1969)	**349**	27

Honolulu, HI

Building	Ht. ft.	Stories
Imperial Plaza (1992)	**400**	40
Waterfront Towers (1990)	**400**	46
Nauru Tower (1991)	**400**	45
Ala Moana Hotel	**396**	38
Pacific Tower	**350**	30
Franklin Towers	**350**	41
Honolulu Tower	**350**	40
Discovery Bay	**350**	42
Hyatt Regency Waikiki	**350**	39
Maile Court Hotel	**350**	43
Regency Tower, 2525 Date St.	**350**	42
Pearlridge Square	**350**	43
Yacht Harbor Towers	**350**	40
Canterbury Place	**350**	40
Royal Iolani	**350**	38
Island Colony	**350**	44
Century Center	**350**	41
Pacific Beach Hotel	**350**	43
Hawaiian Monarch Hotel	**350**	43
Waikiki Hobron	**350**	43
Honolulu Tower 2	**350**	40
Tapa Tower, 2005 Kalia Rd.	**350**	36
Executive Center, 1088 Bishop St.	**350**	41
1001 Bishop	**350**	28

Houston, TX

Building	Ht. ft.	Stories
Texas Commerce Tower (1981)	**1,002**	75
First Interstate Plaza (1983)	**992**	71
Transco Tower (1983)	**901**	64
NationsBank Center (1983)	**780**	56
Heritage Plaza, 1111 Bagby	**762**	53
InterFirst Plaza (1980)	**744**	55
1600 Smith St. (1984)	**729**	54
Chevron Tower, 1301 McKinney (1982)	**725**	52
One Shell Plaza (not incl. 285-ft. TV tower) (1970)	**714**	50
Enron Bldg. (1983)	**692**	50
Capital Natl. Bank Plaza	**685**	50
One Houston Center (1978)	**678**	47
First City, Tex. Financial Center (1984)	**662**	47
1100 Milam Bldg. (1973)	**651**	47
San Felipe Plaza (1984)	**620**	45
Exxon Bldg. (1962)	**606**	44
The America Tower	**577**	42
Marathon Oil Tower (1983)	**572**	41
Two Houston Center (1974)	**570**	40
Kellogg Tower (1973)	**550**	40
1415 Louisiana Tower (1983)	**550**	44
Pennzoil, 700 Milam (2 bldgs.) (1975)	**523**	36
Two Allen Center (1978)	**521**	36
1201 Louisiana Bldg. (1971)	**518**	35
Huntington	**506**	34
Tenneco Bldg. (1962)	**502**	33
Conoco Tower (1973)	**465**	32
One Allen Center (1974)	**452**	34
Summit Tower West (1979)	**441**	31
Coastal Tower (1978)	**441**	31
Four Leafs Towers (2 bldgs.)	**439**	40
Phoenix Tower (1984)	**434**	34
Chevron Bldg.	**428**	37
The Spires	**426**	41
Central Tower (4 Oaks Place)	**420**	30
First City Natl. Bank (1960)	**410**	32
Houston Lighting & Power (1968)	**410**	27
Niels Esperson Bldg. (1927)	**409**	31
Hyatt Regency Houston (1972)	**401**	34

Indianapolis, IN

Building	Ht. ft.	Stories
Bank One Tower (1989)	**728**	51
AUL Tower (1981)	**533**	38
Market Tower (1988)	**515**	32
Indiana Natl. Bank Tower (1969)	**504**	35
Riley Towers (2 bldgs.) (1963)	**427**	30
300 N Meridian Bldg. (1988)	**408**	28

Jacksonville, FL

Building	Ht. ft.	Stories
Barnett Center (1990)	**617**	42
Independent Life Bldg. (1975)	**535**	37
Southern Bell (1983)	**447**	32
Gulf Life Tower (1967)	**432**	28
American Heritage Life (1989)	**357**	23

Kansas City, MO

Building	Ht. ft.	Stories
One Kansas City Place	**626**	42
AT&T Town Pavilion	**590**	38
Hyatt Regency	**504**	40
Kansas City Power and Light Bldg.	**476**	32
City Hall	**443**	29
Federal Office Bldg.	**413**	35
Commerce Tower	**402**	32
City Center Sq.	**402**	30
Southwest Bell Telephone Bldg.	**394**	27
Pershing Road Associates	**352**	28

Las Vegas, NV

Building	Ht. ft.	Stories
*Vegas World Tower	**771**	...
Landmark Hotel	**356**	31
Las Vegas Hilton	**345**	31

Lexington, KY

Building	Ht. ft.	Stories
Lexington Financial Center (1986)	**410**	30
Kincaid Tower (1980)	**333**	22

Little Rock, AK

Building	Ht. ft.	Stories
TCBY Towers (1986)	**546**	40
First Commercial Bank (1975)	**454**	30
Worthen Bank & Trust (1969)	**375**	24
Stephens Bldg. (1985)	**365**	35
Tower Bldg. (1960)	**350**	18

Los Angeles, CA

Building	Ht. ft.	Stories
First Interstate World Center (1989)	**1,017**	73
First Interstate Bank	**858**	62
California Plaza 11A	**750**	57
Wells Fargo Tower	**750**	54
Security Pacific Plaza	**735**	55
S California Gas Center (1990)	**733**	55
777 Tower	**725**	52
Mitsui Fudosan (1990)	**716**	52
Atlantic Richfield Tower	**699**	52
Bank of America Tower	**699**	52
444 S Flower St.	**625**	48
AT&T Bldg.	**620**	42
One California Plaza	**578**	42
Century Plaza Towers (2 bldgs.)	**571**	44
IBM Tower	**560**	45
Citicorp Plaza	**534**	42
1999 Ave. of the Stars (1989)	**533**	39
Manulife Tower (1990)	**517**	37
Union Bank Square	**516**	41
MCA-Getty	**506**	36
WTC Bldg.	**496**	36
Fox Plaza	**492**	34
ARCO Center	**462**	33
City Hall	**454**	28
Equitable Life Bldg.	**454**	34
Transamerica Center	**452**	32
Mutual Benefit Life Ins. Bldg.	**435**	31
Warner Center Plaza III	**415**	25
Broadway Plaza	**414**	33
1900 Ave. of Stars	**398**	27
One Wilshire Bldg.	**395**	28
The Evian	**390**	31
400 S Hope St.	**375**	26
Westin Bonaventure Hotel	**367**	35
Beaudry Center	**365**	29
California Fed. Savings & Loan Bldg.	**363**	28
Century City North	**363**	26
Home Savings Tower	**356**	25

Building	Ht. ft.	Stories
Louisville, KY		
First Natl. Bank (1972)	**512**	40
Citizen's Plaza (1971)	**420**	30
Humana Bldg.	**350**	27
Meidinger Tower (1982)	**338**	26
Brown & Williamson Tower (1982)	**338**	26
Memphis, TN		
100 N Main Bldg.	**430**	37
Commerce Square	**396**	31
Sterick Bldg.	**365**	31
Clark, 5100 Poplar	**365**	32
First Tennessee Bldg.	**332**	25
Miami, FL		
First Union Financial Center (1983)	**764**	55
International Place (1987)	**562**	35
Metro-Dade Administration Bldg.	**510**	30
Florida National Tower (1986)	**484**	35
One Biscayne Tower	**456**	38
Barnett Tower (1986)	**450**	33
Courthouse Center (1986)	**405**	30
Sunbank International Center (1973)	**375**	31
Bristol	**371**	41
Hotel Inter-Continental Miami	**366**	35
Venitia, 1635 Bayshore Dr.	**365**	42
Dade County Court House	**357**	28
Milwaukee, WI		
Firstar Center	**625**	42
100 E Wisconsin (1989)	**549**	37
Milwaukee Center	**425**	29
411 E Wisconsin	**385**	30
Northwestern Mutual Tower (1989)	**350**	19
City Hall	**350**	9
Minneapolis, MN		
IDS Center (1973)	**776**	51
First Bank Place	**775**	53
Norwest (1988)	**773**	57
Multifoods Tower (1983)	**608**	51
Piper Jaffray Tower (1984)	**627**	42
Dain Bosworth Plaza	**539**	40
Pillsbury Center, 200 S 6th St. (1981)	**530**	40
150 South Fifth	**498**	36
Metropolitan Center, 333 S 7th (1987)	**496**	31
Plaza VII, 45 S 7th (1987)	**468**	36
Foshay Tower, not including 163-ft. antenna tower (1929)	**447**	31
Hennepin Co. Govt. Center (1974)	**413**	25
Marriott Hotel (1983)	**379**	33
100 South Fifth (1987)	**347**	26
Telephone Bldg. (1931)	**345**	27
Montreal, Quebec		
1100 Rue de la Gauchetiere	**669**	45
1250 Boulevard Rene Levesque	**640**	45
Place Victoria (1963)	**624**	47
Place Ville Marie (1962)	**620**	45
Canadian Imperial Bank of Commerce (1962)	**590**	45
Le Complexe Desjardins		
La Tour du Sud	**498**	40
La Tour du L'Est	**428**	32
La Tour du Nord	**355**	27
Les Cooperants (1987)	**479**	34
Place Montreal Trust (1988)	**449**	32
Chateau Champlain Hotel (1967)	**420**	38
Port Royal Apts.	**400**	33
Royal Bank Tower	**397**	22
Sun Life Bldg.	**390**	26
500 Place d'Armes	**390**	32
Nashville, TN		
South Central Bell Bldg.	**617**	33
Third National Financial Center	**490**	30
American General Center	**452**	31
Landmark Center	**409**	30
Nashville City Center (1987)	**402**	27
James K. Polk State Office Bldg.	**392**	32
Stouffer Hotel (1987)	**385**	35
First American Center	**354**	28
One Nashville Plaza	**346**	23
Newark, NJ		
Natl. Newark & Essex Bldg.	**465**	36
Raymond-Commerce	**448**	37
Park Plaza Bldg.	**400**	26
Prudential Plaza	**370**	24
Public Service Elec. & Gas	**360**	26
Prudential Ins. Co., 753 Broad St.	**360**	26
AT&T Bldg.	**359**	31
Gateway 1	**355**	28

Building	Ht. ft.	Stories
New Orleans, LA		
One Shell Square (1972)	**697**	51
Place St. Charles (1985)	**645**	53
Plaza Tower (1969)	**531**	45
Energy Centre (1984)	**530**	39
LL&E Tower (1987)	**481**	36
Sheraton Hotel (1985)	**478**	47
Marriott Hotel (1972)	**450**	42
Texaco Bldg. (1983)	**442**	33
Canal Place One (1979)	**439**	32
1010 Common (1971)	**438**	31
Int'l. Trade Mart Bldg.	**407**	33
225 Baronne St. (1965)	**362**	28
One Poydras Plaza (1983)	**360**	28
Hibernia Bank Bldg. (1920)	**355**	23
Hyatt-Regency Hotel (1976)	**353**	32
New York, NY		
World Trade Center (2 towers) (1973)	**1,368/ 1,362**	110/110
Empire State, 34th St. & 5th Ave.	**1,250**	102
TV tower, 164 ft., makes total (1931)	**1,414**	...
Chrysler, Lexington & 43d (1930)	**1,046**	77
Amer. International, 70 Pine (1932)	**950**	67
40 Wall Tower (1929)	**927**	71
Citicorp Center (1977)	**914**	46
G.E. Bldg., Rockefeller Center (1933)	**850**	70
Chase Manhattan Plaza (1960)	**813**	60
MetLife Bldg. (1963)	**808**	59
Cityspire (1989)	**802**	72
Woolworth, 233 Broadway (1913)	**792**	60
One Worldwide Plaza	**778**	47
One Penn Plaza (1972)	**764**	57
Carnegie Tower	**756**	59
Exxon, 1251 Ave. of Americas (1971)	**750**	54
Equitable Center Tower West (1985)	**750**	58
60 Wall St. (1989)	**745**	50
One Liberty Plaza (1972)	**743**	50
Citibank (1907)	**741**	57
World Financial Center, Tower C (1988)	**739**	54
One Astor Plaza (1969)	**730**	54
Solow Bldg. (1979)	**725**	50
Marine Midland	**724**	52
Metropolitan Tower (1988)	**716**	66
Union Carbide Bldg. (1960)	**707**	52
General Motors Bldg. (1968)	**705**	50
Metropolitan Life (1909)	**700**	50
500 5th Ave. (1928)	**697**	58
Chem. Bank, NY. Trust Bldg. (1963)	**687**	50
55 Water St.	**687**	53
1585 Broadway	**685**	42
Four Seasons Hotel (1993)	**682**	52
Chanin, Lexington & 42d (1929)	**680**	56
15 Columbus Circle (1970)	**679**	44
McGraw Hill, 1221 Ave. of Am. (1972)	**674**	51
Citicorp (Queens) (1990)	**673**	50
Lincoln, 60 E 42d Street (1939)	**673**	53
1633 Broadway	**670**	48
Trump Tower, 725 5th Ave. (1983)	**664**	68
599 Lexington Ave. (1988)	**653**	47
Museum Tower Apts. (1985)	**650**	58
712 5th Ave. (1990)	**650**	56
American Brands, 245 Park Ave.	**648**	47
550 Madison Ave. (1983)	**648**	37
World Financial Center Tower B (1986)	**645**	50
General Electric, 570 Lexington (1931)	**640**	50
Irving Trust, 1 Wall St. (1932)	**640**	50
345 Park Ave.	**634**	44
Grace Plaza, 1114 Ave. of Am.	**630**	50
One New York Plaza (1969)	**630**	50
Home Insurance Co. Bldg.	**630**	44
NYNEX, 1095 Ave. of Am.	**630**	40
Central Park Place (1988)	**628**	56
888 7th Ave.	**628**	42
One Hammarskjold Plaza	**628**	50
Waldorf-Astoria, 301 Park Ave. (1931)	**625**	47
Burlington House (1970)	**625**	50
Olympic Tower, 645 5th Ave. (1976)	**620**	51
10 E 40th St.	**620**	48
101 Park Ave.	**618**	50
750 7th Ave.	**615**	35
New York Life, 51 Madison Ave. (1928)	**615**	40
Rihga Royal Hotel	**610**	54
17 State St.	**610**	41
Penney Bldg., 1301 Ave. of Am.	**609**	46
IBM, 590 Madison Ave. (1983)	**603**	41
780 3d Ave.	**600**	50
Celanese Bldg. (1973)	**592**	45

Building	Ht. ft.	Stories
U.S. Court House, 505 Pearl St. (1976)	**590**	37
Kalikow Hotel	**588**	58
Federal Bldg., Foley Square	**587**	41
Time & Life, 1271 Ave. of Am. (1959)	**587**	47
Cooper Bregstein Bldg., 1250 Bway.	**580**	40
Stevens Tower, 1185 Ave. of Am.	**580**	42
Municipal Bldg. (1919)	**580**	34
520 Madison Ave. (1983)	**577**	42
One Madison Square Plaza (1968)	**576**	42
World Financial Center Tower A (1986)	**575**	42
One Financial Sq. (1987)	**575**	37
Park Ave. Plaza (1981)	**575**	44
Westvaco Bldg. 299 Park Ave.	**574**	42
Marriott Marquis Hotel (1985)	**574**	42
Socony Mobil Bldg., East 42d St.	**572**	45
Sperry Rand Bldg., 1290 Ave. of Am.	**570**	43
600 3d Ave.	**570**	42
Helmsley Bldg., 230 Park (1929)	**565**	35
One Bankers Trust Plaza	**565**	40
Hemsley Palace Hotel (1980)	**563**	51
30 Broad St.	**562**	48
Park Ave Tower (1986)	**561**	36
Sherry-Netherland, 5th Ave. & 59th St.	**560**	40
Continental Can, 633 3d Ave. (1983)	**557**	39
Sperry & Hutchinson, 330 Madison	**555**	39
Continental Corp., 180 Maiden Lane	**555**	41
Galleria, 117 E 57th St. (1975)	**552**	57
Interchem Bldg., 1133 Ave. of Am.	**552**	45
151 E 44th St.	**550**	44
NYNEX, 323 Bway. (1979)	**550**	45
919 3d Ave.	**550**	47
Burroughs Bldg., 605 3d Ave.	**550**	44
Bankers Trust, 33 E 48 St. (1963)	**547**	41
Transportation Bldg., 225 Bway.	**546**	45
Equitable, 120 Broadway (1915)	**545**	42
One Brooklyn Bridge Plaza (1976)	**540**	42
Paine Webber Bldg. (1961)	**540**	42
Ritz Tower, Park Ave. & 57th St.	**540**	41
Bankers Trust, 6 Wall St.	**540**	39
1166 Ave. of Americas	**540**	44
1700 Broadway	**533**	41
Downtown Athletic Club, 19 West St.	**530**	45
Nelson Towers, 7th Ave. & 34th St.	**525**	45
767 3d Ave.	**525**	39
Hotel Pierre, 5th Ave. & 61st St. (1928)	**525**	44
House of Seagram (1958)	**525**	38
7 World Trade Center (1985)	**525**	44
Random House, 825 3d Ave.	**522**	40
3 Park Ave.	**522**	42
North American Plywood, 800 3d Ave.	**520**	41
Du Mont Bldg., 515 Madison Ave.	**520**	42
26 Broadway	**520**	31
Newsweek Bldg., 444 Madison Ave.	**518**	43
Sterling Drug Bldg., 90 Park Ave.	**515**	41
Citibank	**515**	41
Bank of New York, 48 Wall St.	**513**	32
Navarre, 512 7th Ave.	**513**	43
Manhattan Savings Bank (Bklyn.)	**512**	42
ITT—American, 437 Madison Ave.	**512**	40
International, Rockefeller Ctr.	**512**	41
1407 Broadway Realty Corp.	**512**	44
United Nations, 405 E 42 St. (1953)	**505**	39
Oakland, CA		
Ordway Bldg., 2150 Valdez St.	**404**	28
Kaiser Bldg.	**390**	28
Lake Merritt Plaza	**371**	27
Federal Bldg. (2 bldgs.)	**368**	19
American President Lines (1990)	**360**	29
Oklahoma City, OK		
Liberty Tower (1971)	**500**	36
First National Center (1974)	**493**	28
City Place (1985)	**440**	33
First Oklahoma Tower (1982)	**425**	31
Kerr-McGee Center (1973)	**393**	30
Mid America Tower (1981)	**362**	19
Omaha, NE		
Woodmen Tower (1969)	**469**	30
Enron Building (1960)	**400**	18
Masonic Manor (1963)	**320**	22
First Natl. Center (1971)	**320**	22
Orlando, FL		
*Orange County Courthouse	**522**	25
Sun Bank Center Tower (1988)	**441**	35
DuPont Center Bldg. (1988)	**409**	28

Building	Ht. ft.	Stories
Ottawa, Ontario		
Place de Ville, Tower C	**368**	29
R.H. Coats Bldg.	**341**	26
Philadelphia, PA		
One Liberty Place (1987)	**960**	61
Two Liberty Place (1989)	**845**	52
Mellon Bank Center (1989)	**795**	54
Bell Atlantic Tower (1991)	**739**	53
Blue Cross Tower (1990)	**700**	50
Commerce Sq., #1 (1990)	**572**	40
Commerce Sq., #2 (1992)	**572**	40
City Hall Tower, incl. 37-ft. statue of Wm. Penn. (1901)	**548**	7
1818 Market St. (1974)	**500**	40
Meridan Bank (1972)	**492**	38
Phila. Saving Fund Society (1932)	**492**	39
Provident Mutual Life (1983)	**491**	40
Central Penn Natl. Bank (1970)	**490**	36
Centre Square (2 towers) (1973)	**490/416**	38/32
Industrial Valley Bank (1968)	**482**	32
Philadelphia National Bank (1930)	**475**	25
Two Mellon Plaza (1930)	**450**	30
2000 Market St. (1973)	**435**	29
Two Logan Square (1987)	**435**	34
2 Girard Plaza (1930)	**412**	30
Fidelity Bank Bldg. (1927)	**405**	30
Lewis Tower, 15th & Locust (1929)	**400**	33
One Logan Square (1982)	**400**	32
1500 Locust St. (1973)	**390**	44
Philadelphia Electric Co. (1970)	**384**	29
Academy House, 1420 Locust St.	**377**	37
Penn Mutual Life (1931)	**375**	20
The Drake, 15th & Spruce (1928)	**375**	33
INA Annex	**369**	27
Medical Tower, 255 S 17th (1931)	**364**	33
Phoenix, AZ		
Bank One Center (1972)	**483**	40
Bank of America Bldg. (1976)	**407**	31
Phoenix Plaza I (1989)	**397**	20
Phoenix Plaza II(1990)	**397**	20
First Interstate Bank Plaza (1971)	**372**	26
Phoenix Center (1979)	**361**	28
Norwest Tower (1980)	**356**	26
One Renaissance Sq. (1987)	**347**	26
Two Renaissance Sq. (1989)	**347**	28
Phoenix Corporate Center	**341**	26
Pittsburgh, PA		
USX Towers	**841**	64
One Mellon Bank Center	**725**	54
One PPG Place	**635**	40
Fifth Avenue Place (1987)	**616**	32
One Oxford Centre	**615**	46
Gulf, 7th Ave. and Grant St.	**582**	44
University of Pittsburgh	**535**	42
Mellon Bank Bldg.	**520**	41
One Oliver Plaza	**511**	39
Grant, Grant St. at 3d Ave.	**485**	40
Koppers, 7th Ave. and Grant	**475**	34
Equibank Bldg.	**445**	34
CNG Tower (1987)	**430**	32
Pittsburgh National Bldg.	**424**	30
Alcoa Bldg., 425 Sixth Ave.	**410**	30
Liberty Tower	**358**	29
Westinghouse Bldg.	**355**	23
Oliver, 535 Smithfield St.	**347**	25
Gateway Bldg. No. 3	**344**	24
Centre City Tower	**341**	26
Federal Bldg., 1000 Liberty Ave.	**340**	23
Bell Telephone, 416 7th Ave.	**339**	21
Hilton Hotel	**333**	22
Frick, 437 Grant St.	**330**	20
Portland, OR		
First Interstate Tower	**546**	40
U.S. Bancorp Tower	**536**	42
Koin Tower Plaza	**509**	35
Standard Insurance Center	**367**	29
Pacwest Center	**356**	30
Providence, RI		
Fleet National Bank	**420**	26
Rhode Island Hospital Trust Tower	**410**	30
40 Westminster Bldg.	**301**	24
Raleigh, NC		
BB & T/2 Hanover Sq. (1991)	**431**	29
First Union Capitol Center (1991)	**390**	29

Building	Ht. ft.	Stories
Richmond, VA		
James Monroe Bldg.	**450**	29
City Hall (incl. penthouse)	**425**	17
Crestar Bank Hdqt. Bldg.	**400**	24
Federal Reserve Bank	**393**	26
Nations Bank Center	**333**	25
Rochester, NY		
Xerox Tower (1967)	**443**	30
Lincoln First Tower (1973)	**392**	27
Eastman Kodak Bldg. (1914)	**340**	19
Sacramento, CA		
Wells Fargo Center	**405**	30
Park Plaza Tower	**373**	26
Renaissance Tower	**372**	28
St. Louis, MO		
Gateway Arch (1965)	**630**	...
Metropolitan Square Tower (1989)	**593**	42
One Bell Center (1984)	**588**	44
Mercantile Center Tower (1976)	**540**	36
Boatmen's Plaza	**433**	30
Laclede Gas. Bldg., 8th & Olive	**400**	31
SW Bell Telephone Bldg.	**398**	26
Civil Courts	**390**	13
St. Paul, MN		
First Natl. Bank Bldg., incl. 100-ft. sign	**517**	32
Minn. World Trade Center	**471**	36
Galtier Plaza's Jackson Tower	**440**	46
Osborn Bldg., 320 Wabasha	**368**	20
Kellogg Square Apts.	**366**	32
Northwestern Bell Telephone (2 bldgs.)	**340**	16
Pointe of St. Paul	**340**	34
American National Bank Bldg.	**340**	26
North Central Tower, 445 Minn.	**328**	27
Amhoist/Park Tower	**324**	26
Salt Lake City, UT		
L.D.S. Church Office Bldg.	**420**	30
Beneficial Life Tower	**351**	21
Utah One Center (1992)	**350**	24
San Antonio, TX		
Tower of the Americas (1968)	**622**	...
Marriott Rivercenter (1988)	**546**	38
Weston Centre (1988)	**444**	32
Tower Life (1929)	**404**	30
Nations Bank Plaza (1983)	**387**	28
Nix Professional Bldg. (1931)	**375**	23
San Diego, CA		
One American Plaza (1991)	**500**	34
Symphony Tower (1989)	**499**	34
Hyatt Regency San Diego (1992)	**495**	39
Emerald-Shapery Center (1991)	**450**	30
One Harbor Drive (1992)	**424**	41
First Interstate Bank (1985)	**398**	23
Meridian Condominiums (1985)	**395**	27
Union Bank (1969)	**388**	27
First National Bank (1982)	**379**	27
Imperial Bank	**355**	24
Executive Complex (1963)	**350**	25
Wells Fargo Bldg. (1982)	**348**	20
Great American Bldg. (1974)	**339**	24
San Francisco, CA		
Transamerica Pyramid (1972)	**853**	48
Bank of America (1969)	**778**	52
101 California St. (1986)	**600**	48
5 Fremont Center (1983)	**600**	43
Embarcadero Center, No. 4 (1982)	**570**	45
Security Pacific Bank	**569**	45
One Market Plaza, Spear St. (1976)	**565**	43
Wells Fargo Bldg.	**561**	43
Standard Oil, 575 Market St. (1975)	**551**	39
One Sansome-Citicorp	**550**	39
Shaklee Bldg., 444 Market	**537**	38
Aetna Life	**529**	38
First & Market Bldg. (1973)	**529**	38
Metropolitan Life (1973)	**524**	38
Crocker National Bank	**500**	38
Hilton Hotel	**493**	46
Pacific Gas & Electric (1970)	**492**	34
Union Bank (1972)	**487**	37
Pacific Insurance (1972)	**476**	34
Bechtel Bldg., Fremont St. (1977)	**475**	33

Building	Ht. ft.	Stories
333 Market Bldg. (1979)	**474**	33
Hartford Bldg. (1965)	**465**	33
Mutual Benefit Life (1969)	**438**	32
Russ Bldg. (1928)	**435**	31
Pacific Telephone Bldg. (1925)	**435**	26
Pacific Gateway (1983)	**416**	30
Embarcadero Center, No. 3 (1976)	**412**	31
Embarcadero Center, No. 2 (1974)	**412**	31
595 Market Bldg. (1979)	**410**	31
101 Montgomery St.	**405**	28
California State Automobile Assn. (1974)	**399**	29
Alcoa Bldg.	**398**	27
St. Francis Hotel (1970)	**395**	32
Shell Bldg. (1928)	**386**	29
Del Monte	**378**	28
Meridien Hotel (1984)	**374**	34
Seattle, WA		
Columbia Seafirst Center (1985)	**954**	76
Two Union Square (1989)	**740**	56
Washington Mutual Tower (1988)	**730**	55
AT&T Gateway Tower (1990)	**722**	62
1001 4th Pl. (1969)	**609**	50
Space Needle (1962)	**605**	...
Pacific First Center (1989)	**580**	44
First Interstate Center (1983)	**574**	48
Seafirst 5th Ave. Plaza (1981)	**543**	42
Security Pacific Bank Tower (1977)	**514**	42
Smith Tower (1914)	**500**	42
520 Pike Tower (1984)	**498**	29
Key Tower (1986)	**493**	40
Federal Office Bldg.	**487**	37
US West Communications	**466**	33
One Union Square (1981)	**456**	38
1111 3d Ave. Bldg. (1980)	**454**	35
Westin Bldg., 2001 6th Ave. (1981)	**409**	34
Westin Hotel	**397**	40
Unigard Financial Center (1973)	**389**	27
Century Square (1986)	**379**	30
Sheraton Seattle Hotel	**371**	34
Tampa, FL		
100 N Tampa (1992)	**579**	42
Barnett Plaza (1986)	**577**	42
Tampa City Center (1981)	**537**	38
Landmark Centre (1992)	**525**	36
First Financial Tower (1973)	**458**	35
NCNB Plaza (1988)	**454**	33
Toledo, OH		
Owens-Illinois Corp. HQ. (1962)	**404**	30
Owens-Corning Fiberglas Tower (1970)	**400**	30
Ohio Citizens Bank Bldg. (1932)	**368**	27
One Govt. Center (1983)	**327**	22
Toronto, Ontario		
CN Tower (world's tallest self-supporting structure) (1975)	**1,821**	...
First Canadian Place (1979)	**952**	72
Bay/Adelaide Project (1991)	**951**	57
Scotia Plaza (1988)	**902**	68
Canada Trust Tower (1990)	**869**	52
Commerce Court West (1972)	**784**	57
Toronto-Dominion Tower (TD Centre) (1967)	**758**	56
Bay-Wellington Tower (1990)	**705**	47
Royal Trust Tower (TD Centre) (1969)	**600**	46
Royal Bank Plaza—South Tower (1977)	**589**	41
Manulife Centre (1975)	**545**	53
IBM Tower (TD Centre) (1986)	**520**	36
Two Bloor West (1974)	**488**	34
Exchange Tower (1981)	**480**	36
Commerce Court North (1930)	**476**	34
Simpson Tower (1968)	**473**	33
Eaton Tower (1990)	**471**	34
Cadillac-Fairview Tower (1982)	**466**	36
Palace Point (1991)	**455**	46
Palace Pier (1978)	**453**	46
Continental Bank Bldg. (1980)	**450**	35
Sheraton Centre (1972)	**443**	43
Hudson's Bay Centre (1974)	**442**	35
Royal York Hotel (1929)	**439**	26
Ernst & Yonge Tower (1990)	**438**	31
Old Toronto Exchange Bldg. (1990)	**436**	31
Leaside Towers (2 bldgs.) (1970)	**423**	44
Metro Hall (1991)	**420**	27
Commercial Union Tower (1974)	**420**	32
Maple Leaf Mills Tower	**419**	30
Plaza 2 Hotel	**415**	41
Sun Life Bldg. (1981)	**410**	28

Building	Ht. ft.	Stories
Tulsa, OK		
Bank of Oklahoma Tower	**667**	52
Cityplex Towers	**640**	60
1st National Tower	**516**	41
Mid-Continent Tower	**513**	36
4th Natl. Bank of Tulsa	**412**	33
320 South Boston Bldg.	**400**	24
Occidential Place	**388**	28
Univ. Club Tower	**377**	32
Cityplex Towers	**348**	30
Philtower	**343**	24
Vancouver, British Columbia		
Royal Centre Tower (1973)	**460**	36
Canada Trust Tower, 1055 Melville	**454**	35
Scotiabank Tower	**451**	36
Bentall IV (1981)	**450**	35
Vancouver Center (1977)	**450**	36
Park Place (1984)	**450**	35
T-D Bank Tower (1978)	**440**	30
200 Granville Square (1973)	**438**	28
Harbour Centre (1977)	**428**	21
Bentall III (1974)	**399**	31
Winnipeg, Manitoba		
Toronto Dominion Center (1989)	**413**	33
Richardson Bldg. (1969)	**390**	34
Commodity Exchange Tower (1980)	**384**	31
Winston-Salem, NC		
*Wachovia Bldg.	**460**	28
Wachovia Bldg. (1965)	**410**	27
Southern National Finance Center (1987)	**340**	20
Reynolds Bldg. (1929)	**315**	24

Other Notable Tall Buildings in the U.S.

Cape Canaveral, FL, Vehicle Assembly Bldg., 40 (552′); Amarillo, TX, American Natl. Bank, 33 (374′); Atlantic City, NJ, Taj Mahal, 51 (429′); Charleston, WV, Kanawha Valley Bldg., 20 (384′); Galveston, TX, American National Ins., 20 (358′); Hamilton, Ont., Century Twenty One, 43 (418′); Harrisburg, PA, State Office Tower #2, 21 (334′); Knoxville, TN, United American Bank, 30 (400′); Lincoln, NE, State Capitol (432′); Mobile, AL, First Natl. Bank, 33 (420′); Niagara Falls, Ont., Skylon, (520′); Shreveport LA, Commercial National Tower, 24 (365′); Springfield, MA, Valley Bank Tower, 29 (370′); Tallahassee, FL, State Capitol Tower, 22 (345′).

Notable International Structures

Structure	Ht. ft.	Stories
Central Plaza, Hong Kong (1992)	**1,028**	78
Bank of China, Hong Kong (1989)	**1,001**	70
Eiffel Tower, Paris (1889)	**984**	-
Landmark Tower, Yokohama (1993)	**971**	70
Overseas Union Bank, Singapore (1984)	**919**	63
MesseTurm. Bldg., Frankfurt (1990)	**841**	70
One Canada Sq., London (1991)	**800**	59
Tokyo City Hall (1992)	**797**	59
Metropolitan Tower, Tokyo (1992)	**796**	50
Rialto Tower, Melbourne (1985)	**794**	60
Palace of Science & Culture, Warsaw	**790**	42
Moscow State Univ. (incl. spire)	**787**	39
Treasury Bldg., Singapore (1986)	**770**	52
Seoul Tower, S Korea (1988)	**764**	63
Maine Montparnasse, Paris (1973)	**751**	64
MLC Center, Sydney (1977)	**748**	60
Governor Philip Tower, Sydney (1993)	**745**	54
Raffles City Hotel, Singapore (1986)	**742**	73
Ikebukuro Office Tower, Tokyo (1978)	**742**	60
Bourke Place, Melbourne (1991)	**735**	48
Central Park, Perth (1992)	**733**	51
Carlton Centre, Johannesburg (1973)	**722**	50
Shinjuku Center, Tokyo (1979)	**709**	55
Shinjuku Mitsui, Tokyo	**696**	55
Shinjuku Nomura, Tokyo	**666**	53
Overseas-Chinese Banking Corp., Singapore	**660**	52
Shinjuku Sumitomo, Tokyo	**656**	52
Parque Central Torre Oficinas, Caracas	**656**	56
Ukraine Hotel, Moscow	**650**	60
Natwest Tower, London	**600**	50
Tour Elf Aquitaine, Paris	**578**	48
Ulm Cathedral, Germany	**530**	-
Cologne Cathedral, Germany	**515**	-
Tour du Cite Administrative, Brussels	**492**	36

Notable Bridges in North America

Source: Survey of State Highway Engineers (1994)

Asterisk (*) designates railroad bridge. Double asterisk (**) designates under construction.
Span of a bridge is distance (in feet) between its supports.

Year	Bridge	Location	Longest span
	Suspension		
1964	Verrazano-Narrows	New York, NY	4,260
1937	Golden Gate	San Fran. Bay, CA	4,200
1957	Mackinac	Sts. of Mackinac	3,800
1931	Geo. Washington	Hudson R., NY.- NJ	3,500
1950	Tacoma Narrows	Washington	2,800
1936	[1]Transbay	San Fran. Bay, CA	2,310
1939	Bronx-Whitestone	East R., N.Y.C.	2,300
1970	Pierre Laporte	Quebec	2,190
1951	Del. Memorial	Wilmington, DE	2,150
1968	Del. Mem. (new)	Wilmington, DE	2,150
1957	Walt Whitman	Philadelphia, PA	2,000
1929	Ambassador	Detroit-Canada	1,850
1961	Throgs Neck	Long Is. Sound, NY.	1,800
1926	Benjamin Franklin	Philadelphia, PA	1,750
1924	Bear Mt., NY.	Hudson R.	1,632
1952	[2]William Preston Lane Memorial	Sandy Point, MD	1,600
1903	Williamsburg	East R., N.Y.C.	1,600
1969	Newport	Narragansett Bay, RI	1,600
1883	Brooklyn	East R., N.Y.C.	1,595
1939	Lion's Gate	Burrard Inlet, B.C.	1,550
1930	Mid-Hudson	Poughkeepsie, NY.	1,500
1964	Vincent Thomas	Los Angeles Harbor	1,500
1909	Manhattan	East R., N.Y.C.	1,470
1936	Triboro	East R., N.Y.C.	1,380
1931	St. Johns	Portland, OR	1,207
1929	Mount Hope	Rhode Island	1,200
1960	Ogdensburg, NY	St. Lawrence R.	1,150
1939	Deer Isle	Maine	1,080
1931	Simon Kenton Memorial	Ohio R., KY.	1,060
1867	John A. Roebling	Ohio R., KY.	1,057
1971	Dent	Clearwater Co., ID	1,050
1900	Miampimi	Mexico	1,030
1849	Wheeling, WV	Ohio R.	1,010
	Cantilever		
1917	Quebec	Quebec	1,800
1974	Commodore Barry	Chester, PA	1,622
1958	Mississippi R.	New Orleans, LA	1,575
1988	Mississippi R.	New Orleans, LA	1,575
1936	Transbay	San Fran. Bay	1,400
1968	Mississippi R.	Baton Rouge, LA	1,235
1955	Tappan Zee	Hudson R.	1,212
1930	Lewis and Clark	Longview, WA-OR	1,200
1909	Queensboro	East R., N.Y.C.	1,182
1927	Carquinez Strait	California	1,100
1958	Parallel Span	"	1,100
1930	Jacques Cartier	Montreal, Can.	1,097
1968	Isaiah D. Hart	Jacksonville, FL	1,088
1957	[3]Richmond	San Fran. Bay, CA	1,070
1929	Grace Memorial	Charleston, SC	1,050
1980	Newburgh-Beacon	Hudson R., NY	1,000
1963	Newburgh-Beacon	Hudson R., NY	1,000
1949	Martin Luther King	St. Louis, MO	962
1975	Caruthersville, MO	Mississippi R.	920
1977	Saint Marys	Saint Marys, WV, OH	900
1969	Silver Memorial	Pt. Pleasant, WV, OH	900

Year	Bridge	Location	Longest span
1981	Ravenswood	WV	900
1987	Carl Perkins	Ohio R., KY	900
1986	Mississippi R.	Natchez, MS	875
1940	Mississippi R.	Natchez, MS	875
1938	Blue Water	Pt. Huron, MI	871
1972	Mississippi R.	Vicksburg, MS	870
1972	N Fork American R.	Auburn, CA	862
1940	*Baton Rouge	Mississippi R.	848
1899	*Cornwall	St. Lawrence R.	843
1940	Mississippi R.	Greenville, MS	840
1961	Helena, AR	Mississippi R.	840
1963	Brent Spence	Covington, KY	831
1963	Cincinnati	Ohio R.	830
1963	Mississippi R.	Donaldsonville, LA	825
1940	Mississippi R.	Vicksburg, MS	825
1929	Clark Memorial	Ohio R, KY.	820
1961	Campbellton-Cross Point	New Brunswick-Quebec	815
1935	Rip Van Winkle	Catskill, NY	800
1938	Cairo	Ohio R., IL-KY	800
1932	Washington Mem.	Seattle, WA	800
1936	McCullough	Coos Bay, OR	793
1935	[4]Huey P. Long	New Orleans	790
1916	*Memphis (Harahan)	Mississippi R.	790
1892	*Memphis	Mississippi R.	790
1967	Memphis-Arkansas	Mississippi R.	790
1904	*Mingo Jct., OH	Ohio R.	769
1910	*Beaver, PA	Ohio R.	767
1932	Bi-State Vietnam Gold Star	Henderson, KY	720
1992	Jamestown-Verrazzano	Jamestown, RI	636
1941	Columbia R.	Kettle Falls, WA	600
1954	Columbia R.	Umatilla, OR	600
1954	Columbia R.	The Dalles, OR	573
1968	W 17th St.	Huntington, WV	562

Simple Truss

Year	Bridge	Location	Longest span
1976	Chester	Chester, WV	745
1917	*Metropolis	Ohio R.	720
1929	Irvin S. Cobb	Ohio R.-IL-KY	716
1922	*Tanana R.	Nenana, Alaska	700
1933	*Henderson	Ohio R.-IN-KY	665
1967	I-77, Ohio R.	Williamstown, WV	650
1917	4 MacArthur, IL-MO	St. Louis	647
1919	Louisville	Ohio R.	644
1989	St. Charles	Missouri R.	625
1933	Atchafalaya	Morgan City, LA	608
1924	*Castleton	Hudson R., NY	598
1937	Delaware R.	Easton, PA	550
1930	Swindell Bridge	Pittsburgh, PA	545
1889	*Cincinnati	Ohio R.	542
1952	Allegheny R., Tpk.	Pittsburgh, PA	534
1930	*Martinez	California	528
1951	Rankin	Pittsburgh, PA	525
1914	Old Brownsville	Brownsville, PA	520
1906	Donora-Webster	Donora-Webster, PA	515
1909	Hulton	Pittsburgh, PA	505
1967	Tanana R.	Alaska	500

Steel Truss

Year	Bridge	Location	Longest span
1988	Glade Creek	Raleigh Co., WV	784
1973	Atchafalaya R.	Krotz Springs, LA	780
1972	Piscataqua R.	NH, ME	756
1972	Atchafalaya R.	Simmesport, LA	720
1957	SR-3, Rappahannock R.	Middlesex Co., VA	648
1940	Jamestown	Jamestown, RI	640
1949	Memphis	Mississippi R., AR	621
1978	Atchafalaya R.	Morgan City, LA	607
1938	US-22	Delaware R., NJ	540
1955	Interstate (I-5)	Columbia R., OR-WA	531
1910	[4]McKinley, St. Louis	Mississippi R.	517
1972	Mississippi R.	Muscatine, IA	512
1896	Newport	Ohio R., KY	511
1970	Lake Koocanusa	Lincoln Co., MT	500
1931	Lucy Jefferson Lewis	Cumberland R., KY	500
1958	Lake Oahe	Mobridge, SD	500
1958	Lake Oahe	Gettysburg, SD	500

Continuous Truss

Year	Bridge	Location	Longest span
1966	Columbia R. (Astoria)	OR-WA	1,232
1977	Francis Scott Key	Baltimore, MD	1,200
1995	**Central	Ohio R., KY-OH	850
1943	Dubuque, IA	Mississippi R.	845
1966	Charles Braga	Fall River, MA	840
1956	[5]Earl C. Clements	Ohio R., Ill-KY	825
1953	John E Mathews	Jacksonville, FL	810
1950	Maurice J. Tobin	Boston, MA	801
1940	Gov. Nice Memorial	Potomac River, MD	800
1957	Kingston-Rhinecliff	Hudson R., NY	800
1986	Rochester-Monaca	Rochester-Monaca, PA	780
1918	*Sciotoville	Ohio R.	775
1976	Carroll L. Cropper	Ohio R., IN-KY	750
1981	Sewickley	Sewickley, PA	750
1984	13th St. Bridge, Ohio R.	Ashland, KY	740
1959	Monaca-E. Rochester	Monaca-East Rochester, PA	730
1976	Betsy Ross	Philadelphia, PA	729
1929	Madison-Milton	Ohio R., IN-KY	727
1966	[6]Matthew E. Welsh	Mauckport, IN	725
1994	6th St.	Huntington, WV	720
1977	Bert T. Combs-Lambert	Ohio R.	720
1970	Vanport	Vanport, PA	715
1962	Champlain	Montreal, Que.	707
1964	[7]John F. Kennedy	Louisville, KY	700
1973	Girard Point	Philadelphia, PA	700
1954	PA Tpk., Delaware R.	Philadelphia, PA	682
1949	George Platt	Philadelphia, PA	680
1938	Port Arthur-Orange	TX	680
1929	*Cincinnati	Ohio R.	675
1928	Cape Girardeau, MO	Mississippi R.	672
1946	Chester, IL	Mississippi R.	670
1970	Gulfgate	Port Arthur, TX	664
1994	Williamstown-Marietta	Williamstown, WV	650
1953	Jefferson City	Missouri R.	640
1930	Quincy, IL	Mississippi R.	628
1961	Shippingport	Shippingport, PA	620
1959	US 181, over harbor	Corpus Christi, TX	620
1935	Bourne	Cape Cod Canal, MA	616
1935	Sagamore	Cape Cod Canal, MA	616
1965	Clarion R. (I-80)	Clarion, PA	612
1975	Donora-Monesson	Donora-Monesson, PA	608
1991	Hoffstadt Creek	Mt. St. Helens, WA	600
1957	Blatnik	Duluth, MN	600
1965	Rio Grande Gorge	Taos, NM	600
1987	Jefferson City	Missouri R.	596
1962	W Bridge Feather R.	Oroville, CA	576
1967	Glenwood	Pittsburgh, PA	567
1936	Meredosia	Illinois R.	567
1936	Mark Twain Mem.	Hannibal, MO	562
1957	Mackinac	Mackinac Straits, MI	560
1932	Pulaski Skyway	Passaic R.-Hackensack R., NJ	550

Continuous Box and Plate Girder

Year	Bridge	Location	Longest span
1983	Mississippi R.	Luling, LA	1,222
1982	Houston Ship Chan	Houston, TX	750
1967	San Mateo-Hayward No. 2	San Fran. Bay, CA	750
1977	Intracoastal Canal	Gibbstown, LA	750
1976	Intracoastal Canal	Forked Is., LA	750
1969	[8]San Diego-Coronado	San Diego Bay, CA	660
1987	Columbia R.	Umatilla, OR-WA	660
1994	Acosta	Jacksonville, FL	630
1981	Douglas	Juneau, AK	620
1976	Wax L. Outlet	Calumet, LA	618
1981	Glenn Jackson (I-205)	Columbia R., OR-WA	600
1967	Poplar St.	St. Louis, MO	600
1982	Illinois R.	Pekin, IL	550
1982	I-440	Arkansas R.	540
1980	US-64, Tennessee R.	Savannah, TN	525
1988	Mon City	Monongahela, PA	520
1965	McDonald-Cartier	Ottawa, Ont.	520
1984	Columbia R.	Richland, WA	450
1986	Veterans	Pittsburgh, PA	440
1987	SR 76, Cumberland R.	Dover, TN	440
1987	SR 20, Tennessee R.	Perryville, TN	440
1970	Willamette R., I-205	West Linn, OR	430
1974	I-430	Arkansas R.	430
1984	FAU 3456, TN R.	Chattanooga, TN	420
1965	I-24, Tennessee R.	Marion Co., TN	420
1978	Snake R.	Clarkston, WA	420
1975	36th St.	Charleston, WV	420
1974	Dunbar-S Charleston	S Charleston, WV	420

Continuous Plate

Year	Bridge	Location	Longest span
1973	Ship Channel (I-610)	Houston, TX	630
1971	W Atchafalaya	Henderson, LA	573
1981	Illinois 23	Illinois R., IL	510
1968	Trinity R.	Dallas, TX	480
1978	San Joaquin R.	Antioch, CA	460
1977	Thomas Johnson Mem.	Solomons, MD	451
1975	Lewis	St. Louis, MO	450
1975	I-129	Missouri R., IA	450

Year	Bridge	Location	Longest span
1967	Mississippi R.	La Crosse, WI	450
1972	Whiskey Bay Pilot Channel	Ramah, LA	425
1966	I-480	Missouri R., IA-NE	425
1970	I-435	Missouri R., MO	425
1972	I-80	Missouri R., IA-NE	425
1985	I-435	Missouri R., KS-MO	425
1984	US-36	Missouri R., KS-MO	425
1972	I-635, Kansas City	Missouri R., KS-MO	425
1978	I-24	Cumberland R., KY	420

Cable-Stayed

Year	Bridge	Location	Longest span
1988	Dames Point	Jacksonville, FL	1,300
1994	**Houston Ship Channel	Baytowne-LaPorte,TX	1,250
1987	Sunshine Skyway	Tampa Bay, FL	1,200
1991	Talmadge Mem.	Savannah, GA.	1,100
1979	Columbia River	Pasco-Kennewick, WA	970
1985	E Huntington	Huntington, WV	900
1985	Mississippi R.	Quincy, IL	900
1980	Veterans Mem'l.	WV-OH	820
1991	Neches R.	Port Arthur - Orange, TX	640
1990	James R.	Henrico Co., VA.	630
1972	Sitka Harbor	Sitka, AK.	450

I-Beam Girder

Year	Bridge	Location	Longest span
1980	Shreveport Int.	Louisiana	438
1988	Route 18	Weston's Mill Pond,NJ	276
1954	Fuller Warren	Jacksonville, FL.	224

Steel Arch

Year	Bridge	Location	Longest span
1977	New R. Gorge	Fayetteville, WV	1,817
1931	Kill Van Kull	Bayonne, NJ	1,652
1973	Fremont	Portland, OR	1,255
1964	Port Mann	British Columbia	1,200
1916	*Hell Gate	East R., N.Y.C.	1,038
1959	Glen Canyon	Colorado R.	1,028
1967	Trois-Rivieres	St. Lawrence R., Que.	1,100
1990	Roosevelt Lake	Arizona	1,080
1962	Lewiston-Queenston	Niagara R., Ont.	1,000
1976	Perrine	Twin Falls, ID	993
1941	Rainbow	Niagara Falls	984
1986	Moundsville	Ohio R., WV	912
1984	I-255	Mississippi R., MO	909
1972	[9]I-40, Mississippi R.	Memphis, TN.	900
1936	Henry Hudson	Harlem R., N.Y.C.	840
1967	Lincoln Trail	Ohio R., IN-KY	825
1978	I-57, Cairo, IL	Mississippi R.	821
1980	I-65 Mobile R.	Mobile, AL.	800
1961	Sherman Minton	New Albany, IN	800
1978	I-470 Bridge, Ohio R.	Wheeling, WV	780
1930	West End	Pittsburgh, PA	780

Concrete Arch

Year	Bridge	Location	Longest span
1971	Selah Creek (twin)	Selah, WA.	549
1968	Cowlitz R.	Mossyrock, WA	520
1931	Westinghouse	Pittsburgh, PA	460
1923	Cappelen	Minneapolis, MN	435

Twin Concrete Trestle

Year	Bridge	Location	Longest span
1979	I-55/I-10	Manchae, LA.	181,157
1969	L. Pontchartrain Cswy.	Mandeville, LA.	126,720
1972	Atchafalaya Flwy.	Baton Rouge, LA	93,984
1963	[10]L. Pontchartrain.	Slidell, LA	28,547

Concrete Slab Dam

Year	Bridge	Location	Longest span
1927	Conowingo Dam	Maryland	4,611
1952	SR-4, Roanoke R.	Mecklenburg Co., VA	2,785
1936	Hoover Dam	Lake Mead, AZ-NV	1,324

Drawbridges

Vertical Lift

Year	Bridge	Location	Longest span
1959	*Arthur Kill	NY-NJ	558
1965	Pennsylvania Railroad	Kirkwood-Mt. Pleasant, DE	548
1935	*Cape Cod Canal	Massachusetts	544
1960	*Delair, NJ	Delaware R.	542
1937	Marine Parkway	Jamaica Bay, N.Y.C.	540
1931	Burlington, NJ	Delaware R.	534
1908	*Willamette R.	Portland, OR	521
1968	Second Narrows	Vancouver, B.C.	493
1912	*A-S-B Fratt	Kansas City	428
1945	*Harry S Truman	Kansas City	427
1955	Roosevelt Island	East R., N.Y.C.	418
1980	US-17, James R.	Isle of Wight, Co., VA	415
1932	*M-K-T R.R.	Missouri R.	414
1969	Cape Fear Mem.	Wilmington, NC	408
1930	Aerial	Duluth, MN	386
1941	Main St.	Jacksonville, FL	386
1962	Burlington	Ontario	370
1922	*Cincinnati	Ohio R.	365
1967	SR-156, James R.	Prince George Co., VA	364
1964	Red R.	Alexandria, LA	360
1957	Industrial Canal	New Orleans, LA	360
1950	Red R.	Moncla, LA.	360
1936	Tribo	Harlem R., N.Y.C.	344
1961	[4]Corpus Christi Harbor	Corpus Christi, TX	344
1939	U.S. 1&9, Passaic R.	Newark, NJ	333
1930	*Martinez	California	328
1960	St. Andrews Bay	Panama City, FL.	327
1929	*Penn-Lehigh	Newark Bay	322
1987	Industrial Canal	New Orleans, LA	320
1920	*Chattanooga.	Tennessee R.	310

Bascule

Year	Bridge	Location	Longest span
1969	E Pearl R.	Slidell, LA.	482
1940	Lorain, OH.	Black R.	330
1917	SR-8, Tennessee R.	Chattanooga, TN	306
1956	Duwamish R.	Seattle, WA	300
1955	Chehalis R.	Aberdeen, WA	288
1968	Elizabeth R.	Chesapeake, VA	280
1913	Broadway	Portland, OR	278

Swing Bridges

Year	Bridge	Location	Longest span
1926	[4]Fort Madison.	Mississippi R.	525
1991	SW Spokane St.	Seattle, WA	480
1930	Rigolets Pass.	New Orleans, LA	400
1950	Douglass Memorial.	Wash., DC	386
1945	Lord Delaware	Mattaponi R., VA	252
1957	Eltham.	Pamunkey R., VA	237

Swing Span

Year	Bridge	Location	Longest span
1903	*East Omaha	Missouri R.	519
1952	US-17	York R., VA	500
1897	*Duluth, MN	St. Louis Bay	486
1899	*C.M.&N.R.R.	Chicago	474
1913	Rt. 82, Conn-R.	E Haddam, CT	465
1914	*Coos Bay	Oregon	458

Floating Pontoon

Year	Bridge	Location	Longest span
1963	Evergreen Pt.	Seattle, WA	7,518
1961	Hood Canal	Pt. Gamble, WA	6,471
1993	Lacey V. Murrow-Lake Washington	Seattle, WA	6,543
1989	3rd Lake Washington	Seattle, WA	6,130

(1) The Transbay Bridge has 2 spans of 2,310 ft. each. (2) A second bridge in parallel was completed in 1973. (3) The Richmond Bridge has twin spans 1,070 ft. each. (4) Railroad and vehicular bridge. (5) Two spans each 825 ft. (6) Two spans each 707 ft. (7) Two spans each 700 ft. (8) Two spans each 660 ft. (9) Two spans each 900 ft. (10) Total length of bridge.

Oldest U.S. Bridge in Continuous Use

Completed in 1841, the 178-ft. wood truss (with orthotropic steel deck) covered bridge spans the Housatonic River on Rt. 128 in West Cornwall, CT.

Longest Covered Bridge in the U.S.

Built in 1866, the 449-ft. Cornish Windsor Bridge crosses the Connecticut R. between Cornish, NH, and Windsor, VT.

Notable International Bridges

Span of bridge is distance (in feet) between its supports. Asterisk (*) designates under construction.

Year	Bridge	Location	Longest Span
Suspension			
1998*	Akashi Kaikyo	Japan	6,529
1995*	Store Bælt (East Bridge)	Denmark	5,328
1981	Humber	England	4,626
*	Tsing Ma	Hong Kong	4,518
1988	Minami Bisan-Seto	Japan	3,609
1988	Bosphorus I	Istanbul	3,576
1973	Bosphorus II	Istanbul	3,524
1966	Ponte 25 de Abril	Lisbon	3,323
1964	Forth (road)	Scotland	3,301
1966	Severn	England	3,241
Cantilever			
1917	Quebec	Canada	1,801
1890	Forth[1] (rail)	Scotland	1,709
1974	Nanko	Japan	1,673
Steel Arch			
1932	Sydney Harbour	Australia	1,650
Concrete Arch			
1980	Krk I	Croatia	1,280
1964	Gladesville	Australia	1,001
Steel Plate and Box Girder			
1974	President Costa e Silva	Brazil	984
1956	Sava I	Yugo.	856
1966	Zoobrüke	Germany	850
Steel Cable-Stayed			
1999*	Tatara	Japan	2,920
*	Pont de Normandie	France	2,808
1993	Yangpu	China	1,975
*	Meiko Chuo	Japan	1,936
1991	Skarnsundet	Norway	1,739
1986	Alex Fraser	Canada	1,526
1985	Yokohama	Japan	1,509
1987	Hooghly River	Calcutta	1,499

(1) Two spans of 1,710 ft. each.

Underwater Vehicular Tunnels in North America

(more than 5,000 ft. in length)

Name	Location	Waterway	Feet
BART Trans-Bay Tubes (Rapid Transit)	San Francisco, CA	S.F. Bay	3.6 miles
Brooklyn-Battery	New York, NY	East River	9,117
Holland Tunnel	New York, NY	Hudson River	8,557
Lincoln Tunnel	New York, NY	Hudson River	8,216
Thimble Shoal Channel	Northampton Co., VA	Chesapeake Bay	8,187
Chesapeake Channel	Northampton Co., VA	Chesapeake Bay	7,941
Baltimore Harbor Tunnel	Baltimore, MD	Patapsco River	7,650
Hampton Roads (twin)	Hampton, VA	Hampton Roads	7,479
Fort McHenry Tunnel (2)	Baltimore, MD	Baltimore Harbor	7,200
Queens Midtown	New York, NY	East River	6,414
Sumner Tunnel	Boston, MA	Boston Harbor	5,650
Louis-Hippolyte Lafontaine Tunnel	Montreal, Que.	St. Lawrence River	5,280
Detroit-Windsor	Detroit, MI	Detroit River	5,160
Callahan Tunnel	Boston, MA	Boston Harbor	5,046

Land Vehicular Tunnels in the U.S.

(more than 3,000 ft. in length; asterisk (*) designates under construction)

Name	Location	Feet
E. Johnson Memorial	I-70, CO	8,959
Eisenhower Memorial	I-70, CO	8,941
Allegheny (twin)	PA Turnpike	6,072
Liberty Tubes	Pittsburgh, PA	5,920
Zion Natl. Park	Rte. 9, Utah	5,766
East River Mt. (twin)	Bland Co., VA, Mercer Co., WV	5,412
Tuscarora (twin)	PA Turnpike	5,400
Trans-Koolau	H-3, Hawaii	5,165
Kittatinny (twin)	PA Turnpike	4,660
*Cumberland Gap	Kentucky	4,600
Blue Mountain (twin)	PA Turnpike	4,435
Lehigh[1]	PA Turnpike	4,379
Wawona	Yosemite Natl. Park	4,233
Big Walker Mt.	Bland Co., VA.	4,229
Hanging Lake (twin)	Glenwood Canyon, CO.	4,000
Fort Pitt	Pittsburgh, PA	3,560
Dingess Tunnel	Mingo Co., WV	3,400
Mall Tunnel	Dist. of Columbia	3,400
Caldecott	Oakland, CA	3,371
Cody No. 1	U.S. 14, 16, 20, WY	3,202

(1) twin tunnels

World's Longest Railway Tunnels

Source: Railway Directory & Year Book. Tunnels more than 8 mi. in length.

Tunnel	Date	Miles	Operating railway	Country
Seikan	1985	33.50	Japanese Railway	Japan
English Channel Tunnel	1994	31.04	Eurotunnel	UK - France
Dai-shimizu	1979	14.00	Japanese Railway	Japan
Simplon No. 1 and 2	1906, 1922	12.00	Swiss Fed. & Italian St.	Switz.-Italy
Kanmon	1975	12.00	Japanese Railway	Japan
Apennine	1934	11.00	Italian State	Italy
Rokko	1972	10.00	Japanese Railway	Japan
Mt. MacDonald	1989	9.10	Canadian Pacific	Canada
Gotthard	1882	9.00	Swiss Federal	Switzerland
Lotschberg	1913	9.00	Bern-Lotschberg-Simplon	Switzerland
Hokuriku	1962	9.00	Japanese Railway	Japan
Mont Cenis (Frejus)	1871	8.00	Italian State	France-Italy
Shin-Shimizu	1961	8.00	Japanese Railway	Japan
Aki	1975	8.00	Japanese Railway	Japan
Cascade	1929	8.00	Burlington Northern	U.S.
Flathead	1970	8.00	Burlington Northern	U.S.

The English Channel Tunnel

After more than 6 years of construction and the expenditure of more than $15 billion, the English Channel Tunnel was officially opened May 6, 1994, by Queen Elizabeth II of Britain and President François Mitterrand of France.

Work began on the rail tunnels Dec. 1, 1987. More than 15,000 workers, using a total of 11 tunnel boring machines, drove through soft impermeable (or waterproof) rock called chalk marl, removing more than 9.1 million cubic yards of spoil. Nine work-related deaths occurred during construction.

The Eurotunnel system consists of 3 parallel tunnels—2 single-track tunnels (each 25 ft in diameter) and a service tunnel (16 ft in diameter) between them. The tunnels run for 31 mi at an average depth of 131 ft beneath the channel seabed from terminals in Folkstone, England, and Calais, France. With 24 mi of the system running under the sea, the "Chunnel" is the world's longest underwater tunnel. There are 130 cross-passages (each 11 ft in diameter) 1,230 ft apart linking the service tunnel with the rail tunnels to provide for maintenance and any possible emergency. Two undersea crossovers, which are the largest artificial undersea caverns ever built (each about 520 ft long and 60 ft wide), divide the length of the rail tunnels into 3 equal sections, any of which can be closed off in an emergency. During normal operations, the 2 rail tunnels are completely separated at the crossovers by sliding steel doors.

The Channel Tunnel connects the railway networks of British Rail (BR), French Railways (SNCF), and Belgium Railways (SNCB). The railways' new Eurostar trains carry passengers and freight directly between Britain and continental Europe. The railways also operate special shuttle trains, which can travel at a maximum speed of 87 mph and make the trip from highway to highway in about 1 hour. Each shuttle is more than 1/2 mi long and is composed of 12 single-deck and 12 double-deck carriages with a 7,600-hp electric engine at each end. Le Shuttle, as it is called in French, can carry approximately 130 cars and buses (about 800 passengers). Passengers board Le Shuttle in their vehicles and remain in them throughout the journey. The passenger shuttle is well lit, soundproof, and air-conditioned. Separate freight shuttles carrying as many as 28 trucks each are also in operation

Fares for the Eurostar trains and Le Shuttle vary according to season and time of day.

World's Largest Capacity Hydro Plants

Source: U.S. Committee on Large Dams of the Intl. Commission on Large Dams, 1994

Rank order	Name	Country	Rated capacity now (MW)	Rated capacity planned (MW)
1	Turukhansk (Lower Tunguska)*	Russia		20,000
2	Itaipu	Brazil/Paraguay	7,400	13,320
3	Grand Coulee	U.S.	6,495	10,830
4	Guri (Raúl Leoni)	Venezuela	10,300	10,300
5	Tucuruí	Brazil	2,640	7,260
6	Sayano Shushensk*	Russia	6,400	6,400
7 =	Corpus Posadas	Argentina/Paraguay	4,700	6,000
7 =	Krasnoyarsk	Russia	6,000	6,000
9	La Grande 2	Canada	5,328	5,328
10	Churchill Falls	Canada	5,225	5,225
11	Xingo	Brazil	3,012	5,020
12	Tarbela	Pakistan	1,750	4,678
13 =	Bratsk	Russia	4,500	4,500
13 =	Ust-Ilim	Russia	3,675	4,500
15	Cabora Bassa	Mozambique	2,425	4,150
16	Boguchany	Russia		4,000
17 =	Rogun*	Tajikistan		3,600
17 =	Oak Creek	U.S.	3,600	3,600
19	Paulo Afonso I	Brazil	1,524	3,409
20	Pati*	Argentina		3,300
21 =	Ilha Solteira	Brazil	3,200	3,200
21 =	Brumley Gap*	U.S.	3,200	3,200
23	Chapetón*	Argentina		3,000
24	Gezhouba	China	2,715	2,715
25	John Day	U.S.	2,160	2,700
25 =	Nurek	Tajikistan	900	2,700
25 =	Yacireta*	Argentina/Paraguay		2,700

*Planned or under construction; = Equal rank.

Major Dams of the World

Source: U.S. Committee on Large Dams of the Intl. Commission on Large Dams, 1994

World's Highest Dams

Rank order	Name	Country	Height above lowest formation (m)
1	Rogun*	Tajikistan	335
2	Nurek	Tajikstan	300
3	Grand Dixence	Switzerland	285
4	Inguri	Georgia	272
5	Chicoasén	Mexico	261
6	Tehri*	India	261
7	Kishau*	India	253
8 =	Ertan	China	245
8 =	Sayano-Shushensk*	Russia	245
10	Guavio*	Colombia	243
11	Mica	Canada	242
12	Mauvoisin	Switzerland	237
13	Chivor	Colombia	237
14	El Cajón	Honduras	234
15	Chirkei	Russia	233
16	Oroville	U.S.	230
17	Bhakra	India	226
18	Hoover	U.S.	221
19	Contra	Switzerland	220
20	Mratinje	Yugoslavia	220

*Under construction; = Equal rank.

World's Largest Volume Embankment Dams

Rank order	Name	Country	Volume cubic meters × 1000
1	Tarbela	Pakistan	148,500
2	Fort Peck	U.S.	96,050
3	Tucurui	Brazil	85,200
4	Ataturk*	Turkey	85,000
5	Yacireta*	Argentina	81,000
6	Rogun*	Tajikistan	75,500
7	Oahe	U.S.	70,339
8	Guri	Venezuela	70,000
9	Parambikulam	India	69,165
10	High Island West	Hong Kong	67,000
11	Gardiner	Canada	65,000
12	Afsluitdijk	Netherlands	63,400
13	Mangla	Pakistan	63,379
14	Oroville	U.S.	59,635
15	San Luis	U.S.	59,559
16	Nurek	Tajikistan	58,000
17	Tanda	Pakistan	57,250
18	Garrison	U.S.	50,843
19	Chochiti	U.S.	50,228
20	Oosterschelde	Netherlands	50,000

*Under construction.

World's Largest Capacity Reservoirs

Rank order	Name	Country	Capacity cubic meters × 1,000,000
1	Owen Falls	Uganda	204,800
2	Bratsk	Russia	169,000
3	Aswan (High)	Egypt	162,000
4	Kariba	Zimbabwe/Zambia	160,368
5	Akosombo	Ghana	147,960
6	Daniel Johnson	Canada	141,851
7	Guri	Venezuela	135,000
8	Krasnoyarsk	Russia	73,300
9	W A C Bennett (Portage Mt.)	Canada	70,309
10	Zeya	Russia	68,400
11	Cabora Bassa	Mozambique	63,000
12	La Grande 2	Canada	61,715
13	La Grande 3	Canada	60,020
14	Ust-Ilim	Russia	59,300
15	Boguchany*	Russia	58,200
16	Kuibyshev	Russia	58,000
17	Serra de Mesa	Brazil	54,400
18	Caniapiscau Barrage KA 3	Canada	53,790
19	Bukhtarma	Kazakhstan	49,800
20	Ataturk	Turkey	48,700

*Under construction.

Major U.S. Dams and Reservoirs

Source: Committee on Register of Dams, Corps of Engineers, U.S. Army, 1994

Highest Dams

Order	Dam Name	River	State	Type	Height Feet	Height Meters	Year Complete
1	Oroville	Feather	California	E	754	230	1968
2	Hoover	Colorado	Nevada	A	725	221	1936
3	Dworshak	N Fork Clearwater	Idaho	G	718	219	1973
4	Glen Canyon	Colorado	Arizona	A	708	216	1966
5	New Bullards Bar	North Yuba	California	A	636	194	1970
6	New Melones	Stanislaus	California	R	626	191	1979
7	Swift	Lewis	Washington	E	610	186	1958
8	Mossyrock	Cowlitz	Washington	A	607	185	1968
9	Shasta	Sacramento	California	G	600	183	1945
10	Hungry Horse	S Fork Flathead	Montana	A	564	172	1953
11	Grand Coulee	Columbia	Washington	G	551	168	1942
12	Ross	Skagit	Washington	A	541	165	1949

E= Embankment, Earthfill; R= Embankment, Rockfill; G= Gravity; A= Arch.

Largest Embankment Dams

Order	Dam Name	River	State	Type	Volume Cubic yards X 1000	Volume Cubic Meters X 1000	Year Complete
1	Fort Peck	Missouri	Montana	E	125,624	96,050	1937
2	Oahe	Missouri	South Dakota	E	91,996	70,339	1958
3	Oroville	Feather	California	E	77,997	59,635	1968
4	San Luis	San Luis Creek	California	E	77,897	59,559	1967
5	Garrison	Missouri	North Dakota	E	66,498	50,843	1953
6	Cochiti	Rio Grande	New Mexico	E	65,693	50,228	1975
7	Earthquake Lake	Madison	Montana	E-G	49,998	38,228	1959
8	Fort Randall	Missouri	South Dakota	E	49,962	38,200	1952
9	Castaic	Castaic Creek	California	E	43,998	33,640	1973
10	Ludington P/S	Lake Michigan	Michigan	E	37,699	28,824	1973
11	Kingsley	N Platte	Nebraska	E	31,999	24,466	1941
12	Warm Springs	Dry Creek	California	E	29,977	22,920	1982

E= Embankment, Earthfill; G= Gravity.

Largest Reservoirs

Order	Dam Name	Reservoir	Location	Reservoir Capacity Acre-Feet	Reservoir Capacity Cubic Meters X 1000	Year Completed
1	Hoover	Lake Mead	Nevada	28,253,000	34,850,000	1936
2	Glen Canyon	Lake Powell	Arizona	26,997,000	33,300,000	1966
3	Garrison	Lake Sakakawea	North Dakota	22,635,000	27,920,000	1953
4	Oahe	Lake Oahe	South Dakota	22,238,000	27,430,000	1958
5	Fort Peck	Fort Peck Lake	Montana	17,933,000	22,120,000	1937
6	Grand Coulee	F D Roosevelt Lake	Washington	9,558,000	11,790,000	1942
7	Libby	Lake Koocanusa	Montana	5,813,000	7,170,000	1973
8	Fort Randall	Lake Francis Case	South Dakota	4,621,000	5,700,000	1952
9	Shasta	Lake Shasta	California	4,548,000	5,610,000	1945
10	Toledo Bend	Toledo Bend Lake	Louisiana	4,475,000	5,520,000	1968
11	Wolf Creek	Cumberland Lake	Kentucky	3,997,000	4,930,000	1951
12	Flaming Gorge	Flaming Gorge Reservoir	Utah	3,786,000	4,670,000	1964

1 acre foot = 1 acre of water, 1 foot deep

SOCIAL SECURITY

Social Security Programs

Source: Social Security Administration, U.S. Dept. of Health and Human Services; data as of mid-1994

Old-Age, Survivors, and Disability Insurance; Medicare; Supplemental Security Income

Social Security Benefits

Social Security benefits are based on a worker's primary insurance amount (PIA), which is related by law to the average indexed monthly earnings (AIME) on which Social Security contributions have been paid. The full PIA is payable to a retired worker who becomes entitled to benefits at age 65 and to an entitled disabled worker at any age. Spouses and children of retired or disabled workers and survivors of deceased workers receive set proportions of the PIA subject to a family maximum amount. The PIA is calculated by applying varying percentages to succeeding parts of the AIME. The formula is adjusted annually to reflect changes in average annual wages.

Automatic increases in Social Security benefits are initiated for December of a year whenever the Consumer Price Index (CPI) of the Bureau of Labor Statistics for the third calendar quarter of a year increases relative to the CPI for the base quarter, which is either the third calendar quarter of the preceding year or the quarter in which an increase legislated by Congress becomes effective. The size of the benefit increase is determined by the actual percentage rise of the CPI between the quarters measured.

The average monthly benefit payable to all retired workers was $674.00 in December 1993. The average amount for disabled workers in that month was $642.00.

Minimum and maximum monthly retired-worker benefits payable to individuals who retired at age 65[1]

Year of attainment of age 65[2]	Minimum benefit: Payable at time of retirement	Minimum benefit: Payable effective Dec.1993	Maximum benefit: Payable at time of retirement: Men[3]	Maximum benefit: Payable at time of retirement: Women	Maximum benefit: Payable effective Dec. 1993: Men[3]	Maximum benefit: Payable effective Dec. 1993: Women
1965 ..	$44.00	$267.70	$131.70	$135.90	$715.80	$738.70
1970 ..	64.00	267.70	189.80	196.40	793.30	821.50
1980 ..	133.90	267.70	572.00	...	1,114.40	...
1990 ..	(4)	(4)	975.00	...	1,126.00	...
1993 ..	(4)	(4)	1,128.80	...	1,158.10	...
1994 ..	(4)	(4)	1,147.50	...	...	...

(1) Assumes retirement at beginning of year. (2) The final benefit amount payable after Supplementary Medical Insurance (SMI) premium or any other deductions is rounded to next lower $1 (if not already a multiple of $1). (3) Benefits for both men and women are shown in men's columns except where women's benefit appears separately. (4) Minimum eliminated for workers who reach age 62 after 1981.

Amount of Work Required

To qualify for benefits, the worker must have worked in covered employment long enough to become insured. Just how long depends on when the worker reaches age 62 or, if earlier, when he or she dies or becomes disabled.

A person is fully insured if he or she has one quarter of coverage for every year after 1950 (or year age 21 is reached, if later) up to but not including the year in which the worker reaches age 62, dies, or becomes disabled. In 1994, a person earns one quarter of coverage for each $620.00 of annual earnings in covered employment, up to a maximum of 4 quarters per year.

The law permits special monthly payments under the Social Security program to certain very old persons who are not eligible for regular Social Security benefits since they had little or no opportunity to earn Social Security work credits during their working lifetime.

To get disability benefits, in addition to being fully insured, the worker must also have credit for 20 quarters of coverage out of the 40 calendar quarters before he or she becomes disabled. A disabled blind worker need meet only the fully insured requirement. Persons disabled before age 31 can qualify with a briefer period of coverage. Certain survivor benefits are payable if the deceased worker had 6 quarters of coverage in the 13 quarters preceding death.

Work credit for fully insured status for benefits

Born after 1929; die, become disabled, or reach age 62 in	Years needed
1983	8
1984	8¼
1985	8½
1986	8¾
1987	9
1988	9¼
1989	9½
1990	9¾
1991 and after	10

Contribution and benefit base

Calendar year	OASDI[1] Base	HI[2] Base
1984	$37,800	—
1985	39,600	—
1986	42,000	—
1987	43,800	—
1988	45,000	—
1989	48,000	—
1990	51,300	—
1991	53,400	$125,000[3]
1992	55,500	130,200
1993	57,600	135,000
1994	60,600	no limit

(1) Old-Age, Survivors, and Disability Insurance. (2) Hospital Insurance. (3) Although the OASDI and HI bases were the same prior to 1991, they have differed since that time.

Tax-rate schedule
[Percent of covered earnings]

Year	Total	OASDI	HI
	Employees and employers, each		
1979-80	6.13	5.08	1.05
1981	6.65	5.35	1.30
1982-83	6.70	5.40	1.30
1984	7.00	5.70	1.30
1985	7.05	5.70	1.35
1986-87	7.15	5.70	1.45
1988-89	7.51	6.06	1.45
1990 and after	7.65	6.20	1.45
	Self-employed		
1979-80	8.10	7.05	1.05
1981	9.30	8.00	1.30
1982-83	9.35	8.05	1.30
1984	14.00	11.40	2.60
1985	14.10	11.40	2.70
1986-87	14.30	11.40	2.90
1988-89	15.02	12.12	2.90
1990 and after	15.30	12.40	2.90

What Aged Workers Get

When a person has enough work in covered employment and reaches retirement age (currently 65 for full benefit, 62 for reduced benefit), he or she may retire and get monthly old-age benefits. The age at which unreduced benefits are payable will be increased gradually from 65 to 67 over a 21-year period beginning with workers age 62 in the year 2000 (reduced benefits will still be available as early as age 62 but with a larger reduction at age 62). If a person aged 65 or older continues to work and has earnings of more than $11,160 in 1994, $1 in benefits will be withheld for every $3 above $11,160. The annual exempt amount for people under age 65 is $8,040 in 1994, and $1 in benefits is withheld for every $2 in earnings above the exempt amount for them. The annual exempt amount is raised automatically as the general earnings level rises. The eligible worker who is 70 or over receives the full benefit regardless of earnings.

For workers who reach age 65 from 1982 through 1989, the worker's benefit is raised by 3% for each year for which the worker between 65 and 70 (72 before 1984) did not receive benefits because of earnings from work or because the worker had not applied for benefits. The delayed retirement credit is 1% per year for workers reaching age 65 before 1982. The delayed retirement credit will gradually rise to 8% per year from 1990 through 2008. The rate for workers reaching age 65 in 1992-93 is 4%. The rate for workers reaching age 65 in 1994-1995 is 4.5%.

Effective December 1993, the special benefit for persons aged 72 or over who do not meet the regular coverage requirements is $183.40 a month. Like the monthly benefits, these payments are subject to cost-of-living increases. The special payment is not made to persons on the public assistance or supplemental security income rolls.

Workers retiring before age 65 have their benefits permanently reduced by 5/9 of 1% for each month they receive benefits before age 65. Thus, workers entitled to benefits in the month they reach age 62 receive 80% of the PIA, while a worker retiring at age 65 receives a benefit equal to 100% of the PIA. The nearer to age 65 the worker is when he or she begins collecting a benefit, the larger the benefit will be.

Benefits for Worker's Spouse

The spouse of a worker who is getting Social Security retirement or disability payments may become entitled to a spouse's insurance benefit when he or she reaches 65 of one-half of the worker's PIA. Reduced spouse's benefits are available at age 62 (25/36 of 1% reduction for each month of entitlement before age 65). Benefits are also payable to the aged divorced spouse of an insured worker if he or she was married to the worker for at least 10 years.

Benefits for Children of Retired or Disabled Workers

If a retired or disabled worker has a child under 18, the child will get a benefit that is half of the worker's unreduced benefit, and so will the worker's spouse, even if he or she is under 62 if he or she is caring for an entitled child of the worker who is under 16 or who became disabled before age 22. Total benefits paid on a worker's earnings record are subject to a maximum, and if the total that would be paid to a family exceeds that maximum, the individual dependents' benefits are adjusted downward. (Total benefits paid to the family of a worker who retired in January 1994 at age 65 and who always had the maximum amount of earnings creditable under Social Security can be no higher than $2,007.30.)

When entitled children reach 18, their benefits will generally stop, except that a child disabled before 22 may get a benefit as long as his or her disability meets the definition in the law. Additionally, benefits will be paid to a child until age 19 if the child is in full-time attendance at an elementary or secondary school.

Benefits may also be paid to a grandchild or stepgrandchild of a worker or of his or her spouse, in special circumstances.

OASDI	May 1994	May 1993	May 1992
Monthly beneficiaries, total (in thousands)	**42,518**	**41,784**	**40,956**
Aged 65 and over, total	30,865	30,484	30,030
Retired workers	23,671	23,303	22,889
Survivors and dependents	7,192	7,178	7,137
Special age-72 beneficiaries	2	3	4
Under age 65, total	11,654	11,300	10,926
Retired workers	2,520	2,529	2,536
Disabled workers	3,843	3,571	3,306
Survivors and dependents	5,291	5,200	5,084
Total monthly benefits (in millions)	**$25,869**	**$24,623**	**$23,307**

What Disabled Workers Get

A worker who becomes so severely disabled that he or she is unable to work may be eligible to receive a monthly disability benefit. Benefits continue until it is determined that the individual is no longer disabled. Each beneficiary's eligibility is reviewed periodically. When a disabled-worker beneficiary reaches 65, the disability benefit becomes a retired-worker benefit.

Benefits generally like those provided for dependents of retired-worker beneficiaries may be paid to dependents of disabled beneficiaries. However, the maximum family benefit in disability cases is generally lower than in retirement cases.

Survivor Benefits

If an insured worker should die, one or more types of benefits may be payable to survivors, again subject to a maximum family benefit as described above.

1. If claiming benefits at 65, the surviving spouse will receive a benefit that is 100% of the deceased worker's PIA. The surviving spouse may choose to get the benefit as early as age 60, but the benefit is then reduced by 19/40 of 1% for each month it is paid before age 65. However, for those whose spouses claimed their benefits before 65, the benefit is limited to the reduced amount the worker would be getting if alive but not less than 82 ½% of the worker's PIA. Marriage after the worker's death ends the surviving spouse's benefit rights. However, if he or she marries and the marriage is ended, he or she regains benefit rights (A marriage after age 60, 50 if disabled, is deemed not to have occurred for benefit purposes.). This benefit may also be paid to the divorced spouse if the marriage lasted for at least 10 years.

Disabled widows and widowers may under certain circumstances qualify for benefits after attaining age 50 at the rate of 71.5% of the deceased worker's PIA. The widow or widower must have become totally disabled before or within 7 years after the spouse's death, the last month in which he or she received mother's or father's insurance benefits, or the last month he or she previously received surviving spouse's benefits.

2. A benefit for each child until the child reaches 18. The monthly benefit of each child of a worker who has died is three-quarters of the amount the worker would have received if he or she had lived and drawn full retirement benefits. A child with a disability that began before age 22 may receive benefits. Also, a child may receive benefits until age 19 if he or she is in full-time attendance at an elementary or secondary school.

3. A mother's or father's benefit for the widow(er) if children of the worker under 16 are in his or her care. The benefit is 75% of the PIA, and he or she draws it until the youngest child reaches 16, at which time payments stop even if the child's benefit continues. They may start again when he or she is 60 (50 if disabled) unless he or she is married. If he or she has a disabled child beneficiary aged 16 or over in care, benefits also continue.

4. Dependent parents may be eligible for benefits if they have been receiving at least half their support from the worker before his or her death, have reached age 62, and (except in certain circumstances) have not remarried since the worker's death. Each parent gets 75% of the worker's PIA; if only one parent survives the benefit is 82 ½%.

5. A lump sum cash payment of $255. Payment is made only when there is a spouse who was living with the worker or a spouse or child eligible for immediate monthly survivor benefits.

Self-Employed

A self-employed person who has net earnings of $400 or more in a year must report such earnings for Social Security tax and credit purposes. The person reports net returns from the business. Income from real estate, savings, dividends, loans, pensions, or insurance policies may not be included unless it is part of the business.

A self-employed person gets a quarter of coverage for each $620 (for 1994), up to a maximum of 4 quarters of coverage.

The nonfarm self-employed have the option of reporting their earnings as 2/3 of their gross income from self-employment but not more than $1,600 a year and not less than their actual net earnings. This option can be used only if actual net earnings from self-employment income are less than $1,600 and may be used only 5 times. Also, the self-employed person must have actual net earnings of $400 or more in 2 of the 3 taxable years immediately preceding the year in which he or she uses the option.

When a person has both taxable wages and earnings from self-employment, the wages are credited for Social

Security purposes first; only as much of the self-employment income as will bring total earnings up to the current taxable maximum is subject to the self-employment tax.

Farm Owners and Workers

Self-employed farmers whose gross annual earnings from farming are $2,400 or less may report ⅔ of their gross earnings instead of net earnings for Social Security purposes. Farmers whose gross income is over $2,400 and whose net earnings are less than $1,600 can report $1,600. Cash or crop shares received from a tenant or share farmer count if the owner participated materially in production or management. The self-employed farmer pays contributions at the same rate as other self-employed persons.

Agricultural employees. A worker's earnings from farm work count toward benefits (1) if the employer pays him $150 or more in cash during the year; or (2) if the employer spends $2,500 or more in the year for agricultural labor. Under these rules a person gets credit for one calendar quarter for each $620 in cash pay in 1994 up to 4 quarters.

Foreign farm workers admitted to the United States on a temporary basis are not covered.

Household Workers

Anyone employed as maid, cook, laundry worker, nurse, babysitter, chauffeur, gardener, or other worker in the house of another is covered by Social Security if he or she is paid $50 or more in cash in a calendar quarter by any one employer. Room and board do not count, but transportation costs count if paid in cash. The job does not have to be regular or full time. The employee should get a Social Security card at the Social Security office and show it to the employer.

The employer deducts the amount of the employee's Social Security tax from the worker's pay, adds an identical amount as the employer's Social Security tax, and sends the total amount to the federal government, with the employee's Social Security number.

Medicare

The Medicare health insurance program provides acute-care coverage for Social Security and Railroad Retirement beneficiaries aged 65 and over, for persons entitled for 24 months to receive Social Security disability benefits, and for certain persons with end-stage kidney disease. The Medicare program cost $161 billion in 1993 and served more than 36 million people.

Persons eligible for Medicare may choose to have their covered services provided through a health maintenance organization (HMO).

Hospital insurance. The hospital insurance program pays the cost of covered services for hospital and posthospital care as follows:

- Medicare pays for all necessary inpatient hospital care for the first 60 days of each benefit period, except for a deductible ($696 in 1994). For days 61-90, Medicare pays for covered services except for a coinsurance amount ($174 per day in 1994). After 90 days, the beneficiary has 60 reserve days for which Medicare helps pay. The coinsurance amount for reserve days was $348 in 1994.
- Up to 100 days' care in a skilled-nursing facility (skilled-nursing home) in each benefit period. Hospital insurance pays for all covered services for the first 20 days; for the 21-100th day, the beneficiary pays coinsurance ($87 in 1994).
- Visits by nurses or other health workers (not doctors) from a home health agency.
- Hospice care for terminally ill individuals.

Medical insurance. Aged persons can receive benefits under this supplementary program only if they sign up for them and agree to a monthly premium ($41.10 in 1994). The federal government pays the rest of the cost.

The medical insurance program usually pays 80% of the approved amount (after the first $100 in each calendar year) for the following services:

- Covered services received from a doctor in his or her office, in a hospital, in a skilled-nursing facility, at home, or in other locations.
- Medical and surgical services, including anesthesia.
- Diagnostic tests and procedures that are part of your treatment.
- Radiology and pathology services by doctors while you are a hospital inpatient or outpatient.
- Treatment of mental illness. Medicare payments for nonhospital treatment are limited—you may get the services from doctors, comprehensive outpatient rehabilitation facilities (CORFs), physician assistants, psychologists, and clinical social workers.

These services for nonhospital treatment of a mental illness are subject to a special payment rule. In effect, once the annual deductible is met, Medicare pays only 50% (not 80%) of approved charges for these services. On assigned claims, beneficiaries are responsible for paying the remaining 50%. For unassigned claims, beneficiaries may have to pay more.

Partial hospitalization services for treatment of mental illness are not subject to this special payment rule. Also, brief office visits for the sole purpose of monitoring or changing drug prescriptions used in the treatment of mental illness are not subject to this special payment rule.

- Other services such as:
  - X-rays
  - Services of your doctor's office nurse
  - Drugs and biologicals that cannot be self-administered
  - Transfusions of blood and blood components
  - Medical supplies
  - Physical/occupational therapy and speech pathology services.

To get medical insurance protection, persons approaching age 65 may enroll in the 7-month period that includes 3 months before the 65th birthday, the month of the birthday, and 3 months after the birthday, but if they wish coverage to begin in the month they reach 65, they must enroll in the 3 months before their birthday. Persons not enrolling within their first enrollment period may enroll later, during the first 3 months of each year, but their premium may be 10% higher for each 12-month period elapsed since they first could have enrolled.

The monthly premium is deducted from the cash benefit for persons receiving Social Security, Railroad Retirement, or Civil Service retirement benefits. Income from the medical premiums and the federal matching payments are put in a Supplementary Medical Insurance Trust Fund, from which benefits and administrative expenses are paid.

Medicare card. Persons qualifying for hospital insurance under Social Security receive a health insurance card similar to cards now used by Blue Cross and other health insurers. The card indicates whether the individual has taken out medical insurance protection. It is to be shown to the hospital, skilled-nursing facility, home health agency, doctor, or whoever provides the covered services.

Payments are made only in the 50 states, Puerto Rico, the Virgin Islands, Guam, and American Samoa, except that, in rare cases, inpatient hospital services may be provided in Canada and Mexico.

Social Security Financing

Social Security is paid for by a tax on earnings (for 1994, up to $60,600 for Old Age, Survivors, and Disability Insurance and a tax on all earnings [no upper limit] for Hospital Insurance with the Medicare Program; the taxable earnings bases have been adjusted annually to reflect increases in average wages). The employed worker and his or her employer share the tax equally.

Employers remit amounts withheld from employee wages for Social Security and income taxes to the Internal Revenue Service; employer Social Security taxes are also payable at the same time. (Self-employed workers pay their Social Security taxes along with their regular income tax forms.) The Social Security taxes (along with revenues arising from partial taxation of the Social Security benefits of certain high-income people) are transferred to the Social Security Trust Funds—the Federal Old-Age and Survivors Insurance (OASI) Trust Fund, the Federal Disability Insurance (DI) Trust Fund, and the Federal Hospital Insurance (HI) Trust Fund; they can be used only to pay benefits, the cost of rehabilitation services, and administrative expenses. Money not immediately needed for these purposes is by law invested in obligations of the federal government, which must pay interest on the money borrowed and must repay the principal when the obligations are redeemed or mature.

Supplemental Security Income

On Jan. 1, 1974, the Supplemental Security Income (SSI) program established by the 1972 Social Security Act amendments replaced the former federal grants to states for aid to the needy aged, blind, and disabled in the 50 states and the District of Columbia. The program provides both for federal payments based on uniform national standards and eligibility requirements and for state supplementary payments varying from state to state. The Social Security Administration administers the federal payments financed from general funds of the Treasury—and the state supplements as well, if the state elects to have its supplementary program federally administered. The states may supplement the federal payment for all recipients and must supplement it for persons otherwise adversely affected by the transition from the former public assistance programs. In May 1994, the number of persons receiving federal payments and federally administered state payments was 6,166,394 and the amount of these payments was $2.2 billion.

The maximum monthly federal SSI payment for individuals with no other countable income, living in their own household, was $446.00 in 1994. For couples it was $669.00.

Examples of monthly cash benefit awards for selected beneficiary families with first entitlement in 1994, effective January 1994

Beneficiary Family	Low Earnings ($11,147 in 1994) (45% of average)	Career Earnings Level Average Earnings ($24,772 in 1994)[1]	Maximum Earnings ($60,600 in 1994)
Primary Insurance amount (worker retiring at 65)	$505.00	$829.00	$1,147.00
Maximum family benefit (worker retiring at 65)	758.50	1,510.80	2,007.30
Disability maximum family benefit (worker disabled at 55; in 1993)*	716.80	1,257.10	1,797.80
Disabled worker: (worker disabled at 55)			
Worker alone	508.00	838.00	1,198.00
Worker, spouse, and 1 child	716.00	1,257.00	1,796.00
Retired worker claiming benefits at age 62:			
Worker alone[2]	415.00	685.00	948.00
Worker with spouse claiming benefits at—			
Age 65 or over	757.00	1,243.00	1,720.00
Age 62[2]	609.00	1,006.00	1,392.00
Widow or widower claiming benefits at—			
Age 65 or over[3]	505.00	829.00	1,147.00
Age 60 (spouse died at 65 without receiving reduced benefits)	361.00	593.00	820.00
Disabled widow or widower claiming benefits at age 50-59[4]	361.00	593.00	820.00
1 surviving child	378.00	622.00	860.00
Widow or widower age 65 or over and 1 child[5]	758.00	1,451.00	2,007.00
Widowed mother or father and 1 child[5]	756.00	1,244.00	1,720.00
Widowed mother or father and 2 children[5]	758.00	1,509.00	2,007.00

*Assumes work beginning at age 22. (1) Estimate. (2) Assumes maximum reduction. (3) A widow(er)'s benefit amount is limited to the amount the spouse would have been receiving if still living but not less than 82.5 percent of the PIA. (4) Effective January 1984, disabled widow(er)s claiming benefit at ages 50-59 will receive benefit equal to 71.5 percent of the PIA (based on 1983 Social Security Amendment provision). (5) Based on worker dying at age 65.

Social Security Trust Funds

Old-Age and Survivors Insurance Trust Fund, 1940-1993

(In millions)

	Income					Disbursements						
Fiscal year[1]	Total	Net contributions[2]	Income from taxation of benefits	Payments from the general fund of the Treasury[3]	Net interest[4]	Total	Benefit payments[5]	Administrative expenses	Transfers to Railroad Retirement program	Interfund borrowing transfers[6]	Net increase in fund	Fund at end of period
1940	$592	$550	—	—	$42	$28	$16	$12	—	—	$564	$1,745
1950	2,367	2,106	—	$4	257	784	727	57	—	—	1,583	12,893
1960	10,360	9,843	—	—	517	11,073	10,270	202	$600	—	-713	20,829
1970	31,746	29,955	—	442	1,350	27,321	26,268	474	579	—	4,425	32,616
1980	100,051	97,608	—	557	1,886	103,228	100,626	1,160	1,442	—	-3,177	24,566
1985	179,881	175,305	$3,151	105	1,321	169,210	165,310	1,589	2,310	$-4,364	6,308	33,877
1990	278,607	261,506	2,924	34	14,143	223,481	218,948	1,564	2,969	—	55,126	203,445
1991	293,288	270,841	5,790	-2,089	18,746	241,316	236,195	1,746	3,375	—	51,972	255,417
1992	307,102	278,506	6,019	19	22,557	256,239	251,268	1,823	3,148	—	50,862	306,280
1993	319,298	287,569	5,893	14	25,822	269,934	264,561	2,021	3,353	—	49,364	355,644

(1) Under the Congressional Budget Act of 1974 (Public Law 93-344), fiscal years 1977 and later consist of the 12 months ending on September 30 of each year. Fiscal years prior to 1977 consisted of the 12 months ending on June 30 of each year. (2) Beginning in 1983, includes transfers from general fund of Treasury representing contributions that would have been paid on deemed wage credits for military service in 1957 and later, if such credits were considered covered wages. (3) Includes payments (a) in 1947-52 and in 1967 and later, for costs of noncontributory wage credits for military service performed before 1957; (b) in 1972-83, for costs of deemed wage credits for military service performed after 1956; and (c) in 1969 and later, for costs of benefits to certain uninsured persons who attained age 72 before 1968. (4) Net interest includes net profits or losses on marketable investments. Beginning in 1967, administrative expenses are charged currently to the trust fund on an estimated basis, with a final adjustment, including interest, made in the following fiscal year. The amounts of these interest adjustments are included in net interest. For years prior to 1967, a description of the method of accounting for administrative expenses is contained in the 1970 Annual Report. Beginning in October 1973, the figures shown include relatively small amounts of gifts to the fund. Figures for 1983-86 reflect payments from a borrowing trust fund to a lending trust fund for interest on amounts owed under the interfund borrowing provisions. During 1983-91, interest paid from the trust fund to the general fund on advance tax transfers is reflected. The amounts shown for 1985 and 1986 include interest adjustments of $76.5 million and $11.5 million, respectively, on unnegotiated checks issued before April 1985. (5) Beginning in 1967, includes payments for vocational rehabilitation services furnished to disabled persons receiving benefits because of their disabilities. Beginning in 1983, amounts are reduced by amount of reimbursement for unnegotiated benefit checks. (6) Negative figures represent amounts repaid from the OASI Trust Fund to the DI and HI Trust Funds.

Disability Insurance Trust Fund, 1960-1993

(In millions)

Fiscal year[1]	Income: Total	Net contributions[2]	Income from taxation of benefits	Payments from the general fund of the Treasury[3]	Net interest[4]	Disbursements: Total	Benefit payments[5]	Administrative expenses	Transfers to Railroad Retirement program	Interfund borrowing transfers[6]	Net increase in fund	Fund at end of period
1960	$1,034	$987	—	—	$47	$533	$528	$32	-$27	—	$501	$2,167
1970	4,380	4,141	—	$16	223	2,954	2,795	149	10	—	1,426	5,104
1980	17,376	16,805	—	118	453	15,320	14,998	334	-12	—	2,056	7,680
1985	17,984	16,876	$217	—	891	19,294	18,648	603	43	$2,540	1,230	5,873
1990	28,215	27,291	158	—	766	25,124	24,327	717	80	—	3,091	11,455
1991	29,322	28,953	131	-775	1,014	27,780	26,909	789	82	—	1,543	12,997
1992	31,168	29,871	218	—	1,080	31,285	30,382	845	58	—	-116	12,881
1993	32,056	30,822	268	—	966	34,632	33,615	935	83	—	-2,576	10,305

(1) Under the Congressional Budget Act of 1974 (Public Law 93-344 , fiscal years 1977 and later consist of the 12 months ending on September 30 of each year. The act further provides that the calendar quarter July-September 1976 is a period of transition from fiscal year 1976, which ended on June 30, 1976, to fiscal year 1977, which began on October 1, 1976. (2) Beginning in 1983, includes government contributions on deemed wage credits for military service in 1957 and later. (3) Includes payments (a) in 1967 and later, for costs of noncontributory wage credits for military service performed before 1957; and (b) in 1972-83, for costs of deemed wage credits for military service performed after 1956. (4) Net interest includes net profits or losses on marketable investments. Beginning in 1967, administrative expenses are charged currently to the trust fund on an estimated basis, with a final adjustment, including interest, made in the following fiscal year. The amounts of these interest adjustments are included in net interest. For years prior to 1967, a description of the method of accounting for administrative expenses is contained in the 1970 Annual Report of the Board of Trustees of the Federal Old-Age and Survivors Insurance and Disability Insurance Trust Funds. Beginning in 1983, these figures reflect payments from a borrowing trust fund to a lending trust fund for interest on amounts owed under the interfund borrowing provisions. Also, beginning in 1983, interest paid from the trust fund to the general fund on advance tax transfers is reflected. The amount shown for 1985 includes an interest adjustment of $14.8 million on unnegotiated checks issued before April 1985. (5) Beginning in 1967, includes payments for vocational rehabilitation services furnished to disabled persons receiving benefits because of their disabilities. Beginning in 1983, amounts are reduced by amount of reimbursement for unnegotiated benefit checks. The amount shown for 1983 is reduced by $48 million for all unnegotiated checks issued before 1983; reductions in subsequent years are relatively small. (6) Negative figure represents amounts lent by the DI Trust Fund to the OASI Trust Fund. Positive figures represent repayment of these amounts.

Supplementary Medical Insurance Trust Fund, 1970-1993

(In millions)

Fiscal year[1]	Income: Premium from participants	Government contributions[2]	Interest and other income[3]	Total income	Disbursements: Benefit payments[5]	Administrative expenses	Total disbursements	Balance in fund at end of year[4]
1970	$936	$928	$12	$1,876	$1,979	$217	$2,196	$57
1975	1,887	2,330	105	4,322	3,765	405	4,170	1,424
1980	2,928	6,932	415	10,275	10,144	593	10,737	4,532
1985	5,524	17,898	1,155	24,577	21,808	922	22,730	10,646
1990	11,494[5]	33,210	1,434[5]	46,138[5]	41,498	1,524[5]	43,022[5]	14,527[5]
1991	11,807	34,730	1,629	48,166	45,514	1,505	47,019	15,675
1992	12,748	38,684	1,717	53,149	48,627	1,661	50,288	18,535
1993	14,683	44,227	1,889	60,799	54,214[6]	1,845	56,059	23,276

(1) For 1967 through 1976, fiscal years cover the interval from July 1 through June 30; fiscal years 1977 and later cover the interval from October 1 through September 30. (2) The payments shown as being from the general fund of the Treasury include certain interest-adjustment items. (3) Other income includes recoveries of amounts reimbursed from the trust fund that are not obligations of the trust fund and other miscellaneous income. (4) The financial status of the program depends on both the total net assets and the liabilities of the program. (5) Includes the impact of the Medicare Catastrophic Coverage Act of 1988 (Public Law 100-360). (6) Includes $1,805 million transfer to the HI trust fund, as provided for by Public Law 102-394.

Hospital Insurance Trust Fund, 1970-1993

(In millions)

Fiscal Year[1]	Income: Payroll taxes	Transfers from railroad retirement account	Reimbursement for uninsured persons	Premiums from voluntary enrollees	Payments for military wage credits	Interest on investments and other income[2]	Total income	Disbursements: Benefit payments[3]	Administrative expense[4]	Total disbursements	Trust Fund: Net increase fund	Fund at end of year
1970	$4,785	$64	$617	—	$11	$137	$5,614	$4,804	$149	$4,953	$661	$2,677
1975	11,291	132	481	$6	48	609	12,568	10,353	259	10,612	1,956	9,870
1980	23,244	244	697	17	141	1,072	25,415	23,790	497	24,288	1,127	14,490
1985	46,490	371	766	38	86	3,182	50,933	47,841	813	48,654	4,103[5]	21,277[5]
1990	70,655	367	413	113	107	7,908	79,563	65,912	774	66,687	12,876	95,631
1991	74,655	352	605	367	-1,011[6]	8,969	83,938	68,705	934	69,638	14,299	109,930
1992	80,978	374	621	484	86	10,133	92,677	80,784	1,191	81,974	10,703	120,633
1993	83,147	400	367	622	81	12,484[7]	97,101	90,738	866	91,604	5,497	126,131

(1) Fiscal years 1976 and earlier consist of the 12 months ending on June 30 of each year; fiscal years 1977 and later consist of the 12 months ending on September 30 of each year. (2) Other income includes recoveries of amounts reimbursed from the trust fund that are not obligations of the trust fund and a small amount of miscellaneous income. (3) Includes costs of Peer Review Organizations (beginning with the implementation of the Prospective Payment System on October 1, 1983). (4) Includes costs of experiments and demonstration projects. (5) In fiscal year 1983, $12,437 million was loaned to the Old-Age and Survivors Insurance Trust Fund under the interfund borrowing provisions of the Social Security Act. Repayments of $1,824 million and $10,613 million were made in fiscal years 1985 and 1986, respectively. (6) Includes the lump sum general revenue adjustment of $-1,100 million, as provided for by section 151 of Public Law 98-21. (7) Includes $1,805 million transfer from the SMI catastrophic coverage reserve fund, as provided for by Public Law 102-394. NOTE: Totals do not necessarily equal the sum of rounded components.

Finding Your Target Heart Rate

Source: Carole Casten, EdD, and Peg Jordan, RN, *Aerobics Today*, Aerobic Fitness Association of America

The target heart rate is the heartbeat rate a person should have during aerobic exercise (such as running, fast walking, cycling, or cross-country skiing) to get the full benefit of the exercise for cardiovascular conditioning.

First, determine the intensity level at which one would like to exercise. A sedentary person may want to begin an exercise regimen at the 60% level and work up gradually to the 70% level. Athletes and highly fit individuals must work at the 85-95% level to receive the benefits of exercise.

Second, calculate the target heart rate. One common way of doing this is by using the American College of Sports Medicine Method.

To obtain cardiovascular fitness benefits from aerobic exercise, it is recommended that an individual participate in an aerobic activity at least 3-5 times a week for 20-30 minutes per session, although cardiac patients and very sedentary individuals can obtain benefits with shorter periods (15-20 minutes). Generally, training changes occur in 4-6 weeks but can occur in as little as 2 weeks.

The American College of Sports Medicine Method

Using the American College of Sports Medicine Method to calculate one's target heart rate, an individual should subtract his or her age from 220, then multiply by the desired intensity level of the workout. Then divide the answer by 6 for a 10-second pulse count. (The 10-second pulse count is useful for checking whether the target heart rate is being achieved during the workout. One can easily check one's pulse—at the wrist or side of the neck—counting the number of beats in 10 seconds.)

For example, a 20-year-old wishing to exercise at 70% intensity, would employ the following steps:

Maximum Heart Rate	220 - 20 = 200
Target Heart Rate	200 × .70 =140
10-second Pulse Count	140 ÷ 6 =23

To work at the desired level of intensity, this 20-year old would strive for a target heart rate of 140 beats per minute, or a 10-second pulse count of 23.

Food and Nutrition

Food contains proteins, carbohydrates, fats, water, vitamins, and minerals. Nutrition is the way your body takes in and uses these ingredients to maintain proper functioning.

The U.S. Dept. of Health and Human Services and the Dept. of Agriculture issued dietary guidelines Nov. 5, 1990, that were the most specific ever and covered children age 2 and over, as well as adults. Recommended were: (1) no more than 30 percent of calories from fat, or about 67 grams of fat in a 2,000-calorie daily diet; and no more than 10 percent of calories, or 22 grams of fat, from saturated fats; (2) maximum alcohol consumption of about 1 drink a day for women, 2 for men; (3) daily consumption of vegetables of 3-5 servings; fruits, 2-4; pastas, cereals or breads, 6-11; milk, 2-3; meat, poultry, fish, and eggs, 2-3. (For vegetables, 1 serving=about 1 cup raw leafy greens or one-half cup other kinds; fruit, 1 medium apple, banana, or orange; grains, 1 slice of bread, 1 cup of pasta, or 1 oz. cereal; milk, 1 cup or 1.5 oz. of cheese; meat and poultry, 2-3 oz. cooked lean beef or chicken without skin.)

Protein

Proteins, composed of amino acids, are indispensable in the diet. They build, maintain, and repair the body. Best sources: eggs, milk, fish, meat, poultry, soybeans, nuts. High-quality proteins such as eggs, meat, or fish supply all 8 amino acids needed in the diet. Plant foods can be combined to meet protein needs as well: whole grain breads and cereals, rice, oats, soybeans, other beans, split peas, and nuts.

Fats

Fats provide energy by furnishing calories to the body, and by carrying vitamins A, D, E, and K. They are the most concentrated source of energy in the diet. Best sources of polyunsaturated and monounsaturated fats: margarine, vegetable/plant oils, nuts; meats, cheeses, butter, cream, egg yolks, lard are concentrated sources of saturated fats.

Carbohydrates

Carbohydrates provide energy for body function and activity by supplying immediate calories. The carbohydrate group includes sugars, starches, fiber, and starchy vegetables. Best sources: grains, legumes, potatoes, vegetables, fruits.

Water

Water dissolves and transports other nutrients throughout the body, aiding the processes of digestion, absorption, circulation, and excretion. It helps regulate body temperature.

Vitamins

Vitamin A—promotes good eyesight and helps keep the skin and mucous membranes resistant to infection. Best sources: liver, sweet potatoes, carrots, kale, cantaloupe, turnip greens, collard greens, broccoli, fortified milk.

Vitamin B_1 (thiamine)—prevents beriberi. Essential to carbohydrate metabolism and health of nervous system. Best sources: pork, enriched cereals, grains, soybeans, and nuts.

Vitamin B_2 (riboflavin)—protects skin, mouth, eyes, eyelids, and mucous membranes. Essential to protein and energy metabolism. Best sources: milk, meat, poultry, cheese, broccoli, spinach.

Vitamin B_6 (pyrido xine)—important in the regulation of the central nervous system and in protein metabolism. Best sources: whole grains, meats, fish, poultry, nuts, brewers' yeast.

Vitamin B_{12} (cobalamin)—needed to form red blood cells. Best sources: meat, fish, poultry, eggs, dairy products.

Niacin—maintains the health of skin, tongue, and digestive system. Best sources: poultry, peanuts, fish, enriched flour and bread.

Folic acid (folacin)—required for normal blood cell formation, growth, and reproduction and for important chemical reactions in body cells. Best sources: yeast, orange juice, green leafy vegetables, wheat germ, asparagus, broccoli, nuts.

Other B vitamins—biotin, pantothenic acid.

Vitamin C (ascorbic acid)—maintains collagen, a protein necessary for the formation of skin, ligaments, and bones. It helps heal wounds and mend fractures and aids in resisting some types of viral and bacterial infections. Best sources: citrus fruits and juices, cantaloupe, broccoli, brussels sprouts, potatoes and sweet potatoes, tomatoes, cabbage.

Vitamin D—important for bone development. Best sources: sunlight, fortified milk and milk products, fish-liver oils, egg yolks.

Vitamin E (tocopherol)—helps protect red blood cells. Best sources: vegetable oils, wheat germ, whole grains, eggs, peanuts, margarine, green leafy vegetables.

Vitamin K—necessary for formation of prothrombin, which helps blood to clot. Also made by intestinal bacteria. Best dietary sources: green leafy vegetables, tomatoes.

Minerals

Calcium—the most abundant mineral in the body, works with phosphorus in building and maintaining bones and teeth. Best sources: milk and milk products, cheese, blackstrap molasses, tofu.

Phosphorus—the 2d most abundant mineral, performs more functions than any other mineral, and plays a part in nearly every chemical reaction in the body. Best source: cheese, milk, meats, poultry, fish, tofu.

Iron—Necessary for the formation of myoglobin, which is a reservoir of oxygen for muscle tissue, and hemoglobin, which transports oxygen in the blood. Best sources: lean meats, beans, green leafy vegetables, shellfish, enriched breads and cereals, whole grains.

Other minerals—chromium, cobalt, copper, fluorine, iodine, magnesium, manganese, molybdenum, potassium, selenium, sodium, sulfur, and zinc.

Nutritive Value of Food (Calories, Proteins, etc.)

Source: *Home and Garden Bulletin No. 72*; available from Supt. of Documents, U.S. Government Printing Office, Washington, DC 20402

Food	Measure	Grams	Food Energy (calories)	Protein (grams)	Fat (grams)	Saturated fats (grams)	Carbohydrate (grams)	Calcium (milligrams)	Iron (milligrams)	Sodium (milligrams)	Vitamin A (I.U.)	Ascorbic Acid (milligrams)
Dairy products												
Cheese, cheddar, cut pieces	1 oz.	28	115	7	9	6.0	T	204	0.2	176	300	0
Cheese, cottage, small curd	1 cup	210	215	26	9	6.0	6	126	0.3	850	340	T
Cheese, cream	1 oz.	28	100	2	10	6.2	1	23	0.3	84	400	0
Cheese, Swiss	1 oz.	28	95	7	7	4.5	1	219	0.2	388	230	0
Half-and-half	1 tbsp.	15	20	T	2	1.1	1	16	T	6	70	T
Cream, sour	1 tbsp.	12	25	T	3	1.6	1	14	T	6	90	T
Milk, whole	1 cup	244	150	8	8	5.1	11	291	0.1	120	310	2
Milk, nonfat (skim)	1 cup	245	85	8	T	0.3	12	302	0.1	126	500	2
Milkshake, chocolate	10 oz.	283	355	9	8	4.8	60	374	0.9	314	240	0
Ice cream, hardened	1 cup	133	270	5	14	8.9	32	176	0.1	116	540	1
Sherbet	1 cup	193	270	2	4	2.4	59	103	0.3	88	190	4
Yogurt, fruit-flavored	8 oz.	227	230	10	2	1.6	43	345	0.2	133	100	1
Eggs												
Fried in margarine	1	46	90	6	7	1.9	1	25	0.7	162	390	0
Hard-cooked	1	50	75	6	5	1.6	1	25	0.6	62	280	0
Scrambled (milk added) in margarine	1	61	100	7	7	2.2	1	44	0.7	171	420	T
Fats & oils												
Butter, salted	1 tbsp.	14	100	T	11	7.1	T	3	T	116	430	0
Margarine, salted	1 tbsp.	14	100	T	11	2.2	T	4	T	132	460	T
Olive oil	1 tbsp.	14	125	0	14	1.9	0	0	0	0	0	0
Salad dressing, blue cheese	1 tbsp.	15	75	1	8	1.5	1	12	T	164	30	T
Salad dressing, French, regular	1 tbsp.	16	85	T	9	1.4	1	2	T	188	T	T
Salad dressing, French, low calorie	1 tbsp.	16	25	T	2	0.2	2	6	T	306	T	T
Salad dressing, Italian	1 tbsp.	15	80	T	9	1.3	1	1	T	162	30	T
Mayonnaise	1 tbsp.	14	100	T	11	1.7	T	3	0.1	80	40	0
Fish, meat, poultry												
Clams, raw, meat only	3 oz.	85	65	11	1	0.3	2	59	2.6	102	90	9
Crabmeat, canned	1 cup	135	135	23	3	0.5	1	61	1.1	1,350	50	0
Fish sticks, frozen, reheated	1 fish stick	28	70	6	3	0.8	4	11	0.3	53	20	0
Salmon canned (pink), solids and liquid	3 oz.	85	120	17	5	0.9	0	167	0.7	443	60	0
Sardines, Atlantic, canned in oil, drained solids	3 oz.	85	175	20	9	2.1	0	371	2.6	425	190	0
Shrimp, French fried	3 oz.	85	200	16	10	2.5	11	61	2.0	384	90	0
Trout, broiled, with butter and lemon juice	3 oz.	85	175	21	9	4.1	T	26	1.0	122	230	1
Tuna, canned in oil	3 oz.	85	165	24	7	1.4	0	7	1.6	303	70	0
Bacon, broiled or fried crisp	3 slices	19	110	6	9	3.3	T	2	0.3	303	0	6
Ground beef, broiled, regular	3 oz.	85	245	20	18	6.9	0	9	2.1	70	T	0
Roast beef, relatively lean (lean only)	2.6 oz.	75	135	22	5	1.9	0	3	1.5	46	T	0
Beef steak, lean and fat	3 oz.	85	240	23	15	6.4	0	9	2.6	53	T	0
Beef & vegetable stew	1 cup	245	220	16	11	4.4	15	29	2.9	292	5,690	17
Lamb, chop, broiled loin, lean and fat	2.8 oz.	80	235	22	16	7.3	0	16	1.4	62	T	0
Liver, beef, fried	3 oz.	85	185	23	7	2.5	7	9	5.3	90	30,690	23
Ham, light cure, roasted, lean and fat	3 oz.	85	205	18	14	5.1	0	6	0.7	1,009	0	0
Pork, chop, broiled, lean and fat	3.1 oz.	87	275	24	19	7.0	0	3	0.7	61	10	T
Bologna	2 slices	57	180	7	16	6.1	2	7	0.9	581	0	12
Frankfurter, pork, cooked	1	45	145	5	13	4.8	1	5	0.5	504	0	12
Sausage, pork link, cooked	1 link	13	50	3	4	1.4	T	4	0.2	168	0	T
Veal, cutlet, braised or broiled	3 oz.	85	185	23	9	4.1	0	9	0.8	56	T	0
Chicken, drumstick, fried, bones removed	2.5 oz.	72	195	16	11	3.0	6	12	1.0	194	60	0
Chicken, roasted, half breast, without skin	3 oz.	86	140	27	3	0.9	0	13	0.9	64	20	0
Turkey, roasted, chopped light and dark meat	1 cup	140	240	41	7	2.3	0	35	2.5	98	0	0
Frankfurter, chicken, cooked	1	45	115	6	9	2.5	3	43	0.9	616	60	0
Fruits & fruit products												
Apple, raw, 2-3/4 in. diam.	1	138	80	T	T	0.1	21	10	0.2	T	70	8
Apple juice	1 cup	248	115	T	T	T	29	17	0.9	7	T	2
Apricots, raw	3	106	50	1	T	T	12	15	0.6	1	2,770	11
Banana, raw	1	114	105	1	1	0.2	27	7	0.4	1	90	10
Cherries, sweet, raw	10	68	50	1	1	0.1	11	10	0.3	T	150	5
Cranberry juice cocktail, sweetened	1 cup	253	145	T	T	T	38	8	0.4	10	10	108
Fruit cocktail, canned, in heavy syrup	1 cup	255	185	1	T	T	48	15	0.7	15	520	5
Grapefruit, raw, medium, white	1/2	120	40	1	T	T	10	14	0.1	T	10	41
Grapes, Thompson seedless	10	50	35	T	T	0.1	9	6	0.1	1	40	5
Lemonade, frozen, unsweetened	6 oz.	244	55	1	1	0.1	16	20	0.3	2	30	77
Cantaloupe, 5-in. diam.	1/2	267	95	2	1	0.1	22	29	0.6	24	8,610	113
Orange, 2-5/8 in. diam.	1	131	60	1	T	T	15	52	0.1	T	270	70
Orange juice, frozen, diluted	1 cup	249	110	2	T	T	27	22	0.2	2	190	97
Peach, raw, 2-1/2 in. diam.	1	87	35	1	T	T	10	4	0.1	T	470	6
Raisins, seedless	1 cup	145	435	5	1	0.2	115	71	3.0	17	10	5
Strawberries, whole	1 cup	149	45	1	1	T	10	21	0.6	1	40	84
Watermelon, 4 by 8 in. wedge	1piece	482	155	3	2	0.3	35	39	0.8	10	1,760	46
Grain products												
Bagel, plain	1	68	200	7	2	0.3	38	29	1.8	245	0	0
Biscuit, 2 in. diam., from home recipe	1	28	100	2	5	1.2	13	47	0.7	195	10	T
Bread, pita, enriched, white, 6-1/2 in. diam	1 pita	60	165	6	1	0.1	12	15	0.7	124	0	0
Bread, white, enriched	1 slice	25	65	2	1	0.3	12	32	0.7	129	T	T
Bread, whole-wheat	1 slice	28	70	3	1	0.4	13	20	1.0	180	T	T
Oatmeal or rolled oats, without added salt	1 cup	234	145	6	2	0.4	25	19	1.6	2	40	0
Bran flakes (40% bran), added sugar, salt, iron, vitamins	1 oz.	28	90	4	1	0.1	22	14	8.1	264	1,250	0
Corn flakes, added sugar, salt, iron, vitamins	1 oz.	28	110	2	T	T	24	1	1.8	351	1,250	15
Rice, puffed, added iron, thiamine, niacin	1 oz.	28	110	2	T	T	25	4	1.8	340	1,250	15
Wheat, shredded, plain, 1 biscuit or 2/3 cup.	1 oz.	28	100	3	1	0.1	23	11	1.2	3	0	0
Bulgur, uncooked	1 cup	170	600	19	3	1.2	129	49	9.5	7	0	0
Cake, angel food, 1/12 of cake	1	53	125	3	T	T	29	44	0.2	269	0	0
Cupcake, 2-1/2 in. diam., with chocolate icing	1	35	120	2	4	1.8	20	21	0.7	92	50	T
Plain sheet cake with white, uncooked frosting, 1/9 of cake	1	121	445	4	14	4.6	77	61	1.2	275	240	T

Food	Measure	Grams	Food Energy (calories)	Protein (grams)	Fat (grams)	Saturated fats (grams)	Carbohydrate (grams)	Calcium (milligrams)	Iron (milligrams)	Sodium (milligrams)	Vitamin A (I.U.)	Ascorbic Acid (milligrams)
Fruitcake, dark, 1/32 of loaf	1	43	165	2	7	1.5	25	41	1.2	67	50	16
Cake, pound, 1/17 of loaf	1	29	110	2	5	3.0	15	8	0.5	108	160	0
Cheesecake, 1/12 of 9-in. diam. cake	1	92	280	5	18	9.9	26	52	0.4	204	230	5
Brownies, with nuts, from commercial recipe	1	25	100	1	4	1.6	16	13	0.6	59	70	T
Cookies, chocolate chip, from home recipe	4	40	185	2	11	3.9	26	13	1.0	82	20	0
Crackers, graham, 2-1/2 in. squares	2	14	60	1	1	0.4	11	6	0.4	86	0	0
Crackers, saltines	4	12	50	1	1	0.5	9	3	0.5	165	0	0
Danish pastry, round piece	1	57	220	4	12	3.6	26	60	1.1	218	60	T
Doughnut, cake type	1	50	210	3	12	2.8	24	22	1.0	192	20	T
Macaroni, firm stage (hot)	1 cup	130	190	7	1	0.1	39	14	2.1	1	0	0
Muffin, bran, commercial mix	1	45	140	3	4	1.3	24	27	1.7	385	100	0
Muffin, corn, from home recipe	1	45	145	3	5	1.5	21	66	0.9	169	80	T
Noodles, enriched, cooked	1 cup	160	200	7	2	0.5	37	16	2.6	3	110	0
Pie, apple, 1/6 of pie	1	158	405	3	18	4.6	60	13	1.6	476	50	2
Pie, cherry, 1/6 of pie	1	158	410	4	18	4.7	61	22	1.6	480	700	0
Pie, lemon meringue, 1/6 of pie	1	140	355	5	14	4.3	53	20	1.4	395	240	4
Pie, pecan, 1/6 of pie	1	138	575	7	32	4.7	71	65	4.6	305	220	0
Popcorn, air-popped, plain	1 cup	8	30	1	T	T	6	1	0.2	T	10	0
Pretzels, stick	10	3	10	T	T	T	2	1	0.1	48	0	0
Rolls, enriched, brown & serve	1	28	85	2	2	0.5	14	33	0.8	155	T	T
Rolls, frankfurter & hamburger	1	40	115	3	2	0.5	20	54	1.2	241	T	T
Tortillas, corn	1	30	65	2	1	0.1	13	42	0.6	1	80	0
Legumes, nuts, seeds												
Beans, Black	1 cup	171	225	15	1	0.1	41	47	2.9	1	T	0
Beans, Great Northern, cooked	1 cup	180	210	14	1	0.1	38	90	4.9	13	0	0
Peanuts, roasted in oil, salted	1 cup	145	840	39	71	9.9	27	125	2.8	626	0	0
Peanut butter	1 tbsp.	16	95	5	8	1.4	3	5	0.3	75	0	0
Refried beans, canned	1 cup	290	295	18	3	0.4	51	141	5.1	1,228	0	17
Tofu	1 piece	120	85	9	5	0.7	3	108	2.3	8	0	0
Sunflower seeds, hulled	1 oz.	28	160	6	14	1.5	5	33	1.9	1	10	T
Mixed foods												
Chop suey with beef and pork, home recipe	1 cup	250	300	26	17	4.3	13	60	4.8	1,053	600	33
Enchilada	1	230	235	20	16	7.7	24	97	3.3	1,332	2,720	T
Pizza, cheese, 1/8 of 15 in.-diam. pie	1	120	290	15	9	4.1	39	220	1.6	699	750	2
Spaghetti with meatballs & tomato sauce	1 cup	248	330	19	12	3.9	39	124	3.7	1,009	1,590	22
Sugars & sweets												
Candy, caramels	1 oz.	28	115	1	3	2.2	22	42	0.4	64	T	T
Candy, milk chocolate	1 oz.	28	145	2	9	5.4	16	50	0.4	23	30	T
Fudge, chocolate	1 oz.	28	115	1	3	2.1	21	22	0.3	54	T	T
Gelatin dessert, from prepared powder	1/2 cup	120	70	2	0	0.0	17	2	T	55	0	0
Candy, hard	1 oz.	28	110	0	0	0.0	28	T	0.1	7	0	0
Honey	1 tbsp.	21	65	T	0	0.0	17	1	0.1	1	0	T
Jams & Preserves	1 tbsp.	20	55	T	T	0.0	14	4	0.2	2	T	T
Popsicle, 3 fl. oz.	1	95	70	0	0	0.0	18	0	T	11	0	0
Sugar, white, granulated	1 tbsp.	12	45	0	0	0.0	12	T	T	T	0	0
Vegetables												
Asparagus, spears, cooked from raw	4 spears	60	15	2	T	T	3	14	0.4	2	500	16
Beans, green, from frozen, cuts	1 cup	135	35	2	T	T	8	61	1.1	18	710	11
Broccoli, cooked from raw	1 spear	180	50	5	1	0.1	10	82	2.1	20	2,540	113
Cabbage, raw, coarsely shredded or sliced	1 cup	70	15	1	T	T	4	33	0.4	13	90	33
Carrots, raw, 7-1/2 by 1-1/8 in.	1	72	30	1	T	T	7	19	0.4	25	20,250	7
Cauliflower, cooked, drained, from raw	1 cup	125	30	2	T	T	6	34	0.5	8	20	69
Celery, raw	1 stalk	40	5	T	T	T	1	14	0.2	35	50	3
Collards, cooked from raw	1 cup	190	25	2	T	0.1	5	148	0.8	36	4,220	19
Corn, sweet, yellow, cooked from raw	1 ear	77	85	3	1	0.2	19	2	0.5	13	170	5
Eggplant, cooked, steamed	1 cup	96	25	1	T	T	6	6	0.3	3	60	1
Lettuce, iceberg, chopped	1 cup	55	5	1	T	T	1	10	0.3	5	180	2
Lettuce, looseleaf (such as romaine)	1 cup	56	10	1	T	T	2	38	0.8	5	1,060	10
Mushrooms, raw	1 cup	70	20	1	T	T	3	4	0.9	3	0	2
Onions, raw, chopped	1 cup	160	55	2	T	0.1	12	40	0.6	3	0	13
Peas, green, frozen, cooked	1 cup	160	125	8	T	0.1	23	38	2.5	139	1,070	16
Potatoes, baked, peeled	1	156	145	3	T	T	34	8	0.5	8	0	20
Potatoes, frozen, French fried (oven-heated)	10	50	110	2	4	2.1	17	5	0.7	16	0	5
Potatoes, mashed, milk added	1 cup	210	160	4	1	0.7	37	55	0.6	636	40	14
Potato chips	10	20	105	1	7	1.8	10	5	0.2	94	0	8
Potato salad	1 cup	250	360	7	21	3.6	28	48	1.6	1,323	520	25
Spinach, drained, cooked from raw	1 cup	180	40	5	T	0.1	7	245	6.4	126	14,740	18
Sweet potatoes, baked in skin, peeled	1	114	115	2	T	T	28	32	0.5	11	24,880	28
Tomatoes, raw	1	123	25	1	T	T	5	9	0.6	10	1,390	22
Vegetable juice cocktail, canned	1 cup	242	45	2	T	T	11	27	1.0	883	2,830	67
Miscellaneous												
Beer, regular	12 fl. oz.	360	150	1	0	0.0	13	14	0.1	18	0	0
Gin, rum, vodka, whisky, 86 proof	1-1/2 fl. oz.	42	105	0	0	0.0	T	T	T	T	0	0
Wine, table, white	3-1/2 fl. oz.	102	80	T	0	0.0	3	9	0.3	5	([1])	0
Cola-type beverage	12 fl. oz.	369	160	0	0	0.0	41	11	0.2	18	0	0
Ginger ale	12 fl. oz	366	125	0	0	0.0	32	11	0.1	29	0	0
Coffee, brewed	6 fl. oz.	180	T	T	T	T	T	4	T	2	0	0
Tea, brewed	8 fl. oz.	240	T	T	T	T	T	0	T	1	0	0
Catsup	1 tbsp.	15	15	T	T	T	4	3	0.1	156	210	2
Mustard, prepared, yellow	1 tsp.	5	5	T	T	T	T	4	0.1	63	0	T
Olives, canned, green	4 medium	13	15	T	2	0.2	T	8	0.2	312	40	0
Pickles, dill, whole	1	65	5	T	T	T	1	17	0.7	928	70	4
Relish, finely chopped, sweet	1 tbsp.	15	20	T	T	T	5	3	0.1	107	20	1
Soup, tomato, prepared with milk	1 cup	248	160	6	6	2.9	22	159	1.8	932	850	68
Soup, chicken noodle, prepared with water	1 cup	241	75	4	2	0.7	9	17	0.8	1,106	710	T
Soup, green pea, prepared with water	1 cup	250	165	9	3	1.4	27	28	2.0	988	200	2
Soup, vegetarian, prepared with water	1 cup	241	70	2	2	0.3	12	22	1.1	822	3,010	1

T — Indicates trace ([1]) — Value not determined. **Note:** Values shown here for these foods may be from several different manufacturers and, therefore, may differ somewhat from the values provided by one source.

The New Food Labels

Source: Food Labeling Education Information Center, Beltville, Md.

The federal Nutrition Labeling and Education Act of 1990 established new requirements regarding what information must appear on the labels of processed foods. The effective date of the new regulations was the middle of 1994. The new labels use the heading "Nutrition Facts" on the back or side panel. The new labels offer four basic improvements, according to the U.S. government's Food Labeling Education Information Center:

(1) **You can believe the claims on the package.** Government regulations now define and regulate use of descriptive terms and claims such as low fat or low cholesterol (see below).

(2) **You can more easily compare products.** The information on the label will reflect an average serving in amounts customarily consumed. Since the serving size for each product is defined in the regulations, product comparisons will be easier and more meaningful.

(3) **By using the "% Daily Value," you can quickly determine if a product is high or low in a nutrient.** You can use the % Daily Value column to easily compare one product to another or to make dietary tradeoffs with other foods throughout the day.

(4) **By consulting the Daily Values, you can determine how much (or how little) of the major nutrients you should eat on a daily basis.** Daily Values serve as a reference for dietary guidance. They help consumers understand how much of a nutrient they should eat at a minimum (say for fiber or calcium) or maximum (fat and cholesterol). The Daily Values are listed for people who take in approximately 2,000 calories a day (many older adults, children, and sedentary women) or 2,500 calories a day (active men, teenage boys, and very active women).

Note: The new labeling requirements do not cover restaurant menus. Nor do they cover fresh produce, meat and poultry, and fish. Nutritional information for these products may be available on a voluntary basis at the point of purchase. Beginning July 6, 1994, raw meat, poultry, and fish must bear a label with instructions for the safe handling and preparation of these food products.

Sample of the New Nutrition Labels

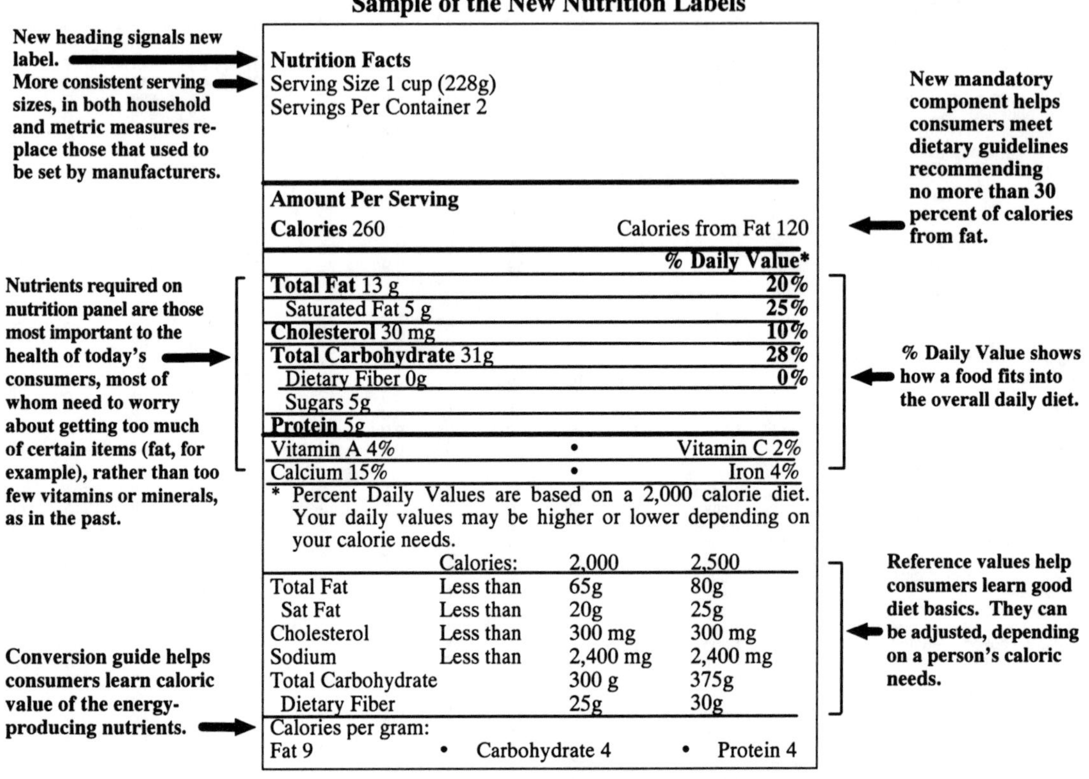

New heading signals new label.
More consistent serving sizes, in both household and metric measures replace those that used to be set by manufacturers.
Nutrients required on nutrition panel are those most important to the health of today's consumers, most of whom need to worry about getting too much of certain items (fat, for example), rather than too few vitamins or minerals, as in the past.
Conversion guide helps consumers learn caloric value of the energy-producing nutrients.
Nutrition Facts
Serving Size 1 cup (228g)
Servings Per Container 2
Amount Per Serving
Calories 260 Calories from Fat 120
% Daily Value*
Total Fat 13 g 20%
Saturated Fat 5 g 25%
Cholesterol 30 mg 10%
Total Carbohydrate 31g 28%
Dietary Fiber 0g 0%
Sugars 5g
Protein 5g
Vitamin A 4% • Vitamin C 2%
Calcium 15% • Iron 4%
* Percent Daily Values are based on a 2,000 calorie diet. Your daily values may be higher or lower depending on your calorie needs.
Calories: 2,000 2,500
Total Fat Less than 65g 80g
Sat Fat Less than 20g 25g
Cholesterol Less than 300 mg 300 mg
Sodium Less than 2,400 mg 2,400 mg
Total Carbohydrate 300 g 375g
Dietary Fiber 25g 30g
Calories per gram:
Fat 9 • Carbohydrate 4 • Protein 4
New mandatory component helps consumers meet dietary guidelines recommending no more than 30 percent of calories from fat.
% Daily Value shows how a food fits into the overall daily diet.
Reference values help consumers learn good diet basics. They can be adjusted, depending on a person's caloric needs.

Other Label Claims and What They Mean

Sugar

Sugar free: Less than 0.5 g per serving

No added sugar; Without added sugar; No sugar added:

- No sugars added during processing or packing, including ingredients that contain sugars (for example, fruit juices, applesauce, or dried fruit).
- Processing does not increase the sugar content above the amount naturally present in the ingredients. (A functionally insignificant increase in sugars is acceptable from the processes used for purposes other than increasing sugar content.)
- The compared food normally contains added sugars.

Reduced sugar: at least 25% less sugar than a compared food

Calories

Calorie free: fewer than 5 calories per serving

Low calorie: 40 calories or less per serving; if the serving is 30 g or less or 2 tablespoons (tbs) or less, 40 calories or less per 50 g of food

Reduced or Fewer calories: at least 25% fewer calories than a compared food

Fat

Fat free: less than 0.5 g of fat per serving

Saturated fat free: less than 0.5 g of saturated fat per serving, and the level of trans fatty acids does not exceed 1% of total fat

Low fat: 3 g or less per serving and, if the serving is 30 g or less or 2 tbs or less, per 50 g of the food

Low saturated fat: 1 g or less per serving and not more than 15% of calories from saturated fatty acids

Reduced or Less fat: at least 25% less per serving than compared food

Cholesterol

Cholesterol free: less than 2 mg of cholesterol and 2 g or less of saturated fat per serving

Low cholesterol: 20 mg or less and 2 g or less of saturated fat per serving and, if the serving is 30 g or less or 2 tbs or less, per 50 g of the food

Reduced or Less cholesterol: at least 25% less than compared food

Sodium

Sodium free: less than 5 mg per serving

Low sodium: 140 mg or less per serving and, if the serving is 30 g or less or 2 tbs or less, per 50 g of the food

Very low sodium: 35 mg or less per serving and, if the serving is 30 g or less or 2 tbs or less, per 50 g of the food

Reduced or Less sodium: at least 25% less per serving than compared food

Fiber

High fiber: 5 g or more per serving. (Also, must meet low-fat definition, or state level of total fat.)

Good source of fiber: 2.5 g to 4.9 g per serving

More or Added fiber: at least 2.5 g more per serving than reference food

Recommended Daily Dietary Allowances

Source: Food and Nutrition Board, Natl. Academy of Sciences—Natl. Research Council; 1989

	Age (years) and sex group	Weight (lbs.)	Protein (grams)	Fat soluble vitamins: Vitamin A*	Vitamin D**	Vitamin E†	Vitamin K	Vitamin C	Water soluble vitamins: Thiamine (mg.)	Riboflavin (mg.)	Niacin (mg.)‡	Vitamin B6 (mg.)	Folate (micrograms)	Vitamin B12 (micrograms)	Minerals: Calcium (mg.)	Phosphorus (mg.)	Magnesium (mg.)	Iron (mg.)	Zinc (mg.)	Iodine (micrograms)	Selenium (micrograms)
Infants . .	to 5 mos.	13	13	375	7.5	3	5	30	0.3	0.4	5	0.3	25	0.3	400	300	40	6	5	40	10
	to 1 yr.	20	14	375	10	4	10	35	0.4	0.5	6	0.6	35	0.5	600	500	60	10	5	50	15
Children .	1-3	29	16	400	10	6	15	40	0.7	0.8	9	1.0	50	0.7	800	800	80	10	10	70	20
	4-6	44	24	500	10	7	20	45	0.9	1.1	12	1.1	75	1.0	800	800	120	10	10	90	20
	7-10	62	28	700	10	7	30	45	1.0	1.2	13	1.4	100	1.4	800	800	170	10	10	120	30
Males . . .	11-14	99	45	1000	10	10	45	50	1.3	1.5	17	1.7	150	2.0	1200	1200	270	12	15	150	40
	15-18	145	59	1000	10	10	65	60	1.5	1.8	20	2.0	200	2.0	1200	1200	400	12	15	150	50
	19-24	160	58	1000	10	10	70	60	1.5	1.7	19	2.0	200	2.0	1200	1200	350	10	15	150	70
	25-50	174	63	1000	5	10	80	60	1.5	1.7	19	2.0	200	2.0	800	800	350	10	15	150	70
	51+	170	63	1000	5	10	80	60	1.2	1.4	15	2.0	200	2.0	800	800	350	10	15	150	70
Females .	11-14	101	46	800	10	8	45	50	1.1	1.3	15	1.4	150	2.0	1200	1200	280	15	12	150	45
	15-18	120	44	800	10	8	55	60	1.1	1.3	15	1.5	180	2.0	1200	1200	300	15	12	150	50
	19-24	128	46	800	10	8	60	60	1.1	1.3	15	1.6	180	2.0	1200	1200	280	15	12	150	55
	25-50	138	50	800	5	8	65	60	1.1	1.3	15	1.6	180	2.0	800	800	280	15	12	150	55
	51+	143	50	800	5	8	65	60	1.0	1.2	13	1.6	180	2.0	800	800	280	10	12	150	55

* Retinol equivalents. ** Micrograms of cholecalciferol. † Milligrams alpha-tocopherol equivalents. ‡ Niacin equivalents.

Recommended Weight Tables

Source: Metropolitan Life Insurance Co., 1983

Weights for people age 25-59 based on lowest mortality. Weight in lbs. according to frame (in indoor clothing weighing 5 lbs. for men, 3 lbs. for women). Heights include shoes with 1-inch heels.

Men: Height Feet	Inches	Small Frame	Medium Frame	Large Frame	Women: Height Feet	Inches	Small Frame	Medium Frame	Large Frame
5	2	128-134	131-141	138-150	4	10	102-111	109-121	118-131
5	3	130-136	133-143	140-153	4	11	103-113	111-123	120-134
5	4	132-138	135-145	142-156	5	0	104-115	113-126	122-137
5	5	134-140	137-148	144-160	5	1	106-118	115-129	125-140
5	6	136-142	139-151	146-164	5	2	108-121	118-132	128-143
5	7	138-145	142-154	149-168	5	3	111-124	121-135	131-147
5	8	140-148	145-157	152-172	5	4	114-127	124-138	134-151
5	9	142-151	148-160	155-176	5	5	117-130	127-141	137-155
5	10	144-154	151-163	158-180	5	6	120-133	130-144	140-159
5	11	146-157	154-166	161-184	5	7	123-136	133-147	143-163
6	0	149-160	157-170	164-188	5	8	126-139	136-150	146-167
6	1	152-164	160-174	168-192	5	9	129-142	139-153	149-170
6	2	155-168	164-178	172-197	5	10	132-145	142-156	152-173
6	3	158-172	167-182	176-202	5	11	135-148	145-159	155-176
6	4	162-176	171-187	181-207	6	0	138-151	148-162	158-179

Some Benefits of Quitting Smoking

Source: American Cancer Society; U.S. Centers for Disease Control and Prevention

Within 20 Minutes
- Blood pressure drops to normal
- Pulse rate drops to normal
- Body temperature of hands and feet increases to normal

Within 8 Hours
- Carbon monoxide level in blood drops to normal
- Oxygen level in blood increases to normal

Within 24 Hours
- Chance of heart attack decreases

Within 48 Hours
- Nerve endings start regrowing
- Ability to smell and taste is enhanced

Within 2 Weeks to 3 Months
- Circulation improves
- Walking becomes easier
- Lung function increases up to 30 percent

Within 1 to 9 Months
- Coughing, sinus congestion, fatigue, shortness of breath decrease
- Cilia regrow in lungs, increasing ability to handle mucus, clean the lungs, reduce infection
- Body's overall energy increases

Within 1 Year
- Excess risk of coronary heart disease is half that of a smoker

Within 5 Years
- Lung cancer death rate for average former smoker (one pack a day) decreases by almost half
- Stroke risk is reduced to that of a nonsmoker 5-15 years after quitting
- Risk of cancer of the mouth, throat, and esophagus is half that of a smoker's

Within 10 Years
- Lung cancer death rate similar to that of nonsmokers
- Precancerous cells are replaced
- Risk of cancer of the mouth, throat, esophagus, bladder, kidney, and pancreas decreases

Within 15 Years
- Risk of coronary heart disease is that of a nonsmoker

Basic First Aid

First aid experts stress that knowing what to do for an injured person until a doctor or trained person gets to an accident scene can save a life, especially in cases of stoppage of breathing, severe bleeding, and shock.

People with special medical problems, such as diabetes, cardiovascular disease, epilepsy, or allergy, are also urged to wear some sort of emblem identifying the problem, as a safeguard against use of medication in an emergency that might be injurious or fatal. Emblems may be obtained from Medic Alert Foundation, Turlock, CA 95380.

Most accidents occur in homes. National Safety Council figures show that home accidents exceed those in other locations, such as in cars, at work, or in public places.

In all cases, get medical assistance as soon as possible.

Animal bite — Wound should be washed with soap under running water and antibiotic ointment and dressing applied. When possible, animal should be caught alive for rabies test.

Asphyxiation — Start rescue breathing immediately after getting patient to fresh air.

Bleeding — Elevate the wound above the heart if possible. Press hard on wound with sterile compress until bleeding stops. Send for doctor if it is severe.

Burn — If mild, with skin unbroken and no blisters, plunge into ice water until pain subsides. Apply a dry dressing if necessary. Send for physician if burn is severe. Apply sterile compresses and keep patient comfortably warm until doctor's arrival. Do not try to clean burn or to break blisters.

Chemical in eye — With patient lying down, pour cupsful of water immediately into corner of eye, letting it run to other side to remove chemicals thoroughly. Cover with sterile compress. Get medical attention immediately.

Choking — See **Abdominal Thrust**.

Convulsions — Place person on back on bed or rug. Loosen clothing. Turn head to side. Do not place a blunt object between the victim's teeth. If convulsions do not stop, get medical attention immediately.

Cut (minor) — Apply mild antiseptic and sterile compress after washing with soap under warm running water.

Fainting — If victim feels faint, lower head to knees. Lay victim down on back with head turned to side if he or she becomes unconscious. Elevate the legs 8 to 10 inches. Loosen clothing and open windows. Keep patient lying quietly for at least 15 minutes after he or she regains consciousness. Call doctor if faint lasts for more than a few minutes.

Foreign body in eye — Touch object with moistened corner of handkerchief if it can be seen. If it cannot be seen or does not come out after a few attempts, take patient to doctor. Do not rub eye.

Frostbite— Handle frostbitten area gently. Do not rub. Soak the affected area in water no warmer than 105°F. Do not allow frostbitten area to touch the container. Soak until frostbitten part looks red and feels warm. Loosely bandage. If fingers or toes are frostbitten, place gauze between them.

Heat Stroke and Heat Exhaustion — Remove the victim from the heat. Loosen any tight clothing and apply cool, wet cloths to the skin. Give the victim cool water, to drink slowly. Call an ambulance if the victim refuses water, vomits, or experiences changes in consciousness.

Hypothermia — Move victim to a warm place. Remove wet clothing and dry victim, if necessary. Warm victim gradually by wrapping the person in warm blankets or clothing. If available, apply heat pads or other heat sources, but not directly to the body. Give the victim warm liquids. Call an ambulance if breathing is slowed or stopped or if the pulse is slow or irregular.

Loss of Limb — If a limb is severed, it is important to properly protect the limb so that it can possibly be reattached to the victim. After the victim is cared for, the limb should be wrapped in a sterile gauze or clean material and placed in a clean plastic bag, garbage can, or other suitable container. Pack ice around the limb on the OUTSIDE of the bag to keep the limb cold. Call ahead to the hospital to alert staff there of the situation.

Poisoning — Call doctor. Use antidote listed on label if container is found. Call local Poison Control Center if possible. Do not give the victim any food or drink or induce vomiting, unless specified on the label or by a medical professional.

Shock (injury-related) — Keep the victim lying down; if uncertain as to his or her injuries, keep the victim flat on the back. Maintain the victim's normal body temperature; if the weather is cold or damp, place blankets or extra clothing over and under the victim; if weather is hot, provide shade.

Snakebite —Wash the injury. Keep the area still and at a lower level than the heart. Keep the victim quiet. If available, use a snakebite kit.

Sprains and fractures — Apply ice to reduce swelling and pain. Do not try to straighten or move broken limbs. Apply a splint to immobilize the injured area if the victim must be transported.

Sting from insect — If possible, remove stinger. Wash the area with soap and water and cover it to keep it clean. Apply a cold pack to reduce pain and swelling. Call physician immediately if body swells or patient collapses.

Unconsciousness — Send for doctor and place person on his or her back. Start rescue breathing if victim stops breathing. Never give food or liquids to an unconscious person.

Abdominal Thrust

The American Red Cross and the American Heart Association both agree that the recommended first aid for choking victims is the abdominal thrust, also known as the Heimlich maneuver, after its creator, Dr. Henry Heimlich. Slaps on the back are no longer advised and may even prove detrimental in an attempt to assist a choking victim.

- Get behind the victim and wrap your arms around him above the waist.
- Make a fist with one hand and place it, with the thumb knuckle pressing inward, just below the point of the "v" of the rib cage.
- Grasp the wrist with the other hand and give one or more upward thrusts or hugs.
- Start rescue breathing if breathing stops.

Rescue Breathing

Stressing that your breath can save a life, the American Red Cross gives the following directions for resuce breathing if the victim is not breathing:

- Determine consciousness by tapping the victim on the shoulder and asking loudly, "Are you okay?"
- Tilt the victim's head back so that the chin is pointing upward. Do not press on the soft tissue under the chin, as this might obstruct the airway. If you suspect that an accident victim might have neck or back injuries, open the airway by placing the tips of your index and middle fingers on the corners of the victim's jaw to lift it forward without tilting the head.
- Place your cheek and ear close to the victim's mouth and nose. Look at the victim's chest to see if it rises and falls. Listen and feel for air to be exhaled for about 5 seconds.
- If there is no breathing, pinch the victim's nostrils shut with the thumb and index finger of your hand that is pressing on the victim's forehead. Another way to prevent leakage of air when the lungs are inflated is to press your cheek against the victim's nose.
- Blow air into victim's mouth by taking a deep breath and then sealing your mouth tightly around the victim's mouth. Initially, give two, quick (approx. 1.5 seconds each), full breaths without allowing the lungs to deflate completely between each breath.
- Watch the victim's chest to see if it rises.
- Stop blowing when the victim's chest is expanded. Raise your mouth; turn your head to the side and listen for exhalation.
- Watch the chest to see if it falls.
- Repeat the blowing cycle until the victim starts breathing.
  Note: Infants (up to one year) and children (1 to 8 years) should be administered rescue breathing as described above, except for the following:
- Do not tilt the head as far back as an adult's head.
- Both the mouth and nose of an infant should be sealed by the mouth.
- Give breaths to a child once every three seconds.
- Blow into the infant's mouth and nose once every three seconds with less pressure and volume than for a child.

Immunization Schedule for Infants and Children

Source: American Academy of Pediatrics, Aug. 3, 1994

By ensuring that your child gets immunized on schedule, you can provide the best defense against dangerous childhood diseases. Childhood immunization means protection from nine major diseases: hepatitis B, polio, measles, mumps, rubella (German measles), pertussis (whooping cough), diphtheria, tetanus (lockjaw), and *Haemophilus influenzae* type b (a bacterium that can cause such serious infections as meningitis and pneumonia).

For the best possible protection against diphtheria, tetanus, and pertussis, your child needs a series of five shots of the combination diphtheria-tetanus-pertussis (DTP) vaccine. The first four doses should be given at 2, 4, 6, and 15 to 18 months of age, with a final booster dose given before school entry (4 to 6 years). For the fourth and fifth dose, the acellular (DTaP) vaccine may be substituted for the DTP vaccine.

For protection against polio, your child needs a series of four oral polio vaccine doses, the first three at 2, 4, and 6 to 18 months and the final dose before school entry (4 to 6 years).

To be completely protected against hepatitis B, your child needs to be vaccinated with a series of three hepatitis B virus (HBV) vaccine shots. The American Academy of Pediatrics recommends that these immunizations be given at birth, at 1 to 2 months, and at 6 to 18 months of age. In some cases your pediatrician may decide to begin the 3-dose schedule after your baby has left the hospital.

Several vaccines are available for protection against *Haemophilus influenzae* type b (Hib). However, only two vaccines—HbOC and PRP-OMP—are approved for children under 15 months of age. The Academy recommends that your child receive either the HbOC vaccine at 2, 4, and 6 months of age, with a final dose at 12 to 15 months or the PRP-OMP vaccine at 2 and 4 months, with a final dose at 12 to 15 months.

At 12 to 15 months, your child should have an immunization for measles, mumps, and rubella (MMR). A second MMR vaccination, primarily to boost measles and mumps immunity, should be given to children 11 to 12 years or older who have not had measles. If there is a measles outbreak in your community or if you live in a high-risk area, the MMR booster may be given just before kindergarten or at an earlier age.

If you do not have a pediatrician, call your local public health department. It usually has supplies of vaccine and may give immunizations free.

	DTP[1]	Polio	Hepatitis B[2]	Measles[3]	Mumps[3]	Rubella[3]	Hib[4]	Tetanus-Diphtheria[5]
Birth			X					
1-2 months			X					
2 months	X	X					X	
4 months	X	X					X	
6 months	X						X	
6-18 months		X	X					
12-15 months				X	X	X	X	
15-18 months	X							
4-6 years	X	X						
11-12 years				X	X	X		
14-16 years								X

(1)For the fourth and fifth doses, the acellular (DTaP) pertussis vaccine may be substituted for the DTP vaccine. (2)Infants of mothers with positive blood tests for hepatitis B must receive hepatitis B immune globulin (HBIG) at or shortly after the first dose. These infants will also require a second hepatitis B vaccine dose at 1 month and a third hepatitis B vaccine injection at 6 months of age. (3)Combined MMR vaccine. Second dose at 11-12 years except where public health authorities require otherwise. (4)The 6-month dose depends on the type of *Haemophilus influenzae* type b vaccine given previously. (5) Repeat every 10 years throughout life.

Heart and Blood Vessel Disease

Source: American Heart Association, Dallas

Warning Signs

Of Heart Attack

- Uncomfortable pressure, fullness, squeezing, or pain in the center of the chest lasting two minutes or longer
- Pain may radiate to the shoulder, arm, neck, or jaw
- Sweating may accompany pain or discomfort
- Nausea and vomiting may also occur
- Shortness of breath, dizziness, or fainting may accompany other signs

The American Heart Association advises immediate action at the onset of these symptoms. The association points out that more than half of heart attack victims die before they reach the hospital and that the average victim waits 2 hours before seeking help.

Of Stroke

- Sudden temporary weakness or numbness of face or limbs on one side of the body
- Temporary loss of speech, or trouble speaking or understanding speech
- Temporary dim or lost vision, especially in one eye
- Unexplained dizziness, unsteadiness, or sudden falls

Some Major Risk Factors

Blood pressure—High blood pressure increases the risk of stroke, heart attack, kidney failure, and congestive heart failure.

Cholesterol—A blood cholesterol level over 240 mg/dl (milligrams of cholesterol per deciliter of blood) approximately doubles the risk of coronary heart disease; about 20% of the U.S. adult population (37.2 mln.) falls into this category. Blood cholesterol levels between 200 and 240 mg/dl are in a zone of moderate and increasing risk. An estimated 26.7 mln. (37%) of youths age 19 and under have levels of 170 mg/dl or higher, comparable to a level of 200 mg/dl in adults.

Cigarettes—Cigarette smokers have more than twice the risk of heart attack and 2-4 times the risk of sudden cardiac death as nonsmokers. Young smokers have a higher risk for early death from stroke.

Obesity—60 mln. adults are 20% or more over their desirable weight (32% of white males, 31.5% of black males, 33.5% of white females, 49.6% of black females).

Cancer's 7 Warning Signals*

Source: American Cancer Society

1. A change in bowel or bladder habits.
2. A sore that does not heal.
3. Unusual bleeding or discharge.
4. Thickening or lump in breast or elsewhere.
5. Indigestion or difficulty in swallowing.
6. Obvious change in wart or mole.
7. Nagging cough or hoarseness.

*If you have a warning signal, see your doctor.

Cancer Prevention

Source: American Cancer Society

PRIMARY PREVENTION: steps that can be taken to avoid those factors that might lead to the development of cancer.

Smoking Cigarette smoking is responsible for 90% of lung cancer cases among men, 79% among women—about 87% overall. Smoking accounts for about 30% of all cancer deaths. Those who smoke two or more packs of cigarettes a day have lung cancer mortality rates 12-25 times greater than nonsmokers.

Nutrition Risk for colon, breast, gallbladder, ovarian, prostate, and uterine cancers increases in obese people. High-fat diets may contribute to the development of certain cancers, particularly those of the breast, colon, and prostate. High-fiber foods may help reduce risk of colon cancer. A varied diet containing plenty of vegetables and fruits rich in vitamins A and C may reduce risk for many cancers. Salt-cured, smoked, and nitrite-cured foods have been linked to esophageal and stomach cancer.

Sunlight Almost all of the more than 700,000 cases of non-melanoma skin cancer diagnosed each year in the U.S. are sun-related. Epidemiological evidence shows that sun exposure is a major factor in the development of melanoma, and the incidence increases for those living near the equator.

Alcohol Oral cancer and cancers of the larynx, throat, esophagus, and liver occur more frequently among heavy drinkers of alcohol, especially when accompanied by cigarette smoking or use of chewing tobacco.

Smokeless Tobacco Use of chewing tobacco or snuff increases risk of cancers of the mouth, larynx, throat, and esophagus.

Estrogen Estrogen treatment to control menopausal symptoms can increase risk of endometrial cancer. However, including progesterone in estrogen replacement therapy helps to minimize this risk. Use of estrogen by menopausal women needs careful discussion by the woman and her physician, while research continues.

Radiation Excessive exposure to ionizing radiation can increase cancer risk. Most medical and dental X rays are adjusted to deliver the lowest dose possible without sacrificing image quality. Excessive radon exposure in the home may increase lung cancer risk, especially in cigarette smokers. If levels are found to be too high, remedial actions should be taken.

Occupational Hazards Exposure to several different industrial agents (including nickel, chromate, asbestos, and vinyl chloride) increases risk of various cancers. Risk of lung cancer from asbestos is greatly increased when combined with smoking.

SECONDARY PREVENTION: steps to be taken to diagnose a cancer or precursor as early as possible after it has developed.

Colorectal Tests The ACS recommends 3 tests for the early detection of colon and rectum cancer in people without symptoms: The digital rectal examination performed by a physician during an office visit, every year after the age of 40; the stool blood test, every year after 50; and the proctosigmoidoscopy examination, every 3 to 5 years, based on the advice of a physician.

Pap Test For cervical cancer, women who are or have been sexually active, or have reached 18 years, should have an annual Pap test and pelvic examination. After a woman has had 3 or more consecutive satisfactory normal exams, the Pap test may be performed less frequently at the discretion of her physician.

Breast Cancer Detection The ACS recommends monthly breast self-examination by women 20 years and older. Examination of the breast by a health-care professional should be done every 3 years from ages 20 to 40, and then every year for women over 40. The ACS recommends a mammogram every year for asymptomatic women age 50 and over. Women age 40-49 should have mammography every 1-2 years, depending on physical and mammographic findings. It is also recommended that women have at least one mammogram prior to age 40.

Prostate Cancer Detection For early detection of prostate cancer, the ACS recommends that men over age 40 should have an annual digital rectal examination. After age 50, men should have an annual prostate-specific antigen blood test.

Diabetes

Source: American Diabetes Association

Diabetes is a chronic disease in which the body does not produce or properly use insulin, a hormone that is needed to convert sugar, starches, and other foods into energy needed for daily life. Both genetics and environment appear to play roles in the onset of the disease. Diabetes, which has no cure, is the 4th-leading cause of death by disease in the U.S. In 1994, more than 160,000 Americans will die from the disease and its related complications.

There are two major types of diabetes:

Insulin dependent (type I)—The body produces very little or no insulin; disease most often begins in childhood or early adulthood. People with type I diabetes must take daily insulin injections to stay alive.

Non-insulin dependent (type II)—The body does not produce enough or cannot properly use insulin. It is the most common form of the disease (90-95% of cases in people over age 20) and often begins later in life.

Warning Signs of Diabetes

Type I Diabetes: (usually occur suddenly)

- frequent urination
- unusual thirst
- extreme hunger
- unusual weight loss
- extreme fatigue
- irritability

Type II Diabetes: (occur less suddenly)

- any type I symptoms
- frequent infections
- blurred vision
- cuts/bruises slow to heal
- tingling/numbness in hands or feet
- recurring skin, gum, or bladder infections

Complications of Diabetes

More than half of all individuals with diabetes do not know that they have the disease until one of its life-threatening complications occurs. Potential complications include:

Blindness. Diabetes is the leading cause of blindness in people ages 25-74. Each year, from 15,000 to 39,000 people lose their sight because of diabetes.

Kidney disease. Ten percent of all people with diabetes develop kidney disease. In 1990, more than 13,000 people initiated treatment for end-stage renal disease (kidney failure) because of diabetes.

Amputations. Diabetes is the most frequent cause of nontraumatic lower limb amputations. The risk of a leg amputation is 27.7 times greater for a person with diabetes than for the average American. Each year, 54,000 people lose a foot or leg to complications brought on by diabetes.

Heart disease and stroke. People with diabetes are 2 to 4 times more likely to have heart disease (more than 77,000 deaths due to heart disease annually). And they are 5 times more likely to suffer a stroke (more than 11,000 diabetes-related stroke-deaths each year).

Health-care and related costs for the treatment of the disease, as well as the cost of lost productivity, total nearly $92 billion annually in the U.S.

Ethics Regarding Care of the Terminally Ill

Physician-assisted suicide for the terminally ill remained a prominent issue. On May 10, 1994, a Michigan court of appeals issued a ruling invalidating, on narrow technical grounds, the Michigan law that had gone into effect in Feb. 1993 that had made it a felony to assist in a suicide. The Michigan law had gained national attention when it was used to arrest Dr. Jack Kevorkian. Kevorkian is a retired Michigan pathologist who had, by mid-1994, assisted the suicides of 20 individuals since he began such procedures in 1990. The appeals court also issued a separate ruling that reinstated two murder charges against Kevorkian for his role in the suicides of Sherry Miller and Marjorie Wantz on Oct. 23, 1991. These deaths were the 2d and 3d that Kevorkian had been present at and had occurred prior to enactment of the struck-down Michigan statute. Both rulings were appealed to the Michigan Supreme Court. Also in May 1994, U.S. District Judge Barbara Rothstein struck down a Washington state law prohibiting assisted suicide, on the grounds that the law violated the 14th Amendment.

In a 1992 survey conducted by the American Society of Internal Medicine, one in five physicians said they had deliberately taken action to cause a patient's death. Another survey of medical practitioners, published in 1993, found that nearly half the attending physicians and nurses and 70 percent of the resident physicians surveyed said they had acted against their own convictions by ignoring requests from terminally ill patients to withhold life support.

Another prominent ethical issue in recent years has involved the questions of whether and under what circumstances life-support for comatose patients with no apparent hope of recovery could be discontinued. The Supreme Court heard its first ever "right-to-die" case on Dec. 6, 1989. *Cruzan v. Missouri Dept. of Health* concerned Nancy Beth Cruzan, 32, who had been unconscious since Jan. 1983, after a car accident. Her parents and a guardian appointed to represent her sought to stop the medical treatment sustaining her in a "persistent vegetative state." On June 25, 1990, the Supreme Court, in a 5-4 ruling, interpreted the 14th Amendment as conferring on patients a right to refuse life-sustaining treatment, but it held that in the case of comatose patients a state could, as Missouri did, require that "clear and convincing" evidence about the patient's previous wishes regarding life-sustaining treatment be presented before such care could be withdrawn. (Since the state courts had found that there was not "clear and convincing" evidence, the Cruzans' request to withdraw their daughter's feeding tube was denied. However, after the family presented further evidence in a new state court proceeding, removal of the feeding tube was permitted, and Nancy Cruzan died in Dec. 1990.)

As of Jan. 1988, hospitals are required by the Joint Commission on Accreditation of Health Care Organizations to have formal policies specifying when doctors and nurses can refrain from trying to resuscitate terminally ill patients. The policy must be developed in consultation with the medical and nursing staff, adopted by the medical staff, and then approved by the hospital's governing body. The policy must define the roles of physicians, nursing personnel, and members of the patient's family in any decision to withhold resuscitation. It must also include "provisions designed to assure that a patient's rights are respected."

In March 1986, the American Medical Association announced that it would be ethical for doctors to withhold "all means of life prolonging medical treatment," including food and water, from permanently unconscious patients even if death was not imminent. The withholding of such therapy should occur only when a patient's unconscious state "is beyond doubt irreversible and there are adequate safeguards to confirm the accuracy of the diagnosis," the association's judicial council said.

In June 1991, the AMA adopted 2 reports of its Council on Ethical and Judicial Affairs dealing with refusal of life-prolonging treatment when patients are incurably ill. The first, "Decisions Near the End of Life," concluded: "the principle of patient autonomy requires that physicians must respect the decision to forego life-sustaining treatment of a patient who possesses decisionmaking capacity." Life-sustaining treatment was defined as "any treatment that serves to prolong life without reversing the underlying medical condition," including "mechanical ventilation, renal dialysis, chemotherapy, antibiotics and artificial nutrition and hydration." The council also reaffirmed its position that "physicians must not perform euthanasia or participate in assisted suicide." The second report, "Decisions to Forego Life-Sustaining Treatment for Incompetent Patients," encouraged the use of advance directives (living wills and the designation of durable power of attorney) by persons to ensure that their interests will be promoted in the event that they become incompetent. When there is no advance directive designating a proxy decisionmaker, the council concluded, the patient's family should become the surrogate decisionmaker. Family was defined as "persons with whom the patient is closely associated." Surrogate decisionmakers should consider the patient's previous values and preferences and base decisions on what the patient would have likely decided had he or she been competent. When this is not possible, decisions should be based on what would objectively be in the best interests of the patient. The council encouraged the establishment and use of ethics committees designed to facilitate sound decisionmaking.

A number of states have advance directive, also known as "living will," statutes that set out a procedure for a mentally competent person to declare his or her wishes about life-sustaining measures. Advance directives may also allow a person to appoint a health-care surrogate to make decisions on his or her behalf in the event that the person is unable to make such a decision. In Oct. 1990, Congress passed the Patient Self-Determination Act, which took effect in December 1991. The Act requires health-care facilities that receive funds from Medicare or Medicaid to provide written information to all patients about advance directives and patients' rights under their state laws and to document whether or not a patient has an advance directive. News media coverage of the deaths of former President Richard M. Nixon and former first lady Jacqueline Kennedy Onassis, both of whom made their feelings regarding their care known through the use of an advance directive, prompted a large increase in requests for information on "living wills." Information on living wills and health-care powers of attorney can be obtained from the American Bar Association's Commission on Legal Problems of the Elderly or from Choice in Dying, Inc., a New York City-based group.

Where to Get Help

Source: Reprinted from Health & Medical Year Book 1994, "Where to Get Help," pp. 279-283.
Copyright ©1994 by P.F. Collier, L.P., Reprinted by permission of the publisher.

Listed below are some of the major U.S. organizations providing information about good health practices generally or about specific conditions and how to deal with them. Where a toll-free number is not available, an address is given when possible.

General Sources

Centers for Disease Control and Prevention Voice Information System
404-332-4555
Tape-recorded information about public health topics, such as AIDS, Lyme disease, and chronic fatigue syndrome. Also, you can request to talk with a CDC expert.

National Health Information Center
800-336-4797; in Maryland, 301-565-4167
Provides phone numbers for more than 1,000 health-related organizations and offers various printed materials.

National Institutes of Health
Bethesda, MD 20892
301-496-4000
Free information, including the latest research findings, on a wide range of diseases.

Tel-Med
Check the phone book for local listings or call Tel-Med headquarters at 909-825-6034
Tape-recorded information on over 600 health topics. Sponsored by local medical societies, health organizations, or hospitals.

Aging

National Association of Area Agencies on Aging's Eldercare Locator
800-677-1116
Provides information and assistance on a wide range of services and programs including adult daycare/respite services, consumer fraud, hospital/nursing home information, legal services, elder abuse/protective services, Medicaid/Medigap information, tax assistance, and transportation.

National Council on the Aging
800-424-9046
Provides information and publications on all aspects of aging.

National Institute on Aging
Public Information Office
Building 31, Room 5C27
Bethesda, MD 20892
301-496-1752
Provides information about disabling conditions, support groups, and community resources.

AIDS

National AIDS Hotline
800-342-AIDS 24 hours;
in Spanish, 800-344-SIDA;
for the hearing impaired, 800-AIDS-TTY
Provides recorded information on the prevention and spread of AIDS.

Alcoholism and Drug Abuse

Alcohol Abuse Emergency
800-ALCOHOL

Alcoholism and Drug Addiction Treatment Center
800-382-4357
Offers referrals to local facilities for adolescents and adults; operates 24 hours.

National Clearinghouse for Alcohol and Drug Information
800-729-6686
Provides federal publications and literature searches.

National Cocaine Hotline
800-COCAINE
Answers questions about cocaine and other drugs, provides referral to drug treatment centers. Operates 24 hours.

National Council on Alcoholism and Drug Dependence Hopeline
800-475-HOPE

National Institute for Drug Abuse
800-662-HELP; in Spanish, 800-66-AYUDA
Makes referrals to support groups and treatment programs.

National Parents' Resource Institute for Drug Education
800-677-7433
Recording gives telephone numbers to call and an address to write to for drug information. Operates 24 hours.

Alzheimer's Disease

Alzheimer's Association
800-621-0379
Makes referrals to local chapters and support groups; offers information on publications available from the association.

Arthritis

Arthritis Foundation
800-283-7800
Provides information, publications, and referrals to local groups.

Asthma and Allergies

Asthma and Allergy Foundation Patient Information Line
800-7-ASTHMA
Provides general information, publications and videos, and referrals to physicians.

Asthma Information Line
800-822-ASMA
Provides written materials on asthma and allergies. Operates 24 hours.

Blindness and Eye Care

American Council of the Blind
800-424-8666; in Washington, D.C., 202-467-5081
Offers information on blindness; provides referrals to clinics and other organizations.

American Foundation for the Blind
800-AF-BLIND; in New York State, 212-620-2147
Gives information on visual impairments and on AFB services, products, and publications.

Blind Children's Center
800-222-3566; in California, 800-222-3567

National Association for Parents of the Visually Impaired
800-562-6265
Offers support and information for parents of individuals who are visually impaired.

National Retinitis Pigmentosa Foundation
800-638-2300; in Maryland, 301-225-9400; for the hearing impaired, 301-225-9409
Answers questions and provides written materials.

Blood Disorders

Cooley's Anemia Foundation
800-221-3571; in New York, 800-522-7222
Provides information on patient care and support groups; makes referrals to local chapters.

Sickle Cell Disease Association of America
800-421-8453; in California, 213-736-5455
Offers genetic counseling and information packet.

Burns

National Burn Victim Foundation
32-34 Scotland Road
Orange, NJ 07050
201-676-7700
Provides 24-hour emergency burn referral service as well as counseling for burn victims and families.

Cancer

American Cancer Society
800-ACS-2345
Provides publications and information about cancer and coping with cancer; makes referrals to local chapters of the American Cancer Society for support services.

National Cancer Institute's Cancer Information Service
800-4-CANCER; 800-638-6070 in Alaska; 808-524-1234 in Oahu, HI (neighboring islands call collect).
Answers questions about cancer; Spanish-speaking staff members available in some areas.

Cerebral Palsy

United Cerebral Palsy Associations
800-USA-5UCP;
in Washington, DC, 202-842-1266
Provides literature about cerebral palsy.

Child Abuse

Childhelp's National Child Abuse Hotline
800-4-A-CHILD
Provides crisis intervention, professional counseling, referrals to local groups offering counseling and to shelters for runaways, and literature in English and Spanish. Operates 24 hours.

National Center for Missing and Exploited Children
800-843-5678; for the hearing impaired, 800-826-7653; in Arlington, VA, 703-235-3900
Operates a hotline for reporting missing children and sightings of missing children. Assists law enforcement agencies.

Crisis

National Adolescent Suicide Hotline
800-621-4000
Provides crisis intervention and referrals for runaways. Operates 24 hours.

National Youth Crisis Hotline
800-HIT-HOME
Provides counseling for youths dealing with drug abuse, pregnancy, molestation, suicide, and child abuse; makes referrals to local drug treatment centers, shelters, and counseling services. Operates 24 hours.

Cystic Fibrosis

Cystic Fibrosis Foundation
800-FIGHT-CF; in Maryland, 301-951-4422
Answers questions and offers literature and referrals to local clinics.

Diabetes

American Diabetes Association
800-ADA-DISC; in Virginia and Washington, DC, 703-549-1500
Provides literature and referrals to local affiliates for information on support groups.

Juvenile Diabetes Foundation Hotline
800-223-1138 or 800-533-2873; in New York City, 212-889-7575
Answers questions, provides literature (some in Spanish), and refers to local chapters, physicians, and clinics.

Digestive Diseases

National Digestive Diseases Information Clearinghouse
Box NDDIC, Bethesda, MD 20892
301-468-6344

National Foundation for Ileitis and Colitis
800-343-3637; in New York, 212-679-1570
Provides educational materials, refers to local support groups and physicians.

Down Syndrome

National Down Syndrome Congress
800-232-6372; in Georgia, 404-633-1555
Answers questions and makes referrals to local organizations.

National Down Syndrome Society Hotline
800-221-4602;
in New York City, 212-460-9330
Provides information and gives referrals for local programs for newborns.

Dyslexia

Orton Dyslexia Society
800-ABCD-123; in Maryland, 410-296-0232
Provides information on testing, tutoring, and computers to aid people with dyslexia and related disorders.

Endometriosis

Endometriosis Association
800-992-ENDO; in Canada, 800-426-2END
Provides a 24-hour recording for callers to request information.

Epilepsy

Epilepsy Foundation of America
800-332-1000
Provides information and referrals to local chapters.

Grief

Grief Recovery Institute
800-445-4808
Provides counseling services on coping with loss.

Handicaps and Disabilities

Library of Congress
800-424-9100;
in Washington, DC, 202-707-5100
Lends braille and audio-recorded books; refers callers to state and local libraries with these services.

National Association for the Craniofacially Handicapped
P.O. Box 11082
Chattanooga, TN 37401
615-266-1632
Offers information on treatment centers, support groups, and financial assistance for individuals with severe facial deformities.

National Information System for Health Related Services
800-922-9234; in South Carolina, 800-922-1107
Makes referrals to support groups and to sources of financial, medical, and legal assistance for developmentally disabled and chronically ill children.

Headaches

National Headache Foundation
800-843-2256; in Illinois, 800-523-8858
Offers literature on headaches and treatment.

National Institute of Neurological Disorders and Stroke
P.O. Box 5801
Bethesda, MD 20824
800-352-9424

Head Injuries

National Head Injury Foundation Family Helpline
800-444-NHIF
Provides informatin on living with head injuries.

Hearing

American Speech-Language-Hearing Association Helpline
800-638-8255; in Maryland call collect, 301-897-0039
Offers materials on hearing aids and on pathologists and audiologists certified by the association.

Dial A Hearing Screening Test
800-222-EARS; in Pennsylvania, 800-345-EARS
Answers questions on hearing problems, makes referrals to local numbers for a two-minute hearing test, as well as to ear, nose, and throat specialists and to organizations with specialized ear and hearing aid information.

Heart Disease

American Heart Association
7272 Greenville Avenue
Dallas, TX 75231
800-242-1793; 214-373-6300

National Heart, Lung, and Blood Institute Information Office
9000 Rockville Pike
Building 31-4A21
Bethesda, MD 20892
301-496-4236

Hospices

Children's Hospice International
800-242-4453; in Virginia, 703-684-0330
Provides information on and referrals to children's hospices.

Hospice Education Institute Hospicelink
800-331-1620; in Connecticut, 203-767-1620
Offers general information about hospice care and makes referrals to local programs.

Huntington's Disease

Huntington's Disease Society of America
800-345-4372; in New York, 212-242-1968
Provides information and referrals to physicians and support groups.

Hysterectomy

Hysterectomy Resources and Services Foundation
422 Bryn Mawr Ave.
Bala-Cynwyd, PA 19004
215-667-7757
Offers peer support for women considering hysterectomy, referrals for second opinions, legal referrals.

Impotence

Impotence Information Center
800-843-4315
Provides information on the causes and treatment of impotence.

Impotence Institute of America Hotline
800-669-1603
Offers literature, physician referrals, and phone numbers of local Impotents Anonymous chapters.

Kidney Diseases

National Kidney and Urologic Diseases Information Clearinghouse
P.O. Box NKUDIC
9000 Rockville Pike
Bethesda, MD 20892
301-468-6345

National Kidney Foundation
800-622-9010
Provides information and referrals.

Lead Exposure

National Lead Information Center Hotline
800-LEAD-FYI
Makes recommendations for reducing a child's exposure to lead, in the home and elsewhere.

Liver Diseases

American Liver Foundation
800-223-0179; in New Jersey, 201-256-2550
Provides information and physician and support group referrals.

Lung Diseases

American Lung Association
Check the phone book for local listings or call the national office at 212-315-8700.

National Jewish Center for Immunology and Respiratory Medicine Information Service
800-222-LUNG; in Denver, 303-355-LUNG
Answers questions on asthma, emphysema, allergies, smoking, and other respiratory and immune system disorders.

Mental Health

American Mental Health Fund
800-433-5959; in Illinois, 800-826-2336
Provides a 24-hour recorded message for callers to request a pamphlet on mental health.

National Depressive and Manic Depressive Association
800-826-3632
Offers support for patients and families, provides emergency assistance, and helps patients seek qualified treatment.

National Foundation for Depressive Illness
800-248-4344
Provides a 24-hour recorded message describing the symptoms of depression and offering an address for more information and physician referral.

National Mental Health Association
800-969-6642
Makes referrals to mental health groups.

Multiple Sclerosis

National Multiple Sclerosis Society
800-532-7667
A 24-hour recording allows callers to request information and leave name and address.

Nutrition

National Center for Nutrition and Dietetics Hotline
800-366-1655
Offers general information on nutrition, answers questions, and provides literature.

University of Alabama at Birmingham Nutrition Information Service
800-231-DIET
Answers questions on healthful eating and food handling.

USDA Food, Safety, and Inspection Service Meat and Poultry Hotline
800-535-4555
Provides information on proper handling, preparation, storage, and cooking of meat, poultry, and eggs.

Organ Donation

Living Bank
800-528-2971
Operates a registry and referral service for people wanting to commit organs to transplantation or research. Operates 24 hours.

Organ Donor Hotline
800-24-DONOR
Offers information and referrals for organ donation and transplantation; handles requests for organ donor cards. Operates 24 hours.

Pain

National Chronic Pain Outreach Association
7979 Old Georgetown Road
Suite 100
Bethesda, MD 20814-2429
301-652-4948
Provides information clearinghouse, makes referrals, and publishes newsletters.

Parkinson's Disease

National Parkinson's Foundation
800-327-4545; in Florida, 800-433-7022; in Miami, 305-547-6666
Answers questions, makes physician referrals, and provides written information.

Parkinson's Educational Program
800-344-7872; in California, 714-250-2975
Provides written materials as well as information on support groups and physician referrals. Operates 24 hours.

Physicians

American Board of Medical Specialties
800-776-2378
Verifies board certification of physicians.

Plastic Surgery

American Society of Plastic and Reconstructive Surgeons, Inc.
800-635-0635
Provides referrals to board-certified plastic surgeons in the United States and Canada; offers written materials on procedures and operations.

Polio

International Polio Network
4502 Maryland Ave.
St. Louis, MO 63108
314-534-0475
Provides an information exchange on coping with the late effects of polio.

Prostate Problems

Prostate Information Line
800-543-9632

Rehabilitation

National Rehabilitation Information Center
800-34-NARIC; in Maryland, 301-588-9284
Provides information on rehabilitation and research on disabilities.

Scleroderma

United Scleroderma Foundation
800-722-HOPE; in California, 408-728-2202
Provides information and referrals to physicians and local chapters.

Sexually Transmitted Diseases

American Social Health Association's National STD Hotline
800-227-8922
Provides information and confidential referrals for treatment.

Sjogren's Syndrome

Sjogren's Syndrome Foundation
382 Main Street
Port Washington, NY 11050
516-767-2866
Provides forum for sharing coping mechanisms and offers opportunities for patients to participate in treatment experiments.

Skin Problems

National Psoriasis Foundation
6600 SW 92d Ave., Suite 300
Portland, OR 97223
503-244-7404
Offers information and referrals.

Speech Disorders

National Center for Stuttering
800-221-2483; in New York State, 212-532-1460
Provides information on stuttering in all age groups.

Stuttering Foundation of America
800-992-9392
Provides referrals to speech pathologists, resource lists, and other publications. Operates 24 hours.

Spina Bifida

Spina Bifida Information and Referral
800-621-3141; in Washington, DC, 202-944-3285.

Spinal Injuries

American Paralysis Association's Spinal Cord Injury Hotline
800-526-3456
Provides literature on spinal cord injuries and makes referrals to organizations and support groups.

National Spinal Cord Injury Association
800-962-9629; in Massachusetts, 617-935-2722
Offers peer counseling and makes referrals to local chapters and other organizations.

Stroke

National Stroke Association
800-787-6537
Provides written and referral information.

Sudden Infant Death Syndrome

American Sudden Infant Death Syndrome Institute
800-232-SIDS; in Georgia, 800-847-7437
Answers questions, distributes literature, and makes referrals to other organizations. Operates 24 hours.

National SIDS Foundation
800-221-SIDS; in Maryland, 410-964-8000
Provides literature on medical information, referrals, and support groups.

Tourette Syndrome

Tourette Syndrome Association
800-237-0717; in New York, 718-224-2999
Provides a 24-hour recording for callers to request information, published in English and Spanish.

Urinary Incontinence

Help for Incontinent People
800-BLADDER
Offers information on bladder control, services available for incontinence, and assistive devices.

Simon Foundation
800-23-SIMON
Offers support and literature on incontinence.

Women's Health

National Women's Health Network
1325 G St. NW
Washington, DC 20005
202-347-1140

National Women's Health Resource Center
2440 M St. NW, Suite 325
Washington, D.C.
202-293-6045

CONSUMER INFORMATION

Consumer Information Catalog

Source: Consumer Information Center, U.S. General Services Administration

The *Consumer Information Catalog* is a free listing of more than 200 of the best federal consumer publications. They range from booklets on financial planning to planning a diet, from learning about federal benefits to getting an education, from fixing a car to dealing effectively with consumer problems. Many of these booklets are free.

The *Consumer Information Catalog* is published quarterly by the Consumer Information Center of the U.S. General Services Administration. For a free copy of the most current *Consumer Information Catalog,* send your name and address to: Consumer Information Catalog, Pueblo, CO 81009. Educators, librarians, and members of other nonprofit groups who are able to distribute 25 or more copies of the *Consumer Information Catalog* on a quarterly basis should write to the same address for an application to be placed on the mailing list. Costs prevent the Consumer Information Center from maintaining a mailing list for individuals.

The free and low-cost booklets listed below are from the *Consumer Information Catalog* and are available as of fall 1994. Quantities of some may be limited. The handling fee is $1.00. To order, send your name and address, the item numbers of the booklets you want, and the $1.00 fee to: S. James, Consumer Information Center, Pueblo, CO 81009.

Some Free and Low-Cost Publications

Children

Helping Your Child Succeed in School. Fifteen fun activities to do with your children (ages 5-11) to help expand their imagination, obey, organize, help others, and much more. 50 pp. (1992) **377A. 50¢.**

Helping Your Child Learn to Read. Fun and practical activities to help you and your child lay a foundation for a lifetime of reading. Primarily for children under 10, but helpful for older children too. 64 pp. (1993) **375A. 50¢.**

Kids Aren't Just Small Adults. Important information about giving nonprescription medicine to your children. 1p. (1992) **509A. Free.**

Helping Your Child Learn Responsible Behavior. Designed for children up to age 9 to help develop fairness, respect, courage, honesty, compassion, and more. 46 pp. (1993) **376A. 50¢.**

Growing Up Drug Free. Shows parents what children should know about drugs, including alcohol and tobacco, at each age level. 55 pp. (1989) **508A. Free.**

Helping Your Child Be Healthy and Fit. Easy and fun activities to do with your children (ages 3-8) to help them build healthy eating and exercise behaviors. 50 pp. (1993) **371A. 50¢.**

Employment

The College Labor Market: Outlook, Current Situation, and Earnings. Describes employment opportunities for college graduates in the 1990s. 27 pp. (1992) **104A. $1.75.**

The GED Diploma. Learn how to earn your General Education Development diploma, including what the tests cover, how to prepare, and where to get more information. 16 pp. (1991) **600A. Free.**

Compliance Guide to the Family and Medical Leave Act. Effective Aug. 5, 1993, the law provides for extended leave without pay under special circumstances. Learn who is eligible and what is required of employees and employers. 22 pp. (1993) **312A. 50¢.**

Handy Reference Guide to the Fair Labor Standards Act. Explains the federal laws on minimum wage, overtime pay, child labor, and more. 16 pp. (1992) **313A. 50¢.**

Federal Benefits Programs

Guide to Health Insurance for People with Medicare. Fill in gaps in Medicare coverage and avoid paying for duplicate benefits. 37 pp. (1994) **605A. Free.**

Medicare and Advance Directives. Explains how to set up a living will or a durable power of attorney to help you receive the medical treatment you want if you become physically or mentally unable to communicate. 4 pp. (1993) **614A. Free.**

Medicare Q & A. Answers 85 commonly asked questions about Medicare—eligibility, enrollment, and who pays deductibles, services, and benefits. 28 pp. (1994) **616A. Free.**

Request for Earnings and Benefit Estimate Statement. A form to complete and return to the Social Security Administration to get your earnings history and an estimate of future benefits. 3 pp. (1993) **517A. Free.**

Understanding Social Security. Explains retirement, disability, survivor's benefits, Medicare coverage, Supplemental Security Income, etc. 41 pp. (1993). **518A. Free.**

Federal Benefits for Veterans and Dependents. Lists medical, educational, home loan guarantees, insurance, compensation, pension, and other benefit programs for survivors and veterans. 80 pp. (1994) **112A. $2.50.**

Health

Cancer Tests You Should Know About: A Guide for People 65 and Over. Describes 6 tests that can help detect cancer early. Checklists included. 16 pp. (1992) **524A. Free.**

Facing Forward: A Guide for Cancer Survivors. Advice on coping with the many effects of this illness. Information on health care, insurance, job concerns, and more. 45 pp. (1990) **527A. Free.**

Silicone Breast Implants. Where to get more information or report problems, and what to do if you already have gel-filled or saline implants. 4 pp. (1992) **532A. Free.**

Menopause. Detailed information about estrogen replacement therapy, cardiovascular diseases, and coping with the emotional ups and downs. 36 pp. (1992) **123A. $2.50.**

Questions and Answers About Breast Lumps. Discusses benign and cancerous growths, questions to ask your doctor, where to get more information, and a self-examination guide. 24 pp. (1992). **547A. Free.**

Skin Cancer. Discusses symptoms, the importance of early detection, and the treatments used by more than 600,000 Americans who develop skin cancer each year. 25 pp. (1993) **604A. Free.**

So You Have High Blood Cholesterol. Revised guidelines for lowering your blood cholesterol through diet, medication, and exercise. 36 pp. (1993) **127A. $1.75.**

Mental Health

A Consumer's Guide to Mental Health Services. Answers common questions, identifies warning signs, discusses treatments, and lists resources for help and information. 28 pp. (1987) **550A. Free.**

Let's Talk About Depression. Helps teenagers learn the symptoms of depression and where to get help. 3 pp. (1991) **621A. Free.**

Panic Disorder. What to do when anxiety or sudden fear seems too much to handle. Lists symptoms, treatments, and where to get help. 7 pp. (1991) **554A. Free.**

You Are Not Alone. Facts about mental health and illness, behavior that may indicate a problem, and how to find help. 12 pp. (1992) **560A. Free.**

Housing

Fair Housing: It's Your Right. Outlines how you are protected against discrimination when buying, selling, or renting a home or an apartment and when applying for a mortgage. Includes a form to use if you think your rights have been violated. 9 pp. (1993) **561A. Free.**

How to Buy a Home with a Low Down Payment. Describes private and federal options for obtaining a low-down-payment mortgage, how to qualify, and how to determine what you can afford. 13 pp. (1993) **563A. Free.**

The Mortgage Money Guide. Explains the various types of mortgages and financing options. Includes a table of monthly mortgage costs at various rates. 18 pp. (1993) **129A. $1.25.**

The Inside Story: A Guide to Indoor Air Quality. Household products, building materials, pets, heating systems, and more can affect your health. Learn how and what to do about it. 32 pp. (1993) **379A. 50¢.**

Repairing Your Flooded Home. Advice on cleaning up and repairing your home and its contents. 55 pp. (1992) **565A. Free.**

Home Buyer's and Seller's Guide to Radon. Learn about testing options and what to do before buying or selling a home. 32 pp. (1993) **131A. $1.50.**

Water Treatment Units. Discusses various options for purifying drinking water and how to avoid deceptive sales. 4 pp. (1993) **332A. 50¢.**

Money Management

Your Credit: A Complete Guide. How to check your credit report, protect your privacy, and avoid fraud. Special help for women and older consumers who may have been denied credit. 43 pp. (1993) **603A. Free.**

The Savings Bonds Question and Answer Book. Savings Bonds purchase, interest, maturity, replacement, redemption, exchange, and taxes. 13 pp. (1994) **347A 50¢.**

A Consumer's Guide to Life Insurance. Learn the types, costs, and coverages. 30 pp. (1992) **345A. 50¢.**

Your Guaranteed Pension. Answers 29 frequently asked questions about the federal agency that insures private pension plans. 14 pp. (1993) **572A. Free.**

Protecting Your Privacy. How to check your credit file and medical record, handle telephone sales, and remove your name from mailing lists. 5 pp. (1990) **583A. Free.**

"900" Numbers. Learn how to protect yourself from unnecessary charges under the new FTC rule. 9 pp. (1993) **380A. 50¢.**

Business Directory

Listed below are major U.S. corporations whose operations—products and services—directly concern the American consumer. At the end of each listing is a **representative sample** of the company's products.

Company...Address...Phone number...Top executive ...Business.

AMR Corp....PO Box 619616, Dallas/Ft. Worth Airport, TX 75261...(817) 963-1234...Robert Crandall...Air transportation (American Airlines).

Abbott Laboratories...One Abbott Park Rd., North Chicago, IL 60064...(708) 937-6100...D. L. Burnham...health care prods.

Aetna Life & Casualty Co....151 Farmington Ave., Hartford, CT 06156...(203) 273-0123...Ronald E. Compton...insurance, financial services.

H. F. Ahmanson & Co....4900 Rivergrade Rd., Irwindale, CA 91706...(818) 814-7986...R. H. Deihi...operates largest S&L assn. in U.S. (Home Savings of America).

Alberto-Culver Co....2525 Armitage Ave., Melrose Park, IL 60160...(708) 450-3000...Leonard H. Lavin...hair care preparations, feminine hygiene products, household and grocery items.

Albertson's Inc....250 Parkcenter Blvd., Boise, ID 83726 ...(208) 385-6200...Gary Michael...supermarkets.

Alexander & Alexander Services Inc....1211 Ave. of the Americas, NY, NY 10036...(212) 840-8500...Frank Zarb...insurance & financial services.

AlliedSignal Inc....Morristown, NJ 07960...(201) 455-2000...Lawrence Bossidy...aerospace, engineered materials, automotive prods.

Alltel Corp....One Allied Dr., Little Rock, AR 72202...(501) 661-8000...J. T. Ford...telephone service in midwest, south, and eastern U.S.

Aluminum Co. of America...425 6th Ave., Pittsburgh, PA 15219...(412) 553-4545...Paul O'Neill...mining, refining, & processing of aluminum.

Amerada Hess Corp....1185 Ave. of the Americas, NY, NY 10036...(212) 997-8500...L. Hess...integrated petroleum co.

American Brands, Inc....1700 E. Putnam Ave., Old Greenwich, CT 06870...(203) 698-5000...W. J. Alley...tobacco (Pall Mall, Carlton, Half and Half, Paleden pipe tobacco), whiskey (Jim Beam), snack foods, life insurance, office prods., food, financial services, toiletries.

American Cyanamid Co....One Cyanamid Plaza, Wayne, NJ 07470...(201) 831-2000...A. J. Costello...medical, agricultural, chemical, and consumer prods.

American Express Co....200 Vesey St., NY, NY 10285...(212) 640-2000...H. Golub...travelers' checks, credit card services, insurance, investment services (Shearson Lehman).

American Greetings Corp....1 American Rd., Cleveland, OH 44144...(216) 252-7300...M. Weiss...greeting cards, stationery, gift items.

American Home Products Corp....5 Giralda Farms, Madison, NJ ...(201) 660-5000...J. R. Stafford...prescription and ethical drugs (Advil, Anacin, Robitussin), household prods. (Woolite, Easy-Off oven cleaner, Black Flag, Wizard air fresheners), food (Chef Boy-ar-dee).

American Stores Co....709 E. South Temple, Salt Lake City, UT 84102...(801) 539-0112...Victor Lund ...retail food markets, dept. & drug stores.

Amoco Corp....200 E. Randolph Dr., Chicago, IL 60601...(312) 856-6111...H. L. Fuller...oil and gas exploration, production, and marketing.

Anheuser-Busch, Inc....One Busch Place, St. Louis, MO 63118...(314) 577-2000...August A. Busch 3d...brewing (Budweiser, Michelob, Bud Light, Natural Light, Busch), theme parks, snack foods (Eagle).

Apple Computer, Inc....20525 Mariani Ave., Cupertino, CA 95014...(408) 974-2421...Michael Spindler...manuf. personal computers.

Archer Daniels Midland Company...4666 Faires Pkwy., Decatur, IL 62526...(217) 424-5200...Dwayne Andreas...agricultural commodities.

Armstrong World Industries...PO Box 3001, 313 W. Liberty St., Lancaster, PA 17604...(717) 397-0611...George Lorch...interior furnishings.

Arvin Industries, Inc....1531 13th St., Columbus, IN 47201...(812) 379-3000...J. K. Baker...auto emission & noise control systems.

Ashland Oil, Inc....PO Box 391, Ashland, KY 41101...(606) 329-3333...J. R. Hall...petroleum refiner, chemicals.

Atlantic Richfield Co....515 S. Flower St., Los Angeles, CA 90071...(213) 486-3511...L. M. Cook...petroleum, chemicals, other natural resources.

AT&T Corp....32 Ave. of the Americas, NY, NY 10013...(212) 387-5400...Robert Allen...communications, financial services.

Avery Dennison Corp....150 N. Orange Grove Blvd., Pasadena, CA 91103...(818) 304-2000...Charles D. Miller... self-adhesive labels, office prods., specialty chemicals.

Avon Products, Inc....9 West 57th St., NY, NY 10019...(212) 546-6015...J. E. Preston...cosmetics, fragrances, toiletries, health care.

Bausch & Lomb...One Lincoln First Square, Rochester, NY 14601...(716) 338-6000...D. E. Gill...manuf. of vision care products, accessories.

Baxter International Inc....One Baxter Pkwy., Deerfield, IL 60015...(708) 948-2000...Vernon R. Loucks, Jr....health care prods. & services.

Bell Atlantic Corp....1717 Arch St., Philadelphia, PA 19103...(215) 963-6000...R. W. Smith...telephone service in mid-Atlantic region.

BellSouth Corp....1155 Peachtree St. NE, Atlanta, GA 30367...(404) 249-2000...J. L. Clendenin...telephone service in the South.

Bethlehem Steel Corp....Bethlehem, PA 18016...(215) 694-2424...C. H. Barnette...steel & steel prods.

Bic Corporation...500 Bic Dr., Milford, CT 06460...(203) 783-2070...Bruno Bich...writing instruments, disposable lighters, shavers, and correction fluid (wite•out).

Black & Decker Corp....701 E. Joppa Rd., Towson, MD 21204...(410) 716-3900...N. D. Archibald...manuf. power tools, household prods., small appliances.

H & R Block, Inc....4410 Main St., Kansas City, MO 64111...(816) 753-6900...Henry W. Bloch...tax preparation.

Blockbuster Entertainment Corp....901 East Las Olas Blvd., Ft. Lauderdale, FL 33301...(305) 524-8200...H. Wayne Huizenga...video rental superstores.

Boeing Company...7755 E. Marginal Way S., Seattle, WA 98108...(206) 655-2121...F. A. Shrontz...aircraft manuf.

Boise Cascade Corp....One Jefferson Square, Boise, ID 83728...(208) 384-6161...J. B. Fery...timber, paper, wood prod.

Borden, Inc....277 Park Ave., NY, NY 10172...(212) 573-4000...E. Shames...food, cheese and cheese products, snacks (Cracker Jack), beverages, adhesives (Elmer's, Krazy Glue), pasta (Prince, Creamette), pasta sauce (Aunt Millie's, Classico).

Bristol-Myers Squibb Co....345 Park Ave., NY, NY 10022...(212) 546-4000...Richard L. Gelb...toiletries (Ban antiperspirant), hair items (Clairol), drugs (Bufferin, Comtrex, Excedrin), household prods. (Drano, Windex), infant formula (Enfamil).

Brown-Forman Corp....PO Box 1080, Louisville, KY 40201...(502) 585-1100...Owsley Brown 2d...distilled spirits (Jack Daniel's, Early Times), wines (Bolla, Fontana Candida), champagne (Korbel), liquor (Southern Comfort), Lenox china and crystal.

Brown Group, Inc....8400 Maryland Ave., St. Louis, MO 63105...(314) 854-4000...B. A. Bridgewater, Jr....manuf. and wholesaler of women's and children's shoes (Buster Brown, Naturalizer); specialty retailing.

Brunswick Corp....One N. Field Ct., Lake Forest, IL 60045...(708) 735-4700...J. F. Reichert...marine, recreation prods., bowling centers & equip., fishing equip.

Burlington Coat Factory Warehouse Corp....1830 Route 130 N., Burlington, NJ 08016...(609) 387-7800...M. G. Milstein...discount apparel stores.

Burlington Northern Inc....777 Main St., Ft. Worth, TX 76102...(817) 333-2000...G. Grinstein...rail transportation.

CBS Inc....51 W. 52d St., NY, NY 10019...(212) 975-4321...L. A. Tisch...broadcasting.

CPC International, Inc....International Plaza, Englewood Cliffs, NJ 07632...(201) 894-4000...Charles Shoemate...branded food items (Hellmann's mayonnaise, Best Foods, Mazola corn oil, Skippy peanut butter, Knorr soups, Thomas' English muffins, Mueller pasta prods., Arnold breads).

Caesar's World, Inc....1801 Century Park East, Los Angeles, CA 90067...(213) 552-2711...H. Gluck...hotels & casinos, resort hotels.

Caldor Corp....20 Glover Ave., Norwalk, CT 06856...(203) 849-2000...D. R. Clarke...discount retailer.

Campbell Soup Co....Campbell Pl., Camden, NJ 08103...(609) 342-4800...D. W. Johnson...canned soups, spaghetti (Franco-American), vegetable juice (V-8), pork and beans, pet foods, confections, Swanson frozen dinners, Prego spaghetti sauce, Mrs. Paul's frozen fish, Pepperidge Farm breads.

Capital Cities/ABC, Inc....77 W. 66th St., NY, NY 10023...(212) 456-7777...D. B. Burke...operates television and radio stations, cable TV (ESPN); newspapers, specialized business and consumer periodicals.

Carter-Wallace, Inc....1345 Ave. of the Americas, NY, NY 10105...(212) 339-5000...H. H. Hoyt, Jr....personal care items, antiperspirant (Arrid), shave lathers (Rise), tooth polish (Pearl Drops), condoms (Trojan), laxative (Carter's Pills), pet prods. (Victory flea collars).

Caterpillar Inc....100 N.E. Adams St., Peoria, IL 61629...(309) 675-1000...Donald Fites...heavy duty earth-moving equip.

Chase Manhattan Corp....1 Chase Manhattan Plaza, NY, NY 10081...(212) 552-2222...Thomas Labrecque ...bank holding co.

Chevron Corp....225 Bush St., San Francisco, CA 94104...(415) 894-7700...K. T. Derr...integrated oil co.

Chrysler Corp....Highland Pk., MI 48288...(313) 956-5252...R. J. Eaton...cars, trucks.

Church & Dwight Co., Inc....469 N. Harrison St., Princeton, NJ 08543...(609) 683-5900...D. C. Minton...consumer prods. (Arm & Hammer).

Circuit City Stores, Inc....9950 Maryland Dr., Richmond, VA 23233...(804) 527-4000...R. L. Sharp...retailer of electronic equip., consumer appliances.

Circus Circus Enterprises, Inc....2880 Las Vegas Blvd. S., Las Vegas, NV 89109...(702) 734-0410...Clyde Turner...casino operator.

Citicorp...399 Park Ave., NY, NY 10043...(212) 559-1000...J. S. Reed...largest U.S. commercial bank.

Clayton Homes...PO Box 15169, Knoxville, TN 37901...(615) 970-7200...J. L. Clayton...produces & sells manufactured homes.

Clorox Co....1221 Broadway, Oakland, CA 94612...(510) 271-7000...C. R. Weaver...retail consumer prods. (Formula 409, Pine-Sol, Kingsford charcoal briquets, Deer Park bottled water, Combat insecticides, Hidden Valley Ranch salad dressing, Soft Scrub cleanser).

Coachman Industries Inc....601 E. Beardsley Ave., Elkhart, IN 46514...(219) 262-0123...T. H. Corson...manuf. recreational vehicles.

Coastal Corp....9 Greenway Plaza, Houston, TX 77046...(713) 877-1400...O. S. Wyatt...oil refineries, natural gas pipeline systems.

Coca-Cola Co....One Coca-Cola Plaza N.W., Atlanta, GA 30313...(404) 676-2121...R. C. Goizueta...soft drinks (Coca-Cola, Sprite, Nestea), syrups, citrus and fruit juices (Minute Maid, Hi-C).

Colgate-Palmolive Co....300 Park Ave., NY, NY 10022...(212) 310-2000...R. Mark...soaps (Palmolive, Irish Spring), detergents (Fab, Ajax, Fresh Start), toothpaste (Colgate, Ultra Brite), household prods. (Handy Wipes, Curad bandages).

Compaq Computer Corp....20555 SH 249, Houston, TX 77070...(713) 370-0670...E. Pfeiffer...portable and desktop computers.

Con Agra...1 Con Agra Dr....Omaha, NE 68102...(402) 595-4000...Philip Fletcher...food processor.

Adolph Coors Co....Golden, CO 80401...(303) 279-6565...W. K. Coors...brewery.

Corning, Inc....One Riverfront Plaza, Corning, NY 14831...(607) 974-9000...J. R. Houghton ...glass mfg.

Crane Co....100 First Stamford Place, Stamford, CT 06902...(203) 363-7300...R. S. Evans...manuf. fluid control devices, vending machines, fiberglass panels, aircraft brakes.

A. T. Cross Co....One Albion Rd., Lincoln, RI 02865...(401) 333-1200...B. R. Boss...writing instruments.

Culbro Corp....387 Park Ave. S., NY, NY 10016...(212) 561-8700...E. M. Cullman...cigars (Corina, Robert Burns, White Owl, Tiparillo's), snack foods.

Dana Corp....4500 Dorr St., Toledo, OH 43615...(419) 535-4500...S. J. Morcott...truck and auto parts supplies.

Data General Corp....4400 Computer Dr., Westboro, MA 01580...(508) 898-5000...R. L. Skates...computer & communications sytems manuf.

Dayton Hudson Corp....777 Nicollet Mall, Minneapolis, MN 55402...(612) 370-6948...K. A. Macke...department, specialty stores.

Deere & Co....John Deere Rd., Moline, IL 61265...(309) 765-8000...H. W. Becherer...farm, industrial, and outdoor power equip.

Delta Air Lines, Inc....Hartsfield Atlanta Intl. Airport, Atlanta, GA 30320...(404) 715-2600...Ronald W. Allen...air transportation.

Dial Corp....Dial Tower, Phoenix, AZ 85077...(602) 207-4000...J. W. Teets...consumer prods. (Dial, Purex detergents, Armour Star meats, Breck shampoo), contract and fast food services.

Diebold, Inc....PO Box 8230, Canton, OH 44711...(216) 489-4000...R. W. Mahoney...manuf. equip. for financial insts.

Digital Equipment Corp....146 Main St., Maynard, MA 01754...(508) 493-5111...R. B. Palmer...computer systems manuf.

Walt Disney Co....500 S. Buena Vista St., Burbank, CA 91521...(818) 560-1000...M. D. Eisner...motion pictures, cable television, theme parks (Walt Disney World, Disneyland) and resorts, publishing, recordings, retailing (Disney stores).

Dole Food Co....31355 Oak Crest Drive, Westlake Village, CA 91361...(818) 879-6600...David Murdock...food products, fresh fruits and vegetables, real estate.

R. R. Donnelley & Sons Co....77 W. Wacker Dr., Chicago, IL 60601...(312) 326-8000...J. R. Walter...largest commercial printer.

Dow Chemical Co....2030 Dow Center, Midland, MI 48674...(517) 636-1000...F. P. Popoff...chemicals, plastics, metals, consumer prods. (Ziploc, Saran Wrap, Fantastik).

Dow Jones & Co....200 Liberty St., NY, NY 10281...(212) 416-2000...P. R. Kann...financial news service, publishing (Wall Street Journal, Barron's, Ottaway Newspapers).

Dun & Bradstreet Corp....299 Park Ave., NY, NY 10171...(212) 593-6800...C. W. Moritz...business information and computer services, publishing, broadcasting.

E. I. du Pont de Nemours & Co....1007 Market St., Wilmington, DE 19898...(302) 774-1000...Edgar Woolard, Jr....chemicals, petroleum, consumer prods., coal.

Duracell Intl. Inc....Berkshire Industrial Park, Bethel, CT 06801...(203) 796-4000...C. R. Kidder...manuf. batteries.

Eastman Kodak Co....343 State St., Rochester, NY 14650...(716) 724-5492...G. Fisher...photographic prods., information systems, health care.

Eaton Corp....1111 Superior Ave., Cleveland, OH 44114...(216) 523-5000...W. E. Butler...manuf. of electronic, electrical prods., vehicle components.

Emerson Electric Co....8000 W. Florissant Ave., St. Louis, MO 63136...(314) 553-2000...C. F. Knight...electrical, electronics products & systems.

Ethyl Corp....330 S. 4th St., Richmond, VA 23217...(804) 788-5000...B. C. Gottwald...petroleum and industrial chemicals.

Exxon Corp....225 E. John W. Carpenter Freeway, Irving, TX 75062...(214) 444-1900...L. R. Raymond...oil, natural gas, coal, chemicals.

Fabri-Centers of America, Inc...5555 Darrow Rd., Hudson, OH 44236...(216) 656-2600...Alan Rosskamm...specialty fabric stores.

Family Dollar Stores, Inc....PO Box 1017, Charlotte, NC 28201...(704) 847-6961...L. Levine...discount variety stores.

Fedders Corp....158 Highway 206, PO Box 265, Peapack, NJ 07977...(908) 234-2100...S. Giordano, Jr....manuf. of room air conditioners.

Federal Express Corp....Box 727, Memphis, TN 38194 ...(901) 369-3600...F. W. Smith...express delivery service.

Fieldcrest Cannon, Inc....Eden, NC 27288...(919) 627-3000...J. M. Fitzgibbons...household textile prods., rugs (Karastan).

First Brands Corp....83 Wooster Hts. Rd., Danbury, CT 06813...(203) 731-2300...A. E. Dudley...consumer prods. (Glad plastic bags, Scoop-Away cat litter, Prestone auto prods.).

Fleetwood Enterprises, Inc....PO Box 7638, Riverside, CA 92523...(909) 351-3500...John C. Crean...manufactured homes, recreational vehicles.

Fluor Corp....3333 Michelson Dr., Irvine, CA 92730...(714) 975-6961...L. G. McCraw...engineering and construction.

Ford Motor Co....The American Rd., Dearborn, MI 48121...(313) 845-8540...Alexander Trotman...motor vehicles, Ford Tractor, Lincoln-Mercury.

Fruit of the Loom, Inc....5000 Sears Tower, Chicago, IL 60606...(312) 876-1724...W. Farley...manuf. of underwear.

GTE Corp....One Stamford Forum, Stamford, CT 06904...(203) 965-2000...C. R. Lee...largest U.S. local exchange telephone co., cellular telephone operator.

Gannett Co., Inc....1100 Wilson Blvd., Arlington, VA 22234...(703) 284-6000...J. J. Curley...newspaper publishing (USA Today), TV stations, outdoor advertising.

The GAP, Inc....1 Harrison, San Francisco, CA 94105...(415) 952-4400...D. G. Fisher...casual and activewear retailer.

Gencorp...175 Ghent Rd., Fairlawn, OH 44333...(216) 869-4200...A. W. Reynolds...aerospace, auto prods., polymer prods.

General Dynamics Corp....3190 Fairview Park Dr., Falls Church, VA 22042...(703) 876-3000...J. R. Mellor...nuclear submarines, armored vehicles.

General Electric Co....3135 Easton Ave., Fairfield, CT 06431...(203) 373-2211...J. F. Welch, Jr....electrical, electronic equip., radio, television (NBC), aircraft engines.

General Host Corp....22 Gate House Rd., Stamford, CT 06904...(203) 357-9900...H. J. Ashton...crafts, lawn and garden retail stores (Frank's Nursery & Crafts).

General Mills, Inc....PO Box 1113, Minneapolis, MN 55440...(612) 540-2444...H. B. Atwater, Jr....foods (Total, Bisquick, Wheaties, Cheerios, Hamburger Helper, Gorton's, Betty Crocker), restaurants (Red Lobster, Olive Garden).

General Motors Corp....3044 W. Grand Blvd., Detroit, MI 48202...(313) 556-5000...John G. Smale....world's largest auto manuf.

Genesco, Inc....Genesco Park, Nashville, TN 37202...(615) 367-7000...E. D. Grindstaff...footwear and men's clothing manuf. and retailer.

Genuine Parts Co....2999 Circle 75 Pkwy., Atlanta, GA 30339...(404) 953-1700...L. L. Prince...distributes auto replacement parts (NAPA).

Georgia-Pacific Corp....133 Peachtree St. NE, Atlanta, GA 30303...(404) 521-5210...A. D. Correll....building prods., pulp, paper.

Giant Food, Inc....6300 Sheriff Rd., Landover, MD 20785...(301) 341-4100...I. Cohen...supermarkets.

Gillette Co....Prudential Tower Bldg., Boston, MA 02199...(617) 421-7000...Alfred Zeier...razors, pens (Paper Mate), toiletries (Right Guard deodorants, Foamy shaving cream, Earth Born shampoo), hair products (Toni, Adorn).

Goodyear Tire & Rubber Co....1144 E. Market St., Akron, OH 44316...(216) 796-8576...Stanley Gault...tires and other auto products.

W. R. Grace & Co....One Town Center Rd., Boca Raton, FL 33486...(407) 362-2000...J. P. Bolduc...chemicals, natural resources, health care.

Great Atlantic & Pacific Tea Co....2 Paragon Dr., Montvale, NJ 07645...(201) 573-9700...James Wood...supermarket chain.

Hannaford Bros. Co....145 Pleasant Hill Rd., Scarborough, ME 04074...(207) 883-2911...Hugh G. Farrington...operates supermarkets, drug stores.

Harley-Davidson, Inc....3700 W. Juneau Ave., Milwaukee, WI 53208...(414) 342-4680...R. F. Teerlink...manuf. of motorcycles, parts & accessories.

Hartmarx...101 N. Wacker Dr., Chicago, IL 60606...(312) 372-6300...E. O. Hand...apparel manufacturer and retailer (Hickey-Freeman, Hart Schaffner & Marx).

Hasbro, Inc....1027 Newport Ave., Pawtucket, RI 02862...(401) 431-8697...A. G. Hassenfeld...toy manuf. & marketer (Milton Bradley, Playskool, G. I. Joe, Parker Bros. games, Tonka trucks, Play-Doh).

H. J. Heinz Co....PO Box 57, Pittsburgh, PA 15230...(412) 456-6014...Anthony J. F. O'Reilly...foods (Star-Kist, Ore-Ida, '57 Varieties), 9-Lives cat food, Weight Watchers.

Helene Curtis...325 N. Wells St., Chicago, IL 60610...(312) 661-0222...R. J. Gidwitz...hair care prods. (Finesse, Suave, Salon Selectives), antiperspirant (Degree).

Hershey Foods Corp....100 Crystal A Dr., Hershey, PA 17033...(717) 534-6799...Kenneth Wolfe...chocolate & confectionery prods. (Reese's peanut butter cups, Kit Kat, Peter Paul Mounds, Almond Joy), pasta (San Giorgio, Ronzoni).

Hewlett-Packard Co....300 Hanover St., Palo Alto, CA 94304...(415) 857-1501...L. E. Platt...manuf. electronic prods. and systems.

Hillenbrand Industries, Inc....Highway 46, Batesville, IN 47006...(812) 934-7000...D. A. Hillenbrand...manuf. burial caskets, electronically operated hospital beds, luggage.

Home Depot, Inc....2727 Paces Ferry Rd., Atlanta, GA 30339...(404) 433-8211...Bernard Marcus...retailer of building materials & home improvement prods.

Honeywell, Inc....Honeywell Plaza, Minneapolis, MN 55408...(612) 951-1000...Michael Bonsignore...industrial systems & controls, aerospace guidance systems, information systems.

Geo. A. Hormel & Co....501 16th Ave. N.E., Austin, MN 55912...(507) 437-5611...R. L. Knowlton...meat packaging, pork and beef prods. (Spam, Dinty Moore, Mary Kitchen).

Houghton Mifflin Co....One Beacon St., Boston, MA 02108...(617) 725-5000...Nader F. Darehshori...book publishing.

Household International Inc....2700 Sanders Rd., Prospect Heights, IL 60070...(708) 564-5000...D. C. Clark...financial and insurance services.

Huffy Corp....7701 Byers Rd., Miamisburg, OH 45342...(513) 866-6251...Richard Molen...bicycles, sports and hardware equip. manuf.

Humana, Inc....500 W. Main St., Louisville, KY 40202...(502) 580-1000...D. A. Jones...operates hospitals, provides health care plans.

IBP, Inc....IBP Ave., PO Box 515, Dakota City, NE 68731...(402) 494-2061...Robert Peterson...processor of beef and pork.

Intel Corp....2200 Mission College Blvd., Santa Clara, CA 95052...(408) 765-8080...G. E. Moore...manuf. integrated circuits.

International Business Machines Corp....Old Orchard Rd., Armonk, NY 10504...(914) 765-1900...Louis Gerstner, Jr. ...information processing systems, equip., and services.

International Paper Co....2 Manhattanville Rd., Purchase, NY 10577...(914) 397-1500...J. A. Georges...paper, wood prods.

ITT Corp....1330 Ave. of the Americas, NY, NY 10022...(212) 258-1000...R. V. Araskog...manuf., installs communication and electronic equip., auto equip., insurance, financial services, hotels, educational services.

Johnson Controls...5757 N. Green Bay Ave., Milwaukee, WI 53201...(414) 228-1200...James Keyes...fire protection services, auto seats and batteries, beverage containers.

Johnson & Johnson...501 George St., New Brunswick, NJ 08903...(908) 524-0400...R. S. Larsen...surgical dressings, pharmaceuticals (Tylenol), toiletries.

Jostens, Inc....5501 Norman Center Dr., Minneapolis, MN 55437...(612) 830-3300...R. Buhrmaster...school rings, yearbooks.

Kellogg Co....One Kellogg Sq., Battle Creek, MI 49016...(616) 961-2000...Arnold G. Langbo...ready-to-eat cereals & other food prods.

Kimberly-Clark Corp....PO Box 619100, Dallas, TX 75261...(214) 830-1200...Wayne R. Sanders...paper and lumber prods., consumer prods. (Kleenex, Huggies, Depend).

King World Productions, Inc....1700 Broadway, NY, NY 10019...(212) 315-4000...M. King...syndicator of TV programs (Oprah Winfrey Show, Wheel of Fortune, Jeopardy, Inside Edition).

Kmart Corp....3100 W. Big Beaver Rd., Troy, MI 48084...(313) 643-1000...J. E. Antonini...largest U.S. chain of discount stores, book stores (Waldenbooks, Borders), cafeterias, drug stores (Payless Drug Stores), home improvement retail stores.

Knight-Ridder, Inc....One Herold Plaza, Miami, FL 33101...(305) 376-3838...J. K. Batten...newspaper publishing, TV broadcasting, book publishing, information services.

Kroger Co....1014 Vine St., Cincinnati, OH 45201...(513) 762-4000...Joseph Pichler...grocery chain.

L.A. Gear, Inc....2850 Ocean Park Blvd., Santa Monica, CA 90405...(310) 822-1995...Stanley P. Gold...athletic & leisure footwear, casual apparel.

La-Z-Boy Chair Co....1284 N. Telegraph Rd., Monroe, MI 48161...(313) 242-1444...C. T. Knabusch...reclining chair mfg.

Lands' End, Inc....Lands' End Lane, Dodgeville, WI 53595...(608) 935-9341...William End...direct-mail catalog co.

Eli Lilly & Company...Lilly Corp. Center, Indianapolis, IN 46285...(317) 276-2000...R. L. Tobias...mfg. health and agricultural products.

The Limited, Inc....Two Limited Pkwy., Columbus, OH 43216...(614) 479-7000...L. H. Wexner...women's apparel stores (Lane Bryant, Lerner, Victoria's Secret), Abercrombie & Fitch.

Litton Industries, Inc....360 N. Crescent Dr., Beverly Hills, CA 90210...(310) 859-5000...A. J. Brann...industrial systems & services, advanced electronic systems, electronic & electrical prods., marine engineering.

Lockheed Martin Corp....6801 Rockledge Dr., Bethesda, MD 20817...(301) 897-6000...D. M. Tellep...commercial and military aircraft, electronics, missiles.

Loews Corp....667 Madison Ave., NY, NY 10021...(212) 545-2000...Laurence A. Tisch...tobacco prods. (Kent, Newport, True), watches, hotels, insurance.

Longs Drug Stores, Inc....141 North Civic Dr., Walnut Creek, CA 94596...(510) 937-1170...R. M. Long...drug store chain.

Lowe's Cos., Inc....Box 1111, North Wilkesboro, NC 28656...(919) 651-4000...L. G. Herring...retailer of building materials & related prods.

Luby's Cafeterias, Inc....2211 Northeast Loop 410, San Antonio, TX 78265...(210) 654-9000...R. Erben...operates cafeterias in Southwest U.S.

Manor Care, Inc....10750 Columbia Pike, Silver Spring, MD 20901...(301) 681-9400...S. Bainum, Jr....operates nursing homes.

Marriott Corp....Marriott Dr., Washington, DC 20058...(301) 380-9000...J. Willard Marriott, Jr....hotels, food service.

Mattel, Inc....333 Continental Blvd., El Segundo, CA 90245...(213) 524-2000...J. W. Amerman...toy & hobby prods. (Barbie doll, Hot Wheels).

May Department Stores Co....611 Olive St., St. Louis, MO 63101...(314) 342-6300...D. C. Farrell...department stores (Hecht's, Lord & Taylor, Foley's).

Maytag Corp....Newton, IA 50208...(515) 792-8000...L. A. Hadley...manuf. home laundry equip., appliances (Magic Chef, Admiral).

McDonald's Corp....McDonald's Plaza, Oak Brook, IL 60521...(708) 575-7428...M. R. Quinlan...fast-food restaurants.

McDonnell Douglas Corp....PO Box 516, St. Louis, MO 63166...(314) 232-0232...J. F. McDonnell...commercial & military aircraft, space systems & missiles.

McGraw-Hill, Inc....1221 Ave. of the Americas, NY, NY 10020...(212) 512-2000...J. L. Dionne...book, magazine publishing (Business Week), information & financial services (Standard and Poor's), TV stations.

Mead Corporation...Courthouse Plaza NE, Dayton, OH 45463...(513) 495-6323...S. C. Mason...printing and writing paper, paperboard, packaging, shipping containers, pulp and lumber.

Media General, Inc....333 E. Grace St., Richmond, VA 23219...(804) 649-6000...J. S. Bryan 3d...broadcasting, newspaper publishing.

Medtronic, Inc....7000 Central Ave. NE, Minneapolis, MN 55432...(612) 574-4000...W. W. George...manuf. prosthetic and pacemaker devices.

Melville Corp....1 Theall Rd., Rye, NY 10580...(914) 925-4000...S. P. Goldstein...shoe stores (Thom McAn), apparel (Marshalls, Chess King), drug stores.

Merck & Co., Inc....PO Box 100, Whitehouse Station, NJ 08889...(908) 423-1000...P. Roy Vagelos...human & animal health care prods.

Meredith Corp....1716 Locust St., Des Moines, IA 50336...(515) 284-3000...J. D. Rehm...magazine publishing (Better Homes and Gardens, Ladies Home Journal), book publishing, broadcasting.

Merrill Lynch & Co., Inc....World Financial Center, N. Tower, NY, NY 10281...(212) 449-1000...Daniel P. Tully...securities broker, financial services.

Microsoft Corp....One Microsoft Way, Redmond, WA 98052...(206) 882-8080...William H. Gates...the world's largest computer software company.

Minnesota Mining & Manuf. Co....3M Center, St. Paul, MN 55144...(612) 733-1110...L. D. DeSimone...abrasives, adhesives, building services & chemicals, electrical, health care, photographic, printing, recording materials, consumer prods. (Scotch Tape, Post-It).

Mirage Resorts, Inc....3400 Las Vegas Blvd. S, Las Vegas, NV 89109...(702) 385-7111...S. A. Wynn...hotel-casino operator (Mirage, Treasure Island, Golden Nugget).

Mobil Corp....3225 Gallows Rd., Fairfax, VA 22037...(703) 846-3000...L. A. Noto...international oil co., chemicals.

Monsanto Company...800 N. Lindbergh Blvd., St. Louis, MO 63167...(314) 694-1000...R. J. Mahoney...chemicals, agricultural prods., pharmaceuticals, consumer prods. (NutraSweet).

Motorola, Inc....1303 E. Algonquin Rd., Schaumburg, IL 60196...(708) 576-5000...G. L. Tooker...electronic equipment and components.

National Medical Enterprises, Inc....PO Box 4070, Santa Monica, CA 90411...(310) 998-8000...J. C. Barbakow...operates hospitals.

National Semiconductor Corp....2900 Semiconductor Dr., Santa Clara, CA 95052...(408) 721-5000...P. Sprague...manuf. of semiconductors.

Navistar Intl. Corp....455 N. Cityfront Plaza Dr., Chicago, IL 60611...(312) 836-2000...J. C. Cotting...manuf. heavy duty trucks, parts.

New York Times Co....229 W. 43d St., NY, NY 10036...(212) 556-3660...A. O. Sulzberger...newspapers, radio, CATV stations, magazines (Family Circle, Golf Digest).

Nike, Inc....One Bowerman Dr., Beaverton, OR 97005...(503) 671-6453...Philip Knight...athletic & leisure footware.

Norfolk Southern Corp....3 Commercial Place, Norfolk, VA 23510...(804) 629-2640...D. R. Goode...operates Norfolk & Southern railways, freight carrier (North American Van Lines).

Northrop Grumman Corp....1840 Century Park E, Los Angeles, CA 90067...(213) 553-6262...K. Kresa...aircraft, electronics, communications.

Nynex Corp....1095 Ave. of the Americas, NY, NY 10036...(212) 370-7400...W. C. Ferguson...telephone co. in northeast U.S.

Occidental Petroleum Corp....10889 Wilshire Blvd., Los Angeles, CA 90024...(213) 879-1700...Ray Irani...oil, gas, chemicals, coal, agriculture.

Office Depot, Inc....2200 Old Germantown Rd., Delray Beach, FL 33445...(407) 278-4800...D. I. Fuente...retail office supply stores.

Ogden Corp....2 Pennsylvania Plaza, NY, NY 10121...(212) 868-6100...R. E. Ablon...transportation, foods, metals, financial services.

Olin Corp....120 Long Ridge Rd., Stamford, CT 06904...(203) 356-2000...J. W. Johnstone, Jr....chemicals, water treatment prods., aerospace.

Olsten Corp....One Merrick Ave., Westbury, NY 11590...(516) 832-8200...F. N. Liguori...provides temporary workers.

Outboard Marine Corp....100 Sea-Horse Dr., Waukegan, IL 60085...(708) 689-6200...J. C. Chapman...outboard motors (Evinrude, Johnson), boats.

Owens-Corning Fiberglas Corp....Fiberglas Tower, Toledo, OH 43659...(419) 248-8000...G. H. Hiner...glass fiber and related prods.

Oxford Industries, Inc....222 Piedmont Ave. NE, Atlanta, GA 30308...(404) 659-2424...J. H. Lanier...manuf. men's and women's apparel.

Pacific Telesis Group...130 Kearny St., San Francisco, CA 94108...(415) 394-3000...Philip Quigley...telephone service.

J. C. Penney Co....14841 N. Dallas Pkwy., PO Box 659000, Dallas, TX 75265...(214) 591-1000...W. R. Howell...dept. stores, catalog sales, drug stores, insurance.

Pennzoil Co....PO Box 2967, Houston, TX 77252...(713) 546-4000...J. L. Pate...integrated oil and gas co.

Pep Boys—Manny, Moe & Jack...3111 W. Allegheny Ave., Philadelphia, PA 19132...(215) 229-9000...M. G. Leibovitz...automotive parts and accessories, retail stores.

PepsiCo, Inc....PepsiCo. World HQ, Purchase, NY 10577...(914) 253-2000...D. W. Calloway...soft drinks (Pepsi-Cola, Slice), snack foods (Ruffles, Lays, Sunchips, Doritos), restaurants (Pizza Hut, KFC, Taco Bell).

Perry Drug Stores, Inc....5400 Perry Dr., PO Box 436021, Pontiac, MI 48343...(313) 334-1300...J. A. Robinson...drug stores, health care.

Petrie Stores Corp....70 Enterprise Ave., Secaucus, NJ 07094...(201) 866-3600...M. J. Petrie...operates chain of women's specialty stores.

Pfizer, Inc....235 E. 42d St., NY, NY 10017...(212) 573-2323...W. C. Steere, Jr....pharmaceutical, hospital, agricultural, chemical prods., consumer prods. (Visine eye drops, Ben-Gay pain relief).

Philip Morris Cos., Inc....120 Park Ave., NY, NY 10017 ...(212) 880-5000...Geoffrey Bible...cigarettes (Marlboro, Virginia Slims), beer (Miller High Life, Lowenbrau brands), packaged foods (Jell-O, Entenmann baked goods, Maxwell House coffee, Kool Aid, Oscar Mayer meats, Tang, Cheez Whiz & Velveeta cheese prods).

Phillips-Van Heusen Corp....1290 Ave. of the Americas, NY, NY 10104...(212) 541-5200...L. S. Phillips...manuf. apparel for men & women; operates retail stores.

Pitney Bowes, Inc....Wheeler Dr., Stamford, CT 06926...(203) 356-5000...G. B. Harvey...postage meters, mail handling equip., office equipment.

Playboy Enterprises, Inc....680 N. Lake Shore Dr., Chicago, IL 60611...(312) 751-8000...C. Hefner...magazine publishing, CATV, merchandising.

Polaroid Corp....Technology Sq., Cambridge, MA 02139 ...(617) 386-2000...I. M. Booth...photographic equip., supplies, and optical goods.

PPG Industries, Inc....One PPG Place, Pittsburgh, PA 15272...(412) 434-3131...Jerry Dempsey...glass prods., paints, chemicals.

Premark Intl., Inc....1717 Deerfield Rd., Deerfield, IL 60015...(708) 405-6000...W. L. Batts...consumer prods.

Procter & Gamble Co....One Proctor & Gamble Plaza, Cincinnati, OH 45202...(513) 983-1100...E. L. Artzt...soap & detergent (Ivory, Cheer, Tide, Mr. Clean, Comet, Spic and Span, Zest), toiletries (Crest toothpaste, Prell, Head and Shoulders shampoos, Noxzema, Oil of Olay, Old Spice), pharmaceuticals (Pepto-Bismol); Pampers disposable diapers, Folgers coffee, Hawaiian Punch, Ultra Charmin toilet tissues, Bounty towels, Vicks cough medicines, Crisco shortening, Duncan Hines cakes.

Promus Cos. Inc....1023 Cherry Rd., Memphis, TN 38117...(901) 762-8852...M. D. Rose...casinos (Harrah), lodging (Hampton Inn, Embassy Suites).

Quaker Oats Co....Quaker Tower, PO Box 9001, Chicago, IL 60604...(312) 222-7818...William D. Smithburg...cereal (Quaker Oat Bran, Life, Cap'n Crunch, Puffed Wheat, Puffed Rice), foods (Aunt Jemima, Celeste pizza, Van Camp's pork and beans, Gatorade), pet foods (Ken-L-Ration, Gaines).

Quaker State Corp....255 Elm St., Oil City, PA 16301...(814) 676-7676...H. M. Baum...refining, marketing petroleum prods., filters, mining & marketing coal.

Ralston Purina Co....Checkerboard Sq., St. Louis, MO 63164...(314) 982-2161...W. K. Stiritz...pet and livestock food (Purina), consumer prods. (Chex cereal, Beech-Nut baby food, Wonder bread, Hostess baked goods, Eveready and Energizer batteries).

Raytheon Company...141 Spring St., Lexington, MA 02173...(617) 862-6600...Dennis J. Picard...electronics, aviation, appliances; Amana Refrigeration, Beech Aircraft.

Reader's Digest Assn....Pleasantville, NY 10570...(914) 238-1000...James Schadt...magazines, books.

Reebok Intl. Ltd....100 Technology Ctr. Dr., Stoughton, MA 02072...(617) 341-5000...P. B. Fireman...athletic & casual footwear, sportswear.

Reynolds Metals Co....6601 W. Broad St., Richmond, VA 23230...(804) 281-2000...Richard G. Holder...aluminum prods.

Rite Aid Corp....PO Box 3165, Harrisburg, PA 17105...(717) 761-2633...Martin Grass...discount drug stores, beauty aid stores.

RJR Nabisco Holdings Corp....1301 Ave. of the Americas, NY, NY 10019...(212) 258-5600...C. M. Harper...cigarettes (Winston, Salem, Camel), foods (Oreos, Ritz crackers).

Rockwell Intl. Corp....625 Liberty Ave., Pittsburgh, PA 15222 ...(412) 565-2000...(213) 647-5000...D. R. Beall...aerospace, electronic, automotive prods.

Rubbermaid Inc....1147 Akron Rd., Wooster, OH 44691...(216) 264-6464...W. R. Schmitt...rubber and plastic consumer prods.

Russell Corp....Alexander City, AL 35010...(205) 329-4000...J. C. Adams...manuf. leisure apparel, athletic uniforms.

Ryder System, Inc....3600 NW 82d Ave., Miami, FL 33166...(305) 593-3726...M. A. Burns...truck-leasing service.

Santa Fe Pacific Corp....1700 E. Golf Rd., Schaumburg, IL 60173...(708) 995-6000...Robert D. Krebs...railroad, real estate, construction, natural resources.

Sara Lee Corp....3 First National Plaza, Chicago, IL 60602...(312) 726-2600...J. H. Bryan...baked goods, fresh and processed meats, fresh and frozen fruits and vegetables and other packaged foods, beverages, tobacco products, hosiery, intimate apparel and knitwear (Hanes, Kiwi, Shasta, Hillshire Farm, L'eggs, Isotoner).

Schering-Plough Corp....One Giralda Farms, Madison, NJ 07940...(201) 822-7000...R. P. Luciano...pharmaceuticals, consumer prods.

Scott Paper Co....Scott Plaza, Philadelphia, PA 19113...(215) 522-5000...P. E. Lippincott...bathroom tissue, paper towels, napkins.

Sears, Roebuck & Co....Sears Tower, Chicago, IL 60684...(312) 875-2500...E. A. Brennan...merchandising, insurance (Allstate).

Service Merchandise, Inc....PO Box 246000, Nashville, TN 37202...(615) 660-6000...R. Zimmerman... operates catalog showrooms.

Shaw Industries, Inc....616 E. Walnut Ave., Dalton, GA 30720...(706) 278-3812...R. E. Shaw...manuf. tufted carpeting (Magee, Philadelphia).

Sherwin-Williams Co....101 Prospect Ave. NW, Cleveland, OH 44115...(216) 566-2000...John G. Breen...paint manuf. (Dutch Boy, Kem-Tone).

Sizzler Intl., Inc....12655 W. Jefferson Blvd., Los Angeles, CA 90066...(310) 827-2300...Kevin Perkins...quick-service restaurants.

Skyline Corp....2520 By-Pass Rd., Elkhart, IN 46515...(219) 294-6521...Arthur J. Decio...mfg. housing and recreational vehicles.

Smucker (J. M.) Co....Strawberry Lane, Orrville, OH 44667 ...(216) 682-3000...R. K. Smucker...preserves, jams, jellies, toppings.

Snap-on, Inc....2801 80th St., Kenosha, WI 53140...(414) 656-5449...R. A. Cornog...manuf. mechanic's tools, equip.

Southwest Airlines Co....PO Box 36611, Dallas, TX 75235...(214) 904-4000...H. D. Kelleher...air transportation.

Southwestern Bell Corp....PO Box 2933, San Antonio, TX 78299...(210) 351-2044...E. E. Whitacre, Jr....telephone services.

Sprint Corp....PO Box 11315 Plaza Station, Kansas City, MO 64112...(913) 624-3000...W. T. Esrey...long-distance telecommunications.

Stanley Works...1000 Stanley Dr., PO Box 7000, New Britain, CT 06050...(203) 225-5111...R. H. Ayers...hand tools, hardware, door-opening equip.

Stride Rite Corp....5 Cambridge Center, Cambridge, MA 02142...(617) 491-8800...Robert Siegel...children's footwear.

Sun Company, Inc....1801 Market St., Philadelphia, PA 19103...(215) 977-3000...R. H. Campbell...energy resources co.

Tambrands Inc....777 Westchester Ave., White Plains, NY 10604...(914) 696-6000...Edward Fogarty...feminine hygiene products (Tampax, Maxithins).

Tandem Computers...19333 Vallco Pkwy., Cupertino, CA 95014...(408) 285-6000...J. Treybig...supplier of computer systems and networks.

Tandy Corp....1800 One Tandy Center, Fort Worth, TX 76102...(817) 390-3700...J. F. Roach...consumer electronics retailing (Computer City, Radio Shack).

Teledyne, Inc....1901 Ave. of the Stars, Los Angeles, CA 90067...(310) 551-4268...William Rutledge...electronics, aerospace prods., industrial prods., insurance, finance.

Tenneco, Inc....PO Box 2511, Houston, TX 77252...(713) 757-2131...D. Mead...oil, natural gas pipelines, shipbuilding, farm equip.

Texaco Inc....2000 Westchester Ave., White Plains, NY 10650...(914) 253-4000...A. C. DeCrane...petroleum and petroleum prods.

Texas Instruments Inc....13500 N. Central Expressway, Dallas, TX 75265...(214) 995-3773...Jerry Junkins...electrical & electronics prods.

Textron Inc....40 Westminster St., Providence, RI 02903...(401) 421-2800...J. F. Handymon...aerospace, consumer, industrial, metal prods., consumer finance, insurance, management services.

Tiffany & Co....727 5th Ave., NY, NY 10022...(212) 755-8000...W. R. Chaney...designs, manuf., and distributes jewelry & gift items.

Time Warner Inc....Time & Life Bldg., Rockefeller Center, NY, NY 10020...(212) 522-1212...G. M. Levin...magazine publisher (Time, Sports Illustrated, Fortune, Money, People), CATV (HBO, Cinemax), book publishing (Little, Brown, Warner Books), motion pictures (Warner Bros.).

Tootsie Roll Industries, Inc....7401 S. Cicero Ave., Chicago, IL 60629...(312) 838-3400...M. J. Gordon...candy (Tootsie Roll, Mason Dots, Charms).

Toro Co....8111 Lyndale Ave. S, Bloomington, MN 55420...(612) 888-8801...K. B. Melrose...lawn and turf maintenance (Lawn-Boy); snow removal equipment.

Toys "R" Us...461 From Rd., Paramus, NJ 07652...(201) 262-7800...Charles Lazarus...toy retailer, clothing stores (Kids "R" Us).

Transamerica Corp....600 Montgomery St., San Francisco, CA 94111...(415) 983-4000...Frank C. Herringer...insurance, financial services.

Travelers Corp....65 E. 55th St., NY, NY 10022...(212) 891-8900...James Dimon...insurance.

Tribune Co....435 N. Michigan Ave., Chicago, IL 60611...(312) 222-3883...C. T. Brumback...newpaper publishing, broadcasting, entertainment (Chicago Cubs baseball team).

Trinity Industries, Inc....2525 Stemmons Freeway, Dallas, TX 75356...(214) 631-4420...W. R. Wallace...manufactures variety of metal products.

TRW Inc....1900 Richmond Rd., Cleveland, OH 44124...(216) 291-7000...J. T. Gorman...car and truck operations, electronics, and space systems.

Turner Broadcasting System, Inc....1 CNN Center, Atlanta, GA 30303...(404) 827-1700...R. E. Turner...operates cable TV networks: CNN, TBS, TNT; owns MGM film library; owns Atlanta Braves, Hawks.

Tyson Foods, Inc....2210 W. Oaklawn, Springdale, AR 72764...(501) 756-4000...Don Tyson...fresh and processed poultry prods.

USAIR Group, Inc....1911 Jefferson Davis Hwy., Arlington, VA 22202...(703) 418-7000...Seth E. Schofield...air carrier of passengers, property, and mail.

UST Inc....100 W. Putnam Ave., Greenwich, CT 06830...(203) 661-1100...Vincent Gierer...smokeless tobacco (Copenhagen, Skoal, Happy Days), pipes, pipe tobacco.

USX-U.S. Steel Group...600 Grant St., Pittsburgh, PA 15230...(412) 433-1121...C. A. Corry...steel manuf.

Union Carbide Corp....39 Old Ridgebury Rd., Danbury, CT 06817...(203) 794-2000...R. D. Kennedy...chemicals, industrial gases.

Union Pacific Corp....Martin Tower, Bethlehem, PA 18018 ...(215) 861-3200...D. Lewis...railroad, natural resources.

Unisys Corp....PO Box 500, Blue Bell, PA 19424...(215) 986-6999...James Unruh...computer-based information systems.

U.S. Shoe Corp....One Eastwood Dr., Cincinnati, OH 45227...(513) 527-7000...B. B. Hudson...apparel, retailer (Casual Corner), shoes (Red Cross, Joyce), eye-care stores (LensCrafters).

United Technologies Corp....United Technologies Bldg., Hartford, CT 06101...(203) 728-7000...George David... aerospace, industrial prods. & services, Carrier Corp., Otis Elevator, Pratt & Whitney, Sikorsky Aircraft.

Univar Corp....6100 Carillon Pt., Kirkland, WA 98033...(206) 899-3400...J. W. Bernard...industrial and agricultural chemicals, laboratory and graphic arts products distributor, home furnishing supplies and fabrics distributors.

Universal Foods Corp....433 E. Michigan St., Milwaukee, WI 53202...(414) 271-6755...G. A. Osborn...yeast products, cheese products, dehydrated seasonings, food colors and flavors, imported gourmet foods.

Unocal Corp....1201 W. 5th St., Los Angeles, CA 90052...(213) 977-7600...R. J. Stegmeirer...oil, chemicals, geothermal energy.

Upjohn Co....700 Portage Rd., Kalamazoo, MI 49001...(616) 323-4000...John Zabriskie...pharmaceuticals (Motrin, Nuprin, Halcion), chemicals, agricultural and health care prods.

VF Corp....1047 N. Park Rd., Wyomissing, PA 19610...(215) 378-1151...L. R. Pugh...apparel, Vanity Fair, Lee, Wrangler jeans, Jantzen.

Viacom, Inc....200 Elm St., Dedham, MA 02026...(617) 461-1600...Frank Biondi...TV broadcast stations and cable systems, channels (Showtime, MTV); book publishing (Simon & Schuster); produces, dist. movies, TV shows.

Walgreen Co....200 Wilmot Rd., Deerfield, IL 60015...(708) 940-2500...Charles R. Walgreen 3d...retail drug chain.

Wal-Mart Stores Inc....Box 116, Bentonville, AR 72716...(501) 273-4000...D. D. Glass...retail dept. stores (Sam's Wholesale Clubs).

Warner-Lambert Co....201 Tabor Rd., Morris Plains, NJ 07950...(201) 540-2000...M. R. Goodes,....health care prods. (Benadryl), consumer prods. (Efferdent dental cleanser, Hall cough tablets, Schick razors, Rolaids antacid, Listerine mouthwash).

Washington Post Co....1150 15th St., NW, Washington, DC 20071...(202) 334-6000...D. E. Graham...newspapers, magazines (Newsweek), TV stations.

Weis Markets, Inc....1000 S. 2d St., Sunbury, PA 17801 ...(717) 286-4571...S. Weis...operates supermarkets, distributes frozen foods and grocery items.

Wells Fargo & Co....420 Montgomery St., San Francisco, CA 94163...(415) 396-3606...C. E. Reichardt...banking.

Wendy's Intl., Inc....4288 W. Dublin-Granville Rd., Dublin, OH 43017...(614) 764-3100...J. W. Near...quick-service restaurants.

Westinghouse Electric Corp....Westinghouse Bldg., Gateway Center, Pittsburgh, PA 15222...(412) 244-2000...Michael H. Jordan...manuf. electrical, mechanical equip.; radio and television stations.

Westvaco Corp....299 Park Ave., NY, NY 10171...(212) 688-5000...J. A. Luke, Jr....manufactures paper for graphic reproduction, communications, and packaging.

Weyerhaeuser Co....Tacoma, WA 98477...(206) 924-2345...John W. Creighton, Jr....manuf., distribution of forest prods.

Whirlpool Corp....Benton Harbor, MI 49022...(616) 923-5000...D. R. Whitwam...major home appliances.

Whitman Corp....111 Crossroads of Commerce, 3501 Algonquin Rd., Rolling Meadows, IL 60008...(708) 818-5000...Bruce S. Chelberg...diversified prods. and services, consumer prods., food, auto prods. (Midas).

Winn-Dixie Stores, Inc....5050 Edgewood Ct., Jacksonville, FL 32205...(904) 783-5000...A. D. Davis....supermarket chain.

Winnebago Industries, Inc....PO Box 152, Forest City, IA 50436...(515) 582-3535...J. K. Hanson....manuf. of motor homes, recreation vehicles.

Wolverine World Wide Corp....9341 Courtland Dr., Rockford, MI 49351...(616) 866-5500...Geoffrey Bloom...manuf. footwear (Hush Puppies).

Woolworth Corp....233 Broadway, NY, NY 10279...(212) 553-2000...W. K. Lavin...variety stores, shoe stores (Kinney), men's clothing (Richman Brothers), children's apparel (Kid's Mart), athletic footwear (Foot Locker).

Wm. Wrigley Jr. Co....410 N. Michigan Ave., Chicago, IL 60611...(312) 644-2121...William Wrigley...chewing gum.

Xerox Corp....PO Box 1600, Stamford, CT 06904...(203) 968-3000...Paul Allaire...equip. for reproduction, reduction, and transmission of business prods. & systems.

Zenith Electronics Corp....1000 Milwaukee Ave., Glenview, IL 60025...(708) 391-8181...Jerry K. Pearlman...TVs and video recorders.

Who Owns What: Familiar Consumer Products

Listed below are familiar consumer products and their parent companies. The parent company address can be found on pp. 713-18.

Admiral appliances: Maytag
Advil: American Home Products
Ajax cleanser: Colgate-Palmolive
Anacin: American Home Products
Arm & Hammer: Church & Dwight
Arrid antiperspirant: Carter-Wallace
Arnold breads: CPC International
Aunt Millie's pasta sauce: Borden
Ban antiperspirant: Bristol-Myers
Beech Aircraft: Raytheon
Beechnut baby food: Ralston Purina
Ben-Gay: Pfizer
Betty Crocker products: General Mills
Breck shampoo: Dial
Budweiser beer: Anheuser-Busch
Bufferin: Bristol-Myers Squibb
Business Week magazine: McGraw-Hill
Buster Brown shoes: Brown Group
Cap'n Crunch cereal: Quaker Oats
Carrier air conditioners: United Technologies
Celeste Pizza: Quaker Oats
Charmin toilet tissues: Procter & Gamble
Cheer detergent: Procter & Gamble
Cheerios cereal: General Mills
Chef Boy-ar-dee products: American Home Products
Clairol hair products: Bristol-Myers Squibb
Clorets breath freshener: Warner-Lambert
Combat insecticides: Clorox
Comet cleanser: Procter & Gamble
Copenhagen snuff: UST
Cracker Jack: Borden
Crest toothpaste: Procter & Gamble
Crisco shortening: Procter & Gamble
Degree antiperspirant: Helene Curtis
Doritos chips: PepsiCo
Drano: Bristol-Myers Squibb
Dristan: American Home Products
Duncan Hines cakes: Procter & Gamble
Efferdent dental cleanser: Warner-Lambert
ESPN: Capital Cities/ABC
Eveready batteries: Ralston Purina
Excedrin: Bristol-Myers
Fab detergent: Colgate-Palmolive
Family Circle magazine: New York Times
Foamy shaving cream: Gillette
Folger's coffee: Procter & Gamble
Formula 409 spray cleaner: Clorox
Franco-American foods: Campbell Soup
Frito-Lay snacks: PepsiCo
Gatorade: Quaker Oats
Gleem toothpaste: Procter & Gamble
Halcion: Upjohn
Hanes hosiery: Sara Lee
Hawaiian Punch: Procter & Gamble
Head and Shoulders shampoo: Procter & Gamble
Hellmann's mayonnaise: CPC International
Hi-C fruit drinks: Coca-Cola
Hillshire Farms meats: Sara Lee
Home Box Office: Time Warner
Hostess baked goods: Ralston Purina
Huggies: Kimberley-Clarke
Hush Puppies shoes: Wolverine World Wide
Ivory soap products: Procter & Gamble
Jack Daniel's bourbon: Brown-Forman
Jell-O: Philip Morris
Jim Beam whiskey: American Brands
Ken-L-Ration pet foods: Quaker Oats
Kent cigarettes: Loews
Kinney shoe stores: Woolworth
Kleenex: Kimberley-Clarke
Knorr soups: CPC International
Kool-Aid: Philip Morris
Ladies Home Journal magazine: Meredith
Lee jeans: VF Corp.
Lenox china: Brown-Forman
LensCrafters: U.S. Shoe
Lerner stores: The Limited
Listerine mouthwash: Warner-Lambert
Log Cabin syrup: Philip Morris
Lord & Taylor dept. stores: May Dept. Stores
Marlboro cigarettes: Philip Morris
Mazola oil: CPC International
Maxwell House coffee: Philip Morris
Michelob beer: Anheuser-Busch
Midas automotive centers: Whitman
Miller beer: Philip Morris
Milton Bradley games: Hasbro
Minute Rice: Philip Morris
Mrs. Paul's frozen fish: Campbell Soup
NBC Broadcasting: General Electric
Newsweek magazine: Washington Post
9 Lives cat food: H.J. Heinz
North American Van Lines: Norfolk Southern
NutraSweet: Monsanto
Old Spice: Procter & Gamble
Olive Garden restaurants: General Mills
Ore-Ida frozen foods: H.J. Heinz
Oreo cookies: RJR Nabisco
Pampers: Procter & Gamble
Paper Mate pens: Gillette
People magazine: Time Warner
Pepto-Bismol: Procter & Gamble
Pepperidge Farm products: Campbell Soup
Pizza Hut restaurants: PepsiCo
Playskool toys: Hasbro
Post-It stickers: Minn. Min. & Manuf.
Prego spaghetti sauce: Campbell Soup
Prell shampoo: Procter & Gamble
Prentice-Hall publishing: Viacom
Prestone auto products: First Brands
Prozac: Eli Lilly
Purex detergent: Dial
Radio Shack retail outlets: Tandy
Red Lobster Inns: General Mills
Reese's peanut butter cups: Hershey
Right Guard deodorant: Gillette
Ritz crackers: RJR Nabisco
Robitussin: American Home Products
Rolaids antacid: Warner-Lambert
Ruffles chips: PepsiCo
San Giorgio pasta: Hershey
Saran Wrap: Dow Chemical
Scholl's foot products: Schering-Plough
Scotch tape: Minn. Min. & Manuf.
Skippy peanut butter: CPC International
Simon & Schuster publishing: Viacom
Southern Comfort liquor: Brown-Forman
Sports Illustrated magazine: Time Warner
Sprite soda: Coca-Cola
Sugar Twin: Alberto-Culver
Swanson frozen dinners: Campbell Soup
Taco Bell restaurants: PepsiCo
Thomas' English muffins: CPC International
Tide detergent: Procter & Gamble
Tonka trucks: Hasbro
Trojan condoms: Carter-Wallace
Tupperware: Premark
Tylenol: Johnson & Johnson
Ultra Brite toothpaste: Colgate-Palmolive
V-8 vegetable juice: Campbell Soup
Vanity Fair apparel: VF Corp.
Velveeta cheese prods.: Philip Morris
Vicks cough medicines: Procter & Gamble
Victory flea collars: Carter-Wallace
Virginia Slims cigarettes: Philip Morris
Wall Street Journal: Dow Jones
Weight Watchers: H.J. Heinz
Wheaties cereal: General Mills
White Owl cigars: Culbro
Wise snacks: Borden

Interest Laws and Consumer Finance Loan Rates

Source: Revised by Christian T. Jones, Editor, Consumer Finance Law Bulletin, Chicago, IL

All states have laws regulating interest rates. These laws fix a legal or conventional rate, which applies when there is no contract for interest. They also fix a general maximum contract rate, but there are so many exceptions that the general contract maximum actually applies only to exceptional cases. Also, federal law has preempted state limits on first home mortgages, subject to each state's right to reinstate its own law, and has given depository institutions parity with other state lenders.

Legal rate of interest. The legal or conventional rate of interest applies to money obligations when no interest rate is contracted for and also to judgments. The rate is usually somewhat below the general interest rate.

General maximum contract rates. General interest laws in most states set the maximum rate between 8% and 16% per year. The general maximum is fixed by the state constitution at 5% over the Federal Reserve discount rate in Arkansas. Loans to corporations are frequently exempted or subject to a higher maximum. In recent years, it has also been common to provide special rates for home mortgage loans and variable usury rates that are indexed to market rates.

Specific enabling acts. In many states special statutes permit industrial loan companies, second mortgage lenders, and banks to charge 1.5% a month or more. Laws regulating revolving loans, charge accounts, and credit cards generally limit rates to between 1.5% and 2% per month plus annual fees for credit cards. Rates for installment sales contracts in most states are somewhat higher. Credit unions may generally charge 1% to 1.5% a month. Pawnbrokers' rates vary widely. Savings and loan associations and loans insured by federal agencies are also specially regulated. A number of states allow regulated lenders to charge any rate agreed to with the customer either for all credit or for credit over a certain dollar amount.

Consumer finance loan statutes. Most consumer finance loan statutes are based on early models drafted by the Russell Sage Foundation (1916-42) to provide small loans to wage earners under license and other protective regulations. Since 1969 the model has frequently been the Uniform Consumer Credit Code, which applies to credit sales and loans for consumer purposes. In general, licensed lenders may charge 3% a month and reduced rates for additional amounts. An add-on of 17% ($17 per $100) per year yields about 2.5% per month if paid in equal monthly installments. Discount rates produce higher yields than add-on rates of the same amount. In the table below, unless otherwise stated, monthly and annual rates are based on reducing principal balances, annual add-on rates are based on the original principal for the full term, and 2 or more rates apply to different portions of the balance or original principal.

States (and Puerto Rico) with consumer finance loan laws and the rates of charge as of Aug. 1, 1994

Maximum monthly rates computed on unpaid balances, unless otherwise stated.

AL..... Annual add-on: 15% to $750, 10% to $2,000 (min. 1.5% on unpaid balances). Higher rates for loans up to $749. Over $2,000, any agreed rate. Fee: 4% (max. $25); 5% real estate.

AK..... 3% to $850, 2% to $10,000. Over $10,000, any agreed rate.

AZ..... To $1,000: 3%. Over $1,000: 3% to $500, 2% to $10,000. Over $10,000, any agreed rate. Fee: 4% for real estate credit.

CA .... 2.5% to $225, 2% to $900, 1.5% to $1,650, 1% to $2,500 (1.6% min.). Over $2,500, any agreed rate. 5% fee (max. $50) to $2,500.

CO .... 36% per year to $630, 21% to $2,100, 15% to $25,000 (21% min.).

CT..... Annual add-on: 17% to $600, 11% to $5,000; 11% over $1,800 to $5,000 for certain secured loans. Any agreed rate for 2d mortgages.

DE .... Any agreed rate.

DC .... 24% per year.

FL..... 30% per year to $1,000, 24% to $2,000, 18% to $25,000.

GA .... 10% per year discount to 18 months, add-on to 36½ months; 8% fee to $600, 4% on excess plus $2 per month. Over $3,000, any agreed rate.

HI..... 3.5% to $100, 2.5% to $300; 2% on entire balance over $300 or discount rates.

ID..... Any agreed rate.

IL..... Any agreed rate.

IN..... 36% per year to $870, 21% to $2,900, 15% to $25,000 (21% min.).

IA..... 3% to $1,000, 2% to $2,800, 1.5% to $10,000; or equivalent flat rate. Over $10,000, 21% per year.

KS..... 36% per year to $780, 21% to $2,600, 14.45% to $25,000 (18% min.). Fee: 2% (max. $100); 3% real estate.

KY..... 3% to $1,000, 2% to $3,000. Over $3,000, 2%.

LA..... 36% per year to $1,400, 27% to $4,000, 24% to $7,000, 21% over $7,000, plus $25 fee.

ME .... 30% per year to $1,000, 21% to $2,800, 15% to $25,000 (18% min.).

MD .... 2.75% to $1,000, 2% to $2,000. Over $2,000, 2%.

MA .... 23% per year plus $20 annual fee to $6,000; any agreed rate over $6,000.

MI..... 22% per year to $8,000; 18% for 2d mortgages, plus 2% fee (max. $200).

MN .... 33% per year to $750, 19% over $750 (21.75% min.).

MS .... 36% per year to $1,000, 33% to $1,800, 24% to $5,000, 14% over $5,000. Over $25,000, 18%; 2% fee (max. $50).

MO .... 2.218% to $1,200, 1.67% over $1,200, plus 5% fee (max. $15); 1.67% plus 2% for 2d mortgages.

MT .... Any agreed rate.

NE .... 24% per year to $1,000. 21% over, plus fee of 7% to $2,000 and 5% over (max. $500). Any agreed rate for real estate loans of $7,500 or more.

NV .... Any agreed rate.

NH .... 2% to $600, 1.5% to $1,500; any agreed rate over $1,500 or for real estate mortgages.

NJ..... 30% per year to $5,000 or for 2d mortgages.

NM .... Any agreed rate.

NY..... 25% per year.

NC .... 2.5% to $1,000, 1.5% to $7,500; 1.5% on entire amount to $10,000. 1.5% or variable plus 2% fee for 2d mortgages.

ND .... 2.5% to $250, 2% to $500, 1.75% to $750, 1.5% to $1,000; any agreed rate over $1,000.

OH .... 28% per year to $1,000, 22% to $5,000; 25% on entire amount over $5,000; plus fee.

OK .... 30% per annum to $900, 21% to $3,000, 15% to $45,000 (21% min.). Special rates to $500.

OR .... Any agreed rate.

PA .... 9.5% per year discount to 48 months, 6% for remaining time plus 2% fee (max. $100); or 2% on unpaid balances; 1.85% for 2d mortgages over $5,000, plus 2% fee.

PR .... Variable: 25% max., 19% min.

RI..... 3% to $300, 2.5% for loans between $300 and $800; 2% for larger loans to $5,000. 1.75% over $5,000.

SC .... Any agreed and posted rate.

SD .... Any agreed rate.

TN .... Over $100, 24% per year or discount rates plus fees.

TX..... Annual add-on: 18% to $1,260, 8% to $10,500 or formula rate (18% to 24% per year on unpaid balances)

UT .... Any agreed rate.

VT..... 2% to $1,000, 1% to $3,000 (min. 1.5%); 1.5% for 2d mortgages.

VA .... 2.75% to $800, 2% to $2,000, 1.5% to $3,500; or annual add-on of 17% to $800, 15% to $2,000, 12% to $3,500; 2% fee. Any agreed rate over $3,500 for 2d mortgages, plus 2% fee.

WA .... 25% per year plus fees.

WV .... 36% per year to $500, 24% to $1,500, 18% to $2,000. Over $2,000, 27% per year to $2,000, 25% to $10,000, 18% on remainder, plus 2% fee.

WI..... Any agreed rate.

WY .... 36% per year to $1,000, 21% to $25,000. No limit over $25,000.

How to Check Your Credit File

Any individual can investigate the contents of his or her credit file by directly contacting one or more of the approximately 2,000 credit bureaus, or consumer credit clearinghouses, in the United States. The nearest ones can be found by calling a local Better Business Bureau or by looking in the telephone Yellow Pages under "Credit Rating or Reporting Agencies."

Although the Fair Credit Reporting Act requires that a bureau give a person no more than an oral or written credit history review, many bureaus will go beyond the technical requirements of the law and furnish the same computer-generated compilation of facts that they give the banks, retailers, and other companies that subscribe to their service. An individual who has been denied credit on the basis of negative information from a credit bureau can obtain this review without charge within 30 days of the denial. Sometimes a small fee is charged for such a credit check.

After inspecting this record of past credit behavior, a consumer can question any item believed to be inaccurate, misleading, or vague. The credit bureau must then investigate and remove any item that cannot be substantiated.

When a bureau affirms, rather than removes, a questionable item, an individual can present a 100-word explanation that must be placed in his or her file. And whenever an adverse item is deleted from the file or an explanatory statement is added to one, a consumer may request that the credit bureau inform every credit grantor who received a report within the last 6 months.

Credit Card Rates

Source: Christian T. Jones, Editor, Consumer Finance Law Bulletin, Chicago, IL
(As of Aug. 1, 1994)

Nearly all states have special laws dealing with rates charged for credit cards issued by state banks and other financial institutions. Although some state laws apply only to banks, under federal parity law, the same charges can be made by other financial institutions. A bank can charge the highest rates allowed for revolving credit extended by any other creditor in the state where the bank is located for similar types of credit, and such rates may also be charged to residents of any other state. Maximum rates and fees are shown below; rates are yearly unless otherwise stated.

AL. . . No limit.
AK . . 17% plus fee.
AZ. . . No limit.
AK . . 5% over FRB discount rate (max. 17%).
CA . . No limit.
CO . . 21%.
CT. . . 19.8%; $35 annual fee.
DC . . 24%.
DE . . No limit.
FL. . . No limit.
GA . . No limit on rate or fee.
HI . . . 24%.
ID . . . No limit.
IL . . . No limit; plus fee.
IN . . . 36-21-15%, @ $870, $2,900; or 21%.
IA . . . No limit.
KS . . 18-14.45% @ $1,000.
KY . . 21%; $20 annual fee.
LA. . . 18%; 4% cash advance and $12 annual fee.
ME. . No limit; plus annual fee.
MD . 24%; 2% fee.
MA. . 18% or formula rate.
MI . . 18%; no limit on annual fee.
MN . 18%; $50 annual fee.
MS. . 21%; or 18% plus $12 annual fee.
MO . 22-10% @ $1,000.
MT. . No limit.
NE. . No limit; plus fees.
NV. . No limit.
NH. . No limit.
NJ . . 30%; $15 annual fee or $50 over $5,000.
NM . No limit.
NY. . 25% plus annual fee.
NC. . 18%; $24 annual fee.
ND. . No limit.
OH. . 25% to 1/1/96.
OK. . 30-21-15% @ $870, $2,900; or 21%.
OR. . No limit.
PA . . 12% loans; 18% purchases to 7/1/98; $15 annual fee.
PR . . 2.17% per mo.
RI . . 18%.
SC . . No limit.
SD . . No limit.
TN . . 24%.
TX . . Set by rule (max. 22%, min. 14%).
UT . . No limit.
VT . . 18%; no limit on annual fee.
VA . . No limit.
WA. . 25% loan; no limit for purchases; fees.
WV. . 18%.
WI . . No limit.
WY. . 36-21% @ $1,000; no limit over $25,000.

The Cost of Raising a Child

Source: Family Economics Research Group, U.S. Dept. of Agriculture

Estimated annual expenditures in 1993 dollars for a child born in 1993, by income group. Estimates are for the younger child in a 2-parent family with 2 children for the overall U.S.

Year	Age of child	Low	Middle	High
		Income group[1]		
1993	under 1 . . .	$4,960	$6,870	$10,210
1994	1.	5,260	7,280	10,820
1995	2.	5,570	7,720	11,470
1996	3.	6,260	8,600	12,660
1997	4.	6,640	9,120	13,420
1998	5.	7,040	9,660	14,230
1999	6.	7,830	10,580	15,250
2000	7.	8,300	11,220	16,160
2001	8.	8,800	11,890	17,130
2002	9.	$8,570	$11,790	$17,230
2003	10	9,080	12,500	18,270
2004	11	9,620	13,250	19,360
2005	12	11,070	14,870	21,490
2006	13	11,730	15,760	22,780
2007	14	12,430	16,710	24,150
2008	15	15,000	19,890	28,260
2009	16	15,900	21,080	29,950
2010	17	16,860	22,350	31,750
Total		**$170,920**	**$231,140**	**$334,590**

(1) Low income is less than $32,000 in 1993; middle income is $32,000 to $54,100; high income is $54,100 or more. The projected annual inflation rate is 6%.

Customs Exemptions and Advice to Travelers

Source: U.S. Dept. of the Treasury, U.S. Customs Service

U.S. residents returning after a stay abroad of at least 48 hr are usually granted customs exemptions of $400 each. The duty-free articles must accompany the traveler at the time of his or her return, be for personal or household use, have been acquired as an incident of the trip, and be properly declared to Customs. Not more than one liter of alcoholic beverages nor more than 100 cigars and 200 cigarettes (one carton) may be included in the $400 exemption. The exemption for alcoholic beverages is accorded only when the returning resident has attained 21 years of age at the time of arrival. Cuban cigars may be included only if purchased in Cuba.

If a U.S. resident arrives directly or indirectly from a U.S. insular possession — American Samoa, Guam, or the U.S. Virgin Islands — a customs exemption of $1,200 is allowed. One thousand cigarettes may be included, but only 200 of them may have been purchased elsewhere. If a U.S. resident returns from any one of the following beneficiary countries, the customs exemption is $600, based on fair market value: Antigua and Barbuda, Aruba, Bahamas, Barbados, Belize, British Virgin Islands, Costa Rica, Dominica, Dominican Republic, El Salvador, Grenada, Guatemala, Guyana, Haiti, Honduras, Jamaica, Montserrat, Netherlands Antilles, Nicaragua, Panama, St. Kitts and Nevis, St. Lucia, St. Vincent and the Grenadines, Trinidad and Tobago.

The $400, $600, or $1,200 exemption may be granted only if the exemption or any part of it has not been used within the preceding 30-day period and the stay abroad was for at least 48 hr. The 48-hr absence requirement does not apply to travelers returning from Mexico or the U.S. Virgin Islands. If you cannot claim the $400, $600, or $1,200 exemption because of the 30-day or 48-hr minimum limitations, you may bring in free of duty and tax articles acquired abroad for your personal or household use if the total fair retail value does not exceed $25.

Bona fide gifts of not more than $50 in fair retail value where shipped can be received by friends and relations in the U.S. free of duty and tax if the same person does not receive more than $50 in gift shipments in one day. (Shipping of alcoholic beverages by mail is prohibited by U.S. postal laws. Alcoholic beverages include wine and beer as well as distilled spirits.) These gifts are not declared by you upon your return to the U.S.

The U.S. Customs Service booklet *Know Before You Go* answers frequently asked customs questions and is available free by writing U.S. Customs, KBYG, PO Box 7407, Washington, DC 20044.

U.S. Passport, Visa, and Health Requirements

Source: Bureau of Consular Affairs, U.S. Dept. of State, as of Aug. 1994.

Passports are issued by the U.S. Department of State to citizens and nationals of the U.S. for the purpose of documenting them for foreign travel and identifying them as Americans.

How to Obtain a Passport

Applicants who have never been issued a passport in their own name must execute an application in person before (1) a passport agent; (2) a clerk of any federal court or state court of record or a judge or clerk of any probate court accepting applications; (3) a postal employee designated by the postmaster at a post office that has been selected to accept passport applications; or (4) a U.S. diplomatic or consular officer abroad. A DSP-11 is the correct form to use for applicants who must apply in person. All persons are required to obtain individual passports in their own name. An applicant who is 13 years of age or older is required to appear in person before the clerk or agent executing the application. A parent or legal guardian must execute the application for children under 13.

A full validity passport previously issued to the applicant or one in which he or she was included will be accepted as proof of U.S. citizenship. If the applicant has no prior passport and was born in the U.S., a certified copy of his/her birth certificate shall be presented to the agent accepting the passport application. To be acceptable, the certificate must show the given name and surname, the date and place of birth, and that the birth record was filed shortly after birth. A delayed birth certificate (a record filed more than 1 year after the date of birth) is acceptable provided that it shows that acceptable secondary evidence was used for creating this record. Contact the nearest Dept. of State passport agency for more information concerning acceptable secondary evidence.

If a birth certificate is not obtainable, a notice from a state registrar shall be submitted stating that no birth record exists. The notice shall be accompanied by the best obtainable secondary evidence, such as a baptismal certificate or a hospital birth record.

A naturalized citizen with no previous passport must present a Certificate of Naturalization. A person born abroad claiming U.S. citizenship through either a native-born or naturalized citizen parent must submit a Certificate of Citizenship issued by the Immigration and Naturalization Service; or a Consular Report of Birth or Certification of Birth Abroad issued by the Dept. of State. If one of the above documents has not been obtained, evidence of citizenship of the parent(s) through whom citizenship is claimed and evidence that would establish the parent/child relationship must be submitted. Additionally, if citizenship is derived through birth to citizen parent(s), the following documents will be required: parents' marriage certificate plus an affidavit from parent(s) showing periods and places of residence or physical presence in the U.S. and abroad, specifying periods spent abroad in the employment of the U.S. government, including the armed forces, or with certain international organizations. If citizenship is derived through naturalization of parents, evidence of admission to the U.S. for permanent residence also will be required.

Persons who possess the most recent passport issued within the last 12 years and after their 18th birthday may be eligible to apply for a new passport by mail. A form DSP-82, Application for Passport by Mail, must be filled out and mailed to the address shown on the form, together with the previous passport, 2 recent identical photographs, and a fee of $55.00. The DSP-82 may not be used if the most recent passport has been altered or mutilated.

Photographs, Fees, and Identity

Photographs—Submit 2 identical photographs that are sufficiently recent (normally not more than 6 months old) and that are a good likeness of and satisfactorily identify the applicant. Photographs should be 2 × 2 in. in size. The image size measured from the bottom of the chin to the top of the head (including hair) should not be less than one in. nor more than 1-3/8 in. Photographs should be portrait-type prints. They must be clear, front view, full face, with a plain white or off-white background. Photographs that depict the applicant as relaxed and smiling are encouraged.

Fees—The fee is $30.00 for passports issued to persons under 18 years of age. These passports are valid for 5 years from the date of issue. The fee is $55.00 for passports issued to persons 18 and older. These passports are valid for 10 years from the date of issuance. An additional fee of $10.00 is charged for the execution of the application. There is no execution fee when using DSP-82, Application for Passport by Mail. Applicants eligible to use this form pay only the $55.00 passport fee.

Identity—Applicants must also establish their identity to the satisfaction of the person accepting the application and to Passport Services. Generally acceptable documents of identity include a previous U.S. passport, a Certificate of Naturalization, a Certificate of Citizenship, a valid driver's license, or a government identification card. Applicants may not use a Social Security card, learner's or temporary driver's license, credit card, or expired identity card. Extremely old documents cannot be used by themselves. Applicants unable to establish identity must present some documentation in their own name (e.g., Social Security card) and must be accompanied by a person who has known the applicant for at least 2 years and who is a U.S. citizen or legal U.S. permanent resident alien. That person must sign an affidavit before the individual who executes the passport application. The witness will be required to establish his or her own identity.

The loss or theft of a valid passport is a serious matter and should be reported immediately in writing to Passport Services, 1111 19th St., NW, Dept. of State, Washington, DC 20524-1705, telephone: (202) 647-0518, or to the nearest passport agency or the nearest U.S. embassy or consulate when abroad. For more information, the booklet *Passports—Applying for the Easy Way* is available for 50¢ from the Consumer Information Center, Pueblo, CO 81009.

Foreign Regulations

A visa, usually rubber stamped in a passport by a representative of the country to be visited, indicates that the bearer of the passport is permitted to enter that country for a certain purpose and length of time. In most instances, you must obtain necessary visas before you leave the U.S. Apply directly to the embassy or nearest consulate of each country you plan to visit, or consult a travel agent. The State Dept.'s *Foreign Entry Requirements* contains entry requirements and application instructions for most foreign countries and is also available for 50¢ from the Consumer Information Center. The process may take several weeks, so it is important to apply well in advance and verify requirements with the embassy or nearest consulate of each country before applying.

How to Obtain Birth, Marriage, Death Records

The pamphlet *Where to Write for Vital Records: Births, Deaths, Marriages, and Divorces* (Pub. #93-1142, Stock # 017-022-01196-4) is available from the Superintendent of Documents, Government Printing Office, Washington, DC 20402; advance payment of $2.25 is required. *Genealogical Research in the National Archives* is sold by the National Archives Trust Fund Board, PO Box 100793, Atlanta, GA 30384.

Copyright Law of the United States

Source: Copyright Office, Library of Congress

What Copyright Is

Copyright is a form of protection provided by the laws of the U.S. (title 17, U.S. Code) to the authors of "original works of authorship," including literary, dramatic, musical, artistic, and certain other intellectual works. This protection is available to both published and unpublished works. Section 106 of the Copyright Act generally gives the owner of copyright the exclusive right to do and to authorize others to do the following:

• *To reproduce* the copyrighted work in copies or phonorecords;

• *To prepare derivative works* based upon the copyrighted work;

• *To distribute copies or phonorecords* of the copyrighted work to the public by sale or other transfer of ownership, or by rental, lease, or lending;

• *To perform the copyrighted work publicly,* in the case of literary, musical, dramatic, and choreographic works, pantomimes, and motion pictures and other audiovisual works; and

• *To display the copyrighted work publicly,* in the case of literary, musical, dramatic, and choreographic works, pantomimes, and pictorial, graphic, or sculptural works, including the individual images of a motion picture or other audiovisual work.

It is illegal for anyone to violate any of the rights provided by the act to the owner of copyright. These rights, however, are not unlimited in scope. Sections 107 through 119 of the Copyright Act establish limitations on these rights. In some cases, these limitations are specified exemptions from copyright liability. One major limitation is the doctrine of "fair use," which is given a statutory basis by section 107 of the act. In other instances, the limitation takes the form of a "compulsory license" under which certain limited uses of copyrighted works are permitted upon payment of specified royalties and compliance with statutory conditions.

Copyright protection subsists from the time the work is created in fixed form; that is, it is an incident of the process of authorship. The copyright in the work of authorship *immediately* becomes the property of the author who created it. Only the author or those deriving their rights from the author can rightfully claim copyright.

In the case of works made for hire, the employer and not the employee is presumptively considered the author. Section 101 of the copyright statute defines a "work made for hire" as:

(1) a work prepared by an employee within the scope of his or her employment; or

(2) a work specially ordered or commissioned for use as a contribution to a collective work, as a part of a motion picture or other audiovisual work, as a translation, as a supplementary work, as a compilation, as an instructional text, as a test, as answer material for a test, or as an atlas, if the parties expressly agree in a written instrument signed by them that the work shall be considered a work made for hire.

The authors of a joint work are co-owners of the copyright in the work, unless there is an agreement to the contrary.

Copyright in each separate contribution to a periodical or other collective work is distinct from copyright in the collective work as a whole and vests initially with the author of the contribution.

Works published on or after Jan. 1, 1978, are subject to protection under the copyright statute if, on the date of first publication, one or more of the authors is a national or domiciliary of the U.S., or is a national, domiciliary, or sovereign authority of a foreign nation that is a party to a copyright treaty to which the U.S. is also a party, or is a stateless person, regardless of domicile, or if the work is first published either in the U.S. or in a foreign nation that on the date of first publication is a party to the Universal Copyright Convention or the Berne Union.

Which Works Are Protected

Copyright protects "original works of authorship" that are fixed in a tangible form of expression. The fixation need not be directly perceptible, as long as it may be communicated with the aid of a machine or device. Copyrightable works include the following categories:

(1) literary works;
(2) musical works, including any accompanying words;
(3) dramatic works, including any accompanying music;
(4) pantomimes and choreographic works;
(5) pictorial, graphic, and sculptural works;
(6) motion pictures and other audiovisual works;
(7) sound recordings; and
(8) architectural works.

These categories should be viewed quite broadly: for example, computer programs and most "compilations" are registrable as "literary works"; maps and architectural plans are registrable as "pictorial, graphic, and sculptural works."

Which Works Are Not Protected

Several categories of material are generally not eligible for statutory copyright protection. These include among others:

• Works that have *not* been fixed in a tangible form of expression. For example: choreographic works that have not been notated or recorded, or improvisational speeches or performances that have not been written or recorded.

• Titles, names, short phrases, and slogans; familiar symbols or designs; mere variations of typographic ornamentation, lettering, or coloring; mere listings of ingredients or contents.

• Ideas, procedures, methods, systems, processes, concepts, principles, discoveries, or devices, as distinguished from a description, explanation, or illustration.

• Works consisting *entirely* of information that is common property and containing no original authorship. For example: standard calendars, height and weight charts, tape measures and rulers, and lists or tables taken from public documents or other common sources.

Notice of Copyright

For works first published on and after Mar. 1, 1989, use of the copyright notice is optional, though highly recommended. Before Mar. 1, 1989, the use of the notice was mandatory on all published works, and any work first published before that date *must* bear a notice or risk loss of copyright protection.

Use of the notice is recommended because it informs the public that the work is protected by copyright, identifies the copyright owner, and shows the year of first publication. Furthermore, in the event that a work is infringed, if the work carries a proper notice, the court will not allow a defendant to claim "innocent infringement"—that is, that he or she did not realize that the work is protected. (A successful innocent infringement claim may result in a reduction in damages that the copyright owner would otherwise receive.)

The use of the copyright notice is the responsibility of the copyright owner and does not require advance permission from, or registration with, the Copyright Office.

For visually perceptible copies, the form of the notice consists of the following: © (the letter C in a circle), the word "Copyright," or "Copr.," and the year of first publication, and the name of the owner of copyright in the work. Example: © 1995 Judy Smith. The notice must be affixed in such manner and location as to give reasonable notice of the claim of copyright.

The notice of copyright prescribed for all published phonorecords of sound recordings consists of the letter ℗ in a circle, the year of first publication of the sound recording, and the name of the owner of copyright in the sound recording.

Example ℗ 1995 XYZ Records, Inc. The notice on phonorecords may appear on the surface of the phonorecord or on the phonorecord label or container, provided the manner of placement and location give reasonable notice of the claim.

How Long Copyright Protection Endures

Works Originally Created on or After Jan. 1, 1978

A work that is created (fixed in tangible form for the first time) on or after Jan. 1, 1978, is automatically protected from the moment of its creation and is ordinarily given a term enduring for the author's life, plus an additional 50 years after the author's death. In the case of "a joint work prepared by 2 or more authors who did not work for hire," the term lasts for 50 years after the last surviving author's death. For works made for hire and for anonymous and pseudonymous works (unless the author's identity is revealed in Copyright Office records) the duration of copyright is 75 years from publication or 100 years from creation, whichever is shorter.

Works that were created but not published or registered for copyright before Jan. 1, 1978, have been automatically brought under the statute and are now given federal copyright protection. The duration of copyright in these works will generally be computed in the same way as for works created on or after Jan. 1, 1978: the life-plus-50 or 75/100-year terms will apply to them as well. The law provides that in no case will the term of copyright for works in this category expire before Dec. 31, 2002, and for works published on or before Dec. 31, 2002, the term of copyright will not expire before Dec. 31, 2027.

Works Created and Published or Registered Before Jan. 1, 1978

Under the law in effect before 1978, copyright was secured either on the date a work was published or on the date of registration if the work was registered in unpublished form. In either case, the copyright endured for a first term of 28 years from the date it was secured. During the last (28th) year of the first term, the copyright was eligible for renewal. The current copyright law has extended the renewal term from 28 to 47 years for copyrights that were subsisting on Jan. 1, 1978, making these works eligible for a total term of protection of 75 years. On June 26, 1992, President George Bush signed Public Law 102-307, which amends the Copyright Law to extend automatically the term of copyrights secured between Jan. 1, 1964, and Dec. 31, 1977, to a further term of 47 years and increases the filing fee from $12.00 to $20.00. This fee increase applies to all renewal applications filed on or after June 29, 1992.

PL 102-307 makes renewal registration optional. An author need not file the renewal in order to extend the original 28-year copyright term to the full 75 years. It may be beneficial, however, to re-registration during the 28th year of the original term. (For more information on copyright renewal, request Circular 15 from the Copyright Office.)

International Copyright Protection

There is no such thing as an "international copyright" that will automatically protect an author's writings throughout the entire world. Protection against unauthorized use in a particular country depends, basically, on the national laws of that country. However, most countries do offer protection to foreign works under certain conditions, and these conditions have been greatly simplified by international copyright treaties and conventions. The U.S. belongs to both global, multilateral copyright treaties—the Universal Copyright Convention (UCC) and the Berne Convention for the Protection of Literary and Artistic Works.

A work by a national or a resident of a country that is a member of the UCC or a work first published in a UCC country may claim protection under the UCC. If the work bears the notice of copyright in the form and position specified by the UCC, this notice will satisfy and substitute for any other formalities a UCC member country would otherwise impose as a condition of copyright. A UCC notice should consist of the symbol © accompanied by the name of the copyright proprietor and the year of first publication. U.S. authors have protection in all member nations of the Berne Union with which the U.S. formerly had either no copyright relations or had bilateral treaty arrangements. Members of the Berne Union agree to a certain minimum level of copyright protection and agree to treat nationals of other member countries like their own nationals for purposes of copyright. A work first published in the U.S. or another Berne Union country (or first published in a non-Berne country, followed by publication within 30 days in a Berne country) is eligible for protection in all Berne member countries.

For a list of countries that maintain copyright relations with the U.S., write or call the Copyright Office and ask for Circular 38a.

Copyright Registration

Copyright registration is a legal formality intended to make a public record of the basic facts of a particular copyright. Except in specific situations, registration is not a condition for protection, but the copyright law provides several inducements or advantages to encourage copyright owners to register. Among these are the following:

- Registration establishes a public record of the copyright claim.
- Before an infringement suit may be filed in court, registration is necessary for works of U.S. origin and for foreign works not originating in a Berne Union country. (For more information on when a work is of U.S. origin, request Circular 93 from the Copyright Office).
- If made before or within 5 years of publication, registration will establish prima facie evidence in court of the validity of the copyright and of the facts stated in the certificate.
- If registration is made within 3 months after publication of the work or prior to an infringement of the work, statutory damages and attorney's fees will be available to the copyright owner in court actions. Otherwise, only an award of actual damages and profits is available to the copyright owner.

Copyright registration allows the owner of the copyright to record the registration with the U.S. Customs Service for protection against the importation of infringing copies. For additional information, request Publication No. 563 from:

Commissioner of Customs
ATTN: IPR Branch,
Room 2104
U.S. Customs Service
1301 Constitution Avenue, NW
Washington, DC 20229

Registration may be made at any time within the life of the copyright. When a work has been registered in unpublished form, making another registration when the work becomes published is unnecessary (although the copyright owner may register the published edition, if desired).

The process of registration is simple. Request an appropriate form from the Copyright Office and complete it. Returned it to the Copyright Office along with a $20 nonrefundable filing fee and the appropriate deposit(s) of the work for which registration is sought. In a common example—a published book—the deposit is 2 copies of the best edition of the book. The Copyright Office sends a certificate of registration when the paperwork is completed, a process that usually takes 12 to 16 weeks because of the large volume of registrations the Office must handle.

Although a copyright registration is not required, the Copyright Act establishes a mandatory deposit requirement for works published in the U.S. In general, the owner of copyright or the owner of the exclusive right of publication in the work has a legal obligation to deposit in the Copyright Office, within 3 months of publication in the U.S., 2 copies (or, in the case of sound recordings, 2 phonorecords) for the use of the Library of Congress. Failure to deposit these copies can result in fines and other penalties but does not affect copyright protection. Certain categories of works are exempt entirely from the mandatory deposit requirements, and the obligation is reduced for certain other categories.

Information on registration and application forms may be obtained free of charge by writing the Copyright Office, Information Section, LM-401, Library of Congress, Washington, DC 20559. Registration application forms and circulars may be ordered on a 24-hr basis by calling (202) 707-9100. Request Circular 1 for additional general information on copyright, including a list of which application forms to use when registering specific types of works.

Birthstones

Source: Jewelry Industry Council

Month	Ancient	Modern
January	Garnet	Garnet
February	Amethyst	Amethyst
March	Jasper	Bloodstone or Aquamarine
April	Sapphire	Diamond
May	Agate	Emerald
June	Emerald	Pearl, Moonstone, or Alexandrite
July	Onyx	Ruby
August	Carnelian	Sardonyx or Peridot
September	Chrysolite	Sapphire
October	Aquamarine	Opal or Tourmaline
November	Topaz	Topaz
December	Ruby	Turquoise or Zircon

Wedding Anniversaries

The traditional names for wedding anniversaries go back many years in social usage. As such names as wooden, crystal, silver, and golden were applied to anniversary years, it was considered proper to present the married couple with gifts made of these products or of something related. The list of traditional gifts, with a few allowable revisions in parentheses, is presented below, followed by modern gifts in **boldface.**

1st	Paper, **clocks**
2d	Cotton, **china**
3d	Leather, **crystal, glass**
4th	Linen (silk), **appliances**
5th	Wood, **silverware**
6th	Iron, **wood**
7th	Wool (copper), **desk sets**
8th	Bronze, **linens, lace**
9th	Pottery (china), **leather**
10th	Tin, aluminum, **diamond**
11th	Steel, **fashion jewelry**
12th	Silk, **pearl, colored gems**
13th	Lace, **textiles, furs**
14th	Ivory, **gold jewelry**
15th	Crystal, **watches**
20th	China, **platinum**
25th	Silver, **sterling silver**
30th	Pearl, **diamond**
35th	Coral (jade), **jade**
40th	Ruby, **ruby**
45th	Sapphire, **sapphire**
50th	Gold, **gold**
55th	Emerald, **emerald**
60th	Diamond, **diamond**

Mortgage Payment Tables

Source: *The Mortgage Money Guide,* Federal Trade Commission

8% Annual Percentage Rate

Monthly payments (principal and interest)

Amount financed	10 Years	15 Years	20 Years	25 Years	30 Years
$ 25,000	303.32	238.91	209.11	192.95	183.44
35,000	424.65	334.48	292.75	270.14	256.82
45,000	545.97	430.04	376.40	347.32	330.19
50,000	606.64	477.83	418.22	385.91	366.88
60,000	727.97	573.39	501.86	463.09	440.26
70,000	849.29	668.96	585.51	540.27	513.64
80,000	970.62	764.52	669.15	617.45	587.01
90,000	1091.95	860.09	752.80	694.63	660.39
100,000	1213.28	955.65	836.44	771.82	733.76
120,000	1455.94	1146.78	1003.72	926.18	880.52
140,000	1698.58	1337.92	1171.02	1080.54	1027.28
160,000	1941.24	1529.04	1338.30	1234.90	1174.02
180,000	2183.90	1720.18	1505.60	1389.26	1320.78
200,000	2426.56	1911.30	1672.88	1543.64	1467.52

10% Annual Percentage Rate

Monthly payments (principal and interest)

Amount financed	10 Years	15 Years	20 Years	25 Years	30 Years
$25,000	330.38	268.65	241.26	227.18	219.39
35,000	462.53	376.11	337.76	318.05	307.15
45,000	594.68	483.57	434.26	408.92	394.91
50,000	660.75	537.30	482.51	454.35	438.79
60,000	792.90	644.76	579.01	545.22	526.54
70,000	925.06	752.22	675.52	636.09	614.30
80,000	1057.20	859.68	772.02	726.96	702.06
90,000	1189.36	967.14	868.52	817.83	789.81
100,000	1321.51	1074.61	965.02	908.70	877.57
120,000	1585.80	1289.52	1158.02	1090.44	1053.08
140,000	1850.12	1504.44	1351.04	1272.18	1228.60
160,000	2114.40	1719.36	1544.04	1453.92	1404.12
180,000	2378.72	1934.28	1737.04	1635.66	1579.62
200,000	2643.02	2149.22	1930.04	1817.40	1755.14

9% Annual Percentage Rate

Monthly payments (principal and interest)

Amount financed	10 Years	15 Years	20 Years	25 Years	30 Years
$25,000	316.69	253.57	224.93	209.80	201.16
35,000	443.36	354.99	314.90	293.72	281.62
45,000	570.04	456.42	404.88	377.64	362.08
50,000	633.38	507.13	449.86	419.60	402.31
60,000	760.05	608.56	539.84	503.52	482.77
70,000	886.73	709.99	629.81	587.44	563.24
80,000	1013.41	811.41	719.78	671.36	643.70
90,000	1140.08	912.84	809.75	755.28	724.16
100,000	1266.76	1014.27	899.73	839.20	804.62
120,000	1520.10	1217.12	1079.68	1007.04	965.54
140,000	1773.46	1419.98	1259.62	1174.88	1126.48
160,000	2026.82	1622.82	1439.56	1342.72	1287.40
180,000	2280.16	1825.68	1619.50	1510.56	1448.32
200,000	2533.52	2028.54	1799.46	1678.40	1609.24

11% Annual Percentage Rate

Monthly payments (principal and interest)

Amount financed	10 Years	15 Years	20 Years	25 Years	30 Years
$25,000	344.38	284.15	258.05	245.03	238.08
35,000	482.13	397.81	361.27	343.04	333.31
45,000	619.88	511.47	464.48	441.05	428.55
50,000	688.75	568.30	516.09	490.06	476.16
60,000	826.50	681.96	619.31	588.07	571.39
70,000	964.25	795.62	722.53	686.08	666.63
80,000	1102.00	909.28	825.75	784.09	761.86
90,000	1239.75	1022.94	928.97	882.10	857.09
100,000	1377.50	1136.60	1032.19	980.11	952.32
120,000	1653.00	1363.92	1238.62	1176.14	1142.78
140,000	1928.50	1591.24	1445.06	1372.16	1333.26
160,000	2204.00	1818.56	1651.50	1568.18	1523.72
180,000	2479.50	2045.88	1857.94	1764.20	1714.18
200,000	2755.00	2273.20	2064.38	1960.22	1904.64

Median Price of Existing Single-Family Homes

Source: National Association of Realtors; data as of midyear 1994

City[1]	Apr. 1992	Apr. 1993	Apr. 1994
Akron, OH	$75,500	$77,400	$81,600
Albuquerque, NM	86,700	94,400	103,100
Anaheim/Santa Ana, CA[2]	235,100	222,200	209,500
Atlanta, GA	85,800	NA	93,200
Baltimore, MD	111,500	113,200	115,700
Baton Rouge, LA	71,800	72,800	78,400
Birmingham, AL	89,500	89,000	99,500
Boston, MA	168,200	165,200	170,600
Bradenton, FL	80,400	84,300	86,400
Buffalo, NY	79,700	84,200	82,400
Charleston, SC	82,000	86,200	91,300
Chicago, IL	131,100	131,200	135,500
Cincinnati, OH	87,500	85,600	93,600
Cleveland, OH	88,100	89,200	94,200
Columbia, SC	85,100	82,300	82,900
Columbus, OH	90,300	89,300	92,800
Corpus Christi, TX	62,500	66,600	71,700
Dallas, TX	90,500	89,600	95,100
Daytona Beach, FL	63,600	67,600	66,200
Denver, CO	91,300	96,300	111,200
Des Moines, IA	71,200	71,600	77,400
Detroit, MI	77,500	92,200	84,500
El Paso, TX	65,900	67,900	73,600
Grand Rapids, MI	73,000	73,900	76,600
Hartford, CT	141,500	135,500	132,900
Honolulu, HI	342,000	347,000	355,000
Houston, TX	78,200	78,000	84,800
Indianapolis, IN	80,100	83,800	90,500
Jacksonville, FL	75,100	74,100	79,700
Kansas City, MO	76,100	79,100	84,900
Knoxville, TN	78,300	82,400	88,600
Las Vegas, NV	101,400	105,200	110,400
Los Angeles, CA[2]	218,000	199,700	188,500
Louisville, KY	$69,700	$69,900	77,400
Madison, WI	89,400	97,700	111,500
Memphis, TN	83,600	84,200	85,600
Miami, FL	97,300	98,000	105,000
Milwaukee, WI	96,100	98,400	106,500
Minneapolis, MN	94,800	96,400	100,000
Mobile, AL	63,300	66,200	69,500
Nashville, TN	89,000	87,000	95,200
New Haven, CT	142,400	142,600	137,600
New Orleans, LA	68,400	73,000	75,400
New York, NY	169,300	168,000	170,300
Oklahoma City, OK	59,800	61,100	67,600
Omaha, NE	67,400	64,300	72,800
Orlando, FL	86,200	86,900	89,900
Philadelphia, PA	119,800	108,900	116,800
Phoenix, AZ	84,700	86,300	89,200
Pittsburgh, PA	74,800	75,900	80,000
Portland, OR	92,300	99,600	111,200
Providence, RI	120,300	112,500	115,600
Sacramento, CA[2]	135,600	130,400	127,300
St. Louis, MO	81,600	80,900	83,100
Salt Lake City, UT	73,000	79,000	92,800
San Antonio, TX	68,000	72,600	76,800
San Diego, CA[2]	182,700	175,500	177,800
San Francisco, CA[2]	243,900	249,300	246,900
Seattle, WA	141,300	145,000	152,900
Spokane, WA	71,300	79,100	90,700
Syracuse, NY	77,400	86,100	82,100
Tampa, FL	70,100	69,900	74,300
Toledo, OH	74,000	65,700	72,800
Tulsa, OK	68,500	68,200	73,500
Washington, DC	152,500	153,500	154,900

(1) All areas are metropolitan statistical areas as defined by the U.S. Office of Management and Budget. They include the named central city and surrounding suburban areas. (2) Data provided by the California Association of Realtors. NA=not available.

Housing Affordability

Source: National Association of Realtors; data as of midyear 1994

	Median-priced existing home	Average mortgage rate[1]	Monthly principal and interest payment	Payment as percentage of median income
1983	$70,300	12.85%	$616	30.1%
1984	72,400	12.49	618	28.2
1985	75,500	11.74	609	26.2
1986	80,300	10.25	563	23.0
1987	85,600	9.28	565	21.9
1988	90,600	9.31	591	22.0
1989	$93,100	10.11%	$660	23.1%
1990	97,500	10.04	673	22.7
1991	99,700	9.51	671	22.3
1992	100,900	8.48	620	20.0
1993	106,100	7.30	582	18.8
1994	107,600	7.01	573	18.0

(1)The average mortgage rate is based on the effective rate on loans closed on existing homes monitored by the Federal Housing Finance Board.

Income Needed to Get a Mortgage

Source: National Association of Realtors

The following shows the minimum annual gross income needed for various size home loans at different rates. The figures are based on a 30-year loan and assume that the borrower's monthly payments cannot exceed 28% of gross income, the ceiling most lenders use. The figures do not include property taxes and insurance as part of the monthly payment.

Interest rate (percent)	Loan amount: $50,000	$75,000	$100,000	$150,000	$200,000
	Income needed				
8	$15,724	$23,586	$31,447	$47,171	$62,895
8 ½	16,477	24,715	32,954	49,430	65,907
9	17,242	25,863	34,484	51,726	68,968
9 ½	18,018	27,028	36,037	54,055	72,074
10	18,085	28,208	37,611	56,415	75,221
10 ½	19,602	29,403	39,203	58,805	78,406
11	20,407	30,611	40,814	61,221	81,628
11 ½	21,221	31,831	42,441	63,662	84,883
12	22,042	33,063	44,084	66,125	88,167
12 ½	22,870	34,305	45,740	68,610	91,479
13	23,704	35,556	47,409	71,113	94,817

Marriage Laws

Source: Gary N. Skoloff, Skoloff & Wolfe, Livingston, NJ; as of Sept. 1, 1994

State	Age with parental consent		Age without consent		Physical exam & blood test for male and female			
					Maximum period between exam and license	Scope of medical exam	Waiting period	
	Male	Female	Male	Female			Before license	After license
Alabama*	14a	14a	18	18	—	b	—	s
Alaska	16z	16z	18	18	—	—	3 days, w	—
Arizona	16z	16z	18	18	—	—	—	—
Arkansas	17c	16c	18	18	—	—	v	—
California	aa	aa	18	18	30 days, w	zz	—	h
Colorado*	16z	16z	18	18	—	—	—	s
Connecticut	16z	16z	18	18	—	bb	4 days, w	ttt
Delaware	18c	16c	18	18	—	—	—	e, s
Florida	16a, c	16a, c	18	18	—	—	3 days	s
Georgia*	16c,z	16c,z	16	16	—	b	3 days, g	s*
Hawaii	15	15	16	16	—	bb	—	—
Idaho*	16z	16z	18	18	—	zzz	—	—
Illinois	16	16	18	18	30 days	n	1 day	ee
Indiana	17c	17c	18	18	—	bb	72 hr	t
Iowa*	18z	18z	18	18	—	—	3 days, v	tt
Kansas*[y]	18z	18z	18	18	—	—	3 days, w	—
Kentucky	18c, z	18c, z	18	18	—	—	—	—
Louisiana	18z	18z	18	18	10 days	b	72 hr, w	—
Maine	16z	16z	18	18	—	—	3 days, v, w	h
Maryland	16c, f	16c, f	18	18	—	—	48 hr, w	ff
Massachusetts	14j	12j	18	18	60 days	bb	3 days, v	—
Michigan	16	16	18	18	30 days	b	3 days, w	—
Minnesota	16z	16z	18	18	—	—	5 days, w	—
Mississippi	17	15	17	15	30 days	b	3 days, w	—
Missouri	15d, 18z	15d, 18z	18	18	—	—	—	—
Montana[yy]	16	16	18	18	—	b	—	ff
Nebraska[yy]	17	17	19	19	—	bb	—	—
Nevada	16z	16z	18	18	—	—	—	1 yr
New Hampshire	14j	13j	18	18	—	l,zz	3 days, v	h
New Jersey	16z, c	16z, c	18	18	30 days	b	72 hr, w	s
New Mexico[y]	16d, c	16d, c	18	18	30 days	b	—	—
New York	16z	16z	18	18	—	nn	—	24 hr, w, t
North Carolina	16c, g	16c, g	18	18	—	m	—	—
North Dakota	16	16	18	18	—	—	—	t
Ohio*	18c, z	16c, z	18	18	30 days	b	5 days,w	t
Oklahoma*	16c	16c	18	18	30 days, w	b	—	s
Oregon	17	17	18	18	—	—	3 days, w	—
Pennsylvania*	16d	16d	18	18	30 days	b	3 days, w	t
Puerto Ricoy	18c, d, z	16c, d, z	21	21	—	b	—	—
Rhode Island*	18d	16d	18	18	—	bb	—	—
South Carolina*	16c	14c	18	18	—	—	1 day	—
South Dakota	16c	16c	18	18	—	—	—	tt
Tennesee	16d	16d	18	18	—	—	3 days, cc	s
Texas*[y]	14j, k	14j, k	18	18	—	—	—	s
Utah*	18a	18a	18x	18x	30 days	b	—	s
Vermont	16z	16z	18	18	30 days	b	1 day, w	—
Virginia	16a, c	16a, c	18	18	—	zz	—	t
Washington	17d	17d	18	18	—	bbb	3 days	t
West Virginia	18c	18c	18	18	—	b	3 days, w	—
Wisconsin	16d	16d	18	18	—	—	5 days, w	s
Wyoming	16d	16d	18	18	—	bb	—	—
Dist. of Columbia*	16a	16a	18	18	30 days	b	3 days w	—

*Indicates 1987 common-law marriage recognized; in many states, such marriages are only recognized if entered into many years before. (a) Parental consent not required if minor was previously married. (aa) No age limits. (b) Venereal diseases. (bb) Venereal diseases and rubella (for female). In CO and WY, rubella for female under 45 and Rh type. (bbb) No medical exam required; however, applicants must file affidavit showing non-affliction of contagious venereal disease. (c) Younger parties may obtain license in case of pregnancy or birth of child. (cc) Unless parties are over 18 years of age. (d) Younger parties may obtain license in special circumstances. (e) Residents before expiration of 24-hr waiting period; non-residents formerly residents, before expiration of 96-hr waiting period; others 96 hr. (ee) License effective 1 day after issuance, unless court orders otherwise, valid for 60 days only. (f) If parties are at least 16 years of age, proof of age and the consent of parents in person is required. If a parent is ill, an affidavit by the incapacitated parent and a physician's affidavit to that effect required. (ff) License valid for 180 days only. (g) Unless parties are 18 years of age or more, or female is pregnant, or applicants are the parents of a living child born out of wedlock. (h) License valid for 90 days only. (j) Parental consent and/or permission of judge required. (k) Below age of consent parties need parental consent and permission of judge. (l) With each certificate issued to couples, a list of family planning agencies and services available to them is provided. (m) Mental incompetence, infectious tuberculosis, venereal diseases, and rubella (certain counties only). (n) Venereal diseases; test for sickle cell anemia given at request of examining physician. (nn) Tests for sickle cell anemia may be required for certain applicants. Marriage prohibited unless it is established that procreation is not possible. (s) License valid for 30 days only. (t) License valid for 60 days only. (tt) License valid for 20 days only. (ttt) License valid for 65 days. (v) Parties must file notice of intention to marry with local clerk. (w) Waiting period may be avoided. (x) Authorizes counties to provide for premarital counseling as a requisite to issuance of license to persons under 19 and persons previously divorced. (y) Marriages by proxy are valid. (yy) Proxy marriages are valid under certain conditions. (z) Younger parties may marry with parental consent and/or permission of judge. In CT, judicial approval. (zz) Required offer of HIV test, and/or must be provided with information on AIDS. (zzz) Applicants must receive information on AIDS and certify having read it.

Divorce Laws

Source: Gary N. Skoloff, Skoloff & Wolfe, Livingston, NJ; as of Sept. 1, 1994. Important: Almost all states also have other laws as well as qualifications of the laws shown below and proposed divorce-reform laws pending. It would be wise to consult a lawyer in conjunction with the use of this chart.

Some grounds for absolute divorce[1]

	Residence	Adultery	Cruelty	Desertion	Alcoholism	Impotency	Non-support	Insanity	Pregnancy at marriage	Bigamy	Separation	Felony conviction or imprisonment	Drug addiction	Fraud force, duress
PR	1 yr.	Yes	Yes	1 yr.	Yes	Yes	No	Yes	No	A	2 yrs.	Yes*	Yes	No
AL	6 mos.*	Yes	Phys. only	1 yr.	Yes	Yes*	2 yrs.	5 yrs.	Yes	A	2 yrs.*	2 yrs*	Yes	A
AK	*	Yes	Yes	1 yr.	1 yr.	Yes	No	18 mos.	No	A	No	Yes	Yes	A
AZ	90 days	No	No	No	No	No	No	No	No	No	No	No	No	No
AR	60 days	Yes	Yes	No	1 yr.	Yes	Yes	3 yrs.	No	No	18 mos.	Yes	No	A
CA	6 mos.	No	No	No	No	A	No	Yes, A	No	A	No	No	No	A
CO	90 days	No	No	No	A	A	No	No	No	A	No	No	A	A
CT	1 yr.*	Yes	Yes	1 yr.	Yes	No	No	5 yrs.	No	A	18 mos.*	life*	No	Yes
DE	6 mos.	Yes	Yes	Yes	Yes	A	No	Yes	No	Yes	Yes	Yes	Yes	A
FL	6 mos.	No	No	No	No	No	No	3 yrs.	No	No	No	No	No	A
GA	6 mos.	Yes	Yes	1 yr.	Yes	Yes	No	2 yrs.	Yes	A	No	Yes*	Yes	Yes
HI	6 mos.*	No	No	No	No	No	No	A	No	A	2 yrs.*	No	No	A
ID	6 wks.	Yes	Yes	Yes	Yes	A	Yes	3 yrs.	No	A	5 yrs.	Yes	No	A
IL	90 days	Yes	Yes	1 yr.	2 yrs.	Yes	No	No	No	Yes	2 yrs.*	Yes	2 yrs.	No
IN	6 mos.*	No	No	No	No	Yes	No	2 yrs.	No	A	No	Yes	No	A
IA	1 yr.*	No	No	No	No	A	No	A	No	A	No	No	No	No
KS	60 days	No	No	No	No	No	Yes	2 yrs.	No	A	No	No	No	A
KY	180 days	No	No	No	No	A	No	No	No	A	No	No	No	A
LA	1 yr.*	Yes	No	No	No	No	No	No	No	A	6 mos.	Yes*	No	A
ME	6 mos.*	Yes	Yes	3 yrs.	Yes	Yes	Yes	A	No	A	No	No	Yes	No
MD	1 yr.*	Yes	No	1 yr.*	No	No	No	3 yrs.	No	A	1 yr.*	1 yr.*	No	No
MA	1 yr.*	Yes	Yes	1 yr.	Yes	Yes	No	A	No	A	No	5 yrs.	Yes	No
MI	180 days	No	No	No	No	No	No	No	No	No	No	No	A	A
MN	180 days	No	No	No	No	No	No	No	No	No	No	No	No	A
MS	6 mos.	Yes	Yes	1 yr.	Yes	Yes	No	3 yrs.	Yes	A	No	Yes*	Yes	A
MO	90 days	No	No	No	No	No	No	No	No	A	No	No	No	A
MT	90 days	No	No	No	No	A	No	No	No	A	180 days*	No	No	A
NE	1 yr.*	No	No	No	No	A	No	No	No	A	No	No	No	A
NV	6 wks.	No	No	No	No	No	No	2 yrs.	No	A	1 yr.	No	No	A
NH	1 yr.*	Yes	Yes	2 yrs.	2 yrs.	Yes	2 yrs.	No	No	A	2 yrs.	1 yr.*	No	No
NJ	1 yr.*	Yes	Yes	1 yr.	1 yr.	A	No	2 yrs.	No	A	18 mos.	18 mos.	1 yr.	A
NM	6 mos.	Yes	Yes	Yes*	No	No	No	No	No	No	No	No	No	No
NY	1 yr.*	Yes	Yes	1 yr.	No	No	A	No	No	A	1 yr.	3 yrs.	No	A
NC	6 mos.	No	No	No	No	A	No	3 yrs.	No	A	1 yr.	No	No	No
ND	6 mos.	Yes	Yes	1 yr.	1 yr.	A	1 yr.	5 yrs.*	No	A	No	Yes	1 yr.	A
OH	6 mos.	Yes	Yes	1 yr.	Yes	Yes	Yes	No	No	Yes, A	1 yr.	Yes	No	Yes, A
OK	6 mos.	Yes	Yes	1 yr.	Yes	Yes	Yes	5 yrs.	Yes	Yes	No	Yes	No	Yes
OR	6 mos.*	No	No	No	No	No	No	No	No	No	No	No	No	A
PA	6 mos.	Yes	Yes	1 yr.	No	No	No	18 mos.*	No	Yes	2 yrs.*	Yes	No	No
RI	1 yr.	Yes	Yes	5 yrs.*	Yes	Yes	1 yr.	No	No	Yes	3 yrs.	Yes	Yes	No
SC	1 yr.*	Yes	Phys. only	1 yr.	Yes	No	No	No	No	No	1 yr.	No	Yes	No
SD	none*	Yes	Yes	1 yr.	1 yr.	A	1 yr.	5 yrs.	No	A	No	Yes	No	A*
TN	6 mos.*	Yes	Yes	1 yr.	Yes	Yes	Yes	No	Yes	Yes	2 yrs.	Yes	Yes	A
TX	6 mos.*	Yes	Yes	1 yr.	*	A	No	3 yrs.	No	No	3 yrs.	1 yr.	No	No
UT	3 mos.*	Yes	Yes	1 yr.	Yes	Yes	Yes	Yes	No	A	3 yrs.*	Yes	No	No
VT	6 mos.*	Yes	Yes	7 yrs.*	No	No	Yes	5 yrs.	No	A	6 mos.	3 yrs.	No	A
VA	6 mos.*	Yes	Yes*	1 yr.	No	A	No	A	A	A	1 yr.*	1 yr.*	A*	A
WA	bona fide resident	No	No	No	No	No	No	No	No	A*	No	No	No	A*
WV	1 yr.*	Yes	Yes	6 mos.	Yes	A	No	3 yrs.	A	A	1 yr.	Yes	Yes	No
WI	6 mos.	No	No	No	A	A	No	No	No	A	1 yr.	No	A	A
WY	60 days*	No	No	No	No	A*	No	2 yrs.	No	A	No	No	No	A
DC	6 mos.	No	No	No	No	A	No	A*	No	A	6 mos.-1 yr.	No	No	A

(1) Almost all states have "no-fault" divorce laws. Conduct that constitutes "no-fault" divorce may vary from state to state. (*) Indicates qualification; check local statutes. (A) Indicates grounds for annulment.

RELIGIOUS INFORMATION

Census of Religious Groups in the U.S.

Source: *1994 Yearbook of American & Canadian Churches;* World Almanac research

Membership figures generally are based on reports made by group leaders rather than "head counts" of the population. In many cases, groups keep careful records; others make only estimates. Not all groups report annually. Christian church membership figures reported in this table are inclusive and refer to those who are full communicants or confirmed members plus other members baptized, nonconfirmed, or noncommunicant. Only data reported within the past 10 years are included.

The number of congregations appears in parentheses. * Indicates that the group declines to publish membership figures.

Group	Members
Adventist churches:	
Advent Christian Ch. (335)	28,000
Church of God General Conf. (Oregon, IL) (87)	5,336
Primitive Advent Christian Ch. (10)	340
Seventh-day Adventists (4,261)	748,687
American Rescue Workers (16)	**35,000**
Apostolic Christian Ch. (Nazarene) (48)	**2,799**
Apostolic Christian Churches of America (80)	**11,450**
Baha'i Faith (1,700)	**50,000**
Baptist churches:	
American Baptist Assn. (1,705)	250,000
American Baptist Chs. in U.S.A. (5,845)	1,534,078
Baptist Bible Fellowship Intl. (3,500)	1,500,000
Baptist General Conference (821)	134,658
Baptist Missionary Assn. of America (1,362)	236,604
Conservative Baptist Assn. of America (1,084)	200,000
Free Will Baptists, Natl. Assn. of (2,495)	209,223
General Assn. of Regular Baptist Chs. (1,532)	160,123
General Baptists, General Assn. of (876)	74,156
Liberty Baptist Fellowship (100)	*
Natl. Baptist Convention of America (2,500)	3,500,000
Natl. Baptist Convention, U.S.A. (33,000)	8,200,000
Natl. Missionary Baptist Convention of America (*)	2,500,000
North American Baptist Conference (289)	43,446
Progressive National Baptist Convention (1,400)	2,500,000
Separate Baptists in Christ (100)	8,000
Seventh Day Baptist General Conference (90)	5,250
Southern Baptist Convention (38,401)	15,358,866
Sovereign Grace Baptists (300)	3,000
Brethren (German Baptists):	
Brethren Ch. (Ashland, Ohio) (124)	13,132
Fellowship of Grace Brethren (308)	36,220
Old German Baptist Brethren (56)	5,477
Brethren, River:	
Brethren in Christ Ch. (184)	16,697
United Zion Ch. (13)	850
Buddhist Churches of America (67)	**590,000**
Christian Brethren (1,150)	**98,000**
Christian Catholic Church (5)	**2,000**
Christian Church (Disciples of Christ) (3,996)	**1,011,502**
Christian Churches and Churches of Christ (5,579)	**1,070,616**
Christian Congregation (1,437)	**111,324**
Christian Nation Church U.S.A. (5)	**200**
Christian Union (240)	**9,790**
Church of Christ, Scientist (2,500)	*
Churches of Christ:	
Church of the Living God (170)	42,000
Churches of Christ (13,174)	1,684,872
Churches of God:	
Chs. of God, General Conference (359)	33,096
Ch. of God (Anderson, Ind.) (2,330)	214,743
Ch. of God (Seventh Day), Denver, CO (153)	5,749
Church of God by Faith (145)	8,235
Church of God in Christ Which He Purchased With His Own Blood (7)	800
Church of the Nazarene (5,172)	**573,834**
Community Churches, Intl. Council of (410)	**500,000**
Congregational Christian Chs. (405)	**90,000**
Conservative Congregational Christian Conference (188)	**30,387**
Eastern Orthodox churches:	
Albanian Orthodox Diocese of America (2)	1,873
American Carpatho-Russian Orthodox Greek Catholic Ch. (72)	18,611
Antiochian Orthodox Christian Archdiocese of North America (160)	250,000
Apostolic Catholic Assyrian Ch. of the East, N.A. Diocese (22)	120,000
Armenian Apostolic Ch. of America (30)	150,000
Armenian Church of Amer., Diocese of the (72)	414,000
Bulgarian Eastern Orthodox Ch. (9)	1,100
Coptic Orthodox Ch. (85)	180,000
Greek Orthodox Archdiocese of North and South America (555)	1,500,000
Orthodox Ch. in America (700)	600,000
Patriarchal Parishes of the Russian Orthodox Ch. in the U.S.A. (38)	9,780
Romanian Orthodox Episcopate of America (37)	65,000
Serbian Orthodox Ch. of U.S.A. & Canada (68)	67,000
Syrian Orthodox Ch. of Antioch (Archdiocese of the U.S.A. and Canada) (16)	33,000
True Orthodox Church of Greece (7)	1,000
Ukrainian Orthodox Ch. in America (Ecumenical Patriarchate) (27)	5,000
Episcopal Church (7,367)	**2,471,880**
Ethical Culture Movement (21)	**3,212**
Evangelical Church (43)	**3,336**
Evangelical Congregational Church (155)	**24,437**
Evangelical Covenant Church (596)	**89,648**
Evangelical Free Church of America (1,173)	**214,186**
Fellowship of Fundamental Bible Churches (25)	**2,090**
Fire Baptized Holiness Church (Wesleyan) (49)	**692**
Friends:	
Evangelical Friends International, North American (246)	26,322
Friends General Conference (520)	30,902
Friends United Meeting (526)	50,803
Religious Society of Friends (Conservative) (28)	1,744
Grace Gospel Fellowship (128)	**60,000**
Hindu	**340,000**
Independent Fundamental Churches of America (708)	**71,672**
Islam	**†3,332,000**
Jehovah's Witnesses (9,890)	**914,079**
Jewish organizations:	
Union of American Hebrew Congregations (Reform) (848)	1,300,000
Union of Orthodox Jewish Congregations of America (1,200)	1,000,000
United Synagogue of America (Conservative) (800)	2,000,000
Latter-day Saints:	
Ch. of Jesus Christ (Bickertonites) (63)	2,707
Ch. of Jesus Christ of Latter-day Saints (Mormon) (9,654)	4,430,000
Reorganized Ch. of Jesus Christ of Latter Day Saints (1,001)	150,143
Liberal Catholic Ch.-Province of the U.S.A. (34)	**2,800**
Lutheran churches:	
Apostolic Lutheran Ch. of America (60)	9,500
Ch. of the Lutheran Brethren of America (110)	12,182
Ch. of the Lutheran Confession (70)	8,798
Conservative Lutheran Assn. (12)	1,530
Estonian Evangelical Lutheran Ch. (24)	7,298
Evangelical Lutheran Ch. in America (11,055)	5,234,568
Evangelical Lutheran Synod (126)	21,525
Free Lutheran Congregations, Assn. of (225)	28,469
Latvian Evangelical Lutheran Church of America (56)	12,553
Lutheran Ch.-Missouri Synod (5,369)	2,609,905
Lutheran Chs., American Assn. of (78)	15,150
Protestant Conference (Lutheran) (7)	1,150
Wisconsin Evangelical Lutheran Synod (1,211)	420,039
Mennonite churches:	
Beachy Amish Mennonite Chs. (95)	6,968
Church of God in Christ (Mennonite) (79)	10,234
Evangelical Mennonite Ch. (27)	4,130
Fellowship of Evangelical Bible Churches (14)	1,925
Hutterian Brethren (95)	6,700
Mennonite Brethren Chs., The Conf. of (144)	16,843
Mennonite Church (1,056)	99,446
Mennonite Ch., The General Conference (227)	34,040
Old Order Amish Ch. (873)	78,570
Methodist churches:	
African Methodist Episcopal Ch. (8,000)	3,500,000
African Methodist Episcopal Zion Ch. (3,000)	1,200,000
Allegheny Wesleyan Methodist Connection (122)	2,060
Evangelical Methodist Ch. (132)	8,500

Group	Members
Free Methodist Ch. of North America (1,055)	74,168
Fundamental Methodist Ch. (12)	1,075
Primitive Methodist Ch., U.S.A. (81)	7,677
Southern Methodist Ch. (133)	7,745
United Methodist Ch. (37,100)	8,789,101
The Wesleyan Church (U.S.A.) (1,612)	114,174
Metropolitan Community Churches, Universal Fellowship of (291)	**30,000**
Moravian churches:	
Moravian Ch. Northern Province (97)	29,469
Moravian Ch. in America Southern Province (56)	21,513
Unity of the Brethren (26)	3,615
Natl. Organization of the New Apostolic Ch. of North America (549)	**41,201**
Natl. Spiritualist Assn. of Churches (137)	**3,883**
Old Catholic churches:	
Christ Catholic Ch. (12)	1,558
North American Old Roman Catholic Church-N.Y. Archdiocese (5)	400
Pentecostal churches:	
Apostolic Faith Mission (Portland, OR) (55)	4,500
Apostolic Faith Mission Ch. of God (53)	14,000
Apostolic Overcoming Holy Church of God (192)	1,463
Assemblies of God (11,689)	2,257,846
Bible Church of Christ (6)	6,700
Christian Church of N.A., Gen. Council (104)	13,500
Church of God (Cleveland, TN) (5,776)	672,008
Church of God in Christ (15,300)	5,499,875
Church of God of Prophecy (2,072)	72,465
Congregational Holiness Ch. (176)	7,116
Elim Fellowship (66)	*
Gen. Council, Christian Ch. of N. America (104)	13,500
Intl. Ch. of the Foursquare Gospel (1,558)	207,455
Open Bible Standard Chs. (368)	40,000
Pentecostal Assemblies of the World (1,170)	101,786
Pentecostal Church of God (1,160)	92,060
Pentecostal Free-Will Baptist Ch. (150)	18,000
United Pentecostal Ch. Intl. (3,728)	550,000
Presbyterian churches:	
Associate Reformed Presbyterian Ch. (General Synod) (196)	38,763
Cumberland Presbyterian Ch. (782)	92,240
Evangelical Presbyterian Ch. (174)	55,008
Korean Presbyterian Church in America (203)	26,988
Orthodox Presbyterian Ch. (170)	18,137
Presbyterian Ch. in America (1,212)	239,500
Presbyterian Ch. (U.S.A.) (11,456)	3,758,085
Reformed Presbyterian Ch. of N. America (68)	5,174
Reformed churches:	
Christian Reformed Ch. in N. America (736)	223,617
Hungarian Reformed Ch. in America (27)	9,780
Netherlands Reformed Congregations (15)	5,336
Reformed Ch. in America (927)	274,521
Reformed Ch. in the U.S. (34)	3,778
United Church of Christ (6,264)	1,555,382
Reformed Episcopal Church (83)	**6,565**
Roman Catholic Church (19,863)	**59,220,723**
Salvation Army (1,151)	**446,403**
Schwenkfelder Church (5)	**2,489**
Swedenborgian Church (50)	**2,475**
Unitarian Universalist Assn. (1,020)	**141,315**
United Brethren:	
United Brethren in Christ (251)	26,879
United Christian Ch. (12)	420
Vedanta Societies (13)	**2,500**

† Figure is for Northern America. Estimates vary.

Headquarters of Selected Religious Groups in the United States

Source: 1994 *Yearbook of American & Canadian Churches*
Year organized in parentheses

Adventists, Seventh-day (1863), 12501 Old Columbia Pike, Silver Spring, MD 20904; Pres., Robert Folkenberg

American Rescue Workers (1884), 2827 Frankford Ave., PO Box 4766, Philadelphia, PA 19134; Commander-in-Chief & President, Gen. Paul E. Martin

Armenian Church of America, Diocese of the (1889), **Eastern Diocese**: 630 Second Ave., New York, NY 10016; Primate, Archbishop Khajag Barsamian; **Western Diocese**: 1201 N. Vine St., Hollywood, CA 90038; Primate, His Eminence Archbishop Vatche Hovespian

Assemblies of God (1914), 1445 Boonville Ave., Springfield, MO 65802; General Supt., Thomas E. Trask

Baha'i Faith, 536 Sheridan Rd., Wilmette, IL 60091

Baptist Bible Fellowship Intl. (1950), PO Box 191, Springfield, MO 65801; Pres., Parker Daily

Baptist Churches in the U.S.A., American (1907), PO Box 851, Valley Forge, PA 19482; Pres., Hector Gonzales

Baptist Convention of America, Inc., National (1880), 777 S.R.L. Thornton Freeway, Ste. 205, Dallas, TX 75203; Pres., Dr. E. Edward Jones

Baptist Convention of America, Natl. Missionary (1988), 6717 Centennial Blvd., Nashville, TN 37209; General Sec., Dr. S. J. Gilbert, Sr.

Baptist Convention, U.S.A., National (1880), 1700 Baptist World Center Dr., Nashville, TN 37207; Pres., Dr. T. J. Jemison

Baptist Convention, Progressive Natl. (1961), 601 50th St. NE, Washington, DC 20019; Pres., Dr. Charles G. Adams

Baptist Convention, Southern (1845), 901 Commerce St., Nashville, TN 37203; Pres., H. Edwin Young

Brethren in Christ Church (1778), PO Box 290, Grantham, PA 17027; Moderator, Rev. Harvey R. Sider

Brethren, Fellowship of Grace (1882), PO Box 386, Winona Lake, IN 46590; Moderator, Robert Fetterhoff

Buddhist Churches of America (1899), 1710 Octavia St., San Francisco, CA 94109

Christian Church (Disciples of Christ) (1809), 222 S. Downey Ave., Indianapolis, IN 46206; Gen. Minister, Richard L. Hamm

Christian Churches and Churches of Christ, 4201 Bridgetown Rd., Box 11326, Cincinnati, OH 45211

Christian and Missionary Alliance (1897), PO Box 35000, Colorado Springs, CO 80935; Pres., Rev. David Rambo, Ph.D

Churches of Christ, PO Box 726, Kosciusko, MO 39090

Church of Christ, Scientist (1879), 175 Huntington Ave., Boston, MA 02115; Pres., K. Dieter Förster

Church of God (Cleveland, TN) (1886), PO Box 2430, Cleveland, TN 37320; Gen. Overseer, R. Lamar Vest

Church of God in Christ (1907), Mason Temple, 939 Mason St., Memphis, TN 38126; Presiding Bishop, Rt. Rev. L. H. Ford

Church of Jesus Christ of the Latter Day Saints (Mormon) (1830), 50 E. North Temple St., Salt Lake City, UT 84150; Pres., Howard W. Hunter

Church of the Nazarene (1907), 6401 The Paseo, Kansas City, MO 64131; General Sec., Dr. Jack Stone

Coptic Orthodox Church, 427 West Side Ave., Jersey City, NJ 07304; Archpriest, Very Reverend Fr. Gabriel Avdelsayed

Episcopal Church (1789), 815 Second Ave., New York, NY 10017; Bishop, Most Rev. Edmond L. Browning

Evangelical Free Church of America (1884), 901 E. 78th St., Minneapolis, MN 55420; Pres., Dr. Paul Cedar

Friends General Conference (1900), 1216 Arch St., Philadelphia, PA 19107; Gen. Secretary, Bruce Birchard

Greek Orthodox Archdiocese of North and South America (1864), 8-10 E. 79th St., New York, NY 10021; Chairperson, Archbishop Iakovos

International Church of the Foursquare Gospel (1927), 1910 W. Sunset Blvd., Ste. 200, Los Angeles, CA 90026; Pres., Dr. John R. Holland

Islamic Association in the U.S. and Canada, Federation of, 25351 Five Mile Rd., Redford Township, MI 48239; Sec., Nihad Hamed

Jehovah's Witnesses (1879) 25 Columbia Heights, Brooklyn, NY 11201; Pres., Milton Henschel

Lutheran Church in America, Evangelical (1987), 8765 W. Higgins Rd., Chicago, IL 60631; Bishop, Rev. Dr. Herbert W. Chilstrom

Lutheran Church - Missouri Synod (1847), 1333 S. Kirkwood, St. Louis, MO 63122; Pres., A. L. Barry

Mennonite Church (1525), 421 S. Second St., Elkhart, IN 46516; Moderator, Donella Clemens

Mennonite Church, The General Conference (1860), 722 Main St., Newton, KS 67114; Moderator, Darrell Fast

Methodist Episcopal Church, Christian (1870), 4466 Elvis Presley Blvd., Memphis, TN 38116; Executive Secretary, Dr. Clyde Williams

Methodist Episcopal Church, African (1787), 1134 11th St. NW, Washinton, DC 20001

Methodist Episcopal Zion Church, African (1796), PO Box 32843, Charlotte, NC 28232; Senior Bishop, Ruben L. Speaks

Methodist Church, United (1968), PO Box 320, Nashville, TN 37202; Pres., Bishop J. Woodrow Hearn

Moravian Church (1735), **Northern Province:** 1021 Center St., Bethlehem, PA 18016; Pres., Gordon L. Sommers; **Southern Province:** 459 S. Church St., Winston-Salem, NC 27108; Pres., Rev. Graham H. Rights

Orthodox Christian Archdiocese of North America, Antiochian (1895), 358 Mountain Rd., Englewood, NJ 07631; Primate, Metropolitan Philip Saliba

Orthodox Church in America (1794), PO Box 675, Syosset, NY 11791; Primate, The Most Blessed Theodosius

Pentecostal Church Intl., United (1925), 8855 Dunn Rd., Hazelwood, MO 63042; General Superintendent, Rev. Nathaniel A. Urshan

Presbyterian Church in America (1973), 1852 Century Pl., Atlanta, GA 30345; Moderator, G. Richard Hostetter

Presbyterian Church (USA), (1983), 100 Witherspoon St., Louisville, KY 40202; Moderator, David Dobler

Presbyterian Church, Cumberland (1810), 1978 Union Ave., Memphis, TN 38104; Moderator, Dr. Robert M. Shelton

Reformed Church in North America, Christian (1857), 2850 Kalamazoo Ave. SE, Grand Rapids, MI 49560; Gen. Secretary, Rev. Leonard J. Hofman

Reformed Church in America (1628), 475 Riverside Dr., New York, NY 10115; Pres., Warren D. Burgess

Roman Catholic Church, The (National Conference of Catholic Bishops), 3211 Fourth St., Washington, DC 20017; Pres., Archbishop William H. Keeler

Salvation Army, The (1880), 615 Slaters Lane, Alexandria, VA 22313; National Cammander, Commissioner Kenneth Hodder

Union of American Hebrew Congregations (Reform), 838 5th Ave., New York, NY; Pres., Rabbi Alexander M. Schindler

Union of Orthodox Jewish Congregations of America 333 7th Ave., New York, NY 10001; Pres., Sheldon Rudoff

Unitarian Universalist Association (1793), 25 Beacon St., Boston, MA 02108

United Church of Christ (1957), 700 Prospect Ave., Cleveland, OH 44115; Pres., Reverend Paul H. Sherry

United Synagogue of America (Conservative), 155 5th Ave., New York, NY 10010; Pres., Alan Tichnor

Vedanta Societies (1893), 34 W. 71st St., New York, NY 10023

Wesleyan Church (1843), PO Box 50434, Indianapolis, IN 46250; General Sec., Dr. Ronald Brannon

Adherents of All Religions by Continental Areas, Mid-1993

Source: *1994 Encyclopaedia Britannica Book of the Year*

	Africa	Asia	Europe	Latin America	Northern America	Oceania	Former USSR	World
Christians	341,208,000	300,383,000	409,653,000	443,056,000	241,147,000	22,686,000	111,618,000	1,869,751,000
Roman Catholics	128,167,000	130,102,000	260,034,000	412,366,000	97,892,000	8,229,000	5,711,000	1,042,501,000
Protestants	91,070,000	85,764,000	73,206,000	17,550,000	97,176,000	7,537,000	10,071,000	382,374,000
Orthodox	29,771,000	3,847,000	35,777,000	1,793,000	6,062,000	577,000	95,733,000	173,560,000
Anglicans	28,013,000	744,000	32,629,000	1,322,000	7,404,000	5,734,000	1,000	75,847,000
Other Christians	64,187,000	79,926,000	8,007,000	10,025,000	32,614,000	609,000	102,000	195,470,000
Muslims	284,844,000	668,298,000	13,633,000	1,400,000	3,332,000	104,000	42,761,000	1,014,372,000
Nonreligious	2,578,000	721,113,000	57,542,000	18,444,000	24,718,000	3,572,000	84,907,000	912,874,000
Hindus	1,569,000	746,512,000	707,000	916,000	1,285,000	369,000	2,000	751,360,000
Buddhists	22,000	332,143,000	273,000	561,000	565,000	26,000	412,000	334,002,000
Atheists	336,000	167,217,000	16,669,000	3,343,000	1,336,000	549,000	52,402,000	241,852,000
Chinese folk religionists	14,000	140,661,000	60,000	76,000	123,000	21,000	1,000	140,956,000
New-Religionists	22,000	121,693,000	50,000	550,000	1,439,000	10,000	1,000	123,765,000
Tribal religionists	70,000,000	28,654,000	1,000	971,000	41,000	69,000	0	99,736,000
Sikhs	28,000	19,318,000	232,000	8,000	257,000	9,000	1,000	19,853,000
Jews	359,000	6,264,000	1,475,000	1,132,000	6,850,000	100,000	1,973,000	18,153,000
Shamanists	1,000	10,591,000	2,000	1,000	1,000	1,000	257,000	10,854,000
Confucians	1,000	6,204,000	2,000	2,000	26,000	1,000	2,000	6,230,000
Baha'is	1,591,000	2,774,000	91,000	830,000	370,000	79,000	7,000	5,742,000
Jains	56,000	3,847,000	15,000	4,000	4,000	1,000	0	3,927,000
Shintoists	0	3,332,000	1,000	1,000	1,000	1,000	0	3,336,800
Other religionists	461,000	12,714,000	1,475,000	3,701,000	491,000	4,000	337,000	19,183,000
Total Population	**703,090,000**	**3,291,718,000**	**501,881,000**	**474,996,000**	**281,986,000**	**27,602,000**	**294,681,000**	**5,575,954,000**

Notes:

Adherents: As defined and enumerated for each of the world's countries in *World Christian Encyclopedia* (1982), projected to mid-1993, adjusted for recent data.

Christians: Followers of Jesus Christ affiliated with churches (church members, including children: 1,726,420,000) plus persons professing in censuses or polls though not so affiliated.

Other Christians: Catholics (non-Roman), marginal Protestants, crypto-Christians, and adherents of African, Asian, black, and Latin-American indigenous churches.

Muslims: 83% Sunnites, 16% Shi'ites, 1% other schools. Up to 1990 the former ethnic Muslims in the USSR who had embraced Communism were not included as Muslims in this table. After the collapse of Communism in 1990-91, these ethnic Muslims are once again enumerated as Muslims where they have returned to Islamic profession and practice.

Nonreligious: Persons professing no religion, nonbelievers, agnostics, freethinkers, dereligionized secularists indifferent to all religion.

Hindus: 70% Vaishnavites, 25% Shaivites, 2% neo-Hindus and reform Hindus.

Buddhists: 56% Mahayana, 38% Theravada (Hinayana), 6% Tantrism (Lamaism).

Atheists: Persons professing atheism, skepticism, disbelief, or irreligion, including antireligious (opposed to all religion).

Chinese folk-religionists: Followers of traditional Chinese religion (local deities, ancestor veneration, Confucian ethics, Taoism, universism, divination, some Buddhist elements).

New-Religionists: Followers of Asian 20th-cent. New Religions, New Religious movements, radical new crisis religions, and non-Christian syncretistic mass religions, all founded since 1800 and mostly since 1945.

(continued)

Jews: Estimates of the Jewish population worldwide differ widely; for detailed discussion see the annual "World Jewish Populations" article in the American Jewish Committee's *American Jewish Year Book.*
Confucians: Non-Chinese followers of Confucius and Confucianism, mostly Koreans in Korea.
Other religionists: Including 70 minor world religions and a large number of spiritist religions, New Age religions, quasi religions, pseudo religions, para-religions, religious or mystic systems, and religious and semireligious brotherhoods.
Total Population: UN medium variant figures for mid-1993, as given in *World Population Prospects 1990* (UN, 1991).

Episcopal Church Liturgical Colors and Calendar

Source: The Episcopal Church Center, New York City

White—from Christmas Day through the First Sunday after Epiphany; Maundy Thursday (as an alternative to crimson at the Eucharist); from the Vigil of Easter to the Day of Pentecost (Whitsunday); Trinity Sunday; Feasts of the Lord (except Holy Cross Day); the Confession of St. Peter; the Conversion of St. Paul; St. Joseph; St. Mary Magdalene; St. Mary the Virgin; St. Michael and All Angels; All Saints' Day; St. John the Evangelist; memorials of other saints who were not martyred; Independence Day and Thanksgiving Day; weddings and funerals. **Red**—the Day of Pentecost; Holy Cross Day; feasts of apostles and evangelists (except those listed above); feasts and memorials of martyrs (including Holy Innocents' Day). **Violet**—Advent and Lent. **Crimson** (dark red)—Holy Week. **Green**—the seasons after Epiphany and after Pentecost. **Black**—optional alternative for funerals. Alternative colors used in some churches: **Blue**—Advent; **Lenten White**—Ash Wednesday to Palm Sunday.

In the Episcopal Church the days of fasting are Ash Wednesday and Good Friday. Other days of special devotion (abstinence) are the 40 days of Lent and all Fridays of the year, except those in Christmas and Easter seasons and any Feasts of the Lord that occur on a Friday or during Lent. Ember Days (optional) are days of prayer for the church's ministry. They fall on the Wednesday, Friday, and Saturday after the first Sunday in Lent, the Day of Pentecost, Holy Cross Day, and the Third Sunday of Advent. Rogation Days (also optional) are the 3 days before Ascension Day and are days of prayer for God's blessing on the crops, on commerce and industry, and for the conservation of the earth's resources.

Days, etc.	1994	1995	1996	1997	1998
Golden Number	19	1	2	3	4
Sunday Letter	B	A	GF	E	D
Sundays after Epiphany	6	8	7	5	7
Ash Wednesday	Feb. 16	Mar. 1	Feb. 21	Feb. 12	Feb. 25
First Sunday in Lent	Feb. 20	Mar. 5	Feb. 25	Feb. 16	Feb. 29
Passion/Palm Sunday	Mar. 27	Apr. 9	Mar. 31	Mar. 23	Apr. 5
Good Friday	Apr. 1	Apr. 14	Apr. 5	Mar. 28	Apr. 10
Easter Day	Apr. 3	Apr. 16	Apr. 7	Mar. 30	Apr. 12
Ascension Day	May 12	May 25	May 16	May 8	May 21
The Day of Pentecost	May 22	June 4	May 26	May 18	May 31
Trinity Sunday	May 29	June 11	June 2	May 25	June 7
Numbered Proper of 2 Pentecost	#5	#6	#5	#4	#6
First Sunday of Advent	Nov. 27	Dec. 3	Dec. 1	Nov. 30	Nov. 29

Greek Orthodox Movable Ecclesiastical Dates

	1994	1995	1996	1997	1998
Triódion begins	February 20	February 12	February 4	February 16	February 8
Sat. of Souls	March 5	February 25	February 17	March 1	February 21
Meat Fare	March 6	February 26	February 18	March 2	February 22
2d Sat. of Souls	March 12	March 4	February 24	March 8	February 28
Lent Begins	March 14	March 6	February 26	March 10	March 2
St. Theodore 3d Sat. of Souls	March 19	March 11	March 2	March 15	March 7
Sunday of Orthodoxy	March 20	March 12	March 3	March 16	March 8
Sat. of Lazarus	April 23	April 15	April 6	April 19	April 11
Palm Sunday	April 24	April 16	April 7	April 20	April 12
Holy (Good) Friday	April 29	April 21	April 12	April 25	April 17
Western Easter	April 3	April 16	April 7	March 30	April 12
Orthodox Easter	May 1	April 23	April 14	April 27	April 19
Ascension	June 9	June 1	May 23	June 5	May 28
Sat. of Souls	June 18	June 10	June 1	June 14	June 6
Pentecost	June 19	June 11	June 2	June 15	June 7
All Saints	June 26	June 18	June 9	June 22	June 14

Islamic (Muslim) Calendar 1994-99 (1415-19)

The Islamic calendar is a lunar reckoning from the year of the *hegira* AD 622, when Muhammad moved from Mecca to Medina. It runs in cycles of 30 years, of which the 2d, 5th, 7th, 10th, 13th, 16th, 18th, 21st, 24th, 26th, and 29th are leap years; 1415 is the 5th year of the cycle. Common years have 354 days, leap years 355, the extra day being added to the last month, Dhû al-Hijjah. Except for this case, the 12 months beginning with Muharram have alternately 30 and 29 days.

	1994-95 (1415)		1995-96 (1416)		1996-97 (1417)		1997-98 (1418)		1998-99 (1419)	
Muharram (New Year)	June 10	Fri.	May 21	Sun.	May 19	Sun.	May 9	Fri.	Apr. 28	Tue.
Safar	July 10	Sun.	June 30	Fri.	June 18	Tue.	June 8	Sun.	May 28	Thu.
Rabia I	Aug. 8	Mon.	July 29	Sat.	July 17	Wed.	July 7	Mon.	June 26	Fri.
Rabia II	Sept. 7	Wed.	Aug. 28	Mon.	Aug. 16	Fri.	Aug. 6	Wed.	July 26	Sun.
Jamada I	Oct. 6	Thu.	Sept. 26	Tue.	Sept. 14	Sat.	Sept. 4	Thu.	Aug. 24	Mon.
Jamada II	Nov. 5	Sat.	Oct. 26	Thu.	Oct. 14	Mon.	Oct. 4	Sat.	Sept. 23	Wed.
Rajab	Dec. 12	Mon.	Nov. 24	Fri.	Nov. 12	Tue.	Nov. 2	Sun.	Oct. 22	Thu.
Shabân	Jan. 3	Tue.	Dec. 24	Sun.	Dec. 12	Thu.	Dec. 2	Tue.	Nov. 21	Sat.
Rhamadân	Feb. 2	Thu.	Jan. 22	Mon.	Jan. 10	Fri.	Dec. 31	Wed.	Dec. 20	Sun.
Shawwâi	Mar. 3	Fri.	Feb. 21	Wed.	Feb. 9	Sun.	Jan. 30	Fri.	Jan. 19	Tue.
Dhû al-Qa'da	Apr. 4	Tue.	Mar. 21	Thu.	Mar. 10	Mon.	Feb. 27	Fri.	Feb. 17	Wed.
Dhû al-Hijjah	May 1	Mon.	Apr. 20	Sat.	Apr. 9	Wed.	Mar. 30	Mon.	Mar. 19	Fri.

Jewish Holy Days, Festivals, and Fasts

	1994 (5754-55)	1995 (5755-56)	1996 (5756-57)	1997 (5757-58)	1998 (5758-59)
Tu B'Shvat	Jan. 27 Thu.	Jan. 16 Mon.	Feb. 5 Mon.	Jan. 23 Thu.	Feb. 11 Wed.
Ta'anis Esther (Fast of Esther)	Feb. 24 Thu.	Mar. 15 Wed.	Mar. 4 Mon.	Mar. 20 Thu.*	Mar. 11 Wed.
Purim	Feb. 25 Fri.	Mar. 16 Thu.	Mar. 5 Tue.	Mar. 23 Sun.	Mar. 12 Thu.
Passover	Mar. 27 Sun.	Apr. 15 Sat.	Apr. 4 Thu.	Apr. 22 Tue.	Apr. 11 Sat.
	Apr. 3 Sun.	Apr. 22 Sat.	Apr. 11 Thu.	Apr. 29 Tue.	Apr. 18 Sat.
Lag B'Omer	Apr. 29 Fri.	May 18 Thu.	May 7 Tue.	May 25 Sun.	May 14 Thu.
Shavuot	May 16 Mon.	June 4 Sun	May 24 Fri.	June 11 Sun.	May 31 Sun.
	May 17 Tue.	June 5 Mon.	May 25 Sat.	June 12 Mon.	June 1 Mon.
Fast of the 17th Day of Tammuz	June 26 Sun.	July 16 Sun.*	July 4 Thu.	July 22 Tue.	July 12 Sun.*
Fast of the 9th Day of Av	July 17 Sun.	Aug. 6 Sun.	July 25 Thu.	Aug. 12 Tue.	Aug. 2 Sun.*
Rosh Hashanah	Sept. 6 Tue.	Sept. 25 Mon.	Sept. 14 Sat.	Oct. 2 Thu.	Sept. 21 Mon.
	Sept 7 Wed.	Sept. 26 Tue.	Sept. 15 Sun.	Oct. 3 Fri.	Sept. 22 Tue.
Fast of Gedalya	Sept. 8 Thu.	Sept. 27 Wed.	Sept. 16 Mon.	Oct. 5 Sun.*	Sept. 23 Wed.
Yom Kippur	Sept. 15 Thu.	Oct. 4 Wed.	Sept 23 Mon.	Oct. 11 Sat.	Sept. 30 Wed.
Sukkot	Sept. 20 Tue.	Oct. 9 Mon.	Sept. 28 Sat.	Oct. 16 Thu.	Oct. 5 Mon.
	Sept. 26 .Mon.	Oct. 15 Sun.	Oct. 4 Fri.	Oct. 22 Wed	Oct. 11 Sun.
Shmini Atzeret	Sept. 27 Tue.	Oct. 16 Mon.	Oct. 5 Sat.	Oct. 23 Thu.	Oct. 12 Mon.
	Sept. 28 Wed.	Oct. 17 Tue.	Oct. 6 Sun.	Oct. 24 Fri.	Oct. 13 Tue.
Chanukah	Nov. 28 Mon.	Dec. 18 Mon.	Dec. 6 Fri.	Dec. 24 Wed.	Dec. 14 Mon.
	Dec. 5 Mon.	Dec. 25 Mon.	Dec. 13 Fri.	Dec. 31 Wed.	Dec. 21 Mon.
Fast of the 10th of Tevet	Dec. 13 Tue.	Jan. 2 Tue.	Dec. 20 Fri.	Jan. 8 Thu.	Dec. 29 Tue.

The months of the Jewish year are: 1) Tishri; 2) Cheshvan (also Marcheshvan); 3) Kislev; 4) Tebet (also Tebeth); 5) Shebat (also Shebhat); 6) Adar; 6a) Adar Sheni (II) added in leap years; 7) Nisan; 8) Iyar; 9) Sivan; 10) Tammuz; 11) Av (also Abh); 12) Elul. All Jewish holy days, etc., begin at sunset on the previous day. *Date changed to avoid Sabbath.

Ash Wednesday and Easter Sunday

Year	Ash Wed.	Easter Sunday	Year	Ash Wed.	Easter Sunday	Year	Ash Wed.	Easter Sunday	Year	Ash Wed.	Easter Sunday
1901	Feb. 20	Apr. 7	1951	Feb. 7	Mar. 25	2001	Feb. 28	Apr. 15	2051	Feb. 15	Apr. 2
1902	Feb. 12	Mar. 30	1952	Feb. 27	Apr. 13	2002	Feb. 13	Mar. 31	2052	Mar. 6	Apr. 21
1903	Feb. 25	Apr. 12	1953	Feb. 18	Apr. 5	2003	Mar. 5	Apr. 20	2053	Feb. 19	Apr. 6
1904	Feb. 17	Apr. 3	1954	Mar. 3	Apr. 18	2004	Feb. 25	Apr. 11	2054	Feb. 11	Mar. 29
1905	Mar. 8	Apr. 23	1955	Feb. 23	Apr. 10	2005	Feb. 9	Mar. 27	2055	Mar. 3	Apr. 18
1906	Feb. 28	Apr. 15	1956	Feb. 15	Apr. 1	2006	Mar. 1	Apr. 16	2056	Feb. 16	Apr. 2
1907	Feb. 13	Mar. 31	1957	Mar. 6	Apr. 21	2007	Feb. 21	Apr. 8	2057	Mar. 7	Apr. 22
1908	Mar. 4	Apr. 19	1958	Feb. 19	Apr. 6	2008	Feb. 6	Mar. 23	2058	Feb. 27	Apr. 14
1909	Feb. 24	Apr. 11	1959	Feb. 11	Mar. 29	2009	Feb. 25	Apr. 12	2059	Feb. 12	Mar. 30
1910	Feb. 9	Mar. 27	1960	Mar. 2	Apr. 17	2010	Feb. 17	Apr. 4	2060	Mar. 3	Apr. 18
1911	Mar. 1	Apr. 16	1961	Feb. 15	Apr. 2	2011	Mar. 9	Apr. 24	2061	Feb. 23	Apr. 10
1912	Feb. 21	Apr. 7	1962	Mar. 7	Apr. 22	2012	Feb. 22	Apr. 8	2062	Feb. 8	Mar. 26
1913	Feb. 5	Mar. 23	1963	Feb. 27	Apr. 14	2013	Feb. 13	Mar. 31	2063	Feb. 28	Apr. 15
1914	Feb. 25	Apr. 12	1964	Feb. 12	Mar. 29	2014	Mar. 5	Apr. 20	2064	Feb. 20	Apr. 6
1915	Feb. 17	Apr. 4	1965	Mar. 3	Apr. 18	2015	Feb. 18	Apr. 5	2065	Feb. 11	Mar. 29
1916	Mar. 8	Apr. 23	1966	Feb. 23	Apr. 10	2016	Feb. 10	Mar. 27	2066	Feb. 24	Apr. 11
1917	Feb. 21	Apr. 8	1967	Feb. 8	Mar. 26	2017	Mar. 1	Apr. 16	2067	Feb. 16	Apr. 3
1918	Feb. 13	Mar. 31	1968	Feb. 28	Apr. 14	2018	Feb. 14	Apr. 1	2068	Mar. 7	Apr. 22
1919	Mar. 5	Apr. 20	1969	Feb. 19	Apr. 6	2019	Mar. 6	Apr. 21	2069	Feb. 27	Apr. 14
1920	Feb. 18	Apr. 4	1970	Feb. 11	Mar. 29	2020	Feb. 26	Apr. 12	2070	Feb. 12	Mar. 30
1921	Feb. 9	Mar. 27	1971	Feb. 24	Apr. 11	2021	Feb. 17	Apr. 4	2071	Mar. 4	Apr. 19
1922	Mar. 1	Apr. 16	1972	Feb. 16	Apr. 2	2022	Mar. 2	Apr. 17	2072	Feb. 24	Apr. 10
1923	Feb. 14	Apr. 1	1973	Mar. 7	Apr. 22	2023	Feb. 22	Apr. 9	2073	Feb. 8	Mar. 26
1924	Mar. 5	Apr. 20	1974	Feb. 27	Apr. 14	2024	Feb. 14	Mar. 31	2074	Feb. 28	Apr. 15
1925	Feb. 25	Apr. 12	1975	Feb. 12	Mar. 30	2025	Mar. 5	Apr. 20	2075	Feb. 20	Apr. 7
1926	Feb. 17	Apr. 4	1976	Mar. 3	Apr. 18	2026	Feb. 18	Apr. 5	2076	Mar. 4	Apr. 19
1927	Mar. 2	Apr. 17	1977	Feb. 23	Apr. 10	2027	Feb. 10	Mar. 28	2077	Feb. 24	Apr. 11
1928	Feb. 22	Apr. 8	1978	Feb. 8	Mar. 26	2028	Mar. 1	Apr. 16	2078	Feb. 16	Apr. 3
1929	Feb. 13	Mar. 31	1979	Feb. 28	Apr. 15	2029	Feb. 14	Apr. 1	2079	Mar. 8	Apr. 23
1930	Mar. 5	Apr. 20	1980	Feb. 20	Apr. 6	2030	Mar. 6	Apr. 21	2080	Feb. 21	Apr. 7
1931	Feb. 18	Apr. 5	1981	Mar. 4	Apr. 19	2031	Feb. 26	Apr. 13	2081	Feb. 12	Mar. 30
1932	Feb. 10	Mar. 27	1982	Feb. 24	Apr. 11	2032	Feb. 11	Mar. 28	2082	Mar. 4	Apr. 19
1933	Mar. 1	Apr. 16	1983	Feb. 16	Apr. 3	2033	Mar. 2	Apr. 17	2083	Feb. 17	Apr. 4
1934	Feb. 14	Apr. 1	1984	Mar. 7	Apr. 22	2034	Feb. 22	Apr. 9	2084	Feb. 9	Mar. 26
1935	Mar. 6	Apr. 21	1985	Feb. 20	Apr. 7	2035	Feb. 7	Mar. 25	2085	Feb. 28	Apr. 15
1936	Feb. 26	Apr. 12	1986	Feb. 12	Mar. 30	2036	Feb. 27	Apr. 13	2086	Feb. 13	Mar. 31
1937	Feb. 10	Mar. 28	1987	Mar. 4	Apr. 19	2037	Feb. 18	Apr. 5	2087	Mar. 5	Apr. 20
1938	Mar. 2	Apr. 17	1988	Feb. 17	Apr. 3	2038	Mar. 10	Apr. 25	2088	Feb. 25	Apr. 11
1939	Feb. 22	Apr. 9	1989	Feb. 8	Mar. 26	2039	Feb. 23	Apr. 10	2089	Feb. 16	Apr. 3
1940	Feb. 7	Mar. 24	1990	Feb. 28	Apr. 15	2040	Feb. 15	Apr. 1	2090	Mar. 1	Apr. 16
1941	Feb. 26	Apr. 13	1991	Feb. 13	Mar. 31	2041	Mar. 6	Apr. 21	2091	Feb. 21	Apr. 8
1942	Feb. 18	Apr. 5	1992	Mar. 4	Apr. 19	2042	Feb. 19	Apr. 6	2092	Feb. 13	Mar. 30
1943	Mar. 10	Apr. 25	1993	Feb. 24	Apr. 11	2043	Feb. 11	Mar. 29	2093	Feb. 25	Apr. 12
1944	Feb. 23	Apr. 9	1994	Feb. 16	Apr. 3	2044	Mar. 2	Apr. 17	2094	Feb. 17	Apr. 4
1945	Feb. 14	Apr. 1	1995	Mar. 1	Apr. 16	2045	Feb. 22	Apr. 9	2095	Mar. 9	Apr. 24
1946	Mar. 6	Apr. 21	1996	Feb. 21	Apr. 7	2046	Feb. 7	Mar. 25	2096	Feb. 29	Apr. 15
1947	Feb. 19	Apr. 6	1997	Feb. 12	Mar. 30	2047	Feb. 27	Apr. 14	2097	Feb. 13	Mar. 31
1948	Feb. 11	Mar. 28	1998	Feb. 25	Apr. 12	2048	Feb. 19	Apr. 5	2098	Mar. 5	Apr. 20
1949	Mar. 2	Apr. 17	1999	Feb. 17	Apr. 4	2049	Mar. 3	Apr. 18	2099	Feb. 25	Apr. 12
1950	Feb. 22	Apr. 9	2000	Mar. 8	Apr. 23	2050	Feb. 23	Apr. 10	2100	Feb. 10	Mar. 28

The Ten Commandments

According to Judeo-Christian tradition, as related in the Bible, the Ten Commandments were revealed by God to Moses and form the basic moral component of God's covenant with Israel. The Ten Commandments appear in 2 places in the Old Testament—Exodus 20:1-17 and Deuteronomy 5:6-21; the phrasing is similar but not identical. Most Protestant, Anglican, and Orthodox Christians enumerate the commandments differently from Roman Catholics and Lutherans. Jewish tradition considers the introduction, "I am the Lord..." the first commandment and makes the prohibition against "other gods" and idolatry the second.

Following is abridged text of the Ten Commandments in Exodus 20:1-17

I. I am the Lord your God, who brought you out of the land of Egypt, out of the house of bondage. You shall have no other gods before me.
II. You shall not make for yourself a graven image. You shall not bow down to them or serve them.
III. You shall not take the name of the Lord your God in vain.
IV. Remember the sabbath day, to keep it holy.
V. Honor your father and your mother.
VI. You shall not kill.
VII. You shall not commit adultery.
VIII. You shall not steal.
IX. You shall not bear false witness against your neighbor.
X. You shall not covet.

Books of the Bible

Old Testament—Standard Protestant English Versions

Genesis	II Chronicles	Daniel
Exodus	Ezra	Hosea
Leviticus	Nehemiah	Joel
Numbers	Esther	Amos
Deuteronomy	Job	Obadiah
Joshua	Psalms	Jonah
Judges	Proverbs	Micah
Ruth	Ecclesiastes	Nahum
I Samuel	Song of Solomon	Habakkuk
II Samuel	Isaiah	Zephaniah
I Kings	Jeremiah	Haggai
II Kings	Lamentations	Zechariah
I Chronicles	Ezekiel	Malachi

New Testament—Standard Protestant English Versions

Matthew	Ephesians	Hebrews
Mark	Phillippians	James
Luke	Colossians	I Peter
John	I Thessalonians	II Peter
Acts	II Thessalonians	I John
Romans	I Timothy	II John
I Corinthians	II Timothy	III John
II Corinthians	Titus	Jude
Galatians	Philemon	Revelation

Catholic Versions

All the Catholic books of the Bible (Old Testament and New Testament) have the same names as Protestant Versions. A Catholic Version (and Pre-Reformation Bibles) simply has the books **Tobit, Judith, Wisdom, Sirach (Ecclesiasticus), Baruch, I Maccabees,** and **II Maccabees** as part of the Old Testament. These books are called Deuterocanonical Books.

Roman Catholic Hierarchy

Source: U.S. Catholic Conference; as of mid-1994

Supreme Pontiff

At the head of the Roman Catholic Church is the Supreme Pontiff, Pope John Paul II, Karol Wojtyla, born at Wadowice (Krakow), Poland, May 18, 1920; ordained priest Nov. 1, 1946; appointed bishop July 4, 1958; promoted to archbishop of Krakow Jan. 13, 1964; proclaimed cardinal June 26, 1967; elected pope as successor of Pope John Paul I Oct. 16, 1978; installed as pope Oct. 22, 1978.

College of Cardinals

Members of the Sacred College of Cardinals are chosen by the pope to be his chief assistants and advisers in the administration of the church. Among their duties is the election of the pope when the Holy See becomes vacant.

In its present form, the College of Cardinals dates from the 12th century. The first cardinals, from about the 6th century, were deacons and priests of the leading churches of Rome and were bishops of neighboring dioceses. The title of cardinal was limited to members of the college in 1567. The number of cardinals was set at 70 in 1586 by Pope Sixtus V. From 1959 Pope John XXIII began to increase the number; however, the number of cardinals eligible to participate in papal elections was limited to 120. There were lay cardinals until 1918, when the Code of Canon Law specified that all cardinals must be priests. Pope John XXIII in 1962 established that all cardinals must be bishops. The first age limits were set in 1971 by Pope Paul VI, who decreed that at age 80 cardinals must retire from curial departments and offices and from participation in papal elections. They continue as members of the college, with all rights and privileges.

U.S. Cardinals

Name	Office	Born	Named Cardinal
Baum, William W.	Major Penitentiary of Apostolic Penitentiary, the Vatican	1926	1976
Bernardin, Joseph L.	Archbishop of Chicago	1928	1983
Bevilacqua, Anthony J.	Archbishop of Philadelphia	1923	1991
Carberry, John J. *	Archbishop emeritus of St. Louis	1904	1969
Hickey, James A.	Archbishop of Washington	1920	1988
Krol, John J. *	Archbishop emeritus of Philadelphia	1910	1967
Law, Bernard F.	Archbishop of Boston	1931	1985
Mahony, Roger	Archbishop of Los Angeles	1936	1991
O'Connor, John J.	Archbishop of New York	1920	1985
Szoka, Edmund C.	Pres. of Prefecture of Economic Affairs of Holy See, the Vatican	1927	1988

* Indicates cardinals ineligible to take part in papal elections.

Chronological List of Popes

Source: Annuario Pontificio. Table lists year of accession of each pope.

The Roman Catholic Church names the Apostle Peter as founder of the church in Rome. He arrived there c. 42, was martyred there c. 67, and was raised to sainthood.

The pope's temporal title is: Sovereign of the State of Vatican City.

The pope's spiritual titles are: Bishop of Rome, Vicar of Jesus Christ, Successor of St. Peter, Prince of the Apostles, Supreme Pontiff of the Universal Church, Patriarch of the West, Primate of Italy, Archbishop and Metropolitan of the Roman Province.

The names of antipopes are in *italics.* Antipopes were illegitimate claimants of or pretenders to the papal throne.

Year	Pope
	St. Peter
67	St. Linus
76	St. Anacletus or Cletus
88	St. Clement I
97	St. Evaristus
105	St. Alexander I
115	St. Sixtus I
125	St. Telesphorus
136	St. Hyginus
140	St. Pius I
155	St. Anicetus
166	St. Soter
175	St. Eleutherius
189	St. Victor I
199	St. Zephyrinus
217	St. Callistus I
217	*St. Hippolytus*
222	St. Urban I
230	St. Pontian
235	St. Anterus
236	St. Fabian
251	St. Cornelius
251	*Novatian*
253	St. Lucius I
254	St. Stephen I
257	St. Sixtus II
259	St. Dionysius
269	St. Felix I
275	St. Eutychian
283	St. Caius
296	St. Marcellinus
308	St. Marcellus I
309	St. Eusebius
311	St. Melchiades
314	St. Sylvester I
336	St. Marcus
337	St. Julius I
352	Liberius
355	*Felix II*
366	St. Damasus I
366	*Ursinus*
384	St. Siricius
399	St. Anastasius I
401	St. Innocent I
417	St. Zosimus
418	St. Boniface I
418	*Eulalius*
422	St. Celestine I
432	St. Sixtus III
440	St. Leo I
461	St. Hilary
468	St. Simplicius
483	St. Felix III (II)
492	St. Gelasius I
496	Anastasius II
498	St. Symmachus
498	*Lawrence (501-505)*
514	St. Hormisdas
523	St. John I, Martyr
526	St. Felix IV (III)
530	Boniface II
530	*Dioscorus*
533	John II
535	St. Agapitus I
536	St. Silverius, Martyr
537	Vigilius
556	Pelagius I
561	John III
575	Benedict I
579	Pelagius II
590	St. Gregory I
604	Sabinian
607	Boniface III
608	St. Boniface IV
615	St. Deusdedit or Adeodatus
619	Boniface V
625	Honorius I
640	Severinus
642	Theodore I
649	St. Martin I, Martyr
654	St. Eugene I
657	St. Vitalian
672	Adeodatus II
676	Donus
678	St. Agatho
682	St. Leo II
684	St. Benedict II
685	John V
686	Conon
687	*Theodore*
687	*Paschal*
687	St. Sergius I
701	John VI
705	John VII
708	Sisinnius
708	Constantine
715	St. Gregory II
731	St. Gregory III
741	St. Zachary
752	Stephen II (III)
757	St. Paul I
767	*Constantine*
768	*Philip*
768	Stephen III (IV)
772	Adrian I
795	St. Leo III
816	Stephen IV (V)
817	St. Paschal I
824	Eugene II
827	Valentine
827	Gregory IV
844	*John*
844	Sergius II
847	St. Leo IV
855	Benedict III
855	*Anastasius*
858	St. Nicholas I
867	Adrian II
872	John VIII
882	Marinus I
884	St. Adrian III
885	Stephen V (VI)
891	Formosus
896	Boniface VI
896	Stephen VI (VII)
897	Romanus
897	Theodore II
898	John IX
900	Benedict IV
903	Leo V
903	*Christopher*
904	Sergius III
911	Anastasius III
913	Landus
914	John X
928	Leo VI
928	Stephen VII (VIII)
931	John XI
936	Leo VII
939	Stephen VIII (IX)
942	Marinus II
946	Agapitus II
955	John XII
963	Leo VIII
964	Benedict V
965	John XIII
973	Benedict VI
974	*Boniface VII*
974	Benedict VII
983	John XIV
985	John XV
996	Gregory V
997	*John XVI*
999	Sylvester II
1003	John XVII
1004	John XVIII
1009	Sergius IV
1012	Benedict VIII
1012	*Gregory*
1024	John XIX
1032	Benedict IX
1045	Sylvester III
1045	Benedict IX
1045	Gregory VI
1046	Clement II
1047	Benedict IX
1048	Damasus II
1049	St. Leo IX
1055	Victor II
1057	Stephen IX (X)
1058	*Benedict X*
1059	Nicholas II
1061	Alexander II
1061	*Honorius II*
1073	St. Gregory VII
1080	*Clement III*
1086	Bl. Victor III
1088	Bl. Urban II
1099	Paschal II
1100	*Theodoric*
1102	*Albert*
1105	*Sylvester IV*
1118	Gelasius II
1118	*Gregory VIII*
1119	Callistus II
1124	Honorius II
1124	*Celestine II*
1130	Innocent II
1130	*Anacletus II*
1138	*Victor IV*
1143	Celestine II
1144	Lucius II
1145	Bl. Eugene III
1153	Anastasius IV
1154	Adrian IV
1159	Alexander III
1159	*Victor IV*
1164	*Paschal III*
1168	*Callistus III*
1179	*Innocent III*
1181	Lucius III
1185	Urban III
1187	Clement III
1187	Gregory VIII
1191	Celestine III
1198	Innocent III
1216	Honorius III
1227	Gregory IX
1241	Celestine IV
1243	Innocent IV
1254	Alexander IV
1261	Urban IV
1265	Clement IV
1271	Bl. Gregory X
1276	Bl. Innocent V
1276	Adrian V
1276	John XXI
1277	Nicholas III
1281	Martin IV
1285	Honorius IV
1288	Nicholas IV
1294	St. Celestine V
1294	Boniface VIII
1303	Bl. Benedict XI
1305	Clement V
1316	John XXII
1328	*Nicholas V*
1334	Benedict XII
1342	Clement VI
1352	Innocent VI
1362	Bl. Urban V
1370	Gregory XI
1378	Urban VI
1378	*Clement VII*
1389	Boniface IX
1394	*Benedict XIII*
1404	Innocent VII
1406	Gregory XII
1409	*Alexander V*
1410	*John XXIII*
1417	Martin V
1431	Eugene IV
1439	*Felix V*
1447	Nicholas V
1455	Callistus III
1458	Pius II
1464	Paul II
1471	Sixtus IV
1484	Innocent VIII
1492	Alexander VI
1503	Pius III
1503	Julius II
1513	Leo X
1522	Adrian VI
1523	Clement VII
1534	Paul III
1550	Julius III
1555	Marcellus II
1555	Paul IV
1559	Pius IV
1566	St. Pius V
1572	Gregory XIII
1585	Sixtus V
1590	Urban VII
1590	Gregory XIV
1591	Innocent IX
1592	Clement VIII
1605	Leo XI
1605	Paul V
1621	Gregory XV
1623	Urban VIII
1644	Innocent X
1655	Alexander VII
1667	Clement IX
1670	Clement X
1676	Bl. Innocent XI
1689	Alexander VIII
1691	Innocent XII
1700	Clement XI
1721	Innocent XIII
1724	Benedict XIII
1730	Clement XII
1740	Benedict XIV
1758	Clement XIII
1769	Clement XIV
1775	Pius VI
1800	Pius VII
1823	Leo XII
1829	Pius VIII
1831	Gregory XVI
1846	Pius IX
1878	Leo XIII
1903	St. Pius X
1914	Benedict XV
1922	Pius XI
1939	Pius XII
1958	John XXIII
1963	Paul VI
1978	John Paul I
1978	John Paul II

Census of Religious Groups in Canada

Source: *1994 Yearbook of American and Canadian Churches*

Number of churches in parentheses; groups with fewer than 1,000 members not included. *Indicates church declines to publish membership figures.

Religious Body	Members
Anglican Church of Canada (1,767)	848,256
Antiochian Orthodox Christian Archdiocese of North America (13)	100,000
Apostolic Church in Canada (14)	1,600
Apostolic Church of Pentecost of Canada Inc. (129)	14,500
Associated Gospel Churches (126)	9,284
Baha'i Faith (398)	27,000
Baptist Convention of Ontario and Quebec (372)	44,713
Baptist General Conference of Canada (70)	6,066
Baptist Union of Western Canada (162)	20,660
Brethren in Christ Church, Canadian Conference (39)	3,173
Canadian and American Reformed Churches (44)	13,536
Canadian Baptist Federation (1,150)	131,349
Canadian Convention of Southern Baptists (104)	6,743
Canadian Yearly Meeting of the Religious Society of Friends (23)	1,095
Central Canada Baptist Conference (37)	*
Christian and Missionary Alliance in Canada (348)	80,681
Christian Brethren (also known as Plymouth Brethren) (60)	*
Christian Church (Disciples of Christ) in Canada (35)	4,066
Christian Churches and Churches of Christ in Canada (140)	7,500
Christian Reformed Church in North America (240)	86,281
Church of God (Anderson, IN) (50)	3,421
Church of God (Cleveland, TN) (99)	6,670
Church of God of Prophecy in Canada (28)	4,232
Church of Jesus Christ of Latter-day Saints in Canada (391)	130,000
Church of the Nazarene (161)	10,915
Churches of Christ in Canada (147)	7,181
Conference of Mennonites in Canada (150)	37,008
Coptic Church in Canada (12)	*
Estonian Evangelical Lutheran Church (13)	6,478
Evangelical Baptist Churches in Canada, Fellowship of (500)	61,572
Evangelical Church in Canada (46)	3,688
Evangelical Covenant Church in Canada (23)	1,278
Evangelical Free Church of Canada (133)	13,699
Evangelical Lutheran Church in Canada (656)	203,937
Evangelical Mennonite Conference (49)	6,358
Evangelical Mennonite Mission Conference (27)	3,389
Foursquare Gospel Church of Canada (53)	2,354
Free Methodist Church in Canada (147)	7,479
Greek Orthodox Diocese of Toronto (Canada) (58)	230,000
Italian Pentecostal Church of Canada (21)	3,300
Jehovah's Witnesses (1,312)	106,052
Latvian Evangelical Lutheran Church in America (8)	2,380
Lutheran Church–Canada (326)	79,645
Mennonite Brethren Churches, Canadian Conference of (193)	27,597
Metropolitan Community Churches, Universal Fellowship (12)	1,500
Missionary Church of Canada (92)	6,431
Moravian Church in America, Northern Province, Canadian District of (9)	2,126
Netherlands Reformed Congregations of North America (9)	4,762
North American Baptist Conference (127)	17,943
Old Order Amish Church (17)	*
Open Bible Standard Churches of Canada (4)	1,000
Orthodox Church in America (Canada Section) (59)	*
Pentecostal Assemblies of Canada (976)	194,972
Pentecostal Assemblies of Newfoundland (160)	33,700
Presbyterian Church in Canada (998)	233,335
Reformed Church in Canada (42)	6,236
Reformed Doukhobors, Christian Community and Brotherhood of (1)	2,108
Reorganized Church of Jesus Christ of Latter Day Saints (82)	11,111
Roman Catholic Church in Canada (11,286)	11,852,350
Romanian Orthodox Episcopate of America (Jackson, MI) (13)	8,600
Russian Orthodox Church in Canada, Patriarchal Parishes (24)	7,000
Salvation Army in Canada (402)	99,658
Seventh-day Adventist Church in Canada (328)	42,083
Ukranian Orthodox Church of Canada (258)	120,000
Union D'Eglises Baptistes Francaises Au Canada (24)	1,169
Unitarian Universalist Association (40)	6,003
United Baptist Convention of the Atlantic Provinces (546)	66,484
United Church of Canada (4,019)	1,984,307
United Pentecostal Church in Canada (213)	*
Wesleyan Church of Canada (82)	5,256

Women and Blacks Enrolled in Seminaries, 1972-93[1]

Source: *Fact Book on Theological Education 1993-94*

	Women			Blacks		
Year	Number of students	Percentage annual change	Percentage of total enrollment	Number of students	Percentage annual change	Percentage of total enrollment
1972	3,358	NA	10.2	1,061	+ 16.9	3.2
1973	4,021	+ 19.7	11.8	1,210	+ 14.0	3.6
1974	5,255	+ 30.7	14.3	1,246	+ 3.0	3.4
1975	6,505	+ 23.8	15.9	1,365	+ 9.6	3.3
1976	7,349	+ 13.0	17.1	1,524	+ 11.6	3.5
1977	8,371	+ 13.9	18.5	1,759	+ 15.4	3.9
1978	8,972	+ 7.2	19.3	1,919	+ 9.1	4.1
1979	10,204	+ 13.7	21.1	2,043	+ 6.5	4.2
1980	10,830	+ 6.1	21.8	2,205	+ 7.9	4.4
1981	11,683	+ 7.9	23.1	2,371	+ 7.5	4.7
1982	12,473	+ 6.8	23.7	2,576	+ 8.6	4.9
1983	13,451	+ 7.8	24.4	2,881	+ 11.8	5.2
1984	14,142	+ 5.1	25.0	2,917	+ 1.2	5.2
1985	14,572	+ 3.0	25.8	3,046	+ 4.4	5.4
1986	14,864	+ 2.0	26.4	3,277	+ 7.6	5.8
1987	15,310	+ 3.0	27.0	3,379	+ 3.1	6.0
1988	16,344	+ 6.8	29.3	3,662	+ 8.4	6.6
1989	16,461	+ 0.7	29.3	3,961	+ 8.2	7.1
1990	17,571	+ 6.7	29.7	4,303	+ 8.6	7.3
1991	18,384	+ 4.6	30.6	4,671	+ 8.6	7.8
1992	19,653	+ 6.9	31.1	5,554	+ 18.9	8.8
1993	19,798	+ 0.7	31.1	5,235	−5.7	8.2

(1) Data cover U.S. and Canadian seminaries that are members of the Assn. of Theological Schools. NA=not available.

The Major World Religions

Source: Reviewed by Anthony Padovano, Ph.D., S.T.D., prof. of lit., Ramapo College, NJ, adj. prof. of theol. and rel. studies, Fordham U., NYC

Buddhism

Founded: About 525 BC, reportedly near Benares, India.
Founder: Gautama Siddhartha (c 563-483), the Buddha, who achieved enlightenment through intense meditation.
Sacred Texts: The Tripitaka, a collection of the Buddha's teachings, rules of monastic life, and philosophical commentaries on the teachings; also a vast body of Buddhist teachings and commentaries, many of which are called *sutras.*
Organization: The basic institution is the *sangha*, or monastic order through which the traditions are passed to each generation. Monastic life tends to be democratic and anti-authoritarian. Large lay organizations have developed in some sects.
Practice: Varies widely according to the sect, and ranges from austere meditation to magical chanting and elaborate temple rites. Many practices, such as exorcism of devils, reflect pre-Buddhist beliefs.
Divisions: A variety of sects grouped into 3 primary branches: Theravada (sole survivor of the ancient Hinayana schools), which emphasizes the importance of pure thought and deed; Mahayana (includes Zen and Soka-gakkai), which ranges from philosophical schools to belief in the saving grace of higher beings or ritual practices and to practical meditative disciplines; and Tantrism, an unusual combination of belief in ritual magic and sophisticated philosophy.
Location: Throughout Asia, from Sri Lanka to Japan. Zen and Soka-gakkai have several thousand adherents in the U.S.
Beliefs: Life is misery and decay, and there is no ultimate reality in it or behind it. The cycle of endless birth and rebirth continues because of desire and attachment to the unreal "self." Right meditation and deeds will end the cycle and achieve Nirvana, the Void, nothingness.

Hinduism

Founded: About 500 BC by Aryan invaders of India where their Vedic religion intermixed with the practices and beliefs of the natives.
Sacred texts: The *Veda,* including the *Upanishads,* a collection of rituals and mythological and philosophical commentaries; a vast number of epic stories about gods, heroes, and saints, including the *Bhagavadgita,* a part of the *Mahabharata,* and the *Ramayana;* and a great variety of other literature.
Organization: None, strictly speaking. Generally, rituals should be performed or assisted by Brahmins, the priestly caste, but in practice simpler rituals can be performed by anyone. Brahmins are the final judges of ritual purity, the vital element in Hindu life. Temples and religious organizations are usually presided over by Brahmins.
Practice: A variety of private rituals, primarily passage rites (for example, initiation, marriage, death, etc.) and daily devotions, and a similar variety of public rites in temples. Of the latter, the *puja,* a ceremonial dinner for a god, is the most common.
Divisions: There is no concept of orthodoxy in Hinduism, which presents a variety of sects, most of them devoted to the worship of one of the many gods. The 3 major living traditions are those devoted to the gods Vishnu and Shiva and to the goddess Shakti; each is divided into further subsects. Numerous folk beliefs and practices, often in amalgamation with the above groups, exist side by side with sophisticated philosophic schools and exotic cults.
Location: Mainly India, Nepal, Malaysia, Guyana, Suriname, Sri Lanka.
Beliefs: There is only one divine principle; the many gods are only aspects of that unity. Life in all its forms is an aspect of the divine, but it appears as a separation from the divine, a meaningless cycle of birth and rebirth (*samsara*) determined by the purity or impurity of past deeds (*karma*). To improve one's *karma* or escape *samsara* by pure acts, thought, and/or devotion is the aim of every Hindu.

Islam

Founded: AD 622 in Medina, Arabian peninsula.
Founder: Muhammad (c 570-632), the Prophet.
Sacred texts: Koran, the words of God; *Hadith,* collections of the sayings of the Prophet.
Organization: Theoretically, the state and religious community are one, administered by a caliph. In practice, Islam is a loose collection of congregations united by a very conservative tradition. Islam is basically egalitarian and nonauthoritarian.
Practice: Every Muslim has 5 duties: to make the profession of faith ("There is no god but Allah ..."), to pray 5 times a day, to give a regular portion of his goods to charity, to fast during the day in the month of Ramadan, and to make at least one pilgrimage to Mecca if possible.
Divisions: The 2 major sects of Islam are the Sunni (orthodox) and the Shia. The Shia believe in 12 *imams,* perfect teachers, who still guide the faithful from Paradise. Shia practice tends toward the ecstatic; however, the Sunni is staid and simple. The Shia affirm human free will; the Sunni are deterministic. The mystic tradition in Islam is Sufism. A Sufi adept is someone who believes he or she has acquired a special inner knowledge direct from Allah.
Location: From the west coast of Africa to the Philippines across a broad band that includes Tanzania, Central Asia and western China, India, Malaysia, and Indonesia. Islam has several million adherents in the U.S.
Beliefs: Strictly monotheistic. God is creator of the universe, omnipotent, just, and merciful. The human being is God's highest creation, but limited and commits sins. Humans are misled by Satan, an evil spirit. God revealed the Koran to Muhammad to guide humans to the truth. Those who repent and sincerely submit to God return to a state of sinlessness. In the end, the sinless go to Paradise, a place of physical and spiritual pleasure, and the wicked burn in Hell.

Judaism

Founded: About 1300 BCE.
Founder: Abraham is regarded as the founding patriarch, but the Torah of Moses is the basic source of the teachings.
Sacred Texts: The 5 books of Moses constitute the written Torah. Special sanctity is also assigned other writings of the Hebrew Bible—the teachings of oral Torah are recorded in the Talmud, in the Midrash, and in various commentaries.
Organization: Originally theocratic, Judaism has evolved a congregational polity. The basic institution is the local synagogue, operated by the congregation and led by a rabbi of their choice. Chief rabbis in France and Great Britain have authority only over those who accept it; in Israel, the 2 chief rabbis have civil authority in family law.
Practice: Among traditional practitioners, almost all areas of life are governed by strict religious discipline. Sabbath and holidays are marked by special observances, and attendance at public worship is regarded as especially important then. The chief annual observances are Passover, celebrating the liberation of the Israelites from Egypt and marked by the ritual Seder meal in the home, and the 10 days from Rosh Hashana (New Year) to Yom Kippur (Day of Atonement), a period of fasting and penitence.
Divisions: Judaism is an unbroken spectrum from ultra conservative to ultra liberal, largely reflecting different points of view regarding the binding character of the prohibitions and duties—particularly the dietary and Sabbath observations—prescribed in the daily life of the Jew.
Location: Almost worldwide, with concentrations in Israel and the U.S.
Beliefs: Strictly monotheistic. God is the creator and absolute ruler of the universe. Men and women are free to choose to rebel against God's rule. God established a particular relationship with the Hebrew people: by obeying a divine law God gave them, they would be a special witness to God's mercy and justice. The emphasis in Judaism is on ethical behavior (and, among the traditional, careful ritual obedience) as the true worship of God.

(See following pages for discussion of Christian denominations.)

Major Christian Denominations:

Italics indicate that area which, generally speaking, most

Source: Reviewed by Anthony Padovano, Ph.D., S.T.D., prof. of lit.,

Denomination	Origins	Organization	Authority	Special rites
Baptists	In radical Reformation objections to infant baptism, demands for church and state separation; John Smyth, English Separatist in 1609; Roger Williams, 1638, Providence, RI.	Congregational; each local church is autonomous.	Scripture; some Baptists, particularly in the South, interpret the Bible literally.	Baptism, usually early teen years and after, by total immersion; Lord's Supper.
Church of Christ (Disciples)	Among evangelical Presbyterians in KY (1804) and PA (1809), in distress over Protestant factionalism and decline of fervor; organized 1832.	Congregational.	*"Where the Scriptures speak, we speak; where the Scriptures are silent, we are silent."*	Adult baptism; Lord's Supper (weekly).
Episcopalians	Henry VIII separated English Catholic Church from Rome, 1534, for political reasons; Protestant Episcopal Church in U.S. founded 1789.	*Bishops, in apostolic succession, are elected by diocesan representatives; part of Anglican Communion, symbolically headed by the Archbishop of Canterbury.*	Scripture as interpreted by tradition, especially *39 Articles* (1563); not dogmatic; tri-annual convention of bishops, priests, and laypeople.	Infant baptism, Eucharist, and other sacraments; sacrament is symbolic, but has real spiritual effect.
Jehovah's Witnesses	1870 in PA by Charles Taze Russell; incorporated as Watch Tower Bible and Tract Society of PA, 1884; name Jehovah's Witnesses adopted, 1931.	A governing body located in NY coordinates worldwide activities; each congregation cared for by a body of elders; each Witness considered a minister.	The Bible.	Baptism by immersion; annual Lord's Meal ceremony.
Lutherans	By Martin Luther in Wittenberg, Germany, 1517; objection to Catholic doctrine of salvation by merit and sale of indulgences; break complete, 1519.	Varies from congregational to episcopal; in U.S. a combination of regional synods and congregational polities is most common.	*Scripture, and tradition as spelled out in Augsburg Confession (1530) and other creeds; these confessions of faith are binding although interpretations vary.*	Infant baptism; Lord's Supper; Christ's true body and blood present "in, with, and under the bread and wine."
Methodists	Rev. John Wesley began movement, 1738, within Church of England; first U.S. denomination, Baltimore, 1784.	Conference and superintendent system; *in United Methodist Church, general superintendents are bishops—not a priestly order, only an office —who are elected for life.*	Scripture as interpreted by tradition, reason, and experience.	Baptism of infants or adults; Lord's Supper commanded; other rites include marriage, ordination, solemnization of personal commitments.
Mormons	In visions of the Angel Moroni by Joseph Smith, 1827, in NY, in which he received new revelation on golden tablets: The Book of Mormon.	Theocratic; all male adults are in priesthood, which culminates in Council of 12 Apostles and 1st Presidency (1st President, 2 counselors).	The Bible, Book of Mormon, *and other revelations to Smith, and certain pronouncements of the 1st Presidency.*	Baptism, at age 8, laying on of hands (which confers the gift of the Holy Spirit); Lord's Supper; temple rites: baptism for the dead, marriage for eternity, others.
Orthodox	Original Christian proselytizing in 1st century; broke with Rome, 1054, after centuries of doctrinal disputes and diverging traditions.	Synods of bishops in autonomous, usually national, churches elect a patriarch, archbishop or metropolitan; these men, as a group, are the heads of the church.	Scripture, tradition, and the first 7 church councils up to Nicaea II in 787; bishops in council have authority in doctrine and policy.	Seven sacraments: infant baptism and anointing, Eucharist (both bread and wine), ordination, penance, anointing of the sick, and marriage.
Pentecostal	In Topeka, KS (1901) and Los Angeles (1906), in reaction to loss of evangelical fervor among Methodists and other denominations.	Originally a movement, not a formal organization, Pentecostalism now has a variety of organized forms and continues also as a movement.	Scripture; individual charismatic leaders, the teachings of the Holy Spirit.	*Spirit baptism, especially as shown in "speaking in tongues"; healing and sometimes exorcism; adult baptism; Lord's Supper.*
Presbyterians	In 16th-cent. Calvinist Reformation; differed with Lutherans over sacraments, church government; John Knox founded Scotch Presbyterian church about 1560.	*Highly structured representational system of ministers and laypersons (presbyters) in local, regional, and national bodies (synods).*	Scripture.	Infant baptism; Lord's Supper; bread and wine symbolize Christ's spiritual presence.
Roman Catholics	Traditionally, by Jesus who named St. Peter the 1st vicar; historically, in early Christian proselytizing and the conversion of imperial Rome in the 4th century.	Hierarchy with supreme power vested in pope elected by cardinals; councils of bishops advise on matters of doctrine and policy.	*The pope, when speaking for the whole church in matters of faith and morals, and tradition, which is partly recorded in scripture and expressed in church councils.*	Seven sacraments: baptism, reconciliation, confirmation, Eucharist, marriage, ordination, and anointing of the sick (unction).
United Church of Christ	*By ecumenical union, 1957, of Congregationalists and Evangelical & Reformed, representing both Calvinist* and *Lutheran traditions.*	Congregational; a General Synod, representative of all congregations, sets general policy.	Scripture.	Infant baptism; Lord's Supper.

How Do They Differ?

distinguishes that denomination from any other.

Ramapo College, NJ, adj. prof. of theol. and rel. studies, Fordham U., NYC

Practice	Ethics	Doctrine	Other	Denomination
Worship style varies from staid to evangelistic; extensive missionary activity.	Usually opposed to alcohol and tobacco; sometimes tends toward a perfectionist ethical standard.	*No creed; true church is of believers only, who are all equal.*	Because no authority can stand between the believer and God, the Baptists are strong supporters of church and state separation.	**Baptists**
Tries to avoid any rite or doctrine not explicitly part of the 1st-century church; some congregations may reject instrumental music.	Some tendency toward perfectionism; increasing interest in social action programs.	Simple New Testament faith; avoids any elaboration not firmly based on Scripture.	Highly tolerant in doctrinal and religious matters; strongly supportive of scholarly education.	**Church of Christ (Disciples)**
Formal, based on *Book of Common Prayer* (1549); services range from austerely simple to highly elaborate.	Tolerant, sometimes permissive; some social action programs.	*Apostles' Creed* is basic; otherwise, considerable variation ranges from rationalist and liberal to acceptance of most Roman Catholic dogma.	Strongly ecumenical, holding talks with all other branches of Christendom.	**Episcopalians**
Meetings are held in Kingdom Halls and members' homes for study and worship; extensive door-to-door visitations.	High moral code; stress marital fidelity and family values; avoid tobacco and blood transfusions.	*God, by his first creation, Christ, will soon destroy all wickedness; 144,000 faithful ones will rule in heaven with Christ over others on a paradise earth.*	Total allegiance only to God's kingdom or heavenly government by Christ, thus remain politically neutral; main periodical *The Watchtower* is printed in 115 languages.	**Jehovah's Witnesses**
Relatively simple, formal liturgy with emphasis on the sermon.	Generally, conservative in personal and social ethics; doctrine of "2 kingdoms" (worldly and holy) supports conservatism in secular affairs.	Salvation by faith alone through grace; Lutheranism has made major contributions to Protestant theology.	Though still somewhat divided along ethnic lines (German, Swede, etc.), main divisions are between fundamentalists and liberals.	**Lutherans**
Worship style varies widely by denomination, local church, geography.	Originally pietist and perfectionist; always strong social activist elements.	No distinctive theological development; 25 Articles abridged from Church of England's 39 not binding.	In 1968, The United Methodist Church was formed by the union of The Methodist Church and The Evangelical United Brethren Church.	**Methodists**
Staid service with hymns, sermon; secret temple ceremonies may be more elaborate; strong missionary activity.	Temperance; strict tithing; combine a strong work ethic with communal self-reliance.	God is a material being; he created the universe out of pre-existing matter; all persons can be saved and many will become divine; most other beliefs are traditionally Christian.	Mormons regard mainline churches as apostate and corrupt; reorganized Church (founded 1860) rejects most Mormon doctrine and practice except the Book of Mormon.	**Mormons**
Elaborate liturgy, usually in the vernacular, though extremely traditional; the liturgy is the essence of Orthodoxy; veneration of icons.	Tolerant; very little social action; divorce, remarriage permitted in some cases; bishops are celibate; priests need not be.	Emphasis on Christ's resurrection, rather than crucifixion; the Holy Spirit proceeds from God the Father only.	Orthodox Church in America originally under Patriarch of Moscow, was granted autonomy in 1970; Greek Orthodox do not recognize this autonomy.	**Orthodox**
Loosely structured service with rousing hymns and sermons, culminating in spirit baptism.	Usually, emphasis on perfectionism with varying degrees of tolerance.	Simple traditional beliefs, usually Protestant, with emphasis on the immediate presence of God in the Holy Spirit.	Once confined to lower-class "holy rollers," Pentecostalism now appears in mainline churches and has established middle-class congregations.	**Pentecostal**
A simple, sober service in which the sermon is central.	Traditionally, a tendency toward strictness with firm church- and self-discipline, otherwise tolerant.	Emphasizes the sovereignty and justice of God; no longer doctrinaire.	Although traces of belief in predestination (that God has foreordained salvation for the "elect") remain, this idea is no longer a central element in Presbyterianism.	**Presbyterians**
Relatively elaborate ritual; wide variety of public and private rites, mass, rosary recitation, processions, novenas.	Theoretically very strict; tolerant in practice on most issues; divorce and remarriage not accepted; celibate clergy, except in Eastern rite.	Highly elaborated; salvation by merit gained through faith; dogmatic; unique development of doctrines surrounding Mary, the mother of Jesus Christ.	Roman Catholicism went through a period of relatively rapid change as a result of Vatican Council II.	**Roman Catholics**
Usually simple services with emphasis on the sermon.	Tolerant; some social action emphasis.	Standard Protestant; *Statement of Faith* (1959) is not binding.	The 2 main churches in the 1957 union represented earlier unions with small groups of almost every Protestant denomination.	**United Church of Christ**

NATIONS OF THE WORLD

As of mid-1994

The nations of the world are listed in alphabetical order. Initials in the following articles include UN (United Nations), OAS (Org. of American States), NATO (North Atlantic Treaty Org.), EU (European Union, or Common Market), OAU (Org. of African Unity), ILO (Intl. Labor Org.), FAO (Food & Agriculture Org.), WHO (World Health Org.), IMF (Intl. Monetary Fund), GATT (General Agreement on Tariffs & Trade), CIS (Commonwealth of Independent States), FY (fiscal year). **Sources:** U.S. Census Bureau: *World Population Profile;* Population Reference Bureau; Central Intelligence Agency: *The World Factbook;* Encyclopaedia Britannica and Encyclopaedia Britannica Book of the Year; International Monetary Fund; International Institute for Strategic Studies: *The Military Balance;* Facts on File; Keesing's Record of World Events; Current History; Collier's Encyclopedia and Collier's Year Book; Encyclopedia Americana Yearbook; Who's Who in the World; U.S. Dept. of State; UN Statistical Yearbook; UN Demographic Yearbook; The Statesman's Year-Book; Funk & Wagnalls New Encyclopedia. Population figures are mid-1994 estimates, unless otherwise noted. Gross Domestic Product/Gross National Product: * denotes purchasing power equivalent. Otherwise, exchange rate conversions were used, which may account for significant variation from year to year. National Budget measures expenditures, unless otherwise noted. Comm. (commercial) vehicles include trucks and buses. All embassy addresses are Wash., DC; area codes (202), unless otherwise noted. Literacy rates are usually based on the ability to read and write on a lower elementary school level. The concept of literacy is changing in the industrialized countries, where literacy is defined as the ability to read instructions necessary for a job or a license. By these standards, illiteracy may be more common than present rates suggest. Per-person figures in communications and health sections are post-1988.

See pages 481-496 for full-color maps and flags.

Afghanistan

Republic of Afghanistan

De Afghanistan Jamhuriat

People: Population: 16,903,000. **Pop. density:** 67 per sq. mi. **Urban:** 18%. **Ethnic groups:** Pashtun 38%, Tajik 25%, Uzbek 6%, Hazara 19%. **Principal languages:** Pashtu 35%, Dari Persian (spoken by Tajiks, Hazaras) 50%, Uzbek (Turkic) 11%. **Religions:** Sunni Muslim 84%, Shi'a Muslim 15%.

Geography: Area: 251,825 sq. mi., about the size of Texas. **Location:** In SW Asia, NW of the Indian subcontinent. **Neighbors:** Pakistan on E, S, Iran on W, Turkmenistan, Tajikistan, Uzbekistan on N; the NE tip touches China. **Topography:** The country is landlocked and mountainous, much of it over 4,000 ft. above sea level. The Hindu Kush Mts. tower 16,000 ft. above Kabul and reach a height of 25,000 ft. to the E. Trade with Pakistan flows through the 35-mile-long Khyber Pass. The climate is dry, with extreme temperatures, and there are large desert regions, though mountain rivers produce intermittent fertile valleys. **Capital:** Kabul. **Cities** (1988 est.): Kabul 1.4 mln.

Government: Type: In transition. **Head of state:** Pres. Burhanuddin Rabbani; in office: June 28, 1992. **Local divisions:** 30 provinces. **Defense:** 15% of GDP (1990).

Economy: Industries: Textiles, furniture, cement. **Chief crops:** Nuts, wheat, fruits. **Minerals:** Copper, coal, zinc, iron. **Other resources:** Wool, hides, karacul pelts. **Arable land:** 12%. **Livestock** (1992): cattle: 1.6 mln.; sheep: 13 mln. **Electricity prod.** (1992): 1.0 bln. kWh. **Labor force:** agriculture supports about 80% of the population.

Finance: Monetary unit: Afghani (Mar. 1994: 50.60 = $1 US). **Gross domestic product** (1989): $3 bln. **Per capita GDP:** $200. **Imports** (1991): $874 mln.; partners: CIS 55%, Jap. 8%. **Exports** (1991): $236 mln.; partners: CIS 72%. **International reserves less gold** (Feb. 1992): $229 mln. **Gold:** 965,000 oz t. **Consumer prices** (change in 1991): 56%.

Transport: Motor vehicles: in use: 31,800 passenger cars, 30,900 comm. vehicles. **Civil aviation::** 121 mln. passenger-mi.

Communications: Television sets: 1 per 181 persons; **Radios:** 1 per 12 persons. **Telephones:** 1 per 443 persons. **Daily newspaper circ.:** 11 per 1,000 pop.

Health: Life expectancy at birth (1994): 46 male; 44 female. **Births** (per 1,000 pop.): 43. **Deaths** (per 1,000 pop.): 19. **Natural increase:** 2.5%. **Hospital beds:** 1 per 2,054 persons. **Physicians:** 1 per 4,797 persons. **Infant mortality** (per 1,000 live births 1994): 156.

Education (1990): **Literacy:** 29%. Over 88% of adults have no formal schooling.

Major International Organizations: UN (World Bank, IMF)

Embassy: 2341 Wyoming Ave. NW 20008; 234-3770.

Afghanistan, occupying a favored invasion route since antiquity, has been variously known as Ariana or Bactria (in ancient times) and Khorasan (in the Middle Ages). Foreign empires alternated rule with local emirs and kings until the 18th century, when a unified kingdom was established. In 1973, a military coup ushered in a republic.

Pro-Soviet leftists took power in a bloody 1978 coup and concluded an economic and military treaty with the USSR. In Dec. 1979 the USSR began a massive airlift into Kabul and backed a new coup, leading to installation of a more pro-Soviet leader. Soviet troops fanned out over Afghanistan and became engaged in a protracted guerrilla war with Muslim rebels, in which some 15,000 Soviet troops reportedly died.

A UN-mediated agreement was signed Apr. 14, 1988, providing for withdrawal of Soviet troops, a neutral Afghan state, and repatriation of refugees. Afghan rebels rejected the pact, vowing to continue fighting while "Soviets and their puppets" remained in Afghanistan. The Soviets completed their troop withdrawal Feb. 15, 1989; fighting between Afghan rebels and government forces ensued.

Communist Pres. Najibullah resigned Apr. 16, 1992, as competing guerrilla forces advanced on Kabul. The rebels achieved power Apr. 28, ending 14 years of Soviet-backed regimes. More than 2 million Afghans had been killed and 6 million had left the country since 1979.

Following the rebel victory there were clashes between moderates and Islamic fundamentalist forces. Burhanuddin Rabbani, a guerrilla leader, became president June 28, 1992. Fierce fighting continued around Kabul and elsewhere in 1993 and 1994. As of mid-1994 there were still more than 3 million Afghan refugees in Pakistan and Iran.

Albania

Republic of Albania

Republika e Shqipërisë

People: Population: 3,374,000. **Pop. density:** 304 per sq. mi. **Urban:** 36%. **Ethnic groups:** Albanians (Gegs in N, Tosks in S) 90%, Greeks 8%. **Principal languages:** Albanian, Greek. **Religions:** Muslim 70%, Greek Orthodox 20%, Roman Catholic 10%.

Geography: Area: 11,100 sq. mi., slightly larger than Maryland. **Location:** On SE coast of Adriatic Sea. **Neighbors:** Greece on S, Yugoslavia on N, Macedonia on E. **Topography:** Apart from a narrow coastal plain, Albania consists of hills and mountains covered with scrub forest, cut by small E-W rivers. **Capital:** Tiranë. **Cities** (1990 est.): Tiranë 243,000; Durres 85,000; Elbasin 83,000.

Government: Type: Democracy. **Head of state:** Pres. Sali Berisha; in office: Apr. 9, 1992. **Head of government:** Prem. Alexander Meksi; in office: Apr. 13, 1992. **Local divisions:** 26 districts. **Defense:** 2.3% of GNP (1992).

Economy: Industries: Cement, textiles, food processing. **Chief crops:** Corn, wheat, cotton, potatoes, tobacco, fruits. **Minerals:** Chromium, coal, oil. **Other resources:** Forests. **Arable land:** 21%. **Livestock** (1991): 650,000 cattle; 1.6 mln. sheep. **Electricity prod.** (1992): 5.0 bln. kWh. **Labor force:** 47% agric.; 53% ind. & comm.

Finance: Monetary unit: Lek (Nov. 1992: 109 = $1 US). **Gross national product** (1992): $2.5 bln.* **Per capita GNP:**

$760. **Imports** (1991): $147 mln.; partners: Czech., Yugoslavia, Rom. **Exports** (1991): $80 mln.; partners: Czech., Yugoslavia, Italy. **National budget** (1991): $1.4 bln.

Chief ports: Durres, Vlone, Sarande.

Communications: Television sets: 1 per 13 persons. **Radios:** 1 per 16 persons. **Daily newspaper circ.:** 42 per 1,000 pop.

Health: Life expectancy at birth (1994): 70 male; 77 female. **Births** (per 1,000 pop.): 22. **Deaths** (per 1,000 pop): 5. **Natural increase:** 1.7%. **Hospital beds:** 1 per 173 persons. **Physicians:** 1 per 585 persons. **Infant mortality** (per 1,000 live births 1994): 30.

Major International Organizations: UN (FAO, WHO).

Education (1989): **Literacy:** 92%. Free and compulsory ages 7-15.

Embassy: 1511 K St. NW 20005; 223-4942.

Ancient Illyria was conquered by Romans, Slavs, and Turks (15th century); the latter Islamized the population. Independent Albania was proclaimed in 1912, republic was formed in 1920. King Zog I ruled 1925-39, until Italy invaded.

Communist partisans took over in 1944, allied Albania with USSR, then broke with USSR in 1960 over de-Stalinization. Strong political alliance with China followed, leading to several billion dollars in aid, which was curtailed after 1974. China cut off aid in 1978 when Albania attacked its policies after the death of Chinese ruler Mao Zedong. Large-scale purges of officials occurred during the 1970s.

Enver Hoxha, the nation's ruler for 4 decades, died Apr. 11, 1985. Eventually the new regime introduced some liberalization, including measures in 1990 providing for freedom to travel abroad. Efforts were begun to improve ties with the outside world. Mar. 1991 elections left the former Communists in power, but a general strike and urban opposition led to the formation of a coalition cabinet including non-Communists.

Albania's former Communists were routed in elections Mar. 1992, amid economic collapse and social unrest. Sali Berisha was elected as the first non-Communist president since World War II.

Algeria

Democratic and Popular Republic of Algeria

al-Jumhuriya al-Jazairiya ad-Dimuqratiya ash-Shabiya

People: Population: 27,895,000. **Age distrib.** (%): <15: 44; 65+: 4. **Pop. density:** 30 per sq. mi. **Urban:** 50%. **Ethnic groups:** Arab-Berber 99%. **Principal languages:** Arabic (official), French Berber (indigenous language). **Religions:** Sunni Muslim (state religion) 99%.

Geography: Area: 919,595 sq. mi., more than 3 times the size of Texas. **Location:** In NW Africa, from Mediterranean Sea into Sahara Desert. **Neighbors:** Morocco on W, Mauritania, Mali, Niger on S, Libya, Tunisia on E. **Topography:** The Tell, located on the coast, comprises fertile plains 50-100 miles wide, with a moderate climate and adequate rain. Two major chains of the Atlas Mts., running roughly E-W, and reaching 7,000 ft., enclose a dry plateau region. Below lies the Sahara, mostly desert with major mineral resources. **Capital:** Algiers (El Djazair). **Cities** (1987 est.): El Djazair 1,483,000; Wahran 590,000; Qacentina 483,000.

Government: Type: Republic. **Head of state:** Pres. Liamine Zeroual; in office: Jan. 31, 1994. **Head of government:** Prime Min. Mokdad Sifi; in office: Apr. 11, 1994. **Local divisions:** 48 provinces. **Defense:** 2.5% of GDP (1993 est.).

Economy: Industries: Oil, light industry, food processing. **Chief crops:** Grains, wine-grapes, potatoes, dates, olives, oranges. **Minerals:** Mercury, iron, zinc, lead. **Crude oil reserves** (1987): 4.8 bln. bbls. **Other resources:** Cork trees. **Arable land:** 3%; **Livestock** (1991): cattle: 1.4 mln.; sheep: 13 mln. **Electricity prod.** (1992): 16.8 bln. kWh. **Labor force:** 24% agric.; 40% ind. and commerce; 24% government & services.

Finance: Monetary Unit: Dinar (Mar. 1994: 25.94 = $1 US). **Gross domestic product** (1992): $42 bln. **Per capita GDP:** $1,570. **Imports** (1991): $9.2 bln.; partners: EEC 64%. **Exports** (1991): $11.7 bln.; partners: EEC 74%. **National budget** (1992 est.): $14.6 bln. **International reserves less gold** (Mar. 1994): $1.1 bln. **Gold:** 5.5 mln. oz t. **Consumer prices** (change in 1992): 33.7%

Transport: Railroads: Length: 2,668 mi. **Motor vehicles:** in use: 760,000 passenger cars, 510,000 comm. vehicles. **Chief ports:** El Djazair.

Communications: Television sets: 1 per 13 persons. **Radios:** 1 per 7.7 persons. **Telephones:** 1 per 23 persons. **Daily newspaper circ.:** 51 per 1,000 pop.

Health: Life expectancy at birth (1994): 67 male; 69 female. **Births** (per 1,000 pop.): 30. **Deaths** (per 1,000 pop.): 6. **Natural increase:** 2.3%. **Hospital beds:** 1 per 393 persons. **Physicians:** 1 per 1,062 persons. **Infant mortality** (per 1,000 live births 1994): 52.

Education (1991): **Literacy:** 52%.

Major International Organizations: UN (FAO, IMF, WHO), OAU, Arab League, OPEC.

Embassy: 2118 Kalorama Rd. NW 20008; 265-2800.

Earliest known inhabitants were ancestors of Berbers, followed by Phoenicians, Romans, Vandals, and, finally, Arabs. Turkey ruled 1518 to 1830, when France took control.

Large-scale European immigration and French cultural inroads did not prevent an Arab nationalist movement from launching guerrilla war. Peace, and French withdrawal, was negotiated with French Pres. Charles de Gaulle. One million Europeans left. Independence came July 5, 1962. Ahmed Ben Bella was the victor of infighting and ruled until 1965, when an army coup installed Col. Houari Boumedienne as leader.

In 1967, Algeria declared war on Israel, broke ties with U.S., and moved toward eventual military and political ties with the USSR. Some 500 died in riots protesting economic hardship in 1988. In 1989, voters approved a new constitution which cleared the way for a multiparty system.

The government canceled Jan. 1992 elections Islamic fundamentalists were expected to win and banned all nonreligious activities at Algeria's 10,000 mosques. Pres. Mohammed Boudiaf was assassinated June 29, 1992. There were repeated attacks on high-ranking officials, security forces, foreigners, and others by militant Muslim fundamentalists over the next 2 years; thousands were killed. Pro-government death squads also were active.

Andorra

Principality of Andorra

Principat d'Andorra

People: Population: 64,000. **Pop. density:** 353 per sq. mi. **Ethnic groups:** Spanish 61%, Andorran 30%, French 6%. **Principal languages:** Catalan (official), French, Castillian. **Religions:** Roman Catholic.

Geography: Area: 181 sq. mi., half the size of New York City. **Location:** In Pyrenees Mtns. **Neighbors:** Spain on S, France on N. **Topography:** High mountains and narrow valleys over the country. **Capital:** Andorra la Vella.

Government: Type: Parliamentary democracy. **Head of government:** Oscar Ribas Reig; in office: May 4, 1992. **Local divisions:** 7 parishes.

Economy: Industries: Tourism, tobacco products. **Labor force:** 20% agric.; 80% ind. and commerce; services; government.

Finance: Monetary unit: French franc, Spanish peseta. **Gross domestic product** (1992): $760 mln.* **Per capita GDP:** $14,000. **National budget** (1990): $190 mln.

Communications: Television sets: 1 per 8.6 persons. **Radios:** 1 per 5.7 persons. **Telephones:** 1 per 2.5 persons.

Health: Births (per 1,000 pop.): 13. **Deaths** (per 1,000 pop.): 7. **Natural increase:** 0.6%.

Education (1992): **Literacy:** 99%. School compulsory to age 16.

Major International Organizations: UN.

Andorra was a co-principality, with joint sovereignty by France and the bishop of Urgel, from 1278 to 1993.

Tourism, especially skiing, is the economic mainstay. A free port, allowing for an active trading center, draws some 10 million tourists annually. The ensuing economic prosperity, accompanied by Andorra's virtual law-free status, gave rise to calls for reform. Andorra voters chose to end a feudal system that had been in place for 715 years and adopt a parliamentary system of government Mar. 14, 1993.

Angola

Republic of Angola

República de Angola

People: Population: 9,804,000. **Pop. density:** 20 per sq. mi. **Urban:** 28%. **Ethnic groups:** Ovimbundu 37%, Kimbundu 25%; Bakongo 13%. **Urban:** 28%. **Principal languages:** Portuguese (official), various Bantu languages. **Religions:** Roman Catholic 38%, Protestant 15%, indigenous beliefs 47%.

Geography: Area: 481,354 sq. mi., larger than Texas and California combined. **Location:** In SW Africa on Atlantic coast. **Neighbors:** Namibia on S, Zambia on E, Zaire on N; Cabinda, an enclave separated from rest of country by short Atlantic coast of Zaire, borders Congo Republic. **Topography:** Most of Angola consists of a plateau elevated 3,000 to 5,000 feet above sea level, rising from a narrow coastal strip. There is also a temperate highland area in the west-central region, a desert in the S, and a tropical rain forest covering Cabinda. **Capital:** Luanda (1988 est.): 1.1 mln.

Government: Type: Republic. **Head of state:** Pres. José Eduardo dos Santos; b Aug. 28, 1942; in office: Sept. 20, 1979. Prime Min. Marcolino Moco; in office: Dec. 2, 1992. **Local divisions:** 18 provinces. **Defense:** NA.

Economy: Industries: Food processing, textiles, mining, tires, petroleum. **Chief crops:** Coffee, bananas. **Minerals:** Iron, diamonds (over 2 mln. carats a year), copper, phosphates, oil. **Livestock** (1992): cattle: 3.2 mln.; goats: 1.5 mln. **Crude oil reserves** (1987): 1.9 bln. bbls. **Arable land:** 2%. **Fish catch** (1991): 75,062 metric tons. **Electricity prod.** (1991): 800 mln. kWh. **Labor force:** 85% agric., 15% industry.

Finance: Monetary unit: Kwanza (Nov. 1992: 550 = $1 US). **Gross domestic product** (1991): $5.1 bln. **Per capita GDP:** $950. **Imports** (1991): $1.3 bln.; partners: Portugal 29%, Fra. 9%; U.S. 9%. **Exports** (1991): $3.4 bln.; partners: U.S. 56%. **National budget** (1991 est.): $3.6 bln.

Transport: Motor vehicles: in use: 120,000 passenger cars, 40,000 comm. vehicles. **Chief ports:** Cabinda, Lobito, Luanda.

Communications: Television sets: 1 per 210 persons. **Radios:** 1 per 24 persons. **Telephones:** 1 per 132 persons. **Daily newspaper circ.:** 11 per 1,000 pop.

Health: Life expectancy at birth (1994): 44 male; 48 female. **Births** (per 1,000 pop.): 45. **Deaths** (per 1,000 pop.): 19. **Natural increase:** 2.7%. **Hospital beds:** 1 per 845 persons. **Physicians:** 1 per 15,136 persons. **Infant mortality** (per 1,000 live births 1994): 145.

Education (1992): **Literacy:** 40%.

Major International Organizations: UN (ILO, WHO), OAU.

From the early centuries AD to 1500, Bantu tribes penetrated most of the region. Portuguese came in 1583, allied with the Bakongo kingdom in the north, and developed the slave trade. Large-scale colonization did not begin until the 20th century, when 400,000 Portuguese immigrated.

A guerrilla war begun in 1961 lasted until 1975, when Portugal granted independence. Fighting then erupted between three rival rebel groups —the National Front, based in Zaire, the Soviet-backed Popular Movement for the Liberation of Angola (MPLA), and the National Union for the Total Independence of Angola (UNITA), aided by the U.S. and S Africa. The civil war killed thousands of blacks, drove most whites to emigrate, and completed economic ruin. Cuban troops and Soviet aid helped the MPLA win control of most of the country by 1976 and gain wide recognition as the government of Angola.

An agreement was signed in Dec. 1988 between Angola, Cuba, and S Africa on a timetable for withdrawal of Cuban troops, completed May 25, 1991. The 16-year war was officially ended May 1, 1991, as the government and UNITA signed a peace agreement.

Elections were held in Sept. 1992, but fighting again broke out, as UNITA rejected the presidential election results, and continued into 1993 and 1994, with UNITA forces holding most of the countryside. Large numbers of civilians died from war-related causes, especially starvation. Rebels signed an accord with the government, June 28, 1994. The U.S. formally recognized the government of Angola, May 19, 1993, for the first time since independence.

Antigua and Barbuda

People: Population: 65,000. **Urban:** 31%. **Ethnic groups:** Mostly African. **Principal languages:** English (official). **Religion:** Predominantly Church of England.

Geography: Area: 171 sq. mi. **Location:** Eastern Caribbean. **Neighbors:** approx. 30 mi. north of Guadeloupe. **Capital:** St. John's, (1988 est.) 27,000.

Government: Type: Constitutional monarchy with British-style parliament. **Head of state:** Queen Elizabeth II; represented by James Carlisle. **Head of government:** Prime Min. Lester Bird; b 1940; in office: Mar. 1994. **Defense:** 1% of GDP (FY 1990-91).

Economy: Industries: Manufacturing, tourism. **Arable land:** 18%.

Finance: Monetary unit: East Caribbean dollar (Mar. 1994): 3.81 = $1 US. **Gross domestic product** (1991): $424 mln.**Per capita GDP:** $6,600. **National Budget** (1992): $161 mln.

Health: Births (per 1,000 pop.): 17. **Deaths** (per 1,000 pop.): 5. **Natural increase:** 1.2%.

Education (1990): **Literacy:** 90%.

Major International Organizations: UN, Commonwealth of Nations.

Embassy: 3400 International Dr., NW 20008; 362-5211.

Columbus landed on Antigua in 1493. The British colonized it in 1632.

The British associated state of Antigua achieved independence as Antigua and Barbuda on Nov. 1, 1981. The government maintains close relations with the U.S., United Kingdom, and Venezuela.

Argentina

Argentine Republic

República Argentina

People: Population: 33,913,000. **Age distrib.** (%): <15: 30; 65+: 9. **Pop. density:** 31 per sq. mi. **Urban:** 86%. **Ethnic groups:** white 85% (Spanish, Italian), Mestizos, Indians. **Principal languages:** Spanish (official), English, Italian. **Religions:** Roman Catholic 90%.

Geography: Area: 1,073,518 sq. mi., 4 times the size of Texas, second largest in S America. **Location:** Occupies most of southern S America. **Neighbors:** Chile on W, Bolivia, Paraguay on N, Brazil, Uruguay on NE. **Topography:** The mountains in W: the Andean, Central, Misiones, and Southern. Aconcagua is the highest peak in the western hemisphere, alt. 22,834 ft. E of the Andes are heavily wooded plains, called the Gran Chaco in the N, and the fertile, treeless Pampas in the central region. Patagonia, in the S, is bleak and arid. Rio de la Plata, 170 by 140 mi., is mostly fresh water, from 2,485-mi. Parana and 1,000-mi. Uruguay rivers. **Capital:** Buenos Aires. (The Senate has approved the moving of the capital to the Patagonia Region). **Cities** (1991 est.): Buenos Aires 12,582,000 met.; Cordoba 1.1 mln.; Rosario 1.0 mln. (met.).

Government: Type: Republic. **Head of state:** Pres. Carlos Saúl Menem; b July 2, 1930; in office: July 8, 1989. **Local divisions:** 28 provinces, 1 federal dist. **Defense:** 1.7% of GDP (1992).

Economy: Industries: Food processing, flour milling, chemicals, textiles, machinery, autos. **Chief crops:** Grains, corn, grapes, linseed, sugar, tobacco, rice, soybeans, citrus fruits. **Minerals:** Oil, lead, zinc, iron, copper, tin, uranium. **Crude oil reserves** (1987): 2.1 bln. bbls. **Arable land:** 9%. **Livestock** (1992): cattle: 50 mln.; sheep: 23 mln. **Fish catch** (1991): 640,636 metric tons. **Electricity prod.** (1992): 51.3 bln. kWh. **Labor force:** 19% agric.; 36% ind. and comm.; 20% services.

Finance: Monetary unit: Peso (Mar. 1994: .99 = $1 US). **Gross domestic product** (1992): $112 bln. **Per capita GDP:** $3,400. **Imports** (1991): $8.0 bln.; partners: U.S. 21%, W Ger. 9%, Braz. 16%, Jap. 7%. **Exports** (1991): $12.3 bln.; partners: CIS 13%, Neth. 9%, U.S. 12%. **Tourism** (1990): receipts: $903 mln. **National budget** (1992): $35.8 bln. **International reserves less gold** (Feb. 1994): $14 bln. **Gold:** 4.37 mln. oz t. **Consumer prices** (change in 1993): 10.6%.

Transport: Railroads: Length: 21,198 mi. **Motor vehicles:** in use: 4.1 mln. passenger cars, 1.5 mln. comm. vehicles. **Civil aviation::** 5 bln. passenger-mi. **Chief ports:** Buenos Aires, Bahia Blanca, La Plata.

Communications: Television sets: 1 per 4.6 persons. **Radios:** 1 per 1.5 persons. **Telephones:** 1 per 7 persons. **Daily newspaper circ.:** 124 per 1,000 pop.

Health: Life expectancy at birth (1994): 68 male; 75 female. **Births** (per 1,000 pop.): 20. **Deaths** (per 1,000 pop.): 9. **Natural increase:** 1.1%. **Hospital beds:** 1 per 205 persons. **Physicians:** 1 per 326 persons. **Infant mortality** (per 1,000 live births 1994): 29.

Education (1992): **Literacy:** 95%. **Years compulsory:** 7.

Major International Organizations: UN (WHO, IMF, FAO), OAS.

Embassy: 1600 New Hampshire Ave. NW 20009; 939-6400.

Nomadic Indians roamed the Pampas when Spaniards arrived, 1515-16, led by Juan Diaz de Solis. Nearly all the Indians were killed by the late 19th century. The colonists won independence, 1816, and a long period of disorders ended in a strong centralized government.

Large-scale Italian, German, and Spanish immigration in the decades after 1880 spurred modernization. Social reforms were enacted in the 1920s, but military coups prevailed 1930-46, until the election of Gen. Juan Perón as president.

Perón, with his wife, Eva Duarte (d 1952), effected labor reforms, but also suppressed speech and press freedoms, closed religious schools, and ran the country into debt. A 1955 coup exiled Perón, who was followed by a series of military and civilian regimes. Perón returned in 1973, and was once more elected president. He died 10 months later, succeeded by his wife Isabel, who had been elected vice president, and who became the first woman head of state in the western hemisphere.

A military junta ousted Mrs. Perón in 1976 amid charges of corruption. Under a continuing state of siege, the army battled guerrillas and leftists, killed 5,000 people, and jailed and tortured others. On Dec. 9, 1985, after a trial of 5 months and nearly 1,000 witnesses, 5 former junta members were found guilty of murder and human rights abuses.

Argentine troops seized control of the British-held Falkland Islands on Apr. 2, 1982. Both countries had claimed sovereignty over the islands, located 250 miles off the Argentine coast, since 1833. The British dispatched a task force and declared a total air and sea blockade around the Falklands. Fighting began May 1; several hundred lost their lives as the result of the destruction of a British destroyer and the sinking of an Argentine cruiser.

British troops landed on East Falkland Island May 21 and eventually surrounded Stanley, the capital city and Argentine stronghold. The Argentine troops surrendered, June 14; Argentine Pres. Leopoldo Galtieri resigned June 17.

Democratic rule returned to Argentina in 1983 as Raul Alfonsín's Radical Civic Union gained an absolute majority in the presidential electoral college and Congress. By 1989 the nation was plagued by severe financial problems as inflation reached crisis levels of over 6,000%. The hyperinflation sparked looting and rioting in several cities. The government of Perónist Pres. Carlos Saúl Menem, installed 1989, unveiled harsh economic measures in an effort to combat spiraling inflation, control government spending, and restructure the foreign debt.

About 100 people were killed in the terrorist bombing of a Jewish cultural center in Buenos Aires, July 18, 1994.

Armenia

Republic of Armenia

Haikakan Hanrapetoutioun

People: Population: 3,522,000. **Pop. density:** 306 per sq. mi. **Urban:** 68%. **Ethnic groups:** Armenian 93%. **Principal languages:** Armenian 96%. **Religions:** Armenian Orthodox 94%.

Geography: Area: 11,500 sq. mi., slightly larger than Maryland. **Neighbors:** Georgia on N, Azerbaijan on E, Iran on S, Turkey on W. **Topography:** Mountainous with many peaks above 10,000 ft. **Capital:** Yerevan.

Government: Type: Republic. **Head of state:** Pres. Levon Ter-Petrosyan; b Jan. 9, 1945; in office: Oct. 16, 1991. **Head of government:** Hrand Bagratian; in office: Feb. 12, 1993.

Economy: Industries: Mining, chemicals. **Chief crops:** Cotton, figs, grain. **Minerals:** Copper, zinc. **Arable land:** 29%.

Finance: Monetary unit: Ruble.

Transport: Vehicles: 230,100 passenger cars.

Communications: Television sets: 1 per 5 persons. **Radios:** 1 per 5.6 persons. **Telephones:** 1 per 5.3 persons. **Daily newspaper circ.:** 496 per 1,000 pop.

Health: Life expectancy at birth (1994): 69 male; 76 female. **Births** (per 1,000 pop.): 24. **Deaths** (per 1,000 pop.): 7. **Natural increase:** 1.7%. Physicians: 1 per 246 persons. **Hospital beds:** 1 per 117 persons. **Infant mortality** (per 1,000 live births 1994): 35.

Major International Organizations: UN (IMF), CIS.

Embassy: 122 C St. NW 20001; 628-5766.

Armenia is an ancient country, parts of which are now in Turkey and Iran. Present-day Armenia was set up as a Soviet Republic Apr. 2, 1921. It joined Georgian and Azerbaijan SSRs Mar. 12, 1922, to form the Transcaucasian SFSR, which became part of the USSR Dec. 30, 1922. Armenia became a constituent republic of the USSR Dec. 5, 1936. An earthquake struck Armenia Dec. 7, 1988; more than 55,000 were killed and several cities and towns were left in ruins.

Armenia declared independence Sept. 23, 1991, and became an independent state when the USSR disbanded Dec. 26, 1991. Fighting between mostly Christian Armenia and mostly Muslim Azerbaijan escalated in 1992 and continued in 1993 and 1994. Each country claimed Nagorno-Karabakh, an enclave in Azerbaijan that has a majority population of ethnic Armenians. A temporary cease-fire was announced in May 1994, with Armenian forces in control of the enclave.

Australia

Commonwealth of Australia

People: Population: 18,077,000. **Age distrib.** (%): <15: 22; 65+: 12. **Pop. density:** 6.1 per sq. mi. **Urban:** 85%. **Ethnic groups:** Caucasian 95%, Asian 4%, aborigines (including mixed) 1%. **Principal languages:** English, aboriginal languages. **Religions:** Anglican 26%, Roman Catholic 26%, other Christian 24%.

Geography: Area: 2,966,200 sq. mi., almost as large as the continental U.S. **Location:** SE of Asia, Indian O. is W and S, Pacific O. (Coral, Tasman seas) is E; they meet N of Australia in Timor and Arafura seas: Tasmania lies 150 mi. S of Victoria state, across Bass Strait. **Neighbors:** Nearest are Indonesia, Papua New Guinea on N, Solomons, Fiji, and New Zealand on E. **Topography:** An island continent. The Great Dividing Range along the E coast has Mt. Kosciusko, 7,310 ft. The W plateau rises to 2,000 ft., with arid areas in the Great Sandy and Great Victoria deserts. The NW part of Western Australia and Northern Terr. are arid and hot. The NE has heavy rainfall and Cape York Peninsula has jungles. The Murray R. rises in New South Wales and flows 1,600 mi. to the Indian O. **Capital:** Canberra. **Cities** (1991 est.): Sydney 3.5 mln.; Melbourne 3.0 mln.; Brisbane 1.3 mln.; Perth 1.1 mln.; Adelaide 1.0 mln.

Government: Type: Democratic, federal state system. **Head of state:** Queen Elizabeth II, represented by Gov.-Gen. William Hayden; in office: Feb. 16, 1989. **Head of government:** Prime Min. Paul Keating; b Jan. 18, 1944; in office: Dec. 20, 1991. **Local divisions:** 6 states, 2 territories. **Defense:** 2.4% of GDP (FY 1992-93).

Economy: Industries: Iron, steel, textiles, electrical equip., chemicals, autos, aircraft, ships, machinery. **Chief crops:** Wheat (a leading export), barley, oats, corn, hay, sugar, wine, fruit, vegetables. **Minerals:** Coal, copper, iron, lead, tin, uranium, zinc. **Crude oil reserves** (1987): 1.6 bln. bbls. **Other resources:** Wool (30% of world output). **Arable land:** 6%. **Livestock** (1992): cattle: 23 mln.; sheep: 148 mln.; pigs: 2.7 mln. **Fish catch** (1991): 227,300 metric tons. **Electricity prod.** (1992): 150 bln. kWh. **Labor force:** 6% agric.; 33% finance & services; 36% trade & manuf.

Finance: Monetary unit: Dollar (Mar. 1994: 1.00 = $.71 US). **Gross domestic product** (1992): $293.5 bln.* **Per capita income:** $16,700. **Imports** (1992): $37.8 bln.; partners: U.S. 24%, Jap. 19%, UK 6%. **Exports** (1992): $41.7 bln.; partners: Jap. 26%, U.S. 11%, NZ 6%. **Tourism** (1990): $3.7 bln. receipts. **National budget** (1992): $78 bln. **International reserves less gold** (Mar. 1994): $11.5 bln. **Gold:** 7.90 mln. oz t. **Consumer prices** (change in 1993): 1.8%.

Transport: Railroads: Length: 22,050 mi. **Motor vehicles:** in use: 7.7 mln. passenger cars, 1.9 mln. comm. vehicles. **Civil aviation::** 23.0 bln. passenger-mi.; 441 airports with scheduled flights. **Chief ports:** Sydney, Melbourne, Newcastle, Port Kembla, Fremantle, Geelong.

Communications: Television sets: 1 per 2.2 persons. **Radios:** 1 per 0.9 persons. **Telephones:** 1 per 2.1 persons. **Daily newspaper circ.:** 249 per 1,000 pop.

Health: Life expectancy at birth (1994): 74 male; 81 female. **Births** (per 1,000 pop.): 14. **Deaths** (per 1,000 pop.): 7. **Natural increase:** .7%. **Hospital beds:** 1 per 199 persons. **Physicians:** 1 per 438 persons. **Infant mortality** (per 1,000 live births 1994): 7.

Education (1992): **Literacy:** 99%. **Years compulsory:** to age 15; attendance 94%.

Major International Organizations: UN and all its specialized agencies, OECD, Commonwealth of Nations.

Embassy: 1601 Massachusetts Ave NW 20036; 797-3000.

Capt. James Cook explored the E coast in 1770, when the continent was inhabited by a variety of different tribes. The first settlers, beginning in 1788, were mostly convicts, soldiers, and government officials. By 1830, Britain had claimed the entire continent, and the immigration of free settlers began to accelerate. The commonwealth was proclaimed Jan. 1, 1901. Northern Terr. was granted limited self-rule July 1, 1978.

States/Territory, Capital	Area (sq. mi.)	Population (1991 cen.)
New South Wales, Sydney	309,500	5,731,926
Victoria, Melbourne	87,900	4,243,719
Queensland, Brisbane	666,990	2,976,617
Western Aust., Perth	975,100	1,586,393
South Aust., Adelaide	379,900	1,400,656
Tasmania, Hobart	26,200	452,847
Aust. Capital Terr., Canberra	900	280,085
Northern Terr., Darwin	519,800	175,253

Racially discriminatory immigration policies were abandoned in 1973, after 3 million Europeans (half British) had entered since 1945. The 50,000 aborigines and 150,000 part-aborigines are mostly detribalized, but there are several preserves in the Northern Territory. They remain economically disadvantaged.

Australia's agricultural success makes the country among the top exporters of beef, lamb, wool, and wheat. Major mineral deposits have been developed as well, largely for exports. Industrialization has been completed.

Australia harbors many plant and animal species not found elsewhere, including the kangaroo, koalas, platypus, dingo (wild dog), Tasmanian devil (racoon-like marsupial), wombat (bear-like marsupial), and barking and frilled lizards.

The nation suffered through a deep recession 1990-93. Unemployment was 11.1% in Feb. 1993. A year later it was down somewhat, to 10.5%.

The Labor Party won a majority in Feb. 1983 general elections and was reelected in 1984, 1987, 1990, and 1993.

Australian External Territories

Norfolk Is., area 13½ sq. mi., pop. (1990) 1,800, was taken over, 1914. The soil is very fertile, suitable for citrus fruits, bananas, and coffee. Many of the inhabitants are descendants of the Bounty mutineers, moved to Norfolk 1856 from Pitcairn Is. Australia offered the island limited home rule, 1978.

Coral Sea Is. Territory, 1 sq. mi., is administered from Norfolk Is.

Territory of Ashmore and Cartier Is., area 2 sq. mi., in the Indian O. came under Australian authority 1934 and are administered as part of Northern Territory. **Heard** and **McDonald Is.** are administered by the Dept. of Science.

Cocos (Keeling) Is., 27 small coral islands in the Indian O. 1,750 mi. NW of Australia. Pop. (1990) 600, area: 5½ sq. mi. The residents voted to become part of Australia, Apr. 1984.

Christmas Is. 52 sq. mi., pop. 1,700 (1991), 230 mi. S of Java, was transferred by Britain in 1958. It has phosphate deposits.

Australian Antarctic Territory was claimed by Australia in 1933, including 2,362,000 sq. mi. of territory S of 60th parallel S Lat. and between 160th-45th meridians E Long. It does not include Adelie Coast.

Austria

Republic of Austria

Republik Österreich

People: Population: 7,955,000. **Age distrib.** (%): <15: 18; 65+: 15. **Pop. density:** 245 per sq. mi. **Urban:** 54%. **Ethnic groups:** German 99%, Croatian Slovene. **Principal languages:** German. **Religions:** Roman Catholic 85%, Protestant 6%.

Geography: Area: 32,378 sq. mi., slightly smaller than Maine. **Location:** In S Central Europe. **Neighbors:** Switzerland, Liechtenstein on W, Germany, Czech Rep., Slovakia on N, Hungary on E, Slovenia, Italy on S. **Topography:** Austria is primarily mountainous, with the Alps and foothills covering the western and southern provinces. The eastern provinces and Vienna are located in the Danube River Basin. **Capital:** Vienna. **Cities** (1991 est.): Vienna 1,539,000.

Government: Type: Parliamentary democracy. **Head of state:** Pres. Thomas Klestil; b Nov. 4, 1932; in office: July 8, 1992. **Head of government:** Chancellor Franz Vranitzky; b Oct. 4, 1937; in office: June 16, 1986. **Local divisions:** 9 lander (states), each with a legislature. **Defense:** 0.9% of GDP (1993 est.).

Economy: Industries: Steel, machinery, autos, electrical and optical equip., glassware, sport goods, paper, textiles, chemicals, cement. **Chief crops:** Grains, potatoes, beets. **Minerals:** Iron ore, oil, magnesite. **Other resources:** Forests, hydro power. **Arable land:** 17%. **Livestock** (1991): cattle: 2.5 mln.; pigs: 3.6 mln. **Electricity prod.** (1992): 49.5 bln. kWh. **Labor force:** 8% agric.; 35% ind. & comm.; 56% service.

Finance: Monetary unit: Schilling (Mar. 1994: 11.90 = $1 US). **Gross domestic product** (1992): $141.3 bln.* **Per capita GDP:** $18,000. **Imports** (1991): $54.1 bln.; partners: EU 70%. **Exports** (1992): $44.4 bln.; partners: EU 68%. **Tourism** (1990): receipts: $13.0 bln. **National budget** (1992 est.): $53 bln. **International reserves less gold** (Mar. 1994): $16.5 bln. **Gold:** 18.62 mln. oz t. **Consumer prices** (change in 1993): 3.6%.

Transport: Railroads: Length: 4,136 mi. **Motor vehicles:** in use: 3.1 mln. passenger cars, 268,000 comm. **Civil aviation::** 2.9 bln. passenger-mi.; 6 airports with scheduled flights.

Communications: Television sets: 1 per 2.9 persons. **Radios:** 1 per 1.7 persons. **Telephones:** 1 per 1.7 persons. **Daily newspaper circ.:** 357 per 1,000 pop.

Health: Life expectancy at birth (1994): 73 male; 80 female. **Births** (per 1,000 pop.): 11. **Deaths** (per 1,000 pop.): 10. **Natural increase:** .1% **Hospital beds:** 1 per 105 persons. **Physicians:** 1 per 327 persons. **Infant mortality** (per 1,000 live births 1994): 7.

Education (1992): **Literacy:** 99%. **School years compulsory:** 9; attendance 95%.

Major International Organizations: UN and all of its specialized agencies, EFTA, OECD.

Embassy: 3524 International Court NW 20008; 895-6700.

Rome conquered Austrian lands from Celtic tribes around 15 BC. In 788 the territory was incorporated into Charlemagne's empire. By 1300, the House of Hapsburg had gained control; they added vast territories in all parts of Europe to their realm in the next few hundred years.

Austrian dominance of Germany was undermined in the 18th century and ended by Prussia by 1866. But the Congress of Vienna, 1815, confirmed Austrian control of a large empire in southeast Europe consisting of Germans, Hungarians, Slavs, Italians, and others. The dual Austro-Hungarian monarchy was established in 1867, giving autonomy to Hungary and almost 50 years of peace.

World War I, started after the June 28, 1914, assassination of Archduke Franz Ferdinand, the Hapsburg heir, by a Serbian nationalist, destroyed the empire. By 1918 Austria was reduced to a small republic, with the borders it has today.

Nazi Germany invaded Austria Mar. 13, 1938. The republic was reestablished in 1945, under Allied occupation. Full independence and neutrality were restored in 1955. Austria was to join the European Union (formerly European Community) on Jan. 1, 1995.

Azerbaijan

Azerbaijani Republic

Azerbaijchan Respublikasy

People: Population: 7,684,000; **Pop. density:** 230 per sq. mi. **Urban:** 54%. **Ethnic groups:** Azeri 83%, Russian 6%, Armenian 6%. **Principal languages:** Azeri 82%, Russian 7%, Armenian 5%. **Religions:** mostly Muslim.

Geography: Area: 33,400 sq. mi., slightly larger than Maine. **Neighbors:** Russia, Georgia on N, Iran on S, Armenia on W, Caspian Sea on E. **Capital:** Baku.

Government: Type: in transition. **Head of state:** Pres. Geidar A. Aliyev; in office: June 30, 1993. **Head of government:** Prime Min. Surat Huseynov; in office: June 30, 1993. **Defense:** 1.9% of GDP (1992).

Economy: Industries: Oil refining. **Chief crops:** Grain, cotton, rice, silk. **Minerals:** Iron, copper, lead, zinc. **Livestock** (1992): cattle: 1.8 mln., goats & sheep: 5.1 mln. **Electricity prod.** (1992): 22.3 bln. kWh.

Finance: Monetary unit: Manat (1 manat=10 rubles).

Transport: Vehicles: 235,600 passenger cars.

Communications: Daily newspaper circ.: 416 per 1,000 pop.

Health: Life expectancy at birth (1994): 67 male; 75 female. **Births** (per 1,000 pop.): 23. **Deaths** (per 1,000 pop.): 7. **Natural increase:** 1.6%. Physicians: 1 per 255 persons. **Hospital beds:** 1 per 98 persons. **Infant mortality** (per 1,000 live births 1994): 35.

Major International Organizations: UN.

Azerbaijan was the home of Scythian tribes and part of the Roman Empire. It was overrun by Turks in the 11th century and conquered by Russia in 1806 and 1813. It joined the USSR Dec. 30, 1922, and became a constituent republic in 1936. Azerbaijan declared independence Aug. 30, 1991 and became an independent state when the Soviet Union disbanded Dec. 26, 1991.

Fighting between mostly Muslim Azerbaijan and mostly Christian Armenia escalated in 1992 and continued in 1993 and 1994. Each country claimed Nagorno-Karabakh, an enclave in Azerbaijan with a majority population of ethnic Armenians. A temporary cease-fire was announced in May 1994, with Armenian forces in control of the enclave.

A National Council ousted Communist Pres. Mutaibov and took power May 19, 1992. Abulfez Elchibey became the nation's first democratically elected president June 7, but was ousted from office by Surat Huseynov, commander of a private militia, June 30, 1993. Huseynov became prime minister, and Geidar Aliyev, a pro-Russian former Communist, became president.

The Bahamas

The Commonwealth of the Bahamas

People: Population: 273,000. **Age distrib.** (%): <15: 30; 65+: 5. **Pop. density:** 50 per sq. mi. **Urban:** 64%. **Ethnic groups:** black 85%, white (British, Canadian, U.S.) 15%. **Principal languages:** English, Creole. **Religions:** Baptist 32%, Anglican 20%, Roman Catholic 19%.

Geography: Area: 5,382 sq. mi., about the size of Connecticut. **Location:** In Atlantic O., E of Florida. **Neighbors:** Nearest are U.S. on W, Cuba on S. **Topography:** Nearly 700 islands (30 inhabited) and over 2,000 islets in the western Atlantic extend 760 mi. NW to SE. **Capital:** Nassau. **Cities:** (1990 est.) Nassau 172,000; Freeport 26,000.

Government: Type: Independent commonwealth. **Head of state:** Queen Elizabeth II, represented by Gov.-Gen. Clifford Darling. **Head of government:** Prime Min. Hubert Ingraham; b 1947; in office: Aug. 21, 1992. **Local divisions:** 21 districts. **Defense:** 2.7% of GDP (1990).

Economy: Industries: Tourism (50% of GDP), rum, banking, pharmaceuticals. **Chief crops:** Fruits, vegetables. **Minerals:** Salt. **Other resources:** Lobsters. **Arable land:** 1%. **Electricity prod.** (1992): 929 mln. kWh. **Labor force:** 5% agric.; 25% tourism; 30% government.

Finance: Monetary unit: Dollar (Mar. 1994: 1 = $1 US). **Gross domestic product** (1991): $2.6 bln. **Per capita income:** $10,200. **Imports** (1991): $1.1 bln.; partners: U.S. 35%, Nigeria 21%. **Exports** (1991): $306 mln.; partners: U.S. 41%, Norway 30%. **Tourism** (1990): $1.1 bln. **National budget** (1992 est.): $727.5 mln. **International reserves less gold** (Feb. 1994): $237 mln. **Consumer prices** (change in 1993): 2.7%.

Transport: Motor vehicles: in use: 70,000 passenger cars, 15,000 comm. vehicles. **Chief ports:** Nassau, Freeport.

Communications: Radios: 1 per 1.3 persons. **Television sets:** 1 per 4.4 persons. **Telephones:** 1 per 1.8 persons. **Daily newspaper circ.:** 135 per 1,000 pop.

Health: Life expectancy at birth (1994): 68 male; 75 female. **Births** (per 1,000 pop.): 19. **Deaths** (per 1,000 pop.): 5. **Natural increase:** 1.3%. **Infant mortality** (per 1,000 live births 1994): 34.

Education (1992): **Literacy:** 95%; School compulsory through age 14.

Major International Organizations: UN (World Bank, IMF, WHO), OAS.

Embassy: 2220 Massachusetts Ave. NW 20008.

Christopher Columbus first set foot in the New World on San Salvador (Watling I.) in 1492, when Arawak Indians inhabited the islands. British settlement began in 1647; the islands became a British colony in 1783. Internal self-government was granted in 1964; full independence within the Commonwealth was attained July 10, 1973.

International banking and investment management has become a major industry alongside tourism, despite controversy over financial irregularities.

Bahrain

State of Bahrain

Dawlat al-Bahrayn

People: Population: 586,000. **Age distrib.** (%): <15: 32; 65+: 2. **Pop. density:** 2,186 per sq. mi. **Urban:** 81%. **Ethnic groups:** Bahraini 63%, Asian 13%, other Arab 10%, Iranian 8%. **Principal languages:** Arabic (official), English, Farsi, Urdu. **Religions:** Shi'a Muslim 70%, Sunni Muslim 30%.

Geography: Area: 268 sq. mi., smaller than New York City. **Location:** In Persian Gulf. **Neighbors:** Nearest are Saudi Arabia on W, Qatar on E. **Topography:** Bahrain Island, and several adjacent, smaller islands, are flat, hot and humid, with little rain. **Capital:** Manama. **Cities** (1988 est.): Manama 151,000.

Government: Type: Traditional monarchy. **Head of state:** Amir Isa bin Sulman al-Khalifa; b July 3, 1933; in office: Nov. 2, 1961. **Head of government:** Prime Min. Kahlifa bin Sulman al–Khalifa; b 1935; in office: Jan. 19, 1970. **Local divisions:** 12 districts. **Defense:** 6.0% of GDP (1990).

Economy: Industries: Oil products, aluminum smelting. **Chief crops:** Fruits, vegetables. **Minerals:** Oil, gas. **Crude oil reserves** (1985): 173 mln. bbls. **Arable land:** 2%. **Electricity prod.** (1992): 4.7 bln. kWh. **Labor force:** 5% agric.; 85% ind. and commerce; 5% services; 3% gov.

Finance: Monetary unit: Dinar (Mar. 1994: 1.00 = $2.66 US). **Gross domestic product** (1992): $4.3 bln. **Per capita income:** $7,800. **Imports** (1991): $4.0 bln.; partners: Sau. Ar. 60%, UK 6%, U.S. 9%. **Exports** (1991): $3.4 bln.; partners: UAE 18%, Jap. 12%, Sing. 10%, U.S. 6%. **National budget** (1989): $1.3 bln. **International reserves less gold** (Mar. 1994): $1.2 bln. **Gold:** 150,000 oz t. **Consumer prices** (change in 1992): -0.2%.

Transport: Motor vehicles: in use: 107,000 passenger cars, 24,000 comm. vehicles. **Chief ports:** Sitra.

Communications: Television sets: 1 per 2.0 persons. **Radios:** 1 per 1.7 persons. **Telephones:** 1 per 3.1 persons.

Health: Life expectancy at birth (1994): 71 male; 76 female. **Births** (per 1,000 pop.): 27. **Deaths** (per 1,000 pop.): 4. **Natural increase:** 2.3%. Medical services are free. **Infant mortality** (per 1,000 live births 1994): 19.

Education (1992): **Literacy:** 77%.

Major International Organizations: UN (GATT, IMF, WHO), Arab League.

Embassy: 3502 International Dr. NW 20008; 342-0741.

Long ruled by the Khalifa family, Bahrain was a British protectorate from 1861 to Aug. 15, 1971, when it regained independence.

Pearls, shrimp, fruits, and vegetables were the mainstays of the economy until oil was discovered in 1932. By the 1970s, oil reserves were depleted; international banking thrived.

Bahrain took part in the 1973-74 Arab oil embargo against the U.S. and other nations. The government bought controlling interest in the oil industry in 1975.

Bangladesh

People's Republic of Bangladesh

Gama Prajatantrï Bangladesh

People: Population: 125,149,000. **Age distrib.** (%): <15: 44; 65+: 3. **Pop. density:** 2,184 per sq. mi. **Urban:** 14%. **Ethnic groups:** Bengali 98%, Bihari, tribesmen. **Principal languages:** Bangla (official), English. **Religions:** Muslim 83%, Hindu 16%.

Geography: Area: 57,295 sq. mi. slightly smaller than Wisconsin. **Location:** In S Asia, on N bend of Bay of Bengal. **Neighbors:** India nearly surrounds country on W, N, E; Myanmar on SE. **Topography:** The country is mostly a low plain cut by the Ganges and Brahmaputra rivers and their delta. The land is alluvial and marshy along the coast, with hills only in the extreme SE and NE. A tropical monsoon climate prevails, among the rainiest in the world. **Capital:** Dhaka. **Cities** (1991 est.): Dhaka (met.) 6.1 mln.; Chittagong (met.) 2.0 mln.; Khulna (met.) 877,000.

Government: Type: Parliamentary democracy. **Head of state:** Pres. Abdur Rahman Biswas in office: Oct. 10, 1991. **Head of government:** Prime Min. Khaleda Zia; b Nov. 1944; in office: Mar. 20, 1991. **Local divisions:** 64 districts. **Defense:** 1.5% of GDP (FY 1992-93).

Economy: Industries: Food processing, jute, textiles, fertilizers, petroleum products. **Chief crops:** Jute (most of world output), rice, tea. **Minerals:** Natural gas, offshore oil, coal. **Arable land:** 67%. **Livestock** (1992): cattle: 23 mln.; goats: 18 mln. **Fish catch** (1991): 892,700 metric tons. **Electricity prod.** (1992): 9 bln. kWh. **Labor force:** 74% agric; 11% ind.; 15% services.

Finance: Monetary unit: Taka (Mar. 1994: 40.15 = $1 US). **Gross domestic product** (1992): $23.8 bln. **Per capita GDP:** $200. **Imports** (1991): $3.6 bln.; partners: Jap. 9%, U.S. 6%. **Exports** (1991): $1.6 bln.; partners: U.S. 31%, It. 9%; Pak 5%. **Tourism** (1990): $11.0 mln. receipts. **National budget** (1992): $3.7 bln. **International reserves less gold** (Mar. 1994): $2.7 bln. **Gold:** 94,000 oz t. **Consumer prices** (change in 1992): 4.3%.

Transport: Railroads: Length: 1,706 mi. **Motor vehicles:** in use: 67,000 passenger cars, 63,000 comm. vehicles. **Chief ports:** Chittagong, Chalna.

Communications: Radios: 1 per 25 persons. **Television sets:** 1 per 316 persons. **Telephones:** 1 per 427 persons.

Health: Life expectancy at birth (1994): 55 male; 55 female. **Births** (per 1,000 pop.): 35. **Deaths** (per 1,000 pop.): 12. **Natural increase:** 2.3%. **Hospital beds:** 1 per 3,218 persons. **Physicians:** 1 per 5,264 persons. **Infant mortality** (per 1,000 live births 1994): 107.

Education (1992): **Literacy:** 47%. **Attendance:** 73% primary school; 26% secondary school.

Major International Organizations: UN (GATT, IMF, WHO).

Embassy: 2201 Wisconsin Ave. NW 20007; 342-8372.

Muslim invaders conquered the formerly Hindu area in the 12th century. British rule lasted from the 18th century to 1947, when East Bengal became part of Pakistan.

Charging West Pakistani domination, the Awami League, based in the East, won National Assembly control in 1971. Assembly sessions were postponed; riots broke out. Pakistani troops attacked Mar. 25; Bangladesh independence was proclaimed the next day. In the ensuing civil war, one million died and 10 million fled to India.

War between India and Pakistan broke out Dec. 3, 1971. Pakistan surrendered in the East on Dec. 15. Sheikh Mujibur Rahman became prime minister. The country moved into the Indian and Soviet orbits in response to U.S. support of Pakistan, and much of the economy was nationalized. Bangladesh adopted a parliamentary system of government in 1991.

Chronic destitution in the densely crowded population has been worsened by the decline of jute as a world commodity.

On May 30, 1981, Pres. Ziaur Rahman was killed in an unsuccessful coup attempt by army rivals. Vice President Abdus Sattar assumed the presidency but was ousted in a coup led by army chief of staff Gen. H.M. Ershad, Mar. 1982. Ershad declared Bangladesh an Islamic Republic in 1988. Taslima Nasrin, a Bangladeshi feminist writer charged in court with offending the Muslim faith and threatened with death by Islamic militants, left the country for Sweden, Aug. 10, 1994.

Bangladesh is subject to devastating storms and floods that kill thousands. A cyclone struck Apr. 1991, killing over 131,000 people and causing $2.7 billion in damages.

Barbados

People: Population: 256,000. **Age distrib.** <15: 25; 65+: 11. **Pop. density:** 1,542 per sq. mi. **Urban:** 38%. **Ethnic groups:** African 80%, mixed 16%, European 4%. **Principal languages:** English. **Religions:** Protestant 67%, Roman Catholic 4%.

Geography: Area: 166 sq. mi. **Location:** In Atlantic, farthest E of W Indies. **Neighbors:** Nearest are Trinidad, Grenada on SW. **Topography:** The island lies alone in the Atlantic almost completely surrounded by coral reefs. Highest point is Mt. Hillaby, 1,115 ft. **Capital:** Bridgetown. **Cities** (1990): Bridgetown 6,000.

Government: Type: Parliamentary democracy. **Head of state:** Queen Elizabeth II, represented by Gov.-Gen. Dame Nita Barrow; in office: June 6, 1990. **Head of government:** Prime Min. Owen Arthur; in office: Sept. 9, 1994. **Local divisions:** 11 parishes and Bridgetown. **Defense:** 0.7% of GDP (1989).

Economy: Industries: Sugar, tourism. **Chief crops:** Sugar, cotton. **Minerals:** Lime. **Other resources:** Fish. **Arable land:** 77%. **Electricity prod.** (1992): 540 mln. kWh. **Labor force:** 8% agric.; 22% ind. and comm.; 37% services and government.

Finance: Monetary unit: Dollar (Mar. 1994: 2.01 = $1 US). **Gross domestic product** (1991): $1.8 bln. **Per capita GDP** $7,000. **Imports** (1991): $694 mln.; partners: U.S. 35%, CARACOM 12%. **Exports** (1991): $205 mln.; partners: U.S. 21%, CARACOM 30%. **Tourism** (1990): $502 mln. receipts. **National budget** (FY1992-93): $620 mln. **International reserves less gold** (Mar. 1994): $171 mln. **Consumer prices** (change in 1993): 1.1%.

Transport: Motor vehicles: in use: 39,000 passenger cars; 9,000 comm. vehicles. **Chief ports:** Bridgetown.

Communications: Television sets: 1 per 3.7 persons. **Radios:** 1 per 1.3 persons. **Telephones:** 1 per 2.4 persons. **Daily newspaper circ.:** 160 per 1,000 pop.

Health: Life expectancy at birth (1994): 71 male; 77 female. **Births** (per 1,000 pop.): 16. **Deaths** (per 1,000 pop.): 8. **Natural increase:** 0.7%. **Hospital beds:** 1 per 121 persons. **Physicians:** 1 per 1,042 persons. **Infant mortality** (per 1,000 live births 1994): 20.

Education (1992): **Literacy:** 99%. **Years compulsory:** to age 16.

Major International Organizations: UN (FAO, GATT, ILO, IMF, WHO), OAS.

Embassy: 2144 Wyoming Ave. NW 20008; 939-9200.

Barbados was probably named by Portuguese sailors in reference to bearded fig trees. An English ship visited in 1605, and British settlers arrived on the uninhabited island in 1627. Slaves worked the sugar plantations until slavery was abolished in 1834. Self-rule came gradually, with full independence proclaimed Nov. 30, 1966. British traditions have remained.

Belarus

Republic of Belarus

Respublika Belarus

People: Population: 10,405,000. **Pop. density:** 130 per sq. mi. **Urban:** 67%. **Ethnic groups:** Belarussian 80%, Russian 13%. **Principal languages:** Byelorusian, Russian.

Geography: Area: 80,134 sq. mi. **Neighbors:** Poland on W, Latvia, Lithuania on N, Russia on E, Ukraine on S. **Capital:** Minsk. **Cities** (1991): Minsk 1.6 mln., Homel 503,000.

Government: Republic. **Head of state:** Pres. Aleksandr Lukashenko; in office: July 1994. **Head of government:** Prime Min. Mikhail M. Chygir; b May 24, 1948; in office July 21, 1994. **Local divisions:** 6 regions. **Defense:** 4.5% of GDP (1992).

Economy: Industries: Food processing, chemicals, machine-tool & agricultural machinery. **Chief crops:** Grain, flax, potatoes, sugar beets. **Livestock** (1992): cattle: 6.6 mln. pigs: 4.7 mln. **Electricity prod.** (1992): 37.6 bln. kWh.

Finance: Monetary unit: Belarus ruble.

Transport: Railroads: Length: 3,472 mi. **Passenger cars:** 498,000.

Communications: Television sets: 1 per 2.9 persons. **Radios:** 1 per 3.3 persons. **Telephones:** 1 per 5.8 persons. **Daily newspaper circ.:** 286 per 1,000 pop.

Health: Life expectancy at birth (1994): 66 male; 76 female. **Birth** (per 1,000 pop.): 13. **Deaths** (per 1,000 pop.): 11. **Natural increase:** 0.2%. **Physicians:** 1 per 248 persons. **Hospital beds:** 1 per 76 persons. **Infant mortality** (per 1,000 live births 1994): 19.

Major International Organizations: UN, CIS.

Embassy: 1511 K St. NW 20036; 638-2954.

The region was subject to Lithuanians and Poles in medieval times, and was a prize of war between Russia and Poland beginning in 1503. It became part of the USSR in 1922 although the western part of the region was controlled by Poland. Belarus was overrun by German armies in 1941; recovered by Soviet troops in 1944. Following World War II, Belarus increased in area through Soviet annexation of part of NE Poland. Belarus declared independence Aug. 25, 1991. It became an independent state when the Soviet Union disbanded Dec. 26, 1991. A new constitution was adopted, Mar. 15, 1994, and a new president was chosen in elections concluding July 10, 1994.

Belgium

Kingdom of Belgium

Koninkrijk België (Dutch)
Royaume de Belgique (French)

People: Population: 10,063,000. **Age distrib.** (%): <15: 18; 65+: 15. **Pop. density:** 853 per sq. mi. **Urban:** 97%. **Ethnic groups:** Fleming 55%, Walloon 33%. **Principal languages:** Flemish (Dutch) 56%, French 32%, German. **Religions:** Roman Catholic 75%.

Geography: Area: 11,787 sq. mi., slightly larger than Maryland. **Location:** In NW Europe, on N Sea. **Neighbors:** France on W, S, Luxembourg on SE, Germany on E, Netherlands on N. **Topography:** Mostly flat, the country is trisected by the Scheldt and Meuse, major commercial rivers. The land becomes hilly and forested in the SE (Ardennes) region. **Capital:** Brussels. **Cities** (1991 est.): Brussels (met.) 951,000; Antwerp (met.) 465,000; Ghent 230,000; Charleroi 206,000; Liege 196,000.

Government: Type: Parliamentary democracy under a constitutional monarch. **Head of state:** King Albert II; b June 6, 1934; in office: Aug. 9, 1993. **Head of government:** Premier Jean-Luc Dehaene; b Aug. 7, 1940; in office: Mar. 7, 1992. **Local divisions:** 9 provinces; 3 regions; 3 cultural communities. **Defense:** 2% of GDP (1992).

Economy: Industries: Steel, glassware, diamond cutting, textiles, chemicals. **Chief crops:** Wheat, potatoes, sugar beets. **Minerals:** Coal. **Other resources:** Forests. **Arable land**: 24%. **Livestock:** (1992): cattle: 3.3 mln.; pigs: 6.5 mln. **Fish catch** (1991): 40,226 metric tons. **Electricity prod.** (1992): 68 bln. kWh. **Labor force:** 2% agric.; 28% industry; 64% services.

Finance: Monetary unit: Franc (Mar. 1994: 34.86 = $1 US). **Gross domestic product** (1992): $177.9 bln. **Per capita GDP** $17,800. *Note:* the following trade and tourism data includes Luxembourg. **Imports** (1992): $120 bln.; partners: EU 73%. **Exports** (1992): $118 bln.; partners: EU 74%. **Tourism** (1990): receipts: $3.5 bln. **National budget** (1989): $109.3 bln. **International reserves less gold** (Mar. 1994): $13.0 bln. **Gold:** 25.04 mln. oz t. **Consumer prices** (change in 1993): 2.8%.

Transport: Railroads: Length: 2,162 mi. **Motor vehicles:** in use: 3.9 mln. passenger cars, 596,000 comm. vehicles. **Civil aviation::** 3.8 bln. passenger-mi.; 3 airports with scheduled flights. **Chief ports:** Antwerp, Zeebrugge, Ghent.

Communications: Television sets: 1 per 2.4 persons. **Radios:** 1 per 2.2 persons. **Telephones:** 1 per 1.8 persons. **Daily newspaper circ.:** 305 per 1,000 pop.

Health: Life expectancy at birth (1994): 74 male; 80 female. **Births** (per 1,000 pop.): 12. **Deaths** (per 1,000 pop.): 10. **Natural increase** 0.1%. **Hospital beds:** 1 per 103 persons. **Physicians:** 1 per 298 persons. **Infant mortality** (per 1,000 live births 1994): 7.

Education (1992): **Literacy:** 98%. School compulsory to age 18.

Major International Organizations: UN and all of its specialized agencies, NATO, EU, OECD.

Embassy: 3330 Garfield St. NW 20008; 333-6900

Belgium derives its name from the Belgae, the first recorded inhabitants, probably Celts. The land was conquered by Julius Caesar, and was ruled for 1800 years by conquerors, including Rome, the Franks, Burgundy, Spain, Austria, and France. After 1815, Belgium was made a part of the Netherlands, but it became an independent constitutional monarchy in 1830.

Belgian neutrality was violated by Germany in both world wars. King Leopold III surrendered to Germany, May 28, 1940. After the war, he was forced by political pressure to abdicate in favor of his son, King Baudouin.

The Flemings of northern Belgium speak Dutch, while French is the language of the Walloons in the south. The language difference has been a perennial source of controversy and led to antagonism between the 2 groups. Parliament has passed measures aimed at transferring power from the central government to 3 regions—Wallonia, Flanders, and Brussels.

Belgium lives by its foreign trade; about 50% of its entire production is sold abroad.

Belize

People: Population: 209,000. **Age distrib.** (%): <15: 44; 65+: 4. **Pop. density:** 23 per sq. mi. **Ethnic groups:** Mestizo 44%, Creole 30%, Maya 11%, Garifuna 7%. **Principal languages:** English (official), Spanish, Maya/Garifuna (Carib). **Religions:** Roman Catholic 62%, Protestant 30%.

Geography: Area: 8,867 sq. mi. **Location:** eastern coast of Central America. **Neighbors:** Mexico on N, Guatemala on W and S. **Capital:** Belmopan. **Cities:** (1991 est.): Belize City 45,000.

Government: Type: Parliamentary democracy. **Head of state:** Gov.-Gen. Colville Young. **Head of government:** Prime Min. Manuel Esquivel; b May 2, 1940; in office: July 2, 1993. **Local divisions:** 6 districts. **Defense:** 2% of GDP (1992).

Economy: Sugar is the main export.

Finance: Monetary unit: Belize dollar (Mar. 1994) 2 = $1 U.S. **Gross domestic product** (1990): $373 mln. **Per capita GDP:** $1,635. **Imports** (1992): $273 mln.; partners: U.S. 55%, UK 8%. **Exports:** (1992): $102 mln.; partners: U.S. 46%, UK 31%. **National budget** (1991): $123.1 mln.

Health: Life expectancy at birth (1994): 66 male, 70 female. **Births** (per 1,000 pop.): 35. **Deaths** (per 1,000 pop.): 6. **Natural increase:** 2.9%. **Hospital beds:** 1 per 332 persons. **Physicians:** 1 per 2,021 persons. **Infant mortality** (per 1,000 live births 1994): 36.

Education: (1991) **Literacy:** 93%. **Years compulsory:** 9; attendance 55%.

Major International Organizations: OAS, UN (IMF, World Bank), Commonwealth of Nations.

Embassy: 2535 Massachusetts Ave. NW 20008; 332-9636.

Belize (formerly British Honduras) was Britain's last colony on the American mainland. The country achieved independence Sept. 21, 1981. British troops in Belize guarantee security.

Benin

Republic of Benin

République du Benin

People: Population: 5,342,000. **Age distrib.** (%): <15: 47; 65+: 3. **Pop. density:** 122 per sq. mi. **Urban:** 38%. **Ethnic groups:** African (Fon, Adja, Bariba, Yoruba) 99%. **Principal languages:** French (official), Fon, Yoruba. **Religions:** indigenous beliefs 70%, Muslim 15%, Christian 15%.

Geography: Area: 43,500 sq. mi., slightly smaller than Pennsylvania. **Location:** In W Africa on Gulf of Guinea. **Neighbors:** Togo on W, Burkina Faso, Niger on N, Nigeria on E. **Topography:** most of Benin is flat and covered with dense vegetation. The coast is hot, humid, and rainy. **Capital:** Porto-Novo. **Cities** (1985 est.): Cotonou 402,000.

Government: Type: Democracy. **Head of state:** Nicéphore Soglo; b Nov. 29, 1934; in office: Apr. 4, 1991. **Local divisions:** 6 provinces. **Defense:** 1.7% of GDP (1988 est.).

Economy: Chief crops: Palm products, peanuts, cotton, coffee, tobacco. **Minerals:** Oil. **Arable land:** 12%. **Livestock** (1992): sheep: 920,000; goats: 1.1 mln. **Fish catch** (1991): 41,000 metric tons. **Electricity prod.** (1991): 25 mln. kWh. **Labor force:** 60% agric; 38% transport, commerce, public service.

Finance: Monetary unit: CFA franc (Mar. 1994: 576 = $1 US). **Gross domestic product** (1991): $2 bln. **Per capita GDP:** $410. **Imports** (1990): $428 mln.; partners: Fr. 34%. **Exports** (1990): $263 mln.; partners: EU. **National budget** (1990): $390 bln. **International reserves less gold** (Dec. 1993): $244 mln.

Transport: Railroads: Length: 359 mi. **Chief ports:** Cotonou.

Communications: Radios: 1 per 14 persons. **Televisions:** 1 per 246 persons. **Daily newspaper circ.:** 3 per 1,000 pop.

Health: Life expectancy at birth (1994): 50 male; 54

female. **Births** (per 1,000 pop.): 48. **Deaths** (per 1,000 pop.): 14. **Natural increase:** 3.3%. **Hospital beds:** 1 per 749 persons. **Physicians:** 1 per 11,306 persons. **Infant mortality** (per 1,000 live births 1994): 110.

Education (1991): **Literacy:** 28%. Years compulsory 6; attendance 43%.

Major International Organizations: UN (GATT, IMF, WHO), OAU.

Embassy: 2737 Cathedral Ave. NW 20008; 232-6656.

The Kingdom of Abomey, rising to power in wars with neighboring kingdoms in the 17th century, came under French domination in the late 19th century and was incorporated into French West Africa by 1904.

Under the name Dahomey, the country became independent Aug. 1, 1960. The name was changed to Benin in 1975. In the fifth coup since independence Col. Ahmed Kerekou took power in 1972; two years later he declared a socialist state with a "Marxist-Leninist" philosophy. In Dec. 1989, Kerekou announced that Marxism-Leninism would no longer be the state ideology. In 1991, Kerekou was defeated in Benin's first free presidential elections in 30 years by Nicéphore Soglo.

The economy relies on the development of agriculturally based industries.

Bhutan

Kingdom of Bhutan

Druk-Yul

People: Population: 1,739,000. **Age distrib.** (%): <15: 39; 65+: 4. **Pop. density:** 96 per sq. mi. **Ethnic groups:** Bhote 50%, Nepalese 35%. **Principal languages:** Dzongkha (official), Gurung, Assamese. **Religions:** Lamaistic Buddhist (state religion) 75%, Hindu 25%.

Geography: Area: 18,147 sq. mi., the size of Vermont and New Hampshire combined. **Location:** In eastern Himalayan Mts. **Neighbors:** India on W (Sikkim) and S, China on N. **Topography:** Bhutan is comprised of very high mountains in the N, fertile valleys in the center, and thick forests in the Duar Plain in the S. **Capital:** Thimphu (Paro Dzong is administrative capital). **City** (1987 est.): Thimphu 20,000.

Government: Type: Monarchy. **Head of state:** King Jigme Singye Wangchuk; b Nov. 11, 1955; in office: July 21, 1972. **Local divisions:** 18 districts.

Economy: Industries: Handicrafts, chemicals. **Chief crops:** Rice, corn, wheat. **Other resources:** Timber. **Arable land:** 2%. **Labor force:** 93% agric.

Finance: Monetary unit: Ngultrum (Mar. 1994: 31.37 = $1 US). (Indian Rupee also used). **Gross domestic product** (1991): $320 mln. **Per capita GDP:** $200. **Tourism** (1990): 2.0 mln. **Imports** (1991): $138 mln.; partners: India 67%. **Exports** (1989): $70 mln.; partners: India 93%. **National budget** (1991 est.): $121 mln.

Communications: Radios: 1 per 54 persons. **Telephones:** 1 per 669 persons.

Health: Life expectancy at birth (1994): 51 male; 50 female. **Births** (per 1,000 pop.): 39. **Deaths** (per 1,000 pop.): 16. **Natural increase:** 2.3%. **Hospital beds:** 1 per 1,492 persons. **Physicians:** 1 per 8,969 persons. **Infant mortality** (per 1,000 live births 1994): 121.

Education (1989): **Literacy:** 15%. School attendance: 25%.

Major International Organizations: UN (IMF, World Bank).

The region came under Tibetan rule in the 16th century. British influence grew in the 19th century. A monarchy, set up in 1907, became a British protectorate by a 1910 treaty. The country became independent in 1949, with India guiding foreign relations and supplying aid.

Links to India have been strengthened by airline service and a road network. Most of the population engages in subsistence agriculture.

Bolivia

Republic of Bolivia

República de Bolivia

People: Population: 7,719,000. **Age distrib.** (%): <15: 42; 65+: 40. **Pop. density:** 18 per sq. mi. **Urban:** 58%. **Ethnic groups:** Quechua 30%, Aymara 25%, mixed 25–30%, European 5–15%. **Principal languages:** Spanish, Quechua, Aymara (all official). **Religions:** Roman Catholic 95%.

Geography: Area: 424,164 sq. mi., the size of Texas and California combined. **Location:** In central Andes Mtns. **Neighbors:** Peru, Chile on W, Argentina, Paraguay on S, Brazil on E and N. **Topography:** The great central plateau, at an altitude of 12,000 ft., over 500 mi. long, lies between two great cordilleras having 3 of the highest peaks in S America. Lake Titicaca, on Peruvian border, is highest lake in world on which steamboats ply (12,506 ft.). The E central region has semitropical forests; the llanos, or Amazon-Chaco lowlands are in E. **Capitals**: La Paz (administrative), Sucre (judicial). **Cities** (1992 est.): La Paz 711,000; Santa Cruz 694,000; Cochabamba 404,000.

Government: Type: Republic. **Head of state:** Pres. Gonzalo Sánchez de Lozada; in office: Aug. 6, 1993. **Local divisions:** 9 departments. **Defense:** 1.6% of GDP (1990 est.).

Economy: Industry: Textiles, food processing, mining, clothing. **Chief crops:** Potatoes, sugar, coffee, corn, coca (sold for cocaine processing). **Minerals:** Antimony, tin, tungsten, silver, zinc, oil, gas, iron. **Crude oil reserves** (1985): 157 mln. bbls. **Other resources:** rubber, cinchona bark. **Arable land:** 3%. **Livestock** (1991): cattle: 5.6 mln.; sheep: 12.3 mln.; pigs: 630,000. **Electricity prod.** (1992): 1.8 bln. kWh. **Labor force:** 50% agric., 10% ind. & comm, 26% serv. & utilities.

Finance: Monetary unit: Bolivianos (Feb. 1994: 4.51 = $1 US). **Gross domestic product** (1992): $4.9 bln. **Per capita GDP:** $670. **Imports** (1991): $760 mln.; partners: U.S. 20%, Jap. 10%, Arg. 14%, Braz. 20%. **Exports** (1991): $970 mln.; partners: U.S. 19%. **National budget** (1993 est.): $1.57 bln. **International reserves less gold** (Jan. 1994): $232 mln. **Gold:** 894,000 oz t. **Consumer prices** (change in 1993): 8.5%.

Transport: Railroads: Length: 2,264 mi. **Motor vehicles:** in use: 265,000 passenger cars, 60,000 comm. vehicles. **Civil aviation::** 739 mln. passenger-mi.; 19 airports with scheduled flights.

Communications: Television sets: 1 per 12 persons. **Radios:** 1 per 1.9 persons. **Telephones:** 1 per 38 persons. **Daily newspaper circ.:** 55 per 1,000 pop.

Health: Life expectancy at birth (1994): 61 male; 66 female. **Births** (per 1,000 pop.): 32. **Deaths** (per 1,000 pop.): 8. **Natural increase:** 2.4%. **Hospital beds:** 1 per 1,183 persons. **Physicians:** 1 per 2,124 persons. **Infant mortality** (per 1,000 live births 1994): 74.

Education (1991): **Literacy:** 78%. **Years compulsory:** ages 7-14; attendance 82%.

Major International Organizations: UN (IMF, FAO, WHO), OAS.

Embassy: 3014 Massachusetts Ave. NW 20008; 483-4410.

The Incas conquered the region from earlier Indian inhabitants in the 13th century. Spanish rule began in the 1530s and lasted until Aug. 6, 1825. The country is named after Simon Bolivar, independence fighter.

In a series of wars, Bolivia lost its Pacific coast to Chile, the oil-bearing Chaco to Paraguay, and rubber-growing areas to Brazil, 1879-1935.

Economic unrest, especially among the militant mine workers, has contributed to continuing political instability. A reformist government under Victor Paz Estenssoro, 1951-64, nationalized tin mines and attempted to improve conditions for the Indian majority but was overthrown by a military junta. A series of coups and countercoups continued through 1981, until the military junta elected Gen. Villa as president.

In July 1982, the military junta assumed power amid a growing economic crisis and foreign debt difficulties. The junta resigned in Oct. and allowed the Congress, elected democratically in 1980, to take power.

U.S. pressure on the government to reduce the country's output of coca, the raw material for cocaine, has led to clashes between police and coca growers and increased anti-U.S. feeling among Bolivians.

Bosnia and Herzegovina

People: Population: 4,651,000. **Pop. density:** 235 per sq. mi. **Ethnic groups:** Muslim 44%, Serbian 31%, Croatian 17%. **Principal languages:** Serbo-Croatian (official) 99%. **Religions:** Muslim 40%, Orthodox 31%, Catholic 15% .

Geography: Area: 19,741 sq. mi. **Location:** in SE Europe. **Neighbors:** Yugoslavia, Croatia, Adriatic Sea. **Topography:** Hilly with some mountains. About 50% of the land is forested. **Capital:** Sarajevo.

Government: Type: In transition. **Head of state:** Pres. Alija Izetbegovic; b 1925; in office: Dec. 1990.

Economy: Industries: Textiles, rugs, timber. **Chief crops:** Corn, wheat, oats, barley. **Minerals:** Bauxite, iron ore, coal.

Finance: Monetary unit: New Yugoslav Dinar. **Gross domestic product** (1991): $14 bln.* **Per capita GDP:** $3,200.

Health: Births (per 1,000 pop.): 13. **Deaths** (per 1,000 pop.): 6. **Natural increase:** 0.7%. **Physicians:** 1 per 624 persons. **Hospital beds:** 1 per 219 persons.

Education: Literacy (1991): 90%.

International Organizations: UN.

Bosnia was ruled by Croatian kings c. 958 AD, and by Hungary 1000-1200. It became organized c. 1200 and later took control of Herzegovina. The kingdom disintegrated from 1391, with the southern part becoming the independent duchy Herzegovina. It was conquered by Turks in 1463 and made a Turkish province. The area was placed under control of Austria-Hungary in 1878, and made part of the province of **Bosnia and Herzegovina,** which was formally annexed to Austria-Hungary 1908, and it became a province of Yugoslavia in 1918. It was reunited with Herzegovina as a federated republic in the 1946 constitution.

The Bosnia and Herzegovina parliament adopted a declaration of sovereignty Oct. 15, 1991. A referendum for independence was passed Feb. 29, 1992. Ethnic Serbs' opposition to the referendum spurred violent clashes and bombings. The U.S. and EU recognized the republic Apr. 7. Fierce three-way fighting continued between Bosnia's Serbs, Muslims, and Croats. Serb forces massacred thousands of Bosnian Muslims and engaged in "ethnic cleansing" (the expulsion of Muslims and other non-Serbs from areas under Bosnian Serb control). The capital, Sarajevo, was surrounded and besieged by Bosnian Serb forces.

Muslims and Croats in Bosnia reached a cease-fire Feb. 23, 1994, and signed an accord, Mar. 18, to create a Muslim-Croat confederation in Bosnia. The Bosnian and Croatian governments agreed to link this confederation loosely with Croatia. Heavy Muslim-Serb fighting continued, with many civilian casualties. More than 60 were killed Feb. 5 when a mortar shell exploded in a Sarajevo marketplace. On Feb. 17-20, Bosnian Serbs removed most heavy weapons from around Sarajevo in response to a NATO ultimatum. On Feb. 28, NATO aircraft shot down Bosnian Serb aircraft reportedly violating a no-fly zone over Bosnia.

As of mid-1994, Bosnian Serbs had control of more than 70% of the country. An international peace plan that would give Serbs 49% of a partitioned Bosnia, and the Muslim-Croat confederation 51%, was repeatedly rejected by Bosnian Serbs.

Botswana

Republic of Botswana

People: Population: 1,359,000. **Age distrib.** (%): <15: 48; 65+: 30. **Pop. density:** 6 per sq. mi. **Urban:** 26%. **Ethnic groups:** Batswana 95%, Kalanga, others. **Principal languages:** English (official), Setswana. **Religions:** indigenous beliefs 50%, Christian 50%.

Geography: Area: 224,607 sq. mi., slightly smaller than Texas. **Location:** In southern Africa. **Neighbors:** Namibia on N and W, S Africa on S, Zimbabwe on NE; Botswana claims border with Zambia on N. **Topography:** The Kalahari Desert, supporting nomadic Bushmen and wildlife, spreads over SW; there are swamplands and farming areas in N, and rolling plains in E where livestock are grazed. **Capital:** Gaborone. **Cities** (1991): Gaborone 133,000.

Government: Type: Parliamentary republic. **Head of state:** Pres. Quett Masire; b 1925; in office: July 13, 1980. **Local divisions:** 10 district councils and 4 town councils. **Defense:** 4.9% of GDP (FY1993-94).

Economy: Industries: Livestock processing, mining. **Chief crops:** Corn, sorghum, beans. **Minerals:** Copper, coal, nickel, diamonds. **Other resources:** Big game. **Arable land:** 2%. **Electricity prod.** (1991): 1.1 bln. kWh. **Labor force:** 70% agric.

Finance: Monetary unit: Pula (Mar. 1994: 1.00 = $.38 US). **Gross domestic product** (1992): $3.6 bln. **Per capita GDP:** $2,450. **Imports** (1991): $2.2 bln.; partners: S Africa 88%. **Exports** (1991): $2.7 bln.; partners: Europe 67%, U.S. 17%, S Africa 7%. **National budget** (1994): $1.99 bln. **International reserves less gold** (Dec. 1993): $4.1 bln. **Consumer prices** (change in 1993): 14.3%.

Transport: Railroads: Length: 551 mi. **Motor vehicles:** in use: 17,000 passenger cars, 28,000 comm. vehicles.

Communications: Radios: 1 per 1.2 persons. **Telephones:** 1 per 23 persons. **Daily newspaper circ.:** 14 per 1,000 pop.

Health: Life expectancy at birth (1994): 60 male; 66 female. **Births** (1,000 pop.): 32. **Deaths** (per 1,000 pop.): 8. **Natural increase:** 2.4%. **Hospital beds:** 1 per 395 persons. **Physicians:** 1 per 5,417 persons. **Infant mortality** (per 1,000 live births 1994): 39.

Education (1990): **Literacy:** 23%.

Major International Organizations: UN (GATT, IMF, WHO), OAU, Commonwealth of Nations.

Embassy: 3400 International Dr. NW 20008; 244-4990.

First inhabited by bushmen, then by Bantus, the region became the British protectorate of Bechuanaland in 1886, halting encroachment by Boers and Germans from the south and southwest. The country became fully independent Sept. 30, 1966, changing its name to Botswana.

Cattle raising and mining (diamonds, copper, nickel) have contributed to the country's economic growth. The economy is closely tied to S Africa.

Brazil

Federative Republic of Brazil

República Federativa do Brasil

People: Population: 158,739,000. **Age distrib.** (%): <15: 35; 65+: 5. **Pop. density:** 48 per sq. mi. **Urban:** 76%. **Ethnic groups:** Portuguese, Africans, and mulattoes make up the vast majority; Italians, Germans, Japanese, Indians, Jews, Arabs. **Principal languages:** Portuguese (official), Spanish, French, English. **Religions:** Roman Catholic 90%.

Geography: Area: 3,286,470 sq. mi., larger than contiguous 48 U.S. states; largest country in S America. **Location:** Occupies eastern half of S America. **Neighbors:** French Guiana, Suriname, Guyana, Venezuela on N, Colombia, Peru, Bolivia, Paraguay, Argentina on W, Uruguay on S. **Topography:** Brazil's Atlantic coastline stretches 4,603 miles. In N is the heavily wooded Amazon basin covering half the country. Its network of rivers navigable for 15,814 mi. The Amazon itself flows 2,093 miles in Brazil, all navigable. The NE region is semiarid scrubland, heavily settled and poor. The S central region, favored by climate and resources, has almost half of the population, produces 75% of farm goods and 80% of industrial output. The narrow coastal belt includes most of the major cities. Almost the entire country has a tropical or semitropical climate. **Capital:** Brasília. **Cities** (1991 est.): São Paulo 15.2 mln.; Rio de Janeiro 9.6 mln.; Brasília 1.6 mln.; Salvador 2.0 mln.

Government: Type: Federal republic. **Head of state:** Pres. Fernando Henrique Cardoso; b June 18, 1931; in office: Jan. 1, 1995. **Local divisions:** 26 states, federal district (Brasília). **Defense:** 3% of GDP (1990).

Economy: Industries: Steel, autos, ships, appliances, petrochemicals, machinery. **Chief crops:** Coffee (largest grower), cotton, soybeans, sugar, cocoa, rice, corn, fruits. **Minerals:** Chromium, iron, manganese, diamonds, gold, nickel, gem stones, tin, bauxite, oil. **Crude oil reserves** (1991): 2.8 bln. bbls. **Arable land:** 7%. **Livestock** (1992): cattle: 153 mln.; pigs: 33 mln.; sheep: 19.5 mln. **Fish catch** (1991): 800,000 metric tons. **Electricity prod.** (1992): 242 bln. kWh. **Labor force:** 42% services, 31% agric., 27% ind.

Finance: Monetary unit: Cruzeiro (Mar. 1994: 768 = $1 US). **Gross domestic product** (1992): $369 bln. **Per capita GDP:** $2,350. **Imports** (1992): $23 bln.; partners: U.S. 21%, EU 23%. **Exports** (1992): $36 bln.; partners: U.S. 26%, EU 27%. **Tourism** (1991): receipts: $1.4 bln. **National budget** (1991): $170 bln. **International reserves less gold** (Jan. 1994): $33.7 bln. **Gold:** 2.93 mln. oz t. **Consumer prices** (change in 1993): 2,148%.

Transport: Railroads: Length: 18,721 mi. **Motor vehicles:** in use: 12 mln. passenger cars, 900,000. **Civil aviation:**17.3 bln. passenger-mi.; 110 airports with scheduled flights. **Chief ports:** Santos, Rio de Janeiro, Vitoria, Salvador, Rio Grande, Recife.

Communications: Television sets: 1 per 5 persons. **Radios:** 1 per 2.5 persons. **Telephones:** 1 per 10 persons. **Daily newspaper circ.:** 54 per 1,000 pop.

Health: Life expectancy at birth (1994): 57 male; 67 female. **Births** (per 1,000 pop.): 21. **Deaths** (per 1,000 pop.): 9. **Natural increase:** 1.3%. **Hospital beds:** 1 per 270 persons. **Physicians:** 1 per 848 persons. **Infant mortality** (per 1,000 live births 1994): 60.

Education (1991): **Literacy:** 81%.

Major International Organizations: UN and most of its specialized agencies, OAS.

Embassy: 3006 Massachusetts Ave. NW 20008; 745-2700.

Pedro Alvares Cabral, a Portuguese navigator, is generally credited as the first European to reach Brazil, in 1500. The country was thinly settled by various Indian tribes. Only a few have survived to the present, mostly in the Amazon basin.

In the next centuries, Portuguese colonists gradually pushed inland, bringing along large numbers of African slaves. Slavery was not abolished until 1888.

The King of Portugal, fleeing before Napoleon's army, moved the seat of government to Brazil in 1808. Brazil thereupon became a kingdom under Dom Joao VI. After his return to Portugal, his son Pedro proclaimed the independence of Brazil, Sept. 7, 1822, and was acclaimed emperor. The second emperor, Dom Pedro II, was deposed in 1889, and a republic proclaimed, called the United States of Brazil. In 1967 the country was renamed the Federative Republic of Brazil.

A military junta took control in 1930; dictatorial power was assumed by Getulio Vargas, until finally forced out by the military in 1945. A democratic regime prevailed 1945-64, during which time the capital was moved from Rio de Janeiro to Brasília.

In 1964, Pres. Joao Belchoir Marques Goulart instituted economic policies that aggravated Brazil's inflation; he was overthrown by an army revolt. The next 5 presidents were all military leaders. Censorship was imposed, and much of the opposition was suppressed amid charges of torture. In 1974 elections, the official opposition party made gains in the chamber of deputies; some relaxation of censorship occurred.

Since 1930, successive governments have pursued industrial and agricultural growth and the development of interior areas. Exploiting vast mineral resources, fertile soil in several regions, and a huge labor force, Brazil became the leading industrial power of Latin America by the 1970s, while agricultural output soared.

However, income maldistribution and inflation led to severe economic recession. Foreign debt is among the largest in the world. Brazil and its principal commercial bank lenders agreed to restructure the nation's $44 billion commercial debts, July 1992. The 1991 census revealed that population growth dipped below 2 percent for the first time in half a century.

Brazil unveiled a comprehensive environmental program for the Amazon region in 1989, amid an international outcry by environmentalists and others concerned about the ongoing destruction of the Amazon ecosystem. Brazil hosted delegates from 178 countries at the Earth Summit June 3-14, 1992.

Democratic presidential elections were held in 1985 as the nation returned to civilian rule. Fernando Collor de Mello was elected president in Dec. 1989. In Sept. 1992, Pres. Collor was impeached for corruption. He resigned on Dec. 29 as his trial was beginning, and Itamar Franco, who had been acting president, was sworn in as president. In elections held on Oct. 3, 1994, sociology professor and former foreign minister and finance minister Fernando Henrique Cardoso was elected president by the widest popular margin in Brazil since 1945.

Brunei

State of Brunei Darussalam

Negara Brunei Darussalam

People: Population: 285,000. **Pop. density:** 128 per sq. mi. **Ethnic groups:** Malay 64%, Chinese 20%. **Principal languages:** Malay (official), English, Chinese. **Religion:** Muslim 63%, Buddhist 14%, Christian 8%.

Geography: Area: 2,226 sq. mi.; larger than Delaware. **Location:** on the north coast of the island of Borneo; it is surrounded on its landward side by the Malaysian state of Sarawak. **Capital:** Bandar Seri Begawan. **Cities** (1982 est.): Bandar Seri Begawan 51,000.

Government: Type: Independent sultanate. **Head of government:** Sultan Sir Muda Hassanal Bolkiah Mu'izzadin Waddaulah; b July 15, 1946; in office: Jan. 1, 1984. **Local divisions:** 4 districts. **Defense:** 9% of GDP (1990).

Economy: Industries: petroleum (about 90% of revenue is derived from oil exports). **Chief crops:** rice, bananas, cassava.

Finance: Monetary unit: Brunei dollar (Jan. 1993: 1.65 = $1 US). **Gross domestic product** (1990): $3.5 bln. **Per capita GDP:** $8,800.

Transport: Motor vehicles: in use: 115,000 passenger cars, 13,000 commercial vehicles.

Communications: Television sets: 1 per 4 persons. **Radios:** 1 per 2.7 persons. **Telephones:** 1 per 4.9 persons.

Education (1987): **Literacy:** 95% among young.

Health: Life expectancy at birth: (1994): 69 male; 73 female. **Births** (per 1,000 pop.): 26. **Deaths** (per 1,000 pop.): 5. **Natural increase**: 2.1%. **Infant mortality** (per 1,000 live births 1994): 25.

Major International Organizations: UN and some of its specialized agencies.

The Sultanate of Brunei was a powerful state in the early 16th century, with authority over all of the island of Borneo as well as parts of the Sulu Islands and the Philippines. In 1888, a treaty placed the state under the protection of Great Britain.

Brunei became a fully sovereign and independent state on Jan. 1, 1984.

The Sultan of Brunei donated $10 million to the Nicaraguan *contras* in 1987; the subsequent misplacement of the funds generated much media attention in the U.S.

Bulgaria

Republic of Bulgaria

Republika Bulgaria

People: Population: 8,800,000. **Age distrib.** (%): <15: 20; 65+: 14. **Pop. density:** 205 per sq. mi. **Urban:** 67%. **Ethnic groups:** Bulgarian 85%, Turk 8.5%. **Principal languages:** Bulgarian. **Religions:** Bulgarian Orthodox 85%, Muslim 13%.

Geography: Area: 42,855 sq. mi., about the size of Ohio. **Location:** In eastern Balkan Peninsula on Black Sea. **Neighbors:** Romania on N, Yugoslavia, Macedonia on W, Greece, Turkey on S. **Topography:** The Stara Planina (Balkan) Mts. stretch E-W across the center of the country, with the Danubian plain on N, the Rhodope Mts. on SW, and Thracian Plain on SE. **Capital:** Sofia. **Cities** (1991 est.): Sofia 1.1 mln.; Plovdiv 379,000; Varna 316,000.

Government: Type: Republic. **Head of state:** Pres. Zhelyu Zhelev; b Mar. 3, 1935; in office: Aug. 1, 1990. **Head of government:** Prem. Lyuben Berov; in office: Dec. 30, 1992. **Local divisions:** 9 provinces. **Defense:** 5.7% of GNP (1992).

Economy: Industries: Chemicals, machinery, metals, textiles, processed food. **Chief crops:** Grains, fruit, corn, potatoes, tobacco. **Minerals:** Lead, manganese, lignite, coal. **Arable land:** 34%. **Livestock** (1993): cattle: 974,000; pigs: 2.6 mln.; sheep: 4.8 mln. **Fish catch** (1992): 27,000 metric tons. **Electricity prod.** (1992): 45 bln. kWh. **Labor force:** 20% agric.; 33% ind.

Finance: Monetary unit: Lev (Jan. 1993: 24.56 = $1 US). **Gross national product** (1992): $34.1 bln.* **Per capita GNP:** $3,800. **Imports** (1990): $9.6 bln.; partners: CIS 56%. **Exports** (1990): $8.4 bln.; partners: CIS 70%. **Tourism** (1989): revenues: $362 mln. **National budget** (1991 est.): $5 bln.

Transport: Railroads: Length: 4,076 mi. **Motor vehicles:** in use: 1.3 mln. passenger cars, 133,000 commercial vehicles. **Civil aviation:** 1.8 bln. passenger-mi.; 3 airports. **Chief ports:** Burgas, Varna.

Communications: Television sets: 1 per 2.9 persons. **Radios:** 1 per 3.0 persons. **Telephones:** 1 per 3.0 persons. **Daily newspaper circ.:** 451 per 1,000 pop.

Health: Life expectancy at birth (1994): 70 male; 77 female. **Births** (per 1,000 pop): 12. **Deaths** (per 1,000 pop.): 11. **Hospital beds:** 1 per 97 persons. **Physicians:** 1 per 312 persons. **Infant mortality** (per 1,000 live births 1994): 12.

Education (1990): **Literacy:** 98%.

Major International Organizations: UN.

Embassy: 1621-22d St. NW 20008; 387-7969.

Bulgaria was settled by Slavs in the 6th century. Turkic Bulgars arrived in the 7th century, merged with the Slavs, became

Christians by the 9th century, and set up powerful empires in the 10th and 12th centuries. The Ottomans prevailed in 1396 and remained for 500 years.

A revolt in 1876 led to an independent kingdom in 1908. Bulgaria expanded after the first Balkan War but lost its Aegean coastline in World War I, when it sided with Germany. Bulgaria joined the Axis in World War II but withdrew in 1944. Communists took power with Soviet aid; the monarchy was abolished Sept. 8, 1946.

On Nov. 10, 1989, Communist Party leader and head of state Todor Zhivkov, who had held power for 35 years, resigned. Zhivkov was imprisoned, Jan. 1990, and convicted, Sept. 1992, of corruption and abuse of power. In Jan. 1990, Parliament voted to revoke the constitutionally guaranteed dominant role of the Communist Party.

Burkina Faso

People: Population: 10,135,000. **Pop. density:** 95 per sq. mi. **Urban:** 21%. **Ethnic groups:** Gurunsi, Senufo, Lobi, Mossi, Bobo, Mande, Fulani. **Principal languages:** French (official), Sudanic tribal languages. **Religions:** indigenous beliefs 65%, Muslim 25%, Christian 10%.

Geography: Area: 105,946 sq. mi., the size of Colorado. **Location:** In W Africa, S of the Sahara. **Neighbors:** Mali on NW, Niger on NE, Benin, Togo, Ghana, Côte d'Ivoire on S. **Topography:** Landlocked Burkina Faso is in the savannah region of W Africa. The N is arid, hot, and thinly populated. **Capital:** Ouagadougou. **Cities** (1990): Ouagadougou 441,000; Bobo-Dioulasso 228,000.

Government: Type: Military. **Head of state:** Pres. Blaise Compaoré; in office: Oct. 15, 1987. **Head of government:** Prime Min. Roch Christian Kabore; in office: Mar. 20, 1994. **Local divisions:** 30 provinces. **Defense:** 4.3% of GDP (1992).

Economy: Chief crops: Millet, sorghum, rice, peanuts, grain. **Minerals:** Manganese, gold, limestone. **Arable land:** 10%. **Electricity prod.** (1991): 320 mln. kWh. **Labor force:** 82% agric.

Finance: Monetary unit: CFA Franc (Mar. 1994: 576 = $1 US). **Gross domestic product** (1991): $3.3 bln. **Per capita GDP:** $350. **Imports** (1989): $322 mln.; partners: EU, Côte d' Ivoire. **Exports** (1989): $95 mln.; partners: Côte d'Ivoire, EU, China. **National budget** (1991): $786 mln. **International reserves less gold** (Dec. 1993): $382 mln. **Gold:** 11,000 oz t. **Consumer prices** (change in 1992): -1.4%.

Transport: Motor vehicles: in use: 12,000 passenger cars, 13,000 comm. vehicles.

Communications: Television sets: 1 per 209 persons. **Radios:** 1 per 48 persons. **Telephones:** 1 per 485 persons.

Health: Life expectancy at birth (1994): 46 male; 48 female. **Births** (per 1,000 pop.): 48. **Deaths** (per 1,000 pop.): 18. **Natural increase:** 3.0%. **Hospital beds:** 1 per 1,359 persons. **Physicians:** 1 per 29,914 persons. **Infant mortality** (per 1,000 live births 1994): 118.

Education (1991): **Literacy:** 18%. Only 8% attend school.

Major International Organizations: UN and many of its specialized agencies, OAU.

Embassy: 2340 Massachusetts Ave. NW 20008; 332-5577.

The Mossi tribe entered the area in the 11th to 13th centuries. Their kingdoms ruled until defeated by the Mali and Songhai empires.

French control came by 1896, but Upper Volta (renamed Burkina Faso on Aug. 4, 1984) was not established as a separate territory until 1947. Full independence came Aug. 5, 1960, and a pro-French government was elected. The military seized power in 1980. A 1987 coup established the current regime, which restored limited democracy in the early 1990s.

Several hundred thousand farm workers migrate each year to Côte d'Ivoire and Ghana. Burkina Faso is heavily dependent on foreign aid.

Burma

(See Myanmar)

Burundi

Republic of Burundi

Republika y'Uburundi

People: Population: 6,125,000. **Age distrib.** (%): <15: 46; 65+: 4. **Pop. density:** 570 per sq. mi. **Urban:** 6%. **Ethnic groups:** Hutu 85%, Tutsi 14%, Twa (pygmy) 1%. **Principal languages:** French, Kirundi (both official), Swahili. **Religions:** Roman Catholic 62%, indigenous beliefs 32%.

Geography: Area: 10,740 sq. mi., the size of Maryland. **Location:** In central Africa. **Neighbors:** Rwanda on N, Zaire on W, Tanzania on E. **Topography:** Much of the country is grassy highland, with mountains reaching 8,900 ft. The southernmost source of the White Nile is located in Burundi. Lake Tanganyika is the second deepest lake in the world. **Capital:** Bujumbura. **Cities** (1991 est.): Bujumbura 240,000.

Government: Type: Republic. **Head of state:** Interim Pres. Sylvestre Ntibantunganya; in office: Apr. 8, 1994. **Head of government:** Prem. Anatole Kanyenkiko; in office: 1994. **Local divisions:** 15 provinces. **Defense:** 3.7% of GDP (1989).

Economy: Chief crops: Coffee (87% of exports), cotton, tea. **Minerals:** Nickel. **Arable land:** 43%. **Electricity prod.** (1991): 105 mln. kWh. **Labor force:** 93% agric.

Finance: Monetary unit: Franc (Mar. 1994: 264 = $1 US). **Gross domestic product** (1991): $1.23 bln. **Per capita GDP:** $205. **Imports** (1991): $248 mln.; partners: Belg.-Lux. 17%; Ger. 18%. **Exports** (1991): $90 mln.; partners: Ger. 31%, Belg. 20%. **Tourism** (1990): $4 mln. receipts. **National budget** (1991 est.): $326 mln. **International reserves less gold** (Mar. 1994): $212 mln. **Gold:** 17,000 oz t. **Consumer prices** (change in 1993): 9.7%.

Transport: Motor vehicles: in use: 13,000 passenger cars, 14,000 comm. vehicles.

Communications: Radios: 1 per 11 persons. **Telephones:** 1 per 506 persons.

Health: Life expectancy at birth (1994): 38 male; 42 female. **Births** (per 1,000 pop.): 44. **Deaths** (per 1,000 pop.): 21. **Natural increase:** 2.3%. **Hospital beds:** 1 per 515 persons. **Physicians:** 1 per 31,777 persons. **Infant mortality** (per 1,000 live births 1994): 114.

Education (1991): **Literacy:** 50%. **Years compulsory:** 6. **Attendance:** 45%.

Major International Organizations: UN (GATT, IMF, WHO), OAU.

Embassy: 2233 Wisconsin Ave. NW 20007; 342-2574.

The pygmy Twa were the first inhabitants, followed by Bantu Hutus, who were conquered in the 16th century by the Tutsi (Watusi), probably from Ethiopia. Under German control in 1899, the area fell to Belgium in 1916, which exercised successively a League of Nations mandate and UN trusteeship over Ruanda-Urundi (now the two countries of Rwanda and Burundi).

Independence came in 1962.

An unsuccessful Hutu rebellion in 1972-73 left 10,000 Tutsi and 150,000 Hutu dead. Over 100,000 Hutu fled to Tanzania and Zaire. In the 1980s, Burundi's Tutsi-dominated regime pledged itself to ethnic reconciliation and democratic reform. In the nation's first democratic presidential election, in June 1993, a Hutu was elected, but he was killed in an attempted coup, Oct. 21, 1993, setting off new waves of ethnic violence in which thousands were killed. Pres. Cyprien Ntaryamira, elected Jan. 1994, was killed with the president of Rwanda in a mysterious plane crash, Apr. 6. The incident sparked massive carnage in Rwanda; violence in Burundi was, at least initially, far more limited.

Cambodia

State of Cambodia

Roat Kampuchea

People: Population: 10,265,000. **Pop. density:** 146 per sq. mi. **Urban:** 13%. **Ethnic groups:** Khmer 90%, Vietnamese 5%, Chinese 1%. **Principal languages:** Khmer (official), French. **Religions:** Theravada Buddhism 95%.

Geography: Area: 70,238 sq. mi., the size of Missouri. **Location:** In Indochina Peninsula. **Neighbors:** Thailand on W, N, Laos on NE, Vietnam on E. **Topography:** The central area, formed by the Mekong R. basin and Tonle Sap lake, is level. Hills and mountains are in SE, a long escarpment separates the country from Thailand on NW. 75% of the area is forested. **Capital:** Phnom Penh. **Cities** (1990 est.): Phnom Penh 800,000.

Government: Type: Constitutional monarchy. **Head of state:** King Norodom Sihanouk; b Oct. 31, 1922; in office: Sept. 24, 1993. **Head of government:** First Prime Min. Prince

Norodom Ranariddh; in office: Sept. 24, 1993. **Local divisions:** 19 provinces and 2 cities. **Defense:** 4.8% of GNP (1992).

Economy: Industries: Rice milling, wood & rubber. **Chief crops:** Rice, corn. **Minerals:** Iron, copper, manganese. **Other resources:** Forests, rubber. **Arable land:** 16%. **Livestock** (1992): cattle: 2.2 mln. pigs: 1.7 mln. **Fish catch** (1991): 110,000 metric tons. **Electricity prod.** (1991): 200 mln. kWh. **Labor force:** 74% agri.

Finance: Monetary unit: Riel (Jan. 1993: 1,508 = $1 US). **Gross domestic product** (1991 est.): $2 bln. **Per capita GDP:** $280. **Imports** (1988): $147 mln. **Exports** (1988): $32 mln.

Transport: Railroads: Length: 403 mi. **Motor vehicles:** in use: 4,000 passenger cars, 7,000 trucks. **Chief ports:** Kompong Som.

Communications: Television sets: 1 per 129 persons. **Radios:** 1 per 11 persons. **Telephones:** 1 per 3,300 persons.

Health: Life expectancy at birth (1994): 48 male; 51 female. **Births** (per 1,000 pop.): 45. **Deaths** (per 1,000 pop.): 16. **Natural increase:** 2.9. **Hospital beds:** 1 per 632 persons. **Physicians:** 1 per 27,000 persons. **Infant Mortality** (per 1,000 live births 1994): 111.

Education (1990): **Literacy:** 50%.

Major International Organizations: UN.

Early kingdoms dating from that of Funan in the 1st century AD culminated in the great Khmer empire which flourished from the 9th century to the 13th, encompassing present-day Thailand, Cambodia, Laos, and southern Vietnam. The peripheral areas were lost to invading Siamese and Vietnamese, and France established a protectorate in 1863. Independence came in 1953.

Prince Norodom Sihanouk, king 1941-1955 and head of state from 1960, tried to maintain neutrality. Relations with the U.S. were broken in 1965, after South Vietnam planes attacked Vietcong forces within Cambodia. Relations were restored in 1969, after Sihanouk charged Viet Communists with arming Cambodian insurgents.

In 1970, pro-U.S. Prem. Lon Nol seized power, demanding removal of 40,000 North Viet troops; the monarchy was abolished. Sihanouk formed a government-in-exile in Peking, and open war began between the government and Khmer Rouge. The U.S. provided heavy military and economic aid.

Khmer Rouge forces captured Phnom Penh Apr. 17, 1975. The new government evacuated all cities and towns, and shuffled the rural population, sending virtually the entire population to clear jungle, forest, and scrub. Over one million people were killed in executions and enforced hardships.

Severe border fighting broke out with Vietnam in 1978 and developed into a full-fledged Vietnamese invasion. Formation of a backed government was announced, Jan. 8, 1979, one day after the Vietnamese capture of Phnom Pehn. Thousands of refugees flowed into Thailand and widespread starvation was reported.

On Jan. 10, 1983, Vietnam launched an offensive against rebel forces in the west. They overran a refugee camp, Jan. 31, driving 30,000 residents into Thailand. In Mar., Vietnam launched a major offensive against camps on the Cambodian-Thailand border, engaged Khmer Rouge guerrillas, and crossed the border instigating clashes with Thai troops. Vietnam announced that it would withdraw all its troops by Sept. 1989.

Following UN-sponsored elections in Cambodia that ended May 28, 1993, the 2 leading parties agreed to share power in an interim government until a new constitution was adopted. On Sept. 21, a constitution that created a constitutional monarchy was adopted by the National Assembly. It went into effect on Sept. 24, 1993, with Norodom Sihanouk as king. The Khmer Rouge, which had boycotted the elections, opposed the new government, and some armed violence continued.

Cameroon

Republic of Cameroon

People: Population: 13,132,000. **Age distrib.** (%): <15: 45; 65+: 3. **Pop. density:** 71 per sq. mi. **Urban:** 41%. **Ethnic groups:** Cameroon Highlanders 31%, Equatorial Bantu 19%, Kirdi 11%, Fulani 10%. **Principal languages:** English, French (both official), numerous African groups. **Religions:** indigenous beliefs 51%, Christian 33%, Muslim 16%.

Geography: Area: 183,569 sq. mi., somewhat larger than California. **Location:** Between W and central Africa. **Neighbors:** Nigeria on NW, Chad, Central African Republic on E, Congo, Gabon, Equatorial Guinea on S. **Topography:** A low coastal plain with rain forests is in S; plateaus in center lead to forested mountains in W, including Mt. Cameroon, 13,000 ft.; grasslands in N lead to marshes around Lake Chad. **Capital:** Yaoundé. **Cities** (1988 est.): Douala 852,000; Yaoundé 700,000.

Government: Type: Republic. **Head of state:** Pres. Paul Biya; b Feb. 13, 1933; in office: Nov. 6, 1982. **Head of government:** Prime Min. Simon Achidi Achu; in office: Apr. 9, 1992. **Local divisions:** 10 provinces. **Defense:** 1.7% of GDP (1990).

Economy: Industries: Aluminum processing, oil prod., palm products. **Chief crops:** Cocoa, coffee, cotton. **Crude oil reserves** (1985): 531 mln. bbls. **Other resources:** Timber. **Arable land:** 13%. **Livestock** (1992): cattle: 4.7 mln.; sheep: 3.5 mln.; pigs: 1.3 mln. **Fish catch** (1990): 77,000 metric tons. **Electricity prod.** (1991): 2.1 bln. kWh. **Labor force:** 74% agric., 11% ind. and transport.

Finance: Monetary unit: CFA franc (Mar. 1994: 576 = $1 US). **Gross domestic product** (1991): $11.6 bln. **Per capita GDP:** $1,010. **Imports** (1990): $2.1 bln.; partners: Fr. 42%. **Exports** (1990): $928 mln.; partners: EU 50%. **National budget** (1990): $2.1 bln. **International reserves less gold** (Dec. 1993): $2.4 mln. **Gold:** 30,000 oz t.

Transport: Railroads: Length: 686 mi. **Motor vehicles:** in use: 94,000 passenger cars, 82,000 comm. vehicles. **Chief ports:** Douala.

Communications: Radios: 1 per 6.3 persons. **Telephones:** 1 per 185 persons.

Health: Life expectancy at birth (1994): 55 male; 59 female. **Births** (per 1,000 pop.): 41. **Deaths** (per 1,000 pop.): 11. **Natural increase:** 2.9%. **Hospital beds:** 1 per 377 persons. **Physicians:** 1 per 12,540 persons. **Infant mortality** (per 1,000 live births 1994): 77.

Education (1991): **Literacy:** 65%. About 70% attend school.

Major International Organizations: UN, OAU, EU (Associate).

Embassy: 2349 Massachusetts Ave. NW 20008; 265-8790.

Portuguese sailors were the first Europeans to reach Cameroon, in the 15th century. The European and American slave trade was very active in the area. German control lasted from 1884 to 1916, when France and Britain divided the territory, later receiving League of Nations mandates and UN trusteeships. French Cameroon became independent Jan. 1, 1960; one part of British Cameroon joined Nigeria in 1961, the other part joined Cameroon. Stability has allowed for development of roads, railways, agriculture, and petroleum production.

Pres. Paul Biya retained his office in Oct. 1992 elections, but the results were widely disputed.

Canada

People: Population: 28,114,000. **Age distrib.** (%): <15: 21; 65+: 12. **Pop. density:** 7 per sq. mi. **Urban:** 77%. **Ethnic groups:** British 40%; French 27%; other European 20%; indigenous Indian and Eskimo 1.5%. **Principal languages:** English, French (both official). **Religions:** Roman Catholic 46%, United Church 16%, Anglican 10%.

Geography: Area: 3,849,674 sq. mi., the largest country in land size in the western hemisphere. Canada stretches 3,426 miles from east to west and extends southward from the North Pole to the U.S. border. Its seacoast includes 36,356 miles of mainland and 115,133 miles of islands, including the Arctic islands almost from Greenland to near the Alaskan border. Climate, while generally temperate, varies from freezing winter cold to blistering summer heat. **Capital:** Ottawa. **Cities** (met. 1991 est.): Toronto 3.8 mln.; Montreal 3.1 mln.; Vancouver 1.6 mln.; Ottawa-Hull 920,000; Winnipeg 652,000; Edmonton 839,000; Calgary 754,000; Quebec 645,000.

Government: Type: Confederation with parliamentary democracy. **Head of state:** Queen Elizabeth II, represented by Gov.-Gen. Ramon Hnatyshyn; b Mar. 16, 1934; in office: Jan. 29, 1990. **Head of government:** Prime Min. Jean Chrétien; b Jan. 11, 1934; in office: Nov. 4, 1993. **Local divisions:** 10 provinces, 2 territories. **Defense:** 2% of GDP (FY 1992-93).

Economy: Minerals: Nickel, zinc, copper, gold, lead, molybdenum, potash, silver. **Crude oil reserves** (1991): 6.4 bln. barrels. **Arable land:** 5%. **Livestock** (1992): cattle: 13.0 mln.; pigs: 10.3 mln.; sheep: 914,000. **Fish catch** (1991): 1.5 mln. metric tons. **Electricity prod.** (1992): 493 bln. kWh. **Labor force:** 4% agric., 75% services, 14% manufacturing.

Finance: Monetary unit: Dollar (Mar. 1994: 1.36 = $1 US). **Gross domestic product** (1992): $537.1 bln. **Per capita GDP:** $19,600. **Imports** (1992): $124 bln.; partners: U.S. 69%, EU 8%, Jap. 5%. **Exports** (1992): $134 bln.; partners: U.S. 75%, EU 9%, Jap. 5%. **Tourism** (1990): receipts: $6.3 bln. **National budget** (FY 1990): $138.3 bln. **International reserves less gold** (Mar. 1994): $10.9 bln. **Gold:** 5.71 mln. oz t. **Consumer prices** (change in 1993): 1.8%.

Transport: Railroads: Length: 56,771 mi. **Motor vehicles:** in use: 12.8 mln. passenger cars, 3.4 mln. comm. vehicles. **Civil aviation:** 29 bln. passenger-mi.: 106 airports with scheduled flights.

Communications: Television sets: 1 per 1.6 persons. **Radios:** 1 per 1.2 persons. **Telephones:** 1 per 1.3 persons. **Daily newspaper circ.:** 187 per 1,000 pop.

Health: Life expectancy at birth (1994): 75 male; 82 female. **Births** (per 1,000 pop.): 14. **Deaths** (per 1,000 pop.): 7. **Natural increase:** .7%. **Hospital beds:** 1 per 143 persons. **Physicians:** 1 per 449 persons. **Infant mortality** (per 1,000 live births 1994): 7.

Education (1991): **Literacy:** 99%.

Major International Organizations: UN and all of its specialized agencies, NATO, OECD, Commonwealth of Nations.

Embassy: 501 Pennsylvania Ave. NW 20001; 682-1740.

French explorer Jacques Cartier, who reached the Gulf of St. Lawrence in 1534, is generally regarded as the founder of Canada. But English seaman John Cabot sighted Newfoundland 37 years earlier, in 1497, and Vikings are believed to have reached the Atlantic coast centuries before either explorer.

Canadian settlement was pioneered by the French who established Quebec City (1608) and Montreal (1642) and declared New France a colony in 1663.

Britain acquired Acadia (later Nova Scotia) in 1717 and, through military victory over French forces in Canada, captured Quebec (1759) and obtained control of the rest of New France in 1763. The French, through the Quebec Act of 1774, retained the rights to their own language, religion, and civil law. The British presence in Canada increased during the American Revolution when many colonials, proudly calling themselves United Empire Loyalists, moved north to Canada.

Fur traders and explorers led Canadians westward across the continent. Sir Alexander Mackenzie reached the Pacific in 1793 and scrawled on a rock by the ocean, "from Canada by land."

In Upper and Lower Canada (later called Ontario and Quebec) and in the Maritimes, legislative assemblies appeared in the 18th century and reformers called for responsible government. But the War of 1812 intervened. The war, a conflict between Great Britain and the United States fought mainly in Upper Canada, ended in a stalemate in 1814.

In 1837 political agitation for more democratic government culminated in rebellions in Upper and Lower Canada. Britain sent Lord Durham to investigate; in a famous report (1839), he recommended union of the 2 parts into one colony called Canada. The union lasted until Confederation, July 1, 1867, when proclamation of the British North America (BNA) Act launched the Dominion of Canada, consisting of Ontario, Quebec, and the former colonies of Nova Scotia and New Brunswick.

Since 1840 the Canadian colonies had held the right to internal self-government. The BNA act, which became the country's written constitution, established a federal system of government on the model of a British parliament and cabinet structure under the crown. Canada was proclaimed a self-governing Dominion within the British Empire in 1931. In 1982 Canada severed its last formal legislative link with Britain by obtaining the right to amend its constitution (the British North America Act of 1867).

The so-called Meech Lake Agreement was signed (subject to provincial ratification) June 3, 1987. The accord would have assured constitutional protection for Quebec's efforts to preserve its French language and culture. Critics charged that it did not make any provision for other minority groups and that it gave Quebec too much power, which might enable Quebec to override the nation's 1982 Charter of Rights and Freedoms. The accord died June 22, 1990.

Its failure sparked a separatist revival in Quebec which culminated in Aug. 1992 in the Charlottetown agreement. This called for changes to the constitution, such as recognition of Quebec as a "distinct society" within the Canadian confederation. It was defeated in a national referendum on Oct. 26, 1992.

In May 1992 voters in the Northwest Territories approved the creation of a self-governing homeland for the 17,500 Inuit living in the territories. The area—to be known as Nunavut, "Our Land"—would cover an area of 136,493 sq. mi. and take effect by 1999.

Canada became the first nation to ratify the North American Free Trade Agreement between Canada, Mexico, and the U.S., June 23, 1993. It went into effect Jan. 1, 1994.

On Feb. 24, 1993, Brian Mulroney resigned as prime minister after more than 8 years in office; he was succeeded by Kim Campbell. In elections Oct. 25, 1993, the ruling Conservatives were defeated in a landslide that left them only 2 of the 295 seats in the House of Commons. Jean Chrétien became prime minister.

Canadian Provinces

	Sq. mi.	Population, 1991 cen.
Alberta	255,287	2,545,553
British Columbia	365,947	3,282,061
Manitoba	250,947	1,091,942
New Brunswick	28,355	723,900
Newfoundland	156,949	568,474
Nova Scotia	21,425	899,942
Ontario	412,581	10,084,885
Prince Edward Island	2,185	129,765
Quebec	594,860	6,895,963
Saskatchewan	251,866	988,928
Territories		
Northwest Territories	1,322,909	57,649
Yukon	186,661	27,797

Prime Ministers of Canada

Canada is a constitutional monarchy with a parliamentary system of government. It is also a federal state. Canada's official head of state, Queen Elizabeth II, is represented by a resident Governor-General. However, in practice the nation is governed by the Prime Minister, leader of the party that commands the support of a majority of the House of Commons, dominant chamber of Canada's bicameral Parliament.

Name	Party	Term
Sir John A. MacDonald	Conservative	1867-1873
		1878-1891
Alexander Mackenzie	Liberal	1873-1878
Sir John J. C. Abbott	Conservative	1891-1892
Sir John S. D. Thompson	Conservative	1892-1894
Sir Mackenzie Bowell	Conservative	1894-1896
Sir Charles Tupper	Conservative	1896
Sir Wilfrid Laurier	Liberal	1896-1911
Sir Robert L. Borden	Cons. Union.	1911-1920
Arthur Meighen	Cons. Union.	1920-1921
W.L. Mackenzie King	Liberal	1921-1930[1]
		1935-1948
R. B. Bennett	Conservative	1930-1935
Louis St. Laurent	Liberal	1948-1957
John G. Diefenbaker	Prog. Cons.	1957-1963
Lester B. Pearson	Liberal	1963-1968
Pierre Elliott Trudeau	Liberal	1968-1979
Joe Clark	Prog. Cons.	1979-1980
Pierre Elliott Trudeau	Liberal	1980-1984
John Turner	Liberal	1984
Brian Mulroney	Prog. Cons.	1984-1993
Kim Campbell	Prog. Cons.	1993
Jean Chrétien	Liberal	1993-

(1) King served 2 terms in these years, interrupted June 26-Sept. 25, 1926, when Arthur Meighen served as prime minister.

Cape Verde

Republic of Cape Verde

República de Cabo Verde

People: Population: 423,000. **Age distrib.** (%): <15: 44; 65+: 5. **Pop. density:** 271 per sq. mi. **Urban:** 44%. **Ethnic groups:** Creole (mulatto) 71%, African 28%, European 1%. **Principal languages:** Portuguese (official), Crioulo. **Religions:** Roman Catholic fused with indigenous beliefs.

Geography: Area: 1,557 sq. mi., a bit larger than Rhode Island. **Location:** In Atlantic O., off western tip of Africa. **Neighbors:** Nearest are Mauritania, Senegal. **Topography:** Cape Verde Islands are 15 in number, volcanic in origin (active crater on Fogo). The landscape is eroded and stark, with vegetation mostly in interior valleys. **Capital:** Praia. **Cities** (1990 est.): Mindelo 47,000; Praia 61,000.

Government: Type: Republic. **Head of state:** Pres. Antonio Mascarenhas Monteiro; in office: Mar. 17, 1991. **Head of government:** Prime Min. Carlos Veiga; in office: Apr. 4, 1991. **Local divisions:** 14 administrative districts.

Economy: Chief crops: Bananas, coffee, beets, corn, beans. **Minerals:** Salt. **Other resources:** Fish. **Arable land:** 9%. **Electricity prod.** (1991): 15 mln. kWh.

Finance: Monetary unit: Escudo (Dec. 1993: 85.99 = $1 US). **Gross domestic product** (1990): $310 mln. **Per capita GDP:** $800. **Imports** (1989): $108 mln.; partners: Port. 33%, Neth. 12%. **Exports** (1989): $10.9 mln.; partners: Port. 32%, Ang. 21%. **National budget** (1990 est.): $800 mln.

Transport: Motor vehicles: in use: 10,000 passenger cars, 5,000 comm. vehicles. **Chief ports:** Mindelo, Praia.

Communications: Radios: 1 per 6.9 persons. **Telephones:** 1 per 38 persons.

Health: Life expectancy at birth (1994): 61 male; 65 female. **Births** (per 1,000 pop.): 46. **Deaths** (per 1,000 pop.): 9. **Natural increase:** 3.7%. **Hospital beds:** 1 per 550 persons. **Physicians:** 1 per 4,208 persons. **Infant mortality** (per 1,000 live births 1994): 58.

Education (1989): **Literacy:** 37%.

Major International Organizations: UN (GATT, IMF, WHO), OAU.

Embassy: 3415 Massachusetts Ave. NW 20007; 965-6820.

The uninhabited Cape Verdes were discovered by the Portuguese in 1456 or 1460. The first Portuguese colonists landed in 1462; African slaves were brought soon after, and most Cape Verdeans descend from both groups. Cape Verde independence came July 5, 1975. Antonio Mascarenhas Monteiro won the nation's first free presidential election in 1991.

Central African Republic

République Centrafricaine

People: Population: 3,142,000. **Pop. density:** 13 per sq. mi. **Urban:** 47%. **Ethnic groups:** Baya 34%, Banda 27%, Mandjia 21%, Sara 10%. **Principal languages:** French (official), local dialects. **Religions:** Protestant 25%, Roman Catholic 25%, indigenous beliefs 24%, Muslim 15%.

Geography: Area: 240,324 sq. mi., slightly smaller than Texas. **Location:** In central Africa. **Neighbors:** Chad on N, Cameroon on W, Congo, Zaire on S, Sudan on E. **Topography:** Mostly rolling plateau, average altitude 2,000 ft., with rivers draining S to the Congo and N to Lake Chad. Open, well-watered savanna covers most of the area, with an arid area in NE, and tropical rainforest in SW. **Capital:** Bangui. **Cities** (1988 est.): Bangui (met.) 596,000.

Government: Type: Republic. **Head of state:** Pres. Ange Patasse; b Jan. 25, 1937; in office: Sept. 27, 1993. **Head of government:** Prime Min. Jean-Luc Mandaba; in office: Oct. 25, 1993. **Local divisions:** 16 prefectures. **Defense:** 1.8% of GDP (1989 est.).

Economy: Industries: Textiles, light manuf., mining. **Chief crops:** Cotton, coffee, peanuts, tobacco. **Minerals:** Diamonds (chief export), uranium. **Other resources:** Timber. **Arable land:** 3%. **Electricity prod.** (1991): 95 mln. kWh. **Labor force:** 85% agric.

Finance: Monetary unit: CFA Franc (Mar. 1994: 576 = $1 US). **Gross domestic product** (1990): $1.3 bln. **Per capita GDP:** $440. **Imports** (1990): $214 mln.; partners: Fr. 44%. **Exports** (1990): $151 mln.; partners: Fr. 53%, Belg.-Lux. 23%. **National budget** (1991 est.): $312 mln. **International reserves less gold** (Dec. 1993): $112 mln. **Gold:** 11,000 oz t.

Transport: Motor vehicles: in use: 10,000 passenger cars, 8,000 comm. vehicles.

Communications: Radios: 1 per 5.3 persons. **Telephones:** 1 per 391 persons.

Health: Life expectancy at birth (1994): 41 male; 44 female. **Births** (per 1,000 pop.): 42. **Deaths** (per 1,000 pop.): 21. **Natural increase:** 2.2%. **Hospital beds:** 1 per 695 persons. **Physicians:** 1 per 16,447 persons. **Infant mortality** (per 1,000 live births 1994): 137.

Education (1991): **Literacy:** 27%. **Attendance:** primary school 79%; secondary school 18%.

Major International Organizations: UN (GATT, IMF, WHO), OAU.

Embassy: 1618 22d St. NW 20008; 483-7800.

Various Bantu tribes migrated through the region for centuries before French control was asserted in the late 19th century, when the region was named Ubangi-Shari. Complete independence was attained Aug. 13, 1960.

All political parties were dissolved in 1960, and the country became a center for Chinese political influence in Africa. Relations with China were severed after 1965. Pres. Jean-Bedel Bokassa, who seized power in a 1965 military coup, proclaimed himself constitutional emperor of the renamed Central African Empire Dec. 1976.

Bokassa's rule was characterized by ruthless and cruel authoritarianism and human rights violations. He was ousted in a bloodless coup aided by the French government, Sept. 20, 1979. In 1981, Gen. André Kolingba became head of state in another bloodless coup. Multiparty legislative and presidential elections were held in Oct. 1992 but were canceled by the government when Kolingba was losing. New elections were ultimately held in Aug. and Sept. 1993, leading to the installation of a civilian government.

Chad

Republic of Chad

République du Tchad

People: Population: 5,467,000. **Age distrib.** (%): <15: 41; 65+: 3. **Pop. density:** 11 per sq. mi. **Urban:** 32%. **Ethnic groups:** 200 distinct groups. **Principal languages:** French, Arabic (both official), some 100 other languages. **Religions:** Muslim 44%, Christian 33%, indigenous beliefs 23%.

Geography: Area: 495,755 sq. mi., four-fifths the size of Alaska. **Location:** In central N Africa. **Neighbors:** Libya on N, Niger, Nigeria, Cameroon on W, Central African Republic on S, Sudan on E. **Topography:** Wooded savanna, steppe, and desert in the S; part of the Sahara in the N. Southern rivers flow N to Lake Chad, surrounded by marshland. **Capital:** N'Djamena. **Cities** (1992 est.): N'Djamena 687,000.

Government: Type: Republic. **Head of state:** Pres. Idriss Déby; in office: Dec. 4, 1990. **Head of government:** Prime Min. Delwa Kassire Koumakoye; in office: Nov. 6, 1993. **Local divisions:** 14 prefectures. **Defense:** 5.6% of GDP (1990).

Economy: Chief crops: Cotton. **Minerals:** Uranium, salt. **Arable land:** 2%. **Fish catch** (1991): 60,000 metric tons. **Electricity prod.** (1991): 70 mln. kWh. **Labor force:** 85% agric.

Finance: Monetary unit: CFA franc (Mar. 1994: 576 = $1 US). **Gross domestic product** (1992): $1.0 bln. **Per capita GDP:** $190. **Imports** (1990): $264 mln.; partners: Fr. 47%. **Exports** (1990): $174 mln.; partners Fra. **National budget** (1991 est.): $412 mln. **International reserves less gold** (Dec. 1993): $39 mln. **Gold:** 11,000 oz t.

Transport: Motor vehicles: in use: 8,000 passenger cars, 6,000 comm. vehicles.

Communications: Radios: 1 per 4.7 persons. **Telephones:** 1 per 716 persons.

Health: Life expectancy at birth (1994): 40 male; 42 female. **Births** (per 1,000 pop.): 42. **Deaths** (per 1,000 pop.): 21. **Natural increase:** 2.2%. **Infant mortality** (per 1,000 live births 1994): 132.

Education (1991): **Literacy:** 30%.

Major International Organizations: UN, (GATT, IMF, WHO), OAU, EEC.

Embassy: 2002 R St. NW 20009; 462-4009.

Chad was the site of paleolithic and neolithic cultures before the Sahara Desert formed. A succession of kingdoms and Arab slave traders dominated Chad until France took control around 1900. Independence came Aug. 11, 1960.

Northern Muslim rebels have fought animist and Christian southern government and French troops from 1966, despite numerous cease-fires and peace pacts.

Libyan troops entered the country at the request of a pro-Libyan Chad government, Dec. 1980. The troops were withdrawn from Chad in Nov. 1981. Rebel forces, led by Hissène Habré, captured the capital and forced Pres. Goukouni Oueddei to flee the country in June 1982.

In 1983, France sent some 3,000 troops to Chad to assist Pres. Habré in opposing Libyan-backed rebels. France and Libya agreed to a simultaneous withdrawal of troops from Chad in Sept. 1984, but Libyan forces remained in the north until Mar. 1987, when Chad forces drove them from their last major stronghold. In Dec. 1990, Habré was overthrown by a Libyan-supported insurgent group, the Patriotic Salvation Movement.

On Feb. 3, 1994, the World Court dismissed a long-standing territorial claim by Libya to the mineral-rich Aozou Strip, on the Libyan border. Libyan troops reportedly withdrew at the end of May.

Chile

Republic of Chile

República de Chile

People: Population: 13,951,000. **Age distrib.** (%): <15: 31; 65+: 6. **Pop. density:** 47 per sq. mi. **Urban:** 85%. **Ethnic groups:** European and European-Indian 95%, Indian 3%. **Principal languages:** Spanish. **Religions:** Roman Catholic 89%, Protestant 11%.

Geography: Area: 292,135 sq. mi., twice the size of California. **Location:** Occupies western coast of southern S America. **Neighbors:** Peru on N, Bolivia on NE, Argentina on E. **Topography:** Andes Mtns. are on E border including some of the world's highest peaks; on W is 2,650-mile Pacific Coast. Width varies between 100 and 250 miles. In N is Atacama Desert, in center are agricultural regions, in S are forests and grazing lands. **Capital:** Santiago. **Cities** (1992 metro est.): Santiago 5.1 mln.

Government: Type: Republic. **Head of state:** Pres. Eduardo Frei Ruíz Tagle; in office: Mar. 11, 1994. **Local divisions:** 13 regions. **Defense:** 3.4% of GDP (1991).

Economy: Industries: Fish processing, wood products, iron, steel. **Chief crops:** Grain, onions, beans, potatoes, peas, fruits. **Minerals:** Copper (about half of export revenues), molybdenum, nitrates, iodine (half world output), iron, coal, oil, gas, gold, cobalt, zinc, manganese, borate, mica, mercury, salt, sulphur, marble, onyx. **Other resources:** Water, forests. **Arable land:** 7%. **Livestock** (1992): cattle: 3.3 mln.; sheep: 6.6 mln.; pigs: 1.7 mln. **Fish catch** (1991): 6.1 mln. metric tons. **Electricity prod.** (1992): 22.0 bln. kWh. **Labor force:** 19% agric., forestry, fishing; 34% ind & comm.; 38% serv.

Finance: Monetary unit: Peso (Mar. 1994: 430 = $1 US). **Gross domestic product** (1992): $34.7 bln. **Per capita GDP:** $2,550. **Imports** (1991): $7.6 bln.; partners: U.S. 19%, EU 23%. **Exports** (1991): $9.0 bln.; partners: EU 34%, U.S. 18%. **Tourism** (1990): $548 mln. receipts. **National budget** (1993): $10.9 bln. **International reserves less gold** (Mar. 1994): $10.2 bln. **Gold:** 1.86 mln. oz. t. **Consumer prices** (change in 1993): 12.7%.

Transport: Railroads: Length: 2,778 mi. **Motor vehicles:** in use: 792,000 passenger cars, 412,000 comm. vehicles. **Civil aviation::** 1.8 bln. passenger-mi.; 16 airports with scheduled flights. **Chief ports:** Valparaiso, Arica, Antofagasta.

Communications: Television sets: 1 per 6.7 persons. **Radios:** 1 per 3.1 persons. **Telephones:** 1 per 11 persons.

Health: Life expectancy at birth (1994): 72 male; 78 female. **Births** (per 1,000 pop.): 21. **Deaths** (per 1,000 pop.): 5. **Natural increase:** 1.5%. **Hospital beds:** 1 per 303 persons. **Physicians:** 1 per 895 persons. **Infant mortality** (per 1,000 live births 1994): 15.

Education (1991): **Literacy:** 92%. Compulsory ages 6-14.

Major International Organizations: UN and all of its specialized agencies, OAS.

Embassy: 1732 Massachusetts Ave. NW 20036; 785-1746.

Northern Chile was under Inca rule before the Spanish conquest, 1536-40. The southern Araucanian Indians resisted until the late 19th century. Independence was gained 1810-18, under José de San Martin and Bernardo O'Higgins; the latter, as supreme director 1817-23, sought social and economic reforms until deposed. Chile defeated Peru and Bolivia in 1836-39 and 1879-84, gaining mineral-rich northern land.

In 1970, Salvador Allende Gossens, a Marxist, became president with a third of the national vote. The Allende government improved conditions for the poor. But illegal and violent actions by extremist supporters of the government, the regime's failure to attain majority support, and poorly planned socialist economic programs led to political and financial chaos.

A military junta seized power Sept. 11, 1973, and said Allende had killed himself. The junta named a mostly military cabinet and announced plans to "exterminate Marxism." Repression continued during the 1980s with little sign of any political liberalization.

In a plebiscite held Oct. 5, 1988, voters rejected the incumbent president, Gen. Augusto Pinochet Ugarte. He agreed to presidential elections. In Dec. 1989 voters removed Pinochet from office and elected a civilian president. In Mar. 1994 a Chilean human rights organization announced a revised estimate of more than 3,100 deaths from human rights violations during Pinochet's rule.

Tierra del Fuego is the largest (18,800 sq. mi.) island in the archipelago of the same name at the southern tip of South America, an area of majestic mountains, tortuous channels, and high winds. It was discovered 1520 by Magellan and named the Land of Fire because of its many Indian bonfires. Part of the island is in Chile, part in Argentina. Punta Arenas, on a mainland peninsula, is a center of sheep raising and the world's southernmost city (pop. about 70,000); Puerto Williams is the southernmost settlement.

China

People's Republic of China

Zhonghua Renmin Gonghe Guo

People: Population: 1,190,431,000. **Age distrib.** (%): <15: 28; 65+: 6. **Pop. density:** 322 per sq. mi. **Urban:** 28%. **Ethnic groups:** Han Chinese 91.9%, Mongol, Korean, Manchu, others. **Principal languages:** Mandarin (official), Yue, Wu, Hakka, Xiang, Gan, Minbei, Minnan. **Religions:** officially atheist; Buddhism, Taoism are traditional.

Geography: Area: 3,696,100 sq. mi., slightly larger than the U.S. **Location:** Occupies most of the habitable mainland of E Asia. **Neighbors:** Mongolia on N, Russia on NE and NW, Afghanistan, Pakistan, Tajikistan, Kazakhstan on W, India, Nepal, Bhutan, Myanmar, Laos, Vietnam on S, N Korea on NE. **Topography:** Two-thirds of the vast territory is mountainous or desert, and only one-tenth is cultivated. Rolling topography rises to high elevations in the N in the Daxinganlingshanmai separating Manchuria and Mongolia; the Tienshan in Xinjiang; the Himalayan and Kunlunshanmai in the SW and in Tibet. Length is 1,860 mi. from N to S, width E to W is more than 2,000 mi. The eastern half of China is one of the best-watered lands in the world. Three great river systems, the Changjiang, the Huanghe, and the Xijiang provide water for vast farmlands. **Capital:** Beijing. **Cities** (1990 est.): Shanghai 7.5 mln.; Beijing 5.7 mln.; Tianjin 4.5 mln.; Shenyang 3.6 mln.; Wuhan 3.2 mln.; Canton 2.9 mln.

Government: Type: Communist Party-led state. **Head of state:** Pres. Jiang Zemin; b Aug. 17, 1926; in office: Mar. 27, 1993. **Head of government:** Premier Li Peng; b Oct. 1928; in office: Apr. 9, 1989. **Local divisions:** 22 provinces, 5 autonomous regions, and 3 cities. **Defense:** 5.0% of GNP (1992).

Economy: Industries: Iron and steel, textiles, agriculture implements, trucks. **Chief crops:** Grain, rice, cotton, tea. **Minerals:** tungsten, antimony, coal, iron, lead, manganese, molybdenum, tin. **Crude oil reserves** (1991): 30.8 bln. barrels. **Other resources:** Silk. **Arable land:** 10%. **Livestock** (1991): cattle: 81 mln.; pigs: 363 mln.; sheep: 112 mln. **Fish catch** (1990): 12.0 mln. metric tons. **Electricity prod.** (1992): 740 bln. kWh. **Labor force:** 60% agric.; 25% ind. & comm.

Finance: Monetary unit: Yuan (Mar. 1994): 8.7 = $1 US). **Gross national product** (1989): $393 bln. **Per capita GNP:** $360. **Imports** (1992): $76.3 bln.; partners: Jap. 20%, U.S. 11%, Hong Kong 20%. **Exports** (1992): $80.5 bln.; partners: Hong Kong 38%, Jap. 16%, U.S. 7%. **Tourism** (1991): $2.8 bln. receipts. **National budget** (1992): $16.3 bln. deficit. **International reserves less gold** (Nov. 1993): $22 bln. **Gold:** 12.7 mln. oz t. **Consumer prices** (change in 1991): 5.1%.

Transport: Railroads: Length: 42,261 mi. **Motor vehicles:** in use: 1.8 mln. passenger cars, 4.2 mln. comm. vehicles.

departure from rigid central planning and the stressing of market-oriented socialism. **Civil aviation::** 24.8 bln. passenger-mi., 86 airports with scheduled flights. **Chief ports:** Shanghai, Qinhuangdao, Dalian, Canton.

Communications: Television sets: 1 per 32 persons. **Radios:** 1 per 5.4 persons. **Telephones:** 1 per 77 persons.

Health: Life expectancy at birth (1994): 67 male; 69 female. **Births** (per 1,000 pop.): 18. **Deaths** (per 1,000 pop.): 7. **Natural increase:** 1.1%. **Hospital beds:** 1 per 427 persons. **Physicians:** 1 per 648 persons. **Infant mortality** (per 1,000 live births 1994): 52.

Education (1987): **Literacy:** 70%. Years compulsory 9; first grade enrollment 93%.

Major International Organizations: UN (IMF, FAO, WHO).

Embassy: 2300 Conn. Ave. NW 20008; 328-2500.

History. Remains of various humanlike creatures who lived as early as several hundred thousand years ago have been found in many parts of China. Neolithic agricultural settlements dotted the Huanghe basin from about 5000 BC. Their language, religion, and art were the sources of later Chinese civilization.

Bronze metallurgy reached a peak and Chinese pictographic writing, similar to today's, was in use in the more developed culture of the Shang Dynasty (c. 1500 BC-c. 1000 BC), which ruled much of North China.

A succession of dynasties and interdynastic warring kingdoms ruled China for the next 3,000 years. They expanded Chinese political and cultural domination to the south and west, and developed a brilliant technologically and culturally advanced society. Rule by foreigners (Mongols in the Yuan Dynasty, 1271-1368, and Manchus in the Ch'ing Dynasty, 1644-1911) did not alter the underlying culture.

A period of relative stagnation left China vulnerable to internal and external pressures in the 19th century. Rebellions left tens of millions dead, and Russia, Japan, Britain, and other powers exercised political and economic control in large parts of the country. China became a republic Jan. 1, 1912, following the Wuchang Uprising inspired by Dr. Sun Yat-sen.

For a period of 50 years, 1894-1945, China was involved in conflicts with Japan. In 1895, China ceded Korea, Taiwan, and other areas. On Sept. 18, 1931, Japan seized the Northeastern Provinces (Manchuria) and set up a puppet state called Manchukuo. The border province of Jehol was cut off as a buffer state in 1933. Japan invaded China proper July 7, 1937. After its defeat in World War II, Japan gave up all seized land.

Following World War II, internal disturbances arose involving the Kuomintang, Communists, and other factions. China came under domination of Communist armies, 1949-1950. The Kuomintang government moved to Taiwan, 90 mi. off the mainland, Dec. 8, 1949.

The People's Republic of China was proclaimed in Beijing (Peking) Sept. 21, 1949, by the Chinese People's Political Consultative Conference under Mao Zedong. China and the USSR signed a 30-year treaty of "friendship, alliance and mutual assistance," Feb. 15, 1950. The U.S. refused recognition of the new regime. On Nov. 26, 1950, the People's Republic sent armies into Korea against U.S. troops and forced a stalemate in the Korean War.

By the 1960s, relations with the USSR deteriorated, with disagreements on borders, ideology, and leadership of world Communism. The USSR cancelled aid accords, and China, with Albania, launched anti-Soviet propaganda drives.

On Oct. 25, 1971, the UN General Assembly ousted the Taiwan government from the UN and seated the People's Republic in its place. The U.S. had supported the mainland's admission but opposed Taiwan's expulsion.

U.S. Pres. Richard Nixon visited China Feb. 21-28, 1972, on invitation from Premier Zhou Enlai, ending years of antipathy between the 2 nations. China and the U.S. opened liaison offices in each other's capitals, May-June 1973. The U.S., Dec. 15, 1978, formally recognized the People's Republic of China as the sole legal government of China; diplomatic relations between the 2 nations were established, Jan. 1, 1979.

Internal developments. After an initial period of consolidation, 1949-52, industry, agriculture, and social and economic institutions were forcibly molded according to Maoist ideals. However, frequent drastic changes in policy and violent factionalism interfered with economic development. In 1957, Mao Zedong admitted an estimated 800,000 people had been executed 1949-54; opponents claimed much higher figures.

The Great Leap Forward, 1958-60, tried to force the pace of economic development through intensive labor on huge new rural communes, and through emphasis on ideological purity. The program caused resistance and was largely abandoned.

The Great Proletarian Cultural Revolution, 1965, was an attempt to oppose pragmatism and bureaucratic power and instruct a new generation in revolutionary principles. Massive purges took place. A program of forcibly relocating millions of urban teenagers into the countryside was launched. By 1968 the movement had run its course; many purged officials returned to office in subsequent years, and reforms that had placed ideology above expertise were gradually weakened.

Mao died Sept. 9, 1976. In a continuing "reassessment" of his policies his widow, Jiang Quing, and other "Gang of Four" leftists were convicted of "committing crimes during the 'Cultural Revolution,' " Jan. 25, 1981.

The new ruling group modified Maoist policies in education, culture, and industry, and sought better ties with non-Communist countries. By the mid-1980s, China had enacted far-reaching economic reforms highlighed by the

Some 100,000 students and workers staged a march in Beijing to demand democratic reforms, May 4, 1989. The demonstrations continued during a visit to Beijing by Soviet leader Mikhail Gorbachev May 15-18. It was the first Sino-Soviet summit since 1959. A million people gathered in Beijing to demand reforms and the removal of Deng and other leaders. There were protests in at least 20 other Chinese cities. Martial law was imposed, May 20, but was mostly ignored by protesters.

Chinese army troops entered Beijing, June 3-4, and crushed the pro-democracy protests. Tanks and armored personnel carriers attacked Tiananmen Square, outside the Great Hall of the People, which was the main scene of the demonstrations and hunger strikes. It is estimated that 5,000 died, 10,000 were injured, and hundreds of students and workers arrested. Human rights violations continued in succeeding years. The U.S. nevertheless unconditionally renewed most-favored-nation trading status for China, May 26, 1994.

China's population, the world's largest, is still increasing, but with more couples following the government's one-child policy some experts predict that the nation's population will actually decline after peaking in the early 21st century.

Manchuria. Home of the Manchus, rulers of China 1644-1911, Manchuria has accommodated millions of Chinese settlers in the 20th century. Under Japanese rule 1931-45, the area became industrialized. China no longer uses the name Manchuria for the region, which is divided into the 3 NE provinces of Heilongjiang, Jilin, and Liaoning.

Guangxi is in SE China, bounded on N by Kweichow and Hunan provinces, E and S by Kwangtung, on SW by North Vietnam, and on W by Yunnan. It produces rice in the river valleys and has valuable forest products.

Inner Mongolia was organized by the People's Republic in 1947. Its boundaries have undergone frequent changes, reaching its greatest extent (and restored in 1979) in 1956, with an area of 454,000 sq. mi., allegedly in order to dilute the minority Mongol population. Chinese settlers outnumber the Mongols more than 10 to 1. Pop. (1990 cen.): 21.4 mln. Capital: Hohhot.

Xinjiang, in Central Asia, is 633,802 sq. mi., pop. (1990 cen.): 15.1 mln. (75% Uygurs, a Turkic Muslim group, with a heavy Chinese increase in recent years). Capital: Urumqi. It is China's richest region in strategic minerals.

Tibet, 470,000 sq. mi., is a thinly populated region of high plateaus and massive mountains, the Himalayas on the S, the Kunluns on the N. High passes connect with India and Nepal; roads lead into China proper. Capital: Lhasa. Average altitude is 15,000 ft. Jiachan, 15,870 ft., is believed to be the highest inhabited town on earth. Agriculture is primitive. Pop. (1990 cen.): 2.1 mln. (of whom about 500,000 are Chinese). Another 4 million Tibetans form the majority of the population of vast adjacent areas that have long been incorporated into China.

China ruled all of Tibet from the 18th century, but independence came in 1911. China reasserted control in 1951, and a Communist government was installed in 1953, revising the theocratic Lamaist Buddhist rule. Serfdom was abolished, but all land remained collectivized.

A Tibetan uprising within China in 1956 spread to Tibet in 1959. The rebellion was crushed with Chinese troops, and Buddhism was almost totally suppressed. The Dalai Lama and 100,000 Tibetans fled to India.

Colombia

Republic of Colombia

República de Colombia

People: Population: 35,578,000. **Age distrib.** (%): <15: 34; 65+: 4. **Pop. density:** 80 per sq. mi. **Urban:** 68%. **Ethnic groups:** Mestizo 58%, white 20%, Mulatto 14%. **Principal languages:** Spanish. **Religions:** Roman Catholic 95%.

Geography: Area: 440,831 sq. mi., about the size of Texas, and New Mexico combined. **Location:** At the NW corner of S America. **Neighbors:** Panama on NW, Ecuador, Peru on S, Brazil, Venezuela on E. **Topography:** Three ranges of Andes, the Western, Central, and Eastern Cordilleras, run through the country from N to S. The eastern range consists mostly of high table lands, densely populated. The Magdalena R. rises in Andes, flows N to Caribbean, through a rich alluvial plain. Sparsely-settled plains in E are drained by Orinoco and Amazon systems. **Capital:** Bogota. **Cities** (1993 est.): Bogota 5.0 mln.; Medellin 1.6 mln.; Cali 1.6 mln.; Barranquilla 1.0 mln.

Government: Type: Republic. **Head of state:** Pres. Ernesto Samper Pizano; in office: Aug. 7, 1994. **Local divisions:** 23 departments, 8 national territories, and special district of Bogota. **Defense:** 1.3% of GDP (1993 est.).

Economy: Industries: Textiles, processed goods, hides, steel, cement, chemicals. **Chief crops:** Coffee (50% of exports), rice, corn, cotton, sugar, bananas. **Minerals:** Oil, gas, emeralds (90% world output), gold, copper, lead, coal, iron, nickel, salt. **Crude oil reserves** (1991): 1.8 bln. bbls. **Other resources:** Rubber, balsam, dye-woods, copaiba, hydro power. **Arable land:** 4%. **Livestock** (1992): cattle: 24.7 mln.; pigs: 2.6 mln.; sheep: 2.5 mln. **Fish catch** (1991): 108,000 metric tons. **Electricity prod.** (1992): 36 bln. kWh. **Labor force:** 30% agric.; 24% ind.; 46% services.

Finance: Currency: Peso (Feb. 1994: 929 = $1 US). **Gross domestic product** (1992): $51 bln. **Per capita GDP:** $1,500. **Imports** (1991): $6.1 bln.; partners: U.S. 36%, EU 16%. **Exports** (1991): $7.5 bln.; partners: U.S. 40%, EU 21%. **Tourism** (1990): $362 mln. receipts. **National budget** (1991 est.): $5.1 bln. **International reserves less gold** (June 1993): $7.9 bln. **Gold:** 382,000 oz t. **Consumer prices** (change in 1992): 27.0%.

Transport: Railroads: Length: 2,011 mi. **Motor vehicles:** in use: 936,000 passenger cars, 364,000. **Civil aviation::** 2.8 bln. passenger-mi.; 63 airports with scheduled flights. **Chief ports:** Buena Ventura, Santa Marta, Barranquilla, Cartagena.

Communications: Television sets: 1 per 6.1 persons. **Radios:** 1 per 1 persons. **Telephones:** 1 per 8.7 persons. **Daily newspaper circ.:** 23 per 1,000 pop.

Health: Life expectancy at birth (1994): 69 male; 75 female. **Births** (per 1,000 pop.): 23. **Deaths** (per 1,000 pop.): 5. **Natural increase:** 1.8%. **Physicians:** 1 per 1,061 persons. **Infant mortality** (per 1,000 live births 1994): 28.

Education (1990): **Literacy:** 80%. Only 28% finish primary school.

Major International Organizations: UN (World Bank, GATT), OAS.

Embassy: 2118 Leroy Pl. NW, 20008; 387-8338.

Spain subdued the local Indian kingdoms (Funza, Tunja) by the 1530s and ruled Colombia and neighboring areas as New Granada for 300 years. Independence was won by 1819. Venezuela and Ecuador broke away in 1829-30, and Panama withdrew in 1903.

One of the Latin American democracies, Colombia is plagued by rural and urban violence, though scaled down from "La Violencia" of 1948-58, which claimed 200,000 lives. Attempts at land and social reform and progress in industrialization have not succeeded in reducing massive social problems.

The government's increased activity against local drug traffickers sparked a series of retaliation killings. On Aug. 18, 1989, Luis Carlos Galán, the ruling party's presidential hopeful for the 1990 election, was assassinated. In 1990, 2 other presidential candidates were assassinated, as drug traffickers carried on a campaign of intimidation. Pablo Esocobar, head of the Medellín drug cartel, escaped from prison in July 1992, allegedly with aid from military and prison officials. He was killed by government troops Dec. 1, 1993.

Comoros

Federal Islamic Republic of the Comoros

Jumhurīyat al-Qumur al-Itthadīyah al-Islamīyah

People: Population: 530,000. **Pop. density:** 737 per sq. mi. **Ethnic groups:** Arabs, Africans, East Indians. **Principal languages:** Arabic, French (both official), Comoran. **Religions:** Sunni Muslim 86%, Roman Catholic 14%.

Geography: Area: 719 sq. mi., less than half the size of Delaware. **Location:** 3 islands (Grande Comore, Anjouan, and Moheli) in the Mozambique Channel between NW Madagascar and SE Africa. **Neighbors:** Nearest are Mozambique on W, Madagascar on E. **Topography:** The islands are of volcanic origin, with an active volcano on Grand Comoro. **Capital:** Moroni. **Cities** (1992 est.): Moroni (met.) 30,000.

Government: Type: Republic. **Head of state:** Pres. Said Mohammed Djohar; in office: Nov. 26, 1989. **Head of government:** Mohamed Abdou Mahdi; in office: Jan. 2, 1994. **Local divisions:** each of the 3 main islands is a prefecture.

Economy: Industries: Perfume. **Chief crops:** Vanilla, copra, perfume plants, fruits. **Arable land:** 35%. **Electricity prod.** (1991): 25 mln. kWh. **Labor force:** 80% agric.

Finance: Monetary unit: CFA franc (Mar. 1994: 432 = $1 US). **Gross domestic product** (1991): $260 mln. **Per capita GDP:** $540. **Imports** (1990): $41 mln.; partners: Fr. 22%. **Exports** (1990): $16 mln.; partners: Fr. 41%, U.S. 53%. **National budget** (1991 est.): $88 mln.

Transport: Chief ports: Dzaoudzi.

Communications: Radios: 1 per 9.9 persons. **Telephones:** 1 per 93 persons.

Health: Life expectancy at birth (1994): 56 male; 60 female. **Births** (per 1,000 pop.): 46. **Deaths** (per 1,000 pop.): 11. **Natural increase:** 3.6%. **Infant mortality** (per 1,000 live births 1994): 80.

Education: (1989): **Literacy:** 15%; less than 20% attend secondary school.

Major International Organizations: UN (IMF, World Bank); OAU.

Embassy: 336 E. 45th St., New York, NY 10017; (212) 972-8010.

The islands were controlled by Muslim sultans until the French acquired them 1841-1909. They became a French overseas territory in 1947. A 1974 referendum favored independence, with only the Christian island of Mayotte preferring association with France. The French National Assembly decided to allow each of the islands to decide its own fate. The Comoro Chamber of Deputies declared independence July 6, 1975, with Ahmed Abdallah as president. In a referendum in 1976, Mayotte voted to remain French. A leftist regime that seized power from Abdallah in 1975 was deposed in a pro-French 1978 coup in which he regained the presidency.

In Nov. 1989, Pres. Abdallah was assassinated.

Congo

Republic of Congo

République du Congo

People: Population: 2,447,000. **Pop. density:** 18 per sq. mi. **Urban:** 41%. **Ethnic groups:** Kongo 48%, Sangha 20%, Teke 17%, others. **Principal languages:** French (official), African languages. **Religions:** Christians 50% (two-thirds Roman Catholic), indigenous beliefs 48%, Muslim 2%.

Geography: Area: 132,047 sq. mi., slightly smaller than Montana. **Location:** In western central Africa. **Neighbors:** Gabon, Cameroon on W, Central African Republic on N, Zaire on E, Angola on SW. **Topography:** Much of the Congo is covered by thick forests. A coastal plain leads to the fertile Niari Valley. The center is a plateau; the Congo R. basin consists of flood plains in the lower and savanna in the upper portion. **Capital:** Brazzaville. **Cities** (1992 est.): Brazzaville (met.) 937,000; Pointe-Noire 576,000; Loubomo 83,000.

Government: Type: Democracy. **Head of state:** Pres. Pascal Lissouba; in office: Aug. 20, 1992. **Head of government:** Prime Min. Jacques-Joachim Yhombi-Opango; in office: June 23, 1993. **Local divisions:** 9 regions and capital district. **Defense:** 3.8% of GDP (1992).

Economy: Chief crops: Palm oil and kernels, cocoa,

coffee, tobacco. **Minerals:** Gold, lead, copper, zinc. **Crude oil reserves** (1988): 750 mln. bbls. **Arable land:** 2%. **Fish catch** (1991): 45,000 metric tons. **Electricity prod.** (1991): 315 mln. kWh. **Labor force:** 75% agric.

Finance: Monetary unit: CFA franc (Mar. 1994: 576 = $1 US). **Gross domestic product** (1991): $2.5 bln. **Per capita GDP:** $1,070. **Imports** (1990): $621 mln.; partners: Fr. 52%. **Exports** (1990): $981 mln.; partners: U.S. 45%, Fr. 15%. **Tourism** (1990): $7 mln. receipts. **National budget** (1990): $952 mln. **International reserves less gold** (Dec. 1993): $1.3 mln. **Gold:** 11,000 oz t.

Transport: Railroads: Length: 494 mi. **Motor vehicles:** in use: 27,000 passenger cars, 15,000 comm. vehicles. **Chief ports:** Pointe-Noire, Brazzaville.

Communications: Television sets: 1 per 317 persons. **Radios:** 1 per 11 persons. **Telephones:** 1 per 86 persons.

Health: Life expectancy at birth (1994): 46 male; 49 female. **Births** (per 1,000 pop.): 40. **Deaths** (per 1,000 pop.): 16. **Natural increase:** 2.4%. **Hospital beds:** 1 per 456 persons. **Physicians:** 1 per 3,873 persons. **Infant mortality** (per 1,000 live births 1994): 111.

Education (1991): **Literacy:** 57%. Years compulsory 10; attendance 80%.

Major International Organizations: UN (GATT, IMF, WHO), OAU.

Embassy: 4891 Colorado Ave. NW 20011; 726-5500.

The Loango Kingdom flourished in the 15th century, as did the Anzico Kingdom of the Batekes; by the late 17th century they had become weakened. France established control by 1885. Independence came Aug. 15, 1960.

After a 1963 coup sparked by trade unions, the country adopted a Marxist-Leninist stance, with the USSR and China vying for influence. France remained a dominant trade partner and source of technical assistance, however, and French-owned private enterprise retained a major economic role.

In 1990, Marxism was renounced and opposition parties legalized. In 1991 the country's name was changed to Republic of Congo, and a new constitution was approved. A democratically elected government came into office in 1992; one of its key problems was a resurgence of ethnic and regional hostilities, often erupting into violence.

Costa Rica

Republic of Costa Rica

República de Costa Rica

People: Population: 3,342,000. **Age distrib.** (%): <15: 36; 65+: 5. **Pop. density:** 169 per sq. mi. **Urban:** 44%. **Ethnic groups:** white (with Mestizo minority) 96%. **Principal languages:** Spanish (official). **Religions:** Roman Catholic 95%.

Geography: Area: 19,730 sq. mi., smaller than W Virginia. **Location:** In central America. **Neighbors:** Nicaragua on N, Panama on S. **Topography:** Lowlands by the Caribbean are tropical. The interior plateau, with an altitude of about 4,000 ft., is temperate. **Capital:** San José. **Cities** (1992 met. est.): San José (met.) 1.0 mln.

Government: Type: Democratic republic. **Head of state:** Pres. José María Figueres Olsen; in office: May 8, 1994. **Local divisions:** 7 provinces. **Defense:** 0.5% of GDP (1989).

Economy: Industries: Furniture, food processing, aluminum, textiles, fertilizers, roofing, cement. **Chief crops:** Coffee (chief export), bananas, sugar, cocoa, cotton, hemp. **Minerals:** Gold, salt, sulphur, iron. **Other resources:** Fish, forests. **Arable land:** 6%. **Livestock** (1992): cattle: 1.7 mln. **Fish catch** (1990): 21,000 metric tons. **Electricity prod.** (1992): 3.6 bln. kWh. **Labor force:** 27% agric.; 35% ind. & comm.; 33% service and government.

Finance: Monetary unit: Colones (Feb. 1994: 152 = $1 US). **Gross domestic product** (1992): $6.4 bln. **Per capita GDP:** $2,000. **Imports** (1992): $2.5 bln.; partners: U.S. 38%, CACM 10%, Jap. 10%. **Exports** (1992): $1.8 bln.; partners: U.S. 45%, CACM 18%. **Tourism** (1989): receipts: $206 mln. **National budget** (1991 est.): $1.34 bln. **International reserves less gold** (Mar. 1994): $977 mln. **Gold:** 35,000 oz t. **Consumer prices** (change in 1993): 9.8%.

Transport: Motor vehicles: in use: 168,000 passenger cars, 95,000 comm. vehicles. **Civil aviation::** 787 mln. passenger-mi.; 13 airports with scheduled flights. **Chief ports:** Limon, Puntarenas, Golfito.

Communications: Television sets: 1 per 9.2 persons. **Radios:** 1 per 12 persons. **Telephones:** 1 per 6.9 persons. **Daily newspaper circ.:** 102 per 1,000 pop.

Health: Life expectancy at birth (1994): 76 male; 80 female. **Births** (per 1,000 pop.): 25. **Deaths** (per 1,000 pop.): 4. **Natural increase:** 2.2%. **Hospital beds:** 1 per 442 persons. **Physicians:** 1 per 981 persons. **Infant mortality** (per 1,000 live births 1994): 11.

Education (1992): **Literacy:** 93%. Years compulsory 6; attendance 99%.

Major International Organizations: UN (FAO, ILO, IMF, WHO), OAS.

Embassy: 1825 Connecticut Ave. NW, 20009; 234-2945.

Guaymi Indians inhabited the area when Spaniards arrived, 1502. Independence came in 1821. Costa Rica seceded from the Central American Federation in 1838. Since the civil war of 1948-49, there has been little violent social conflict, and free political institutions have been preserved. During 1993 there was an unusual wave of kidnappings and hostage-taking, some of it related to the international cocaine trade.

Costa Rica, though still a largely agricultural country, has achieved a relatively high standard of living and social services, and land ownership is widespread.

Côte d'Ivoire

Ivory Coast

République de la Côte d'Ivoire

People: Population: 14,296,000. **Age distrib.** (%): <15: 47; 65+: 2. **Pop. density:** 114 per sq. mi. **Urban:** 39%. **Ethnic groups:** Baoule 23%, Bete 18%, Senoufou 15%, Malinke 11%, over 60 tribes. **Principal languages:** French (official), Dioula, Akan, Kru, Voltaic, Malinke. **Religions:** indigenous 63%, Muslim 25%, Christian 12%.

Geography: Area: 124,504 sq. mi., slightly larger than New Mexico. **Location:** On S coast of W Africa. **Neighbors:** Liberia, Guinea on W, Mali, Burkina Faso on N, Ghana on E. **Topography:** Forests cover the W half of the country, and range from a coastal strip to halfway to the N on the E. A sparse inland plain leads to low mountains in NW. **Capital:** Yamoussoukro (official); Abidjan (de facto). **Cities** (1990 est.): Abidjan 2.7 mln.

Government: Type: Republic. **Head of state:** Henri Konan Bédié; b 1934; in office: Dec. 7, 1993. **Head of government:** Prime Min. Daniel Kablan Duncan; in office: Dec. 1993. **Local divisions:** 49 departments. **Defense:** 2.3% of GDP (1988).

Economy: Chief crops: Coffee, cocoa. **Minerals:** Diamonds, manganese. **Other resources:** Timber, rubber, petroleum. **Arable land:** 9%. **Livestock** (1992): goats: 919,000; sheep: 1.2 mln.; cattle: 1.1 mln. **Fish catch** (1991): 85,000 metric tons. **Electricity prod.** (1991): 1.9 bln. kWh. **Labor force:** 85% agric., forestry.

Finance: Monetary unit: CFA franc (Mar. 1994: 576 = $1 US). **Gross domestic product** (1991): $10 bln. **Per capita GDP:** $800. **Imports** (1989): $2.1 bln.; partners: Fr. 31%, Jap. 5%, U.S. 5%. **Exports** (1989): $2.8 bln.; partners: Fr. 14%, Neth. 19%, U.S. 11%, It. 8%. **Tourism** (1990): $48 mln. receipts. **National budget** (1990 est.): $3.6 bln. **International reserves less gold** (Dec. 1993): $2.3 mln. **Gold:** 45,000 oz t. **Consumer prices** (changed in 1993): 2.8%.

Transport: Railroads: Length: 410 mi. **Motor vehicles:** in use: 168,000 passenger cars, 91,000 comm. vehicles. **Chief ports:** Abidjan, Sassandra.

Communications: Television sets: 1 per 16 persons. **Radios:** 1 per 8.6 persons. **Telephones:** 1 per 80 persons.

Health: Life expectancy at birth (1994): 47 male; 51 female. **Births** (per 1,000 pop.): 47. **Deaths** (per 1,000 pop.): 15. **Natural increase:** 3.2%. **Hospital beds** (1982): 10,062. **Physicians** (1982): 502. **Infant mortality** (per 1,000 live births 1994): 95.

Education (1990): **Literacy:** 45%. **Years compulsory:** none; attendance 75%.

Major International Organizations: UN and all of its specialized agencies, OAU.

Embassy: 2424 Massachusetts Ave. NW 20008; 483-0300.

A French protectorate from 1842, Côte d'Ivoire became independent in 1960. It is the most prosperous of the tropical African nations, as a result of diversification of agriculture for export, close ties to France, and encouragement of foreign investment. About 20% of the population are workers from neighboring countries. Côte d'Ivoire officially changed its name from Ivory Coast in Oct. 1985.

Students and workers protested, Feb. 1990, demanding the ouster of longtime Pres. Félix Houphouët-Boigny and multiparty democracy. Côte d'Ivoire held its first multiparty presidential election Oct. 1990, and Houphouët-Boigny retained his office. He died Dec. 7, 1993. The National Assembly named a successor, pending elections planned for 1995.

Croatia

Republic of Croatia

Republika Hrvatska

People: Population: 4,698,000. **Pop. density:** 215 per sq. mi. **Ethnic groups:** Croatian 78%, Serbian 12%. **Principal languages:** Serbo-Croatian 96%. **Religions:** Roman Catholic 77%.

Geography: Area: 21,829 sq. mi., slightly smaller than W Virginia. **Location:** in SE Europe. **Neighbors:** Slovenia, Bosnia and Herzegovina, Hungary, Yugoslavia, and the Adriatic Sea. Over 33 percent is forested. **Capital:** Zagreb.

Government: Type: Parliamentary democracy. **Head of state:** Pres. Franjo Tudjman; b 1922; in office: May 1990. **Head of government:** Prime Min. Nikica Valentic; in office: Apr. 3, 1993. **Local divisions:** 102 districts.

Economy: Industries: Textiles, chemicals, aluminum prods., paper. **Chief crops:** Olives, wine. **Minerals:** Bauxite, copper, coal. **Arable land:** 32%. **Electricity prod.** (1992): 11.5 bln. kWh.

Finance: Monetary unit: Croatian Dinar (Jan. 1993: 365 = $1 US). **Gross domestic product** (1991): $26.3 bln. **Per capita GDP:** $5,600. **Imports** (1990): $4.4 bln. **Exports** (1990): 2.9 bln.

Transport: Motor vehicles: in use: 865,000 passenger cars, 72,000 commercial vehicles.

Communications: Television sets: 1 per 4.6 persons. **Radios:** 1 per 6.3 persons. **Telephones:** 1 per 4.2 persons. **Daily newspaper circ.:** 133 per 1,000 pop.

Health: Life expectancy at birth (1994): 70 male; 77 female. **Births** (per 1,000 pop.): 12. **Deaths** (per 1,000 pop.): 11. **Hospital beds:** 1 per 153 persons. **Physicians:** 1 per 535 persons. **Infant mortality** (per 1,000 live births 1994): 9.

Education (1991): **Literacy:** 96%.

International Organizations: UN.

Embassy: 2356 Massachusetts Ave. NW 20036; 543-5586.

From the 7th century the area was inhabited by Croats, a south Slavic people. It was formed into a kingdom under Tomislav in 924, and joined with Hungary in 1102. The Croats became westernized and separated from Slavs under Austro-Hungarian influence. The Croats retained autonomy under the Hungarian crown. Slavonia was taken by Turks in the 16th century; the northern part was restored by the Treaty of Karlowitz in 1699. Croatia helped Austria put down the Hungarian revolution 1848-49 and as a result was set up with Slavonia as the separate Austrian crownland of Croatia and Slavonia, which was reunited to Hungary as part of *Ausgleich* in 1867. It united with other Yugoslav areas to proclaim the kingdom of Serbs, Croats, and Slovenes in 1918. At the reorganization of Yugoslavia in 1929, Croatia and Slavonia became Savska co., which in 1939 was united with Primorje co. to form the county of Croatia. A nominally independent state between 1941-45, it became a constituent republic in the 1946 constitution.

On June 25, 1991, Croatia declared independence from Yugoslavia. Fighting began between ethnic Serbs and Croats, with the former gaining control of about 30% of Croatian territory. A cease-fire was declared in Jan. 1992, but new hostilities broke out in 1993. A cease-fire with Serb rebels forming a self-declared republic of Krajina was agreed to Mar. 30, 1994.

Cuba

Republic of Cuba

República de Cuba

People: Population: 11,064,000. **Age distrib.** (%): <15: 23; 65+: 9. **Pop. density:** 258 per sq. mi. **Urban:** 73%. **Ethnic groups:** mulatto 51%, white 37%, black 11%. **Principal languages:** Spanish. **Religions:** Roman Catholic 85% prior to Castro.

Geography: Area: 42,804 sq. mi., nearly as large as Pennsylvania. **Location:** Westernmost of West Indies. **Neighbors:** Bahamas, U.S. on N, Mexico on W, Jamaica on S, Haiti on E. **Topography:** The coastline is about 2,500 miles. The N coast is steep and rocky, the S coast low and marshy. Low hills and fertile valleys cover more than half the country. Sierra Maestra, in the E is the highest of 3 mountain ranges. **Capital:** Havana. **Cities** (1989 est.): Havana 2.0 mln.; Santiago de Cuba 397,000; Camagüey 279,000.

Government: Type: Communist state. **Head of state:** Pres. Fidel Castro Ruz; b Aug. 13, 1926; in office: Dec. 3, 1976 (formerly prime min. since Feb. 16, 1959). **Local divisions:** 14 provinces, Havana. **Defense:** 6.0% of GNP (1989).

Economy: Industries: Cement, food processing, sugar. **Chief crops:** Sugar (75% of exports), tobacco, rice, coffee, tropical fruit. **Minerals:** Cobalt, nickel, iron, copper, manganese, salt. **Other resources:** Forests. **Arable land:** 23%. **Livestock** (1992): cattle: 4.7 mln.; pigs: 1.8 mln. **Fish catch** (1991): 165,000 metric tons. **Electricity prod.** (1992): 16.2 bln. kWh. **Labor force:** 20% agric.; 33% ind. & comm.; 30% services & govt.

Finance: Monetary unit: Peso (1.00 = $1.00 US). **Gross national product** (1992 est.): $14.9 bln. **Per capita GNP:** $1,370. **Imports** (1991): $3.7 bln. **Exports** (1991): $3.6 bln. **Tourism** (1990): $250 mln. revenues. **National budget** (1990): $14.4 bln.

Transport: Railroads: Length: 3,033 mi. **Motor vehicles:** in use: 241,000 passenger cars, 208,000 comm. vehicles. **Civil aviation::** 1.9 bln. passenger-mi.; 10 airports with scheduled flights. **Chief ports:** Havana, Matanzas, Cienfuegos, Santiago de Cuba.

Communications: Television sets: 1 per 4.3 persons. **Radios:** 1 per 5.1 persons. **Telephones:** 1 per 18 persons. **Daily newspaper circ.:** 124 per 1,000 pop.

Health: Life expectancy at birth (1994): 75 male; 79 female. **Births** (per 1,000 pop.): 17. **Deaths** (per 1,000 pop.): 7. **Natural increase:** 1.0%. **Hospital beds:** 1 per 141 persons. **Physicians:** 1 per 303 persons. **Infant mortality** (per 1,000 live births 1994): 10.

Education (1992): **Literacy:** 99%. 92% of those between ages 6–14 attend school.

Major International Organizations: UN (UNESCO, WHO).

Some 50,000 Indians lived in Cuba when it was reached by Columbus in 1492. Its name derives from the Indian Cubanacan. Except for British occupation of Havana, 1762-63, Cuba remained Spanish until 1898. A slave-based sugar plantation economy developed from the 18th century, aided by early mechanization of milling. Sugar remains the chief product and chief export despite government attempts to diversify.

A ten-year uprising ended in 1878 with guarantees of rights by Spain, which Spain failed to carry out. A full-scale movement under Jose Marti began Feb. 24, 1895.

The U.S. declared war on Spain in Apr. 1898, after the sinking of the USS *Maine* in Havana harbor, and defeated it in the Spanish-American War. Spain gave up all claims to Cuba. U.S. troops withdrew in 1902, but under 1903 and 1934 agreements, the U.S. leases a site at Guantánamo Bay in the SE as a naval base. U.S. and other foreign investments acquired a dominant role in the economy. In 1952, former Pres. Fulgencio Batista seized control and established a dictatorship, which grew increasingly harsh and corrupt. Fidel Castro assembled a rebel band in 1956; guerrilla fighting intensified in 1958. Batista fled Jan. 1, 1959, and in the resulting political vacuum Castro took power, becoming premier Feb. 16.

The government began a program of sweeping economic and social changes, without restoring promised liberties. Opponents were imprisoned, and some were executed. Some 700,000 Cubans emigrated in the first years after the Castro takeover, mostly to the U.S.

Cattle and tobacco lands were nationalized, while a system of cooperatives was instituted. By 1960 all banks and industrial companies had been nationalized, including over $1 billion worth of U.S.-owned properties, mostly without compensation.

Poor sugar crops resulted in collectivization of farms, stringent labor controls, and rationing, despite continued aid from the USSR and other Communist countries. The U.S. imposed an export embargo in 1962, severely damaging the economy.

In 1961, some 1,400 Cubans, trained and backed by the U.S. Central Intelligence Agency, unsuccessfully tried to invade and overthrow the regime. In the fall of 1962, the U.S. learned that the USSR had brought nuclear missiles to Cuba. After an Oct. 22 warning from Pres. John F. Kennedy, the missiles were removed.

In 1977, Cuba and the U.S. signed agreements to exchange diplomats, without restoring full ties, and to regulate offshore fishing. In 1978, and again in 1980, the U.S. agreed to accept political prisoners released by Cuba, some of whom were criminals and mental patients. A 1987 agreement provided for 20,000 Cubans to emigrate to the U.S. each year; Cuba agreed to take back some 2,500 jailed in the U.S. since 1980.

In 1975-78, Cuba sent troops to aid one faction in the Angola civil war; the last Cuban troops were withdrawn by May 1991. Cuba's involvement in Central America, Africa, and the Caribbean contributed to poor relations with the U.S.

Cuba resisted the social and economic reforms that took place in the late 1980s and 1990s in the Soviet Union and its successor states and in Eastern Europe. Cuba's economy, formerly propped up by preferential trading status within the Communist bloc, was severely shaken by its collapse. Stiffer trading sanctions enacted by the U.S. in 1992 made things worse. Antigovernment demonstrations in Aug. 1994 prompted Castro to loosen emigration restrictions. As the tide of boat refugees rapidly rose, the U.S. announced Aug. 18 that future Cuban refugees would be detained, not granted free entry as in the past. A new U.S.-Cuba emigration agreement in Sept. 1994 ended the exodus of "boat people" after more than 30,000 had left Cuba.

Cyprus

Republic of Cyprus

Kypriaki Dimokratia (Greek)

Kibris Cumhuriyeti (Turkish)

People: Population: 730,000. **Age distrib.** (%): <15: 26; 65+: 10. **Pop. density:** 204 per sq. mi. **Urban:** 62%. **Ethnic groups:** Greeks 78%, Turks 18%. **Principal languages:** Greek, Turkish (both official), English. **Religions:** Greek Orthodox 78%, Muslim 18%.

Geography: Area: 3,572 sq. mi., smaller than Connecticut. **Location:** In eastern Mediterranean Sea, off Turkish coast. **Neighbors:** Nearest are Turkey on N, Syria, Lebanon on E. **Topography:** Two mountain ranges run E-W, separated by a wide, fertile plain. **Capital:** Nicosia. **Cities** (1992 est.): Nicosia 166,000.

Government: Type: Republic. **Head of state:** Pres. Glafcos Clerides; b Apr. 24, 1919; in office: Mar. 1, 1993. **Local divisions:** 6 districts. **Defense:** 5% of GDP (1990 est.).

Economy: Industries: Light manuf. **Chief crops:** Grains, grapes, carobs, citrus fruits, potatoes, olives. **Minerals:** Copper, pyrites, asbetos. **Arable land:** 40%. **Electricity prod.** (1990): 1.6 mln. kWh. **Labor force:** 21% agric., 22% ind., 57% serv.

Finance: Monetary unit: Pound (Mar. 1994: 1.00 = $1.96 US). **Gross domestic product** (1990): $5.3 bln. **Per capita GDP:** $7,585. **Imports** (1991): $2.2 bln.; partners: UK 13%, Itl. 12%. **Exports** (1991): $838 mln.; partners: UK 21%, Libya 9%. **Tourism** (1991): receipts: $990 mln. **National budget** (1993): $2.2 bln. **International reserves less gold** (Nov. 1993): $1.1 bln. **Gold:** 459,000 oz t. **Consumer prices** (change in 1993): 4.9%.

Transport: Motor vehicles: in use: 189,000 passenger cars, 84,000 comm. vehicles. **Civil aviation::** 1.3 bln. passenger-mi.; 1 airport. **Chief ports:** Famagusta, Limassol.

Communications: Television sets: 1 per 3.2 persons. **Radios:** 1 per 2.8 persons. **Telephones:** 1 per 1.6 persons. **Daily newspaper circ.:** 111 per 1,000 pop.

Health: Life expectancy at birth (1994): 74 male; 79 female. **Births** (per 1,000 pop.): 17. **Deaths** (per 1,000 pop.): 8. **Natural increase:** 0.9%. **Hospital beds:** 1 per 168 persons. **Physicians:** 1 per 476 persons. **Infant mortality** (per 1,000 live births 1994): 9.

Education (1991): **Literacy:** 95%. **Years compulsory:** 9; attendance 99%.

Major International Organizations: UN (GATT, IMF, WHO), Commonwealth of Nations, EU (Assoc.).

Embassy: 2211 R St. NW, 20008; 462-5772.

Agitation for enosis (union) with Greece increased after World War II, with the Turkish minority opposed, and broke into violence in 1955-56. In 1959, Britain, Greece, Turkey, and Cypriot leaders approved a plan for an independent republic, with constitutional guarantees for the Turkish minority and permanent division of offices on an ethnic basis. Greek and Turkish Communal Chambers dealt with religion, education, and other matters.

Archbishop Makarios III, formerly the leader of the enosis movement, was elected president, and full independence became final Aug. 16, 1960. Further communal strife led the United Nations to send a peacekeeping force in 1964; its mandate has been repeatedly renewed.

The Cypriot National Guard, led by officers from the army of Greece, seized the government July 15, 1974. On July 20, Turkey invaded the island; Greece mobilized its forces but did not intervene. A cease-fire was arranged but collapsed. By Aug. 16, Turkish forces had occupied the NE 40% of the island, despite the presence of UN peacekeeping forces.

Turkish Cypriots voted overwhelmingly, June 8, 1975, to form a separate Turkish Cypriot federated state. A president and assembly were elected in 1976. Some 200,000 Greeks have been expelled from the Turkish-controlled area, replaced by thousands of Turks, some from the mainland.

Turkish Republic of Northern Cyprus

A declaration of independence was announced by Turkish-Cypriot leader Rauf Denktash, Nov. 15, 1983. The state is not internationally recognized although it does have trade relations with some countries. TRNC contains 1,295 sq mi., pop. (1992 est.): 176,000, 99% Turkish.

Czech Republic

(Figures prior to 1993 are for the Czech and Slovak Federal Republic)

People: Population: 10,408,000. **Age distrib.** (%): <15: 21; 65+: 13. **Pop. density:** 342 per sq. mi. **Urban:** 73%. **Ethnic groups:** Czechs 94%, Slovaks 3%. **Principal languages:** Czech. **Religions:** atheist 39.8%, Roman Catholic 39.2%, Protestant 4.6%.

Geography: Area: 30,449 sq. mi. **Location:** In E central Europe. **Neighbors:** Poland on N, Germany on N, W, Austria on S, Slovakia on E, SE. **Topography:** Bohemia, in W, is a plateau surrounded by mountains; Moravia is hilly. **Capital:** Prague. **Cities** (1992 est.): Prague 1.2 mln.; Brno 391,000; Ostrava 331,000.

Government: Type: Republic. **Head of state:** Vaclav Havel; b Oct. 5, 1936; in office: Feb. 15, 1993. **Head of government:** Prime Min. Vaclav Klaus; in office: July 1993. **Defense:** 2.2% of GDP (1992).

Economy: Industries: Machinery, oil products, iron and steel, glass, chemicals, motor vehicles, cement. **Chief crops:** Wheat, sugar beets, potatoes, rye, corn, barley. **Minerals:** coke, coal, iron. **Livestock:** (1991): cattle: 2.5 mln.; pigs: 4.5 mln.; sheep: 254,000. **Electricity prod.** (1991): 89.0 bln. kWh. **Labor force:** 8% agric.; 38% ind.

Finance: Monetary unit: Koruny (Mar. 1994: 29.59 = $1 US). **Gross domestic product** (1992): $75.3 bln.* **Per capita GDP:** $7,300. **Imports** (1991): $10.4 bln.; partners: USSR 31%, Ger. 19%, Pol. 6%. **Exports** (1991): $10.8 bln.; partners: USSR 35%, Ger. 7%, Pol. 7%. **Tourism** (1989): $689 mln. receipts. **National budget** (1991): $16.8 bln. **International reserves less gold** (Feb. 1994): $4 bln. **Gold:** 1.95 mln. oz t. **Consumer prices** (change in 1992): 10.8%.

Transport: Railroads: Length: 5,874 mi. **Motor vehicles:** in use: 2.4 mln. passenger cars, 232,000 comm. vehicles. **Civil aviation::** 1.4 bln. passenger-mi.; 4 airports.

Communications: Television sets: 1 per 3.2 persons. **Radios:** 1 per 3.5 persons. **Telephones:** 1 per 3.2 persons. **Daily newspaper circ.:** 368 per 1,000 pop.

Health: Life expectancy at birth (1994): 69 male; 77 female. **Births** (per 1,000 pop.): 13. **Deaths** (per 1,000 pop.): 11. **Natural increase:** .2%. **Hospital beds:** 1 per 98 persons. **Physicians:** 1 per 319 persons. **Infant mortality** (per 1,000 live births 1994): 9.

Education (1992): **Literacy:** 99%.

Major International Organizations: UN (GATT, WHO).

Embassy: 3900 Spring of Freedom St. NW 20008; 363-6315.

Bohemia and Moravia were part of the Great Moravian Empire in the 9th century and later became part of the Holy Roman Empire. Under the kings of Bohemia, Prague in the 14th century was the cultural center of Central Europe. Bohemia and Hungary became part of Austria-Hungary.

In 1914-18 Thomas G. Masaryk and Eduard Benes formed a provisional government with the support of Slovak leaders including Milan Stefanik. They proclaimed the Republic of Czechoslovakia Oct. 28, 1918.

Czechoslovakia

By 1938 Nazi Germany had worked up disaffection among German-speaking citizens in Sudetenland and demanded its cession. Prime Min. Neville Chamberlain of Britain, with the acquiescence of France, signed with Hitler at Munich, Sept. 30, 1938, an agreement to the cession, with a guarantee of peace by Hitler and Mussolini. Germany occupied Sudetenland Oct. 1-2.

Hitler on Mar. 15, 1939, dissolved Czechoslovakia, made protectorates of Bohemia and Moravia, and supported the autonomy of Slovakia, proclaimed independent Mar. 14, 1939.

Soviet troops with some Czechoslovak contingents entered eastern Czechoslovakia in 1944 and reached Prague in May 1945; Benes returned as president. In May 1946 elections, the Communist Party won 38% of the votes, and Benes accepted Klement Gottwald, a Communist, as prime minister.

In Feb. 1948, the Communists seized power in advance of scheduled elections. In May 1948 a new constitution was approved. Benes refused to sign it. On May 30 the voters were offered a one-slate ballot and the Communists won full control. Benes resigned June 7 and Gottwald became president. A harsh Stalinist period followed, with complete and violent suppression of all opposition.

In Jan. 1968 a liberalization movement spread explosively through Czechoslovakia. Antonin Novotny, long the Stalinist ruler of the nation, was deposed as party leader and succeeded by Alexander Dubcek, a Slovak, who supported democratic reforms. On Mar. 22 Novotny resigned as president and was succeeded by Gen. Ludvik Svoboda. On Apr. 6, Prem. Joseph Lenart resigned and was succeeded by Oldrich Cernik, a reformer.

In July 1968 the USSR and 4 Warsaw Pact nations demanded an end to liberalization. On Aug. 20, the Soviet, Polish, East German, Hungarian, and Bulgarian armies invaded Czechoslovakia. Despite demonstrations and riots by students and workers, press censorship was imposed, liberal leaders were ousted from office and promises of loyalty to Soviet policies were made by some old-line Communist Party leaders.

On Apr. 17, 1969, Dubcek resigned as leader of the Communist Party and was succeeded by Gustav Husak. In Jan. 1970, Cernik was ousted. Censorship was tightened, and the Communist Party expelled a third of its members. In 1973, amnesty was offered to some of the 40,000 who fled the country after the 1968 invasion, but repressive policies continued.

More than 700 leading Czechoslovak intellectuals and former party leaders signed a human rights manifesto in 1977, called Charter 77, prompting a renewed crackdown by the regime.

The police crushed the largest antigovernment protests since 1968, when tens of thousands of demonstrators took to the streets of Prague, Nov. 17, 1989. As protesters demanded free elections, the Communist Party leadership resigned Nov. 24; millions went on strike Nov. 27.

On Dec. 10, 1989 the first cabinet in 41 years without a Communist majority took power; Vaclav Havel, playwright and human rights campaigner, was chosen president, Dec. 29. Havel failed to win reelection July 3, 1992; his bid was blocked by a Slovak-led coalition.

Slovakia declared sovereignty, July 17. Czech and Slovak leaders agreed, July 23, on a basic plan for a peaceful division of Czechoslovakia into 2 independent states.

Czech Republic

Czechoslovakia split into 2 separate states—the Czech Republic and Slovakia—on Jan. 1, 1993. Havel was elected president, Jan. 26, 1993.

Denmark

Kingdom of Denmark

Kongeriget Danmark

People: Population: 5,188,000. **Age distrib.** (%): <15: 17; 65+: 16. **Pop. density:** 311 per sq. mi. **Urban:** 85%. **Ethnic groups:** Almost all Scandinavian. **Principal languages:** Danish, Faroese. **Religions:** Evangelical Lutheran 91%.

Geography: Area: 16,639 sq. mi., the size of Massachusetts and New Hampshire combined. **Location:** In northern Europe, separating the North and Baltic seas. **Neighbors:** Germany on S, Norway on NW, Sweden on NE. **Topography:** Denmark consists of the Jutland Peninsula and about 500 islands, 100 inhabited. The land is flat or gently rolling, and is almost all in productive use. **Capital:** Copenhagen. **Cities** (1991, met.): Copenhagen 1.3 mln. (met.).

Government: Type: Constitutional monarchy. **Head of state:** Queen Margrethe II; b Apr. 16, 1940; in office: Jan. 14, 1972. **Head of government:** Prime Min. Poul Nyrup Rasmussen; b June 15, 1943; in office: Jan. 25, 1993. **Local divisions:** 14 counties and one city (Copenhagen). **Defense:** 2% of GDP (1992).

Economy: Industries: Machinery, textiles, furniture, electronics. **Chief crops:** Dairy products. **Arable land:** 61%. **Livestock** (1987): cattle: 2.3 mln.; pigs: 9.2 mln. **Fish catch** (1992): 1.8 mln. metric tons. **Electricity prod.** (1992): 34 bln. kWh. **Labor force:** 6% agric.; 67% serv. & govt.; 20% manuf. & mining.

Finance: Monetary unit: Krone (Mar. 1994: 6.63 = $1 US). **Gross domestic product** (1992): $94.2 bln.* **Per capita GDP:** $18,200. **Imports** (1992): $32.3 bln.; partners: EU 52%, Swe. 10%. **Exports** (1992): $39.6 bln.; partners: EU 54%, Swe. 11%. **Tourism** (1991): $3.4 bln. receipts. **National budget** (1992): $55.3 bln. **International reserves less gold** (Mar. 1994): $9.5 bln. **Gold:** 2.0 mln. oz t. **Consumer prices** (change in 1993): 1.3%.

Transport: Railroads: Length: 1,763 mi. **Motor vehicles:** in use: 1.6 mln. passenger cars, 315,000 comm. vehicles. **Civil aviation::** 2.4 bln. passenger-mi.; 11 airports with scheduled flights. **Chief ports:** Copenhagen, Alborg, Arhus, Odense.

Communications: Television sets: 1 per 2.1 persons. **Radios:** 1 per 2.3 persons. **Telephones:** 1 per 1 person. **Daily newspaper circ.:** 352 per 1,000 pop.

Health: Life expectancy at birth (1994): 73 male; 79 female. **Births** (per 1,000 pop.): 12. **Deaths** (per 1,000 pop.): 11. **Hospital beds:** 1 per 184 persons. **Physicians:** 1 per 360 persons. **Infant mortality** (per 1,000 live births 1994): 7.

Education (1991): **Literacy:** 99%. Years compulsory 9; attendance 100%.

Major International Organizations: UN and all of its specialized agencies, OECD, EU, NATO.

Embassy: 3200 Whitehaven St. NW 20008; 234-4300.

The origin of Copenhagen dates back to ancient times, when the fishing and trading place named Havn (port) grew up on a cluster of islets, but Bishop Absalon (1128-1201) is regarded as the actual founder of the city.

Danes formed a large component of the Viking raiders in the early Middle Ages. The Danish kingdom was a major north European power until the 17th century, when it lost its land in southern Sweden. Norway was separated in 1815, and Schleswig-Holstein in 1864. Northern Schleswig was returned in 1920.

Voters ratified the Maastricht Treaty on greater European Community unity, May 1993, after having rejected it in 1992.

The **Faeroe Islands** in the N Atlantic, about 300 mi. NE of the Shetlands, and 850 mi. from Denmark proper, 18 inhabited, have an area of 540 sq. mi. and pop. (1987) of 46,000. They are self-governing in most matters.

Greenland

(Kalaallit Nunaat)

Greenland, a huge island between the N Atlantic and the Polar Sea, is separated from the North American continent by Davis Strait and Baffin Bay. Its total area is 840,000 sq. mi., 84% of which is ice-capped. Most of the island is a lofty plateau 9,000 to 10,000 ft. in altitude. The average thickness of the cap is 1,000 ft. The population (1994) is 57,000. Under the 1953 Danish constitution the colony became an integral part of the realm with representatives in the Folketing. The Danish parliament, 1978, approved home rule for Greenland, effective May 1, 1979. Accepting home rule the islanders elected a socialist-dominated legislature, Apr. 4th. With home rule, Greenlandic place names came into official use. The technically correct name for Greenland is now Kalaallit Nunaat; its capital is Nuuk, rather than Gothab. Fish is the principal export.

Djibouti

Republic of Djibouti

Jumhouriyya Djibouti

People: Population: 413,000. **Pop. density:** 46. **Urban:** 77%. **Ethnic groups:** Somali 60%; Afar 35%. **Principal**

languages: French, Arabic (both official); Afar, Somali. **Religions:** Muslim 94%, Christian 6%.

Geography: Area: 8,950 sq. mi., about the size of New Hampshire. **Location:** On E coast of Africa, separated from Arabian Peninsula by the strategically vital strait of Bab el-Mandeb. **Neighbors:** Ethiopia on W, NW, Eritrea on NW, Somalia on S. **Topography:** The territory, divided into a low coastal plain, mountains behind, and an interior plateau, is arid, sandy, and desolate. The climate is generally hot and dry. **Capital:** Djibouti. **Cities** (1989): Djibouti (met.) 450,000.

Government: Type: Republic. **Head of state:** Pres. Hassan Gouled Aptidon; b 1916; in office: June 24, 1977. **Head of government:** Prem. Barkat Gourad Hamadou; in office: Sept. 30, 1978. **Local divisions:** 5 districts.

Economy: Minerals: Salt. **Electricity prod.** (1991): 200 mln. kWh.

Finance: Monetary unit: Franc (Mar. 1994: 177=$1 US). **Gross domestic product** (1990): $358 mln. **Per capita GDP:** $1,030. **Imports** (1990): $311 mln.; partners: EU 36%. **Exports** (1990): $190 mln.; partners: Middle East 50%. **National budget** (1991 est.): $203 mln.

Transport: Motor vehicles: in use: 13,000 passenger cars, 2,000 commercial vehicles. **Chief ports:** Djibouti.

Communications: Television sets: 1 per 33 persons. **Radios:** 1 per 19 persons. **Telephones:** 1 per 40 persons.

Health: Life expectancy at birth (1994): 47 male; 51 female. **Births** (per 1,000 pop.): 43. **Deaths** (per 1,000 pop.): 16. **Natural increase:** 2.7%. **Infant mortality** (per 1,000 live births 1994): 111.

Education (1991): **Literacy:** 48%.

Major International Organizations: UN, OAU, Arab League.

Embassy: 1156 15th St. NW 20005; 331-0270.

France gained control of the territory in stages between 1862 and 1900.

Ethiopia and Somalia have renounced their claims to the area, but each has accused the other of trying to gain control. There were clashes between Afars (ethnically related to Ethiopians) and Issas (related to Somalis) in 1976. Immigrants from both countries continued to enter the country up to independence, which came June 27, 1977.

French aid is the mainstay of the economy, as well as assistance from the U.S.

Dominica

Commonwealth of Dominica

People: Population: 88,000. **Pop. density:** 303 per sq. mi. **Ethnic groups:** nearly all African or mulatto, Caribs. **Principal languages:** English (official), French patois. **Religions:** Roman Catholic 77%.

Geography: Area: 290 sq. mi., about one-fourth the size of Rhode Island. **Location:** In Eastern Caribbean, most northerly Windward Is. **Neighbors:** Guadeloupe to N, Martinique to S. **Topography:** Mountainous, a central ridge running from N to S, terminating in cliffs; volcanic in origin, with numerous thermal springs; rich deep topsoil on leeward side, red tropical clay on windward coast. **Capital** Roseau. **Cities** (1991 est.): Roseau 16,000.

Government: Type: Parliamentary democracy. **Head of state:** Pres. Crispin Anselm Sorhaindo; in office: Oct. 25, 1993. **Head of government:** Prime Min. Mary Eugenia Charles; b 1919; in office: July 21, 1980. **Local divisions:** 10 parishes.

Economy: Industries: Agriculture, tourism. **Chief crops:** Bananas, citrus fruits, coconuts. **Minerals:** Pumice. **Other resources:** Forests. **Arable land:** 9%. **Electricity prod.** (1992): 16 mln. kWh. **Labor force:** 40% agric.; 32% ind & comm.; 28% services.

Finance: Monetary unit: East Caribbean dollar (Mar. 1994: 2.70 = $1 US). **Gross domestic product** (1991): $174 mln. **Per capita GDP:** $2,100. **Imports** (1992): $111 mln.; partners: UK 17%, U.S. 23%. **Exports** (1992): $56 mln.; partners: UK 70%. **Tourism** (1989): $19 mln. receipts. **National budget** (1991 est.): $84 mln. **Consumer prices** (change in 1992): 5.3%.

Transport: Chief ports: Roseau.

Communications: Telephones: 1 per 5.8 persons.

Health: Life expectancy at birth (1994): 74 male; 80 female. **Births** (per 1,000 pop.): 20. **Deaths** (per 1,000 pop.): 5. **Natural increase:** 1.5%. **Hospital beds:** 1 per 247 persons. **Physicians:** 1 per 1,947 persons. **Infant mortality** (per 1,000 live births 1994): 10.

Education: Literacy: 90%.

Major International Organizations: UN, OAS.

A British colony since 1805, Dominica was granted self-government in 1967. Independence was achieved Nov. 3, 1978.

Hurricane David struck, Aug. 30, 1979, devastating the island and destroying the banana plantations, Dominica's economic mainstay. Coups were attempted in 1980 and 1981.

Dominica took a leading role in the instigation of the 1983 U.S.-led invasion of Grenada.

Dominican Republic

República Dominicana

People: Population: 7,826,000. **Age distrib.** (%): <15: 38; 65+: 3. **Pop. density:** 418 per sq. mi. **Urban:** 60%. **Ethnic groups:** mixed 73%, white 16%, black 11%. **Principal languages:** Spanish. **Religions:** Roman Catholic 95%.

Geography: Area: 18,704 sq. mi., the size of Vermont and New Hampshire combined. **Location:** In West Indies, sharing I. of Hispaniola with Haiti. **Neighbors:** Haiti on W. **Topography:** The Cordillera Central range crosses the center of the country, rising to over 10,000 ft., highest in the Caribbean. The Cibao valley to the N is major agricultural area. **Capital:** Santo Domingo. **Cities** (1991 est.): Santo Domingo 2.4 mln.; Santiago de Los Caballeros 490,000.

Government: Type: Representative democracy. **Head of state:** Pres. Joaquín Balaguer; b Sept. 1, 1907; in office: Aug. 16, 1986. **Local divisions:** 29 provinces and Santo Domingo. **Defense:** 0.7% of GDP (1993 est.).

Economy: Industries: Sugar refining, cement, pharmaceuticals. **Chief crops:** sugar, cocoa, coffee, tobacco, rice. **Minerals:** Nickel, gold, silver. **Other resources:** Timber. **Arable land:** 23%. **Livestock** (1991): cattle: 2.2 mln.; pigs: 431,000. **Electricity prod.** (1992): 5.0 bln. kWh. **Labor force:** 49% agric.; 18% ind.; 33% serv. & govt.

Finance: Monetary unit: Peso (Mar. 1994: 13.03 = $1 US). **Gross domestic product** (1992): $8.4 bln. **Per capita GDP:** $1,120. **Imports** (1991): $1.8 bln.; partners: U.S. 50%. **Exports** (1991): $775 mln.; partners: U.S. 59%, EU 19%. **Tourism** (1990): $750 mln. receipts. **National budget** (1993 est.): $1.8 bln. **International reserves less gold** (Mar. 1994): $493 mln. **Gold:** 18,000 oz t. **Consumer prices** (change in 1992): 4.6%

Transport: Motor vehicles: in use: 160,000 passenger cars, 110,000 comm. vehicles. **Civil aviation::** 154 mln. passenger-mi.; 5 airports. **Chief ports:** Santo Domingo, San Pedro de Macoris, Puerto Plata.

Communications: Television sets: 1 per 10 persons. **Radios:** 1 per 6.5 persons. **Telephones:** 1 per 14 persons. **Daily newspaper circ.:** 32 per 1,000 pop.

Health: Life expectancy at birth (1994): 66 male; 71 female. **Births** (per 1,000 pop.): 25. **Deaths** (per 1,000 pop.): 6. **Natural increase:** 1.9%. **Hospital beds:** 1 per 508 persons. **Physicians:** 1 per 934 persons. **Infant mortality** (per 1,000 live births 1994): 52.

Education (1991): **Literacy:** 83%. Years compulsory 6; attendance 70%.

Major International Organizations: UN (World Bank, IMF, GATT), OAS.

Embassy: 1715 22d St. NW 20008; 332-6280.

Carib and Arawak Indians inhabited the island of Hispaniola when Columbus landed in 1492. The city of Santo Domingo, founded 1496, is the oldest settlement by Europeans in the hemisphere and has the supposed ashes of Columbus in an elaborate tomb in its ancient cathedral.

The western third of the island was ceded to France in 1697. Santo Domingo itself was ceded to France in 1795. Haitian leader Toussaint L'Ouverture seized it, 1801. Spain returned intermittently 1803-21, as several native republics came and went. Haiti ruled again, 1822-44, and Spanish occupation occurred 1861-63.

The country was occupied by U.S. Marines from 1916 to 1924, when a constitutionally elected government was installed.

In 1930, Gen. Rafael Leonidas Trujillo Molina was elected

president. Trujillo ruled brutally until his assassination in 1961. Pres. Joaquín Balaguer, appointed by Trujillo in 1960, resigned under pressure in 1962.

Juan Bosch, elected president in the first free elections in 38 years, was overthrown in 1963. On Apr. 24, 1965, a revolt was launched by followers of Bosch and others, including a few Communists. Four days later U.S. Marines intervened against the pro-Bosch forces. Token units were later sent by 5 South American countries as a peacekeeping force. A provisional government supervised a June 1966 election, in which Balaguer defeated Bosch. Balaguer remained in office for most of the next 28 years, but his May 1994 reelection was widely denounced as fraudulent, and he promised new elections for 1995.

Continued depressed world prices have affected the main export commodity, sugar.

Ecuador

Republic of Ecuador

República del Ecuador

People: Population: 10,677,000. **Age distrib.** (%): <15: 39; 65+: 4. **Pop. density:** 101 per sq. mi. **Urban:** 57%. **Ethnic groups:** Mestizo 55%, Indians 25%, Spanish 10%, African 10%. **Principal languages:** Spanish (official), Quechuan, Jivaroan. **Religions:** Roman Catholic 95%.

Geography: Area: 105,037 sq. mi., the size of Colorado. **Location:** In NW S America, on Pacific coast, astride Equator. **Neighbors:** Colombia to N, Peru to E and S. **Topography:** Two ranges of Andes run N and S, splitting the country into 3 zones: hot, humid lowlands on the coast; temperate highlands between the ranges; and rainy, tropical lowlands to the E. **Capital:** Quito. **Cities** (1991 est.): Guayaquil 2.0 mln.; Quito 1.5 mln.

Government: Type: Republic. **Head of state:** Pres. Sixto Durán Ballén; b 1922; in office: Aug. 10, 1992. **Local divisions:** 21 provinces. **Defense:** 2.2% of GDP (1992).

Economy: Industries: Food processing, wood prods., textiles. **Chief crops:** Bananas (largest exporter), coffee, rice, sugar, corn. **Minerals:** Oil, copper, iron, lead, silver, sulphur. **Crude oil reserves** (1991): 1.8 bln. bbls. **Other resources:** Rubber, bark. **Arable land:** 6%. **Livestock** (1992): cattle: 4.6 mln.; pigs: 2.4 mln.; sheep: 1.5 mln. **Fish catch** (1991): 383,000 metric tons. **Electricity prod.** (1992): 7.6 bln. kWh. **Labor force:** 35% agric., 21% ind., 28% services.

Finance: Monetary unit: Sucre (July 1993: 1,875 = $1 US). **Gross domestic product** (1992): $11.8 bln. **Per capita GDP:** $1,100. **Imports** (1992): $2.4 bln.; partners: U.S. 34%. **Exports** (1992): $3.0 bln.; partners: U.S. 60%. **Tourism** (1990): $193 mln. receipts. **National budget** (1992): $1.9 bln. **International reserves less gold** (Oct. 1993): $1.3 bln. **Gold:** 414,000 oz t. **Consumer prices** (change in 1993): 45.0%.

Transport: Railroads: Length: 600 mi. **Motor vehicles:** in use: 165,000 passenger cars, 207,000 comm. vehicles. **Civil aviation::** 746 mln. passenger-mi.; 14 airports. **Chief ports:** Guayaquil, Manta, Esmeraldas, Puerto Bolivar.

Communications: Television sets: 1 per 12 persons. **Radios:** 1 per 3.5 persons. **Telephones:** 1 per 20 persons. **Daily newspaper circ.:** 87 per 1,000 pop.

Health: Life expectancy at birth (1994): 67 male, 73 female. **Births** (per 1,000 pop.): 26. **Deaths** (per 1,000 pop.): 6. **Natural increase:** 2.0%. **Hospital beds:** 1 per 598 persons. **Physicians:** 1 per 1,039. **Infant mortality** (per 1,000 live births 1994): 39.

Education (1991): **Literacy:** 88%. **Attendance:** through 6th grade—76% urban, 33% rural.

Major International Organizations: UN (IMF, WHO), OAS.

Embassy: 2535 15th St. NW 20009; 234-7200.

Spain conquered the region, which was the northern Inca empire, in 1633. Liberation forces defeated the Spanish May 24, 1822, near Quito. Ecuador became part of the Great Colombia Republic but seceded, May 13, 1830.

Ecuador had been ruled by civilian and military dictatorships since 1968. A peaceful transfer of power from the military junta to the democratic civilian government took place, 1979.

Since 1972, the economy has revolved around its petroleum exports, which have declined since 1982 causing severe economic problems. Ecuador suspended interest payments for 1987 on its estimated $8.2 billion foreign debt following a Mar. 5-6 earthquake which left 20,000 homeless, and destroyed a stretch of the country's main oil pipeline.

Ecuadoran Indians staged a number of protests in the 1990s to demand greater rights.

The **Galapagos Islands,** 600 mi. to the W, are the home of huge tortoises and other unusual animals.

Egypt

Arab Republic of Egypt

Jumhurīyah Misr al-Arabiyah

People: Population: 59,325,000. **Age distrib** (%) <15: 40; 65+: 4. **Pop. density:** 154 per sq. mi. **Urban:** 45%. **Ethnic groups:** Eastern Hamitic stock 90%, Greek, Italian, Syro-Lebanese. **Principal languages:** Arabic (official), English, French. **Religions:** Sunni Muslim 94%.

Geography: Area: 385,229 sq. mi, about the size of Texas, Oklahoma, and Arkansas combined. **Location:** NE corner of Africa. **Neighbors:** Libya on W, Sudan on S, Israel on E. **Topography:** Almost entirely desolate and barren, with hills and mountains in E and along Nile. The Nile Valley, where most of the people live, stretches 550 miles. **Capital:** Cairo. **Cities** (1991 est.): Cairo 6.6 mln.; Alexandria 3.3 mln.; al-Jizah 2.1 mln.

Government: Type: Republic. **Head of state:** Pres. Hosni Mubarak; b May 4, 1928; in office: Oct. 14, 1981. **Head of government:** Atef Sedki; in office: Nov. 10, 1986. **Local divisions:** 26 governorates. **Defense:** 5% of GDP (FY 1992-93).

Economy: Industries: Textiles, chemicals, petrochemicals, food processing, cement. **Chief crops:** Cotton (one of largest producers), rice, beans, fruits, grains, vegetables, sugar, corn. **Minerals:** Oil, phosphates, gypsum, iron, manganese, limestone. **Crude oil reserves** (1991): 6.2 bln. bbls. **Arable land:** 3%. **Livestock** (1991): cattle: 3.5 mln.; sheep: 4.2 mln. **Fish catch** (1991): 298,000 metric tons. **Electricity prod.** (1992): 47 bln. kWh. **Labor force:** 34% agric.; 36% govt.

Finance: Monetary unit: Pound (Mar. 1994: 3.38 = $1 US). **Gross domestic product** (1992): $41.2 bln. **Per capita GDP:** $730. **Imports** (1991): $11.5 bln.; partners: U.S. 19%, Ger. 10%, It. 8%, France 8%. **Exports** (1991): $4.5 bln.; partners: It. 22%, Rom. 12%. **Tourism** (1990): $1.9 bln. receipts. **National budget** (1992 est.): $15.2 bln. **International reserves less gold** (Jan. 1994): $12.6 bln. **Gold:** 2.43 mln. oz t. **Consumer prices** (change in 1993): 12.1%.

Transport: Railroads: Length: 5,489 mi. **Motor vehicles:** in use: 826,000 passenger cars, 550,000 comm. vehicles. **Civil aviation::** 3.2 bln. passenger-mi.; 10 airports. **Chief ports:** Alexandria, Port Said, Suez.

Communications: Television sets: 1 per 11 persons. **Radios:** 1 per 4 persons.**Telephones:** 1 per 22 persons. **Daily newspaper circ.:** 57 per 1,000 pop.

Health: Life expectancy at birth (1994): 59 male; 63 female. **Births** (per 1,000 pop.): 32. **Deaths** (per 1,000 pop.): 9. **Natural increase:** 2.3%. **Hospital beds:** 1 per 504 persons. **Physicians:** 1 per 1,698 persons. **Infant mortality** (per 1,000 live births 1994): 76.

Education (1990): **Literacy:** 44%. Compulsory ages 6-12.

Major International Organizations: UN (IMF, World Bank, GATT), OAU.

Embassy: 2310 Decatur Pl. NW 20008; 232-5400.

Archaeological records of ancient Egyptian civilization date back to 4000 BC. A unified kingdom arose around 3200 BC, and extended its way south into Nubia and north as far as Syria. A high culture of rulers and priests was built on an economic base of serfdom, fertile soil, and annual flooding of the Nile banks.

Imperial decline facilitated conquest by Asian invaders (Hyksos, Assyrians). The last native dynasty fell in 341 BC to the Persians, who were in turn replaced by Greeks (Alexander and the Ptolemies), Romans, Byzantines, and Arabs, who introduced Islam and the Arabic language. The ancient Egyptian language is preserved only in the liturgy of the Coptic Christians.

Egypt was ruled as part of larger Islamic empires for several centuries. The Mamluks, a military caste of Caucasian origin, ruled Egypt from 1250 until defeat by the Ottoman Turks in 1517. Under Turkish sultans the khedive as hereditary viceroy had wide authority. Britain intervened in 1882 and took control of administration, though nominal allegiance to the Ottoman Empire continued until 1914.

The country was a British protectorate from 1914 to 1922. A 1936 treaty strengthened Egyptian autonomy, but Britain retained bases in Egypt and a condominium over the Sudan.

Britain fought German and Italian armies from Egypt, 1940-42. In 1951 Egypt abrogated the 1936 treaty. The Sudan became independent in 1956.

The uprising of July 23, 1952, led by the Society of Free Officers, named Maj. Gen. Mohammed Naguib commander in chief and forced King Farouk to abdicate. When the republic was proclaimed June 18, 1953, Naguib became its first president and premier. Lt. Col. Gamal Abdel Nasser removed Naguib and became premier in 1954. In 1956, he was voted president. Nasser died in 1970 and was replaced by Vice Pres. Anwar Sadat.

The Aswan High Dam, completed 1971, provides irrigation for more than a million acres of land. Artesian wells, drilled in the Western Desert, reclaimed 43,000 acres, 1960-66.

When the state of Israel was proclaimed in 1948, Egypt joined other Arab nations invading Israel and was defeated.

After terrorist raids across its border, Israel invaded Egypt's Sinai Peninsula, Oct. 29, 1956. Egypt rejected a cease-fire demand by Britain and France; on Oct. 31 the 2 nations dropped bombs and on Nov. 5-6 landed forces. Egypt and Israel accepted a UN cease-fire; fighting ended Nov. 7.

A UN Emergency Force guarded the 117-mile-long border between Egypt and Israel until May 19, 1967, when it was withdrawn at Nasser's demand. Egyptian troops entered the Gaza Strip and the heights of Sharm el Sheikh and 3 days later closed the Strait of Tiran to all Israeli shipping. Full-scale war broke out June 5; before it ended under a UN cease-fire June 10, Israel had captured Gaza and the Sinai Peninsula, controlled the east bank of the Suez Canal, and reopened the gulf. After sporadic fighting, Israel and Egypt agreed, Aug. 7, 1970, to a new cease-fire.

In a surprise attack Oct. 6, 1973, Egyptian forces crossed the Suez Canal into the Sinai. (At the same time, Syrian forces attacked Israelis on the Golan Heights.) Egypt was supplied by a USSR military airlift; the U.S. responded with an airlift to Israel. Israel counterattacked, crossed the canal, surrounded Suez City. A UN cease-fire took effect Oct. 24.

A disengagement agreement was signed Jan. 18, 1974. Under it, Israeli forces withdrew from the canal's W bank; limited numbers of Egyptian forces occupied a strip along the E bank. A second accord was signed in 1975, with Israel yielding Sinai oil fields. Pres. Sadat's surprise visit to Jerusalem, Nov. 1977, opened the prospect of peace with Israel. On Mar. 26, 1979, Egypt and Israel signed a formal peace treaty, ending 30 years of war, and establishing diplomatic relations. Israel returned control of the Sinai to Egypt in Apr. 1982.

Tension between Muslim fundamentalists and Christians in 1981 caused street riots and culminated in a nationwide security crackdown in Sept. Pres Sadat was assassinated on Oct. 6.

Egypt was a political and military supporter of the Allied forces in their defeat of Iraq in the Persian Gulf War, 1991.

Egypt saw a rising tide of Islamic fundamentalist violence in the 1990s. Egyptian security forces conducted raids against Islamic militants, some of whom were apprehended and convicted of terrorism.

The **Suez Canal,** 103 mi. long, links the Mediterranean and Red seas. It was built by a French corporation 1859-69, but Britain obtained controlling interest in 1875. The last British troops were removed June 13, 1956. On July 26, Egypt nationalized the canal.

El Salvador

Republic of El Salvador

República de El Salvador

People: Population: 5,753,000. **Age distrib.** (%): <15: 44; 65+: 4. **Pop. density:** 708 per sq. mi. **Urban:** 45%. **Ethnic groups:** Mestizo 94%, Indian 5%. **Principal languages:** Spanish (official). **Religions:** Roman Catholic 75%.

Geography: Area: 8,124 sq. mi., the size of Massachusetts. **Location:** In Central America. **Neighbors:** Guatemala on W, Honduras on N. **Topography:** A hot Pacific coastal plain in the south rises to a cooler plateau and valley region, densely populated. The N is mountainous, including many volcanoes. **Capital:** San Salvador. **Cities** (1993 est.): San Salvador 1.4 mln.

Government: Type: Republic. **Head of state:** Pres. Armando Calderón Sol; in office: June 1, 1994. **Local divisions:** 14 departments. **Defense:** 3-4% of GDP (1993 est.).

Economy: Industries: Food and beverages, textiles, petroleum products. **Chief crops:** Coffee (45% of exports), cotton, corn, sugar. **Other resources:** Rubber, forests. **Arable land:** 27%. **Livestock** (1992): cattle: 1.2 mln.; pigs: 320,000. **Electricity prod.** (1992): 2.1 bln. kWh. **Labor force:** 40% agric.; 16% commerce.

Finance: Monetary unit: Colon (Mar. 1994: 8.72 = $1 US). **Gross domestic product** (1992): $5.9 bln. **Per capita GDP:** $1,060. **Imports** (1992): $1.5 bln.; partners: U.S. 41%, CACM 22%. **Exports** (1992): $683 mln.; partners: U.S. 41%, EU 30%, CACM 10%. **Tourism** (1990): $70 mln. receipts. **National budget** (1992 est.): $890 mln. **International reserves less gold** (Mar. 1994): $579 mln. **Gold:** 469,000 oz t. **Consumer prices** (change in 1992): 11.2%.

Transport: Railroads: Length: 374 mi. **Motor vehicles:** in use: 80,000 passenger cars, 80,000 comm. vehicles. **Chief ports:** La Union, Acajutla.

Communications: Television sets: 1 per 11 persons. **Radios:** 1 per 2.8 persons. **Telephones:** 1 per 21 persons. **Daily newspaper circ.:** 87 per 1,000 pop.

Health: Life expectancy at birth (1994): 64 male; 70 female. **Births** (per 1,000 pop.): 33. **Deaths** (per 1,000 pop.): 6. **Natural increase:** 2.6%. **Hospital beds:** 1 per 973 persons. **Physicians:** 1 per 1,322 persons. **Infant mortality** (per 1,000 live births 1994): 41.

Education (1991): **Literacy:** 75%. Years compulsory 6; attendance 82%.

Major International Organizations: UN (IMF, WHO, ILO), OAS, CACM.

Embassy: 2308 California St. NW 20008; 265-9671.

El Salvador became independent of Spain in 1821, and of the Central American Federation in 1839.

A fight with Honduras in 1969 over the presence of 300,000 Salvadoran workers left 2,000 dead.

A military coup overthrew the government of Pres. Carlos Humberto Romero in 1979, but the ruling military-civilian junta failed to quell a rebellion by leftist insurgents, armed by Cuba and Nicaragua. Extreme right-wing death squads organized to eliminate suspected leftists were blamed for thousands of deaths in the 1980s. The Reagan administration staunchly supported the government with military aid.

Voters turned out in large numbers in the May 1984 presidential election. Christian Democrat José Napoleon Duarte, a moderate, was victorious, with 54% of the vote.

The 12-year civil war ended Jan. 16, 1992, as the government and leftist rebels signed a formal peace treaty. The civil war had taken the lives of some 75,000 people. The treaty provided for military and political reforms.

Nine soldiers, including 3 officers, were indicted Jan. 1990 in the Nov. 1989 slaying of 6 Jesuit priests in San Salvador. Two of the officers received maximum 30-year jail sentences. They were released Mar. 20, 1993, when the National Assembly passed a sweeping amnesty.

Equatorial Guinea

Republic of Equatorial Guinea

República de Guinea Ecuatorial

People: Population: 410,000. **Age distrib.** (%): <15: 43; 65+: 4. **Pop. density:** 38 per sq. mi. **Ethnic groups:** Fangs 80%, Bubi 15%. **Principal languages:** Spanish (official), Fang, Bubi. **Religions:** Mostly Roman Catholic.

Geography: Area: 10,831 sq. mi., the size of Maryland. **Location:** Bioko Is. off W Africa coast in Gulf of Guinea, and Rio Muni, mainland enclave. **Neighbors:** Gabon on S, Cameroon on E, N. **Topography:** Bioko Is. consists of 2 volcanic mountains and a connecting valley. Rio Muni, with over 90% of the area, has a coastal plain and low hills beyond. **Capital:** Malabo. **Cities** (1989 est.): Malabo 38,000.

Government: Type: in transition. **Head of state:** Pres., Supreme Military Council Teodoro Obiang Nguema Mbasogo; b June 5, 1942; in office: Oct. 10, 1979. **Head of government:** Prime Min. Silvestre Siale Bileka; In office: Mar. 4, 1992. **Local divisions:** 7 provinces.

Economy: Chief crops: Cocoa, coffee, bananas, sweet potatoes. **Other resources:** Timber. **Arable land:** 8%. **Electricity prod.** (1991): 60 mln. kWh. **Labor force:** 66% agric.; 11% ind.

Finance: Monetary unit: CFA franc (Mar. 1994: 576 = $1

US). **Gross domestic product** (1991): $144 mln. **Per capita GDP:** $380. **Imports** (1990): 68 mln.; partners: Fra. 26%, Sp. 21%. **Exports** (1990): $37 mln.; partners: Sp. 38%, Neth. 12%. **National budget** (1991 est.): $30 mln.

Transport: Chief ports: Malabo, Bata.

Communications: Radios: 1 per 3.7 persons.

Health: Life expectancy at birth (1994): 50 male; 54 female. **Births** (per 1,000 pop.): 41. **Deaths** (per 1,000 pop.): 15. **Natural increase:** 2.6%. **Hospital beds** (1982): 3,200. **Physicians:** 1 per 3,622 persons. **Infant mortality** (per 1,000 live births 1994): 103.

Education (1991): **Literacy:** 55%. About 65% attend primary school.

Major International Organizations: UN (IMF, World Bank), OAU.

Embassy: 57 Magnolia Ave., Mount Vernon, NY 10553; (914) 667-9664.

Fernando Po (now Bioko) Island was reached by Portugal in the late 15th century and ceded to Spain in 1778. Independence came Oct. 12, 1968. Riots occurred in 1969 over disputes between the island and the more backward Rio Muni province on the mainland. Masie Nguema Biyogo, himself from the mainland, became president for life in 1972.

Masie's reign was one of the most brutal in Africa, resulting in a bankrupted nation. Most of the nation's 7,000 Europeans emigrated. He was ousted in a military coup, Aug. 1979, and Teodoro Mbasogo, leader of the coup, became president. His regime eventually agreed to elections, held Nov. 21, 1993. These were nominally won by the ruling party, but boycotted by opposition parties that maintained the rules were rigged.

The nation is heavily dependent on external aid.

Eritrea

State of Eritrea

People: Population: 3,200,000. **Pop. density:** 70 per sq. mi. **Ethnic groups:** Tigrays 50%, Tigre and Kunama 40%, Afar 4%. **Principal languages:** 7 native languages. **Religions:** about evenly split between Muslim and Christian.

Geography: Area: 45,300 sq. mi., slightly larger than Ohio. **Location:** in E Africa. **Neighbors:** Ethiopia on S, Djibouti on E, Sudan on W, Red Sea on N. **Topography:** includes many islands of the Dahlak Archipelago, low coastal plains in S, mountain range with peaks to 9,000 ft. in N. **Capital:** Asmera.

Government: Type: in transition. **Head of state:** Issaias Afwerki; b 1945; in office: May 24, 1993.

Economy: no industry. **Chief crops:** Cotton, coffee, tobacco.

Finance: Gross domestic product (1992): $400 mln. **Per capita GDP:** $115.

Transport: Chief ports: Masewa, Aseb.

Communications: no telephones outside the capital.

Major International Organizations: UN.

Eritrea was part of the Ethiopian kingdom of Aksum. It was an Italian colony from 1890 to 1941, when it was captured by the British. Following a period of British and UN supervision, Eritrea was awarded to Ethiopia as part of a federation in 1952. Ethiopia annexed Eritrea as a province in 1962. This led to a 31-year struggle for independence, which ended when Eritrea formally declared itself an independent nation May 24, 1993.

Estonia

Republic of Estonia

Eesti Vabariik

People: Population: 1,617,000. **Pop. density:** 93 per sq. mi. **Urban:** 71%. **Ethnic groups:** Estonian 62%, Russian 30%. **Principal languages:** Estonian (official), Latvian, Lithuanian, Russian. **Religions:** Lutheran.

Geography: Area: 17,413 sq. mi. **Neighbors:** bounded on N, W by the Baltic Sea, E by Russia, S by Latvia. **Capital:** Tallinn. **Cities** (1992 est.): Tallinn 471,000.

Government: Type: Republic. **Head of state:** Pres. Lennart Meri; b Mar. 29, 1929; in office: Oct. 5, 1992. **Head of government:** Prime Min. Mart Laar; b 1960; in office: Oct. 8, 1992. **Local divisions:** 15 districts, 33 towns, 26 urban settlements.

Economy: Industries: Agricultural machinery, electric motors. **Chief crops:** Grain, vegetables. **Arable land:** 22%. **Livestock** (1991): cattle: 708,000, sheep: 143,000. **Electricity prod.** (1992): 22.9 bln. kWh. **Labor force:** Ind. & const. 42%, agric. 20%.

Finance: Monetary unit: Kroon (Jan. 1993: 11.26 = $1 US). **National budget** (1992): $223 mln. revenues.

Transport: Railroads: Length: 638 mi. **Motor vehicles:** in use: 260,000 passenger cars. **Chief port:** Tallinn.

Communications: Television sets: 1 per 2.6 persons. **Radios:** 1 per 1.7 persons. **Telephones:** 1 per 3.9 persons.

Health: Life expectancy at birth (1994): 65 male, 75 female. **Births** (per 1,000 pop.): 14. **Deaths** (per 1,000 pop.): 12. **Natural increase:** 0.2%. **Hospital beds:** 1 per 83 persons.

Education: 11-year school curriculum.

Major International Organizations: UN, IMF.

Embassy: 630 Fifth Ave., New York, NY 10111; (212) 247-2131.

Estonia was a province of imperial Russia before World War I, was independent between World Wars I and II, but was conquered by the USSR in 1940. Estonia declared itself an "occupied territory," and proclaimed itself a free nation Mar. 1990. During an abortive Soviet coup, Estonia declared immediate full independence, Aug. 20, 1991; the Soviet Union recognized its independence in Sept. 1991. The first free elections in over 50 years were held Sept. 20, 1992. The last occupying Russian troops were withdrawn by Aug. 31, 1994.

Ethiopia

(Figures prior to 1993 include Eritrea)

People: Population: 58,710,000. **Age distrib.** (%): <15: 49; 65+: 3. **Pop. density:** 134 per sq. mi. **Urban:** 15%. **Ethnic groups:** Oromo 40%, Amhara and Tigre 32%, Sidamo 9%. **Principal languages:** Amharic (official), Tigre (Semitic languages), Galla (Hamitic). **Religions:** Muslim 45–50%, Ethiopian Orthodox 35–40%,

Geography: Area: 437,794 sq. mi., about three-quarters the size of Alaska. **Location:** In E Africa. **Neighbors:** Sudan on W, Kenya on S, Somalia, Djibouti on E, Eritrea on N. **Topography:** A high central plateau, between 6,000 and 10,000 ft. high, rises to higher mountains near the Great Rift Valley, cutting in from the SW. The Blue Nile and other rivers cross the plateau, which descends to plains on both W and SE. **Capital:** Addis Ababa. **Cities** (1988 est.): Addis Ababa 1.6 mln.

Government: Type: In transition. **Head of state:** Pres. Meles Zenawi; in office: May 28, 1991. **Head of government:** Prime Min. Timirat Layne; in office: June 6, 1991. **Local divisions:** 13 provinces. **Defense:** 8.9% of GDP (1991).

Economy: Industries: Food processing, cement, textiles. **Chief crops:** Coffee (over 50% export earnings), grains. **Minerals:** Platinum, gold, copper, potash. **Arable land:** 12%. **Livestock** (1992): cattle: 31 mln.; sheep: 23 mln. **Electricity prod.** (1991): 650 mln. kWh. **Labor force:** 80% agric.

Finance: Monetary unit: Birr (Mar. 1994: 5.00 = $1 US). **Gross domestic product** (1992): $6.6 bln. **Per capita GDP:** $130. **Imports** (1991): $472 mln.; partners: USSR 22%, U.S. 15%, Italy 10%, Jap. 6%, Ger. 10%. **Exports** (1991): $189 mln.; partners: U.S. 20%, Ger. 18%, Italy 7%. **National budget** (1991): $2.3 bln. **International reserves less gold** (Mar. 1994): $460 mln. **Gold:** 113,000 oz t. **Consumer prices** (change in 1992): 10.5%.

Transport: Railroads: Length: 486 mi. **Motor vehicles:** in use: 37,000 passenger cars, 15,000 comm. vehicles. **Civil aviation::** 977 mln. passenger-mi.; 29 airports with scheduled flights.

Communications: Television sets: 1 per 541 persons. **Radios:** 1 per 16 persons. **Telephones:** 1 per 316 persons.

Health: Life expectancy at birth (1994): 51 male; 54 female. **Births** (per 1,000 pop.): 45. **Deaths** (per 1,000 pop.): 14. **Natural increase:** 3.1%. **Hospital beds:** 1 per 3,873 persons. **Physicians:** 1 per 36,660 persons. **Infant mortality** (per 1,000 live births 1994): 106.

Education (1985): **Literacy:** 18%.

Major International Organizations: UN (IMF, WHO), OAU.

Embassy: 2134 Kalorama Rd. NW 20008; 234-2281.

Ethiopian culture was influenced by Egypt and Greece. The ancient monarchy was invaded by Italy in 1880 but maintained its independence until another Italian invasion in 1936. British forces freed the country in 1941.

The last emperor, Haile Selassie I, established a parliament and judiciary system in 1931 but barred all political parties.

A series of droughts in the 1970s killed hundreds of thousands. An army mutiny, strikes, and student demonstrations led to the dethronement of Selassie in 1974. The ruling junta pledged to form a one-party socialist state and instituted a successful land reform; opposition was violently suppressed. The influence of the Coptic Church, embraced in 330 AD, was curbed, and the monarchy was abolished in 1975.

The regime, torn by bloody coups, faced uprisings by tribal and political groups in part aided by Sudan and Somalia. Ties with the U.S., once a major ally, deteriorated, while cooperation accords were signed with the USSR in 1977. In 1978, Soviet advisers and Cuban troops helped defeat Somalian forces. Ethiopia and Somalia signed a peace agreement in 1988.

A worldwide relief effort began in 1984, as an extended drought caused millions to face starvation and death. In 1988, victories by Eritrean guerrillas led the government to curtail the work of foreign aid workers in drought-stricken regions. In 1994 Ethiopia again faced possible severe famine as a result of drought.

The Ethiopian People's Revolutionary Democractic Front (EPRDF), an umbrella group of 6 rebel armies, launched a major push against government forces, Feb. 1991. In May, Pres. Mengistu Haile Mariam resigned and left the country. The EPRDF took over and set up a transitional government.

Eritrea, a province on the Red Sea, declared its independence May 24, 1993.

Fiji

Republic of Fiji

People: Population: 764,000. **Age distrib.** (%): <15: 38; 65+: 3. **Pop. density:** 108 per sq. mi. **Urban:** 39%. **Ethnic groups:** Fijian (Melanesian-Polynesian) 49%, Indian 46%, Europeans. **Principal languages:** English (official), Fijian, Hindustani. **Religions:** Christian 52%, Hindu 38%, Muslim 8%.

Geography: Area: 7,056 sq. mi., the size of Massachusetts. **Location:** In western S Pacific O. **Neighbors:** Nearest are Solomons on NW, Tonga on E. **Topography:** 322 islands (106 inhabited), many mountainous, with tropical forests and large fertile areas. Viti Levu, the largest island, has over half the total land area. **Capital:** Suva. **Cities** (1986 est.): Suva 69,000.

Government: Type: Republic. **Head of state:** Pres. Ratu Sir Kamisese Mara; b May 13, 1920; in office: Jan. 18, 1994. **Head of government:** Prime Min. Sitiveni Rabuka; in office: June 2, 1992. **Local divisions:** 4 divisions, 1 dependency. **Defense:** 2% of GDP (FY 1991-92).

Economy: Industries: Sugar refining, light industry, tourism. **Chief crops:** Sugar, bananas, ginger. **Minerals:** Gold. **Other resources:** Timber. **Arable land:** 8%. **Electricity prod.** (1992): 420 mln. kWh. **Labor force:** 67% agric.

Finance: Monetary unit: Dollar (Mar. 1994: 1.49 = $1.00 US). **Gross domestic product** (1992): $1.4 bln. **Per capita GDP:** $1,900. **Imports** (1991): $840 mln.; partners: Austral. 29%, Jap. 12%, N.Z. 19%. **Exports** (1991): $646 mln.; partners: EU 32%, Aust. 21%. **Tourism** (1990): $320 mln. receipts. **National budget** (1993 est.): $546 mln. **International reserves less gold** (Feb. 1994): $260 mln. **Gold:** 10,000 oz t. **Consumer prices** (change in 1993): 5.2%.

Transport: Motor vehicles: in use: 42,000 passenger cars, 29,000 comm. vehicles. **Civil aviation::** 548 mln. passenger-mi.; 19 airports with scheduled flights. **Chief ports:** Suva, Lautoka.

Communications: Televisions: 1 per 73 persons. **Radios:** 1 per 1.7 persons. **Telephones:** 1 per 9.6 persons. **Daily newspaper circ.:** 35 per 1,000 pop.

Health: Life expectancy at birth (1994): 63 male; 68 female. **Births** (per 1,000 pop.): 24. **Deaths** (per 1,000 pop.): 7. **Natural increase:** 1.8%. **Hospital beds:** 1 per 413 persons. **Physicians:** 1 per 2,438 persons. **Infant mortality** (per 1,000 live births 1994): 18.

Education (1990): **Literacy:** 85%. 95% attend school.

Major International Organizations: UN (IMF, WHO).

Embassy: 2233 Wisconsin Ave. NW 20007; 337-8320.

A British colony since 1874, Fiji became an independent parliamentary democracy Oct. 10, 1970.

Cultural differences between the majority Indian community, descendants of contract laborers brought to the islands in the 19th century, and the less modernized native Fijians, who by law own 83% of the land in communal villages, have led to political polarization.

In 1987, a military coup ousted the government; order was restored May 21 when a compromise was reached granting Lt. Col. Sitveni Rabuka, the coup's leader, increased power. Rabuka staged a second coup Sept. 25 and declared Fiji a republic. A civilian government was restored to power in Dec., and a democratic constitution was drafted.

Finland

Republic of Finland

Suomen Tasavalta

People: Population: 5,069,000. **Age distrib.** (%): <15: 19; 65+: 14. **Pop. density:** 38 per sq. mi. **Urban:** 80%. **Ethnic groups:** Finns 94%, Swedes, Lapps. **Principal languages:** Finnish, Swedish (both official). **Religions:** Evangelical Lutheran 89%.

Geography: Area: 130,559 sq. mi., slightly smaller than Montana. **Location:** In northern Europe. **Neighbors:** Norway on N, Sweden on W, Russia on E. **Topography:** South and central Finland are mostly flat areas with low hills and many lakes. The N has mountainous areas, 3,000-4,000 ft. **Capital:** Helsinki. **Cities** (1993 est.): Helsinki 501,000; Espoo 178,000; Tampere 175,000.

Government: Type: Constitutional republic. **Head of state:** Pres. Martii Ahtisaari; in office: Mar. 1, 1994. **Head of government:** Prime Min. Esko Aho: b 1954; in office: Apr. 26, 1991. **Local divisions:** 12 laanit (provinces). **Defense:** 2% of GDP (1992).

Economy: Industries: Machinery, metal, shipbuilding, textiles, clothing. **Chief crops:** Grains, potatoes, dairy prods. **Minerals:** Copper, iron, zinc. **Other resources:** Forests (40% of exports). **Arable land:** 8%. **Livestock** (1991): cattle; 1.3 mln. pigs: 1.3 mln. **Fish catch** (1990): 97,000 metric tons. **Electricity prod.** (1992): 55.3 bln. kWh. **Labor force:** 9% agric.; 46% ind., comm. & finance.

Finance: Monetary unit: Markka (Mar. 1994: 5.53 = $1 US). **Gross domestic product** (1992): $79.4 bln.* **Per capita GDP:** $15,900. **Imports** (1992): $21.2 bln.; partners: EU 45%. **Exports** (1992): $23.8 bln.; partners: EU 50%. **Tourism** (1991): $1.2 bln. receipts. **National budget** (1992): $40.6 bln. **International reserves less gold** (Mar. 1994): $5.4 bln. **Gold** 2.0 mln. oz t. **Consumer prices** (change in 1993): 2.1%.

Transport: Railroads: Length: 3,646 mi. **Motor vehicles:** in use: 1.9 mln. passenger cars, 273,000 comm. vehicles. **Civil aviation:** 6.1 bln. passenger-mi.; 24 airports. **Chief ports:** Helsinki, Turku.

Communications: Television sets: 1 per 2.6 persons. **Radios:** 1 per person. **Telephones:** 1 per 1.3 persons. **Daily newspaper circ.:** 559 per 1,000 pop.

Health: Life expectancy at birth (1994): 72 male; 80 female. **Births** (per 1,000 pop.): 12. **Deaths** (per 1,000 pop.): 10. **Natural increase:** .3%. **Hospital beds:** 1 per 80 persons. **Physicians:** 1 per 406 persons. **Infant mortality** (per 1,000 live births 1994): 5.

Education (1991): **Literacy:** 99%. Years compulsory 9; attendance 99%.

Major International Organizations: UN (IMF, GATT), EFTA, OECD.

Embassy: 3216 New Mexico Ave. NW 20016; 363-2430.

The early Finns probably migrated from the Ural area at about the beginning of the Christian era. Swedish settlers brought the country into Sweden, 1154 to 1809, when Finland became an autonomous grand duchy of the Russian Empire. Russian exactions created a strong national spirit; on Dec. 6, 1917, Finland declared its independence and in 1919 became a republic.

On Nov. 30, 1939, the Soviet Union invaded, and the Finns were forced to cede 16,173 sq. mi. of territory. After World War II, further cessions were exacted. In 1948, Finland signed a treaty of mutual assistance with the USSR; Finland and Russia nullified this treaty with a new pact in Jan. 1992.

Finnish voters were to decide in an Oct. 16 referendum whether to approve membership in the European Union (formerly European Community), effective Jan. 1, 1995.

Aland, constituting an autonomous department, is a group of small islands, 590 sq. mi., in the Gulf of Bothnia, 25 mi. from Sweden, 15 mi. from Finland. Mariehamn is the principal port.

France
French Republic
République Francaise

People: Population: 57,840,000. **Age distrib.** (%): <15: 20; 65+: 15. **Pop. density:** 275 per sq. mi. **Urban:** 74%. **Ethnic groups:** A mixture of various European and Mediterranean groups. **Principal languages:** French (official); minorities speak Breton, Alsatian German, Flemish, Italian, Basque, Catalan. **Religions:** Roman Catholic 90%.

Geography: Area: 210,026 sq. mi., four-fifths the size of Texas. **Location:** In western Europe, between Atlantic O. and Mediterranean Sea. **Neighbors:** Spain on S, Italy, Switzerland, Germany on E, Luxembourg, Belgium on N. **Topography:** A wide plain covers more than half of the country, in N and W, drained to W by Seine, Loire, Garonne rivers. The Massif Central is a mountainous plateau in center. In E are Alps (Mt. Blanc is tallest in W Europe, 15,771 ft.), the lower Jura range, and the forested Vosges. The Rhone flows from Lake Geneva to Mediterranean. Pyrenees are in SW, on border with Spain. **Capital:** Paris. **Cities** (1990 est.): Paris 2,152,000; Marseille 801,000; Lyon 415,000; Toulouse 359,000; Nice 342,000; Strasbourg 252,000; Nantes 245,000; Bordeaux 201,000.

Government: Type: Republic. **Head of state:** Pres. François Mitterrand; b Oct. 26, 1916; in office: May 21, 1981. **Head of government:** Prime Min. Edouard Balladur; in office: Mar. 29, 1993. **Local divisions:** 22 administrative regions containing 95 departments. **Defense:** 3.1% of GDP (1993 est.).

Economy: Industries: Steel, chemicals, textiles, wine, perfume, aircraft, electronic equipment. **Chief crops:** Grains, corn, rice, fruits, vegetables. France is largest food producer, exporter, in W Eur. **Minerals:** Bauxite, iron, coal. **Crude oil reserves** (1985): 221 mln. bbls. **Other resources:** Forests. **Arable land:** 32%. **Livestock** (1992): cattle: 20.9 mln.; pigs: 12.3 mln.; sheep: 10.6 mln. **Fish catch** (1991): 812,000 metric tons. **Electricity prod.** (1992): 426 bln. kWh. **Labor force:** 7% agric.; 31% ind. & comm.; 62% services.

Finance: Monetary unit: Franc (Mar. 1994: 5.76 = $1 US). **Gross domestic product** (1992): $1.08 trl.* **Per capita GDP:** $18,900. **Imports** (1992): $239 bln.; partners: EU 51%. **Exports** (1992): $235 bln.; partners: EU 50%, U.S. 6%. **Tourism** (1990): $21.6 bln. receipts. **National budget** (1993): $249.1 bln. **International reserves less gold** (Feb. 1994): $23.8 bln. **Gold:** 81.89 mln. oz t. **Consumer prices** (change in 1993): 2.1%.

Transport: Railroads: Length: 21,173 mi. **Motor vehicles:** in use: 23.8 mln. passenger cars, 5.1 mln. **Civil aviation::** 20.2 bln. passenger-mi.; 64 airports with scheduled flights. **Chief ports:** Marseille, LeHavre, Nantes, Bordeaux, Rouen.

Communications: Television sets: 1 per 2 persons. **Radios:** 1 per 1.2 persons. **Telephones:** 1 per 1.6 persons. **Daily newspaper circ.:** 210 per 1,000 pop.

Health: Life expectancy at birth (1994): 74 male; 82 female. **Births** (per 1,000 pop.): 13. **Deaths** (per 1,000 pop.): 9. **Natural increase:** .4%. **Hospital beds:** 1 per 81 persons. **Physicians:** 1 per 374 persons. **Infant mortality** (per 1,000 live births 1994): 7.

Education (1991): **Literacy:** 99%. Years compulsory 10.

Major International Organizations: UN and most of its specialized agencies, OECD, EU, NATO.

Embassy: 4101 Reservoir Rd. NW 20007; 944-6000.

Celtic Gaul was conquered by Julius Caesar 58-51 BC; Romans ruled for 500 years. Under Charlemagne, Frankish rule extended over much of Europe. After his death France emerged as one of the successor kingdoms.

The monarchy was overthrown by the French Revolution (1789-93) and succeeded by the First Republic; followed by the First Empire under Napoleon (1804-15), a monarchy (1814-48), the Second Republic (1848-52), the Second Empire (1852-70), the Third Republic (1871-1946), the Fourth Republic (1946-58), and the Fifth Republic (1958 to present).

France suffered severe losses in manpower and wealth in the first World War, 1914-18, when it was invaded by Germany. By the Treaty of Versailles, France exacted return of Alsace and Lorraine, French provinces seized by Germany in 1871. Germany invaded France again in May, 1940, and signed an armistice with a government based in Vichy. After France was liberated by the Allies Sept. 1944, Gen. Charles de Gaulle became head of the provisional government, serving until 1946.

De Gaulle again became premier in 1958, during a crisis over Algeria, and obtained voter approval for a new constitution, ushering in the Fifth Republic. Using strong executive powers, he promoted French economic and technological advances in the context of the European Economic Community and guarded French foreign policy independence.

France had withdrawn from Indochina in 1954, and from Morocco and Tunisia in 1956. Most of its remaining African territories were freed 1958-62. In 1966, France withdrew all its troops from the integrated military command of NATO, though 60,000 remained stationed in Germany.

In May 1968 rebellious students in Paris and other centers rioted, battled police, and were joined by workers who launched nationwide strikes. The government awarded pay increases to the strikers May 26. De Gaulle resigned from office in Apr. 1969, after losing a nationwide referendum on constitutional reform.

On May 10, 1981, France elected François Mitterrand, a Socialist candidate, president. In Sept., the government nationalized 5 major industries and most private banks. From 1986 to 1993, however, France pursued a privatization program in which many state-owned companies were sold. Mitterrand was elected to a 2d 7-year term in 1988.

In 1993, France set tighter rules for entry into the country and made it easier for the government to expel foreigners. In June 1994, France sent troops to Rwanda in an effort to help protect civilians there from ongoing massacres.

The international terrorist known as Carlos the Jackal (Ilich Ramirez Sánchez) was arrested in Sudan Aug. 14, 1994, and extradited to France, where he had been sentenced in absentia to life imprisonment.

The island of **Corsica,** in the Mediterranean W of Italy and N of Sardinia, is an official region of France comprising 2 departments. Area: 3,369 sq. mi.; pop. (1990 cen.): 249,700. The capital is Ajaccio, birthplace of Napoleon.

Overseas Departments

French Guiana is on the NE coast of South America with Suriname on the W and Brazil on the E and S. Its area is 43,740 sq. mi.; pop. (1991): 101,000. Guiana sends one senator and one deputy to the French Parliament. Guiana is administered by a prefect and has a Council General of 16 elected members; capital is Cayenne.

The famous penal colony, Devil's Island, was phased out between 1938 and 1951.

Immense forests of rich timber cover 90% of the land. Placer gold mining is the most important industry. Exports are shrimp, timber, and machinery.

Guadeloupe, in the West Indies' Leeward Islands, consists of 2 large islands, Basse-Terre and Grande-Terre, separated by the Salt River, plus Marie Galante and the Saintes group to the S and, to the N, Desirade, St. Barthelemy, and over half of St. Martin (the Netherlands portion is St. Maarten). A French possession since 1635, the department is represented in the French Parliament by 2 senators and 3 deputies; administration consists of a prefect (governor) and an elected general and regional councils.

Area of the islands is 660 sq. mi.; pop. (1991 est.) 395,000, mainly descendants of slaves; capital is Basse-Terre on Basse-Terre Is. The land is fertile; sugar, rum, and bananas are exported; tourism is an important industry.

Martinique, the northernmost of the Windward Islands, in the West Indies, has been a possession since 1635, and a department since Mar. 1946. It is represented in the French Parliament by 2 senators and 3 deputies. The island was the birthplace of Napoleon's Empress Josephine.

It has an area of 425 sq. mi.; pop. (1991 est.) 365,000, mostly descendants of slaves. The capital is Fort-de-France (pop. 1991: 101,000). It is a popular tourist stop. The chief exports are rum, bananas, and petroleum products.

Réunion is a volcanic island in the Indian O. about 420 mi. E of Madagascar, and has belonged to France since 1665. Area, 969 sq. mi.; pop. (1992 est.) 626,000, 30% of French extraction. Capital: Saint-Denis. The chief export is sugar. It elects 3 deputies, 2 senators to the French Parliament.

Territorial Collectivities

Mayotte, claimed by Comoros and administered by France, voted in 1976 to become a territorial collectivity of France. An island NW of Madagascar, area is 144 sq. mi., pop. (1992 est.) 86,000.

St. Pierre and Miquelon, formerly an Overseas Territory (1816-1976) and department (1976-85), made the transition to territorial collectivity in 1985. It consists of 2 groups of rocky islands near the SW coast of Newfoundland, inhabited by fishermen. The exports are chiefly fish products. The St. Pierre group has an area of 10 sq. mi.; Miquelon, 83 sq. mi. Total pop. (1992 est.), 6,513. The capital is St. Pierre. A deputy and a senator are elected to the French Parliament.

Overseas Territories

French Polynesia Overseas Territory, comprises 130 islands widely scattered among 5 archipelagos in the South Pacific; administered by a governor. Territorial Assembly and a Council with headquarters at Papeete, Tahiti, one of the **Society Islands** (which include the **Windward** and **Leeward** islands). A deputy and a senator are elected to the French Parliament.

Other groups are the **Marquesas Islands,** the **Tuamotu Archipelago,** including the **Gambier Islands,** and the **Austral Islands.**

Total area of the islands administered from Tahiti is 1,544 sq. mi.; pop. (1991 est.), 195,000, more than half on Tahiti. Tahiti is picturesque and mountainous with a productive coastline bearing coconut, banana and orange trees, sugar cane and vanilla.

Tahiti was visited by Capt. James Cook in 1769 and by Capt. Bligh in the Bounty, 1788-89. Its beauty impressed Herman Melville, Paul Gauguin, and Charles Darwin.

French Southern and Antarctic Lands Overseas Territory comprises **Adelie Land,** on Antarctica, and 4 island groups in the Indian O. Adelie, reached 1840, has a research station, a coastline of 185 mi. and tapers 1,240 mi. inland to the South Pole. The U.S. does not recognize national claims in Antarctica. There are 2 huge glaciers, Ninnis, 22 mi. wide, 99 mi. long, and Mentz, 11 mi. wide, 140 mi. long. The Indian O. groups are:

Kerguelen Archipelago, visited 1772, consists of one large and 300 small islands. The chief is 87 mi. long, 74 mi. wide, and has Mt. Ross, 6,429 ft. tall. Principal research station is Port-aux-Français. Seals often weigh 2 tons; there are blue whales, coal, peat, semi-precious stones. **Crozet Archipelago,** reached 1772, covers 195 sq. mi. Eastern Island rises to 6,560 ft. **Saint Paul,** in southern Indian O., has warm springs with earth at places heating to 120° to 390° F. **Amsterdam** is nearby; both produce cod and rock lobster.

New Caledonia and its dependencies, an overseas territory, are a group of islands in the Pacific O. about 1,115 mi. E of Australia and approx. the same distance NW of New Zealand. Dependencies are the **Loyalty Islands,** the **Isle of Pines, Huon Islands,** and the **Chesterfield Islands.**

New Caledonia, the largest, has 6,530 sq. mi. Total area of the territory is 8,548 sq. mi.; population (1991 est.) 172,000. The group was acquired by France in 1853.

The territory is administered by a governor and government council. There is a popularly elected Territorial Assembly. A deputy and a senator are elected to the French Parliament. Capital: Noumea.

Mining is the chief industry. New Caledonia is one of the world's largest nickel producers. Other minerals found are chrome, iron, cobalt, manganese, silver, gold, lead, and copper. Agricultural products include coffee, copra, cotton, manioc (cassava), corn, tobacco, bananas, and pineapples.

In 1987, New Caledonian voters chose by referendum to remain within the French Republic. There were clashes between French and Melanesians (Kanaks) in 1988.

Wallis and Futuna Islands, 2 archipelagos raised to status of overseas territory July 29, 1961, are in the SW Pacific S of the Equator between Fiji and Samoa. The islands have a total area of 106 sq. mi. and population (1988 est.) of 15,400. **Alofi,** attached to Futuna, is uninhabited. Capital: Mata-Utu. Chief products are copra, yams, taro roots, bananas. A senator and a deputy are elected to the French Parliament.

Gabon

Gabonese Republic

République Gabonaise

People: Population: 1,139,000. **Pop. density:** 11 per sq. mi. **Urban:** 46%. **Ethnic groups:** Fang 25%, Bapounou 10%, others. **Principal languages:** French (official), Bantu dialects. **Religions:** Mostly Christian, minority follow traditional beliefs.

Geography: Area: 103,347 sq. mi., the size of Colorado. **Location:** On Atlantic coast of central Africa. **Neighbors:** Equatorial Guinea, Cameroon on N, Congo on E, S. **Topography:** Heavily forested, the country consists of coastal lowlands plateaus in N, E, and S, mountains in N, SE, and center. The Ogooue R. system covers most of Gabon. **Capital:** Libreville. **Cities** (1991 est.): Libreville 275,000.

Government: Type: Republic. **Head of state:** Pres. Omar Bongo; b Dec. 30, 1935; in office: Dec. 2, 1967. **Head of government:** Prime Min. Casimir Oye Mba; in office: May 3, 1990. **Local divisions:** 9 provinces. **Defense:** 3.2% of GDP (1990 est.).

Economy: Industries: Oil products. **Chief crops:** Cocoa, coffee, rice, peanuts, palm products, cassava, bananas. **Minerals:** Manganese, uranium, oil, iron, gas. **Crude oil reserves** (1985): 623 mln. bbls. **Other resources:** Timber. **Arable land:** 1%. **Electricity prod.** (1991): 995 mln. kWh. **Labor force:** 65% agric.; 30% ind. & comm.

Finance: Monetary unit: CFA franc (Mar. 1994: 576 = $1 US). **Gross domestic product** (1991): $4.6 bln. **Per capita income:** $4,200. **Imports** (1990): $780 mln.; partners: Fr. 51%. **Exports** (1990): $1.1 bln.; partners: Fr. 53%, U.S. 22%. **Tourism receipts** (1990): $4 mln. **National budget** (1991): $1.8 bln. **Consumer prices** (change in 1992): -9.6%.

Transport: Motor vehicles: in use: 19,000 passenger cars, 15,000 comm. vehicles. **Civil aviation::** 276 mln. passenger-mi.; 18 airports. **Chief ports:** Port-Gentil, Owendo, Mayumba.

Communications: Television sets: 1 per 31 persons. **Radios:** 1 per 5 persons. **Telephones:** 1 per 57 persons.

Health: Life expectancy at birth (1994): 52 male; 58 female. **Births** (per 1,000 pop.): 28. **Deaths** (per 1,000 pop.): 14. **Natural increase:** 1.5%. **Hospital beds** (1985): 4,617. **Physicians** (1985): 265. **Infant mortality** (per 1,000 live births 1994): 95.

Education (1991): **Literacy:** 70%. Compulsory to age 16; attendance: 100% primary, 14% secondary.

Major International Organizations: UN (World Bank), OAU, OPEC.

Embassy: 2034 20th St NW 20009; 797-1000.

France established control over the region in the second half of the 19th century. Gabon became independent Aug. 17, 1960. A multiparty political system was introduced in 1990, and a new constitution was enacted in 1991. However, the reelection of longtime Pres. Omar Bongo, on Dec. 5, 1993, prompted rioting and charges of vote fraud. In Feb. 1994 clashes between security forces and demonstrators led to 9 deaths.

Gabon is one of the most prosperous black African countries, thanks to abundant natural resources, foreign private investment, and government development programs.

The Gambia

Republic of The Gambia

People: Population: 959,000. **Age distrib.** (%): <15: 45; 65+: 2. **Pop. density:** 232 per sq. mi. **Urban:** 26%. **Ethnic groups:** Mandinka 42%, Fula 18%, Wolof 16%, others. **Principal languages:** English (official), Mandinka, Wolof. **Religions:** Muslim 90%, Christian 9%.

Geography: Area: 4,127 sq. mi., smaller than Connecticut. **Location:** On Atlantic coast near western tip of Africa. **Neighbors:** Surrounded on 3 sides by Senegal. **Topography:** A narrow strip of land on each side of the lower Gambia. **Capital:** Banjul. **Cities** (1993 est.): Banjul 40,000.

Government: Type: Military. **Head of state and government:** Lieut. Yahya Jammeh; in office: July 23, 1994. **Local divisions:** 5 divisions and Banjul.

Economy: Industries: Tourism, peanut processing. **Chief crops:** Peanuts (main export), rice. **Arable land:** 16%. **Fish catch** (1991): 23,000 metric tons. **Electricity prod.** (1991): 65 mln. kWh. **Labor force:** 75% agric.; 19% ind., comm., serv.

Finance: Monetary unit: Dalasi (Nov. 1993: 9.44 = $1.00 US). **Gross domestic product** (1991): $292 mln. **Per capita GDP:** $325. **Imports** (1991): $167 mln.; partners: EU 53%. **Exports** (1991): $122 mln.; partners: Japan 60%. **Tourism** (1990): $26 mln. receipts. **National budget** (1990): $95 mln. expenditures. **International reserves less gold** (Nov. 1993): $104 mln. **Consumer prices** (change in 1993): 6.5%.

Transport: Motor vehicles: in use: 19,000 passenger cars, 15,000 comm. vehicles. **Chief ports:** Banjul.

Communications: Radios: 1 per 5.1 persons. **Telephones:** 1 per 92 persons.

Health: Life expectancy at birth (1994): 48 male; 52 female. **Births** (per 1,000 pop.): 46. **Deaths** (per 1,000 pop.): 16. **Natural increase:** 3.1%. **Physicians:** 1 per 14,536 persons. **Infant mortality** (per 1,000 live births 1994): 124.

Education (1993): **Literacy:** 30%.

Major International Organizations: UN (GATT, IMF, WHO), OAU.

Embassy: 1030 15th St. 20005; 842-1356.

The tribes of Gambia were at one time associated with the West African empires of Ghana, Mali, and Songhay. The area became Britain's first African possession in 1588.

Independence came Feb. 18, 1965; republic status within the Commonwealth was achieved in 1970. After a coup attempt in 1981, The Gambia formed the confederation of Senegambia with Senegal that lasted until 1989. The country suffered from severe famine in the 1970s.

On July 23, 1994, after 24 years in power, Pres. Dawda K. Jawara was deposed in a bloodless coup by Lieut. Yahya Jammeh. Jammeh barred political activity, detained potential opponents, and governed by decree, while promising a transition to democracy.

Georgia

Republic of Georgia

Sakartvelos Respublica

People: Population: 5,681,000. **Pop. density:** 211 per sq. mi. **Urban:** 56%. **Ethnic groups:** Georgian 70%, Armenian 8%, Russian 6%. **Principal languages:** Georgian (official), Russian. **Religions:** Georgia Orthodox 65%, Muslim 11%, Russian Orthodox 10%.

Geography: Area: 26,900 sq. mi., slightly larger than S.C. **Neighbors:** Black Sea on W, Russia on N, NE, Turkey, Armenia on S, Azerbaijan on SE. **Topography:** Separated from Russia on NE by main range of the Caucasus mts. **Capital:** Tbilisi. **Cities** (1991): Tbilisi 1.2 mln.

Government: Type: Republic. **Head of state:** Pres. Eduard A. Shevardnadze; b Jan. 25, 1928; in office: Nov. 6, 1992. **Head of government:** Prime Min. Otar Patsatsia; in office: Aug. 1993.

Economy: Industries: Manganese mining. **Chief crops:** Citrus fruits, wheat, grapes. **Livestock** (1992): cattle: 1.1 mln., sheep: 1.5 mln.

Finance: Monetary unit: Ruble. **Imports** (1990): $1.5 bln. **Exports** (1990): $176 mln.

Transport: Railroads: Length: 976 mi. **Motor vehicles:** in use: 427,000 passenger cars.

Communications: Daily newspaper circ.: 671 per 1,000 pop.

Health: Life expectancy at birth (1994): 69 male; 77 female. **Births** (per 1,000 pop.): 16. **Deaths** (per 1,000 pop.): 9. **Natural increase**: .7%. **Infant mortality** (per 1,000 live births 1994): 23. **Physicians:** 1 per 170 persons; **Hospital beds:** 1 per 90 persons.

The region contained the ancient kingdoms of Colchis and Iberia. It was Christianized in the 4th century and conquered by Arabs in the 8th century. The region expanded to include area from the Black Sea to Caspian and parts of Armenia and Persia before its disintegration under the impact of Mongol and Turkish invasions. The annexation to Russia in 1801 caused the Russian war with Persia, 1804-1813. Georgia entered the USSR in 1922 and became a constituent republic in 1936.

In 1989, strong nationalist feelings led the USSR to attempts at repression; Soviet troops attacked nationalist demonstrators in April, killing some 20 persons. Georgia declared independence Apr. 9, 1991. It became an independent state when the Soviet Union disbanded Dec. 26, 1991.

There was fighting during 1991 between rebel forces and loyalists of Pres. Zviad Gamsakhurdia, who fled the capital Jan. 6, 1992. The ruling Military Council picked former Soviet Foreign Minister Eduard A. Shevardnadze to chair a newly created State Council. An attempted coup by forces loyal to Gamsakhurdia was crushed June 24,.1992. Shevardnadze was later elected president. Gamsakhurdia died Jan. 1994, reportedly by suicide.

In Abkhazia, an autonomous region within Georgia, ethnic Abkhazis, reportedly aided by Russia, launched a bloody military campaign and, by late 1993, had gained control of much of the region. A cease-fire providing for Russian peacekeepers was signed in Moscow May 14, 1994.

On Feb. 3, 1994, Georgia signed agreements with Russia for economic and military cooperation. On Mar. 1, Georgia's Supreme Council ratified membership by Georgia in the Commonwealth of Independent States.

Germany

Federal Republic of Germany

Bundesrepublik Deutschland

(Figures prior to 1990 for original 11 states)

People: Population: 81,088,000. **Age distrib.** (%): <15: 16; 65+: 15. **Pop. density:** 588 per sq. mi. **Urban:** 85%. **Ethnic groups:** German 95%. **Principal languages:** German. **Religions:** Protestant 45%, Roman Catholic 37%.

Geography: Area: 137,735 sq. mi. **Location:** In central Europe. **Neighbors:** Denmark on N, Netherlands, Belgium, Luxembourg, France on W, Switzerland, Austria on S, Czech Rep., Poland on E. **Topography:** Germany is flat in N, hilly in center and W, and mountainous in Bavaria. Chief rivers are Elbe, Weser, Ems, Rhine, and Main, all flowing toward North Sea, and Danube, flowing toward Black Sea. **Capital:** Berlin. **Cities** (1991 est.): Berlin 3.4 mln.; Hamburg 1.6 mln.; Munich 1.2 mln.; Cologne 955,000; Essen 626,000; Frankfurt 647,000; Dortmund 600,000; Dusseldorf 576,000; Stuttgart 583,000; Leipzig 507,000; Nürnberg 495,000; Dresden 488,000.

Government: Type: Federal republic. **Head of state:** Pres. Roman Herzog; in office: July 1, 1994. **Head of government:** Chan. Helmut Kohl; b Apr. 3, 1930; in office: Oct. 1, 1982. **Local divisions:** 16 laender (states) with substantial powers. **Defense:** 2.2% of GDP (1992).

Economy: Industries: Steel, ships, vehicles, machinery, electronics, coal, chemicals. **Chief crops:** Grains, potatoes, sugar beets. **Minerals:** Coal, potash, lignite, iron, uranium. **Arable land:** 34%. **Livestock** (1990): cattle: 15.3 mln.; pigs: 10.0 mln.; sheep: 1.2 mln. **Fish catch** (1991): 241,000 metric tons. **Electricity prod.** (1992): 580 bln. kWh. **Labor force:** 6% agric.; 41% ind.

Finance: Monetary unit: Mark (Mar. 1994: 1.69 = $1 US). **Gross domestic product** (1992): $1,398 trl.* **Per capita GDP:** $17,400. **Imports** (1992): $402 bln.; partners: EU 52%; other European 16%. **Exports** (1992): $422 bln.; partners: EU 55%; other European 19%. **Tourism** (1989): receipts $8.6 bln. **National budget** (1990): $704 bln.. **International reserves less gold** (Mar. 1994): $80 bln. **Gold:** 95.18 mln. oz t. **Consumer prices** (change in 1993): 4.1%.

Transport: Railroads: Length: 56,397 mi. **Motor vehicles:** in use: 35.5 mln. passenger cars, 2.7 mln. comm. **Civil aviation:** 62.8 bln. passenger-mi.; 40 airports with scheduled flights. **Chief ports:** Hamburg, Bremen, Bremerhaven, Lubeck.

Communications: Television sets: 1 per 2.6 persons. **Radios:** 1 per 2.6 persons. **Telephones:** 1 per 1.7 persons. **Daily newspaper circ.:** 424 per 1,000 pop.

Health: Life expectancy at birth (1994): 73 male; 80 female. **Births** (per 1,000 pop.): 11. **Deaths** (per 1,000 pop.): 11. **Hospital beds:** 1 per 121 persons. **Physicians:** 1 per 319 persons. **Infant mortality** (per 1,000 live births 1994): 7.

Education (1991): **Literacy:** 99%. **Years compulsory:** 10; attendance 100%.

Major International Organizations: UN and all of its specialized agencies, EU, OECD, NATO.

Embassy: 4645 Reservoir Rd. NW 20007; 298-4000.

Germany, prior to World War II, was a central European nation composed of numerous states which had a common language and traditions and which had been united in one country since 1871; since World War II until 1990, had been split in 2 parts.

History and government. Germanic tribes were defeated by Julius Caesar, 55 and 53 BC, but Roman expansion N of the Rhine was stopped in 9 AD. Charlemagne, ruler of the Franks, consolidated Saxon, Bavarian, Rhenish, Frankish, and other lands; after him the eastern part became the German Empire. The Thirty Years' War, 1618-1648, split Germany into small principalities and kingdoms. After Napoleon, Austria contended with Prussia for dominance, but lost the Seven Weeks' War to Prussia, 1866. Otto von Bismarck, Prussian chancellor, formed the North German Confederation, 1867.

In 1870 Bismarck maneuvered Napoleon III into declaring war. After the quick defeat of France, Bismarck formed the

German Empire and on Jan. 18, 1871, in Versailles, proclaimed King Wilhelm I of Prussia German emperor (Deutscher kaiser).

The German Empire reached its peak before World War I in 1914, with 208,780 sq. mi., plus a colonial empire. After that war Germany ceded Alsace-Lorraine to France; West Prussia and Posen (Poznan) province to Poland; part of Schleswig to Denmark; lost all of its colonies and the ports of Memel and Danzig.

Republic of Germany, 1919-1933, adopted the Weimar constitution; met reparation payments and elected Friedrich Ebert and Gen. Paul von Hindenburg presidents.

Third Reich, 1933-1945, Adolf Hitler led the National Socialist German Workers' (Nazi) party after World War I. In 1923 he attempted to unseat the Bavarian government and was imprisoned. Pres. von Hindenburg named Hitler chancellor Jan. 30, 1933; on Aug. 3, 1934, the day after Hindenburg's death, the cabinet joined the offices of president and chancellor and made Hitler fuehrer (leader). Hitler abolished freedom of speech and assembly, and began a long series of persecutions climaxed by the murder of millions of Jews and opponents.

Hitler repudiated the Versailles treaty and reparations agreements. He remilitarized the Rhineland (1936) and annexed Austria (Anschluss, 1938). At Munich he made an agreement with Neville Chamberlain, British prime minister, which permitted Germany to annex part of Czechoslovakia. He signed a nonaggression treaty with the USSR, 1939. He declared war on Poland Sept. 1, 1939, precipitating World War II.

With total defeat near, Hitler committed suicide in Berlin Apr. 1945. The victorious Allies voided all acts and annexations of Hitler's Reich.

Postwar changes. The zones of occupation administered by the Allied Powers and later relinquished gave the USSR Saxony, Saxony-Anhalt, Thuringia, and Mecklenburg, and the former Prussian provinces of Saxony and Brandenburg. The territory E of the Oder-Neisse line within 1937 boundaries, comprising Silesia, Pomerania, and the southern part of East Prussia, was taken by Poland. Northern East Prussia was taken by the USSR.

The Western Allies ended the state of war with Germany in 1951. The USSR did so in 1955.

There was also created the area of Greater Berlin, within but not part of the Soviet zone, administered by the 4 occupying powers under the Allied Command. In 1948 the USSR withdrew, established its single command in East Berlin, and cut off supplies. The Allies utilized a gigantic airlift to bring food to West Berlin, 1948-49. In Aug. 1961 the East Germans built a wall dividing Berlin, after over 3 million E Germans had emigrated.

On Nov. 9, 1989 the E German government announced the decision to open the border with the West, signaling the end of the infamous Berlin Wall.

A New Era: As Communism was being rejected in E Germany, talks began concerning German reunification. At a meeting in Ottawa, Feb. 1990, the foreign ministers of the World War II "Big Four" Allied nations—U.S., USSR, UK, and France—and of E Germany and W Germany reached agreement on a format for high-level talks on German reunification.

In May, NATO ministers adopted a package of proposals on reunification, including the inclusion of the united Germany as a full member of NATO and the barring of the new Germany from having its own nuclear, chemical, or biological weapons. In July, the USSR agreed to conditions that would allow Germany to become a member of NATO.

The 2 nations agreed to monetary unification under the W German mark beginning in July. The merger of the 2 Germanys took place on Oct. 3, 1990, and the first all-German elections since 1932 were held Dec. 2, 1990.

In 1992, neo-Nazi groups intensified their campaign against refugees. Parliament approved constitutional changes to restrict foreigners' rights to seek asylum in Germany, May 1993.

Germany's highest court ruled, July 12, 1994, that German troops could participate in international military missions abroad, when approved by Parliament. Ceremonies were held marking the final withdrawal of Russian troops from Germany, Aug. 31, 1994. Ceremonies were held the following week marking the final withdrawal of American, British, and French troops from Berlin.

East Germany

The German Democratic Republic was proclaimed in the Soviet sector of Berlin Oct. 7, 1949. It was proclaimed fully sovereign in 1954, but Soviet troops remained on grounds of security and the 4-power Potsdam agreement.

Coincident with the entrance of W Germany into the European defense community in 1952, the E German government decreed a prohibited zone 3 miles deep along its 600-mile border with W Germany and cut Berlin's telephone system in two. Berlin was further divided by erection of a fortified wall in 1961, but an exodus of refugees to the West continued, though on a smaller scale.

E Germany suffered severe economic problems at least until the mid-1960s. Then a "new economic system" was introduced, easing central planning controls and allowing factories to make profits provided they were reinvested in operations or redistributed to workers as bonuses. By the early 1970s, the economy was highly industrialized; and the nation was credited with the highest standard of living among Warsaw Pact countries. But growth slowed in the late 1970s, because of shortages of natural resources and labor, and a huge debt to lenders in the West. Comparison with the lifestyle in the West caused many of the young to leave the country.

The government firmly resisted following the USSR's policy of *glasnost,* but by Oct. 1989, was faced with nationwide demonstrations demanding reform. Pres. Erich Honecker, in office since 1976, was forced to resign, Oct. 18. On Nov. 4, the border with Czechoslovakia was opened and permission granted for refugees to travel on to the West. On Nov. 9, the decision was made to open the border with the West, signaling the end of the "Berlin Wall," which separated the 2 Germanys and was the supreme emblem of the cold war.

On Aug. 23, 1990, the E German Parliament agreed to formal unification with W Germany; this took place on Oct. 3.

West Germany

The Federal Republic of Germany was proclaimed May 23, 1949, in Bonn, after a constitution had been drawn up by a consultative assembly formed by representatives of the 11 laender (states) in the French, British, and American zones. Later reorganized into 9 units, the laender numbered 10 with the addition of the Saar, 1957. Berlin also was granted land (state) status, but the 1945 occupation agreements placed restrictions on it.

The occupying powers, the U.S., Britain, and France, restored the civil status, Sept. 21, 1949. The U.S. resumed diplomatic relations July 2, 1951. The powers lifted controls and the republic became fully independent May 5, 1955.

Dr. Konrad Adenauer, Christian Democrat, was made chancellor Sept. 15, 1949, reelected 1953, 1957, 1961. Willy Brandt, heading a coalition of Social Democrats and Free Democrats, became chancellor Oct. 21, 1969. (He resigned May 1974 because of a spy scandal.)

In 1970 Brandt signed friendship treaties with the USSR and Poland. In 1971, the U.S., Britain, France, and the USSR signed an agreement on Western access to West Berlin. In 1972 E and W Germany signed their first formal treaty, implementing the agreement easing access to West Berlin. In 1973 a W Germany-Czechoslovakia pact normalized relations and nullified the 1938 "Munich Agreement."

W Germany experienced strong economic growth since the 1950s. The country led Europe in provisions for worker participation in the management of industry.

A NATO decision to deploy medium-range nuclear missiles in Western Europe sparked a demonstration by some 400,000 protesters in 1983. In 1989, Chancellor Helmut Kohl's call for early negotiations with the Soviets on reducing short-range missiles caused a rift with NATO allies.

In 1989, the changes in the E German government and the opening of the Berlin Wall sparked talk of reunification of the 2 Germanys. In 1990, under the leadership of Chancellor Kohl, W Germany moved rapidly to reunite with E Germany.

Helgoland, an island of 130 acres in the North Sea, was taken from Denmark by a British Naval Force in 1807 and later ceded to Germany to become a part of Schleswig-Holstein province in return for rights in East Africa. The heavily fortified island was surrendered to UK, May 23, 1945, demilitarized in 1947, and returned to W Germany, Mar 1, 1952. It is a free port.

Ghana

Republic of Ghana

People: Population: 17,225,000. **Age distrib.** (%): <15: 45; 65+: 3. **Pop. density:** 187 per sq. mi. **Urban:** 34%. **Ethnic**

groups: Akan 44%, Moshi-Dagomba 16%, Ewe 13%, Ga 8%, others. **Principal languages:** English (official), Akan, Moshi-Dagomba, Ewe, Ga. **Religions:** indigenous beliefs 38%, Muslim 30%, Christian 24%.

Geography: Area: 92,098 sq. mi., slightly smaller than Oregon. **Location:** On southern coast of W Africa. **Neighbors:** Côte D'Ivoire on W, Burkina Faso on N, Togo on E. **Topography:** Most of Ghana consists of low fertile plains and scrubland, cut by rivers and by the artificial Lake Volta. **Capital:** Accra. **Cities** (1988 est.): Accra 949,000.

Government: Type: Military. **Head of state and government:** Pres. Jerry Rawlings; b 1947; in office: Dec. 31, 1981. **Local divisions:** 10 regions. **Defense:** Less than 1% of GDP (1989 est.).

Economy: Industries: Aluminum, light industry. **Chief crops:** Cocoa, coffee. **Minerals:** Gold, manganese, industrial diamonds, bauxite. **Crude oil reserves:** (1980): 7 mln. bbls. **Other resources:** Timber, rubber. **Arable land:** 5%. **Livestock** (1992): cattle: 1.4 mln.; sheep: 2.6 mln. **Fish catch** (1991): 364,000 metric tons. **Electricity prod.** (1991): 4.5 bln. kWh. **Labor force:** 55% agric.; 19% ind.

Finance: Monetary unit: Cedi (Oct. 1993: 713 = $1.00 US). **Gross domestic product** (1992): $6.6 bln. **Per capita GDP:** $410. **Imports** (1991): $1.2 bln.; partners: UK 10%, Ger. 12%, Nigeria 12%. **Exports** (1991): $843 mln.; partners: U.S. 23%, Neth. 9%, Ger. 9%. **National budget** (1991 est.): $905 mln. **International reserves less gold** (Mar. 1993): $399 mln. **Gold:** 275,000 oz t. **Consumer prices** (change in 1992): 10.1%.

Transport: Railroads: Length: 592 mi. **Motor vehicles:** in use: 57,000 passenger cars, 30,000 comm. vehicles. **Civil aviation:** 253 mln. passenger-mi.; 3 airports with scheduled flights. **Chief ports:** Tema, Takoradi.

Communications: Television sets: 1 per 61 persons. **Radios:** 1 per 4.2 persons.**Telephones:** 1 per 185 persons.

Health: Life expectancy at birth (1994): 54 male; 58 female. **Births** (per 1,000 pop.): 44. **Deaths** (per 1,000 pop.): 12. **Natural increase:** 3.2%. **Physicians:** 1 per 22,452 persons. **Infant mortality** (per 1,000 live births 1994): 83.

Education (1991): **Literacy:** 60%.

Major International Organizations: UN and all of its specialized agencies, OAU.

Embassy: 3512 International Dr., 20008; 686-4520.

Named for an African empire along the Niger River, 400-1240 AD, Ghana was ruled by Britain for 113 years as the Gold Coast. The UN in 1956 approved merger with the British Togoland trust territory. Independence came March 6, 1957. Republic status within the Commonwealth was attained in 1960.

Pres. Kwame Nkrumah built hospitals and schools, promoted development projects like the Volta R. hydroelectric and aluminum plants but ran the country into debt, jailed opponents, and was accused of corruption. A 1964 referendum gave Nkrumah dictatorial powers and set up a one-party socialist state.

Nkrumah was overthrown in 1966 by a police-army coup, which expelled Chinese and East German teachers and technicians. Elections were held in 1969, but 4 further coups occurred in 1972, 1978, 1979, and 1981. The 1979 and 1981 coups, led by Flight Lieut. Jerry Rawlings, were followed by suspension of the constitution and banning of political parties. A new constitution, which allowed for multiparty politics, was approved in April 1992.

In Feb. 1993 more than 1,000 people were killed in ethnic clashes in northern Ghana.

Greece

Hellenic Republic

Elliniki Dimokratia

People: Population: 10,565,000. **Age distrib.** (%): <15: 19; 65+: 14. **Pop. density:** 207 per sq. mi. **Urban:** 58%. **Ethnic groups:** Greeks 98%. **Principal languages:** Greek (official), English, French. **Religions:** Greek Orthodox 98% (official).

Geography: Area: 50,949 sq. mi., the size of Alabama. **Location:** Occupies southern end of Balkan Peninsula in SE Europe. **Neighbors:** Albania, Macedonia, Bulgaria on N, Turkey on E. **Topography:** About 75% of Greece is nonarable, with mountains in all areas. Pindus Mts. run through the country N to S. The heavily indented coastline is 9,385 mi. long. Of over 2,000 islands, only 169 are inhabited, among them Crete, Rhodes, Milos, Kerkira (Corfu), Chios, Lesbos, Samos, Euboea, Delos, Mykonos. **Capital:** Athens. **Cities** (1991 est.): Athens 748,000; Thessaloniki 377,000.

Government: Type: Presidential parliamentary republic. **Head of state:** Pres. Konstantinos Karamanlis; b Mar. 8, 1907; in office: May, 1990. **Head of government:** Prime Min. Andreas Papandreou; b Feb. 5, 1919; in office: Oct. 13, 1993. **Local divisions:** 51 prefectures. **Defense:** 5.1% of GDP (1992).

Economy: Industries: Textiles, chemicals, metals, wine, food processing, cement. **Chief crops:** Grains, corn, rice, cotton, tobacco, olives, citrus fruits, raisins, figs. **Minerals:** Bauxite, lignite, oil, manganese. **Crude oil reserves** (1985): 35 mln. bbls. **Arable land:** 23%. **Livestock** (1991): sheep: 9.7 mln.; goats: 5.9 mln. **Fish catch** (1990): 128,000 metric tons. **Electricity prod.** (1992): 36.4 bln. kWh. **Labor force:** 27% agric.; 28% ind., 45% service.

Finance: Monetary unit: Drachma (Mar. 1994: 246 = $1 US). **Gross domestic product** (1992): $82.9 bln.* **Per capita GDP:** $8,200. **Imports** (1991): $21.5 bln.; partners: Ger. 21%, It. 15%, Fr. 7%. **Exports** (1991): $8.6 bln.; partners: Ger. 20%, It. 17%, Fra. 10%. **Tourism** (1990): $2.5 bln. receipts. **National budget** (1993): $45.1 bln. **International reserves less gold** (Mar. 1994): $9.2 bln. **Gold:** 3.4 mln. oz t. **Consumer prices** (change in 1993): 14.4%.

Transport: Railroads: Length: 1,570 mi. **Motor vehicles:** in use: 1.7 mln. passenger cars, 817,000 comm. vehicles. **Civil aviation:** 3.8 bln. passenger-mi.; 34 airports with scheduled flights. **Chief ports:** Piraeus, Thessaloniki, Patrai.

Communications: Television sets: 1 per 4.5 persons. **Radios:** 1 per 2.5 persons. **Telephones:** 1 per 2.1 persons. **Daily newspaper circ.:** 140 per 1,000 pop.

Health: Life expectancy at birth (1994): 75 male; 80 female. **Births** (per 1,000 pop.): 11. **Deaths** (per 1,000 pop.): 9. **Natural increase:** .1%. **Hospital beds:** 1 per 199 persons. **Physicians:** 1 per 303 persons. **Infant mortality** (per 1,000 live births 1994): 9.

Education (1991): **Literacy:** men 96%, women 89%. **Years compulsory:** 9.

Major International Organizations: UN (GATT, IMF, WHO, ILO), EU, NATO, OECD.

Embassy: 2221 Massachusetts Ave. NW 20008; 939-5800.

The achievements of ancient Greece in art, architecture, science, mathematics, philosophy, drama, literature, and democracy became legacies for succeeding ages. Greece reached the height of its glory and power, particularly in the Athenian city-state, in the 5th century BC.

Greece fell under Roman rule in the 2d and 1st centuries BC. In the 4th century AD it became part of the Byzantine Empire and, after the fall of Constantinople to the Turks in 1453, part of the Ottoman Empire.

Greece won its war of independence from Turkey 1821-1829, and became a kingdom. A republic was established 1924; the monarchy was restored, 1935, and George II, King of the Hellenes, resumed the throne. In Oct. 1940, Greece rejected an ultimatum from Italy. Nazi support resulted in its defeat and occupation by Germans, Italians, and Bulgarians. By the end of 1944 the invaders withdrew. Communist resistance forces were defeated by Royalist and British troops. A plebiscite again restored the monarchy.

Communists waged guerrilla war 1947-49 against the government but were defeated with the aid of the U.S. A period of reconstruction and rapid development followed, mainly with conservative governments under Premier Constantine Karamanlis. The Center Union, led by George Papandreou, won elections in 1963 and 1964, but King Constantine, who acceded in 1964, forced Papandreou to resign. A period of political maneuvers ended in the military takeover of April 21, 1967, by Col. George Papadopoulos. King Constantine tried to reverse the consolidation of the harsh dictatorship Dec. 13, 1967, but failed and fled to Italy. Papadopoulos was ousted Nov. 25, 1973.

Greek army officers serving in the National Guard of Cyprus staged a coup on the island July 15, 1974. Turkey invaded Cyprus a week later, precipitating the collapse of the Greek junta, which was implicated in the Cyprus coup. Democratic government returned (and in 1975 the monarchy was abolished).

The 1981 electoral victory of the Panhellenic Socialist Movement (Pasok) of Andreas Papandreou brought about substantial changes in Greece's internal and external policies. A scandal centered on George Kostokas, a banker and publisher, led to the arrest or investigation of leading Socialists, implicated Papandreou, and contributed to the defeat of the

Socialists at the polls in 1989. However, Papandreou, who was narrowly acquitted Jan. 1992 of corruption charges, led the Socialists to a comeback victory in general elections Oct. 10, 1993.

Grenada

People: Population: 94,000. **Pop. density:** 706 per sq. mi. **Ethnic groups:** Mostly African descent. **Principal languages:** English (official), French patois. **Religions:** Roman Catholic 64%, Anglican 22%.

Geography: Area: 133 sq. mi., twice the size of Washington, D.C. **Location:** 90 mi. N of Venezuela. **Topography:** Main island is mountainous; country includes Carriacon and Petit Martinique islands. **Capital:** St. George's. **Cities** (1991 est.): St. George's 30,000.

Government: Type: Parliamentary democracy. **Head of state:** Queen Elizabeth II, represented by Gov.-Gen. Reginald Palmer. **Head of government:** Prime Min.: Nicholas Brathwaite; in office: Mar. 13, 1990. **Local divisions:** 6 parishes and one dependency.

Economy: Industries: Rum. **Chief crops:** Nutmeg, bananas, cocoa, mace. **Arable land:** 15%. **Electricity prod.** (1992): 26 mln. kWh. **Labor force:** 24% agric.; 31% services.

Finance: Monetary unit: East Caribbean dollar (Mar. 1994: 2.70 = $1 US). **Gross domestic product** (1992): $250 mln. **Per capita GDP:** $3,000. **Imports** (1989): $200 mln.; partners: UK 19%, Trin./Tob. 12%, U.S. 24%. **Exports** (1990): $26 mln.; partners: UK 23%, CARICOM countries 38%. **Tourism** (1991): $38 mln. receipts. **National budget** (1991 est.): $78 mln. revenues. **International reserves less gold** (Jan. 1994): $25 mln.

Transport: Chief ports: Saint George's.

Communications: Radios: 1 per 1.1 persons. **Telephones:** 1 per 3.4 persons.

Health: Life expectancy at birth (1994): 68 male; 73 female. **Births** (per 1,000 pop.): 30. **Deaths** (per 1,000 pop.): 6. **Natural increase:** 2.4%. **Infant mortality** (per 1,000 live births 1994): 12.

Education (1991): **Literacy:** 95%; **Years compulsory:** 6.

Major International Organizations: UN (IMF, WHO), OAS.

Embassy: 1701 New Hampshire Ave. NW 20009; 265-2561.

Columbus sighted the island 1498. First European settlers were French, 1650. The island was held alternately by France and England until final British occupation, 1784. Grenada became fully independent Feb. 7, 1974 during a general strike. It is the smallest independent nation in the western hemisphere.

On Oct. 14, 1983, a military coup ousted Prime Minister Maurice Bishop, who was put under house arrest, later freed by supporters, rearrested, and, finally, on Oct. 19, executed. U.S. forces, with a token force from 6 area nations, invaded Grenada, Oct. 25. Resistance from the Grenadian army and Cuban advisors was quickly overcome as most of the population welcomed the invading forces. U.S. troops left Grenada in June 1985.

Guatemala

Republic of Guatemala

República de Guatemala

People: Population: 10,721,000. **Age distrib.** (%): <15: 45; 65+: 3. **Pop. density:** 255 per sq. mi. **Urban:** 38%. **Ethnic groups:** Mestizos 56%, Indian 44%. **Principal languages:** Spanish (official), Mayan languages. **Religions:** Mostly Roman Catholics.

Geography: Area: 42,042 sq. mi., the size of Tennessee. **Location:** In Central America. **Neighbors:** Mexico N, W, El Salvador on S, Honduras, Belize on E. **Topography:** The central highland and mountain areas are bordered by the narrow Pacific coast and the lowlands and fertile river valleys on the Caribbean. There are numerous volcanoes in S, more than half a dozen over 11,000 ft. **Capital:** Guatemala City. **Cities** (1993 est.): Guatemala City 1.1 mln.

Government: Type: Republic. **Head of state and government:** Pres. Ramiro de León Carpio; in office: June 6, 1993. **Local divisions:** Guatemala City and 22 departments. **Defense:** 1% of GDP (1993).

Economy: Industries: Prepared foods, tires, textiles. **Chief crops:** Coffee (one third of exports), sugar, bananas, cotton, corn. **Minerals:** Oil, nickel. **Crude oil reserves** (1985): 500 mln. bbls. **Other resources:** Rare woods, fish, chicle. **Arable land:** 12%. **Electricity prod.** (1991): 2.5 bln. kWh. **Labor force:** 60% agric.; 13% service.

Finance: Monetary unit: Quetzal (Mar. 1994: 5.82 = $1 US). **Gross domestic product** (1992): $12.6 bln. **Per capita GDP:** $1,300. **Imports** (1992): $2.4 bln.; partners: U.S. 37%, CACM 8%. **Exports** (1992): $1.0 bln.; partners: U.S. 28%, CACM 20%. **Tourism** (1990): $185 mln. **National budget** (1990 est.): $808 mln. **International reserves less gold** (Feb. 1994): $899 mln. **Gold:** 209,000 oz t. **Consumer prices** (change in 1992): 10.0%.

Transport: Motor vehicles: in use: 145,000 passenger cars, 105,000 comm. vehicles. **Civil aviation:** 143 mln. passenger-mi; 2 airports with scheduled flights. **Chief ports:** Puerto Barrios, San Jose.

Communications: Television sets: 1 per 20 persons. **Radios:** 1 per 24 persons. **Telephones:** 1 per 36 persons. **Daily newspaper circ.:** 21 per 1,000 pop.

Health: Life expectancy at birth (1994): 62 male; 67 female. **Births** (per 1,000 pop.): 35. **Deaths** (per 1,000 pop.): 8. **Natural increase:** 2.8%. **Physicians:** 1 per 2,356 persons. **Infant mortality** (per 1,000 live births 1994): 54.

Education (1991): **Literacy:** 55%. **Years compulsory:** 6. **Attendance:** 35%.

Major International Organizations: UN (IMF, World Bank), OAS.

Embassy: 2220 R St. NW 20008; 745-4952.

The old Mayan Indian empire flourished in what is today Guatemala for over 1,000 years before the Spanish.

Guatemala was a Spanish colony 1524-1821; briefly a part of Mexico and then of the U.S. of Central America, the republic was established in 1839.

Since 1945 when a liberal government was elected to replace the long-term dictatorship of Jorge Ubico, the country has seen a variety of military and civilian governments and periods of civil unrest.

Dissident army officers seized power Mar. 23, 1982, denouncing a presidential election as fraudulent and pledging to restore "authentic democracy" to the nation. Political violence caused large numbers of Guatemalans to seek refuge in Mexico. Another military coup occurred Oct. 8, 1983. The nation returned to civilian rule in 1986.

The crisis-ridden government of Pres. Jorge Serrano Elías was ousted by the military June 1, 1993. Ramiro de León Carpio was elected president by Congress June 6. Limited electoral reforms were approved Jan. 30, 1994, in a referendum.

Guinea

Republic of Guinea

République de Guinée

People: Population: 6,392,000. **Pop. density:** 67 per sq. mi. **Urban:** 26%. **Ethnic groups:** Fulani 35%, Malinke 30%, Soussou 20%, 15 other tribes. **Principal languages:** French (official), Peul, Mande. **Religions:** Muslim 85%, Christian 8%.

Geography: Area: 94,926 sq. mi., slightly smaller than Oregon. **Location:** On Atlantic coast of W Africa. **Neighbors:** Guinea-Bissau, Senegal, Mali on N, Côte d'Ivoire on E, Liberia on S. **Topography:** A narrow coastal belt leads to the mountainous middle region, the source of the Gambia, Senegal, and Niger rivers. Upper Guinea, farther inland, is a cooler upland. The SE is forested. **Capital:** Conakry. **Cities** (1989 est.): Conakry 705,000; Labe 273,000; N'Zerekore 250,000; Kankan 278,000.

Government: Type: Republic. **Head of state and government:** Pres. Brig. Gen. Lansana Conté; b 1944; in office: Apr. 5, 1984. **Local divisions:** 33 administrative regions. **Defense:** 1.2% of GDP (1988).

Economy: Chief crops: Bananas, pineapples, rice, corn, palm nuts, coffee, honey. **Minerals:** Bauxite, iron, diamonds. **Arable land:** 6%. **Electricity prod.** (1991) 300 mln. kWh. **Labor force:** 82% agric.; 11% ind. & comm.

Finance: Monetary unit: Franc (Jan. 1993: 811 = $1 US). **Gross domestic product** (1990): $3.0 bln. **Per capita GDP:** $410. **Imports** (1990): $692 mln.; partners: U.S. 16%. **Exports** (1990): $788 mln.; partners: U.S. 33%. **National budget** (1990): $708 mln.

Transport: Motor vehicles: in use: 13,000 passenger cars, 13,000 comm. vehicles. **Chief ports:** Conakry.

Communications: Radios: 1 per 56 persons. **Telephones:** 1 per 382 persons.

Health: Life expectancy at birth (1994): 42 male; 46 female. **Births** (per 1,000 pop.): 44. **Deaths** (per 1,000 pop.): 20. **Natural increase:** 2.4%. **Physicians:** 1 per 9,732 persons. **Infant mortality** (per 1,000 live births 1994): 139.

Education (1989): **Literacy:** 35% (in French). **Years compulsory:** 8. **Attendance:** 36% primary, 15% secondary.

Major International Organizations: UN and most specialized agencies, OAU.

Embassy: 2112 Leroy Pl. NW 20008; 483-9420.

Part of the ancient West African empires, Guinea fell under French control 1849-98. Under Sékou Touré, it opted for full independence in 1958, and France withdrew all aid.

Touré turned to Communist nations for support and set up a militant one-party state. Thousands of opponents were jailed in the 1970s, in the aftermath of an unsuccessful Portuguese invasion. Many were tortured and killed.

The military took control in a bloodless coup after the March 1984 death of Touré. A new constitution was approved in 1991, but movement toward democracy was slow. When presidential elections were finally held, in Dec. 1993, the incumbent, Gen. Lansana Conté, was the official winner; outside monitors denounced the elections as flawed.

Guinea-Bissau

Republic of Guinea-Bissau

Republica da Guiné-Bissau

People: Population: 1,098,000. **Pop. density:** 78 per sq. mi. **Ethnic groups:** Balanta 30%, Fula 20%, Manjaca 14%, Mandinga 13%. **Principal languages:** Portuguese (official), Criolo, tribal languages. **Religions:** indigenous beliefs 65%, Muslim 30%, Christian 5%.

Geography: Area: 13,948 sq. mi. about the size of Connecticut and New Hampshire combined. **Location:** On Atlantic coast of W Africa. **Neighbors:** Senegal on N, Guinea on E, S. **Topography:** A swampy coastal plain covers most of the country; to the east is a low savanna region. **Capital:** Bissau. **Cities** (1988 est.): Bissau 138,000.

Government: Type: Republic. **Head of state:** Brig.-Gen. Joao Bernardo Vieira; b 1939; in office: Nov. 14, 1980. **Head of government:** Prime Min. Carlos Correia; in office: Dec. 27, 1991. **Local divisions:** 9 regions. **Defense:** 5%-6% of GDP (1987).

Economy: Chief crops: Peanuts, cotton, rice. **Minerals:** Bauxite. **Arable land:** 11%. **Electricity prod.** (1991): 30 mln. kWh. **Labor force:** 90% agric.

Finance: Monetary unit: Peso (Mar. 1994: 12,068 = $1 US). **Gross domestic product** (1991): $210 mln. **Per capita GDP:** $210. **Imports** (1989): $69 mln.; partners: Port. 20%, It. 27%. **Exports** (1989): $14 mln.; partners: Port. 35%. **National budget** (1991 est.): $44.8 mln.

Transport: Motor vehicles: in use: 3,200 passenger cars, 2,400 commercial vehicles.

Communications: Radios: 1 per 29 persons.

Health: Life expectancy at birth (1994): 46 male; 49 female. **Births** (per 1,000 pop.): 41. **Deaths** (per 1,000 pop.): 17. **Natural increase:** 2.4%. **Infant mortality** (per 1,000 live births 1994): 120.

Education (1991): **Literacy:** 36%. **Years compulsory:** 4.

Major International Organizations: UN, OAU.

Embassy: 918 16th St. NW 20006; 872-4222.

Portuguese mariners explored the area in the mid-15th century; the slave trade flourished in the 17th and 18th centuries, and colonization began in the 19th.

Beginning in the 1960s, an independence movement waged a guerrilla war and formed a government in the interior that achieved international support. Full independence came Sept. 10, 1974, after the Portuguese regime was overthrown.

The November 1980 coup gave Vieira absolute power. Vieira eventually initiated political liberalization; multiparty elections were scheduled for 1994.

Guyana

Co-operative Republic of Guyana

People: Population: 729,000. **Age distrib.** (%): <15: 33; 65+: 4. **Pop. density:** 9 per sq. mi. **Urban:** 33%. **Ethnic groups:** East Indians 51%, black and mixed 43%. **Principal languages:** English (official), Amerindian dialects. **Religions:** Christian 57%, Hindu 33%, Muslim 9%.

Geography: Area: 83,044 sq. mi., the size of Idaho. **Location:** On N coast of S America. **Neighbors:** Venezuela on W, Brazil on S, Suriname on E. **Topography:** Dense tropical forests cover much of the land, although a flat coastal area up to 40 mi. wide, where 90% of the population lives, provides rich alluvial soil for agriculture. A grassy savanna divides the 2 zones. **Capital:** Georgetown. **Cities** (1985 est.): Georgetown 195,000.

Government: Type: Republic. **Head of state:** President Cheddi Jagan; in office: Oct. 9, 1992. **Head of Government:** Prime Min. Sam Hinds; in office: Oct. 9, 1992. **Local divisions:** 10 regions. **Defense:** 6% of GDP (1989).

Economy: Industries: Mining, textiles. **Chief crops:** Sugar, rice, citrus and other fruits. **Minerals:** Bauxite, diamonds. **Other resources:** Timber, shrimp. **Arable land:** 3%. **Electricity prod.** (1992): 276 mln. kWh. **Labor force:** 34% agric.; 45% ind. & comm.; 21% services.

Finance: Monetary unit: Dollar (Mar. 1994: 132 = $1 US). **Gross domestic product** (1992): $267.5 mln. **Per capita GDP:** $370. **Imports** (1991): $246 mln.; partners: U.S. 33%, CARICOM 10%. **Exports** (1991): $189 mln.; partners: UK 31%, U.S. 23%. **National budget** (1990 est): $225 mln. **International reserves less gold** (Jan. 1994): $228 mln. **Consumer prices** (change in 1992): 2.6%.

Transport: Motor vehicles: in use: 24,000 passenger cars, 9,000 comm. vehicles. **Chief ports:** Georgetown.

Communications: Radios: 1 per 2.4 persons. **Telephones:** 1 per 23 persons. **Daily newspaper circ.:** 101 per 1,000 pop.

Health: Life expectancy at birth (1994): 62 male; 68 female. **Births** (per 1,000 pop.): 20. **Deaths** (per 1,000 pop.): 7. **Natural increase:** 1.3% **Hospital beds:** 1 per 341 persons. **Physicians:** 1 per 2,552 persons. **Infant mortality** (per 1,000 live births 1994): 49.

Education (1991): **Literacy:** 95%. **Years compulsory:** ages 5-14.

Major International Organizations: UN (GATT, ILO, IMF, World Bank), Commonwealth of Nations, OAS.

Embassy: 2490 Tracy Pl. NW 20008; 265-6900.

Guyana became a Dutch possession in the 17th century, but sovereignty passed to Britain in 1815. Indentured servants from India soon outnumbered African slaves. Ethnic tension has affected political life.

Guyana became independent May 26, 1966. A Venezuelan claim to the western half of Guyana was suspended in 1970 but renewed in 1982. The Suriname border is also disputed. The government has nationalized most of the economy which has remained severely depressed.

The Port Kaituma ambush of U.S. Rep. Leo J. Ryan and others investigating mistreatment of American followers of the Rev. Jim Jones' People's Temple cult triggered a mass suicide-execution of 911 cultists at Jonestown in the Guyana jungle, Nov. 18, 1978.

The People's National Congress, the party in power since Guyana became independent, was voted out of office with the election of Cheddi Jagan in Oct. 1992.

Haiti

Republic of Haiti

Républiqe d'Haiti

People: Population: 6,491,000. **Age distrib.** (%): <15: 40; 65+: 4. **Pop. density:** 607 per sq. mi. **Urban:** 31%. **Ethnic groups:** black 95%. **Principal languages:** French (official), Creoleo. **Religions:** Roman Catholic 80%, Protestant 16%; Voodoo widely practiced.

Geography: Area: 10,695 sq. mi., the size of Maryland. **Location:** In West Indies, occupies western third of I. of Hispaniola. **Neighbors:** Dominican Republic on E, Cuba on W **Topography:** About two-thirds of Haiti is mountainous. Much of the rest is semiarid. Coastal areas are warm and moist. **Capital:** Port-au-Prince. **Cities** (1992 est.): Port-au-Prince 752,000.

Government: Type: Republic. **Head of state:** Pres. Jean-Bertrand Aristide; b July 15, 1953; in office Feb. 7, 1991 (ousted in military coup Sept. 30, 1991; restored to office Oct. 15, 1994). **Local divisions:** 9 departments. **Defense:** 2.1% of GDP (1992).

Economy: Industries: Sugar refining, textiles. **Chief crops:** Coffee, sugar, bananas, cocoa, tobacco, rice. **Minerals:** Bauxite. **Other resources:** Timber. **Arable land:** 20%. **Livestock** (1991): cattle: 1.4 mln.; goats: 1.2 mln. **Fish catch** (1990): 7,500 metric tons. **Electricity prod.** (1992): 480 mln. kWh. **Labor force:** 66% agric.; 9% ind. & comm.; 25% services.

Finance: Monetary unit: Gourde (Dec. 1992: 5.00 = $1 US). **Gross domestic product** (1991): $2.2 bln. **Per capita GDP:** $340. **Imports** (1991): $347 mln.; partners: U.S. 64%. **Exports** (1991): $103 mln.; partners: U.S. 84%. **Tourism** (1991): receipts $66 mln. **National budget** (1990): $416 mln. **Consumer prices** (change in 1991): 15.4%.

Transport: Motor vehicles: in use: 33,000 passenger cars, 22,000 comm. vehicles. **Chief ports:** Port-au-Prince, Les Cayes.

Communications: Television sets: 1 per 271 persons. **Radios:** 1 per 2.3 persons. **Telephones:** 1 per 126 persons. **Daily newspaper circ.:** 7 per 1,000 pop.

Health: Life expectancy at birth (1994): 43 male; 47 female. **Births** (per 1,000 pop.): 40. **Deaths** (per 1,000 pop.): 19. **Natural increase:** 2.1%. **Hospital beds:** 1 per 1,258 persons. **Physicians:** 1 per 6,083 persons. **Infant mortality rate** (per 1,000 live births 1994): 109.

Education (1991): **Literacy:** 53%.

Major International Organizations: UN and some of its specialized agencies, OAS.

Embassy: 2311 Massachusetts Ave. NW 20008; 332-4090.

Haiti, visited by Columbus, 1492, and a French colony from 1677, attained its independence, 1804, following the rebellion led by former slave Toussaint L'Ouverture. Following a period of political violence, the U.S. occupied the country 1915-34.

Francois Duvalier was voted president in 1957; in 1964 he was named president for life. Upon his death in 1971, he was succeeded by his son, Jean-Claude. Drought in 1975-77 brought famine, and Hurricane Allen in 1980 destroyed most of the rice, bean, and coffee crops. Following several weeks of unrest, President Jean Claude Duvalier fled Haiti aboard a U.S. Air Force jet Feb. 7, 1986, ending the 28-year dictatorship by the Duvalier family.

A military-civilian council headed by Gen. Henri Namphy assumed control. In 1987, voters approved a new constitution, but the Jan. 1988 elections were marred by violence and boycotted by the opposition.

Gen. Namphy seized control, June 20, but was ousted by a military coup in Sept. By mid-1990, there had been 5 governments since Duvalier fled.

Father Jean-Bertrand Aristide was elected president Dec. 1990. A coup led by leaders of the Tonton Macoutes, the private militia of the Duvalier family, was crushed by loyalist army forces, Jan. 1991. The attempted coup sparked riots that left some 70 dead. In Sept. 1991, Aristide was arrested by the military and expelled from the country.

Some 35,000 Haitian refugees were intercepted by the U.S. Coast Guard as they tried to enter the U.S., 1991-92. Most were returned to Haiti. There was a new upsurge of refugees starting in late 1993.

The UN imposed a worldwide oil, arms, and financial embargo on Haiti June 23, 1993. The embargo was suspended when the military agreed to Aristide's return to power on Oct. 30, but the military effectively blocked his return. After renewed sanctions, the UN Security Council authorized, July 31, 1994, an invasion of Haiti by a multinational force. With U.S. invasion forces already en route, an invasion was averted, Sept. 18, by a new agreement for military leaders to step down and Aristide to resume office. As part of the agreement, thousands of U.S. troops began arriving in Haiti, Sept. 19. Aristide returned to Haiti and was restored in office Oct. 15.

Honduras

Republic of Honduras

República de Honduras

People: Population: 5,315,000. **Age distrib.** (%): <15: 47; 65+: 4. **Pop. density:** 122 per sq. mi. **Urban:** 44%. **Ethnic groups:** Mestizo 90%, Indian 7%. **Principal languages:** Spanish (official). **Religions:** Roman Catholic 97%.

Geography: Area: 43,277 sq. mi., slightly larger than Tennessee. **Location:** In Central America. **Neighbors:** Guatemala on W, El Salvador, Nicaragua on S. **Topography:** The Caribbean coast is 500 mi. long. Pacific coast, on Gulf of Fonseca, is 40 mi. long. Honduras is mountainous, with wide fertile valleys and rich forests. **Capital:** Tegucigalpa. **Cities** (1989 est.): Tegucigalpa 608,000; San Pedro Sula 300,000.

Government: Type: Democratic constitutional republic. **Head of State:** Pres. Carlos Roberta Reina; in office: Jan. 27, 1994. **Local divisions:** 18 departments. **Defense:** 1% of GDP (1993 est.).

Economy: Industries: Textiles, wood prods. **Chief crops:** Bananas (chief export), coffee, corn, beans. **Minerals:** Gold, silver, copper, lead, zinc, iron, antimony, coal. **Other resources:** Timber. **Arable land:** 14%. **Livestock** (1992): cattle: 2.3 mln. **Electricity prod.** (1992): 2.0 bln. kWh. **Labor force:** 62% agric.; 20% services; 9% manuf.

Finance: Monetary unit: Lempira (Dec. 1993: 7.26 = $1 US). **Gross domestic product** (1992): $5.5 bln. **Per capita GDP:** $1,090. **Imports** (1989): $981 mln.; partners: U.S. 39%, Jap. 8%. **Exports** (1989): $940 mln.; partners: U.S. 54%, Europe 34%. **Tourism** (1989): $28 mln. receipts. **National budget** (1990 est.): $1.9 bln. **International reserves less gold** (Mar. 1994): $78 mln. **Gold:** 21,000 oz t. **Consumer prices** (change in 1992): 10.7%.

Transport: Motor vehicles: in use: 89,000 passenger cars, 18,000 comm. vehicles. **Civil aviation:** 321 mln. passenger-mi.; 9 airports with scheduled flights. **Chief ports:** Puerto Cortes, La Ceiba.

Communications: Television sets: 1 per 31 persons. **Radios:** 1 per 2.8 persons. **Telephones:** 1 per 51 persons. **Daily newspaper circ.:** 39 per 1,000 pop.

Health: Life expectancy at birth (1994): 65 male; 70 female. **Births** (per 1,000 pop.): 35. **Deaths** (per 1,000 pop.): 6. **Natural increase:** 2.9%. **Hospital beds:** 1 per 818 persons. **Physicians:** 1 per 1,586 persons. **Infant mortality** (per 1,000 live births 1994): 45.

Education (1991): **Literacy:** 73%. **Years compulsory:** 6; attendance 70%.

Major International Organizations: UN, (IMF, WHO, ILO), OAS.

Embassy: 3007 Tilden St. NW 20008; 966-7700.

Mayan civilization flourished in Honduras in the 1st millennium AD. Columbus arrived in 1502. Honduras became independent after freeing itself from Spain, 1821 and from the Fed. of Central America, 1838.

Gen. Oswaldo Lopez Arellano, president for most of the period 1963-75 by virtue of one election and 2 coups, was ousted by the army in 1975 over charges of pervasive bribery by United Brands Co. of the U.S. The government has resumed land distribution, raised minimum wages, and started a literacy campaign. An elected civilian government took power in 1982.

Some 3,200 U.S. troops were sent to Honduras after the Honduran border was violated by Nicaraguan forces, Mar. 1988.

Honduras is one of the poorest countries in the western hemisphere.

Hungary

Republic of Hungary

Magyar Köztársaság

People: Population: 10,319,000. **Age distrib.** (%): <15: 19; 65+: 14. **Pop. density:** 287 per sq. mi. **Urban:** 63%. **Ethnic groups:** Hungarian 89.9%, Gypsy 4%, German 2.6%. **Principal languages:** Hungarian (Magyar). **Religions:** Roman Catholic 67%, Calvinist 20%, Lutheran 5%.

Geography: Area: 35,919 sq. mi., slightly smaller than Indiana. **Location:** In East Central Europe. **Neighbors:** Slovakia, Ukraine on N, Austria on W, Slovenia, Yugoslavia, Croatia on S, Romania, on E. **Topography:** The Danube R. forms the Slovak border in the NW, then swings S to bisect the country. The eastern half of Hungary is mainly a great fertile plain, the Alfold; the W and N are hilly. **Capital:** Budapest. **Cities** (1992 est.): Budapest 2.0 mln.; Miskolc 191,000; Debrecen 214,000.

Government: Type: Parliamentary democracy. **Head of state:** Pres. Arpad Goncz; in office: May 2, 1990. **Head of government:** Prime Min. Gyula Horn; b July 5, 1932; in office: July 1994. **Local divisions:** 19 counties, 1 capital. **Defense:** 3.5% of GDP (1992).

Economy: Industries: Iron and steel, machinery, pharmaceuticals, vehicles, communications equip., milling, distilling. **Chief crops:** Grains, vegetables, fruits, grapes. **Minerals:** Bauxite, coal, natural gas. **Arable land:** 51%. **Livestock** (1992): cattle: 1.1 mln.; pigs: 5.3 mln.; sheep: 1.7 mln. **Electricity prod.** (1992): 30.0 bln. kWh. **Labor force:** 16% agric.; 30% ind.

Finance: Monetary unit: Forint (Mar. 1994: 101 = $1 US).

Gross domestic product (1992): $55.4 bln.* **Per capita GDP:** $5,380. **Imports** (1991): $11.7 bln.; partners: CIS 34%, EU 21%. **Exports** (1991): $10.2 bln.; partners: CIS 30%, EU 32%. **National budget** (1993 est.): $15.4 bln. **Tourism** (1990): $1 bln. receipts. **International reserves less gold** (Dec. 1993): $6.7 bln. **Consumer prices** (change in 1992): 22.9%.

Transport: Railroads: Length: 8,200 mi. **Motor vehicles:** in use: 2.0 mln. passenger cars, 225,000 comm. vehicles. **Civil aviation:** 799 mln. passenger-mi.; 1 airport with scheduled flights.

Communications: Television sets: 1 per 2.4 persons. **Radios:** 1 per 1.7 persons. **Telephones:** 1 per 5.3 persons. **Daily newspaper circ.:** 233 per 1,000 pop.

Health: Life expectancy at birth (1994): 67 male; 76 female. **Births** (per 1,000 pop.): 12. **Deaths** (per 1,000 pop.): 13. **Hospital beds:** 1 per 100 persons. **Physicians:** 1 per 262 persons. **Infant mortality** (per 1,000 live births 1994): 13.

Education (1992): **Literacy:** 98%. **Years compulsory:** to age 16; attendance 96%.

Major International Organizations: UN (IMF, World Bank, GATT).

Embassy: 3910 Shoemaker St. NW 20008; 362-6730.

Earliest settlers, chiefly Slav and Germanic, were overrun by Magyars from the east. Stephen I (997-1038) was made king by Pope Sylvester II in 1000 AD. The country suffered repeated Turkish invasions in the 15th-17th centuries. After the defeats of the Turks, 1686-1697, Austria dominated, but Hungary obtained concessions until it regained internal independence in 1867, with the emperor of Austria as king of Hungary in a dual monarchy with a single diplomatic service. Defeated with the Central Powers in 1918, Hungary lost Transylvania to Romania, Croatia and Bacska to Yugoslavia, Slovakia and Carpatho-Ruthenia to Czechoslovakia, all of which had large Hungarian minorities. A republic under Michael Karolyi and a bolshevist revolt under Bela Kun were followed by a vote for a monarchy in 1920 with Admiral Nicholas Horthy as regent.

Hungary joined Germany in World War II, and was allowed to annex most of its lost territories. Russian troops captured the country, 1944-1945. By terms of an armistice with the Allied powers Hungary agreed to give up territory acquired by the 1938 dismemberment of Czechoslovakia and to return to its borders of 1937.

A republic was declared Feb. 1, 1946; Zoltan Tildy was elected president. In 1947 the communists forced Tildy out. Premier Imre Nagy, in office since mid-1953, was ousted for his moderate policy of favoring agriculture and consumer production, April 18, 1955.

In 1956, popular demands for the ousting of Erno Gero, Communist Party secretary, and for formation of a government by Nagy, resulted in the latter's appointment Oct. 23; demonstrations against communist rule developed into open revolt. On Nov. 4 Soviet forces launched a massive attack against Budapest with 200,000 troops, 2,500 tanks and armored cars.

About 200,000 persons fled the country. Nagy was executed, and thousands were arrested. In the spring of 1963 the regime freed many captives from the 1956 revolt.

Hungarian troops participated in the 1968 Warsaw Pact invasion of Czechoslovakia. Major economic reforms were launched early in 1968, switching from a central planning system to one in which market forces and profit control much of production.

In 1989 Parliament passed legislation legalizing freedom of assembly and association as Hungary shifted away from communism. In Oct. the Communist Party was formally dissolved. The last Soviet troops left Hungary June 19, 1991.

Iceland

Republic of Iceland

Lýoveldio Island

People: Population: 264,000. **Age distrib.** (%): <15: 25; 65+: 11. **Pop. density:** 7 per sq. mi. **Urban:** 91%. **Ethnic groups:** Homogeneous, descendants of Norwegians, Celts. **Principal languages:** Icelandic (Islenska). **Religions:** Evangelical Lutheran 96%.

Geography: Area: 36,699 sq. mi., the size of Virginia. **Location:** At N end of Atlantic O. **Neighbors:** Nearest is Greenland. **Topography:** Iceland is of recent volcanic origin. Three-quarters of the surface is wasteland: glaciers, lakes, a lava desert. There are geysers and hot springs, and the climate is moderated by the Gulf Stream. **Capital:** Reykjavik. **Cities** (1992 est.): Reykjavik 101,000.

Government: Type: Constitutional republic. **Head of state:** Pres. Vigdis Finnbogadottir; b Apr. 15, 1930; in office: Aug. 1, 1980. **Head of government:** Prime Min. David Oddsson; in office: Apr. 30, 1991. **Local divisions:** 23 counties, 14 ind. towns.

Economy: Industries: Fish products (some 80% of exports), aluminum. **Chief crops:** Potatoes, turnips, hay. **Arable land:** 1%. **Livestock** (1992): sheep: 487,000. **Fish catch** (1991): 991,000 metric tons. **Electricity prod.** (1992): 5.1 bln. kWh. **Labor force:** 4% agric.; 60% comm. & services, 12% fish.

Finance: Monetary unit: Kronur (Mar. 1994: 72.17 = $1 US). **Gross domestic product** (1992): $4.5 bln.* **Per capita GDP:** $17,400. **Imports** (1992): $1.7 bln.; partners: EU 50%. **Exports** (1992): $1.6 bln.; partners: EU 67%. **Tourism** (1991): receipts: $223 mln. **National budget** (1992): $1.9 bln. **International reserves less gold** (Mar. 1994): $545.9 mln. **Gold:** 49,000 oz t. **Consumer prices** (change in 1993): 4.1%.

Transport: Motor vehicles: in use: 120,000 passenger cars, 16,000 comm. vehicles. **Civil aviation:** 1.1 bln. passenger-mi.; 19 airports with scheduled flights. **Chief ports:** Reykjavik.

Communications: Television sets: 1 per 3.4 persons. **Radios:** 1 per 1.7 persons. **Telephones:** 1 per 1.9 persons. **Daily newspaper circ.:** 572 per 1,000 pop.

Health: Life expectancy at birth (1994): 77 male; 81 female. **Births** (per 1,000 pop.): 16. **Deaths** (per 1,000 pop.): 7. **Natural increase:** 1.0%. **Hospital beds:** 1 per 58 persons. **Physicians:** 1 per 355 persons. **Infant mortality** (per 1,000 live births 1994): 4.

Education (1992): **Literacy:** 99%. **Years compulsory:** 8; **Attendance:** 99%.

Major International Organizations: UN (GATT), NATO, EFTA, OECD.

Embassy: 2022 Connecticut Ave. NW 20008; 265-6653.

Iceland was an independent republic from 930 to 1262, when it joined with Norway. Its language has maintained its purity for 1,000 years. Danish rule lasted from 1380-1918; the last ties with the Danish crown were severed in 1941. The Althing, or assembly, is the world's oldest surviving parliament.

India

Republic of India

Bharat

People: Population: 919,903,000. **Age distrib.** (%): <15: 36; 65+: 4. **Pop. density:** 752 per sq. mi. **Urban:** 26%. **Ethnic groups:** Indo-Aryan groups 72%, Dravidians 25%, Mongoloids 3%. **Principal languages:** 16 languages, including Hindi (official) and English (associate official). **Religions:** Hindu 83%, Muslim 11%, Christian 2%, Sikh 2%.

Geography: Area: 1,222,559 sq. mi., one-third the size of the U.S. **Location:** Occupies most of the Indian subcontinent in S Asia. **Neighbors:** Pakistan on W, China, Nepal, Bhutan on N, Myanmar, Bangladesh on E. **Topography:** The Himalaya Mts., highest in world, stretch across India's northern borders. Below, the Ganges Plain is wide, fertile, and among the most densely populated regions of the world. The area below includes the Deccan Peninsula. Close to one quarter the area is forested. The climate varies from tropical heat in S to near-Arctic cold in N. Rajasthan Desert is in NW; NE Assam Hills get 400 in. of rain a year. **Capital:** New Delhi. **Cities** (1991 met. est.): Calcutta 11.0 mln.; Bombay 12.5 mln.; Delhi 8.4 mln.; Madras 5.4 mln.; Bangalore 4.1 mln.; Hyderabad 4.2 mln.

Government: Type: Federal republic. **Head of state:** Pres. Shankar Dayal Sharma; b. Aug. 19, 1918; in office: July 26, 1992. **Head of government:** Prime Min. P. V. Narasimha Rao; b June 28, 1921; in office: June 21, 1991. **Local divisions:** 25 states, 7 union territories. **Defense:** 2.4% of GNP (FY 1993-94).

Economy: Industries: Textiles, steel, processed foods, cement, machinery, chemicals, fertilizers, consumer appliances, autos. **Chief crops:** Rice, grains, coffee, sugar cane, spices, tea, cashews, cotton, copra, coir, juta, linseed. **Minerals:** Chromium, coal, iron, manganese, mica salt, bauxite, gypsum, oil. **Crude oil reserves** (1991): 4.2 bln. bbls. **Other resources:** Rubber, timber. **Arable land:** 55%. **Livestock** (1991): cattle: 198 mln.; sheep: 55 mln. **Fish catch** (1990): 3.6 mln. metric tons. **Electricity prod.** (1992): 310 bln. kWh. **Labor force:** 67% agric.

Finance: Monetary unit: Rupee (Mar. 1994: 31.37 = $1 US). **Gross domestic product** (1993): $240 bln. **Per capita GDP:** $270. **Imports** (1991): $25.2 bln.; partners: Jap. 8%, U.S. 12%, EU 33%. **Exports** (1991): $20.2 bln.; partners: U.S. 16%, EU 25%, CIS 19%. **Tourism** (1991): receipts: $1.4 bln. **National budget** (FY 1992): $41.06 bln. **International reserves less gold** (Mar. 1994): $15.4 bln. **Gold:** 11.8 mln. oz t. **Consumer prices** (change in 1993): 6.4%.

Transport: Railroads: Length: 38,752 mi. **Motor vehicles:** in use: 2.3 mln. passenger cars, 1.4 mln. comm. vehicles. **Civil aviation:** 10.2 bln. passenger-mi.; 98 airports with scheduled flights. **Chief ports:** Calcutta, Bombay, Madras, Cochin, Vishakhapatnam.

Communications: Television sets: 1 per 44 persons. **Radios:** 1 per 16 persons. **Telephones:** 1 per 145 persons. **Daily newspaper circ.:** 21 per 1,000 pop.

Health: Life expectancy at birth (1994): 58 male; 59 female. **Births** (per 1,000 pop.): 28. **Deaths** (per 1,000 pop.): 10. **Natural increase:** 1.8%. **Hospital beds:** 1 per 1,324 persons. **Physicians:** 1 per 2,337 persons. **Infant mortality** (per 1,000 live births 1994): 78.

Education (1991): **Literacy:** 48%. **Years compulsory:** to age 14.

Major International Organizations: UN (IMF, World Bank).

Embassy: 2107 Massachusetts Ave. NW 20008; 939-7000.

India has one of the oldest civilizations in the world. Excavations trace the Indus Valley civilization back for at least 5,000 years. Paintings in the mountain caves of Ajanta, richly carved temples, the Taj Mahal in Agra, and the Kutab Minar in Delhi are among relics of the past.

Aryan tribes, speaking Sanskrit, invaded from the NW around 1500 BC, and merged with the earlier inhabitants to create classical Indian civilization.

Asoka ruled most of the Indian subcontinent in the 3d century BC, and established Buddhism. But Hinduism revived and eventually predominated. During the Gupta kingdom, 4th-6th century AD, science, literature, and the arts enjoyed a "golden age."

Arab invaders established a Muslim foothold in the W in the 8th century, and Turkish Muslims gained control of North India by 1200. The Mogul emperors ruled 1526-1857.

Vasco de Gama established Portuguese trading posts 1498-1503. The Dutch followed. The British East India Co. sent Capt. William Hawkins, 1609, to get concessions from the Mogul emperor for spices and textiles. Operating as the East India Co. the British gained control of most of India. The British parliament assumed political direction; under Lord Bentinck, 1828-35, rule by rajahs was curbed. After the Sepoy troops mutinied, 1857-58, the British supported the native rulers.

Nationalism grew rapidly after World War I. The Indian National Congress and the Muslim League demanded constitutional reform. A leader emerged in Mohandas K. Gandhi (called Mahatma, or Great Soul), born Oct. 2, 1869, assassinated Jan. 30, 1948. He advocated self-rule, non-violence, removal of untouchability. In 1930 he launched "civil disobedience," including boycott of British goods and rejection of taxes without representation.

In 1935 Britain gave India a constitution providing a bicameral federal congress. Mohammed Ali Jinnah, head of the Muslim League, sought creation of a Muslim nation, Pakistan.

The British government partitioned British India into the dominions of India and Pakistan. India became a self-governing member of the Commonwealth and a member of the UN. It became a democratic republic, Jan. 26, 1950.

More than 12 million Hindu & Muslim refugees crossed the India-Pakistan borders in a mass transferral of some of the 2 peoples during 1947; about 200,000 were killed in communal fighting.

After Pakistan troops began attacks on Bengali separatists in East Pakistan, Mar. 25, 1971, some 10 million refugees fled into India. India and Pakistan went to war Dec. 3, 1971, on both the East and West fronts. Pakistan troops in the east surrendered Dec. 16; Pakistan agreed to a cease-fire in the west Dec. 17. In Aug. 1973 India released 93,000 Pakistanis held prisoner since 1971. The 2 countries resumed full relations in 1976.

Mrs. Indira Gandhi, was named prime minister Jan. 19, 1966. Threatened with adverse court rulings and an opposition protest campaign, Gandhi invoked emergency provisions of the constitution June 1975. Thousands of opponents were arrested and press censorship imposed. These and other actions, including the enforcement of coercive birth control measures in some areas, were widely resented. Opposition parties, united in the Janata coalition, turned Gandhi's New Congress Party from power in federal and state parliamentary elections in 1977.

Gandhi became prime minister for the second time, Jan. 14, 1980. She was assassinated by 2 of her Sikh bodyguards Oct. 31, 1984. Widespread rioting followed. Thousands of Sikhs were killed and some 50,000 left homeless.

The assassination was in response to the government suppression of a Sikh uprising in Punjab in June 1984 which included an assault on the Golden Temple, the holiest Sikh shrine. Rajiv, Indira Gandhi's son, replaced her as prime minister. He was swept from office in 1989 amid charges of incompetence and corruption. He was assassinated May 21, 1991 during an election campaign to regain the prime ministership.

Sikhs ignited several violent clashes during the 1980s. The government's May 1987 decision to bring the state of Punjab under the rule of the central government led to violence. Many died during a government siege of the Golden Temple at Amritsar, May 1988. Another trouble spot was Assam in NW India, where thousands were killed in ethnic violence in Feb. 1993; a renewed outburst in July 1994 led to more than 60 deaths there.

In the biggest wave of criminal violence in Indian history, a series of bombings jolted Bombay and Calcutta, Mar. 12-19, 1993, leaving over 300 dead and some 1,200 injured. The explosions came in the wake of nationwide riots prompted by the destruction of a 16th century mosque by Hindu militants in Dec. 1992.

Sikkim, bordered by Tibet, Bhutan, and Nepal, formerly British protected, became a protectorate of India in 1950. Area, 2,740 sq. mi.; pop. 1991 cen. 405,000; capital, Gangtok. In Sept. 1974 India's parliament voted to make Sikkim an associate Indian state, absorbing it into India.

Kashmir, a predominantly Muslim region in the NW, has been in dispute between India and Pakistan since 1947. A cease-fire was negotiated by the UN Jan. 1, 1949; it gave Pakistan control of one-third of the area, in the west and northwest, and India the remaining two-thirds, the Indian state of Jammu and Kashmir, which enjoys internal autonomy.

In the 1990s there were repeated clashes between Indian army troops and pro-independence demonstrators triggered by India's decision to impose central government rule. The clashes strained relations between India and Pakistan which India charged was aiding the Muslim separatists. Talks on the issue in early 1994 were inconclusive.

France, 1952-54, peacefully yielded to India its 5 colonies, former French India, comprising Pondicherry, Karikal, Mahe, Yanaon (which became Pondicherry Union Territory, area 185 sq. mi., pop. 1991, 807,000) and Chandernagor (which was incorporated into the state of West Bengal).

Indonesia

Republic of Indonesia

Republik Indonesia

People: Population: 200,410,000. **Age distrib.** (%): <15: 37; 65+: 4. **Pop. density:** 270 per sq. mi. **Urban:** 31%. **Ethnic groups:** Javanese 45%, Sundanese 14%, Madurese 7.5%, Malay 7.5%. **Principal languages:** Bahasa Indonesian (Malay) (official), English, Dutch, Javanese. **Religions:** Muslim 87%.

Geography: Area: 741,052 sq. mi. **Location:** Archipelago SE of Asia along the Equator. **Neighbors:** Malaysia on N, Papua New Guinea on E. **Topography:** Indonesia comprises some 17,000 islands, including Java (one of the most densely populated areas in the world with 1,500 persons to the sq. mi.), Sumatra, Kalimantan (most of Borneo), Sulawesi (Celebes), and West Irian (Irian Jaya, the W half of New Guinea). Also: Bangka, Billiton, Madura, Bali, Timor. The mountains and plateaus on the major islands have a cooler climate than the tropical lowlands. **Capital:** Jakarta. **Cities** (1990 est.): Jakarta 8.2 mln.; Surabaya 2.4 mln.; Bandung 2.0 mln.; Medan 1.7 mln.

Government: Type: Republic. **Head of state:** Pres. Suharto; b June 8, 1921; in office: Mar. 6, 1967. **Local divisions:** 24 provinces, 3 special regions. **Defense:** 1.5% of GDP (FY 1993-94 est.).

Economy: Industries: Food processing, textiles, cement, light industry. **Chief crops:** Rice, coffee, sugar. **Minerals:** Nickel, tin, oil, bauxite, copper, natural gas. **Crude oil reserves** (1991): 10.7 bln. bbls. **Other resources:** Rubber. **Arable land:** 8%. **Livestock** (1992): cattle: 11.0 mln.; sheep: 5.9 mln. **Fish catch** (1991): 3.1 mln. metric tons. **Electricity prod.** (1991): 38 bln. kWh. **Labor force:** 55% agric.; 10% manuf.

(continued on page 785)

Change in South Africa

AP/WIDEWORLD PHOTOS

Voters line up in large numbers (below) to cast ballots in South Africa's first election open to all races. At right, Nelson Mandela, whose African National Congress won the most votes, is sworn in May 10 as the nation's president.

GORDEN HODGE/SYGMA

World Events

Rwanda's capital was littered with corpses (below) after massive ethnic violence broke out in April. Hundreds of thousands fled across the border to face hunger and disease in refugee camps in Zaire (inset).

REUTERS/BETTMANN; INSET, ROGER JOB/GAMMA LIAISON

Cuban refugees aboard makeshift rafts sight a U.S. Coast Guard helicopter. In August and September 1994, the Coast Guard intercepted more than 30,000 Cubans attempting to reach U.S. shores, before a new U.S.-Cuba immigration accord took effect.

GAMMA LIAISON

North Korean strongman Kim Il Sung (left) died July 8 at age 82, leaving a son, Kim Jong Il, as his chosen heir.

AP/WIDE WORLD PHOTOS

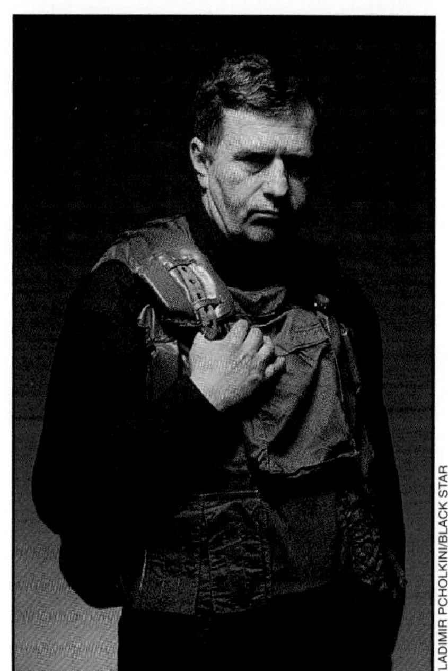

VLADIMIR PCHOLKINI/BLACK STAR

Ultranationalists, like Vladimir Zhirinovsky (left, in bulletproof vest), and pro-Communist hard-liners posed challenges to reformers in Russia.

MOSHE MILNER/SYGMA

As the Mideast peace process continued, self-rule began in occupied territories (at right, Palestinian police enter Jericho in May), and Jordan ended its state of war with Israel (below, Jordan's King Hussein and Israel's Yitzhak Rabin shake hands at the White House in July).

MARKEL/LIAISON

ARTS AND ENTERTAINMENT

Kurt Cobain, leader of the rock group Nirvana, died April 8 of a self-inflicted gunshot wound.

AP/WIDE WORLD PHOTOS

AP/WIDE WORLD PHOTOS

Perhaps the most talked-about TV show was the gritty police drama *NYPD Blue.* The original cast included, at left, David Caruso (who later left the series) and Dennis Franz.

JOAN MARCUS/MARC BRYAN-BROWN

Beauty and the Beast, with Susan Egan and Terrence Mann in the title roles, was Disney's Broadway debut—and, at $11.9 million, the most expensive Broadway musical ever.

Steven Spielberg (inset) picked up best director and best picture Oscars March 21 for *Schindler's List*, a moving film about the Holocaust, starring Liam Neeson (left) and Ben Kingsley.

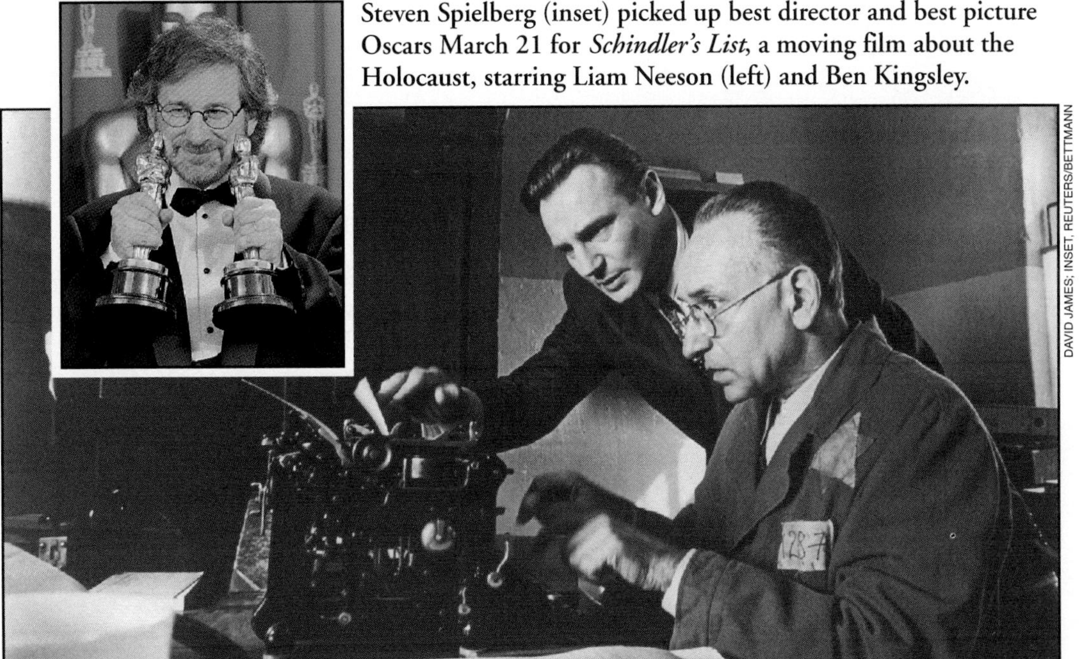

DAVID JAMES; INSET, REUTERS/BETTMANN

SYGMA

Russian writer Aleksandr Solzhenitsyn returned to his homeland after 20 years of exile; here he walks with his wife, Natalya, in Vladivostok.

Returning to the concert circuit after more than 20 years, Barbra Streisand, shown performing at London's Wembley stadium in April, proved she was still a superstar.

SYGMA

Sports Highlights

MVP Emmitt Smith (carrying the ball) helped the Dallas Cowboys defeat the Buffalo Bills and take the Super Bowl for the second year in a row.

FOCUS ON SPORTS

Scotty Thurman sinks a shot to help Arkansas overcome Duke, April 4, to win the NCAA championship.

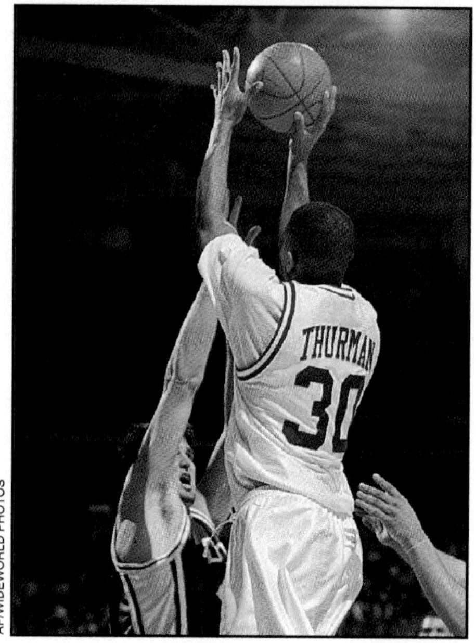

AP/WIDEWORLD PHOTOS

The New York Rangers won the Stanley Cup for the first time since 1940, defeating the Vancouver Canucks in a seven-game championship series.

SPORTS ILLUSTRATED © TIME INC.

Houston Rockets MVP Hakeem Olajuwon goes up for a shot during the NBA finals, in which the Rockets beat the New York Knicks to win their first title.

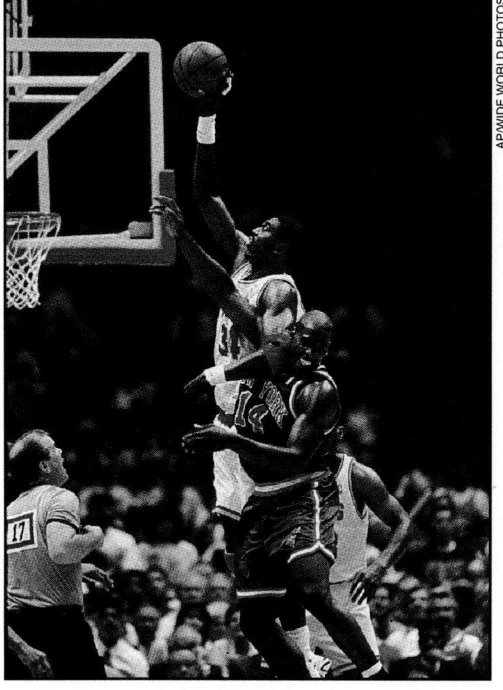

AP/WIDE WORLD PHOTOS

© DUOMO 1994

Pete Sampras triumphed at Wimbledon in July, becoming the first man to win back-to-back titles there since Boris Becker in 1986.

AP/WIDE WORLD PHOTOS

Though fans showed signs of distress, major league baseball players went out on strike in August.

Dunga scores the winning penalty kick for Brazil, in a shoot-out against Italy for soccer's World Cup, July 17 in Pasadena, CA.

AP/WIDE WORLD PHOTOS

The Winter Olympics

The Olympic torch is passed to a ski jumper, at opening ceremonies for the XVII Winter Olympics, February 12 in Lillehammer, Norway.

AP/WIDE WORLD PHOTOS

FOCUS ON SPORTS

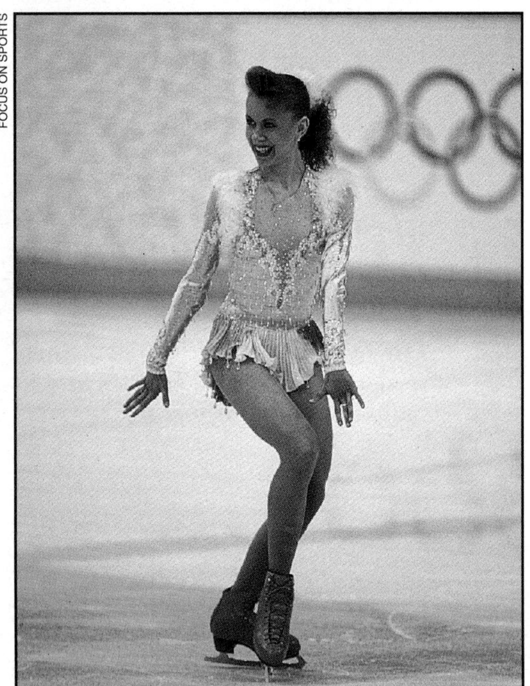

In the headline-grabbing women's figure skating competition, Ukrainian Oksana Baiul (left) won the gold, and American Nancy Kerrigan, the silver.

DOUG BEGHTEL/SYGMA

Finance: Monetary unit: Rupiah (Mar. 1994: 2,140 = $1 US). **Gross domestic product** (1992): $133 bln. **Per capita GDP:** $680. **Imports** (1991): $25.8 bln.; partners: Jap. 23%, U.S. 12%, Sing. 6%. **Exports** (1991): $29.5 bln.; partners: Jap. 41%, U.S. 16%, Sing. 10%. **Tourism** (1990): $1.8 bln. receipts. **National budget** (1991): $23.4 bln. **International reserves less gold** (Jan. 1994): $11.3 bln. **Gold:** 3.10 mln. oz t. **Consumer prices** (change in 1993): 9.7%.

Transport: Railroads: Length: 4,090 mi. **Motor vehicles:** in use: 1.3 mln. passenger cars, 1.5 mln. comm. vehicles **Civil aviation:** 9.2 bln. passenger-mi.; 117 airports. **Chief ports:** Jakarta, Surabaya, Medan, Palembang, Semarang.

Communications: Television sets: 1 per 17 persons. **Radios:** 1 per 8.4 persons. **Telephones:** 1 per 122 persons.

Health: Life expectancy at birth (1994): male 59; female 63 years. **Births** (per 1,000 pop.): 24. **Deaths** (per 1,000 pop.): 9. **Natural increase:** 1.6%. **Hospital beds:** 1 per 688 persons. **Physicians:** 1 per 2,685 persons. **Infant mortality** (per 1,000 live births 1994): 67.

Education (1990): **Literacy:** 85%. **Attendance:** 84% attend primary school.

Major International Organizations: UN and all of its specialized agencies, ASEAN, OPEC.

Embassy: 2020 Massachusetts Ave. NW 20036; 775-5200.

Hindu and Buddhist civilization from India reached the peoples of Indonesia nearly 2,000 years ago, taking root especially in Java. Islam spread along the maritime trade routes in the 15th century, and became predominant by the 16th century. The Dutch replaced the Portuguese as the most important European trade power in the area in the 17th century. They secured territorial control over Java by 1750. The outer islands were not finally subdued until the early 20th century, when the full area of present-day Indonesia was united under one rule for the first time.

Following Japanese occupation, 1942-45, nationalists led by Sukarno and Hatta declared independence. The Netherlands ceded sovereignty Dec. 27, 1949, after 4 years of fighting. A republic was declared, Aug. 17, 1950, with Sukarno as president. West Irian, on New Guinea, remained under Dutch control.

After the Dutch in 1957 rejected proposals for new negotiations over West Irian, Indonesia stepped up the seizure of Dutch property. A U.S. mediator's plan was adopted in 1962. In 1963 the UN turned the area over to Indonesia, which promised a plebiscite. In 1969, voting by tribal chiefs favored staying with Indonesia, despite an uprising and widespread opposition.

Sukarno suspended Parliament in 1960, and was named president for life in 1963. He made close alliances with Communist governments. Russian-armed Indonesian troops staged raids in 1964 and 1965 into Malaysia, whose formation Sukarno had opposed.

In 1965 an attempted coup in which several military officers were murdered was successfully put down. The regime blamed the coup on the Communist Party, some of whose members were known to have been involved. In its wake more than 300,000 alleged Communists were killed in army-initiated massacres.

Gen. Suharto, head of the army, was named president in 1968 and was reelected for a 6th consecutive 5-year term in 1993. He developed a strong government party, restricted the opposition, and allied the country with the West. Muslim opposition parties made gains in 1977 elections but lost ground subsequently. The military retained a predominant role.

In 1966 Indonesia and Malaysia signed an agreement ending hostility. In Dec. 1975, Indonesia invaded East Timor as Portuguese rule collapsed there, annexing it in 1976, despite international condemnation.

Oil exports and political stability have made Indonesia's economy stable.

Iran

Islamic Republic of Iran

Jomhori-e-Islami-e-Irân

People: Population: 65,612,000. **Age distrib.** (%): <15: 47; 65+: 4. **Pop. density:** 103 per sq. mi. **Urban:** 57%. **Ethnic groups:** Persian 51%, Azerbaijani 24%, Kurd 7%. **Principal languages:** Persian, Turkic, Kurdish, Luri. **Religions:** Shi'a Muslim 95%.

Geography: Area: 632,457 sq. mi., slightly larger than Alaska. **Location:** Between the Middle East and S Asia. **Neighbors:** Turkey, Iraq on W, Armenia, Azerbaijan, Turkmenistan on N, Afghanistan, Pakistan on E. **Topography:** Interior highlands and plains are surrounded by high mountains, up to 18,000 ft. Large salt deserts cover much of the area, but there are many oases and forest areas. Most of the population inhabits the N and NW. **Capital:** Tehran. **Cities** (1986 cen.): Tehran 6.0 mln.; Esfahan 1.0 mln.; Mashhad 1.4 mln.; Tabriz 971,000; Shiraz 848,000.

Government: Type: Islamic republic. **Religious head:** Ayatollah Sayyed Ali Khamenei; b 1939; in office: June 4, 1989. **Head of state:** Pres. Hashemi Rafsanjani; in office: Aug 3, 1989. **Local divisions:** 24 provinces. **Defense:** 15% of GNP (1991).

Economy: Industries: Cement, sugar refining, carpets. **Chief crops:** Grains, rice, fruits, sugar beets, cotton, grapes. **Minerals:** Chromium, oil, gas. **Crude oil reserves** (1991): 63 bln. barrels. **Other resources:** Gums, wool, silk, caviar. **Arable land:** 8%. **Livestock** (1991): cattle: 6.9 mln.; sheep: 45.0 mln. **Electricity prod.** (1992): 43.6 bln. kWh. **Labor force:** 33% agric.; 21% manuf.

Finance: Monetary unit: Rial (Mar. 1994: 1,747 = $1 US). **Gross national product** (1992): $90 bln. **Per capita GNP** (1991): $1,500. **Imports** (1991): $21.6 bln.; partners: Ger. 20%, Jap. 10%, UK 6%. **Exports** (1991): $15.9 bln.; partners: Jap. 13%, Neth. 12%. **National budget** (1990): $80 bln. **Consumer prices** (change in 1993): 20.3%.

Transport: Motor vehicles: in use: 1.6 mln. passenger cars, 600,000 comm. vehicles. **Civil aviation:** 3.3 bln. passenger-mi.; 19 airports. **Chief ports:** Bandar Abbas.

Communications: Television sets: 1 per 26 persons. **Radios:** 1 per 5 persons. **Telephones:** 1 per 25 persons. **Daily newspaper circ.:** 27 per 1,000 pop.

Health: Life expectancy at birth (1994): 65 male; 67 female. **Births** (per 1,000 pop.): 42. **Deaths** (per 1,000 pop.): 8. **Natural increase:** 3.5%. **Hospital beds:** 1 per 688 persons. **Physicians:** 1 per 2,685 persons. **Infant mortality** (per 1,000 live births 1994): 60.

Education (1990): **Literacy:** 54%.

Major International Organizations: UN (IMF, WHO), OPEC.

Iran was once called Persia. The Iranians, who supplanted an earlier agricultural civilization, came from the E during the 2d millennium BC; they were an Indo-European group related to the Aryans of India.

In 549 BC Cyrus the Great united the Medes and Persians in the Persian Empire, conquered Babylonia in 538 BC, restored Jerusalem to the Jews. Alexander the Great conquered Persia in 333 BC, but Persians regained their independence in the next century under the Parthians, themselves succeeded by Sassanian Persians in 226 AD. Arabs brought Islam to Persia in the 7th century, replacing the indigenous Zoroastrian faith. After Persian political and cultural autonomy was reasserted in the 9th century, the arts and sciences flourished for several centuries.

Turks and Mongols ruled Persia in turn from the 11th century to 1502, when a native dynasty reasserted full independence. The British and Russian empires vied for influence in the 19th century, and Afghanistan was severed from Iran by Britain in 1857.

Reza Khan abdicated as shah, 1941, and was succeeded by his son, Mohammad Reza Pahlavi. Under his rule, Iran underwent economic and social change but political opposition was not tolerated.

Conservative Muslim protests led to 1978 violence. Martial law in 12 cities was declared Sept. 8. A military government was appointed Nov. 6 to deal with striking oil workers. Prime Min. Shahpur Bakhtiar was designated by the shah to head a regency council in his absence. The shah left Iran Jan. 16, 1979.

Exiled religious leader Ayatollah Ruhollah Khomeini named a provisional government council in preparation for his return to Iran, Jan. 31. Clashes between Khomeini's supporters and government troops culminated in a rout of Iran's elite Imperial Guard Feb. 11, leading to the fall of Bakhtiar's government.

The Iranian revolution was marked by revolts among the ethnic minorities and by a continuing struggle between the clerical forces and westernized intellectuals and liberals. The Islamic Constitution established final authority to be vested in a Faghi, the Ayatollah Khomeini.

Iranian militants seized the U.S. embassy, Nov. 4, 1979, and took hostages including 62 Americans. Despite international condemnations and U.S. efforts, including an abortive Apr. 1980 rescue attempt, the crisis continued. The U.S. broke diplomatic relations with Iran, Apr. 7. The shah died in Egypt, July

27. The hostage drama finally ended Jan. 21, 1981, when an accord, involving the release of frozen Iranian assets, was reached.

A dispute over the Shatt al-Arab waterway that divides the two countries brought Iran and Iraq, Sept. 22, 1980, into open warfare. Iraqi planes attacked Iranian air fields including Tehran airport. Iranian planes bombed Iraqi bases. Iraqi troops occupied Iranian territory including the port city of Khorramshahr in October. Iranian troops recaptured the city and drove Iraqi troops back across the border, May 1982. Iraq, and later Iran, attacked several oil tankers in the Persian Gulf during 1984. Saudi Arabian war planes shot down 2 Iranian jets, June 5, which they felt were threatening Saudi shipping. In Aug. 1988, Iran agreed to accept a UN resolution calling for a cease-fire.

In Nov. 1986, senior U.S. officials secretly visited Iran and exchanged arms for Iran's help in obtaining the release of U.S. hostages held by terrorists in Lebanon. The exchange sparked a major scandal in the Reagan administration.

A U.S. Navy warship shot down an Iranian commercial airliner, July 3, 1988, after mistaking it for an F-14 fighter jet; all 290 aboard the plane died.

A major earthquake struck northern Iran June 21, 1990, killing more than 45,000, injuring 100,000, and leaving 400,000 homeless. A U.S. offer of assistance was accepted by the Iranian government.

Some one million Kurdish refugees crossed Iran's border to escape Iraqi forces following the Persian Gulf War.

Iraq

Republic of Iraq

al Jumhouriya al 'Iraqia

People: Population: 19,890,000. **Age distrib.** (%): <15: 48; 65+: 3. **Pop. density:** 118 per sq. mi. **Urban:** 70%. **Ethnic groups:** Arabs 75–80%, Kurds 15–20%, Turks. **Principal languages:** Arabic (official), Kurdish. **Religions:** Muslim 97% (Shi'a 60–65%, Sunnis 32–37%), Christian or other 3%.

Geography: Area: 167,975 sq. mi., larger than California. **Location:** In the Middle East, occupying most of historic Mesopotamia. **Neighbors:** Jordan, Syria on W, Turkey on N, Iran on E, Kuwait, Saudi Arabia on S. **Topography:** Mostly an alluvial plain, including the Tigris and Euphrates rivers, descending from mountains in N to desert in SW. Persian Gulf region is marshland. **Capital:** Baghdad. **Cities** (1985 est.): Baghdad (met.) 3.8 mln., Basra 616,000, Mosul 570,000.

Government: Type: Republic. **Head of state:** Pres. Saddam Hussein At-Takriti, b. Apr. 29, 1937; in office: July 16, 1979; also assumed post of prime minister, May 29, 1994. **Local divisions:** 18 provinces. **Defense:** 18% of GNP (1990).

Economy: Industries: Textiles, petrochemicals, oil refining, cement. **Chief crops:** Grains, rice, dates, cotton. **Minerals:** Oil, gas. **Crude oil reserves** (1991): 100 bln. barrels. **Other resources:** Wool, hides. **Arable land:** 12%. **Livestock** (1992): cattle: 1.4 mln.; sheep: 9.0 mln. **Fish catch** (1991): 12,000 metric tons. **Electricity prod.** (1991): 3.8 bln. kWh. **Labor force:** 30% agric.; 48% services; 22% ind.

Finance: Monetary unit: Dinar (Mar. 1994: 1.00 = $3.21 US). **Gross national product** (1989): $35 bln. **Per capita GNP:** $1,940. **Imports** (1990): $6.6 bln.; partners: Tur. 2%, U.S. **Exports** (1990): $10.4 bln.; partners: U.S., Tur., Jap. **National budget** (1990): $35 bln. expenditures.

Transport: Railroads: Length: 1,484 mi. **Motor vehicles:** in use: 744,000 passenger cars, 295,000 comm. vehicles. **Chief ports:** Basra.

Communications: Television sets: 1 per 19 persons. **Radios:** 1 per 5.4 persons. **Telephones:** 1 per 25 persons. **Daily newspaper circ.:** 34 per 1,000 pop.

Health: Life expectancy at birth (1994): 65 male; 67 female. **Births** (per 1,000 pop.): 44. **Deaths** (per 1,000 pop.): 7. **Natural increase:** 3.7%. **Hospital beds:** 1 per 568 persons. **Physicians:** 1 per 1,922 persons. **Infant mortality** (per 1,000 live births 1994): 67.

Major International Organizations: UN (IMF, ILO), Arab League, OPEC.

Education (1991): **Literacy:** 60%. Compulsory age 6 to grade 6.

The Tigris-Euphrates valley, formerly called Mesopotamia, was the site of one of the earliest civilizations in the world. The Sumerian city-states of 3,000 BC originated the culture later developed by the Semitic Akkadians, Babylonians, and Assyrians.

Mesopotamia ceased to be a separate entity after the conquests of the Persians, Greeks, and Arabs. The latter founded Baghdad, from where the caliph ruled a vast empire in the 8th and 9th centuries. Mongol and Turkish conquests led to a decline in population, the economy, cultural life, and the irrigation system.

Britain secured a League of Nations mandate over Iraq after World War I. Independence under a king came in 1932. A leftist, pan-Arab revolution established a republic in 1958, which oriented foreign policy toward the USSR. Most industry has been nationalized, and large land holdings broken up.

A local faction of the international Baath Arab Socialist party has ruled by decree since 1968. Russia and Iraq signed an aid pact in 1972, and arms were sent along with several thousand advisers. The 1978 execution of 21 communists and a shift of trade to the West signalled a more neutral policy, straining relations with the USSR. In the 1973 Arab-Israeli war Iraq sent forces to aid Syria. Within a month of assuming power, Saddam Hussein instituted a bloody purge in the wake of a reported coup attempt against the new regime.

Years of battling with the Kurdish minority resulted in total defeat for the Kurds in 1975, when Iran withdrew support. The fighting led to Iraqi bombing of Kurdish villages in Iran, causing relations with Iran to deteriorate.

After skirmishing intermittently for 10 months over the sovereignty of the disputed Shatt al-Arab waterway that divides the two countries, Iraq and Iran, Sept. 22, 1980, entered into open warfare when Iraqi fighter-bombers attacked 10 Iranian airfields, including Tehran airport, and Iranian planes retaliated with strikes on 2 Iraqi bases. In the following days, there was heavy ground fighting around Abadan and the port of Khorramshahr as Iraq pressed its attack on Iran's oil-rich province of Khuzistan. In May 1982, Iraqi troops were driven back across the border.

Israeli airplanes destroyed a nuclear reactor near Baghdad on June 7, 1981, claiming that it could be used to produce nuclear weapons.

Iraq and Iran expanded their war to the Persian Gulf in Apr. 1984. There were several attacks on oil tankers. An Iraqi warplane launched a missile attack on the U.S.S. *Stark,* a U.S. Navy frigate on patrol in the Persian Gulf, May 17, 1987; 37 U.S. sailors died. Iraq apologized for the attack, claiming it was inadvertent. The fierce war ended Aug. 1988, when Iraq accepted a UN resolution for a cease-fire.

Iraq attacked and overran Kuwait Aug. 2, 1990, sparking an international crisis. The United Nations, Aug. 6, imposed a ban on all trade with Iraq and called on member countries to protect the assets of the legitimate government of Kuwait. Iraq declared Kuwait its 19th province, Aug. 28. A campaign of looting, murder, and pillage was mounted against Kuwaiti civilians. Westerners caught in Iraq and Kuwait were initially held as hostages, but by the end of 1990, all were released.

A U.S.-led coalition launched air and missile attacks on Iraq, Jan. 16, 1991, after the expiration of a UN Security Council deadline for Iraq to withdraw from Kuwait. Iraq retaliated by firing scud missiles at Saudi Arabia and Israel. The coalition began a ground attack to retake Kuwait Feb. 23. Iraqi forces showed little resistance and were soundly defeated in 4 days. Some 175,000 Iraqis were taken prisoner, and casualties were estimated at over 85,000. As part of the cease-fire agreement, Iraq agreed to scrap all poison gas and germ weapons and allow UN observers to inspect the sites. UN trade sanctions would remain in effect until Iraq complied with all terms.

In the aftermath of the war, there were revolts against Pres. Saddam Hussein throughout Iraq. In Feb., Iraqi troops drove Kurdish insurgents and civilians to the Iran and Turkey borders, causing a refugee crisis. The U.S. and allies established havens inside Iraq for the Kurds.

Tensions heightened over the UN's efforts to dismantle Iraq's arms-production program, July 5, 1992, when a UN inspection team was denied entrance to a ministry building in Baghdad. Iraq allowed the team access July 26; the team found no arms-related evidence. In Feb. 1994, Iraq agreed to cooperate with the UN in inspection of long-range weapons. The Iraqi economy remained crippled by 4 years of trade sanctions.

The U.S. launched a missile attack aimed at Iraq's intelligence headquarters in Baghdad June 26, 1993. The U.S. justified the attack by citing evidence that Iraq had sponsored a plot to kill former Pres. George Bush during his visit to Kuwait in Apr. 1993.

Ireland

Eire

People: Population: 3,539,000. **Age distrib.** (%): <15: 27; 65+: 11. **Pop. density:** 130 per sq. mi. **Urban:** 56%. **Ethnic**

groups: Celtic, English minority. **Principal languages:** English predominates, Irish (Gaelic) spoken by minority. **Religions:** Roman Catholic 93%, Anglican 3%.

Geography: Area: 27,137 sq. mi. slightly larger than W Va. **Location:** In the Atlantic O. just W of Great Britain. **Neighbors:** United Kingdom (Northern Ireland). **Topography:** Ireland consists of a central plateau surrounded by isolated groups of hills and mountains. The coastline is heavily indented by the Atlantic O. **Capital:** Dublin. **Cities** (1991 est.): Dublin 477,000; Cork 127,000.

Government: Type: Parliamentary republic. **Head of State:** Pres. Mary Robinson; b May 21, 1944; in office: Dec. 3, 1990. **Head of government:** Prime Min. Albert Reynolds; b Nov. 3, 1935; in office: Feb. 11, 1992. **Local divisions:** 26 counties. **Defense:** 1.6% of GDP (1992).

Economy: Industries: Food processing, textiles, chemicals, brewing, machinery, tourism. **Chief crops:** Potatoes, grain, sugar beets, fruits, vegetables. **Minerals:** Zinc, lead, silver, gas. **Arable land:** 14%. **Livestock** (1991): cattle: 7.1 mln.; pigs: 1.0 mln.; sheep: 9.0 mln. **Fish catch** (1990): 230,000 metric tons. **Electricity prod.** (1992): 14.5 bln. kWh. **Labor force:** 14% agric.; 28% ind., 57% services.

Finance: Monetary unit: Punt (Mar. 1994: 0.70 = $1 US). **Gross domestic product** (1992): $42.4 bln.* **Per capita GDP:** $12,000. **Imports** (1991): $24.5 bln.; partners: UK 41%, U.S. 14%, other EU 25%. **Exports** (1991): $27.8 bln.; partners: UK 34%, other EU 40%, U.S. 8%. **Tourism** (1990): receipts: $1.4 bln. **National budget** (1992 est.): $16.6 bln. **International reserves less gold** (Mar. 1994): $6.3 bln. **Gold:** 360,000 oz t. **Consumer prices** (change in 1993): 1.4%.

Transport: Railroads: Length: 1,749 mi. **Motor vehicles:** in use: 836,000 passenger cars, 152,000 comm. vehicles. **Civil aviation:** 2.3 bln. passenger-mi.; 10 airports. **Chief ports:** Dublin, Cork.

Communications: Television sets: 1 per 3.5 persons. **Radios:** 1 per 1.8 persons. **Telephones:** 1 per 3.4 persons. **Daily newspaper circ.:** 159 per 1,000 pop.

Health: Life expectancy at birth (1994): 73 male; 79 female. **Births** (per 1,000 pop.): 14. **Deaths** (per 1,000 pop.): 9. **Natural increase:** .6%. **Hospital beds:** 1 per 255 persons. **Physicians:** 1 per 681 persons. **Infant mortality** (per 1,000 live births 1994): 7.

Education (1991): **Literacy:** 99%. **Years compulsory:** 9; attendance 91%.

Major International Organizations: UN (GATT, IMF, World Bank), EU, OECD.

Embassy: 2234 Massachusetts Ave. NW 20008; 462-3939.

Celtic tribes invaded the islands about the 4th century BC; their Gaelic culture and literature flourished and spread to Scotland and elsewhere in the 5th century AD, the same century in which St. Patrick converted the Irish to Christianity. Invasions by Norsemen began in the 8th century, ended with defeat of the Danes by the Irish King Brian Boru in 1014. English invasions started in the 12th century; for over 700 years the Anglo-Irish struggle continued with bitter rebellions and savage repressions.

The Easter Monday Rebellion (1916) failed but was followed by guerrilla warfare and harsh reprisals by British troops, the "Black and Tans." The Dail Eireann, or Irish parliament, reaffirmed independence in Jan. 1919. The British offered dominion status to Ulster (6 counties) and southern Ireland (26 counties) Dec. 1921. The constitution of the Irish Free State, a British dominion, was adopted Dec. 11, 1922. Northern Ireland remained part of the United Kingdom.

A new constitution adopted by plebiscite came into operation Dec. 29, 1937. It declared the name of the state Eire in the Irish language (Ireland in the English) and declared it a sovereign democratic state.

On Dec. 21, 1948, an Irish law declared the country a republic rather than a dominion and withdrew it from the Commonwealth. The British Parliament recognized both actions, 1949, but reasserted its claim to incorporate the 6 northeastern counties in the United Kingdom. This claim has not been recognized by Ireland. *(See United Kingdom — Northern Ireland.)*

Irish governments have favored peaceful unification of all Ireland. Ireland cooperated with Britain against terrorist groups. On Dec. 15, 1993, the Irish and British governments agreed on outlines of a peace plan to resolve the Northern Ireland issue. Much of it was rejected July 24, 1994, by Sinn Fein, the political wing of the Irish Republican Army, a terrorist group dedicated to the unification of Ireland. On Aug. 31, however, the I.R.A. issued a cease-fire announcement, saying that it would abandon warfare and would instead rely on peace talks and political means to accomplish its objectives.

Israel

State of Israel

Medinat Israel

People: Population: 5,051,000. **Age distrib.** (%): <15: 31; 65+: 9. **Pop. density:** 632 per sq. mi. **Urban:** 90%. **Ethnic groups:** Jewish 83%, non-Jewish (mostly Arab) 17%. **Principal languages:** Hebrew and Arabic (official). **Religions:** Jewish 82%, Muslim 14%.

Geography: Area: 7,992 sq. mi. about the size of New Jersey. **Location:** On eastern end of Mediterranean Sea. **Neighbors:** Lebanon on N, Syria, Jordan on E, Egypt on W. **Topography:** The Mediterranean coastal plain is fertile and well-watered. In the center is the Judean Plateau. A triangular-shaped semi-desert region, the Negev, extends from south of Beersheba to an apex at the head of the Gulf of Aqaba. The eastern border drops sharply into the Jordan Rift Valley, including Lake Tiberias (Sea of Galilee) and the Dead Sea, which is 1,312 ft. below sea level, lowest point on the earth's surface. **Capital:** Jerusalem. Most countries maintain their embassy in Tel Aviv. **Cities** (1992 est.): Jerusalem 544,000; Tel Aviv-Yafo 353,000; Haifa 251,000.

Government: Type: Republic. **Head of state:** Pres. Ezer Weizman; b June 15, 1924; in office: May 13, 1993. **Head of government:** Prime Min. Yitzhak Rabin; b Mar. 1, 1922; in office: July 13, 1992. **Local divisions:** 6 districts. **Defense:** 18% of GDP (1993 est.).

Economy: Industries: Diamond cutting, textiles, electronics, machinery, food processing. **Chief crops:** Citrus fruit, vegetables. **Minerals:** Potash, copper, phosphate, manganese, sulphur. **Arable land:** 17%. **Livestock** (1992): cattle: 349,000; sheep: 360,000. **Fish catch** (1991): 20,000 metric tons. **Electricity prod.** (1992): 21.8 bln. kWh. **Labor force:** 6% agric.; 23% ind., 29% public services.

Finance: Monetary unit: New Sheqalim (Mar. 1994: 2.97 = $1 US). **Gross domestic prod.** (1992): $57.4 bln.* **Per capita GDP:** $12,100. **Imports** (1991): $18.1 bln.; partners: U.S. 16%, W Ger. 13%, UK 9%. **Exports** (1991): $12.1 bln.; partners: U.S. 30%, W Ger. 5%, UK 7%. **Tourists** (1990): receipts $1.4 bln. **National budget** (1993): $36.8 bln. **International reserves less gold** (Feb. 1994): $6.1 bln. **Gold:** 9,000 oz t. **Consumer prices** (change in 1993): 10.9%.

Transport: Railroads: Length: 357 mi. **Motor vehicles:** in use: 848,000 passenger cars, 165,000 comm. vehicles. **Civil aviation:** 4.3 bln. passenger-mi.; 7 airports with scheduled flights. **Chief ports:** Haifa, Ashdod, Eilat.

Communications: Television sets: 1 per 3.5 persons. **Radios:** 1 per 2.3 persons. **Telephones:** 1 per 2.0 persons. **Daily newspaper circ.:** 261 per 1,000 pop.

Health: Life expectancy at birth (1994): 76 male; 80 female. **Births** (per 1,000 pop.): 21. **Deaths** (per 1,000 pop.): 6. **Natural increase:** 1.4%. **Hospital beds:** 1 per 177 persons. **Physicians:** 1 per 345 persons. **Infant mortality** (per 1,000 live births 1994): 9.

Education (1991): **Literacy:** 92% (Jewish), 70% (Arab).

Major International Organizations: UN (GATT).

Embassy: 3514 International Dr. NW 20008; 364-5500.

Occupying the SW corner of the ancient Fertile Crescent, Israel contains some of the oldest known evidence of agriculture and of primitive town life. A more advanced civilization emerged in the 3d millennium BC. The Hebrews probably arrived early in the 2d millennium BC. Under King David and his successors (c.1000 BC-597 BC), Judaism was developed and secured. After conquest by Babylonians, Persians, and Greeks, an independent Jewish kingdom was revived, 168 BC, but Rome took effective control in the next century, suppressed Jewish revolts in 70 AD and 135 AD, and renamed Judea Palestine, after the earlier coastal inhabitants, the Philistines.

Arab invaders conquered Palestine in 636. The Arabic language and Islam prevailed within a few centuries, but a Jewish minority remained. The land was ruled from the 11th century as a part of non-Arab empires by Seljuks, Mamluks, and Ottomans (with a crusader interval, 1098-1291).

After 4 centuries of Ottoman rule, during which the population declined to a low of 350,000 (1785), the land was taken in 1917 by Britain, which in the Balfour Declaration that year pledged to support a Jewish national homeland there, as foreseen by the Zionists. In 1920 a British Palestine Mandate was recognized; in 1922 the land east of the Jordan was detached.

Jewish immigration, begun in the late 19th century, swelled in the 1930s with refugees from the Nazis; heavy Arab immigration from Syria and Lebanon also occurred. Arab opposition to Jewish immigration turned violent in 1920, 1921, 1929, and 1936. The UN General Assembly voted in 1947 to partition Palestine into an Arab and a Jewish state. Britain withdrew in May 1948.

Israel was declared an independent state May 14, 1948; the Arabs rejected partition. Egypt, Jordan, Syria, Lebanon, Iraq, and Saudi Arabia invaded, but failed to destroy the Jewish state, which gained territory. Separate armistices with the Arab nations were signed in 1949; Jordan occupied the West Bank, Egypt occupied Gaza, but neither granted Palestinian autonomy.

After persistent terrorist raids, Israel invaded Egypt's Sinai, Oct. 29, 1956, aided briefly by British and French forces. A UN cease-fire was arranged Nov. 6.

An uneasy truce between Israel and the Arab countries, supervised by a UN Emergency Force, prevailed until May 19, 1967, when the UN force withdrew at the demand of Egypt's Pres. Gamal Abdel Nasser. Egyptian forces reoccupied the Gaza Strip and closed the Gulf of Aqaba to Israeli shipping. In a 6-day war that started June 5, the Israelis took the Gaza Strip, occupied the Sinai Peninsula to the Suez Canal, and captured East Jerusalem, Syria's Golan Heights, and Jordan's West Bank. The fighting was halted June 10 by UN-arranged cease-fire agreements.

Egypt and Syria attacked Israel, Oct. 6, 1973 (Yom Kippur, most solemn day on the Jewish calendar). Israel counterattacked, driving the Syrians back, and crossed the Suez Canal.

A cease-fire took effect Oct. 24; a UN peacekeeping force went to the area. A disengagement agreement was signed Jan. 18, 1974. Israel withdrew from the canal's west bank. A second withdrawal was completed in 1976; Israel returned the Sinai to Egypt in 1982.

Israeli forces raided Entebbe, Uganda, July 3, 1976, and rescued 103 hostages seized by Arab and German terrorists.

In 1977, the conservative opposition, led by Menachem Begin, was voted into office for the first time. Egypt's Pres. Anwar al-Sadat visited Jerusalem Nov. 1977, and on Mar. 26, 1979, Egypt and Israel signed a formal peace treaty, ending 30 years of war and establishing diplomatic relations.

Israel invaded S Lebanon, Mar. 1978, following a Lebanon-based terrorist attack in Israel. Israel withdrew in favor of a 6,000-man UN force, but continued to aid Christian militiamen. Violence on the Israeli-occupied West Bank rose in 1982 when Israel announced plans to build new Jewish settlements. Israel affirmed the entire city of Jerusalem as its capital, July 1980, encompassing the annexed East Jerusalem.

On June 7, 1981, Israeli jets destroyed an Iraqi atomic reactor near Baghdad that, Israel claimed, would have enabled Iraq to manufacture nuclear weapons.

Israeli jets bombed Palestine Liberation Organization (PLO) strongholds in Lebanon Apr.-May 1982. In reaction to the wounding of the Israeli ambassador to Great Britain, Israeli forces in a coordinated land, sea, and air attack invaded Lebanon, June 6, to destroy PLO strongholds in that country. Israeli forces encircled Beirut June 14. Following massive Israeli bombing of West Beirut, the PLO agreed to evacuate the city.

Israeli troops entered West Beirut after newly elected Lebanese Pres. Bashir Gemayel was assassinated on Sept. 14. Israel received widespread condemnation when Lebanese Christian forces, Sept. 16, entered two West Beirut refugee camps and slaughtered hundreds of Palestinian refugees.

In 1989, violence escalated over the Israeli military occupation of the West Bank and Gaza Strip; Palestinian protesters and Israeli troops clashed frequently. Israeli police and stone-throwing Palestinians clashed, Oct. 8, 1990, around the al-Aqsa mosque on the Temple Mount in Jerusalem. Some 20 Palestinians died.

During the Persian Gulf War, Iraq fired a series of scud missiles at Israel; most were intercepted by U.S. Patriot missiles. Israel agreed in Aug. 1991 to take part in a U.S.-Soviet sponsored Middle East peace conference.

The Labor Party of Yitzhak Rabin won a clear victory in elections held June 23, 1992. Rabin called for peace and reconciliation with Israel's Arab neighbors.

A Jewish gunman opened fire on Arab worshippers at a mosque in Hebron, Feb. 25, 1994, killing at least 29 before he himself was killed.

Ongoing peace talks produced historic agreements between Israel and the Palestine Liberation Organization in Sept. 1993. The latter recognized Israel's right to exist, and Israel recognized the PLO as the representative of the Palestinians; the two sides then signed, Sept. 13, an agreement for limited Palestinian self-rule in Gaza and in the West Bank, beginning with the city of Jericho. An accord formally initiating self-rule was signed in Cairo, May 4, 1994. Israel and Jordan signed, July 25, 1994, in Washington, DC, a declaration ending their 46-year state of war.

Gaza: Population (1994 est.): 731,000. **Area:** 140 sq. mi.

West Bank: Population (1994 est.): 1,444,000. **Area:** 2,270 sq. mi.

Italy

Italian Republic

Repubblica Italiana

People: Population: 58,138,000. **Age distrib.** (%): <15: 16; 65+: 15. **Pop. density:** 499 per sq. mi. **Urban:** 68%. **Ethnic groups:** Italians, small minorities of Germans, Slovenes, Albanians. **Principal languages:** Italian. **Religions:** Predominantly Roman Catholic.

Geography: Area: 116,333 sq. mi., about the size of Florida and Georgia combined. **Location:** In S Europe, jutting into Mediterranean S. **Neighbors:** France on W, Switzerland, Austria on N, Slovenia on E. **Topography:** Occupies a long boot-shaped peninsula, extending SE from the Alps into the Mediterranean, with the islands of Sicily and Sardinia offshore. The alluvial Po Valley drains most of N. The rest of the country is rugged and mountainous, except for intermittent coastal plains, like the Campania, S of Rome. Apennine Mts. run down through center of peninsula. **Capital:** Rome. **Cities** (1991 est.): Rome 2.8 mln.; Milan 1.4 mln.; Naples 1.2 mln.; Turin 1.0 mln.

Government: Type: Republic. **Head of state:** Pres. Oscar Luigi Scalfaro; b Sept. 9, 1918; in office: May 28, 1992. **Head of government:** Prime Min. Silvio Berlusconi; b Sept. 29, 1936; in office: May 11, 1994. **Local divisions:** 20 regions with some autonomy, 94 provinces. **Defense:** 2% of GDP (1992).

Economy: Industries: Steel, machinery, autos, textiles, shoes, machine tools, chemicals. **Chief crops:** Grapes, olives, citrus fruits, vegetables, wheat, rice. **Minerals:** Mercury, potash, sulphur. **Crude oil reserves** (1991): 700 mln. bbls. **Arable land:** 32%. **Livestock** (1992): cattle: 8.6 mln.; pigs: 9.5 mln.; sheep: 11.6 mln. **Fish catch** (1991): 355,000 metric tons. **Electricity prod.** (1992): 235 bln. kWh. **Labor force:** 10% agric.; 32% ind. and comm.; 58% services and govt.

Finance: Monetary unit: Lira (Mar. 1994: 1,667 = $1 US). **Gross domestic product** (1992): $1.01 bln.* **Per capita GDP:** $17,500. **Imports** (1991): $181 bln.; partners: EU 58%, Fr. 15%, U.S. 7%. **Exports** (1991): $170 bln.; partners: EU 58%. **Tourism** (1990): receipts $19.7 bln. **National budget** (1992 est.): $581 bln. **International reserves less gold** (Mar. 1994): $31.9 bln. **Gold:** 66.67 mln. oz t. **Consumer prices** (change in 1993): 4.2%.

Transport: Railroads: Length: 12,176 mi. **Motor vehicles:** in use: 28.2 mln. passenger cars, 2.5 mln. comm. vehicles. **Civil aviation:** 13.4 bln. passenger-mi.; 32 airports. **Chief ports:** Genoa, Venice, Trieste, Taranto, Naples, La Spezia.

Communications: Television sets: 1 per 3.4 persons. **Radios:** 1 per 3.8 persons. **Telephones:** 1 per 1.8 persons. **Daily newspaper circ.:** 107 per 1,000 pop.

Health: Life expectancy at birth (1994): 74 male; 81 female. **Births** (per 1,000 pop.): 11. **Deaths** (per 1,000 pop.): 10. **Natural increase:** .1%. **Hospital beds:** 1 per 153 persons. **Physicians:** 1 per 228 persons. **Infant mortality** (per 1,000 live births 1994): 8.

Education (1991): **Literacy:** 98%. **Years compulsory:** 8.

Major International Organizations: UN and all of its specialized agencies, NATO, OECD, EU.

Embassy: 1601 Fuller St. NW 20009; 328-5500.

Rome emerged as the major power in Italy after 500 BC, dominating the more civilized Etruscans to the N and Greeks to the S. Under the Empire, which lasted until the 5th century AD, Rome ruled most of Western Europe, the Balkans, the Near East, and North Africa. In 1988, archaeologists unearthed evidence showing Rome as a dynamic society in the 6th and 7th centuries BC.

After the Germanic invasions, lasting several centuries, a high civilization arose in the city-states of the N, culminating in the Renaissance. But German, French, Spanish, and Austrian intervention prevented the unification of the country. In 1859 Lombardy came under the crown of King Victor Emmanuel II of Sardinia. By plebiscite in 1860, Parma, Modena, Romagna, and Tuscany joined, followed by Sicily and Naples, and by the Marches and Umbria. The first Italian Parliament declared Victor Emmanuel king of Italy Mar. 17, 1861. Mantua and Venetia were added in 1866 as an outcome of the Austro-Prussian war. The Papal States were taken by Italian troops Sept. 20, 1870, on the withdrawal of the French garrison. The states were annexed to the kingdom by plebiscite. Italy recognized the State of Vatican City as independent Feb. 11, 1929.

Fascism appeared in Italy Mar. 23, 1919, led by Benito Mussolini, who took over the government at the invitation of the king Oct. 28, 1922. Mussolini acquired dictatorial powers. He made war on Ethiopia and proclaimed Victor Emmanuel III emperor, defied the sanctions of the League of Nations, sent troops to fight for Franco against the Republic of Spain, and joined Germany in World War II.

After Fascism was overthrown in 1943, Italy declared war on Germany and Japan and contributed to the Allied victory. It surrendered conquered lands and lost its colonies. Mussolini was killed by partisans Apr. 28, 1945. Victor Emmanuel III abdicated May 9, 1946; his son Humbert II was king until June 10, when Italy became a republic after a referendum, June 2-3.

Italy has enjoyed growth in industry and living standards since World War II, in part a result of membership in the European Community.

A wave of left-wing political violence began in the late 1970s with kidnappings and assassinations and continued into the 1980s. Christian Democratic leader and former Prime Min. Aldo Moro was murdered May 1978 by Red Brigade terrorists.

By mid-1991, some 20,000 Albanian refugees had entered Italy as the result of political unrest in their homeland. In Aug. an additional wave of 18,000 Albanians reached Italy. They were rounded up and sent back to Albania.

Italian voters in a referendum and Italy's Parliament approved, in 1993, electoral reforms, amid growing political corruption scandals. Under the reforms, most members of Parliament were to be elected from single districts, rather than in a proportional representation system that fragmented power among several major parties. In Mar. 27-28, 1994, elections, right-wing parties won a majority, dislodging Italy's long-powerful Christian Democratic Party; Silvio Berlusconi, an industrialist and head of the party Forza Italia, became premier.

Sicily, 9,926 sq. mi., pop. (1990) 5,172,000, is an island 180 by 120 mi., seat of a region that embraces the island of **Pantelleria,** 32 sq. mi., and the **Lipari** group, 44 sq. mi., 63 14,000, including 2 active volcanoes: **Vulcano,** 1,637 ft. and **Stromboli,** 3,038 ft. From prehistoric times Sicily has been settled by various peoples; a Greek state had its capital at Syracuse. Rome took Sicily from Carthage 215 BC. **Mt. Etna,** 11,053 ft. active volcano, is tallest peak.

Sardinia, 9,301 sq. mi., pop. (1990) 1,657,000, lies in the Mediterranean, 115 mi. W of Italy and 7½ mi. S of Corsica. It is 160 mi. long, 68 mi. wide, and mountainous, with mining of coal, zinc, lead, copper. In 1720 Sardinia was added to the possessions of the Dukes of Savoy in Piedmont and Savoy to form the Kingdom of Sardinia. Giuseppe Garibaldi is buried on the nearby isle of Caprera. **Elba,** 86 sq. mi., lies 6 mi. W of Tuscany. Napoleon I lived in exile on Elba 1814-1815.

Trieste. An agreement, signed Oct. 5, 1954, by Italy and Yugoslavia, confirmed, Nov. 10, 1975, gave Italy provisional administration over the northern section and the seaport of Trieste, and Yugoslavia the part of Istrian peninsula it has occupied.

Jamaica

People: Population: 2,555,000. **Age distrib.** (%): <15: 33; 65+: 8. **Pop. density:** 602 per sq. mi. **Urban:** 52%. **Ethnic groups:** African 76%, Afro-European 15%, Chinese, Caucasians, East Indians. **Principal languages:** English (official), Jamaican Creole. **Religions:** Protestant 56%.

Geography: Area: 4,244 sq. mi., slightly smaller than Connecticut. **Location:** In West Indies. **Neighbors:** Nearest are Cuba on N, Haiti on E. **Topography:** The country is four-fifths covered by mountains. **Capital:** Kingston. **Cities** (1991 est.): Kingston (met.) 587,000.

Government: Type: Parliamentary democracy. **Head of state:** Queen Elizabeth II, represented by Gov.-Gen. Howard Cooke; in office: Aug. 1, 1991. **Head of government:** Prime Min. Percival J. Patterson; in office: Mar. 30, 1992. **Local divisions:** 14 parishes; Kingston and St. Andrew corporate area. **Defense:** 1% of GDP (FY 1991-92).

Economy: Industries: Rum, molasses, mining, tourism. **Chief crops:** Sugar cane, coffee, bananas, coconuts, citrus fruits. **Minerals:** Bauxite, limestone, gypsum. **Arable land:** 19%. **Livestock** (1991): cattle: 250,000; goats: 440,000. **Electricity prod.** (1992): 2.7 bln. kWh. **Labor force:** 23% agric.; 41% services; 19% ind.

Finance: Monetary unit: Dollar (Dec. 1993: 31.26 = $1 US). **Gross domestic product** (1992): $3.7 bln. **Per capita GDP:** $1,500. **Imports** (1991): $1.8 bln.; partners: U.S. 48%. **Exports** (1991): $1.2 bln.; partners: U.S. 36%. **Tourism** (1990): receipts: $740 mln. **National budget** (1991): $736 mln. **Consumer prices** (change in 1992): 77.3%.

Transport: Railroads: Length: 129 mi. **Motor vehicles:** in use: 97,000 passenger cars, 18,000 comm. vehicles. **Civil aviation:** 888 mln. passenger-mi.; 4 airports with scheduled flights. **Chief ports:** Kingston, Montego Bay.

Communications: Television sets: 1 per 5.1 persons. **Radios:** 1 per 1.6 persons. **Telephones:** 1 per 13 persons. **Daily newspaper circ.:** 63 per 1,000 pop.

Health: Life expectancy at birth (1994): 72 male; 77 female. **Births** (per 1,000 pop.): 22. **Deaths:** (per 1,000 pop.): 6. **Natural increase:** 1.6%. **Hospital beds:** 1 per 457 persons. **Physicians:** 1 per 6,159 persons. **Infant mortality** (per 1,000 live births 1994): 17.

Education (1990): **Literacy:** 98%. Compulsory to age 14.

Major International Organizations: UN (World Bank, GATT), OAS.

Embassy: 1850 K St. NW 20006; 452-0660.

Jamaica was visited by Columbus, 1494, and ruled by Spain (under whom Arawak Indians died out) until seized by Britain, 1655. Jamaica won independence Aug. 6, 1962.

In 1974 Jamaica sought an increase in taxes paid by U.S. and Canadian bauxite mines. The socialist government acquired 50% ownership of the companies' Jamaican interests in 1976, and was reelected that year. Rudimentary welfare state measures were passed. Relations with the U.S. improved greatly in the 1980s following the election of Edward Seaga, which marked the beginning of a more conservative era.

Japan

Nippon

People: Population: 125,107,000. **Age distrib.** (%): <15: 17; 65+: 14. **Pop. density:** 857 per sq. mi. **Urban:** 77%. **Ethnic groups:** Japanese 99.4%, other (mostly Korean) 0.6%. **Principal languages:** Japanese. **Religions:** Buddhism, Shintoism shared by large majority.

Geography: Area: 145,850 sq. mi., slightly smaller than California. **Location:** Archipelago off E coast of Asia. **Neighbors:** USSR on N, S Korea on W. **Topography:** Japan consists of 4 main islands: Honshu ("mainland"), 87,805 sq. mi.; Hokkaido, 30,144 sq. mi.; Kyushu, 14,114 sq. mi.; and Shikoku, 7,049 sq. mi. The coast, deeply indented, measures 16,654 mi. The northern islands are a continuation of the Sakhalin Mts. The Kunlun range of China continues into southern islands, the ranges meeting in the Japanese Alps. In a vast transverse fissure crossing Honshu E-W rises a group of volcanoes, mostly extinct or inactive, including 12,388 ft. Fuji-San (Fujiyama) near Tokyo. **Capital:** Tokyo. **Cities** (1992 est.): Tokyo 8.1 mln.; Osaka 2.6 mln.; Yokohama 3.3 mln.; Nagoya 2.1 mln.; Kyoto 1.4 mln.; Kobe 1.5 mln.; Sapporo 1.7 mln.; Kitakyushu 1 mln.; Kawasaki 1.2 mln.; Fukuoka 1.2 mln.

Government: Type: Parliamentary democracy. **Head of state:** Emp. Akihito; b Dec. 23, 1933; in office: Jan. 7, 1989. **Head of government:** Prime Min. Tomiichi Murayama; b Mar. 23, 1924; in office: June 30, 1994. **Local divisions:** 47 prefectures. **Defense:** 0.94% of GDP (FY 1993-94 est.).

Economy: Industries: Electrical & electronic equip., autos, machinery, chemicals. **Chief crops:** Rice, grains, vegetables, fruits. **Minerals:** negligible. **Arable land:** 13%. **Livestock** (1992): cattle: 4.9 mln.; pigs: 10.9 mln. **Fish catch** (1991): 9.3 mln. metric tons. **Electricity prod.** (1992): 835 bln. kWh. **Labor**

force: 7% agric.; 33% manuf. & mining; 54% services & trade.

Finance: Monetary unit: Yen (Mar. 1994: 105 = $1 US). **Gross domestic product** (1992): $2.47 trl.* **Per capita GDP:** $19,800. **Imports** (1992): $233 bln.; partners: U.S. 22%, Middle East 26%, SE Asia 22%, EU 6%. **Exports** (1992): $339 bln.; partners: U.S. 33%, EU 20%, SE Asia 23%. **Tourism** (1990): $3.6 bln. receipts. **National budget** (1993): $579 bln. **International reserves less gold** (Mar. 1994): $104.7 bln. **Gold:** 24.23 mln. oz t. **Consumer prices** (change in 1993): 1.3%.

Transport: Railroads: Length: 23,690 mi. **Motor vehicles:** in use: 37.0 mln. passenger cars, 22.9 mln. comm. vehicles. **Civil aviation:** 59.2 bln. passenger-mi.; 71 airports with scheduled flights. **Chief ports:** Yokohama, Tokyo, Kobe, Osaka, Nagoya, Chiba, Kawasaki, Hakodate.

Communications: Television sets: 1 per 1.2 persons. **Radios:** 1 per 1.3 persons. **Telephones:** 1 per 1.8 persons. **Daily newspaper circ.:** 587 per 1,000 pop.

Health: Life expectancy at birth (1994): 76 male; 82 female. **Births** (per 1,000 pop.): 10. **Deaths** (per 1,000 pop.): 7. **Natural increase:** 0.3%. **Hospital beds:** 1 per 74 persons. **Physicians:** 1 per 588 persons. **Infant mortality** (per 1,000 live births 1994): 4.

Education (1991): **Literacy:** 99%. Most attend school for 12 years.

Major International Organizations: UN (IMF, GATT, ILO), OECD.

Embassy: 2520 Massachusetts Ave. NW 20008; 939-6700.

According to Japanese legend, the empire was founded by Emperor Jimmu, 660 BC, but earliest records of a unified Japan date from 1,000 years later. Chinese influence was strong in the formation of Japanese civilization. Buddhism was introduced before the 6th century.

A feudal system, with locally powerful noble families and their samurai warrior retainers, dominated from 1192. Central power was held by successive families of shoguns (military dictators), 1192-1867, until recovered by the Emperor Meiji, 1868. The Portuguese and Dutch had minor trade with Japan in the 16th and 17th centuries; U.S. Commodore Matthew C. Perry opened it to U.S. trade in a treaty ratified 1854. Japan fought China, 1894-95, gaining Taiwan. After war with Russia, 1904-05, Russia ceded S half of Sakhalin and gave concessions in China. Japan annexed Korea 1910. In World War I Japan ousted Germany from Shantung, took over German Pacific islands. Japan took Manchuria 1931, started war with China 1932. Japan launched war against the U.S. by attack on Pearl Harbor Dec. 7, 1941. Japan surrendered Aug. 14, 1945.

In a new constitution adopted May 3, 1947, Japan renounced the right to wage war; the emperor gave up claims to divinity; the Diet became the sole law-making authority.

The U.S. and 48 other non-communist nations signed a peace treaty and the U.S. a bilateral defense agreement with Japan, in San Francisco Sept. 8, 1951, restoring Japan's sovereignty as of April 28, 1952.

On June 26, 1968, the U.S. returned to Japanese control the Bonin Is., the Volcano Is. (including Iwo Jima) and Marcus Is. On May 15, 1972, Okinawa, the other Ryukyu Is., and the Daito Is. were returned to Japan by the U.S.; it was agreed the U.S. would continue to maintain military bases on Okinawa.

Industrialization was begun in the late 19th century. After World War II, Japan emerged as one of the most powerful economies in the world, and as a leader in technology.

The U.S. and EU member nations have criticized Japan for its restrictive policy on imports, which has given Japan a substantial trade surplus.

The Recruit scandal, the nation's worst political scandal since World War II, which involved illegal political donations and stock trading, led to the resignation of Premier Noboru Takeshita in May 1989. A series of scandals rocked Japan's financial sector in 1991.

Following new political scandals, the Liberal Democratic Party was denied a majority in general elections July 18, 1993. The LDP had held power since it was founded in 1955. Morihiro Hosokawa, a reformer, was chosen prime minister Aug. 6; he initiated reforms but resigned Apr. 8, 1994, because of controversy over his financial connections. His replacement, Tsutomu Hata, resigned June 25, to be replaced by Japan's first Socialist premier since 1947-48, Tomiichi Murayama.

Jordan

Hashemite Kingdom of Jordan

al Mamlaka al Urduniya al Hashemiyah

Population: 3,961,000. **Age distrib.** (%): <15: 41; 65+: 3. **Pop. density:** 115 per sq. mi. **Urban:** 70%. **Ethnic groups:** Arab 98%. **Principal languages:** Arabic (official). **Religions:** Sunni Muslim 92%, Christian 8%.

Geography: Area: 34,342 sq. mi., slightly larger than Indiana. **Location:** In W Asia. **Neighbors:** Israel on W, Saudi Arabia on S, Iraq on E, Syria on N. **Topography:** About 88% of Jordan is arid. Fertile areas are in W. Only port is on short Aqaba Gulf coast. Country shares Dead Sea (1,296 ft. below sea level) with Israel. **Capital:** Amman. **Cities** (1989 est.): Amman 936,000; az-Zarqa 318,000; Irbid 167,000.

Government: Type: Constitutional monarchy. **Head of state:** King Hussein I; b Nov. 14, 1935; in office: Aug. 11, 1952. **Head of government:** Prime Min. Abdel Salman al-Majali; in office: May 1993. **Local divisions:** 8 governorates. **Defense:** 7.9% of GDP (1993 est.).

Economy: Industries: Textiles, cement, food processing. **Chief crops:** Grains, olives, vegetables, fruits. **Minerals:** Phosphate, potash. **Arable land:** 4%. **Electricity prod.** (1992): 3.8 bln. kWh. **Labor force:** 20% agric. 20% manuf. & mining.

Finance: Monetary unit: Dinar (Mar. 1994: 1.00 = $1.43 US). **Gross domestic product** (1991): $3.6 bln. **Per capita GDP:** $1,100. **Imports** (1991): $2.3 bln.; partners: Saudi Ar. 6%, U.S. 11%, Jap. 8%. **Exports** (1991): $1.0 bln.; partners: Saudi Ar. 12%, Ind. 13%, Iraq. 18%. **Tourism** (1989): receipts: $546 mln. **National budget** (1992 est.): $1.9 bln. **International reserves less gold** (Mar. 1994): $458 mln. **Gold:** 793,000 oz t. **Consumer prices** (change in 1993): 4.7%.

Transport: Motor vehicles: in use: 173,000 passenger cars, 65,000 comm. vehicles. **Civil aviation:** 1.7 bln. passenger-mi.; 2 airports with scheduled flights. **Chief ports:** Aqaba.

Communications: Television sets: 1 per 15 persons. **Radios:** 1 per 5.2 persons. **Telephones:** 1 per 10 persons. **Daily newspaper circ.:** 56 per 1,000 pop.

Health: Life expectancy at birth (1994): 70 male; 74 female. **Births** (per 1,000 pop.): 39. **Deaths** (per 1,000 pop.): 4. **Natural increase:** 3.5%. **Hospital beds:** 1 per 571 persons. **Physicians:** 1 per 813 persons. **Infant mortality** (per 1,000 live births 1994): 32.

Education (1989): **Literacy:** 71%.

Major International Organizations: UN (WHO, IMF), Arab League.

Embassy: 3504 International Dr. NW 20008; 966-2664.

From ancient times to 1922 the lands to the E of the Jordan River were culturally and politically united with the lands to the W. Arabs conquered the area in the 7th century; the Ottomans took control in the 16th. Britain's 1920 Palestine Mandate covered both sides of the Jordan. In 1921, Abdullah, son of the ruler of Hejaz in Arabia, was installed by Britain as emir of an autonomous Transjordan, covering two-thirds of Palestine. An independent kingdom was proclaimed, 1946.

During the 1948 Arab-Israeli war the West Bank and East Jerusalem were added to the kingdom, which changed its name to Jordan. All these territories were lost to Israel in the 1967 war, which swelled the number of Arab refugees on the East Bank. A 1974 Arab summit conference designated the Palestine Liberation Organization as the sole representative of Arabs on the West Bank. In 1988 Jordan cut legal and administrative ties with the Israeli-occupied West Bank. Jordan and Israel signed, Sept. 14, 1993, a framework accord, intended to lead to a peace treaty, and officially agreed, July 25, 1994, to end their state of war.

Some 700,000 refugees entered Jordan following Iraq's invasion of Kuwait, Aug. 1990. Jordan was viewed as supporting Iraq during the 1990-1991 Persian Gulf crisis.

Kazakhstan

Republic of Kazakhstan

Kazak Respublikasy

People: Population: 17,268,000. **Pop. density:** 16 per sq. mi. **Urban:** 58%. **Ethnic groups:** Kazakh 42%, Russian 37%,

Ukrainian 5%, German 4%. **Principal languages:** Kazakh (official), Russian. **Religions:** Muslim 47%, Russian Orthodox 15%.

Geography: Area: 1,049,200 sq. mi. **Neighbors:** Russia on N, China on E, Kyrgyzstan, Uzbekistan, Turkmenistan on S, Caspian Sea on W. **Topography:** Extends from the lower reaches of Volga in Europe to the Altai Mtns. on the Chinese border. **Capital:** Almaty (Alma-Ata). **Cities** (1991): Almaty (Alma-Ata) 1.1 mln., Qaraghandy 608,000.

Government: Type: Republic. **Head of state:** Pres. Nursultan A. Nazarbayev; b July 6, 1940. **Head of government:** Prime Min. Sergei Tereshchenko. **Defense:** 3.8% of GDP (1992).

Economy: Industries: Steel, cement, footwear, textiles. **Chief crops:** Grain, cotton. **Minerals:** Coal, tungsten, copper, lead, zinc. **Livestock** (1992): cattle: 9.5 mln.; sheep and goats: 34.5 mln.; pigs: 2.9 mln.

Finance: Monetary unit: Ruble.

Transport: Railroads: Length: 13,200 mi. **Motor vehicles:** 734,000 passenger cars. **Civil aviation:** 7.8 bln. passenger-mi.; 6 airports with scheduled flights.

Communications: Television: 1 per 3.5 persons. **Radios:** 1 per 4.0 persons. **Telephones:** 1 per 4.8 persons. **Daily newspaper circ:** 512 per 1,000 pop.

Health: Life expectancy at birth (1994): 63 male; 73 female. **Birth rate** (per 1,000 pop.): 19. **Death rate** (per 1,000 pop.): 8. **Natural increase:** 1.1%. **Hospital beds:** 1 per 75 persons. **Physicians:** 1 per 254 persons. **Infant mortality** (per 1,000 live births 1994): 41.

Major International Organizations: UN, CIS.

Embassy: 3421 Massachusetts Ave. NW 20007; 333-4504.

The region came under the Mongols in the 13th century and gradually came under Russian rule, 1730-1853. It was admitted to the USSR as a constituent republic 1936. Kazakhstan declared independence Dec. 16, 1991. It became an independent state when the Soviet Union dissolved Dec. 26, 1991. The party chief, Nursultan Nazarbayev, was elected president unopposed. In legislative elections Mar. 7, 1994, criticized by international monitors, his party won a sweeping victory. Kazakhstan agreed, Feb. 14, to dismantle nuclear missiles and adhere to the 1968 Nuclear Nonproliferation Treaty; the U.S. pledged increased aid. A privatization program was launched Apr. 29.

Kenya

Republic of Kenya

Jamhuri ya Kenya

People: Population: 28,241,000. **Age distrib.** (%): <15: 49; 65+: 2. **Pop. density:** 125 per sq. mi. **Urban:** 25%. **Ethnic groups:** Kikuyu 21%, Luhya 14%, Luo 13%, Kalenjin 11%, Kamba 11%, others, including Asians, Arabs, Europeans. **Principal languages:** Swahili, English (both official), Kikuyu, Luhya, Luo, Meru. **Religions:** Roman Catholic 28%, Protestant 26%, indigenous beliefs 18%, Muslim 6%.

Geography: Area: 224,961 sq. mi., slightly smaller than Texas. **Location:** On Indian O. coast of E Africa. **Neighbors:** Uganda on W, Tanzania on S, Somalia on E, Ethopia, Sudan on N. **Topography:** The northern three-fifths of Kenya is arid. To the S, a low coastal area and a plateau varying from 3,000 to 10,000 ft. The Great Rift Valley enters the country N-S, flanked by high mountains. **Capital:** Nairobi. **Cities** (1987 est.): Nairobi 959,000; Mombasa 401,000.

Government: Type: Republic. **Head of state:** Pres. Daniel arap Moi, b. Sept. 1924; in office: Aug. 22, 1978. **Local divisions:** Nairobi and 7 provinces. **Defense:** 4.9% of GDP (1989 est.).

Economy: Industries: Tourism, light industry, petroleum prods. **Chief crops:** Coffee, corn, tea, cereals, cotton, sisal. **Minerals:** Gold, limestone, diatomite, salt, barytes, magnesite, feldspar, sapphires, fluorspar, garnets. **Other resources:** Timber, hides. **Arable land:** 3%. **Livestock** (1992): cattle: 11 mln. **Fish catch** (1991): 198,000 metric tons. **Electricity prod.** (1991): 2.8 bln. kWh. **Labor force:** 19% agric.; 55% service.

Finance: Monetary unit: Shilling (Mar. 1994: 66 = $1 US). **Gross domestic product** (1992): $8.3 bln. **Per capita GDP:** $320. **Imports** (1991): $1.9 bln.; partners: EU 45%. **Exports** (1991): $1.0 bln.; partners: EU 44%. **Tourism** (1992): receipts: $295 mln. **National budget** (1990): $2.8 bln. **International reserves less gold** (Oct. 1993): $146 mln. **Gold:** 80,000 oz t. **Consumer prices** (change in 1993): 45.8%.

Transport: Motor vehicles: in use: 157,000 passenger cars, 172,000 comm. vehicles. **Civil aviation:** 828 mln. passenger-mi.; 14 airports with scheduled flights. **Chief ports:** Mombasa.

Communications: Television sets: 1 per 104 persons. **Radios:** 1 per 6.4 persons. **Telephones:** 1 per 66 persons. **Daily newspaper circ.:** 15 per 1,000 pop.

Health: Life expectancy at birth (1994): 51 male; 55 female. **Births** (per 1,000 pop.): 42. **Deaths** (per 1,000 pop.): 12. **Natural increase:** 3.1%. **Hospital beds:** 1 per 734 persons. **Physicians:** 1 per 7,313 persons. **Infant mortality** (per 1,000 live births 1994): 74.

Education (1989): **Literacy:** 50%. 86% attend primary school.

Major International Organizations: UN and all of its specialized agencies, OAU, Commonwealth of Nations.

Embassy: 2249 R St. NW 20008; 387-6101.

Arab colonies exported spices and slaves from the Kenya coast as early as the 8th century. Britain obtained control in the 19th century. Kenya won independence Dec. 12, 1963, 4 years after the end of the violent Mau Mau uprising.

Kenya had steady growth in industry and agriculture under a modified private enterprise system, and enjoyed a relatively free political life. But stability was shaken in 1974-75, with opposition charges of corruption and oppression. Jomo Kenyatta, the country's leader since independence, died Aug. 22, 1978. He was succeeded by his vice-president, Daniel arap Moi.

Tribal clashes in the western provinces claimed thousands of lives in the early 1990s and left tens of thousands homeless. The unrest was the worst since independence in 1963. Several western nations issued travel advisories for Kenya.

In the 1990s, Kenya suffered from widespread unemployment and high inflation. Pres. Moi won a third term in Dec. 1992 elections, which were marred by wide-scale violence and charges of corruption.

Kiribati

Republic of Kiribati

People: Population: 78,000. **Pop. density:** 249 per sq. mi. **Ethnic groups:** nearly all Micronesian, some Polynesians. **Principal languages:** English (official), Gilbertese. **Religions:** evenly divided between Protestant and Roman Catholic.

Geography: Area: 313 sq. mi., approx. the size of New York City. **Location:** 33 Micronesian islands (the Gilbert, Line, and Phoenix groups) in the mid-Pacific scattered in a 2-mln. sq. mi. chain around the point where the International Date Line cuts the Equator. **Neighbors:** Nearest are Nauru to SW, Tuvalu and Tokelau Is. to S. **Topography:** except Banaba (Ocean) I., all are low-lying, with soil of coral sand and rock fragments, subject to erratic rainfall. **Capital** (1990): Tarawa 25,000.

Government: Type: Republic. **Head of state and government:** Pres. Teatao Teannaki; in office: July 3, 1991.

Economy: Industries: Copra. **Chief crops:** Coconuts, breadfruit, pandanus, bananas, paw paw. **Other resources:** Fish. **Electricity prod.** (1990): 13 mln. kWh.

Finance: Monetary unit: Australian dollar. **Gross domestic product** (1990): $36 mln. **Per capita GDP:** $525. **National budget** (1990 est.): $16.3 mln.

Transport: Chief port: Tarawa.

Communications: Radios: 1 per 7.5 persons. **Telephones:** 1 per 46 persons.

Health: Births (per 1,000 pop.): 32. **Deaths** (per 1,000 pop.): 12. **Natural increase:** 1.9%. **Hospital beds:** 1 per 253 persons. **Physicians:** 1 per 4,483 persons.

Education: Literacy (1985): 90%.

A British protectorate since 1892, the Gilbert and Ellice Islands colony was completed with the inclusion of the Phoenix Islands, 1937. Self-rule was granted 1971; the Ellice Islands separated from the colony 1975 and became independent Tuvalu, 1978. Kiribati (pronounced *Kiribass)* independence was attained July 12, 1979. Under a treaty of friendship the U.S. relinquished its claims to several of the Line and Phoenix islands, including Christmas (Kiritimati), Canton, and Enderbury.

Tarawa Atoll was the scene of some of the bloodiest fighting in the Pacific during World War II.

Korea, North
Democratic People's Republic of Korea
Chosun Minchu-chui Inmin Konghwa-guk

People: Population: 23,067,000. **Age distrib.** (%): <15: 29; 65+: 4. **Pop. density:** 486 per sq. mi. **Urban:** 60%. **Ethnic groups:** Korean. **Principal languages:** Korean. **Religions:** activities almost nonexistent; traditionally Buddhism, Confucianism, Chondogyo.

Geography: Area: 47,399 sq. mi., slightly smaller than Mississippi. **Location:** In northern E Asia. **Neighbors:** China, Russia on N, S Korea on S. **Topography:** Mountains and hills cover nearly all the country, with narrow valleys and small plains in between. The N and the E coast are the most rugged areas. **Capital:** Pyongyang. **Cities** (1987 est.): Pyongyang 2.3 mln.

Government: Type: Communist state. **Leader:** Kim Jong Il; b Feb. 16, 1948; in power: July 1994. **Local divisions:** 9 provinces, 3 special cities. **Defense:** 8% of GNP (1991 est.).

Economy: Industries: Textiles, petrochemicals, food processing. **Chief crops:** Corn, potatoes, fruits, vegetables, rice. **Minerals:** Coal, lead tungsten, graphite, magnesite, iron, copper, gold, phosphate, salt, fluorspar. **Arable land:** 18%. **Livestock** (1992): cattle: 1.3 mln.; pigs: 3.3 mln. **Fish catch** (1991): 1.7 mln. metric tons. **Electricity prod.** (1992): 26 bln. kWh. **Labor force:** 36% agric.

Finance: Monetary unit: Won (Mar. 1993: 2.15 = $1 US). **Gross national product** (1992): $22 bln.* **Per capita GNP:** $1,000. **Imports** (1990): $2.6 bln.; partners: China 17%, USSR 36%, Jap. 19%. **Exports** (1990): $2.0 bln.; partners: USSR 43%, China 13%, Jap. 15%. **National budget** (1992): $18.4 bln.

Communications: Television sets: 1 per 87 persons. **Radios:** 1 per 4.7 persons.

Transport: Chief ports: Chonglin, Hamhung, Nampo.

Health: Life expectancy at birth (1994): 67 male; 73 female. **Births** (per 1,000 pop.): 24. **Deaths** (per 1,000 pop.): 6. **Natural increase:** 1.8%. **Hospital beds:** 1 per 74 persons. **Physicians:** 1 per 370 persons. **Infant mortality** (per 1,000 live births 1994): 28.

Education (1991): **Literacy:** 99%. **Years compulsory:** 11.

Major International Organizations: UN.

The Democratic People's Republic of Korea was founded May 1, 1948, in the zone occupied by Russian troops after World War II. Its armies tried to conquer the south, 1950. After 3 years of fighting, with Chinese and U.S. intervention, a cease-fire was proclaimed.

Industry, begun by the Japanese during their 1910-45 occupation, and nationalized in the 1940s, had grown substantially, using N Korea's abundant mineral and hydroelectric resources.

In Mar. 1993, N Korea became the first nation to formally withdraw from the Nuclear Nonproliferation Treaty, the international pact designed to limit the spread of nuclear weapons. The nation suspended its withdrawal in June in reaction to threats of UN economic sanctions, but was widely believed to be developing nuclear weapons. The U.S. and N Korea reached an interim agreement, Aug. 13, 1994, intended to resolve the nuclear issue, and further negotiations followed

Kim Il Sung, who in 1948 had been one of the founders of the state of N Korea and who had ruled over it for more than 40 years, died July 8, 1994. He was apparently succeeded by his son, Kim Jong Il.

Korea, South
Republic of Korea
Taehan Min'guk

People: Population: 45,083,000. **Age distrib.** (%): <15: 24; 65+: 5. **Pop. density:** 1,176 per sq. mi. **Urban:** 74%. **Ethnic groups:** Korean. **Principal languages:** Korean. **Religions:** Christian 49%, Buddhist 47%.

Geography: Area: 38,330 sq. mi., slightly larger than Indiana. **Location:** In Northern E Asia. **Neighbors:** N Korea on N. **Topography:** The country is mountainous, with a rugged east coast. The western and southern coasts are deeply indented, with many islands and harbors. **Capital:** Seoul. **Cities** (1990 est.): Seoul 10.6 mln.; Pusan 3.8 mln.; Taegu 2.2 mln.; Inchon 1.8 mln.; Kwangju 1.1 mln.

Government: Type: Republic, with power centralized in a strong executive. **Head of state:** Pres. Kim Young Sam; b Dec. 20, 1927; in office: Feb. 25, 1993. **Head of government:** Prime Min. Lee Yung Duk; in office: Apr. 1994. **Local divisions:** 9 provinces and 6 special cities. **Defense:** 3.6% of GNP (1993 est.).

Economy: Industries: Electronics, ships, textiles, clothing, motor vehicles. **Chief crops:** Rice, barley, vegetables, wheat. **Minerals:** Tungsten, coal, graphite. **Arable land:** 21%. **Livestock** (1991): cattle: 2.1 mln.; pigs: 4.5 mln. **Fish catch:** (1991): 2.9 mln. metric tons. **Electricity prod.** (1992): 105 bln. kWh. **Labor force:** 21% agric.; 27% manuf. & mining; 52% services.

Finance: Monetary unit: Won (Mar. 1994: 807 = $1 US). **Gross national product** (1992): $287 bln.* **Per capita GNP:** $6,500. **Imports** (1992): $81 bln.; partners: Jap. 26%, U.S. 21%. **Exports** (1992): $72 bln.; partners: U.S. 26%, Jap. 18%. **Tourism** (1990): receipts: $3.5 bln. **National budget** (1993): $48.4 bln. **International reserves less gold** (Feb. 1994): $20.7 bln. **Gold:** 324,000 oz t. **Consumer prices** (change in 1993): 4.8%.

Transport: Railroads: Length: 4,092 mi. **Motor vehicles:** in use: 2.7 mln. passenger cars, 1.5 mln. comm. vehicles. **Civil aviation:** 12.4 bln. passenger-mi.; 12 airlines with scheduled flights. **Chief ports:** Pusan, Inchon.

Communications: Television sets: 1 per 5.0 persons. **Radios:** 1 per 1.0 persons. **Telephones:** 1 per 2.5 persons. **Daily newspaper circ.:** 280 per 1,000 pop.

Health: Life expectancy at birth (1994): 67 male; 74 female. **Births** (per 1,000 pop.): 16. **Deaths** (per 1,000 pop.): 6. **Natural increase:** 1.0%. **Hospital beds:** 1 per 429 persons. **Physicians:** 1 per 1,007 persons. **Infant mortality** (per 1,000 live births 1994): 22.

Education (1991): **Literacy:** 96%. **Attendance:** High school 90%, college 14%.

Major International Organizations: UN.

Embassy: 2370 Massachusetts Ave. NW 20008; 939-5600.

Korea, once called the Hermit Kingdom, has a recorded history since the 1st century BC. It was united in a kingdom under the Silla Dynasty, 668 AD. It was at times associated with the Chinese empire; the treaty that concluded the Sino-Japanese war of 1894-95 recognized Korea's complete independence. In 1910 Japan forcibly annexed Korea as Chosun.

At the Potsdam conference, July, 1945, the 38th parallel was designated as the line dividing the Soviet and the American occupation. Russian troops entered Korea Aug. 10, 1945, U.S. troops entered Sept. 8, 1945. The Soviet military organized socialists and Communists and blocked efforts to let the Koreans unite their country. *(See Index for Korean War.)*

The South Koreans formed the Republic of Korea in May 1948 with Seoul as the capital. Dr. Syngman Rhee was chosen president, but a movement spearheaded by college students forced his resignation Apr. 26, 1960.

In an army coup May 16, 1961, Gen. Park Chung Hee became chairman of the ruling junta. He was elected president, 1963; a 1972 referendum allowed him to be reelected for 6-year terms unlimited times. Park was assassinated by the chief of the Korean CIA, Oct. 26, 1979. The calm of the new government was halted by the rise of Gen. Chun Doo Hwan, head of the military intelligence, who reinstated martial law.

In July 1972 South and North Korea agreed on a common goal of reunifying the 2 nations by peaceful means. But there was no sign of a thaw in relations between the two regimes until 1985, when they agreed to discuss economic issues. In 1988, radical students demanding reunification clashed with police.

On June 10, 1987, middle-class office workers, shopkeepers, and business executives joined students in antigovernment protests in Seoul calling for democratic reforms. Following weeks of rioting and violence, Chun, July 1, agreed to permit election of the next president by direct popular vote and other constitutional reforms. In Dec., Roh Tae Woo was elected president. In 1990, the nation's 3 largest political parties merged; some 100,000 students demonstrated, charging that the merger was undemocratic.

Kim Young Sam took office in 1993 as the first civilian president since 1961.

Kuwait
State of Kuwait
Dowlat al-Kuwait

People: Population: 1,819,000. **Age distrib.** (%): <15: 43; 65+: 2. **Pop. density:** 264 per sq. mi. **Urban:** 95%. **Ethnic**

groups: Kuwaiti 45%, other Arab 35%, Iranians, Indians, Pakistanis. **Principal languages:** Arabic (official). **Religions:** Muslim 85%.

Geography: Area: 6,880 sq. mi., slightly smaller than New Jersey. **Location:** In Middle East, at N end of Persian Gulf. **Neighbors:** Iraq on N, Saudi Arabia on S. **Topography:** The country is flat, very dry, and extremely hot. **Capital:** Kuwait City. **Cities** (1985 est.): Hawalli 145,000; as-Salimiyah 153,000.

Government: Type: Constitutional monarchy. **Head of state:** Emir Sheikh Jabir al-Ahmad al-Jabir as-Sabah; b 1928; in office: Jan. 1, 1978. **Head of government:** Prime Min. Sheikh Saad Abdulla as-Salim as-Sabah; in office: Feb. 8, 1978. **Local divisions:** 5 governorates. **Defense:** 7.3% of GDP (1993).

Economy: Industries: Oil products. **Minerals:** Oil, gas. **Crude oil reserves** (1990): 94 bln. barrels. **Cultivated land:** 1%. **Electricity prod.** (1991): 3.1 bln. kWh. **Labor force:** social services 45%; construction 20%.

Finance: Monetary unit: Dinar (Mar. 1994: 1.00 = $3.36 US). **Gross domestic product** (1992): $15.3 bln. **Per capita GDP:** $11,000. **Imports** (1991): $4.7 bln.; partners: Jap. 21%, U.S. 9%. **Exports** (1989): $11.4 bln.; partners: Jap. 16%, It. 10%. **Tourism** (1990): $180 mln. receipts. **National budget** (1992): $21 bln. **International reserves less gold** (Mar. 1994): $4.1 bln. **Gold:** 2.53 mln. oz t.

Transport: Motor vehicles: in use: 500,000 passenger cars, 110,000 comm. vehicles. **Civil aviation:** 1.1 bln. passenger-mi.; 1 airport with scheduled flights. **Chief ports:** Mina al-Ahmadi.

Communications: Television sets: 1 per 1.5 persons. **Radios:** 1 per 1.4 persons. **Telephones:** 1 per 5.5 persons. **Daily newspaper circ.:** 221 per 1,000 pop.

Health: Life expectancy at birth (1994): 73 male; 77 female. **Births** (per 1,000 pop.): 29. **Deaths** (per 1,000 pop.): 2. **Natural increase:** 2.7%. **Hospital beds:** 1 per 347 persons. **Physicians:** 1 per 515 persons. **Infant mortality** (per 1,000 live births 1994): 13.

Education (1989): **Literacy:** 71%. **Years compulsory:** 8.

Major International Organizations: UN (World Bank, IMF, GATT), Arab League, OPEC.

Embassy: 2940 Tilden St. NW 20008; 966-0702.

Kuwait is ruled by the Al-Sabah dynasty, founded 1759. Britain ran foreign relations and defense from 1899 until independence in 1961. The majority of the population is non-Kuwaiti, with many Palestinians, and cannot vote.

Oil is the fiscal mainstay, providing most of Kuwait's income. Oil pays for free medical care, education, and social security. There are no taxes, except customs duties.

Kuwaiti oil tankers came under frequent attack by Iran because of Kuwait's support of Iraq in the Iran-Iraq War. In July 1987, U.S. Navy warships began escorting Kuwaiti tankers in the Persian Gulf.

Kuwait was attacked and overrun by Iraqi forces Aug. 2, 1990. The emir and senior members of the ruling family fled to Saudi Arabia to establish a government in exile. On Aug. 28, Iraq announced that Kuwait was its 19th province. Following several weeks of aerial attacks on Iraq and Iraqi forces in Kuwait, a U.S.-led coalition began a ground attack Feb. 23, 1991. By Feb. 27, Iraqi forces were routed and Kuwait liberated. Following liberation, there were reports of abuse of Palestinians and others suspected of collaborating with Iraqi occupiers.

Former U.S. Pres. George Bush visited Kuwait, Apr. 14-16, 1993, and was honored as the leader of the Persian Gulf War alliance that expelled Iraqi troops. Kuwaiti authorities arrested 14 Iraqis and Kuwaitis for allegedly plotting to assassinate Bush during his visit. Thirteen were convicted and sentenced to prison or death, June 4, 1994.

Kyrgyzstan

Republic of Kyrgyzstan

Kyrgyz Respublikasy

People: Population: 4,698,000. **Pop density:** 61 per sq. mi. **Urban:** 37%. **Ethnic groups:** Kirghiz 52%, Russian 22%, Uzbek 13%. **Principal languages:** Kirghiz (official), Russian. **Religions:** Muslim 70%.

Geography: Area: 76,642 sq. mi. **Neighbors:** Kazakhstan on N, China on E, Uzbekistan on W, Tajikistan on S. **Capital:** Bishkek. **Cities** (1991): Bishkek 631,000; Osh 218,000.

Government: Type: Republic. **Head of state:** Pres. Askar Akayev; b 1944. **Head of government:** Prime Min. Apas Jumagulov; in office: Dec. 1993. **Local divisions:** 6 oblasts.

Economy: Industries: Tanning, tobacco, textiles, mining. **Chief crops:** Wheat, sugar beets, tobacco. **Livestock** (1992): cattle: 1.2 mln.; sheep and goats: 9.5 mln.

Finance: Monetary unit: Som (May 1993): 1.00 = $.24 US.

Transport: Railroads: Length: 490 mi. **Motor vehicles:** in use: 173,000 passenger cars. **Civil aviation:** 2.3 bln. passenger-mi.; 1 airport.

Communications: Telephones: 1 per 12 persons. **Daily newspaper circ.:** 367 per 1,000 pop.

Health: Life expectancy at birth (1994): 64 male; 72 female. **Birth rate** (per 1,000 pop.): 26. **Death rate** (per 1,000 pop.): 7. **Natural increase:** 1.9%. **Hospital beds:** 1 per 82 persons. **Physicians:** 1 per 271 persons. **Infant mortality** (per 1,000 live births 1994): 47.

Major International Organizations: UN (IMF), CIS.

The region was inhabited around the 13th century by the Kirghiz. It was annexed to Russia 1864. After 1917, it was nominally a Kara-Kirghiz autonomous area, which was reorganized 1926, and made a constituent republic of the USSR in 1936. Kyrgyzstan declared independence Aug. 31, 1991. It became an independent state when the USSR disbanded Dec. 26, 1991.

Laos

Lao People's Democratic Republic

Sathalanalat Paxathipatai Paxaxon Lao

People: Population: 4,702,000. **Pop. density:** 51 per sq. mi. **Urban:** 19%. **Ethnic groups:** Lao 50%, tribal Thai 20%, Phoutheung 15%, Meo, Hmong, Yao, others. **Principal languages:** Lao (official), French, English. **Religions:** Buddhist 85%, animist and other 15%.

Geography: Area: 91,429 sq. mi., slightly larger than Utah. **Location:** In Indochina Peninsula in SE Asia. **Neighbors:** Myanmar, China on N, Vietnam on E, Cambodia on S, Thailand on W. **Topography:** Landlocked, dominated by jungle. High mountains along the eastern border are the source of the E-W rivers slicing across the country to the Mekong R., which defines most of the western border. **Capital:** Vientiane. **Cities** (1985 cen.): Vientiane 377,000.

Government: Type: Communist. **Head of state:** Pres. Nouhak Phoumsavan; in office: Nov. 25, 1992. **Head of government:** Prime Min. Khamtai Siphandon; in office: Aug. 15, 1991. **Local divisions:** 17 provinces, 1 municipality. **Defense:** 6.1% of GDP (1992).

Economy: Industries: Wood products, mining. **Chief crops:** Rice, corn, tobacco, cotton, opium, citrus fruits, coffee. **Minerals:** Tin. **Other resources:** Forests. **Arable land:** 4%. **Livestock** (1991): pigs: 1.3 mln. **Fish catch** (1990): 20,000 metric tons. **Electricity prod.** (1992): 990 mln. kWh. **Labor force:** 85% agric.; 6% ind.

Finance: Monetary unit: New kip (Dec. 1992: 714 = $1 US). **Gross domestic product** (1991): $900 mln. **Per capita GDP:** $200. **Imports** (1990): $240 mln.; partners: Thai. 45%, Jap. 20%. **Exports** (1990): $72 mln.; partners: Thai, Viet, USSR.

Transport: Motor vehicles: in use: 21,000 passenger cars, 14,000 comm. vehicles.

Communications: Radios: 1 per 10 persons.

Health: Life expectancy at birth (1994): 50 male; 53 female. **Births** (per 1,000 pop.): 43. **Deaths** (per 1,000 pop.): 15. **Natural increase:** 2.8%. **Hospital beds:** 1 per 402 persons. **Physicians:** 1 per 3,555 persons. **Infant mortality** (per 1,000 live births 1994): 102.

Education: (1991): **Literacy:** 45%.

Major International Organizations: UN (FAO, IMF, WHO).

Embassy: 2222 S St. NW 20008; 332-6416.

Laos became a French protectorate in 1893, but regained independence as a constitutional monarchy July 19, 1949.

Conflicts among neutralist, communist, and conservative factions created a chaotic political situation. Armed conflict increased after 1960.

The 3 factions formed a coalition government in June 1962, with neutralist Prince Souvanna Phouma as premier. A 14-nation conference in Geneva signed agreements, 1962, guaranteeing neutrality and independence. By 1964 the Pathet Lao had withdrawn from the coalition, and, with aid from N

Vietnamese troops, renewed sporadic attacks. U.S. planes bombed the Ho Chi Minh trail, supply line from N Vietnam to Communist forces in Laos and S Vietnam.

In 1970 the U.S. stepped up air support and military aid. After Pathet Lao military gains, Souvanna Phouma in May 1975 ordered government troops to cease fighting; the Pathet Lao took control. A Lao People's Democratic Republic was proclaimed Dec. 3, 1975.

Latvia
Republic of Latvia
Latvijas Republika

People: Population: 2,749,000. **Pop density:** 110 per sq. mi. **Urban:** 70%. **Ethnic groups:** Latvian 52%, Russian 34%. **Principal languages:** Latvian (official), Lithuanian, Russian. **Religions:** Lutheran, Roman Catholic, Russian Orthodox.

Geography: Area: 24,900 sq. mi., slightly larger than W Va. **Neighbors:** Estonia & Baltic Sea on N., Baltic Sea on W., Lithuania & Belarus on S., Russia on E. **Capital:** Riga. **Cities** (1992): Riga 897,000.

Government: Type: Republic. **Head of state:** Pres. Guntis Ulmanis; in office: July 1993. **Head of government:** Prime Min. Valdis Birkavs; in office: Aug. 3, 1993. **Local divisions:** 26 districts, 56 towns, 37 urban settlements.

Economy: Industries: Electric railway passenger cars, paper. **Chief crops:** oats, barley, potatoes. **Livestock** (1991): cattle 1.3 mln. **Arable land:** 27%. **Electricity prod.** (1992): 5.8 bln. kWh. **Labor force:** 16% agric. & forestry; 41% ind. & comm.

Finance: Monetary unit: Lat. **Imports** (1990): $9.0 bln. **Exports** (1990): $239 mln.

Transport: Railroads: Length: 1,489 mi. **Motor vehicles:** in use: 328,000 passenger cars, 14,000 comm. vehicles. **Civil aviation:** 3.7 bln. passenger-mi.; 1 airport. **Chief port:** Riga.

Communications: Television sets: 1 per 2.2 persons. **Radios:** 1.9 per household. **Telephones:** 1 per 3.2 persons. **Daily newspaper circ.:** 1,637 per 1,000 pop.

Health: Life expectancy at birth (1994): 64 male, 75 female. **Births** (per 1,000 pop.): 14. **Deaths** (per 1,000 pop.): 13. **Natural increase:** .1%. **Hospital beds:** 1 per 74 persons. **Physicians:** 1 per 219 persons. **Infant mortality rates** (per 1,000 live births 1994): 22.

Embassy: 4325 17th St. NW 20011; 726-8213.

Prior to 1918, Latvia was occupied by the Russians and Germans. It was an independent republic, 1918-39. The Aug. 1939 Soviet-German agreement assigned it to the Soviet sphere of influence. It was officially accepted as part of the USSR on Aug. 5, 1940. It was overrun by the German army, but retaken in 1945.

During an abortive Soviet coup, Latvia declared independence, Aug. 21, 1991. The Soviet Union recognized Latvia's independence in Sept. 1991. The last Russian troops in Latvia withdrew by Aug. 31, 1994.

Lebanon
Republic of Lebanon
al-Jumhouriya al-Lubnaniya

People: Population: 3,620,000. **Age distrib.** (%): <15: 33; 65+: 5. **Pop. density:** 916 per sq. mi. **Urban:** 86%. **Ethnic groups:** Arab 95%, Armenian 4%. **Principal languages:** Arabic, French (both official). **Religions:** Muslim 70%, Christian 30%.

Geography: Area: 3,950 sq. mi., smaller than Connecticut. **Location:** On Eastern end of Mediterranean Sea. **Neighbors:** Syria on E Israel on S. **Topography:** There is a narrow coastal strip, and 2 mountain ranges running N-S enclosing the fertile Beqaa Valley. The Litani R. runs S through the valley, turning W to empty into the Mediterranean. **Capital:** Beirut. **Cities** (1991 est.): Beirut 1.1 mln.; Tripoli 240,000.

Government: Type: Republic. **Head of state:** Pres. Elias Hrawi; b 1930; in office: Nov. 24, 1989. **Head of government:** Prime Min. Rafiq al-Hariri; in office: Oct. 31, 1992. **Local divisions:** 5 governorates. **Defense:** 8.2% of GDP (1992).

Economy: Industries: Trade, food products, textiles, cement, oil products. **Chief crops:** Fruits, olives, tobacco, grapes, vegetables, grains. **Minerals:** Iron. **Arable land:** 21%. **Livestock** (1992): goats: 465,000; sheep: 230,000. **Electricity prod.** (1992): 3.4 bln. kWh. **Labor force:** 11% agric.; 79% ind., comm., services.

Finance: Monetary unit: Pound (Mar. 1994: 1,697 = $1 US). **Gross domestic product** (1991): $4.8 bln. **Per capita GDP:** $1,400. **Imports** (1990): $1.9 bln.; partners: It. 15%, Fr. 10%, U.S. 6%. **Exports** (1990): $700 mln.; partners: Saudi Ar. 16%, Jor. 6%, Kuw. 8%. **National budget** (1991): $1.3 bln. **International reserves less gold** (Mar. 1994): $3.3 bln. **Gold:** 9.22 mln. oz t.

Transport: Motor vehicles: in use: 473,000 passenger cars, 50,000 comm. vehicles. **Civil aviation:** 934 mln. passenger-mi.; 2 airports with scheduled flights. **Chief ports:** Beirut, Tripoli, Sidon.

Communications: Television sets: 1 per 2.5 persons. **Radios:** 1 per 1.3 persons. **Telephones:** 1 per 9.1 persons. **Daily newspaper circ.:** 118 per 1,000 pop.

Health: Life expectancy at birth (1994): 67 male; 72 female. **Births** (per 1,000 pop.): 28. **Deaths** (per 1,000 pop.): 7. **Natural increase:** 2.1%. **Hospital beds:** 1 per 263 persons. **Physicians:** 1 per 771 persons. **Infant mortality** (per 1,000 live births 1994): 40.

Education: (1991): **Literacy:** 75%. **Years compulsory:** 5; attendance 93%.

Major International Organizations: UN (IMF, ILO, WHO).

Embassy: 2560 28th St. NW 20008; 939-6300.

Formed from 5 former Turkish Empire districts, Lebanon became an independent state Sept. 1, 1920, administered under French mandate 1920-41. French troops withdrew in 1946.

Under the 1943 National Covenant, all public positions were divided among the various religious communities, with Christians in the majority. By the 1970s, Muslims became the majority and demanded a larger political and economic role.

U.S. Marines intervened, May-Oct. 1958, during a Syrian-aided revolt. Continued raids against Israeli civilians, 1970-75, brought Israeli attacks against guerrilla camps and villages. Israeli troops occupied S Lebanon, Mar. 1978, and again in Apr. 1980.

An estimated 60,000 were killed and billions of dollars in damage inflicted in a 1975-76 civil war. Palestinian units and leftist Muslims fought against the Maronite militia, the Phalange, and other Christians. Several Arab countries provided political and arms support to the various factions, while Israel aided Christian forces. Up to 15,000 Syrian troops intervened in 1976, and fought Palestinian groups. Arab League troops from several nations tried to impose a cease-fire.

Clashes between Syrian troops and Christian forces erupted, Apr. 1, 1981, bringing to an end the cease-fire. By Apr. 22, fighting had also broken out between two Muslim factions. In July, Israeli air raids on Beirut killed or wounded some 800 persons.

Israeli forces invaded Lebanon June 6, 1982, in a coordinated land, sea, and air attack aimed at crushing strongholds of the Palestine Liberation Organization (PLO). Israeli and Syrian forces engaged in the Bekaa Valley. By June 14, Israeli troops had encircled Beirut. On Aug. 21, the PLO evacuated west Beirut following massive Israeli bombings of the city. Israeli troops entered west Beirut following the Sept. 14 assassination of newly elected Lebanese Pres. Bashir Gemayel. On Sept. 16, Lebanese Christian troops entered 2 refugee camps and massacred hundreds of Palestinian refugees. Israeli troops withdrew from Lebanon in June 1985.

In 1983, terrorist bombings became a way of life in Beirut as some 50 people were killed in an explosion at the U.S. Embassy, Apr. 18; 241 U.S. servicemen and 58 French soldiers died in separate Muslim suicide attacks, Oct. 23.

There was heavy fighting between Shiite militiamen and Palestinian guerrillas in May 1985. In June, Beirut Airport was the scene of a hostage crisis where Shiite terrorists held U.S. citizens for 17 days. Fierce artillery duels between Christian east Beirut and Muslim west Beirut, Mar.-Apr. 1989, left some 200 dead and 700 wounded.

Kidnapping of foreign nationals by Islamic militants became common in the 1980s. U.S., British, French, and Soviet citizens were victims. All were released by 1992.

A treaty signed May 22, 1991, between Lebanon and Syria recognized Lebanon as a separate and independent state for the first time since the 2 countries gained independence in 1943.

Israeli forces conducted air raids and artillery strikes against guerrilla bases and villages in S Lebanon, causing over 200,000 to flee their homes July 25-29, 1993.

Lesotho
Kingdom of Lesotho

People: Population: 1,944,000. **Age distrib.** (%): <15: 41; 65+: 4. **Pop. density:** 166 per sq. mi. **Ethnic groups:** Sotho

99.7%. **Principal languages:** English (official), Sesotho. **Religions:** Christian 80%.

Geography: Area: 11,716 sq. mi., slightly larger than Maryland. **Location:** In Southern Africa. **Neighbors:** Completely surrounded by Republic of South Africa. **Topography:** Landlocked and mountainous, with altitudes ranging from 5,000 to 11,000 ft. **Capital:** Maseru. **Cities** (1990 est.): Maseru 109,000.

Government: Type: Parliamentary democracy under constitutional monarchy. **Head of state:** King Letsie 3d; in office: Nov. 12, 1990. **Head of government:** Government run by provisional council, pending elections. **Local divisions:** 10 districts. **Defense:** 13% of GDP (1990 est.).

Economy: Industries: Food processing. **Chief crops:** Corn, grains, peas, beans. **Other resources:** Diamonds. **Arable land:** 10%. **Labor force:** 40% agric.

Finance: Monetary unit: Maloti (Mar. 1994: 1.00 = $.28 US). **Gross domestic product** (1991): $620 mln. **Per capita GDP:** $340. **Imports** (1990): $600 mln.; partners: Mostly So. Afr. **Exports** (1990): $60 mln.; partners: Mostly So. Afr. **National budget** (1993): $399 mln.

Transport: Motor vehicles: in use: 6,000 passenger cars, 15,000 comm. vehicles.

Communications: Radios: 1 per 4.4 persons. **Daily newspaper circ.:** 11 per 1,000 pop.

Health: Life expectancy at birth (1994): 60 male; 64 female. **Births** (per 1,000 pop.): 34. **Deaths** (per 1,000 pop.): 9. **Natural increase:** 2.5%. **Hospital beds:** 1 per 672 persons. **Physicians:** 1 per 15,728 persons. **Infant mortality** (per 1,000 live births 1994): 70.

Education (1990): **Literacy:** 59%.

Major International Organizations: UN (IMF, UNESCO, WHO), OAU.

Embassy: 2511 Massachusetts Ave. NW 20008; 797-5534.

Lesotho (once called Basutoland) became a British protectorate in 1868 when Chief Moshesh sought protection against the Boers. Independence came Oct. 4, 1966. Elections were suspended in 1970. Most of Lesotho's GNP is provided by citizens working in S Africa. Livestock raising is the chief industry; diamonds are the chief export.

S Africa imposed a blockade, Jan. 1, 1986, because of Lesotho's giving sanctuary to rebel groups fighting to overthrow the S African government. The blockade sparked a Jan. 20 military coup, and was lifted, Jan. 25, when the new leaders agreed to expel the rebels.

In 1990, King Moshoeshoe was sent into exile by the military government. In Mar. 1993, Ntsu Mokhehle, a civilian, was elected prime minister, ending 23 years of military rule. Rival army factions engaged in heavy street fighting Jan. 1994. In Apr., mutinous soldiers kidnapped 4 government ministers and killed a deputy prime minister. After new disturbances, the king dissolved Parliament Aug. 17, pending elections.

Liberia

Republic of Liberia

People: Population: 2,973,000. **Age distrib.** (%): <15: 45; 65+: 4. **Pop. density:** 77 per sq. mi. **Urban:** 43%. **Ethnic groups:** indigenous tribes 95%, Americo-Liberians 5%. **Principal languages:** English (official), tribal dialects. **Religions:** traditional beliefs 70%, Muslim 20%, Christian 10%.

Geography: Area: 38,250 sq. mi., slightly smaller than Pennsylvania. **Location:** On SW coast of W Africa. **Neighbors:** Sierra Leone on W, Guinea on N, Côte d'Ivoire on E. **Topography:** Marshy Atlantic coastline rises to low mountains and plateaus in the forested interior; 6 major rivers flow in parallel courses to the ocean. **Capital:** Monrovia. **Cities** (1987 est.): Monrovia 400,000.

Government: Type: In transition. **Head of state:** David Kpormakor, head of transitional Council of State; in office: Mar. 7, 1994. **Local divisions:** 13 counties. **Defense:** 3.8% of GDP (1987).

Economy: Industries: Food processing, mining. **Chief crops:** Rice, cassava, coffee, cocoa, sugar. **Minerals:** Iron, diamonds, gold. **Other resources:** Rubber, timber. **Arable land:** 1%. **Fish catch** (1991): 9,620 metric tons. **Electricity prod.** (1991): 750 mln. kWh. **Labor force:** 71% agric.

Finance: Monetary unit: Dollar (Mar. 1994: 1.00 = $1 US). **Gross national product** (1989): $1.0 bln. **Per capita GNP:** $440. **Imports** (1989): $394 mln.; partners: U.S. 32%, W Ger. 10%, Jap. 6%, Neth. 7%. **Exports** (1989): $505 mln.; partners: W Ger. 31%, U.S. 20%, It. 14%, Fr. 9%. **National budget** (1989): $435 mln.

Transport: Motor vehicles: in use: 7,000 passenger cars, 4,000 comm. vehicles. **Chief ports:** Monrovia, Buchanan, Greenville.

Communications: Television sets: 1 per 62 persons. **Radios:** 1 per 4.6 persons. **Telephones:** 1 per 86 persons. **Daily newspaper circ.:** 14 per 1,000 pop.

Health: Life expectancy at birth (1994): 55 male; 60 female. **Births** (per 1,000 pop.): 43. **Deaths** (per 1,000 pop.): 12. **Natural increase:** 3.1%. **Infant mortality** (per 1,000 live births 1994): 113.

Education (1990): **Literacy:** 40%; 35% attend primary school.

Major International Organizations: UN and most specialized agencies, OAU.

Embassy: 5201 16th St. NW 20011; 723-0437.

Liberia was founded in 1822 by U.S. black freedmen who settled at Monrovia with the aid of colonization societies. It became a republic July 26, 1847, with a constitution modeled on that of the U.S. Descendants of freedmen dominated politics.

Charging rampant corruption, an Army Redemption Council of enlisted men staged a bloody predawn coup, April 12, 1980, in which Pres. Tolbert was killed and replaced as head of state by Sgt. Samuel Doe. Doe was chosen president in a disputed election, and survived a subsequent coup, in 1985.

A civil war began Dec. 1989. Rebel forces seeking to depose Pres. Doe made major territorial gains and advanced on the capital, June 1990. In Sept., Doe was captured and put to death. A series of cease-fires failed to hold; a new accord in July 1993 called for gradual disarmament under a reconstituted peacekeeping force with troops from several countries. A 17-member coalition transition government was instituted May 16, 1994. More than half of the nation's population became refugees as a result of the civil war.

Libya

Socialist People's Libyan Arab Jamahiriya

al-Jamahiriyah al-Arabiya al-Libya al-Shabiya al-Ishtirakiya

People: Population: 5,057,000. **Age distrib.** (%): <15: 47; 65+: 3. **Pop. density:** 7 per sq. mi. **Urban:** 76%. **Ethnic groups:** Arab-Berber 97%. **Principal languages:** Arabic. **Religions:** Sunni Muslim 97%.

Geography: Area: 679,359 sq. mi., larger than Alaska. **Location:** On Mediterranean coast of N Africa. **Neighbors:** Tunisia, Algeria on W, Niger, Chad on S, Sudan, Egypt on E. **Topography:** Desert and semidesert regions cover 92% of the land, with low mountains in N, higher mountains in S, and a narrow coastal zone. **Capital:** Tripoli. **Cities** (1988 est.): Tripoli 591,000.

Government: Type: Islamic Arabic Socialist "Mass-State." **Leader:** Col. Muammar al-Qaddafi; b Sept. 1942; in power: Sept. 1969. **Local divisions:** 25 municipalities. **Defense:** 15% of GDP (1989 est.).

Economy: Industries: Carpets, textiles, petroleum. **Chief crops:** Dates, olives, citrus and other fruits, grapes, wheat. **Minerals:** Gypsum, oil, gas. **Crude oil reserves** (1987): 22 bln. bbls. **Arable land:** 2%. **Livestock** (1992): sheep: 5.6 mln.; goats: 1.2 mln. **Electricity prod.** (1992): 14.3 bln. kWh. **Labor force:** 18% agric.; 31% ind.; 27% services; 24% govt.

Finance: Monetary unit: Dinar (Mar. 1994: 1.00 = $3.16 US). **Gross domestic product** (1992): $26.1 bln. **Per capita GDP:** $5,800. **Imports** (1990): $7.6 bln.; partners: It. 21%, W Ger. 11%, Fr. 6%. **Exports** (1990): $11.0 bln.; partners: It. 57%, W Ger. 27%, Sp. 13%. **National budget** (1989): $9.8 bln. **International reserves less gold** (Mar. 1993): $6.1 bln. **Gold:** 3.6 mln. oz t.

Transport: Motor vehicles: in use: 448,000 passenger cars, 322,000 comm. vehicles. **Chief ports:** Tripoli, Benghazi.

Communications: Television sets: 1 per 8.9 persons. **Radios:** 1 per 4.4 persons. **Daily newspaper circ.:** 15 per 1,000 pop.

Health: Life expectancy at birth (1994): 62 male; 66 female. **Births** (per 1,000 pop.): 45. **Deaths** (per 1,000 pop.): 8. **Natural increase:** 3.7%. **Infant mortality** (per 1,000 live births 1994): 63.

Education (1991): **Literacy:** 64%. **Years compulsory:** 7. **Attendance:** 90%.

Major International Organizations: UN, Arab League, OAU, OPEC.

First settled by Berbers, Libya was ruled in succession by Carthage, Rome, the Vandals, and the Ottomans. Italy ruled from 1912, and Britain and France after WW II. Libya became an independent constitutional monarchy Jan. 2, 1952. In 1969 a junta led by Col. Muammar al-Qaddafi seized power.

Libya and Egypt fought several air and land battles along their border in July 1977. Chad charged Libya with military occupation of its uranium-rich northern region in 1977. Libyan troops were driven from their last major stronghold by Chad forces in 1987, leaving over $1 billion in military equipment behind.

Libya reportedly helped arm violent revolutionary groups in Egypt and Sudan and aided terrorists of various nationalities.

On Jan. 7, 1986, the U.S., in response, imposed economic sanctions against Libya, ordered all Americans to leave that country, and froze all Libyan assets in the U.S. The U.S. commenced flight operations over the Gulf of Sidra, Jan. 27, and a U.S. Navy task force began conducting exercises in the Gulf, Mar. 23. When Libya fired antiaircraft missiles at American warplanes, the U.S. responded by sinking 2 Libyan ships and bombing a missile installation in Libya. The U.S. withdrew from the Gulf, Mar. 27.

The U.S. accused Qaddafi of having ordered the Apr. 5, 1986, bombing of a West Berlin discotheque, which killed 3, including a U.S. serviceman. In response, the U.S. sent warplanes to attack terrorist-related targets in Tripoli and Benghazi, Libya, Apr. 14.

The UN imposed limited sanctions, Apr. 15, 1992, for Libya's failure to extradite 2 intelligence agents linked to the 1988 bombing of Pan American World Airways Flight 103 over Lockerbie, Scotland, and 4 others linked to an airplane bombing over Niger. Sanctions were tightened as of Dec. 1, 1993.

Liechtenstein

Principality of Liechtenstein

Furstentum Liechtenstein

People: Population: 30,000. **Age distrib.** (%): <15: 19; 65+: 10. **Pop. density:** 484 per sq. mi. **Ethnic groups:** Alemannic 95%, Italian 5%. **Principal languages:** German (official), Alemannic dialect. **Religions:** Roman Catholic 87%, Protestant 8%.

Geography: Area: 62 sq. mi., the size of Washington, D.C. **Location:** In the Alps. **Neighbors:** Switzerland on W, Austria on E. **Topography:** The Rhine Valley occupies one-third of the country, the Alps cover the rest. **Capital:** Vaduz. **Cities** (1991 cen.): Vaduz 4,874, Schaan 4,930.

Government: Type: Hereditary constitutional monarchy. **Head of state:** Prince Hans Adam; in office: Nov. 13, 1989. **Head of government:** Mario Frick; in office: Dec. 15, 1993. **Local divisions:** 2 districts, 11 communities.

Economy: Industries: Machines, instruments, chemicals, furniture, ceramics. **Arable land:** 25%. **Labor force:** 54% industry, trade, and building; 45% services; 2% agric., fishing, forestry.

Finance: Monetary unit: Swiss Franc. **Gross domestic product** (1990): $630 mln.* **Per capita GDP:** $22, 300.* **National budget** (1990): $292 mln.

Communications: Radios: 1 per 2.8 persons. **Telephones:** 1 per 1.7 persons. **Daily newspaper circ.:** 307 per 1,000 pop.

Health: Births (per 1,000 pop.): 13. **Deaths** (per 1,000 pop.): 7. **Natural increase:** .6%. **Infant mortality** (per 1,000 live births 1994): 5.

Education (1992): **Literacy:** 100%. **Years compulsory** 9; attendance 100%.

Liechtenstein became sovereign in 1866. Austria administered Liechtenstein's ports up to 1920; Switzerland has administered its postal services since 1921. Liechtenstein is united with Switzerland by a customs and monetary union. Taxes are low; many international corporations have headquarters there. Foreign workers comprise a third of the population.

Lithuania

Republic of Lithuania

Lietuvos Respublika

People: Population: 3,848,000. **Pop. density:** 152 per sq. mi. **Urban:** 69%. **Ethnic groups:** Lithuanian 80%, Russian 9%, Polish 8%. **Principal languages:** Lithuanian (official), Polish, Russian. **Religions:** mostly Roman Catholic.

Geography: Area: 25,213 sq. mi. **Neighbors:** Latvia on N, Belarus on E, S, Poland, Russia, & Baltic Sea on W. **Capital:** Vilnius. **Cities** (1993): Vilnius 590,000; Kaunas 429,000.

Government: Type: Republic. **Head of state:** Pres. Algirdas Brazauskas; in office: Feb. 25, 1993. **Head of government:** Prime Min. Adolfas Slezevicius; in office: Mar. 1993. **Defense:** 5.5% of GDP (1993 est.).

Economy: Industries: Engineering, shipbuilding. **Chief crops:** grain, potatoes, vegetables. **Arable land:** 49%. **Livestock** (1993): cattle: 1.7 mln., pigs: 1.3 mln. **Electricity prod.** (1992): 25 bln. kWh. **Labor force:** 18% agric., 42% ind.

Finance: Monetary unit: Lit. **National budget** (1992 est.): $270.2 mln.

Transport: Railroads: Length: 1,862 mi. **Motor vehicles:** in use: 480,000 passenger cars, 90,000 comm. vehicles. **Civil aviation:** 569 mln. passenger-mi.; 1 airport. **Chief ports:** Klaipeda.

Communications: Television sets: 1 per 2.7 persons. **Radios:** 1 per 2.7 persons. **Telephones:** 1 per 2.3 persons.

Health: Life expectancy at birth (1994): 67 male, 76 female. **Births** (per 1,000 pop.): 15. **Deaths** (per 1,000 pop.): 11. **Natural increase:** .4%. **Hospital beds:** 1 per 85 persons. **Physicians:** 1 per 274 persons. **Infant mortality rate** (per 1,000 live births 1994): 17.

Major international organizations: UN.

Embassy: 2622 16th St. NW 20009; 234-5860.

Lithuania, was occupied by the German Army, 1914-18. It was annexed by the Soviet Russian army, but the Soviets were overthrown, 1919. Lithuania was a democratic republic until 1926 when the regime was ousted by a coup. In 1939, the Soviet-German treaty assigned most of Lithuania to the Soviet sphere of influence. It was annexed by the USSR Aug. 3, 1940. Lithuania formally declared its independence from the Soviet Union Mar. 11, 1990. During an abortive Soviet coup in Aug., the Western nations recognized Lithuania's independence, which was recognized by the Soviet Union in Sept. 1991. The last Russian troops withdrew on Aug. 31, 1993.

In 1992 elections, former Communists won an absolute majority in the legislature.

Luxembourg

Grand Duchy of Luxembourg

Grand-Duché de Luxembourg

People: Population: 402,000. **Age distrib.** (%): <15: 17; 65+: 13. **Pop. density:** 402 per sq. mi. **Urban:** 86%. **Ethnic groups:** Mixture of French and Germans predominate. **Principal languages:** French, German (both official), Luxembourgisch. **Religions:** Roman Catholic 97%.

Geography: Area: 999 sq. mi., smaller than Rhode Island. **Location:** In W Europe. **Neighbors:** Belgium on W, France on S, Germany on E. **Topography:** Heavy forests (Ardennes) cover N, S is a low, open plateau. **Capital:** Luxembourg. **Cities** (1991 est.): Luxembourg 75,000.

Government: Type: Constitutional monarchy. **Head of state:** Grand Duke Jean; b Jan. 5, 1921; in office: Nov. 12, 1964. **Head of government:** Prime Min. Jacques Santer; in office: July 21, 1984. **Local divisions:** 3 districts. **Defense:** 1.2% of GDP (1992).

Economy: Industries: Steel, chemicals, beer, tires, tobacco, metal products, cement. **Chief crops:** Corn, wine. **Minerals:** Iron. **Arable land:** 24%. **Electricity prod.** (1990): 1.3 bln. kWh. **Labor force:** 3% agric.; 32% ind. & comm.; 65% services.

Finance: Monetary unit: Franc (Mar. 1994: 34.86 = $1 US). **Gross domestic product** (1992): $8.5 bln.* **Per capita GDP:** $21,700. **Note:** trade and tourism data included in Belgian statistics. **Tourism** (1989): $286 mln. receipts. **National budget** (1992): $3.5 bln. **Consumer prices** (change in 1993): 3.6%.

Transport: Railroads: Length: 168 mi. **Motor vehicles:** in use: 200,000 passenger cars, 20,000 comm. vehicles.

Communications: Television sets: 1 per 3.9 persons. **Radios:** 1 per 1.7 persons. **Telephones:** 1 per 2.0 persons. **Daily newspaper circ.:** 389 per 1,000 pop.

Health: Life expectancy at birth (1994): 73 male; 81 female. **Births** (per 1,000 pop.): 13. **Deaths** (per 1,000 pop.): 9. **Natural increase:** .3%. **Hospital beds:** 1 per 87 persons. **Physicians:** 1 per 496 persons. **Infant mortality** (per 1,000 live births 1994): 7.

Education (1989): **Literacy:** 100%. **Years compulsory** 9; attendance 100%.

Major International Organizations: UN, OECD, EU, NATO.

Embassy: 2200 Massachusetts Ave. NW 20008; 265-4171.

Luxembourg, founded about 963, was ruled by Burgundy, Spain, Austria, and France from 1448 to 1815. It left the Germanic Confederation in 1866. Overrun by Germany in 2 world wars, Luxembourg ended its neutrality in 1948, when a customs union with Belgium and Netherlands was adopted.

Macedonia

The Former Yugoslav Republic of Macedonia

People: Population: 2,214,000. **Pop. density:** 223 per sq. mi. **Ethnic groups:** Macedonian 67%, Albanian 21%. **Principal languages:** Macedonian, Albanian, Turkish, Serbo-Croatian. **Religions:** mostly Eastern Orthodox, Muslim.

Geography: Area: 9,928 sq. mi., slightly larger than Vermont. **Location:** In SE Europe. **Neighbors:** Bulgaria on E, Greece on S, Albania on W, Yugoslavia on N. **Capital:** Skopje. **Cities** (1991 met. est.): Skopje 563,000, Tetova 180,000.

Government: Type: Republic. **Head of state:** Pres. Kiro Gligorov; b May 3, 1917. **Head of government:** Prime Min. Branko Crvenkovski. **Local divisions:** 30 districts.

Economy: Industries: Steel, cement. **Chief crops:** Wheat, cotton, tobacco. **Livestock** (1992): 2.2 mln. sheep. **Electricity prod.** (1992): 6.3 bln. kWh.

Finance: Monetary unit: Denar. **Gross domestic product** (1991): $7.1 bln.* **Per capita GDP:** $3,110.

Transport: Railroads: Length: 431 mi. **Vehicles:** in use: 230,000 passenger cars, 22,000 comm. vehicles. **Civil aviation:** 1 airport.

Communications: Television sets: 1 per 6.1 persons. **Radios:** 1 per 5.5 persons. **Telephones:** 1 per 5.7 persons. **Daily newspaper circ.:** 26 per 1,000 pop.

Health: Births (per 1,000 pop.): 11. **Deaths** (per 1,000 pop.): 11. **Hospital beds:** 1 per 171 persons. **Physicians:** 1 per 464 persons. **Infant mortality** (per 1,000 live births 1994): 28.

Education (1990): **Literacy:** 90%.

Major International Organizations: UN.

Macedonia, as part of a larger region also called Macedonia, was ruled by Muslim Turks from 1389 to 1912, when native Greeks, Bulgarians, and Slavs won independence. Serbia received the largest part of the territory, with the rest going to Greece and Bulgaria. The area was incorporated in Serbia in 1918.

Macedonia declared its independence from Yugoslavia, Sept. 8, 1991, and was admitted to the UN under a provisional name in 1993. A UN force, which included 300 U.S. troops, was deployed there to deter the warring factions in Bosnia from carrying their dispute into other areas of the Balkans. In Feb. 1994 both Russia and the U.S. recognized Macedonia, while Greece, which objected to Macedonia's use of what it considered a Hellenic name and symbols, imposed a trade blockade on the landlocked country.

Madagascar

Democratic Republic of Madagascar

Repoblika Demokratika Malagasy

People: Population: 13,428,000. **Pop. density:** 59 per sq. mi. **Urban:** 22%. **Ethnic groups:** 18 Malayan-Indonesian tribes (Merina 26%), with Arab and African presence. **Principal languages:** Malagasy, French (both official). **Religions:** indigenous beliefs 52%, Christian 41%, Muslim 7%.

Geography: Area: 226,658 sq. mi., slightly smaller than Texas. **Location:** In the Indian O., off the SE coast of Africa. **Neighbors:** Comoro Is., Mozambique (across Mozambique Channel). **Topography:** Humid coastal strip in the E, fertile valleys in the mountainous center plateau region, and a wider coastal strip on the W. **Capital:** Antananarivo. **Cities** (1990 est.): Antananarivo 802,000.

Government: Type: Republic. **Head of state:** Pres. Albert Zafy; in office: Feb. 10, 1993. **Head of government:** Prime Min. Francisque Ravony; in office: Aug. 1993. **Local divisions:** 6 provinces. **Defense:** 2.2% of GDP (1991 est.).

Economy: Industries: Food processing, textiles. **Chief crops:** Coffee (over 50% of exports), cloves, vanilla, rice, sugar, sisal, tobacco, peanuts. **Minerals:** Chromium, graphite, coal, bauxite. **Arable land:** 4%. **Livestock** (1992): cattle: 10.2 mln.; pigs: 1.4 mln. **Fish catch** (1991): 101,000 metric tons. **Electricity prod.** (1991): 450 mln. kWh. **Labor force:** 90% agric.

Finance: Monetary unit: Franc (Jan. 1994: 1,965 = $1 US). **Gross domestic product** (1992): $2.5 bln. **Per capita GDP:** $200. **Imports** (1991): $442 mln.; partners: Fr. 32%, U.S. 15%. **Exports** (1991): $305 mln.; partners: Fr. 34%, U.S. 14%. **Tourism** (1990): $28 mln. receipts. **National budget** (1991): $265 mln. **International reserves less gold** (Jan. 1993): $89 mln. **Consumer prices** (change in 1992): 14.5%.

Transport: Railroads: Length: 655 mi. **Motor vehicles:** in use: 46,000 passenger cars, 33,000 comm. vehicles. **Civil aviation:** 319 mln. passenger-mi.; 50 airports with scheduled flights. **Chief ports:** Tamatave, Diego-Suarez, Majunga, Tulear.

Communications: Television sets: 1 per 98 persons. **Radios:** 1 per 8.5 persons. **Telephones:** 1 per 203 persons.

Health: Life expectancy at birth (1994): 52 male; 56 female. **Births** (per 1,000 pop.): 45. **Deaths** (per 1,000 pop.): 13. **Natural increase:** 3.2%. **Physicians:** 1 per 8,610 persons. **Infant mortality** (per 1,000 live births 1994): 89.

Education (1987): **Literacy:** 53%. **Years compulsory:** 5; attendance 83%.

Major International Organizations: UN (GATT, WHO, IMF), OAU.

Embassy: 2374 Massachusetts Ave. NW 20008; 265-5525.

Madagascar was settled 2,000 years ago by Malayan-Indonesian people, whose descendants still predominate. A unified kingdom ruled the 18th and 19th centuries. The island became a French protectorate, 1885, and a colony 1896. Independence came June 26, 1960.

Discontent with inflation and French domination led to a coup in 1972. The new regime nationalized French-owned financial interests, closed French bases and a U.S. space tracking station, and obtained Chinese aid. The government conducted a program of arrests, expulsion of foreigners, and repression of strikes, 1979.

In 1990, Madagascar ended a ban on multiparty politics that had been in place since 1975. Albert Zafy was elected president in 1993, ending the 17-year rule of Adm. Didier Ratsiraka.

Malawi

Republic of Malawi

People: Population: 9,732,000. **Age distrib.** (%): <15: 48; 65+: 3. **Pop. density:** 212 per sq. mi. **Urban:** 17%. **Ethnic groups:** Chewa 90%, Nyanja, Lomwe, other Bantu tribes. **Principal languages:** English, Chichewa (both official), Lomwe, Yao. **Religions:** Christian 75%, Muslim 20%.

Geography: Area: 45,747 sq. mi., the size of Pennsylvania. **Location:** In SE Africa. **Neighbors:** Zambia on W, Mozambique on SE, Tanzania on N. **Topography:** Malawi stretches 560 mi. N-S along Lake Malawi (Lake Nyasa), most of which belongs to Malawi. High plateaus and mountains line the Rift Valley the length of the nation. **Capital:** Lilongwe. **Cities** (1987 est.): Blantyre 333,000; Lilongwe 223,000.

Government: Type: Republic. **Head of state and government:** Pres. Bakili Muluzi; b Mar. 17, 1943; in office: May 21, 1994. **Local divisions:** 24 districts. **Defense:** 1.6% of GDP (1989 est.).

Economy: Industries: Textiles, sugar, cement. **Chief crops:** Tea, tobacco, sugar, coffee. **Other resources:** Rubber. **Arable land:** 25%. **Fish catch** (1991): 63,000 metric tons. **Electricity prod.** (1992): 620 mln. kWh. **Labor force:** 43% agric.; 25% ind. and comm.; 15% services.

Finance: Monetary unit: Kwacha (Nov. 1993: 4.45 = $1 US). **Gross domestic product** (1992): $1.9 bln. **Per capita GDP:** $200. **Imports** (1992): $720 mln.; partners: So. Afr. 29%, UK 24%, Jap. 6%. **Exports** (1992): $392 mln.; partners: UK 27%, S Afr. 8%., Ger. 10%. **National budget** (1991): $510 mln. **International reserves less gold** (Mar. 1993): $45 mln. **Gold:**

13,000 oz t. **Consumer prices** (change in 1992): 22.7%.

Transport: Railroads: Length: 495 mi. **Motor vehicles:** in use: 16,000 passenger cars, 17,000 comm. vehicles.

Communications: Radios: 1 per 8.9 persons. **Telephones:** 1 per 184 persons.

Health: Life expectancy at birth (1994): 39 male; 41 female. **Births** (per 1,000 pop.): 50. **Deaths** (per 1,000 pop.): 23. **Natural increase:** 2.7%. **Hospital beds:** 1 per 627 persons. **Physicians:** 1 per 27,094 persons. **Infant mortality** (per 1,000 live births 1994): 141.

Education (1989): **Literacy:** 25%. About 45% attend school.

Major International Organizations: UN (World Bank, IMF), OAU, Commonwealth of Nations.

Embassy: 2408 Massachusetts Ave. NW 20008; 797-1007.

Bantus came in the 16th century, Arab slavers in the 19th. The area became the British protectorate Nyasaland in 1891. It became independent July 6, 1964, and a republic in 1966. After 3 decades as a one-party state under Pres. Hastings Kamuzu Banda, the country adopted a new constitution and, in multiparty elections May 17, 1994, chose a new leader.

Malaysia

People: Population: 19,283,000. **Age distrib.** (%): <15: 36; 65+: 4. **Pop. density:** 151 per sq. mi. **Urban:** 51%. **Ethnic groups:** Malays 59%, Chinese 32%, Indian 9%. **Principal languages:** Malay (official), English, Chinese, Indian languages. **Religions:** Muslim, Hindu, Buddhist, Confucian, Taoist, local religions.

Geography: Area: 127,584 sq. mi., slightly larger than New Mexico. **Location:** On the SE tip of Asia, plus the N coast of the island of Borneo. **Neighbors:** Thailand on N, Indonesia on S. **Topography:** Most of W Malaysia is covered by tropical jungle, including the central mountain range that runs N-S through the peninsula. The western coast is marshy, the eastern, sandy. E Malaysia has a wide, swampy coastal plain, with interior jungles and mountains. **Capital:** Kuala Lumpur. **Cities** (1991 est.): Kuala Lumpur 1 mln.

Government: Type: Federal parliamentary democracy with a constitutional monarch. **Head of state:** Paramount Ruler Sultan Jaafar bin Abdul Rahman; in office: Apr. 26, 1994. **Head of government:** Prime Min. Datuk Seri Mahathir bin Mohamad; b Dec. 20, 1925; in office: July 16, 1981. **Local divisions:** 13 states and 2 federal terr. **Defense:** 5% of GDP (1992).

Economy: Industries: Rubber goods, steel, electronics. **Chief crops:** Palm oil, copra, rice, pepper. **Minerals:** Tin (35% world output), iron. **Crude oil reserves** (1987): 3.2 bln. bbls. **Other resources:** Rubber (35% world output). **Arable land:** 3%. **Livestock** (1991): pigs: 2.4 mln. **Fish catch** (1990): 604,000 metric tons. **Electricity prod.** (1992): 30 bln. kWh. **Labor force:** 18% agric.; 11% tourism & trade; 10% govt.

Finance: Monetary unit: Ringgit (Mar. 1994: 2.71 = $1 US). **Gross domestic product** (1992): $54.5 bln. **Per capita GDP:** $2,960. **Imports** (1991): $38.7 bln.; partners: Jap. 21%, U.S. 18%, Sing. 14%. **Exports** (1991): $35.4 bln.; partners: Jap. 20%, U.S. 17% Sing. 19%, Neth. 6%. **Tourism** (1990): $1.6 bln. receipts. **National budget** (1992 est.): $18.0 bln. **International reserves less gold** (Dec. 1993): $27.2 bln. **Gold:** 2.39 mln. oz t. **Consumer prices** (change in 1993): 3.4%.

Transport: Railroads: Length: 1,381 mi. **Motor vehicles:** in use: 2.0 mln. passenger cars, 400,000 comm. vehicles. **Civil aviation:** 9.2 bln. passenger-mi.; 39 airports with scheduled flights. **Chief ports:** George Town, Kelang, Melaka, Kuching.

Communications: Television sets: 1 per 9.3 persons. **Radios:** 1 per 5.3 persons. **Telephones:** 1 per 8.9 persons. **Daily newspaper circ.:** 140 per 1,000 pop.

Health: Life expectancy at birth (1994): 66 male; 72 female. **Births** (per 1,000 pop.): 28. **Deaths** (per 1,000 pop.): 6. **Natural increase:** 2.3%. **Hospital beds:** 1 per 457 persons. **Physicians:** 1 per 2,638 persons. **Infant mortality** (per 1,000 live births 1994): 26.

Education (1991): **Literacy:** 80%. **Attendance:** 96% primary, 65% secondary.

Major International Organizations: UN (World Bank, IMF, GATT), ASEAN.

Embassy: 2401 Massachusetts Ave. NW 20008; 328-2700.

European traders appeared in the 16th century; Britain established control in 1867. Malaysia was created Sept. 16, 1963. It included Malaya (which had become independent in 1957 after the suppression of Communist rebels), plus the formerly-British Singapore, Sabah (N Borneo), and Sarawak (NW Borneo). Singapore was separated in 1965, in order to end tensions between Chinese, the majority in Singapore, and Malays in control of the Malaysian government.

A monarch is elected by a council of hereditary rulers of the Malayan states every 5 years.

Abundant natural resources have assured prosperity, and foreign investment has aided industrialization.

Maldives

Republic of Maldives

Divehi Jumhuriya

People: Population: 252,000. **Age distrib.** (%): <15: 47; 65+: 3. **Pop. density:** 2,191 per sq. mi. **Urban:** 26%. **Ethnic groups:** Sinhalese, Dravidian, Arab mixture. **Principal languages:** Divehi (Sinhalese dialect). **Religions:** Sunni Muslim.

Geography: Area: 115 sq. mi., twice the size of Washington, D.C. **Location:** In the Indian O. SW of India. **Neighbors:** Nearest is India on N. **Topography:** 19 atolls with 1,087 islands, about 200 inhabited. None of the islands are over 5 sq. mi. in area, and all are nearly flat. **Capital:** Male. **Cities** (1991 est.): Male 55,000.

Government: Type: Republic. **Head of state:** Pres. Maumoon Abdul Gayoom; b Dec. 29, 1939; in office: Nov. 11, 1978. **Local divisions:** 19 districts.

Economy: Industries: Fish processing, tourism. **Chief crops:** Coconuts, fruit, millet. **Other resources:** Shells. **Arable land:** 10%. **Fish catch** (1991): 80,000 metric tons. **Electricity prod.** (1991): 11.0 mln. kWh. **Labor force:** 80% fishing, agriculture, & manufacturing.

Finance: Monetary unit: Rufiyaa (Mar. 1994: 11.21 = $1 US). **Gross domestic product** (1991): $140 mln. **Per capita GDP:** $620. **Imports** (1990): $128 min.; partners: Sing., Ger., Sri Lan. **Exports** (1990): $52 mln.; partners: U.S., U.K.. **Tourism** (1990): $142 mln. receipts. **National budget** (1991 est.): $83 mln.

Transport: Chief ports: Male Atoll.

Communications: Radios: 1 per 9.2 persons. **Telephones:** 1 per 75 persons.

Health: Life expectancy at birth (1994): 63 male; 66 female. **Births** (per 1,000 pop.): 44. **Deaths** (per 1,000 pop.): 7. **Natural increase:** 3.6%. **Infant morality** (per 1,000 live births 1994): 54.

Education (1989): **Literacy:** 93%. Only 6% of those aged 11-15 attend school.

Major International Organizations: UN.

The islands had been a British protectorate since 1887. The country became independent July 26, 1965. Long a sultanate, the Maldives became a republic in 1968. Natural resources and tourism are being developed; however, it remains one of the world's poorest countries.

Mali

Republic of Mali

République du Mali

People: Population: 9,113,000. **Age distrib.** (%): <15: 46; 65+: 4. **Pop. density:** 19 per sq. mi. **Urban:** 22%. **Ethnic groups:** Mande (Bambara, Malinke, Sarakole) 50%, Peul 17%, Voltaic 12%, Songhai 6%, Tuareg and Moor 10%. **Principal languages:** French (official), Bambara, Senufo. **Religions:** Muslim 90%.

Geography: Area: 482,077 sq. mi., about the size of Texas and California combined. **Location:** In the interior of W Africa. **Neighbors:** Mauritania, Senegal on W, Guinea, Côte d'Ivoire, Burkina Faso on S, Niger on E, Algeria on N. **Topography:** A landlocked grassy plain in the upper basins of the Senegal and Niger rivers, extending N into the Sahara. **Capital:** Bamako. **Cities** (1989 est.): Bamako (met.) 800,000.

Government: Type: Republic. **Head of state:** Pres. Alpha Oumar Konare; b 1946; in office: June 8, 1992. **Head of government:** Prime Min. Ibrahim Boubakar Keita; in office: Feb. 4, 1994. **Local divisions:** 8 regions. **Defense:** 2% of GDP (1989).

Economy: Chief crops: Millet, rice, peanuts, cotton. **Other resources:** Bauxite, iron, gold. **Arable land:** 2%. **Livestock** (1992): sheep and goats: 13.3 mln.; cattle: 5.3 mln. **Fish catch** (1991): 60,000 metric tons. **Electricity prod.** (1991): 750 mln. kWh. **Labor force:** 80% agric.; 19% services.

Finance: Monetary unit: Franc (Mar. 1994: 576 = $1 US). **Gross domestic product** (1991): $2.3 bln. **Per capita GDP:** $265. **Imports** (1989): $513 mln.; partners: Fr. 22%, Côte d'Ivoire 25%. **Exports** (1989): $285 mln.; partners: Belg.-Lux. 25%, Fr. 15%. **Tourism** (1990): $37 mln. receipts. **National budget** (1989): $519 mln. **International reserves less gold** (Dec. 1993): $332 mln. **Gold:** 19,000 oz t.

Transport: Railroads: Length: 401 mi. **Motor vehicles:** in use: 22,000 passenger cars, 9,000 comm. vehicles.

Communications: Radios: 1 per 56 persons. **Telephones:** 1 per 564 persons.

Health: Life expectancy at birth (1994): 44 male; 48 female. **Births** (per 1,000 pop.): 52. **Deaths** (per 1,000 pop.): 20. **Natural increase:** 3.1%. **Hospital beds** (1983): 4,215. **Physicians** (1983): 283. **Infant mortality** (per 1,000 live births 1994): 106.

Education (1991): **Literacy:** 25%. **Attendance:** 21% attend primary school.

Major International Organizations: UN and all of its specialized agencies, OAU, EU.

Embassy: 2130 R St. NW 20008; 332-2249.

Until the 15th century the area was part of the great Mali Empire. Timbuktu was a center of Islamic study. French rule was secured, 1898. The Sudanese Rep. and Senegal became independent as the Mali Federation June 20, 1960, but Senegal withdrew, and the Sudanese Rep. was renamed Mali.

Mali signed economic agreements with France and, in 1963, with Senegal. In 1968, a coup ended the socialist regime. Famine struck in 1973-74, killing as many as 100,000 people. Drought conditions returned in the 1980s.

The military, Mar. 26, 1991, overthrew the government of Pres. Amadou Toumani Traoré, who had been in power since 1968. Oumar Konare, a leader in the coup, was elected president, Apr. 26, 1992.

Malta

Repubblika Ta' Malta

People: Population: 367,000. **Age distrib.** (%): <15: 23; 65+: 10. **Pop. density:** 3,008 per sq. mi. **Ethnic groups:** Italian, Arab, French. **Principal languages:** Maltese, English (both official). **Religions:** Mainly Roman Catholic.

Geography: Area: 122 sq. mi., twice the size of Washington, D.C. **Location:** In center of Mediterranean Sea. **Neighbors:** Nearest is Italy on N. **Topography:** Island of Malta is 95 sq. mi.; other islands in the group: Gozo, 26 sq. mi., Comino, 1 sq. mi. The coastline is heavily indented. Low hills cover the interior. **Capital:** Valletta. **Cities** (1992 est.): Birkirkara 21,000, Qormi 19,000.

Government: Type: Parliamentary democracy. **Head of state:** Pres. Ugo Mifsud Bonnici; b July 17, 1933; in office: Apr. 4, 1994. **Head of government:** Prime Min. Edward Fenech-Adami; b Feb. 7, 1934; in office: May 12, 1987. **Local divisions:** 13 electoral districts. **Defense:** 1.3% of GNP (1989 est.).

Economy: Industries: Textiles, machinery, food & beverages, tourism. **Chief crops:** Potatoes, tomatoes. **Arable land:** 38%. **Electricity prod.** (1992): $1.1 bln. kWh. **Labor force:** 2% agric.; 22% manuf.; 26% services; 37% gov.

Finance: Monetary unit: Maltese Lira (Mar. 1994: 1.00 = $2.57 US). **Gross domestic product** (1991): $2.7 bln. **Per capita GDP:** $7,600. **Imports** (1991): $2.1 bln.; partners: UK 16%, It. 30%, Ger. 14%, U.S. 4%. **Exports** (1991): $1.2 bln.; partners: Ger. 23%, UK 11%, It. 30%. **Tourism** (1989): receipts: $475 mln. **National budget** (1992 est.): $1.1 bln. **International reserves less gold** (Feb. 1994): 1.3 bln. **Gold:** 100,000 oz t. **Consumer prices** (change in 1993): 4.1%.

Transport: Motor vehicles: in use: 104,000 passenger cars, 19,000 comm. vehicles. **Civil aviation:** 693 mln. passenger-mi.; 1 airport. **Chief ports:** Valletta.

Communications: Television sets: 1 per 2.7 persons. **Radios:** 1 per 4.0 persons. **Telephones:** 1 per 1.9 persons.

Health: Life expectancy at birth (1994): 75 male; 79 female. **Births** (per 1,000 pop.): 14. **Deaths** (per 1,000 pop.): 7. **Natural increase:** .6%. **Hospital beds:** 1 per 107 persons. **Physicians:** 1 per 444 persons. **Infant mortality** (per 1,000 live births 1994): 8.

Education (1988): **Literacy:** 90%. **Compulsory:** until age 16.

Major International Organizations: UN (GATT, WHO, IMF), Commonwealth of Nations.

Embassy: 2017 Connecticut Ave. NW 20008; 462-3611.

Malta was ruled by Phoenicians, Romans, Arabs, Normans, the Knights of Malta, France, and Britain (since 1814). It became independent Sept. 21, 1964. Malta became a republic in 1974. The withdrawal of the last British sailors, Apr. 1, 1979, ended 179 years of British military presence on the island.

Marshall Islands

Republic of the Marshall Islands

People: Population: 54,000. **Pop. density:** 771 per sq. mi. **Ethnic groups:** Micronesian. **Principal languages:** English (official), Marshallese, Japanese. **Religions:** Protestant 90%.

Geography: Area: 70 sq. mi. **Location:** In central Pacific Ocean; comprised of 2 800-mi-long parallel chains of coral atolls. **Capital:** Majuro.

Government: Type: Republic. **Head of state:** Pres. Amata Kabua.

Economy: Agriculture and tourism are mainstays of the economy. **Electricity prod.** (1990): 80 mln. kWh.

Finance: Monetary unit: U.S. dollar. **Gross domestic product** (1989): $63 mln. **Per capita GDP:** $1,500. **Imports** (1988): 34 mln. **Exports** (1988): $2 mln.

Transport: 24 airports with scheduled flights. **Port:** Majuro.

Communications: Telephones: 1 per 57 persons.

Health: Life expectancy at birth (1994): 62 male; 65 female. **Births** (per 1,000 pop.): 46. **Deaths** (per 1,000 pop.): 8. **Natural increase:** 3.9%. **Infant mortality** (per 1,000 live births 1994): 49.

Education (1990): **Literacy:** 86%.

Major International Organizations: UN.

The Marshall Islands were a German possession until World War I and were administered by Japan between the World Wars. After WW II, they were administered as part of the UN Trust Territory of the Pacific Islands by the U.S.

The Marshall Islands secured international recognition as an independent nation on Sept. 17, 1991.

Mauritania

Islamic Republic of Mauritania

République Islamique de Mauritanie

People: Population: 2,193,000. **Age distrib.** (%): <15: 44; 65+: 4. **Pop. density:** 5 per sq. mi. **Urban:** 39%. **Ethnic groups:** mixed Maur/black 40%, Maur 30%, black 30%. **Principal languages:** Hassanya Arabic, Wolof (offical), Pular, Soninke. **Religions:** Nearly 100% Muslim.

Geography: Area: 398,000 sq. mi., the size of Texas and California combined. **Location:** In W Africa. **Neighbors:** Morocco on N, Algeria, Mali on E, Senegal on S. **Topography:** The fertile Senegal R. valley in the S gives way to a wide central region of sandy plains and scrub trees. The N is arid and extends into the Sahara. **Capital:** Nouakchott. **Cities** (1992 est.): Nouakchott 550,000; Nouadhibou 70,000; Kaedi 74,000.

Government: Type: Islamic republic. **Head of state:** Pres. Maaouya Ould Sidi Ahmed Taya; b 1943; in office: Apr. 18, 1992. **Head of government:** Prime Min. Sidi Mohamed Ould Boubacar; in office: Apr. 18, 1992. **Local divisions:** 12 regions, one capital district. **Defense:** 4.2% of GDP (1989).

Economy: Chief crops: Dates, grain. **Industries:** Iron mining. **Minerals:** Iron, ore, gypsum. **Livestock** (1992): sheep: 5.4 mln.; goats: 3.6 mln.; cattle: 1.4 mln. **Fish catch** (1991): 90,000 metric tons. **Electricity prod.** (1991): 135 mln. kWh. **Labor force:** 47% agric., 14% ind. & comm., 29% services.

Finance: Monetary unit: Ouguiya (Mar. 1994: 123 = $1 US). **Gross domestic product** (1991): $1.1 bln. **Per capita GDP:** $555. **Imports** (1990): $639 mln.; partners: EU 60%. **Exports** (1990): $437 mln.; partners: EU 43%, Jap. 27%. **International reserves less gold** (Mar. 1994): $44 mln.

Transport: Motor vehicles: in use: 10,000 passenger cars, 5,000 comm. vehicles. **Chief ports:** Nouakchott, Nouadhibou.

Communications: Radios: 1 per 7.0 persons. **Telephones:** 1 per 268 persons.

Health: Life expectancy at birth (1994): 45 male; 51 female. **Births** (per 1,000 pop.): 46. **Deaths** (per 1,000 pop.): 16. **Natural increase:** 3.2%. **Hospital beds:** 1 per 1,217 persons. **Physicians:** 1 per 13,167 persons. **Infant mortality** (per 1,000 live births 1994): 85.

Education (1991): **Literacy:** 30%. **Attendance:** 79% in primary school, 18% in secondary school.

Major International Organizations: UN (GATT, IMF, WHO), OAU, Arab League.

Embassy: 2129 Leroy Pl. NW 20008; 232-5700.

Mauritania was a French protectorate from 1903. It became independent Nov. 28, 1960. It annexed the south of former Spanish Sahara in 1976. Saharan guerrillas stepped up attacks in 1977; 8,000 Moroccan troops and French bomber raids aided the government. Mauritania signed a peace treaty with the Polisario Front, 1980, resumed diplomatic relations with Algeria while breaking a defense treaty with Morocco, and renounced sovereignty over its share of former Spanish Sahara. Morocco annexed the territory.

Mauritius

People: Population: 1,117,000. **Age distrib.** (%): <15: 30; 65+: 5. **Pop. density:** 1,417 per sq. mi. **Urban:** 39%. **Ethnic groups:** Indo-Mauritian 68%, Creole 27%, others. **Principal languages:** English (official), French, Creole, Bhojpoori. **Religions:** Hindu 52%, Christian 28%, Muslim 17%.

Geography: Area: 788 sq. mi., about the size of Rhode Island. **Location:** In the Indian O., 500 mi. E of Madagascar. **Neighbors:** Nearest is Madagascar on W. **Topography:** A volcanic island nearly surrounded by coral reefs. A central plateau is encircled by mountain peaks. **Capital:** Port Louis. **Cities** (1991 est.): Port Louis 142,000.

Government: Type: Republic. **Head of state:** Pres. Cassam Uteem; b Mar. 22, 1941; in office: June 30, 1992. **Head of government:** Prime Min. Aneerood Jugnauth; in office: June 12, 1982. **Local divisions:** 9 districts, 3 dependencies.

Economy: Industries: Tourism, food processing. **Chief crops:** Sugar cane, tea. **Arable land:** 54%. **Electricity prod.** (1992): 630 mln. kWh. **Labor force:** 27% agric. & fishing; 22% manuf.; 29% govt. services.

Finance: Monetary unit: Rupee (Mar. 1994: 18.34 = $1 US). **Gross domestic product** (1991): $2.5 bln. **Per capita GDP:** $2,300. **Imports** (1991): $1.5 bln.; partners: UK 9%, Fr. 12%, So. Afr. 9%. **Exports** (1991): $1.1 bln.; partners: UK 50%, Fr. 22%, U.S. 8%. **Tourists** (1990): $264 mln. receipts. **National budget** (1990): $607 mln. **International reserves less gold** (Mar. 1994): $788 mln. **Gold:** 62,000 oz t. **Consumer prices** (change in 1993): 10.5%.

Transport: Motor vehicles: in use: 50,000 passenger cars, 16,000 comm. vehicles. **Chief ports:** Port Louis.

Communications: Television sets: 1 per 7.8 persons. **Radios:** 1 per 4.3 persons. **Telephones:** 1 per 15 persons. **Daily newspaper circ.:** 74 per 1,000 pop.

Health: Life expectancy at birth (1994): 67 male; 75 female. **Births** (per 1,000 pop.): 19. **Deaths** (per 1,000 pop.): 6. **Natural increase:** 1.3%. **Hospital beds:** 1 per 351 persons. **Physicians:** 1 per 996 persons. **Infant mortality** (per 1,000 live births 1994): 18.

Education (1989): **Literacy:** 94%. **Attendance:** almost all children attend school.

Major International Organizations: UN and all of its specialized agencies, OAU, Commonwealth of Nations.

Embassy: 4301 Connecticut Ave. NW 20008; 244-1491.

Mauritius was uninhabited when settled in 1638 by the Dutch, who introduced sugar cane. France took over in 1721, bringing African slaves. Britain ruled from 1810 to Mar. 12, 1968, bringing Indian workers for the sugar plantations.

Mauritius formally severed its association with the British crown Mar. 12, 1992.

Mexico

United Mexican States

Estados Unidos Mexicanos

People: Population: 92,202,000. **Age distrib.** (%): <15: 38; 65+: 4. **Pop. density:** 122 per sq. mi. **Urban:** 71%. **Ethnic groups:** Mestizo 60%, American Indian 30%, Caucasian 9%. **Principal languages:** Spanish (official), Ameridian languages. **Religions:** Roman Catholic 89%.

Geography: Area: 756,066 sq. mi., three times the size of Texas. **Location:** In southern N America. **Neighbors:** U.S. on N, Guatemala, Belize on S. **Topography:** The Sierra Madre Occidental Mts. run NW-SE near the west coast; the Sierra Madre Oriental Mts., run near the Gulf of Mexico. They join S of Mexico City. Between the 2 ranges lies the dry central plateau, 5,000 to 8,000 ft. alt., rising toward the S, with temperate vegetation. Coastal lowlands are tropical. About 45% of land is arid. **Capital:** Mexico City. **Cities** (1991 est.): Mexico City (metro) 20 mln.; Guadalajara (metro) 3 mln.; Monterrey (metro) 2.7 mln.

Government: Type: Federal republic. **Head of state:** Pres. Carlos Salinas de Gortari; b Apr. 3, 1948; in office: Dec. 1, 1988. **Local divisions:** Federal district and 31 states. **Defense:** 0.5% of GDP (1992).

Economy: Industries: Steel, chemicals, electric goods, textiles, rubber, petroleum, tourism. **Chief crops:** Cotton, coffee, wheat, rice, sugar cane, vegetables, corn. **Minerals:** Silver, lead, zinc, gold, oil, natural gas. **Crude oil reserves** (1991): 51 bln. barrels. **Arable land:** 12%. **Livestock** (1992): cattle: 32 mln.; pigs: 13 mln.; sheep: 6 mln. **Fish catch** (1991): 1.1 mln. metric tons. **Electricity prod.** (1992): 120 bln. kWh. **Labor force:** 28% agric.; 11% manuf.; 32% services; 15% comm.

Finance: Monetary unit: New peso (Mar. 1994: 3,115 = $1 US). **Gross domestic product** (1992): $328 bln. **Per capita GDP:** $3,600. **Imports** (1991): $36.7 bln.; partners: U.S. 69%, EU 13%. **Exports** (1991): $27 bln.; partners: U.S. 68%, EU 14%. **Tourism** (1992): receipts: $6.6 bln. **National budget** (1991): $48.3 bln. **International reserves less gold** (Oct. 1993): $23.2 bln. **Gold:** 500,000 oz t. **Consumer prices** (change in 1993): 9.8%.

Transport: Railroads: Length: 16,363 mi. **Motor vehicles:** in use: 6.8 mln. passenger cars, 3.0 mln. comm. **Civil aviation:** 10.8 bln. passenger-mi.; 54 airports. **Chief ports:** Veracruz, Tampico, Mazatlan, Coatzacoalcos.

Communications: Television sets: 1 in 6.7 persons. **Radios:** 1 in 5.2 persons. **Telephones:** 1 in 8.0 persons. **Daily newspaper circ.:** 127 per 1,000 pop.

Health: Life expectancy at birth (1994): 69 male; 77 female. **Births** (per 1,000 pop.): 27. **Deaths** (per 1,000 pop.): 5. **Natural increase:** 2.2%. **Hospital beds:** 1 per 1,367 persons. **Physicians:** 1 per 885 persons. **Infant mortality** (per 1,000 live births 1994): 27.

Education (1993): **Literacy:** 90%. **Years compulsory:** 8.

Major International Organizations: UN (IMF, GATT), OAS.

Embassy: 1911 Pennsylvania Ave. NW 20006; 728-1600.

Mexico was the site of advanced Indian civilizations. The Mayas, an agricultural people, moved up from Yucatan, built immense stone pyramids, invented a calendar. The Toltecs were overcome by the Aztecs, who founded Tenochtitlan 1325 AD, now Mexico City. Hernando Cortes, Spanish conquistador, destroyed the Aztec empire, 1519-1521.

After 3 centuries of Spanish rule the people rose, under Fr. Miguel Hidalgo y Costilla, 1810, Fr. Morelos y Payon, 1812, and Gen. Agustin Iturbide, who made himself emperor as Agustin I, 1821. A republic was declared in 1823.

Mexican territory extended into the present American Southwest and California until Texas revolted and established a republic in 1836; the Mexican legislature refused recognition but was unable to enforce its authority there. After numerous clashes, the U.S.-Mexican War, 1846-48, resulted in the loss by Mexico of the lands north of the Rio Grande.

French arms supported an Austrian archduke on the throne of Mexico as Maximilian I, 1864-67, but pressure from the U.S. forced France to withdraw. A dictatorial rule by Porfirio Diaz, president 1877-80, 1884-1911, led to fighting by rival forces until the new constitution of Feb. 5, 1917, provided social reform. Since then Mexico has developed large-scale programs of social security, labor protection, and school improvement. A constitutional provision requires management to share profits with labor.

The Institutional Revolutionary Party (PRI) has been dominant in politics since 1929. Radical opposition, including some guerrilla activity, has been contained by strong measures.

Some gains in agriculture, industry, and social services have been achieved. The land is rich, but the rugged topography and lack of sufficient rainfall are major obstacles. Economic prospects brightened with the discovery of vast oil reserves, perhaps the world's greatest. But much of the work force is jobless or underemployed. Inflation and a drop in world oil prices aggravated the country's economic problems in the 1980s. An antipoverty program was launched in 1989.

Mexico reached agreement with the U.S. and Canada on the North American Free Trade Agreement Aug. 12, 1992; it went into effect Jan. 1, 1994.

Guerrillas of the Zapatista National Liberation Army (EZLN) launched an uprising, Jan. 1, 1994, in southern Mexico. A tentative peace accord was reached Mar. 2.

The presidential candidate of the governing PRI, Luis Donaldo Colosio Murrieta, was assassinated at a political rally in Tijuana, Mar. 23, 1994. The new PRI candidate, Ernesto Zedillo Ponce de León, won election Aug. 21. He was to be inaugurated Dec. 1.

Micronesia

Federated States of Micronesia

People: Population: 120,000. **Pop. density:** 442 per sq. mi. **Ethnic groups:** 9 ethnic Micronesian and Polynesian groups. **Principal languages:** English (official). **Religions:** Mostly Christian.

Geography: Area: 271 sq. mi. The Federation consists of 607 islands in the W Pacific Ocean. **Capital:** Palikir.

Government: Type: Republic. **Head of state:** Bailey Olter; in office: May 21, 1991. **Local divisions:** 4 states.

Economy: Chief crops: Tropical fruits, vegetables, coconuts.

Finance: Monetary unit: U.S. dollar. **Gross national product** (1989): $150 mln.* **Per capita GDP:** $1,500. **Imports** (1988): 67 mln. **Exports** (1988): 3 mln.

Transport: 4 airports with scheduled flights.

Communications: Television sets: 1 per 15 persons. **Radios:** 1 per 1.5 persons. **Telephones:** 1 per 37 persons.

Health: Life expectancy at birth (1994): 66 male; 70 female. **Births** (per 1,000 pop.): 28. **Deaths** (per 1,000 pop.): 6. **Natural increase:** 2.2%. **Hospital beds:** 1 per 309 persons. **Physicians:** 1 per 3,084 persons. **Infant mortality** (per 1,000 live births 1994): 37.

Education (1991): **Literacy:** 90%.

Major International Organizations: UN.

The Federated States of Micronesia, formerly known as the Caroline Islands, was ruled successively by Spain, Germany, Japan, and the U.S. It was internationally recognized as an independent nation Sept. 17, 1991.

Moldova

Republic of Moldova

Republica Moldoveneasca

People: Population: 4,473,000. **Pop. density:** 343 per sq. mi. **Urban:** 48%. **Ethnic groups:** Moldovan/Romanian 65%, Ukrainian 14%, Russian 13%. **Principal languages:** Moldovan (official), Russian. **Religions:** Eastern Orthodox 99%.

Geography: Area: 13,012 sq. mi. **Neighbors:** Romania on W, Ukraine on N, E, and S. **Capital:** Chisinau. **Cities** (1991): Chisinau 753,000; Tiraspol 186,000.

Government: Type: Republic. **Head of state:** Pres. Mircea Snegur; b Jan. 17, 1940; in office: Sept. 1990. **Head of government:** Prime Min. Andre Sangheli; in office: July 1, 1992.

Economy: Industries: Canning, wine making, textiles. **Chief crops:** Grain, grapes. **Minerals:** Lignite, gypsum. **Livestock** (1992): cattle: 1.0 mln., pigs: 1.4 mln., sheep: 1.1 mln. **Electricity prod.** (1992): 11 bln. kWh.

Finance: Monetary unit: Ruble.

Transport: Railroads: Length: 715 mi. **Motor vehicles:** in use: 210,000 passenger cars. **Civil aviation:** 1.4 bln. passenger-mi.; 1 airport.

Communications: Telephones: 1 per 7.6 persons. **Daily newspaper circ.:** 561 per 1,000 pop.

Health: Life expectancy at birth (1994): 65 male; 72 female. **Births** (per 1,000 pop.): 16. **Deaths** (per 1,000 pop.): 10. **Natural increase:** .6%. **Hospital beds:** 1 per 77 persons. **Physicians:** 1 per 251 persons. **Infant mortality** (per 1,000 live births 1994): 30.

Major International Organizations: UN, CIS.

In 1918, Romania annexed all of Bessarabia which Russia had acquired from Turkey in 1812 by the Treaty of Bucharest. In 1924, the Soviet Union established the Moldavian Autonomous Soviet Socialist Republic on the eastern bank of the Dniester. It was merged with the Romanian-speaking districts of Bessarabia in 1940 to form the Moldavian SSR.

During World War II, Romania, allied with Germany, occupied the area. It was recaptured by the USSR in 1944. Moldova declared independence Aug. 27, 1991. It became an independent state when the Soviet Union disbanded Dec. 26, 1991. Fighting erupted between Moldovan security forces and Slavic separatists—ethnic Russians and ethnic Ukrainians—Mar. 1992. The Slavs feared that Moldovans, who are Romanian in language and culture, would merge with neighboring Romania. In a plebiscite on Mar. 6, 1994, however, the electorate supported independence, without unification with Romania.

Monaco

Principality of Monaco

People: Population: 31,000. **Pop. density:** 41,333 per sq. mi. **Ethnic groups:** French 47%, Italian 16%, Monégasque 16%. **Principal languages:** French (official). **Religions:** Predominantly Roman Catholic.

Geography: Area: 0.75 sq. mi. **Location:** On the NW Mediterranean coast. **Neighbors:** France to W, N, E. **Topography:** Monaco-Ville sits atop a high promontory, the rest of the principality rises from the port up the hillside. **Capital:** Monaco.

Government: Type: Constitutional monarchy. **Head of state:** Prince Rainier III; b May 31, 1923; in office: May 9, 1949. **Head of government:** Min. of State Jacques Dupont.

Economy: Industries: Tourism, gambling, chemicals, precision instruments, plastics.

Finance: Monetary unit: French franc or Monégasque franc. **Gross domestic product** (1991): $475 mln. **Per capita GDP:** $16,000. **National budget** (1991): $424 mln. revenues.

Transport: Chief ports: La Condamine.

Communications: Television sets: 1 per 1.5 persons. **Telephones:** 1 per 0.6 persons.

Health: Births (per 1,000 pop.): 11. **Deaths** (per 1,000 pop.): 12. **Natural increase:** -.2%. **Infant mortality** (per 1,000 live births 1994): 7.

Education: (1989): **Literacy:** 99%. **Years compulsory:** 10; attendance 99%.

Major International Organizations: UN.

An independent principality for over 300 years, Monaco has belonged to the House of Grimaldi since 1297, except during the French Revolution. It was placed under the protectorate of Sardinia in 1815, and under that of France, 1861. The Prince of Monaco was an absolute ruler until a 1911 constitution.

Monaco's fame as a tourist resort is widespread. It is noted for its mild climate and magnificent scenery.

Mongolia

People: Population: 2,430,000. **Pop. density:** 4 per sq. mi. **Urban:** 57%. **Ethnic groups:** Mongol 90%. **Principal languages:** Mongolian (official). **Religions:** traditionally Tibetan Buddhism.

Geography: Area: 604,800 sq. mi., more than twice the size of Texas. **Location:** In E Central Asia. **Neighbors:** Russia N, China on S. **Topography:** Mostly a high plateau with mountains, salt lakes, and vast grasslands. Arid lands in the S are part of the Gobi Desert. **Capital:** Ulaanbaatar. **Cities** (1991 est.): Ulaanbaatar 536,000, Darhan 80,000.

Government: Type: In transition. **Head of state:** Pres. Punsalmaagiyn Ochirbat; b 1942; in office: Mar. 21, 1990. **Head of government:** Prime Min. Puntsagiyn Jasray; in office: July 21, 1992. **Local divisions:** 18 provinces, 3 municipalities. **Defense:** 1% of GDP (1992).

Economy: Industries: Food processing, textiles, chemicals, cement. **Chief crops:** Grain. **Minerals:** Coal, tungsten, copper, molybdenum, gold, tin. **Arable land:** 1%. **Livestock** (1991): sheep: 15 mln.; cattle 2.9 mln. **Electricity prod.** (1992): 3.7 bln. kWh. **Labor force:** 52% agric.; 10% manuf.

Finance: Monetary unit: Tughrik (Jan. 1993: 120 = $1 US). **Gross domestic product** (1992): $1.8 bln. **Per capita GDP:** $800. **Imports** (1991): $360 mln.; partners: CIS 91%. **Exports** (1991): $279 mln.; partners: CIS 80%.

Transport: Railroads: Length: 1,445 mi.

Communications: Television sets: 1 per 18 persons. **Radios:** 1 per 12 persons. **Telephones:** 1 per 31 persons. **Daily newspaper circ.:** 74 per 1,000 pop.

Health: Life expectancy at birth (1994): 64 male; 69 female. **Births** (per 1,000 pop.): 33. **Deaths** (per 1,000 pop.): 7. **Natural increase:** 2.6%. **Hospital beds:** 1 per 83 persons. **Physicians:** 1 per 340 persons. **Infant mortality** (per 1,000 live births 1994): 43.

Major International Organizations: UN (ILO, WHO).

Education (1990): **Literacy:** 89%.

One of the world's oldest countries, Mongolia reached the zenith of its power in the 13th century when Genghis Khan and his successors conquered all of China and extended their influence as far west as Hungary and Poland. In later centuries, the empire dissolved and Mongolia became a province of China.

With the advent of the 1911 Chinese revolution, Mongolia, with Russian backing, declared its independence. A Mongolian Communist regime was established July 11, 1921.

In 1990, the Mongolian Communist Party surrendered its monopoly on power. Free elections were held July 1990; the Communists were victorious.

Morocco

Kingdom of Morocco

al-Mamlaka al-Maghrebia

People: Population: 28,559,000. **Age distrib.** (%): <15: 40; 65+: 4. **Pop. density:** 161 per sq. mi. **Urban:** 47%. **Ethnic groups:** Arab-Berber 99%. **Principal languages:** Arabic (official), Berber. **Religions:** Sunni Muslims 99%.

Geography: Area: 177,117 sq. mi., larger than California. **Location:** on NW coast of Africa. **Neighbors:** W Sahara on S, Algeria on E. **Topography:** Consists of 5 natural regions: mountain ranges (Riff in the N, Middle Atlas, Upper Atlas, and Anti-Atlas); rich plains in the W; alluvial plains in SW; well-cultivated plateaus in the center; a pre-Sahara arid zone extending from SE. **Capital:** Rabat. **Cities** (1984): Casablanca 2,600,000, Rabat 556,000, Fes 852,000.

Government: Type: Constitutional monarchy. **Head of state:** King Hassan II; b July 9, 1929; in office: Mar. 3, 1961. **Head of government:** Prime Min. Abdellatif Filali; in office: May 25, 1994. **Local divisions:** 37 provinces, 5 municipalities. **Defense:** 3.8% of GDP (1993).

Economy: Industries: Carpets, clothing, leather goods, mining, tourism. **Chief crops:** Grain, fruits, dates, grapes. **Minerals:** Copper, cobalt, manganese, phosphates, lead, oil. **Crude oil reserves** (1980): 100 mln. bbls. **Arable land:** 18%. **Livestock** (1992): cattle: 3.3 mln.; sheep; 17 mln.; goats: 5.5 mln. **Fish catch** (1991): 592,000 metric tons. **Electricity prod.** (1992): 8.8 bln. kWh. **Labor force:** 50% agric., 26% services; 15% ind.

Finance: Monetary unit: Dirham (Mar. 1994: 9.48 = $1 US). **Gross domestic product** (1992): $28.1 bln. **Per capita GDP:** $1,060. **Imports** (1991): $6.0 bln.; partners: EU 53%, U.S. 11%. **Exports** (1991): $4.1 bln.; partners: EU 58%. **Tourism** (1990): $1.2 bln. receipts. **National budget** (1992): $7.7 bln. **International reserves less gold** (Feb. 1994): $3.5 bln. **Gold:** 704,000 oz t. **Consumer prices** (change in 1993): 4.6%.

Transport: Railroads: Length: 1,176 mi. **Motor vehicles:** in use: 669,000 passenger cars, 282,000 comm. vehicles. **Civil aviation:** 1.7 bln. passenger-mi.; 16 airports. **Chief ports:** Tangier, Casablanca, Kenitra.

Communications: Television sets: 1 per 21 persons. **Radios:** 1 per 5.8 persons. **Telephones:** 1 per 46 persons. **Daily newspaper circ.:** 13 per 1,000 pop.

Health: Life expectancy at birth (1994): 66 male; 70 female. **Births** (per 1,000 pop.): 29. **Deaths** (per 1,000 pop.): 6. **Natural increase:** 2.2%. **Hospital beds:** 1 per 959 persons. **Physicians:** 1 per 4,415 persons. **Infant mortality** (per 1,000 live births 1994): 50.

Education (1990): **Literacy:** 50%.

Major International Organizations: UN (ILO, IMF, WHO), OAU, Arab League.

Embassy: 1601 21st St. NW 20009; 462-7979.

Berbers were the original inhabitants, followed by Carthaginians and Romans. Arabs conquered in 683. In the 11th and 12th centuries, a Berber empire ruled all NW Africa and most of Spain from Morocco.

Part of Morocco came under Spanish rule in the 19th century; France controlled the rest in the early 20th. Tribal uprisings lasted from 1911 to 1933. The country became independent Mar. 2, 1956. Tangier, an internationalized seaport, was turned over to Morocco, 1956. Ifni, a Spanish enclave, was ceded in 1969.

Morocco annexed over 70,000 sq. mi. of phosphate-rich land Apr. 14, 1976, two-thirds of former Spanish Sahara, with the remainder annexed by Mauritania. Spain had withdrawn in February. Polisario, a guerrilla movement, proclaimed the region independent Feb. 27, and launched attacks with Algerian support. When Mauritania signed a treaty with the Polisario Front and gave up its portion of the former Spanish Sahara, Morocco occupied the area, 1980.

After years of bitter fighting, Morocco controlled the main urban areas, but the Polisario Front's guerrillas moved freely in the vast, sparsely populated deserts. The 2 sides signed a cease-fire agreement in 1990. The UN planned to conduct a referendum in Western Sahara on whether the territory should become independent or remain part of Morocco.

Mozambique

Republic of Mozambique

República de Mocambique

People: Population: 17,346,000. **Age distrib.** (%): <15: 44; 65+: 3. **Pop. density:** 55 per sq. mi. **Ethnic groups:** Bantu tribes. **Principal languages:** Portuguese (official), Makua, Malawl, Shona, Tsonga. **Religions:** indigenous beliefs 60%, Christian 30%, Muslim 10%.

Geography: Area: 313,661 sq. mi., about the size of Texas. **Location:** On SE coast of Africa. **Neighbors:** Tanzania on N, Malawi, Zambia, Zimbabwe on W, South Africa, Swaziland on S. **Topography:** Coastal lowlands comprise nearly half the country with plateaus rising in steps to the mountains along the western border. **Capital:** Maputo. **Cities:** (1991 est.): Maputo 931,000, Beira 298,000.

Government: Type: Republic. **Head of state:** Pres. Joaquim Chissano; b Oct. 22, 1939; in office: Oct. 19, 1986. **Head of government:** Mario de Graca Machungo; in office: July 17, 1986. **Local divisions:** 10 provinces. **Defense:** 8% of GDP (1993 est.).

Economy: Industries: Cement, alcohol, textiles. **Chief crops:** Cashews, cotton, sugar, copra, tea. **Minerals:** Coal, titanium. **Arable land:** 4%. **Livestock** (1992): cattle: 1.2 mln. **Fish catch** (1991): 34,000 metric tons. **Electricity prod.** (1991): 1.7 bln. kWh. **Labor force:** 90% agric.

Finance: Monetary unit: Metical (Dec. 1993: 5,369 = $1 US). **Gross domestic product** (1992): $1.75 bln. **Per capita GDP:** $115. **Imports** (1990): $870 mln.; partners: So. Afr. 11%, U.S. 8%, USSR 12%, It. 10%. **Exports** (1990): $117 mln.; partners: Sp. 21%, U.S. 16%, Jap. 15%. **National budget** (1992 est.): $607 mln.

Transport: Railroads: Length: 1,857 mi. **Motor vehicles:** in use: 24,000 passenger cars, 42,000 comm. vehicles. **Chief ports:** Maputo, Beira, Nacala, Quelimane.

Communications: Television sets: 1 per 428 persons. **Radios:** 1 per 30 persons. **Telephones:** 1 per 211 persons.

Health: Life expectancy at birth (1994): 47 male; 50 female. **Births** (per 1,000 pop.): 45. **Deaths** (per 1,000 pop.): 16. **Natural increase:** 2.9%. **Hospital beds:** 1 per 1,227 persons. **Physicians:** 1 per 43,536 persons. **Infant mortality** (per 1,000 live births 1994): 129.

Education (1989): **Literacy:** 14%.

Major International Organization: UN (IMF, World Bank), OAU.

Embassy: 1990 M St. NW 20036; 293-7146.

The first Portuguese post on the Mozambique coast was established in 1505, on the trade route to the East. Mozambique became independent June 25, 1975, after a ten-year war against Portuguese colonial domination. The 1974 revolution in Portugal had paved the way for the orderly transfer of power to Frelimo (Front for the Liberation of Mozambique). Frelimo took over local administration Sept. 20, 1974, over the opposition, in part violent, of some blacks and whites.

The new government, led by Maoist Pres. Samora Machel, provided for a gradual transition to a communist system. Economic problems included the emigration of most of the country's whites, a politically untenable economic dependence on white-ruled South Africa, and a large external debt.

In the 1980s, severe drought and civil war caused famine and heavy loss of life.

The ruling party formally abandoned Marxist-Leninism in 1989, and a new constitution, effective Nov. 30, 1990, provided for multiparty elections and a free-market economy. Elections were scheduled for Oct. 27-28, 1994.

On Oct. 4, 1992, a peace agreement was signed aimed at ending hostilities between the government and the rebel Mozambique National Resistance (MNR).

Myanmar (Formerly Burma)

Union of Myanmar

Pyidaungzu Myanma Naingngandaw

People: Population: 44,277,000. **Age distrib.** (%): <15: 36; 65+: 4. **Pop. density:** 169 per sq. mi. **Urban:** 25%. **Ethnic groups:** Burmese (related to Tibetans) 68%, Shan 9%, Karen 7%, Rakhine 4%. **Principal languages:** Burmese (official), Karen, Shan. **Religions:** Buddhist 89%, animist, Christian.

Geography: Area: 261,228 sq. mi., nearly as large as Texas. **Location:** Between S and S.E. Asia, on Bay of Bengal. **Neighbors:** Bangladesh, India on W, China, Laos, Thailand on E. **Topography:** Mountains surround Myanmar on W, N, and E, and dense forests cover much of the nation. N-S rivers provide habitable valleys and communications, especially the Irrawaddy, navigable for 900 miles. The country has a tropical monsoon climate. **Capital:** Yangôn. **Cities** (1983 est.): Yangôn 2.5 mln.; Mandalay 532,000.

Government: Type: Military. **Head of state and government:** Gen. Than Shwe; in office: Apr. 24, 1992. **Local divisions:** 7 states and 7 divisions. **Defense:** 3.1% of GDP (1992).

Economy: Industries: mining, textiles, footwear, petroleum, refining. **Chief crops:** Rice, sugarcane, peanuts, beans. **Minerals:** Oil, lead, silver, tin, tungsten, precious stones. **Crude oil reserves** (1985): 733 mln. bbls. **Other resources:** Rubber, teakwood. **Arable land:** 15%. **Livestock** (1992): cattle: 9.4 mln.; pigs: 2.5 mln. **Fish catch** (1991): 769,000 metric tons. **Electricity prod.** (1992): 2.8 bln. kWh. **Labor force:** 65% agric.; 14% ind.

Finance: Monetary unit: Kyat (Mar. 1994: 6.13 = $1 US). **Gross domestic product** (1992): $28 bln. **Per capita GDP:** $660. **Imports** (1991): $1.1 bln.; partners: Jap. 50%, EU 20%. **Exports** (1991): $568 mln.; partners: SE Asian countries 30%; EU 12%. **Tourism** (1990): $5 mln. receipts. **National budget** (1992): $11.6 bln. **International reserves less gold** (Feb. 1994): $346 mln. **Gold:** 251,000 oz t. **Consumer prices** (change in 1993): 31.8%.

Transport: Railroads: Length: 1,949 mi. **Motor vehicles:** in use: 35,000 passenger cars, 35,000 comm. vehicles. **Civil aviation:** 137 mln. passenger-mi.; 20 airports with scheduled flights. **Chief ports:** Yangôn, Bassein, Moulmein.

Communications: Television sets: 1 per 43 persons. **Radios:** 1 per 14 persons. **Telephones:** 1 per 501 persons.

Health: Life expectancy at birth (1994): 58 male; 62 female. **Births** (per 1,000 pop.): 28. **Deaths** (per 1,000 pop.): 10. **Natural increase:** 1.9%. **Hospital beds:** 1 per 1,602 persons. **Physicians:** 1 per 3,389 persons. **Infant mortality** (per 1,000 live births 1994): 64.

Education (1990): **Literacy:** 81%. **Years compulsory:** 4. **Attendance:** 84%.

Major International Organizations: UN (World Bank, IMF, GATT).

Embassy: 2300 S St. NW 20008; 332-9044.

The Burmese arrived from Tibet before the 9th century, displacing earlier cultures, and a Buddhist monarchy was established by the 11th. Burma was conquered by the Mongol dynasty of China in 1272, then ruled by Shans as a Chinese tributary, until the 16th century.

Britain subjugated Burma in 3 wars, 1824-84, and ruled the country as part of India until 1937, when it became self-governing. Independence outside the Commonwealth was achieved Jan. 4, 1948.

Gen. Ne Win dominated politics from 1962 to 1988, first as military ruler then as constitutional president. His regime drove Indians from the civil service and Chinese from commerce. Socialization of the economy was advanced, isolation from foreign countries enforced. In 1987 Burma, once the richest nation in SE Asia, was granted less developed status by the UN.

Ne Win resigned July 1988, following waves of antigovernment riots. Rioting and street violence continued, and in Sept. the military seized power, under Gen. Saw Maung. In 1989 the country's name was changed to Myanmar.

The first free multiparty elections in 30 years took place May 27, 1990, with the main opposition party winning a decisive victory, but the military refused to hand over power. A key opposition leader, Aung San Suu Kyi, had been put under house arrest before elections; still under house arrest, she was awarded the Nobel Peace Prize in 1991.

Namibia

Republic of Namibia

People: Population: 1,596,000. **Pop density:** 5 per sq. mi. **Urban:** 33%. **Ethnic groups:** Ovambo 50%, Kavango 9%, Herero 7%, Damara 7%. **Principal languages:** Afrikaans, English (official), several indigenous languages. **Religions:** Lutheran 50%, other Christian 30%.

Geography: Area: 318,146 sq. mi., slightly more than half the size of Alaska. **Location:** In S Africa on the coast of the Atlantic Ocean. Angola on the N, Botswana on the E, and South Africa on the S. **Capital:** Windhoek. **Cities** (1990 est.): Windhoek, 114,000.

Government: Type: Republic. **Head of state:** Pres. Sam Nujoma; b May 12, 1929; in office: Mar. 21, 1990. **Head of government:** Prime Min. Hage Geingob. **Local divisions:** 14 regions. **Defense:** 3.4% of GDP (1992).

Economy: Mining accounts for over 40% of GDP. **Minerals:** Diamonds. **Fish catch** (1991): 204,000 metric tons. **Electricity prod.** (1991): 1.2 mln. kWh.

Finance: Monetary unit: Dollar (Mar. 1994: 3.45 = $1 US). **Gross domestic product** (1992): $2.0 bln. **Per capital GDP:** $1,300. **Imports** (1989): $894 mln. **Exports** (1989): $1.0 bln. **National budget** (1992): $1.1 bln. **International reserves less gold** (Feb. 1994): $206 mln.

Transport: Railroads: Length: 1,481 mi.

Communications: Television sets: 1 per 53 persons. **Radios:** 1 per 5.6 persons. **Telephones:** 1 per 16 persons.

Health: Life expectancy at birth (1994): 59 male; 64 female. **Births** (per 1,000 pop.): 43. **Deaths** (per 1,000 pop.): 9. **Natural increase:** 3.5. **Hospital beds:** 1 per 166 persons. **Physicians:** 1 per 4,594 persons. **Infant mortality** (per 1,000 live births 1994): 62.

Education (1989): **Literacy:** 16% nonwhite.

Embassy: 1605 New Hampshire Ave. NW 20009; 986-0540.

Namibia was declared a protectorate by Germany in 1890 and officially called South-West Africa. South Africa seized the territory from Germany in 1915 during World War I; the League of Nations gave South Africa a mandate over the territory in 1920. In 1966, the Marxist South-West Africa People's Organization (SWAPO) launched a guerrilla war for independence.

In 1968 the UN General Assembly gave the area the name Namibia.

After many years of guerrilla warfare and failed diplomatic efforts, S Africa, Angola, and Cuba signed a U.S.-mediated agreement Dec. 22, 1988, to end S African administration of Namibia and provide for a cease-fire and transition to independence, in accordance with a 1978 UN plan. A separate accord between Cuba and Angola provided for a phased withdrawal of Cuban troops from Namibia. SWAPO later endorsed the plan. Elections were held for a constituent assembly, and a constitution providing for multiparty government was adopted Feb. 9, 1990. Namibia became an independent nation Mar. 21, 1990.

Walvis Bay, the principal deepwater port, had been turned over to S African administration in 1922. It remained in S African hands after independence, but S Africa turned control of the port back to Namibia, as of Mar. 1, 1994.

Nauru

Republic of Nauru

Naoero

People: Population: 10,000. **Pop density:** 1,219 per sq. mi. **Ethnic groups:** Nauruans 58%, Pacific Islanders 26%,

Chinese 8%, European 8%. **Principal languages:** Nauruan (official). **Religions:** Predominantly Christian.

Geography: Area: 8.2 sq. mi. **Location:** In Western Pacific O. just S of Equator. **Neighbors:** Nearest are Solomon Is. **Topography:** Mostly a plateau bearing high grade phosphate deposits, surrounded by a coral cliff and a sandy shore in concentric rings. **Capital:** Yaren.

Government: Type: Republic. **Head of state:** Pres. Bernard Dowiyogo; b Feb. 14, 1946; in office: Dec. 12, 1989. **Local divisions:** 14 districts.

Economy: Phosphate mining. **Electricity prod.** (1990): 50 mln. kWh.

Finance: Monetary unit: Australian dollar. **Gross national product** (1989): $90 mln.

Communications: Radios: 1 per 2.4 persons. **Telephones:** 1 per 5.9 persons.

Health: Births (per 1,000 pop.): 18. **Deaths** (per 1,000 pop.): 5. **Natural increase:** 1.3%. **Infant mortality** (per 1,000 live births 1994): 41.

Education (1988): **Literacy:** 99%; compulsory ages 6-16.

The island was discovered in 1798 by the British but was formally annexed to the German Empire in 1886. After World War I, Nauru became a League of Nations mandate administered by Australia. During World War II the Japanese occupied the island and shipped 1,200 Nauruans to the fortress island of Truk as slave laborers.

In 1947 Nauru was made a UN trust territory, administered by Australia. Nauru became an independent republic Jan. 31, 1968.

Phosphate exports provide Nauru with one of the world's highest per capita revenues.

Nepal

Kingdom of Nepal

Nepal Adhirajya

People: Population: 21,042,000. **Age distrib.** (%): <15: 44; 65+: 3. **Pop. density:** 370 per sq. mi. **Urban:** 8%. **Ethnic groups:** The many tribes are descendants of Indian, Tibetan, and Central Asian migrants. **Principal languages:** Nepali (official) (an Indic language), many others. **Religions:** Hindu (official) 90%, Buddhist 5%, Muslim 3%.

Geography: Area: 56,827 sq. mi., the size of North Carolina. **Location:** Astride the Himalaya Mts. **Neighbors:** China on N, India on S. **Topography:** The Himalayas stretch across the N, the hill country with its fertile valleys extends across the center, while the southern border region is part of the flat, subtropical Ganges Plain. **Capital:** Kathmandu. **Cities** (1991 est.): Kathmandu 419,000; Biratnagar 130,000; Lalitpur 117,000; Pokhara 95,000.

Government: Type: Constitutional monarchy. **Head of state:** King Birendra Bir Bikram Shah Dev; b Dec. 28, 1945; in office: Jan. 31, 1972. **Head of government:** Prime Min. Giriga Prasad Koirala; in office: May 26, 1991. **Local divisions:** 14 zones. **Defense:** 2% of GDP (1992).

Economy: Industries: Sugar, jute mills, tourism. **Chief crops:** Jute, rice, grain. **Minerals:** Quartz. **Other resources:** Forests. **Arable land:** 17%. **Livestock** (1991): cattle: 6.3 mln. **Electricity prod.** (1992): 1 bln. kWh. **Labor force:** 93% agric.

Finance: Monetary unit: Rupee (Mar. 1994: 49 = $1 US). **Gross domestic product** (1992): $3.4 bln. **Per capita GDP:** $165. **Imports** (1991): $545 mln.; partners: India 47%, Jap. 25%. **Exports** (1991): $180 mln.; partners: India 68%. **Tourism** (1990): receipts: $57 mln. **National budget** (1992): $672 mln. **International reserves less gold** (Oct. 1993): $602 mln. **Gold:** 153,000 oz t. **Consumer prices** (change in 1992): 17.1%.

Transport: Civil aviation: 439 mln. passenger-mi.

Communications: Radios: 1 per 33 persons. **Telephones:** 1 per 275 persons.

Health: Life expectancy at birth (1994): 52 male; 53 female. **Births** (per 1,000 pop.): 38. **Deaths** (per 1,000 pop.): 13. **Natural increase:** 2.4%. **Hospital beds:** 1 per 4,015 persons. **Physicians:** 1 per 16,007 persons. **Infant mortality** (per 1,000 live births 1994): 84.

Education (1989): **Literacy:** 29%. **Years compulsory:** 3; Attendance: 79% primary, 22% secondary.

Major International Organizations: UN (IMF).

Embassy: 2131 Leroy Pl. NW 20008; 667-4550.

Nepal was originally a group of petty principalities, the inhabitants of one of which, the Gurkhas, became dominant about 1769. In 1951 King Tribhubana Bir Bikram, member of the Shah family, ended the system of rule by hereditary premiers of the Ranas family, who had kept the kings virtual prisoners, and established a cabinet system of government.

Virtually closed to the outside world for centuries, Nepal is now linked to India and Pakistan by roads and air service and to Tibet by road. Polygamy, child marriage, and the caste system were officially abolished in 1963.

The government announced the legalization of political parties in 1990. Multiparty elections were held in 1991.

Netherlands

Kingdom of the Netherlands

Koninkrijk der Nederlanden

People: Population: 15,368,000. **Age distrib.** (%): <15: 18; 65+: 13. **Pop. density:** 958 per sq. mi. **Urban:** 89%. **Ethnic groups:** Dutch 96%. **Principal languages:** Dutch. **Religions:** Roman Catholic 36%, Protestant 27%.

Geography: Area: 16,033 sq. mi., the size of Mass., Conn., and R.I. combined. **Location:** In NW Europe on North Sea. **Topography:** The land is flat, an average alt. of 37 ft. above sea level, with much land below sea level reclaimed and protected by some 1,500 miles of dikes. Since 1920 the government has been draining the IJsselmeer, formerly the Zuider Zee. **Capital:** Amsterdam. **Cities** (1992): Amsterdam 713,000; Rotterdam 589,000; The Hague 445,000.

Government: Type: Parliamentary democracy under a constitutional monarch. **Head of state:** Queen Beatrix; b Jan. 31, 1938; in office: Apr. 30, 1980. **Head of government:** Prime Min. Ruud Lubbers; in office: Nov. 4, 1982. **Seat of govt.:** The Hague. **Local divisions:** 12 provinces. **Defense:** 3% of GDP (1992).

Economy: Industries: Metals, machinery, chemicals, oil refinery, diamond cutting, electronics, tourism. **Chief crops:** Grains, potatoes, sugar beets, vegetables, fruits, flowers. **Minerals:** Natural gas, oil. **Crude oil reserves** (1987): 195 mln. bbls. **Arable land:** 26%. **Livestock** (1992): cattle: 4.9 mln.; pigs: 14.1 mln. **Fish catch** (1989): 421,000 metric tons. **Electricity prod.** (1992): 63.5 bln. kWh. **Labor force:** 6% agric.; 50% services; 16% govt.

Finance: Monetary unit: Guilder (Mar. 1994: 1.90 = $1 US). **Gross domestic product** (1992): $259.8 bln.* **Per capita GDP:** $17,200. **Imports** (1992): $156 bln.; partners: Ger. 26%, Belg. 14%, U.S. 9%, U.K. 9%. **Exports**(1992): $160 bln.; partners: Ger. 26%, Belg. 14%, Fr. 10%, UK 9%. **Tourism** (1990): receipts: $3.6 bln. **National budget** (1992 est.): $122.1 bln. **International reserves less gold** (Mar. 1994): $32.7 bln. **Gold:** 33.39 mln. oz t. **Consumer prices** (change in 1993): 2.1%.

Transport: Railroads: Length: 1,727 mi. **Motor vehicles:** in use: 5.6 mln. passenger cars, 797,000 comm. vehicles. **Civil aviation:** 17.1 bln. passenger-mi.; 5 airports. **Chief ports:** Rotterdam, Amsterdam, IJmuiden.

Communications: Television sets: 1 per 2.5 persons. **Radios:** 1 per 1.3 persons. **Telephones:** 1 per 1.4 persons. **Daily newspaper circ.:** 311 per 1,000 pop.

Health: Life expectancy at birth (1994): 75 male; 81 female. **Births** (per 1,000 pop.): 13. **Deaths** (per 1,000 pop.): 9. **Natural increase:** .4%. **Hospital beds:** 1 per 170 persons. **Physicians:** 1 per 400 persons. **Infant mortality** (per 1,000 live births 1994): 6.

Education (1991): **Literacy:** 99%. **Years compulsory:** 10; attendance: 100%.

Major International Organizations: UN and all of its specialized agencies, NATO, EU, OECD.

Embassy: 4200 Linnean Ave. NW 20008; 244-5300.

Julius Caesar conquered the region in 55 BC, when it was inhabited by Celtic and Germanic tribes.

After the empire of Charlemagne fell apart, the Netherlands (Holland, Belgium, Flanders) split among counts, dukes and bishops, passed to Burgundy and thence to Charles V of Spain. His son, Philip II, tried to check the Dutch drive toward political freedom and Protestantism (1568-1573). William the Silent, prince of Orange, led a confederation of the northern provinces, called Estates, in the Union of Utrecht, 1579. The Estates retained individual sovereignty, but were represented jointly in the States-General, a body that had control of foreign affairs and defense. In 1581 they repudiated allegiance to Spain. The rise of the Dutch republic to naval, economic, and artistic eminence came in the 17th century.

The United Dutch Republic ended 1795 when the French formed the Batavian Republic. Napoleon made his brother Louis king of Holland, 1806; Louis abdicated 1810 when Napoleon annexed Holland. In 1813 the French were expelled. In 1815 the Congress of Vienna formed a kingdom of the Netherlands, including Belgium, under William I. In 1830, the Belgians seceded and formed a separate kingdom.

The constitution, promulgated 1814, and subsequently revised, provides for a hereditary constitutional monarchy.

The Netherlands maintained its neutrality in World War I, but was invaded and brutally occupied by Germany, 1940-45.

In 1949, after several years of fighting, the Netherlands granted independence to Indonesia. In 1963, West New Guinea was turned over to Indonesia.

The independence of former Dutch colonies has instigated mass emigrations to the Netherlands.

Though the Netherlands has been heavily industrialized, its small farms export large quantities of pork and dairy foods. Rotterdam, located along the principal mouth of the Rhine, handles the most cargo of any ocean port in the world. Canals, of which there over 3,400 miles, are important in transportation.

Netherlands Antilles

The **Netherlands Antilles,** constitutionally on a level of equality with the Netherlands homeland within the kingdom, consist of 2 groups of islands in the West Indies. **Curacao, Aruba,** and **Bonaire** are near the South American coast; **St. Eustatius, Saba,** and the southern part of **St. Maarten** are SE of Puerto Rico. Northern two-thirds of St. Maarten belong to French Guadeloupe; the French call the island St. Martin. Total area of the 2 groups is 385 sq. mi., including: Aruba 75, Bonaire 111, Curacao 171, St. Eustatius 11, Saba 5, St. Maarten (Dutch part) 13.

Aruba was separated from The Netherlands Antilles on Jan. 1, 1986; it is an autonomous member of The Netherlands, the same status as the Netherland Antilles.

Total pop. (est. 1992) was 184,000. Willemstad, on Curacao, is the capital. Principal industry is the refining of crude oil from Venezuela. Tourism is an important industry, as is shipbuilding.

New Zealand

People: Population: 3,389,000. **Age distrib.** (%): <15: 23; 65+: 11 **Pop. density:** 32 per sq. mi. **Urban:** 85%. **Ethnic groups:** European (mostly British) 88%, Polynesian (mostly Maori) 9%. **Principal languages:** English (official), Maori. **Religions:** Anglican 24%, Presbyterian 18%, Roman Catholic 15%, others.

Geography: Area: 104,454 sq. mi., the size of Colorado. **Location:** In SW Pacific O. **Neighbors:** Nearest are Australia on W, Fiji, Tonga on N. **Topography:** Each of the 2 main islands (North and South Is.) is mainly hilly and mountainous. The east coasts consist of fertile plains, especially the broad Canterbury Plains on South Is. A volcanic plateau is in center of North Is. South Is. has glaciers and 15 peaks over 10,000 ft. **Capital:** Wellington. **Cities** (1992 est.): Auckland 316,000; Christchurch 293,000; Wellington 150,000; Manukau 229,000.

Government: Type: Parliamentary democracy. **Head of state:** Queen Elizabeth II, represented by Gov.-Gen. Dame Catherine Tizard. **Head of government:** Prime Min. Jim Bolger; b 1935; in office: Oct. 27, 1990. **Local divisions:** 93 counties, 12 towns & districts. **Defense:** 2% of GDP (1992).

Economy: Industries: Food processing, textiles, machinery, fish, forest prods. **Chief crops:** Grains, fruits. **Minerals:** Oil, gas, iron, coal **Crude oil reserves** (1987): 182 mln. bbls. **Other resources:** Wool, timber. **Arable land:** 2%. **Livestock** (1992): cattle: 8.1 mln.; sheep: 52.5 mln. **Fish catch** (1991): 609,000 metric tons. **Electricity prod.** (1992): 31.0 bln. kWh. **Labor force:** 20% manuf.; 67% services and gov.

Finance: Monetary unit: Dollar (Mar. 1994: 1.00 = $.57 US). **Gross domestic product** (1992): $49.8 bln.* **Per capita GDP:** $14,900. **Imports** (1992): $9.2 bln.; partners: Austral. 22%, U.S. 16%, Jap. 20%. **Exports** (1992): $9.8 bln.; partners: UK 9%, U.S. 15%, Jap. 15%, Austral. 16%. **Tourism** (1990): receipts $900,000 mln. **National budget** (1992): $15.2 bln. **International reserves less gold** (Feb. 1994): $4.0 bln. **Consumer prices** (change in 1993): 1.3%.

Transport: Railroads: Length: 2,627 mi. **Motor vehicles:** in use: 1.5 mln. passenger cars; 309,000 comm. vehicles. **Civil aviation:** 6.6 bln. passenger-mi.; 36 airports. **Chief ports:** Auckland, Wellington, Lyttleton, Tauranga.

Communications: Television sets: 1 per 3.2 persons. **Radios:** 1 per 1.1 persons. **Telephones:** 1 per 1.4 persons. **Daily newspaper circ.:** 324 per 1,000 pop.

Health: Life expectancy at birth (1994): 73 male; 80 female. **Births** (per 1,000 pop.): 16. **Deaths** (per 1,000 pop.): 8. **Natural increase:** .7%. **Hospital beds:** 1 per 114 persons. **Physicians:** 1 per 359 persons. **Infant mortality** (per 1,000 live births 1994): 9.

Education (1991): **Literacy:** 99%. Compulsory ages 6-15; attendance: 100%.

Major International Organizations: UN (GATT, World Bank, IMF), Commonwealth of Nations, OECD.

Embassy: 37 Observatory Cir. NW 20008; 328-4800.

The Maoris, a Polynesian group from the eastern Pacific, reached New Zealand before and during the 14th century. The first European to sight New Zealand was Dutch navigator Abel Janszoon Tasman, but Maoris refused to allow him to land. British Capt. James Cook explored the coasts, 1769-1770.

British sovereignty was proclaimed in 1840, with organized settlement beginning in the same year. Representative institutions were granted in 1853. Maori Wars ended in 1870 with British victory. The colony became a dominion in 1907, and is an independent member of the Commonwealth.

In July 1985, the *Rainbow Warrior,* flagship of the Greenpeace organization, was bombed and sunk in Auckland harbor by French secret service agents.

A progressive tradition in politics dates back to the 19th century, when New Zealand was internationally known for social experimentation. Private ownership is basic to the economy, but state ownership or regulation affects many industries. In recent years, the Labor and National parties have had alternating periods in power. The National Party, led by Jim Bolger, won general elections in 1990 and 1993.

The native Maoris number about 325,000. Four of 97 members of the House of Representatives are elected directly by the Maori people.

New Zealand comprises **North Island,** 44,035 sq. mi.; **South Island,** 58,304 sq. mi.; **Stewart Island,** 674 sq. mi.; **Chatham Islands,** 372 sq. mi.

In 1965, the **Cook Islands** (pop. 1986 est., 17,185; area 93 sq. mi.) became self-governing although New Zealand retains responsibility for defense and foreign affairs. **Niue** attained the same status in 1974; it lies 400 mi. to W (pop. 1987 est., 2,500; area 100 sq. mi.). **Tokelau Is.,** (pop. 1987 est., 1,600; area 4 sq. mi.) are 300 mi. N of Samoa.

Ross Dependency, administered by New Zealand since 1923, comprises 160,000 sq. mi. of Antarctic territory.

Nicaragua

Republic of Nicaragua

República de Nicaragua

People: Population: 4,097,000. **Age distrib.** (%): <15: 46; 65+: 3. **Pop. density:** 80 per sq. mi. **Urban:** 62%. **Ethnic groups:** Mestizo 69%, white 17%, black 9%, Indian 5%. **Principal languages:** Spanish (official). **Religions:** Roman Catholic 95%.

Geography: Area: 50,880 sq. mi., about the size of Iowa. **Location:** In Central America. **Neighbors:** Honduras on N, Costa Rica on S. **Topography:** Both Atlantic and Pacific coasts are over 200 mi. long. The Cordillera Mtns., with many volcanic peaks, runs NW-SE through the middle of the country. Between this and a volcanic range to the E lie Lakes Managua and Nicaragua. **Capital:** Managua. **Cities** (1986): Managua 1 mln.

Government: Type: Republic. **Head of state and government:** Pres. Violeta Barrios de Chamorro; b 1929; in office Apr. 25, 1990. **Local divisions:** 16 departments. **Defense:** 2.7% of GDP (1992).

Economy: Industries: Oil refining, food processing, chemicals, textiles. **Chief crops:** Bananas, cotton, fruit, yucca, coffee, sugar, corn, beans, cocoa, rice, sesame, tobacco, wheat. **Minerals:** Gold, silver, copper, tungsten. **Other resources:** Forests, shrimp. **Arable land:** 9%. **Livestock** (1992): cattle: 1.6 mln.; pigs: 709,000. **Electricity prod.** (1992): 1.1 bln. kWh. **Labor force:** 44% agric.; 13% ind.; 43% services.

Finance: Monetary unit: Cordoba (May 1993: 5.00 = $1 US). **Gross domestic product** (1992): $1.7 bln. **Per capita GDP:** $425. **Imports** (1991): $738 mln.; partners: U.S. 25%, Latin Amer. 30%, EU 20%. **Exports** (1991): $342 mln.; partners: OECD 75%. **National budget** (1991): $499 mln. **Consumer prices** (change in 1992): 20%.

Transport: Railroads: Length: 186 mi. **Motor vehicles:** in use: 35,000 passenger cars, 35,000 comm. vehicles. **Chief ports:** Corinto, Puerto Somoza, San Juan del Sur.

Communications: Television sets: 1 per 20 persons. **Radios:** 1 per 4.8 persons. **Telephones:** 1 per 81 persons. **Daily newspaper circ.:** 65 per 1,000 pop.

Health: Life expectancy at birth (1994): 61 male; 67 female. **Births** (per 1,000 pop.): 35. **Deaths** (per 1,000 pop.): 7. **Natural increase:** 2.8%. **Hospital beds:** 1 per 804 persons. **Physicians:** 1 per 1,882 persons. **Infant mortality** (per 1,000 live births 1994): 53.

Education (1991): **Literacy:** 57%. **Years compulsory:** 11 years or 16 years old.

Major International Organizations: UN and all of its specialized agencies, OAS.

Embassy: 1627 New Hampshire Ave. NW 20009; 939-6570.

Nicaragua, inhabited by various Indian tribes, was conquered by Spain in 1552. After gaining independence from Spain, 1821, Nicaragua was united for a short period with Mexico, then with the United Provinces of Central America, finally becoming an independent republic, 1838.

U.S. Marines occupied the country at times in the early 20th century, the last time from 1926 to 1933.

Gen. Anastasio Somoza Debayle was elected president 1967. He resigned 1972, but was elected president again in 1974. Martial law was imposed in Dec. 1974, after officials were kidnapped by the Marxist Sandinista guerrillas. Violent opposition spread to nearly all classes in 1978; nationwide strikes called against the government touched off a state of civil war. Months of simmering civil war ended when Somoza fled, July 19, 1979.

Relations with the U.S. were strained as a result of Nicaragua's aid to leftist guerrillas in El Salvador and U.S. backing of anti-Sandinista contra guerrilla groups.

In 1983, the contras launched their first major offensive; the Sandinistas imposed rule by decree. In 1985, the U.S. House rejected Pres. Reagan's request for military aid to the contras. The subsequent diversion of funds to the contras from the proceeds of a secret arms sale to Iran caused a major scandal in the U.S.

In a stunning upset, Violeta Barrios de Chamorro defeated Ortega in national elections, Feb. 25, 1990. Ortega remained leader of the Sandinista party.

Niger

Republic of Niger

République du Niger

People: Population: 8,635,000. **Age distrib.** (%): <15: 49; 65+: 3. **Pop. density:** 17 per sq. mi. **Urban:** 15%. **Ethnic groups:** Hausa 56%, Djerma 22%, Fula 9%, Tuareg 8%. **Principal languages:** French (official), Hausa, Djerma. **Religions:** Sunni Muslim 80%.

Geography: Area: 497,000 sq. mi., almost 3 times the size of California. **Location:** In the interior of N Africa. **Neighbors:** Libya, Algeria on N, Mali, Burkina Faso on W, Benin, Nigeria on S, Chad on E. **Topography:** Mostly arid desert and mountains. A narrow savanna in the S and the Niger R. basin in the SW contain most of the population. **Capital:** Niamey. **Cities** (1988 est.): Niamey 392,000.

Government: Type: Republic. **Head of state:** Pres. Mahamane Ousmane; in office: Mar. 1993. **Head of government:** Prime Min. Mahamadou Issoufou; in office: Apr. 1993. **Local divisions:** 7 departments. **Defense:** 1.3% of GDP (1989).

Economy: Chief crops: Peanuts, cotton. **Minerals:** Uranium, coal, iron. **Arable land:** 3%. **Livestock** (1992): cattle: 1.8 mln.; sheep: 3.4 mln.; goats: 5.4 mln. **Electricity prod.** (1991): 230 mln. kWh. **Labor force:** 90% agric.

Finance: Monetary unit: CFA franc (Mar. 1994: 576 = $1 US). **Gross domestic product** (1991): $2.3 bln. **Per capita GDP:** $290. **Imports** (1990): $439 mln.; partners: Fr. 32%. **Exports** (1990): $320 mln.; partners: Fr. 65%, Nig. 11%. **National budget** (1991): $355 mln. **International reserves less gold** (Dec. 1993): $192 mln. **Gold:** 11,000 oz t. **Consumer prices** (change in 1992): -4.5%.

Transport: Motor vehicles: in use: 31,000 passenger cars, 8,000 comm. vehicles.

Communications: Television sets: 1 per 330 persons. **Radios:** 1 per 21 persons. **Telephones:** 1 per 541 persons.

Health: Life expectancy at birth (1994): 43 male; 46 female. **Births** (per 1,000 pop.): 57. **Deaths** (per 1,000 pop.): 22. **Natural increase:** 3.5%. **Infant mortality** (per 1,000 live births 1994): 111.

Education (1991): **Literacy:** 28%. **Years compulsory:** 6; attendance: 15%.

Major International Organizations: UN (GATT, IMF, WHO, FAO), OAU.

Embassy: 2204 R St. NW 20008; 483-4224.

Niger was part of ancient and medieval African empires. European explorers reached the area in the late 18th century. The French colony of Niger was established 1900-22, after the defeat of Tuareg fighters, who had invaded the area from the N a century before. The country became independent Aug. 3, 1960. The next year it signed a bilateral agreement with France.

In 1993, Niger held its first free and open elections since independence. An opposition leader, Mahamane Ousmane, won the presidency.

Nigeria

Federal Republic of Nigeria

People: Population: 98,091,000. **Pop. density:** 275 per sq. mi. **Urban:** 16%. **Ethnic groups:** Hausa 21%, Yoruba 20%, Ibo 17%, Fulani 9%, others. **Principal languages:** English (official), Hausa, Yoruba, Ibo. **Religions:** Muslim 50% (in N), Christian 40% (in S), others.

Geography: Area: 356,669 sq. mi., more than twice the size of California. **Location:** On the S coast of W Africa. **Neighbors:** Benin on W, Niger on N, Chad, Cameroon on E. **Topography:** 4 E-W regions divide Nigeria: a coastal mangrove swamp 10-60 mi. wide, a tropical rain forest 50-100 mi. wide, a plateau of savanna and open woodland, and semidesert in the N. **Capital:** Abuja. **Cities:** (1992): Lagos 1.3 mln.; Ibadan 1.3 mln.

Government: Type: In transition. **Head of state and government:** Pres. Gen. Sani Abacha; in office: Nov. 17, 1993. **Local divisions:** 30 states plus federal capital territory. **Defense:** 1% of GDP (1992).

Economy: Industries: Crude oil (95% of export), food processing, assembly of vehicles, textiles. **Chief crops:** Cocoa (main export crop), tobacco, palm products, peanuts, cotton, soybeans. **Minerals:** Oil, gas, coal, iron, limestone, columbium, tin. **Crude oil reserves** (1991): 17.4 bln. bbls. **Other resources:** Timber, rubber, hides. **Arable land:** 31%. **Livestock** (1992): cattle: 15.7 mln.; goats: 24 mln.; sheep: 13 mln. **Fish catch** (1991): 266,000 metric tons. **Electricity prod.** (1991): 8.3 bln. kWh. **Labor force:** 54% agric., 19% ind., comm., and serv.

Finance: Monetary unit: Naira (Feb. 1994: 21.99 = $1 US). **Gross domestic product** (1992): $35 bln. **Per capita GDP:** $300. **Imports** (1990): $9.5 bln.; partners: U.S., EU. **Exports** (1990): $13.0 bln.; partners: U.S., EU. **Tourism receipts** (1990): $21 mln. **National budget** (1992 est.): $10.8 bln. **International reserves less gold** (Nov. 1993): $1.3 bln. **Gold:** 687,000 oz t. **Consumer prices** (change in 1993): 57.2%.

Transport: Motor vehicles: in use: 785,000 passenger cars, 625,000 comm. vehicles. **Civil aviation:** 481 mln. passenger-mi.; 14 airports. **Chief ports:** Port Harcourt, Lagos, Warri, Calabar.

Communications: Television sets: 1 per 21 persons. **Radios:** 1 per 9 persons. **Telephones:** 1 per 118 persons. **Daily newspaper circ.:** 16 per 1,000 pop.

Health: Life expectancy at birth (1994): 54 male; 57 female. **Births** (per 1,000 pop.): 44. **Deaths** (per 1,000 pop.): 12. **Natural increase:** 3.1%. **Hospital beds:** 1 per 1,160 persons. **Physicians:** 1 per 6,573 persons. **Infant mortality** (per 1,000 live births 1994): 75.

Education (1991): **Literacy:** 51%. **Primary school attendance:** 42%.

Major International Organizations: UN (GATT, IMO, WHO), OPEC, OAU, Commonwealth of Nations.

Embassy: 2201 M St. NW 20037; 822-1500.

Early cultures in Nigeria date back to at least 700 BC. From the 12th to the 14th centuries, more advanced cultures developed in the Yoruba area, at Ife, and in the north, where Muslem influence prevailed.

Portuguese and British slavers appeared from the 15th-16th centuries. Britain seized Lagos, 1861, and gradually extended control inland until 1900. Nigeria became independent Oct. 1, 1960, and a republic Oct. 1, 1963.

On May 30, 1967, the Eastern Region seceded, proclaiming itself the Republic of Biafra, plunging the country into civil war. Casualties in the war were estimated at over 1 million, including many "Biafrans" (mostly Ibos) who died of starvation despite international efforts to provide relief. The secessionists, after steadily losing ground, capitulated Jan. 12, 1970.

Oil revenues have made possible a massive economic development program, largely using private enterprise, but agriculture has lagged.

After 13 years of military rule, the nation experienced a peaceful return to civilian government, Oct., 1979. However, military rule resumed, Dec. 31, 1983, as a coup ousted the democratically elected government. A second coup came in 1985. The new regime, headed by Gen. Ibrahim Babangida, promised elections but voided the result of a presidential election on June 23, 1993; riots followed in which many were killed.

Babangida resigned and appointed a civilian to head an interim government, Aug, 26, 1993, but that government was ousted in a military coup, Nov. 17. In June 1994 the presumed winner of the 1993 presidential election, Moshood Abiola, declared himself president. He was jailed, and a wave of strikes were launched in response.

Norway

Kingdom of Norway

Kongeriket Norge

People: Population: 4,315,000. **Age distrib.** (%): <15: 19; 65+: 16. **Pop. density:** 34 per sq. mi. **Urban:** 72%. **Ethnic groups:** Germanic (Nordic, Alpine, Baltic), minority Lapps. **Principal languages:** Norwegian (official). **Religions:** Evangelical Lutheran 88%.

Geography: Area: 125,050 sq. mi., slightly larger than New Mexico. **Location:** Occupies the W part of Scandinavian peninsula in NW Europe (extends farther north than any European land). **Neighbors:** Sweden, Finland, Russia on E. **Topography:** A highly indented coast is lined with tens of thousands of islands. Mountains and plateaus cover most of the country, which is only 25% forested. **Capital:** Oslo. **Cities** (1993): Oslo 473,000; Bergen 218,000.

Government: Type: Hereditary constitutional monarchy. **Head of state:** King Harald V; b Feb. 21, 1937; in office: Jan. 17, 1991. **Head of government:** Prime Min. Gro Harlem Brundtland; in office: Nov. 3, 1990. **Local divisions:** Oslo, Svalbard and 18 fylker (counties). **Defense:** 3.4% of GDP (1992).

Economy: Industries: Paper, shipbuilding, engineering, metals, chemicals, food processing oil, gas. **Chief crops:** Grains, potatoes, fruits. **Minerals:** Oil, copper, pyrites, nickel, iron, zinc, lead. **Crude oil reserves** (1987): 11.1 bln. bbls. **Other resources:** Timber. **Arable land:** 3%. **Livestock** (1992): sheep: 1.0 mln.; cattle: 981,000; pigs: 763,000. **Fish catch** (1991): 2.3 mln. metric tons. **Electricity prod.** (1992): 111 bln. kWh. **Labor force:** 6% agric.; 47% ind., banking, comm.; 39% services.

Finance: Monetary unit: Kroner (Mar. 1994: 7.34 = $1 US). **Gross domestic product** (1992): $76.1 bln.* **Per capita GDP:** $17,700. **Imports** (1992): $25.9 bln.; partners: EU 47%. **Exports** (1992): $35.1 bln.; partners: EU 65%. **Tourism** (1990): receipts: $1.5 bln. **National budget** (1992): $57 bln. **International reserves less gold** (Mar. 1994): $20.0 bln. **Gold:** 1.18 mln. oz t. **Consumer prices** (change in 1993): 2.3%.

Transport: Railroads: Length: 2,502 mi. **Motor vehicles:** in use: 1.6 mln. passenger cars, 390,000 comm. vehicles. **Civil aviation:** 4.4 bln. passenger-mi.; 47 airports. **Chief ports:** Bergen, Stavanger, Oslo, Tonsberg.

Communications: Television sets: 1 per 2.9 persons. **Radios:** 1 per 1.3 persons. **Telephones:** 1 per 1.6 persons. **Daily newspaper circ.:** 614 per 1,000 pop.

Health: Life expectancy at birth (1994): 74 male; 81 female. **Births** (per 1,000 pop.): 13. **Deaths** (per 1,000 pop.): 10. **Natural increase:** .3%. **Hospital beds:** 1 per 177 persons. **Physicians:** 1 per 305 persons. **Infant mortality** (per 1,000 live births 1994): 6.

Education (1991): **Literacy:** 99%. **Years Compulsory:** 9.

Major International Organizations: UN and all of its specialized agencies, NATO, OECD.

Embassy: 2720 34th St. NW 20008; 333-6000.

The first ruler of Norway was Harald the Fairhaired, who came to power in 872 AD. Between 800 and 1000, Norway's Vikings raided and occupied widely dispersed parts of Europe.

The country was united with Denmark 1381-1814, and with Sweden, 1814-1905. In 1905, the country became independent with Prince Charles of Denmark as king.

Norway remained neutral during World War I. Germany attacked Norway Apr. 9, 1940, and held it until liberation May 8, 1945. The country abandoned its neutrality after the war, and joined the NATO alliance. Norway was scheduled to join the European Union (formerly European Community), Jan. 1, 1995, provided that Norwegians approved membership in a referendum scheduled for Nov. 28, 1994.

Abundant hydroelectric resources provided the base for Norway's industrialization, producing one of the highest living standards in the world.

Norway's merchant marine is one of the world's largest.

Svalbard is a group of mountainous islands in the Arctic O., c. 23,957 sq. mi., pop. varying seasonally from 1,500 to 3,600. The largest, Spitsbergen (formerly called West Spitsbergen), 15,060 sq. mi., seat of governor, is about 370 mi. N of Norway. By a treaty signed in Paris, 1920, major European powers recognized the sovereignty of Norway, which incorporated it in 1925.

Oman

Sultanate of Oman

Saltanat 'Uman

People: Population: 1,701,000. **Pop. density:** 14 per sq. mi. **Urban:** 12%. **Ethnic groups:** Omani Arab 74%, Pakistani 21%. **Principal languages:** Arabic (official). **Religions:** Ibadhi Muslim 75%, Sunni Muslim.

Geography: Area: 118,150 sq. mi., about the size of New Mexico. **Location:** On SE coast of Arabian peninsula. **Neighbors:** United Arab Emirates, Saudi Arabia, Yemen on W. **Topography:** Oman has a narrow coastal plain up to 10 mi. wide, a range of barren mountains reaching 9,900 ft., and a wide, stony, mostly waterless plateau, avg. alt. 1,000 ft. Also the tip of the Ruus-al-Jebal peninsula controls access to the Persian Gulf. **Capital:** Muscat. **Cities** (1990 est.): Muscat 85,000.

Government: Type: Absolute monarchy. **Head of state and government:** Sultan Qabus bin Said; b Nov. 18, 1942; in office: July 23, 1970. **Defense:** 16% of GDP (1993 est.).

Economy: Chief crops: Dates, fruits, vegetables, wheat, bananas. **Minerals:** Oil (95% of exports). **Crude oil reserves** (1987): 4.5 bln. bbls. **Fish catch** (1991): 117,000 metric tons. **Electricity prod.** (1992): 5.1 bln. kWh. **Labor force:** 60% agric. & fishing.

Finance: Monetary unit: Rial Omani (Mar. 1994: .38 = $1 US). **Gross domestic product** (1991): $10.2 bln. **Per capita GDP:** 6,670. **Imports** (1990): $2.6 bln.; partners: Jap. 21%, UAE 17%, UK 14%. **Exports** (1990): $2.6 bln.; partners: Jap. 58%, Europe 30%. **National budget** (1991): $4.8 bln. **International reserves less gold** (Mar. 1993): $1.6 bln. **Gold:** 289,000 oz t.

Transport: Motor vehicles: in use: 96,000 passenger cars, 70,000 comm. vehicles. **Civil aviation:** 1.0 bln. passenger-mi.; 6 airports. **Chief ports:** Matrah, Muscat.

Communications: Television sets: 1 per 1.1 persons. **Radios:** 1 per 1.8 persons. **Telephones:** 1 per 6.1 persons.

Health: Life expectancy at birth (1994): 66 male; 70 female. **Births** (per 1,000 pop.): 40. **Deaths** (per 1,000 pop.): 6. **Natural increase:** 3.5%. **Hospital beds:** 1 per 380 persons. **Physicians:** 1 per 1,078 persons. **Infant mortality** (per 1,000 live births 1994): 37.

Education (1989): **Literacy:** 20%. **Attendance:** 80% primary, 30% secondary.

Major International Organizations: UN (World Bank, IMF), Arab League.

Embassy: 2342 Massachusetts Ave. NW 20008; 387-1980.

A long history of rule by other lands, including Portugal in the 16th century, ended with the ouster of the Persians in 1744. By the early 19th century, Muscat and Oman was one of the most important countries in the region, controlling much of the

Persian and Pakistan coasts, and ruling far-away Zanzibar, which was separated in 1861 under British mediation.

British influence was confirmed in a 1951 treaty, and Britain helped suppress an uprising by traditionally rebellious interior tribes against control by Muscat in the 1950s.

On July 23, 1970, Sultan Said bin Taimur was overthrown by his son, who changed the nation's name to Sultanate of Oman.

Oil is the major source of income.

Oman opened its air bases to Western forces following the Iraqi invasion of Kuwait on Aug. 2, 1990.

Pakistan

Islamic Republic of Pakistan

Islam-i Jamhuriya-e Pakistan

People: Population: 121,856,000. **Age distrib.** (%): <15: 44; 65+: 3. **Pop. density:** 379 per sq. mi. **Urban:** 28%. **Ethnic groups:** Punjabi 66%, Sindhi 13%, Pathan 8.5%, Urdu 7.6%, Baluchi 2.5%, others. **Principal languages:** Urdu, English (both official), Punjabi, Sindhi, Pashtu, Balochi, Brahvi. **Religions:** Muslim 97%.

Geography: Area: 339,697 sq. mi., about the size of Texas. **Location:** In W part of South Asia. **Neighbors:** Iran on W, Afghanistan, China on N, India on E. **Topography:** The Indus R. rises in the Hindu Kush and Himalaya Mtns. in the N (highest is K2, or Godwin Austen, 28,250 ft., 2d highest in world), then flows over 1,000 mi. through fertile valley and empties into Arabian Sea. Thar Desert, Eastern Plains flank Indus Valley. **Capital:** Islamabad. **Cities** (1992 est.): Karachi 7.0 mln.; Lahore 3.5 mln.; Faisalabad 2.0 mln.; Hyderabad 795,000; Rawalpindi 928,000.

Government: Type: Parliamentary democracy in a federal setting. **Head of state:** Pres. Farooq Ahmed Leghari; in office: Nov. 14, 1993. **Head of government:** Prime Min. Benazir Bhutto; b June 21, 1953; in office: Oct. 19, 1993. **Local divisions:** Federal capital, 4 provinces, tribal areas. **Defense:** 6% of GDP (1992).

Economy: Industries: Textiles, food processing, chemicals, petroleum prods. **Chief crops:** Rice, wheat. **Minerals:** Natural gas, iron ore. **Crude oil reserves** (1987): 116 mln. bbls. **Other resources:** Wool. **Arable land:** 26%. **Livestock** (1991): cattle: 17.7 mln.; sheep: 30.1 mln.; goats: 36.6 mln. **Fish catch** (1990): 479,000 metric tons. **Electricity prod.** (1992): 43 bln. kWh. **Labor force:** 54% agric.; 13% mining & manuf.; 33% services.

Finance: Monetary unit: Rupee (Mar. 1994: 30.49 = $1 US). **Gross national product** (1992): $48.3 bln. **Per capita GNP**: $410. **Imports** (1991): $7.9 bln.; partners: EU 21%, Jap. 13%, U.S. 16%. **Exports** (1991): $6.0 bln.; partners: EU 31%, Jap. 10%, U.S. 10%. **Tourism** (1990): $156 mln. receipts. **National budget** (1993): $10.9 bln. **International reserves less gold** (Feb. 1994): $1.3 bln. **Gold:** 2.0 mln. oz t. **Consumer prices** (change in 1993): 4.2%.

Transport: Railroads: Length: 5,453 mi. **Motor vehicles:** in use: 721,000 passenger cars, 200,000 comm. vehicles. **Civil aviation:** 5.6 bln. passenger-mi.; 35 airports with scheduled flights. **Chief ports:** Karachi.

Communications: Television sets: 1 per 63 persons. **Radios:** 1 per 13 persons. **Telephones:** 1 per 95 persons. **Daily newspaper circ.:** 15 per 1,000 pop.

Health: Life expectancy at birth (1994): 57 male; 58 female. **Births** (per 1,000 pop.): 42. **Deaths** (per 1,000 pop.): 12. **Natural increase:** 3.0%. **Hospital beds:** 1 per 1,706 persons. **Physicians:** 1 per 2,364 persons. **Infant mortality** (per 1,000 live births 1994): 102.

Education (1991): **Literacy:** 35%.

Major International Organizations: UN (GATT, ILO, IMF, WHO).

Embassy: 2315 Massachusetts Ave. NW 20008; 939-6200.

Present-day Pakistan shares the 5,000-year history of the India-Pakistan subcontinent. At present day Harappa and Mohenjo Daro, the Indus Valley Civilization, with large cities and elaborate irrigation systems, flourished c. 4,000-2,500 BC.

Aryan invaders from the NW conquered the region around 1,500 BC, forging a Hindu civilization that dominated Pakistan as well as India for 2,000 years.

Beginning with the Persians in the 6th century BC, and continuing with Alexander the Great and with the Sassanians, successive nations to the west ruled or influenced Pakistan, eventually separating the area from the Indian cultural sphere.

The first Arab invasion, 712 AD, introduced Islam. Under the Mogul empire (1526-1857), Muslims ruled most of India, yielding to British encroachment and resurgent Hindus.

After World War I the Muslims of British India began agitation for minority rights in elections. Mohammad Ali Jinnah (1876-1948) was the principal architect of Pakistan. A leader of the Muslim League from 1916, he worked for dominion status for India; from 1940 he advocated a separate Muslim state.

When the British withdrew Aug. 14, 1947, the Islamic majority areas of India acquired self-government as Pakistan, with dominion status in the Commonwealth. Pakistan was divided into 2 sections, West Pakistan and East Pakistan. The 2 areas were nearly 1,000 mi. apart on opposite sides of India. Pakistan became a republic in 1956.

In Oct. 1958, Gen. Mohammad Ayub Khan took power in a coup. He was elected president in 1960, reelected in 1965. He resigned Mar. 25, 1969, after several months of violent rioting and unrest, most of it in East Pakistan, which demanded autonomy. The government was turned over to Gen. Agha Mohammad Yahya Khan and martial law was declared.

The Awami League, which sought regional autonomy for East Pakistan, won a majority in Dec. 1970 elections to a constituent assembly. In March 1971 Yahya postponed the assembly. Rioting and strikes broke out in the East.

On Mar. 25, 1971, government troops launched attacks in the East. The Easterners, aided by India, proclaimed the independent nation of Bangladesh. In months of widespread fighting, countless thousands were killed. Some 10 million Easterners fled into India.

Full-scale war between India and Pakistan had spread to both the East and West fronts by Dec. 3. Pakistan troops in the East surrendered Dec. 16; Pakistan agreed to a cease-fire in the West Dec. 17. On July 3, 1972, Pakistan and India signed a pact agreeing to withdraw troops from their borders and seek peaceful solutions to all problems.

Zulfikar Ali Bhutto, leader of the Pakistan People's Party, which had won the most West Pakistan votes in the Dec. 1970 elections, became president Dec. 20.

Bhutto was overthrown in a military coup July 1977. Convicted of complicity in a 1974 political murder, he was executed Apr. 4, 1979. Benazir Bhutto, his daughter, returned to Pakistan from exile in Europe in 1986. Her efforts to relaunch the Pakistan People's Party sparked violence and riots.

Pres. Mohammad Zia ul-Haq was killed when his plane exploded in Aug. 1988. Following Nov. elections, Benazir Bhutto was named prime minister, becoming the first woman leader of a Muslim nation. She was accused of corruption and dismissed by the president, Aug. 1990, and her party was soundly defeated in the Oct. 1990 elections. However, she was returned to power after elections in Oct. 1993.

Panama

Republic of Panama

República de Panamá

People: Population: 2,630,000. **Age distrib.** (%): <15: 35; 65+: 5. **Pop. density:** 90 per sq. mi. **Urban:** 49%. **Ethnic groups:** Mestizo 70%, West Indian 14%, white 10%, Indian 6%. **Principal languages:** Spanish (official), English. **Religions:** Roman Catholic 85%, Protestant 15%.

Geography: Area: 29,157 sq. mi., slightly larger than West Virginia. **Location:** In Central America. **Neighbors:** Costa Rica on W., Colombia on E. **Topography:** 2 mountain ranges run the length of the isthmus. Tropical rain forests cover the Caribbean coast and eastern Panama. **Capital:** Panama City. **Cities** (1990 est.): Panama City 413,000.

Government: Type: Constitutional democracy. **Head of state and government:** Pres. Ernesto Pérez Balladares; in office: Sept. 1, 1994. **Local divisions:** 9 provinces, 1 territory. **Defense:** 1.7% of GDP (1993 est.).

Economy: Industries: Oil refining, international banking. **Chief crops:** Bananas, pineapples, cocoa, corn, coconuts, sugar. **Minerals:** Copper. **Other resources:** Forests (mahogany), shrimp. **Arable land:** 6%. **Livestock** (1991): cattle: 1.4 mln.; pigs: 256,000. **Electricity prod.** (1992): 4.3 mln. kWh. **Labor force:** 27% agric. & fishing; 32% govt. & community services.

Finance: Monetary unit: Balboa (Apr. 1994: 1.00 = $1 US). **Gross domestic product** (1992): $6 bln. **Per capita GDP:** $2,400. **Imports** (1991): $1.5 bln.; partners: U.S. 37%. **Exports** (1991): $380 mln.; partners: U.S. 44%. **Tourism** (1990): $167 mln. receipts. **National budget** (1992 est.): $1.9 bln. **International reserves less gold** (Feb. 1994): $611 mln. **Consumer prices** (change in 1993): 0.5%.

Transport: Motor vehicles: in use: 150,000 passenger cars, 72,000 comm. vehicles. **Civil aviation:** 169 mln. passenger-mi.; 8 airports with scheduled flights. **Chief ports:** Balboa, Cristobal.

Communications: Television sets: 1 per 12 persons. **Radios:** 1 per 5.6 persons. **Telephones:** 1 per 9.1 persons. **Daily newspaper circ.:** 70 per 1,000 pop.

Health: Life expectancy at birth (1994): 72 male; 78 female. **Births** (per 1,000 pop.): 25. **Deaths** (per 1,000 pop.): 5. **Natural increase:** 2.0%. **Hospital beds:** 1 per 333 persons. **Physicians:** 1 per 871 persons. **Infant mortality** (per 1,000 live births 1994): 17.

Education (1991): **Literacy:** 87%. **Primary school attendance:** almost 100%.

Major International Organizations: UN (IMF, IMO, World Bank), OAS.

Embassy: 2862 McGill Terrace NW 20008; 483-1407.

The coast of Panama was sighted by Rodrigo de Bastidas, sailing with Columbus for Spain in 1501, and was visited by Columbus in 1502. Vasco Nunez de Balboa crossed the isthmus and "discovered" the Pacific O. Sept. 13, 1513. Spanish colonies were ravaged by Francis Drake, 1572-95, and Henry Morgan, 1668-71. Morgan destroyed the old city of Panama which had been founded in 1519. Freed from Spain, Panama joined Colombia in 1821.

Panama declared its independence from Colombia Nov. 3, 1903, with U.S. recognition. U.S. naval forces deterred action by Colombia. Panama granted use, occupation, and control of the Canal Zone to the U.S. by treaty, ratified Feb. 26, 1904. In 1978, a new treaty provided for a gradual takeover by Panama of the canal, and withdrawal of U.S. troops, to be completed by 1999. U.S. payments were substantially increased in the interim.

President Delvalle was ousted by the National Assembly, Feb. 26, 1988, after he tried to fire the head of the Panama Defense Forces, Gen. Manuel Antonio Noriega. Noriega had been indicted by 2 U.S. federal grand juries on drug charges. A general strike followed. Despite U.S.-imposed economic sanctions Noriega remained in power. Voters went to the polls to elect a new president May 7, 1989. Noriega claimed victory, but foreign observers said that the opposition had won overwhelmingly. The government voided the election May 10, charging foreign interference. There was an attempted coup against Noriega Oct. 3.

U.S. troops invaded Panama Dec. 20, 1989, following a series of incidents, including the killing of a U.S. Marine by Panamanian soldiers. The operation had as its chief objective the capture of Noriega. He took refuge in the Vatican diplomatic mission, but surrendered to U.S. officials Jan. 3, 1990. He was convicted on 8 counts of racketeering and drug trafficking in a U.S. District Court in Miami, FL, Apr. 9, 1992.

Papua New Guinea

People: Population: 4,197,000. **Age distrib.** (%): <15: 40; 65+: 4. **Pop. density:** 23 per sq. mi. **Urban:** 13%. **Ethnic groups:** Papuans (in S and interior), Melanesian (N,E), pygmies, minorities of Chinese, Australians, Polynesians. **Principal languages:** English (official), Melanesian languages, Papuan languages. **Religions:** Protestant 44%, Roman Catholic 22%, local religions.

Geography: Area: 178,704 sq. mi., slightly larger than California. **Location:** Occupies eastern half of island of New Guinea. **Neighbors:** Indonesia (West Irian) on W, Australia on S. **Topography:** Thickly forested mtns. cover much of the center of the country, with lowlands along the coasts. Included are some of the nearby islands of Bismarck and Solomon groups, including Admiralty Is., New Ireland, New Britain, and Bougainville. **Capital:** Port Moresby. **Cities** (1991): Port Moresby 193,000; Lae 80,000.

Government: Type: Parliamentary democracy. **Head of state:** Queen Elizabeth II, represented by Gov. Gen. Wiwa Korowi; in office: Oct. 4, 1991. **Head of government:** Prime Min. Paias Wingti; in office: Sept. 24, 1993. **Local divisions:** 20 provinces. **Defense:** approx. 1.8% of GDP (1993 est.).

Economy: Chief crops: Coffee, coconuts, cocoa. **Minerals:** Gold, copper, silver. **Arable land:** 1%. **Livestock** (1992): pigs: 1.0 mln. **Electricity prod.** (1992): 1.6 bln. kWh. **Labor force:** 82% agric., 3% ind. and commerce, 8% services.

Finance: Monetary unit: Kina (Mar. 1994: 1.00 = $1.02 US). **Gross domestic product** (1992): $3.4 bln. **Per capita GDP:** $850. **Imports** (1992): $1.5 bln.; partners: Austral. 40%, Jap. 17%; U.S. 9%. **Exports** (1992): $1.8 bln.; partners: Jap. 26%, W Ger. 36%, Austral. 8%. **National budget** (1993 est.): $1.49 bln. **International reserves less gold** (Jan. 1994): $140 mln. **Gold:** 63,000 oz t. **Consumer prices** (change in 1992): 4.3%.

Transport: Motor vehicles: in use: 17,000 passenger cars, 29,000 comm. vehicles. **Chief ports:** Port Moresby, Lae.

Communications: Television sets: 1 per 383 persons. **Radios:** 1 per 16 persons. **Telephones:** 1 per 59 persons. **Daily newspaper circ.:** 13 per 1,000 pop.

Health: Life expectancy at birth (1994): 56 male; 57 female. **Births** (per 1,000 pop.): 34. **Deaths** (per 1,000 pop.): 10. **Natural increase:** 2.3%. **Hospital beds:** 1 per 234 persons. **Physicians:** 1 per 9,953 persons. **Infant mortality** (per 1,000 live births 1994): 63.

Education (1991): **Literacy:** 52%. **Attendance:** 65% primary school; 13% secondary school.

Major International Organizations: UN (GATT), Commonwealth of Nations.

Embassy: 1615 New Hampshire Ave. NW 20009; 745-3680.

Human remains have been found in the interior of New Guinea dating back at least 10,000 years and possibly much earlier. Successive waves of peoples probably entered the country from Asia through Indonesia. Europeans visited in the 15th century, but land claims did not begin until the 19th century, when the Dutch took control of the western half of the island.

The southern half of eastern New Guinea was first claimed by Britain in 1884, and transferred to Australia in 1905. The northern half was claimed by Germany in 1884, but captured in World War I by Australia, which was granted a League of Nations mandate and then a UN trusteeship over the area. The 2 territories were administered jointly after 1949, given self-government Dec. 1, 1973, and became independent Sept. 16, 1975.

The indigenous population consists of a huge number of tribes, many living in almost complete isolation with mutually unintelligible languages.

Prime Min. Paias Wingti, who came to power in July 1992, resigned in Sept. 1993 and then was promptly reelected and re-installed; this tactic enabled him to avoid a vote of confidence.

Paraguay

Republic of Paraguay

República del Paraguay

People: Population: 5,214,000. **Age distrib.** (%): <15: 40; 65+: 4. **Pop. density:** 33 per sq. mi. **Urban:** 51%. **Ethnic groups:** Mestizo 95%, small white, Indian, black minorities. **Principal languages:** Spanish (official), Guarani. **Religions:** Roman Catholic (official) 90%.

Geography: Area: 157,048 sq. mi., the size of California. **Location:** One of the 2 landlocked countries of S America. **Neighbors:** Bolivia on N, Argentina on S, Brazil on E. **Topography:** Paraguay R. bisects the country. To E are fertile plains, wooded slopes, grasslands. To W is the Chaco plain, with marshes and scrub trees. Extreme W is arid. **Capital:** Asunción. **Cities** (1992 est.): Asunción 502,000.

Government: Type: Republic. **Head of state:** Pres. Juan Carlos Wasmosy; in office: Aug. 15, 1993. **Local divisions:** 19 departments. **Defense:** 1.4% of GDP (1988 est.).

Economy: Industries: Food processing, wood products, textiles, cement. **Chief crops:** Corn, cotton, beans, sugar cane. **Minerals:** Iron, manganese, limestone. **Other resources:** Forests. **Arable land:** 20%. **Livestock** (1992): cattle: 7.8 mln.; pigs: 2.6 mln. **Electricity prod.** (1992): 16.2 bln. kWh. **Labor force:** 44% agric., 34% ind. and commerce, 18% services.

Finance: Monetary unit: Guarani (Mar. 1994: 1,887 = $1 US). **Gross domestic product** (1992): $7.3 bln. **Per capita GDP:** $1,500. **Imports** (1991): $1.8 bln.; partners: Braz. 32%,

EU 20%. **Exports** (1991): $642 mln.; partners: EU 37%, Braz. 25%. **Tourism** (1990): $113 mln. receipts. **National budget** (1991): $1.2 bln. **International reserves less gold** (Mar. 1993): $561 mln. **Gold:** 35,000 oz t. **Consumer prices** (change in 1992): 15.1%.

Transport: Motor vehicles: in use: 117,000 passenger cars, 3,000 comm. vehicles. **Civil aviation:** 355 mln. passenger-mi.; 1 airport with scheduled flights. **Chief ports:** Asuncion.

Communications: Television sets: 1 per 13 persons. **Radios:** 1 per 5.8 persons. **Telephones:** 1 per 33 persons. **Daily newspaper circ.:** 39 per 1,000 pop.

Health: Life expectancy at birth (1994): 72 male; 75 female. **Births** (per 1,000 pop.): 34. **Deaths** (per 1,000 pop.): 4. **Natural increase:** 2.8%. **Hospital beds:** 1 per 816 persons. **Physicians:** 1 per 1,470 persons. **Infant mortality** (per 1,000 live births 1994): 25.

Education (1991): **Literacy:** 90%. **Years compulsory:** 7. **Attendance:** 83%.

Major International Organizations: UN (IMF, WHO, ILO), OAS.

Embassy: 2400 Massachusetts Ave. NW 20008; 483-6960.

The Guarani Indians were settled farmers speaking a common language before the arrival of Europeans.

Visited by Sebastian Cabot in 1527 and settled as a Spanish possession in 1535, Paraguay gained its independence from Spain in 1811. It lost much of its territory to Brazil, Uruguay, and Argentina in the War of the Triple Alliance, 1865-1870. Large areas were won from Bolivia in the Chaco War, 1932-35.

Gen. Alfredo Stroessner, who ruled since 1954, was ousted in a military coup led by Gen. Andrés Rodríguez on Feb. 3, 1989. Rodríguez was elected president May 1. Juan Carlos Wasmosy was elected president May 9, 1993, becoming the nation's first civilian head of state in many years.

Peru

Republic of Peru

República del Peru

People: Population: 23,651,000. **Age distrib.** (%): <15: 38; 65+: 4. **Pop. density:** 47 per sq. mi. **Urban:** 71%. **Ethnic groups:** Indians 45%, Mestizos 37%, whites 15%, blacks, Asians. **Principal languages:** Spanish, Quechua (both official), Aymara. **Religions:** Roman Catholic 90%.

Geography: Area: 496,225 sq. mi., slightly larger than Alaska. **Location:** On the Pacific coast of S America. **Neighbors:** Ecuador, Colombia on N, Brazil, Bolivia on E, Chile on S. **Topography:** An arid coastal strip, 10 to 100 mi. wide, supports much of the population thanks to widespread irrigation. The Andes cover 27% of land area. The uplands are well-watered, as are the eastern slopes reaching the Amazon basin, which covers half the country with its forests and jungles. **Capital:** Lima. **Cities** (1990 est.): Lima 6.1 mln.; Arequipa 621,000; Callao 572,000.

Government: Type: in transition. **Head of state:** Pres. Alberto Fujimori; b July 28, 1938; in office: July 28, 1990. **Head of government:** Prime Min. Efrain Goldenberg Schreiver; in office: Feb. 1994. **Local divisions:** 24 departments, 1 province. **Defense:** 2% of GDP (1991).

Economy: Industries: Fish meal, mineral processing, light industry, textiles. **Chief crops:** Cotton, sugar, coffee, corn. **Minerals:** Copper, lead, molybdenum, silver, zinc, iron, oil. **Crude oil reserves** (1987): 535 mln. bbls. **Other resources:** Wool, sardines. **Arable land:** 3%. **Livestock** (1992): cattle: 3.9 mln.; pigs: 2.4 mln.; sheep: 12.0 mln. **Fish catch** (1991): 6.9 mln. metric tons. **Electricity prod.** (1992): 17.4 bln. kWh. **Labor force:** 37% agric.; 19% ind. and mining; 44% govt. and other services.

Finance: Monetary unit: Nuevo Sol (Mar. 1994: 2.17 = $1 US). **Gross domestic product** (1992): $25 bln. **Per capita GDP:** $1,100. **Imports** (1991): $3.5 bln.; partners: U.S. 32%, EU 17%. **Exports** (1991): $3.3 bln.; partners: U.S. 20%, EU 28%, Jap. 13%. **Tourism** (1990): $353 mln. receipts. **National budget** (1992 est.): $2.7 bln. **International reserves less gold** (Dec. 1993): $3.4 bln. **Gold:** 1.3 mln. oz t. **Consumer prices** (change in 1993): 48.6%.

Transport: Railroads: Length: 2,157 mi. **Motor vehicles:** in use: 399,000 passenger cars, 235,000 comm. vehicles. **Civil aviation:** 1.0 bln. passenger-mi.; 25 airports. **Chief ports:** Callao, Chimbate, Mollendo.

Communications: Television sets: 1 per 11 persons. **Radios:** 1 per 5.1 persons. **Telephones:** 1 per 28 persons. **Daily newspaper circ.:** 79 per 1,000 pop.

Health: Life expectancy at birth (1994): 63 male; 68 female. **Births** (per 1,000 pop.): 26. **Deaths** (per 1,000 pop.): 7. **Natural increase:** 1.9%. **Hospital beds:** 1 per 625 persons. **Physicians:** 1 per 997 persons. **Infant mortality** (per 1,000 live births 1994): 54.

Education (1991): **Literacy:** 85%. **Years compulsory:** 10.

Major International Organizations: UN and all of its specialized agencies, OAS.

Embassy: 1700 Massachusetts Ave. NW 20036; 833-9860.

The powerful Inca empire had its seat at Cuzco in the Andes covering most of Peru, Bolivia, and Ecuador, as well as parts of Colombia, Chile, and Argentina. Building on the achievements of 800 years of Andean civilization, the Incas had a high level of skill in architecture, engineering, textiles, and social organization.

A civil war had weakened the empire when Francisco Pizarro, Spanish conquistador, began raiding Peru for its wealth, 1532. In 1533 he had the seized ruling Inca, Atahualpa, filled a room with gold as a ransom, then executed him and enslaved the natives.

Lima was the seat of Spanish viceroys until the Argentine liberator, José de San Martin, captured it in 1821; Spanish forces were ultimately routed by Simón Bolívar, 1824.

On Oct. 3, 1968, a military coup ousted Pres. Fernando Belaunde Terry. In 1968-74, the military government started socialist programs. Food shortages, escalating foreign debt, and strikes led to another coup, Aug. 29, 1976.

After 12 years of military rule, Peru returned to democratic leadership in 1980 but was plagued by economic problems and terrorism by left-wing Sendero Luminosa (Shining Path) guerrillas. Pres. Alberto Fujimoro, elected in June 1990, dissolved the National Congress, suspended parts of the constitution, and initiated press censorship, Apr. 5, 1992. The leader of Sendero Luminosa was captured Sept. 12, 1993.

Philippines

Republic of the Philippines

People: Population: 69,809,000. **Age distrib.** (%): <15: 39; 65+: 4. **Pop. density:** 602 per sq. mi. **Urban:** 44%. **Ethnic groups:** Malays the large majority, Chinese, Americans, Spanish are minorities. **Principal languages:** Pilipino (based on Tagalog), English (both official), Cebuano, Bicol, Ilocano, Pampango, many others. **Religions:** Roman Catholics 83%, Protestants 9%, Muslims 5%.

Geography: Area: 115,860 sq. mi., slightly larger than Arizona. **Location:** An archipelago off the SE coast of Asia. **Neighbors:** Nearest are Malaysia, Indonesia on S, Taiwan on N. **Topography:** The country consists of some 7,100 islands stretching 1,100 mi. N-S. About 95% of area and population are on 11 largest islands, which are mountainous, except for the heavily indented coastlines and for the central plain on Luzon. **Capital:** Manila. **Cities** (1990 est.): Manila 1.8 mln.; Quezon City 1.5 mln.; Cebu 610,000.

Government: Type: Republic. **Head of state:** Pres. Fidel V. Ramos; b 1928; in office: June 30, 1992. **Local divisions:** 72 provinces, 61 cities. **Defense:** 1.9% of GNP (1991).

Economy: Industries: Food processing, textiles, clothing, drugs, wood prods., appliances. **Chief crops:** Sugar, rice, corn, pineapple, coconut. **Minerals:** Cobalt, copper, gold, nickel, silver, iron, petroleum. **Other resources:** Forests (42% of area). **Arable land:** 26%. **Livestock** (1992): buffalo: 2.5 mln.; cattle: 1.6 mln.; pigs: 8.0 mln. **Fish catch** (1991): 2.3 mln. metric tons. **Electricity prod.** (1992): 28 bln. kWh. **Labor force:** 46% agric., 16% ind. and comm., 19% services.

Finance: Monetary unit: Peso (Mar. 1994: 27.54 = $1 US). **Gross national product** (1992): $54.1 bln. **Per capita GNP:** $860. **Imports** (1991): $12.3 bln.; partners: U.S. 25%, Jap. 16%. **Exports** (1991): $8.7 bln.; partners: U.S. 35%, Jap. 17%, EU 19%. **Tourism** (1990): $1.3 bln. receipts. **National budget** (1992 est.): $12 bln. **International reserves less gold** (Feb. 1994): $4.7 bln. **Gold:** 3.18 mln. oz t. **Consumer prices** (change in 1993): 7.6%.

Transport: Railroads: Length: 658 mi. **Motor vehicles:** in use: 456,000 passenger cars, 848,000 comm. vehicles. **Civil aviation:** 8.0 bln. passenger-mi.; 21 airports with scheduled flights. **Chief ports:** Cebu, Manila, Iloilo, Davao.

Communications: Television sets: 1 per 9.1 persons. **Radios:** 1 per 16 persons. **Telephones:** 1 per 57 persons. **Daily newspaper circ.:** 54 per 1,000 pop.

Health: Life expectancy at birth (1994): 63 male; 68 female. **Births** (per 1,000 pop.): 27. **Deaths** (per 1,000 pop.): 7. **Natural increase:** 2.0%. **Hospital beds:** 1 per 683 persons.

Physicians: 1 per 1,062 persons. **Infant mortality** (per 1,000 live births 1994): 51.

Education (1989): **Literacy:** 88%. **Attendance:** 97% in elementary, 55% secondary.

Major International Organizations: UN (World Bank, IMF, GATT), ASEAN.

Embassy: 1617 Massachusetts Ave. NW 20036; 483-1414

The Malay peoples of the Philippine Islands, whose ancestors probably migrated from Southeast Asia, were mostly hunters, fishers, and unsettled cultivators when first visited by Europeans.

The archipelago was visited by Magellan, 1521. The Spanish founded Manila, 1571. The islands, named for King Philip II of Spain, were ceded by Spain to the U.S. for $20 million, 1898, following the Spanish-American War. U.S. troops suppressed a guerrilla uprising in a brutal 6-year war, 1899-1905.

Japan attacked the Philippines Dec. 8, 1941 and occupied the islands during WW II. On July 4, 1946, independence was proclaimed in accordance with an act passed by the U.S. Congress in 1934. A republic was established.

Riots by radical youth groups and terrorism by leftist guerrillas and outlaws increased from 1970. On Sept. 21, 1972, Pres. Ferdinand Marcos declared martial law. Ruling by decree, he ordered some land reform and stabilized prices. But opposition was suppressed, and a high population growth rate aggravated poverty and unemployment. Political corruption was widespread. On Jan. 17, 1973, Marcos proclaimed a new constitution with himself as president. His wife, Imelda, received wide powers in 1978 to supervise planning and development.

Government troops battled Muslim (Moro) secessionists, 1973-76, in southern Mindanao. Fighting resumed, 1977, after a Libyan-mediated agreement on autonomy was rejected by the region's mainly Christian voters.

Martial law was lifted Jan. 17, 1981, but Marcos retained broad emergency powers. He was reelected in June to a new 6-year term as president.

The assassination of prominent opposition leader Benigno S. Aquino Jr, Aug. 21, 1983, sparked demonstrations calling for the resignation of Marcos. A bitter presidential election campaign ended Feb. 7, 1986, as elections were held amid allegations of widespread fraud. On Feb. 16, Marcos was declared the victor over Corazon Aquino, widow of the slain opposition leader. She proclaimed herself president and announced a nonviolent "active resistance" to overthrow the Marcos government.

On Feb. 24, Marcos declared a state of emergency as his military and religious support eroded. He ended his 20-year tenure as president Feb. 26 and fled the country. Aquino was recognized as president by the U.S. and other nations.

In 1987, Aquino announced the start of land reforms. Candidates endorsed by Aquino won large majorities in legislative elections held in May. She was plagued, however, by a weak economy, widespread poverty, Communist insurgents, and lukewarm support from the military. Rebel troops seized military bases, TV stations, and bombed the presidential palace, Dec. 1, 1989. Government forces defeated the attempted coup with the aid of air cover provided by U.S. F-4s. Aquino endorsed Fidel Ramos in the May 1992 presidential election, which he won.

The U.S. vacated the Subic Bay Naval Station at the end of 1992, ending its long military presence in the Philippines.

The government signed a cease-fire agreement, Jan. 30, 1994, with Muslim separatist guerrillas.

The archipelago has a coastline of 10,850 mi. Manila Bay, with an area of 770 sq. mi., and a circumference of 120 mi., is the finest harbor in the Far East.

Poland

Republic of Poland

Rzeczpospolita Polska

People: Population: 38,655,000. **Age distrib.** (%): <15: 25; 65+: 10. **Pop. density:** 320 per sq. mi. **Urban:** 62%. **Ethnic groups:** Polish 98%, Germans, Ukrainians, Belarusians. **Principal languages:** Polish. **Religions:** Roman Catholic 95%.

Geography: Area: 120,727 sq. mi., slightly smaller than New Mexico. **Location:** On the Baltic Sea in E Central Europe. **Neighbors:** Germany on W, Czech Rep., Slovakia on S, Lithuania, Belarus, Ukraine on E. **Topography:** Mostly lowlands forming part of the Northern European Plain. The Carpathian Mts. along the southern border rise to 8,200 ft. **Capital:** Warsaw. **Cities** (1992 est.): Warsaw 1.6 mln., Lodz 844,000, Kracow 751,000.

Government: Type: Democratic state. **Head of state:** Pres. Lech Walesa; b Sept. 29, 1943; in office: Dec. 22, 1990. **Head of government:** Prime Min. Waldemar Pawlak; in office: Oct. 26, 1993. **Local divisions:** 49 provinces. **Defense:** 1.8% of GNP (1993 est.).

Economy: Industries: Shipbuilding, chemicals, metals, autos, food processing. **Chief crops:** Grains, potatoes, sugar beets, tobacco, flax. **Minerals:** Coal, copper, zinc, silver, zinc, sulphur, natural gas. **Arable land:** 46%. **Livestock** (1992): cattle: 8.2 mln.; pigs: 22.1 mln. **Fish catch** (1991): 457,000 metric tons. **Electricity prod.** (1992): 137 bln. kWh. **Labor force:** 27% agric.; 34% ind. & constr.

Finance: Monetary unit: Zloty (Feb. 1994: 21,926 = $1 US). **Gross domestic product** (1992): $167.6 bln.* **Per capita GDP:** $4,400. **Imports** (1991): $15.7 bln.; partners: CIS 18%, Ger. 15%, Czech. 5%. **Exports** (1991): $14.9 bln.; partners: CIS 25%, E Ger. 14%, Czech. 6%. **Tourism** (1990): $266 mln. receipts. **National budget** (1992 est.): $22 bln. **International reserves less gold** (Feb. 1994): $4.1 bln. **Gold:** 473,000. **Consumer prices** (change in 1993): 36.9%.

Transport: Railroads: Length: 16,061 mi. **Motor vehicles:** in use: 6.1 mln. passenger cars, 1.3 mln. comm. vehicles. **Civil aviation:** 3.4 bln. passenger-mi.; 12 airports. **Chief ports:** Gdansk, Gdynia, Szczecin.

Communications: Television sets: 1 per 3.8 persons. **Radios:** 1 per 3.7 persons. **Telephones:** 1 per 7.0 persons. **Daily newspaper circ.:** 127 per 1,000 pop.

Health: Life expectancy at birth (1994): 69 male; 77 female. **Births** (per 1,000 pop.): 13. **Deaths** (per 1,000 pop.): 9. **Natural increase:** .4%. **Hospital beds:** 1 per 118 persons. **Physicians:** 1 per 464 persons. **Infant mortality** (per 1,000 live births 1994): 13.

Education (1991): **Literacy:** 98%. **Years compulsory:** 8; attendance 97%.

Major International Organizations: UN (GATT, WHO).

Embassy: 2640 16th St. NW 20009; 234-3800.

Slavic tribes in the area were converted to Latin Christianity in the 10th century. Poland was a great power from the 14th to the 17th centuries. In 3 partitions (1772, 1793, 1795) it was apportioned among Prussia, Russia, and Austria. Overrun by the Austro-German armies in World War I, it declared its independence on Nov. 11, 1918, and was recognized as independent by the Treaty of Versailles, June 28, 1919. Large territories to the east were taken in a war with Russia, 1921.

Germany and the USSR invaded Poland Sept. 1-27, 1939, and divided the country. During the war, some 6 million Polish citizens, half of them Jews, were killed by the Nazis. With Germany's defeat, a Polish government-in-exile in London was recognized by the U.S., but the USSR pressed the claims of a rival group. The election of 1947 was completely dominated by the Communists.

In compensation for 69,860 sq. mi. ceded to the USSR, 1945, Poland received approx. 40,000 sq. mi. of German territory E of the Oder-Neisse line comprising Silesia, Pomerania, West Prussia, and part of East Prussia.

In 12 years of rule by Stalinists, large estates were abolished, industries nationalized, schools secularized, and Roman Catholic prelates jailed. Farm production fell off. Harsh working conditions caused a riot in Poznan, June 28-29, 1956. A new Politburo, committed to a more independent Polish Communism, was named Oct. 1956, with Wladyslaw Gomulka as first secretary of the party. Collectivization of farms was ended.

In Dec. 1970 workers in port cities rioted because of price rises and new incentive wage rules. On Dec. 20 Gomulka resigned as party leader; he was succeeded by Edward Gierek. The incentive rules were dropped; price rises were revoked. In 1956 Gomulka agreed to permit religious liberty and religious publications, provided the church kept out of politics.

After 2 months of labor turmoil had crippled the country, the Polish government, Aug. 30, 1980, met the demands of striking workers at the Lenin Shipyard, Gdansk. Among the 21 concessions granted were the right to form independent trade unions and the right to strike. By 1981, 9.5 mln. workers had joined the independent trade union (Solidarity). Solidarity leaders proposed, Dec. 12, a nationwide referendum on establishing a non-Communist government if the government failed to agree to a series of demands.

Spurred by the fear of Soviet intervention, the government, Dec. 13, imposed martial law. Lech Walesa and other Solidarity leaders were arrested. The U.S. imposed economic sanctions, which were lifted when martial law was suspended Dec. 1982. On Apr. 5, 1989, an accord was reached between the government and opposition factions on a broad range of political and economic reforms including free elections. Candidates endorsed by Solidarity swept the parliamentary elections, June 4. Lech Walesa became president, 1990.

A radical economic program designed to transform the economy into a free-market system drew protests from unions, farmers, and miners because it resulted in inflation and unemployment. In Sept. 1993 elections former Communists and other leftists won a majority of seats in the lower house of Parliament.

Portugal

Republic of Portugal

República Portuguesa

People: Population: 10,524,000. **Age distrib.** (%): <15: 20; 65+: 13. **Pop. density:** 295 per sq. mi. **Urban:** 34%. **Ethnic groups:** Homogeneous Mediterranean stock with small African minority. **Principal languages:** Portuguese. **Religions:** Roman Catholics 97%.

Geography: Area: 35,672 sq. mi., incl. the Azores and Madeira Islands, slightly smaller than Indiana. **Location:** At SW extreme of Europe. **Neighbors:** Spain on N, E. **Topography:** Portugal N of Tajus R, which bisects the country NE-SW, is mountainous, cool and rainy. To the S there are drier, rolling plains, and a warm climate. **Capital:** Lisbon. **Cities** (1988 est.): Lisbon 2 mln. (met.), Oporto, 1.5 mln. (met.).

Government: Type: Parliamentary democracy. **Head of state:** Pres. Mario Soares; b Dec. 7, 1924; in office: Mar. 9, 1986. **Head of government:** Prime Min. Anibal Cavaco Silva; in office: Nov. 6, 1985. **Local divisions:** 18 districts, 2 autonomous regions, one dependency. **Defense:** 2.9% of GDP (1992).

Economy: Industries: Textiles, footwear, cork, chemicals, fish canning, wine, paper. **Chief crops:** Grains, potatoes, rice, grapes, olives, fruits. **Minerals:** Tungsten, uranium, copper, iron. **Other resources:** Forests (world leader in cork production). **Arable land:** 32%. **Livestock** (1992): sheep: 5.8 mln.; pigs: 2.5 mln.; cattle: 1.3 mln. **Fish catch** (1991): 325,000 metric tons. **Electricity prod.** (1992): 26.4 bln. kWh. **Labor force:** 20% agric.; 35% ind. and comm.; 45% services and govt.

Finance: Monetary unit: Escudo (Mar. 1994: 171 = $1 US). **Gross domestic product** (1992): $93.7 bln.* **Per capita GDP:** $9,000. **Imports** (1992): $30.0 bln.; partners: Ger. 12%, UK 8%, Fr. 11%. **Exports** (1992): $18.2 bln.; partners: UK 15%, Ger. 13%, Fr. 13%. **Tourism** (1990): $3.5 bln. receipts. **National budget** (1991): $33.2 bln. **International reserves less gold** (Jan. 1994): $16.1 bln. **Gold:** 16.0 mln. oz t. **Consumer prices** (change in 1993): 6.5%.

Transport: Railroads: Length: 2,229 mi. **Motor vehicles:** in use: 1.8 mln. passenger cars, 648,000 comm. vehicles. **Civil aviation:** 4.3 bln. passenger-mi.; 13 airports. **Chief ports:** Lisbon, Setubal, Leixoes.

Communications: Television sets: 1 per 5.6 persons. **Radios:** 1 per 4.0 persons. **Telephones:** 1 per 3.2 persons. **Daily newspaper circ.:** 38 per 1,000 pop.

Health: Life expectancy at birth (1994): 72 male; 79 female. **Births** (per 1,000 pop.): 12. **Deaths** (per 1,000 pop.): 10. **Natural increase:** .2%. **Hospital beds:** 1 per 221 persons. **Physicians:** 1 per 348 persons. **Infant mortality** (per 1,000 live births 1994): 10.

Education (1990): **Literacy:** 83%. **Years compulsory:** 6; attendance 60%.

Major International Organizations: UN (GATT, IMF, WHO), NATO, EU, OECD.

Embassy: 2125 Kalorama Rd. NW 20008; 328-8610.

Portugal, an independent state since the 12th century, was a kingdom until a revolution in 1910 drove out King Manoel II and a republic was proclaimed.

From 1932 a strong, repressive government was headed by Premier Antonio de Oliveira Salazar. Illness forced his retirement in Sept. 1968.

On Apr. 25, 1974, the government was seized by a military junta led by Gen. Antonio de Spinola, who was named president.

The new government reached agreements providing independence for Guinea-Bissau, Mozambique, Cape Verde Islands, Angola, and São Tomé and Príncipe. Despite a 64% victory for democratic parties in Apr. 1975, the Soviet-supported Communist Party increased its influence. Banks, insurance companies, and other industries were nationalized.

Parliament approved, June 1, 1989, a package of reforms that did away with the socialist economy and created a "democratic" economy, denationalizing industries.

Azores Islands, in the Atlantic, 740 mi. W of Portugal, have an area of 868 sq. mi. and a pop. (1992) of 236,000. A 1951 agreement gave the U.S. rights to use defense facilities in the Azores. The **Madeira Islands,** 350 mi. off the NW coast of Africa, have an area of 307 sq. mi. and a pop. (1992) of 253,000. Both groups were offered partial autonomy in 1976.

Macau, area of 6 sq. mi., is an enclave, a peninsula and 2 small islands, at the mouth of the Canton R. in China. Portugal granted broad autonomy in 1976. In 1987, Portugal and China agreed that Macau would revert to China in 1999. Macau, like Hong Kong, was guaranteed 50 years of noninterference in its way of life and capitalist system. Pop. (1992 est.): 367,000.

Qatar

State of Qatar

Dawlet al-Qatar

People: Population: 513,000. **Pop. density:** 116 per sq. mi. **Ethnic groups:** Arab 40%, Pakistani 18%, Indian 18%, Iranian 10%, others. **Principal languages:** Arabic (official), English. **Religions:** Muslim 95%.

Geography: Area: 4,412 sq. mi., smaller than Connecticut and Rhode Island combined. **Location:** Occupies peninsula on W coast of Persian Gulf. **Neighbors:** Saudi Arabia on W, United Arab Emirates on S. **Topography:** Mostly a flat desert, with some limestone ridges, vegetation of any kind is scarce. **Capital:** Doha. **Cities** (1987 est.): Doha 236,000.

Government: Type: Traditional monarchy. **Head of state and head of government:** Emir & Prime Min. Khalifah ibn Hamad ath-Thani; b 1932; in office: Feb. 22, 1972 (emir), 1970 (prime min.) **Defense:** 8.0% of GDP (1989).

Economy: Arable land: 2.9%. **Electricity prod.** (1992): 4.8 bln. kWh. **Labor force:** 10% agric., 70% ind., services and commerce.

Finance: Monetary unit: Riyal (Mar. 1994: 3.64 = $1.00 US). **Gross domestic product** (1991): $8.1 bln. **Per capita GDP:** $17,000. **Imports** (1990): $1.4 bln.; partners: Jap. 11%, UK 13%, U.S. 9%. **Exports** (1990): $3.2 bln.; partners: Jap. 61%. **National budget** (1992): $3.0 bln.

Transport: Chief ports: Doha, Musayid.

Communications: Television sets: 1 per 2.1 persons. **Radios:** 1 per 2.1 persons. **Telephones:** 1 per 3.5 persons.

Health: Life expectancy at birth (1994): 70 male; 75 female. **Births** (per 1,000 pop.): 19. **Deaths** (per 1,000 pop.): 4. **Natural increase:** 1.5%. **Hospital beds:** 1 per 459 persons. **Physicians:** 1 per 660 persons. **Infant mortality** (per 1,000 live births 1994): 22.

Education (1991): **Literacy:** 76%. **Years compulsory:** ages 6-16; attendance: 98%.

Major International Organizations: UN (FAO, GATT, IMF, World Bank), Arab League, OPEC.

Embassy: 600 New Hampshire Ave. NW 20037; 338-0111.

Qatar was under Bahrain's control until the Ottoman Turks took power, 1872 to 1915. In a treaty signed 1916, Qatar gave Great Britain responsibility for its defense and foreign relations. After Britain announced it would remove its military forces from the Persian Gulf area by the end of 1971, Qatar sought a federation with other British protected states in the area; this failed and Qatar declared itself independent, Sept. 1, 1971.

Oil revenues give Qatar a per capita income among the highest in the world, but lack of skilled labor hampers development.

Romania

People: Population: 23,181,000. **Age distrib.** (%): <15: 22; 65+: 11. **Pop. density:** 252 per sq. mi. **Urban:** 54%. **Ethnic groups:** Romanians 89%, Hungarians 9%. **Principal lan-**

guages: Romanian (official), Hungarian, German. **Religions:** Romanian Orthodox 70%, Roman Catholic 6%.

Geography: Area: 91,699 sq. mi., slightly smaller than Oregon. **Location:** In SE Europe on the Black Sea. **Neighbors:** Moldova on E, Ukraine on N, Hungary, Yugoslavia on W, Bulgaria on S. **Topography:** The Carpathian Mts. encase the north-central Transylvanian plateau. There are wide plains S and E of the mountains, through which flow the lower reaches of the rivers of the Danube system. **Capital:** Bucharest. **Cities** (1992 est.): Bucharest 2.0 mln.; Constanta 350,000; Iasi 342,000; Timisoara 334,000.

Government: Type: Republic. **Head of state:** Pres. Ion Iliescu; b Mar. 30, 1930; in office: Dec. 25, 1989. **Head of government:** Prime Min. Nicolae Vacaroiu; in office; Nov. 4, 1992. **Local divisions:** Bucharest and 40 counties. **Defense:** 3% of GDP (1993).

Economy: Industries: Steel, metals, machinery, oil products, chemicals, textiles, shoes, tourism. **Chief crops:** Grains, sunflower, vegetables, potatoes. **Minerals:** Oil, gas, coal. **Other resources:** Timber. **Arable land:** 43%. **Livestock** (1991): cattle: 5.3 mln.; pigs:12.0 mln.; sheep: 14.0 mln. **Fish catch** (1990): 127,000 metric tons. **Electricity prod.** (1992): 59 bln. kWh. **Crude steel prod.** (1991): 7 mln. metric tons. **Labor force:** 28% agric.; 38% ind.

Finance: Monetary unit: Lei (Mar. 1994: 1,601 = $1 US). **Gross domestic product** (1992): $63.4 bln.* **Per capita GDP:** $2,700. **Imports** (1991): $15.4 bln.; partners: CIS 50%. **Exports** (1991): $14.0 bln.; partners: CIS 30%. **Tourism** (1990): $106 mln. receipts. **National budget** (1991): $20 bln. **International reserves less gold** (Feb. 1994): $916 mln. **Gold:** $2.38 mln. oz t. **Consumer prices** (change in 1993): 255.2%.

Transport: Railroads: Length: 6,887 mi. **Motor vehicles:** in use: 1.3 mln. passenger cars; 332,000 comm. vehicles. **Civil aviation:** 2.3 bln. passenger-mi.; 14 airports. **Chief ports:** Constanta, Galati, Braila.

Communications: Television sets: 1 per 5.8 persons. **Radios:** 1 per 7.3 persons. **Telephones:** 1 per 7.3 persons. **Daily newspaper circ.:** 134 per 1,000 pop.

Health: Life expectancy at birth (1994): 69 male; 75 female. **Births** (per 1,000 pop.): 14. **Deaths** (per 1,000 pop.): 10. **Natural increase:** .4%. **Hospital beds:** 1 per 106 persons. **Physicians:** 1 per 549 persons. **Infant mortality** (per 1,000 live births 1994): 20.

Education (1991): **Literacy:** 96%. **Years compulsory:** 10; attendance 98%.

Major International Organizations: UN (World Bank, IMF, GATT).

Embassy: 1607 23d St. NW 20008; 232-4747.

Romania's earliest known people merged with invading Proto-Thracians, preceding by centuries the Dacians. The Dacian kingdom was occupied by Rome, 106 AD-271 AD; people and language were Romanized. The principalities of Wallachia and Moldavia, dominated by Turkey, were united in 1859, became Romania in 1861. In 1877 Romania proclaimed independence from Turkey, became an independent state by the Treaty of Berlin, 1878, a kingdom, 1881, under Carol I. In 1886 Romania became a constitutional monarchy with a bicameral legislature.

Romania helped Russia in its war with Turkey, 1877-78. After World War I it acquired Bessarabia, Bukovina, Transylvania, and Banat. In 1940 it ceded Bessarabia and Northern Bukovina to the USSR, part of southern Dobrudja to Bulgaria, and northern Transylvania to Hungary.

In 1941, Romanian Prem. Marshal Ion Antonescu led his country in support of Germany against the USSR. In 1944 he was overthrown by King Michael and Romania joined the Allies.

After occupation by Soviet troops a People's Republic was proclaimed, Dec. 30, 1947; Michael was forced to abdicate. Land owners were dispossessed; most banks, factories and transportation units were nationalized.

On Aug. 22, 1965, a new constitution proclaimed Romania a Socialist, rather than a People's Republic.

Internal policies were oppressive. Ethnic Hungarians protested cultural and job discrimination, which led to strained relations with Hungary. Romania became industrialized, but lagged in consumer goods and in personal freedoms. All industry was state owned, and state farms and cooperatives owned almost all the arable land.

On Dec. 16, 1989, security forces opened fire on antigovernment demonstrators in Timisoara; hundreds were buried in mass graves. President Nicolae Ceausescu declared a state of emergency as protests spread to other cities. On Dec. 21, in Bucharest, security forces fired on protesters. Army units joined the rebellion, Dec. 22, and a group known as the Council of National Salvation announced that it had overthrown the government. Fierce fighting took place between the army, which backed the new government, and forces loyal to Ceausescu.

Ceausescu and his wife were captured and, following a trial in which they were found guilty of genocide, were executed Dec. 25. The U.S. and USSR quickly recognized the new government. Former Communists dominated the government in succeeding years.

Russia

Russian Federation

(Figures prior to 1992 are for the former USSR)

People: Population: 149,609,000. **Age distrib.** (%): <15: 22; 65+: 11. **Pop. density:** 22 per sq. mi. **Urban:** 73%. **Ethnic groups:** Russians 82%, Tatar 4%. **Principal languages:** Russian (official), Ukrainian, Belorussian, Uzbek, Armenian, Azerbaijani, Georgian, many others. **Religions:** Russian Orthodox 25%, nonreligious 60%.

Geography: Area: 6,592,800 sq. mi., over 76% of the total area of the former USSR and is the largest country in the world. **Location:** Stretches from E Europe across N Asia to the Pacific O. **Neighbors:** Finland, Poland, Norway, Estonia, Belarus, Ukraine on W, Georgia, Azerbaijan, Kazakhstan, China, Mongolia, N Korea on S. **Topography:** Russia contains every type of climate except the distinctly tropical, and has a varied topography.

The European portion is a low plain, grassy in S, wooded in N, with Ural Mtns. on the E, and Caucasus Mts. on the S. Urals stretch N-S for 2,500 mi. The Asiatic portion is also a vast plain, with mountains on the S and in the E; tundra covers extreme N, with forest belt below; plains, marshes are in W, desert in SW. **Capital:** Moscow. **Cities** (1992 est.): Moscow 8.8 mln.; St. Petersburg 4.4 mln.; Samara 1.2 mln.; Nizhniy Novgorod 1.4 mln.

Government: Type: Federation. **Head of state:** Pres. Boris Yeltsin; b Feb. 1, 1931; in office: July 10, 1991. **Head of government:** Prime Min. Viktor Chernomyrdin; in office: Dec. 14, 1992. **Local divisions:** 20 autonomous republics, 49 oblasts, 6 krays. **Defense:** 11% of GNP (1991).

Economy: Industries: Steel, machinery, machine tools, vehicles, chemicals, cement, textiles, appliances, paper. **Chief crops:** Grain, cotton, sugar beets, potatoes, vegetables, sunflowers. **Minerals:** Manganese, mercury, potash, bauxite, cobalt, chromium, copper, coal, gold, lead, molybdenum, nickel, phosphates, silver, tin, tungsten, zinc, oil, potassium salts. **Other resources:** Forests. **Arable land:** 11%. **Livestock** (1992): cattle: 54 mln.; sheep: 52 mln.; pigs: 35 mln.; goats 3.1 mln. **Fish catch** (1992): 6.9 mln. metric tons. **Electricity prod.** (1992): 1,014 bln. kWh. **Crude steel prod.** (1988): 164 mln. metric tons. **Labor force:** 84% production & serv.; 16% govt.

Finance: Monetary unit: Ruble (Aug. 1993: 987 = $1 US). **Gross national product** (1991): $479 bln. **Per capita GNP:** $3,220. **Imports** (1991): $43.5 bln.; partners: EU, CIS. **Exports** (1991): $58.7 bln.; partners: EU, CIS. **National budget** (1989): $310 bln. **Tourism** (1988): receipts: $216 mln.

Transport: Railroads: Length: 99,900 mi. **Motor vehicles:** in use: 8.9 mln. passenger cars, 484,000 comm. vehicles. **Civil aviation:** 95 bln. passenger-mi.; 58 airports with scheduled flights. **Chief ports:** St. Petersburg, Murmansk, Tver, Archangelsk.

Communications: Television sets: 1 per 2.7 persons. **Radios:** 1 per 1.7 persons. **Telephones:** 1 per 6.1 persons. **Daily newspaper circ.:** 1,119 per 1,000 pop.

Health: Life expectancy at birth (1994): 64 male; 74 female. **Births** (per 1,000 pop.): 13. **Deaths** (per 1,000 pop.): 11. **Natural increase:** .1%. **Hospital beds:** 1 per 74 persons. **Physicians:** 1 per 226 persons. **Infant mortality** (per 1,000 live births 1994): 27.

Education (1993): **Literacy:** 99%. Most receive 11 years of schooling.

Major International Organizations: UN (ILO, IMF, UNESCO, WHO), CIS.

Embassy: 1125 16th St. NW 20036; 628-7551.

History. Slavic tribes began migrating into Russia from the

W in the 5th century AD. The first Russian state, founded by Scandinavian chieftains, was established in the 9th century, centering in Novgorod and Kiev. In the 13th century the Mongols overran the country. It recovered under the grand dukes and princes of Muscovy, or Moscow, and by 1480 freed itself from the Mongols. Ivan the Terrible was the first to be formally proclaimed Tsar (1547). Peter the Great (1682-1725) extended the domain and, in 1721, founded the Russian Empire.

Western ideas and the beginnings of modernization spread through the huge Russian empire in the 19th and early 20th centuries. But political evolution failed to keep pace.

Military reverses in the 1905 war with Japan and in World War I led to the breakdown of the Tsarist regime. The 1917 Revolution began in March with a series of sporadic strikes for higher wages by factory workers. A provisional democratic government under Prince Georgi Lvov was established but was quickly followed in May by the second provisional government, led by Alexander Kerensky. The Kerensky government and the freely-elected Constituent Assembly were overthrown in a Communist coup led by Vladimir Ilyich Lenin Nov. 7.

Soviet Union

Lenin's death Jan. 21, 1924, resulted in an internal power struggle from which Joseph Stalin eventually emerged on top. Stalin secured his position at first by exiling opponents, but from the 1930s to 1953, he resorted to a series of "purge" trials, mass executions, and mass exiles to work camps. These measures resulted in millions of deaths, according to most estimates.

Germany and the Soviet Union signed a non-aggression pact Aug. 1939; Germany launched a massive invasion of the Soviet Union, June 1941. Notable heroic episode was the "900 days" siege of Leningrad, lasting to Jan. 1944, and causing a million deaths; the city was never taken. Russian winter counterthrusts, 1941-42 and 1942-43, stopped the German advance. Turning point was the failure of German troops to take and hold Stalingrad, Sept. 1942 to Feb. 1943. With British and U.S. Lend-Lease aid sustaining great casualties, the Russians drove the German forces from eastern Europe and the Balkans in the next 2 years.

After Stalin died, Mar. 5, 1953, Nikita Khrushchev was elected first secretary of the Central Committee. In 1956 he condemned Stalin. "De-Stalinization" of the country was begun.

Under Khrushchev the open antagonism of Poles and Hungarians toward domination by Moscow was brutally suppressed in 1956. He advocated peaceful co-existence with the capitalist countries, but continued arming the Soviet Union with nuclear weapons. He aided the Cuban revolution under Fidel Castro but withdrew Soviet missiles from Cuba during confrontation by U.S. Pres. Kennedy, Sept.-Oct. 1962. Khrushchev was suddenly deposed, Oct. 1964, and replaced by Leonid I. Brezhnev.

In Aug. 1968 Russian, Polish, East German, Hungarian, and Bulgarian military forces invaded Czechoslovakia to put a curb on liberalization policies of the Czech government.

Massive Soviet military aid to North Vietnam in the late 1960s and early 1970s helped assure Communist victories throughout Indo-China. Soviet arms aid and advisers were sent to several African countries in the 1970s.

In 1979, Soviet forces entered Afghanistan to support that government against rebels. In 1988, the Soviets announced withdrawal of their troops, ending a futile 8-year war.

Mikhail Gorbachev was chosen gen. secy. of the Communist Party, Mar. 1985. He was the youngest member of the Politburo and signaled a change in Soviet leadership. He held 4 summit meetings with U.S. Pres. Reagan. In 1987, in Washington, a treaty was signed eliminating intermediate–range nuclear missiles from Europe.

In 1987, Gorbachev initiated a program of reforms, including expanded freedoms and the democratization of the political process, through openness (*glasnost*) and restructuring (*perestroika*). The reforms were opposed by some Eastern bloc countries and many old-line Communists in the USSR. Gorbachev faced economic problems as well as ethnic and nationalist unrest in the republics.

On Aug. 19, 1991, it was announced that the vice president had taken over the country because of Gorbachev's ilness. A state of emergency was imposed for 6 months. The Russian republic's pres. Boris Yeltsin denounced the coup and called for a general strike. Some 50,000 demonstrated at the Russian Parliament in support of Yeltsin. By Aug. 21, the coup had failed and Gorbachev was restored as pres. On Aug. 24, Gorbachev resigned as leader of the Communist Party and recommended that its central committee be disbanded. Several republics declared their independence, including Russia, Ukraine, and Kazakhstan. On Aug. 29, the Soviet Parliament voted to suspend all activities of the Communist Party.

On Sept. 2, Gorbachev declared that the nation was "on the brink of catastrophe," and proposed to transfer all central authority to himself, the leaders of 10 republics, and an appointed legislative council in order to form a new kind of Soviet Union.

The Soviet Union officially broke up Dec. 26, 1991, one day after Gorbachev resigned. The Soviet hammer and sickle flying over the Kremlin was lowered and replaced by the flag of Russia, ending the domination of the Communist Party over all areas of national life since 1917.

Russian Federation

In a first major step in radical economic reform, Russia eliminated state subsidies of most goods and services, Jan. 1992. The effect was to allow prices to soar far beyond the means of ordinary workers. In June 1992, Pres. Yeltsin and then-U.S. Pres. George Bush agreed to massive arms reductions.

Russia launched a drive to privatize thousands of large and medium-sized state-owned enterprises in 1993. Pres. Yeltsin narrowly survived an impeachment vote by the Congress of People's Deputies, Mar. 28. He received strong support from voters in a countrywide referendum Apr. 25, but he continued to face a legislature dominated by conservatives and former Communists.

On Sept. 21, 1993, Yeltsin called early elections and dissolved Parliament, which in turn declared him deposed. Anti-Yeltsin legislators then barricaded themselves in the Parliament building. On Oct. 3, anti-Yeltsin forces attacked some facilities in Moscow and broke into the Parliament building. Yeltsin ordered the army to attack and seize the building. About 140 people were killed in the fighting, according to medical authorities. More than 150 were arrested.

In elections Dec. 12, 1993, a Yeltsin-supported constitution was approved, but ultranationalists and Communist hard-liners made strong showings in legislative contests.

Rwanda
Republic of Rwanda
Republika y'u Rwanda

Note: Statistics do not account for the massive mortalities, emigration, and displacement that followed the April 6, 1994 death of Pres. Habyarimana. These are detailed at the end of this entry.

People: Population: 8,374,000. **Age distrib.** (%): <15: 48; 65+: 3. **Pop. density:** 823 per sq. mi. **Urban:** 5%. **Ethnic groups:** Hutu 90%, Tutsi 9%, Twa (pygmies) 1%. **Principal languages:** French, Kinyarwanda (both official). **Religions:** Christian 74%, traditional 25%, Muslim 1%.

Geography: Area: 10,169 sq. mi., the size of Maryland. **Location:** In E central Africa. **Neighbors:** Uganda on N, Zaire on W, Burundi on S, Tanzania on E. **Topography:** Grassy uplands and hills cover most of the country, with a chain of volcanoes in the NW. The source of the Nile R. has been located in the headwaters of the Kagera (Akagera) R., SW of Kigali. **Capital:** Kigali. **Cities** (1991 est.): Kigali 237,000.

Government: Type: In transition. **Head of state:** Pres. Pasteur Bizimungu; in office: July 19, 1994. **Head of government:** Prime Min. Faustin Twagiramungu; in office: July 19, 1994. **Local divisions:** 10 prefectures. **Defense:** 1.6% of GDP (1988 est.).

Economy: Chief crops: Coffee, tea. **Minerals:** Tin, gold, wolframite. **Arable land:** 29%. **Electricity prod.** (1991): 130 mln. kWh. **Labor force:** 93% agric.

Finance: Monetary unit: Franc (Feb. 1994: 145 = $1 US). **Gross domestic product** (1992): $2.35 bln. **Per capita GDP:** $310. **Imports** (1990): $279.2 mln.; partners: Ken. 21%, Belg. 16%, Jap. 12%, W Ger. 9%. **Exports** (1990): $111.7 mln.; partners: EU, Ugan. **National budget** (1992 est.): $453.7 mln. **International reserves less gold** (Feb. 1994): $47 mln. **Consumer prices** (change in 1993): 12.4%.

Transport: Motor vehicles: in use: 8,000 passenger cars, 2,000 comm. vehicles.

Communications: Radios: 1 per 12 persons. **Telephones:** 1 per 480 persons.

Health: Life expectancy at birth (1994): 39 male; 41 female. **Births** (per 1,000 pop.): 49. **Deaths** (per 1,000 pop.): 21. **Natural increase:** 2.8%. **Hospital beds** (1984): 9,000. **Physicians** (1984): 177. **Infant mortality** (per 1,000 live births 1994): 119.

Education (1991): **Literacy:** 50%. **Years compulsory:** 8; **attendance:** 70%.

Major International Organizations: UN (GATT, IMF, WHO), OAU.

Embassy: 1714 New Hampshire Ave. NW 20009; 232-2882.

For centuries, the Tutsi (an extremely tall people) dominated the Hutus (90% of the population). A civil war broke out in 1959 and Tutsi power was ended. Many Tutsi went into exile. A referendum in 1961 abolished the monarchic system. Rwanda, which had been part of the Belgian UN trusteeship of Rwanda-Urundi, became independent July 1, 1962.

In 1963 Tutsi exiles invaded in an unsuccessful coup; a large-scale massacre of Tutsi followed. Rivalries among Hutu led to a bloodless coup July 1973 in which Juvénal Habyarimana took power. After an invasion and coup attempt by Tutsi exiles in 1990, a multiparty democracy was established.

Renewed ethnic strife led to an Aug. 1993 peace accord between the government and rebels of the Tutsi-led Rwandan Patriotic Front (RPF). But after Habyarimana and the president of Burundi were killed Apr. 6, 1994, in a suspicious plane crash, massive violence broke out. An estimated 200,000 or more died in massacres, mainly of Tutsi by Hutu militias, and in civil warfare as the RPF sought power. An estimated 2 million Tutsi and Hutu fled to camps in Zaire and other countries, where many died of cholera and other natural causes. French troops under a UN mandate moved into SW Rwanda June 23 to establish a so-called safe zone. The RPF claimed victory, installing a government in July led by a moderate Hutu president. French troops pulled out Aug. 22; a small African peacekeeping force remained.

Saint Kitts and Nevis

Federation of Saint Kitts & Nevis

People: Population: 41,000. **Pop. density:** 394 per sq. mi. **Ethnic groups:** black African 95%. **Principal languages:** English. **Religions:** Protestant 76%.

Geography: Area: 104 sq. mi. in the northern part of the Leeward group of the Lesser Antilles in the eastern Caribbean Sea. **Capital:** Basseterre (1990): 15,000.

Government: Constitutional monarchy. **Head of state:** Queen Elizabeth represented by Sir Clement Arrindell. **Head of government:** Prime Min. Kennedy A. Simmonds; b Apr. 12, 1936; in office: Sept. 19, 1983.

Economy: Sugar is the principal industry.

Finance: Monetary unit: E Caribbean Dollar (Mar. 1994: 2.70 = $1 US). **Gross domestic product** (1991): $142 mln. **Tourism** (1990): $63 mln. receipts.

Communications: Telephones: 1 per 4.6 persons.

Health: Births (per 1,000 pop.): 24. **Deaths** (per 1,000 pop.): 10. **Natural increase:** 1.4%. **Infant mortality** (per 1,000 live births 1994): 20.

Education: Literacy (1991): 98%.

St. Kitts (known by the natives as Liamuiga) and Nevis were reached (and named) by Columbus in 1493. They were settled by Britain in 1623, but ownership was disputed with France until 1713. They were part of the Leeward Islands Federation, 1871-1956, and the Federation of the W Indies, 1958-62. The colony achieved self-government as an Associated State of the UK in 1967, and became fully independent Sept. 19, 1983.

Saint Lucia

People: Population: 145,000. **Age distrib.** (%): <15: 44; 65+: 6. **Pop. density:** 609 per sq. mi. **Ethnic groups:** Predominantly African descent. **Principal languages:** English (official), French patois. **Religions:** Roman Catholic 90%.

Geography: Area: 238 sq. mi., about one-fifth the size of Rhode Island. **Location:** In Eastern Caribbean, 2d largest of the Windward Is. **Neighbors:** Martinique to N, St. Vincent to SW. **Topography:** Mountainous, volcanic in origin; Soufriere, a volcanic crater, in the S. Wooded mountains run N-S to Mt. Gimie, 3,145 ft., with streams through fertile valleys. **Capital:** Castries. **Cities:** Castries (1991 est.): 45,000.

Government: Type: Parliamentary democracy. **Head of state:** Queen Elizabeth II, represented by Gov.-Gen. S.A. James; **Head of government:** Prime Min. John Compton; in office: May 3, 1982. **Local divisions:** 11 quarters.

Economy: Industries: Agriculture, tourism, manufacturing. **Chief crops:** Bananas, coconuts, cocoa, citrus fruits. **Other resources:** Forests. **Arable land:** 8%. **Electricity prod.** (1992): 112 mln. kWh. **Labor force:** 43% agric., 18% ind. & commerce, 39% services.

Finance: Monetary unit: East Caribbean dollar (Mar. 1994: 2.70 = $1 US). **Gross domestic product** (1991): $250 mln. **Per capita GDP:** $1,650. **Imports** (1990): $270 mln.; partners: U.S. 36%, UK 12%, Trin./Tob. 11%. **Exports** (1990): $127 mln.; partners: U.S. 19%, UK 51%. **Tourism** (1990): receipts: $155 mln.

Transport: Motor vehicles: in use: 7,000 passenger cars, 4,000 comm. vehicles. **Chief ports:** Castries, Vieux Fort.

Communications: Television sets: 1 per 5.3 persons. **Radios:** 1 per 1.5 persons. **Telephones:** 1 per 5.6 persons.

Health: Life expectancy at birth (1994): 67 male; 72 female. **Births** (per 1,000 pop.): 23. **Deaths** (per 1,000 pop.): 6. **Natural increase:** 1.7%. **Hospital beds:** 1 per 283 persons. **Physicians:** 1 per 2,521 persons. **Infant mortality** (per 1,000 live births 1994): 19.

Education: Literacy (1989): 78%; **Years compulsory:** ages 5-15; **Attendance:** 80%.

Major International Organizations: UN (IMF, ILO), CARICOM, OAS.

St. Lucia was ceded to Britain by France at the Treaty of Paris, 1814. Self-government was granted with the West Indies Act, 1967. Independence was attained Feb. 22, 1979.

Saint Vincent and the Grenadines

People: Population: 115,000. **Pop. density:** 766 per sq. mi. **Ethnic groups:** Mainly of African descent. **Principal languages:** English, French patois. **Religions:** Methodist, Anglican, Roman Catholic.

Geography: Area: 150 sq. mi., about twice the size of Washington, D.C. **Location:** In the eastern Caribbean, St. Vincent (133 sq. mi.) and the northern islets of the Grenadines form a part of the Windward chain. **Neighbors:** St. Lucia to N, Barbados to E, Grenada to S. **Topography:** St. Vincent is volcanic, with a ridge of thickly wooded mountains running its length. **Capital:** Kingstown. **Cities** (1991 est.): Kingstown 15,000.

Government: Type: Constitutional monarchy. **Head of state:** Queen Elizabeth II, represented by Gov.-Gen. David Jack; in office: Sept. 20 1989. **Head of government:** Prime Min. James Mitchell; in office: July 30, 1984.

Economy: Industries: Agriculture, tourism. **Chief crops:** Bananas (62% of exports), arrowroot, coconuts. **Arable land:** 38%. **Electricity prod.** (1992): 64 mln. kWh. **Labor force:** 30% agric.

Finance: Monetary unit: East Caribbean dollar (Mar. 1994: 2.70 = $1 US). **Gross domestic product** (1992): $171 mln. **Per capita GDP:** $1,500. **Tourism** (1991): $53 mln. receipts. **National budget** (1990): $67 mln.

Transport: Motor vehicles: in use: 5,000 passenger cars, 2,800 comm. vehicles. **Chief port:** Kingstown.

Communications: Telephones: 1 per 6.4 persons.

Health: Life expectancy at birth (1994): 71 male; 74 female. **Births** (per 1,000 pop.): 20. **Deaths** (per 1,000 pop.): 5. **Natural increase:** 1.5%. **Infant mortality** (per 1,000 live births 1994): 17.

Education (1989): **Literacy:** 85%.

Columbus landed on St. Vincent on Jan. 22, 1498 (St. Vincent's Day). Britain and France both laid claim to the island in the 17th and 18th centuries; the Treaty of Versailles, 1783, finally ceded it to Britain. Associated State status was granted 1969; independence was attained Oct. 27, 1979.

San Marino

Most Serene Republic of San Marino
Serenissima Repubblica di San Marino

People: Population: 24,000. **Age distrib.** (%): <15: 16; 65+: 14. **Pop. density:** 1,000 per sq. mi. **Urban:** 90%. **Ethnic**

groups: Sanmarinese 80%, Italian 18%. **Principal languages:** Italian. **Religions:** mostly Roman Catholic.

Geography: Area: 24 sq. mi. **Location:** In N central Italy near Adriatic coast. **Neighbors:** Completely surrounded by Italy. **Topography:** The country lies on the slopes of Mt. Titano. **Capital:** San Marino. **Cities** (1993 est.): San Marino 2,397.

Government: Type: Republic. **Head of state:** Two co-regents appt. every 6 months. **Local divisions:** 9 municipalities.

Economy: Industries: Postage stamps, tourism, woolen goods, paper, cement, ceramics. **Arable land:** 17%.

Finance: Monetary unit: Italian lira. **Gross domestic product** (1992): $465 mln.* **Tourism** (1991): 3.1 mln. arrivals.

Communications: Television sets: 1 per 2.9 persons. **Radios:** 1 per 1.9 persons. **Telephones:** 1 per 1.5 persons.

Births (per 1,000 pop.): 11. **Deaths** (per 1,000 pop.): 7. **Natural increase:** 0.4%. **Infant mortality** (per 1,000 live births 1994): 6.

Education (1991): **Literacy:** 97%. **Years compulsory:** 8. **Attendance:** 93%.

Major International Organizations: UN.

San Marino claims to be the oldest state in Europe and to have been founded in the 4th century. A Communist-led coalition ruled 1947-57; a similar coalition ruled 1978-86. It has had a treaty of friendship with Italy since 1862.

São Tomé and Príncipe

Democratic Republic of São Tomé and Príncipe

República Democrática de São Tomé e Príncipe

People: Population: 137,000. **Pop. density:** 354 per sq. mi. **Ethnic groups:** Portuguese-African mixture, African minority (Angola, Mozambique immigrants). **Principal languages:** Portuguese (official). **Religions:** Christian 80%.

Geography: Area: 386 sq. mi., slightly larger than New York City. **Location:** In the Gulf of Guinea about 125 miles off W Central Africa. **Neighbors:** Gabon, Equatorial Guinea on E. **Topography:** São Tomé and Príncipe islands, part of an extinct volcano chain, are both covered by lush forests and croplands. **Capital:** São Tomé. **Cities** (1993 est.): São Tomé 43,000.

Government: Type: Republic. **Head of state:** Pres. Miguel Trovoada; in office: Apr. 3, 1991. **Head of government:** Prime Min. Norberto Jose D'Alva Costa Alegre Daio; in office: May 16, 1992. **Local divisions:** 2 districts.

Economy: Chief crops: Cocoa (82% of exports), coconut products. **Arable land:** 1%; **Permanent crops:** 20%. **Electricity prod.** (1991): 10 mln. kWh.

Finance: Monetary unit: Dobra (Jan. 1993: 240 = $1 US). **Gross domestic product** (1992): $41.4 mln. **Per capita GDP:** $315. **Imports** (1990): $21.3 mln.; partners: Port. 61%, Angola 13%. **Exports** (1990): $4.4 mln.; partners: Neth. 52%, Port. 33%, Ger. 8%.

Transport: Chief ports: São Tomé, Santo Antonio.

Communications: Radios: 1 per 4.0 persons.

Health: Births (per 1,000 pop.): 35. **Deaths** (per 1,000 pop.): 9. **Natural increase:** 2.6%. **Physicians:** 1 per 2,819 persons. **Infant mortality** (per 1,000 live births 1994): 64.

Education (1988): **Literacy:** 50%.

Major International Organizations: UN, OAU.

Embassy: 801 2d Ave., New York, NY 10017; 212-697-4211.

The islands were discovered in 1471 by the Portuguese, who brought the first settlers — convicts and exiled Jews. Sugar planting was replaced by the slave trade as the chief economic activity until coffee and cocoa were introduced in the 19th century.

Portugal agreed, 1974, to turn the colony over to the Gabon-based Movement for the Liberation of São Tomé and Príncipe, which proclaimed as first president its East German-trained leader, Manuel Pinto da Costa. Independence came July 12, 1975. Democratic reforms were instituted in 1987. In 1991 Miguel Trovoada won the first free presidential election following the withdrawal of Pres. da Costa.

Saudi Arabia

Kingdom of Saudi Arabia

al-Mamlaka al-'Arabiya as-Sa'udiya

People: Population: 18,197,000. **Age distrib.** (%): <15: 43; 65+: 2. **Pop. density:** 21 per sq. mi. **Urban:** 79%. **Ethnic groups:** Arab tribes, immigrants from other Arab and Muslim countries. **Principal languages:** Arabic. **Religions:** Muslim 100%.

Geography: Area: 865,000 sq. mi., one-third the size of the U.S. **Location:** Occupies most of Arabian Peninsula in Middle East. **Neighbors:** Kuwait, Iraq, Jordan on N, Yemen, Oman on S, United Arab Emirates, Qatar on E. **Topography:** The highlands on W, up to 9,000 ft., slope as an arid, barren desert to the Persian Gulf. **Capital:** Riyadh. **Cities** (1986 est.): Riyadh 1.3 mln.; Jidda 1.2 mln.; Mecca 463,000.

Government: Type: Monarchy with council of ministers. **Head of state and government:** King Fahd ibn Abdul Aziz; b 1922; in office: June 13, 1982 (prime min. since 1982). **Local divisions:** 14 emirates. **Defense:** 13% of GDP (1993).

Economy: Industries: Oil products. **Chief crops:** Dates, wheat, barley, fruit. **Minerals:** Oil, gas, gold, copper, iron. **Crude oil reserves** (1990): 255 bln. barrels. **Arable land:** 1%. **Livestock** (1992): sheep: 6.0 mln.; goats: 3.3 mln. **Electricity prod.** (1992): 63 bln. kWh. **Labor force:** 16% agric.; 34% govt.; 28% industry & oil; 22% services.

Finance: Monetary unit: Riyal (Mar. 1994: 3.74 = $1 US). **Gross domestic product** (1992): $111 bln. **Per capita GDP:** $6,500. **Imports** (1990): $21.5 bln.; partners: US 15%, Jap. 12%, UK 14%. **Exports** (1990): $28.3 bln.; partners: U.S. 22%, Jap. 20%. **National budget** (1993 est.): $52.5 bln. **International reserves less gold** (Mar. 1994): $5.2 bln. **Gold:** 4.59 mln. oz t. **Consumer prices** (change in 1993): 1.1%.

Transport: Railroads: Length: 555 mi. **Motor vehicles:** in use: 2.3 mln. passenger cars, 2.1 mln. comm. vehicles. **Civil aviation:** 16.0 bln. passenger-mi.; 25 airports. **Chief ports:** Jidda, Ad-Dammam, Ras Tannurah.

Communications: Television sets: 1 per 3.7 persons. **Radios:** 1 per 3.4 persons. **Telephones:** 1 per 11 persons. **Daily newspaper circ.:** 42 per 1,000 pop.

Health: Life expectancy at birth (1994): 66 male; 70 female. **Births** (per 1,000 pop.): 38. **Deaths** (per 1,000 pop.): 6. **Natural increase:** 3.2%. **Hospital beds:** 1 per 359 persons. **Physicians:** 1 per 523 persons. **Infant mortality** (per 1,000 live births 1994): 52.

Education (1990): **Literacy:** 62%.

Major International Organizations: UN (IMF, WHO, FAO), Arab League, OPEC.

Embassy: 601 New Hampshire Ave. NW 20037; 342-3800.

Arabia was united for the first time by Mohammed, in the early 7th century. His successors conquered the entire Near East and North Africa, bringing Islam and the Arabic language. But Arabia itself soon returned to its former status.

Nejd, long an independent state and center of the Wahhabi sect, fell under Turkish rule in the 18th century, but in 1913 Ibn Saud, founder of the Saudi dynasty, overthrew the Turks and captured the Turkish province of Hasa; took the Hejaz in 1925 and by 1926, most of Asir. The discovery of oil in the 1930s transformed the new country.

Crown Prince Khalid was proclaimed king on Mar. 25, 1975, after the assassination of King Faisal. Fahd became king on June 13, 1982, following Khalid's death. There is no constitution and no parliament. The king exercises authority together with a Council of Ministers. The Islamic religious code is the law of the land. Alcohol and public entertainments are restricted, and women have an inferior legal status.

Saudi units fought against Israel in the 1948 and 1973 Arab-Israeli wars. Billions of dollars of advanced arms have been purchased from Britain, France, and the U.S. Beginning with the 1967 Arab-Israeli war, Saudi Arabia provided large annual financial gifts to Egypt; aid was later extended to Syria, Jordan, and Palestinian guerrilla groups, as well as to other Muslim countries.

Faisal played a leading role in the 1973-74 Arab oil embargo against the U.S. and other nations in an attempt to force them to adopt an anti-Israel policy. Saudi Arabia joined most other Arab states, 1979, in condemning Egypt's peace treaty with Israel.

In the 1980s, Saudi Arabia's moderate position on crude oil prices often prevailed at OPEC meetings.

Two Saudi oil tankers were attacked May 1984, as Iran and Iraq began air attacks against shipping in the Persian Gulf. On May 29, the U.S., citing grave concern over the growing escalation of the Iran-Iraq war in the Persian Gulf, authorized the sale of 400 Stinger antiaircraft missiles.

The Hejaz contains the holy cities of Islam — Medina, where the Mosque of the Prophet enshrines the tomb of Mohammed, and Mecca, his birthplace. More than 600,000 Muslims from 60 nations pilgrimage to Mecca annually.

In 1987, Iranians making a pilgrimage to Mecca clashed with anti-Iranian pilgrims and Saudi police; over 400 were killed. Saudi Arabia broke diplomatic relations with Iran in 1988. Some 1,426 Muslim pilgrims died July 2, 1990, in a stampede in a pedestrian tunnel leading to Mecca. Nearly 300 pilgrims were killed in a stampede in Mecca, May 26, 1994.

Following Iraq's attack on Kuwait, Aug. 2, 1990, Saudi Arabia accepted the Kuwait royal family and over 400,000 Kuwaiti refugees. King Fahd invited Western and Arab troops to deploy on its soil in support of Saudi defense forces. During the Persian Gulf War, Iraq fired a series of Scud missiles at Saudi Arabia; most were intercepted by U.S. Patriot missiles, although 28 U.S. soldiers were killed when a Scud hit their barracks in Dhahran, Feb. 25. The nation's northern Gulf coastline suffered severe pollution as a result of Iraqi sabotage of the Kuwaiti oil fields.

Senegal

Republic of Senegal

République du Sénégal

People: Population: 8,731,000. **Age distrib.** (%): <15: 47; 65+: 3. **Pop. density:** 115 per sq. mi. **Urban:** 39%. **Ethnic groups:** Wolof 36%, Serer 17%, Fulani 17%, Diola 9%, Toucouleur 9%, Mandingo 9%. **Principal languages:** French (official), Wolof, Serer, Peul, Tukulor, others. **Religions:** Muslim 92%, Christian 2%.

Geography: Area: 75,951 sq. mi., the size of South Dakota. **Location:** At western extreme of Africa. **Neighbors:** Mauritania on N, Mali on E, Guinea, Guinea-Bissau on S, Gambia surrounded on three sides. **Topography:** Low rolling plains cover most of Senegal, rising somewhat in the SE. Swamp and jungles are in SW. **Capital:** Dakar. **Cities** (1992): Dakar 1.7 mln.; Thies 201,000; Kaolack 179,000.

Government: Type: Republic. **Head of state:** Pres. Abdou Diouf; b Sept. 7, 1935; in office: Jan. 1, 1981. **Head of government:** Habib Thiam; in office: Apr. 8, 1991. **Local divisions:** 10 regions. **Defense:** 2% of GDP (1989 est.).

Economy: Industries: Food processing, fishing. **Chief crops:** Peanuts, millet, rice. **Minerals:** Phosphates. **Arable land:** 27%. **Livestock** (1992): cattle: 2.8 mln.; sheep: 3.6 mln.; goats: 2.4 mln. **Fish catch** (1991): 319,000 metric tons. **Electricity prod.** (1991): 760 mln. kWh. **Labor force:** 77% agric.

Finance: Monetary unit: CFA franc (Mar. 1994: 576 = $1 US). **Gross domestic product** (1991): $5.4 bln. **Per capita GDP:** $780. **Imports** (1990): $1.0 bln.; partners Fr. 37%, U.S. 6%. **Exports** (1990): $814 mln.; partners Fr. 25%, UK 6%. **Tourism** (1990): $152 mln. receipts. **National budget** (1989): $1.0 bln. **International reserves less gold** (Mar. 1994): $5.2 bln. **Gold:** 29,000 oz t. **Consumer prices** (change in 1992): -0.1%.

Transport: Railroads: Length: 562 mi. **Motor vehicles:** in use: 90,000 passenger cars, 37,000 comm. vehicles. **Chief ports:** Dakar, Saint-Louis.

Communications: Television sets: 1 per 126 persons. **Radios:** 1 per 9.0 persons. **Telephones:** 1 per 157 persons.

Health: Life expectancy at birth (1994): 55 male, 58 female. **Births** (per 1,000 pop.): 43. **Deaths** (per 1,000 pop.): 12. **Natural increase:** 3.1%. **Hospital beds:** 1 per 1,134 persons. **Physicians:** 1 per 17,072 persons. **Infant mortality** (per 1,000 live births 1994): 76.

Education (1988): **Literacy:** 10%. **Attendance:** 48% primary, 11% secondary.

Major International Organizations: UN and all of its specialized agencies, OAU.

Embassy: 2112 Wyoming Ave. NW 20008; 234-0540.

Portuguese settlers arrived in the 15th century, but French control grew from the 17th century. The last independent Muslim state was subdued in 1893. Dakar became the capital of French West Africa.

Independence as part, along with the Sudanese Rep., of the Mali Federation, came June 20, 1960. Senegal withdrew Aug. 20. French political and economic influence remained strong.

Senegal, Dec. 17, 1981, signed an agreement with The Gambia for confederation of the 2 countries, without loss of individual sovereignty, under the name of Senegambia. The confederation collapsed in 1989, although in 1991 the 2 nations signed a friendship and cooperation treaty.

Seychelles

Republic of Seychelles

People: Population: 72,000. **Age distrib.** (%): <15: 35; 65+: 6. **Pop. density:** 409 per sq. mi. **Urban:** 50%. **Ethnic groups:** Seychellois (mixture of Asians, Africans, and French) predominate. **Principal languages:** English, French (both official). **Religions:** Roman Catholic 90%.

Geography: Area: 176 sq. mi. **Location:** In the Indian O. 700 miles NE of Madagascar. **Neighbors:** Nearest are Madagascar on SW, Somalia on NW. **Topography:** A group of 86 islands, about half of them composed of coral, the other half granite, the latter predominantly mountainous. **Capital:** Victoria. **Cities** (1987): Victoria 24,000.

Government: Type: Republic. **Head of state:** Pres. France-Albert René, b. Nov. 16, 1935; in office: June 5, 1977. **Local divisions:** 23 districts. **Defense:** 4% of GDP (1990 est.).

Economy: Industries: Food processing. **Chief crops:** Coconut products, cinnamon, vanilla, patchouli. **Electricity prod.** (1991): 80 mln. kWh. **Labor force:** 12% agric.; 31% industry & comm.; 20% govt; 21% services.

Finance: Monetary unit: Rupee (Mar. 1994: 5.16 = $1 US). **Gross domestic product** (1991): $350 mln. **Per capita GDP:** $5,200. **Imports** (1991): $172 mln.; partners: UK 20%, So. Afr. 13%. **Exports** (1991): $48 mln.; partners: Pak. 38%, Jap. 26%. **National budget** (1989): $202 mln. **Tourism** (1991): $97 mln. receipts. **International reserves less gold** (Feb. 1994): $31 mln. **Consumer prices** (change in 1993): 1.3%.

Transport: Motor vehicles: in use: 4,700 passenger cars, 1,600 comm. vehicles. **Chief ports:** Victoria.

Communications: Radios: 1 per 2.4 persons. **Telephones:** 1 per 8.7 persons. **Daily newspaper circ.:** 47 per 1,000 pop.

Health: Life expectancy at birth (1994): 66 male; 73 female. **Births** (per 1,000 pop.): 22. **Deaths** (per 1,000 pop.): 7. **Natural increase:** 1.5%. **Hospital beds:** 1 per 172 persons. **Physicians:** 1 per 1,164 persons. **Infant mortality** (per 1,000 live births 1994): 12.

Education (1991): **Literacy:** 85%. **Years compulsory** 9; attendance 98%.

Major International Organizations: UN, OAU, Commonwealth of Nations.

The islands were occupied by France in 1768, and seized by Britain in 1794. Ruled as part of Mauritius from 1814, the Seychelles became a separate colony in 1903. The ruling party had opposed independence as impractical, but pressure from the OAU and the UN became irresistible, and independence was declared June 29, 1976. The first president was ousted in a coup a year later by a socialist leader.

A new constitution, approved June 1993, provided for a multiparty state.

Sierra Leone

Republic of Sierra Leone

People: Population: 4,630,000. **Age distrib.** (%): <15: 45; 65+: 3. **Pop. density:** 167 per sq. mi. **Urban:** 32%. **Ethnic groups:** Temne 30%, Mende 30%, others. **Principal languages:** English (official), tribal languages. **Religions:** indigenous beliefs 30%, Muslim 30%, Christian 10%.

Geography: Area: 27,699 sq. mi., slightly smaller than South Carolina. **Location:** On W coast of W Africa. **Neighbors:** Guinea on N, E, Liberia on S. **Topography:** The heavily-indented, 210-mi. coastline has mangrove swamps. Behind are wooded hills, rising to a plateau and mountains in the E. **Capital:** Freetown. **Cities** (1985 est.): Freetown 469,000; Koidu-New Sembehun 80,000; Bo, Kenema, Makeni.

Government: Type: Military. **Head of government:** Capt.

Valentine E. M. Strasser; in office: May 7, 1992. **Local divisions:** 4 provinces. **Defense:** 0.7% of GDP (1988 est.).

Economy: Industries: Mining, tourism. **Chief crops:** Cocoa, coffee, palm kernels, rice, ginger. **Minerals:** Diamonds, bauxite. **Arable land:** 25%. **Fish catch** (1991): 50,000 metric tons. **Electricity prod.** (1991): 185 mln. kWh. **Labor force:** 65% agric.; 35% ind. & serv.

Finance: Monetary unit: Leone (Mar. 1994: 576 = $1.00 US). **Gross domestic product** (1992): $1.4 bln. **Per capita GDP:** $330. **Imports** (1992): $131 mln.; partners: UK 22%, Fr. 11%. **Exports** (1992): $145 mln.; partners: Neth. 31%; UK 15%, U.S. 9%. **National budget** (1992 est.): $118 mln. **International reserves less gold** (Feb. 1994): $30 mln. **Consumer prices** (change in 1992): 65.5%.

Transport: Motor vehicles: in use: 29,000 passenger cars, 10,000 comm. vehicles. **Chief ports:** Freetown, Bonthe.

Communications: Television sets: 1 per 175 persons. **Radios:** 1 per 4.9 persons. **Telephones:** 1 per 125 persons.

Health: Life expectancy at birth (1994): 44 male; 49 female. **Births** (per 1,000 pop.): 45. **Deaths** (per 1,000 pop.): 19. **Natural increase:** 2.6%. **Hospital beds:** 1 per 980 persons. **Physicians:** 1 per 13,150 persons. **Infant mortality** (per 1,000 live births 1994): 142.

Education (1991): **Literacy:** 21%.

Major International Organizations: UN (GATT, IMF, WHO), Commonwealth of Nations, OAU.

Embassy: 1701 19th St. NW 20009; 939-9261.

Freetown was founded in 1787 by the British government as a haven for freed slaves. Their descendants, known as Creoles, number more than 60,000.

Successive steps toward independence followed the 1951 constitution. Full independence arrived Apr. 27, 1961. Sierra Leone became a republic Apr. 19, 1971. A one-party state approved by referendum 1978, brought political stability, but the economy has been plagued by inflation, corruption, and dependence upon the International Monetary Fund and creditors.

Mutinous soldiers ousted Pres. Joseph Momoh Apr. 30, 1992. The new regime promised a gradual transition back to civilian rule.

Singapore

Republic of Singapore

People: Population: 2,859,000. **Age distrib.** (%): <15: 23; 65+: 6. **Pop. density:** 11,574 per sq. mi. **Ethnic groups:** Chinese 77%, Malays 15%, Indians 6%. **Principal languages:** Chinese, Malay, Tamil, English (all official). **Religions:** Buddhism 29%, Christian 19%, Muslim 16%, Taoism 13%.

Geography: Area: 247 sq. mi., smaller than New York City. **Location:** Off tip of Malayan Peninsula in SE Asia. **Neighbors:** Nearest are Malaysia on N, Indonesia on S. **Topography:** Singapore is a flat, formerly swampy island. The nation includes 40 nearby islets. **Capital:** Singapore.

Government: Type: Republic. **Head of state:** Pres. Ong Teng Cheong; in office: Sept. 2, 1993. **Head of government:** Prime Min. Goh Chok Tong; b May 20, 1941; in office: Nov. 28, 1990. **Defense:** 4% of GDP (1990 est.).

Economy: Industries: Shipbuilding, oil refining, electronics, banking, textiles, food, rubber, lumber processing, tourism. **Arable land:** 4%. **Livestock** (1989): pigs: 321,000. **Fish catch** (1992): 9,000 metric tons. **Electricity prod.** (1992): 18 bln. kWh. **Labor force:** 1% agric.; 59% ind. & comm.; 30% services.

Finance: Monetary unit: Dollar (Mar. 1994: 1.58 = $1 US). **Gross domestic product** (1992): $45.9 bln. **Per capita GDP:** $16,500. **Imports** (1992): $72.1 bln.; partners: Jap. 18%, Malay. 13%, U.S. 17%, Sau. Ar. 9%. **Exports** (1992): $63.4 bln., partners: U.S. 20%, Malay. 16%, Jap. 11%, HK 6%. **Tourism** (1990): $4.3 bln. receipts. **National budget** (1993): $9.4 bln. **International reserves less gold** (Jan. 1994): $49.5 bln. **Consumer prices** (change in 1993): 2.4%.

Transport: Motor vehicles: in use: 302,000 passenger cars, 128,000 comm. vehicles. **Civil aviation:** 23 bln. passenger-mi.; 1 airport.

Communications: Television sets: 1 per 5.1 persons. **Radios:** 1 per 3.5 persons. **Telephones:** 1 per 2.2 persons. **Daily newspaper circ.:** 280 per 1,000 pop.

Health: Life expectancy at birth (1994): 73 male; 79 female. **Births** (per 1,000 pop.): 17. **Deaths** (per 1,000 pop.): 5. **Natural increase:** 1.1%. **Hospital beds:** 1 per 282 persons. **Physicians:** 1 per 757 persons. **Infant mortality** (per 1,000 live births 1994): 6.

Education (1990): **Literacy:** 87%. **Years compulsory:** none; attendance 94%.

Major International Organizations: UN (GATT, IMF, WHO), ASEAN.

Embassy: 1824 R St. NW 20009; 667-7555.

Founded in 1819 by Sir Thomas Stamford Raffles, Singapore was a British colony until 1959, when it became autonomous within the Commonwealth. On Sept. 16, 1963, it joined with Malaya, Sarawak, and Sabah to form the Federation of Malaysia. Tensions between Malayans, dominant in the federation, and ethnic Chinese, dominant in Singapore, led to an agreement under which Singapore became a separate nation, Aug. 9, 1965.

Singapore is one of the world's largest ports. Standards in health, education, and housing are high. International banking has grown. The government, dominated by a single party, has taken strong actions to suppress dissent.

Despite appeals from U.S. President Bill Clinton and others, Michael Fay, 18, a U.S. citizen, was flogged with a cane May 5, 1994, after being convicted of vandalism by a Singapore court.

Slovakia

Slovensko

People: Population: 5,404,000. **Pop. density:** 285 per sq. mi. **Ethnic groups:** Slovak 86%, Hungarian 11%. **Principal languages:** Slovak (official), Hungarian. **Religions:** Roman Catholic 60%, Protestant 8%.

Geography: Area: 18,933 sq. mi. **Location:** In E central Europe. **Neighbors:** Poland on N, Hungary on S, Austria, Czech Rep. on W, Ukraine on E. **Topography:** mountains (Carpathians) in N, fertile Danube plane in S. **Capital:** Bratislava. **Cities** (1991 est.): Bratislava 441,000, Kosice 234,000.

Government: Type: Republic. **Head of state:** Pres. Michal Kovac; b 1931; in office: Feb. 2, 1993. **Head of government:** Prime Min. Jozef Moravcik; in office: Mar. 16, 1994.

Economy: Industries: Iron and steel, glass, chemicals, cement. **Chief crops:** Wheat potatoes, rye, corn.

Finance: Monetary unit: new Koruna (Feb. 1993: 29.00 = $1 US). **Gross domestic product** (1992): $32.1 bln.* **Per capita GDP:** $6,100.

Transport: Railroads: Length: 2,275 mi. **Motor vehicles:** in use: 906,000 passenger cars, 109,000 comm. vehicles.

Communications: Radios: 1 per 3.3 persons. **Telephones:** 1 per 3.0 persons.

Health: Births (per 1,000 pop.): 15. **Deaths** (per 1,000 pop.): 9. **Natural increase:** .5%.

Education (1993): **Literacy:** 99%.

Major International Organizations: UN.

Embassy: 3900 Spring of Freedom St. NW 20008; 363-6315.

Slovakia was originally settled by Illyrian, Celtic, and Germanic tribes and was incorporated into Great Moravia in the 9th century. It became part of Hungary in the 11th century. Overrun by Czech Hussites in the 15th century, it was restored to Hungarian rule in 1526. The Slovaks disassociated themselves from Hungary following World War I and joined the Czechs of Bohemia to form the Republic of Czechoslovakia, Oct. 28, 1918.

Germany invaded Czechoslovakia, 1939, and declared Slovakia independent. Slovakia rejoined Czechoslovakia in 1945.

Czechoslovakia split into 2 separate states—the Czech Republic and Slovakia—on Jan. 1, 1993. Slovakia, with its less developed economy, faced difficult times ahead.

Slovenia

Republic of Slovenia

Republica of Slovenija

People: Population: 1,972,000. **Pop. density:** 252 per sq. mi. **Ethnic groups:** Slovenes 91%. **Principal languages:** Slovenian, Serbo-Croatian. **Religions:** Mostly Roman Catholic.

Geography: Area: 7,821 sq. mi., slightly larger than New

Jersey. **Location:** in SE Europe. **Neighbors:** Italy, Austria, Hungary, Croatia. **Topography:** mostly hilly; 42% of the land is forested. **Capital:** Ljubljana. **Cities** (1991): Ljubljana 276,000.

Government: Type: Republic. **Head of state:** Pres. Milan Kucan; b Jan. 14, 1941; in office: Apr. 1990. **Head of government:** Janez Drnovsek; in office: May 14, 1992. **Defense:** 4.5% of GDP (1993).

Economy: Industries: Steel, textiles. **Minerals:** Coal, mercury. **Chief crops:** Wheat, potatoes. **Livestock** (1992): cattle: 484,000; pigs: 529,000. **Electricity prod.** (1992): 10 bln. kWh.

Finance: Monetary unit: Tolar. **Gross domestic product** (1991): $21 bln.* **Per capita GDP:** $10,700. **Imports** (1990): $4.6 bln. **Exports** (1990): $4.1 bln.

Transport: Motor vehicles: in use: 583,000 passenger cars.

Communications: Television sets: 1 per 4.4 persons. **Telephones:** 1 per 3 persons. **Daily newspaper circ.:** 115 per 1,000 pop.

Health: Life expectancy at birth (1994): 70 male; 78 female. **Births** (per 1,000 pop.): 12. **Deaths** (per 1,000 pop.): 10. **Natural increase:** .2%. **Hospital beds:** 1 per 167 persons. **Physicians:** 1 per 481 persons. **Infant mortality:** (per 1,000 live births 1994): 8.

Education: Literacy (1991): 90%.

Major International Organizations: UN.

The Slovenes settled in their current territory in the period from the 6th to the 8th centuries. They fell under German domination as early as the 9th century. Modern Slovenian political history began after 1848 when the Slovenes, who were divided among several Austrian provinces, began their struggle for political and national unification. With the establishment of Yugoslavia in 1918, this unification was largely achieved when the majority of the Slovenes entered the new state, which became the Kingdom of the Serbs, Croats, and Slovenes.

Slovenia declared independence June 25, 1991.

Solomon Islands

People: Population: 386,000. **Pop. density:** 35 per sq. mi. **Urban:** 13%. **Ethnic groups:** Melanesian 93%, Polynesian 4%. **Principal languages:** English (official), Papuan, Melanesian, Polynesian languages. **Religions:** Anglican 34%, Roman Catholic 19%, Baptist 17%, traditional religions.

Geography: Area: 10,954 sq. mi., slightly larger than Maryland. **Location:** Melanesian archipelago in the western Pacific O. **Neighbors:** Nearest is Papua New Guinea on W. **Topography:** 10 large volcanic and rugged islands and 4 groups of smaller ones. **Capital:** Honiara. **Cities:** (1988): Honiara 30,000.

Government: Type: Parliamentary democracy within the Commonwealth of Nations. **Head of state:** Queen Elizabeth II, represented by Gov.-Gen. George Lepping. **Head of government:** Prime Min. Billy Hilly; in office: June 1993. **Local divisions:** 7 provinces and Honiara.

Economy: Industries: Fish canning. **Chief crops:** Coconuts, rice, bananas, yams. **Other resources:** Forests, marine shell. **Arable land:** 1%. **Fish catch** (1992): 40,000 metric tons. **Electricity prod.** (1991): 39 mln. kWh. **Labor force:** 32% agric., 25% services, 12% ind. & comm.

Finance: Monetary unit: Dollar (Mar. 1994: 3.24 = $1 US). **Gross domestic product** (1990): $200 mln. **Per capita GDP:** $600. **Imports** (1990): $92 mln.; partners: Austral. 31%, Jap. 14%, Sing. 18%. **Exports** (1990): $70 mln.; partners: Jap. 37%, UK 11%.

Communications: Radios: 1 per 8.9 persons. **Telephones:** 1 per 46 persons.

Health: Life expectancy at birth (1994): 68 male; 73 female. **Births:** (per 1,000 pop.): 39. **Deaths** (per 1,000 pop.): 5. **Natural increase:** 3.4%. **Infant mortality** (per 1,000 live births 1994): 28.

Education (1989): **Literacy:** 60%. **Attendence:** primary school 78%, secondary school 21%.

Major International Organizations: UN, Commonwealth of Nations.

The Solomon Islands were sighted in 1568 by an expedition from Peru. Britain established a protectorate in the 1890s over most of the group, inhabited by Melanesians. The islands saw major World War II battles. Self-government came Jan. 2, 1976, and independence was formally attained July 7, 1978.

Somalia
Somali Democratic Republic
Jamhuriyadda Dimugradiga Somaliya

People: Population: 6,667,000. **Pop. density:** 27 per sq. mi. **Urban:** 24%. **Ethnic groups:** mainly Somalis, others. **Principal languages:** Somali (official), Arabic, Italian, English. **Religions:** Sunni Muslims 99%.

Geography: Area: 246,300 sq. mi., slightly smaller than Texas. **Location:** Occupies the eastern horn of Africa. **Neighbors:** Djibouti, Ethiopia, Kenya on W. **Topography:** The coastline extends for 1,700 mi. Hills cover the N; the center and S are flat. **Capital:** Mogadishu. **Cities** (1986 est.): Mogadishu 700,000.

Government: Type: In transition. **Local divisions:** 16 regions.

Economy: Chief crops: Incense, sugar, bananas, sorghum, corn, gum. **Minerals:** Iron, tin, gypsum, bauxite, uranium. **Arable land:** 2%. **Livestock** (1992): cattle: 1.0 mln.; goats: 6.0 mln.; sheep: 4 mln. **Fish catch** (1991): 16,000 metric tons. **Electricity prod.** (1991): 60 mln. kWh. **Labor force:** 70% agric.

Finance: Monetary unit: Shilling (Dec. 1992: 4,200 = $1 US). **Gross domestic product** (1989): $1.7 bln. **Per capita GDP** (1989): $170. **Imports** (1990): $249 mln.; partners: It. 29%, Fra. 18%. **Exports** (1990): $58 mln.; partners: It. 17%.

Transport: Motor vehicles: in use: 20,000 passenger cars, 12,000 comm. vehicles. **Chief ports:** Mogadishu, Berbera.

Communications: Radios: 1 per 20 persons.

Health: Life expectancy at birth (1994): 54 male; 55 female. **Births** (per 1,000 pop.): 46. **Deaths** (per 1,000 pop.): 14. **Natural increase:** 3.2%. **Hospital beds:** 1 per 1,053 persons. **Physicians:** 1 per 19,071 persons. **Infant mortality** (per 1,000 live births 1994): 126.

Education (1990): **Literacy:** 24%. **Attendance:** 50% attend primary school, 7% attend secondary school.

Major International Organizations: UN, OAU, Arab League.

Embassy: 600 New Hampshire Ave. NW 20037; 342-1575.

The UN in 1949 approved eventual creation of Somalia as a sovereign state, and in 1950 Italy took over the trusteeship held by Great Britain since World War II.

British Somaliland was formed in the 19th century in the NW. Britain gave it independence June 26, 1960; on July 1 it joined with the former Italian part to create the independent Somali Republic.

On Oct. 21, 1969, a Supreme Revolutionary Council seized power in a bloodless coup, named a Council of Secretaries of State, and abolished the Assembly. In May 1970, several foreign companies were nationalized.

Somalia has laid claim to Ogaden, the huge eastern region of Ethiopia, peopled mostly by Somalis. Ethiopia battled Somali rebels in 1977. Some 11,000 Cuban troops with Soviet arms defeated Somali army troops and ethnic Somali rebels in Ethiopia, 1978. As many as 1.5 mln. refugees entered Somalia. Guerrilla fighting in Ogaden continued until 1988, when a peace agreement was reached with Ethiopia.

Twenty-one years of one-man rule ended in Jan. 1991 with the flight of Gen. Muhammad Siyad Barre from the capital. Fighting between rival factions caused 40,000 casualties in 1991 and 1992, and by mid-1992 the civil war, drought, and banditry combined to produce a famine that threatened some 1.5 million people with starvation. In July 1992 the UN secretary general declared Somalia to be a country without a government.

In Dec. 1992 the UN accepted a U.S. offer of troops to safeguard the delivery of food to the starving. The UN took control of the multinational relief effort from the U.S. May 4, 1993. While the operation helped alleviate the famine, efforts to establish a viable government and to capture warlord Gen. Mohammed Farah Aidid, who opposed the UN role in Somalia, floundered, and there were significant U.S. and other casualties. The U.S. withdrew its peacekeeping troops Mar. 25, 1994; some UN forces remained to monitor distribution of relief aid. A peace accord was signed June 19, 1994, by 19 Somali leaders, but violence continued.

South Africa
Republic of South Africa
Republiek van Suid-Afrika

People: Population: 43,931,000. **Age distrib.** (%): <15: 39; 65+: 4. **Pop. density:** 92 per sq. mi. **Urban:** 57%. **Ethnic**

groups: black 75%, white 14%, Coloured 9%, Indian 3%. **Principal languages:** Afrikaans, English (both official), Nguni, Sotho languages. **Religions:** Mainly Christian, Hindu, Muslim minorities.

Geography: Area: 473,290 sq. mi., about twice the size of Texas. **Location:** At the southern extreme of Africa. **Neighbors:** Namibia, Botswana, Zimbabwe on N, Mozambique, Swaziland on E; surrounds Lesotho. **Topography:** The large interior plateau reaches close to the country's 2,700-mi. coastline. There are few major rivers or lakes; rainfall is sparse in W, more plentiful in E. **Capitals:** Cape Town (legislative). Pretoria (administrative), and Bloemfontein (judicial). **Cities** (1991 met.): Durban 1.1 mln.; Cape Town 1.9 mln.; Johannesburg 1.9 mln.; Pretoria 1.0 mln.

Government: Type: Federal republic with bicameral Parliament and universal suffrage. **Head of state and government:** Pres. Nelson Mandela; b July 1918; in office: May 10, 1994. Deputy presidents: Thabo Mbeki, F.W. de Klerk. **Local divisions:** 9 provinces. **Defense:** 2.5% of GDP (1993).

Economy: Industries: Steel, tires, motors, textiles, plastics. **Chief crops:** Corn, wool, dairy products, grain, tobacco, sugar, fruit, peanuts, grapes. **Minerals:** Gold (largest producer), chromium, antimony, coal, iron, manganese, nickel, phosphates, tin, uranium, gem diamonds, platinum, copper, vanadium. **Other resources:** Wool. **Arable land:** 10%. **Livestock** (1989): cattle: 11.8 mln.; sheep: 30.3 mln. **Fish catch** (1991): 498,000 metric tons. **Electricity prod.** (1991): 180 bln. kWh. **Labor force:** 10% agric.; 20% ind.; 55% services.

Finance: Monetary unit: Rand (Mar. 1994: 1.00 = $.29 US). **Gross domestic product** (1992): $115 bln. **Per capita GDP** $2,800. **Imports** (1992): $21.2 bln.; partners: Ger. 19%, U.S. 68%, UK. 12%. **Exports** (1992): $23.8 bln.; partners: U.S. 43%, Jap. 9%. **Tourism** (1990): $1.0 bln. receipts. **National budget** (1993): $36 bln. **International reserves less gold** (Feb. 1994): $956 mln. **Gold:** 4.84 mln. oz t. **Consumer prices** (change in 1993): 9.7%.

Transport: Railroads: Length: 13,432 mi. **Motor vehicles:** in use: 3.4 mln. passenger cars, 1.5 mln. comm. vehicles. **Civil aviation:** 5.2 bln. passenger-mi. **Chief ports:** Durban, Cape Town, East London, Port Elizabeth.

Communications: Television sets: 1 per 11 persons. **Radios:** 1 per 3.9 persons. **Telephones:** 1 per 7.5 persons. **Daily newspaper circ.:** 38 per 1,000 pop.

Health: Life expectancy at birth (1994): 62 male; 68 female. **Births** (per 1,000 pop.): 34. **Deaths** (per 1,000 pop.): 8. **Natural increase:** 2.6%. **Physicians:** 1 per 1,271 persons. **Infant mortality** (per 1,000 live births 1994) 47.

Education (1990): **Literacy:** 99% (whites), 69% (Asians), 62% (Coloureds), 50% (Africans).

Major International Organizations: UN (GATT).

Embassy: 3051 Massachusetts Ave. NW 20008; 232-4400.

Bushmen and Hottentots were the original inhabitants. Bantus, including Zulu, Xhosa, Swazi, and Sotho, had occupied the area from Transvaal to south of Transkei before the 17th century.

The Cape of Good Hope area was settled by Dutch, beginning in the 17th century. Britain seized the Cape in 1806. Many Dutch trekked north and founded 2 republics, the Transvaal and the Orange Free State. Diamonds were discovered, 1867, and gold, 1886. The Dutch (Boers) resented encroachments by the British and others; the Anglo-Boer War followed, 1899-1902. Britain won and, effective May 31, 1910, created the Union of South Africa, incorporating the British colonies of the Cape and Natal, the Transvaal and the Orange Free State. After a referendum, the Union became the Republic of South Africa, May 31, 1961, and withdrew from the Commonwealth.

With the election victory of Daniel Malan's National Party in 1948, the policy of separate development of the races, or apartheid, already existing unofficially, became official. This called for separate development, separate residential areas, and ultimate political independence for the whites, Bantus, Asians, and Coloureds. In 1959 the government passed acts providing the eventual creation of several Bantu nations or Bantustans on 13% of the country's land area, though most black leaders opposed the plan.

Under apartheid, blacks were severely restricted to certain occupations, and paid far lower wages than whites for similar work. Only whites could vote or run for public office. There was an advisory Indian Council, partly elected, partly appointed. In 1969, a Coloured People's Representative Council was created.

At least 600 persons, mostly Bantus, were killed in 1976 riots protesting apartheid. Black protests continued as violence broke out in several black townships. A new constitution was approved by referendum, Nov. 1983, which extended the parliamentary franchise to the Coloured and Asian minorities. Laws banning interracial sex and marriage were repealed in 1985.

In 1963, the Transkei, an area in the SE, became the first of the partially self-governing black territories or "Homelands." Transkei became independent on Oct. 26, 1976, Bophuthatswana on Dec. 6, 1977, and Venda on Sept. 13, 1979; none received international recognition.

In 1981, So. Africa launched military operations in Angola and Mozambique to combat terrorists groups; So. African troops attacked the South West African People's Organization (SWAPO) guerrillas in Angola, Mar. 1982. South Africa and Mozambique signed a non-aggression pact in 1984.

In 1986, Nobel Peace Prize winner Bishop Desmond Tutu called for Western nations to apply sanctions against So. Africa to force an end to apartheid. President Botha announced in Apr. the end to the nation's system of racial pass laws and offered blacks an advisory role in government. On May 19, So. Africa attacked 3 neighboring countries—Zimbabwe, Botswana, Zambia—to strike at guerrilla strongholds of the black nationalist African National Congress. A nationwide state of emergency was declared June 12, giving almost unlimited power to the security forces. As confrontation between blacks and government increased, there was widespread support in Western nations for a complete trade embargo on So. Africa.

Some 2 million South African black workers staged a massive strike, June 6-8, 1988. P.W. Botha, head of the government since 1978, resigned Aug. 14, 1989, and was replaced by Frederik W. de Klerk.

In 1990, the government lifted its ban on the ANC. On Feb. 11, black nationalist leader Nelson Mandela was freed after more than 27 years in prison. In Oct. the Separate Amenities Act was repealed, ending the legal basis of segregation in public places. In Feb. 1991, Pres. de Klerk announced plans to end all apartheid laws. In June the race registration law was repealed.

A band of marauders swept through the township of Boipatong, June 17, 1992, killing some 40 blacks and prompting the ANC to temporarily break off constitutional talks with the white-minority government. Violence involving rival black groups continued later in the year. Violence flared in several black townships following the assassination of Chris Hani, head of the South African Communist Party, Apr. 10, 1993.

In 1993 the nation's negotiating parties, led by the ANC and the National Party, agreed on basic principles for a new constitution, with elections in which all races could vote. A multiracial transition committee was instituted in Dec. to oversee certain government operations prior to elections. Voters would determine party composition of a National Assembly and provincial assemblies. The former would elect the president, enact legislation, and approve a permanent constitution. Under the new system, S Africa's homelands were abolished as such, incorporated into the national system of 9 provinces.

In elections Apr. 26-29, 1994, the ANC won 62.7% of the vote, enabling Mandela to become president. The National Party won 20.4%. The Inkatha Freedom Party won 10.5% and control of the legislature in a predominantly Zulu province.

Spain

España

People: Population: 39,303,000. **Age distrib.** (%): <15: 19; 65+: 14. **Pop. density:** 201 per sq. mi. **Urban:** 78%. **Ethnic groups:** Spanish (Castilian, Valencian, Andalusian, Asturian) 72.8%, Catalan 16.4%, Galician 8.2%, Basque 2.3%. **Principal languages:** Spanish (official), Catalan, Galician, Basque. **Religions:** Roman Catholic 99%.

Geography: Area: 194,898 sq. mi., the size of Arizona and Utah combined. **Location:** In SW Europe. **Neighbors:** Portugal on W, France on N. **Topography:** The interior is a high, arid plateau broken by mountain ranges and river valleys. The NW is heavily watered, the south has lowlands and a Mediterranean climate. **Capital:** Madrid. **Cities** (1991 est.): Madrid 2.9 mln.; Barcelona 1.6 mln.; Valencia 752,000; Seville 659,000.

Government: Type: Constitutional monarchy. **Head of state:** King Juan Carlos I de Borbon y Borbon, b. Jan. 5, 1938; in office: Nov. 22, 1975. **Head of government:** Prime Min.

Felipe González Márquez; in office: Dec. 2, 1982. **Local divisions:** 17 automonous communities. **Defense:** 1.6% of GDP (1992).

Economy: Industries: Machinery, steel, textiles, shoes, autos, processed foods. **Chief crops:** Grains, olives, grapes, citrus fruits, vegetables, olives. **Minerals:** Lignite, uranium, lead, iron, copper, zinc, coal. **Other resources:** Forests (cork). **Arable land:** 31%. **Livestock** (1992): cattle: 4.9 mln.; pigs: 17.2 mln.; sheep: 24.6 mln. **Fish catch** (1991): 1.3 mln. metric tons. **Electricity prod.** (1992): 157 bln. kWh. **Labor force:** 14% agric.; 24% ind. and comm.; 53% serv.

Finance: Monetary unit: Peseta (Mar. 1994: 138.91 = $1 US). **Gross domestic product** (1992): $514.9 bln.* **Per capita GDP:** $13,200. **Imports** (1992): $99.7 bln.; partners: U.S. 8%, EU 57%. **Exports** (1992): $64.3 bln.; partners: EU 71%, U.S. 6%. **Tourism** (1990): $18.5 bln. receipts. **National budget** (1992 est.): $140.2 bln. **International reserves less gold** (Mar. 1994): $41.6 bln. **Gold:** 15.62 mln. oz t. **Consumer prices** (change in 1993): 4.6%.

Transport: Railroads: Length: 7,806 mi. **Motor vehicles:** in use: 12.5 mln. passenger cars, 2.6 mln. comm. vehicles. **Civil aviation:** 16.9 bln. passenger-mi.; 24 airports with scheduled flights. **Chief ports:** Barcelona, Bilbao, Valencia, Cartagena, Gijon.

Communications: Television sets: 1 per 2.3 persons. **Radios:** 1 per 3.1 persons. **Telephones:** 1 per 2.5 persons. **Daily newspaper circ.:** 82 per 1,000 pop.

Health: Life expectancy at birth (1994): 74 male; 81 female. **Births** (per 1,000 pop.): 11. **Deaths** (per 1,000 pop.): 9. **Natural increase:** .2%. **Hospital beds:** 1 per 234 persons. **Physicians:** 1 per 257 persons. **Infant mortality** (per 1,000 live births 1994): 7.

Education (1991): **Literacy:** 97%. **Years compulsory:** to age 16.

Major International Organizations: UN and all of its specialized agencies, NATO, OECD, EU.

Embassy: 2700 15th St. NW 20009; 265-0190.

Spain was settled by Iberians, Basques, and Celts, partly overrun by Carthaginians, conquered by Rome c. 200 BC. The Visigoths, in power by the 5th century AD, adopted Christianity but by 711 AD lost to the Islamic invasion from Africa. Christian reconquest from the N led to a Spanish nationalism. In 1469 the kingdoms of Aragon and Castile were united by the marriage of Ferdinand II and Isabella I, and the last Moorish power was broken by the fall of the kingdom of Granada, 1492.

Spain obtained a colonial empire with the discovery of America by Columbus, 1492, the conquest of Mexico by Cortes, and Peru by Pizarro. It also controlled the Netherlands and parts of Italy and Germany. Spain lost its American colonies in the early 19th century. It lost Cuba, the Philippines, and Puerto Rico during the Spanish-American War, 1898.

Primo de Rivera became dictator in 1923. King Alfonso XIII revoked the dictatorship, 1930, but was forced to leave the country 1931. A republic was proclaimed which disestablished the church, curtailed its privileges, and secularized education. A conservative reaction occurred 1933 but was followed by a Popular Front (1936-1939) composed of socialists, Communists, republicans, and anarchists.

Army officers under Francisco Franco revolted against the government, 1936. In a destructive 3-year war, in which some one million died, Franco received massive help and troops from Italy and Germany, while the USSR, France, and Mexico supported the republic. War ended Mar. 28, 1939. Franco was named caudillo, leader of the nation. Spain was neutral in World War II, but its relations with fascist countries caused its exclusion from the UN until 1955.

In July 1969, Franco and the Cortes (Parliament) designated Prince Juan Carlos as the future king and chief of state. After Franco's death, Nov. 20, 1975, Juan Carlos was sworn in as king. He presided over the formal dissolution of the institutions of the Franco regime. In free elections June 1977, moderates and democratic socialists emerged as the largest parties.

In 1981 a coup attempt by right-wing military officers was thwarted by the king. The Socialist Workers' Party, under Felipe González Márquez, won 4 consecutive general elections from 1982 to 1993.

Catalonia and the Basque country were granted autonomy, Jan. 1980, following overwhelming approval in home-rule referendums. Basque extremists, however, have continued their campaign for independence.

The **Balearic Islands** in the western Mediterranean, 1,935 sq. mi., are a province of Spain; they include **Majorca** (Mallorca), with the capital, Palma; **Minorca, Cabrera, Ibiza** and **Formentera.** The **Canary Islands,** 2,807 sq. mi., in the Atlantic W of Morocco, form 2 provinces, including the islands of **Tenerife, Palma, Gomera, Hierro, Grand Canary, Fuerteventura,** and **Lanzarote** with Las Palmas and Santa Cruz thriving ports. **Ceuta** and **Melilla,** small enclaves on Morocco's Mediterranean coast, are part of Metropolitan Spain.

Spain has sought the return of Gibraltar, in British hands since 1704.

Sri Lanka

Democratic Socialist Republic of Sri Lanka
Sri Lanka Prajathanthrika Samajavadi Janarajaya

People: Population: 18,033,000. **Age distrib.** (%): <15: 35; 65+: 4. **Pop. density:** 711 per sq. mi. **Urban:** 22%. **Ethnic groups:** Sinhalese 74%, Tamils 18%, Moors 7%. **Principal languages:** Sinhalese (official), Tamil. **Religions:** Buddhist 69%, Hindu 15%, Christian 8%, Muslim 8%.

Geography: Area: 25,332 sq. mi. about the size of W Va. **Location:** In Indian O. off SE coast of India. **Neighbors:** India on NW. **Topography:** The coastal **a** and the northern half are flat; the S-central area is hilly and mountainous. **Capital:** Colombo. **Cities** (1990): Colombo 615,000.

Government: Type: Republic. **Head of state:** Pres. Dingiri Banda Wijetunga; b 1923; in office: May 7, 1993. **Head of government:** Prime Min. Chandrika Bandaranaike Kumaratunga; in office: Aug. 19, 1994. **Local divisions:** 9 provinces, 24 districts. **Defense:** 4.7% of GDP (1992).

Economy: Industries: Plywood, paper, milling, chemicals, textiles. **Chief crops:** Tea, coconuts, rice. **Minerals:** Graphite, limestone, gems, phosphate. **Other resources:** Forests, rubber. **Arable land:** 16%. **Livestock** (1992): cattle: 1.5 mln. **Fish catch** (1991): 198,000 metric tons. **Electricity prod.** (1992): 3.6 bln. kWh. **Labor force:** 46% agric.; 13% mining & manuf.

Finance: Monetary unit: Rupee (Mar. 1994: 49 = $1 US). **Gross domestic product** (1992): $7.75 bln. **Per capita GDP:** $440. **Imports** (1991): $3.0 bln.; partners: Jap. 15%, UK 7%. **Exports** (1991): $2.3 bln.; partners: U.S. 22%, UK 7%. **Tourism** (1990): $125 mln. receipts. **National budget** (1992): $3.7 bln. **International reserves less gold** (Mar. 1994): $1.8 bln. **Gold:** 145,000 oz t. **Consumer prices** (change in 1993): 11.7%.

Transport: Railroads: Length: 884 mi. **Motor vehicles:** in use: 180,000 passenger cars, 146,000 comm. vehicles. **Civil aviation:** 2.5 bln. passenger-mi.; 1 airport. **Chief ports:** Colombo, Trincomalee, Galle.

Communications: Television sets: 1 per 25 persons. **Radios:** 1 per 7.9 persons. **Telephones:** 1 per 101 persons.

Health: Life expectancy at birth (1994): 69 male; 74 female. **Births** (per 1,000 pop.): 18. **Deaths** (per 1,000 pop.): 6. **Natural increase:** 1.2%. **Hospital beds:** 1 per 356 persons. **Physicians:** 1 per 5,823 persons. **Infant mortality** (per 1,000 live births 1994): 22.

Education (1990): **Literacy:** 90%. **Years compulsory:** to age 12; attendance 98%.

Major International Organizations: UN (World Bank, IMF), Commonwealth of Nations.

Embassy: 2148 Wyoming Ave. NW 20008; 483-4025.

The island was known to the ancient world as Taprobane (Greek for copper-colored) and later as Serendip (from Arabic). Colonists from northern India subdued the indigenous Veddahs about 543 BC; their descendants, the Buddhist Sinhalese, still form most of the population. Hindu descendants of Tamil immigrants from southern India account for one-fifth of the population. Parts were occupied by the Portuguese in 1505 and by the Dutch in 1658. The British seized the island in 1796. As Ceylon it became an independent member of the Commonwealth in 1948. On May 22, 1972, Ceylon became the Republic of Sri Lanka.

Prime Min. W. R. D. Bandaranaike was assassinated Sept. 25, 1959. In new elections, the Freedom Party was victorious under Mrs. Sirimavo Bandaranaike, widow of the former prime minister.

After May 1970 elections, Mrs. Bandaranaike became prime

minister again. In 1971 the nation suffered economic problems and terrorist activities by ultra-leftists, thousands of whom were executed. Massive land reform and nationalization of foreign-owned plantations was undertaken in the mid-1970s. Mrs. Bandaranaike was ousted in 1977 elections. The powers of the presidency were increased in 1978 in an effort to restore stability.

Tension between the Sinhalese and Tamil separatists erupted into violence repeatedly in the 1980s. In 1987, hundreds died in an attack by Tamil rebels Apr. 17. Sri Lankan government forces retaliated in June with attacks on the rebel-held Jaffna peninsula. Over 35,000 have died in the civil war, which continued into the 1990s. Pres. Ranasinghe Premadasa was assassinated May 1, 1993, by a Tamil rebel.

Mrs. Bandaranaike's daughter, Chandrika Kumaratunga, became prime minister after Aug. 16, 1994, general elections.

Sudan

Republic of the Sudan

Jamhuryat as-Sudan

People: Population: 29,420,000. **Pop. density:** 30 per sq. mi. **Urban:** 23%. **Ethnic groups:** black 52%, Arab 39%, Beja 6%. **Principal languages:** Arabic (official), Dinka, Nubian, Nuer, Beja, others. **Religions:** Sunni Muslim 70%, indigenous beliefs 25%, Christians 5%.

Geography: Area: 966,757 sq. mi., the largest country in Africa, over one-fourth the size of the U.S. **Location:** At the E end of Sahara desert zone. **Neighbors:** Egypt on N, Libya, Chad, Central African Republic on W, Zaire, Uganda, Kenya on S, Ethiopia and Eritrea on E. **Topography:** The N consists of the Libyan Desert in the W, and the mountainous Nubia desert in E, with narrow Nile valley between. The center contains large, fertile, rainy areas with fields, pasture, and forest. The S has rich soil, heavy rain. **Capitals:** Khartoum (executive), Omdurman (legislative). **Cities** (1983 est.): Khartoum 476,000; Omdurman 526,000; North Khartoum 341,000; Port Sudan 206,000.

Government: Type: Military. **Head of state and government:** Pres. Gen. Omar Al-Bashir; in office: June 30, 1989. **Local divisions:** 9 states. **Defense:** 2.2% of GDP (1989 est.).

Economy: Industries: Textiles, food processing. **Chief crops:** Gum arabic (principal world source), durra (sorghum), cotton (main export), sesame, peanuts, rice, coffee, sugar cane, wheat, dates. **Minerals:** Chrome, copper, **Other resources:** Mahogany. **Arable land:** 5%. **Livestock** (1992): cattle: 67 mln.; sheep: 21 mln.; goats: 18 mln. **Electricity prod.** (1991): 905 mln. kWh. **Labor force:** 80% agric.; 10% ind., comm.

Finance: Monetary unit: Pound (Jan. 1993: 124 = $1 US). **Gross domestic product** (1992): $5.2 bln. **Per capita GDP:** $184. **Imports** (1991): $1.4 bln.; partners: EU 32%, U.S. 13%. **Exports** (1991): $325 mln.; partners: EU 46%. **National budget** (1991): $2.1 bln. **International reserves less gold** (Nov. 1993): $43 mln. **Consumer prices** (change in 1992): 117.6%.

Transport: Railroads: Length: 3,029 mi. **Motor vehicles:** in use: 116,000 passenger cars, 57,000 comm. vehicles. **Civil aviation:** 317 mln. passenger-mi.; 13 airports with scheduled flights. **Chief ports:** Port Sudan.

Communications: Television sets: 1 per 120 persons. **Radios:** 1 per 5.0 persons. **Telephones:** 1 per 343 persons. **Daily newspaper circ.:** 24 per 1,000 pop.

Health: Life expectancy at birth (1994): 53 male; 55 female. **Births** (per 1,000 pop.): 42. **Deaths** (per 1,000 pop.): 12. **Natural increase:** 3.0%. **Hospital beds:** 1 per 1,222 persons. **Physicians: 1** per 9,439 persons **Infant mortality** (per 1,000 live births 1994): 80.

Education (1991): **Literacy:** 27%. **Years compulsory:** 9; attendance 50%.

Major International Organizations: UN (IMF, WHO, FAO), Arab League, OAU.

Embassy: 2210 Massachusetts Ave. NW 20008; 338-8565.

Northern Sudan, ancient Nubia, was settled by Egyptians in antiquity, and was converted to Coptic Christianity in the 6th century. Arab conquests brought Islam in the 15th century.

In the 1820s Egypt took over Sudan, defeating the last of earlier empires, including the Fung. In the 1880s a revolution was led by Mohammed Ahmed, who called himself the Mahdi (leader of the faithful), and his followers, the dervishes.

In 1898 an Anglo-Egyptian force crushed the Mahdi's successors. In 1951 the Egyptian Parliament abrogated its 1899 and 1936 treaties with Great Britain and amended its constitution to provide for a separate Sudanese constitution. Sudan voted for complete independence as a parliamentary government effective Jan. 1, 1956.

In 1969, a Revolutionary Council took power, but a civilian premier and cabinet were appointed; the government announced it would create a socialist state. The northern 12 provinces are predominantly Arab-Muslim and have been dominant in the central government. The 3 southern provinces are populated largely by black Christians and animists. The 2 halves of the nation began a civil war in 1988.

Economic problems plagued the nation in the 1980s and 1990s, aggravated by continuing civil war and influxes of refugees from neighboring countries. After 16 years in power, Pres. Jaafar al-Nimeiry was overthrown in a bloodless military coup, Apr. 6, 1985. Sudan held its first democratic parliamentary elections in 18 years in 1986, but the elected government was overthrown in a bloodless coup June 30, 1989.

Close to 300,000 people died as a result of drought and famine in 1988. Sudan agreed to allow large-scale UN relief efforts in 1991, as millions were threatened with famine. The UN suspended aid to southern Sudan in 1992 because of the fighting. In 1993, Amnesty International accused Sudan of practicing "ethnic cleansing" against the Nuba people in the South, and Sudan was among several countries cited for human rights violations by the UN Human Rights Commission Mar. 9, 1994. During 1994 millions were again reported in danger of famine, as war and drought conditions escalated.

Suriname

Republic of Suriname

People: Population: 423,000. **Pop. density:** 6 per sq. mi. **Ethnic groups** Hindustanis 37%, Creole 31%, Javanese 15%. **Principal languages:** Dutch (official), Sranan Tonga, English. **Religions:** Christian 48%, Hindu 27%, Muslim 20%.

Geography: Area: 63,251 sq. mi., slightly larger than Georgia. **Location:** On N shore of S America. **Neighbors:** Guyana on W, Brazil on S, French Guiana on E. **Topography:** A flat Atlantic coast, where dikes permit agriculture. Inland is a forest belt; to the S, largely unexplored hills cover 75% of the country. **Capital:** Paramaribo. **Cities** (1989): Paramaribo 192,000.

Government: Type: Republic. **Head of state:** Pres. Roland Venetiaan; in office: Sept. 16, 1991. **Head of government:** Prime Min. Jules Adjodhia; in office: Sept. 16, 1991. **Local divisions:** 10 districts.

Economy: Industries: Aluminum. **Chief crops:** Rice, sugar, fruits. **Minerals:** Bauxite. **Other resources:** Forests, shrimp. **Arable land:** 1%. **Electricity prod.** (1992): 2.0 bln. kWh. **Labor force:** 29% agric.; 15% ind. and commerce; 42% govt.

Finance: Monetary unit: Guilder (Mar. 1994: 1.78 = $1 US). **Gross domestic product** (1991): $1.35 bln. **Per capita GDP:** $3,300. **Imports** (1990): $370 mln.; partners: U.S. 37%, Neth. 15%, Trin./Tob. 9%. **Exports** (1990): $472 mln.; partners: Nor. 33%, U.S. 13%, Neth. 26%. **Tourism** (1990): receipts: $11 mln. **National budget** (1990): $716 mln. **Gold:** 54,000 oz t.

Transport: Motor vehicles: in use: 36,000 passenger cars, 14,000 comm. vehicles. **Chief ports:** Paramaribo, Nieuw-Nickerie.

Communications: Television sets: 1 per 9.4 persons. **Radios:** 1 per 1.6 persons. **Telephones:** 1 per 7.5 persons. **Daily newspaper circ.:** 95 per 1,000 pop.

Health: Life expectancy at birth (1994): 67 male; 72 female. **Births** (per 1,000 pop.): 25. **Deaths** (per 1,000 pop.): 6. **Natural increase:** 1.9%. **Infant mortality** (per 1,000 live births 1994): 31.

Education (1989): **Literacy:** 65%; compulsory ages 6–12.

Major International Organizations: UN (WHO, ILO, FAO, World Bank, IMF), OAS.

Embassy: 2600 Virginia Ave. NW 20037; 338-6980.

The Netherlands acquired Suriname in 1667 from Britain, in exchange for New Netherlands (New York). The 1954 Dutch constitution raised the colony to a level of equality with the Netherlands and the Netherlands Antilles. Independence was granted Nov. 25, 1975, despite objections from East Indians. Some 40% of the population (mostly East Indians) emigrated to the Netherlands in the months before independence.

The National Military Council took over control of the government, Feb. 1982. The government came under democratic leadership in 1988.

Swaziland

Kingdom of Swaziland

People: Population: 936,000. **Age distrib.** (%): <15: 47; 65+: 3. **Pop. density:** 143 per sq. mi. **Urban:** 23%. **Ethnic groups:** African 97%, European 3%, other African, non-African groups. **Principal languages:** siSwati, English (both official). **Religions:** Christians 60%, indigenous beliefs 40%.

Geography: Area: 6,704 sq. mi., slightly smaller than New Jersey. **Location:** In southern Africa, near Indian O. coast. **Neighbors:** South Africa on N, W, S, Mozambique on E. **Topography:** The country descends from W-E in broad belts, becoming more arid in the low veld region, then rising to a plateau in the E. **Capital:** Mbabane. **Cities** (1990 est.): Mbabane 46,000; Manzini 53,000.

Government: Type: Monarchy. **Head of state:** King Mswati 3d; in office: Apr. 25, 1986. **Head of government:** Prime Min. Prince Jameson Mbilini Dlamini; in office: Feb. 16, 1994. **Local divisions:** 4 districts, 2 municipalities, 40 regions.

Economy: Industries: Wood pulp. **Chief crops:** Sugar, corn, cotton, rice, pineapples, sugar, citrus fruits. **Minerals:** Asbestos, iron, coal. **Other resources:** Forests. **Arable land:** 8%. **Electricity prod.** (1991): 155 mln. kWh. **Labor force:** 36% agric.; 20% community & social service.

Finance: Monetary unit: Lilangeni (Mar. 1994: 1.00 = $.29 US). **Gross domestic product** (1991): $700 mln. **Per capita GDP:** $800. **Imports** (1992): $746 mln.; partners: So. Afr., 92%. **Exports** (1990): $543 mln.; partners: So. Afr. 40%. **National budget** (1994 est.): $410 mln. **International reserves less gold** (Mar. 1994): $258 mln. **Consumer prices** (change in 1993): 17.0%.

Transport: Motor vehicles: in use: 25,000 passenger cars, 8,000 comm. vehicles.

Communications: Radios: 1 per 13 persons. **Telephones:** 1 per 31 persons.

Health: Life expectancy at birth (1994): 52 male; 61 female. **Births** (per 1,000 pop.): 43. **Deaths** (per 1,000 pop.): 11. **Natural increase:** 3.2%. **Hospital beds** (1984): 1,608. **Physicians** (1984): 80. **Infant mortality rate** (per 1,000 live births 1994): 93.

Education (1990): **Literacy:** 65%. 82% attend primary school.

Major International Organizations: UN (IMF, WHO, FAO), OAU, Commonwealth of Nations.

Embassy: 3400 International Dr. NW 20008; 362-6683.

The royal house of Swaziland traces back 400 years, and is one of Africa's last ruling dynasties. The Swazis, a Bantu people, were driven to Swaziland from lands to the N by the Zulus in 1820. Their autonomy was later guaranteed by Britain and Transvaal, with Britain assuming control after 1903. Independence came Sept. 6, 1968. In 1973 the king repealed the constitution and assumed full powers.

Under the constitution political parties are forbidden; parliament's role in government is limited to debate and advice.

Sweden

Kingdom of Sweden

Konungariket Sverige

People: Population: 8,778,000. **Age distrib.** (%): <15: 18; 65+: 18. **Pop. density:** 50 per sq. mi. **Urban:** 83%. **Ethnic groups:** Swedish 91%, Finnish 3%, Lapps, European immigrants. **Principal languages** Swedish. **Religions:** Evangelical Lutheran (official) 94%.

Geography: Area: 173,732 sq. mi., larger than California. **Location:** On Scandinavian Peninsula in N Europe. **Neighbors:** Norway on W, Denmark on S (across Kattegat), Finland on E. **Topography:** Mountains along NW border cover 25% of Sweden, flat or rolling terrain covers the central and southern areas, which includes several large lakes. **Capital:** Stockholm. **Cities** (1993): Stockholm 684,000; Göteborg 433,000; Malmö 236,000.

Government: Type: Constitutional monarchy. **Head of state:** King Carl XVI Gustaf; b Apr. 30, 1946; in office: Sept. 19, 1973. **Head of government:** Prime Min. Ingvar Carlssen; b Nov. 9, 1934; in office: Oct. 7, 1994. **Local divisions:** 24 provinces. **Defense:** 3.8% of GDP (FY 1993-94).

Economy: Industries: Steel, machinery, instruments, autos, shipbuilding, shipping, paper. **Chief crops:** Grains, potatoes, sugar beets. **Minerals:** Zinc, iron, lead, copper, gold, silver. **Other resources:** Forests (half the country); yield one-fourth exports. **Arable land:** 7%. **Livestock** (1992): cattle: 1.7 mln.; pigs: 2.0 mln. **Fish catch** (1991): 227,000 metric tons. **Electricity prod.** (1992): 142 bln. kWh. **Crude steel prod.** (1991): 4.2 mln. metric tons. **Labor force:** 3% agric.; 21% manuf. & mining; 38% social services.

Finance: Monetary unit: Krona (Mar. 1994: 7.90 = $1 US). **Gross domestic product** (1992): $145.6 bln.* **Per capita GDP:** $16,900. **Imports** (1992): $49.7 bln.; partners: EU 56%. **Exports** (1992): $56.1 bln.; partners: EU 55%. **Tourism** (1990): $2.8 bln. receipts. **National budget** (1992): $82.5 bln. **International reserves less gold** (Jan. 1994): $19.3 bln. **Gold:** 6.06 mln. oz t. **Consumer prices** (change in 1993): 4.6%.

Transport: Railroads: Length: 6,960 mi. **Motor vehicles:** in use: 3.6 mln. passenger cars, 329,000 comm. vehicles. **Civil aviation:** 4.1 bln. passenger-mi.; 42 airports. **Chief ports:** Göteborg, Stockholm, Malmö.

Communications: Television sets: 1 per 2.3 persons. **Radios:** 1 per 1.2 persons. **Telephones:** 1 per 1.1 persons. **Daily newspaper circ.:** 533 per 1,000 pop.

Health: Life expectancy at birth (1994): 75 male; 81 female. **Births** (per 1,000 pop.): 14. **Deaths** (per 1,000 pop.): 11. **Natural increase:** .3%. **Hospital beds:** 1 per 175 persons. **Physicians:** 1 per 395 persons. **Infant mortality** (per 1,000 live births (1994): 6.

Education (1991): **Literacy:** 99%. **Years compulsory:** 12; attendance 100%.

Major International Organizations: UN and all of its specialized agencies, EFTA, OECD.

Embassy: 600 New Hampshire Ave. NW 20037; 944-5600.

The Swedes have lived in present-day Sweden for at least 5,000 years, longer than nearly any other European people. Gothic tribes from Sweden played a major role in the disintegration of the Roman Empire. Other Swedes helped create the first Russian state in the 9th century.

The Swedes were Christianized from the 11th century, and a strong centralized monarchy developed. A parliament, the Riksdag, was first called in 1435, the earliest parliament on the European continent, with all classes of society represented.

Swedish independence from rule by Danish kings (dating from 1397) was secured by Gustavus I in a revolt, 1521-23; he built up the government and military and established the Lutheran Church. In the 17th century Sweden was a major European power, gaining most of the Baltic seacoast, but its international position subsequently declined.

The Napoleonic wars, in which Sweden acquired Norway (it became independent 1905), were the last in which Sweden participated. Armed neutrality was maintained in both world wars.

Over 4 decades of Social Democratic rule was ended in 1976 parliamentary elections. The party was returned to power in the 1982 elections, but Carl Bildt, a non-Socialist, became prime minister Oct. 1991. His coalition government sought to turn the nation away from long-established economic and social programs. The Social Democrats returned to power following 1994 elections. Sweden was to enter the European Union (formerly European Community) Jan. 1, 1995, if Swedish voters endorsed membership in a Nov. 1994 referendum.

Switzerland

Swiss Confederation

People: Population: 7,040,000. **Age distrib.** (%): <15: 16; 65+: 15. **Pop. density:** 441 per sq. mi. **Urban:** 68%. **Ethnic groups:** Mixed European stock. **Principal languages:** German, French, Italian (all official). **Religions:** Roman Catholic 48%, Protestant 44%.

Geography: Area: 15,943 sq. mi., as large as Mass., Conn., and R.I., combined. **Location:** In the Alps Mts. in Central Europe. **Neighbors:** France on W, Italy on S, Austria on E, Germany on N. **Topography:** The Alps cover 60% of the land area, the Jura, near France, 10%. Running between, from NE to SW, are midlands, 30%. **Capitals:** Bern (administrative), Lausanne (judicial). **Cities** (1991): Zurich 341,000; Basel 171,000; Geneva 167,000; Bern 135,000.

Government: Type: Federal republic. **Head of government:** Pres. Otto Stich; in office: Jan. 1, 1994. **Local divisions:** 20 full cantons, 6 half cantons. **Defense:** 1.7% of GDP (1993 est.).

Economy: Industries: Machinery, machine tools, steel, instruments, watches, textiles, foodstuffs (cheese, chocolate), banking, tourism. **Chief crops:** Grains, potatoes, sugar beets, vegetables, tobacco. **Minerals:** Salt. **Other resources:** Hydro power potential. **Arable land:** 10%. **Livestock** (1991): cattle: 1.8 mln.; pigs: 1.7 mln. **Electricity prod.** (1992): 56 bln. kWh. **Crude steel prod.** (1988): 825,000 metric tons. **Labor force:** 33% ind. and crafts, 6% agric., 50% serv.

Finance: Monetary unit: Franc (Mar. 1994: 1.42 = $1 US). **Gross domestic product** (1992): $152.3 bln.* **Per capita GDP:** $22,300. **Imports** (1992): $61.7 bln.; partners: EU 71%. **Exports** (1992): $61.3 bln.; partners: EU 56%. **Tourism** (1990); receipts: $6.8 bln. **National budget** (1990): $23.8 bln. **International reserves less gold** (Mar. 1994): $31.2 bln. **Gold:** 83.28 mln. oz t. **Consumer prices** (change in 1993): 3.3%.

Transport: Railroads: Length: 3,126 mi. **Motor vehicles:** in use: 3.0 mln. passenger cars, 291,000 comm. vehicles. **Civil aviation:** 10.0 bln. passenger-mi.; 6 airports with scheduled flights.

Communications: Television sets: 1 per 3.2 persons. **Radios:** 1 per 2.6 persons. **Telephones:** 1 per 1.1 persons. **Daily newspaper circ.:** 463 per 1,000 pop.

Health: Life expectancy at birth (1994): 75 male; 82 female. **Births** (per 1,000 pop.): 12. **Deaths** (per 1,000 pop.): 9. **Natural increase:** .3%. **Physicians:** 1 per 311 persons. **Infant mortality** (per 1,000 live births 1994): 7.

Education (1991): **Literacy:** 99%. **Years compulsory:** 9; attendance 100%.

Major International Organizations: Many UN specialized agencies (though not a member).

Embassy: 2900 Cathedral Ave. NW 20008; 745-7900.

Switzerland, the Roman province of Helvetia, is a federation of 23 cantons (20 full cantons and 6 half cantons), 3 of which in 1291 created a defensive league and later were joined by other districts. Voters in the French-speaking part of Canton Bern voted for self-government, 1978; Canton Jura was created Jan. 1, 1979.

In 1648 the Swiss Confederation obtained its independence from the Holy Roman Empire. The cantons were joined under a federal constitution in 1848, with large powers of local control retained by each canton.

Switzerland has maintained an armed neutrality since 1815, and has not been involved in a foreign war since 1515. It is the seat of many UN and other international agencies.

Switzerland is a leading world banking center; stability of the currency brings funds from many quarters. The nation's famed secret bank accounts were phased out in 1992.

Syria

Syrian Arab Republic

al-Jumhuriyah al-Arabiyah

People: Population: 14,887,000. **Age distrib.** (%): <15: 48; 65+: 3. **Pop. density:** 208 per sq. mi. **Urban:** 51%. **Ethnic groups:** Arab 90%, Kurd, Armenian, others. **Principal languages:** Arabic (official), Kurdish, Armenian. **Religions:** Sunni Muslim 74%, other Muslim 16%, Christian 10%.

Geography: Area: 71,498 sq. mi., slightly larger than North Dakota. **Location:** At eastern end of Mediterranean Sea. **Neighbors:** Lebanon, Israel on W, Jordan on S, Iraq on E, Turkey on N. **Topography:** Syria has a short Mediterranean coastline, then stretches E and S with fertile lowlands and plains, alternating with mountains and large desert areas. **Capital:** Damascus. **Cities** (1992 est.): Damascus 1.4 mln.; Aleppo 1.4 mln.; Homs 518,000.

Government: Type: Republic (under military regime). **Head of state:** Pres. Hafez al-Assad; b Mar. 1930; in office: Feb. 22, 1971. **Head of government:** Prime Min. Mahmoud Zuabi; in office: Nov. 1, 1987. **Local divisions:** Damascus and 13 provinces. **Defense:** 6% of GDP (1992).

Economy: Industries: Oil products, textiles, tobacco, glassware, brassware. **Chief crops:** Cotton, grain, olives, fruits, vegetables. **Minerals:** Oil, phosphate, gypsum. **Crude oil reserves** (1987): 1.4 bln. bbls. **Other resources:** Wool. **Arable land:** 28%. **Livestock** (1992): sheep: 15.7 mln., goats: 986,000. **Electricity prod.** (1992): 11.9 bln. kWh. **Labor force:** 32% agric.; 32% ind. & constr.; 36% services.

Finance: Monetary unit: Pound (Mar. 1994: 11.22 = $1 US). **Gross domestic product** (1991): $30.0 bln. **Per capita GDP:** $2,300. **Imports** (1991): $2.7 bln.; partners: EU 42%. **Exports** (1991): $3.6 bln.; partners: E Europe 42%, EU 31%. **Tourism** (1990): receipts: $244 mln. **National budget** (1991): $7.5 bln. **Consumer prices** (change in 1993): 10.6%.

Transport: Railroads: Length: 948 mi. **Motor vehicles:** in use: 117,000 passenger cars, 138,000 comm. vehicles. **Civil aviation:** 719 mln. passenger-mi.; 5 airports with scheduled flights. **Chief ports:** Latakia, Tartus.

Communications: Television sets: 1 per 19 persons. **Radios:** 1 per 4.5 persons. **Telephones:** 1 per 18 persons. **Daily newspaper circ.:** 22 per 1,000 pop.

Health: Life expectancy at birth (1994): 65 male; 68 female. **Births** (per 1,000 pop.): 44. **Deaths** (per 1,000 pop.): 6. **Natural increase:** 3.7%. **Hospital beds:** 1 per 891 persons. **Physicians:** 1 per 1,037 persons. **Infant mortality** (per 1,000 live births 1994): 43.

Education (1990): **Literacy:** 64%. **Years compulsory:** 6; attendance: 94%.

Major International Organizations: UN (IMF, WHO, FAO), Arab League.

Embassy: 2215 Wyoming Ave. NW 20008; 232-6313.

Syria contains some of the most ancient remains of civilization. It was the center of the Seleucid empire, but later became absorbed in the Roman and Arab empires. Ottoman rule prevailed for 4 centuries, until the end of World War I.

The state of Syria was formed from former Turkish districts, separated by the Treaty of Sevres, 1920, and divided into the states of Syria and Greater Lebanon. Both were administered under a French League of Nations mandate 1920-1941.

Syria was proclaimed a republic by the occupying French Sept. 16, 1941, and exercised full independence effective Apr. 17, 1946. Syria joined in the Arab invasion of Israel in 1948.

Syria joined Egypt Feb. 1958 in the United Arab Republic but seceded Sept. 1961. The Socialist Baath party and military leaders seized power Mar. 1963. The Baath, a pan-Arab organization, became the only legal party. The government has been dominated by members of the minority Alawite sect.

In the Arab-Israeli war of June 1967, Israel seized and occupied the Golan Heights area inside Syria, from which Israeli settlements had for years been shelled by Syria. On Oct. 6, 1973, Syria joined Egypt in an attack on Israel. Arab oil states agreed in 1974 to give Syria $1 billion a year to aid anti-Israel moves. Some 30,000 Syrian troops entered Lebanon in 1976 to mediate in a civil war. They fought Palestinian guerrillas and, later, Christian militiamen. Syrian troops again battled Christian forces in Lebanon, Apr. 1981, ending a cease-fire that had been in place.

Following the June 6, 1982 Israeli invasion of Lebanon, Israeli planes destroyed 17 Syrian antiaircraft missile batteries in the Bekka Valley, June 9. Some 25 Syrian planes were downed during the engagement. Israel and Syria agreed to a cease-fire June 11. In 1983, Syria backed the PLO rebels who ousted Yasir Arafat's forces from Tripoli.

Syria's role in promoting international terrorism led to the breaking of diplomatic relations with Great Britain and to limited sanctions by the European Community in 1986.

Syria condemned the Aug. 1990 Iraqi invasion of Kuwait and sent troops to help Allied forces in the Gulf War. In 1991, Syria accepted U.S. proposals for the terms of an Arab-Israeli peace conference. Syria subsequently participated in peace negotiations with Israel. In Jan. 1994, Syria held out the prospect that the 2 countries might normalize relations.

Taiwan

Republic of China

Chung-hua Min-kuo

People: Population: 21,299,000. **Age distrib.** (%): <15: 26; 65+: 7. **Pop. density:** 1,524 per sq. mi. **Urban:** 75%. **Ethnic groups:** Taiwanese 84%, Chinese 14%. **Principal languages:** Mandarin Chinese (official), Taiwanese, Hakka dialects. **Religions:** Buddhism, Taoism, Confucianism prevail.

Geography: Area: 13,969 sq. mi., about the size of Connecticut & New Hampshire combined. **Location:** Off SE coast of China, between E and S China Seas. **Neighbors:** Nearest is China. **Topography:** A mountain range forms the backbone of the island; the eastern half is very steep and craggy, the western slope is flat, fertile, and well cultivated. **Capital:** Taipei. **Cities** (1993): Taipei (met.) 2.7 mln.; Kaohsiung 1.4 mln.; Taichung 802,000; Tainan 696,000.

Government: Type: Democracy. **Head of state and Nationalist Party chmn.:** Pres. Lee Teng-hui; b Jan. 15, 1923; in office: Jan. 13, 1988. **Head of government:** Prime Min. Lien Chan; in office: Feb. 10, 1993. **Local divisions:** 16 counties, 5 cities, Taipei & Kao-Hsiung. **Defense:** 5.4% of GNP (FY 1993-94 est.).

Economy: Industries: Textiles, clothing, electronics, processed foods, chemicals, plastics. **Chief crops:** Rice, bananas, pineapples, sugar cane, sweet potatoes, peanuts. **Minerals:** Coal, limestone, marble. **Crude oil reserves** (1987): 10 mln. bbls. **Arable land:** 24%. **Livestock** (1991): pigs: 10.0 mln. **Fish catch** (1991): 1.3 mln. metric tons. **Electricity prod.** (1992): 98.5 bln. kWh. **Labor force:** 16% agric.; 53% ind. & comm.; 22% services.

Finance: Monetary unit: New Taiwan dollar (July 1993: 26.28 = $1 US). **Gross national product** (1992): $209 bln.* **Per capita GNP:** $10,000. **Imports** (1992): $72 bln.; partners: U.S. 23%, Jap. 30%. **Exports** (1992): $81 bln.; partners: U.S. 39%, Jap. 13%, Hong Kong 8%. **Tourism** (1990): $1.7 bln. receipts. **National budget** (1991): $30.1 bln.

Transport: Motor vehicles: in use: 3.0 mln. passenger cars, 751,000 commercial vehicles. **Civil aviation:** 20.9 bln. passenger-mi.; 12 airports. **Chief ports:** Kaohsiung, Keelung, Hualien, Taichung.

Communications: Television sets: 1 per 3.1 persons. **Radios:** 1 per 1.5 persons. **Telephones:** 1 per 2.4 persons. **Daily newspaper circ.:** 202 per 1,000 pop.

Health: Life expectancy at birth (1994): 72 male; 79 female. **Births** (per 1,000 pop.): 16. **Deaths** (per 1,000 pop.): 6. **Natural increase:** 1.0%. **Physicians:** 1 per 868 persons. **Hospital beds:** 1 per 221 persons. **Infant mortality** (per 1,000 live births 1994): 6.

Education (1991): **Literacy:** 90%. **Years compulsory:** 9; attendance 99%.

Large-scale Chinese immigration began in the 17th century. The island came under mainland control after an interval of Dutch rule, 1620-62. Taiwan (also called Formosa) was ruled by Japan 1895-1945. Two million Kuomintang supporters fled to Taiwan in 1949. Both the Taipei and Beijing governments consider Taiwan an integral part of China. Taiwan has rejected Beijing's efforts at reunification, but unofficial dealings with the mainland have grown more flexible.

The U.S., upon its recognition of the People's Republic of China, Dec. 15, 1978, severed diplomatic ties with Taiwan. It maintains the unofficial American Institute in Taiwan, while Taiwan has established the Coordination Council for North American Affairs in Washington, DC.

Land reform, government planning, U.S. aid and investment, and free universal education have brought huge advances in industry, agriculture, and mass living standards. In 1987, martial law was lifted after 38 years, and in 1991, the 43-year period of emergency rule ended. The ruling Nationalist Party has faced increasing challenge from opposition parties.

Taiwan has one of the world's strongest economies and is among the 10 leading capital exporters.

The Penghu (Pescadores), 50 sq. mi., pop. 120,000, lie between Taiwan and the mainland. **Quemoy** and **Matsu,** pop. (1990) 70,000 lie just off the mainland.

Tajikistan

Republic of Tajikistan

Respubliki i Tojikiston

People: Population: 5,995,000. **Age distrib.** (%): <15: 43; 65+: 3. **Pop. density:** 108 per sq. mi. **Urban:** 31%. **Ethnic groups:** Tajik 65%, Uzbek 25%, Russian 4%. **Principal languages:** Tajik (official). **Religions:** Mostly Sunni Muslim.

Geography: Area: 55,300 sq. mi., slightly smaller than Wisconsin. **Neighbors:** Uzbekistan and Kyrgyzstan on N and W, China on E, Afghanistan on S and E. **Topography:** Mountainous region which contains the Pamirs, Trans Alai mountain system. **Capital:** Dushanbe.

Government: Type: Parliamentary republic. **Head of state:** Acting Pres. Ali Rakhmanov; in office: Dec. 1, 1993. **Head of government:** Acting Prime Min. Abdujalil Samadov; in office: Dec. 1993. **Defense:** 3.7% of GDP (1992).

Economy: Industries: Cement, knitwear, footwear. **Chief crops:** Barley, cotton, wheat, vegetables. **Minerals:** Coal, lead, zinc. **Livestock** (1992): cattle: 1.4 mln., sheep: 3.4 mln. **Electricity prod.** (1992): 16.8 bln. kWh.

Finance: Monetary Unit: Ruble. **Imports** (1990): 1.3 bln. **Exports** (1990): $706 mln.

Transportation: Railroads: Length: 554 mi. **Civil aviation:** 3.2 bln. passenger-mi.; 1 airport.

Communications: Television sets: 1 per 6.3 persons. **Telephones:** 1 per 19 persons. **Daily newspaper circ.:** 309 per 1,000 pop.

Health: Life expectancy at birth (1994): 66 male; 72 female. **Births** (per 1,000 pop.): 35. **Deaths** (per 1,000 pop.): 7. **Natural increase:** 2.8%. **Hospital beds:** 1 per 93 persons. **Physicians:** 1 per 362 persons. **Infant mortality** (per 1,000 live births 1994): 62.

Major International Organizations: UN, CIS.

There were settled societies in the region from about 3000 BC. Throughout history, the region has undergone invasions by Iranians (Arabs who converted the population to Islam), Mongols, Uzbeks, Afghans, and Russians. In 1924, the Tadzhik ASSR was created within the Uzbek SSR. The Tadzhik SSR was proclaimed in 1929.

Tajikistan declared independence Sept. 9, 1991. It became an independent state when the Soviet Union disbanded Dec. 26, 1991. Conservative Communist Pres. Rakhmon Nabiyev was forced to resign, Sept. 1992, by a coalition of Islamic, nationalist, and Western-oriented parties, but factional fighting led to the installation of a pro-Communist regime, Jan. 1993. Muslim rebels, reportedly armed by Afghanistan, continued to fight the regime.

Tanzania

United Republic of Tanzania

Jamhuri ya Mwungano wa Tanzania

People: Population: 27,986,000. Age distrib. (%): <15: 47; 65+: 3. **Pop. density:** 76 per sq. mi. **Urban:** 21%. **Ethnic groups:** African. **Principal languages:** Swahili, English (both official), many others. **Religions:** Christians 40%, Muslims 33%, indigenous beliefs 25%.

Geography: Area: 364,017 sq. mi., more than twice the size of California. **Location:** On coast of E Africa. **Neighbors:** Kenya, Uganda on N, Rwanda, Burundi, Zaire on W, Zambia, Malawi, Mozambique on S. **Topography:** Hot, arid central plateau, surrounded by the lake region in the W, temperate highlands in N and S, the coastal plains. Mt. Kilimanjaro, 19,340 ft., is highest in Africa. **Capital:** Dar-es-Salaam. **Cities** (1992 est): Dar-es-Salaam 1.4 mln.

Government: Type: Republic. **Head of state:** Pres. Ali Hassan Mwinyi; b May 8, 1925; in office: Nov. 5, 1985. **Head of government:** Prime Min. John Malecela; in office: Nov. 9, 1990. **Local divisions:** 25 regions. **Defense:** 3.9% of GDP (1992).

Economy: Industries: Food processing, clothing. **Chief crops:** Sisal, cotton, coffee, tea, tobacco. **Minerals:** Diamonds, gold, nickel. **Other resources:** Hides. **Arable land:** 5%. **Livestock** (1992): cattle: 13.2 mln.; goats: 9.0 mln.; sheep: 3.7 mln. **Fish catch** (1991): 400,000 metric tons. **Electricity prod.** (1991): 600 mln. kWh. **Labor force:** 90% agric., 10% ind., comm. & govt.

Finance: Monetary unit: Shilling (Jan. 1994: 486 = $1 US). **Gross domestic product** (1992): $7.2 bln. **Per capita GDP:** $260. **Imports** (1991): $1.5 bln.; partners: UK 14%, Jap. 12%, Ger. 10%. **Exports** (1991): $418 mln.; partners: Ger. 15%, UK 13%. **Tourism** (1990): $63 mln. receipts. **National budget** (1990): $631 mln. **International reserves less gold** (Jan. 1994): $191 mln. **Consumer prices** (change in 1992): 22.1%.

Transport: Motor vehicles: in use: 45,000 passenger cars; 55,000 comm. vehicles. **Civil aviation:** 174 mln. passenger-mi.; 19 airports. **Chief ports:** Dar-es-Salaam, Mtwara, Tanga.

Communications: Radios: 1 per 6.5 persons. **Telephones:** 1 per 177 persons.

Health: Life expectancy at birth (1994): 42 male; 45 female. **Births** (per 1,000 pop.): 45. **Deaths** (per 1,000 pop.): 19. **Natural increase:** 2.6%. **Hospital beds** (1984): 22,800. **Physicians** (1984): 1,065. **Infant mortality** (per 1,000 live births 1994): 110.

Education (1987): **Literacy:** 85%. **Attendance:** 87% attend primary school.

Major International Organizations: UN and all of its specialized agencies, OAU, Commonwealth of Nations.

Embassy: 2139 R. St. NW 20008; 939-6125.

The Republic of Tanganyika in E Africa and the island Republic of Zanzibar, off the coast of Tanganyika, both of which had recently gained independence, joined into a single nation, the United Republic of Tanzania, Apr. 26, 1964. Zanzibar retains internal self-government.

Until resigning as president in 1985, Julius K. Nyerere, a former Tanganyikan independence leader, dominated Tanzania's politics, which emphasized government planning and control of the economy, with single-party rule. In 1992 the constitution was amended to allow opposition parties to participate in elections. Privatization of the economy was undertaken in the 1990s.

Tanganyika. Arab colonization and slaving began in the 8th century AD; Portuguese sailors explored the coast by about 1500. Other Europeans followed.

In 1885 Germany established German East Africa of which Tanganyika formed the bulk. It became a League of Nations mandate and, after 1946, a UN trust territory, both under Britain. It became independent Dec. 9, 1961, and a republic within the Commonwealth a year later.

Zanzibar, the Isle of Cloves, lies 23 mi. off the coast of Tanganyika; its area is 621 sq. mi. The island of **Pemba,** 25 mi. to the NE, area 380 sq. mi., is included in the administration. The total population (1990 est.) is 375,000.

Chief industry is the production of cloves and clove oil of which Zanzibar and Pemba produce the bulk of the world's supply.

Zanzibar was for centuries the center for Arab slave-traders. Portugal ruled for 2 centuries until ousted by Arabs around 1700. Zanzibar became a British Protectorate in 1890; independence came Dec. 10, 1963. Revolutionary forces overthrew the Sultan Jan. 12, 1964. The new government ousted Western diplomats and newsmen, slaughtered thousands of Arabs, and nationalized farms. Union with Tanganyika followed.

Thailand

Kingdom of Thailand

Muang Thai or Prathet Thai

People: Population: 59,510,000. **Age distrib.** (%): <15: 29; 65+: 5. **Pop. density:** 300 per sq. mi. **Urban:** 19%. **Ethnic groups:** Thai 75%, Chinese 14%, others 11%. **Principal languages:** Thai (official), Chinese, Malay, regional dialects. **Religions:** Buddhist 95%, Muslim 4%.

Geography: Area: 198,115 sq. mi., about the size of Texas. **Location:** On Indochinese and Malayan Peninsulas in SE Asia. **Neighbors:** Myanmar on W Laos on N, Cambodia on E, Malaysia on S. **Topography:** A plateau dominates the NE third of Thailand, dropping to the fertile alluvial valley of the Chao Phraya R. in the center. Forested mountains are in N, with narrow fertile valleys. The southern peninsula region is covered by rain forests. **Capital:** Bangkok. **Cities** (1991 est.): Bangkok (met.): 5.6 mln.

Government: Type: Constitutional monarchy. **Head of state:** King Bhumibol Adulyadej; b Dec. 5, 1927; in office: June 9, 1946. **Head of government:** Prime Min. Chuan Leekpai; in office: Sept. 23, 1992. **Local divisions:** 72 provinces. **Defense:** 2% of GNP (FY 1992-93).

Economy: Industries: Textiles, mining, wood prods., tourism. **Chief crops:** Rice (a major export), corn tapioca, sugarcane. **Minerals:** Antimony, tin (among largest producers), tungsten, iron, gas. **Other resources:** Forests (teak is exported), rubber. **Arable land:** 34%. **Livestock** (1992): cattle: 6.8 mln.; pigs: 5.1 mln. **Fish catch** (1991): 3.0 mln. metric tons. **Electricity prod.** (1992): 43.7 bln. kWh. **Labor force:** 62% agric.; 24% ind. & comm.; 14% serv. & govt.

Finance: Monetary unit: Baht (Mar. 1994: 25.29 = $1 US). **Gross national product** (1992): $103 bln. **Per capita GNP:** $1,800. **Imports** (1991): $39.0 bln.; partners: Jap. 30%, U.S. 11%. **Exports** (1991): $27.5 bln.; partners: Jap. 17%, U.S. 22%. **Tourism** (1990): $4.3 mln. receipts. **National budget** (1993 est.): $22.4 bln. **International reserves less gold** (Mar. 1994): $25.7 bln. **Gold:** 2.47 mln. oz t. **Consumer prices** (change in 1993): 3.6%.

Transport: Railroads: Length: 2,399 mi. **Motor vehicles:** in use: 735,000 passenger cars, 1.9 mln. comm. vehicles. **Civil aviation:** 12.7 bln. passenger-mi.; 26 airports with scheduled flights. **Chief ports:** Bangkok, Sattahip.

Communication: Television sets: 1 per 17 persons. **Radios:** 1 per 5.7 persons. **Telephones:** 1 per 36 persons. **Daily newspaper circ.:** 72 per 1,000 pop.

Health: Life expectancy at birth (1994): 65 male; 72 female. **Births** (per 1,000 pop.): 19. **Deaths** (per 1,000 pop.): 6. **Natural increase:** 1.3%. **Hospital beds:** 1 per 604 persons. **Physicians:** 1 per 4,377 persons. **Infant mortality** (per 1,000 live births 1994): 37.

Education (1991): **Literacy:** 89%. **Years compulsory:** 6; attendance 96%.

Major International Organizations: UN (GATT, World Bank).

Embassy: 2300 Kalorama Rd. NW 20008; 483-7200.

Thais began migrating from southern China in the 11th century. Thailand is the only country in SE Asia never taken over by a European power, thanks to King Mongkut and his son King Chulalongkorn—who ruled from 1851 to 1910, modernized the country, and signed trade treaties with both Britain and France. A bloodless revolution in 1932 limited the monarchy.

Japan occupied the country in 1941.

The military took over the government in a bloody 1976 coup. Kriangsak Chomanan, prime minister resigned, Feb. 1980, under opposition over soaring inflation, oil price increases, labor unrest, and growing crime. Chatichai Choonhavan was chosen prime minister in a democratic election, Aug. 1988. In Feb. 1991, the military ousted Choonhavan in a bloodless coup. A violent crackdown on street demonstrations in May 1992 led to more than 50 deaths. Elections were held Sept. 1992; Chuan Leekpai was chosen prime minister.

Vietnamese troops had crossed the border and been repulsed by Thai forces in the 1980s.

Togo

Republic of Togo

République Togolaise

People: Population: 4,255,000. **Age distrib.** (%): <15: 49; 65+: 2. **Pop. density:** 194 per sq. mi. **Urban:** 29%. **Ethnic groups:** Ewe 35%, Mina 6%, Kabye 22%. **Principal languages:** French (official), Gur & Kwa languages. **Religions:** indigenous beliefs 70%, Christian 20%, Muslim 10%.

Geography: Area: 21,925 sq. mi., slightly smaller than West Virginia. **Location:** On S coast of W Africa. **Neighbors:** Ghana on W, Burkina Faso on N, Benin on E. **Topography:** A range of hills running SW-NE splits Togo into 2 savanna plains regions. **Capital:** Lomé. **Cities** (1989 est.): Lomé 600,000.

Government: Type: in transition. **Head of state:** Pres. Gnassingbé Eyadéma; b Dec. 26, 1937; in office: Apr. 14, 1967. **Head of government:** Prime Min. Edem Kodjo; in office: Apr. 4, 1994. **Local divisions:** 21 prefectures. **Defense:** 3% of GDP (1989).

Economy: Industries: Textiles, shoes. **Chief crops:** Coffee, cocoa, yams, manioc, millet, rice. **Minerals:** Phosphates. **Arable land:** 25%. **Electricity prod.** (1991): 209 mln. kWh. **Labor force:** 78% agric.; 22% industry.

Finance: Monetary unit: CFA franc (Mar. 1994: 576 = $1 US). **Gross domestic product** (1991): $1.5 bln. **Per capita GDP:** $400. **Imports** (1990): $502 mln.; partners: EU 61%. **Exports** (1990): $363 mln.; partners: EU 70%. **Tourism** (1990): $23 mln. receipts. **National budget** (1991 est.): $407 mln. **International reserves less gold** (Dec. 1993): $156 mln. **Gold:** 13,000 oz t. **Consumer prices** (change in 1993): -1.0%.

Transport: Railroads: Length: 326 mi. **Chief ports:** Lomé.

Communications: Television sets: 1 per 161 persons. **Radios:** 1 per 5.3 persons. **Telephones:** 1 per 170 persons.

Health: Life expectancy at birth (1994): 55 male; 59 female. **Births** (per 1,000 pop.): 47. **Deaths** (per 1,000 pop.): 11. **Natural increase:** 3.6%. **Hospital beds:** 1 per 752 persons.

Physicians: 1 per 12,992 persons. **Infant mortality** (per 1,000 live births 1994): 89.

Education (1990): **Literacy:** 45%.

Major International Organizations: UN (GATT, IMF), OAU.

Embassy: 2208 Massachusetts Ave. NW 20008; 234-4212.

The Ewe arrived in southern Togo several centuries ago. The country later became a major source of slaves. Germany took control in 1884. France and Britain administered Togoland as UN trusteeships. The French sector became the republic of Togo Apr. 27, 1960.

The population is divided between Bantus in the S and Hamitic tribes in the N. Togo has actively promoted regional integration, as a means of stimulating the economy.

In Jan. 1993 police fired on antigovernment demonstrators, killing at least 22. Some 25,000 people fled to Ghana and Benin as a result of civil unrest. In Jan. 1994 at least 40 people were killed when gunmen reportedly attacked an army base.

Tonga

Kingdom of Tonga

Pule 'anga Tonga

People: Population: 105,000. **Pop. density:** 348 per sq. mi. **Ethnic groups:** Polynesian, European. **Principal languages:** Tongan, English (both official). **Religions:** Free Wesleyan 47%, Roman Catholics 14%, Free Church of Tonga 14%, Mormons 9%, Church of Tonga 9%.

Geography: Area: 301 sq. mi., the size of New York City. **Location:** In western S Pacific O. **Neighbors:** Nearest is Fiji, on W, New Zealand, on S. **Topography:** Tonga comprises 169 volcanic and coral islands, 45 inhabited. **Capital:** Nuku'alofa. **Cities** (1986): Nuku'alofa (met.) 29,000.

Government: Type: Constitutional monarchy. **Head of state:** King Taufa'ahau Tupou IV; b July 4, 1918; in office: Dec. 16, 1965. **Head of government:** Prime Min. Baron Vaea; in office: Aug. 21, 1991. **Local divisions:** 3 main island groups.

Economy: Industries: Tourism. **Chief crops:** Coconut-products, bananas are exported. **Other resources:** Fish. **Arable land:** 25%. **Electricity prod.** (1991): 8 mln. kWh. **Labor force:** 70% agric.

Finance: Monetary unit: Pa'anga (Feb. 1994: 1.34 = $1 US). **Gross domestic product** (1990): $92 mln. **Imports** (1991): $59 mln.; partners: N Z 39%, Aust. 25%. **Exports** (1991): $13 mln.; partners: Aust. 29%, N Z 56%. **Tourism** (1991): $7.6 mln. receipts.

Transport: Motor vehicles: in use: 1,000 passenger cars, 2,400 comm. vehicles. **Chief ports:** Nuku'alofa.

Communications: Radios: 1 per 1.5 persons. **Telephones:** 1 per 19 persons.

Health: Life expectancy at birth (1992): 65 male; 70 female. **Births** (per 1,000 pop.): 25. **Deaths** (per 1,000 pop.): 7. **Natural increase:** 1.8%. **Infant mortality** (per 1,000 live births 1994): 21.

Education (1988): **Literacy:** 99%. **Years compulsory:** 8. **Attendance:** 77%.

The islands were first visited by the Dutch in the early 17th century. A series of civil wars ended in 1845 with establishment of the Tupou dynasty. In 1900 Tonga became a British protectorate. On June 4, 1970, Tonga became independent and a member of the Commonwealth.

Trinidad and Tobago

Republic of Trinidad and Tobago

People: Population: 1,328,000. **Age distrib.** (%): <15: 32; 65+: 6. **Pop. density:** 670 per sq. mi. **Ethnic groups:** blacks 43%, East Indians 40%, mixed 14%. **Principal languages:** English (official). **Religions:** Roman Catholic 32%, Protestant 29%, Hindu 24%, Muslim 6%.

Geography: Area: 1,980 sq. mi., the size of Delaware. **Location:** Off eastern coast of Venezuela. **Neighbors:** Nearest is Venezuela on SW. **Topography:** Three low mountain ranges cross Trinidad E-W, with a well-watered plain between N and Central Ranges. Parts of E and W coasts are swamps. Tobago, 116 sq. mi., lies 20 mi. NE. **Capital:** Port-of-Spain. **Cities** (1990 met. est.): Port-of-Spain 300,000; San Fernando 50,000.

Government: Type: Parliamentary democracy. **Head of state:** Pres. Noor Hassanali; b Aug. 13, 1918; in office: Mar. 19, 1987. **Head of government:** Prime Min. Patrick Manning; in office: Dec. 17, 1991. **Local divisions:** 8 counties, 3 municipalities. **Defense:** 1%-2% of GDP (1989 est.).

Economy: Industries: Oil products, rum, cement, tourism. **Chief crops:** Sugar, cocoa, coffee, citrus fruits, bananas. **Minerals:** Asphalt, oil, **Crude oil reserves** (1987): 567 mln. bbls. **Arable land:** 14%. **Electricity prod.** (1991): 3.4 bln. kWh. **Labor force:** 18% construction & utilities, 15% manuf. & mining.

Finance: Monetary unit: Dollar (Mar. 1994: 5.79 = $1 US). **Gross domestic product** (1991): $5 bln. **Per capita GDP:** $3,800. **Imports** (1991): $1.6 bln.; partners: U.S. 51%, UK 8%. **Exports** (1991): $1.9 bln.; partners: U.S. 53%. **Tourism** (1990): $122 mln. receipts. **National budget** (1993 est.): $1.6 bln. **International reserves less gold** (Mar. 1993): $172 mln. **Gold:** 54,000 oz t. **Consumer prices** (change in 1993): 10.8%.

Transport: Motor vehicles: in use: 150,000 passenger cars, 60,000 comm. vehicles. **Civil aviation:** 1.9 bln. passenger-mi.; 2 airports. **Chief ports:** Port-of-Spain.

Communications: Television sets: 1 per 5.1 persons. **Radios:** 1 per 1.8 persons. **Telephones:** 1 per 5.3 persons. **Daily newspaper circ.:** 140 per 1,000 pop.

Health: Life expectancy at birth (1994): 68 male; 73 female. **Births** (per 1,000 pop.): 20. **Deaths** (per 1,000 pop.): 6. **Natural increase:** 1.3%. **Hospital beds:** 1 per 318 persons. **Physicians:** 1 per 1,543 persons. **Infant mortality** (per 1,000 pop. 1994): 17.

Education (1988): **Literacy:** 97%. **Years compulsory:** 8.

Major International Organizations: UN (GATT, IMF, WHO), Commonwealth of Nations, OAS.

Embassy: 1708 Massachusetts Ave. NW 20036; 467-6490.

Columbus sighted Trinidad in 1498. A British possession since 1802, Trinidad and Tobago won independence Aug. 31, 1962. It became a republic in 1976. The People's National Movement party has held control of the government since 1956.

The nation is one of the most prosperous in the Caribbean. Oil production has increased with offshore finds. Middle Eastern oil is refined and exported, mostly to the U.S.

In July 1990, some 120 Muslim extremists captured the Parliament building and TV station and took about 50 hostages, including Prime Min. Arthur Robinson, who was beaten, shot in the legs, and tied to explosives. After a 6-day siege, the rebels surrendered.

Tunisia

Republic of Tunisia

al Jumhuriyah at-Tunisiyah

People: Population: 8,727,000. **Age distrib.** (%) <15: 37; 65+: 5. **Pop. density:** 137 per sq. mi. **Ethnic groups:** Arab-Berber 98%. **Principal languages:** Arabic (official), French. **Religions:** Muslim 98%.

Geography: Area: 63,378 sq. mi., about the size of Missouri. **Location:** On N coast of Africa. **Neighbors:** Algeria on W, Libya on E. **Topography:** The N is wooded and fertile. The central coastal plains are given to grazing and orchards. The S is arid, approaching Sahara Desert. **Capital:** Tunis. **Cities** (1989 est.): Tunis 620,000, Sfax 221,000.

Government: Type: Republic. **Head of state:** Pres. Gen. Zine al-Abidine Ben Ali; b Sept 3, 1936; in office: Nov. 7, 1987. **Head of government:** Prime Min. Hamed Karoui; in office: Sept. 27, 1989. **Local divisions:** 23 governorates. **Defense:** 3.7% of GDP (1993 est.).

Economy: Industries: Food processing, textiles, oil products, mining, construction materials. **Chief crops:** Grains, dates, olives, citrus fruits, figs, vegetables, grapes. **Minerals:** Phosphates, iron, oil, lead, zinc. **Crude oil reserves** (1987): 1.7 bln. bbls. **Arable land:** 20%. **Livestock** (1991): sheep: 6.2 mln.; goats: 1.3 mln. **Fish catch** (1990): 92,000 metric tons. **Electricity prod.** (1992): 5.0 bln. kWh. **Labor force:** 32% agric.

Finance: Monetary unit: Dinar (Mar. 1994: 1.04 = $1 US). **Gross domestic product** (1992): $13.6 bln. **Per capita GDP:** $1,650. **Imports** (1992): $6.4 bln.; partners: EU 68%. **Exports** (1992): $4.0 bln.; partners: EU 73%. **Tourism** (1990): $953 mln. receipts. **National budget** (1993 est.): $5.5 bln. **International reserves less gold** (Feb. 1994): $806 mln. **Gold:** 215,000 oz t. **Consumer prices** (change in 1992): 5.4%.

Transport: Railroads: Length: 1,343 mi. **Motor vehicles:**

in use: 321,000 passenger cars, 208,000 comm. vehicles. **Civil aviation:** 875 mln. passenger-mi.; 5 airports. **Chief ports:** Tunis, Sfax, Bizerte.

Communications: Television sets: 1 per 13 persons. **Radios:** 1 per 4.9 persons. **Telephones:** 1 per 18 persons. **Daily newspaper circ.:** 37 per 1,000 pop.

Health: Life expectancy at birth (1994): 71 male; 75 female. **Births** (per 1,000 pop.): 23. **Deaths** (per 1,000 pop.): 5. **Natural increase:** 1.8%. **Hospital beds:** 1 per 510 persons. **Physicians:** 1 per 1,834 persons. **Infant mortality** (per 1,000 pop. live births 1994): 34.

Education (1990): **Literacy:** 62%. **Years compulsory:** 8; attendance 85%.

Major International Organizations: UN, Arab League, OAU.

Embassy: 1515 Massachusetts Ave. NW 20005; 862-1850.

Site of ancient Carthage and a former Barbary state under the suzerainty of Turkey, Tunisia became a protectorate of France under a treaty signed May 12, 1881. The nation became independent Mar. 20, 1956, and ended the monarchy the following year. Habib Bourguiba, an independence leader, served as president until 1987, when he was deposed by his prime minister, Zine al-Abidine Ben Ali.

Tunisia has actively repressed Islamic fundamentalism.

Turkey

Republic of Turkey

Turkiye Cumhuriyeti

People: Population: 62,154,000. **Age distrib.** (%): <15: 35; 65+: 4. **Pop. density:** 206 per sq. mi. **Urban:** 61%. **Ethnic groups:** Turks 80%, Kurds 20%. **Principal languages:** Turkish (official), Kurdish, Arabic. **Religions:** Muslim 99.8%.

Geography: Area: 300,948 sq. mi., twice the size of California. **Location:** Occupies Asia Minor, and stretches into continental Europe; borders on Mediterranean and Black seas. **Neighbors:** Bulgaria, Greece on W, Georgia, Armenia on N, Iran on E, Iraq, Syria on S. **Topography:** Central Turkey has wide plateaus, with hot, dry summers and cold winters. High mountains ring the interior on all but W, with more than 20 peaks over 10,000 ft. Rolling plains are in W; mild, fertile coastal plains are in S, W. **Capital:** Ankara. **Cities** (1990 est.): Istanbul 6.6 mln.; Ankara 2.5 mln.; Izmir 1.7 mln.; Adana 916,000.

Government: Type: Republic. **Head of state:** Pres. Suleyman Demirel; b 1924; in office: May 16, 1993. **Head of government:** Prime Min. Tansu Ciller; in office: July 5, 1993. **Local divisions:** 73 provinces. **Defense:** 3.9% of GDP (1992).

Economy: Industries: Iron, steel, machinery, metal prods., cars, processed foods. **Chief crops:** Tobacco, cereals, cotton, barley, corn, fruits, potatoes, sugar beets. **Minerals:** Chromium, mercury, boron, copper, coal. **Crude oil reserves** (1987): 139 mln. bbls. **Other resources:** Wool, silk, forests. **Arable land:** 30%. **Livestock** (1991): cattle: 11.3 mln.; sheep: 40 mln. **Fish catch** (1990): 382,000 metric tons. **Electricity prod.** (1991): 44 bln. kWh. **Labor force:** 50% agric.; 15% ind. and comm.; 35% serv.

Finance: Monetary unit: Lira (Mar. 1994: 20,581 = $1 US). **Gross domestic product** (1992): $219 bln.* **Per capita GDP:** $3,670. **Imports** (1991): $21.0 bln.; partners: EU 49%, U.S. 7%. **Exports** (1991): $13.5 bln.; partners: EU 49%. **Tourism** (1991): $2.5 bln. receipts. **National budget** (1993): $46.8 bln. **International reserves less gold** (Nov. 1993): $7.2 bln. **Gold:** 4.0 mln. oz t. **Consumer prices** (change in 1993): 66.1%.

Transport: Railroads: Length: 5,238 mi. **Motor vehicles:** in use: 1.8 mln. passenger cars, 756,000 comm. vehicles. **Civil aviation:** 3.4 bln. passenger-mi.; 24 airports with scheduled flights. **Chief ports:** Istanbul, Izmir, Mersin, Samsun.

Communications: Television sets: 1 per 5.6 persons. **Radios:** 1 per 8.3 persons. **Telephones:** 1 per 5.7 persons.

Health: Life expectancy at birth (1994): 69 male; 73 female. **Births** (per 1,000 pop.): 26. **Deaths** (per 1,000 pop.): 6. **Natural increase:** 2.0%. **Hospital beds:** 1 per 465 persons. **Physicians:** 1 per 1,108 persons. **Infant mortality** (per 1,000 live births 1994): 49.

Education (1990): **Literacy:** 81%. **Years compulsory:** 6; attendance 95%.

Major International Organizations: UN (GATT, WHO, IMF), NATO, OECD, EU.

Embassy: 1714 Massachusetts Ave. NW 20036; 659-8200.

Ancient inhabitants of Turkey were among the worlds first agriculturalists. Such civilizations as the Hittite, Phrygian, and Lydian flourished in Asiatic Turkey (Asia Minor), as did much of Greek civilization. After the fall of Rome in the 5th century, Constantinople was the capital of the Byzantine Empire for 1,000 years. It fell in 1453 to Ottoman Turks, who ruled a vast empire for over 400 years.

Just before World War I, Turkey, or the Ottoman Empire, ruled what is now Syria, Lebanon, Iraq, Jordan, Israel, Saudi Arabia, Yemen, and islands in the Aegean Sea.

Turkey joined Germany and Austria in World War I and its defeat resulted in loss of much territory and fall of the sultanate. A republic was declared Oct. 29, 1923. The Caliphate (spiritual leadership of Islam) was renounced 1924.

Long embroiled with Greece over Cyprus, off Turkey's south coast, Turkey invaded the island July 20, 1974, after Greek officers seized the Cypriot government as a step toward unification with Greece. Turkey sought a new government for Cyprus, with Greek Cypriot and Turkish Cypriot zones. In reaction to Turkey's moves, the U.S. cut off military aid in 1975. Turkey, in turn, suspended the use of most U.S. bases. Aid was restored in 1978. There was a military takeover, Sept. 12, 1980.

Religious and ethnic tensions and active left and right extremists have caused endemic violence. Martial law, imposed in 1978, was lifted in 1984. The military formally transferred power to an elected Parliament in 1983.

Turkey was a member of the Allied forces which ousted Iraq from Kuwait, 1991. In the aftermath of the war, millions of Kurdish refugees fled to Turkey's border to escape Iraqi forces. The Turkish government mounted sporadic offensives against separatist Kurds in this border area; casualties among guerrillas and civilians alike have been heavy.

Kurdish militants raided Turkish diplomatic missions in some 25 Western European cities June 24, 1993. The militants were demanding an independent state for the Kurds.

Turkmenistan

Republic of Turkmenistan

People: Population: 3,995,000. **Pop. density:** 21 per sq. mi. **Urban:** 45%. **Ethnic groups:** Turkmen 73%, Russian 10%, Uzbek 9%. **Principal languages:** Turkmen, Russian, Uzbek. **Religions:** Muslim 87%.

Geography: Area: 188,417 sq. mi., slightly larger than California. **Neighbors:** Uzbekistan, Kazakhstan on N, NE, Afghanistan and Iran on S. The Kara Kum desert occupies 80% of the area. **Capital:** Ashgabat. **Cities** (1991): Ashkgabat 416,000.

Government: Type: Republic. **Head of state:** Pres. Saparmurad Niyazov; b 1940; in office: 1991. **Head of government:** Prime Min. Khan A. Akhmedov. **Local divisions:** 5 regions.

Economy: Industries: Mining, textiles. **Chief crops:** Grain, cotton, grapes. **Minerals:** Coal, sulfur, salt. **Livestock** (1992): sheep and goats: 5.6 mln. **Electricity prod.** (1992): 13.1 bln. kWh.

Finance: Monetary unit: Ruble. **Imports** (1990): $970 mln. **Exports** (1990): $239 mln.

Transportation: Railroads: Length: 1,317 mi.

Communications: Telephones: 1 per 14 persons.

Health: Life expectancy at birth (1994): 62 male; 69 female. **Births** (per 1,000 pop.): 30. **Deaths** (per 1,000 pop.): 7. **Natural increase:** 2.3%. **Hospital beds:** 1 per 86 persons. **Physicians:** 1 per 274 persons. **Infant mortality** (1 per 1,000 live births 1994): 70.

Major International Organizations: UN, CIS.

The region has been inhabited by Turki tribes since the 10th century. It became part of Russian Turkistan 1881, and a constituent republic of the USSR 1925. Turkmenistan declared independence Oct. 27, 1991, and became an independent state when the Soviet Union disbanded Dec. 26, 1991.

Extensive oil and gas reserves place Turkmenistan in a more favorable economic position than other former Soviet republics. Power remained mainly with the former Communist Party apparatus; Pres. Saparmurad Niyazov became the object of a strong personality cult.

Tuvalu

People: Population: 10,000. **Pop. density:** 1,063 per sq. mi. **Ethnic group:** Polynesian. **Principal languages:** Tuvaluan, English. **Religions:** Church of Tuvalu (Congregationalist) 97%.

Geography: Area: 9.4 sq. mi., less than one-half the size of Manhattan. **Location:** 9 islands forming a NW-SE chain 360 mi. long in the SW Pacific O. **Neighbors:** Nearest are Samoa on SE, Fiji on S. **Topography:** The islands are all low-lying atolls, nowhere rising more than 15 ft. above sea level, composed of coral reefs. **Capital:** Funafuti (pop. 1985): 2,800.

Government: Head of state: Queen Elizabeth II, represented by Gov.-Gen. Toaripi Lauti; in office: Oct. 1, 1990. **Head of government:** Prime Min. Kamuta Laatasi; in office: Dec. 1993. **Local divisions:** 8 island councils on the permanently inhabited islands.

Economy: Industries: Copra. **Chief crops:** Coconuts. **Labor force:** Approx. 1,500 Tuvaluans work overseas in the Gilberts' phosphate industry, or as overseas seamen.

Finance: Monetary unit: Australian dollar.

Transport: Chief port: Funafuti.

Health: (including former Gilbert Is.) **Life expectancy at birth** (1994): 62 male; 64 female. **Births** (per 1,000 pop.): 26. **Deaths** (per 1,000 pop.): 9. **Natural increase:** 1.7%. **Infant mortality** (per 1,000 live births 1994): 27.

Education: Literacy (1990): 96%.

The Ellice Islands separated from the British Gilbert and Ellice Islands colony in 1975 and became independent Tuvalu, Oct. 1, 1978.

Uganda

Republic of Uganda

People: Population: 19,859,000. **Age distrib.** (%): <15: 47; 65+: 3. **Pop. density:** 213 per sq. mi. **Urban:** 11%. **Ethnic groups:** Bantu, Nilotic, Nilo-Hamitic, Sudanic tribes. **Principal languages:** English (official), Luganda, Swahili. **Religions:** Christian 66%, Muslim 16%, indigenous beliefs.

Geography: Area: 93,070 sq. mi., slightly smaller than Oregon. **Location:** In E Central Africa. **Neighbors:** Sudan on N, Zaire on W, Rwanda, Tanzania on S, Kenya on E. **Topography:** Most of Uganda is a high plateau 3,000-6,000 ft. high, with high Ruwenzori range in W (Mt. Margherita 16,750 ft.), volcanoes in SW, NE is arid, W and SW rainy. Lakes Victoria, Edward, Albert form much of borders. **Capital:** Kampala. **Cities** (1991): Kampala 773,000.

Government: Type: Republic. **Head of state:** Pres. Yoweri Kaguta Museveni; b 1944; in office: Jan. 29, 1986. **Head of government:** Prime Min. George Cosmas Adyebo; in office: Jan. 22, 1991. **Local divisions:** 10 provinces. **Defense:** 15% of budget (FY 1989-90).

Economy: Chief crops: Coffee, cotton, tea, corn, bananas, sugar. **Minerals:** Copper, cobalt. **Arable land:** 23%. **Livestock** (1992): cattle: 5.1 mln.; goats: 3.3 mln.; sheep: 1.9 mln. **Fish catch** (1991): 254,000 metric tons. **Electricity prod.** (1991): 610 mln. kWh. **Labor force:** 80% agric.

Finance: Monetary unit: Shilling (Jan. 1994: 1,112 = $1 US). **Gross domestic product** (1992): $6 bln. **Per capita GDP:** $300. **Imports** (1991): $196 mln.; partners: Kenya 24%, U.K. 17%. **Exports** (1991): $200 mln.; partners: U.S. 14%, U.K. 12%, Neth. 15%. **National budget** (1989 est.): $545 mln. **International reserves less gold** (Dec. 1993): $145 mln. **Consumer prices** (change in 1993): 6.1%.

Transport: Motor vehicles: in use: 35,000 passenger cars, 14,000 comm. vehicles.

Communications: Television sets: 1 per 150 persons. **Radios:** 1 per 4.9 persons. **Telephones:** 1 per 287 persons.

Health: Life expectancy at birth (1994): 37 male; 38 female. **Births** (per 1,000 pop.): 49. **Deaths** (per 1,000 pop.): 24. **Natural increase:** 2.6%. **Hospital beds:** 1 per 817 persons. **Physicians:** 1 per 20,000 persons. **Infant mortality** (per 1,000 live births 1994): 112.

Education (1989): **Literacy:** 52%. About 50% attend primary school.

Major International Organizations: UN (GATT, WHO, IMF), OAU, Commonwealth of Nations.

Embassy: 5909 16th St. NW 20011; 726-7100.

Britain obtained a protectorate over Uganda in 1894. The country became independent Oct. 9, 1962, and a republic within the Commonwealth a year later. In 1967, the traditional kingdoms, including the powerful Buganda state, were abolished and the central government strengthened. (In 1993 the government authorized restoration of the Buganda and other monarchies, but as ceremonial only.)

Gen. Idi Amin seized power from Prime Min. Milton Obote in 1971. As many as 300,000 of his opponents were reported killed in subsequent years. Amin was named president for life in 1976.

In 1972 Amin expelled nearly all of Uganda's 45,000 Asians. In 1973 the U.S. withdrew all diplomatic personnel. Amid worsening economic and domestic crises, Uganda's troops exchanged invasion attacks with long-standing foe Tanzania, 1978 to 1979. Tanzanian forces, coupled with Ugandan exiles and rebels, ended the dictatorial rule of Amin, Apr. 11, 1979.

A draft constitution was issued in late 1992 providing for transition to a multiparty democracy.

Ukraine

Ukrayina

People: Population: 51,847,000. **Age distrib.** (%): <15: 21; 65+: 12. **Pop. density:** 222 per sq. mi. **Urban:** 68%. **Ethnic groups:** Ukrainian 73%, Russian 22%. **Principal languages:** Ukrainian, Russian. **Religions:** Orthodox 76%, Ukrainian Catholic 13.5%, Muslim 8.2%.

Geography: Area: 233,100 sq. mi. **Location:** In SE Europe. **Neighbors:** Belarus on N, Russia on NE and E, Moldova and Romania on SW, Hungary, Slovakia, and Poland on W. **Topography:** Part of the E European plain. Mountainous areas include the Carpathians in the SW and the Crimean chain in the S. Arable black soil constitutes a large part of the country. **Climate:** Average temperature range from 21F in Jan. to 66F in July. Annual precipitation averages 27.5 in. in the W part of the country and less than 11 in. in the East. **Capital:** Kiev. **Cities** (1992 est.): Kiev 2.6 mln.; Kharkiv 1.6 mln.; Donetsk 1.1 mln.; Dnipropetrovsk 1.1 mln.; Odessa 1.1 mln.

Government: Type: Constitutional republic. **Head of state:** Pres. Leonid J. Kuchma; b 1938; in office: July 19, 1994. **Head of government:** Vitaly A. Masoi; in office: June 16, 1994. **Local divisions:** 24 provinces (oblasts), 1 autonomous province. **Defense:** 3.8% of GNP (1992).

Economy: Industries: Steel, chemicals, machinery, vehicles, cement. **Chief crops:** Grains, sugar beets, potatoes. **Minerals:** Iron, manganese, chromium, copper, coal, lead, gold, nickel, potassium salts. **Other resources:** Forests. **Arable land:** 56%. **Livestock** (1992): cattle: 7.9 mln.; sheep and goats: 2.3 mln. **Fish catch** (1992): 1.3 mln. metric tons. **Electricity prod.** (1992): 281 bln. kWh. **Labor force:** 19% agric.; 41% ind. & constr.; 28% services.

Finance: Monetary unit: Karbovanet (May 1993: 3,000 = $1 US). **Gross national product** (1990): $47.6 bln. **Per capita income** (1987): $2,500. **Imports** (1990): $16.7 bln. **Exports** (1990): $13.5 bln. **National budget** (1990): $8 bln.

Transport: Railroads: Length: 770 mi. **Civil aviation:** 10.0 bln. passenger-mi., 20 airports. **Chief ports:** Odessa, Kherson, Zhdanov, Sevastopil, Berdiansk.

Communications: Television sets: 1 per 3 persons. **Radios:** 1 per 3.5 persons. **Telephones:** 1 per 6.4 persons. **Daily newspaper circ.:** 251 per 1,000 pop.

Health: Life expectancy at birth (1994): 65 male; 75 female. **Births** (per 1,000 pop.): 12. **Deaths** (per 1,000 pop.): 13. **Hospital beds:** 1 per 75 persons. **Physicians:** 1 per 228 persons. **Infant mortality** (per 1,000 live births 1994): 21.

Education (1990): **Literacy:** 99%.

Major International Organizations: UN, CIS.

Embassy: 3350 M St. NW 20007; 333-0606.

The ancient ancestors of Ukrainians, the Trypilians, flourished along the Dnipro River, Ukraine's main artery, from 6000-1000 BC. The Slavic ancestors of the Ukrainians inhabited modern Ukrainian territory well before the first century AD.

The princes of Kyyiv established a strong state called Kyyivan Rus in the 9th century. A strong dynasty was established, with ties to virtually all major European royal families. St. Volodymyr the Great, ruler of Kyyivan Ukraine, accepted Christianity as the national faith in 988. At the crossroads of European trade routes, Kyyivan Rus reached its zenith under Iaroslav the Wise (1019-1054). While directly absorbing most of the Asian invasion of Europe in the 13th century, the Ukrainian state slowly disintegrated and was divided mainly between Russia and Poland.

The Ukrainian Cossack State, founded in the late 16th century, waged numerous wars of liberation against the occupiers of Ukraine: Russia, Poland, and Turkey. By the late 18th century, Ukrainian independence was lost. Ukraine's neighbors once again divided its territory. At the turn of the last century, Ukraine was occupied by Russia and Austria-Hungary.

An independent Ukrainian National Republic was proclaimed on January 22, 1918. In 1921, Ukraine's neighbors occupied and divided Ukrainian territory. In 1932-33, the Soviet government engineered a man-made famine in eastern Ukraine, resulting in the deaths of 7-10 million Ukrainians.

In March 1939, independent Carpatho-Ukraine was the first European state to wage war against Nazi-led aggression in the region. During WW2 the Ukrainian nationalist underground and its Ukrainian Insurgent Army (UPA) fought both Nazi German and Soviet forces. The restoration of Ukrainian independence was declared on June 30, 1941. Over 5 million Ukrainians lost their lives during the war. With the reoccupation of Ukraine by Soviet troops in 1944 came a renewed wave of mass arrests, executions, and deportations of Ukrainians.

The world's worst nuclear power plant disaster occurred in Chernobyl, Ukraine, in April 1986.

Ukrainian independence was restored in Dec. 1991 with the dissolution of the Soviet Union.

Ukraine remained burdened by hyperinflation, a deteriorating infrastructure, and unproductive state enterprises. The Ukrainian Parliament ratified Feb. 3, 1994, a Jan. 14 agreement with Russia and the U.S. calling for deactivation of Ukraine's large nuclear arsenal.

United Arab Emirates

Ittihad al-Imarat al-Arabiyah

People: Population: 2,791,000. **Pop. density:** 93 per sq. mi. **Ethnic groups:** Arab, Iranian, Pakistani, Indian. **Principal languages:** Arabic (official), several others. **Religions:** Muslim 96%, Christian, Hindu.

Geography: Area: 30,000 sq. mi., the size of Maine. **Location:** On the S shore of the Persian Gulf. **Neighbors:** Qatar on N, Saudi Ar. on W, S, Oman on E. **Topography:** A barren, flat coastal plain gives way to uninhabited sand dunes on the S. Hajar Mtns. are on E. **Capital:** Abu Dhabi. **Cities** (1990 est.): Abu Dhabi 722,000; Dubavy 266,000.

Government: Type: Federation of emirates. **Head of state:** Pres. Zaid ibn Sultan an-Nahayan b. 1923; in office: Dec. 2, 1971. **Head of government:** Prime Min. Sheikh Maktum ibn Rashid al-Maktum; in office: Nov. 20, 1990. **Local divisions:** 7 autonomous emirates: Abu Dhabi, Ajman, Dubai, Fujaira, Ras al-Khaimah, Sharjah, Umm al-Qaiwain. **Defense:** 5.3% of GDP (1989 est.).

Economy: Chief crops: Vegetables, dates, limes. **Minerals:** Oil. **Crude oil reserves** (1991): 66 bln. barrels. **Arable land:** 1%. **Electricity prod.** (1992): 17.8 bln. kWh. **Labor force:** 5% agric.; 85% ind. and commerce; 5% serv.; 5% gvt.

Finance: Monetary unit: Dirham (Mar. 1994: 3.67 = $1 US). **Gross domestic product** (1992): $34.9 bln. **Per capita GDP:** $13,800. **Imports** (1992): $13.7 bln.; partners: Jap. 14%, UK 11%, Ger. 6%. **Exports** (1990): $21.3 bln.; partners: Jap. 36%. **National budget** (1993): $4.8 bln. **International reserves less gold** (Nov. 1993): $5.7 bln. **Gold:** 798,000 oz t.

Transport: Motor Vehicles: 302,000 passenger cars; 157,000 commercial vehicles. **Civil aviation:** 2.4 bln. passenger-mi., 4 airports with scheduled flights. **Chief ports:** Dubavy, Abu Dhabi.

Communications: Television sets: 1 per 12 persons. **Radios:** 1 per 4.7 persons. **Telephones:** 1 per 2.5 persons.

Health: Life expectancy at birth (1994): 70 male, 74 female. **Births** (per 1,000 pop.): 28. **Deaths** (per 1,000 pop.): 3. **Natural increase:** 2.5%. **Hospital beds:** 1 per 292 persons. **Physicians:** 1 per 618 persons. **Infant mortality** (per 1,000 live births 1994): 22.

Education (1989): **Literacy:** 68%. **Years compulsory:** ages 6-12.

Major International Organizations: UN (World Bank, IMF, ILO), Arab League, OPEC.

Embassy: 600 New Hampshire Ave. NW 20037; 338-6500.

The 7 "Trucial Sheikdoms" gave Britain control of defense and foreign relations in the 19th century. They merged to become an independent state Dec. 2, 1971.

The Abu Dhabi Petroleum Co. was fully nationalized in 1975. Oil revenues have given the UAE one of the highest per capita GDPs in the world. International banking has grown in recent years.

United Kingdom of Great Britain and Northern Ireland

People: Population: 58,135,000. **Age distrib.** (%): <15: 19; 65+: 16. **Pop. density:** 616 per sq. mi. **Urban:** 92%. **Ethnic groups:** English 81.5%, Scottish 9.6%, Irish 2.4%, Welsh 1.9%, Ulster 1.8%; West Indian, Indian, Pakistani over 2%; others. **Principal languages:** English, Welsh spoken in western Wales. **Religions:** Church of England, Roman Catholic.

Geography: Area: 94,251 sq. mi., slightly smaller than Oregon. **Location:** Off the NW coast of Europe, across English Channel, Strait of Dover, and North Sea. **Neighbors:** Ireland to W, France to SE. **Topography:** England is mostly rolling land, rising to Uplands of southern Scotland; Lowlands are in center of Scotland, granite Highlands are in N. Coast is heavily indented, especially on W. British Isles have milder climate than N Europe due to the Gulf Stream and ample rainfall. Severn, 220 mi., and Thames, 215 mi., are longest rivers. **Capital:** London. **Cities** (1991 est.): London 6.8 mln.; Birmingham 994,000; Glasgow 687,000; Leeds 706,000; Sheffield 520,000; Liverpool 474,000; Manchester 432,000; Edinburgh 438,000; Bradford 468,000; Bristol 392,000.

Government: Type: Constitutional monarchy. **Head of state:** Queen Elizabeth II; b Apr. 21, 1926; in office: Feb. 6, 1952. **Head of government:** Prime Min. John Major; b Mar. 29, 1943; in office: Nov. 28, 1990. **Local divisions:** England and Wales: 47 non-metro counties, 7 metro counties, Greater London; Scotland: 9 regions, 3 island areas; N Ireland: 26 districts. **Defense:** 3.8% of GDP (FY 1992-93).

Economy: Industries: Steel, metals, vehicles, shipbuilding, banking, textiles, chemicals, electronics, aircraft, machinery, distilling. **Chief crops:** Grains, sugar beets, fruits, vegetables. **Minerals:** Coal, tin, oil, gas, limestone, iron, salt, clay. **Crude oil reserves** (1991): 4.0 bln. bbls. **Arable land:** 29%. **Livestock** (1992): cattle: 11.6 mln.; pigs: 7.5 mln.; sheep: 28.9 mln. **Fish catch** (1991): 823,000 metric tons. **Electricity prod.** (1992): 317 bln. kWh. **Labor force:** 1% agric.; 25% manuf. & constr.; 63% services.

Finance: Monetary unit: Pound (Mar. 1994: 1.00 = $1.49 US). **Gross domestic product** (1992): $920.6 bln.* **Per capita GDP:** $15,900. **Imports** (1992): $221 bln.; partners: EU 52%, U.S. 10%. **Exports** (1992): $190 bln.; partners: EU 53%, U.S. 13%. **Tourism** (1991): receipts: $18.8 bln. **National budget** (FY 1992 est.): $439.3 bln. **International reserves less gold** (Dec. 1993): $36.7 bln. **Gold:** 18.45 mln. oz t. **Consumer prices** (change in 1993): 1.6%.

Transport: Railroads: Length: 23,518 mi. **Motor vehicles:** in use: 19.7 mln. passenger cars, 2.8 mln. comm. vehicles. **Civil aviation:** 54 bln. passenger-mi.; 53 airports with scheduled flights. **Chief ports:** London, Liverpool, Glasgow, Southampton, Cardiff, Belfast.

Communications: Television sets: 1 per 2.9 persons. **Radios:** 1 per 0.8 person. **Telephones:** 1 per 1.9 persons. **Daily newspaper circ.:** 395 per 1,000 pop.

Health: Life expectancy at birth: (1994): 74 male; 80 female. **Births:** (per 1,000 pop.): 13. **Deaths:** (per 1,000 pop.): 11. **Natural increase:** .3%. **Hospital beds:** 1 per 146 persons. **Physicians:** 1 per 611 persons. **Infant mortality:** (per 1,000 live births 1994): 7.

Education (1991): **Literacy:** 99%. **Years compulsory:** 12; attendance 99%.

Major International Organizations: UN and all of its specialized agencies, NATO, EU, OECD.

Embassy: 3100 Massachusetts Ave. NW 20008; 462-1340.

The United Kingdom of Great Britain and Northern Ireland comprises England, Wales, Scotland, and Northern Ireland.

Queen and Royal Family. The ruling sovereign is Elizabeth II of the House of Windsor, born Apr. 21, 1926, elder daughter of King George VI. She succeeded to the throne Feb. 6, 1952, and was crowned June 2, 1953. She was married Nov. 20, 1947, to Lt. Philip Mountbatten, born June 10, 1921, former Prince of Greece. He was created Duke of Edinburgh, Earl of Merioneth, and Baron Greenwich, and given the style H.R.H.,

Nov. 19, 1947; he was given the title Prince of the United Kingdom and Northern Ireland Feb. 22, 1957. Prince Charles Philip Arthur George, born Nov. 14, 1948, is the Prince of Wales and heir apparent. His son, William Philip Arthur Louis, born June 21, 1982, is second in line to the throne.

Parliament is the legislative governing body for the United Kingdom, with certain powers over dependent units. It consists of 2 houses: The **House of Lords** includes 763 hereditary and 314 life peers and peeresses, certain judges, 2 archbishops and 24 bishops of the Church of England. Total membership is over 1,000. The **House of Commons** has 650 members, who are elected by direct ballot and divided as follows: England 516; Wales 36; Scotland 71; Northern Ireland 12.

Resources and Industries. Great Britain's major occupations are manufacturing and trade. Metals and metal-using industries contribute more than 50% of the exports. Of about 60 million acres of land in England, Wales, and Scotland, 46 million are farmed, of which 17 million are arable, the rest pastures.

Large oil and gas fields have been found in the North Sea. Commercial oil production began in 1975. There are large deposits of coal.

Britain imports all of its cotton, rubber, sulphur, about 80% of its wool, half of its food and iron ore, also certain amounts of paper, tobacco, chemicals. Manufactured goods made from these basic materials have been exported since the industrial age began. Main exports are machinery, chemicals, woolen and synthetic textiles, clothing, autos and trucks, iron and steel, locomotives, ships, jet aircraft, farm machinery, drugs, radio, TV, radar and navigation equipment, scientific instruments, arms, whisky.

Religion and Education. The Church of England is Protestant Episcopal. The queen is its temporal head, with rights of appointments to archbishoprics, bishoprics, and other offices. There are 2 provinces, Canterbury and York, each headed by an archbishop. The most famous church is Westminster Abbey (1050-1760), site of coronations, tombs of Elizabeth I, Mary of Scots, kings, poets, and of the Unknown Warrior.

The most celebrated British universities are Oxford and Cambridge, each dating to the 13th century. There are about 40 other universities.

History. Britain was part of the continent of Europe until about 6,000 BC, but migration of peoples across the English Channel continued long afterward. Celts arrived 2,500 to 3,000 years ago. Their language survives in Welsh, and Gaelic enclaves.

England was added to the Roman Empire in 43 AD. After the withdrawal of Roman legions in 410, waves of Jutes, Angles, and Saxons arrived from German lands. They contended with Danish raiders for control from the 8th through 11th centuries. The last successful invasion was by French speaking Normans in 1066, who united the country with their dominions in France.

Opposition by nobles to royal authority forced King John to sign the Magna Carta in 1215, a guarantee of rights and the rule of law. In the ensuing decades, the foundations of the parliamentary system were laid.

English dynastic claims to large parts of France led to the Hundred Years War, 1338-1453, and the defeat of England. A long civil war, the War of the Roses, lasted 1455-85, and ended with the establishment of the powerful Tudor monarchy. A distinct English civilization flourished. The economy prospered over long periods of domestic peace unmatched in continental Europe. Religious independence was secured when the Church of England was separated from the authority of the pope in 1534.

Under Queen Elizabeth I, England became a major naval power, leading to the founding of colonies in the new world and the expansion of trade with Europe and the Orient. Scotland was united with England when James VI of Scotland was crowned James I of England in 1603.

A struggle between Parliament and the Stuart kings led to a bloody civil war, 1642-49, and the establishment of a republic under the Puritan Oliver Cromwell. The monarchy was restored in 1660, but the "Glorious Revolution" of 1688 confirmed the sovereignty of Parliament: a Bill of Rights was granted 1689.

In the 18th century, parliamentary rule was strengthened. Technological and entrepreneurial innovations led to the Industrial Revolution. The 13 North American colonies were lost, but replaced by growing empires in Canada and India. Britain's role in the defeat of Napoleon, 1815, strengthened its position as the leading world power.

The extension of the franchise in 1832 and 1867, the formation of trade unions, and the development of universal public education were among the drastic social changes which accompanied the spread of industrialization and urbanization in the 19th century. Large parts of Africa and Asia were added to the empire during the reign of Queen Victoria, 1837-1901.

Though victorious in World War I, Britain suffered huge casualties and economic dislocation. Ireland became independent in 1921, and independence movements became active in India and other colonies. The country suffered major bombing damage in World War II, but held out against Germany singlehandedly for a year after the fall of France in 1940.

Industrial growth continued in the postwar period, but Britain lost its leadership position to other powers. Labor governments passed socialist programs nationalizing some basic industries and expanding social security. The Conservative government of Prime Min. Margaret Thatcher, however, tried to increase the role of private enterprise. In 1987, Thatcher became the first British leader in 160 years to be elected to a 3d consecutive term as prime minister. Falling on unpopular times, she resigned as prime minister in Nov. 1990. Her successor, John Major, led Conservatives to an upset victory at the polls, Apr. 9, 1993.

The UK supported the UN resolutions against Iraq and sent military forces to the Persian Gulf War.

The Channel Tunnel linking Britain to the Continent was officially inaugurated May 6, 1994.

Wales

The Principality of Wales in western Britain has an area of 8,019 sq. mi. and a population (1991 cen.) of 2,798,000. Cardiff is the capital, pop. (1981 est.) 273,856.

England and Wales are administered as a unit. Less than 20% of the population of Wales speak both English and Welsh; about 32,000 speak Welsh solely. A 1979 referendum rejected, 4-1, the creation of an elected Welsh Assembly.

Early Anglo-Saxon invaders drove Celtic peoples into the mountains of Wales, terming them Waelise (Welsh, or foreign). There they developed a distinct nationality. Members of the ruling house of Gwynedd in the 13th century fought England but were crushed, 1283. Edward of Caernarvon, son of Edward I of England, was created Prince of Wales, 1301.

Scotland

Scotland, a kingdom now united with England and Wales in Great Britain, occupies the northern 37% of the main British island, and the Hebrides, Orkney, Shetland, and smaller islands. Length, 275 mi., breadth approx. 150 mi., area, 30,405 sq. mi., population (1991 cen.) 4,957,000.

The Lowlands, a belt of land approximately 60 mi. wide from the Firth of Clyde to the Firth of Forth, divide the farming region of the Southern Uplands from the granite Highlands of the North, contain 75% of the population and most of the industry. The Highlands, famous for hunting and fishing, have been opened to industry by many hydroelectric power stations.

Edinburgh, pop. (1986 est.) 439,000, is the capital. Glasgow, pop. (1986 est.) 733,000, is Britain's greatest industrial center. It is a shipbuilding complex on the Clyde and an ocean port. Aberdeen, pop. (1986 est.) 215,000, NE of Edinburgh, is a major port, center of granite industry, fish processing, and North Sea oil exploration. Dundee, pop. (1986 est.) 177,000, NE of Edinburgh, is an industrial and fish processing center. About 90,000 persons speak Gaelic as well as English.

History. Scotland was called Caledonia by the Romans who battled early Celtic tribes and occupied southern areas from the 1st to the 4th centuries. Missionaries from Britain introduced Christianity in the 4th century; St. Columba, an Irish monk, converted most of Scotland in the 6th century.

The Kingdom of Scotland was founded in 1018. William Wallace and Robert Bruce both defeated English armies 1297 and 1314, respectively.

In 1603 James VI of Scotland, son of Mary, Queen of Scots, succeeded to the throne of England as James I, and effected the Union of the Crowns. In 1707 Scotland received representation in the British Parliament, resulting from the union of former separate Parliaments. Its executive in the British cabinet is the Secretary of State for Scotland. The growing Scottish National Party urges independence. A 1979 referendum on the creation of an elected Scotland Assembly was defeated.

Memorials of Robert Burns, Sir Walter Scott, John Knox, Mary, Queen of Scots draw many tourists, as do the beauties of the Trossachs, Loch Katrine, Loch Lomond, and abbey ruins.

Industries. Engineering products are the most important industry, with growing emphasis on office machinery, autos, electronics, and other consumer goods. Oil has been discovered offshore in the North Sea, stimulating on-shore support industries.

Scotland produces fine woolens, worsteds, tweeds, silks, fine linens, and jute. It is known for its special breeds of cattle and sheep. Fisheries have large hauls of herring, cod, whiting. Whisky is the biggest export.

The Hebrides are a group of c. 500 islands, 100 inhabited, off the W coast. The Inner Hebrides include **Skye, Mull,** and **Iona,** the last famous for the arrival of St. Columba, 563 AD. The Outer Hebrides include **Lewis** and **Harris.** Industries include sheep raising and weaving. The **Orkney Islands,** c. 90, are to the NE. The capital is Kirkwall, on Pomona Is. Fish curing, sheep raising, and weaving are occupations. NE of the Orkneys are the 200 **Shetland Islands,** 24 inhabited, home of Shetland pony. The Orkneys and Shetlands have become centers for the North Sea oil industry.

Northern Ireland

Six of the 9 counties of Ulster, the NE corner of Ireland, constitute Northern Ireland, with the parliamentary boroughs of Belfast and Londonderry. Area 5,463 sq. mi., 1991 cen. pop. 1,570,000, capital and chief industrial center, Belfast, (1990 est.) 297,000.

Industries. Shipbuilding, including large tankers, has long been an important industry, centered in Belfast, the largest port. Linen manufacture is also important, along with apparel, rope, and twine. Growing diversification has added engineering products, synthetic fibers, and electronics. There are large numbers of cattle, hogs, and sheep. Potatoes, poultry, and dairy foods are also produced.

Government. An act of the British Parliament, 1920, divided Northern from Southern Ireland, each with a parliament and government. When Ireland became a dominion, 1921, and later a republic, Northern Ireland chose to remain a part of the United Kingdom. It elects 12 members to the British House of Commons.

During 1968-69, large demonstrations were conducted by Roman Catholics who charged they were discriminated against in voting rights, housing, and employment. The Catholics, a minority comprising about a third of the population, demanded abolition of property qualifications for voting in local elections. Violence and terrorism intensified, involving branches of the Irish Republican Army (outlawed in the Irish Republic), Protestant groups, police, and British troops.

A succession of Northern Ireland prime ministers pressed reform programs but failed to satisfy extremists on both sides. Over 2,000 were killed in over 15 years of bombings and shootings through 1990, many in England itself. Britain suspended the Northern Ireland parliament Mar. 30, 1972, and imposed direct British rule. A coalition government was formed in 1973 when moderates won election to a new one-house Assembly. But a Protestant general strike overthrew the government in 1974 and direct rule was resumed.

The turmoil and agony of Northern Ireland was dramatized in 1981 by the deaths of 10 imprisoned Irish nationalist hunger strikers in Maze Prison near Belfast. The inmates had starved themselves to death in an attempt to achieve status as political prisoners, but the British government refused to yield to their demands. In 1985, the Hillsborough agreement gave the Rep. of Ireland a voice in the governing of Northern Ireland; the accord was strongly opposed by Ulster loyalists. On Dec. 12, 1993, Britain and Ireland announced a declaration of principles aimed at leading to a political settlement of the Northern Ireland issue. On Aug. 31, 1994, the IRA announced a cease-fire, saying it would rely on political means to achieve its objectives.

Education and Religion. Northern Ireland is 2/3 Protestant, 1/3 Roman Catholic. Education is compulsory through age 15.

Channel Islands

The Channel Islands, area 75 sq. mi., est. pop. 1986 145,000, off the NW coast of France, the only parts of the onetime Dukedom of Normandy belonging to England, are **Jersey, Guernsey** and the dependencies of Guernsey — **Alderney, Brechou, Great Sark, Little Sark, Herm, Jethou and Lihou.** Jersey and Guernsey have separate legal existences and lieutenant governors named by the Crown. The islands were the only British soil occupied by German troops in World War II.

Isle of Man

The Isle of Man, area 227 sq. mi., 1991 cen. pop. 69,788, is in the Irish Sea, 20 mi. from Scotland, 30 mi. from Cumberland. It is rich in lead and iron. The island has its own laws and a lieutenant governor appointed by the Crown. The Tynwald (legislature) consists of the Legislative Council, partly elected, and House of Keys, elected. Capital: Douglas. Farming, tourism, fishing (kippers, scallops) are chief occupations. Man is famous for the Manx tailless cat.

Gibraltar

Gibraltar, a dependency on the southern coast of Spain, guards the entrance to the Mediterranean. The Rock has been in British possession since 1704. The Rock is 2.75 mi. long, 3/4 of a mi. wide and 1,396 ft. in height; a narrow isthmus connects it with the mainland. Est. pop. 1992, 29,651.

Gibraltar has historically been an object of contention between Britain and Spain. Residents voted with near unanimity to remain under British rule, in a 1967 referendum held in pursuance of a UN resolution on decolonization. A new constitution, May 30, 1969, increased Gibraltarian control of domestic affairs (the UK continues to handle defense and internal security matters). Following a 1984 agreement between Britain and Spain, the border, closed by Spain in 1969, was fully reopened in Feb. 1985. A UN General Assembly resolution requested Britain to end Gibraltar's colonial status by Oct. 1, 1996. No settlement has been reached.

British West Indies

Swinging in a vast arc from the coast of Venezuela NE, then N and NW toward Puerto Rico are the Leeward Islands, forming a coral and volcanic barrier sheltering the Caribbean from the open Atlantic. Many of the islands are self-governing British possessions. Universal suffrage was instituted 1951-54; ministerial systems were set up 1956-1960.

The **Leeward Islands,** still associated with the UK are **Montserrat** (1987 pop. 11,600, area 32 sq. mi., capital Plymouth), the small **British Virgin Islands** (pop. 1991 cen.: 16,749), and **Anguilla** (pop. 1990 est.: 7,000), the most northerly of the Leeward Islands.

The three **Cayman Islands,** a dependency, lie S of Cuba, NW of Jamaica. Pop. 23,000 (1987), most of it on Grand Cayman. It is a free port; in the 1970s Grand Cayman became a tax-free refuge for foreign funds and branches of many Western banks were opened there. Total area 102 sq. mi., capital Georgetown.

The **Turks and Caicos Islands,** at the SE end of the Bahama Islands, are a separate possession. There are about 30 islands, only 6 inhabited (pop. 1990 cen.: 11,696; area 193 sq. mi.; capital Grand Turk). Salt, crayfish, and conch shells are the main exports.

Bermuda

Bermuda is a British dependency governed by a royal governor and an assembly, dating from 1620, the oldest legislative body among British dependencies. Capital is Hamilton.

It is a group of 360 small islands of coral formation, 20 inhabited, comprising 20.6 sq. mi. in the western Atlantic, 580 mi. E of North Carolina. Pop., 1992 est., was 60,213 (about 61% of African descent). Density is high.

The U.S. has air and naval bases under long-term lease, and a NASA tracking facility.

Bermuda boasts many resort hotels. The government raises most revenue from import duties. Exports: petroleum products, medicine.

South Atlantic

Falkland Islands and Dependencies, a British dependency, lies 300 mi. E of the Strait of Magellan at the southern end of South America.

The Falklands or Islas Malvinas include about 200 islands, area 4,700 sq. mi., pop. (1991 cen.) 2,121. Sheep-grazing is the main industry; wool is the principal export. There are indications of large oil and gas deposits. The islands are also claimed by Argentina though 97% of inhabitants are of British origin. Argentina invaded the islands Apr. 2, 1982. The British responded by sending a task force to the area, landing their main force on the Falklands, May 21, and forcing an Argentine surrender at Port Stanley, June 14.

British Antarctic Territory, south of 60° S lat., was made a separate colony in 1962 and comprises mainly the **South Shetland Islands,** the **South Orkneys** and **Graham's Land.** A chain of meteorological stations is maintained.

St. Helena, an island 1,200 mi. off the W coast of Africa and 1,800 E of South America, has 47 sq. mi. and est. pop., 1985, of 5,400. Flax, lace and rope making are the chief industries. After Napoleon Bonaparte was defeated at Waterloo the Allies exiled him to St. Helena, where he lived from Oct. 16, 1815, to his death, May 5, 1821. Capital is Jamestown.

Tristan da Cunha is the principal of a group of islands of volcanic origin, total area 40 sq. mi., halfway between the Cape of Good Hope and South America. A volcanic peak 6,760 ft. high erupted in 1961. The 262 inhabitants were removed to England, but most returned in 1963. The islands are dependencies of St. Helena.

Ascension is an island of volcanic origin, 34 sq. mi. in area, 700 mi. NW of St. Helena, through which it is administered. It is a communications relay center for Britain, and has a U.S. satellite tracking center. Est. pop., 1985, was 1,500, half of them communications workers. The island is noted for sea turtles.

Hong Kong

A Crown Colony at the mouth of the Canton R. in China, 90 mi. S of Canton. Its nucleus is Hong Kong Is., 35½ sq. mi., acquired from China 1841, on which is located Victoria, the capital. Opposite is Kowloon Peninsula, 3 sq. mi. and Stonecutters Is., ¼ sq. mi., added, 1860. An additional 355 sq. mi. known as the New Territories, a mainland area and islands, were leased from China, 1898, for 99 years. Britain and China, Dec. 19, 1984, signed an agreement under which Hong Kong would be allowed to keep its capitalist system for 50 years after 1997, the year that the 99-year lease will expire. During 1994 the Hong Kong legislature approved democratic reforms, which were opposed by China. Total area of the colony is 409 sq. mi., with a population, 1992 est., of 5.8 million, including fewer than 20,000 British. From 1949 to 1962 Hong Kong absorbed more than a million refugees from China.

Hong Kong harbor was long an important British naval station and one of the world's great trans-shipment ports.

Principal industries are textiles and apparel; also tourism, $4.9 bln. expenditures (1991), shipbuilding, iron and steel, fishing, cement, and small manufactures.

Spinning mills, among the best in the world, and low wages compete with textiles elsewhere and have resulted in the protective measures in some countries. Hong Kong also has a booming electronics industry.

British Indian Ocean Territory

Formed Nov. 1965, embracing islands formerly dependencies of Mauritius or Seychelles: the Chagos Archipelago (including Diego Garcia), Aldabra, Farquhar and Des Roches. The latter 3 were transferred to Seychelles, which became independent in 1976. Area 22 sq. mi. No civilian population remains.

Pacific Ocean

Pitcairn Island is in the Pacific, halfway between South America and Australia. The island was discovered in 1767 by Carteret but was not inhabited until 23 years later when the mutineers of the Bounty landed there. The area is 1.7 sq. mi. and 1991 pop. was 59. It is a British colony and is administered by a British Representative in New Zealand and a local Council. The uninhabited islands of **Henderson, Ducie,** and **Oeno** are in the Pitcairn group.

United States of America

People: Population: 260,714,000 (incl. 50 states & Dist. of Columbia). **Age distrib.**(%): <15: 22; 65+: 13. **Pop. density:** 69 per sq. mi. **Urban:** 75%.

Geography: 3,787,318 sq. mi. (incl. 50 states and D. of C.). Vast central plain, mountains in west, hills and low mountains in east.

Government: Federal republic, strong democratic tradition. **Head of state:** Pres. Bill Clinton; b Aug. 19, 1946; in office: Jan. 20, 1993. **Administrative divisions:** 50 states and Dist. of Columbia. **Defense:** 5.3% of GDP (1992).

Economy: Minerals: Coal, copper, lead, molybdenum, phosphates, uranium, bauxite, gold, iron, mercury, nickel, potash, silver, tungsten, zinc. **Crude oil reserves** (1991): 26 bln. barrels. **Arable land:** 20%. **Livestock** (1992): cattle: 99 mln.; pigs: 57 mln.; sheep: 10.7 mln. **Fish catch** (1992): 3.3 mln. metric tons. **Electricity prod.** (1992): 3,230 bln. kWh. **Crude steel prod.** (1992): 84.3 mln. metric tons.

Finance: Gross domestic product (1992): 5.95 trl.* **Per capita GDP:** $23,400. **Imports** (1992): $553 bln.; partners: Can. 17%, Jap. 20%, Mex. 6%. **Exports** (1992): $447 bln.; partners: Can. 22%, Jap. 12%, Mex. 6%, UK 5%. **Tourism** (1991): receipts $45.5 bln. **International reserves less gold** (Mar. 1994): $65.7 bln. **Gold:** 261.77 mln. oz t. **Consumer prices** (change in 1993): 3.0%.

Transport: Railroads: Length: 172,893 mi. **Motor vehicles:** in use: 143 mln. passenger cars, 45 mln. comm. vehicles. **Civil aviation:** 475 bln. passenger-mi.; 834 airports with scheduled flights.

Communications: Television sets: 1 per 1.2 persons. **Radios:** 1 per 0.5 persons. **Telephones:** 1 per 1.3 persons. **Daily newspaper circ.:** 250 per 1,000 pop.

Health: Life expectancy at birth (1992): 72 male; 79 female. **Births** (per 1,000 pop.): 15. **Deaths** (per 1,000 pop.): 9. **Natural increase:** .7%. **Hospital beds:** 1 per 211 persons. **Physicians:** 1 per 406 persons. **Infant mortality** (per 1,000 live births 1992): 10.

Major International Organizations: UN (GATT, IMF, WHO, FAO), OAS, NATO, OECD.

Education (1991): **Literacy:** 97%.

Uruguay

Republic of Uruguay

República del Uruguay

People: Population: 3,199,000. **Age distrib.** (%): <15: 26; 65+: 12. **Pop. density:** 47 per sq. mi. **Urban:** 89%. **Ethnic groups:** whites (Iberians, Italians) 88%, mestizos 8%, black. **Principal languages:** Spanish. **Religions:** Roman Catholic 66%.

Geography: Area: 68,037 sq. mi., the size of Washington State. **Location:** In southern S America, on the Atlantic O. **Neighbors:** Argentina on W, Brazil on N. **Topography:** Uruguay is composed of rolling, grassy plains and hills, well-watered by rivers flowing W to Uruguay R. **Capital:** Montevideo. **Cities** (1991 est.): Montevideo 1.4 mln.

Government: Type: Republic. **Head of state:** Pres. Luis Alberto Lacalle; in office: Nov. 26, 1989. **Local divisions:** 19 departments. **Defense:** 2.3% of GDP (1991 est.).

Economy: Industries: Meat-packing, textiles, wine, cement, oil products. **Chief crops:** Corn, wheat, citrus fruits, rice, oats, linseed. **Arable land:** 8%. **Livestock** (1992): cattle: 9.5 mln.; sheep: 25.7 mln. **Fish catch** (1991): 143,000 metric tons. **Electricity prod.** (1992): 5.9 bln. kWh. **Labor force** 11% agric.; 19% manuf.; 21% serv.; 25% govt.; 12% comm.

Finance: Monetary unit: Peso (Jan. 1994: 4.47 = $1 US). **Gross domestic product** (1992): $9.8 bln. **Per capita GDP:** $3,100. **Imports** (1991): $1.3 bln.; partners: EU 27%, Braz. 24%, Arg. 14%, U.S. 8%. **Exports** (1991): $1.6 bln.; partners: Braz. 28%, U.S. 11%, EU 23%. **Tourism** (1990): $261 mln. receipts. **National budget** (1991): $3.0 bln. **International reserves less gold** (Jan. 1994): $773 mln. **Gold:** 1.70 mln. oz t. **Consumer prices** (change in 1993): 54.1%

Transport: Railroads: Length: 1,865 mi. **Motor vehicles:** in use: 379,000 passenger cars, 49,000 comm. vehicles. **Civil aviation:** 293 mln. passenger-mi.; 7 airports. **Chief ports:** Montevideo.

Communications: Television sets: 1 per 5.2 persons. **Radios:** 1 per 1.7 persons. **Telephones:** 1 per 5.4 persons. **Daily newspaper circ.:** 233 per 1,000 pop.

Health: Life expectancy at birth (1994): 71 male; 77 female. **Births** (per 1,000 pop.): 18. **Deaths** (per 1,000 pop.): 9. **Natural increase:** .8%. **Hospital beds:** 1 per 127 persons. **Physicians:** 1 per 341 persons. **Infant mortality** (per 1,000 live births 1994): 17.

Education (1990): **Literacy:** 96%.

Major International Organizations: UN (GATT, IMF, WHO), OAS.

Embassy: 1918 F St. NW 20006; 331-1313.

Spanish settlers did not begin replacing the indigenous Charrua Indians until 1624. Portuguese from Brazil arrived later, but Uruguay was attached to the Spanish Viceroyalty of Rio de la Plata in the 18th century. Rebels fought against Spain beginning in 1810. An independent republic was declared Aug. 25, 1825.

Socialist measures were adopted as far back as 1911. The state owns the power, telephone, railroad, cement, oil-refining, and other industries.

Uruguay's standard of living was one of the highest in South America, and political and labor conditions among the freest. Economic stagnation, inflation, floods and drought, and a general strike in the late 1960s brought government attempts to strengthen the economy through devaluation of the peso and wage and price controls.

Terrorist activities led to Pres. Juan Maria Bordaberry agreeing to military control of his administration Feb. 1973. In June he abolished Congress and set up a Council of State in its place. Bordaberry was removed by the military in a 1976 coup. Civilian government was restored to the country in 1985.

Uzbekistan

Republic of Uzbekistan

Ozbekiston Republikasy

People: Population: 22,609,000. **Age distrib.** (%): <15: 41; 65+: 4. **Pop. density:** 130 per sq. mi. **Urban:** 40%. **Ethnic groups:** Uzbek 71%, Russian 8%. **Principal languages:** Uzbek, Russian. **Religions:** Mostly Sunni Muslim.

Geography: Area: 172,700 sq. mi., slightly larger than California. **Neighbors:** Kazakhstan on N and W, Kyrgyzstan and Tajikistan on E, Afghanistan and Turkmenistan on S. **Topography:** mostly plains and desert. **Capital:** Tashkent.

Government: Type: Republic. **Head of state:** Pres. Islam A. Karimov; b 1938. **Head of government:** Prime Min. Abdulkhashim Mutalov; in office: Jan. 8, 1992. **Local divisions:** 11 oblasts, 1 autonomous republic.

Economy: Industries: Steel, tractors, cars, textiles. **Chief crops:** Cotton, rice. **Minerals:** Coal, copper. **Livestock** (1992): cattle: 5.1 mln., sheep: 9.2 mln. **Electricity prod.** (1992): 51 bln. kWh. **Labor force:** 39% agric. & forestry; 24% ind. & constr.

Finance: Monetary unit: Ruble. **Imports** (1990): $3.5 bln. **Exports** (1990): $1.5 bln.

Transportation: Railroads: Length: 4,200 mi. **Civil aviation:** 6.5 bln. passenger-mi.; 1 airport.

Communications: Television sets: 1 per 6.3 persons. **Telephones:** 1 per 14 persons.

Health: Life expectancy at birth (1994): 65 male; 72 female. **Births** (per 1,000 pop.): 30. **Deaths** (per 1,000 pop.): 7. **Natural increase:** 2.4%. **Hospital beds:** 1 per 83 persons. **Physicians:** 1 per 300 persons. **Infant mortality rate** (per 1,000 live births 1994): 53.

Major International Organizations: UN, CIS.

Embassy: 200 Pennsylvania Ave. NW 20006; 778-0107.

The region was overrun by the Mongols under Genghis Khan in 1220. In the 14th century, Uzbekistan became the center of a native empire—that of the Timurids. In later centuries Muslim feudal states emerged. Russian military conquest began in the 19th century.

The Uzbek SSR became a Soviet Union republic in 1925. Uzbekistan declared independence Aug. 29, 1991. It became an independent republic when the Soviet Union disbanded Dec. 26, 1991. Subsequently, the government of Uzbekistan was dominated by former Communists.

Vanuatu

Republic of Vanuatu

Ripablik Blong Vanuatu

People: Population: 170,000. **Pop. density:** 36 per sq. mi. **Ethnic groups:** Mainly Melanesian, some European, Polynesian, Micronesian. **Principal languages:** French, English, (both official), Bislama. **Religions:** Presbyterian 37%, Anglican 15%, Roman Catholic 15%, indigenous beliefs 8%.

Geography: Area: 4,707 sq. mi., slightly larger than Connecticut. **Location:** SW Pacific, 1,200 mi. NE of Brisbane, Australia. **Topography:** dense forest with narrow coastal strips of cultivated land. **Capital:** Vila. **Cities:** Vila (1990): 19,000.

Government: Type: Republic. **Head of state:** Pres. Jean-Marie Leye; in office: Mar. 2, 1994. **Head of gov't:** Prime Min. Maxime Carlot Korman; in office: Dec. 16, 1991.

Economy: Industries: Fish-freezing, meat canneries, tourism. **Chief crops:** Copra (38% of export), cocoa, coffee. **Minerals:** Manganese. **Other resources:** Forests, cattle. **Fish catch** (1991): 3,200 metric tons.

Finance: Monetary unit: Vatu (Sept. 1993): 123 = $1 US). **Gross domestic product** (1990): $142 mln. **Imports** (1990): $60 mln.; partners: Aus. 36%, Fr. 8%, Japan 13%. **Exports** (1990): $15 mln.; partners: Neth. 34%, Jap. 17%, Fr. 27%.

Health: Life expectancy at birth (1994): 58 male, 61 female. **Births** (per 1,000 pop.): 32. **Deaths** (per 1,000 pop.): 9. **Natural increase:** 2.3%. **Infant mortality** (per 1,000 live births 1994): 68.

Education: Literacy (1990): 90%. Education not compulsory, but 85-90% of children of primary school age attend primary schools.

The Anglo-French condominium of the New Hebrides, administered jointly by France and Great Britain since 1906, became the independent Republic of Vanuatu on July 30, 1980.

Vatican City

The Holy See

People: Population: 811. **Ethnic groups:** Italians, Swiss. **Principal languages:** Italian, Latin.

Geography: Area: 108.7 acres. **Location:** In Rome, Italy. **Neighbors:** Completely surrounded by Italy.

Monetary unit: Lira.

Apostolic Nunciature in U.S.: 3339 Massachusetts Ave. NW 20008; 333-7121.

The popes for many centuries, with brief interruptions, held temporal sovereignty over mid-Italy (the so-called Papal States), comprising an area of some 16,000 sq. mi., with a population in the 19th century of more than 3 million. This territory was incorporated in the new Kingdom of Italy, the sovereignty of the pope being confined to the palaces of the Vatican and the Lateran in Rome and the villa of Castel Gandolfo, by an Italian law, May 13, 1871. This law also guaranteed to the pope and his successors a yearly indemnity of over $620,000. The allowance, however, remained unclaimed.

A Treaty of Conciliation, a concordat and a financial convention were signed Feb. 11, 1929, by Cardinal Gasparri and Premier Mussolini. The documents established the independent state of Vatican City, and gave the Catholic religion special status in Italy. The treaty (Lateran Agreement) was made part of the Constitution of Italy (Article 7) in 1947. Italy and the Vatican reached preliminary agreement in 1976 on revisions of the concordat, that would eliminate Roman Catholicism as the state religion and end required religious education in Italian schools.

Vatican City includes St. Peter's, the Vatican Palace and Museum covering over 13 acres, the Vatican gardens, and neighboring buildings between Viale Vaticano and the Church. Thirteen buildings in Rome, outside the boundaries, enjoy extraterritorial rights; these buildings house congregations or officers necessary for the administration of the Holy See.

The legal system is based on the code of canon law, the apostolic constitutions, and the laws especially promulgated for the Vatican City by the pope. The Secretariat of State represents the Holy See in its diplomatic relations. By the Treaty of Conciliation the pope is pledged to a perpetual neutrality unless his mediation is specifically requested. This, however, does not prevent the defense of the Church whenever it is persecuted.

The present sovereign of the State of Vatican City is the Supreme Pontiff John Paul II, Karol Wojtyla, born in Wadowice, Poland, May 18, 1920, elected Oct. 16, 1978 (the first non-Italian to be elected Pope in 456 years).

The U.S. restored formal relations in 1984 after the U.S.

Congress repealed an 1867 ban on diplomatic relations with the Vatican. The Vatican and Israel agreed to establish formal relations Dec. 30, 1993.

Venezuela

Republic of Venezuela

Republica de Venezuela

People: Population: 20,562,000. **Age distrib.** (%): <15: 38; 65+: 4. **Pop. density:** 58 per sq. mi. **Urban:** 84%. **Ethnic groups:** Mestizo 67%, white (Spanish, Portuguese, Italian) 21%, black 10%, Indian 2%. **Principal languages:** Spanish (official). **Religions:** Roman Catholic 96%.

Geography: Area: 352,144 sq. mi., more than twice the size of California. **Location:** On the Caribbean coast of S America. **Neighbors:** Colombia on W, Brazil on S, Guyana on E. **Topography:** Flat coastal plain and Orinoco Delta are bordered by Andes Mtns. and hills. Plains, called llanos, extend between mountains and Orinoco. Guyana Highlands and plains are S of Orinoco, which stretches 1,600 mi. and drains 80% of Venezuela. **Capital:** Caracas. **Cities** (1990 est.): Caracas 1.3 mln.; Maracaibo 1.2 mln.; Barquisimeto 723,000; Valencia 955,000.

Government: Type: Federal republic. **Head of state:** Pres. Rafael Caldera Rodríguez; b Jan. 24, 1916; in office: Feb. 2, 1994. **Local divisions:** 21 states, territory, federal district, federal dependency. **Defense:** 4% of GDP (1991).

Economy: Industries: Steel, oil products, textiles, containers, paper. **Chief crops:** Coffee, rice, fruits, sugar. **Minerals:** Oil, iron (extensive reserves and production), gold. **Crude oil reserves** (1991): 60 bln. barrels. **Arable land:** 3%. **Livestock** (1992): cattle: 14.1 mln. **Fish catch** (1991): 352,000 metric tons. **Electricity prod.** (1992): 58.5 bln. kWh. **Labor force:** 16% agric.; 28% ind.; 56% services.

Finance: Monetary unit: Bolivar (Mar. 1994: 112 = $1 US). **Gross domestic product** (1992): $57.8 bln. **Per capita GDP:** $2,800. **Imports** (1991): $10.2 bln.; partners: U.S. 44%. **Exports** (1991): $15.1 bln.; partners: U.S. 50%. **Tourism** (1990): $359 mln. receipts. **National budget** (1992): $13.1 bln. **International reserves less gold** (Mar. 1994): $7.5 bln. **Gold:** 11.46 mln. oz t. **Consumer prices** (change in 1993): 38.1%.

Transport: Railroads: Length: 226 mi. **Motor vehicles:** in use: 1.6 mln. passenger cars, 319,000 comm. vehicles. **Civil aviation:** 3.6 bln. passenger-mi.; 31 airports with scheduled flights. **Chief ports:** Maracaibo, La Guaira, Puerto Cabello.

Communications: Television sets: 1 per 5.5 persons. **Radios:** 1 per 2.5 persons. **Telephones:** 1 per 11 persons. **Daily newspaper circ.:** 142 per 1,000 pop.

Health: Life expectancy at birth (1994): 70 male; 76 female. **Births** (per 1,000 pop.): 26. **Deaths** (per 1,000 pop.): 5. **Natural increase:** 2.1%. **Hospital beds:** 1 per 370 persons. **Physicians:** 1 per 576 persons. **Infant mortality** (per 1,000 live births 1994): 28.

Education (1991): **Literacy:** 88%. **Years compulsory:** 8; attendance 82%.

Major International Organizations: UN (IMF, WHO, FAO), OAS, OPEC.

Embassy: 1099 30th St. NW 20007; 342-2214.

Columbus first set foot on the South American continent on the peninsula of Paria, Aug. 1498. Alonso de Ojeda, 1499, found Lake Maracaibo, called the land Venezuela, or Little Venice, because natives had houses on stilts. Venezuela was under Spanish domination until 1821. The republic was formed after secession from the Colombian Federation in 1830.

Military strongmen ruled Venezuela for most of the 20th century. They promoted the oil industry; some social reforms were implemented. Since 1959, the country has had democratically elected governments.

Venezuela helped found the Organization of Petroleum Exporting Countries (OPEC). The government, Jan. 1, 1976, nationalized the oil industry with compensation. Oil accounts for much of total export earnings and the economy suffered a severe cash crisis in the 1980s and 1990s as a result of falling oil revenues.The government has attempted to reduce dependence on oil.

A coup attempt, led by midlevel military officers, was thwarted by loyalist troops Feb. 4, 1992. A second coup attempt was thwarted in Nov. Pres. Carlos Andrés Pérez was suspended from office and charged with misappropriating government funds, May 1993. Pres. Rafael Caldera Rodríguez, a populist elected Dec. 5, 1993, suspended many constitutional rights in June-July 1994, citing economic crisis.

Vietnam

Socialist Republic of Vietnam

Cong Hoa Xa Hoi Chu Nghia Viet Nam

People: Population: 73,104,000. **Age distrib.** (%): <15: 39; 65+: 5. **Pop. density:** 574 per sq. mi. **Urban:** 21%. **Ethnic groups:** Vietnamese 85–90%, Chinese 3%, remainder Muong, Thai, Meo, Khmer, Man, Cham. **Principal languages:** Vietnamese (official), French, Chinese. **Religions:** Buddhists, Taoists most numerous, Roman Catholics, indigenous beliefs, Muslims, Protestants.

Geography: Area: 127,246 sq. mi., the size of New Mexico. **Location:** On the E coast of the Indochinese Peninsula in SE Asia. **Neighbors:** China on N, Laos, Cambodia on W. **Topography:** Vietnam is long and narrow, with a 1,400-mi. coast. About 24% of country is readily arable, including the densely settled Red R. valley in the N, narrow coastal plains in center, and the wide, often marshy Mekong R. Delta in the S. The rest consists of semi-arid plateaus and barren mountains, with some stretches of tropical rain forest. **Capital:** Hanoi. **Cities** (1992): Ho Chi Minh City 4.0 mln.; Hanoi 2.0 mln.

Government: Type: Communist. **Head of state:** Pres. Le Duc Anh; in office: Sept. 23, 1992. **Head of government:** Prime Min. Vo Van Kiet; in office: Aug. 8, 1991. **Local divisions:** 50 provinces, 3 municipalities. **Defense:** 11% of GNP (1992).

Economy: Industries: Food processing, textiles, cement, chemical fertilizers. **Chief crops:** Rice, rubber, fruits and vegetables, corn, manioc, sugar cane. **Minerals:** Phosphates, coal, iron, manganese, bauxite, apatite, chromate. **Other resources:** Forests. **Arable land:** 22%. **Livestock** (1992): cattle: 3.1 mln.; pigs: 12.1 mln. **Fish catch** (1991): 877,000 metric tons. **Electricity prod.** (1992): 9.0 bln. kWh. **Labor force:** 65% agric.; 35% ind. and service.

Finance: Monetary unit: Dong (Jan. 1993: 10,881 = $1 US). **Gross national product** (1992): $16 bln. **Per capita GNP:** $230. **Imports** (1991): $1.9 bln.; partners: CIS, Jap. **Exports** (1991): $1.8 bln.; partners: CIS. **National budget** (1990): $1.9 bln.

Transport: Railroads: Length: 2,001 mi. **Civil aviation:** 6.3 bln. passenger-mi.; 4 airports with scheduled flights. **Chief ports:** Ho Chi Minh City, Haiphong, Da Nang.

Communications: Television sets: 1 per 31 persons. **Radios:** 1 per 12 persons. **Telephones:** 1 per 544 persons. **Daily newspaper circ.:** 9 per 1,000 pop.

Health: Life expectancy at birth (1994): 63 male; 68 female. **Births** (per 1,000 pop.): 27. **Deaths** (per 1,000 pop.): 8. **Natural increase:** 1.9%. **Hospital beds:** 1 per 298 persons. **Physicians:** 1 per 2,843 persons. **Infant mortality** (per 1,000 live births 1994): 46.

Education (1989): **Literacy:** 88%.

Major International Organizations: UN (IMF, WHO).

Vietnam's recorded history began in Tonkin before the Christian era. Settled by Viets from central China, Vietnam was held by China, 111 BC-939 AD, and was a vassal state during subsequent periods. Vietnam defeated the armies of Kublai Khan, 1288. Conquest by France began in 1858 and ended in 1884 with the protectorates of Tonkin and Annam in the N and the colony of Cochin-China in the S.

In 1940 Vietnam was occupied by Japan; nationalist aims gathered force. A number of groups formed the Vietminh (Independence) League, headed by Ho Chi Minh, Communist guerrilla leader. In Aug. 1945 the Vietminh forced out Bao Dai, former emperor of Annam, head of a Japan-sponsored regime. France, seeking to reestablish colonial control, battled Communist and nationalist forces, 1946-1954, and was finally defeated at Dienbienphu, May 8, 1954. Meanwhile, on July 1, 1949, Bao Dai had formed a State of Vietnam, with himself as chief of state, with French approval. China backed Ho Chi Minh.

A cease-fire signed in Geneva July 21, 1954, provided for a buffer zone, withdrawal of French troops from the North, and elections to determine the country's future. Under the agreement the Communists gained control of territory north of the

17th parallel, with its capital at Hanoi and Ho Chi Minh as president. South Vietnam came to comprise the 39 southern provinces. Some 900,000 North Vietnamese fled to South Vietnam.

On Oct. 26, 1955, Ngo Dinh Diem, premier of the interim government of South Vietnam, proclaimed the Republic of Vietnam and became its first president.

The North, adopted a constitution Dec. 31, 1959, based on Communist principles and calling for reunification of all Vietnam. North Vietnam sought to take over South Vietnam beginning in 1954. Fighting persisted from 1956, with the Communist Vietcong, aided by North Vietnam, pressing war in the South. Northern aid to Vietcong guerrillas was intensified in 1959, and large-scale troop infiltration began in 1964, with Soviet and Chinese arms assistance. Large Northern forces were stationed in border areas of Laos and Cambodia.

A serious political conflict arose in the South in 1963 when Buddhists denounced authoritarianism and brutality. This paved the way for a military coup Nov. 1-2, 1963, which overthrew Diem. Several other military coups followed.

In 1964, the U.S. began air strikes against North Vietnam. Beginning in 1965, the raids were stepped up and U.S. troops became combatants. U.S. troop strength in Vietnam, which reached a high of 543,400 in Apr. 1969, was ordered reduced by President Nixon in a series of withdrawals, beginning in June 1969. U.S. bombings were resumed in 1972-73.

A cease-fire agreement was signed in Paris Jan. 27, 1973 by the U.S., North and South Vietnam, and the Vietcong. It was never implemented.

North Vietnamese forces launched attacks against remaining government outposts in the Central Highlands in the first months of 1975. Government retreats turned into a rout, and the Saigon regime surrendered April 30. North Vietnam assumed control, and began transforming society along Communist lines.

The war's toll included — Combat deaths: U.S. 47,369; South Vietnam over 200,000; other allied forces 5,225. Total U.S. fatalaties numbered more than 58,000. Vietnamese civilian casualties were over a million. Displaced war refugees in South Vietnam totaled over 6.5 million.

The country was officially reunited July 2, 1976. The Northern capital, flag, anthem, emblem, and currency were applied to the new state. Nearly all major government posts went to officials of the former Northern government.

Heavy fighting with Cambodia took place, 1977-80, amid mutual charges of aggression and atrocities against civilians. Increasing numbers of Vietnamese civilians, ethnic Chinese, escaped the country, via the sea, or the overland route across Cambodia. Vietnam launched an offensive against Cambodian refugee strongholds along the Thai-Cambodian border in 1985; they also engaged Thai troops.

Relations with China soured as 140,000 ethnic Chinese left Vietnam charging discrimination; China cut off economic aid. Reacting to Vietnam's invasion of Cambodia, China attacked 4 Vietnamese border provinces, Feb. 1979, instigating heavy fighting.

Vietnam announced a package of reforms aimed at reducing central control of the economy in 1987, as many of the old revolutionary followers of Ho Chi Minh were removed from office.

Citing Vietnamese cooperation in returning remains of U.S. soldiers killed in the Vietnam War, the U.S. announced an end Feb. 3, 1994, to a 19-year-old U.S. embargo on trade with Vietnam.

Western Samoa

Independent State of Western Samoa

Malotuto'atasi o Samoa i Sisifo

People: Population: 204,000. **Age distrib.** (%): <15: 41; 65+: 3. **Pop. density:** 186 per sq. mi. **Urban:** 21%. **Ethnic groups:** Samoan (Polynesian) 93%, Euronesian (mixed) 7%, European, other Pacific Islanders. **Principal languages:** Samoan, English (both official). **Religions:** Protestant 70%, Roman Catholic 20%.

Geography: Area: 1,093 sq. mi., the size of Rhode Island. **Location:** In the S Pacific O. **Neighbors:** Nearest are Fiji on W, Tonga on S. **Topography:** Main islands, Savai'i (670 sq. mi.) and Upolu (429 sq. mi.), both ruggedly mountainous, and small islands Manono and Apolima. **Capital:** Apia. **Cities** (1983 est.): Apia 35,000.

Government: Type: Constitutional monarchy. **Head of state:** Malietoa Tanumafili II; b Jan. 4, 1913; in office: Jan. 1, 1962. **Head of government:** Prime Min. Toflau Eti Alesana; in office: Apr. 11, 1988. **Local divisions:** 11 districts.

Economy: Chief crops: Cocoa, copra, bananas. **Other resources:** Hardwoods, fish. **Arable land:** 43%. **Electricity prod.** (1991): 45 mln. kWh. **Labor force:** 67% agric.

Finance: Monetary unit: Tala (Mar. 1994: 1.00 = $.39 US). **Gross domestic product** (1990): $115 mln. **Per capita GDP:** $690. **Imports** (1992): $113 mln.; partners: NZ 28% Austral. 20%, Jap. 13%, U.S. 5%. **Exports** (1992): $6.0 mln.; partners: EU 28%. **International reserves less gold** (Feb. 1994): $51 mln. **Consumer prices** (change in 1993): 1.7%.

Transport: Motor vehicles: in use: 2,500 passenger cars, 3,000 comm. vehicles. **Chief ports:** Apia, Asau.

Communications: Radios: 1 per 2.5 persons. **Telephones:** 1 per 30 persons.

Health: Life expectancy at birth (1994): 66 male; 70 female. **Births** (per 1,000 pop.): 32. **Deaths** (per 1,000 pop.): 6. **Natural increase:** 2.6%. **Hospital beds:** 1 per 255 persons. **Physicians:** 1 per 3,584 persons. **Infant mortality** (per 1,000 live births 1994): 37.

Education (1989): **Literacy:** 90%. 95% attend elementary school.

Major International Organizations: UN (IMF, World Bank), Commonwealth of Nations.

Western Samoa was a German colony, 1899 to 1914, when New Zealand landed troops and took over. It became a New Zealand mandate under the League of Nations and, in 1945, a New Zealand UN Trusteeship.

An elected local government took office in Oct. 1959 and the country became fully independent Jan. 1, 1962.

Yemen

Republic of Yemen

al-Jumhurīyah al Yamanīyah

People: Population: 11,105,000. **Pop. density:** 54 per sq. mi. **Urban:** 31%. **Ethnic groups:** Arabs, Indians, some Negroids. **Principal languages:** Arabic. **Religions:** Muslim (Sha'fi, Sunni, Zaydi Shi'a).

Geography: Area: 205,356 sq. mi., slightly smaller than France. **Location:** On the southern coast of the Arabian Peninsula. **Neighbors:** Saudi Arabia on NE, Oman on the E. **Topography:** A sandy coastal strip leads to well-watered fertile mountains in interior. **Capital:** Sanaa. **Cities** (1986 est.): Sanaa 427,000; Aden 318,000.

Government: Type: Republic. **Head of state:** Pres. Ali Abdullah Saleh, b. 1942; in office: July 17, 1978. **Head of government:** Acting Prime Min. Mohamed al-Attar; in office: May 1994. **Local divisions:** 17 provinces. **Defense:** 10% of GDP (1992).

Economy: Industries: Food processing, mining, petroleum refining. **Chief crops:** Wheat, sorghum, fruits, coffee, cotton. **Minerals:** Salt. **Crude oil reserves** (1984): 600 mln. bbls. **Arable land:** 6%. **Livestock** (1992): goats: 3.4 mln.; sheep: 3.8 mln. **Fish catch** (1991): 85,000 metric tons. **Electricity prod.** (1992): 1.2 bln. kWh. **Labor force:** 45% agric.; 11% ind.; 21% services.

Finance: Monetary unit: Rial (Jan. 1993: 16.50 = $1 US). **Gross domestic product** (1992): $8 bln. **Per capita GDP:** $775. **Imports** (1990): $2.1 bln.; partners: Saudi Ar. 20%, Fr. 8%, Jap. 16%. **Exports** (1990): $908 mln.; partners: S Yemen 23%, Saudi Ar. 8%, Pak. 19%.

Transport: Motor vehicles in use: 165,000 passenger cars, 237,000 commercial vehicles. **Civil aviation:** 641 mln. passenger-mi.; 12 airports with scheduled flights. **Chief ports:** Al-Hudaydah, Al-Mukha, Aden.

Communications: Television sets: 1 per 34 persons. **Radios:** 1 per 37 persons. **Telephones:** 1 per 87 persons.

Health: Life expectancy at birth (1992): 49 male; 51 female. **Births** (per 1,000 pop.): 51. **Deaths** (per 1,000 pop.): 15. **Natural increase:** 3.6%. **Hospital beds:** 1 per 995 persons. **Physicians:** 1 per 5,531 persons. **Infant mortality** (per 1,000 live births 1994): 113.

Education (1990): **Literacy:** 38%. **Primary school attendance:** 59%.

Major International Organizations: UN (IMF, WHO), Arab League.

Embassy: 600 New Hampshire Ave. NW 20037; 965-4760.

Yemen's territory once was part of the ancient Kindgom of Sheba, or Saba, a prosperous link in trade between Africa and India. A Biblical reference speaks of its gold, spices, and precious stones as gifts borne by the Queen of Sheba to King Solomon.

Yemen became independent in 1918, after years of Ottoman Turkish rule, but remained politically and economically backward. Imam Ahmed ruled 1948-1962. Army officers headed by Brig. Gen. Abdullah al-Salal declared the country to be the Yemen Arab Republic.

The Imam Ahmed's heir, the Imam Mohamad al-Badr, fled to the mountains where tribesmen joined royalist forces; internal warfare between them and the republican forces continued. About 150,000 people died in the fighting.

There was a bloodless coup Nov. 5, 1967. In April 1970 hostilities ended with an agreement between Yemen and Saudi Arabia. On June 13, 1974, an army group, led by Col. Ibrahim al-Hamidi, seized the government. He was assassinated in 1977.

Meanwhile, South Yemen won independence from Britain in 1967, formed out of the British colony of Aden and the British protectorate of South Arabia. It became the Arab world's only Marxist state, taking the name People's Democratic Republic of Yemen in 1970 and signing a friendship treaty with the USSR in 1979 that allowed for the stationing of Soviet troops.

More than 300,000 Yemenis fled from the south to the north after independence, contributing to 2 decades of hostility between the 2 states that flared into warfare twice in the 1970s.

An Arab League-sponsored agreement between North and South Yemen on unification of the 2 countries was signed Mar. 29, 1979. An agreement providing for widespread political and economic cooperation was signed in 1988.

The 2 countries were formally united on May 21, 1990, but regional clan-based rivalries led to full-scale civil war in 1994. Secessionists declared a breakaway state in S Yemen, May 21, 1994. However, northern troops captured the former southern capital of Aden in July.

Yugoslavia

Federal Republic of Yugoslavia

Federativna Republika Jugoslavija

(Data prior to 1992 include former republics Croatia, Slovenia, Bosnia and Herzegovina, and Macedonia)

People: Population: 10,760,000. **Age distrib.** (%): <15: 23; 65+: 10. **Pop. density:** 272 per sq. mi. **Urban:** 47%. **Ethnic groups:** Serbs 63%, Albanians 14%. **Principal languages:** Serbo-Croatian (official), Macedonian, Hungarian, Albanian. **Religions:** Orthodox 65%, Roman Catholic, Muslim.

Geography: Area: 39,449 sq. mi. **Location:** On the Balkan Peninsula in SE Europe. Present-day Yugoslavia consists of the former republics of Serbia and Montenegro. **Neighbors:** Croatia, Bosnia and Herzegovina on W, Hungary on N, Romania, Bulgaria on E, Greece, Albania, Macedonia on S. **Capital:** Belgrade. **Cities** (1992 est.): Belgrade 1.5 mln.

Government: Type: Republic. **Head of state:** Pres. Zoran Lilic; in office: June 1993. **Head of government:** Mirko Marjanovic; in office: Feb. 1994. **Local divisions:** 2 republics. **Defense:** 4%-6% of GDP (1992 est.).

Economy: Industries: Steel, wood products. **Chief crops:** Corn, grains, tobacco, sugar beets. **Minerals:** Antimony, bauxite, lead, mercury, coal, iron, copper, chrome, zinc, salt. **Arable land:** 30%. **Livestock** (1992): cattle: 1.9 mln.; pigs: 3.8 mln.; sheep: 2.7 mln. **Fish catch:** (1991): 36,000 metric tons. **Electricity prod.** (1992): 42.0 bln. kWh. **Labor force:** 5% agric.; 40% ind. & mining.

Finance: Monetary unit: Dinar (Feb. 1993: 225 = $1 US). **Gross national product** (1992): $27-$37 bln. **Per capita GNP:** $2,500-$3,500. **Imports** (1990): $19.1 bln.; partners: EU 54%, USSR 15%. **Exports** (1990): $14.6 bln.; partners: EU 54%, USSR 17%. **Tourism** (1990): $2.7 bln. receipts. **National budget:** NA. **International reserves less gold** (Mar. 1993): $1.4 bln. **Gold:** 1.90 mln. oz t. **Consumer prices** (change in 1991): 117.4%.

Transport: Motor vehicles: in use: 1.4 mln. passenger cars, 132,000 comm. vehicles. **Civil aviation:** 7 airports.

Communications: Television sets: 1 per 3.6 persons. **Radios:** 1 per 6 persons. **Telephones:** 1 per 4.9 persons. **Daily newspaper circ.:** 98 per 1,000 pop.

Health: Life expectancy at birth (1994): 71 male; 76 female. **Births** (per 1,000 pop. 1991): 14. **Deaths** (per 1,000 pop. 1991): 9. **Natural increase:** .6%. **Hospital beds:** 1 per 163 persons. **Physicians:** 1 per 490 persons. **Infant mortality** (per 1,000 live births 1994): 21.

Education (1991): **Literacy:** 90%. Almost all attend primary school.

Major International Organizations: UN (IMF, World Bank).

Embassy: 2410 California St. NW 20008; 462-6566.

Serbia, which had since 1389 been a vassal principality of Turkey, was established as an independent kingdom by the Treaty of Berlin, 1878. Montenegro, independent since 1389, also obtained international recognition in 1878. After the Balkan wars Serbia's boundaries were enlarged by the annexation of Old Serbia and Macedonia, 1913.

When the Austro-Hungarian empire collapsed after World War I, the Kingdom of the Serbs, Croats, and Slovenes was formed from the former provinces of Croatia, Dalmatia, Bosnia, Herzegovina, Slovenia, Voyvodina, and the independent state of Montenegro. The name was later changed to Yugoslavia.

Nazi Germany invaded in 1941. Many Yugoslav partisan troops continued to operate. Among these were the Chetniks led by Draja Mikhailovich, who fought other partisans led by Josip Broz, known as Marshal Tito. Tito, backed by the USSR and Britain from 1943, was in control by the time the Germans had been driven from Yugoslavia in 1945. Mikhailovich was executed July 17, 1946, by the Tito regime.

A constituent assembly proclaimed Yugoslavia a republic Nov. 29, 1945. It became a federated republic Jan. 31, 1946, and Marshal Tito, a Communist, became head of the government. The Stalin policy of dictating to all Communist nations was rejected by Tito. He accepted economic aid and military equipment from the U.S. and received aid in foreign trade also from France and Great Britain. Tito also supported the liberal government of Czechoslovakia in 1968 before the Soviet invasion.

A separatist movement among Croatians brought arrests and a change of leaders in the Croatian Republic in Jan. 1972. Violence by Croatian nationalists and fears of Soviet political intervention led to restrictions on political and intellectual dissent.

Beginning in 1965, reforms designed to decentralize the administration of economic development and to force industries to produce more efficiently were introduced, and considerable trade with the West was developed.

Pres. Tito died May 4, 1980; with his death, the post as head of the Collective Presidency and also that as head of the League of Communists became a rotating system of succession among the members representing each republic.

On Jan. 22, 1990, a Communist Party conference renounced its constitutionally guaranteed leading role in society and called on Parliament to enact "political pluralism, including a multiparty system."

Croatia and Slovenia formally declared independence June 25, 1991. In Croatia, fighting began between Croats and ethnic Serbs. Serbia sent arms and medical supplies to the Serb rebels in Croatia. There were numerous clashes between Croatian forces and Yugoslavian army units and their Serb supporters.

The republics of Serbia and Montenegro proclaimed a new "Federal Republic of Yugoslavia" Apr. 17, 1992. Serbia, under Pres. Slobodan Milosevic, was the main supplier of arms to the ethnic Serb fighters in Bosnia and Herzegovina. The UN imposed sweeping international sanctions on the new Yugoslavia (Serbia and Montenegro) as a means of ending the bloodshed in Bosnia, May 30, 1992. On Aug. 4, 1994, Yugoslavia said it was cutting off support for Bosnian Serbs because they rejected an international partition plan for Bosnia. This prompted the UN to vote for a conditional easing of sanctions, Sept. 23, 1994.

Kosovo: An area in southern Serbia (4,203 sq. mi.), with a population of about 2,000,000, mostly Albanians. The capital is Pristina. The Albanian majority has declared its independence, which Serbia has not recognized.

Vojvodina: An area in northern Serbia (3,304 sq. mi.), with a population of about 2,000,000, mostly Serbian. The capital is Novi Sad.

Zaire

Republic of Zaire

République du Zaïre

People: Population: 42,684,000. **Age distrib.** (%): <15: 45; 65+: 3. **Pop. density:** 47 per sq. mi. **Urban:** 40%. **Ethnic groups:** Bantu tribes 80%, over 200 other tribes. **Principal languages:** French (official), Kongo, Luba, Mongo, Rwanda, others. **Religions:** Christian 70%, Muslim 10%.

Geography: Area: 905,446 sq. mi., one-fourth the size of the U.S. **Location:** In central Africa. **Neighbors:** Congo on W, Central African Republic, Sudan on N, Uganda, Rwanda, Burundi, Tanzania on E, Zambia, Angola on S. **Topography:** Zaire includes the bulk of the Zaire (Congo) R. Basin. The vast central region is a low-lying plateau covered by rain forest. Mountainous terraces in the W, savannas in the S and SE, grasslands toward the N, and the high Ruwenzori Mtns. on the E surround the central region. A short strip of territory borders the Atlantic O. The Zaire R. is 2,718 mi. long. **Capital:** Kinshasa. **Cities** (1991 est.): Kinshasa 3.8 mln.; Lubumbashi 739,000.

Government: Type: Republic with strong presidential authority (in transition). **Head of state:** Pres. Mobutu Sese Seko; b Oct. 14, 1930; in office: Nov. 25, 1965. **Head of government:** Prime Min. Kengo Wa Dondo; named: June 17, 1994. **Local divisions:** 10 regions, Kinshasa. **Defense:** 0.8% of GDP (1988).

Economy: Chief crops: Coffee, rice, sugar cane, bananas, plantains, manioc, mangoes, tea, cocoa, palm oil. **Minerals:** Cobalt (60% of world reserves), copper, cadmium, gold, silver, tin, germanium, zinc, iron, manganese, uranium, radium. **Crude oil reserves** (1987): 111 mln. bbls. **Other resources:** Forests, rubber, ivory. **Arable land:** 3%. **Livestock** (1992): cattle: 1.6 mln.; goats: 3.0 mln. **Fish catch** (1991): 160,000 metric tons. **Electricity prod.** (1991): 6.0 bln. kWh. **Labor force:** 75% agric.

Finance: Monetary unit: Zaire (Feb. 1994: 90.98 = $1 US). **Gross domestic product** (1990): $6.6 bln. **Per capita GDP:** $180. **Imports** (1991): $710 mln.; partners: Chi. 38%, Belg. 16%, Ger. 7%, Fra. 7%. **Exports** (1991): $828 mln.; partners: Belg.-Lux. 36%, U.S. 19%. **National budget** (1990): $1.1 bln. **International reserves less gold** (Nov. 1993): $151 mln. **Gold:** 30,000 oz t. **Consumer prices** (change in 1992): 4,129.2%.

Transport: Railroads: Length: 3,193 mi. **Motor vehicles:** in use: 100,000 passenger cars, 90,000 comm. vehicles. **Civil aviation:** 89 mln. passenger-mi.; 24 airports with scheduled flights. **Chief ports:** Matadi, Boma.

Communications: Television sets: 1 per 1,870 persons. **Radios:** 1 per 12 persons. **Telephones:** 1 per 1,026 persons. **Daily newspaper circ.:** 1 per 1,000 pop.

Health: Life expectancy at birth (1994): 46 male; 49 female. **Births** (per 1,000 pop.): 48. **Deaths** (per 1,000 pop.): 17. **Natural increase:** 3.2%. **Hospital beds:** 1 per 476 persons. **Physicians:** 1 per 23,193 persons. **Infant mortality** (per 1,000 live births 1994): 111.

Education (1990): **Literacy:** 72%.

Major International Organizations: UN and all of its specialized agencies, OAU.

Embassy: 1800 New Hampshire Ave. NW 20009; 234-7690.

The earliest inhabitants of Zaire may have been the pygmies, followed by Bantus from the E and Nilotic tribes from the N. The large Bantu Bakongo kingdom ruled much of Zaire and Angola when Portuguese explorers visited in the 15th century.

Leopold II, king of the Belgians, formed an international group to exploit the Congo in 1876. In 1877 Henry M. Stanley explored the Congo, and in 1878 the king's group sent him back to organize the region and win over the native chiefs. The Conference of Berlin, 1884-85, organized the Congo Free State with Leopold as king and chief owner. Exploitation of native laborers on the rubber plantations caused international criticism and led to granting of a colonial charter, 1908.

Belgian and Congolese leaders agreed Jan. 27, 1960, that the Congo would become independent June 30. In the first general elections, May 31, the National Congolese movement of Patrice Lumumba won 35 of 137 seats in the National Assembly. He was appointed premier June 21, and formed a coalition cabinet.

Widespread violence caused Europeans and others to flee. The UN Security Council Aug. 9, 1960, called on Belgium to withdraw its troops and sent a UN contingent. President Kasavubu removed Lumumba as premier; he was murdered in 1961.

The last UN troops left the Congo June 30, 1964, and Moise Tshombe became president.

On Sept. 7, 1964, leftist rebels set up a "People's Republic" in Stanleyville. Tshombe hired foreign mercenaries and sought to rebuild the Congolese Army. In Nov. and Dec. 1964 rebels killed scores of white hostages and thousands of Congolese; Belgian paratroops, dropped from U.S. transport planes, rescued hundreds. By July 1965 the rebels had lost their effectiveness.

In 1965 Gen. Joseph D. Mobutu was named president. He later changed his name to Mobutu Sese Seko. The country changed its name to Republic of Zaire on Oct. 27, 1971.

Economic difficulties, amid charges of corruption by government officials, plagued Zaire in the 1980s and worsened in the 1990s. In 1990, Pres. Mobutu announced an end to a 20-year ban on multiparty politics. He sought to retain power despite economic collapse, outside pressure, and widespread internal opposition.

During 1994, Zaire was inundated with refugees from the massive ethnic bloodshed in Rwanda.

Zambia

Republic of Zambia

People: Population: 9,188,000. **Age distrib.** (%): <15: 48; 65+: 2. **Pop. density:** 31 per sq. mi. **Urban:** 49%. **Ethnic groups:** Mostly Bantu tribes. **Principal languages:** English (official), Bantu dialects. **Religions:** Christian 50–75%, Hindu, Muslim minorities.

Geography: Area: 290,586 sq. mi., larger than Texas. **Location:** In southern central Africa. **Neighbors:** Zaire on N, Tanzania, Malawi, Mozambique on E, Zimbabwe, Namibia on S, Angola on W. **Topography:** Zambia is mostly high plateau country covered with thick forests, and drained by several important rivers, including the Zambezi. **Capital:** Lusaka. **Cities** (1992): Lusaka 982,000; Kitwe 348,000; Ndola 376,000.

Government: Type: Republic. **Head of state:** Pres. Frederick Chiluba; b 1943; in office: Nov. 2, 1991. **Local divisions:** 9 provinces. **Defense:** 1% of GDP (1992 est.).

Economy: Chief crops: Corn, tobacco, peanuts, cotton, sugar. **Minerals:** Cobalt, copper, zinc, gold, lead, vanadium, manganese, coal. **Other resources:** Rubber, ivory. **Arable land:** 7%. **Livestock** (1992): cattle: 3.0 mln. **Fish catch** (1991): 65,000 metric tons. **Electricity prod.** (1991): 12 bln. kWh. **Labor force:** 85% agric.; 15% ind. and commerce.

Finance: Monetary unit: Kwacha (Mar. 1994: 1.00 = $.01 US). **Gross domestic product** (1992): $4.7 bln. **Per capita GDP:** $380. **Imports** (1991): $1.3 bln.; S Af. 13%, Ger. 6%, U.S. 7%. **Exports** (1991): $1.1 bln.; partners: Jap. 4%, UK 3%, U.S. 10%, Ger. 9%. **National budget** (1991 est.): $767 mln. **International reserves less gold** (Jan. 1992): $184 mln. **Gold:** 15,000 oz t. **Consumer prices** (change in 1993): 187.2%.

Transport: Motor vehicles: in use: 100,000 passenger cars, 70,000 comm. vehicles. **Civil aviation:** 200 mln. passenger-mi.; 8 airports with scheduled flights.

Communications: Television sets: 1 per 41 persons. **Radios:** 1 per 5.0 persons. **Telephones:** 1 per 78 persons. **Daily newspaper circ.:** 12 per 1,000 pop.

Health: Life expectancy at birth (1994): 44 male; 45 female. **Births** (per 1,000 pop.): 46. **Deaths** (per 1,000 pop.): 18. **Natural increase:** 2.8%. **Hospital beds:** 1 per 349 persons. **Physicians:** 1 per 8,437 persons. **Infant mortality** (per 1,000 live births 1994): 85.

Education (1991): **Literacy:** 54%. **Attendance:** less than 50% in grades 1–7.

Major International Organizations: UN (GATT, IMF, WHO), OAU, Commonwealth of Nations.

Embassy: 2419 Massachusetts Ave. NW 20008; 265-9717.

As Northern Rhodesia, the country was under the administration of the South Africa Company, 1889 until 1924, when the office of governor was established, and, subsequently, a legislature. The country became an independent republic within the Commonwealth Oct. 24, 1964.

After the white government of Rhodesia declared its independence from Britain Nov. 11, 1965, relations between Zambia and Rhodesia became strained.

As part of a program of government participation in major industries, a government corporation in 1970 took over 51% of the ownership of 2 foreign-owned copper mining companies. Privately-held land and other enterprises were nationalized in 1975. In the 1980s and 1990s lowered copper prices hurt the economy and severe drought caused famine.

Food riots erupted in June 1990, as the nation suffered its worst violence since independence.

Elections held Oct. 1991 resulted in an end to one-party rule. The new government made efforts to sell off state enterprises.

Zimbabwe

Republic of Zimbabwe

People: Population: 10,975,000. **Age distrib.** (%): <15: 48; 65+: 3. **Pop. density:** 73 per sq. mi. **Urban:** 27%. **Ethnic groups:** Shona 71%, Ndebele 16%. **Principal languages:** English (official), Shona, Sindebele. **Religions:** Predominantly traditional tribal beliefs, Christian minority.

Geography: Area: 150,872 sq. mi., slightly larger than Montana. **Location:** In southern Africa. **Neighbors:** Zambia on N, Botswana on W, S Africa on S, Mozambique on E. **Topography:** Zimbabwe is high plateau country, rising to mountains on eastern border, sloping down on the other borders. **Capital:** Harare. **Cities** (1992 met. est.): Harare 1.2 mln.; Bulawayo 621,000.

Government: Type: Parliamentary democracy. **Head of state:** Pres. Robert Mugabe; b Feb. 21, 1924; in office: Jan. 1, 1988. **Local divisions:** 8 provinces. **Defense:** 6% of GDP (1991).

Economy: Industries: Clothing, chemicals, light industries. **Chief crops:** Tobacco, sugar, cotton, corn, wheat. **Minerals:** Chromium, gold, nickel, asbestos, copper, iron, coal. **Arable land:** 7%. **Livestock** (1992): cattle: 4.7 mln.; goats: 2.5 mln. **Electricity prod.** (1991): 8.9 bln. kWh. **Labor force:** 74% agric.; 16% serv.

Finance: Monetary unit: Dollar (Mar. 1994: 1.00 = $.12 US). **Gross domestic product** (1992): $6.2 bln. **Per capita GDP:** $545. **Imports** (1991): $1.6 bln. partners: EU 31%, So. Afr. 21%. **Exports** (1991): $1.8 bln.; partners: EU 40%. **National budget** (1991): $3.3 bln. **Total reserves less gold** (Mar. 1994): $500 mln. **Consumer prices** (change in 1993): 27.6%.

Transport: Motor vehicles: in use: 178,000 passenger cars, 82,000 comm. vehicles. **Civil aviation:** 491 mln. passenger-mi.; 6 airports with scheduled flights.

Communications: Television sets: 1 per 72 persons. **Radios:** 1 per 19 persons. **Telephones:** 1 per 31 persons. **Daily newspaper circ.:** 21 per 1,000 pop.

Health: Life expectancy at birth (1994): 40 male; 44 female. **Births** (per 1,000 pop.): 37. **Deaths** (per 1,000 pop.): 18. **Natural increase:** 1.9%. **Physicians:** 1 per 6,951 persons. **Infant mortality** (per 1,000 live births 1994): 74.

Education (1990): **Literacy:** 67%. **Attendance:** 90% primary, 15% secondary for Africans; higher for whites, Asians.

Major International Organizations: UN (IMF, World Bank), OAU, Commonwealth of Nations.

Embassy: 1608 New Hampshire Ave. NW 20009; 332-7100.

Britain took over the area as Southern Rhodesia in 1923 from the British South Africa Co. (which, under Cecil Rhodes, had conquered the area by 1897) and granted internal self-government. Under a 1961 constitution, voting was restricted to maintain whites in power. On Nov. 11, 1965, Prime Min. Ian D. Smith announced his country's unilateral declaration of independence. Britain termed the act illegal and demanded Zimbabwe (known as Rhodesia until 1980) broaden voting rights to provide for eventual rule by the majority Africans.

Urged by Britain, the UN imposed sanctions, including embargoes on oil shipments to Zimbabwe. Some oil and gasoline reached Zimbabwe, however, from South Africa and Mozambique, before the latter became independent in 1975. In May 1968, the UN Security Council ordered a trade embargo.

A new constitution came into effect, Mar. 2, 1970. The election law effectively prevented full black representation through income tax requirements.

Intermittent negotiations between the government and various black nationalist groups failed to prevent increasing skirmishes. An "internal settlement" signed Mar. 1978 in which Smith and 3 popular black leaders share control until transfer of power to the black majority was rejected by guerrilla leaders.

In the country's first universal-franchise election, Apr. 21, 1979, Bishop Abel Muzorewa's United African National Council gained a bare majority control of the black-dominated Parliament. Britain, 1979, began efforts to normalize its relationship with Zimbabwe. A British cease-fire was accepted by all parties, Dec. 5. Independence was finally achieved Apr. 18, 1980.

Pres. Robert Mugabe declared Zimbabwe's drought a national disaster and appealed to foreign donors for food, money, and medicine, Mar. 6, 1992. An economic adjustment program caused widespread hardship.

Area and Population of the World

Source: Bureau of the Census, U.S. Dept. of Commerce; prior to 1950, Rand McNally & Co.

Continent or Region	Area (1,000 sq. mi.)	% of Earth	Population (est., thousands) 1650	1750	1850	1900	1950	1980	1994	% World Total, 1994
North America	9,400	16.2	5,000	5,000	39,000	106,000	166,000	252,000	289,000	5.1
South America	6,900	11.9	8,000	7,000	20,000	38,000	—	—	—	—
Latin America, Caribbean	—	—	—	—	—	—	166,000	364,000	474,000	8.4
Europe	3,800	6.6	100,000	140,000	265,000	400,000	392,000	484,000	509,000	9.0
Asia	17,400	30.1	335,000	476,000	754,000	932,000	1,368,000	2,494,000	3,344,000	59.2
Africa	11,700	20.2	100,000	95,000	95,000	118,000	281,000	594,000	701,000	12.4
Former USSR	—	—	—	—	—	—	180,000	266,000	296,000	5.2
Oceania, incl. Australia	3,300	5.7	2,000	2,000	2,000	6,000	12,000	23,000	28,000	0.5
Antarctica	5,400	9.3	Uninhabited							
World	**57,900**	**—**	**550,000**	**725,000**	**1,175,000**	**1,600,000**	**2,564,000**	**4,478,000**	**5,642,000**	**—**

Figures may not add to total because of independent rounding.

Leading Countries in Population and Area in 1994

China has the highest population in the world, with 1.19 billion inhabitants, more than one-fifth of the world's population. India had more than 900 million people and was expected to reach 1 billion by the end of the decade. The United States had the third-largest population, with over 260 million, followed by Indonesia, Brazil, and Russia. Russia is the largest country in area, with over 6.5 million square miles, followed by Canada, China, the United States, and Brazil.

Population of World's Largest Cities

Source: Bureau of the Census, U.S. Dept. of Commerce

The table below represents one attempt at comparing the world's largest cities. The cities are defined as population clusters of continuous built-up areas with a population density of a least 5,000 persons per square mile. The boundary of the city was determined by examining detailed maps of each city in conjunction with the most recent official population statistics. Exclaves of areas exceeding the minimum population density were added to the city if the intervening gap was less than one mile. To the extent practical, nonresidential areas such as parks, airports, industrial complexes, and water were excluded from the area reported for each city, thus making the population density reflective of the concentrations in the residential portions of the city. By using a consistent definition for the city, it is possible to make comparisons of the cities on the basis of total population, area, and population density.

The population of each city was projected based on projected country populations and the proportion of each city population to the total population of the country at the time of the last 2 censuses. Figures in the table below may differ from city population figures elsewhere in *The World Almanac* because of different methods of determining population. NA = not available.

City, Country	1991 (thousands)	2000 (thousands projected)	Area (sq. mi.)	Density 1991 (pop per sq. mi.)
Tokyo-Yokohama, Japan	27,245	29,971	1,089	25,019
Mexico City, Mexico	20,899	27,872	522	40,037
São Paulo, Brazil	18,701	25,354	451	41,466
Seoul, South Korea	16,792	21,976	342	49,101
New York, U.S.	14,625	14,648	1,274	11,480
Osaka-Kobe-Kyoto, Japan	13,872	14,287	495	28,025
Bombay, India	12,101	15,357	95	127,461
Calcutta, India	11,898	14,088	209	56,927
Rio de Janeiro, Brazil	11,688	14,169	260	44,952
Buenos Aires, Argentina	11,657	12,911	535	21,790
Moscow, Russia	10,446	11,121	379	27,562
Manila, Philippines	10,156	12,846	188	54,024
Los Angeles, U.S.	10,130	10,714	1,110	9,126
Cairo, Egypt	10,099	12,512	104	97,106
Jakarta, Indonesia	9,882	12,804	76	130,026
Tehran, Iran	9,779	14,251	112	87,312
London, U.K.	9,115	8,574	874	10,429
Delhi, India	8,778	11,849	138	63,612
Paris, France	8,720	8,803	432	20,185
Karachi, Pakistan	8,014	11,299	190	42,179
Lagos, Nigeria	7,998	12,528	56	142,821
Essen, Germany	7,452	7,239	704	10,585
Shanghai, China	6,936	7,540	78	88,924
Lima, Peru	6,815	9,241	120	56,794
Taipei, Taiwan	6,695	8,516	138	48,517
Istanbul, Turkey	6,678	8,875	165	40,476
Chicago, U.S.	6,529	6,568	762	8,568
Bangkok, Thailand	5,955	7,587	102	58,379
Bogotá, Colombia	5,913	7,935	79	74,851
Madras, India	5,896	7,384	115	51,270
Beijing, China	5,762	5,993	151	38,156
Hong Kong	5,693	5,956	23	247,501
Santiago, Chile	5,378	6,294	128	40,018
Pusan, South Korea	5,008	6,700	54	92,735
Tianjin, China	4,850	5,298	49	98,990
Bangalore, India	4,802	6,764	50	96,041
Nagoya, Japan	4,791	5,303	307	15,606
Milan, Italy	4,749	4,839	344	13,806
St. Petersburg, Russia	4,672	4,738	139	33,614
Madrid, Spain	4,513	5,104	66	68,385
Dhaka, Bangladesh	4,419	6,492	32	138,108
Lahore, Pakistan	4,376	5,864	57	76,779
Shenyang, China	4,289	4,684	39	109,974
Barcelona, Spain	4,227	4,834	87	48,584
Baghdad, Iraq	4,059	5,239	97	41,843
Manchester, U.K.	4,030	3,827	357	11,287
Philadelphia, U.S.	4,003	3,979	471	8,499
San Francisco, U.S.	3,986	4,214	428	9,315
Belo Horizonte, Brazil	3,812	5,125	79	48,249
Kinshasa, Zaire	3,747	5,646	57	65,732
Ho Chi Minh City, Vietnam	3,725	4,481	31	120,168
Ahmadabad, India	3,709	4,837	32	115,893
Hyderabad, India	3,673	4,765	88	41,741
Sydney, Australia	3,536	3,708	338	10,460
Athens, Greece	3,507	3,866	116	30,237
Miami, U.S.	3,471	3,894	448	7,748
Guadalajara, Mexico	3,370	4,451	78	43,205
Guangzhou, China	3,360	3,652	79	42,537
Surabaya, Indonesia	3,248	3,632	43	75,544
Caracas, Venezuela	3,217	3,435	54	59,582
Wuhan, China	3,200	3,495	65	49,225
Toronto, Canada	3,145	3,296	154	20,420
Porto Alegre, Brazil	3,114	4,109	231	13,479
Rome, Italy	3,033	3,129	69	43,949
Berlin, Germany	3,021	3,006	274	11,026
Naples, Italy	2,978	3,134	62	48,032
Casablanca, Morocco	2,973	3,795	35	84,953
Detroit, U.S.	2,969	2,735	468	6,343
Alexandria, Egypt	2,941	3,304	35	84,022
Monterrey, Mexico	2,939	3,974	77	38,169
Montreal, Canada	2,916	3,071	164	17,779
Melbourne, Australia	2,915	2,968	327	8,914
Ankara, Turkey	2,872	3,777	55	52,221
Yangon, Myanmar	2,864	3,332	47	60,927
Kiev, Ukraine	2,796	3,237	62	45,095
Dallas, U.S.	2,787	3,257	419	6,652
Singapore, Singapore	2,719	2,913	78	34,856
Taegu, South Korea	2,651	4,051	NA	NA
Harbin, China	2,643	2,887	30	88,110
Washington, U.S.	2,565	2,707	357	7,184
Poona, India	2,547	3,647	NA	NA
Boston, U.S.	2,476	2,485	303	8,172
Lisbon, Portugal	2,426	2,717	NA	NA
Tashkent, Uzbekistan	2,418	2,947	NA	NA
Chongqing, China	2,395	2,961	NA	NA
Chengdu, China	2,372	2,591	25	94,870
Vienna, Austria	2,344	2,647	NA	NA
Houston, U.S.	2,329	2,651	310	7,512
Budapest, Hungary	2,303	2,335	138	16,691
Salvador, Brazil	2,298	3,286	NA	NA

Current Population and Projections for All Countries: 1994, 2010, and 2020

Source: Bureau of the Census, U.S. Dept. of Commerce

(in thousands)

Country	1994	2010	2020
Afghanistan	16,903	32,889	41,518
Albania	3,374	4,016	4,424
Algeria	27,895	38,186	44,096
Andorra	64	79	78
Angola	9,804	14,982	19,272
Antigua and Barbuda	65	74	80
Argentina	33,913	39,947	43,190
Armenia	3,522	3,854	3,959
Australia	18,077	21,151	22,724
Austria	7,955	8,259	8,329
Azerbaijan	7,684	8,995	9,689
Bahamas	273	332	356
Bahrain	586	849	1,008
Bangladesh	125,149	176,902	210,248
Barbados	256	272	284
Belarus	10,405	10,864	11,047
Belgium	10,063	10,135	10,015
Belize	209	299	356
Benin	5,342	8,955	11,920
Bhutan	1,739	2,474	3,035
Bolivia	7,719	10,671	12,547
Bosnia and Herzegovina	4,651	5,039	5,117
Botswana	1,359	1,871	2,187
Brazil	158,739	183,742	197,466
Brunei	285	410	491
Bulgaria	8,800	8,757	8,642
Burkina Faso	10,135	14,478	18,123
Burundi	6,125	8,382	10,734
Cambodia	10,265	15,679	20,208
Cameroon	13,132	21,165	28,329

Country	1994	2010	2020
Canada	28,114	32,265	34,347
Cape Verde	423	646	812
Central African Republic	3,142	3,898	4,561
Chad	5,467	7,680	9,396
Chile	13,951	17,266	19,225
China	1,190,431	1,348,429	1,424,725
Colombia	35,578	44,504	49,266
Comoros	530	919	1,249
Congo	2,447	3,219	3,775
Costa Rica	3,342	4,537	5,257
Côte d'Ivoire	14,296	22,924	29,705
Croatia	4,698	4,729	4,647
Cuba	11,064	12,274	12,755
Cyprus	730	829	883
Czech Republic	10,408	10,892	10,991
Denmark	5,188	5,311	5,307
Djibouti	413	588	751
Dominica	88	107	118
Dominican Republic	7,826	9,931	11,153
Ecuador	10,677	13,990	15,894
Egypt	59,325	82,478	97,434
El Salvador	5,753	7,603	8,763
Equatorial Guinea	410	615	783
Eritrea	—	—	—
Estonia	1,617	1,776	1,880
Ethiopia	58,710	94,496	124,294
Fiji	764	933	1,037
Finland	5,069	5,246	5,283
France	57,840	61,001	61,793
Gabon	1,139	1,445	1,675
The Gambia	959	1,561	2,073
Georgia	5,681	6,253	6,506
Germany	81,088	82,837	82,385
Ghana	17,225	27,305	35,877
Greece	10,565	10,920	10,689
Grenada	94	115	141
Guatemala	10,721	15,284	18,131
Guinea	6,392	9,303	11,664
Guinea-Bissau	1,098	1,579	1,925
Guyana	729	767	833
Haiti	6,491	8,121	9,499
Honduras	5,315	7,643	9,042
Hungary	10,319	10,477	10,449
Iceland	264	293	306
India	919,903	1,173,621	1,320,746
Indonesia	200,410	250,033	276,474
Iran	65,612	107,676	143,624
Iraq	19,890	34,545	46,260
Ireland	3,539	3,846	4,034
Israel	5,051	6,241	6,934
Italy	58,138	59,089	57,844
Jamaica	2,555	3,110	3,446
Japan	125,107	129,361	126,062
Jordan	3,961	6,213	7,595
Kazakhstan	17,268	18,794	19,404
Kenya	28,241	37,990	44,240
Kiribati	78	95	98
Korea, North	23,067	28,491	30,969
Korea, South	45,083	51,677	54,014
Kuwait	1,819	3,220	4,091
Kyrgyzstan	4,698	5,810	6,490
Laos	4,702	7,168	8,923
Latvia	2,749	3,009	3,194
Lebanon	3,620	4,973	5,748
Lesotho	1,944	2,771	3,314
Liberia	2,973	4,903	6,449
Libya	5,057	8,913	12,391
Liechtenstein	30	34	36
Lithuania	3,848	4,263	4,505
Luxembourg	402	428	436
Macedonia	2,214	2,478	2,578
Madagascar	13,428	22,064	29,362
Malawi	9,732	13,233	16,697
Malaysia	19,283	26,589	31,681
Maldives	252	423	554
Mali	9,113	14,966	20,427
Malta	367	404	420
Marshall Islands	54	100	144
Mauritania	2,193	3,630	4,859
Mauritius	1,117	1,322	1,428
Mexico	92,202	120,115	136,096
Micronesia	120	141	143
Moldova	4,473	4,738	4,880
Monaco	31	33	34
Mongolia	2,430	3,545	4,309
Morocco	28,559	38,112	43,701
Mozambique	17,346	27,381	35,240
Myanmar	44,277	57,720	65,914
Namibia	1,596	2,705	3,638
Nauru	10	11	12
Nepal	21,042	30,783	37,767
Netherlands	15,368	16,140	16,222
New Zealand	3,389	3,543	3,586
Nicaragua	4,097	5,864	6,945
Niger	8,635	14,652	20,166
Nigeria	98,091	161,969	215,893
Norway	4,315	4,424	4,446
Oman	1,701	2,991	4,175
Pakistan	128,856	195,108	251,330
Panama	2,630	3,422	3,886
Papua New Guinea	4,197	5,925	7,044
Paraguay	5,214	7,730	9,474
Peru	23,651	30,483	34,340
Philippines	69,809	90,316	101,530
Poland	38,655	41,332	42,474
Portugal	10,524	10,997	11,038
Qatar	513	645	713
Romania	23,181	23,950	24,337
Russia	149,609	155,933	159,263
Rwanda[1]	8,374	11,755	15,006
Saint Kitts and Nevis	41	50	57
Saint Lucia	145	169	193
Saint Vincent and the Grenadines	115	136	152
San Marino	24	26	27
São Tomé and Príncipe	137	196	232
Saudi Arabia	18,197	30,494	42,085
Senegal	8,731	14,318	19,127
Seychelles	72	81	86
Sierra Leone	4,630	7,041	9,036
Singapore	2,859	3,206	3,335
Slovakia	5,404	5,883	6,078
Slovenia	1,972	2,025	2,008
Solomon Islands	386	620	767
Somalia	6,667	12,588	16,832
South Africa	43,931	65,850	82,502
Spain	39,303	40,682	40,421
Sri Lanka	18,033	20,972	22,463
Sudan	29,420	46,167	58,090
Suriname	423	534	598
Swaziland	936	1,566	2,128
Sweden	8,778	9,228	9,469
Switzerland	7,040	7,519	7,696
Syria	14,887	25,768	34,309
Taiwan	21,299	24,092	25,122
Tajikistan	5,995	8,619	10,429
Tanzania	27,986	38,651	48,526
Thailand	59,510	64,181	62,941
Togo	4,255	7,401	10,146
Tonga	105	119	128
Trinidad and Tobago	1,328	1,583	1,722
Tunisia	8,727	10,937	12,144
Turkey	62,154	81,790	93,362
Turkmenistan	3,995	5,277	6,116
Tuvalu	10	12	15
Uganda	19,859	26,997	34,106
Ukraine	51,847	52,280	52,337
United Arab Emirates	2,791	4,873	6,080
United Kingdom	58,135	59,617	60,042
United States	260,714	298,621	323,113
Uruguay	3,199	3,594	3,822
Uzbekistan	22,609	30,380	35,422
Vanuatu	170	230	266
Venezuela	20,562	27,407	31,312
Vietnam	73,104	91,729	102,359
Western Samoa	204	288	341
Yemen	11,105	18,985	25,907
Yugoslavia	10,760	11,625	11,881
Zaire	42,684	69,079	91,860
Zambia	9,188	12,614	15,828
Zimbabwe	10,975	12,990	14,620
Regions			
Africa	701,327	1,060,838	1,351,270
Asia	3,344,623	4,165,409	4,659,792
Latin America and Caribbean	474,155	587,345	652,416
North America	288,952	331,027	357,611
Europe	508,828	528,083	530,148
Former Soviet Union	296,000	320,844	335,119
Oceania inc. Australia	28,265	34,109	37,369
World[2]	**5,642,151**	**7,027,656**	**7,923,725**

(1) Numbers for Rwanda do not include massive mortalities and dislocations beginning in Apr. 1994. (2) Figures may not add to total due to rounding and exclusion of certain pseudo-national entities.

Reported AIDS Cases and Estimated HIV Infection by Region, 1993

Source: World Health Organization

The interval between infection with the human immunodeficiency virus (HIV) and development of acquired immune deficiency syndrome (AIDS) is estimated to be 7-10 years. The actual number of AIDS cases is estimated to be 2.5 million—4 times the number of reported cases—because of underdiagnosis, underreporting, and the use of different surveillance case definitions of AIDS in different countries.

Region	Cumulative AIDS Cases (Jan. 1993)	Estimated Total HIV[1] (mid-1993)
Sub-Saharan Africa	210,376	8,000,000+
South/Southeast Asia	1,445	1,500,000+
Latin America and Caribbean	64,048	1,500,000
North America	249,035	1,000,000+
Western Europe	78,049	500,000
North Africa/Middle East	1,160	75,000
Eastern Europe/Central Asia	2,850	50,000
Oceania, inc. Australia	3,963	25,000+
East Asia/Pacific	663	25,000+
World	**611,589**	**13,000,000+**

(1) Estimated cumulative HIV prevalence in adults. According to WHO, 1 million children had been infected with HIV by mid-1993.

The World's Refugees

(as of Dec. 31, 1992)

Source: *World Refugee Survey 1993,* U.S. Committee for Refugees, a nonprofit corp. The refugees in this table include only those who are in need of protection and/or assistance and do not include refugees who have resettled.

Place of asylum	Mostly from	Number
Total Africa		**5,825,000**
Algeria	W. Sahara, Mali	121,000[1]
Benin	Togo	120,000
Burundi	Rwanda, Zaire	110,000[1]
Côte d'Ivoire	Liberia	250,000
Ethiopia	Somalia, Sudan	156,000[1]
Ghana	Togo, Liberia	133,000
Guinea	Liberia, Sierra Leone	570,000[1]
Kenya	Somalia, Sudan, Ethiopia	332,000[1]
Liberia	Sierra Leone	110,000
Malawi	Mozambique	700,000
Rwanda	Burundi	370,000
S. Africa	Mozambique	300,000[1]
Sudan	Eritrea, Ethiopia, Chad	633,000[1]
Tanzania	Burundi, Mozambique	479,500
Uganda	Sudan, Rwanda	257,000[1]
Zaire	Angola, Sudan, Burundi	452,000
Zambia	Angola, Mozambique, Zaire	158,500
Zimbabwe	Mozambique	200,000
Total East Asia/Pacific		**468,000**
China	Vietnam	296,900[1]
Thailand	Myanmar, Laos, Vietnam	108,300
Total Europe & No. America		**2,785,000**
Armenia	Azerbaijan	290,000[1]
Azerbaijan	Armenia, Uzbekistan	251,000[1]
Croatia	Former Yugoslavia	280,000[1]
Germany	Former Yugoslavia, other	529,100
Russia	various	347,500[1]
United States	various	150,400
Yugoslavia[2]	Former Yugoslavia	357,000[1]
Total Latin America/Caribbean		**102,000**
Total Middle East/South & Central Asia		**7,075,000**
Bangladesh	Myanmar	199,000
India	Tibet, Sri Lanka, Bangladesh	325,600[1]
Iran	Afghanistan, Iraq	1,995,000[1]
Jordan	Palestinians	1,073,600
Pakistan	Afghanistan	1,482,300
Syria	Palestinians	319,200
West Bank	Palestinians	479,000
Total Refugees		**16,255,000**

(1) Significant variance among sources in number reported. (2) Serbia/Montenegro.

Principal Sources of Refugees

Afghanistan	3,429,800[1]
Palestinians	2,801,300
Mozambique	1,332,000[1]
Former Yugoslavia	1,319,650[1]
Burundi	780,000
Liberia	701,000[1]
Somalia	491,200[1]
Eritrea	421,500[1]
Sudan	373,000
Angola	335,000
Vietnam	303,500
Azerbaijan	290,000[1]
Myanmar	289,500[1]
Rwanda	275,000[1]
Sierra Leone	260,000[1]
Togo	240,000
Ethiopia	232,200
Armenia	200,000[1]
Tajikistan	153,000[1]
Georgia	143,000[1]

(1) Significant variance among sources in number reported.

U.S. Immigration Law

Source: Immigration and Naturalization Service, U.S. Dept. of Justice

The Immigration Act of 1990 became law when it was signed by Pres. George Bush on Nov. 29, 1990. Bush called the bill the "most comprehensive reform of U.S. immigration laws in 66 years." Most of its provisions amend the Immigration and Nationality Act, which remains the basic law. The new law raised the total number of numerically limited immigrants entering the U.S. annually in FY 1992-94 to 700,000 (excluding refugees whose admission numbers are announced annually and some others not subject to limitation). The visas would be distributed as follows:

- 465,000 for family immigrants;
- 55,000 for the spouses and children of aliens legalized under IRCA (see below);
- 140,000 for employment-based immigrants;
- 40,000 for nationals from "adversely affected" countries.

Beginning in FY 1995 the number drops from 700,000 to 675,000. These visas would be distributed as follows:

- 480,000 for family immigrants;
- 140,000 for employment-based immigrants;
- 55,000 for "diversity immigrants."

Family Immigrants

Fiscal year 1992-94: 465,000 minus the number of "immediate relatives" admitted the previous fiscal year, *plus* any numbers unused by the employment-based preference system. During this period, the number of family-sponsored visas could not fall below 226,000 (10,000 visas higher than the previous allocation). If visa availability dipped below this new floor, the shortfall would be made up from the category below.

During this period, 55,000 additional visas would be made available to the spouses and children of aliens legalized under the Immigration Reform and Control Act (IRCA) of 1986.

Fiscal year 1995 and beyond: 480,000 minus the number of "immediate relatives" admitted during the previous fiscal year, plus any unused numbers under the employment-based preference system. The number of family-sponsored visas cannot drop below a floor of 226,000.

New Family Preference System

First preference—unmarried sons and daughters of U.S. citizens: 23,400 visas plus unused visas from the 4th preference.

Second preference—spouses and unmarried children of Lawful Permanent Residents (LPRs): 114,200 visas, plus any visas available above the floor of 226,000 family preference visas, plus any unused visas from the previous preference.

The category is subdivided as follows: A minimum of 77% of the visas allocated to the category goes to the spouses and minor children of LPRs; 75% of the visas are issued without regard to per country ceilings; these visas are distributed in the order in which the petitions were filed; a maximum of 23% of the category visa allocation goes to the unmarried sons and daughters of LPRs. This group of visas continues to be subject to per country ceilings.

Third preference—married sons and daughters of U.S. citizens; 23,400 visas plus unused visas from all earlier preferences.

Fourth preference—brothers and sisters of U.S. citizens: 65,000 plus unused visas from all earlier preferences.

Employment-Based Immigrants

A total of 140,000 plus, beginning in 1994, any unused numbers under the family-sponsored system. These visas would be distributed as follows:

First preference—Priority Workers—28.6% of the employment-based limit plus visas unused by the fourth and fifth employment-based preferences "investors" and "special immigrants." The category is subdivided as follows: (1) extraordinary ability, demonstrated by sustained national or international acclaim, in the sciences, arts, education, business, and athletics; no U.S. employer required; (2) outstanding, internationally recognized and with at least 3 years of experience, professors and researchers seeking to enter in senior positions; U.S. employer required; (3) executives and managers of multinationals—requires one year of prior service with the firm during the preceding 3 years; the terms are extensively defined; U.S. employer required.

Second preference—Professionals with advanced degrees and aliens of exceptional ability—28.6% of the employment-based limit plus any unused "priority worker" visas. A U.S. employer and labor certification are required—although the Attorney General can waive both requirements. Members of the professions with advanced degrees or exceptional ability in the sciences, arts, or business. The possession of a degree, certificate, or license is not by itself considered sufficient evidence of exceptional ability.

Third preference—Skilled workers, professionals, and "other workers"—40,000 visas plus any visas unused by the 2 previous categories. Requires a U.S. employer and labor certification. Skilled workers must be in an occupation that requires at least 2 years training or experience. Professionals need a bachelor's degree. "Other workers" refers to unskilled workers. Their numbers are limited to no more than 10,000 visas per year.

Fourth preference—Special immigrants—7.1% of the employment-based limit. This category includes ministers of religion and persons working for religious organizations for at least 2 years, foreign medical graduates, employees of the U.S. government abroad including certain employees of the U.S. mission in Hong Kong who file for admission as special immigrants before Jan. 1, 2002, retired employees of international organizations, etc.

Fifth preference—7.1% of the employment-based limit—7,000 for investors of $1 million in urban areas and 3,000 for investors of no less than $500,000 in rural or high-unemployment areas. The Attorney General may increase the required investment amount up to $3 million for high employment areas. Investment must create employment for at least 10 U.S. workers.

Diversity Immigrant (DV) Category

The Immigration and Nationality Act provides 55,000 immigrant visas each fiscal year (beginning with FY 1995) to provide immigration opportunities for persons from countries other than the principal sources of current immigration to the US. DV visas are divided among six geographic regions. Not more than 3,850 visas (7% of the 55,000 visa limit) may be provided to immigrants from any one country.

The allotment of FY 1995 visa numbers for each region is as follows: Africa, 20,200; Asia, 6,837; Europe, 24,549; North America (Bahamas), 8; South America, Central America, and the Caribbean, 2,589; and Oceania, 817.

Diversity Immigrant Visa Lottery (DV) Drawing

On Aug. 12, 1994, the National Visa Center in Portsmouth, NH, began the selection of winners of the DV lottery. The first notices were sent to the winners in September.

The DV registration mail-in was held June 1-30, 1994. During this one-month period, the National Visa Center received approximately 6.5 million qualified entries. An additional 1.5 million entries received during those dates were disqualified for not providing the requested information or following published guidelines.

In order to issue all 55,000 visas in FY 1995, the National Visa Center planned to notify 110,000 principal applicants. Persons whose entries were not selected were not notified. Winners were sent instructions on how to apply for an immigrant visa. During the visa interview, applicants must provide proof of a high school education or its equivalent or must show two years of work experience within the past five years in an occupation that requires at least two years of training or experience.

Those selected needed to act on their immigrant visa applications quickly. As soon as 55,000 visas were issued, the program for FY 1995 would end.

Naturalization: How to Become an American Citizen

Source: Federal Statutes

A person who desires to be naturalized as a citizen of the United States may obtain the necessary application form as well as detailed information from the nearest office of the Immigration and Naturalization Service or from the clerk of a court handling naturalization cases.

An applicant must be at least 18 years old and must have been a lawful resident of the United States continuously for 5 years. For husbands and wives of U.S. citizens the period is 3 years in most instances. Special provisions apply to certain veterans of the armed forces.

An applicant must have been physically present in the country for at least half of the required 5 years' residence.

Every applicant for naturalization must:

(1) demonstrate an understanding of the English language, including an ability to read, write, and speak words in ordinary usage in the English language (persons physically unable to do so and persons who, on the date of their examinations, are over 55 years of age and have been lawful permanent residents of the United States for 15 years or more are exempt);

(2) have been a person of good moral character, attached to the principles of the Constitution, and well disposed to the good order and happiness of the United States for 5 years just before filing the petition or for whatever other period of residence is required in the particular case and continue to be such a person until admitted to citizenship; and

(3) demonstrate a knowledge and understanding of the fundamentals of the history, and the principles and form of government, of the United States. This can be done at private, designated testing entities or at the interview before an immigration examiner.

At the interview the applicant may be represented by a lawyer or social service agency. There is a 30-day wait. If action is favorable, there is a swearing in ceremony conducted administratively or judicially. At that ceremony the following oath of allegiance is administered:

I hereby declare, on oath, that I absolutely and entirely renounce and abjure all allegiance and fidelity to any foreign prince, potentate, state or sovereignty, to whom or which I have heretofore been a subject or citizen; that I will support and defend the Constitution and laws of the United States of America against all enemies, foreign and domestic; that I will bear true faith and allegiance to the same; that I will bear arms on behalf of the United States when required by the law; that I will perform noncombatant service in the armed forces of the United States when required by the law; that I will perform work of national importance under civilian direction when required by the law; and that I take this obligation freely without any mental reservation or purpose of evasion; so help me God.

Major International Organizations

As of mid-1994

Association of Southeast Asian Nations (ASEAN), formed in 1967 to promote economic, social, and cultural cooperation and development among the non-Communist states of the region. Members in 1994 were Brunei, Indonesia, Malaysia, Philippines, Singapore, and Thailand. Annual ministerial meetings set policy; a central Secretariat in Jakarta and specialized intergovernmental committees work in trade, transportation, communications, agriculture, science, finance, and culture.

Caribbean Community and Common Market (CARICOM), established July 4, 1973. Its function is to further cooperation in economics, health, education, culture, science and technology, and tax administration, as well as the coordination of foreign policy. Members in 1994 were Antigua and Barbuda, Bahamas, Barbados, Belize, Dominica, Grenada, Guyana, Jamaica, Montserrat, Saint Kitts and Nevis, Saint Lucia, Saint Vincent and the Grenadines, and Trinidad and Tobago.

Commonwealth of Independent States (CIS), created Dec. 1991 upon the disbanding of the Soviet Union. It is made up of 12 of the 15 former Soviet constituent republics. Members in 1994 were Armenia, Azerbaijan, Belarus, Georgia, Kazakhstan, Kyrgyzstan, Moldova, Russia, Tajikistan, Turkmenistan, Ukraine, and Uzbekistan. The commonwealth is not in itself a state but an alliance of fully independent states. Commonwealth policy is set through coordinating bodies such as a Council of Heads of State and Council of Heads of Government. The capital of the commonwealth is Minsk, Belarus.

The Commonwealth, originally called the British Commonwealth of Nations, and then the Commonwealth of Nations, an association of nations and dependencies loosely joined by a common interest based on having been parts of the old British Empire. The British monarch is the symbolic head of the Commonwealth.

There are 51 self-governing independent nations in the Commonwealth, plus various colonies and protectorates. As of 1994, the members were the United Kingdom of Great Britain and Northern Ireland and 15 other nations recognizing the British monarch, represented by a governor-general, as their head of state: Antigua and Barbuda, Australia, The Bahamas, Barbados, Belize, Canada, Grenada, Jamaica, New Zealand, Papua New Guinea, Saint Kitts and Nevis, Saint Lucia, Saint Vincent and the Grenadines, Solomon Islands, and Tuvalu (special member); and 35 countries with their own heads of state: Bangladesh, Botswana, Brunei, Cyprus, Dominica, The Gambia, Ghana, Guyana, India, Kenya, Kiribati, Lesotho, Malawi, Malaysia, The Maldives, Malta, Mauritius, Namibia, Nauru (special member), Nigeria, Pakistan, Seychelles, Sierra Leone, Singapore, South Africa, Sri Lanka, Swaziland, Tanzania, Tonga, Trinidad and Tobago, Uganda, Vanuatu, Western Samoa, Zambia, and Zimbabwe.

The Commonwealth facilitates consultation among member states through meetings of prime ministers and finance ministers, and through a permanent Secretariat. Members consult on economic, scientific, educational, financial, legal, and military matters, and try to coordinate policies.

European Union (EU)—known as the European Community (EC) until 1994—the collective designation of three organizations with common membership: the European Economic Community (Common Market), the European Coal and Steel Community, and the European Atomic Energy Community (Euratom). The 12 full members in 1994 were Belgium, Denmark, France, Germany, Greece, Ireland, Italy, Luxembourg, Netherlands, Portugal, Spain, and United Kingdom. Four more nations—Austria, Finland, Norway, and Sweden—were scheduled to enter the Union on Jan. 1, 1995, pending 1994 referendum votes in each country. Austrian voters approved EU membership by a 2 to 1 margin on June 12, 1994. Some 60 nations in Africa, the Caribbean, and the Pacific are affiliated under the Lomé Convention.

A merger of the 3 communities' executives went into effect July 1, 1967, though the component organizations date back to 1951 and 1958. The Council of Ministers, the Commission of the European Communities, the European Parliament, and the European Court of Justice comprise the permanent structure. The EU aims to integrate the economies, coordinate social developments, and bring about political union of the democratic states of Europe. Effective Dec. 31, 1992, there are no restrictions on the movement of goods, services, capital, workers, and tourists within the EU. There are also common agricultural, fisheries, and nuclear research policies.

Leaders of the 12 member nations met Dec. 9–11, 1991, in Maastricht, the Netherlands. Treaties on monetary union and political union and accompanying protocols agreed upon by the leaders:

- Committed the organization to launching a common currency for at least some nations by 1999. Britain and, later, Denmark were allowed to "opt out" of joining.
- Sought to establish common foreign policies for the members.
- Laid the groundwork for a common defense policy.
- Expanded the policy issues in which the organization would have a voice.
- Gave the organization a leading role in social policy. Britain was not included in this plan.
- Pledged increased aid for the 4 poorest member nations—Ireland, Greece, Spain, and Portugal.
- Slightly increased the powers of the 567-member European Parliament.

The treaties went into effect Nov. 1, 1993, following ratification by all 12 members.

European Free Trade Association (EFTA), created May 3, 1960, to promote expansion of free trade. Current members are Austria, Finland, Iceland, Liechtenstein, Norway, Sweden, and Switzerland. By Dec. 31, 1966, tariffs and quotas between member nations had been eliminated. Members of the association entered into free trade agreements with the EU in 1972 and 1973. In 1992 the EFTA and EU concluded an agreement to create a single market—with free flow of goods, services, capital, and labor—encompassing the nations of the two organizations.

Group of Seven (G-7), organization of seven major industrial democracies who meet periodically to discuss world economic and other issues. Established Sept. 22, 1985. Members are Canada, France, Germany, Italy, Japan, United Kingdom, and United States.

International Criminal Police Organization (Interpol), created June 13, 1956, to ensure and promote the widest possible mutual assistance between all police authorities within the limits of the law existing in the different countries and in the spirit of the Universal Declaration of Human Rights. There were 159 members (independent nations), plus 5 subbureaus (dependencies), in 1994.

Arab League (League of Arab States), created Mar. 22, 1945. Members in 1994 were Algeria, Bahrain, Djibouti, Egypt, Iraq, Jordan, Kuwait, Lebanon, Libya, Mauritania, Morocco, Oman, The Palestine Liberation Org., Qatar, Saudi Arabia, Somalia, Sudan, Syria, Tunisia, United Arab Emirates, and Yemen. The League promotes economic, social, political, and military cooperation and mediates disputes among the Arab states; it represents Arab states in certain international negotiations. The league's headquarters is in Cairo.

North Atlantic Treaty Organization (NATO), created by treaty (signed Apr. 4, 1949; in effect Aug. 24, 1949). Members in 1994 were Belgium, Canada, Denmark, France, Germany, Greece, Iceland, Italy, Luxembourg, Netherlands, Norway, Portugal, Spain, Turkey, United Kingdom, and United States. The members agreed to settle disputes by peaceful means; to develop their individual and collective capacity to resist armed attack; to regard an attack on one as an attack on all; and to take necessary action to repel an attack under Article 51 of the United Nations Charter.

The NATO structure consists of a Council and a Military Committee of 3 commands (Allied Command Europe, Allied Command Atlantic, Allied Command Channel) and the Canada-U.S. Regional Planning Group.

With the dissolution of the Soviet Union and the end of the cold war in the early 1990s, NATO members sought to modify the organization's mission, putting greater stress on political action and creating a rapid deployment force to react to local crises. Former Warsaw Pact members were no longer considered adversaries, and Hungary gained associate membership in 1991. In 1994, Russia joined 20 other nations, including former Soviet republics, in a "partnership for peace" agreement with NATO, providing for limited joint military exercises, peacekeeping missions, and information exchange.

Organization of African Unity (OAU), formed May 25, 1963, by 32 African countries (53 members in 1994) to promote peace and security as well as economic and social development. It holds annual conferences of heads of state. Headquarters is in Addis Ababa, Ethiopia.

Organization of American States (OAS), formed in Bogotá, Colombia, Apr. 30, 1948. Headquarters is in Washington, DC. It has a Permanent Council, Inter-American Economic and Social Council, Inter-American Council for Education, Science, and Culture, Juridical Committee, and Commission on Human Rights. The Permanent Council can call meetings of foreign ministers to deal with urgent security matters. A General Assembly meets annually. A secretary general and assistant are elected for 5-year terms. There are 35 members, each with one vote in the various organizations: Antigua and Barbuda, Argentina, The Bahamas, Barbados, Belize, Bolivia, Brazil, Canada, Chile, Colombia, Costa Rica, Cuba, Dominica, Dominican Republic, Ecuador, El Salvador, Grenada, Guatemala, Guyana, Haiti, Honduras, Jamaica, Mexico, Nicaragua, Panama, Paraguay, Peru, Saint Kitts and Nevis, Saint Lucia, Saint Vincent and the Grenadines, Suriname, Trinidad and Tobago, United States, Uruguay, and Venezuela. In 1962, the OAS excluded Cuba from OAS activities but not from membership.

Organization for Economic Cooperation and Development (OECD), established Sept. 30, 1961, to promote economic and social welfare in member countries, and to stimulate and harmonize efforts on behalf of developing nations. The OECD collects and disseminates economic and environmental information. Members in 1994 were Australia, Austria, Belgium, Canada, Denmark, Finland, France, Germany, Greece, Iceland, Ireland, Italy, Japan, Luxembourg, Netherlands, New Zealand, Norway, Portugal, Spain, Sweden, Switzerland, Turkey, United Kingdom, and United States. Headquarters is in Paris.

Organization of Petroleum Exporting Countries (OPEC), created Sept. 14, 1960. The group attempts to set world oil prices by controlling oil production. It is also involved in advancing members' interests in trade and development dealings with industrialized oil-consuming nations. Members in 1994 were Algeria, Gabon, Indonesia, Iran, Iraq, Kuwait, Libya, Nigeria, Qatar, Saudi Arabia, United Arab Emirates, and Venezuela.

United Nations

The 49th regular session of United Nations General Assembly opened in September 1994.

UN headquarters is in New York, NY, between First Ave. and Roosevelt Drive and E. 42d St. and E. 48th St. The General Assembly Bldg., Secretariat, Conference and Library bldgs. are interconnected.

A European office at Geneva includes Secretariat and agency staff members. Other offices of UN bodies and related organizations with a staff of some 23,000 from some 150 countries are scattered throughout the world.

The UN has a post office originating its own stamps.

Proposals to establish an organization of nations for maintenance of world peace led to the United Nations Conference on International Organization at San Francisco, Apr. 25-June 26, 1945, where the charter of the United Nations was drawn up. It was signed June 26 by 50 nations, and by Poland, one of the original 51 UN members, on Oct. 15, 1945. The charter came into effect Oct. 24, 1945, upon ratification by the permanent members of the Security Council and a majority of other signatories.

Purposes: To maintain international peace and security; to develop friendly relations among nations; to achieve international cooperation in solving economic, social, cultural, and humanitarian problems and in promoting respect for human rights and fundamental freedoms; to be a center for harmonizing the actions of nations in attaining these common ends.

Visitors to the UN: Headquarters is open to the public every day of the year except Christmas and New Year's Day. Guided tours are given approximately every half hour from 9:15 AM to 4:15 PM daily. Groups of 15 or more persons should write to the Group Program Unit, Visitors' Service, Room GA-56, United Nations, New York, NY 10017, or telephone (212) 963-4440. Children under 5 are not permitted on tours.

Roster of the United Nations

The 184 members of the United Nations, with the years in which they became members; as of Sept. 1994

Member	Year	Member	Year	Member	Year	Member	Year
Afghanistan	1946	Canada	1945	Georgia	1992	Lebanon	1945
Albania	1955	Cape Verde	1975	Germany	1973	Lesotho	1966
Algeria	1962	Central Afr. Rep.	1960	Ghana	1957	Liberia	1945
Andorra	1993	Chad	1960	Greece	1945	Libya	1955
Angola	1976	Chile	1945	Grenada	1974	Liechtenstein	1990
Antigua and Barbuda	1981	China[1]	1945	Guatemala	1945	Lithuania	1991
Argentina	1945	Colombia	1945	Guinea	1958	Luxembourg	1945
Armenia	1992	Comoros	1975	Guinea-Bissau	1974	Macedonia[5]	1993
Australia	1945	Congo	1960	Guyana	1966	Madagascar	1960
Austria	1955	Costa Rica	1945	Haiti	1945	Malawi	1964
Azerbaijan	1992	Côte d'Ivoire	1960	Honduras	1945	Malaysia[6]	1957
Bahamas	1973	Croatia	1992	Hungary	1955	Maldives	1965
Bahrain	1971	Cuba	1945	Iceland	1946	Mali	1960
Bangladesh	1974	Cyprus	1960	India	1945	Malta	1964
Barbados	1966	Czech Rep.[2]	1993	Indonesia[4]	1950	Marshall Islands	1991
Belarus	1945	Denmark	1945	Iran	1945	Mauritania	1961
Belgium	1945	Djibouti	1977	Iraq	1945	Mauritius	1968
Belize	1981	Dominica	1978	Ireland	1955	Mexico	1945
Benin	1960	Dominican Rep.	1945	Israel	1949	Micronesia	1991
Bhutan	1971	Ecuador	1945	Italy	1955	Moldova	1992
Bolivia	1945	Egypt[3]	1945	Jamaica	1962	Monaco	1993
Bosnia and Herzegovina	1992	El Salvador	1945	Japan	1956	Mongolia	1961
Botswana	1966	Equatorial Guinea	1968	Jordan	1955	Morocco	1956
Brazil	1945	Eritrea	1993	Kazakhstan	1992	Mozambique	1975
Brunei	1984	Estonia	1991	Kenya	1963	Myanmar (Burma)	1948
Bulgaria	1955	Ethiopia	1945	Korea, N.	1991	Namibia	1990
Burkina Faso	1960	Fiji	1970	Korea, S.	1991	Nepal	1955
Burundi	1962	Finland	1955	Kuwait	1963	Netherlands	1945
Cambodia	1955	France	1945	Kyrgyzstan	1992	New Zealand	1945
Cameroon	1960	Gabon	1960	Laos	1955	Nicaragua	1945
		Gambia, The	1965	Latvia	1991	Niger	1960

(continued)

Member	Year	Member	Year	Member	Year	Member	Year
Nigeria	1960	Saint Lucia	1979	South Africa[7]	1945	Uganda	1962
Norway	1945	Saint Vincent and the Grenadines	1980	Spain	1955	Ukraine	1945
Oman	1971	Samoa (Western)	1976	Sri Lanka	1955	United Arab Emirates	1971
Pakistan	1947	San Marino	1992	Sudan	1956	United Kingdom	1945
Panama	1945	São Tomé and Príncipe	1975	Suriname	1975	United States	1945
Papua New Guinea	1975	Saudi Arabia	1945	Swaziland	1968	Uruguay	1945
Paraguay	1945	Senegal	1960	Sweden	1946	Uzbekistan	1992
Peru	1945	Seychelles	1976	Syria[3]	1945	Vanuatu	1981
Philippines	1945	Sierra Leone	1961	Tajikistan	1992	Venezuela	1945
Poland	1945	Singapore[6]	1965	Tanzania[8]	1961	Vietnam	1977
Portugal	1955	Slovakia[2]	1993	Thailand	1946	Yemen[9]	1947
Qatar	1971	Slovenia	1992	Togo	1960	Yugoslavia[10]	1945
Romania	1955	Solomon Islands	1978	Trinidad and Tobago	1962	Zaire	1960
Russia	1945	Somalia	1960	Tunisia	1956	Zambia	1964
Rwanda	1962			Turkey	1945	Zimbabwe	1980
Saint Kitts and Nevis	1983			Turkmenistan	1992		

(1) The General Assembly voted in 1971 to expel the Chinese government on Taiwan and admit the Beijing government in its place. (2) Czechoslovakia, which split into the separate nations of the Czech Republic and Slovakia on Jan. 1, 1993, was a UN member from 1945 to 1992. (3) Egypt and Syria were original members of the UN. In 1958, the United Arab Republic was established by a union of Egypt and Syria and continued as a single member of the UN. In 1961, Syria resumed its separate membership. (4) Indonesia withdrew from the UN in 1965 and rejoined in 1966. (5) Admitted under the provisional name of The Former Yugoslav Republic of Macedonia. (6) Malaya joined the UN in 1957. In 1963, its name was changed to Malaysia following the accession of Singapore, Sabah, and Sarawak. Singapore became an independent UN member in 1965. (7) In 1994, the General Assembly accepted the credentials of the South African delegation, which had been rejected for 24 years because of the country's former apartheid policies. (8) Tanganyika was a member of the United Nations from 1961 and Zanzibar was a member from 1963. Following the ratification in 1964 of Articles of Union between Tanganyika and Zanzibar, the United Republic of Tanganyika and Zanzibar continued as a single member of the United Nations, later changing its name to United Republic of Tanzania. (9) The Yemen Arab Republic was admitted in 1947; the People's Republic of Yemen, in 1967. The two nations merged in 1990. (10) The Socialist Federal Republic of Yugoslavia became a member in 1945. After four of its six republics (Bosnia and Herzegovina, Croatia, Macedonia, and Slovenia) declared independence in 1991-92, the two remaining republics, Montenegro and Serbia, reconstituted themselves as the Federal Republic of Yugoslavia, which assumed Yugoslavia's UN seat Apr. 8, 1992. The General Assembly suspended Yugoslavia in September 1992 for violating UN resolutions relating to the civil wars in the former Yugoslav republics.

United Nations Secretaries General

Year	Secretary, Nation	Year	Secretary, Nation	Year	Secretary, Nation
1946	Trygve Lie, Norway	1961	U Thant, Burma	1982	Javier Perez de Cuellar, Peru
1953	Dag Hammarskjold, Sweden	1972	Kurt Waldheim, Austria	1992	Boutros Boutros-Ghali, Egypt

U.S. Representatives to the United Nations

The U.S. Representative to the United Nations is the Chief of the U.S. Mission to the United Nations in New York and holds the rank and status of Ambassador Extraordinary and Plenipotentiary.

Year	Representative	Year	Representative	Year	Representative
1946	Edward R. Stettinius, Jr.	1968	George W. Ball	1977	Andrew Young
1946	Herschel V. Johnson (act.)	1968	James Russell Wiggins	1979	Donald McHenry
1947	Warren R. Austin	1969	Charles W. Yost	1981	Jeane J. Kirkpatrick
1953	Henry Cabot Lodge, Jr.	1971	George Bush	1985	Vernon A. Walters
1960	James J. Wadsworth	1973	John A. Scali	1989	Thomas R. Pickering
1961	Adlai E. Stevenson	1975	Daniel P. Moynihan	1992	Edward J. Perkins
1965	Arthur J. Goldberg	1976	William W. Scranton	1993	Madeleine K. Albright

Organization of the United Nations

The text of the UN Charter may be obtained from the Office of Public Information, United Nations, New York, NY 10017.

General Assembly. The General Assembly is composed of representatives of all the member nations. Each nation is entitled to one vote.

The General Assembly meets in regular annual sessions and in special session when necessary. Special sessions are convoked by the Secretary General at the request of the Security Council or of a majority of the members of the UN.

On important questions a two-thirds majority of members present and voting is required; on other questions a simple majority is sufficient.

The General Assembly must approve the budget and apportion expenses among members. A member in arrears will have no vote if the amount of arrears equals or exceeds the amount of the contributions due for the preceding 2 full years.

Security Council. The Security Council consists of 15 members, 5 with permanent seats. The remaining 10 are elected for 2-year terms by the General Assembly; they are not eligible for immediate reelection.

Permanent members of the Council are: China, France, Russia, United Kingdom, United States.

Nonpermanent members are: (with terms expiring Dec. 31, 1994) Brazil, Djibouti, New Zealand, Pakistan, Spain; (with terms expiring Dec. 31, 1995) Argentina, Czech Republic, Nigeria, Oman, Rwanda.

The Security Council has the primary responsibility within the UN for maintaining international peace and security. The Council may investigate any dispute that threatens international peace and security.

Any member of the UN at UN headquarters may participate in its discussions and a nation not a member of the UN may appear if it is a party to a dispute.

Decisions on procedural questions are made by an affirmative vote of 9 members. On all other matters the affirmative vote of 9 members must include the concurring votes of all permanent members; it is this clause which gives rise to the so-called veto power of permanent members. A party to a dispute must refrain from voting.

The Security Council directs the various peacekeeping forces deployed throughout the world.

Economic and Social Council. The Economic and Social Council consists of 54 members elected by the General Assembly for 3-year terms of office. The council is responsible under the General Assembly for carrying out the functions of the United Nations with regard to international economic, social, cultural, educational, health, and related matters. The council meets once a year.

Trusteeship Council. The administration of trust territories is under UN supervision.

Secretariat. The Secretary General is the chief administrative officer of the UN. He may bring to the attention of the Security Council any matter that threatens international peace. He reports to the General Assembly.

Budget: The General Assembly approved a total budget for 1994-95 of $2.58 billion.

International Court of Justice (World Court). The International Court of Justice is the principal judicial organ of the United Nations. All members are *ipso facto* parties to the statute of the Court. Other states may become parties to the Court's statute.

The jurisdiction of the Court comprises cases which the parties submit to it and matters especially provided for in the charter or in treaties. The Court gives advisory opinions and renders judgments. Its decisions are binding only between the parties concerned and in respect to a particular dispute. If any party to a case fails to heed a judgment, the other party may have recourse to the Security Council.

The 15 judges are elected for 9-year terms by the General Assembly and the Security Council. Retiring judges are eligible for reelection. The Court remains permanently in session, except during vacations. All questions are decided by majority. The Court sits in The Hague, Netherlands.

Selected Specialized and Related Agencies

These agencies are autonomous, with their own memberships and organs, and have a functional relationship or working agreement with the UN (headquarters), except for UNICEF and UNHCR, which report directly to the Economic and Social Council and to the General Assembly.

Food and Agriculture Organization (FAO), aims to increase production from farms, forests, and fisheries; improve food distribution and marketing, nutrition, and the living conditions of rural people. (Viale delle Terme di Caracalla, 00100 Rome, Italy.)

General Agreement on Tariffs and Trade (GATT), the only treaty setting rules for world trade, provides a forum for settling trade disputes and negotiating trade liberalization. (Centre William Rappard, 154 rue de Lausanne, 1211 Geneva 21, Switzerland.)

International Atomic Energy Agency (IAEA), aims to promote the safe, peaceful uses of atomic energy. (Vienna International Centre, PO Box 100, A-1400, Vienna, Austria.)

International Bank for Reconstruction and Development (IBRD) (World Bank), provides loans and technical assistance for economic development projects in developing member countries; encourages cofinancing for projects from other public and private sources. The **International Development Association (IDA),** an affiliate of the Bank, provides funds for development projects on concessionary terms to the poorer developing member countries. The **International Finance Corporation (IFC),** an affiliate of the Bank, promotes the growth of the private sector in developing member countries; encourages the development of local capital markets; stimulates the international flow of private capital. (1818 H St., NW, Washington, DC 20433.)

International Civil Aviation Organization (ICAO), promotes international civil aviation standards and regulations. (1000 Sherbrooke St. W., Montreal, Quebec, Canada H3A 2R2.)

International Fund for Agricultural Development (IFAD), aims to mobilize funds for agricultural and rural projects in developing countries. (107 Via del Serafico, Rome, Italy.)

International Labor Organization (ILO), aims to promote employment; improve labor conditions and living standards. (4 route de Morillons, CH-1211 Geneva 22, Switzerland.)

International Maritime Organization (IMO), aims to promote cooperation on technical matters affecting international shipping. (4 Albert Embankment, London SE1 7SR, England.)

International Monetary Fund (IMF), aims to promote international monetary cooperation and currency stabilization and expansion of international trade. (700 19th St., NW, Washington, DC 20431.)

International Telecommunication Union (ITU), establishes international regulations for radio, telegraph, telephone, and space radio-communications, allocates radio frequencies. (Place des Nations, 1211 Geneva 20, Switzerland.)

United Nations Children's Fund (UNICEF), provides aid and development assistance to programs for children and mothers in developing countries. (1 UN Plaza, New York, NY 10017.)

United Nations Educational, Scientific, and Cultural Organization (UNESCO), aims to promote collaboration among nations through education, science, and culture. (7 Place de Fontenoy, 75352 Paris 07SP, France.)

United Nations High Commissioner for Refugees (UNHCR), provides essential assistance for refugees. (Place des Nations, 1211 Geneva 10, Switzerland.)

Universal Postal Union (UPU), aims to perfect postal services and promote international collaboration. (Weltpoststrasse 4, 3000 Berne, 15 Switzerland.)

World Health Org. (WHO), aims to aid the attainment of the highest possible level of health. (1211 Geneva 27, Switzerland.)

World Intellectual Property Organization (WIPO), seeks to protect, through international cooperation, literary, industrial, scientific, and artistic works. (34, Chemin des Colom Bettes, 1211 Geneva, Switzerland.)

World Meteorological Org. (WMO), aims to coordinate and improve world meteorological work. (Case Postale 5, CH-1211 Geneva 20, Switzerland.)

Geneva Conventions

The Geneva Conventions are 4 international treaties governing the protection of civilians in time of war, the treatment of prisoners of war, and the care of the wounded and sick in the armed forces. The first convention, covering the sick and wounded, was concluded in Geneva, Switzerland, in 1864; it was amended and expanded in 1906. A third convention, in 1929, covered prisoners of war. Outrage at the treatment of prisoners and civilians during World War II by some belligerents, notably Germany and Japan, prompted the conclusion, in August 1949, of 4 new conventions. Three of these restated and strengthened the previous conventions, and the fourth codified general principles of international law governing the treatment of civilians in wartime.

The 1949 convention for civilians provided for special safeguards for the wounded, children under 15, pregnant women, and the elderly. Discrimination was forbidden on racial, religious, national, or political grounds. Torture, collective punishment, reprisals, the unwarrented destruction of property, and the forced use of civilians for an occupier's armed forces were also prohibited.

Also included in the new 1949 treaties was a pledge to treat prisoners humanely, feed them adequately, and deliver relief supplies to them. They were not to be forced to disclose more than minimal information.

Most countries have formally accepted all or most of the humanitarian conventions as binding. A nation is not free to withdraw its ratification of the conventions during wartime. However, there is no permanent machinery in place to apprehend, try, or punish violators.

Ambassadors and Envoys

As of mid-1994

The address of U.S. embassies abroad is the appropriate foreign capital. The U.S. does not have diplomatic relations with the following countries: Liechtenstein, Maldives, Cambodia,[1] Taiwan,[2] Cuba,[3] Iran,[4] Libya,[5] Vietnam,[1] N. Korea, Iraq,[6] Solomon Islands. There are informal relations with Bhutan and Vanuatu.

Countries	Envoys from United States	Envoys to United States
Afghanistan	Vacancy	Abdul Rahim, Chargé
Albania	William E. Ryerson, Amb.	Roland Bimo, Amb.
Algeria	Mary Ann Casey, Amb.	Nourredine Zerhouni, Amb.
Angola	Vacancy	Jose G.M. Patricio, Amb.
Antigua & Barbuda	Bryant J. Salter, Chargé	Patrick A. Lewis, Amb.
Argentina	James R. Cheek, Amb.	Raul Enrique Granillo Ocampo, Amb.
Armenia	Harry J. Gilmore, Amb.	Rouben Robert Shugarian, Amb.
Australia	Edward J. Perkins, Amb	Donald Eric Russell, Amb.
Austria	Swanee G. Hunt, Amb.	Helmut Turk, Amb.
Azerbaijan	Richard D. Kauzlarich, Amb.	Hafiz Mir Jalal Oglu Pashayev, Amb.
Bahamas	Sidney Williams, Amb.	Timothy B. Donaldson, Amb.
Bahrain	David S. Robins, Chargé	Muhammad Abdul Ghaffar, Amb.
Bangladesh	David N. Merrill, Amb.	Humayun Kabir, Amb.
Barbados	Jeanette W. Hyde, Amb.	Rudi V. Webster, Amb.
Belarus	George Krol, Chargé.	Serguei Martynov, Amb.
Belgium	Alan J. Blinker, Amb.	Jean Cassiers, Amb.
Belize	Eugene L. Scassa, Amb.	Dean Russell Lindo, Amb.
Benin	Ruth A. Davis, Amb.	Candide Pierre Ahouansou, Amb.
Bolivia	Charles R. Bowers, Amb.	Andres Petricevic, Amb.
Bosnia and Herzegovina	Victor Jackovich, Amb.	Sven Alkalaj, Chargé
Botswana	Howard F. Jeter, Amb.	Botsweletse K. Sebele, Amb.
Brazil	Mark Lore, Chargé	Paulo-Tarso Flecha de Lima, Amb.
Brunei	Theresa A. Tull, Amb.	H.J. bin Abdul Latif, Amb.
Bulgaria	William D. Montgomery, Amb.	Ognian R. Pishev, Amb.
Burkina Faso	Donald J. McConnell, Amb.	Gaetan R. Ouegraogo, Amb.
Burundi	Leonard J. Lange, Chargé	Jacques Bacamurwanko, Amb.
Cameroon	Harriet W. Isom, Amb.	Jerome Mendouga, Amb.
Canada	James J. Blanchard, Amb.	Raymond A.J. Chretien, Amb.
Cape Verde	Joseph M. Segars, Amb.	Jose Eduardo Barbosa, Chargé.
Central African Rep.	Robert E. Gribbon 3d, Amb.	Jean-Pierre Sohahong-Kombet, Amb.
Chad	Laurence E. Pope II, Amb.	Lemaye Favitso-Boulandi, Chargé
Chile	Curtis W. Kamman, Amb.	Patricio Silva, Amb.
China	J. Stapleton Roy, Amb.	Zi Daoyu, Amb.
Colombia	Morris D. Busby, Amb.	Gabriel Silva, Amb.
Comoros	Kenneth N. Peltier, Amb.	Amini Ali Moumin, Amb.
Congo	William C. Ramsay, Amb.	Pierre Boussoukou-Boumba, Amb.
Costa Rica	Joseph Becelia, Chargé	Jose Antonio Munoz, Chargé
Côte d'Ivoire	Hume A. Horan, Amb.	Charles Gomis, Amb.
Croatia	Peter W. Galbraith, Amb.	Peter A. Sarcevic, Amb.
Cyprus	Richard A. Boucher, Amb.	Andrew J. Jacovides, Amb.
Czech Rep.	Adrian A. Basora, Amb.	Michael Zantovsky, Amb.
Denmark	Edward E. Elson, Amb.	Peter P. Dyvig, Amb.
Djibouti	Martin L. Cheshes, Amb.	Roble Olhaye, Amb.
Dominica	Jeanette W. Hyde, Amb.	Edward I. Watty, Amb.
Dominican Republic	Robert S. Pastorino, Amb.	Jose del Carmen Ariza, Amb.
Ecuador	Peter F. Romero, Amb.	Edgar Teran-Teran, Amb.
Egypt	Edmund J. Hull, Chargé	Ahmed Maher El Sayed, Amb.
El Salvador	Alan H. Flanigan, Amb.	Ana Cristina Sol, Amb.
Equatorial Guinea	John E. Bennett, Amb.	Biyogo Nsue, Chargé
Eritrea	Robert G. Houdek, Amb.	Arefaine Berhe, Chargé
Estonia	Robert C. Frasure, Amb.	Tomas Hendrik Ives, Amb.
Ethiopia	Marc Baas, Amb.	Berhane Gebre-Chirstos, Amb.
Fiji	Michael W. Marine, Chargé	Pita Kewa Nacuva, Amb.
Finland	John H. Kelly, Amb.	Jukka Valtasaari, Amb.
France	Pamela C. Harriman, Amb.	Jacques Andreani, Amb.
Gabon	Joseph C. Wilson 4th, Amb.	Paul Boundoukou-Latha, Amb.
Gambia, The	Andrew J. Winter, Amb.	Ousman A. Sallah, Amb.
Georgia	Kent N. Brown, Amb.	Peter Chkhefdze, Amb.
Germany	Richard C. Holbrooke, Amb.	Immo Stabreit, Amb.
Ghana	Kenneth L. Brown, Amb.	Nana Effah-Apenteng, Chargé
Greece	Thomas Niles, Amb.	Loucas Tsilas, Amb.
Grenada	Ollie P. Anderson Jr., Chargé	Denneth Modeste, Amb.
Guatemala	Marilyn McAfee, Amb.	Edmond A. Mulet, Amb.
Guinea	Joseph A. Saloom 3d, Amb.	Boubacar Barry, Amb.
Guinea-Bissau	Rogert A. McGuire, Amb.	Alfredo Lopes Cabral, Amb.
Guyana	George F. Jones, Amb.	Mohammed Ali Odeen Ishmael, Amb.
Haiti	William Lacy Swing, Amb.	Jean Casimir, Amb.
Honduras	William T. Pryce, Amb.	Lopez Villamil, Chargé
Hungary	Donald M. Blinken, Amb.	Pal Tar, Amb.
Iceland	Parker W. Borg, Amb.	Einar Benediktsson, Amb.
India	Kenneth C. Brill, Chargé	Siddhartha S. Ray, Amb.
Indonesia	Robert L. Barry, Amb.	Arifin Mohamad Siregar, Amb.
Ireland	Jean Kennedy Smith, Amb.	Dermot A. Gallagher, Amb.
Israel	Edward P. Djerejian, Amb.	Itamar Rabinovich, Amb.
Italy	Reginald Bartholomew, Amb.	Boris Biancheri, Amb.
Jamaica	Lacy A. Wright Jr., Chargé	Richard L. Bernal, Amb.
Japan	Walter F. Mondale, Amb.	Takakazu Kuriyama, Amb.
Jordan	Wesley W. Egan Jr., Amb.	Fayez A. Tarawneh, Amb.
Kazakhstan	William H. Courtney, Amb.	Almaz N. Khamzaev, Chargé
Kenya	Aurelia Brazeal, Amb.	Benjamin Edward Kipkorir, Amb.

Countries	Envoys from United States	Envoys to United States
Kiribati	Evelyn I.H. Teegen, Amb.	Vacancy
Korea, South	James T. Laney, Amb.	Seung-Soo Han, Amb.
Kuwait	Georgia Debell, Chargé	Mohammed Sabah Salim Al-Sabah, Amb.
Kyrgyzstan	Edward Hurwitz, Amb.	Almas Chukin, Chargé
Laos	Victor L. Tomseth, Amb.	Hiem Phommachanh, Amb.
Latvia	Ints M. Silins, Amb.	Ojars E. Kalnins, Amb.
Lebanon	Mark G. Hambley, Amb.	Raid Tabbarahf, Amb.
Lesotho	Karl Hoffman, Chargé	Teboho E. Kitleli, Amb.
Liberia	William P. Twaddell, Chargé	Konah Blackett, Chargé
Lithuania	Darryl N. Johnson, Amb.	Alfonsas Eidintas, Amb.
Luxembourg	William T. Harris, Chargé	Alphonse Berns, Amb.
Madagascar	Dennis P. Barrett, Amb.	Pierrot J. Rajaonarivelo, Amb.
Malawi	Michael T. F. Pistor, Amb.	Robert Mbaya, Amb.
Malaysia	John S. Wolf, Amb.	Dato Abdul Majid, Amb.
Mali	William H. Dameron 3d, Amb.	Siragatou Cisse, Amb.
Malta	William A. Moffitt, Chargé	Borg Olivier de Puget, Amb.
Marshall Islands	David C. Fields, Amb.	Wilfred Kendall, Amb.
Mauritania	Gordon S. Brown, Amb.	Mohammed Fall Ainini, Amb.
Mauritius	Leslie M. Alexander, Amb.	Anund Priyay Neewoor, Amb.
Mexico	James R. Jones, Amb.	Jorge Montano, Amb.
Micronesia	March Fong Eu, Amb.	Jesse B. Marehalau, Amb.
Moldova	Mary C. Pendleton, Amb.	Nicolae Tau, Amb.
Mongolia	Donald C. Johnson, Amb.	Luvsandorj Dawagiv, Amb.
Morocco	Marc C. Ginsberg, Amb.	Mohamed Beneissar, Amb.
Mozambique	Dennis Coleman Jett, Amb.	Hipolito Patricio, Amb.
Myanmar	Franklin P. Huddle Jr., Chargé	U Thaung, Amb.
Namibia	Marshall F. McCallie, Amb.	Tuliameni Kalomoh, Amb.
Nauru	Marilyn A. Meyers, Chargé	Vacancy
Nepal	Sandra L. Vogelgesang, Amb.	Pradeep Khatiwada, Chargé
Netherlands	K. Terry Dornbush, Amb.	Adriaan P.R.J.de Szeged, Amb.
New Zealand	Josiah Horton Beeman, Amb.	L. John Wood, Amb.
Nicaragua	John Maisto, Amb.	Roberto G. Mayorga-Cortes, Amb.
Niger	John S. Davison, Amb.	Adamou Seydou, Amb.
Nigeria	Walter C. Carrington, Amb.	Zubair Kazaure, Amb.
Norway	Thomas A. Loftus, Amb.	Kjeld Vibe, Amb.
Oman	David J. Dunford, Amb.	Roshid Mubarik R. Al-Ghilani, Chargé
Pakistan	John C. Monjo, Amb.	Maleeha Lodhi, Amb.
Panama	Oliver P. Garza, Chargé	Jaime F. Boyd, Amb.
Papua New Guinea	Richard W. Teare, Amb.	Kepas Isimel Watangia, Amb.
Paraguay	Jon David Glassman, Amb.	Otazu Gimenez, Chargé
Peru	Alvin P. Adams Jr., Amb.	Ricardo V. Luna, Amb.
Philippines	John D. Negroponte, Amb.	Raul Rabe, Amb.
Poland	Nicholas Andrew Rey, Amb.	Maciej Kozlowsjum, Chargé
Portugal	Sharon P. Wilkinson, Chargé	Francisco Knopfli, Amb.
Qatar	Kenton W. Keith, Amb.	Abdulrahman bin Saud al-Thani, Amb.
Romania	John R. Davis Jr., Amb.	Vasile Puscas, Chargé
Russia	Thomas R. Pickering, Amb.	Vladimir I. Chkhikvishvili, Chargé
Rwanda	David P. Rawson, Amb.	Aloys Uwimana, Amb.
St. Kitts & Nevis	Jeanette W. Hyde, Amb.	Erstein Mallet Edwards, Amb.
St. Lucia	Jeanette W. Hyde, Amb.	Joseph E. Edmunds, Amb.
St. Vincent and The Grenadines	Jeanette W. Hyde, Amb.	Kingsley C.A. Layne, Amb.
Sao Tome and Principe	Joseph C. Wilson, Amb.	Vacancy
Saudi Arabia	C. David Welch, Chargé	Bandar Bin Sultan, Amb.
Senegal	Mark Johnson, Amb.	Mamadou Mansour Seck, Amb.
Seychelles	F. Stephen Malott, Chargé	Marc Marengo, Amb.
Sierra Leone	Lauralee M. Peters, Amb.	Thomas Kahota Kargbo, Amb.
Singapore	Ralph L. Boyce Jr., Chargé	S.R. Nathan, Amb.
Slovakia	Theodore E. Russel, Amb.	Branislav Lichardus, Amb.
Slovenia	E. Allan Wendt, Amb.	Ernest Petric, Amb.
Somalia	Richard W. Bogosian, Amb.	Vacancy
South Africa	Princeton N. Lyman, Amb.	Harry H. Schwarz, Amb.
Spain	Richard N. Gardner, Amb.	Jaime de Ojeda, Amb.
Sri Lanka	Teresita C. Schaffer, Amb.	Anada W. P. Guruge, Amb.
Sudan	David K. Petterson, Amb.	Ahmed Suliman, Amb.
Suriname	Roger R. Gamble, Amb.	Willem A. Udenhout, Amb.
Swaziland	John T. Sprott, Amb.	Absalom V. Mamba, Amb.
Sweden	Thomas L. Siebert, Amb.	Henrik Sihver Lfljegren, Amb.
Switzerland	M. Larry Lawrence, Amb.	Carlo Jagmetti, Amb.
Syria	Christopher W. S. Ross, Amb.	Walid Al-Moualem, Amb.
Tajikistan	Stanley T. Escudero, Amb.	Vacancy
Tanzania	Peter Jon de Vos, Amb.	Charles M. Nyirabu, Amb.
Thailand	David F. Lambertson, Amb.	Busba Bunnag, Chargé
Togo	Harmon E. Kirby, Amb.	Edem F. Hegbe, Chargé
Tonga	Evelyn I.H. Teegan, Amb.	Sione Kite, Amb.
Trinidad and Tobago	Sally G. Cowal, Amb.	Corinne A. McKnight, Amb.
Tunisia	John T. McCarthy, Amb.	Ismail Khelil, Amb.
Turkey	Richard C. Barkley, Amb.	Nuzhet Kandemir, Amb.
Turkmenistan	Joseph S. Hulings 3d, Amb.	Halil Ugar, Amb.
Tuvalu	Evelyn I.H. Teegan, Amb.	Vacancy
Uganda	Johnnie Carson, Amb.	Stephen K. Katenta-Apuli, Amb.
Ukraine	William Green Miller, Amb.	Oleh H. Bilorus, Amb.
United Arab Emirates	William A. Rugh, Amb.	Mohammad bin Hussein Al-Shaali, Amb.
United Kingdom	Raymond G.H. Seitz, Amb.	Robin R. Renwick, Amb.
Uruguay	Thomas J. Dodd, Amb.	Eduardo MacGillycuddy
Uzbekistan	Henry L. Clarke, Amb.	Fatikh Teshabaev, Amb.
Vatican	Raymond L. Flynn, Amb.	Agostino Cacciavillan, Pro-Nuncio
Venezuela	Jeffrey Davidow, Amb.	Victor Rodriguez Cedeno, Chargé
Western Samoa	Josiah Horton Beeman, Amb.	Tuiloma Neroni Slade, Amb.

Countries	Envoys from United States	Envoys to United States
Yemen	Arthur H. Hughes, Amb.	Mohsin A. Alaini, Amb.
Yugoslavia	Rudolf V. Perina, Chargé	Dusan Paunovic, Chargé
Zaire	John M. Yates, Chargé	Tatanene Manata, Amb.
Zambia	Roland K. Kuchel, Amb.	Dustin W. Kamana, Amb.
Zimbabwe	E. Gibson Lanpher, Amb.	Amos Bernard Muvengwa Midzi, Amb.

Special Missions

U.S. Mission to NATO, Brussels—Vacancy; U.S. Mission to the European Union, Brussels—Stuart E. Eizenstat; U.S. Mission to the UN, New York—Madeleine K. Albright, Amb.; U.S. Mission to the European Office of the UN, Geneva—Morris B. Abram, Amb.; U.S. Mission to the OECD, Paris—David L. Aaron; U.S. Mission to the Organization of American States, Washington—Harriet C. Babbit, Amb.

(1) U.S. embassy closed in 1975. (2) U.S. severed relations in 1978; unofficial relations are maintained. (3) Relations severed in 1961; limited ties restored in 1977. (4) U.S. severed relations on Apr. 7, 1980. (5) Embassy closed on May 2, 1980. U.S. closed the Libyan mission on May 6, 1981. (6) Operations temporarily suspended.

Codes for International Direct Dial Calling From the U.S.

Station-to-station: 011+country code (below)+city code+local number.

Person-to-person (operator assisted, collect calls, credit card calls, and calls billed to another number): 01+country code (below)+city code+local number.

Note: The dialing code for all of the former Soviet Republics is 7.

For countries not listed, contact your long distance company.

Country	Code
Afghanistan	93
Albania	355
Algeria	213
American Samoa	684
Andorra	33
Angola	244
Anguilla	809 *
Antigua & Barbuda	809 *
Argentina	54
Aruba	297
Australia	61
Austria	43
Bahamas	809 *
Bahrain	973
Bangladesh	880
Barbados	809 *
Belgium	32
Belize	501
Benin	229
Bermuda	809 *
Bhutan	975
Bolivia	591
Bosnia & Herzegovina	38
Botswana	267
Brazil	55
British Virgin Islands	809 *
Brunei Darussalam	673
Bulgaria	359
Burkina Faso	226
Burundi	257
Cameroon	237
Canada	Use Area Codes
Cape Verde	238
Cayman Islands	809 *
Central African Republic	236
Chad	235
Chile	56
China	86
Colombia	57
Comoros	269
Congo	242
Costa Rica	506
Côte d'Ivoire	225
Croatia	38
Cyprus	357
Czech. Rep.	42
Denmark	45
Djibouti	253
Dominica	809 *
Dominican Republic	809 *
Ecuador	593
Egypt	20
El Salvador	503
Equatorial Guinea	240
Ethiopia	251
Fiji	679
Finland	358
France	33
Gabon	241
Gambia	220
Germany	49
Ghana	233
Gibraltar	350
Greece	30
Greenland	299
Grenada	809 *
Guam	671
Guantanamo	53
Guatemala	502
Guinea	224
Guinea-Bissau	245
Guyana	592
Haiti	509
Honduras	504
Hong Kong	852
Hungary	36
Iceland	354
India	91
Indonesia	62
Iran	98
Iraq	964
Ireland	353
Israel	972
Italy	39
Jamaica	809 *
Japan	81
Jordan	962
Kenya	254
Kiribati	686
Korea, South	82
Kuwait	965
Lebanon	961
Lesotho	266
Liberia	231
Libya	218
Liechtenstein	41
Luxembourg	352
Madagascar	261
Malawi	265
Malaysia	60
Maldives	960
Mali	223
Malta	356
Marshall Islands	692
Mauritania	222
Mauritius	230
Mexico	52
Micronesia	691
Monaco	33
Montserrat	809 *
Morocco	212
Mozambique	258
Myanmar	95
Namibia	264
Nauru	674
Nepal	977
Netherlands	31
New Zealand	64
Nicaragua	505
Niger	227
Nigeria	234
Northern Mariana Islands	670
Norway	47
Oman	968
Pakistan	92
Panama	507
Papua New Guinea	675
Paraguay	595
Peru	51
Philippines	63
Poland	48
Portugal	351
Puerto Rico	809 *
Qatar	974
Romania	40
Russia (Moscow)	7
Rwanda	250
St. Kitts & Nevis	809 *
St. Lucia	809 *
St. Vincent & the Grenadines	809 *
San Marino	39
São Tomé & Príncipe	23
Saudi Arabia	966
Senegal	221
Seychelles	248
Sierra Leone	232
Singapore	65
Slovakia	42
Slovenia	38
Solomon Islands	677
Somalia	252
South Africa	27
Spain	34
Sri Lanka	94
Sudan	249
Suriname	597
Swaziland	268
Sweden	46
Switzerland	41
Syria	963
Taiwan	886
Tanzania	255
Thailand	66
Togo	228
Tonga	676
Trinidad & Tobago	809 *
Tunisia	216
Turkey	90
Turks & Caicos Islands	809 *
Tuvalu	688
Uganda	256
United Arab Emirates	971
United Kingdom	44
Uruguay	598
Vanuatu	678
Vatican City	39
Venezuela	58
Virgin Islands (U.S.)	809 *
Western Samoa	685
Yemen	967
Yugoslavia	38
Zaire	243
Zambia	260
Zimbabwe	263

* Follow Domestic Dialing instructions: dial "1" + 809 + number you're calling.

U.S. Aid to Foreign Nations in 1993

Source: Bureau of Economic Analysis, U.S. Dept. of Commerce

Figures are in millions of dollars (*Less than $500,000.) Data include military supplies and services furnished under the Foreign Assistance Act and direct Defense Department appropriations, and include credits extended to private entities.

Net grants and credits take into account all known returns to the U.S., including reverse grants, returns of grants, and payments of principal. A minus sign (-) indicates that the total of these returns is greater than the total of grants or credits. Nations with net grants or credits under $2 million (+ or -) are included with "Other and Unspecified."

Other Assistance represents the transfer of U.S. farm products in exchange for foreign currencies, less the government's disbursements of such currencies as grants, credits, or for purchases.

Amounts do not include investments in the following: Asian Development Bank, $50 mln.; Inter-American Development Bank, $68 mln.; International Development Assn., $782 mln.; International Bank for Reconstruction and Development, $59 mln.; African Development Fund, $103 mln.; International Finance Corp., $38 mln.; European Bank for Reconstruction and Development, $33 mln.

UNRWA = United Nations Relief Works Agency (aid for Palestinian refugees)

	Total	Net grants	Net credits	Net other
Total	**14,092**	**15,184**	**-1,083**	**-8**
Western Europe	**153**	**503**	**-351**	**(*)**
Bosnia and Herzegovina	8	8	—	—
Croatia	6	6	—	—
Finland	-26	—	-26	—
Ireland	-8	26	-34	—
Macedonia	4	4	—	—
Portugal	51	90	-39	—
Spain	-114	(*)	-114	(*)
United Kingdom	-118	(*)	-118	—
Yugoslavia	-8	8	-16	—
Other & Unspecified	358	360	-3	(*)
Eastern Europe	2,224	663	1,580	—
Albania	10	10	—	—
Armenia	19	19	—	—
Belarus	17	10	7	—
Bulgaria	15	1	15	—
Czechoslovakia	15	1	14	—
Hungary	2	2	—	—
Kazakhstan	8	8	—	—
Kyrgyzstan	11	11	—	—
Lithuania	24	(*)	24	—
Moldova	11	1	10	—
Poland	20	21	(*)	—
Romania	13	3	10	—
Russia	1,581	123	1,438	—
Tajikistan	14	—	14	—
Turkmenistan	9	(*)	9	—
Ukraine	36	17	20	—
Former USSR - Regional	248	248	—	—
Other & Unspecified	190	190	(*)	—
Near East & South Asia	6,939	7,322	-381	-2
Afghanistan	42	42	—	(*)
Bangladesh	72	58	13	—
Cyprus	14	14	(*)	(*)
Egypt	2,734	2,766	-32	1
Greece	154	(*)	183	1
India	57	177	-120	(*)
Israel	2,886	3,080	-194	—
Jordan	113	58	54	(*)
Lebanon	6	8	-2	—
Nepal	20	20	(*)	(*)
Oman	20	7	13	—
Pakistan	-40	119	-156	-3
Sri Lanka	34	31	3	(*)
Turkey	592	744	-151	(*)
UNRWA	140	140	—	—
West Bank - Gaza	19	19	—	—
Yemen	20	12	8	—
Other & Unspecified	26	26	—	—
Africa	1,738	1,858	-119	(*)
Algeria	-11	2	-13	—
Angola	9	21	-13	—
Benin	12	12	—	—
Botswana	14	16	-1	—
Burkina Faso	18	18	—	(*)
Burundi	19	19	—	—
Cameroon	23	23	—	—
Cape Verde, Republic of	5	5	—	—
Central African Republic	3	3	—	—
Chad	20	20	—	—
Djibouti	2	2	—	—
Eritrea	4	4	—	—
Ethiopia	156	152	4	—
Gambia, The	14	14	—	—
Ghana	45	45	(*)	(*)
Guinea	31	26	6	—
Guinea-Bissau	6	6	—	—
Ivory Coast	21	12	9	(*)
Kenya	73	59	14	—
Lesotho	7	7	—	—
Liberia	71	71	—	—
Madagascar	28	25	—	—
Malawi	42	42	—	—
Mali	36	36	(*)	(*)
Mauritania	5	8	1	—
Morocco	-21	61	-81	(*)
Mozambique	68	55	1	—
Namibia	9	9	—	—
Niger	25	29	(*)	—
Nigeria	16	16	3	—
Rwanda	29	29	—	—
Senegal	49	49	(*)	(*)
Sierra Leone	5	7	-2	—
Somalia	492	492	—	—
South Africa	66	66	—	—
Sudan	35	35	(*)	—
Swaziland	14	16	(*)	—
Tanzania	28	24	4	—
Togo	7	7	—	—
Tunisia	-7	9	-16	(*)
Uganda	57	57	—	—
Zaire	9	6	(*)	—
Zambia	52	59	-37	—
Zimbabwe	30	26	3	—
Other & Unspecified	117	119	-1	—
East Asia & Pacific	**-16**	**655**	**-673**	**1**
Burma	-2	1	-3	—
Cambodia	29	29	(*)	—
China, Mainland	14	(*)	14	—
Federated States of Micronesia	45	45	—	—
Fiji	2	2	—	—
Indonesia	-64	65	-129	—
Korea, Republic of	-431	(*)	-431	—
Marshall Islands, Republic of	24	24	—	—
Mongolia	14	14	—	—
Palau	83	83	—	—
Papua New Guinea	2	1	1	—
Philippines	137	318	-181	(*)
Singapore	3	3	—	—
Taiwan	-9	—	-10	1
Thailand	84	19	65	—
Other & Unspecified	52	52	(*)	—
Western Hemisphere	**514**	**1,643**	**-1,119**	**-9**
Argentina	79	6	73	—
Belize	12	5	4	—
Bolivia	105	105	3	(*)
Brazil	-159	3	-192	—
Canada	-41	—	-41	—
Chile	-33	30	-63	—
Colombia	-227	60	-256	—
Costa Rica	13	23	-6	-4
Dominican Republic	161	26	135	(*)
Ecuador	12	21	-9	—
El Salvador	215	648	-433	—
Guatemala	73	54	20	-1
Guyana	3	5	-1	—
Haiti	60	59	(*)	(*)
Honduras	83	63	20	(*)
Jamaica	56	147	-86	-4
Mexico	-183	12	-195	—
Nicaragua	30	33	-3	—
Panama	50	59	-9	—
Peru	89	96	-7	(*)
Suriname	4	—	4	—
Trinidad and Tobago	-11	(*)	-11	(*)
Other & Unspecified	151	185	-34	(*)
Intl. Orgs. & Unspecified	**2,540**	**2,540**	**(*)**	**—**

SPORTS

Ten Most Dramatic Sports Events, Nov. 1, 1993-Nov. 5, 1994

Strikes shook American sports, as the eighth Major League Baseball work stoppage in 22 years resulted in the cancellation of the remainder of the 1994 regular season, the playoffs, and the World Series. It was the first time in 90 years that no World Series was played. The strike, which began after the conclusion of the Aug. 11 games, ended a season in which historic records had appeared within the reach of a number of players. Similar labor disputes in the National Hockey League led to a lockout Oct. 1, which would have been the first day of the 1994-95 season.

Women's figure skating dominated the spotlight at the 1994 Winter Olympic Games, held in Lillehammer, Norway, in February, as 16-year-old Ukrainian Oksana Baiul edged out Nancy Kerrigan for the gold medal. The event followed an attack on Kerrigan orchestrated by associates of U.S. teammate Tonya Harding. Harding, who later pleaded guilty to conspiracy charges (although she denied prior knowledge of the attack), finished out of medal contention.

The New York Rangers captured the Stanley Cup, June 14, ending a 54-year drought by defeating the Vancouver Canucks, 2-0, in game 7 of the NHL championship series.

The Dallas Cowboys repeated as Super Bowl champions, sending the Buffalo Bills to an unprecedented 4th consecutive Super Bowl defeat, 30-13, in Atlanta, Jan. 30.

Brazil outscored Italy, 3-2, in a tie-breaking shootout round, to capture its 4th World Cup, July 17. Neither team had been able to score in 90 minutes of regular time or 30 minutes of extra time. The 1994 World Cup was the first ever held in the U.S., as well as the first decided by a penalty kick shootout.

With a short, straight, right-hand shot to Michael Moorer's mouth, 45-year-old George Foreman stunned the boxing world by reclaiming a share of the heavyweight title that he had lost to Muhammad Ali 20 years before. The victory, a tenth-round knockout, Nov. 5, 1994, in Las Vegas, gave Foreman the WBA and IBF heavyweight titles, making him the oldest heavyweight champion in history.

The Houston Rockets captured their first NBA title, June 22, defeating the New York Knicks, 90-84, in the 7th game of a physical, low-scoring championship series.

Florida State's 18-16 victory over Nebraska in the Orange Bowl, Jan. 1, propelled FSU to the top spot in the final polls, giving coach Bobby Bowden his first national collegiate football championship. The two teams traded go-ahead field goals in the last 2 minutes of play, but Nebraska missed a 45-yard kick in the closing seconds that would have given it the win.

"The Great One," Wayne Gretzky, became the NHL's all-time leading goal-scorer, breaking Gordie Howe's record of 801 career goals. Gretzky scored number 802 on March 23 against one of the best, Vancouver goaltender Kirk McLean. The record was the last major offensive mark that Gretzky did not already own.

Arkansas beat Duke, 76-72, Apr. 4, to claim its first national collegiate basketball championship. Arkansas guard Scotty Thurman hit a 3-point shot with 50 seconds remaining to break a 70-70 tie and put his team up for good, denying Duke its third title in 4 years.

OLYMPICS

Winter Olympic Games Champions, 1924-1994

Sites of Games

1924	Chamonix, France	**1956**	Cortina d'Ampezzo, Italy	**1980**	Lake Placid, N.Y.
1928	St. Moritz, Switzerland	**1960**	Squaw Valley, Cal.	**1984**	Sarajevo, Yugoslavia
1932	Lake Placid, N.Y.	**1964**	Innsbruck, Austria	**1988**	Calgary, Alberta
1936	Garmisch-Partenkirchen, Germany	**1968**	Grenoble, France	**1992**	Albertville, France
1948	St. Moritz, Switzerland	**1972**	Sapporo, Japan	**1994**	Lillehammer, Norway
1952	Oslo, Norway	**1976**	Innsbruck, Austria	**1998**	Nagano, Japan

In 1992, the Unified Team represented the former Soviet republics of Russia, Ukraine, Belarus, Kazakhstan, and Uzbekistan.

Bobsledding

(Driver in parentheses)

4-Man Bob

		Time
1924	Switzerland (Eduard Scherrer)	5:45.54
1928	United States (William Fiske) (5-man)	3:20.50
1932	United States (William Fiske)	7:53.68
1936	Switzerland (Pierre Musy)	5:19.85
1948	United States (Francis Tyler)	5:20.10
1952	Germany (Andreas Ostler)	5:07.84
1956	Switzerland (Franz Kapus)	5:10.44
1964	Canada (Victor Emery)	4:14.46
1968	Italy (Eugenio Monti) (2 races)	2:17.39
1972	Switzerland (Jean Wicki)	4:43.07
1976	E. Germany (Meinhard Nehmer)	3:40.43
1980	E. Germany (Meinhard Nehmer)	3:59.92
1984	E. Germany (Wolfgang Hoppe)	3:20.22
1988	Switzerland (Ekkehard Fasser)	3:47.51
1992	Austria (Ingo Appelt)	3:53.90
1994	Germany (Wolfgang Hoppe)	3:27.28

2-Man Bob

		Time
1932	United States (Hubert Stevens)	8:14.74
1936	United States (Ivan Brown)	5:29.29
1948	Switzerland (F. Endrich)	5:29.20
1952	Germany (Andreas Ostler)	5:24.54
1956	Italy (Dalla Costa)	5:30.14
1964	Great Britain (Anthony Nash)	4:21.90
1968	Italy (Eugenio Monti)	4:41.54
1972	W. Germany (Wolfgang Zimmerer)	4:57.07
1976	E. Germany (Meinhard Nehmer)	3:44.42
1980	Switzerland (Erich Schaerer)	4:09.36
1984	E. Germany (Wolfgang Hoppe)	3:25.56
1988	USSR (Janis Kipours)	3:54.19
1992	Switzerland (Gustav Weber)	4:03.26
1994	Switzerland (Gustav Weber)	3:30.81

Luge

	Men's Singles	Time
1964	Thomas Keohler, Germany	3:26.77
1968	Manfred Schmid, Austria	2:52.48
1972	Wolfgang Scheidel, E. Germany	3:27.58
1976	Detlef Guenther, E. Germany	3:27.688
1980	Bernhard Glass, E. Germany	2:54.796
1984	Paul Hildgartner, Italy	3:04.258
1988	Jens Mueller, E. Germany	3:05.548
1992	Georg Hackl, Germany	3:02.363
1994	Georg Hackl, Germany	3:21.571

	Men's Pairs	Time
1964	Austria	1:41.62
1968	E. Germany	1:35.85
1972	Italy, E. Germany (tie)	1:28.35
1976	E. Germany	1:25.604
1980	E. Germany	1:19.331
1984	W. Germany	1:23.620
1988	E. Germany	1:31.940
1992	Germany	1:32.053
1994	Italy	1:36.720

	Women's Singles	Time
1964	Ortun Enderlein, Germany	3:24.67
1968	Erica Lechner, Italy	2:28.66
1972	Anna M. Muller, E. Germany	2:59.18
1976	Margit Schumann, E. Germany	2:50.621
1980	Vera Zozulya, USSR	2:36.537
1984	Steffi Martin, E. Germany	2:46.570
1988	Steffi Walter, E. Germany	3:03.973
1992	Doris Neuner, Austria	3:06.696
1994	Gerda Weissensteiner, Italy	3:15.517

Biathlon

	Men's 10 Kilometers	Time
1980	Frank Ullrich, E. Germany	32:10.69
1984	Eirik Kvalfoss, Norway	30:53.80
1988	Frank-Peter Roetsch, E. Germany	25:08.10
1992	Mark Kirchner, Germany	26:02.30
1994	Serguei Tchepikov, Russia	28:07.00

	Men's 20 Kilometers	Time
1960	Klas Lestander, Sweden	1:33:21.6
1964	Vladimir Melanin, USSR	1:20:26.8
1968	Magnar Solberg, Norway	1:13:45.9
1972	Magnar Solberg, Norway	1:15:55.50
1976	Nikolai Kruglov, USSR	1:14:12.26
1980	Anatoly Aljabiev, USSR	1:08:16.31
1984	Peter Angerer, W. Germany	1:11:52.7
1988	Frank-Peter Roetsch, E. Germany	0:56:33.33
1992	Yevgeny Redkine, Unified Team	0:57:34.4
1994	Serguei Tarasov, Russia	0:57:25.3

	Men's 30-Kilometer Relay	Time
1968	USSR, Norway, Sweden (40 km)	2:13:02.4
1972	USSR, Finland, E. Germany (40 km)	1:51:44.92
1976	USSR, Finland, E. Germany (40 km)	1:57:55.64
1980	USSR, E. Germany, W. Germany	1:34:03.27
1984	USSR, Norway, W. Germany	1:38:51.70
1988	USSR, W. Germany, Italy	1:22:30.00
1992	Germany, Unified Team, Sweden	1:24:43.50
1994	Germany, Russia, France	1:30:22.1

	Women's 7.5 Kilometers	Time
1992	Anfissa Restsova, Unified Team	24:29.20
1994	Myriam Bedard, Canada	26:08.8

	Women's 15 Kilometers	Time
1992	Antje Misersky, Germany	51:47.2
1994	Myriam Bedard, Canada	52:06.6

	Women's 22.5 Kilometer Relay	Time
1992	France, Germany, Unified Team	1:15:55.6

	Women's 30 Kilometer Relay	Time
1994	Russia, Germany, France	1:47:19.5

Figure Skating

	Men's Singles
1908	Ulrich Salchow, Sweden
1920	Gillis Grafstrom, Sweden
1924	Gillis Grafstrom, Sweden
1928	Gillis Grafstrom, Sweden
1932	Karl Schaefer, Austria
1936	Karl Schaefer, Austria
1948	Richard Button, U.S.
1952	Richard Button, U.S.
1956	Hayes Alan Jenkins, U.S.
1960	David W. Jenkins, U.S.
1964	Manfred Schnelldorfer, Germany
1968	Wolfgang Schwartz, Austria
1972	Ondrej Nepela, Czechoslovakia
1976	John Curry, Great Britain
1980	Robin Cousins, Great Britain
1984	Scott Hamilton, U.S.
1988	Brian Boitano, U.S.
1992	Viktor Petrenko, Unified Team
1994	Aleksei Urmanov, Russia

	Women's Singles
1908	Madge Syers, Great Britain
1920	Magda Julin-Mauroy, Sweden
1924	Herma von Szabo-Planck, Austria
1928	Sonja Henie, Norway
1932	Sonja Henie, Norway
1936	Sonja Henie, Norway
1948	Barbara Ann Scott, Canada
1952	Jeanette Altwegg, Great Britain
1956	Tenley Albright, U.S.
1960	Carol Heiss, U.S.
1964	Sjoukje Dijkstra, Netherlands
1968	Peggy Fleming, U.S.
1972	Beatrix Schuba, Austria
1976	Dorothy Hamill, U.S.
1980	Anett Poetzsch, E. Germany
1984	Katarina Witt, E. Germany
1988	Katarina Witt, E. Germany
1992	Kristi Yamaguchi, U.S.
1994	Oksana Baiul, Ukraine

	Pairs
1908	Anna Hubler & Heinrich Burger, Germany
1920	Ludovika & Walter Jakobsson, Finland
1924	Helene Engelman & Alfred Berger, Austria
1928	Andree Joly & Pierre Brunet, France
1932	Andree Joly & Pierre Brunet, France
1936	Maxi Herber & Ernst Baier, Germany
1948	Micheline Lannoy & Pierre Baugniet, Belgium
1952	Ria and Paul Falk, Germany
1956	Elisabeth Schwartz & Kurt Oppelt, Austria
1960	Barbara Wagner & Robert Paul, Canada
1964	Ludmila Beloussova & Oleg Protopopov, USSR
1968	Ludmila Beloussova & Oleg Protopopov, USSR
1972	Irina Rodnina & Alexei Ulanov, USSR
1976	Irina Rodnina & Aleksandr Zaitzev, USSR
1980	Irina Rodnina & Aleksandr Zaitzev, USSR
1984	Elena Valova & Oleg Vassiliev, USSR
1988	Ekaterina Gordeeva & Sergei Grinkov, USSR
1992	Natalia Mishkutienok & Artur Dimitriev, Unified Team
1994	Ekaterina Gordeeva & Sergei Grinkov, Russia

	Ice Dancing
1976	Ludmila Pakhomova & Aleksandr Gorschkov, USSR
1980	Natalya Linichuk & Gennadi Karponosov, USSR
1984	Jayne Torvill & Christopher Dean, Great Britain
1988	Natalia Bestemianova & Andrei Bukin, USSR
1992	Marina Klimova & Sergei Ponomarenko, Unified Team
1994	Oksana Grichtchuk & Yevgeny Platov, Russia

Ice Hockey

1920	Canada, U.S., Czechoslovakia
1924	Canada, U.S., Great Britain
1928	Canada, Sweden, Switzerland
1932	Canada, U.S., Germany
1936	Great Britain, Canada, U.S.
1948	Canada, Czechoslovakia, Switzerland
1952	Canada, U.S., Sweden
1956	USSR, U.S., Canada
1960	U.S., Canada, USSR
1964	USSR, Sweden, Czechoslovakia
1968	USSR, Czechoslovakia, Canada
1972	USSR, U.S., Czechoslovakia,
1976	USSR, Czechoslovakia, W. Germany
1980	U.S., USSR, Sweden
1984	USSR, Czechoslovakia, Sweden
1988	USSR, Finland, Sweden
1992	Unified Team, Canada, Czechoslovakia
1994	Sweden, Canada, Finland

Alpine Skiing

Men's Downhill		Time
1948	Henri Oreiller, France	2:55.0
1952	Zeno Colo, Italy	2:30.8
1956	Anton Sailer, Austria	2:52.2
1960	Jean Vuarnet, France	2:06.0
1964	Egon Zimmermann, Austria	2:18.16
1968	Jean-Claude Killy, France	1:59.85
1972	Bernhard Russi, Switzerland	1:51.43
1976	Franz Klammer, Austria	1:45.73
1980	Leonhard Stock, Austria	1:45.50
1984	Bill Johnson, U.S.	1:45:59
1988	Pirmin Zurbriggen, Switzerland	1:59.63
1992	Patrick Ortlieb, Austria	1:50.37
1994	Tommy Moe, U.S.	1:45.75

Men's Super Giant Slalom		Time
1988	Franck Piccard, France	1:39.66
1992	Kjetil-Andre Aamodt, Norway	1:13.04
1994	Markus Wasmeier, Germany	1:32.53

Men's Giant Slalom		Time
1952	Stein Eriksen, Norway	2:25.0
1956	Anton Sailer, Austria	3:00.1
1960	Roger Staub, Switzerland	1:48.3
1964	Francois Bonlieu, France	1:46.71
1968	Jean-Claude Killy, France	3:29.28
1972	Gustavo Thoeni, Italy	3:09.62
1976	Heini Hemmi, Switzerland	3:26.97
1980	Ingemar Stenmark, Sweden	2:40.74
1984	Max Julen, Switzerland	2:41.18
1988	Alberto Tomba, Italy	2:06:37
1992	Alberto Tomba, Italy	2:06.98
1994	Markus Wasmeier, Germany	2:52.46

Men's Slalom		Time
1948	Edi Reinalter, Switzerland	2:10.3
1952	Othmar Schneider, Austria	2:00.0
1956	Anton Sailer, Austria	194.7 (pts.)
1960	Ernst Hinterseer, Austria	2:08.9
1964	Josef Stiegler, Austria	2:11.13
1968	Jean-Claude Killy, France	1:39.73
1972	Francisco Fernandez Ochoa, Spain	1:49.27
1976	Piero Gros, Italy	2:03.29
1980	Ingemar Stenmark, Sweden	1:44.26
1984	Phil Mahre, U.S.	1:39.41
1988	Alberto Tomba, Italy	1:39.47
1992	Finn Christian Jagge, Norway	1:44.39
1994	Thomas Stangassinger, Austria	2:02.02

Men's Combined		Points
1988	Hubert Strolz, Austria	36.55
1992	Josef Polig, Italy	14.58
1994	Lasse Kjus, Norway	14.58

Women's Downhill		Time
1948	Hedi Schlunegger, Switzerland	2:28.3
1952	Trude Jochum-Beiser, Austria	1:47.1
1956	Madeleine Berthod, Switzerland	1:40.7
1960	Heidi Biebl, Germany	1:37.6
1964	Christl Haas, Austria	1:55.39
1968	Olga Pall, Austria	1:40.87
1972	Marie Therese Nadig, Switzerland	1:36.68
1976	Rosi Mittermaier, W. Germany	1:46.16
1980	Annemarie Proell Moser, Austria	1:37.52
1984	Michela Figini, Switzerland	1:13.36
1988	Marina Kiehl, W. Germany	1:25.86
1992	Kerrin Lee-Gartner, Canada	1:52.55
1994	Katja Seizinger, Germany	1:35.93

Women's Super Giant Slalom		Time
1988	Sigrid Wolf, Austria	1:19.03
1992	Deborah Compagnoni, Italy	1:21.22
1994	Diann Roffe-Steinrotter, U.S.	1:22.15

Women's Giant Slalom		Time
1952	Andrea Mead Lawrence, U.S.	2:06.8
1956	Ossi Reichert, Germany	1:56.5
1960	Yvonne Ruegg, Switzerland	1:39.9
1964	Marielle Goitschel, France	1:52.24
1968	Nancy Greene, Canada	1:51.97
1972	Marie Therese Nadig, Switzerland	1:29.90
1976	Kathy Kreiner, Canada	1:29.13
1980	Hanni Wenzel, Liechtenstein (2 runs)	2:41.66
1984	Debbie Armstrong, U.S.	2:20.98
1988	Vreni Schneider, Switzerland	2:06.49
1992	Pernilla Wiberg, Sweden	2:12.74
1994	Deborah Compagnoni, Italy	2:30.97

Women's Slalom		Time
1948	Gretchen Fraser, U.S.	1:57.2
1952	Andrea Mead Lawrence, U.S.	2:10.6
1956	Renee Colliard, Switzerland	112.3 pts.
1960	Anne Heggtveigt, Canada	1:49.6
1964	Christine Goitschel, France	1:29.86
1968	Marielle Goitschel, France	1:25.86
1972	Barbara Cochran, U.S.	1:31.24
1976	Rosi Mittermaier, W. Germany	1:30.54
1980	Hanni Wenzel, Liechtenstein	1:25.09
1984	Paoletta Magoni, Italy	1:36.47
1988	Vreni Schneider, Switzerland	1:36.69
1992	Petra Kronberger, Austria	1:32.68
1994	Vreni Schneider, Switzerland	1:56.01

Women's Combined		Time
1988	Anita Wachter, Austria	29.25 (pts.)
1992	Petra Kronberger, Austria	2.55 (pts.)
1994	Pernilla Wiberg, Sweden	3:05.16

Freestyle Skiing

Men's Moguls		Points
1992	Edgar Grospiron, France	25.81
1994	Jean-Luc Brassard, Canada	27.24

Men's Aerials		Points
1994	Andreas Schoenbaechler, Switzerland	234.67

Women's Moguls		Points
1992	Donna Weinbrecht, U.S.	23.69
1994	Stine Lise Hattestad, Norway	25.97

Women's Aerials		Points
1994	Lina Tcherjazova, Uzbekistan	166.84

Cross-Country Skiing

Men's Events

10 kilometers (6.2 miles)		Time
1992	Vegard Ulvang, Norway	27:36.0
1994	Bjorn Daehlie, Norway	24:20.1

15 kilometers (9.3 miles)		Time
1924	Thorleif Haug, Norway	1:14:31
1928	Johan Grottumsbraaten, Norway	1:37:01
1932	Sven Utterstrom, Sweden	1:23:07
1936	Erik-August Larsson, Sweden	1:14:38
1948	Martin Lundstrom, Sweden	1:13:50
1952	Hallgeir Brenden, Norway	1:01:34
1956	Hallgeir Brenden, Norway	49:39.0
1960	Haakon Brusveen, Norway	51:55.5
1964	Eero Maentyranta, Finland	50:54.1
1968	Harald Groenningen, Norway	47:54.2
1972	Sven-Ake Lundback, Sweden	45:28.24
1976	Nikolai Balukov, USSR	43:58.47
1980	Thomas Wassberg, Sweden	41:57.63
1984	Gunde Svan, Sweden	41:25.6
1988	Mikhail Deviatiarov, USSR	41:18.9
1992	Bjorn Daehlie, Norway	38:01.9
1994	Bjorn Daehlie, Norway	35:48.8

(Note: approx. 18-km. course 1924-1952)

30 kilometers (18.6 miles)		Time
1956	Veikko Hakulinen, Finland	1:44:06.0
1960	Sixten Jernberg, Sweden	1:51:03.9
1964	Eero Maentyranta, Finland	1:30:50.7
1968	Franco Nones, Italy	1:35:39.2
1972	Vyacheslav Vedenine, USSR	1:36:31.15
1976	Sergei Saveliev, USSR	1:30:29.38
1980	Nikolai Zimyatov, USSR	1:27:02.80
1984	Nikolai Zimyatov, USSR	1:28:56.3
1988	Aleksei Prokourorov, USSR	1:24:26.3
1992	Vegard Ulvang, Norway	1:22:27.8
1994	Thomas Alsgaard, Norway	1:12:26.4

50 kilometers (31.2 miles)		Time
1924	Thorleif Haug, Norway	3:44:32.0
1928	Per Erik Hedlund, Sweden	4:52:03.0
1932	Veli Saarinen, Finland	4:28:00.0

1936	Elis Wiklund, Sweden	3:30:11.0
1948	Nils Karlsson, Sweden	3:47:48.0
1952	Veikko Hakulinen, Finland	3:33:33.0
1956	Sixten Jernberg, Sweden	2:50:27.0
1960	Kalevi Hamalainen, Finland	2:59:06.3
1964	Sixten Jernberg, Sweden	2:43:52.6
1968	Ole Ellefsaeter, Norway	2:28:45.8
1972	Paal Tyldum, Norway	2:43:14.75
1976	Ivar Formo, Norway	2:37:30.05
1980	Nikolai Zimyatov, USSR	2:27:24.60
1984	Thomas Wassberg, Sweden	2:15:55.8
1988	Gunde Svan, Sweden	2:04:30.9
1992	Bjorn Daehlie, Norway	2:03:41.5
1994	Vladimir Smirnov, Kazakhstan	2:07:20.3

	40-km. Relay	Time
1936	Finland, Norway, Sweden	2:41:33.0
1948	Sweden, Finland, Norway	2:32:08.0
1952	Finland, Norway, Sweden	2:20:16.0
1956	USSR, Finland, Sweden	2:15:30.0
1960	Finland, Norway, USSR	2:18:45.6
1964	Sweden, Finland, USSR	2:18:34.6
1968	Norway, Sweden, Finland	2:08:33.5
1972	USSR, Norway, Switzerland	2:04:47.94
1976	Finland, Norway, USSR	2:07:59.72
1980	USSR, Norway, Finland	1:57:03.46
1984	Sweden, USSR, Finland	1:55:06.30
1988	Sweden, USSR, Czechoslovakia	1:43:58.60
1992	Norway, Italy, Finland	1:39:26.00
1994	Italy, Norway, Finland	1:41:15.00

	Combined Cross-Country & Jumping	Points
1924	Thorleif Haug, Norway	453.800
1928	Johan Grottumsbraaten, Norway	427.800
1932	Johan Grottumsbraaten, Norway	446.000
1936	Oddbjorn Hagen, Norway	430.300
1948	Heikki Hasu, Finland	448.800
1952	Simon Slattvik, Norway	451.621
1956	Sverre Stenersen, Norway	455.000
1960	Georg Thoma, Germany	457.952
1964	Tormod Knutsen, Norway	469.280
1968	Franz Keller, W. Germany	449.040
1972	Ulrich Wehling, E. Germany	413.340
1976	Ulrich Wehling, E. Germany	423.390
1980	Ulrich Wehling, E. Germany	432.200
1984	Tom Sandberg, Norway	422.595
1988	Hippolyt Kempf, Switzerland	235.8
1992	Fabrice Guy, France	426.470
1994	Fred Barre Lundberg, Norway	457.970

	Team Ski Jumping (90 meters)	Points
1988	Finland, Yugoslavia, Norway	634.4
1992	Finland, Austria, Czechoslovakia	644.4
1994	Germany, Japan, Austria	970.1

	Ski Jumping (90 meters)	Points
1924	Jacob Thams, Norway	227.5
1928	Alfred Andersen, Norway	230.5
1932	Birger Ruud, Norway	228.1
1936	Birger Ruud, Norway	232.0
1948	Petter Hugsted, Norway	228.1
1952	Arnfinn Bergmann, Norway	226.0
1956	Antti Hyvarinen, Finland	227.0
1960	Helmut Recknagel, Germany	227.2
1964	Toralf Engan, Norway	230.7
1968	Vladimir Beloussov, USSR	231.3
1972	Wojiech Fortuna, Poland	219.9
1976	Karl Schnabl, Austria	234.8
1980	Jouko Tormanen, Finland	271.0
1984	Matti Nykaenen, Finland	231.2
1988	Matti Nykaenen, Finland	224.0
1992	Ernst Vettori, Austria	222.8
1994	Espen Bredesen, Norway	282.0

	Ski Jumping (120 meters)	Points
1992	Toni Nicminen, Finland	239.5
1994	Jens Weissflog, Germany	274.5

	Team Nordic Combined	Time
1988	W. Germany, Switzerland, Austria	1:20:46.0
1992	Japan, Norway, Austria	1:23:36.5
1994	Japan, Norway, Switzerland	1,368.860 (pts.)

Women's Events

	5 kilometers (approx. 3.1 miles)	Time
1964	Claudia Boyarskikh, USSR	17:50.5
1968	Toini Gustafsson, Sweden	16:45.2
1972	Galina Koulacova, USSR	17:00.50
1976	Helena Takalo, Finland	15:48.69
1980	Raisa Smetanina, USSR	15:06.92
1984	Marja-Liisa Haemaelainen, Finland	17:04.0
1988	Marjo Matikainen, Finland	15:04.0
1992	Marjut Lukkarinen, Finland	14:13.8
1994	Ljubov Egorova, Russia	14:08.8

	10 kilometers (6.2 miles)	Time
1952	Lydia Wideman, Finland	41:40.0
1956	Lyubov Kosyreva, USSR	38:11.0
1960	Maria Gusakova, USSR	39:46.6
1964	Claudia Boyarskikh, USSR	40:24.3
1968	Toini Gustafsson, Sweden	36:46.5
1972	Galina Koulacova, USSR	34:17.82
1976	Raisa Smetanina, USSR	30:13.41
1980	Barbara Petzold, E. Germany	30:31.54
1984	Marja-Liisa Haemaelainen, Finland	31:44.2
1988	Vida Ventsene, USSR	30:08.3
1992	Lyubov Egorova, Unified Team	25:53.7
1994	Lyubov Egorova, Russia	27:30.1

	15 kilometers (9.3 miles)	Time
1992	Lyubov Egorova, Unified Team	42:20.8
1994	Manuela Di Centa, Italy	39:44.5

	30 kilometers (18.6 miles)	Time
1992	Stefania Belmondo, Italy	1:22:30.1
1994	Manuela Di Centa, Italy	1:25:41.6

	20-km. Relay	Time
1956	Finland, USSR, Sweden (15 km.)	1:09:01.0
1960	Sweden, USSR, Finland (15 km.)	1:04:21.4
1964	USSR, Sweden, Finland (15 km.)	59:20.2
1968	Norway, Sweden, USSR (15 km.)	57:30.0
1972	USSR, Finland, Norway (15 km.)	48:46.15
1976	USSR, Finland, E. Germany	1:07:49.75
1980	E. Germany, USSR, Norway	1:02:11.1
1984	Norway, Czechoslovakia, Finland	1:06:49.7
1988	USSR, Norway, Finland	59:51.1
1992	United Team, Norway, Italy	59:34.8
1994	Russia, Norway, Italy	57:12.5

Speed Skating

	Men's 500 meters	Time
1924	Charles Jewtraw, U.S.	0:44.0
1928	Thunberg, Finland & Evensen, Norway (tie)	0:43.4
1932	John A. Shea, U.S.	0:43.4
1936	Ivar Ballangrud, Norway	0:43.4
1948	Finn Helgesen, Norway	0:43.1
1952	Kenneth Henry, U.S.	0:43.2
1956	Evgeniy Grishin, USSR	0:40.2
1960	Evgeniy Grishin, USSR	0:40.2
1964	Terry McDermott, U.S.	0:40.1
1968	Erhard Keller, W. Germany	0:40.3
1972	Erhard Keller, W. Germany	0:39.44
1976	Evgeny Kulikov, USSR	0:39.17
1980	Eric Heiden, U.S.	0:38.03
1984	Sergei Fokichev, USSR	0:38.19
1988	Uwe-Jens Mey, E. Germany	0:36.45
1992	Uwe-Jens Mey, Germany	0:37.14
1994	Aleksandr Golubev, Russia	0:36.33

	Men's 1,000 meters	Time
1976	Peter Mueller, U.S.	1:19.32
1980	Eric Heiden, U.S.	1:15.18
1984	Gaetan Boucher, Canada	1:15.80
1988	Nikolai Guiliaev, USSR	1:13.03
1992	Olaf Zinke, Germany	1:14.85
1994	Dan Jansen, U.S.	1:12.43

	Men's 1,500 meters	Time
1924	Clas Thunberg, Finland	2:20.8
1928	Clas Thunberg, Finland	2:21.1
1932	John A. Shea, U.S.	2:57.5
1936	Charles Mathiesen, Norway	2:19.2
1948	Sverre Farstad, Norway	2:17.6
1952	Hjalmar Andersen, Norway	2:20.4
1956	Grishin, & Mikhailov, both USSR (tie)	2:08.6
1960	Aas, Norway & Grishin, USSR (tie)	2:10.4
1964	Ants Anston, USSR	2:10.3
1968	Cornetis Verkerk, Netherlands	2:03.4
1972	Ard Schenk, Netherlands	2:02.96
1976	Jan Egil Storholt, Norway	1:59.38
1980	Eric Heiden, U.S.	1:55.44
1984	Gaetan Boucher, Canada	1:58.36
1988	Andre Hoffmann, E. Germany	1:52.06
1992	Johann Koss, Norway	1:54.81
1994	Johann Koss, Norway	1:51.29

Men's 5,000 meters

Year	Winner	Time
1924	Clas Thunberg, Finland	8:39.0
1928	Ivar Ballangrud, Norway	8:50.5
1932	Irving Jaffee, U.S.	9:40.8
1936	Ivar Ballangrud, Norway	8:19.6
1948	Reidar Liaklev, Norway	8:29.4
1952	Hjalmar Andersen, Norway	8:10.6
1956	Boris Shilkov, USSR	7:48.7
1960	Viktor Kosichkin, USSR	7:51.3
1964	Knut Johannesen, Norway	7:38.4
1968	F. Anton Maier, Norway	7:22.4
1972	Ard Schenk, Netherlands	7:23.61
1976	Sten Stensen, Norway	7:24.48
1980	Eric Heiden, U.S.	7:02.29
1984	Sven Tomas Gustafson, Sweden	7:12.28
1988	Tomas Gustafson, Sweden	6:44.63
1992	Geir Karlstad, Norway	6:59.97
1994	Johann Koss, Norway	6:34.96

Men's 10,000 meters

Year	Winner	Time
1924	Julius Skutnabb, Finland	18:04.8
1928	Event not held, thawing of ice	
1932	Irving Jaffee, U.S.	19:13.6
1936	Ivar Ballangrud, Norway	17:24.3
1948	Ake Seyffarth, Sweden	17:26.3
1952	Hjalmar Andersen, Norway	16:45.8
1956	Sigvard Ericsson, Sweden	16:35.9
1960	Knut Johannesen, Norway	15:46.6
1964	Jonny Nilsson, Sweden	15:50.1
1968	Jonny Hoeglin, Sweden	15:23.6
1972	Ard Schenk, Netherlands	15:01.35
1976	Piet Kleine, Netherlands	14:50.59
1980	Eric Heiden, U.S.	14:28.13
1984	Igor Malkov, USSR	14:39.90
1988	Tomas Gustafson, Sweden	13:48.20
1992	Bart Veldkamp, Netherlands	14:12.12
1994	Johann Koss, Norway	13:30.55

Women's 500 meters

Year	Winner	Time
1960	Helga Haase, Germany	0:45.9
1964	Lydia Skoblikova, USSR	0:45.0
1968	Ludmila Titova, USSR	0:46.1
1972	Anne Henning, U.S.	0:43.33
1976	Sheila Young, U.S.	0:42.76
1980	Karin Enke, E. Germany	0:41.78
1984	Christa Rothenburger, E. Germany	0:41.02
1988	Bonnie Blair, U.S.	0:39.10
1992	Bonnie Blair, U.S.	0:40.33
1994	Bonnie Blair, U.S.	0:39.25

Women's 1,000 meters

Year	Winner	Time
1960	Klara Guseva, USSR	1:34.1
1964	Lydia Skoblikova, USSR	1:33.2
1968	Carolina Geijssen, Netherlands	1:32.6
1972	Monika Pflug, W. Germany	1:31.40
1976	Tatiana Averina, USSR	1:28.43
1980	Natalya Petruseva, USSR	1:24.10
1984	Karin Enke, E. Germany	1:21.61
1988	Christa Rothenburger, E. Germany	1:17.65
1992	Bonnie Blair, U.S.	1:21.90
1994	Bonnie Blair, U.S.	1:18.74

Women's 1,500 meters

Year	Winner	Time
1960	Lydia Skoblikova, USSR	2:52.2
1964	Lydia Skoblikova, USSR	2:22.6
1968	Kaija Mustonen, Finland	2:22.4
1972	Dianne Holum, U.S.	2:20.85
1976	Galina Stepanskaya, USSR	2:16.58
1980	Anne Borckink, Netherlands	2:10.95
1984	Karin Enke, E. Germany	2:03.42
1988	Yvonne van Gennip, Netherlands	2:00.68
1992	Jacqueline Boerner, Germany	2:05.87
1994	Emese Hunyady, Austria	2:02.19

Women's 3,000 meters

Year	Winner	Time
1960	Lydia Skoblikova, USSR	5:14.3
1964	Lydia Skoblikova, USSR	5:14.9
1968	Johanna Schut, Netherlands	4:56.2
1972	Christina Baas-Kaiser, Netherlands	4:52.14
1976	Tatiana Averina, USSR	4:45.19
1980	Bjoerg Eva Jensen, Norway	4:32.13
1984	Andrea Schoene, E. Germany	4:24.79
1988	Yvonne van Gennip, Netherlands	4:11.94
1992	Gunda Niemann, Germany	4:19.90
1994	Svetlana Bazhanova, Russia	4:17.43

Women's 5,000 meters

Year	Winner	Time
1988	Yvonne van Gennip, Netherlands	7:14.13
1992	Gunda Niemann, Germany	7:31.57
1994	Claudia Pechstein, Germany	7:14.37

Short Track Speed Skating

Men's 1,000 meters

Year	Winner	Time
1992	Kim Ki-Hoon, S. Korea	1:30.76
1994	Kim Ki-Hoon, S. Korea	1:34.57

Men's 5,000-meter relay

Year	Winner	Time
1992	S. Korea, Canada, Japan	7:14.02
1994	Italy, U.S., Australia	7:11.74

Women's 500 meters

Year	Winner	Time
1992	Cathy Turner, U.S.	47:04
1994	Cathy Turner, U.S.	45.98

Women's 3,000-meter relay

Year	Winner	Time
1992	Canada, U.S., Unified Team	4:36.62
1994	S. Korea, Canada, U.S.	4:26.64

Winter Olympic Games in 1994

Lillehammer, Norway, Feb. 12-27, 1994

The 1994 Olympic Winter Games were held only 2 years after the 1992 games, due to an International Olympic Committee decision to switch to a two-year cycle between summer and winter Olympics. The next Summer Games will be held in 1996 (in Atlanta, GA) and the next Winter Games in 1998 (in Nagano, Japan). The 17th Olympic Winter Games, held in Lillehammer, Norway, featured 1,884 athletes from 67 countries, including 11 former Soviet republics now competing as independent countries. Athletes from host-country Norway, whose speed skater Johann Olav Koss broke 3 Olympic records, won a games-high 26 medals. U.S. speed skater Bonnie Blair took home 2 gold medals, giving her a career total of 5 gold medals, the most of any female American Olympian. Team USA captured 13 medals, more than in any previous Olympic Winter Games.

For the first time, the U.S. Olympic Committee rewarded athletes' superior performances by handing out prizes of $15,000 for a gold medal, $10,000 for a silver, $7,500 for a bronze, and $5,000 for a fourth-place finish.

Final Medal Standings

	Gold	Silver	Bronze	Total
Norway	10	11	5	**26**
Germany	9	7	8	**24**
Russia	11	8	4	**23**
Italy	7	5	8	**20**
U.S.	6	5	2	**13**
Canada	3	6	4	**13**
Switzerland	3	4	2	**9**
Austria	2	3	4	**9**
N. Korea	4	1	1	**6**
Finland	0	1	5	**6**
Japan	1	2	2	**5**
France	0	1	4	**5**
Netherlands	0	1	3	**4**
Sweden	2	1	0	**3**
Kazakhstan	1	2	0	**3**
China	0	1	2	**3**
Slovenia	0	0	3	**3**
Ukraine	1	0	1	**2**
Belarus	0	2	0	**2**
Great Britain	0	0	2	**2**
Uzbekistan	1	0	0	**1**
Australia	0	0	1	**1**

Summer Olympic Games in 1992

Barcelona, Spain, July 25–Aug. 9, 1992

More than 14,000 athletes gathered in Barcelona, Spain, in July and August, 1992, for 16 days to compete in the Games of the XXV Olympiad. The athletes represented a record 172 nations, 11 more than had participated in any previous Olympics, and competed for medals in 257 events.

The 1992 games will be remembered mostly for the appearance of the Dream Team—the United States basketball team—featuring, for the first time, the stars of the National Basketball Association. As expected, the team crushed all its opponents on the way to a gold medal. Other notable events at the games were the victory in the long jump for Carl Lewis, his third consecutive gold medal in the event; the successful defense in the heptathlon by Jackie Joyner-Kersee; and the domination in men's gymnastics by Vitaly Shcherbo of the Unified Team. Perhaps the biggest surprise was the failure of world-record holder Sergei Bubka (Ukraine) to win a medal in the pole vault. Also notable was the appearance of South African athletes after missing 7 consecutive Olympiads.

The Unified Team, made up of athletes of 12 republics of the former Soviet Union, won the most gold medals, 45, and the most medals, 112. The United States finished second with 37 gold medals and 108 medals overall.

Final Medal Standings

	Gold	Silver	Bronze	Total
Unified Team[1]	45	38	29	**112**
United States	37	34	37	**108**
Germany	33	21	28	**82**
China	16	22	16	**54**
Cuba	14	6	11	**31**
Hungary	11	12	7	**30**
South Korea	12	5	12	**29**
France	8	5	16	**29**
Australia	7	9	11	**27**
Spain	13	7	2	**22**
Japan	3	8	11	**22**
Britain	5	3	12	**20**
Italy	6	5	8	**19**
Poland	3	6	10	**19**
Canada	6	5	7	**18**
Romania	4	6	8	**18**
Bulgaria	3	7	6	**16**
Netherlands	2	6	7	**15**
Sweden	1	7	4	**12**
New Zealand	1	4	5	**10**
North Korea	4	0	5	**9**
Kenya	2	4	2	**8**
Czechoslovakia	4	2	1	**7**
Norway	2	4	1	**7**
Turkey	2	2	2	**6**
Denmark	1	1	4	**6**
Indonesia	2	2	1	**5**
Finland	1	2	2	**5**
Jamaica	0	3	1	**4**
Nigeria	0	3	1	**4**
Brazil	2	1	0	**3**
Morocco	1	1	1	**3**

	Gold	Silver	Bronze	Total
Ethiopia	1	0	2	**3**
Latvia	0	2	1	**3**
Croatia	0	1	2	**3**
Belgium	0	1	2	**3**
Iran	0	1	2	**3**
I.O.P.[2]	0	1	2	**3**
Greece	2	0	0	**2**
Ireland	1	1	0	**2**
Algeria	1	0	1	**2**
Estonia	1	0	1	**2**
Lithuania	1	0	1	**2**
Austria	0	2	0	**2**
Namibia	0	2	0	**2**
South Africa	0	2	0	**2**
Israel	0	1	1	**2**
Mongolia	0	0	2	**2**
Slovenia	0	0	2	**2**
Switzerland	1	0	0	**1**
Mexico	0	1	0	**1**
Peru	0	1	0	**1**
Taiwan	0	1	0	**1**
Argentina	0	0	1	**1**
Bahamas	0	0	1	**1**
Colombia	0	0	1	**1**
Ghana	0	0	1	**1**
Malaysia	0	0	1	**1**
Pakistan	0	0	1	**1**
Philippines	0	0	1	**1**
Puerto Rico	0	0	1	**1**
Qatar	0	0	1	**1**
Suriname	0	0	1	**1**
Thailand	0	0	1	**1**

(1) Athletes from 12 former Soviet republics. (2) Independent Olympic Participants (athletes from Serbia, Montenegro, Macedonia).

Summer Olympic Games Records

The modern Olympic Games, first held in Athens, Greece, in 1896, were the result of efforts by Baron Pierre de Coubertin, a French educator, to promote interest in education and culture, also to foster better international understanding through the universal medium of youth's love of athletics.

His source of inspiration for the Olympic Games was the ancient Greek Olympic Games, most notable of the four Panhellenic celebrations. The games were combined patriotic, religious, and athletic festivals held every four years. The first such recorded festival was held in 776 B.C., the date from which the Greeks began to keep their calendar by "Olympiads," or four-year spans between the games.

The first Olympiad is said to have consisted merely of a 200-yard foot race near the small city of Olympia, but the games gained in scope and became demonstrations of national pride. Only Greek citizens — amateurs — were permitted to participate. Winners received laurel, wild olive, and palm wreaths and were accorded many special privileges. Under the Roman emperors, the games deteriorated into professional carnivals and circuses. Emperor Theodosius banned them in AD 394.

Baron de Coubertin enlisted 9 nations to send athletes to the first modern Olympics in 1896; now more than 170 nations compete. Winter Olympic Games were started in 1924.

Sites of Olympic Games

1896	Athens, Greece	**1920**	Antwerp, Belgium	**1952**	Helsinki, Finland	**1976**	Montreal, Canada
1900	Paris, France	**1924**	Paris, France	**1956**	Melbourne, Australia	**1980**	Moscow, USSR
1904	St. Louis, U.S.	**1928**	Amsterdam, Netherlands	**1960**	Rome, Italy	**1984**	Los Angeles, U.S.
1906	Athens *, Greece	**1932**	Los Angeles, U.S.	**1964**	Tokyo, Japan	**1988**	Seoul, S. Korea
1908	London, England	**1936**	Berlin, Germany	**1968**	Mexico City, Mexico	**1992**	Barcelona, Spain
1912	Stockholm, Sweden	**1948**	London, England	**1972**	Munich, W. Germany	**1996**	Atlanta, U.S.
						2000	Sydney, Australia

* Games not recognized by International Olympic Committee. Games 6 (1916), 12 (1940), and 13 (1944) were not celebrated. The 1980 games were boycotted by 62 nations, including the U.S. The 1984 games were boycotted by the USSR and most eastern bloc nations. East and West Germany competed separately 1968-88. The 1992 Unified Team consisted of 12 former Soviet republics. The 1992 Independent Olympic Participants (I.O.P.) were athletes from Serbia, Montenegro, and Macedonia.

Olympic Games Champions, 1896-1992

(*Indicates Gold Medal-Winning Record)

Track and Field — Men

100-Meter Run

1896	Thomas Burke, United States	12s
1900	Francis W. Jarvis, United States	11.0s
1904	Archie Hahn, United States	11s
1908	Reginald Walker, South Africa	18s
1912	Ralph Craig, United States	10.8s
1920	Charles Paddock, United States	10.8s
1924	Harold Abrahams, Great Britain	10.6s
1928	Percy Williams, Canada	10.8s
1932	Eddie Tolan, United States	10.3s
1936	Jesse Owens, United States	10.3s
1948	Harrison Dillard, United States	10.3s
1952	Lindy Remigino, United States	10.4s
1956	Bobby Morrow, United States	10.5s
1960	Armin Hary, Germany	10.2s
1964	Bob Hayes, United States	10.0s
1968	Jim Hines, United States	9.95s
1972	Valery Borzov, USSR	10.14s
1976	Hasely Crawford, Trinidad	10.06s
1980	Allan Wells, Great Britain	10.25s
1984	Carl Lewis, United States	9.99s
1988	Carl Lewis, United States	9.92s*
1992	Linford Christie, Great Britain	9.96s

200-Meter Run

1900	Walter Tewksbury, United States	22.2s
1904	Archie Hahn, United States	21.6s
1908	Robert Kerr, Canada	22.6s
1912	Ralph Craig, United States	21.7s
1920	Allan Woodring, United States	22s
1924	Jackson Scholz, United States	21.6s
1928	Percy Williams, Canada	21.8s
1932	Eddie Tolan, United States	21.2s
1936	Jesse Owens, United States	20.7s
1948	Mel Patton, United States	21.1s
1952	Andrew Stanfield, United States	20.7s
1956	Bobby Morrow, United States	20.6s
1960	Livio Berruti, Italy	20.5s
1964	Henry Carr, United States	20.3s
1968	Tommie Smith, United States	19.83s
1972	Valeri Borzov, USSR	20.00s
1976	Donald Quarrie, Jamaica	20.23s
1980	Pietro Mennea, Italy	20.19s
1984	Carl Lewis, United States	19.80s
1988	Joe DeLoach, United States	19.75s*
1992	Mike Marsh, United States	20.01s

400-Meter Run

1896	Thomas Burke, United States	54.2s
1900	Maxey Long, United States	49.4s
1904	Harry Hillman, United States	49.2s
1908	Wyndham Halswelle, Great Britain, walkover	50s
1912	Charles Reidpath, United States	48.2s
1920	Bevil Rudd, South Africa	49.6s
1924	Eric Liddell, Great Britain	47.6s
1928	Ray Barbuti, United States	47.8s
1932	William Carr, United States	46.2s
1936	Archie Williams, United States	46.5s
1948	Arthur Wint, Jamaica	46.2s
1952	George Rhoden, Jamaica	45.9s
1956	Charles Jenkins, United States	46.7s
1960	Otis Davis, United States	44.9s
1964	Michael Larrabee, United States	45.1s
1968	Lee Evans, United States	43.8s
1972	Vincent Matthews, United States	44.66s
1976	Alberto Juantorena, Cuba	44.26s
1980	Viktor Markin, USSR	44.60s
1984	Alonzo Babers, United States	44.27s
1988	Steven Lewis, United States	43.87s
1992	Quincy Watts, United States	43.50s*

800-Meter Run

1896	Edwin Flack, Australia	2m. 11s
1900	Alfred Tysoe, Great Britain	2m. 1.2s
1904	James Lightbody, United States	1m. 56s
1908	Mel Sheppard, United States	1m. 52.8s
1912	James Meredith, United States	1m. 51.9s
1920	Albert Hill, Great Britain	1m. 53.4s
1924	Douglas Lowe, Great Britain	1m. 52.4s
1928	Douglas Lowe, Great Britain	1m. 51.8s
1932	Thomas Hampson, Great Britain	1m. 49.8s
1936	John Woodruff, United States	1m. 52.9s
1948	Mal Whitfield, United States	1m. 49.2s
1952	Mal Whitfield, United States	1m. 49.2s
1956	Thomas Courtney, United States	1m. 47.7s
1960	Peter Snell, New Zealand	1m. 46.3s
1964	Peter Snell, New Zealand	1m. 45.1s
1968	Ralph Doubell, Australia	1m. 44.3s
1972	Dave Wottle, United States	1m. 45.9s
1976	Alberto Juantorena, Cuba	1m. 43.50s
1980	Steve Ovett, Great Britain	1m. 45.40s
1984	Joaquim Cruz, Brazil	1m. 43.00s*
1988	Paul Ereng, Kenya	1m. 43.45s
1992	William Tanui, Kenya	1m. 43.66s

1,500-Meter Run

1896	Edwin Flack, Australia	4m. 33.2s
1900	Charles Bennett, Great Britain	4m. 6.2s
1904	James Lightbody, United States	4m. 5.4s
1908	Mel Sheppard, United States	4m. 3.4s
1912	Arnold Jackson, Great Britain	3m. 56.8s
1920	Albert Hill, Great Britain	4m. 1.8s
1924	Paavo Nurmi, Finland	3m. 53.6s
1928	Harry Larva, Finland	3m. 53.2s
1932	Luigi Beccali, Italy	3m. 51.2s
1936	Jack Lovelock, New Zealand	3m. 47.8s
1948	Henri Eriksson, Sweden	3m. 49.8s
1952	Joseph Barthel, Luxemburg	3m. 45.2s
1956	Ron Delany, Ireland	3m. 41.2s
1960	Herb Elliott, Australia	3m. 35.6s
1964	Peter Snell, New Zealand	3m. 38.1s
1968	Kipchoge Keino, Kenya	3m. 34.9s
1972	Pekka Vasala, Finland	3m. 36.3s
1976	John Walker, New Zealand	3m. 39.17s
1980	Sebastian Coe, Great Britain	3m. 38.4s
1984	Sebastian Coe, Great Britain	3m. 32.53s*
1988	Peter Rono, Kenya	3m. 35.96s
1992	Fermin Cacho Ruiz, Spain	3m. 40.12s

3,000-Meter Steeplechase

1920	Percy Hodge, Great Britain	10m. 0.4s
1924	Willie Ritola, Finland	9m. 33.6s
1928	Toivo Loukola, Finland	9m. 21.8s
1932	Volmari Iso-Hollo, Finland	10m. 33.4s
	(About 3,450 mtrs. extra lap by error)	
1936	Volmari Iso-Hollo, Finland	9m. 3.8s
1948	Thore Sjoestrand, Sweden	9m. 4.6s
1952	Horace Ashenfelter, United States	8m. 45.4s
1956	Chris Brasher, Great Britain	8m. 41.2s
1960	Zdzislaw Krzyszkowiak, Poland	8m. 34.2s
1964	Gaston Roelants, Belgium	8m. 30.8s
1968	Amos Biwott, Kenya	8m. 51s
1972	Kipchoge Keino, Kenya	8m. 23.6s
1976	Anders Garderud, Sweden	8m. 08.2s
1980	Bronislaw Malinowski, Poland	8m. 09.7s
1984	Julius Korir, Kenya	8m. 11.8s
1988	Julius Kariuki, Kenya	8m. 05.51s*
1992	Matthew Birir, Kenya	8m. 08.84s

5,000-Meter Run

1912	Hannes Kolehmainen, Finland	14m. 36.6s
1920	Joseph Guillemot, France	14m. 55.6s
1924	Paavo Nurmi, Finland	14m. 31.2s
1928	Willie Ritola, Finland	14m. 38s
1932	Lauri Lehtinen, Finland	14m. 30s
1936	Gunnar Hockert, Finland	14m. 22.2s
1948	Gaston Reiff, Belgium	14m. 17.6s
1952	Emil Zatopek, Czechoslovakia	14m. 6.6s
1956	Vladimir Kuts, USSR	13m. 39.6s
1960	Murray Halberg, New Zealand	13m. 43.4s
1964	Bob Schul, United States	13m. 48.8s
1968	Mohamed Gammoudi, Tunisia	14m. 05.0s
1972	Lasse Viren, Finland	13m. 26.4s
1976	Lasse Viren, Finland	13m. 24.76s
1980	Miruts Yifter, Ethiopia	13m. 21.0s
1984	Said Aouita, Morocco	13m. 05.59s*
1988	John Ngugi, Kenya	13m. 11.70s
1992	Dieter Baumann, Germany	13m. 12.52s

10,000-Meter Run

1912	Hannes Kolehmainen, Finland	31m. 20.8s
1920	Paavo Nurmi, Finland	31m. 45.8s
1924	Willie Ritola, Finland	30m. 23.2s
1928	Paavo Nurmi, Finland	30m. 18.8s
1932	Janusz Kusocinski, Poland	30m. 11.4s
1936	Ilmari Salminen, Finland	30m. 15.4s
1948	Emil Zatopek, Czechoslovakia	29m. 59.6s
1952	Emil Zatopek, Czechoslovakia	29m. 17.0s
1956	Vladimir Kuts, USSR	28m. 45.6s
1960	Pyotr Bolotnikov, USSR	28m. 32.2s
1964	Billy Mills, United States	28m. 24.4s
1968	Naftali Temu, Kenya	29m. 27.4s
1972	Lasse Viren, Finland	27m. 38.4s
1976	Lasse Viren, Finland	27m. 40.38s
1980	Miruts Yifter, Ethiopia	27m. 42.7s
1984	Alberto Cova, Italy	27m. 47.54s
1988	Brahim Boutaib, Morocco	27m. 21.46s*
1992	Khalid Skah, Morocco	27m. 46.70s

Marathon

1896	Spiridon Loues, Greece	2h. 58m. 50s
1900	Michel Theato, France	2h. 59m. 45s
1904	Thomas Hicks, United States	3h. 28m. 63s
1908	John J. Hayes, United States	2h. 55m. 18.4s
1912	Kenneth McArthur, South Africa	2h. 36m. 54.8s
1920	Hannes Kolehmainen, Finland	2h. 32m. 35.8s
1924	Albin Stenroos, Finland	2h. 41m. 22.6s
1928	A.B. El Ouafi, France	2h. 32m. 57s
1932	Juan Zabala, Argentina	2h. 31m. 36s
1936	Kijung Son, Japan (Korean)	2h. 29m. 19.2s
1948	Delfo Cabrera, Argentina	2h. 34m. 51.6s
1952	Emil Zatopek, Czechoslovakia	2h. 23m. 03.2s
1956	Alain Mimoun, France	2h. 25m.
1960	Abebe Bikila, Ethiopia	2h. 15m. 16.2s
1964	Abebe Bikila, Ethiopia	2h. 12m. 11.2s
1968	Mamo Wolde, Ethiopia	2h. 20m. 26.4s
1972	Frank Shorter, United States	2h. 12m. 19.8s
1976	Waldemar Cierpinski, E. Germany	2h. 09m. 55s
1980	Waldemar Cierpinski, E. Germany	2h. 11m. 03s
1984	Carlos Lopes, Portugal	2h. 09m. 21 s*
1988	Gelindo Bordin, Italy	2h. 10m. 32s
1992	Hwang Young-Cho, S. Korea	2h. 13m. 23s

20 Kilometer Walk

1956	Leonid Spirin, USSR	1h. 31m. 27.4s
1960	Vladimir Golubnichy, USSR	1h. 33m. 7.2s
1964	Kenneth Mathews, Great Britain	1h. 29m. 34.0s
1968	Vladimir Golubnichy, USSR	1h. 33m. 58.4s
1972	Peter Frenkel, E. Germany	1h. 26m. 42.4s
1976	Daniel Bautista, Mexico	1h. 24m. 40.6s
1980	Maurizio Damilano, Italy	1h. 23m. 35.5s
1984	Ernesto Canto, Mexico	1h. 23m. 13.0s
1988	Josef Pribilinec, Czech.	1h. 19m. 57.0s*
1992	Daniel Plaza Montero, Spain	1h. 21m. 45.0s

50-Kilometer Walk

1932	Thomas W. Green, Great Britain	4h. 50m. 10s
1936	Harold Whitlock, Great Britain	4h. 30m. 41.4s
1948	John Ljunggren, Sweden	4h. 41m. 52s
1952	Giuseppe Dordoni, Italy	4h. 28m. 07.8s
1956	Norman Read, New Zealand	4h. 30m. 42.8s
1960	Donald Thompson, Great Britain	4h. 25m. 30s
1964	Abdon Pamich, Italy	4h. 11m. 12.4s
1968	Christoph Hohne, E. Germany	4h. 20m. 13.6s
1972	Bern Kannenberg, W. Germany	3h. 56m. 11.6s
1980	Hartwig Gauter, E. Germany	3h. 49m. 24.0s
1984	Raul Gonzalez, Mexico	3h. 47m. 26.0s
1988	Vayachselav Ivanenko, USSR	3h. 38m. 29.0s*
1992	Andrei Perlov, Unified Team	3h. 50m. 13.0s

110-Meter Hurdles

1896	Thomas Curtis, United States	17.6s
1900	Alvin Kraenzlein, United States	15.4s
1904	Frederick Schule, United States	16s
1908	Forrest Smithson, United States	15s
1912	Frederick Kelly, United States	15.1s
1920	Earl Thomson, Canada	14.8s
1924	Daniel Kinsey, United States	15s
1928	Sydney Atkinson, South Africa	14.8s
1932	George Saling, United States	14.6s
1936	Forrest Towns, United States	14.2s
1948	William Porter, United States	13.9s
1952	Harrison Dillard, United States	13.7s
1956	Lee Calhoun, United States	13.5s
1960	Lee Calhoun, United States	13.8s
1964	Hayes Jones, United States	13.6s
1968	Willie Davenport, United States	13.3s
1972	Rod Milburn, United States	13.24s
1976	Guy Drut, France	13.30s
1980	Thomas Munkelt, E. Germany	13. 39s
1984	Roger Kingdom, United States	13.20s
1988	Roger Kingdom, United States	12.98s*
1992	Mark McCoy, Canada	13.12s

400-Meter Hurdles

1900	J.W.B. Tewksbury, United States	57.6s
1904	Harry Hillman, United States	53s
1908	Charles Bacon, United States	55s
1920	Frank Loomis, United States	54s
1924	F. Morgan Taylor, United States	52.6s
1928	Lord Burghley, Great Britain	53.4s
1932	Robert Tisdall, Ireland	51.7s
1936	Glenn Hardin, United States	52.4s
1948	Roy Cochran, United States	51.1s
1952	Charles Moore, United States	50.8s
1956	Glenn Davis, United States	50.1s
1960	Glenn Davis, United States	49.3s
1964	Rex Cawley, United States	49.6s
1968	Dave Hemery, Great Britain	48.12s
1972	John Akii-Bua, Uganda	47.82s
1976	Edwin Moses, United States	47.64s
1980	Volker Beck, E. Germany	48.70s
1984	Edwin Moses, United States	47.75s
1988	Andre Phillips, United States	47.19s
1992	Kevin Young, United States	46.78s*

High Jump

1896	Ellery Clark, United States	5ft. 11 1-4 in.
1900	Irving Baxter, United States	6ft. 2 4-5 in.
1904	Samuel Jones, United States	5ft. 11 in.
1908	Harry Porter, United States	6ft. 3 in.
1912	Alma Richards, United States	6ft. 4 in.
1920	Richmond Landon, United States	6ft. 4 in.
1924	Harold Osborn, United States	6ft. 6 in.
1928	Robert W. King, United States	6ft. 4 1-2 in.
1932	Duncan McNaughton, Canada	6ft. 5 5-8 in.
1936	Cornelius Johnson, United States	6ft. 8 in.
1948	John L. Winter, Australia	6ft. 6 in.
1952	Walter Davis, United States	6ft. 8.32 in.
1956	Charles Dumas, United States	6ft. 11 1-2 in.
1960	Robert Shavlakadze, USSR	7ft. 1 in.
1964	Valery Brumel, USSR	7ft. 1 3-4 in.
1968	Dick Fosbury, United States	7ft. 4 1-4 in.
1972	Yuri Tarmak, USSR	7ft. 3 3-4 in.
1976	Jacek Wszola, Poland	7ft. 4 1-2 in.
1980	Gerd Wessig, E. Germany	7ft. 8 3-4 in.
1984	Dietmar Mogenburg, W. Germany	7ft. 8 1-2 in.
1988	Guennadi Avdeenko, USSR	7ft. 9 1-2 in.*
1992	Javier Sotomayor, Cuba	7ft. 8 in.

Long Jump

1896	Ellery Clark, United States	20ft. 10 in.
1900	Alvin Kraenzlein, United States	23ft. 6 3-4 in.
1904	Myer Prinstein, United States	24ft. 1 in.
1908	Frank Irons, United States	24ft. 6 1-2 in.
1912	Albert Gutterson, United States	24ft. 11 1-4 in.
1920	William Petterssen, Sweden	23ft. 5 1-2 in.
1924	DeHart Hubbard, United States	24ft. 5 in.
1928	Edward B. Hamm, United States	25ft. 4 1-2 in.
1932	Edward Gordon, United States	25ft. 3-4 in.
1936	Jesse Owens, United States	26ft. 5 1-2 in.
1948	William Steele, United States	25ft. 8 in.
1952	Jerome Biffle, United States	24ft. 10 in.
1956	Gregory Bell, United States	25ft. 8 1-4 in.
1960	Ralph Boston, United States	26ft. 7 3-4 in.
1964	Lynn Davies, Great Britain	26ft. 5 3-4 in.
1968	Bob Beamon, United States	29ft. 2 1-2 in.*
1972	Randy Williams, United States	27ft. 1-2 in.
1976	Arnie Robinson, United States	27ft. 4 1-2 in.
1980	Lutz Dombrowski, E. Germany	28ft. 1-4 in.
1984	Carl Lewis, United States	28ft. 1-4 in.
1988	Carl Lewis, United States	28ft. 7 1-4 in.
1992	Carl Lewis, United States	28ft. 5 1-2 in.

400-Meter Relay

1912	Great Britain	42.4s
1920	United States	42.2s
1924	United States	41s

1928	United States	41s
1932	United States	40s
1936	United States	39.8s
1948	United States	40.6s
1952	United States	40.1s
1956	United States	39.5s
1960	Germany (U.S. disqualified)	39.5s
1964	United States	39.0s
1968	United States	38.2s
1972	United States	38.19s
1976	United States	38.33s
1980	USSR	38.26s
1984	United States	37.83s
1988	USSR (U.S. disqualified)	38.19s
1992	United States	37.40s*

1,600-Meter Relay

1908	United States	3m. 29.4s
1912	United States	3m. 16.6s
1920	Great Britain	3m. 22.2s
1924	United States	3m. 16s
1928	United States	3m. 14.2s
1932	United States	3m. 8.2s
1936	Great Britain	3m. 9s
1948	United States	3m. 10.4s
1952	Jamaica	3m. 03.9s
1956	United States	3m. 04.8s
1960	United States	3m. 02.2s
1964	United States	3m. 00.7s
1968	United States	2m. 56.16s
1972	Kenya	2m. 59.8s
1976	United States	2m. 58.65s
1980	USSR	3m. 01.1s
1984	United States	2m. 57.91s
1988	United States	2m. 56.16s
1992	United States	2m. 55.74s*

Pole Vault

1896	William Hoyt, United States	10ft. 10 in.
1900	Irving Baxter, United States	10ft. 10 in.
1904	Charles Dvorak, United States	11ft. 5 3-4 in.
1908	A. C. Gilbert, United States	
	Edward Cook Jr., United States	12ft. 2 in.
1912	Harry Babcock, United States	12ft. 11 1-2 in.
1920	Frank Foss, United States	13ft. 5 in.
1924	Lee Barnes, United States	12ft. 11 1-2 in.
1928	Sabin W. Carr, United States	13ft. 9 1-4 in.
1932	William Miller, United States	14ft. 1 3-4 in.
1936	Earle Meadows, United States	14ft. 3 1-4 in.
1948	Guinn Smith, United States	14ft. 1 1-4 in.
1952	Robert Richards, United States	14ft. 11 in.
1956	Robert Richards, United States	14ft. 11 1-2 in.
1960	Don Bragg, United States	15ft. 5 in.
1964	Fred Hansen, United States	16ft. 8 3-4 in.
1968	Bob Seagren, United States	17ft. 8 1-2 in.
1972	Wolfgang Nordwig, E. Germany	18ft. 1-2 in.
1976	Tadeusz Slusarski, Poland	18ft. 1-2 in.
1980	Wladyslaw Kozakiewicz, Poland	18ft. 11 1-2 in.
1984	Pierre Quinon, France	18ft. 10 1-4 in.
1988	Sergei Bubka, USSR	19ft. 9 1-4 in.*
1992	Maksim Tarassov, Unified Team	19ft. 1-4 in.

Hammer Throw

1900	John Flanagan, United States	163ft. 1 in.
1904	John Flanagan, United States	168ft. 1 in.
1908	John Flanagan, United States	170ft. 4 1-4 in.
1912	Matt McGrath, United States	179ft. 7 1-8 in.
1920	Pat Ryan, United States	173ft. 5 5-8 in.
1924	Fred Tootell, United States	174ft. 10 1-8 in.
1928	Patrick O'Callaghan, Ireland	168ft. 7 1-2 in.
1932	Patrick O'Callaghan, Ireland	176ft. 11 1-8 in.
1936	Karl Hein, Germany	185ft. 4 in.
1948	Imre Nemeth, Hungary	183ft. 11 1-2 in.
1952	Jozsef Csermak, Hungary	197ft. 11 9-16 in.
1956	Harold Connolly, United States	207ft. 3 1-2 in.
1960	Vasily Rudenkov, USSR	220ft. 1 5-8 in.
1964	Romuald Klim, USSR	228ft. 9 1-2 in.
1968	Gyula Zsivotsky, Hungary	240ft. 8 in.
1972	Anatoli Bondarchuk, USSR	247ft. 8 in.
1976	Yuri Syedykh, USSR	254ft. 4 in.
1980	Yuri Syedykh, USSR	268ft. 4 1-2 in.
1984	Juha Tiainen, Finland	256ft. 2 in.
1988	Sergei Litinov, USSR	278ft. 2 1-2 in.*
1992	Andrey Abduvaliyev, Unified Team.	270ft. 9 1-2 in.

Discus Throw

1896	Robert Garrett, United States	95ft. 7 1-2 in.
1900	Rudolf Bauer, Hungary	118ft. 3 in.
1904	Martin Sheridan, United States	128ft. 10 1-2 in.
1908	Martin Sheridan, United States	134ft. 2 in.
1912	Armas Taipale, Finland	148ft. 3 in.
	Both hands—Armas Taipale, Finland	271ft. 10 1-4 in.
1920	Elmer Niklander, Finland	146ft. 7 in.
1924	Clarence Houser, United States	151ft. 4 in.
1928	Clarence Houser, United States	155ft. 3 in.
1932	John Anderson, United States	162ft. 4 in.
1936	Ken Carpenter, United States	165ft. 7 in.
1948	Adolfo Consolini, Italy	173ft. 2 in.
1952	Sim Iness, United States	180ft. 6.85 in.
1956	Al Oerter, United States	184ft. 10 1-2 in.
1960	Al Oerter, United States	194ft. 2 in.
1964	Al Oerter, United States	200ft. 1 1-2 in.
1968	Al Oerter, United States	212ft. 6 1-2 in.
1972	Ludvik Danek, Czechoslovakia	211ft. 3 in.
1976	Mac Wilkins, United States	221ft. 5.4 in.
1980	Viktor Rashchupkin, USSR	218ft. 8 in.
1984	Rolf Dannenberg, W. Germany	218ft. 6 in.
1988	Jurgen Schult, E. Germany	225ft. 9 1-4 in.*
1992	Romas Ubartas, Lithuania	213ft. 7 3-4 in.

Triple Jump

1896	James Connolly, United States	44ft. 11 3-4 in.
1900	Myer Prinstein, United States	47ft. 5 3-4 in.
1904	Myer Prinstein, United States	47 ft.
1908	Timothy Ahearne, Great Britain, Ireland	48ft. 11 1-4 in.
1912	Gustaf Lindblom, Sweden	48ft. 5 1-4 in.
1920	Vilho Tuulos, Finland	47ft. 7 in.
1924	Anthony Winter, Australia	50ft. 11 1-4 in.
1928	Mikio Oda, Japan	49ft. 11 in.
1932	Chuhei Nambu, Japan	51ft. 7 in.
1936	Naoto Tajima, Japan	52ft. 6 in.
1948	Arne Ahman, Sweden	50ft. 6 1-4 in.
1952	Adhemar da Silva, Brazil	53ft. 2 3-4 in.
1956	Adhemar da Silva, Brazil	53ft. 7 3-4 in.
1960	Jozef Schmidt, Poland	55ft. 2 in.
1964	Jozef Schmidt, Poland	55ft. 3 1-2 in.
1968	Viktor Saneev, USSR	57ft. 3-4 in.
1972	Viktor Saneev, USSR	56ft. 11 in.
1976	Viktor Saneev, USSR	56ft. 8 3-4 in.
1980	Jaak Uudmae, USSR	56ft. 11 1-4 in.
1984	Al Joyner, United States	56ft. 7 1-2 in.
1988	Hristo Markov, Bulgaria	57ft. 9 1-4 in.
1992	Mike Conley, United States	59ft. 7 1-2 in.

16-lb. Shot Put

1896	Robert Garrett, United States	36ft. 9 3-4 in.
1900	Richard Sheldon, United States	46ft. 3 1-4 in.
1904	Ralph Rose, United States	48ft. 7 in.
1908	Ralph Rose, United States	46ft. 7 1-2 in.
1912	Pat McDonald, United States	50ft. 4 in.
	Both hands—Ralph Rose, United States	90ft. 5 1-2 in.
1920	Ville Porhola, Finland	48ft. 7 1-4 in.
1924	Clarence Houser, United States	49ft. 2 1-4 in.
1928	John Kuck, United States	52ft. 3-4 in.
1932	Leo Sexton, United States	52ft. 6 in.
1936	Hans Woellke, Germany	53ft. 1 3-4 in.
1948	Wilbur Thompson, United States	56ft. 2 in.
1952	Parry O'Brien, United States	57ft. 1-2 in.
1956	Parry O'Brien, United States	60ft. 11 1-4 in.
1960	William Nieder, United States	64ft. 6 3-4 in.
1964	Dallas Long, United States	66ft. 8 1-2 in.
1968	Randy Matson, United States	67ft. 4 3-4 in.
1972	Wladyslaw Komar, Poland	69ft. 6 in.
1976	Udo Beyer, E. Germany	69ft. 3-4 in.
1980	Vladimir Kiselyov, USSR	70ft. 1-2 in.
1984	Alessandro Andrei, Italy	69ft. 9 in.
1988	Ulf Timmermann, E. Germany	73ft. 8 3-4 in.
1992	Michael Stulce, United States	71ft. 2 1-4 in.

Javelin

1908	Erik Lemming, Sweden	178ft. 7 1-2 in.
	Held in middle—Erik Lemming, Sweden	179ft. 10 1-2 in.
1912	Erik Lemming, Sweden	198ft. 11 1-4 in.
	Both hands, Julius Saaristo, Finland	358ft. 11 7-8 in.
1920	Jonni Myyra, Finland	215ft. 9 3-4 in.
1924	Jonni Myyra, Finland	206ft. 6 3-4 in.
1928	Eric Lundkvist, Sweden	218ft. 6 1-8 in.
1932	Matti Jarvinen, Finland	238ft. 6 in.

1936	Gerhard Stoeck, Germany	235ft. 8 5-16 in.
1948	Tapio Rautavaara, Finland	228ft. 10 1-2 in.
1952	Cy Young, United States	242ft. 0.79 in.
1956	Egil Danielson, Norway	281ft. 2 1-4 in.
1960	Viktor Tsibulenko, USSR	277ft. 8 3-8 in.
1964	Pauli Nevala, Finland	271ft. 2 1-2 in.
1968	Janis Lusis, USSR	295ft. 7 1-4 in.
1972	Klaus Wolfermann, W. Germany	296ft. 10 in.
1976	Miklos Nemeth, Hungary	310ft. 4 in.
1980	Dainis Kula, USSR.	299ft. 2 3-8 in.
1984	Arto Haerkoenen, Finland	284ft. 8 in.
1988	Tapio Korjus, Finland	276ft. 6 in.
1992	Jan Zelezny, Czech.	294ft. 2 in.

Decathlon

1912	Hugo Wieslander, Sweden	7,724.49 pts.(a)
1920	Helge Lovland, Norway	6,804.35 pts.
1924	Harold Osborn, United States	7,710.77 pts.
1928	Paavo Yrjola, Finland	8,053.29 pts.
1932	James Bausch, United States	8,462.23 pts.
1936	Glenn Morris, United States	7,900 pts.
1948	Robert Mathias, United States	7,139 pts.
1952	Robert Mathias, United States	7,887 pts.
1956	Milton Campbell, United States	7,937 pts.
1960	Rafer Johnson, United States	8,392 pts.
1964	Willi Holdorf, Germany	7,887 pts.(c)
1968	Bill Toomey, United States	8,193 pts.
1972	Nikolai Avilov, USSR	8,454 pts.
1976	Bruce Jenner, United States	8,617 pts.
1980	Daley Thompson, Great Britain	8,495 pts.
1984	Daley Thompson, Great Britain	8,798 pts.*(b)
1988	Christian Schenk, E. Germany	8,488 pts.
1992	Robert Zmelik, Czech.	8,611 pts.

(a) Jim Thorpe of the U.S. won the 1912 Decathlon with 8,413 pts. but was disqualified and had to return his medals because he had played professional baseball prior to the Olympic games. The medals were restored posthumously in 1982. (b) Scoring change effective Apr. 1985. (c) Former point systems used prior to 1964.

Track and Field—Women

100-Meter Run

1928	Elizabeth Robinson, United States	12.2s
1932	Stella Walsh, Poland	11.9s
1936	Helen Stephens, United States	11.5s
1948	Francina Blankers-Koen, Netherlands	11.9s
1952	Marjorie Jackson, Australia	11.5s
1956	Betty Cuthbert, Australia	11.5s
1960	Wilma Rudolph, United States	11.0s
1964	Wyomia Tyus, United States.	11.4s
1968	Wyomia Tyus, United States.	11.0s
1972	Renate Stecher, E. Germany	11.07s
1976	Annegret Richter, W. Germany.	11.08s
1980	Lyudmila Kondratyeva, USSR	11.6s
1984	Evelyn Ashford, United States	10.97s
1988	Florence Griffith-Joyner, United States	10.54s*
1992	Gail Devers, United States	10.82s

200-Meter Run

1948	Francina Blankers-Koen, Netherlands	24.4s
1952	Marjorie Jackson, Australia	23.7s
1956	Betty Cuthbert, Australia	23.4s
1960	Wilma Rudolph, United States	24.0s
1964	Edith McGuire, United States.	23.0s
1968	Irena Szewinska, Poland	22.5s
1972	Renate Stecher, E. Germany	22.40s
1976	Barbel Eckert, E. Germany	22.37s
1980	Barbel Wockel, E. Germany	22.03s
1984	Valerie Brisco-Hooks, United States	21.81s
1988	Florence Griffith-Joyner, United States	21.34s*
1992	Gwen Torrence, United States	21.81s

400-Meter Run

1964	Betty Cuthbert, Australia	52s
1968	Colette Besson, France	52s
1972	Monika Zehrt, E. Germany	51.08s
1976	Irena Szewinska, Poland	49.29s
1980	Marita Koch, E. Germany	48.88s
1984	Valerie Brisco-Hooks, United States	48.83s
1988	Olga Bryzgina, USSR	48.65s*
1992	Marie-Jose Perec, France	48.83s

800-Meter Run

1928	Lina Radke, Germany	2m. 16.8s
1960	Ludmila Shevtsova, USSR	2m. 4.3s
1964	Ann Packer, Great Britain	2m. 1.1s
1968	Madeline Manning, United States	2m. 0.9s
1972	Hildegard Falck, W. Germany	1m. 58.6s
1976	Tatyana Kazankina, USSR	1m. 54.94s
1980	Nadezhda Olizayrenko, USSR	1m. 53.5s*
1984	Doina Melinte, Romania	1m. 57.6s
1988	Sigrun Wodars, E. Germany	1m. 56.10s
1992	Ellen Van Langen, Netherlands	1m. 55.54s

1,500-Meter Run

1975	Lyudmila Bragina, USSR	4m. 01.4s
1976	Tatyana Kazankina, USSR	4m. 05.48s
1980	Tatyana Kazankina, USSR	3m. 56.6s
1984	Gabriella Dorio, Italy	4m. 03.25s
1988	Paula Ivan, Romania	3m. 53.96s*
1992	Hassiba Boulmerka, Algeria	3m. 55.30s

3,000-Meter Run

1984	Maricica Puica, Romania	8m. 35.96s
1988	Tatyana Samolenko, USSR	8m. 26.53s*
1992	Elena Romanova, Unified Team	8m. 46.04s

10,000-Meter Run

1988	Olga Boldarenko, USSR	31m. 44.69s
1992	Derartu Tulu, Ethiopia	31m. 06.02s*

400-Meter Relay

1928	Canada	48.4s
1932	United States	46.9s
1936	United States	46.9s
1948	Netherlands	47.5s
1952	United States	45.9s
1956	Australia	44.5s
1960	United States	44.5s
1964	Poland	43.6s
1968	United States	42.8s
1972	West Germany	42.81s
1976	East Germany	42.55s
1980	East Germany	41.60s*
1984	United States	41.65s
1988	United States	41.98s
1992	United States	42.11s

1,600-Meter Relay

1972	East Germany	3m. 23s
1976	East Germany	3m. 19.23s
1980	USSR	3m. 20.02s
1984	United States	3m. 18.29s
1988	USSR	3 m. 15.18s*
1992	Unified Team	3m. 20.20s

100-Meter Hurdles

1972	Annelie Ehrhardt, E. Germany	12.59s
1976	Johanna Schaller, E. Germany	12.77s
1980	Vera Komisova, USSR	12.56s
1984	Benita Brown-Fitzgerald, United States	12.84s
1988	Jordanka Donkova, Bulgaria	12.38s*
1992	Paraskevi Patoulidou, Greece	12.64s

400-Meter Hurdles

1984	Nawal el Moutawakii, Morocco	54.61s
1988	Debra Flintoff-King, Australia	53.17s*
1992	Sally Gunnell, Great Britain	53.23s

Heptathlon

1984	Glynis Nunn, Australia	6,390 pts.
1988	Jackie Joyner-Kersee, United States	7,215 pts.*
1992	Jackie Joyner-Kersee, United States	7,044 pts.

High Jump

1928	Ethel Catherwood, Canada	5ft. 2 1-2 in.
1932	Jean Shiley, United States	5ft. 5 1-4 in.
1936	Ibolya Csak, Hungary	5ft. 3 in.
1948	Alice Coachman, United States	5ft. 6 1-8 in.
1952	Esther Brand, South Africa	5ft. 5 3-4 in.

1956	Mildred L. McDaniel, United States	5ft. 9 1-4 in.
1960	Iolanda Balas, Romania	6ft. 3-4 in.
1964	Iolanda Balas, Romania	6ft. 2 3-4 in.
1968	Miloslava Reskova, Czechoslovakia	5ft. 11 1-2 in.
1972	Ulrike Meyfarth, W. Germany	6ft. 4 in.
1976	Rosemarie Ackermann, E. Germany	6ft. 3 3-4 in.
1980	Sara Simeoni, Italy	6ft. 5 1-2 in.
1984	Ulrike Meyfarth, W. Germany	6ft. 7 1-2 in.
1988	Louise Ritter, United States	6ft. 8 in.*
1992	Heike Henkel, Germany	6ft. 7 1-2 in.

Discus Throw

1928	Helena Konopacka, Poland	129ft. 11 3-4 in.
1932	Lillian Copeland, United States	133ft. 2 in.
1936	Gisela Mauermayer, Germany	156ft. 3 in.
1948	Micheline Ostermeyer, France	137ft. 6 1-2 in.
1952	Nina Romaschkova, USSR	168ft. 8 in.
1956	Olga Fikotova, Czechoslovakia	176ft. 1 in.
1960	Nina Ponomareva, USSR	180ft. 8 1-4 in.
1964	Tamara Press, USSR	187ft. 10 in.
1968	Lia Manoliu, Romania	191ft. 2 in.
1972	Faina Melnik, USSR	218ft. 7 in.
1976	Evelin Schlaak, E. Germany	226ft. 4 in.
1980	Evelin Jahl, E. Germany	229ft. 6 in.
1984	Ria Stalman, Netherlands	214ft. 5 in.
1988	Martina Hellmann, E. Germany	237ft. 2 1-4 in.*
1992	Maritza Marten Garcia, Cuba	222ft. 10 in.

Javelin Throw

1932	"Babe" Didrikson, United States	143ft. 4 in.
1936	Tilly Fleischer, Germany	148ft. 2 3-4 in.
1948	Herma Bauma, Austria	149ft. 6 in.
1952	Dana Zatopkova, Czechoslovakia	165ft. 7 in.
1956	Inese Jaunzeme, USSR	176ft. 8 in.
1960	Elvira Ozolina, USSR	183ft. 8 in.
1964	Mihaela Penes, Romania	198ft. 7 1-2 in.
1968	Angela Nemeth, Hungary	198ft. 1-2 in.
1972	Ruth Fuchs, E. Germany	209ft. 7 in.
1976	Ruth Fuchs, E. Germany	216ft. 4 in.
1980	Maria Colon, Cuba	224ft. 5 in.
1984	Tessa Sanderson, Great Britain	228ft. 2 in.
1988	Petra Felke, E. Germany	245ft.*
1992	Silke Renke, Germany	224ft. 2 1-2 in.

Shot Put (8lb., 13oz.)

1948	Micheline Ostermeyer, France	45ft. 1 1-2 in.
1952	Galina Zybina, USSR	50ft. 1 3-4 in.
1956	Tamara Tishkyevich, USSR	54ft. 5 in.
1960	Tamara Press, USSR	56ft. 10 in.
1964	Tamara Press, USSR	59ft. 6 1-4 in.
1968	Margitta Gummel, E. Germany	64ft. 4 in.
1972	Nadezhda Chizova, USSR	69ft.
1976	Ivanka Hristova, Bulgaria	69ft. 5 1-4 in.
1980	Ilona Slupianek, E. Germany	73ft. 6 1-4 in.*
1984	Claudia Losch, W. Germany	67ft. 2 1-4 in.
1988	Natalya Lisovskaya, USSR	72ft. 11 1-2 in.
1992	Svetlana Kriveleva, Unified Team	69ft. 1 1-2in.

Long Jump

1948	Olga Gyarmati, Hungary	18ft. 8 1-4 in.
1952	Yvette Williams, New Zealand	20ft. 5 3-4 in.
1956	Elzbieta Krzeskinska, Poland	20ft. 9 3-4 in.
1960	Vyera Krepkina, USSR	20ft. 10 3-4 in.
1964	Mary Rand, Great Britain	22ft. 2 1-4 in.
1968	Viorica Viscopoleanu, Romania	22ft. 4 1-2 in.
1972	Heidemarie Rosendahl, W. Germany	22ft. 3 in.
1976	Angela Voigt, E. Germany	22ft. 3-4 in.
1980	Tatyana Kolpakova, USSR	23ft. 2 in.
1984	Anisoara Stanciu, Romania	22ft. 10 in.
1988	Jackie Joyner-Kersee, United States	24ft. 3 1-2 in.
1992	Helke Drechsler, Germany	23ft. 5 1-4 in.*

Marathon

1984	Joan Benoit, United States	2h. 24m. 52s*
1988	Rosa Mota, Portugal	2h. 25m. 40s
1992	Valentina Yegorova, Unified Team	2h. 32m. 41s

Swimming and Diving—Men

50-Meter Freestyle

1988	Matt Biondi, U.S.	22.14
1992	Alexandre Popov, Unified Team	21.91*

100-Meter Freestyle

1896	Alfred Hajos, Hungary	1:22.2
1904	Zoltan de Halmay, Hungary (100 yards)	1:02.8
1908	Charles Daniels, U.S.	1:05.6
1912	Duke P. Kahanamoku, U.S.	1:03.4
1920	Duke P. Kahanamoku, U.S.	1:01.4
1924	John Weissmuller, U.S.	59.0
1928	John Weissmuller, U.S.	58.6
1932	Yasuji Miyazaki, Japan	58.2
1936	Ferenc Csik, Hungary	57.6
1948	Wally Ris, U.S.	57.3
1952	Clark Scholes, U.S.	57.4
1956	Jon Henricks, Australia	55.4
1960	John Devitt, Australia	55.2
1964	Don Schollander, U.S.	53.4
1968	Mike Wenden, Australia	52.2
1972	Mark Spitz, U.S.	51.22
1976	Jim Montgomery, U.S.	49.99
1980	Jorg Woithe, E. Germany	50.40
1984	Rowdy Gaines, U.S.	49.80
1988	Matt Biondi, U.S.	48.63*
1992	Alexandre Popov, Unified Team	49.02

200-Meter Freestyle

1968	Mike Wenden, Australia	1:55.2
1972	Mark Spitz, U.S.	1:52.78
1976	Bruce Furniss, U.S.	1:50.29
1980	Sergei Kopliakov, USSR	1:49.81
1984	Michael Gross, W. Germany	1:47.44
1988	Duncan Armstrong, Australia	1:47.25
1992	Yevgeny Sadovyi, Unified Team	1:46.70*

400-Meter Freestyle

1904	C. M. Daniels, U.S. (440 yards)	6:16.2
1908	Henry Taylor, Great Britain	5:36.8
1912	George Hodgson, Canada	5:24.4
1920	Norman Ross, U.S.	5:26.8
1924	John Weissmuller, U.S.	5:04.2
1928	Albert Zorilla, Argentina	5:01.6
1932	Clarence Crabbe, U.S.	4:48.4
1936	Jack Medica, U.S.	4:44.5
1948	William Smith, U.S.	4:41.0
1952	Jean Boiteux, France	4:30.7
1956	Murray Rose, Australia	4:27.3
1960	Murray Rose, Australia	4:18.3
1964	Don Schollander, U.S.	4:12.2
1968	Mike Burton, U.S.	4:09.0
1972	Brad Cooper, Australia	4:00.27
1976	Brian Goodell, U.S.	3:51.93
1980	Vladimir Salnikov, USSR	3:51.31
1984	George DiCarlo, U.S	3:51.23
1988	Ewe Dassler, E. Germany	3:46.95
1992	Yevgeny Sadovyi, Unified Team	3:45.00*

1,500-Meter Freestyle

1908	Henry Taylor, Great Britain	22:48.4
1912	George Hodgson, Canada	22:00.0
1920	Norman Ross, U.S.	22:23.2
1924	Andrew Charlton, Australia	20:06.6
1928	Arne Borg, Sweden	19:51.8
1932	Kusuo Kitamura, Japan	19:12.4
1936	Noboru Terada, Japan	19:13.7
1948	James McLane, U.S.	19:18.5
1952	Ford Konno, U.S.	18:30.3
1956	Murray Rose, Australia	17:58.9
1960	Jon Konrads, Australia	17:19.6
1964	Robert Windle, Australia	17:01.7
1968	Mike Burton, U.S.	16:38.9
1972	Mike Burton, U.S.	15:52.58

1976	Brian Goodell, U.S.	15:02.40
1980	Vladimir Salnikov, USSR	14:58.27
1984	Michael O'Brien, U.S.	15:05.20
1988	Vladimir Salnikov, USSR	15:00.40
1992	Kieren Perkins, Australia	14:43.48*

400-Meter Medley Relay

1960	United States	4:05.4
1964	United States	3:58.4
1968	United States	3:54.9
1972	United States	3:48.16
1976	United States	3:42.22
1980	Australia	3:45.70
1984	United States	3:39.30
1988	United States	3:36.93*
1992	United States	3:36.93*

400-Meter Freestyle Relay

1964	United States	3:31.2
1968	United States	3:31.7
1972	United States	3:26.42
1984	United States	3:19.03
1988	United States	3:16.53*
1992	United States	3:16.74

800-Meter Freestyle Relay

1908	Great Britain	10:55.6
1912	Australia	10:11.6
1920	United States	10:04.4
1924	United States	9:53.4
1928	United States	9:36.2
1932	Japan	8:58.4
1936	Japan	8:51.5
1948	United States	8:46.0
1952	United States	8:31.1
1956	Australia	8:23.6
1960	United States	8:10.2
1964	United States	7:52.1
1968	United States	7:52.33
1972	United States	7:35.78
1976	United States	7:23.22
1980	USSR	7:23.50
1984	United States	7:15.69
1988	United States	7:12.51
1992	Unified Team	7:11.95*

100-Meter Backstroke

1904	Walter Brack, Germany (100 yds.)	1:16.8
1908	Arno Bieberstein, Germany	1:24.6
1912	Harry Hebner, U.S.	1:21.2
1920	Warren Kealoha, U.S.	1:15.2
1924	Warren Kealoha, U.S.	1:13.2
1928	George Kojac, U.S.	1:08.2
1932	Masaji Kiyokawa, Japan	1:08.6
1936	Adolph Kiefer, U.S.	1:05.9
1948	Allen Stack, U.S.	1:06.4
1952	Yoshi Oyakawa, U.S.	1:05.4
1956	David Thiele, Australia	1:02.2
1960	David Thiele, Australia	1:01.9
1968	Roland Matthes, E. Germany	58.7
1972	Roland Matthes, E. Germany	56.58
1976	John Naber, U.S.	55.49
1980	Bengt Baron, Sweden	56.33
1984	Rick Carey, U.S.	55.79
1988	Daichi Suzuki, Japan	55.05
1992	Mark Tewksbury, Canada	53.98*

200-Meter Backstroke

1964	Jed Graef, U.S.	2:10.3
1968	Roland Matthes, E. Germany	2:09.6
1972	Roland Matthes, E. Germany	2:02.82
1976	John Naber, U.S.	1:59.19
1980	Sandor Wladar, Hungary	2:01.93
1984	Rick Carey, U.S.	2:00.23
1988	Igor Polianski, USSR	1:59.37
1992	Martin Lopez-Zubero, Spain	1:58.47*

100-Meter Breaststroke

1968	Don McKenzie, U.S.	1:07.7
1972	Nobutaka Taguchi, Japan	1:04.94
1976	John Hencken, U.S.	1:03.11
1980	Duncan Goodhew, Great Britain	1:03.44
1984	Steve Lundquist, U.S.	1:01.65
1988	Adrian Moorhouse, Great Britain	1:02.04
1992	Nelson Diebel, U.S.	1:01.50*

200-Meter Breaststroke

1908	Frederick Holman, Great Britain	3:09.2
1912	Walter Bathe, Germany	3:01.8
1920	Haken Malmroth, Sweden	3:04.4
1924	Robert Skelton, U.S.	2:56.6
1928	Yoshiyuki Tsuruta, Japan	2:48.8
1932	Yoshiyuki Tsuruta, Japan	2:45.4
1936	Tetsuo Hamuro, Japan	2:41.5
1948	Joseph Verdeur, U.S.	2:39.3
1952	John Davies, Australia	2:34.4
1956	Masura Furukawa, Japan	2:34.7
1960	William Mulliken, U.S.	2:37.4
1964	Ian O'Brien, Australia	2:27.8
1968	Felipe Munoz, Mexico	2:28.7
1972	John Hencken, U.S.	2:21.55
1976	David Wilkie, Great Britain	2:15.11
1980	Robertas Zhulpa, USSR	2:15.85
1984	Victor Davis, Canada	2:13.34
1988	Jozsef Szabo, Hungary	2:13.52
1992	Mike Barrowman, U.S.	2:10.16*

100-Meter Butterfly

1968	Doug Russell, U.S.	55.9
1972	Mark Spitz, U.S.	54.27
1976	Matt Vogel, U.S.	54.35
1980	Par Arvidsson, Sweden	54.92
1984	Michael Gross, W. Germany	53.08
1988	Anthony Nesty, Suriname	53.00*
1992	Pablo Morales, U.S.	53.32

200-Meter Butterfly

1956	William Yorzyk, U.S.	2:19.3
1960	Michael Troy, U.S.	2:12.8
1964	Kevin J. Berry, Australia	2:06.6
1968	Carl Robie, U.S.	2:08.7
1972	Mark Spitz, U.S.	2:00.70
1976	Mike Bruner, U.S.	1:59.23
1980	Sergei Fesenko, USSR	1:59.76
1984	Jon Sieben, Australia	1:57.04
1988	Michael Gross, W. Germany	1:56.94
1992	Mel Stewart, U.S.	1:56.26*

200-Meter Individual Medley

1968	Charles Hickcox, U.S.	2:12.0
1972	Gunnar Larsson, Sweden	2:07.17
1984	Alex Baumann, Canada	2:01.42
1988	Tamas Darnyi, Hungary	2:00.17*
1992	Tamas Darnyi, Hungary	2:00.76

400-Meter Individual Medley

1964	Dick Roth, U.S.	4:45.4
1968	Charles Hickcox, U.S.	4:48.4
1972	Gunnar Larsson, Sweden	4:31.98
1976	Rod Strachan, U.S.	4:23.68
1980	Aleksandr Sidorenko, USSR	4:22.89
1984	Alex Baumann, Canada	4:17.41
1988	Tamas Darnyi, Hungary	4:14.75
1992	Tamas Darnyi, Hungary	4:14.23*

Springboard Diving

		Points
1908	Albert Zurner, Germany	85.5
1912	Paul Guenther, Germany	79.23
1920	Louis Kuehn, U.S.	.675.40
1924	Albert White, U.S.	97.46
1928	Pete Desjardins, U.S.	185.04
1932	Michael Galitzen, U.S.	161.38
1936	Richard Degener, U.S.	163.57
1948	Bruce Harlan, U.S.	163.64
1952	David Browning, U.S.	205.29
1956	Robert Clotworthy, U.S.	159.56
1960	Gary Tobian, U.S.	170.00
1964	Kenneth Sitzberger, U.S.	159.90
1968	Bernie Wrightson, U.S.	170.15
1972	Vladimir Vasin, USSR	594.09
1976	Phil Boggs, U.S.	619.52
1980	Aleksandr Portnov, USSR	905.02
1984	Greg Louganis, U.S.	754.41
1988	Greg Louganis, U.S.	730.80
1992	Mark Lenzi, U.S.	676.530

Platform Diving

		Points
1904	Dr. G.E. Sheldon, U.S.	12.75
1908	Hjalmar Johansson, Sweden	83.75
1912	Erik Adlerz, Sweden	73.94

1920	Clarence Pinkston, U.S.	100.67
1924	Albert White, U.S.	97.46
1928	Pete Desjardins, U.S.	98.74
1932	Harold Smith, U.S.	124.80
1936	Marshall Wayne, U.S.	113.58
1948	Sammy Lee, U.S.	130.05
1952	Sammy Lee, U.S.	156.28
1956	Joaquin Capilla, Mexico	152.44
1960	Robert Webster, U.S.	165.56
1964	Robert Webster, U.S.	148.58
1968	Klaus Dibiasi, Italy	164.18
1972	Klaus Dibiasi, Italy	504.12
1976	Klaus Dibiasi, Italy	600.51
1980	Falk Hoffmann, E. Germany	835.65
1984	Greg Louganis, U.S.	710.91
1988	Greg Louganis, U.S.	638.61
1992	Sun Shuwei, China	677.310

Swimming and Diving—Women

50-Meter Freestyle

1988	Kristin Otto, E. Germany	25.49
1992	Yang Wenyi, China	24.76*

100-Meter Freestyle

1912	Fanny Durack, Australia	1:22.2
1920	Ethelda Bleibtrey, U.S.	1:13.6
1924	Ethel Lackie, U.S.	1:12.4
1928	Albina Osipowich, U.S.	1:11.0
1932	Helene Madison, U.S.	1:06.8
1936	Hendrika Mastenbroek, Holland	1:05.9
1948	Greta Andersen, Denmark	1:06.3
1952	Katalin Szoke, Hungary	1:06.8
1956	Dawn Fraser, Australia	1:02.0
1960	Dawn Fraser, Australia	1:01.2
1964	Dawn Fraser, Australia	59.5
1968	Jan Henne, U.S.	1:00.0
1972	Sandra Neilson, U.S.	58.59
1976	Kornelia Ender, E. Germany	55.65
1980	Barbara Krause, E. Germany	54.79
1984	(tie) Carrie Steinseifer, U.S.	55.92
	Nancy Hogshead, U.S.	55.92
1988	Kristin Otto, E. Germany	54.93
1992	Zhuang Yong, China	54.64*

200-Meter Freestyle

1968	Debbie Meyer, U.S.	2:10.5
1972	Shane Gould, Australia	2:03.56
1976	Kornelia Ender, E. Germany	1:59.26
1980	Barbara Krause, E. Germany	1:58.33
1984	Mary Wayte, U.S.	1:59.23
1988	Heike Friedrich, E. Germany	1:57.65*
1992	Nicole Haislett, U.S.	1:57.90

400-Meter Freestyle

1924	Martha Norelius, U.S	6:02.2
1928	Martha Norelius, U.S.	5:42.8
1932	Helene Madison, U.S.	5:28.5
1936	Hendrika Mastenbroek, Netherlands	5:26.4
1948	Ann Curtis, U.S.	5:17.8
1952	Valerie Gyenge, Hungary	5:12.1
1956	Lorraine Crapp, Australia	4:54.6
1960	Susan Chris von Saltza, U.S.	4:50.6
1964	Virginia Duenkel, U.S.	4:43.3
1968	Debbie Meyer, U.S.	4:31.8
1972	Shane Gould, Australia	4:19.44
1976	Petra Thuemer E. Germany	4:09.89
1980	Ines Diers, E. Germany	4:08.76
1984	Tiffany Cohen, U.S.	4:07.10
1988	Janet Evans, U.S.	4:03.85*
1992	Dagmar Hase, Germany	4:07.18

800-Meter Freestyle

1968	Debbie Meyer, U.S.	9:24.0
1972	Keena Rothhammer, U.S.	8:53.68
1976	Petra Thuemer, E. Germany	8:37.14
1980	Michelle Ford, Australia	8:28.90
1984	Tiffany Cohen, U.S.	8:24.95
1988	Janet Evans, U.S.	8:20.20*
1992	Janet Evans, U.S.	8:25.52

100-Meter Backstroke

1924	Sybil Bauer, U.S.	1:23.2
1928	Marie Braun, Netherlands	1:22.0
1932	Eleanor Holm, U.S.	1:19.4
1936	Dina Senff, Netherlands	1:18.9
1948	Karen Harup, Denmark	1:14.4
1952	Joan Harrison, South Africa	1:14.3
1956	Judy Grinham, Great Britain	1:12.9
1960	Lynn Burke, U.S.	1:09.3
1964	Cathy Ferguson, U.S.	1:07.7
1968	Kaye Hall, U.S.	1:06.2
1972	Melissa Belote, U.S.	1:05.78
1976	Ulrike Richter, E. Germany	1:01.83
1980	Rica Reinisch, E. Germany	1:00.86
1984	Theresa Andrews, U.S.	1:02.55
1988	Kristin Otto, E. Germany	1:00.89
1992	Krisztina Egerszegi, Hungary	1:00.68*

200-Meter Backstroke

1968	Pokey Watson, U.S.	2:24.8
1972	Melissa Belote, U.S.	2:19.19
1976	Ulrike Richter, E. Germany	2:13.43
1980	Rica Reinisch, E. Germany	2:11.77
1984	Jolanda De Rover, Netherlands	2:12.38
1988	Krisztina Egerszegi, Hungary	2:09.29
1992	Krisztina Egerszegi, Hungary	2:07.06*

100-Meter Breaststroke

1968	Djurdjica Bjedov, Yugoslavia	1:15.8
1972	Cathy Carr, U.S.	1:13.58
1976	Hannelore Anke, E. Germany	1:11:16
1980	Ute Geweniger, E. Germany	1:10.22
1984	Petra Van Staveren, Netherlands	1:09.88
1988	Tania Dangalakova, Bulgaria	1:07.95*
1992	Elena Roudkovskaia, Unified Team	1:08.00

200-Meter Breaststroke

1924	Lucy Morton, Great Britain	3:33.2
1928	Hilde Schrader, Germany	3:12.6
1932	Clare Dennis, Australia	3:06.3
1936	Hideko Maehata, Japan	3:03.6
1948	Nelly Van Vliet, Netherlands	2:57.2
1952	Eva Szekely, Hungary	2:51.7
1956	Ursula Happe, Germany	2:53.1
1960	Anita Lonsbrough, Great Britain	2:49.5
1964	Galina Prozumenschikova, USSR	2:46.4
1968	Sharon Wichman, U.S.	2:44.4
1972	Beverly Whitfield, Australia	2:41.71
1976	Marina Koshevaia, USSR	2:33.35
1980	Lina Kachushite, USSR	2:29.54
1984	Anne Ottenbrite, Canada	2:30.38
1988	Silke Hoerner, E. Germany	2:26.71
1992	Kyoko Iwasaki, Japan	2:26.65*

200-Meter Individual Medley

1968	Claudia Kolb, U.S.	2:24.7
1972	Shane Gould, Australia	2:23.07
1984	Tracy Caulkins, U.S.	2:12.64
1988	Daniela Hunger, E. Germany	2:12.59
1992	Lin Li, China	2:11.65*

400-Meter Individual Medley

1964	Donna de Varona, U.S.	5:18.7
1968	Claudia Kolb, U.S.	5:08.5
1972	Gail Neall, Australia	5:02.97
1976	Ulrike Tauber, E. Germany	4:42.77
1980	Petra Schneider, E. Germany	4:36.29*
1984	Tracy Caulkins, U.S.	4:39.24
1988	Janet Evans, U.S.	4:37.76
1992	Krisztina Egerszegi, Hungary	4:36.54

100-Meter Butterfly

1956	Shelley Mann, U.S.	1:11.0
1960	Carolyn Schuler, U.S.	1:09.5
1964	Sharon Stouder, U.S.	1:04.7

1968	Lynn McClements, Australia	1:05.5
1972	Mayumi Aoki, Japan	1:03.34
1976	Kornelia Ender, E. Germany	1:00.13
1980	Caren Metschuck, E. Germany	1:00.42
1984	Mary T. Meagher, U.S.	59.26
1988	Kristin Otto, E. Germany	59.00
1992	Qian Hong, China	58.62*

200-Meter Butterfly

1968	Ada Kok, Netherlands	2:24.7
1972	Karen Moe, U.S.	2:15.57
1976	Andrea Pollack, E. Germany	2:11.41
1980	Ines Geissler, E. Germany	2:10.44
1984	Mary T. Meagher, U.S.	2:06.90*
1988	Kathleen Nord, E. Germany	2:09.51
1992	Summer Sanders, U.S.	2:08.67

400-Meter Medley Relay

1960	United States	4:41.1
1960	United States	4:33.9
1968	United States	4:28.3
1972	United States	4:20.75
1976	East Germany	4:07.95
1980	East Germany	4:06.67
1984	United States	4:08.34
1988	East Germany	4:03.74
1992	United States	4:02.54*

400-Meter Freestyle Relay

1912	Great Britain	5:52.8
1920	United States	5:11.6
1924	United States	4:58.8
1928	United States	4:47.6
1932	United States	4:38.0
1936	Netherlands	4:36.0
1948	United States	4:29.2
1952	Hungary	4:24.4
1956	Australia	4:17.1
1960	United States	4:08.9
1964	United States	4:03.8
1968	United States	4:02.5
1972	United States	3:55.19
1976	United States	3:44.82
1980	East Germany	3:42.71
1984	United States	3:43.43
1988	East Germany	3:40.63
1992	United States	3:39.46*

Springboard Diving

		Points
1920	Aileen Riggin, U.S.	539.90
1924	Elizabeth Becker, U.S.	474.50
1928	Helen Meany, U.S.	78.62
1932	Georgia Coleman U.S.	87.52
1936	Marjorie Gestring, U.S.	89.27
1948	Victoria M. Draves, U.S.	108.74
1952	Patricia McCormick, U.S.	147.30
1956	Patricia McCormick, U.S.	142.36
1960	Ingrid Kramer, Germany	155.81
1964	Ingrid Engel-Kramer, Germany	145.00
1968	Sue Gossick, U.S.	150.77
1972	Micki King, U.S.	450.03
1976	Jenni Chandler, U.S.	506.19
1980	Irina Kalinina, USSR	725.91
1984	Sylvie Bernier, Canada	530.70
1988	Gao Min, China	580.23
1992	Gao Min, China	572.400

Platform Diving

		Points
1912	Greta Johansson, Sweden	39.90
1920	Stefani Fryland-Clausen, Denmark	34.60
1924	Caroline Smith, U.S.	33.20
1928	Elizabeth B. Pinkston, U.S.	31.60
1932	Dorothy Poynton, U.S.	40.26
1936	Dorothy Poynton Hill, U.S.	33.93
1948	Victoria M. Draves, U.S.	68.87
1952	Patricia McCormick, U.S.	79.37
1956	Patricia McCormick, U.S.	84.85
1960	Ingrid Kramer, Germany	91.28
1964	Lesley Bush, U.S.	99.80
1968	Milena Duchkova, Czech.	109.59
1972	Ulrika Knape, Sweden	390.00
1976	Elena Vaytsekhouskaya, USSR	406.59
1980	Martina Jaschke, E. Germany	596.25
1984	Zhou Jihong, China	435.51
1988	Xu Yanmei, China	445.20
1992	Fu Mingxia, China	461.430

Boxing

Light Flyweight (106 lbs)

1968 Francisco Rodriguez, Venezuela
1972 Gyorgy Gedo, Hungary
1976 Jorge Hernandez, Cuba
1980 Shamil Sabyrov, USSR
1984 Paul Gonzalez, U.S.
1988 Ivailo Hristov, Bulgaria
1992 Rogelio Marcelo, Cuba

Flyweight (112 lbs)

1904 George Finnegan, U.S.
1920 William Di Gennara, U.S.
1924 Fidel LaBarba, U.S.
1928 Antal Kocsis, Hungary
1932 Istvan Enekes, Hungary
1936 Willi Kaiser, Germany
1948 Pascual Perez, Argentina
1952 Nathan Brooks, U.S.
1956 Terence Spinks, Great Britain
1960 GyulaTorok, Hungary
1964 Fernando Atzori, Italy
1968 Ricardo Delgado, Mexico
1972 Georgi Kostadinov, Bulgaria
1976 Leo Randolph, U.S.
1980 Peter Lessov, Bulgaria
1984 Steve McCrory, U.S.
1988 Kim Kwang Sun, S. Korea
1992 Su Choi Choi, N. Korea

Bantamweight (119 lbs)

1904 Oliver Kirk, U.S.
1908 A Henry Thomas, Great Britain
1920 Clarence Walker, South Africa
1924 William Smith, South Africa
1928 Vittorio Tamagnini, Italy
1932 Horace Gwynne, Canada
1936 Ulderico Sergo, Italy
1948 Tibor Csik, Hungary
1952 Pentti Hamalainen, Finland
1956 Wolfgang Behrendt, E. Germany
1960 Oleg Grigoryev, USSR
1964 Takao Sakurai, Japan
1968 Valery Sokolov, USSR
1972 Orlando Martinez, Cuba
1976 Yong-Jo Gu, N. Korea
1980 Juan Hernandez, Cuba
1984 Maurizio Stecca, Italy
1988 Kennedy McKinney, U.S.
1992 Joel Casamayor, Cuba

Featherweight (126 lbs)

1904 Oliver Kirk, U.S.
1908 Richard Gunn, Great Britain
1920 Paul Fritsch, France
1924 John Fields, U.S.
1928 Lambertus van Klaveren, Netherlands
1932 Carmelo Robledo, Argentina
1936 Oscar Casanovas, Argentina
1948 Ernesto Formenti, Italy
1952 Jan Zachara, Czech.
1956 Vladimir Safronov, USSR
1960 Francesco Musso, Italy
1964 Stanislav Stephashkin, USSR
1968 Antonin Roldan, Mexico
1972 Boris Kousnetsov, USSR
1976 Angel Herrera, Cuba
1980 Rudi Fink, E. Germany
1984 Meldrick Taylor, U.S.
1988 Giovanni Parisi, Italy
1992 Andreas Tews, Germany

Lightweight (132 lbs)

1904 Harry Spanger, U.S.
1908 Frederick Grace, Great Britain
1920 Samuel Mosberg, U.S.
1924 Hans Nielsen, Denmark
1928 Carlo Orlandi, Italy
1932 Lawrence Stevens, South Africa
1936 Imre Harangi, Hungary
1948 Gerald Dreyer, South Africa
1952 Aureliano Bolognesi, Italy
1956 Richard McTaggart, Great Britain
1960 Kazimierz Pazdzior, Poland
1964 Jozef Grudzien, Poland
1968 Ronald Harris, U.S.
1972 Jan Szczepanski, Poland
1976 Howard Davis, U.S.
1980 Angel Herrera, Cuba
1984 Pernell Whitaker, U.S.
1988 Andreas Zuelow, E. Germany
1992 Oscar De La Hoya, U.S.

Light Welterweight (140 lbs)

1952 Charles Adkins, U.S.
1956 Vladimir Yengibaryan, USSR
1960 Bohumil Nemecek, Czech.
1964 Jerzy Kulej, Poland
1968 Jerzy Kulej, Poland
1972 Ray Seales, U.S.
1976 Ray Leonard, U.S.
1980 Patrizio Oliva, Italy

1984 Jerry Page, U.S.
1988 Viatcheslav Janovski, USSR
1992 Hector Vinent, Cuba

Welterweight (147 lbs)

1904 Albert Young, U.S.
1920 Albert Schneider, Canada
1924 Jean Delarge, Belgium
1928 Edward Morgan, New Zealand
1932 Edward Flynn, U.S.
1936 Sten Suvio, Finland
1948 Julius Torma, Czech.
1952 Zygmunt Chychia, Poland
1956 Nicolae Linca, Romania
1960 Giovanni Benvenuti, Italy
1964 Marian Kasprzyk, Poland
1968 Manfred Wolke, E. Germany
1972 Emilio Correa, Cuba
1976 Jochen Bachfeld, E. Germany
1980 Andres Aldama, Cuba
1984 Mark Breland, U.S.
1988 Robert Wangila, Kenya
1992 Michael Carruth, Ireland

Light Middleweight (157 lbs)

1952 Laszlo Papp, Hungary
1956 Laszlo Papp, Hungary
1960 Wilbert McClure, U.S.
1964 Boris Lagutin, USSR
1968 Boris Lagutin, USSR
1972 Dieter Kottysch, W. Germany
1976 Jerzy Rybicki, Poland
1980 Armando Martinez, Cuba
1984 Frank Tate, U.S.
1988 Park Si Hun, S. Korea
1992 Juan Lemus, Cuba

Middleweight (165 lbs)

1904 Charles Mayer, U.S.
1908 John Douglas, Great Britain
1920 Harry Mallin, Great Britain
1924 Harry Mallin, Great Britain
1928 Piero Toscani, Italy
1932 Carmen Barth, U.S.
1936 Jean Despeaux, France
1948 Laszlo Papp, Hungary
1952 Floyd Patterson, U.S.
1956 Gennady Schatkov, USSR
1960 Edward Crook, U.S.
1964 Valery Popenchenko, USSR
1968 Christopher Finnegan, Great Britain
1972 Vyacheslav Lemechev, USSR
1976 Michael Spinks, U.S.
1980 Jose Gomez, Cuba
1984 Joon-Sup Shin, S. Korea
1988 Henry Maske, E. Germany
1992 Ariel Hernandez, Cuba

Light Heavyweight (179 lbs)

1920 Edward Eagan, U.S.
1924 Harry Mitchell, Great Britain
1928 Victor Avendano, Argentina
1932 David Carstens, South Africa
1936 Roger Michelot, France
1948 George Hunter, South Africa
1952 Norvel Lee, U.S.
1956 James Boyd, U.S.
1960 Cassius Clay, U.S.
1964 Cosimo Pinto, Italy
1968 Dan Poznyak, USSR
1972 Mate Parlov, Yugoslavia
1976 Leon Spinks, U.S.
1980 Slobodan Kacar, Yugoslavia
1984 Anton Josipovic, Yugoslavia
1988 Andrew Maynard, U.S.
1992 Torsten May, Germany

Heavyweight (201 lbs)

1984 Henry Tillman, U.S.
1988 Ray Mercer, U.S.
1992 Felix Savon, Cuba

Super Heavyweight (Unlimited)
(known as heavyweight from 1904-80)

1904 Samuel Berger, U.S.
1908 Albert Oldham, Great Britain
1920 Ronald Rawson, Great Britain
1924 Otto von Porat, Norway
1928 Arturo Rodriguez Jurado, Argentina
1932 Santiago Lovell, Argentina
1936 Herbert Runge, Germany
1948 Rafael Inglesias, Argentina
1952 H. Edward Sanders, U.S.
1956 T. Peter Rademacher, U.S.
1960 Franco De Piccoli, Italy
1964 Joe Frazier, U.S.
1968 George Foreman, U.S.
1972 Teofilo Stevenson, Cuba
1976 Teofilo Stevenson, Cuba
1980 Teofilo Stevenson, Cuba
1984 Tyrell Biggs, U.S.
1988 Lennox Lewis, Canada
1992 Roberto Balado, Cuba

Other Summer Olympics Gold Medalists in 1992

Archery

Men's 70-Meter Individual—Sebastien Flute, France.
Men's Team—Spain.
Women's 70-Meter Individual—Cho Youn Jeong, S. Korea.
Women's Team—S. Korea.

Badminton

Men's Singles—Alan Budi Kusuma, Indonesia.
Men's Doubles—Kim Moon Soo and Park Joo Bong, S. Korea.
Women's Singles—Susi Susanti, Indonesia.
Women's Doubles—Hwang Hye Young and Chung So-Young, S. Korea.

Baseball

G-Cuba; S-Taiwan; B-Japan.

Basketball

Men—G-U.S.; S-Croatia; B-Lithuania.
Women—G-Cuba; S-China; B-U.S.

Canoe/Kayak

Men

Single Kayak Slalom—Pierpaolo Ferrazzi, Italy.
Kayak 500M Singles—Mikko Yrjoe Kolehmainen, Finland.
Kayak 500M Doubles—Germany.
Kayak 1,000M Singles—Clint Robinson, Australia.
Kayak 1,000M Doubles—Germany.
Kayak 1,000M Fours—Germany.
Double Canoe Slalom—U.S.
Canoe Slalom—Lukas Pollert, Czechoslovakia.
Canoe 500M Singles—Nikolai Boukhalov, Bulgaria.
Canoe 500M Doubles—Unified Team.
Canoe 1,000M Singles—Nikolai Boukhalov, Bulgaria.
Canoe 1,000M Doubles—Germany.

Women

Kayak Slalom—Elisabeth Micheler, Germany.
Kayak 500M Singles—Birgit Schmidt, Germany.
Kayak 500M Doubles—Germany.
Kayak 500M Fours—Hungary.

Cycling

Men

Individual Road Race—Fabio Casartelli, Italy.
Sprint—Jens Fiedler, Germany.
Individual Points Race—Giovanni Lombardi, Italy.
4,000 Team Pursuit—Germany.
4K Individual Pursuit—Chris Boardman, Great Britain.
1 KM Time Trial—Jose Moreno, Spain.
Road Race—Germany.

Women

Sprint—Erika Salumae, Estonia.
Individual Pursuit—Petra Rossner, Germany.
Individual Road Race—Kathryn Watt, Australia.

Diving

Men's Platform—Sun Shuwei, China.
Men's Springboard—Mark Lenzi, U.S.
Women's Platform—Fu Mingxia, China.
Women's Springboard—Gao Min, China.

Equestrian

Ind. Three-Day Event—Matthew Ryan, Australia.
Team Three-Day Event—Australia.
Individual Dressage—Nicole Uphoff, Germany.
Team Dressage—Germany.
Individual Jumping—Ludger Beerbaum, Germany.
Team Jumping—Netherlands.

Fencing

Men

Individual Foil—Philippe Omnes, France.
Team Foil—Germany.
Individual Saber—Bence Szabo, Hungary.
Team Saber—Unified Team.
Individual Épée—Eric Srecki, France.
Team Épée—Germany.

Women

Individual Foil—Giovanna Trillini, Italy.
Team Foil—Italy.

Field Hockey

Men—G-Germany; S-Australia; B-Pakistan.
Women—G-Spain; S-Germany; B-Great Britain.

Gymnastics

Men

Floor Exercise—Li Xiaosahuang, China.
Horizontal Bar—Trent Dimas, U.S.
Parallel Bars—Vitaly Shcherbo, Unified Team.
Pommel Horse—(tie) Vitaly Shcherbo, Unified Team; Pae Gil Su, N. Korea.
Rings—Vitaly Shcherbo, Unified Team.
Vault—Vitaly Shcherbo, Unified Team.
Individual All-Around—Vitaly Shcherbo, Unified Team.
Team—Unified Team.

Women

Balance Beam— Tatiana Lisenko, Unified Team.
Floor Exercise—Lavinia Corina Milosovici, Romania.
Uneven Bars—Lu Li, China.
Vault—(tie) Henrietta Onodi, Hungary; Lavinia Corina Milosovici, Romania.
All-Around—Tatiana Gutsu, Unified Team.
Team Artistic—Unified Team.

Rhythmic Gymnastics

Alexandra Timoshenko, Unified Team.

Judo

Men

132 Pounds—Nazim Gousseinov, Unified Team.
143 Pounds—Rogerio Sampalo Cardoso, Brazil.
157 Pounds—Toshihiko Koga, Japan.
172 Pounds—Hidehiko Yoshida, Japan.
198 Pounds—Waldemar Legien, Poland.
209 Pounds—Antal Kovacs, Hungary.
Heavyweight—David Khakhaleichvili, Unified Team.

Women

106 Pounds—Cecile Nowak, France.
115 Pounds—Almudena Munoz Martinez, Spain.
123 Pounds—Miriam Blasco Soto, Spain.
134 Pounds—Catherine Fleury, France.
146 Pounds—Odalis Reve Jimenez, Cuba.
159 Pounds—Kim Mi Jung, S. Korea.
Over 159 Pounds—Zhuang Xiaoyan, China.

Modern Pentathlon

Individual—Arkadiusz Skrzypaszek, Poland.
Team—Poland.

Rowing

Men

Single Sculls—Thomas Lange, Germany.
Double Sculls—Australia.
Coxless Pairs—Great Britain.
Coxed Pairs—Great Britain.
Coxed Fours—Romania.
Coxless Fours—Australia.
Quadruple Sculls—Germany.
Coxed Eights—Canada.

Women

Single Sculls—Elisabeta Lipa, Romania.
Double Sculls—Germany.
Coxless Pairs—Canada.
Coxless Fours—Canada.
Quadruple Sculls—Germany.
Coxed Eights—Canada.

Shooting

Men

Running Game Target—Michael Jakosits, Germany.
Rapid Fire Pistol—Ralf Schumann, Germany.
Three-Position Rifle—Gratchia Petikiane, Unified Team.
Free Rifle—Lee Eun Chul, S. Korea.
Air Pistol—Wang Yifu, China.
Air Rifle—Iouri Fedkine, Unified Team.
Free Pistol—Konstantine Loukachik, Unified Team.

Women

Air Pistol—Marina Logvinenko, Unified Team.
Three-Position Rifle—Launi Meili, U.S.
Sport Pistol—Marina Logvinenko, Unified Team.
Air Rifle—Yeo Kab Soon, S. Korea.

Mixed

Trap—Petr Hrdlicka, Czechoslovakia.
Skeet—Zhang Shan, China.

Soccer

G-Spain; S-Poland; B-Ghana.

Synchronized Swimming

Solo—Kristen Babb-Sprague, U.S.
Duet—Karen Josephson and Sarah Josephson, U.S.

Table Tennis

Men's Singles—Jan Waldner, Sweden.
Men's Doubles—Lu Lin and Wang Tao, China.
Women's Singles—Deng Yaping, China.
Women's Doubles—Deng Yaping and Qiao Hong, China.

Team Handball

Men—G-Unified Team; S-Sweden; B-France.
Women—G-S. Korea; S-Norway; B-Unified Team.

Tennis

Men's Singles—Marc Rosset, Switzerland.
Men's Doubles—Boris Becker and Michael Stich, Germany.
Women's Singles—Jennifer Capriati, U.S.
Women's Doubles—Gigi Fernandez and Mary Joe Fernandez, U.S.

Volleyball

Men—G-Brazil; S-Netherlands; B-U.S.
Women—G-Cuba; S-Unified Team; B-U.S.

Water Polo

G-Italy; S-Spain; B-Unified Team.

Weight Lifting

115 Pounds—Ivan Ivanov, Bulgaria.
123 Pounds—Chun Byung Kwan, S. Korea.
132 Pounds—Naim Suleymanoglu, Turkey.
148 Pounds—Israel Militossian, Unified Team.
165 Pounds—Fedor Kassapu, Unified Team.
180 Pounds—Pyrros Dimas, Greece.
198 Pounds—Kakhi Kakhiachvili, Unified Team.
220 Pounds—Victor Tregoubov, Unified Team.
243 Pounds—Ronny Weller, Germany.
Over 243 Pounds—Aleksandr Kourlovitch, Unified Team.

Wrestling

Freestyle

106 Pounds—Kim Il, N. Korea.
115 Pounds—Li Hak Son, S. Korea.
126 Pounds—Alejandro Puerto Diaz, Cuba.
137 Pounds—John Smith, U.S.
150 Pounds—Arsen Fadzaev, Unified Team.
163 Pounds—Park Jang Soon, S. Korea.
182 Pounds—Kevin Jackson, U.S.
198 Pounds—Makharbek Khadartsev, Unified Team.
220 Pounds—Leri Khabelov, Unified Team.
286 Pounds—Bruce Baumgartner, U.S.

Greco-Roman

106 Pounds—Oleg Koutherenko, Unified Team.
115 Pounds—Jon Ronningen, Norway.
126 Pounds—An Han Bong, S. Korea.
137 Pounds—M. Akif Pirim, Turkey.
150 Pounds—Attila Repka, Hungary.
163 Pounds—Mnatsakan Iskandarian, Unified Team.
181 Pounds—Peter Farkas, Hungary.
198 Pounds—Maik Bullmann, Germany.
220 Pounds—Hector Milian Perez, Cuba.
286 Pounds—Aleksandr Karelin, Unified Team.

Yachting

Soling—Denmark.
Finn—Jose Van Der Ploeg, Spain.
Tornado—France.
Europe—Linda Anderson, Norway.
Flying Dutchman—Spain.
Star—U.S.
Men's Sailboard—Franck David, France.
Women's Sailboard—Barbara Kendall, New Zealand.
Men's 470—Spain.
Women's 470—Spain.

Olympic Information

Symbol: Five rings or circles, linked together to represent the sporting friendship of all peoples. The rings also symbolize 5 geographic areas—Europe, Asia, Africa, Australia, and America. Each ring is a different color—blue, yellow, black, green, and red.

Flag: The symbol of the 5 rings on a plain white background.

Motto: "Citius, Altius, Fortius." Latin meaning "faster, higher, braver," or the modern interpretation "swifter, higher, stronger." The motto was coined by Father Didon, a French educator, in 1895.

Creed: "The most important thing in the Olympic Games is not to win but to take part, just as the most important thing in life is not the triumph but the struggle. The essential thing is not to have conquered but to have fought well."

Oath: An athlete of the host country recites the following at the opening ceremony. "In the name of all competitors I promise that we will take part in these Olympic Games, respecting and abiding by the rules which govern them, in the true spirit of sportsmanship for the glory of sport and the honor of our teams." Both the oath and the creed were composed by Pierre de Coubertin, the founder of the modern Games.

Flame: Symbolizes the continuity between the ancient and modern Games. The modern version of the flame was adopted in 1936. The torch used to kindle the flame is first lit by the sun's rays at Olympia, Greece, and then carried to the site of the Games by relays of runners. Ships and planes are used when necessary.

TRACK AND FIELD

World Track and Field Records

As of Oct. 1, 1994

The International Amateur Atheletic Federation, the world body of track and field, recognizes only records in metric distances except for the mile.

Men's Records

Running

Event	Record	Holder	Country	Date	Where made
100 meters	**9.85 s.**	Leroy Burrell	U.S.	July 6, 1994	Lausanne, Switz.
200 meters	**19.72 s.**	Pietro Mennea	Italy	Sept. 12, 1979	Mexico City
400 meters	**43.29 s.**	Butch Reynolds	U.S.	Aug. 16, 1988	Zurich
800 meters	**1 m., 41.73 s.**	Sebastian Coe	Gr. Britain	June 10, 1981	Florence, Italy
1,000 meters	**2 m., 12.18 s.**	Sebastian Coe	Gr. Britain	July 11, 1981	Oslo
1,500 meters	**3 m., 28.86 s.**	Noureddine Morceli	Algeria	Sept. 6, 1992	Rieti, Italy
1 mile	**3 m., 44.39 s.**	Noureddine Morceli	Algeria	Sept. 5, 1993	Rieti, Italy
2,000 meters	**4 m., 50.81 s.**	Said Aouita	Morocco	July 16, 1987	Paris
3,000 meters	**7 m., 25.11 s.**	Noureddine Morceli	Algeria	Aug. 2, 1994	Monte Carlo
5,000 meters	**12 m., 56.96 s.**	Haile Gebreselasie	Ethiopia	June 4, 1994	Netherlands
10,000 meters	**26 m., 52.23 s.**	William Sigei	Kenya	July 22,1994	Oslo
20,000 meters	**56 m., 55.6 s.**	Arturo Barrios	Mexico	Mar. 30, 1991	France
25,000 meters	**1 hr., 13 m., 55.8 s.**	Toshihiko Seko	Japan	Mar. 22, 1981	New Zealand
3,000 meter stpl.	**8 m., 02.08 s.**	Moses Kiptanui	Kenya	Aug. 19, 1992	Zurich
Marathon	**2 hr., 6 m., 50 s.**	Belayneh Densimo	Ethiopia	Apr. 17, 1988	Rotterdam

Hurdles

Event	Record	Holder	Country	Date	Where made
110 meters	**12.91 s.**	Colin Jackson	Gr. Britain	Aug. 20, 1993	Stuttgart
400 meters	**46.78 s.**	Kevin Young	U.S.	Aug. 6, 1992	Barcelona

Relay Races

Event	Record	Holder	Country	Date	Where made
400 mtrs. (4x100)	**37.40 s.**	(Marsh, Burrell, Mitchell, Lewis)	U.S.	Aug. 8, 1992	Barcelona
		(Drummond, Cason, Mitchell, Burrell)	U.S.	Aug. 22, 1993	Stuttgart
800 mtrs. (4×200)	**1 m., 18.68 s.**	(Marsh, Burrell, Heard, Lewis)	U.S.	Apr. 17, 1994	Walnut, Calif.
1,600 mtrs. (4×400)	**2 m., 54.29 s.**	(Valmon, Watts, Reynolds, Johnson)	U.S.	Aug. 22, 1993	Stuttgart
3,200 mtrs. (4×800)	**7 m., 03.89 s.**	(Elliott, Cook, Cram, Coe)	Gr. Britain	Aug. 30, 1982	London

Field Events

Event	Record	Holder	Country	Date	Where made
High jump	**8 ft., ½ in.**	Javier Sotomayor	Cuba	July 27, 1993	Salamanca, Spain
Long jump	**29 ft., 4½ in.**	Mike Powell	U.S.	Aug. 30, 1991	Tokyo
Triple jump	**58 ft., 11½ in.**	Willie Banks	U.S.	June 16, 1985	Indianapolis
Pole vault	**20 ft., 1¾ in.**	Sergei Bubka	Ukraine	July 31, 1994	Sestriere, Italy
16 lb. shot put	**75 ft., 10¼ in.**	Randy Barnes	U.S.	May 20, 1990	Los Angeles
Discus	**243 ft.**	Juergen Schult	E. Germany	June 6, 1986	E. Germany
Javelin	**313 ft., 10 in.**	Jan Zelezny	Czech Rep.	Aug. 29, 1993	Sheffield, England
16 lb. hammer	**284 ft., 7 in.**	Yuri Sedykh	USSR	Aug. 30, 1986	Stuttgart
Decathlon	**8,891 pts.**	Dan O'Brien	U.S.	Sept. 4-5, 1992	Talence, France

Women's Records

Running

Event	Record	Holder	Country	Date	Where made
100 meters	**10.49 s.**	Florence Griffith Joyner	U.S.	July 16, 1988	Indianapolis
200 meters	**21.34 s.**	Florence Griffith Joyner	U.S.	Sept. 29, 1988	Seoul
400 meters	**47.60 s.**	Marita Koch	E. Germany	Oct. 6, 1985	Canberra
800 meters	**1 m., 53.28 s.**	Jarmila Kratochvilova	Czech.	July 26, 1983	Munich
1,000 meters	**2 m., 30.67 s.**	Christine Wachtel	E. Germany	Aug. 17, 1990	Berlin
1,500 meters	**3 m., 50.46 s.**	Qu Yunxia	China	Sept. 11, 1993	Beijing
1 mile	**4 m., 15.61 s.**	Paula Ivan	Romania	July 10, 1989	Nice, France
2,000 meters	**5 m., 25.36 s.**	Sonia O'Sullivan	Ireland	July 9, 1994	Edinburgh
3,000 meters	**8 m., 06.11 s.**	Wang Junxia	China	Sept. 13, 1993	Beijing
5,000 meters	**14 m., 37.33 s.**	Ingrid Kristiansen	Norway	Aug. 5, 1986	Stockholm
10,000 meters	**29 m., 31.78 s.**	Wang Junxia	China	Sept. 8, 1993	Beijing
Marathon	**2 h., 21 m., 06 s.**	Ingrid Kristiansen	Norway	Apr. 21, 1985	London

Hurdles

Event	Record	Holder	Country	Date	Where made
100 meters	**12.21 s.**	Yordanka Donkova	Bulgaria	Aug. 21, 1988	Bulgaria
400 meters	**52.74 s.**	Sally Gunnell	Gr. Britain	Aug. 19, 1993	Stuttgart

Field Events

Event	Record	Holder	Country	Date	Where made
High jump	**6 ft., 10¼ in.**	Stefka Kostadinova	Bulgaria	Aug. 30, 1987	Rome
Shot put	**74 ft., 3 in.**	Natalya Lisovskaya	USSR	June 7, 1987	Moscow
Long jump	**24 ft., 8¼ in.**	Galina Chistyakova	USSR	June 11, 1988	Leningrad
Triple Jump	**49 ft., 6¼ in.**	Ana Biryukova	Russia	Aug. 21, 1993	Stuttgart
Discus	**252 ft.**	Gabriele Reinsch	E. Germany	July 9, 1988	E. Germany
Javelin	**262 ft., 5 in.**	Petra Felke	E. Germany	Sept. 9, 1988	E. Germany
Heptathlon	**7,291 pts.**	Jackie Joyner-Kersee	U.S.	Sept. 23-24, 1988	Seoul

Relay Races

Event	Record	Holder	Country	Date	Where made
400 mtrs. (4×100)	**41.37 s.**	National team	E. Germany	Oct. 6, 1985	Canberra
800 mtrs. (4×200)	**1 m., 28.15 s.**	National team	E. Germany	Aug. 9, 1980	E. Germany
1,600 mtrs. (4×400)	**3 m., 15.17 s.**	National team	USSR	Oct. 1, 1988	Seoul
3,200 mtrs. (4×800)	**7 m., 50.17 s.**	National team	USSR	Aug. 5, 1984	Moscow

World Track and Field Indoor Records

As of Oct. 1, 1994

The International Amateur Athletic Federation began recognizing world indoor track and field records as official on January 1, 1987. Prior to that, there were only unofficial world indoor bests. World indoor bests set prior to January 1, 1987, are subject to approval as world records providing they meet the prescribed IAAF world records criteria, including drug testing. To be accepted as a world indoor record, a performance must meet the same criteria as a world record outdoors except that a track performance cannot be set on an indoor track larger than 200 meters. *Record pending.

Men

Event	Record	Holder	Country	Date	Where made
50 meters	**5.61**	Manfred Kokot	E. Germany	Feb. 4, 1973	E. Berlin
		James Sanford	U.S.	Feb. 20, 1981	San Diego
60 meters	**6.41**	Andre Cason	U.S.	Feb. 14, 1992	Madrid
200 meters	**20.36**	Bruno Marie-Rose	France	Feb. 22, 1987	Lievin, France
400 meters	**45.02**	Danny Everett	U.S.	Feb. 2, 1992	Stuttgart
800 meters	**1:44.84**	Paul Ereng	Kenya	Mar. 4, 1989	Budapest
1,000 meters	**2:15.26**	Noureddine Morceli	Algeria	Feb. 22, 1992	Birmingham, England
1,500 meters	**3:34.16**	Noureddine Morceli	Algeria	Feb. 28, 1991	Seville, Spain
1 mile	**3:49.78**	Eamonn Coghlan	Ireland	Feb. 27, 1983	E. Rutherford, N.J.
3,000 meters	**7:37.31**	Moses Kiptanui	Kenya	Feb. 20, 1992	Seville, Spain
5,000 meters	**13:20.40**	Suleiman Nyambui	Tanzania	Feb. 6, 1981	New York
50-meter hurdles	**6.25**	Mark McKoy	Canada	Mar. 5, 1986	Kobe, Japan
60-meter hurdles	***7.30**	Colin Jackson	Gr. Britain	Mar. 6, 1994	Germany
High jump	**7 ft., 11¼ in.**	Javier Sotomayor	Cuba	Mar. 4, 1989	Budapest
Pole vault	**20 ft., 2 in.**	Sergei Bubka	Ukraine	Feb. 21, 1993	Ukraine
Long jump	**28 ft., 10¼ in.**	Carl Lewis	U.S.	Jan. 27, 1984	New York
Triple jump	***58 ft., 3¾ in.**	Leonid Voloshin	Russia	Feb. 6, 1994	Grenoble, France
Shot put	**74 ft., 4¼ in.**	Randy Barnes	U.S.	Jan. 20, 1989	Los Angeles

Women

Event	Record	Holder	Country	Date	Where made
50 meters	**6.00**	Merlene Ottey	Jamaica	Feb. 4, 1994	Moscow
60 meters	**6.92**	Irina Privalova	Russia	Feb. 11, 1993	Madrid
200 meters	**21.87**	Merlene Ottey	Jamaica	Feb. 13, 1993	Lievin, France
400 meters	**49.59**	Jarmila Kratochvilova	Czechoslovakia	Mar. 7, 1982	Milan
800 meters	**1:56.40**	Christine Wachtel	E. Germany	Feb. 13, 1988	Vienna
1,000 meters	**2:34.8**	Brigitte Kraus	W. Germany	Feb. 19, 1978	W. Germany
1,500 meters	**4:00.27**	Doina Melinte	Romania	Feb. 9, 1990	E. Rutherford, N.J.
1 mile	**4:17.14**	Doina Melinte	Romania	Feb. 9, 1990	E. Rutherford, N.J.
3,000 meters	**8:33.82**	Elly van Hulst	Netherlands	Mar. 4, 1989	Budapest
5,000 meters	**15:03.17**	Liz McColgan	Gr. Britain	Feb. 22, 1992	Birmingham, England
50-meter hurdles	**6:58**	Cornelia Oschkenat	E. Germany	Feb. 20, 1988	Berlin
60-meter hurdles	**7.69**	Lyudmila Narozhilenko	USSR	Feb 4, 1990	Chelyabinsk, USSR
High jump	**6 ft., 9½ in.**	Heike Henkel	Germany	Feb. 8, 1992	Germany
Long jump	**24 ft., 2¼ in.**	Heike Drechsler	E. Germany	Feb. 13, 1988	Vienna
Triple jump	***48 ft., 10¾ in.**	Inna Lasovskaya	Russia	Feb. 13, 1994	Lievin, France
Shot put	**73 ft., 10 in.**	Helena Fibingerova	Czechoslovakia	Feb. 19, 1977	Czechoslovakia

NATIONAL FOOTBALL LEAGUE

Expansion Teams

The NFL announced the addition of 2 new teams in 1993, both scheduled to begin play in the 1995 season. The Carolina Panthers were awarded a franchise on Oct. 26, 1993, and will be based in a new 72,000-seat stadium in Charlotte, NC. The Jacksonville Jaguars were awarded a franchise on Nov. 30, 1993, and will play their home games in the renovated 73,000-seat Gator Bowl.

Final 1993 Standings

American Football Conference

Eastern Division

	W	L	T	Pct.	Pts.	Opp.
Buffalo	12	4	0	.750	329	242
Miami	9	7	0	.563	349	351
N.Y. Jets	8	8	0	.500	270	247
New England	5	11	0	.313	238	286
Indianapolis	4	12	0	.250	189	378

Central Division

	W	L	T	Pct.	Pts.	Opp.
Houston	12	4	0	.750	368	238
Pittsburgh	9	7	0	.563	308	281
Cleveland	7	9	0	.438	304	307
Cincinnati	3	13	0	.188	187	319

Western Division

	W	L	T	Pct.	Pts.	Opp.
Kansas City	11	5	0	.688	328	291
L.A. Raiders	10	6	0	.625	306	326
Denver	9	7	0	.563	373	284
San Diego	8	8	0	.500	322	290
Seattle	6	10	0	.375	280	314

National Football Conference

Eastern Division

	W	L	T	Pct.	Pts.	Opp.
Dallas	12	4	0	.750	376	229
N.Y. Giants	11	5	0	.688	288	205
Philadelphia	8	8	0	.500	293	315
Phoenix	7	9	0	.438	326	269
Washington	4	12	0	.250	230	345

Central Division

	W	L	T	Pct.	Pts.	Opp.
Detroit	10	6	0	.625	298	292
Minnesota	9	7	0	.563	277	290
Green Bay	9	7	0	.563	340	282
Chicago	7	9	0	.438	236	230
Tampa Bay	5	11	0	.313	237	376

Western Division

	W	L	T	Pct.	Pts.	Opp.
San Francisco	10	6	0	.625	465	273
New Orleans	8	8	0	.500	317	343
Atlanta	6	10	0	.375	316	385
L.A. Rams	5	11	0	.313	221	367

AFC Playoffs—Kansas City 27, Pittsburgh 24 (OT); L.A. Raiders 42, Denver 24; Buffalo 29, L.A. Raiders 23; Kansas City 28, Houston 20; Buffalo 30, Kansas City 13.

NFC Playoffs—Green Bay 28, Detroit 24; N.Y. Giants 17, Minnesota 10; San Francisco 44, N.Y. Giants 3; Dallas 27, Green Bay 17; Dallas 38, San Francisco 21.

National Football League Champions

Year	East Winner (W-L-T)	West Winner (W-L-T)	Playoff
1933	New York Giants (11-3-0)	Chicago Bears (10-2-1)	Chicago Bears 23, New York 21
1934	New York Giants (8-5-0)	Chicago Bears (13-0-0)	New York 30, Chicago Bears 13
1935	New York Giants (9-3-0)	Detroit Lions (7-3-2)	Detroit 26, New York 7
1936	Boston Redskins (7-5-0)	Green Bay Packers (10-1-1)	Green Bay 21, Boston 6
1937	Washington Redskins (8-3-0)	Chicago Bears (9-1-1)	Washington 28, Chicago Bears 21
1938	New York Giants (8-2-1)	Green Bay Packers (8-3-0)	New York 23, Green Bay 17
1939	New York Giants (9-1-1)	Green Bay Packers (9-2-0)	Green Bay 27, New York 0
1940	Washington Redskins (9-2-0)	Chicago Bears (8-3-0)	Chicago Bears 73, Washington 0
1941	New York Giants (8-3-0)	Chicago Bears (10-1-1)(a)	Chicago Bears 37, New York 9
1942	Wash. Redskins (10-1-1)	Chicago Bears (11-0-0)	Washington 14, Chicago Bears 6
1943	Wash. Redskins (6-3-1)(a)	Chicago Bears (8-1-1)	Chicago Bears, 41, Washington 21
1944	New York Giants (8-1-1)	Green Bay Packers (8-2-0)	Green Bay 14, New York 7
1945	Wash. Redskins (8-2-0)	Cleveland Rams (9-1-0)	Cleveland 15, Washington 14
1946	New York Giants (7-3-1)	Chicago Bears (8-2-1)	Chicago Bears 24, New York 14
1947	Philadelphia Eagles (8-4-0)(a)	Chicago Cardinals (9-3-0)	Chicago Cardinals 28, Philadelphia 21
1948	Philadelphia Eagles (9-2-1)	Chicago Cardinals (11-1-0)	Philadelphia 7, Chicago Cardinals 0
1949	Philadelphia Eagles (11-1-0)	Los Angeles Rams (8-2-2)	Philadelphia 14, Los Angeles 0
1950	Cleveland Browns (10-2-0)(a)	Los Angeles Rams (9-3-0)(a)	Cleveland 30, Los Angeles 28
1951	Cleveland Browns (11-1-0)	Los Angeles Rams (8-4-0)	Los Angeles 24, Cleveland 17
1952	Cleveland Browns (8-4-0)	Detroit Lions (9-3-0)(a)	Detroit 17, Cleveland 7
1953	Cleveland Browns (11-1-0)	Detroit Lions (10-2-0)	Detroit 17, Cleveland 16
1954	Cleveland Browns (9-3-0)	Detroit Lions (9-2-1)	Cleveland 56, Detroit 10
1955	Cleveland Browns (9-2-1)	Los Angeles Rams (8-3-1)	Cleveland 38, Los Angeles 14
1956	New York Giants (8-3-1)	Chicago Bears (9-2-1)	New York 47, Chicago Bears 7
1957	Cleveland Browns (9-2-1)	Detroit Lions (8-4-0)(a)	Detroit 59, Cleveland 14
1958	New York Giants (9-3-0)(a)	Baltimore Colts (9-3-0)	Baltimore 23, New York 17(b)
1959	New York Giants (10-2-0)	Baltimore Colts (9-3-0)	Baltimore 31, New York 16
1960	Philadelphia Eagles (10-2-0)	Green Bay Packers (8-4-0)	Philadelphia 17, Green Bay 13
1961	New York Giants (10-3-1)	Green Bay Packers (11-3-0)	Green Bay 37, New York 0
1962	New York Giants (12-2-0)	Green Bay Packers (13-1-0)	Green Bay 16, New York 7
1963	New York Giants (11-3-0)	Chicago Bears (11-1-2)	Chicago 14, New York 10
1964	Cleveland Browns (10-3-1)	Baltimore Colts (12-2-0)	Cleveland 27, Baltimore 0
1965	Cleveland Browns (11-3-0)	Green Bay Packers (10-3-1)(a)	Green Bay 23, Cleveland 12
1966	Dallas Cowboys (10-3-1)	Green Bay Packers (12-2-0)	Green Bay 34, Dallas 27

(a) Won divisional playoff. (b) Won at 8:15 of sudden death overtime period.

Year	Conference	Division	Winner (W-L-T)	Playoff
1967	East	Century	Cleveland (9-5-0)	Dallas 52, Cleveland 14
		Capitol	Dallas (9-5-0)	
	West	Central	Green Bay (9-4-1)	Green Bay 28, Los Angeles 7
		Coastal	Los Angeles (11-1-2)(a)	Green Bay 21, Dallas 17

(continued)

Year	Conference	Division	Winner (W-L-T)	Playoff
1968	East	Century	Cleveland (10-4-0)	Cleveland 31, Dallas 20
		Capitol	Dallas (12-2-0)	
	West	Central	Minnesota (8-6-0)	Baltimore 24, Minnesota 14
		Coastal	Baltimore (13-1-0)	Baltimore 34, Cleveland 0
1969	East	Century	Cleveland (10-3-1)	Cleveland 38, Dallas 14
		Capitol	Dallas (11-2-1)	
	West	Central	Minnesota (12-2-0)	Minnesota 23, Los Angeles 20
		Coastal	Los Angeles (11-3-0)	Minnesota 27, Cleveland 7
1970	American	Eastern	Baltimore (11-2-1)	Baltimore 17, Cincinnati 0
		Central	Cincinnati (8-6-0)	Oakland 21, Miami 14
		Western	Oakland (8-4-2)	Baltimore 27, Oakland 17
	National	Eastern	Dallas (10-4-0)	Dallas 5, Detroit 0
		Central	Minnesota (12-2-0)	San Francisco 17, Minnesota 14
		Western	San Francisco (10-3-1)	Dallas 17, San Francisco 10
1971	American	Eastern	Miami (10-3-1)	Miami 27, Kansas City 24
		Central	Cleveland (9-5-0)	Baltimore 20, Cleveland 3
		Western	Kansas City (10-3-1)	Miami 21, Baltimore 0
	National	Eastern	Dallas (11-3-0)	Dallas 20, Minnesota 12
		Central	Minnesota (11-3-0)	San Francisco 24, Washington 20
		Western	San Francisco (9-5-0)	Dallas 14, San Francisco 3
1972	American	Eastern	Miami (14-0-0)	Miami 20, Cleveland 14
		Central	Pittsburgh (11-3-0)	Pittsburgh 13, Oakland 7
		Western	Oakland (10-3-1)	Miami 21, Pittsburgh 17
	National	Eastern	Washington (11-3-0)	Washington 16, Green Bay 3
		Central	Green Bay (10-4-0)	Dallas 30, San Francisco 28
		Western	San Francisco (8-5-1)	Washington 26, Dallas 3
1973	American	Eastern	Miami (12-2-0)	Miami 34, Cincinnati 16
		Central	Cincinnati (10-4-0)	Oakland 33, Pittsburgh 14
		Western	Oakland (9-4-1)	Miami 27, Oakland 10
	National	Eastern	Dallas (10-4-0)	Dallas 27, Los Angeles 16
		Central	Minnesota (12-2-0)	Minnesota 27, Washington 20
		Western	Los Angeles (12-2-0)	Minnesota 27, Dallas 10
1974	American	Eastern	Miami (11-3-0)	Oakland 28, Miami 26
		Central	Pittsburgh (10-3-1)	Pittsburgh 32, Buffalo 14
		Western	Oakland (12-2-0)	Pittsburgh 24, Oakland 13
	National	Eastern	St. Louis (10-4-0)	Minnesota 30, St. Louis 14
		Central	Minnesota (10-4-0)	Los Angeles 19, Washington 10
		Western	Los Angeles (10-4-0)	Minnesota 14, Los Angeles 10
1975	American	Eastern	Baltimore (10-4-0)	Pittsburgh 28, Baltimore 10
		Central	Pittsburgh (12-2-0)	Oakland 31, Cincinnati 28
		Western	Oakland (11-3-0)	Pittsburgh 16, Oakland 10
	National	Eastern	St. Louis (11-3-0)	Dallas 17, Minnesota 14
		Central	Minnesota (12-2-0)	Los Angeles 35, St. Louis 23
		Western	Los Angeles (12-2-0)	Dallas 37, Los Angeles 7
1976	American	Eastern	Baltimore (11-3-0)	Pittsburgh 40, Baltimore 14
		Central	Pittsburgh (10-4-0)	Oakland 24, New England 21
		Western	Oakland (13-1-0)	Oakland 24, Pittsburgh 7
	National	Eastern	Dallas (11-3-0)	Minnesota 35, Washington 20
		Central	Minnesota (11-2-1)	Los Angeles 14, Dallas 12
		Western	Los Angeles (10-3-1)	Minnesota 24, Los Angeles 13
1977	American	Eastern	Baltimore (10-4-0)	Oakland 37, Baltimore 31
		Central	Pittsburgh (9-5-0)	Denver 34, Pittsburgh 21
		Western	Denver (12-2-0)	Dallas 37, Chicago 7
	National	Eastern	Dallas (12-2-0)	Minnesota 14, Los Angeles 7
		Central	Minnesota (9-5-0)	Denver 20, Oakland 17
		Western	Los Angeles (10-4-0)	Dallas 23, Minnesota 6
1978	American	Eastern	New England (11-5-0)	Pittsburgh 33, Denver 10
		Central	Pittsburgh (14-2-0)	Houston 31, New England 14
		Western	Denver (10-6-0)	Pittsburgh 34, Houston 5
	National	Eastern	Dallas (12-4-0)	Dallas 27, Atlanta 20
		Central	Minnesota (8-7-1)	Los Angeles 34, Minnesota 10
		Western	Los Angeles (12-4-0)	Dallas 28, Los Angeles 0
1979	American	Eastern	Miami (10-6-0)	Houston 17, San Diego 14
		Central	Pittsburgh (12-4-0)	Pittsburgh 34, Miami 14
		Western	San Diego (12-4-0)	Pittsburgh 27, Houston 13
	National	Eastern	Dallas (11-5-0)	Tampa Bay 24, Philadelphia 17
		Central	Tampa Bay (10-6-0)	Los Angeles 21, Dallas 19
		Western	Los Angeles (9-7-0)	Los Angeles 9, Tampa Bay 0
1980	American	Eastern	Buffalo (11-5-0)	San Diego 20, Buffalo 14
		Central	Cleveland (11-5-0)	Oakland 14, Cleveland 12
		Western	San Diego (11-5-0)	Oakland 34, San Diego 27
	National	Eastern	Philadelphia (12-4-0)	Philadelphia 31, Minnesota 16
		Central	Minnesota (9-7-0)	Dallas 30, Atlanta 27
		Western	Atlanta (12-4-0)	Philadelphia 20, Dallas 7
1981	American	Eastern	Miami (11-4-1)	San Diego 41, Miami 38
		Central	Cincinnati (12-4-0)	Cincinnati 28, Buffalo 21
		Western	San Diego (10-6-0)	Cincinnati 27, San Diego 7
	National	Eastern	Dallas (12-4-0)	Dallas 38, Tampa Bay 0
		Central	Tampa Bay (9-7-0)	San Francisco 38, N.Y. Giants 24
		Western	San Francisco (13-3-0)	San Francisco 28, Dallas 27
1982	American		L.A. Raiders (8-1-0)	
	National		Washington (8-1-0)	Strike-shortened season

AFC playoffs—Miami 28, New England 13; L.A. Raiders 27, Cleveland 10; N.Y. Jets 44, Cincinnati 17; San Diego 31, Pittsburgh 28; N.Y. Jets 17, L.A. Raiders 14; Miami 34, San Diego 13; Miami 14, N.Y. Jets 0. **NFC playoffs**—Washington 31, Detroit 7; Green Bay 41, St. Louis 16; Dallas 30, Tampa Bay 17; Minnesota 30, Atlanta 24; Washington 21, Minnesota 7; Dallas 37, Green Bay 26; Washington 31, Dallas 17.

Year	Conference	Division	Winner (W-L-T)	Playoff
1983	American	Eastern	Miami (12-4-0)	Seattle 27, Miami 20
		Central	Pittsburgh (10-6-0)	L.A. Raiders 38, Pittsburgh 10
		Western	L.A. Raiders (12-4-0)	L.A. Raiders 30, Seattle 14

Year	Conference	Division	Winner (W-L-T)	Playoff
	National	Eastern	Washington (14-2-0)	Washington 51, L.A. Rams 7
		Central	Detroit (9-7-0)	San Francisco 24, Detroit 23
		Western	San Francisico (10-6-0)	Washington 24, San Francisco 21
1984	American	Eastern	Miami (14-2-0)	Miami 31, Seattle 10
		Central	Pittsburgh (9-7-0)	Pittsburgh 24, Denver 17
		Western	Denver (13-3-0)	Miami 45, Pittsburgh 28
	National	Eastern	Washington (11-5-0)	Chicago 23, Washington 19
		Central	Chicago (10-6-0)	San Francisco 21, N.Y. Giants 10
		Western	San Francisco (15-1-0)	San Francisco 23, Chicago 0
1985	American	Eastern	Miami (12-4-0)	New England 27, L.A. Raiders 20
		Central	Cleveland (8-8-0)	Miami 24, Cleveland 21
		Western	L.A. Raiders (12-4-0)	New England 31, Miami 14
	National	Eastern	Dallas (10-6-0)	Chicago 21, N.Y. Giants 0
		Central	Chicago (15-1-0)	L.A. Rams 20, Dallas 0
		Western	L.A. Rams (11-5-0)	Chicago 24, L.A. Rams 0
1986	American	Eastern	New England (11-5-0)	Denver 22, New England 17
		Central	Cleveland (12-4-0)	Cleveland 23, N.Y. Jets 20
		Western	Denver (11-5-0)	Denver 23, Cleveland 20
	National	Eastern	N.Y. Giants (14-2-0)	N.Y. Giants 49, San Francisco 3
		Central	Chicago (14-2-0)	Washington 27, Chicago 13
		Western	San Francisco (10-5-1)	N.Y. Giants 17, Washington 0
1987	American	Eastern	Indianapolis (9-6-0)	Cleveland 38, Indianapolis 21
		Central	Cleveland (10-5-0)	Denver 34, Houston 10
		Western	Denver (10-4-1)	Denver 38, Cleveland 33
	National	Eastern	Washington (11-4-0)	Washington 21, Chicago 17
		Central	Chicago (11-4-0)	Minnesota 36, San Francisco 24
		Western	San Francisco (13-2-0)	Washington 17, Minnesota 10
1988	American	Eastern	Buffalo (12-4-0)	Buffalo 17, Houston 10
		Central	Cincinnati (12-4-0)	Cincinnati 21, Seattle 13
		Western	Seattle (9-7-0)	Cincinnati 21, Buffalo 10
	National	Eastern	Philadelphia (10-6-0)	Chicago 20, Philadelphia 12
		Central	Chicago (12-4-0)	San Francisco 34, Minnesota 9
		Western	San Francisco (10-6-0)	San Francisco 28, Chicago 3
1989	American	Eastern	Buffalo (9-7-0)	Cleveland 34, Buffalo 30
		Central	Cleveland (9-6-1)	Denver 24, Pittsburgh 23
		Western	Denver (11-5-0)	Denver 37, Cleveland 21
	National	Eastern	N.Y. Giants (12-4-0)	San Francisco 41, Minnesota 13
		Central	Minnesota (10-6-0)	L.A. Rams 19, N.Y. Giants 13
		Western	San Francisco (14-2-0)	San Francisco 30, L.A. Rams 3
1990	American	Eastern	Buffalo (13-3-0)	L.A. Raiders 20, Cincinnati 10
		Central	Cincinnati (9-7-0)	Buffalo 44, Miami 34
		Western	L.A. Raiders (12-4-0)	Buffalo 51, L.A. Raiders 3
	National	Eastern	N.Y. Giants (13-3-0)	San Francisco 28, Washington 10
		Central	Chicago (11-5-0)	N.Y. Giants 31, Chicago 3
		Western	San Francisco (14-2-0)	N.Y. Giants 15, San Francisco 13
1991	American	Eastern	Buffalo (13-3-0)	Denver 26, Houston 24
		Central	Houston (11-5-0)	Buffalo 37, Kansas City 14
		Western	Denver (12-4-0)	Buffalo 10, Denver 7
	National	Eastern	Washington (14-2-0)	Washington 24, Atlanta 7
		Central	Detroit (12-4-0)	Detroit 38, Dallas 6
		Western	New Orleans (11-5-0)	Washington 41, Detroit 10
1992	American	Eastern	Miami (11-5-0)	Miami 31, San Diego 0
		Central	Pittsburgh (11-5-0)	Buffalo 24, Pittsburgh 3
		Western	San Diego (11-5-0)	Buffalo 29, Miami 10
	National	Eastern	Dallas (13-3-0)	Dallas 34, Philadelphia 10
		Central	Minnesota (11-5-0)	San Francisco 20, Washington 13
		Western	San Francisco (14-2-0)	Dallas 30, San Francisco 20
1993	American	Eastern	Buffalo (12-4-0)	Buffalo 29, L.A. Raiders 23
		Central	Houston (12-4-0)	Kansas City 28, Houston 20
		Western	Kansas City (11-5-0)	Buffalo 30, Kansas City 13
	National	Eastern	Dallas (12-4-0)	Dallas 27, Green Bay 17
		Central	Detroit (10-6-0)	San Francisco 44, N.Y. Giants 3
		Western	San Francisco (10-6-0)	Dallas 38, San Francisco 21

NFL Head Coaches at Start of 1994 Season

AFC

Buffalo—Marv Levy
Cincinnati—David Shula
Cleveland—Bill Belichick
Denver—Wade Phillips
Houston—Jack Pardee
Indianapolis—Ted Marchibroda
Kansas City—Marty Schottenheimer
L.A. Raiders—Art Shell
Miami—Don Shula
New England—Bill Parcells
N.Y. Jets—Pete Carroll
Pittsburgh—Bill Cowher
San Diego—Bobby Ross
Seattle—Tom Flores

NFC

Arizona—Buddy Ryan
Atlanta—June Jones
Chicago—Dave Wannstedt
Dallas—Barry Switzer
Detroit—Wayne Fontes
Green Bay—Mike Holmgren
L.A. Rams—Chuck Knox
Minnesota—Dennis Green
New Orleans—Jim Mora
N.Y. Giants—Dan Reeves
Philadelphia—Rich Kotite
San Francisco—George Seifert
Tampa Bay—Sam Wyche
Washington—Norv Turner

Cowboys Defeat Bills in Super Bowl

The Dallas Cowboys took control of the game in the second half and defeated the Buffalo Bills 30-13 to win Super Bowl XXVIII on Jan. 30, 1994. The Cowboys became the fifth team to win consecutive Super Bowls, while the Bills became the first team in the history of major American sports to lose in 4 straight championships. Dallas running back Emmitt Smith was named the game's most valuable player.

Score by Quarters

Dallas	6	0	14	10—30
Buffalo	3	10	0	0—13

Scoring

Dallas—Murray 41 yd field goal
Buffalo—Christie 54 yd field goal
Dallas—Murray 24 yd field goal
Buffalo—T. Thomas 4 yd run (Christie kick)
Buffalo—Christie 28 yd field goal
Dallas—J. Washington 46 yd fumble return (Murray kick)
Dallas—E. Smith 15 yd run (Murray kick)
Dallas—E. Smith 1 yd run (Murray kick)
Dallas—Murray 20 yd field goal

Individual Statistics

Rushing —Dallas, E. Smith 30-132, K. Williams 1-6, Aikman 1-3, Johnston 1-0, Kosar 1-(minus 1), Coleman 1-(minus 3). Buffalo, K. Davis 9-38, T. Thomas 16-37, Kelly 2-12.

Passing —Dallas, Aikman 19-27-1-207. Buffalo, Kelly 31-50-1-260.

Receiving —Dallas, Irvin 5-66, Novacek 5-26, E. Smith 4-26, Harper 3-75, Johnston 2-14. Buffalo, Brooks 7-63, T. Thomas 7-52, Reed 6-75, Beebe 6-60, K. Davis 3-(minus 5), Metzelaars 1-8, McKeller 1-7.

Team Statistics

	Dallas	Buffalo
First downs	20	22
Rushes-yards	35-137	27-87
Passing yards	204	227
Punt returns-yards	1-5	1-5
Kickoff returns-yards	2-72	6-144
Interception returns-yards	1-12	1-41
Comp.-att.-int.	19-27-1	31-50-1
Sacked-yards lost	2-3	3-33
Punts-average	4-44	5-38
Fumbles-lost	0-0	3-2
Penalties-yards	6-50	1-10
Time of possession	34:29	25:31

Super Bowl

Year	Winner	Loser	Winning coach	Site
1967	Green Bay Packers, 35	Kansas City Chiefs, 10	Vince Lombardi	Los Angeles Coliseum
1968	Green Bay Packers, 33	Oakland Raiders, 14	Vince Lombardi	Orange Bowl, Miami
1969	New York Jets, 16	Baltimore Colts, 7	Weeb Ewbank	Orange Bowl, Miami
1970	Kansas City Chiefs, 23	Minnesota Vikings, 7	Hank Stram	Tulane Stadium, New Orleans
1971	Baltimore Colts, 16	Dallas Cowboys, 13	Don McCafferty	Orange Bowl, Miami
1972	Dallas Cowboys, 24	Miami Dolphins, 3	Tom Landry	Tulane Stadium, New Orleans
1973	Miami Dolphins, 14	Washington Redskins, 7	Don Shula	Los Angeles Coliseum
1974	Miami Dolphins, 24	Minnesota Vikings, 7	Don Shula	Rice Stadium, Houston
1975	Pittsburgh Steelers, 16	Minnesota Vikings, 6	Chuck Noll	Tulane Stadium, New Orleans
1976	Pittsburgh Steelers, 21	Dallas Cowboys, 17	Chuck Noll	Orange Bowl, Miami
1977	Oakland Raiders, 32	Minnesota Vikings, 14	John Madden	Rose Bowl, Pasadena
1978	Dallas Cowboys, 27	Denver Broncos, 10	Tom Landry	Superdome, New Orleans
1979	Pittsburgh Steelers, 35	Dallas Cowboys, 31	Chuck Noll	Orange Bowl, Miami
1980	Pittsburgh Steelers, 31	Los Angeles Rams, 19	Chuck Noll	Rose Bowl, Pasadena
1981	Oakland Raiders, 27	Philadelphia Eagles, 10	Tom Flores	Superdome, New Orleans
1982	San Francisco 49ers, 26	Cincinnati Bengals, 21	Bill Walsh	Silverdome, Pontiac, Mich.
1983	Washington Redskins, 27	Miami Dolphins, 17	Joe Gibbs	Rose Bowl, Pasadena
1984	Los Angeles Raiders, 38	Washington Redskins, 9	Tom Flores	Tampa Stadium
1985	San Francisco 49ers, 38	Miami Dolphins, 16	Bill Walsh	Stanford Stadium, Palo Alto, Cal.
1986	Chicago Bears, 46	New England Patriots, 10	Mike Ditka	Superdome, New Orleans
1987	New York Giants, 39	Denver Broncos, 20	Bill Parcells	Rose Bowl, Pasadena
1988	Washington Redskins, 42	Denver Broncos, 10	Joe Gibbs	San Diego Stadium
1989	San Francisco 49ers, 20	Cincinnati Bengals, 16	Bill Walsh	Joe Robbie Stadium, Miami
1990	San Francisco 49ers, 55	Denver Broncos, 10	George Seifert	Superdome, New Orleans
1991	New York Giants, 20	Buffalo Bills, 19	Bill Parcells	Tampa Stadium
1992	Washington Redskins, 37	Buffalo Bills, 24	Joe Gibbs	Metrodome, Minneapolis
1993	Dallas Cowboys, 52	Buffalo Bills, 17	Jimmy Johnson	Rose Bowl, Pasadena
1994	Dallas Cowboys, 30	Buffalo Bills, 13	Jimmy Johnson	Georgia Dome, Atlanta

Super Bowl MVPs

1967	Bart Starr, Green Bay	1977	Fred Biletnikoff, Oakland	1986	Richard Dent, Chicago
1968	Bart Starr, Green Bay	1978	Randy White, Harvey Martin, Dallas	1987	Phil Simms, N.Y. Giants
1969	Joe Namath, N.Y. Jets	1979	Terry Bradshaw, Pittsburgh	1988	Doug Williams, Washington
1970	Len Dawson, Kansas City	1980	Terry Bradshaw, Pittsburgh	1989	Jerry Rice, San Francisco
1971	Chuck Howley, Dallas	1981	Jim Plunkett, Oakland	1990	Joe Montana, San Francisco
1972	Roger Staubach, Dallas	1982	Joe Montana, San Francisco	1991	Ottis Anderson, N.Y. Giants
1973	Jake Scott, Miami	1983	John Riggins, Washington	1992	Mark Rypien, Washington
1974	Larry Csonka, Miami	1984	Marcus Allen, L.A. Raiders	1993	Troy Aikman, Dallas
1975	Franco Harris, Pittsburgh	1985	Joe Montana, San Francisco	1994	Emmitt Smith, Dallas
1976	Lynn Swann, Pittsburgh				

American Football League

Year	Eastern Division	Western Division	Playoff
1960	Houston Oilers (10-4-0)	L. A. Chargers (10-4-0)	Houston 24, Los Angeles 16
1961	Houston Oilers (10-3-1)	San Diego Chargers (12-2-0)	Houston 10, San Diego 3
1962	Houston Oilers (11-3-0)	Dallas Texans (11-3-0)	Dallas 20, Houston 17(b)
1963	Boston Patriots (8-6-1)(a)	San Diego Chargers (11-3-0)	San Diego 51, Boston 10
1964	Buffalo Bills (12-2-0)	San Diego Chargers (8-5-1)	Buffalo 20, San Diego 7
1965	Buffalo Bills (10-3-1)	San Diego Chargers (9-2-3)	Buffalo 23, San Diego 0
1966	Buffalo Bills (9-4-1)	Kansas City Chiefs (11-2-1)	Kansas City 31, Buffalo 7
1967	Houston Oilers (9-4-1)	Oakland Raiders (13-1-0)	Oakland 40, Houston 7
1968	New York Jets (11-3-0)	Oakland Raiders (12-2-0)(a)	New York 27, Oakland 23
1969	New York Jets (10-4-0)	Oakland Raiders (12-1-1)	Kansas City 17, Oakland 7(c)

(a) Won divisional playoff. (b) Won at 2:45 of second overtime. (c) Kansas City defeated Jets to make playoffs.

American Football Conference Leaders

(American Football League, 1960-1969)

Passing						Pass-Receiving			
Player, team	**Atts**	**Com**	**YG**	**TD**	**Year**	**Player, team**	**Ct**	**YG**	**TD**
Jack Kemp, Los Angeles	406	211	3,018	20	**1960**	Lionel Taylor, Denver	92	1,235	12
George Blanda, Houston	362	187	3,330	36	**1961**	Lionel Taylor, Denver	100	1,176	4
Len Dawson, Dallas	310	189	2,759	29	**1962**	Lionel Taylor, Denver	77	908	4
Tobin Rote, Kansas City	286	170	2,510	20	**1963**	Lionel Taylor, Denver	78	1,101	10
Len Dawson, Kansas City	354	199	2,879	30	**1964**	Charley Hennigan, Houston	101	1,546	8
John Hadl, San Diego	348	174	2,798	20	**1965**	Lionel Taylor, Denver	85	1,131	6
Len Dawson, Kansas City	284	159	2,527	26	**1966**	Lance Alworth, San Diego	73	1,383	13
Daryle Lamonica, Oakland	425	220	3,228	30	**1967**	George Sauer, N.Y. Jets	75	1,189	6
Len Dawson, Kansas City	224	131	2,109	17	**1968**	Lance Alworth, San Diego	68	1,312	10
Greg Cook, Cincinnati	197	106	1,854	15	**1969**	Lance Alworth, San Diego	64	1,003	4
Daryle Lamonica, Oakland	356	179	2,516	22	**1970**	Marlin Briscoe, Buffalo	57	1,036	8
Bob Griese, Miami	263	145	2,089	19	**1971**	Fred Biletnikoff, Oakland	61	929	9
Earl Morrall, Miami	150	83	1,360	11	**1972**	Fred Biletnikoff, Oakland	58	802	7
Ken Stabler, Oakland	260	163	1,997	14	**1973**	Fred Willis, Houston	57	371	1
Ken Anderson, Cincinnati	328	213	2,667	18	**1974**	Lydell Mitchell, Baltimore	72	544	2
Ken Anderson, Cincinnati	377	228	3,169	21	**1975**	Reggie Rucker, Cleveland	60	770	3
						Lydell Mitchell, Baltimore	60	554	4
Ken Stabler, Oakland	291	194	2,737	27	**1976**	MacArthur Lane, Kansas City	66	686	1
Bob Griese, Miami	307	180	2,252	22	**1977**	Lydell Mitchell, Baltimore	71	620	4
Terry Bradshaw, Pittsburgh	368	207	2,915	28	**1978**	Steve Largent, Seattle	71	1,168	8
Dan Fouts, San Diego	530	332	4,082	24	**1979**	Joe Washington, Baltimore	82	750	3
Brian Sipe, Cleveland	554	337	4,132	30	**1980**	Kellen Winslow, San Diego	89	1,290	9
Ken Anderson, Cincinnati	479	300	3,754	29	**1981**	Kellen Winslow, San Diego	88	1,075	10
Ken Anderson, Cincinnati	309	218	2,495	12	**1982**	Kellen Winslow, San Diego	54	721	6
Dan Marino, Miami	296	173	2,210	20	**1983**	Todd Christensen, L.A. Raiders	92	1,247	12
Dan Marino, Miami	564	362	5,084	48	**1984**	Ozzie Newsome, Cleveland	89	1,001	5
Ken O'Brien, N.Y. Jets	488	297	3,888	25	**1985**	Lionel James, San Diego	86	1,027	6
Dan Marino, Miami	623	378	4,746	44	**1986**	Todd Christensen, L.A. Raiders	95	1,153	8
Bernie Kosar, Cleveland	389	241	3,033	22	**1987**	Al Toon, N.Y. Jets	68	976	5
Boomer Esiason, Cincinnati	388	223	3,572	28	**1988**	Al Toon, N.Y. Jets	93	1,067	5
Boomer Esiason, Cincinnati	455	258	3,525	28	**1989**	Andre Reed, Buffalo	88	1,312	9
Jim Kelly, Buffalo	346	219	2,829	24	**1990**	Haywood Jeffires, Houston	74	1,048	8
						Drew Hill, Houston	74	1,019	5
Jim Kelly, Buffalo	474	304	3,844	33	**1991**	Haywood Jeffires, Houston	100	1,181	7
Warren Moon, Houston	346	224	2,521	18	**1992**	Haywood Jeffires, Houston	90	913	9
John Elway, Denver	551	348	4,030	25	**1993**	Reggie Langhorne, Indianapolis	85	1,038	3

Scoring						Rushing			
Player, team	**TD**	**PAT**	**FG**	**Pts**	**Year**	**Player, team**	**Yds**	**Atts**	**TD**
Gene Mingo, Denver	6	33	18	123	**1960**	Abner Haynes, Dallas	875	156	9
Gino Cappelletti, Boston	8	48	17	147	**1961**	Billy Cannon, Houston	948	200	6
Gene Mingo, Denver	4	32	27	137	**1962**	Cookie Gilchrest, Buffalo	1,096	214	13
Gino Cappelletti, Boston	2	35	22	113	**1963**	Clem Daniels, Oakland	1,099	215	3
Gino Cappelletti, Boston	7	36	25	155	**1964**	Cookie Gilchrest, Buffalo	981	230	6
Gino Cappelletti, Boston	9	27	17	132	**1965**	Paul Lowe, San Diego	1,121	222	7
Gino Cappelletti, Boston	6	35	16	119	**1966**	Jim Nance, Boston	1,458	299	11
George Blanda, Oakland	0	56	20	116	**1967**	Jim Nance, Boston	1,216	269	7
Jim Turner, N.Y. Jets	0	43	34	145	**1968**	Paul Robinson, Cincinnati	1,023	238	8
Jim Turner, N.Y. Jets	0	33	32	129	**1969**	Dick Post, San Diego	873	182	6
Jan Stenerud, Kansas City	0	26	30	116	**1970**	Floyd Little, Denver	901	209	3
Garo Yepremian, Miami	0	33	28	117	**1971**	Floyd Little, Denver	1,133	284	6
Bobby Howfield, N.Y. Jets	0	40	27	121	**1972**	O.J. Simpson, Buffalo	1,251	292	6
Roy Gerela, Pittsburgh	0	36	29	123	**1973**	O.J. Simpson, Buffalo	2,003	332	12
Roy Gerela, Pittsburgh	0	33	20	93	**1974**	Otis Armstrong, Denver	1,407	263	9
O.J. Simpson, Buffalo	23	0	0	138	**1975**	O.J. Simpson, Buffalo	1,817	329	16
Toni Linhart, Baltimore	0	49	20	109	**1976**	O.J. Simpson, Buffalo	1,503	290	8
Errol Mann, Oakland	0	39	20	99	**1977**	Mark van Eeghen, Oakland	1,273	324	7
Pat Leahy, N.Y. Jets	0	41	22	107	**1978**	Earl Campbell, Houston	1,450	302	13
John Smith, New England	0	46	23	115	**1979**	Earl Campbell, Houston	1,697	368	19
John Smith, New England	0	51	26	129	**1980**	Earl Campbell, Houston	1,934	373	13
Jim Breech, Cincinnati	0	49	22	115	**1981**	Earl Campbell, Houston	1,376	361	10
Marcus Allen, L.A. Raiders	14	0	0	84	**1982**	Freeman McNeil, N.Y. Jets	786	151	6
Gary Anderson, Pittsburgh	0	38	27	119	**1983**	Curt Warner, Seattle	1,446	335	13
Gary Anderson, Pittsburgh	0	45	24	117	**1984**	Earnest Jackson, San Diego	1,179	296	8
Gary Anderson, Pittsburgh	0	40	33	139	**1985**	Marcus Allen, L.A. Raiders	1,759	380	11
Tony Franklin, New England	0	44	32	140	**1986**	Curt Warner, Seattle	1,481	319	13
Jim Breech, Cincinnati	0	25	24	97	**1987**	Eric Dickerson, L.A. Rams, Indianapolis	1,288*	283	6
Scott Norwood, Buffalo	0	33	32	129	**1988**	Eric Dickerson, Indianapolis	1,659	388	14
David Treadwell, Denver	0	39	27	120	**1989**	Christian Okoye, Kansas City	1,480	370	12
Nick Lowery, Kansas City	0	37	34	139	**1990**	Thurman Thomas, Buffalo	1,297	271	11
Pete Stoyanovich, Miami	0	28	31	121	**1991**	Thurman Thomas, Buffalo	1,407	288	7
Pete Stoyanovich, Miami	0	34	30	124	**1992**	Barry Foster, Pittsburgh	1,690	390	11
Jeff Jaeger, L.A. Raiders	0	27	35	132	**1993**	Thurman Thomas, Buffalo	1,315	355	6

* 1,011 AFC yards led conference.

National Football Conference Leaders

(National Football League, 1960-69)

Passing / Pass-Receiving

Player, team	Atts	Com	YG	TD	Year	Player, team	Ct	YG	TD
Milt Plum, Cleveland	250	151	2,297	21	**1960**	Raymond Berry, Baltimore	74	1,298	10
Milt Plum, Cleveland	302	177	2,416	18	**1961**	Jim Phillips, L.A. Rams	78	1,092	5
Bart Starr, Green Bay	285	178	2,438	12	**1962**	Bobby Mitchell, Washington	72	1,384	11
Y.A. Tittle, N.Y. Giants	367	221	3,145	36	**1963**	Bobby Joe Conrad, St. Louis	73	967	10
Bart Starr, Green Bay	272	163	2,144	15	**1964**	Johnny Morris, Chicago	93	1,200	10
Rudy Bukich, Chicago	312	176	2,641	20	**1965**	Dave Parks, San Francisco	80	1,344	12
Bart Starr, Green Bay	251	156	2,257	14	**1966**	Charley Taylor, Washington	72	1,119	12
Sonny Jurgensen, Washington	508	288	3,747	31	**1967**	Charley Taylor, Washington	70	990	9
Earl Morrall, Baltimore	317	182	2,909	26	**1968**	Clifton McNeil, San Francisco	71	994	7
Sonny Jurgensen, Washington	442	274	3,102	22	**1969**	Dan Abramowicz, New Orleans	73	1,015	7
John Brodie, San Francisco	378	223	2,941	24	**1970**	Dick Gordon, Chicago	71	1,026	13
Roger Staubach, Dallas	211	126	1,882	15	**1971**	Bob Tucker, Giants	59	791	4
Norm Snead, N.Y. Giants	325	196	2,307	17	**1972**	Harold Jackson, Philadelphia	62	1,048	4
Roger Staubach, Dallas	286	179	2,428	23	**1973**	Harold Carmichael, Philadelphia	67	1,116	9
Sonny Jurgensen, Washington	167	107	1,185	11	**1974**	Charles Young, Philadelphia	63	696	3
Fran Tarkenton, Minnesota	425	273	2,294	25	**1975**	Chuck Foreman, Minnesota	73	691	9
James Harris, Los Angeles	158	91	1,460	8	**1976**	Drew Pearson, Dallas	58	806	6
Roger Staubach, Dallas	361	210	2,620	18	**1977**	Ahmad Rashad, Minnesota	51	681	2
Roger Staubach, Dallas	413	231	3,190	25	**1978**	Rickey Young, Minnesota	88	704	5
Roger Staubach, Dallas	461	267	3,586	27	**1979**	Ahmad Rashad, Minnesota	80	1,156	9
Ron Jaworski, Philadelphia	451	257	3,529	27	**1980**	Earl Cooper, San Francisco	83	567	4
Joe Montana, San Francisco	488	311	3,565	19	**1981**	Dwight Clark, San Francisco	85	1,105	4
Joe Thiesmann, Washington	252	161	2,033	13	**1982**	Dwight Clark, San Francisco	60	913	5
Steve Bartkowski, Atlanta	423	274	3,167	22	**1983**	Roy Green, St. Louis	78	1,227	14
						Charlie Brown, Washington	78	1,225	8
						Earnest Gray, N.Y. Giants	78	1,139	5
Joe Montana, San Francisco	432	279	3,630	28	**1984**	Art Monk, Washington	106	1,372	7
Joe Montana, San Francisco	494	303	3,653	27	**1985**	Roger Craig, San Francisco	92	1,016	6
Tommy Kramer, Minnesota	372	208	3,000	24	**1986**	Jerry Rice, San Francisco	86	1,570	15
Joe Montana, San Francisco	398	266	3,054	31	**1987**	J.T. Smith, St. Louis	91	1,117	8
Wade Wilson, Minnesota	332	204	2,746	15	**1988**	Henry Ellard, L.A. Rams	86	1,414	10
Joe Montana, San Francisco	386	271	3,521	26	**1989**	Sterling Sharpe, Green Bay	90	1,423	12
Phil Simms, N.Y. Giants	311	184	2,284	15	**1990**	Jerry Rice, San Francisco	100	1,502	13
Steve Young, San Francisco	279	180	2,517	17	**1991**	Michael Irvin, Dallas	93	1,523	8
Steve Young, San Francisco	402	268	3,465	25	**1992**	Sterling Sharpe, Green Bay	108	1,461	13
Steve Young, San Francisco	462	314	4,023	29	**1993**	Sterling Sharpe, Green Bay	112	1,274	11

Scoring / Rushing

Player, team	TD	PAT	FG	Pts	Year	Player, team	Yds	Atts	TD
Paul Hornung, Green Bay	15	41	15	176	**1960**	Jim Brown, Cleveland	1,257	215	9
Paul Hornung, Green Bay	10	41	15	146	**1961**	Jim Brown, Cleveland	1,408	305	8
Jim Taylor, Green Bay	19	0	0	114	**1962**	Jim Taylor, Green Bay	1,474	272	19
Don Chandler, N.Y. Giants	0	52	18	106	**1963**	Jim Brown, Cleveland	1,863	291	12
Lenny Moore, Baltimore	20	0	0	120	**1964**	Jim Brown, Cleveland	1,446	280	7
Gale Sayers, Chicago	22	0	0	132	**1965**	Jim Brown, Cleveland	1,544	289	17
Bruce Gossett, L.A. Rams	0	29	28	113	**1966**	Gale Sayers, Chicago	1,231	229	8
Jim Bakken, St. Louis	0	36	27	117	**1967**	Leroy Kelly, Cleveland	1,205	235	11
Leroy Kelly, Cleveland	20	0	0	120	**1968**	Leroy Kelly, Cleveland	1,239	248	16
Fred Cox, Minnesota	0	43	26	121	**1969**	Gale Sayers, Chicago	1,032	236	8
Fred Cox, Minnesota	0	35	30	125	**1970**	Larry Brown, Washington	1,125	237	5
Curt Knight, Washington	0	27	29	114	**1971**	John Brockington, Green Bay	1,105	216	4
Chester Marcol, Green Bay	0	29	33	128	**1972**	Larry Brown, Washington	1,216	285	8
David Ray, Los Angeles	0	40	30	130	**1973**	John Brockington, Green Bay	1,144	265	3
Chester Marcol, Green Bay	0	19	25	94	**1974**	Lawrence McCutcheon, Los Angeles	1,109	236	3
Chuck Foreman, Minnesota	22	0	0	132	**1975**	Jim Otis, St. Louis	1,076	269	5
Mark Moseley, Washington	0	31	22	97	**1976**	Walter Payton, Chicago	1,390	311	13
Walter Payton, Chicago	16	0	0	96	**1977**	Walter Payton, Chicago	1,852	339	14
Frank Corrall, Los Angeles	0	31	29	118	**1978**	Walter Payton, Chicago	1,395	333	11
Mark Moseley, Washington	0	39	25	114	**1979**	Walter Payton, Chicago	1,610	369	14
Ed Murray, Detroit	0	35	27	116	**1980**	Walter Payton, Chicago	1,460	317	15
Ed Murray, Detroit	0	46	25	121	**1981**	George Rogers, New Orleans	1,674	378	13
Wendell Tyler, L.A. Rams	13	0	0	78	**1982**	Tony Dorsett, Dallas	745	177	5
Mark Moseley, Washington	0	62	33	161	**1983**	Eric Dickerson, L.A. Rams	1,808	390	18
Ray Wersching, San Francisco	0	56	25	131	**1984**	Eric Dickerson, L.A. Rams	2,105	379	14
Kevin Butler, Chicago	0	51	31	144	**1985**	Gerald Riggs, Atlanta	1,719	397	10
Kevin Butler, Chicago	0	36	28	120	**1986**	Eric Dickerson, L.A. Rams	1,821	404	11
Jerry Rice, San Francisco	23	0	0	138	**1987**	Charles White, L.A. Rams	1,374	324	11
Mike Cofer, San Francisco	0	40	27	121	**1988**	Herschel Walker, Dallas	1,514	361	5
Mike Cofer, San Francisco	0	49	29	136	**1989**	Barry Sanders, Detroit	1,470	280	14
Chip Lohmiller, Washington	0	41	30	131	**1990**	Barry Sanders, Detroit	1,304	255	13
Chip Lohmiller, Washington	0	56	31	149	**1991**	Emmitt Smith, Dallas	1,563	365	12
Morten Andersen, New Orleans	0	33	29	120	**1992**	Emmitt Smith, Dallas	1,713	373	18
Chip Lohmiller, Washington	0	30	30	120					
Jason Hanson, Detroit	0	28	34	130	**1993**	Emmitt Smith, Dallas	1,486	283	9

1993 NFL Individual Leaders

American Football Conference

Passing

	Att	Comp	Pct comp	Yds	Avg gain	TD	Pct TD	Int	Rating points
Elway, John, Denver	551	348	63.2	4,030	7.31	25	4.5	10	92.8
Montana, Joe, Kansas City	298	181	60.7	2,144	7.19	13	4.4	7	87.4
Testaverde, Vinny, Cleveland	230	130	56.5	1,797	7.81	14	6.1	9	85.7
Esiason, Boomer, N.Y. Jets	473	288	60.9	3,421	7.23	16	3.4	11	84.5
Mitchell, Scott, Miami	233	133	57.1	1,773	7.61	12	5.2	8	84.2
Hostetler, Jeff, L.A. Raiders	419	236	56.3	3,242	7.74	14	3.3	10	82.5
Kelly, Jim, Buffalo	470	288	61.3	3,382	7.20	18	3.8	18	79.9
O'Donnell, Neil, Pittsburgh	486	270	55.6	3,208	6.60	14	2.9	7	79.5
George, Jeff, Indianapolis	407	234	57.5	2,526	6.21	8	2.0	6	76.3
DeBerg, Steve, T.B.-Miami	227	136	59.9	1,707	7.52	7	3.1	10	75.3
Moon, Warren, Houston	520	303	58.3	3,485	6.70	21	4.0	21	75.2
Friesz, John, San Diego	238	128	53.8	1,402	5.89	6	2.5	4	72.8

Rushing

	Att	Yds	Avg	Long	TD
Thomas, Thurman, Buffalo	355	1,315	3.7	27	6
Russell, Leonard, New England	300	1,088	3.6	21	7
Warren, Chris, Seattle	273	1,072	3.9	45td	7
Brown, Gary, Houston	195	1,002	5.1	26	6
Johnson, Johnny, N.Y. Jets	198	821	4.1	57td	3
Bernstine, Rod, Denver	223	816	3.7	24	4
Allen, Marcus, Kansas City	206	764	3.7	39	12
Thompson, Leroy, Pittsburgh	205	763	3.7	36	3
Butts, Marion, San Diego	185	746	4.0	27	4
Foster, Barry, Pittsburgh	177	711	4.0	38	8

Pass Receiving

	No	Yds	Avg	Long	TD
Langhorn, Reggie, Indianapolis	85	1,038	12.2	72td	3
Miller, Anthony, San Diego	84	1,162	13.8	66td	7
Sharpe, Shannon, Denver	81	995	12.3	63	9
Brown, Tim, L.A. Raiders	80	1,180	14.8	71td	7
Blades, Brian, Seattle	80	945	11.8	41	3
Slaughter, Webster, Houston	77	904	11.7	41	5
Kirby, Terry, Miami	75	874	11.7	47	3
Harmon, Ronnie, San Diego	73	671	9.2	37	2
Givins, Ernest, Houston	68	887	13.0	80td	4
Metzelaars, Pete, Buffalo	68	609	9.0	51	4

Scoring-Touchdowns

	TD	Rush	Pass	Pts
Allen, Marcus, Kansas City	15	12	3	90
Foster, Barry, Pittsburgh	9	8	1	54
Sharpe, Shannon, Denver	9	0	9	54
Brown, Gary, Houston	8	6	2	48
Brown, Tim, L.A. Raiders	7	0	7	48[1]
Coates, Ben, New England	8	0	8	48
Delpino, Robert, Denver	8	8	0	48
Jackson, Michael, Cleveland	8	0	8	48
Means, Natrone, San Diego	8	8	0	48

(1) Includes 1 punt return for a touchdown.

Scoring-Kicking

	PAT	FG	Pts
Jaeger, Jeff, L.A. Raiders	27/29	35/44	132
Del Greco, Al, Houston	39/40	29/34	126
Carney, John, San Diego	31/33	31/40	124
Elam, Jason, Denver	41/42	26/35	119
Anderson, Gary, Pittsburgh	32/32	28/30	116

Interceptions

	No	Yds	Avg	Long	TD
Robinson, Eugene, Seattle	9	80	8.9	28	0
Odomes, Nate, Buffalo	9	65	7.2	25	0
Woodson, Rod, Pittsburgh	8	138	17.3	63td	1
Robertson, Marcus, Houston	7	137	19.6	69	0
Carrington, Darren, San Diego	7	104	14.9	28	0

Kickoff Returns

	No	Yds	Avg	Long	TD
Ismail, Raghib, L.A. Raiders	25	605	24.2	66	0
McDuffie, O. J., Miami	32	755	23.6	48	0
Ball, Eric, Cincinnati	23	501	21.8	45	0
Verdin, Clarence, Indianapolis	50	1,050	21.0	38	0
Crittenden, Ray, New England	23	478	20.8	44	0

Punt Returns

	No	FC	Yds	Avg	Long	TD
Metcalf, Eric, Cleveland	36	11	464	12.9	91td	2
Gordon, Darrien, San Diego	31	15	395	12.7	54	0
Brown, Tim, L.A. Raiders	40	20	465	11.6	74td	1
McDuffie, O. J., Miami	28	22	317	11.3	72td	2
Milburn, Glyn, Denver	40	11	425	10.6	54	0

Punting

	No	Yds	Long	Avg
Montgomery, Greg, Houston	54	2,462	77	45.6
Rouen, Tom, Denver	67	3,017	62	45.0
Tuten, Rick, Seattle	90	4,007	64	44.5
Hansen, Brian, Cleveland	82	3,632	72	44.3
Johnson, Lee, Cincinnati	90	3,954	60	43.9

Sacks

	No
Smith, Neil, Kansas City	15.0
Smith, Bruce, Buffalo	14.0
Fletcher, Simon, Denver	13.5
Jones, Sean, Houston	13.0
Greene, Kevin, Pittsburgh	12.5
Smith, Anthony, L.A. Raiders	12.5

National Football Conference

Passing

	Att	Comp	Pct comp	Yds	Avg gain	TD	Pct TD	Int	Rating points
Young, Steve, San Francisco	462	314	68.0	4,023	8.71	29	6.3	16	101.5
Aikman, Troy, Dallas	392	271	69.1	3,100	7.91	15	3.8	6	99.0
Simms, Phil, N.Y. Giants	400	247	61.8	3,038	7.60	15	3.8	9	88.3
Brister, Bubby, Philadelphia	309	181	58.6	1,905	6.17	14	4.5	5	84.9
Hebert, Bobby, Atlanta	430	263	61.2	2,978	6.93	24	5.6	17	84.0
Beuerlein, Steve, Phoenix	418	258	61.7	3,164	7.57	18	4.3	17	82.5
McMahon, Jim, Minnesota	331	200	60.4	1,968	5.95	9	2.7	8	76.2
Favre, Brett, Green Bay	522	318	60.9	3,303	6.33	19	3.6	24	72.2
Harbaugh, Jim, Chicago	325	200	61.5	2,002	6.16	7	2.2	11	72.1
Wilson, Wade, New Orleans	388	221	57.0	2,457	6.33	12	3.1	15	70.1
Peete, Rodney, Detroit	252	157	62.3	1,670	6.63	6	2.4	14	66.4
Erickson, Craig, Tampa Bay	457	233	51.0	3,054	6.68	18	3.9	21	66.4

Rushing

	Att	Yds	Avg	Long	TD
Smith, Emmitt, Dallas	283	1,486	5.3	62td	9
Bettis, Jerome, L.A. Rams	294	1,429	4.9	71td	7
Pegram, Erric, Atlanta	292	1,185	4.1	29	3
Sanders, Barry, Detroit	243	1,115	4.6	42	3
Hampton, Rodney, N.Y. Giants	292	1,077	3.7	20	5
Brooks, Reggie, Washington	223	1,063	4.8	85td	3
Moore, Ron, Phoenix	263	1,018	3.9	20	9
Watters, Ricky, San Francisco	208	950	4.6	39	10
Walker, Herschel, Philadelphia	174	746	4.3	35	1
Brown, Derek, New Orleans	180	705	3.9	60	2

Receiving

	No	Yds	Avg	Long	TD
Sharpe, Sterling, Green Bay	112	1,274	11.4	54	11
Rice, Jerry, San Francisco	98	1,503	15.3	80td	15
Irvin, Michael, Dallas	88	1,330	15.1	61td	7
Rison, Andre, Atlanta	86	1,242	14.4	53td	15
Carter, Cris, Minnesota	86	1,071	12.5	58	9
Walker, Herschel, Philadelphia	75	610	8.1	55	3
Prichard, Mike, Atlanta	74	736	9.9	34	7
Haynes, Michael, Atlanta	72	778	10.8	98td	4
Jones, Brent, San Francisco	68	735	10.8	29	3
Martin, Eric, New Orleans	66	950	14.4	54td	3

Scoring-Touchdowns

	TD	Rush	Pass	Pts
Rice, Jerry, San Francisco	16	1	15	96
Rison, Andre, Atlanta	15	0	15	90
Sharpe, Sterling, Green Bay	11	0	11	66
Watters, Ricky, San Francisco	11	10	1	66
Bennett, Edgar, Green Bay	10	9	1	60
Smith, Emmitt, Dallas	10	9	1	60
Williams, Calvin, Philadelphia	10	0	10	60

Scoring-Kicking

	PAT	FG	Pts
Hanson, Jason, Detroit	28/28	34/43	130
Jacke, Chris, Green Bay	35/35	31/37	128
Murray, Eddie, Dallas	38/38	28/33	122
Andersen, Morten, New Orleans	33/33	28/35	117
Johnson, Norm, Atlanta	34/34	26/27	112

Interceptions

	No	Yds	Avg	Long	TD
Sanders, Deion, Atlanta	7	91	13.0	41	0
Allen, Eric, Philadelphia	6	201	33.5	94td	4
Butler, LeRoy, Green Bay	6	131	21.8	39	0
Smith, Kevin, Dallas	6	56	9.3	32td	1
Carter, Tom, Washington	6	54	9.0	29	0

Kickoff Returns

	No	Yds	Avg	Long	TD
Brooks, Robert, Green Bay	23	611	26.6	95td	1
Hughes, Tyrone, New Orleans	30	753	25.1	99td	1
Smith, Tony, Atlanta	38	948	24.9	97td	1
Gray, Mel, Detroit	28	688	24.6	95td	1
Bailey, Johnny, Phoenix	31	699	22.5	48	0

Punt Returns

	No	FC	Yds	Avg	Long	TD
Hughes, Tyrone, New Orleans	37	21	503	13.6	83td	2
Carter, Dexter, San Francisco	34	20	411	12.1	72td	1
Williams, Kevin, Dallas	36	14	381	10.6	64td	2
Meggett, David, N.Y. Giants	32	20	331	10.3	75td	1
Gray, Mel, Detroit	23	14	197	8.6	35	0

Punting

	No	Yds	Long	Avg
Arnold, Jim, Detroit	72	3,207	68	44.5
Roby, Reggie, Washington	78	3,447	60	44.2
Camarillo, Rich, Phoenix	73	3,189	61	43.7
Barnhardt, Tommy, New Orleans	77	3,356	58	43.6
Alexander, Harold, Atlanta	72	3,114	75	43.3

Sacks

	No
Turnbull, Renaldo, New Orleans	13.0
White, Reggie, Green Bay	13.0
Dent, Richard, Chicago	12.5
Doleman, Chris, Minnesota	12.5
Randle, John, Minnesota	12.5

MVP, Defensive Player of the Year, Rookie of the Year

The Jim Thorpe Trophy goes to the most valuable player as chosen by the NFL Players Association. The George Halas Trophy is awarded annually to the outstanding defensive player in the NFL as chosen by a panel of sports experts. Rookie of the Year is one of many awards given out annually by *The Sporting News*.

MVP

1955 Harlon Hill, Chicago
1956 Frank Gifford, N.Y. Giants
1957 John Unitas, Baltimore
1958 Jim Brown, Cleveland
1959 Charley Conerly, N.Y. Giants
1960 Norm Van Brocklin, Philadelphia
1961 Y.A. Tittle, N.Y. Giants
1962 Jim Taylor, Green Bay
1963 Jim Brown, Cleveland; Y.A. Tittle, N.Y. Giants
1964 Lenny Moore, Baltimore
1965 Jim Brown, Cleveland
1966 Bart Starr, Green Bay
1967 John Unitas, Baltimore
1968 Earl Morrall, Baltimore
1969 Roman Gabriel, L.A. Rams
1970 John Brodie, San Francisco
1971 Bob Griese, Miami
1972 Larry Brown, Washington
1973 O.J. Simpson, Buffalo
1974 Ken Stabler, Oakland
1975 Fran Tarkenton, Minnesota
1976 Bert Jones, Baltimore
1977 Walter Payton, Chicago
1978 Earl Campbell, Houston
1979 Earl Campbell, Houston
1980 Earl Campbell, Houston
1981 Ken Anderson, Cincinnati
1982 Dan Fouts, San Diego
1983 Joe Theismann, Washington
1984 Dan Marino, Miami
1985 Walter Payton, Chicago
1986 Phil Simms, N.Y. Giants
1987 Jerry Rice, San Francisco
1988 Roger Craig, San Francisco
1989 Joe Montana, San Francisco
1990 Warren Moon, Houston
1991 Thurman Thomas, Buffalo
1992 Steve Young, San Francisco
1993 Emmitt Smith, Dallas

Defensive Player

1966 Larry Wilson, St. Louis
1967 Deacon Jones, Los Angeles
1968 Deacon Jones, Los Angeles
1969 Dick Butkus, Chicago
1970 Dick Butkus, Chicago
1971 Carl Eller, Minnesota
1972 Joe Greene, Pittsburgh
1973 Alan Page, Minnesota
1974 Joe Greene, Pittsburgh
1975 Curley Culp, Houston
1976 Jerry Sherk, Cleveland
1977 Harvey Martin, Dallas
1978 Randy Gradishar, Denver
1979 Lee Roy Selmon, Tampa Bay
1980 Lester Hayes, Oakland
1981 Joe Klecko, N.Y. Jets
1982 Mark Gastineau, N.Y. Jets
1983 Jack Lambert, Pittsburgh
1984 Mike Haynes, L.A. Raiders
1985 Howie Long, L.A. Raiders
Andre Tippett, New England
1986 Lawrence Taylor, N.Y. Giants
1987 Reggie White, Philadelphia
1988 Mike Singletary, Chicago
1989 Tim Harris, Green Bay
1990 Bruce Smith, Buffalo
1991 Pat Swilling, New Orleans
1992 Junior Seau, San Diego
1993 Bruce Smith, Buffalo

Rookie of the Year

1964 Charley Taylor, Washington
1965 Gale Sayers, Chicago
1966 Tommy Nobis, Atlanta
1967 Mel Farr, Detroit
1968 Earl McCullouch, Detroit
1969 Calvin Hill, Dallas
1970 NFC: Bruce Taylor, San Francsico
AFC: Dennis Shaw, Buffalo
1971 NFC: John Brockington, Green Bay
AFC: Jim Plunkett, New England
1972 NFC: Chester Marcol, Green Bay
AFC: Franco Harris, Pittsburgh
1973 NFC: Chuck Foreman, Minnesota
AFC: Boobie Clark, Cincinnati
1974 NFC: Wilbur Jackson, San Francisco
AFC: Don Woods, San Diego
1975 NFC: Steve Bartkowski, Atlanta
AFC: Robert Brazile, Houston
1976 NFC: Sammy White, Minnesota
AFC: Mike Haynes, New England
1977 NFC: Tony Dorsett, Dallas
AFC: A. J. Duhe, Miami
1978 NFC: Al Baker, Detroit
AFC: Earl Campbell, Houston
1979 NFC: Ottis Anderson, St. Louis
AFC: Jerry Butler, Buffalo
1980 Billy Sims, Detroit
1981 George Rogers, New Orleans
1982 Marcus Allen, L.A. Raiders
1983 Dan Marino, Miami
1984 Louis Lipps, Pittsburgh
1985 Eddie Brown, Cincinnati
1986 Rueben Mayes, New Orleans
1987 Robert Awalt, St. Louis
1988 Keith Jackson, Philadelphia
1989 Barry Sanders, Detroit
1990 Richmond Webb, Miami
1991 Mike Croel, Denver
1992 Santana Dotson, Tampa Bay
1993 Jerome Bettis, L.A. Rams

Number One NFL Draft Choices, 1936-1994

Year	Team	Player, Pos., College
1936	Philadelphia	Jay Berwanger, HB, Chicago
1937	Philadelphia	Sam Francis, FB, Nebraska
1938	Cleve.Rams	Corbett Davis, FB, Indiana
1939	Chi. Cards	Ki Aldrich, C, TCU
1940	Chi. Cards	George Cafego, HB, Tennessee
1941	Chi. Bears	Tom Harmon, HB, Michigan
1942	Pittsburgh	Bill Dudley, HB, Virginia
1943	Detroit	Frank Sinkwich, HB, Georgia
1944	Boston Yanks	Angelo Bertelli, QB, Notre Dame
1945	Chi. Cards	Charley Trippi, HB, Georgia
1946	Boston Yanks	Frank Dancewicz, QB, Notre Dame
1947	Chi. Bears	Bob Fenimore, HB, Okla. A&M
1948	Washington	Harry Gilmer, QB, Alabama
1949	Philadelphia	Chuck Bednarik, C, Penn
1950	Detroit	Leon Hart, E, Notre Dame
1951	N.Y. Giants	Kyle Rote, HB, SMU
1952	L.A. Rams	Bill Wade, QB, Vanderbilt
1953	San Francisco	Harry Babcock, E, Georgia
1954	Cleveland	Bobby Garrett, QB, Stanford
1955	Baltimore	George Shaw, QB, Oregon
1956	Pittsburgh	Gary Glick, DB, Col. A&M
1957	Green Bay	Paul Hornung, QB, Notre Dame
1958	Chi. Cards	King Hill, QB, Rice
1959	Green Bay	Randy Duncan, QB, Iowa
1960	L.A. Rams	Billy Cannon, HB, LSU
1961	Minnesota	Tommy Mason, HB, Tulane
1962	Washington	Ernie Davis, HB, Syracuse
1963	L.A. Rams	Terry Baker, QB, Oregon St.
1964	San Francisco	Dave Parks, E, Texas Tech
1965	N.Y. Giants	Tucker Frederickson, HB, Auburn
1966	Atlanta	Tommy Nobis, LB, Texas
1967	Baltimore	Bubba Smith, DT, Michigan St.
1968	Minnesota	Ron Yary, T, USC
1969	Buffalo	O.J. Simpson, RB, USC
1970	Pittsburgh	Terry Bradshaw, QB, La.Tech
1971	New England	Jim Plunkett, QB, Stanford
1972	Buffalo	Walt Patulski, DE, Notre Dame
1973	Houston	John Matuszak, DE, Tampa
1974	Dallas	Ed "Too Tall" Jones, Tenn.St.
1975	Atlanta	Steve Bartkowski, QB, Cal.
1976	Tampa Bay	Lee Roy Selmon, DE, Oklahoma
1977	Tampa Bay	Ricky Bell, RB, USC
1978	Houston	Earl Campbell, RB, Texas
1979	Buffalo	Tom Cousineau, LB, Ohio St.
1980	Detroit	Billy Sims, RB, Oklahoma
1981	New Orleans	George Rogers, RB, S.Carolina
1982	New England	Kenneth Sims, DT, Texas
1983	Baltimore	John Elway, QB, Stanford
1984	New England	Irving Fryar, WR, Nebraska
1985	Buffalo	Bruce Smith, DE, Va.Tech
1986	Tampa Bay	Bo Jackson, RB, Auburn
1987	Tampa Bay	Vinny Testaverde, QB, Miami (FL)
1988	Atlanta	Aundray Bruce, LB, Auburn
1989	Dallas	Troy Aikman, QB, UCLA
1990	Indianapolis	Jeff George, QB, Illinois
1991	Dallas	Russell Maryland, DL, Miami (FL)
1992	Indianapolis	Steve Emtman, DL, Washington
1993	New England	Drew Bledsoe, QB, Washington St.
1994	Cincinnati	Dan Wilkinson, DT, Ohio St.

First-Round Selections in the 1994 NFL Draft

Team	Player	Pos	College
1—Cincinnati	Dan Wilkinson	DT	Ohio State
2—Indianapolis	Marshall Faulk	RB	San Diego State
3—Washington	Heath Shuler	QB	Tennessee
4—New Enlgand	Willie McGinest	DE	Southern Cal
5—Indianapolis	Trev Alberts	LB	Nebraska
6—Tampa Bay	Trent Dilfer	QB	Fresno State
7—San Francisco	Bryant Young	DT	Notre Dame
8—Seattle	Sam Adams	DE	Texas A&M
9—Cleveland	Antonio Langham	DB	Alabama
10—Arizona	Jamir Miller	LB	UCLA
11—Chicago	John Thierry	LB	Alcorn State
12—N.Y. Jets	Aaron Glenn	DB	Texas A&M
13—New Orleans	Joe Johnson	DE	Louisville
14—Philadelphia	Bernard Williams	T	Georgia
15—L.A. Rams	Wayne Gandy	T	Auburn
16—Green Bay	Aaron Taylor	T	Notre Dame
17—Pittsburgh	Charles Johnson	WR	Colorado
18—Minnesota	Dewayne Washington	CB	North Carolina State
19—Minnesota	Todd Steussie	T	California
20—Miami	Tim Bowens	DT	Mississippi
21—Detroit	Johnnie Morton	WR	Southern Cal
22—L.A. Raiders	Rob Fredrickson	LB	Michigan State
23—Dallas	Shante Carver	DE	Arizona State
24—N.Y. Giants	Thomas Lewis	WR	Indiana
25—Kansas City	Greg Hill	RB	Texas A&M
26—Houston	Henry Ford	DE	Arkansas
27—Buffalo	Jeff Burris	DB	Notre Dame
28—San Francisco	William Floyd	RB	Florida State
29—Cleveland	Derrick Alexander	WR	Michigan

Pro Football Hall of Fame, Canton, Ohio

Herb Adderley
Lance Alworth
Doug Atkins
Morris "Red" Badgro
Lem Barney
Cliff Battles
Sammy Baugh
Chuck Bednarik
Bert Bell
Bobby Bell
Raymond Berry
Charles Bidwell
Fred Biletnikoff
George Blanda
Mel Blount
Terry Bradshaw
Jim Brown
Paul Brown
Roosevelt Brown
Willie Brown
Buck Buchanan
Dick Butkus
Earl Campbell
Tony Canadeo
Joe Carr
Guy Chamberlin
Jack Christiansen
Dutch Clark
George Connor
Jim Conzelman
Larry Csonka
Al Davis
Willie Davis
Len Dawson
Mike Ditka
Art Donovan
Tony Dorsett
Paddy Driscoll
Bill Dudley
Turk Edwards
Weeb Ewbank
Tom Fears
Ray Flaherty
Len Ford
Dr. Daniel Fortmann
Dan Fouts
Frank Gatski
Bill George
Frank Gifford
Sid Gillman
Otto Graham
Red Grange
Joe Greene
Forrest Gregg
Bob Griese
Lou Groza
Joe Guyon
George Halas
Jack Ham
John Hannah
Franco Harris
Ed Healey
Mel Hein
Ted Hendricks
Pete Henry
Arnold Herber
Bill Hewitt
Clarke Hinkle
Elroy "Crazy Legs" Hirsch
Paul Hornung
Ken Houston
Cal Hubbard
Sam Huff
Lamar Hunt
Don Hutson
Jimmy Johnson[1]
John Henry Johnson
Deacon Jones
Stan Jones
Sonny Jurgensen
Leroy Kelly
Walt Kiesling
Frank "Bruiser" Kinard
Curly Lambeau
Jack Lambert
Tom Landry
Dick "Night Train" Lane
Jim Langer
Willie Lanier
Yale Lary
Dante Lavelli
Bobby Layne
Tuffy Leemans
Bob Lilly
Larry Little
Vince Lombardi
Sid Luckman
Link Lyman
John Mackey
Tim Mara
Gino Marchetti
George Marshall
Ollie Matson
Don Maynard
George McAfee
Mike McCormack
Hugh McElhenny
John "Blood" McNally
Mike Michalske
Wayne Millner
Bobby Mitchell
Ron Mix
Lenny Moore
Marion Motley
George Musso
Bronko Nagurski
Joe Namath
Greasy Neale
Ernie Nevers
Ray Nitschke
Chuck Noll
Leo Nomellini
Merlin Olsen
Jim Otto
Steve Owen
Alan Page
Clarence "Ace" Parker
Jim Parker
Walter Payton
Joe Perry
Pete Pihos
Hugh "Shorty" Ray
Dan Reeves
John Riggins
Jim Ringo
Andy Robustelli
Art Rooney
Pete Rozelle
Bob St. Clair
Gale Sayers
Joe Schmidt
Tex Schramm
Art Shell
O.J. Simpson
Jackie Smith
Bart Starr
Roger Staubach
Ernie Stautner
Jan Stenerud
Ken Strong
Joe Stydahar
Fran Tarkenton
Charlie Taylor
Jim Taylor
Jim Thorpe
Y.A. Tittle
George Trafton
Charlie Trippi
Emlen Tunnell
Clyde "Bulldog" Turner
Johnny Unitas
Gene Upshaw
Norm Van Brocklin
Steve Van Buren
Doak Walker
Bill Walsh
Paul Warfield
Bob Waterfield
Arnie Weinmeister
Randy White
Bill Willis
Larry Wilson
Alex Wojciechowicz
Willie Wood

(1) Johnson is a former 49ers cornerback, not the former Cowboys coach.

All-Time NFL Coaching Victories

(at start of 1994 season; *active through 1993)

Coach	Years	Teams	Regular Season W	L	T	Pct	Career W	L	T	Pct
Don Shula*	31	Colts, Dolphins	309	143	6	.684	327	158	6	.672
George Halas	40	Bears	318	148	31	.671	324	151	31	.671
Tom Landry	29	Cowboys	250	162	6	.605	270	178	6	.601
Curly Lambeau	33	Packers, Cardinals, Redskins	226	132	22	.624	229	134	22	.623
Chuck Noll	23	Steelers	193	148	1	.566	209	156	1	.572
Chuck Knox*	21	Rams, Bills, Seahawks	182	135	1	.574	189	146	1	.564
Paul Brown	21	Browns, Bengals	166	100	6	.621	170	109	6	.607
Bud Grant	18	Vikings	158	96	5	.620	168	109	5	.605
Steve Owen	23	Giants	151	100	17	.595	154	108	17	.582
Joe Gibbs*	12	Redskins	124	60	0	.674	140	65	0	.683
Hank Stram	17	Chiefs, Saints	131	97	10	.571	136	100	10	.573
Weeb Ewbank	20	Colts, Jets	130	129	7	.502	134	130	7	.507
Dan Reeves*	13	Broncos, Giants	121	78	1	.608	129	85	1	.602
Sid Gillman	18	Rams, Chargers, Oilers	122	99	7	.550	123	104	7	.541
George Allen	12	Rams, Redskins	116	47	5	.705	120	54	5	.684
Marv Levy*	13	Chiefs, Bills	110	81	0	.576	120	87	0	.580
Don Coryell	14	Cardinals, Chargers	111	83	1	.572	114	89	1	.561
John Madden	10	Raiders	103	32	7	.750	112	39	7	.731
Mike Ditka	11	Bears	106	62	0	.631	112	68	0	.622
Buddy Parker	15	Cardinals, Lions, Steelers	104	75	9	.577	107	77	9	.578

All-Time Professional Football Records

NFL and AFL

(at start of 1994 season; *active through 1993)

Leading Lifetime Rushers

Player	League	Yrs	Att	Yards	Avg
Walter Payton	NFL	13	3,838	16,726	4.4
Eric Dickerson*	NFL	11	2,996	13,259	4.4
Tony Dorsett	NFL	12	2,936	12,739	4.3
Jim Brown	NFL	9	2,359	12,312	5.2
Franco Harris	NFL	13	2,949	12,120	4.1
John Riggins	NFL	14	2,916	11,352	3.9
O.J. Simpson	AFL-NFL	11	2,404	11,236	4.7
Ottis Anderson	NFL	14	2,562	10,273	4.0
Earl Campbell	NFL	8	2,187	9,407	4.3
Marcus Allen*	NFL	12	2,296	9,309	4.1
Jim Taylor	NFL	10	1,941	8,597	4.4
Joe Perry	NFL	14	1,737	8,378	4.8
Gerald Riggs	NFL	10	1,989	8,188	4.1
Larry Csonka	AFL-NFL	11	1,891	8,081	4.3
Freeman McNeil	NFL	12	1,798	8,074	4.5
Roger Craig*	NFL	11	1,991	8,189	4.1
James Brooks	NFL	12	1,685	7,962	4.7
Thurman Thomas*	NFL	6	1,731	7,631	4.4
Herschel Walker*	NFL	8	1,794	7,468	4.2
Mike Pruitt	NFL	11	1,844	7,378	4.0

Most Yards Gained, Season — 2,105, Eric Dickerson, Los Angeles Rams, 1984.
Most Yards Gained, Game — 275, Walter Payton, Chicago Bears vs. Minnesota Vikings, Nov. 20, 1977.
Most Touchdowns Rushing, Career — 110, Walter Payton, Chicago Bears, 1975-1987.
Most Touchdowns Rushing, Season — 24, John Riggins, Washington Redskins, 1983.
Most Touchdowns Rushing, Game — 6, Ernie Nevers, Chicago Cardinals vs. Chicago Bears, Nov. 8, 1929.
Most Rushing Attempts, Game — 45, Jamie Morris, Washington Redskins vs. Cincinnati Bengals, Dec. 17, 1988 (overtime game).
Longest Run From Scrimmage — 99 yds., Tony Dorsett, Dallas vs. Minnesota, Jan. 3, 1983 (scored touchdown).

Leading Lifetime Passers

(Minimum 1,500 attempts)

Player	League	Yrs	Att	Comp	Yds	Pts†
Joe Montana*	NFL	14	4,898	3,110	37,268	93.1
Steve Young*	NFL	9	1,968	1,222	15,900	93.0
Dan Marino*	NFL	11	5,434	3,219	40,720	88.1
Jim Kelly*	NFL	8	3,494	2,112	26,413	86.0
Roger Staubach	NFL	11	2,958	1,685	22,700	83.4
Neil Lomax	NFL	8	3,153	1,817	22,771	82.7
Sonny Jurgensen	NFL	18	4,262	2,433	32,224	82.6
Len Dawson	NFL-AFL	19	3,741	2,136	28,711	82.6
Boomer Esiason*	NFL	10	3,851	2,185	29,092	82.1
Dave Krieg*	NFL	14	4,178	2,431	30,485	82.0
Ken Anderson	NFL	16	4,475	2,654	32,838	81.9
Bernie Kosar*	NFL	9	3,213	1,889	22,314	81.9
Danny White	NFL	13	2,950	1,761	21,959	81.7
Troy Aikman*	NFL	5	1,920	1,191	13,627	81.0
Bart Starr	NFL	16	3,149	1,808	24,718	80.5
Fran Tarkenton	NFL	18	6,467	3,686	47,003	80.4
Ken O'Brien*	NFL	11	3,602	2,110	25,094	80.4
Warren Moon*	NFL	10	4,546	2,632	33,685	80.4
Randall Cunningham*	NFL	9	2,751	1,540	19,043	80.3

†Rating points based on performances in the following categories: Percentage of completions, percentage of touchdown passes, percentage of interceptions, and average gain per pass attempt.

Most Yards Gained, Season — 5,084, Dan Marino, Miami Dolphins, 1984.
Most Yards Gained, Game — 554, Norm Van Brocklin, Los Angeles Rams vs. New York Yankees, Sept. 18, 1951 (27 completions in 41 attempts).
Most Touchdowns Passing, Career — 342, Fran Tarkenton, Minnesota Vikings, 1961-66; N.Y. Giants, 1967-71; Vikings, 1972-78.
Most Touchdowns Passing, Season — 48, Dan Marino, Miami Dolphins, 1984.
Most Touchdowns Passing, Game — 7, Sid Luckman, Chicago Bears vs. New York Giants, Nov. 14, 1943; Adrian Burk, Philadelphia Eagles vs. Washington Redskins, Oct. 17, 1954; George Blanda, Houston Oilers vs. New York Titans, Nov. 19, 1961; Y.A. Tittle, New York Giants vs. Washington Redskins, Oct. 28, 1962; Joe Kapp, Minnesota Vikings vs. Baltimore Colts, Sept. 28, 1969.
Most Passes Completed, Season — 404, Warren Moon, Houston Oilers, 1991.
Most Passes Completed, Game — 42, Richard Todd, N.Y. Jets vs. San Francisco 49ers, Sept. 21, 1980.

Leading Lifetime Receivers

Player	League	Yrs	No	Yds	Avg
Art Monk*	NFL	14	888	12,026	13.5
Steve Largent	NFL	14	819	13,089	16.0
James Lofton*	NFL	16	764	14,004	18.3
Charlie Joiner	AFL-NFL	18	750	12,146	16.2
Jerry Rice*	NFL	9	708	11,776	16.6
Ozzie Newsome	NFL	13	662	7,980	12.1
Charley Taylor	NFL	13	649	9,110	14.0
Drew Hill*	NFL	14	634	9,831	15.5
Don Maynard	AFL-NFL	15	633	11,834	18.7
Raymond Berry	NFL	13	631	9,275	14.7
Gary Clark*	NFL	9	612	9,560	15.6
Henry Ellard*	NFL	11	593	9,761	16.5
Harold Carmichael	NFL	14	590	8,985	15.2
Fred Biletnikoff	AFL-NFL	14	589	8,974	15.2
Andre Reed*	NFL	9	586	8,233	14.0
Mark Clayton*	NFL	11	582	8,974	15.4
Harold Jackson	NFL	16	579	10,372	17.9
Lionel Taylor	AFL-NFL	10	567	7,195	12.7
Roger Craig*	NFL	11	566	4,911	8.7
Wes Chandler	NFL	11	559	8,966	16.0
Roy Green	NFL	14	559	8,965	16.0

Most Yards Gained, Season — 1,746, Charley Hennigan, Houston Oilers, 1961.
Most Yards Gained, Game — 336, Flipper Anderson, L.A. Rams vs. New Orleans, Nov. 26, 1989.
Most Pass Receptions, Season — 112, Sterling Sharpe, Green Bay Packers, 1993.
Most Pass Receptions, Game — 18, Tom Fears, Los Angeles Rams vs. Green Bay Packers, Dec. 3, 1950 (189 yards).
Most Touchdown Passes, Season — 22, Jerry Rice, San Francisco 49ers, 1987.
Most Touchdown Passes, Game — 5, Bob Shaw, Chicago Cardinals vs. Baltimore Colts, Oct. 2, 1950; Kellen Winslow, San Diego vs. Oakland, Nov. 22, 1981; Jerry Rice, San Francisco vs. Atlanta, Oct. 14, 1990.

Leading Lifetime Scorers

Player	League	Yrs	TD	PAT	FG	Total
George Blanda	AFL-NFL	26	9	943	335	2,002
Jan Stenerud	AFL-NFL	19	0	580	373	1,699
Nick Lowery*	NFL	15	0	486	329	1,473
Pat Leahy	NFL	18	0	558	304	1,470
Jim Turner	AFL-NFL	16	1	521	304	1,439
Mark Moseley	NFL	16	0	482	300	1,382
Jim Bakken	NFL	17	0	534	282	1,380
Fred Cox	NFL	15	0	519	282	1,365
Lou Groza	NFL	17	1	641	234	1,349
Eddie Murray*	NFL	13	0	432	277	1,263
Jim Breech*	NFL	14	0	517	243	1,246
Gary Anderson*	NFL	12	0	384	285	1,239
Chris Bahr	NFL	14	0	490	241	1,213
Matt Bahr*	NFL	15	0	459	250	1,209
Morten Anderson*	NFL	12	0	380	274	1,202
Gino Cappelletti	AFL	11	42	350	176	1,130
Ray Wersching	NFL	15	0	456	222	1,122
Norm Johnson*	NFL	12	0	444	222	1,110
Don Cockroft	NFL	13	0	432	216	1,080
Garo Yepremian	AFL-NFL	14	0	444	210	1,074

Most Points, Season — 176, Paul Hornung, Green Bay Packers, 1960 (15 TD's, 41 PAT's, 15 FG's).
Most Points, Game — 40, Ernie Nevers, Chicago Cardinals vs. Chicago Bears, Nov. 28, 1929 (6 TD's, 4 PAT's).
Most Touchdowns, Season — 24, John Riggins, Washington Redskins, 1984 (24 rushing).
Most Touchdowns, Game — 6, Ernie Nevers, Chicago Cardinals vs. Chicago Bears, Nov. 28, 1929 (6 rushing); Dub Jones, Cleveland Browns vs. Chicago Bears, Nov. 25, 1951 (4 rushing, 2 pass receptions); Gale Sayers, Chicago Bears vs. San Francisco 49ers, Dec. 12, 1965 (4 rushing, 1 pass reception, 1 punt return).
Most Points After Touchdown, Season — 66, Uwe von Schamann, Miami Dolphins, 1984.
Most Consecutive Points After Touchdown — 234, Tommy Davis, San Francisco 49ers, 1959-1969.
Most Field Goals, Game — 7, Jim Bakken, St. Louis Cardinals vs. Pittsburgh Steelers, Sept. 24, 1967; Rich Karlis, Minnesota Vikings vs. L.A. Rams, Nov. 5, 1989.
Longest Field Goal — 63 yds., Tom Dempsey, New Orleans Saints vs. Detroit Lions, Nov. 8, 1970.

NFL Stadiums

Name, location (built)	Capacity
Anaheim Stadium, Anaheim, Cal. (1966)	69,008
Arrowhead Stadium, Kansas City, Mo. (1972)	77,872
Astrodome, Houston, Tex. (1965)	59,905
Candlestick Park, San Francisco, Cal. (1960)	68,491
Cleveland Stadium (1931)	78,512
Foxboro Stadium, Mass. (1971)	60,290
Georgia Dome, Atlanta (1992)	71,280
Giants Stadium, E. Rutherford, N.J. (1976)	77,121
Robert F. Kennedy Stadium, Wash., D.C. (1961)	56,454
Kingdome, Seattle, Wash. (1976)	66,400
Lambeau Field, Green Bay, Wis. (1957)	59,543
Los Angeles Memorial Coliseum (1923)	67,800
Louisiana Superdome, New Orleans (1975)	69,065
Metrodome, Minneapolis (1982)	63,000
Mile High Stadium, Denver, Col. (1948)	76,273
Milwaukee County Stadium (1953)	56,051
Pontiac Silverdome, Mich. (1975)	80,365
RCA Dome, Indianapolis, Ind. (1984)	60,127
Rich Stadium, Buffalo, N.Y. (1973)	80,091
Riverfront Stadium, Cincinnati, Oh. (1970)	60,389
Joe Robbie Stadium, Miami, Fla. (1987)	74,916
San Diego Jack Murphy Stadium (1967)	60,789
Soldier Field, Chicago, Ill. (1924)	66,949
Sun Devil Stadium, Tempe, Ariz. (1958)	73,521
Tampa Stadium, Tampa, Fla. (1967)	74,296
Texas Stadium, Irving, Tex. (1971)	65,024
Three Rivers Stadium, Pittsburgh, Pa. (1970)	59,600
Veterans Stadium, Philadelphia, Pa. (1971)	65,178

NFL All-Time Team

As part of ceremonies to commemorate its 75th anniversary, the NFL, which began in August 1920 as the American Professional Football Conference, named the following players to its all-time, all-star team in August 1994:

Offense—QB: Sammy Baugh, Otto Graham, Joe Montana, and Johnny Unitas; RB: Jim Brown, Marion Motley, Bronko Nagurski, Walter Payton, Gale Sayers, O. J. Simpson, and Steve Van Buren; WR: Lance Alworth, Raymond Berry, Don Hutson, and Jerry Rice; TE: Mike Ditka and Kellen Winslow; T: Roosevelt Brown, Forrest Gregg, and Anthony Munoz; G: John Hannah, Jim Parker, and Gene Upshaw; C: Mel Hein and Mike Webster. **Defense**—LB: Dick Butkus, Jack Ham, Ted Hendricks, Jack Lambert, Willie Lanier, Ray Nitschke, and Lawrence Taylor; E: Deacon Jones, Gino Marchetti, and Reggie White; T: Joe Greene, Bob Lilly, and Merlin Olsen; CB: Mel Blount, Mike Haynes, Dick Lane, and Rod Woodson; S: Ken Houston, Ronnie Lott, and Larry Wilson. **Special Teams**—PK: Jan Stenerud; P: Ray Guy; PR: Billy (White Shoes) Johnson; KR: Gale Sayers.

CANADIAN FOOTBALL LEAGUE

Grey Cup Championship Game

1954 Edmonton Eskimos 26, Montreal Alouettes 25
1955 Edmonton Eskimos 34, Montreal Alouettes 19
1956 Edmonton Eskimos 50, Montreal Alouettes 27
1957 Hamilton Tiger-Cats 32, Winnipeg Blue Bombers 7
1958 Winnipeg Blue Bombers 35, Hamilton Tiger-Cats 28
1959 Winnipeg Blue Bombers 21, Hamilton Tiger-Cats 7
1960 Ottawa Rough Riders 16, Edmonton Eskimos 6
1961 Winnipeg Blue Bombers 21, Hamilton Tiger-Cats 14
1962 Winnipeg Blue Bombers 28, Hamilton Tiger-Cats 27
1963 Hamilton Tiger-Cats 21, British Columbia Lions 10
1964 British Columbia Lions 34, Hamilton Tiger-Cats 24
1965 Hamilton Tiger-Cats 22, Winnipeg Blue Bombers 16
1966 Saskatchewan Roughriders 29, Ottawa Rough Riders 14
1967 Hamilton Tiger-Cats 24, Saskatchewan Roughriders 1
1968 Ottawa Rough Riders 24, Calgary Stampeders 21
1969 Ottawa Rough Riders 29, Saskatchewan Roughriders 11
1970 Montreal Alouettes 23, Calgary Stampeders 10
1971 Calgary Stampeders 14, Toronto Argonauts 11
1972 Hamilton Tiger-Cats 13, Saskatchewan Roughriders 10
1973 Ottawa Rough Riders 22, Edmonton Eskimos 18
1974 Montreal Alouettes 20, Edmonton Eskimos 7
1975 Edmonton Eskimos 9, Montreal Alouettes 8
1976 Ottawa Rough Riders 23, Saskatchewan Roughriders 20
1977 Montreal Alouettes 41, Edmonton Eskimos 6
1978 Edmonton Eskimos 20, Montreal Alouettes 13
1979 Edmonton Eskimos 17, Montreal Alouettes 9
1980 Edmonton Eskimos 48, Hamilton Tiger-Cats 10
1981 Edmonton Eskimos 26, Ottawa Rough Riders 23
1982 Edmonton Eskimos 32, Toronto Argonauts 16
1983 Toronto Argonauts 18, B.C. Lions 17
1984 Winnipeg Blue Bombers 47, Hamilton Tiger-Cats 17
1985 B.C. Lions 37, Hamilton Tiger-Cats 24
1986 Hamilton Tiger-Cats 39, Edmonton Eskimos 15
1987 Edmonton Eskimos 38, Toronto Argonauts 36
1988 Winnipeg Blue Bombers 22, B.C. Lions 21
1989 Saskatchewan Roughriders 43, Hamilton Tiger-Cats 40
1990 Winnipeg Blue Bombers 50, Edmonton Eskimos 11
1991 Toronto Argonauts 36, Calgary Stampeders 21
1992 Calgary Stampeders 24, Winnipeg Blue Bombers 10
1993 Edmonton Eskimos 33, Winnipeg Blue Bombers 23

CFL Teams, Divisions

(at start of 1994 season)

Western Division
British Columbia Lions
Calgary Stampeders
Edmonton Eskimos
Sacramento Gold Miners
Saskatchewan Roughriders
Las Vegas Posse

Eastern Division
Baltimore CFL's*
Hamilton Tiger-Cats
Ottawa Rough Riders
Shreveport Pirates
Toronto Argonauts
Winnipeg Blue Bombers

*Provisional name pending legal action with the NFL over the name Colts.

All-Time CFL Records

(through 1993 season)

Longest Run—The Canadian Football League features 3 downs, 12 players on a side, and a field that is 110 yards long. George Dixon of the Montreal Alouettes made full use of the longer field with a 109-yard run against Ottawa on Sept. 2, 1963. Willie Fleming of the British Columbia Lions did the same against Edmonton on Oct. 17, 1964.

Leading Lifetime Rushers

	Seasons	No	Yds	Avg	Long	TDs
George Reed, Sask.	13	3,243	16,116	5.0	71	134
Johnny Bright, Calg.-Edm.	13	1,969	10,909	5.5	90	69
Normie Kwong, Calg.-Edm.	13	1,745	9,022	5.2	60	78
Leo Lewis, Wpg.	11	1,351	8,861	6.5	92	48
Dave Thelen, Ott.-Tor.	9	1,530	8,463	5.5	77	47
Jim Evenson, B.C.-Ott.	7	1,460	7,060	4.8	68	37
Earl Lunsford, Calg.	6	1,199	6,994	5.8	85	55
Dick Shatto, Tor.	12	1,322	6,958	5.3	67	39
Lovell Coleman, Calg.-Ott.-B.C.	10	1,135	6,566	5.8	85	42
Willie Burden, Calg.	8	1,242	6,234	5.0	71	32

Leading Lifetime Passers

(ranked by total yards passing)

	Seasons	Att	Comp	Yds	Pct	Avg	Lg	TDs
Ron Lancaster, Ott.-Sask.	19	6,233	3,384	50,535	54.3	14.9	102	333
Tom Clements, Ott.-Sask.-Ham.-Wpg.	12	4,657	2,807	39,041	60.3	13.9	105	252
Dieter Brock, Wpg.-Ham.	11	4,535	2,602	34,830	57.4	13.4	98	210
Matt Dunigan, Edm.-B.C.-Tor.-Wpg.	11	4,191	2,329	33,256	55.6	14.3	89	226
Kent Austin, Sask.	7	3,413	1,984	26,626	57.5	13.6	107	162
Sam Etcheverry, Mtl.	7	2,829	1,630	25,582	57.6	15.7	109	183
Tom Burgess, Ott.-Sask.-Wpg.	8	3,316	1,739	25,284	52.4	14.5	104	164
Condredge Holloway, Ott.-Tor.-B.C.	13	3,013	1,710	25,193	56.8	14.7	80	166
Russ Jackson, Ott.	12	2,530	1,356	24,592	53.6	18.1	107	185
Bernie Faloney, Edm.-Ham.-Mtl.-B.C.	12	2,876	1,493	24,264	51.9	16.3	96	161
Roy Dewalt, B.C.-Wpg.-Ott.	9	3,130	1,803	24,147	57.6	13.4	90	132
Damon Allen, Edm.-Ott.-Ham.	9	3,121	1,588	24,021	50.8	18.1	102	151
Joe Kapp, Calg.-B.C.	8	2,709	1,476	22,725	54.5	16.4	106	136
Tom Wilkinson, Tor.-B.C.-Edm.	15	2,662	1,613	22,579	60.6	14.0	87	154
Joe Paopao, B.C.-Sask.-Ott.	11	3,008	1,721	22,474	57.2	13.1	94	117
Doug Flutie, B.C.-Calg.	4	2,513	1,485	21,616	59.1	14.6	89	130
John Hufnagel, Calg.-Sask.-Wpg.	12	2,694	1,495	21,594	55.5	14.4	85	127
Tracy Ham, Edm.-Tor.	7	2,635	1,362	21,387	51.7	15.7	85	150
Peter Liske, Tor.-Calg.-B.C.	7	2,571	1,449	21,266	56.4	14.7	104	130
Warren Moon, Edm.	6	2,382	1,369	21,228	57.5	15.5	91	144

Leading Lifetime Receivers

	Seasons	Number
Rocky DiPietro, Ham.	14	706
Ray Elgaard, Sask.	11	694
Tommy Joe Coffey, Edm.-Ham.-Tor.	14	650
Tom Scott, Wpg.-Edm.-Calg.	11	649
Tony Gabriel, Ham.-Ont.	11	614
Terry Evanshen, Mtl.-Calg.-Tor.	14	600
Craig Ellis, Wpg.-Calg.-Sask.-Tor.-Edm.	10	580
Brian Kelly, Edm.	9	575
James Murphy, Wpg.	8	573
Tom Forzani, Calg.	11	553

COLLEGE FOOTBALL

Annual Results of Major Bowl Games

(Note: Dates indicate the year that the game was played.)

Rose Bowl, Pasadena

1902 Michigan 49, Stanford 0
1916 Wash. State 14, Brown 0
1917 Oregon 14, Pennsylvania 0
1918-19 Service teams
1920 Harvard 7, Oregon 6
1921 California 28, Ohio State 0
1922 Wash. & Jeff. 0, California 0
1923 Southern Cal 14, Penn State 3
1924 Navy 14, Washington 14
1925 Notre Dame 27, Stanford 10
1926 Alabama 20, Washington 19
1927 Alabama 7, Stanford 7
1928 Stanford 7, Pittsburgh 6
1929 Georgia Tech 8, California 7
1930 Southern Cal 47, Pittsburgh 14
1931 Alabama 24, Wash. State 0
1932 Southern Cal 21, Tulane 12
1933 Southern Cal 35, Pittsburgh 0
1934 Columbia 7, Stanford 0
1935 Alabama 29, Stanford 13
1936 Stanford 7, So. Methodist 0
1937 Pittsburgh 21, Washington 0
1938 California 13, Alabama 0
1939 Southern Cal 7, Duke 3
1940 Southern Cal 14, Tennessee 0
1941 Stanford 21, Nebraska 13
1942* Oregon St. 20, Duke 16
1943 Georgia 9, UCLA 0
1944 Southern Cal 29, Washington 0
1945 Southern Cal 25, Tennessee 0
1946 Alabama 34, Southern Cal 14
1947 Illinois 45, UCLA 14
1948 Michigan 49, Southern Cal 0
1949 Northwestern 20, California 14
1950 Ohio State 17, California 14
1951 Michigan 14, California 6
1952 Illinois 40, Stanford 7
1953 Southern Cal 7, Wisconsin 0
1954 Mich. State 28, UCLA 20
1955 Ohio State 20, Southern Cal 7
1956 Mich. State 17, UCLA 14
1957 Iowa 35, Oregon St. 19
1958 Ohio State 10, Oregon 7
1959 Iowa 38, California 12
1960 Washington 44, Wisconsin 8
1961 Washington 17, Minnesota 7
1962 Minnesota 21, UCLA 3
1963 Southern Cal 42, Wisconsin 37
1964 Illinois 17, Washington 7
1965 Michigan 34, Oregon St. 7
1966 UCLA 14, Mich. State 12
1967 Purdue 14, Southern Cal 13
1968 Southern Cal. 14, Indiana 3
1969 Ohio State 27, Southern Cal 16
1970 Southern Cal 10, Michigan 3
1971 Stanford 27, Ohio State 17
1972 Stanford 13, Michigan 12
1973 Southern Cal 42, Ohio State 17
1974 Ohio State 42, Southern Cal 21
1975 Southern Cal 18, Ohio State 17
1976 UCLA 23, Ohio State 10
1977 Southern Cal 14, Michigan 6
1978 Washington 27, Michigan 20
1979 Southern Cal 17, Michigan 10
1980 Southern Cal 17, Ohio State 16
1981 Michigan 23, Washington 6
1982 Washington 28, Iowa 0
1983 UCLA 24, Michigan 14
1984 UCLA 45, Illinois 9
1985 Southern Cal 20, Ohio State 17
1986 UCLA 45, Iowa 28
1987 Arizona St. 22, Michigan 15
1988 Mich. State 20, Southern Cal 17
1989 Michigan 22, Southern Cal 14
1990 Southern Cal. 17, Michigan 10
1991 Washington 46, Iowa 34
1992 Washington 34, Michigan 14
1993 Michigan 38, Washington 31
1994 Wisconsin 21, UCLA 16

*Played at Durham, NC

Orange Bowl, Miami

1935 Bucknell 26, Miami (FL) 0
1936 Catholic U. 20, Mississippi 19
1937 Duquesne 13, Miss. State 12
1938 Auburn 6, Mich. State 0
1939 Tennessee 17, Oklahoma 0
1940 Georgia Tech 21, Missouri 7
1941 Miss. State 14, Georgetown 7
1942 Georgia 40, TCU 26
1943 Alabama 37, Boston Coll. 21
1944 LSU 19, Texas A&M 14
1945 Tulsa 26, Georgia Tech 12
1946 Miami (FL) 13, Holy Cross 6
1947 Rice 8, Tennessee 0
1948 Georgia Tech 20, Kansas 14
1949 Texas 41, Georgia 28
1950 Santa Clara 21, Kentucky 13
1951 Clemson 15, Miami (FL) 14
1952 Georgia Tech 17, Baylor 14
1953 Alabama 61, Syracuse 6
1954 Oklahoma 7, Maryland 0
1955 Duke 34, Nebraska 7
1956 Oklahoma 20, Maryland 6
1957 Colorado 27, Clemson 21
1958 Oklahoma 48, Duke 21
1959 Oklahoma 21, Syracuse 6
1960 Georgia 14, Missouri 0
1961 Missouri 21, Navy 14
1962 LSU 25, Colorado 7
1963 Alabama 17, Oklahoma 0
1964 Nebraska 13, Auburn 7
1965 Texas 21, Alabama 17
1966 Alabama 39, Nebraska 28
1967 Florida 27, Georgia Tech 12
1968 Oklahoma 26, Tennessee 24
1969 Penn State 15, Kansas 14
1970 Penn State 10, Missouri 3
1971 Nebraska 17, Louisiana St. 12
1972 Nebraska 38, Alabama 6
1973 Nebraska 40, Notre Dame 6
1974 Penn State 16, Louisiana St. 9
1975 Notre Dame 13, Alabama 11
1976 Oklahoma 14, Michigan 6
1977 Ohio State 27, Colorado 10
1978 Arkansas 31, Oklahoma 6
1979 Oklahoma 31, Nebraska 24
1980 Oklahoma 24, Florida St. 7
1981 Oklahoma 18, Florida St. 17
1982 Clemson 22, Nebraska 15
1983 Nebraska 21, Louisiana St. 20
1984 Miami (FL) 31, Nebraska 30
1985 Washington 28, Oklahoma 17
1986 Oklahoma 25, Penn State 10
1987 Oklahoma 42, Arkansas 8
1988 Miami (FL) 20, Oklahoma 14
1989 Miami (FL) 23, Nebraska 3
1990 Notre Dame 21, Colorado 6
1991 Colorado 10, Notre Dame 9
1992 Miami (FL) 22, Nebraska 0
1993 Florida St. 27, Nebraska 14
1994 Florida St. 18, Nebraska 16

Sugar Bowl, New Orleans

1935 Tulane 20, Temple 14
1936 TCU 3, LSU 2
1937 Santa Clara 21, LSU 14
1938 Santa Clara 6, LSU 0
1939 TCU 15, Carnegie Tech 7
1940 Texas A&M 14, Tulane 13
1941 Boston Col. 19, Tennessee 13
1942 Fordham 2, Missouri 0
1943 Tennessee 14, Tulsa 7
1944 Georgia Tech 20, Tulsa 18
1945 Duke 29, Alabama 26
1946 Oklahoma A&M 33, St. Mary's 13
1947 Georgia 20, N. Carolina 10
1948 Texas 27, Alabama 7
1949 Oklahoma 14, N. Carolina 6
1950 Oklahoma 35, LSU 0
1951 Kentucky 13, Oklahoma 7
1952 Maryland 28, Tennessee 13
1953 Georgia Tech 24, Mississippi 7
1954 Georgia Tech 42, West Virginia 19
1955 Navy 21, Mississippi 0
1956 Georgia Tech 7, Pittsburgh 0
1957 Baylor 13, Tennessee 7
1958 Mississippi 39, Texas 7
1959 LSU 7, Clemson 0
1960 Mississippi 21, LSU 0
1961 Mississippi 14, Rice 6
1962 Alabama 10, Arkansas 3
1963 Mississippi 17, Arkansas 13
1964 Alabama 12, Mississippi 7
1965 LSU 13, Syracuse 10
1966 Missouri 20, Florida 18
1967 Alabama 34, Nebraska 7
1968 LSU 20, Wyoming 13
1969 Arkansas 16, Georgia 2
1970 Mississippi 27, Arkansas 22
1971 Tennessee 34, Air Force 13
1972 (Jan.) Oklahoma 40, Auburn 22
1972* (Dec.) Okla. 14, Penn State 0
1973 Notre Dame 24, Alabama 23
1974 Nebraska 13, Florida 10
1975 Alabama 13, Penn St. 6
1977 (Jan.) Pittsburgh 27, Georgia 3
1978 Alabama 35, Ohio State 6
1979 Alabama 14, Penn State 7
1980 Alabama 24, Arkansas 9
1981 Georgia 17, Notre Dame 10
1982 Pittsburgh 24, Georgia 20
1983 Penn State 27, Georgia 23
1984 Auburn 9, Michigan 7
1985 Nebraska 28, Louisiana St. 10
1986 Tennessee 35, Miami (FL) 7
1987 Nebraska 30, Louisiana St. 15
1988 Syracuse 16, Auburn 16
1989 Florida St. 13, Auburn 7
1990 Miami 33, Alabama 25
1991 Tennessee 23, Virginia 22
1992 Notre Dame 39, Florida 28
1993 Alabama 34, Miami (FL) 13
1994 Florida 41, West Virginia 7

* Penn St. awarded game by forfeit

Fiesta Bowl, Tempe

1971 Arizona St. 45, Florida St. 38
1972 Arizona St. 49, Missouri 35
1973 Arizona St. 28, Pittsburgh 7
1974 Okla. St. 16, Brigham Young 6
1975 Arizona St. 17, Nebraska 14
1976 Oklahoma 41, Wyoming 7
1977 Penn St. 42, Arizona St. 30
1978 UCLA 10, Arkansas 10
1979 Pittsburgh 16, Arizona 10
1980 Penn St. 31, Ohio St. 19
1982 (Jan.) Penn St. 26, USC 10
1983 Arizona St. 32, Oklahoma 21
1984 Ohio State 28, Pittsburgh 23
1985 UCLA 39, Miami (FL) 37
1986 Michigan 27, Nebraska 23
1987 Penn St. 14, Miami (FL) 10
1988 Florida St. 31, Nebraska 28
1989 Notre Dame 34, W. Virginia 21
1990 Florida St. 41, Nebraska 17
1991 Louisville 34, Alabama 7
1992 Penn St. 42, Tennessee 17
1993 Syracuse 26, Colorado 22
1994 Arizona 29, Miami (FL) 0

Hall of Fame Bowl, Tampa

1986 (Dec.) Boston Coll. 27, Georgia 24
1988 (Jan.) Michigan 28, Alabama 24
1989 Syracuse 23, LSU 10
1990 Auburn 31, Ohio St. 14
1991 Clemson 30, Illinois 0
1992 Syracuse 24, Ohio St. 17
1993 Tennessee 38, Boston College 23
1994 Michigan 42, North Carolina St. 7

Cotton Bowl, Dallas

1937 TCU 16, Marquette 6
1938 Rice 28, Colorado 14
1939 St. Mary's 20, Texas Tech 13
1940 Clemson 6, Boston Col. 3
1941 Texas A&M 13, Fordham 12
1942 Alabama 29, Texas A&M 21
1943 Texas 14, Georgia Tech 7
1944 Randolph Field 7, Texas 7
1945 Oklahoma A&M 34, TCU 0
1946 Texas 40, Missouri 27
1947 Arkansas 0, LSU 0
1948 So. Methodist 13, Penn State 13
1949 So. Methodist 21, Oregon 13
1950 Rice 27, No. Carolina 13
1951 Tennessee 20, Texas 14
1952 Kentucky 20, TCU 7
1953 Texas 16, Tennessee 0
1954 Rice 28, Alabama 6
1955 Georgia Tech 14, Arkansas 6
1956 Mississippi 14, TCU 13
1957 TCU 28, Syracuse 27
1958 Navy 20, Rice 7
1959 TCU 0, Air Force 0
1960 Syracuse 23, Texas 14
1961 Duke 7, Arkansas 6
1962 Texas 12, Mississippi 7
1963 LSU 13, Texas 0
1964 Texas 28, Navy 6
1965 Arkansas 10, Nebraska 7
1966 (Jan.) LSU 14, Arkansas 7
1966 (Dec.) Georgia 24, SMU 9
1968 (Jan.) Texas A&M 20, Ala. 16
1969 Texas 36, Tennessee 13
1970 Texas 21, Notre Dame 17
1971 Notre Dame 24, Texas 11
1972 Penn State 30, Texas 6
1973 Texas 17, Alabama 13
1974 Nebraska 19, Texas 3
1975 Penn State 41, Baylor 20
1976 Arkansas 31, Georgia 10
1977 Houston 30, Maryland 21
1978 Notre Dame 38, Texas 10
1979 Notre Dame 35, Houston 34
1980 Houston 17, Nebraska 14
1981 Alabama 30, Baylor 2
1982 Texas 14, Alabama 12
1983 SMU 7, Pittsburgh 3
1984 Georgia 10, Texas 9
1985 Boston Coll. 45, Houston 28
1986 Texas A&M 36, Auburn 16
1987 Ohio St. 28, Texas A&M 12
1988 Texas A&M 35, Notre Dame 10
1989 UCLA 17, Arkansas 3
1990 Tennessee 31, Arkansas 27
1991 Miami (FL) 46, Texas 3
1992 Florida St. 10, Texas A&M 2
1993 Notre Dame 28, Texas A&M 3
1994 Notre Dame 24, Texas A&M 21

John Hancock Bowl, El Paso (Sun Bowl until 1989)

1936 Hardin-Simmons 14, New Mexico St. 14
1937 Hardin-Simmons 34, Texas Mines 6
1938 West Virginia 7, Texas Tech 6
1939 Utah 26, New Mexico 0
1940 Catholic U. 0, Arizona St. 0
1941 Western Reserve 26, Arizona St. 13
1942 Tulsa 6, Texas Tech 0
1943 2d Air Force 13, Hardin-Simmons 7
1944 Southwestern (TX) 7, New Mexico 0
1945 Southwestern (TX) 35, U. of Mexico 0
1946 New Mexico 34, Denver 24
1947 Cincinnati 18, Virginia Tech 6
1948 Miami (OH) 13, Texas Tech 12
1949 West Virginia 21, Texas Mines 12
1950 Texas Western 33, Georgetown 20
1951 West Texas St. 14, Cincinnati 13
1952 Texas Tech 25, Pacific (CA) 14
1953 Pacific (CA) 26, Southern Miss. 7
1954 Texas Western 37, Southern Miss. 14
1955 Texas Western 47, Florida St. 20
1956 Wyoming 21, Texas Tech 14
1957 Geo. Washington 13, Texas Western 0
1958 (Jan.)Louisville 34, Drake 20
1958 (Dec.) Wyoming 14, Hardin-Simmons 6
1959 New Mexico St. 28, N. Texas St. 8
1960 New Mexico St. 20, Utah State 13
1961 Villanova 17, Wichita 9
1962 West Texas St. 15, Ohio U. 14
1963 Oregon 21, So. Methodist 14
1964 Georgia 7, Texas Tech 0
1965 Texas Western 13, TCU 12
1966 Wyoming 28, Florida St. 20
1967 UTex El Paso 14, Mississippi 7
1968 Auburn 34, Arizona 10
1969 Nebraska 45, Georgia 6
1970 Georgia Tech. 17, Texas Tech 9
1971 LSU 33, Iowa State 15
1972 North Carolina 32, Texas Tech 28
1973 Missouri 34, Auburn 17
1974 Mississippi St. 26, N. Carolina 24
1975 Pittsburgh 33, Kansas 19
1977 (Jan.) Texas A&M 37, Florida 14
1977 (Dec.) Stanford 24, Louisiana St. 14
1978 Texas 42, Maryland 0
1979 Washington 14, Texas 7
1980 Nebraska 31, Mississippi St. 17
1981 Oklahoma 40, Houston 14
1982 North Carolina 26, Texas 10
1983 Alabama 28, SMU 7
1984 Maryland 28, Tennessee 27
1985 Georgia 13, Arizona 13
1986 Alabama 28, Washington 6
1987 Oklahoma St. 35, West Virginia 33
1988 Alabama 29, Army 28
1989 Pittsburgh 31, Texas A&M 28
1990 Michigan St. 17, USC 16
1991 UCLA 6, Illinois 3
1992 Baylor 20, Arizona 15
1993 Oklahoma 41, Texas Tech 10

Gator Bowl, Jacksonville

1946 Wake Forest 26, S. Carolina 14
1947 Oklahoma 34, NC State 13
1948 Maryland 20, Georgia 20
1949 Clemson 24, Missouri 23
1950 Maryland 20, Missouri 7
1951 Wyoming 20, Wash. & Lee 7
1952 Miami (FL) 14, Clemson 0
1953 Florida 14, Tulsa 13
1954 (Jan.) Tex. Tech 35, Auburn 13
1954 (Dec.) Auburn 33, Baylor 13
1955 Vanderbilt 25, Auburn 13
1956 Georgia Tech 21, Pittsburgh 14
1957 Tennessee 3, Texas A&M 0
1958 Mississippi 7, Florida 3
1960 (Jan.) Arkansas 14, Ga.Tech 7
1960 (Dec.) Florida 13, Baylor 12
1961 Penn State 30, Georgia Tech 15
1962 Florida 17, Penn State 7
1963 N. Carolina 35, Air Force 0
1965 (Jan.) Florida St. 36, Okla.19
1965 (Dec.) Georgia Tech 31, Texas Tech 21
1966 Tennessee 18, Syracuse 12
1967 Penn State 17, Florida St. 17
1968 Missouri 35, Alabama 10
1969 Florida 14, Tennessee 13
1971 (Jan.) Auburn 35, Mississippi 28
1971 (Dec.) Georgia 7, N. Carolina 3
1972 Auburn 24, Colorado 3
1973 Tex. Tech 28, Tenn. 19
1974 Auburn 27, Texas 3
1975 Maryland 13, Florida 0
1976 Notre Dame 20, Penn State 9
1977 Pittsburgh 34, Clemson 3
1978 Clemson 17, Ohio State 15
1979 N. Carolina 17, Michigan 15
1980 Pittsburgh 37, S. Carolina 9
1981 N. Carolina 31, Arkansas 27
1982 Florida St. 31, West Virginia 12
1983 Florida 14, Iowa 6
1984 Oklahoma St. 21, S. Carolina 14
1985 Florida St. 34, Oklahoma St. 23
1986 Clemson 27, Stanford 21
1987 LSU 30, S. Carolina 13
1989 (Jan.) Georgia 34, Michigan St. 27
1989 (Dec.) Clemson 27, W. Va. 7
1991 (Jan.) Michigan 35, Mississippi 3
1991 (Dec.) Oklahoma 48, Virginia 14
1992 Florida 27, NC State 10
1993 Alabama 24, N. Carolina 10

Liberty Bowl, Memphis

1959 Penn State 7, Alabama 0
1960 Penn State 41, Oregon 12
1961 Syracuse 15, Miami 14
1962 Oregon State 6, Villanova 0
1963 Miss. State 16, NC State 12
1964 Utah 32, West Virginia 6
1965 Mississippi 13, Auburn 7
1966 Miami (FL) 14, Virginia Tech 7
1967 N.C. State 14, Georgia 7
1968 Mississippi 34, Virginia Tech 17
1969 Colorado 47, Alabama 33
1970 Tulane 17, Colorado 3
1971 Tennessee 14, Arkansas 13
1972 Georgia Tech 31, Iowa State 30
1973 N. Carolina St. 31, Kansas 18
1974 Tennessee 7, Maryland 3
1975 USC 20, Texas A&M 0
1976 Alabama 36, UCLA 6
1977 Nebraska 21, N. Carolina 17
1978 Missouri 20, Louisiana St. 15
1979 Penn St. 9, Tulane 6
1980 Purdue 28, Missouri 25
1981 Ohio State 31, Navy 28
1982 Alabama 21, Illinois 15
1983 Notre Dame 19, Boston Coll. 18
1984 Auburn 21, Arkansas 15
1985 Baylor 21, Louisiana St. 7
1986 Tennessee 21, Minnesota 14
1987 Georgia 20, Arkansas 17
1988 Indiana 34, S. Carolina 10
1989 Mississippi 42, Air Force 29
1990 Air Force 23, Ohio State 11
1991 Air Force 38, Mississippi St. 15
1992 Mississippi 13, Air Force 0
1993 Louisville 18, Michigan St. 7

Freedom Bowl, Anaheim

1984 Iowa 55, Texas 17
1985 Washington 20, Colorado 17
1986 UCLA 31, Brigham Young 10
1987 Arizona St. 33, Air Force 28
1988 Brigham Young 20, Colorado 17
1989 Washington 34, Florida 7
1990 Colorado St. 32, Oregon 31
1991 Tulsa 28, San Diego St. 17
1992 Fresno St. 24, USC 7
1993 Southern Cal 28, Utah 21

Copper Bowl, Tucson

1989 Arizona 17, NC St. 10
1990 California 17, Wyoming 15
1991 Indiana 24, Baylor 0
1992 Washington St. 31, Utah 28
1993 Kansas St. 52, Wyoming 17

Independence Bowl, Shreveport

1976 McNeese St. 20, Tulsa 16
1977 Louisiana Tech 24, Louisiville 14
1978 E. Carolina 35, La. Tech 13
1979 Syracuse 31, McNeese St. 7
1980 So. Miss. 16, McNeese St. 14
1981 Texas A&M 33, Oklahoma St. 16
1982 Wisconsin 14, Kansas St. 3
1983 Air Force 9, Mississippi 3
1984 Air Force 23, Virginia Tech 7
1985 Minnesota 20, Clemson 13
1986 Mississippi 20, Texas Tech 17
1987 Washington 24, Tulane 12
1988 So. Mississippi 38, UTEP 18
1989 Oregon 27, Tulsa 24
1990 Louisiana Tech 34, Maryland 34
1991 Georgia 24, Arkansas 15
1992 Wake Forest 39, Oregon 35
1993 Virginia Tech 45, Indiana 20

Citrus Bowl, Orlando (Tangerine Bowl until 1983)

1947 Catawba 31, Maryville 6
1948 Catawba 7, Marshall 0
1949 Murray State 21, Sul Ross St. 21
1950 St. Vincent 7, Emory & Henry 6
1951 Morris Harvey 35, Emory & Henry 14
1952 Stetson 35, Arkansas St. 20
1953 East Texas St. 33, Tenn. Tech 0
1954 East Texas St. 7, Arkansas St. 7
1955 Neb.-Omaha 7, E. Kentucky 6
1956 Juniata 6, Missouri Valley 6
1957 West Texas St. 20, So. Miss. 13
1958 East Texas St. 10, So. Miss. 9
1958 (Dec.) East Texas St. 26, Missouri Valley 7
1960 (Jan.) Middle Tenn. 21, Presbyterian 12
1960 (Dec.) Citadel 27, Tenn. Tech 0
1961 Lamar 21, Middle Tennessee 14
1962 Houston 49, Miami (OH) 21
1963 Western Ky. 27, Coast Guard 0
1964 E. Carolina 14, Massachusetts 13
1965 East Carolina 31, Maine 0
1966 Morgan State 14, West Chester 6
1967 Tenn.-Martin 25, West Chester 8
1968 Richmond 49, Ohio U. 42
1969 Toledo 56, Davidson 33
1970 Toledo 40, William & Mary 12
1971 Toledo 28, Richmond 3
1972 Tampa 21, Kent State 18
1973 Miami (OH) 16, Florida 7
1974 Miami (OH) 21, Georgia 10
1975 Miami (OH) 20, S. Carolina 7
1976 Okla. St. 49, Brigham Young 21
1977 Florida St. 40, Texas Tech 17
1978 NC State 30, Pittsburgh 17
1979 LSU 34, Wake Forest 10
1980 Florida 35, Maryland 20
1981 Missouri 19, Southern Miss. 17
1982 Auburn 33, Boston College 26
1983 Tennessee 30, Maryland 23
1984 Georgia 17, Florida St. 17
1985 Ohio St. 10, Brigham Young 7
1987 (Jan.) Auburn 16, USC 7
1988 Clemson 35, Penn St. 10
1989 Clemson 13, Oklahoma 6
1990 Illinois 31, Virginia 21
1991 Georgia Tech 45, Nebraska 21
1992 California 37, Clemson 13
1993 Georgia 21, Ohio St. 14
1994 Penn St. 31, Tennessee 13

Peach Bowl, Atlanta

1968 LSU 31, Florida St. 27
1969 West Virginia 14, S. Carolina 3
1970 Arizona St. 48, N. Carolina 26
1971 Mississippi 41, Georgia Tech 18
1972 N. Carolina St. 49, W. Va. 13
1973 Georgia 17, Maryland 16
1974 Vanderbilt 6, Texas Tech 6
1975 W. Virginia 13, N. Carolina St. 10
1976 Kentucky 21, North Carolina 0
1977 N. Carolina St. 24, Iowa St. 14
1978 Purdue 41, Georgia Tech 21
1979 Baylor 24, Clemson 18
1981 (Jan.) Miami (FL) 20, Virginia Tech 10
1981 (Dec.) West Virginia 26, Florida 6
1982 Iowa 28, Tennessee 22
1983 Florida St. 28, North Carolina 3
1984 Virginia 27, Purdue 22
1985 Army 31, Illinois 29
1986 Virginia Tech 25, NC State 24
1988 (Jan.) Tennessee 28, Indiana 22
1988 (Dec.) NC State 28, Iowa 23
1989 Syracuse 19, Georgia 18
1990 Auburn 27, Indiana 23
1992 (Jan.) E. Carolina 37, NC State 34
1993 (Jan.) North Carolina 21, Mississippi St. 17
1993 (Dec.) Clemson 14, Kentucky 13

Holiday Bowl, San Diego

1978 Navy 23, Brigham Young 16
1979 Indiana 38, Brigham Young 37
1980 Brigham Young 46, SMU 45
1981 Brigham Young 38, Wash. St. 36
1982 Ohio State 47, Brigham Young 17
1983 Brigham Young 21, Missouri 17
1984 Brigham Young 24, Michigan 17
1985 Arkansas 18, Arizona St. 17
1986 Iowa 39, San Diego St. 38
1987 Iowa 20, Wyoming 19
1988 Oklahoma St. 62, Wyoming 14
1989 Penn St. 50, Brigham Young 39
1990 Texas A&M 65, Brigham Young 14
1991 Iowa 13, Brigham Young 13
1992 Hawaii 27, Illinois 17
1993 Ohio St. 28, Brigham Young 21

Aloha Bowl, Honolulu

1982 Washington 21, Maryland 20
1983 Penn State 13, Washington 10
1984 SMU 27, Notre Dame 20
1985 Alabama 24, USC 3
1986 Arizona 30, North Carolina 21
1987 UCLA 20, Florida 16
1988 Washington St. 24, Houston 22
1989 Michigan St. 33, Hawaii 13
1990 Syracuse 28, Arizona 0
1991 Georgia Tech 18, Stanford 17
1992 Kansas 23, Brigham Young 20
1993 Colorado 41, Fresno St. 30

Carquest Bowl, Miami (Blockbuster Bowl until 1993)

1990 Florida St. 24, Penn St. 17
1991 Alabama 30, Colorado 25
1993 (Jan.) Stanford 24, Penn St. 3
1994 Boston College 31, Virginia 13

Las Vegas Bowl, Las Vegas

1992 Bowling Green 35, Nevada 34
1993 Utah St. 42, Ball St. 33

Selected College Division I Football Teams

Team	Nickname	Team colors	Conference	Coach	1993 record (W-L-T)
Air Force	Falcons	Blue & silver	Western Athletic	Fisher De Berry	4-8-0
Akron	Zips	Blue & gold	Mid-American	Gerry Faust	5-6-0
Alabama	Crimson Tide	Crimson & white	Southeastern	Gene Stallings	8-3-1
Arizona	Wildcats	Cardinal & navy	Pacific Ten	Dick Tomey	9-2-0
Arizona State	Sun Devils	Maroon & gold	Pacific Ten	Bruce Snyder	6-5-0
Arkansas	Razorbacks	Cardinal & white	Southeastern	Danny Ford	5-5-1
Arkansas State	Indians	Scarlet & black	Big West	John Bobo	2-8-1
Army	Cadets	Black, gold, gray	Independent	Bob Sutton	6-5-0
Auburn	Tigers	Burnt orange & navy	Southeastern	Terry Bowden	11-0-0
Ball State	Cardinals	Cardinal & white	Mid-American	Paul Schudel	8-2-1
Baylor	Bears	Green & gold	Southwest	Chuck Reedy	5-6-0
Boston College	Eagles	Maroon & gold	Big East	Dan Henning	8-3-0
Boston Univ.	Terriers	Scarlet & white	Yankee	Dan Allen	11-0-0
Bowling Green	Falcons	Orange & brown	Mid-American	Gary Blackney	6-3-2
Brigham Young	Cougars	Royal blue & white	Western Athletic	LaVell Edwards	6-5-0
Brown	Bears	Brown, cardinal, white	Ivy	Mark Whipple	4-6-0
California	Golden Bears	Blue & gold	Pacific Ten	Keith Gilbertson	8-4-0
Central Michigan	Chippewas	Maroon & gold	Mid-American	Dick Flynn	5-6-0
Cincinnati	Bearcats	Red & black	Independent	Rick Minter	8-3-0
Citadel	Bulldogs	Blue & white	Southern	Charles Taaffe	5-6-0
Clemson	Tigers	Purple & orange	Atlantic Coast	Tommy West	8-3-0
Colgate	Red Raiders	Maroon	Patriot	Ed Sweeney	3-7-1
Colorado	Buffaloes	Silver, gold & black	Big Eight	Bill McCartney	7-3-1
Colorado State	Rams	Green & gold	Western Athletic	Sonny Lubick	5-6-0
Cornell	Big Red	Carnelian & white	Ivy	Jim Hofher	4-6-0
Dartmouth	Big Green	Dartmouth green & white	Ivy	John Lyons	7-3-0
Delaware	Fightin' Blue Hens	Blue & gold	Yankee	Harold Raymond	8-3-0
Delaware State	Hornets	Red & blue	Mid-Eastern	William Collick	6-5-0
Duke	Blue Devils	Royal blue & white	Atlantic Coast	Fred Goldsmith	3-8-0
East Carolina	Pirates	Purple & gold	Independent	Steve Logan	2-9-0
East Tennessee St.	Buccaneers	Blue & gold	Southern	Mike Cavan	5-6-0
Eastern Illinois	Panthers	Blue & gray	Gateway	Bob Spoo	3-7-1
Eastern Kentucky	Colonels	Maroon & white	Ohio Valley	Roy Kidd	8-3-0
Eastern Michigan	Eagles	Green & white	Mid-American	Ron Cooper	4-7-0
Eastern Washington	Eagles	Red & white	Big Sky	Mike Kramer	7-3-0
Florida	Gators	Orange & blue	Southeastern	Steve Spurrier	10-2-0
Florida A&M	Rattlers	Orange & green	Mid-Eastern	Billy Joe	5-6-0
Florida State	Seminoles	Garnet & gold	Atlantic Coast	Bobby Bowden	11-1-0
Fresno State	Bulldogs	Cardinal & blue	Western Athletic	Jim Sweeney	8-3-0
Furman	Paladins	Purple & white	Southern	Bobby Johnson	5-5-1
Georgia	Bulldogs	Red & black	Southeastern	Ray Goff	5-6-0
Georgia Southern	Eagles	Blue & white	Southern	Tim Stowers	9-2-0
Georgia Tech	Yellow Jackets	Old gold & white	Atlantic Coast	Bill Lewis	5-6-0
Grambling	Tigers	Black & gold	Southwestern	Eddie Robinson	7-4-0
Harvard	Crimson	Crimson	Ivy	Tim Murphy	3-7-0
Hawaii	Rainbow Warriors	Green & white	Western Athletic	Bob Wagner	6-6-0
Holy Cross	Crusaders	Royal purple	Patriot	Peter Vaas	3-8-0
Houston	Cougars	Scarlet & white	Southwest	Kim Helton	1-9-1
Howard	Bison	Blue & white	Mid-Eastern	Steve Wilson	11-0-0
Idaho	Vandals	Silver & gold	Big Sky	John L. Smith	9-2-0
Idaho State	Bengals	Orange & black	Big Sky	Brian McNeely	2-9-0
Illinois	Fighting Illini	Orange & blue	Big Ten	Lou Tepper	5-6-0
Illinois State	Redbirds	Red & white	Gateway	Jim Heacock	6-4-1
Indiana	Hoosiers	Cream & crimson	Big Ten	Bill Mallory	8-3-0
Indiana State	Sycamores	Blue & white	Gateway	Dennis Raetz	4-7-0
Iowa	Hawkeyes	Old gold & black	Big Ten	Hayden Fry	6-5-0
Iowa State	Cyclones	Cardinal & gold	Big Eight	Jim Walden	3-8-0
Jackson State	Tigers	Blue & white	Southwestern	James Carson	5-5-1
James Madison	Dukes	Purple & gold	Yankee	Rip Scherer	6-5-0
Kansas	Jayhawks	Crimson & blue	Big Eight	Glen Mason	5-7-0
Kansas State	Wildcats	Purple & white	Big Eight	Bill Snyder	8-2-1
Kent	Golden Flashes	Blue & gold	Mid-American	Jim Corrigall	0-11-0
Kentucky	Wildcats	Blue & white	Southeastern	Bill Curry	6-5-0
Lafayette	Leopards	Maroon & white	Patriot	Bill Russo	5-4-2
Lehigh	Engineers	Brown & white	Patriot	Kevin Higins	7-4-0
Liberty	Flames	Red, white, blue	Independent	Sam Rutigliano	6-5-0
Louisiana State	Fighting Tigers	Purple & gold	Southeastern	Curley Hallman	5-6-0
Louisiana Tech	Bulldogs	Red & blue	Big West	Joe Raymond Peace	2-9-0
Louisville	Cardinals	Red, black, white	Independent	Howard Schnellenberger	8-3-0
Maine	Black Bears	Blue & white	Yankee	Jack Cosgrove	3-8-0
Marshall	Thundering Herd	Green & white	Southern	Jim Donnan	8-3-0
Maryland	Terps	Red, white, black & gold	Atlantic Coast	Mark Duffner	2-9-0
Massachusetts	Minutemen	Maroon & white	Yankee	Mike Hodges	8-3-0

Team	Nickname	Team colors	Conference	Coach	1993 record (W-L-T)
McNeese State	Cowboys	Blue & gold	Southland	Bobby Keasler	9-2-0
Memphis State	Tigers	Blue & gray	Independent	Chuck Stobart	6-5-0
Miami (Florida)	Hurricanes	Orange, green, white	Big East	Dennis Erickson	9-2-0
Miami (Ohio)	Redskins	Red & white	Mid-American	Randy Walker	4-7-0
Michigan	Wolverines	Maize & blue	Big Ten	Gary Moeller	7-4-0
Michigan State	Spartans	Green & white	Big Ten	George Perles	6-5-0
Middle Tennessee St.	Blue Raiders	Blue & white	Ohio Valley	Boots Donnelly	5-6-0
Minnesota	Golden Gophers	Maroon & gold	Big Ten	Jim Wacker	4-7-0
Mississippi	Rebels	Red & blue	Southeastern	Billy Brewer	5-6-0
Mississippi State	Bulldogs	Maroon & white	Southeastern	Jackie Sherrill	3-6-2
Mississippi Valley	Delta Devils	Green & white	Southwestern	Larry Dorsey	4-4-2
Missouri	Tigers	Old gold & black	Big Eight	Larry Smith	3-7-1
Montana	Grizzlies	Copper, silver, gold	Big Sky	Don Read	10-1-0
Montana State	Bobcats	Blue & gold	Big Sky	Cliff Hyself	7-4-0
Morehead State	Eagles	Blue & gold	Ohio Valley	Matt Ballard	3-8-0
Morgan State	Bears	Blue & orange	Mid-Eastern	Ricky Diggs	2-9-0
Murray State	Racers	Blue & gold	Ohio Valley	Houston Nutt	4-7-0
Navy	Midshipmen	Navy blue & gold	Independent	George Chaump	4-7-0
Nebraska	Cornhuskers	Scarlet & cream	Big Eight	Tom Osborne	11-0-0
Nevada-Las Vegas	Rebels	Scarlet & gray	Big West	Jeff Horton	3-8-0
Nevada-Reno	Wolf Pack	Silver & blue	Big West	Chris Ault	7-4-0
New Hampshire	Wildcats	Blue & white	Yankee	Bill Bowes	6-5-0
New Mexico	Lobos	Cherry & silver	Western Athletic	Dennis Franchione	6-5-0
New Mexico State	Aggies	Crimson & white	Big West	Jim Hess	5-6-0
Nicholls St.	Colonels	Red & grey	Southland	Rick Rhoades	3-8-0
North Carolina	Tar Heels	Blue & white	Atlantic Coast	Mack Brown	10-2-0
North Carolina A & T	Aggies	Blue & gold	Mid-Eastern	Bill Hayes	8-3-0
North Carolina State	Wolfpack	Red & white	Atlantic Coast	Mike O'Cain	7-4-0
North Texas	Mean Green, Eagles	Green & white	Southland	Matt Simon	4-7-0
Northeast Louisiana	Indians	Maroon & gold	Southland	Ed Zaunbrecher	9-2-0
Northeastern	Huskies	Red & black	Yankee	Barry Gallup	2-9-0
Northern Arizona	Lumberjacks	Blue & gold	Big Sky	Steve Axman	7-4-0
Northern Illinois	Huskies	Cardinal & black	Big West	Charlie Sadler	4-7-0
Northern Iowa	Panthers	Purple & old gold	Gateway	Terry Allen	8-3-0
Northwestern	Wildcats	Purple & white	Big Ten	Gary Barnett	2-9-0
Northwestern State	Demons	Purple & white	Southland	Sam Goodwin	5-6-0
Notre Dame	Fighting Irish	Gold & blue	Independent	Lou Holtz	10-1-0
Ohio	Bobcats	Green & white	Mid-American	Tom Lichtenberg	4-7-0
Ohio State	Buckeyes	Scarlet & gray	Big Ten	John Cooper	9-1-1
Oklahoma	Sooners	Crimson & cream	Big Eight	Gary Gibbs	8-3-0
Oklahoma State	Cowboys	Orange & black	Big Eight	Pat Jones	3-8-0
Oregon	Ducks	Green & yellow	Pacific Ten	Rich Brooks	5-6-0
Oregon State	Beavers	Orange & black	Pacific Ten	Jerry Pettibone	4-7-0
Pacific	Tigers	Orange & black	Big West	Chuck Shelton	3-8-0
Penn State	Nittany Lions	Blue & white	Big Ten	Joe Paterno	9-2-0
Pennsylvania	Red & Blue, Quakers	Red & blue	Ivy	Al Bagnoli	10-0-0
Pittsburgh	Panthers	Gold & blue	Big East	Johnny Majors	3-8-0
Princeton	Tigers	Orange & black	Ivy	Steve Tosches	8-2-0
Purdue	Boilermakers	Old gold & black	Big Ten	Jim Colletto	1-10-0
Rhode Island	Rams	Blue & white	Yankee	Floyd Keith	3-8-0
Rice	Owls	Blue & gray	Southwest	Ken Hatfield	6-5-0
Richmond	Spiders	Red & blue	Yankee	Jim Marshall	5-6-0
Rutgers	Scarlet Knights	Scarlet	Big East	Doug Graber	4-7-0
Sam Houston State	Bearkats	Orange & white	Southland	Ron Randleman	4-7-0
Samford	Bulldogs	Crimson & blue	Independent	Pete Hurt	5-6-0
San Diego State	Aztecs	Scarlet & black	Western Athletic	Ted Tollner	6-6-0
San Jose State	Spartans	Gold & white	Big West	John Ralston	2-9-0
South Carolina	Fighting Gamecocks	Garnet & black	Southeastern	Brad Scott	4-7-0
South Carolina State	Bulldogs	Garnet & blue	Mid-Eastern	Willie Jeffries	8-3-0
SE Missouri St.	Indians	Red & black	Ohio Valley	John Mumford	3-8-0
Southern-Baton Rouge	Jaguars	Blue & gold	Southwestern	Pete Richardson	10-1-0
Southern California	Trojans	Cardinal & gold	Pacific Ten	John Robinson	7-5-0
Southern Illinois	Salukis	Maroon & white	Gateway	Shawn Watson	2-9-0
Southern Methodist	Mustangs	Red & blue	Southwest	Tom Rossley	2-7-2
Southern Mississippi	Golden Eagles	Black & gold	Independent	Jeff Bower	2-8-1
SW Missouri St.	Bears	Maroon & white	Gateway	Jesse Branch	7-4-0
SW Texas St.	Bobcats	Maroon & gold	Southland	Jim Bob Helduser	2-9-0
SW Louisiana	Ragin' Cajuns	Vermillion & white	Big West	Nelson Stokley	8-3-0
Stanford	Cardinal	Cardinal & white	Pacific Ten	Bill Walsh	4-7-0
Stephen F. Austin St.	Lumberjacks	Purple & white	Southland	John Pearce	8-3-0
Syracuse	Orangemen	Orange	Big East	Paul Pasqualoni	6-4-1
Temple	Owls	Cherry & white	Big East	Ron Dickerson	1-10-0
Tennessee	Volunteers	Orange & white	Southeastern	Philip Fulmer	9-1-1
Tenn.-Chattanooga	Moccasins	Navy blue & gold	Southern	Buddy Green	4-7-0
Tenn.-Martin	Pacers	Orange, white, blue	Ohio Valley	Don McLeary	6-5-0
Tennessee State	Tigers	Blue & white	Ohio Valley	Bill Davis	4-7-0
Tennessee Tech	Golden Eagles	Purple & gold	Ohio Valley	Jim Ragland	8-3-0

Team	Nickname	Team colors	Conference	Coach	1993 record (W-L-T)
Texas	Longhorns	Orange & white	Southwest	John Mackovic	5-5-1
Texas A & M	Aggies	Maroon & white	Southwest	R.C. Slocum	10-1-0
Texas Christian	Horned Frogs	Purple & white	Southwest	Pat Sullivan	4-7-0
Texas Southern	Tigers	Maroon & gray	Southwestern	Bill Thomas	2-9-0
Texas Tech	Red Raiders	Scarlet & black	Southwest	Spike Dykes	6-5-0
Toledo	Rockets	Blue & gold	Mid-American	Gary Pinkel	4-7-0
Towson St.	Tigers	Gold & white	Independent	Gordy Combs	8-2-0
Tulane	Green Wave	Olive green & sky blue	Independent	Buddy Teevens	3-9-0
Tulsa	Golden Hurricane	Blue & gold	Independent	Dave Rader	4-6-1
UCLA	Bruins	Blue & gold	Pacific Ten	Terry Donahue	8-3-0
Utah	Utes	Crimson & white	Western Athletic	Ron McBride	7-5-0
Utah State	Aggies	Navy blue & white	Big West	Charlie Weatherbie	6-5-0
UTEP	Miners	Orange, blue, white	Western Athletic	Charlie Bailey	1-11-0
Vanderbilt	Commodores	Black & gold	Southeastern	Gerry DiNardo	4-7-0
Villanova	Wildcats	Blue & white	Yankee	Andy Talley	3-8-0
Virginia	Cavaliers	Orange & blue	Atlantic Coast	George Welsh	7-4-0
VMI	Keydets	Red, white & yellow	Southern	Bill Stewart	1-10-0
Virginia Tech.	Gobblers, Hokies	Orange & maroon	Big East	Frank Beamer	8-3-0
Wake Forest	Demon Deacons	Old gold & black	Atlantic Coast	Jim Caldwell	2-9-0
Washington	Huskies	Purple & gold	Pacific Ten	Jim Lambright	7-4-0
Washington State	Cougars	Crimson & gray	Pacific Ten	Mike Price	5-6-0
Weber State	Wildcats	Purple & white	Big Sky	Dave Arsianian	7-4-0
West Virginia	Mountaineers	Old gold & blue	Big East	Don Nehlen	11-0-0
Western Carolina	Catamounts	Purple & gold	Southern	Steve Hodgin	6-5-0
Western Illinois	Leathernecks	Purple & gold	Gateway	Randy Ball	4-7-0
Western Kentucky	Hilltoppers	Red & white	Independent	Jack Harbaugh	8-3-0
Western Michigan	Broncos	Brown & gold	Mid-American	Al Molde	7-3-1
William & Mary	Tribe	Green, gold & silver	Yankee	Jimmye Laycock	9-2-0
Wisconsin	Badgers	Cardinal & white	Big Ten	Barry Alvarez	9-1-1
Wyoming	Cowboys	Brown & yellow	Western Athletic	Joe Tiller	8-3-0
Yale	Bulldogs, Elis	Yale blue & white	Ivy	Carmen Cozza	3-7-0
Youngstown St.	Penguins	Red & white	Independent	Jim Tressel	9-2-0

Heisman Trophy Winners

Awarded annually to the nation's outstanding college football player.

1935 Jay Berwanger, Chicago, HB
1936 Larry Kelley, Yale, E
1937 Clinton Frank, Yale, HB
1938 David O'Brien, Tex. Christian, QB
1939 Nile Kinnick, Iowa, HB
1940 Tom Harmon, Michigan, HB
1941 Bruce Smith, Minnesota, HB
1942 Frank Sinkwich, Georgia, HB
1943 Angelo Bertelli, Notre Dame, QB
1944 Leslie Horvath, Ohio State, QB
1945 Felix Blanchard, Army, FB
1946 Glenn Davis, Army, HB
1947 John Lujack, Notre Dame, QB
1948 Doak Walker, SMU, HB
1949 Leon Hart, Notre Dame, E
1950 Vic Janowicz, Ohio State, HB
1951 Richard Kazmaier, Princeton, HB
1952 Billy Vessels, Oklahoma, HB
1953 John Lattner, Notre Dame, HB
1954 Alan Ameche, Wisconsin, FB
1955 Howard Cassady, Ohio St., HB
1956 Paul Hornung, Notre Dame, QB
1957 John Crow, Texas A & M, HB
1958 Pete Dawkins, Army, HB
1959 Billy Cannon, LA State, HB
1960 Joe Bellino, Navy, HB
1961 Ernest Davis, Syracuse, HB
1962 Terry Baker, Oregon State, QB
1963 Roger Staubach, Navy, QB
1964 John Huarte, Notre Dame, QB
1965 Mike Garrett, USC, HB
1966 Steve Spurrier, Florida, QB
1967 Gary Beban, UCLA, QB
1968 O. J. Simpson, USC, RB
1969 Steve Owens, Oklahoma, RB
1970 Jim Plunkett, Stanford, QB
1971 Pat Sullivan, Auburn, QB
1972 Johnny Rodgers, Nebraska, RB-R
1973 John Cappelletti, Penn State, RB
1974 Archie Griffin, Ohio State, RB
1975 Archie Griffin, Ohio State, RB
1976 Tony Dorsett, Pittsburgh, RB
1977 Earl Campbell, Texas, RB
1978 Billy Sims, Oklahoma, RB
1979 Charles White, USC, RB
1980 George Rogers, S. Carolina, RB
1981 Marcus Allen, USC, RB
1982 Herschel Walker, Georgia, RB
1983 Mike Rozier, Nebraska, RB
1984 Doug Flutie, Boston College, QB
1985 Bo Jackson, Auburn, RB
1986 Vinny Testaverde, Miami, QB
1987 Tim Brown, Notre Dame, WR
1988 Barry Sanders, Oklahoma St., RB
1989 Andre Ware, Houston, QB
1990 Ty Detmer, BYU, QB
1991 Desmond Howard, Michigan, WR
1992 Gino Torretta, Miami, QB
1993 Charlie Ward, Florida St., QB

Outland Award

Honoring the outstanding interior lineman selected by the Football Writers Association of America.

1946 George Connor, Notre Dame, T
1947 Joe Steffy, Army, G
1948 Bill Fischer, Notre Dame, G
1949 Ed Bagdon, Michigan St., G
1950 Bob Gain, Kentucky, T
1951 Jim Weatherall, Oklahoma, T
1952 Dick Modzelewski, Maryland, T
1953 J. D. Roberts, Oklahoma, G
1954 Bill Brooks, Arkansas, G
1955 Calvin Jones, Iowa, G
1956 Jim Parker, Ohio State, G
1957 Alex Karras, Iowa, T
1958 Zeke Smith, Auburn, G
1959 Mike McGee, Duke, T
1960 Tom Brown, Minnesota, G
1961 Merlin Olsen, Utah State, T
1962 Bobby Bell, Minnesota, T
1963 Scott Appleton, Texas, T
1964 Steve Delong, Tennessee, T
1965 Tommy Nobis, Texas, G
1966 Loyd Phillips, Arkansas, T
1967 Ron Yary, Southern Cal, T
1968 Bill Stanfill, Georgia, T
1969 Mike Reid, Penn State, DT
1970 Jim Stillwagon, Ohio State, MG
1971 Larry Jacobson, Nebraska, DT
1972 Rich Glover, Nebraska, MG
1973 John Hicks, Ohio State, OT
1974 Randy White, Maryland, DE
1975 Lee Roy Selmon, Oklahoma, DT
1976 Ross Browner, Notre Dame, DE
1977 Brad Shearer, Texas, DT
1978 Greg Roberts, Oklahoma, G
1979 Jim Ritcher, N. Carolina St., C
1980 Mark May, Pittsburgh, OT
1981 Dave Rimington, Nebraska, C
1982 Dave Rimington, Nebraska, C
1983 Dean Steinkuhler, Nebraska, G
1984 Bruce Smith, Virginia Tech, DT
1985 Mike Ruth, Boston College, NG
1986 Jason Buck, BYU, DT
1987 Chad Hennings, Air Force, DT
1988 Tracy Rocker, Auburn, DT
1989 Mohammed Elewonibi, BYU, G
1990 Russell Maryland, Miami (FL) DT
1991 Steve Emtman, Washington, DT
1992 Will Shields, Nebraska, G
1993 Rob Waldrop, Arizona, NG

All-Time Division I-A Percentage Leaders

(Classified as Division I-A for the last 10 years; record includes bowl games; ties computed as half won and half lost)

	Years	Won	Lost	Tied	Pct.	Bowl Games W	Bowl Games L	Bowl Games T
Notre Dame	105	723	211	41	.762	13	6	0
Michigan	114	739	242	36	.749	12	13	0
Alabama	99	691	237	44	.734	26	17	3
Oklahoma	99	659	240	52	.720	20	10	1
Texas	101	687	273	32	.709	16	16	2
Ohio St.	104	659	265	53	.702	13	13	0
USC	101	630	254	52	.701	23	13	0
Nebraska	104	673	290	40	.691	14	18	0
Penn St.	107	674	291	41	.690	18	10	2
Tennessee	97	636	276	53	.687	18	16	0
Central Michigan	93	480	255	36	.646	3	1	0
Florida St.	47	316	176	16	.638	14	7	2
Washington	104	562	310	49	.637	12	8	1
Army	104	588	327	50	.635	2	1	0
Miami (Ohio)	105	546	308	42	.633	5	2	0
Louisiana St.	100	573	325	46	.631	11	16	1
Georgia	100	589	333	53	.631	15	13	3
Arizona St	81	444	255	24	.631	9	5	1
Auburn	101	558	335	46	.619	12	9	2
Colorado	104	557	348	36	.611	6	12	0
Miami (Florida)	67	411	260	19	.609	10	10	0
Michigan St.	97	521	328	43	.608	5	6	0
Bowling Green	75	389	242	52	.608	2	3	0
UCLA	75	437	280	37	.604	10	8	1
Minnesota	110	555	359	43	.602	2	3	0

All-Time Division I-A Coaching Victories (Incl. Bowl Games)

Paul "Bear" Bryant 323
Glenn "Pop" Warner 319
Amos Alonzo Stagg 314
*Joe Paterno 257
*Bobby Bowden 239
Woody Hayes 238
Bo Schembechler 234
Jess Neely 207
*Tom Osborne 206
Warren Woodson 203
Eddie Anderson 201
Vince Dooley 201
*Hayden Fry 200
Dana Bible 198
Dan McGugin 197
*LaVell Edwards 197
Fielding Yost 196
Howard Jones 194
*Lou Holtz 193
John Vaught 190
*Jim Sweeney 186
John Heisman 185
Darrell Royal 184
Carl Snavely 180
Gil Dobie 180
Jerry Claiborne 179
Ben Schwartzwalder 178

Active coaches are denoted by an asterisk (*). Eddie Robinson of Grambling State Univ. holds the record for most college football victories with 388 at the start of the 1994 season.

National College Football Champions

The unofficial national champion as selected each year by the AP poll of writers and the USA Today-CNN (until 1992 the UPI) poll of coaches. When the polls disagree both teams are listed. The AP poll originated in 1936 and the UPI poll in 1950.

1936 Minnesota
1937 Pittsburgh
1938 Texas Christian
1939 Texas A&M
1940 Minnesota
1941 Minnesota
1942 Ohio State
1943 Notre Dame
1944 Army
1945 Army
1946 Notre Dame
1947 Notre Dame
1948 Michigan
1949 Notre Dame
1950 Oklahoma
1951 Tennessee
1952 Michigan State
1953 Maryland
1954 Ohio State, UCLA
1955 Oklahoma
1956 Oklahoma
1957 Auburn, Ohio State
1958 Louisiana State
1959 Syracuse
1960 Minnesota
1961 Alabama
1962 Southern Cal
1963 Texas
1964 Alabama
1965 Alabama, Mich. State
1966 Notre Dame
1967 Southern Cal
1968 Ohio State
1969 Texas
1970 Nebraska, Texas
1971 Nebraska
1972 Southern Cal
1973 Notre Dame, Alabama
1974 Oklahoma, Southern Cal
1975 Oklahoma
1976 Pittsburgh
1977 Notre Dame
1978 Alabama, Southern Cal
1979 Alabama
1980 Georgia
1981 Clemson
1982 Penn State
1983 Miami (FL)
1984 Brigham Young
1985 Oklahoma
1986 Penn State
1987 Miami (FL)
1988 Notre Dame
1989 Miami (FL)
1990 Colorado, Georgia Tech
1991 Miami (FL), Washington
1992 Alabama
1993 Florida St.

College Football Coach of the Year

The Division I-A Coach of the Year has been selected by the American Football Coaches Assn. since 1935 and selected by the Football Writers Assn. of America since 1957. When polls disagree, both winners are indicated.

1935 Lynn Waldorf, Northwestern
1936 Dick Harlow, Harvard
1937 Edward Mylin, Lafayette
1938 Bill Kern, Carnegie Tech
1939 Eddie Anderson, Iowa
1940 Clark Shaughnessy, Stanford
1941 Frank Leahy, Notre Dame
1942 Bill Alexander, Georgia Tech
1943 Amos Alonzo Stagg, Pacific
1944 Carroll Widdoes, Ohio St.
1945 Bo McMillin, Indiana
1946 Earl "Red" Blaik, Army
1947 Fritz Crisler, Michigan
1948 Bennie Oosterbaan, Michigan
1949 Bud Wilkinson, Oklahoma
1950 Charlie Caldwell, Princeton
1951 Chuck Taylor, Stanford
1952 Biggie Munn, Michigan St.
1953 Jim Tatum, Maryland
1954 Henry "Red" Sanders, UCLA
1955 Duffy Daugherty, Michigan St.
1956 Bowden Wyatt, Tennessee
1957 Woody Hayes, Ohio St.
1958 Paul Dietzel, LSU
1959 Ben Schwartzwalder, Syracuse
1960 Murray Warmath, Minnesota
1961 Paul "Bear" Bryant, Alabama (AFCA); Darrell Royal, Texas (FWAA)
1962 John McKay, USC
1963 Darrell Royal, Texas
1964 Ara Parseghian, Notre Dame, and Frank Broyles, Arkansas (AFCA); Ara Parseghian (FWAA)
1965 Tommy Prothro, UCLA (AFCA); Duffy Daugherty, Michigan St. (FWAA)
1966 Tom Cahill, Army
1967 John Pont, Indiana
1968 Joe Paterno, Penn St. (AFCA); Woody Hayes, Ohio St. (FWAA)
1969 Bo Schembechler, Michigan
1970 Charles McClendon, LSU, and Darrell Royal, Texas (AFCA); Alex Agase, Northwestern (FWAA)
1971 Paul "Bear" Bryant, Alabama (AFCA); Bob Devaney, Nebraska (FWAA)
1972 John McKay, USC
1973 Paul "Bear" Bryant, Alabama (AFCA); Johnny Majors, Pittsburgh (FWAA)
1974 Grant Teaff, Baylor
1975 Frank Kush, Arizona St. (AFCA); Woody Hayes, Ohio St. (FWAA)
1976 Johnny Majors, Pittsburgh
1977 Don James, Washington (AFCA); Lou Holtz, Arkansas (FWAA)
1978 Joe Paterno, Penn St.
1979 Earle Bruce, Ohio St.
1980 Vince Dooley, Georgia
1981 Danny Ford, Clemson
1982 Joe Paterno, Penn St.
1983 Ken Hatfield, Air Force (AFCA);

Howard Schnellenberger, Miami (FL) (FWAA)
1984 LaVell Edwards, Brigham Young
1985 Fisher De Berry, Air Force
1986 Joe Paterno, Penn St.
1987 Dick MacPherson, Syracuse
1988 Don Nehlen, W. Virginia (AFCA); Lou Holtz, Notre Dame (FWAA)
1989 Bill McCartney, Colorado
1990 Bobby Ross, Georgia Tech
1991 Don James, Washington
1992 Gene Stallings, Alabama
1993 Barry Alvarez, Wisconsin (AFCA); Terry Bowden, Auburn (FWAA)

Longest Division I-A Winning Streaks

(includes Bowl Games)

Wins	Team	Years	Ended by	Score
47	Oklahoma	1953-57	Notre Dame	7-0
39	Washington	1908-14	Oregon State	0-0
37	Yale	1890-93	Princeton	6-0
37	Yale	1887-89	Princeton	10-0
35	Toledo	1969-71	Tampa	21-0
34	Pennsylvania	1894-96	Lafayette	6-4
31	Oklahoma	1948-50	Kentucky	13-7
31	Pittsburgh	1914-18	Cleveland Naval Reserve	10-9
31	Pennsylvania	1896-98	Harvard	10-0
30	Texas	1968-70	Notre Dame	24-11
29	Miami (FL)	1990-93	Alabama	34-13
29	Michigan	1901-03	Minnesota	6-6
28	Alabama	1991-93	Tennessee	17-17
28	Alabama	1978-80	Mississippi State	6-3
28	Oklahoma	1973-75	Kansas	23-3
28	Michigan State	1950-53	Purdue	6-0

College Football Conference Champions

	Atlantic Coast	Ivy	Big Eight	Big Ten
1979	N. Carolina St.	Yale	Oklahoma	Ohio State
1980	North Carolina	Yale	Oklahoma	Michigan
1981	Clemson	Yale, Dartmouth	Nebraska	Iowa, Ohio State
1982	Clemson	Harvard, Dartmouth, Penn	Nebraska	Michigan
1983	Maryland	Harvard, Penn	Nebraska	Illinois
1984	Maryland	Penn	Nebraska, Oklahoma	Ohio State
1985	Maryland	Penn	Oklahoma	Iowa
1986	Clemson	Penn	Oklahoma	Michigan, Ohio State
1987	Clemson	Harvard	Oklahoma	Michigan St.
1988	Clemson	Penn, Cornell	Nebraska	Michigan
1989	Virginia, Duke	Yale, Princeton	Colorado	Michigan
1990	Georgia Tech	Dartmouth	Colorado	Iowa, Illinois, Michigan, Michigan St.
1991	Clemson	Dartmouth	Nebraska, Colorado	Michigan
1992	Florida St.	Dartmouth, Princeton	Nebraska	Michigan
1993	Florida St.	Penn	Nebraska	Ohio St., Wisconsin

	Mid-America	Southern	Southeastern	Southwest
1979	Central Michigan	Tenn.-Chattanooga	Alabama	Houston, Arkansas
1980	Central Michigan	Furman	Georgia	Baylor
1981	Toledo	Furman	Georgia, Alabama	SMU
1982	Bowling Green	Furman	Georgia	SMU
1983	Northern Illinois	Furman	Auburn	Texas
1984	Toledo	Tenn.-Chattanooga	Florida (title vacated)	SMU, Houston
1985	Bowling Green	Furman	Tennessee	Texas A&M
1986	Miami	Appalachian St.	LSU	Texas A&M
1987	E. Michigan	Appalachian St.	Auburn	Texas A&M
1988	W. Michigan	Marshall, Furman	Auburn, LSU	Arkansas
1989	Ball State	Furman	Alabama, Tennessee, Auburn	Arkansas
1990	Central Michigan	Furman	Tennessee	Texas
1991	Bowling Green	Appalachian St.	Florida	Texas A&M
1992	Bowling Green	Citadel	Alabama	Texas A&M
1993	Ball State	Georgia Southern	Florida, Auburn	Texas A&M

	Pacific Ten	Western Athletic	Big West
1979	USC	Brigham Young	San Jose St.
1980	Washington	Brigham Young	Long Beach State
1981	Washington	Brigham Young	San Jose State
1982	UCLA	Brigham Young	Fresno State
1983	UCLA	Brigham Young	Cal State-Fullerton
1984	USC	Brigham Young	Nevada-Las Vegas
1985	UCLA	Brigham Young, Air Force	Fresno State
1986	Arizona State	San Diego State	San Jose State
1987	UCLA, USC	Wyoming	San Jose State
1988	USC	Wyoming	Fresno State
1989	USC	Brigham Young	Fresno State
1990	Washington	Brigham Young	San Jose State
1991	Washington	Brigham Young	San Jose St., Fresno St.
1992	Washington, Stanford	Hawaii, Brigham Young, Fresno St.	Nevada-Reno
1993	UCLA	Wyoming, Fresno St., Brigham Young	Southwestern Louisiana, Utah St.

HOCKEY

National Hockey League, 1993–94

Final Standings

Eastern Conference

Northeast Division

	W	L	T	GF	GA	PTS
Pittsburgh . .	44	27	13	299	285	101
Boston	42	29	13	289	252	97
Montreal . . .	41	29	14	283	248	96
Buffalo	43	32	9	282	218	95
Quebec. . . .	34	42	8	277	292	76
Hartford. . . .	27	48	9	227	288	63
Ottawa	14	61	9	201	397	37

Atlantic Division

	W	L	T	GF	GA	PTS
N.Y. Rangers	52	24	8	299	231	112
New Jersey .	47	25	12	306	220	106
Washington .	39	35	10	277	263	88
N.Y. Islanders	36	36	12	282	264	84
Florida	33	34	17	233	233	83
Philadelphia	35	39	10	294	314	80
Tampa Bay .	30	43	11	224	251	71

Western Conference

Central Division

	W	L	T	GF	GA	PTS
Detroit	46	30	8	356	275	100
Toronto	43	29	12	280	243	98
Dallas	42	29	13	286	265	97
St. Louis. . . .	40	33	11	270	283	91
Chicago	39	36	9	254	240	87
Winnipeg . . .	24	51	9	245	344	57

Pacific Division

	W	L	T	GF	GA	PTS
Calgary	42	29	13	302	256	97
Vancouver . .	41	40	3	279	276	85
San Jose . . .	33	35	16	252	265	82
Anaheim . . .	33	46	5	229	251	71
Los Angeles .	27	45	12	294	322	66
Edmonton . .	25	45	14	261	305	64

Rangers Win Stanley Cup Championship

The New York Rangers won the 1994 Stanley Cup by defeating the Vancouver Canucks in the final game of the 7 game series. The win ended a drought of more than half a century, as the Rangers captured their first Stanley Cup championship since 1940. Rangers defenseman Brian Leetch won the Conn Smythe Trophy as the most valuable player in the playoffs.

Stanley Cup Playoff Results

Eastern Conference

N.Y. Rangers defeated N.Y. Islanders 4–0
Washington defeated Pittsburgh 4–2
New Jersey defeated Buffalo 4–3
Boston defeated Montreal 4–3
N.Y. Rangers defeated Washington 4–1
New Jersey defeated Boston 4–2
N.Y. Rangers defeated New Jersey 4–3

Western Conference

San Jose defeated Detroit 4–3
Vancouver defeated Calgary 4–3
Toronto defeated Chicago 4–2
Dallas defeated St. Louis 4–0
Toronto defeated San Jose 4–3
Vancouver defeated Dallas 4–1
Vancouver defeated Toronto 4–1

Finals

N.Y. Rangers defeated Vancouver 4–3

Stanley Cup Champions Since 1927

Year	Champion	Coach	Final opponent
1927	Ottawa	Dave Gill	Boston
1928	N.Y. Rangers	Lester Patrick	Montreal
1929	Boston	Cy Denneny	N.Y. Rangers
1930	Montreal	Cecil Hart	Boston
1931	Montreal	Cecil Hart	Chicago
1932	Toronto	Dick Irvin	N.Y. Rangers
1933	N.Y. Rangers	Lester Patrick	Toronto
1934	Chicago	Tommy Gorman	Detroit
1935	Montreal Maroons	Tommy Gorman	Toronto
1936	Detroit	Jack Adams	Toronto
1937	Detroit	Jack Adams	N.Y. Rangers
1938	Chicago	Bill Stewart	Toronto
1939	Boston	Art Ross	Toronto
1940	N.Y. Rangers	Frank Boucher	Toronto
1941	Boston	Cooney Weiland	Detroit
1942	Toronto	Hap Day	Detroit
1943	Detroit	Jack Adams	Boston
1944	Montreal	Dick Irvin	Chicago
1945	Toronto	Hap Day	Detroit
1946	Montreal	Dick Irvin	Boston
1947	Toronto	Hap Day	Montreal
1948	Toronto	Hap Day	Detroit
1949	Toronto	Hap Day	Detroit
1950	Detroit	Tommy Ivan	N.Y. Rangers
1951	Toronto	Joe Primeau	Montreal
1952	Detroit	Tommy Ivan	Montreal
1953	Montreal	Dick Irvin	Boston
1954	Detroit	Tommy Ivan	Montreal
1955	Detroit	Jimmy Skinner	Montreal
1956	Montreal	Toe Blake	Detroit
1957	Montreal	Toe Blake	Boston
1958	Montreal	Toe Blake	Boston
1959	Montreal	Toe Blake	Toronto
1960	Montreal	Toe Blake	Toronto
1961	Chicago	Rudy Pilous	Detroit
1962	Toronto	Punch Imlach	Chicago
1963	Toronto	Punch Imlach	Detroit
1964	Toronto	Punch Imlach	Detroit
1965	Montreal	Toe Blake	Chicago
1966	Montreal	Toe Blake	Detroit
1967	Toronto	Punch Imlach	Montreal
1968	Montreal	Toe Blake	St. Louis
1969	Montreal	Claude Ruel	St. Louis
1970	Boston	Harry Sinden	St. Louis
1971	Montreal	Al MacNeil	Chicago
1972	Boston	Tom Johnson	N.Y. Rangers
1973	Montreal	Scotty Bowman	Chicago
1974	Philadelphia	Fred Shero	Boston
1975	Philadelphia	Fred Shero	Buffalo
1976	Montreal	Scotty Bowman	Philadelphia
1977	Montreal	Scotty Bowman	Boston
1978	Montreal	Scotty Bowman	Boston
1979	Montreal	Scotty Bowman	N.Y. Rangers
1980	N.Y. Islanders	Al Arbour	Philadelphia
1981	N.Y. Islanders	Al Arbour	Minnesota
1982	N.Y. Islanders	Al Arbour	Vancouver
1983	N.Y. Islanders	Al Arbour	Edmonton
1984	Edmonton	Glen Sather	N.Y. Islanders
1985	Edmonton	Glen Sather	Philadelphia
1986	Montreal	Jean Perron	Calgary
1987	Edmonton	Glen Sather	Philadelphia
1988	Edmonton	Glen Sather	Boston
1989	Calgary	Terry Crisp	Montreal
1990	Edmonton	John Muckler	Boston
1991	Pittsburgh	Bob Johnson	Minnesota
1992	Pittsburgh	Scotty Bowman	Chicago
1993	Montreal	Jacques Demers	Los Angeles
1994	N.Y. Rangers	Mike Keenan	Vancouver

Individual Leaders

Points

Wayne Gretzky, Los Angeles, 130; Sergei Fedorov, Detroit, 120; Adam Oates, Boston, 112; Doug Gilmour, Toronto, 111; Pavel Bure, Vancouver, 107; Mark Recchi, Philadelphia, 107; Jeremy Roenick, Chicago, 107.

Goals

Pavel Bure, Vancouver, 60; Brett Hull, St. Louis, 57; Sergei Fedorov, Detroit, 56; Dave Andreychuk, Toronto, 53; Adam Graves, N.Y. Rangers, 52; Brendan Shanahan, St. Louis, 52; Ray Sheppard, Detroit, 52.

Assists

Wayne Gretzky, Los Angeles, 92; Doug Gilmour, Toronto, 84; Adam Oates, Boston, 80; Sergei Zubov, N.Y. Rangers, 77; Ray Bourque, Boston, 71.

Power-play goals

Pavel Bure, Vancouver, 25; Brett Hull, St.Louis, 25; Luc Robitaille, Los Angeles, 24; Jeremy Roenick, Chicago, 24; Keith Tkachuk, Winnipeg, 22.

Shorthanded goals

Brendan Shanahan, St. Louis, 7; 8 players tied with 5.

Shooting percentage

(minimum 84 shots)

Cam Neely, Boston, 27.0; Martin Straka, Pittsburgh, 23.1; Eric Lindros, Philadelphia, 22.3; Mike Ricci, Quebec, 21.7; Gary Roberts, Calgary, 20.3.

Plus/Minus

Scott Stevens, New Jersey, 53; Sergei Fedorov, Detroit, 48; Nicklas Lidstrom, Detroit, 43; Frank Musil, Calgary, 38; Gary Roberts, Calgary, 37.

GOALTENDING LEADERS

(minimum 27 games)

Goals against average

Dominik Hasek, Buffalo, 1.95; Martin Brodeur, New Jersey, 2.40; Patrick Roy, Montreal, 2.50; John Vanbiesbrouck, Florida, 2.53; Mike Richter, N.Y. Rangers, 2.57.

Wins

Mike Richter, N.Y. Rangers, 42; Ed Belfour, Chicago, 37; Curtis Joseph, St. Louis, 36; Patrick Roy, Montreal, 35; Felix Potvin, Toronto, 34.

Save percentage

Dominik Hasek, Buffalo, .930; John Vanbiesbrouck, Florida, .924; Patrick Roy, Montreal, .918; Martin Brodeur, New Jersey, .915; Mark Fitzpatrick, Florida, .914.

Shutouts

Ed Belfour, Chicago, 7; Dominik Hasek, Buffalo, 7; Patrick Roy, Montreal, 7; Ron Hextall, N.Y. Islanders, 5; Mike Richter, N.Y. Rangers, 5.

Individual Scoring

(40 or more games played)

Mighty Ducks of Anaheim

	GP	G	A	Pts	PIM	+/-
Terry Yake	82	21	31	52	44	2
Bob Corkum	76	23	28	51	18	4
Garry Valk	78	18	27	45	100	8
Tim Sweeney	78	16	27	43	49	3
Bill Houlder	80	14	25	39	40	18–
Joe Sacco	84	19	18	37	61	11–
Peter Douris	74	12	22	34	21	5–
Shaun Van Allen	80	8	25	33	64	0
Anatoli Semenov	49	11	19	30	12	4–
Sean Hill	68	7	20	27	78	12–
Stephan Lebeau	56	15	11	26	22	4–
Patrik Carnback	73	12	11	23	54	8–
Bobby Dollas	77	9	11	20	55	20
David Williams	56	5	15	20	42	8
Troy Loney	62	13	6	19	88	5–
Todd Ewen	76	9	9	18	272	7–
Randy Ladouceur	81	1	9	10	74	7
Mark Ferner	50	3	5	8	30	16–
Stu Grimson	77	1	5	6	199	6–
Guy Hebert	52	0	0	0	2	0

Coach—Ron Wilson

Boston Bruins

	GP	G	A	Pts	PIM	+/-
Adam Oates	77	32	80	112	45	10
Ray Bourque	72	20	71	91	58	26
Cam Neely	49	50	24	74	54	12
Al Iafrate	79	15	43	58	163	16
Glen Wesley	81	14	44	58	64	1
Ted Donato	84	22	32	54	59	0
Bryan Smolinksi	83	31	20	51	82	4
Glen Murray	81	18	13	31	48	1–
Brent Hughes	77	13	11	24	143	10
Jozef Stumpel	59	8	15	23	14	4
Dave Reid	83	6	17	23	25	10
Stephen Heinze	77	10	11	21	32	2–
Don Sweeney	75	6	15	21	50	29
Stephen Leach	42	5	10	15	74	10–
Paul Stanton	71	3	7	10	54	7–
David Shaw	55	1	9	10	85	11–
Cameron Stewart	57	3	6	9	66	6–
Glen Featherstone	58	1	8	9	152	5–
Gordie Roberts	59	1	6	7	40	13–
Jon Casey	57	0	2	2	14	0

Coach—Brian Sutter

Buffalo Sabres

	GP	G	A	Pts	PIM	+/-
Dale Hawerchuk	81	35	51	86	91	10
Alexander Mogilny	66	32	47	79	22	8
Donald Audette	77	29	30	29	41	2
Yuri Khmylev	72	27	31	58	49	13
Derek Plante	77	21	35	56	24	4
Brad May	84	18	27	45	171	6–
Richard Smehlik	84	14	27	41	69	22
Doug Bodger	75	7	32	39	76	8
Randy Wood	84	22	16	39	71	11
Wayn Presley	65	17	8	25	103	18
Bob Sweeney	60	11	14	25	94	3
Ken Sutton	78	4	20	24	71	6–
Dave Hannan	83	6	15	21	53	10
Petr Svoboda	60	2	14	16	89	11
Craig Muni	82	2	12	14	66	31
Randy Moller	78	2	11	13	154	5–
Rob Ray	82	3	4	7	274	2
Dominik Hasek	58	0	3	3	6	0

Coach—John Muckler

Calgary Flames

	GP	G	A	Pts	PIM	+/-
Robert Reichel	84	40	53	93	58	20
Theoren Fleury	83	40	45	85	186	30
Gary Roberts	73	41	43	84	145	37
Al MacInnis	75	28	54	82	95	35
Joe Nieuwendyk	64	36	39	75	51	19
Michael Nylander	73	13	42	55	30	8
Zarley Zalapski	69	10	37	47	74	6–
German Titov	76	27	18	45	28	20
Wes Walz	53	11	27	38	16	20
James Patrick	68	10	25	35	40	5–
Kelly Kisio	51	7	23	30	28	6–
Ronnie Stern	71	9	20	29	243	6
Joel Otto	81	11	12	23	92	17–
Michel Petit	63	2	21	23	110	5
Dan Keczmer	69	1	21	22	60	8–
Trent Yamney	58	6	15	21	60	21
Chris Dahlquist	77	1	11	12	52	5
Paul Kruse	68	3	8	11	185	6–
Sandy McCarthy	79	5	5	10	173	3–
Mike Sullivan	45	4	5	9	10	1–
Frank Musil	75	1	8	9	50	38
Mike Vernon	48	0	0	0	14	0

Coach—Dave King

Chicago Blackhawks

	GP	G	A	Pts	PIM	+/-
Jeremy Roenick	84	46	61	107	125	21
Joe Murphy	81	31	39	70	111	1
Chris Chelios	76	16	44	60	212	12
Tony Amonte	79	17	25	42	37	0
Brent Sutter	73	9	29	38	43	17
Paul Ysebaert	71	14	21	35	26	7–
Dirk Graham	67	15	18	33	45	13
Michel Goulet	56	16	14	30	26	1
Christian Ruuttu	54	9	20	29	68	4–
Patrick Poulin	67	14	14	28	51	8–

Eric Weinrich	62	4	24	28	35	1
Steve Smith	57	5	22	27	174	5–
Rich Sutter	83	12	14	26	108	8–
Randy Cunneyworth	79	13	11	24	100	1–
Gary Suter	41	6	12	18	38	12–
Jeff Shantz	52	3	13	16	30	14–
Neil Wilkinson	72	3	9	12	114	2
Cam Russell	67	1	7	8	200	10
Darin Kimble	65	4	2	6	133	2
Robert Dirk	71	2	3	5	131	18
Ed Belfour	70	0	4	4	61	0
Greg Smyth	61	1	1	2	183	4–

Coach—Darryl Sutter

Dallas Stars

	GP	G	A	Pts	PIM	+/-
Mike Modano	76	50	43	93	54	8–
Russ Courtnall	84	23	57	80	59	6
Dave Gagner	76	32	29	61	83	13
Neal Broten	79	17	35	52	62	10
Grant Ledyard	84	9	37	46	42	7
Paul Cavallini	74	11	33	44	82	13
Dean Evason	80	11	33	44	66	12–
Trent Klatt	61	14	24	38	30	13
Mike Craig	72	13	24	37	139	14–
Mike McPhee	79	20	15	35	36	8
Brent Gilchrist	76	17	14	31	31	0
Derian Hatcher	83	12	19	31	211	19
Paul Broten	64	12	12	24	30	18
Mike Tinordi	61	6	18	24	143	6
Pelle Eklund	53	3	17	20	10	2–
Craig Ludwig	84	1	13	14	123	1–
Shane Churla	69	6	7	13	333	8–
Alan May	51	5	7	12	115	3–
Doug Zmolek	75	1	4	5	133	8–
Andy Moog	55	0	1	1	16	0

Coach—Bob Gainey

Detroit Red Wings

	GP	G	A	Pts	PIM	+/-
Sergei Fedorov	82	56	64	120	34	48
Ray Sheppard	82	52	41	93	26	13
Steve Yzerman	58	24	58	82	36	11
Paul Coffey	80	14	63	77	106	28
Vyacheslav Kozlov	77	34	39	73	50	27
Keith Primeau	78	31	42	73	173	34
Dino Ciccarelli	66	28	29	57	73	10
Nicklas Lidstrom	84	10	46	56	26	43
Steve Chiasson	82	13	33	46	122	17
Vladimir Konstantinov	80	12	21	33	138	30
Mike Sillinger	62	8	21	29	10	2
Darren McCarty	67	9	17	26	181	12
Mark Howe	44	4	20	24	8	16
Shawn Burr	51	10	12	22	31	12
Bob Probert	66	7	10	17	275	1–
Greg Johnson	52	6	11	17	22	7–
Martin Lapointe	50	8	8	16	55	7
Sheldon Kennedy	61	6	7	13	30	2–
Micah Aivazoff	59	4	4	8	38	1–
Terry Carkner	68	1	6	7	130	13
Sergei Bautin	60	0	7	7	78	12–
Bob Essensa	69	0	2	2	6	0

Coach—Scotty Bowman

Edmonton Oilers

	GP	G	A	Pts	PIM	+/-
Doug Weight	84	24	50	74	47	22–
Jason Arnott	78	33	35	68	104	1
Zdeno Ciger	84	22	35	57	8	11–
Shayne Corson	64	25	29	54	118	8–
Igor Kravchuk	81	12	38	50	16	12–
Bob Beers	82	11	32	43	86	22–
Scott Pearson	72	19	18	37	165	4–
Fredrik Olausson	73	11	24	35	30	7–
Steven Rice	63	17	15	32	36	10–
Boris Mironov	79	7	24	31	110	33–
Ilya Byakin	44	8	20	28	30	3–
Dean McAmmond	45	6	21	27	16	12
Mike Stapleton	81	12	13	25	46	5–
Kelly Buchberger	84	3	18	21	199	20–
Kirk Maltby	68	11	8	19	74	2–
Vladimir Vujtek	40	4	15	19	14	7–
Scot Thornton	61	4	7	11	104	15–
Louie DeBrusk	48	4	6	10	185	9–
Adam Bennett	48	3	6	9	49	8–
Luke Richardson	69	2	6	8	131	13–

Coach—George Burnett

Florida Panthers

	GP	G	A	Pts	PIM	+/-
Bob Kudelski	86	40	30	70	24	33–
Scott Mellanby	80	30	30	60	149	0
Jesse Belanger	70	17	33	50	16	4–
Stu Barnes	77	23	24	47	38	4
Andrei Lomakin	76	19	28	47	26	1
Gord Murphy	84	14	29	43	71	11–
Brian Skrudland	79	15	25	40	136	13
Dave Lowry	80	15	22	37	64	4–
Tom Fitzgerald	83	18	14	32	54	3–
Brian Benning	73	6	24	30	107	7–
Mike Hough	78	6	23	29	62	3
Jody Hull	69	13	13	26	8	6
Rob Niedermayer	65	9	17	26	51	11–
Bill Lindsay	84	6	6	12	97	2–
Keith Brown	51	4	8	12	60	11
Brent Severyn	67	4	7	11	156	1–
Joe Cirella	63	1	9	10	99	8
Mike Foligno	43	4	5	9	53	7
Geoff Smith	77	1	8	9	50	13–
Jeff Daniels	70	3	5	8	20	1–
John Vanbiesbrouck	57	0	0	0	38	0

Coach—Roger Neilson

Hartford Whalers

	GP	G	A	Pts	PIM	+/-
Pat Verbeek	84	37	38	75	177	15–
Geoff Sanderson	82	41	26	67	42	13–
Andrew Cassels	79	16	42	58	37	21–
Robert Kron	77	24	26	50	8	0
Chris Pronger	81	5	25	30	113	3–
Brian Propp	65	12	17	29	44	3
Jocelyn Lemieux	82	18	9	27	82	3–
Paul Ranheim	82	10	17	27	22	18–
Alexander Godynyuk	69	3	19	22	75	13
Frantisek Kucera	76	5	16	21	48	3–
Ted Drury	50	6	12	18	36	15–
Adam Burt	63	1	17	18	75	4–
Jim Storm	68	6	10	16	27	4
Bryan Marchment	55	4	11	15	166	14–
Mark Janssens	84	2	10	12	137	13–
Brad McCrimmon	65	1	5	6	72	7–
Marc Potvin	54	2	3	5	272	8–

Coach—Paul Holmgren

Los Angeles Kings

	GP	G	A	Pts	PIM	+/-
Wayne Gretzky	81	38	92	130	20	25–
Luc Robitaille	83	44	42	86	86	20–
Jark Kurri	81	31	46	77	48	24–
Rob Blake	84	20	48	68	137	7–
Alexei Zhitnik	81	12	40	52	101	11–
Mike Donnelly	81	21	21	42	34	2
Darryl Sydor	84	8	27	35	94	9–
John Druce	55	14	17	31	50	16
Marty McSorley	65	7	24	31	194	12–
Pat Conacher	77	15	13	28	71	0
Kevin Todd	47	8	14	22	24	3–
Tony Granato	50	7	14	21	150	2–
Warren Rychel	80	10	9	19	322	19–
Charlie Huddy	79	5	13	18	71	4
Dixon Ward	67	12	3	15	82	22–
Tim Watters	60	1	9	10	67	11–
Donald Dufresne	60	2	6	8	58	7–
Doug Houda	61	2	6	8	188	19–
Gary Shuchuk	56	3	4	7	30	8–
Jim Paek	59	1	5	6	18	8–
Kelly Hrudey	64	0	1	1	6	0

Coach—Barry Melrose

Montreal Canadiens

	GP	G	A	Pts	PIM	+/-
Vincent Damphousse	84	40	51	91	75	0
Brian Bellows	77	33	38	71	36	9
Kirk Muller	76	23	34	57	96	1–
Matt Schneider	75	20	32	52	62	15
Mike Keane	80	16	30	46	119	6
Gilbert Dionne	74	19	26	45	31	9–
John LeClair	74	19	24	43	32	17
Lyle Odelein	79	11	29	40	276	8
Guy Carbonneau	79	14	24	38	48	16
Eric Desjardins	84	12	23	35	97	1–
Paul Di Pietro	70	13	20	33	37	2–

Benoit Brunet	71	10	20	30	20	14
Oleg Petrov.	55	12	15	27	2	7
Patrice Brisebois . . .	53	2	21	23	63	5
Ed Ronan	61	6	8	14	42	3
Peter Popovic	47	2	12	14	26	10
J.J. Daigneault.	68	2	12	14	73	16
Kevin Haller.	68	4	9	13	118	3
Ron Wilson	48	2	10	12	12	2–
Pierre Sevigny.	43	4	5	9	42	6
Patrick Roy	68	0	1	1	30	0

Coach—Jacques Demers

New Jersey Devils

	GP	G	A	Pts	PIM	+/–
Scott Stevens . . .	83	18	60	78	112	53
Stephane Richer .	80	36	36	72	16	31
John MacLean. . .	80	37	33	70	95	30
Valeri Zelepukin. .	82	26	31	57	70	36
Corey Millen	78	20	30	50	52	24
Bernie Nicholls. . .	61	19	27	46	86	24
Scott Niedermayer	81	10	36	46	42	34
Bill Guerin	81	25	19	44	101	14
Claude Lemieux. .	79	18	26	44	86	13
Tom Chorske. . . .	76	21	20	41	32	14
Bobby Holik.	70	13	20	33	72	28
Bob Carpenter. . .	76	10	23	33	51	7
Bruce Driver	66	8	24	32	63	29
Alexander Semak	54	12	17	29	22	6
Randy McKay . . .	78	12	15	27	244	24
Mike Peluso.	69	4	16	20	238	19
Tommy Albelin. . .	62	2	17	19	36	20
Jaroslav Modry . .	41	2	15	17	18	10
Viacheslav Fetisov	52	1	14	15	30	14
Ken Daneyko. . . .	78	1	9	10	176	27
Jason Smith	41	0	5	5	43	7
Chris Terreri	44	0	2	2	4	0
Martin Brodeur. . .	47	0	0	0	2	0

Coach—Jacques Lemaire

New York Islanders

	GP	G	A	Pts	PIM	+/–
Pierre Turgeon . . .	69	38	56	94	18	14
Steve Thomas . . .	78	42	33	75	139	9–
Derek King	78	30	40	70	59	18
Benoit Hogue	83	36	33	69	73	7–
Vladimir Malakhov .	76	10	47	57	80	29
Marty McInnis	81	25	31	56	24	31
Ray Ferraro.	82	21	32	53	83	1
Patrick Flatley	64	12	30	42	40	12
Travis Green	83	18	22	40	44	16
Tom Kurvers	66	9	31	40	47	7
Brad Dalgarno	73	11	19	30	62	14
Uwe Krupp	41	7	14	21	30	11
Scott Lachance . . .	74	3	11	14	70	5–
Dennis Vaske	65	2	11	13	76	21
Darius Kasparaitis .	76	1	10	11	142	6–
Keith Acton	77	2	7	9	71	5–
David Maley	56	0	6	6	104	7–
Mick Vukota.	72	3	1	4	237	5–
Ron Hextall	65	0	3	3	52	0

Coach—Lorne Henning

New York Rangers

	GP	G	A	Pts	PIM	+/–
Sergei Zubov	78	12	77	89	39	20
Mark Messier	76	26	58	84	76	25
Adam Graves	84	52	27	79	127	27
Brian Leetch	84	23	56	79	67	28
Steve Larmer	68	21	39	60	41	14
Alexei Kovalev	76	23	33	56	154	18
Esa Tikkanen	83	22	32	54	114	5
Sergei Nemchinov. .	76	22	27	49	36	13
Glenn Anderson . . .	85	21	20	41	62	5–
Brian Noonan	76	18	23	41	69	7
Stephane Matteau. .	77	19	19	38	57	15
Craig MacTavish. . .	78	20	13	33	91	14–
Kevin Lowe.	71	5	14	19	70	4
Alexander Karpovtsev	67	3	15	18	58	12
Jeff Beukeboom . . .	68	8	8	16	170	18
Greg Gilbert	76	4	11	15	29	3–
Mike Hudson.	48	4	7	11	47	5–
Jay Wells	79	2	7	9	110	4
Nick Kypreos	56	3	5	8	139	16–
Joey Kocur	71	2	1	3	129	9–
Mike Richter	68	0	0	0	2	0

Coach—Mike Keenan

Ottawa Senators

	GP	G	A	Pts	PIM	+/–
Alexei Yashin	83	30	49	79	22	49–
Alexandre Daigle. . . .	84	20	31	51	40	45–
Dave McLlwain	66	17	26	43	48	40–
Sylvain Turgeon	47	11	15	26	52	25–
Troy Mallette.	82	7	16	23	166	33–
Brad Shaw	66	4	19	23	59	41–
Norm Maciver	53	3	20	23	26	26–
Gord Dineen	77	0	21	21	89	52–
Evgeny Davydov	61	7	13	20	46	9–
Andrew McBain.	55	11	8	19	64	41–
Scot Levins.	62	8	11	19	162	26–
Vladimir Ruzicka	42	5	13	18	14	21–
Kerry Huffman.	62	4	14	18	40	28–
Darren Rumble	70	6	9	15	116	50–
Dennis Vial	55	2	5	7	214	9–
Bill Huard	63	2	2	4	162	19–
Claude Boivin	41	2	1	3	95	17–
Darcy Loewen.	44	0	3	3	52	11–
Craig Billington	63	0	0	0	8	0

Coach—Rick Bowness

Philadelphia Flyers

	GP	G	A	Pts	PIM	+/–
Mark Recchi	84	40	67	107	46	2–
Eric Lindros.	65	44	53	97	103	16
Rod Brind'Amour . .	84	35	62	97	85	9–
Mikael Renberg . . .	83	38	44	82	36	8
Garry Galley	81	10	60	70	91	11–
Yves Racine	67	9	43	52	48	11–
Josef Beranek	80	28	21	49	85	2–
Kevin Dineen.	71	19	23	42	113	9–
Brent Fedyk	72	20	18	38	74	14–
Mark Lamb	85	12	24	36	72	44–
Dimitri Yushkevich .	75	5	25	30	86	8–
Rob DiMaio	53	11	12	23	46	4–
Dave Tippett	73	4	11	15	38	20–
Jeff Finley.	55	1	8	9	24	16
Allan Conroy	62	4	3	7	65	12–
Rob Zettler	75	0	7	7	134	26–
Jason Bowen	56	1	5	6	87	12
Dave Brown	71	1	4	5	137	12–
Ryan McGill	50	1	3	4	112	5–
Stewart Malgunas .	67	1	3	4	86	2
Dominic Roussel . .	60	0	1	1	4	0

Coach—Terry Murray

Pittsburgh Penguins

	GP	G	A	Pts	PIM	+/–
Jaromir Jagr	80	32	67	99	61	15
Ron Francis	82	27	66	93	62	3–
Kevin Stevens. . . .	83	41	47	88	155	24–
Larry Murphy.	84	17	56	73	44	10
Joe Mullen	84	38	32	70	41	9
Martin Straka.	84	30	34	64	24	24
Tomas Sandstrom .	78	23	35	58	83	7–
Doug Brown	77	18	37	55	18	19
Shawn McEachern.	76	20	22	42	34	14
Rick Tocchet.	51	14	26	40	134	15–
Mario Lemieux. . . .	22	17	20	37	32	2–
Greg Hawgood . . .	64	6	28	34	36	9
Ulf Samuelsson. . .	80	5	24	29	199	23
Bryan Trottier	41	4	11	15	36	12–
Peter Taglianetti . .	60	2	12	14	142	5
Kjell Samuelsson. .	59	5	8	13	118	18
Markus Naslund . .	71	4	7	11	27	3–
Jim McKenzie	71	3	5	8	146	7–
Grant Jennings . . .	61	2	4	6	126	10–
Mike Ramsey	65	2	2	4	22	4–
Ken Wregget.	42	0	1	1	8	0
Tom Barrasso	44	0	1	1	42	0

Coach—Eddie Johnston

Quebec Nordiques

	GP	G	A	Pts	PIM	+/–
Joe Sakic	84	28	64	92	18	8–
Mats Sundin	84	32	53	85	60	1
Valeri Kamensky . .	76	28	37	65	42	12
Mike Ricci	83	30	21	51	113	9–
Scott Young	76	26	25	51	14	4–
Ron Sutter	73	15	25	40	90	2
Iain Fraser	60	17	20	37	23	5–
Andrei Kovalenko .	58	16	17	33	46	5–
Martin Rucinsky. . .	60	9	23	32	58	4
Bob Bassen	83	13	15	28	99	17–

	GP	G	A	Pts	PIM	+/-
Claude Lapointe . .	59	11	17	28	70	2
Alexei Gusarov . . .	76	5	20	25	38	3
Curtis Leschyshyn .	72	5	17	22	65	2–
Garth Butcher	77	4	15	19	143	7–
Dave Karpa.	60	5	12	17	148	0
Steven Finn.	80	4	13	17	159	9–
Craig Wolanin	63	6	10	16	80	16
Mike McKee	48	3	12	15	41	5
Adam Foote	45	2	6	8	67	3
Paul MacDermid . .	44	2	3	5	35	3–
Tony Twist.	49	0	4	4	101	1–
Stephane Fiset . . .	50	0	3	3	8	0

Coach—Marc Crawford

St. Louis Blues

	GP	G	A	Pts	PIM	+/-
Brendan Shanahan .	81	52	50	102	211	9–
Brett Hull.	81	57	40	97	38	3–
Craig Janney.	69	16	68	84	24	14–
Kevin Miller	75	23	25	48	83	6
Vitali Prokhorov	55	15	10	25	20	6–
Philippe Bozon	80	9	16	25	42	4
Alexei Kasatonov. . .	63	4	20	24	62	3–
Vitali Karamnov	59	9	12	21	51	3–
Jim Montgomery . . .	67	6	14	20	44	1–
Igor Korolev.	73	6	10	16	40	12–
Murray Baron.	77	5	9	14	123	14–
Rick Zombo.	74	2	8	10	85	15–
Doug Crossman. . . .	50	2	7	9	10	1
Tom Tilley	48	1	7	8	32	3
Kelly Chae.	68	2	5	7	278	5–
Basil McRae	40	1	2	3	103	7–
Curtis Joseph	71	0	3	3	4	0

Coach—Bob Berry

San Jose Sharks

	GP	G	A	Pts	PIM	+/-
Ulf Dahlen.	78	25	44	69	10	1–
Sergei Makarov .	80	30	38	68	78	11
Todd Elik.	79	25	41	66	95	3–
Sandis Ozolinsh.	81	26	38	64	24	16
Igor Larionov	60	18	38	56	40	20
Pat Falloon	83	22	31	53	18	3–
Johan Garpenlov	80	18	35	53	28	9
Ray Whitney . . .	61	14	26	40	14	2
Jeff Norton	64	7	33	40	36	16
Rob Gaudreau. .	84	15	20	35	28	10–
Bob Errey	64	12	18	30	126	11–
Gaetan Duchesne	84	12	18	30	28	8
Tom Pederson. .	74	6	19	25	31	3
Viacheslav Butsayev	59	12	11	23	68	0
Jeff Odgers	81	13	8	21	222	13–
Jamie Baker . . .	65	12	5	17	38	2
Mike Rathje	47	1	9	10	59	9–
Dale Craigwell . .	58	3	6	9	16	13–
Jay More.	49	1	6	7	63	5–
Arturs Irbe	74	0	2	2	16	0

Coach—Kevin Constantine

Tampa Bay Lightning

	GP	G	A	Pts	PIM	+/-
Brian Bradley . .	78	24	40	64	56	8–
Petr Klima	75	28	27	55	76	15–
Denis Savard. . .	74	18	28	46	106	1–
Danton Cole . . .	81	20	23	43	32	7
Chris Gratton. . .	84	13	29	42	123	25–
John Tucker. . . .	66	17	23	40	28	9
Shawn Chambers	66	11	23	34	23	6–
Chris Joseph . . .	76	11	20	31	136	21–
Pat Elynuik.	67	13	15	28	64	21–
Mikael Andersson	76	13	12	25	23	8
Roman Hamrlik .	64	3	18	21	135	14–
Adam Creighton.	53	10	10	20	37	7–
Marc Bergevin . .	83	1	15	16	87	5–
Marc Bureau . . .	75	8	7	15	30	9–
Gerard Gallant. .	51	4	9	13	74	6–
Rob Zamuner . .	59	6	6	12	42	9–
Rudy Poeschek .	71	3	6	9	118	3
Enrico Ciccone .	57	1	2	3	226	4–
Daren Puppa. . .	63	0	1	1	2	0

Coach—Terry Crisp

Toronto Maple Leafs

	GP	G	A	Pts	PIM	+/-
Doug Gilmour	83	27	84	111	105	25
Dave Andreychuk .	83	53	45	98	98	22
Wendel Clark.	64	46	30	76	115	10
Mike Gartner.	81	34	30	64	62	20
Dave Ellett	68	7	36	43	42	6
Dmitri Mironov. . . .	76	9	27	36	78	5
Nikolai Borschevsky	45	14	21	35	10	6
John Cullen.	53	13	17	30	64	2–
Rob Pearson.	67	12	18	30	189	6–
Jamie Macoun. . . .	82	3	27	30	115	5–
Todd Gill.	45	4	23	27	44	8
Mark Osborne	73	9	16	25	145	2
Bill Berg	83	8	11	19	93	3–
Mike Eastwood . . .	54	8	10	18	28	2
Peter Zezel	41	8	8	16	19	5
Kent Manderville . .	67	7	9	16	63	5
Bob Rouse	63	5	11	16	101	8
Mark Greig	44	6	7	13	41	5–
Mike Krushelnyski .	54	5	6	11	28	5–
Sylvain Lefebvre . .	84	2	9	11	79	33
Drake Berehowsky.	49	2	8	10	63	3–
Ken Baumgartner .	64	4	4	8	185	6–
Felix Potvin	66	0	4	4	4	0

Coach—Pat Burns

Vancouver Canucks

	GP	G	A	Pts	PIM	+/-
Pavel Bure	76	60	47	107	86	1
Geoff Courtnall .	82	26	44	70	123	15
Cliff Ronning . . .	76	25	43	68	42	7
Jeff Brown.	74	14	52	66	56	11–
Trevor Linden . .	84	32	29	61	73	6
Murray Craven .	78	15	40	55	30	5
Jyrki Lumme . . .	83	13	42	55	50	3
Jiri Slegr	78	5	33	38	86	0
Greg Adams	68	13	24	37	20	1–
Dave Babych. . .	73	4	28	32	52	0
Gino Odjick	76	16	13	29	271	13
Martin Gelinas . .	64	14	14	28	34	8–
Jimmy Carson . .	59	11	17	28	24	15–
Sergio Momesso	68	14	13	27	149	2–
Dana Murzyn. . .	80	6	14	20	109	4
Brian Glynn. . . .	64	2	13	15	53	19–
Bret Hedican . . .	69	0	12	12	64	7–
Gerald Diduck . .	55	1	10	11	72	2
Adrien Plavsic . .	47	1	9	10	6	5–
John McIntyre . .	62	3	6	9	38	9–
Nathan LaFayette	49	3	4	7	18	7–
Tim Hunter	56	3	4	7	171	7–
Kirk McLean . . .	52	0	4	4	2	0
Shawn Antoski .	55	1	2	3	190	11–

Coach—Pat Quinn

Washington Capitals

	GP	G	A	Pts	PIM	+/-
Joe Juneau	74	19	66	85	41	11
Mike Ridley	81	26	44	70	24	15
Dimitri Khristich .	83	29	29	58	73	2–
Sylvain Cote . . .	84	16	35	51	66	30
Michal Pivonka .	82	14	36	50	38	2
Peter Bondra. . .	69	24	19	43	40	22
Randy Burridge .	78	25	17	42	73	1–
Calle Johansson	84	9	33	42	59	3
Kevin Hatcher . .	72	16	24	40	108	13–
Kelly Miller	84	14	25	39	32	8
Dale Hunter. . . .	52	9	29	38	131	4–
Keith Jones. . . .	68	16	19	35	149	4
Todd Krygier . . .	66	12	18	30	60	4–
Pat Peake.	49	11	18	29	39	1
Steve Konowalchuk	62	12	14	26	33	9
Dave Poulin . . .	63	6	19	25	52	1–
Joe Reekie	85	1	16	17	156	15
John Slaney . . .	47	7	9	16	27	3
Craig Berube. . .	84	7	7	14	305	4–
Tim Bergland. . .	54	6	5	11	10	15–
Shawn Anderson	50	0	9	9	12	1–
Jim Johnson . . .	61	0	7	7	63	7–
Don Beaupre. . .	53	0	1	1	16	0

Coach—Jim Schoenfeld

Winnipeg Jets

	GP	G	A	Pts	PIM	+/-
Keith Tkachuk . .	84	41	40	81	255	12–
Nelson Emerson .	83	33	41	74	80	38–
Alexei Zhamnov.	61	26	45	71	62	20–
Darrin Shannon.	77	21	37	58	87	18–
Teemu Selanne.	51	25	29	54	22	23–
Thomas Steen. .	76	19	32	51	32	38–
Dallas Drake . . .	62	13	27	40	49	1–

	GP	G	A	Pts	PIM	+/-
Stephane Quintal	81	8	18	26	119	25–
Teppo Numminen	57	5	18	23	28	23–
Dave Manson . .	70	4	17	21	191	14–
Tie Domi	81	8	11	19	347	8–
Luciano Borsato.	75	5	13	18	28	11–
Igor Ulanov	74	0	17	17	165	11–
Wayne McBean .	50	3	13	16	40	34–
Randy Gilhen . .	60	7	7	14	50	12–
Mike Eagles . . .	73	4	8	12	96	20–
Kris King.	83	4	8	12	205	22–
Dean Kennedy .	76	2	8	10	164	22–
Tim Cheveldae .	44	0	1	1	2	0

Coach—John Paddock

Individual Goaltending

(top goalie for each team by games played)

Player	GP	GAA	W	L	T	SO	SV%
Hebert, Ana.	52	2.83	20	27	3	2	.907
Casey, Bos.	57	2.88	30	15	9	4	.881
Hasek, Buf..	58	1.95	30	20	6	7	.930
Vernon, Cgy..	48	2.81	26	17	5	3	.892
Belfour, Chi.	70	2.67	37	24	6	7	.906
Moog, Dal.	55	3.27	24	20	7	2	.894
Osgood, Det.	41	2.86	23	8	5	2	.895
Ranford, Edm.	71	3.48	22	34	11	1	.898
Vanbiesbrouck, Fla.	57	2.53	21	25	11	1	.924
Burke, Hfd.	47	2.99	17	24	5	2	.906
Hrudey, L.A.	64	3.68	22	31	7	1	.897
Roy, Mon..	68	2.50	35	17	11	7	.918
Brodeur, N.J.	47	2.40	27	11	8	3	.915
Hextall, N.Y.I. . .	65	3.08	27	26	6	5	.898
Richter, N.Y.R. .	68	2.57	42	12	6	5	.910
Billington, Ott. . . .	63	4.59	11	41	4	0	.859
Roussel, Phila. .	60	3.34	29	20	5	1	.896
Barrasso, Pitts. .	44	3.36	22	15	5	2	.893
Fiset, Que.	50	3.39	20	25	4	2	.890
Joseph, St.L.. . . .	71	3.10	36	23	11	1	.911
Irbe, S.J..	74	2.84	30	28	16	3	.899
Puppa, T.B.	63	2.71	22	33	6	4	.899
Potvin, Tor..	66	2.89	34	22	9	3	.907
McLean, Van. . .	52	2.99	23	26	3	3	.891
Beaupre, Wash.	53	2.84	24	16	8	2	.880
Essensa, Winn.	56	3.85	19	30	6	1	.883

Ross Trophy (Leading Scorer)

1927 Bill Cook, N.Y. Rangers
1928 Howie Morenz, Montreal
1929 Ace Bailey, Toronto
1930 Cooney Weiland, Boston
1931 Howie Morenz, Montreal
1932 Harvey Jackson, Toronto
1933 Bill Cook, N.Y. Rangers
1934 Charlie Conacher, Toronto
1935 Charlie Conacher, Toronto
1936 Dave Schriner, N.Y. Americans
1937 Dave Schriner, N.Y. Americans
1938 Gordie Drillon, Toronto
1939 Toe Blake, Montreal
1940 Milt Schmidt, Boston
1941 Bill Cowley, Boston
1942 Bryan Hextall, N.Y. Rangers
1943 Doug Bentley, Chicago
1944 Herbie Cain, Boston
1945 Elmer Lach, Montreal
1946 Max Bentley, Chicago
1947 Max Bentley, Chicago
1948 Elmer Lach, Montreal
1949 Roy Conacher, Chicago
1950 Ted Lindsay, Detroit
1951 Gordie Howe, Detroit
1952 Gordie Howe, Detroit
1953 Gordie Howe, Detroit
1954 Gordie Howe, Detroit
1955 Bernie Geoffrion, Montreal
1956 Jean Beliveau, Montreal
1957 Gordie Howe, Detroit
1958 Dickie Moore, Montreal
1959 Dickie Moore, Montreal
1960 Bobby Hull, Chicago
1961 Bernie Geoffrion, Montreal
1962 Bobby Hull, Chicago
1963 Gordie Howe, Detroit
1964 Stan Mikita, Chicago
1965 Stan Mikita, Chicago
1966 Bobby Hull, Chicago
1967 Stan Mikita, Chicago
1968 Stan Mikita, Chicago
1969 Phil Esposito, Boston
1970 Bobby Orr, Boston
1971 Phil Esposito, Boston
1972 Phil Esposito, Boston
1973 Phil Esposito, Boston
1974 Phil Esposito, Boston
1975 Bobby Orr, Boston
1976 Guy Lafleur, Montreal
1977 Guy Lafleur, Montreal
1978 Guy Lafleur, Montreal
1979 Bryan Trottier, N.Y. Islanders
1980 Marcel Dionne, Los Angeles
1981 Wayne Gretzky, Edmonton
1982 Wayne Gretzky, Edmonton
1983 Wayne Gretzky, Edmonton
1984 Wayne Gretzky, Edmonton
1985 Wayne Gretzky, Edmonton
1986 Wayne Gretzky, Edmonton
1987 Wayne Gretzky, Edmonton
1988 Mario Lemieux, Pittsburgh
1989 Mario Lemieux, Pittsburgh
1990 Wayne Gretzky, Los Angeles
1991 Wayne Gretzky, Los Angeles
1992 Mario Lemieux, Pittsburgh
1993 Mario Lemieux, Pittsburgh
1994 Wayne Gretzky, Los Angeles

James Norris Memorial Trophy (Outstanding Defenseman)

1954 Red Kelly, Detroit
1955 Doug Harvey, Montreal
1956 Doug Harvey, Montreal
1957 Doug Harvey, Montreal
1958 Doug Harvey, Montreal
1959 Tom Johnson, Montreal
1960 Doug Harvey, Montreal
1961 Doug Harvey, Montreal
1962 Doug Harvey, N.Y. Rangers
1963 Pierre Pilote, Chicago
1964 Pierre Pilote, Chicago
1965 Pierre Pilote, Chicago
1966 Jacques Laperriere, Montreal
1967 Harry Howell, N.Y. Rangers
1968 Bobby Orr, Boston
1969 Bobby Orr, Boston
1970 Bobby Orr, Boston
1971 Bobby Orr, Boston
1972 Bobby Orr, Boston
1973 Bobby Orr, Boston
1974 Bobby Orr, Boston
1975 Bobby Orr, Boston
1976 Denis Potvin, N.Y. Islanders
1977 Larry Robinson, Montreal
1978 Denis Potvin, N.Y. Islanders
1979 Denis Potvin, N.Y. Islanders
1980 Larry Robinson, Montreal
1981 Randy Carlyle, Pittsburgh
1982 Doug Wilson, Chicago
1983 Rod Langway, Washington
1984 Rod Langway, Washington
1985 Paul Coffey, Edmonton
1986 Paul Coffey, Edmonton
1987 Ray Bourque, Boston
1988 Ray Bourque, Boston
1989 Chris Chelios, Montreal
1990 Ray Bourque, Boston
1991 Ray Bourque, Boston
1992 Brian Leetch, N.Y. Rangers
1993 Chris Chelios, Chicago
1994 Ray Bourque, Boston

*Vezina Trophy (Leading Goalie)

1927 George Hainsworth, Montreal
1928 George Hainsworth, Montreal
1929 George Hainsworth, Montreal
1930 Tiny Thompson, Boston
1931 Roy Worters, N.Y. Americans
1932 Charlie Gardiner, Chicago
1933 Tiny Thompson, Boston
1934 Charlie Gardiner, Chicago
1935 Lorne Chabot, Chicago
1936 Tiny Thompson, Boston
1937 Normie Smith, Detroit
1938 Tiny Thompson, Boston
1939 Frank Brimsek, Boston
1940 Dave Kerr, N.Y. Rangers
1941 Turk Broda, Toronto
1942 Frank Brimsek, Boston
1943 Johnny Mowers, Detroit
1944 Bill Durnan, Montreal
1945 Bill Durnan, Montreal
1946 Bill Durnan, Montreal
1947 Bill Durnan, Montreal
1948 Turk Broda, Toronto
1949 Bill Durnan, Montreal
1950 Bill Durnan, Montreal
1951 Al Rollins, Toronto
1952 Terry Sawchuk, Detroit
1953 Terry Sawchuk, Detroit
1954 Harry Lumley, Toronto
1955 Terry Sawchuk, Detroit
1956 Jacques Plante, Montreal
1957 Jacques Plante, Montreal
1958 Jacques Plante, Montreal
1959 Jacques Plante, Montreal
1960 Jacques Plante, Montreal
1961 John Bower, Toronto
1962 Jacques Plante, Montreal
1963 Glenn Hall, Chicago
1964 Charlie Hodge, Montreal
1965 Sawchuk, Bower, Toronto
1966 Worsley, Hodge, Montreal
1967 Hall, DeJordy, Chicago
1968 Worsley, Vachon, Montreal
1969 Hall, Plante, St. Louis
1970 Tony Esposito, Chicago
1971 Giacomin, Villemure, N.Y. Rangers
1972 Esposito, Smith, Chicago
1973 Ken Dryden, Montreal
1974 Bernie Parent, Philadelphia; Tony Esposito, Chicago
1975 Bernie Parent, Philadelphia
1976 Ken Dryden, Montreal
1977 Dryden, Larocque, Montreal
1978 Dryden, Larocque, Montreal
1979 Dryden, Larocque, Montreal
1980 Sauve, Edwards, Buffalo
1981 Sevigny, Larocque, Herron, Montreal
1982 Bill Smith, N.Y. Islanders
1983 Pete Peeters, Boston
1984 Tom Barrasso, Buffalo
1985 Pelle Lindbergh, Philadelphia
1986 John Vanbiesbrouck, N.Y. Rangers
1987 Ron Hextall, Philadelphia
1988 Grant Fuhr, Edmonton
1989 Patrick Roy, Montreal
1990 Patrick Roy, Montreal
1991 Ed Belfour, Chicago
1992 Patrick Roy, Montreal
1993 Ed Belfour, Chicago
1994 Dominik Hasek, Buffalo

*Awarded to goalie who played a minimum 25 games for the team that allowed the fewest goals; since 1982, awarded to outstanding goalie.

Calder Memorial Trophy (Rookie of the Year)

1933 Carl Voss, Detroit
1934 Russ Blinco, Montreal Maroons
1935 Dave Schriner, N.Y. Americans
1936 Mike Karakas, Chicago
1937 Syl Apps, Toronto
1938 Cully Dahlstrom, Chicago
1939 Frank Brimsek, Boston
1940 Kilby Macdonald, N.Y. Rangers
1941 John Quilty, Montreal
1942 Grant Warwick, N.Y. Rangers
1943 Gaye Stewart, Toronto
1944 Gus Bodnar, Toronto
1945 Frank McCool, Toronto
1946 Edgar Laprade, N.Y. Rangers
1947 Howie Meeker, Toronto
1948 Jim McFadden, Detroit
1949 Pentti Lund, N.Y. Rangers
1950 Jack Gelineau, Boston
1951 Terry Sawchuk, Detroit
1952 Bernie Geoffrion, Montreal
1953 Gump Worsley, N.Y. Rangers
1954 Camille Henry, N.Y. Rangers
1955 Ed Litzenberger, Chicago
1956 Glenn Hall, Detroit
1957 Larry Regan, Boston
1958 Frank Mahovlich, Toronto
1959 Ralph Backstrom, Montreal
1960 Bill Hay, Chicago
1961 Dave Keon, Toronto
1962 Bobby Rousseau, Montreal
1963 Kent Douglas, Toronto
1964 Jacques Laperriere, Montreal
1965 Roger Crozier, Detroit
1966 Brit Selby, Toronto
1967 Bobby Orr, Boston
1968 Derek Sanderson, Boston
1969 Danny Grant, Minnesota
1970 Tony Esposito, Chicago
1971 Gilbert Perreault, Buffalo
1972 Ken Dryden, Montreal
1973 Steve Vickers, N.Y. Rangers
1974 Denis Potvin, N.Y. Islanders
1975 Eric Vail, Atlanta
1976 Bryan Trottier, N.Y. Islanders
1977 Willi Plett, Atlanta
1978 Mike Bossy, N.Y. Islanders
1979 Bobby Smith, Minnesota
1980 Ray Bourque, Boston
1981 Peter Stastny, Quebec
1982 Dale Hawerchuk, Winnipeg
1983 Steve Larmer, Chicago
1984 Tom Barrasso, Buffalo
1985 Mario Lemieux, Pittsburgh
1986 Gary Suter, Calgary
1987 Luc Robitaille, Los Angeles
1988 Joe Nieuwendyk, Calgary
1989 Brian Leetch, N.Y. Rangers
1990 Sergei Makarov, Calgary
1991 Ed Belfour, Chicago
1992 Pavel Bure, Vancouver
1993 Teemu Selanne, Winnipeg
1994 Martin Brodeur, New Jersey

Lady Byng Memorial Trophy (Most Gentlemanly Player)

1925 Frank Nighbor, Ottawa
1926 Frank Nighbor, Ottawa
1927 Billy Burch, N.Y. Americans
1928 Frank Boucher, N.Y. Rangers
1929 Frank Boucher, N.Y. Rangers
1930 Frank Boucher, N.Y. Rangers
1931 Frank Boucher, N.Y. Rangers
1932 Joe Primeau, Toronto
1933 Frank Boucher, N.Y. Rangers
1934 Frank Boucher, N.Y. Rangers
1935 Frank Boucher, N.Y. Rangers
1936 Doc Romnes, Chicago
1937 Marty Barry, Detroit
1938 Gordie Drillon, Toronto
1939 Clint Smith, N.Y. Rangers
1940 Bobby Bauer, Boston
1941 Bobby Bauer, Boston
1942 Syl Apps, Toronto
1943 Max Bentley, Chicago
1944 Clint Smith, Chicago
1945 Bill Mosienko, Chicago
1946 Toe Blake, Montreal
1947 Bobby Bauer, Boston
1948 Buddy O'Connor, N.Y. Rangers
1949 Bill Quackenbush, Detroit
1950 Edgar Laprade, N.Y. Rangers
1951 Red Kelly, Detroit
1952 Sid Smith, Toronto
1953 Red Kelly, Detroit
1954 Red Kelly, Detroit
1955 Sid Smith, Toronto
1956 Earl Reibel, Detroit
1957 Andy Hebenton, N.Y. Rangers
1958 Camille Henry, N.Y. Rangers
1959 Alex Delvecchio, Detroit
1960 Don McKenney, Boston
1961 Red Kelly, Toronto
1962 Dave Keon, Toronto
1963 Dave Keon, Toronto
1964 Ken Wharram, Chicago
1965 Bobby Hull, Chicago
1966 Alex Delvecchio, Detroit
1967 Stan Mikita, Chicago
1968 Stan Mikita, Chicago
1969 Alex Delvecchio, Detroit
1970 Phil Goyette, St. Louis
1971 John Bucyk, Boston
1972 Jean Ratelle, N.Y. Rangers
1973 Gil Perreault, Buffalo
1974 John Bucyk, Boston
1975 Marcel Dionne, Detroit
1976 Jean Ratelle, N.Y. R.–Boston
1977 Marcel Dionne, Los Angeles
1978 Butch Goring, Los Angeles
1979 Bob MacMillan, Atlanta
1980 Wayne Gretzky, Edmonton
1981 Rick Kehoe, Pittsburgh
1982 Rick Middleton, Boston
1983 Mike Bossy, N.Y. Islanders
1984 Mike Bossy, N.Y. Islanders
1985 Jari Kurri, Edmonton
1986 Mike Bossy, N.Y. Islanders
1987 Joe Mullen, Calgary
1988 Mats Naslund, Montreal
1989 Joe Mullen, Calgary
1990 Brett Hull, St. Louis
1991 Wayne Gretzky, Los Angeles
1992 Wayne Gretzky, Los Angeles
1993 Pierre Turgeon, N.Y. Islanders
1994 Wayne Gretzky, Los Angeles

Frank J. Selke Trophy (Best Defensive Forward)

1978 Bob Gainey, Montreal
1979 Bob Gainey, Montreal
1980 Bob Gainey, Montreal
1981 Bob Gainey, Montreal
1982 Steve Kasper, Boston
1983 Bobby Clarke, Philadelphia
1984 Doug Jarvis, Washington
1985 Craig Ramsay, Buffalo
1986 Troy Murray, Chicago
1987 Dave Poulin, Philadelphia
1988 Guy Carbonneau, Montreal
1989 Guy Carbonneau, Montreal
1990 Rick Meagher, St. Louis
1991 Dirk Graham, Chicago
1992 Guy Carbonneau, Montreal
1993 Doug Gilmour, Toronto
1994 Sergei Fedorov, Detroit

Hart Memorial Trophy (MVP)

1927 Herb Gardiner, Montreal
1928 Howie Morenz, Montreal
1929 Roy Worters, N.Y. Americans
1930 Nels Stewart, Montreal Maroons
1931 Howie Morenz, Montreal
1932 Howie Morenz, Montreal
1933 Eddie Shore, Boston
1934 Aurel Joliat, Montreal
1935 Eddie Shore, Boston
1936 Eddie Shore, Boston
1937 Babe Siebert, Montreal
1938 Eddie Shore, Boston
1939 Toe Blake, Montreal
1940 Ebbie Goodfellow, Detroit
1941 Bill Cowley, Boston
1942 Tom Anderson, N.Y. Americans
1943 Bill Cowley, Boston
1944 Babe Pratt, Toronto
1945 Elmer Lach, Montreal
1946 Max Bentley, Chicago
1947 Maurice Richard, Montreal
1948 Buddy O'Connor, N.Y. Rangers
1949 Sid Abel, Detroit
1950 Chuck Rayner, N.Y. Rangers
1951 Milt Schmidt, Boston
1952 Gordie Howe, Detroit
1953 Gordie Howe, Detroit
1954 Al Rollins, Chicago
1955 Ted Kennedy, Toronto
1956 Jean Beliveau, Montreal
1957 Gordie Howe, Detroit
1958 Gordie Howe, Detroit
1959 Andy Bathgate, N.Y. Rangers
1960 Gordie Howe, Detroit
1961 Bernie Geoffrion, Montreal
1962 Jacques Plante, Montreal
1963 Gordie Howe, Detroit
1964 Jean Beliveau, Montreal
1965 Bobby Hull, Chicago
1966 Bobby Hull, Chicago
1967 Stan Mikita, Chicago
1968 Stan Mikita, Chicago
1969 Phil Esposito, Boston
1970 Bobby Orr, Boston
1971 Bobby Orr, Boston
1972 Bobby Orr, Boston
1973 Bobby Clarke, Philadelphia
1974 Phil Esposito, Boston
1975 Bobby Clarke, Philadelphia
1976 Bobby Clarke, Philadelphia
1977 Guy Lafleur, Montreal
1978 Guy Lafleur, Montreal
1979 Bryan Trottier, N.Y. Islanders
1980 Wayne Gretzky, Edmonton
1981 Wayne Gretzky, Edmonton
1982 Wayne Gretzky, Edmonton
1983 Wayne Gretzky, Edmonton
1984 Wayne Gretzky, Edmonton
1985 Wayne Gretzky, Edmonton
1986 Wayne Gretzky, Edmonton
1987 Wayne Gretzky, Edmonton
1988 Mario Lemieux, Pittsburgh
1989 Wayne Gretzky, Los Angeles
1990 Mark Messier, Edmonton
1991 Brett Hull, St. Louis
1992 Mark Messier, N.Y. Rangers
1993 Mario Lemieux, Pittsburgh
1994 Sergei Fedorov, Detroit

Conn Smythe Trophy (MVP in Playoffs)

1965 Jean Beliveau, Montreal
1966 Roger Crozier, Detroit
1967 Dave Keon, Toronto
1968 Glenn Hall, St. Louis
1969 Serge Savard, Montreal
1970 Bobby Orr, Boston
1971 Ken Dryden, Montreal
1972 Bobby Orr, Boston
1973 Yvan Cournoyer, Montreal
1974 Bernie Parent, Philadelphia
1975 Bernie Parent, Philadelphia
1976 Reg Leach, Philadelphia
1977 Guy Lafleur, Montreal
1978 Larry Robinson, Montreal
1979 Bob Gainey, Montreal
1980 Bryan Trottier, N.Y. Islanders
1981 Butch Goring, N.Y. Islanders
1982 Mike Bossy, N.Y. Islanders
1983 Billy Smith, N.Y. Islanders
1984 Mark Messier, Edmonton
1985 Wayne Gretzky, Edmonton
1986 Patrick Roy, Montreal
1987 Ron Hextall, Philadelphia
1988 Wayne Gretzky, Edmonton
1989 Al MacInnis, Calgary
1990 Bill Ranford, Edmonton
1991 Mario Lemieux, Pittsburgh
1992 Mario Lemieux, Pittsburgh
1993 Patrick Roy, Montreal
1994 Brian Leetch, N.Y. Rangers

Most NHL Goals in a Season

Player	Team	Season	Goals
Wayne Gretzky	Edmonton	1981–82	92
Wayne Gretzky	Edmonton	1983–84	87
Brett Hull	St. Louis	1990–91	86
Mario Lemieux	Pittsburgh	1988–89	85
Phil Esposito	Boston	1970–71	76
Alexander Mogilny	Buffalo	1992–93	76
Teemu Selanne	Winnipeg	1992–93	76
Wayne Gretzky	Edmonton	1984–85	73
Brett Hull	St. Louis	1989–90	72
Wayne Gretzky	Edmonton	1982–83	71
Jari Kurri	Edmonton	1984–85	71
Mario Lemieux	Pittsburgh	1987–88	70
Bernie Nicholls	Los Angeles	1988–89	70
Bret Hull	St. Louis	1991–92	70
Mike Bossy	N.Y. Islanders	1978–79	69
Mario Lemieux	Pittsburgh	1992–93	69
Phil Esposito	Boston	1973–74	68
Mike Bossy	N.Y. Islanders	1980–81	68
Jari Kurri	Edmonton	1985–86	68
Phil Esposito	Boston	1971–72	66
Lanny McDonald	Calgary	1982–83	66
Steve Yzerman	Detroit	1988–89	65
Mike Bossy	N.Y. Islanders	1981–82	64
Luc Robitaille	Los Angeles	1992–93	63
Wayne Gretzky	Edmonton	1986–87	62
Steve Yzerman	Detroit	1989–90	62
Mike Bossy	N.Y. Islanders	1985–86	61
Phil Esposito	Boston	1974–75	61
Reggie Leach	Philadelphia	1975–76	61
Mike Bossy	N.Y. Islanders	1982–83	60
Guy Lafleur	Montreal	1977–78	60
Steve Shutt	Montreal	1976–77	60
Dennis Maruk	Washington	1981–82	60
Pavel Bure	Vancouver	1992–93	60
Pavel Bure	Vancouver	1993–94	60

NCAA Hockey Champions

1948 Michigan
1949 Boston College
1950 Colorado College
1951 Michigan
1952 Michigan
1953 Michigan
1954 RPI
1955 Michigan
1956 Michigan
1957 Colorado College
1958 Denver
1959 North Dakota
1960 Denver
1961 Denver
1962 Michigan Tech
1963 North Dakota
1964 Michigan
1965 Michigan Tech
1966 Michigan State
1967 Cornell
1968 Denver
1969 Denver
1970 Cornell
1971 Boston Univ.
1972 Boston Univ.
1973 Wisconsin
1974 Minnesota
1975 Michigan Tech
1976 Minnesota
1977 Wisconsin
1978 Boston Univ.
1979 Minnesota
1980 North Dakota
1981 Wisconsin
1982 North Dakota
1983 Wisconsin
1984 Bowling Green
1985 RPI
1986 Michigan State
1987 North Dakota
1988 Lake Superior St.
1989 Harvard
1990 Wisconsin
1991 N. Michigan
1992 Lake Superior St.
1993 Maine
1994 Lake Superior St.

THOROUGHBRED RACING

Triple Crown Winners

Since 1920, colts have carried 126 lbs. in triple crown events; fillies 121 lbs.

(Kentucky Derby, Preakness, and Belmont Stakes)

Year	Horse	Jockey	Trainer
1919	Sir Barton	J. Loftus	H. G. Bedwell
1930	Gallant Fox	E. Sande	J. Fitzsimmons
1935	Omaha	W. Sanders	J. Fitzsimmons
1937	War Admiral	C. Kurtsinger	G. Conway
1941	Whirlaway	E. Arcaro	B.A. Jones
1943	Count Fleet	J. Longden	G.D. Cameron
1946	Assault	W. Mehrtens	M. Hirsch
1948	Citation	E. Arcaro	H.A. Jones
1973	Secretariat	R. Turcotte	L. Laurin
1977	Seattle Slew	J. Cruguet	W.H. Turner Jr.
1978	Affirmed	S. Cauthen	L.S. Barrera

Kentucky Derby

Churchill Downs, Louisville, KY; inaugurated 1875; distance 1-1/4 miles; 1-1/2 miles until 1896. 3-year olds. Best time: 1:59.2, Secretariat, 1973.

Year	Winner	Jockey
1875	Aristides	O. Lewis
1876	Vagrant	R. Swim
1877	Baden Baden	W. Walker
1878	Day Star	J. Carter
1879	Lord Murphy	C. Schauer
1880	Fonso	G. Lewis
1881	Hindoo	J. McLaughlin
1882	Apollo	B. Hurd
1883	Leonatus	W. Donohue
1884	Buchanan	I. Murphy
1885	Joe Cotton	E. Henderson
1886	Ben Ali	P. Duffy
1887	Montrose	I. Lewis
1888	Macbeth II	G. Covington
1889	Spokane	T. Kiley
1890	Riley	I. Murphy
1891	Kingman	I. Murphy
1892	Azra	A. Clayton
1893	Lookout	E. Kunze
1894	Chant	F. Goodale
1895	Halma	J. Perkins
1896	Ben Brush	W. Simms
1897	Typhoon II	F. Garner
1898	Plaudit	W. Simms
1899	Manuel	F. Taral
1900	Lieut. Gibson	J. Boland
1901	His Eminence	J. Winkfield
1902	Alan-a-Dale	J. Winkfield
1903	Judge Himes	H. Booker
1904	Elwood	F. Prior
1905	Agile	J. Martin
1906	Sir Huon	R. Troxler
1907	Pink Star	A. Minder
1908	Stone Street	A. Pickens
1909	Wintergreen	V. Powers
1910	Donau	F. Herbert
1911	Meridian	G. Archibald
1912	Worth	C.H. Shilling
1913	Donerail	R. Goose
1914	Old Rosebud	J. McCabe
1915	Regret*	J. Notter
1916	George Smith	J. Loftus
1917	Omar Khayyam	C. Borel
1918	Exterminator	W. Knapp
1919	Sir Barton	J. Loftus
1920	Paul Jones	T. Rice
1921	Behave Yourself	C. Thompson
1922	Morvich	A. Johnson
1923	Zev	E. Sande
1924	Black Gold	J. D. Mooney
1925	Flying Ebony	E. Sande
1926	Bubbling Over	A. Johnson
1927	Whiskery	L. McAtee
1928	Reigh Count	C. Lang
1929	Clyde Van Dusen	L. McAtee
1930	Gallant Fox	E. Sande
1931	Twenty Grand	C. Kurtsinger
1932	Burgoo King	E. James
1933	Brokers Tip	D. Meade
1934	Cavalcade	M. Garner
1935	Omaha	W. Saunders
1936	Bold Venture	I. Hanford
1937	War Admiral	C. Kurtsinger
1938	Lawrin	E. Arcaro
1939	Johnstown	J. Stout
1940	Gallahadion	C. Bierman
1941	Whirlaway	E. Arcaro
1942	Shut Out	W. D. Wright
1943	Count Fleet	J. Longden
1944	Pensive	C. McCreary
1945	Hoop, Jr.	E. Arcaro
1946	Assault	W. Mehrtens
1947	Jet Pilot	E. Guerin
1948	Citation	E. Arcaro
1949	Ponder	S. Brooks
1950	Middleground	W. Boland
1951	Count Turf	C. McCreary
1952	Hill Gail	E. Arcaro
1953	Dark Star	H. Moreno
1954	Determine	R. York
1955	Swaps	W. Shoemaker
1956	Needles	D. Erb
1957	Iron Liege	W. Hartack
1958	Tim Tam	I. Valenzuela
1959	Tomy Lee	W. Shoemaker
1960	Venetian Way	W. Hartack
1961	Carry Back	J. Sellers
1962	Decidedly	W. Hartack
1963	Chateaugay	B. Baeza
1964	Northern Dancer	W. Hartack
1965	Lucky Debonair	W. Shoemaker
1966	Kauai King	D. Brumfield
1967	Proud Clarion	R. Ussery
1968	Dancer's Image (a)	R. Ussery
1969	Majestic Prince	W. Hartack
1970	Dust Commander	M. Manganello
1971	Canonero II	G. Avila
1972	Riva Ridge	R. Turcotte
1973	Secretariat	R. Turcotte
1974	Cannonade	A. Cordero
1975	Foolish Pleasure	J. Vasquez
1976	Bold Forbes	A. Cordero
1977	Seattle Slew	J. Cruguet
1978	Affirmed	S. Cauthen
1979	Spectacular Bid	R. Franklin
1980	Genuine Risk*	J. Vasquez
1981	Pleasant Colony	J. Velasquez
1982	Gato del Sol	E. Delahoussaye
1983	Sunny's Halo	E. Delahoussaye
1984	Swale	L. Pincay
1985	Spend a Buck	A. Cordero
1986	Ferdinand	W. Shoemaker
1987	Alysheba	C. McCarron
1988	Winning Colors*	G. Stevens
1989	Sunday Silence	P. Valenzuela
1990	Unbridled	C. Perret
1991	Strike the Gold	C. Antley
1992	Lil E. Tee	P. Day
1993	Sea Hero	J. Bailey
1994	Go for Gin	C. McCarron

(a) Dancer's Image was disqualified from purse money after tests disclosed that he had run with a pain-killing drug, phenylbutazone, in his system. All wagers were paid on Dancer's Image. Forward Pass was awarded first place money.

The Kentucky Derby has been won five times by two jockeys, Eddie Arcaro, 1938, 1941, 1945, 1948, and 1952; and Bill Hartack, 1957, 1960, 1962, 1964, and 1969; four times by Willie Shoemaker, 1955, 1959, 1965, and 1986; and three times by each of three jockeys, Isaac Murphy, 1884, 1890, and 1891; Earle Sande, 1923, 1925, and 1930; and Angel Cordero in 1974, 1976, and 1985. * Regret, Genuine Risk, and Winning Colors are the only fillies to win the Derby.

Preakness

Pimlico, Baltimore, MD; inaugurated 1873; distance 1-3/16 miles. 3-year olds. Best time: 1:53.2, Tank's Prospect, 1985.

Year	Winner	Jockey
1873	Survivor	G. Barbee
1874	Culpepper	M. Donohue
1875	Tom Ochiltree	L. Hughes
1876	Shirley	G. Barbee
1877	Cloverbrook	C. Holloway
1878	Duke of Magenta	C. Holloway
1879	Harold	L. Hughes
1880	Grenada	L. Hughes
1881	Saunterer	W. Costello
1882	Vanguard	W. Costello
1883	Jacobus	G. Barbee
1884	Knight of Ellerslie	S. H. Fisher
1885	Tecumseh	J. McLaughlin
1886	The Bard	S. H. Fisher
1887	Dunboyne	W. Donohue
1888	Refund	F. Littlefield
1889	Buddhist	G. Anderson
1890	Montague	W. Martin
1894	Assignee	F. Taral
1895	Belmar	F. Taral
1896	Margrave	H. Griffin
1897	Paul Kauvar	C. Thorpe
1898	Sly Fox	W. Simms
1899	Half Time	R. Clawson
1900	Hindus	H. Spencer
1901	The Parader	F. Landry
1902	Old England	L. Jackson
1903	Flocarline	W. Gannon
1904	Bryn Mawr	E. Hildebrand
1905	Cairngorm	W. Davis
1906	Whimsical	W. Miller
1907	Don Enrique	G. Mountain
1908	Royal Tourist	E. Dugan
1909	Effendi	W. Doyle
1910	Layminster	R. Estep
1911	Watervale	E. Dugan
1912	Colonel Holloway	C. Turner
1913	Buskin	J. Butwell
1914	Holiday	A. Schuttinger
1915	Rhine Maiden	D. Hoffman
1916	Damrosch	L. McAtee
1917	Kalitan	E. Haynes

Year	Winner	Jockey	Year	Winner	Jockey	Year	Winner	Jockey
1918	War Cloud	J. Loftus	1943	Count Fleet	J. Longden	1969	Majestic Prince	W. Hartack
	Jack Hare Jr.	C. Peak	1944	Pensive	C. McCreary	1970	Personality	E. Belmonte
1919	Sir Barton	J. Loftus	1945	Polynesian	W.D. Wright	1971	Canonero II	G. Avila
1920	Man o' War	C. Kummer	1946	Assault	W. Mehrtens	1972	Bee Bee Bee	E. Nelson
1921	Broomspun	F. Coltiletti	1947	Faultless	D. Dodson	1973	Secretariat	R. Turcotte
1922	Pillory	L. Morris	1948	Citation	E. Arcaro	1974	Little Current	M. Rivera
1923	Vigil	B. Marinelli	1949	Capot	T. Atkinson	1975	Master Derby	D. McHargue
1924	Nellie Morse	J. Merimee	1950	Hill Prince	E. Arcaro	1976	Elocutionist	J. Lively
1925	Coventry	C. Kummer	1951	Bold	E. Arcaro	1977	Seattle Slew	J. Cruguet
1926	Display	J. Malben	1952	Blue Man	C. McCreary	1978	Affirmed	S. Cauthen
1927	Bostonian	A. Abel	1953	Native Dancer	E. Guerin	1979	Spectacular Bid	R. Franklin
1928	Victorian	R. Workman	1954	Hasty Road	J. Adams	1980	Codex	A. Cordero
1929	Dr. Freeland	L. Schaefer	1955	Nashua	E. Arcaro	1981	Pleasant Colony	J. Velasquez
1930	Gallant Fox	E. Sande	1956	Fabius	W. Hartack	1982	Aloma's Ruler	J. Kaenel
1931	Mate	G. Ellis	1957	Bold Ruler	E. Arcaro	1983	Deputed Testamony	D. Miller
1932	Burgoo King	E. James	1958	Tim Tam	I. Valenzuela	1984	Gate Dancer	A. Cordero
1933	Head Play	C. Kurtsinger	1959	Royal Orbit	W. Harmatz	1985	Tank's Prospect	P. Day
1934	High Quest	R. Jones	1960	Bally Ache	R. Ussery	1986	Snow Chief	A. Solis
1935	Omaha	W. Saunders	1961	Carry Back	J. Sellers	1987	Alysheba	C. McCarron
1936	Bold Venture	G. Woolf	1962	Greek Money	J.L. Rotz	1988	Risen Star	E. Delahoussaye
1937	War Admiral	C. Kurtsinger	1963	Candy Spots	W. Shoemaker	1989	Sunday Silence	P. Valenzuela
1938	Dauber	M. Peters	1964	Northern Dancer	W. Hartack	1990	Summer Squall	P. Day
1939	Challedon	G. Seabo	1965	Tom Rolfe	R. Turcotte	1991	Hansel	J. Bailey
1940	Bimelech	F.A. Smith	1966	Kauai King	D. Brumfield	1992	Pine Bluff	C. McCarron
1941	Whirlaway	E. Arcaro	1967	Damascus	W. Shoemaker	1993	Prairie Bayou	M. Smith
1942	Alsab	B. James	1968	Forward Pass	I. Valenzuela	1994	Tabasco Cat	P. Day

Belmont Stakes

Belmont Park, Elmont, NY; inaugurated 1867; distance 1-1/2 miles. 3-year olds. Best time: 2:24, Secretariat, 1973.

Year	Winner	Jockey	Year	Winner	Jockey	Year	Winner	Jockey
1867	Ruthless	J. Gilpatrick	1909	Joe Madden	E. Dugan	1953	Native Dancer	E. Guerin
1868	General Duke	R. Swim	1910	Sweep	J. Butwell	1954	High Gun	E. Guerin
1869	Fenian	C. Miller	1913	Prince Eugene	R. Troxler	1955	Nashua	E. Arcaro
1870	Kingfisher	W. Dick	1914	Luke McLuke	M. Buxton	1956	Needles	D. Erb
1871	Harry Bassett	W. Miller	1915	The Finn	G. Byrne	1957	Gallant Man	W. Shoemaker
1872	Joe Daniels	J. Rowe	1916	Friar Rock	E. Haynes	1958	Cavan	P. Anderson
1873	Springbok	J. Rowe	1917	Hourless	J. Butwell	1959	Sword Dancer	W. Shoemaker
1874	Saxon	G. Barbee	1918	Johren	F. Robinson	1960	Celtic Ash	W. Hartack
1875	Calvin	R. Swim	1919	Sir Barton	J. Loftus	1961	Sherluck	B. Baeza
1876	Algerine	W. Donohue	1920	Man o' War	C. Kummer	1962	Jaipur	W. Shoemaker
1877	Cloverbrook	C. Holloway	1921	Grey Lag	E. Sande	1963	Chateaugay	B. Baeza
1878	Duke of Magenta	L. Hughes	1922	Pillory	C.H. Miller	1964	Quadrangle	M. Ycaza
1879	Spendthrift	S. Evans	1923	Zev	E. Sande	1965	Hail to All	J. Sellers
1880	Grenada	L. Hughes	1924	Mad Play	E. Sande	1966	Amberoid	W. Boland
1881	Saunterer	T. Costello	1925	American Flag	A. Johnson	1967	Damascus	W. Shoemaker
1882	Forester	J. McLaughlin	1926	Crusader	A. Johnson	1968	Stage Door Johnny	H. Gustines
1883	George Kinney	J. McLaughlin	1927	Chance Shot	E. Sande	1969	Arts and Letters	B. Baeza
1884	Panique	J. McLaughlin	1928	Vito	C. Kummer	1970	High Echelon	J.L. Rotz
1885	Tyrant	P. Duffy	1929	Blue Larkspur	M. Garner	1971	Pass Catcher	W. Blum
1886	Inspector B.	J. McLaughlin	1930	Gallant Fox	E. Sande	1972	Riva Ridge	R. Turcotte
1887	Hanover	J. McLaughlin	1931	Twenty Grand	C. Kurtsinger	1973	Secretariat	R. Turcotte
1888	Sir Dixon	J. McLaughlin	1932	Faireno	T. Malley	1974	Little Current	M. Rivera
1889	Eric	W. Hayward	1933	Hurryoff	M. Garner	1975	Avatar	W. Shoemaker
1890	Burlington	S. Barnes	1934	Peace Chance	W.D. Wright	1976	Bold Forbes	A. Cordero
1891	Foxford	E. Garrison	1935	Omaha	W. Saunders	1977	Seattle Slew	J. Cruguet
1892	Patron	W. Hayward	1936	Granville	J. Stout	1978	Affirmed	S. Cauthen
1893	Comanche	W. Simms	1937	War Admiral	C. Kurtsinger	1979	Coastal	R. Hernandez
1894	Henry of Navarre	W. Simms	1938	Pasteurized	J. Stout	1980	Temperence Hill	E. Maple
1895	Belmar	F. Taral	1939	Johnstown	J. Stout	1981	Summing	G. Martens
1896	Hastings	H. Griffin	1940	Bimelech	F.A. Smith	1982	Conquistador Cielo	L. Pincay
1897	Scottish Chieftain	J. Scherrer	1941	Whirlaway	E. Arcaro	1983	Caveat	L. Pincay
1898	Bowling Brook	F. Littlefield	1942	Shut Out	E. Arcaro	1984	Swale	L. Pincay
1899	Jean Bereaud	R.R. Clawson	1943	Count Fleet	J. Longden	1985	Creme Fraiche	E. Maple
1900	Ildrim	N. Turner	1944	Bounding Home	G.L. Smith	1986	Danzig Connection	C. McCarron
1901	Commando	H. Spencer	1945	Pavot	E. Arcaro	1987	Bet Twice	C. Perret
1902	Masterman	J. Bullman	1946	Assault	W. Mehrtens	1988	Risen Star	E. Delahoussaye
1903	Africander	J. Bullman	1947	Phalanx	R. Donoso	1989	Easy Goer	P. Day
1904	Delhi	G. Odom	1948	Citation	E. Arcaro	1990	Go and Go	M. Kinane
1905	Tanya	E. Hildebrand	1949	Capot	T. Atkinson	1991	Hansel	J. Bailey
1906	Burgomaster	L. Lyne	1950	Middleground	W. Boland	1992	A.P. Indy	E. Delahoussaye
1907	Peter Pan	G. Mountain	1951	Counterpoint	D. Gorman	1993	Colonial Affair	J. Krone
1908	Colin	J. Notter	1952	One Count	E. Arcaro	1994	Tabasco Cat	P. Day

Annual Leading Jockey—Money Won

Year	Jockey	Dollars	Year	Jockey	Dollars	Year	Jockey	Dollars
1957	Bill Hartack	3,060,501	1970	Laffit Pincay Jr.	2,626,526	1983	Angel Cordero Jr.	10,116,697
1958	Willie Shoemaker	2,961,693	1971	Laffit Pincay Jr.	3,784,377	1984	Chris McCarron	12,045,813
1959	Willie Shoemaker	2,843,133	1972	Laffit Pincay Jr.	3,225,827	1985	Laffit Pincay Jr.	13,353,299
1960	Willie Shoemaker	2,123,961	1973	Laffit Pincay Jr.	4,093,492	1986	Jose Santos	11,329,297
1961	Willie Shoemaker	2,690,819	1974	Laffit Pincay Jr.	4,251,060	1987	Jose Santos	12,375,433
1962	Willie Shoemaker	2,916,844	1975	Braulio Baeza	3,695,198	1988	Jose Santos	14,877,298
1963	Willie Shoemaker	2,526,925	1976	Angel Cordero Jr.	4,709,500	1989	Jose Santos	13,838,389
1964	Willie Shoemaker	2,649,553	1977	Steve Cauthen	6,151,750	1990	Gary Stevens	13,881,198
1965	Braulio Baeza	2,582,702	1978	Darrel McHargue	6,029,885	1991	Chris McCarron	14,441,083
1966	Braulio Baeza	2,951,022	1979	Laffit Pincay Jr.	8,193,535	1992	Kent Desormeaux	14,193,006
1967	Braulio Baeza	3,088,888	1980	Chris McCarron	7,663,300	1993	Mike Smith	14,024,815
1968	Braulio Baeza	2,835,108	1981	Chris McCarron	8,397,604			
1969	Jorge Velasquez	2,542,315	1982	Angel Cordero Jr.	9,483,590			

Breeders' Cup

The Breeders' Cup was inaugurated in 1984 and consists of seven races at one track on one day late in the year to determine thoroughbred racing's champion contenders.

Juvenile

Distances: one mile 1984-85, 87; 1-1/16 miles 1986 and since 1988

Year		Jockey	Year		Jockey	Year		Jockey
1984	Chief's Crown	Don MacBeth	1988	Is It True	Laffit Pincay Jr.	1992	Gilded Time	Chris McCarron
1985	Tasso	Laffit Pincay Jr.	1989	Rhythm	Craig Perre	1993	Brocco	Gary Stevens
1986	Capote	Laffit Pincay Jr.	1990	Fly So Free	Jose Santos	1994	Timber Country	Pat Day
1987	Success Express	Jose Santos	1991	Arazi	Pat Valenzuela			

Juvenile Fillies

Distances: one mile 1984-85, 87; 1-1/16 miles 1986 and since 1988

Year		Jockey	Year		Jockey	Year		Jockey
1984	*Outstandingly	Walter Guerra	1988	Open Mind	Angel Cordero Jr.	1992	Eliza	Pat Valenzuela
1985	Twilight Ridge	Jorge Velasquez	1989	Go for Wand	Randy Romero	1993	Phone Chatter	Laffit Pincay Jr.
1986	Brave Raj	Pat Valenzuela	1990	Meadow Star	Jose Santos	1994	Flanders	Pat Day
1987	Epitome	Pat Day	1991	Pleasant Stage	Eddie Delahoussaye			

*By disqualification.

Sprint

Distance: six furlongs

Year		Jockey	Year		Jockey	Year		Jockey
1984	Eillo	Craig Perret	1988	Gulch	Angel Cordero Jr.	1991	Sheikh Albadou	Pat Eddery
1985	Precisionist	Chris McCarron	1989	Dancing Spree	Angel Cordero Jr.	1992	Thirty Slews	Eddie Delahoussaye
1986	Smile	Jacinto Vasquez	1990	Safely Kept	Craig Perret	1993	Cardmania	Eddie Delahoussaye
1987	Very Subtle	Pat Valenzuela				1994	Cherokee Run	Mike Smith

Mile

Year		Jockey	Year		Jockey	Year		Jockey
1984	Royal Heroine	Fernando Toro	1988	Miesque	Freddie Head	1991	Opening Verse	Pat Valenzuela
1985	Cozzene	Walter Guerra	1989	Steinlen	Jose Santos	1992	Lure	Mike Smith
1986	Last Tycoon	Yves St.-Martin	1990	Royal Academy	Lester Piggott	1993	Lure	Mike Smith
1987	Miesque	Freddie Head				1994	Barathea	Lanfranco Dettori

Distaff

Distances: 1-1/4 miles 1984-87; 1-1/8 miles since 1988

Year		Jockey	Year		Jockey	Year		Jockey
1984	Princess Rooney	Eddie Delahoussaye	1988	Personal Ensign	Randy Romero	1992	Paseana	Chris McCarron
1985	Life's Magic	Angel Cordero Jr.	1989	Bayakoa	Laffit Pincay Jr.	1993	Hollywood Wildcat	Eddie Delahoussaye
1986	Lady's Secret	Pat Day	1990	Bayakoa	Laffit Pincay Jr.	1994	One Dreamer	Gary Stevens
1987	Sacahuista	Randy Romero	1991	Dance Smartly	Pat Day			

Turf

Distance: 1-1/2 miles

Year		Jockey	Year		Jockey	Year		Jockey
1984	Lashkari	Yves St.-Martin	1988	Great Communicator	Ray Sibille	1991	Miss Alleged	Eric Legrix
1985	Pebbles	Pat Eddery	1989	Prized	Eddie Delahoussaye	1992	Fraise	Pat Valenzuela
1986	Manila	Jose Santos	1990	In The Wings	Gary Stevens	1993	Kotashaan	Kent Desormeaux
1987	Theatrical	Pat Day				1994	Tikkanen	Mike Smith

Classic

Distance: 1-1/4 miles

Year		Jockey	Year		Jockey	Year		Jockey
1984	Wild Again	Pat Day	1988	Alysheba	Chris McCarron	1991	Black Tie Affair	Jerry Bailey
1985	Proud Truth	Jorge Velasquez	1989	Sunday Silence	Chris McCarron	1992	A.P. Indy	Eddie Delahoussaye
1986	Skywalker	Laffit Pincay Jr.	1990	Unbridled	Pat Day	1993	Arcangues	Jerry Bailey
1987	Ferdinand	Willie Shoemaker				1994	Concern	Jerry Bailey

Eclipse Awards

The Eclipse Awards, honoring the Horse of the Year and other champions of the sport, began in 1971 and are sponsored by the *Daily Racing Form,* the Thoroughbred Racing Associations and the National Turf Writers Assn. Prior to 1971, the DRF (1936-70) and the TRA (1950-70) issued separate selections for horse of the year.

Eclipse Awards in 1993

Horse of the Year—Kotashaan
2-year-old colt—Dehere
2-year-old filly—Phone Chatter
3-year-old colt—Prairie Bayou
3-year-old filly—Hollywood Wildcat
Colt, horse, or gelding (4-year-olds & up)—Bertrando
Filly or mare (4-year-olds & up)—Paseana
Male turf horse—Kotashaan
Turf filly or mare—Flawlessly
Sprinter—Cardmania
Steeplechase horse—Lonesome Glory
Trainer—Bobby Frankel
Jockey—Mike Smith
Apprentice jockey—Juan Umana
Breeder—Allen Paulson

Horse of the Year

Year	Horse	Year	Horse	Year	Horse	Year	Horse
1936	Granville	1951	Counterpoint	1964	Kelso	1978	Affirmed
1937	War Admiral	1952	One Count (DRF)	1965	Roman Brother (DRF)	1979	Affirmed
1938	Seabiscuit		Native Dancer (TRA)		Moccasin (TRA)	1980	Spectacular Bid
1939	Challedon	1953	Tom Fool	1966	Buckpasser	1981	John Henry
1940	Challedon	1954	Native Dancer	1967	Damascus	1982	Conquistador Cielo
1941	Whirlaway	1955	Nashua	1968	Dr. Fager	1983	All Along
1942	Whirlaway	1956	Swaps	1969	Arts and Letters	1984	John Henry
1943	Count Fleet	1957	Bold Ruler (DRF)	1970	Fort Marcy (DRF)	1985	Spend A Buck
1944	Twilight Tear		Dedicate (TRA)		Personality (TRA)	1986	Lady's Secret
1945	Busher	1958	Round Table	1971	Ack Ack	1987	Ferdinand
1946	Assault	1959	Sword Dancer	1972	Secretariat	1988	Alysheba
1947	Armed	1960	Kelso	1973	Secretariat	1989	Sunday Silence
1948	Citation	1961	Kelso	1974	Forego	1990	Criminal Type
1949	Capot	1962	Kelso	1975	Forego	1991	Black Tie Affair
1950	Hill Prince	1963	Kelso	1976	Forego	1992	A.P. Indy
				1977	Seattle Slew	1993	Kotashaan

HARNESS RACING

Harness Horse of the Year

(Chosen by the U.S. Trotting Assn. and the U.S. Harness Writers Assn.)

1951	Pronto Don	1962	Su Mac Lad	1973	Sir Dalrae	1984	Fancy Crown
1952	Good Time	1963	Speedy Scot	1974	Delmonica Hanover	1985	Nihilator
1953	Hi Lo's Forbes	1964	Bret Hanover	1975	Savior	1986	Forrest Skipper
1954	Stenographer	1965	Bret Hanover	1976	Keystone Ore	1987	Mack Lobell
1955	Scott Frost	1966	Bret Hanover	1977	Green Speed	1988	Mack Lobell
1956	Scott Frost	1967	Nevele Pride	1978	Abercrombie	1989	Matt's Scooter
1957	Torpid	1968	Nevele Pride	1979	Niatross	1990	Beach Towel
1958	Emily's Pride	1969	Nevele Pride	1980	Niatross	1991	Precious Bunny
1959	Bye Bye Byrd	1970	Fresh Yankee	1981	Fan Hanover	1992	Artsplace
1960	Adios Butler	1971	Albatross	1982	Cam Fella	1993	Staying Together
1961	Adios Butler	1972	Albatross	1983	Cam Fella		

The Hambletonian (3-year-old trotters)

Year	Winner	Driver	Year	Winner	Driver
1965	Egyptian Candor	Del Cameron	1980	Burgomeister	Bill Haughton
1966	Kerry Way	Frank Ervin	1981	Shiaway St. Pat	Ray Remmen
1967	Speedy Streak	Del Cameron	1982	Speed Bowl	Tommy Haughton
1968	Nevele Pride	Stanley Dancer	1983	Duenna	Stanley Dancer
1969	Lindy's Pride	Howard Beissinger	1984	Historic Freight	Ben Webster
1970	Timothy T	John Simpson Sr.	1985	Prakas	Bill O'Donnell
1971	Speedy Crown	Howard Beissinger	1986	Nuclear Kosmos	Ulf Thoresen
1972	Super Bowl	Stanley Dancer	1987	Mack Lobell	John Campbell
1973	Flirth	Ralph Baldwin	1988	Armbro Goal	John Campbell
1974	Christopher T	Bill Haughton	1989	Park Avenue Joe	Ron Waples
1975	Bonefish	Stanley Dancer	1990	Harmonious	John Campbell
1976	Steve Lobell	Bill Haughton	1991	Giant Victory	Jack Moiseyev
1977	Green Speed	Bill Haughton	1992	Alf Palema	Mickey McNicholl
1978	Speedy Somolli	Howard Beissinger	1993	American Winner	Ron Pierce
1979	Legend Hanover	George Sholty	1994	Victory Dream	Michael La Chance

BOWLING

Professional Bowlers Association

Hall of Fame

Performance

Bill Allen
Glenn Allison
Earl Anthony
Barry Asher
Ray Bluth
Roy Buckley
Nelson Burton Jr.
Don Carter
Pat Colwell
Steve Cook
Dave Davis
Gary Dickinson
Mike Durbin
Buzz Fazio
Skee Foremsky
Jim Godman
Johnny Guenther
Billy Hardwick
Tommy Hudson
Don Johnson
Joe Joseph
Larry Laub
Mike Limongello
Don McCune
Mike McGrath
George Pappas
Johnny Petraglia
Dick Ritger
Mark Roth
Jim St. John
Carmen Salvino
Bob Strampe
Harry Smith
Dave Soutar
Jim Stefanich
Brian Voss
Wayne Webb
Dick Weber
Billy Welu
Wayne Zahn

Meritorious service

Joe Antenora
John Archibald
Chuck Clemons
Eddie Elias
Frank Esposito
Dick Evans
Raymond Firestone
E. A. "Bud" Fisher
Lou Frantz
Harry Golden
Ted Hoffman Jr.
John Jowdy
Joe Kelley
Steve Nagy
Chuck Pezzano
Jack Reichert
Joe Richards
Chris Schenkel
Lorraine Stilzlein
Al Thompson

Tournament of Champions

Year	Winner	Year	Winner	Year	Winner	Year	Winner
1965	Billy Hardwick	1973	Jim Godman	1980	Wayne Webb	1988	Mark Williams
1966	Wayne Zahn	1974	Earl Anthony	1981	Steve Cook	1989	Del Ballard Jr.
1967	Jim Stefanich	1975	Dave Davis	1982	Mike Durbin	1990	Dave Ferraro
1968	Dave Davis	1976	Marshall Holman	1983	Joe Berardi	1991	David Ozio
1969	Jim Godman	1977	Mike Berlin	1984	Mike Durbin	1992	Marc McDowell
1970	Don Johnson	1978	Earl Anthony	1985	Mark Williams	1993	George Branham 3d
1971	Johnny Petraglia	1979	George Pappas	1986	Marshall Holman	1994	Norm Duke
1972	Mike Durbin			1987	Pete Weber		

PBA Leading Money Winners

Total winnings are from PBA, ABC Masters, and BPAA All-Star tournaments only, and do not include numerous other tournaments or earnings from special television shows and matches.

Year	Bowler	Amount	Year	Bowler	Amount	Year	Bowler	Amount
1962	Don Carter	$49,972	1974	Earl Anthony	$99,585	1985	Mike Aulby	$201,200
1963	Dick Weber	46,333	1975	Earl Anthony	107,585	1986	Walter Ray Williams Jr.	145,550
1964	Bob Strampe	33,592	1976	Earl Anthony	110,833	1987	Pete Weber	175,491
1965	Dick Weber	47,674	1977	Mark Roth	105,583	1988	Brian Voss	225,485
1966	Wayne Zahn	54,720	1978	Mark Roth	134,500	1989	Mike Aulby	298,237
1967	Dave Davis	54,165	1979	Mark Roth	124,517	1990	Amleto Monacelli	204,775
1968	Jim Stefanich	67,377	1980	Wayne Webb	116,700	1991	David Ozio	225,585
1969	Billy Hardwick	64,160	1981	Earl Anthony	164,735	1992	Marc McDowell	174,215
1970	Mike McGrath	52,049	1982	Earl Anthony	134,760	1993	Walter Ray Williams Jr.	296,370
1971	Johnny Petraglia	85,065	1983	Earl Anthony	135,605			
1972	Don Johnson	56,648	1984	Mark Roth	158,712			
1973	Don McCune	69,000						

Leading PBA Averages by Year

Year	Bowler	Average	Year	Bowler	Average	Year	Bowler	Average
1962	Don Carter	212.844	1973	Earl Anthony	215.799	1984	Marshall Holman	213.911
1963	Billy Hardwick	210.346	1974	Earl Anthony	219.394	1985	Mark Baker	213.718
1964	Ray Bluth	210.512	1975	Earl Anthony	219.060	1986	John Gant	214.378
1965	Dick Weber	211.895	1976	Mark Roth	215.970	1987	Marshall Holman	216.801
1966	Wayne Zahn	208.663	1977	Mark Roth	218.174	1988	Mark Roth	218.036
1967	Wayne Zahn	212.342	1978	Mark Roth	219.834	1989	Pete Weber	215.432
1968	Jim Stefanich	211.895	1979	Mark Roth	221.662	1990	Amleto Monacelli	218.158
1969	Bill Hardwick	212.957	1980	Earl Anthony	218.535	1991	Norm Duke	218.208
1970	Nelson Burton Jr.	214.908	1981	Mark Roth	216.699	1992	Dave Ferraro	219.702
1971	Don Johnson	213.977	1982	Marshall Holman	212.844	1993	Walter Ray Williams Jr.	222.980
1972	Don Johnson	215.290	1983	Earl Anthony	216.645			

American Bowling Congress Masters Tournament Champions

Year	Winner	Year	Winner	Year	Winner
1980	Neil Burton, St. Louis, MO	1985	Steve Wunderlich, St. Louis, MO	1990	Chris Warren, Dallas, TX
1981	Randy Lightfoot, St. Charles, MO	1986	Mark Fahy, Chicago, IL	1991	Doug Kent, Canandaigua, NY
1982	Joe Berardi, Brooklyn, NY	1987	Rick Steelsmith, Wichita, KS	1992	Ken Johnson, N. Richmond Hills, TX
1983	Mike Lastowski, Havre de Grace, MD	1988	Del Ballard Jr., Richardson, TX	1993	Norm Duke, Oklahoma City, OK
1984	Earl Anthony, Dublin, CA	1989	Mike Aulby, Indianapolis, IN	1994	Steve Fehr, Cincinnati, OH

Most Sanctioned 300 Games

Mike Whalin, Cincinnati, OH 48
Bob Learn Jr., Erie, PA 45
Jim Johnson Jr., Wilmington, DE. . . 43
Joe Jimenez, Saginaw, MI 34
Ron Woolet, Louisville, KY. 33
John Wilcox Jr., Shavertown, PA . . 32
Doug Spicer, W. Bloomfield, MI . . . 30
Bob Buckery, McAdoo, PA. 28
Elvin Mesger, Sullivan, MO 27
Steve Gehringer, Reading, PA . . . 27
Jim Ewald Jr., Louisville, KY. 26
Ralph Burley Jr., Dayton, OH 26
Mark Stibora, Cleveland, OH 25
Alan Hulsizer, Reading, PA 25
Tony Torrice, Wolcott, CT 24
Jerry Kessler, Dayton, OH 23
Teata Semiz, Fairfield, NJ 23
Mitch Jabczenski, Detroit, MI 23
Jerome Penxa, Detroit, MI 23
Anthony Juliano, Margate, FL. 22
Don Anthony, Columbus, OH 22
Jeff Jensen, Wichita, KS 22
Dave Soutar, Kansas City, MO. . . . 22
Randy Choat, Granite City, IL. 22
Steve Carson, Oklahoma City, OK . 21
Dave Heller, Highland Falls, NY . . . 21
Bob Goike, Belleville, MI 21
Gary Barney, St. Louis, MO 21
John Chako Jr., Larksville, PA 21
Joe Vito Buenrostro, San Antonio, TX 20
Paul Cannon, Binghamton, NY. . . . 20
Nicolas Wissinger, Detroit, MI. 20
Jim Doherty, Oklahoma City, OK . . 18

Women's International Bowling Congress

Champions in 1994

Queens Tournament—Anne Marie Duggan, Edmond, OK
Singles Event—Vicki Fifield, El Paso, TX
All Events—Wendy Macpherson-Papanos, Henderson, NV
Doubles Event—(tie) Lucy Giovinco, Norcross, GA and Cindy Coburn-Carroll, Tonawanda, NY; Rachael Perez, San Antonio, TX and Kim Straub, Beatrice, NE
Team—Strike Zone Pro Shop, Rolling, IL

Most Sanctioned 300 Games

Jeanne Maiden-Naccarato, Tacoma, WA. 21
Tish Johnson, Panorama City, CA . 19
Aleta Sill, Dearborn, MI 17
Vicki Fischel, Wheat Ridge, CO . . . 15
Leanne Barrette, Youkon, OK 14
Betty Morris, Stockton, CA. 12
Donna Adamek, Apple Valley, CA. . 11
Cheryl Daniels, Detroit, MI 11
Cindy Coburn-Carroll, Tonawanda, NY 10
Robin Romeo, Van Nuys, CA. 9

Figure Skating Champions

U.S. Champions		World Champions		
Men	**Women**	**Year**	**Men**	**Women**
Dick Button	Tenley Albright	**1952**	Dick Button, U.S.	Jacqueline du Bief, France
Hayes Jenkins	Tenley Albright	**1953**	Hayes Jenkins, U.S.	Tenley Albright, U.S.
Hayes Jenkins	Tenley Albright	**1954**	Hayes Jenkins, U.S.	Gundi Busch, W. Germany
Hayes Jenkins	Tenley Albright	**1955**	Hayes Jenkins, U.S.	Tenley Albright, U.S.
Hayes Jenkins	Tenley Albright	**1956**	Hayes Jenkins, U.S.	Carol Heiss, U.S.
Dave Jenkins	Carol Heiss	**1957**	Dave Jenkins, U.S.	Carol Heiss, U.S.
Dave Jenkins	Carol Heiss	**1958**	Dave Jenkins, U.S.	Carol Heiss, U.S.
Dave Jenkins	Carol Heiss	**1959**	Dave Jenkins, U.S.	Carol Heiss, U.S.
Dave Jenkins	Carol Heiss	**1960**	Alain Giletti, France	Carol Heiss, U.S.
Bradley Lord	Laurence Owen	**1961**	none	none
Monty Hoyt	Barbara Roles Pursley	**1962**	Don Jackson, Canada	Sjoukje Dijkstra, Neth.
Tommy Litz	Lorraine Hanlon	**1963**	Don McPherson, Canada	Sjoukje Dijkstra, Neth.
Scott Allen	Peggy Fleming	**1964**	Manfred Schnelldorfer, W. Germany	Sjoukje Dijkstra, Neth.
Gary Visconti	Peggy Fleming	**1965**	Alain Calmat, France	Petra Burka, Canada
Scott Allen	Peggy Fleming	**1966**	Emmerich Danzer, Austria	Peggy Fleming, U.S.
Gary Visconti	Peggy Fleming	**1967**	Emmerich Danzer, Austria	Peggy Fleming, U.S.
Tim Wood	Peggy Fleming	**1968**	Emmerich Danzer, Austria	Peggy Fleming, U.S.
Tim Wood	Janet Lynn	**1969**	Tim Wood, U.S.	Gabriele Seyfert, E. Germany
Tim Wood	Janet Lynn	**1970**	Tim Wood, U.S.	Gabriele Seyfert, E. Germany
John Misha Petkevich	Janet Lynn	**1971**	Ondrej Nepela, Czech.	Beatrix Schuba, Austria
Ken Shelley	Janet Lynn	**1972**	Ondrej Nepela, Czech.	Beatrix Schuba, Austria
Gordon McKellen Jr.	Janet Lynn	**1973**	Ondrej Nepela, Czech.	Karen Magnussen, Canada
Gordon McKellen Jr.	Dorothy Hamill	**1974**	Jan Hoffmann, E. Germany	Christine Errath, E. Germany
Gordon McKellen Jr.	Dorothy Hamill	**1975**	Sergei Volkov, USSR	Dianne de Leeuw, Neth.-U.S.
Terry Kubicka	Dorothy Hamill	**1976**	John Curry, Gr. Britain	Dorothy Hamill, U.S.
Charles Tickner	Linda Fratianne	**1977**	Vladimir Kovalev, USSR	Linda Fratianne, U.S.
Charles Tickner	Linda Fratianne	**1978**	Charles Tickner, U.S.	Anett Poetzsch, E. Germany
Charles Tickner	Linda Fratianne	**1979**	Vladimir Kovalev, USSR	Linda Fratianne, U.S.
Charles Tickner	Linda Fratianne	**1980**	Jan Hoffmann, E. Germany	Anett Poetzsch, E. Germany
Scott Hamilton	Elaine Zayak	**1981**	Scott Hamilton, U.S.	Denise Biellmann, Switzerland
Scott Hamilton	Rosalynn Sumners	**1982**	Scott Hamilton, U.S.	Elaine Zayak, U.S.
Scott Hamilton	Rosalynn Sumners	**1983**	Scott Hamilton, U.S.	Rosalynn Sumners, U.S.
Scott Hamilton	Rosalynn Sumners	**1984**	Scott Hamilton, U.S.	Katarina Witt, E. Germany
Brian Boitano	Tiffany Chin	**1985**	Aleksandr Fadeev, USSR	Katarina Witt, E. Germany
Brian Boitano	Debi Thomas	**1986**	Brian Boitano, U.S.	Debi Thomas, U.S.
Brian Boitano	Jill Trenary	**1987**	Brian Orser, Canada	Katarina Witt, E. Germany
Brian Boitano	Debi Thomas	**1988**	Brian Boitano, U.S.	Katarina Witt, E. Germany
Christopher Bowman	Jill Trenary	**1989**	Kurt Browning, Canada	Midori Ito, Japan
Todd Eldredge	Jill Trenary	**1990**	Kurt Browning, Canada	Jill Trenary, U.S.
Todd Eldredge	Tonya Harding	**1991**	Kurt Browning, Canada	Kristi Yamaguchi, U.S.
Christopher Bowman	Kristi Yamaguchi	**1992**	Viktor Petrenko, Ukraine	Kristi Yamaguchi, U.S.
Scott Davis	Nancy Kerrigan	**1993**	Kurt Browning, Canada	Oksana Baiul, Ukraine
Scott Davis	vacant[1]	**1994**	Elvis Stojko, Canada	Yuka Sato, Japan

(1) Tonya Harding was stripped of title.

James E. Sullivan Memorial Trophy Winners

The James E. Sullivan Memorial Trophy, named after the former president of the AAU and inaugurated in 1930, is awarded annually by the AAU to the athlete who "by his or her performance, example and influence as an amateur, has done the most during the year to advance the cause of sportsmanship."

Year	Winner	Sport
1930	Bobby Jones	Golf
1931	Barney Berlinger	Track
1932	Jim Bausch	Track
1933	Glenn Cunningham	Track
1934	Bill Bonthron	Track
1935	Lawson Little	Golf
1936	Glenn Morris	Track
1937	Don Budge	Tennis
1938	Don Lash	Track
1939	Joe Burk	Rowing
1940	Greg Rice	Track
1941	Leslie MacMitchell	Track
1942	Cornelius Warmerdam	Track
1943	Gilbert Dodds	Track
1944	Ann Curtis	Swimming
1945	Doc Blanchard	Football
1946	Arnold Tucker	Football
1947	John Kelly Jr.	Rowing
1948	Robert Mathias	Track
1949	Dick Button	Skating
1950	Fred Wilt	Track
1951	Rev. Robert Richards	Track
1952	Horace Ashenfelter	Track
1953	Dr. Sammy Lee	Diving
1954	Mal Whitfield	Track
1955	Harrison Dillard	Track
1956	Patricia McCormick	Diving
1957	Bobby Joe Morrow	Track
1958	Glenn Davis	Track
1959	Parry O'Brien	Track
1960	Rafer Johnson	Track
1961	Wilma Rudolph Ward	Track
1962	James Beatty	Track
1963	John Pennel	Track
1964	Don Schollander	Swimming
1965	Bill Bradley	Basketball
1966	Jim Ryun	Track
1967	Randy Matson	Track
1968	Debbie Meyer	Swimming
1969	Bill Toomey	Track
1970	John Kinsella	Swimming
1971	Mark Spitz	Swimming
1972	Frank Shorter	Track
1973	Bill Walton	Basketball
1974	Rick Wohlhutter	Track
1975	Tim Shaw	Swimming
1976	Bruce Jenner	Track
1977	John Naber	Swimming
1978	Tracy Caulkins	Swimming
1979	Kurt Thomas	Gymnastics
1980	Eric Heiden	Speed Skating
1981	Carl Lewis	Track
1982	Mary Decker	Track
1983	Edwin Moses	Track
1984	Greg Louganis	Diving
1985	Joan Benoit Samuelson	Marathon
1986	Jackie Joyner-Kersee	Track
1987	Jim Abbott	Baseball
1988	Florence Griffith Joyner	Track
1989	Janet Evans	Swimming
1990	John Smith	Wrestling
1991	Mike Powell	Track
1992	Bonnie Blair	Speed Skating
1993	Charlie Ward	Football, Basketball

Professional Sports Directory

Major League Baseball

Commissioner's Office
350 Park Ave.
New York, NY 10022

National League

National League Office
350 Park Ave.
New York, NY 10022

Atlanta Braves
521 Capitol Ave. SW
Atlanta, GA 30312

Chicago Cubs
Wrigley Field
Chicago, IL 60613

Cincinnati Reds
100 Riverfront Stadium
Cincinnati, OH 45202

Colorado Rockies
1700 Broadway
Denver, CO 80290

Florida Marlins
2267 NW 199th St.
Miami, FL 33056

Houston Astros
PO Box 288
Houston, TX 77001

Los Angeles Dodgers
Dodger Stadium
Los Angeles, CA 90012

Montreal Expos
PO Box 500, Station M
Montreal, Que. H1V 3P2

New York Mets
Shea Stadium
Flushing, NY 11368

Philadelphia Phillies
PO Box 7575
Philadelphia, PA 19101

Pittsburgh Pirates
Three Rivers Stadium
Pittsburgh, PA 15212

St. Louis Cardinals
Busch Memorial Stadium
St. Louis, MO 63102

San Diego Padres
PO Box 2000
San Diego, CA 92112

San Francisco Giants
Candlestick Park
San Francisco, CA 94124

American League

American League Office
350 Park Ave.
New York, NY 10022

Baltimore Orioles
333 W. Camden St.
Baltimore, MD 21202

Boston Red Sox
24 Yawkey Way
Boston, MA 02215

California Angels
Anaheim Stadium
Anaheim, CA 92803

Chicago White Sox
333 W. 35th St.
Chicago, IL 60616

Cleveland Indians
2401 Ontario St.
Cleveland, OH 44115

Detroit Tigers
Tiger Stadium
Detroit, MI 48216

Kansas City Royals
P.O. Box 419969
Kansas City, MO 64141

Milwaukee Brewers
Milwaukee County Stadium
Milwaukee, WI 53214

Minnesota Twins
501 Chicago Ave. South
Minneapolis, MN 55415

New York Yankees
Yankee Stadium
Bronx, NY 10451

Oakland Athletics
Oakland Coliseum
Oakland, CA 94621

Seattle Mariners
PO Box 4100
Seattle, WA 98104

Texas Rangers
PO Box 90111
Arlington, TX 76004

Toronto Blue Jays
1 Blue Jays Way
Toronto, Ont. M5V 1J1

National Basketball Association

League Office
645 5th Ave.
New York, NY 10022

Atlanta Hawks
One CNN Center
Atlanta, GA 30303

Boston Celtics
151 Merrimac St.
Boston, MA 02114

Charlotte Hornets
100 Hive Drive
Charlotte, NC 28217

Chicago Bulls
1901 W. Madison St.
Chicago, IL 60612

Cleveland Cavaliers
1 Center Court
Cleveland, OH 44115

Dallas Mavericks
777 Sports St.
Dallas, TX 75207

Denver Nuggets
1635 Clay St.
Denver, CO 80204

Detroit Pistons
Two Championship Dr.
Auburn Hills, MI 48326

Golden State Warriors
7000 Oakland Coliseum Way
Oakland, CA 94621

Houston Rockets
Ten Greenway Plaza
Houston, TX 77277

Indiana Pacers
300 E. Market St.
Indianapolis, IN 46204

Los Angeles Clippers
3939 S. Figueroa
Los Angeles, CA 90037

Los Angeles Lakers
3900 W. Manchester Blvd.
Inglewood, CA 90306

Miami Heat
The Miami Arena
Miami, FL 33136

Milwaukee Bucks
1001 N. 4th St.
Milwaukee, WI 53203

Minnesota Timberwolves
600 First Ave. N.
Minneapolis, MN 55403

New Jersey Nets
405 Murray Hill Parkway
E. Rutherford, NJ 07073

New York Knickerbockers
Two Pennsylvania Plaza
New York, NY 10121

Orlando Magic
One Magic Place
Orlando, FL 32801

Philadelphia 76ers
Veterans Stadium
Philadelphia, PA 19147

Phoenix Suns
208 E. Jefferson
Phoenix, AZ 85004

Portland Trail Blazers
700 NE Multnomah St.
Portland, OR 97232

Sacramento Kings
One Sports Parkway
Sacramento, CA 95834

San Antonio Spurs
100 Montana St.
San Antonio, TX 78203

Seattle SuperSonics
190 Queen Ann Ave. N.
Seattle, WA 98109

Utah Jazz
301 West S. Temple
Salt Lake City, UT 84101

Washington Bullets
USAir Arena
Landover, MD 20785

National Hockey League

League Headquarters
1251 Ave. of the Americas
New York, NY 10020

Mighty Ducks of Anaheim
2695 E. Katella Ave.
Anaheim, CA 92803

Boston Bruins
150 Causeway St.
Boston, MA 02114

Buffalo Sabres
140 Main St.
Buffalo, NY 14202

Calgary Flames
P.O. Box 1540
Calgary, Alta. T2P 3B9

Chicago Blackhawks
1901 W. Madison St.
Chicago, IL 60612

Dallas Stars
901 Main St.
Dallas, TX 75202

Detroit Red Wings
600 Civic Center Drive
Detroit, MI 48226

Edmonton Oilers
Northlands Coliseum
Edmonton, Alta. T5B 4M9

Florida Panthers
100 NE Third Ave.
Ft. Lauderdale, FL 33301

Hartford Whalers
242 Trumbull St.
Hartford, CT 06103

Los Angeles Kings
3900 W. Manchester Blvd.
Inglewood, CA 90306

Montreal Canadiens
2313 St. Catherine St. W
Montreal, Quebec H3H 1N2

New Jersey Devils
PO Box 504
E. Rutherford, NJ 07073

New York Islanders
Nassau Coliseum
Uniondale, NY 11553

New York Rangers
4 Pennsylvania Plaza
New York, NY 10001

Ottawa Senators
301 Moodie Dr.
Nepean, Ont. K2H 9C4

Philadelphia Flyers
Pattison Place
Philadelphia, PA 19148

Pittsburgh Penguins
Civic Arena
Pittsburgh, PA 15219

Quebec Nordiques
2205 Ave. du Colisee
Quebec, Que. G1L 4W7

St. Louis Blues
1401 Clark
St. Louis, MO 63103

San Jose Sharks
525 W. Santa Clara St.
San Jose, CA 95113

Tampa Bay Lightning
501 E. Kennedy Blvd.
Tampa, FL 33602

Toronto Maple Leafs
60 Carlton St.
Toronto, Ont. M5B 1L1

Vancouver Canucks
100 North Renfrew St.
Vancouver, B.C. V5K 3N7

Washington Capitals
USAir Arena
Landover, MD 20785

Winnipeg Jets
15-1430 Maroons Road
Winnipeg, Man. R3G 0L5

National Football League

League Office
410 Park Avenue
New York, NY 10022

Arizona Cardinals
PO Box 888
Phoenix, AZ 85001

Atlanta Falcons
2745 Burnett Road
Suwanee, GA 30174

Buffalo Bills
One Bills Drive
Orchard Park, NY 14127

Chicago Bears
250 N. Washington Rd.
Lake Forest, IL 60045

Cincinnati Bengals
200 Riverfront Stadium
Cincinnati, OH 45202

Cleveland Browns
80 First Ave.
Berea, OH 44017

Dallas Cowboys
One Cowboys Pkwy.
Irving, TX 75063

Denver Broncos
13655 E. Dove Valley Pkwy.
Englewood, CO 80112

Detroit Lions
1200 Featherstone Rd.
Pontiac, MI 48342

Green Bay Packers
PO Box 10628
Green Bay, WI 54307

Houston Oilers
6910 Fannin St.
Houston, TX 77030

Indianapolis Colts
PO Box 53500
Indianapolis, IN 46253

Kansas City Chiefs
One Arrowhead Drive
Kansas City, MO 64129

Los Angeles Raiders
332 Center St.
El Segundo, CA 90245

Los Angeles Rams
2327 W. Lincoln Ave.
Anaheim, CA 92801

Miami Dolphins
2269 NW 199 St.
Miami, FL 33056

Minnesota Vikings
9520 Viking Dr.
Eden Prairie, MN 55344

New England Patriots
60 Washington St.
Foxboro, MA 02035

New Orleans Saints
6928 Saints Dr.
Metairie, LA 70003

New York Giants
Giants Stadium
E. Rutherford, NJ 07073

New York Jets
1000 Fulton Ave.
Hempstead, NY 11550

Philadelphia Eagles
3501 S. Broad St.
Philadelphia, PA 19148

Pittsburgh Steelers
300 Stadium Circle
Pittsburgh, PA 15212

San Diego Chargers
P.O. Box 609609
San Diego, CA 92160

San Francisco 49ers
4949 Centennial Blvd.
Santa Clara, CA 95054

Seattle Seahawks
11220 NE 53d St.
Kirkland, WA 98033

Tampa Bay Buccaneers
One Buccaneer Place
Tampa, FL 33607

Washington Redskins
PO Box 17247
Washington, DC 20041

Other Sports Organizations

Amateur Athletic Union
3600 W. 86th St.
Indianapolis, IN 46268

Amateur Softball Assn.
2801 NE 50th St.
Oklahoma City, OK 73111

American Horse Show Assn.
220 E. 42d St.
New York, NY 10017

American Kennel Club
51 Madison Ave.
New York, NY 10010

American Water Ski Assn.
799 Overlook Dr. SE
Winter Haven, FL 33884

Canadian Football League
110 Eglinton Ave. W
Toronto, Ont. M4R 1A3

IndyCar
390 Enterprise Court
Bloomfield, MI 48302

Intl. Game Fish Assn.
1301 E. Atlantic Blvd.
Pompano Beach, FL 33060

LPGA
2570 Volusra Ave.
Daytona Beach, FL 32114

Little League Baseball
PO Box 3485
Williamsport, PA 17701

National Archery Assn.
One Olympic Plaza
Colorado Springs, CO 80909

NASCAR
PO Box 2875
Daytona Beach, FL 32120

NCAA
6201 College Blvd.
Overland Park, KS 66211

National Rifle Assn.
11250 Waples Mill Rd.
Fairfax, VA 22030

Pro Bowlers Assn.
1720 Merriman Rd.
Akron, OH 44334

PGA
100 Ave. of the Champions
Palm Beach Gardens, FL 33418

Pro Rodeo Cowboys Assn.
101 Pro Rodeo Dr.
Colorado Springs, CO 80919

Special Olympics
1350 New York Ave. NW
Washington, DC 20005

Thoroughbred Racing Assns.
420 Fair Hill Dr.
Elkton, MD 21921

USA Track & Field
One Hoosier Dome
Indianapolis, IN 46225

U.S. Auto Club
4910 W. 16th St.
Speedway, IN 46224

U.S. Figure Skating Assn.
20 First St.
Colorado Springs, CO 80906

U.S. Olympic Committee
One Olympic Plaza
Colorado Springs, CO 80909

U.S. Skiing Assn.
PO Box 100
Park City, UT 84060

U.S. Tennis Assn.
Flushing Meadow
Flushing York, NY 11368

U.S. Trotting Assn.
750 Michigan Ave.
Columbus, OH 43215

NCAA Wrestling Champions

Year	Champion	Year	Champion	Year	Champion	Year	Champion	Year	Champion
1964	Oklahoma State	1970	Iowa State	1976	Iowa	1982	Iowa	1988	Arizona State
1965	Iowa State	1971	Oklahoma State	1977	Iowa State	1983	Iowa	1989	Oklahoma State
1966	Oklahoma State	1972	Iowa State	1978	Iowa	1984	Iowa	1990	Oklahoma State
1967	Michigan State	1973	Iowa State	1979	Iowa	1985	Iowa	1991	Iowa
1968	Oklahoma State	1974	Oklahoma	1980	Iowa	1986	Iowa	1992	Iowa
1969	Iowa State	1975	Iowa	1981	Iowa	1987	Iowa State	1993	Iowa
								1994	Oklahoma State

World Swimming Records

As of Aug. 1993

Men's Records

Freestyle

Distance	Time	Holder	Country	Where made	Date
50 meters	**0:21.81**	Tom Jager	U.S.	Nashville, TN	Mar. 24, 1990
100 meters	**0:48.21**	Alexander Popov	Russia	Monte Carlo	June 18, 1994
200 meters	**1:46.69**	Giorgio Lamberti	Italy	Bonn	Aug. 15, 1989
400 meters	**3:43.80**	Kieren Perkins	Australia	Rome	Sept. 9, 1994
800 meters	**7:46.00**	Kieren Perkins	Australia	Victoria, Canada	Aug. 24, 1994
1,500 meters	**14:41.66**	Kieren Perkins	Australia	Victoria, Canada	Aug. 24, 1994

Breaststroke

Distance	Time	Holder	Country	Where made	Date
100 meters	**1:00.95**	Karolyi Guttler	Hungary	Sheffield, Gr. Britain	Aug. 5, 1994
200 meters	**2:10.16**	Mike Barrowman	U.S.	Barcelona	July 29, 1992

Butterfly

Distance	Time	Holder	Country	Where made	Date
100 meters	**0:52.84**	Pablo Morales	U.S.	Orlando, FL	June 23, 1986
200 meters	**1:55.69**	Melvin Stewart	U.S.	Perth, Australia	Jan. 12, 1991

Backstroke

Distance	Time	Holder	Country	Where made	Date
100 meters	**0:53.86**	Jeff Rouse	U.S.	Barcelona	July 29, 1992
200 meters	**1:56.57**	Martin Lopez-Zubero	Spain	Tuscaloosa, AL	Nov. 23, 1991

Individual Medley

Distance	Time	Holder	Country	Where made	Date
200 meters	**1:58.16**	Jani Sievinen	Finland	Rome	Sept. 11, 1994
400 meters	**4:12.30**	Tom Dolan	U.S.	Rome	Sept. 6, 1994

Freestyle Relays

Distance	Time	Holder	Country	Where made	Date
400 m. (4×100)	**3:16.53**	(Jacobs, Dalbey, Jager, Biondi)	U.S.	Seoul	Sept. 23, 1988
800 m. (4×200)	**7:11.95**	(Lepikov, Pychnenko, Taianovitch, Sadovyi)	Unified Team	Barcelona	July 27, 1992

Medley Relays

Distance	Time	Holder	Country	Where made	Date
400 m. (4×100)	**3:36.93**	(Berkoff, Schroeder, Jacobs, Biondi)	U.S.	Seoul	Sept. 25, 1988
		(Rouse, Diebel, Morales, Olsen)	U.S.	Barcelona	July 31, 1992

Women's Records

Freestyle

Distance	Time	Holder	Country	Where made	Date
50 meters	**0:24.51**	Jingyi Le	China	Rome	Sept. 11, 1994
100 meters	**0:54.01**	Jingyi Le	China	Rome	Sept. 5, 1994
200 meters	**1:56.78**	Franziska Van Almsick	Germany	Rome	Sept. 6, 1994
400 meters	**4:03.85**	Janet Evans	U.S.	Seoul	Sept. 22, 1988
800 meters	**8:16.22**	Janet Evans	U.S.	Tokyo	Aug. 20, 1989
1,500 meters	**15:52.10**	Janet Evans	U.S.	Orlando, FL	Mar. 26, 1988

Breaststroke

Distance	Time	Holder	Country	Where made	Date
100 meters	**1:07.69**	Samatha Riley	Australia	Rome	Sept. 9, 1994
200 meters	**2:24.76**	Rebecca Brown	Australia	Queensland, Australia	Mar. 16, 1994

Butterfly

Distance	Time	Holder	Country	Where made	Date
100 meters	**0:57.93**	Mary T. Meagher	U.S.	Brown Deer, WI	Aug. 16, 1981
200 meters	**2:05.96**	Mary T. Meagher	U.S.	Brown Deer, WI	Aug. 13, 1981

Backstroke

Distance	Time	Holder	Country	Where made	Date
100 meters	**1:00.16**	Cihong He	China	Rome	Sept. 10, 1994
200 meters	**2:06.62**	Krisztina Egerszegi	Hungary	Athens	Aug. 25, 1991

Individual Medley

Distance	Time	Holder	Country	Where made	Date
200 meters	**2:11.65**	Lin Li	China	Barcelona	July 30, 1992
400 meters	**4:36.10**	Petra Schneider	E. Germany	Ecuador	Aug. 1, 1982

Freestyle Relays

Distance	Time	Holder	Country	Where made	Date
400 m. (4×100)	**3:37.91**	Jingyi Le, Shan Ying, Ying Le, Lu Bin	China	Rome	Sept. 7, 1994

Medley Relays

Distance	Time	Holder	Country	Where made	Date
400 m. (4×100)	**4:01.67**	Cihong He, Guohong Dai, Limin Liu, Jingyi Le	China	Rome	Sept. 10, 1994

NATIONAL BASKETBALL ASSOCIATION

Final Standings, 1993-94 Season

Eastern Conference

Atlantic Division

	W	L	Pct	GB
New York	57	25	.695	—
Orlando	50	32	.610	7
New Jersey	45	37	.549	12
Miami	42	40	.512	15
Boston	32	50	.390	25
Philadelphia	25	57	.305	32
Washington	24	58	.293	33

Central Division

	W	L	Pct	GB
Atlanta	57	25	.695	—
Chicago	55	27	.671	2
Cleveland	47	35	.573	10
Indiana	47	35	.573	10
Charlotte	41	41	.500	16
Detroit	20	62	.244	37
Milwaukee	20	62	.244	37

Western Conference

Midwest Division

	W	L	Pct	GB
Houston	58	24	.707	—
San Antonio	55	27	.671	3
Utah	53	29	.646	5
Denver	42	40	.512	16
Minnesota	20	62	.244	38
Dallas	13	69	.159	45

Pacific Division

	W	L	Pct	GB
Seattle	63	19	.768	—
Phoenix	56	26	.683	7
Golden State	50	32	.610	13
Portland	47	35	.573	16
L.A. Lakers	33	49	.402	30
Sacramento	28	54	.341	35
L.A. Clippers	27	55	.329	36

NBA Regular Season Individual Highs in 1993-94

Most minutes played, season — 3,533: Latrell Sprewell, Golden State.

Most points, game — 71: David Robinson, San Antonio v. L.A. Clippers, Apr. 24.

Most field goals made, game — 26: David Robinson, San Antonio v. L.A. Clippers, Apr. 24.

Most field goal attempts, game — 41: David Robinson, San Antonio v. L.A. Clippers, Apr. 24.

3-point field goals made, highest percentage (min. 50 made), season — .459: Tracy Murray, Portland.

Most free throws made, game — 20: Kenny Anderson, New Jersey v. Detroit, Apr. 15 (OT). Non-overtime — 18: David Robinson, San Antonio v. L.A. Clippers, Apr. 24.

Most rebounds, game — 32: Dennis Rodman, San Antonio v. Dallas, Jan. 22.

Most offensive rebounds, season — 453: Dennis Rodman, San Antonio.

Most defensive rebounds, season — 914: Dennis Rodman, San Antonio.

Most assists, game — 25: Kevin Johnson, Phoenix v. San Antonio, Apr. 6.

Most steals, game — 10: Kevin Johnson, Phoenix v. Washington, Dec. 9.

Most personal fouls, season — 312: Shawn Kemp, Seattle.

Most games disqualified, season — 11: Shawn Kemp, Seattle; Rik Smits, Indiana.

Rockets Win First Championship by Beating Knicks in Seven Games

The Houston Rockets won their first National Basketball Association championship by defeating the New York Knicks 4 games to 3. For the first time since the 24-second shot clock was introduced in the 1954-55 season, neither team scored 100 points in any of the championship games. Houston center Hakeem Olajuwon won Finals MVP honors, becoming the first player ever to be named Defensive Player of the Year, regular-season MVP, and NBA Finals MVP in the same season.

Houston Rockets

	FG A-M	FT A-M	Reb O-D	Ast	Avg
Olajuwon	150-75	43-37	13-51	25	26.9
Maxwell	96-35	22-15	3-20	20	13.4
Horry	74-24	21-13	13-30	26	10.3
Cassel	45-19	27-25	6-16	20	10.0
Thorpe	52-27	22-11	23-56	23	9.3
Herrera	38-22	8-6	8-17	3	7.1
Smith	36-14	6-6	2-8	22	5.6
Bullard	10-2	4-2	2-4	0	4.0
Elie	20-5	6-5	3-4	7	2.4
Cureton	0-0	0-0	0-0	0	0.0
Jent	2-0	0-0	0-1	0	0.0

New York Knicks

	FG A-M	FT A-M	Reb O-D	Ast	Avg
Ewing	160-58	21-15	32-55	12	18.9
Starks	106-39	39-30	3-19	41	17.7
Harper	90-42	17-14	7-14	42	16.4
Oakley	64-31	18-15	29-54	17	11.0
Smith	59-26	19-13	14-16	12	9.3
Mason	47-22	25-16	14-34	9	8.6
Anthony	31-10	2-2	3-3	17	3.3
Bonner	2-2	1-0	1-1	0	2.0
Davis	10-2	6-3	2-0	2	1.6
Williams	1-0	0-0	0-0	0	0.0

1994 NBA Playoff Results

Eastern Division

Atlanta defeated Miami 3 games to 2
New York defeated New Jersey 3 games to 1
Chicago defeated Cleveland 3 games to 0
Indiana defeated Orlando 3 games to 0
New York defeated Chicago 4 games to 3
Indiana defeated Atlanta 4 games to 2
New York defeated Indiana 4 games to 3

Western Division

Denver defeated Seattle 3 games to 2
Houston defeated Portland 3 games to 1
Phoenix defeated Golden State 3 games to 0
Utah defeated San Antonio 3 games to 1
Houston defeated Phoenix 4 games to 3
Utah defeated Denver 4 games to 3
Houston defeated Utah 4 games to 1

Championship

Houston defeated New York 4 games to 3

MVP in Playoffs

1969 Jerry West, Los Angeles
1970 Willis Reed, New York
1971 Lew Alcindor, Milwaukee
1972 Wilt Chamberlain, Los Angeles
1973 Willis Reed, New York
1974 John Havlicek, Boston
1975 Rick Barry, Golden State
1976 Jo Jo White, Boston
1977 Bill Walton, Portland
1978 Wes Unseld, Washington
1979 Dennis Johnson, Seattle
1980 Magic Johnson, Los Angeles
1981 Cedric Maxwell, Boston
1982 Magic Johnson, Los Angeles
1983 Moses Malone, Philadelphia
1984 Larry Bird, Boston
1985 Kareem Abdul-Jabbar, L.A. Lakers
1986 Larry Bird, Boston
1987 Magic Johnson, L.A. Lakers
1988 James Worthy, L.A. Lakers
1989 Joe Dumars, Detroit
1990 Isiah Thomas, Detroit
1991 Michael Jordan, Chicago
1992 Michael Jordan, Chicago
1993 Michael Jordan, Chicago
1994 Hakeem Olajuwon, Houston

NBA Scoring Leaders

Year	Scoring champion	Pts	Avg
1947	Joe Fulks, Philadelphia	1,389	23.2
1948	Max Zaslofsky, Chicago	1,007	21.0
1949	George Mikan, Minneapolis	1,698	28.3
1950	George Mikan, Minneapolis	1,865	27.4
1951	George Mikan, Minneapolis	1,932	28.4
1952	Paul Arizin, Philadelphia	1,674	25.4
1953	Neil Johnston, Philadelphia	1,564	22.3
1954	Neil Johnston, Philadelphia	1,759	24.4
1955	Neil Johnston, Philadelphia	1,631	22.7
1956	Bob Pettit, St. Louis	1,849	25.7
1957	Paul Arizin, Philadelphia	1,817	25.6
1958	George Yardley, Detroit	2,001	27.8
1959	Bob Pettit, St. Louis	2,105	29.2
1960	Wilt Chamberlain, Philadelphia	2,707	37.9
1961	Wilt Chamberlain, Philadelphia	3,033	38.4
1962	Wilt Chamberlain, Philadelphia	4,029	50.4
1963	Wilt Chamberlain, San Francisco	3,586	44.8
1964	Wilt Chamberlain, San Francisco	2,948	36.5
1965	Wilt Chamberlain, San Fran., Phila.	2,534	34.7
1966	Wilt Chamberlain, Philadelphia	2,649	33.5
1967	Rick Barry, San Francisco	2,775	35.6
1968	Dave Bing, Detroit	2,142	27.1
1969	Elvin Hayes, San Diego	2,327	28.4
1970	Jerry West, Los Angeles	2,309	31.2
1971	Lew Alcindor, Milwaukee	2,596	31.7
1972	Kareem Abdul-Jabbar (Alcindor), Milwaukee	2,822	34.8
1973	Nate Archibald, Kansas City-Omaha	2,719	34.0
1974	Bob McAdoo, Buffalo	2,261	30.6
1975	Bob McAdoo, Buffalo	2,831	34.5
1976	Bob McAdoo, Buffalo	2,427	31.1
1977	Pete Maravich, New Orleans	2,273	31.1
1978	George Gervin, San Antonio	2,232	27.2
1979	George Gervin, San Antonio	2,365	29.6
1980	George Gervin, San Antonio	2,585	33.1
1981	Adrian Dantley, Utah	2,452	30.7
1982	George Gervin, San Antonio	2,551	32.3
1983	Alex English, Denver	2,326	28.4
1984	Adrian Dantley, Utah	2,418	30.6
1985	Bernard King, New York	1,809	32.9
1986	Dominique Wilkins, Atlanta	2,366	30.3
1987	Michael Jordan, Chicago	3,041	37.1
1988	Michael Jordan, Chicago	2,868	35.0
1989	Michael Jordan, Chicago	2,633	32.5
1990	Michael Jordan, Chicago	2,753	33.6
1991	Michael Jordan, Chicago	2,580	31.5
1992	Michael Jordan, Chicago	2,404	30.1
1993	Michael Jordan, Chicago	2,541	32.6
1994	David Robinson, San Antonio	2,383	29.8

NBA Most Valuable Player

1956 Bob Pettit, St. Louis
1957 Bob Cousy, Boston
1958 Bill Russell, Boston
1959 Bob Pettit, St. Louis
1960 Wilt Chamberlain, Philadelphia
1961 Bill Russell, Boston
1962 Bill Russell, Boston
1963 Bill Russell, Boston
1964 Oscar Robertson, Cincinnati
1965 Bill Russell, Boston
1966 Wilt Chamberlain, Philadelphia
1967 Wilt Chamberlain, Philadelphia
1968 Wilt Chamberlain, Philadelphia
1969 Wes Unseld, Baltimore
1970 Willis Reed, New York
1971 Lew Alcindor, Milwaukee
1972 Kareem Abdul-Jabbar (Alcindor), Milwaukee
1973 Dave Cowens, Boston
1974 Kareem Abdul-Jabbar, Milwaukee
1975 Bob McAdoo, Buffalo
1976 Kareem Abdul-Jabbar, Los Angeles
1977 Kareem Abdul-Jabbar, Los Angeles
1978 Bill Walton, Portland
1979 Moses Malone, Houston
1980 Kareem Abdul-Jabbar, Los Angeles
1981 Julius Erving, Philadelphia
1982 Moses Malone, Houston
1983 Moses Malone, Philadelphia
1984 Larry Bird, Boston
1985 Larry Bird, Boston
1986 Larry Bird, Boston
1987 Magic Johnson, L.A. Lakers
1988 Michael Jordan, Chicago
1989 Magic Johnson, L.A. Lakers
1990 Magic Johnson, L.A. Lakers
1991 Michael Jordan, Chicago
1992 Michael Jordan, Chicago
1993 Charles Barkley, Phoenix
1994 Hakeem Olajuwon, Houston

NBA Champions 1947-94

	Regular season		Playoffs		
Year	Eastern Conference	Western Conference	Winner	Coach	Runner-up
1947	Washington	Chicago	Philadelphia	Ed Gottlieb	Chicago
1948	Philadelphia	St. Louis	Baltimore	Buddy Jeannette	Philadelphia
1949	Washington	Rochester	Minneapolis	John Kundla	Washington
1950	Syracuse	Minneapolis	Minneapolis	John Kundla	Syracuse
1951	Philadelphia	Minneapolis	Rochester	Lester Harrison	New York
1952	Syracuse	Rochester	Minneapolis	John Kundla	New York
1953	New York	Minneapolis	Minneapolis	John Kundla	New York
1954	New York	Minneapolis	Minneapolis	John Kundla	Syracuse
1955	Syracuse	Ft. Wayne	Syracuse	Al Cervi	Ft. Wayne
1956	Philadelphia	Ft. Wayne	Philadelphia	George Senesky	Ft. Wayne
1957	Boston	St. Louis	Boston	Red Auerbach	St. Louis
1958	Boston	St. Louis	St. Louis	Alex Hannum	Boston
1959	Boston	St. Louis	Boston	Red Auerbach	Minneapolis
1960	Boston	St. Louis	Boston	Red Auerbach	St. Louis
1961	Boston	St. Louis	Boston	Red Auerbach	St. Louis

	Regular season		Playoffs		
Year	Eastern Conference	Western Conference	Winner	Coach	Runner-up
1962	Boston	Los Angeles	Boston	Red Auerbach	Los Angeles
1963	Boston	Los Angeles	Boston	Red Auerbach	Los Angeles
1964	Boston	San Francisco	Boston	Red Auerbach	San Francisco
1965	Boston	Los Angeles	Boston	Red Auerbach	Los Angeles
1966	Philadelphia	Los Angeles	Boston	Red Auerbach	Los Angeles
1967	Philadelphia	San Francisco	Philadelphia	Alex Hannum	San Francisco
1968	Philadelphia	St. Louis	Boston	Bill Russell	Los Angeles
1969	Baltimore	Los Angeles	Boston	Bill Russell	Los Angeles
1970	New York	Atlanta	New York	Red Holzman	Los Angeles

	Atlantic	Central	Midwest	Pacific	Winner	Coach	Runner-up
1971	New York	Baltimore	Milwaukee	Los Angeles	Milwaukee	Lady Costello	Baltimore
1972	Boston	Baltimore	Milwaukee	Los Angeles	Los Angeles	Bill Sharman	New York
1973	Boston	Baltimore	Milwaukee	Los Angeles	New York	Red Holzman	Los Angeles
1974	Boston	Capital	Milwaukee	Los Angeles	Boston	Tom Heinsohn	Milwaukee
1975	Boston	Washington	Chicago	Golden State	Golden State	Al Attles	Washington
1976	Boston	Cleveland	Milwaukee	Golden State	Boston	Tom Heinsohn	Phoenix
1977	Philadelphia	Houston	Denver	Los Angeles	Portland	Jack Ramsay	Philadelphia
1978	Philadelphia	San Antonio	Denver	Portland	Washington	Dick Motta	Seattle
1979	Washington	San Antonio	Kansas City	Seattle	Seattle	Len Wilkens	Washington
1980	Boston	Atlanta	Milwaukee	Los Angeles	Los Angeles	Paul Westhead	Philadelphia
1981	Boston	Milwaukee	San Antonio	Phoenix	Boston	Bill Fitch	Houston
1982	Boston	Milwaukee	San Antonio	Los Angeles	Los Angeles	Pat Riley	Philadelphia
1983	Philadelphia	Milwaukee	San Antonio	Los Angeles	Philadelphia	Billy Cunningham	Los Angeles
1984	Boston	Milwaukee	Utah	Los Angeles	Boston	K.C. Jones	Los Angeles
1985	Boston	Milwaukee	Denver	L.A. Lakers	L.A. Lakers	Pat Riley	Boston
1986	Boston	Milwaukee	Houston	L.A. Lakers	Boston	K.C. Jones	Houston
1987	Boston	Atlanta	Dallas	L.A. Lakers	L.A. Lakers	Pat Riley	Boston
1988	Boston	Detroit	Denver	L.A. Lakers	L.A. Lakers	Pat Riley	Detroit
1989	New York	Detroit	Utah	L.A. Lakers	Detroit	Chuck Daly	L. A. Lakers
1990	Philadelphia	Detroit	San Antonio	L.A. Lakers	Detroit	Chuck Daly	Portland
1991	Boston	Chicago	San Antonio	Portland	Chicago	Phil Jackson	L. A. Lakers
1992	Boston	Chicago	Utah	Portland	Chicago	Phil Jackson	Portland
1993	New York	Chicago	Houston	Phoenix	Chicago	Phil Jackson	Phoenix
1994	New York	Atlanta	Houston	Seattle	Houston	Rudy Tomjanovich	New York

NBA Coach of the Year, 1963-94

1963 Harry Gallatin, St. Louis Hawks
1964 Alex Hannum, San Francisco Warriors
1965 Red Auerbach, Boston Celtics
1966 Dolph Schayes, Philadelphia 76ers
1967 Johnny Kerr, Chicago Bulls
1968 Richie Guerin, St. Louis Hawks
1969 Gene Shue, Baltimore Bullets
1970 Red Holzman, New York Knicks
1971 Dick Motta, Chicago Bulls
1972 Bill Sharman, Los Angeles Lakers
1973 Tom Heinsohn, Boston Celtics
1974 Ray Scott, Detroit Pistons
1975 Phil Johnson, Kansas City-Omaha Kings
1976 Bill Fitch, Cleveland Cavaliers
1977 Tom Nissalke, Houston Rockets
1978 Hubie Brown, Atlanta Hawks
1979 Cotton Fitzsimmons, Kansas City Kings
1980 Bill Fitch, Boston Celtics
1981 Jack McKinney, Indiana Pacers
1982 Gene Shue, Washington Bullets
1983 Don Nelson, Milwaukee Bucks
1984 Frank Layden, Utah Jazz
1985 Don Nelson, Milwaukee Bucks
1986 Mike Fratello, Atlanta Hawks
1987 Mike Schuler, Portland Trail Blazers
1988 Doug Moe, Denver Nuggets
1989 Cotton Fitzsimmons, Phoenix Suns
1990 Pat Riley, Los Angeles Lakers
1991 Don Chaney, Houston Rockets
1992 Don Nelson, Golden State Warriors
1993 Pat Riley, New York Knicks
1994 Lenny Wilkens, Atlanta Hawks

NBA All-League Team in 1994

First team	Position	Second team
Scottie Pippen, Chicago	Forward	Shawn Kemp, Seattle
Karl Malone, Utah	Forward	Charles Barkley, Phoenix
Hakeem Olajuwon, Houston	Center	David Robinson, San Antonio
John Stockton, Utah	Guard	Mitch Richmond, Sacramento
Latrell Sprewell, Golden State	Guard	Kevin Johnson, Phoenix

NBA Statistical Leaders, 1993-94

Scoring
(Minimum 70 games or 1,400 pts.)

	G	FG	Pts	Avg
Robinson, San Antonio. .	80	840	2383	29.8
O'Neal, Orlando.	81	953	2377	29.3
Olajuwon, Houston.	80	894	2184	27.3
Wilkins, Atl.-LAC	74	698	1923	26.0
K. Malone, Utah.	82	772	2063	25.2
Ewing, New York	79	745	1939	24.5
Richmond, Sacramento .	78	635	1823	23.4
Pippen, Chicago	72	627	1587	22.0
Barkley, Phoenix	65	518	1402	21.6
Rice, Miami	81	663	1708	21.1

Rebounds per Game
(Minimum 70 games or 800 rebounds)

	G	Def	Tot	Avg
Rodman, San Antonio . .	79	914	1367	17.3
O'Neal, Orlando	81	688	1072	13.2
Willis, Atlanta	80	628	963	12.0
Olajuwon, Houston	80	726	955	11.9
Polynice, Det.-Sac.	68	510	809	11.9
Mutombo, Denver	82	685	971	11.8
Oakley, New York	82	616	965	11.8
K. Malone, Utah	82	705	940	11.5
Coleman, New Jersey . .	77	608	870	11.3
Ewing, New York	79	666	885	11.2

Field Goal Percentage
(Minimum 300 field goals made)

	FG	FGA	Pct
O'Neal, Orlando	953	1591	.599
Mutombo, Denver	365	642	.569
Thorpe, Houston	449	801	.561
Webber, Golden State	572	1037	.552
Kemp, Seattle	533	990	.538
Vaught, L.A. Clippers	373	695	.537
Ceballos, Phoenix	425	795	.535
Smits, Indiana	493	923	.534
D. Davis, Indiana	308	582	.529
Olajuwon, Houston	894	1694	.528
Stockton, Utah	458	868	.528

Free Throw Percentage
(Minimum 125 free throws made)

	FT	FTA	Pct
Abdul-Rauf, Denver	219	229	.956
Miller, Indiana	403	444	.908
Pierce, Seattle	189	211	.896
Threatt, L.A. Lakers	138	155	.890
Price, Cleveland	238	268	.888
Rice, Miami	250	284	.880
Hornacek, Phi.-Utah	260	296	.878
Skiles, Orlando	195	222	.878
Porter, Portland	204	234	.872
Smith, Houston	135	155	.871

3-Point Field Goal Percentage
(Minimum 50 made)

	FG	FGA	Pct
Murray, Portland	50	109	.459
Armstrong, Chicago	60	135	.444
Miller, Indiana	123	292	.421
Kerr, Chicago	52	124	.419
Skiles, Orlando	68	165	.412
Murdock, Milwaukee	69	168	.411
Richmond, Sacremento	127	312	.407
Smith, Houston	89	220	.405
Curry, Charlotte	152	378	.402
Davis, New York	53	132	.402

Assists
(Minimum 70 games or 400 assists)

	G	Ast	Avg
Stockton, Utah	82	1031	12.6
Bogues, Charlotte	77	780	10.1
Blaylock, Atlanta	81	789	9.7
K. Anderson, New Jersey	82	784	9.6
K. Johnson, Phoenix	67	637	9.5
Strickland, Portland	82	740	9.0
Douglas, Boston	78	683	8.8
Jackson, L.A. Clippers	79	678	8.6
Price, Cleveland	76	589	7.8
M. Williams, Minnesota	71	512	7.2

Steals
(Minimum 70 games or 125 steals)

	G	Stl	Avg
McMillan, Seattle	73	216	2.96
Pippen, Chicago	72	211	2.93
Blaylock, Atlanta	81	212	2.62
Stockton, Utah	82	199	2.43
Murdock, Milwaukee	82	197	2.40
Hardaway, Orlando	82	190	2.32
Payton, Seattle	82	188	2.29
Gugliotta, Washington	78	172	2.21
Sprewell, Golden State	82	180	2.20
Brown, Boston	77	156	2.03

Blocked Shots
(Minimum 70 games or 100 blocked shots)

	G	Blk	Avg
Mutombo, Denver	82	336	4.10
Olajuwon, Houston	80	297	3.71
Robinson, San Antonio	80	265	3.31
Mourning, Charlotte	60	188	3.13
Bradley, Philadelphia	49	147	3.00
O'Neal, Orlando	81	231	2.85
Ewing, New York	79	217	2.75
Miller, Phoenix	69	156	2.26
Webber, Golden State	76	164	2.16
Kemp, Seattle	79	166	2.10

NBA Rookie of the Year

Year	Player
1953	Don Meineke, Ft. Wayne
1954	Ray Felix, Baltimore
1955	Bob Pettit, Milwaukee
1956	Maurice Stokes, Rochester
1957	Tom Heinsohn, Boston
1958	Woody Sauldsberry, Philadelphia
1959	Elgin Baylor, Minneapolis
1960	Wilt Chamberlain, Philadelphia
1961	Oscar Robertson, Cincinnati
1962	Walt Bellamy, Chicago
1963	Terry Dischinger, Chicago
1964	Jerry Lucas, Cincinnati
1965	Willis Reed, New York
1966	Rick Barry, San Francisco
1967	Dave Bing, Detroit
1968	Earl Monroe, Baltimore
1969	Wes Unseld, Baltimore
1970	Lew Alcindor, Milwaukee
1971	Dave Cowens, Boston; Geoff Petrie, Portland (tie)
1972	Sidney Wicks, Portland
1973	Bob McAdoo, Buffalo
1974	Ernie DiGregorio, Buffalo
1975	Keith Wilkes, Golden State
1976	Alvan Adams, Phoenix
1977	Adrian Dantley, Buffalo
1978	Walter Davis, Phoenix
1979	Phil Ford, Kansas City
1980	Larry Bird, Boston
1981	Darrell Griffith, Utah
1982	Buck Williams, New Jersey
1983	Terry Cummings, San Diego
1984	Ralph Sampson, Houston
1985	Michael Jordan, Chicago
1986	Patrick Ewing, New York
1987	Chuck Person, Indiana
1988	Mark Jackson, New York
1989	Mitch Richmond, Golden State
1990	David Robinson, San Antonio
1991	Derrick Coleman, New Jersey
1992	Larry Johnson, Charlotte
1993	Shaquille O'Neal, Orlando
1994	Chris Webber, Golden State

Individual Statistics, 1993-94
(Over 600 minutes played)

Atlanta Hawks

	Min	FG%	FT%	Reb	Ast	Pts	Avg
Wilkins	1687	.432	.854	305	114	1196	24.4
Manning	2520	.488	.669	465	261	1403	20.6
Willis	2867	.499	.713	963	150	1531	19.1
Augmon	2605	.510	.764	394	187	1212	14.8
Blaylock	2915	.411	.730	424	789	1118	13.8
Ehlo	2147	.446	.727	279	273	821	10.0
Ferrell	1155	.485	.783	129	65	513	7.1
Lang	1608	.469	.689	313	51	504	6.1
Keefe	763	.451	.730	201	34	273	4.3
Koncak	1823	.431	.667	365	102	342	4.2
Whatley	1004	.508	.788	99	181	292	3.6

Coach—Lenny Wilkens

Boston Celtics

	Min	FG%	FT%	Reb	Ast	Pts	Avg
Brown	2867	.480	.831	300	347	1192	15.5
Radja	2303	.521	.751	577	114	1208	15.1
Douglas	2789	.462	.641	193	683	1040	13.3
Parish	1987	.491	.740	542	82	866	11.7
Gamble	1880	.458	.817	159	149	864	11.5
McDaniel	1971	.461	.676	400	126	928	11.3
Fox	2096	.467	.757	355	217	887	10.8
Earl	1149	.406	.675	247	12	410	5.5
Pinckney	1524	.522	.736	478	62	394	5.2

Coach—Chris Ford

Charlotte Hornets

	Min	FG%	FT%	Reb	Ast	Pts	Avg
Mourning	2018	.505	.762	610	86	1287	21.5
L. Johnson	1757	.515	.695	448	184	834	16.4
Curry	2173	.455	.873	262	221	1335	16.3
Hawkins	2648	.460	.862	377	216	1180	14.4
Brickowski	2094	.488	.768	404	222	935	13.2
E. Johnson	1460	.459	.780	224	125	836	11.5
Bogues	2746	.471	.806	313	780	835	10.8
Gattison	1644	.524	.646	358	95	592	7.7
Wingate	1005	.481	.667	134	104	310	6.2
Burrell	767	.419	.657	132	62	244	4.8
Ellis	680	.484	.662	188	24	221	4.4
Bennett	983	.399	.733	90	163	248	3.4

Coach—Allan Bristow

Chicago Bulls

	Min	FG%	FT%	Reb	Ast	Pts	Avg
Pippen . .	2759	.491	.660	629	403	1587	22.0
Grant . . .	2570	.524	.596	769	236	1057	15.1
Armstrong	2770	.476	.855	170	323	1212	14.8
Kukoc . . .	1808	.431	.743	297	252	814	10.9
Kerr	2036	.497	.856	131	210	709	8.6
Myers . . .	2030	.455	.701	181	245	650	7.9
Williams .	638	.483	.612	181	39	289	7.6
Wennington	1371	.488	.818	353	70	542	7.1
Longley . .	1502	.471	.720	433	109	528	6.9
Cartwright	780	.513	.684	152	57	235	5.6
Blount . . .	690	.437	.613	194	56	198	3.0

Coach—Phil Jackson

Cleveland Cavaliers

	Min	FG%	FT%	Reb	Ast	Pts	Avg
Price	2386	.478	.888	228	589	1316	17.3
Daugherty	1838	.488	.785	508	149	848	17.0
Wilkins . .	2768	.457	.776	303	255	1170	14.3
Williams .	2660	.478	.728	575	193	1040	13.7
Nance . . .	909	.487	.753	227	49	370	11.2
Hill	1447	.543	.668	499	46	603	10.6
Mills	2022	.419	.778	401	128	743	9.4
Phills. . . .	1531	.471	.720	212	133	598	8.3
Brandon .	1548	.420	.858	159	277	606	8.3
Battle . . .	814	.476	.753	39	83	338	6.6
Ferry. . . .	965	.446	.884	141	74	350	5.0

Coach—Mike Fratello

Dallas Mavericks

	Min	FG%	FT%	Reb	Ast	Pts	Avg
Jackson .	3066	.445	.821	388	374	1576	19.2
Mashburn	2896	.406	.699	353	266	1513	19.2
Rooks . . .	1255	.491	.714	259	49	536	11.4
Smith . . .	1684	.435	.835	349	119	698	8.8
Campbell.	1214	.443	.783	186	82	555	8.8
Legler . . .	1322	.438	.840	128	120	656	8.3
Lever . . .	1947	.408	.765	283	213	555	6.9
Jones . . .	1773	.479	.729	605	99	468	5.8
Harris . . .	1165	.421	.731	157	106	418	5.4
Williams .	716	.445	.429	217	25	110	2.9
Dreiling . .	685	.500	.711	170	31	132	2.4

Coach—Quinn Buckner

Denver Nuggets

	Min	FG%	FT%	Reb	Ast	Pts	Avg
Abdul-Rauf	2617	.460	.956	168	362	1437	18.0
Ellis	2699	.502	.674	682	167	1215	15.4
R. Williams	2654	.412	.733	392	300	1065	13.0
Stith	2853	.450	.829	349	199	1023	12.5
Mutombo.	2853	.569	.583	971	127	986	12.0
Pack	1382	.443	.758	123	356	631	9.6
Rogers . .	1406	.439	.672	226	101	640	8.1
B. Williams	1507	.541	.649	446	50	639	8.0
Hammonds	877	.500	.683	199	34	301	4.1

Coach—Dan Issel

Detroit Pistons

	Min	FG%	FT%	Reb	Ast	Pts	Avg
Dumars . .	2591	.452	.836	151	261	1410	20.4
Mills	2773	.511	.797	672	177	1381	17.3
Thomas. .	1750	.417	.702	159	399	856	14.8
Elliott . . .	2409	.455	.803	263	197	885	12.1
Hunter. . .	2172	.375	.732	189	390	843	10.3
Houston .	1519	.405	.824	120	100	668	8.5
Anderson	1624	.543	.571	571	51	491	6.4
Chilcutt .	1365	.453	.631	371	86	450	5.9
Wood . . .	1182	.459	.756	239	51	322	4.1
Jones . . .	877	.462	.559	235	29	91	2.2

Coach—Don Chaney

Golden State Warriors

	Min	FG%	FT%	Reb	Ast	Pts	Avg
Sprewell .	3533	.433	.774	401	385	1720	21.0
Webber . .	2438	.552	.532	694	272	1333	17.5
Mullin . . .	2324	.472	.753	345	315	1040	16.8
Owens . .	2738	.507	.610	640	326	1186	15.0
Johnson .	2332	.492	.704	176	433	890	10.9
Alexander	1318	.530	.527	308	66	602	8.7
Gatling . .	1296	.588	.620	397	41	671	8.2
Grayer . .	1096	.526	.602	191	62	455	6.8
Jennings .	1097	.404	.833	89	218	432	5.7
Houston .	866	.458	.611	194	32	196	2.8

Coach—Don Nelson

Houston Rockets

	Min	FG%	FT%	Reb	Ast	Pts	Avg
Olajuwon .	3277	.528	.716	955	287	2184	27.3
Thorpe . . .	2909	.561	.657	870	189	1149	14.0
Maxwell . .	2571	.389	.749	229	380	1023	13.6
Smith	2209	.480	.871	138	327	906	11.6
Horry	2370	.459	.732	440	231	803	9.9
Elie	1606	.446	.860	181	208	626	9.3
Cassell. . .	1122	.418	.841	134	192	440	6.7
Brooks . . .	1225	.491	.871	102	149	381	5.2
Herrera . .	1292	.458	.711	285	37	353	4.7
Bullard . . .	725	.345	.769	84	64	226	3.5

Coach—Rudy Tomjanovich

Indiana Pacers

	Min	FG%	FT%	Reb	Ast	Pts	Avg
Miller	2638	.503	.908	212	248	1574	19.9
Smits	2113	.534	.793	483	156	1224	15.7
McKey . . .	2613	.500	.756	402	327	911	12.0
D. Davis . .	2292	.529	.527	718	100	771	11.7
Scott	1197	.467	.805	110	133	696	10.4
Richardson	1022	.452	.610	110	237	370	10.0
A. Davis . .	1732	.508	.642	505	55	626	7.7
Workman .	1714	.424	.802	204	404	501	7.7
Sealy	623	.405	.678	118	48	285	6.6
Fleming . .	1053	.462	.736	123	173	358	6.5
Williams . .	982	.488	.703	205	52	427	6.3
Mitchell . .	1084	.458	.745	190	65	362	4.8

Coach—Larry Brown

Los Angeles Clippers

	Min	FG%	FT%	Reb	Ast	Pts	Avg
Wilkins . . .	2635	.440	.847	481	169	1923	26.0
Harper . . .	2856	.426	.715	460	344	1508	20.1
Vaught . . .	2118	.537	.720	656	74	877	11.7
Jackson . .	2711	.452	.791	348	678	865	10.9
Aguirre . . .	859	.468	.694	116	104	413	10.6
Spencer . .	1930	.533	.599	415	75	673	8.9
Ellis	923	.545	.711	153	31	424	8.7
Grant	1533	.449	.855	142	291	588	7.5
Outlaw . . .	871	.587	.592	212	36	257	6.9
Williams . .	725	.431	.667	127	97	191	5.6
Dehere. . .	759	.377	.753	68	78	342	5.3
Tolbert . . .	640	.418	.733	108	30	187	3.8

Coach—Bob Weiss

Los Angeles Lakers

	Min	FG%	FT%	Reb	Ast	Pts	Avg
Divac	2685	.506	.686	851	307	1123	14.2
Peeler	923	.430	.803	109	94	423	14.1
Van Exel . .	2700	.394	.781	238	466	1099	13.6
Campbell . .	2253	.462	.689	519	86	934	12.3
Threatt	2278	.482	.890	153	344	965	11.9
Christie . . .	1515	.434	.697	235	136	672	10.3
Worthy	1597	.406	.741	181	154	812	10.2
Lynch.	1762	.508	.596	410	96	681	9.6
Smith	1617	.441	.714	195	148	645	8.8
Rambis . . .	635	.518	.648	189	32	164	3.3

Coach—Randy Pfund; Magic Johnson

Miami Heat

	Min	FG%	FT%	Reb	Ast	Pts	Avg
Rice.	2999	.467	.880	434	184	1708	21.1
Smith	2776	.456	.835	352	394	1346	17.3
Seikaly. . .	2410	.488	.720	740	136	1088	15.1
Long	2201	.446	.786	495	170	788	11.4
Miner	1358	.477	.828	156	95	661	10.5
Shaw	2037	.417	.719	350	385	693	9.0
Coles	1726	.449	.779	159	263	588	7.7
Salley . . .	1910	.477	.729	407	135	582	7.7
Geiger . . .	1199	.574	.779	303	32	521	7.2
Burton . . .	697	.438	.759	136	39	371	7.0

Coach—Kevin Loughery

Milwaukee Bucks

	Min	FG%	FT%	Reb	Ast	Pts	Avg
Murdock. .	2533	.468	.813	261	546	1257	15.3
Baker. . . .	2560	.501	.569	621	163	1105	13.5
Day	2127	.415	.698	310	138	966	12.7
Norman . .	2539	.448	.503	500	222	979	11.9
Edwards. .	2322	.478	.799	329	171	953	11.6
Strong . . .	1131	.413	.772	281	48	444	6.6
Barry	1242	.414	.795	146	168	445	6.2
Mayberry .	1472	.415	.690	101	215	433	5.3
Lohaus. . .	962	.363	.690	150	62	270	4.0

Coach—Mike Dunleavy

Minnesota Timberwolves

	Min	FG%	FT%	Reb	Ast	Pts	Avg
Laettner .	2428	.448	.783	602	307	1173	16.8
Rider. . . .	2415	.468	.811	315	202	1313	16.6
West. . . .	2182	.487	.810	231	172	1056	14.7
M. Williams	2206	.457	.839	221	512	971	13.7
Person . .	2029	.422	.759	253	185	894	11.6
King	1053	.428	.684	241	58	385	7.9
Bailey . . .	1297	.510	.799	215	54	583	7.4
Smith . . .	1617	.435	.674	122	285	473	5.9
Maxey. . .	626	.533	.714	199	10	248	4.5
Brown. . .	1921	.427	.653	447	72	299	3.6
Frank . . .	959	.419	.711	220	57	188	2.8

Coach—Sidney Lowe

New Jersey Nets

	Min	FG%	FT%	Reb	Ast	Pts	Avg
Coleman .	2778	.447	.774	870	262	1559	20.2
K. Anderson	3135	.417	.818	322	784	1538	18.8
Edwards .	2727	.458	.770	281	232	1144	14.0
Gilliam . .	1969	.510	.759	500	69	970	11.8
Morris . . .	1349	.447	.720	228	83	544	10.9
Newman .	1697	.471	.809	180	72	832	10.3
Benjamin.	1817	.480	.710	499	44	718	9.3
Brown. . .	1950	.415	.757	493	93	450	5.7
Williams .	877	.427	.605	263	26	322	4.6

Coach—Chuck Daly

New York Knickerbockers

	Min	FG%	FT%	Reb	Ast	Pts	Avg
Ewing . . .	2972	.496	.765	885	179	1939	24.5
Starks. . .	2057	.420	.754	185	348	1120	19.0
Oakley . .	2932	.478	.776	965	218	969	11.8
Davis . . .	1333	.471	.825	67	165	614	11.0
Smith . . .	1105	.443	.719	165	50	447	10.4
Harper . .	2204	.407	.687	141	334	791	9.6
Anthony .	1994	.394	.774	189	365	628	7.9
Blackman	969	.436	.906	93	76	400	7.3
Mason. . .	1903	.476	.720	427	151	528	7.2
Bonner . .	1402	.563	.476	344	88	374	5.1
Williams .	774	.442	.643	182	28	233	3.3

Coach—Pat Riley

Orlando Magic

	Min	FG%	FT%	Reb	Ast	Pts	Avg
O'Neal . .	3224	.599	.554	1072	195	2377	29.3
Hardaway	3015	.466	.742	439	544	1313	16.0
Anderson	2811	.478	.672	476	294	1277	15.8
Scott. . . .	2283	.405	.774	218	216	1046	12.8
Skiles . . .	2303	.429	.878	189	503	815	9.9
Royal . . .	1357	.501	.740	248	61	547	7.4
Turner. . .	1536	.467	.778	271	60	451	6.6
Avent . . .	1371	.377	.724	338	65	389	5.3
Krystkowiak	682	.480	.795	123	35	173	5.1
Bowie . . .	948	.481	.837	120	102	320	4.6

Coach—Brian Hill

Philadelphia 76ers

	Min	FG%	FT%	Reb	Ast	Pts	Avg
Weatherspoon	3147	.483	.693	832	192	1506	18.4
J. Malone . . .	2560	.486	.830	199	125	1262	16.4
Barros.	2519	.469	.800	196	424	1075	13.3
Woolridge . . .	1955	.471	.689	298	139	937	12.7
Bradley	1385	.409	.607	306	98	504	10.3
Perry.	2336	.435	.580	404	94	719	9.0
Dawkins	1343	.418	.840	123	263	475	6.6
M. Malone. . .	618	.440	.769	226	34	294	5.3
Leckner.	1163	.486	.646	282	86	362	5.1
Graham.	889	.400	.836	86	66	338	4.8
Kidd	884	.592	.547	233	19	247	3.6

Coach—Fred Carter

Phoenix Suns

	Min	FG%	FT%	Reb	Ast	Pts	Avg
Barkley	2298	.495	.704	727	296	1402	21.6
K. Johnson .	2449	.487	.819	167	637	1340	20.0
Ceballos . . .	1602	.535	.724	344	91	1010	19.1
Majerle	3207	.418	.739	349	275	1320	16.5
Green.	2825	.502	.735	753	137	1204	14.7
Miller.	1786	.609	.584	476	244	636	9.2
Ainge	1555	.417	.830	131	180	606	8.9
West.	1236	.566	.500	295	33	382	4.7
F. Johnson .	875	.448	.783	82	148	324	4.6
Kleine	848	.488	.769	193	45	285	3.9

Coach—Paul Westphal

Portland Trail Blazers

	Min	FG%	FT%	Reb	Ast	Pts	Avg
C. Robinson	2853	.457	.765	550	159	1647	20.1
Drexler. . .	2334	.428	.777	445	333	1303	19.2
Strickland.	2889	.483	.749	370	740	1411	17.2
Porter . . .	2074	.416	.872	215	401	1010	13.1
Grant. . . .	2112	.460	.641	351	107	798	10.4
Williams . .	2636	.555	.679	843	80	783	9.7
Murray . . .	820	.470	.694	111	31	434	6.6
Kersey . . .	1276	.433	.748	331	75	508	6.5
Bryant . . .	1441	.482	.692	315	37	442	5.6
J. Robinson	673	.365	.672	78	68	276	4.8

Coach—Rick Adelman

Sacramento Kings

	Min	FG%	FT%	Reb	Ast	Pts	Avg
Richmond.	2897	.445	.834	286	313	1823	23.4
Tisdale. . .	2557	.501	.808	560	139	1319	16.7
Simmons .	2702	.438	.777	562	305	1129	15.1
Webb. . . .	2567	.460	.813	222	528	1005	12.7
Polynice . .	2402	.523	.508	809	41	789	11.6
Williams . .	1356	.390	.635	235	132	638	11.2
Wilson . . .	1221	.482	.554	273	72	466	8.2
Chilcutt . .	974	.463	.596	271	71	335	7.3
Smith. . . .	877	.405	.750	84	109	332	5.0
Brown . . .	1041	.438	.609	112	133	273	4.5
Causwell .	674	.518	.588	186	11	182	4.4
Peplowski.	667	.539	.545	169	24	176	3.2

Coach—Garry St. Jean

San Antonio Spurs

	Min	FG%	FT%	Reb	Ast	Pts	Avg
Robinson .	3241	.507	.749	855	381	2383	29.8
Ellis	2590	.494	.776	255	80	1170	15.2
Anderson .	2488	.471	.848	242	347	955	11.9
Del Negro.	1949	.487	.824	161	320	773	10.0
Knight . . .	1438	.474	.810	103	197	595	9.2
Reid.	1344	.491	.699	220	73	627	9.0
Cummings	1133	.428	.589	297	50	429	7.3
Daniels . .	980	.376	.719	111	94	370	5.7
Rodman. .	2989	.534	.520	1367	184	370	5.4
Floyd	737	.335	.667	70	101	200	3.8

Coach—John Lucas

Seattle SuperSonics

	Min	FG%	FT%	Reb	Ast	Pts	Avg
Kemp. . . .	2597	.538	.741	851	207	1431	18.1
Payton . . .	2881	.504	.595	269	494	1349	16.5
Schrempf .	2728	.493	.769	454	275	1212	15.0
Pierce . . .	1022	.471	.896	83	91	739	14.5
Gill.	2435	.443	.782	268	275	1111	14.1
Perkins . .	2170	.438	.801	366	111	999	12.3
Askew . . .	1690	.481	.829	184	194	727	9.1
McMillan. .	1887	.447	.564	283	387	437	6.0
Cage	1708	.545	.486	444	45	378	4.6

Coach—George Karl

Utah Jazz

	Min	FG%	FT%	Reb	Ast	Pts	Avg
K. Malone. .	3329	.497	.694	940	328	2063	25.2
Hornacek . .	2820	.470	.878	279	419	1274	15.9
Stockton. . .	2969	.528	.805	258	1031	1236	15.1
Chambers .	1838	.440	.786	326	79	893	11.2
Spencer . . .	2210	.505	.607	658	43	677	8.6
Corbin	2149	.456	.813	389	122	659	8.0
Humphries .	1619	.436	.750	127	219	561	7.5
Benoit	1070	.385	.773	260	23	358	6.5
Russell. . . .	1121	.484	.614	181	54	334	5.0

Coach—Jerry Sloan

Washington Bullets

	Min	FG%	FT%	Reb	Ast	Pts	Avg
Chapman . .	2025	.498	.816	146	185	1094	18.2
MacLean . .	2487	.502	.824	467	160	1365	18.2
Gugliotta . .	2795	.466	.685	728	276	1333	17.1
Adams	2337	.408	.830	183	480	849	12.1
Cheaney . .	1604	.470	.770	190	126	779	12.0
Ellison	1178	.469	.722	242	70	344	7.3
Butler.	1321	.495	.578	225	77	518	6.9
Duckworth .	1485	.417	.667	325	56	456	6.6
Price	1035	.433	.782	90	213	400	6.2
Muresan. . .	650	.545	.676	192	18	304	5.6
Walker	1397	.482	.696	289	33	351	4.8
Overton . . .	749	.403	.827	69	92	218	3.6

Coach—Wes Unseld

1994 NBA Player Draft, First Round Picks

Milwaukee—Glenn Robinson, Purdue
Dallas—Jason Kidd, California
Detroit—Grant Hill, Duke
Minnesota—Donyell Marshall, Connecticut
Washington—Juwan Howard, Michigan
Philadelphia—Sharone Wright, Clemson
L.A. Clippers—Lamond Murray, California
Sacramento—Brian Grant, Xavier
Boston—Eric Montross, North Carolina
L.A. Lakers—Eddie Jones, Temple
Seattle—Carlos Rogers, Tennessee State
Miami—Khalid Reeves, Arizona
Denver—Jalen Rose, Michigan
New Jersey—Yinka Dare, George Washington
Indiana—Eric Piatkowski, Nebraska
Golden State—Clifford Rozier, Louisville
Portland—Aaron McKee, Temple
Milwaukee—Eric Mobley, Pittsburgh
Dallas—Tony Dumas, Missouri-Kansas City
Philadelphia—B. J. Tyler, Texas
Chicago—Dickey Simpkins, Providence
San Antonio—Bill Curley, Boston College
Phoenix—Wesley Person, Auburn
New York—Monty Williams, Notre Dame
L.A. Clippers—Greg Minor, Louisville
New York—Charlie Ward, Florida State
Orlando—Brooks Thompson, Oklahoma State

Number One First Round NBA Draft Picks, 1966-94

Year	Team	Player, college
1966	New York	Cazzie Russell, Michigan
1967	Detroit	Jimmy Walker, Providence
1968	Houston	Elvin Hayes, Houston
1969	Milwaukee	Lew Alcindor[1], UCLA
1970	Detroit	Bob Lanier, St. Bonaventure
1971	Cleveland	Austin Carr, Notre Dame
1972	Portland	LaRue Martin, Loyola-Chicago
1973	Philadelphia	Doug Collins, Illinois St.
1974	Portland	Bill Walton, UCLA
1975	Atlanta	David Thompson[2], N.C. State
1976	Houston	John Lucas, Maryland
1977	Milwaukee	Kent Benson, Indiana
1978	Portland	Mychal Thompson, Minnesota
1979	L.A. Lakers	Magic Johnson, Michigan St.
1980	Golden State	Joe Barry Carroll, Purdue
1981	Dallas	Mark Aguirre, DePaul
1982	L.A. Lakers	James Worthy, N. Carolina
1983	Houston	Ralph Sampson, Virginia
1984	Houston	Akeem Olajuwon, Houston
1985	New York	Patrick Ewing, Georgetown
1986	Cleveland	Brad Daugherty, N. Carolina
1987	San Antonio	David Robinson, Navy
1988	L.A. Clippers	Danny Manning, Kansas
1989	Sacramento	Pervis Ellison, Louisville
1990	New Jersey	Derrick Coleman, Syracuse
1991	Charlotte	Larry Johnson, UNLV
1992	Orlando	Shaquille O'Neal, LSU
1993	Orlando	Chris Webber[3], Michigan
1994	Milwaukee	Glenn Robinson, Purdue

(1) Later Kareem Abdul-Jabbar. (2) Signed with Denver of the ABA. (3) Traded to Golden State.

NBA All-Defensive Team in 1994

First team	Position	Second team
Scottie Pippen, Chicago	Forward	Dennis Rodman, San Antonio
Charles Oakley, New York	Forward	Horace Grant, Chicago
Hakeem Olajuwon, Houston	Center	David Robinson, San Antonio
Gary Payton, Seattle	Guard	Nate McMillan, Seattle
Mookie Blaylock, Atlanta	Guard	Latrell Sprewell, Golden State

All-Time NBA Statistical Leaders

(At the start of the 1994-95 season. *Player active in 1993-94 season.)

Scoring Average
(Minimum 400 games or 10,000 points)

	G	Pts.	Avg
Michael Jordan	667	21,541	32.3
Wilt Chamberlain	1,045	31,419	30.1
Elgin Baylor	846	23,149	27.4
Jerry West	932	25,192	27.0
*Dominique Wilkins	907	24,019	26.5
Bob Pettit	792	20,880	26.4
George Gervin	791	20,708	26.2
*Karl Malone	734	19,050	26.0
Oscar Robertson	1,040	26,710	25.7
Kareem Abdul-Jabbar	1,560	38,387	24.6

Field Goal Percentage
(Minimum 2,000 field goals made)

	FGA	FGM	Pct.
Artis Gilmore	9,570	5,732	.599
*Mark West	3,568	2,113	.592
Steve Johnson	4,965	2,841	.572
Darryl Dawkins	6,079	3,477	.572
James Donaldson	5,368	3,061	.570
Jeff Ruland	3,734	2,105	.564
*Charles Barkley	11,144	6,259	.562
Kareem Abdul-Jabbar	28,307	15,837	.559
*Otis Thorpe	8,834	4,898	.554
*Buck Williams	10,198	5,653	.554

Free Throw Percentage
(Minimum 1,200 free throws made)

	FTA	FTM	Pct.
*Mark Price	1,916	1,735	.906
Rick Barry	4,243	3,818	.900
Calvin Murphy	3,864	3,445	.892
*Scott Skiles	1,529	1,361	.890
Larry Bird	4,471	3,960	.886
Bill Sharman	3,559	3,143	.883
*Ricky Pierce	3,353	2,940	.877
*Reggie Miller	3,197	2,803	.877
Kiki Vandeweghe	3,997	3,484	.872
*Jeff Malone	3,292	2,867	.871

Points

Kareem Abdul-Jabbar	38,387
Wilt Chamberlain	31,419
*Moses Malone	27,360
Elvin Hayes	27,313
Oscar Robertson	26,710
John Havlicek	26,395
Alex English	25,613
Jerry West	25,192
*Dominique Wilkins	24,019
Adrian Dantley	23,177

Games Played

Kareem Abdul-Jabbar	1,560
*Robert Parish	1,413
*Moses Malone	1,312
Elvin Hayes	1,303
John Havlicek	1,270
Paul Silas	1,254
Alex English	1,193
Hal Greer	1,122
*James Edwards	1,112
Jack Sikma	1,107

Assists

Magic Johnson	9,921
Oscar Robertson	9,887
*John Stockton	9,383
*Isiah Thomas	9,061
Maurice Cheeks	7,392
Len Wilkens	7,211
Bob Cousy	6,955
Guy Rodgers	6,917
Nate Archibald	6,476
John Lucas	6,454

Field Goals Made

Kareem Abdul-Jabbar	15,837
Wilt Chamberlain	12,681
Elvin Hayes	10,976
Alex English	10,659
John Havlicek	10,513
Oscar Robertson	9,508
*Moses Malone	9,422
*Robert Parish	9,265
*Dominique Wilkins	9,020
Jerry West	9,016

Rebounds

Wilt Chamberlain	23,924
Bill Russell	21,620
Kareem Addul-Jabbar	17,440
Elvin Hayes	16,279
*Moses Malone	16,166
Nate Thurmond	14,464
Walt Bellamy	14,241
*Robert Parish	13,973
Wes Unseld	13,769
Jerry Lucas	12,942

Individuals in the Basketball Hall of Fame

Springfield, Mass.

Players
Archibald, Nate
Arizin, Paul
Barlow, Thomas
Barry, Rick
Baylor, Elgin
Beckman, John
Bellamy, Walt
Belov, Sergei
Bing, Dave
Blazejowski, Carol
Borgmann, Bennie
Bradley, Bill
Brennan, Joseph
Cervi, Al
Chamberlain, Wilt
Cooper, Charles
Cousy, Bob
Cowens, Dave
Cunningham, Billy
Davies, Bob
DeBernardi, Forrest
DeBusschere, Dave
Dehnert, Dutch
Endacott, Paul
Erving, Julius
Foster, Bud
Frazier, Walt
Friedman, Max
Fulks, Joe
Gale, Lauren
Gallatin, Harry
Gates, Pop
Gola, Tom
Greer, Hal
Gruenig, Ace
Hagan, Cliff
Hanson, Victor
Harris, Luisa
Havlicek, John
Hawkins, Connie
Hayes, Elvin
Heinsohn, Tom
Holman, Nat
Houbregs, Bob
Hyatt, Chuck
Issel, Dan
Jeannette, Buddy
Johnson, William
Johnston, Neil
Jones, K.C.
Jones, Sam
Krause, Moose
Kurland, Bob
Lanier, Bob
Lapchick, Joe
Lovellette, Clyde
Lucas, Jerry
Luisetti, Hank
Macauley, Ed
Maravich, Pete
Martin, Slater
McCracken, Branch
McCracken, Jack
McDermott, Bobby
McGuire, Dick
Meyers, Ann
Mikan, George
Monroe, Earl
Murphy, Calvin
Murphy, Stretch
Page, Pat
Pettit, Bob
Phillip, Andy
Pollard, Jim
Ramsey, Frank
Reed, Willis
Robertson, Oscar
Roosma, John S.
Russell, Bill
Russell, Honey
Schayes, Adolph
Schmidt, Ernest
Schommer, John
Sedran, Barney
Semyonova, Ulyona
Sharman, Bill
Steinmetz, Christian
Thompson, Cat
Thurmond, Nate
Twyman, Jack
Unseld, Wes
Vandivier, Fuzzy
Wachter, Edward
Walton, Bill
Wanzer, Bobby
West, Jerry
White, Nera
Wilkins, Lenny
Wooden, John

Coaches
Anderson, Harold
Auerbach, Red
Barry, Sam
Blood, Ernest
Cann, Howard
Carlson, Dr. H. C.
Carnesecca, Lou
Carnevale, Ben
Case, Everett
Crum, Denny
Daly, Chuck
Dean, Everett
Diddle, Edgar
Drake, Bruce
Gaines, Clarence
Gardner, Jack
Gill, Slats
Harshman, Marv
Hickey, Edgar
Hobson, Howard
Holzman, Red
Iba, Hank
Julian, Alvin
Keaney, Frank
Keogan, George
Knight, Bob
Lambert, Ward
Litwack, Harry
Loeffler, Kenneth
Lonborg, Dutch
McCutchan, Arad
McGuire, Al
McGuire, Frank
Meanwell, Dr. W.E.
Meyer, Ray
Miller, Ralph
Ramsay, Jack
Rupp, Adolph
Sachs, Leonard
Shelton, Everett
Smith, Dean
Taylor, Fred
Teague, Bertha
Wade, Margaret
Watts, Stan
Wooden, John
Woolpert, Phil

Referees
Enright, James
Hepburn, George
Hoyt, George
Kennedy, Matthew
Leith, Lloyd
Mihalik, Red
Nucatola, John
Quigley, Ernest
Shirley, J. Dallas
Tobey, David
Walsh, David

Contributors
Abbott, Senda B.
Allen, Phog
Bee, Clair
Brown, Walter
Bunn, John
Douglas, Bob
Duer, Al O.
Fagan, Cliff
Fisher, Harry
Fleisher, Larry
Gottlieb, Edward
Gulick, Dr. L. H.
Harrison, Lester
Hepp, Dr. Ferenc
Hickox, Edward
Hinkle, Tony
Irish, Ned
Jones, R. W.
Kennedy, Walter
Liston, Emil
McLendon, John
Mokray, Bill
Morgan, Ralph
Morgenweck, Frank
Naismith, Dr. James
Newell, Pete
O'Brien, John
O'Brien, Larry
Olsen, Harold
Podoloff, Maurice
Porter, H. V.
Reis, William
Ripley, Elmer
St. John, Lynn
Saperstein, Abe
Schabinger, Arthur
Stagg, Amos Alonzo
Stankovich, Boris
Steitz, Edward
Taylor, Chuck
Tower, Oswald
Trester, Arthur
Wells, Clifford
Wilke, Lou

All-Time NBA Coaching Victories

(*Active through 1993-94 season)

Coach	W-L	Pct.
Red Auerbach	938-479	.662
Lenny Wilkens*	926-774	.545
Jack Ramsay	864-783	.525
Dick Motta	856-863	.498
Bill Fitch	845-877	.491
Cotton Fitzsimmons	805-745	.519
Don Nelson*	803-573	.584
Gene Shue	784-861	.477
John MacLeod	707-657	.518
Pat Riley*	701-272	.720
Red Holzman	696-604	.535
Doug Moe	628-529	.543
Chuck Daly*	564-379	.598
Alvin Attles	557-518	.518
K.C. Jones	522-252	.674
Larry Brown*	481-377	.561
Alex Hannum	471-412	.533
Kevin Loughery*	457-633	.419
Billy Cunningham	454-196	.698
Larry Costello	430-300	.589
Tom Heinsohn	427-263	.619
John Kundla	423-302	.583
Jerry Sloan*	398-292	.577
Mike Fratello*	371-288	.563
Hubie Brown	341-410	.454
Bill Russell	341-290	.540
Bill Sharman	333-240	.581
Del Harris	332-341	.493
Richie Guerin	327-291	.529
Al Cervi	326-241	.575
Joe Lapchick	326-247	.569
Fred Schaus	315-245	.563
Stan Albeck	307-267	.535
Lester Harrison	295-181	.620
Phil Jackson*	295-115	.720
Rick Adelman*	291-154	.654
Frank Layden	277-294	.485
Paul Seymour	271-241	.529
Butch van Breda Kolff	266-253	.513
George Karl*	264-237	.527

NBA Home Courts

Team	Name (built)	Capacity
Atlanta	The Omni (1972)	16,365
Boston	Boston Garden (1928)	14,890
	Hartford Civic Center (1975)	15,418
Charlotte	Charlotte Coliseum (1988)	23,698
Chicago	United Center (1994)	21,500
Cleveland	Gund Arena (1994)	20,562
Dallas	Reunion Arena (1980)	17,502
Denver	McNichols Sports Arena (1975)	17,171
Detroit	Palace of Auburn Hills (1988)	21,454
Golden State	Oakland Coliseum Arena (1966)	15,025
Houston	The Summit (1975)	16,311
Indiana	Market Square Arena (1974)	16,530
L.A. Clippers	L.A. Memorial Sports Arena (1959)	16,005
L.A. Lakers	The Great Western Forum (1967)	17,505
Miami	Miami Arena (1988)	15,200
Milwaukee	Bradley Center (1988)	18,633
Minnesota	Target Center (1990)	19,006
New Jersey	Meadowlands Arena (1981)	20,029
New York	Madison Square Garden (1968)	19,763
Orlando	Orlando Arena (1989)	16,010
Philadelphia	The Spectrum (1967)	18,168
Phoenix	America West Arena (1992)	19,023
Portland	Memorial Coliseum (1960)	12,888
Sacramento	Arco Arena (1988)	17,317
San Antonio	Alamodome (1993)	20,662
Seattle	Seattle Center Coliseum (1962)	17,500
	Tacoma Dome (1983)	16,300
Utah	Delta Center (1991)	19,911
Washington	USAir Arena (1973)	18,756
	Baltimore Arena (1962)	12,756

COLLEGE BASKETBALL

Final Division I Conference Standing, 1993–94

Atlantic Coast

	Conference W	Conference L	Overall W	Overall L
Duke	12	4	28	6
North Carolina	11	5	28	7
Wake Forest	9	7	21	12
Virginia	8	8	18	13
Maryland	8	8	18	12
Georgia Tech	7	9	16	13
Florida St.	6	10	13	14
Clemson	6	10	18	16
North Carolina St.	5	11	11	19

Tournament Champion—North Carolina`

Atlantic 10

	Conference W	Conference L	Overall W	Overall L
Massachusetts	14	2	28	7
Temple	12	4	23	8
George Washington	8	8	18	12
West Virginia	8	8	17	12
Duquesne	8	8	17	13
Rhode Island	7	9	11	16
Rutgers	6	10	11	16
St. Joseph's (Pa.)	5	11	14	14
St. Bonaventure	4	12	10	17

Tournament Champion—Massachusetts

Big East

	Conference W	Conference L	Overall W	Overall L
Connecticut	16	2	29	5
Syracuse	13	5	23	7
Boston College	11	7	23	11
Providence	10	8	20	10
Villanova	10	8	20	12
Georgetown	10	8	19	12
Seton Hall	8	10	17	13
Pittsburgh	7	11	13	14
St. John's (N.Y.)	5	13	12	17
Miami (Fla.)	0	18	7	20

Tournament Champion—Providence

Big Eight

	Conference W	Conference L	Overall W	Overall L
Missouri	14	0	28	4
Oklahoma St.	10	4	24	10
Kansas	9	5	27	8
Nebraska	7	7	20	10
Oklahoma	6	8	15	13
Kansas St.	4	10	20	14
Iowa St.	4	10	14	13
Colorado	2	12	10	17

Tournament Champion—Nebraska

Big Sky

	Conference W	Conference L	Overall W	Overall L
Weber St.	10	4	20	10
Idaho St.	10	4	18	9
Idaho	9	5	18	10
Montana St.	8	6	16	11
Boise St.	7	7	17	13
Montana	6	8	19	9
Northern Arizona	6	8	13	13
E. Washington	0	14	5	21

Tournament Champion—Boise St.

Big South*

	Conference W	Conference L	Overall W	Overall L
Towson St.	16	2	21	9
Campbell	14	4	20	9
Radford	13	5	20	8
Liberty	13	5	18	12
N.C.-Greenville	11	7	15	12
Charleston So.	8	10	9	18
Md.-Baltimore County	6	12	6	21
Winthrop	5	13	4	23
N.C.-Asheville	3	15	3	24
Coastal Carolina	1	17	15	11

Tournament Champion—Liberty

Big Ten

	Conference W	Conference L	Overall W	Overall L
Purdue	14	4	29	5
Michigan	13	5	24	8
Indiana	12	6	21	9
Illinois	10	8	17	11
Minnesota	10	8	21	12
Michigan St.	10	8	20	12
Wisconsin	8	10	18	11
Ohio St.	6	12	13	16
Penn St.	6	12	13	14
Northwestern	5	13	15	14
Iowa	5	13	11	16

Big West

	Conference W	Conference L	Overall W	Overall L
New Mexico St.	12	6	23	8
Utah St.	11	7	14	13
Long Beach St.	11	7	17	10
San Jose St.	11	7	15	12
UNLV	10	8	15	13
Pacific (Cal.)	10	8	17	14
UC Santa Barbara	9	9	13	17
Cal St. Fullerton	6	12	8	19
Nevada	6	12	11	17
UC Irvine	4	14	10	20

Tournament Champion—New Mexico St.

Colonial Athletic

	Conference W	Conference L	Overall W	Overall L
Old Dominion	10	4	21	10
James Madison	10	4	20	10
N.C.-Wilmington	9	5	18	10
Richmond	8	6	14	14
East Carolina	7	7	15	12
George Mason	5	9	10	17
American	5	9	8	19
William & Mary	2	12	4	23

Tournament Champion—James Madison

East Coast

	Conference W	Conference L	Overall W	Overall L
Troy St.	5	0	13	14
Northeastern Ill.	4	1	17	11
Buffalo	3	2	10	18
Chicago St.	2	3	4	23
Hofstra	1	4	9	20
Central Conn. St.	0	5	4	22

Tournament Champion—Hofstra

Great Midwest

	Conference W	Conference L	Overall W	Overall L
Marquette	10	2	24	9
St. Louis	8	4	23	6
Ala.-Birmingham	8	4	22	8
Cincinnati	7	5	22	10
DePaul	4	8	16	12
Memphis St.	4	8	13	16
Dayton	1	11	6	21

Tournament Champion—Cincinnati

Ivy League

	Conference W	Conference L	Overall W	Overall L
Pennsylvania	14	0	25	3
Princeton	11	3	18	8
Yale	7	7	10	16
Brown	6	8	12	14
Dartmouth	6	8	10	16
Harvard	5	9	9	17
Columbia	4	10	6	20
Cornell	3	11	8	18

Metropolitan

	Conference W	Conference L	Overall W	Overall L
Louisville	10	2	28	8
N.C.-Charlotte	7	5	16	13
Tulane	7	5	18	11
Virginia Tech	6	6	18	10
Va. Commonwealth	5	7	14	13
Southern Miss.	5	7	15	15
South Florida	2	10	10	17

Tournament Champion—Louisville

Metro Atlantic Athletic

	Conference W	Conference L	Overall W	Overall L
Canisius	12	2	22	7
Siena	10	4	25	8
Manhattan	10	4	19	11
St. Peter's	8	6	14	13
Loyola (Md.)	6	8	17	13
Fairfield	4	10	8	19
Iona	3	11	7	20
Niagara	3	11	6	21

Tournament Champion—Loyola (Md.)

Mid-American

	Conference W	Conference L	Overall W	Overall L
Ohio	14	4	25	8
Bowling Green	12	6	18	10
Miami (Ohio)	12	6	19	11
Ball St.	11	7	16	12
Toledo	10	8	15	12
Eastern Michigan	10	8	15	12
Kent	8	10	13	14
Western Michigan	7	11	14	14
Central Michigan	4	14	5	21
Akron	2	16	8	18

Tournament Champion—Ohio

Mid-Continent

	Conference W	Conference L	Overall W	Overall L
Wis.-Green Bay	15	3	27	7
Valparaiso	14	4	20	8
Illinois-Chicago	14	4	20	9
Cleveland St.	9	9	14	15
Wright St.	9	9	12	18
Eastern Illinois	7	11	12	15
Northern Illinois	7	11	10	17
Wis.-Milwaukee	7	11	10	17
Western Illinois	5	13	7	20
Youngstown St.	3	15	5	21

Tournament Champion—Wisconsin-Green Bay

Mid-Eastern Athletic

	Conference W	Conference L	Overall W	Overall L
Coppin St.	16	0	22	8
Md.-East. Shore	10	6	16	12
North Carolina A&T	10	6	16	14
South Carolina St.	10	6	16	13
Bethune-Cookman	8	8	9	18
Howard	7	9	10	17
Delaware St.	5	11	8	19
Morgan St.	4	12	8	21
Florida A&M	2	14	4	23

Tournament Champion—North Carolina A&T

Midwestern Collegiate

	Conference W	Conference L	Overall W	Overall L
Xavier (Ohio)	8	2	22	8
Evansville	6	4	21	11
Butler	6	4	16	13
Detroit Mercy	5	5	16	13
La Salle	4	6	11	16
Loyola (Ill.)	1	9	8	19

Tournament Champion—Detroit Mercy

Missouri Valley

	Conference W	Conference L	Overall W	Overall L
Southern Illinois	16	4	23	7
Tulsa	16	4	23	8
Bradley	15	5	23	8
Illinois St.	12	7	16	11
Northern Iowa	12	8	16	13
Southwest Mo. St.	7	12	12	15
Wichita St.	6	13	9	18
Drake	6	13	11	16
Creighton	3	15	7	22
Indiana St.	3	15	4	22

Tournament Champion—Southern Illinois

North Atlantic

	Conference W	Conference L	Overall W	Overall L
Drexel	12	2	25	5
Maine	11	3	20	9
Hartford	9	5	16	12
New Hampshire	8	6	15	13
Delaware	7	7	14	13
Boston U.	4	10	11	16
Vermont	3	11	12	15
Northeastern	2	12	5	22

Tournament Champion—Drexel

Northeast

	Conference W	Conference L	Overall W	Overall L
Rider	14	4	21	9
Monmouth (N.J.)	13	5	18	11
Robert Morris	11	7	14	14
Wagner	11	7	16	12
FDU-Teaneck	10	8	14	13
Marist	10	8	14	13
Mt. St. Mary's (Md.)	9	9	14	14
St. Francis (N.Y.)	9	9	13	15
LIU-Brooklyn	2	16	3	24
St. Francis (Pa.)	1	17	1	26

Tournament Champion—Rider

Ohio Valley

	Conference W	Conference L	Overall W	Overall L
Murray St.	15	1	23	6
Tennessee St.	12	4	19	12
Austin Peay	10	6	11	16
Eastern Kentucky	9	7	13	14
Morehead St.	8	8	14	14
Southeast Mo. St.	5	11	10	17
Tennessee Tech	5	11	10	21
Middle Tenn. St.	5	11	8	19
Tennessee-Martin	3	13	5	22

Tournament Champion—Tennessee St.

Pacific-10	Conf. W	Conf. L	Overall W	Overall L
Arizona	14	4	29	6
UCLA	13	5	21	7
California	13	5	22	8
Washington St.	10	8	20	11
Stanford	10	8	17	11
Arizona St.	10	8	15	13
Southern Cal.	9	9	16	12
Oregon	6	12	10	17
Washington	3	15	5	22
Oregon St.	2	16	6	21

Patriot	Conf. W	Conf. L	Overall W	Overall L
Navy	9	5	17	13
Fordham	9	5	12	15
Colgate	9	5	17	12
Holy Cross	9	5	14	14
Bucknell	6	8	10	17
Lehigh	6	8	10	17
Lafayette	4	10	9	19
Army	4	10	7	20

Tournament Champion—Navy

Southeastern

Eastern Division	Conf. W	Conf. L	Overall W	Overall L
Florida	12	4	29	8
Kentucky	12	4	27	7
Vanderbilt	9	7	20	12
Georgia	7	9	14	16
South Carolina	4	12	9	19
Tennessee	2	14	5	22
Western Division				
Arkansas	14	2	31	3
Alabama	12	4	20	10
Mississippi St.	9	7	18	11
Mississippi	7	9	14	13
Louisiana St.	5	11	11	16
Auburn	3	13	11	17

Tournament Champion—Kentucky

Southern	Conf. W	Conf. L	Overall W	Overall L
Tenn.-Chattanooga	14	4	23	7
Davidson	13	5	22	8
East Tennessee St.	13	5	16	14
Appalachian St.	12	6	16	11
Georgia Southern	9	9	14	14
Western Carolina	8	10	12	16
Marshall	7	11	9	18
Citadel	6	12	11	16
Furman	6	12	10	18
Virginia Military	2	16	5	23

Tournament Champion—Tenn.-Chattanooga

Southland	Conf. W	Conf. L	Overall W	Overall L
Northeast Lousiana	15	3	19	9
Southwest Tex. St.	14	4	25	7
Nicholls St.	12	6	19	9
North Texas	9	9	14	15
McNeese St.	9	9	11	16
Texas-San Antonio	8	10	12	15
Sam Houston St.	7	11	7	20
Stephen F. Austin	6	12	9	18
Northwestern St.	6	12	11	15
Texas-Arlington	4	14	7	22

Tournament Champion—Southwest Texas State

Southwest	Conf. W	Conf. L	Overall W	Overall L
Texas	12	2	26	8
Texas A&M	10	4	19	11
Texas Tech.	10	4	17	11
Baylor	7	7	16	11
Rice	6	8	15	14
Houston	5	9	8	19
Southern Methodist	3	11	6	21
Texas Christian	3	11	7	20

Tournament Champion—Texas

Southwestern Athletic	Conf. W	Conf. L	Overall W	Overall L
Texas Southern	12	2	19	11
Jackson St.	11	3	19	10
Alabama St.	10	4	19	10
Southern-B.R.	8	6	16	11
Mississippi Valley	6	8	10	17
Grambling	4	10	9	18
Alcorn St.	3	11	3	24
Prairie View	2	12	5	22

Tournament Champion—Texas Southern

Sun Belt	Conf. W	Conf. L	Overall W	Overall L
Western Kentucky	14	4	20	11
Southwestern La.	13	5	22	8
New Orleans	12	6	20	10
Jacksonville	11	7	17	11
Arkansas St.	10	8	15	12
South Alabama	9	9	13	14
Tex.-Pan American	9	9	16	12
Ark.-Little Rock	6	12	13	15
Lamar	6	12	10	17
Louisiana Tech.	0	18	2	25

Tournament Champion—Southwestern Louisiana

Trans America Athletic	Conf. W	Conf. L	Overall W	Overall L
Charleston (S.C.)	14	2	24	4
Central Florida	11	5	21	9
Stetson	9	7	14	15
Georgia St.	9	7	13	14
Centenary	8	8	16	12
Florida Int'l.	7	9	11	16
Southeastern La.	7	9	10	17
Samford	4	12	10	18
Mercer	3	13	5	24
Florida Atlantic	-	-	3	24

Tournament Champion—Central Florida

West Coast	Conf. W	Conf. L	Overall W	Overall L
Gonzaga	12	2	22	8
Pepperdine	8	6	19	11
San Francisco	8	6	17	11
San Diego	7	7	18	11
Portland	6	8	13	17
Santa Clara	6	8	13	14
St. Mary's (Cal.)	5	9	13	14
Loyola Marymount	4	10	6	21

Tournament Champion—Pepperdine

Western Athletic	Conf. W	Conf. L	Overall W	Overall L
New Mexico	14	4	23	8
Fresno St.	13	5	21	11
Brigham Young	12	6	22	10
Hawaii	11	7	18	15
UTEP	8	10	18	12
Colorado St.	8	10	15	13
Utah	8	10	14	14
Wyoming	7	11	14	14
San Diego St.	6	12	12	16
Air Force	3	15	8	18

Tournament Champion—Hawaii

Independents	W	L
Southern Utah St.	16	11
Missouri-Kansas City	12	17
Notre Dame	12	17
Cal St. Northridge	8	18
Oral Roberts	6	21
Cal St. Sacramento	1	26

*Coastal Carolina had to forfeit 14 Big South Conference games. Conference records for all Big South teams show the adjustment; however, overall records remain as played.

Major College Basketball Tournaments

The National Invitation Tournament (NIT), first played in 1938, is the nation's oldest basketball tournament. The National Collegiate Athletic Association's (NCAA) national championship tournament was first played a year later. Selections for both tournaments are made in March, with the NCAA selecting first from among the top Division I teams.

National Invitation Tournament Champions

Year	Champion	Year	Champion	Year	Champion	Year	Champion
1938	Temple	1952	LaSalle	1966	Brigham Young	1980	Virginia
1939	Long Island Univ.	1953	Seton Hall	1967	Southern Illinois	1981	Tulsa
1940	Colorado	1954	Holy Cross	1968	Dayton	1982	Bradley
1941	Long Island Univ.	1955	Duquesne	1969	Temple	1983	Fresno State
1942	West Virginia	1956	Louisville	1970	Marquette	1984	Michigan
1943	St. John's	1957	Bradley	1971	North Carolina	1985	UCLA
1944	St. John's	1958	Xavier (Ohio)	1972	Maryland	1986	Ohio State
1945	De Paul	1959	St. John's	1973	Virginia Tech	1987	Southern Mississippi
1946	Kentucky	1960	Bradley	1974	Purdue	1988	Connecticut
1947	Utah	1961	Providence	1975	Princeton	1989	St. John's
1948	St. Louis	1962	Dayton	1976	Kentucky	1990	Vanderbilt
1949	San Francisco	1963	Providence	1977	St. Bonaventure	1991	Stanford
1950	CCNY	1964	Bradley	1978	Texas	1992	Virginia
1951	Brigham Young	1965	St. John's	1979	Indiana	1993	Minnesota
						1994	Villanova

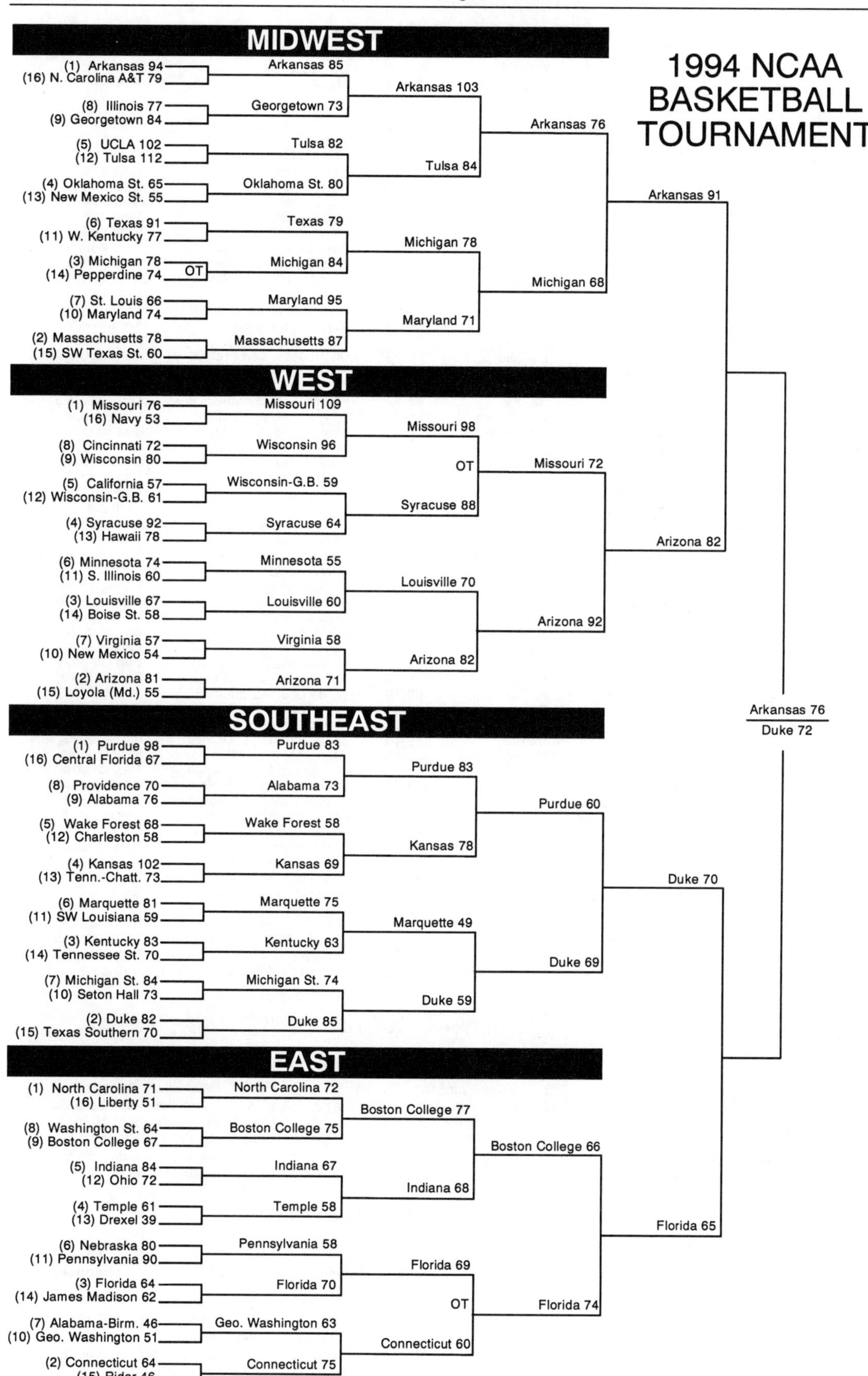
1994 NCAA BASKETBALL TOURNAMENT
MIDWEST
(1) Arkansas 94
(16) N. Carolina A&T 79
(8) Illinois 77
(9) Georgetown 84
(5) UCLA 102
(12) Tulsa 112
(4) Oklahoma St. 65
(13) New Mexico St. 55
(6) Texas 91
(11) W. Kentucky 77
(3) Michigan 78
(14) Pepperdine 74
OT
(7) St. Louis 66
(10) Maryland 74
(2) Massachusetts 78
(15) SW Texas St. 60
Arkansas 85
Georgetown 73
Tulsa 82
Oklahoma St. 80
Texas 79
Michigan 84
Maryland 95
Massachusetts 87
Arkansas 103
Tulsa 84
Michigan 78
Maryland 71
Arkansas 76
Michigan 68
Arkansas 91
WEST
(1) Missouri 76
(16) Navy 53
(8) Cincinnati 72
(9) Wisconsin 80
(5) California 57
(12) Wisconsin-G.B. 61
(4) Syracuse 92
(13) Hawaii 78
(6) Minnesota 74
(11) S. Illinois 60
(3) Louisville 67
(14) Boise St. 58
(7) Virginia 57
(10) New Mexico 54
(2) Arizona 81
(15) Loyola (Md.) 55
Missouri 109
Wisconsin 96
Wisconsin-G.B. 59
Syracuse 64
Minnesota 55
Louisville 60
Virginia 58
Arizona 71
Missouri 98
OT
Syracuse 88
Louisville 70
Arizona 82
Missouri 72
Arizona 92
Arizona 82
Arkansas 76
Duke 72
SOUTHEAST
(1) Purdue 98
(16) Central Florida 67
(8) Providence 70
(9) Alabama 76
(5) Wake Forest 68
(12) Charleston 58
(4) Kansas 102
(13) Tenn.-Chatt. 73
(6) Marquette 81
(11) SW Louisiana 59
(3) Kentucky 83
(14) Tennessee St. 70
(7) Michigan St. 84
(10) Seton Hall 73
(2) Duke 82
(15) Texas Southern 70
Purdue 83
Alabama 73
Wake Forest 58
Kansas 69
Marquette 75
Kentucky 63
Michigan St. 74
Duke 85
Purdue 83
Kansas 78
Marquette 49
Duke 59
Purdue 60
Duke 69
Duke 70
EAST
(1) North Carolina 71
(16) Liberty 51
(8) Washington St. 64
(9) Boston College 67
(5) Indiana 84
(12) Ohio 72
(4) Temple 61
(13) Drexel 39
(6) Nebraska 80
(11) Pennsylvania 90
(3) Florida 64
(14) James Madison 62
(7) Alabama-Birm. 46
(10) Geo. Washington 51
(2) Connecticut 64
(15) Rider 46
North Carolina 72
Boston College 75
Indiana 67
Temple 58
Pennsylvania 58
Florida 70
Geo. Washington 63
Connecticut 75
Boston College 77
Indiana 68
Florida 69
OT
Connecticut 60
Boston College 66
Florida 74
Florida 65

NCAA Division I Champions

Year	Champion	Coach	Final opponent	Score	Outstanding player	Site
1939	Oregon	Howard Hobson	Ohio St.	46-33	None	Evanston, Ill.
1940	Indiana	Branch McCracken	Kansas	60-42	Marvin Huffman, Indiana	Kansas City, Mo.
1941	Wisconsin	Harold Foster	Washington St.	39-34	John Kotz, Wisconsin	Kansas City, Mo.
1942	Stanford	Everett Dean	Dartmouth	53-38	Howard Dallmar, Stanford	Kansas City, Mo.
1943	Wyoming	Everett Shelton	Georgetown	46-34	Ken Sailors, Wyoming	New York, N.Y.
1944	Utah	Vadal Peterson	Dartmouth	42-40(1)	Arnold Ferrin, Utah	New York, N.Y.
1945	Oklahoma St.(2)	Henry Iba	NYU	49-45	Bob Kurland, Oklahoma St.	New York, N.Y.
1946	Oklahoma St.(2)	Henry Iba	N. Carolina	43-40	Bob Kurland, Oklahoma St.	New York, N.Y.
1947	Holy Cross	Alvin Julian	Oklahoma	58-47	George Kaftan, Holy Cross	New York, N.Y.
1948	Kentucky	Adolph Rupp	Baylor	58-42	Alex Groza, Kentucky	New York, N.Y.
1949	Kentucky	Adolph Rupp	Oklahoma St.	46-36	Alex Groza, Kentucky	Seattle, Wash.
1950	CCNY	Nat Holman	Bradley	71-68	Irwin Dambrot, CCNY	New York, N.Y.
1951	Kentucky	Adolph Rupp	Kansas St.	68-58	None	Minneapolis, Minn.
1952	Kansas	Forrest Allen	St. John's	80-63	Clyde Lovellette, Kansas	Seattle, Wash.
1953	Indiana	Branch McCracken	Kansas	69-68	B.H. Born, Kansas	Kansas City, Mo.
1954	La Salle	Kenneth Loeffler	Bradley	92-76	Tom Gola, La Salle	Kansas City, Mo.
1955	San Francisco	Phil Woolpert	LaSalle	77-63	Bill Russell, San Francisco	Kansas City, Mo.
1956	San Francisco	Phil Woolpert	Iowa	83-71	Hal Lear, Temple	Evanston, Ill.
1957	N. Carolina	Frank McGuire	Kansas	54-53(1)	Wilt Chamberlain, Kansas	Kansas City, Mo.
1958	Kentucky	Adolph Rupp	Seattle	84-72	Elgin Baylor, Seattle	Louisville, Ky.
1959	California	Pete Newell	W. Virginia	71-70	Jerry West, W. Virginia	Louisville, Ky.
1960	Ohio St.	Fred Taylor	California	75-55	Jerry Lucas, Ohio St.	San Francisco, Cal.
1961	Cincinnati	Edwin Jucker	Ohio St.	70-65(1)	Jerry Lucas, Ohio St.	Kansas City, Mo.
1962	Cincinnati	Edwin Jucker	Ohio St.	71-59	Paul Hogue, Cincinnati	Louisville, Ky.
1963	Loyola (Ill.)	George Ireland	Cincinnati	60-58(1)	Art Heyman, Duke	Louisville, Ky.
1964	UCLA	John Wooden	Duke	98-83	Walt Hazzard, UCLA	Kansas City, Mo.
1965	UCLA	John Wooden	Michigan	91-80	Bill Bradley, Princeton	Portland, Ore.
1966	Texas-El Paso(3)	Don Haskins	Kentucky	72-65	Jerry Chambers, Utah	College Park, Md.
1967	UCLA	John Wooden	Dayton	79-64	Lew Alcindor, UCLA	Louisville, Ky.
1968	UCLA	John Wooden	N. Carolina	78-55	Lew Alcindor, UCLA	Los Angeles, Cal.
1969	UCLA	John Wooden	Purdue	92-72	Lew Alcindor, UCLA	Louisville, Ky.
1970	UCLA	John Wooden	Jacksonville	80-69	Sidney Wicks, UCLA	College Park, Md.
1971	UCLA	John Wooden	Villanova*	68-62	Howard Porter, Villanova*	Houston, Tex.
1972	UCLA	John Wooden	Florida St.	81-76	Bill Walton, UCLA	Los Angeles, Cal.
1973	UCLA	John Wooden	Memphis St.	87-66	Bill Walton, UCLA	St. Louis, Mo.
1974	N. Carolina St.	Norm Sloan	Marquette	76-64	David Thompson, N.C. St.	Greensboro, N.C.
1975	UCLA	John Wooden	Kentucky	92-85	Richard Washington, UCLA	San Diego, Cal.
1976	Indiana	Bob Knight	Michigan	86-68	Kent Benson, Indiana	Philadelphia, Pa.
1977	Marquette	Al McGuire	N. Carolina	67-59	Butch Lee, Marquette	Atlanta, Ga.
1978	Kentucky	Joe Hall	Duke	94-88	Jack Givens, Kentucky	St. Louis, Mo.
1979	Michigan St.	Jud Heathcote	Indiana St.	75-64	Magic Johnson, Michigan St.	Salt Lake City, Ut.
1980	Louisville	Denny Crum	UCLA*	59-54	Darrell Griffith, Louisville	Indianapolis, Ind.
1981	Indiana	Bob Knight	N. Carolina	63-50	Isiah Thomas, Indiana	Philadelphia, Pa.
1982	N. Carolina	Dean Smith	Georgetown	63-62	James Worthy, N. Carolina	New Orleans, La.
1983	N. Carolina St.	Jim Valvano	Houston	54-52	Hakeem Olajuwon, Houston	Albuquerque, N.M.
1984	Georgetown	John Thompson	Houston	84-75	Patrick Ewing, Georgetown	Seattle, Wash.
1985	Villanova	Rollie Massimino	Georgetown	66-64	Ed Pinckney, Villanova	Lexington, Ky.
1986	Louisville	Denny Crum	Duke	72-69	Pervis Ellison, Louisville	Dallas, Tex.
1987	Indiana	Bob Knight	Syracuse	74-73	Keith Smart, Indiana	New Orleans, La.
1988	Kansas	Larry Brown	Oklahoma	83-79	Danny Manning, Kansas	Kansas City, Mo.
1989	Michigan	Steve Fisher	Seton Hall	80-79(1)	Glen Rice, Michigan	Seattle, Wash.
1990	UNLV	Jerry Tarkanian	Duke	103-73	Anderson Hunt, UNLV	Denver, Col.
1991	Duke	Mike Krzyzewski	Kansas	72-65	Christian Laettner, Duke	Indianapolis, Ind.
1992	Duke	Mike Krzyzewski	Michigan	71-51	Bobby Hurley, Duke	Minneapolis, Minn.
1993	N. Carolina	Dean Smith	Michigan	77-71	Donald Williams, N. Carolina	New Orleans, La.
1994	Arkansas	Nolan Richardson	Duke	76-72	Corliss Williamson, Arkansas	Charlotte, N.C.

*Declared ineligible subsequent to the tournament. (1) Overtime. (2) Known as Oklahoma A&M at that time. (3) Known as Texas Western at that time.

John R. Wooden Award

Awarded annually to the nation's outstanding college basketball player by the United States Basketball Writers Assn.

Year	Player	Year	Player	Year	Player
1977	Marques Johnson, UCLA	1983	Ralph Sampson, Virginia	1989	Sean Elliott, Arizona
1978	Phil Ford, North Carolina	1984	Michael Jordan, North Carolina	1990	Lionel Simmons, La Salle
1979	Larry Bird, Indiana State	1985	Chris Mullin, St. John's	1991	Larry Johnson, UNLV
1980	Darrell Griffith, Louisville	1986	Walter Berry, St. John's	1992	Christian Laettner, Duke
1981	Danny Ainge, Brigham Young	1987	David Robinson, Navy	1993	Calbert Cheaney, Indiana
1982	Ralph Sampson, Virginia	1988	Danny Manning, Kansas	1994	Glenn Robinson, Purdue

NCAA Division I Women's Champions

Year	Champion	Coach	Final opponent	Year	Champion	Coach	Final opponent
1982	Louisiana Tech	Sonja Hogg	Cheyney	1989	Tennessee	Pat Summitt	Auburn
1983	USC	Linda Sharp	Louisiana Tech	1990	Stanford	Tara VanDerveer	Auburn
1984	USC	Linda Sharp	Tennessee	1991	Tennessee	Pat Summitt	Virginia
1985	Old Dominion	Marianne Stanley	Georgia	1992	Stanford	Tara VanDerveer	W. Kentucky
1986	Texas	Jody Conradt	USC	1993	Texas Tech	Marsha Sharp	Ohio St.
1987	Tennessee	Pat Summitt	Louisiana Tech	1994	North Carolina	Sylvia Hatchell	Louisiana Tech
1988	Louisiana Tech	Leon Barmore	Auburn				

Selected Division I Basketball Coaches in 1994

College	Coach	College	Coach	College	Coach
Akron	Coleman Crawford	Indiana St.	Sherman Dillard	Richmond	Bill Dooley
Alabama	David Hobbs	Iowa	Tom Davis	Rutgers	Bob Wenzel
Ala.-Birmingham	Gene Bartow	Iowa St.	Tim Floyd	St. Bonaventure	Jim Baron
American	Chris Knoche	James Madison	Lefty Driesell	St. John's (N.Y.)	Brian Mahoney
Arizona	Lute Olson	Kansas	Roy Williams	St. Joseph's (Pa.)	John Griffin
Arizona St.	Bill Frieder	Kansas St.	Tom Asbury	St. Louis	Charlie Spoonhour
Arkansas	Nolan Richardson	Kent	Dave Grube	St. Mary's (Cal.)	Ernie Kent
Army	Dino Gaudio	Kentucky	Rick Pitino	San Diego	Brad Holland
Auburn	Cliff Ellis	Long Beach St.	Seth Greenberg	San Diego St.	Fred Trenkle
Austin Peay	Dave Loos	LSU	Dale Brown	San Francisco	Jim Brovelli
Ball St.	Ray McCallum	Louisville	Denny Crum	San Jose St.	Stan Morrison
Baylor	Darrel Johnson	Loyola (Cal.)	John Olive	Santa Clara	Dick Davey
Boise St.	Bobby Dye	Loyola (Ill.)	Ken Burmeister	Seton Hall	George Blaney
Boston Coll.	Jim O'Brien	Marquette	Mike Dean	S. Carolina	Eddie Folger
Bowling Green	Jim Larranaga	Maryland	Gary Williams	S. Florida	Bobby Paschal
Bradley	Jim Molinari	Massachusetts	John Calipari	SE Mo. St.	Ron Shumate
BYU	Roger Reid	Memphis	Larry Finch	USC	George Raveling
Brown	Frank Dobbs	Miami (Fla.)	Leonard Hamilton	So. Illinois	Rick Herrin
Butler	Barry Collier	Miami (Oh.)	Herb Sendek	SMU	John Shumate
California	Todd Bozeman	Michigan	Steve Fisher	So. Mississippi	M. K. Turk
Cal. St. Fullerton	Bob Hawking	Michigan St.	Jud Heathcote	SW Mo. St.	Mark Bernsen
UC Irvine	Rod Baker	Middle Tenn. St.	David Farrar	Stanford	Mike Montgomery
UC Santa Barbara	Jerry Pimm	Minnesota	Clem Haskins	Syracuse	Jim Boeheim
Central Mich.	Leonard Drake	Mississippi	Rob Evans	Temple	John Chaney
Cincinnati	Bob Huggins	Mississippi St.	Richard Williams	Tennessee	Kevin O'Neill
Clemson	Rick Barnes	Missouri	Norm Stewart	Tennessee St.	Frankie Allen
Cleveland St.	Mike Boyd	Montana	Blaine Taylor	Tennessee Tech	Frank Harrell
Colorado	Joe Harrington	Montana St.	Mick Durham	Tennessee-Chatt.	Mack McCarthy
Colorado St.	Stew Morrill	Morehead St.	Dick Fick	Tennessee-Martin	Calvin C. Luther
Columbia	Jack Rohan	Murray St.	Scott Edgar	Texas	Tom Penders
Connecticut	Jim Calhoun	Nebraska	Danny Nee	Texas A&M	Tony Barone
Cornell	Al Walker	Nevada	Pat Foster	Tex. Christian	Billy Tubbs
Creighton	Dana Altman	UNLV	to be named	Tex.-Arlington	Eddie McCarter
Dartmouth	Dave Faucher	New Mexico	Dave Bliss	UTEP	Don Haskins
Dayton	Oliver Purnell	New Mexico St.	Neil McCarthy	Toledo	Larry Gipson
DePaul	Joey Meyer	North Carolina	Dean Smith	Tulane	Perry Clark
Detroit Mercy	Perry Watson	N.C. A&T	Roy Thomas	Tulsa	Tubby Smith
Drake	Rudy Washington	N.C. State	Les Robinson	UCLA	Jim Harrick
Duke	Mike Krzyzewski	N.C.-Charlotte	Jeff Mullins	Utah	Rick Majerus
E. Carolina	Eddie Payne	N.C.-Wilmington	Jerry Wainwright	Utah St.	Larry Eustachy
E. Illinois	Rick Samuels	N. Arizona	Ben Howland	Valparaiso	Homer Drew
E. Kentucky	Mike Calhoun	N. Illinois	Brian Hammel	Vanderbilt	Jan van Breda Kolff
E. Michigan	Ben Braun	N. Iowa	Eldon Miller	Villanova	Steve Lappas
E. Washington	John Wade	Northwestern	Ricky Byrdsong	Virginia	Jeff Jones
Evansville	Jim Crews	Notre Dame	John MacLeod	Va. Commonwealth	Sonny Smith
Florida	Lon Kruger	Ohio	Larry Hunter	Va. Tech	Bill Foster
Florida St.	Pat Kennedy	Ohio St.	Randy Ayers	Wake Forest	Dave Odem
Fresno St.	Gary Colson	Oklahoma	Kelvin Sampson	Washington	Bob Bender
George Mason	Paul Westhead	Oklahoma St.	Eddie Sutton	Washington St.	Kevin Eastman
Geo. Washington	Mike Jarvis	Old Dominion	Jeff Capel	Weber St.	Ron Abegglen
Georgetown	John Thompson	Oregon	Jerry Green	W. Virginia	Gale Catlett
Georgia	Hugh Durham	Oregon St.	Jim Anderson	W. Illinois	Jim Kerwin
Georgia Tech	Bobby Cremins	Pacific (Cal.)	Bob Thomason	W. Kentucky	Matt Kilcullen
Gonzaga	Dan Fitzgerald	Pennsylvania	Fran Dunphy	W. Michigan	Bob Donewald
Harvard	Frank Sullivan	Penn St.	Bruce Parkhill	Wichita St.	Scott Thompson
Hawaii	Riley Wallace	Pepperdine	Tony Fuller	William & Mary	Charlie Woollum
Houston	Alvin Brooks	Pittsburgh	Ralph Willard	Wisconsin	Stan Van Gundy
Idaho	Joe Cravens	Portland	Rob Chavez	Wis.-Green Bay	Dick Bennett
Idaho St.	Herb Williams	Princeton	Pete Carril	Wright St.	Ralph Underhill
Illinois	Lou Henson	Providence	Pete Gillen	Wyoming	Joby Wright
Illinois St.	Kevin Stallings	Purdue	Gene Keady	Xavier (Oh.)	Skip Prosser
Illinois-Chi.	Bob Hallberg	Rhode Island	Al Skinner	Yale	Dick Kuchen
Indiana	Bob Knight	Rice	Willis Wilson		

Most Coaching Victories in the NCAA Tournament Through 1994

Coach, school, years	Wins	Tournaments
Dean Smith, North Carolina, 1967-94	56	24
John Wooden, UCLA, 1950-75	47	16
Bob Knight, Indiana, 1973-94	40	18
Mike Krzyzewski, Duke, 1984-94	39	11
Denny Crum, Louisville, 1972-94	37	18
Jerry Tarkanian, Long Beach State and UNLV, 1970-91	31	16
Adolph Rupp, Kentucky, 1942-72	30	20
John Thompson, Georgetown, 1975-94	29	17
Guy Lewis, Houston, 1961-84	26	14
Jim Boeheim, Syracuse, 1976-94	21	15
Eddie Sutton, Creighton, Arkansas, Kentucky, Oklahoma St., 1974-94	21	16

NCAA Division I Basketball Statistical Trends

Averages and percentages are for both teams, per game.

Year	Games	FG Made	FG Att.	Pct.	FT Made	FT Att.	Pct.	PF	Pts.
1948	3945	40.6	138.7	29.3	25.3	42.2	59.8	36.9	106.5
1950	3659	43.2	136.8	31.6	28.7	46.5	61.8	39.0	115.1
1952	4009	47.5	140.6*	33.7	31.6	50.5	62.6	44.9*	126.6
1953	3754	48.0	138.1	34.7	42.1	65.8*	64.0	42.5	138.1
1955	3829	51.1	138.6	36.9	43.1*	64.7	66.5	37.9	145.3
1958	4153	51.6	134.2	38.4	33.6	50.5	66.4	36.4	136.8
1960	4295	52.6	132.3	39.8	34.7	51.5	67.4	36.7	139.9
1963	4180	53.2	127.6	41.7	32.6	47.8	68.2	36.4	139.0
1965	4520	58.3	135.4	43.1	34.7	50.3	69.0	38.5	151.4
1971	5232	60.2	135.6	44.4	35.0	51.3	68.1	38.5	155.4*
1973	5582	62.3*	139.2	44.8	26.2	38.3	68.4	38.4	150.9
1975	6147	62.9	136.7	46.0	27.4	39.7	69.0	40.3	153.1
1979	7131	59.2	124.1	47.7	29.5	42.2	69.7*	41.1	147.9
1983	7957	54.3	114.0	47.7	29.0	42.3	68.5	39.7	138.7
1985	8269	54.5	113.9	47.9*	29.3	42.5	68.9	39.3	138.3
1986	8360	54.7	114.6	47.7	29.4	42.5	69.1	39.1	138.7
1987	8580	54.4	117.3	46.6	29.7	43.0	69.1	39.3	145.5
1988	8587	54.8	116.6	47.0	30.2	43.8	68.9	39.4	147.8
1989	8677	55.7	118.5	47.0	31.1	45.0	69.1	40.2	151.4
1990	8646	54.7	118.9	46.0	31.1	45.1	68.9	39.6	149.8
1991	8720	55.6	121.3	45.8	31.7	46.3	68.5	39.2	152.9
1992	8803*	53.0	116.6	45.5	31.6	46.4	68.1	40.0	147.6
1993	8528	52.9	117.2	45.2	30.8	45.5	67.7	39.1	147.2
1994	8630	53.7	121.1	44.3	31.2	46.4	67.1	39.7	150.0

*All-time high

Skiing

World Cup Alpine Champions

Men

1967 Jean Claude Killy, France
1968 Jean Claude Killy, France
1969 Karl Schranz, Austria
1970 Karl Schranz, Austria
1971 Gustavo Thoeni, Italy
1972 Gustavo Thoeni, Italy
1973 Gustavo Thoeni, Italy
1974 Piero Gros, Italy
1975 Gustavo Thoeni, Italy
1976 Ingemar Stenmark, Sweden
1977 Ingemar Stenmark, Sweden
1978 Ingemar Stenmark, Sweden
1979 Peter Luescher, Switzerland
1980 Andreas Wenzel, Liechtenstein
1981 Phil Mahre, U.S.
1982 Phil Mahre, U.S.
1983 Phil Mahre, U.S.
1984 Pirmin Zurbriggen, Switzerland
1985 Marc Girardelli, Luxembourg
1986 Marc Girardelli, Luxembourg
1987 Pirmin Zurbriggen, Switzerland
1988 Pirmin Zurbriggen, Switzerland
1989 Marc Girardelli, Luxembourg
1990 Pirmin Zurbriggen, Switzerland
1991 Marc Girardelli, Luxembourg
1992 Paul Accola, Switzerland
1993 Marc Girardelli, Luxembourg
1994 Marc Girardelli, Luxembourg

Women

1967 Nancy Greene, Canada
1968 Nancy Greene, Canada
1969 Gertrud Gabl, Austria
1970 Michele Jacot, France
1971 Annemarie Proell, Austria
1972 Annemarie Proell, Austria
1973 Annemarie Proell, Austria
1974 Annemarie Proell, Austria
1975 Annemarie Proell, Austria
1976 Rose Mittermaier, W. Germany
1977 Lise-Marie Morerod, Switzerland
1978 Hanni Wenzel, Liechtenstein
1979 Annemarie Proell Moser, Austria
1980 Hanni Wenzel, Liechtenstein
1981 Marie-Theres Nadig, Switzerland
1982 Erika Hess, Switzerland
1983 Tamara McKinney, U.S.
1984 Erika Hess, Switzerland
1985 Michela Figini, Switzerland
1986 Maria Walliser, Switzerland
1987 Maria Walliser, Switzerland
1988 Michela Figini, Switzerland
1989 Vreni Schneider, Switzerland
1990 Petra Kronberger, Austria
1991 Petra Kronberger, Austria
1992 Petra Kronberger, Austria
1993 Anita Wachter, Austria
1994 Vreni Schneider, Switzerland

Westminster Kennel Club

Year	Best-in-show	Breed	Owner
1985	Ch. Braeburn's Close Encounter	Scottish terrier	Sonnie Novick
1986	Ch. Marjetta National Acclaim	Pointer	Mrs. Alan Robson & Michael Zollo
1987	Ch. Covy Tucker Hill's Manhattan	German shepherd	Shirley Braunstein & Jane Firestone
1988	Ch. Great Elms Prince Charming II	Pomeranian	Skip Piazza & Olga Baker
1989	Ch. Royal Tudor's Wild As The Wind	Doberman	Sue & Art Kemp, Richard & Carolyn Vida, Beth Wilhite
1990	Ch. Wendessa Crown Prince	Pekingese	Ed Jenner
1991	Ch. Whisperwind on a Carousel	Poodle	Joan & Frederick Hartsock
1992	Ch. Registry's Lonesome Dove	Fox terrier	Marion & Sam Lawrence
1993	Ch. Salilyn's Condor	English springer spaniel	Donna & Roger Herzig
1994	Ch. Chidley Willum	Norwich terrier	Ruth Cooper & Patricia Lussier

Iditarod Trail Sled Dog Race in 1994

Martin Buser won the 1994 Iditarod Trail Sled Dog Race on March 15, 1994, in a record time of 10 days 13 hours 2 minutes. It was Buser's second win in 3 years. By winning the 1,159-mile race from Anchorage to Nome, Buser received $50,000 in prize money and a pickup truck valued at about $25,000. Rick Mackey finished second, and Jeff King finished third.

IGFA Saltwater & Freshwater All-Tackle World Records

Source: International Game Fish Association; records confirmed to Sept. 1994

Saltwater Fish

Species	Weight	Where caught	Date	Angler
Albacore	88 lbs. 2 oz.	Pt. Mogan, Canary Islands	Nov. 19, 1977	Siegfried Dickemann
Amberjack, greater	155 lbs. 10 oz.	Bermuda	June 24, 1981	Joseph Dawson
Barracuda, great	85 lbs.	Christmas Island	Apr. 11, 1992	John Helfrich
Barracuda, Mexican	21 lbs.	Costa Rica	Mar. 27, 1987	E. Greg Kent
Barracuda, Pacific	6 lbs. 3 oz.	Pt. Loma, San Diego, Cal.	Apr. 4, 1992	James Seibert
Bass, barred sand	13 lbs. 3 oz.	Huntington Beach, Cal.	Aug. 29, 1988	Robert Halal
Bass, black sea	9 lbs. 8 oz.	Virginia Beach, Va.	Jan. 9, 1987	Joe Mizelle Jr.
		Virginia Beach, Va.	Dec. 22, 1990	Jack Stallings, Jr.
Bass, giant sea	563 lbs. 8 oz.	Anacaba Island, Cal.	Aug. 20, 1968	James D. McAdam Jr.
Bass, striped	78 lbs. 8 oz.	Atlantic City, N.J.	Sept. 21, 1982	Albert McReynolds
Bass, white	6 lbs. 13 oz.	L. Orange, Va.	July 31, 1989	Ronald Sprouse
Bluefish	31 lbs. 12 oz.	Hatteras Inlet, N.C.	Jan. 30, 1972	James M. Hussey
Bonefish	19 lbs.	Zululand, S. Africa	May 26, 1962	Brian W. Batchelor
Bonito, Atlantic	18 lbs. 14 oz.	Fayal I., Azores	July 8, 1953	D. G. Higgs
Bonito, Pacific	14 lbs. 12 oz.	San Benitos Is., Mexico	Oct. 12, 1980	Jerome Rilling
Cabezon	23 lbs.	Juan De Fuca Strait, Wash.	Aug. 4, 1990	Wesley Hunter
Cobia	135 lbs. 9 oz.	Shark Bay, Australia	July 9, 1985	Peter W. Goulding
Cod, Atlantic	98 lbs. 12 oz.	Isle of Shoals, N.H.	June 8, 1969	Alphonse Bielevich
Cod, Pacific	30 lbs.	Andrew Bay, Alaska	June 7, 1984	Donald Vaughn
Conger	110 lbs. 8 oz.	Plymouth, England	Aug. 20, 1991	Hans Clausen
Dolphin	87 lbs.	Papagallo Gulf, Costa Rica	Sept. 25, 1976	Manual Salazar
Drum, black	113 lbs. 1 oz.	Lewes, Del.	Sept. 15, 1975	Gerald Townsend
Drum, red	94 lbs. 2 oz.	Avon, N.C.	Nov. 7, 1984	David Deuel
Eel, American	8 lbs. 8 oz.	Brewster, Mass.	May 17, 1992	Gerald LaPierre
Eel, marbled	36 lbs. 1 oz.	Hazelmere Dam, S. Africa	June 10, 1984	Ferdie van Nooten
Flounder, southern	20 lbs. 9 oz.	Nassau Sound, Fla.	Dec. 23, 1983	Larenza Mungin
Flounder, summer	22 lbs. 7 oz.	Montauk, N.Y.	Sept. 15, 1975	Charles Nappi
Grouper, Warsaw	436 lbs. 12 oz.	Gulf of Mexico, Destin, Fla.	Dec. 22, 1985	Steve Haeusler
Halibut, Atlantic	255 lbs. 4 oz.	Gloucester, Mass.	July 28, 1989	Sonny Manley
Halibut, California	53 lbs. 4 oz.	Santa Rosa Is., Cal.	July 7, 1988	Russell Harmon
Halibut, Pacific	368 lbs.	Gustavus, Alaska	July 5, 1991	Celia Deuitt
Jack, crevalle	57 lbs. 5 oz.	Barra co Kwanza, Angola	Oct. 10, 1992	Cam Nicoldon`
Jack, horse-eye	24 lbs. 8 oz.	Miami, Fla.	Dec. 20, 1982	Tito Schnau
Jack, Pacific crevalle	29 lbs. 8 oz.	Playa Zancudo, Costa Rica	Jan. 1, 1994	Ronald C. Snody
Jewfish	680 lbs.	Fernandina Beach, Fla.	May 20, 1961	Lynn Joyner
Kawakawa	29 lbs.	Clarion Is., Mexico	Dec. 17, 1986	Ronald Nakamura
Lingcod	69 lbs.	Langara Is., B.C.	June 16, 1992	Murray Romer
Mackerel, cero	17 lbs. 2 oz.	Islamorada, Fla.	Apr. 5, 1986	G. Michael Mills
Mackerel, king	90 lbs.	Key West, Fla.	Feb. 16, 1976	Norton Thomton
Mackerel, Spanish	13 lbs.	Ocracoke Inlet, N.C.	Nov. 4, 1987	Robert Cranton
Marlin, Atlantic blue	1,402 lbs. 2 oz.	Vitoria, Brazil	Feb. 29, 1992	Paulo Amorim
Marlin, black	1,560 lbs.	Cabo Blanco, Peru	Aug. 4, 1953	A. C. Glassell Jr.
Marlin, Pacific blue	1,376 lbs.	Kaaiwa Pt., Hawaii	May 31, 1982	J.W. deBeaubien
Marlin, striped	494 lbs.	Tutukaka, New Zealand	Jan. 16, 1986	Bill Boniface
Marlin, white	181 lbs. 14 oz.	Vitoria, Brazil	Dec. 8, 1979	Evandro Luiz Caser
Permit	53 lbs. 4 oz.	Lake Worth Inlet, Fla.	March 25, 1994	Roy Brooker
Pollack	27 lbs. 6 oz.	Devon, England	Jan. 16, 1986	Robert Milkins
Pollock	46 lbs. 10 oz.	Perkins Cove, Me.	Oct. 24, 1990	Linda Paul
Pompano, African	50 lbs. 8 oz.	Daytona Beach, Fla.	Apr. 21, 1990	Tom Sargent
Roosterfish	114 lbs.	La Paz, Mexico	June 1, 1960	Abe Sackheim
Runner, blue	8 lbs. 4 oz.	Bimini, Bahamas	Sept. 9, 1990	Brent Rowland
Runner, rainbow	37 lbs. 9 oz.	Clarion Is., Mexico	Nov. 21, 1991	Tom Pfleger
Sailfish, Atlantic	135 lbs. 5 oz.	Lagos, Nigeria	Nov. 10, 1991	Ron King
Sailfish, Pacific	221 lbs.	Santa Cruz Is., Ecuador	Feb. 12, 1947	C. W. Stewart
Seabass, white	83 lbs. 12 oz.	San Felipe, Mexico	Mar. 31, 1953	L.C. Baumgardner
Seatrout, spotted	16 lbs.	Mason's Beach, Va.	May 28, 1977	William Katko
Shark, bigeye thresher	802 lbs.	Tutukaka, New Zealand	Feb. 8, 1981	Dianne North
Shark, blue	437 lbs.	Catherine Bay, N.S.W. Australia	Oct. 2, 1976	Peter Hyde
Shark, great hammerhead	991 lbs.	Sarasota, Fla.	May 30, 1982	Allen Ogle
Shark, Greenland	1,708 lbs. 9 oz.	Trondheim, Norway	Oct. 18, 1987	Terje Nordtvedt
Shark, man-eater or white	2,664 lbs.	Ceduna, Australia	Apr. 21, 1959	Alfred Dean
Shark, porbeagle	465 lbs.	Cornwall, England	July 23, 1976	Jorge Potier
Shark, shortfin mako	1,115 lbs.	Black R., Mauritius	Nov. 16, 1988	Patrick Guillanton
Shark, tiger	1,780 lbs.	Cherry Grove, S.C.	June 14, 1964	Walter Maxwell
Skipjack, black	26 lbs.	Baja, Mexico	Oct. 23, 1991	Clifford Hamishi
Snapper, cubera	121 lbs. 8 oz.	Cameron, La.	July 5, 1982	Mike Hebert
Snook	53 lbs. 10 oz.	Costa Rica	Oct. 18, 1978	Gilbert Ponzi
Spearfish, Mediterranean	90 lbs. 13 oz.	Madeira Island, Portugal	June 2, 1980	Joseph Larkin
Swordfish	1,182 lbs.	Iquique, Chile	May 7, 1953	L. Marron
Tarpon	283 lbs. 4 oz.	Sierra Leone	Apr. 16, 1991	Yvon Sebag
Tautog	24 lbs.	Wachapreagee, Va.	Aug. 25, 1987	Gregory Bell
Tope	72 lbs. 12 oz.	Parengarenga Harbor, New Zealand	Dec. 19, 1986	Melanie Feldman
Trevally, bigeye	15 lbs. 8 oz.	Waianae, Hawaii	Mar. 6, 1992	Darryl Bailey
Trevally, giant	145 lbs. 8 oz.	Makena, Hawaii	Mar. 28, 1991	Russell Mori
Tuna, Atlantic bigeye	375 lbs. 8 oz.	Ocean City, Md.	Aug. 26, 1977	Cecil Browne
Tuna, blackfin	42 lbs.	Bermuda	June 2, 1978	Alan J. Card
		Bermuda	July 18, 1989	Gilbert Pearman
Tuna, bluefin	1,496 lbs.	Aulds Cove, Nova Scotia	Oct. 26, 1979	Ken Fraser
Tuna, longtail	79 lbs. 2 oz.	Montague Is., N.S.W., Australia	Apr. 12, 1982	Tim Simpson
Tuna, Pacific bigeye	435 lbs.	Cabo Blanco, Peru	Apr. 17, 1957	Dr. Russel Lee

Species	Weight	Where caught	Date	Angler
Tuna, skipjack	41 lbs. 14 oz.	Mauritius	Nov. 12, 1985	Edmund Heinzen
Tuna, southern bluefin	348 lbs. 5 oz.	Whakatane, New Zealand	Jan. 16, 1981	Rex Wood
Tuna, yellowfin	388 lbs. 12 oz.	San Benedicto Island, Mexico	Apr. 1, 1977	Curt Wiesenhutter
Tunny, little	35 lbs. 2 oz.	Cap de Garde, Algeria	Dec. 14, 1988	Jean Yves Chatard
Wahoo	155 lbs. 8 oz.	Bahamas	Apr. 3, 1990	William Bourne
Weakfish	19 lbs. 2 oz.	Jones Beach Inlet, N.Y.	Oct. 11, 1984	Dennis Rooney
		Delaware Bay, Delaware	May 20, 1989	William Thomas
Yellowtail, California	79 lbs. 4 oz.	Alijos Rocks, Mexico	July 2, 1991	Robert Walker
Yellowtail, southern	114 lbs. 10 oz.	Tauranga, New Zealand	Feb. 5, 1984	Mike Godfrey

Freshwater Fish

Species	Weight	Where caught	Date	Angler
Barramundi	63 lbs. 2 oz.	Normah R., Australia	Apr. 28, 1991	Scott Barnsley
Bass, largemouth	22 lbs. 4 oz.	Montgomery Lake, Ga.	June 2, 1932	George W. Perry
Bass, peacock	26 lbs. 8 oz.	Matevini R., Colombia	Jan. 26, 1982	Rod Neubert
Bass, redeye	8 lbs. 3 oz.	Flint River, Ga.	Oct. 23, 1977	David A. Hubbard
Bass, rock	3 lbs.	York River, Ont.	Aug. 1, 1974	Peter Gulgin
Bass, smallmouth	11 lbs. 15 oz.	Dale Hollow Lake, Ky.	July 9, 1955	David L. Hayes
Bass, Suwannee	3 lbs. 14 oz.	Suwannee River, Fla.	Mar. 2, 1985	Ronnie Everett
Bass, white	6 lbs. 13 oz.	L. Orange, Va.	July 31, 1989	Ronald Sprouse
Bass, whiterock	24 lbs. 3 oz.	Leesville L., Va.	May 12, 1989	David Lambert
Bass, yellow	2 lbs. 4 oz.	Lake Monroe, Ind.	Mar. 27, 1977	Donald L. Stalker
Bluegill	4 lbs. 12 oz.	Ketona Lake, Ala.	Apr. 9, 1950	T.S. Hudson
Bowfin	21 lbs. 8 oz.	Florence, S.C.	Jan. 29, 1980	Robert Harmon
Buffalo, bigmouth	70 lbs. 5 oz.	Bastrop, La.	Apr. 21, 1980	Delbert Sisk
Buffalo, black	55 lbs. 8 oz.	Cherokee L., Tenn.	May 3, 1984	Edward McLain
Buffalo, smallmouth	68 lbs. 8 oz.	L. Hamilton, Ark.	May 16, 1984	Jerry Dolezal
Bullhead, brown	5 lbs. 8 oz.	Veal Pond, Ga.	May 22, 1975	Jimmy Andrews
Bullhead, yellow	4 lbs. 4 oz.	Mormon Lake, Ariz.	May 11, 1984	Emily Williams
Burbot	18 lbs. 4 oz.	Pickford, Mich.	Jan. 31, 1980	Thomas Courtemanche
Carp	75 lbs. 11 oz.	Lac de St. Cassien, France	May 21, 1987	Leo van der Gugten
Catfish, blue	109 lbs. 4 oz.	Cooper R., S.C.	Mar. 14, 1991	George Lijewski
Catfish, channel	58 lbs.	Santee-Cooper Res., S.C.	July 7, 1964	W.B. Whaley
Catfish, flathead	91 lbs. 4 oz.	L. Lewisville, Tex.	Mar. 28, 1982	Mike Rogers
Catfish, white	18 lbs. 14 oz.	Withlacoochee R., Fla.	Sept. 21, 1991	Jim Miller
Char, Arctic	32 lbs. 9 oz.	Tree River, Canada	July 30, 1981	Jeffrey Ward
Crappie, white	5 lbs. 3 oz.	Enid Dam, Miss.	July 31, 1957	Fred L. Bright
Dolly Varden	18 lbs. 9 oz.	Mashutuk R., Alaska	July 13, 1993	Richard B. Evans
Dorado	51 lbs. 5 oz.	Corrientes, Argentina	Sept. 27, 1984	Armando Giudice
Drum, freshwater	54 lbs. 8 oz.	Nickajack Lake, Tenn.	Apr. 20, 1972	Benny E. Hull
Gar, alligator	279 lbs.	Rio Grande River, Tex.	Dec. 2, 1951	Bill Valverde
Gar, Florida	21 lbs. 3 oz.	Boca Raton, Fla.	June 3, 1981	Jeff Sabol
Gar, longnose	50 lbs. 5 oz.	Trinity River, Tex.	July 30, 1954	Townsend Miller
Gar, shortnose	5 lbs.	Sally Jones L., Oklahoma	Apr. 26, 1985	Buddy Croslin
Gar, spotted	8 lbs. 12 oz.	Tennessee R., Ala.	Aug. 26, 1987	Winston Baker
Grayling, Arctic	5 lbs. 15 oz.	Katseyedie River, N.W.T.	Aug. 16, 1967	Jeanne P. Branson
Inconnu	53 lbs.	Pah R., Alaska	Aug. 20, 1986	Lawrence Hudnall
Kokanee	9 lbs. 6 oz.	Okanagan Lake, Vernon, B.C.	June 18, 1988	Norm Kuhn
Muskellunge	65 lbs.	Blackstone Harbor, Ont.	Oct. 16, 1988	Kenneth O'Brien
Muskellunge, tiger	51 lbs. 3 oz.	Lac Vieux-Desert, Wis., Mich.	July 16, 1919	John Knobla
Perch, Nile	191 lbs. 8 oz.	L. Victoria, Kenya	Sept. 5, 1991	Andy Davison
Perch, white	4 lbs. 12 oz.	Messalonskee Lake, Me.	June 4, 1949	Mrs. Earl Small
Perch, yellow	4 lbs. 3 oz.	Bordentown, N.J.	May, 1865	Dr. C.C. Abbot
Pickerel, chain	9 lbs. 6 oz.	Homerville, Ga.	Feb. 17, 1961	Baxley McQuaig Jr.
Pike, northern	55 lbs. 1 oz.	Lake of Grefeern, W. Germany	Oct. 16, 1986	Lothar Louis
Redhorse, greater	9 lbs. 3 oz.	Salmon R., Pulaski, N.Y.	May 11, 1985	Jason Wilson
Redhorse, silver	11 lbs. 7 oz.	Plum Creek, Wis.	May 29, 1985	Neal Long
Salmon, Atlantic	79 lbs. 2 oz.	Tana River, Norway	1928	Henrik Henriksen
Salmon, chinook	97 lbs. 4 oz.	Kenai R., Alas.	May 17, 1985	Les Anderson
Salmon, chum	32 lbs.	Behm Canal, Alas.	June 7, 1985	Fredrick Thynes
Salmon, coho	33 lbs. 4 oz.	Salmon R., Pulaski, N.Y.	Sept. 27, 1989	Jerry Lifton
Salmon, pink	13 lbs. 1 oz.	St. Mary's R., Ontario	Sept. 23, 1992	Ray Higaki
Salmon, sockeye	15 lbs. 3 oz.	Kenai R., Alaska	Aug. 9, 1987	Stan Roach
Sauger	8 lbs. 12 oz.	Lake Sakakawea, N.D.	Oct. 6, 1971	Mike Fischer
Shad, American	11 lbs. 4 oz.	Connecticut R., Mass.	May 19, 1986	Bob Thibodo
Sturgeon, white	468 lbs.	Benicia, Cal.	July 9, 1983	Joey Pallotta 3d
Sunfish, green	2 lbs. 2 oz.	Stockton Lake, Mo.	June 18, 1971	Paul M. Dilley
Sunfish, redbreast	1 lb. 12 oz.	Suwannee R., Fla.	May 29, 1984	Alvin Buchanan
Sunfish, redear	4 lbs. 13 oz.	Marianna, Fla.	Mar. 13, 1986	Joey Floyd
Tigerfish, giant	97 lbs.	Zaire R., Kinshasa, Zaire	July 9, 1988	Raymond Houtmans
Tilapia	6 lbs.	L. Okeechobee, Fla.	June 24, 1989	Joseph M. Tucker
Trout, Apache	5 lb. 3 oz.	Apache Res., Ariz.	May 29, 1991	John Baldwin
Trout, brook	14 lbs. 8 oz.	Nipigon River, Ont.	July 1916	Dr. W.J. Cook
Trout, brown	40 lbs. 4 oz.	Little Red R., Ark.	May 9, 1992	Howard Collins
Trout, bull	32 lbs.	L. Pend Oreille, Ida.	Oct. 27, 1949	N.L. Higgins
Trout, cutthroat	41 lbs.	Pyramid Lake, Nev.	Dec. 1925	J. Skimmerhorn
Trout, golden	11 lbs.	Cook's Lake, Wyo.	Aug. 5, 1948	Charles S. Reed
Trout, lake	66 lbs. 8 oz.	Great Bear Lake, N.W.T.	July 19, 1991	Rodney Harback
Trout, rainbow	42 lbs. 2 oz.	Bell Island, Alas.	June 22, 1970	David Robert White
Trout, tiger	20 lbs. 13 oz.	Lake Michigan, Wis.	Aug. 12, 1978	Pete Friedland
Walleye	25 lbs.	Old Hickory Lake, Tenn.	Aug. 1, 1960	Mabry Harper
Warmouth	2 lbs. 7 oz.	Yellow R., Holt, Fla.	Oct. 19, 1985	Tony D. Dempsey
Whitefish, lake	14 lbs. 6 oz.	Meaford, Ont.	May 21, 1984	Dennis Laycock
Whitefish, mountain	5 lbs. 6 oz.	Rioh R., Sask.	June 15, 1988	John Bell
Whitefish, river	11 lbs. 2 oz.	Nymoua, Sweden	Dec. 9, 1984	Jorgen Larsson
Whitefish, round	6 lbs.	Putahow R., Manitoba	June 14, 1984	Allen Ristori
Zander	22 lbs. 2 oz.	Trosa, Sweden	June 12, 1986	Harry Lee Tennison

GOLF

United States Open Winners

Year	Winner	Year	Winner	Year	Winner	Year	Winner
1903	Willie Anderson	1926	Bobby Jones*	1951	Ben Hogan	1973	Johnny Miller
1904	Willie Anderson	1927	Tommy Armour	1952	Julius Boros	1974	Hale Irwin
1905	Willie Anderson	1928	John Farrell	1953	Ben Hogan	1975	Lou Graham
1906	Alex Smith	1929	Bobby Jones*	1954	Ed Furgol	1976	Jerry Pate
1907	Alex Ross	1930	Bobby Jones*	1955	Jack Fleck	1977	Hubert Green
1908	Fred McLeod	1931	Wm. Burke	1956	Cary Middlecoff	1978	Andy North
1909	George Sargent	1932	Gene Sarazen	1957	Dick Mayer	1979	Hale Irwin
1910	Alex Smith	1933	John Goodman*	1958	Tommy Bolt	1980	Jack Nicklaus
1911	John McDermott	1934	Olin Dutra	1959	Billy Casper	1981	David Graham
1912	John McDermott	1935	Sam Parks Jr.	1960	Arnold Palmer	1982	Tom Watson
1913	Francis Ouimet*	1936	Tony Manero	1961	Gene Littler	1983	Larry Nelson
1914	Walter Hagen	1937	Ralph Guldahl	1962	Jack Nicklaus	1984	Fuzzy Zoeller
1915	Jerome Travers*	1938	Ralph Guldahl	1963	Julius Boros	1985	Andy North
1916	Chick Evans*	1939	Byron Nelson	1964	Ken Venturi	1986	Ray Floyd
1917-18	(Not played)	1940	Lawson Little	1965	Gary Player	1987	Scott Simpson
1919	Walter Hagen	1941	Craig Wood	1966	Billy Casper	1988	Curtis Strange
1920	Edward Ray	1942-45	(Not played)	1967	Jack Nicklaus	1989	Curtis Strange
1921	Jim Barnes	1946	Lloyd Mangrum	1968	Lee Trevino	1990	Hale Irwin
1922	Gene Sarazen	1947	L. Worsham	1969	Orville Moody	1991	Payne Stewart
1923	Bobby Jones*	1948	Ben Hogan	1970	Tony Jacklin	1992	Tom Kite
1924	Cyril Walker	1949	Cary Middlecoff	1971	Lee Trevino	1993	Lee Janzen
1925	Willie MacFarlane	1950	Ben Hogan	1972	Jack Nicklaus	1994	Ernie Els

* Amateur

Professional Golfer's Association Championship Winners

Year	Winner	Year	Winner	Year	Winner	Year	Winner
1922	Gene Sarazen	1940	Byron Nelson	1959	Bob Rosburg	1977	Lanny Wadkins
1923	Gene Sarazen	1941	Victor Ghezzi	1960	Jay Hebert	1978	John Mahaffey
1924	Walter Hagen	1942	Sam Snead	1961	Jerry Barber	1979	David Graham
1925	Walter Hagen	1944	Bob Hamilton	1962	Gary Player	1980	Jack Nicklaus
1926	Walter Hagen	1945	Byron Nelson	1963	Jack Nicklaus	1981	Larry Nelson
1927	Walter Hagen	1946	Ben Hogan	1964	Bob Nichols	1982	Ray Floyd
1928	Leo Diegel	1947	Jim Ferrier	1965	Dave Marr	1983	Hal Sutton
1929	Leo Diegel	1948	Ben Hogan	1966	Al Geiberger	1984	Lee Trevino
1930	Tommy Armour	1949	Sam Snead	1967	Don January	1985	Hubert Green
1931	Tom Creavy	1950	Chandler Harper	1968	Julius Boros	1986	Bob Tway
1932	Olin Dutra	1951	Sam Snead	1969	Ray Floyd	1987	Larry Nelson
1933	Gene Sarazen	1952	James Turnesa	1970	Dave Stockton	1988	Jeff Sluman
1934	Paul Runyan	1953	Walter Burkemo	1971	Jack Nicklaus	1989	Payne Stewart
1935	Johnny Revolta	1954	Melvin Harbert	1972	Gary Player	1990	Wayne Grady
1936	Denny Shute	1955	Doug Ford	1973	Jack Nicklaus	1991	John Daly
1937	Denny Shute	1956	Jack Burke	1974	Lee Trevino	1992	Nick Price
1938	Paul Runyan	1957	Lionel Hebert	1975	Jack Nicklaus	1993	Paul Azinger
1939	Henry Picard	1958	Dow Finsterwald	1976	Dave Stockton	1994	Nick Price

Masters Golf Tournament Winners

Year	Winner	Year	Winner	Year	Winner	Year	Winner
1934	Horton Smith	1951	Ben Hogan	1966	Jack Nicklaus	1981	Tom Watson
1935	Gene Sarazen	1952	Sam Snead	1967	Gay Brewer Jr.	1982	Craig Stadler
1936	Horton Smith	1953	Ben Hogan	1968	Bob Goalby	1983	Seve Ballesteros
1937	Byron Nelson	1954	Sam Snead	1969	George Archer	1984	Ben Crenshaw
1938	Henry Picard	1955	Cary Middlecoff	1970	Billy Casper	1985	Bernhard Langer
1939	Ralph Guldahl	1956	Jack Burke	1971	Charles Coody	1986	Jack Nicklaus
1940	Jimmy Demaret	1957	Doug Ford	1972	Jack Nicklaus	1987	Larry Mize
1941	Craig Wood	1958	Arnold Palmer	1973	Tommy Aaron	1988	Sandy Lyle
1942	Byron Nelson	1959	Art Wall Jr.	1974	Gary Player	1989	Nick Faldo
1943-1945	(Not played)	1960	Arnold Palmer	1975	Jack Nicklaus	1990	Nick Faldo
1946	Herman Keiser	1961	Gary Player	1976	Ray Floyd	1991	Ian Woosnam
1947	Jimmy Demaret	1962	Arnold Palmer	1977	Tom Watson	1992	Fred Couples
1948	Claude Harmon	1963	Jack Nicklaus	1978	Gary Player	1993	Bernhard Langer
1949	Sam Snead	1964	Arnold Palmer	1979	Fuzzy Zoeller	1994	Jose Maria Olazabal
1950	Jimmy Demaret	1965	Jack Nicklaus	1980	Seve Ballesteros		

British Open Winners

Year	Winner	Year	Winner	Year	Winner	Year	Winner
1931	Tommy Armour	1951	Max Faulkner	1966	Jack Nicklaus	1981	Bill Rogers
1932	Gene Sarazen	1952	Bobby Locke	1967	Roberto de Vicenzo	1982	Tom Watson
1933	Denny Shute	1953	Ben Hogan	1968	Gary Player	1983	Tom Watson
1934	Henry Cotton	1954	Peter Thomson	1969	Tony Jacklin	1984	Seve Ballesteros
1935	Alf Perry	1955	Peter Thomson	1970	Jack Nicklaus	1985	Sandy Lyle
1936	Alf Padgham	1956	Peter Thomson	1971	Lee Trevino	1986	Greg Norman
1937	T.H. Cotton	1957	Bobby Locke	1972	Lee Trevino	1987	Nick Faldo
1938	R.A. Whitcombe	1958	Peter Thomson	1973	Tom Weiskopf	1988	Seve Ballesteros
1939	Richard Burton	1959	Gary Player	1974	Gary Player	1989	Mark Calcavecchia
1940-45	(Not played)	1960	Kel Nagle	1975	Tom Watson	1990	Nick Faldo
1946	Sam Snead	1961	Arnold Palmer	1976	Johnny Miller	1991	Ian Baker-Finch
1947	Fred Daly	1962	Arnold Palmer	1977	Tom Watson	1992	Nick Faldo
1948	Henry Cotton	1963	Bob Charles	1978	Jack Nicklaus	1993	Greg Norman
1949	Bobby Locke	1964	Tony Lema	1979	Seve Ballesteros	1994	Nick Price
1950	Bobby Locke	1965	Peter Thomson	1980	Tom Watson		

Professional Golf Tournaments in 1994

Men

Date	Event	Winner	Score	Prize
Jan. 9	Mercedes Tournament of Champions, Carlsbad, CA	Phil Mickelson	*276	$180,000
Jan. 16	Hawaiian Open, Honolulu. HI	Brett Ogle	269	216,000
Jan. 23	Northern Telecom Open, Tucson, AZ	Andrew Magee	270	198,000
Jan. 30	Phoenix Open, AZ	Bill Glasson	268	216,000
Feb. 6	A.T.&T. National Pro-Am, Pebble Beach, CA	Johnny Miller	281	225,000
Feb. 13	Los Angeles Open	Corey Pavin	271	180,000
Feb. 20	Bob Hope Classic, Indian Wells, CA	Scott Hoch	334	198,000
Feb. 27	Buick Invitational, San Diego, CA	Craig Stadler	268	198,000
Mar. 6	Doral Ryder Open, Miami, FL	John Huston	274	252,000
Mar. 14	Honda Classic, Ft. Lauderdale, FL	Nick Price	276	198,000
Mar. 20	Nestle Invitational, Orlando, FL	Loren Roberts	275	216,000
Mar. 27	Tournament Players Championship, Ponte Vedra, FL	Greg Norman	264	450,000
Apr. 10	Masters Tournament, Augusta, GA	Jose Maria Olazabal	279	360,000
Apr. 17	Heritage Classic, Hilton Head, SC	Hale Irwin	266	225,000
Apr. 24	Greater Greensboro Open, NC	Mike Springer	275	270,000
May 8	BellSouth Classic, Marietta, GA	John Daly	274	216,000
May 15	GTE Byron Nelson Classic, Dallas, TX	Neal Lancaster	†132	216,000
May 22	Memorial Tournament, Dublin, OH	Tom Lehman	268	270,000
June 5	Kemper Open, Potomac, MD	Mark Brooks	271	234,000
June 12	Buick Classic, Harrison, NY	Lee Janzen	268	216,000
June 20	U.S. Open, Oakmont, PA	Ernie Els	*279	320,000
June 26	Greater Hartford Open, Cromwell, CT	David Frost	268	216,000
July 3	Western Open, Lemont, IL	Nick Price	277	216,000
July 10	Anheuser-Busch Classic, Williamsburg, VA	Mark McCumber	267	198,000
July 24	New England Classic, Sutton, MA	Kenny Perry	268	180,000
July 31	Federal Express Classic, Memphis, TN	Dicky Pride	*267	225,000
Aug. 7	Buick Open, Grand Blanc, MI	Fred Couples	270	198,000
Aug. 14	PGA Championship, Tulsa, OK	Nick Price	269	310,000
Aug. 21	The International, Castle Rock, CO	Steve Lowery	*35 pts	252,000
Aug. 28	World Series of Golf, Akron, OH	Jose Maria Olazabal	269	360,000
Sept. 4	Greater Milwaukee Open	Mike Springer	268	180,000
Sept. 11	Canadian Open, Oakville, Ontario	Nick Price	275	234,000
Sept. 18	B.C. Open, Endicott, NY	Mike Sullivan	266	162,000
Sept. 25	Hardee's Classic, Coal Valley, IL	Mike McCumber	265	180,000

Women

Date	Event	Winner	Score	Prize
Feb. 20	Hawaiian Open, Honolulu HI	Marta Figueras-Dotti	209	$75,000
Mar. 13	Ping-Welch's Championship, Tucson, AZ	Donna Andrews	276	63,750
Mar. 20	Standard Register Classic, Phoenix, AZ	Laura Davies	277	105,000
Mar. 27	Nabisco Dinah Shore Classic, Rancho Mirage, CA	Donna Andrews	276	105,000
Apr. 17	Atlanta Women's Championship	Val Skinner	206	97,500
May 1	Sprint Championship, Daytona, FL	Sherri Steinhauer	273	180,000
May 8	Sara Lee Classic, Nashville, TN	Laura Davies	203	78,750
May 15	McDonald's LPGA Championship, Wilmington, DE	Laura Davies	279	165,000
May 29	Corning Classic, Corning, NY	Beth Daniel	278	75,000
June 5	Oldsmobile Classic, East Lansing, MI	Beth Daniel	268	90,000
June 12	Minnesota Classic, Brooklyn Park, MN	Liselotte Neumann	205	75,000
June 19	Rochester International, Pittsford, NY	Lisa Kiggens	273	75,000
June 26	ShopRite Classic, Somers Pt., NJ	Donna Andrews	207	75,000
July 3	Warren Classic, Warren, OH	Tammie Green	206	82,500
July 10	Jamie Farr Toledo Classic, OH	Kelly Robbins	*204	75,000
July 18	Big Apple Classic, New Rochelle, NY	Beth Daniel	*276	97,500
July 24	U.S. Women's Open, Lake Orion, MI	Patty Sheehan	277	155,000
July 31	Ping-Welch's Championship, Canton, MA	Helen Alfredsson	274	67,500
Aug. 7	McCall's Classic, Stratton Mountain, VT	Carolyn Hill	275	75,000
Aug. 21	*Chicago Sun-Times* Challenge, Naperville, IL	Jane Geddes	272	75,000
Aug. 28	Du Maurier Ltd. Classic, Ottawa, Ontario	Martha Nause	279	120,000
Sept. 4	Rail Charity Classic, Springfield, IL	Barb Mucha	203	78,750
Sept. 11	Ping-Cellular One Championship, Portland, OR	Missie McGeorge	207	75,000
Sept. 18	Safeco Classic, Kent, WA	Deb Richard	276	75,000

* Won playoff. † Shortened due to weather.

U.S. Women's Open Golf Champions

Year	Winner	Year	Winner	Year	Winner	Year	Winner
1948	"Babe" Zaharias	1960	Betsy Rawls	1972	Susie Maxwell Berning	1984	Hollis Stacy
1949	Louise Suggs	1961	Mickey Wright	1973	Susie Maxwell Berning	1985	Kathy Baker
1950	"Babe" Zaharias	1962	Murle Lindstrom	1974	Sandra Haynie	1986	Jane Geddes
1951	Betsy Rawls	1963	Mary Mills	1975	Sandra Palmer	1987	Laura Davies
1952	Louise Suggs	1964	Mickey Wright	1976	JoAnne Carner	1988	Liselotte Neumann
1953	Betsy Rawls	1965	Carol Mann	1977	Hollis Stacy	1989	Betsy King
1954	"Babe" Zaharias	1966	Sandra Spuzich	1978	Hollis Stacy	1990	Betsy King
1955	Fay Crocker	1967	Catherine Lacoste*	1979	Jerilyn Britz	1991	Meg Mallon
1956	Mrs. K. Cornelius	1968	Susie Maxwell Berning	1980	Amy Alcott	1992	Patty Sheehan
1957	Betsy Rawls	1969	Donna Caponi	1981	Pat Bradley	1993	Lauri Merten
1958	Mickey Wright	1970	Donna Caponi	1982	Janet Alex	1994	Patty Sheehan
1959	Mickey Wright	1971	JoAnne Carner	1983	Jan Stephenson		

*Amateur

PGA Leading Money Winners

Year	Player	Dollars	Year	Player	Dollars	Year	Player	Dollars
1946	Ben Hogan	$42,556	1962	Arnold Palmer	$81,448	1978	Tom Watson	$362,429
1947	Jimmy Demaret	27,936	1963	Arnold Palmer	128,230	1979	Tom Watson	462,636
1948	Ben Hogan	36,812	1964	Jack Nicklaus	113,284	1980	Tom Watson	530,808
1949	Sam Snead	31,593	1965	Jack Nicklaus	140,752	1981	Tom Kite	375,699
1950	Sam Snead	35,758	1966	Billy Casper	121,944	1982	Craig Stadler	446,462
1951	Lloyd Mangrum	26,088	1967	Jack Nicklaus	188,988	1983	Hal Sutton	426,668
1952	Julius Boros	37,032	1968	Billy Casper	205,168	1984	Tom Watson	476,260
1953	Lew Worsham	34,002	1969	Frank Beard	175,223	1985	Curtis Strange	542,321
1954	Bob Toski	65,819	1970	Lee Trevino	157,037	1986	Greg Norman	653,296
1955	Julius Boros	65,121	1971	Jack Nicklaus	244,490	1987	Curtis Strange	925,941
1956	Ted Kroll	72,835	1972	Jack Nicklaus	320,542	1988	Curtis Strange	1,147,644
1957	Dick Mayer	65,835	1973	Jack Nicklaus	308,362	1989	Tom Kite	1,395,278
1958	Arnold Palmer	42,407	1974	Johnny Miller	353,201	1990	Greg Norman	1,165,477
1959	Art Wall Jr.	53,167	1975	Jack Nicklaus	323,149	1991	Corey Pavin	979,430
1960	Arnold Palmer	75,262	1976	Jack Nicklaus	266,438	1992	Fred Couples	1,344,188
1961	Gary Player	64,540	1977	Tom Watson	310,653	1993	Nick Price	1,478,557

LPGA Leading Money Winners

Year	Player	Dollars	Year	Player	Dollars	Year	Player	Dollars
1954	Patty Berg	$16,011	1968	Kathy Whitworth	$48,379	1982	JoAnne Carner	$310,399
1955	Patty Berg	16,492	1969	Carol Mann	49,152	1983	JoAnne Carner	291,404
1956	Marlene Hagge	20,235	1970	Kathy Whitworth	30,235	1984	Betsy King	266,771
1957	Patty Berg	16,272	1971	Kathy Whitworth	41,181	1985	Nancy Lopez	416,472
1958	Beverly Hanson	12,629	1972	Kathy Whitworth	65,063	1986	Pat Bradley	492,021
1959	Betsy Rawls	26,774	1973	Kathy Whitworth	82,854	1987	Ayako Okamoto	466,034
1960	Louise Suggs	16,892	1974	JoAnne Carner	87,094	1988	Sherri Turner	347,255
1961	Mickey Wright	22,236	1975	Sandra Palmer	94,805	1989	Betsy King	654,132
1962	Mickey Wright	21,641	1976	Judy Rankin	150,734	1990	Beth Daniel	863,578
1963	Mickey Wright	31,269	1977	Judy Rankin	122,890	1991	Pat Bradley	763,118
1964	Mickey Wright	29,800	1978	Nancy Lopez	189,813	1992	Dottie Mochrie	693,335
1965	Kathy Whitworth	28,658	1979	Nancy Lopez	215,987	1993	Betsy King	595,992
1966	Kathy Whitworth	33,517	1980	Beth Daniel	231,000			
1967	Kathy Whitworth	32,937	1981	Beth Daniel	206,977			

Rifle and Pistol Individual Championships in 1994

Source: National Rifle Association

National Outdoor Rifle and Pistol Championships

Pistol—MSG Steve Reiter, USAR, Sparks, NV, 2651-128X
Civilian Pistol—Al Dorman, Princeton, WV, 2632-120X
Woman Pistol—Ruby Fox, Parker, AZ, 2632-121X
Smallbore Rifle Prone—CPL Kenneth Johnson, Columbus, GA, 6394-505X
Civilian Smallbore Rifle Prone—T.R. Bishop, Lenoir, NC, 6392-454X
Smallbore Rifle NRA 3-Position—CPT Michael Anti, Columbus, GA, 2302-91X
Civilian Smallbore Rifle NRA 3-Position—Kenneth Benyo, Ne Tripoli, PA, 2276-87X
Woman Smallbore Rifle NRA 3-Position—1LT Kristin Ann Frazer, Columbus, GA, 2264
High Power Rifle—Mitchell Maxberry, Philport, KY, 2372-98X
Civilian High Power Rifle—Mitchell Maxberry, Philport, KY, 2372-98X
Woman High Power Rifle—Nancy H. Tompkins-Gallagher, Prescott, AZ 2366-06X

National Indoor Rifle and Pistol Championships

Smallbore Rifle 4-Position—Glenn Dubis, Ft. Benning, GA, 800
Woman Smallbore Rifle 4-Position—Karen E. Monez, Weatherford, TX, 799
Smallbore Rifle NRA 3-Position—Glenn Dubis, Ft. Benning, Ga., 1192
Woman Smallbore Rifle NRA 3-Position—Karen E. Monez, Weatherford, TX, 1165
Smallbore Rifle International—Robert E. Harbison, Phenix City, AL, 1185
Woman Smallbore Rifle International—Ann Pfiffner, Dubuque, IA, 1177
Air Rifle—Tammie Deangelis, Colorado Springs, CO, 595
Conventional Pistol—Albert J. Turner, Plano, TX, 887
Woman Conventional Pistol—Karen S. Bowker, Tustin, CA, 868
International Free Pistol—James Robert Lee, Jr., Auburn, CA, 548
Woman International Free Pistol—Janine Lavallee, New London, CT, 505
International Standard Pistol—James Robert Lee, Jr., Auburn, CA, 565
Woman International Standard Pistol—Lois Wilson, Tacoma, WA, 542
Air Pistol—Daryl L. Szarenski, Ft. Benning, GA, 575
Woman Air Pistol—Janine Lavallee, New London, CT, 559

NRA Bianchi Cup National Action Pistol Championships

Action Pistol—John H. Pride, La Verne, CA, 1920
Woman Action Pistol—Judith A. Woolley, Plains, MT, 1906
Junior Action Pistol— Chad L. Dietrich, Bismarck, ND, 1902

American Power Boat Assn. Gold Cup Champions

Year	Boat	Driver	Year	Boat	Driver
1975	Pay 'N Pak	George Henley	1985	Miller American	Chip Hanauer
1976	Miss U.S.	Tom D'Eath	1986	Miller American	Chip Hanauer
1977	Atlas Van Lines	Bill Muncey	1987	Miller American	Chip Hanauer
1978	Atlas Van Lines	Bill Muncey	1988	Miller American	Chip Hanauer
1979	Atlas Van Lines	Bill Muncey	1989	Miss Budweiser	Tom D'Eath
1980	Miss Budweiser	Dean Chenoweth	1990	Miss Budweiser	Tom D'Eath
1981	Miss Budweiser	Dean Chenoweth	1991	Winston Eagle	Mark Tate
1982	Atlas Van Lines	Chip Hanauer	1992	Miss Budweiser	Chip Hanauer
1983	Atlas Van Lines	Chip Hanauer	1993	Miss Budweiser	Chip Hanauer
1984	Atlas Van Lines	Chip Hanauer	1994	Smokin' Joe's	Mark Tate

Notable Sports Personalities

Henry (Hank) Aaron, b. 1934: Milwaukee-Atlanta outfielder hit record 755 home runs; led NL 4 times.
Kareem Abdul-Jabbar, b. 1947: Milwaukee, L.A. Lakers center; MVP 6 times; leading scorer twice; playoff MVP, 1971, 1985; all-time leading NBA scorer.
Grover Cleveland Alexander, (1887-1950): pitcher won 374 NL games; pitched 16 shutouts, 1916.
Muhammad Ali, b. 1942: 3-time heavyweight champion.
Mario Andretti, b. 1940: won Indy 500, 1969; Grand Prix champ, 1978.
Eddie Arcaro, b. 1916: jockey rode 4,779 winners including the Kentucky Derby 5 times; the Preakness and Belmont Stakes 6 times each.
Henry Armstrong, (1912-1988): boxer held feather-, welter-, light-weight titles simultaneously, 1937-38.
Arthur Ashe, (1943-1993): U.S. singles champ, 1968; Wimbledon champ, 1975.
Red Auerbach, b. 1917: coached Boston Celtics to 9 NBA championships.
Ernie Banks, b. 1931: Chicago Cubs slugger hit 512 NL homers; twice MVP.
Roger Bannister, b. 1929: Briton ran first sub 4-minute mile, May 6, 1954.
Rick Barry, b. 1944: NBA scoring leader, 1967; ABA, 1969.
Sammy Baugh, b. 1914: Washington Redskins quarterback held numerous records upon retirement after 16 pro seasons.
Elgin Baylor, b. 1934: L.A. Lakers forward; 1st team all-star 10 times.
Boris Becker, b. 1967: German tennis star; won U.S. Open 1989; Wimbledon champ 3 times.
Jean Beliveau, b. 1931: Montreal Canadiens center scored 507 goals; twice MVP.
Johnny Bench, b. 1947: Cincinnati Reds catcher; MVP twice; led league in home runs twice, RBIs 3 times.
Patty Berg, b. 1918: won more than 80 golf tournaments; AP Woman Athlete-of-the-Year 3 times.
Yogi Berra, b. 1925: N.Y. Yankees catcher; MVP 3 times; played in 14 World Series.
Raymond Berry, b. 1933: Baltimore Colts receiver caught 631 passes.
Matt Biondi, b. 1965: swimmer won 5 gold medals at 1988 Olympics.
Larry Bird, b. 1956: Boston Celtics forward; chosen MVP 1984-86; playoff MVP, 1984, 1986.
George Blanda, b. 1927: quarterback, kicker; 26 years as active player, scoring record 2,002 points.
Wade Boggs, b. 1958: AL batting champ, 1983, 1985-88.
Bjorn Borg, b. 1956: led Sweden to first Davis Cup, 1975; Wimbledon champion 5 times.
Mike Bossy, b. 1957; N.Y. Islanders right wing scored more than 50 goals 8 times.
Ray Bourque, b. 1960: Boston Bruins defenseman won Norris Trophy 4 times.
Terry Bradshaw, b. 1948; Pittsburgh Steelers quarterback led team to 4 Super Bowl titles.
George Brett, b. 1953: Kansas City Royals infielder led AL in batting, 1976, 1980, 1990; MVP, 1980.
Lou Brock, b. 1939: St. Louis Cardinals outfielder stole NL record 118 bases, 1974; led NL 8 times.
Jim Brown, b. 1936: Cleveland Browns fullback ran for 12,312 career yards; MVP 3 times.
Paul Brown, (1908-1991), football owner, coach; led Cleveland Browns to 3 NFL championships.
Paul "Bear" Bryant, (1913-1983), college football coach with 323 victories.
Sergei Bubka, b. 1963: Ukrainian pole vaulter; first to clear 20 feet both indoors and outdoors.
Maria Bueno, b. 1939: U.S. singles champ 4 times; Wimbledon champ 3 times.
Dick Butkus, b. 1942: Chicago Bears linebacker twice chosen best NFL defensive player.
Dick Button, b. 1929: figure skater won 1948, 1952 Olympic gold medals; world titlist, 1948-52.
Walter Camp, (1859-1925): Yale football player, coach, athletic director; established many rules; promoted All-America designations.
Roy Campanella, (1921-1993): Brooklyn Dodgers catcher; MVP 3 times.
Earl Campbell, b. 1955: NFL running back; NFL MVP 1978-80.
Rod Carew, b. 1945: AL infielder won 7 batting titles; MVP, 1977.
Steve Carlton, b. 1944: NL pitcher won 20 games 5 times, Cy Young award 4 times.
Billy Casper, b. 1931: PGA Player-of-the-Year 3 times; U.S. Open champ twice.
Wilt Chamberlain, b. 1936: center was NBA leading scorer 7 times; MVP 4 times.
Bobby Clarke, b. 1949: Philadelphia Flyers center led team to 2 Stanley Cup championships; MVP 3 times.
Roger Clemens, b. 1962: Boston Red Sox pitcher; AL MVP 1986; Cy Young award 1986, 1987, 1991.
Roberto Clemente, (1934-1972): Pittsburgh Pirates outfielder won 4 batting titles; MVP, 1966.
Ty Cobb, (1886-1961): Detroit Tigers outfielder had record .367 lifetime batting average, 12 batting titles.
Sebastian Coe, b. 1956: Briton won Olympic 1,500-meter run, 1980, 1984.
Nadia Comaneci, b. 1961: Romanian gymnast won 3 gold medals, achieved 7 perfect scores, 1976 Olympics.
Maureen Connolly, (1934-1969): won tennis "grand slam," 1953; AP Woman-Athlete-of-the-Year 3 times.
Jimmy Connors, b. 1952: U.S. singles champ 5 times; Wimbledon champ twice.
James J. Corbett, (1866-1933): heavyweight champion, 1892-97; credited with being the first "scientific" boxer.
Angel Cordero, b. 1942: leading money winner, 1976, 1982-83; rode 3 Kentucky Derby winners.
Margaret Smith Court, b. 1942: Australian won U.S. singles championship 5 times; Wimbledon champ 3 times.
Bob Cousy, b. 1928: Boston Celtics guard led team to 6 NBA championships; MVP, 1957.
Andre Dawson, b. 1954: slugger led NL in home runs, MVP, 1987.
Dizzy Dean, (1911-1974): colorful pitcher for St. Louis Cardinals "Gashouse Gang" in the '30s; MVP, 1934.
Jack Dempsey, (1895-1983): heavyweight champion, 1919-26.
Eric Dickerson, b. 1960: running back ran for NFL record 2,105 yds., 1984; led NFC 3 times, AFC twice.
Joe DiMaggio, b. 1914: N.Y. Yankees outfielder hit safely in record 56 consecutive games, 1941; MVP 3 times.
Leo Durocher, (1906-1991): manager won 3 NL pennants.
Stefan Edberg, b. 1966: U.S. singles champ 1991, 1992; Wimbledon champ 1988, 1990.
Gertrude Ederle, b. 1906: first woman to swim English Channel, broke existing men's record, 1926.
Julius Erving, b. 1950: MVP and leading scorer in ABA 3 times; NBA MVP, 1981.
Phil Esposito, b. 1942: NHL scoring leader 5 times.
Chris Evert, b. 1954: U.S. singles champ 6 times, Wimbledon champ 3 times.
Patrick Ewing, b. 1962: center led Georgetown Univ. to 1984 NCAA championship.
Ray Ewry, (1873-1937): track and field star won 8 gold medals, 1900, 1904, and 1908 Olympics.
Nick Faldo, 1957: British golfer won Masters, 1989-90; British Open 3 times.
Juan Fangio, b. 1911: World Grand Prix champion 5 times.
Bob Feller, b. 1918: Cleveland Indians pitcher won 266 games; pitched 3 no-hitters, 12 one-hitters.
Peggy Fleming, b. 1948: world figure skating champion, 1966-68; gold medalist 1968 Olympics.
Whitey Ford, b. 1928: N.Y. Yankees pitcher won record 10 World Series games.
Dick Fosbury, b. 1947: high jumper won 1968 Olympic gold medal; developed the "Fosbury Flop."
Jimmie Foxx, (1907-1967): Red Sox, Athletics slugger; MVP 3 times; triple crown, 1933.
A.J. Foyt, b. 1935: won Indy 500 4 times; U.S. Auto Club champ 7 times.
Joe Frazier, b. 1944: heavyweight champion, 1970-73.
Lou Gehrig, (1903-1941): N.Y. Yankees 1st baseman played record 2,130 consecutive games; MVP, 1927, 1936.
George Gervin, b. 1952: leading NBA scorer, 1978-80, 1982.
Althea Gibson, b. 1927: twice U.S. and Wimbledon singles champ.
Bob Gibson, b. 1935: St. Louis Cardinals pitcher won Cy Young award twice; struck out 3,117 batters.
Frank Gifford, b. 1930: N.Y. Giants back; MVP, 1956.
Dwight Gooden, b. 1964: N.Y. Mets pitcher was NL Rookie of Year, 1984; Cy Young award, 1985.
Steffi Graf, b. 1969: German won tennis "grand slam," 1988; U.S. champ 1988, 1989, 1993; Wimbledon champ 5 times.
Otto Graham, b. 1921: Cleveland Browns quarterback; all-pro 4 times.
Red Grange, (1903-1991): All-America at Univ. of Illinois 1923-25; played for Chicago Bears, 1925-35.
Joe Greene, b. 1946: Pittsburgh Steelers lineman; twice NFL outstanding defensive player.
Wayne Gretzky, b. 1961: all-time leading scorer in NHL history; MVP, 1980-87, 1989.

Florence Griffith Joyner, b. 1959: sprinter won 3 gold medals at 1988 Olympics.
Lefty Grove, (1900-1975): pitcher won 300 AL games; 20-game winner 8 times.
Tony Gwynn, b. 1960: NL batting champ, 1984, 1987-89, 1994.
Walter Hagen, (1892-1969): won PGA championship 5 times; British Open 4 times.
George Halas, (1895-1983): founder-coach of Chicago Bears; won 5 NFL championships.
Bill Hartack, b. 1932: jockey rode 5 Kentucky Derby winners.
John Havlicek, b. 1940: Boston Celtics forward scored more than 26,000 NBA points.
Rickey Henderson, b. 1958; AL outfielder stole record 130 bases, 1982; record lifetime steals; AL MVP, 1990.
Sonja Henie, (1912-1969): world champion figure skater, 1927-36; Olympic gold medalist, 1928, 1932, 1936.
Ben Hogan, b. 1912: won 4 U.S. Open championships, 2 PGA, 2 Masters.
Rogers Hornsby, (1896-1963): NL 2d baseman batted record .424 in 1924; twice won triple crown; batting leader, 1920-25.
Paul Hornung, b. 1935: Green Bay Packers runner-placekicker scored record 176 points, 1960.
Gordie Howe, b. 1928: hockey forward; NHL MVP 6 times.
Carl Hubbell, (1903-1988): N.Y. Giants pitcher; 20-game winner 5 consecutive years, 1933-37.
Bobby Hull, b. 1939: NHL all-star 10 times.
Brett Hull, b. 1964: St. Louis Blues forward led NHL in goals, 1990-92; MVP 1991.
Catfish Hunter, b. 1946: pitched perfect game, 1968; 20-game winner 5 times.
Don Hutson, b. 1913: Green Bay Packers receiver caught 99 NFL touchdown passes.
Reggie Jackson, b. 1946: slugger led AL in home runs 4 times; MVP, 1973; hit 5 World Series home runs, 1977.
Jack Johnson, (1878-1946): heavyweight champion, 1910-15.
Jimmy Johnson, b. 1943: football coach, led Univ. of Miami (Fla.) to national championship in 1987, and Dallas Cowboys to consecutive Super Bowl wins.
Magic Johnson, b. 1959: NBA MVP 1987, 1989, 1990; Playoff MVP 1980, 1982, 1987; record 9,921 career assists.
Walter Johnson, (1887-1946): Washington Senators pitcher won 416 games.
Bobby Jones, (1902-1971): won "grand slam of golf" 1930; U.S. Amateur champ 5 times, U.S. Open champ 4 times.
Deacon Jones, b. 1938: L.A. Rams lineman; twice NFL outstanding defensive player.
Michael Jordan, b. 1963: NBA leading scorer, 1987-93; MVP, 1988, 1991, 1992; Playoff MVP, 1991, 1992, 1993.
Jackie Joyner-Kersee, b. 1962; Olympic gold medalist in heptathlon, 1988, 1992.
Sonny Jurgensen, b. 1934: quarterback named all-pro 5 times.
Duke Kahanamoku, (1890-1968): swimmer won 1912, 1920 Olympic gold medals in 100-meter freestyle; surfing pioneer.
Harmon Killebrew, b. 1936: Minnesota Twins slugger led AL in home runs 6 times.
Jean Claude Killy, b. 1943: French skier won 3 1968 Olympic gold medals.
Ralph Kiner, b. 1922: Pittsburgh Pirates slugger led NL in home runs 7 consecutive years, 1946-52.
Billie Jean King, b. 1943: U.S. singles champ 4 times; Wimbledon champ 6 times.
Bob Knight, b. 1940: Indiana U. basketball coach led team to NCAA championships, 1976, 1981, 1987.
Olga Korbut, b. 1955: Soviet gymnast won 3 1972 Olympic gold medals.
Sandy Koufax, b. 1935: Dodgers pitcher won Cy Young award 3 times; lowest ERA in NL, 1962-66; pitched 4 no-hitters, one a perfect game.
Mike Krzyzewski, b. 1947: basketball coach, led Duke Univ. to national championships in 1991 and 1992.
Guy Lafleur, b. 1951: forward led NHL in scoring 3 times; MVP, 1977, 1978.
Tom Landry, b. 1924: Dallas Cowboys head coach 1960-88.
Rod Laver, b. 1938: Australian won tennis "grand slam," 1962, 1969; Wimbledon champ 4 times.
Mario Lemieux, b. 1965: NHL leading scorer, 1988-89, 1992-93; MVP, 1988, 1993; Playoff MVP, 1991, 1992.
Ivan Lendl, b. 1960: U.S. singles champ, 1985-87.
Sugar Ray Leonard, b. 1956: boxer held titles in 5 different weight classes.
Carl Lewis, b. 1961: track and field star won 8 Olympic gold medals in sprinting and the long jump.
Vince Lombardi, (1913-1970): Green Bay Packers coach led team to 5 NFL championships and 2 Super Bowl victories.
Joe Louis, (1914-1981): heavyweight champion, 1937-49.
Sid Luckman, b. 1916: Chicago Bears quarterback led team to 4 NFL championships; MVP, 1943.
Connie Mack, (1862-1956): Philadelphia Athletics manager, 1901-50; won 9 pennants, 5 championships.
Greg Maddux, b. 1966: first pitcher ever to win 3 consecutive Cy Young awards, 1992-94.
Bill Madlock, b. 1951: NL batting leader 4 times.
Moses Malone, b. 1955: NBA center was MVP 1979, 1982, 1983.
Mickey Mantle, b. 1931: N.Y. Yankees outfielder; triple crown, 1956; 18 World Series home runs; MVP 3 times.
Pete Maravich (1948-1988): guard scored NCAA record 44.2 ppg during collegiate career; led NBA in scoring, 1977.
Rocky Marciano, (1923-1969): heavyweight champion, 1952-56; retired undefeated.
Dan Marino, b. 1961: Miami Dolphins quarterback passed for NFL record 5,084 yds, 1984.
Roger Maris, (1934-1985): N.Y. Yankees outfielder hit record 61 home runs, 1961; MVP, 1960 and 1961.
Eddie Mathews, b. 1931: Milwaukee-Atlanta 3d baseman hit 512 career home runs.
Christy Mathewson, (1880-1925): N.Y. Giants pitcher won 373 games.
Bob Mathias, b. 1930: decathlon gold medalist, 1948, 1952.
Don Mattingly, b. 1961: N.Y. Yankees 1st baseman won 1984 AL batting title; MVP, 1985.
Willie Mays, b. 1931: N.Y.-S.F. Giants center fielder hit 660 home runs; led NL 4 times; twice MVP.
Willie McCovey, b. 1938: S.F. Giants slugger hit 521 home runs; led NL 3 times; MVP, 1969.
John McEnroe, b. 1959: U.S. singles champ, 1979-81, 1984; Wimbledon champ, 1981, 1983-84.
John McGraw, (1873-1934): N.Y. Giants manager led team to 10 pennants, 3 championships.
Mark Messier, b. 1961: center chosen NHL MVP, 1990; Conn Smythe Trophy, 1984.
George Mikan, b. 1924: Minn. Lakers center considered the best basketball player of the first half of the century.
Stan Mikita, b. 1940: Chicago Black Hawks center led NHL in scoring 4 times; MVP twice.
Joe Montana, b. 1956: quarterback was Super Bowl MVP, 1982, 1985, 1990.
Archie Moore, b. 1913: world light-heavyweight champion, 1952-62.
Howie Morenz, (1902-1937): Montreal Canadiens forward considered the best hockey player of the first half of the century.
Joe Morgan, b. 1943: National League MVP, 1975, 1976.
Thurman Munson, (1947-1979): N.Y. Yankees catcher; MVP, 1976.
Dale Murphy, b. 1956: outfielder chosen NL MVP 1982, 1983.
Stan Musial, b. 1920: St. Louis Cardinals star won 7 NL batting titles; MVP 3 times.
Bronko Nagurski, (1908-1990): Chicago Bears fullback and tackle; gained more than 4,000 yds. rushing.
Joe Namath, b. 1943: quarterback led N.Y. Jets to 1969 Super Bowl title.
Martina Navratilova, b. 1956: Wimbledon champ 8 times, U.S. champ 1983-84, 1986-87.
Byron Nelson, b. 1912: won 11 consecutive golf tournaments in 1945; twice Masters and PGA titlist.
Ernie Nevers, (1903-1976): Stanford star selected the best college fullback to play between 1919-69.
John Newcombe, b. 1943: Australian twice U.S. singles champ; Wimbledon titlist 3 times.
Jack Nicklaus, b. 1940: PGA Player-of-the-Year, 1967, 1972; leading money winner 8 times; won Masters 6 times.
Chuck Noll, b. 1931: coach led Pittsburgh Steelers to 4 Super Bowl titles.
Paavo Nurmi, (1897-1973): Finnish distance runner won 6 Olympic gold medals, 1920, 1924, 1928.
Al Oerter, b. 1936: discus thrower won gold medal at 4 consecutive Olympics, 1956-68.
Bobby Orr, b. 1948: Boston Bruins defenseman; Norris Trophy 8 times; led NHL in scoring twice, assists 5 times.
Mel Ott, (1909-1958): N.Y. Giants outfielder hit 511 home runs; led NL 6 times.
Jesse Owens, (1913-1980): track and field star won 4 1936 Olympic gold medals.
Satchel Paige, (1906-1982): pitcher starred in Negro leagues, 1924-48; entered major leagues at age 42.
Arnold Palmer, b. 1929: golf's first $1 million winner; won 4 Masters, 2 British Opens.
Jim Palmer, b. 1945: Baltimore Orioles pitcher; Cy Young award 3 times; 20-game winner 7 times.
Floyd Patterson, b. 1935: twice heavyweight champion.
Walter Payton, b. 1954: Chicago Bears running back has most rushing yards in NFL history; leading NFC rusher, 1976-80.
Pele, b. 1940: Brazilian soccer star scored 1,281 goals during 22-year career.
Bob Pettit, b. 1932: first NBA player to score 20,000 points; twice NBA scoring leader.

Richard Petty, b. 1937: NASCAR national champ 7 time; 7-time Daytona 500 winner.
Laffit Pincay Jr., b. 1946: leading money-winning jockey, 1970-74, 1979.
Jacques Plante, (1929-1986): goalie, 7 Vezina trophies; first goalie to wear a mask in a game.
Kirby Puckett, b. 1961: Minn. Twins outfielder won AL batting title, 1989; led AL in hits, 1987-89, 1992; RBIs, 1994.
Willis Reed, b. 1942: N.Y. Knicks center; MVP, 1970; playoff MVP, 1970, 1973.
Jerry Rice, b. 1962: S.F. 49ers receiver chosen 1989 Super Bowl MVP.
Jim Rice, b. 1953: Boston Red Sox outfielder led AL in home runs, 1977-78, 1983; MVP 1978.
Maurice Richard, b. 1921: Montreal Canadiens forward scored 544 regular season goals, 82 playoff goals.
Branch Rickey, (1881-1965): executive instrumental in breaking baseball's color barrier, 1947; initiated farm system, 1919.
Pat Riley, b. 1945: coached L.A. Lakers to 4 NBA championships.
Cal Ripken Jr., b. 1961: Baltimore Orioles shortstop; AL MVP 1983, 1991.
Oscar Robertson, b. 1938: guard averaged career 25.7 points per game; 2d most career assists; MVP, 1964.
Brooks Robinson, b. 1937: Baltimore Orioles 3d baseman played in 4 World Series; MVP, 1964.
Frank Robinson, b. 1935: slugger MVP in both NL and AL; triple crown winner, 1966; first black manager in majors.
Jackie Robinson, (1919-1972): broke baseball's color barrier with Brooklyn Dodgers, 1947; MVP, 1949.
Larry Robinson, b. 1951: NHL defenseman won Norris Trophy, 1977, 1980.
Sugar Ray Robinson, (1920-1989): middleweight champion 5 times, welterweight champion.
Knute Rockne, (1888-1931): Notre Dame football coach, 1918-31; revolutionized game by stressing forward pass.
Pete Rose, b. 1941: won 3 NL batting titles; hit safely in 44 consecutive games, 1978; has most major league hits.
Wilma Rudolph, b. 1940: sprinter won 3 1960 Olympic gold medals.
Bill Russell, b. 1934: Boston Celtics center led team to 11 NBA titles; MVP 5 times; first black coach of major pro sports team.
Babe Ruth, (1895-1948): N.Y. Yankees outfielder hit 60 home runs, 1927; 714 lifetime; led AL 12 times.
Johnny Rutherford, b. 1938: auto racer won Indy 500 3 times.
Nolan Ryan, b. 1947: pitcher struck out record 383 batters, 1973; record 5,714 career; pitched record 7 no-hitters; won 324 major league games.
Bret Saberhagen, b. 1964: pitcher won AL Cy Young award, 1985, 1989; World Series MVP, 1985.
Gene Sarazen, b. 1902: won PGA championship 3 times, U.S. Open twice; developer of sand wedge.
Gale Sayers, b. 1943: Chicago Bears back twice led NFC in rushing.
Mike Schmidt, b. 1949: Phillies 3d baseman led NL in home runs, 1974-76, 1980-81, 1983-84, 1986; NL MVP, 1980, 1981, 1986.
Tom Seaver, b. 1944: pitcher won NL Cy Young award 3 times, won 311 major league games.
Monica Seles, b. 1973; U.S. Open champ 1991, 1992.
Bill Shoemaker, b. 1931: jockey rode 3 Kentucky Derby and 5 Belmont Stakes winners; leading career money winner.
Eddie Shore, (1902-1985): Boston Bruins defenseman; MVP 4 times, first-team all-star 7 times.
Don Shula, b. 1930: all-time winningest NFL coach.
Al Simmons, (1902-1956): AL outfielder had lifetime .334 batting average.
O.J. Simpson, b. 1947: running back rushed for 2,003 yds., 1973; AFC leading rusher 4 times.
George Sisler, (1893-1973): St. Louis Browns 1st baseman had record 257 hits, 1920; batted .340 lifetime.
Billy Smith, b. 1950: N.Y. Islanders goalie led team to 4 Stanley Cup championships.
Sam Snead, b. 1912: PGA and Masters champ 3 times each.
Warren Spahn, b. 1921: pitcher won 363 NL games; 20-game winner 13 times; Cy Young award, 1957.
Tris Speaker, (1885-1958): AL outfielder batted .344 over 22 seasons; hit record 793 career doubles.
Mark Spitz, b. 1950: swimmer won 7 1972 Olympic gold medals.
Amos Alonzo Stagg, (1862-1965): coached Univ. of Chicago football team for 41 years, including 5 undefeated seasons; introduced huddle, man-in-motion, and end-around play.
Bart Starr, b. 1934: Green Bay Packers quarterback led team to 5 NFL titles and 2 Super Bowl victories.
Roger Staubach, b. 1942: Dallas Cowboys quarterback; leading NFC passer 5 times.
Casey Stengel, (1890-1975): managed Yankees to 10 pennants, 7 championships, 1949-60.
Jackie Stewart, b. 1939: Scot auto racer retired with 27 Grand Prix victories.
John L. Sullivan, (1858-1918): last bareknuckle heavyweight champion, 1882-1892.
Fran Tarkenton, b. 1940: quarterback holds career passing records for touchdowns, completions, yardage.
Lawrence Taylor, b. 1959; linebacker led N.Y. Giants to 2 Super Bowl titles; played in 10 Pro Bowls.
Gustavo Thoeni, b. 1951: Italian 4-time world alpine ski champ.
Jim Thorpe, (1888-1953): football All-America, 1911, 1912; won pentathlon and decathlon, 1912 Olympics.
Bill Tilden, (1893-1953): U.S. singles champ 7 times; played on 11 Davis Cup teams.
Y.A. Tittle, b. 1926: N.Y. Giants quarterback; MVP, 1961, 1963.
Lee Trevino, b. 1939: won the U.S. and British Open championships twice.
Bryan Trottier, b. 1956: center played on 6 Stanley Cup championship teams.
Wyomia Tyus, b. 1945: sprinter won 1964, 1968 Olympic 100-meter dash.
Johnny Unitas, b. 1933: Baltimore Colts quarterback passed for more than 40,000 yds.; MVP, 1957, 1967.
Al Unser, b. 1939: Indy 500 winner 4 times.
Bobby Unser, b. 1934: Indy 500 winner 3 times.
Norm Van Brocklin, (1926-1983): quarterback passed for game record 554 yds., 1951; MVP, 1960.
Honus Wagner, (1874-1955): Pittsburgh Pirates shortstop won 8 NL batting titles.
Tom Watson, b. 1949: golfer won British Open 5 times.
Johnny Weissmuller, (1903-1984): swimmer won 52 national championships, 5 Olympic gold medals; set 67 world records.
Jerry West, b. 1938: L.A. Lakers guard had career average 27 points per game; first team all-star 10 times.
Kathy Whitworth, b. 1939: women's golf leading money winner 8 times; first woman to earn more than $300,000.
Ted Williams, b. 1918: Boston Red Sox outfielder won 6 batting titles; last major leaguer to hit over .400: .406 in 1941; .344 lifetime batting average.
Katarina Witt, b. 1965: German figure skater; won Olympic gold medal, 1984, 1988.
John Wooden, b. 1910: coached UCLA basketball team to 10 national championships.
Mickey Wright, b. 1935: won LPGA championship 4 times, Vare Trophy 5 times; twice AP Woman-Athlete-of-the-Year.
Carl Yastrzemski, b. 1939: Boston Red Sox slugger won 3 batting titles; triple crown, 1967.
Cy Young, (1867-1955): pitcher won record 511 major league games.
Babe Didrikson Zaharias, (1914-1956): track star won 2 1932 Olympic gold medals; won numerous golf tournaments.

Tour de France in 1994

On July 24, Miguel Indurain of Spain won the Tour de France, the world's most prestigious bicycle race, for the fourth consecutive year. His margin of victory in the 81st Tour de France was 5 minutes 39 seconds, and he completed the 23-day, 2,474-mile race in a total time of 103 hours, 38 minutes, 38 seconds. Pyotr Ugrumov of Latvia finished second.

World Gymnastics Championships in 1994

Ivan Ivankov of Belarus won the men's all-around title at the World Gymnastics Championship in Brisbane, Australia. Shannon Miller of Edmond, Okla., won the women's all-around title for the second consecutive year.

TENNIS

U.S. Open Champions

Men's Singles

Year	Champion	Final opponent
1910	William Larned	T. C. Bundy
1911	William Larned	Maurice McLoughlin
1912	Maurice McLoughlin	Wallace Johnson
1913	Maurice McLoughlin	Richard Williams
1914	Richard Williams	Maurice McLoughlin
1915	William Johnston	Maurice McLoughlin
1916	Richard Williams	William Johnston
1917	R. L. Murray	N. W. Niles
1918	R. L. Murray	Bill Tilden
1919	William Johnston	Bill Tilden
1920	Bill Tilden	William Johnston
1921	Bill Tilden	Wallace Johnson
1922	Bill Tilden	William Johnston
1923	Bill Tilden	William Johnston
1924	Bill Tilden	William Johnston
1925	Bill Tilden	William Johnston
1926	Rene Lacoste	Jean Borotra
1927	Rene Lacoste	Bill Tilden
1928	Henri Cochet	Francis Hunter
1929	Bill Tilden	Francis Hunter
1930	John Doeg	Francis Shields
1931	H. Ellsworth Vines	George Lott
1932	H. Ellsworth Vines	Henri Cochet
1933	Fred Perry	John Crawford
1934	Fred Perry	Wilmer Allison
1935	Wilmer Allison	Sidney Wood
1936	Fred Perry	Don Budge
1937	Don Budge	Baron G. von Cramm
1938	Don Budge	C. Gene Mako
1939	Robert Riggs	S. Welby Van Horn
1940	Don McNeill	Robert Riggs
1941	Robert Riggs	F. L. Kovacs
1942	F. R. Schroeder Jr.	Frank Parker
1943	Joseph Hunt	Jack Kramer
1944	Frank Parker	William Talbert
1945	Frank Parker	William Talbert
1946	Jack Kramer	Thomas Brown Jr.
1947	Jack Kramer	Frank Parker
1948	Pancho Gonzales	Eric Sturgess
1949	Pancho Gonzales	F. R. Schroeder Jr.
1950	Arthur Larsen	Herbert Flam
1951	Frank Sedgman	E. Victor Seixas Jr.
1952	Frank Sedgman	Gardnar Mulloy
1953	Tony Trabert	E. Victor Seixas Jr.
1954	E. Victor Seixas Jr.	Rex Hartwig
1955	Tony Trabert	Ken Rosewall
1956	Ken Rosewall	Lewis Hoad
1957	Malcolm Anderson	Ashley Cooper
1958	Ashley Cooper	Malcolm Anderson
1959	Neale A. Fraser	Alejandro Olmedo
1960	Neale A. Fraser	Rod Laver
1961	Roy Emerson	Rod Laver
1962	Rod Laver	Roy Emerson
1963	Rafael Osuna	F. A. Froehling 3d
1964	Roy Emerson	Fred Stolle
1965	Manuel Santana	Cliff Drysdale
1966	Fred Stolle	John Newcombe
1967	John Newcombe	Clark Graebner
1968	Arthur Ashe	Tom Okker
1969	Rod Laver	Tony Roche
1970	Ken Rosewall	Tony Roche
1971	Stan Smith	Jan Kodes
1972	Ilie Nastase	Arthur Ashe
1973	John Newcombe	Jan Kodes
1974	Jimmy Connors	Ken Rosewall
1975	Manuel Orantes	Jimmy Connors
1976	Jimmy Connors	Bjorn Borg
1977	Guillermo Vilas	Jimmy Connors
1978	Jimmy Connors	Bjorn Borg
1979	John McEnroe	Vitas Gerulaitis
1980	John McEnroe	Bjorn Borg
1981	John McEnroe	Bjorn Borg
1982	Jimmy Connors	Ivan Lendl
1983	Jimmy Connors	Ivan Lendl
1984	John McEnroe	Ivan Lendl
1985	Ivan Lendl	John McEnroe
1986	Ivan Lendl	Miloslav Mecir
1987	Ivan Lendl	Mats Wilander
1988	Mats Wilander	Ivan Lendl
1989	Boris Becker	Ivan Lendl
1990	Pete Sampras	Andre Agassi
1991	Stefan Edberg	Jim Courier
1992	Stefan Edberg	Pete Sampras
1993	Pete Sampras	Cedric Pioline
1994	Andre Agassi	Michael Stich

Women's Singles

Year	Champion	Final opponent
1926	Molla B. Mallory	Elizabeth Ryan
1927	Helen Wills	Betty Nuthall
1928	Helen Wills	Helen Jacobs
1929	Helen Wills	M. Watson
1930	Betty Nuthall	L. A. Harper
1931	Helen Wills Moody	E. B. Whittingstall
1932	Helen Jacobs	Carolin A. Babcock
1933	Helen Jacobs	Helen Wills Moody
1934	Helen Jacobs	Sarah H. Palfrey
1935	Helen Jacobs	Sarah Palfrey Fabyan
1936	Alice Marble	Helen Jacobs
1937	Anita Lizana	Jadwiga Jedrzejowska
1938	Alice Marble	Nancye Wynne
1939	Alice Marble	Helen Jacobs
1940	Alice Marble	Helen Jacobs
1941	Sarah Palfrey Cooke	Pauline Betz
1942	Pauline Betz	Louise Brough
1943	Pauline Betz	Louise Brough
1944	Pauline Betz	Margaret Osborne
1945	Sarah Palfrey Cooke	Pauline Betz
1946	Pauline Betz	Doris Hart
1947	Louise Brough	Margaret Osborne
1948	Margaret Osborne duPont	Louise Brough
1949	Margaret Osborne duPont	Doris Hart
1950	Margaret Osborne duPont	Doris Hart
1951	Maureen Connolly	Shirley Fry
1952	Maureen Connolly	Doris Hart
1953	Maureen Connolly	Doris Hart
1954	Doris Hart	Louise Brough
1955	Doris Hart	Patricia Ward
1956	Shirley Fry	Althea Gibson
1957	Althea Gibson	Louise Brough
1958	Althea Gibson	Darlene Hard
1959	Maria Bueno	Christine Truman
1960	Darlene Hard	Maria Bueno
1961	Darlene Hard	Ann Haydon
1962	Margaret Smith	Darlene Hard
1963	Maria Bueno	Margaret Smith
1964	Maria Bueno	Carole Graebner
1965	Margaret Smith	Billie Jean Moffitt
1966	Maria Bueno	Nancy Richey
1967	Billie Jean King	Ann Haydon Jones
1968	Virginia Wade	Billie Jean King
1969	Margaret Smith Court	Nancy Richey
1970	Margaret Smith Court	Rosemary Casals
1971	Billie Jean King	Rosemary Casals
1972	Billie Jean King	Kerry Melville
1973	Margaret Smith Court	Evonne Goolagong
1974	Billie Jean King	Evonne Goolagong
1975	Chris Evert	Evonne Goolagong
1976	Chris Evert	Evonne Goolagong
1977	Chris Evert	Wendy Turnbull
1978	Chris Evert	Pam Shriver
1979	Tracy Austin	Chris Evert Lloyd
1980	Chris Evert Lloyd	Hana Mandlikova
1981	Tracy Austin	Martina Navratilova
1982	Chris Evert Lloyd	Hana Mandlikova
1983	Martina Navratilova	Chris Evert Lloyd
1984	Martina Navratilova	Chris Evert Lloyd
1985	Hana Mandlikova	Martina Navratilova
1986	Martina Navratilova	Helena Sukova
1987	Martina Navratilova	Steffi Graf
1988	Steffi Graf	Gabriela Sabatini
1989	Steffi Graf	Martina Navratilova
1990	Gabriela Sabatini	Steffi Graf
1991	Monica Seles	Martina Navratilova
1992	Monica Seles	Arantxa Sanchez Vicario
1993	Steffi Graf	Helena Sukova
1994	Arantxa Sanchez Vicario	Steffi Graf

All-England Champions, Wimbledon

Men's Singles

Year	Champion	Final opponent	Year	Champion	Final opponent
1933	Jack Crawford	Ellsworth Vines	1967	John Newcombe	Wilhelm Bungert
1934	Fred Perry	Jack Crawford	1968	Rod Laver	Tony Roche
1935	Fred Perry	Gottfried von Cramm	1969	Rod Laver	John Newcombe
1936	Fred Perry	Gottfried von Cramm	1970	John Newcombe	Ken Rosewall
1937	Donald Budge	Gottfried von Cramm	1971	John Newcombe	Stan Smith
1938	Donald Budge	Wilfred Austin	1972	Stan Smith	Ilie Nastase
1939	Bobby Riggs	Elwood Cooke	1973	Jan Kodes	Alex Metreveli
1940-45	not held		1974	Jimmy Connors	Ken Rosewall
1946	Yvon Petra	Geoff E. Brown	1975	Arthur Ashe	Jimmy Connors
1947	Jack Kramer	Tom P. Brown	1976	Bjorn Borg	Ilie Nastase
1948	Bob Falkenburg	John Bromwich	1977	Bjorn Borg	Jimmy Connors
1949	Ted Schroeder	Jaroslav Drobny	1978	Bjorn Borg	Jimmy Connors
1950	Budge Patty	Frank Sedgman	1979	Bjorn Borg	Roscoe Tanner
1951	Dick Savitt	Ken McGregor	1980	Bjorn Borg	John McEnroe
1952	Frank Sedgman	Jaroslav Drobny	1981	John McEnroe	Bjorn Borg
1953	Vic Seixas	Kurt Nielsen	1982	Jimmy Connors	John McEnroe
1954	Jaroslav Drobny	Ken Rosewall	1983	John McEnroe	Chris Lewis
1955	Tony Trabert	Kurt Nielsen	1984	John McEnroe	Jimmy Connors
1956	Lew Hoad	Ken Rosewall	1985	Boris Becker	Kevin Curren
1957	Lew Hoad	Ashley Cooper	1986	Boris Becker	Ivan Lendl
1958	Ashley Cooper	Neale Fraser	1987	Pat Cash	Ivan Lendl
1959	Alex Olmedo	Rod Laver	1988	Stefan Edberg	Boris Becker
1960	Neale Fraser	Rod Laver	1989	Boris Becker	Stefan Edberg
1961	Rod Laver	Chuck McKinley	1990	Stefan Edberg	Boris Becker
1962	Rod Laver	Martin Mulligan	1991	Michael Stich	Boris Becker
1963	Chuck McKinley	Fred Stolle	1992	Andre Agassi	Goran Ivanisevic
1964	Roy Emerson	Fred Stolle	1993	Pete Sampras	Jim Courier
1965	Roy Emerson	Fred Stolle	1994	Pete Sampras	Goren Ivanisevic
1966	Manuel Santana	Dennis Ralston			

Women's Singles

Year	Champion	Year	Champion	Year	Champion	Year	Champion
1946	Pauline Betz	1959	Maria Bueno	1971	Evonne Goolagong	1983	Martina Navratilova
1947	Margaret Osborne	1960	Maria Bueno	1972	Billie Jean King	1984	Martina Navratilova
1948	Louise Brough	1961	Angela Mortimer	1973	Billie Jean King	1985	Martina Navratilova
1949	Louise Brough	1962	Karen Hantze-Susman	1974	Chris Evert	1986	Martina Navratilova
1950	Louise Brough	1963	Margaret Smith	1975	Billie Jean King	1987	Martina Navratilova
1951	Doris Hart	1964	Maria Bueno	1976	Chris Evert	1988	Steffi Graf
1952	Maureen Connolly	1965	Margaret Smith	1977	Virginia Wade	1989	Steffi Graf
1953	Maureen Connolly	1966	Billie Jean King	1978	Martina Navratilova	1990	Martina Navratilova
1954	Maureen Connolly	1967	Billie Jean King	1979	Martina Navratilova	1991	Steffi Graf
1955	Louise Brough	1968	Billie Jean King	1980	Evonne Goolagong	1992	Steffi Graf
1956	Shirley Fry	1969	Ann Haydon-Jones	1981	Chris Evert Lloyd	1993	Steffi Graf
1957	Althea Gibson	1970	Margaret Smith Court	1982	Martina Navratilova	1994	Conchita Martinez
1958	Althea Gibson						

Davis Cup Challenge Round

Year	Result	Year	Result	Year	Result
1900	United States 5, British Isles 0	1933	Great Britain 3, France 2	1966	Australia 4, India 1
1901	(not played)	1934	Great Britain 4, United States 1	1967	Australia 4, Spain 1
1902	United States 3, British Isles 2	1935	Great Britain 5, United States 0	1968	United States 4, Australia
1903	British Isles 4, United States 1	1936	Great Britain 3, Australia 2	1969	United States 5, Romania 0
1904	British Isles 5, Belgium 0	1937	United States 4, Great Britain 1	1970	United States 5, W. Germany 0
1905	British Isles 5, United States 0	1938	United States 3, Australia 2	1971	United States 3, Romania 2
1906	British Isles 5, United States 0	1939	Australia 3, United States 2	1972	United States 3, Romania 2
1907	Australia 3, British Isles 2	1940-45	(not played)	1973	Australia 5, United States 0
1908	Australasia 3, United States 2	1946	United States 5, Australia 0	1974	South Africa (default by India)
1909	Australasia 5, United States 0	1947	United States 4, Australia 1	1975	Sweden 3, Czechoslovakia 2
1910	(not played)	1948	United States 5, Australia 0	1976	Italy 4, Chile 1
1911	Australasia 5, United States 0	1949	United States 4, Australia 1	1977	Australia 3, Italy 1
1912	British Isles 3, Australasia 2	1950	Australia 4, United States 1	1978	United States 4, Great Britain 1
1913	United States 3, British Isles 2	1951	Australia 3, United States 2	1979	United States 5, Italy 0
1914	Australasia 3, United States 2	1952	Australia 4, United States 1	1980	Czechoslovakia 4, Italy 1
1915-18	(not played)	1953	Australia 3, United States 2	1981	United States 3, Argentina 1
1919	Australasia 4, British Isles 1	1954	United States 3, Australia 2	1982	United States 3, France, 0
1920	United States 5, Australasia 0	1955	Australia 5, United States 0	1983	Australia 3, Sweden 1
1921	United States 5, Japan 0	1956	Australia 5, United States 0	1984	Sweden 3, United States 0
1922	United States 4, Australasia 1	1957	Australia 3, United States 2	1985	Sweden 3, W. Germany 2
1923	United States 4, Australasia 1	1958	United States 3, Australia 2	1986	Australia 3, Sweden 2
1924	United States 5, Australasia 0	1959	Australia 3, United States 2	1987	Sweden 5, India 0
1925	United States 5, France 0	1960	Australia 4, Italy 1	1988	W. Germany 4, Sweden 1
1926	United States 4, France 1	1961	Australia 5, Italy 0	1989	W. Germany 3, Sweden 2
1927	France 3, United States 2	1962	Australia 5, Mexico 0	1990	United States 3, Australia 2
1928	France 4, United States 1	1963	United States 3, Australia 2	1991	France 3, United States 1
1929	France 3, United States 2	1964	Australia 3, United States 2	1992	United States 3, Switzerland 1
1930	France 4, United States 1	1965	Australia 4, Spain 1	1993	Germany 4, Australia 1
1931	France 3, Great Britain 2				
1932	France 3, United States 2				

French Open Singles Champions

Year	Men	Women	Year	Men	Women
1969	Rod Laver	Margaret Smith Court	1982	Mats Wilander	Martina Navratilova
1970	Jan Kodes	Margaret Smith Court	1983	Yannick Noah	Chris Evert Lloyd
1971	Jan Kodes	Evonne Goolagong	1984	Ivan Lendl	Martina Navratilova
1972	Andres Gimeno	Billie Jean King	1985	Mats Wilander	Chris Evert Lloyd
1973	Ilie Nastase	Margaret Smith Court	1986	Ivan Lendl	Chris Evert Lloyd
1974	Bjorn Borg	Chris Evert	1987	Ivan Lendl	Steffi Graf
1975	Bjorn Borg	Chris Evert	1988	Mats Wilander	Steffi Graf
1976	Adriano Panatta	Sue Barker	1989	Michael Chang	Arantxa Sanchez Vicario
1977	Guillermo Vilas	Mima Jausovec	1990	Andres Gomez	Monica Seles
1978	Bjorn Borg	Virginia Ruzici	1991	Jim Courier	Monica Seles
1979	Bjorn Borg	Chris Evert Lloyd	1992	Jim Courier	Monica Seles
1980	Bjorn Borg	Chris Evert Lloyd	1993	Sergi Bruguera	Steffi Graf
1981	Bjorn Borg	Hana Mandlikova	1994	Sergi Bruguera	Arantxa Sanchez Vicario

Australian Open Singles Champions

Year*	Men	Women	Year*	Men	Women
1969	Rod Laver	Margaret Smith Court	1982	Johan Kriek	Chris Evert Lloyd
1970	Arthur Ashe	Margaret Smith Court	1983	Mats Wilander	Martina Navratilova
1971	Ken Rosewall	Margaret Smith Court	1984	Mats Wilander	Chris Evert Lloyd
1972	Ken Rosewall	Virginia Wade	1985	Stefan Edberg	Martina Navratilova
1973	John Newcombe	Margaret Smith Court	1986	Not held	Not held
1974	Jimmy Connors	Evonne Goolagong	1987	Stefan Edberg	Hana Mandlikova
1975	John Newcombe	Evonne Goolagong	1988	Mats Wilander	Steffi Graf
1976	Mark Edmondson	Evonne Goolagong	1989	Ivan Lendl	Steffi Graf
1977	Roscoe Tanner	Kerry Reid	1990	Ivan Lendl	Steffi Graf
	Vitas Gerulaitis	Evonne Goolagong	1991	Boris Becker	Monica Seles
1978	Guillermo Vilas	Chris O'Neill	1992	Jim Courier	Monica Seles
1979	Guillermo Vilas	Barbara Jordan	1993	Jim Courier	Monica Seles
1980	Brian Teacher	Hana Mandlikova	1994	Pete Sampras	Steffi Graf
1981	Johan Kriek	Martina Navratilova			

* Two tournaments were held in 1977 (Jan. & Dec.). Tournament moved back to Jan. in 1987, so no championship was decided in 1986.

AUTO RACING

Indianapolis 500 Winners

Year	Winner, Car	MPH
1911	Ray Harroun, Marmon Wasp	74.59
1912	Joe Dawson, National	78.72
1913	Jules Goux, Peugeot	75.933
1914	Rene Thomas, Delage	82.47
1915	Ralph DePalma, Mercedes	89.84
1916	Dario Resta, Peugeot	84.00
1917-18	race not held	
1919	Howdy Wilcox, Peugeot	88.05
1920	Gaston Chevrolet, Monroe	88.16
1921	Tommy Milton, Frontenac	89.62
1922	Jimmy Murphy, Murphy Special	94.48
1923	Tommy Milton, H.C.S.	90.95
1924	L.L. Corum-Joe Boyer, Duesenberg	98.23
1925	Pete DePaolo, Duesenberg	101.13
1926	Frank Lockhart, Miller	95.904
1927	George Souders, Duesenberg	97.545
1928	Louis Meyer, Miller	99.482
1929	Ray Keech, Simplex	97.585
1930	Billy Arnold, Miller-Hartz	100.448
1931	Louis Schneider, Bowes Seal Fast	96.629
1932	Fred Frame, Miller-Hartz	104.144
1933	Louis Meyer, Tydol	104.162
1934	Bill Cummings, Boyle Products	104.863
1935	Kelly Petillo, Gilmore Speedway	106.240
1936	Louis Meyer, Ring Free	109.069
1937	Wilbur Shaw, Shaw-Gilmore	113.580
1938	Floyd Roberts, Burd Piston Ring	117.200
1939	Wilbur Shaw, Boyle	115.035
1940	Wilbur Shaw, Boyle	114.277
1941	Floyd Davis-Mauri Rose, Knock-Out-Hose Clip	115.117
1942-45	race not held	
1946	George Robson, Thorne Engineering	114.820
1947	Mauri Rose, Blue Crown Special	116.338
1948	Mauri Rose, Blue Crown Special	119.814
1949	Bill Holland, Blue Crown Special	121.327
1950	Johnny Parsons, Wynn Kurtis Kraft	124.002
1951	Lee Wallard, Belanger	126.224
1952	Troy Ruttman, Agajanian	128.922
1953	Bill Vukovich, Fuel Injection	128.740
1954	Bill Vukovich, Fuel Injection	130.840
1955	Bob Sweikert, John Zink Special	128.209
1956	Pat Flaherty, John Zink Special	128.490

Year	Winner, Car	MPH
1957	Sam Hanks, Belond Exhaust	135.601
1958	Jimmy Bryan, Belond A.P.	133.791
1959	Rodger Ward, Leader Card Special	135.857
1960	Jim Rathmann, Ken Paul Special	138.767
1961	A.J. Foyt, Bowes Seal Fast	139.130
1962	Rodger Ward, Leader Card Special	140.293
1963	Parnelli Jones, Agajanian Special	143.137
1964	A.J. Foyt, Sheraton-Thompson Special	147.350
1965	Jim Clark, Lotus-Ford	150.686
1966	Graham Hill, American Red Ball	144.317
1967	A.J. Foyt, Sheraton-Thompson Special	151.207
1968	Bobby Unser, Rislone Special	152.882
1969	Mario Andretti, STP Oil Treatment Special	156.867
1970	Al Unser, Johnny Lightning Special	155.749
1971	Al Unser, Johnny Lightning Special	157.735
1972	Mark Donohue, Sunoco McLaren	162.962
1973	Gordon Johncock, STP Double Oil Filter	159.036
1974	Johnny Rutherford, McLaren	158.589
1975	Bobby Unser, Jorgenson Eagle	149.213
1976	Johnny Rutherford, Hygain McLaren	148.725
1977	A.J. Foyt, Gilmore Coyote-Ford	161.331
1978	Al Unser, Lola Cosworth	161.363
1979	Rick Mears, Penske-Cosworth	158.899
1980	Johnny Rutherford, Chaparral-Cosworth	142.862
1981	Bobby Unser, Penske-Cosworth	139.085
1982	Gordon Johncock, Wildcat-Cosworth	162.026
1983	Tom Sneva, March-Cosworth	162.117
1984	Rick Mears, March-Cosworth	163.621
1985	Danny Sullivan, March-Cosworth	152.982
1986	Bobby Rahal, March-Cosworth	170.722
1987	Al Unser, March-Cosworth	162.175
1988	Rick Mears, Penske-Chevy V8	144.809
1989	Emerson Fittipaldi, Penske PC 18-Chevy	167.581
1990	Arie Luyendyk, Lola-Chevy	185.984
1991	Rick Mears, Penske-Chevy	176.457
1992	Al Unser Jr., Galmer-Chevy A	134.477
1993	Emerson Fittipaldi, Penske-Chevy C	157.207
1994	Al Unser Jr., Penske-Mercedes	160.872

The race was less than 500 miles in the following years: 1916 (300 mi.), 1926 (400 mi.), 1950 (345 mi.), 1973 (332.5 mi.), 1975 (435 mi.), 1976 (255 mi.). Race record —185.984 MPH, Arie Luyendyk, 1990.

Notable One-Mile Speed Records

Date	Driver	Car	MPH
1/26/06	Marriott	Stanley (Steam)	127.659
3/16/10	Oldfield	Benz	131.724
4/23/11	Burman	Benz	141.732
2/12/19	DePalma	Packard	149.875
4/27/20	Milton	Dusenberg	155.046
4/28/26	Parry-Thomas	Thomas Spl.	170.624
3/29/27	Seagrave	Sunbeam	203.790
4/22/28	Keech	White Triplex	207.552
3/11/29	Seagrave	Irving-Napier	231.446
2/5/31	Campbell	Napier-Campbell	246.086
2/24/32	Campbell	Napier-Campbell	253.96
2/22/33	Campbell	Napier-Campbell	272.109
9/3/35	Campbell	Bluebird Special	301.13
11/19/37	Eyston	Thunderbolt 1	311.42
9/16/38	Eyston	Thunderbolt 1	357.5
8/23/39	Cobb	Railton	368.9
9/16/47	Cobb	Railton-Mobil	394.2
8/5/63	Breedlove	Spirit of America	407.45
10/27/64	Arfons	Green Monster	536.71
11/15/65	Breedlove	Spirit of America	600.601
10/23/70	Gabelich	Blue Flame	622.407
10/9/79	Barrett	Budweiser Rocket	638.637*
10/4/83	Noble	Thrust 2	633.6

*Not recognized as official by sanctioning bodies.

IndyCar Champions

(U.S. Auto Club Champions prior to 1979; Cart Champions, 1979-94)

Year	Driver
1960	A. J. Foyt
1961	A. J. Foyt
1962	Rodger Ward
1963	A. J. Foyt
1964	A. J. Foyt
1965	Mario Andretti
1966	Mario Andretti
1967	A. J. Foyt
1968	Bobby Unser
1969	Mario Andretti
1970	Al Unser
1971	Joe Leonard
1972	Joe Leonard
1973	Roger McCluskey
1974	Bobby Unser
1975	A. J. Foyt
1976	Gordon Johncock
1977	Tom Sneva
1978	Tom Sneva
1979	Rick Mears
1980	Johnny Rutherford
1981	Rick Mears
1982	Rick Mears
1983	Al Unser
1984	Mario Andretti
1985	Al Unser
1986	Bobby Rahal
1987	Bobby Rahal
1988	Danny Sullivan
1989	Emerson Fittipaldi
1990	Al Unser Jr.
1991	Michael Andretti
1992	Bobby Rahal
1993	Nigel Mansell
1994	Al Unser Jr.

Le Mans 24-Hour Race in 1994

Hurley Haywood (U.S.), Yannick Dalmas (France), and Mauro Baldi (Italy) drove their Dauer Porche 962 to victory in the 1994 Le Mans 24-hour race. They traveled the 2,906.8 miles at an average of 121.117 mph.

World Grand Prix Champions

Year	Driver
1951	Juan Fangio, Argentina
1952	Alberto Ascari, Italy
1953	Alberto Ascari, Italy
1954	Juan Fangio, Argentina
1955	Juan Fangio, Argentina
1956	Juan Fangio, Argentina
1957	Juan Fangio, Argentina
1958	Mike Hawthorne, England
1959	Jack Brabham, Australia
1960	Jack Brabham, Australia
1961	Phil Hill, United States
1962	Graham Hill, England
1963	Jim Clark, Scotland
1964	John Surtees, England
1965	Jim Clark, Scotland
1966	Jack Brabham, Australia
1967	Denis Hulme, New Zealand
1968	Graham Hill, England
1969	Jackie Stewart, Scotland
1970	Jochen Rindt, Austria
1971	Jackie Stewart, Scotland
1972	Emerson Fittipaldi, Brazil
1973	Jackie Stewart, Scotland
1974	Emerson Fittipaldi, Brazil
1975	Niki Lauda, Austria
1976	James Hunt, England
1977	Niki Lauda, Austria
1978	Mario Andretti, U.S.
1979	Jody Scheckter, So. Africa
1980	Alan Jones, Australia
1981	Nelson Piquet, Brazil
1982	Keke Rosberg, Finland
1983	Nelson Piquet, Brazil
1984	Niki Lauda, Austria
1985	Alain Prost, France
1986	Alain Prost, France
1987	Nelson Piquet, Brazil
1988	Ayrton Senna, Brazil
1989	Alain Prost, France
1990	Ayrton Senna, Brazil
1991	Ayrton Senna, Brazil
1992	Nigel Mansell, Britain
1993	Ayrton Senna, Brazil

Grand Prix Races for Formula 1 Cars in 1994

Grand Prix	Winner, car
Belgian	Damon Hill, Williams-Renault
Brazilian	Michael Schumacher, Benetton-Ford
British	Damon Hill, Williams-Renault
Canadian	Michael Schumacher, Benetton-Ford
European	Michael Schumacher, Benetton-Ford
French	Michael Schumacher, Benetton-Ford
German	Gerhardt Berger, Ferrari
Hungarian	Michael Schumacher, Benetton-Ford
Italian	Damon Hill, Williams-Renault
Monaco	Michael Schumacher, Benetton-Ford
Pacific	Michael Schumacher, Benetton-Ford
Portugal	Damon Hill, Williams-Renault
San Marino	Michael Schumacher, Benetton-Ford
Spanish	Damon Hill, Williams-Renault

Winston Cup Champions (NASCAR)

Year	Driver
1949	Red Byron
1950	Bill Rexford
1951	Herb Thomas
1952	Tim Flock
1953	Herb Thomas
1954	Lee Petty
1955	Tim Flock
1956	Buck Baker
1957	Buck Baker
1958	Lee Petty
1959	Lee Petty
1960	Rex White
1961	Ned Jarrett
1962	Joe Weatherly
1963	Joe Weatherly
1964	Richard Petty
1965	Ned Jarrett
1966	David Pearson
1967	Richard Petty
1968	David Pearson
1969	David Pearson
1970	Bobby Isaac
1971	Richard Petty
1972	Richard Petty
1973	Benny Parsons
1974	Richard Petty
1975	Richard Petty
1976	Cale Yarborough
1977	Cale Yarborough
1978	Cale Yarborough
1979	Richard Petty
1980	Dale Earnhardt
1981	Darrell Waltrip
1982	Darrell Waltrip
1983	Bobby Allison
1984	Terry Labonte
1985	Darrell Waltrip
1986	Dale Earnhardt
1987	Dale Earnhardt
1988	Bill Elliott
1989	Rusty Wallace
1990	Dale Earnhardt
1991	Dale Earnhardt
1992	Alan Kulwicki
1993	Dale Earnhardt

Daytona 500 Winners

Year	Driver, car	Avg. MPH	Year	Driver, car	Avg. MPH
1959	Lee Petty, Oldsmobile	135.521	1978	Bobby Allison, Ford	159.730
1960	Junior Johnson, Chevrolet	124.740	1979	Richard Petty, Oldsmobile	143.977
1961	Marvin Panch, Pontiac	149.601	1980	Buddy Baker, Oldsmobile	177.602
1962	Fireball Roberts, Pontiac	152.529	1981	Richard Petty, Buick	169.651
1963	Tiny Lund, Ford	151.566	1982	Bobby Allison, Buick	153.991
1964	Richard Petty, Plymouth	154.334	1983	Cale Yarborough, Pontiac	155.979
1965	Fred Lorenzen, Ford (a)	141.539	1984	Cale Yarborough, Chevrolet	150.994
1966	Richard Petty, Plymouth (b)	160.627	1985	Bill Elliott, Ford	172.265
1967	Mario Andretti, Ford	146.926	1986	Geoff Bodine, Chevrolet	148.124
1968	Cale Yarborough, Mercury	143.251	1987	Bill Elliott, Ford	176.263
1969	Lee Roy Yarborough, Ford	160.875	1988	Bobby Allison, Buick	137.531
1970	Pete Hamilton, Plymouth	149.601	1989	Darrell Waltrip, Chevrolet	148.466
1971	Richard Petty, Plymouth	144.456	1990	Derrike Cope, Chevrolet	165.761
1972	A. J. Foyt, Mercury	161.550	1991	Ernie Irvan, Chevrolet	148.148
1973	Richard Petty, Dodge	157.205	1992	Davey Allison, Ford	160.256
1974	Richard Petty, Dodge (c)	140.894	1993	Dale Jarrett, Chevrolet	154.972
1975	Benny Parsons, Chevrolet	153.649	1994	Sterling Marlin, Chevrolet	156.931
1976	David Pearson, Mercury	152.181			
1977	Cale Yarborough, Chevrolet	153.218			

(a) 322.5 miles. (b) 495 miles. (c) 450 miles.

NASCAR Racing in 1994

Winston Cup Races

Date	Race, site	Winner	Car
Feb. 20	Daytona 500, Daytona Beach, FL	Sterling Marlin	Chevrolet
Feb. 27	Goodwrench 500, Rockingham, NC	Rusty Wallace	Ford
Mar. 6	Pontiac Excitement 400, Richmond, VA	Ernie Irvan	Ford
Mar. 13	Purolator 500, Atlanta, GA	Ernie Irvan	Ford
Mar. 27	Transouth Finanacial 400, Darlington, SC	Dale Earnhardt	Chevrolet
Apr. 10	Food City 500, Bristol, TN	Dale Earnhardt	Chevrolet
Apr. 17	First Union 400, N. Wilkesboro, NC	Terry Labonte	Pontiac
Apr. 24	Hanes 500, Martinsville, VA	Rusty Wallace	Ford
May 1	Winston Select 500, Talladega, AL	Dale Earnhardt	Chevrolet
May 29	Coca Cola 600, Concord, NC	Jeff Gordon	Chevrolet
June 5	Budweiser 500, Dover, DE	Rusty Wallace	Ford
June 12	Pocono 500, Pocono, PA	Rusty Wallace	Ford
June 19	Miller Genuine Draft 400, Brooklyn, MI	Rusty Wallace	Ford
July 2	Pepsi 400, Daytona Beach, FL	Jimmy Spencer	Ford
July 17	Miller Genuine Draft 500, Pocono, PA	Geoff Bodine	Ford
July 24	Die-Hard 500, Talladega, AL	Jimmy Spencer	Ford
Aug. 14	Budweiser at The Glen, Watkins Glen, NY	Mark Martin	Ford
Aug. 21	GM Goodwrench 400, Brooklyn, MI	Geoff Bodine	Ford
Aug. 27	Goody's 500, Bristol, TN	Rusty Wallace	Ford
Sept. 4	Southern 500, Darlington, SC	Bill Elliott	Ford
Sept. 10	Miller Genuine Draft 400, Richmond, VA	Terry Labonte	Pontiac
Sept. 18	Spitfire Spark Plug 500, Dover, DE	Rusty Wallace	Ford
Sept. 25	Goody's 500, Martinsville, VA	Rusty Wallace	Ford

LACROSSE

Lacrosse Champions in 1994

World Lacrosse Championship (held every 4 years)—Manchester, England, July 30: U.S. 21, Australia 7.

U.S. Club Lacrosse Association Championship—Baltimore, MD, June 11: Long Island-Hofstra 11, Mount Washington 9.

NCAA Division I Championship—College Park, MD, May 30: Princeton 9, Virginia 8 (OT).

NCAA Division II Championship—Brookville, NY, May 15: Springfield College 15, New York I T 12.

NCAA Division III Championship—College Park, MD, May 29: Salisbury State (MD) 15, Hobart 9.

USILA Division I All-Star Game—Baltimore, MD, June 10: South 11, North 10.

National Junior College Championship—Arnold, MD, May 8: Herkimer (NY) 19, Anne Arundel (MD) 13.

NCAA Women's Division I Championship—College Park, MD, May 22: Princeton 10, Maryland 7.

NCAA Women's Division III Championship—College Park, MD, May 22: Trenton State 29, William Smith 11.

USILA Division I All America Team

Attack: Kevin Lowe, Princeton; Terry Riordan, Johns Hopkins; David Evans, Brown.

Midfield: Scott Reinhardt, Princeton; Dom Fin, Syracuse; Ryan Wade, N. Carolina; Roy Colsey, Syracuse.

Defense: Reid Jackson, Rutgers; Todd Higgins, Princeton; Ric Beardsley, Syracuse.

Goal: Scott Bacigalupo, Princeton.

Coach of the Year: Peter Lasagna, Brown.

Note: 4 midfielders selected for the 3 midfield positions

NCAA Division I Champions

Year	Champion	Year	Champion	Year	Champion	Year	Champion
1972	Virginia	1978	Johns Hopkins	1984	Johns Hopkins	1990	Syracuse
1973	Maryland	1979	Johns Hopkins	1985	Johns Hopkins	1991	North Carolina
1974	Johns Hopkins	1980	Johns Hopkins	1986	North Carolina	1992	Princeton
1975	Maryland	1981	North Carolina	1987	Johns Hopkins	1993	Syracuse
1976	Cornell	1982	North Carolina	1988	Syracuse	1994	Princeton
1977	Cornell	1983	Syracuse	1989	Syracuse		

BOXING

Champions by Classes

There are numerous governing bodies in boxing, including the World Boxing Council, the World Boxing Assn., the International Boxing Federation, the United States Boxing Assn., the North American Boxing Federation, and the European Boxing Union. Other organizations are recognized by TV networks and the print media. All the governing bodies have their own champions and assorted boxing divisions. The following are the recognized champions—generally as of mid-1994, heavyweights as of Nov. 1994—in the principal divisions of the WBC, WBA, and IBF.

Class, Weight limit	WBC	WBA	IBF
Heavyweight	Oliver McCall, U.S.	George Foreman, U.S.	George Foreman, U.S.
Cruiserweight (195 lbs.)	Anaclet Wamba, France	Orlin Norris, U.S.	Al Cole, U.S.
Light Heavyweight (175 lbs.)	Jeff Harding, Australia	Virgil Hill, U.S.	Henry Maske, Germany
Super Middleweight (168 lbs.)	Nigel Benn, U.K.	Steve Little, U.S.	James Toney, U.S.
Middleweight (160 lbs.)	Gerald McClellan, U.S.	Vacant	Roy Jones, U.S.
Jr. Middleweight (154 lbs.)	Terry Norris, U.S.	Julio Cesar Vasquez, Argentina	Gianfranco Rosi, Italy
Welterweight (147 lbs.)	Pernell Whitaker, U.S.	Crisanto Espana, N. Ireland	Felix Trinidad, Puerto Rico
Jr. Welterweight (140 lbs.)	Julio Cesar Chavez, Mexico	Juan Coggi, Argentina	Jake Rodriguez, U.S.
Lightweight (135 lbs.)	Miguel Angel Gonzalez, Mexico	Nazarov Olzubek, Japan	Rafael Ruelas, U.S.
Jr. Lightweight (130 lbs.)	Jessie James Leija, U.S.	Genaro Hernandez, U.S.	John-John Molina, Puerto Rico
Featherweight (126 lbs.)	Kevin Kelley, U.S.	Eloy Rojas, Venezuela	Tom Johnson, U.S.
Jr. Featherweight (122 lbs.)	Tracy Patterson, U.S.	Wilfredo Vasquez, Puerto Rico	Kennedy McKinney, U.S.
Bantamweight (118 lbs.)	Yasuei Yakushiji, Japan	John Michael Johnson, U.S.	Orlando Canizales, U.S.
Flyweight (112 lbs.)	Yuri Arbachakov, Russia	San Sow Ploenchit, Thailand	Phichit Sithbangprachan, Thailand
Jr. Flyweight (108 lbs.)	Humberto Gonzalez, Mexico	Leo Gomez, Venezuela	Humberto Gonzalez, Mexico

Ring Champions by Years

*Abandoned title

Heavyweights

1882-1892	John L. Sullivan (a)
1892-1897	James J. Corbett (b)
1897-1899	Robert Fitzsimmons
1899-1905	James J. Jeffries* (c)
1905-1906	Marvin Hart
1906-1908	Tommy Burns
1908-1915	Jack Johnson
1915-1919	Jess Willard
1919-1926	Jack Dempsey
1926-1928	Gene Tunney*
1928-1930	vacant
1930-1932	Max Schmeling
1932-1933	Jack Sharkey
1933-1934	Primo Carnera
1934-1935	Max Baer
1935-1937	James J. Braddock
1937-1949	Joe Louis*
1949-1951	Ezzard Charles
1951-1952	Joe Walcott
1952-1956	Rocky Marciano*
1956-1959	Floyd Patterson
1959-1960	Ingemar Johansson
1960-1962	Floyd Patterson
1962-1964	Sonny Liston
1964-1967	Cassius Clay* (Muhammad Ali) (d)
1970-1973	Joe Frazier
1973-1974	George Foreman
1974-1978	Muhammad Ali
1978	Leon Spinks (e); Ken Norton (WBC); Larry Holmes (WBC) (f); Muhammad Ali* (WBA)
1979	John Tate (WBA)
1980	Mike Weaver (WBA)
1982	Michael Dokes (WBA)
1983	Gerrie Coetzee (WBA)
1984	Tim Witherspoon (WBC); Pinklon Thomas (WBC); Greg Page (WBA)
1985	Tony Tubbs (WBA); Michael Spinks (IBF)
1986	Tim Witherspoon (WBA); Trevor Berbick (WBC); Mike Tyson (WBC); James "Bonecrusher" Smith (WBA)
1987	Mike Tyson (WBA, 1988—IBF)
1990	James "Buster" Douglas (WBA, WBC, IBF); Evander Holyfield (WBA, WBC, IBF)
1992	Riddick Bowe (WBA, IBF, WBC); Lennox Lewis (WBC) (g)
1993	Evander Holyfield (WBA, IBF)
1994	Michael Moorer (WBA, IBF); Oliver McCall (WBC); George Foreman (WBA, IBF)

(a) London Prize Ring (bare knuckle champion).

(b) First Marquis of Queensberry champion.

(c) Jeffries abandoned the title (1905) and designated Marvin Hart and Jack Root as logical contenders. Hart defeated Root in 12 rounds (1905) and in turn was defeated by Tommy Burns (1906) who laid claim to the title. Jack Johnson defeated Burns (1908) and was recognized as champion. He clinched the title by defeating Jeffries in an attempted comeback (1910).

(d) Title declared vacant by the WBA and other groups in 1967 after Clay's refusal to fulfill his military obligation. Joe Frazier was recognized as champion by 6 states, Mexico, and So. America. Jimmy Ellis was declared champion by the WBA. Frazier KOd Ellis, Feb. 16, 1970.

(e) After Spinks defeated Ali, the WBC recognized Ken Norton as champion. Ali defeated Spinks in a rematch to win the WBA title and subsequently retired in 1979.

(f) Holmes was stripped of his WBC title in 1984. He was the IBF champion when he lost to Michael Spinks in 1985.

(g) Lewis was named WBC champion when Bowe refused to fight him.

Light Heavyweights

1903	Jack Root, George Gardner
1903-1905	Bob Fitzsimmons
1905-1912	Philadelphia Jack O'Brien*
1912-1916	Jack Dillon
1916-1920	Battling Levinsky
1920-1922	George Carpentier
1922-1923	Battling Siki
1923-1925	Mike McTigue
1925-1926	Paul Berlenbach
1926-1927	Jack Delaney*
1927-1929	Tommy Loughran*
1930-1934	Maxey Rosenbloom
1934-1935	Bob Olin
1935-1939	John Henry Lewis*
1939	Melio Bettina
1939-1941	Billy Conn*
1941	Anton Christoforidis (won NBA title)
1941-1948	Gus Lesnevich, Freddie Mills
1948-1950	Freddie Mills
1950-1952	Joey Maxim
1952-1960	Archie Moore
1961-1962	vacant
1962-1963	Harold Johnson
1963-1965	Willie Pastrano
1965-1966	Jose Torres
1966-1968	Dick Tiger
1968-1974	Bob Foster*
1974-1977	John Conteh (WBC); Victor Galindez (WBA)
1977	Miguel Cuello (WBC)
1978	Mike Rossman (WBA); Mate Parlov (WBC); Marvin Johnson (WBC)
1979	Matthew Saad Muhammad (WBC); Victor Galindez (WBA); Marvin Johnson (WBA)
1980	Eddie Mustafa Muhammad (WBA)
1981	Michael Spinks (WBA); Dwight Braxton (WBC)
1983-1985	Michael Spinks*
1985	J. B. Williamson (WBC)
1986	Marvin Johnson (WBA); Dennis Andries (WBC)
1987	Thomas Hearns* (WBC); Leslie Stewart (WBA); Virgil Hill (WBA); Don Lalonde (WBC)

1988 Ray Leonard* (WBC)
1989 Dennis Andries (WBC); Jeff Harding (WBC)
1990 Dennis Andries (WBC)
1991 Thomas Hearns (WBA); Jeff Harding (WBC)
1992 Iran Barkley* (WBA); Virgil Hill (WBA)

Middleweights

1884-1891 Jack "Nonpareil" Dempsey
1891-1897 Bob Fitzsimmons*
1897-1907 Tommy Ryan*
1907-1908 Stanley Ketchel, Billy Papke
1908-1910 Stanley Ketchel
1911-1913 vacant
1913 Frank Klaus; George Chip
1914-1917 Al McCoy
1917-1920 Mike O'Dowd
1920-1923 Johnny Wilson
1923-1926 Harry Greb
1926-1931 Tiger Flowers; Mickey Walker
1931-1932 Gorilla Jones (NBA)
1932-1937 Marcel Thil
1938 Al Hostak (NBA); Solly Krieger (NBA)
1939-1940 Al Hostak (NBA)
1941-1947 Tony Zale
1947-1948 Rocky Graziano
1948 Tony Zale; Marcel Cerdan
1949-1951 Jake LaMotta
1951 Ray Robinson; Randy Turpin; Ray Robinson*
1953-1955 Carl (Bobo) Olson
1955-1957 Ray Robinson
1957 Gene Fullmer; Ray Robinson; Carmen Basilio
1958 Ray Robinson
1959 Gene Fullmer (NBA); Ray Robinson (N.Y.)
1960 Gene Fullmer (NBA); Paul Pender (New York and Mass.)
1961 Gene Fullmer (NBA); Terry Downes (New York, Mass., Europe)
1962 Gene Fullmer; Dick Tiger (NBA); Paul Pender (New York and Mass.)*
1963 Dick Tiger (universal)
1963-1965 Joey Giardello
1965-1966 Dick Tiger
1966-1967 Emile Griffith
1967 Nino Benvenuti
1967-1968 Emile Griffith
1968-1970 Nino Benvenuti
1970-1977 Carlos Monzon*
1977-1978 Rodrigo Valdez
1978-1979 Hugo Corro
1979-1980 Vito Antuofermo
1980 Alan Minter; Marvin Hagler
1987 Ray Leonard* (WBC); Thomas Hearns (WBC); Sumbu Kalambay (WBA)
1988 Iran Barkley (WBC)
1989 Mike McCallum (WBA); Roberto Duran (WBC)
1991 Julian Jackson (WBC)
1992 Reggie Johnson (WBA)
1993 Gerald McClellan (WBC)

Welterweights

1892-1894 Mysterious Billy Smith
1894-1896 Tommy Ryan
1896 Kid McCoy*
1900 Rube Ferns; Matty Matthews
1901 Rube Ferns
1901-1904 Joe Walcott
1904-1906 Dixie Kid; Joe Walcott; Honey Mellody
1907-1911 Mike Sullivan
1911-1915 vacant
1915-1919 Ted Lewis
1919-1922 Jack Britton
1922-1926 Mickey Walker
1926 Pete Latzo
1927-1929 Joe Dundee
1929 Jackie Fields
1930 Jack Thompson; Tommy Freeman
1931 Freeman; Thompson; Lou Brouillard
1932 Jackie Fields
1933 Young Corbett; Jimmy McLarnin
1934 Barney Ross; Jimmy McLarnin
1935-1938 Barney Ross
1938-1940 Henry Armstrong
1940-1941 Fritzie Zivic
1941-1946 Fred Cochrane
1946-1946 Marty Servo*; Ray Robinson (a)
1946-1950 Ray Robinson*
1951 Johnny Bratton (NBA)
1951-1954 Kid Gavilan
1954-1955 Johnny Saxton
1955 Tony De Marco; Carmen Basilio
1956 Carmen Basilio; Johnny Saxton; Basilio
1957 Carmen Basilio*
1958-1960 Virgil Akins, Don Jordan
1960 Benny Paret
1961 Emile Griffith; Benny Paret
1962 Emile Griffith
1963 Luis Rodriguez; Emile Griffith
1964-1966 Emile Griffith*
1966-1969 Curtis Cokes
1969-1970 Jose Napoles; Billy Backus
1971-1975 Jose Napoles
1975-1976 John Stracey (WBC); Angel Espada (WBA)
1976-1979 Carlos Palomino (WBC); Jose Cuevas (WBA)
1979 Wilfredo Benitez (WBC); Sugar Ray Leonard (WBC)
1980 Roberto Duran (WBC); Thomas Hearns (WBA); Sugar Ray Leonard (WBC)
1981-1982 Sugar Ray Leonard*
1983 Donald Curry (WBA); Milton McCrory (WBC)
1985 Donald Curry
1986 Lloyd Honeyghan (WBC)
1987 Mark Breland (WBA); Marlon Starling (WBA); Jorge Vaca (WBC).
1988 Tomas Molinares (WBA); Lloyd Honeyghan (WBC)
1989 Marlon Starling (WBC); Mark Breland (WBA)
1990 Maurice Blocker (WBC); Aaron Davis (WBA)
1991 Meldrick Taylor (WBA); Simon Brown (WBC); Buddy McGirt (WBC)
1992 Crisanto Espana (WBA)
1993 Pernell Whitaker (WBC)

(a) Robinson gained the title by defeating Tommy Bell in an elimination agreed to by the NY Commission and the NBA. Both claimed Robinson waived his title when he won the middleweight crown from LaMotta in 1951.

Lightweights

1896-1899 Kid Lavigne
1899-1902 Frank Erne
1902-1908 Joe Gans
1908-1910 Battling Nelson
1910-1912 Ad Wolgast
1912-1914 Willie Ritchie
1914-1917 Freddie Welsh
1917-1925 Benny Leonard*
1925 Jimmy Goodrich; Rocky Kansas
1926-1930 Sammy Mandell
1930 Al Singer; Tony Canzoneri
1930-1933 Tony Canzoneri
1933-1935 Barney Ross*
1935-1936 Tony Canzoneri
1936-1938 Lou Ambers
1938 Henry Armstrong
1939 Lou Ambers
1940 Lew Jenkins
1941-1943 Sammy Angott
1944 S. Angott (NBA); J. Zurita (NBA)
1945-1951 Ike Williams (NBA: later universal)
1951-1952 James Carter
1952 Lauro Salas; James Carter
1953-1954 James Carter
1954 Paddy De Marco; James Carter
1955 James Carter; Bud Smith
1956 Bud Smith; Joe Brown
1956-1962 Joe Brown
1962-1965 Carlos Ortiz
1965 Ismael Laguna
1965-1968 Carlos Ortiz
1968-1969 Teo Cruz
1969-1970 Mando Ramos
1970 Ismael Laguna; Ken Buchanan (WBA)
1971 Mando Ramos (WBC); Pedro Carrasco (WBC)
1972-1979 Roberto Duran* (WBA)
1972 Pedro Carrasco; Mando Ramos; Chango Carmona; Rodolfo Gonzalez (all WBC)
1974-1976 Guts Ishimatsu (WBC)
1976-1977 Esteban De Jesus (WBC)
1979 Jim Watt (WBC); Ernesto Espana (WBA)
1980 Hilmer Kenty (WBA)
1981 Alexis Arguello (WBC); Sean O'Grady (WBA); Arturo Frias (WBA)
1982-1984 Ray Mancini (WBA)
1983 Edwin Rosario (WBC)
1984 Livingstone Bramble (WBA); Jose Luis Ramirez (WBC)
1985 Hector (Macho) Camacho (WBC)
1986 Edwin Rosario (WBA); Jose Luis Ramirez (WBC)

1987	Julio Cesar Chavez (WBA)
1989	Edwin Rosario (WBA); Pernell Whitaker (WBC)
1990	Juan Nazario (WBA); Pernell Whitaker (WBA)
1992	Joey Gamache (WBA)
1992	Tony Lopez (WBA); Miguel Angel Gonzalez (WBC)
1993	Dingaan Thobela (WBA); Nazarov Olzubek (WBA)

Featherweights

1892-1900	George Dixon (disputed)
1900-1901	Terry McGovern; Young Corbett*
1901-1912	Abe Attell
1912-1923	Johnny Kilbane
1923	Eugene Criqui; Johnny Dundee
1923-1925	Johnny Dundee*
1925-1927	Kid Kaplan*
1927-1928	Benny Bass; Tony Canzoneri
1928-1929	Andre Routis
1929-1932	Battling Battalino*
1932-1934	Tommy Paul (NBA)
1933-1936	Freddie Miller
1936-1937	Petey Sarron
1937-1938	Henry Armstrong*
1938-1940	Joey Archibald (a)
1940-41	Harry Jeffra
1942-1948	Willie Pep
1948-1949	Sandy Saddler
1949-1950	Willie Pep
1950-1957	Sandy Saddler*
1957-1959	Hogan (Kid) Bassey
1959-1963	Davey Moore
1963-1964	Sugar Ramos
1964-1967	Vicente Saldivar*
1968-1971	Paul Rojas (WBA); Sho Saijo (WBA)
1971	Antonio Gomez (WBA); Kuniaki Shibada (WBC)
1972	Ernesto Marcel* (WBA); Clemente Sanchez* (WBC); Jose Legra (WBC)
1973	Eder Jofre (WBC)
1974	Ruben Olivares (WBA); Alexis Arguello (WBA); Bobby Chacon (WBC)
1975	Ruben Olivares (WBC); David Kotey (WBC)
1976	Danny Lopez (WBC)
1977	Rafael Ortega (WBA)
1978	Cecilio Lastra (WBA); Eusebio Pedrosa (WBA)
1980	Salvador Sanchez (WBC)
1982	Juan LaPorte (WBC)
1984	Wilfredo Gomez (WBC); Azumah Nelson (WBC)
1985	Barry McGuigan (WBA)
1986	Steve Cruz (WBA)
1987	Antonio Esparragoza (WBA)
1988	Jeff Fenech (WBC)
1990	Marcos Villasana (WBC)
1991	Park Yung Kyun (WBA)
1991	Paul Hodkinson (WBC)
1993	Goyo Vargas (WBC); Kevin Kelley (WBC); Eloy Rojas (WBA)

(a) After Petey Scalzo knocked out Archibald in an overweight match and was refused a title bout, the NBA named Scalzo champion. The NBA title succession: Scalzo, 1938-1941; Richard Lemos, 1941; Jackie Wilson, 1941-1943; Jackie Callura, 1943; Phil Terranova, 1943-1944; Sal Bartolo, 1944-1946.

History of Heavyweight Championship Bouts

(Bouts in which title changed hands)

1889—July 8—John L. Sullivan def. Jake Kilrain, 75, Richburg, Miss. Last championship bare knuckles bout.

1892—Sept. 7—James J. Corbett def. John L. Sullivan, 21, New Orleans. Big gloves used for first time.

1897—Bob Fitzsimmons def. James J. Corbett, 14, Carson City, Nev.

1899—June 9—James J. Jeffries def. Bob Fitzsimmons, 11, Coney Island, N.Y.

1905—James J. Jeffries retired, July 3—Marvin Hart KOd Jack Root, 12, Reno. Jeffries refereed and presented the title to the victor. Jack O'Brien also claimed the title.

1906—Feb. 23—Tommy Burns def. Marvin Hart, 20, Los Angeles.

1908—Dec. 26—Jack Johnson KOd Tommy Burns, 14, Sydney, Australia. Police halted contest.

1915—April 5—Jess Willard KOd Jack Johnson, 26, Havana. Cuba.

1919—July 4—Jack Dempsey KOd Jess Willard, Toledo, Oh. Willard failed to answer bell for 4th round.

1926—Sept. 23—Gene Tunney def. Jack Dempsey, 10, Philadelphia.

1930—June 12—Max Schmeling def. Jack Sharkey, 4, New York. Sharkey fouled Schmeling in a bout which was generally considered to have resulted in the election of a successor to Gene Tunney, New York.

1932—June 21—Jack Sharkey def. Max Schmeling, 15, New York.

1933—June 29— Primo Carnera KOd Jack Sharkey, 6, New York.

1934—June 14—Max Baer KOd Primo Carnera, 11, New York.

1935—June 13—James J. Braddock def. Max Baer, 15, New York.

1937—June 22—Joe Louis KOd James J. Braddock, 8, Chicago.

1949—June 22—Following Joe Louis' retirement Ezzard Charles def. Joe Walcott, 15, Chicago, NBA recognition only.

1951—July 18—Joe Walcott KOd Ezzard Charles, 7, Pittsburgh.

1952—Sept. 23—Rocky Marciano KOd Joe Walcott, 13, Philadelphia.

1956—Nov. 30—Floyd Patterson KOd Archie Moore, 5, Chicago.

1959—June 26—Ingemar Johansson KOd Floyd Patterson, 3, New York.

1960—June 20—Floyd Patterson KOd Ingemar Johansson, 5, New York. First heavyweight in boxing history to regain title.

1962—Sept. 25—Sonny Liston KOd Floyd Patterson, 1, Chicago.

1964—Feb. 25—Cassius Clay KOd Sonny Liston, 7, Miami Beach.

1967—Clay was stripped of his title by the WBA and others for refusing military service.

1970—Feb. 16—Joe Frazier KOd Jimmy Ellis, 5, New York.

1971—Mar. 8—Joe Frazier def. Cassius Clay (Muhammad Ali), 15, New York.

1973—Jan. 22—George Foreman KOd Joe Frazier, 2, Kingston, Jamaica.

1974—Oct. 30—Muhammad Ali KOd George Foreman, 8, Zaire.

1978—Feb. 15—Leon Spinks def. Muhammad Ali, 15, Las Vegas.

1978—June 9—(WBC) Larry Holmes def. Ken Norton, 15, Las Vegas.

1978—Sept. 15—(WBA) Muhammad Ali def. Leon Spinks, 15, New Orleans. Ali retired in 1979.

1980—Mar. 31—(WBA) Mike Weaver KOd John Tate, 15, Knoxville.

1982—Dec. 10—(WBA) Michael Dokes KOd Mike Weaver, 1, Las Vegas.

1983—Sept. 23—(WBA) Gerrie Coetzee KOd Michael Dokes, 10, Richfield, Oh.

1984—Mar. 10—(WBC) Tim Witherspoon def. Greg Page, 12, Las Vegas, Nev.

1984—Aug. 31—(WBC) Pinklon Thomas def. Tim Witherspoon, 12, Las Vegas, Nev.

1984—Dec. 2—(WBA) Greg Page KOd Gerrie Coetzee, 8, Sun City, Bophuthatswana

1985—Apr. 29—(WBA) Tony Tubbs def. Greg Page, 15, Buffalo, N.Y.

1985—Sept. 21—(IBF) Michael Spinks def. Larry Holmes, 15, Las Vegas, Nev.

1986—Jan. 17—(WBA) Tim Witherspoon def. Tony Tubbs, 15, Atlanta, Ga.

1986—Mar. 23—(WBC) Trevor Berbick def. Pinklon Thomas, 12, Miami, Fla.

1986—Nov. 22—(WBC) Mike Tyson KOd Trevor Berbick, 2, Las Vegas.

1986—Dec. 12—(WBA) James (Bonecrusher) Smith KOd Tim Witherspoon, 1, New York.

1987—Mar. 7—(WBA) Mike Tyson def. James (Bonecrusher) Smith, 12, Las Vegas.

1988—June 27—(IBF) Mike Tyson KOd Michael Spinks, 1, Atlantic City.

1990—Feb. 11—(WBA, WBC, IBF) James "Buster" Douglas KOd Mike Tyson, 10, Tokyo.

1990—Oct. 25—(WBA, WBC, IBF) Evander Holyfield KOd James "Buster" Douglas, 3, Las Vegas.

1992—Nov. 13—(WBA, WBC, IBF) Riddick Bowe def. Evander Holyfield, 12, Las Vegas. Lennox Lewis was named WBC champion when Bowe refused to fight him.

1993—Nov. 6—(WBA, IBF) Evander Holyfield def. Riddick Bowe, 12, Las Vegas.

1994—Apr. 22—(WBA, IBF) Michael Moorer def. Evander Holyfield, 12, Las Vegas.

1994—Sept. 24—(WBC) Oliver McCall KOd Lennox Lewis, 2, London.

1994—Nov. 5—(WBA, IBF) George Foreman KOd Michael Moorer, 10, Las Vegas.

Pro Rodeo Championship Standings in 1993

Event	Winner	Money won
All Around	Ty Murray, Stephenville, Tex. . .	$297,896
Saddle Bronc	Dan Mortenson, Manhattan, Kan.	$150,062
Bareback	Deb Greenough, Red Lodge, Mont.	$128,740
Bull Riding	Ty Murray, Stephenville, Tex. . .	$124,563
Calf Roping	Joe Beaver, Huntsville, Tex. . . .	$122,863
Steer Wrestling	Steve Duhon, Opelousas, La. . .	$113,450
Steer Roping	Guy Allen, Vinita, Okla.	$ 52,322
Team Roping	Bobby Hurley, Clarksville, Ark. . .	$ 86,858
Women's Barrel Racing	Charmayne Rodman, Galt, Cal. .	$103,609

Pro Rodeo Cowboy All Around Champions

Year	Winner	Money won
1972	Phil Lyne, George West, Tex. . . .	$60,852
1973	Larry Mahan, Dallas, Tex.	64,447
1974	Tom Ferguson, Miami, Okla. . . .	66,929
1975	Leo Camarillo, Oakdale, Cal. . . .	50,300
	Tom Ferguson, Miami, Okla. . . .	50,300
1976	Tom Ferguson, Miami, Okla. . . .	87,908
1977	Tom Ferguson, Miami, Okla. . . .	76,730
1978	Tom Ferguson, Miami, Okla. . . .	103,734
1979	Tom Ferguson, Miami, Okla. . . .	96,272
1980	Paul Tierney, Rapid City, S.D. . .	105,568
1981	Jimmie Cooper, Monument, N.M.	105,862
1982	Chris Lybbert, Coyote, Cal.	123,709
1983	Roy Cooper, Durant, Okla.	$153,391
1984	Dee Pickett, Caldwell, Ida.	122,618
1985	Lewis Feild, Elk Ridge, Ut.	130,347
1986	Lewis Feild, Elk Ridge, Ut.	166,042
1987	Lewis Feild, Elk Ridge, Ut.	144,335
1988	Dave Appleton, Arlington, Tex. . .	121,546
1989	Ty Murray, Odessa, Tex.	134,806
1990	Ty Murray, Stephenville, Tex. . . .	213,772
1991	Ty Murray, Stephenville, Tex. . . .	244,230
1992	Ty Murray, Stephenville, Tex. . . .	225,992
1993	Ty Murray, Stephenville, Tex. . . .	297,896

The America's Cup

In the 1992 America's Cup match the United States yacht *America^3* defeated the Italian yacht *Il Moro di Venezia* 4-1 in the waters off San Diego, CA. *America^3* was skippered by Bill Koch. The next America's Cup competition is scheduled for 1995 in San Diego.

Competition for the America's Cup grew out of the first contest to establish a world yachting championship, one of the carnival features of the London Exposition of 1851. The race, open to all classes of yachts from all over the world, covered a 60-mile course around the Isle of Wight; the prize was a cup worth about $500, donated by the Royal Yacht Squadron of England, known as the "America's Cup" because it was first won by the United States yacht *America.*

Winners of the America's Cup

1851 America
1870 Magic defeated Cambria, England, (1-0)
1871 Columbia (first three races) and Sappho (last two races) defeated Livonia, England, (4-1)
1876 Madeline defeated Countess of Dufferin, Canada, (2-0)
1881 Mischief defeated Atalanta, Canada, (2-0)
1885 Puritan defeated Genesta, England, (2-0)
1886 Mayflower defeated Galatea, England, (2-0)
1887 Volunteer defeated Thistle, Scotland, (2-0)
1893 Vigilant defeated Valkyrie II, England, (3-0)
1895 Defender defeated Valkyrie III, England, (3-0)
1899 Columbia defeated Shamrock, England, (3-0)
1901 Columbia defeated Shamrock II, England, (3-0)
1903 Reliance defeated Shamrock III, England, (3-0)
1920 Resolute defeated Shamrock IV, England, (3-2)
1930 Enterprise defeated Shamrock V, England, (4-0)
1934 Rainbow defeated Endeavour, England, (4-2)
1937 Ranger defeated Endeavour II, England, (4-0)
1958 Columbia defeated Sceptre, England, (4-0)
1962 Weatherly defeated Gretel, Australia, (4-1)
1964 Constellation defeated Sovereign, England, (4-0)
1967 Intrepid defeated Dame Pattie, Australia, (4-0)
1970 Intrepid defeated Gretel II, Australia, (4-1)
1974 Courageous defeated Southern Cross, Australia, (4-0)
1977 Courageous defeated Australia, Australia, (4-0)
1980 Freedom defeated Australia, Australia, (4-1)
1983 Australia II, Australia defeated Liberty, (4-3)
1987 Stars & Stripes defeated Kookaburra III, Australia, (4-0)
1988 Stars & Stripes defeated New Zealand, New Zealand, (2-0)
1992 America^3 defeated Il Moro di Venezia, Italy, (4-1)

The World Cup

In 1994 the World Cup, emblematic of international soccer supremacy, was held in the U.S. for the first time. Brazil captured an unprecedented 4th World Cup by defeating Italy on July 17, 1994, at the Rose Bowl in Pasadena Calif. For the first time ever, the final was decided in the tie-breaking, penalty-kick round, in which Brazil outscored Italy 3-2, after neither team had been able to score in 90 minutes of regulation time and an additional 30 minutes of extra time. The 1998 World Cup is scheduled to be held in France. Winners and sites of all World Cup tournaments follow:

Year	Winner	Final opponent	Site
1930	Uruguay	Argentina	Uruguay
1934	Italy	Czechoslovakia	Italy
1938	Italy	Hungary	France
1950	Uruguay	Brazil	Brazil
1954	W. Germany	Hungary	Switzerland
1958	Brazil	Sweden	Sweden
1962	Brazil	Czechoslovakia	Chile
1966	England	W. Germany	England
1970	Brazil	Italy	Mexico
1974	W. Germany	Netherlands	W. Germany
1978	Argentina	Netherlands	Argentina
1982	Italy	W. Germany	Spain
1986	Argentina	W. Germany	Mexico
1990	W. Germany	Argentina	Italy
1994	Brazil	Italy	U.S.

1994 World Cup Tournament

Germany, as the defending champion, and the United States, as the host country, received automatic berths in the 1994 World Cup finals. More than 100 national teams competed for the remaining 22 slots. The 24 finalists were divided into 6 groups for the first round, a round robin in which each team played 3 different teams from its group. The top 2 finishers from each group, along with the 4 teams with the next best records, advanced into the single elimination rounds.

The games were played at the following 9 sites: the Rose Bowl in Pasadena, Calif.; Giants Stadium in East Rutherford, N.J.; Foxboro Stadium in Foxboro, Mass.; the Cotton Bowl in Dallas, Tex.; the Citrus Bowl in Orlando, Fla.; RFK Stadium in Washington, D.C.; the Silverdome in Pontiac, Mich.; Stanford Stadium in Palo Alto, Calif.; and Soldier Field in Chicago.

1994 World Cup — First Round

Group A
U.S. 2, Colombia 1
U.S. 1, Switzerland 1
Romania 1, U.S. 0
Romania 3, Colombia 1
Switzerland 4, Romania 1
Colombia 2, Switzerland 0

Group B
Cameroon 2, Sweden 2
Brazil 2, Russia 0
Brzail 3, Cameroon 0
Sweden 3, Russia 1
Russia 6, Cameroon 1
Brazil 1, Sweden 1

Group C
Germany 1, Bolivia 0
Spain 2, South Korea 2
Germany 1, Spain 1
South Korea 0, Bolivia 0
Germany 3, South Korea 2
Spain 3, Bolivia 1

Group D
Argentina 4, Greece 0
Nigeria 3, Bulgaria 0
Argentina 2, Nigeria 1
Bulgaria 4, Greece 0
Nigeria 2, Greece 0
Bulgaria 2, Argentina 0

Group E
Ireland 1, Italy 0
Norway 1, Mexico 0
Italy 1, Norway 0
Mexico 2, Ireland 1
Ireland 0, Norway 0
Italy 1, Mexico 1

Group F
Belgium 1, Morocco 0
Netherlands 2, Saudi Arabia 1
Belgium 1, Netherlands 0
Saudi Arabia 2, Morocco 1
Netherlands 2, Morocco 1
Saudi Arabia 1, Belgium 0

1994 World Cup — Elimination Rounds

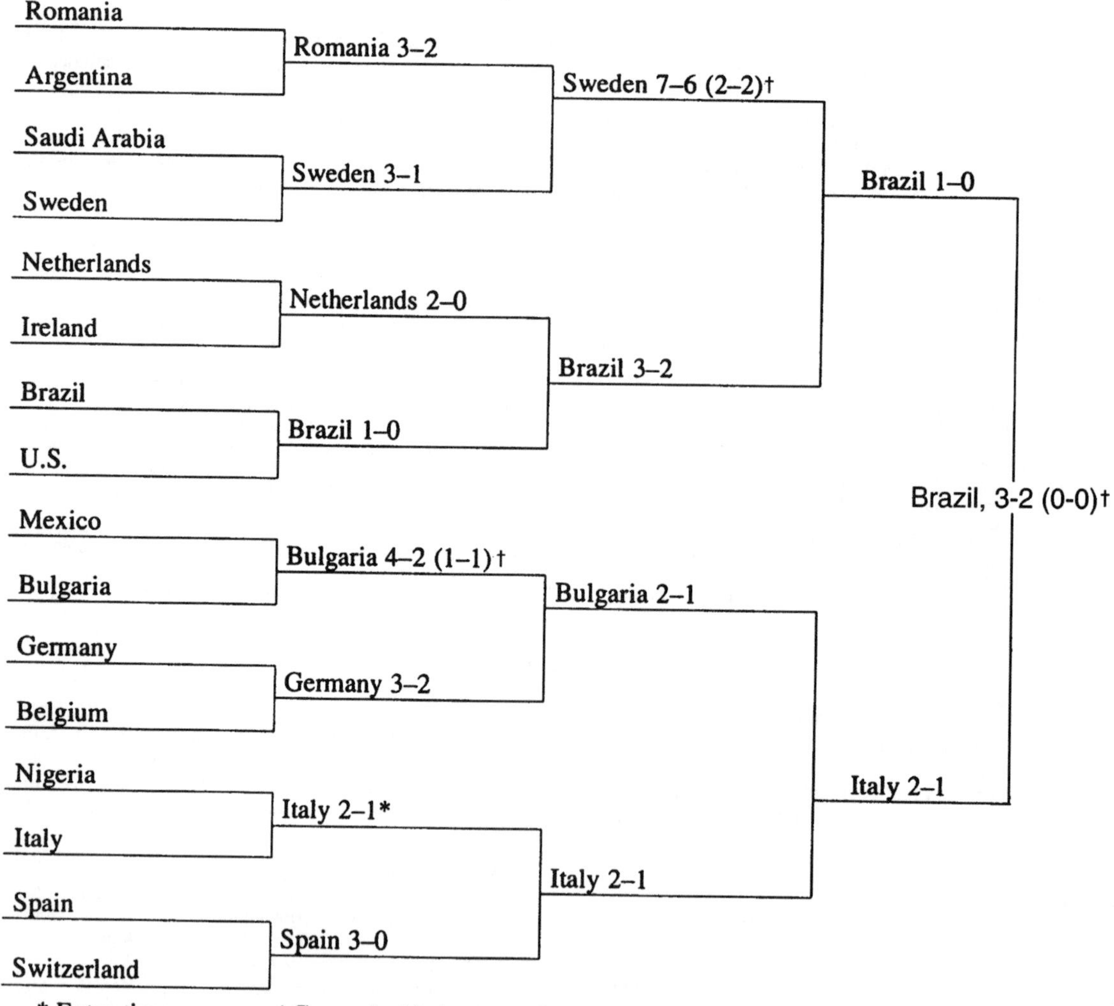

* Extra-time game. † Game decided on penalty kicks.

BASEBALL

Strike Ends 1994 Season, Kills Playoffs and World Series

Acting Major League Baseball Commissioner Allan H. (Bud) Selig announced the end of the 1994 baseball season at a Sept. 14, 1994, press conference in Milwaukee, WI. The players had gone on strike after the games of Aug. 11 over owner plans to impose a salary cap. Intermittent negotiations between the two sides served only to underline the differences in their positions.

The strike was the eighth work stoppage in 22 years, but it was the first to result in the cancellation of the full remainder of the season and the postseason. It marked the first time since 1904 that there would be no World Series. The strike ended a promising season, in which a number of historic records might have fallen. Matt Williams was the closest of several players within striking distance of Roger Maris's record 61 home runs in a season, Tony Gwynn was hitting just below .400, and Frank Thomas and Albert Belle were contending for a possible AL Triple Crown (best in home runs, runs batted in, and batting average). Just over two-thirds of the scheduled 162 games were played. League leaders and award winners are marked with an asterisk (*) in this section to denote the shortened season.

Major League Pennant Winners, 1901–1994

	National League						American League				
Year	**Winner**	**Won**	**Lost**	**Pct**	**Manager**	**Year**	**Winner**	**Won**	**Lost**	**Pct**	**Manager**
1901	Pittsburgh	90	49	**.647**	Clarke	1901	Chicago	83	53	**.610**	Griffith
1902	Pittsburgh	103	36	**.741**	Clarke	1902	Philadelphia	83	53	**.610**	Mack
1903	Pittsburgh	91	49	**.650**	Clarke	1903	Boston	91	47	**.659**	Collins
1904	New York	106	47	**.693**	McGraw	1904	Boston	95	59	**.617**	Collins
1905	New York	105	48	**.686**	McGraw	1905	Philadelphia	92	56	**.622**	Mack
1906	Chicago	116	36	**.763**	Chance	1906	Chicago	93	58	**.616**	Jones
1907	Chicago	107	45	**.704**	Chance	1907	Detroit	92	58	**.613**	Jennings
1908	Chicago	99	55	**.643**	Chance	1908	Detroit	90	63	**.588**	Jennings
1909	Pittsburgh	110	42	**.724**	Clarke	1909	Detroit	98	54	**.645**	Jennings
1910	Chicago	104	50	**.675**	Chance	1910	Philadelphia	102	48	**.680**	Mack
1911	New York	99	54	**.647**	McGraw	1911	Philadelphia	101	50	**.669**	Mack
1912	New York	103	48	**.682**	McGraw	1912	Boston	105	47	**.691**	Stahl
1913	New York	101	51	**.664**	McGraw	1913	Philadelphia	96	57	**.627**	Mack
1914	Boston	94	59	**.614**	Stallings	1914	Philadelphia	99	53	**.651**	Mack
1915	Philadelphia	90	62	**.592**	Moran	1915	Boston	101	50	**.669**	Carrigan
1916	Brooklyn	94	60	**.610**	Robinson	1916	Boston	91	63	**.591**	Carrigan
1917	New York	98	56	**.636**	McGraw	1917	Chicago	100	54	**.649**	Rowland
1918	Chicago	84	45	**.651**	Mitchell	1918	Boston	75	51	**.595**	Barrow
1919	Cincinnati	96	44	**.686**	Moran	1919	Chicago	88	52	**.629**	Gleason
1920	Brooklyn	93	60	**.604**	Robinson	1920	Cleveland	98	56	**.636**	Speaker
1921	New York	94	56	**.614**	McGraw	1921	New York	98	55	**.641**	Huggins
1922	New York	93	61	**.604**	McGraw	1922	New York	94	60	**.610**	Huggins
1923	New York	95	58	**.621**	McGraw	1923	New York	98	54	**.645**	Huggins
1924	New York	93	60	**.608**	McGraw	1924	Washington	92	62	**.597**	Harris
1925	Pittsburgh	95	58	**.621**	McKechnie	1925	Washington	96	55	**.636**	Harris
1926	St. Louis	89	65	**.578**	Hornsby	1926	New York	91	63	**.591**	Huggins
1927	Pittsburgh	94	60	**.610**	Bush	1927	New York	110	44	**.714**	Huggins
1928	St. Louis	95	59	**.617**	McKechnie	1928	New York	101	53	**.656**	Huggins
1929	Chicago	98	54	**.645**	McCarthy	1929	Philadelphia	104	46	**.693**	Mack
1930	St. Louis	92	62	**.597**	Street	1930	Philadelphia	102	52	**.662**	Mack
1931	St. Louis	101	53	**.656**	Street	1931	Philadelphia	107	45	**.704**	Mack
1932	Chicago	90	64	**.584**	Grimm	1932	New York	107	47	**.695**	McCarthy
1933	New York	91	61	**.599**	Terry	1933	Washington	99	53	**.651**	Cronin
1934	St. Louis	95	58	**.621**	Frisch	1934	Detroit	101	53	**.656**	Cochrane
1935	Chicago	100	54	**.649**	Grimm	1935	Detroit	93	58	**.616**	Cochrane
1936	New York	91	62	**.597**	Terry	1936	New York	102	51	**.667**	McCarthy
1937	New York	95	57	**.625**	Terry	1937	New York	102	52	**.662**	McCarthy
1938	Chicago	89	63	**.586**	Hartnett	1938	New York	99	53	**.651**	McCarthy
1939	Cincinnati	97	57	**.630**	McKechnie	1939	New York	106	45	**.702**	McCarthy
1940	Cincinnati	100	53	**.654**	McKechnie	1940	Detroit	90	64	**.584**	Baker
1941	Brooklyn	100	54	**.649**	Durocher	1941	New York	101	53	**.656**	McCarthy
1942	St. Louis	106	48	**.688**	Southworth	1942	New York	103	51	**.669**	McCarthy
1943	St. Louis	105	49	**.682**	Southworth	1943	New York	98	56	**.636**	McCarthy
1944	St. Louis	105	49	**.682**	Southworth	1944	St. Louis	89	65	**.578**	Sewell
1945	Chicago	98	56	**.636**	Grimm	1945	Detroit	88	65	**.575**	O'Neill
1946	St. Louis	98	58	**.628**	Dyer	1946	Boston	104	50	**.675**	Cronin
1947	Brooklyn	94	60	**.610**	Shotton	1947	New York	97	57	**.630**	Harris
1948	Boston	91	62	**.595**	Southworth	1948	Cleveland	97	58	**.626**	Boudreau
1949	Brooklyn	97	57	**.630**	Shotton	1949	New York	97	57	**.630**	Stengel
1950	Philadelphia	91	63	**.591**	Sawyer	1950	New York	98	56	**.636**	Stengel
1951	New York	98	59	**.624**	Durocher	1951	New York	98	56	**.636**	Stengel
1952	Brooklyn	96	57	**.627**	Dressen	1952	New York	95	59	**.617**	Stengel
1953	Brooklyn	105	49	**.682**	Dressen	1953	New York	99	52	**.656**	Stengel
1954	New York	97	57	**.630**	Durocher	1954	Cleveland	111	43	**.721**	Lopez
1955	Brooklyn	98	55	**.641**	Alston	1955	New York	96	58	**.623**	Stengel
1956	Brooklyn	93	61	**.604**	Alston	1956	New York	97	57	**.630**	Stengel
1957	Milwaukee	95	59	**.617**	Haney	1957	New York	98	56	**.636**	Stengel
1958	Milwaukee	92	62	**.597**	Haney	1958	New York	92	62	**.597**	Stengel
1959	Los Angeles	88	68	**.564**	Alston	1959	Chicago	94	60	**.610**	Lopez
1960	Pittsburgh	95	59	**.617**	Murtaugh	1960	New York	97	57	**.630**	Stengel
1961	Cincinnati	93	61	**.604**	Hutchinson	1961	New York	109	53	**.673**	Houk
1962	San Francisco	103	62	**.624**	Dark	1962	New York	96	66	**.593**	Houk
1963	Los Angeles	99	63	**.611**	Alston	1963	New York	104	57	**.646**	Houk
1964	St. Louis	93	69	**.574**	Keane	1964	New York	99	63	**.611**	Berra
1965	Los Angeles	97	65	**.599**	Alston	1965	Minnesota	102	60	**.630**	Mele
1966	Los Angeles	95	67	**.586**	Alston	1966	Baltimore	97	63	**.606**	Bauer
1967	St. Louis	101	60	**.627**	Schoendienst	1967	Boston	92	70	**.568**	Williams
1968	St. Louis	97	65	**.599**	Schoendienst	1968	Detroit	103	59	**.636**	Smith

National League

Year	East Winner	W	L	Pct	Manager	West Winner	W	L	Pct	Manager	Playoff winner
1969	N.Y. Mets	100	62	**.617**	Hodges	Atlanta	93	69	**.574**	Harris	New York
1970	Pittsburgh	89	73	**.549**	Murtaugh	Cincinnati	102	60	**.630**	Anderson	Cincinnati
1971	Pittsburgh	97	65	**.599**	Murtaugh	San Francisco	90	72	**.556**	Fox	Pittsburgh
1972	Pittsburgh	96	59	**.619**	Virdon	Cincinnati	95	59	**.617**	Anderson	Cincinnati
1973	N.Y. Mets	82	79	**.509**	Berra	Cincinnati	99	63	**.611**	Anderson	New York
1974	Pittsburgh	88	74	**.543**	Murtaugh	Los Angeles	102	60	**.630**	Alston	Los Angeles
1975	Pittsburgh	92	69	**.571**	Murtaugh	Cincinnati	108	54	**.667**	Anderson	Cincinnati
1976	Philadelphia	101	61	**.623**	Ozark	Cincinnati	102	60	**.630**	Anderson	Cincinnati
1977	Philadelphia	101	61	**.623**	Ozark	Los Angeles	98	64	**.605**	Lasorda	Los Angeles
1978	Philadelphia	90	72	**.556**	Ozark	Los Angeles	95	67	**.586**	Lasorda	Los Angeles
1979	Pittsburgh	98	64	**.605**	Tanner	Cincinnati	90	71	**.559**	McNamara	Pittsburgh
1980	Philadelphia	91	71	**.562**	Green	Houston	93	70	**.571**	Virdon	Philadelphia
1981(a)	Philadelphia	34	21	**.618**	Green	Los Angeles	36	21	**.632**	Lasorda	(c)
1981(b)	Montreal	30	23	**.566**	Williams, Fanning	Houston	33	20	**.623**	Virdon	Los Angeles
1982	St. Louis	92	70	**.568**	Herzog	Atlanta	89	73	**.549**	Torre	St. Louis
1983	Philadelphia	90	72	**.556**	Corrales, Owens	Los Angeles	91	71	**.562**	Lasorda	Philadelphia
1984	Chicago	96	65	**.596**	Frey	San Diego	92	70	**.568**	Williams	San Diego
1985	St. Louis	101	61	**.623**	Herzog	Los Angeles	95	67	**.586**	Lasorda	St. Louis
1986	N.Y. Mets	108	54	**.667**	Johnson	Houston	96	66	**.593**	Lanier	New York
1987	St. Louis	95	67	**.586**	Herzog	San Francisco	90	72	**.556**	Craig	St. Louis
1988	N.Y. Mets	100	60	**.625**	Johnson	Los Angeles	94	67	**.584**	Lasorda	Los Angeles4
1989	Chicago	93	69	**.571**	Zimmer	San Francisco	92	70	**.568**	Craig	San Francisco
1990	Pittsburgh	95	67	**.586**	Leyland	Cincinnati	91	71	**.562**	Piniella	Cincinnati4
1991	Pittsburgh	98	64	**.605**	Leyland	Atlanta	94	68	**.580**	Cox	Atlanta
1992	Pittsburgh	96	66	**.593**	Leyland	Atlanta	98	64	**.605**	Cox	Atlanta
1993	Philadelphia	97	65	**.599**	Fregosi	Atlanta	104	58	**.642**	Cox	Philadelphia
1994	No pennants										

American League

Year	East Winner	W	L	Pct	Manager	West Winner	W	L	Pct	Manager	Playoff winner
1969	Baltimore	109	53	**.673**	Weaver	Minnesota	97	65	**.599**	Martin	Baltimore
1970	Baltimore	108	54	**.667**	Weaver	Minnesota	98	64	**.605**	Rigney	Baltimore
1971	Baltimore	101	57	**.639**	Weaver	Oakland	101	60	**.627**	Williams	Baltimore
1972	Detroit	86	70	**.551**	Martin	Oakland	93	62	**.600**	Williams	Oakland
1973	Baltimore	97	65	**.599**	Weaver	Oakland	94	68	**.580**	Williams	Oakland
1974	Baltimore	91	71	**.562**	Weaver	Oakland	90	72	**.556**	Dark	Oakland
1975	Boston	95	65	**.594**	Johnson	Oakland	98	64	**.605**	Dark	Boston
1976	New York	97	62	**.610**	Martin	Kansas City	90	72	**.556**	Herzog	New York
1977	New York	100	62	**.617**	Martin	Kansas City	102	60	**.630**	Herzog	New York
1978	New York	100	63	**.613**	Martin, Lemon	Kansas City	92	70	**.568**	Herzog	New York
1979	Baltimore	102	57	**.642**	Weaver	California	88	74	**.543**	Fregosi	Baltimore
1980	New York	103	59	**.636**	Howser	Kansas City	97	65	**.599**	Frey	Kansas City
1981(a)	New York	34	22	**.607**	Michael	Oakland	37	23	**.617**	Martin	(d)
1981(b)	Milwaukee	31	22	**.585**	Rodgers	Kansas City	30	23	**.566**	Frey, Howser	New York
1982	Milwaukee	95	67	**.586**	Rodgers, Kuenn	California	93	69	**.574**	Mauch	Milwaukee
1983	Baltimore	98	64	**.605**	Altobelli	Chicago	99	63	**.611**	LaRussa	Baltimore
1984	Detroit	104	58	**.642**	Anderson	Kansas City	84	78	**.519**	Howser	Detroit
1985	Toronto	99	62	**.615**	Cox	Kansas City	91	71	**.562**	Howser	Kansas City
1986	Boston	95	66	**.590**	McNamara	California	92	70	**.568**	Mauch	Boston
1987	Detroit	98	64	**.605**	Anderson	Minnesota	85	77	**.525**	Kelly	Minnesota
1988	Boston	89	73	**.549**	McNamara, Morgan	Oakland	104	58	**.642**	LaRussa	Oakland
1989	Toronto	89	73	**.549**	Williams, Gaston	Oakland	99	63	**.611**	LaRussa	Oakland
1990	Boston	88	74	**.543**	Morgan	Oakland	103	59	**.636**	LaRussa	Oakland
1991	Toronto	91	71	**.562**	Gaston	Minnesota	95	67	**.586**	Kelly	Minnesota
1992	Toronto	96	66	**.593**	Gaston	Oakland	96	66	**.593**	LaRussa	Toronto
1993	Toronto	95	67	**.586**	Gaston	Chicago	94	68	**.580**	Lamont	Toronto
1994	No pennants										

(a) First half; (b) Second half; (c) Montreal and L.A. won the divisional playoffs; (d) N.Y. and Oakland won the divisional playoffs.

The Sporting News Gold Glove Awards in 1993

National League

Mark Grace, Chicago, first base
Robby Thompson, San Francisco, second base
Matt Williams, San Francisco, third base
Jay Bell, Pittsburgh, shortstop
Barry Bonds, San Francisco, outfield
Larry Walker, Montreal, outfield
Marquis Grissom, Montreal, outfield
Kirt Manwaring, San Francisco, catcher
Greg Maddux, Atlanta, pitcher

American League

Don Mattingly, New York, first base
Roberto Alomar, Toronto, second base
Robin Ventura, Chicago, third base
Omar Vizquel, Seattle, shortstop
Ken Griffey Jr., Seattle, outfield
Devon White, Toronto, outfield
Kenny Lofton, Cleveland, outfield
Ivan Rodriguez, Texas, catcher
Mark Langston, California, pitcher

The following are the players at each position who have won the most Gold Gloves since the award was instituted in 1957.

First base:	Keith Hernandez	11
	Don Mattingly	8
	George Scott	8
Second base:	Ryne Sandberg	9
	Bill Mazeroski	8
	Frank White	8
Third base:	Brooks Robinson	16
	Mike Schmidt	10
Shortstop:	Ozzie Smith	13
	Luis Aparicio	9
Outfield:	Roberto Clemente	12
	Willie Mays	12
	Al Kaline	10
	Paul Blair	8
	Dwight Evans	8
	Garry Maddox	8
Catcher:	Johnny Bench	10
	Bob Boone	7
Pitcher:	Jim Kaat	16
	Bob Gibson	9

Home Run Leaders

National League			American League		
Year	Player, Club	HR	Year	Player, Club	HR
1901	Sam Crawford, Cincinnati	16	1901	Napoleon Lajoie, Philadelphia	14
1902	Thomas Leach, Pittsburgh	6	1902	Socks Seybold, Philadelphia	16
1903	James Sheckard, Brooklyn	9	1903	Buck Freeman, Boston	13
1904	Harry Lumley, Brooklyn	9	1904	Harry Davis, Philadelphia	10
1905	Fred Odwell, Cincinnati	9	1905	Harry Davis, Philadelphia	8
1906	Timothy Jordan, Brooklyn	12	1906	Harry Davis, Philadelphia	12
1907	David Brain, Boston	10	1907	Harry Davis, Philadelphia	8
1908	Timothy Jordan, Brooklyn	12	1908	Sam Crawford, Detroit	7
1909	Red Murray, New York	7	1909	Ty Cobb, Detroit	9
1910	Fred Beck, Bos., Frank Schulte, Chi.	10	1910	Jake Stahl, Boston	10
1911	Frank Schulte, Chicago	21	1911	J. Franklin Baker, Philadelphia	11
1912	Henry Zimmerman, Chicago	14	1912	J. Franklin Baker, Philadelphia, Tris Speaker, Boston	10
1913	Gavvy Cravath, Philadelphia	19	1913	J. Franklin, Baker, Philadelphia	12
1914	Gavvy Cravath, Philadelphia	19	1914	J. Franklin, Baker, Philadelphia	9
1915	Gavvy Cravath, Philadelphia	24	1915	Robert Roth, Chicago-Cleveland	7
1916	Dave Robertson, N.Y., Fred (Cy) Williams, Chi.	12	1916	Wally Pipp, New York	12
1917	Dave Robertson, N.Y., Gavvy Cravath, Phil.	12	1917	Wally Pipp, New York	9
1918	Gavvy Cravath, Philadelphia	8	1918	Babe Ruth, Bos., Tilly Walker, Phil.	11
1919	Gavvy Cravath, Philadelphia	12	1919	Babe Ruth, Boston	29
1920	Cy Williams, Philadelphia	15	1920	Babe Ruth, New York	54
1921	George Kelly, New York	23	1921	Babe Ruth, New York	59
1922	Rogers Hornsby, St. Louis	42	1922	Ken Williams, St. Louis	39
1923	Cy Williams, Philadelphia	41	1923	Babe Ruth, New York	41
1924	Jacques Fournier, Brooklyn	27	1924	Babe Ruth, New York	46
1925	Rogers Hornsby, St. Louis	39	1925	Bob Meusel, New York	33
1926	Hack Wilson, Chicago	21	1926	Babe Ruth, New York	47
1927	Hack Wilson, Chicago; Cy Williams, Philadelphia.	30	1927	Babe Ruth, New York	60
1928	Hack Wilson, Chicago; Jim Bottomley, St. Louis	31	1928	Babe Ruth, New York	54
1929	Chuck Klein, Philadelphia	43	1929	Babe Ruth, New York	46
1930	Hack Wilson, Chicago	56	1930	Babe Ruth, New York	49
1931	Chuck Klein, Philadelphia	31	1931	Babe Ruth, Lou Gehrig, New York	46
1932	Chuck Klein, Philadelphia, Mel Ott, New York	38	1932	Jimmie Foxx, Philadelphia	58
1933	Chuck Klein, Philadelphia	28	1933	Jimmie Foxx, Philadelphia	48
1934	Rip Collins, St. Louis; Mel Ott, New York	35	1934	Lou Gehrig, New York	49
1935	Walter Berger, Boston	34	1935	Jimmie Foxx, Philadelphia, Hank Greenberg, Detroit	36
1936	Mel Ott, New York	33	1936	Lou Gehrig, New York	49
1937	Mel Ott, New York; Joe Medwick, St. Louis	31	1937	Joe DiMaggio, New York	46
1938	Mel Ott, New York	36	1938	Hank Greenberg, Detroit	58
1939	John Mize, St. Louis	28	1939	Jimmie Foxx, Boston	35
1940	John Mize, St. Louis	43	1940	Hank Greenberg, Detroit	41
1941	Dolph Camilli, Brooklyn	34	1941	Ted Williams, Boston	37
1942	Mel Ott, New York	30	1942	Ted Williams, Boston	36
1943	Bill Nicholson, Chicago	29	1943	Rudy York, Detroit	34
1944	Bill Nicholson, Chicago	33	1944	Nick Etten, New York	22
1945	Tommy Holmes, Boston	28	1945	Vern Stephens, St. Louis	24
1946	Ralph Kiner, Pittsburgh	23	1946	Hank Greenberg, Detroit	44
1947	Ralph Kiner, Pittsburgh; John Mize, New York.	51	1947	Ted Williams, Boston	32
1948	Ralph Kiner, Pittsburgh; John Mize, New York.	40	1948	Joe DiMaggio, New York	39
1949	Ralph Kiner, Pittsburgh	54	1949	Ted Williams, Boston	43
1950	Ralph Kiner, Pittsburgh	47	1950	Al Rosen, Cleveland	37
1951	Ralph Kiner, Pittsburgh	42	1951	Gus Zernial, Chicago-Philadelphia	33
1952	Ralph Kiner, Pittsburgh; Hank Sauer, Chicago.	37	1952	Larry Doby, Cleveland	32
1953	Ed Mathews, Milwaukee	47	1953	Al Rosen, Cleveland	43
1954	Ted Kluszewski, Cincinnati	49	1954	Larry Doby, Cleveland	32
1955	Willie Mays, New York	51	1955	Mickey Mantle, New York	37
1956	Duke Snider, Brooklyn	43	1956	Mickey Mantle, New York	52
1957	Hank Aaron, Milwaukee	44	1957	Roy Sievers, Washington	42
1958	Ernie Banks, Chicago	47	1958	Mickey Mantle, New York	42
1959	Ed Mathews, Milwaukee	46	1959	Rocky Colavito, Cleve., Harmon Killebrew, Wash.	42
1960	Ernie Banks, Chicago	41	1960	Mickey Mantle, New York	40
1961	Orlando Cepeda, San Francisco	46	1961	Roger Maris, New York	61
1962	Willie Mays, San Francisco	49	1962	Harmon Killebrew, Minnesota	48
1963	Hank Aaron, Milwaukee, Willie McCovey, S.F.	44	1963	Harmon Killebrew, Minnesota	45
1964	Willie Mays, San Francisco	47	1964	Harmon Killebrew, Minnesota	49
1965	Willie Mays, San Francisco	52	1965	Tony Conigliaro, Boston	32
1966	Hank Aaron, Atlanta	44	1966	Frank Robinson, Baltimore	49
1967	Hank Aaron, Atlanta	39	1967	Carl Yastrzemski, Boston, Harmon Killebrew, Minn.	44
1968	Willie McCovey, San Francisco	36	1968	Frank Howard, Washington	44
1969	Willie McCovey, San Francisco	45	1969	Harmon Killebrew, Minnesota	49
1970	Johnny Bench, Cincinnati	45	1970	Frank Howard, Washington	44
1971	Willie Stargell, Pittsburgh	48	1971	Bill Melton, Chicago	33
1972	Johnny Bench, Cincinnati	40	1972	Dick Allen, Chicago	37
1973	Willie Stargell, Pittsburgh	44	1973	Reggie Jackson, Oakland	32
1974	Mike Schmidt, Philadelphia	36	1974	Dick Allen, Chicago	32
1975	Mike Schmidt, Philadelphia	38	1975	George Scott, Milwaukee; Reggie Jackson, Oakland	36
1976	Mike Schmidt, Philadelphia	38	1976	Graig Nettles, New York	32
1977	George Foster, Cincinnati	52	1977	Jim Rice, Boston	39
1978	George Foster, Cincinnati	40	1978	Jim Rice, Boston	46
1979	Dave Kingman, Chicago	48	1979	Gorman Thomas, Milwaukee	45
1980	Mike Schmidt, Philadelphia	48	1980	Reggie Jackson, New York; Ben Oglivie, Milwaukee	41
1981	Mike Schmidt, Philadelphia	31	1981	Bobby Grich, California; Tony Armas, Oakland; Dwight Evans, Boston; Eddie Murray, Baltimore	22
1982	Dave Kingman, New York	37	1982	Gorman Thomas, Milwaukee; Reggie Jackson, Cal.	39

(continued)

National League

Year	Player, Club	RBI
1983	Mike Schmidt, Philadelphia	40
1984	Mike Schmidt, Phil.; Dale Murphy, Atlanta	36
1985	Dale Murphy, Atlanta	37
1986	Mike Schmidt, Philadelphia	37
1987	Andre Dawson, Chicago	49
1988	Darryl Strawberry, New York	39
1989	Kevin Mitchell, San Francisco	47
1990	Ryne Sandberg, Chicago	40
1991	Howard Johnson, New York	38
1992	Fred McGriff, San Diego	35
1993	Barry Bonds, San Francisco	46
1994	*Matt Williams, San Francisco	43

American League

Year	Player, Club	RBI
1983	Jim Rice, Boston	39
1984	Tony Armas, Boston	43
1985	Darrell Evans, Detroit	40
1986	Jesse Barfield, Toronto	40
1987	Mark McGwire, Oakland	49
1988	Jose Canseco, Oakland	42
1989	Fred McGriff, Toronto	36
1990	Cecil Fielder, Detroit	51
1991	Cecil Fielder, Detroit; Jose Canseco, Oakland	44
1992	Juan Gonzalez, Texas	43
1993	Juan Gonzalez, Texas	46
1994	*Ken Griffey Jr., Seattle	40

Runs Batted In Leaders

National League

Year	Player, Club	RBI
1907	Honus Wagner, Pittsburgh	91
1908	Honus Wager, Pittsburgh	106
1909	Honus Wager, Pittsburgh	102
1910	Sherwood Magee, Philadelphia	116
1911	Frank Schulte, Chicago	121
1912	Henry Zimmerman, Chicago	98
1913	Gavvy Cravath, Philadelphia	118
1914	Sherwood Magee, Philadelphia	101
1915	Gavvy Cravath, Philadelphia	118
1916	Hal Chase, Cincinnati	94
1917	Henry Zimmerman, New York	100
1918	Frederick Merkle, Chicago	71
1919	Hi Myers, Boston	72
1920	George Kelly, N.Y., Rogers Hornsby, St. Louis	94
1921	Rogers Hornsby, St. Louis	126
1922	Rogers Hornsby, St. Louis	152
1923	Emil Meusel, New York	125
1924	George Kelly, New York	136
1925	Rogers Hornsby, St. Louis	143
1926	Jim Bottomley, St. Louis	120
1927	Paul Waner, Pittsburgh	131
1928	Jim Bottomley, St. Louis	136
1929	Hack Wilson, Chicago	159
1930	Hack Wilson, Chicago	190
1931	Chuck Klein, Philadelphia	121
1932	Don Hurst, Philadelphia	143
1933	Chuck Klein, Philadelphia	120
1934	Mel Ott, New York	135
1935	Walter Berger, Boston	130
1936	Joe Medwick, St. Louis	138
1937	Joe Medwick, St. Louis	154
1938	Joe Medwick, St. Louis	122
1939	Frank McCormick, Cincinnati	128
1940	John Mize, St. Louis	137
1941	Adolph Camilli, Brooklyn	120
1942	John Mize, New York	110
1943	Bill Nicholson, Chicago	128
1944	Bill Nicholson, Chicago	122
1945	Dixie Walker, Brooklyn	124
1946	Enos Slaughter, St. Louis	130
1947	John Mize, New York	138
1948	Stan Musial, St. Louis	131
1949	Ralph Kiner, Pittsburgh	127
1950	Del Ennis, Philadelphia	126
1951	Monte Irvin, New York	121
1952	Hank Sauer, Chicago	121
1953	Roy Campanella, Brooklyn	142
1954	Ted Kluszewski, Cincinnati	141
1955	Duke Snider, Brooklyn	136
1956	Stan Musial, St. Louis	109
1957	Hank Aaron, Milwaukee	132
1958	Ernie Banks, Chicago	129
1959	Ernie Banks, Chicago	143
1960	Hank Aaron, Milwaukee	126
1961	Orlando Cepeda, San Francisco	142
1962	Tommy Davis, Los Angeles	153
1963	Hank Aaron, Milwaukee	130
1964	Ken Boyer, St. Louis	119
1965	Deron Johnson, Cincinnati	130
1966	Hank Aaron, Atlanta	127
1967	Orlando Cepeda, St. Louis	111
1968	Willie McCovey, San Francisco	105
1969	Willie McCovey, San Francisco	126
1970	Johnny Bench, Cincinnati	148
1971	Joe Torre, St. Louis	137
1972	Johnny Bench, Cincinnati	125
1973	Willie Stargell, Pittsburgh	119

American League

Year	Player, Club	RBI
1907	Ty Cobb, Detroit	116
1908	Ty Cobb, Detroit	101
1909	Ty Cobb, Detroit	115
1910	Sam Crawford, Detroit	115
1911	Ty Cobb, Detroit	144
1912	J. Franklin Baker, Philadelphia	133
1913	J. Franklin Baker, Philadelphia	126
1914	Sam Crawford, Detroit	112
1915	Sam Crawford, Detroit	116
1916	Wally Pipp, New York	99
1917	Robert Veach, Detroit	115
1918	George Burns, Phila., Robert Veach, Detroit	74
1919	Babe Ruth, Boston	112
1920	Babe Ruth, New York	137
1921	Babe Ruth, New York	171
1922	Ken Williams, St. Louis	155
1923	Babe Ruth, New York	131
1924	Goose Goslin, Washington	129
1925	Bob Meusel, New York	138
1926	Babe Ruth, New York	145
1927	Lou Gehrig, New York	175
1928	Babe Ruth, N.Y., Lou Gehrig, N.Y.	142
1929	Al Simmons, Philadelphia	157
1930	Lou Gehrig, New York	174
1931	Lou Gehrig, New York	184
1932	Jimmie Foxx, Philadelphia	169
1933	Jimmie Foxx, Philadelphia	163
1934	Lou Gehrig, New York	165
1935	Hank Greenberg, Detroit	170
1936	Hal Trosky, Cleveland	162
1937	Hank Greenberg, Detroit	183
1938	Jimmie Foxx, Boston	175
1939	Ted Williams, Boston	145
1940	Hank Greenberg, Detroit	150
1941	Joe DiMaggio, New York	125
1942	Ted Williams, Boston	137
1943	Rudy York, Detroit	118
1944	Vern Stephens, St. Louis	109
1945	Nick Etten, New York	111
1946	Hank Greenberg, Detroit	127
1947	Ted Williams, Boston	114
1948	Joe DiMaggio, New York	155
1949	Ted Williams, Bos., Vern Stephens, Bos.	159
1950	Walt Dropo, Bos., Vern Stephens, Bos.	144
1951	Gus Zernial, Chicago-Philadelphia	129
1952	Al Rosen, Cleveland	105
1953	Al Rosen, Cleveland	145
1954	Larry Doby, Cleveland	126
1955	Ray Boone, Detroit, Jackie Jensen, Boston	116
1956	Mickey Mantle, New York	130
1957	Roy Sievers, Washington	114
1958	Jackie Jensen, Boston	122
1959	Jackie Jensen, Boston	112
1960	Roger Maris, New York	112
1961	Roger Maris, New York	142
1962	Harmon Killebrew, Minnesota	126
1963	Dick Stuart, Boston	118
1964	Brooks Robinson, Baltimore	118
1965	Rocky Colavito, Cleveland	108
1966	Frank Robinson, Baltimore	122
1967	Carl Yastrzemski, Boston	121
1968	Ken Harrelson, Boston	109
1969	Harmon Killebrew, Minnesota	140
1970	Frank Howard, Washington	126
1971	Harmon Killebrew, Minnesota	119
1972	Dick Allen, Chicago	113
1973	Reggie Jackson, Oakland	117

National League

Year	Player, Club	RBI
1974	Johnny Bench, Cincinnati	129
1975	Greg Luzinski, Philadelphia	120
1976	George Foster, Cincinnati	121
1977	George Foster, Cincinnati	149
1978	George Foster, Cincinnati	120
1979	Dave Winfield, San Diego	118
1980	Mike Schmidt, Philadelphia	121
1981	Mike Schmidt, Philadelphia	91
1982	Dale Murphy, Atlanta; Al Oliver, Montreal	109
1983	Dale Murphy, Atlanta	121
1984	Mike Schmidt, Phil.; Gary Carter, Montreal	106
1985	Dave Parker, Cincinnati	125
1986	Mike Schmidt, Philadelphia	119
1987	Andre Dawson, Chicago	137
1988	Will Clark, San Francisco	109
1989	Kevin Mitchell, San Francisco	125
1990	Matt Williams, San Francisco	122
1991	Howard Johnson, New York	117
1992	Darren Daulton, Philadelphia	109
1993	Barry Bonds, San Francisco	123
1994	*Jeff Bagwell, Houston	116

American League

Year	Player, Club	RBI
1974	Jeff Burroughs, Texas	118
1975	George Scott, Milwaukee	109
1976	Lee May, Baltimore	109
1977	Larry Hisle, Minnesota	119
1978	Jim Rice, Boston	139
1979	Don Baylor, California	139
1980	Cecil Cooper, Milwaukee	122
1981	Eddie Murray, Baltimore	78
1982	Hal McRae, Kansas City	133
1983	Cecil Cooper, Milwaukee; Jim Rice, Boston	126
1984	Tony Armas, Boston	123
1985	Don Mattingly, New York	145
1986	Joe Carter, Cleveland	121
1987	George Bell, Toronto	134
1988	Jose Canseco, Oakland	124
1989	Ruben Sierra, Texas	119
1990	Cecil Fielder, Detroit	132
1991	Cecil Fielder, Detroit	133
1992	Cecil Fielder, Detroit	124
1993	Albert Belle, Cleveland	129
1994	*Kirby Puckett, Minnesota	112

Batting Champions

National League

Year	Player	Club	Pct.
1901	Jesse C. Burkett	St. Louis	**.382**
1902	Clarence Beaumont	Pittsburgh	**.357**
1903	Honus Wagner	Pittsburgh	**.355**
1904	Honus Wagner	Pittsburgh	**.349**
1905	James Seymour	Cincinnati	**.377**
1906	Honus Wagner	Pittsburgh	**.339**
1907	Honus Wagner	Pittsburgh	**.350**
1908	Honus Wagner	Pittsburgh	**.354**
1909	Honus Wagner	Pittsburgh	**.339**
1910	Sherwood Magee	Philadelphia	**.331**
1911	Honus Wagner	Pittsburgh	**.334**
1912	Henry Zimmerman	Chicago	**.372**
1913	Jacob Daubert	Brooklyn	**.350**
1914	Jacob Daubert	Brooklyn	**.329**
1915	Larry Doyle	New York	**.320**
1916	Hal Chase	Cincinnati	**.339**
1917	Edd Roush	Cleveland	**.341**
1918	Zach Wheat	Brooklyn	**.335**
1919	Edd Roush	Cincinnati	**.321**
1920	Rogers Hornsby	St. Louis	**.370**
1921	Rogers Hornsby	St. Louis	**.397**
1922	Rogers Hornsby	St. Louis	**.401**
1923	Rogers Hornsby	St. Louis	**.384**
1924	Rogers Hornsby	St. Louis	**.424**
1925	Rogers Hornsby	St. Louis	**.403**
1926	Eugene Hargrave	Cincinnati	**.353**
1927	Paul Waner	Pittsburgh	**.380**
1928	Rogers Hornsby	Boston	**.387**
1929	Lefty O'Doul	Philadelphia	**.398**
1930	Bill Terry	New York	**.401**
1931	Chick Hafey	St. Louis	**.349**
1932	Lefty O'Doul	Brooklyn	**.368**
1933	Chuck Klein	Philadelphia	**.368**
1934	Paul Waner	Pittsburgh	**.362**
1935	Arky Vaughan	Pittsburgh	**.385**
1936	Paul Waner	Pittsburgh	**.373**
1937	Joe Medwick	St. Louis	**.374**
1938	Ernie Lombardi	Cincinnati	**.342**
1939	John Mize	St. Louis	**.349**
1940	Debs Garms	Pittsburgh	**.355**
1941	Pete Reiser	Brooklyn	**.343**
1942	Ernie Lombardi	Boston	**.330**
1943	Stan Musial	St. Louis	**.357**
1944	Dixie Walker	Brooklyn	**.357**
1945	Phil Cavarretta	Chicago	**.355**
1946	Stan Musial	St. Louis	**.365**
1947	Harry Walker	Philadelphia	**.363**
1948	Stan Musial	St. Louis	**.376**
1949	Jackie Robinson	Brooklyn	**.342**
1950	Stan Musial	St. Louis	**.346**
1951	Stan Musial	St. Louis	**.355**
1952	Stan Musial	St. Louis	**.336**
1953	Carl Furillo	Brooklyn	**.344**
1954	Willie Mays	New York	**.345**
1955	Richie Ashburn	Philadelphia	**.338**
1956	Hank Aaron	Milwaukee	**.328**
1957	Stan Musial	St. Louis	**.351**
1958	Richie Ashburn	Philadelphia	**.350**

American League

Year	Player	Club	Pct.
1901	Napoleon Lajoie	Philadelphia	**.422**
1902	Ed Delahanty	Washington	**.376**
1902	Napoleon Lajoie	Cleveland	**.355**
1904	Napoleon Lajoie	Cleveland	**.381**
1905	Elmer Flick	Cleveland	**.308**
1906	George Stone	St. Louis	**.358**
1907	Ty Cobb	Detroit	**.350**
1908	Ty Cobb	Detroit	**.324**
1909	Ty Cobb	Detroit	**.377**
1910	Ty Cobb	Detroit	**.385**
1911	Ty Cobb	Detroit	**.420**
1912	Ty Cobb	Detroit	**.410**
1913	Ty Cobb	Detroit	**.390**
1914	Ty Cobb	Detroit	**.368**
1915	Ty Cobb	Detroit	**.369**
1916	Tris Speaker	Cleveland	**.386**
1917	Ty Cobb	Detroit	**.383**
1918	Ty Cobb	Detroit	**.382**
1919	Ty Cobb	Detroit	**.384**
1920	George Sisler	St. Louis	**.407**
1921	Harry Heilmann	Detroit	**.394**
1922	George Sisler	St. Louis	**.420**
1923	Harry Heilmann	Detroit	**.403**
1924	Babe Ruth	New York	**.378**
1925	Harry Heilmann	Detroit	**.393**
1926	Henry Manush	Detroit	**.378**
1927	Harry Heilmann	Detroit	**.398**
1928	Goose Goslin	Washington	**.379**
1929	Lew Fonseca	Cleveland	**.369**
1930	Al Simmons	Philadelphia	**.381**
1931	Al Simmons	Philadelphia	**.390**
1932	Dale Alexander	Detroit-Boston	**.367**
1933	Jimmie Foxx	Philadelphia	**.356**
1934	Lou Gehrig	New York	**.363**
1935	Buddy Myer	Washington	**.349**
1936	Luke Appling	Chicago	**.388**
1937	Charlie Gehringer	Detroit	**.371**
1938	Jimmie Foxx	Boston	**.349**
1939	Joe DiMaggio	New York	**.381**
1940	Joe DiMaggio	New York	**.352**
1941	Ted Williams	Boston	**.406**
1942	Ted Williams	Boston	**.356**
1943	Luke Appling	Chicago	**.328**
1944	Lou Boudreau	Cleveland	**.327**
1945	George Stirnweiss	New York	**.309**
1946	Mickey Vernon	Washington	**.353**
1947	Ted Williams	Boston	**.343**
1948	Ted Williams	Boston	**.369**
1949	George Kell	Detroit	**.343**
1950	Billy Goodman	Boston	**.354**
1951	Ferris Fain	Philadelphia	**.344**
1952	Ferris Fain	Philadelphia	**.327**
1953	Mickey Vernon	Washington	**.337**
1954	Roberto Avila	Cleveland	**.341**
1955	Al Kaline	Detroit	**.340**
1956	Mickey Mantle	New York	**.353**
1957	Ted Williams	Boston	**.388**
1958	Ted Williams	Boston	**.328**

(continued)

National League

Year	Player, Club		RBI
1959	Hank Aaron	Milwaukee	.355
1960	Dick Groat	Pittsburgh	.325
1961	Roberto Clemente	Pittsburgh	.351
1962	Tommy Davis	Los Angeles	.346
1963	Tommy Davis	Los Angeles	.326
1964	Roberto Clemente	Pittsburgh	.339
1965	Roberto Clemente	Pittsburgh	.329
1966	Matty Alou	Pittsburgh	.342
1967	Roberto Clemente	Pittsburgh	.357
1968	Pete Rose	Cincinnati	.335
1969	Pete Rose	Cincinnati	.348
1970	Rico Carty	Atlanta	.366
1971	Joe Torre	St. Louis	.363
1972	Billy Williams	Chicago	.333
1973	Pete Rose	Cincinnati	.338
1974	Ralph Garr	Atlanta	.353
1975	Bill Madlock	Chicago	.354
1976	Bill Madlock	Chicago	.339
1977	Dave Parker	Pittsburgh	.338
1978	Dave Parker	Pittsburgh	.334
1979	Keith Hernandez	St. Louis	.344
1980	Bill Buckner	Chicago	.324
1981	Bill Madlock	Pittsburgh	.341
1982	Al Oliver	Montreal	.331
1983	Bill Madlock	Pittsburgh	.323
1984	Tony Gwynn	San Diego	.351
1985	Willie McGee	St. Louis	.353
1986	Tim Raines	Montreal	.334
1987	Tony Gwynn	San Diego	.369
1988	Tony Gwynn	San Diego	.313
1989	Tony Gwynn	San Diego	.336
1990	Willie McGee	St. Louis	.335
1991	Terry Pendleton	Atlanta	.319
1992	Gary Sheffield	San Diego	.330
1993	Andres Galarraga	Colorado	.370
1994	*Tony Gwynn	San Diego	.394

American League

Year	Player, Club		RBI
1959	Harvey Kuenn	Detroit	.353
1960	Pete Runnels	Boston	.320
1961	Norm Cash	Detroit	.361
1962	Pete Runnels	Boston	.326
1963	Carl Yastrzemski	Boston	.321
1964	Tony Oliva	Minnesota	.323
1965	Tony Oliva	Minnesota	.321
1966	Frank Robinson	Baltimore	.316
1967	Carl Yastrzemski	Boston	.326
1968	Carl Yastrzemski	Boston	.301
1969	Rod Carew	Minnesota	.332
1970	Alex Johnson	California	.328
1971	Tony Oliva	Minnesota	.337
1972	Rod Carew	Minnesota	.318
1973	Rod Carew	Minnesota	.350
1974	Rod Carew	Minnesota	.364
1975	Rod Carew	Minnesota	.359
1976	George Brett	Kansas City	.333
1977	Rod Carew	Minnesota	.388
1978	Rod Carew	Minnesota	.333
1979	Fred Lynn	Boston	.333
1980	George Brett	Kansas City	.390
1981	Carney Lansford	Boston	.336
1982	Willie Wilson	Kansas City	.332
1983	Wade Boggs	Boston	.361
1984	Don Mattingly	New York	.343
1985	Wade Boggs	Boston	.368
1986	Wade Boggs	Boston	.357
1987	Wade Boggs	Boston	.363
1988	Wade Boggs	Boston	.366
1989	Kirby Puckett	Minnesota	.339
1990	George Brett	Kansas City	.329
1991	Julio Franco	Texas	.342
1992	Edgar Martinez	Seattle	.343
1993	John Olerud	Toronto	.363
1994	*Paul O'Neill	New York	.359

Triple Crown Hitters

National League

Player, Club	Year	HR	RBI	BA
Paul Hines, Providence	1878	4	50	.358
Hugh Duffy, Boston	1894	18	145	.438
Heinie Zimmerman, Chicago[1]	1912	14	103	.372
Rogers Hornsby, St. Louis	1922	42	152	.401
	1925	39	143	.403
Chuck Klein, Philadelphia	1933	28	120	.368
Joe Medwick, St. Louis	1937	31	154	.374

(1) RBI lead disputed.

American League

Player, Club	Year	HR	RBI	BA
Nap Lajoie, Philadelphia	1901	14	125	.422
Ty Cobb, Detroit	1909	9	115	.377
Jimmie Foxx, Philadelphia	1933	48	163	.356
Lou Gehrig, New York	1934	49	165	.363
Ted Williams, Boston	1942	36	137	.356
	1947	32	114	.343
Mickey Mantle, New York	1956	52	130	.353
Frank Robinson, Baltimore	1966	49	122	.316
Carl Yastrzemski, Boston	1967	44	121	.326

Cy Young Award Winners

Year	Player, Club
1956	Don Newcombe, Dodgers
1957	Warren Spahn, Braves
1958	Bob Turley, Yankees
1959	Early Wynn, White Sox
1960	Vernon Law, Pirates
1961	Whitey Ford, Yankees
1962	Don Drysdale, Dodgers
1963	Sandy Koufax, Dodgers
1964	Dean Chance, Angels
1965	Sandy Koufax, Dodgers
1966	Sandy Koufax, Dodgers
1967	(NL) Mike McCormick, Giants
	(AL) Jim Lonborg, Red Sox
1968	(NL) Bob Gibson, Cardinals
	(AL) Dennis McLain, Tigers
1969	(NL) Tom Seaver, Mets
	(AL) (tie) Dennis McLain, Tigers
	Mike Cuellar, Orioles
1970	(NL) Bob Gibson, Cardinals
	(AL) Jim Perry, Twins
1971	(NL) Ferguson Jenkins, Cubs
	(AL) Vida Blue, A's
1972	(NL) Steve Carlton, Phillies
	(AL) Gaylord Perry, Indians
1973	(NL) Tom Seaver, Mets
	(AL) Jim Palmer, Orioles
1974	(NL) Mike Marshall, Dodgers
	(AL) Jim (Catfish) Hunter, A's
1975	(NL) Tom Seaver, Mets
	(AL) Jim Palmer, Orioles
1976	(NL) Randy Jones, Padres
	(AL) Jim Palmer, Orioles
1977	(NL) Steve Carlton, Phillies
	(AL) Sparky Lyle, Yankees
1978	(NL) Gaylord Perry, Padres
	(AL) Ron Guidry, Yankees
1979	(NL) Bruce Sutter, Cubs
	(AL) Mike Flanagan, Orioles
1980	(NL) Steve Carlton, Phillies
	(AL) Steve Stone, Orioles
1981	(NL) Fernando Valenzuela, Dodgers
	(AL) Rollie Fingers, Brewers
1982	(NL) Steve Carlton, Phillies
	(AL) Pete Vuckovich, Brewers
1983	(NL) John Denny, Phillies
	(AL) LaMarr Hoyt, White Sox
1984	(NL) Rick Sutcliffe, Cubs
	(AL) Willie Hernandez, Tigers
1985	(NL) Dwight Gooden, Mets
	(AL) Bret Saberhagen, Royals
1986	(NL) Mike Scott, Astros
	(AL) Roger Clemens, Red Sox
1987	(NL) Steve Bedrosian, Phillies
	(AL) Roger Clemens, Red Sox
1988	(NL) Orel Hershiser, Dodgers
	(AL) Frank Viola, Twins
1989	(NL) Mark Davis, Padres
	(AL) Bret Saberhagan, Royals
1990	(NL) Doug Drabek, Pirates
	(AL) Bob Welch, A's
1991	(NL) Tom Glavine, Braves
	(AL) Roger Clemens, Red Sox
1992	(NL) Greg Maddux, Cubs
	(AL) Dennis Eckersley, A's
1993	(NL) Greg Maddux, Braves
	(AL) Jack McDowell, White Sox
1994	(NL) *Greg Maddux, Braves
	(AL) *David Cone, Royals

Pitchers With 300 Major League Wins

Cy Young	511	Warren Spahn	363	Steve Carlton	329	Nolan Ryan	324	Mickey Welch	311
Walter Johnson	416	Pud Galvin	361	Eddie Plank	327	Phil Niekro	318	Old Hoss Radbourn	308
Christy Mathewson	373	Kid Nichols	360	John Clarkson	326	Gaylord Perry	314	Lefty Grove	300
Grover Alexander	373	Tim Keefe	344	Don Sutton	324	Tom Seaver	311	Early Wynn	300

Most Valuable Player

Baseball Writers' Association

National League

Year	Player, team	Year	Player, team	Year	Player, team
1931	Frank Frisch, St. Louis	1953	Roy Campanella, Brooklyn	1974	Steve Garvey, Los Angeles
1932	Charles Klein, Philadelphia	1954	Willie Mays, New York	1975	Joe Morgan, Cincinnati
1933	Carl Hubbell, New York	1955	Roy Campanella, Brooklyn	1976	Joe Morgan, Cincinnati
1934	Dizzy Dean, St. Louis	1956	Don Newcombe, Brooklyn	1977	George Foster, Cincinnati
1935	Gabby Hartnett, Chicago	1957	Hank Aaron, Milwaukee	1978	Dave Parker, Pittsburgh
1936	Carl Hubbell, New York	1958	Ernie Banks, Chicago	1979	(tie)Willie Stargelll, Pittsburgh Keith Hernandez, St. Louis
1937	Joe Medwick, St. Louis	1959	Ernie Banks, Chicago		
1938	Ernie Lombardi, Cincinnati	1960	Dick Groat, Pittsburgh	1980	Mike Schmidt, Philadelphia
1939	Bucky Walters, Cincinnati	1961	Frank Robinson, Cincinnati	1981	Mike Schmidt, Philadelphia
1940	Frank McCormick, Cincinnati	1962	Maury Wills, Los Angeles	1982	Dale Murphy, Atlanta
1941	Dolph Camilli, Brooklyn	1963	Sandy Koufax, Los Angeles	1983	Dale Murphy, Atlanta
1942	Mort Cooper, St. Louis	1964	Ken Boyer, St. Louis	1984	Ryne Sandberg, Chicago
1943	Stan Musial, St. Louis	1965	Willie Mays, San Francisco	1985	Willie McGee, St. Louis
1944	Martin Marion, St. Louis	1966	Roberto Clemente, Pittsburgh	1986	Mike Schmidt, Philadelphia
1945	Phil Cavarretta, Chicago	1967	Orlando Cepeda, St. Louis	1987	Andre Dawson, Chicago
1946	Stan Musial, St. Louis	1968	Bob Gibson, St. Louis	1988	Kirk Gibson, Los Angeles
1947	Bob Elliott, Boston	1969	Willie McCovey, San Francisco	1989	Kevin Mitchell, San Francisco
1948	Stan Musial, St. Louis	1970	Johnny Bench, Cincinnati	1990	Barry Bonds, Pittsburgh
1949	Jackie Robinson, Brooklyn	1971	Joe Torre, St. Louis	1991	Terry Pendleton, Atlanta
1950	Jim Konstanty, Philadelphia	1972	Johnny Bench, Cincinnati	1992	Barry Bonds, Pittsburgh
1951	Roy Campanella, Brooklyn	1973	Pete Rose, Cincinnati	1993	Barry Bonds, San Francisco
1952	Hank Sauer, Chicago			1994	*Jeff Bagwell, Houston

American League

Year	Player, team	Year	Player, team	Year	Player, team
1931	Lefty Grove, Philadelphia	1953	Al Rosen, Cleveland	1974	Jeff Burroughs, Texas
1932	Jimmie Foxx, Philadelphia	1954	Yogi Berra, New York	1975	Fred Lynn, Boston
1933	Jimmie Foxx, Philadelphia	1955	Yogi Berra, New York	1976	Thurman Munson, New York
1934	Mickey Cochrane, Detroit	1956	Mickey Mantle, New York	1977	Rod Carew, Minnesota
1935	Hank Greenberg, Detroit	1957	Mickey Mantle, New York	1978	Jim Rice, Boston
1936	Lou Gehrig, New York	1958	Jackie Jensen, Boston	1979	Don Baylor, California
1937	Charley Gehringer, Detroit	1959	Nellie Fox, Chicago	1980	George Brett, Kansas City
1938	Jimmie Foxx, Boston	1960	Roger Maris, New York	1981	Rollie Fingers, Milwaukee
1939	Joe DiMaggio, New York	1961	Roger Maris, New York	1982	Robin Yount, Milwaukee
1940	Hank Greenberg, Detroit	1962	Mickey Mantle, New York	1983	Cal Ripken Jr., Baltimore
1941	Joe DiMaggio, New York	1963	Elston Howard, New York	1984	Willie Hernandez, Detroit
1942	Joe Gordon, New York	1964	Brooks Robinson, Baltimore	1985	Don Mattingly, New York
1943	Spurgeon Chandler, New York	1965	Zoilo Versalles, Minnesota	1986	Roger Clemens, Boston
1944	Hal Newhouser, Detroit	1966	Frank Robinson, Baltimore	1987	George Bell, Toronto
1945	Hal Newhouser, Detroit	1967	Carl Yastrzemski, Boston	1988	Jose Canseco, Oakland
1946	Ted Williams, Boston	1968	Denny McLain, Detroit	1989	Robin Yount, Milwaukee
1947	Joe DiMaggio, New York	1969	Harmon Killebrew, Minnesota	1990	Rickey Henderson, Oakland
1948	Lou Boudreau, Cleveland	1970	John (Boog) Powell, Baltimore	1991	Cal Ripken Jr., Baltimore
1949	Ted Williams, Boston	1971	Vida Blue, Oakland	1992	Dennis Eckersley, Oakland
1950	Phil Rizzuto, New York	1972	Dick Allen, Chicago	1993	Frank Thomas, Chicago
1951	Yogi Berra, New York	1973	Reggie Jackson, Oakland	1994	*Frank Thomas, Chicago
1952	Bobby Shantz, Philadelphia				

Rookie of the Year

Baseball Writers' Association

1947—Combined selection—Jackie Robinson, Brooklyn, 1b; 1948—Combined selection—Alvin Dark, Boston, N.L., ss

National League

Year	Player, team	Year	Player, team	Year	Player, team
1949	Don Newcombe, Brooklyn, p	1965	Jim Lefebvre, Los Angeles, 2b	1980	Steve Howe, Los Angeles, p
1950	Sam Jethroe, Boston, of	1966	Tommy Helms, Cincinnati, 2b	1981	Fernando Valenzuela, Los Angeles, p
1951	Willie Mays, New York, of	1967	Tom Seaver, New York, p		
1952	Joe Black, Brooklyn, p	1968	Johnny Bench, Cincinnati, c	1982	Steve Sax, Los Angeles, 2b
1953	Jim Gilliam, Brooklyn, 2b	1969	Ted Sizemore, Los Angeles, 2b	1983	Darryl Strawberry, New York, of
1954	Wally Moon, St. Louis, of	1970	Carl Morton, Montreal, p	1984	Dwight Gooden, New York, p
1955	Bill Virdon, St. Louis, of	1971	Earl Williams, Atlanta, c	1985	Vince Coleman, St. Louis, of
1956	Frank Robinson, Cincinnati, of	1972	Jon Matlack, New York, p	1986	Todd Worrell, St. Louis, p
1957	Jack Sanford, Philadelphia, p	1973	Gary Matthews, S.F., of	1987	Benito Santiago, San Diego, c
1958	Orlando Cepeda, S.F., 1b	1974	Bake McBride, St. Louis, of	1988	Chris Sabo, Cincinnati, 3b
1959	Willie McCovey, S.F., 1b	1975	John Montefusco, S.F., p	1989	Jerome Walton, Chicago, of
1960	Frank Howard, Los Angeles, of	1976	(tie)Butch Metzger, San Diego, p Pat Zachry, Cincinnati, p	1990	Dave Justice, Atlanta, 1b
1961	Billy Williams, Chicago, of			1991	Jeff Bagwell, Houston, 1b
1962	Ken Hubbs, Chicago, 2b	1977	Andre Dawson, Montreal, of	1992	Eric Karros, Los Angeles, 1b
1963	Pete Rose, Cincinnati, 2b	1978	Bob Horner, Atlanta, 3b	1993	Mike Piazza, Los Angeles, c
1964	Richie Allen, Philadelphia, 3b	1979	Rick Sutcliffe, Los Angeles, p	1994	*Raul Mondesi, Los Angeles, of

American League

Year	Player, team	Year	Player, team	Year	Player, team
1949	Roy Sievers, St. Louis, of	1965	Curt Blefary, Baltimore, of	1980	Joe Charboneau, Cleveland, of
1950	Walt Dropo, Boston, 1b	1966	Tommie Agee, Chicago, of	1981	Dave Righetti, New York, p
1951	Gil McDougald, New York, 3b	1967	Rod Carew, Minnesota, 2b	1982	Cal Ripken Jr., Baltimore, ss
1952	Harry Byrd, Philadelphia, p	1968	Stan Bahnsen, New York, p	1983	Ron Kittle, Chicago, of
1953	Harvey Kuenn, Detroit, ss	1969	Lou Piniella, Kansas City, of	1984	Alvin Davis, Seattle, 1b
1954	Bob Grim, New York, p	1970	Thurman Munson, New York, c	1985	Ozzie Guillen, Chicago, ss
1955	Herb Score, Cleveland, p	1971	Chris Chambliss, Cleveland, 1b	1986	Jose Canseco, Oakland, of
1956	Luis Aparicio, Chicago, ss	1972	Carlton Fisk, Boston, c	1987	Mark McGwire, Oakland, 1b
1957	Tony Kubek, New York, if-of	1973	Al Bumbry, Baltimore, of	1988	Walt Weiss, Oakland, ss
1958	Albie Pearson, Washington, of	1974	Mike Hargrove, Texas, 1b	1989	Gregg Olson, Baltimore, p
1959	Bob Allison, Washington, of	1975	Fred Lynn, Boston, of	1990	Sandy Alomar Jr., Cleveland, c
1960	Ron Hansen, Baltimore, ss	1976	Mark Fidrych, Detroit, p	1991	Chuck Knoblauch, Minnesota, 2b
1961	Don Schwall, Boston, p	1977	Eddie Murray, Baltimore, dh	1992	Pat Listach, Milwaukee, ss
1962	Tom Tresh, New York, if-of	1978	Lou Whitaker, Detroit, 2b	1993	Tim Salmon, California, of
1963	Gary Peters, Chicago, p	1979	(tie)John Castino, Minnesota, 3b Alfredo Griffin, Toronto, ss	1994	*Bob Hamelin, Kansas City, dh
1964	Tony Oliva, Minnesota, of				

National League Records, 1994

Final standings for strike-shortened season

Eastern Division

	W	L	Pct.	GB	Home	vs. RHP	Grass	Night
Montreal	74	40	.649	—	32-20	56-32	27-13	53-26
Atlanta	68	46	.596	6	31-24	50-30	56-30	44-35
New York	55	58	.487	18½	23-30	37-44	49-45	37-40
Philadelphia	54	61	.470	20½	34-26	39-45	15-26	39-40
Florida	51	64	.443	23½	25-34	40-34	44-49	37-49

Central Division

	W	L	Pct.	GB	Home	vs. RHP	Grass	Night
Cincinnati	66	48	.579	—	37-22	50-36	20-18	44-32
Houston	66	49	.574	½	37-22	46-37	14-17	49-31
Pittsburgh	53	61	.465	13	32-29	38-49	13-14	38-44
St. Louis	53	61	.465	13	23-33	39-41	19-14	41-42
Chicago	49	64	.434	16½	20-39	34-47	36-45	21-25

Western Division

	W	L	Pct.	GB	Home	vs. RHP	Grass	Night
Los Angeles	58	56	.509	—	33-22	43-46	47-40	38-42
San Francisco	55	60	.478	3½	29-31	41-44	44-44	25-29
Colorado	53	64	.453	6½	25-32	45-52	42-50	30-40
San Diego	47	70	.402	12½	26-31	34-46	39-50	30-51

Team Batting

	Avg	AB	R	H	HR	RBI
Cincinnati	**.286**	3999	609	1142	124	569
Houston	**.278**	3955	602	1099	120	573
Montreal	**.278**	4000	585	1111	108	542
San Diego	**.275**	4068	479	1117	92	445
Colorado	**.274**	4006	573	1098	125	540
Los Angeles	**.270**	3904	532	1055	115	505
Atlanta	**.267**	3861	542	1031	137	510
Florida	**.266**	3926	468	1043	94	451
St. Louis	**.263**	3902	535	1026	108	506
Philadelphia	**.262**	3927	521	1028	80	484
Chicago	**.259**	3918	500	1015	109	464
Pittsburgh	**.259**	3864	466	1001	80	435
New York	**.250**	3869	506	966	117	477
San Francisco	**.249**	3869	504	963	123	472

Team Pitching

	ERA	IP	H	BB	SO	SV
Montreal	**3.56**	1036⅔	970	288	805	46
Atlanta	**3.57**	1026⅓	929	378	865	26
Cincinnati	**3.78**	1038⅓	1037	339	799	27
Philadelphia	**3.85**	1024⅓	1028	377	699	30
Houston	**3.97**	1029⅔	1043	367	739	29
San Francisco	**3.99**	1025⅓	1014	372	655	33
San Diego	**4.08**	1045⅔	1008	393	862	27
New York	**4.13**	1023	1069	332	640	35
Los Angeles	**4.17**	1014	1041	354	732	20
Chicago	**4.47**	1023⅔	1054	392	717	27
Florida	**4.50**	1015	1069	428	649	30
Pittsburgh	**4.64**	1005⅔	1094	370	650	24
St. Louis	**5.14**	1018	1154	355	632	29
Colorado	**5.15**	1031	1185	448	703	28

Individual Batting (at least 125 at-bats); Individual Pitching (at least 50 innings or 6 saves)

Atlanta Braves

Batting	AB	R	H	HR	RBI	Avg
McGriff	424	81	135	34	94	**.318**
Justice	352	61	110	19	59	**.313**
Lemke	350	40	103	3	31	**.294**
R. Kelly	434	73	127	9	45	**.293**
Klesko	245	42	68	17	47	**.278**
Tarasco	132	16	36	5	19	**.273**
Blauser	380	56	98	6	45	**.258**
Pendleton	309	25	78	7	30	**.252**
Lopez	277	27	68	13	35	**.245**
O'Brien	152	24	37	8	28	**.243**
Gallagher	152	27	34	2	14	**.224**

Pitching	W	L	ERA	IP	H	BB	SO
Maddux	16	6	**1.56**	202.0	150	31	156
Merckert	9	4	**3.45**	112.1	90	45	111
McMichael	4	6	**3.84**	58.2	66	19	47
Glavine	13	9	**3.97**	165.1	173	70	140
Avery	8	3	**4.04**	151.2	127	55	122
Smoltz	6	10	**4.14**	134.2	120	48	113
Wohlers	7	2	**4.59**	51.0	51	33	58

Manager—Bobby Cox

Chicago Cubs

Batting	AB	R	H	HR	RBI	Avg
Sosa	426	59	128	25	70	**.300**
Grace	403	55	120	6	44	**.298**
Hill	269	48	80	10	38	**.297**
Sanchez	291	26	83	0	24	**.285**
May	345	43	98	8	51	**.284**
Dunston	331	38	92	11	35	**.278**
Hernandez	132	18	32	1	9	**.242**
Buechele	339	33	82	14	52	**.242**
Sandberg	223	36	53	5	24	**.238**
Rhodes	269	39	63	8	19	**.234**
Wilkins	313	44	71	7	39	**.227**

Pitching	W	L	ERA	IP	H	BB	SO
Foster	3	4	**2.89**	81.0	70	35	75
Trachsel	9	7	**3.21**	146.0	133	54	108
Bullinger	6	2	**3.60**	100.0	87	34	72
Myers	1	5	**3.79**	40.1	40	16	32
Bautista	4	5	**3.89**	69.1	75	17	45
Young	4	6	**3.92**	114.2	103	46	65
Crim	5	4	**4.48**	64.1	69	24	43
Plesac	2	3	**4.61**	54.2	61	13	53
Banks	8	12	**5.40**	138.1	139	56	91
Morgan	2	10	**6.69**	80.2	111	35	57

Manager—Tom Trebelhorn

Cincinnati Reds

Batting	AB	R	H	HR	RBI	Avg
Morris	436	60	146	10	78	**.335**
Mitchell	310	57	101	30	77	**.326**
Boone	381	59	122	12	68	**.320**
Taubensee	187	29	53	8	21	**.283**
D. Sanders	375	58	106	4	28	**.283**
Fernandez	366	50	102	8	50	**.279**
Larkin	427	78	119	9	52	**.279**
Howard	178	24	47	5	24	**.264**
R. Sanders	400	66	105	17	62	**.263**
Dorsett	216	21	53	5	26	**.245**
Hunter	256	34	60	15	57	**.234**

Pitching	W	L	ERA	IP	H	BB	SO
Carrasco	5	6	**2.24**	56.1	42	30	41
McElroy	1	2	**2.34**	57.2	52	15	38
Brantley	6	6	**2.48**	65.1	46	28	63
Rijo	9	6	**3.08**	172.1	177	52	171
Ruffin	7	2	**3.09**	70.0	57	27	44
Smiley	11	10	**3.86**	158.2	169	37	112
Schourek	7	2	**4.09**	81.1	90	29	69
Hanson	5	5	**4.11**	122.2	137	23	101
Roper	6	2	**4.50**	92.0	90	30	51

Manager—Dave Johnson

Colorado Rockies

Batting	AB	R	H	HR	RBI	Avg
Kingery	301	56	105	4	41	**.349**
Castilla	130	16	43	3	18	**.331**
Burks	149	33	48	13	24	**.322**
Galarraga	417	77	133	31	85	**.319**
Bichette	484	74	147	27	95	**.304**
Hayes	423	46	122	10	50	**.288**
Girardi	330	47	91	4	34	**.276**
Young	228	37	62	7	30	**.272**
Liriano	255	39	65	3	31	**.255**
Weiss	423	58	106	1	32	**.251**
Johnson	227	30	48	10	40	**.211**

Pitching	W	L	ERA	IP	H	BB	SO
Freeman	10	2	**2.80**	112.2	113	23	67
Reed	3	2	**3.94**	61.0	79	26	51
Ruffin	4	5	**4.04**	55.2	55	30	65
Nied	9	7	**4.80**	122.0	137	47	74
Reynoso	3	4	**4.82**	52.1	54	22	25
Ritz	5	6	**5.62**	73.2	88	35	53
Harkey	1	6	**5.79**	91.2	125	35	39
Blair	0	5	**5.79**	77.2	98	39	68
Painter	4	6	**6.11**	73.2	91	26	41
Harris	3	12	**6.65**	130.0	154	52	82

Manager—Don Baylor

Florida Marlins

Batting	AB	R	H	HR	RBI	Avg
Conine	451	60	144	18	82	**.319**
Colbrunn	155	17	47	6	31	**.303**
Barberie	372	40	112	5	31	**.301**
Browne	329	42	97	3	30	**.295**
Sheffield	322	61	89	27	78	**.276**
Magadan	211	30	58	1	17	**.275**
Santiago	337	35	92	11	41	**.273**
Carr	433	61	114	2	30	**.263**
Carrillo	136	13	34	0	9	**.250**
Abbott	345	41	86	9	33	**.249**
Destrade	130	12	27	5	15	**.208**

Pitching	W	L	ERA	IP	H	BB	SO
Hernandez	3	3	**2.70**	23.1	16	14	13
Nen	5	5	**2.95**	58.0	46	17	60
Hammond	4	4	**3.07**	73.1	79	23	40
Aquino	2	1	**3.73**	50.2	39	22	22
Rapp	7	8	**3.85**	133.1	132	69	75
Gardner	4	4	**4.87**	92.1	97	30	57
Hough	5	9	**5.15**	113.2	118	52	65
Harvey	0	0	**5.23**	10.1	12	4	10
Weathers	8	12	**5.27**	135.0	166	59	72
Lewis	1	4	**5.67**	54.0	62	38	45

Manager—Rene Lachemann

Houston Astros

Batting	AB	R	H	HR	RBI	Avg
Bagwell	400	104	147	39	116	**.368**
Biggio	437	88	139	6	56	**.318**
Bass	203	37	63	6	35	**.310**
Eusebio	159	18	47	5	30	**.296**
Caminiti	406	63	115	18	75	**.283**
Finley	373	64	103	11	33	**.276**
Thompson	241	34	66	4	33	**.274**
Gonzalez	392	57	107	8	67	**.273**
Cedeno	342	38	90	9	49	**.263**
Mouton	310	43	76	2	16	**.245**
Servais	251	27	49	9	41	**.195**

Pitching	W	L	ERA	IP	H	BB	SO
Jones	5	2	**2.72**	72.2	52	26	63
Drabek	12	6	**2.84**	164.2	132	45	121
Hudek	0	2	**2.97**	39.1	24	18	39
Reynolds	8	5	**3.05**	124.0	128	21	110
Swindell	8	9	**4.37**	148.1	175	26	74
Kile	9	6	**4.57**	147.2	153	82	105
Harnisch	8	5	**5.40**	95.0	100	39	62
B. Williams	6	5	**5.74**	78.1	112	41	49
M. Williams	1	4	**7.65**	20.0	21	24	21

Manager—Terry Collins

Los Angeles Dodgers

Batting	AB	R	H	HR	RBI	Avg
Piazza	405	64	129	24	92	**.319**
Butler	417	79	131	8	33	**.314**
Mondesi	434	63	133	16	56	**.306**
Wallach	414	68	116	23	78	**.280**
Rodriguez	306	33	82	8	49	**.268**
Karros	406	51	108	14	46	**.266**
DeShields	320	51	80	2	33	**.250**
Snyder	153	18	36	6	18	**.235**
Offerman	243	27	51	1	25	**.210**

Pitching	W	L	ERA	IP	H	BB	SO
Gross	9	7	**3.60**	157.1	162	43	124
Hershiser	6	6	**3.79**	135.1	146	42	72
Martinez	12	7	**3.97**	170.0	160	56	119
Candiotti	7	7	**4.12**	153.0	149	54	102
Worrell	6	5	**4.29**	42.0	37	12	44
Astacio	6	8	**4.29**	149.0	142	47	108
Dreifort	0	5	**6.21**	29.0	45	15	22

Manager—Tommy Lasorda

Montreal Expos

Batting	AB	R	H	HR	RBI	Avg
M. Alou	422	81	143	22	78	**.339**
Walker	395	76	127	19	86	**.322**
Cordero	415	65	122	15	63	**.294**
Grissom	475	96	137	11	45	**.288**
Floyd	334	43	94	4	41	**.281**
Berry	320	43	89	11	41	**.278**
Webster	143	13	39	5	23	**.273**
Frazier	140	25	38	0	14	**.271**
Lansing	394	44	105	5	35	**.266**
Fletcher	285	28	74	10	57	**.260**

Pitching	W	L	ERA	IP	H	BB	SO
Henry	8	3	**2.43**	107.1	97	20	70
Scott	5	2	**2.70**	53.1	51	18	37
Wetteland	4	6	**2.83**	63.2	46	21	68
Fassero	8	6	**2.99**	138.2	119	40	119
Hill	16	5	**3.32**	154.2	145	44	85
Rojas	3	2	**3.32**	84.0	71	21	84
Martinez	11	5	**3.42**	144.2	115	45	142
Heredia	6	3	**3.46**	75.1	85	13	62
Shaw	5	2	**3.88**	67.1	67	15	47
Rueter	7	3	**5.17**	92.1	106	23	50

Manager—Felipe Alou

New York Mets

Batting	AB	R	H	HR	RBI	Avg
Brogna	131	16	46	7	20	**.351**
Kent	415	53	121	14	68	**.292**
Bonilla	403	60	117	20	67	**.290**
Lindeman	137	18	37	7	20	**.270**
Orsulak	292	39	76	8	42	**.260**
Vizcaino	410	47	105	3	33	**.256**
McReynolds	180	23	46	4	21	**.256**
Stinnett	150	20	38	2	14	**.253**
Segui	336	46	81	10	43	**.241**
Burnitz	143	26	34	3	15	**.238**
Hundley	291	45	69	16	42	**.237**
Thompson	334	39	75	18	59	**.225**

Pitching	W	L	ERA	IP	H	BB	SO
Jacome	4	3	**2.67**	54.0	54	17	30
Franco	1	4	**2.70**	50.0	47	19	42
Saberhagen	14	4	**2.74**	177.1	169	13	143
Jones	12	7	**3.15**	160.0	157	56	80
Mason	3	5	**3.75**	60.0	55	25	33
Linton	6	2	**4.47**	50.1	74	20	29
Remlinger	1	5	**4.61**	54.2	55	35	33
Gozzo	3	5	**4.83**	69.0	86	28	33
Smith	4	10	**5.55**	131.1	145	42	62

Manager—Dallas Green

Philadelphia Phillies

Batting	AB	R	H	HR	RBI	Avg
Kruk	255	35	77	5	38	**.302**
Eisenreich	290	42	87	4	43	**.300**
Daulton	257	43	77	15	56	**.300**
Morandini	274	40	80	2	26	**.292**
Jordan	220	29	62	8	37	**.282**
Stocker	271	38	74	2	28	**.273**
Dykstra	315	68	86	5	24	**.273**
Duncan	347	49	93	8	48	**.268**
Hatcher	134	15	33	2	13	**.246**
Longmire	139	10	33	0	17	**.237**
Batiste	209	17	49	1	13	**.234**
Incaviglia	244	28	56	13	32	**.230**
Hollins	162	28	36	4	26	**.222**

Pitching	W	L	ERA	IP	H	BB	SO
Jones	2	4	**2.17**	54.0	55	6	38
Munoz	7	5	**2.67**	104.1	101	35	59
Slocumb	5	1	**2.86**	72.1	75	28	58
Jackson	14	6	**3.26**	179.1	183	46	129
West	4	10	**3.55**	99.0	74	61	83
Edens	5	1	**4.33**	54.0	59	18	39
Schilling	2	8	**4.48**	82.1	87	28	58
Williams	2	4	**5.01**	50.1	61	20	29
Boskie	4	6	**5.01**	88.0	88	29	61

Manager—Jim Fregosi

Pittsburgh Pirates

Batting	AB	R	H	HR	RBI	Avg
Clark	223	37	66	10	46	**.296**
Slaught	240	21	69	2	21	**.288**
Martin	276	48	79	9	33	**.286**
Garcia	412	49	114	6	28	**.277**
Bell	424	68	117	9	45	**.276**
Merced	386	48	105	9	51	**.272**
Parrish	126	10	34	3	16	**.270**
King	339	36	89	5	42	**.263**
Van Slyke	374	41	92	6	30	**.246**

Pitching	W	L	ERA	IP	H	BB	SO
Smith	10	8	**3.27**	157.0	162	34	57
Dewey	2	1	**3.68**	51.1	61	19	30
Lieber	6	7	**3.73**	108.2	116	25	71
White	4	5	**3.82**	75.1	79	17	38
Manzanillo	4	2	**4.14**	50.0	45	42	39
Wagner	7	8	**4.59**	119.2	136	50	86
Pena	3	2	**5.02**	28.2	22	10	27
Cooke	4	11	**5.02**	134.1	157	46	74
Neagle	9	10	**5.12**	137.0	135	49	122

Manager—Jim Leyland

St. Louis Cardinals

Batting	AB	R	H	HR	RBI	Avg
Jefferies	397	52	129	12	55	**.325**
Whiten	334	57	98	14	53	**.293**
Alicea	205	32	57	5	29	**.278**
Pagnozzi	243	21	66	7	40	**.272**
Zeile	415	62	111	19	75	**.267**
Lankford	416	89	111	19	57	**.267**
Oquendo	129	13	34	0	9	**.264**
O. Smith	381	51	100	3	30	**.262**
Jordan	178	14	46	5	15	**.258**
Pena	213	33	54	11	34	**.254**
Gilkey	380	52	96	6	45	**.253**

Pitching	W	L	ERA	IP	H	BB	SO
Arocha	4	4	**4.01**	83.0	94	21	62
Rodriguez	3	5	**4.03**	60.1	62	26	43
Palacios	3	8	**4.44**	117.2	104	43	95
Eversgerd	2	3	**4.52**	67.2	75	20	47
Urbani	3	7	**5.15**	80.1	98	21	43
Tewksbury	12	10	**5.32**	155.2	190	22	79
Watson	6	5	**5.52**	115.2	130	53	74
Olivares	3	4	**5.74**	73.2	84	37	26
Sutcliffe	6	4	**6.52**	67.2	93	32	26
Perez	2	3	**8.71**	31.0	52	10	20

Manager—Joe Torre

San Diego Padres

Batting	AB	R	H	HR	RBI	Avg
Gwynn	419	79	165	12	64	**.394**
Shipley	240	32	80	4	30	**.333**
Williams	175	32	58	11	42	**.331**
Roberts	403	52	129	2	31	**.320**
Bell	434	54	135	14	54	**.311**
Lopez	235	29	65	2	20	**.277**
Livingstone	180	11	49	2	10	**.272**
Ausmus	327	45	82	7	24	**.251**
Gutierrez	275	27	66	1	28	**.240**
Plantier	341	44	75	18	41	**.220**
Cianfrocco	146	9	32	4	13	**.219**
Bean	135	7	29	0	14	**.215**
Clark	149	14	32	5	20	**.215**

Pitching	W	L	ERA	IP	H	BB	SO
Hoffman	4	4	**2.57**	56.0	39	20	68
P. Martinez	3	2	**2.90**	68.1	52	49	52
Hamilton	9	6	**2.98**	108.2	98	29	61
Ashby	6	11	**3.40**	164.1	145	43	121
Benes	6	14	**3.86**	172.1	155	51	189
Sanders	4	8	**4.78**	111.0	103	48	109
Whitehurst	4	7	**4.92**	64.0	84	26	43

Manager—Jim Riggleman

San Francisco Giants

Batting	AB	R	H	HR	RBI	Avg
Bonds	391	89	122	37	81	**.312**
McGee	156	19	44	5	23	**.282**
Williams	445	74	119	43	96	**.267**
Benzinger	328	32	87	9	31	**.265**
Lewis	451	70	116	4	29	**.257**
Manwaring	316	30	79	1	29	**.250**
Martinez	235	23	58	4	27	**.247**
Patterson	240	36	57	3	32	**.238**
Clayton	385	38	91	3	30	**.236**
Thompson	129	13	27	2	7	**.209**

Pitching	W	L	ERA	IP	H	BB	SO
Beck	2	4	**2.77**	48.2	49	13	39
Swift	8	7	**3.38**	109.1	109	31	62
Van Landingham	8	2	**3.54**	84.0	70	43	56
Burkett	6	8	**3.62**	159.1	176	36	85
Portugal	10	8	**3.93**	137.1	135	45	87
Burba	3	6	**4.38**	74.0	59	45	84
Black	4	2	**4.47**	54.1	50	16	28
Hickerson	4	8	**5.40**	98.1	118	38	59
Torres	2	8	**5.44**	84.1	95	34	42

Manager—Dusty Baker

American League Records, 1994

Final standings for strike-shortened season

Eastern Division

	W	L	Pct.	GB	Home	vs. RHP	Grass	Night
New York	70	43	.619	—	33-24	42-26	60-34	45-23
Baltimore	63	49	.563	6½	28-27	46-38	55-41	43-36
Toronto	55	60	.478	16	33-26	34-44	14-27	34-45
Boston	54	61	.470	17	31-33	38-43	48-53	31-40
Detroit	53	62	.461	18	34-24	40-49	46-51	34-36

Central Division

	W	L	Pct.	GB	Home	vs. RHP	Grass	Night
Chicago	67	46	.593	—	34-19	46-33	62-36	46-34
Cleveland	66	47	.584	1	35-16	52-28	57-38	46-30
Kansas City	64	51	.557	4	35-24	48-35	21-22	45-37
Minnesota	53	60	.469	14	32-27	35-45	17-22	35-45
Milwaukee	53	62	.461	15	24-32	41-47	45-52	36-41

Western Division

	W	L	Pct.	GB	Home	vs. RHP	Grass	Night
Texas	52	62	.456	—	31-32	39-43	49-49	42-43
Oakland	51	63	.447	1	24-32	24-41	41-57	32-39
Seattle	49	63	.438	2	22-22	28-47	22-33	34-41
California	47	68	.409	5½	23-40	31-44	42-61	36-49

Team Batting

	Avg	AB	R	H	HR	RBI
New York	**.290**	3986	670	1155	139	632
Cleveland	**.290**	4022	679	1165	167	647
Chicago	**.287**	3942	633	1133	121	602
Texas	**.280**	3983	613	1114	124	582
Minnesota	**.276**	3952	594	1092	103	556
Baltimore	**.272**	3856	589	1047	139	557
Seattle	**.269**	3883	569	1045	153	549
Kansas City	**.269**	3911	574	1051	100	538
Toronto	**.269**	3962	566	1064	115	534
Detroit	**.265**	3955	652	1048	161	622
California	**.264**	3943	543	1042	120	518
Boston	**.263**	3940	552	1038	120	523
Milwaukee	**.263**	3978	547	1045	99	510
Oakland	**.260**	3885	549	1009	113	515

Team Pitching

	ERA	IP	H	BB	SO	Sv
Chicago	**3.96**	1011⅓	964	377	754	20
Kansas City	**4.23**	1031⅔	1018	392	717	38
Baltimore	**4.31**	997⅔	1005	351	666	37
New York	**4.34**	1019⅔	1045	398	656	31
Cleveland	**4.36**	1018⅔	1097	404	666	21
Milwaukee	**4.62**	1036	1071	421	577	23
Toronto	**4.70**	1025	1053	482	832	26
Oakland	**4.80**	1003⅓	979	510	732	23
Boston	**4.93**	1029⅓	1104	450	729	30
Seattle	**4.99**	984	1051	486	763	21
Detroit	**5.38**	1018	1139	449	560	20
California	**5.42**	1027	1149	436	682	21
Texas	**5.45**	1023	1176	394	683	26
Minnesota	**5.68**	1005	1197	388	602	29

Individual Batting (at least 125 at-bats); Individual Pitching (at least 50 innings or 6 saves)

Baltimore Orioles

Batting	AB	R	H	HR	RBI	Avg
Palmeiro	436	82	139	23	76	**.319**
Ripken	444	71	140	13	75	**.315**
Hammonds	250	45	74	8	31	**.296**
Baines	326	44	96	16	54	**.294**
D. Smith	196	31	55	8	30	**.281**
Gomez	285	46	78	15	56	**.274**
Anderson	453	78	119	12	48	**.263**
McLemore	343	44	88	3	29	**.257**
Sabo	258	41	66	11	42	**.256**
Hoiles	332	45	82	19	53	**.247**
Voigt	141	15	34	3	20	**.241**
Devereaux	301	35	61	9	33	**.203**

Pitching	W	L	ERA	IP	H	BB	SO
Eichhorn	6	5	**2.15**	71.0	62	19	35
Mussina	16	5	**3.06**	176.1	163	42	99
Le. Smith	1	4	**3.29**	38.1	34	11	42
Williamson	3	1	**4.01**	67.1	75	17	28
McDonald	14	7	**4.06**	157.1	151	54	94
Moyer	5	7	**4.77**	149.0	158	38	87
Fernandez	6	6	**5.15**	115.1	109	46	95
Rhodes	3	5	**5.81**	52.2	51	30	47
Oquist	3	3	**6.17**	58.1	75	30	39

Manager—John Oates

Boston Red Sox

Batting	AB	R	H	HR	RBI	Avg
Valentin	301	53	95	9	49	**.316**
Vaughn	394	65	122	26	82	**.310**
Rodriguez	174	15	50	1	13	**.287**
Cooper	369	49	104	13	53	**.282**
Naehring	297	41	82	7	42	**.276**
Nixon	398	60	109	0	25	**.274**
Greenwell	327	60	88	11	45	**.269**
Berryhill	255	30	67	6	34	**.263**
Chamberlain	164	13	42	4	20	**.256**
Hatcher	164	24	40	1	18	**.244**
Dawson	292	34	70	16	48	**.240**
Brunasky	205	24	48	10	34	**.234**
Fletcher	185	31	42	3	11	**.227**
Tinsley	144	27	32	2	14	**.222**

Pitching	W	L	ERA	IP	H	BB	SO
Ryan	2	3	**2.44**	48.0	46	17	32
Clemens	9	7	**2.85**	170.2	124	71	168
Sele	8	7	**3.83**	143.1	140	60	105
Hesketh	8	5	**4.26**	114.0	117	46	83
Darwin	7	5	**6.30**	75.2	101	24	54
Nabholz	3	5	**7.64**	53.0	67	38	28

Manager—Butch Hobson

California Angels

Batting	AB	R	H	HR	RBI	Avg
Davis	392	72	122	26	84	**.311**
Owen	268	30	83	3	37	**.310**
Salmon	373	67	107	23	70	**.287**
Fabregas	127	12	36	0	16	**.283**
Jackson	201	23	56	13	43	**.279**
Edmonds	289	35	79	5	37	**.273**
DiSarcina	389	53	101	3	33	**.260**
Curtis	453	67	116	11	50	**.256**
Myers	126	10	31	2	8	**.246**
Turner	149	23	36	1	12	**.242**
Reynolds	207	33	48	0	11	**.232**
Snow	223	22	49	8	30	**.220**
Easley	316	41	68	6	30	**.215**
Perez	129	10	27	5	16	**.209**

Pitching	W	L	ERA	IP	H	BB	SO
Finley	10	10	**4.32**	183.1	178	71	148
Langston	7	8	**4.68**	119.1	121	54	109
Leiter	4	7	**4.72**	95.1	99	35	71
B. Anderson	7	5	**5.22**	101.2	120	27	47
Leftwich	5	10	**5.68**	114.0	127	42	67
Dopson	1	4	**6.14**	58.2	67	26	33
Grahe	2	5	**6.65**	43.1	68	18	26
Magrane	2	6	**7.30**	74.0	89	51	33

Manager—Buck Rodgers; Marcel Lachemann

Chicago White Sox

Batting	AB	R	H	HR	RBI	Avg
Thomas	399	106	141	38	101	**.353**
Franco	433	72	138	20	98	**.319**
Jackson	369	43	115	10	51	**.312**
Guillen	365	46	105	1	39	**.288**
Ventura	401	57	113	18	78	**.282**
LaValliere	139	6	39	1	24	**.281**
L. Johnson	412	56	114	3	54	**.277**
Cora	312	55	86	2	30	**.276**
Martin	131	19	36	1	16	**.275**
Raines	384	80	102	10	52	**.266**
Karkovice	207	33	44	11	29	**.213**

Pitching	W	L	ERA	IP	H	BB	SO
DeLeon	3	2	**3.36**	67.0	48	31	67
McCaskill	1	4	**3.42**	52.2	51	22	37
Alvarez	12	8	**3.45**	161.2	147	62	108
McDowell	10	9	**3.73**	181.0	186	42	127
Bere	12	2	**3.81**	141.2	119	80	127
Fernandez	11	7	**3.86**	170.1	163	50	122
Hernandez	4	4	**4.91**	47.2	44	19	50
Sanderson	8	4	**5.09**	92.0	110	12	36

Manager—Gene Lamont

Cleveland Indians

Batting	AB	R	H	HR	RBI	Avg
Belle	412	90	147	36	101	**.357**
Lofton	459	105	160	12	57	**.349**
Baerga	442	81	139	19	80	**.314**
Kirby	191	33	56	5	23	**.293**
Alomar	292	44	84	14	43	**.288**
Sorrento	322	43	90	14	62	**.280**
Vizquel	286	39	78	1	33	**.273**
Ramirez	290	51	78	17	60	**.269**
Thome	321	58	86	20	52	**.268**
Murray	433	57	110	17	76	**.254**
Espinoza	231	27	55	1	19	**.238**

Pitching	W	L	ERA	IP	H	BB	SO
Plunk	7	2	**2.54**	71.0	61	37	73
Nagy	10	8	**3.45**	169.1	175	48	108
Martinez	11	6	**3.52**	176.2	166	44	92
Clark	11	3	**3.82**	127.1	133	40	60
Mesa	7	5	**3.82**	73.0	71	26	63
Grimsley	5	2	**4.57**	82.2	91	34	59
Russell	1	6	**5.09**	40.2	43	16	28
Morris	10	6	**5.60**	141.1	163	67	100

Manager—Mike Hargrove

Detroit Tigers

Batting	AB	R	H	HR	RBI	Avg
Samuel	136	32	42	5	21	**.309**
Felix	301	54	92	13	49	**.306**
Whitaker	322	67	97	12	43	**.301**
Phillips	438	91	123	19	61	**.281**
Gibson	330	71	91	23	72	**.276**
Trammell	292	38	78	8	28	**.267**
Fryman	464	66	122	18	85	**.263**
Fielder	425	67	110	28	90	**.259**
Gomez	296	32	76	8	53	**.257**
Tettleton	339	57	84	17	51	**.248**
Kreuter	170	17	38	1	19	**.224**

Pitching	W	L	ERA	IP	H	BB	SO
Wells	5	7	**3.96**	111.1	113	24	71
Boever	9	2	**3.98**	81.1	80	37	49
Gardiner	2	2	**4.14**	58.2	53	23	31
Henneman	1	3	**5.19**	34.2	43	17	27
Moore	11	10	**5.42**	154.1	152	89	62
Belcher	7	15	**5.89**	162.0	192	78	76
Gullickson	4	5	**5.93**	115.1	156	25	65
Doherty	6	7	**6.48**	101.1	139	26	28

Manager—Sparky Anderson

Kansas City Royals

Batting	AB	R	H	HR	RBI	Avg
Joyner	363	52	113	8	57	**.311**
Jose	366	56	111	11	55	**.303**
Gaetti	327	53	94	12	57	**.287**
Hamelin	312	64	88	24	65	**.282**
B. McRae	436	71	119	4	40	**.273**
Lind	290	34	78	1	31	**.269**
Gagne	375	39	97	7	51	**.259**
Mayne	144	19	37	2	20	**.257**
Macfarlane	314	53	80	14	47	**.255**
Henderson	198	27	49	5	31	**.247**
Shumpert	183	28	44	8	24	**.240**
Coleman	438	61	105	2	33	**.240**

Pitching	W	L	ERA	IP	H	BB	SO
Cone	16	5	**2.94**	171.2	130	54	132
Meacham	3	3	**3.73**	50.2	51	12	36
Appier	7	6	**3.83**	155.0	137	63	145
Montgomery	2	3	**4.03**	44.2	48	15	50
Gordon	11	7	**4.35**	155.1	136	87	126
Gubicza	7	9	**4.50**	130.0	158	26	59
Pichardo	5	3	**4.92**	67.2	82	24	36
Milacki	0	5	**6.14**	55.2	68	20	17

Manager—Hal McRae

Milwaukee Brewers

Batting	AB	R	H	HR	RBI	Avg
Seitzer	309	44	97	5	49	**.314**
Harper	251	23	73	4	32	**.291**
Nilsson	397	51	109	12	69	**.275**
Reed	399	48	108	2	37	**.271**
Hamilton	141	23	37	1	13	**.262**
Surhoff	134	20	35	5	22	**.261**
Mieske	259	39	67	10	38	**.259**
Vaughn	370	59	94	19	55	**.254**
Spiers	214	27	54	0	17	**.252**
Diaz	187	17	47	1	17	**.251**
Jaha	291	45	70	12	39	**.241**
Valentin	285	47	68	11	46	**.239**
Cirillo	126	17	30	3	12	**.238**
Ward	367	55	85	9	45	**.232**

Pitching	W	L	ERA	IP	H	BB	SO
Fetters	1	4	**2.54**	46.0	41	27	31
Bones	10	9	**3.43**	170.2	166	45	57
Scanlan	2	6	**4.11**	103.0	117	28	65
Wegman	8	4	**4.51**	115.2	140	26	59
Eldred	11	11	**4.68**	179.0	158	84	98
Navarro	4	9	**6.62**	89.2	115	35	65
Higuera	1	5	**7.06**	58.2	74	36	35

Manager—Phil Garner

Minnesota Twins

Batting	AB	R	H	HR	RBI	Avg
Mack	303	55	101	15	61	**.333**
Puckett	439	79	139	20	112	**.317**
Knoblauch	445	85	139	5	51	**.312**
Cole	345	68	102	4	23	**.296**
Munoz	244	35	72	11	36	**.295**
Hrbek	274	34	74	10	53	**.270**
Meares	229	29	61	2	24	**.266**
Hale	118	13	31	1	11	**.263**
McCarty	131	21	34	1	12	**.260**
Reboulet	189	28	49	3	23	**.259**
Winfield	294	35	74	10	43	**.252**
Leius	350	57	86	14	49	**.246**
Walbeck	338	31	69	5	35	**.204**

Pitching	W	L	ERA	IP	H	BB	SO
Aguilera	1	4	**3.63**	44.2	57	10	46
Tapani	11	7	**4.62**	156.0	181	39	91
Mahomes	9	5	**4.73**	120.0	121	62	53
Erickson	8	11	**5.44**	144.0	173	59	104
Willis	2	4	**5.92**	59.1	89	12	37
Pulido	3	7	**5.98**	84.1	87	40	32
Guthrie	4	2	**6.14**	51.1	65	18	38
Deshaies	6	12	**7.39**	130.1	170	54	78

Manager—Tom Kelly

New York Yankees

Batting	AB	R	H	HR	RBI	Avg
O'Neill	368	68	132	21	83	**.359**
Boggs	366	61	125	11	55	**.342**
Polonia	350	62	109	1	36	**.311**
Mattingly	372	62	113	6	51	**.304**
Stanley	290	54	87	17	57	**.300**
B. Williams	408	80	118	12	57	**.289**
Kelly	286	35	80	3	41	**.280**
Velarde	280	47	78	9	34	**.279**
Leyritz	249	47	66	17	58	**.265**
Tartabull	399	68	102	19	67	**.256**
Gallego	306	39	73	6	41	**.239**

Pitching	W	L	ERA	IP	H	BB	SO
Howe	3	0	**1.80**	40.0	28	7	18
Wickman	5	4	**3.09**	70.0	54	27	56
Key	17	4	**3.27**	168.0	177	52	97
Kamieniecki	8	6	**3.76**	117.1	115	59	71
Perez	9	4	**4.10**	151.1	134	58	109
Abbott	9	8	**4.55**	160.1	167	64	90
Hernandez	4	4	**5.85**	40.0	48	21	37
Mulholland	6	7	**6.49**	120.2	150	37	72
Harris	3	5	**7.99**	50.2	64	26	48

Manager—Buck Showalter

Oakland Athletics

Batting	AB	R	H	HR	RBI	Avg
Berroa	340	55	104	13	65	**.306**
Steinbach	369	51	105	11	57	**.285**
Gates	233	29	66	2	24	**.283**
Javier	419	75	114	10	44	**.272**
Sierra	426	71	114	23	92	**.268**
Neel	278	43	74	15	48	**.266**
Henderson	296	66	77	6	20	**.260**
Bordick	391	38	99	2	37	**.253**
McGwire	135	26	34	9	25	**.252**
Aldrete	178	23	43	4	18	**.242**
Brosius	324	31	77	14	49	**.238**
Hemond	198	23	44	3	20	**.222**

Pitching	W	L	ERA	IP	H	BB	SO
Ontiveros	6	4	**2.65**	115.1	93	26	56
Reyes	0	3	**4.15**	78.0	71	44	57
Eckersley	5	4	**4.26**	44.1	49	13	47
Darling	10	11	**4.50**	160.0	162	59	108
Witt	8	10	**5.04**	135.2	151	70	111
Van Poppel	7	10	**6.09**	116.2	108	89	83
Welch	3	6	**7.08**	68.2	79	43	44

Manager—Tony LaRussa

Seattle Mariners

Batting	AB	R	H	HR	RBI	Avg
Jefferson	162	24	53	8	32	**.327**
Griffey	433	94	140	40	90	**.323**
Fermin	379	52	120	1	35	**.317**
Blowers	270	37	78	9	49	**.289**
E. Martinez	326	47	93	13	51	**.285**
Buhner	358	74	100	21	68	**.279**
Sojo	213	32	59	6	22	**.277**
Amaral	228	37	60	4	18	**.263**
T. Martinez	329	42	86	20	61	**.261**
Anthony	262	31	62	10	30	**.237**
Mitchell	128	21	29	5	15	**.227**
Wilson	282	24	61	3	27	**.216**

Pitching	W	L	ERA	IP	H	BB	SO
Ayala	4	3	**2.86**	56.2	42	26	76
Johnson	13	6	**3.19**	172.0	132	72	204
Risley	9	6	**3.44**	52.1	31	19	61
Bosio	4	10	**4.32**	125.0	137	40	67
Cummings	2	4	**5.63**	64.0	66	37	33
Fleming	7	11	**6.46**	117.0	152	65	65
Hibbard	1	5	**6.69**	80.2	115	31	39
Salkeld	2	5	**7.17**	59.0	76	45	46

Manager—Lou Piniella

Texas Rangers

Batting	AB	R	H	HR	RBI	Avg
Clark	389	73	128	13	80	**.329**
Frye	205	37	67	0	18	**.327**
Greer	277	36	87	10	46	**.314**
Rodriguez	363	56	108	16	57	**.298**
Beltre	131	12	37	0	12	**.282**
Canseco	429	88	121	31	90	**.282**
Lee	335	41	93	2	38	**.278**
Gonzalez	422	57	116	19	85	**.275**
McDowell	183	34	48	1	15	**.262**
James	133	28	34	7	19	**.256**
Hulse	310	58	79	1	19	**.255**
Palmer	342	50	84	19	59	**.246**
Strange	226	26	48	5	26	**.212**

Pitching	W	L	ERA	IP	H	BB	SO
Oliver	4	0	**3.42**	50.0	40	35	50
Henke	3	6	**3.79**	38.0	33	12	39
Dettmer	0	6	**4.33**	54.0	63	20	27
Rogers	11	8	**4.46**	167.1	169	52	120
Brown	7	9	**4.82**	170.0	218	50	123
Whiteside	2	2	**5.02**	61.0	68	28	37
Carpenter	2	5	**5.03**	59.0	69	20	39
Helling	3	2	**5.88**	52.0	62	18	25
Fajardo	5	7	**6.91**	83.1	95	26	45
Pavlik	2	5	**7.69**	50.1	61	30	31

Manager—Kevin Kennedy

Toronto Blue Jays

Batting	AB	R	H	HR	RBI	Avg
Molitor	454	86	155	14	75	**.341**
Alomar	392	78	120	8	38	**.306**
Huff	207	31	63	3	25	**.304**
Olerud	384	47	114	12	67	**.297**
Carter	435	70	118	27	103	**.271**
White	403	67	109	13	49	**.270**
Schofield	325	38	83	4	32	**.255**
Borders	295	24	73	3	26	**.247**
Sprague	405	38	97	11	44	**.240**
Delgado	130	17	28	9	24	**.215**
Coles	143	15	30	4	15	**.210**

Pitching	W	L	ERA	IP	H	BB	SO
Castillo	5	2	**2.51**	68.0	66	28	43
Hentgen	13	8	**3.40**	174.2	158	59	147
Hall	2	3	**3.41**	31.2	26	14	28
Williams	1	3	**3.64**	59.1	44	33	56
Stottlemyre	7	7	**4.22**	140.2	149	48	105
Leiter	6	7	**5.08**	111.2	125	65	100
Guzman	12	11	**5.68**	147.1	165	76	124
Stewart	7	8	**5.87**	133.1	151	62	111

Manager—Cito Gaston

National Baseball Hall of Fame and Museum, Cooperstown, N.Y.

Aaron, Hank
Alexander, Grover Cleveland
Alston, Walt
Anson, Cap
Aparicio, Luis
Appling, Luke
Averill, Earl
Baker, Home Run
Bancroft, Dave
Banks, Ernie
Barlick, Al
Barrow, Edward G.
Beckley, Jake
Bell, Cool Papa
Bench, Johnny
Bender, Chief
Berra, Yogi
Bottomley, Jim
Boudreau, Lou
Bresnahan, Roger
Brock, Lou
Brouthers, Dan
Brown, Mordecai (Three Finger)
Bulkeley, Morgan C.
Burkett, Jesse C.
Campanella, Roy
Carew, Rod
Carey, Max
Carlton, Steve
Cartwright, Alexander
Chadwick, Henry
Chance, Frank
Chandler, Happy
Charleston, Oscar
Chesbro, John
Clarke, Fred
Clarkson, John
Clemente, Roberto
Cobb, Ty
Cochrane, Mickey
Collins, Eddie
Collins, James
Combs, Earle
Comiskey, Charles A.
Conlan, Jocko
Connolly, Thomas H.
Connor, Roger
Coveleski, Stan
Crawford, Sam
Cronin, Joe
Cummings, Candy
Cuyler, Kiki
Dandridge, Ray
Dean, Dizzy
Delahanty, Ed
Dickey, Bill
DiHigo, Martin
DiMaggio, Joe
Doerr, Bobby
Drysdale, Don
Duffy, Hugh
Durocher, Leo
Evans, Billy
Evers, John
Ewing, Buck
Faber, Urban
Feller, Bob
Ferrell, Rick
Fingers, Rollie
Flick, Elmer H.
Ford, Whitey
Foster, Andrew
Foxx, Jimmie
Frick, Ford
Frisch, Frank
Galvin, Pud
Gehrig, Lou
Gehringer, Charles
Gibson, Bob
Gibson, Josh
Giles, Warren
Gomez, Lefty
Goslin, Goose
Greenberg, Hank
Griffith, Clark
Grimes, Burleigh
Grove, Lefty
Hafey, Chick
Haines, Jesee
Hamilton, Bill
Harridge, Will
Harris, Bucky
Hartnett, Gabby
Heilmann, Harry
Herman, Billy
Hooper, Harry
Hornsby, Rogers
Hoyt, Waite
Hubbard, Cal
Hubbell, Carl
Huggins, Miller
Hunter, Catfish
Irvin, Monte
Jackson, Reggie
Jackson, Travis
Jenkins, Ferguson
Jennings, Hugh
Johnson, Byron
Johnson, William (Judy)
Johnson, Walter
Joss, Addie
Kaline, Al
Keefe, Timothy
Keeler, William
Kell, George
Kelley, Joe
Kelly, George
Kelly, King
Killebrew, Harmon
Kiner, Ralph
Klein, Chuck
Klem, Bill
Koufax, Sandy
Lajoie, Napoleon
Landis, Kenesaw M.
Lazzeri, Tony
Lemon, Bob
Leonard, Buck
Lindstrom, Fred
Lloyd, Pop
Lombardi, Ernie
Lopez, Al
Lyons, Ted
Mack, Connie
MacPhail, Larry
Mantle, Mickey
Manush, Henry
Maranville, Rabbit
Marichal, Juan
Marquard, Rube
Mathews, Eddie
Mathewson, Christy
Mays, Willie
McCarthy, Joe
McCarthy, Thomas
McCovey, Willie
McGinnity, Joe
McGowan, Bill
McGraw, John
McKechnie, Bill
Medwick, Joe
Mize, Johnny
Morgan, Joe
Musial, Stan
Newhouser, Hal
Nichols, Kid
O'Rourke, James
Ott, Mel
Paige, Satchel
Palmer, Jim
Pennock, Herb
Perry, Gaylord
Plank, Ed
Radbourn, Charlie
Reese, Pee Wee
Rice, Sam
Rickey, Branch
Rixey, Eppa
Rizzuto, Phil (Scooter)
Roberts, Robin
Robinson, Brooks
Robinson, Frank
Robinson, Jackie
Robinson, Wilbert
Roush, Edd
Ruffing, Red
Rusie, Amos
Ruth, Babe
Schalk, Ray
Schoendienst, Red
Seaver, Tom
Sewell, Joe
Simmons, Al
Sisler, George
Slaughter, Enos
Snider, Duke
Spahn, Warren
Spalding, Albert
Speaker, Tris
Stargell, Willie
Stengel, Casey
Terry, Bill
Thompson, Sam
Tinker, Joe
Traynor, Pie
Vance, Dazzy
Vaughan, Arky
Veeck, Bill
Waddell, Rube
Wagner, Honus
Wallace, Roderick
Walsh, Ed
Waner, Lloyd
Waner, Paul
Ward, John
Weiss, George
Welch, Mickey
Wheat, Zach
Wilhelm, Hoyt
Williams, Billy
Williams, Ted
Wilson, Hack
Wright, George
Wright, Harry
Wynn, Early
Yastrzemski, Carl
Yawkey, Tom
Young, Cy
Youngs, Ross

Hall of Famers Chosen in First Year of Eligibility

1962	Jackie Robinson, Bob Feller
1966	Ted Williams
1969	Stan Musial
1972	Sandy Koufax
1973	Warren Spahn
1974	Mickey Mantle
1977	Ernie Banks
1979	Willie Mays
1980	Al Kaline
1981	Bob Gibson
1982	Hank Aaron, Frank Robinson
1983	Brooks Robinson
1985	Lou Brock
1986	Willie McCovey
1988	Willie Stargell
1989	Johnny Bench, Carl Yastrzemski
1990	Jim Palmer, Joe Morgan
1992	Tom Seaver
1993	Reggie Jackson
1994	Steve Carlton

All-Star Baseball Games, 1933-1994

Year	Winner	Score	Location
1933	American	**4-2**	Chicago
1934	American	**9-7**	New York
1935	American	**4-1**	Cleveland
1936	National	**4-3**	Boston
1937	American	**8-3**	Washington
1938	National	**4-1**	Cincinnati
1939	American	**3-1**	New York
1940	National	**4-0**	St. Louis
1941	American	**7-5**	Detroit
1942	American	**3-1**	New York
1943*	American	**5-3**	Philadelphia
1944*	National	**7-1**	Pittsburgh
1945	Not played		
1946	American	**12-0**	Boston
1947	American	**2-1**	Chicago
1948	American	**5-2**	St. Louis
1949	American	**11-7**	New York
1950	National (1)	**4-3**	Chicago
1951	National	**8-3**	Detroit
1952	National	**3-2**	Philadelphia
1953	National	**5-1**	Cincinnati
1954	American	**11-9**	Cleveland
1955	National (2)	**6-5**	Milwaukee
1956	National	**7-3**	Washington
1957	American	**6-5**	St. Louis
1958	American	**4-3**	Baltimore
1959	National	**5-4**	Pittsburgh
1959	American	**5-3**	Los Angeles
1960	National	**5-3**	Kansas City
1960	National	**6-0**	New York
1961	National (3)	**5-4**	San Francisco
1961	Called-rain	**1-1**	Boston
1962	National (3)	**3-1**	Washington
1962	American	**9-4**	Chicago
1963	National	**5-3**	Cleveland
1964	National	**7-4**	New York
1965	National	**6-5**	Minnesota
1966	National (3)	**2-1**	St. Louis
1967	National (4)	**2-1**	Anaheim
1968*	National	**1-0**	Houston
1969	National	**9-3**	Washington
1970*	National (2)	**5-4**	Cincinnati
1971*	American	**6-4**	Detroit
1972*	National	**4-3**	Atlanta
1973*	National	**7-1**	Kansas City
1974*	National	**7-2**	Pittsburgh
1975*	National	**6-3**	Milwaukee
1976*	National	**7-1**	Philadelphia
1977*	National	**7-5**	New York
1978*	National	**7-3**	San Diego
1979*	National	**7-6**	Seattle
1980*	National	**4-2**	Los Angeles
1981*	National	**5-4**	Cleveland
1982*	National	**4-1**	Montreal
1983*	American	**13-3**	Chicago
1984*	National	**3-1**	San Francisco
1985*	National	**6-1**	Minneapolis
1986*	American	**3-2**	Houston
1987*	National (5)	**2-0**	Oakland
1988*	American	**2-1**	Cincinnati
1989*	American	**5-3**	Anaheim
1990*	American	**2-0**	Chicago
1991*	American	**4-2**	Toronto
1992*	American	**13-6**	San Diego
1993*	American	**9-3**	Baltimore
1994*	National	**8-7**	Pittsburgh

(1) 14 innings. (2) 12 innings. (3) 10 innings. (4) 15 innings. (5) 13 innings. * Night game.

Major League Leaders in 1994

Final statistics for strike-shortened season

American League

Batting

O'Neill, New York, .359; Belle, Cleveland, .357; Thomas, Chicago, .353; Lofton, Cleveland, .349; Boggs, New York, .342.

Runs

Thomas, Chicago, 106; Lofton, Cleveland, 105; Griffey, Seattle, 94; Phillips, Detroit, 91; Belle, Cleveland, 90.

Runs Batted In

Puckett, Minnesota, 112; Carter, Toronto, 103; Thomas, Chicago, 101; Belle, Cleveland, 101; Franco, Chicago, 98.

Hits

Lofton, Cleveland, 160; Molitor, Toronto, 155; Belle, Cleveland, 147; Thomas, Chicago, 141; Griffey, Seattle, 140.

Doubles

Knoblauch, Minnesota, 45; Belle, Cleveland, 35; Thomas, Chicago, 34; Fryman, Detroit, 34; Lofton, Cleveland, 32.

Triples

L. Johnson, Chicago, 14; Coleman, Kansas City, 12; Lofton, Cleveland, 9; A. Diaz, Milwaukee, 7; McRae, Kansas City, 6.

Home Runs

Griffey, Seattle, 40; Thomas, Chicago, 38; Belle, Cleveland, 36; Canseco, Texas, 31; Fielder, Detroit, 28.

Stolen Bases

Lofton, Cleveland, 60; Coleman, Kansas City, 50; Nixon, Boston, 42; Knoblauch, Minnesota, 35; By. Anderson, Baltimore, 31.

Pitching (12 Decisions)

Bere, Chicago, 12-2, .857, 3.81; Key, New York, 17-4, .810, 3.27; M. Clark, Cleveland, 11-3, .786, 3.82; Mussina, Baltimore, 16-5, .762, 3.06; Cone, Kansas City, 16-5, .762, 2.94.

Strikeouts

R. Johnson, Seattle, 204; Clemens, Boston, 168; Finley, California, 148; Hentgen, Toronto, 147; Appier, Kansas City, 145.

Saves

Le. Smith, Baltimore, 33; Montgomery, Kansas City, 27; Aguilera, Minnesota, 23; Eckersley, Oakland, 19; Ayala, Seattle, 18.

National League

Batting

Gwynn, San Diego, .394; Bagwell, Houston, .367; Alou, Montreal, .339; Morris, Cincinnati, .335; Mitchell, Cincinnati, .326.

Runs

Bagwell, Houston, 104; Grissom, Montreal, 96; Lankford, St. Louis, 89; Bonds, San Francisco, 89; Biggio, Houston, 88.

Runs Batted In

Bagwell, Houston, 116; Matt Williams, San Francisco, 96; Bichette, Colorado, 95; McGriff, Atlanta, 94; Piazza, Los Angeles, 92.

Hits

Gwynn, San Diego, 165; Bagwell, Houston, 147; Bichette, Colorado, 147; Morris, Cincinnati, 146; Conine, Florida, 144.

Doubles

Biggio, Houston, 44; L. Walker, Montreal, 44; J. Bell, Pittsburgh, 35; Gwynn, San Diego, 35; Bichette, Colorado, 33.

Triples

D. Lewis, San Francisco, 9; Butler, Los Angeles, 9; Mondesi, Los Angeles, 8; R. Sanders, Cincinnati, 8; Kingery, Colorado, 8.

Home Runs

Matt Williams, San Francisco, 43; Bagwell, Houston, 39; Bonds, San Francisco, 37; McGriff, Atlanta, 34; Galaragga, Colorado, 31.

Stolen Bases

Biggio, Houston, 39; D. Sanders, Cincinnati, 38; Grissom, Montreal, 36; Carr, Florida, 32; D. Lewis, San Francisco, 30.

Pitching (12 Decisions)

Freeman, Colorado, 10-2, .833, 2.80; Saberhagen, New York, 14-4, .778, 2.74; K. Hill, Montreal, 16-5, .762, 3.32; G. Maddux, Atlanta, 16-6, .727, 1.56; Dn. Jackson, Philadelphia, 14-6, .700, 3.26.

Strikeouts

Benes, San Diego, 189; Rijo, Cincinnati, 171; G. Maddux, Atlanta, 156; Saberhagen, New York, 143; P.J. Martinez, Montreal, 142.

Saves

Franco, Mets, 30; Beck, San Francisco, 28; D. Jones, Philadelphia, 27; Wetteland, Montreal, 25; McMichael, Atlanta, 21.

Earned Run Average Leaders

National League					American League				
Year	Player, club	G	IP	ERA	Year	Player, club	G	IP	ERA
1972	Steve Carlton, Philadelphia	41	346	**1.98**	1972	Luis Tiant, Boston	43	179	**1.91**
1973	Tom Seaver, New York	36	290	**2.07**	1973	Jim Palmer, Baltimore	38	296	**2.40**
1974	Buzz Capra, Atlanta	39	217	**2.28**	1974	Catfish Hunter, Oakland	41	318	**2.49**
1975	Randy Jones, San Diego	37	285	**2.24**	1975	Jim Palmer, Baltimore	39	323	**2.09**
1976	John Denny, St. Louis	30	207	**2.52**	1976	Mark Fidrych, Detroit	31	250	**2.34**
1977	John Candelaria, Pittsburgh	33	231	**2.34**	1977	Frank Tanana, California	31	241	**2.54**
1978	Craig Swan, New York	29	207	**2.43**	1978	Ron Guidry, New York	35	274	**1.74**
1979	J. R. Richard, Houston	38	292	**2.71**	1979	Ron Guidry, New York	33	236	**2.78**
1980	Don Sutton, Los Angeles	32	212	**2.21**	1980	Rudy May, New York	41	175	**2.47**
1981	Nolan Ryan, Houston	21	149	**1.69**	1981	Steve McCatty, Oakland	22	186	**2.32**
1982	Steve Rogers, Montreal	35	277	**2.40**	1982	Rick Sutcliffe, Cleveland	34	216	**2.96**
1983	Atlee Hammaker, San Francisco	23	172	**2.25**	1983	Rick Honeycutt, Texas	25	174	**2.42**
1984	Alejandro Pena, Los Angeles	28	199	**2.48**	1984	Mike Boddicker, Baltimore	34	261	**2.79**
1985	Dwight Gooden, New York	35	276	**1.53**	1985	Dave Stieb, Toronto	36	265	**2.48**
1986	Mike Scott, Houston	37	275	**2.22**	1986	Roger Clemens, Boston	33	254	**2.48**
1987	Nolan Ryan, Houston	34	211	**2.76**	1987	Jimmy Key, Toronto	36	261	**2.76**
1988	Joe Magrane, St. Louis	24	165	**2.18**	1988	Allan Anderson, Minnesota	30	202	**2.45**
1989	Scott Garrelts, San Francisco	30	193	**2.28**	1989	Bret Saberhagen, Kansas City	36	262	**2.16**
1990	Danny Darwin, Houston	48	162	**2.21**	1990	Roger Clemens, Boston	31	228	**1.93**
1991	Dennis Martinez, Montreal	31	222	**2.39**	1991	Roger Clemens, Boston	35	271	**2.62**
1992	Bill Swift, San Francisco	30	164	**2.08**	1992	Roger Clemens, Boston	32	246	**2.41**
1993	Greg Maddux, Atlanta	36	267	**2.36**	1993	Kevin Appier, Kansas City	34	238	**2.56**
1994	*Greg Maddux, Atlanta	25	202	**1.56**	1994	*Steve Ontiveros, Oakland	27	115	**2.65**

ERA is computed by multiplying earned runs allowed by 9, then dividing by innings pitched.

All-Time Major League Leaders

(Includes 1994 season)

Games		At Bats		Runs Batted In		Stolen Bases (since 1898)	
Pete Rose	3,562	Pete Rose	14,043	Hank Aaron	2,297	Rickey Henderson	1,117
Carl Yastrzemski	3,308	Hank Aaron	12,364	Babe Ruth	2,204	Lou Brock	938
Hank Aaron	3,298	Carl Yastrzemski	11,988	Lou Gehrig	1,990	Ty Cobb	892
Ty Cobb	3,033	Ty Cobb	11,429	Ty Cobb	1,961	Tim Raines	764
Stan Musial	3,026	Robin Yount	11,008	Stan Musial	1,951	Eddie Collins	742
Willie Mays	2,992	Stan Musial	10,972	Jimmie Foxx	1,922	Max Carey	738
Rusty Staub	2,951	Dave Winfield	10,888	Willie Mays	1,903	Honus Wagner	703
Dave Winfield	2,927	Willie Mays	10,881	Mel Ott	1,860	Vince Coleman	698
Brooks Robinson	2,896	Brooks Robinson	10,654	Carl Yastrzemski	1,844	Joe Morgan	689
Robin Yount	2,856	Honus Wagner	10,427	Ted Williams	1,839	Willie Wilson	668
Runs		**Hits**		**Strikeouts**		**Shutouts**	
Ty Cobb	2,245	Pete Rose	4,256	Nolan Ryan	5,714	Walter Johnson	110
Hank Aaron	2,174	Ty Cobb	4,191	Steve Carlton	4,136	Grover C. Alexander	90
Babe Ruth	2,174	Hank Aaron	3,771	Bert Blyleven	3,701	Christy Mathewson	83
Pete Rose	2,165	Stan Musial	3,630	Tom Seaver	3,640	Cy Young	77
Willie Mays	2,062	Tris Speaker	3,515	Don Sutton	3,574	Eddie Plank	69
Stan Musial	1,949	Honus Wagner	3,430	Gaylord Perry	3,534	Warren Spahn	63
Lou Gehrig	1,888	Carl Yastrzemski	3,419	Walter Johnson	3,508	Mordecai Brown	63
Tris Speaker	1,881	Eddie Collins	3,309	Phil Niekro	3,340	Tom Seaver	61
Mel Ott	1,859	Willie Mays	3,283	Ferguson Jenkins	3,192	Nolan Ryan	61
Frank Robinson	1,829	Nap Lajoie	3,244	Bob Gibson	3,117	Bert Blyleven	60

All-Time Home Run Leaders

Player	HR	Player	HR	Player	HR	Player	HR
Hank Aaron	755	Jimmy Foxx	534	Dave Winfield	463	Dale Murphy	398
Babe Ruth	714	Ted Williams	521	Eddie Murray	458	Graig Nettles	390
Willie Mays	660	Willie McCovey	521	Carl Yastrzemski	452	Johnny Bench	389
Frank Robinson	586	Ed Mathews	512	Dave Kingman	442	Dwight Evans	385
Harmon Killebrew	573	Ernie Banks	512	Andre Dawson	428	Frank Howard	382
Reggie Jackson	563	Mel Ott	511	Billy Williams	426	Jim Rice	382
Mike Schmidt	548	Lou Gehrig	493	Darrell Evans	414	Orlando Cepeda	379
Mickey Mantle	536	Stan Musial	475	Duke Snider	407	Tony Perez	379
		Willie Stargell	475	Al Kaline	399		

Players With 3,000 Major League Hits

Player	Hits	Player	Hits	Player	Hits
Pete Rose	4,256	Carl Yastrzemski	3,419	Dave Winfield	3,088
Ty Cobb	4,191	Eddie Collins	3,309	Cap Anson	3,081
Hank Aaron	3,771	Willie Mays	3,283	Rod Carew	3,053
Stan Musial	3,630	Nap Lajoie	3,244	Lou Brock	3,023
Tris Speaker	3,515	George Brett	3,154	Al Kaline	3,007
Honus Wagner	3,430	Paul Waner	3,152	Roberto Clemente	3,000
		Robin Yount	3,142		

Baseball Stadiums

National League

Team	Stadium (built)	Surface	Home run distances (ft.) LF	Center	RF	Seating capacity
Atlanta Braves	Atlanta-Fulton County Stadium (1965)	Grass	330	402	330	52,003
Chicago Cubs	Wrigley Field (1914)	Grass	355	400	353	38,710
Cincinnati Reds	Riverfront Stadium (1970)	Artificial	330	404	330	52,952
Colorado Rockies	Mile High Stadium (1948)	Artificial	335	423	370	76,100
Florida Marlins	Joe Robbie Stadium (1987)	Grass	335	410	345	48,000
Houston Astros	Astrodome (1965)	Artificial	325	400	325	54,816
Los Angeles Dodgers	Dodger Stadium (1962)	Grass	330	395	330	56,000
Montreal Expos	Olympic Stadium (1976)	Artificial	325	404	325	43,739
New York Mets	Shea Stadium (1964)	Grass	338	410	338	55,601
Philadelphia Phillies	Veterans Stadium (1971)	Artificial	330	408	330	62,382
Pittsburgh Pirates	Three Rivers Stadium (1970)	Artificial	335	400	335	58,727
St. Louis Cardinals	Busch Stadium (1966)	Artificial	330	402	330	56,227
San Diego Padres	Jack Murphy Stadium (1967)	Grass	327	405	327	59,022
San Francisco Giants	Candlestick Park (1960)	Grass	335	400	330	62,000

American League

Team	Stadium (built)	Surface	LF	Center	RF	Seating capacity
Baltimore Orioles	Camden Yards (1992)	Grass	333	400	318	48,041
Boston Red Sox	Fenway Park (1912)	Grass	315	390	302	34,142
California Angels	Anaheim Stadium (1966)	Grass	333	404	333	64,593
Chicago White Sox	Comiskey Park (1991)	Grass	347	400	347	44,702
Cleveland Indians	Jacob's Field (1994)	Grass	325	405	325	42,400
Detroit Tigers	Tiger Stadium (1912)	Grass	340	440	325	52,416
Kansas City Royals	Kauffman Stadium (1973)	Artificial	330	410	330	40,625
Milwaukee Brewers	Milwaukee County Stadium (1953)	Grass	315	402	315	53,192
Minnesota Twins	Hubert H. Humphrey Metrodome (1982)	Artificial	343	408	327	55,883
New York Yankees	Yankee Stadium (1923)	Grass	318	408	314	57,545
Oakland A's	Oakland Alameda County Coliseum (1968)	Grass	330	400	330	47,313
Seattle Mariners	Kingdome (1976)	Artificial	331	405	312	59,702
Texas Rangers	The Ballpark (1994)	Grass	332	400	325	49,292
Toronto Blue Jays	Sky-Dome (1989)	Artificial	328	400	328	50,516

World Series Results, 1903-1994

1903	Boston AL 5, Pittsburgh NL 3
1904	No series
1905	New York NL 4, Philadelphia AL 1
1906	Chicago AL 4, Chicago NL 2
1907	Chicago NL 4, Detroit AL 0, 1 tie
1908	Chicago NL 4, Detroit AL 1
1909	Pittsburgh NL 4, Detroit AL 3
1910	Philadelphia AL 4, Chicago NL 1
1911	Philadelphia AL 4, New York NL 2
1912	Boston AL 4, New York NL 3, 1 tie
1913	Philadelphia AL 4, New York NL 1
1914	Boston NL 4, Philadelphia AL 0
1915	Boston AL 4, Philadelphia NL 1
1916	Boston AL 4, Brooklyn NL 1
1917	Chicago AL 4, New York NL 2
1918	Boston AL 4, Chicago NL 2
1919	Cincinnati NL 5, Chicago AL 3
1920	Cleveland AL 5, Brooklyn NL 2
1921	New York NL 5, New York AL 3
1922	New York NL 4, New York AL 0, 1 tie
1923	New York AL 4, New York NL 2
1924	Washington AL 4, New York NL 3
1925	Pittsburgh NL 4, Washington AL 3
1926	St. Louis NL 4, New York AL 3
1927	New York AL 4, Pittsburgh NL 0
1928	New York AL 4, St. Louis NL 0
1929	Philadelphia AL 4, Chicago NL 1
1930	Philadelphia AL 4, St. Louis NL 2
1931	St. Louis NL 4, Philadelphia AL 3
1932	New York AL 4, Chicago NL 0
1933	New York NL 4, Washington AL 1
1934	St. Louis NL 4, Detroit AL 3
1935	Detroit AL 4, Chicago NL 2
1936	New York AL 4, New York NL 2
1937	New York AL 4, New York NL 1
1938	New York AL 4, Chicago NL 0
1939	New York AL 4, Cincinnati NL 0
1940	Cincinnati NL 4, Detroit AL 3
1941	New York AL 4, Brooklyn NL 1
1942	St. Louis NL 4, New York AL 1
1943	New York AL 4, St. Louis NL 1
1944	St. Louis NL 4, St. Louis AL 2
1945	Detroit AL 4, Chicago NL 3
1946	St. Louis NL 4, Boston AL 3
1947	New York AL 4, Brooklyn NL 3
1948	Cleveland AL 4, Boston NL 2
1949	New York AL 4, Brooklyn NL 1
1950	New York AL 4, Philadelphia NL 0
1951	New York AL 4, New York NL 2
1952	New York AL 4, Brooklyn NL 3
1953	New York AL 4, Brooklyn NL 2
1954	New York NL 4, Cleveland AL 0
1955	Brooklyn NL 4, New York AL 3
1956	New York AL 4, Brooklyn NL 3
1957	Milwaukee NL 4, New York AL 3
1958	New York AL 4, Milwaukee NL 3
1959	Los Angeles NL 4, Chicago AL 2
1960	Pittsburgh NL 4, New York AL 3
1961	New York AL 4, Cincinnati NL 1
1962	New York AL 4, San Francisco NL 3
1963	Los Angeles NL 4, New York AL 0
1964	St. Louis NL 4, New York AL 3
1965	Los Angeles NL 4, Minnesota AL 3
1966	Baltimore AL 4, Los Angeles NL 0
1967	St. Louis NL 4, Boston AL 3
1968	Detroit AL 4, St. Louis NL 3
1969	New York NL 4, Baltimore AL 1
1970	Baltimore AL 4, Cincinnati NL 1
1971	Pittsburgh NL 4, Baltimore AL 3
1972	Oakland AL 4, Cincinnati NL 3
1973	Oakland AL 4, New York NL 3
1974	Oakland AL 4, Los Angeles NL 1
1975	Cincinnati NL 4, Boston AL 3
1976	Cincinnati NL 4, New York AL 0
1977	New York AL 4, Los Angeles NL 2
1978	New York AL 4, Los Angeles NL 2
1979	Pittsburgh NL 4, Baltimore AL 3
1980	Philadelphia NL 4, Kansas City AL 2
1981	Los Angeles NL 4, New York AL 2
1982	St. Louis NL 4, Milwaukee AL 3
1983	Baltimore AL 4, Philadelphia NL 1
1984	Detroit AL 4, San Diego NL 1
1985	Kansas City AL 4, St. Louis NL 3
1986	New York NL 4, Boston AL 3
1987	Minnesota AL 4, St. Louis NL 3
1988	Los Angeles NL 4, Oakland AL 1
1989	Oakland AL 4, San Francisco NL 0
1990	Cincinnati NL 4, Oakland AL 0
1991	Minnesota AL 4, Atlanta NL 3
1992	Toronto AL 4, Atlanta NL 2
1993	Toronto AL 4, Philadelphia NL 2
1994	No series

Major League Franchise Shifts and Additions

1953—Boston Braves (NL) became Milwaukee Braves.
1954—St. Louis Browns (AL) became Baltimore Orioles.
1955—Philadelphia Athletics (AL) became Kansas City Athletics.
1958—New York Giants (NL) became San Francisco Giants.
1958—Brooklyn Dodgers (NL) became Los Angeles Dodgers.
1961—Washington Senators (AL) became Minnesota Twins.
1961—Los Angeles Angels (later renamed the California Angels) enfranchised by the American League.
1961—Washington Senators enfranchised by the American League (a new team, replacing the former Washington club, whose franchise was moved to Minneapolis-St. Paul).
1962—Houston Colt .45's (later renamed the Houston Astros) enfranchised by the National League.
1962—New York Mets enfranchised by the National League.
1966—Milwaukee Braves (NL) became Atlanta Braves.
1968—Kansas City Athletics (AL) became Oakland Athletics.
1969—Kansas City Royals and Seattle Pilots enfranchised by the American League; Montreal Expos and San Diego Padres enfranchised by the National League.
1970—Seattle Pilots became Milwaukee Brewers.
1971—Washington Senators became Texas Rangers (Dallas-Fort Worth area).
1977—Toronto Blue Jays and Seattle Mariners enfranchised by the American League.
1993—Colorado Rockies (Denver) and Florida Marlins (Miami) enfranchised by the National League.

NCAA Baseball Champions

1960	Minnesota
1961	USC
1962	Michigan
1963	USC
1964	Minnesota
1965	Arizona St.
1966	Ohio St.
1967	Arizona St.
1968	USC
1969	Arizona St.
1970	USC
1971	USC
1972	USC
1973	USC
1974	USC
1975	Texas
1976	Arizona
1977	Arizona St.
1978	USC
1979	Cal. St.-Fullerton
1980	Arizona
1981	Arizona St.
1982	Miami, Fla.
1983	Texas
1984	Cal. St.-Fullerton
1985	Miami, Fla.
1986	Arizona
1987	Stanford
1988	Stanford
1989	Wichita St.
1990	Georgia
1991	LSU
1992	Pepperdine
1993	LSU
1994	Oklahoma

Little League World Series

The Little League World Series is played annually in Williamsport, PA. The team from Maracaibo, Venezuela, won the 1994 Little League World Series by defeating the team from Northridge, CA, 4-3, on Aug. 27.

Year	Winning / Losing Team	Score
1947	Williamsport, PA; Lock Haven, PA	16-7
1948	Lock Haven, PA; St. Petersburg, FL	6-5
1949	Hammonton, NJ; Pensacola, FL	5-0
1950	Houston, TX; Bridgeport, CT	2-1
1951	Stamford, CT; Austin, TX	3-0
1952	Norwalk, CT; Monongahela, PA	4-3
1953	Birmingham, AL; Schenectady, NY	1-0
1954	Schenectady, NY; Colton, CA	7-5
1955	Morrisville, PA; Merchantville, NJ	4-3
1956	Roswell, NM; Delaware, NJ	3-1
1957	Mexico; La Mesa, CA	4-0
1958	Mexico; Kankakee, IL	10-1
1959	Hamtramck, MI; Auburn, CA	12-0
1960	Levittown, PA; Ft. Worth, TX	5-0
1961	El Cajon, CA; El Campo, TX	4-2
1962	San Jose, CA; Kankakee, IL	3-0
1963	Granada Hills, CA; Stratford, CT	2-1
1964	Staten Island, NY; Mexico	4-0
1965	Windsor Locks, CT; Ontario, Canada	3-1
1966	Houston, TX; W. New York, NJ	8-2
1967	Tokyo, Japan; Chicago, IL	4-1
1968	Osaka, Japan; Richmond, VA	1-0
1969	Taiwan; Santa Clara, CA	5-0
1970	Wayne, NJ; Campbell, CA	2-0
1971	Taiwan; Gary, IN	12-3
1972	Taiwan; Hammond, IN	6-0
1973	Taiwan; Tucson, AZ	12-0
1974	Taiwan; Red Bluff, CA	12-1
1975	Lakewood, NJ; Tampa, FL	4-3
1976	Tokyo, Japan; Campbell, CA	10-3
1977	Taiwan; El Cajon, CA	7-2
1978	Taiwan; Danville, CA	11-1
1979	Taiwan; Campbell, CA	2-1
1980	Taiwan; Tampa, FL	4-3
1981	Taiwan; Tampa, FL	4-2
1982	Kirkland, WA; Taiwan	6-0
1983	Marietta, GA; Dominican Rep.	3-1
1984	South Korea; Altamonte Springs, FL	6-2
1985	South Korea; Mexico	7-1
1986	Taiwan; Tucson, AZ	12-0
1987	Chinese Taipei; Irvine, CA	21-1
1988	Chinese Taipei; Pearl City, HI	10-0
1989	Trumbull, CT; Chinese Taipei	5-2
1990	Chinese Taipei; Shippensburg, PA	9-0
1991	Chinese Taipei; Danville, CA	11-0
1992	Long Beach, CA; Philippines	6-0
1993	Long Beach, CA; Panama	3-2
1994	Venezuela; Northridge, CA	4-3

Chess

World Chess Champions

Source: U.S. Chess Federation

Chess dates back to antiquity, its exact origin unknown. The best players of their time, regarded by later generations as world champions, were Francois Philidor, Alexandre Deschappelles, Louis de la Bourdonnais, all France; Howard Staunton, England; Adolph Anderssen, Germany; and Paul Morphy, U.S. In 1866 Wilhelm Steinitz defeated Adolph Anderssen and claimed the world champion title. Official world champions since the title was first used follow:

1866-1894	Wilhelm Steinitz, Austria
1894-1921	Emanuel Lasker, Germany
1921-1927	Jose R. Capablanca, Cuba
1927-1935	Alexander A. Alekhine, France
1935-1937	Max Euwe, Netherlands
1937-1946	Alexander A. Alekhine, France (a)
1948-1957	Mikhail Botvinnik, USSR
1957-1958	Vassily Smyslov, USSR
1958-1959	Mikhail Botvinnik, USSR
1960-1961	Mikhail Tal, USSR
1961-1963	Mikhail Botvinnik, USSR
1963-1969	Tigran Petrosian, USSR
1969-1972	Boris Spassky, USSR
1972-1975	Bobby Fischer, U.S. (b)
1975-1985	Anatoly Karpov, USSR
1985-1993	Gary Kasparov, USSR/Russia (c)
1993-	Anatoly Karpov, Russia

(a) After Alekhine died in 1946, the title was vacant until 1948, when Botvinnik won the first championship match sanctioned by the International Chess Federation (FIDE). (b) Defaulted championship after refusal to accept FIDE rules for a championship match, April 1975. (c) Kasparov broke with FIDE, Feb. 26, 1993. FIDE stripped Kasparov of his title Mar. 23. Kasparov defeated Nigel Short of Great Britain in a world championship match played Sept.-Oct. 1993 under the auspices of a new organization the two had founded, the Professional Chess Association. FIDE held a championship match between Anatoly Karpov (Russia) and Jan Timman (the Netherlands), which Karpov won in Nov. 1993.

United States Chess Champions

Unofficial champions	
1857-1871	Paul Morphy
1871-1876	George Mackenzie
1876-1880	James Mason
1880-1889	George Mackenzie
1889-1890	S. Lipschutz
1890	Jackson Showalter
Official champions	
1891-1892	Jackson Showalter
1892-1894	S. Lipschutz
1894	Jackson Showalter
1894-1895	Albert Hodges
1895-1897	Jackson Showalter
1897-1906	Harry Pillsbury
1906-1909	vacant
1909-1936	Frank Marshall
1936-1944	Samuel Reshevsky
1944-1946	Arnold Denker
1946-1948	Samuel Reshevsky
1948-1951	Herman Steiner
1951-1954	Larry Evans
1954-1957	Arthur Bisguier
1957-1961	Bobby Fischer
1961-1962	Larry Evans
1962-1968	Bobby Fischer
1968-1969	Larry Evans
1969-1972	Samuel Reshevsky
1972-1973	Robert Byrne
1973-1974	Lubomir Kavalek, John Grefe
1974-1977	Walter Browne
1978-1980	Lubomir Kavalek
1980-1981	(tie) Larry Evans, Larry Christiansen, Walter Browne
1981-1983	(tie) Walter Browne, Yasser Seirawan
1983	(tie) Walter Browne, Larry Christiansen, Roman Dzindzichashvili
1984-1985	Lev Alburt
1986	Yasser Seirawan
1987	(tie) Joel Benjamin, Nick DeFirmian
1988	Michael Wilder
1989	(tie) Stuart Rachels, Yasser Seirawan, Roman Dzindzichashvili
1990	Lev Alburt
1991	Gata Kamsky
1992	Patrick Wolff
1993	(tie) Alexander Shabaloz, Alex Yermolinsky
1994	Boris Gulko

Special Olympics

Special Olympics is an international program of year-round sports training and athletic competition for children and adults with mental retardation. All 50 U.S. states, Washington, DC, and Guam have chapter offices. In addition, there are accredited Special Olympics programs in more than 100 countries. Persons wishing to volunteer or find out more about Special Olympics can contact Special Olympics International Headquarters, 1350 New York Ave. NW, Washington, DC 20005.

1995 Special Olympics World Games

The ninth Special Olympics World Games will be held July 1-9, 1995, in New Haven, CT. A total of 6,700 athletes from more than 130 countries are expected to participate, along with 2,000 coaches and 15,000 family members and friends. In addition to an estimated half-million spectators, television coverage will bring the games to viewers worldwide. Athletes will compete in the following sports:

Aquatics
Badminton
Basketball
Bocce
Bowling
Croquet
Cycling
Equestrian
Golf
Gymnastics
Powerlifting
Roller Skating
Rowing
Sailing
Soccer
Softball
Table Tennis
Team Handball
Tennis
Track & Field
Volleyball

Marathons

Boston Marathon in 1994

Cosmos N'Deti of Kenya won the 1994 Boston Marathon on April 18—his second straight victory in the event—with a time of 2 hours 7 minutes 15 seconds. Uta Pippig of Germany won for the women in 2:21:45. Both set course records, aided by comfortable temperatures and a steady 20 mph wind at their backs.

New York Marathon in 1994

German Silva of Mexico overcame a wrong turn late in the 1994 New York Marathon, held Nov. 6, to win in the closest finish in race history. Silva's time of 2 hours 11 minutes 21 seconds was only 2 seconds ahead of second-place finisher Benjamin Paredes, also of Mexico. Tegla Loroupe of Kenya had no trouble finding the finish line, winning the women's race in 2:27:37.

VITAL STATISTICS

Births, Deaths, Marriages, and Divorces in the U.S., First Quarter 1994

Source: National Center for Health Statistics, U.S. Dept. of Health and Human Services

Births

According to provisional statistics for the first quarter of 1994, there were 993,000 births, a slight increase from the number reported for the same 3-month period in 1993 (992,000). The birthrate declined by 1%, from 15.7 per 1,000 population in the first quarter of 1993 to 15.5 in the first quarter of 1994.

During the 12 months ending with March 1994, there were an estimated 4,040,000 live births, 1% less than reported for the comparable period ending a year earlier (4,078,000). The birthrate was 15.6 per 1,000 population, 2% below the rate for the 12 months ending with March 1993 (15.9).

Marriages

The total number of marriages for the first quarter of 1994 was 410,000, a decrease of 1% from the number for the comparable period in 1993 (415,000). The marriage rate was 6.5 per 1,000 population, a decrease of 2% from the first quarter of 1993.

During the 12 months ending with March 1994, an estimated 2,329,000 couples married, a decrease of 1% from the previous 12-month period (2,353,000). The 12-month marriage rate was 9.0, down 2% from the rate for the 12 months ending with March 1993.

Divorces

A total of 287,000 couples divorced during the first quarter of 1994, a 2% decrease compared to the first quarter of 1993 (292,000). The divorce rate was 4.5 per 1,000 population, a decrease of less than 1% from the first quarter of 1993 (4.6).

During the 12 months ending with March 1994, an estimated 1,182,000 couples divorced, 2% less than the 1,206,000 divorces granted during the 12 months ending March 1993; and the rate declined from 4.7 to 4.6 per 1,000.

Deaths

According to provisional statistics, there were 628,000 deaths during the first quarter of 1994, 4% more than for the first quarter of 1993 (601,000). The death rate was 9.8 per 1,000 population, 3% higher than the Jan.-March 1993 rate. Among the deaths for the first quarter of 1994 were 8,300 deaths at ages under 1 year, yielding an infant mortality rate of 8.4 per 1,000 live births, compared with a rate of 8.6 for the first quarter of 1993. This change in infant mortality was not statistically significant.

The death rate for the 12 months ending with March 1994 (8.9 deaths per 1,000 population) was 3% higher than the rate of 8.6 for the comparable 12-month period a year earlier. The infant mortality rate for this 12-month period was 8.2 per 1,000 live births, less than 1% lower than the rate of 8.3 for the 12 months ending with March 1993.

Provisional Statistics

12 months ending with March

	Number		Rate*	
	1994	1993	1994	1993
Live births	4,040,000	4,078,000	15.6	15.9
Deaths	2,294,000	2,190,000	8.9	8.6
Natural increase	1,746,000	1,888,000	6.7	7.3
Marriages	2,329,000	2,353,000	9.0	9.2
Divorces	1,182,000	1,206,000	4.6	4.7
Infant deaths	32,900	33,700	8.2	8.3

*Per 1,000 population. **Note:** Figures include revisions.

Annual Report for the Year 1993 (Provisional Statistics)

Source: National Center for Health Statistics, U.S. Dept. of Health and Human Services

Highlights

Provisional data for 1993 show that the number of live births increased 1 percent from the number reported for 1992. The provisional number of marriages and divorces in 1993 decreased from the comparable figures for 1992. The declining divorce rate reversed a pattern of increase that had been observed since 1964.

Births

An estimated 4,039,000 babies were born in the United States in 1993, a decline of 1% from the 4,084,000 births in 1992. The birthrate of 15.7 per 1,000 population was 2% lower than the rate of 16.0 for the preceding year. The fertility rate (the number of live births per 1,000 women aged 15-44 years) for 1993 was 68.3, 1% lower than the rate for 1992 (69.2).

Deaths

The provisional count of deaths during 1993 was 2,268,000, about 4% more than in the previous year (2,177,000). The death rate of 879.3 deaths per 100,000 population was 3% higher than the rate of 853.3 for 1992. About 33,300 of these deaths were to infants under 1 year of age. The infant mortality rate was 828.8 per 100,000 live births, 2% lower than the rate of 848.7 for 1992.

Natural Increase

As a result of natural increase, the excess of births over deaths, an estimated 1,771,000 persons were added to the population in 1993. This rate was 6.9 per 1,000 population, 8% lower than the rate of 7.5 for 1992, and was the lowest rate since 1987. The decline in the rate of natural increase is due to a decrease in the birthrate and an increase in the death rate.

Marriages

An estimated 2,334,000 marriages were performed in 1993. This is the smallest number of marriages performed since 1979 (2,331,337). The marriage rate per 1,000 population also dropped for the 3d straight year; in 1993 it was 9.0, the lowest rate since 1964.

Divorces

The number of divorces granted in 1993 (1,187,000) was 2% lower than in 1992 (1,215,000). The divorce rate per 1,000 population was also lower in 1993 (4.6) than in 1992 (4.8) and was the lowest rate since 1974.

Births and Deaths in the U.S.

Source: National Center for Health Statistics, U.S. Dept. of Health and Human Services

Refers only to events occurring within the U.S. Excludes fetal deaths. Rates per 1,000 population enumerated as of April 1 for 1960 and 1970; estimated as of July 1 for all other years. Beginning 1970 excludes births and deaths occurring to nonresidents of the U.S.

	Births		Deaths	
Year	Total number	Rate	Total number	Rate
1960	4,257,850	23.7	1,711,982	9.5
1970	3,731,386	18.4	1,921,031	9.5
1980	3,612,258	15.9	1,986,000	8.7
1990	4,179,000	16.7	2,162,000	8.6
1991	4,111,000	16.3	2,165,000	8.6
1992	4,084,000	16.0	2,177,000	8.5
1993	4,039,000	15.7	2,268,000	8.8

Births and Deaths by States and Regions, 1992-93

Source: National Center for Health Statistics, U.S. Dept. of Health and Human Services

Area	Live births 1992 Number	Live births 1992 Rate	Live births 1993 Number	Live births 1993 Rate	Deaths 1992 Number	Deaths 1992 Rate	Deaths 1993 Number	Deaths 1993 Rate
New England	**189,276**	**14.3**	**183,678**	**13.9**	**116,218**	**8.8**	**120,492**	**9.1**
Maine	15,623	12.7	15,027	12.1	10,900	8.8	11,479	9.3
New Hampshire	15,719	14.1	14,952	13.3	8,555	7.7	8,919	7.9
Vermont	7,625	13.4	7,286	12.6	4,732	8.3	4,868	8.5
Massachusetts	88,185	14.7	86,317	14.4	54,292	9.1	56,460	9.4
Rhode Island	14,789	14.7	14,275	14.3	9,444	9.4	9,709	9.7
Connecticut	47,335	14.4	45,821	14.0	28,295	8.6	29,057	8.9
Middle Atlantic	**570,697**	**15.1**	**560,516**	**14.7**	**359,395**	**9.5**	**369,956**	**9.7**
New York	285,568	15.8	278,307	15.3	164,869	9.1	170,203	9.4
New Jersey	119,923	15.4	123,020	15.6	71,201	9.1	72,776	9.2
Pennsylvania	165,206	13.8	159,189	13.2	123,325	10.3	126,977	10.5
East North Central	**654,228**	**15.3**	**645,299**	**15.0**	**372,449**	**8.7**	**387,135**	**9.0**
Ohio	169,067	15.3	156,748	14.1	99,601	9.0	100,678	9.1
Indiana	83,832	14.8	84,644	14.8	50,144	8.9	52,210	9.1
Illinois	192,483	16.5	191,042	16.3	101,590	8.7	107,563	9.2
Michigan	138,968	14.7	143,576	15.1	79,307	8.4	82,651	8.7
Wisconsin	69,878	14.0	69,289	13.8	41,807	8.3	44,033	8.7
West North Central	**259,737**	**14.5**	**258,692**	**14.3**	**162,094**	**9.0**	**171,929**	**9.5**
Minnesota	65,477	14.6	63,761	14.1	34,909	7.8	36,236	8.0
Iowa	38,120	13.6	37,044	13.2	27,002	9.6	27,862	9.9
Missouri	75,437	14.5	77,424	14.8	50,447	9.7	56,305	10.8
North Dakota	8,935	14.0	8,746	13.8	5,797	9.1	5,925	9.3
South Dakota	11,281	15.9	10,830	15.1	6,927	9.7	6,863	9.6
Nebraska	23,003	14.3	22,847	14.2	14,852	9.2	15,401	9.6
Kansas	37,484	14.9	38,040	15.0	22,160	8.8	23,337	9.2
South Atlantic	**680,220**	**15.1**	**673,147**	**14.7**	**403,745**	**9.0**	**423,762**	**9.3**
Delaware	10,902	15.8	10,555	15.1	5,937	8.6	6,116	8.7
Maryland	76,173	15.5	75,526	15.2	37,806	7.7	43,087	8.7
District of Columbia	10,052	17.1	9,780	16.9	6,578	11.2	6,713	11.6
Virginia	97,600	15.3	95,161	14.7	49,541	7.8	51,773	8.0
West Virginia	22,123	12.2	22,044	12.1	20,107	11.1	19,929	11.0
North Carolina	103,047	15.1	100,597	14.5	59,478	8.7	62,580	9.0
South Carolina	56,635	15.7	53,997	14.8	30,609	8.5	31,404	8.6
Georgia	111,397	16.5	112,400	16.2	53,288	7.9	55,851	8.1
Florida	192,291	14.3	193,087	14.1	140,401	10.4	146,309	10.7
East South Central	**234,462**	**15.1**	**231,361**	**14.7**	**147,410**	**9.5**	**154,664**	**9.8**
Kentucky	53,906	14.4	52,256	13.8	35,341	9.4	36,921	9.7
Tennessee	74,048	14.7	73,613	14.4	47,149	9.4	49,628	9.7
Alabama	63,021	15.2	63,332	15.1	39,630	9.6	41,540	9.9
Mississippi	43,487	16.6	42,160	16.0	25,290	9.7	26,575	10.1
West South Central	**479,421**	**17.4**	**481,374**	**17.2**	**224,221**	**8.1**	**234,665**	**8.4**
Arkansas	34,967	14.6	34,248	14.1	25,202	10.5	26,371	10.9
Louisiana	71,743	16.7	69,819	16.3	37,446	8.7	40,117	9.3
Oklahoma	47,850	14.9	46,711	14.5	30,626	9.5	32,574	10.1
Texas	324,861	18.4	330,596	18.3	130,947	7.4	135,603	7.5
Mountain	**245,352**	**17.1**	**246,110**	**16.7**	**103,301**	**7.2**	**108,143**	**7.3**
Montana	11,551	14.0	11,450	13.6	7,151	8.7	7,502	8.9
Idaho	17,475	16.4	17,162	15.6	8,063	7.6	8,345	7.6
Wyoming	6,823	14.6	6,662	14.2	3,333	7.2	3,544	7.5
Colorado	54,586	15.7	54,817	15.4	22,528	6.5	23,722	6.7
New Mexico	28,463	18.0	27,658	17.1	11,561	7.3	11,861	7.3
Arizona	66,698	17.4	70,770	18.0	30,659	8.0	32,090	8.2
Utah	37,411	20.6	36,462	19.6	9,904	5.5	10,193	5.5
Nevada	22,345	16.8	21,129	15.2	10,102	7.6	10,886	7.8
Pacific	**756,915**	**18.6**	**733,461**	**17.8**	**287,474**	**7.1**	**296,347**	**7.2**
Washington	79,300	15.4	71,437	13.6	37,272	7.3	41,986	8.0
Oregon	41,606	14.0	42,195	13.9	25,862	8.7	27,275	9.0
California	604,393	19.6	589,685	18.9	215,206	7.0	217,559	7.0
Alaska	11,706	19.9	10,555	17.6	2,225	3.8	2,247	3.8
Hawaii	19,910	17.2	19,589	16.7	6,909	6.0	7,280	6.2

Note: Data are provisional estimates, reported by state of residence. Figures include revisions, and so may differ from those previously published. Rates for births and deaths are per 1,000 population. Rates for deaths in 1992 have been recomputed based on revised population estimates.

Deaths Under 1 Year and Infant Mortality Rates, for 10 Selected Causes, 1993-94

Source: National Center for Health Statistics, U.S. Dept. of Health and Human Services

Age and cause of death	1994 Number	1994 Rate	1993 Number	1993 Rate
Total, under 1 year	**33,100**	**826.1**	**33,900**	**835.8**
Under 28 days	21,420	534.5	21,590	532.8
28 days to 11 months	11,690	291.7	12,280	303.0
Certain gastrointestinal diseases	220	5.5	310	7.6
Pneumonia and influenza	430	10.7	570	14.1
Congenital anomalies	6,700	167.2	7,570	186.8
Disorders relating to short gestation and unspecified low birthweight	4,130	103.1	3,840	94.8
Birth trauma	180	4.5	150	3.7
Intrauterine hypoxia and birth asphyxia	660	16.5	690	17.0
Respiratory distress syndrome	2,070	51.7	2,210	54.5
Other conditions originating in the perinatal period	8,340	208.1	8,270	204.1
Sudden infant death syndrome	4,290	107.1	4,070	100.4
All other causes	6,080	151.7	6,200	153.0

Notes: Data are provisional, estimated from a 10% sample of deaths for a 12-month period ending in Feb. of the year cited. Rates are on an annual basis per 100,000 live births. Due to rounding of estimates, figures may not add to totals.

Infant Mortality Rates, by Race and Sex, 1960-91[1]

Source: National Center for Health Statistics, U.S. Dept. of Health and Human Services

Year	All races Both sexes	All races Male	All races Female	White Both sexes	White Male	White Female	Black Both sexes	Black Male	Black Female
1960	26.0	29.3	22.6	22.9	26.0	19.6	44.3	49.1	39.4
1970	20.0	22.4	17.5	17.8	20.0	15.4	32.6	36.2	29.0
1980	12.6	13.9	11.2	11.0	12.3	9.6	21.4	23.3	19.4
1981	11.9	13.1	10.7	10.5	11.7	9.2	20.0	21.7	18.3
1982	11.5	12.8	10.2	10.1	11.2	8.9	19.6	21.5	17.7
1983	11.2	12.3	10.0	9.7	10.8	8.6	19.2	21.1	17.2
1984	10.8	11.9	9.6	9.4	10.5	8.3	18.4	19.8	16.9
1985	10.6	11.9	9.3	9.3	10.6	8.0	18.2	19.9	16.5
1986	10.4	11.5	9.1	8.9	10.0	7.8	18.0	20.0	16.0
1987	10.1	11.2	8.9	8.6	9.6	7.6	17.9	19.6	16.0
1988	10.0	11.0	8.9	8.5	9.5	7.4	17.6	19.0	16.1
1989	9.8	10.8	8.8	8.1	9.0	7.1	18.6	20.0	17.2
1990	9.2	10.3	8.1	7.6	8.5	6.6	18.0	19.6	16.2
1991	8.9	10.0	7.8	7.3	8.3	6.3	17.6	19.4	15.7

(1) Final data. Rates per 1,000 live births.

The 10 Leading Causes of Death, 1993[1]

Source: National Center for Health Statistics, U.S. Dept. of Health and Human Services

Rank	Cause of death	Number	Death rate[2]	Percentage of total deaths
	All causes	**2,268,000**	**879.3**	**100.0**
1	Heart Disease	739,860	286.9	32.6
2	Cancer	530,870	205.8	23.4
3	Stroke	149,740	58.1	6.6
4	Chronic obstructive lung diseases and allied conditions	101,090	39.2	4.5
5	Accidents and adverse effects	88,630	34.4	3.9
	Motor vehicle accidents	40,880	15.9	1.8
	All other accidents and adverse effects	47,750	18.5	2.1
6	Pneumonia and influenza	81,730	31.7	3.6
7	Diabetes mellitus	55,110	21.4	2.4
8	Human immunodeficiency virus (HIV) infection[3]	38,500	14.9	1.7
9	Suicide	31,230	12.1	1.4
10	Homicide and legal intervention	25,470	9.9	1.1

(1) Data are provisional, estimated from a 10% sample of deaths. Figures may not add to totals due to rounding. Rates have been recomputed based on revised population estimates. (2) Per 100,000 population. (3) HIV is the virus that causes AIDS.

U.S. Abortions, by State, 1988-92

Source: Alan Guttmacher Institute, New York, NY

State	Number of reported abortions[1] 1988	1991	1992	Rate per 1,000 women[2] 1988	1991	1992	Percentage change 1988-92
Total	**1,590,750**	**1,556,510**	**1,528,930**	**27.3**	**26.3**	**25.9**	**–5**
Alabama	18,220	17,400	17,450	18.7	18.2	18.2	–3
Alaska	2,390	2,400	2,370	18.2	16.9	16.5	–10
Arizona	23,070	19,690	20,600	28.8	23.2	24.1	–16
Arkansas	6,250	7,150	7,130	11.6	13.6	13.5	16
California	311,720	320,960	304,230	45.9	44.4	42.1	–8
Colorado	18,740	21,010	19,880	22.4	25.3	23.6	6
Connecticut	23,630	20,530	19,720	31.2	26.7	26.2	–16
Delaware	5,710	5,720	5,730	35.7	34.9	35.2	–1
District of Columbia	26,120	21,510	21,320	163.3	136.1	138.4	–15
Florida	82,850	84,570	84,680	31.5	29.9	30.0	–5
Georgia	36,720	39,720	39,680	23.5	24.2	24.0	2
Hawaii	11,170	12,130	12,190	43.0	45.9	46.0	7
Idaho	1,920	1,740	1,710	8.2	7.5	7.2	–12
Illinois	72,570	64,990	68,420	26.4	24.1	25.4	–4
Indiana	15,760	15,940	15,840	11.9	12.1	12.0	1
Iowa	9,420	7,200	6,970	14.6	11.7	11.4	–22
Kansas	11,440	12,770	12,570	20.1	22.9	22.4	11
Kentucky	11,520	8,270	10,000	13.0	9.5	11.4	–12
Louisiana	17,340	13,930	13,600	16.3	13.7	13.4	–18
Maine	4,620	4,210	4,200	16.2	14.7	14.7	–9
Maryland	32,670	33,000	31,260	28.6	27.5	26.4	–8
Massachusetts	43,720	44,150	40,660	30.2	30.2	28.4	–6
Michigan	63,410	55,800	55,580	28.5	25.1	25.2	–11
Minnesota	18,580	16,880	16,180	18.2	16.3	15.6	–14
Mississippi	5,120	8,160	7,550	8.4	13.5	12.4	48
Missouri	19,490	15,770	13,510	16.4	13.5	11.6	–29
Montana	3,050	3,680	3,300	16.5	20.6	18.2	11
Nebraska	6,490	6,230	5,580	17.7	17.5	15.7	–11
Nevada	10,190	14,450	13,300	40.3	49.0	44.2	10
New Hampshire	4,710	4,260	3,890	17.5	15.7	14.6	–17
New Jersey	63,900	55,800	55,320	35.1	30.9	31.0	–12
New Mexico	6,810	6,190	6,410	19.1	17.2	17.7	–7

(continued)

State	Number of reported abortions[1] 1988	1991	1992	Rate per 1,000 women[2] 1988	1991	1992	Percentage change 1988-92
New York	183,980	190,410	195,390	43.3	44.5	46.2	7
North Carolina	39,720	37,210	36,180	25.4	23.2	22.4	–12
North Dakota	2,230	1,600	1,490	14.9	11.4	10.7	–28
Ohio	53,400	52,030	49,520	21.0	20.4	19.5	–7
Oklahoma	12,120	9,130	8,940	16.2	12.8	12.5	–23
Oregon	15,960	16,580	16,060	23.9	24.9	23.9	0
Pennsylvania	51,830	51,780	49,740	18.9	19.2	18.6	–2
Rhode Island	7,190	7,500	6,990	30.6	31.5	30.0	–2
South Carolina	14,160	13,520	12,190	16.7	15.8	14.2	–15
South Dakota	900	980	1,040	5.7	6.4	6.8	19
Tennessee	22,090	19,840	19,060	18.9	16.9	16.2	–14
Texas	100,690	95,930	97,400	24.8	23.0	23.1	–7
Utah	5,030	4,250	3,940	12.8	10.4	9.3	–27
Vermont	3,580	3,110	2,900	25.8	22.7	21.2	–18
Virginia	35,420	35,170	35,020	23.7	22.8	22.7	–5
Washington	31,220	32,640	33,190	27.6	27.6	27.7	0
West Virginia	3,270	2,590	3,140	7.5	6.3	7.7	2
Wisconsin	18,040	15,510	15,450	16.0	13.6	13.6	–15
Wyoming	600	520	460	5.1	4.9	4.3	–16

(1) Numbers of abortions are rounded to the nearest 10. (2) Only women aged 15-44 years old.

Suicides by Age, Race, and Sex, 1993

Source: National Center for Health Statistics, U.S. Dept. of Health and Human Services

	All ages	1-14 yrs.	15-24 yrs.	25-34 yrs.	35-44 yrs.	45-54 yrs.	55-64 yrs.	65-74 yrs.	75-84 yrs.	85 yrs. & over	Age not stated
All races, both sexes[1]	31,230	310	4,960	6,240	5,910	4,040	2,980	3,400	2,520	860	10
Male	24,990	260	4,110	5,130	4,670	3,020	2,250	2,680	2,130	720	10
Female	6,250	50	850	1,110	1,250	1,010	730	720	390	140	(—)
White, both sexes	28,060	230	4,060	5,360	5,370	3,710	2,860	3,140	2,490	840	10
Male	22,460	190	3,370	4,400	4,210	2,790	2,160	2,510	2,100	720	10
Female	5,600	40	690	950	1,160	920	700	630	390	120	(—)
Black, both sexes	2,280	60	630	700	400	230	50	170	30	10	(—)
Male	2,000	50	580	650	360	170	30	140	30	(—)	(—)
Female	280	10	50	50	40	60	20	30	(—)	10	(—)

(—) = Data represent zero. **Note:** Data are provisional, estimated from a 10% sample of deaths. Due to rounding of estimates, figures may not add to totals. (1) All races includes races other than white and black.

Families in the U.S., 1993

Source: Bureau of the Census, U.S. Dept. of Commerce

Note: Totals may not add due to rounding. A household consists of all persons who occupy a house, apartment, or other group of rooms that has its own eating facilities. A family consists of two persons or more related by birth, marriage, or adoption who reside together.

•There were 96.4 million households in the U.S. in 1993, a net increase of 722,000 since 1992. In the 1990s, the number of households increased by about 1.1% per year, a rate slightly lower than that for the 1980s and well below the average annual increase for the 1970s.

•Less than half of the nation's 68.1 million families had children present in the home in 1993. The most recent year in which a majority of families included children was 1982. Two-parent families accounted for 36% of family households in 1993, down from 50% in 1970.

•There were about 28.2 million nonfamily households in 1993, most of which were one-person households. People living alone made up 84% of the nonfamily households in the nation.

•The average number of persons per household was 2.63 in 1993. There has not been a significant change in household size since 1989.

•The median age of householders was 45.9 years old, representing a slight increase since 1990 as Baby Boomers grew older.

•The number of married persons increased from 95 million to 114.5 million between 1970 and 1993, although the increase in unmarried adults was greater (from 37.5 million to 72.6 million). The number of never-married persons doubled from 21.4 million to 42.3 million during the same time period; never-married persons accounted for the largest share of unmarried adults.

•The median age at first marriage continued to increase. In 1993, it was 26.5 for men and 24.5 for women, versus 23.2 and 20.8 respectively in 1970.

•In 1993, 22% of black women between the ages of 40-44 had never married, compared with 7% of whites and 9% of Hispanics.

•The number of unmarried-couple households was 3.5 million in 1993, 7 times larger than the number of such households in 1970 (523,000).

•More than one in every 8 people 15 years of age or older lived alone in 1993 (23.6 million). Over the past 2 decades, the number of women living alone rose 94% (from 7.3 to 14.2 million), while the number of men living alone rose 167% (from 3.5 to 9.4 million).

•Nearly 30% of all family groups with children were maintained by single parents in 1993, a significant increase from 12% in 1970. A child in a one-parent situation was just slightly more likely to be living with a divorced parent (37%) in 1993 than with a never-married parent (35%). A decade earlier, a child was twice as likely to be living with a divorced parent as with a never-married parent. Single mothers raising children outnumbered single fathers raising children by 6 to 1.

•Although two-thirds of all single parents were white, one-parent situations were much more common among black Americans than whites. About 63% of all black family groups with children were maintained by single parents, versus 25% of comparable white family groups. Among Hispanics, single parents represented 35% of family groups with children.

•In 1993, there were 3.4 million grandchildren under 18 years of age living in the home of their grandparent(s). This represented 5% of all children under 18 years of age, up only slightly from 3% of all children in 1970.

Persons Living Alone, 1970-93

Source: Bureau of the Census, U.S. Dept. of Commerce

Sex and age	Number of persons (1,000) 1970	1980	1993	Percent distribution 1970	1980	1993
Both sexes	**10,851**	**18,296**	**23,642**	**7.3**	**10.6**	**12.0**
15 to 24 years old[1]	556	1,726	1,186	1.4	4.2	3.4
25 to 34 years old	893	3,259	3,735	3.6	8.9	8.9
35 to 44 years old	711	1,470	3,286	3.1	5.8	8.1
45 to 54 years old	1,303	1,705	3,048	5.6	7.5	10.7
55 to 64 years old	2,319	2,809	3,033	12.4	13.1	14.3
65 to 74 years old	2,815	3,851	4,330	22.8	25.2	23.6
75 years old and over	2,256	3,477	5,025	30.0	39.1	40.2
Male	**3,532**	**6,966**	**9,436**	**5.0**	**8.5**	**9.9**
15 to 24 years old[1]	274	947	665	1.5	4.6	3.9
25 to 34 years old	535	1,975	2,282	4.4	10.9	10.9
35 to 44 years old	398	945	1,972	3.5	7.6	9.9
45 to 54 years old	513	804	1,465	4.6	7.4	10.6
55 to 64 years old	639	809	1,057	7.2	8.1	10.4
65 to 74 years old	611	775	1,046	11.3	11.6	12.9
75 years old and over	563	711	948	19.1	21.6	20.1
Female	**7,319**	**11,330**	**14,206**	**9.4**	**12.6**	**13.9**
15 to 24 years old[1]	282	779	521	1.4	3.7	3.0
25 to 34 years old	358	1,284	1,451	2.8	6.9	6.9
35 to 44 years old	313	525	1,313	2.6	4.0	6.4
45 to 54 years old	790	901	1,583	6.6	7.7	10.8
55 to 64 years old	1,680	2,000	1,976	17.1	17.4	17.9
65 to 74 years old	2,204	3,076	3,284	31.6	35.6	32.0
75 years old and over	1,693	2,766	4,078	37.0	49.3	52.3

(1)1970, persons 14 to 24 years old.

Child Care Arrangements of Employed Mothers, 1991

Source: Bureau of the Census, U.S. Dept. of Commerce; as of fall 1991

Type of arrangement	Children Under 15 years of age Number (1,000)	Percentage	Children Under 5 years of age Number (1,000)	Percentage	Children 5-14 years of age Number (1,000)	Percentage
Total	**31,074**	**100.0**	**9,854**	**100.0**	**21,220**	**100.0**
Care in child's home	5,785	18.6	3,522	35.7	2,263	10.7
By father	3,384	10.9	1,974	20.0	1,411	6.6
By grandparent	971	3.1	708	7.2	263	1.2
By other relative	709	2.3	313	3.2	396	1.9
By nonrelative	720	2.3	527	5.4	193	0.9
Care in another home	3,809	12.3	3,052	31.0	757	3.6
By grandparent	1,095	3.5	846	8.6	249	1.2
By other relative	645	2.1	443	4.5	203	1.0
By nonrelative	2,069	6.7	1,763	17.9	305	1.4
Organized child care facilities	2,673	8.6	2,268	23.0	405	1.9
Day/group care center	1,852	6.0	1,553	15.8	299	1.4
Nursery/preschool	822	2.6	716	7.3	106	0.5
School-based activity	689	2.2	52	0.5	638	3.0
Kindergarten/grade school	16,281	52.4	105	1.1	16,176	76.2
Child care for self	566	1.8	NA	NA	566	2.7
Mother cares for child at work[1]	1,271	4.1	855	8.7	416	2.0

NA = Not applicable; number represents zero. (1) Includes women working at home.

Living Arrangements of Children, 1970-93

Source: Bureau of the Census, U.S. Dept. of Commerce

(as of March; excludes persons under 18 years of age who maintained households or resided in group quarters)

Race, Hispanic origin, and year	Number (1,000)	Both parents	Percent living with— Mother only: Total	Divorced	Married spouse absent	Single[1]	Widowed	Father only	Neither parent
White									
1970	58,790	90	8	3	3	Z	2	1	2
1980	52,242	83	14	7	4	1	2	2	2
1990	51,390	79	16	8	4	3	1	3	2
1991	51,918	79	17	8	5	3	1	3	2
1993	53,042	77	17	8	4	4	1	4	2
Black									
1970	9,422	59	30	5	16	4	4	2	10
1980	9,375	42	44	11	16	13	4	2	12
1990	10,018	38	51	10	12	27	2	4	8
1991	10,209	36	54	10	11	31	2	4	7
1993	10,649	36	54	10	12	31	1	3	7
Hispanic[2]									
1970	4,006[3]	78	NA	NA	NA	NA	NA	NA	NA
1980	5,459	75	20	6	8	4	2	2	4
1990	7,174	67	27	7	10	8	2	3	3
1991	7,462	66	27	7	10	9	2	3	4
1993	7,773	64	28	7	9	11	1	4	4

NA=Not available. Z=Less than 0.5%. (1) Never married. (2) Hispanic persons may be of any race. (3) All persons under 18 years old.

Children Living With Grandparents, by Race and Hispanic Origin, 1970-93

Source: Bureau of the Census, U.S. Dept. of Commerce

(in thousands)

Living arrangement	1993 Total	1993 White	1993 Black	1993 Hispanic[1]	1980 Total	1970 Total
Total children under 18 years of age	66,893	53,075	10,660	7,776	63,369	69,276
Grandchild of householder	3,368	1,947	1,290	460	2,306	2,214
Percentage of all children under 18 years of age	5.0	3.7	12.1	5.9	3.6	3.2
With both parents present	475	395	56	107	310	363
With mother only present	1,647	904	683	218	922	817
With father only present	229	163	52	29	86	78
With neither parent present	1,017	485	499	105	988	957
Percentage of all grandchildren living with grandparents						
With both parents present	14.1	20.3	4.3	23.3	13.4	16.4
With mother only present	48.9	46.4	52.9	47.4	40.0	36.9
With father only present	6.8	8.4	4.0	6.3	3.7	3.5
With neither parent present	30.2	24.9	38.7	22.8	42.8	43.2

(1) Persons of Hispanic origin may be of any race.

Living Arrangements of Adopted Children, by Race and Hispanic Origin, 1991

Source: Bureau of the Census, U.S. Dept. of Commerce; as of summer 1991

Characteristics	Number in thousands	Percentage
Adopted children	1,062	100.0
Race:		
White	805	75.8
Black	130	12.2
Other	127	12.0
Ethnic origin[1]:		
Hispanic	65	6.1
Not Hispanic	997	93.9

Characteristics	Number in thousands	Percentage
Living arrangements:		
Two parents	936	88.1
Two adoptive parents	581	54.7
One adoptive parent and one biological	324	30.5
One adoptive and one other	31	2.9
One parent	126	11.9
Mother only	110	10.4
Father only	16	1.5

(1) Persons of Hispanic origin may be of any race.

Unmarried-Couple Households, by Presence of Children, 1970-93

Source: Bureau of the Census, U.S. Dept. of Commerce

(in thousands)

Year	married couples	Unmarried couples: Total	Unmarried couples: Without children under 15 years of age	Unmarried couples: With children under 15 years of age	Ratio of unmarried couples per 100 married couples
1970	44,593	523	327	196	1
1980	49,714	1,589	1,159	431	3
1985	51,114	1,983	1,380	603	4
1990	56,112	2,856	1,966	891	5
1993	54,199	3,510	2,274	1,236	6

Children in Blended Families,[1] by Race and Hispanic Origin, 1991

Source: Bureau of the Census, U.S. Dept. of Commerce; as of summer 1991

(in thousands)

Living arrangements	All races	White	Black	Hispanic origin[2]
Children living in a blended family	9,807	7,298	2,101	1,016
Percentage of all children under 18 years of age	14.9	14.0	19.9	13.5
Child living with a parent and:				
Stepparent	2,068	1,848	152	166
Stepsibling	235	55	173	5
Half-sibling	4,966	3,271	1,485	593
Stepparent and stepsibling	517	409	62	32
Stepsibling and half-sibling	1,794	1,540	176	203
Stepparent and half-sibling	13	(–)	13	(–)
Stepparent, stepsibling, and half-sibling	216	175	40	16
Percentage of all blended families that include a natural parent and:				
Stepparent	21.1	25.3	7.2	16.3
Stepsibling	2.4	0.8	8.2	0.5
Half-sibling	50.6	44.8	70.7	58.4
Stepparent and stepsibling	5.3	5.6	3.0	3.1
Stepparent and half-sibling	18.3	21.1	8.4	20.0
Stepsibling and half-sibling	(–)	(–)	0.6	(–)
Stepparent, stepsibling, and half-sibling	2.2	2.4	1.9	1.6

(–) = Equals zero or a number that rounds to zero. (1) Blended families must include a biological parent and child and at least one stepparent, stepsibling, and/or half-sibling. Stepsiblings do not share a common biological parent; the biological parent of one child is the stepparent of the other. Half-siblings share only one biological parent. (2) Persons of Hispanic origin may be of any race.

Drug Use: America's Students

Source: Univ. of Michigan Inst. for Social Research, National Institute on Drug Abuse

Middle and High School Students

Drug use among American young people was increasing in 1993 according to the results of the University of Michigan's 19th annual survey of American high school seniors and 3d annual survey of 8th and 10th graders. While drug use was still not at the peak levels reached in the 1970s, there was evidence to support a reversal of the declines recorded for more than a decade. Researchers reported a sharp rise in marjiuana use throughout the country at all 3 grade levels, as well as an increase in the use of stimulants, LSD, and inhalants.

Marijuana remained the most popular of illegal drugs among the 10th graders and seniors. In 1993, the proportion of students that reported using marijuana in the past year rose to 9% of 8th graders, 19% of 10th graders, and 26% of seniors.

After alcohol and tobacco, inhalants were the most widely abused substance among 8th graders in 1993. Eleven percent of 8th graders reported past-year use of inhalants, compared with 8.4% of 10th graders and 7% of 12th graders.

Cigarette smoking remained quite high among all 3 grade levels in 1993. Sixteen percent of 8th graders, 22% of 10th graders, and 28% of 12th graders reported having smoked during the 30 days before they responded to the survey. Eighth graders showed some modest, but not statistically significant, increases in alcohol use.

Although the surveys missed the 15-20% of a class group that drops out of school early, investigators said there was little reason to believe trends would differ among this group, although it would undoubtedly have higher rates of use overall.

In 1993, around 17,000 seniors in 139 public and private high schools participated in the survey, along with 15,500 10th graders in 128 schools and 18,500 8th graders in 159 schools.

College Students

A 1992 survey of 1,500 college students found that the long-term decline in illicit drug use by such students had halted. It was found that 30.6% of the college students used some illicit drugs at least once in the prior 12 months—a slight increase over the 29.2% figure for 1991. The change was attributed largely to an increase in the percentage of college students using marijuana, for which use rose from 26% to 27%.

One in every eight college students (13%) reported using an illicit drug other than marijuana, representing virtually no change from 1991. However, the use of one class of illicit drugs did rise: Hallucinogen use rose among college students for the third year in a row. In 1989, 5.1% reported using a hallucinogen; by 1992, 6.8% reported such use. LSD use accounted for most or all of this increase, rising from 3.4% to 5.7% between 1989 and 1992.

The popularity of cocaine (excluding crack) continued to decline, with use dropping from 3.6% of college students surveyed in 1991 to 3% of the 1992 students.

Crack, stimulants, barbiturates, tranquilizers, inhalants, heroin, opiates other than heroine, and other illicitly used drugs showed little or no further decline in active use among college students in 1992, although a number of them had been declining previously.

Drug Use: America's High School Seniors

Source: Univ. of Michigan Inst. for Social Research

Percentage ever used

	Class of 1975	Class of 1980	Class of 1985	Class of 1986	Class of 1987	Class of 1988	Class of 1990	Class of 1991	Class of 1992	Class of 1993	'92-'93 change
Marijuana/hashish	47.3	60.3	54.2	50.9	50.2	47.2	40.7	36.7	32.6	35.3	+2.7 s
Inhalants	NA	11.9	15.4	15.9	17.0	16.7	18.0	17.6	16.6	17.4	+0.8
Inhalants adjusted[1]	NA	17.3	18.1	20.1	18.6	17.5	18.5	18.0	17.0	17.7	+0.7
Amyl & butyl nitrites	NA	11.1	7.9	8.6	4.7	3.2	2.1	1.6	1.5	1.4	–0.1
Hallucinogens	16.3	13.3	10.3	9.7	10.3	8.9	9.4	9.6	9.2	10.9	+1.7 ss
Hallucinogens adjusted[2]	NA	15.6	12.1	11.9	10.6	9.2	9.7	10.0	9.4	11.3	+1.9 ss
LSD	11.3	9.3	7.5	7.2	8.4	7.7	8.7	8.8	8.6	10.3	+1.7 ss
PCP	NA	9.6	4.9	4.8	3.0	2.9	2.8	2.9	2.4	2.9	+0.5
Cocaine	9.0	15.7	17.3	16.9[5]	15.2	12.1	9.4	7.8	6.1	6.1	0.0
"Crack"	NA	NA	NA	NA	5.4	4.8	3.5	3.1	2.6	2.6	0.0
Heroin	2.2	1.1	1.2	1.1	1.2	1.1	1.3	0.9	1.2	1.1	–0.1
Other opiates[3]	9.0	9.8	10.2	9.0	9.2	8.6	8.3	6.6	6.1	6.4	+0.3
Stimulants[3,4]	22.3	26.4	26.2	23.4	21.6	19.8	17.5	15.4	13.9	15.1	+1.2
Sedatives[3]	18.2	14.9	11.8	10.4	8.7	7.8	7.5	6.7	6.1	6.4	+0.3
Barbiturates[3]	16.9	11.0	9.2	8.4	7.4	6.7	6.8	6.2	5.5	6.3	+0.8
Methaqualone[3]	8.1	9.5	6.7	5.2	4.0	3.3	2.3	1.3	1.6	0.8	–0.8 s
Tranquilizers[3]	17.0	15.2	11.9	10.9	10.9	9.4	7.2	7.2	6.0	6.4	+0.4
Alcohol	90.4	93.2	92.2	91.3	92.2	92.0	89.5	88.0	87.5	87.0	–0.5
Cigarettes	73.6	71.0	68.8	67.6	67.2	66.4	64.4	63.1	61.8	61.9	+0.1

NA=Not available. Level of significance between the two most recent classes: s=0.05, ss=0.01. (1) Adjusted for underreporting of amyl and butyl nitrites. (2) Adjusted for underreporting of PCP. (3) Only drug use that was not under a doctor's orders. (4) Adjusted for overreporting of the nonprescription stimulants. (5) In 1986, three-fourths of those who used cocaine used it in powder form; the remainder used the "crack" form.

Drug Use in the General U.S. Population

Source: Bureau of Justice Statistics, U.S. Dept. of Justice

According to the Substance Abuse and Mental Health Administration's 1993 National Household Survey on Drug Abuse, an estimated 77 mil. (37.2%) Americans 12 years of age and older had used an illicit drug at least once during their lifetimes, 11.8% used one during the previous year, and 5.6% used one in the month before the survey was conducted. Among those 25 years of age and under, an estimated 1.6 mil. used cocaine (including crack), and 8.6 mil. used marijuana at least once within the previous year. Among those 26 years of age and over, 2.9 mil. used cocaine (including crack), and 10 mil. used marijuana at least once within the previous year.

The National Institute on Drug Abuse's Drug Abuse Warning Network reported an estimated 433,493 admissions to hospital emergency rooms nationwide that involved drug abuse in 1992. A total of 7,532 drug-abuse-related deaths were reported in 1992 by 137 medical examiners in 38 metropolitan areas.

Principal Types of Accidental Deaths, 1970-93

Source: National Safety Council

Year	Motor vehicle	Falls	Poison (solid, liquid)	Drowning	Fires, burns	Injestion of food, object	Firearms	Poison (gases)
1970	54,633	16,926	3,679	7,860	6,718	2,753	2,406	1,620
1975	45,853	14,896	4,694	8,000	6,071	3,106	2,380	1,577
1980	53,172	13,294	3,089	7,257	5,822	3,249	1,955	1,242
1985	45,901	12,001	4,091	5,316	4,938	3,551	1,649	1,079
1990	46,300	12,400	5,700	5,200	4,300	3,200	1,400	800
1991	43,500	12,200	5,600	4,600	4,200	2,900	1,400	800
1992	40,300	12,400	5,200	4,300	4,000	2,700	1,400	700
1993	42,000	13,500	6,500	4,800	4,000	2,900	1,600	700
			Death rates per 100,000 population					
1970	26.8	8.3	1.8	3.9	3.3	1.4	1.2	0.8
1975	21.3	6.9	2.2	3.7	2.8	1.4	1.1	0.7
1980	23.4	5.9	1.4	3.2	2.6	1.4	0.9	0.5
1985	19.2	5.0	1.7	2.2	2.1	1.5	0.7	0.5
1990	18.8	5.0	2.3	2.1	1.7	1.3	0.6	0.3
1991	17.2	4.8	2.2	1.8	1.7	1.1	0.6	0.3
1992	15.8	4.9	2.0	1.7	1.6	1.1	0.5	0.3
1993	16.3	5.2	2.5	1.9	1.6	1.1	0.6	0.3

Note: There were 14,000 other accidental deaths in 1993; the most frequently occurring types were medical complications, machinery, air transport, water transport, mechanical suffocation, and excessive cold.

Motor Vehicle Accidents, 1993

Source: National Safety Council

Motor vehicle deaths increased 3% in 1993 compared to 1992. In the same period, mileage driven increased 2%, the number of vehicles on the road increased 1 percent, and the population increased by 1 percent. The death rate per 100 million vehicle-miles was 1.83, one of the lowest on record. Motor vehicle accidents in 1993 caused 42,000 deaths and at least 2 million disabling injuries.

Almost 2 out of 3 deaths in 1993 occurred in places classified as rural. In urban areas, nearly one-fourth of the victims were pedestrians. More than one-half of all deaths occurred in night accidents.

About 45% of all traffic fatalities in 1992 involved an intoxicated or alcohol-impaired driver or nonoccupant. Of these 17,695 alcohol-related traffic fatalities, an estimated 14,125 occurred in accidents in which a driver or nonoccupant was intoxicated, and the remainder involved a driver or nonoccupant who had been drinking but was not legally intoxicated. Alcohol was also a factor in about 10% of serious injury accidents and 5% of property damage accidents. The estimated cost of all alcohol-related motor vehicle accidents in 1993 was $26.7 billion. Alcohol-related deaths declined 27% between 1982 and 1992.

	Death total	Percentage change from 1992	Death rate[1]
All motor vehicle accidents	**42,000**	**+3**	**16.3**
Urban	14,600	0	
Rural	27,400	+5	
Collision between motor vehicles	**17,900**	**+4**	**6.9**
Urban	5,000	−11	
Rural	12,900	+11	
Collision with fixed object	**11,900**	**+3**	**4.6**
Urban	4,000	+14	
Rural	7,900	−1	
Pedestrian accidents	**6,200**	**−5**	**2.4**
Urban	3,400	−15	
Rural	2,800	+17	

	Death total	Percentage change from 1992	Death rate[1]
Noncollision accidents	**4,500**	**+2**	**1.7**
Urban	1,500	+67	
Rural	3,000	−14	
Collision with pedalcycle	**800**	**+14**	**0.3**
Urban	400	0	
Rural	400	+33	
Collision with railroad train	**600**	**+20**	**0.2**
Urban	300	+50	
Rural	300	0	
Other collision (animal, animal-drawn vehicles, street cars)	**100**	**0**	(2)

(1) Deaths per 100,000 population. (2) Death rate was less than 0.05.

Improper Driving Reported in Accidents, 1993

Source: National Safety Council

	Fatal Accidents			Injury Accidents			All Accidents		
	Total %	Urban %	Rural %	Total %	Urban %	Rural %	Total %	Urban %	Rural %
Improper driving	**57.7**	**54.7**	**59.4**	**72.7**	**74.3**	**69.6**	**68.6**	**69.8**	**66.1**
Speed too fast or unsafe	16.5	14.4	17.7	13.5	11.8	17.6	12.2	11.1	15.4
Right of way	12.7	17.0	10.1	25.0	28.8	15.5	20.6	23.2	13.7
Failed to yield	7.8	9.4	6.8	17.3	19.3	12.3	15.1	16.6	11.3
Passed stop sign	2.7	2.7	2.7	2.7	3.0	1.9	2.0	2.1	1.4
Disregarded signal	2.2	4.9	0.6	5.0	6.5	1.3	3.5	4.5	1.0
Drove left of center	7.6	3.2	10.1	2.1	1.3	4.0	1.8	1.1	3.4
Improper overtaking	1.2	0.6	1.5	1.0	0.8	1.4	1.3	1.1	1.7
Made improper turn	2.9	2.7	3.0	3.4	3.3	3.7	4.5	4.6	4.2
Followed too closely	0.5	0.4	0.6	6.2	7.2	3.7	5.5	6.2	3.6
Other improper driving	16.3	16.4	16.4	21.5	21.1	23.7	22.7	22.5	24.1
No improper driving stated	**42.3**	**45.3**	**40.6**	**27.3**	**25.7**	**30.4**	**31.4**	**30.2**	**33.9**

Note: Based on reports from 11 state traffic authorities. When a driver was under the influence of alcohol or drugs, the accident was considered a result of the driver's physical condition—not a driving error. For this reason, accidents in which the driver was reported to be under the influence are classified under "no improper driving."

Deaths Involving Firearms, by Age, 1991

Source: National Safety Council

After motor vehicles, firearms were the 2d leading cause of injury deaths (both intentional and unintentional) in the U.S. in 1991. Although firearm deaths decreased 11% from 1980 to 1985, the trend then reversed. From 1986 to 1991, firearm deaths increased 9%. Recent increases in firearm mortality have been the greatest among adolescents and young adults. From 1988 to 1991, the firearm death rate for persons 15-24 years of age increased 40% to a rate of 28.9 deaths per 100,000 persons. Large differences exist between firearm death rates for whites and blacks. The firearm death rate for black persons 15-34 years of age was almost 5 times the death rate for non-Hispanic white persons. Hispanic and American Indian persons also had higher firearm death rates than non-Hispanic whites.

	All Ages	Under 5	5-14	15-24	25-44	45-64	65-74	75 & Over
Total Firearm Deaths[1]	**38,077**	**105**	**707**	**10,430**	**15,505**	**6,365**	**2,549**	**2,416**
Male	32,651	57	567	9,306	13,038	5,299	2,179	2,205
Female	5,426	48	140	1,124	2,467	1,066	370	211
Accidents	**1,441**	**24**	**203**	**542**	**387**	**175**	**55**	**55**
Male	1,304	13	183	507	351	155	47	48
Female	137	11	20	35	36	20	8	7
Suicide	**18,526**	**0**	**156**	**3,109**	**6,627**	**4,298**	**2,166**	**2,170**
Male	16,120	0	125	2,786	5,607	3,659	1,901	2,042
Female	2,406	0	31	323	1,020	639	265	128
Homicide	**17,746**	**81**	**339**	**6,642**	**8,350**	**1,839**	**316**	**179**
Male	14,926	44	251	5,897	6,968	1,439	222	105
Female	2,820	37	88	745	1,382	400	94	74
Undetermined[2]	**364**	**0**	**9**	**137**	**141**	**53**	**12**	**12**
Male	301	0	8	116	112	46	9	10
Female	63	0	1	21	29	7	3	2

(1) Excludes firearm deaths by legal intervention. These deaths totaled 259 in 1991. (2) Undetermined means the intentionality of the death (accident, suicide, homicide) cannot be determined.

Home Accident Deaths, 1950-93

Source: National Safety Council

Year	Total	Falls	Poison (solid, liquid)	Fires, burns[1]	Suffo., ingesting object	Firearms	Suffo., mech-anical	Poison (gases)	All Other[2]
1950	29,000	14,800	1,300	5,000	([3])	950	1,600	1,250	4,100
1960	28,000	12,300	1,350	6,350	1,850	1,200	1,500	900	2,550
1970	27,000	9,700	3,000	5,600	1,800[4]	1,400[4]	1,100[4]	1,100	3,300[4]
1980	22,800	7,100	2,500	4,800	2,000	1,100	500	700	4,100[5]
1990	21,500	6,700	4,000	3,400	2,300	800	600	500	3,200
1991	22,100	6,900	4,500	3,400	2,200	800	700	500	3,100
1992[6]	21,000	6,500	4,600	3,300	1,800	800	800	400	2,800
1993[7]	22,500	7,100	5,300	3,200	1,900	800	800	400	3,000

(1) Includes deaths resulting from conflagration, regardless of nature of injury. (2) Includes drowning in swimming pools and bathtubs. (3) Included in All Other. (4) Data for this year and subsequent years not comparable with previous years due to classification changes. (5) Includes about 1,000 excessive deaths due to summer heat wave. (6) Revised. (7) Data are preliminary.

Worldwide Airline Fatalities, 1980-93

Source: National Safety Council

Year	Aircraft accidents[1]	Passenger deaths	Death rate[2]	Year	Aircraft accidents[1]	Passenger deaths	Death rate[2]
1980	22	814	0.14	1987	24	890	0.10
1981	21	362	0.06	1988	25	699	0.08
1982	26	764	0.13	1989	27	817	0.08
1983	20	809	0.13	1990	22	440	0.04
1984	16	223	0.03	1991	25	510	0.05
1985	22	1,066	0.15	1992	25	990	0.09
1986	17	331	0.04	1993[3]	31	801	0.07

(1) Involving a passenger fatality. (2) Passenger deaths per 100 million passenger miles. (3) Preliminary.

Cost of Unintentional Injuries, 1993

Source: National Safety Council, estimates

Every 10 minutes unintentional injuries cost Americans approximately $7,800,000. On the average, there are 10 unintentional-injury deaths and about 2,080 disabling injuries every hour.

The cost of...	is equivalent to...
...all injuries ($407.5 billion)	80 cents of every dollar paid in 1993 federal personal income taxes, *or*
	62 cents of every dollar spent on food in the U.S. in 1993.
...motor vehicle accidents ($167.3 billion)	purchasing 800 gallons of gasoline per registered vehicle in the U.S., *or*
	a $19,200 rebate on each new car sold in 1993.
...work injuries ($111.9 billion)	66 cents of every dollar of 1993 corporate dividends to stockholders, *or*
	25 cents of every dollar of property taxes paid in 1993.
...home injuries ($86.5 billion)	a $76,800 rebate on each new single-family home built in 1993, *or*
	46 cents of every dollar of property taxes paid in 1993.
...public injuries[1] ($58.9 billion)	a $6.5 million grant to each public library in the U.S., *or*
	an $84,300 bonus for each police officer and firefighter.

(1) Any accident, other than a motor vehicle or a work-related accident, that occurs in public use of any premises, such as accidents during recreation (swimming, hunting, etc.), due to natural disasters, or in a public building.

U.S. Fires, 1992

Source: National Fire Protection Assn.

Fires
- Public fire departments responded to 1,964,500 fires in 1992, a decrease of 3.8% from 1991.
- There were 637,500 structure fires in 1992, virtually no change from 1991.
- 74% of all structure fires, or 472,000 fires, occurred in residential properties.
- There were 405,000 vehicle fires in 1992, a decrease of 5.5% from 1991.
- The number of fires in outside properties decreased by 5.2%, to 922,000 fires.
- The South and the Northeast—with 9.2 and 9.1 fires per 1,000 population, respectively—had the highest fire incidence rates in the nation.

Civilian deaths
- The number of civilian fire deaths increased by 5.9%, to 4,730.
- About 78% of all fire deaths occurred in homes.
- There were 3,705 home fire deaths in 1992, an increase of 5.9% from 1991.
- The South had the highest regional death rate, with 24.1 civilian deaths per million population, followed closely by the North Central region, with 21.4 deaths per million.

Civilian injuries
- There were 28,700 civilian fire injuries in 1992, a decrease of 2.3% from the year before. The actual number of injuries may have been higher, however, because of underreporting of civilian injuries to the fire service.
- 21,600 civilian injuries, or 75.3%, occurred in residential properties; 9.5%, or 2,725 injuries, occurred in nonresidential structure fires.
- The Northeast had the highest civilian injury rate, with 160.9 civilian injuries per million population.

Property damage
- Property damage resulting from fires in 1992 decreased by 12.4%, to an estimated $8.295 billion. The higher figure in 1991 reflected the Oakland Hills, California, fire, which resulted in an estimated $1.5 billion loss.
- Structure fires accounted for 84% of all property damage, or $6.957 billion.
- 56% of all structure property loss occurred in residential properties. The cost totaled $3.880 billion.
- The West had the highest property loss rate in the nation: $35.3 per person.

Incendiary and suspicious fires
- 14.7% of all structure fires, or an estimated 94,000 fires, were deliberately set or suspected of having been deliberately set. This represented a decrease from 1991.
- Incendiary or suspicious structure fires resulted in the deaths of 605 people in 1992, an increase of 23.5% from the year before. These fires cost $1.999 billion in property damage, representing 28.7% of all property loss from structure fires and an increase of 30.6% from 1991. The increase was almost entirely attributable to the Los Angeles riots that began on Apr. 29, 1992, in which set fires resulted in $567,371,476 in property damage.
- Vehicle fires of incendiary or suspicious origin decreased by 10.2%, to 44,000. They caused $158 million in property damage, down 13.2% from the previous year.

Physicians by Age, Sex, and Specialty

Source: American Medical Assn., Jan. 1, 1992

	Total Physicians[1]		Under 35 yrs.		35–44 yrs.		45–54 yrs.		55–64 yrs.	
	Male	Female	Male	Female	Male	Female	Male	Female	Male	Female
All Specialties	**534,543**	**118,519**	**93,287**	**40,431**	**153,921**	**44,336**	**110,790**	**18,026**	**80,288**	**7,224**
Aerospace Medicine	650	41	103	15	208	20	151	4	122	2
Allergy & Immunology	2,889	552	198	96	868	248	813	123	600	48
Anesthesiology	22,978	5,170	5,379	1,408	8,044	1,958	4,757	1,144	3,288	460
Cardiovascular Disease	15,563	915	1,923	210	6,288	469	4,024	160	2,179	48
Child Psychiatry	2,981	1,637	269	245	999	688	889	397	577	204
Colon/Rectal Surgery	840	29	47	7	304	18	235	3	135	1
Dermatology	6,006	1,906	745	716	1,838	805	1,777	265	1,020	88
Diagnostic Radiology	14,354	2,899	3,628	1,165	5,389	1,296	3,690	336	1,217	78
Emergency Medicine	13,111	2,359	2,543	788	6,378	1,133	2,716	331	978	77
Family Practice	41,261	9,708	8,556	4,104	16,661	4,135	6,828	971	5,377	314
Forensic Pathology	325	98	15	8	100	46	83	26	83	14
Gastroenterology	7,438	508	1,040	136	3,242	287	2,052	72	784	9
General Practice	18,391	2,328	367	111	1,998	625	3,170	721	5,297	455
General Preventive Med.	877	299	102	75	254	130	213	48	160	22
General Surgery	36,380	2,831	9,737	1,623	8,694	940	7,656	179	6,147	57
Internal Medicine	67,138	18,701	22,286	9,573	21,321	6,531	10,279	1,770	7,579	558
Neurological Surgery	4,355	146	785	53	1,196	73	1,139	16	834	3
Neurology	8,110	1,632	1,273	464	3,238	784	2,141	250	1,078	101
Nuclear Medicine	1,156	216	91	41	349	96	358	58	271	17
Obstetrics/Gynecology	23,497	8,090	3,802	3,607	6,914	3,028	6,099	1,013	4,566	302
Occupational Medicine	2,465	322	107	35	539	148	424	61	659	45
Ophthalmology	14,691	1,742	2,245	643	4,322	742	4,049	219	2,670	82
Orthopedic Surgery	20,126	514	4,056	228	6,192	225	5,305	40	3,241	9
Otolaryngology	7,882	491	1,425	206	2,209	226	2,228	35	1,388	17
Pathology-Anat./Clin.	12,849	4,156	1,722	1,069	3,590	1,646	3,243	934	2,966	336
Pediatric Cardiology	829	211	116	59	302	68	219	46	143	25
Pediatrics	23,842	16,573	5,191	6,761	7,415	5,824	5,410	2,625	3,649	885
Physical Med./Rehab.	3,124	1,345	857	398	1,030	494	580	272	397	138
Plastic Surgery	4,354	334	352	59	1,532	183	1,456	64	754	20
Psychiatry	27,377	9,028	3,315	2,360	7,092	3,243	7,003	1,832	5,887	960
Public Health	1,505	479	41	24	316	136	350	92	350	103
Pulmonary Diseases	5,777	560	746	146	2,757	272	1,491	82	507	36
Radiation Oncology	2,447	566	501	157	776	237	679	130	344	30
Radiology	7,064	784	231	90	962	268	2,387	261	2,312	119
Thoracic Surgery	2,090	30	150	7	514	17	571	5	543	1
Urological Surgery	9,290	162	1,341	70	2,490	73	2,796	14	1,812	5
Other	6,304	991	364	111	1,618	372	1,345	216	1,483	152
Unspecified	6,024	2,085	3,680	1,373	1,168	484	446	139	327	53

(1) Includes physicians 65 and over, those living in U.S. possessions, those "Inactive," "Not Classified," and "Address Unknown."

Ownership of Life Insurance in the U.S. and Assets of U.S. Life Insurance Companies

Source: American Council of Life Insurance

(millions of dollars)

Year	Purchases of life insurance				Insurance in force					Assets
	Ordinary	Group	Industrial	Total	Ordinary	Group	Industrial	Credit	Total	
1940	6,689	691	3,350	10,730	79,346	14,938	20,866	380	115,530	30,802
1950	17,326	6,068	5,402	28,796	149,116	47,793	33,415	3,844	234,168	64,020
1960	52,883	14,645	6,880	74,408	341,881	175,903	39,563	29,101	586,448	119,576
1965	83,485	51,385*	7,296	142,166*	499,638	308,078	39,818	53,020	900,554	158,884
1970	122,820	63,690*	6,612	193,122*	734,730	551,357	38,644	77,392	1,402,123	207,254
1975	188,003	95,190*	6,729	289,922*	1,083,421	904,695	39,423	112,032	2,139,571	289,304
1980	385,575	183,418	3,609	572,602	1,760,474	1,579,355	35,994	165,215	3,541,038	479,210
1985	910,944	319,503	722	1,231,169	3,247,289	2,561,595	28,250	215,973	6,053,107	825,901
1987	986,660	365,529	324	1,352,513	4,139,071	3,043,782	26,668	242,977	7,452,498	1,044,459
1989	1,020,719	420,707	252	1,441,678	4,939,964	3,469,498	24,446	260,107	8,694,015	1,299,756
1990	1,069,660	459,271	220	1,529,151	5,366,982	3,753,506	24,071	248,038	9,392,597	1,408,402
1991	1,041,508	573,953*	198	1,615,659*	5,677,777	4,057,606	22,475	228,478	9,986,336	1,551,201
1992	1,048,135	440,143	222	1,488,500	5,941,810	4,240,919	20,973	202,090	10,405,792	1,664,531
1993	1,101,327	576,823	149	1,678,299	6,428,434	4,456,338	20,451	199,518	11,104,741	1,839,127

*Includes Servicemen's Group Life Insurance $27.8 billion in 1965, $17.1 billion in 1970, $1.7 billion in 1975, and $166.7 billion in 1991.

Health Insurance Coverage, 1991

Source: Bureau of the Census, U.S. Dept. of Commerce

(monthly average, first through fourth quarters)

	Quarter 1	Quarter 2	Quarter 3	Quarter 4
All persons	**249,038**	**249,595**	**250,203**	**250,894**
% Covered by Private or Gvt. Health Insurance				
Total	**86.1**	**86.8**	**87.1**	**86.7**
Age				
Less than 16 years	85.8	86.3	86.8	86.6
16 to 24 years	78.7	79.9	80.1	79.4
25 to 34 years	80.2	81.4	81.9	81.3
35 to 44 years	85.7	86.5	86.7	86.4
45 to 54 years	88.4	88.2	88.3	87.8
55 to 64 years	89.1	89.8	89.9	89.0
65 years and over	99.3	99.5	99.6	99.5
Race and Hispanic Origin				
White	87.2	87.8	88.1	87.6
Black	80.9	82.2	82.2	81.5
Hispanic origin[1]	70.0	72.5	72.6	70.3
% Covered by Private Health Insurance				
Total	**74.5**	**75.2**	**75.5**	**75.1**
Age				
Less than 16 years	68.7	69.1	69.6	69.8
16 to 24 years	69.6	70.3	71.0	70.3
25 to 34 years	71.7	73.0	73.6	73.2
35 to 44 years	79.6	80.4	80.4	80.1
45 to 54 years	82.3	82.2	82.2	81.7
55 to 64 years	81.3	82.0	81.6	80.6
65 years and over	76.8	77.6	77.6	77.7
Race and Hispanic Origin				
White	78.0	78.6	78.7	78.3
Black	53.8	55.5	56.7	56.0
Hispanic origin[1]	49.6	51.9	51.9	49.8

	Quarter 1	Quarter 2	Quarter 3	Quarter 4
% Covered by Private Health Insurance Related to Employment of Self or Other Family Member				
Total	**60.1**	**60.4**	**60.5**	**60.3**
Age				
Less than 16 years	57.2	57.1	57.5	58.0
16 to 24 years	54.5	54.9	54.7	54.1
25 to 34 years	64.6	65.6	66.2	66.0
35 to 44 years	72.3	72.7	72.4	72.3
45 to 54 years	72.8	73.0	72.4	71.9
55 to 64 years	66.7	66.9	67.0	65.5
65 years and over	34.1	34.3	33.8	34.1
Race and Hispanic Origin				
White	62.8	63.0	62.8	62.6
Black	44.5	46.2	47.1	46.0
Hispanic origin[1]	42.0	44.0	44.1	43.0
% Covered by Medicaid				
Total	**8.7**	**9.0**	**9.2**	**9.1**
Age				
Less than 16 years	17.1	17.5	17.8	17.8
16 to 24 years	8.5	9.0	9.0	9.1
25 to 34 years	6.7	7.1	6.9	6.8
35 to 44 years	4.3	4.5	4.8	4.9
45 to 54 years	3.5	3.5	3.8	3.7
55 to 64 years	4.6	4.6	5.1	5.0
65 years and over	8.3	8.5	8.6	8.6
Race and Hispanic Origin				
White	6.2	6.6	6.9	6.8
Black	23.9	23.5	23.2	23.7
Hispanic origin[1]	18.8	19.4	19.2	19.0

(1) Persons of Hispanic origin may be of any race.

Selected Health Services: Estimated Sources of Revenue, 1992

Source: Bureau of the Census, U.S. Dept. of Commerce; in millions of dollars

Source of revenue	Kind of business: Health practitioners		Offices and clinics of MDs		Offices and clinics of dentists		Nursing and personal care	
	Revenue	Percent of total revenue	Revenue	Percent of total revenue	Revenue	Percent of total revenue	Revenue	Percent of total revenue
Total	**$203,208**	**100.0**	**$150,129**	**100.0**	**$33,021**	**100.0**	**$42,462**	**100.0**
Medicare	36,772	18.1	34,115	22.7	258	0.8	3,470	8.2
Medicaid	10,544	5.2	9,175	6.1	701	2.1	23,026	54.2
Other government	3,687	1.8	2,882	1.9	NA	NA	911	2.1
Private insurance	88,268	43.4	64,714	43.1	15,246	46.2	1,819	4.3
Patient	52,552	25.9	29,840	19.9	15,988	48.4	10,746	25.3
Other	11,372	5.6	9,403	6.3	NA	NA	2,489	5.9

NA = not available. **Note:** Estimates are obtained from a sample of employer firms only and, therefore, do not include nonemployer receipts. Estimates are for taxable and tax-exempt firms and organizations. Totals may include kinds of business not shown separately. Detail may not add due to rounding.

Health Services: Estimated Annual Revenue, 1991-92

Source: Bureau of the Census, U.S. Dept. of Commerce

Kind of business	Revenue (millions of dollars) 1991	1992	Percent change 1991-92
Health services	**$575,410**	**$625,084**	**8.6**
Offices and clinics of MDs	137,948	150,129	8.8
Offices and clinics of dentists	29,993	32,878	9.6
Offices and clinics of osteopaths	2,599	2,736	5.3
Offices and clinics of other health practitioners	15,628	17,323	10.8
Offices and clinics of chiropractors	4,986	5,787	16.1
Offices and clinics of optometrists	4,430	4,649	4.9
Offices and clinics of podiatrists	1,826	1,961	7.4
Nursing and personal care facilities	**39,319**	**42,462**	**8.0**

Kind of business	Revenue (millions of dollars) 1991	1992	Percent change 1991-92
Hospitals	**$310,355**	**$335,190**	**8.0**
General medical and surgical hospitals	279,446	303,737	8.7
Psychiatric hospitals	15,341	14,876	–3.0
Specialty hospitals, except psychiatric	15,568	16,577	6.5
Medical and dental laboratories	**10,527**	**11,115**	**5.6**
Medical laboratories	8,849	9,336	5.5
Dental laboratories	1,678	1,779	6.0
Home health care services	**11,240**	**13,705**	**2.2**
Miscellaneous health and allied services	**17,659**	**19,403**	**9.9**
Kidney dialysis centers	1,911	2,332	22.0
Specialty outpatient facilities	9,715	10,201	5.0

U.S. Health Expenditures, 1960-91

Source: Health Care Financing Administration, Office of the Actuary; data from Office of National Health Statistics

(in billions of dollars)

Type of expenditure	1960	1970	1980	1985	1986	1987	1988	1989	1990	1991
National health expenditures	**$27.1**	**$74.4**	**$250.1**	**$422.6**	**$454.8**	**$494.1**	**$546.0**	**$604.3**	**$675.0**	**$751.8**
Health services & supplies	**25.4**	**69.1**	**238.9**	**407.2**	**438.9**	**476.9**	**526.2**	**583.6**	**652.4**	**728.6**
Personal health care	23.9	64.9	219.4	369.7	400.8	439.3	482.8	530.9	591.5	660.2
Hospital care	9.3	27.9	102.4	168.3	179.8	194.2	212.0	232.4	258.1	288.6
Physician services	5.3	13.6	41.9	74.0	82.1	93.0	105.1	116.1	128.8	142.0
Dental services	2.0	4.7	14.4	23.3	24.7	27.1	29.4	31.6	34.1	37.1
Other professional services	0.6	1.5	8.7	16.6	18.6	21.1	23.8	27.1	30.7	35.8
Home health care	0.0	0.1	1.3	3.8	4.0	4.1	4.5	5.6	7.6	9.8
Drugs & other medical nondurables	4.2	8.8	21.6	36.2	39.7	43.2	46.3	50.5	55.6	60.7
Vision products & other medical durables	0.8	2.0	4.6	7.1	8.1	9.1	10.1	10.4	11.7	12.4
Nursing home care	1.0	4.9	20.0	34.1	36.7	39.7	42.8	47.5	53.3	59.9
Other personal health care	0.7	1.4	4.6	6.4	7.1	7.8	8.7	9.8	11.5	14.0
Program administration & net cost of private health insurance	1.2	2.8	12.2	25.2	24.6	23.0	26.9	33.8	38.9	43.9
Government public health activities	0.4	1.4	7.2	12.3	13.5	14.6	16.6	18.9	22.0	24.5
Research & construction	**1.7**	**5.3**	**11.3**	**15.4**	**16.0**	**17.3**	**19.8**	**20.7**	**22.7**	**23.1**
Research[1]	0.7	2.0	5.4	7.8	8.5	9.0	10.3	11.0	11.9	12.6
Construction	1.0	3.4	5.8	7.6	7.4	8.2	9.5	9.7	10.8	10.6
	Average annual % change from previous year shown									
National health expenditures	**—**	**10.6**	**12.9**	**11.1**	**7.6**	**8.6**	**10.5**	**10.7**	**11.7**	**11.4**
Health services & supplies	**—**	**10.5**	**13.2**	**11.3**	**7.8**	**8.6**	**10.3**	**10.9**	**11.8**	**11.7**
Personal health care	—	10.5	13.0	11.0	8.4	9.6	9.9	10.0	11.4	11.6
Hospital care	—	11.7	13.9	10.4	6.8	8.0	9.2	9.6	11.1	11.8
Physician services	—	9.9	11.9	12.1	10.9	13.3	13.1	10.4	11.0	10.2
Dental services	—	9.1	11.9	10.1	6.4	9.6	8.5	7.5	7.7	8.8
Other professional services	—	9.6	19.1	13.8	12.0	13.6	12.4	13.8	13.5	16.7
Home health care	—	14.5	25.2	23.3	3.6	3.4	9.9	24.4	34.4	29.0
Drugs & other medical nondurables	—	7.6	9.4	10.8	9.9	8.6	7.2	9.1	10.3	9.0
Vision products & other medical durables	—	9.6	8.5	9.4	13.0	12.3	11.8	2.8	12.6	5.4
Nursing home care	—	17.4	15.2	11.3	7.6	8.0	7.8	11.1	12.3	12.4
Other personal health care	—	7.1	12.8	6.9	11.1	10.0	12.1	11.8	17.4	21.9
Program administration & net cost of private health insurance	—	9.0	16.0	15.5	–2.5	–6.6	16.8	25.7	15.3	12.7
Government public health activities	—	13.9	18.0	11.3	9.6	8.3	13.5	14.3	16.0	11.6
Research & construction	**—**	**12.1**	**7.8**	**6.4**	**3.7**	**8.2**	**14.9**	**4.2**	**9.6**	**2.1**
Research[1]	—	10.9	10.8	7.4	9.5	5.7	14.5	6.2	8.0	6.1
Construction	—	12.8	5.6	5.4	–2.4	11.1	15.3	1.9	11.5	–2.2

Note: Numbers may not add to totals because of rounding. (1) Research and development expenditures of drug companies and other manufacturers and providers of medical equipment and supplies are excluded from "research expenditures," but included in the expenditure class in which the product falls.

Top 20 Reasons Given by Patients for Emergency Room Visits, 1992

Source: National Center for Health Statistics, U.S. Dept. of Health and Human Services

Principal reason for visit	Number of visits (1,000)	Percentage of total
All visits to emergency rooms	**89,796**	**100.0**
Stomach and abdominal pain, cramps, and spasms	4,955	5.5
Chest pain and related symptoms	4,625	5.2
Fever	3,678	4.1
Headache, pain in the head	2,545	2.8
Laceration and cuts—upper extremity	2,347	2.6
Shortness of breath	2,025	2.3
Cough	1,997	2.2
Back symptoms	1,959	2.2
Symptoms referable to throat	1,957	2.2
Vomiting	1,877	2.1
Pain, site not referable to a specific body system	1,812	2.0
Earache or ear infection	1,614	1.8
Laceration and cuts—facial area	1,485	1.7
Hand and finger symptoms	1,390	1.5
Neck symptoms	1,325	1.5
Skin rash	1,305	1.5
Labored or difficult breathing (dyspnea)	1,239	1.4
Leg symptoms	1,154	1.3
Knee symptoms	1,102	1.2
Foot and toe symptoms	1,085	1.2
All other reasons	48,322	53.8

Top 20 Reasons Given by Patients for Physicians' Office Visits, 1992

Source: National Center for Health Statistics, U.S. Dept. of Health

Principal reason for visit	Number of visits (1,000)	Percentage distribution		
		Total	Female	Male
All visits	**762,045**	**100.0**	**100.0**	**100.0**
General medical examination	33,973	4.5	4.7	4.1
Cough	30,226	4.0	3.7	4.3
Routine prenatal examination	28,036	3.7	6.1	NA
Progress visit, not otherwise specified	25,771	3.4	3.4	3.4
Symptoms referable to throat	20,839	2.7	2.9	2.6
Postoperative visit	20,060	2.6	2.6	2.7
Earache or ear infection	15,292	2.0	1.9	2.1
Back symptoms	13,899	1.8	1.6	2.1
Vision dysfunctions	13,414	1.8	1.7	1.8
Skin rash	13,379	1.8	1.5	2.1
Fever	12,790	1.7	1.4	2.1
Stomach pain, cramps, and spasms	11,985	1.6	1.9	1.1
Head cold, upper respiratory infection (coryza)	10,986	1.4	1.3	1.6
Headache, pain in the head	10,854	1.4	1.7	1.1
Well-baby examination	10,799	1.4	1.2	1.8
Knee symptoms	10,630	1.4	1.3	1.6
Nasal congestion	10,538	1.4	1.3	1.5
Hypertension	8,716	1.1	1.2	1.1
Depression	8,344	1.1	1.2	1.0
All other reasons	451,513	59.3	57.4	61.9

NA = not applicable.

The 20 Drugs Most Frequently Prescribed in Physicians' Offices, 1991

Source: National Center for Health Statistics, U.S. Dept. of Health and Human Services; in thousands

Rank	Name of drug and principal generic substance[1]	Number of times prescribed	Therapeutic use
1.	Amoxicillin	20,554	Antibiotic
2.	Amoxil (amoxicillin)	17,492	Antibiotic
3.	Lasix (furosemide)	13,543	Diuretic, antihypertensive
4.	Ceclor (cefaclor)	9,607	Antibiotic
5.	Zantac (ranitidine)	9,037	Duodenal or gastric ulcer
6.	Vasotec (enalapril)	9,022	Antihypertensive
7.	Premarin (estrogens)	8,814	Estrogen replacement therapy
8.	Prednisone	8,808	Steroid replacement therapy, anti-inflammatory agent
9.	Naprosyn (naproxen)	8,541	Nonsteroidal anti-inflammatory agent
10.	Synthroid (levothyroxine)	8,278	Thyroid hormone therapy
11.	Tylenol (acetaminophen)	8,226	Analgesic
12.	Seldane (terfenadine)	7,771	Antihistaminic
13.	Cardizem (ditiazem)	7,604	Cardiotonic/calcium channel blocking agent
14.	Lanoxin (digoxin)	7,593	Cardiotonic/digitalis
15.	Ventolin (albuterol)	7,490	Bronchodilator
16.	Motrin (ibuprofen)	6,918	Nonsteroidal anti-inflammatory agent
17.	Proventil (albuterol)	9,735	Bronchodilator
18.	Diphtheria tetanus toxoids pertussis	6,176	Immunization
19.	Xanax (alprazolam)	6,027	Anxiety disorders
20.	Poliomyelitis vaccine	5,761	Immunization

(1) The trade or generic name used by the physician on the prescription or other medical records. The use of trade names is for identification only and does not imply endorsement by the Public Health Service or the U.S. Department of Health and Human Services. Because of their nonspecific nature, the entries "Allergy relief or shots," with 6,183,286 mentions, and "Prenatal formula (vitamins)" with 5,584,932 mentions, are omitted.

Estimated New Cancer Cases and Deaths, by Sex, for Leading Sites, 1994

Source: American Cancer Society

The estimates of new cancer cases are offered as a rough guide and should not be regarded as definitive. About 700,000 basal and squamous cell skin cancers and 100,000 carcinoma in situ cases are not included in the totals. About 2,300 nonmelanoma skin cancer deaths occurred in 1994.

Estimated New Cases

Total		Women		Men	
All Sites	1,208,000	All Sites	576,000	All Sites	632,000
Prostate	200,000	Breast	182,000	Prostate	200,000
Breast	183,000	Colorectal	74,000	Lung	100,000
Lung	172,000	Lung	72,000	Colorectal	75,000
Colorectal	149,000	Uterus	46,000	Bladder	38,000
Lymphoma	53,900	Ovary	24,000	Lymphoma	29,400

Estimated Deaths

Total		Women		Men	
All Sites	538,000	All Sites	255,000	All Sites	283,000
Lung	153,000	Lung	59,000	Lung	94,000
Colorectal	56,000	Breast	46,000	Prostate	38,000
Breast	46,300	Colorectal	28,200	Colorectal	27,800
Prostate	38,000	Ovary	13,600	Pancreas	12,400
Pancreas	25,900	Pancreas	13,500	Lymphoma	12,100

Trends in Cancer Death Rates, 1958-60 and 1988-90

Source: American Cancer Society

Sites	Sex	Death rate[1] 1958-60	Death rate[1] 1988-90	Percentage change	Number of deaths 1960	Number of deaths 1990
All Sites	Male	180.9	218.0	21	143,498	268,283
	Female	136.8	140.8	†	124,084	237,039
Colon and rectum	Male	25.2	23.5	–7	19,127	28,635
	Female	22.8	16.1	–30	20,265	28,895
Colon	Male	17.0	20.0	17	13,010	24,385
	Female	17.4	14.1	–19	15,527	25,325
Rectum	Male	8.2	3.5	–58	6,117	4,250
	Female	5.4	2.0	–63	4,738	3,570
Lung	Male	36.4	74.2	104	31,257	91,091
	Female	5.5	30.6	452	5,163	50,194
Melanoma of skin	Male	1.4	3.0	120	1,194	3,844
	Female	1.0	1.5	48	989	2,576
Breast	Male	0.3	0.2	–33	215	272
	Female	25.7	27.4	7	23,755	43,391
Cervix uteri	Female	9.4	3.0	–68	8,487	4,627
Other uterus	Female	6.6	3.5	–47	5,929	6,052
Ovary	Female	8.8	7.9	–10	8,046	12,762
Prostate	Male	20.5	25.3	23	14,452	32,378
Bladder	Male	7.2	5.6	–22	5,440	6,910
	Female	2.7	1.7	–38	2,425	3,431
Non-Hodgkin's lymphoma	Male	4.8	7.7	62	4,015	9,795
	Female	3.2	5.0	58	2,839	8,806
Hodgkin's lymphoma	Male	2.2	0.7	–67	1,877	956
	Female	1.3	0.4	–68	1,198	676

†Not statistically significant. **Note:** Even though the death rates declined or remained stable, the number of deaths increased because the population has become larger and older. The U.S. population increased 38% from 1960-1990. (1) Death rates are per 100,000 persons and were adjusted to the age distribution of the 1970 U.S. census population.

Cardiovascular Diseases Statistical Summary, 1992

Source: American Heart Association, Dallas, TX

Prevalence — 58,920,000 Americans had one or more forms of heart and blood vessel disease.

- high blood pressure — 50,000,000
- coronary heart disease — 11,200,000
- stroke — 3,080,000
- rheumatic heart disease — 1,350,000

Hypertension (high blood pressure) — afflicted 50,000,000 Americans age 6 and above, including about 1 in 4 adults, in 1992.

Mortality[1] — 925,079 in 1992 (42.5% of all deaths).

- Someone died from cardiovascular disease every 34 seconds in the U.S. in 1992.

Congenital or inborn heart defects —

- Mortality from heart defects was 5,600 in 1992.

Coronary heart disease (heart attack) — caused 480,170 deaths in 1992.

- 11,200,000 people alive today have a history of heart attack and/or angina pectoris.
- As many as 1,500,000 Americans had a heart attack in 1992, about one-third of them fatal.

Stroke — killed about 143,640 in 1992; afflicted 3,080,000.

Rheumatic heart disease — afflicted 1,350,000 in 1992.

- killed 5,960 in 1992.

(1) Mortality estimates for 1992 are based on provisional data released by National Center for Health Statistics, U.S. Dept. of Health and Human Services.

AIDS Deaths and New AIDS Cases in the U.S., 1985-93

Source: *Health United States 1993,* National Center for Health Statistics, U.S. Dept. of Health and Human Services

	All years[1]	1985	1987	1988	1989	1990	1991	1992	1993[2]
TOTAL DEATHS	**197,727**	**6,704**	**15,504**	**19,773**	**26,005**	**29,022**	**32,573**	**34,228**	**16,885**
NEW AIDS CASES									
All races	**328,392**	**8,189**	**21,048**	**30,648**	**33,511**	**41,558**	**43,574**	**45,603**	**83,814**
Male									
All males, 13 years and older	**285,063**	**7,538**	**19,047**	**27,049**	**29,549**	**36,300**	**37,530**	**38,917**	**70,396**
White, not Hispanic	160,861	4,787	12,034	16,008	17,470	20,903	20,613	20,763	36,336
Black, not Hispanic	82,110	1,704	4,315	7,153	8,031	10,268	11,082	12,107	23,047
Hispanic	38,914	987	2,245	3,647	3,714	4,731	5,403	5,540	10,125
American Indian[3]	614	7	24	34	60	72	75	97	223
Asian or Pacific Islander[4]	1,992	48	131	163	214	255	259	83	540
13–19 years	934	31	67	84	90	102	99	94	299
20–29 years	51,945	1,468	3,784	5,449	5,692	6,814	6,459	6,350	12,052
30–39 years	131,858	3,610	8,855	12,581	13,868	16,802	17,332	17,819	32,116
40–49 years	70,729	1,657	4,283	6,105	6,809	8,908	9,628	10,337	18,935
50–59 years	21,657	605	1,474	1,990	2,240	2,651	2,896	3,079	5,289
60 years and over	7,940	167	584	840	850	1,023	1,116	1,238	1,705
Female									
All females, 13 years and over	**38,684**	**522**	**1,682**	**3,034**	**3,370**	**4,540**	**5,375**	**5,942**	**12,789**
White, not Hispanic	10,288	141	544	854	948	1,225	1,358	1,454	3,379
Black, not Hispanic	21,707	285	894	1,650	1,893	2,539	3,109	3,398	7,171
Hispanic	6,285	92	230	497	493	736	859	1,024	2,091
American Indian[3]	103	3	3	6	9	10	11	15	43
Asian or Pacific Islander[4]	228	1	11	22	17	19	25	37	86
13–19 years	418	4	11	23	29	63	55	57	157
20–29 years	9,418	173	480	768	889	1,104	1,223	1,370	2,962
30–39 years	18,224	236	750	1,503	1,615	2,091	2,538	2,715	6,131
40–49 years	6,919	44	229	411	507	788	995	1,245	2,523
50–59 years	2,148	26	92	151	172	275	342	344	681
60 years and over	1,557	39	120	178	158	219	222	211	335
Children									
All children, under 13 years	**4,645**	**129**	**319**	**565**	**592**	**718**	**669**	**744**	**629**
White, not Hispanic	979	27	85	149	111	159	146	128	110
Black, not Hispanic	2,680	83	160	300	339	384	403	470	380
Hispanic	937	19	71	112	135	168	113	137	128
American Indian[3]	14	–	2	–	2	3	2	3	2
Asian or Pacific Islander[4]	22	–	1	4	3	4	4	1	4
Under 1 year	1,820	54	141	190	241	284	247	302	224
1–12 years	2,825	75	178	375	351	434	422	442	405

Note: The AIDS case definition was changed in 1985, 1987, and 1993, as more was learned about AIDS-associated diseases and conditions and to expand the spectrum of human immunodeficiency virus-associated diseases reportable as AIDS. Excludes residents of U.S. territories. Data are updated periodically because of reporting delays. Data for all years have been updated through Sept. 30, 1993. (1) Includes cases and deaths prior to 1985 and years not shown. (2) Jan. to Sept. 1993. (3) Includes Aleut and Eskimo. (4) Includes Chinese, Japanese, Filipino, Hawaiian and part-Hawaiian, and other Asian or Pacific Islander.

New AIDS Cases in the U.S., 1985-93, by Transmission Category

Source: *Health United States 1993,* National Center for Health Statistics, U.S. Dept. of Health and Human Services

Sex and transmission category	All years[1]	1985	1987	1988	1989	1990	1991	1992	1993[2]
Male	285,063	7,538	19,047	27,049	29,549	36,300	37,530	38,917	70,396
Men who have sex with men	181,468	5,419	13,536	17,811	19,632	23,863	23,879	24,116	40,054
Injecting drug use	55,900	1,108	2,691	5,279	5,429	6,993	7,652	7,972	16,006
Men who have sex with men and injecting drug use	20,376	592	1,564	2,063	2,237	2,452	2,593	2,605	4,595
Hemophilia/coagulation disorder	2,855	73	201	291	279	326	302	303	910
Born in Caribbean/African countries	2,596	107	187	263	237	303	324	279	528
Heterosexual contact[3]	6,169	28	162	328	507	726	889	1,276	2,175
Sex with injecting drug user	3,317	25	116	227	367	461	515	650	901
Transfusion[4]	3,496	111	395	487	435	460	408	381	528
Undetermined[5]	12,203	100	311	527	793	1,177	1,483	1,985	5,547
Female	38,684	522	1,682	3,034	3,370	4,540	5,375	5,942	12,789
Injecting drug use	19,037	284	838	1,626	1,774	2,277	2,715	2,783	5,983
Hemophilia/coagulation disorder	71	2	4	4	7	9	9	3	25
Born in Caribbean/African countries	1,160	31	74	107	130	111	166	169	280
Heterosexual contact[3]	12,847	116	488	865	1,005	1,526	1,854	2,229	4,414
Sex with injecting drug user	7,541	81	331	638	701	1,038	1,177	1,287	2,042
Transfusion[4]	2,283	59	216	324	283	328	243	261	431
Undetermined[5]	3,286	30	62	108	171	289	388	497	1,656

Note: The AIDS case definition was changed in 1985, 1987, and 1993, as more was learned about AIDS-associated diseases and conditions and to expand the spectrum of human immunodeficiency virus-associated diseases reportable as AIDS. Excludes residents of U.S. territories. Data are updated periodically because of reporting delays. Data for all years have been updated through Sept. 30, 1993. (1) Includes cases prior to 1985 and years not shown. (2) Jan. to Sept. 1993. (3) Includes persons who have had heterosexual contact with a person with human immunodeficiency virus (HIV) infection or at risk of HIV infection. (4) Receipt of blood transfusion, blood components, or tissue. (5) Includes persons for whom risk information is incomplete, persons still under investigation, men reported only to have had heterosexual contact with prostitutes, and interviewed persons for whom no specific risk is identified.

Years of Life Expected at Birth

Source: National Center for Health Statistics

Year[1]	All Races Total	All Races Male	All Races Female	White Total	White Male	White Female	Black and Other Total	Black and Other Male	Black and Other Female
1920	54.1	53.6	54.6	54.9	54.4	55.6	45.3	45.5	45.2
1930	59.7	58.1	61.6	61.4	59.7	63.5	48.1	47.3	49.2
1940	62.9	60.8	65.2	64.2	62.1	66.6	53.1	51.5	54.9
1950	68.2	65.6	71.1	69.1	66.5	72.2	60.8	59.1	62.9
1960	69.7	66.6	73.1	70.6	67.4	74.1	63.6	61.1	66.3
1965	70.2	66.8	73.7	71.0	67.6	74.7	64.1	61.1	67.4
1970	70.8	67.1	74.7	71.7	68.0	75.6	65.3	61.3	69.4
1975	72.6	68.8	76.6	73.4	69.5	77.3	68.0	63.7	72.4
1976	72.9	69.1	76.8	73.6	69.9	77.5	68.4	64.2	72.7
1977	73.3	69.5	77.2	74.0	70.2	77.9	68.9	64.7	73.2
1978	73.5	69.6	77.3	74.1	70.4	78.0	68.1	63.7	72.4
1979	73.9	70.0	77.8	74.6	70.8	78.4	69.8	65.4	74.1
1980	73.7	70.0	77.5	74.4	70.7	78.1	69.5	65.3	73.6
1981	74.2	70.4	77.8	74.8	71.1	78.4	70.3	66.2	74.4
1982	74.5	70.9	78.1	75.1	71.5	78.7	70.9	66.8	74.9
1983	74.6	71.0	78.1	75.2	71.7	78.7	70.9	67.0	74.7
1984	74.7	71.2	78.2	75.3	71.8	78.7	71.1	67.2	74.9
1985	74.7	71.2	78.2	75.3	71.9	78.7	67.0	64.8	69.3
1986	74.8	71.3	78.3	75.4	72.0	78.8	70.9	66.8	74.9
1987	75.0	71.5	78.4	75.6	72.2	78.9	66.9	65.0	69.1
1988	74.9	71.5	78.3	75.6	72.3	78.9	70.8	66.7	74.8
1989	75.1	71.7	78.5	75.9	72.5	79.2	70.9	66.7	74.9
1990	75.4	71.8	78.8	76.1	72.9	79.4	71.2	67.0	75.2
1991	75.5	72.0	78.9	76.3	72.9	79.2	71.5	67.4	75.5
1992[p]	75.7	72.3	79.0	76.5	73.2	79.7	71.8	67.8	75.6
1993[p]	75.5	72.1	78.9	76.5	73.0	79.5	71.5	67.4	75.5

p= preliminary. (1) Data prior to 1940 for death-registration states only.

Average Height and Weight for Children

Source: *Physicians Handbook,* 1990

Boys Age Years	Height ft	Height in	cm	Weight lb	Weight kg	Girls Age Years	Height ft	Height in	cm	Weight lb	Weight kg
(Birth)	1	8	50.8	7 ½	3.4	(Birth)	1	8	50.8	7 ½	3.4
½	2	2	66.0	17	7.7	½	2	2	66.0	16	7.2
1	2	5	73.6	21	9.5	1	2	5	73.6	20	9.1
2	2	9	83.8	26	11.8	2	2	9	83.8	25	11.3
3	3	0	91.4	31	14.0	3	3	0	91.4	30	13.6
4	3	3	99.0	34	15.4	4	3	3	99.0	33	15.0
5	3	6	106.6	39	17.7	5	3	5	104.1	38	17.2
6	3	9	114.2	46	20.9	6	3	8	111.7	45	20.4
7	3	11	119.3	51	23.1	7	3	11	119.3	49	22.2
8	4	2	127.0	57	25.9	8	4	2	127.0	56	25.4
9	4	4	132.0	63	28.6	9	4	4	132.0	62	28.1
10	4	6	137.1	69	31.3	10	4	6	137.1	69	31.3
11	4	8	142.2	77	34.9	11	4	8	142.2	77	34.9
12	4	10	147.3	83	37.7	12	4	10	147.3	86	39.0
13	5	0	152.4	92	41.7	13	5	0	152.4	98	45.5
14	5	2	157.5	107	48.5	14	5	2	157.5	107	48.5

This table gives a general picture of American children at specific ages. Heights and weights given represent the mean of those children in the study. When used as a standard, the individual variation in children's growth should not be overlooked. In most cases the height-weight relationship is probably a more valid index of weight status than a weight-for-age assessment.

Overweight Adults, by Age, 1960-91

Source: *Health United States 1993,* National Center for Health Statistics, U.S. Dept. of Health and Human Services

Overweight is defined for men as body mass index greater than or equal to 27.8 kilograms/meter^2, and for women as body mass index greater than or equal to 27.3 kilograms/meter^2. These cut points were used because they represent the sex-specific 85th percentiles of all persons 20-29 years of age in the 1976-80 National Health and Nutrition Examination Survey. Height was measured without shoes; two pounds were deducted from the 1960-62 data to allow for weight of clothing. Pregnant women were excluded from the survey.

Overweight persons, 20 years of age and older	1960-62	1971-74	1976-80	1988-91
	Percentage of U.S. population			
Male				
20-34 years of age	19.6	19.2	17.3	22.2
35-44 years of age	22.8	29.4	28.9	35.3
45-54 years of age	28.1	27.6	31.0	35.6
55-64 years of age	26.9	24.8	28.1	40.1
65-74 years of age	21.8	23.0	25.2	42.9
75 years and older	NA	NA	NA	26.4
Female				
20-34 years of age	13.2	14.8	16.8	25.1
35-44 years of age	24.1	27.3	27.0	36.9
45-54 years of age	30.7	32.3	32.5	41.6
55-64 years of age	43.2	38.5	37.0	48.5
65-74 years of age	42.9	38.0	38.4	39.8
75 years and older	NA	NA	NA	30.9

NA = not available.

OBITUARIES

Deaths, Oct. 16, 1993–Oct. 31, 1994

A

Akins, Claude, 67; character actor in films and television; Altadena, CA, Jan. 27, 1994.

Ameche, Don, 85; actor on radio and TV and in movies, and on stage, famous for his role as Alexander Graham Bell; Scottsdale, AZ, Dec. 6, 1993.

Anderson, Lindsay, 71; film and stage director; Dordogne region, France, Aug. 29, 1994.

Anderson, Paul, 61; weightlifter, 1956 Olympic gold medalist, who still held record for lifting 6,270 lb; Vidalia, GA, Aug. 15, 1994.

Arcel, Ray, 94; boxing trainer who handled many champions; New York, Mar. 7, 1994.

B

Baker, Benny, 87; chubby-cheeked comedian who made a career of playing bellboys, Western Union messengers, and bank clerks in more than 75 films, including *Papa's Delicate Condition*; Woodland Hills, CA, Sept. 20, 1994.

Ball, George, 84; investment banker, international affairs specialist; as undersecretary of state opposed Vietnam War; New York, May 26, 1994.

Barrault, Jean-Louis, 83; actor, director; Paris, Jan. 22, 1994.

Basquette, Lina, 87; silent-film star and professional dog breeder; Wheeling, WV, Sept. 30, 1994.

Beck, Dave, 99; Teamsters union president imprisoned for tax evasion and embezzlement; Seattle, WA, May 26, 1994.

Belluschi, Pietro, 94; architect who designed New York's Pan Am Building (now MetLife Bldg.) and other large urban structures; Portland, OR, Feb. 14, 1994.

Benson, Ezra Taft, 94; secretary of agriculture, 1953-61, and leader since 1985 of the Church of Jesus Christ of Latter Day Saints; Salt Lake City, UT, May 30, 1994.

Bich, Marcel, 79; inventor of Bic disposable pen; Paris, May 30, 1994.

Bixby, Bill, 59; TV actor in *My Favorite Martian* and *The Incredible Hulk;* Century City, CA, Nov. 21, 1993.

Bloch, Robert, 77; prolific mystery writer whose works included the novel *Psycho;* Los Angeles, Sept. 23, 1994.

Booke, Sorrell, 64; actor who played Boss Hogg in *The Dukes of Hazzard*; Sherman Oaks, CA, Feb. 11, 1994.

Boros, Julius, 74; golfer who won 2 U.S. Open championships; Fort Lauderdale, FL, May 28, 1994.

Boulle, Pierre, 81; author of *The Bridge Over the River Kwai* and *Planet of the Apes*; Paris, Jan. 30, 1994.

Burgess, Anthony, 76; author of plays, scripts, screenplays, and 50 books, including *A Clockwork Orange*; London, Nov. 22, 1993.

C

Callen, Michael, 38; writer, singer, and AIDS activist; Los Angeles, Dec. 27, 1993.

Candy, John, 43; film actor in comic roles; Mexico, Mar. 4, 1994.

Canetti, Elias, 89; novelist, playwright, who won Nobel Prize in literature; Zurich, Switzerland, Aug. 13, 1994.

Carey, Macdonald, 81; actor in films and in radio and TV soap operas; Beverly Hills, CA, Mar. 21, 1994.

Childress, Alice, 77; actress and writer of plays and novels, including *A Hero Ain't Nothin' but a Sandwich*; New York, Aug. 14, 1994.

Clavell, James, 69; author of novels with exotic settings, including *Tai-Pan* and *Shogun*; Vevey, Switzerland, Sept. 6, 1994.

Clay, Lucius, Jr., 74; general who directed Air Force combat operations in Vietnam; Alexandria, VA, Feb. 7, 1994.

Cobain, Kurt, 27; singer, guitarist, and songwriter, who created grunge rock sound that dominated popular music for several years; Seattle, WA, Apr. 5, 1994.

Collins, Dorothy, 67; singer who starred on TV's *Your Hit Parade*; Watervliet, NY, July 21, 1994.

Conrad, William, 73; TV actor in *Jake and the Fatman* and *Cannon*; North Hollywood, CA, Feb. 11, 1994.

Corrigan, Daniel N., 93; Episcopal bishop whose long career was marked by campaigns for peace and human rights; Santa Barbara, CA, Sept. 21, 1994.

Cotten, Joseph, 88; stage and screen actor known for strong dramatic roles; Los Angeles, Feb. 6, 1994.

Curry, John, 44; 1976 Olympic champion who infused ice skating with the form of ballet; Stratford-upon-Avon, England, Apr. 15, 1994.

D

Dandridge, Ray, 79; Hall of Fame 3d baseman in Negro leagues; Palm Bay, FL, Feb. 12, 1994.

DeFore, Don, 80; actor in TV comedies, including *Hazel* and *Ozzie and Harriet;* Santa Monica, CA, Dec. 22, 1993.

Dickey, Bill, 86; Baseball Hall of Fame catcher for New York Yankees; Little Rock, AR, Nov. 12, 1993.

Duke, Doris, 80; tobacco heiress, philanthropist, once known as "richest girl in the world"; Beverly Hills, CA, Oct. 28, 1993.

E

Ellison, Ralph, 80; author whose acclaimed novel *Invisible Man* recounted the struggle of a young black against racial discrimination; New York, Apr. 16, 1994.

Ellul, Jacques, 82; theologian and author who warned of dangers of technological society; Bordeaux, France, May 19, 1994.

Erikson, Erik, 91; psychoanalyst, pioneer thinker in child development and resolution of conflicts within humans, coined phrase "identity crisis"; Harwich, MA, May 12, 1994.

Ewell, Tom, 85; actor, starred in *The Seven Year Itch* on stage and in film; Woodland Hills, CA, Sept. 12, 1994.

F

Feeney, Charles, 72; president of baseball's National League, 1970-86; San Francisco, Jan. 10, 1994.

Fellini, Federico, 73; preeminent director of films with offbeat themes and styles, including *La Dolce Vita, La Strada*, and *Amarcord*; Rome, Oct. 31, 1993.

Fisher, Avery, 87; founder of electronics company, philanthropist; New Milford, CT, Feb. 26, 1994.

Flood, Daniel, 90; U.S. House member who pleaded guilty to accepting payoffs; Wilkes-Barre, PA, May 28, 1994.

Fowler, Joseph, 99; admiral, builder of warships and theme parks, including, Disneyland and Disney World; Orlando, FL, Dec. 3, 1993.

Furness, Betty, 78; actress who gained fame for her Westinghouse commercials on TV and then as a consumer advocate; New York, Apr. 2, 1994.

G

Gamsakhurdia, Zviad, 54; president of Georgia who was ousted from office; western Georgia, Dec. 31, 1993.

Ganiau, Penaia, 75; president of Fiji; Washington, DC, Dec. 15, 1993.

Gerulaitis, Vitas, 40; tennis player, won Wimbledon doubles (1975) and Australian Open (1977); Southampton, NY, Sept. 18, 1994.

H

Habyarimana, Juvenal, 57; president of Rwanda; Kigali, Rwanda, Apr. 6, 1994.

Haldeman, H. R., 67; Pres. Richard Nixon's top aide who served prison term for his role in Watergate affair; Santa Barbara, CA, Nov. 12, 1993.

Hall, Adelaide, 92; jazz singer and cabaret entertainer; London, Nov. 8, 1993.

Hoad, Lew, 59; tennis player who won 5 Wimbledon titles; Marbella, Spain, July 3, 1994.

Hodgkin, Dorothy, 84; Nobel prize-winning chemist, discovered structure of penicillin, vitamin B12, insulin; Shipston-on-Stour, England, July 29, 1994.

Honecker, Erich, 81; Marxist ruler of East Germany for 18 years; Chile, May 29, 1994.

Houphouet-Boigny, Felix, 88; president of Côte d'Ivoire since 1960; Yamoussoukro, Côte d'Ivoire, Dec. 7, 1993.

I

Ionesco, Eugene, 84; playwright whose innovative works, including *Rhinoceros* and *The Bald Soprano,* satirized modern society; Paris, Mar. 28, 1994.

J

Judd, Donald, 65; sculptor whose sleek, simple designs made him a major figure in Minimal Art; New York, Feb. 12, 1994.

Judd, Walter, 95; missionary in China and U.S. House member; Mitchellville, MD, Feb. 13, 1994.

Julia, Raul, 54; acclaimed actor who distinguished himself in the classics, in comedy, and in musicals; Manhasset, NY, Oct. 24, 1994.

K

Kabibble, Ish, 86; comic actor; Joshua Tree, CA, June 5, 1994.

Kahn, E. J., Jr., 77; author and a staff writer for *The New Yorker* (1937-94); Holyoke, MA, May 28, 1994.

Kelley, Virginia Clinton, 70; mother of Pres. Bill Clinton; Hot Springs, AR, Jan. 6, 1994.

Kim Il Sung, 82; leader of North Korea since 1948, a communist who was revered almost as a god by his people; Pyongyang, North Korea, July 8, 1994.

Kirk, Russell, 75; author of *The Conservative Mind*, regarded as a founder of the modern U.S. conservative political movement; Mecosta, MI, Apr. 29, 1994.

L

Lancaster, Burt, 80; rugged former acrobat and Oscar-winning actor, well known for his performance in *From Here to Eternity;* Century City, CA, Oct. 20, 1994.

Langton, David, 82; actor best known for *Upstairs, Downstairs* role; Stratford-upon-Avon, England, Apr. 25, 1994.

Lantz, Walter, 93; animator and producer who created Woody Woodpecker; Burbank, CA, Mar. 22, 1994.

Lasker, Mary, 93; philanthropist who supported research on cancer and on heart and eye diseases; Greenwich, CT, Feb. 21, 1994.

Lazar, Irving "Swifty," 86; talent agent who negotiated big contracts for leading entertainers and authors; Beverly Hills, CA, Dec. 30, 1993.

Lebow, Fred, 62; creator and developer of the New York City Marathon; New York, Oct. 9, 1994.

Lee, Robert E., 75; playwright, coauthor of *Inherit the Wind* and *Auntie Mame*; Los Angeles, July 8, 1994.

Lejeune, Jerome, 67; discovered chromosome abnormality that causes Down's syndrome; Paris, Apr. 3, 1994.

Levitt, William, 86; developer who built inexpensive houses in large tracts ("Levittowns") that were popular with soldiers returning from World War II; Manhasset, NY, Jan. 28, 1994.

Linblad, Lars-Eric, 67; pioneer in organizing adventure vacations to remote areas of the world; Stockholm, Sweden, July 8, 1994.

Loy, Myrna, 88; urbane actress best known for role as Nora Charles in *The Thin Man* and its sequels; New York, Dec. 14, 1993.

M

MacKendrick, Alexander, 81; director of motion pictures, including *The Man in the White Suit, The Ladykillers,* and *The Sweet Smell of Success*; Los Angeles, Dec. 21, 1993.

Mancini, Henry, 70; composer and conductor of music for films and TV who wrote "Moon River" and "Days of Wine and Roses"; Beverly Hills, CA, June 14, 1994.

Masina, Giulietta, 73; actress who starred in *La Strada*, directed by her husband, Federico Fellini; Rome, Mar. 23, 1994.

Massieu, José Francisco Ruiz, 48; secretary general of the Institutional Revolutionary Party, the governing party of Mexico; Mexico City, Sept. 28, 1994.

May, Rollo, 85; innovative psychologist and psychotherapist, known for his writings, which were particularly accessible to lay people; Tiburon, CA, Oct. 22, 1994.

Mercouri, Melina, 68; actress in *Never on Sunday*, culture minister of Greece; New York, Mar. 6, 1994.

Mitchell, Cameron, 75; theater, film, and television actor; Pacific Palisades, CA, July 6, 1994.

Moore, Charles, 68; architect and educator, whose eclectic designs borrowed from several schools; Austin, TX, Dec. 16, 1993.

Moore, Garry, 78; TV entertainer who was the host of *I've Got a Secret* and *To Tell the Truth*; Hilton Head Island, SC, Nov. 28, 1993.

Morgan, Henry, 79; sharp-tongued radio and TV comedian who often ridiculed sponsors; New York, May 19, 1994.

Morris, William, 80; publishing executive and lexicographer who edited *The American Heritage Dictionary of the English Language*; Columbus, OH, Jan. 2, 1994.

Morrow, E. Frederic, 88; aide to Pres. Dwight Eisenhower, 1st black in high White House position; New York, July 19, 1994.

N

Natcher, William, 84; U.S. House member who cast a record 18,401 consecutive roll call votes; Washington, DC, Mar. 29, 1994.

Nelson, Harriet, 85; actress who with her husband, Ozzie, and her sons, David and Ricky, became a symbol of American family life through their 14-year TV series *The Adventures of Ozzie and Harriet*; Laguna Beach, CA, Oct. 2, 1994.

Nilsson, Harry, 52; singer, composer known for "salon rock" style; Agoura Hills, CA, Jan. 15, 1994.

Nixon, Richard M., 81; 37th president of U.S. (1969-74), whose administration ended U.S. role in Vietnam War and scored diplomatic breakthroughs with China and the Soviet Union; resigned as result of Watergate scandal; New York, Apr. 22, 1994.

Ntaryamira, Cyprien, 39; president of Burundi; Kigali, Rwanda, Apr. 6, 1994.

O

Onassis, Jacqueline Bouvier Kennedy, 64; widow of Pres. John Kennedy and Greek shipping tycoon Aristotle Onassis, she was U.S. first lady from 1961 to 1963; New York, May 19, 1994.

O'Neill, Thomas P., 81; ex-Speaker of U.S. House and advocate of political liberalism; Boston, Jan. 5, 1994.

P

Parish, Sister, 84; interior designer who originated "American country style"; Dark Harbor, ME, Sept. 8, 1994.

Pauling, Linus, 93; winner of Nobel prizes in chemistry and in peace—the latter for opposition to nuclear weaponry; advocated heavy doses of vitamin C to fight common cold; Big Sur, CA, Aug.19,1994.

Peale, Norman Vincent, 95; minister of Marble Collegiate Church in New York for 52 years, whose assertion in his book *The Power of Positive Thinking* that optimism could lead to material success brought him a wide following; Pawling, NY, Dec. 24, 1993.

Peppard, George, 65; film and TV actor who starred in *Breakfast at Tiffany's*; Los Angeles, May 8, 1994.

Phoenix, River, 23; motion picture actor; Los Angeles, Oct. 31, 1993.

Pluckett, Roy, 83; inventor of Teflon, which revolutionized plastics and cookware industries; Corpus Christi, TX, May 12, 1994.

Preus, Jacob A. O., 74; minister whose belief that Bible was historically true caused split in Lutheran Church-Missouri Synod; Burnsville, MN, Aug. 13, 1994.

Price, Vincent, 82; actor whose forte was the portrayal of sinister villians in horror films; Los Angeles, Oct. 25, 1993.

Puller, Lewis, Jr., 48; Vietnam War hero who won Pulitzer Prize for his autobiography *Favorite Son*; Mount Vernon, VA, May 11, 1994.

R

Ray, Dixy Lee, 79; former head of Atomic Energy Commission and governor of Washington; Fox Island, WA, Jan. 2, 1994.

Raye, Martha, 78; big-mouthed, big-hearted comic who traveled thousands of mi through 3 wars entertaining American troops; Los Angeles, Oct. 19, 1994.

Rey, Fernando, 76; actor who played villains and cosmopolitan men; Madrid, Spain, Mar. 9, 1994.

Rodney, Red, 66; jazz trumpeter and band leader; Boynton Beach, FL, May 27, 1994.

Roland, Gilbert, 88; actor from silent films to TV, who played dashing romantic leads and character roles; Beverly Hills, CA, May 15, 1994.

Romero, Cesar, 86; suave film actor who also played the Joker in TV's *Batman*; Santa Monica, CA, Jan. 1, 1994.

Ryan, Sheelah, 69; winner of a $55.2 million Florida lottery in 1988 who spent the rest of her life giving the money away to charitable causes; Sept. 24, 1994.

S

Savalas, Telly, 70; film actor in tough-guy roles who also starred as Kojak on TV; Los Angeles, Jan. 22, 1994.

Scarry, Richard, 74; author and illustrator of children's books; Gstaad, Switzerland, Apr. 30, 1994.

Schneerson, Menachem Mendel, 92; rabbi, leader of the Lubavitcher Hasidic Jewish sect based in Brooklyn, NY; New York, June 12, 1994.

Senna, Ayrton, 34; 3-time Formula One auto-racing champion; Imola, Italy, May 1, 1994.

Sharkey, Jack, 91; world heavyweight boxing champion 1932-33; Beverly, MA, Aug. 17, 1994.

Sharrock, Sonny, 53; free-jazz guitarist; Ossining, NY, May 26, 1994.

Shilts, Randy, 42; journalist whose books included *And the Band Played On: Politics, People and the AIDS Epidemic* and *Conduct Unbecoming: Lesbians and Gays in the U.S. Military*; Guerneville, CA, Feb. 17, 1994.

Shirer, William L., 89; war correspondent and historian who wrote *The Rise and Fall of the Third Reich*; Boston, Dec. 28, 1994.

Shore, Dinah, 76; singer and entertainer whose charm and vitality made her one of TV's biggest stars; Beverly Hills, CA, Feb. 24, 1994.

Smith, John, 55; leader of the British Labour Party; London, May 12, 1994.

Spadolini, Giovanni, 69; historian, journalist, prime minister of Italy; Rome, Aug. 4, 1994.

Spivak, Lawrence E., 93; journalist who originated and was first moderator of TV's "Meet the Press"; Washington, DC, Mar. 9, 1994.

Stone, Ezra, 76; actor and director who played Henry Aldrich on radio; Perth Amboy, NJ, Mar. 3, 1994.

Styne, Jule, 88; versatile, prolific songwriter and composer whose hits included "Three Coins in the Fountain," "People," *Gypsy*, and *Funny Girl;* New York, Sept. 20, 1994.

T

Tanaka, Kakuei, 75; premier of Japan, 1972-74, who was later convicted of bribery; Dec. 16, 1993.

Tandy, Jessica, 85; theater and film actress, often opposite husband Hume Cronyn, originated Blanche DuBois role in *Streetcar Named Desire*, won Oscar for *Driving Miss Daisy*; Easton, CT, Sept. 11, 1994.

Taylor, Dub, 87; actor who played grizzled character and sidekicks and whose 60-year movie career included roles in *Bonnie and Clyde* and *Maverick*; Westlake Village, CA, Oct. 3, 1994.

Thomas, Lewis, 80; doctor and writer whose essays were collected in *Lives of a Cell* and *The Medusa and the Snail*; New York, Dec. 3, 1993.

Tully, Alice, 91; ex-singer, philanthropist who donated millions of dollars to the arts; New York, Dec. 10, 1994.

V

Vazgen I, 85; Catholicos, or head, of Armenian Apostolic Church; Yerevan, Armenia, Aug. 18, 1994.

Vera Cruz, Philip, 89; co-founder of the United Farm Workers Union; Bakersfield, CA, June 11, 1994.

W

Walcott, "Jersey Joe", 80; heavyweight boxing champion, oldest—at age 37—to win title; Camden, NJ, Feb. 25, 1994.

Wanamaker, Sam, 74; film and stage actor and director who led effort to rebuild Globe Theatre; London, Dec. 18, 1993.

Washington, Fredi, 90; pioneering black actress in films and on stage; Stamford, CT, June 28, 1994.

Watson, Thomas, 79; president who led IBM into computer era; Greenwich, CT, Dec. 31, 1993.

Wells, Frank, 62; president of Walt Disney Company; central Nevada, Apr. 3, 1994.

Wilkinson, Bud, 77; college football coach, led Univ. of Oklahoma to a still-record 47 straight victories and 3 national championships; St. Louis, Feb. 9, 1994.

Williams, Marion, 66; gospel singer; Philadelphia, July 2, 1994.

Winfrey, Bill, 77; trainer of thoroughbreds; Lake Forest, CA, Apr. 14, 1994.

Worner, Manfred, 59; German defense minister, NATO secretary general; Brussels, Aug. 13, 1994.

Z

Zappa, Frank, 52; prolific composer, guitarist, band leader, and producer who excelled in a range of pop genres; Los Angeles, Dec. 4, 1993.

Offbeat News Stories of 1994

Getting High on Nature—In the summer of 1994, Arizona's newest recreation was toad licking, a poisonous, dangerous, and illegal activity. The object of affection was the Colorado River toad (*Bufo alvarius*), which secretes a milky white substance that includes a powerful combination of bufotenine (a psychoactive drug according to Arizona law) and a drug called dimethyltryptamine. Some licked the toads directly; the squeamish dried the secretion and then smoked it.

But She Doesn't Look a Day Over 1,800—The body of a 2,000-year-old frozen woman was found in the Siberian permafrost by Russian archaeologists in July 1993. A year later she was undergoing a make-over by the same scientists who helped preserve Ho Chi Minh and Lenin. When found, Lady (as she has been named by her reconstructionists) was elegantly laid out in a white silk blouse, a red skirt, and white stockings. She had been buried in a hollow tree trunk alongside horse harnesses, a mirror, dishes, and a small container of cannabis, which archaeologists believe was smoked for pleasure and used in pagan rituals. Intricate tattoos covered her left arm. To preserve her as a mummy, her vital organs had been removed and replaced with moss and peat. At 5 ft 4 in, she was tall for her time and had long legs. Scientists have not been able to determine the cause of her death at about the age of 18. When their work is complete, she will be displayed in Novosibirsk, near where she was found.

Frequent Flier Miles—Over a 12-day period in July 1994, Tabitha the cat logged 30,000 mi aboard a Tower Air Boeing 747. Her travels took her to New York, Los Angeles, Miami, and San Juan, PR, but she was unable to disembark at any of those destinations because, unknown to pilot, crew, and passengers, she was stowed away in a 7-in-high, 60-ft-long space above the cargo hold's drop ceiling. Apparently she slipped out of her carrier in the cargo hold of the plane while en route with her owner on a flight from New York to Los Angeles. During her 12-day plight, some 100 airline workers looked for her for some 1,000 hours. Finally, her owner, Carol Ann Timmel, filed suit to ground the plane for a 24-hr search. Nine hours into the search Tabitha was found, fit but hungry. On her next and she hoped final flight, Tabitha sat in a free first class seat beside her owner, going home to California.

Do You Believe in the Loch Ness Monster?—In March 1994, London's *Sunday Telegraph* reported that the famous 1934 snapshot of Scotland's Loch Ness Monster is a fake. The last of 5 pranksters who created it confessed just before dying that Nessie was actually a toy submarine fitted with a plastic head and neck. One poll showed that only about 14% ever believed the monster was real anyway.

There's an Airplane in Your Basement—While mowing the lawn at his new home in Vermont, Tom Hutchins looked up to find the Civil Air Patrol from 4 states looking for an airplane in his basement. The search was triggered when moving a box in Hutchins's basement set off a brick-sized Emergency Locator Transmitter (ELT) that sent a radio distress signal to a satellite. The ELT was apparently left by a former homeowner who was a pilot. When the ELT began sending out its message, Civil Air Patrol volunteers began a night-long rescue search.

Baby Think It Over—This high-tech 8-lb doll is programmed to shriek at random intervals day and night. The only way to stop the crying is to hold a key in its back for 20 minutes, just about the length of time it takes to feed a newborn. Developed and distributed by Richard Jurmain, Baby Think It Over is being used in schools and health clinics around the U.S. to give teenagers a realistic view of what it's like to spend day and night with an infant. Usually, they get the doll for a 3-night assignment. Its maker insists that the doll doesn't teach values but that it does teach sleeplessness. A microprocessor in the doll monitors how long the baby cried before it stopped and if it was handled roughly.

Ted, the Forecasting Fowl—Ted the Rooster, a half bantam, half fighting cock, famed for predicting the winners of sporting events, passed away Mar. 24, 1994, while watching *The Young and the Restless*. His prognosticating procedure was to peck at kernels of corn placed in front of cards with team names and numbers from 1 to 20. In 1988, Ted had an accuracy rate of 88% in picking winners in the NCAA men's basketball tournament. At his death, he had an accuracy rate of 75% for the year.

Miscellaneous Facts

—On Aug. 1, 1964, Hasbro Inc. introduced GI Joe. A year later, sales were at 2 million, and by the time of his 30th birthday in 1994 more than 250 million GI Joe "action figures" had been sold. GI Joe is 11½ in tall. If he were real, he would be 5 ft 9 in. He originally cost $4; the 1994 price was $18. Other names originally considered for him were Salty the Sailor, Ace the Pilot, and Rocky the Marine. His creation was inspired by the 1945 movie *The Story of GI Joe,* starring Robert Mitchum.

—Almost $400 billion was wagered in the U.S. in 1993, an increase of more than 17% from 1992, according to *Gaming & Wagering Business* magazine. And where did people bet? Mostly in casinos (close to $300 billion). The rest was spread out among (in descending order) lotteries, Indian reservations, horse racing, card rooms, charitable games, charitable bingo, greyhound racing, bookmaking, and jai alai.

—The answer is:

114,381,625,757,888,867,669,235,779,976,146,612,010,
218,296,721,242,362,562,561,842,935,706,935,245,733,
897,830,597,123,563,958,705,058,989,075,147,599,290,
026,879,543, 541 = 3,490, 529,510,847,650,949,147,
849,619,903,898,133,417,764,638,493,387,843,990,820,
577 × 32,769,132,993,266,709,549,961,988,190,834,
461,413,177,642,967,992,942, 539,798,288,533

The question was: What is the factor of R.S.A. 129, the 129-digit number linked to a popular computer coding system that was said to be proof of the system's security?

The inventors of R.S.A. 129 had predicted 17 years ago that it would take 40 quadrillion years to factor it with the methods of the time. In 1993-94, several computer scientists and some 600 volunteers on the Internet factored the number in 8 months. They said it took 100 quadrillion calculations. Their reward was $100 offered by the inventors and the pleasure of reading the encoded message: "The magic words are squeamish ossifrage."

—American Sign Language, the hand language used by 500,000 people to communicate with the deaf, has been updated to become more politically correct. For example, the sign for Japanese, which was a twist of the little finger at the corner of the eye, denoting a slant eye, has been replaced with a hand signal that shows the shape of the Japanese islands. And the sign for African-American, which was flattening the nose with the index finger, has been replaced with a gesture that indicates a map of Africa.

—The U.S. government spends more than $25 billion a year on computers and related services, and it takes the government almost 4 years to purchase computers, compared with 13 months in the private sector. Thirty years ago the government bought more than 62% of the output of the U.S. computer industry; today it accounts for less than 4%.

—The African pigmy hedgehog is being called the designer pet of the '90s. By mid-1994 some 3,000 of the spiny critters were being kept domestically. They like to be petted along the quills, live in wood-chip-filled boxes, don't smell, need to eat only once a day (they prefer pet food or mealworms), and cost about $250 a pair.

QUICK REFERENCE INDEX

ABBREVIATIONS, U.S. POSTAL . . . 589
ACADEMY AWARDS . . . 327-329
ACTORS, ACTRESSES . . . 357-372
AEROSPACE . . . 292-299
AGRICULTURE . . . 134-141
AIDS . . . 842, 971
AIR MAIL, INTERNATIONAL . . . 590-591
ANIMALS . . . 188-190
AREA CODES, U.S. . . . 387-417
INTERNATIONAL . . . 850
ARTISTS, PHOTOGRAPHERS, SCULPTORS . . . 344-346
ARTS AND MEDIA . . . 300-313
ASSOCIATIONS AND SOCIETIES . . . 575-586
ASTRONOMICAL DATA, 1995 . . . 251-285
AWARDS, MEDALS, PRIZES . . . 70, 174, 314-330
BASEBALL . . . 938-955
BASKETBALL . . . 907-920
BIRTHSTONES . . . 725
BOOKS . . . 303-304, 324, 330
BOXING . . . 934-936
BRIDGES . . . 690-693
BUDGET, U.S. . . . 107-108
BUILDINGS, TALL . . . 684-690
BUSINESS DIRECTORY . . . 713-718
CABINET, U.S. . . . 98-102
CALENDARS . . . 251-254, 274-291, 732-733
CHEMICAL ELEMENTS . . . 177-178
CHRONOLOGY, 1993-94 . . . 40-69
CITIES OF THE U.S. . . . 380-381, 674-683
CLINTON ADMINISTRATION . . . 72-75
COLLEGES . . . 226-250
COMPOSERS . . . 352-354
COMPUTER GLOSSARY . . . 170-172
CONGRESS . . . 76-85, 103, 634-635
CONSTITUTION . . . 455-463
CONSUMER INFORMATION . . . 712-728
COPYRIGHT LAW . . . 723-725
COST OF LIVING . . . 109-111
COUNTIES, U.S. . . . 378-380, 418-436
CRIME . . . 213-218
DEATHS . . . 367-370, 973-974
DECLARATION OF INDEPENDENCE . . . 453-455
DISASTERS . . . 565-574
DIVORCE LAWS . . . 728
DRUG USE . . . 963
ECONOMIC AND FINANCIAL GLOSSARY . . . 132-133
ECONOMICS . . . 107-133
EDUCATION . . . 219-250
ELECTIONS . . . 33-34, 76-84, 90-94, 601-633
EMMY AWARDS . . . 325
EMPLOYMENT . . . 142-154
ENDANGERED SPECIES . . . 188-189
ENERGY . . . 164-168
ENVIRONMENT . . . 187-192
EXPLORATION AND GEOGRAPHY . . . 543-556
FIRST AID . . . 706
FLAGS OF THE WORLD (COLOR) . . . 481-484
FOODS, NUTRITIVE VALUE . . . 702-703
FOOTBALL . . . 870-889
FORMS OF ADDRESS . . . 597
GEOGRAPHICAL DATA . . . 497-500, 545-556
GOVERNORS . . . 93-97
GRAMMY AWARDS . . . 329-330
HEADS OF STATE . . . 534-542, 740-776, 785-839
HEALTH . . . 38-39, 701-711, 966-972
WHERE TO GET HELP . . . 710-711
HEIGHT AND WEIGHT TABLES . . . 705
HISTORICAL ANNIVERSARIES . . . 105-106
HISTORICAL FIGURES . . . 534-542
HISTORY . . . 438-470, 508-533
HOCKEY . . . 890-897
HOLIDAYS . . . 289, 291, 732-733
HOUSE OF REPRESENTATIVES, U.S. . . . 78-84, 103
IMMIGRATION LAW . . . 842-843
IMMUNIZATION . . . 707
INDEX, GENERAL . . . 4-32
INFORMATION SUPERHIGHWAY . . . 35-36
INTEREST LAWS, RATES . . . 720-721
INVENTIONS AND DISCOVERIES . . . 174-178
JUDICIARY, U.S. . . . 86-89
LABOR UNION DIRECTORY . . . 153-154
LANGUAGE . . . 592-600
LATITUDE, LONGITUDE, & ALTITUDE OF CITIES . . . 550-552
MAGAZINES . . . 306
MAPS (COLOR) . . . 485-496
MARRIAGE LAWS . . . 727
MAYORS . . . 90-93
MEASURES, WEIGHTS . . . 557-564
MEDICINE . . . 707-709, 966-969
METEOROLOGICAL DATA . . . 179-186
METRIC SYSTEM . . . 557-561
MILEAGE, AIR . . . 212
ROAD . . . 211
MILITARY . . . 155-163
MINERALS . . . 129-131
MISCELLANEOUS FACTS . . . 975
MONEY . . . 117-118
MONUMENTS, NATIONAL . . . 672-673
MORTGAGE RATES . . . 725
MOUNTAINS . . . 546-548
MOVIES . . . 300-302, 327-329
MUSIC AND MUSICIANS . . . 307-309, 329-330, 352-356
NATIONAL DEFENSE . . . 155-163
NATIONAL PARKS . . . 503-506
NATIONS OF THE WORLD . . . 740-776, 785-851
NEWSPAPERS . . . 305
NEWS PHOTOS, 1994 (COLOR) . . . 193-200, 777-784
NEWS STORIES, 1993-1994 . . . 40-69
NOBEL PRIZES . . . 70, 314-316
NORTH AMERICAN FREE TRADE AGREEMENT . . . 204
NUTRITION . . . 701-705
OBITUARIES . . . 973-974
OFF-BEAT NEWS STORIES . . . 975
OLYMPICS . . . 852-868
PASSPORTS . . . 722
PEN NAMES . . . 598
PERSONALITIES, NOTED . . . 331-372
PLANETS . . . 254-262, 267
POPES . . . 735
POPULATION, U.S. . . . 373-437
U.S. TERRITORIES . . . 436, 669-671
WORLD . . . 740-776, 785-841
POSTAL INFORMATION . . . 587-591
PRESIDENTIAL ELECTIONS . . . 601-633
PRESIDENTS, U.S. . . . 471-480, 632-635
PULITZER PRIZES . . . 316-324
QUOTES OF THE YEAR . . . 104
RECORDINGS . . . 309, 329-330
RELIGIOUS INFORMATION . . . 729-739
RIVERS . . . 553-554
SCIENCE AND TECHNOLOGY . . . 169-178
SCIENTISTS . . . 314-315, 349-351
SENATE, U.S. . . . 76-77, 103
SOCIAL SECURITY . . . 696-700
SPACE FLIGHTS, NOTABLE . . . 292-294
SPORTS . . . 852-956
PERSONALITIES . . . 926-928
DRAMATIC EVENTS, 1994 . . . 852
STATE NAMES, ORIGIN . . . 501
STATES OF THE UNION . . . 643-668
STOCK MARKETS . . . 127-128
SUPREME COURT, JUSTICES . . . 86
DECISIONS . . . 70, 464-465
TAXES . . . 636-642
TELEVISION . . . 310-312, 325
THEATER . . . 300-301, 307, 325
TIME DIFFERENCES . . . 290-291
TONY AWARDS . . . 325
TOP TEN NEWS STORIES, 1994 . . . 33
TRACK AND FIELD . . . 868-869
TRADE AND TRANSPORTATION . . . 201-212
TUNNELS . . . 693-694
UNITED NATIONS . . . 845-847
UNIVERSITIES . . . 226-250
U.S. CAPITAL . . . 668-669, 672-673
U.S. FACTS . . . 497-507
U.S. FLAG . . . 466-468
U.S. GOVERNMENT . . . 72-103
U.S. HISTORY . . . 438-470
VICE PRESIDENTS . . . 632-635
VITAL STATISTICS . . . 957-972
VOLCANOES . . . 545-546
WEATHER . . . 179-186
WEDDING ANNIVERSARIES . . . 725
WEIGHTS AND MEASURES . . . 557-564
WORLD HISTORY . . . 508-533
WORLD WAR II 50th ANNIVERSARY . . . 37
WRITERS . . . 334-335, 341-344
ZIP CODES . . . 387-417, 436
ZOOLOGICAL PARKS . . . 191

For complete Index, see pp. 4-32

DUE	RETURNED	DUE	RETURNED
1.		13.	
2.		14.	
3.		15.	
4.		16.	
5.		17.	
6.		18.	
7.		19.	
8.		20.	
9.		21.	
10.		22.	
11.		23.	
12.		24.	

Withdrawn From
Ohio Northern
University Library

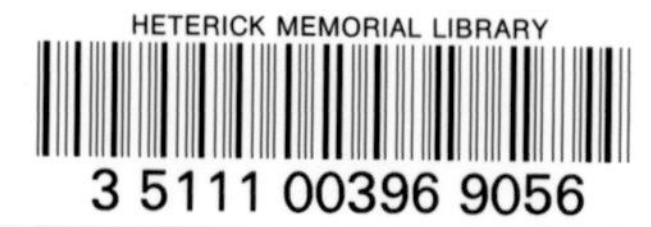

Heterick Memorial Library
Ohio Northern University
Ada, Ohio 45810